DATE DUE

DEMCO 38-296

TOTAL

BASEBALL
SECOND EDITION

EDITED BY

John Thorn and Pete Palmer

with David Reuther

A BASEBALL INK BOOK

WARNER BOOKS

A Time Warner Company

Total Baseball Staff
Second Edition

Editors
John Thorn   Pete Palmer

Project Manager
David Reuther

Associate Editor
Richard Puff

Assistant Editor
Val Poletto

Book Design
Marc Cheshire

Managing Editor
Gypsy da Silva

Fact Checkers
Bill Deane   Richard Topp   David Pietrusza

Copy Editors & Proofreaders
Scott Kurtz
Carol Catt   Andrew Hafitz   Barbara Hanson

Typographer
Gendell Graphics
Peter Bird, President

Warner Books
Laurence J. Kirshbaum, President
Rick Horgan, Senior Editor
Milton Batalion, V.P., Manufacturing

(W) A Time Warner Company

Printed in the United States of America
First Printing: April 1991
1 3 5 7 9 10 8 6 4 2

Library of Congress Cataloging-in-Publication Data

Total baseball / edited by John Thorn and Pete Palmer
with David Reuther. — 2nd ed.
p.   cm. — (A Baseball ink book)
ISBN 0-446-51620-1
1. Baseball—United States—History.   I. Thorn, John, 1947-
II. Palmer, Pete.   III. Reuther, David.   IV. Series.
GV863.A1T68   1991
796.357′ 0973—dc20   90-50531
CIP

This book is dedicated to the great pioneer
of baseball history and record keeping,
Henry Chadwick,
and to today's keepers of the flame,
the Society for American Baseball Research.

Contents

Acknowledgments   ix

PART ONE

Introduction   3

The History

1. The History of Major League Baseball, *David Q. Voigt*   7
2. Team Histories, *Frederick Ivor-Campbell*   59
3. Postseason Play, *Frederick Ivor-Campbell* 109
4. The All-Star Game, *Frederick Ivor-Campbell* 259
5. Ballparks, *Philip J. Lowry* 276

The Players

6. Lives of the Players, *John B. Holway and Bob Carroll* 301
7. Phantom Ballplayers, *Clifford S. Kachline* 399
8. Baseball Families, *Larry Amman* 403
9. No Minor League Experience, *Cappy Gagnon* 410
10. Scandals and Controversies, *Stephen S. Hall* 413
11. Tragedies and Shortened Careers, *Joseph M. Overfield* 425
12. The Pinch Hitters, *L. Robert Davids* 439
13. Two-Sport Stars, *Stan Grosshandler* 445
14. Managers and Coaches, *Fred Stein* 452
15. Umpires, *Larry R. Gerlach* 463

The Highlights of the Game

16. Streaks and Feats, *Jack Kavanagh* 471
17. Awards and Honors, *Bill Deane* 496
18. Baseball Lore, *Eliot Cohen* 529

Other Leagues

19. Black Ball, *Jules Tygiel* 551
20. The Minor Leagues, *Bob Hoie* 567
21. Japanese Baseball, *Yoichi Nagata and John B. Holway* 579
22. Baseball in the Caribbean, Rob Ruck 593
23. Baseball in Canada, *Bruce L. Prentice and Merritt Clifton* 601
24. College Baseball, *Cappy Gagnon* 605
25. Baseball and the Armed Services, *Harrington E. Crissey, Jr.* 608
26. Women in Baseball, *Debra A. Shattuck* 616

The Game Off the Field

27. The Business of Baseball, *Steve Mann and David Pietrusza* 621
28. Baseball and the Law, *Gary D. Hailey* 638
29. The Farm System, *Bob Hoie* 644
30. Baseball Reporting, *Jack Lang* 648
31. Baseball on the Air, *Paul D. Adomites* 654
32. Baseball Collecting, *Barry Halper with Bill Madden* 657

PART TWO

Introduction   665
Sabermetrics   682

The Player Register

The Player Register   695

The Pitcher Register

The Pitcher Register 1403

The Fielding Register

The Fielding Register 1887

The Annual Record

The Annual Record 2115

The All-Time Leaders

The All-Time Leaders 2347
        Lifetime Leaders 2349
        Single Season Leaders 2382

The Rosters

The Team Rosters 2413
The Manager Roster 2469
The Coach Roster 2495
The Umpire Roster 2503
The Owners and Officials Roster 2510

Home-Road Statistics

Home-Road Statistics 2517

Appendices

1. Rules and Scoring, *Dennis Bingham and Thomas R. Heitz* 2553
2. Forfeits and No-Decision Games 2609
3. Pitcher Lifetime Fielding 2613

Notes on Contributors 2617
Glossary of Statistical Terms 2621
Team and League Abbreviations 2629

Acknowledgments

A book as large and complex as this second edition of *Total Baseball* could not have been published without the assistance of a legion of writers, researchers, and editorial/production staff. The principal contributors in these areas are credited on the preceding staff page and table of contents; others may be acknowledged within the text or in the separate introductions to the various sections of Part 2. Still others provided vital inspiration, investigative tips, and production help, yet go unmentioned in the body of the book; this page is for them, especially.

We are indebted to David Reuther, our friend and associate in many other books, and tireless project manager for this one. His contributions to the editorial, production, and business aspects of *Total Baseball*—both the original and this revised edition—were truly indispensable.

Richard Puff joined Baseball Ink after the publication of *Total Baseball 1* and played a vital role in all the new features that mark its successor, from updating and correcting the original edition to handling the torrents of information that flowed through our hands daily. In the final months of production he was ably assisted by Val Poletto. Laura Burnett, Susan Ray, and Elaine Fiore also chipped in.

Marc Cheshire designed the first edition masterfully and this time around added some refinements that aided legibility and general usefulness. He also created designs for new elements such as the Fielding Register.

The burden that Marc endured by doubling as Production Chief for *Total Baseball 1*—the inhuman hours, the unreasonable demands, the editors' vacillations and blunders—was, for this book, dropped on the shoulders of Gypsy da Silva, made sturdy through previous Baseball Ink books. As Casey Stengel would have said, she did splendid. Gypsy coordinated the copy-editing and proofreading talents of a far-flung staff that included Scott Kurtz, Carol Catt, Andrew Hafitz, and Barbara Hanson.

Peter Bird, president of Gendell Graphics, supervised the mammoth job of setting *Total Baseball* in both its editions. We thank him and his extraordinary staff for going the extra mile for us, especially in the final weeks of production.

Without the enthusiasm and commitment of Larry Kirshbaum, president of Warner Books, this book would have remained just another good idea in search of a publisher. Larry believed in *Total Baseball* from the moment he heard of it, and he put the prodigious energies and skills of Warner behind us. Rick Horgan, senior editor at Warner Books, offered critical guidance and support that made this second edition a better book than its forebear. Milton Batalion, vice president for manufacturing, could have thrown up his hands in dismay at the prospect of printing the biggest baseball book ever in less time than is conventionally given to a midsize novel; instead, he found a way to do it. And to all the other good folks at Warner who lent a hand, we extend our admiration and thanks.

Our friend Dick Perez provided a baker's dozen of his typically wonderful sketches to embellish the title pages and part-titles. Dick is the preeminent artist of baseball in whatever medium he chooses to work, and we appreciate his unique enhancement of *Total Baseball*.

The editors and writers of this book know a thing or two about baseball, yet we are still liable to an occasional lapse. Helping to keep these to a minimum were three experts for whose fact-checking services we are grateful: Bill Deane, senior associate of the National Baseball Library in Cooperstown; Richard Topp, baseball historian and president of the Society for American Baseball Research (SABR); and David Pietrusza, author and executive secretary of the World Baseball Hall of Fame. Also helpful in these areas were baseball experts Peter Bjarkman, Harold Dellinger, Tim Harkness, Bill Himmelman, David Kempt, and Jon Scher.

For research help, particularly into the years before 1920, we extend heartfelt thanks to (alphabetically) SABR colleagues Bill Carle, Bob McConnell, David Neft, Bob Tiemann, and Frank Williams. Bill Carle helped us with biographical data, especially debut dates. Bob McConnell lent his personal expertise and his knowledge of the John Tattersall research collection to clear up a variety of perplexing areas. David Neft supplied us with heretofore unknown RBI data for the National League of 1880–1885 and inspired us by his example, as the man who headed the Information Concepts, Inc., team that produced *The Baseball Encyclopedia* of 1969. Bob Tiemann provided game scores and sites for a host of pre-1900 games that were most helpful in deriving, for the first time, home-road stats for the nineteenth century; he also headed the SABR research project that yielded the National Association data described below. And Frank Williams continued his remarkable efforts in correcting pitcher won-lost records before 1920.

Particularly helpful to Pete Palmer in the preparation of this second edition were, in addition to those mentioned above, Jim Beck, Bob Hoie, Eddie Epstein, Ray Gonzalez, Warren Johnson, Joe Wayman, and Walt Wilson. Michael Stagno's massive compilation of box scores and play-by-plays of the National Association years, 1871–1875, is at the core of all the new data for that period, which is presented to the public for the first time here. Jerry Kahn, Walter Nissen, Jr., Tom Ruane, and Ed Yerha suggested new features and broad areas of potential improvement that are reflected in the book. And a veritable legion of readers took us up on our invitation to write with their corrections and suggestions, from the mathematical to the typographical; we thank them in the aggregate here and list them by name in the Notes on Contributors near the end of the book.

Other SABR members whose research is represented in *Total Baseball* include Bob Davids, the society's founder and the man who, in the words of Bill James, "has done more for baseball research than anyone else living"; and John Schwartz and Alex Haas, who combined with Davids to compile hit-by-pitch information from early newspaper box scores. The aid of Cliff Kachline, that extraordinary font of baseball knowledge, was invaluable even before this book began to take shape and continued to be so at many points in its development.

And last, we thank some giants of baseball research whose work informs these pages but who are no longer with us to receive the tribute: in no particular order, Ernie Lanigan, John Tattersall, S. C. Thompson, Alex Haas, Preston D. Orem, Len Gettelson, and Lee Allen.

PART ONE

Introduction

When it first appeared, in 1989, *Total Baseball* was the most complete, most authoritative, and most informative—not to mention the biggest—baseball book ever published. It came into being because its creators saw that there was nothing else like it and because its publishers had faith that fans would want such a book: a virtual baseball library in one volume. (A dozen conventional books could be bound between these covers.) In fact, it could be said that *Total Baseball* was the first true baseball encyclopedia because it offers not only the game's numbers but also the stories behind them. In this, its second incarnation, *Total Baseball* builds upon that foundation to provide new stories, new stats, and a painstaking review of all the data that went into the first edition.

This book is divided into two parts. The first consists of prose features on subjects of interest to all baseball fans, from the general reader who wishes to know more about the game's trivia and lore to the advanced fan who wants to know about its business and law. The origins of the farm system; black baseball before Jackie Robinson; complete balloting for the Hall of Fame, MVP, Cy Young, and Rookie of the Year awards; women in baseball; scandals and controversies; . . . but why tease you with the pleasures that await you while (we hope) holding you captive with this Introduction? Simply be assured that *Total Baseball* will be totally absorbing, whether you begin with David Voigt's "History of Major League Baseball" and read straight through to the end of Part 1, or scan the Table of Contents for what appeals at the moment. The writers gathered together here are the experts in their fields, as befits an encyclopedic reference work, and even the most erudite reader will learn countless new things about this great game. Among the new prose features are chapters on baseball reporting, collecting, pinch hitting, and ballparks.

The same holds true for Part 2, which contains the playing and pitching registers, a variety of rosters, a year-by-year statistical summary of major league play since 1871, home-road statistics and more. The stats newly developed for this book—like the Clutch Hitting Index or Relief Ranking—will please the devotee of sabermetrics, who may know about Runs Created, Production, and the whole Linear Weights System but who has never before been offered these stats applied to all of baseball's 13,490

players. The traditional computations will appeal to baseball scholars, who know what a tangle of briars the historical record has become over the last 20 years, as individual player records have been altered without making corresponding changes to other players on the same team. (For more on this, see the much longer Introduction to Part 2.) And the cornucopia of stats old and new—for everyone from all-time leaders to cup-of-coffee nonentities—will provide days, months, and years of archaeological delight for baseball fans of all stripes. New to this edition are the massive Fielding Register; the revamped Manager Roster; newly figured—and more revealing—tabulations of Park Factor and Fielding Runs; and nearly complete data for the formerly sparse National Association years, 1871–75.

Total Baseball joins the game's most knowledgeable writers, most of them members of the Society for American Baseball Research (SABR), with the game's great historical database, the one built up over two decades by Pete Palmer. Benefiting from the painstaking research of hundreds of friends and colleagues in SABR, we have corrected many errors and omissions in the eighth edition of Macmillan's *Baseball Encyclopedia*, relying not upon the numbers enshrined by tradition or official edict but upon the evidence. How many hours have been spent scanning the handwritten official records of the early years of the century or reviewing box scores and scoresheets and game summaries! It would have been easier not to bother, to accept, for example, a game mistakenly entered twice in the record for 1910 so that Ty Cobb could keep his 1910 batting championship and career total of 4,191 hits. But there can be no statute of limitations on historical error; the researcher and historian must go where the evidence leads them, and if the result upsets some commonly held notions, so be it.

This book is as good as we know how to make it, but we do want to hear from you about our blunders (we know there will be some, as there were in the first edition) or about your research (which may be as important to the third edition of *Total Baseball* as that of, say, Walt Wilson or Bob Tiemann was for this). We believe that history is process, not product, and our aim has been for *Total Baseball* to reflect the state of the art in baseball research and to convey its editors' love for the game. We hope you'll let us know if we succeeded.

The History

The History of Major League Baseball
David Q. Voigt

An Evolving Game: The Formative Years of Major League Baseball

Deeply embedded in the folklore of American sports is the story of baseball's supposed invention by a young West Point cadet, Abner Doubleday, in the summer of 1839 at the village of Cooperstown, New York. The yarn originated in 1907, in the final report of a committee commissioned by major league executives to inquire into the origins of "America's National Game."

The claim that the game was invented by the late Doubleday, who also won enduring fame as a Union general in the Civil War, was based on the dubious testimony of Abner Graves, a retired mining engineer. Indeed, Graves claimed to have actually witnessed the long-ago event. The Graves account appealed to committeeman Albert G. Spalding, a former star player and club owner, and concurrently a famous sporting goods tycoon and a fervently patriotic American. He persuaded his colleagues to accept the Doubleday invention account without further ado. With the release of the final version of the committee's report, the legend of baseball's immaculate conception began to worm its way into American mythology.

Ever since then, sports historians have repeatedly and futilely assailed the Doubleday account, arguing that Abner Doubleday never visited Cooperstown in 1839, that his diaries contain no reference to the game, and that the form of baseball he supposedly invented far too closely resembled the game as it was played in the early 1900s.

Indeed, sports historians have marshaled impressive evidence showing that American baseball, far from being an independent invention, evolved out of various ball-and-stick games that had been played in many areas of the world since the beginnings of recorded history. Among many suggested precursors of baseball, a Russian ball-and-stick game called *lapta* has been recently advanced by Soviet propagandists. But in early America, precursors of baseball included informal games of English origin such as paddleball, trap ball, one-old-cat, rounders, and town ball. The latter was a popular game in colonial New England and was played by adults and children with a bat and ball on an open field. Moreover, printed references to "base ball" in America date back to the eighteenth century. Among these accounts is one of Albigence Waldo, a surgeon with Washington's troops at Valley Forge who poetically told of soldiers batting balls and running bases in their free time. And in the early 1820s, the grandfather of the late novelist Samuel Hopkins Adams vividly re-

called playing "base ball" on Mr. Mumford's pasture lot. Similarly in 1834 Robin Carver's *Book of Sports* related that an American version of rounders called 'base' or 'goal ball' was rivaling cricket in popularity among Americans. Indeed, cricket played a role in the evolution of organized baseball. From this British game came umpires and innings, and early baseball writers like Henry Chadwick used cricket terminology such as "batsman," "playing for the side," and "excellent field" in describing early baseball games. Likewise, the pioneer baseball innovator Harry Wright, a cricket professional turned baseball manager, drew heavily on his cricket background in promoting baseball as a professional team sport in the United States.

As an evolutionary blend of informal bat-and-ball games and the formal game of cricket, baseball needed no immaculate conception to become a popular American field sport. By the 1840s various forms of baseball vied for acceptance, including the popular Massachusetts and New York versions of the game. The Massachusetts game utilized an irregular four-sided field of play, with the four bases located at fixed, asymmetrical distances from each other and the "striker's," or batter's position away from the home base. "Scouts," or fielders, put men out by fielding a batted ball on the fly or on the first bounce, or by hitting a runner with a thrown ball. But this lively version of the game was overshadowed in the late 1840s by the "New York game," a popular version of which was devised by the members of the New York Knickerbocker Club. Organized in 1845 by a band of aspiring gentlemen and baseball enthusiasts, the Knickerbocker version was devised by one of their members, Alexander J. Cartwright. Cartwright prescribed a diamond-shaped infield with bases at ninety feet apart, a standard which has stood the test of time. The pitching distance was set at forty-five feet from the home base, and a pitcher was required to "pitch" a ball in a stiff-armed, underhanded fashion. The three-strikes-are-out rule was adopted, and a batter could also be put out by a fielder catching a batted ball in the air, or on the first bounce, or by throwing a fielded ball to the first baseman before the runner arrived. Other innovations included the nine-man team and three outs ending a team's batting in their half of an inning. Thus Cartwright's version of baseball became the basis of the game as presently played. Over the years, other innovations were added, including the nine-inning standard for games, changes in the pitching distance, and so on.

Once it was published and propagated by the Knickerbockers, the "New York game" was speedily adopted by other baseball clubs that sprang up in the New York City area and in other towns and cities of antebellum America.

In the 1850s the rise of baseball clubs and team competition helped to meet the recreational needs of Americans who were caught up in an increasingly urban and industrial society. By the 1860s one of every six Americans lived in towns or cities, and by then newspapers were covering games and noting the booming popularity of baseball. Mostly a northern and midwestern phenomenon, baseball fever ran highest in the New York City area, where in the 1850s games were being played "on every available green plot within a ten-mile circuit of the city." Spearheading the baseball boom were formally organized clubs with officers, clubhouses and playing grounds. Among the many clubs, the Knickerbockers sought to rule the game by posing as arbiters of play, rules, and decorum. Since no leagues or playing schedules existed, formal games in the 1850s were arranged by correspondence between club secretaries. The lordly Knickerbockers resisted such overtures, preferring to play among themselves, yet insisting on their preeminence over all other clubs. But the dynamic American game was not to be bound by gentlemanly monopolists or by arbitrary codes of amateurism. By the end of the 1850s, victories and the prospect of gate receipts were becoming more important factors. As more clubs embraced these goals, greater emphasis was placed on obtaining good players at whatever affronts to amateur standards.

In 1858 the Knickerbockers were dethroned as would-be overlords of baseball by the newly organized National Association of Base Ball Players. That year, representatives of twenty-five clubs formed the Association for the ostensible purpose of codifying rules and establishing guidelines for organized clubs and team competition. But the Association speedily established itself as the new arbiter of the game. Among its early rulings were the establishment of a pitcher's box and the standardization of the nine-inning game. The Association also approved the practice of charging paid admissions at games and that year saw 1,500 spectators pay 50¢ each to watch a game played between Brooklyn and New York "all-star" teams. Although the Association established no league or formal playing schedules, its authority was accepted and it lasted until 1871, when it was replaced by a lame organization called the National Association of Amateur Base Ball Players—to differentiate it from the newly founded National Association of Professional Base Ball Players. Meanwhile, by 1860 some sixty clubs had joined the first National Association; mostly they came from the East and Midwest, but a sprinkling of college teams was included. By then, the mounting hostilities between the North and South account for the absence of southern clubs.

American baseball's popularity was at high tide when the Civil War broke out, but the South was excluded from major league baseball competition for many years. Indeed, one of the smaller legacies of the war between the states was major league baseball's east-west alignment of its franchises. And yet the war, which claimed 600,000 American lives, also popularized the game in all sections of the country, as soldiers in both armies played the game in camps and in prison compounds. This infusion of interest in the game set the stage for an even greater baseball boom which swept the North in the immediate postwar era.

Meanwhile, as the war raged toward its conclusion, baseball's popularity diminished for a time on the northern home front. Still, strong teams like the Brooklyn Excelsiors, the Brooklyn Eckfords, and the Brooklyn Atlantics delighted fans by their spirited competition. At the time, pitcher Jim Creighton of the Excelsiors became a popular hero by leading his team on a victorious eastern tour in 1860. In 1862 and 1863 the Eckfords laid claim to being America's best team, and the Brooklyn Atlantics, led by Dickey Pearce, boasted consecutive unbeaten seasons in 1864 and 1865.

The game's popularity among returning soldiers helped to inspire a major baseball boom in post–Civil War America. By 1865 the game was widely touted as America's "national game," and its growing popularity was evidenced by the proliferation of organized clubs. In 1865, ninety-one clubs had joined the Association; the following year membership swelled to nearly two hundred; and 1867 saw more than three hundred clubs enrolled, including more than a hundred from midwestern towns and cities. At their own expense, the powerful Washington Nationals embarked on an unprecedented midwestern tour in 1867; they were beaten in one game by the previously unheralded Rockford (Illinois) Forest City nine. Although the Nationals' tour suggested that some type of organized competition was needed, it failed to produce such reforms as an organized league or a fixed playing schedule. However, editor Frank Queen of the *New York Clipper*, a popular sporting journal, hit upon the idea of giving gold awards annually to the best team and the nine best players. But such judgments were arbitrary and inadequate. Meanwhile, the style of play continued to improve in the late 1860s. Pitchers became more than passive servers as one of them, Arthur "Candy" Cummings, popularized a wrist-twisting, curved-ball delivery. Moreover, fielders became more mobile, baserunners took to sliding to avoid fielders' tags, and a rule change outlawed the one-bounce-and-out catch.

But baseball's dynamic postwar growth also confronted the shaky National Association with vexing problems. Rampant commercialism was one of them. As more clubs charged admission to games, many took to dividing receipts among the players. This trend swelled the ranks of "professional" players, whose presence posed a serious threat to the Association's amateur code. In 1863 Association leaders debated the problem, but vacillated by grudgingly allowing professionals to retain their memberships. The following year the Association defined a professional player as one who "plays base ball for money, place, or emolument." The definition embraced many players, some of whom drew straight salaries, or shared gate receipts, or occupied jobs that were awarded as a subterfuge to conceal their ball-playing activities. What's more, some of the professionals were jumping their contracts for better offers from other clubs. Dubbed "revolvers," they posed a major threat to the shaky authority of the National Association.

The Cincinnati Reds of 1869

By the late 1860s baseball was becoming more of a business, and playing competitive baseball was becoming a recognized career. As baseball writer Henry Chadwick observed in 1868, a new rank ordering among ball players was evidenced by the makeup of the Brooklyn Atlantics club. At the top was the club's elite professional team, followed by the club's amateur nine, with the lowly "muffins," or third-rate players, at the bottom. As baseball clubs came to be dominated by professional interests, some clubs financed their operations by selling stock shares and becoming joint stock companies, while others, which depended on shared gate receipts, operated as "cooperative nines."

Until 1869 the professional movement in baseball was mainly a covert trend, but in that year the Cincinnati Red Stocking club boldly announced its intention of fielding an all-salaried team which would compete against the top teams in the land. This forthright move was the brainchild of club president Aaron B. Champion, a Cincinnati businessman and local booster. The Reds were not the first professional team, nor the first all-salaried team, nor the first team to go undefeated over a season. But as the first openly announced all-salaried team, the Reds, led by player-manager Harry Wright, who became known as the "Father of Professional Baseball," toured the country in 1869, winning some 60 games without a loss. The following year, the well-drilled Reds won another 24 before losing in June to the host Brooklyn Atlantics by an 8–7 score in eleven innings. Although the Reds' effort was financially unremunerative to its stockholders, who voted to return to amateur play after the 1870 season, the experiment inspired an enduring myth that professional baseball in America arose out of this episode. In truth the professional movement was already strongly entrenched. But the Reds' example inspired imitators and brought the smouldering amateur-professional controversy to a head. Thus when the National Association, at its annual meeting in 1870, sought to curb the professional movement, the professional delegates withdrew and formed their own organization in March 1871. This successful coup stunned the amateur National Association, which never recovered and died in 1874. It also marked the beginning of major league baseball in America. From 1871 to the present day, most changes in American baseball rules and style of play would be inspired by the professional major leagues.

The First Major League: The National Association of Professional Base Ball Players

America's first professional baseball league, the National Association of Professional Base Ball Players, was also the first major league. In its ranks were the strongest teams and the best players. The players controlled the league and enjoyed full freedom of contract and movement. Financial support came to those clubs whose stockholders or investors derived more prestige than monetary rewards from their sponsorship. And in this artist-patron relationship, player salaries had a higher priority than investor profits.

The National Association was created by a single evening's work on March 17, 1871. Structurally the league resembled the old amateur National Association, whose constitution was modified to serve professional interests and whose playing rules were adopted. Admission to the professional league required the payment of a ten-dollar entry fee, in stark contrast to the multimillion-dollar price tag now placed on a major league franchise. Like its predecessor, the professional National Association lacked a fixed schedule of games; each team was expected to play each rival five times in a season, with playing dates to be arranged by secretarial correspondence. The championship pennant was awarded to the team with the most victories, and a championship committee was empowered to rule on any disputed claims.

Although the National Association dominated organized baseball in 1871–1875, its structural defects portended its coming demise. The player-run organization wielded little control over players or teams. The easy admission policy made for a chronic dropout problem as disenchanted teams found it easy to turn their backs on ten dollars. Because of the absence of a fixed playing schedule, few contending teams played their required quota of games. Disputes over officiating stemmed from a reliance on volunteer umpires. Teams also quarreled over ticket pricing and the division of gate receipts. Indeed, most teams lost money, and such losses fueled the tension between players and investors. Critics accused the player-controlled league of failing to discipline players, especially the contract jumpers, drunkards, and alleged game fixers. Unresolved problems like these sowed the seeds of the league's eventual collapse, but while it lasted, the National Association also provided spectators with a sprightly brand of baseball.

Campaigns of the National Association, 1871–1875

The Association's 1871 campaign featured an exciting three-way battle between the Chicago White Stockings, Philadelphia Athletics, and Harry Wright's Boston Red Stockings. The Chicago team, which was housed in a new 7,000-seat wooden park and which boasted a $4,500 salaried star among its players, set a fast pace until the city's tragic fire destroyed the park. Forced to play their remaining games on the road, the White Stockings finished third and dropped out of the league until 1874. At the season's end, the Athletics and Red Stockings each had won 22 games, but the championship committee awarded the pennant to the Athletics, who had fewer losses. Harry Wright's plea that his Boston Reds had come closer to meeting their scheduled obligations was disallowed. Thus in spite of continuing controversy and a devastating fire, the National Association enjoyed an auspicious debut. Most clubs profited, and only one dropped out of the race. At the Association's annual meeting, the professionals tightened their hold on the league by electing one of their own, Bob Ferguson of the Brooklyn Atlantics, to serve as president.

Eleven clubs entered the lists for the 1872 campaign, but hopes for a wide-open race were crushed by Harry Wright's powerful Boston team, which rolled to the championship on a 39–8 record. Stocked with stars like pitcher Al Spalding, infielder Ross Barnes (whose bunting prowess permitted him to take maximum advantage of the then-prevailing fair-foul hitting rule), and shortstop George Wright, the Red Stockings won the first of four consecutive pennants. They were the first of many powerful major league dynasties to come—a phenomenon which, over the course of major league baseball history, consistently made a mockery of the idea of competitive balance.

With nine teams competing in 1873, the Reds won a second pennant by staging a late-season drive to overtake the front-running Philadelphia "Phillies," or "Whites." Two Boston newcomers, catcher Jim White and outfielder Jim O'Rourke, contributed to the Reds' 43–16 winning gait. Although overall league revenues were disappointing, only one club dropped from contention during the course of the season.

In 1874, Wright's Reds posted a 52–18 record, to lap the New York Mutuals by 7½ games. That year Wright's team was the only one to play its full schedule of games, an impressive feat considering that Wright's team, in company with the Philadelphia Athletics, embarked upon a six-week baseball tour of Britain in hopes of persuading English sportsmen to adopt America's "national game." Like this first baseball mission, the Association's 1874 season was a financial bust. Although only one club dropped out of the race, accusations of gambling and fixed games clouded the league's reputation.

The 1875 season was the last campaign of the National Association. Thirteen teams entered the fray, but Boston's juggernaut, headed by Spalding, Barnes, O'Rourke, White, and George Wright, buried all rivals. With four Boston men topping the league's hitters, the Reds posted a 71–8 record to finish 15 games up on their nearest pursuers. Of the thirteen contenders, seven failed to finish the 1875 season.

Now in full disarray, the sullied National Association reeled under problems of competitive imbalance, financial losses, and excessive player freedom. The time was ripe for a reformist coup, and a new breed of club directors, headed by William A. Hulbert of the Chicago White Stockings, moved to raise a rival major league that would better serve the interests of the club owners.

But the pioneering National Association was by no means a failure. For all its weaknesses, the Association had popularized professional baseball. Supporters like Henry Chadwick, the innovative sportswriter who now wore the title of "Father of Base Ball," publicized the league by his coverage of games and by his statistics-laden guidebooks. Chadwick's game coverage provided detailed accounts of games with box scores, including a lasting version which he devised in 1876. Such coverage enhanced the game's popularity and inspired widespread coverage by leading newspapers. Chadwick also served on the Association's rules committee, which approved a pitching change that allowed the underhanded pitchers to utilize wrist-snapping curveballs. But Chadwick's quixotic proposal to make baseball a ten-man game failed.

The Association's most solid innovator was Harry Wright, who set high standards for professional promotion. Wright's Boston payroll was baseball's highest until the early 1880s. As Boston's manager, Wright presided over a $35,000 annual budget and dealt creatively with such problems as proper groundskeeping, equipment design and procurement, advertising, and the recruiting and training of players. Wright's mastery paid off in his team's astonishing success. He was honored in these years as the "Father of Professional Base Ball," and his envious colleagues also referred to the National Association as "Harry Wright's League."

The First Stable Major League: The National League, 1876–1879

President William A. Hulbert of the Chicago White Stockings was the driving force behind the coup that dethroned the National Association. Determined to field a strong team in Chicago, Hulbert in 1875 signed Boston pitcher Al Spalding to play with Chicago the following season, along with three other Boston stars: Ross Barnes, Jim White, and Cal McVey. Hulbert also signed Adrian Anson of the Athletics, who later became Chicago's longtime player-manager and the first major league hitter to notch over 3,000 hits.

Fearing possible reprisals from the player-run National Association, Hulbert moved to create a new league run by business-minded club investors. Backed by representatives from the St. Louis, Louisville, and Cincinnati clubs, Hulbert met with representatives of several eastern clubs—New York, Philadelphia, Boston, and Hartford—in February 1876. Out of this meeting came the National League of Professional Base Ball Clubs. The first permanent major league embraced Hulbert's thirteen-point plan of organization. In keeping with its title, the league emphasized the interests of member clubs over those of the players. Admitted as members were well-financed, joint-stock company clubs, each of which paid annual dues of $100 which were used to finance the league administrative body's handling of disputes, recordkeeping, and officiating fees. The latter expense went for a staff of umpires, each to be paid $5 a game.

The eight charter clubs of the new National League were aligned on an east-west basis, and each team was granted a monopoly over its territory. For the 1876 season, each team agreed to play each rival ten times, with expulsion from the league the penalty for failing to do so. Adopting a high moral stance, NL leaders ordered member clubs to ban gambling, liquor sales, and Sunday games, and to draw up tightly written contracts aimed at preventing players from "revolving." For the players this was tough medicine, but with the strongest teams enrolled in the new league, there was little to do but submit. Indeed, the National Association never survived the NL coup and collapsed in 1876.

As the "Father of the National League," Hulbert presided over its fortunes from 1877 until his death in 1882. However, this most powerful of NL presidents to date owed much to his chief lieutenant, Al Spalding, who retired from the field to become the NL's most powerful advocate and defender. As a reward for his loyal support, Spalding's fledgling sporting goods company received the contract to supply the league's balls and to publish its annual guidebook. Beginning in 1877, Chadwick became the perennial editor of the league's official *Spalding Guide*.

Although its debut was auspicious, the NL's first four campaigns were marred by flagging profits, a major scandal, and opposition from a strong rival in the International Association. In 1876 Spalding pitched and managed the Chicago White Stockings to a 52–14 record, topping their closest pursuer by six games. Because of this runaway, attendance tailed off, prompting two teams, the Philadelphia Athletics and New York Mutuals, to forgo playing their final games in the west. For this breach of rules,

Hulbert expelled the pair, thereby depriving the NL of franchises in the populous Philadelphia and New York areas until 1883. However, Hulbert made no effort to replace the two; hence only six teams took the field in 1877, the year the NL adopted a formal schedule of games. Spalding's decision to quit pitching that year dashed Chicago's hopes, but Louisville's hopes ran high until late in the season, when Wright's Boston Reds overtook them and won by seven games. But revelations that gamblers had bribed four Louisville players to lose key games marred Boston's victory. Faced with a major crisis, Hulbert responded by banishing the four players (Jim Devlin, George Hall, William Craver, and Al Nichols) for life. In the wake of the scandal, Louisville dropped from the league, followed by Hartford and St. Louis. To replace them, Indianapolis, Milwaukee, and Providence clubs joined the league. Meanwhile the NL also faced strong competition from the rival International Association. A loose league of mostly cooperative (gate-receipt-sharing) teams, the International Association threat prompted NL leaders to form a "League Alliance" of independent teams. By paying fees of ten dollars a year, League Alliance teams won the right to play exhibitions with NL teams, and the NL also pledged to honor their territorial rights and player contracts.

The hard-pressed NL suffered another profitless season in 1878, with Boston winning a second pennant by four games over Cincinnati. Still challenged by the International Association, the NL retaliated by raiding the circuit's teams and playing rosters. Over the winter of 1878–1879, Syracuse and Buffalo were persuaded to quit the Association for memberships in the NL, while Milwaukee and Indianapolis were dropped from the NL. Troy and Cleveland were also admitted to bring the number of NL teams back to its original eight. Such tactics undermined the International Association, which fielded an enfeebled minor league called the National Association in 1879.

In returning to an eight-team format in 1879, NL teams imposed rigid austerity measures. Among them, salaries were slashed and players compelled to buy their own uniforms and share the costs of meals. Moreover, player mobility was limited by the adherence to a reserve clause in player contracts. Limited to five players per team in 1879, by 1883 the reserve system was applied to most player contracts. Thereafter the reserve clause became a major bone of contention between owners and players. Meanwhile Providence won the 1879 pennant race; managed by George Wright and paced by John M. Ward's pitching, the Providence Grays won by 5 games over Wright's Boston Reds.

Major League Baseball's Golden Age, 1880–1889

As the decade of the 1880s dawned, major league baseball was only a pale reflection of the enormously popular spectacle that it would soon become. In 1880 the NL reigned supreme, but the league's financial performance was dismal. Thus far no NL club had matched the profits of Wright's 1875 Boston Reds, player salaries barely exceeded those of the 1869 Cincinnati Reds, annual membership changes underscored the league's instability, and

the NL was unrepresented in the populous New York and Philadelphia areas.

At this point, however, a powerful stimulus came from the nation's booming economic and urban growth, and professional baseball expanded vigorously. The first to prosper was the NL, but its rising fortunes inspired rivals like the American Association (AA), which was recognized as a major league under the 1883 National Agreement. The following year another rival, the Union Association, vied for major league status, but the NL and AA joined forces to crush the pretender and maintain the dual major league system. The dual major league system lasted from 1883 to 1891, when it was replaced by a single major league. But in its heyday the dual major league system, with its annual World Series competition between the two leagues, proved to be popular and profitable. By 1889 leading clubs from both circuits counted annual profits of over $100,000. While most of the profits went to club owners, player salaries increased, averaging $2,000 a season, with a few stars getting as much as $5,000. Such gains by players were modest enough, but club owners still sought to limit player salaries. In opposing salary ceilings, players banded together under the Brotherhood of Professional Base Ball Players, which also opposed the unwritten reserve clause, unreasonable fines, and the sale of players from one club to another. In this decade the NL's Chicago team received $10,000 apiece from the sale of "King" Kelly and John Clarkson to the Boston club.

The prosperity of the major league game was further evidenced by the expanded seasonal playing schedule. From 84 games a season in 1880 the NL increased its schedule to 132 games by 1889, while the AA upped its seasonal schedule to 140 games in 1889. To accommodate growing numbers of fans, including the 2 million who attended major league games in 1889, clubs erected new wooden parks with double-decked stands. To serve them, concessionaire Harry M. Stevens introduced the now classic baseball lunch of hot dogs, soda pop, and peanuts. And to sate the public's hunger for baseball news, daily newspapers expanded their coverage of games, and two weekly journals devoted to baseball—*Sporting Life* and *The Sporting News*—sprang to vigorous life in this decade. Moreover, at the peak of baseball's popularity, Spalding dispatched, in 1888–1889, two major league squads on a world tour in hopes of spreading the American game to other lands.

If Spalding's mission fell short of its goal abroad, at home the professional game was spreading to all corners of the land. In 1889 some 15 minor leagues were operating. Under the National Agreement of 1883, and its subsequent revisions, minor leagues were recognized as a part of organized baseball. Territorial rights and player rosters of such teams were protected by the major leagues. But black players and teams were increasingly excluded from organized baseball. In the past, gentlemen's agreements barred black teams from the amateur National Association and the professional National Association. At this time a few blacks played briefly in the major AA and in some minor leagues, but the presence of the segregated Negro league in Pennsylvania, in 1889, plus the existence of all-black independent professional teams, signaled the trend toward segregation of black players from organized baseball. Not until 1946 would the color barrier be lifted.

In this dynamic golden age, professional baseball's maturation as a field sport was speeded by a rash of rule changes. In 1881 the pitching distance was extended to fifty feet; in 1884 overhand pitching was legalized; in 1887 a uniform strike zone was established; in 1888 the three-strikes rule and in 1889 the four-balls rule were permanently adopted. These and other changes in playing rules resulted from pragmatic experiments by major league rules committees, whose constant tinkerings kept the game in a state of flux. Some short-lived changes, like the 1887 rule scoring bases on balls as hits and employing a modified four-strike rule, aimed at correcting the pitching-batting imbalance. But these quixotic rules inflated batting averages and produced sixteen .400 hitters before they were discarded at the close of the 1887 season.

NL Campaigns of the 1880s

As the sole major league in 1880, the NL saw its fortunes rise with those of the Chicago dynasty. Winners of three consecutive pennants over the years 1880–1882, the Chicago team was led by player-manager Cap Anson, a popular hero and the leading hitter of the nineteenth century. Fielding a nucleus of stars, including colorful Mike "King" Kelly, pitchers Larry Corcoran and Fred Goldsmith, and catcher Frank "Silver" Flint, Chicago topped Providence by 15 games in 1880, by nine games in 1881, and by three games in 1882. In an unofficial postseason encounter with the rival American Association's Cincinnati champs, the two teams split a pair of games before AA officials canceled this 1882 harbinger of the World Series.

The rise of the AA threatened the dominant NL, which was left leaderless by Hulbert's death in 1882. At Spalding's suggestion, A. G. Mills was elected president. That fall the NL strengthened its position by dropping Troy and Worcester and planting teams in New York and Philadelphia. The NL playing schedule was increased to 98 games.

In the hotly contested 1883 race, Boston ended Chicago's reign by edging Anson's team by four games. That fall Mills ended the AA war by negotiating the National Agreement of 1883, which conceded major league status to the rival AA. Under the agreement, the AA adopted the reserve clause, the two leagues ceased raiding each other's players, and postseason World Series play between the two leagues was accepted. The agreement provided for major league control over lower levels of professional baseball by recognizing the territorial rights of minor league signatories. With frequent changes, this National Agreement remained in force until the American Association war of 1891.

In 1884 the two major leagues faced competition from another major league aspirant. To combat this Union Association incursion, the NL and AA extended reserve coverage to all players and upped their playing schedules to 112 games. The surfeit of major league games contributed to lower attendance for all three embattled leagues, but the Union Association suffered more and was driven out. Least damaged was the NL, whose sprightly 1884 campaign saw pitcher Charles "Old Hoss" Radbourn employ the new rule legalizing overhand pitching with telling effect. Radbourn won 60 games to lead Providence to

10½-game victory over runner-up Boston. And in the first officially sanctioned World Series, Radbourn defeated the AA champion Mets in three straight games.

The following year Anson's White Stockings regained the heights as they won the first of two consecutive pennants. With ace pitcher John Clarkson winning 53 games, Chicago held off the New York Giants by two games to land the 1885 NL pennant. The Giants' surge owed to a piece of skullduggery by its owner. Having acquired a financial interest in the AA New York Mets, the Giants plucked ace pitcher Tim Keefe from them, and Keefe won 32 games for the Giants in 1885. Such trickery by the NL now had AA leaders wary of their rival, but in the World Series of 1885 AA prestige rose when the St. Louis Browns tied the powerful Chicagoans, and it soared further in 1886, when the Browns defeated Chicago in the $15,000 winner-take-all World Series of that year. The loss blighted Chicago's gritty 2½-game victory over Detroit in the 1886 NL campaign. Following the loss, Spalding sold King Kelly to Boston for $10,000. The sale electrified baseball fans, but it also signaled the end of the Chicago dynasty.

In the memorable 1887 campaign, Detroit won the pennant by 3½ games over the Philadelphia Phillies. Wildly inflated batting averages resulted from rule changes that modified the third-strike rule and scored bases on balls as hits. Detroit feasted under the new rules as Sam Thompson and the "big four" of Dan Brouthers, Jack Rowe, Hardie Richardson, and Jim White keyed a league-leading .343 (.299 when adjusted for that year's counting of walks as hits) team batting average. In World Series play, Detroit thrashed the Browns, winning ten of the fifteen games. That fall the rules committee scuttled the average-inflating rules and the NL increased its playing schedule to 132 games.

As Detroit faded, the New York Giants captured the next two NL pennants. Managed by Jim Mutrie and captained by John Ward, the well-balanced Giants defeated Chicago by 9 games and humbled the Browns in the 1888 World Series. The following year the Giants repeated, edging Boston by a single game and then trouncing the Brooklyn Bridegrooms in the World Series.

The profitable 1889 season marked the passing of the first golden age in major baseball history. Over the next two seasons the NL fought two costly interleague wars that overshadowed the pennant races. In 1890, as the NL battled the serious challenge of the Players League, the Brooklyn Bridegrooms, who were enticed to jump the AA for the NL, won by 6½ games over Anson's Chicago Colts. And in 1891, as the NL battled the AA, manager Frank Selee's Boston Bean-eaters defeated Chicago by 3½ games. By then the interleague wars had ended with the NL the victor in both frays. Thus as the 1892 season dawned, the NL once again reigned supreme over major league baseball.

Rival Major Leagues of the 1880s: American and Union Associations and Players League

The NL's most formidable nineteenth-century rival, the American Association of Base Ball Clubs, was organized by promoters who opposed the NL's monopoly. In wooing prospective clubs, the AA promoters saw an opportunity: New York, Philadelphia, Cincinnati, and St. Louis were good baseball cities that were not represented in the league. They also established a basic 25¢ admission price and allowed member clubs the option of selling booze and playing Sunday games. To entice good players, the AA promoters rejected the NL's reserve clause; and to ensure orderly play, a salaried corps of umpires was hired—an innovation soon imitated by the NL.

In its maiden season of 1882, the AA's six teams (Cincinnati, Louisville, St. Louis, Pittsburgh, Philadelphia, and Baltimore) prospered. All six finished the season, with Cincinnati winning the pennant by 11½ games over Philadelphia. Emergent stars of the AA included pitcher Will White and second baseman Bid McPhee of Cincinnati, first baseman Charles Comiskey of St. Louis, and outfielder Pete Browning and pitcher Tony Mullane of Louisville among the contenders.

In 1883 the AA expanded to eight clubs by adding Columbus and the New York Mets. By opposing the NL's reserve clause, the AA lured a number of disgruntled NL players into its ranks. Thus strengthened, the AA staged another profitable campaign, which saw the Philadelphia Athletics edge the St. Louis Browns by a single game. The AA's sprightly season prompted the NL to accommodate its rival. That fall NL president Mills and AA president Denny McKnight negotiated the National Agreement of 1883, which recognized the AA as a major league and instituted World Series play between the two leagues. For its part, the AA adopted the reserve clause.

The agreement between the NL and AA was barely concluded when a new league made a bid for major league recognition. The rival Union Association of Base Ball Clubs was organized in Pittsburgh in the fall of 1883. To entice players from the established majors, the UA leaders proclaimed their opposition to the reserve clause. A few major league players jumped to the new league, but most remained with the clubs out of fear of blacklisting, or in some cases because they were bought off by salary increases. With mostly unknown players in their ranks, the eight-team UA commenced playing a 128-game schedule in 1884. From the start the league suffered from unbalanced funding and talent distribution. The UA's principal backer, Henry V. Lucas, poured most of his money into his St. Louis Maroons, a team which won its first twenty-one games and made a shambles of the pennant race. Plagued by financial losses, only five charter teams survived the campaign. Nevertheless, the UA drained attendance from the established majors—especially the AA, which unwisely expanded to counter the threat. In the fall of 1884, the UA folded when Lucas accepted an offer to enroll his St. Louis Maroons in the NL.

The collapse of the UA left the dual major league system intact, but relations between the NL and AA were strained. AA leaders accused their NL allies of duplicity for persuading the AA to expand to twelve teams to counter the UA's incursion. As a result the AA suffered heavier financial losses in its 1884 campaign, which the New York Mets won by 6½ games over Columbus. The Mets' victory was soured by their loss to Providence in the first officially sanctioned World Series. But even more damaging to the AA was the revelation the the Mets had come under the ownership of the NL New York Giants. Moreover, AA suspicions of NL duplicity were heightened by the UA peace settlement which brought the St. Louis Maroons into the NL, where they competed directly with the AA's St. Louis Browns.

As it turned out, the Maroons were no match for the Browns, whose profitable formula of cheap baseball, liquor sales, sideshows, Sunday games, and winning baseball was making a folk hero of the Browns' colorful president, Chris Von der Ahe. Beginning in 1885, player-manager Charles Comiskey led his team to four consecutive AA pennants. In 1885 the Browns won by 16 games over Cincinnati; in 1886, by 12 over Pittsburgh; in 1887, by 14 over Cincinnati; and in 1888, by 6½ over a beefed-up Brooklyn team. Star players like infielder Arlie Latham, outfielder Tip O'Neill, and pitchers Dave Foutz and Bob Caruthers paced the Browns to the first three pennants. Then, when Von der Ahe sold Foutz and Caruthers to Brooklyn in 1888, Comiskey came up with pitcher Silver King, whose 45 victories helped land a fourth consecutive pennant. In World Series play the Browns tied Chicago in 1885 and defeated Anson's team in 1886. But the team was drubbed by Detroit in 1887 and by the Giants in 1888.

Bitter rivalry between the Browns and Brooklyn Bridegrooms dominated the 1889 race, which ended with the Bridegrooms on top of the Browns by 2 games. But the Bridegrooms lost to the Giants in World Series play. Over the winter the St. Louis and Brooklyn factions battled over the choice of a new AA president, and in the stormy aftermath Brooklyn and Cincinnati joined the National League. The loss of these clubs, together with the loss of key players to the newly organized Players' League, crippled the AA. Forced to field weak teams in 1890, the AA ran a poor third to the NL and the Players' League. The AA's dismal race was won by Louisville, which only the year before had finished dead last in the AA with a 27–111 record.

The Players League War of 1890

The Players League of 1890 arose out of the long smoldering hostilities between major league players and owners, dating back to the NL seizure of power in 1876. Under NL control, players lost money and freedom of movement, and were subjected to harsh disciplinary codes backed by threats of expulsion and blacklisting. To the list of player grievances was added the reserve clause in player contracts, which players viewed as a device for lowering salaries and a denial of one's right to sell his services to the highest bidder. For their part, owners credited the clause for stabilizing teams and increasing profits. Although legal challenges sustained the players' position, such victories were too limited to overturn the reserve clause. Nor were players helped when rival leagues attacked the clause because the AA soon embraced the clause and the UA was driven out of business. Frustrated on these fronts, in 1885 the players resorted to collective action by forming the Brotherhood of Professional Base Ball Players. Initially organized as a benevolent association, the Brotherhood, under the leadership of star player and lawyer John Ward, became a collective-bargaining agency by 1887. In confronting the major league owners, the Brotherhood sought redress on such matters as the reserve clause, the sale of players, and the

threatened salary ceiling, known as the Brush classification plan.

In 1888 protracted negotiations between the Brotherhood and the owners broke down when the NL owners
refused to budge on the salary ceiling issue, which had
been accepted by the AA as part of the National Agreement. When the owners rejected Ward's ultimatum on the
key issues, the Brotherhood moved to field a rival major
league in 1890. With most of the best players in the fold,
the Players' League attracted financial backers who accepted Ward's plan of sharing profits and power with the
players. In 1890 the eight-team PL opened play with well-
stocked teams in every NL city except Cincinnati.

Faced with a head-to-head battle for survival, the NL
relied upon its war committee headed by Spalding. Spalding met the PL head-on by scheduling games on the same
dates as PL teams, bribing PL players to jump ranks,
initiating costly lawsuits over the reserve clause, lowering
ticket prices, cajoling press support by threats to withdraw advertising, and raiding the AA and minor league
rosters for players. Loyal managers like Anson, Wright,
Bill McGunnigle, and Jim Mutrie persuaded good players
to stay with the NL. Roster raids on AA teams lured stars
like Billy Hamilton and Tommy Tucker; and promising
rookies like pitchers Kid Nichols and Cy Young, infielder
Bobby Lowe and outfielder Jess Burkett beefed up the
NL teams.

Although beaten in the courts and at the turnstiles by
the PL, which finished its season with Mike Kelly's Boston team beating out Ward's Brooklyn team by 6½ games,
the PL's financial losses were too much for its backers to
bear. In the fall of 1890, the disenchanted PL backers
broke ranks and sued for peace. Magnanimous in victory,
Spalding imposed no reprisals on PL players, but he gave
no ground on the key issues. With the NL girding for war
with the AA in the upcoming 1891 season, the salary
ceiling implementation was delayed until the latest struggle was over.

The collapse of the PL afforded little relief for the
stricken AA. In 1891 all-out war erupted between the NL
and AA over the return of players and the relocation of
franchises. When the AA's weak Cincinnati club folded,
its popular manager Mike Kelly joined the Boston AA
team, but after a few days he joined the Boston Nationals.
With Kelly gone, the Boston AA team won the pennant by
8½ games over the Browns, but Boston fans flocked to
watch Kelly captain the Boston Nationals to the NL
pennant.

The 1891 season was the last for the AA. That fall four
AA clubs, St. Louis, Louisville, Baltimore and Washington, quit the dying circuit to join the expanded twelve-
club National League.

The "Big League": The National League, 1892–1899

The defeat of the AA in 1891 saddled the NL with a
$130,000 debt, which was incurred by buying out four of
the defeated circuit's clubs. The remaining four AA
teams—Baltimore, Louisville, St. Louis, and Washington—were added to the NL to form the twelve-club National League and American Association of Professional

Base Ball Clubs. From 1892 to 1899 this monopolistic
"big league" represented major league baseball. En-
thralled by their newly created baseball "trust," the
league's owners styled themselves as magnates presiding
over a million-dollar entertainment industry. The magnates fully expected their monopoly league to produce
unprecedented cash and glory. But such dreams were
dashed by external factors, including a chronic national
recession, the 1898 war with Spain, and the league's competitive imbalance. Eight seasons of play under the
twelve-club format underscored its imbalance. With Boston, Baltimore, and Brooklyn winning all the races, fans in
other cities lost interest. As profits dwindled, owners imposed a $2,400 ceiling on player salaries and battled one
another over the division of gate receipts. Lacking strong
leadership, each individual owner ran his club like a feudal fiefdom. Indeed, the blustering antics of the owners
often upstaged players in newspaper accounts of this
time. Some magnates hatched grandiose schemes aimed
at making the monopoly league work more efficiently.
Thus Andrew Freedman of the Giants advocated the annual pooling and redistribution of players and profits,
provided that the "strongest and most lucrative franchises" got the best players. And another, Cincinnati
owner John T. Brush, proposed harsh disciplinary measures aimed at curbing rowdy players, while also experi-
menting with minor league farm systems as a cheap
source of talent.

Indeed, owner infighting over these and other issues
damaged the big league's image, but the biggest threat to
the league's credibility was the "syndicate" issue. The
term "syndicatism" used at this time referred to interlocking club ownership schemes. Following bitter debate in
1898, two such interlocking directorates were approved
by the owners. One of these schemes permitted owner
Frank Robison of the Cleveland and St. Louis teams to
transfer his best players to St. Louis; the other allowed
owners Ferdinand Abell and Harry Vonderhorst of the
Brooklyn and Baltimore teams to stock the Brooklyn team
with the pick of those two squads. These operations made
a farce of the 1899 pennant race and prompted the NL to
return to an eight-club format in 1900; the cutback was
accomplished by dropping Cleveland, Baltimore, Washington, and St. Louis from the NL.

The return to the eight-club format ended eight wayward seasons of major league baseball played under one
unwieldy league format. Nevertheless, major league baseball continued to mature in the 1890s. Surprisingly
enough, there were no franchise changes in these years. In
1898 the 154-game playing schedule was introduced, a
format which dominated until 1961. And in 1893 a major
change in playing rules fixed the pitching distance at
60′6″ from home plate and also replaced the pitching box
with a rubber slab atop a mound. This permanent change
was introduced that year to correct the pitching-batting
imbalance, a desirable goal which to this day remains
elusive. The immediate effect of the lengthened pitching
distance was not to give a mild boost to batting averages,
but to send them soaring.

Thus in 1894 the Phillies posted a .349 team batting
average, with the four-man outfield of Ed Delahanty, Sam
Thompson, Billy Hamilton, and Tuck Turner combining
for a .400-plus batting average. Sluggers also prospered,

as Thompson hit 129 homers in this era, and Washington outfielder Buck Freeman hit 25 homers in 1899; both these records endured for twenty years. (Later recounts gave the career record to Roger Connor and the single season mark to Ned Williamson who had 27 tainted homers in 1884.) It took pitchers several seasons to adapt to the increased distance, but they did so by developing curves, changeups, and ball-doctoring trick deliveries to go with their fastballs. Meanwhile two offensive styles vied for acceptance in this era. For a brief time the "manly slugging" style feasted on pitchers, but the "scientific style" mastered by the Baltimore and Boston teams, which stressed bunting, stealing, sacrificing, and the hit-and-run, became the dominant offensive style of the next twenty years.

At this time other rule changes allowed player substitutions, established the infield fly rule, treated foul bunts as strikes, defined sacrifice flies and bunts, and introduced the pentagon-shaped home plate. On the playing fields, players wore stylized uniforms and most sported gloves, with catchers employing the big "Decker" mitt and wearing masks and chest protectors. When in action, teams played heady ball, using signals to trigger offensive and defensive movements. Defensively, infielders aligned themselves to turn double plays and outfielders coordinated their play by using backups, cutoffs and relays. Offensively, bunting, sacrificing, sliding, stealing, and hit-and-run plays were familiar tactics. But when teams like the Baltimore Orioles and Cleveland Spiders augmented their play with roughhouse tactics like spiking and jostling runners, baiting umpires, and bench jockeying, this "rowdy" brand of ball stirred the ire of reformers like Indianapolis owner John Brush. But hard-nosed baseball survived its critics, as did Sunday baseball. Despite fervent opposition from Sabbatarians, Sunday games were permitted by local option, although eastern cities held out against such games for twenty years. By then, major league clubs had outgrown the wooden parks of this era. A spate of ballpark fires late in this era inspired tougher safety codes that soon prompted the replacement of the vulnerable old wooden parks with concrete-and-steel edifices.

Big League Campaigns: The NL, 1892–1899

During the big league's eight-year existence, pennant monopolizing was the rule as only Boston, Baltimore, and Brooklyn teams won pennants. Managed by Frank Selee, the powerful Boston Beaneaters won back-to-back pennants in 1892–1893 and in 1897–1898. Paced by pitcher Kid Nichols (who won 297 games in this decade), Boston won the 1892 race played under a split-season format. Boston easily won the first half, but lost the second half by 3 games to manager Pat Tebeau's Cleveland Spiders, whose ace pitcher was the great Cy Young. In the postseason playoff, after the two teams played a scoreless tie, Boston swept the rest of the games to land the 1892 pennant.

In 1893 the unprofitable split-season format was dropped and the pitching distance was increased to 60′6″. In a campaign marked by heavy hitting, Boston won by 5 games over Pittsburgh. Pittsburgh's Frank Killen won 34 games to lead hurlers, and outfielder Billy Hamilton batted .380. The following year saw Boston fall to the Baltimore Orioles, who rebounded from an eighth-place finish in 1893 to win the first of three consecutive pennants. Although plagued by poor pitching, the offense-minded Orioles batted .343, with every regular topping the .300 mark at the plate. Future Hall of Famers on this star-studded team included Dan Brouthers, Hugh Jennings, John McGraw, Joe Kelley, Willie Keeler, and Wilbert Robinson. The Orioles won the 1894 pennant by 3 games over the Giants, but lost the first postseason Temple Cup Series, played between the first- and second-place finishers. In this inaugural Temple Cup Series, manager John Ward's Giants swept the Orioles in four straight games.

The following year manager Ned Hanlon's Orioles repeated as NL champions by edging the Cleveland Spiders by 3 games. A .324 team batting average and a brilliant 54–14 home won-loss record keyed the 1895 Orioles. But once again the Orioles failed in Temple Cup play, this time falling to the Spiders by four games to one. In 1896 the Orioles won a third consecutive NL pennant by 9½ games over the Spiders and swept their rivals in postseason Temple Cup play.

Bolstered by newcomers Billy Hamilton, Chick Stahl, and Jimmy Collins, Boston regained the heights in 1897–1898. Nichols won 30 games as the 1897 Beaneaters edged the Orioles by 2 games. But the Orioles won the postseason Temple Cup four games to one, the last year of this unremunerative and "shabby spectacle" which, one observer said, no more resembled the old World Series than a "crabapple does . . . a pippin."

Boston repeated in 1898, in a baseball campaign overshadowed by the Spanish-American War, beating the Orioles by 6 games. But by then the unprofitable "big league" was in its last throes. In a race marred by ludicrous syndicate ventures, in 1899 the Brooklyn Superbas won by 8 games over Boston. A syndicate team, the Superbas were managed by Hanlon, who stocked the Brooklyn team with the best players from the Brooklyn and Baltimore rosters. A similar venture that season had Robison's St. Louis-Cleveland syndicate loading the St. Louis team with the pick of these two clubs. But Robison's venture failed miserably as St. Louis finished fifth while the Cleveland team's 20–134 record was the worst by any major league team playing a 154-game schedule.

In the aftermath of the 1899 campaign, the owners scuttled the twelve-club big league and cut back to eight teams. Baltimore, Cleveland, Washington, and Louisville were dropped at a cost of $100,000, a buyout shared by the eight surviving teams. Born in debt, the monopoly big league died in debt, but the dawning twentieth century soon saw major league baseball prospering under a revived dual league format.

Major League Baseball's Silver Age, 1903–1920

The American League War, 1900–1902

The American League's struggle for major league recognition began in 1900, a propitious time for such an incursion. The NL owners had recently shed four teams, which left many unemployed players and some promising territories. Moreover, NL owners were distracted by an abortive attempt by other outsiders to revive the American Association, and by the NL's prosperous season of 1900. With a hefty boost from the nation's booming economy, most NL teams made money that year. In a close race the Brooklyn Superbas repeated as NL champs by beating a strong Pittsburgh team by 4½ games.

Such distractions favored the cause of the American League schemers. Prior to 1900, the newly proclaimed American League had operated as the Western League, a strong minor league based in the Midwest. Since 1894 the Western League's president, the able, dictatorial, and hard-drinking Byron "Ban" Johnson, had dreamed of making his circuit into a major league. To this end he had battled with NL owners over the drafting of his league's players, a practice which underscored his league's inferior status. Johnson's opportunity to press toward his goal came in 1899, when the NL cut back to eight teams. With the backing of lieutenants like Charles Comiskey and Connie Mack, Johnson renamed his circuit the American League, his clubs snapped up surplus NL players, and Comiskey moved his team to Chicago, where his White Stockings boldly confronted the NL's Cubs. With solid financial backing and a new ballpark, Comiskey's team of major league castoffs and promising youngsters captured the first AL pennant in a profitable campaign.

Emboldened by the AL's successful 1900 campaign, Johnson took note of the expiring National Agreement and unilaterally proclaimed the AL to be a major league. This 1901 declaration formally opened the American League war, and Johnson's promoters commenced hostilities by invading the NL's Philadelphia and Boston territories and occupying the former NL sites of Baltimore, Washington, Cleveland, and Detroit. To stock their teams, Johnson's financiers offered higher salaries to NL players, and in 1901 over a hundred NL players snapped at the bait. The jumpers included a bevy of stars, among them Cy Young, Clark Griffith, Jimmy Collins, and Nap Lajoie. Then, in a hotly contested and profitable pennant race, Comiskey's Chicago team edged Boston by 4 games to capture the 1901 AL pennant.

The timing of the AL's assault was excellent. In 1901–1902 the leaderless NL owners were locked in a bitter struggle over the choice of a league president. Two factions, one headed by owner Andrew Freedman of the Giants and the other by Spalding, battled to a standstill. In 1902 a temporary Control Commission headed the NL, which finally elected Henry Clay Pulliam as its president. In a complicated settlement the controversial Freedman sold his New York Giants interests for $125,000, on the condition that one of his cronies be permitted to plant an AL franchise in New York in 1903. By then, the AL had concluded another profitable season. With more NL players joining AL ranks, Connie Mack's Philadelphia Athletics landed the 1902 AL pennant by beating the Browns by 5 games.

In the fall of 1902, with most war-weary NL owners favoring a return to the dual major league structure, the NL sued for peace with the AL. Early in 1903 Johnson and Comiskey met with Pulliam and Cincinnati owner August "Garry" Herrmann and negotiated the National Agreement of 1903. Under its terms, the NL and AL would operate as separate but equal major leagues, bound by common playing rules, harmonized playing schedules, and mutually recognized territories and player contracts. The player contract accord restored the reserve clause and ended the AL's roster raids. The agreement also allowed an AL franchise to be located in New York, which Johnson secured by moving the financially shaky Baltimore Orioles to Manhattan, where in time the team prospered as the New York Yankees. Among other points, the Agreement reclassified the minor leagues and set new rules for the drafting of minor league players. Indeed, in this era minor league baseball grew lustily, reaching an all-time peak in 1913, when 46 leagues started the season. But if the National Agreement stimulated the growth of organized baseball, it did little to empower major league players. Major league players were denied representation on the controlling National Commission, and over the years 1902–1913 two attempts by players to organize unions were beaten down. And if the National Agreement included no salary ceiling plank, the Agreement unequivocally embraced the reserve clause and asserted the right of the National Commission to control baseball "by its own decrees . . . enforcing them without the aid of law, and [making it] answerable to no power outside its own."

The power to enforce these baseball laws came via a master stroke when the negotiators created a three-member National Commission charged with enforcing the National Agreement and keeping peace between the rival major leagues. As earlier demonstrated by the uneasy coexistence that marked the dual major league system of the 1880s, some such high-level executive and judicial body was needed to settle disputes between two independent and highly competitive major leagues. It was a challenge that the National Commission successfully met for seventeen years.

Heading the National Commission were league presidents Johnson and Pulliam and Cincinnati magnate Garry Herrmann, who served as the Commission's permanent chairman. On the face of it, this gave the NL two votes, but Johnson and Herrmann were close friends. Together they served during the lifetime of the National Commission, while four relatively weak presidents represented the NL, whose owners feared to empower any president. By contrast Johnson reigned as the most powerful president in major league history. As the AL's entrenched "czar," Johnson used his powers to safeguard his league against any NL treachery. In defending his league, Johnson personally held all AL franchise leases, ruled on ownership changes, fixed playing schedules, set basic admission prices, and imposed his standards on owners and players. Inevitably such powers incurred enmities among AL owners, but until the Black Sox Scandal of 1919, Johnson's domination of the AL held firm.

Over the years 1903–1920, with Herrmann's support, Johnson dominated the National Commission. In those years the Commission functioned as baseball's Supreme Court, settling disputes between clubs (mostly involving rights to player services), supporting the interests of club owners, disciplining players, defending umpires, fending off Federal League interlopers, defusing a players' union threat, and overseeing relations with the minor leagues. But the most important achievement of the National Commission was its profitable administration of the revived World Series. Initially revived in 1903, the World

Series got off to a shaky start when the Giants refused to play the AL champion in 1904. But in 1905 the two leagues adopted a new World Series format that placed the conduct of the classic under the control of the National Commission. With 10 percent of World Series revenues set aside for financing National Commission activities, the Commission faced a stern test. By capable administration the Commission met the challenge and the annual World Series became a profitable and permanent part of each major league season. By 1910 profits from World Series games had increased tenfold over those of 1905. But the Commission was responsible for any World Series chicanery; thus the rigged World Series of 1919 precipitated the downfall of the National Commission.

Peace and Prosperity: 1903–1920

By reviving the dual major league system with World Series play, the framers of the National Agreement harked back to the successful format of the golden 1880s. To that profitable format was added a National Commission charged with keeping the peace between the two major leagues. The combination launched the major leagues on a stable course which produced no franchise changes for the next fifty years. In the 1903–1919 era the pattern was set and the two major leagues enjoyed a silver age of popularity and prosperity. In these years the popularity of the national pastime was buoyed by rising attendance, increased media coverage including motion pictures, and the ever-popular song, "Take Me Out to the Ball Game," introduced in 1908. The game's increasing popularity swelled annual profits, but as always these were unevenly distributed. In these years attendance at major league games increased steadily; from 4.7 million in 1903, attendance rose to 10 million in 1911, before falling under the impact of the Federal League incursion and the nation's involvement in the First World War. To house the growing numbers of fans, durable ballparks constructed of concrete and steel were built during the construction boom of 1909–1911. Capable of housing 30,000 or more fans, these parks served until the post–World War Two construction boom. At this time increasing profits boosted player salaries. By 1910 annual salaries ranged from $900 to $12,000, and by 1915 salaries of superstars like Ty Cobb, Tris Speaker, and Walter Johnson approached $20,000.

In this era stability also characterized the style of play. Only a few rule changes were made. Among them, a rule limited the height of pitching mounds to fifteen inches above the baseline level, the infield fly rule was invoked, a foul bunt on a third strike was ruled a strikeout, and earned run averages by pitchers were included in annual records. On the playing fields teams employed the deadball style of play that resembled the "scientific game" of the 1890s. With new balls seldom being introduced into games, pitchers took command, using a variety of deliveries including spitballs and defacing balls with other foreign substances. In this era, earned run averages of 3.00 or below were seasonal norms, and seasonal batting averages, now affected by bigger parks and improved gloves, hovered around the .250 mark. Offensively, teams relied heavily on bunts, hit-and-run tactics, and base stealing to produce a few runs which power pitchers protected.

Not surprisingly, pitching masters like Cy Young, Walter Johnson, Christy Mathewson, Grover Cleveland Alexander, Eddie Plank, and spitball artist Ed Walsh sparkled among the leading stars of this era. But pitted against these dominant hurlers were some of the greatest hitters of all time. The masters of the deadball offense included Detroit's Ty Cobb, who won thirteen AL batting titles while scoring runs and stealing bases at unprecedented rates, and Pittsburgh's Honus Wagner, who won eight NL batting titles and stole 722 bases. Other hitting stars included Eddie Collins, Tris Speaker, Nap Lajoie, Sam Crawford, and the ill-fated Joe Jackson. The decline of the "deadball style" was foreshadowed by the 1910 introduction of the cork-centered ball. When widely used later in the era, it ended the conservative style of offensive play. The transformation was signaled in 1919, when Babe Ruth of the Red Sox hit 29 homers to set a new seasonal homer mark.

By 1919 the stability of the silver age had been undermined by a series of disturbing events. In 1913 interlopers launched the Federal League and vied for major league recognition. That fall President James Gilmore lined up enough wealthy backers to plant Federal League teams in Chicago, Baltimore, Buffalo, Pittsburgh, Indianapolis, Brooklyn, St. Louis, and Kansas City. Over the next two seasons, the "Feds" took to raiding major league rosters with offers of higher salaries. The surfeit of games in 1914 and 1915 lowered major league revenues, but the Federal League invaders suffered more. There were two Federal League campaigns; Indianapolis won the 1914 pennant and Chicago took honors in 1915. The 1915 season was the last gasp of the Feds. Staggered by financial losses, the Feds surrendered when the established majors paid $5 million in compensation and awarded major league franchises to two Federal owners. But an antitrust suit pressed by dissident Baltimore owners against the majors eventually reached the U.S. Supreme Court. In 1922, Justice Oliver Wendell Holmes, speaking for a unanimous court, dismissed the suit and judged major league baseball to be mainly a sport and not a commonly accepted form of interstate commerce. But the 1922 decision was not a definitive ruling, and the major leagues would have to defend the reserve clause against future attacks in the courts and in the Congress of the United States. Nevertheless the FL challenge was the last full-scale incursion by a rival major league against the established majors.

Soon after the Federal League war, major league baseball faced another crisis brought on by America's entry into World War One. In supporting the nation's total war effort, dozens of major league players entered the armed services, and clubs staged patriotic displays, donating money and equipment to troops. For all that, in 1918 the provost marshal ruled major league baseball to be nonessential to the war effort, but his ruling permitted the majors to play a shortened 1918 campaign. That year attendance sank to 3 million, prompting tremulous owners to vote to shorten the 1919 playing schedule. However, to their surprise the war ended, and the attenuated 1919 campaign attracted 6.5 million fans. Caught short by this unexpected boom, officials sought to recoup money by upping the World Series schedule to a best-of-nine-games format.

As it turned out the expanded 1919 World Series precipitated the final crisis that ended the commissioner system. Embittered over their low salaries, eight Chicago White Sox players accepted bribes from gamblers to throw the World Series to the NL champion Cincinnati Reds. When revelations of this "Black Sox Scandal" came to light, it destroyed the National Commission and ended the old National Agreement. Chairman Herrmann resigned early in 1920, and that fall Federal Judge Kenesaw M. Landis was named the game's sole commissioner, an action confirmed by the new National Agreement of 1921. As the autocratic Landis defused the Black Sox Scandal by barring the eight accused Chicago players from organized baseball for life, the major league game lurched into a new golden age of cash and glory.

Deadball Dynasties: The American League, 1903–1920

Over the years 1903–1920, Ban Johnson's "great American League" surpassed its NL rival in attendance and also took an enduring lead over its rival in World Series victories. However, such dominance was not a result of the league's competitive balance; indeed, this dream was never realized in any era of major league history until the early 1980s. In this early phase of AL history, four teams—Boston, Philadelphia, Chicago, and Detroit—dominated all AL pennant races.

The first of the AL minidynasties, the Boston Pilgrims relied in 1903 on the pitching of Cy Young, Bill Dineen, and Tom Hughes to trample the Philadelphia Athletics by 14½ games and then go on to win the first modern World Series over Pittsburgh. The following year Boston repeated, winning a close race by 1½ games over the New York Highlanders. That year manager John McGraw of the Giants refused to meet the Pilgrims in World Series play, but the controversy was resolved over the winter of 1904 with the establishment of a permanent World Series format.

In 1905 manager Connie Mack's Philadelphia Athletics got 87 victories from the pitching corps of Rube Waddell, Eddie Plank, Andy Coakley and Chief Bender, to edge the White Sox by 2 games. But with league-leading pitcher Waddell sidelined by an injury, the A's fell to the Giants in the World Series. As the A's faded in 1906, the most impotent of all pennant winners, the weak-hitting Chicago White Sox, won a close race by 3 games over the Highlanders. In winning, the White Sox batted .230 and scored a mere 570 runs. Yet in World Series play against the Cubs, whose 116 victories were the most ever by a team playing a 154-game schedule, the White Sox prevailed, winning four of the six games.

The next three AL pennants were captured by the Detroit Tigers, the league's most formidable dynasty to date. Managed by Hugh Jennings and powered by outfielders Sam Crawford and Ty Cobb, the latter the Georgia sensation who won the first of a record nine consecutive AL batting titles, the 1907 Tigers defeated Mack's Athletics by 1½ games. The following year the Tigers eked out a half-game win over player-manager Nap Lajoie's Cleveland team, and in 1909 the Tigers held off the Athletics by 3½ games. But in World Series action the Tigers resembled kittens. In 1907 and again in 1908 they fell to the Cubs, and in 1909 they lost to the Pirates. Those three consecutive World Series losses infuriated

AL president Johnson, but four straight AL victories over the years 1910–1913 restored the aplomb of the portly czar. In 1910 Mack's revamped Athletics, newly located in Shibe Park, used the pitching of Plank, Bender, Jack Coombs, and Cy Morgan, and the offensive and defensive skills of his "$100,000 infield" of Stuffy McGinnis, Eddie Collins, Jack Barry, and Frank "Home Run" Baker, to lap the Yankees by 14½ games and topple the Cubs in the World Series. The following year the A's repeated; this time they crushed the Tigers by 13½ games and then beat the Giants in World Series play.

Mack's A's faded to third in 1912, but the renamed Boston Red Sox, now playing in their new Fenway Park, breezed to a 14-game win over the Senators. "Smokey Joe" Wood's 34–5 pitching and Tris Speaker's .383 batting led the Red Sox, who followed their league win with a victory over the Giants in the World Series. With this latest Series, the AL took a lead in this fall competition, which they hold to this day.

The Federal League war was beginning when Mack led his resurgent A's to a 6½-game win over the Senators and another victory over the Giants in the 1913 World Series. In 1914 the Mackmen captured their fourth AL pennant in five years as they outran the Red Sox by 8½ games, but then they lost the World Series to the sweeping "miracle" Boston Braves who had come from last place on July 4 to take the NL flag. That fall, racked by heavy financial losses incurred by the Federal League war, Mack sought to recoup by selling some of his stars. As a result, Mack's emasculated A's spent the next seven seasons in the AL cellar.

As the A's collapsed, the Red Sox and White Sox, both strengthened by player purchases from Mack, monopolized the next five AL races. By purchasing Jack Barry from Mack and snapping up minor league pitcher Babe Ruth, whom Mack had passed over, Boston was the first to cash in. The Red Sox won the 1915 pennant by 2½ games over the Tigers and went on to trounce the Phillies in World Series action. In this the last year of the Federal League war, Boston was one of only seven major league clubs to show a profit. But with the Feds out of the way in 1916, prosperity returned to the major leagues. Despite dealing Speaker to Cleveland, where his .386 batting ended Cobb's skein of nine straight AL batting titles, the Red Sox repeated. Ruth's 23 pitching victories led Boston to a 2-game victory over the White Sox and 5-game victory over the Dodgers in the World Series.

America's entry into the First World War in 1917 sent major league attendance plummeting as manager Clarence "Pants" Rowland drove his White Sox to a 9-game win over Boston. Shine-ball pitcher Eddie Cicotte's 28 victories led all AL hurlers, and Eddie Collins, Joe Jackson, and Happy Felsch supplied the power as the White Sox capped their victory with a win over the Giants in the World Series. But major league profits were low in 1917, and they touched rock bottom the following year, when the war effort forced the majors to cut their playing schedules to 128 games. The Red Sox rebounded to win the 1918 campaign by 2½ games over Cleveland. And by drubbing the Cubs in the World Series, the Red Sox notched their fifth World Series title in as many tries. However, at this point the Red Sox fell victim to their impecunious owner, Harry Frazee, whose player sales soon divested the team of its ablest stars, including Ruth. As the Red Sox faded, so did their record of World Series triumphs. To this day Red Sox fans are still waiting for a sixth World Series victory.

Boston's collapse opened the way for the powerful White Sox to win the shortened 1919 race by 3½ games over the surging Cleveland Indians. In the wake of the White Sox victory came the sordid World Series of 1919, which saw eight Chicago players conspire with gamblers to throw the extended Series to the Cincinnati Reds. In 1920 the much-publicized revelations of that piece of skullduggery forced owner Charles Comiskey to suspend his eight Black Sox players in the last week of the red-hot 1920 pennant campaign.

Stripped of their stars, the White Sox finished second, a game ahead of the Yankees and two games behind the victorious Cleveland Indians. The gritty Indians lost their star shortstop Ray Chapman when he was fatally beaned by pitcher Carl Mays of the Yankees. To the present day, this remains the only fatality in major league history that was the direct result of a playing field accident. In the memorable World Series of 1920, Cleveland and Brooklyn were tied at two games apiece when Indian second-sacker Bill Wambsganss busted a promising Dodger rally by pulling off the first and only unassisted triple play in World Series history. And in that same game Indian outfielder Elmer Smith hit the first World Series grand-slam homerun. Such heroics, plus three pitching victories by Stan Coveleski, boosted the Indians to a five-games-to-two triumph in the 1920 fall classic. Cleveland's victory also ended the Boston, Philadelphia, Chicago pennant monopoly of the AL's deadball era, while Ruth's 59 homers as a Yankee in 1920 heralded the incoming "big-bang" style of play that would characterize the coming decade of the 1920s.

Deadball Dynasties: The National League, 1901–1920

A similar pattern of competitive imbalance also marked the NL campaigns of the silver age. In this era three NL mini-dynasties—those of Pittsburgh, Chicago, and New York — monopolized the first 14 NL campaigns. Moreover, even as outsiders rose up to win three consecutive pennants over the years 1914–1916, the Giants and Cubs came back to win pennants in 1917–1918 before yielding to the Reds and Dodgers in this era's final two campaigns. Of the three monopolists, the Giants were the most dominating team. Under manager John McGraw, "the Napoleonic genius" who jumped the AL in 1902 to skipper the moribund Giants, the New Yorkers won six pennants, finished second eight times, and suffered only one losing season.

In 1901 the first of this dynastic trio, the Pittsburgh Pirates, won the first of three consecutive NL pennants. Pittsburgh's rise began in 1900, the year the NL cut back to eight teams. When his Louisville team was dropped in the NL's cutback, owner Barney Dreyfuss purchased the Pittsburgh club, which he strengthened by adding Louisville stars Fred Clarke and Honus Wagner to his Pirate team. Powered by player-manager Clarke and Wagner, and unscathed by the disastrous roster raids by AL teams that were weakening his opponents, Pittsburgh won the 1901 NL race by 7½ games over the Phillies; they then

won the 1902 race by an awesome 27½ games over runner-up Brooklyn, and captured the 1903 flag by 6½ games over the Giants. In each of these campaigns, both Wagner and Clarke topped the .300 mark in batting. Moreover, Wagner's .355 hitting won the 1903 batting title while outfielder Ginger Beaumont's .357 batting won the 1902 batting title. The Pirate pitching staff was fronted by Deacon Phillippe, who won 66 games in these years, and by Jack Chesbro, who won 49 games in two seasons before jumping to the AL in 1903. In postseason play, the 1903 Pirates lost the first modern World Series to the Boston Red Sox.

Pittsburgh sank to fourth place in 1904 as the Giants surfaced to win consecutive pennants in 1904–1905. In 1904 the Giants won 106 games to beat the runner-up Chicago Cubs by 13 games. Power pitching by "Ironman" Joe McGinnity (35–8), Christy Mathewson (33–12), and "Dummy" Taylor (21–15) paced the light-hitting Giants to victory. But in the aftermath of the win, manager McGraw refused to meet the AL champion Boston Pilgrims in World Series play. That issue was resolved in 1905, the year McGraw drove his team to a 9-game win over the Pirates and then to an easy conquest of the Philadelphia Athletics in the World Series, with Mathewson tossing three shutouts.

The following year, the Chicago Cubs emerged as the third NL dynasty of the deadball era. Pennant-starved since 1886, the Chicagoans recouped with a vengeance, winning an astonishing 530 games over the years 1906–1910. Such mastery was good enough to land four pennants in those five years. Skippered by player-manager Frank Chance, who, along with fellow infielders Johnny Evers and Joe Tinker, is now immortalized in baseball folklore, the 1906 Cubs won their record 116 games. Powered by Chance and third baseman Harry Steinfeldt, and armed by Mordecai "Three-Finger" Brown's 26–6 pitching, this superb team buried the Giants by 20 games, but lost the World Series to their hometown AL rivals, the "hitless wonder" White Sox.

The Cubs made it three victories in a row by winning in 1907–1908. The 1907 Cubs crushed Pittsburgh by 17 games, and in the unforgettable season of 1908, the Cubs edged the Giants by a single game. With two weeks remaining in the 1908 season, the Giants, Cubs, and Pirates were locked in a close race. Then, in a fateful encounter with the Cubs at the Polo Grounds, Fred Merkle of the Giants blundered by failing to touch second base as his Giants were scoring what looked like the winning run. In the stormy aftermath of this play, Umpire Hank O'Day ruled Merkle out for failing to touch the base and declared the game a tie because the swirling masses of Giant fans on the field made resumption of play impossible. Later NL president Harry Pulliam supported O'Day's decision and ruled that if necessary the game would be replayed at the close of the season. As it turned out, this was necessary because the Cubs and the Giants finished the season in a dead heat. To settle the outcome, the controversial game was replayed on October 8 at the Polo Grounds. The Cubs won the sudden-death game 4–2, as Brown outpitched Mathewson. In baseball folklore the Giant defeat permanently stigmatized "Bonehead" Fred Merkle as the blamesake of the Giants' defeat. As for the Cubs, they took full advantage of their quirky victory by defeating the Tigers for a second straight time in World Series action.

In 1909 the Cubs won 104 games, with Brown pitching 27 victories. But the Pirates won 110 that year to beat Chance's men by 6½ games. Wagner led the league in hitting, and pitchers Vic Willis and Howie Camnitz combined for 48 wins. In World Series action, the Pirates hung a third straight loss on the AL champion Tigers. But the Cubs rebounded in 1910, winning 104 games for a second straight year. This time it was enough to lap the Giants by 13, but the Cubs then fell to the Athletics in the World Series.

Over the years 1911–1913 the Giants dominated NL play. In winning three consecutive pennants, they piled up 303 victories; pitchers Mathewson and Rube Marquard accounted for 147 of these, while Giant hitters led the NL in batting each year. But in World Series appearances McGraw's men repeatedly swooned, losing to the Athletics in 1911 and 1913 and to the Red Sox in 1912.

Over the years 1914–1916, a whiff of competitive balance settled over the NL as three outsiders wrested pennants from the three dynasty teams. In 1914 the "miracle" Boston Braves stormed from 10 games back in mid-July to win 60 of their last 76 games; the surge was enough to crush the Giants by 10½ games. The following year, the Philadelphia Phillies landed their first NL pennant on the strength of 31 wins by pitcher Grover Cleveland Alexander and 24 homers by Gavvy Cravath. The Phillies beat out the Boston Braves by 7 games. And in 1916, manager Wilbert Robinson's Dodgers got 25 victories from pitcher Ed Pfeffer as they edged the Phillies by 2½ games. But this trio of outsiders produced only one World Series victory, which came when the Braves swept Mack's Athletics to win the 1914 classic. As for the other interlopers, both the Phillies and Dodgers fell to the Boston Red Sox.

Like the AL's, the NL's wartime campaigns of 1917–1918 were plagued by poor attendance which caused some tremulous owners to sell players in hopes of recouping losses. But the pennant monopolists held firm. The Giants won the 1917 race by 10 games over the Phillies, but then fell for a fourth straight time in World Series play as the White Sox prevailed. And in 1918, after winning the attenuated NL race by 10½ games over the Giants, the Cubs bowed to the Red Sox in the World Series.

The deadball era was drawing to a close in 1919, which was the year that manager Pat "Whiskey Face" Moran drove his Cincinnati Reds to their first NL pennant. The Reds won by 9 games over the runner-up Giants as future Hall of Fame outfielder Edd Roush batted .321 to lead the league. The Reds also won the World Series, but the stench of the Black Sox Scandal sullied their victory. As breaking news stories of that scandal overshadowed stories of the 1920 pennant race, in progress when the news broke, the Brooklyn Dodgers went on to defeat the Giants by 7 games. But the Dodgers lost to an inspired Cleveland Indians team in the World Series. In the atmosphere of gloom caused by the Black Sox Scandal revelations, it was also apparent that the deadball era of stylized baseball play was ending. But a new era was unfolding in the 1920s that would launch the major leagues into new uplands of cash and glory.

Baseball's Second Golden Age, 1921–1931

Over the winter of 1920–1921, crestfallen club owners slavishly chose Federal Judge Kenesaw Mountain Landis to be baseball's high commissioner and empowered him to restore the game's scandal-sullied image. At the time few observers could have predicted that major league baseball was moving into another golden age of cash and glory that would be highlighted by the dazzling exploits of Babe Ruth, who already was enthralling fans by his mastery of the new "big-bang" offensive style. But the sparkling turnabout in baseball's fortunes was also buoyed by the optimistic spirit of America's "roaring twenties." This was a decade of booming prosperity, an expanding urban population, declining work hours, and hefty increases in recreational spending by the American people. By 1929, indeed, Americans were annually spending $4.9 billion for recreational pursuits. To be sure, much of this spending was diverted into movies, radios, and automobiles, but major sports like baseball, football, basketball, boxing, golf, and tennis were attracting millions of hero-worshiping fans. Such adulation made demigods of athletes like Red Grange, Jack Dempsey, Bobby Jones, and Bill Tilden, but all of these sporting heroes were overshadowed by Babe Ruth, who now became the most photographed American of the decade.

During baseball's "guilty season" of 1920, it was the fun-loving Ruth, not the stern moralist Commissioner Landis, who diverted the attention of fans from the Black Sox Scandal. In 1920 the Babe accomplished this feat by smacking 54 homers to break his own seasonal mark, which he had set only the year before. Ruth's latest achievement fully justified the astonishing $125,000 which the Yankees shelled out before the 1920 season to obtain the former Red Sox pitching ace, whose batting achievements caused him to be assigned to regular duty as an outfielder.

With the Yankees, the charismatic Ruth bestrode the baseball scene like a young colossus. The very embodiment of the big-bang offensive style, Ruth notched ten AL homer titles over the years 1920–1931. In the last six of those seasons, he smacked 302 homers, including a record 60 blows in 1927. At the close of the 1931 season Ruth's homer output exceeded 600, and when he retired in 1935, he had raised his total to 714, along with a lifetime batting average of .342.

Inspired by Ruth's example, the big-bang style dominated major league baseball offensives of this and all subsequent eras. While no other team matched the consistent power of the Yankees, in this era NL teams outslugged their AL counterparts. And if no player surpasses Ruth's consistent power, sluggers like Cy Williams, Hack Wilson, Chuck Klein, Harry Heilmann, and Rogers Hornsby ably mastered the big-bang style. In 1930 Wilson hit 56 homers to set an NL seasonal mark, but for sheer all-around batting consistency Hornsby and Heilmann had no peers. Over the years 1921–1927 Tiger outfielder Heilmann topped .390 four times, hit 104 homers, and won four AL batting titles.

Incredibly Hornsby bettered this performance. Over the years 1920–1925, Hornsby won six NL batting titles, topped the .400 mark in batting three times, and won two Triple Crowns. Hornsby's lifetime batting average of .358

is the best of any right-handed batter in major league history.

Such heroics by players of this era were the highlights of all-out seasonal offensives that dwarfed those of the deadball era. In this decade seasonal batting averages in both major leagues topped .280, with NL batters averaging a whopping .303 in 1930. At the same time, league-wide homer production, averaging 540 a season in the NL and 490 in the AL, helped raise per-game scoring to an average of five runs per team, while relegating base stealing to the status of a secondary tactic. Abetting the big-bang offensives of this era were innovations in technology and in pitching rules. Technology provided livelier balls, which were more frequently changed during games; indeed, fans were now permitted to keep balls hit into the stands. Meanwhile, rule changes of 1920–1921 barred the use of spitters and other doctored balls by all pitchers except for a few specified veterans. Such changes made for much battered pitchers with ERAs of 4.00 now regarded as an acceptable level of pitching performance. To cope with the situation, managers now relied more heavily on relief pitchers. Nevertheless, virtuoso starting pitchers like Johnson, Alexander, Grimes, Grove, Pennock, Hoyt, and Vance ranked among the top stars of this decade.

That fans welcomed the new offensive style was evidenced by the record-setting attendance marks of this era. Despite the lurid exposés of the Black Sox Scandal, a record 9.1 million fans attended major league games in 1920. Then, after falling below that mark for three seasons, attendance soared to an average of 9.6 million a season over the years 1924–1929 and peaked at 10.1 million in 1930. Helping to swell attendance in this era were Sunday games, which were legalized in all cities outside of Pennsylvania. Such support boosted revenues by 40 percent over the previous era and raised annual player salaries to an average of $7,000 by 1930. However, such average figures are misleading. In the NL, the Giants, Dodgers, Pirates, and Cardinals got most of the profits, and the AL Yankees alone accounted for 25 percent of that circuit's annual attendance. Player salaries also varied widely, ranging from less than $2,000 for fringe players to Ruth's princely $80,000 for the season of 1930; moreover, in this era the Yankee and Cub payrolls topped those of other teams.

That the Cardinals ranked with the most profitable NL clubs at this time owed to the genius of General Manager Branch Rickey. One of baseball's greatest innovators, Rickey had an impact on the game that extended far beyond this decade. At this time Rickey made a contender out of the impecunious Cardinals by reviving the farm system and using minor league farm clubs to develop and train young players. By purchasing minor league clubs and establishing working agreements with others, and by deploying scouts to sign young players at low costs, Rickey built and stocked a network of minor league farm clubs which supplied the Cardinals with a steady flow of star players. Despite opposition from Landis, Rickey's farm network flourished and was widely imitated. By cornering the market on young talent and selling surplus players to other major league teams, the Cardinals profited despite poor attendance. For his part, Rickey profited by reaping a percentage from each player sale.

As a baseball innovator, Rickey had a much more enduring impact on the game than Commissioner Landis. By banishing the Black Sox, disciplining players, and presiding in watchdog fashion over annual World Series games, Landis contributed to restoring the game's honest image. But Landis's autocratic posturing grated on major league owners, some of whom resented his opposition to farm systems and his conservative approach to the sale of World Series radio broadcasting rights. Landis also stubbornly opposed the racial integration of organized baseball. Thus in this era outcast black players turned to their own leader, Andrew "Rube" Foster, who founded the Negro National League in 1920. In 1923 the Eastern Colored League took to the field as a second black major league, but gave way in 1928 to the Negro American League, which lasted until 1950. Such leagues fielded great black stars like future Hall of Famers Satchel Paige, Pop Lloyd, "Cool Papa" Bell, the slugging Josh Gibson, and Ray Dandridge. In this decade postseason exhibition games played between white and black major leaguers drew attention to the black stars, whose abilities matched and often surpassed those of white major leaguers.

But the limited exposure afforded to black stars contrasted starkly with the broad media coverage now lavished on the white majors. For this golden era of major league baseball history was gilded by newspaper coverage which touted the games and the player-heroes in romanticized style. Moreover, motion pictures and radio coverage opened new dimensions for promoting the game that suspicious owners of the age were slow to exploit. Conservative owners also took a dim view of the night baseball games which pioneer promoters were staging in the minors and in the black leagues. However, when the golden age ended amidst the worst economic depression of this century, such innovations would enable hard-pressed owners to better cope with the austerities of the 1930s.

Golden Age Campaigns: The AL, 1921–1931

In this era dreams of a competitively balanced AL went for naught as three teams—the Yankees, Senators, and Athletics—dominated the eleven pennant races. Foremost among these powers, the lordly Yankees used Ruth's explosive power to win six pennants and three world titles, while outdrawing all other AL teams by a wide margin. Once established, the Yankee dynasty lasted for forty years, during which time no more than three seasons passed by without the Yankees hoisting another AL pennant. In laying the foundations for this awesome domination, Yankee owners Jake Ruppert and Cap Huston repeatedly took advantage of their financially strapped Boston colleague, Harry Frazee, to denude the latter's Boston Red Sox of its ablest stars. In 1919 the Yankees pried pitcher Carl Mays from Frazee, and at the end of that year, the Yankee owners paid Frazee $125,000 upfront money and also a $300,000 loan to snag their biggest catch of all in Babe Ruth. What's more, over the next few years Frazee paid off the loan by sending more players to New York. By then, picking the right Boston players was the job of General Manager Ed Barrow, who left his former post as Boston field manager to come to the Yankees. After joining the Yankees at the close of the 1920 season, Barrow's dealings with Frazee over the next three seasons made Yankees of such Boston stars as pitchers Waite Hoyt, Sam Jones, Joe Bush, Herb Pennock, and George Pipgras, catcher Wally Schang, and infielders Everett Scott and Joe Dugan.

Over the years 1921–1923, these acquisitions helped to carry the Yankees to three consecutive pennants while burying the once-proud Red Sox. In 1921, with Ruth smashing 59 homers and driving in 171 runs, and Mays pitching 27 victories, the Yankees defeated the Indians by 4½ games. The following year ex–Red Sox players Jones, Bush, and Scott were on hand to help the Yankees edge the Browns by a single game. However, consecutive World Series losses to the rival New York Giants, whose Polo Grounds the Yankees shared as tenants, blighted these victories. But in 1923 the Yankees, now owned outright by Ruppert, moved into their brand-new Yankee Stadium, where Ruth's opening-day homer signaled a coming turnabout. With Ruth batting .393 that season, leading the league in homers, and sharing the lead in RBIs, the Yankees swept to an easy 16-game romp over the runner-up Tigers. And then, after dropping two of the first three games of the 1923 World Series, the Yankees swept the Giants to land their first world title.

This initial display of Yankee dominance ended in 1924, when the team lost to the Washington Senators by two games. It was Washington's first AL pennant. Led by their "boy manager," second baseman Bucky Harris, the Senators went on to down the Giants in a seven-game World Series struggle. Pitching in relief, the veteran Walter Johnson notched the victory in the final game. The following year the Senators repeated, using a powerful .303 batting assault to top the Athletics by 8½ games. But in World Series action the 1925 Senators blew a three-games-to-one lead and lost to the Pirates in seven games.

As the AL's 1926 season began, any likelihood of a Yankee resurgence seemed a remote possibility. Only the year before, the Yankees languished in seventh place, as illness and insubordination tolled on Ruth's performance. But a contrite Ruth came back as strong as ever, and young infielders Lou Gehrig, Tony Lazzeri, and Mark Koenig revitalized the team. In a close race the Yankees edged the Indians by 3 games, but lost to the Cardinals in a memorable seven-game World Series battle. Rebounding from that defeat, the 1927 Yankees mounted one of the most devastating assaults in major league history. In crushing the runner-up Athletics by 19 games, the Yankees batted .307 and led the AL in all major offensive categories. Ruth's 60 homers set a seasonal mark that lasted for 34 years, and Gehrig weighed in with 47 homers and 175 RBIs. In World Series action the Yankees easily dispatched the Pirates in four games. The following year the Yankees repeated, although they were pressed hard by the Athletics, who finished 2½ games behind. Still the 1928 Yankees finished their season in fine fettle by scoring an avenging four-game sweep of the Cardinals in the World Series.

The Yankees' latest stranglehold on the AL ended in 1929, when manager Connie Mack's power-packed Athletics captured the first of three consecutive pennants. The resurrection of the once-powerful Athletic dynasty was a triumph of patient rebuilding by Mack. After the veteran owner-manager broke up his formidable 1914 team, the Athletics spent the next seven years in the AL

cellar. After quitting the depths in 1922, the team improved steadily. In 1928 the Athletics came close to dethroning the Yankees, and in 1929 the Mackmen mounted an offensive which rivaled that of the 1927 Yankees as they crushed the New Yorkers by 18 games. The team's .296 batting average was led by outfielder Al Simmons, who batted .365 with 34 homers and a league-leading 157 RBIs, and by first baseman Jimmy Foxx's .354-33-117 performance. The pitching staff, led by Lefty Grove (20–6), George Earnshaw (24–8), and Rube Walberg (18–11), was the league's best. In World Series play the Athletics crushed the Cubs in five games; one of the team's victories included a devastating 10-run outburst that turned an 8–0 deficit into a 10–8 victory.

Over the next two seasons, the Athletics continued their dominance. In 1930 they defeated the Senators by 8 games, and in 1931 they crushed the runner-up Yankees by 13½ games. In postseason action, the Athletics beat the Cardinals in six games to win the 1930 World Series, but in 1931 the team lost a seven-game struggle to the Cardinals. Indeed, the 1931 AL pennant was to be the last for manager Mack and for the Philadelphia Athletics. Financial losses caused by the nation's deepening Depression forced the aging manager to sell star players to weather the storm. In the past such drastic measures had worked, and Mack had been able to rebuild his team. But advancing age and changing baseball fortunes now conspired against Mack.

Golden Age Campaigns: The NL, 1921–1931

Although upstaged by Ruth and the Yankees and bested in six of eleven World Series clashes, NL teams of this era more than held their own against AL rivals. Indeed, NL sluggers outslugged their AL counterparts in nine of these seasons, NL pitchers posted better ERAs than AL hurlers, and in the inflationary 1930 season NL batters outhit and outslugged their rivals by wide margins. That year NL batters averaged .303 to the AL's .288, and NL sluggers powered 892 homers to 673 for the junior circuit.

And yet in this era the NL was no better balanced competitively than the AL. Of the eleven NL campaigns of this era, the Giants and Cardinals each won four, the Pirates won two, and the Cubs won the other. In 1924 manager McGraw's Giants became the first major league team of this century to win four consecutive pennants. This was a feat matched only by Harry Wright's Boston Red Stockings of the 1870s and by Charley Comiskey's St. Louis Browns of the 1880s. For their part, the Giants of this era turned the trick with a potent batting attack; in their four-year sway, Giant hitters averaged better than .300 and smashed 335 homers.

In stocking his first pennant winner, McGraw pulled off astute trades with the moribund Braves and Phillies to obtain pitcher Art Nehf, shortstop Dave Bancroft, and outfielders Irish Meusel and Casey Stengel. These acquisitions joined with future Hall of Famers Frank Frisch and Ross Youngs to lead the Giants to the 1921 pennant. That year the Giants edged the Pirates by 4 games, and in 1922 they repeated, beating the runner-up Reds by 7 games. In both years the Giants met and defeated the Yankees in World Series play. In 1923 the Giants won a third straight flag by edging the Reds by 4½ games, but they lost the World Series to the Yankees. In 1924, with the addition of first baseman and future Hall of Famer Bill Terry, the Giants eked a narrow 1½-game victory over the Dodgers. In World Series play the Giants lost to the Senators in seven games. The 1924 pennant was McGraw's last as the Giants' manager and the last by a Giant team in this era.

As sicknesses took their toll on McGraw, coach Hugh Jennings, and outfielder Ross Youngs, the Pirates ended the Giants' four-year reign with an 8½-game victory over the New Yorkers. Future Hall of Famers—third baseman Harold "Pie" Traynor, and outfielders Max Carey and Hazen "Ki Ki" Cuyler—led the Pirates, who went on to score a dramatic come-from-behind victory over the Senators in the 1925 World Series.

As the squabbling Pirates faded to third place in 1926, the hitherto unsung Cardinals won their first NL pennant. It was the first of four championships in this era by this emergent new dynasty. The rise of the Cardinals was the handiwork of general manager Branch Rickey. From Rickey's expanding farm system came stalwarts like infielders Jim Bottomley and Tom Thevenow and outfielders Chick Hafey and Taylor Douthit. In 1921 player-manager Rogers Hornsby led the team to a 2-game victory over the Cincinnati Reds. And in a classic seven-game struggle, the Cardinals went on to defeat the Yankees in the World Series.

That fall Rickey enraged Cardinal fans by dealing the contentious Hornsby to the Giants for second baseman Frank Frisch. Frisch batted .337 to lead the 1927 Cardinals, while Hornsby batted .361 with the Giants. Nevertheless, both teams came up short, as the Pirates edged the runner-up Cardinals by 1½ games. Pittsburgh's .305 team batting average was sparked by future Hall of Fame outfielders Paul and Lloyd Waner; Paul's .380 clouting led the league, and brother Lloyd batted .355. But the Pirates were crushed by the Yankees in the 1927 World Series.

Under manager Bill McKechnie, the resilient Cardinals rebounded to win the 1928 campaign by 2 games over the Giants. But like the 1927 Pirates, the Cardinals too were swept by the Yankees in the World Series. As the Cardinals slipped to fourth place in 1929, the Cubs won their only pennant of this era. Managed by Joe McCarthy, the Cub revival was powered by a .303 team batting attack. Newly acquired Rogers Hornsby, who was pried loose from the Braves in a mammoth deal, led the Cubs with a .380 batting average. Behind Hornsby the team's power-packed outfield weighed in with Riggs Stephenson hitting .362, Hack Wilson batting .345 and driving in 159 runs, and "Ki Ki" Cuyler batting .360. The assault boosted the Cubs to a 10½-game victory over the Pirates, but the Chicagoans were no match for the rampaging Athletics in the World Series.

As the golden era ended, manager Gabby Street drove the Cardinals to consecutive pennants in 1930–1931. In 1930 the Cardinals struggled to a 2-game victory over the Cubs, who dumped manager McCarthy in the wake of the loss. In this vintage year of NL hitting, the Cardinals batted .314, but were outhit by the Giants, who smote .319 as a team! Every Cardinal starter in 1930 topped the .300 mark, and in World Series play the Cardinals outhit the Athletics. Nevertheless, the Athletics won the World

Series in six games. The following year, as NL batting mirrored the falling national economy by dropping to .277, the Cardinals coasted to a 13-game victory over the Giants. A .286 team batting average and stout pitching by "Wild Bill" Hallahan, Burleigh Grimes, Paul Derringer, and Jess Haines paced the Cardinals, who defeated the Athletics in the World Series, four games to three. But falling attendance caused by the deepening Depression marred the 1931 NL season. Indeed, the decline signaled the end of the latest golden age and the beginning of a long era of austerity in major league baseball.

Austerity Baseball, 1932-1945

In company with most industrialized nations, America during these years suffered the calamitous effects of a lingering economic Depression followed hard after by years of total war. In America the great Depression blighted the 1930s by creating millions of jobless workers, holding wages far below their 1929 level, slowing population growth, and, of course, drastically reducing recreational spending. Although abetted by federal remedial programs, the national economy languished until 1940, when federal defense-spending programs spurred an economic revival. But the following year the nation faced a second ordeal, when it embarked upon four years of total war against the Axis powers.

Major league baseball felt the effects of the gathering Depression in 1931, when the AL suffered losses while the NL barely broke even. Once engulfed by the economic storm, both major leagues were hard hit as attendance fell to 8.1 million in 1932 and hit rock bottom with an overall total of 6.3 million in 1933. Thereafter attendance improved, but not until 1940 did annual attendance totals reach 10 million. A similar sickening decline affected the minor leagues. But the minors recovered strongly after 1933 and zoomed to a record total attendance of 18 million in 1940.

Since major league baseball's fate was at its gates, declining attendance translated into financial losses. In the AL, six previous years of domination by the Yankees and Athletics had the junior circuit trailing the NL in overall revenues. After losing a total of $156,000 in 1931, the AL suffered three desperate years during which overall losses topped $2 million. Slow improvement began with the 1935 season, but as always revenues were unevenly distributed. Strong clubs like the Yankees and Tigers fared far better than the financially battered Athletics, Browns, and Senators. Nor were conditions much better in the NL, which also lost heavily during the years 1932–1934. In that three-year span every NL team suffered at least two seasons of red ink. A turnabout began with the 1935 season, but over the next six seasons annual profits only twice totaled $500,000. Moreover, like those of the AL, NL revenues were unevenly distributed. The Cubs, Giants, Cardinals, and Reds fared far better than did the woebegone Braves and Phillies.

Under such financial pressures, salaries of major league players were slashed. Annual salary spending in the majors fell from $4 million in 1929 to $3 million in 1933, and as late as 1940 total payrolls still lagged behind the 1929 figure. Such cuts dropped the average player's salary to

$6,000 in 1933, and the 1939 average salary of $7,300 still lagged behind the $7,500 figure of 1929. While such pay was good for those desperate times, job insecurity was rife among big league players of this era. Most players of this era needed no reminders that budget-slashing owners could easily find cheap replacements in the minor leagues. But for the time being, the great stars of the black majors, which also suffered from Depression austerities, posed no competitive threat. However, winds of change were stirring against segregated institutions in America, including major league baseball's unwritten color bar.

Of course, owners also faced a survival-of-the-fittest struggle in this depressed decade. Better-located clubs like the Yankees, Tigers, Cubs, and Giants adapted far better than did the owners of the financially strapped Athletics, Senators, Browns, Braves, and Phillies. Caught up in a vicious cycle, these poorer owners were forced to sell players to better-heeled clubs, a policy which had the effect of worsening attendance. However, one club, the Cardinals, managed to sell players to much better advantage. Although plagued by poor attendance, including three seasons which produced an aggregate home attendance total of fewer than 900,000, and one of those a world championship season which attracted only 325,000 fans at home, the Cardinals still managed to hold their own financially. Player sales from Rickey's well-stocked minor league farm system enabled the Cardinals to recoup financially and at the same time field strong teams.

At this time eager purchasers of players included Tom Yawkey, the wealthy new owner of the Red Sox. In this decade Yawkey spent $1 million on players. As a result Red Sox attendance rose while that of his moribund NL rival the Boston Braves worsened. Other bullish owners included the owners of the Cubs, Reds, Tigers, and Dodgers. But the well-financed Yankees emulated Rickey's example and built an efficient farm system of their own. Directed by the ruthlessly efficient George Weiss, the Yankee farms strengthened the Yankees' stranglehold on the AL.

Still, Depression-imposed austerities challenged all clubs of this era to find new ways to beef up revenues. Perhaps the most drastic of these was the plan of the owner of the St. Louis Browns to move the club to the West Coast, a strategy which was aborted by the outbreak of World War Two. But for the most part promoters tried to find ways of wringing more money from ballpark fans. Among these, expanding concession sales, utilizing promotional schemes, and staging night baseball games were tactics borrowed from minor league promoters and the black majors. But night baseball proved to be the wave of the future for the major leagues. When introduced to the majors in 1935 by Cincinnati general manager Larry MacPhail, the popularity of night baseball had most major league clubs following suit by 1940. Yet another source of profits came from the sale of local radio rights to broadcast accounts of games, a scheme which some owners had tried, but most had stubbornly resisted back in the twenties. By 1939 radio income totaled 7.3 percent of club revenues, up from a negligible 0.3 percent in 1930. Similarly, sales of World Series radio rights, a windfall shared by all major league clubs, now fetched higher prices. And at the close of the decade, the new medium of television showed promise, but the onslaught of World War Two delayed its profitable exploitation.

In the near future such innovations would profoundly alter the major league scene, but for now survival dictated sticking to more conservative measures. Thus in this era no privately financed ballparks were constructed (as, indeed, had been the case in the 1920s with the exception of Yankee Stadium), but Cleveland's publicly financed Municipal Stadium foreshadowed a future building boom that would replace most of the aging major league parks with modern facilities financed by public monies. When that day dawned, black players at last would be playing alongside whites in organized baseball. But in this era Commissioner Landis and his supporters continued their stubborn resistance in the face of mounting public support for organized baseball's integration. The breakthrough came, a year after Landis's death in 1945, as the first black player in this century signed a major league contract. Ironically, the integration of the white majors dealt a death blow to the flourishing black major leagues.

However, such impending changes were only dimly perceived by owners of this era. On the whole the 1930s were conservative years, with no significant rule changes invoked. In these years teams continued to master the big-bang style of play, with annual homer barrages, and pitching ERAs surpassing those of the 1920s. And if Ruth's departure in 1935 deprived the game of its most colorful hero of all time, new slugging stars like Hank Greenberg, Ted Williams, and Joe DiMaggio proved to be worthy successors. Their accomplishments and those of this era's teams were lavishly covered by sportswriters and by a new breed of radio sportscasters, whose ranks included some ex-players. Such coverage broadened baseball's appeal. So did the 1939 opening of the Baseball Hall of Fame at Cooperstown, New York, and the annual ritual of electing baseball immortals to the select circle. Indeed, the first annual election conducted in January of 1936 selected Ty Cobb, Babe Ruth, Honus Wagner, Christy Mathewson, and Walter Johnson as the five charter members. Over the years the number of enshrined players swelled to over 200, including stars from the segregated black majors. And so did the numbers of fans who annually made the pilgrimage to the Hall of Fame; from a few thousand a year in this era, the number of visitors now exceeds 250,000 annually.

The Crisis of World War Two

The major leagues were recovering from Depression-imposed austerities when the nation's entry into World War Two posed a second major crisis. From 1942 until the Allied victory in 1945, the nation's total war effort sapped baseball's manpower and threatened to curtail the 1945 playing season. Among the 12 million Americans summoned to military service during the war years were some 500 major league players and 3,500 minor leaguers. This talent drain shrank the minor leagues to nine circuits at one point, while only President Roosevelt's "green light" enabled the major leagues to continue playing throughout the war years.

That the major leagues continued playing the game in the face of wartime austerities owed to the resilience of its promoters and the continuing support of the fans. Although annual attendance fell from 10 million in 1941 to

8.8 million in 1942 and to a low point of 7.7 million in 1943, the numbers rebounded to 9 million in 1944 and then soared to a record 11.1 million in 1945. Indeed, baseball's continuing popularity won the support of political figures like J. Edgar Hoover and Senator A. B. Chandler, who were convinced that the game was serving the war effort by boosting morale, both on the homefront and among the troops abroad.

Nevertheless, it was no easy task keeping the game of baseball afloat amidst a total war effort. In these years owners were hard-pressed to find ways of coping with a variety of shortages. Among them, a crunching transportation and hotel accommodation shortage forced promoters to cancel spring training programs in the southlands. And in 1945 the same problems forced the cancellation of that year's All-Star Game. Meanwhile a rubber shortage forced the major leagues to go with a dead "balata" ball (with a hard plastic at the core) in 1943, and all during the war a shortage of wood affected the quality of bats. Early in the war the threat of submarine attacks on coastal shipping also curtailed night games in East Coast centers, but by 1944 the restriction was lifted. Indeed, night games came to be welcomed by government officials, who regarded them as good recreation for defense workers.

But the worst shortage of all was in manpower. Indeed, never before nor since did the major leagues face a talent shortage of such proportions as occurred then. As draft boards denuded team rosters of able players, club officials scoured the land for draft rejects and other ineligibles; at this time, overage and underaged players were welcomed along with aliens. In questing after talented alien players, scouts turned up a mother lode in Latin America. Cuba turned out to be especially rich in prospects and at this time some fifty Cuban players were recruited. Indeed, at one point a young minor league promoter and war hero, Bill Veeck, proposed to buy the sickly NL Phillies franchise and stock it with black players from the Negro Leagues. Landis nixed the proposal.

For their part, owners needed stout hearts and a love of the game to keep going in the face of financial losses. In 1943 the majors lost $240,000, with the Cardinals and Tigers faring better than most other clubs. Hardest hit were the owners of the NL Phillies, who declared bankruptcy. The franchise was sold to the NL for $50,000, and after one abortive sale attempt NL officials sold the club to one of the DuPont Company heirs. Thus in the affluent hands of Bob Carpenter, this chronically weak NL franchise was soon revitalized.

At this time each owner was obliged to do his bit for the war effort. In response, clubs staged war bond sales, admitted servicemen free of charge to games, and allowed radio broadcasts of games to be transmitted free of charge to military bases. Although costly, such gestures paid off by increasing baseball's popularity. By 1944 the worst of the financial reverses caused by the war ended, and when the 1945 season returned overall profits of $1.2 million, it was apparent that major league baseball was once again on the upswing.

Such was not the case for the players who took a financial beating in each of these years. A government edict of 1943, which was part of a general effort to halt inflation by stabilizing wages, froze player salaries. The salary freezes came at a time when player salaries, which aver-

aged $6,400 in 1942, were already at a low point. When the freeze on salaries continued through 1946, it stirred strong unionist sentiments among grousing players that erupted in the first postwar season.

Other changes unleashed by the war forced far-reaching changes on major league baseball. Fair employment policies adopted by the federal government and by some states now threatened major league baseball's long-established practice of racial segregation. Sensing the new trend toward racial integration, Branch Rickey in 1945 signed black major leaguer Jackie Robinson to a Dodger contract. Rickey also sent his scouts in search of other promising talent in the black majors. This was a timely move because Judge Landis's death in 1944 had removed a major stumbling block to the integration of the major leagues.

When the war ended in 1945 with a complete victory over the Axis powers, the prospects for major league baseball looked bright. But that year also brought news of the sale of the Yankees to a triumvirate of owners who paid $2.8 million for the club. And as it turned out, the postwar era would usher in yet another phase of Yankee domination.

Austerity Campaigns: The AL, 1932–1945

In the Depression era of 1932–1941, the AL extended its domination over the NL by winning seven of ten World Series encounters and six of the first nine All-Star Games. The annual All-Star Game was instituted in 1933 and quickly became a popular spectacle that marked the midpoint of each seasonal campaign. Meanwhile in the seasonal campaigns of this decade, AL batters topped their NL counterparts in batting average, homers, RBIs, and stolen bases, while NL hurlers posted lower ERAs than did AL pitchers. But there was an illusory quality to this apparent pattern of mastery. This was because the AL's dominance owed most to the powerful Yankees, who captured six of the AL's seven world titles in these years.

After a three-year hiatus, the Yankees recaptured the AL heights in 1932, crushing the Athletics by 13 games. Gehrig and Ruth combined for 75 homers and Yankee hitters batted .286. Under Manager Joe McCarthy, who was destined to become one of baseball's most victorious managers, pitching superiority also became a Yankee hallmark. In 1932, with Lefty Gomez leading the Yankees staff with 24 wins, the Yankee mound corps led the AL in ERA with 3.98. Thus fortified, the versatile Yankees went on to sweep the Cubs in a legendary World Series matchup, highlighted by Ruth's much-debated "called shot" homerun in the third game. And over the winter George Weiss was hired to build a Yankee farm system, a task which Weiss handled effectively. Within a few years the Yankee farm system laid the foundation for an awesome phase of Yankee domination.

Meanwhile, the other AL teams enjoyed a brief respite, as the Yankees fell behind the front-running Senators and Tigers over the next three seasons. As age tolled on Yankee stars like Ruth, the Senators, now skippered by another young player-manager, shortstop Joe Cronin, defeated the Yankees by 7 games to win the 1933 pennant race. League-leading hitting and sturdy pitching by Al Crowder and Earl Whitehill, who combined for 46 victories, carried the Senators, who went on to lose the World Series in five games to the Giants. Worse yet, in this rock-bottom Depression year, the Senators attracted only 437,000 home fans. Confronted with financial losses, owner Clark Griffith sold outfield star Goose Goslin to the Tigers. Goslin's loss dashed the Senators' hopes for 1934, and when the team slipped to the second division that year, Griffith sold Cronin—his son-in-law—to the Red Sox for $250,000.

As the Senators suffered, the Detroit Tigers prospered. In addition to landing Goslin in 1934, the Tigers also purchased catcher Mickey Cochrane from the Athletics. Installed as the Tigers' player-manager, Cochrane headed a Tiger resurgence that saw the team rise from a fifth-place finish in 1933 to consecutive AL titles in 1934–1935. In 1934 Cochrane and Goslin teamed with Hank Greenberg and Charley Gehringer to spearhead a .300 team batting attack. What's more, pitchers School-boy Rowe and Tommy Bridges combined for 46 wins as the Tigers defeated the Yankees by 7 games. The sprightly effort attracted 919,000 home fans, who watched Detroit land its first AL pennant since 1909. Unhappily for the fans, they also saw the Tigers extend their World Series losing streak to four as the Cardinals prevailed in a seven-game struggle. But in 1935 the Tigers repeated as AL champions, edging the runner-up Yankees by 3 games. Greenberg led the team's .290 batting offensive by batting in 170 runs, and the purchase of Crowder from the Senators beefed up the team's pitching staff. Although a late-season injury kept Greenberg out of action in the 1935 World Series, the Tigers downed the Cubs in five games. It was Detroit's first World Series victory since 1887. But as it turned out, this victory was also the last World Series triumph by any AL team but the Yankees until 1945.

The second phase of Yankee domination over the AL began in 1936. The year before, Ruth's departure had removed the club's greatest drawing card, but this year young Joe DiMaggio appeared. Purchasing him from the San Francisco Seals of the Pacific Coast League for $25,000 and five other ballplayers, the Yankees were taking a chance that DiMaggio would be able to play effectively in spite of his injured knee. Indeed, he was, although the outfielder did prove to be injury-prone. But in 1936 the highly touted DiMaggio was an immediate sensation. In his freshman year he hit .323 with 29 homers and 125 RBIs. That year Gehrig's 49 homers led the league and the Yankees batted .300 as a team with 182 homers. The Yankee assault lapped the runner-up Tigers by 19½ games and in World Series action the Yankees downed the Giants in six games. It was the first of four consecutive World Series titles by the Bronx Bombers. During this record-setting streak, Weiss's farm system provided a steady flow of talented replacements. Included were pitchers Spud Chandler, Steve Sundra, Marius Russo, and Atley Donald; outfielders Tommy Henrich and Charley Keller; and second baseman Joe Gordon. In 1937 the Yankees repeated by topping the Tigers by 13 games; in 1938 they beat out the beefed-up Red Sox by 9½ games; and in 1939 the Red Sox trailed the all-conquering Yankees by 17 games. In each of these seasons the Yankees blasted at least 166 homers. And in World Series play their mastery of their NL rivals increased steadily; in 1937 the Giants fell in five games, and in 1938 and 1939 the Yankees swept the Cubs and the Reds. Landing four consecutive world titles was an unprecedented achievement, but such domination also kindled an enduring wave of anti-Yankee hostility among fans and rival teams.

Mercifully for the rest of the AL contenders, a year's respite from Yankee domination came in 1940. The year before, Lou Gehrig's tragic illness ended the career of the great first baseman, whose "iron man" record of having played in 2,130 consecutive games still stands. In 1940 Gehrig's absence was keenly felt, and it enabled the Tigers and Indians to battle the Yankees on even terms. Cleveland's fireballing pitching ace, Bob Feller, won 27 games to lead his team's assault, but tensions between the Indian players and manager Oscar Vitt adversely affected the team's morale. Such tensions enabled the hard-hitting Tigers to close the gap. Batting a league-leading .286, the Tigers were paced by future Hall of Famer Hank Greenberg; the big outfielder batted .340 with a league-leading 41 homers and 150 RBIs. First baseman Rudy York weighed in with a .316 batting average, and his 33 homers and 134 RBIs complemented Greenberg's production. Second baseman Charley Gehringer, another destined Hall of Famer, batted .313 and drove in 81 runs, and outfielder Barney McCosky batted .340. To top it off, portly pitcher Bobo Newsom enjoyed a vintage season with a 21–5 record. In the last week of the season the Tigers deadlocked the Indians, and on the last day of the campaign the Tigers defeated the Indians to win the hotly contested race. In the decisive game, won by the Tigers 2–0, rookie Tiger pitcher Floyd Giebell outpitched the great Feller. Ironically it was Giebell's last major league victory. But in World Series action the Tigers lost to the Cincinnati Reds in seven games.

Hard after that defeat, the gathering storm of World War Two dealt the Tigers a crushing blow. After playing 19 games of the 1941 season, slugger Greenberg was drafted into the Army. As the Tigers slumped, the Yankees rebounded and romped to a runaway 17-game victory over the second-place Red Sox. But this last peacetime AL campaign was fraught with memorable events. For one, by hitting safely in 56 consecutive games, Yankee outfielder Joe DiMaggio sparked the Yankee surge and established an enduring major league record. For another, by batting .406 over the season, Boston outfielder Ted Williams became the last major league player to this day to top the .400 mark. And in the unforgettable World Series of 1941, by missing a third strike with two out in the ninth inning, thereby opening the floodgates for a game-winning Yankee rally in the fourth game, Dodger catcher Mickey Owen won enduring notoriety as the blamesake for the latest Yankee victory. The 1941 Series victory was the eighth straight by Yankee teams.

In the wake of the 1941 major league season, the Japanese attack on Pearl Harbor plunged the nation into full-scale war with the Axis powers. Soon thereafter, the military drafts sapped the playing strength of all teams, but the efficient Yankee farm system enabled the Yankees to retain enough able players to land two more pennants in 1942 and 1943. In 1942 the Yankees led the league in homers, fielding, and pitching to defeat the bridesmaid Red Sox by nine games. Yankee pitcher Ernie Bonham led all AL hurlers with a 21–5 mark, while Red Sox outfielder Ted Williams followed his brilliant 1941 season by notching a rare Triple Crown effort; Williams batted .356 with 36 homers and 137 RBIs. However, Yankee hopes of extending their World Series winning streak came a cropper as the Cardinals downed the New Yorkers in five games.

But the resilient Yankees bounced back in 1943. League-leading slugging and pitching, the latter fronted by Spud Chandler's 20–4, 1.64 ERA performance, carried the Yankees to a 13½-game win over the Washington Senators. To top off the victory, in World Series action the Yankees scored an avenging victory over the Cardinals, who were beaten in five games.

In 1944 the military draft finally denuded the Yankees, who fell to third. As the Yankees sagged, the Browns and the Tigers battled for the top position, and the struggle ended with the St. Louis Browns winning their first and only AL pennant. In edging the Tigers by a single game, the Browns' .252 team batting mark ranked near the bottom of the league. But stout pitching by Jack Kramer, Nelson Potter, and reliever George Caster, and shortstop Vern Stephens's league-leading 109 RBIs made the difference. Matched against their hometown rivals in World Series play, the Browns fell to the Cardinals in six games.

In the last wartime campaign, the 1945 Tigers eked a 1½-game victory over the Senators. Although the Tigers were outhit by five other teams, pitcher Hal Newhouser's 25–9, 1.81 ERA pitching and slugger Greenberg's timely return from military service sparked the Tigers. After missing four seasons of play, Greenberg returned to play in 78 games, during which he batted .311 and drove in 60 runs. In World Series play Greenberg's .304 batting and his two homers led the Tigers to victory over the Cubs in seven games, in what has been described as "the worst World Series ever played."

Austerity Campaigns: The NL, 1932–1945

Although offensively outclassed by the AL, the NL boasted the best pitching in these years. Indeed, pitching decided eight of the first ten NL campaigns of this era while also contributing to the senior circuit's better competitive balance. Over the years 1932–1941 the NL campaigns featured nine close races with five different pennant winners. Thus the longest reign of any would-be dynasty was two years, a feat achieved by the New York Giants and the Cincinnati Reds.

In 1932 the Chicago Cubs rose to the top of the NL and continued a quirky pattern, dating back to 1929, of winning a pennant every three years. In August the embattled Cubs replaced manager Rogers Hornsby with first baseman Charlie Grimm, a timely move that rallied the Cubs. Player-manager Grimm, in company with infielder Billy Herman and outfielders Riggs Stephenson and Johnny Moore, led the .278 team batting attack, while pitcher Lon Warneke (22–6) fronted the team's league-leading pitching staff. The Cubs went on to defeat the Pirates by four games, but were swept by the Yankees in the World Series.

As the Cubs swooned in 1933, another player-manager, first baseman Bill Terry, led the Giants to their first NL pennant since 1924. They did it by scoring a five-game

victory over the Pirates. Terry batted .322, and outfielder Mel Ott's 23 homers keyed the Giants' league-leading homer assault. The pitching staff, fronted by lefty Carl Hubbell's 23 victories, was the league's best. And in World Series action the Giants beat the Senators in five games.

The following year the Giants again boasted league-leading pitching, but the hard-hitting Cardinals overtook the New Yorkers in the final week to win by 2 games. Dubbed the "Gas House Gang," these Cardinals symbolized the Depression austerities that affected the nation in this worst year of the economic hard times. The Cardinals drew only 325,000 home fans, but player-manager Frank Frisch, in company with Rip Collins, Ernie Orsatti, Joe Medwick, and Spud Davis, topped the .300 mark in batting to pace the team's league-leading .288 batting effort. But the brightest star was pitcher Dizzy Dean, who won 30 games to become the last major league hurler to crack the 30-game barrier for over thirty years; moreover, Dean's brother Paul won 19. In World Series play, the Cardinals rebounded from a 3–2 deficit in games to beat the Tigers.

The folksy Arkansas country boy Dizzy Dean won 28 games in 1935, but the Cubs trumped the Cardinal ace with their league-leading pitching staff. At the close of the campaign, the Cubs led the Cardinals by four games. Heading the Cub hurlers were Lon Warneke and Bill Lee, each a 20-game winner. Five Cub regulars topped the .300 mark, including infielders Stan Hack and Billy Herman, outfielders Frank Demaree and Augie Galan, and catcher Gabby Hartnett, to pace the team's .288 batting offensive. And outfielder Chuck Klein, a timely acquisition from the moribund Phillies, powered 21 homers. But the Cubs were no match for the Tigers in World Series play; the Tigers defeated the Chicagoans in six games.

Over the next two seasons, Cub hitters topped all NL teams in batting, but each time the team finished second behind the Giants. Dominant pitching, paced by Carl Hubbell's 26 wins and Ott's league-leading 33 homers, led the 1936 Giants to a five-game win over the Cubs and Cardinals. In the second half of the campaign, many eyes were on lefty Hubbell, as the Giant hurler finished the season with 16 consecutive victories to threaten the record seasonal streak of 19 owned by Rube Marquard of the old Giants. Hubbell won the opener of the 1936 World Series, but the Yankees beat the lefty in the fourth game and went on to down the Giants in six games.

But postseasonal play was discounted, and Hubbell went on to add another eight victories in 1937. When the ace finally lost one on Memorial Day, his record (over two seasons) of 24 consecutive victories stood as the best by a major league pitcher. But more important to the Giants' cause in 1937, Hubbell went on to win 22 games and rookie Cliff Melton won 20 as the Giants hung on to beat the runner-up Cubs by 3 games. It was the second straight conquest for the Giants, but in World Series action they again fell to the Yankees, this time losing in five games.

For a last time in 1938, the Cubs used their magical three-year formula to land the NL pennant. In an epic campaign that saw Cincinnati Reds' pitcher Johnny Vander Meer pitch two consecutive no-hit games, and the front-running Pirates blow a big lead, the Cubs mounted a remarkable September surge to overhaul and topple the

Pirates by 2 games. In a decisive game played in late September's gathering darkness at Wrigley Field, player-manager Gabby Hartnett hit his legendary "homer in the gloaming" as part of a three-game Cub sweep of the Pirates. Although the Cubs batted only .269 that year, the team's pitching staff was the best in the league. Nevertheless, the well-armed Cubs were swept by the Yankees in the 1938 World Series.

As the punchless Cubs sank to fourth place in 1939, manager Bill McKechnie drove the Cincinnati Reds to their first NL pennant since 1919. Since that victory, the Reds had been remembered primarily for pioneering night baseball and for Johnny Vander Meer's double no-hit feat. But recently the club had come under the ownership of radio tycoon Powel Crosley, whose player purchases were strengthening the team. Included were a prize pair of pitchers: Paul Derringer, who was purchased from the Cardinals, and Bucky Walters, who came via the Phillies. In 1939 this duo combined for 52 victories and headed the league's best pitching staff. Supported by sturdy hitting from outfielder Ival Goodman, first baseman Frank McCormick, and catcher Ernie Lombardi, the Reds held off the Cardinals to win by 4½ games. However, the Reds suffered the same fate as did the 1938 Cubs when the Yankees swept them in World Series play. Regrouping after this defeat, the Reds repeated in 1940 as they downed the rebuilt Dodgers by 12 games. For the winning Reds, mediocre hitting was overcome by league-leading pitching and fielding. And in the 1940 World Series it was the Reds who outlasted the Tigers in a seven-game struggle.

In the NL's last peacetime campaign before the outbreak of the Second World War, the Reds fell behind the rising Dodgers and the perennially contending Cardinals. In a close race the Dodgers held on to win by 2½ games over the Cardinals. In rebuilding the Dodgers, general manager Larry MacPhail persuaded the club's banker trustees to bankroll the purchases of players from the Phillies and Cardinals. From the Cardinals came pitcher Curt Davis, and outfielders Medwick and young Pete Reiser. Snagging Reiser from the Cardinals' farm system was a real coup as he led the league in batting with a .343 mark. From the Phillies, MacPhail obtained pitcher Kirby Higbe and first baseman Dolph Camilli; and in 1941 Camilli's 34 homers and 120 RBIs led the league. With additional acquisitions, the 1941 Dodgers fielded few home-grown players. Indeed, player-manager Leo Durocher was a former Cardinal hand. But the Dodger assemblage of mercenaries led the NL in pitching and homers and tied with the Cardinals in hitting. During the frenzied campaign, the Dodgers attracted a million home fans, most of whom mourned their "Bums'" heart-breaking loss to the Yankees in the 1941 World Series.

As wartime exigencies riddled NL teams of playing talent, the Cardinals retained enough players to land three consecutive pennants over the years 1942–1944. Although Rickey left the Cardinals in 1942 to join the Dodgers as that team's general manager, his efficient farm system fueled the Cardinals. In dominating the NL, the Cardinals won 316 games in these years, each time leading the league in hitting and pitching. Managed by Billy Southworth, the 1942 Cardinals needed 106 wins to edge the Dodgers by 2 games. The following year 105 victories

enabled the Cardinals to romp to an 18-game win over the runner-up Reds. And in 1944 another 105 victories easily carried the Redbirds to a 14½-game win over the second-place Pirates. In World Series play the Cardinals split with the Yankees, winning in five games in 1942 and losing by the same count in 1943. And in 1944 the Cardinals thrashed the Browns in six games. In these years young outfielder Stan Musial emerged as a superstar with the Cardinals, winning the first of what would be seven NL batting titles with a .357 mark in 1943.

It was the loss of Musial to military service in 1945 which helped the Cubs end the Cardinals' pennant monopoly. League-leading batting, fronted by first baseman Phil Cavaretta's major-league-leading .355 batting, and league-leading pitching carried the Cubs to a 3-game victory over the Cardinals. But the victory was soured by defeat at the hands of the Tigers in the 1945 World Series. Worse still, Cub fans to this day are still looking for another NL pennant.

Baseball's Postwar Era, 1946–1961

Victory in World War Two unleashed a host of pent-up changes which altered American society. Among the most welcomed was a steadily expanding economy which increased jobs, wages, and consumer spending. Bolstered by such growth industries as housing, television, and automobile production, the tide of economic prosperity transformed the nation into an affluent society of dynamic abundance. Moreover, most Americans shared in the fruits of this abundance. With plenty of discretionary income, Americans spent ever-increasing amounts for leisure and recreational purposes. From a total of $11 billion spent in 1946 on such pursuits, such spending topped $18 billion by 1960. By then, the most popular leisure activity was television viewing, with nearly 80 percent of American households of 1960 boasting at least one TV set. And the number of American households increased sharply along with the nation's booming population. A postwar marriage boom fueled a fifteen-year-long baby boom to add to the nation's population growth. And in this era, millions of Americans forsook older cities for new suburban homes, a trend that sped the growth of new urban regions.

But postwar America was also faced with disturbing and controversial changes. At home, long-festering opposition to racial discrimination and segregation now saw black Americans using political action movements to batter away at sources of inequality. Similarly, increased union activity by organized workers was aimed at securing bigger shares of the fruits of abundance. And on the international front, the nation found itself thrust into a role as defender of the free world against Communist expansion. At this time a mounting arms race with the Soviet Union had America and the Russians stockpiling nuclear weapons and extending their rivalry into space exploration. This international ideological struggle translated at home into increased federal spending for defense and space programs, a continuation of the military draft, and a pervasive fear of Communism which spilled over into political campaigns.

At this time most of these forces and others impacted

upon major league baseball. For openers, the rising national prosperity boosted attendance and revenues, but shifting population centers now tempted some club owners to abandon old sites for greener pastures elsewhere. By 1958 five such franchise shifts had occurred. In 1953 the NL Braves became the first breakaway franchise when they abandoned their traditional Boston haunts for Milwaukee; in 1954 the penurious AL Browns departed St. Louis for Baltimore, and the following year the equally penurious AL Athletics moved from Philadelphia to Kansas City. Such moves were controversial, for they destroyed a long-standing, fifty-year-old status quo in major league baseball. But the biggest public uproar echoed from Brooklyn and New York City, when fans of the NL Dodgers and Giants saw these teams move to the West Coast, respectively to Los Angeles and San Francisco. Following upon those moves, a rival major league, the Continental League, threatened to plant teams in some abandoned cities, but mostly in new population centers that now hungered for major league baseball. The urgent need to defuse the Continental League threat and the lesser need to assuage bereft New York fans prompted major league owners to expand the major leagues at the end of this era.

Meanwhile, these breakaway franchise movements, while increasing major league attendance and revenues, were weakening the minor leagues by pre-empting some of the strongest minor league territories. At the same time attendance at minor league games was being undermined by the increasing radio and television broadcasts of major league games. For the minor leagues, such blows were crushers. From an all-time peak in 1949, when the minors fielded 59 leagues with over 7,800 players and attracted 40 million fans, the number of minor leagues steadily dwindled. By the early 1960s, the number of minor leagues had shrunk to nineteen, with fewer than 2,500 players and total annual attendance of less than 20 million fans. By then, major league owners were learning that there was a piper to pay; for the decline of the minors confronted the major leagues with a chronic, persistent problem of talent scarcity. To cope with the knotty talent shortage problem, major league clubs engaged in costly bidding wars for the services of promising young players. And in addition to bidding for "bonus babies," major league clubs recruited black players both at home and in Latin America. Since such moves failed to solve the problem of talent scarcity, by the end of this era the majors were challenged to find ways of subsidizing the surviving minor leagues, to prevent these vital nurseries of playing talent from drying up.

But baseball's talent scarcity problem was also aggravated by the television revolution. As television producers soon learned that other sports attracted viewers, they took to subsidizing rival team sports such as professional football and basketball. As these and other sports gained in popularity, young athletes turned to them in increasing numbers. Indeed, at many schools and colleges baseball now ranked as a minor sport. But television bestowed blessings as well as problems upon baseball. In 1950 baseball telecasting provided $2.3 million in new revenues and by 1960 such annual income topped $12 million. As television income enhanced the value of major league franchises, its potential now became a major consideration in the relocation of franchises. For now, as at the present time, owners clung to the policy of negotiating their own local television contracts. But owners of this era worried over television's impact on live attendance at games. In 1946 a record 18.1 million fans attended major league games and in 1948 rising annual attendance peaked at 21.3 million. Thereafter annual attendance sagged, falling below the 20 million mark during the 1950s. For this turnabout, some owners blamed television for making a free show of the games. But aging parks, located in congested and declining center cities whose populations were shifting to suburban areas, also accounted for the decline. In other ways television altered the game. The steadily increasing number of night games now transformed major league baseball into a primarily nocturnal spectacle— except at Wrigley Field in Chicago. Night baseball was a trend encouraged by the televising of games as producers found night games to be more profitable. And by making celebrities of players, television triggered a rise in player salaries which would reach astonishing proportions in later years. Moreover, by scooping newspapers on the coverage of the outcome of games, television forced baseball writers to adopt a new, more probing style of baseball coverage. But such mixed blessings failed to deter owners of this era from reaping revenues from local and national television contracts. However, it is unlikely that any owner of this era could have envisioned a coming time when television revenue would exceed that of ticket sales at games.

Nor could many owners at the dawn of this era envision the revolutionary impact of the racial integration of baseball. Nevertheless, in 1947 major league baseball became a major front in the ongoing battle for racial equality. That year Branch Rickey's "great experiment" introduced Jackie Robinson as the first known black player in this century to play in the major leagues. Playing first base for the Brooklyn Dodgers that year, Robinson endured a trying ordeal of acceptance, but he passed the test magnificently. A .297 batting average sparked a championship season for the Dodgers and won Robinson the Rookie of the Year honors. More important, his success paved the way for other black stars to follow in his footsteps. By 1958 some hundred black Americans and some eighty black Hispanics played in the major leagues, mostly with NL teams, where their feats helped to exalt the NL over the AL. In Robinson's footsteps there followed such future Hall of Famers as Willie Mays, Roy Campanella, Ernie Banks, and Roberto Clemente. However, the opening of doors into the white major leagues doomed the black major leagues to extinction. By 1950 the era of the great black majors was over. As for the white majors, the recruitment of black players only temporarily alleviated the growing talent shortage.

Meanwhile, the postwar surge in labor union activity in the nation at large was exerting its influence on the major leagues. In 1946 a mounting number of grievances against owners prompted major league players to organize under the newly formed American Baseball Guild. Headed by Boston attorney Robert Murphy, this fourth unionizing attempt by major league players now had players forming chapters on each team, electing player representatives, and demanding higher salaries, fringe benefits, and a pension plan. A strike threat that year was defused when owners conceded a minimum salary of $5,000, some fringe benefits, and a pension plan to be funded by national radio and television income. The latter concession was portentous; not only were owners committed to the pension principle, but an important precedent was set by giving players a share in national media revenue. Such concessions undercut the Guild, which soon died out. But when the owners attempted to abolish the pension system in 1953, player representatives from the sixteen clubs hired New York attorney J. Norman Lewis to represent their cause. Out of this crisis came the Major League Players Association; under Lewis's leadership, the Association fought a successful battle to retain the pension system. But the Association languished after this struggle and late in this era came under the leadership of Robert Cannon, who ran the Association as a company union until 1966. Then, under Marvin Miller's efficient leadership, the Association became a formidable collective-bargaining agency for the players.

Meanwhile, the Mexican League crisis of 1946 added to the growing tensions between players and owners. That year Mexican League promoters enticed a handful of major league players to jump to Mexican League teams with offers of high salaries. When Commissioner A. B. Chandler blacklisted the jumpers, one of them, Danny Gardella, sued in the federal courts. When a Circuit Court of Appeals found for Gardella, the threat to baseball's reserve clause was serious enough to persuade the owners to settle the case out of court. Subsequently, congressional investigations into baseball's monopolistic practices also threatened the reserve clause, but no legislation followed the work of Congressman Emmanuel Celler's probings.

Nevertheless, by creating the Major League Players Association and by linking pension payments to national television revenues, the militant players of this era laid the groundwork for massive salary breakthroughs to be reaped by a future generation of players. But for now the players had to content themselves with salaries which at least topped those of their forebears. During the 1950s, 75 percent of player salaries ranged from $10,000 to $25,000 a season. However, three superstars—Joe DiMaggio, Ted Williams, and Stan Musial—received annual salaries of $100,000 a season.

But if organized players showed signs of gaining wealth and power, the powers of baseball commissioners were waning. Indeed, when Landis died in 1944, it soon became apparent that the owners would not abide another powerful commissioner. Thus Landis's successor, Commissioner Chandler, was denied a second term in 1951. For his part, Chandler blamed his assertive stance on such issues as his support of the pension plan, his opposition to Sunday night ball, and his defense of the rights of minor league players, for his ouster. Be that as it may, the flamboyant Chandler was replaced by Ford Frick, who served for fourteen years as the compliant tool of the owners. At this time the changing ranks of club owners included a new breed of wealthy businessmen who deferred to powerful owners like Walter O'Malley of the Dodgers and Dan Topping of the Yankees. By wielding influence on the owners' powerful executive committee, their powers far exceeded those of the commissioner.

Among the playing rule changes of this era, the 1950 recodification narrowed the strike zone and a 1954 rule permanently restored the sacrifice fly rule. Of important future significance was a 1959 rule which reacted to the designs of new, publicly financed ballparks in Milwaukee, Kansas City, Baltimore, San Francisco, and Los Angeles, and which anticipated the coming new park-building boom. This rule ordained that parks constructed after 1959 must conform to minimum distances of 325 feet from home plate to the right and left field fences.

On the playing fields, improved fielding was attributed to bigger, more flexible gloves. And the homer production of this era owed much to players wielding lighter, more tapered bats, to the required use of batting helmets, and to the frequent replacement of balls. A team now used as many as 12,000 balls in a season. Offensively such changes resulted in unprecedented homer barrages, with NL hitters averaging more than 1,100 homers a season during the 1950s. What's more, NL hitters regularly also bested AL batters in batting averages and stolen bases. Credit for this turnabout went to the greater number of black stars in the NL. Robinson became the first black star to win a Most Valuable Player Award, and after Robinson received that award in 1949, seven black stars, including sluggers Roy Campanella, Ernie Banks, and Willie Mays, won NL MVP awards in the 1950s. But the most celebrated stars of this era were DiMaggio, Williams, and Musial. DiMaggio retired after the 1951 season with a .325 lifetime batting average, while Williams and Musial starred throughout this era. When he retired in 1960, Williams, despite years lost for service in World War Two and the Korean conflict, owned a .344 lifetime batting average, six AL batting titles, 521 homers, and a pair of Triple Crowns. And when Musial retired in 1963, his credentials showed a .331 lifetime batting average, seven NL batting titles, and an NL record of 3,630 lifetime hits, evenly divided at home and on the road.

For the battered pitchers these postwar years were nightmarish. ERAs hovered around 4.00 in the NL and just below that seasonal mark in the AL. To cope with their batting tormentors, pitchers now relied more upon sliders and some clandestinely employed illegal deliveries like the spitball. Managers responded by deploying relief pitchers. At this time "short relievers," capable of dousing late-inning rallies, now became valued specialists whose exploits were measured by saves and honored late in the era with annual "Fireman of the Year" awards. Among the best of this era's "firemen" were Joe Page of the Yankees, Jim Konstanty of the Phillies, Roy Face of the Pirates, and the much-traveled Hoyt Wilhelm. Indeed, the knuckleball-throwing Wilhelm lasted twenty-one seasons. When he retired in 1972, he had appeared in 1,070 games, with 227 saves and a lifetime ERA of 2.52. But able starters were by no means extinct at this time. Among the very best, lefty Warren Spahn of the Braves went on to win 20 or more games in a dozen seasons, and retired with 363 lifetime victories. To honor the outstanding pitchers of each season, in 1956 the annual Cy Young Award was instituted. The first recipient was Don Newcombe, the black pitching ace of the Brooklyn Dodgers. From 1956 through the 1966 season, only one award was given annually in the major leagues, but thereafter the best pitcher of the year in each league received a Cy Young Award.

Postwar Campaigns: The AL, 1946–1960

In this era the AL lagged behind the NL both in offensive performance and in annual attendance. For this reversal of fortunes, some observers faulted AL owners for taking a back seat to their NL counterparts in the signing of black stars and in the occupation of such choice sites as Los Angeles and San Francisco. But the AL's biggest problem was the overwhelming superiority of its own New York Yankees. By winning eleven of fifteen postwar-era campaigns, the Yankees made a mockery of the concept of competitive balance. Moreover, by their perennial dominance, the New Yorkers attracted the lion's share of AL attendance, to the detriment of their overmatched competitors. Indeed, such was the magnitude of the Yankee oppression that after 1948 no AL team but the Yankees won a World Series until 1966. For their part, the Yankees won nine world titles, thus singlehandedly maintaining the AL's domination in the annual test of strength between the two majors. Nevertheless, by the end of this era, the growing strength of the NL was evidenced by their team's victories in three of the last five World Series encounters and by victories in nine of this era's seventeen All Star Games.

But when each of the first three AL postwar campaigns produced a new champion, prospects for competitive balance looked bright. In 1946 the Boston Red Sox won their first AL pennant since 1918 to help foster this illusion. League-leading hitting by Red Sox batters, fronted by Ted Williams's .342-38-123 stickwork, and 45 wins posted by pitchers Dave "Boo" Ferriss and Tex Hughson, boosted the Red Sox to 104 wins and a 12-game romp over the defending Detroit Tigers. But after the Red Sox lost a hard-fought seven-game World Series battle at the hands of the Cardinals, another two decades would pass by before this club won another AL pennant.

As the Red Sox faded to third in 1947, the Yankees rebounded from a third-place finish to notch their first postwar pennant. DiMaggio batted .315 with 20 homers and 97 RBIs to lead the team's .271 batting assault. Besides leading the league in homers and batting, the Yankees also fielded the league's best pitching staff; Allie Reynolds, newly acquired from Cleveland, won 19, and rookies Specs Shea and Vic Raschi combined for 21 wins. Reliever Joe Page won 14 and tied for league leadership in saves with 17. It was enough to carry manager Bucky Harris's charges to a 12-game win over the second-place Tigers. Then, for a second time, the Yankees downed the Dodgers in World Series play.

The following year the Yankees, Red Sox, and Indians hooked up in a furious pennant struggle that ended in a tie between the Indians and Red Sox. To settle this first seasonal deadlock in AL history, the two teams played a sudden-death playoff game in Boston. By downing the Red Sox 8–3 in that game, Cleveland won the 1948 AL pennant and went on to beat the Boston Braves in the World Series. League-leading team batting (.282), homer production (155), pitching, and fielding powered the Indians, whose home attendance of more than 2 million fans was unsurpassed in this era. Player-manager Lou Boudreau led the Indians with a .355 average; outfielder Dale Mitchell batted .336, and outfielder Larry Doby, who joined the team in 1947 as the first black player in the

AL, hit .301. Pitchers Bob Lemon, Bob Feller, and Gene Bearden accounted for 59 victories, but the pitching staff got an important boost when owner Bill Veeck acquired the legendary and aging Satchel Paige from the black majors. Paige contributed 6 victories and a save to the team's winning cause.

At this point the resurging Yankees dashed all hopes of continuing the league's pattern of competitive balance. Regrouping under manager Casey Stengel, the Yankees snatched ten of the next twelve AL pennants, including a record five in a row beginning with the 1949 conquest. In the torrid 1949 race, the injury-ridden Yankees edged the Red Sox by a game. Needing a pair of victories to overtake and conquer the Red Sox, the Yankees hosted the Bostonians in the closing days of the campaign and won both games. Key performances included relief pitcher Joe Page's 27 saves and 13 victories, and a .346-14-67 offensive effort by the ailing DiMaggio. Though he was sidelined much of the season by injuries, the Yankee Clipper's heroics helped to offset Williams's tremendous performance for the Red Sox. Williams's .343 batting average was barely edged out by George Kell, and his 43 homers and 159 RBIs led all rivals.

Over the next three seasons, the Yankees prevailed in three close races, edging the Tigers by 3 games in 1950, the Indians by 5 games in 1951, and the Indians by 2 games in 1952. Nor did they stop there. In winning for a fifth straight season in 1953, the Yankees enjoyed their only comfortable edge in their record skein as they downed the perennial bridesmaid Indians by 8½ games. In winning a record five consecutive AL pennants, the great Yankee pitching triumvirate of Allie Reynolds, Vic Raschi, and lefty Ed Lopat combined for a sparkling 255–117 won-loss record. That victory total included two no-hitters pitched by Reynolds in the 1951 campaign. In 1950, future Hall of Famer Ed "Whitey" Ford joined the Yankee staff; Ford's 9–1 pitching performance was a decisive factor in the team's winning stretch drive of that season. Offensively, manager Stengel relied on star performers like DiMaggio and catcher Yogi Berra and successfully platooned such able hitters as outfielders Hank Bauer and Gene Woodling. When age tolled on the great DiMaggio, who retired after the 1951 season, or when the Korean War military draft snagged young stars like Ford and Billy Martin, general manager George Weiss summoned rising stars like Mickey Mantle and Gil McDougald from the Yankee farm system. Shrewd trades by Weiss also landed key performers like Johnny Mize, pitcher Ed Lopat, and relief pitcher Bob Kuzava. In World Series action, the relentless Yankees captured five classics in a row. Three times, in 1949, 1952, and 1953, they toppled the Dodgers. In 1950 they swept the "Whiz Kid" Phillies, and in 1951 they defeated the "Miracle Giants" in six games. In two of these encounters, Kuzava's relief pitching was a deciding factor. And at the pinnacle of their success in 1953, the Yankees could boast of having won their last seven World Series encounters.

The following year, the Yankees won 103 games, their best record under Stengel's leadership, but manager Al Lopez's Cleveland Indians won the 1954 pennant with an AL record-breaking 111 victories. Second baseman Bobby Avila's .341 hitting won the league's batting title, and Larry Doby's league-leading 32 homers and 126

RBIs headed the team's league-leading 156 homer barrage. With a 2.78 ERA the team's pitching staff was unmatched; the starting trio of Early Wynn, Bob Lemon, and Mike Garcia accounted for 65 victories. But like the 1906 Chicago Cubs, who lost the World Series of that year after winning a major league record 116 games, the Indians fell to the New York Giants, who swept to victory in the 1954 World Series.

The 1954 victory was also Cleveland's last AL pennant to this day. What followed was another assertion of Yankee tyranny. Regrouping in 1955, the Yankees went on to win a string of four consecutive AL pennants. By this time most of the heroes of the 1949–1953 Yankees were gone. To replace the great pitching trio of Reynolds, Raschi, and Lopat, Weiss traded for pitchers Bob Turley and Don Larsen and summoned catcher Elston Howard, the first black player to wear a Yankee uniform, from the farm system. In a close race the 1955 Yankees edged the Indians by 3 games, with Berra winning his third MVP award for his latest offensive performance. Berra batted a workmanlike .272, and his 27 homers drove in 108 runs. Outfielder Mantle batted .306, and his league-leading 37 homers were accompanied by 99 RBIs. And Ford's 18 wins led AL hurlers. But in World Series action the Dodgers finally turned on their Yankee tormentors as they won the fall classic in seven games.

In 1956 Mantle's Triple Crown performance (.353-52-130) and Ford's 19 pitching victories paced the Yankees to an 8-game victory over the Indians. In the aftermath of that victory, the Yankees faced the Brooklyn Dodgers for a seventh and last subway World Series. The next time these two rivals met, the breakaway Dodgers would represent the West Coast city of Los Angeles. What followed was an epochal struggle which the Yankees won in seven games. But Larsen's brilliant pitching in the fifth game stamped this World Series with the mark of immortality. With the Series tied at two games, Larsen pitched a perfect game; it was the first no-hitter in World Series history and the first perfect game pitched in the majors in over thirty years. But the stubborn Dodgers carried the Series another two games before succumbing.

Over the next two seasons the Yankees won two more AL pennants. In 1957 the Bronx Bombers wielded league-leading batting and pitching to down the runner-up White Sox by 8 games. Mantle's .365-34-94 performance won the switch-hitting superstar another MVP Award. Rookie shortstop Tony Kubek's .297 hitting won him Rookie of the Year honors, and rookie Tom Sturdivant's 16 victories led the pitching staff. Nevertheless, the 1957 Yankees lost the World Series in seven games to the transplanted Milwaukee Braves. But the 1958 Yankees avenged that loss. Winning easily by 10 games over manager Al Lopez's White Sox, the Yankees led the AL in team batting, homers, and pitching. Turley's 21 victories led AL pitchers and Mantle's 42 homers led the league's sluggers. Then, in a rematch with the Braves, the gritty Yankees overcame a three-games-to-one deficit to win the 1958 World Series in seven games.

The following year slumping performances by Mantle and Turley contributed to the Yankee's third-place finish. The collapse enabled perennial runner-up manager Al Lopez to drive his Chicago White Sox to a 5-game victory over the Indians. The White Sox batted a weak .250, but they led the league in stolen bases, fielding, and pitching. Veteran pitcher Early Wynn, a future Hall of Famer, notched 22 victories in his last great seasonal performance, and relievers Turk Lown and George Staley fronted the league's best bullpen crew. But the White Sox lost the 1959 World Series to the Los Angeles Dodgers.

That fall the decision by AL owners to expand the league to ten teams in 1961 sounded the knell for the league's hallowed eight-club format and 154-game seasons. As the postwar era ended with the 1960 campaign, the Yankees rebounded to win by 8 games over the Baltimore Orioles. Although soon to pass from the Yankee scene, general manager Weiss pulled off another canny deal by obtaining outfielder Roger Maris from the Kansas City Athletics. With Maris leading the league in RBIs, and Mantle in homers, the well-armed Yankees faced the Pirates in the 1960 World Series. Yet despite a World Series record .338 team batting average, which produced three crushing victories over the Pirates, the Yankees lost the classic in seven games. Hard after this defeat, Weiss and manager Stengel were forced into retirement, although the pair soon surfaced in their familiar capacities with the NL's expansion New York Mets. Meanwhile, with the passing of the 1960 season, the AL prepared to enter the dawning era of expansion.

Postwar Campaigns: The NL, 1946–1961

In this era much of the credit for boosting NL stock above that of the AL belonged to Branch Rickey and Walter O'Malley of the Dodgers. Dodger general manager Rickey built the superb farm system which fueled the Dodger dynasty, and it was Rickey too who successfully pulled off the coup of baseball's racial integration. When Jackie Robinson made his successful debut in 1947, Rickey enjoyed a temporary corner on the market of black players whom his scouts recruited from the fading black majors and from Latin American countries. Moreover, when Dodger owner O'Malley engineered Rickey's ouster in 1950, the aging genius joined the Pirates and laid the groundwork for that forlorn team's rise to power. And as a final touch, it was Rickey's presence among the would-be promoters of the rival Continental League movement in 1959 that goaded major league owners into expanding their circuit in order to deflect the threat.

But the 1957 West Coast move of the Brooklyn Dodgers and New York Giants was O'Malley's doing. Indeed, these moves stirred the Continental League movement. And it was O'Malley, the most powerful and influential owner of this era, who persuaded his colleagues to embark upon the expansionist course. Thus while Rickey and O'Malley plied different courses of action, these embattled rivals together forced major league baseball to adapt to a changing American society.

But the rise of the Brooklyn Dodger dynasty in the NL of this era was mostly Rickey's handiwork. And an effective piece of domination it was. Of the sixteen NL campaigns of this era, the Dodgers won seven and narrowly missed winning three others. And yet the Dodgers, who won only two world titles, were upstaged by an even greater Yankee dynasty. Nevertheless, the Dodgers lorded over other NL teams. In these years the Braves won three pennants and a World Series; the Giants won two pennants and a World Series; and the four one-time winners—the Cardinals, Phillies, Pirates, and Reds—accounted for two World Series victories. At least it made the NL a better-balanced circuit than the Yankee-dominated AL of this era.

As the NL's postwar era unfolded, the outcomes of the first three campaigns produced an illusion of competitive balance similar to that in the AL. Here too the first three races produced three different winners. The 1946 race pitted the Dodgers against a Cardinal team which Rickey had assembled in his previous tenure at St. Louis. In a donnybrook race, the two teams finished the season in a dead heat. To settle the issue of this first true deadlock in NL history, a best-of-three playoff series was set, which the Cardinals won by sweeping the first two games. Overall, the Cardinals used league-leading pitching, batting, and fielding to assert their superiority. Pitcher Howie Pollet's league-leading 21 victories and 2.01 ERA led the pitching staff. And a pair of outfielders powered the Cardinal offensive: Musial's .365 hitting won the league batting crown, and Enos Slaughter's 130 RBIs topped all others. In the World Series the Cardinals toppled the favored Red Sox in seven games.

As it turned out, St. Louis fans would have to wait another seventeen seasons before a Cardinal team again scaled the heights. Meanwhile in 1947 attention of fans everywhere riveted upon the Dodgers and Jackie Robinson's debut as the first black player of the century to play in the majors. When Commissioner Chandler suspended manager Leo Durocher, Burt Shotton took over the reins of the club and stationed Robinson at first base. Advised by Rickey to turn his cheek against racist slurs, which came mostly from the Cardinals and Phillies, Robinson responded stoically and successfully. His .297 batting that year won him NL Rookie of the Year honors, and his example opened the way for more black players to follow. With outfielders Pete Reiser and Dixie Walker topping the .300 mark at bat, and with pitcher Ralph Branca winning a league-leading 21 games and bullpen master Hugh Casey saving a league-leading 18 games, the Dodgers beat the Cardinals by 5 games. That year the Dodgers also had the satisfaction of seeing their hated rivals, the Giants, finish in fourth place despite a record 221-homer barrage. But in World Series play, another local rival, the Yankees, downed the Dodgers in a grueling seven-game struggle.

In 1948 the Dodgers slipped to third as ex-Cardinal manager Billy Southworth drove the Boston Braves to a 6½-game victory over his former Redbird team. It was Boston's first NL pennant since 1914 and its last as a Beantown franchise. Boston's pitching trio of Johnny Sain (whose 24 victories led all NL hurlers), Warren Spahn, and Vern Bickford fronted the NL's most effective staff. And the team's league-leading .275 batting attack was fronted by outfielder Tommy Holmes (.325), and by infielders Al Dark (.322) and Bob Elliott (100 RBIs). But when the Braves met the Indians in World Series play, the Indians dispatched the Braves in five games. Landing the 1948 NL pennant was the last gasp of this faltering franchise, which five years later would move to more profitable pastures in Milwaukee.

As the Braves faded in 1949, the Dodgers asserted their dynastic power. Over the next five seasons the Dodgers won three NL races and lost two others by heartbreakingly narrow margins. In 1949 Robinson's league-leading .342 hitting helped the Dodgers eke a 1-game victory over the Cardinals. Joining the MVP Award-winning Robinson were black stars Roy Campanella, who batted .287, and pitcher Don Newcombe, whose 17 wins paced the staff. Outfielder Carl Furillo batted .322 and outfielder Duke Snider and first baseman Gil Hodges, who combined for 46 homers and 207 RBIs, paced the team's league-leading homer assault. But then, for a third time, the Dodgers bowed to the Yankees in the World Series.

In 1950 the Dodger "Boys of Summer" lost by 2 games to the Phillies' "Whiz Kids." Phillies' ace Robin Roberts averted a possible deadlock by outpitching Newcombe on the final day of the season. With youngsters Roberts and Curt Simmons combining for 37 wins, and relief ace Jim Konstanty winning 16 and saving 22 for a Most Valuable Player Award performance, the Phillies boasted the league's best pitching. At the plate the team was powered by Del Ennis, who drove in a league-leading 126 runs, and by young Richie Ashburn, who batted .303. But late in the season the team lost pitcher Simmons to the Korean War military draft. His absence tolled on the Phillies, who were swept by the Yankees in the World Series.

Over the winter of 1950, Dodger owner O'Malley forced Rickey out of his general manager post, but Rickey's departure spared him the agonies of the Dodgers' 1951 season. As the fateful campaign unfolded, the Dodgers soared to a 13½-game lead in early August. But in the September stretch, the "miracle" New York Giants rose to deadlock the Dodgers at the season's end. In the unforgettable playoff series between these traditional rivals, the Giants rallied to win the decisive game on outfielder Bobby Thomson's dramatic ninth-inning homer. In baseball folklore, Thomson's winning blast is immortalized as "the shot heard round the world." Indeed, it was a miraculous season as the Dodgers, paced by the hitting of Robinson and Campanella, led Giant hitters by 15 points. But black stars Monte Irvin (who batted .312-24-121) and rookie Willie Mays (who hit 20 homers) powered the Giants, who also got a .303 performance from team leader Al Dark and a .293 performance with 32 homers from the heroic Thomson. Moreover, Giant pitchers Sal Maglie and Larry Jansen each won 23 games, to pace the league-leading Giant pitching staff. However, the Giants' celebrated "Miracle of Coogan's Bluff" was tarnished by defeat at the hands of the Yankees in the 1951 World Series.

But at this point the snakebit Dodgers picked themselves up and went on to capture the next two NL pennants. In 1952 they outlasted the Giants by 4½ games, and the following year they coasted to a 13-game win over the transplanted Milwaukee Braves. In the hard-fought 1952 race the Giants suffered the loss of Mays to the military draft. It was a crushing blow for the Giants, but Dodger crushers led the league in homers. Snider, Hodges, and Campanella combined for 75, and this trio drove in nearly 300 runs. The pitching was shaky. Able starters Preacher Roe, Carl Erskine, and Billy Loes won 38 games, but reliever Joe Black made the difference. With a 15–4 record and 15 saves, Black enjoyed the best season of his brief career. The following year, Erskine picked up after the slumping Black and posted a 20–6 record to lead the staff. Behind him the mature Boys of

Summer beat a hefty tattoo, leading the league in batting (.285) and homers (208). Rebounding from his previous year's slump, Furillo batted .344 to lead the league, and Campanella's .312-41-142 record won him another MVP Award. It added up to a two-year domination of the NL, but in World Series play the Dodger champs twice fell to their Yankee nemesis; in 1952 they lost the Series in seven games, and the following year they fell in six games.

Shortly after the 1953 Series loss, O'Malley picked the little-known Walter Alston to skipper the club. Although Alston would manage the team for twenty-three seasons, a longer skein than any of his managerial colleagues, his 1954 debut was inauspicious. That year the Dodgers lost to the Giants by 5 games. Offensively the Dodgers outbatted and outscored their rivals, but the Giants matched the Dodgers in homer production and fielded the league's best pitching staff. Returning from military service, Willie Mays led the league in hitting with a .345 mark, and his 41 homers and 110 RBIs firmly established his credentials as one of the leading stars of the decade. That year also saw the ex–bonus baby Johnny Antonelli come into his own as a pitcher. His 21 victories and 2.30 ERA paced the Giant pitching staff, which was the league's best. But the Giants were cast as underdogs in the World Series against the powerful Cleveland Indians. However, a sensational fielding play by outfielder Mays doused a promising Indian rally in the first game, and key pinch hits by "Dusty" Rhodes in each of the first three games triggered winning rallies. The result was a four-game sweep of the Indians.

But the Giant victory was also the team's last as longtime residents of New York. Over the next two seasons, the battle-wise Dodgers rebounded to win another pair of back-to-back pennants. Each year it was the Braves who finished second; in 1955 the Dodgers lapped the Milwaukee Braves by 13½ games, and the following year they held off their rivals by a single game. In 1955 outfielders Snider (.309-42-136) and Furillo (.314), and catcher Campanella (.318-32-107) paced the offensive. For his heroics, Campanella won his third MVP Award of the decade. Newcombe's 20 wins headed the dominant pitching staff. In the aftermath of the easy victory, the Dodgers also managed to defeat their Yankee tormentors for the first time as they won the 1955 World Series in seven games.

For the team's fanatical followers, this was to be the first and only world title they would see flying over Ebbets Field. In 1956 the Dodgers repeated, but only by the narrowest margin. League-leading performances by pitcher Newcombe (27 wins) and Clem Labine (19 saves) and a league-leading 43 homers by Duke Snider were needed to atone for the team's .258 batting. And in the aftermath of the grueling 1956 campaign, New York–area fans witnessed the last subway World Series matchup between the Yankees and Dodgers. Although the Dodgers won the first two games, they lost the Series in seven games. What's more, this Dodger team became the victims of the first no-hit game in World Series history when Yankee hurler Don Larsen hurled his perfect game in the fifth game.

As owner O'Malley laid plans for his team's postseasonal move to Los Angeles in 1957, his Dodger team fell to third. The following season, the team's first in Los

Angeles, they fell further, to seventh place. In these years there was no stopping the well-balanced Milwaukee Braves. As the first breakaway franchise to win a major league pennant in this century, the 1957 Braves attracted over 2 million home fans, who saw the team down the Cardinals by 8 games. Outfielder Hank Aaron's 44 homers and 132 RBIs led the league's hitters, and veteran pitcher Spahn's 21 wins led the league's pitchers. Third baseman Ed Mathews supplied additional power with 32 homers and 94 RBIs, and starting pitchers Lew Burdette and Bob Buhl combined for 35 victories. Then in World Series play the underdog Braves treated their fans to Milwaukee's only world title to this date by downing the Yankees in seven games. The following year the Braves repeated, scoring an 8-game victory over the rising Pirates. Spahn's 22 victories again led NL hurlers and Burdette added 20 victories. At the bat Aaron showed the way with .326-30-95 hitting, with Mathews adding 31 homers and first baseman Frank Torre batting .309. But in a World Series rematch with the Yankees, the Braves blew a commanding three-games-to-one lead, and the avenging Yankees won in seven games. To the Yankees went the honor of becoming the first team in over thirty years to rebound from such a deficit in World Series play.

As the decade of the fifties drew to a close, the transplanted Los Angeles Dodgers recovered from their seventh-place finish of 1958 to end the Braves' two-year reign. In a brilliant September stretch drive, the Dodgers won thirteen of fourteen games to deadlock the Braves at the end of the campaign. And for a change the Dodgers won the playoff series by sweeping the Braves in two games to claim the NL pennant. The Braves outhit, outhomered, and outpitched the Dodgers, but the Dodgers led the league in fielding, and outfielders Duke Snider (.308-23-88) and Wally Moon (.302-19-74) supplied power enough, and the bullpen saved 26 games. In World Series action against the White Sox, the Dodgers won in six games. The Dodgers' victories included a sweep of its three home games, which were played at the Los Angeles Coliseum, where a record 270,000 fans jammed the converted football stadium to witness the triumphs.

But the Dodgers fell to fourth in 1960 as the Pirates, a team constructed by Rickey, beat the Braves by 7 games. Manager Danny Murtaugh's "Bucs" batted a league-leading .276; shortstop Dick Groat's .325 batting led the NL hitters, and future Hall of Fame outfielder Roberto Clemente batted .314. Vern Law's 20 pitching victories led the starters, but reliever Roy Face was the bellwether of the staff. Face appeared in a league-leading 68 games, won 10 and saved 24, and posted an ERA of 2.90. In World Series play the Pirates were thrice battered by the Yankees, but they won the 1960 classic in seven games. Second baseman Bill Mazeroski's tenth-inning homer in the finale at Forbes Field secured Pittsburgh's first world title in thirty-five years.

The AL had already expanded to ten teams in 1961, when the NL played its last season under the traditional eight-club format with its hallowed 154-game schedule. In a close race the 1961 Cincinnati Reds edged the Dodgers by 4 games. Stout pitching, paced by starters Joey Jay, whose 21 wins led NL pitchers, and Jim O'Toole (19 wins), and 40 saves by the relief corps headed by Jim Brosnan and Bill Henry, carried the team. At bat the

Reds batted .270, with outfielders Frank Robinson (.323-37-124) and Vada Pinson (.343-16-87) powering the attack. But when the Reds met the Yankees in World Series play, they succumbed in five games.

The Expansion Era Begins, 1961–1968

In this turbulent decade of American history, major league baseball's tradition-breaking expansion ranked as one of the lesser social disturbances. A time of massive social unrest, the strident sixties saw most established institutions targeted by would-be reformers. Sparking the fires of unrest were the assassinations of the Kennedy brothers and Martin Luther King, the great black civil rights leader. In the wake of these tragedies came storms of protest demonstrations supportive of increased freedom for individuals and for oppressed minorities. But as the decade wore on, the major focus of the protests centered on the nation's involvement in the Vietnam War. This country's latest struggle against the spread of international Communism began in the mid-1960s and lasted until 1973. An unpopular war, the Vietnam involvement consumed over 50,000 American soldiers' lives, polarized the nation into factions embattled over the morality of the war, and ended in a political and military defeat. Moreover, the violent protests against the war spilled over into other social institutions. Thus demonstrations and protest movements by black Americans aimed at securing civil rights and economic betterment erupted at times into urban riots. And among other discontented minorites, many women organized into protest movements and demanded economic and political equality. At this time the widespread consciousness-raising appealed to many Americans, who supported such slogans as "Freedom Now" and affected new lifestyles in social relations, speech, clothing, and hairstyles. And by the end of the decade such supporters included numbers of major league ballplayers, who sought relief from long-established paternal controls imposed upon them by baseball law and custom.

Meanwhile, other forces of change were reshaping the nation and its national game. In this decade the nation's population soared past 200 million, with nearly half that number concentrated in some thirteen sprawling urban regions. Thus even as major league owners embarked upon an initial expansion course in 1960–1961, these new demographics portended further expansion of the two leagues along with the possible relocation of teams now situated in deteriorating urban areas.

Nevertheless, amidst all the disturbing changes the nation's economy continued to prosper. Although they were sapped by continuing inflation, the average wages of all workers rose to an annual figure of $8,000 by the end of the decade. As a result, annual spending for recreation rose to $18 billion, with television viewing continuing to reign as the most popular leisure outlet.

The continuing popularity of televised sports programs, now shown in color with ever-improving visual effects, was a boon to professional sports. While baseball profited from this popular medium, so did half a dozen rival sports. Among these, professional football expanded rapidly under the impetus of hefty national TV contracts which clubowners shared equally. By occupying most of the major urban regions, pro football now threatened baseball's pre-eminent position among the nation's favorite team sports. Indeed, in 1967 professional football's Super Bowl outscored the World Series in television ratings.

In stark contrast to pro football's bold expansionist course was major league baseball's limited expansion movement of these years. Baseball's initial expansion took place over the years 1961–1962 and was primarily an attempt to undercut the threat of the rival Continental League. Under this expansion, each major league added two teams and upped its seasonal playing schedule to 162. A significant departure, the addition of eight more games to playing schedules would drastically affect statistical comparisons of seasonal performances. Moreover, each new franchise owner paid $2 million, which was divided among the eight established clubs of each major league, and also participated in an expansion draft, which was used to enable the owners to stock their teams with players. But since established teams were permitted to withhold their best twenty-five players from the pool of eligibles, the new owners were forced to purchase unprotected cullings.

Under these procedures, the AL took the first expansion plunge in 1961. That year the AL added the Los Angeles Angels and a new edition of the Washington Senators. At the request of owner Cal Griffith, the original Senators relocated to Bloomington, Minnesota, where they became the Minnesota Twins. The furor evoked by that breakaway move forced AL owners to admit the new Washington Senators. It was an unwise move, as the franchise languished under weak ownership and poor attendance. In 1972 the Senators moved to Arlington, Texas, where they fared better as the Texas Rangers. Nor did the AL Angels fare well in Los Angeles, where they were upstaged by O'Malley's Dodgers. However, this well-financed team found prosperity when it was moved to nearby Anaheim in 1965.

For its part the NL did better under its 1962 expansion. That year the NL occupied Houston, where the Colt .45s occupied temporary quarters while awaiting the construction of their new all-weather indoor Astrodome Stadium. When the Astrodome opened in 1965, this expansion team took on a new identity as the Houston Astros. Meanwhile, as part of a deal which allowed the AL to occupy the Los Angeles territory, the NL reoccupied the New York area by admitting the New York Mets. Although the Mets lost 120 games in their first season of play, the team was generously supported by suffering fans, who rejoiced in the return of NL baseball to the Gotham area. After playing its first two seasons in the old Polo Grounds, the Mets moved into newly built Shea Stadium, located in Queens.

Thus did the major leagues move into their first phase of expansion. But each passing season underscored the inadequacy of the ten-club format. Like the twelve-club NL of the 1890s, the ten-club array of the 1960s produced too many losers each season. Annual attendance was disappointing. By 1968, overall major league attendance topped that of 1960 by only 3 million admissions. And added to the problems of this phase of expansion were two controversial franchise shifts. In 1966 the NL's

Milwaukee Braves abandoned that city for Atlanta, and in 1968 the AL's Athletics departed Kansas City for Oakland, California, where they poached upon the territory of the NL Giants. Each of these breakaway moves aroused protests from fans of the abandoned sites, and each prompted lawsuits which affected future expansion moves.

Meanwhile major league teams continued to face a growing shortage of playing talent. At most schools and colleges, where baseball now ranked as a minor sport, scouts complained that major sports like football and basketball were getting the best athletes. With the minor leagues shrinking alarmingly, major league owners in 1962 adopted a remedial Player Development Plan. Under this scheme, the minor leagues were reclassified, and each major league team agreed to subsidize at least five minor league teams. And to equitably distribute the limited supply of young prospects, the majors in 1965 adopted the radical plan of an annual free agent (rookie) draft. Under its provisions, each major league club in turn picked from a nationwide pool of high school and college prospects. Thus except for prospecting in foreign countries, the annual rookie draft ended the long and colorful era of free-enterprise scouting in America.

Along with the prevailing national mood of liberation for oppressed groups, the chronic player shortage helped to kindle reformist sentiments among this generation of major league players. More pampered and better trained, doctored, and defended than past generations of players, players of this decade demanded improved salaries, pensions, and working conditions. In these years player disdain for traditional authority was rife, and this was candidly spelled out in revelatory books, including bestsellers authored by pitchers Jim Brosnan and Jim Bouton. And in a precedent-shattering move in 1966, Dodger pitchers Sandy Koufax and Don Drysdale, acting on the advice of a lawyer, staged a successful joint holdout for hefty salary increases. That same year, player representatives strengthened the moribund Major League Players Association (MLPA) by successfully engineering the election of Marvin Miller, an experienced labor negotiator, to serve as the Association's executive director. Landing Miller proved to be a master stroke for the players' cause. By rallying the players and by invoking federal labor relations laws, Miller forced the clubowners to recognize and to bargain collectively with the MLPA. During his seventeen years as executive director, Miller negotiated five Basic Agreements, or labor contracts, which wrung from owners unprecedented concessions and benefits. The Basic Agreements of 1966 and 1969 increased pension benefits and raised minimum salaries along with other gains. Thus by 1970 average player salaries, which totaled $17,000 in 1965, rose to $25,000. At the same time some twenty players were being paid annual salaries of at least $100,000 a year. But Miller's greatest coup of this decade was to win the solid support of major league players behind the MLPA. And by the end of this decade, major league umpires also won recognition and bargaining rights under their newly formed Major League Umpires Association.

Among the deserving recipients of increasing salaries were the growing numbers of black players in major league uniforms. By the end of the sixties, well over a hundred black Americans and scores of Latin Americans were playing in the majors. What's more, their offensive production made a reality of the prevailing Afro-American protest slogan that "black is beautiful." In these years black hitters dominated major league offenses. In the NL, black stars won seven homer titles, as many MVP awards, and six batting titles. And in the AL, blacks won three batting titles and three MVP awards. Among the reigning black superstars, Willie Mays of the Giants was voted Player of the Decade by *The Sporting News;* indeed, Mays posted a remote threat to overtake Ruth's lifetime homer mark, and at the end of his career he had powered 660 homers. But by the end of the decade more observers were touting Braves' outfielder Hank Aaron's chances of bettering Ruth. Meanwhile at this time, Frank Robinson became the first player to win an MVP Award in each major league, and outfielder Roberto Clemente of the Pirates won three NL batting titles.

Sparkling alongside such stars were white prodigies like Roger Maris, who blasted 61 homers in 162 games in 1961, to set a new seasonal mark for homer production; or Carl Yastrzemski, who won an AL Triple Crown; or Pete Rose, who broke in as a rookie in 1963 with the Cincinnati Reds and would later break Cobb's lifetime total of 4,191 hits.

Indeed, such offensive performances occurred despite the hitting famine caused by the dominant pitchers of this era. Abetting the hitting famine was the rule that expanded the strike zone for the 1963 season. But improved coaching techniques, improved gloves and defensive strategies, and, above all, the astute deployment of specialized relief pitchers tolled on hitters of the era. As a result, pitching ERAs averaged 3.30 in this era, and in 1968, the notorious "year of the pitcher," hurlers combined to produce an overall ERA of 2.98, which was the lowest earned run mark in nearly forty years. Not surprisingly, the impact of such virtuosity on hitting was traumatic. In 1967 major league hitters averaged .242, and in 1968 batting bottomed to a nadir of .237. It was that puny mark which prompted remedial action by the rules committee, whose members voted to narrow strike zones and lower pitching mounds for the 1969 season. Such medicine broke the hitting famine, but while it lasted star pitchers made the most of their skills. In 1968 Cardinal ace Bob Gibson posted a 1.12 ERA and fanned a record 35 batters in three appearances in the World Series that fall. That same year, Denny McLain of the Tigers became the first hurler in over thirty years to break the 30-game victory barrier with a 31-6 performance; and Don Drysdale of the Dodgers posted a record 58 consecutive shutout innings. Moreover, in this decade fifteen pitchers would go on to join the ranks of the twenty all-time strikeout leaders.

However, many observers blamed the dominant pitching for lowering seasonal attendance marks in these years. From a record of 15 million in 1966, NL attendance slipped to 11.7 million in 1968, "the year of the pitcher." Nevertheless, annual NL attendance consistently bettered that of the AL; overall NL attendance of this era topped that of the AL by 16 million admissions. But a major factor accounting for NL attendance strength was the greater number of new ballparks in the senior circuit. In this decade, seven of the ten newly constructed parks were occupied by NL teams. Of these, nine were publicly financed, but the privately financed Dodger Stadium now attracted the lion's share of NL attendance.

But rising television revenues dispelled some of the anxieties over falling attendance. By 1967, revenues from local and national television contracts rose to $25 million, with no sign of abating. On the other hand, by urging more night games, by raising the value of major league franchises, by making celebrities of players, and by the presence of television entrepreneurs in the ranks of club owners, television was reshaping the game. To some alarmists television's influence was menacing. In 1964 the sale of the Yankees to the powerful CBS Network fed fears of excessive television influence. However, such fears were allayed by the declining fortunes of the Yankees under CBS management and by the 1973 resale of the team to private interests.

Campaigns of the Sixties: The AL, 1961–1968

By first expanding to ten teams in 1961, the AL led the NL both in attendance and in hitting. But when the NL followed suit in 1962, the AL was annually worsted in both categories. And when the hitting famine ravaged the major leagues late in this era, except for their leadership in homer hitting, AL batters suffered more.

To add to AL woes, the Yankees continued to monopolize pennants and overall attendance. Four more victories over the years 1961–1964 extended the Yankee's latest consecutive string of pennants to five, during which time the New Yorkers attracted 40 percent of the league's attendance. However, the latest Yankee surge was marred by losses in their last two World Series appearances. And in the wake of their loss to the Cardinals in the 1964 World Series, the Yankees collapsed suddenly and ignominiously. Thereafter, another twelve seasons would pass before a Yankee team again rose to the top of the league. But if rival clubs welcomed the tyrant's fall, they also discovered the draining impact of a weakened Yankee club on AL attendance.

In the AL's first expansion campaign, the 1961 Yankees powered their way to an 8-game win over the Tigers. With Roger Maris bashing a new seasonal record of 61 homers and Mantle poling 54, the Yankees unleashed a record seasonal team barrage of 240 homers. Maris also led the league in RBIs with 142, and Mantle knocked in 128. Ace pitcher Whitey Ford's 25 victories led the league's hurlers and reliever Luis Arroyo's 29 saves was tops in the league. While some observers blamed the Yankee power explosion on the expansion draft, which supposedly weakened pitching staffs around the league, the Yankees had no trouble downing the NL champion Reds in six games in the 1961 World Series.

In 1962 the Yankees won again, beating the Twins by 5 games. League-leading .267 batting and pitcher Ralph Terry's league-leading 23 victories spearheaded the attack. The switch-hitting Mantle's .321 batting topped the team, but this time around the Maris-Mantle slugging combination tailed off to a more modest 63 homers and 189 RBIs. Then, in a seven-game struggle that was drawn out by unprecedented rain delays, the Yankees defeated the Giants in the 1962 World Series. In the dramatic final game, Terry pitched a 1–0 shutout, but second baseman

Bobby Richardson gloved a screaming liner by Giant slugger Willie McCovey to save the Yankee victory.

In retrospect the Yankee glory years ended with the 1962 victory. With Mantle sidelined much of the 1963 season, the Yankees batted only .252, but still romped to an easy 10½-game victory over the hard-hitting Twins. Superb pitching by Ford (whose 24 wins led the league) and by Bouton (who won 21 games) sparked the drive. But in World Series play the Yankees were swept by the Dodgers. Still, the Yankees mounted one last winning effort in 1964. Rallying from six games back in the late going, the team overtook the White Sox and Orioles to win by 1 game over the White Sox. Mantle's last great batting effort (.303-35-111) powered the team, and Ford, Bouton, and Al Downing combined for 48 pitching victories. But it took a nine-game winning streak in September, highlighted by the pitching of rookie Mel Stottlemyre, to turn the trick. However, the Yankees again fell in World Series play, this time losing to the Cardinals in seven games.

In the wake of that loss, like the wonderful one-hoss shay, the aging Yankees collapsed "all at once and nothing first." In 1965 the team sank to sixth place and in 1966 they finished last. The suddenness of the team's collapse was reflected in AL attendance figures; in 1965 AL attendance lagged 5 million behind that of the NL. Into the breach left by the faltering Yankees rushed other contenders, but no team held the heights for more than a single season. First to reach the top were the Minnesota Twins, who won the 1965 race by 7 games over the White Sox. Outfielder Tony Oliva topped all hitters with .321 batting and paced the team's league-leading .254 hitting. Aging slugger and future Hall of Famer Harmon Killebrew hit 25 homers. Pitcher Jim "Mudcat" Grant's 21 wins led all pitchers; Jim Kaat won 18, and reliever Al Worthington won 10 and saved 21. But for a third consecutive time the NL prevailed in World Series action, as the Twins lost to the Dodgers in seven games.

The AL ended its string of World Series losses in 1966, and with this victory the league's teams weaned themselves of Yankee dependence. Indeed, over the preceding eighteen seasons no AL team but the Yankees had won a world title. In exorcising that bugaboo, the Baltimore Orioles began by dispatching the Twins by 9 games. Outfielder Frank Robinson keyed the team's .258 batting assault with league-leading .316-49-122 hitting. The performance won Robinson a Triple Crown and placed him in the records as the first player ever to win an MVP Award in both major leagues. Infielders Brooks Robinson and John "Boog" Powell combined to drive in 209 runs, and the Oriole bullpen corps saved 51 games to make life easier for the young starting pitchers. But in the 1966 World Series three of these pitching prodigies—Jim Palmer, Wally Bunker, and Steve Barber—hurled consecutive shutouts as the Orioles swept the favored Dodgers.

The rising Orioles were destined to become the AL's winningest team of the next 20 years, but in 1967 they slumped to sixth place, which opened the door of opportunity to yet another contender. In a close race the Boston Red Sox won their first pennant since 1946 by edging the Tigers by a game. In winning the Red Sox overcame the loss of promising young outfielder Tony Conigliaro, who suffered a career-threatening beaning; at the time of his accident, Conigliaro had 20 homers and 67 RBIs. But future Hall of Fame outfielder Carl Yastrzemski won a Triple Crown on .326-44-121 batting to front the team's league leadership in batting (.255) and homers (158). Pitcher Jim Lonborg's 22 wins led the league and reliever John Wyatt saved 20 games. But like their forebears of 1946, the 1967 Red Sox lost to the Cardinals in a seven-game World Series encounter.

In the last year of the ten-club format, the AL race produced the weakest seasonal hitting of this century. As the Red Sox faded, the Detroit Tigers won by 12 games over the reviving Orioles. Although batting a mere .235 as a team, the Tigers led the league in homers, paced by outfielder Willie Horton, who slugged 36. And considering that the best hitting team in the league that year, the Oakland Athletics, batted .240, the Tigers' offensive was proportionally respectable. Moreover, the Tigers boasted pitcher Denny McLain, who won 31 games and lost 6 with a 1.96 ERA. Matched against the Cardinals in the 1968 World Series, the Tigers lost three of the first four games. But pitcher Mickey Lolich won two of the next three, to spark the Tigers to a dramatic comeback victory. It was Detroit's first world title since the war year of 1945.

As the year of 1968 ended, the owners voted to join with the NL in expanding the circuit to twelve teams beginning in 1969. Mercifully for beleaguered batters, the owners also accepted a rules committee proposal to penalize pitchers. Thenceforth in both major leagues the strike zone would be narrowed and pitching mounds would be lowered.

Campaigns of the Sixties: The NL, 1962–1968

Although the NL expanded a year after the AL took the first step, the senior circuit was quick to reassert its offensive superiority. In its brief seven-season span as a ten-team circuit, the NL won four of the seven World Series encounters and seven of eight All-Star Games. Moreover, in six of the seven seasons NL batters topped AL batters in hitting and in stolen bases. And although the AL was better-balanced competitively in this era, as the Dodgers and Cardinals were monopolizing six of the seven NL races, attendance at NL games far surpassed AL attendance.

In 1962 the NL opened its first season as an expanded circuit, with most teams drained of their reserve strength by the expansion draft. In the ensuing campaign, the Dodgers and Giants staged a torrid race. But a late September losing streak by the Dodgers enabled the Giants to draw even at the close of the playing season. To settle the issue, the fourth postseason playoff in NL history was scheduled, with the Dodgers astonishingly involved in all of them. And when Dodger relief pitchers blew a 4–2 lead in the ninth inning of the decisive third game, the Dodgers lost a playoff for the third time. For their part, the Dodgers were led that season by pitcher Don Drysdale, whose 25 wins led all pitchers, and by outfielder Tommy Davis, whose .346 batting and 153 RBIs led all NL hitters. But the hard-hitting Giants led the league in batting (.278) and in homers (204). Superstar Willie Mays led the Giant attack with .304 batting, 141 RBIs, and a league-leading 49 homers. Fellow outfielders Felipe Alou and Harvey Kuenn topped the .300 mark, and first baseman Orlando

Cepeda weighed in with .306 batting, 35 homers, and 114 RBIs. Pitcher Jack Sanford won 24 games, and Juan Marichal and Billy O'Dell combined for 37, while reliever Stu Miller saved 19. However, the Giants lost a seven-game World Series duel to the Yankees.

Thereafter the Dodgers and Cardinals divided the remaining six NL championships of this era. In 1963 the Dodgers won by 6 games over the Cardinals. The team batted a modest .251, but Tommy Davis batted .326 to notch his second straight NL batting title, and shortstop Maury Wills batted .302 and led the league in stolen bases with 40. What really counted was the pitching, as the staff's 2.85 ERA was the league's best. That year lefty Sandy Koufax began a four-year skein of mastery that would propel him into the Hall of Fame. The ace's 25 wins and 1.88 ERA topped all hurlers, and reliever Ron Perranoski's 21 saves was the league's second best mark. In the 1963 World Series, the team's dominant pitching limited Yankee batters to a .171 batting average as the Dodgers swept to victory.

Dodger pitching again topped the league in 1964, with Koufax winning 19 and leading all hurlers with a 1.74 ERA, but poor hitting consigned Alston's men to sixth place. In a hotly contested five-team race, the Phillies led the pack by 6½ games with 12 games remaining on the schedule. But ten consecutive losses dropped the Phillies into a second-place tie with the Reds. The Phillies' swoon opened the gate for the Cardinals, who won 28 of their last 30 games. This brilliant stretch drive enabled the Redbirds to eke a one-game victory over the Phillies and Reds. The Cardinals' league-leading .272 batting made the difference. Infielders Bill White and Ken Boyer combined for 45 homers and 221 RBIs, and outfielder Curt Flood batted .311. But the timely acquisition of outfielder Lou Brock from the Cubs was decisive. Brock batted .348 in 103 games for the Cardinals and his 43 stolen bases ranked just behind Wills's total. And starting pitchers Bob Gibson, Ray Sadecki, and Curt Simmons combined to win 57 games. Yet so unexpected was the Cardinal victory that team manager Johnny Keane had signed a midseason pact to manage the Yankees the following year. The situation raised eyebrows when the Cardinals squared off against the Yankees in the 1964 World Series, but lame-duck Keane led the Cardinals to a seven-game victory over the Yankees.

In the wake of Keane's departure, the 1965 Cardinals dropped to seventh place. Into the power vacuum rushed the Dodgers, who gained the high ground and held it for two seasons against determined opposition from the Giants. Each Dodger victory was a near thing; in 1965 the Dodgers edged the Giants by 2 games, and the following year by 1½. In winning the 1965 pennant, the Dodgers batted a skimpy .245, with nary a .300 hitter in the regular lineup. But once again the Dodger pitching was superb; lefty Koufax won 26 on a 2.04 ERA, to top all NL hurlers, and Don Drysdale added 23 wins. And it was Koufax's shutout pitching in the seventh game of the World Series which led the team to victory over the Twins.

Over the winter Koufax and Drysdale staged an unprecedented joint holdout for salaries that were commensurate with their worth to the team. The two aces won salaries in the $100,000 range although these were grudgingly granted by owner O'Malley. But with Dodger home attendance topping the 2 million mark for the past eight seasons, such salaries were affordable. And in the case of Koufax, it was money well spent. In the close race of 1966 the lefty won 27 games with a 1.73 ERA, both league-leading figures. Drysdale slipped to 13–16, but reliever Phil "the Vulture" Regan saved 21 games. Such heroics were needed as the team batted only .256 with only Tommy Davis, in limited duty, topping the .300 mark. And in the 1966 World Series, the team's poor batting tolled as they were swept by the Orioles.

At the close of the 1966 campaign, the chronic arthritis in Koufax's pitching arm forced the ace to retire at the peak of his career. Thus disarmed, the weak-hitting Dodgers fell from contention. Not so the Cardinals, who perched atop the NL for the next two seasons as they twice drubbed the perennial bridesmaid Giants. In 1967 the Cardinals won by 10½ games, and in 1968 they won by 9. With Gibson sidelined for much of the 1967 season, the Cardinal bullpen responded by leading the league in saves. At bat the Cardinals hit .263, with Flood batting .335 and first baseman Orlando Cepeda batting .325 and driving in a league-leading 111 runs. Outfielder Lou Brock weighed in with .299 batting, and his 52 stolen bases led the league. In the 1967 World Series, Brock's .414 batting and seven stolen bases, and Gibson's three pitching wins and 26 strikeouts, highlighted the Cardinals' victory in the seven-game struggle with the Red Sox.

The following year a healthy Gibson won 22 games with a league-leading ERA of 1.12. In support of the black ace, pitchers Nelson Briles, Steve Carlton, and Ray Washburn combined to pitch 46 victories. Offensively, Brock's 62 steals led the league and Flood batted .301. As a team the Cardinals batted only .249, but in this "year of the pitcher," when overall NL batting stood at .243, it was enough. In the 1968 World Series, Gibson fanned a record 35 batters, but Flood's misjudging of Jim Northrup's fly ball in the seventh game allowed the Tigers to break through and complete their memorable come-from-behind victory.

As the curtain descended on the 1968 season, the major league owners now embarked on a second phase of expansion that would usher in a rich era of cash and glory for the major league game.

The Expanding Majors, 1969–1980

As the stormy sixties drew to a close, the nation united in applauding the successful moon landing by American astronauts in the summer of 1969. And if the strident countercultural protests lingered into the new decade, they lost their steam when the Vietnam War ended in 1973. The nation still had to weather a major political storm in 1974, when the Watergate scandal forced the resignation of President Richard Nixon, but the passing of that crisis marked the ending of the era of social turbulence. By then, a conservative reaction was ascendant and was marked by such themes as religious and patriotic revival and continuing fears of Communist expansionism.

In retrospect, mounting economic problems turned public attention from social protests to the harsh realities of earning a living. In 1973–1974 the nation suffered its worst economic recession since the thirties. A frightening accompaniment to the recession was mounting "stagflation"—a combination of inflation and rising unemployment. Indeed, by the end of the seventies an estimated 24 million Americans were living at or near the poverty level. To cope with the problem, millions of wives and mothers entered the labor force. As a result, the nation's birthrate declined sharply over the years 1973–1979. Nevertheless, abetted by the falling death rate, the population continued to grow; from a level of 204 million in 1970, the population reached 226 million by 1980.

The trend toward dual-income families in this era translated into rising incomes (albeit, inflated dollars) for most Americans. Nor did rising prices for consumer goods dampen the people's ardor for leisure and recreational pursuits. By the end of the decade, annual spending for recreation reached $40 billion. And because watching televised sports maintained its status as one of the most favored leisure outlets, the popularity of major team sports like baseball increased. For major league club owners of this era, this translated into heftier profits from television sources and surging attendance at the turnstiles.

Happily for major league baseball interests, such increasing prosperity followed hard after its latest expansion movement. In 1968 major league owners voted to add two teams to each league, thus increasing the 1969 major league membership to twenty-four teams. Under the new format, which imitated professional football's earlier and successful experiment, each league was realigned into six-team Eastern and Western Divisions. The 162-game seasonal schedule was retained, with each team playing its intradivisional opponents eighteen times and outsiders twelve times. At the close of a season, the new format called for the two divisional winners in each league to meet in a best-of-five-game playoff series to determine the league championship. Afterward, the champions of each league would meet in the usual World Series competition to determine the ultimate winner.

Supporters of this revolutionary new format touted its successful precedent in pro football and its competitive advantage over the recent ten-team system. Proponents also counted on the lure of each season's divisional races to sustain public interest; after all, such races would return four winners each season instead of two. Furthermore, a divisional winning team got to fly a pennant even if it subsequently lost out in the league championship playoffs. Finally, with six teams competing in each division, the worst any team might do was finish a season in sixth place. It was nice sleight-of-hand logic, and it worked.

Events speedily demonstrated the wisdom of such logic. For their part, baseball fans welcomed the new format once they got used to the new teams with their strange-sounding totems, including the presence of a Canadian team, the Montreal Expos, in the major league ranks. In the NL, the Expos joined the Eastern Division along with the Cardinals, Cubs, Mets, Phillies, and Pirates; in the NL's Western Division, the San Diego Padres were grouped with the Astros, Braves, Dodgers, Giants, and Reds. For its part, the AL installed its two new teams in its Western Division. There the newcoming Kansas

City Royals and Seattle Pilots vied with the Angels, Athletics, Twins, and White Sox. However, this made for a perennially stronger Eastern Division, where the established Indians, Orioles, Red Sox, Senators, Tigers, and Yankees were now arrayed.

For the privilege of obtaining one of the new franchises, each newly admitted NL owner paid $10 million and each new AL owner paid $5.6 million; these initiation fees were divided as a windfall among the established clubs of each league. To stock the new teams with players, another expansion draft was held in each league. The latest draft allowed the new owners to purchase unprotected cullings from the rosters of established teams. And like the first expansion draft, this latest one placed the newcomers at a competitive disadvantage. In the NL the Expos and Padres long languished in their divisional cellars, and neither entry won a divisional pennant in this era. But such was not the case with the AL's newcoming Kansas City Royals club. In their first campaign the Royals finished fourth, and over the years 1975–1980 the Royals won four divisional races and a league championship. But on the other hand, the AL's new Seattle Pilots turned out to be a financial disaster. After finishing last in the AL West in 1969, the bankrupt club was sold to Milwaukee interests. There the Brewers prospered, but the relocation had the AL pulling NL chestnuts out of a legal fire. For having earlier allowed the Braves to abandon Milwaukee, the NL faced a menacing lawsuit (State of Wisconsin v. Milwaukee Braves), which was quashed by the AL's decision to relocate the Pilots. But in abandoning Seattle, the AL soon incurred a lawsuit by Seattle interests, a threat that the AL deflected by admitting a new Seattle team, the Mariners, in 1977. That year the AL's unilateral expansion move added two new teams, which raised the league's membership to fourteen clubs while that of the NL remained the same. In addition to the newly admitted Mariners, who joined the Western Division, the AL then added the Toronto Blue Jays to its Eastern Division. This precipitous move resulted in an unbalanced major league format which exists to this day; moreover, since 1977 AL teams have annually played a skewed 162-game schedule.

However, this mini-expansion ploy and another bold move of this era enabled the AL to gain parity with its NL rival. Indeed, drastic measures were needed to restore the AL's attendance deficit, which, over the years 1970–1976, lagged some 24 million admissions behind that of the NL. In an early effort to regain parity, AL owners in 1972 allowed the moribund Washington Senators to move to Arlington, Texas, where they played as the Texas Rangers in the league's Western Division. And to balance that move, the Milwaukee Brewers were relocated in the Eastern Division.

But the most controversial of all AL parity measures was the league's 1973 unilateral adoption of the designated hitter rule. An experiment that was successfully pioneered in the minors, the rule allowed a designated hitter to bat in place of a pitcher in a team's lineup. It must be admitted that the designated hitter rule helped to remedy the AL's chronic problem of weak hitting. Only the year before, overall AL batting had averaged an anemic .239. In 1973, with AL teams playing designated hitters, the seasonal batting average rose to .259. Thenceforth AL batting averages always surpassed seasonal NL

figures. But the NL stubbornly resisted the innovation, and over the years 1973–1985 the use of designated hitters in World Series competition was limited to alternate years.

Meanwhile, the AL quest for parity was aided by a spate of new ballparks. Early in this era the NL opened five new parks. Belatedly, the AL followed suit, with four new parks and a major refurbishing of Yankee Stadium completed over the years 1972–1977. A new feature of some of the new parks, which affected fielding and batting, was the use of artificial playing surfaces. At the present time, ten major league parks are equipped with artificial playing surfaces. In the NL, where the Houston Astros pioneered in artificial surfacing in 1965, the Phillies, Pirates, Cardinals, Expos, and Reds now use artificial surfacing. In the AL, the Mariners, Royals, Twins, and Blue Jays now play home games on synthetic turfs.

Along with new parks, other innovations such as promotional giveaways and expanded concession sales and in-park entertainments contributed to soaring attendance at major league games in this era. After holding at 30 million admissions annually over the years 1973–1975, annual attendance at major league games soared to 43 million by 1980. But if rising attendance stimulated rising revenues, so did television. By 1980 income from national and local TV contracts accounted for 30 percent of baseball's $500 million in revenues of that year. Indeed, throughout the decade baseball's income from national network TV (which all clubs shared) increased steadily. From $17.5 million in 1971, such contracts returned $27.5 million in 1980. In 1980 this translated into a $1.8 million annual windfall for each team. And considering that such contracts covered only World Series games, league championship playoff games, the annual All-Star Game, and selected weekly and weekend games, such figures were impressive.

Indeed, major league owners might have wrung much more money from network TV sources had they not hewed to the policy of allowing clubs to contract individually with local TV stations. In 1975 local TV revenue totaled $31 million, and by 1980 this figure had nearly doubled. However, local TV income was unevenly distributed, which tended to favor some clubs over others. Thus clubs situated in more lucrative local television markets got the lion's share of this source of revenue. Still, at the close of this era local TV markets represented the fastest-growing segment of the television industry.

Nor was television income an unalloyed blessing. In this era some critics charged baseball owners with selling out to television interests when they permitted nocturnal broadcasts of World Series games. But the popularity of such games was evinced when an estimated 75 million TV fans witnessed the dramatic seventh game of the 1975 World Series. But if this demonstration of the game's popularity silenced some critics, others inveighed against the medium's impact on other areas of the game. Among such criticisms was the charge that TV was transforming ballplayers into highly paid and pampered celebrity entertainers.

Certainly player salaries in this decade soared to heights undreamed of by past generations of players. Even allowing for the bugaboo of inflation, the spiraling salary trend was dazzling. At the outset of this era, both a

$100,000 salaried player and a $1 million total player payroll were exceptional. In 1971 player salaries averaged $34,000. But thereafter the average rose to $52,000 in 1976, to $90,000 in 1978, to $100,000 in 1979, and to an astonishing $185,000 in 1980. By 1980, indeed, payrolls of $10 million were common and were defended by director Marvin Miller of the Players Association, who noted salaries amounted to less than 20 percent of revenues.

Truth to tell, much of the credit for enriching players of this era belonged to Miller. By threatening to lead his united players in a strike in 1969, Miller was able to negotiate a second Basic Agreement, which raised the minimum salary, increased the pension fund, and won for players the right to use agents in bargaining for salaries with owners. Then when this contract expired and negotiations for a new Basic Agreement bogged down in 1972, the Players Association staged a thirteen-day strike which shortened that season's playing schedule by forcing the cancellation of games. In the aftermath of that strike, Miller negotiated a third Basic Agreement, which won for players the right to arbitrate their salary disputes. In retrospect it was this important concession that really fueled the spiraling salary trend.

In 1975 the players scored another major coup, when the Messersmith-McNally case was decided in their favor. That year Dodger pitcher Andy Messersmith refused to sign his 1975 contract and, after playing the season under his former contract, claimed his right to free agency under the existing reserve-clause procedure. Messersmith's appeal (along with that of pitcher Dave McNally, who chose to retire after the 1975 season) went to a three-member arbitration panel which upheld the players' claim by a 2–1 vote. Professional arbiter Peter Seitz joined with Miller in supporting Messersmith's appeal against the negative vote cast by owners' representative John Gaherin. Certainly the implications of this "Seitz decision" were far-reaching. The decision effectively circumvented the long-established reserve clause which had recently been tested by player Curt Flood *(Flood* v. *Kuhn)* before the U.S. Supreme Court. At the time, in 1972, the court rejected Flood's appeal by a 5–3 vote, but the court's ruling suggested that the players might overturn the reserve clause by means of collective bargaining or by legislation. The Messersmith decision was the outcome of collective bargaining. And when the owners failed to overturn the Seitz decision on a legal appeal, they staged a lockout of spring training camps in 1976, claiming that the latest Basic Agreement had expired with no new labor contract in place. However, a compromise reached by the embattled players and owners allowed the 1976 playing season to open on time. And over the following summer, negotiations produced a fourth Basic Agreement, which conceded free agency to six-year veterans. The latest Agreement instituted an annual re-entry draft procedure which enabled qualifying players to auction their services anew. As compensation for losing a veteran player in one of the re-entry drafts, an owner received an extra choice in the annual rookie draft. Thus over the years 1976–1980, some owners bid high prices for the services of veteran free agents. And in turn the gains scored by players in these annual drafts helped to boost the salaries granted by players who opted for salary arbitration procedures.

The combination of re-entry draft bids and salary arbitration awards resulted in spiraling salaries and produced a new breed of player plutocrats. In the first re-entry draft of 1976, outfielder Reggie Jackson received a five-year contract worth $2.93 million from Yankee owner George Steinbrenner. In 1979 the Houston Astros plucked pitcher Nolan Ryan from the re-entry draft by giving the hurler a $1 million annual contract. That same year outfielder Dave Parker wrung a five-year pact worth $900,000 annually from his Pittsburgh owners to dissuade him from entering the re-entry draft. Thus it was hardly surprising that when the fourth Basic Agreement expired in 1980 the owners determined to halt the salary spiral. Among their demands, owners wanted a veteran player in compensation for a player lost via the re-entry draft. And when negotiations broke down, the threat of another player strike darkened the 1980 season. But in the nick of time a compromise between the embattled groups postponed the debacle for a season.

Meanwhile, the plutocratic players basked in a suntime of cash and glory. As television celebrities, players of this era stood as a breed apart from those of past generations. More glamorized by television exposure, far more wealthy, and more pampered, some players now indulged in illegal drugs to the point of self-abuse. At this time baseball's growing problem of drug abuse mirrored a national epidemic of drug abuse which was one of the unhappier legacies from that decade of self-involvement, the embattled sixties.

Yet another survival from that feverish era was the hirsute appearance of many players of this decade. In addition to wearing gaudier uniforms, many players now sported long hair, mustaches, and beards in the fashion of nineteenth-century players. Formerly a symbol of social protest in the sixties, such hirsute appearances now became a widespread affectation of American males. Although some clubs opposed the trend, owner Charles Finley of the Oakland Athletics encouraged it by paying his players $300 apiece to grow facial hair. Once established, the trend spread widely among players and continues to this day. But appearances aside, this breed of players was more pampered, better doctored and trained, and more ably defended than any of their forebears. Indeed, lesser-paid managers were now hard pressed to discipline their charges. Moreover, players of the seventies were less easily replaced. In this era the total number of minor leaguers competing for big league jobs averaged about 3,000 in any season.

Continuing the trend of the last two decades, blacks and Hispanics predominated among the splendid performers of these years. In 1974 the number of black major league players peaked at 26 percent, but the figure leveled off at 20 percent by 1979. By then, Hispanic players comprised 10 percent of the major league players. As before, blacks and Hispanics continued to lead the majors in stolen bases, with superstar Lou Brock of the Cardinals setting a new seasonal mark of 118 thefts while en route to shattering Ty Cobb's lifetime total of 892 bases stolen. In 1974, Hank Aaron broke Ruth's lifetime homer mark and went on to set a new lifetime mark of 755 clouts. But in toppling the Babe's record, Aaron went to bat 3,965 more times than the great Yankee slugger. And when Willie Mays retired in 1973, his lifetime total of 660 homers ranked third on the all-time slugging list; behind Mays in the fourth position was Frank Robinson, who retired with 586. And in this decade, Aaron, Al Kaline, Mays, Brock, and Roberto Clemente joined the 3,000 hit club, while Rod Carew captured seven AL batting titles, including four in a row over the years 1972–1975. Moreover, in these years twelve black and Hispanic stars won MVP Awards, and pitchers Bob Gibson and Juan Marichal hurled their ways into baseball's Hall of Fame. Finally, it was fitting that the leading player celebrity of this era was Reggie Jackson, a slugging outfielder of mixed black and Hispanic parentage. Widely acclaimed for his homer clouting, Jackson's seven homers in two World Series appearances with the Yankees won him the sobriquet of "Mr. October" and a short-lived "Reggie" candy bar was named for him.

Although they were justly rewarded and celebrated for their feats on the playing fields, black players still faced lingering forms of discrimination. At this time studies showed that black players had to be better-than-average players to make it into the majors. Thus there were few marginal black players on team rosters; moreover, teams were fearful of playing too many black players in a game lest it affect attendance. And retired black players seldom found jobs in baseball as field managers or in top administrative posts. However, Frank Robinson became the first black manager to be hired (and fired) — hired by the Cleveland Indians in 1975, fired in 1977 — and a few token black umpires also debuted in this era.

At the end of this era, *The Sporting News* chose the versatile white star Pete Rose as the recipient of its Player of the Decade Award. It was well deserved. In this era, Rose won a pair of NL batting titles and led the league in total hits four times. In 1978 the Cincinnati infielder, who was dubbed "Charlie Hustle," tied the NL's consecutive-game hitting record by batting safely in 44 consecutive games. That same year Rose joined the 3,000-hit club and continued his relentless drive to topple Ty Cobb's lifetime record of 4,191 hits.

White stars also predominated among pitchers of this era. In these years, Gaylord Perry, Tom Seaver, Phil Niekro, Don Sutton, and Steve Carlton hurled themselves to ultimate memberships in the exclusive 300-victory club. Carlton, Seaver, Perry, Sutton, and Nolan Ryan also were compiling strikeout totals that would later eclipse Walter Johnson's all-time mark. But with pitching ERAs now hovering above the 3.50 mark each season, managers continued to rely on specialized relief pitchers to bail out starters. Most prized were rally-busting short relievers like Mike Marshall of the Dodgers. In 1974 Marshall appeared in a record 106 games; by winning 15 and saving 21, Marshall won both the NL's Cy Young and Fireman of the Year awards for his efforts. Other acclaimed short relievers included Rollie Fingers of the Athletics, who won three Fireman of the Year awards, while saving 244 games. Fireballing Goose Gossage thrice led the AL in saves, and in 1978 he fanned 122 batters in his role as Yankee fireman. Sparky Lyle, who pitched for four different clubs in this era, saved 230 games. And late in this era, Bruce Sutter saved 133 games in five seasons with the Cubs.

With pitchers now penalized by a narrower strike zone and lowered mounds, such heroics were needed to cope with the batting resurgence. Offensively teams plied the big-bang tactic with gusto. At this time AL teams regained their power advantage and outhomered their NL rivals in eleven of the twelve seasons. Of course, the AL's 1977 mini-expansion made this a foregone conclusion. In the first year of that expansion, AL sluggers hammered a record 2,013 homers. By then, hitters in both leagues were swinging at cowhide-covered balls instead of the traditional horsehide-covered spheres. But this necessary innovation failed to produce the overall batting surge forecast by alarmed pundits. Except for the AL's unilateral adoption of the designated hitter rule, there were no significant rule changes in these years; most rule changes addressed statistical compilations. And at this time the major league policy of subsidizing the minor leagues was working. With each team spending at least $1.5 million a year to finance up to five minor league teams, by 1977 the minor leagues were stabilized at 17 leagues and 121 teams.

Internally the major leagues were mightily affected by the shift in the balance of power toward players and umpires. The powerful Players Association upset the power balance, as did the Major League Umpires Association. Indeed, umpires had long endured poor pay and job insecurity. But umpires of the 1970s had come a long way since the single-umpire system of the nineteenth century. Not until 1911 did both major leagues adopt a dual-umpire system for every game and the 1930s first saw both major leagues employ three-man crews to work regular season games. By the 1969–1980 era, four-man crews worked each seasonal game and crews for postseasonal games numbered six. More important, the Major League Umpires Association (MLUA) now became a powerful bargaining agency. After winning collective-bargaining rights in 1970, the MLUA waged a successful strike in 1979, a walkout that lasted until mid-May. When the strike ended, the umpires could celebrate a major victory. Among the concessions they wrung from owners was a maximum salary of $50,000 for twenty-year veteran umps, hefty increases in expense allowances, safeguards against arbitrary dismissals, guaranteed pay for forty-five days in the event of a player strike, and—wonder of wonders—a two-week paid vacation. How the late Bill Klem, who earlier in this century worked each game behind the plate for thirteen seasons, would have welcomed that concession! What's more, umpire Ron Luciano became a minor celebrity and, in company with others, became the author of books.

Against such power blocs, the owners now deployed their power committees and hired negotiators. As for Commissioner Bowie Kuhn, he continued to occupy what by now was largely a ceremonial post, one mainly responsive to the wishes of the owners. In 1979 Walter O'Malley's death removed a powerful figure from the owners' camp. In passing, O'Malley left his enormously profitable franchise as his chief legacy; by 1977 the Dodgers were valued at $50 million, twice the value of most franchises. Thus as the decade of the 1980s dawned, baseball owners were challenged to find a new leader of O'Malley's stripe and new tactics to restore the balance of power in their favor.

Campaigns of the Seventies: the AL, 1969–1980

Upstaged by the NL in the first two expansion moves, the AL was forced to take drastic measures to gain parity with the NL in attendance and offensive performances. To this end such measures as new park construction and franchise shifts contributed, but most decisive were two bold unilateral moves whereby the AL adopted the designated hitter rule in 1973 and undertook its mini-expansion in 1977. By these strokes the AL ensured its perennial domination, both at bat and at the turnstiles.

But if AL leaders expected the new divisional format of the 1969 expansion move to produce competitive balance, they were disillusioned. Indeed, throughout this era pennant monopoly was the rule in both AL divisions. Over the twelve campaigns of 1969–1980, the Orioles and Yankees dominated the Eastern Division, while the Athletics and Royals ruled the West. By winning six Eastern Division races and finishing second four times, the Orioles now reigned as the winningest team in the majors. For their part, the reviving Yankees won four Eastern races, which left but two for outsiders to divide. In the AL West, it was much the same story. There the Oakland Athletics won five races, the Kansas City Royals won four, and the Minnesota Twins won two—leaving only one for an outsider to claim.

In the first expansion season of 1969, the Baltimore Orioles asserted their balanced power, which made them the most victorious major league team of this era. Under sophomore manager Earl Weaver, the Orioles stormed the Eastern Division, their 109 victories lapping the runner-up Tigers by 19 games. It was the first of three consecutive Eastern titles for the Birds, with top-ranked pitching the key to each success. In 1969 the Oriole staff was the league's best, with Mike Cuellar (23–11) and Dave McNally (20–7) setting the pace. At bat the Orioles were powered by first baseman Boog Powell (.304-37-121) and outfielder Frank Robinson (.308-32-100). In the West, meanwhile, the Twins were winning the first of two consecutive titles. Victors by 9 games over the Athletics that year, the Twins led the league in batting and relief pitching. Offensive standouts included Rod Carew, whose .332 hitting topped the league, and Harmon Killebrew, whose league-leading 49 homers and 140 RBIs won the veteran slugger the MVP Award. But when the divisional titlists squared off in the first American League Championship Series, the Orioles brushed the Twins aside in three games. The sweep gave the Orioles a fourteen-game winning streak to take to the World Series. But after winning the opening game against the New York Mets, the Orioles surprisingly lost the next four.

In 1970 the crestfallen Orioles came back nearly as strong and downed the Yankees by 15 games to repeat as Eastern champs. Once again manager Earl Weaver's pitching corps was the league's best. Starters Mike Cuellar and Dave McNally each won 24 and Jim Palmer won 20. At the plate the Orioles batted .257, with outfielder Merv Rettenmund's .322 leading the team batting, and Powell (35-114) and Frank Robinson (25-78) supplying the power. In the West, the Twins also repeated, again topping the Athletics by 9 games and again leading the league in hitting and relief pitching. This time the team batted .262, but Killebrew (41-113) again powered the

club. An injury to Carew limited his play, but even so the infielder batted .366. Taking up the slack this year were outfielders Tony Oliva (.325-23-107) and Cesar Tovar, who hit .300. However, when the Twins met the Orioles in LCS play, they were again swept. And this time the Orioles went on to score an avenging victory in World Series play. In crushing the Reds in five games, the Orioles blasted fifty hits; the star Oriole performer was future Hall of Famer Brooks Robinson, who batted .429 and dazzled the Reds with his brilliant fielding at third base.

It was a glorious victory for the Orioles, but astonishingly this well-armed team would not win another world title in this era. In 1971 the Orioles captured a third straight Eastern title by thrashing the Tigers by 12 games. It was a vintage season for Baltimore, which could boast league-leading hitting and pitching, including a quartet of 20-game winning pitchers in Cuellar, McNally, Palmer, and Pat Dobson. Offensively, outfielder Rettenmund (.318) fronted the team's .261 batting attack, and Powell, Frank Robinson, and Brooks Robinson powered the assault with a combined 70 homers and 283 RBIs. In the West, the fading Twins now yielded to the surging Oakland Athletics, who notched the first of five consecutive Western titles in 1971. In matching the Orioles' victory total of 101 games, the Athletics crushed the expansion Kansas City Royals by 16 games. For the A's, rookie pitcher Vida Blue won 24 games with a league-leading 1.82 ERA, and Jim "Catfish" Hunter won 21. Hunter's nickname was hung on the hurler by the team's flamboyant owner, Charley Finley, who also tried unsuccessfully to get Blue to change his first name to "True." Offensively, the A's lacked a .300 hitter, but third baseman Sal Bando (24-94) and outfielder Reggie Jackson (32-80) provided power aplenty. But when the Athletics met the Orioles in LCS play, they were swept by the Orioles. It was the third consecutive LCS sweep by the Orioles. However, the Orioles lost a seven-game World Series struggle to the Pittsburgh Pirates, led by MVP Roberto Clemente.

In the wake of that loss, the Orioles fell from the top, and the balance of power now shifted to the West, where the volatile Athletics won the first of three consecutive AL championships. In the strike-shortened season of 1972, the A's won the Western title by 5½ games over the Chicago White Sox. Left fielder Joe Rudi batted .305, and first baseman Mike Epstein and outfielder Reggie Jackson combined for 51 homers as the A's rolled up 93 wins to head the AL. Moreover, the pitching staff was the league's best; Hunter and Ken Holtzman combined for 40 victories, and reliever Rollie Fingers won 11 and saved 21 games. In the East the strike-shortened schedule enabled the Tigers to eke a half-game victory over the runner-up Red Sox by dint of playing and winning one more game than the Bostonians. Manager Billy Martin's Tigers batted a mere .237, with no .300 hitter among the regulars, but lefty Mickey Lolich's 22 wins fronted the league's second-best pitching corps. In LCS play the weak-hitting Tigers held out for five games before succumbing to the A's, who went on to defeat the Reds in a seven-game World Series struggle. With slugger Jackson sidelined by an injury, unheralded catcher Gene Tenace took up the offensive slack. Tenace batted .348 and won three World Series games with timely hits.

Over the next two seasons, the Athletics continued their winning ways, twice downing the Orioles in LCS play and twice defeating NL contenders in World Series action. In 1973 the garishly clad A's defeated the Royals by 6 games in the West. Jackson's league-leading 32 homers and 117 RBIs powered the team, which also got superb pitching from Hunter (21–5), Holtzman (21–13), Blue (20–9), and reliever Fingers, who saved 22 games with a 1.92 ERA. That year the Orioles returned to the top in the East by downing the Red Sox by 8 games. In this first season under the designated hitter rule, the Orioles were paced by DH Tommy Davis, who batted .306 and drove in 89 runs. Palmer headed the pitching staff, which was the league's best, with a 22–9 mark; Cuellar won 18; and McNally and young Doyle Alexander combined for 29 wins. In the aftermath the Orioles battled the A's in a tense LCS matchup which went the full five games before Hunter's shutout pitching decided the issue. Then, in World Series action against the New York Mets, the Athletics rallied from a 3–2 deficit to land a second world title. Home runs by Reggie Jackson and Bert Campeneris settled the issue in Game Seven.

In 1974 the Athletics won a third consecutive World Series banner, a feat thus far unmatched under the major leagues' divisional format. In winning the Western race by 5 games over the Texas Rangers, the light-hitting (.247) A's were backed by the best pitching corps in the majors. Hunter's league-leading 25 wins and 2.49 ERA led the staff, who also got 19 wins from Holtzman, 17 wins from Blue, and 18 saves from the redoubtable Fingers. Although lacking a .300 hitter, the team was powered by Bando (22-103), Jackson (29-93), and outfielder Joe Rudi (.293-22-99). In the East, the Orioles won a fifth divisional flag by 2 games over the Yankees. League-leading fielding and sturdy pitching from Cuellar (22–10), McNally (16–10), and Ross Grimsley (18–13) carried the Orioles. In LCS competition the A's lost the opening game, but swept the next three to claim the league pennant. Pitted against the Dodgers in the World Series, the bickering Athletics, who squabbled among themselves and with their owner, nevertheless downed the Dodgers in five games. It was the A's third straight World Series victory, and astonishingly the team's bullpen saved or won all twelve of the games won by the Athletics in their remarkable three-season skein.

But the 1974 league championship was the last by an Athletic team until 1988. Years of bickering between the players and owner Charley Finley wore on the team, and the loss of pitcher Hunter to the Yankees was a crushing blow. Hunter's loss was Finley's fault; after Finley reneged on the terms of Hunter's contract, Hunter sought arbitration, and the ruling allowed the pitcher to become a free agent. Nevertheless, in 1975 the A's won the Western title for a fifth straight year as they outlasted the Royals by 7 games. Despite the loss of Hunter, the team's pitching was the league's second best. Blue won 22 games, Holtzman 18, and Fingers won 10 and saved 24. Offensively, outfielder Claudell Washington led the team with .308 batting, and Jackson drove in 104 runs and hit a league-leading 36 homers. However, the league's power balance now shifted eastward, where the next five AL champions would be crowned. First of the Eastern powers to emerge were the 1975 Red Sox, who defeated the

Orioles by 4½ games. The team's pitching was mediocre, but hefty .275 batting bolstered the assault. Rookie outfielder Fred Lynn's .331-21-105 hitting won him both Rookie of the Year and MVP honors, but outfielder Jim Rice (.309-22-102) came close to matching Lynn's production, while DH Cecil Cooper and catcher Carlton Fisk each topped the .300 mark. In the LCS faceoff, the Red Sox ended Oakland's domination with a three-game sweep. But in World Series action, the Red Sox lost an epochal seven-game struggle to the Cincinnati Reds.

Boston slipped to third in 1976, as another power rose in the AL East. After a twelve-year hiatus, the Yankees regained the heights and held the high ground for the next three seasons. For the Yankee renaissance much of the credit belonged to the team's wealthy and erratic owner, George Steinbrenner. After purchasing the team from the CBS Network in 1973, Steinbrenner brashly promised Yankee fans a pennant within three years, and in 1976 his words rang true. Moreover, the timing was propitious. In 1976 the team returned to its newly refurbished Yankee Stadium after spending two seasons at Shea Stadium in Queens. Under brash manager Billy Martin, whom Steinbrenner would fire and rehire five times, the Yankees romped over the runner-up Orioles by 10½ games. League-leading pitching, including 53 wins from starters Hunter, Dock Ellis, and Ed Figueroa, and a league-leading 23 saves from reliever Sparky Lyle eased the way. The team's .269 batting effort was led by outfielder Mickey Rivers, who batted .312, catcher Thurman Munson's .302 and 105 RBIs, and third baseman Graig Nettles's league-leading 32 homers. Meanwhile, the surging Kansas City Royals were breaking Oakland's stranglehold in the West. In downing owner Finley's decimated A's by 2½ games, the Royals matched the .269 batting mark of the Yankees. Third baseman George Brett's .333 topped the league's hitters, but DH Hal McRae was only a point behind at .332, and his 73 RBIs bettered Brett's total. The 1976 victory was the first of three straight Western titles by the Royals, who became the first of the AL's 1969 expansion teams to win a divisional pennant. In LCS play the Royals and Yanks battled for five games before first baseman Chris Chambliss won the pennant for the Yankees with a ninth-inning homer in the final game at Yankee Stadium. However, the Yankees were no match for Cincinnati's powerful "Big Red Machine," which swept to a four-game victory in the World Series.

Over the winter Steinbrenner strengthened his team by acquiring slugger Reggie Jackson in the re-entry draft. Jackson responded by batting .286 with 32 homers and 110 RBIs as the Yankees edged the Orioles by 2½ games in the 1977 Eastern race. Overall the team batted .281, with Rivers's .326 batting leading the team, Munson weighing in with .308-18-100 stickwork, and Nettles driving in 107 runs on 37 homers. Young Ron Guidry (16–7) led the starting pitchers, with Figueroa winning 16, newly acquired Don Gullett winning 14, and reliever Lyle saving 26. In the West, meanwhile, the Royals repeated as they downed the Texas Rangers by 8 games. The Royals batted .277, with outfielder Al Cowens (.312-23-112) leading the team, Brett batting .312, and McRae adding 21 homers and 92 RBIs. The Royal pitching staff was the league's best; Dennis Leonard won 20 games to lead the league, Paul Splittorff won 16, and the bullpen posted a league-leading 42 saves. In another LCS donnybrook, the Yankees edged the Royals in five games to land a second consecutive AL pennant. And in World Series action the Yankees trounced the Dodgers in six games. For the Yankees, the highlight came in the final game at the Stadium, when Jackson slugged three homers. In the afterglow of the victory, a candy bar was named for Jackson, who also wore the sobriquet of "Mr. October" for the remainder of his colorful career.

In an unforgettable encore performance, the Yankees repeated in 1978 after staging one of the most storied comebacks in baseball history. During much of the turbulent campaign, the Yankees trailed the slugging Red Sox. Midway in the campaign Steinbrenner sacked the volatile Martin for insubordination and replaced him with Bob Lemon. Under Lemon, the Yankees recuperated from a spate of injuries and crushed the Red Sox in two series to gain a tie by the season's end. In the sudden-death playoff game for the Eastern title, pitchers Ron Guidry and Goose Gossage held off the Red Sox, while homers by Jackson and shortstop Bucky Dent capped a 5–4 victory at Fenway Park. That year the Yankee pitchers posted a league-leading 3.10 ERA; Guidry's 25 wins (he lost only 3) and 1.74 ERA were the league's best, and Gossage won 10 and saved 27 games. Outfielder Lou Piniella's .314 batting led the team, which was powered by Jackson (27-97), Nettles (27-93), and Chambliss (who drove in 90 runs). Meanwhile, the upstaged Royals were winning a third consecutive Western title, this time by 5 games over the California Angels. With no .300 hitter in the regular lineup, the Royals batted .268; outfielder Amos Otis led the hitters with .298-22-96 batting. Starting pitchers Leonard and Splittorff combined for 40 victories, and reliever Al Hrabosky saved 20 as the Royals compiled the league's second-best pitching record. But the Yankees toppled the Royals in four games in LCS play. When World Series play began, the Yankees lost the first two games to the Dodgers, but then swept the next four games to cap a legendary campaign with a second straight world title.

Although Steinbrenner continued to spend heavily on free agents, the 1979 Yankees fell to fourth place in the Eastern Division. By winning 102 games, manager Earl Weaver led the Orioles to an 8-game win over the second-place Milwaukee Brewers. League-leading pitching, paced by Mike Flanagan's 23–9 effort, led the Orioles, whose offense was powered by first baseman Eddie Murray (.295-25-99) and outfielder Ken Singleton (.295-35-111). While the Orioles winged to the top in the AL East, the California Angels ended the Royals' Western reign by scoring a 3-game victory. The Angels' victory ended years of frustration for owner Gene Autry, who had spent $15 million on playing talent since 1961. In 1978 two of Autry's recent acquisitions paid off as Rod Carew batted .318 and Don Baylor won the MVP Award for his .296-36-139 production. But the Angels' pitching corps compiled a vulnerable 4.34 ERA, and in LCS play the Orioles dispatched the Angels in four games. But the Orioles now faced their old Pirate tormentors in the World Series. In an eerie repeat of their 1971 matchup, after leading by three games to one in this 1979 encounter, the Orioles lost to the Pirates in seven games.

As the era ended, the Yankees rebounded to edge the Orioles by 3 games in the East. In the close race, Stein-

brenner's latest re-entry draft acquisitions, infielder Bob Watson and pitcher Rudy May, made the difference. May won 15 games, and his 2.47 ERA led the league; Tommy John won 22, Guidry won 17, and the fireballing Gossage saved 33 games in relief. Watson's .307 batting led the hitters, but Jackson batted .300 and his 111 RBIs came with a league-leading 41 homers. This year, however, the Yankees were outmatched by the Royals. Rebounding to win the Western Division by 14 games over the Athletics, the Royals batted a league-leading .286. Brett's .390 batting, which included 24 homers and 118 RBIs, was the best batting mark in the majors since 1941. Outfielder Willie Wilson batted .326 and catcher-outfielder John Wathan batted .305. Pitcher Leonard won 20, and a Yankee castoff, lefty Larry Gura, won 18, with relief ace Dan Quisenberry saving 33 games to tie Gossage for the league lead. In LCS play the Royals, who had feasted on the Yankees during the season, swept the New Yorkers. In the wake of that loss, owner Steinbrenner sacked manager Dick Howser, despite the 103 victories the Yankees had compiled under Howser's leadership. By then, the Royals had lost to the Phillies in six games in the 1980 World Series. Thus the era ended with the NL boasting two straight World Series triumphs which the senior circuit would extend to four in the early 1980s.

Campaigns of the Seventies: the NL, 1969–1980

In this era the NL also failed to achieve the competitive balance envisioned by its 1969 expansion. Over the twelve NL campaigns of these years, both divisions were ruled by powerful dynasties. In the East, the Pirates won six races, the Phillies four, and the Mets two. In the West, the Reds won six races, the Dodgers three, with the Braves, Giants, and Astros as single-season winners.

Yet it was one of the league's lesser powers, the New York Mets, who made a rousing success of the first NL campaign under the new divisional format. Like the moonwalking American astronauts of that summer, the Mets also realized an "impossible dream," and their unlikely triumph became the sports story of that memorable year in the nation's history. In a baseball version of Horatio Alger's rags-to-riches yarns, the forlorn Mets shook off the effects of their horrendous 394–737 won-loss record, which the team had painfully compiled over seven zany seasons of NL play, and won the 1969 Eastern Division race by 8 games over a cocky Chicago Cub team. What's more, the Mets turned the trick by winning 38 of their last 49 games, mostly due to good pitching. Young Tom Seaver's league-leading 25 victories and Jerry Koosman's 17 headed a pitching staff whose 2.99 ERA ranked second in the league. However, a puny .242 team batting average, fronted by outfielder Cleon Jones's .340-12-75, afforded little hope against the Western champion Atlanta Braves, winners by 3 games over the Giants. For the Braves, who led the NL in fielding, Hank Aaron's .300-44-97 batting, and Rico Carty's .342-16-58 effort in limited action, excelled. Pitcher Phil Niekro won 23 and Ron Reed won 18 as the staff turned in a 3.53 ERA. But in the NL's first League Championship Series, the impotent Mets turned tartars; scoring 27 runs in three games, they swept the favored Braves. However, the Mets appeared to be ludicrously mismatched against the versatile Orioles in the following World Series. But after losing the opening game, the Mets swept the Orioles in the next four games to realize their "impossible dream." In the afterglow, an outpouring of "Metomania" swept the country, and a dozen hastily written books celebrating the team's victory were churned out.

But the following year the powerful Pittsburgh Pirates ruthlessly banished any hopes of a continuing competitive balance in the NL East. Over the next six seasons, the Pirates captured five Eastern pennants, including three in a row over the years 1970–1972. In 1970 the Pirates baptized their newly occupied Three Rivers Stadium by downing the Cubs by 5 games and raising their first divisional flag. The Pirates batted .270, with Roberto Clemente hitting .352 and catcher Manny Sanguillen batting .325. With a 3.70 ERA, their pitching was shaky, but reliever Dave Giusti saved 26 games. Coincident with the Pirates' rise, another power moved to the top in the West as the Cincinnati Reds, now ensconced in their new Riverfront Stadium, scored a crushing 14½-game win over the runner-up Dodgers. At the plate the Reds matched the Pirates' batting, while leading the league in homers with 191. Catcher Johnny Bench's 45 homers and 148 RBIs led all sluggers and won him MVP honors. Infielders Pete Rose (.316) and Tony Perez (.317-40-129), and outfielder Bob Tolan (.316) added to the hit parade which was needed to bolster the pitching staff. The team's starting pitchers completed only 32 games, which inspired the bullpen to compile a league-leading 60 saves. And yet the staff's 3.71 ERA was only a point above that of the Pirates. In the LCS that year, the Reds swept the Pirates, but then the Reds fell to the avenging Orioles in the 1970 World Series.

The following year manager Danny Murtaugh led his Pirates to a 7-game win over the Cardinals in the NL East. At the plate the Pirates upped their batting to .274 as Clemente (.341) and Sanguillen (.319) maintained their pace, while outfielder Willie Stargell's league-leading 48 homers powered the team's league-leading 154-homer assault. In the West, poor pitching consigned the Reds to fourth place, leaving the field to the Giants and Dodgers. After leading most of the way, the Giants faltered in the stretch, but hung on to win by a game over the Dodgers. League-leading fielding buoyed the Giants, who batted only .247. Outfielder Bobby Bonds's .288-33-102 was the best effort by a regular. Future Hall of Fame pitcher Juan Marichal and Gaylord Perry combined for 34 victories as the staff's 3.33 ERA came close to matching the Pirates' mark of 3.31. In LCS play the Pirates lost the opening game, but swept to victory. And when matched against the Orioles in the World Series, the Pirates lost the first two games, but then rebounded to win in seven. The Pirate victory triggered a spate of destructive riots in Pittsburgh, but any fears by city fathers of future riots to come were banished by the shortcomings of the Pirate teams.

Although the 1972 Pirates romped to an 11-game victory over the Cubs in the East, another six seasons would pass before the Bucs won another NL pennant. Future Hall of Famer Roberto Clemente batted .312 and notched his 3,000th career hit as the Pirates matched their .274 batting mark of 1971. Outfielder Al Oliver batted .312 and infielder Richie Hebner batted .300, while Stargell

powered the attack with 33 homers and 112 RBIs. Led by starting pitcher Steve Blass (19–8) and reliever Giusti (22 saves), the pitching staff posted a 2.81 ERA. In the West, meanwhile, the Reds rebounded to win by 10½ games over the Houston Astros. The acquisition of infielder Joe Morgan strengthened the Reds, who also got another MVP performance from Bench. The catcher's 40 homers and 125 RBIs led the league, and infielder Rose batted .307. But the pitching staff completed only 25 games. The best effort by a starter was Gary Nolan's 15–5 mark, but the bullpen, led by Clay Carroll's league-leading 37 saves, saved 60 games. In LCS action the Reds rallied from a 2–1 deficit to win the league pennant in five games. In the decisive game, played in Cincinnati, the Reds won 4–3. In the ninth inning of that game, Pirate reliever Bob Moose wild-pitched the winning run home. But when the Reds faced a 3–1 deficit in the World Series, their rally fell short as the Athletics hung on to win the world title in seven games.

Over the winter, Clemente's tragic death while on a mercy mission to Nicaragua was a crushing blow to the Pirate cause. Even so, the 1973 Pirates hung close, finishing third in a weak Eastern Division. On the strength of a lackluster 82–79 record, the Mets edged the Cardinals by 1½ games. Offensively the Mets batted a meager .246 with only 85 homers, but Seaver's 19–10 pitching and league-leading 2.08 ERA and reliever Tug McGraw's 25 saves compensated. In the West the Reds outlasted the Dodgers by 3½ games to win the divisional pennant. Led by Rose's league-leading .338 hitting, the Reds batted .254 and hit 137 homers. Perez batted .314-27-101, Morgan batted .290-26-82, and Bench drove in 104 runs. The Reds also led the league in stolen bases and fielding, and the pitching staff ranked fourth, just behind the Mets. Not surprisingly, the Reds were touted as LCS favorites, but the Mets edged them in five games to emerge as the NL's standard bearer in the World Series. Astonishingly the Mets took a 3–2 lead in the first five Series games against the Athletics. Had they hung on to win with their puny seasonal record, it would have gone into the record books as a quirky record. But the A's quashed this prospect by snagging the final two games to win the 1973 World Series.

As the impotent Mets faded in 1974, the Pirates rose again to win the next two Eastern races before yielding to the rising Phillies. Unsurpassed .274 team batting boosted the Pirates to a thin 1½-game win over the Cardinals in the East. Outfielders Richie Zisk (.313-17-100), Al Oliver (.321 and 85 RBIs), and Stargell (.301-25-96) powered the team, whose pitching staff posted a 3.49 ERA. But the league's balance of power was shifting westward, where the Dodgers and Reds would monopolize the next five NL pennants. In the 1974 Western Division race, the Dodgers defeated the Reds by 4 games. Backed by the most durable infield in baseball history, in Steve Garvey, Dave Lopes, Bill Russell, and Ron Cey, the 1974 Dodgers batted .272. First baseman Garvey, who would set an NL record in consecutive games played, led the assault that year with a .312-21-111 performance which won him MVP honors. Outfielder Jim Wynn added 32 homers and 108 RBIs. Pitchers Andy Messersmith and Don Sutton combined for 39 wins to head the league's top-ranked pitching staff, but reliever Mike Marshall won the pitching honors with his 15 victories and 21 saves. What's more, fireman Marshall appeared in a record 106 games. In the LCS playoff the Dodgers dispatched the Pirates in four games, but the Dodgers lost the World Series to the Athletics in five games.

It was the third consecutive Series victory for the Athletics, but the powerful Cincinnati Reds reversed the trend in 1975–1976. Dubbed "the Big Red Machine," the perennially pitching-poor Reds got only 22 complete games from their starters in 1975, but the team's crushing offense buried the runner-up Dodgers by 20 games. Heading the team's .271 batting offensive was second baseman Joe Morgan, who won MVP honors for his .327 batting and 94 RBIs. Third baseman Rose and outfielders Ken Griffey and George Foster topped .300 at bat, and first baseman Tony Perez and catcher Bench drove in a combined 219 runs. In the East the Pirates beat the Phils by 6½ games to win a second straight divisional title. The Pirates batted .263 and led the league in homers. Outfielder Dave Parker (.308-25-101) and first baseman Stargell (.295-22-90) powered the team, and catcher Manny Sanguillen batted .328. And the pitching staff's 3.02 ERA bettered the Reds. But the Reds swept the Pirates in LCS play and went on to beat the Red Sox in a tense seven-game World Series classic. In the final game at Boston the Reds overcame a 3–0 Boston lead. Morgan's single in the ninth inning provided the margin of victory as the Reds won 4–3. The victory was the Reds' first World Series triumph since 1940.

Nor did they stop there. The following year, as the NL celebrated its hundredth anniversary, the all-conquering Reds downed the Dodgers by 10 games in the West on the strength of league leadership in batting, homers, RBIs, stolen bases, and fielding. Morgan's .320-27-111 batting won the infielder a second straight MVP Award, Rose batted .323, and the outfield of Griffey (.336), Cesar Geronimo (.307), and George Foster (.306) all topped the .300 mark. Foster's 121 RBIs led the league, and the bullpen fronted by Rollie Eastwick led the league in saves. In the East it was the Phillies' misfortune to have to face this wrecking crew in LCS play. That year the Phillies finally won an Eastern title, the first of three consecutive victories, all coming at the expense of the Pirates. In 1976 the Phillies trounced the Pirates by 9 games. Slugging third baseman Mike Schmidt led the league in homers with 38 and drove in 107 runs, and the outfield of Jay Johnstone, Garry Maddox, and Greg Luzinski all topped the .300 mark, with Luzinski batting in 95 runs. Steve Carlton (20–7) headed a pitching staff that bettered the mediocre Reds' staff, but otherwise needed the 36 saves posted by the relief corps of Ron Reed, Tug McGraw, and Gene Garber. The LCS matchup between the Reds and the Phillies was a foregone conclusion which the Reds decided with a sweep. The Reds then went on to sweep the Yankees in the World Series to become the first NL team since 1922 to win back-to-back world titles.

But the Big Red Machine blew a gasket in 1977. The loss of ace pitcher Don Gullett to the re-entry draft (and the Yankees) and a dubious trade which sent first baseman Perez to the Expos created weaknesses that not even the mid-season acquisition of pitcher Tom Seaver from the Mets could assuage. Nor could Foster's herculean batting, which produced a league-leading 52 homers and

149 RBIs together with a .320 batting average. As the pitching-poor Reds faltered, the Dodgers brushed them aside to win the Western title by 10 games. League leadership in homers (191) and pitching buoyed the Dodgers. A successful arm operation gave a new life to lefty Tommy John, whose 20 victories led the pitching staff. Offensively, outfielder Reggie Smith's .302-32-87 led the attack, with outfielder Dusty Baker and infielders Garvey and Ron Cey each topping the 30 mark in homers. Meanwhile, the Phillies repeated in the East, their 101 victories leading the league and topping the runner-up Pirates by 5 games. The Phillies led the league in batting at .279. Outfielder Luzinski's .309-30-130 was his best effort, and Schmidt again powered 38 homers while driving in 101 runs. Carlton led the pitchers with 23 victories, and Larry Christenson's 19–6 mark was his best in the majors; moreover, the bullpen's 43 saves topped the league. Still, the Dodgers defeated the Phillies in four games in the LCS. However, the Dodgers got their comeuppance from the Yankees, who won the 1977 World Series in six games.

Although the victory margin for both teams was skimpier, the 1978 divisional races repeated the scenario of the previous year. In the West the Dodgers repeated by edging the Reds by 2½ games. Once again the pitching staff was the league's best (3.12 ERA). Starters Burt Hooton, Tommy John, Don Sutton, and Doug Rau won 66 games, and reliever Terry Foster saved 22. Garvey headed the team's .264 batting attack with .316-21-113 stickwork; and Cey, Reggie Smith, and Rick Monday combined for 71 homers to head the team's league-leading homer barrage. In the East the Phillies won for a third straight year, but by a skimpy 1½-game margin over the Pirates. Luzinski's 35 homers and 101 RBIs paced a weak .258 batting assault; and Carlton (with 16 wins) and Dick Ruthven (with 13 wins), and relievers Ron Reed and McGraw led the Phils' pitching staff, which was the best in the Eastern Division, but a far cry from the Dodgers' mark of 1978. In LCS play the Dodgers again trounced the Phillies in four games, but again the Dodgers fell to their old Yankee nemesis in six games.

As the decade waned, the Pirates returned to power in the East by edging the runner-up Expos by 2 games. It was the sixth Eastern title of this era for the Pirates, who batted a lusty .272 but whose mediocre pitching staff depended heavily on its superb bullpen headed by Kent Tekulve, who appeared in 94 games and saved 31. Third baseman Bill Madlock's .328 batting led the team along with Parker (.310-25-94) and Stargell, whose 32 homers helped drive in 82 runs. At the same time in the West, the Reds also won their sixth divisional title of the era, beating the Astros by 1½ games. With Rose gone by way of the re-entry draft, his replacement Ray Knight batted .318 and, along with outfielders Griffey (.316) and Foster (.302-30-98), paced the team's .264 batting. Seaver's 16 victories led the team's mediocre pitching staff. The two rival dynasties met for a last time to date in LCS play with the Pirates sweeping the Reds. In World Series action the Pirates fell behind the Orioles three games to one, but swept the last three games for a stunning victory.

In 1980 the Phillies ended a thirty-year drought by winning an NL pennant. Goaded by manager Dallas Green, the Phillies won 21 of their last 28 games to eke a 1-game victory over the Expos in the East. An MVP performance by slugger Schmidt, who hit 48 homers and drove in 121 runs, powered the Phils, who also got .309 batting from outfielder Bake McBride, and .282 batting and inspired leadership from the transplanted Pete Rose. Lefty Carlton's 24 wins led the league and won him the Cy Young Award, and Dick Ruthven won 17, while bullpen stalwart Tug McGraw saved 20 games. In the West the Dodgers and Astros finished in a dead heat as the front-running Astros lost their last three games to the visiting Dodgers. But in a sudden-death playoff for the Eastern Division title, Joe Niekro pitched the Astros to a 7–1 victory over the Dodgers at Dodger Stadium. The Astros got .309 hitting from outfielder Cesar Cedeno, and the team batted .261, but the punchless offense produced only 75 homers. But the Astros' pitching staff was the league's best. Joe Niekro won 20 games, Nolan Ryan won 11, and Vern Ruhle won 12. Ruhle's pitching compensated for the loss of power pitcher J. R. Richard, who had compiled a 10–4, 1.89 record when he sustained a career-ending stroke. In LCS play the Phils and Astros battled through five games, with the rebounding Phillies scoring two extra-inning victories in Houston to land the pennant. Thus emboldened, the Phillies went on to beat the Royals in a six-game World Series tussle. It was the Phillies' first world championship in the club's ninety-seven-year history as an NL team.

But in the season after Philadelphia's momentous victory, which saw the local police deploying mounted troopers and guard dogs to restrain the delirious Philadelphia fans, the major leagues were staggered by a crippling player strike.

Baseball's Embattled Decade, 1981–1990

The conservative mood that gripped the nation in the late 1970s also held sway during these years and helped to catapult Ronald Reagan to landslide victories in the presidential elections of 1980 and 1984. Indeed, ex–movie actor Reagan was no stranger to baseball fans, many of whom saw him play the role of ex–pitching great Grover Cleveland Alexander on the silver screen. And now, as an avowed conservative, President Reagan sought to divert the nation's economy toward a free-enterprise course by such tactics as cutting federal taxes and reducing federal domestic spending programs. At the same time Reagan advocated a powerful national defense posture aimed at combating the spread of international communism.

But Reagan's first term was darkened by an economic recession which contributed to high unemployment. Especially hard hit by unemployment were minorities and blue-collar workers in declining industries. Among the declining industries were such former bellwether industries as steel and mining, whose sagging production was attributed to foreign competition. However, the American economy in the main continued to shift from its former heavy-industrial base to its present emphasis on high technology and information and services production.

Nevertheless, before Reagan's first term ended, such factors as federal tax cuts and falling inflation and interest rates spurred an economic recovery which continued into 1987. The boomlet reduced unemployment, but for most workers wage increases were small, and some 20 million

Americans still remained at or near the poverty level in 1987. Indeed, some critics faulted Reagan's economic policies for favoring the well-to-do, whose ranks by 1987 included a million millionaires and a score of billionaires among a population of 240 million.

But prospects for continuing affluence dimmed as the year 1987 closed amidst fears of an impending recession. In October the nation's burgeoning national debt (estimated at $2.6 trillion) and a chronic foreign-trade imbalance triggered financial panics in domestic and foreign stock markets. Aggravated by the festering Iran-Contra scandal and the naval confrontation with Iran in the Persian Gulf, the economic crisis boded ill for the Reagan Administration and for the nation's future.

Moreover, other menacing problems clouded the nation's future. Among them was the epidemic of drug abuse which defied efforts at punitive control. According to a 1985 estimate, the multibillion-dollar illegal drug industry was being supported by 20 million American consumers. Included were scores of professional athletes who confronted their officials with the knotty problem of disciplining abusers without violating their civil rights.

And yet for all the sobering national problems, most Americans of these years enjoyed moderately prosperous lifestyles. For this accomplishment, the two-paycheck family trend was largely responsible. By 1987 working women, whose ranks included most wives, accounted for more than half of the American labor force. Buoyed by the additional income, most Americans continued to spend lavishly on leisure and recreational activities. According to one report, Americans in 1987 were spending well over $50 billion a year on gambling, sports betting, and physical activities alone. And among the host of available leisure activities, television viewing, especially televised sports programs, maintained a leading position.

Certainly America's continuing infatuation with major sports was a blessing for baseball as revenues from live attendance and television continued to grow at a record-setting pace. At the same time, however, spiraling player salaries pitted players against owners in a series of pitched battles on the labor front.

Indeed, embattled relations between players and owners was a leitmotif of this era. In 1981 the failure of owners and players to agree on a new labor contract triggered a crippling baseball strike—the worst in the history of major league baseball since the 1890 debacle. A major bone of contention was the owners' demand that a club receive a veteran player as compensation for losing a player in one of the annual re-entry drafts. When the deadline for an agreement expired with no compromise, the players struck on June 11, 1981. Once the strike began, it lasted some fifty days and wiped out a third of the season's playing schedule. The strike cost the united players at least $30 million in lost salaries, and the owners lost an estimated $116 million in revenues. However, the owners were partly compensated by $50 million in strike insurance. On the last day of July, a compromise ended the great player strike. The owners won their point on the player compensation issue, but they had to settle for an indirect approach. Thus when a team lost a player in a re-entry draft, the team got to choose a veteran player from a pool of surplus players provided by all major league teams. For their part, the players also successfully fended off the owners' demand for a ceiling on salaries. Agreement on these and lesser issues produced a fifth Basic Agreement, which ran through the season of 1984. The eleventh-hour agreement saved what was left of the 1981 season, but the salvage format devised by Commissioner Bowie Kuhn drew much criticism. Kuhn's plan called for a split-season campaign, a format which had been tried and discarded as unsatisfactory in 1892. Under Kuhn's scheme, the first-half winners were those teams which led their divisions at the time of the June 11 player walkout. The second-half winners would be the teams that led the divisions at the close of the campaign after the resumption of play in August. By ruling first-half winners ineligible to repeat as champions, Kuhn's plan of scheduling a round of playoffs to decide the divisional championships in each league was assured. Thus a separate best-of-five playoff series was scheduled to settle first the matter of the 1981 divisional championships. Thereafter, the winners engaged in the usual best-of-five game series to determine the champions of each league. Although the format worked as planned, it was faulted for producing lackadaisical play on the part of three of the four first-half winners and for reducing attendance in the second half of what writer Red Smith called "the dishonest season."

Nor did the great strike of 1981 end the tensions between the embattled players and owners. When the fifth Basic Agreement expired at the end of 1984 with no agreement in place, a new strike threat loomed in 1985. With salaries continuing their upward spiral, averaging $363,000 in 1984 with 36 players paid at least a million dollars that year, the owners determined to arrest the trend. Correctly zeroing in on salary arbitration as the cause of runaway salaries, the owners demanded that a player wait more than the current two-year period before becoming eligible for salary arbitration. In addition, the owners renewed their demand for a ceiling on salaries. Naturally the players resisted, and when no agreement was reached, the players struck on August 6, 1985. But this time the walkout lasted only two days; obviously neither side wanted a repeat of the 1981 ordeal. Following the resumption of negotiations, a sixth Basic Agreement was promulgated. The new contract compromised on the major issues. For their part, the owners failed to get a salary ceiling, but the players agreed to wait three years instead of two to become eligible for salary arbitration. The players won increased pension benefits, which now would pay a retired veteran with ten years of major league service an annual pension of $91,000! And the owners also won their demand to increase the popular League Championship Series playoffs to a best-of-seven-games format beginning with the 1985 season.

Still, the new four-year Basic Agreement failed to end the hostilities between players and owners. As salaries continued to soar, the owners unilaterally cut team player rosters to twenty-four men and proceeded to boycott the re-entry drafts of 1985–1987. Despite the presence of veteran stars on the auction blocks in those years, there were no bidders. In retaliation, the Players Association charged collusion and filed separate grievances for each of the two boycotted drafts. In September 1987 arbiter Thomas Roberts ruled in favor of the players in the first of those suits, that of 1985. Shortly thereafter, arbiter George Nicolau ruled against the owners in the 1986 and 1987 cases of alleged grievances. The rulings awarded damages in the range of $100 million to the players involved. As a result the chastened owners engaged in open bidding in the re-entry markets of 1988 and 1989. But the Players Association insisted on further collusion protection, which became part of the seventh Basic Agreement that was negotiated after the 1990 lockout. A proviso in that agreement imposed triple damages for any repetition of owner collusion in the signing of free agents.

Still, whatever the outcome of this impending struggle, the players of this era were obvious winners on the salary front. In 1982, the year after the great strike, salaries averaged $250,000. Two years later the average salary climbed to $330,000, almost the same as that of the highest-paid manager, Tom Lasorda of the Dodgers. Then in 1986 the average salary peaked at $412,000 before falling slightly to $410,000 in 1987. The decrease was due in part to teams releasing veteran players and calling up minor leaguers, some of whom could be paid the minimum salary of $62,500. But the decrease was a minor one as annual payrolls for major league clubs in 1987 topped $295 million. Of course, payrolls varied from team to team; in 1987 the Yankee payroll of $18.5 million topped all others, while the $5.6 million payroll of the Seattle Mariners was the lowest of the twenty-six teams.

Average figures also failed to tell the full story of player gains of this era. Boosting average salary figures were the growing number of million-dollar-a-year players. In 1984 there were twenty; in 1985, thirty-six; in 1986, fifty-eight; and in 1987, fifty-seven. Among these plutocrats were a number of $2-million-a-year men, including slugger Mike Schmidt of the Phillies. In signing a two-year contract late in 1987, Schmidt successfully bucked the rumored attempt by owners to hold salaries at $2 million. In Schmidt's words, "I wanted the salary to read $2.25 million probably more for negotiating reasons for my fellow players. . . . I want my fellow players to know that's what top dollar is now." Small wonder then that salaries of baseball players now exceeded those of any rival team sports in America.

In defense of these astronomical player salaries, one could cite major league baseball's continuing prosperity. In this era, annual attendance at major league games repeatedly set new records. After the jarring strike of 1981 limited attendance to 22 million, attendance rebounded to a record 45 million the following year. And despite the national recession, that record fell in 1983. And, after falling by a mere 800,000 in 1984, attendance continued upward. In 1986 annual attendance totaled 47,500,000 and in 1987 it topped 52 million. As in every year since its mini-expansion in 1977, the AL led in attendance, and in 1987 the AL outdrew the NL by 2.5 million. But as always, attendance was unevenly distributed among the clubs. Until 1987 only the Dodgers had topped the 3 million mark in annual attendance, which they did on several occasions, but that year the NL Mets and Cardinals also cracked that barrier. Meanwhile, no AL team had broken the 3 million attendance barrier, but in 1987 the Toronto Blue Jays neared the mark, and in 1988 the Twins surpassed it. Moreover, the attendance picture was brightening for teams located in older cities like Chicago, Boston, New York, San Francisco, Cleveland, St. Louis, and Milwaukee, where demographic reports showed a reversal of population losses.

However, revenues from soaring attendance alone could not have supported the astonishing salaries of this era. What made the difference was television revenue, which some critics blamed for stimulating the trend by casting ballplayers in the company of highly paid TV celebrities. Be that as it may, in 1983 major league officials negotiated a $1.1 billion, six-year network television contract. When the contract took effect in 1984, revenues from network and local TV sources exceeded those of ticket sales. Although revenues from local TV contracts tended to favor teams that were located in the more lucrative local TV markets, the network TV contract in its final year of 1989 promised a hefty $230 million for all clubs to divide. Nevertheless, it was too soon to write *finis* to the old adage that "at the gate is baseball's fate." In 1985 a reported decline in network TV advertising sales raised the specter that the overexposure of televised sports programs would reverse the trend. Should ratings of televised sports programs decline further, the amount of revenue from network TV would be further reduced.

At this time critics blamed drug abuse by players for lessening the popularity of major sports. But surprisingly baseball's popularity was little affected by revelations of drug abuse by players of this era. In 1980 director Ken Moffett of the Players Association admitted that as many as 40 percent of major league players might be drug abusers. In 1983 the problem reached serious proportions when three Kansas City Royals players were sentenced to jail terms as convicted users. That same year a Dodger pitcher was suspended, and in 1985 a San Diego Padres player was traded for similar offenses. And in 1985 baseball's public image was further tarnished by revelations coming from two Pittsburgh court trials of drug sellers. The testimony named seventeen players as drug users. Although these revelations had no discernible impact on the game's popularity, Commissioner Peter Ueberroth chose to treat the matter as a major scandal. But the commissioner's attempt to force all players to submit to periodic drug tests ran afoul of the Players Association, which insisted that the issue be addressed through collective-bargaining procedures. Still, Ueberroth suspended the accused players and, as a condition for reinstatement, forced each player to donate up to 10 percent of his salary to charities and to engage in antidrug campaigns. After ruling on this matter, Ueberroth announced at the opening of the 1986 season that the drug problem in baseball was solved. But this face-saving claim ignored the reality of the national epidemic of drug abuse and was mocked by the failure of President Reagan's vaunted 1986 antidrug crusade. Indeed, it is most unlikely that the game has been purged of drug abuse, and the problem of devising a punitive policy continued to be an unresolved issue facing the game as it entered the decade of the 1990s.

That major league baseball's popularity was so little troubled by drug scandals, strikes, soaring salaries, or even the economic recession owed much to the dazzling style of play. Indeed, fans of this era witnessed the apotheosis of the big-bang offensives. In the AL, where sluggers consistently outhomered NL swingers by wide margins, homer records fell like sheaves. Over this seven-year span AL sluggers averaged 2,000 homers a year, with record-breaking seasons succeeding each other over the years

1985–1987. In 1985 AL sluggers bashed 2,178; in 1986, 2,240; and in 1987, a gargantuan 2,634 homers were struck. What's more, NL sluggers in 1987 weighed in with 1,824 homers to break their league's 1970 record.

Major league baseball's 1987 cannonade saw twenty-eight players hit 30 or more homers, including twenty American leaguers. Rookie Mark McGwire of the Oakland Athletics led the AL with 49—an all-time seasonal mark by a yearling, the feat won McGwire a unanimous vote for Rookie of the Year honors. Meanwhile, Andre Dawson of the Cubs matched McGwire's output and won the NL MVP Award despite his team's last-place finish in the NL East. Among the most consistent sluggers of this era, Mike Schmidt of the Phillies led NL sluggers four times, while Dale Murphy of the Braves twice topped the league. By the end of the 1988 season, Schmidt's total of 542 homers ranked him with the all-time leading clouters and following his retirement early in the 1989 season, Schmidt was named Player of the Decade by *The Sporting News*. And at the end of the 1987 season, Reggie Jackson retired from the AL wars with a lifetime total of 563 homers. Jackson's passing from the game left a lonesome gap in AL power circles which young Goliaths like McGwire, Pete Incaviglia, Jose Canseco, George Bell, and Jesse Barfield seemed destined to fill.

But if this era's homer production was unprecedented, seasonal batting achievements were ordinary. Thanks to its designated hitter rule, AL batters annually surpassed NL hitters, with seasonal AL averages topping .260 while those of the NL hovered around the .255 mark. In the NL, black stars continued their batting leadership. Black stars won all of the NL batting titles of this era, with veteran Bill Madlock of the Pirates capturing a pair and young Tony Gwynn of the Padres winning three. It was otherwise in the AL, where a single dominating hitter, third baseman Wade Boggs of the Red Sox, captured four batting titles. An ideal leadoff hitter, the lefty-swinging Boggs batted .349 as a rookie in 1982. Over the next five seasons Boggs averaged a Cobbian .368. Moreover, in 1987 Boggs belted 24 homers to triple his best seasonal homer output thus far. In 1989, he became the first AL player to post seven consecutive 200-hit seasons.

Among the memorable batting feats of this era, Pete Rose gained immortality on September 4, 1985, when the Cincinnati player-manager's single off pitcher Eric Show of the Padres broke Cobb's lifetime record of 4,191 hits. To be sure, Rose needed 2,300 more at bats than Cobb did to turn the trick, but the forty-four-year-old sparkplug put his feat into proper perspective when he said, "I might not be the best player, but I got the most hits." Indeed, and when Rose retired from active play at the end of the 1986 season, he had extended the total hit record to 4,256. While nothing touched Rose's accomplishment, the explosive 1987 season saw Don Mattingly of the Yankees match Dale Long's feat of homering in eight consecutive games, while Paul Molitor of the Brewers hit safely in 39 consecutive games, and rookie catcher Benito Santiago of the Padres hit safely in 34. Santiago's feat won for him NL Rookie of the Year honors.

In the offensive category of stolen bases, NL speedsters perennially topped their AL counterparts. At this time the newly crowned prince of thieves was outfielder Vince Coleman of the Cardinals. In 1985 Coleman set a rookie record with 110 steals, and at the end of the 1987 season he became the first player ever to swipe 100 or more bases in three consecutive seasons. However, Coleman had yet to top the latest seasonal record of 130 thefts, set by outfielder Rickey Henderson of the Oakland Athletics in 1982. Indeed, in 1990 Henderson broke Ty Cobb's AL record for the most steals, zipped by the mark of Sliding Billy Hamilton, and zeroed in on Lou Brock's major league record.

Not surprisingly the offensive pyrotechnics of these years had pundits wondering whatever had happened to pitching. Indeed, seasonal ERAs skyrocketed in both leagues, with the AL average well above 4.00 and that of the NL above 3.70. Of course this meant that the always volatile pitching-batting equilibrium was again out of whack. For the latest imbalance, observers proffered such explanations as livelier balls, narrowed strike zones, pitchers' fears of retaliation if they threw inside to batters, pitchers relying too much on breaking pitches, and managers relying more on their bullpen and demanding too little of their starters. Indeed, the numbers of complete games pitched by starting pitchers declined as managers relied more on specialized relief pitchers. Among the bullpen specialists, the most celebrated continued to be the firemen who were counted to come on late in a game to save a victory. Among the best were Dan Quisenberry, Goose Gossage, Bruce Sutter (all of whom bowed out in 1990), Todd Worrell, Dave Righetti, Gene Garber (who notched his 200th career save in 1987), and Lee Smith, who set a record by recording 30 or more saves in three consecutive seasons.

Still, it seemed evident that more than yeomanlike relief work was needed to restore pitching to a proper balance with hitting. For now, managers complained of poorly trained pitchers, while pitchers blamed prevailing rules for favoring batters. Nor was it surprising that some pitchers were smuggling in illegal scuffed-ball and spitball deliveries.

However, good pitchers were by no means extinct. In this era Nolan Ryan hurled a record-setting fifth no-hitter in 1981. And at the end of the 1988 season, the forty-one-year-old fireballer, who had lost little of his earlier velocity, extended his all-time leading strikeout total to 4,775 whiffs. Indeed, in 1987 Ryan's 270 strikeouts led the NL, and his 2.76 ERA hardly justified his 8–16 won-loss record. In 1989, the forty-two-year-old Ryan fanned 301 batters and topped the 5000 mark in strikeouts. And in 1990 the venerable fireballer hurled a sixth no-hitter to break his earlier record of five. Among the promising younger pitchers, Dwight Gooden of the Mets blazed his way to a 24–4, 1.53 ERA, with 268 strikeouts in 1985. And the following year Roger Clemens of the Red Sox also went 24–4 to become the first starting pitcher in fifteen years to win the AL MVP Award. Naturally Clemens also won the Cy Young Award that year, and when the ace went 20–9 in 1987, despite early-season ineffectiveness caused by his salary holdout, Clemens won a second Cy Young Award. By winning two straight, Clemens joined the select company of Sandy Koufax, Denny McLain, and Jim Palmer as the only pitchers to win back-to-back Cy Young Awards. And in 1988 Orel Hershiser's performance from August through October was unprecedented.

Recent Campaigns: The AL, 1981–1990

The long unrealized dream of an era of competitive balance now became something of a reality in the AL, as each of the first seven campaigns produced a new league champion. Moreover, eleven different teams won divisional titles in these years. However, in the West the Oakland Athletics won three divisional championships and captured consecutive league championships in 1988–1989. And the Tigers, Royals, Red Sox, and Angels each won a pair of divisional pennants in this era.

The AL's free-for-all pattern began with the singular campaign of 1981. When the long player strike gutted the middle of that season, a split-season format was adopted in hopes of renewing fan support for the arrested campaign. Under this format, the first half of the season ended when the players walked out on June 11, and the second half ran from the resumption of play in mid-August to the end of the regular playing schedule. Because the June 11 strike date had the Yankees leading the Orioles by 2 games in the East, and the Athletics leading the Rangers by 1½ games in the West, these teams were declared the first-half winners of their divisions. But when the split-season plan barred first-half winners from repeating as divisional champs, the Yankees dawdled to a sixth-place finish in the East's second-half race. Thus the Milwaukee Brewers won the second-half Eastern race by 1½ games over the Red Sox. In the West, the Athletics lost the second half to the Royals by 1 game.

At this point, the split-season script called for a best-of-five-games playoff series to determine the divisional championships. In the East the series went the full five games before the Yankees defeated the Brewers, but in the West the scrappy Athletics swept the Royals. Then in the ensuing League Championship Series the Yankees swept the Athletics. Although the Yankees won the 1981 AL pennant, their overall record was bettered by two other teams. The Yankee victory owed to its pitching staff, whose 2.90 ERA led the league; starters Ron Guidry and Dave Righetti combined for 19 wins, and reliever Goose Gossage saved 20 games. As for the Athletics, whose overall record was the AL's best, they led the league in homers. The Athletics were led by outfielder Rickey Henderson, who batted .319 and led the league in stolen bases, and pitcher Steve McCatty, whose 14 wins and 2.32 ERA led the league. As for the Yankees, their comeuppance came in the World Series. Matched against the resilient Dodgers, the Yankees took the first two games, but then were ignominiously swept. And by losing three games in relief, Yankee pitcher George Frazier added his name to the annals of World Series goats.

In the dog-eat-dog competition of the next six AL seasons, the Yankees failed to win another divisional title. In 1982 the Brewers squeaked to a 1-game win over the Orioles in the East. In winning, the Brewers batted .279 and the team's 216 homers topped the majors, with shortstop Robin Yount winning MVP honors for his .331-29-114 batting exploits. Outfielder Gorman Thomas led the league with 39 homers and drove in 112 runs. And infielders Cecil Cooper (.331-32-121) and Paul Molitor (.302-19-71) complemented Yount's stickwork. But the pitching was shaky, except for starters Pete Vuckovich and Mike Caldwell, who combined for 35 victories. Veteran reliever

Rollie Fingers saved 29 games, so the late-season injury that sidelined this mustachioed ace was a crusher. In the West, the California Angels won a close race by 3 games over the Royals. A good hitting team, the Angels finished right behind the Brewers in hitting and homers, and their pitching bettered the Brewers. Starter Geoff Zahn's 18 wins led the staff. Offensively, a quartet of expensive recent acquisitions paced the attack, including infielders Rod Carew (.319) and Doug DeCinces (.301-30-97), and outfielders Fred Lynn (.299) and Reggie Jackson (39 homers and 102 RBIs). Jackson's 39 homers tied Thomas for the league leadership, and the veteran drove in 101 runs. When these two well-matched teams met in LCS play, for a time it seemed likely that Angel manager Gene Mauch might win his first pennant. The Angels took the first two games at home, but were swept by the Brewers in Milwaukee. Thus the Brewers became the first major league team to win an LCS after losing the first two games. But in World Series play it was the Cardinals who rebounded from a 3–2 deficit to defeat the Brewers. This latest loss was the fourth in a row by an AL entry.

But over the next three seasons, three different AL teams ended the NL streak by winning world titles. In 1983 the Orioles drove to a 6-game victory over the runner-up Tigers in the Eastern Division. Pitchers Scott McGregor (18–7), Mike Boddicker (16–8), Storm Davis (13–7), and reliever Tippy Martinez (with 21 saves) headed the league's second-best pitching staff. At bat the Orioles hit .269, and the team's 168 homers led the majors. Shortstop Cal Ripken, Jr.'s .318-27-102 batting won him MVP honors, while first baseman Eddie Murray weighed in with .306-33-111 clouting. Meanwhile, in the West the long-dormant Chicago White Sox stormed to a 20-game victory over the Royals. In landing their first divisional title, the White Sox drew 2 million fans, who saw young Ron Kittle win Rookie of the Year honors with his 35 homers and 100 RBIs. Although lacking a .300 hitter, the White Sox got plentiful power from outfielder Harold Baines (20-99), catcher Carlton Fisk (26-86), and DH Greg Luzinski (32-95). What's more, the White Sox boasted a pair of 20-game winners in Cy Young Award winner LaMarr Hoyt (24–10) and Rich Dotson (22–7). Behind Hoyt, the White Sox won the first LCS game, but the Orioles swept the next three games to win the pennant. The Orioles then dropped the opening game of the 1983 World Series at home, but then swept the Phillies to end the AL's humiliating losing streak.

The following year another new champion surfaced in the AL East, which was now being touted as the strongest division in the majors. Riding the momentum of a 35–5 breakaway gait, the Detroit Tigers went on to win 104 games, enough to lap the Toronto Blue Jays by 15 games. It was indeed a vintage year for manager Sparky Anderson's all-conquering Tigers. Offensively the Tigers led the league in hitting (.271) and homers (187). Shortstop Alan Trammell batted .314, and outfielder Kirk Gibson and catcher Lance Parrish combined to produce 60 homers and 189 RBIs. To top it off, the Tigers also fielded the league's best pitching staff. Starters Jack Morris, Dan Petry, and Milt Wilcox turned in 54 victories and reliever Willie Hernandez, a recent acquisition from the Phillies, saved 32 games. In 32 of his 33 game-saving situations, Hernandez met the test—an achievement that won him

both the Cy Young and MVP awards. Meanwhile, in the weaker Western Division the Royals eked a 3-game win over the Angels and Twins, but the Royals won only six more games than they lost. The Royals batted .268, with outfielder Willie Wilson and DH Hal McRae topping the .300 mark. But the pitching was mediocre and the staff depended heavily on reliever Dan Quisenberry, who saved 44 games. When the Tigers and Royals faced off in LCS play, the Tigers won the 1984 AL pennant by dispatching the Royals in three games. And in World Series action, the Tigers easily defeated the San Diego Padres in five games. By skippering the Tigers to victory, Sparky Anderson became the first manager to win World Series titles in both the American and National leagues.

But the Tigers' view from the top was a brief one. In 1985 they fell 15 games off the pace, leaving the Eastern field to the Blue Jays and Yankees. And at the close of the season, the Blue Jays topped the Yankees by 2 games, to win their first divisional title since joining the AL in the mini-expansion of 1977. The rise of the Blue Jays owed much to general manager Pat Gillick, who, by dint of shrewd trades and canny selections in annual surplus-player drafts, swiftly assembled a pennant contender. In 1985 the Blue Jays' pitching staff led the league, and outfielder Jesse Barfield (.289-27-84) powered an offense that produced a .269 team batting average and 158 homers. Pitcher Dave Stieb's 2.48 ERA led the league's pitchers, although his 14–13 record was disappointing. Starters Doyle Alexander and Jimmy Key combined for 31 victories, and Dennis Lamp posted an 11–0 record in relief. In the lightly regarded Western Division, meanwhile, the Royals became the only AL team of this brief era to repeat as divisional champs. In winning by a single game over the Angels, the Royals batted only .252, but powered 154 homers. Third baseman George Brett's .335-30-112 led the hitters, and first baseman Steve Balboni drove in 88 runs and hit 36 homers. The pitching was good. Young Bret Saberhagen's 20–6, 2.87 ERA won him the Cy Young Award, Charlie Leibrandt's 17 wins came on the league's second-best ERA, and reliever Dan Quisenberry saved 37 games. When the Blue Jays and Royals squared off in the newly extended seven-game LCS, the Blue Jays took a 3–1 lead, but the gritty Royals came on to win in seven games, beating the Blue Jays in their home roost the last two games. In the World Series, the resilient Royals staged yet another memorable comeback against the favored Cardinals. After losing the first two games at home, the Royals fell behind 3–1, but rallied to win the next three games. This latest World Series victory extended the AL's winning streak to three.

In another topsy-turvy campaign, the 1986 Red Sox dethroned the Blue Jays in the East. The Red Sox took the lead in June and hung on to win the division pennant by 5½ games over the Yankees. A .271 team batting assault was fronted by batting champ Wade Boggs (.357-8-71) and outfielder Jim Rice (.324-20-110). Boston's overall pitching was mediocre, but starter Roger Clemens led all pitchers with a 24–4, 2.48 effort that won the big righthander both the MVP and Cy Young awards. While the Red Sox were winning in the East, the Royals faded in the West as arm miseries tolled on young Saberhagen. Thus the Angels won the division by 5 games over the Texas Rangers. Rookie first baseman Wally Joyner, who replaced the great Carew, batted .299-22-100 to head the Angels' weak .255 batting. But Angel pitching ranked second in the AL, with Mike Witt winning 18 on a sparkling 2.84 ERA, Kirk McCaskill and veteran Don Sutton combining for 32 wins, and reliever Donnie Moore saving 21 games. When the Angels took a 3–1 lead over the Red Sox in LCS play, it now appeared as if manager Gene Mauch might win his first pennant in twenty-five years at the helm of major league teams. Indeed, in the fifth game Mauch's Angels were one pitch away from a league title, but the Red Sox rallied to win the game on heroics by Dave Henderson. The Red Sox then took the next two games at home to land the 1986 AL pennant. In the World Series the Red Sox jumped to a 3–2 lead over the Mets and appeared on the verge of winning their first world title since 1918, but the Mets crushed the dream by winning the last two games at Shea Stadium.

As a climax to the eighty-six-year history of the AL, the 1987 season provided a storied campaign. In a frenetic season which saw AL sluggers set yet another homer mark and attendance climb to new heights, both divisional races were fiercely contested. In the East waged an epic struggle that ended in a 2-game victory by the Tigers. With seven games to play, the Blue Jays led by 3½ games, but incredibly they lost all seven, including three vital games to the Tigers in Detroit. Hefty .272 batting and a major-league-leading 225 homer barrage powered the Tigers, whose shaky pitching staff was bolstered by the September acquisition of veteran Doyle Alexander from the Braves. By posting a 5–0 record with the Tigers, Alexander was named Pitcher of the Month by *The Sporting News*. Among the offensive standouts, shortstop Alan Trammell batted .343-28-105, young catcher Matt Nokes, who replaced the departed Parrish, batted .289-32-87, and forty-year-old first baseman Darrell Evans hit 34 homers and drove in 99 runs. With Anderson's Tigers posting the best record in the majors, scant hope was afforded the Western-winning Minnesota Twins, who defeated the Royals by 2 games to win their first divisional title. Indeed, the Twins surrendered more runs (806) than they scored (786). But the Twins batted .261 and poled 196 homers; outfielder Kirby Puckett (.332-28-99) led the hitters, with outfielder Tom Brunansky and infielders Kent Hrbek and Gary Gaetti combining for 97 homers and 284 RBIs. On the other hand, Twins' pitchers allowed a horrendous 4.63 ERA. But the staff's most respectable member, Frank Viola, stood out as the winningest left-handed pitcher in the majors over the past four seasons. In 1986 Viola posted a 17–10, 2.90 ERA, and veteran Bert Blyleven recorded a 15–12 mark.

Matched against the Tigers in LCS play, the Twins were scorned as hometown dependents whose outstanding home record owed to the vagaries of their much-maligned domed stadium. But the Twins thrashed the Tigers in five games to win their first AL pennant in twenty-two years. Moreover, they went on to beat the crippled Cardinals in a seven-game World Series struggle by scoring all of their victories in their cozy "homer dome" before capacity crowds of screaming, hankie-waving fans. Thus the 1987 World Series stood out as the first where all victories were won on home fields. And the Twins were indeed fortunate to have hosted four of the games in their favorite bailiwick.

In 1988 a timely rule change which redefined the strike zone helped to quell the raging homer epidemic. In an anticlimactic season that saw batting and power hitting tail off, the well-balanced Oakland Athletics dominated the AL West from the start. The A's 104 victories topped the majors and lapped the runner-up Minnesota Twins by 13 games. League-leading pitching, paced by Dave Stewart's 21 wins and reliever Dennis Eckersley's 45 saves, carried the A's who were powered by young outfielder Jose Canseco's .307-42-124 batting. Canseco also stole 40 bases to become the first player to notch at least 40 homers and as many stolen bases. Meanwhile the AL East saw the only hotly contested divisional race in the majors, as the Boston Red Sox edged the Detroit Tigers by a single game; only 3½ games separated the Red Sox from the sixth place Yankees. Barely playing .500 ball at the All-Star break, the Red Sox changed managers—from John McNamara to Joe Morgan—and staged an extended winning streak that carried them to the top. Despite a late-season slump, they hung on to win. Leading the Boston attack, perennial batting champ Wade Boggs batted .366 to lead the majors and outfielder Mike Greenwell weighed in with a .325-22-119 performance. Ace pitchers Roger Clemens and Bruce Hurst each won 18 games and newly acquired reliever Lee Smith saved 29; still, the Red Sox needed the timely pitching of Mike Boddicker, who joined the staff from the Orioles late in the season and won seven games for Boston. However, the Red Sox were mismatched against the A's, who stormed to a sweeping victory in LCS play on the strength of Canseco's 3 homers and Eckersley's four saves in relief of the starters. In the World Series the A's were held in check by the Los Angeles Dodgers' pitchers, notably Orel Hershiser—whose three hits in Game 2 exceeded the Series total of Canseco and Mark McGwire combined.

But the resilient A's came back with a vengeance in 1989. Newcomers included outfielder Rickey Henderson, acquired from the Yankees, and veteran pitcher Mike Moore, picked up in the re-entry draft. Moore signed for $1.9 million, which he repaid by winning 19 games with a nifty 2.61 ERA. Moore buttressed a pitching staff headed by Dave Stewart, whose 21 victories marked the third consecutive year he matched or topped 20 wins. Bob Welch added 17 victories and reliever Dennis Eckersley saved 33 games. Offensively, Henderson led the league in stolen bases (72) and tied for the lead in runs scored (113). Henderson's production offset the loss of slugger Canseco, who missed 88 games because of an injury. Returning to action, Canseco hit 17 homers to augment the 33 hit by McGwire, who drove in 95 runs. Manager Tony LaRussa's team batted .261 with 127 homers. Meanwhile in the AL East, Manager Frank Robinson took over the helm of the hapless Orioles, who won but 54 games in 1988, and drove them to within two games of the divisional championship. For this achievement Robinson was voted AL Manager of the Year, thus becoming the first black manager to win the award in both major leagues. But the AL East championship went to the Toronto Blue Jays, who were skippered by Cito Gaston. In 1989 Gaston took over a 12–24 team and drove them to a 2-game victory over the Orioles, thus becoming the first black manager to land a divisional title. Toronto's pitching staff was the best in the East, but ranked only fourth in the AL. Dave Stieb's 17–8 pitching led the hurlers, while six Blue Jay sluggers, led by AL homer champ Fred McGriff's 36 blows, reached double figures in homer production. But when the Blue Jays faced the A's in LCS play, the A's crushed them in five games. And matched against the NL Giants in the earthquake-ravaged Bay Area World Series, the A's swept to victory. For pitching two of the four victories, Stewart was named the Series MVP.

Recent Campaigns: The NL, 1981–1990

Although less competitively balanced than the AL, the NL campaigns of this era were hotly contested. Each one of the twelve teams won a divisional title in these years. But the Dodgers won four Western titles and captured two league pennants and two world titles, and in the East the Cardinals won three divisional races and three league championships, yet won only one World Series. Dual divisional titles were won by the Mets, Giants, and Cubs, and singletons were won by the Expos, Padres, Phillies, Braves, Astros, Pirates, and Reds.

When the long players' strike of 1981 gutted team playing schedules by an average of 55 games, the split-season format was unveiled upon resumption of play in August in hopes of salvaging the campaign. By dint of their 1½-game lead over the Cardinals on the June 11 strike day, the Phillies were declared first-half winners in the East; and by virtue of a mere half-game lead over the Reds on that fatal date, the Dodgers became the first-half winners in the West. These were close calls to be sure, but no closer than the results of the second-half races. In the NL East, the Montreal Expos finished a half-game up on the luckless Cardinals, while the Houston Astros edged the snakebit Reds by 1½ games in the West. As frustrated runners-up in two close calls, the Cardinals and Reds with the best overall record in the NL received no recognition. However, the defiant Reds later raised their own home-made pennant as a symbol of protest. In the playoffs for the divisional titles, the Expos beat the Phillies in five games to win in the East, and the Dodgers rallied from a 2–1 deficit in games to beat the Astros in the West. The division-winning Expos and Dodgers then met in the usual League Championship Series, which the Dodgers won. Once again rallying from a 2–1 deficit, manager Lasorda's men edged the Expos. In winning the NL's forlorn 1981 championship, the Dodgers batted .262, led the league in homers with 82, and fielded the league's second-ranked pitching staff. Rookie pitcher Fernando Valenzuela won his first eight games and finished with a 13–7 mark to pace the staff, while outfielders Pedro Guerrero (.300-12-48) and Dusty Baker (.320-9-49) led the batting attack. In World Series play, the Dodgers once again dug themselves a hole by losing the first two games. But once again they rebounded, this time sweeping their old Yankee tormentors to win the 1981 world title.

With the game's image blighted by the "dishonest season" of 1981, the NL sorely needed a dramatic flourish to regain its credibility. Mercifully this was supplied by the extremely close divisional races of 1982. In the NL East a four-team struggle ended with the Cardinals topping the Phillies by 3 games. At bat the Cardinals hit .264, but with scant power (67 homers). Outfielder Lonnie Smith

was the only regular to top the .300 mark, but first baseman Keith Hernandez batted .299 and drove in 94 runs, and outfielder George Hendrick powered the team with his .282-19-104 hitting. By way of compensation, the Cardinals led the league in fielding and stolen bases, and owned the league's second-best mound corps. Starters Joaquin Andujar and Bob Forsch each won 15 games, and ace reliever Bruce Sutter won 9 and saved a league-leading 36 games. In the West, meanwhile, the Braves won their first 13 games and hung on for dear life thereafter to edge the Dodgers by a game. Offensively, the Braves batted only .256, but led the league in homers with 146. Outfielder Dale Murphy's 36 homers generated a league-leading 109 RBIs, and third baseman Bob Horner hit 32 homers and drove in 97 runs. Veteran knuckleball hurler Phil Niekro's 17–4 effort headed the pitching staff, which needed every one of reliever Gene Garber's 30 saves. In LCS play the Braves' mediocre pitching tolled as the Cardinals swept to victory. In ensuing World Series play, the Cardinals fell behind the heavy-hitting Brewers 3–2, but rallied to win the final two games at home. This latest World Series victory was the fourth straight for NL contenders.

When the Cardinals succumbed to poor pitching in 1983, the Phillies snatched the Eastern title by 6 games over the Pirates. The Phillies did it with a brilliant stretch drive, winning twenty-one of their last twenty-five games. Offensively, the aging Phillies batted only .249, but third baseman Mike Schmidt's 40 homers led the league, and his 109 RBIs led the team. A sound pitching staff, fronted by John Denny's Cy Young Award-winning 19–6 effort and reliever Al Holland's 25 saves was a decisive factor in the victory. Meanwhile, in the West the Dodgers also mounted a September stretch drive to topple the Braves by 3 games. Like the Phillies, the Dodgers' .250 hitting was lackluster, but the team led the league in homers (146); outfielder Guerrero's 32 homers and 103 RBIs headed the assault. A major factor was the team's pitching staff, whose 3.10 ERA was the league's best. Valenzuela and Bob Welch combined for 30 victories, and reliever Steve Howe saved 18. In LCS play, veteran hurler Steve Carlton's two victories paced the Phillies to victory in four games. However, the Philadelphia "Wheeze Kids" fell to the Orioles in five games in the 1983 World Series.

As the Phillies sank to fourth place in 1984, the long-suffering Chicago Cubs notched their first pennant of any sort since 1945. In downing the Mets by 6½ games in the East, the Cubs staged a second-half rally, fronted by ex-Phillie infielder Ryne Sandberg's MVP-winning .314 batting. Dodger castoff Ron Cey contributed 25 homers and 97 RBIs, and young first baseman Leon "Bull" Durham weighed in with 23 homers and 96 RBIs. And the pitching staff was bolstered by yet another recent acquisition, Rick Sutcliffe, whose 16–1 record won him the Cy Young Award. Starter Steve Trout chipped in with 13 victories, and reliever Lee Smith won 9 games and saved 33. While the Cubs were winning in the East, another newcomer, the San Diego Padres, easily won the Western title by 12 games over the runner-up Braves. The Padres batted .259, with young outfielder Tony Gwynn leading the league with his .351 batting. The team's modest total of 109 homers was augmented by third baseman Graig Nettles and outfielder Kevin McReynolds, each of whom poled 20. More distinguished was the pitching staff, whose 3.48 ERA ranked third in the league. Able starters Eric Show, Ed Whitson, and Mark Thurmond combined for 43 victories, and veteran reliever Goose Gossage won 10 and saved 25 games. In LCS play the Cubs pounded out a pair of early victories at Wrigley Field, but the surprising Padres swept the next three games at home to become the first NL team ever to win an LCS after losing the first two games. Sad to say, however, the Padres' world title hopes went aglimmering as the Tigers trounced them in five games in the 1984 World Series.

The following year the Cardinals won another NL pennant. In fending off the rising New York Mets by 3 games in the East, the Cardinals relied on league-leading batting and base stealing. Outfielder Willie McGee's league-leading .353 batting won him the MVP Award, and outfielder Vince Coleman won Rookie of the Year honors by stealing 110 bases—a new record for a rookie. Among other stalwarts, second baseman Tom Herr batted .302; first baseman Jack Clark, recently acquired from the Giants, hit 22 homers and drove in 87 runs; and shortstop Ozzie Smith, who won the league's Gold Glove Award for a sixth straight year, batted .276. What's more, Cardinal pitching ranked second in the league, with ex-Pirate John Tudor leading the hurlers with a 21–8, 1.93 ERA performance. Starters Andujar (21 wins) and Danny Cox (18 wins) lent sturdy support, as did relievers Jeff Lahti and Ken Dayley. The pair's 30 saves compensated for the loss of free agent Sutter. As the Cardinals were winning in the East, the Dodgers went on to win the Western title by 5½ games over the Reds. Offensively, the Dodgers' .261 hitting was led by outfielder Guerrero's .320-33-87 hitting. Better still, the Dodger pitching corps led the majors with a 2.96 ERA. The starting quartet of Orel Hershiser, Bob Welch, Jerry Reuss, and Fernando Valenzuela produced 64 wins, and the bullpen saved 31 games. In LCS play, the well-armed Dodgers took the first two games of the newly established seven-game format, but the Cardinals swept the next four to win the NL pennant. Pitted against the underdog Royals in the 1985 World Series, the Cardinals won three of the first four games, including the first two in the Royals' home lair. But the Royals won the fifth game at St. Louis and the final two games back home. The sixth game was marred by a disputed call at first base that gave the Royals a life of which they took full advantage. The Royals then won the final game in an 11–0 laugher, and their victory extended the recent AL World Series winning streak to three years.

The following year the New York Mets ended the AL's victory flurry with a dramatic win. In dominating the NL East, the 1986 Mets won 108 games to lap the runner-up Phillies by 21½ games. Offensively, the versatile Mets led the league in hitting (.263), poled 148 homers, and stole 118 bases. First baseman Keith Hernandez (.310-13-83) headed the charge, with outfielder Darryl Strawberry and catcher Gary Carter powering a combined 51 homers and 198 RBIs. As icing on their victory cake, the Mets fielded the best pitching staff in the majors. Starters Bob Ojeda (18–5), Dwight Gooden (17–6), Sid Fernandez (16–6) and Ron Darling (15–6) were formidable, as was the bullpen duo of Roger McDowell (14 wins, 22 saves) and Jesse Orosco (8 wins, 21 saves). While the Mets were

compiling the best record in the majors, the Houston Astros were winning the Western Division by 10 games over the Reds. Offensively, the Astros batted .255 with 125 homers. Outfielder Kevin Bass batted .311-20-79 to head the hitters, while first baseman Glenn Davis powered 31 homers and drove in 101 runs. Backing the hitters was the league's second-best pitching staff, fronted by Mike Scott's 18–10 hurling, which was accompanied by a league-leading 2.22 ERA. While the outcome of the LCS appeared to be a foregone conclusion, the Astros hung tough before losing in six games to the Mets. The Red Sox also fell to the Mets in World Series play, but not before throwing a scare into manager Davey Johnson's crew. Indeed, the Red Sox took a 3–2 lead in games before the Mets rallied to win the final two games at Shea Stadium.

The following year most observers picked the swaggering Mets to repeat, but the resilient Cardinals took the 1987 Eastern title by 3 games. Although outhit by the league-leading Met batters, the Cardinals mustered .263 hitting, which they backed by stout relief pitching to pull off their victory. Offensively, the Cardinals' 94 homers were the fewest by any major league team this season, but first baseman Jack Clark bashed 35 and drove in 106 runs. Third baseman Terry Pendleton drove in 96 runs, while shortstop Ozzie Smith drove home 75 runs with nary a homer to his credit. But the Cardinals atoned with a sprightly running game led by outfielder Vince Coleman, who topped 100 seasonal steals for the third straight season. Likewise the shaky pitching staff that completed only ten games was backed by a redoubtable relief crew whose ace, Todd Worrell, saved 33 games. Meanwhile in the NL West, the Giants won over the bridesmaid Reds by 6 games. The Giant victory was a dramatic turnabout for a team that in 1985 had finished last in their division with 100 losses. A fine balance of hitting and pitching made the difference in 1987. At the plate the Giants batted .260 with 205 homers and were led by first baseman Will Clark's .308-35-91 pyrotechnics. Moreover, the pitching staff boasted the league's best ERA, even if the Giant starters completed only 28 games. What mattered was that relievers Scott Garrelts and Jeff Robinson combined for 22 wins and 31 saves. When the Giants met the Cardinals in LCS play, injuries to Jack Clark and Pendleton cast the Cardinals as underdogs. But the Cardinals won their third NL title of the era by overcoming a 3–2 deficit in games with a pair of home-field victories. In World Series play, it was the crippled Cardinals who were favored over the unheralded Twins, but the American Leaguers won four games, all of them in their cozy domed stadium, to edge the Cardinals in seven games.

The pitching rule modification that stemmed the homer tide in 1988 wreaked havoc with NL batters in 1988 as only five regulars attained the .300 mark. Although no New York Met batter joined this circle, Darryl Strawberry boomed a league-leading 39 homers and drove in 101 runs and outfield mate Kevin McReynolds produced a .288-27-99; they powered the Mets to 100 victories and an easy 15-game victory over the Pirates in the NL East. With a 2.91 ERA, the Mets also boasted the best pitching staff in the majors. David Cone led the starters at 20-3 and Dwight Gooden and Ron Darling combined for 35 wins. Relievers Randy Myers and Roger McDowell saved 42 games. In the West, meanwhile, the

Los Angeles Dodgers took the lead in July and hung on to win by 7 games over the Cincinnati Reds who along the way got a rare perfect-game pitching performance from Tom Browning. But the Dodgers held claim to the best individual pitching performance of the year when their ace, Orel Hershiser, finished the regular season with a new record of 59 scoreless innings. In addition to a 23–8 record Hershiser led all NL pitchers in innings pitched, complete games, and shutouts. Offensively the modest Dodger attack was powered by newly acquired free agent Kirk Gibson (.290-25-76) and veteran outfielder Mike Marshall (.277-20-82). The lightly regarded Dodgers were afforded little chance against the Mets in LCS play. But the Dodgers prevailed in seven games with Hershiser starting three games and relieving in another. And then they upset the Oakland Athletics in the World Series, despite crippling injuries to Gibson, pitcher John Tudor, and catcher Mike Scioscia.

But there was no encore to such heroics, and the 1989 Dodgers fell to fourth place in the NL West. An impotent .240 batting average that included only 89 homers sabotaged the pitching staff's major league-leading 2.95 ERA. Hershiser again led the league in innings pitched and finished second in ERA, but was held to a 15–15 performance. And the workload took its toll on the Dodger ace, who was sidelined by a crippling shoulder injury at the outset of the 1990 season.

As the struggling Dodgers fell from grace, the Giants and the Padres battled for the 1989 Western title. The talent-laden Reds struggled in fifth, as the investigation of their manager, Pete Rose, culminated in his expulsion from the game. San Diego's reliever Mark Davis saved a league-leading 44 games for the Padres. Offensively, Tony Gwynn's league-leading .336 batting and 203 hits and Jack Clark's 26 homers, 94 RBIs, and a major-league-leading 132 walks fronted a Padre attack that fell three games short of their goal. The victory went to manager Roger Craig's Giants, whose pitching staff, headed by Scott Garrelts's league-leading 14–5 winning percentage and 2.28 ERA, ranked third in the league. At bat, out-fielder-third baseman Kevin Mitchell won MVP honors by blasting a matchless 47 homers and 125 RBIs. First baseman Will Clark weighed in with a .333 batting mark and scored 104 runs to lead the league. That the Giants' .250 team batting average ranked fourth in the league underscored the NL's impotent batting, which averaged .246 and produced only five .300-plus batters. While the Giants eked out a narrow victory in the West, manager Don Zimmer's Chicago Cubs coasted to a six-game victory over the much-touted, but underachieving Mets in the East. A league-leading .261 batting attack, paced by first baseman Mark Grace's .314 hitting and second baseman Ryne Sandberg's .290 batting, compensated for the pitching staff's sixth-place ranking in the league.

In LCS play the Giants downed the Chicagoans in five games, but then were victimized by the Oakland A's, who swept to victory in the World Series of 1989.

Scanning the Future: Baseball's Problems and Prospects

Carping purists notwithstanding, domed stadiums like Minnesota's Metrodome, which contributed to the Twins'

stunning 1987 World Series victory, are likely to become a familiar part of baseball's future landscape. In 1989 the Toronto Blue Jays occupied their new Toronto Skydome; and St. Petersburg, Florida, whose officials are eyeing a future major league franchise, will open their Florida-Suncoast Dome in the near future. Moreover, domed structures are under consideration in St. Louis, Chicago, Atlanta, and Tampa; the latter site, like St. Petersburg, is another beckoning location for future major league expansion.

As baseball's architecture has changed dramatically over five score years of major league baseball history, so have other aspects of the national game. Indeed, if major league baseball's history offers any enduring lesson, it is that change is essential for sustaining the game's continuing growth and popularity. Thus as the game moves into the last decade of the twentieth century, its leaders cannot afford to assume complacently that its present popularity and prosperity are guaranteed to continue. The game's history teaches that in the past baseball has had to endure dismal busts along with dazzling booms. Indeed, the recent shock waves that buffeted the nation's economy must pose a grim reminder of the forces that nearly sixty years ago plunged the nation's economy and its national game into a decade of Depression.

To nurture the game's continuing growth, baseball leaders should keep wary eyes fixed on baseball's alliance with television. With half of major league baseball's annual revenues now coming from television, there is some cause for alarm in recent reports warning that televised sports programming may be reaching a saturation point. However, in 1990 the latest $1 billion, four-year network television contract with CBS paid each owner $10 million a season and was augmented by a four-year national cable contract that delivered another $2 million to each franchise. Ironically, the CBS contract delivered fewer televised games to national audiences, a circumstance that had some critics faulting baseball owners for depriving the host of fans who were not served by local broadcasts of opportunities for viewing their favorite pastime.

Indeed, baseball's overall popularity shows few signs of declining. On the contrary, baseball's elevation to the status of a medal sport in the 1992 Olympic Games should boost interest in the game at the all-important school and college grassroots. Moreover, another round of major league expansion is looming. The 1990 Basic Agreement paved the way for the NL to add two cities by 1992, thus ending the structural imbalance between the two leagues that has persisted since 1977.

Like the issue of future expansion, the matter of resolving the designated hitter controversy also cries out for enlightened statesmanship by leaders of the two major leagues. Toward this end, in 1986 Commissioner Ueberroth moved to clarify the use of designated hitters in World Series play. Instead of the old practice of allowing the DH rule to be employed every other year, designated hitters now perform each year at World Series games played in AL parks. A reasonable compromise, it could be followed by wider accord on this divisive problem. Yet, as baseball history also shows, the two major leagues have always jealously guarded their independence. For this reason, overall statesmanlike leadership has always been hampered.

Still, such enlightened leadership is needed to resolve these and other knotty problems besetting the game. For one, the pitching-batting equation needs to be addressed anew. As the homer barrages of 1987 tolled on pitchers, rules makers were challenged to strike a balance in favor of the pitching side of the game. In 1988, the pendulum seemed to swing forcefully—at least in the NL—back toward the pitchers.

On the labor front, continuing animosity plagued the latest negotiations between owners and players for a new Basic Agreement. With tensions heightened by the owners' conspiracy against free agents over the years 1985–1987, players and owners staged a crippling struggle in 1990—the centennial anniversary of the great strike of 1890. When the sixth Basic Agreement expired with no new contract in place, the owners locked the players out of the spring training camps on February 15.

The owners sought to impose revenue-sharing and pay-for-performance plans. For their part, the players rejected these and demanded a return to a two-year requirement for salary arbitration eligibility, the restoration of twenty-five-man playing rosters, protection from owner collusion, and increases in the minimum salary and owner contributions to the pension plan. With the battlelines drawn, the lockout lasted thirty-two days, affecting spring training and the opening of the championship season. When a settlement was reached on March 19, the new agreement compromised on the salary arbitration issue, raised the minimum salary to $100,000, increased the owners' annual contribution to the pension plan, and provided for punitive damages in the event of any further collusion by owners against free agent players. The owners dropped their revenue-sharing and pay-for-performance plans, and the players approved the expansion of the NL to fourteen clubs. In the aftermath of the long dispute, an attenuated spring training program began March 20 and the opening of the playing season was delayed a week. The 162-game schedule was preserved by extending the regular season by three days to allow for the replaying of canceled games. The new Basic Agreement promised four years of peace, but the continuing growth of the game is seriously threatened by such confrontations.

With baseball's hostilities returning to their natural habitat of the playing fields, fans were treated to a season of unpredictable events and performances. For one, the 1990 season saw a record nine no-hitters tossed by major league pitchers, a total that matched the number produced in some *decades* of this century (purists may elect not to count Melido Perez's rain-shortened job). Among the nine, ageless Nolan Ryan's latest masterpiece extended his record total to six. The veteran also enhanced his all-time record of most strikeouts of batters by fanning another 232. And among relief pitchers, Bobby Thigpen of the White Sox posted a new seasonal mark with 57 saves and Yankee stopper Dave Righetti broke the all-time save mark for lefthanded relievers.

In the AL such pitching pyrotechnics reduced the number of .300 batters to six, but slugger Cecil Fielder of the Detroit Tigers, who played in Japan during the 1989 season, walloped 51 home runs to become the first to top the 50 mark since 1977. In 1990, too, perennial league batting champions Wade Boggs and Tony Gwynn faltered, enabling veterans George Brett and Willie Mc-

Gee to claim titles. The thirty-seven-year-old Brett won the AL title, and McGee won the NL crown with a .335 mark, which held up despite his being traded to the Oakland A's in August. And the season also saw Commissioner Fay Vincent bar Yankee owner George Steinbrenner from running the team. The Yankees finished last in the AL East with the worst record in the AL. The team also suffered the ignominy of being swept in their twelve encounters with the Oakland A's.

Indeed, in 1990 the talent-rich Oakland A's were heavily favored to repeat as World Champions. With star pitchers Bob Welch and Dave Stewart winning 27 and 22 games and reliever Dennis Eckersley saving 48 games, the A's overcame a mediocre .254 team batting average to win 103 games, the best mark in the majors. But in the Western division, the A's were pursued by the Chicago White Sox who, though finishing 9 games back, attracted over 3 million fans while playing their last season in Comiskey Park. By winning 94 games the White Sox posted the third best record in the majors.

In the weaker AL East neither the Boston Red Sox nor the Toronto Blue Jays approached Chicago's record. But these teams staged the closest race in any division, a race that ended with Boston on top by two games. A .272 team batting mark carried the Red Sox, along with pitcher Roger Clemens's 21–6 effort that included a major-league-leading 1.93 ERA. But in LCS play, Boston's vulnerable relief corps, the worst in the majors, faltered. In sweeping the Red Sox, the Oakland A's won a third consecutive AL pennant.

If the status quo ruled in the AL, it was otherwise in the NL, where the reigning division winners were dethroned by a pair of fifth-place finishers of the previous year. In seizing the heights in the NL East, the Pittsburgh Pirates won by 4 games over the underachieving New York Mets. Outfielder Barry Bonds batted .301-33-114 and stole 52 bases, and first baseman Bobby Bonilla added 32 homers and 120 RBIs to propel the Pirates. Overall the Pirates' .259 batting ranked fifth in the NL and the pitching staff ranked third. A 22-game winner, Doug Drabek, led the staff, which received a 6–2 boost from Zane Smith, acquired from the Montreal Expos in August.

In the NL West the Cincinnati Reds won four fewer games than the Pirates, but the team's 91–71 log topped the Los Angeles Dodgers by 5 games. In winning the Western title the Reds took over on day one and after winning their first seven games, they clung to the top all the way to become the first NL team to accomplish this feat since the inauguration of the 162-game schedule in 1962.

League-leading .265 batting fronted the Reds' assault, which also included a 3.39 pitching ERA, the second best by any NL staff. Starters Jose Rijo and Tom Browning combined for 29 wins, but the Reds' bullpen crew, the self-styled "nasty boys" Ron Dibble and Randy Myers, saved 42 games. Among the hitters, rookie Hal Morris played in 107 games and batted .340 and regulars Barry Larkin and Mariano Duncan batted .300. Chris Sabo and Eric Davis combined for 49 homers, and a key acquisition from the Pirates, Billy Hatcher, batted .276. Manager Lou Piniella, one of many Steinbrenner castoffs, replaced Pete Rose, who watched the Reds' fall exploits from prison.

When the Pirates and Reds clashed in LCS play, the Pirates won the opener but fell to the Reds in six games. Given little chance against the Oakland A's, the NL champion Reds opened World Series play by shutting out their rivals 7–0 behind Jose Rijo. Then with Rijo adding another victory and Hatcher delivering 9 hits in 12 at bats for a new World Series batting mark, the Reds swept the A's! This unexpected victory, reminiscent of the 1914 sweep of the Philadelphia A's by the lowly Boston Braves, brightened a season that appeared to be ill-starred at its outset by the acrimonious labor strife.

On baseball's still-festering racial front, the Commissioner—first A. Bartlett Giamatti, then Fay Vincent—has struck a hopeful note by fostering the integration of minority group members, including black ex-players, into the game's managerial and administrative posts. Toward this end the Baseball Network was working at the close of the decade. Critics decried the slow pace of reform, but the task is a formidable one, since blacks and other minorities occupied fewer than 5 percent of these positions by 1990.

In pondering the game's present and future problems and prospects, baseball leaders would do well to survey the game's illustrious past. Since 1871, more than 13,000 players have played in the major leagues, and well over a billion fans have passed through turnstiles at major league ballparks. Indeed, the game's greatest assets always have been its players and devoted fans. With expansion looming, baseball faces a formidable challenge to maintain the quality of its players. To do this would ensure the steady support of its fans, whose devotion has always been to those who played the game.

Team Histories

Frederick Ivor-Campbell

There are today 26 major-league baseball teams—12 in the National League and 14 in the American—and their number will grow to 28 with the addition of two clubs to the National League in 1993. From the organization of the first professional league—the National Association—in 1871, 108 clubs (plus those of the Negro major leagues) have played major-league ball at one time or another. Some played for as little as a few games in a single season, but others have played for more than a century, and one—the present Atlanta Braves—has played every season from 1871 to the present. The only existing franchise older than Atlanta's (which originated as the Boston Red Stockings, then became the Boston and Milwaukee Braves before moving to Atlanta) is the Chicago Cubs, which organized in 1870, a year before league play began. The White Stockings (as they were first known) missed two seasons (1872–1873) in the aftermath of the great Chicago fire, but have since then continuously represented the same city longer than any other club in baseball history.

Here are brief histories of the 26 current big-league clubs, arranged alphabetically by city or state. These are followed by summary histories of the 82 other clubs—now defunct—that at one time also represented their cities in the major leagues.

Atlanta Braves

The Atlanta Braves, who first played in 1871 as Boston's Red Stockings, are the only club to field a team every season of professional league baseball. When the game's first openly professional club, the Cincinnati Red Stockings, decided to revert to amateur status, manager/outfielder Harry Wright and three of his teammates took their talents (and club nickname) to Boston, where, with infielders Ross Barnes and Harry Schafer and pitcher Al Spalding, they formed the nucleus of a team that would dominate the five-year history of the first professional league, the National Association. After a close third-place finish in their first year, the Red Stockings won four pennants in convincing fashion, including a 71–8 record in 1875 with an .899 winning percentage that has never since been approached in major league ball.

When the National League replaced the NA in 1876, four of Boston's best players (including Spalding and Barnes) deserted the club for Chicago. But after a fourth-place finish in 1876, the Red Stockings lured pitcher Tommy Bond from Hartford and finished at the top in 1877 and '78. Bond dominated NL pitching, winning 80 games (40 each year), 22 more than his nearest rival. Although he won another 43 in 1879, Boston slipped to second.

In 1880 the Red Stockings suffered their first losing season as they fell to sixth. After another sixth-place finish the next year, Wright left to manage Providence, but Boston rebounded to third in 1882 and surprised everyone in 1883 by outplaying favored Chicago and Providence to capture their seventh pennant.

Providence knocked them out of the race late in 1884, and Boston remained out of contention the next four seasons. In 1889, though, with several players signed from the defunct Detroit Wolverines (including batting champ Dan Brouthers), and 49 wins from pitcher John Clarkson, the Beaneaters (as they were now more commonly known) waged a two-team race for the championship with the New York Giants. Boston won as many games as the Giants, but lost two more and finished a game back.

Frank Selee, who had managed two straight minor league pennant winners, was hired from Omaha along with his star pitcher, Charles "Kid" Nichols. Their arrival in 1890 ushered in Boston's second golden era. Before they left the club twelve years later, the Beaneaters had won five more NL pennants. Nichols won 27 games in his rookie season, but Boston—decimated by defections to the outlaw Players League—finished only fifth. With the return of some of the defectors in 1891, Clarkson won 33 games, Nichols recorded the first of seven consecutive 30-win seasons, and the Beaneaters returned to the top.

When the NL expanded in 1892 from eight teams to twelve, the schedule too was expanded, and the season divided into two halves. Boston won the first half, and the Cleveland Spiders the second. In a World Series to determine the league champion, the Beaneaters (who at 102–48 had the best over-all season record) defeated the Spiders.

The split season was abandoned and the schedule reduced in 1893—and Boston captured its third straight pennant. Center fielder Hugh Duffy hit .363. The next year, when hitters exploded for a league BA of .309, Duffy led the way with a .438 that is still the major-league record. His Beaneaters didn't win the pennant, but they became the first club in a decade (and the last until 1920) to hit over 100 home runs. Five Beaneaters drove in 100 runs or more, and the team set a big league record for runs scored (1,222) that still stands.

Boston dropped out of contention for a couple of years, but bounced back in 1897 to edge Baltimore for the pennant by two games. In the Temple Cup series, though (played between the first- and second-place teams for the world title), the Orioles overwhelmed Boston four games to one. The next year the schedule was expanded again, and again (as in 1892) Boston won 102 games to lead the league, winning their twelfth pennant. But as the league had abandoned the four-year-old Temple Cup play, there was no World Series.

After coming in second in 1899, Boston dropped out of pennant contention for fourteen years, finishing as far back as 66½ games (in 1906) and losing as many as 108 (in 1909). Five times the club finished last, including the four years from 1909 to 1912. The Braves (as they were now known) rose to fifth in 1913 under new manager George Stallings, but seemed through the first half of 1914 to be securing for themselves another bed in the cellar.

In mid-July they stood a last-place eighth in a tight field. Six days and six wins later they were third. By mid-August they had climbed to second; on August 26 they replaced the New York Giants in first. For two weeks they alternated between first and second, then took off to win the pennant by 10½ games.

Boston's heroes were pitchers Dick Rudolph and Bill James, both in only their second full big league seasons. Rudolph won 27 games in 1914 and James won 26; then they added two more each in the Braves' World Series sweep of the heavily favored Philadelphia Athletics. But Rudolph crafted only one more 20-win season, and James won only 5 games in two final major-league campaigns.

Classy fielding kept the Braves competitive the next two years. In 1915 they spurted once again out of the cellar—but only to second place this time. They began their climb earlier the next year, but a seven-game losing streak in early September dropped them out of a tie for first. They rallied, but finished third. It was the Braves' last close race for thirty-two years.

In the twenty-nine years from 1917 through 1945 the Braves finished only three seasons as high as fourth, and only once as close as nine games from the top. With four years in the cellar and eleven in seventh place, the team finished near the bottom of the league more than half the time. In 1935 slugger Wally Berger led the league in home runs and RBIs, but the Braves lost a club-record 115 games in their worst season ever.

In 1946, with dynamic new ownership headed by contractor Lou Perini, a new manager—Billy Southworth, who had led the Cardinals to three pennants and two world championships—and the return of war veterans like pitchers Warren Spahn and John Sain, the Braves neared the end of their long depression with their first winning season in eight years. At the end of the season Boston acquired third baseman Bob Elliott from Pittsburgh. He enjoyed a career year in 1947, powering the Braves to third place. Spahn and Sain won 21 games each.

Spahn dropped to 15 wins in 1948, but Sain won 24. Four veterans—plus rookie shortstop Alvin Dark—hit over .300. With the league's best pitching and hitting, the Braves moved out in front in June, and shook off their last challengers with a September spurt that left them at the end champions by 6½ games.

But from there on, the Braves' path in Boston was downhill. Cleveland beat them in the World Series, and the club dropped to fourth for the next three years. South-

worth resigned part way into the 1951 season. In 1952 the team fell to seventh; home attendance was less than one-fifth what it had been four years earlier. The next spring Perini moved the franchise to Milwaukee in the league's first realignment since 1900.

The move was a spectacular success. Not only did the Braves rebound to second place, but attendance jumped 649 percent over their previous year in Boston to set an NL record of more than 1.8 million. The league's best pitching staff was led by the trio that would anchor Milwaukee's years of greatness: veteran Warren Spahn, sophomore Lew Burdette, and rookie Bob Buhl. Sophomore third baseman Eddie Mathews led the league in home runs; with outfielder Henry Aaron, who came up the next year, Mathews would give the Braves a consistent source of power through their Milwaukee years.

A July-August surge in 1954 pulled the Braves within a few games of the top before they slipped back, but they set another attendance record and became the first NL club to draw more than two million at home in a season. In 1955 the Braves finished a distant second to the Dodgers, but 1956 produced a great three-way race that found the Braves slightly ahead through much of the season until five straight losses in early September brought them even with the surging Dodgers. It was a dogfight the rest of the way, not settled until the final day, when a Dodger victory over Pittsburgh left Milwaukee a game back in second.

The acquisition of veteran second baseman Red Schoendienst from St. Louis in June 1957 steadied the infield and gave the team a frequent baserunner for Mathews and Aaron to drive in. In August the Braves drew away from the pack, and recovered from a September slump to win the pennant by a convincing 8 games over St. Louis. The Yankees took them to seven games in the World Series, but Burdette's shutout in the finale brought the Braves their first world championship in forty-three years.

Milwaukee repeated as league champions just as convincingly in 1958, but in the autumn classic, after taking the first two games from the Yankees, they lost the Series in seven. The race was much tighter in 1959 until the Giants moved away from the Dodgers and Braves in August. But in September the Giants faltered as the others surged past them, and the season ended with the Braves and Dodgers tied. In a best-of-three playoff, the Dodgers took the pennant in two games—but both by only one run and the second only after twelve innings.

A portent for the Braves' future could be seen in the crowd of under 20,000 that attended the first playoff game in Milwaukee. After setting a third NL record in 1957, Milwaukee attendance had gradually declined, dropping below two million in 1958, the club's second pennant year, and even farther in this year of the tight pennant race. As the Braves declined on the field to a more distant second in 1960, then successively to fourth, fifth, and sixth, so too did the decline continue in the stands to well under a million. Perini sold his majority interest in the club. A tighter race in 1964 stirred a little more fan interest, but when attendance dropped in 1965 to a new Milwaukee low of just over half a million, the club pulled up stakes again and moved to Atlanta.

The Braves' won-lost records in 1965 and '66 were nearly identical. But in Atlanta attendance improved by almost a million. Of the Braves who had brought glory to Milwaukee, most were gone from the club or in decline. But Aaron was still at the height of his powers, and younger players were beginning to make their mark. Reliever Phil Niekro, for example, was converted to a starter in 1967 and responded with the league's best ERA.

After finishing no higher than fifth in their first three seasons in Atlanta, the Braves celebrated 1969, the first year of divisional play, with a late-season drive that carried them out of a tight five-team race to the championship of the West. Veteran Orlando Cepeda, newly acquired from St. Louis, joined Aaron in supplying power, and Niekro won 23 games as the Braves won ten in a row to clinch the title in their next-to-last game. In the league's first Championship Series, though, the "Miracle" Mets of New York swept Atlanta in three games.

Aaron remained a presence in Atlanta for five more years, and Niekro, after a relatively dismal season in 1970, established himself over the years as one of the game's most durable and effective pitchers. But the team went nowhere. When they enjoyed an occasional good season (as in 1974, when they won 88 games), at least two other clubs did much better. Aaron returned to Milwaukee (to the AL Brewers) in 1975, and attendance sank to an Atlanta low. Yachtsman Ted Turner bought the club in 1976 and attendance rose, but the team sank to the bottom of the division for four years.

In 1982, though, with power from outfielder Dale Murphy and third baseman Bob Horner, and exceptional pitching from Niekro (17–4) and reliever Gene Garber (30 saves, a club record), Atlanta grabbed the division lead with a season-opening 13-game winning streak, and recovered from a midsummer collapse to edge Los Angeles by one game for their second divisional crown. But they were swept in the LCS, this time by St. Louis.

For the next two seasons Murphy's league-leading slugging carried the Braves to second place—a close 3 games behind Los Angeles in 1983 (in a race which pushed Atlanta attendance over two million for the first time), and a tie with Houston 12 games behind San Diego the next year. By 1986, though, they had sunk into the division cellar. Murphy boosted them up a notch in 1987 with the most productive season of his career, but as his power at the plate dropped the next year, the Braves sunk to their worst finish in fifty-three years. Fans fell away, and Atlanta became the first big-league club in three seasons to attract fewer than a million spectators to its home games.

Veteran outfielder Lonnie Smith broke out of a five-year slump in 1989, his second Atlanta season, to become one of baseball's most potent hitters, and in 1990 strong seasons by young sluggers Ron Gant and rookie Dave Justice gave Atlanta hope for the future. But Dale Murphy, in the third year of his decline, was traded to Philadelphia in August, and the Braves, mired in the cellar for their third straight season, remained the weakest draw in major league baseball.

Baltimore Orioles

The history of major league baseball in Baltimore dates back to 1872, to the Lord Baltimores of the National Association, and includes the great National League Orioles of the 1890s. The city was also represented in the American League's first big league seasons, 1901–1902. But when those Orioles moved to New York in 1903 and became the Highlanders (later the Yankees), Baltimore was left without a big league club for more than half a century, until the transfer of the Browns from St. Louis in 1954.

The current Orioles didn't get their start in St. Louis, though. Their first home was Milwaukee, where they finished in the AL cellar in 1901. When they moved to St. Louis the next year, they lured several valuable players from the city's NL Cardinals—including 1901 batting champ Jesse Burkett, star shortstop Bobby Wallace, and the Cards' three best pitchers. They also took on the Cardinals' discarded nickname: becoming the new St. Louis Browns.

The Browns finished a strong second to the Philadelphia Athletics in their first St. Louis season, but fell to sixth the next year and, except for a fourth-place finish in 1908 (thanks to the pitching of newly acquired veteran Rube Waddell), remained mired in the second division until 1920. Late in the 1913 season a young Branch Rickey was hired to manage the Browns. In his two full seasons he was unable to lift the club out of the second division, but he did sign college star George Sisler (whom he had coached at the University of Michigan), who became, as the Browns' first baseman, one of the game's all-time greats.

In 1916, his first full season, Sisler led the Browns in hitting as they caught fire in August to record their first winning season in eight years. Pitcher Urban Shocker was obtained from the Yankees two years later and by 1920 had developed into a 20-game winner. Also in 1920, Sisler connected for what is still a major league record 257 hits and batted .407 to help move the Browns up to fourth, their first finish that high since 1908 (though their won-lost record of 76–77 remained on the losing side). The next year Shocker's 27 victories brought them a winning season and third place. And in 1922 the team recorded its finest record ever in St. Louis: 93 wins and a .604 winning percentage.

The 1922 Browns, led by Sisler's sizzling .420 BA, hit .313 as a team to lead the league. Left fielder Ken Williams ran away with the RBI title and beat out Babe Ruth and Tilly Walker for the home run crown. (Ruth, to be honest, did miss nearly a third of the season that year.) Sisler and Williams even finished one-two in AL stolen bases. And though Shocker slipped a bit to 24 wins, he led a pitching staff that recorded the league's lowest ERA. The team led the league in the standings throughout July and into August before the Yankees nudged ahead of them. The Browns hung close, but didn't regain the lead, remaining second, a heartbreaking single game back, at season's end.

Falling back to fifth the next year, as Sisler missed the whole season with a sinus infection, the Browns remained out of contention for the next twenty-one years, dropping to their lowest point in 1939, 64½ games out of first, with 111 losses. They recovered for three winning seasons in the war years 1942–1945, finishing a distant third in 1942, and capturing their only St. Louis pennant in 1944, edging the Detroit Tigers on the final day after trailing them through most of September. The World Series—an all-St. Louis affair—proved anticlimactic for the Browns as they lost to the Cardinals in six games.

The Browns finished third in 1945 before sinking back into the second division. Even the club's purchase by the dynamic Bill Veeck in July 1951 couldn't rouse them out of the depths. (A month after buying the Browns, Veeck made his best-remembered move; bringing in midget Eddie Gaedel for one plate appearance—he walked.)

Unable to earn either victories or money in St. Louis, Veeck in September 1953 sold the club to a Baltimore group, who moved the Browns and renamed them the Orioles. The new owners hired the brilliant Paul Richards to rebuild the team as manager, both in the front office and on the field. It took him (and Lee MacPhail, who became general manager and president in 1958) several years to move the Orioles above .500, but in 1960, young third baseman Brooks Robinson found he could hit as well as field, and rookie Jim Gentile drove in 98 runs; the team made its first run for the pennant since 1944. In first place in early September, they finished second when the Yanks won fifteen straight to pass them by.

The next year the O's did even better, winning six more games than they had in 1960 as Gentile hit 46 home runs and drove in 141. But it was an even better year for New York and Detroit, and Baltimore finished a distant third.

When Hank Bauer was brought in to manage the Orioles in 1964, the team entered its golden decades—twenty years which saw them win seven division titles, six pennants, and three world championships, with only two finishes below third. With Robinson driving in runs and left fielder Boog Powell slugging at a league-leading pace, the O's finished 1964 with wins in seven of their final eight games. But the White Sox won their last nine and the Yankees put together an eleven-game streak near the end to take the flag and leave Baltimore third, two games back.

After another third-place finish in 1965, the Orioles acquired slugging Frank Robinson from Cincinnati and moved second-year pitcher Jim Palmer into the starting rotation. Palmer won 15 to lead a balanced staff, and Frank Robinson captured the Triple Crown. With both Robinsons and Powell driving in 100 runs or more, the O's romped to their first Baltimore pennant. They continued the romp in the World Series, holding Los Angeles to a total of just two runs as they swept to their first world title.

A drop in offensive production and the loss of Palmer to injuries for most of the season plunged Baltimore into a tie for sixth in 1967. Palmer was out the next year, too, but pitchers Dave McNally and Jim Hardin burst to the forefront with fine seasons to lift the club back to second.

Baltimore coach Earl Weaver, a pennant-winning manager in the O's farm system, replaced Hank Bauer at the Orioles' helm in mid-1968 to begin what became one of the longest and most successful managerial tenures of recent times. In fourteen full seasons Weaver led his club to six Eastern Division titles and six second-place finishes, with one season each in third and fourth. His teams featured fine hitters and fielders, but it is the pitching that stands out above the rest. In seven of the fourteen years the Oriole staff compiled the league's lowest ERA, including five consecutive seasons (1969-1973). Oriole pitchers put together in those fourteen years twenty-one 20-win

seasons (eight of them by Jim Palmer), and garnered six Cy Young Awards.

In the first three years of divisional play (1969-71) Baltimore ran away with the East championship and swept to the pennant each time in the League Championship Series. The 1969 team (despite an embarrassingly easy loss to the New York Mets in the World Series) is often ranked among the greatest of all time. With overwhelming pitching and fielding, the Orioles took the division crown by 19 games, winning a club-record 109. In fielding, seven percentage points separated the AL's second-best team from the worst; the Orioles fielded three points better than the second-best team. And Oriole pitchers gave up nearly a run less per game than the league average.

Baltimore's performance in 1970 was nearly as impressive. Mike Cuellar and Dave McNally won 24 games each, and Jim Palmer contributed 20 more wins to the O's total of 108. This year they won the World Series as well as the pennant, rolling over Cincinnati in five games.

In the 1971 World Series, though, Pittsburgh came back from losses in the first two games to defeat the Orioles by a run in game seven. The O's captured divisional titles in 1973 and '74, but it was 1979 before they again triumphed in the LCS. Once again, however, they faced the Pirates in the World Series, and once again took the Series lead, only to fall again in the seventh game.

The 1979 pennant was Weaver's last, as late-season Oriole surges in 1980 and '82 fell just short. But in 1983 the O's—paced by the pitching of veteran Scott McGregor and rookie Mike Boddicker, and the hitting and fielding of Cal Ripken, Jr., and Eddie Murray at short and first—made new manager Joe Altobelli look good. After a comfortable divisional win, they trounced Chicago's White Sox in the LCS and the Philadelphia Phillies in the World Series.

Declining after 1983 despite the return of Earl Weaver in 1985–1986, the Orioles finished last in the East in 1986. Though they rose to sixth in 1987, their .414 winning percentage was their lowest in thirty-two years. Then in 1988 they hit rock bottom, not only finishing last but also beginning the season with an AL record-setting twenty-one consecutive defeats.

Baltimore's rebound was even more startling than its plummet. Under manager Frank Robinson (who had been handed the hapless O's early in the 1988 season) the 1989 Orioles took over first place in late April, held the lead through August, and stayed within the reach of the division title until Toronto defeated them in the season's penultimate game to clinch the crown. The newly potent bat of catcher Mickey Tettleton and splendid relief from rookie Gregg Olson highlighted the Baltimore resurgence. Olson remained effective in 1990, but the offense faltered, and an August-September slide dropped the Orioles out of the race.

Boston Red Sox

Since the end of World War Two, the Red Sox have won the American League pennant four times, only to lose the World Series each time in the seventh game. It was not always thus. In their first two decades they were the league's most successful club, winners of six pennants and five world championships. (No World Series was played the year of their second pennant.)

Organized in 1901 as one of four new eastern clubs in Ban Johnson's newly major league AL, Boston's Americans (or Pilgrims, Puritans, Plymouth Rocks, or Somersets, as they were variously called) quickly established themselves as one of the game's strongest teams. Star third baseman Jimmy Collins was lured from Boston's NL club to manage the new Americans, and he assembled a team that included such former NL standouts as slugger Buck Freeman and pitcher Cy Young. Finishing a strong second in the AL's inaugural major league season, the Pilgrims quickly supplanted their mediocre NL counterparts in the hearts and wallets of Boston fans.

After a third-place finish in 1902, the Pilgrims ran away from the rest of the league in 1903 to take their first pennant by 14½ games over Philadelphia. Young led the league in victories for the third straight season, Freeman took titles in home runs, total bases, and RBIs, and second-year outfielder Patsy Dougherty finished first in hits and runs scored. In the first modern World Series, Boston overcame Pittsburgh's favored Pirates, thereby confirming in the public mind the AL's claim to major league status.

Boston repeated as pennant winners in 1904, but by a much narrower margin, after a struggle with New York's Highlanders that wasn't settled until the next-to-last day of the season. The NL Giants refused to play Boston in a World Series that year.

Over the next few years, as the Pilgrims dropped into the league cellar, new owner John I. Taylor (whose father, *Boston Globe* publisher Charles Taylor, was said to have bought the club for his son to give him something useful to do) rid the team of many of the players who had brought it glory. Eventually Taylor was himself maneuvered out of the club presidency, but it turned out he had not been a wanton destroyer. In driving out the old guard he had been making room for new young players: pitcher Joe Wood, for example, and a sprightly outfield of Tris Speaker, Harry Hooper, and Duffy Lewis. The club—now known as the Red Sox—rose out of its depths in the final years of Taylor's presidency, even challenging the league leaders through much of 1909 before dropping away in late August. In 1911, in one of the last acts of his presidency, Taylor had, with his father, purchased land in Boston's Fenway section and built a new ballpark.

Sparked by the spectacular pitching of Joe Wood and Speaker's play at the bat and in center field, the Red Sox of 1912 took the league lead in early June and were never headed, finishing with a club-record 105 victories. In the World Series they edged John McGraw's Giants and Christy Mathewson in one of the most exciting Series ever, four games to three, with one tie. Three years later, with a staff that boasted the AL's four top pitchers in winning percentage (including rookie Babe Ruth), the Sox captured their fourth pennant, staving off a late-season surge by Detroit to finish 2½ games in front. After a first-game loss to the Phillies in the World Series, Boston recovered to sweep the next four by one run apiece.

Joe Wood's ailing arm finally gave out, and Tris Speaker was traded to Cleveland at the start of the 1916 season following a salary dispute. But with Ruth winning 23 games to lead the team, the Sox slid past the White Sox and Tigers in mid-September to take their fifth flag, and waltzed over Brooklyn in the Series.

Incipient disaster struck the Red Sox that December when New York theatrical entrepreneurs Hugh Ward and Harry Frazee bought the club. They put little cash into the deal, counting on future profits to pay the bulk of the purchase price. Ward sailed for Australia, leaving Frazee to run the club. For a while the future looked bright. After a second-place finish in 1917, Frazee hired minor league executive Ed Barrow as manager, and when many of the team's regulars left for military service in World War One, Frazee bought and traded for worthy replacements. In a season shortened a month because of the war, the Sox edged Cleveland for their sixth pennant and defeated the Chicago Cubs for their fifth world championship.

Frazee's theater losses put him in a financial bind and gradually forced him to sell off the best of his players—mostly to the Yankees, who had plenty of money, and an office just a short hop from Frazee's New York theater. Though the Sox fell to sixth place in 1919, Babe Ruth kept attention fixed on the team as he went to the outfield and startled the baseball world with a record 29 home runs. But that winter Frazee sold Ruth to the Yankees for $100,000 and a $300,000 mortgage on Fenway Park.

The Red Sox were embarked on a fifteen-year sojourn in the second division that even a 1923 change in ownership was powerless to end. In the eleven years from 1922 through 1932 the Sox emerged from last place only twice. In 1932 they reached their nadir, losing 111 games and finishing 64 games out of first.

But in 1933, young, wealthy Tom Yawkey bought the club and promptly began what would be a lifetime effort to restore Boston to its former glory. His first efforts to buy success ready-made with such established stars as Lefty Grove, Jimmie Foxx, and Joe Cronin pulled the club out of the cellar but failed to lift it into pennant contention. But as general manager Eddie Collins began turning up young players to join the veterans, the Sox' fortunes rose. The emergence between 1938 and 1942 of players like Bobby Doerr, Ted Williams, and pitcher Tex Hughson brought Boston a level of success not seen since 1918. In four of the five years they finished second to the Yankees, achieving in 1942 their highest winning percentage since 1915.

The loss of most of these newcomers to military service in World War Two delayed further progress. But with the arrival of rookie pitching sensation Dave Ferriss in 1945, and the acquisition of slugging first baseman Rudy York that winter, the club was prepared for its returning war veterans to join in bringing Boston its greatest season since 1912. With 104 victories, the 1946 Sox won their long-delayed seventh pennant by 12 games over second-place Detroit. Only in the World Series was there disappointment as the heavily favored Sox bowed in Game Seven by one run.

The Yankees ran away from the pack in 1947, but the three years that followed saw the Red Sox three times in the throes of pennant fever. In 1948, after falling back a bit in late September, the Sox won four at the very end to tie Cleveland for first—but lost the one-game playoff. The next year they were 12 games behind the Yankees on July 4, but pulled up gradually to take a one-game lead into the final two-game series in New York. One Sox win would give them the flag, but the Yankees took both games. In 1950 Boston played the league's best ball through July and August, to pull within a game of the Yankees on September 18, but then lost four in a row and all hope of the pennant.

In 1951 the Sox collapsed at season's end to finish third, 11 games back. They came no closer for the next fifteen years, finishing with eight consecutive losing seasons from 1959 through 1966, when they suffered their second successive ninth-place finish in a league now expanded to ten teams.

In 1967 the Sox awakened from their long slumber. A ten-game win streak in mid-July shot them out of mediocrity into the midst of a four-team race for the pennant that was not settled until Boston beat Minnesota and Detroit split a doubleheader on the final day, leaving the Sox on top. Carl Yastrzemski, who had replaced Ted Williams in left field seven years earlier, replaced him now in the fans' awe as he clinched the Triple Crown with a game-winning home run and six other hits in the final two must-win games. But Boston lost the World Series to St. Louis in seven games.

It was eight years before the Red Sox won another pennant, but they came close in 1972, losing the AL East crown by half a game to Detroit in the season's final series. They led the division two years later from mid-July through early September, then fell apart and finished third. But the next year, 1975, they maintained to the end the lead they first took in May, and swept Oakland in the League Championship Series for their ninth pennant. Television viewers will long remember Carlton Fisk's home run that won Game Six of the World Series from Cincinnati. But Red Sox fans also remember that the Sox lost Game Seven the next day, 4–3. Owner Tom Yawkey died the following July without the world championship he had sought for more than forty years.

Boston contended seriously in 1977 in a tight three-way race, pulling ahead for a time in June and again in August, but ultimately falling 2½ games short. The next year, though, the Sox pulled off another amazing finish. After blowing a 7½-game late-August lead to fall 3⅓ games behind New York in mid-September, they won their final eight scheduled games to tie the Yankees. But in the playoff, Yankee Bucky Dent's three-run pop-fly homer over Fenway's cozy left field wall proved Boston's ruin. The Sox rallied in the eighth to draw within a run, but with two out and a man on third in the ninth, Yastrzemski popped up and the season was history.

Yaz retired in 1983, full of years and honor, but outfielders Jim Rice and Dwight Evans remained from the 1975 champions. Joined by a new generation that included, in Wade Boggs, baseball's most consistent hitter since Ted Williams, and, in Roger Clemens, Boston's most exciting pitcher since Joe Wood, the Sox in 1986 won their tenth pennant, with an amazing comeback over California from a 3–1 deficit in the League Championship Series. In Game Six of the World Series they were within one pitch of capturing their first world title in 68 years. But they lost the game, and in Game Seven—once again—the Series.

When a pitching decline dropped the Sox to fifth place in 1987, and the All-Star break the next year found them barely above .500, manager John McNamara was re-

placed by coach Joe Morgan. The Sox responded with nineteen wins in their next twenty games and, despite a slump at season's end, took the title in the AL East by one game. In the LCS, though, Oakland swept to the pennant in four games.

In 1989 Boston moved to within half a game of the division lead in August before slipping back to third, but in 1990, with pitcher Clemens back in peak form after a season and a half below par, the Sox arrived at midseason in first place. After trading the lead back and forth with Toronto, they captured the crown of the East on the season's final day. But in the LCS Oakland again swept past them to the pennant.

California Angels

Of the ten teams added to the major leagues in the 1960s and '70s, the Angels were quickest to put together a winning season, finishing third in the American League in only their second year of play.

Former cowboy actor and singer Gene Autry brought the club into being as the Los Angeles Angels in December 1960. Playing their first season, 1961, in Los Angeles's Wrigley Field, a former minor league park with power alleys only five feet deeper than the foul poles, five Angels hit 20 or more home runs. Though the team finished seventh in the standings, they were second in homers only to the mighty Yankees.

What the Angels lost in home runs in 1962 (when they moved out of Wrigley Field into the L.A. Dodgers' new stadium), they more than made up in pitching. Paced by rookie Dean Chance, the Angels nearly doubled their wins on the road, and as late as mid-August stood in second place, within striking distance of New York. Though they tailed off in September, they finished a respectable third, 10 games back.

The team collapsed to ninth the next year, but in 1964 Chance's pitching and splendid relief by rookie Bob Lee overcame the Angels' continuing inertia at the bat to lift them back into the first division. Among Chance's league-leading 11 shutouts were six 1–0 victories.

Los Angeles became the California Angels in 1965 in anticipation of their move south to a new stadium in Anaheim the following year, but neither the name change nor the new location stirred them out of the second division. In 1967, though, with below-average run production but the league's third-best pitching, the Angels in midseason shot up from ninth to third before leveling off to fifth. After dismal seasons in 1968–1969, career years in 1970 by pitcher Clyde Wright (22 wins, including a no-hitter) and newly acquired left fielder Alex Johnson (202 hits and a league-high .329 BA) helped the Angels snap back with an 86–76 record that matched their previous best (1962).

The seven losing seasons which followed 1970 were somewhat redeemed by the arrival in 1972 of pitcher Nolan Ryan, who burst into superstardom as an Angel, setting a modern record of 383 strikeouts in 1973 and hurling four no-hitters in three years (1973–1975). Ryan's effectiveness dipped in 1978, but the club as a whole came to life, contending closely for the Western Division title all season until Kansas City shot ahead in September.

In 1979 Don Baylor became the first (and, so far, only) DH to be named league MVP, as a renewed offense powered California to its first division title. Baltimore stopped the Angels in the LCS, though. The team's run production dropped off dramatically the next year and the club followed up its best season with its worst.

After another losing season in 1981 (during which Jim Fregosi was replaced as manager by twenty-year veteran Gene Mauch), California lured free-agent slugger Reggie Jackson from the Yankees. With Jackson leading a resurgent offense and Geoff Zahn headlining the league's second-best pitching staff, the Angels rebounded to a new team high of 93 wins in 1982, and their second division title. They defeated Milwaukee in the first two games of the LCS, but lost the next three. A disappointed manager Mauch retired.

Again, in 1983, the Angels followed a championship with a poor season—not quite as bad as 1980, but still their third worst ever. In 1984 they rebounded to .500, good enough for second in a weak division. As a foretaste of continuing improvement, pitcher Mike Witt concluded his rise to staff ace with a perfect game on the season's last day.

Gene Mauch came out of retirement to manage the Angels again in 1985. With pitching that featured splendid relief from newly acquired Donnie Moore (31 saves; 1.92 ERA), the team led the division much of the season, but lost three games of four to Kansas City in the final week to fall a game behind the Royals into second.

With Witt's 18 wins and 2.84 ERA pacing the staff and rookie first baseman Wally Joyner leading a revitalized offense, California won the 1986 division crown with ease. In the LCS against Boston, the Angels took three of the first four games, and in Game Five were within one pitch of capturing their first pennant. But the Boston Red Sox rallied to win.

In 1987 California for the third time followed up their division championship with a losing season, this time dropping the season finale to tie for last place in the AL West. Manager Mauch retired again, this time for good. After another losing season brought them home a distant fourth in 1988, the Angels signed Doug Rader to manage the club. They also acquired a veteran pitcher—Bert Blyleven—who led a resurgence of Angel pitching that lifted the club to its third best won-lost record ever. But as the West was now the stronger AL division, the team's 91 wins carried them only into third place, eight games back. In 1990 they dropped just one place in the standings, but finished again below .500, 23 games out of first.

Chicago Cubs

The Chicago Cubs have represented the same city in the major leagues longer than any other club. Organized in 1870 to provide a professional challenge to Cincinnati's Red Stockings, the White Stockings (as they were originally known) were one of the founding members of the game's first professional league—the National Association—the next year.

Despite the great Chicago fire, which destroyed their ballpark, uniforms, and club business records late in the 1871 season, the White Stockings completed their schedule, finishing a close second to the Athletics of Philadelphia. But they dropped out of the NA for the next two years because of the fire's devastation. In 1875, in the midst of a second losing season following their return, the club arranged for four of champion Boston's best players to jump to Chicago for the 1876 season. That winter, White Stocking president William A. Hulbert and pitcher/manager Al Spalding (one of the jumpers) led in forming a new league to replace the NA.

Sparked by its Boston players and infielder Adrian "Cap" Anson (lured from the Athletics), the White Stockings in 1876 outscored their opponents by more than five runs per game and handily won the first championship of the new National League. The next year, though, when Spalding (whose pitching had brought Chicago 47 of its 52 victories in 1876) switched over to first base, the club fell off to fifth.

Spalding retired from the field in 1878 to attend to his young sporting goods firm (though he returned as club president from 1882 through 1891). In 1879 Anson was named to manage the team. Leading the league in batting, he restored the White Stockings to their winning ways, and in 1880 led them back to the top.

For twelve years the White Stockings ranked among baseball's best, garnering five pennants (1880–1882, 1885–1886) and four second-place finishes. Anson's stern morality and strict discipline did not make him popular with his often rowdy teammates, but his consistency as a player set an example, and his innovative management made the most of his players' drive and aggressiveness. Anson's forcefulness, however, contributed to baseball's most grievous setback: his adamant refusal in the mid-1880s to take the field against black players prevented the racial integration of the major leagues that had up to then seemed imminent.

After a close finish behind Boston in 1891, the White Stockings' first era as a National League power ended. In each of the next eleven seasons they fell at least 15 games short of the top. The team's youthful ineptitude was reflected in the nicknames that succeeded "White Stockings": the "Colts," the "Orphans" (in 1898, after Anson—by then known as "Pop"—was fired after nineteen years at the helm), and finally, the "Cubs."

When Frank Selee (who had led Boston to greatness in the 1890s) was hired to manage the Cubs in 1902, he inherited a team that had ended the 1901 season 37 games out, its worst finish up to then. By 1903 he had turned catcher/outfielder Frank Chance into a first baseman, moved Joe Tinker from third to short, and brought up Johnny Evers from Troy to play second. The new double-play combination flourished not only in the field but at the bat. The Cubs finished third in 1903 with their best record in a dozen years.

That winter Selee traded for pitcher Mordecai "Three Finger" Brown, and in 1905 signed rookie hurler Ed Reulbach. After leading the Cubs to second place in 1904, Selee, ill with tuberculosis, took a leave of absence in the middle of the 1905 season. Chance took his place and brought the team to third.

Selee never returned, but he had gone a long way toward building a championship team. Trades for outfielder Jimmy Sheckard and third baseman Harry Steinfeldt, the signing of rookie pitcher Jack Pfiester, and the acquisition during the 1906 season of pitchers Orval Overall and Jack Taylor completed one of the greatest teams of all time. The Cubs passed the Giants to take the lead early in May and kept on rising. New York and Pittsburgh made a race of it through July, but the Cubs won 55 of their final 65 games to finish with a record 116 victories, 20 games ahead of second-place New York. The hitting of Steinfeldt and Chance led the Cubs to the top of the league in batting and slugging, and the club topped all others in fielding. But it was the Cub pitching that stood out most. Brown's 1.04 ERA was the league's best, with those of Pfiester and Reulbach second and third. The team ERA of 1.76 was the first below 2.00 since the pitching distance was increased to 60'6" in 1893. Over all, Chicago scored 80 more runs than its nearest rival, and yielded 89 fewer.

But in the World Series, the crosstown "hitless wonder" White Sox matched the Cubs' hitting and pitched twice as effectively to take the crown in six games. It was the third time the Cubs had failed to win the world title: in two of the earliest Series, they had tied the St. Louis Browns by 3–3–1 in 1885, and lost to them the next year, 2–4.

The Cubs' hitting and run production fell off in 1907, but their pitching did not (ERA: 1.73). With 107 wins, they captured their second straight pennant, by 17 games. This time their dominance carried over into the World Series as they swept Detroit after an opening-game tie.

The pennant race of 1908, in sharp contrast to those of the previous two years, was one of the tightest in baseball history. On September 22 the Cubs won two from the Giants to pull into a virtual tie for first (with Pittsburgh third, 1½ games back). The next day the Giants appeared to have beaten the Cubs with an RBI single in the last of the ninth. But young Fred Merkle, on first when the hit was made, seeing the runner on third cross the plate, failed to continue on to second himself and was forced out by alert Cub second baseman Johnny Evers for the third out, which negated the Giant run. Because of increasing darkness and the mood of excited fans on the field, the game was called and ruled a tie. After another week and a half in which all three teams took turns in front, Chicago defeated Pittsburgh to pull ahead by half a game, leaving the Pirates and Giants tied for second. But New York had one more game—and defeated the Boston Braves to pull into a tie with the Cubs. The "Merkle boner" game thus had to be replayed, and this time the Cubs won to take their third straight pennant. In the World Series they again beat Detroit in five games. Their second straight world title was also, to date, their last.

In 1909 the Cubs won 104 games as their pitching staff for the third time in four years recorded an ERA under 2.00, but the club trailed Pittsburgh throughout the season and finished second. In 1910, however, their 104 wins carried them to another pennant, by a comfortable 13 games. It was their last championship of the Chance era. After a World Series loss to the Philadelphia Athletics, and seasons in second and third place, Chance resigned, protesting the unwillingness of owner Charles Murphy to spend money for top players.

The Cubs got a new owner in 1916, and with him a new ballpark. Charles Weeghman, who had owned the Chicago Whales in the short-lived Federal League, purchased the Cubs when the FL went under, and moved them into the park he had built for the Whales. Although there was talk in the 1980s of moving the Cubs out of what is now Wrigley Field, the introduction of night baseball in 1988 assured continuing play in this crown jewel of ballparks.

The team that next carried Chicago to the pennant, in the war-shortened season of 1918, featured only one name familiar to Cubs fans from earlier championship seasons—Fred Merkle. The man whose rookie boner as a Giant had made possible their pennant in 1908 was now their leading run producer. As in earlier pennant-winning seasons, fine pitching predominated, with veteran James "Hippo" Vaughn the league's best pitcher on the league's top staff.

Several years of decline followed the Cubs' World Series loss to the Boston Red Sox. The club hit bottom in 1925 with its first cellar finish in fifty-three years of league play, but a new era of greatness was at hand. In 1921 wealthy chewing-gum manufacturer William Wrigley had purchased control of the Cubs, with a determination to spend what was needed to produce a winner.

The seeds Wrigley planted eventually bore fruit. In 1926 he hired Joe McCarthy—a successful minor league manager—to lead the club, and drafted outfielder Lewis "Hack" Wilson from Toledo. Wilson immediately became one of the league's leading offensive threats, and the Cubs rebounded to the first division. In 1927 they even led the league through August before dropping back to fourth. A postseason trade brought them outfielder Hazen "Kiki" Cuyler, and a close third-place finish in 1928. Then the Cubs traded with the Braves for second baseman Rogers Hornsby, and in 1929 returned to the top. Led by Wilson's 159 RBIs and Hornsby's 149, five Cubs drove in more than 90 runs each. After battling Pittsburgh for the lead through mid-July, the Cubs hurtled ahead to take the pennant by 10½ games, despite a late-season slump. The slump continued through the World Series, though, as the Athletics humbled the Cubs in five games.

Just four games from the end of the hot pennant race in 1930 (the year Wilson set the major league RBI record with 190), McCarthy—still smarting from criticism arising from the World Series loss—quit as manager. With Hornsby at the helm, the Cubs preserved a second-place finish. They dropped to third the next year, but returned to the top in 1932. Hornsby, near the end of his playing days, was dropped as manager in August, with the Cubs in second, and replaced by first baseman Charlie Grimm. Pitcher Lon Warneke, in his first full season as a starter, led the league in wins and ERA. The club enjoyed a hot streak in August to move out in front of slumping Pittsburgh and hung on to take the flag by four games. The Yankees provided the World Series humiliation this time, a four-game sweep that provided McCarthy (now the Yankee manager) with sweet revenge for the Chicago fans' criticism three years earlier.

It had become a pattern: three years, another pennant. In 1935 a balanced offense (led by catcher "Gabby" Hartnett and second baseman Billy Herman) and the league's best pitching brought the Cubs up from fourth in late June to first in September. They clinched the pennant with three games to go, with their twentieth win of a 21-game streak. In the World Series, Detroit stopped the Cubs in six games.

After two seasons in second, it was time for another pennant. Bill Lee, the Cubs' top pitcher in 1935, was now the league's finest, as was the Cubs' staff. With the club languishing 6½ games back in midseason, Grimm quit as manager and was replaced by catcher Hartnett. In September the Cubs came to life, rising to second early in the month. They overtook Pittsburgh on September 28 with their ninth consecutive win—on Hartnett's homer against the Pirates in the growing darkness with two away in the bottom of the ninth—and clinched the pennant four games later, on the next-to-last day of the season. It was their fourth pennant at three-year intervals—and their sixth straight World Series loss, another Yankee sweep.

In 1940, after fourteen straight winning seasons, the Cubs began a five-year stretch below .500. Jimmie Wilson replaced Hartnett as manager in 1941; then Grimm returned near the start of the 1944 season. The club finished a distant fourth that year, but in 1945, after a middling start, they won twenty-six of thirty midseason games to take a lead they never relinquished. Balanced pitching (sparked by Hank Borowy, who went 11–2 after coming over from the Yankees in July) and the hitting of veteran first baseman Phil Cavarretta (.355) and center fielder Andy Pafko (110 RBIs) held off the pressing St. Louis Cardinals to preserve a sixteenth Cub pennant. But although they battled Detroit through a full seven games in the World Series, they ended up losing again—their ninth defeat in twelve tries.

For the next twenty-three years the Cubs remained out of pennant contention. But in 1969, the first year of divisional play, under the lively management of Leo Durocher, they took an early lead in the NL East. With a potent offense led by veteran sluggers Ron Santo, Ernie Banks, and Billy Williams, the team continued rising through early August. But the New York Mets rose even faster and farther; they didn't pause when Chicago leveled off in late August, and while the Cubs were losing eight straight in September the Mets were winning ten in a row. The Cubs wound up 8 games back.

The next year Chicago started well, slumped in late June, then fought back into the thick of the race in September before fading to another second-place finish. Three years later, in 1973, the Cubs entered July with a substantial lead. Although they fell to fifth by season's end, in the tightly packed division they were only 5 games back. It was to be their closest finish for eleven years.

In 1981 the Wrigley family, no longer able to bankroll a winner, sold the club to the Chicago Tribune Company. Three years later, with a new manager, Jim Frey, and an almost wholly different roster, the new management capped its rebuilding program with the acquisition from Cleveland, in mid-June 1984, of pitcher Rick Sutcliffe. As Sutcliffe fashioned a 16–1 record for his new club, the Cubs moved in front to stay on August 1, and kept on rising to capture their first division title by 6½ games.

Their fall was as rapid as their rise. After winning the first two games of the League Championship Series against San Diego, the pennant was swept out from under them as the Padres took the final three. Four losing seasons followed, in which the Cubs finished no closer than 18½ games behind the division winner.

But in 1989 the team, now managed by Don Zimmer, bounced back to duplicate its 1984 success. With a balanced offense and pitching vastly improved over the previous season, the Cubs took the NL East lead for good on August 7, and finished six games ahead of New York. Once again, though, they were unable to persevere to the pennant, losing the LCS to San Francisco in five games.

Veterans Andre Dawson and Ryne Sandberg enjoyed banner seasons at the bat in 1990. But the pitching faltered and, although the club played well after a poor first half, it took a win on the final day to give the Cubs a tie for fourth place.

Chicago White Sox

When minor league owner Charlie Comiskey transferred his club from St. Paul to Chicago as part of the move to upgrade the American League to major league status, he called it the White Stockings, after the Chicago team that dominated the National League in its early years. The new Chicago team revived memories of the old White Stockings, winning the AL championship in 1900, and repeating the triumph in 1901, the league's first major league season. Manager Clark Griffith (who had jumped to the White Stockings from Chicago's NL Cubs) was the team's star pitcher in 1901, winning 24 of 31 decisions as his team took the lead in May and held off the threatening Boston Somersets the rest of the way.

Griffith's effectiveness fell off in 1902, as did the team, (now called the White Sox) which took a sizable lead in July, only to slide back to fourth in August. Griffith left the next year and the White Sox sank to seventh. It would take eighteen years and baseball's greatest scandal for the Sox to finish that low again.

In 1904, after center fielder Fielder Jones replaced left fielder Nixey Callahan as manager, they rose into first place for a moment in August before settling back to third. The next year they made up a seven-game deficit in September to catch the Philadelphia Athletics, but the loss of two games to the A's stalled their drive and left them in second.

Nothing stalled the White Sox drive in 1906. Although they ranked at the very bottom of the league in hitting and entered June five games below .500, their pitching and hustle pulled them through. "Big Ed" Walsh, who had finally mastered the spitball after two years of trying, won 17 games, including a league-high 10 shutouts. Doc White contributed 18 wins with a league-best 1.52 ERA, and Frank Owen and Nick Altrock won 22 and 20, respectively. The Sox shot to the top in August with a 19-game win streak (including 8 shutouts). Early in September, New York's Highlanders passed them, but after the two teams had traded the lead back and forth for a couple of weeks the Sox spurted to take the pennant by 3 games. If the race was close, so were the individual games: the Sox achieved nearly one-third of their victories by the margin of a single run. The "hitless wonders" carried their momentum through the World Series, shocking the mighty crosstown Cubs (who had won a record 116 games that year) four games to two.

In 1907, after leading the league much of the first half, the Sox slipped to third. The next year Walsh pitched in the final seven games on his way to a career-high 40 wins. In a tight finish he pulled the Sox to within a half game of first-place Detroit before they dropped back to third with a loss to the Tigers on the final day.

It was 1915 before the Sox (piloted by rookie manager Clarence H. "Pants" Rowland) next finished that high, and 1916 before they again challenged seriously for the pennant. Comiskey, though accused of pinching pennies in his payment of players, was willing to spend what was needed to acquire them. After the 1914 season he purchased star second baseman Eddie Collins from the A's, and promising young Oscar "Happy" Felsch from minor league Milwaukee. The following August he acquired the great Joe Jackson from Cleveland. Together with the league's best pitching staff, they carried the Sox into the thick of a three-way race and a close second-place finish in 1916, and in 1917 to the pennant with the best winning percentage the club has ever compiled. Ten-year veteran pitcher Eddie Cicotte enjoyed his first 20-win season with a league-high 28 victories, and a league- and career-best 1.53 ERA. After dueling the Boston Red Sox most of the season, Chicago streaked out of reach in late August to finish with 100 wins and a 9-game lead. In the World Series against the New York Giants they captured their second (and, to date, their last) world title, in six games.

With several key players out much of 1918 for military or civilian war service, the White Sox finished out of the running, a dismal sixth. But in 1919, with the team back at full strength, the race once again went to Chicago. If their pitching didn't have quite the depth of the 1917 squad, its best hurlers were in peak form. Cicotte, after an off-year in 1918, attained a career high with 29 wins, as did Lefty Williams with 23 victories. Collins and Jackson enjoyed their best seasons in several years, and infielder Buck Weaver had never been better. Old-time pitcher/second baseman Kid Gleason was a rookie as a big league manager, but his Sox began strong and, after slipping briefly into second in midseason, pulled ahead in July to stay.

When the Sox lost the World Series to underdog Cincinnati, there were rumors of a fix, but nothing came to light for nearly a year. The White Sox looked better than ever in 1920. Though they fell back in May after a hot April, by mid-August they had risen to the thick of a tight three-team race. Felsch, Collins, and Weaver had never played better, Jackson was enjoying one of his very best seasons, and four pitchers were on their way to more than 20 wins. Chicago might not have caught Cleveland's rampaging Indians, but it didn't help that talk of a White Sox scandal revived late in the season, or that the grand jury convened only eight games from the end, or that eight Sox players were indicted and suspended with just three games to play. The teamed finished two games back, in second place.

The indicted players—among whom were Cicotte, Felsch, Jackson, Weaver, and Williams—were acquitted in court when three crucial confessions disappeared, but they were banned for life from organized baseball by commissioner K. M. Landis. The White Sox did not soon recover from the loss. In 1921 they began fifteen years of wandering in the second division, including three seasons in the cellar and one seventh-place finish (in 1932) that, while not the league's most distant, remains the farthest out Chicago has ever finished, 56½ games behind champion New York.

Two of the club's greatest and most durable players

arrived during these years: pitcher Ted Lyons (who won 260 games for the Sox over twenty-one years) in 1923, and in 1930 shortstop Luke Appling (who averaged .310 in his twenty years with the club). Owner Comiskey died in 1931, in the midst of his Sox's most dismal era, but Lyons and Appling were around long enough to enjoy a few fourth- and third-place seasons. But neither saw the Sox contend seriously for the pennant. After his playing career was over, Lyons managed the team for a few years—until 1948, when the Sox lost 101 games and finished last.

That year Frank Lane was lured from the presidency of the American Association to take charge as Chicago's general manager. He began reshaping the team, and after two more losing seasons the White Sox' fortunes began to rise. When Lane hired Paul Richards to manage the club in 1951, the Sox began what became a seventeen-year string of winning seasons.

In 1951, Richards's first season, the Sox spent a month in first place before drifting down to fourth, and the next year began a five-year stopover in third place. In 1954 they won 94 games but were out of the race by August—that was the year Cleveland won 111 and the second-place Yankees 103. Richards moved on to Baltimore, but Marty Marion, who replaced him, kept the Sox in third place. Their 91 wins in 1955 earned them a much tighter race than '54, one that found them in first place at the start of September, until four straight losses dropped them to third.

Frank Lane left at the end of the 1955 season, and young Chuck Comiskey (one of the grandchildren of Charlie Comiskey who now owned the club) took over the front office. A year later Comiskey replaced Marion with Al Lopez, who had piloted the great Cleveland club of 1954 and whose teams, in his six seasons of managing, had never finished below second. Lopez continued his success in Chicago: the Sox moved up to second (though well behind the Yankees) in 1957 and '58. In March 1959, Bill Veeck (who had in previous years owned the Cleveland Indians and the St. Louis Browns) bought a controlling interest in the White Sox from the Comiskey family and stepped into instant success.

With the Yankees suffering an off-year in 1959, Chicago and Cleveland battled for the lead throughout the summer, until the White Sox pulled away in late August. The same 94–60 record that had given them only a distant third in 1954 now carried them to their first pennant in forty years. The close and successful pennant race, and the club's dynamic new ownership, pushed Sox home attendance up more than 78 percent to a new club record.

As they had in 1906, pitching and hustle won the Sox their 1959 pennant. The league's best staff was led by veteran Early Wynn (enjoying his last big season with a league high of 22 wins) and young Bob Shaw (with a career high of 18), and featured the league's top relievers in Gerry Staley and Turk Lown. Shortstop Luis Aparicio, in the midst of a nine-year reign as stolen-base leader, set a personal high in runs scored as the club went 35–15 in one-run games. But in the World Series, Los Angeles stopped Chicago in six games.

The next year the Sox remained competitive until September, but finished third. After dropping to fourth and fifth the next two years (in a league now expanded to ten teams), they returned to second in 1963. The next year the Sox finished a season-long three-way race with nine straight wins, enough to pull them past Baltimore, but a game short of catching the Yankees, whose eleven-game streak a week earlier had put them out in front. After a third straight second-place finish in 1965, manager Lopez resigned for health reasons.

Under Eddie Stanky—and with the AL's stingiest pitching staff in forty-nine years—the Sox competed into the final week of a hot 1967 race, when five straight losses at the end dropped them to fourth. Only twice in the next thirteen years would they rise above .500; in 1970 they lost a club-record 106 games to finish at the bottom of the AL West. Two years later they took the division lead briefly in late August before dropping back to second, and in 1977 they held the lead through much of the summer before tailing off to third.

Bill Veeck had sold the club and repurchased it in 1976. But in January 1981, after three losing seasons and troubled by poor health and skyrocketing player salaries, he sold the Sox once again, to a group headed by Jerry Reinsdorf and Eddie Einhorn. With Reinsdorf heading the club's baseball operations and lawyer Tony LaRussa piloting the team on the field, the Sox became by 1983 one of the best teams in baseball. With their best record since 1920, the 1983 Sox carried the AL West by 20 games. Rookie slugger Ron Kittle led the attack, backed up by fourth-year outfielder Harold Baines and resurgent old-timers Greg Luzinski and Carlton Fisk. Pitchers La-Marr Hoyt and Rich Dotson attained personal bests to lead the majors in wins (with 24 and 22), and White Sox home attendance for the first time topped two million. In the League Championship Series, though, after a close win over Baltimore in the opener, Chicago lost the next three games and the pennant. The Sox's pitching and offense (except for Baines) collapsed the next season, and the team remained out of serious contention for six years.

Most forecasters predicted another dismal season for the Sox in 1990, but as fans watched a new Comiskey Park arise next door, they also saw their club celebrate its final year in the old yard with an astonishing resurgence. With their best start in decades, the Sox stayed close to mighty Oakland through the first half of the season, and even took over first place for brief periods in June and July before Oakland pulled away. Anchoring a strong bullpen, closer Bobby Thigpen shattered the major league record for saves, passing the old record of 46 with a month to go and finishing with 57.

Cincinnati Reds

The Red Stockings was the nickname of two pioneering Cincinnati ballclubs—the first avowedly professional team, which was undefeated in 1869, and the charter member club in the National League of 1876–1880. After a year on the sidelines, the reformed Reds joined the new American Association and captured the 1882 pennant by 11½ games, with a .688 winning percentage that is still the club record. Seven Reds enjoyed career highs in batting, pitcher Will White led the association with 40 wins, and rookie second baseman John "Bid" McPhee proved himself already one of the game's classiest fielders. The

Reds even won one of a pair of postseason exhibition games with Chicago's White Stockings, champions of the older and stronger National League.

McPhee remained eighteen years with the Reds and established himself as the finest second baseman of the nineteenth century. But the club would go thirty-seven years before it won another pennant. Twice in their seven remaining years in the AA the Reds finished second, and they enjoyed six winning seasons. Transferring from the AA to the NL in 1890, they finished fourth; at 10½ games out of first, it was their closest finish in the thirty-four years between 1884 and their next pennant-winning season, 1919.

The Reds wound up in the cellar for the first time in 1901. The next year club owner John T. Brush sold out to a group of Cincinnati's political bosses, who in mid-August named August "Garry" Herrmann (formerly head of the water works commission) to run it. Herrmann promptly acquired two outfielders from Baltimore—Cy Seymour and Joe Kelley, who was appointed team manager—who helped pull the Reds up to .500 and to fourth place by season's end. Three winning seasons followed, but then came eleven years in which the Reds finished above .500 only once (and then by only one game). Herrmann, meanwhile had found his calling in baseball administration. He not only remained president of the Reds for twenty-five years, but he also chaired the three-man National Commission that oversaw organized baseball, from its establishment in 1903 until 1920 (when his resignation brought about the commission's demise).

A midseason trade in 1916 brought the Reds Christy Mathewson (at the end of his pitching career) to manage the team, plus outfielder Edd Roush. The next year, with Roush leading the league in batting, the Reds edged above .500 and into fourth place. In 1918 an August spurt boosted the Reds into third place, in a season shortened by a month at the end because of the World War. Roush enjoyed another banner year, but Mathewson left for the Army just before the season ended.

First baseman Hal Chase—suspected of throwing games—was traded away after the season and replaced by veteran Jake Daubert. Southpaw Slim Sallee was purchased from the Giants and righthander Ray Fisher from the Yankees. Pat Moran (who had led the Phillies to a pennant in 1915) was hired to replace Mathewson at the Cincinnati helm. Thus fortified, the Reds in 1919 won their second pennant. Three pitchers—Sallee (21–7), Hod Eller (20–9), and Dutch Ruether (19–7, 1.82 ERA)—reached career peaks, Fisher (14–5) enjoyed one of his best years, Roush won another batting title and finished second in NL RBIs, and three Reds finished in the league's top four in runs scored. The Reds broke quickly at the start, but faltered in May and didn't pass the Giants into first place for good until late July. But from then on, they increased their lead to the end, finishing 9 games in front. Rumors of a White Sox fix to throw the World Series clouded the Reds' Series triumph—and spoiled it entirely when, a year later, the scandal became public and the truth of the rumors was confirmed.

In 1920 Cincinnati led the league entering September, but Brooklyn spurted and the Reds slumped to a third-place finish, 10½ games out. They dropped to sixth in 1921, but recovered for five years in the first division, including three second-place finishes. But only in 1926 did the Reds contend closely for the flag. After leading the league much of the first half of the season, they found themselves in the second half tangled in a three-way battle with St. Louis and Pittsburgh. But after surging into a narrow lead with seven straight wins in mid-September, they lost their next five games and wound up 2 games back of the Cardinals in second place.

The Reds finished the eleven years after 1926 in the second division, hitting bottom with four straight cellar finishes in 1931–1934. President Herrmann retired after the 1927 season, and within two years a controlling interest in the Reds was sold to a wealthy Cincinnatian, Sidney Weil. But Weil lost his fortune in the stock market crash of 1929 and the Depression that followed. While he continued to run the Reds for four years, his stock in the club was held by the Central Trust Company. In his efforts to turn the club around, Weil acquired catcher Ernie Lombardi from Brooklyn in March 1932, and pitcher Paul Derringer from the St. Louis Cardinals the following May. Derringer lost 25 games in his first Red season and 21 the next, but both remained with the club long enough to star in its return to glory. Owner Weil, however, relinquished his control to the bank in 1933, at the depth of the Depression and of the team's fortunes.

The bank hired Larry MacPhail (who had rescued minor league Columbus by introducing night baseball there) to run the Reds. MacPhail in turn hired Frank Lane to develop a minor league farm system, and persuaded Cincinnati industrialist Powel Crosley, Jr., to invest in the club. On May 24, 1935, Crosley and MacPhail brought night ball to the major leagues (the Reds, with Derringer pitching, beat the Phillies 2–1), and with it a sharp upswing in attendance at Crosley Field. By June 1936, Crosley's increased investment in the Reds had made him the majority owner. The temperamental MacPhail quit suddenly in mid-September 1936, but the Reds replaced him with another successful minor league executive, Warren Giles, who ran the club until his selection in 1952 as president of the NL.

After rising to sixth place in 1935 and fifth the next year, the Reds dropped back into the cellar in 1937. But the following year, under new manager Bill McKechnie, they rose into the first division once again—even holding second place briefly in September before slipping to fourth. Derringer enjoyed the first of three peak seasons, young Johnny Vander Meer contributed 15 wins (including two consecutive no-hitters) and Bucky Walters, after his acquisition from the Phillies in June, compiled his first winning season since converting from third baseman to pitcher in 1935. Catcher Lombardi led the NL in batting, and first baseman Frank McCormick, in his first full season, led the team in RBIs and the league in hits. The stage was set for the club's first back-to-back pennants.

Several Reds reached the apex of their careers in 1939, among them Walters (27–11) and Derringer (25–7), who between them topped most of the league's pitching stats, and Frank McCormick, who led the league in RBIs and hits and finished second in batting. The club pulled out of the pack to the front before the end of May and held the lead to the end, although St. Louis closed the gap with a late-season surge before slipping 4½ games back. Cincinnati's sweep by the Yankees in the World Series

was something of a shock, but the club had recovered its poise by the next spring. Starting strong and—except for a small dip in August—pushing steadily upward throughout the season, the Reds shook off the persistent Dodgers in midseason and finished 12 games in front with their first 100-win season. McCormick and Lombardi powered the offense, and Walters for the second year in a row took NL crowns in wins and ERA. This time the team's triumph carried through the World Series as Walters and Derringer won two games apiece to edge the Detroit Tigers in seven games.

The Reds' pitching remained strong in 1941, but their hitting and run production fell off and the team struggled to finish third. They remained in the upper division through 1944, but then dropped into an eleven-year trough of losing seasons in which, while they never sank into the cellar, they never rose above fifth.

Ted Kluszewski was in his ninth season as the Reds' slugging first baseman when Cincinnati next offered a serious run for the pennant in 1956 under manager Birdie Tebbetts. Kluszewski led the club in hitting and RBIs, but his 35 home runs were good enough only for third behind rookie Frank Robinson's 38 and Wally Post's 36 on a team that hammered 221 during the season to tie the major league record set nine years earlier by the Giants. The Reds' offense (they led the league in runs scored) kept them in the thick of a three-team race throughout the season, and they finished only 2 games out. That same year, for the first time ever they drew more than a million fans at home.

The Reds dropped out of a tight race in August 1957, and suffered losing seasons the next three years. After the 1960 season, Gabe Paul, who had succeeded Warren Giles as club president and general manager, left to help organize the new Houston club, and the following spring owner Crosley died. Bill DeWitt, who replaced Paul as president (and ultimately purchased control of the club), acquired pitcher Joey Jay from the Milwaukee Braves and third baseman Gene Freese from the White Sox. Jay in 1961 won twelve games more than his previous season high—tying for the league lead with 21, and Freese homered 26 times and drove in 87 runs—both career highs. Most of the team improved on their 1960 stats, and despite a poor start that saw them enter May in last place, the Reds had risen to the top by mid-June. The streaking Dodgers caught them briefly in August, but then fell away as the Reds pushed their pennant-winning margin to 4 games. In the World Series, though, it was the Yankees in five games.

The Reds next threatened in 1964 when, in a wild three-way finish, they won nine straight in late September to take first place for a day before slipping into a tie for second, one game behind St. Louis. In 1965 a young Pete Rose recorded the first of his ten 200-hit seasons as the Reds battled among the leaders through much of the summer before dropping off to fourth.

That December, after a decade of standout offense in Cincinnati, Frank Robinson was traded to Baltimore. The next year, while Robinson won the Triple Crown in assisting his new team to the world championship, the Reds suffered their first losing season in six years and sank to seventh place. That winter, owner DeWitt completed the sale of the team to a group led by Cincinnati newspaper publisher Francis Dale, and including brothers James and William Williams who later acquired a controlling interest in the club.

In 1969, the first year of divisional play, the Reds rose, after a slow start, into the thick of a five-way race in the NL West before stumbling as Atlanta and San Francisco surged in the final three weeks. But the season provided a foretaste of the decade to come as the team captured league crowns in slugging and home runs.

At midseason in 1970 the Reds moved out of Crosley Field—their home for fifty-eight years—into the new Riverfront Stadium. Catcher Johnny Bench and third baseman Tony Perez, with the finest seasons of their long careers, paced an overwhelming Red offense as the team hammered out a new club-high 102 wins to reward rookie manager Sparky Anderson with victory in the NL West by 14½ games, and gain the appelation "Big Red Machine." In the League Championship Series the Reds continued their triumph with a three-game sweep of East winner Pittsburgh. But mighty Baltimore humbled the Reds in the World Series, 4–1.

Cincinnati's hitting and run production fell off sharply the next year, and the club dropped to fourth with their only losing season of the decade. But in 1972—spurred on after a slow start by Johnny Bench's recovery of power, Gary Nolan's finest season on the mound, and the all-around mastery of newly acquired second baseman Joe Morgan—the Reds rebounded after a slow start to take a lead in June and pull away from everyone in July for an easy division win. Victory in the LCS came harder, as powerful Pittsburgh carried the series to the full five games before handing the Reds the pennant with a wild pitch in the last of the ninth inning of the final game. Cincinnati's defeat in the World Series was also close: the Reds won three, and Oakland's four wins were each achieved by a margin of just one run.

The Reds repeated as division titlists in 1973 with a second-half surge from fourth place that carried them past front-runner Los Angeles in September. But the much weaker New York Mets ended Cincinnati's pennant hopes in the LCS, 3–2.

In 1974 the Reds trailed the Dodgers all season and finished 4 games back in second place. But over the next two years the Big Red Machine flattened all opposition. In 1975, after hovering around .500 through mid-May, the Reds began an ascent that carried them to what are still club records: 108 victories and a winning margin of 20 games. The team featured balanced pitching (six starters won ten or more games), a balanced offense in which every regular drove in more than 45 runs (averaging nearly 77 apiece), the best fielding in the majors, and a big NL lead in stolen bases. After a three-game sweep of Pittsburgh in the LCS, the Reds subdued the stubborn Boston Red Sox in seven games for their first world title in thirty-five years, and their third overall.

They won their fourth the next year. Joe Morgan, at the peak of his career, led the NL in slugging, finished second to teammate George Foster in RBIs, and stole 60 bases. Balanced pitching and offense again put the Reds in front to stay in June, carrying the team to 102 wins and a 10-game lead over Los Angeles at the finish. The LCS produced another sweep—of Philadelphia this time. The World Series was also a sweep as the Reds dispatched the Yankees, outscoring them nearly three to one.

Two years of second-place finishes followed, and the Reds replaced Sparky Anderson at the helm with John McNamara, who led the club back to the top of the NL West in 1979. Pete Rose, after sixteen years in Cincinnati, had signed with the Phillies as a free agent, but Ray Knight (who replaced Rose at third base) minimized the loss with a team-high .318 batting average. Houston led the division much of the summer, but a sustained Reds' surge in August brought them even, then pulled them ahead in early September, where they hung on to take the title by just 1½ games. But that was the end of the Reds' decade of splendor, for Pittsburgh swept past them to the pennant in the LCS.

Joe Morgan left the club after the season, returning as a free agent to Houston, whence he had come eight years earlier. In 1980 the Reds dipped in midseason, recovering to make a race of it in August, only to fade a bit and finish third. The next year, in a season shortened and split in two by a players' strike, the Reds compiled the best overall record in the majors. But they came away empty-handed by finishing half a game behind Los Angeles in the first half-season and 1½ games back of Houston in the second half, losing a chance at postseason play when the powers that be decided to pit the half-season winners against each other for the right to play in the LCS.

As a penurious front office continued to trade away its stars or lose them to free agency, the dispirited Reds dropped to the bottom of the NL West in 1982 with a club-worst 101 losses. Manager McNamara yielded in midseason to coach Russ Nixon, who was himself replaced by Vern Rapp after another last-place finish in 1983. Robert Howsam, Sr., whose shrewd trading as general manager had been instrumental in building the mighty Reds of the 1970s, was called out of semiretirement to restore the club to respectability. Howsam signed free-agent slugger Dave Parker from Pittsburgh, and late in the 1984 season brought Pete Rose back as player-manager. Early in 1985 the NL approved the sale of the Reds to Marge Schott, a Cincinnati automobile dealer. With Parker enjoying his most productive seasons in several years, and newcomers Eric Davis and John Franco developing respectively into one of the league's leading run producers and one of its best relief pitchers, owner Schott's public enthusiasm for her team was rewarded with four straight second-place finishes (and a return in 1987 to a home attendance over two million for the first time in seven years). In 1987 the team even spent two months at the top of the NL West, until an August slump dropped them into a hole from which a late-season rally could not extricate them.

Turmoil ruled the Reds in 1989. Disabling injuries to no fewer than twelve players, including such 1988 standouts as pitcher Danny Jackson (whose 23 wins tied for the league high) and infielders Barry Larkin and Chris Sabo, contributed most to the team's drop to fifth place. But baseball's investigation of manager Pete Rose on charges of gambling on baseball games and other offenses—an investigation which resulted in Rose's lifetime banishment from the game in August—did nothing to bolster Cincinnati's play on the field.

The distress of 1989 was all but forgotten in 1990 as the Reds, under new manager Lou Piniella, leaped to a 9–0 start and, surviving threats from San Francisco in August and Los Angeles in September, held on to first place through the entire season. Larkin and Sabo—whole again—anchored a balanced offense, while pitchers Randy Myers (acquired from the Mets in a trade for John Franco) and Rob Dibble provided All-Star relief to a solid core of starters. In the LCS, the Reds overcame an opening-game loss to capture the pennant from Pittsburgh in six games, then startled Oakland's heavily favored Athletics with a four-game sweep.

Cleveland Indians

Cleveland is the only club in the American League East without at least one divisional title. Since the advent of divisional play in 1969, the Indians have enjoyed only four winning seasons, finishing last in the East seven times. Their record was not always this dismal. Though no other major league club with their longevity has won as few pennants, the Indians before 1969 ranked consistently among the league's better teams. They finished in the top half of the league nearly 70 percent of the time through their first sixty-eight years, and only once (in 1914) wound up in the cellar.

The Indians (who were at first called the Blues because of the color of their uniforms) succeeded Cleveland's National League Spiders, who in 1899, their final season, lost a major league record 134 games. When the NL dropped the Spiders at the end of the season, Ban Johnson, president of the emerging American League, grasped the opportunity to move into this major market. In 1901, when Johnson proclaimed the AL a major league, Cleveland lured several players from NL clubs and played much better than the Spiders had, but still finished next-to-last in their first big league season. The next year the Bronchos (as they decided to call themselves) languished in last place through June. But during the season they acquired several players through trade and purchase— most notably star second baseman Napoleon "Nap" Lajoie and pitcher Bill Bernhard—who turned the Bronchos around in midseason and lifted them above .500 (and into fifth place) by season's end.

With Lajoie sparkling in the field and dominating the league at the plate, the fans soon settled on another nickname for the club—the Naps—that lasted as long as Lajoie remained in Cleveland. Late in the 1904 season, Lajoie was named manager. After enjoying moderate success in two of the next three seasons, the Naps in 1908 experienced their best year yet, and one of the team's most exciting finishes ever.

With a ten-game winning streak near the end of the season, they moved from fourth to first, only to be surpassed by Detroit's ten-game streak. Both teams won their season finale, but the Tigers, because they had not made up an earlier rainout, took the pennant by half a game. Cleveland protested that if Detroit had played the missed game and lost, Cleveland would have gained a tie, forcing a playoff that might have brought them the championship. The dispute led to a rules change requiring ties or washouts to be replayed if their outcome could determine the pennant winner.

Poor seasons alternated with good the next few years.

Lajoie quit as manager but remained as player. Pitching ace Addie Joss pitched a second no-hitter (he had hurled a perfect game at the height of the 1908 race), but before the start of the 1911 season, Joss was dead of tubercular meningitis. Outfielder Joe Jackson—acquired from the Athletics—hit .408 in his first full big league season. The club reached bottom in 1914 with a last-place finish that found them 18½ games out of *seventh* place, 48½ out of first. After the season Lajoie was waivered to Philadelphia (the fans then voted to rename the club the Indians), and the next August Jackson was sold to the Chicago White Sox as attendance dropped to its lowest level since 1901.

By the time the 1916 season began, though, new ownership had acquired the great Tris Speaker from Boston and brought up from the minors a pair of promising pitchers, Jim Bagby (Sr.) and Stan Coveleski. The club rose only one place that year, to sixth. But they stayed in the pennant fight through July and wound up winning 20 games more than they had the previous year. Attendance more than tripled over 1915.

Sparked by the three newcomers, the Indians rose to third in 1917, and to close second-place finishes the next two years. In 1920 everything came together. Speaker, who had taken over as manager the previous July, hit .388 and enjoyed one of his best years, as did Coveleski with 24 wins. Bagby, in the finest season of his career, led the league with 31 victories, and veteran pitcher Ray Caldwell (picked up from the Boston Red Sox the previous summer) added another 20. Six regulars hit over .300; the club as a whole hit .303.

Involved from mid-June in a close race with the Yankees, joined in August by the White Sox, Cleveland saw its home attendance climb above 900,000 for the first time, to set a club record that would last twenty-six years. The Yankees dropped back a bit in mid-September, but the White Sox hung close until the final week, when eight of their players were indicted and suspended as suspects in the Black Sox scandal of 1919. The Sox lost two of their final three games and all hope of tying Cleveland to force a playoff. The Indians defeated Brooklyn in a World Series that is best remembered for second baseman Bill Wambsganss's unassisted triple play in Game Five.

Cleveland led much of the way in 1921 before a late slump and a New York surge gave the Yankees their first pennant. Through the next quarter century the Indians came close to a pennant only twice. In 1926, with two veteran Georges—pitcher Uhle and first baseman Burns—enjoying their finest seasons, the Indians came to life in midseason and drew within three games of the Yankees by season's end. Fourteen years later, in 1940, behind the 27 wins of twenty-one-year-old Bob Feller and the inspired play (in the field and at the bat) of second-year shortstop Lou Boudreau, Cleveland made an even closer run for the flag. Throughout the summer the Indians were in or near first place, but six losses in nine games with a resurgent Detroit in late August and September left them a game back at the finish.

Two years later Boudreau, at age twenty-four, was named to manage the Tribe. His team stirred little interest through the war years. But in 1946, with Feller back from military service and pitching his best ever, Cleveland fans boosted home attendance above a million for the first time, even though the team's won-lost record was its worst in eighteen years. The next year, their first full season under new president Bill Veeck, the Indians climbed to fourth. More significantly, Veeck hired the league's first black player, Larry Doby, who became a mainstay of the Indians for the next eight years.

In 1948 the Indians began a nine-year era of excellence with a victory in one of the closest pennant races ever. Through June they ran a three-way race with the Yankees and the surprisingly lively Philadelphia Athletics; in July the Red Sox rose out of nowhere to make it a four-way struggle. In September the A's fell behind, but the three remaining clubs stayed close, and on September 24 found themselves in a three-way tie. Cleveland moved ahead with a four-game win streak, but Boston, after a pair of losses, won their final four (including two to eliminate New York). Cleveland's final-day loss to Detroit left them tied with Boston. In a one-game playoff in Boston the next day (the first playoff in AL history), manager-shortstop Boudreau capped his MVP season with two home runs to help give rookie Gene Bearden his twentieth win and the Tribe their second pennant. The exciting race drew more than 2.6 million Cleveland fans to Municipal Stadium, a new major league record and still Cleveland's season high. By contrast, the World Series against the Boston Braves was anticlimactic—a Cleveland triumph in six games.

By 1951 both owner Veeck and manager Boudreau had moved on, but under new manager Al Lopez the Indians fashioned a six-year stretch in which they finished second to the Yankees five times, and in 1954 they won their third pennant with 111 victories—the most in AL history. The Lopez years, 1951–1956, were punctuated by the power of players like Doby, Luke Easter, Al Rosen, and Vic Wertz. But it was pitching that gave the team its consistency. Bob Lemon and Early Wynn won between 17 and 23 games in every one of the six years, as did Mike Garcia through 1954. As Garcia and Feller (who won 22 in 1951) faded, Art Houtteman was acquired from Detroit for a couple of good years, and Herb Score came along for his two explosive seasons.

The 1954 season—Cleveland's year to break the Yankee grip on the AL—was in fact New York's best season in the eighteen years from 1943 through 1960, a period in which they won twelve pennants. The Yankees kept the race close until the end of July, and finished with 103 wins. But the Indians won an AL-record 111 games to beat New York by 8. Wynn and Lemon tied for the league lead with 23 wins apiece, and Garcia copped the ERA crown. Doby led the league in homers and RBIs, and second baseman Bobby Avila took the batting title. Heavily favored to defeat the Giants in the World Series, the Tribe and their fans were shocked when the NL champs swept them in four games.

After Lopez left to manage the White Sox in 1957, the Indians slipped below .500 for the first time in a decade. Rocky Colavito's power and Cal McLish's pitching brought them back in 1959, when they finished second to Lopez's Sox. Their next highest post-Lopez finish came nine years later, in 1968, when Luis Tiant and Sam McDowell pitched them into third.

From 1969 through 1989 the Indians completed every season in the bottom half of the AL East, rising above .500 in only four seasons while finishing seven years in the division cellar. In 1990, though, with three straight wins

at season's end, they passed Baltimore by half a game to wind up a middle-of-the-divison fourth.

Detroit Tigers

One of the more successful clubs in the American League, the Tigers have enjoyed winning seasons nearly 70 percent of the time. In eighteen of their sixty winning seasons, they have remained in contention into the final days, eleven times emerging triumphant as league or division champions. They have finished last in the league or AL East only four times, and have never had more than four losing seasons in a row.

Detroit was one of the clubs from Ban Johnson's Western League that (renamed the American League) raised itself to major league status in 1901 with a talent raid on the long-established National League. In their first six big league seasons, the Tigers displayed little bite, finishing four times in the second division and never threatening for the league lead.

In 1907 all that changed. Sparked by a young right fielder, Ty Cobb (who in his first full big league season led the league in batting, slugging, hits, RBIs, and stolen bases) and led by a dynamic new manager, Hugh "Eeyah" Jennings (who knew enough not to try to tell Cobb how to play the game), the Tigers clawed their way to the pennant in a four-way race. The outcome might have been different if two late-season games with second-place Philadelphia had not been rained out and tied. Today's rules would require that the games be made up.

The 1908 race was even closer, with four teams contending into late September. The race wasn't settled until the final day, when Detroit beat Chicago to edge Cleveland by half a game. Once again the pennant hinged on a rainout that had not been made up. And once again Cobb dominated the league's hitters (though he slipped to fourth in stolen bases).

The Tigers had a slightly easier time of it the next year. It was a three-way race into September, but Detroit then pulled away to finish 3½ games ahead of Philadelphia. Cobb, in his best season yet, took the Triple Crown and returned to the top in stolen bases. But the Tigers were unable to win a World Series. In 1907, after an opening-game tie, the Chicago Cubs swept the next four. The Cubs lost Game Three the next year, but won the other four. And in 1909 Pittsburgh and Detroit alternated victories, with the Pirates emerging world champions in seven games.

Jennings managed Detroit for eleven more seasons; then Cobb took the reins for six years before leaving for Philadelphia. But the Tigers won no more pennants in the Cobb era. Cobb himself continued to dominate the league offensively through 1919. In 1911 he achieved career highs in most offensive categories, including a batting average of .420, but the Tigers managed no better than a distant second to the Athletics. In 1915 they started strong and remained in the race throughout the season. Cobb stole what was for forty-seven years a modern-record 96 bases, and the team's 100 wins proved to be the highest total in their first thirty-three years. But after running neck and neck with the Red Sox through most of August, the Tigers slumped a bit in early September—

just enough for the Sox to take the flag by 2½ games. A close third-place finish the next year marked the Tigers' last serious challenge for eighteen years.

In 1934, after six straight years in the second division, and only three years after their most distant finish ever (47 games out), the Tigers turned themselves around to win the pennant with a 101–53 record and a .656 winning percentage, the highest in Tiger history. Two newly acquired veterans—manager/catcher Mickey Cochrane and outfielder Goose Goslin—enjoyed fine seasons at the bat, as did first baseman Hank Greenberg (.339, 139 RBIs) in his first full season, and long-time Tiger second baseman Charlie Gehringer (.356, 127 RBIs). The two other infielders, third baseman Marv Owen and shortstop Billy Rogell enjoyed their finest seasons at the plate for a club whose batting average led the league at .300. It took the Tigers a month to get going, but by mid-July they had shot ahead of the Yankees, pulling farther away through August and September to win by 7 games. But once again, victory in the World Series eluded them as the St. Louis Cardinals blew them away 11–0 in Game Seven.

The Tigers' hitting fell off ten points in 1935, but their slugging jumped eleven points. Paced by Greenberg's 170 RBIs, Detroit—after another slow start—shot up so sharply in July and August that even a September slump gave the Yankees no opportunity to catch them. And finally, in their fifth try, the Tigers won a world championship, overcoming Chicago in six games despite the loss of Greenberg, who broke his wrist in Game Two. Part-owner Frank Navin, who had run the club for three decades, had finally seen his Tigers reach the very top. A month later, after falling from a horse, he suffered a heart attack and died.

Del Baker had replaced Cochrane as manager when Detroit next made a run for the pennant in 1940. In a tight race the Tigers caught up with Cleveland in early September and traded the lead with them for two weeks before pulling ahead to stay with two wins in a three-game series. In the pennant clincher, Detroit's Floyd Giebell outdueled Cleveland great Bob Feller 2–0 for his third—and last—big league victory. In the World Series the Tigers lost once again, as Cincinnati came from behind in Game Seven for a 2–1 win.

Two losing seasons followed, and Steve O'Neill replaced Baker at the helm. In 1944, the wartime Tigers, behind the splendid pitching of workhorses Dizzy Trout and Hal Newhouser (one-two in ERA and innings pitched, and winners of 27 and 29 games), joined the race in late August and found themselves tied with the St. Louis Browns for first going into the last game of the season. But the Browns beat the Yankees and Detroit lost to Washington as Trout failed in his try for a twenty-eighth win.

Hank Greenberg's release from military service in mid-1945 sparked another Tiger run for the pennant. They held the lead from mid-June through August, but in September a surging Washington caught up with them. The race once again went down to the final day, and the final inning, when Greenberg's grand slam overcame a St. Louis lead to give Detroit the flag over the idle Senators. Newhouser, with 25 wins and a 1.81 ERA, was named AL MVP for the second straight year. In the World Series his ERA shot up to 6.10, but he still managed to win two

games (including the finale) as the Tigers took the Cubs in seven for their second world title.

In the twenty-three years that passed before their next pennant, the Tigers came close only twice. In 1950 they led the race through the middle of the season, but were caught by the Yankees late in August. After retaking the lead in early September, the two clubs ran neck-and-neck for a while before Detroit fell away to second.

Two years later the Tigers reached their nadir: their first cellar finish, their most losses ever (104), and their lowest winning percentage (.325). After a decade in which they finished no higher than fourth, they rebounded in 1961 as first baseman Norm Cash and left fielder Rocky Colavito both enjoyed the most explosive seasons of their careers. Compiling their best season record since 1934, Detroit led the league through parts of June and July. But this was the year of Maris and Mantle and 109 Yankee victories; when the season ended, the Tigers' 101 wins had earned them only second place.

They came much closer six years later in the great four-way race of 1967 that saw three clubs still contending on the final day, when the Tigers split a doubleheader to tie with Minnesota for second. If 1967 was a scramble, 1968 was all Detroit's. In what is now known as the year of the pitcher, Tiger Denny McLain won 31 games (the last major leaguer to win 30) to lead the team to a 103-win finish, 12 games ahead of Baltimore. Down 1–3 to the Cardinals in the World Series, the pitching of McLain in Game Six and Mickey Lolich in Games Five and Seven brought the Tigers back and gave them their third world championship.

A strike at the start of 1972 contributed to the Tigers' first divisional title, which culminated a four-way race in the AL East. Detroit defeated Boston two games out of three at season's end, to edge the Sox by half a game. But if the strike had not wiped out an unequal number of games, the end of the season could have seen the two clubs tied.

The Tigers lost the pennant to Oakland with a 1–2 loss in the finale of a close League Championship Series, and dropped out of contention for a decade. In 1974 they finished at the bottom of the division, and the next year lost 102 games to post the worst record in the majors.

Finally, after seven seasons in the second division, Detroit put together a strong second half in strike-divided 1981, fading only at the end to tie for second. Three years later the Tigers were back on top with one of their best years. Opening the season with 9 wins, they ended April at 18–2, stretched their mark to 35–5 by late May, and were never headed, finishing a team-record 15 games in front, with 104 wins, their most ever. Their balanced pitching staff led the league in ERA, even though none of their starters finished among the top ten. Tiger newcomer Willie Hernandez (who with Aurelio Lopez compiled a 19–4 record from the bullpen, with 46 saves) earned both Cy Young and MVP awards. After sweeping Kansas City in the LCS, the Tigers took the world championship—their fourth—from San Diego in five games.

In 1987 the Tigers caught Toronto's Blue Jays in the season's final series, tying them for the lead in the first game, moving to the front with a twelve-inning win in the second game, and clinching the division crown in the finale, 1–0. In the LCS, though, Minnesota stopped the favored Tigers, four games to one.

Injuries sidelined veteran keystoners Alan Trammell and Lou Whitaker more than a month each and derailed the season of starter Jeff Robinson in August just as he was emerging as ace of Detroit's pitchers. All the same, the Tigers led the AL East much of the 1988 season before falling back and rallied at season's end to finish second, one game behind Boston.

The next year, though, as new waves of injury broke over an aging lineup, the Tigers dropped into the division cellar in June and kept sinking, finishing with 103 losses and the worst record in the majors. But in 1990 Trammell rebounded from one of his worst seasons with one of his best and, with newly acquired first baseman Cecil Fielder, sparked a Tiger recovery to third place. Fielder, back in the AL after a season in Japan, topped the majors in home runs (with 51, the most in the AL since 1961), slugging percentage, and runs batted in.

Houston Astros

The Colt .45s (as the Astros were originally known) had hoped to begin their history in the Harris County Domed Stadium, but when the start of the vast project was delayed, a temporary outdoor park was built for them next door in time for their 1962 inaugural. Heat, humidity, and giant mosquitoes held Colt home attendance below a million in each of their three outdoor seasons, but when, in 1965, they brought big league baseball indoors for the first time, the fans arrived—more than two million the first year. The original grass under the dome was real, but when the skylight panels were coated over so fielders wouldn't lose sight of high flies, the grass died. In 1966 the club (now known as the Astros) and the stadium (now called the Astrodome) brought to baseball yet another innovation—AstroTurf.

The Houston franchise, conceived as an entry in the abortive Continental League, first took the field instead (along with New York's Mets) in the National League, as part of the league's first expansion since shrinking from twelve teams to eight in 1900. Shrewd player selection by general manager Paul Richards kept the new team from being as bad as the Mets. Although they suffered just as long playing below .500 (seven years), they finished only once below New York in the standings.

When the NL added two more teams in 1969 and split into two divisions, the Astros for the first time made a serious title run. Though they wound up fifth in the West (ahead of only the expansion San Diego Padres), they rose to within two games of the top in August, and again in September, before a six-game losing streak dropped them out of contention. With an 81–81 record, they finished out of the ranks of losers for the first time.

After dropping below .500 again in 1970 and '71, the Astros made their second run for the division title in 1972. At the end of June they were neck and neck with Cincinnati for the lead, but the Reds pulled away over the rest of the season while Houston leveled off for an eventual second-place finish 10½ games back. With a record of 84–69, the Astros had fashioned their first winning season.

In 1975 they endured their worst year ever, losing 97

games to finish at the bottom of the West, 43½ games behind the Reds. But the next year pitcher J. R. Richard, with the first of several fine seasons, brought the club up to third with his 20 wins. By 1979 Richard was the NL's most overwhelming pitcher, leading the league with 313 strikeouts and a 2.71 ERA. His 18 wins and teammate Joe Niekro's 21 sparked a team that spent much of the summer in first place before falling to 1½ games behind Cincinnati at the end.

Houston and Los Angeles battled back and forth for the division lead throughout 1980. Richard began strong and seemed headed for his finest year. With a 10–4 record, he was starting pitcher in the All-Star Game. But shortly after midseason he suffered a stroke that ended his big league career. Led by Joe Niekro and Vern Ruhle (who replaced Richard in the rotation and finished 12–4), the best pitching staff in baseball kept the Astros in the race to season's end, although three straight losses to the Dodgers had left the clubs tied for first. In a one-game playoff, Houston rebounded with a 7–1 win (Niekro's twentieth) to capture the division title. In the League Championship Series, the Astros took the Phillies to the tenth inning of the final game before bowing two games to three.

When a player strike cut the middle out of the 1981 season, intradivisional playoffs were scheduled between the winners of the two halves. Houston, the second-half champion, defeated first-half victor Los Angeles in the first two games, but lost the next three, and with them the division title.

After four years in the middle of the division, the Astros stormed back in 1986 with their best season ever, winning fifteen of their last nineteen games to conquer the West by ten games. Pitcher Mike Scott, who had developed a deceptive split-finger fastball, won 18 to pace a strong Astro staff, leading the league in strikeouts and ERA. On September 25 he clinched the division crown with a no-hitter. In the LCS the Astros lost to the Mets, two games to four—but they held the New Yorkers at bay for fifteen innings of the final game before falling by a run in the sixteenth.

In each of the next three seasons the Astros drew within ½ to 1½ games of first place in August, only to tumble out of the race in the season's final weeks. While the team never challenged for the division lead in 1990, they overcame—with a winning second half—the worst first half in the league to tie for fourth in the NL West.

Kansas City Royals

Two years after the Athletics abandoned Kansas City for the West Coast, patent-medicine millionaire Ewing Kauffman bankrolled an expansion club for the city. Where the A's had been unable in thirteen years to fashion even one winning season, the Royals did it in 1971, their third year (when, ironically, they finished second in the AL West to the newly invincible Oakland A's). One of the most successful of all expansion clubs, the Royals in their first twenty years have finished either first or second in their division fourteen times.

In their fifth season, 1973, the year they moved into new Royals Stadium, the Royals also made their first serious run for the division title. A midsummer spurt carried them into first place in August before they leveled off to another second-place finish behind Oakland.

After a third second-place race with Oakland in 1975 (during which manager Jack McKeon was replaced by Whitey Herzog), the Royals won the division crown in 1976, taking the lead two months into the season and holding it to the end. Third baseman George Brett won his first AL batting championship and carried his hot bat into the League Championship Series, but the Yankees snatched the pennant on Chris Chambliss's home run in the bottom of the ninth inning of the final game.

For two more years the Royals dominated the AL West but failed to stop the Yankees in the LCS. In 1977, with a pitching staff that led the league in ERA and a balanced offense that included four players with more than 20 home runs and 80 RBIs, the Royals compiled a record of 102–60—their finest to date. Though they didn't move into the division lead until mid-August, they were nearly unstoppable the rest of the way. In the LCS they once again battled New York all the way, only to lose the Series and pennant for the second time in the final inning of game five.

The divisional race was a bit tighter in 1978, as California hung close to K.C. through much of August and into September, before the Royals finally pulled away. In the LCS, the Royals tied the Series with a big win in Game Two, but the Yankees came back to take the next two by one run each for their third straight flag.

The Royals slipped to second place in 1979, but the next year (led now by rookie manager Jim Frey) they overwhelmed the rest of a weak division. Despite a month-long decline in September, K.C. finished the season 14 games ahead of Oakland for their fourth divisional title. This was the year Brett chased .400 (ending at .390, the highest major league average since Ted Williams hit .406 in 1941), reliever Dan Quisenberry enjoyed his first big season (12 wins, 33 saves), and starter Dennis Leonard came back from an off-year to record his third 20-win season in four years. It was also the year the Royals finally beat the Yankees to capture their first pennant—with a three-game sweep in the LCS. In the World Series, though, it was Philadelphia in six games.

The player strike of 1981 divided the season into two halves. In the first half the Royals finished fifth, but part way through the second half Dick Howser (who had managed the Yankees to the East title the previous year) replaced Frey as Royals manager and brought the club in first, a game ahead of Oakland. But in the special play-offs, the A's (who had won the first-half race) beat K.C. for the division title with a three-game sweep.

Two more second-place finishes in 1982 (a close race with California) and 1983 (20 games behind the Chicago White Sox) were followed in 1984 by a fifth division championship in a three-way race with California and Minnesota. But Detroit swept away the Royals' pennant hopes in the LCS, in the minimum three games.

For Kansas City, 1985 was a season of catching up. Few picked the Royals to win the West, but with starters Charlie Leibrandt (17–9) and Bret Saberhagen (20–6) finishing two-three in the league ERA race, reliever Quisenberry leading the league in saves for the fourth straight year, and veteran George Brett healthy and en-

joying one of his best seasons ever, the Royals chased California throughout the summer and caught them in the final week to take their sixth division crown by a single game. In the LCS against Toronto, K.C. fell behind 1–3, which would have eliminated them in earlier years. But, saved by the expansion of the Series from five games to seven, they came back with three straight wins for their second pennant. Repeating the suspense in the World Series, the Royals again fell behind 1–3, to St. Louis, before rallying once again to win three straight for their first world championship.

During the 1986 season, manager Howser left the club after he was found to have a brain tumor. The Royals dropped below .500 and finished third, their lowest rank in a dozen years. Howser was unable to return to the helm in 1987 as he had hoped and died during the summer. The Royals rallied at season's end to pull themselves above .500 and finish (for the eighth time) runner-up in the West, 2 games behind Minnesota. Although they improved on their 1987 won-lost record in 1988, they finished in third place.

In 1989 Bret Saberhagen, with his most sparkling season yet (23–6, 2.16 ERA), hurled the Royals to their best record since 1980, but their 92 wins earned them only a ninth second-place finish. Confounding predictions of another strong season, following free agent acquisitions Mark Davis and Storm Davis, the Royals in 1990 floundered in the division cellar much of the summer. They wound up in sixth place, 27½ games out. Thirty-seven-year-old George Brett, though, rallied from the worst start of his career (.200 BA in early May) to hit .329 and capture his third AL batting title.

Los Angeles Dodgers

When the Dodgers left Brooklyn for Los Angeles, an era ended. From baseball's earliest days Brooklyn had been prominent; the city's Atlantics were the nation's best in the mid-1860s, and since 1884 Brooklyn had been home to major league ball. But before the start of the 1958 season, its link to the big time was severed by an owner who saw greener fields to the west. He was right: the Dodgers in Los Angeles are one of the game's most profitable franchises, regularly attracting more than three million fans per year to Dodger Stadium.

The club's origins were modest. After winning the championship of the minor Inter-State League in 1883, Brooklyn moved up to the major league American Association in 1884 and endured three losing seasons in its first four years. But in 1888, after signing three regulars from New York's newly defunct Mets and buying pitching/hitting stars Bob Caruthers and Dave Foutz from the AA champion St. Louis Browns, Brooklyn finished second to St. Louis, and the next year dethroned the Browns for their first big league pennant. In a projected ten-game World Series against the National League champion New York Giants, the Bridegrooms (as the Brooklyns had been nicknamed) won three of the first four games, but lost the next five.

Before the start of the 1890 season, Brooklyn transferred from the AA to the more prestigious NL. Many NL clubs performed below par that year, weakened by the loss of players to the outlaw Players League. But Brooklyn held on to most of its players and swept to its second straight pennant. In postseason play, poor weather and lack of fan support caused the World Series against AA winner Louisville to be called off after each team had won three games and tied one. The next year, with other NL teams renewed by players from the failed PL, Brooklyn finished sixth.

When the AA folded after the 1891 season, Brooklyn picked up slugger Dan Brouthers and pitcher George Haddock from pennant-winning Boston, and rebounded in 1892 to finish second and third in the two halves of a divided season. But for the next five years they finished no higher than fifth, and in 1898 sank to tenth in what was now a twelve-team league.

Help was on the way, however—help that today would be prohibited. Longtime Brooklyn president Charles Byrne had died, and the owners of the Baltimore Orioles—Harry Von der Horst and Ned Hanlon—seeing an opportunity to move into the more lucrative Brooklyn market, purchased a half interest in the Bridegrooms. Hanlon retained his Baltimore presidency, but took over as manager in Brooklyn, bringing along with him the core of his Oriole club—shortstop Hughie Jennings and outfielders Joe Kelley and Willie Keeler—plus its two best pitchers, Jim Hughes and Doc McJames.

The infusion of new talent worked wonders, as Brooklyn in 1899 (with a new nickname, the Superbas) took the NL lead in late May, during a twenty-two game winning streak, and held it the rest of the way. That winter, when Baltimore was dropped as the NL cut back from twelve teams to eight, Hanlon moved more Orioles to Brooklyn (including pitcher Joe "Iron Man" McGinnity), and once again led the Superbas to the pennant. That year they also won their first world championship in a series played with second-place Pittsburgh for the elegant Chronicle-Telegraph Cup.

Slow starts in 1901 and '02 kept the Superbas out of pennant contention, although they finished third and second. During this period Charley Ebbets, who had risen from ticket seller to president, took over majority ownership with the purchase of Von der Horst's stock, thereby quashing Hanlon's proposed move back to Baltimore. But Ebbets's clashes with Hanlon hastened the club's decline. In 1903 the team began a twelve-year sojourn in the second division, including a last-place finish in 1905 with their worst record ever (48–104, 56½ games out). Perhaps the most memorable events of these years were the change in nickname to Dodgers, and their move to brand-new Ebbets Field in 1913.

Hanlon was fired as manager after the disastrous 1905 season, but it was not until Wilbert Robinson took over in 1914 that the team began to pull out of its doldrums. Pitcher Jack Pfeffer, in his first full big-league season, won 23 games for the fifth-place Dodgers that year, and two years later led them to the pennant with 25 wins on a sparkling 1.92 ERA.

But the Dodgers lost the World Series to the Boston Red Sox, and in 1917 fell all the way to seventh. After three years in the second division, they bounced back in 1920, turning a three-way race into a rout with sixteen wins in their final eighteen games. After another World Series loss, to Cleveland, the Dodgers returned to the second division for another three years. In 1924 they began slowly, but leaped from twelve games back to an early-September lead, only to slip 1½ games behind the Giants at the finish.

Charley Ebbets died the following April, and Robinson was named to replace him. In his five years as president the club suffered on the field, finishing sixth each year. Fired as president but retained as manager, "Uncle Robbie" saw his Robins (as the Dodgers were now known) lead the league in 1930 most of the time from mid-May to a mid-August decline, then retake the lead for a day in mid-September before tailing off once more to finish fourth. That was Uncle Robbie's last hurrah. When the Robins provided no serious challenge in their fourth-place run the next year, he resigned after eighteen years at the wheel.

A succession of managers followed, but it was not until the Dodgers brought in the free-spending Larry MacPhail as general manager in 1938 that the club began to pull itself back into contention. The highlight of MacPhail's first year with the Dodgers was not the team's finish (seventh) but the introduction of night baseball to Ebbets Field (on June 15, when Cincinnati's Johnny Vander Meer defeated Brooklyn with his second consecutive no-hitter). MacPhail was also looking for new talent, and over the next couple of years he acquired a combination of youngsters and veterans that turned the Dodgers into one of the best teams in the league.

But MacPhail's most brilliant move may have been his conversion of shortstop Leo Durocher into manager Leo Durocher. The loud, driven Durocher alienated many (including MacPhail himself), but provided inspired leadership and a will to win that overcame complaints against him. After a third-place finish in 1939 and second place in 1940, the Dodgers battled the St. Louis Cardinals through all of 1941 before pulling ahead to clinch the pennant with just two games remaining. Veteran first baseman Dolf Camilli led the league in home runs and RBIs, sophomore outfielder Pete Reiser led the league in batting, slugging, and runs scored, and pitchers Kirby Higbe and Whitlow Wyatt tied for the league lead with 22 wins apiece, as the Dodgers for the first time since 1899 won 100 games. Only their loss to the Yankees in the World Series marred their finest season in forty-two years.

In 1942 they played even better, winning 104 games. But a late-season five-game slump dropped them behind the surging Cardinals, and they finished 2 games short of the flag.

MacPhail and many of his players left for the war, and though the club finished third in 1943 and 1945, it was not until 1946 that the Dodgers again presented a serious challenge. Once again the Cards and Dodgers made a two-team race of it, but this time the race ended in a tie, forcing the first league playoff ever. St. Louis won the pennant with wins in the first two games.

When MacPhail left for the Army, Branch Rickey was hired to run the club. MacPhail had left the club financially sound and a big drawing card; Rickey set about to make it a consistent winner. Famed as the developer of the Cardinal farm system, he was determined at Brooklyn to tap the one source of talent that the major leagues had willfully neglected: black players. He signed Jackie Robinson to Montreal (Brooklyn's leading farm team), and after a year there promoted him to the Dodgers for the 1947 season. Thus began the club's golden Brooklyn decade: ten years in which they won six pennants and—in 1955—a World Series. Two other races went right to the wire; only once did they finish as low as third.

With manager Durocher suspended from baseball for a year for consorting with gamblers, the Dodgers in 1947 were led by grandfatherly Burt Shotton, brought out of his Florida retirement. Robinson's hustle put him at the top of the league in stolen bases and second in runs scored. The team pulled up from fourth in June to first in July, and held the lead to the end. In the World Series they lost to the Yankees in an exciting seven games.

Durocher returned to the helm in 1948, but was replaced by Shotton in midsummer, with the Dodgers in fifth place. Shotton saw the team rise to third that season, then battle back and forth with the Cardinals throughout 1949 before edging them by a game on the final day. Robinson, in his finest season, led the league in hitting and stolen bases, and finished among the leaders in most other offensive categories. Rookie pitcher Don Newcombe led the team in victories with 17, and Preacher Roe led the league in winning percentage. Again the World Series was a loss to the Yankees, this time in only five games.

In 1950 the Dodgers nearly caught the staggering Phillies, losing out only in the tenth inning of the final game. President Rickey left the club for Pittsburgh and was replaced by Walter O'Malley, who replaced manager Shotton with Charlie Dressen. The slugging of catcher Roy Campanella and first baseman Gil Hodges, and 20-win seasons by Roe (22–3) and Newcombe (20–9) kept the Dodgers in front through most of 1951, but New York's surging Giants closed from thirteen games back in August to tie for the lead at the finish. The teams split the first two playoff games. In Game Three the Dodgers were leading by two runs in the last of the ninth when Bobby Thomson's three-run homer gave New York the flag.

The next year, though, the Giants fell short and Brooklyn took the pennant with relative ease. But not the World Series. Although Brooklyn held a 3–2 lead after five games, the Yankees came back to take the final two.

The Dodgers repeated as NL champions in 1953 with their best season ever. Dodger bats overwhelmed the league, hitting 19 points and slugging 63 points above the league average, as the team outscored its nearest rival by more than a run per game. With a club-record 105 wins, the Dodgers cruised to the pennant by 13 games. But again the Yankees took the World Series, in six games.

Dressen wanted a three-year contract and was let go when he turned down another for only one year. Minor league manager Walter Alston wasn't so demanding, and signed for 1954 the first of a historic string of twenty-three one-year Dodger contracts that would see him into the Hall of Fame. After a second-place finish in Alston's rookie season, the Dodgers in 1955 took the lead from the start and—never challenged—walked away with their eleventh pennant. Outfielder Duke Snider, with one of his most productive seasons, led the league's most powerful squad; Newcombe (20–5) paced the league's best pitching staff.

Once more in the World Series, Brooklyn faced the Yankees, and once more the Series went seven games. But this time there was joy in Brooklyn—Johnny Podres shut

out New York in the finale! In an exciting three-way fight in 1956, the Dodgers repeated as pennant-winners, taking their final three games to edge Milwaukee's Braves. Newcombe, in his greatest year, clinched the flag on the final day with his twenty-seventh win. In the World Series, though, it was *déjà vu* time—a sixth Yankee triumph, in seven games. The golden decade was over.

The Dodgers (despite the league's best pitching) vacated the 1957 race in August, finishing third. Before the start of the next season, they had vacated Brooklyn as well, for Los Angeles. Playing in Memorial Coliseum (a converted football stadium) the L.A. Dodgers sank to seventh place in 1958. But the next year the reawakened bats of aging Duke Snider and Gil Hodges, the fiery pitching of young Don Drysdale, and the late-season pitching heroics of Roger Craig (recalled from Spokane) kept the team in the thick of a tight race that found them tied with the Braves at season's end. The Dodgers won the first playoff game in Milwaukee, and captured big league baseball's first West Coast pennant at home the next day, in the twelfth inning. Then they defeated the Chicago White Sox to give the West its first World Series winner.

After finishes of fourth and second, the Dodgers produced record-breaking excitement in 1962 as they moved into brand-new Dodger Stadium in the hills above Los Angeles. Between the new ballpark and the excitement generated on the field, more than 2.75 million fans passed through the turnstiles—a new attendance record that would last until the Dodgers themselves broke it fifteen years later. As pitcher Don Drysdale and left fielder Tommy Davis ignited the league with career-high seasons, and shortstop Maury Wills became the first major leaguer of the century to steal 100 bases, the team locked into a season-long struggle for first place with archrival San Francisco. But after holding a narrow lead much of the season, the Dodgers dropped their last four games to finish in yet another tie—their fourth.

The playoff must have reminded fans of 1951. As they had then, the Giants and Dodgers split the first two games, and the Dodgers once again brought a 4–2 lead into the ninth inning of Game Three. This time, though, it was not a home run that undid them, but a bases-loaded walk.

Sandy Koufax—who had won 14 games in 1962 (and the first of five straight ERA crowns) despite losing half the year with circulation problems in his fingers—rose to dominate the world of pitching the next four years. For three of those years his Dodgers dominated the NL. In 1963 Koufax's 25–5 season carried Los Angeles into the World Series against the Yankees, where two more wins helped put the New Yorkers away in the minimum four games. The next year Koufax slipped to 19 wins, but the Dodgers fell all the way to a tie for sixth.

They rebounded to the top in 1965. Koufax won 26 and Drysdale 23 in a tight four-team race that saw them fall behind the Giants in early September, only to retake the lead for good later in the month with 13 straight wins. The World Series against Minnesota went to the seventh game before Koufax nailed down another world title with his second shutout in three days.

The race in 1966 was just as close as in '65, with three teams switching leads throughout the season. But the Dodgers, third at the end of August, put together streaks of five and seven wins in September to move to the top, where Koufax clinched the pennant on the final day with his twenty-seventh victory. And then it was all over. After a losing effort in Game Two of the World Series (a Baltimore sweep), Koufax, at age thirty, retired because of arthritis in his pitching elbow. The Dodgers sank to eighth the next year and rose only to seventh in 1968.

In 1969, the first season of divisional play, Los Angeles found itself in the thick of a five-team race in the West until eight straight losses in late September dropped them to fourth. No one challenged Cincinnati in 1970, but the next year the Dodgers closed to within a game of the front-running Giants in September before their drive stalled.

A late-season Dodger slump let Cincinnati get to the top in 1973, but the Dodgers held their lead to the end in 1974. Newly acquired veteran outfielder Jimmy Wynn and first baseman Steve Garvey, in his first full season, led the club offensively; pitcher Mike Marshall set a modern major league record with 106 appearances in relief of a staff that was the league's best (which earned him the Cy Young award). The Dodgers beat Pittsburgh handily in the League Championship Series for their fifth Los Angeles pennant, but lost the World Series to Oakland in five games.

Cincinnati proved untouchable in 1975 and '76, but in 1977 the Dodgers—under new manager Tom Lasorda, who moved up from the coaching staff when Alston retired—jumped to an early lead and held it all the way. Garvey's 33 home runs led a balanced offense in which four players hit 30 or more homers and drove in over 85 runs. Again the Dodgers won the LCS (in four games, against Philadelphia), and again they lost the World Series (to the Yankees, in six games).

Although the divisional race was closer— and the Dodgers broke baseball's three million attendance barrier for the first time—1978 was in most respects a replay of 1977. Garvey again led the club offensively, the Dodgers again beat out Cincinnati in the West and Philadelphia in a four-game LCS, and the Yankees again defeated the Dodgers in a six-game World Series.

A season-long back-and-forth battle with Houston in 1980 ended in a tie for first—the fifth tie for the Dodgers, three more than any other club. In the playoff (reduced from three games to one to bring the NL into line with AL practice), Houston won easily.

When the players went out on strike part way through 1981, the Dodgers, paced by the spectacular pitching of rookie Fernando Valenzuela, found themselves half a game in front of Cincinnati. In a special playoff with poststrike leader Houston, the Dodgers defeated the Astros in five games for the division title, and also went the distance in beating Montreal for the pennant—their twenty-first. Facing the Yankees for the eleventh time in World Series play, they lost the first two games, but swept the next four games to capture their sixth world title.

In 1982, after a poor start, the Dodgers fought back to take the lead in August and again in September before dropping back to second, a game out. More successful drives in 1983 and '85 led to their fifth and sixth division titles, but culminated in defeat in the LCS—to Philadelphia in 1983 and St. Louis two years later. In 1986 and '87 they posted identical 73–89 won-lost records—the team's worst performance in two decades.

But then in 1988, with an infusion of talent from the American League—most notably slugger Kirk Gibson and relief ace Jay Howell—and a spectacular season on the mound from starter Orel Hershiser (who concluded his 23–8 year with a major-league record 59 consecutive scoreless innings), the Dodgers bounced back to the top of the NL West. It took them the full seven games to down the favored Mets in the LCS for their twenty-second pennant, but in the World Series they humbled Oakland's powerful Athletics in just five games for their seventh world crown.

Hershiser (whose 15–15 record belied another strong season on the mound) led a 1989 Dodger pitching staff that yielded the fewest runs in the majors, but with an offense last among major league clubs in *scoring* runs, the Dodgers could finish no better than fourth in the West. Hershiser's 1990 season ended almost as soon as it began when he underwent shoulder surgery in late April, but young Ramon Martinez took up the slack, winning 20 games. With a revived offense that topped the NL West in runs scored, the Dodgers bounced back from a slow first half to draw within 3½ games of Cincinnati in late September and finish second, 5 games out.

Milwaukee Brewers

When in 1969 the new Seattle Pilots played their home opener in the refurbished minor league Sick's Stadium, 7,000 seats and the left field fence were still unfinished. The Pilots may not have needed the seats. Fewer than 700,000 fans came to see them play—the third worst attendance in the league—as they drifted into the cellar of the American League West with 98 losses. That winter the Pilots—renamed the Brewers—moved to Milwaukee, where a genuine big league stadium (vacated by the Braves five years earlier) awaited them.

Attendance improved nearly 38 percent in Milwaukee, although the Brewers of 1970 won only one game more than the Pilots had in Seattle. It would be eight more years before they experienced their first winning season. Meanwhile, in 1972, they switched divisions from West to East, trading places with the Washington Senators, who moved West to become the Texas Rangers.

At last—and with power—the Brewers broke their losing pattern in 1978. One key front-office move leading to the turnaround, the signing of free agent Larry Hisle (who the previous year with Minnesota had led the league in RBIs), was also a giant step in the escalation of major league player compensation. With a signing bonus and deferred payments on top of salary, Hisle's six-year contract averaged out to eleven times what he was paid in Minnesota, an annual average figure that would have paid almost 40 percent of the Brewers' player payroll the previous year.

Hisle proved his worth in 1978, leading an offense that sprang to life under rookie manager George Bamberger to top the league in hitting, slugging, homers, and runs scored. On the mound Mike Caldwell won 22 games in the best season of his career. Although the Brewers never threatened the Boston Red Sox or the New York Yankees for the lead, they did rise from below .500 in earl finish a solid third, 24 games above .500.

A shoulder injury the next April marked the beginning of the end of Hisle's career and perhaps cost Milwaukee the division title. Even without Hisle the team compiled what is still their best winning percentage (.590), as out-fielder Gorman Thomas (45 home runs, 123 RBIs) and several other Brewer hitters attained new career peaks of productivity. While they never seriously threatened front-running Baltimore, they rose past Boston in late August to finish second.

Most of the Milwaukee bats remained hot in 1980, but injuries, ragged pitching, and Bamberger's heart attack (which caused him to miss the first part of the season and retire in early September) contributed to a distant third-place finish. In strike-divided 1981, league-leading per-formances by two newly acquired pitchers—starter Pete Vuckovich (14–4) and reliever Rollie Fingers (28 saves)—helped give the Brewers the best overall record in the AL East, and the second-half championship. But in the special intradivisional playoffs with first-half winner New York, the Yankees captured the division crown three games to two.

The Brewers started slowly in 1982; at the end of May they were two games below .500, near the bottom of the division. A day later Buck Rogers, the Milwaukee coach who had replaced Bamberger as manager two years ear-lier, was himself replaced by coach Harvey Kuenn. By mid-July the team had risen to first place, and they led the West by more than six games as September neared. But Baltimore had cut the lead to three games by the time Milwaukee arrived for the season's final four games. One win would give the Brewers their first division champion-ship, but they lost the first three games by five, six, and eight runs. Don Sutton, who had been acquired from Houston a month earlier, faced Oriole Jim Palmer in the season finale: the Brewers made Sutton's job easy, scoring ten runs to Baltimore's two.

Milwaukee's offense—"Harvey's Wallbangers"—had been awesome, scoring more than a run per game above the league average. Just about every offensive category featured one or two Brewers among the league's top three: in hits they took all three top spots. Shortstop Robin Yount, who finished first in slugging, hits, total bases, and doubles, was named major league player of the year.

In postseason play California took a 2–1 lead in the League Championship Series, but Milwaukee came back to take the final two games and the pennant. In the World Series against St. Louis, the Brewers twice took the lead in games, but a Cardinal come-from-behind win in Game Seven ended Brewer hopes.

Milwaukee dropped to fifth in 1983, then to a last-place seventh the next year, 36½ games back—their most dis-tant finish ever. It was not until 1987 that they returned to the winning track, finishing third with 91 victories. Had they remained in the AL West where they started, they would have won the division championship by 6 games.

As veterans Robin Yount and Paul Molitor continued to spark the team's offense, and starter Ted Higuera and reliever Dan Plesac headlined the AL East's best pitching staff, the Brewers in 1988 rose above .500 to stay at the end of August, and finished in a tie for third, just two games behind champion Boston. With Yount and Molitor enjoying even more productive seasons in 1989, and re-

liever Plesac on a club-record pace for saves, the Brewers drew within half a game of first place in August. But injuries and league-worst fielding took their toll, and the club finished fourth, right at .500. In 1990, as poor field-ing led to more than 100 unearned runs, the Brewers dropped to sixth.

Minnesota Twins

The Twins' beginnings as the Washington Senators were inauspicious. When American League president Ban Johnson established the Senators as part of his move in 1901 to raise the league to major league status, he staffed it with the manager and many of the players from his disbanded Kansas City franchise. Within a decade, four of the eight teams in the new major league had won two or more pennants, and three others had enjoyed at least one season in second place. But the Senators, after sixth-place finishes in their first two seasons, spent the next nine years in seventh or eighth. In 1904, their fourth season, they lost 113 games—still the team worst.

Even the arrival of promising young fireballer Walter Johnson didn't seem to help. By 1909 he was the league's second-best strikeout artist, but he lost 25 games and the Senators finished farther back than ever—56 games from the top. Johnson turned his record around the next two years, winning 25 games in 1910 and in 1911, but the team rose only to seventh.

When Clark Griffith—a forty-two-year-old former pitching great and one of the founders of the American League—was hired to manage the Senators after the 1911 season, the club's fortunes took an immediate turn for the better. Griffith revamped the lineup—most strik-ingly in the acquisition of first baseman Chick Gandil from minor league Montreal. The Senators in 1912 won seventeen straight games after Gandil was put into the lineup, and found themselves in the midst of a pennant race. Boston's Red Sox eventually ran away from the field, but the Senators held off Philadelphia for second place. Johnson won 33 games, and his 1.39 ERA led the league.

The next season was Johnson's finest. His league-lead-ing 36 wins, 11 shutouts, and 1.14 ERA were also career bests and enabled Washington to overtake Cleveland late in the season for another second-place finish. But while Johnson continued to top 20 wins per season for several years before beginning to fade, his team was unable to stay competitive, only once in the next decade making a serious run at the pennant (in war-shortened 1918, when they finished 4 games back, in third).

Griffith wanted the Senators to spend more to attract good players; when his demands were rejected, he bought into a controlling interest in the club and named himself president. A year later, in 1921, he retired as field man-ager. Under a succession of veteran player-managers the team showed some improvement over the next three years, but Griffith's surprise appointment of twenty-seven-year-old second baseman Bucky Harris to manage the team in 1924 worked wonders. Left fielder Goose Goslin drove in more runs than Babe Ruth, and Walter Johnson put together his best season in years to head the league's best pitching staff. A hot streak in June shot the team from fifth to first, and a strong stretch drive in August and September brought them to the finish 2 games ahead of the Yankees. In the World Series a ground ball's lucky bounce over the head of the Giants' third baseman brought the Senators victory in the last of the twelfth inning of the seventh game.

Though the Senators, aided by the acquisition of veteran pitcher Stan Coveleski from Cleveland, fought off the A's to repeat as pennant winners in 1925, they were less successful in postseason play. Once again the Series went the full seven games, but this time Pittsburgh won the world title.

The Senators enjoyed winning seasons in five of the next seven years, as Johnson retired from the mound and replaced Harris as manager. But it was not until 1933, when Johnson was replaced by twenty-six-year-old shortstop Joe Cronin, that the team again pursued the pennant beyond midseason. Two veteran pitchers at the top of their form—Alvin "General" Crowder and Earl Whitehill—and a balanced offense led by Cronin and first baseman Joe Kuhel kept the Senators close to New York through July, and then, as the Yankees leveled off in August, shot the team up out of reach. Although they tailed off a bit at the end, the Senators won the pennant handily, compiling a .651 winning percentage that is still the club record. The New York Giants, though, took Washington's measure in the World Series and overcame them in five games.

The following October, after a drop from third place in June to a distant seventh at season's end had plunged home attendance nearly 25 percent below the previous year, Griffith—always close to the edge financially—traded Joe Cronin, his manager, star shortstop, and (since September) son-in-law, to the Boston Red Sox for a lesser shortstop and $225,000.

Only twice in their remaining quarter century in Washington did the Senators rise higher than fourth or finish closer than 17 games from the top. In 1943 they placed second, 13½ games behind the runaway Yankees. And two years later, after a poor start, they caught up with frontrunner Detroit in September, only to stall and finish 1½ games out. In their final six Washington seasons, they wound up in the cellar four times.

Calvin Griffith, Clark's adopted son, assumed the club presidency when his father died in 1955. Within three years he was making plans to move the club to Minneapolis. There were threats from Congress and a plea from President Eisenhower not to move the Senators—and at first the league itself opposed the move. But Washington was not a good baseball town even when the Senators were playing well, and in October 1960 a solution was reached. The league would let Griffith move his club to Minnesota, and Washington would be granted a new expansion team.

Players like outfielders Bob Allison and Harmon Killebrew, and pitcher Camilo Pascual, who had enjoyed productive seasons before the move, were even more productive in Minnesota. Other standouts became regulars or joined the club after the move—Zoilo Versalles at shortstop, Rich Rollins at third, Jim Kaat on the mound, and (arriving in 1964) outfielder Tony Oliva and pitcher Jim "Mudcat" Grant. Infielder Rod Carew began his twelve-year stint with the Twins in 1967.

Former outfielder Sam Mele made his major league managerial debut during 1961, and in 1962 saw his Twins come close to catching the Yankees in mid-September, finishing second. The next year they didn't catch fire until August and wound up third. In 1964 they dropped below .500 into a tie for sixth. But after the end of June 1965 no one challenged them as they breezed to their first Minnesota pennant. Oliva led the league in batting for the second straight year, and Versalles (in what was far and away his finest season) led the league in total bases and runs scored. Mudcat Grant led the league with 21 victories (his only 20-win season) and 6 shutouts, and Kaat's 18 wins were the league's third best. In the World Series it took a three-hitter by Los Angeles's Sandy Koufax to stop the Twins in the seventh game.

After a poor start in 1966 that saw them enter July deep in fifth place, the Twins played better than anyone else the rest of the season to sneak ahead of Detroit into second. Killebrew, who had been injured much of the previous year, returned with his old power in '66, and Kaat enjoyed a career-high season with 25 wins.

The Twins began 1967 with another poor start. With the team in disarray and in sixth place, the easygoing Mele was replaced in June by hard-driving Cal Ermer, a longtime minor league manager. By mid-July the team had risen to second, and a month later (after dropping back to fourth) moved to the top in one of the greatest pennant races ever. Four clubs battled for the title, with three still in the running on the final day. But Boston defeated Minnesota to win the pennant, and Detroit split a doubleheader to tie the Twins for second. The next year Minnesota finished seventh.

Fiery rookie manager Billy Martin replaced Ermer in 1969 and, in this first season of divisional play, piloted the Twins to the championship of the West by a convincing 9 games. Killebrew exploded for the best season of his career (49 home runs, 140 runs driven in), and Carew won the first of his seven batting titles. The first League Championship Series, though, was a disaster for the Twins as Baltimore swept to the pennant in three games. Veteran manager Bill Rigney replaced the difficult Martin at the helm, and piloted Minnesota to an almost identical division crown in 1970, 9 games ahead of Oakland. Pitcher Jim Perry, with 24 victories, enjoyed his second straight 20-win season, and the best of his career. The LCS, though, was another repeat performance—a Baltimore sweep.

For the next thirteen years the Twins remained out of contention, although only in 1981 and '82 did they drop to the bottom of the division. Twice (in 1974 and '76) they recovered from poor starts to make a decent showing, and once (1979) they pushed into first in July before nosediving out of the race. But it was not until the flowering of a new generation of young players in 1984 that a Minnesota title threat could be taken seriously.

The Twins' decline on the field was matched by a decline in attendance, which even their move indoors in 1982 did not significantly redress. The Griffith family, unwilling to risk the high cost of luring proven talent, decided to give up the club after more than sixty years of family ownership. Early in 1984 a buyer was found in Carl Pohlad, a wealthy Minneapolis banker. By the time Pohlad's purchase was completed at the end of July, the

Twins' young team had blossomed into the West's front-runner, paced by pitcher Frank Viola's sudden development into a winner, and by the arrival in May of rookie centerfield sparkplug Kirby Puckett. Although the Twins leveled off in August and lost their final six games, to fall to .500 and a tie for second, they had brought the crowds back to the ballpark. The team in 1984 for the first time ever drew more than 1.5 million fans to their home games, and remained well above a million the next two years despite a pair of losing seasons.

In 1987 the Minnesota fans were rewarded for their faithfulness. Although the Twins lost their last five games to finish only eight above .500 (and two ahead of surging Kansas City), their winning record at home was the best in the league, and their title in the West was never in doubt. More surprising was their decisive triumph over favored Detroit in the LCS, four games to one. In the first World Series to feature indoor play, the Twins won the four games played in their Metrodome to capture Minnesota's first world baseball championship in seven games.

Although the Twins in 1988 improved on their 1987 won-lost record—and Frank Viola, Kirby Puckett, and relief ace Jeff Reardon enjoyed career peaks—they finished well back of Oakland in the race for the division crown. But their home attendance, which had jumped 66 percent in 1987 to top 2 million for the first time, bounded another 45 percent in 1988 to make the Twins the first AL club ever to attract more than 3 million fans in a season.

As the team suffered a general decline in pitching and hitting in 1989, Viola—in the middle of a disappointing season—was traded to the Mets; the Twins finished fifth. Reardon, a free agent, left for Boston after the season. The Twins continued their downhill slide in 1990, slipping from fifth place at midseason to their first cellar finish in eight years.

Montreal Expos

In the spring of 1969, in an unfinished "temporary" ballpark that would be the Expos' home for eight years, major league baseball came to Canada. One of two clubs added to the National League in this first year of divisional play—Montreal in the East and San Diego in the West—the Expos finished 48 games out of first. But although they matched San Diego's 52–110 record and last-place divisional finish, they outdrew the Padres by better than two to one, with a home attendance of more than 1.2 million fans.

After a second last-place (but much improved at 73–89) season in 1970, the Expos moved a notch out of the cellar to fifth in 1971 and '72, and into pennant contention in 1973. Outfielder Ken Singleton became the first Expo to drive in 100 or more runs, rookie pitcher Steve Rogers compiled a sparkling 1.54 ERA (and a 10–5 won-lost record), and reliever Mike Marshall set a new major-league record with 92 pitching appearances (winning 14 games and saving a league-high 31). In the tightest race of the century, all six clubs remained in contention into September, when Philadelphia dropped away. In mid-September Montreal won six straight to catch front-running Pittsburgh, only to lose nine of the next ten and drop back to fifth. Three wins in the final four games lifted them to

fourth place, just 3½ games behind the champion New York Mets.

Center fielder Willie Davis (acquired from Los Angeles in a trade for Mike Marshall) led the Expos' offense in another fourth-place season in 1974, but the club sank back to a tie for last in 1975 and sole possession of the cellar a year later, with a 55–107 record nearly as bad as their first season (and a home attendance little more than half that of 1969).

But with the acquisition of heavy-hitting Tony Perez from Cincinnati, a new manager—the controversial Dick Williams—and strong seasons from catcher Gary Carter, sophomore outfielder Ellis Valentine, and rookie Andre Dawson, the club snapped back in 1977 to win 20 more games than the previous year and rise to fifth. And with their move into the new Olympic Stadium (built for the 1976 Olympics), Expo attendance rebounded from a club low to a new high.

After climbing another notch to fourth in 1978 (as the newly acquired Ross Grimsley became their first—and, to date, only—20-game winner), the Expos put on a run for the title that drove attendance in 1979 to over two million. Third baseman Larry Parrish, with a career-high season, led the club in batting and home runs in a balanced attack that saw five players drive in more than 70 runs. The pitching too was balanced, with six pitchers winning 10 games or more on a staff that compiled the league's lowest ERA. With a fast start in April, the Expos led the East through much of June and into July, when a surging Pittsburgh caught up with them. Both clubs climbed away from the pack to the end of the season. Montreal fell back a bit in August but caught up with the Pirates in September and carried the race to the final day before dropping off to second. The Expos' 95 victories remain the club record to date.

The 1980 race was just as exciting. A three-way struggle with Philadelphia and Pittsburgh through most of the summer narrowed to two teams in September as the Pirates fell away. In a crucial late-September series, the Expos beat the Phillies two games of three to take a half-game lead, but in the final series a week later Philadelphia won two games to clinch the crown.

In a 1981 season divided by a players' strike, Montreal finished the first part of the season in third place, but held off St. Louis to win the second part by half a game. The Expos then won the division championship in a special playoff with first-half winner Philadelphia—their first title—but lost the League Championship Series to Los Angeles.

As the Expos declined gradually over the next five years, most of the regulars left through trade, free agency, or retirement. But in 1987, two 1981 rookies who had remained in Montreal—outfielder Tim Raines and third baseman Tim Wallach—stood out in an Expo comeback that left them in third place, just four games back, with 91 wins and the second-best record in their history.

Strong midsummer surges in 1988 and 1989 propelled the Expos into the thick of the race in the NL East, in 1989 lifting them into the lead for six straight weeks following the acquisition from Seattle of mound ace Mark Langston. But in both years, late-season slumps dropped the club to identical 81–81 finishes. In 1990 strong pitching (despite the loss of free-agents Langston, Bryan

Smith, and Pascual Perez) kept the Expos competitive well into September before they fell out of the race.

New York Mets

Branch Rickey's projected Continental League never materialized, but its New York and Houston franchises were admitted to the National League, expanding the league to ten clubs in 1962. Few major league teams have been as inept as the New York Mets were in their first season. Despite the presence on the club of such New York favorites as manager Casey Stengel, pitcher Roger Craig, and first baseman Gil Hodges, and of players like outfielders Richie Ashburn and Frank Thomas who were still near peak form, the Mets finished at the bottom of the league in batting, fielding, and pitching. They won only one game in four and suffered a twentieth-century record 120 losses. But New York fans—deprived of National League baseball since the defection of the Dodgers and Giants to the West Coast four years earlier—found their ineptitude lovable. By their third season, having moved out of the old Polo Grounds into brand-new Shea Stadium, the last-place Mets were regularly outdrawing the pennant-bound Yankees.

Former New York Giants catcher Wes Westrum replaced the aging Stengel as manager part way through the 1965 season, and the next year saw the club rise out of the cellar for the first time. But they fell back to tenth in 1967 (despite rookie Tom Seaver's 16 wins—a club record), and Westrum was replaced at the helm by Gil Hodges (who had retired from playing after a few games in 1963). With Jerry Koosman joining Seaver in the starting rotation and setting a new club record with 19 victories, Hodges led the Mets in 1968 back up to ninth place with their first season of more than 70 victories.

In 1969 the majors inaugurated divisional play, but the Mets got off to their usual indifferent start. At the end of May, however, they began to win consistently. By early June they were second in the NL East, though well back of the explosive Chicago Cubs. By September, though, the Cubs were faltering. The "Miracle Mets" caught and passed them with a ten-game winning streak and continued on to take the division title by eight games. Among the many Met heroes, Tom Seaver stands out. He won his last ten starts, sparking the team's final push to triumph and finishing with a league-high 25 wins that still stands as the club record. After a three-game sweep of West champion Atlanta in the league's first Championship Series, the Mets faced the mighty Baltimore Orioles—regarded by many as one of baseball's all-time greatest teams—for the world championship. The Met miracle continued as, after an opening game loss, the New Yorkers humbled the Orioles with four straight wins.

The Mets of 1970 remained competitive into mid-September as they sought to repeat their '69 triumph. But they fell back at the end while Pittsburgh spurted, and finished third. Two more third-place finishes followed in 1971 and '72. Just before the start of the 1972 season, Met coach Yogi Berra moved up to manage the club after Hodges suffered a fatal heart attack two days before his forty-eighth birthday.

In 1973 the NL East experienced the tightest major league race of the century. Chicago moved out in front of the pack early in the season, but folded in July and August. So did the Mets, who fell from third to a last-place sixth. But although they were last late in August, they were less than seven games out of first. A series of bursts in September, culminating in a seven-game winning streak, shot the Mets through the division into first place by September 21. Although they finished the season only three games above .500, they topped the division by 1½ games. In the LCS they held off the favored Cincinnati Reds to take the pennant in the maximum five games, but lost the World Series when Oakland overcame a 2–3 deficit to win the final two contests.

The Mets then entered a decade-long decline. Though they won as often in 1975 and '76 as they had in 1973, they didn't come close to winning the East, and dropped into a seven-year trough in 1977 which included five seasons in last place. Seaver was traded to Cincinnati in 1977, and Koosman (after two disastrous seasons) was sent to Minnesota in the fall of 1978 (where he won 20 the next year). The heirs of original owner Joan Whitney Payson (who had died in 1975) sold the club to Nelson Doubleday (of the publishing company) and Fred Wilpon in January 1980. In February the new owners hired Frank Cashen as general manager, hoping he could rebuild the Mets as he had the Baltimore Orioles in the late 1960s.

It took a few years to achieve the right blend, but when outfielder Darryl Strawberry was brought up from the minors early in 1983 and first baseman Keith Hernandez was acquired from St. Louis in June, the mix had nearly all the needed ingredients. In 1984, under new manager Davey Johnson, and with rookie pitchers Dwight Gooden and Ron Darling combining for 29 wins, the Mets rebounded to second place with their second-best season record up till then.

The rise continued in 1985. With catcher Gary Carter (newly acquired from Montreal) leading the club in homers and RBIs, and Gooden cementing his superstardom at age twenty with a phenomenal 24–4, 1.53 ERA season, the Mets won 98 games—eight more than the year before—and came within a game of tying St. Louis late in September before slipping 3 games back at the finish.

When the Mets acquired pitcher Bob Ojeda from the Boston Red Sox after the season, many predicted an easy division title for them in 1986. For once, the pundits were right. With Carter, Strawberry, and Hernandez powering the offense, and Ojeda, Darling, and Gooden all placing among the league's top five pitchers in ERA, the Mets won two of every three games (108 in all) to capture the division title by 21½ games.

The postseason battles were tougher. The Mets won the pennant from Houston with a 16-inning victory in Game Six of the LCS, but came within a strike of elimination by the Red Sox in Game Six of the World Series before rallying to take that game and the next for their second world crown.

Strawberry enjoyed his finest season yet in 1987, and pitchers Terry Leach and Rick Aguilera put together a combined won-lost record of 22–4. But Ojeda was lost to injury early in the season, and the Mets, though they hung close and posted 92 wins, lost out—as in 1985—to St. Louis by 3 games.

David Cone (20–3, 2.22 ERA) emerged in 1988 as the

ace of the league's best pitching staff, which, with the power of Darryl Strawberry and Kevin McReynolds behind it, carried the Mets back to the top of the NL East, 15 games ahead of runner-up Pittsburgh. But after taking a 3-2 lead in the LCS, they lost the pennant to underdog Los Angeles in seven games.

With co-captains Carter and Hernandez injured and in decline, the Mets floundered through 1989, salvaging a narrow second-place finish over St. Louis with four wins in the season's final three days. The two captains were released after the season. Next May, with the Mets mired 9½ games out, manager Davey Johnson was replaced by coach Bud Harrelson. In June the team—ignited by Strawberry's suddenly hot bat—took off: with a flight that included a club-record eleven-game win streak, the Mets propelled themselves into first place before the end of the month. Through July and August the Mets and Pittsburgh lobbed the division lead back and forth, until the Pirates consigned the New Yorkers to second place for good with a three-game sweep in early September.

New York Yankees

In its first twenty seasons, the club that became the New York Yankees won no league championship, and finished second only twice. But for the next forty-four years the Yankees dominated the American League, winning nearly two of every three pennants and twenty World Series. After another pennant drought of eleven years, the club in six years won five division titles, four pennants, and their twenty-first and twenty-second World Series. Their current pennant drought, which has lasted nine years so far, is the third longest in their history.

The Yankees began as the Baltimore Orioles in 1901. But AL president Ban Johnson really wanted a club in New York and, after outmaneuvering the politically influential Giants (who didn't want a competing big league team in their city), Johnson moved the Orioles to the northern end of Manhattan in 1903.

In 1904 the Highlanders (as they were known during their first years in New York because of the high land on which their park was built) chased the Boston Pilgrims through midsummer, catching them in August and trading first place back and forth into October. But after Jack Chesbro defeated Boston 3–2 on October 7 to give New York a half-game lead (it was his forty-first win, a twentieth-century major league record), the Pilgrims came back to win the next two. In the fourth game of the series, with Chesbro again pitching and the score tied 2–2 in the top of the ninth, a wild pitch over the New York catcher's head let in Boston's pennant-clinching run.

The Highlanders again led the league in late September two years later, before tailing off to finish 3 games behind Chicago. But that was the last time they contended seriously for the title for fourteen years. Meanwhile they finished last twice, in 1908 losing a club-worst 103 games, and in 1912 suffering their most distant finish ever—55 games behind pennant-winning Boston.

In 1914 Colonel Jake Ruppert and Tillinghast Huston bought the Yankees, and the next year they purchased pitcher Bob Shawkey from the Philadelphia A's. Shawkey's 24 victories in 1916 led the Yankees to their

first winning season in six years, and in 1919, on returning from military service, his 20 wins (plus the 9 of Carl Mays, who came to the club in a controversial midseason deal with the Red Sox) brought the Yankees to third—at 7½ games out, their closest finish in thirteen years.

That winter, on the recommendation of manager Miller Huggins, the Yankees paid a then-record $125,000 (plus a $300,000 loan) to the Red Sox for Babe Ruth. Ruth, with 54 home runs in 1920, obliterated the record of 29 he had set the year before, and Mays and Shawkey together won 46 games in a three-way pennant race that ended with New York a close third.

At season's end Ruppert hired Ed Barrow as Yankee general manager. While managing the Red Sox, Barrow had converted Ruth from a pitcher to outfielder. His December trade with Boston that gave the Yankees pitcher Waite Hoyt and catcher Wally Schang was just the improvement needed to bring the Yankees their first pennant in 1921. Ruth's 59 homers and his career-high 171 RBIs didn't hurt, either.

The prickly Carl Mays, staff ace in 1921 with a 27–9 record, slipped to 13–14 the next year. But the Yankees continued to decimate the Red Sox roster with trades that brought them pitchers "Bullet Joe" Bush and "Sad Sam" Jones, and infielders Everett Scott and Joe Dugan. Bush's 26 wins in 1922 made up for Mays's decline, and the Yankees captured their second straight league championship.

Both races had been tight two-way struggles—with Cleveland in 1921 and the St. Louis Browns in 1922—and both pennants had been followed by a World Series loss to the Giants. But in 1923 the Yankees at last put everything together. After sharing the Giants' Polo Grounds since 1913, they were at home in brand-new Yankee Stadium just across the Harlem River in the Bronx. With the addition of yet another pitcher from the Red Sox—Herb Pennock—and a .393 year from Ruth, they took the lead from the start and built it over the summer to a 16-game margin by the end. For the third time the Yankees faced the Giants in the World Series; this time they beat them, in six games, for their first world championship.

The Yankees lost a close race to Washington in 1924 and collapsed into seventh place in 1925—a year in which Ruth was lost much of the season to surgery and suspension. There were bright spots, though: center fielder Earle Combs, in his first full season, hit .342 to lead Yankee regulars, left fielder Bob Meusel filled Ruth's shoes as AL home run and RBI leader, and first baseman Lou Gehrig arrived to stay. With Ruth's return to full strength in 1926 and the establishment of a new middle infield of Tony Lazzeri and Mark Koenig, the Yankees took their fourth pennant in a race that was not as close as their 3-game winning margin would suggest. They lost a close World Series to the Cardinals.

Many observers rank the 1927 Yankees as baseball's greatest team ever. Certainly it was the Yankees' greatest team. They won more games (110) than any Yankee team before or since. Ruth hit his 60 home runs, and Gehrig drove in 175. Waite Hoyt led the league in ERA and rookie Wilcy Moore proved the league's premier reliever. As a team the Yankees led the league in hitting (.307) and slugging (.489, still a major league record); their pitchers compiled a 3.20 ERA that was ¾ of a run per game lower than the ERA of the next best team. In the World Series they swept the Pittsburgh Pirates.

The resurgent Athletics made the 1928 race much closer, but New York won three in a row from the A's in mid-September to pull ahead, and held on for their sixth pennant. Another Series sweep (this time against the Cardinals) gave them their third world title.

For three years the A's left the Yankees in the shade. An ill Huggins yielded the club's reins in September 1929 and died before the season had ended. By the time the Yankees returned to the top in 1932, their manager was Joe McCarthy. He had led Chicago's Cubs to the NL pennant in 1929; in fifteen more seasons and seven world championships. Only once would his Yankees finish as low as fourth.

A Yankee pennant and World Series triumph over the Cubs in 1932 was followed by three second-place finishes to Washington (in 1933) and Detroit (in 1934 and 1935). Ruth had retired by the time the Bronx Bombers returned to the top in 1936, but Gehrig was still in top form, catcher Bill Dickey and outfielder George Selkirk developed into formidable sluggers, and Joe DiMaggio arrived to take over center field. New York finished a club-record 19½ games in front and buried the Giants in the World Series.

Three more pennants and three more world titles followed in 1937–1939. Lefty Gomez emerged as the league's premier pitcher in 1937, and DiMaggio picked up the home run and slugging crowns. Again the Giants were vanquished in the World Series. Rookie second baseman Joe Gordon and sophomore outfielder Tommy Henrich joined Dickey, DiMaggio, and a declining Gehrig in leading the slugging Yankees to the 1938 crown and a Series sweep of the Cubs. A balanced attack in 1939 saw seven of the eight starters (including Babe Dahlgren, who replaced the dying Gehrig at first) drive in 80 runs or more as the Yankees won 106 to run away with their eleventh pennant—and eighth World Series, another sweep, with Cincinnati the victim. For the fourth year in a row the offense topped the league in slugging, and overshadowed the steady—if unspectacular—Yankee pitchers, who for the *sixth* consecutive season compiled the league's stingiest ERA.

After catching the leaders with a 19-4 spurt in late summer, the 1940 Yankees fell away to finish a close third. But then came another three convincing pennant wins and a pair of Series triumphs as the nation moved into World War Two. Outfielders DiMaggio and Charlie Keller dominated the Yankee offense in 1941, and rookie shortstop Phil Rizzuto hit .307. Though no Yankee pitcher won more than 15 games, seven won a pair (and reliever Johnny Murphy won 8 while saving a league-high 15). With 101 victories the team was lost from view to the rest of a league in which six of the eight clubs failed to break .500. In the World Series Brooklyn was the loser in five games.

Keller, DiMaggio, and Gordon provided the power, and Tiny Bonham (with 21 wins), Spud Chandler, and rookie Hank Borowy headed the league-leading pitching staff that propelled the Yankees to 103 wins and another easy pennant in 1942. But after winning their previous eight World Series, the Yankees were finally stopped, in five games, by the St. Louis Cardinals.

By 1943 many Yankees were in military service. But pitchers Chandler, Bonham, Borowy, and Murphy were not, and they led the charge to the team's seventh pennant in eight years. In the Series the Yankees reversed the results of the previous year, turning back St. Louis in five.

When Jake Ruppert died in 1939, general manager Barrow succeeded him as president, a position he held until January 1945, when Dan Topping and Del Webb bought the club and installed Larry MacPhail as president, giving him a third of the club and a ten-year contract to run it. The volatile, innovative MacPhail had previously brought new life to Cincinnati and Brooklyn, and did bring night ball to Yankee Stadium. But manager McCarthy, who couldn't get along with MacPhail, quit early in the 1946 season, and the team finished a distant third.

DiMaggio and the others were back from the war by 1946, but it was not until 1947—under new manager Bucky Harris, and with sparkling pitching from Allie Reynolds (acquired from Cleveland), rookie Frank "Spec" Shea, and reliever Joe Page—that the Yankees returned to the top of the heap with an easy pennant win and a narrow World Series triumph over Brooklyn. On the day the Yankees won the Series, though, president MacPhail embarrassed the club and undid himself by brawling in public. Topping and Webb bought out his contract and share of the ownership. Topping took over the presidency, but promoted farm director George Weiss to run the club as general manager.

After the Yankees dropped a pair of season-ending games to the Red Sox to finish third in a tight 1948 race, Weiss replaced manager Harris with Casey Stengel, who in nine years of managing the Braves and Dodgers had only twice seen his club finish as high as fifth. But with Weiss providing a steady stream of talented players via the farm system and canny trades, the Yankees under Stengel proved all but invincible into the '60s.

Stengel's Yankees began by putting together a record string of five world championships. No major league club had ever won five pennants in a row, let alone five World Series, and the Yankees didn't accomplish the feat easily. In 1949, for example, they saw the Red Sox come from 12 games back in midseason to pass them with a three-game series sweep in late September, only to rescue the flag with two close must-win victories over the Sox in the season's final games. In the World Series, Brooklyn was again the victim, in five games.

After losing much of 1949 to injury, DiMaggio returned with power in 1950, shortstop Rizzuto and catcher Yogi Berra enjoyed the finest seasons of their careers, and pitcher Whitey Ford broke into the majors, winning all nine of his decisions as a starter (he lost one game in relief). But the Yankees struggled even harder for the pennant than the year before, battling three other contenders before finally pulling in front to stay with five straight wins near to the end of the season. Though three of the games in the World Series were decided by just one run, New York took the Phillie "Whiz Kids" without a loss.

No Yankee drove in as many as 90 runs in 1951, and Whitey Ford was drafted for two years of military service. But the remaining pitchers doubled their shutout production and lowered the team ERA by more than half a run per game, enough to propel the club ahead of Cleveland in mid-September. In the World Series the Yankees shook the faith of the "miracle" Giants, four games to two. Cleveland challenged once again in 1952, and again fell just short, as did Brooklyn in carrying the World Series to seven games.

Finally, in 1953, Stengel's Yankees won with relative ease. Ford, back from the Army, won 18 to lead the club to a finish 8½ games up. Once again it was Brooklyn in the World Series, and once again the Yankees beat them.

In 1954 New York won 103 games—the most in Stengel's twelve-year tenure. But Cleveland won an AL-record 111 to take the flag by 8 games. In 1955, though, it was back to second place for Cleveland as New York, with Mickey Mantle now established as one of the game's most productive hitters, settled in for another four pennants. As August passed into September, three teams were within a game of each other at the top. But the Chicago White Sox faltered and fell away, leaving the Yankees and Indians to fight it out. With two weeks left, New York won eight straight to pass Cleveland for good. Facing the Dodgers in the World Series for the sixth time, the Yankees finally lost, as Johnny Podres shut them out in Game Seven to give Brooklyn its first world title since 1900.

From 1956 through 1958 the Yankees seldom found themselves out of first place. Only in 1957, when they leveled off in May before surging to the front in June, were they involved in anything resembling a close race. In postseason play, they went the full seven games all three years, winning twice—from the Dodgers in 1956, and from the Milwaukee Braves in 1958, after losing to them the year before.

In 1959 the Yankees started poorly and never did rise much above .500, finishing a distant third with their worst won-lost record in thirty-four years. After the season, Al Weiss sent an aging Hank Bauer to Kansas City in a trade that brought Roger Maris to New York. In 1960 Maris, with AL titles in slugging and RBIs, won the MVP award. He and Mantle dominated the power stats and led the charge back to the top as the Yankees won their final fifteen games to bury the faltering Orioles.

New York's 1960 pennant was the first in another five-flag streak, but it was the last for Stengel. After Pittsburgh toppled the Yankees in the World Series on Bill Mazeroski's famous home run, president Topping retired both the seventy-year-old Stengel and general manager Weiss, sixty-five, who had been with the club for twenty-eight years.

With the season lengthened by eight games in 1961, Maris broke Ruth's home-run record and rookie manager Ralph Houk led the club to 109 wins, just one off the club record. Once again Maris and Mantle finished among the best in offensive power, and once again New York took the pennant by 8 games. Ford enjoyed a splendid 25-4 season and celebrated with two more wins in the World Series as the Yankees humbled Cincinnati in five games.

Pitcher Ralph Terry moved out of Ford's shadow in 1962 with 23 wins. Though the Yankees finished just five games ahead of Minnesota, there was little doubt about the outcome from midseason on. In a close World Series with San Francisco, Terry won two, including the clincher with a four-hit shutout.

Though New York won pennants the next two years, the 1962 world title was to be their last until the Steinbrenner era fifteen years later. Despite the loss to injuries of Mantle and Maris for much of 1963, New York dominated the AL, winning by 10½ games with 104 wins. But in postseason play the Yankees were themselves dominated by the Dodgers (now in Los Angeles), who held them to just four runs in a Series sweep.

Yogi Berra replaced Houk as manager for 1964. In a season-long three-way race with the White Sox and Orioles that found the clubs virtually tied in mid-September, only an eleven-game win streak gave the Yankees the space they needed for their final one-game margin of victory. Pitcher Jim Bouton won a pair in the World Series, but the Cardinals took the crown in seven. Berra was fired.

During the 1964 season Topping had sold the Yankees to CBS. The next year the club, which had gone forty years without a losing season, dropped to sixth place, and in 1966 fell to a last-place tenth, their first cellar finish in more than half a century. Even Houk's return as manager in 1967—though it led to some winning seasons—failed to restore the once-proud club to pennant contention, except once, in 1972, when it was mid-September before they fell out of a tight race to finish fourth.

In January 1973 a syndicate headed by Cleveland shipping magnate George Steinbrenner purchased the Yankees from CBS. Although he had vowed not to take a prominent role in running the club, Steinbrenner soon emerged as one of baseball's most active and intrusive owners. Through a series of shrewd trades, offers of big contracts to free agents, and what became a round robin of managerial changes, Steinbrenner's Yankees became competitive again in 1974 (finishing a close second to Baltimore after streaking from last in July to first in September) and returned to the top with three successive pennants and a pair of world championships.

Billy Martin (a former Yankee second baseman) in 1976, his first full season as manager, led the renewed club to a runaway division title. First baseman Chris Chambliss's homer in the ninth of the final game of the League Championship Series gave the Yankees the pennant by the narrowest of margins over the Kansas City Royals. Cincinnati swept New York in the World Series, but the Yankees came back the next year to edge Baltimore and Boston in a three-way race that saw the teams shift back and forth in the standings throughout the season. Slugger Reggie Jackson, signed as a free agent the previous autumn, turned the club's power trio of Chambliss, Graig Nettles, and Thurman Munson into a quartet as the Yankees recorded their first hundred-victory season in fourteen years. After another ninth-inning win over Kansas City in the LCS finale, New York won the World Series in six games over Los Angeles, and Jackson became "Mr. October" with five home runs—three of them in successive at-bats in the final game.

The 1978 season provided as exciting a race as baseball is likely to see. In mid-July it looked like a Red Sox romp, but the fourth-place Yankees put on a great surge, catching the faltering Sox with a four-game series sweep in early September. Boston dropped 3½ games back, but won their final eight games to catch New York on the final day. In the one-game tiebreaker, Yankee shortstop Bucky

Dent lofted a wind-blown three-run homer over Boston's close left field wall in the seventh, and Jackson homered an inning later for New York's final run in the 5–4 win. Again the Royals were the victims in the LCS, as were the Dodgers in the World Series.

After dropping to fourth in 1979, the Yankees held off Baltimore in 1980 to win their fourth division title—but this time Kansas City swept to the pennant in three games. In 1981 the Yankees found themselves in first place when the players struck in June and were thus admitted to an intradivisional playoff with the season's second-half winner, Milwaukee. Narrowly defeating the Brewers for the division title, New York swept Oakland for the pennant in the LCS. But after taking the first two games from Los Angeles in the World Series, they were stopped cold as the Dodgers won the next four.

The Yankees fell below .500 the next year, and although they revived to win 91 games in 1983, they failed to frighten the division leaders until 1985. First baseman Don Mattingly drove in more runs than any American leaguer since 1953 and newcomer (from Oakland) Rickey Henderson scored more often than any major leaguer since 1949—the team remained in the running until Toronto eliminated them with just one game to go.

But Steinbrenner's constant roster manipulation and managerial rotation (Billy Martin alone was hired and fired five times) at last set in motion a steady drop in Yankee effectiveness. While the team remained in the thick of a tight 1988 divisional race until three season-ending losses set them back into fifth place, their won-lost record showed a third straight season of decline. In 1989 the Yankees sank to their worst finish in twenty-two years and in 1990 they dropped to the floor of the AL East with the club's worst record since 1913.

Before the 1990 season ended, though, Steinbrenner was gone. As penalty for his dealings with gambler Howard Spira in an attempt to gain information damaging to longtime Yankee outfielder Dave Winfield, Steinbrenner relinquished his controlling interest in the club in August. When fans at Yankee Stadium heard the news, they stood and applauded for ninety seconds.

Oakland Athletics

The history of the Athletics is a tale of three cities—a story of the best of teams and of the worst of teams. With a thirteen-year sojourn in Kansas City between residence in Philadelphia and Oakland, the A's are the only club to include a stop in Middle America in their trek from the East Coast to West. They have won fifteen American League pennants (plus three Western Division championships that didn't lead to a pennant), second in the AL only to the incomparable Yankees. But they have also finished last in the league or division twenty-six times, and in sixteen seasons have lost 100 games or more—both AL worsts, by far. A club of extremes, they have been either at the top or at the bottom in nearly one season out of two.

When Ban Johnson in 1901 established four eastern clubs for his American League, he chose Connie Mack to manage the new Philadelphia Athletics and gave him a quarter ownership of the club. Mack, who had been managing the league's Milwaukee franchise, settled in at Philadelphia and set a record for managerial longevity—fifty years—that is unlikely ever to be surpassed.

In his first fourteen years the A's dominated the league, with six pennants and two close second-place finishes. After finishing fourth in 1901, the club won its first pennant the next year, pulling away from the field with spurts in August and September. Rube Waddell led the team with 24 wins, and six regulars hit over .300. The next two years saw the A's fade in August, but in 1905, after forging ahead in early August and hanging on to the lead with two crucial wins over Chicago's surging White Sox in late September, the A's opened October with a five-game winning streak to clinch their second flag. Waddell, with 26 wins, once again led the club (followed closely by Eddie Plank's 25) and compiled a league-leading 1.48 ERA. In the Athletics' first World Series appearance, though, New York's Christy Mathewson provided most of the pitching heroics, shutting out the A's three times in the Giants' 4–1 Series triumph.

Another August decline in 1906 was followed in 1907 by a comeback struggle from fifth place in late May to a 2½-game lead in mid-September. But the loss of a crucial game to Detroit several days later, and the failure to make up a rainout and a tie, left the A's 1½ games behind the Tigers at the finish.

In 1908 the A's suffered their first losing season, but they rebounded in 1909 to chase the Tigers throughout the summer before tailing off to second. In 1910, with a pitching staff that compiled a stunning 1.79 ERA (paced by Jack Coombs, whose 31 wins included 13 shutouts) and with league-leading fielding and hitting, the A's pulled ahead for good in June, increasing their lead through the rest of the season to finish 14½ games in front. In the World Series they continued to dominate, outscoring the Chicago Cubs 35–15 as they took their first world title, in five games. The A's repeated just as convincingly in 1911. With their "$100,000 infield" of Stuffy McInnis, Eddie Collins, Jack Barry, and Frank "Home Run" Baker averaging .323 at the bat, and Jack Coombs winning 28 games to again lead the club (and the league), the A's overtook Detroit in August to win by 13½ games. In the World Series, Baker hit two important home runs against the Giants, and the A's defeated Mathewson twice, avenging their 1905 humiliation with a victory in six games.

A third-place finish in 1912 broke the pennant streak, but the Athletics came back for two more in 1913 and '14, in both seasons pulling away in early June for easy wins. In the 1913 World Series the A's again felled the Giants, this time in just five games, but the next year they were in turn humiliated by the upstart Boston Braves, who stunned Philadelphia with the first sweep since the renewal of World Series play in 1903.

That winter, Mack began to dismantle his championship club, selling second baseman Collins to the White Sox and releasing pitchers Coombs, Eddie Plank, and Chief Bender. (Third baseman Baker, homesick for the country life, sat out the 1915 season before moving on to the Yankees). Though Mack received $50,000 for Collins, his unconditional release of the three pitchers suggests that he had another reason than financial need for purging his club. (Suspicion of corrupt play in the 1914 World Series has been hinted.)

Whatever Mack's reasons, the changes did not help the club. The A's sank immediately to last place, where they remained for seven years. In 1915 they lost 109 games and finished 58½ games out. The next year they lost 117 games to set a league record for ineptitude that has never been equalled.

It was a decade before Mack was able to restore the club to respectability. In 1924 he brought up Al Simmons, and the next year Jimmie Foxx and pitcher Lefty Grove. Thus renewed, the A's in 1925 battled Washington to the end of August before backing off to second. In 1927 they won 91 games, though their second-place finish was 19 games back of the overwhelming Yankees. In 1928 the A's battled from well back of New York in midseason to overtake them for a day or two in September, only to lose three of four games in a critical Yankee series and slip back to second.

From 1929 through 1931, though, the A's interrupted New York's domination of the AL with three spectacular seasons. In 1929 sophomore pitcher George Earnshaw blossomed into the league's big winner with 24 victories and Grove led the league's stingiest staff with a league-low 2.81 ERA. Six players drove in 79 runs or more (led by Simmons' league-high 157) in powering the A's to 104 wins and an impressive finish 18 games ahead of the second-place Yankees.

After swamping the Cubs in the World Series, the A's repeated as pennant winners in 1930. Simmons led the league in batting (.381), and Grove led its pitchers in just about everything: wins (28), ERA, strikeouts—even saves (9). Again the World Series was no contest as the A's downed the Cardinals in six.

Earnshaw won more than 20 games for his third successive season in 1931, Simmons repeated as batting leader (.390), and Grove enjoyed what would be the finest season of his career (31–4, 2.06 ERA) in carrying the A's to 107 wins—their best record ever. But in Game Seven of the World Series their dominance of the baseball world ended in a Cardinal victory.

Following a second-place finish in 1932, Mack began selling off his stars again. This time the reason was primarily economic. Home attendance—never robust—fell off sharply after 1931, as the Great Depression and the A's decline made their impact felt. By 1935 the Athletics were back in the cellar, where they finished in ten of Mack's final sixteen years as manager.

In 1946 Mack, who since 1940 had been the A's majority stockholder, divided his shares among his three sons, provoking a family squabble over control of the club. In 1950 the two eldest, Roy and Earle, bought out Connie Jr. and pressured their eighty-seven-year-old father to retire. But with Connie Sr. gone, attendance (which had risen to new highs in the baseball boom that followed World War Two) dropped off again. When in 1954 the A's finished 60 games behind champion Cleveland and attendance dropped to an eighteen-year low, the Macks sold the club to Chicagoan Arnold Johnson, who moved it to Kansas City.

Attendance jumped more than a million the first season in Kansas City (putting the A's over one million for the first time ever), and the team rose a couple of places to sixth. But 1955 was the high point of their thirteen-year stay in the Midwest; the K.C. A's never again rose above

seventh, and they finished last six times.

Owner Johnson died in March 1960, and that December his heirs sold the club to the enterprising but abrasive Charles O. Finley. Finley brought in a succession of new managers over the next few years, and in 1965 outfitted his players in new bright green-and-yellow uniforms. But with the league's expansion to ten teams in 1961, the A's had two places lower to sink—and did. After finishing tenth in 1967 for the third time in four years, Finley moved the club to Oakland, California.

Attendance was slow to improve in Oakland—unlike the team. In 1968, their first year on the coast, they put together their first winning season in sixteen years. The next year, with the start of divisional play, the A's took second in the AL West. Reggie Jackson, in only his second full big league season, enjoyed his finest year, with 47 home runs, 118 RBIs, and AL highs in slugging (.608) and runs scored (123).

After another second-place finish in 1970, the A's were ready for a return to glory. In the next five years they won five division titles, winning both the AL pennant and the World Series in the three middle years, 1972–1974. In 1971, with a new manager, Dick Williams, and three pitchers (Vida Blue, Catfish Hunter, and reliever Rollie Fingers) who reached their prime all at once, the A's enjoyed their best season in forty years and won the West by 16 games. Baltimore swept them away in the League Championship Series, but they came back to take the West again the next year. Detroit took them to the limit in the LCS, as did Cincinnati in the World Series, but in both series the A's prevailed in the deciding game by the margin of a single run.

The next year, 1973, Jackson led the league in slugging, homers, and RBIs, Ken Holtzman joined Blue and Hunter in the 20-win column, and home attendance crept over a million (by a few hundred souls) for the first time in Oakland as the A's ran their string of Western Division titles to three. Once again they were pushed to the limit in the postseason—by Baltimore in the LCS and the New York Mets in the World Series—and once again they emerged as world champions.

Manager Williams quit in a dispute with Finley and was replaced by Al Dark, but the outcome in 1974 (except for a drop in attendance to under a million) was the same. Hunter bore more of the pitching load and wound up tied for the AL lead with 25 wins. His 2.49 ERA also led the league, as the staff ended Baltimore's five-year hold on the ERA title. The A's toppled the Orioles in the LCS and (in the first World Series held entirely on the West Coast) won their third consecutive world title in five closely fought games with Los Angeles.

Free-agent Catfish Hunter deserted to the Yankees, and Baltimore regained the ERA crown in 1975, but pitchers Paul Lindblad and newcomer Dick Bosman combined for a 20–5 record to supplement the efforts of Blue, Holtzman, and Fingers and carry Oakland to an unprecedented fifth straight division title. But there the magic stopped, as Boston swept to the pennant in the LCS.

In the off-season Finley, with moves reminiscent of Connie Mack, tried to sell off his star players: Blue, Jackson, Fingers, Holtzman, and outfielder/first baseman Joe Rudi, one of the team's steadiest hitters. The proposed sales made some sense: the players planned to leave the club at the end of their 1976 option year, and Finley by disposing of them before they played out their option could at least be compensated for his loss. The Jackson and Holtzman deals were approved, but baseball commissioner Bowie Kuhn blocked the sale of the others, citing the "best interests of baseball."

The weakened A's came back from a poor start to close within 2½ games of the Kansas City Royals in 1976, but they dropped to last place the next year. After another last-place finish in 1979, Finley hired fiery Billy Martin to manage the club. Martin brought the A's in second in 1980, and first in the first half of strike-divided 1981. They won the Western Division championship by sweeping Kansas City in the special intradivisional playoffs, but were in turn swept by the Yankees in the LCS.

Finley's sale of the club in 1981 to the folks who bring us Levi's jeans signaled a turn toward normalcy and popularity. Despite a losing season in 1982, the club set a home attendance record as over 1.7 million fans came to watch Ricky Henderson's successful assault on the stolen-base record. In 1987 the A's finished right at .500—for the first time in their history a perfectly average team.

The next season they inaugurated a new multiyear reign as the league's best. Starter Dave Stewart and closer Dennis Eckersley anchored the league's strongest pitching staff and "bash brothers" Jose Canseco and Mark McGwire headlined an awesome offense. In 1988–90 the A's took title to the AL West with the majors' best won-lost record, then sailed past the East champion to the pennant. In 1988 they built a 13-game margin of victory over runner-up Minnesota, winning 104 games and drawing more than 2 million fans to their home games for the first time. They swept Boston in the ALCS, but faltered in the World Series, losing to underdog Los Angeles in five games.

Injuries to several key players—especially Canseco, who missed the first half of the season with a broken wrist—kept the A's from dominating AL play through most of 1989. But the preseason signing of free agent starter Mike Moore had strengthened the pitching, and a June trade that brought Rickey Henderson back after more than four years with the Yankees gave the A's the push they needed to prevail. At full strength by season's end, the A's overwhelmed Toronto in five games for their fourteenth pennant, then swept San Francisco for their world title.

Only Chicago's surprising White Sox challenged Oakland in 1990, and they too fell away in the latter half of the season as the A's walked to the division title with 103 wins. The potent offense was made even more formidable by the late-season acquisition of Harold Baines from Texas and Willie McGee from St. Louis. But the key to Oakland's dominance was its pitchers, who for the third year in a row compiled the league's lowest earned run average. Bob Welch led the majors with 27 wins, Dave Stewart put together his fourth straight 20-win season, and Dennis Eckersley rebounded from an injury-hampered 1989 with his finest relief year yet. The A's swept over Boston to their third straight pennant, but—shades of 1988!—floundered in the World Series, succumbing in just four games to Cincinnati's aroused Reds.

Philadelphia Phillies

It took the Phillies thirty-two years to win their first pennant, and ninety-seven to win their first world championship. They have finished last in their league or division twenty-eight times—more than one season in four. In the nine years from 1975 through 1983, though, they were one of the most formidable teams in baseball.

Alfred J. Reach, a sporting goods entrepreneur and former player, and Colonel John Rogers, a Philadelphia lawyer and politician, organized the Phillies in 1883 to bring Philadelphia back into the National League after a six-year absence. In their first season, the Phillies won only 17 of 98 decisions to finish an eighth-place last, as far out of seventh as the seventh-place team was from first. Bad as the Phillies have sometimes been since, their 1883 winning percentage of .173 remains their very worst.

Reach hired the respected Harry Wright to manage the Phillies in 1884, and while Wright failed to lead them to a pennant in his ten years at the helm, he did make them respectable. His fourth-place 1886 team, in fact, compiled a winning percentage of .623 that remained the club's best for ninety years. In 1887 the Phillies, with three pitchers winning more than 20 games, finished second, just 3½ games behind Detroit—their closest finish until their first pennant twenty-eight years later.

The Phillies remained in the upper division twelve of the next fourteen years. For five years—1891–1895—they fielded an outfield of Ed Delahanty, Billy Hamilton, and Sam Thompson—Hall of Famers who rank among the top hitters of all time. In the three heavy-hitting seasons that followed the lengthening of the pitching distance to its present 60'6" in 1893, Delahanty, Hamilton, and Thompson—with help from players like catcher Jack Clements (.394 in 1895) and utility outfielder Tuck Turner (.416 in 1894)—sparked the Phillies to three team batting titles with BAs of over .300. In 1894 the big three joined Turner in batting over .400 and the team hit .349—still the major league club record.

In 1899, with Delahanty's .410 leading the way, the Phillies once again topped .300 to lead the league. Though the team finished third, they won 94 games, a club high they would not surpass for seventy-seven years. President Reach sold his interest in the club after a dispute with co-owner Rogers, and Rogers lost star second baseman Larry Lajoie in a salary dispute to the Athletics (Philadelphia's new entry in the rival American League). But the Phillies chased front-runner Pittsburgh through much of 1901. Though they slumped in August, they recovered to finish second.

It was the end of an era. Delahanty deserted to the AL the next season, and the Phillies dropped to seventh. Rogers sold the club to a syndicate. By 1904 the team was in last place, losing 100 games for the first time.

They rose into the first division the next season, but didn't mount a serious pennant run until 1911, when the pitching of rookie Grover Cleveland Alexander kept them in the thick of the race into midseason. Two years later they enjoyed first place through most of June before fading to a distant second.

In 1915 Alexander brought his ERA down more than a run per game to a league- and career-best of 1.22, hurling 12 shutouts among his 31 wins. Right fielder Gavvy

Cravath and first baseman Fred Luderus finished one-two among NL sluggers, and Cravath won home run and RBI crowns. For half a season all eight clubs were in the thick of a tight race, with the Cubs and Phillies at the top of the heap. But in July the Cubs folded, and in August and September the Phillies took off to outdistance the late-surging Boston Braves by 7 games for their first pennant.

The World Series was a Phillies' heartbreak. Four of the five games were decided by a single run—but the runs belonged to the Boston Red Sox, who swept four after the Phillies had taken the opener.

Alexander shut out a record-tying 16 opponents the following year, winning a career-high 33, and teammate Eppa Rixey had his first big year with 22 wins. Through most of the season, the club trailed the leading Dodgers, but caught them in September, only to fall away again in the final week.

After Alexander's 30 wins had brought the Phillies another second-place finish in 1917, the club dealt him to Chicago and embarked on thirty-one years of wandering in the desert. After fourteen losing seasons (eight of them in last place), they climbed to fourth, two games above .500, in 1932, but dropped back the next year into the second division (including nine last-place finishes) for sixteen more years.

Several outstanding players spent time in Philadelphia during these years: Dave Bancroft (a rookie in their pennant season), Cy Williams, Freddy Leach, Chuck Klein, Lefty O'Doul, and Dick Bartell. Of these, only Williams and Klein retired as Phillies. The financially strapped management traded away the others at the height of their careers in deals that included cash as well as players. Even Klein—perhaps the greatest of them all—was sold twice before returning a third time to Philly to end his career.

The Phillies in 1930 produced a season that ranks among the most extraordinary of all time. With Klein and O'Doul leading the way at .386 and .383, every regular hit at least .280, to give the Phillies a team BA of .315. But Phillie pitchers yielded a record 1199 runs while compiling the worst big league ERA ever—6.71. The club lost 102 games and finished last.

The Phillies' move in 1938 out of tiny, antiquated Baker Bowl into the Athletics' Shibe Park did nothing for attendance—or for performance, as the team strung together a club-record five consecutive last-place finishes from 1938 to 1942, in which they averaged 107 losses per season and finished between 43 and 62½ games out of first.

In February 1943 the league took control of the debt-ridden club and sold it to a group headed by New York sportsman William D. Cox. Cox didn't last long; before the year was out he was barred from baseball for betting on the Phillies. His controlling interest was sold to Robert M. Carpenter, who installed his son, Robert Jr., as president. The younger Carpenter hired former pitcher Herb Pennock as general manager with instructions to build a farm system, and a new era began in the club's history.

Outfielder Del Ennis had come up to hit .313 in 1946, but Pennock died (in January 1948) before he could see the full fruits of his labor. First baseman Dick Sisler would be purchased in March; rookie outfielder Richie Ashburn would lead Phillie batters in 1948 with a .333

BA. Willie Jones wouldn't nail down third base for another year, and rookie pitchers Robin Roberts and Curt Simmons wouldn't overawe the opposition for a couple of seasons yet. But the team that would be dubbed the "Whiz Kids" was gathering. Triple-A manager Eddie Sawyer was brought up in late July.

In 1949, the loss of first baseman Eddie Waitkus (shot in the chest by a crazed young woman) and midseason complacency threatened to strand the Phillies in the second division. But Sawyer fired up his players in a special team meeting, and the Phillies rallied to finish third with the club's best record in thirty-two years.

With new red-pinstripe uniforms and a recovered Eddie Waitkus, the 1950 Phillies pulled away from a tightly bunched first division in July and August, but late in September fell to within two games of onrushing Brooklyn. The Dodgers took the first game of a season-ending two-game series to narrow the gap to one. But in the finale the Phillies' Sisler homered to break a tenth-inning tie. When Brooklyn failed to score in the bottom of the tenth, the Whiz Kids had their pennant.

Curt Simmons, who was called up for military service in September after winning 17 games, missed the World Series. As in 1915, the result for Philadelphia was frustration and heartbreak, as the Phillies were swept by the Yankees—in the first three games by a single run.

Roberts's pitching kept the Phillies in the first division for four of the next five years, but the team made no serious run at another pennant. And when Roberts began to lose his effectiveness the team sank farther, to fifth for two years, then to four years in the cellar, culminating in 1961 with the longest big league losing streak of the century: 23 games.

The club stuck with new manager Gene Mauch, and the 1962 Phillies edged above .500 for the first time in nine years (though finishing seventh in a league newly expanded to ten teams). In 1963 they moved up to fourth with a strong second half. In 1964, with the acquisition of pitcher Jim Bunning from Detroit and infielder Richie (later Dick) Allen's productive rookie season, Mauch's Phillies moved way out in front in August. But they blew their lead with ten straight losses in late September while Cincinnati was winning nine and St. Louis eight in a row. Only victories in their final two games salvaged a second-place tie.

The Phillies produced winning seasons the next three years but never challenged the leaders. With Mauch replaced as manager during the 1968 campaign, the team embarked on seven straight losing seasons, including three years at the bottom of the NL East.

Pitcher Steve Carlton, acquired from St. Louis in an off-season trade, accounted for nearly half the Phillies' 59 wins in 1972. His 27 victories for the league's worst team gave the club a ray of hope for the future and earned Carlton the Cy Young Award. Carlton lost a league-high 20 games the next year, but as he regained his form over the next three seasons, so too the Phillies gradually rose to the top of the division.

In 1974 sophomore third baseman Mike Schmidt burst to the forefront of the league's power hitters. The Phillies dropped out of contention in August, but wound up third, their best finish since the league split into divisions in 1969. The next year outfielder Greg Luzinski joined

Schmidt among the league's top sluggers, and the club rose to second, with their first winning season since 1967.

The Phillies had entered their golden age—nine straight winning seasons (a club record), including five division titles, two pennants, and their first world championship. In 1976 they enjoyed their finest regular season ever. With Schmidt and Luzinski providing the power, Carlton returning to the ranks of 20-game winners and Jim Lonborg climaxing a long comeback with 18 wins, the Phillies took the division lead in May and pulled away, recovering from a late-season dive to finish well ahead of Pittsburgh. Their 101 wins, .6235 winning percentage, and nine-game margin of victory remain club records.

The Phillies were swept by Cincinnati in the League Championship Series, but came back the next season to duplicate their record 101 wins for another comfortable first-place finish. Carlton won 23 (and his second Cy Young Award), and Luzinski enjoyed the best season of his career, driving in 130 runs. After defeating Los Angeles in the LCS opener, though, the Phillies lost the pennant with three straight losses.

In 1978, even though Schmidt and Carlton had off-years, the Phillies led much of the season and captured the division title a third straight time. But it was a tight race, and they barely survived a late-season Pittsburgh surge to finish 1½ games in front. For the third time, their triumph in the East was followed by defeat in the LCS—for the second time at the hands of Los Angeles in four games.

Danny Ozark, in his seventh year as Phillies manager, was replaced by Dallas Green late in a disappointing 1979 season that saw the club stumble after a strong start before rallying in September to finish fourth. But Schmidt was back in top form, and Pete Rose had arrived via free agency to add his bat and hustle.

In a three-way race in 1980 that remained close through August, the Phillies hung tight without being able to move into the lead. But as Pittsburgh folded in late August and early September, the Phillies edged in front briefly, then battled back and forth with Montreal. Tied with the Expos as the clubs met in Montreal for the season's final three games, Philadelphia took the first 2–1, then—in eleven innings—the second, to clinch their fourth division title in five years. Schmidt, with perhaps his finest season, drove in 121 runs and was named NL MVP; Carlton, with 24 wins, won his third Cy Young Award; and veteran reliever Tug McGraw enjoyed his best season in years.

In an LCS in which four of the five games went into extra innings, the Phillies prevailed over Houston, capturing their first pennant since the Whiz Kids era thirty years earlier. And in the World Series, fortune finally smiled on the team as they overcame Kansas City in six games.

The Phillies won the first half of the strike-divided 1981 season. In the special intradivisional playoff against Montreal, Philadelphia fought back to tie the series after losing the first two games—only to lose the finale.

The Carpenter family—citing the prohibitive cost of running a major league club—sold the team. Manager Dallas Green also left and was replaced by Pat Corrales, who kept the club in the thick of the 1982 race until the final month, when the Phillies slipped 3½ games back, to second. And Steve Carlton did it again: his 23 wins earned him a record fourth Cy Young trophy.

Mike Schmidt again dominated the Phillies' offense in 1983, but Carlton yielded to John Denny as the team's pitching ace. Newly acquired reliever Al Holland emerged as one of the league's best. After general manager Paul Owens took over for Corrales as manager in midseason, the Phillies came alive and took the division title by 6 games. Carlton dominated the LCS with an 0.66 ERA and two wins as the Phillies won their fourth pennant. But their golden age ended in the World Series, when Baltimore triumphed in five games.

The Phillies dropped to .500 and fourth place in 1984, and suffered a losing fifth-place season in 1985. They rebounded to second in 1986 (but 21½ games behind New York), then dropped back below .500 in 1987. Mike Schmidt continued to power the offense—the only member of the 1980 world champions still a Phillie. Despite an impressive lineup of everyday players in 1988, the Phils collapsed, finishing in the division cellar for the first time in fifteen years.

Unable to recover from a shoulder injury, Mike Schmidt retired in May 1989, and despite several midseason trades the Phillies again finished last in the NL East. In 1990, though, the flaming start of one of the players acquired in mid-1989—outfielder Len Dykstra, who was batting above .400 as late as June—lit the Phillies' competitive fires. But as Dykstra cooled off to mere excellence, the Phillies fell out of contention and finished 18 games back, tied for fourth.

Pittsburgh Pirates

Pittsburgh became a big league city in 1882, when its Allegheny baseball club joined with five other teams to form the American Association. Allegheny president H. D. McKnight was named president of the new league, but Allegheny made little stir until the club hired Horace Phillips to manage it and replaced its team in 1885 with players from the defunct Columbus Club, which had finished second in the AA the year before. The new Alleghenys finished a distant third in 1885, but after purchasing Pud Galvin from Buffalo they improved in 1886 to a respectable second behind the invincible St. Louis Browns.

Flushed with success, Allegheny in 1887 became the first club to desert the AA for the older and more highly regarded National League. There they found the competition stiffer and sank back into the second division. In 1890, when most of the team jumped to the rival Pittsburgh Players' League club, Allegheny (known that year as the Innocents) suffered the worst season in Pittsburgh major league history, finishing last, 66½ games out of first place (and 23 out of seventh), with a won-lost record of 23–113.

When the PL folded after just one season, Allegheny merged with its PL counterpart to form the Pittsburgh Athletic Company, thereby retrieving many of its old regulars. The club also hired a second baseman—Lou Bierbaur—whose signing (or theft, as his old club saw it) gave the Innocents a new and more enduring nickname: the Pirates. The renewed club still finished last in 1891, but thirty-six games closer to the top than the year before, and only fractionally out of seventh place.

In 1893 a rules change moved the pitcher 10½ feet farther back from home plate. Of all the NL clubs, the Pirates benefited most from the change: their batting average jumped 63 points—28 more than that of the league as a whole—while their pitchers suffered less than most. The club finished second, with a .628 winning percentage that was their best of the century. Lefty Frank Killen, a twenty-two-year-old pitcher acquired from Washington, led the club's resurgence with a league-leading 34 wins.

Although catcher Connie Mack was called upon to manage the club toward the end of the 1894 season and led them to winning seasons the next two years, the Pirates did not make another serious run for the pennant until 1900. With a team transformed yet again by players from a defunct club—this time the Louisville Colonels—the Pirates battled Brooklyn's Superbas almost to the end of the season before dropping 4½ games back, a solid second. Although they lost the postseason Chronicle-Telegraph Cup games (that year's World Series) to the Superbas, the Pirates were embarked on an era of greatness.

In the merger that brought the Louisville players to Pittsburgh, the Colonels' owner Barney Dreyfuss acquired half ownership of the Pirates. A year later he bought the other half. His perennial hope for the club was a first-division finish; in twenty-six of his thirty-two years of Pirate ownership his hope was rewarded.

Four of the former Louisville players—outfielder-turned-shortstop Honus Wagner, outfielder/manager Fred Clarke, third baseman/outfielder Tommy Leach, and pitcher Deacon Phillippe—and one carryover from the old Pirates, pitcher Sam Leever, remained with Pittsburgh long enough to help lead them to four pennants and, in 1909, their first world championship. In the sixteen years Clarke managed the Pirates (a club record), they also finished second five times, and slipped out of the first division only in Clarke's final two seasons at the helm.

In contrast to the club's devastation by the Players' League raid of 1890, the Pirates were unaffected in 1901 by raiders from the American League (which that year turned itself into a major league largely by drawing off talent from National League clubs). Only third baseman Jimmy Williams defected to the Americans, and he was ably replaced by Tommy Leach, as the Pirates, with the league's best pitching (Jesse Tannehill and Deacon Phillippe finished one-two in ERA, and Jack Chesbro at 21–10 led in winning percentage), captured their first pennant by a comfortable 7½ games over the Philadelphia Phillies.

The Pirates repeated as pennant winners in 1902 and 1903. The 1902 team was one of the most overwhelming of all time. One Pirate or another led the league in nearly every offensive category: Ginger Beaumont in hits and batting; Tommy Leach in home runs (with 6); and Honus Wagner in slugging, RBIs, runs scored, doubles, and stolen bases. Pitcher Jack Chesbro's 28 wins led the league, and the top five NL pitchers in winning percentage were all Pirates. The club held the lead the whole season, finishing 27½ games ahead of second-place Brooklyn, still a major league record.

Pitchers Chesbro and Tannehill deserted to the AL's New York Highlanders the next season, but their loss merely made Pittsburgh's pennant-winning margin (6½ games) smaller than it might have been. Wagner beat out teammate Fred Clarke for the NL batting crown and finished second to Clarke in slugging. Beaumont took the titles in hits, runs, and total bases. Pitcher Sam Leever, with his finest season, led the club with 25 wins and the league in ERA and winning percentage. Owner Dreyfuss arranged with the AL champion Boston Pilgrims for a best-of-nine World Series—the first between NL and AL champions—but the Pirates lost it in eight games as their tired pitchers at last succumbed to overwork.

Although the Pirates twice finished second over the next four years, they didn't come close to capturing another pennant until 1908, when, in one of the tightest NL races ever, they were edged out by the Chicago Cubs and finished one game back, tied with New York's Giants for second. The following year, though, they moved in June into the new concrete-and-steel Forbes Field and celebrated by returning to the top of the league with a club record 110 wins—holding off the dogged Cubs throughout the season to take the flag by 6½ games. And this time they won the World Series, too, although they needed the full seven games to subdue Detroit's Tigers. Honus Wagner remained the league's dominant offensive force, but aging pitchers Leever and Phillippe were overshadowed by a new crop of standouts: Vic Willis, Howie Camnitz, Nick Maddox, and Lefty Leifield—and the astonishing rookie Babe Adams, who after going 12–3 (with a 1.11 ERA) during the season, won three more games in the World Series.

The Series triumph ended an era. Wagner was past his prime and wound down his long career over the next several seasons as the Pirates dropped out of contention for a dozen years, including four (1914–1917) in the hated second division. Only Babe Adams remained of the world championship team when Pittsburgh next made a contest of the pennant race in 1921, taking an early lead and holding it most of the summer until an August-September decline dropped them to second place, 4 games back.

Former Pirate infielder Bill McKechnie replaced George Gibson as manager during the following season with the club in fifth place, and saw the Pirates spurt to second before fading to third at the finish. Two more third-place seasons—with the Pirates finishing just 3 games out of first in 1924—paved the way for another pennant in 1925.

The 1925 Pirates fielded several stars: shortstop Glenn Wright, who led the club with 121 RBIs; sophomore right fielder Kiki Cuyler, who led the team in hitting (.357) and the league in runs scored; third baseman Pie Traynor, who shone on the field and at the bat; and Max Carey, who beat out Cuyler for the league stolen base title and enjoyed his finest season (.343) at the plate. The team as a whole hit .307 to lead the league and ran away with the pennant, spurting to catch the front-running Giants in midseason and pushing ahead to an 8½-game lead by season's end. The World Series was tougher, but the Pirates prevailed over the Washington Senators, defeating veteran Walter Johnson in a seventh-game slugfest 9–7. Babe Adams, hero of the 1909 Series and now, at forty-three, nearing the end of his long career, pitched one shutout inning in Game Four.

Rookie outfielder Paul Waner arrived the next season and hit .336, but the team, which had led the race going into August, fell into decline late in the month and finished third, 4½ games out. Max Carey sparked an unsuccessful player uprising against the management and was sold to Brooklyn just before the Pirate collapse in August, and manager McKechnie was replaced after the season by former Washington manager Donie Bush.

In 1927, his first season at the helm, Bush sailed the Pirate ship to its sixth pennant, even though Kiki Cuyler was benched for half the season for refusing to bat second in the order. But Paul Waner's younger brother Lloyd arrived to join Paul in the outfield, and the pair tore up the league, finishing one-two in hits (237 and 223) as Paul also took crowns in batting (.380; Lloyd was third at .355), RBIs and total bases, while Lloyd led in runs scored. In and out of first place throughout the season, the Pirates moved into the lead a final time at the start of September and held on to edge the St. Louis Cardinals by 1½ games. In the World Series, though (played with Cuyler on the bench), the Pirates were swept by a Yankee team widely acclaimed as the greatest of all time.

Barney Dreyfuss died in February 1932. Ownership of the Pirates passed to his widow, who named their son-in-law Bill Benswanger president. The team finished a competitive second in 1932 and 1933, but then fell back until 1938, when—with Pie Traynor now manager—they moved out in front in midseason and held their lead comfortably until late September, when ten straight Chicago victories (including three against Pittsburgh) dropped the Pirates to second place, where they finished, 2 games back.

The Pirates showcased some great players in their lean years, like shortstop Arky Vaughan in the 1930s and early '40s, and slugger Ralph Kiner, who won or shared the league home run title all seven of his seasons with Pittsburgh in the 1940s and '50s. But after 1938 the club finished no closer than eight games from the top for twenty-one years. They finished as high as second only twice (in 1944 and 1958), and in the eight years 1950–1957 wound up each season either last or next-to-last, reaching their nadir in 1952 with 112 losses and a last-place finish 54½ games out of first.

The Pirates had been purchased in 1946 by a four-man syndicate that included singer Bing Crosby and real estate tycoon John W. Galbreath. Galbreath later bought a majority interest in the club and, as president, hired Branch Rickey to rebuild the Pirates into contenders. Barney Dreyfuss had resisted the development of minor league farm systems (a Rickey innovation at St. Louis and Brooklyn), preferring to scour unaffiliated minor league teams himself for young talent. Rickey's ministrations helped build a foundation for the Pirate resurgence of 1958–1960.

No one threatened the 1958 Milwaukee Braves' preeminence in the NL after July, but Pittsburgh came closer than anyone, finishing second, eight games back. Six of the eight regulars who would lead the Pirates to their next championship in 1960 were already in the lineup, including Dick Groat, Bill Mazeroski, and Roberto Clemente; and the leading pitchers of 1958—Bob Friend, Vern Law, and reliever Roy Face—topped the 1960 staff, too.

In 1959 the Pirates fell back to fourth place, barely above .500, but the next year they began strong and, shaking off their last challenger in late July, built up a 7-game margin of victory by season's end. League batting champion Groat paced a balanced offense that led the league in hitting, and pitcher Law, with 20 wins, enjoyed the finest season of his career. Facing the Yankees in the World Series, the Pirates were overwhelmed in the three games they lost, but they won the world title with four close wins, capped by Mazeroski's famous home run in the bottom of the ninth inning of the final game.

Pittsburgh again led the league in batting in 1961, with Clemente (whose .351 batting average led the league) and first baseman Dick Stuart (35 home runs, 117 RBIs) enjoying especially fine seasons. But the Pirate pitching fell apart (Vern Law lost most of the season to arm trouble), and the club dropped to sixth place.

When the Pirates next made a serious run for the pennant, in 1966, Harry Walker managed the team and center fielder Matty Alou (newly acquired from San Francisco) won the batting crown. (His brother Felipe of Atlanta was runner-up—the only one-two brother finish ever.) In a season-long three-way race, the Pirates took a lead in August but lost it early in September and finished third, 3 games out. They dropped to sixth again the next season and remained out of the pennant race for three years.

In 1970 the majors experienced their second season of divisional play, John Galbreath's son Daniel was named Pirates' president, and Danny Murtaugh returned a third time to pilot the Pirates. (His second stint was for half a season in 1967.) The team began slowly and entered June with a record under .500. But they were already on their way up, and by mid-July, when they moved out of aging Forbes Field into the brand-new Three Rivers Stadium, they were at the top of the NL East. They slipped into a three-way tangle in mid-September, but shot ahead later in the month to take the division title by 5 games. Most of the team was new since 1960—the power was now supplied by first baseman Bob Robertson and outfielder Willie Stargell. But Roberto Clemente was still in top form, and Bill Mazeroski was still at second base, though nearing the end of his career.

In the 1970 League Championship Series, the Pirates were swept by Cincinnati. But they came back the next season to overwhelm the East in a race that was no race after June, then defeated San Francisco for their eighth pennant, three games to one. Their slugging—paced by Stargell's league-leading 48 home runs—led the league, and reliever Dave Giusti saved a league-leading 30 games in support of a balanced pitching staff. Clemente hit .414 in the World Series (with half his hits going for extra bases) as the Pirates overcame a 0–2 deficit to edge Baltimore in seven games for their fourth world title.

In 1972, after a slow start, Pittsburgh (now managed by their former center fielder Bill Virdon) rocketed to their third straight division championship—by 11 games over Chicago. The club lost, narrowly, to Cincinnati in the LCS, then suffered an even greater loss when Clemente was killed that winter in a plane crash. They played poorly the next season, yet even with a losing record finished third, only 2½ games behind the champion New York Mets in a five-way divisional race. Danny Murtaugh returned as manager a fourth (and final) time late in the season and piloted the club to two more NL East titles the next two years.

The 1974 championship drive featured a comeback from last place in early July to first by late August, followed by a nip-and-tuck race in September with St. Louis that was settled by a tenth-inning Pirate victory over Chicago in the season's final game. Stargell's bat was joined by those of Al Oliver and Richie Zisk as the Pirates outhit the rest of the league. In the LCS, though, the Los Angeles Dodgers overcame Pittsburgh handily, three games to one.

The Pirates won the 1975 race more easily, holding the lead from early June as right fielder Dave Parker, in his first full big league season, led the club in home runs and RBIs, and the league in slugging. But once again, for the fourth time in five tries, Pittsburgh lost the pennant in the LCS—swept this time by the awesome Cincinnati Reds, winners of 108 regular season games.

A distant second-place finish in 1976 was followed that December by manager Murtaugh's untimely death. His successor, Chuck Tanner, kept the Pirates competitive in his first two seasons, steering them to within 5 games of the champion Phillies in 1977, then—with an amazing August-September spurt from way below .500—to within 1½ games of the Phillies in 1978.

In 1979 the Pirates again started slowly but began to move up in May and pushed to the front, ahead of Montreal, in late July. By mid-September, though, the Expos had caught up, and it was not until the final day that an Expo loss and Pirate win gave Pittsburgh its sixth NL East title. Parker and the aging Stargell (now called "Pops") were still the club's big bats, but submariner Kent Tekulve had emerged as the bullpen ace, and one of six Pirate pitchers to win 10 games or more.

In the LCS the Pirates repaid Cincinnati for their 1975 humiliation, sweeping to the pennant in three games. In the World Series they seemed to have met their match in Baltimore, falling behind three games to one. But Pops rallied his "family" to victory in the final three must-win contests, and Pittsburgh for a fifth time reigned at the top of the baseball world.

For seven years the Pirates drifted downhill. The club's family spirit disintegrated, fans deserted the team, and it seemed for a time that the Pirates would leave Pittsburgh. But in 1985 a group of local corporations and individuals purchased the club from the Galbreaths, determined (with the assistance of a loan from the city of Pittsburgh) to keep the Pirates in town. Syd Thrift, a trader of consummate skill, was named general manager, and Chicago White Sox coach Jim Leyland was hired to his first job as a big league pilot. Under the new regime the club improved gradually, until in 1988 it once again proved itself a serious contender for the NL championship of the East. Thrift had built a team second only to New York's mighty Mets, one that drew more than 1.8 million fans at home— a club record. But Thrift's unwillingness to share with his superiors the top-level decision making bulked larger, in the eyes of the Pirate directors, than his achievement and he was fired at the season's end.

Plagued all season by injuries, Pittsburgh plunged to fifth in 1989. But in 1990, as Doug Drabek put together a career season on the mound and the bats of Barry Bonds and Bobby Bonilla burst into full bloom, the Pirates arrived at the All-Star break in first place by half a game over New York. With Drabek and Zane Smith (newly acquired from Montreal) all but unbeatable down the stretch, the Pirates, after exchanging the lead with New York several times, swept a Met series in early September to extend a narrow lead and clinched the NL East title at the end of the month with eight straight wins. In the LCS, though, after coming from behind to take the opener, they fell to Cincinnati in six games.

St. Louis Cardinals

The club that is now the Cardinals first fielded a team in 1881, and the next season became a charter member of the American Association, a new major league formed in part to offer fans the beer and Sunday baseball forbidden by the older National League. Chris Von der Ahe, one of the club's founders and its first president, at first saw in baseball simply a source of customers for his St. Louis saloon and beer garden, but he developed a love for the game itself as his Brown Stockings—or Browns—developed into one of the era's greatest teams.

After a losing season in 1882, Von der Ahe hired Ted Sullivan, a noted judge of baseball talent, to manage the Browns. Sullivan brought in third baseman Arlie Latham and pitcher Tony Mullane to strengthen a team that already boasted a fine pitcher in Jumbo McGinnis (25–18 in 1882) and one of the game's premier first baseman in Charlie Comiskey. Although Sullivan quit before the end of his first season because of the continued interference of the volatile Von der Ahe, the Browns finished second in the AA, just a game behind champion Philadelphia.

When Mullane bolted the Browns in 1884, the club slipped to fourth. But help was on the way. In July Von der Ahe purchased the Bay City, Michigan, club to acquire its heavy-hitting pitcher Dave Foutz, and in September added another hitting pitcher, "Parisian Bob" Caruthers, to the roster. In 1885—with Comiskey now the manager, left fielder Tip O'Neill blossoming into one of baseball's best hitters, and Caruthers and Foutz winning 40 and 33 games—the Browns rose to the top, 16 games ahead of second-place Cincinnati. They finished on top four years in a row, tying Chicago's White Stockings (3–3–1) in the 1885 World Series and defeating them four games to two the next year for the AA's only Series triumph over their NL rivals.

Pitcher Silver King joined the club in 1887, and outfielder Tommy McCarthy arrived the following year. They helped keep the Browns at the top of the AA through 1888 (although the team lost the World Series both years). But Von der Ahe's sale of Foutz and Caruthers to Brooklyn following the 1887 season boosted Brooklyn to second place in 1888. The next year Brooklyn edged the Browns for the pennant, and the club's first era of greatness was over.

When the AA folded after the 1891 season, the Browns were taken into the NL, but fared poorly there, finishing ninth and eleventh of the twelve clubs in the divided season of 1892. They rose no higher than ninth in the remaining years of Von der Ahe's ownership, dropping into the cellar (63½ games out) in 1897 and returning to the bottom with a club-worst 111 losses the next season.

New owners Frank and Stanley Robison (who also controlled the Cleveland club) transferred the best Cleveland players and their manager to St. Louis in 1899. Dubbed the Perfectos, the revitalized St. Louis club fell short of perfection, but did rise to a first-division fifth place that year and (now known as the Cardinals) rose to fourth in 1901 before sinking back into the second division for a dozen years.

After Stanley Robison died in 1911 (his brother Frank had died in 1905), the club passed into the possession of Frank's daughter Helene Britton, who ran it behind the scenes until, in 1916, she sold it to a syndicate headed by her attorney James C. Jones. Jones hired Branch Rickey away from the AL Browns to run the club.

Rickey took over a team with two chief assets: manager Miller Huggins and a promising young infielder, Rogers Hornsby. Huggins had managed the Cards to third place in 1914, before Hornsby arrived, and after a pair of losing seasons brought them up to third again in 1917. Huggins was lost to the New York Yankees the next year, and Rickey left the club temporarily for military service in the Great War. When Rickey returned in 1919, he took over as manager himself, and in 1921 and 1922 saw the team finish third, closer to the leaders than the club had finished since joining the NL in 1891. Led by Hornsby's .397 and .401 batting, the team hit over .300 both seasons.

Sam Breadon, one of the Jones group of owners, increased his investment in the Cardinals until by 1920 he was majority stockholder and club president, with Rickey as vice president and general manager. Breadon moved the Cards out of the inadequate wooden Cardinal Park during the 1920 season into the more modern Sportsman's Park, owned by the Browns (and built on the site of Von der Ahe's original grounds).

Early in the 1925 season, with the Cards in last place, Breadon replaced Rickey as field manager with second baseman Hornsby. The switch worked. In 1925 the Cards rebounded to fourth, and in 1926 they captured their first pennant since the glory days of the old Browns four decades earlier—edging Cincinnati in the final week of the season after an August spurt had shot them into pennant contention. The season was made perfect by victory in the World Series over Miller Huggins's Yankees.

But Breadon and his irascible player-manager had a falling out, and Hornsby found himself traded that winter to the New York Giants for second baseman Frank Frisch and pitcher Jimmy Ring. The trade enraged Cardinal fans, but the team finished a close second in 1927, and returned to the top (under new manager Bill McKechnie) in a tight race the following season.

McKechnie, fired after the Yankees swept the Cards in the 1928 World Series and rehired in the midst of a Cardinal slump the next season, left to manage the Boston Braves in 1930. Former catcher Gabby Street, who replaced him, led the Cards back to the top again for successive pennants in 1930 and 1931, and in 1931 to a World Series victory over the Philadelphia Athletics. The 1930 race saw the club shoot from below .500 in mid-June to 30 games above .500 by season's end, overtaking three other teams to clinch the flag just three games from the finish. The 1931 team ran away with the pennant, leading all the way and finishing 13 games in front. Outfielder

Chick Hafey and first baseman Jim Bottomley finished first and third in NL batting, and pitcher Bill Hallahan led the league in strikeouts (for the second year in a row) and tied for the lead in wins, with 19. Four of the league's top five base stealers—led by Frank Frisch and including outfielder Pepper Martin in his first full season—were Cardinals.

When the Cards dropped to sixth place in 1932 and showed little improvement the following year, Breadon replaced manager Street with Frisch. As when he had named Hornsby to manage, Breadon's move paid immediate dividends. Though the club finished fifth that season, their record improved after Frisch took over, and the next year, in a season-long uphill struggle, the Cards won thirteen of their final fifteen games to pass the front-running New York Giants in the final week.

Writers labeled the 1934 Cardinals the "Gashouse Gang" for their rowdy and daring play. In addition to team veterans Frisch and Martin (who had been shifted from the outfield to third base), the gang included shortstop Leo Durocher, left fielder Joe "Ducky" Medwick, and the team's leading hitter and slugger, first baseman Rip Collins, who in a career-best season led the league in slugging average and tied for first in home runs.

Cardinal pitching was headed by the league-leading Jerome "Dizzy" Dean (30–7) and his rookie brother Paul (19–11). Of the team's final nine wins, Diz and Paul accounted for seven. Each won another pair in the Cards' World Series triumph over Detroit.

The next two seasons the Cardinals moved into the lead late in the season only to wind up second. After the team slipped into the second division in 1938, Breadon replaced Frisch as manager with Ray Blades, who led a late-season run for the flag in 1939 but finished second. When the Cards failed to contend in 1940, Breadon brought up Rochester manager Billy Southworth for a second time. Southworth had failed as McKechnie's replacement in 1929, but this time he stuck, becoming one of the club's greatest helmsmen.

Through all these years Branch Rickey was revolutionizing baseball as he built the game's first and most extensive "farm system" of minor league clubs. The Cardinals' farm teams would—until the other major league clubs caught on and caught up—provide St. Louis with a competitive advantage in the recruitment and development of young players.

In the closing days of the 1941 season, perhaps the Cardinal system's greatest product arrived at the big club: Stan Musial. Southworth brought the club in a close second that year after a season-long back-and-forth struggle with Brooklyn. The next year—Musial's first full season—the Cardinals enjoyed their winningest season ever: 106 victories. They needed them all, too, for Brooklyn won 104 games, leading the race until mid-September, when the Cardinals passed them and held on to a narrow lead by winning twelve of their final thirteen games. St. Louis pitchers Mort Cooper and Johnny Beazley finished one-two in National League wins and ERA, while Enos Slaughter and Musial paced the Cardinal offense. The club maintained its momentum in the World Series, taking the Yankees in five games.

St. Louis retained its preeminence for two more years as baseball gradually lost players to military service in

World War Two. Slaughter and Beazley were gone by 1943. But Cooper remained to compile two more 20-plus winning seasons, and Musial was not called until after the 1944 season. With 105 wins in both 1943 and 1944, the Cards ran away with two more pennants, losing to the Yankees in the 1943 World Series, but taking their sixth world title the next year from their St. Louis landlords, the AL champion Browns.

Owner Breadon had fired Branch Rickey in 1942 (objecting to the personal profit Rickey made from selling the club's unneeded farm players), and Southworth left to manage the Boston Braves after the 1945 season (in which the Cards failed to catch the leading Chicago Cubs, finishing second). Rickey went to head the Brooklyn Dodgers, building for them a farm system and tapping the large reservoir of black players. In 1946, the last year of all-white major league ball, the Cards (managed now by Eddie Dyer) and the Dodgers waged a two-team pennant race, ending the season in the first major league tie for first place. St. Louis won the first two games in a best-of-three playoff and went on to surprise the favored Boston Red Sox in the World Series. With the war over, the team was back at full strength. Slaughter led the league in RBIs, and Musial led it in most other offensive categories; pitcher Howie Pollett led the league in ERA (as he had in 1943 before leaving for the war) and in wins, with 21.

But St. Louis was slow to integrate its club and lost ground to teams like Brooklyn, whose black players brought an immediate upswing in the club's success. The Cards began poorly in 1947, but recovered to finish second to Brooklyn, though never offering a serious challenge for the flag. After the season Breadon sold the club to Fred Saigh and Robert Hannegan (the U.S. Postmaster General). Musial enjoyed his finest season in 1948, but the club finished second again in a lackluster race. The next year, though, the Cards and Dodgers tangled in a season-long struggle for first place that was not resolved until the season's last day—with Brooklyn on top.

The Cardinals threatened to move to Milwaukee, but beer magnate August Busch, Jr., purchased the club early in 1953 and the same year bought Sportsman's Park from the Browns (who were moving to Baltimore). With Busch's infusion of money and enthusiasm, the club slowly revived. They made runs for the pennant in 1957, 1960, and 1963, but each time tailed off sharply in the final week of the season.

The Cards were playing below .500, in seventh place, in mid-June 1964 when the arrival (via a trade with the Cubs) of speedy young Lou Brock sparked a revival of both the team and player. Brock, who had been hitting .251 in Chicago, with 10 stolen bases, hit .348 the rest of the season and stole 33 more bases as the Cards hurtled into the midst of a four-way race for the pennant that was settled only when they took the flag with an 11–5 win on the final day. After surprising the Yankees in the World Series, the Cardinals were themselves surprised when manager Johnny Keane left to take the Yankee helm. The club slipped into the second division for a couple of years under the management of their great former second baseman Red Schoendienst.

But owner Busch built them a striking new stadium in 1966, and the next season the team rebounded to the top again, running away from the field in the last half of the season behind the heavy hitting of Orlando Cepeda, the bat and speed of Lou Brock, and a pitching staff of remarkable breadth and balance. Bob Gibson's three World Series wins over Boston edged the Cards to a ninth world title and set the stage for Gibson's astonishing season the following year.

With his 22 wins leading the Cards to another pennant in 1968, Gibson hurled 13 shutouts and compiled an ERA of just 1.12—both feats the best in more than half a century, both ranking among the top five big league performances ever. After winning two World Series games, Gibson lost Game Seven as Detroit took the crown.

Red Schoendienst continued as Cardinal manager through 1976—a club record twelve years—but led the team to no more championships. When divisional play was inaugurated in 1969, geography was ignored as the Cards were installed in the East to add strength to what seemed the weaker division. But it was fourteen years before they won their first divisional championship. Four times they finished second, losing twice by only 1½ games, in the back-to-back tight races of 1973 and 1974.

Dorrell "Whitey" Herzog was in his first full season as Cardinal manager before the club again finished that near the top. In the strike-shortened divided season of 1981, the Cards compiled the best overall record in the NL East, but because they had finished the two halves of the season second to Philadelphia and Montreal they were ineligible for postseason play.

With the defensive wizard shortstop Ozzie Smith (acquired from San Diego) and rookie speedster Willie McGee bolstering an already strong team, the Cardinals of 1982, after prevailing against the Phillies in the race for the East, swept West champion Atlanta for the pennant and captured their tenth World Series crown in a seven-game struggle with Milwaukee.

After two seasons out of the running, the Cards in 1985 gained the power of veteran Jack Clark (acquired from San Francisco) and the speed of rookie Vince Coleman. With career-best seasons from Willie McGee and newly acquired pitcher John Tudor, the team edged the New York Mets for the division title and defeated Los Angeles for the pennant—but lost the World Series in seven games to Kansas City.

Jack Clark missed two-thirds of the 1986 season to injury, and the Cards finished below .500, but they rebounded to edge the Mets again for the championship of the East in 1987 as Clark and Vince Coleman enjoyed their finest seasons at the bat. But the reinjured Clark made only a token appearance as the Cards edged San Francisco for the league championship, and he missed the World Series entirely as St. Louis bowed to Minnesota in seven games. That winter Clark signed as a free agent with the Yankees and in 1988 the Cardinals dropped to fifth place, 25 games out.

With solid pitching and hitting, and the league's best fielding, the 1989 Cardinals drew within half a game of the division lead on September 8, then fell out of the race with six straight losses, finishing third. As the season drew to its close, long-time owner August Busch, Jr., died at age ninety. The next July, with the club uncharacteristically mired at the bottom of the NL East, manager Whitey Herzog resigned. Under new manager Joe Torre the Cards revived briefly, but then dropped their final seven games to insure their first basement finish in seventy-two years.

San Diego Padres

In their first fifteen years the Padres put together only one winning season. In their sixteenth, they won the National League pennant. Founded in the 1969 expansion that saw the two major leagues divide into East and West divisions, the Padres finished last in the six-team NL West their first six seasons, ending each year from 28½ to 42 games behind the division champion.

Their first season was their worst. With 110 losses, the Padres finished not only 41 games out of first but 29 games out of *fifth*. First baseman Nate Colbert, with 24 home runs, provided San Diego's brightest ray of hope. He proved to be one of the Padres' standout performers through their last-place years, and in 1972 became the first Padre to drive in more than 100 runs.

Big league baseball was not an instant hit in San Diego. Home attendance barely topped half a million in the Padres' first year, and though it rose a little over the next few seasons, the increase was not enough to make the club viable. Owner C. Arnholt Smith decided early in 1974 to sell the franchise to a buyer who planned to move the team to Washington, D.C. New uniforms had been manufactured and the club's files were packed for the move, when the builder of the McDonald's fast-food empire, longtime baseball fan Ray Kroc, stepped in with an offer to buy the Padres for cash and keep them in San Diego. His bid was accepted.

Though Kroc's 1974 Padres finished last with the same 60–102 record they had posted the year before, his sense of showmanship drew spectators. Home attendance shot up 76 percent, rising above a million for the first time. The Padres then began to draw fans on their own merits as they finally pulled themselves out of the cellar. Pitcher Randy Jones, who in 1974 had led the league with 22 losses, turned his record around and for two years shone as one of the game's finest pitchers. He halved his 1974 ERA to a league-leading 2.24, winning 20 games as the Padres rose to fourth place in 1975 and posted a winning percentage over .400 for the first time. The next year Jones won a league-high 22 games and earned the Cy Young Award—the first major award to come to a San Diego player.

Although 1976 proved to be Jones's last winning season, the Padres were by then attracting other top-quality players. Outfielder Dave Winfield came up as a rookie in 1973, and the following year became the team RBI leader, a position he held in six of his seven full seasons with the Padres. Reliever Rollie Fingers signed as a free agent. In each of his four seasons in San Diego (1977–1980) he led the team in saves, twice also leading the league. In 1978 the Padres acquired veteran pitcher Gaylord Perry from Texas and installed rookie Ozzie Smith at shortstop. Perry's sparkling 21–6 season gave San Diego its second Cy Young winner, and together with Smith's play in the field, Winfield's bat (.308, 97 RBIs) and Fingers's 37 saves, brought the Padres their first winning season.

All these stars had gone—and owner Kroc had recently died—by the time the Padres recorded a second winning season six years later, and won the division title and NL pennant with a new blend of experience and youth. Sparked by recently acquired veterans Steve Garvey at first, Graig Nettles at third, and Goose Gossage in the bullpen, and by a bevy of younger stars like batting champ Tony Gwynn and hard-hitting outfielder Kevin McReynolds, the Padres moved into first place to stay in early June. From August 3 to the end of the season, they played only .500 ball but still won the championship of the weak Western Division by 12 games. Underdogs in the League Championship Series, the Padres lost the first two games in Chicago, but pulled themselves together to take the pennant with three come-from-behind wins at home.

Their decline began with their World Series loss to Detroit. The end of 1985 saw them tied for third, and in 1986 they slipped below .500 and into fourth place. In 1987 Gwynn won his second batting title, and rookie catcher Benito Santiago capped the season with a 34-game hitting streak to cop Rookie of the Year honors. But with most of the 1984 standouts faded or traded, the Padres' decline was complete: the club for the ninth time in its nineteen years finished last.

In late May 1988, with the team at 16–30, Padre general manager Jack McKeon took over as field manager from Larry Bowa. Under McKeon the Padres went 67–48, with nine wins in their final ten games, shot from sixth place to third in the NL West.

In 1989 a trio of veteran pitchers—starters Bruce Hurst (lured from Boston as a free agent) and Ed Whitson, and closer Mark Davis—attained new peaks of performance. Slugger Jack Clark (newly acquired from the Yankees) turned on the power after a slow start to complement Tony Gwynn's fourth season as NL batting leader. The Padres stumbled through the first half, arriving at the All-Star break four games below .500, but climbed steadily through the final two months to a second-place finish with their second-best winning percentage ever.

With the loss of free agent Davis in 1990, plus injuries to Clark and catcher Santiago, even the new power of Joe Carter (traded from Cleveland) could not lift the club above a tie for fourth. New owners, headed by TV producer Tom Werner, took control of the Padres from Ray Kroc's widow Joan in mid-June. Jack McKeon resigned his managerial position, which went to coach Greg Riddoch a month later, and was fired as general manager in September.

San Francisco Giants

The expulsion of Troy and Worcester from the National League after the 1882 season cleared the way for the league to reestablish clubs in the major markets of Philadelphia and New York. Manufacturer John B. Day was awarded the New York franchise. Purchasing the defunct Troy club, he divided their players between the new NL Gothams and his other club, the Metropolitans of the American Association, and set them up on adjoining grounds north of Central Park, on a field once used for polo.

The Mets fared better than the Gothams, finishing fourth in 1883 to the Gothams' sixth, and winning the AA pennant the next year while the Gothams rose only to fifth in the NL. Since the NL, with greater prestige and higher ticket prices, offered potentially greater profit, Day switched some of his Mets to the Gothams in 1885, including ace hurler Tim Keefe and manager Jim Mutrie. The results were immediate: the Mets sank to seventh place while the Gothams (dubbed "my Giants" by an enthusiastic Mutrie) rose to the thick of a pennant race with Chicago. At the finish Chicago was on top by two games, but the Giants had won more than three games out of four for a .759 winning percentage that is not only the club's best ever, but one of the highest in major-league history. Pitchers Keefe and Mickey Welch together won 76 of the team's 85 victories, and first-baseman Roger Connor led the league in batting.

The Giants won their first pennant in 1888 by nine games over Chicago, and their second the next year in a one-game squeaker over Boston. Keefe and Welch, still going strong, combined for 61 wins in '88 and 55 in '89. Continuing their winning ways in the World Series, the Giants triumphed easily over St. Louis in 1888, and overcame a 1-3 deficit to vanquish Brooklyn the next year.

In 1890, ravaged by the loss of players to the rival Players League, the Giants finished sixth, but they recovered several players when the PL folded at the end of the season. (They also moved into the PL ballpark, named it after their original Polo Grounds, and played there 67 years). They rose to third in 1891, but Day could no longer afford to maintain the team and sold out to financier Edward Talcott. Talcott brought back former Giant star J. M. Ward to manage the club, and in 1894 saw the team rise to a close second-place finish behind Baltimore. Pitchers Amos Rusie and Jouett Meekin tied for the league lead with 36 wins apiece. In postseason Temple Cup play, the Giants swept Baltimore in four games for their third world championship.

That winter Talcott sold control of the club to Tammany Hall politician Andrew Freedman. Giant fortunes sank under Freedman's abrasive and heavy-handed rule. As he ran through a succession of managers, the Giants fell to ninth (of twelve clubs) in 1895 and—apart from a third-place finish in 1897—rose no higher than seventh while he controlled the franchise. In 1902, his final year of ownership, the Giants suffered their lowest winning percentage—.353—and most distant finish ever—53½ games behind champion Pittsburgh.

In the midst of the 1902 season, though, a skirmish in the war between the NL and the upstart American League led to a Giant turnaround. John T. Brush, owner of the NL Cincinnati Reds, bought the AL Baltimore Orioles, then released Oriole manager John McGraw and several key players to sign with NL clubs. Five joined the Giants, including McGraw, catcher Roger Bresnahan, and pitcher Joe "Iron Man" McGinnity. That winter, Brush sold the Reds and Orioles and bought the Giants.

In 1903, with Bresnahan hitting .350 and McGinnity winning a league-high 31 games (closely followed by third-year Giant Christy Mathewson's 30 wins), manager McGraw saw his Giants win thirty-six more games than they had in 1902 and finish a solid second in the standings. In McGraw's twenty-nine full seasons at the helm, the team would win ten pennants and finish second eleven times.

Just two years after their worst season ever, McGraw in 1904 led the Giants to one of their best. Their 106 wins and 13-game winning margin remain Giant highs to this day. The club led the NL in pitching, hitting, fielding, and base stealing. McGinnity led league pitchers in several categories with a career-best 35–8, 1.61 ERA season. Mathewson, right behind with 33 wins, led the league in strikeouts.

The only Giant disappointment of 1904 was McGraw's refusal to face Boston in a World Series. His rejection of the AL champions as worthy opponents was the last shot fired in the war between the two leagues. By the time the Giants had repeated as NL pennant winners a year later, the World Series was an official and permanent feature of the baseball landscape. Mathewson led NL pitchers in 1905 with 31 wins and an ERA of 1.27, and outfielder "Turkey Mike" Donlin, acquired from Cincinnati the previous July, erupted with the best season of his career, batting a team-high .356 and scoring a league-high 124 runs. The Giants won only one game less than the year before and held a comfortable lead throughout the season. Matty's three shutouts against the Philadelphia Athletics in the World Series secured the club's fourth world crown.

It was 1911 before the Giants won their next pennant. Despite 96 wins in 1906 they finished a distant second to Chicago's mighty Cubs, who won a record 116 games. In 1908 the Giants came within a disputed play of the pennant. On September 23, playing Chicago (with whom they were tied at the top of a three-way race), Giant baserunner Fred Merkle failed to run to second on a single by Al Bridwell that would have driven in the winning run from third. Merkle was forced at second after the ball (or a second ball—the argument still rages) was recovered amid the horde of fans who overran the field. The force out at second negated the run, and the game was ruled a tie. At season's end, when the two clubs found themselves again tied at the top, the "Merkle boner" game was replayed. The Cubs won the game and flag, leaving the Giants in a second-place tie with Pittsburgh.

In 1911 the Giants pulled away from the Cubs in September for the first of three straight pennants. (Early in the season most of the Polo Grounds was rebuilt in concrete after fire destroyed the wooden stands.) The following year the Giants took the lead in May and held it comfortably the rest of the way. In 1913 they didn't move into first until late June, but then quickly put the flag out of reach and finished 12½ games ahead of the faltering Phillies. Mathewson led the team in victories over the three years, with 74, followed closely by Rube Marquard (who with 73 wins enjoyed the three best seasons of his career). Matty led the NL in ERA in 1911 and 1913; Giant rookie Jeff Tesreau took the honors in 1912 (winning 17 games that season and 22 the next). Giant pitching led the league all three seasons, as did their hitting, which featured a balanced offense paced by infielders Larry Doyle and Art Fletcher and catcher John "Chief" Meyers.

In the World Series, though, the Giants three times fell short of the title. Philadelphia's Athletics defeated them handily in 1911 and 1913, but the Giants carried the 1912 Series against the Boston Red Sox to the tenth inning of the final game before a pair of Giant fielding lapses enabled Boston to rally for the win.

Boston's "miracle" Braves, in their 1914 surge from last place to the pennant, passed the front-running Giants for good in early September. The next year, five of the eight NL clubs found themselves bunched within 3½ games of one another at the lower end of the standings as the season ended—with the Giants at the very bottom. And in a 1916 Giant season characterized by dips and surges, even a 26-game winning streak in September couldn't raise the team higher than fourth. But in 1917 a balanced pitching staff—paced by Ferdie Schupp's one big season (21–7, 1.95 ERA)—hurled the Giants to the front early in June and kept them there to the finish. Once more, though, the World Series proved a disappointment, with a loss to the Chicago White Sox in six games.

Three years of second-place finishes followed, in the midst of which the Giants changed owners. Brush had died in 1912 and was succeeded as president by his son-in-law Harry Hempstead. But in January 1919 Brush's heirs sold the club to financier and racehorse fancier Charles A. Stoneham, with manager McGraw a minority stockholder.

In 1921 McGraw brought home the first of four straight winners for Stoneham. Seven regulars hit over .300 (led by third baseman Frank Frisch's .341); first baseman George Kelly's 23 home runs topped the NL. The club hung close to Pittsburgh through August, then broke into a lead which the fading Pirates could not challenge. In postseason play the Giants lost the first two games to the Yankees, but charged back to win their fifth world title. The next year outfielder Emil "Irish" Meusel celebrated his first full season in New York with a team-high 132 RBIs, as the Giants fended off a midseason challenge from St. Louis to pull away to a comfortable margin at the end. The World Series was especially sweet: a four-game sweep of the Yankees.

Cincinnati and Pittsburgh hung just behind the Giants through much of 1923, but never quite caught up. The Giants' league-leading offense was led by individual NL highs in RBIs (Meusel), runs scored (outfielder Ross Youngs), and hits and total bases (Frisch). But the Yankees finally caught the Giants in the World Series, 4–2.

George Kelly took the NL RBI title in 1924. The club's hitting remained the league's best, and by early August the Giants had taken a ten-game lead. But they then leveled off while Brooklyn and Pittsburgh surged. Brooklyn, in fact, took over the lead for a day in early September, but the Giants emerged triumphant at the end by 1½ games. The World Series, though, was as heartbreaking as the pennant race had been heartstopping: the Giants lost to Washington in the last of the twelfth inning of the seventh game when a Senator grounder bounced over the head of rookie third baseman Fred Lindstrom to drive in the Series-ending run.

Close finishes—2 games out—in 1927 and 1928 were the nearest McGraw's Giants came to another pennant. Player relations with the demanding manager had seldom been harmonious, and they had reached a low point when, ill and tired, he quit early in the 1932 season with the team in last place, naming first baseman Bill Terry to replace him. Under Terry the Giants rose only to sixth that season, but McGraw had built a squad fit for a new era of greatness. He had persuaded Terry to leave a career

with Standard Oil for one with the Giants; he had saved Mel Ott's unique but effective batting stance from revision by well-meaning minor league managers by keeping Ott out of the minors; and he had rescued pitcher Carl Hubbell from mediocrity by encouraging the screwball pitch other managers had tried to suppress.

Hubbell and Ott formed the heart of the club that would win a trio of pennants under Terry's management. In 1933 the Giants moved to the front in June and, despite a late-September slump, finished well ahead of runner-up Pittsburgh. Ott, with what was for him an off-year, powered the Giant offense with 23 homers and 103 RBIs, while Hubbell led the league in wins, shutouts, and ERA. Hubbell also hurled two wins against Washington in the World Series, and Ott won it all for New York with a tenth-inning home run in Game Five. McGraw, still the club's vice president, threw a party for "his" Giants after the Series. The following February he died, at age sixty.

As they had the previous season, the Giants of 1934 emerged from the crowd to take and hold first place into late September. They rose higher than they had in 1933 and didn't slump as far at the end. But their five end-of-season losses were enough to drop them 2 games behind the surging Cardinals at the finish. Again in 1935 they led the league much of the season. But they had begun to level off in mid-July and finished the season well back in third. Charles Stoneham died in January 1936, and his son Horace—who at age thirty-three had already run the club for a year—assumed the club presidency.

In 1936, and again in 1937, the Giants came from behind to take the flag. Hubbell sparked their second-half resurgence in 1936, winning his final 16 decisions of the season as the Giants rose from fourth to first. In the World Series, though, Hubbell, after one win, was stopped by the Yankees in his try for a second. The Yankees took the Series in six games.

Again the next year the Giants hid behind the leaders most of the season until a surge in late August coincided with a Chicago decline and shot the Giants to the front. The Cubs recovered, but New York continued its winning ways and finished ahead by 3 games. But again the Yankees dominated the World Series, winning 4–1.

Hubbell's years of greatness were now over, and while the Giants led the NL through the first half of 1938, they finished third, 5 games out. It would be twelve years before they again finished that close to the top. Mel Ott replaced Terry as manager in 1942, but the Giants sank to the cellar in 1943 with their second-worst season ever, and finished last again three years later. One bright spot: in 1947 they rose to fourth with a barrage of 221 home runs (led by Johnny Mize's 51) that remained the major league record (though tied by Cincinnati in 1956) until the 1961 Yankees topped it with 240.

Halfway through the 1948 season the baseball world was startled to learn that Leo Durocher, the fiery manager of the Brooklyn Dodgers, had switched his allegiance to their arch foes, the Giants. Durocher discarded the three top Giant home run hitters of 1947 (but presciently retained the fourth, Bobby Thomson), and added agile infielders Alvin Dark and Eddie Stanky to the roster. By 1950, with the blossoming of Sal Maglie into a first-rank pitcher and the timely midseason purchase of hurler Jim Hearn, the Giants were once more a challenger, spurting in the second half from below .500 to within 5 games of the top.

After losing their first eleven games the next year, the Giants began a long climb. A sixteen-game August winning streak and a seven-game streak at season's end tied them with Brooklyn and forced a three-game playoff. After a win and a loss, the Giants entered the last of the ninth inning of Game Three trailing 1–4. Two singles and a double cut the deficit by a run and brought on Dodger Ralph Branca to face Bobby Thomson, whose two-run homer had provided the Giants' margin of victory in Game One. Thomson homered again, and the Giants won the pennant. Their defeat by the Yankees in the World Series dimmed the miracle a bit, but couldn't detract from the career bests of pitchers Maglie and Larry Jansen, who tied for the NL lead with 23 wins apiece, and of former Negro League great Monte Irvin, who hit .312 and led the league in RBIs.

The next year Irvin was lost until August with a broken ankle, Jansen (with a back problem) fell off to 11–11, and Willie Mays—a promising rookie in 1951—left early in the season for a hitch in the Army. Still, the Giants hung close to Brooklyn for much of the summer and finished second. In 1953, though, they fell apart in midseason and wound up in fifth, 35 games out.

Mays returned in 1954 to enjoy one of his strongest seasons at the bat, and pitchers Johnny Antonelli (newly acquired from Milwaukee), sophomore Ruben Gomez, and reliever Marv Grissom all burst forth with the best seasons of their careers. The Giants pulled away from Brooklyn in July and held on with a late-season rush to finish 5 games up. Underdogs to powerful Cleveland in the World Series, they stunned the Indians (and the rest of the baseball world) with a four-game sweep. It was their eighth world title—and, so far, their last.

Manager Durocher retired after a distant third-place finish in 1955, and Bill Rigney, who replaced him (the first of seven straight rookie managers to be hired by the Giants over the next twenty years), presided over a pair of sixth-place seasons in the club's final years in New York. Persuaded by the Dodgers' Walter O'Malley that California was the land of baseball opportunity, Giant owner Stoneham announced in August 1957 his decision to move the club to San Francisco before the next season.

The move succeeded. Home attendance doubled, even though the team had to play in a former minor league park that seated fewer than 23,000 fans. When new Candlestick Park opened in 1960 attendance climbed to nearly 1.8 million, a new club high. Better still, rookie sensations like Orlando Cepeda in 1958 and Willie McCovey in 1959, plus the continuing mastery of Willie Mays, made the Giants competitive once again. In their first fourteen San Francisco seasons, they compiled winning records—a longer string than they had ever known in New York.

Candlestick Park, though, proved a cold and windy place to watch baseball, and after its inaugural season fans began to drift away. Attendance picked up some in 1962, however, as the Giants battled for first all summer with the Los Angeles Dodgers. Mays, Cepeda, and Felipe Alou headlined the league's best offense, and a pair of veteran pitchers—Jack Sanford and Billy O'Dell—garnered the most wins of their careers (24 and 19) as part of

a balanced staff that also got 16 wins from veteran Billy Pierce and 18 from the emerging great Juan Marichal. Still, the Giants trailed the Dodgers most of the season until a Dodger loss and Giant win on the final day threw the teams into a tie and another playoff. As in 1951, the Giants won the first game and lost the second, and overcame a ninth-inning deficit in the finale to win the pennant. Also as in 1951, they lost the World Series to the Yankees, although this time they held on until the final out of Game Seven before losing their grip on the crown.

The 1963 Giants offered little challenge to the leaders after June, but the next three years found them locked to the end in tight struggles for the flag. Although they finished fourth in 1964, they were still in contention with just two games to play, in one of the closest four-way races ever. The next year they took the lead from the Dodgers early in September, only to lose it in the final week. And in 1966, in a season-long three-way race with the Dodgers and Pirates, the Giants weren't eliminated until the final day.

The turbulence of these races was reflected in the team itself. Cepeda (until traded to St. Louis in 1966) continually railed against his managers and his low pay. Alvin Dark, after four winning seasons as manager, was fired in 1964 when some of his racist comments ended up in print. And Marichal was fined and suspended for nine days in 1965 for hitting Dodger catcher John Roseboro over the head with his bat.

After a pair of distant second-place finishes, the Giants in 1969 (with the fine work of Marichal and McCovey augmented by the speed and power of young outfielder Bobby Bonds) found themselves in the thick of a five-way race for the championship of the newly created NL West. The race wasn't settled until the final week, when Atlanta's ten-game winning streak knocked the Giants out of first. Two years later, with Bonds the chief source of offensive power and fine pitching from starters Marichal and Gaylord Perry and reliever Jerry Johnson, the Giants moved out in front at the start of the season and held their lead all the way. A September slump coinciding with a Dodger surge narrowed the lead to one game in midmonth, but the Giants held on for the division crown. In their first experiences with a League Championship Series, though, they succumbed to Pittsburgh with three losses after an opening-game win.

The LCS loss signaled the end of an era. McCovey was past his prime and Marichal had enjoyed his last big year. Mays, after twenty Giant seasons, was sold to the Mets in 1972 so he could close out his career in New York, where it began. That year the Giants suffered their first losing season in San Francisco, and attendance for the first time dropped below what it had been in their final New York season.

Attendance had reached such a low point by the mid-1970s that Stoneham negotiated the club's sale to a Canadian brewery which planned to move it to Toronto. But San Francisco's mayor George Moscone delayed the sale until a buyer could be found who would keep the Giants in the city. San Francisco realtor Robert Lurie stepped forth with half the purchase price, and Arizona cattleman Arthur "Bud" Herseth provided the rest. (Toronto settled for an expansion club, the Blue Jays.)

After six years out of the running, the Giants in 1978

played at the top of the NL East through much of the summer before dropping to third (and home attendance jumped more than a million above the previous year). But they fell below .500 the next two years—making seven losing seasons in the nine that followed their division title of 1971.

In 1982 the Giants—paced by the slugging of Jack Clark and Greg Minton's sparkling relief pitching—made one of the most impressive comebacks since divisional play was instituted in 1969, driving from ten games below .500 in late June to just 2 games from champion Atlanta at season's end. But they dropped to fifth the following year, and to a last-place sixth in 1984 and 1985.

When Roger Craig was called on to manage the final weeks of the 1985 season, there was no stopping the Giants' slide to a club-record 100 losses. But the next year, inspiring a "can do" spirit among the players, Craig turned the club around. Veteran hurler Mike Krukow won a career-high 20 games, eight players contributed more than 40 RBIs each, and the team captured 26 of their 83 wins in their final at-bat. In first place at midseason, the Giants slipped (in part because of injuries) to third by season's end, but the fans were back—over 700,000 more than a year earlier.

The club set a new home attendance record of more than 1.9 million in 1987 as it returned to the top of the NL West for the first time in sixteen years. Sophomore first baseman Will Clark led a balanced offense, and several shrewd in-season acquisitions by the front office spurred a second-half drive from five games back to a 6-game lead at the finish. But after taking a 3–2 advantage over St. Louis in the LCS, the Giants failed to score in the final two games and the Cardinals captured the flag.

Injuries contributed to the Giants' decline to fourth place the next year, but in 1989 Will Clark enjoyed his strongest season yet, and left fielder Kevin Mitchell erupted with league-high power (47 HRs, 125 RBIs, .635 slugging) to lead another successful Giant assault on the division title. For the first time, the Giants passed the 2 million mark in home attendance. After holding first place from mid-June to the finish, they pushed past the stubborn Cubs in the LCS to their first pennant in twenty-seven years, their nineteenth over all. But the earthquake that delayed Game 3 of the World Series only postponed a sweep by mighty Oakland.

Third baseman Matt Williams joined Clark and Mitchell in the Giant pantheon of power in 1990, but the team, handicapped by a slow start, finished third.

Seattle Mariners

The Mariners are one of only two major-league teams never to have won a pennant or divisional title (the Texas Rangers are the other), the only team without a single winning season or first-division finish—and (at home in Seattle's Kingdome) the only team to have played all its home games indoors. The Mariners have become stronger in recent years. Only once in their first seven years did their winning percentage rise above .450, but in three of the past five seasons it has done so. In 1987, winning eight of their last ten games (including the final four) the Mariners closed the season at 78–84 (.481), only 7 games

behind champion Minnesota, in fourth place—their best record yet.

Organized in 1977, the Mariners returned major league baseball to the Pacific Northwest eight years after the Seattle Pilots had moved to Milwaukee after only one season. With a 64–98 inaugural season, the Mariners avoided last place in the American League West only because the Oakland A's had plummeted faster and farther. The hitting of first baseman Dan Meyer, outfielder Leroy Stanton, and rookie center fielder Ruppert Jones—who combined for 73 home runs—and the relief pitching of rookie Enrique (Romo) Romero, who contributed 16 saves and 8 wins, provided most of the high points of that first season.

There was less to cheer about the next year as the production of the first-season heroes fell off and the Mariners took possession of the cellar from mid-May on, losing a club-record 104 games. They finished 12 games out of sixth place, 35 out of first. Much of the offense that was generated came from outfielder Leon Roberts. Acquired from Houston over the winter, Roberts put together his best season and became the Mariners' first .300 hitter.

The club moved up a notch in 1979, to sixth place. Meyer and Jones regained much of their 1977 power, first baseman Bruce Bochte hit .316 and drove in 100 runs, and DH Willie Horton, near the end of a long career, enjoyed one of his finest seasons, driving in 106 runs and leading the club with 29 homers.

As the Mariners, with the league's weakest hitting, dropped back into the cellar the next season, attendance fell to a new low, and some of the original owners decided to sell out. In January 1981 California real-estate magnate George Argyros purchased control of the club, and later bought out the remaining partners to take sole ownership.

In strike-divided 1981 the Mariners finished sixth and fifth in the two halves of the season. Second baseman Julio Cruz continued among the league's top base stealers, and right fielder Tom Paciorek's second-place .326 BA put a Seattle hitter high among the league's best for the first time. Paciorek was traded away that winter, but his replacement, veteran Al Cowens, came through with one of his best seasons in 1982. And Mariner pitching improved dramatically—from the bottom of the league in ERA in 1981 to fourth best in '82. Newcomers Bill Caudill and rookie Ed Vande Berg, working in relief, combined for 21 wins and 31 saves. Starter Floyd Bannister led the league in strikeouts while winning 12 games (tying Caudill for the team lead), and veteran Gaylord Perry added 10 victories, including his 300th career win in May. The team finished above .450 for the first time, fourth in the AL West, a new high.

Caudill's 26 saves in 1983 couldn't prevent a slide back into last place. But the club's farm system was beginning to produce quality talent, and 1984 saw the arrival of two standouts: first baseman Alvin Davis, whose 27 homers and 116 RBIs earned him AL Rookie of the Year honors, and pitcher Mark Langston, a 17-game winner in 1984 and AL strikeout leader in three of his first four seasons. Rookie third baseman Jim Presley hit 10 home runs in 70 games and proceeded to blossom into one of the Seattle club's leading power hitters the next year.

After sixth-place finishes in 1984 and '85, the Mariners fell off to last again in 1986. Langston's 19 wins led the team's 1987 rebound to fourth, with Lee Guetterman's 11–4 pitching and the power of Davis and Presley providing valuable assists. Infielder Harold Reynolds stole his sixtieth base in the final game to preserve his lead in that department and to give the Mariners their first league leader in an offensive category.

After dropping back into the cellar in 1988 and rising a notch to sixth in 1989, the Mariners revived under new ownership in 1990 to challenge the .500 barrier. Center fielder Ken Griffey, Jr., began to fulfill the promise he had shown as a nineteen-year-old rookie the previous summer. Sophomore hurler Erik Hanson—with 18 wins and an ERA among the league's best—replaced the traded Mark Langston as ace of a young pitching staff that compiled the league's third lowest ERA. The Mariners entered August third in the strong AL West, with a winning record which they maintained through mid-month before stumbling to fifth place with their fourteenth straight losing season.

Texas Rangers

As part of the first American League expansion, a new Washington club was added to the league in November 1960, to replace the old Senators, who were moving to Minnesota to become the Twins. The old Senators had languished in the second division their final 14 years in Washington, and the new Senators scarcely improved on that record. In each of their first four seasons they lost 100 games or more, tying for last place in 1961 and holding down the bottom all by themselves for two years before rising to ninth in 1964.

Although as an expansion team the new Senators had to make do at first with expendable players from the established clubs, they were not devoid of talent. In their first season, pitcher Dick Donovan led the league with a 2.40 earned run average, though injuries and the lack of offensive support held his won-lost record to 10–10. Perhaps their most promising player, he was traded with two teammates to Cleveland for outfielder Jimmy Piersall. Piersall proved a major disappointment in Washington, batting only .244 while Donovan was winning 20 games for his new club.

Not all the Senators' trades proved disastrous. In late 1964 they sent another promising pitcher—Claude Osteen—to the Dodgers in a deal that brought them five players, including third baseman Ken McMullen and outfielder Frank Howard. Osteen blossomed into a consistent winner in Los Angeles, but at the same time, McMullen brought strength to the Washington infield and Howard became one of the league's offensive stars.

The Senators' blend of youth and experience jelled in 1969 under rookie manager Ted Williams, as several key players—including McMullen and Howard—enjoyed career-best seasons. The club finished above .500 for the first time, driving with a late-season spurt to within a game of third-place Boston in the league's Eastern Division.

But 1969 was a one-year phenomenon. After losing seasons in 1970 and '71 (and the loss of much of their fan support), owner Bob Short pulled up stakes and moved the club to Arlington, Texas (midway between Fort Worth and Dallas), where, as the Texas Rangers, they have been ever since. Their first summer in Texas resembled their first in Washington: they lost 100 games (despite a strike-shortened season) and finished last. Williams was replaced by a new rookie manager—Whitey Herzog—but the club did no better in 1973.

Before the season's end Herzog gave way to Billy Martin. Martin came too late to save the Rangers from another lost season, but the next year he spurred the team to the kind of turnaround Williams had managed five years earlier. Behind the 25–12 pitching of Ferguson Jenkins (acquired in the offseason from the Cubs) and the hitting of league MVP Jeff Burroughs and rookie first baseman Mike Hargrove, the Rangers spurted in the second half of 1974 from a sub-.500 record to second place in the American League West, only 5 games behind Oakland.

Since 1974 the Rangers' fortunes have been up and down. After two losing seasons they rebounded in 1977 to their finest season yet (94–68, .580) and second place, behind strong pitching and the blooming of Jim Sundberg as a hitter to go along with his league-leading catching. Fergie Jenkins's return to the club (after two years in Boston), the sparkling 11–5 season of rookie Steve Comer, and a September surge kept the club competitive in 1978. Jim Kern's brilliant relief work the next season helped club recover from a nosedive in July and August to edge Minnesota for a strong third-place finish.

After a losing season in 1980, the Rangers bounced back in 1981 to record their second-best winning percentage ever (.543)—and finishes of second and third in the two halves of the strike-divided season. Then they slipped below .500 again for four more years. Pitcher Charlie Hough's knuckleball, and strong seasons at the bat from Pete O'Brien, Larry Parrish, and rookies Scott Fletcher and Pete Incaviglia helped new manager Bobby Valentine turn the Rangers around once again in 1986, lifting them to the club's fifth second-place finish after last-place seasons in 1984 and '85.

Once more, though, the turnaround was brief: in 1987 losses in their final games of the season dropped the Rangers into a tie at the bottom of the division, and in 1988 they finished only two games out of the cellar, in sixth place.

A group of investors headed by George W. Bush—the President's son—purchased control of the Rangers in March 1989, and strikeout king Nolan Ryan returned to the American League as a Ranger after nine years in Houston. The Rangers returned to the winning side of the ledger featuring Ryan's strong season (which included his 5,000th career strikeout); career years by outfielder Ruben Sierra, second baseman Julio Franco (newly acquired from Cleveland), and reliever Jeff Russell; and a fast start (10–1) that put the club in first place for a month (before they settled back to fourth). In 1990 Ryan—now forty-three years old—hurled his 300th win and a 6th no-hitter, first baseman Rafael Palmeiro peaked at the plate, and pitcher Bobby Witt enjoyed his finest season, with 17 wins. After a slow first half, the Rangers rose from sixth place to third, compiling an 83–79 record identical to that of the year before.

Toronto Blue Jays

For a while, in February 1977, it looked as if the National League's San Francisco Giants would move to Toronto, where there were buyers eager for the club. But when the Giants were sold in March to new owners determined to keep them in San Francisco, the American League jumped in to establish Toronto as an American League city, setting up an expansion club, the Blue Jays.

It took seven years for the Jays to lift themselves out of last place in the seven-team American League East. For five years they had the cellar all to themselves, never finishing closer than 11 games behind the *sixth*-place club.

In their first season, the Jays' 107 losses left them 45½ games out of first, as the team performed at the bottom of the division in hitting, fielding, and pitching. In 1978 their fielding improved dramatically, but the Jays still lost over 100 games, and there was little doubt after April who would finish last.

The next year was the team's worst ever. While every other Eastern Division club was compiling a winning record, Toronto plunged relentlessly downward and, despite a brief rally in September, finished 28½ games out of sixth place (50½ out of first), with 109 losses.

The club's turnaround began in 1980. It was late June before the Jays began their drop away from the rest of the division, and for the first time they finished with fewer than 100 losses. Pitchers Jim Clancy and Dave Stieb lowered their ERAs below 4.00 for the first time, and newly acquired second baseman Damaso Garcia combined with shortstop Alfredo Griffin to form the league's best double-play combination. There were still two more seasons in the cellar, but in strike-divided 1981 the Jays played a creditable second half for the first time, and in 1982 they spurted in September to tie the Indians for sixth at season's end. Garcia in 1982 became a .300 hitter and a leading base stealer, Clancy put together his first winning season and Stieb his second, and Stieb's five shutouts led the league.

In 1983, with seven of the Blue Jays' eight principal pitchers enjoying winning seasons, and the Jays' hitters leading the league in team batting and slugging, Toronto recorded its first winning season—in fourth place, only 9 games out of first. Their balanced pitching and offense carried them to a repeat 89–73 record in 1984—this time for second place (though they finished a distant 15 games behind Detroit).

In 1985 the Blue Jays topped their division with 99 victories, edging the Yankees by 2 games. Their pitching was better than ever. Doyle Alexander won 17 games, Jimmy Key and Dave Stieb contributed 14 each, and reliever Dennis Lamp compiled an impressive 11–0 record. Stieb led the league in ERA, with Key fourth. Tony Fernandez, in his first full big league season, sparkled as expected at short, but also proved unexpectedly solid at the bat. Eight Jays drove in more than 50 runs, with outfielders George Bell (95), Jesse Barfield (84), and Lloyd Moseby (71) pacing the club's balanced attack.

In the LCS the Jays won three of their first four games against Kansas City, but lost the next three—and the pennant. Equally discouraging was their drop to fourth place in 1986. Barfield, Bell, and Fernandez all improved at the plate, but the league-leading pitchers of 1985 dropped back to the middle of the pack in '86 (though rookie Mark Eichorn sparkled in long relief).

Toronto sprang back stronger than ever in 1987. Jim Clancy (15–11, 3.54 ERA) enjoyed his best season yet, as did Jimmy Key (17–8), whose 2.76 ERA led the league. Once again, as in 1985, the team ERA was the league's lowest. And the offense remained strong. (George Bell, league RBI leader with 134, was named the American League MVP at season's end.) The Jays led their division going into the season's final series against second-place Detroit, though four straight losses had reduced the lead to just one game. Needing to win two of the three games to take the AL East title, or one to tie the Tigers and force a playoff, the Jays' slumping bats remained quiet, and Toronto lost the first two games. In the season finale, Jimmy Key hurled a three-hitter, striking out eight. But one of the hits was a home run—the only run of the game, as it turned out. Toronto's seven-game losing streak had cost them what would have been their second title in three years.

In 1988, a rocky season made worse by George Bell's feud with manager Jimy Williams (who wanted the unwilling outfielder to serve as designated hitter), the Jays surged at the end—with six straight wins—into a tie for third place, only two games out of first. The season was highlighted by the emergence of Fred McGriff as one of the game's most powerful batsmen, and by ace Dave Stieb's two successive one-hitters in late September—both of which were no-hitters through 8⅔ innings.

When Toronto's front office replaced manager Williams with batting coach Cito Gaston in mid-May 1989, the Jays were drowning near the bottom of the AL East with a record of 12–24. By mid-August they had bobbed above .500 to stay, and on September 1 replaced Baltimore in first place. With a pair of one-run victories over the Orioles at the end of September, the Jays preserved their narrow lead and clinched the division title. But Oakland outplayed them in the LCS, taking the pennant in five games.

From mid-June 1990 to the final day of the season, the Blue Jays battled Boston for the division lead before settling for second. Dave Stieb (after two more one-hitters in 1989) at last hurled a no-hitter, and third baseman Kelly Gruber confirmed a place with Bell and McGriff among Toronto's power elite. But the brightest Toronto star of 1989–90 was the new Skydome, with its 11,000-ton retractable roof and its restaurants and hotel rooms above the outfield wall. After the Jays moved into the Dome on June 5, 1989, attendance zoomed, and by season's end the club set a new American League home attendance record of nearly 3.4 million. In 1990, with a full season in the Dome, the Jays attracted over a half million more fans than the year before, for a new major league record of 3,885,284.

Defunct Clubs

In addition to the many Negro League teams, some 108 ballclubs have played in the major leagues since the first professional association was formed in 1871. The twenty-six that still do are described above; here are the other eighty-two, listed according to the league and year in which they first played major league ball. Official club names precede the name of the city; nicknames follow.

National Association, 1871–1875

Two of the twenty-three clubs that played at one time or another in baseball's first professional league still play in the majors: the Atlanta Braves (then the Boston Red Stockings) and the Chicago Cubs (then the White Stockings). The other twenty-one:

Athletic of Philadelphia: NA 1871–1875, NL 1876. Organized in 1860 as an amateur club, the Athletics became one of the dominant teams of the decade. As professionals they won the first NA pennant in 1871. After one year in the NL, they were expelled for failing to make the final western trip of the season.

Forest City of Cleveland, NA 1871–1872. In the midst of a second losing season, the club disbanded in August 1872.

Forest City of Rockford, Ill., NA 1871. As an amateur club, Forest City (with its sixteen-year-old pitcher Al Spalding) was the only team to defeat the famous Washington Nationals on their pioneering midwestern tour of 1867. As professionals, Forest City finished seventh of the nine NA teams in 1871.

Kekionga of Fort Wayne, NA 1871. The Kekiongas won the first NA game ever played, but dropped out of the association before the end of the season.

Mutual of New York, NA 1871–1875, NL 1876. Organized as an amateur club in 1857, the Mutuals were said to be backed financially by New York's notorious William M. "Boss" Tweed. Frequently accused of corrupt practices, the club was one of the leading eastern teams of the late 1860s. They were declared national champions of 1868, and proclaimed themselves national champions of 1870. On the demise of the NA the Mutuals entered the NL, but were expelled after one season (along with the Athletics) for failing to play their final games in the West.

Olympic of Washington, D.C., NA 1871–1872. Unsuccessful in 1872 after playing well the year before, the Olympics disbanded about midseason.

Union of Troy, N.Y., NA 1871–1872. The Haymakers, as they were popularly known, dropped out of the NA halfway through the 1872 season.

Atlantic of Brooklyn, NA 1872–1875. One of the greatest of the amateur clubs, the Atlantics (organized in 1855) went undefeated in 1864 and 1865, and won three successive national championships, 1864–1866. But in four NA seasons their combined won-lost record was only 49–139, including a dismal 2–42 in 1875.

Eckford of Brooklyn, NA 1872. Another great early amateur club—like the Atlantics, organized in 1855— they won the national championship in 1862, and again (with an undefeated season of ten games) the next year. The Eckfords actually joined the NA in August 1871, replacing Kekionga, but their 1871 games were later erased from the record because they had failed to enter the association at the start of the season.

Lord Baltimore of Baltimore, NA 1872–1874. After twice finishing third, the Lord Baltimores (or "Canaries," for their yellow silk jerseys) disbanded two games before the end of the 1874 season, while in last place.

Mansfield of Middletown, Ct., NA 1872. Disbanded in late August.

National of Washington, D.C., NA 1872–1873, 1875. Organized as amateurs in 1859, the Nationals were the first eastern club to tour as far west as Chicago and St. Louis. After skipping the 1874 race, the Nationals re-entered the NA in 1875, but dropped out in July.

Maryland of Baltimore, NA 1873. Dropped out after only six games.

Philadelphia, NA 1873–1875. Known successively as the "White Stockings," "Pearls," and "Phillies," the team finished a strong second to Boston in their first season, but slipped to fourth and fifth the next two years.

Resolute of Elizabeth, N.J., NA 1873. Disbanded in August with a 2–21 record.

Hartford Dark Blues, NA 1874–1875, NL 1876–1877. After a weak first year, Hartford finished third in its next three seasons, as standings are reckoned today. But by the 1876 guidelines (which used the number of games won rather than winning percentage), Hartford that year placed second. In 1877 the club played its home games in Brooklyn, N.Y.

Centennial of Philadelphia, NA 1875. Dropped out in late May.

New Haven Elm Citys, NA 1875. Failed to play out their schedule.

St. Louis Brown Stockings, NA 1875, NL 1876–1877. George Bradley pitched all but 5 of the Browns' 39 wins in 1875, when they finished fourth, and all 45 victories in 1876, when they finished a strong third (in number of victories; they were second in winning percentage). With Bradley lost to Chicago the next year, St. Louis dropped below .500—and out of the league.

St. Louis Red Stockings, NA 1875. A successful amateur club that decided to take a fling at pro ball, the Red Stockings played only a few games in the NA.

Western of Keokuk, Iowa, NA 1875. Disbanded in mid-June.

National League, 1876–

When the NL was founded to replace the ill-organized NA, it included six of the stronger NA clubs plus independent clubs in Cincinnati and Louisville. The league's composition was in continual flux to the end of the century as clubs were dropped and added, shrinking the league to as few as six teams and expanding it to as many as twelve. Two clubs that first played major league ball in the NL still do: the Philadelphia Phillies and the San Francisco (originally New York) Giants, both organized in 1883. (The Boston and Chicago franchises—that continue to this day as the Atlanta Braves and Chicago Cubs—had their starts in the National Association.) Those that have not survived:

Cincinnati Red Stockings, NL 1876–1880. From last place in 1876 (and 1877, when their games were not counted because of the club's reorganization and failure to pay its dues), the Reds—with seven new regulars—rose to second in 1878, only to fall back to fifth in 1879, and last again in 1880. That fall, when they refused to accept a new rule abolishing liquor sales and Sunday baseball on club grounds, they were dropped from league membership.

Louisville Grays, NL 1876–1877. The strong Louisville team led the league in mid-August, but seven suspicious losses to chief rivals Boston and Hartford dropped the Grays out of first place. After Boston clinched the pennant, Louisville revived to secure second place, but four players—including pitching ace Jim Devlin—were expelled from baseball for throwing games. Their expulsion showed the NL's determination to wipe out corruption, but it also caused the St. Louis Browns, who had planned to sign three of the four Louisville players for 1878, to resign from the league. Louisville, too, dropped out of the league before the next season, unable to find adequate replacements for the four.

Indianapolis Browns, NL 1878. Finished fifth of six teams.

Milwaukee Grays (or Cream Citys), NL 1878. Finished a last-place sixth.

Providence Grays, NL 1878–1885. One of the great teams in the NL's early years, Providence won pennants in 1879 and 1884, finishing no lower than third in seven of their eight seasons. In 1884, pitcher Charlie "Old Hoss" Radbourn won a record 60 games, then pitched the Grays to victory in baseball's first World Series with a three-game sweep of the American Association champion New York Mets. But as they dropped to fourth place the next year, finishing for the first time below .500, their fans deserted them. Late that autumn the club was dissolved.

Buffalo Bisons, NL 1879–1885. Buffalo moved up to the majors after winning the International Association pennant in 1878. Jim "Pud" Galvin pitched nearly 70 percent of Buffalo's victories as he led them to four first-division finishes in seven big league seasons. First baseman Dan Brouthers, in his five years with Buffalo, twice won the batting title and led NL sluggers five times.

Cleveland Blues, NL 1879–1884. Cleveland's fortunes rested in large measure with pitcher Jim McCormick (who also managed the club their first two seasons). In 1880, their best season, McCormick won a career-high 45 games to bring the Blues in third. In 1883 Cleveland was in first place when McCormick's injured arm put him out for the season after he had won twenty-three games. The Blues dropped to fourth. The club folded after a seventh-place finish in 1884, a season that saw McCormick and two other Blues jump to the UA.

Star of Syracuse, NL 1879. After finishing a close second to Buffalo in the International League in 1878, the Stars moved up with the Bisons to the NL, but disbanded after a single unsuccessful season.

Troy, N.Y., Trojans, NL 1879–1882. After four losing seasons the franchise was expelled to make room for a club in New York City.

Worcester, Mass., Ruby Legs, NL 1880–1882. After a pair of losing minor league seasons, Worcester was admitted to the NL to replace the defunct Stars of Syracuse. After finishing a respectable fifth in 1880, Worcester dropped into the cellar for two seasons before being ousted in 1883 for a new Philadelphia club.

Detroit Wolverines, NL 1881–1888. Buffalo's sale of its "big four" (Dan Brouthers, Hardy Richardson, Jack Rowe, and Deacon White) to Detroit late in 1885 transformed a perennial also-ran into a contender. The club finished second in 1886 and won the pennant in 1887. In a World Series played in ten different cities, the Wolverines

trounced St. Louis ten games to five. In 1888, after finishing fifth, they expired.

Kansas City Cowboys, NL 1886. They finished seventh, 58½ games out.

Washington Senators, NL 1886–1889. In their four seasons, the Senators finished out of the cellar only once: next to last in 1887.

Indianapolis Hoosiers, NL 1887–1889. After dropping below Washington into the cellar in 1887, the Hoosiers and Senators traded places for their final two years.

American Association, 1882–1891

Three of the six clubs that formed the AA in 1882 still represent their cities in the majors today: Allegheny (Pittsburgh), Cincinnati, and St. Louis. Brooklyn, which entered the AA two years later, today represents Los Angeles. The others:

Athletic of Philadelphia, AA 1882–1890. After finishing a distant second in the AA's first season, the Athletics in 1883 took the pennant from St. Louis by a single game. First baseman Harry Stovey, who led AA batters in most offensive categories that year, was even more productive in 1884. But the A's dropped to seventh and never again challenged for the crown. Expelled from the AA after the 1890 season for financial reasons, they were replaced by the Philadelphia club from the defunct Players League.

Baltimore Orioles, AA 1882–1889, 1890–1891, NL 1892–1899. After eight seasons out of pennant contention (including four in last place), the Orioles dropped out of the AA to play minor league ball in 1890. But toward the end of the season, when Brooklyn's new franchise went under, the Orioles returned to complete Brooklyn's season (finishing a combined last). After rising to third in 1891, the AA's final year, the Orioles were invited into the expanding NL, where they dropped to a twelfth-place last (54½ games out) in 1892.

Ned Hanlon, hired to manage Baltimore early in the 1892 season, set about building a championship club. By 1894, with a lineup that included six future Hall of Famers, Hanlon led his club to a narrow pennant victory over New York, though the Giants swept the Orioles in the first Temple Cup World Series, 4–0.

For five years Hanlon's brand of scrappy, hustling play made the Orioles the terror of the NL. Led by shortstop Hughie Jennings and outfielders Willie Keeler and Joe Kelley, the club repeated as NL champions in 1895 and 1896, and finished second to Boston the next two years. They lost the Temple Cup to Cleveland (1–4) in 1895, but swept the Spiders the next year 4–0, and took the cup again in 1897, defeating Boston 4–1 in what turned out to be the Series swan song.

Baltimore owners Hanlon and Harry Von der Horst purchased a half-interest in the Brooklyn club in 1899 (retaining a half-interest in Baltimore), and switched Jennings, Kelley, and Keeler to Brooklyn. Hanlon also went over as manager, leaving third baseman John McGraw in charge of the Orioles. McGraw hit .391 and rookie pitcher Joe McGinnity won 28 games to bring the team in fourth. But Hanlon's Superbas won the pennant, and when the NL cut back to eight teams after the season, Baltimore got the ax.

Eclipse of Louisville/Louisville Colonels (or Cy-

clones), AA 1882–1891, NL 1892–1899. The club, which changed its official name from Eclipse to Louisville after the 1883 season, was one of only two teams to play all ten seasons of the major league AA. (St. Louis—the present Cardinals—was the other.) Louisville finished above .500 in five of its first six years, but only once in that time closed within ten games of the top—in 1884, when Guy Hecker's 52 wins brought the team in third. Slugger Pete Browning paced the Colonel offense in their early years, winning batting titles in 1882 (his rookie season), 1885 and 1886, and hammering a second-best .402 in 1887. (A bat made for him by woodworker John Hillerich inspired the creation of the Louisville Slugger.)

By 1889, though, the club had sunk to last place, finishing 66½ games out of first, with 111 losses. The next year, although Hecker and Browning defected to the outlaw PL, the club was less affected by deserters than other AA teams. The Colonels (paced by the league's best hitter, William "Chicken" Wolf, and its best pitcher, Scott Stratton) made one of the greatest turnarounds in big league history, winning the pennant by 10 games over second-place Columbus. In the World Series against Brooklyn, poor weather and small crowds ended play after the teams had tied once and won three apiece.

Even though the Colonels finished next to last in 1891, they were one of four clubs taken into the NL after the AA folded. They never finished higher than ninth in the NL, and for three straight years (1894–1896) they occupied the cellar. When the league cut back from twelve teams to eight after the 1899 season, Louisville merged with the Pittsburgh Pirates.

Columbus Colts (or Senators), AA 1883–1884. From sixth place in 1883, Columbus climbed to second in 1884 behind the 34–13 pitching of rookie Ed Morris. But when the AA dropped back from twelve clubs to eight in 1885, Columbus was out.

Metropolitan of New York, AA 1883–1887. After success in minor league and independent play since 1880, the Mets entered the AA in 1883 as the association expanded from six clubs to eight. With 41 victories from pitcher Tim Keefe (who was picked up from disbanded Troy), the Mets finished fourth. The next season, with first baseman Dave Orr hitting .354 in his first full major league season and pitcher Jack Lynch matching Keefe with 37 wins apiece, the Mets won the AA pennant handily. But they lost baseball's first World Series to the Providence Grays. When manager Jim Mutrie, third baseman Dude Esterbrook, and pitcher Keefe were transferred in 1885 to the New York Giants (the two clubs had the same owner), the Mets sank to seventh place, where they finished in their final three seasons.

Indianapolis Blues, AA 1884. Finished eleventh of twelve clubs, 46 games behind.

Toledo Blue Stockings, AA 1884. Catcher Fleet Walker (who played in 42 games) and his brother Welday (5 games) were the major leagues' first black players—and the only blacks until Jackie Robinson broke the color bar for good in 1947.

Washington, D.C., AA 1884. The popularity of the city's UA Nationals proved too much for this inept AA club, which went under in early August.

Virginia of Richmond, AA 1884. When Washington disbanded in August, the Wilmington club of the Eastern League was invited to join the AA as its replacement. Wilmington declined (and later jumped to the UA), but Virginia—also a member of the EL—accepted the invitation and took over Washington's remaining games. Washington-Virginia finished a combined 24–81, in last place.

Cleveland Spiders, AA 1887–1888, NL 1889–1899. After two losing seasons in the AA, the Spiders moved to the NL, where they continued below .500 for three more years. But in 1892 Cy Young's league-leading pitching brought them the second-half championship of the league's experimental split season. Cleveland lost the World Series to first-half winner Boston, losing five after tying the first game.

Second-place finishes in 1895 and 1896 qualified the Spiders for the Temple Cup series against champion Baltimore. In 1895 they beat the Orioles for the world title four games to one, but were swept the next year 0–4.

In 1899, when owner Frank Robison transferred all the team's best players to St. Louis (which he also owned), Cleveland suffered the worst season in major league history, winning only 20 games while losing a record 134. They finished 35 games behind eleventh-place Washington and 84 games out of first. After the season the Spiders died, as the NL cut back from twelve teams to eight.

Kansas City Blues, AA 1888–1889. Finished last in 1888, next to last in 1889.

Columbus Colts (or Solons), AA 1889–1891. In 1890, with the AA weakened by the replacement of half its franchises with new clubs and by defections to the outlaw PL, Columbus (which retained several of its regulars) rose from its 1889 sixth-place finish to second behind Louisville. When the PL folded and the defectors returned in 1891, Columbus dropped back to sixth.

Brooklyn Gladiators, AA 1890. Formed as a replacement for the Brooklyn club that forsook the AA for the NL in 1890, the Gladiators floundered and were replaced by Baltimore late in the season.

Rochesters, AA 1890. Played .500 ball, finishing fifth.

Syracuse Stars, AA 1890. Finished sixth.

Toledo Maumees, AA 1890. Finished fourth.

Cincinnati Porkers, AA 1891. Also known as "Kelly's Killers" for their manager Mike "King" Kelly, the club went bankrupt in August and was replaced by Milwaukee.

Milwaukee Brewers, AA 1891. This Western League club moved up to the AA in August. Taking five players and the 43–57 record from the defunct Cincinnati club, Milwaukee went 21–15 the rest of the way to lift the Cincinnati-Milwaukee combination from seventh to fifth by season's end.

Washington Senators, AA 1891, NL 1892–1899. Despite a cellar finish in the AA's final year, the Senators were taken into the expanding NL. Of its nine losing seasons, the best was a tie for sixth in the twelve-team NL of 1897.

Union Association, 1884

Formed in opposition to the reserve rule that governed players in the NL and AA, the UA struggled through one season. The first eight clubs listed here began the season. The other five are listed according to the month they entered the UA as replacement teams. All thirteen—like the UA itself—are long extinct:

Altoona, Pa., Unions, UA 1884. The first of several UA clubs to drop out of competition during the season, Altoona disbanded on May 31, but reorganized as an independent club two days later with many of the same players.

Baltimore Unions, UA 1884. Bill Sweeney's league-leading 40 wins accounted for 70 percent of third-place Baltimore's victories.

Boston Unions, UA 1884. Outfielder Tom McCarthy, the UA's only Hall of Famer, hit .215 in this, his rookie big league season. Boston finished fourth.

Chicago Browns/Pittsburgh Stogies, UA 1884. Financial woes caused the Chicago Browns to relocate in Pittsburgh in late August, but the club quit altogether less than a month later.

Cincinnati Outlaw Reds, UA 1884. With three 20-game winners—including Jim McCormick, who won 21 after defecting from the NL in midseason—Cincinnati compiled a strong 69–36 record, but still finished 21 games behind champion St. Louis.

Keystone of Philadelphia, UA 1884. In early August Keystone dropped out of the league and reorganized as an independent semipro club.

National of Washington, D.C., UA 1884. Finished sixth, 46½ games back.

St. Louis Maroons, UA 1884, NL 1885–1886. Batting 47 points above the league average, the Maroons scored 184 runs more than the next-best club to run away with the pennant. They were the only UA club to survive 1884 as a major league team, but in the NL they were unable to fashion a winning season or finish higher than sixth.

Kansas City Unions, UA 1884. Formed to replace Altoona, Kansas City went 16–63 in its partial season.

Wilmington, Del., UA 1884. After Wilmington had gone 51–12 to sew up the Eastern League championship, they jumped to the UA in August to replace Philadelphia's Keystones. But as several players failed to make the jump with them, the move was a disaster on the field (2–16) and financially. They failed in mid-September.

Milwaukee Grays, UA 1884. One of only two teams left in the deteriorating Northwestern League, Milwaukee moved up to the UA in September to complete the schedule of dropout Wilmington.

St. Paul White Caps, UA 1884. With the disbanding of the Northwestern League in September, St. Paul joined the UA to take over Pittsburgh's remaining games.

Players League, 1890

Formed in rebellion against the Brush classification plan, a scheme to limit players' pay, the PL drew many of the finest players from the NL and AA, and proved the most popular league with the fans. But when only one club turned a profit, the clubs' financial backers deserted and the league died. Two clubs were admitted to the AA, and many of the rest merged with their National League counterparts:

Boston Red Stockings, PL 1890, AA 1891. Boston won the PL pennant with such stars as Dan Brouthers, Old Hoss Radbourne, Hardy Richardson, and manager King Kelly. The only PL club to make money, Boston joined the AA the next year and won another pennant. But when the

popular Kelly defected to Boston's NL Beaneaters (who also won a pennant for the city in 1891), the fans defected too, and the Red Stockings died along with the AA at the end of the season.

Brooklyn Wonders, PL 1890. At the end of a season in which they edged New York for second place, the Wonders merged with Brooklyn's NL pennant-winners.

Buffalo Bisons, PL 1890. After a last-place finish 20 games back of their nearest competitor, the Bisons simply went out of business.

Chicago Pirates, PL 1890. Mark Baldwin, with a league-high 34 wins, and Charles "Silver" King, with 30, pitched Chicago into fourth place. Both went to Pittsburgh the next year, although the franchise was absorbed by Chicago's NL Colts.

Cleveland Infants, PL 1890. Like Cleveland's NL Spiders of 1890, the Infants finished next to last. But one of their three managers, infielder Oliver Wendell "Patsy" Tebeau, would go on to lead the Spiders to their finest seasons.

Philadelphia Quakers, PL 1890, *Athletic* AA 1891. Although they finished sixth in their PL season, the Quakers compiled a winning record. When the Athletics of the AA were expelled following the 1890 season, the Quakers were admitted in their place and awarded the name "Athletic." The team finished fourth in 1891, but was not among the four clubs taken into the NL when the AA folded, because Philadelphia already had an NL team (the Phillies).

New York Giants, PL 1890. Paced by the hitting of first baseman Roger Connor and outfielder Jim O'Rourke, New York's PL Giants finished third. In November the club merged with the city's NL Giants.

Pittsburgh Burghers, PL 1890. After a sixth-place finish, the Pittsburgh PL club and the NL Allegheny Club combined to form the new Pittsburgh Athletic club, which still represents Pittsburgh in the NL.

American League, 1901–

When Western League president Ban Johnson renamed the circuit in 1900 and proclaimed it a major league the next year, he little knew how stable it would be. For over half a century (1903–1953) the same eight clubs represented the same eight cities. Even today, although the league has expanded and several clubs have moved to new cities, not one franchise has perished.

Federal League, 1914–1915

After an inaugural season as a six-team minor league in 1913, the FL expanded to eight teams and declared war on the NL and AL for their players. After two big league seasons, and despite two of the game's most exciting pennant races ever, the league died for lack of patronage, and with it went its eight franchises:

Baltimore Terrapins, FL 1914–1915. Jack Quinn and George Suggs, with 26 and 25 wins, pitched Baltimore to third place in 1914. But when Quinn and Suggs lost their stuff the next year, the club sank out of sight, 24 games behind seventh-place Brooklyn.

Brooklyn Tip-Tops (or Brookfeds), FL 1914–1915. Not even the acquisition of batting and base-stealing champ Benny Kauff could stop Brooklyn from slipping from fifth in 1914 to seventh the next year.

Buffalo Buffeds, FL 1914–1915. Finished fourth in 1914, sixth the next year.

Chicago Chifeds (or Whales), FL 1914–1915. After leading the league through July and much of August in 1914, only to lose out after a late-season struggle with Indianapolis, the Whales came back in 1915 to triumph in an even tighter race that saw the three top teams separated at the finish by only half a game. Owner Charles Weeghman was permitted to buy the NL Cubs in 1916, and many Whales joined the Cubs in play at what was then Weeghman Park and now is known as Wrigley Field.

Indianapolis Federals (or Hoosiers), FL 1914; *Newark Peps*, FL 1915. Five regulars hit over .300 (paced by Benny Kauff's league-leading .370) in 1914, and the team as a whole hit twenty-two points above the league average. From fourth place in August the Hoosiers fought back to capture the flag from Chicago by 1½ games, with seven consecutive wins at the end. The only major league pennant-winner to move to a new city the next year, the Hoosiers became the Peps in 1915. Though they remained competitive into September, an eight-game losing streak dropped them out of the race and they finished fifth.

Kansas City Packers, FL 1914–1915. After a sixth-place finish in 1914, the Packers competed in a five-way race through much of 1915. But from first place on August 21 they dropped to fifth a week later and finished fourth.

Pittsburgh Rebels, FL 1914–1915. After avoiding last place in 1914 only by St. Louis's late-season nosedive, Pittsburgh turned itself around the next year, luring first baseman Ed Konetchy from their NL rival Pirates, and pitcher Frank Allen from the NL Brooklyn Robins. Both enjoyed the best season of their careers to lead the Rebels into first place in late August, where they remained until they were dropped to third by losing three out of four at the end to the champion Whales.

St. Louis Terriers, FL 1914–1915. After finishing last in 1914, St. Louis added veteran pitcher Eddie Plank to its roster. From a club with two 20-game losers, the Terriers became in 1915 a team with three 20-game winners (including Plank), pulling up from fifth late in August to catch the leaders with a nine-game winning streak. At the finish, though, they ranked second—by less than one percentage point, the narrowest big league pennant margin ever. For 1916, Terriers' owner Phil Ball took over the AL St. Louis Browns.

Postseason Play

Frederick Ivor-Campbell

As we all know, major-league baseball doesn't end with the end of the season. There follows the *post-season*—the League Championship Series and the World Series—when even the most casual fan is stirred to follow the games which determine, eventually, the world's best team.

Once there was much more baseball played in the postseason. In the 1880s, for example, nearly every major-league club played a couple of weeks of postseason games, generally exhibitions against clubs they didn't face during the regular season—like teams from the other major league, or a minor league.

Before there was a World Series there were city and regional series. In 1882 Cleveland defeated Cincinnati for the championship of Ohio, and the next year teams in Philadelphia and New York played for the championships of those cities. These were informal series, arranged by the clubs themselves without official league sanction, and varied in the number of games scheduled according to the desires of the clubs involved.

The same held true for the early World Series, which had their beginnings in 1884. Two years earlier, the champions of the National League and the brand-new American Association played a pair of postseason contests (in which each team recorded a shutout against the other). Some would like to call these games the first World Series, but no one in 1882 saw them as more than exhibition games. In fact, because the NL didn't yet recognize the legitimacy of the AA and forbade its clubs to play those of the new league, the NL champion Chicago White Stockings had to release their players from their season contracts so they could face AA champion Cincinnati as technically independent players.

That winter the two major leagues made their peace, and although a proposed series between the 1883 NL and AA titlists was called off, the 1884 champion Providence Grays (NL) and the Metropolitan Club of New York (AA) played three games "for the championship of the United States." The winning Grays were acclaimed in the press as "champions of the world," and the World Series was born.

The brief 1884 Series set the stage for more elaborate World Series to follow. From 1885 through 1890 the NL and AA pennant-winners met in Series that ranged in length from six games to 15.

The demise of the AA after the 1891 season caused a one-year gap in World Series play. When the National League expanded from eight clubs to twelve the next year (by absorbing four teams from the defunct AA), it divided the regular season into two halves, with the first-half winner playing the winner of the second half for the world title. Boston defeated Cleveland in the first official World Series, but the unpopular divided season was not repeated (that is, until the strike year of 1981).

Two years later a new World Series scheme was devised when one William C. Temple offered a prize cup to the winner of a postseason series between the first- and second-place finishers in the NL. For four years these best-of-seven Temple Cup games served as the officially recognized world championship. But by the end of four lopsided Series (only one of which was won by the pennant-winning club), fan interest—never robust—had declined so much that the trophy was returned to its donor and the series abandoned.

In 1900, partisans of second-place Pittsburgh felt that their Pirates were the equal of pennant-winning Brooklyn, and a Pittsburgh newspaper, the *Chronicle-Telegraph*, offered a silver trophy cup to the winner of a best-of-five series between the clubs, to be played entirely in Pittsburgh. Described in the press as the "world's championship series," the games confirmed the superiority of Brooklyn's Superbas, who needed only four games to subdue the hometown Pirates.

The upgrading of the American League from minor- to major-league status in 1901 made a return to interleague World Series play theoretically possible, but it was not until after the NL and AL had made peace in 1903 that the first modern Series was contested. The owners of NL champion Pittsburgh and AL champion Boston arranged a best-of-nine postseason Series in 1903, which proved both popular and financially successful—a firm foundation for future Series. When the NL pennant-winning Giants refused to meet repeating AL titlist Boston in 1904, press and fan disappointment led baseball's National Commission to establish the World Series officially and permanently in 1905.

The end of the 1903 season saw not only the first modern World Series, but also a revival of city and regional series (which had lapsed when the AA folded) in Chicago, Philadelphia, St. Louis, and Ohio. In 1905 the National Commission offered to oversee these series, too, and give them the stability of official sanction. Until the manpower needs of the World War halted the 1918 season a month early (discouraging postseason play apart from the World Series), most of the city and regional series—and occasional series between other clubs, like Cleveland and Pittsburgh, and the Boston Red Sox and New York Giants—were played under National Commission auspices.

After the war's end, only Chicago's Cubs and White Sox resumed a city series; they played 16 series between 1921 and 1942, when World War II intervened. For 26 years thereafter the World Series alone remained of the once multifaceted major-league postseason—until the AL and NL split into two divisions each in 1969 and ushered in a new layer of playoffs: the League Championship Series. (In 1981, to recoup some of the money and fan interest lost during a midseason players' strike that split the season in half, a one-time third layer of postseason playoffs was added, pitting the first-half and second-half winners in each division against each other for the division titles—an aberration that made even more of a mockery of the divisional races than the strike itself had done.) From 1969 through 1984 the LCS were played as best-of-five series, but in 1985 they were expanded to match the best-of-seven World Series.

Key to the Statistics

The statistics in this section of *Total Baseball* are standard—there is little point in applying newer analytical measures to performances that run to seven games or fewer. We do offer, however, stats that were not standard at the time, such as earned run averages for years before 1912 and runs batted in before 1920 (which were determined from box scores and play-by-plays) and saves before 1969. Beyond our powers of reconstruction were the following: runs batted in for the World Series of 1884 and 1885; stolen bases for 1884 and 1885; and batter strikeouts for 1885.

Ignoring the odd 1887 custom of counting walks as base hits, we present the cumulative box score for that year's World Series in accordance with modern practice. Other curiosities of early postseason play include the use of neutral sites for some games in 1885 and 1888 and for the majority of games in 1887, and the use of players who did not appear in so much as an inning for that team during the regular season (Tom Forster, New York Mets, 1884; Bug Holliday, Chicago, 1885; Sy Sutcliffe, Detroit, 1887; Jumbo Davis, Brooklyn 1889).

The length of the World Series varied from three games in 1884 all the way up to fifteen in 1887 and ten the following year. The best-of-seven format came in with the Temple Cup Series of 1894 and has been the norm for World Series ever since (excepting 1900, 1903, and 1919–1921). In recent years this format has become the norm for League Championship Series as well.

If a player appeared at more than one position during the Series, the number of games he played at each is noted (for example, a man who divided seven games at shortstop and third base would carry the notation *ss-4, 3b-3*). Other abbreviations are as follows:

POS	Position	SB	Stolen Bases
AVG	Batting average	W	Wins
G	Games	L	Losses
AB	At bats	ERA	Earned run average
R	Runs	GS	Games started
H	Hits	CG	Complete games
2B	Doubles	SHO	Shutouts
3B	Triples	SV	Saves
HR	Home runs	IP	Innings pitched
RB	Runs batted in	ER	Earned runs
BB	Bases on Balls	SO	Strikeouts

After a flurry of boasts and challenges, Met manager Jim Mutrie and the Grays' Frank Bancroft arranged a three-game series in New York to determine which team was the nation's best. These were not the first games between NL and AA pennant winners. In 1882, the AA's first season, champion Cincinnati met NL titlist Chicago twice as part of its postseason schedule, in games viewed simply as exhibition contests. (Each team won one). The next year a postseason series was proposed between champions Boston (NL) and the Athletics of Philadelphia (AA), but the Athletics fared so poorly in exhibitions against lesser NL teams that they refused to face Boston.

The 1884 Series was touted as "for the championship of the United States," but the influential weekly *Sporting Life* established precedent for future Series hype by naming victorious Providence "Champions of the World." The weather turned cold and windy as the Series got under way. A hardy opening game crowd of 2,500 saw the Grays' great Charlie "Old Hoss" Radbourn blank the Mets on two singles. Met pitcher Tim Keefe, wild at the start, paved the way for two first-inning Providence runs by hitting the first two men to face him and assisted them around the bases with a pair of wild pitches. Paul Hines singled in the third for the Grays' first hit and scored as a passed ball and two more wild pitches brought him home. Keefe yielded only four other hits, but they came back to back in the seventh to produce the Grays' final three runs.

The 1,000 spectators at Game Two witnessed the Series' closest contest. Keefe and Radbourn overwhelmed their opposition for four innings, but in the top of the fifth the Grays bunched three of their five hits for three two-out runs as Jerry Denny homered over the center field fence. The Mets responded with a run in the last of the fifth, but scored no more before darkness ended the game after seven innings.

The Grays had clinched the championship with their second win, and when they saw only a few hundred diehards in the stands for Game Three, they wanted to go home. The Mets must have regretted their insistence on playing the game. Although darkness halted it after only six innings, rookie Met pitcher Buck Becannon (replacing Keefe, who umpired) and awful Mets fielding gave Providence eleven or twelve runs (scorers lost count), while Radbourn held the New Yorkers to a pair of unearned tallies.

Providence Grays (NL), 3; New York Mets (AA), 0

PRO (N)

PLAYER/POS	AVG	G	AB	R	H	2B	3B	HR	RB	BB	SO	SB
Cliff Carroll, of	.100	3	10	2	1	0	0	0		1	1	
Jerry Denny, 3b	.444	3	9	3	4	0	1	1		0	3	
Jack Farrell, 2b	.444	3	9	3	4	2	0	0		0	0	
Barney Gilligan, c	.444	3	9	3	4	2	0	0		0	1	
Paul Hines, of	.250	3	8	5	2	0	0	0		3	0	
Arthur Irwin, ss	.222	3	9	2	2	0	1	0		0	2	
Charlie Radbourn, p	.100	3	10	1	1	0	0	0		3	3	
Paul Radford, of	.000	3	7	1	0	0	0	0		0	1	
Joe Start, 1b	.100	3	10	0	1	0	0	0		0	2	
TOTAL	.235		81	20	19	4	2	1		5	13	

PITCHER	W	L	ERA	G	GS	CG	SV	SHO	IP	H	ER	BB	SO
Charlie Radbourn	3	0	0.00	3	3	3	0	1	22.0	11	0	0	16
TOTAL	3	0	0.00	3	3	3	0	1	22.0	11	0	0	16

NY (A)

PLAYER/POS	AVG	G	AB	R	H	2B	3B	HR	RB	BB	SO	SB
Buck Becannon, p	.500	1	2	0	1	0	0	0		0	0	
Steve Brady, of	.000	3	10	1	0	0	0	0		0	1	
Dude Esterbrook, 3b	.300	3	10	0	3	1	0	0		0	3	
Tom Forster, 2b	.000	1	3	0	0	0	0	0		0	1	
Bill Holbert, c	.000	1	2	0	0	0	0	0		0	1	
Tim Keefe, p	.200	2	5	0	1	0	0	0		0	4	
Ed Kennedy, of	.000	3	7	0	0	0	0	0		0	2	
Candy Nelson, ss	.100	3	10	0	1	0	0	0		0	1	
Dave Orr, 1b	.111	3	9	0	1	0	0	0		0	0	
Charlie Reipschlager, c	.000	2	5	1	0	0	0	0		0	1	
Chief Roseman, of	.333	3	9	1	3	0	0	0		0	1	
Dasher Troy, 2b	.200	2	5	0	1	0	0	0		0	1	
TOTAL	.143		77	3	11	1	0	0		0	16	

PITCHER	W	L	ERA	G	GS	CG	SV	SHO	IP	H	ER	BB	SO
Buck Becannon	0	1	3.00	1	1	1	0	0	6.0	9	2	2	1
Tim Keefe	0	2	3.60	2	2	2	0	0	15.0	10	6	3	12
TOTAL	0	3	3.43	3	3	3	0	0	21.0	19	8	5	13

GAME 1 AT NY OCT 23

NY	000 000 000	0	2	0
PRO	201 000 30X	6	5	2

Pitchers: KEEFE vs RADBOURN
Attendance: 2,500

GAME 2 AT NY OCT 24

PRO	000 030 0	3	5	4
NY	000 010 0	1	3	1

Pitchers: RADBOURN vs KEEFE
Home Runs: Denny-PRO
Attendance: 1,000
(Game called at end of seventh, darkness)

GAME 3 AT NY OCT 25

PRO	120 044	11	9	3
NY	000 011	2	6	9

Pitchers: RADBOURN vs BECANNON
Attendance: 300
(Game called at end of sixth, darkness)

Before the start of the final game, the two clubs agreed to throw out Game Two, which had been forfeited to Chicago, leaving the Series tied at two wins apiece, plus the one tie. But after the Browns won the seventh game for their third victory, Chicago manager Cap Anson decided his club should retain its forfeit win after all, and a select committee agreed, leaving the Series in a tie instead of a White Stocking defeat.

Game One, in Chicago, was called for darkness after eight innings, with the score tied 5–5. The Browns scored first with a run in the second and added four more in the top of the fourth. But Chicago came back with a run in the last of the fourth, and in the bottom of the eighth scored four more on a walk, two singles, and Fred Pfeffer's game-tying three-run homer.

The Series moved to St. Louis for the next three games. Chicago was leading 5–4 in the sixth inning of Game Two when Browns manager Charlie Comiskey pulled his team off the field, objecting to the umpiring of David Sullivan. Umpire Sullivan later forfeited the game to the White Stockings; he worked no more in the Series. The Browns won Game Three, scoring five unearned runs with two out in the top of the first, and holding on for a 7–4 win. Chicago lost again the next day in a much closer game. The Browns scored first with a run in the third inning, but Abner Dalrymple's two-run homer in the fifth gave the White Stockings a 2–1 lead. In the bottom of the eighth, however, St. Louis scored twice and held on for the 3–2 win.

The Series took to the road for its final three games. In Pittsburgh for Game Five, Chicago overwhelmed the Browns 9–2, scoring four runs in the first inning, and their final three just before darkness ended the game after seven innings.

Game Six and Seven were played in Cincinnati. The White Stockings won the sixth game by the same 9–2 score as Game Five. The Browns' two runs were unearned, as Chicago's Jim McCormick stopped St. Louis on just two hits, both singles. The Brown's victory in the finale was a runaway 13–4, called in the eighth for darkness. St. Louis' six-run fourth inning typified the game's sloppy play, the runs scoring on five hits, four errors, and two passed balls.

Chicago White Stockings (NL), 3; St. Louis Browns (AA), 3; tie, 1

CHI (N)

PLAYER/POS	AVG	G	AB	R	H	2B	3B	HR	RB	BB	SO	SB
Cap Anson, 1b	.423	7	26	8	11	1	1	0		2		
Tom Burns, ss-4,3b-3	.080	7	25	3	2	0	1	0		0		
John Clarkson, p-2,of-2	.154	4	13	1	2	1	0	0		0		
Abner Dalrymple, of	.269	7	26	4	7	2	0	1		2		
Silver Flint, c	.143	4	14	0	2	0	0	0		0		
George Gore, of	.000	1	3	1	0	0	0	0		1		
Bug Holliday, of	.000	1	4	0	0	0	0	0		0		
King Kelly, of-4,c-3	.346	7	26	9	9	3	1	0		2		
Jim McCormick, p	.176	5	17	1	3	0	0	0		0		
Fred Pfeffer, 2b	.407	7	27	5	11	2	0	1		0		
Billy Sunday, of	.273	6	22	5	6	2	0	0		2		
N. Williamson, 3b-4,ss-3	.087	7	23	1	2	0	0	0		4		
TOTAL	.243		226	38	55	11	3	2		13		

PITCHER	W	L	ERA	G	GS	CG	SV	SHO	IP	H	ER	BB	SO
John Clarkson	0	1	1.13	2	2	2	0	0	16.0	15	2	1	15
Jim McCormick	3	2	2.00	5	5	5	0	0	36.0	27	8	6	19
TOTAL	3	3	1.73	7	7	7	0	0	52.0	42	10	7	34

STL (A)

PLAYER/POS	AVG	G	AB	R	H	2B	3B	HR	RB	BB	SO	SB
Sam Barkley, 2b	.087	7	23	3	2	0	0	0		2		
Doc Bushong, c	.154	4	13	1	2	0	0	0		0		
Bob Caruthers, p-3,of-2	.200	5	15	1	3	0	1	0		1		
Charlie Comiskey, 1b	.292	7	24	6	7	0	0	0		0		
Dave Foutz, p	.167	4	12	1	2	0	0	0		0		
Bill Gleason, ss	.231	7	26	5	6	2	0	0		1		
Arlie Latham, 3b	.318	7	22	5	7	3	0	0		2		
Hugh Nicol, of	.000	1	2	0	0	0	0	0		0		
Tip O'Neill, of	.208	7	24	4	5	0	0	0		0		
Yank Robinson, of-4,c-3	.174	7	23	5	4	0	1	0		1		
Curt Welch, of	.148	7	27	5	4	1	1	0		0		
TOTAL	.199		211	36	42	6	3	0		7		

PITCHER	W	L	ERA	G	GS	CG	SV	SHO	IP	H	ER	BB	SO
Bob Caruthers	1	1	2.42	3	3	3	0	0	26.0	25	7	4	16
Dave Foutz	2	2	0.61	4	4	4	0	0	29.1	30	2	9	14
TOTAL	3	3	1.46	7	7	7	0	0	55.1	55	9	13	30

GAME 1 AT CHI OCT 14

STL	010 400 00	5	7	2
CHI	000 100 04	5	5	10

Pitchers: CARUTHERS vs CLARKSON
Home Runs: Pfeffer-CHI
Attendance: 2,000
(Game called at end of eighth, darkness)

GAME 2 AT STL OCT 15

CHI	110 003	5	6	5
STL	300 10X	4	2	4

Pitchers: McCORMICK vs FOUTZ
Attendance: 2,000
(Game forfeited to Chicago in bottom of sixth)

GAME 3 AT STL OCT 16

CHI	111 000 001	4	8	7
STL	500 002 00X	7	8	4

Pitchers: CLARKSON vs CARUTHERS
Attendance: 3,000

GAME 4 AT STL OCT 17

CHI	000 020 000	2	8	3
STL	001 000 02X	3	6	7

Pitchers: McCORMICK vs FOUTZ
Home Runs: Dalrymple-CHI
Attendance: 3,000

GAME 5 AT PIT OCT 22

CHI	400 110 3	9	7	1
STL	010 000 1	2	4	7

Pitchers: CLARKSON vs FOUTZ
Attendance: 500
(Game called at end of seventh, darkness)

GAME 6 AT CIN OCT 23

CHI	200 111 040	9	11	7
STL	002 000 000	2	2	7

Pitchers: McCORMICK vs CARUTHERS
Attendance: 1,500

GAME 7 AT CIN OCT 24

CHI	200 020 00	4	9	9
STL	004 621 0X	13	13	5

Pitchers: McCORMICK vs FOUTZ
Attendance: 1,200
(Game called in eighth, darkness)

It was a winner-take-all Series, with the club that won four games pocketing the entire proceeds. Attendance, very good for those days, averaged over 7,000 per game and brought the victorious Browns about $14,000.

The first three games were played in Chicago. The White Stockings won the opener on a sparkling five-hit shutout by their ace John Clarkson. But St. Louis's Bob Caruthers improved on Clarkson's performance the next day, blanking Chicago on just two singles as his Browns turned thirteen hits and thirteen Chicago errors into twelve runs (in a game shortened by darkness to eight innings). The White Stockings improved their fielding in the next game (which was also called after eight innings), and this time their bats came alive. With eleven hits (including home runs by Mike "King" Kelly and George Gore) combining with seven St. Louis errors, they regained the Series advantage with an easy 11–4 win.

When the venue shifted to St. Louis, though, the Browns battled back. In a back-and-forth battle in Game Four, Chicago tied the game at 5–5 with a pair of runs in the sixth, but St. Louis scored three final runs a half inning later, winning when darkness ended play in the middle of the seventh.

Game Five repeated Game Two's innovation: two umpires (instead of the usual one), plus a "referee" who stood between the pitcher and second base. The umpiring satisfied everyone, but Chicago, handicapped by their scheduled pitcher's sore arm, lost when they sent shortstop Ned Williamson and right fielder Jimmy Ryan into the box. In the 6½ innings before dark, St. Louis got to Williamson and Ryan for eleven hits and ten runs as their Nat Hudson held Chicago batters to three hits and three unearned runs.

The finale proved to be the Series' best-played and closest game. Chicago's Clarkson shut out the Browns through seven innings as his mates built a three-run lead—one of them scored on Fred's Pfeffer's homer in the fourth. Rain (and a rowdy crowd which poured onto the field) halted play for a while in the fifth. But the game resumed and the rain subsided. In the last of the eighth, Charlie Comiskey scored the Browns' first run on a single, errant throw and run-scoring fly out, and Arlie Latham tripled home two more runners later in the inning to tie the game. The score remained 3–3 into the last of the tenth, when the Browns' Curt Welch singled (for

only the fourth St. Louis hit), went to second on an infield hit, and took third on a sacrifice. Welch then attempted to steal home but catcher Kelly had smelled out the play and called for a pitch out. Clarkson's delivery was poor and bobbled by Kelly, allowing Welch to steal home with a "$15,000 slide" for the Browns' triumph.

St. Louis Browns (AA), 4; Chicago White Stockings (NL), 2

STL (A)

PLAYER/POS	AVG	G	AB	R	H	2B	3B	HR	RB	BB	SO	SB
Doc Bushong, c	.188	6	16	4	3	1	0	0	2	4	5	0
Bob Caruthers, p-3,of-3	.250	6	24	6	6	1	2	0	5	1	4	1
Charlie Comiskey, 1b	.292	6	24	2	7	1	0	0	2	0	4	0
Dave Foutz, p-2,of-2	.200	4	15	2	3	1	1	0	3	0	3	0
Bill Gleason, ss	.208	6	24	3	5	0	0	0	5	1	3	0
Nat Hudson, p-1,of-1	.167	2	6	1	1	0	1	0	0	1	3	0
Arlie Latham, 3b-6,c-1	.174	6	23	4	4	0	1	0	3	3	4	2
Tip O'Neill, of	.400	6	20	4	8	0	2	2	5	4	5	2
Yank Robinson, 2b	.316	6	19	5	6	1	1	0	3	2	3	2
Curt Welch, of	.350	6	20	7	7	2	0	0	1	3	4	2
TOTAL	.262		191	38	50	7	8	2	29	19	38	9

PITCHER	W	L	ERA	G	GS	CG	SV	SHO	IP	H	ER	BB	SO
Bob Caruthers	2	1	2.42	3	3	3	0	1	26.0	18	7	6	12
Dave Foutz	1	1	3.60	2	2	2	0	0	15.0	16	6	6	7
Nat Hudson	1	0	2.57	1	1	1	0	0	7.0	3	2	3	3
TOTAL	4	2	2.81	6	6	6	0	1	48.0	37	15	15	22

CHI (N)

PLAYER/POS	AVG	G	AB	R	H	2B	3B	HR	RB	BB	SO	SB
Cap Anson, 1b-6,c-2	.238	6	21	3	5	1	0	0	1	4	0	1
Tom Burns, 3b-6,of-1	.286	6	21	2	6	2	1	0	1	0	2	0
John Clarkson, p-4,of-1	.067	4	15	0	1	0	0	0	1	0	2	1
Abner Dalrymple, of	.190	6	21	2	4	1	1	0	2	0	5	1
Silver Flint, c	.000	1	3	0	0	0	0	0	1	0	1	0
George Gore, of	.174	6	23	4	4	0	0	1	2	3	3	0
King Kelly, c-5,ss-2,1b-1,3b-1	.208	6	24	4	5	0	0	1	1	2	2	1
Jim McCormick, p	.000	1	3	0	0	0	0	0	0	0	0	0
Fred Pfeffer, 2b	.286	6	21	7	6	0	0	1	4	2	1	2
Jimmy Ryan, of-6,p-1,ss-1	.250	6	20	4	5	1	0	0	2	0	1	1
Ned Williamson, ss-6,p-2,c-1,of-1	.056	6	18	2	1	0	1	0	3	4	5	1
TOTAL	.195		190	28	37	5	3	3	18	15	22	8

PITCHER	W	L	ERA	G	GS	CG	SV	SHO	IP	H	ER	BB	SO
John Clarkson	2	2	2.01	4	4	3	0	1	31.1	25	7	12	28
Jim McCormick	0	1	6.75	1	1	1	0	0	8.0	13	6	2	4
Jimmy Ryan	0	0	9.00	1	0	0	0	0	5.0	8	5	4	4
Ned Williamson	0	1	4.50	2	1	0	0	0	2.0	4	1	1	2
TOTAL	2	4	3.69	8	6	4	0	1	46.1	50	19	19	38

GAME 1 AT CHI OCT 18

STL	000 000 000	0	5	3
CHI	200 001 03X	6	10	4

Pitchers: FOUTZ vs CLARKSON
Attendance: 6,000

GAME 2 AT CHI OCT 19

STL	200 230 50	12	13	2
CHI	000 000 00	0	2	10

Pitchers: CARUTHERS vs McCORMICK
Home Runs: O'Neill-STL (2)
Attendance: 8,000
(Game called at end of eighth, darkness)

GAME 3 AT CHI OCT 20

CHI	200 112 32	11	11	2
STL	010 002 01	4	9	7

Pitchers: CLARKSON, Williamson (8) vs CARUTHERS
Home Runs: Kelly-CHI, Gore-CHI
Attendance: 6,000
(Game called at end of eighth, darkness)

GAME 4 AT STL OCT 21

CHI	300 002 0	5	6	4
STL	011 033 X	8	7	4

Pitchers: CLARKSON vs FOUTZ
Attendance: 8,000
(Game called in seventh, darkness)

GAME 5 AT STL OCT 22

CHI	011 100 00	3	3	3
STL	214 003 0X	10	11	3

Pitchers: WILLIAMSON, Ryan (2) vs HUDSON
Attendance: 10,000
(Game called in eighth, darkness)

GAME 6 AT STL OCT 23

CHI	010 101 000 0	3	6	2
STL	000 000 030 1	4	5	3

Pitchers: CLARKSON vs CARUTHERS
Home Runs: Pfeffer-CHI
Attendance: 8,000

Even though their star slugger Dan Brouthers was sidelined for all but one game by a sprained ankle, the Wolverines—in baseball's longest World Series, played in ten different cities—followed up their only pennant with an easy triumph over repeating AA champion St. Louis. The Browns won the opener at home, though, 6–1. They played errorless ball (rare in that era) as pitcher Bob Caruthers held Detroit scoreless until the ninth inning, and drove in the Browns' second run himself with a first-inning single.

The Wolverines came back to win the next three games. They took an early lead in Game Two and held on for a 5–3 win in St. Louis to even the Series. Then, in the Series' tightest game (played in Detroit) the Wolverines defeated Caruthers 2–1 in the last of the thirteenth when their pitcher Charlie Getzien led off with a single, advanced to second and third on ground outs, and scored on an infield error. In Game Four (in Pittsburgh) Detroit's Charles "Lady" Baldwin stopped the Browns on two hits for an easy 8–0 win.

Caruthers hurled a seven-hitter in Brooklyn for St. Louis's second win, but Detroit took the next four. Getzien contributed a two-hit shutout in New York, and Baldwin overcame Caruthers 3–1 in Philadelphia the next day. Getzien yielded eight hits the day after that in Boston, but Caruthers gave up thirteen, including two home runs to Sam Thompson, and Detroit took the game 9–2. Back in Philadelphia for Game Nine, St. Louis broke a 1–1 tie with a run in the top of the sixth. But the Wolverines scored two in the seventh and a final run in the eighth. The win gave Detroit a 7–2 Series advantage.

Game Ten, scheduled for the next day in Washington, was postponed because of rain until the following morning. Detroit's Hardy Richardson opened the game with a home run, but the Wolverines lost an opportunity to clinch the Series as the Browns overwhelmed Getzien with sixteen hits for an 11–4 victory featuring a triple play. But that afternoon, in Baltimore, Detroit took the deciding game as decisively as they had lost in the morning, knocking the Browns' Dave Foutz for fourteen hits (including four by Richardson and three—including a home run—by Larry Twitchell) as Baldwin held St. Louis to two hits in a 13–3 win.

The Browns and Wolverines split the final four meaningless games, played in Brooklyn,

Detroit Wolverines (NL), 10; St. Louis Browns (AA), 5

DET (N)

PLAYER/POS	AVG	G	AB	R	H	2B	3B	HR	RB	BB	SO	SB
Lady Baldwin, p	.235	5	17	1	4	1	0	0	1	2	2	1
Charlie Bennett, c-10,1b-3	.262	11	42	6	11	2	1	0	9	3	5	5
Dan Brouthers, 1b	.667	1	3	0	2	0	0	0	0	0	0	0
Pete Conway, p	.000	4	12	0	0	0	0	0	0	0	2	0
Fred Dunlap, 2b	.150	11	40	5	6	0	1	0	1	0	4	4
Charlie Ganzel, 1b-10,c-7	.224	14	58	5	13	1	0	0	2	1	2	3
Charlie Getzien, p	.300	6	20	5	6	2	0	0	2	3	6	1
Ned Hanlon, of	.220	15	50	5	11	1	1	0	4	5	1	7
Hardy Richardson, of-10,2b-5,3b-1	.197	15	66	12	13	5	2	1	4	1	9	7
Jack Rowe, ss	.333	15	63	12	21	1	1	0	7	2	1	5
Cy Sutcliffe, 1b-3,c-1	.091	4	11	1	1	0	0	0	0	1	1	1
Sam Thompson, of	.362	15	58	8	21	2	0	2	7	3	3	5
Larry Twitchell, of	.250	6	20	5	5	1	0	1	3	0	1	1
Deacon White, 3b-14,1b-1	.207	15	58	8	12	1	1	0	3	2	0	2
TOTAL	.243		518	73	126	17	7	4	43	23	37	42

PITCHER	W	L	ERA	G	GS	CG	SV	SHO	IP	H	ER	BB	SO
Lady Baldwin	4	1	1.50	5	5	5	0	1	42.0	28	7	10	4
Pete Conway	2	2	3.00	4	4	4	0	0	33.0	31	11	6	10
Charlie Getzien	4	2	2.48	6	6	6	0	1	58.0	61	16	15	17
TOTAL	10	5	2.30	15	15	15	0	2	133.0	120	34	31	31

STL (A)

PLAYER/POS	AVG	G	AB	R	H	2B	3B	HR	RB	BB	SO	SB
Jack Boyle, c	.208	6	24	1	5	0	0	0	1	0	4	0
Doc Bushong, c	.241	9	29	3	7	0	0	0	1	4	1	0
Bob Caruthers, p-8,of-3	.239	10	46	2	11	0	0	0	3	1	1	3
Charlie Comiskey, 1b-14,of-1	.306	15	62	8	19	2	0	0	2	1	1	4
Dave Foutz, of-11,p-3,1b-1	.169	15	59	4	10	2	1	0	1	2	3	0
Bill Gleason, ss	.163	13	49	3	8	0	0	0	1	3	2	1
Silver King, p	.071	4	14	0	1	0	0	0	0	0	3	0
Arlie Latham, 3b	.293	15	58	12	17	1	0	1	0	9	2	15
Harry Lyons, ss	.286	2	7	3	2	0	0	0	0	1	0	0
Tip O'Neill, of	.200	15	65	7	13	2	1	1	5	0	2	0
Yank Robinson, 2b	.326	15	46	5	15	5	1	0	4	10	6	4
Curt Welch, of	.207	15	58	6	12	3	1	1	6	0	2	1
TOTAL	.232		517	54	120	15	4	2	25	31	27	28

PITCHER	W	L	ERA	G	GS	CG	SV	SHO	IP	H	ER	BB	SO
Bob Caruthers	4	4	2.13	8	8	8	0	0	71.2	64	17	12	19
Dave Foutz	0	3	3.46	3	3	3	0	0	26.0	36	10	9	6
Silver King	1	3	2.03	4	4	4	0	0	31.0	26	7	2	21
TOTAL	5	10	2.38	15	15	15	0	0	128.2	126	34	23	46

Detroit, Chicago, and St. Louis. For the first time in a World Series, two umpires officiated at all the games.

GAME 1 AT STL OCT 10

STL	200 040 000	6 12 0
DET	000 000 001	1 4 5

Pitchers: CARUTHERS vs GETZIEN
Attendance: 4,208

GAME 2 AT STL OCT 11

DET	022 000 100	5 10 2
STL	000 000 120	3 8 7

Pitchers: CONWAY vs FOUTZ
Attendance: 6,408

GAME 3 AT DET OCT 12

STL	010 000 000 000 0	1 13 7
DET	000 000 010 000 1	2 6 1

Pitchers: CARUTHERS vs GETZIEN
Attendance: 4,509

GAME 4 AT PIT OCT 13

DET	410 012 000	8 11 1
STL	000 000 000	0 2 6

Pitchers: BALDWIN vs KING
Attendance: 2,447

GAME 5 AT BRO OCT 14

STL	200 002 100	5 5 4
DET	000 020 000	2 7 5

Pitchers: CARUTHERS vs CONWAY
Attendance: 6,796

GAME 6 AT NY OCT 15

DET	330 000 003	9 12 1
STL	000 000 000	0 2 8

Pitchers: GETZIEN vs FOUTZ
Attendance: 5,797

GAME 7 AT PHI OCT 17

STL	000 000 001	1 8 1
DET	030 000 00X	3 6 1

Pitchers: CARUTHERS vs BALDWIN
Home Runs: O'Neill-STL
Attendance: 6,478

GAME 8 AT BOS OCT 18

DET	031 003 200	9 13 2
STL	100 001 000	2 8 5

Pitchers: GETZIEN vs CARUTHERS
Home Runs: Thompson-DET (2)
Attendance: 2,891

GAME 9 AT PHI OCT 19

STL	000 101 000	2 9 2
DET	000 100 21X	4 6 3

Pitchers: KING vs CONWAY
Attendance: 2,389

GAME 10 AT WAS OCT 21 (AM)

DET	200 010 001	4 8 3
STL	200 031 41X	11 16 5

Pitchers: GETZIEN vs CARUTHERS
Home Runs: Latham-STL, Welch-STL, Richardson-DET
Attendance: 1,261

GAME 11 AT BAL OCT 21 (PM)

STL	110 010 000	3 2 7
DET	100 344 10X	13 14 7

Pitchers: FOUTZ vs BALDWIN
Home Runs: Twitchell-DET
Attendance: 2,707
(Detroit wins best of 15 series 8 to 3)

GAME 12 AT BRO OCT 22

DET	000 100 0	1 5 3
STL	410 000 X	5 10 2

Pitchers: CONWAY vs KING
Attendance: 1,138
(Game called in seventh, darkness)

GAME 13 AT DET OCT 24

DET	020 100 120	6 12 3
STL	100 010 001	3 4 5

Pitchers: BALDWIN vs CARUTHERS
Attendance: 3,389

GAME 14 AT CHI OCT 25

STL	000 002 100	3 10 5
DET	300 010 00X	4 4 4

Pitchers: KING vs GETZIEN
Attendance: 378

GAME 15 AT STL OCT 26

STL	340 110	9 11 5
DET	011 000	2 8 7

Pitchers: CARUTHERS vs BALDWIN
Attendance: 659
(Game called after sixth, cold)

St. Louis, AA champions for the fourth straight year, battled the Giants closely through several games, but blowout losses in Games Six and Eight undid them. The first three games were played in New York. In a splendidly pitched opener, Brown ace Charles "Silver" King held New York to two hits and a walk while Giant ace Tim Keefe limited the Browns to three hits and a walk, striking out nine on his way to a narrow 2–1 win. St. Louis evened the Series in Game Two behind the shutout pitching of Elton "Icebox" Chamberlain. Tommy McCarthy scored the Browns' first run in the second inning when, after singling, he moved around to third on two passed balls by Giant catcher Buck Ewing and came home on Ewing's failed attempt to throw out a runner stealing second. Two more runs in the ninth gave St. Louis more than enough insurance for the win.

The Giants scored twice in the first inning of Game Three, and increased their lead to 4–0 before allowing St. Louis a pair of harmless runs in the final innings. They also scored first and led all the way in Game Four (played in Brooklyn) as another St. Louis rally fell short. The Browns took a 4–1 lead into the bottom of the eighth in Game Five (in New York), but a five-run Giant rally reversed the lead—and the outcome—as the game was called for darkness with St. Louis at bat in the ninth.

Giant Mickey Welch hurled a three-hitter (in Philadelphia) the next day, but St. Louis, capitalizing on walks and a questionable "safe" call at home, carried a 4–1 lead into the sixth inning. New York exploded in the late innings for 11 runs, however, and when darkness ended the game after eight the Giants were just one win away from the title.

The final four games were played in St. Louis. The Browns spoiled New York's hope of quick victory in Game Seven, coming from behind to tie the score with three runs in the fourth, and—after New York had scored twice in the sixth—recovering again with a four-run eighth for a 7–5 lead before darkness again halted play after eight innings. But the Browns' win only delayed the inevitable. The Giants hammered Icebox Chamberlain for twelve hits in Game Eight (including home runs by Buck Ewing and Mike Tiernan) to clinch their first world championship with an 11–3 win.

New York Giants (NL), 6; St. Louis Browns (AA), 4

NY (N)

PLAYER/POS	AVG	G	AB	R	H	2B	3B	HR	RB	BB	SO	SB
Willard Brown, c	.375	2	8	1	3	1	0	0	0	0	0	0
Roger Connor, 1b	.304	7	23	7	7	1	2	0	3	4	0	4
Ed Crane, p	.143	2	7	1	1	0	0	0	2	0	1	0
Buck Ewing, c-6,1b-1	.346	7	26	5	9	0	2	1	6	1	3	5
Bill George, p-1,1b-1	.333	2	9	2	3	1	0	1	4	0	2	0
George Gore, of-2,3b-1	.455	3	11	5	5	1	0	0	0	2	2	2
Gil Hatfield, p-1,2b-1,ss-1	.250	2	8	2	2	0	0	0	1	1	2	1
Tim Keefe, p	.091	4	11	2	1	0	0	0	0	2	2	1
Pat Murphy, c	.100	3	10	1	1	0	0	0	1	0	0	0
Jim O'Rourke, of-7,1b-2,ss-1	.222	10	36	4	8	0	0	0	1	4	2	3
Danny Richardson, 2b	.167	9	36	6	6	2	0	0	6	3	5	3
Mike Slattery, of-10,2b-1	.205	10	39	6	8	2	0	0	5	0	5	6
Mike Tiernan, of	.342	10	38	8	13	0	0	1	6	8	2	5
Ledell Titcomb, p-1,of-1	.500	1	4	1	2	1	0	0	1	0	0	0
Monte Ward, ss	.379	8	29	4	11	1	0	0	6	1	0	6
Mickey Welch, p	.286	2	7	2	2	0	0	0	1	0	0	0
Art Whitney, 3b-9,of-1	.324	10	37	7	12	0	1	0	12	1	4	2
TOTAL	.277		339	64	94	10	5	3	55	27	30	38

PITCHER	W	L	ERA	G	GS	CG	SV	SHO	IP	H	ER	BB	SO
Ed Crane	1	1	2.12	2	2	2	0	0	17.0	15	4	6	12
Bill George	0	1	7.20	1	1	1	0	0	10.0	15	8	3	4
Gil Hatfield	0	0	12.60	1	0	0	0	0	5.0	12	7	3	2
Tim Keefe	4	0	0.51	4	4	4	0	0	35.0	18	2	9	30
Ledell Titcomb	0	1	6.75	1	1	0	0	0	4.0	5	3	2	2
Mickey Welch	1	1	2.65	2	2	2	0	0	17.0	10	5	9	2
TOTAL	6	4	2.97	11	10	9	0	0	88.0	75	29	32	52

STL (A)

PLAYER/POS	AVG	G	AB	R	H	2B	3B	HR	RB	BB	SO	SB
Jack Boyle, c-4,of-1	.438	4	16	4	7	0	1	0	4	2	2	3
Icebox Chamberlain, p	.000	5	13	3	0	0	0	0	0	4	3	1
Charlie Comiskey, 1b-10,of-1	.268	10	41	6	11	1	1	0	3	1	1	4
Jim Devlin, p	.000	1	3	0	0	0	0	0	0	0	0	0
Ed Herr, of	.091	3	11	2	1	0	0	0	0	0	5	1
Silver King, p	.067	5	15	1	1	0	0	0	0	1	6	0
Arlie Latham, 3b	.250	10	40	10	10	0	0	0	3	5	6	11
Harry Lyons, of	.118	5	17	0	2	0	0	0	1	1	5	0
Tommy McCarthy, of	.244	10	41	10	10	1	0	1	9	0	0	6
Jocko Milligan, c-8,1b-1	.400	8	25	5	10	2	1	0	4	3	3	0
Tip O'Neill, of	.243	10	37	8	9	1	0	2	11	6	3	0
Yank Robinson, 2b	.250	10	36	7	9	2	1	0	7	6	12	2
Bill White, ss	.143	10	35	4	5	1	0	0	4	3	6	1
TOTAL	.227		330	60	75	8	4	3	46	32	52	29

PITCHER	W	L	ERA	G	GS	CG	SV	SHO	IP	H	ER	BB	SO
Icebox Chamberlain	2	3	5.32	5	5	5	0	1	44.0	52	26	16	13
Jim Devlin	1	0	2.57	1	0	0	0	0	7.0	5	2	2	5
Silver King	1	3	2.31	5	5	4	0	0	35.0	37	9	9	12
TOTAL	4	6	3.87	11	10	9	0	1	86.0	94	37	27	30

The final two games meant nothing to the outcome, and both clubs used reserve pitchers in Game Nine. But St. Louis rewarded the small crowd with a two-run rally in the ninth to tie the game at 11-all and scored three more runs in the tenth to win it. The finale the next day again featured heavy hitting on both sides, including a trio of home runs (one of them Tip O'Neill's second in two days) and an 18–7 St. Louis romp.

Six wins was the magic number this year, and it was agreed that—unlike most previous Series—play would not continue beyond the deciding game. At first it seemed Brooklyn might prevail, with an assist from the dark of night. The Giants wanted the opening game called for darkness after the seventh inning, when they led 10–8. But the umpires held off until Brooklyn, in the deepening gloom, had scored four runs in the last of the eighth to go ahead 12–10.

The next day, in Brooklyn before more than 16,000 spectators (by far the largest World Series crowd to that time), Giant Ed "Cannonball" Crane held the Grooms to four hits as New York evened the Series. But Brooklyn won the next two for a 3–1 Series advantage. In Game Three, ahead 8–7 in the sixth inning, the Grooms began stalling, waiting for darkness to fall. The score was still 8–7 when the game was finally halted in the top of the ninth with one out and three Giants on base.

Darkness for a third time gave Brooklyn the victory in Game Four. New York overcame a 7–2 Bridegroom lead to tie the score with five runs in the top of the sixth, but in the bottom of the inning Brooklyn's Tom "Oyster" Burns homered in the dark for three runs. The umpires then halted the game.

The five remaining contests went the distance, and the Giants won them all. Cannonball Crane in Game Five gave up eight hits, but homered in his own behalf, driving in two runs in his Giants' 11–3 rout. Game Six was a pitching duel between New York's Hank O'Day and Brooklyn's William "Adonis" Terry. The Grooms scored a run in the second inning, but New York tied the game with two outs in the last of the ninth (when Monte Ward singled, stole second and third, and scored on Roger Connor's single), and won it with two away in the eleventh as Ward drove in a speedy Mike Slattery from second with an infield hit.

Back-to-back homers by Giants Dan Richardson and Jim O'Rourke highlighted an eight-run second inning in Game Seven. The Giants' eventual 11–7 win gave them their first Series advantage. In Game Eight, two of Brooklyn's five hits were home runs. But the Giants outscored the Grooms 12–2 over the first four innings and beat them 16–7.

With their backs to the wall, the Bridegrooms scored first in

New York Giants (NL), 6;
Brooklyn Bridegrooms (AA), 3

NY (N)

PLAYER/POS	AVG	G	AB	R	H	2B	3B	HR	RB	BB	SO	SB
Willard Brown, c	.600	1	5	3	3	0	0	1	2	0	0	0
Roger Connor, 1b	.343	9	35	9	12	2	2	0	12	3	2	8
Ed Crane, p	.278	5	18	3	5	1	1	1	5	1	2	0
Buck Ewing, c	.250	8	36	5	9	4	0	0	7	2	5	1
George Gore, of	.333	5	21	5	7	1	1	0	1	3	0	2
Tim Keefe, p	.500	2	4	1	2	1	0	0	0	1	1	0
Hank O'Day, p	.167	3	6	0	1	0	0	0	0	2	2	0
Jim O'Rourke, of	.389	9	36	7	14	2	2	2	7	2	2	3
Danny Richardson, 2b	.314	9	35	8	11	1	1	3	8	3	5	3
Mike Slattery, of	.188	4	16	6	3	0	0	0	1	3	1	1
Mike Tiernan, of	.289	9	38	12	11	1	1	1	5	5	3	3
Monte Ward, ss	.417	9	36	10	15	0	1	0	7	5	2	10
Mickey Welch, p	.333	1	3	0	1	1	0	0	0	0	0	0
Art Whitney, 3b	.229	9	35	4	8	2	1	0	3	1	0	0
TOTAL	.315		324	73	102	16	10	8	58	31	26	31

PITCHER	W	L	ERA	G	GS	CG	SV	SHO	IP	H	ER	BB	SO
Ed Crane	4	1	3.72	5	5	4	0	0	38.2	29	16	32	19
Tim Keefe	0	1	8.18	2	1	1	1	0	11.0	17	10	2	4
Hank O'Day	2	0	1.17	3	2	2	0	0	23.0	10	3	14	12
Mickey Welch	0	1	9.00	1	1	0	0	0	5.0	11	5	3	1
TOTAL	6	3	3.94	11	9	7	1	0	77.2	67	34	51	36

BRO (A)

PLAYER/POS	AVG	G	AB	R	H	2B	3B	HR	RB	BB	SO	SB
Oyster Burns, of	.229	9	35	8	8	3	0	2	11	5	6	0
Doc Bushong, c	.000	3	8	0	0	0	0	0	0	1	0	0
Bob Caruthers, p	.250	4	8	1	2	0	0	0	1	3	3	0
Bob Clark, c	.417	4	12	3	5	2	0	0	3	2	2	0
Hub Collins, 2b	.371	9	35	13	13	3	0	1	2	7	5	6
Pop Corkhill, of	.208	9	24	4	5	1	0	1	5	6	2	1
Jumbo Davis, ss	.000	1	4	0	0	0	0	0	0	0	0	0
Dave Foutz, 1b-9,p-1	.286	9	35	7	10	2	0	1	9	4	2	3
Mickey Hughes, p	.333	1	3	1	1	1	0	0	0	1	2	0
Tom Lovett, p	.000	1	1	0	0	0	0	0	0	0	0	0
Darby O'Brien, of	.161	9	31	8	5	0	1	0	4	12	6	6
George Pinckney, 3b	.258	9	31	2	8	2	0	0	3	4	2	2
Germany Smith, ss	.172	8	29	2	5	2	1	0	2	3	2	2
Adonis Terry, p-5,1b-1	.167	5	18	1	3	0	0	0	1	1	1	1
Joe Visner, c-3,of-2	.125	5	16	2	2	1	0	0	0	2	3	0
TOTAL	.231		290	52	67	17	2	5	41	51	36	21

PITCHER	W	L	ERA	G	GS	CG	SV	SHO	IP	H	ER	BB	SO
Bob Caruthers	0	2	3.75	4	2	2	1	0	24.0	28	10	6	6
Dave Foutz	0	0	7.20	1	0	0	0	0	5.0	5	4	2	2
Mickey Hughes	1	0	7.71	1	1	0	0	0	7.0	14	6	3	3
Tom Lovett	0	1	24.00	1	1	0	0	0	3.0	8	8	2	1
Adonis Terry	2	3	5.97	5	5	4	0	0	37.2	47	25	18	14
TOTAL	3	6	6.22	12	9	6	1	0	76.2	102	53	31	26

Game Nine and held a 2–1 lead after five innings. But New York tied the score in the sixth and went ahead 3–2 on a passed ball in the seventh. Meanwhile Giant pitcher Hank O'Day (although he walked five batters) blanked the Grooms on just two hits after the first inning to bring New York its second straight world championship.

GAME 1 AT NY OCT 18

NY	020 210 50	10 12 2
BRO	510 000 24	12 16 3

Pitchers: KEEFE vs TERRY
Home Runs: Collins-BRO, Richardson-NY
Attendance: 8,848
(Game called at end of eighth, darkness)

GAME 2 AT BRO OCT 19

NY	111 120 000	6 10 4
BRO	110 000 000	2 4 8

Pitchers: CRANE vs CARUTHERS
Attendance: 16,172

GAME 3 AT NY OCT 22

NY	200 032 00	7 15 2
BRO	023 120 00	8 12 3

Pitchers: WELCH, O'Day (6) vs HUGHES, Caruthers (8)
Home Runs: Corkhill-BRO, O'Rourke-NY
Attendance: 5,181
(Game called at end of eighth, darkness)

GAME 4 AT BRO OCT 23

NY	001 105	7 9 8
BRO	202 033	10 7 1

Pitchers: CRANE vs TERRY
Home Runs: Burns-BRO
Attendance: 3,045
(Game called at end of sixth, darkness)

GAME 5 AT BRO OCT 24

NY	004 040 021	11 12 2
BRO	000 111 000	3 8 2

Pitchers: CRANE vs CARUTHERS
Home Runs: Brown-NY, Richardson-NY, Crane-NY
Attendance: 2,901

GAME 6 AT NY OCT 25

BRO	010 000 000 00	1 6 4
NY	000 000 001 01	2 7 1

Pitchers: TERRY vs O'DAY
Attendance: 2,556

GAME 7 AT NY OCT 26

BRO	004 030 000	7 5 3
NY	180 001 10X	11 14 4

Pitchers: LOVETT, Caruthers (4) vs CRANE, Keefe (5)
Home Runs: Richardson-NY, O'Rourke-NY
Attendance: 3,312

GAME 8 AT BRO OCT 28

NY	541 203 001	16 15 4
BRO	200 000 023	7 5 4

Pitchers: CRANE vs TERRY, Foutz (5)
Home Runs: Foutz-BRO, Tiernan-NY, Burns-BRO
Attendance: 2,584

GAME 9 AT NY OCT 29

BRO	200 000 000	2 4 2
NY	100 001 10X	3 8 5

Pitchers: TERRY vs O'DAY
Attendance: 3,067

The Bridegrooms, AA pennant winners in 1889, switched to the NL and returned to World Series play as champions of their new league. Louisville, meanwhile, rose from a last-place finish in 1889 to replace Brooklyn at the top of the AA. The Series, though, seemed meaningless to many who believed that pennant-winning Boston of the outlaw Players League (which had drawn off many of the best NL and AA players) could beat both Louisville and Brooklyn if given the opportunity.

The first four games of the Series were played in Louisville before an ever decreasing number of spectators. The largest crowd—5,600—saw the Cyclones humiliated in the opener 9–0 as Brooklyn's Adonis Terry stopped them on two singles. The Grooms won the second game, too, breaking a 2–2 tie with a pair of runs in the fourth and holding on for a 5–3 win.

Louisville played catch-up throughout Game Three and entered the last of the eighth still behind 7–4. But a walk, three hits, a sacrifice fly, and a passed ball brought the score to 7-all—where it remained when darkness ended the game. Only 1,050 spectators attended the final contest in Louisville, but they saw the first Louisville win. The Cyclones scored three runs in the first inning, but Brooklyn countered with three an inning later, and both teams scored single runs in the third. Louisville's Red Ehret blanked the Grooms the rest of the way, but Brooklyn's Tom Lovett yielded the Cyclones a winning run in the seventh when Tim Shinnick tripled and was sacrificed home.

Rain postponed the first game in Brooklyn for two days, but when it was played—on a cold, muddy day before a small crowd of 1,000—the Grooms took the lead on Oyster Burns's two-run homer in the first inning and held it all the way for their third win. As the weather grew colder, the crowds declined for the final two games. Louisville captured its second win by a 9–8 margin when a three-run Brooklyn rally in the eighth inning of Game Six stalled one run short of a tie. Only abut 300 diehards saw the Cyclones even the Series in the finale, 6–2 behind Red Ehret's four-hitter. A tie-breaking eighth game seemed called for, but there was not enough interest in playing any further in the bitter cold.

Brooklyn Bridegrooms (NL), 3; Louisville Cyclones (AA), 3; tie, 1

BRO (N)

PLAYER/POS	AVG	G	AB	R	H	2B	3B	HR	RB	BB	SO	SB
Oyster Burns, of-4,3b-3	.222	7	27	6	6	2	0	1	5	3	4	0
Doc Bushong, c	.000	2	6	0	0	0	0	0	0	0	1	0
Bob Caruthers, of	.000	2	6	0	0	0	0	0	0	2	0	0
Bob Clark, c	.667	1	3	2	2	0	1	0	1	0	0	0
Hub Collins, 2b	.310	7	29	7	9	0	1	0	1	3	0	2
Tom Daly, c-6,1b-1	.182	6	22	1	4	2	0	0	3	0	4	2
Patsy Donovan, of	.471	5	17	5	8	1	0	0	3	2	1	3
Dave Foutz, 1b-7,of-1	.300	7	30	6	9	2	1	0	4	0	1	1
Tom Lovett, p-4,of-1	.067	5	15	0	1	0	0	0	0	0	4	0
Darby O'Brien, of	.125	6	24	3	3	0	1	0	3	1	5	3
George Pinckney, 3b	.357	4	14	4	5	0	2	0	3	2	1	1
Germany Smith, ss	.276	7	29	3	8	0	2	0	7	0	3	1
Adonis Terry, p-3,of-3	.050	6	20	5	1	1	0	0	0	6	3	1
TOTAL	.231		242	42	56	8	8	1	30	19	27	14

PITCHER	W	L	ERA	G	GS	CG	SV	SHO	IP	H	ER	BB	SO
Tom Lovett	2	2	2.83	4	4	4	0	0	35.0	29	11	6	14
Adonis Terry	1	1	3.60	3	3	3	0	1	25.0	25	10	10	8
TOTAL	3	3	3.15	7	7	7	0	1	60.0	54	21	16	22

LOU (A)

PLAYER/POS	AVG	G	AB	R	H	2B	3B	HR	RB	BB	SO	SB
Ned Bligh, c	.000	2	3	0	0	0	0	0	0	0	1	0
Ed Daily, of-4,p-2	.136	6	22	1	3	1	1	0	3	1	2	2
Red Ehret, p	.429	3	7	1	3	0	1	0	0	0	0	0
Charlie Hamburg, of	.269	7	26	3	7	1	0	0	2	0	3	0
George Meakim, p	.500	1	2	0	1	0	0	0	0	0	0	0
Harry Raymond, ss-5,ss-3	.148	7	27	5	4	1	1	0	1	2	5	1
John Ryan, c	.053	6	19	0	1	0	0	0	2	0	1	1
Tim Shinnick, 2b	.292	7	24	3	7	1	1	0	3	2	2	2
Scott Stratton, p-3,of-1	.222	4	9	4	2	1	0	0	0	2	1	3
Harry Taylor, 1b	.300	7	30	6	9	1	0	0	2	2	3	3
Phil Tomney, ss	.200	3	5	1	1	0	0	0	0	3	1	0
Farmer Weaver, of	.259	7	27	4	7	1	0	0	4	1	2	5
Pete Weckbecker, c	.000	1	4	0	0	0	0	0	0	0	1	0
Chicken Wolf, 3b-5,of-3	.360	7	25	4	9	3	1	0	8	3	0	2
TOTAL	.235		230	32	54	10	5	0	25	16	22	19

PITCHER	W	L	ERA	G	GS	CG	SV	SHO	IP	H	ER	BB	SO
Ed Daily	0	2	2.65	2	2	2	0	0	17.0	12	5	8	5
Red Ehret	2	0	1.35	3	2	2	1	0	20.0	12	3	6	13
George Meakim	0	0	0.00	1	0	0	0	0	4.0	6	0	1	1
Scott Stratton	1	1	2.37	3	3	1	0	0	19.0	26	5	4	8
TOTAL	3	3	1.95	9	7	5	1	0	60.0	56	13	19	27

GAME 1 AT LOU OCT 17

BRO	300	030	30	9	11	1
LOU	000	000	00	0	2	6

Pitchers: TERRY vs STRATTON
Attendance: 5,600

GAME 2 AT LOU OCT 18

BRO	020	201	000	5	5	3
LOU	101	000	001	3	6	5

Pitchers: LOVETT vs DAILY
Attendance: 2,860

GAME 3 AT LOU OCT 20

BRO	020	130	10	7	10	2
LOU	001	012	03	7	11	3

Pitchers: Terry vs Stratton, Meakim (4)
Attendance: 2,500

GAME 4 AT LOU OCT 21

BRO	031	000	000	4	7	2
LOU	301	000	10X	5	9	2

Pitchers: LOVETT vs EHRET
Attendance: 1,050

GAME 5 AT BRO OCT 25

LOU	010	010	000	2	5	6
BRO	210	200	20X	7	7	0

Pitchers: DAILY vs LOVETT
Home Runs: Burns-BRO
Attendance: 1,000

GAME 6 AT BRO OCT 27

LOU	012	101	220	9	13	3
BRO	100	004	030	8	12	3

Pitchers: STRATTON, Ehret (7) vs TERRY
Attendance: 600

GAME 7 AT BRO OCT 28

LOU	103	000	020	6	8	3
BRO	200	000	000	2	4	1

Pitchers: EHRET vs LOVETT
Attendance: 300

Interleague squabbling prevented a World Series in 1891, and the AA folded before the next season. Four AA clubs were taken into the NL, expanding the NL to twelve teams. To create a postseason championship series, the regular season was divided in half, with first-half winner Boston meeting second-half victor Cleveland for both the league and world titles.

The first game, in Cleveland, was a pitching and fielding classic. Boston's Jack Stivetts and Cleveland's Cy Young blanked the opposition for eleven innings before darkness halted the game. Young yielded just six hits and Stivetts four—all singles. Just as remarkable in an era when errors were commonplace, Cleveland committed only one and Boston none; several outstanding plays were made in the field.

Boston center fielder Hugh Duffy was the offensive and defensive star of Game Two. He drove in three of the Beaneaters' four runs (with a fly out, a triple, and a double), and scored the fourth himself after tripling a second time. And in the bottom of the ninth he snared a leadoff liner with a great running catch. As it was, Cleveland scored once in the inning to pull within a run of a tie; Duffy's catch prevented a certain tie and a possible Cleveland win. Game Three was just as close. Pitchers Stivetts and Young each gave up two early runs, but then blanked their foes until the seventh inning, when Boston's Tommy McCarthy singled in Stivetts (who had doubled) with what proved the winning run.

The Series moved to Boston for the next three games. In Game Four, Boston ace Kid Nichols shut out the Spiders, scattering seven hits and fanning eight. Cleveland's Nig Cuppy yielded only six hits, but one was a home run ball to Hugh Duffy for two runs in the third inning, and another was a two-run single to Joe Quinn in the sixth. Cleveland pitcher John Clarkson helped his own cause the next day with a three-run homer in the Spider's six-run second inning. But Boston pitcher Jack Stivetts—with the score now 7–5 Cleveland in the sixth—tripled in a run and scored the tying run. In the seventh, Stivetts scored Boston's twelfth (and final) run after singling, while holding Cleveland scoreless through the final four innings.

Two days later the Beaneaters brought the Series to an end with their fifth straight win. The Spiders scored first, with a three-run third, but pitcher Kid Nichols

Boston Beaneaters, 5;
Cleveland Spiders, 0; tie, 1

BOS (N)

PLAYER/POS	AVG	G	AB	R	H	2B	3B	HR	RB	BB	SO	SB
Charlie Bennett, c	.286	2	7	2	2	0	0	1	1	0	2	1
Hugh Duffy, of	.462	6	26	3	12	3	2	1	9	1	0	3
Charlie Ganzel, c	.500	2	8	1	4	0	0	0	2	1	0	0
King Kelly, c	.000	2	8	0	0	0	0	0	0	0	2	1
Herman Long, ss	.222	6	27	4	6	0	0	0	1	0	0	2
Bobby Lowe, of	.130	6	23	8	3	0	0	0	0	1	2	1
Tommy McCarthy, of	.381	6	21	2	8	2	0	0	2	6	1	3
Billy Nash, 3b	.167	6	24	3	4	0	0	0	4	2	3	2
Kid Nichols, p	.286	2	7	1	2	0	0	0	2	0	1	1
Joe Quinn, 2b	.286	6	21	2	6	1	1	0	4	1	2	0
Harry Staley, p	.000	1	4	0	0	0	0	0	0	0	3	0
Jack Stivetts, p	.250	3	12	3	3	1	1	0	1	0	2	0
Tommy Tucker, 1b	.261	6	23	2	6	0	0	1	2	0	1	0
TOTAL	.265		211	31	56	7	4	3	28	12	19	14

PITCHER	W	L	ERA	G	GS	CG	SV	SHO	IP	H	ER	BB	SO
Kid Nichols	2	0	1.00	2	2	2	0	1	18.0	17	2	4	13
Harry Staley	1	0	3.00	1	1	1	0	0	9.0	10	3	1	0
Jack Stivetts	2	0	0.93	3	3	3	0	1	29.0	21	3	7	17
TOTAL	5	0	1.29	6	6	6	0	2	56.0	48	8	12	30

CLE (N)

PLAYER/POS	AVG	G	AB	R	H	2B	3B	HR	RB	BB	SO	SB
Jesse Burkett, of	.320	6	25	3	8	1	0	0	1	0	2	4
Cupid Childs, 2b	.409	6	22	3	9	0	2	0	0	5	1	0
John Clarkson, p	.250	2	8	1	2	0	0	1	3	0	1	0
Nig Cuppy, p	.000	1	3	0	0	0	0	0	0	0	2	0
George Davis, 3b-2	.167	3	6	0	1	0	0	0	0	0	1	0
Jimmy McAleer, of	.182	6	22	0	4	0	0	0	1	2	2	1
Ed McKean, ss	.440	6	25	2	11	0	0	0	6	1	3	0
Jack O'Connor, of	.136	6	22	1	3	0	0	0	0	2	3	0
Patsy Tebeau, 3b	.000	5	18	1	0	0	0	0	0	0	2	1
Jake Virtue, 1b	.125	6	24	1	3	0	0	0	0	2	5	1
Cy Young, p	.091	3	11	1	1	0	0	0	0	0	5	0
Chief Zimmer, c	.261	6	23	2	6	1	1	0	2	0	3	0
TOTAL	.230		209	15	48	2	3	1	13	12	30	7

PITCHER	W	L	ERA	G	GS	CG	SV	SHO	IP	H	ER	BB	SO
John Clarkson	0	2	5.29	2	2	2	0	0	17.0	24	10	5	9
Nig Cuppy	0	1	1.13	1	1	1	0	0	8.0	6	1	4	1
Cy Young	0	2	3.00	3	3	3	0	1	27.0	26	9	3	9
TOTAL	0	5	3.46	6	6	6	0	1	52.0	56	20	12	19

held them scoreless after that and singled home Boston's tying and go-ahead runs himself as the Beaneaters tagged Cy Young for eight runs over the final six innings.

GAME 1 AT CLE OCT 17

```
CLE   000 000 000 00    0  4  1
BOS   000 000 000 00    0  6  0
```
Pitchers: YOUNG vs STIVETTS
Attendance: 6,000

GAME 2 AT CLE OCT 18

```
BOS   101 010 010    4 10  2
CLE   001 100 001    3 10  2
```
Pitchers: STALEY vs CLARKSON
Attendance: 6,700

GAME 3 AT CLE OCT 19

```
CLE   200 000 000    2  8  0
BOS   110 000 10X    3  9  2
```
Pitchers: YOUNG vs STIVETTS
Attendance: 5,000

GAME 4 AT BOS OCT 21

```
CLE   000 000 000    0  7  3
BOS   002 002 00X    4  6  0
```
Pitchers: CUPPY vs NICHOLS
Home Runs: Duffy-BOS
Attendance: 6,547

GAME 5 AT BOS OCT 22

```
CLE   060 010 000    7  9  4
BOS   000 324 30X   12 14  3
```
Pitchers: CLARKSON vs STIVETTS
Home Runs: Clarkson-CLE,
   Tucker-BOS
Attendance: 3,466

GAME 6 AT BOS OCT 24

```
CLE   003 000 000    3 10  5
BOS   002 211 11X    8 11  5
```
Pitchers: YOUNG vs NICHOLS
Home Runs: Bennett-BOS
Attendance: 2,300

As the divided season of 1892 was not repeated, no "world series" was held in 1893. But in 1894 Pittsburgh sportsman William C. Temple offered an elegant trophy to the winner of a series between the NL's first- and second-place finishers. For four years the Temple Cup games determined the world championship. In this first matchup, second-place New York swept the feisty pennant-winning Orioles.

Game One, in Baltimore, was a shutout through four innings as New York's Amos Rusie and Baltimore's Duke Esper held their opponents at bay. But Giant George Van Haltren tripled in the fifth inning and scored the game's first run on a fly to left. The Giants also scored single runs in the sixth, seventh, and eighth innings, while Rusie continued his shutout pitching through the eighth. In the ninth Oriole John McGraw singled, and he came around on a sacrifice, stolen base, and single to spoil the shutout. But the Oriole effort was too little to deprive Rusie of his win.

Some two hundred policemen patrolled the second game the next day to protect the umpires and New York's players and fans from the abusive Orioles and the crowd in the stands whom the Oriole players egged on. Baltimore scored first with two runs in the second and, after losing and regaining the lead, completed the eighth inning tied 5–5. But in the top of the ninth, the Giants put together their second four-run inning of the game. Once again the Orioles came up with a run in the last of the ninth, but once again came up short.

More than 22,000 spectators showed up for Game Three as the Series shifted to New York—a huge crowd for that era, even for a Saturday. As in Game One, the Giants' Amos Rusie hurled a 4–1 victory. New York broke a 1–1 tie with a run in the fifth on a throwing error and a ground out, and scored the game's final runs an inning later. Threatening weather held down attendance at Game Four to about 12,000. Baltimore jumped to a quick lead with two runs in the top of the first, but New York pitcher Jouett Meekin held the Orioles to just one run after that as the Giants piled up runs for a 16–3 advantage by the time darkness forced an end to play after eight innings. Meekin, in winning his second game of the Series, connected for three hits himself—half as many as he permitted the whole Oriole team.

New York Giants, 4;
Baltimore Orioles, 0

NY (N)

PLAYER/POS	AVG	G	AB	R	H	2B	3B	HR	RB	BB	SO	SB
Eddie Burke, of	.389	4	18	3	7	1	0	0	2	1	0	1
George Davis, 3b	.313	4	16	5	5	2	2	0	5	2	0	2
Jack Doyle, 1b	.588	4	17	4	10	1	1	0	6	1	1	6
Duke Farrell, c	.400	4	15	5	6	0	0	0	2	1	1	1
Shorty Fuller, ss	.286	4	14	4	4	0	0	0	2	2	0	1
Jouett Meekin, p	.556	2	9	2	5	0	0	0	3	0	1	0
Yale Murphy, of	.000	1	1	0	0	0	0	0	0	0	0	0
Amos Rusie, p	.429	2	7	1	3	1	0	0	1	0	1	0
Mike Tiernan, of	.294	4	17	5	5	0	1	0	3	2	2	0
George Van Haltren, of	.500	4	14	3	7	1	1	0	0	2	2	2
Monte Ward, 2b	.294	4	17	1	5	0	0	0	6	0	0	0
TOTAL	.393		145	33	57	6	5	0	30	11	8	13

PITCHER	W	L	ERA	G	GS	CG	SV	SHO	IP	H	ER	BB	SO
Jouett Meekin	2	0	1.59	2	2	2	0	0	17.0	13	3	8	6
Amos Rusie	2	0	0.50	2	2	2	0	0	18.0	14	1	3	9
TOTAL	4	0	1.03	4	4	4	0	0	35.0	27	4	11	15

BAL (N)

PLAYER/POS	AVG	G	AB	R	H	2B	3B	HR	RB	BB	SO	SB
Frank Bonner, ss-1,of-1	.000	2	5	0	0	0	0	0	0	0	2	0
Steve Brodie, of	.000	4	15	2	0	0	0	0	0	2	1	1
Dan Brouthers, 1b	.188	4	16	2	3	0	0	0	0	1	0	3
Duke Esper, p	.000	1	2	0	0	0	0	0	0	1	1	0
Kid Gleason, p	.200	2	5	0	1	0	1	0	1	0	1	0
Bill Hawke, p	.000	1	2	0	0	0	0	0	0	0	1	0
George Hemming, p	.000	1	3	0	0	0	0	0	0	1	1	0
Hughie Jennings, ss	.143	4	14	0	2	0	0	0	1	0	2	0
Willie Keeler, of	.250	3	12	1	3	0	0	0	1	1	0	0
Joe Kelley, of	.333	4	15	2	5	1	1	0	0	3	2	1
John McGraw, 3b	.250	4	16	2	4	0	0	0	2	0	0	1
Heinie Reitz, 2b	.333	4	15	1	5	0	0	0	4	1	3	1
Wilbert Robinson, c	.267	4	15	1	4	0	0	0	1	1	1	1
TOTAL	.200		135	11	27	1	2	0	10	11	15	8

PITCHER	W	L	ERA	G	GS	CG	SV	SHO	IP	H	ER	BB	SO
Duke Esper	0	1	4.00	1	1	1	0	0	9.0	13	4	1	3
Kid Gleason	0	1	9.69	2	1	1	0	0	13.0	25	14	6	3
Bill Hawke	0	1	9.00	1	1	0	0	0	4.0	9	4	1	0
George Hemming	0	1	1.13	1	1	1	0	0	8.0	10	1	3	2
TOTAL	0	4	6.09	5	4	3	0	0	34.0	57	23	11	8

GAME 1 AT BAL OCT 4

NY	000	011	110	4	13	2
BAL	000	000	001	1	7	1

Pitchers: RUSIE vs ESPER
Attendance: 9,000

GAME 2 AT BAL OCT 5

NY	004	000	014	9	14	3
BAL	022	000	101	6	7	2

Pitchers: MEEKIN vs GLEASON
Attendance: 11,000

GAME 3 AT NY OCT 6

BAL	000	100	000	1	7	4
NY	100	012	00X	4	10	4

Pitchers: HEMMING vs RUSIE
Attendance: 22,000

GAME 4 AT NY OCT 8

BAL	201	000	00	3	6	3
NY	101	351	50	16	20	4

Pitchers: HAWKE, Gleason (5) vs
  MEEKIN
Attendance: 12,000
(Game called at end of eighth, darkness)

Baltimore, repeating as NL pennant winner, returned to Temple Cup play against new runner-up Cleveland. The first 4½ innings of the opener—played in Cleveland—featured a scoreless duel between Baltimore veteran John "Sadie" McMahon and the Spiders' great Cy Young. After Cleveland scored the game's first run in the last of the fifth, the teams traded runs and the lead, completing the eighth inning tied 3–3. In the top of the ninth, doubles by Wilbert Robinson and John McGraw restored the edge to Baltimore. But in the bottom of the inning, four straight Spider hits pushed across the tying run and filled the bases. One runner was forced at home for the first out, but a grounder that just missed being a double-play ball drove in the winning Cleveland run.

The next three games were not so closely contested. A large and enthusiastic Cleveland crowd watched its Spiders jump on Baltimore for three runs in the bottom of the first inning of Game Two and coast to a 7–2 win behind the strong pitching of Nig Cuppy, who held the Orioles to five singles. Cleveland repeated itself in Game Three, again exploding for three runs in the bottom of the first on the way to a seven-run total. Cy Young was just as effective in the box as Cuppy had been, scattering four hits over seven shutout innings before Baltimore put together three singles in the eighth for their only run.

When the teams shifted to Baltimore for Game Four, the Orioles sprang to life. While their pitcher Duke Esper strangled the Spiders on just five singles—only two Cleveland runners advanced as far as second base—Oriole batters tagged Nig Cuppy for five runs and their first Temple Cup win in two years of trying.

It proved to be their only win of the Series. The next day, in the first close struggle since the opener, Cy Young and Baltimore's rookie ace Bill Hoffer dueled scorelessly through six innings. But in the top of the seventh, Young doubled to start what became a three-run rally, and an inning later the Spiders scored twice more. Baltimore scored a single run in the last of the seventh, and, with two out in the ninth, loaded the bases on two walks and a hit batsman. A Cleveland error brought in the Orioles' second run as the bases remained full for Steve Brodie. But despite the pleas of Baltimore partisans to hit a homer or triple, Brodie "failed miserably" and Cleveland copped the cup.

Cleveland Spiders, 4;
Baltimore Orioles, 1

CLE (N)

PLAYER/POS	AVG	G	AB	R	H	2B	3B	HR	RB	BB	SO	SB
Harry Blake, of	.250	5	20	1	5	3	0	0	2	0	2	0
Jesse Burkett, of	.450	5	20	3	9	2	0	0	2	0	0	1
Cupid Childs, 2b	.190	5	21	4	4	1	0	0	2	1	0	1
Nig Cuppy, p	.167	2	6	1	1	1	0	0	1	0	0	0
Jimmy McAleer, of	.286	5	21	2	6	0	0	0	2	0	0	1
Chippy McGarr, 3b	.368	5	19	3	7	2	0	0	1	1	0	2
Ed McKean, ss	.300	5	20	2	6	1	1	0	4	3	0	1
Patsy Tebeau, 1b	.286	5	21	3	6	1	0	0	3	1	1	0
Cy Young, p	.250	3	12	3	3	1	0	0	1	0	1	0
Chief Zimmer, c	.333	4	18	2	6	2	0	0	3	3	4	0
TOTAL	.298		178	24	53	14	1	0	21	9	9*	6

PITCHER	W	L	ERA	G	GS	CG	SV	SHO	IP	H	ER	BB	SO
Nig Cuppy	1	1	3.18	2	2	2	0	0	17.0	14	6	4	6
Cy Young	3	0	2.33	3	3	3	0	0	27.0	28	7	4	2
TOTAL	4	1	2.66	5	5	5	0	0	44.0	42	13	8	8

BAL (N)

PLAYER/POS	AVG	G	AB	R	H	2B	3B	HR	RB	BB	SO	SB
Steve Brodie, of	.200	5	20	1	4	0	0	0	2	0	0	0
Scoops Carey, 1b	.263	5	19	0	5	1	0	0	1	0	0	0
Boileryard Clarke, c	.286	2	7	1	2	0	0	0	0	0	0	2
Duke Esper, p	.000	1	3	0	0	0	0	0	0	1	0	0
Kid Gleason, 2b	.105	5	19	0	2	0	0	0	0	0	1	0
Bill Hoffer, p	.000	2	7	0	0	0	0	0	0	0	2	0
Hughie Jennings, ss	.368	5	19	3	7	2	0	0	2	1	0	1
Willie Keeler, of	.235	5	17	3	4	0	0	0	1	3	1	0
Joe Kelley, of	.368	5	19	1	7	0	0	0	5	1	1	1
John McGraw, 3b	.400	5	20	4	8	2	0	0	1	2	0	2
Sadie McMahon, p	.000	2	7	0	0	0	0	0	0	0	0	0
Wilbert Robinson, c	.250	3	12	1	3	1	0	0	0	0	1	0
TOTAL	.249		169	14	42	6	0	0	12	8	6	6

PITCHER	W	L	ERA	G	GS	CG	SV	SHO	IP	H	ER	BB	SO
Duke Esper	1	0	0.00	1	1	1	0	1	9.0	5	0	0	3
Bill Hoffer	0	2	4.24	2	2	2	0	0	17.0	21	8	6	4
Sadie McMahon	0	2	5.94	2	2	2	0	0	16.2	27	11	3	2
TOTAL	1	4	4.01	5	5	5	0	1	42.2	53	19	9	9

* While the total strikeouts for the team have been confirmed as 9, research has failed, to this point, to identify the missing batter strikeout.

Baltimore captured its third consecutive pennant and for the second year in a row faced runner-up Cleveland in the Temple Cup games. But this time the Orioles emerged triumphant—with a sweep in which their margin of victory was never less than four runs.

Aces Bill Hoffer of Baltimore and the Spiders' Cy Young faced each other in the opener, in Baltimore. Hoffer walked four men, but gave up only five hits while the Orioles bombarded Young for thirteen. When the game ended, Hoffer and Baltimore had a 7–1 win.

Bobby Wallace (who had not yet discovered his role at shortstop that would propel him into the Hall of Fame) pitched for Cleveland in Game Two. He lost the game in the first inning when two Spider errors, a hit batsman, three hits, and a steal of home put four Baltimore runs on the board. The Orioles added two runs in the third and another in the fifth, while their promising twenty-year-old pitcher Joe Corbett held the Spiders to two runs on seven hits.

The Orioles' Hoffer gave up ten hits to Cleveland in Game Three —two more than the Birds made off Spider Nig Cuppy. But all the hits off Hoffer were singles, and he walked only one. Half of Cleveland's hits went toward producing just two runs. Their second run tied the score in the fifth inning, but in the sixth Baltimore regained the lead as John McGraw singled, stole second, took third on an error, and came home on an outfield fly. In the eighth the Orioles bunched four of their eight hits for three insurance runs.

The Series moved to Cleveland for the fourth game. Young Joe Corbett was again sent into the box for Baltimore, this time to face Nig Cuppy. For six innings the game was a scoreless duel. Baltimore hit safely in every inning but the second, but failed to score until the seventh, when Joe Kelley's double and Jack Doyle's single scored the only run they would need. But the Orioles added a second run in that inning and three more in the eighth. Two of the four Cleveland hits against Corbett put men on base in the eighth inning, and Corbett walked two in the ninth to raise Cleveland's hopes. But no Spider scored, and with the 5–0 win the Orioles were world champions at last.

Baltimore Orioles, 4;
Cleveland Spiders, 0

BAL (N)

PLAYER/POS	AVG	G	AB	R	H	2B	3B	HR	RB	BB	SO	SB
Steve Brodie, of	.067	4	15	1	1	0	0	0	3	0	0	1
Joe Corbett, p	.500	2	6	1	3	1	0	0	0	1	1	0
Jack Doyle, 1b	.294	4	17	3	5	1	0	0	4	0	0	2
Bill Hoffer, p	.286	2	7	1	2	0	2	0	0	0	1	0
Hughie Jennings, ss	.333	4	15	5	5	2	0	0	3	1	2	1
Willie Keeler, of	.471	4	17	4	8	1	2	0	4	0	0	1
Joe Kelley, of	.471	4	17	3	8	1	0	0	4	0	1	2
John McGraw, 3b	.267	4	15	4	4	0	0	0	1	0	0	4
Joe Quinn, 3b	.000	1	3	1	0	0	0	0	0	0	0	0
Heinie Reitz, 2b	.133	4	15	1	2	0	0	0	2	1	0	0
Wilbert Robinson, c	.267	4	15	1	4	1	0	0	2	0	3	0
TOTAL	.296		142	25	42	7	4	0	23	3	8	11

PITCHER	W	L	ERA	G	GS	CG	SV	SHO	IP	H	ER	BB	SO
Joe Corbett	2	0	0.50	2	2	2	0	1	18.0	11	1	7	10
Bill Hoffer	2	0	1.50	2	2	2	0	0	18.0	15	3	5	10
TOTAL	4	0	1.00	4	4	4	0	1	36.0	26	4	12	20

CLE (N)

PLAYER/POS	AVG	G	AB	R	H	2B	3B	HR	RB	BB	SO	SB
Harry Blake, of	.071	4	14	1	1	0	0	0	0	1	1	1
Jesse Burkett, of	.333	4	15	1	5	0	0	0	0	2	3	0
Cupid Childs, 2b	.231	4	13	2	3	0	0	0	0	4	0	1
Nig Cuppy, p	.143	2	7	0	1	0	0	0	0	0	1	0
Jimmy McAleer, of	.133	4	15	0	2	0	0	0	1	1	2	1
Chippy McGarr, 3b	.063	4	16	0	1	0	0	0	0	0	3	2
Ed McKean, ss	.313	4	16	0	5	1	1	0	1	1	2	1
Jack O'Connor, 1b	.286	4	14	1	4	0	0	0	1	1	2	0
Patsy Tebeau, 1b	.000	1	1	0	0	0	0	0	0	0	0	0
Bobby Wallace, p-1	.200	3	5	0	1	0	0	0	0	0	0	0
Cy Young, p	.000	1	3	0	0	0	0	0	0	0	0	0
Chief Zimmer, c	.214	4	14	0	3	1	0	0	1	2	6	0
TOTAL	.195		133	5	26	2	1	0	4	12	20	6

PITCHER	W	L	ERA	G	GS	CG	SV	SHO	IP	H	ER	BB	SO
Nig Cuppy	0	2	4.76	2	2	2	0	0	17.0	19	9	0	4
Bobby Wallace	0	1	4.50	1	1	1	0	0	8.0	10	4	2	4
Cy Young	0	1	6.00	1	1	1	0	0	9.0	13	6	1	0
TOTAL	0	4	5.03	4	4	4	0	0	34.0	42	19	3	8

GAME 1 AT BAL OCT 2

BAL	002	001	310	7	13	1
CLE	000	001	000	1	5	4

Pitchers: HOFFER vs YOUNG
Attendance: 4,000

GAME 2 AT BAL OCT 3

BAL	402	010	00	7	10	3
CLE	001	001	00	2	7	3

Pitchers: CORBETT vs WALLACE
Attendance: 3,100
(Game called at end of eighth, darkness)

GAME 3 AT BAL OCT 5

BAL	011	001	030	6	8	2
CLE	001	010	000	2	10	2

Pitchers: HOFFER vs CUPPY
Attendance: 2,000

GAME 4 AT CLE OCT 8

CLE	000	000	000	0	4	2
BAL	000	000	23X	5	11	1

Pitchers: CUPPY vs CORBETT
Attendance: 1,500

Boston had edged Baltimore in a close race for the NL pennant, but the Orioles turned the tables on the Beaneaters in Temple Cup play. The Series was a high-scoring affair, the winner of each game averaging eleven runs, the loser eight.

The opener, in Boston, set the tone for the games. Baltimore sent four runners across the plate in the top of the first inning, and Boston followed in its half with three. The Beaneaters recorded only twelve hits in the game to the Orioles' twenty, but they also received seven walks from Baltimore hurler Jerry Nops, and five of those runners scored. The lead switched back and forth in the middle innings, but Boston scored two final runs in the eighth and hung on for a 13–12 win.

Baltimore's Joe Corbett gave up sixteen hits (one a home run) and four walks in Game Two as Boston scored eleven times. But Boston's two pitchers, Fred Klobedanz and Jack Stivetts, were even more generous, handing out seventeen hits (including three homers—one of them to opposing pitcher Corbett, who also hit a double and two singles) and five walks as the Orioles evened the Series with their thirteen-run attack.

Game Three was the Series' lowest in run production, with Baltimore scoring four in the second inning and another four in the third for an 8–3 win. But rain ended the game before Boston could complete its time at bat in the last of the eighth, which erased from the record four more Oriole runs scored earlier in the inning. Rather than waste the two free days before the Series resumed in Baltimore, the two clubs played a pair of exhibition games in Worcester and Springfield, Massachusetts. Baltimore won them both, 11–10 and 8–6.

The Orioles continued their roll in Series Game Four, with another close but high-scoring victory, 12–11. It looked at first like a blowout as Baltimore scored six runs in the first inning and five more in the second. But Ted Lewis relieved Boston starter Jack Stivetts and held Baltimore to just one further run as the Beaneaters fought back to within one run of a tie before faltering in the ninth.

Boston batters hit Oriole Bill Hoffer safely fifteen times in Game Five, but only three Beaneaters scored. Baltimore, with two fewer hits, garnered six more runs than Boston and, with their fourth win, the right to hold the cup for another year. But at-

tendance at the final game was so small the embarrassed Baltimore management refused to release the figures, and the league gave the cup back to Mr. Temple rather than sponsor another unprofitable Series. There was no postseason championship contest in 1898 or 1899.

Baltimore Orioles, 4; Boston Beaneaters, 1

BAL (N)

PLAYER/POS	AVG	G	AB	R	H	2B	3B	HR	RB	BB	SO	SB
Frank Bowerman, c-1,1b-1	.500	2	8	2	4	0	1	0	4	0	0	0
Boileryard Clarke, c	.563	4	16	5	9	1	1	1	4	1	0	0
Joe Corbett, p	.667	2	6	2	4	1	0	1	2	0	1	0
Jack Doyle, 1b	.526	5	19	7	10	2	0	0	9	0	1	2
Bill Hoffer, p	.250	2	8	2	2	1	0	0	0	0	0	0
Hughie Jennings, ss	.318	5	22	5	7	2	0	0	3	4	0	0
Willie Keeler, of	.391	5	23	5	9	2	0	0	2	4	0	0
Joe Kelley, of	.313	4	16	7	5	3	0	0	5	5	0	0
John McGraw, 3b	.300	5	20	6	6	1	1	0	6	7	0	0
Jerry Nops, p	.286	2	7	0	2	0	0	0	1	1	5	0
Tom O'Brien, of	.400	1	5	2	2	1	0	0	0	0	0	0
Heinie Reitz, 2b	.250	5	20	4	5	1	0	1	4	2	0	0
Jake Stenzel, of	.381	5	21	7	8	1	1	0	3	2	0	2
TOTAL	.382		191	54	73	16	4	3	43	26	7	4

PITCHER	W	L	ERA	G	GS	CG	SV	SHO	IP	H	ER	BB	SO
Joe Corbett	1	0	9.00	2	1	1	0	0	12.0	21	12	8	5
Bill Hoffer	2	0	3.38	2	2	2	0	0	16.0	25	6	4	2
Jerry Nops	1	1	12.86	2	2	1	0	0	14.0	23	20	9	3
TOTAL	4	1	8.14	6	5	4	0	0	42.0	69	38	21	10

BOS (N)

PLAYER/POS	AVG	G	AB	R	H	2B	3B	HR	RB	BB	SO	SB
Marty Bergen, c	.500	1	4	0	2	0	0	0	1	0	1	1
Jimmy Collins, 3b	.182	5	22	2	4	0	0	0	4	1	0	0
Hugh Duffy, of	.524	5	21	6	11	1	0	0	7	1	0	0
Billy Hamilton, of	.500	4	16	6	8	1	0	0	2	5	3	2
Charlie Hickman, p-1,of-1	.250	1	4	0	1	1	0	0	1	0	0	0
Fred Klobedanz, p	1.000	2	5	3	5	0	0	0	0	0	0	0
Fred Lake, c	.000	1	4	0	0	0	0	0	0	0	1	0
Ted Lewis, p	.500	3	6	1	3	1	0	0	1	1	0	0
Herman Long, ss	.286	5	21	4	6	1	1	1	5	2	2	1
Bobby Lowe, 2b	.391	5	23	6	9	2	0	0	6	1	0	1
Kid Nichols, p	.000	1	3	0	0	0	0	0	1	0	0	0
Chick Stahl, of	.400	5	20	6	8	1	0	0	6	3	2	2
Jack Stivetts, p-2,of-1	.000	3	7	1	0	0	0	0	0	1	0	1
Jim Sullivan, p	.000	1	1	0	0	0	0	0	0	0	0	0
Fred Tenney, 1b	.300	5	20	4	6	0	0	0	2	4	1	2
George Yeager, c	.500	3	12	2	6	1	1	0	2	2	0	0
TOTAL	.365		189	41	69	9	2	1	38	21	10	10

PITCHER	W	L	ERA	G	GS	CG	SV	SHO	IP	H	ER	BB	SO
Charlie Hickman	0	1	3.60	1	1	0	0	0	5.0	7	2	2	0
Fred Klobedanz	0	1	9.35	2	1	0	0	0	8.2	12	9	8	0
Ted Lewis	1	1	6.17	3	1	0	0	0	11.2	18	8	9	4
Kid Nichols	0	0	12.00	1	1	0	0	0	6.0	14	8	0	3
Jack Stivetts	0	1	17.55	2	1	0	0	0	6.2	16	13	7	0
Jim Sullivan	0	0	3.00	1	0	0	0	0	3.0	6	1	0	0
TOTAL	1	4	9.00	10	5	0	0	0	41.0	73	41	26	7

GAME 1 AT BOS OCT 4

BAL	401 023 200	12	20	4
BOS	300 125 02X	13	12	4

Pitchers: NOPS vs Nichols, LEWIS (7)
Attendance: 9,600

GAME 2 AT BOS OCT 5

BAL	130 160 110	13	17	2
BOS	002 620 100	11	16	3

Pitchers: CORBETT vs KLOBEDANZ, Stivetts (5)
Home Runs: Reitz-BAL, Clarke-BAL, Corbett-BAL, Long-BOS
Attendance: 6,500

GAME 3 AT BOS OCT 6

BAL	044 000 0	8	9	2
BOS	003 000 0	3	10	2

Pitchers: HOFFER vs LEWIS, Klobedanz (4)
Attendance: 5,000
(Game called in eighth, rain)

GAME 4 AT BAL OCT 9

BOS	000 024 320	11	16	3
BAL	650 001 00X	12	14	3

Pitchers: STIVETTS, Lewis (3) vs NOPS, Corbett (7)
Attendance: 2,500

GAME 5 AT BAL OCT 11

BOS	020 000 001	3	15	3
BAL	023 000 22X	9	13	2

Pitchers: HICKMAN, Sullivan (7) vs HOFFER
Attendance: 700

Pennant-winning Brooklyn led the NL in hitting, but runner-up Pittsburgh claimed the best pitching. Honus Wagner was the only Pirate regular to hit over .300, but he enjoyed what turned out to be his finest season offensively, leading the league with a .381 batting average. Pittsburghers believed their club superior to Brooklyn and a best-of-five "world championship" series was arranged, with all the games to be played in Pittsburgh for a silver cup donated by the *Pittsburgh Chronicle-Telegraph*. Brooklyn, however, proved that its pennant was no fluke.

Two of the game's best pitchers faced off in the opener: Pittsburgh's Rube Waddell, who had led the league in ERA, and Joe "Iron Man" McGinnity, whose 29 regular-season wins totaled nine more than those of the league's runners-up. McGinnity prevailed, shutting out the Pirates until two unearned runs came across in the top of the ninth. Pirate errors also gave Brooklyn a pair of unearned runs, but Waddell lost the game on hits—thirteen in all, including six in the Superbas' three-run third inning.

In Game Two, Brooklyn's Frank Kitson held Pittsburgh to four hits, and although his Superbas scored only one earned run, six Pirate errors gave them their second win, 4–2.

The Pirates staved off a Series sweep with sharp pitching and heavy hitting in Game Three. Deacon Phillippe shut out Brooklyn on six hits as the Pirates jumped on Harry Howell for thirteen. All the Pirate hits were singles, but combined with Brooklyn errors they were good for ten runs, seven of them unearned.

Three Brooklyn singles and a fumble by Pirate pitcher Sam Leever in the fourth inning of Game Four gave the Superbas three runs and a 4–0 lead the Pirates could not overcome. Brooklyn hurler McGinnity scattered nine Pirate hits and, supported by flawless fielding, held Pittsburgh to a single run to bring Brooklyn its first World Series triumph in three tries—and its last until 1955. The Brooklyn players voted to award their trophy to McGinnity for his fine pitching. The cup may be seen today—along with the Temple Cup and the current World Series trophy—at baseball's Hall of Fame in Cooperstown.

Brooklyn Superbas, 3;
Pittsburgh Pirates, 1

BRO (N)

PLAYER/POS	AVG	G	AB	R	H	2B	3B	HR	RB	BB	SO	SB
Lave Cross, 3b	.278	4	18	2	5	0	1	0	1	0	0	1
Bill Dahlen, ss	.176	4	17	3	3	0	1	0	2	0	3	1
Tom Daly, 2b	.154	4	13	2	2	1	0	0	1	3	1	0
Duke Farrell, c	.375	2	8	0	3	0	0	0	1	0	0	1
Harry Howell, p	.000	1	3	0	0	0	0	0	0	0	2	0
Hughie Jennings, 1b	.167	4	18	1	3	1	0	0	2	1	1	0
Fielder Jones, of	.278	4	18	3	5	0	0	0	4	1	1	1
Willie Keeler, of	.353	4	17	0	6	0	0	0	0	1	0	0
Joe Kelley, of	.176	4	17	2	3	0	0	0	1	2	3	0
Frank Kitson, p	.000	1	3	0	0	0	0	0	0	1	2	0
Joe McGinnity, p	.143	2	7	1	1	0	0	0	1	0	2	0
Deacon McGuire, c	.375	2	8	1	3	1	0	0	0	0	1	0
TOTAL	.231		147	15	34	3	2	0	13	9	16	4

PITCHER	W	L	ERA	G	GS	CG	SV	SHO	IP	H	ER	BB	SO
Harry Howell	0	1	3.38	1	1	1	0	0	8.0	13	3	2	3
Frank Kitson	1	0	1.00	1	1	1	0	0	9.0	4	1	1	2
Joe McGinnity	2	0	0.00	2	2	2	0	0	18.0	14	0	3	5
TOTAL	3	1	1.03	4	4	4	0	0	35.0	31	4	6	10

PIT (N)

PLAYER/POS	AVG	G	AB	R	H	2B	3B	HR	RB	BB	SO	SB
Ginger Beaumont, of	.267	4	15	2	4	0	0	0	1	1	0	1
Fred Ely, ss	.286	4	14	1	4	1	0	0	0	1	1	2
Tommy Leach, of	.176	4	17	4	3	0	0	0	1	1	2	0
Sam Leever, p	.250	2	4	0	1	0	0	0	0	0	1	1
Tom O'Brien, 1b	.125	4	16	1	2	1	0	0	2	0	1	0
Jack O'Connor, c	.250	2	4	0	1	0	0	0	1	1	0	0
Deacon Phillippe, p	.000	1	4	1	0	0	0	0	0	0	1	0
Claude Ritchey, 2b	.333	4	15	3	5	1	0	0	1	1	0	0
Pop Schriver, ph	.000	1	1	0	0	0	0	0	0	0	0	0
Rube Waddell, p	.200	2	5	0	1	0	0	0	0	0	1	0
Honus Wagner, of	.400	4	15	2	6	1	0	0	3	0	1	2
Jimmy Williams, 3b	.214	4	14	0	3	0	0	0	0	1	0	0
Chief Zimmer, c	.111	3	9	1	1	0	0	0	1	0	2	1
TOTAL	.233		133	15	31	4	0	0	10	6	10	7

PITCHER	W	L	ERA	G	GS	CG	SV	SHO	IP	H	ER	BB	SO
Sam Leever	0	2	1.38	2	2	1	0	0	13.0	13	2	4	4
Deacon Phillippe	1	0	0.00	1	1	1	0	1	9.0	6	0	2	5
Rube Waddell	0	1	1.93	2	1	1	0	0	14.0	15	3	3	7
TOTAL	1	3	1.25	5	4	3	0	1	36.0	34	5	9	16

GAME 1 AT PIT OCT 15

BRO	003	101	000	5	13	1
PIT	000	000	002	2	5	4

Pitchers: McGINNITY vs WADDELL
Attendance: 4,000

GAME 2 AT PIT OCT 16

BRO	010	003	000	4	7	0
PIT	000	100	100	2	4	6

Pitchers: KITSON vs LEEVER
Attendance: 1,800

GAME 3 AT PIT OCT 17

BRO	000	000	000	0	6	3
PIT	310	020	13X	10	13	1

Pitchers: HOWELL vs PHILLIPPE
Attendance: 2,500

GAME 4 AT PIT OCT 18

BRO	100	311	000	6	8	0
PIT	000	001	000	1	9	3

Pitchers: McGINNITY vs LEEVER, Waddell (6)
Attendance: 2,335

When the Boston Pilgrims of the young American League accepted a challenge from owner Barney Dreyfuss of the National League Pirates, the modern World Series was born. (In 1901–02, the National and American Leagues were warring, and did not stage a postseason series.) Pittsburgh was favored to win but entered the Series weakened by injuries to pitching ace Sam Leever and shortstop Honus Wagner, and by the loss of pitcher Ed Doheny to mental illness.

Deacon Phillippe, the Pirates' one healthy starter, faced Cy Young in the opener, winning handily as Pirate batters, with two out in the top of the first, jumped on Young (and a porous defense) for four runs. Right fielder Jimmy Sebring starred offensively for the Pirates, with four RBIs and the Series's first home run. Boston came back in Game Two as Bill Dinneen shut out the Pirates on three hits. His teammates scored three runs off the sore-armed Leever and reliever Bucky Veil, two coming on homers by Patsy Dougherty. (They were the last World Series home runs for five years.)

Phillippe, with only a day's rest, started Game Three and again pitched Pittsburgh into the Series lead, holding Boston to four hits. After a Sunday travel day to Pittsburgh and a day of rain, Phillippe defeated Boston a third time, though he yielded three ninth-inning runs before emerging with a 5–4 win.

The tide began to turn against the Pirates the next day, as Boston knocked five ground-rule triples into the overflow crowd, scoring ten runs in the sixth and seventh innings to give Young an 11–2 victory. Dinneen bested Leever for a second time in Game Six, holding the Pirates scoreless in eight of their nine innings for a 6–3 win. And in Game Seven, Phillippe finally lost, Young winning his second game as Boston numbered 5 more triples among its 11 hits.

After another travel Sunday and another rainout, Phillippe for the fifth time faced the Pilgrims. He pitched well, giving up three runs (only two of them earned). But Bill Dinneen pitched better, holding the Pirates to four hits as he shut them out for the second time to give Boston the Series.

Boston Pilgrims (AL), 5; Pittsburgh Pirates (NL), 3

BOS (A)

PLAYER/POS	AVG	G	AB	R	H	2B	3B	HR	RB	BB	SO	SB
Jimmy Collins, 3b	.250	8	36	5	9	1	2	0	1	1	1	3
Lou Criger, c	.231	8	26	1	6	0	0	0	4	2	3	0
Bill Dinneen, p	.250	4	12	1	3	0	0	0	0	2	2	0
Patsy Dougherty, of	.235	8	34	3	8	0	2	2	5	2	6	0
Duke Farrell, ph	.000	2	2	0	0	0	0	0	1	0	0	0
Hobe Ferris, 2b	.290	8	31	3	9	0	1	0	5	0	6	0
Buck Freeman, of	.281	8	32	6	9	0	3	0	4	2	2	0
Tom Hughes, p	.000	1	0	0	0	0	0	0	0	0	0	0
Candy La Chance, 1b	.222	8	27	5	6	2	1	0	4	3	2	0
Jack O'Brien, ph	.000	2	2	0	0	0	0	0	0	0	1	0
Freddy Parent, ss	.281	8	32	8	9	0	3	0	4	1	1	0
Chick Stahl, of	.303	8	33	6	10	1	3	0	3	1	2	2
Cy Young, p	.133	4	15	1	2	0	1	0	3	0	3	0
TOTAL	.252		282	39	71	4	16	2	34	14	29	5

PITCHER	W	L	ERA	G	GS	CG	SV	SHO	IP	H	ER	BB	SO
Bill Dinneen	3	1	2.06	4	4	4	0	2	35.0	29	8	8	28
Tom Hughes	0	1	9.00	1	1	0	0	0	2.0	4	2	2	0
Cy Young	2	1	1.85	4	3	3	0	0	34.0	31	7	4	17
TOTAL	5	3	2.15	9	8	7	0	2	71.0	64	17	14	45

PIT (N)

PLAYER/POS	AVG	G	AB	R	H	2B	3B	HR	RB	BB	SO	SB
Ginger Beaumont, of	.265	8	34	6	9	0	1	0	1	2	4	2
Kitty Bransfield, 1b	.207	8	29	3	6	0	2	0	1	1	6	1
Fred Clarke, of	.265	8	34	3	9	2	1	0	2	1	5	1
Brickyard Kennedy, p	.500	1	2	0	1	1	0	0	0	0	0	0
Tommy Leach, 3b	.273	8	33	3	9	0	4	0	7	1	4	1
Sam Leever, p	.000	2	4	0	0	0	0	0	0	0	0	0
Ed Phelps, c-7	.231	8	26	1	6	2	0	0	1	1	6	0
Deacon Phillippe, p	.222	5	18	1	4	0	0	0	1	0	3	0
Claude Ritchey, 2b	.111	8	27	2	3	1	0	0	2	4	7	1
Jimmy Sebring, of	.367	8	30	3	11	0	1	1	3	1	4	0
Harry Smith, c	.000	1	3	0	0	0	0	0	0	0	0	0
Gus Thompson, p	.000	1	1	0	0	0	0	0	0	0	0	0
Bucky Veil, p	.000	1	2	0	0	0	0	0	0	0	2	0
Honus Wagner, ss	.222	8	27	2	6	1	0	0	3	3	4	3
TOTAL	.237		270	24	64	7	9	1	21	14	45	9

PITCHER	W	L	ERA	G	GS	CG	SV	SHO	IP	H	ER	BB	SO
Brickyard Kennedy	0	1	5.14	1	1	0	0	0	7.0	11	4	3	3
Sam Leever	0	2	5.40	2	2	1	0	0	10.0	13	6	3	2
Deacon Phillippe	3	2	2.86	5	5	5	0	0	44.0	38	14	3	22
Gus Thompson	0	0	4.50	1	0	0	0	0	2.0	3	1	0	1
Bucky Veil	0	0	1.29	1	0	0	0	0	7.0	6	1	5	1
TOTAL	3	5	3.34	10	8	6	0	0	70.0	71	26	14	29

GAME 1 AT BOS OCT 1

PIT	401	100	100	7	12	2
BOS	000	000	201	3	6	4

Pitchers: PHILLIPPE vs YOUNG
Home Runs: Sebring-PIT
Attendance: 16,242

GAME 2 AT BOS OCT 2

PIT	000	000	000	0	3	2
BOS	200	001	00X	3	9	0

Pitchers: LEEVER, Vail (2) vs DINNEEN
Home Runs: Dougherty-BOS(2)
Attendance: 9,415

GAME 3 AT BOS OCT 3

PIT	012	000	010	4	7	0
BOS	000	100	010	2	4	2

Pitchers: PHILLIPPE vs HUGHES, Young (3)
Attendance: 18,801

GAME 4 AT PIT OCT 6

BOS	000	010	003	4	9	1
PIT	100	010	30X	5	12	1

Pitchers: DINNEEN vs PHILLIPPE
Attendance: 7,600

GAME 5 AT PIT OCT 7

BOS	000	006	410	11	14	2
PIT	000	000	020	2	6	4

Pitchers: YOUNG vs KENNEDY, Thompson (8)
Attendance: 12,322

GAME 6 AT PIT OCT 8

BOS	003	020	100	6	10	1
PIT	000	000	300	3	10	3

Pitchers: DINNEEN vs LEEVER
Attendance: 11,556

GAME 7 AT PIT OCT 10

BOS	200	202	010	7	11	4
PIT	000	101	001	3	10	3

Pitchers: YOUNG vs PHILLIPPE
Attendance: 17,038

GAME 8 AT BOS OCT 13

PIT	000	000	000	0	4	3
BOS	000	201	00X	3	8	0

Pitchers: PHILLIPPE vs DINNEEN
Attendance: 7,455

After a year's gap caused by the Giants' refusal to play the American League champion Boston Pilgrims, the World Series—now established on an official and permanent basis—resumed with a pitching classic. Even though the A's ERA league leader Rube Waddell had ostensibly injured his shoulder and could not pitch in the Series—rumor had it that gamblers had reached him—the Philadelphia staff recorded a Series ERA of only 1.47. But the Giants' staff—led by Christy Mathewson's three shutouts—registered a matchless ERA of 0.00, permitting only three unearned runs to score in their only Series loss. Every victory in the Series was a shutout.

Mathewson, a 31-game winner in the regular season, continued his winning ways in the Series opener. Though three of the four hits he yielded were doubles, he permitted no more than one hit in any inning, and stopped the only scoring threat, fielding a squeeze bunt to throw out the runner at the plate in the sixth inning.

The A's came back to tie the Series the next day. This time it was Chief Bender's turn to hurl a four-hit shutout. Joe McGinnity also pitched well for the Giants, but New York errors in the third and eighth innings let in three unearned runs—the only runs, as it turned out, to be scored against the Giants in the Series.

Mathewson, pitching with only two days' rest in Game Three, once again permitted only four hits (all singles this time), and Philadelphia's flawed fielding let in seven unearned runs to help give Matty an easy 9–0 win. In Game Four, McGinnity, the hard-luck loser of Game Two, tried again. This time the Giants supported him almost flawlessly, while he gave up only five singles on his way to victory in the Series' tightest game. An A's error led to a single Giant run, and a loss for Eddie Plank, who had pitched even better than McGinnity, giving up only four hits while fanning six.

Chief Bender, the A's winner in Game Two, pitched a five-hitter in Game Six, but he also yielded three walks, all of which contributed to the two Giant runs. Mathewson, though he gave up six hits, walked none, retiring the final ten batters to conclude his record third shutout—and the Series.

New York Giants (NL), 4; Philadelphia Athletics (AL), 1

NY (N)

PLAYER/POS	AVG	G	AB	R	H	2B	3B	HR	RB	BB	SO	SB
Red Ames, p	.000	1	0	0	0	0	0	0	0	0	0	0
Roger Bresnahan, c	.313	5	16	3	5	2	0	0	1	4	0	1
George Browne, of	.182	5	22	2	4	0	0	0	1	0	2	2
Bill Dahlen, ss	.000	5	15	1	0	0	0	0	1	3	2	3
Art Devlin, 3b	.250	5	16	0	4	1	0	0	1	1	3	3
Mike Donlin, of	.263	5	19	4	5	1	0	0	1	2	1	2
Billy Gilbert, 2b	.235	5	17	1	4	0	0	0	2	0	2	1
Christy Mathewson, p	.250	3	8	1	2	0	0	0	0	1	1	0
Dan Mc Gann, 1b	.235	5	17	1	4	2	0	0	4	2	7	0
Joe Mc Ginnity, p	.000	2	5	0	0	0	0	0	0	0	2	0
Sam Mertes, of	.176	5	17	2	3	1	0	0	2	2	5	0
Sammy Strang, ph	.000	1	1	0	0	0	0	0	0	0	1	0
TOTAL	.203		153	15	31	7	0	0	13	15	26	12

PITCHER	W	L	ERA	G	GS	CG	SV	SHO	IP	H	ER	BB	SO
Red Ames	0	0	0.00	1	0	0	0	0	1.0	1	0	1	1
Christy Mathewson	3	0	0.00	3	3	3	0	3	27.0	14	0	1	18
Joe Mc Ginnity	1	1	0.00	2	2	1	0	1	17.0	10	0	3	6
TOTAL	4	1	0.00	6	5	4	0	4	45.0	25	0	5	25

PHI (A)

PLAYER/POS	AVG	G	AB	R	H	2B	3B	HR	RB	BB	SO	SB
Chief Bender, p	.000	2	5	0	0	0	0	0	0	0	1	0
Andy Coakley, p	.000	1	2	0	0	0	0	0	0	0	1	0
Lave Cross, 3b	.105	5	19	0	2	0	0	0	0	1	1	0
Monte Cross, ss	.176	5	17	0	3	0	0	0	0	0	7	0
Harry Davis, 1b	.200	5	20	0	4	1	0	0	0	0	1	0
Topsy Hartsel, of	.294	5	17	1	5	1	0	0	0	2	1	2
Danny Hoffman, ph	.000	1	1	0	0	0	0	0	0	0	1	0
Bris Lord, of	.100	5	20	0	2	0	0	0	2	0	5	0
Danny Murphy, 2b	.188	5	16	0	3	1	0	0	0	0	2	0
Eddie Plank, p	.167	2	6	0	1	0	0	0	0	0	2	0
Mike Powers, c	.143	3	7	0	1	1	0	0	0	0	0	0
Ossee Schreckengost, c	.222	3	9	2	2	1	0	0	0	0	0	0
Socks Seybold, of	.125	5	16	0	2	0	0	0	0	2	3	0
TOTAL	.161		155	3	25	5	0	0	2	5	25	2

PITCHER	W	L	ERA	G	GS	CG	SV	SHO	IP	H	ER	BB	SO
Chief Bender	1	1	1.06	2	2	2	0	1	17.0	9	2	6	13
Andy Coakley	0	1	2.00	1	1	1	0	0	9.0	8	2	5	2
Eddie Plank	0	2	1.59	2	2	2	0	0	17.0	14	3	4	11
TOTAL	1	4	1.47	5	5	5	0	1	43.0	31	7	15	26

GAME 1 AT PHI OCT 9

NY	000	020	001	3	10 1
PHI	000	000	000	0	4 0

Pitchers: MATHEWSON vs PLANK
Attendance: 17,955

GAME 2 AT NY OCT 10

PHI	001	000	020	3	6 2
NY	000	000	000	0	4 2

Pitchers: BENDER vs McGINNITY, Ames (9)
Attendance: 24,992

GAME 3 AT PHI OCT 12

NY	200	050	002	9	9 1
PHI	000	000	000	0	4 5

Pitchers: MATHEWSON vs COAKLEY
Attendance: 10,991

GAME 4 AT NY OCT 13

PHI	000	000	000	0	5 2
NY	000	100	00X	1	4 1

Pitchers: PLANK vs McGINNITY
Attendance: 13,598

GAME 5 AT NY OCT 14

PHI	000	000	000	0	6 0
NY	000	010	01X	2	5 1

Pitchers: BENDER vs MATHEWSON
Attendance: 24,187

The Cubs and White Sox have played more postseason City Series than any other clubs, but this was their only all-Chicago World Series. The Cubs were the clear favorites: league leaders in batting, fielding, and pitching (with a team ERA of only 1.76). They were one of baseball's greatest teams ever, with a still-record 116 wins, finishing 20 games ahead of the second-place Giants. The White Sox, by contrast, although their pitching and fielding were good enough to rank second in the American League, were the junior circuit's weakest hitters, batting as a team only .230, 32 points below the Cubs. But in the Series the "hitless wonders" prevailed. Though they hit only .198 and yielded eight unearned runs to the Cubs' two, the Sox bunched their hits for 20 earned runs—double the Cubs' total. Meanwhile, Sox pitchers held the Cubs to a .196 BA, and produced a team ERA less than half that of Cub pitchers.

Game One was a pitcher's duel as the Cubs' Mordecai (Three Finger) Brown and the Sox' Nick Altrock traded four-hitters and one earned run apiece. But Brown lost the game when his error in the seventh led to the Sox' second run. The Cubs snapped back to take Game Two on Ed Reulbach's one-hit 7–1 win. Although Reulbach issued six walks, he didn't really need the five unearned runs handed his club by Sox errors.

In Game Three the Sox regained the Series lead as Ed Walsh two-hit the Cubs, fanning 12 for the Series' first shutout. The Cubs' Jack Pfiester also pitched shutout ball in eight of his nine innings, but George Rohe's bases-loaded triple in the sixth gave the Sox more than enough to defeat him. Brown brought the Cubs back the next day, evening the Series with a two-hit shutout of his own, winning when Altrock yielded his only run on pairs of singles and sacrifice bunts in the seventh.

The rest of the Series belonged to the hitless wonders, who rocked three Cub pitchers for 12 hits and eight runs to take Game Five, and buried Brown and Orval Overall under 14 hits and another eight runs in Game Six to capture their first world championship.

Chicago White Sox (AL), 4; Chicago Cubs (NL), 2

CHI (A)

PLAYER/POS	AVG	G	AB	R	H	2B	3B	HR	RB	BB	SO	SB
Nick Altrock, p	.250	2	4	0	1	0	0	0	0	1	1	0
George Davis, ss	.308	3	13	4	4	3	0	0	6	0	1	1
Jiggs Donahue, 1b	.333	6	18	0	6	2	1	0	4	3	3	0
Patsy Dougherty, of	.100	6	20	1	2	0	0	0	1	3	4	2
Eddie Hahn, of	.273	6	22	4	6	0	0	0	0	1	1	0
Frank Isbell, 2b	.308	6	26	4	8	4	0	0	4	0	6	1
Fielder Jones, of	.095	6	21	4	2	0	0	0	0	3	3	0
Ed Mc Farland, ph	.000	1	1	0	0	0	0	0	0	0	0	0
Bill O'Neill, of	.000	1	1	1	0	0	0	0	0	0	0	0
Frank Owen, p	.000	1	2	0	0	0	0	0	0	0	1	0
George Rohe, 3b	.333	6	21	2	7	1	2	0	4	3	1	2
Billy Sullivan, c	.000	6	21	0	0	0	0	0	0	0	9	0
Lee Tannehill, ss	.111	3	9	1	1	0	0	0	0	0	2	0
Babe Towne, ph	.000	1	1	0	0	0	0	0	0	0	0	0
Ed Walsh, p	.000	2	4	1	0	0	0	0	0	0	3	0
Doc White, p	.000	3	3	0	0	0	0	0	0	1	0	0
TOTAL	.198		187	22	37	10	3	0	19	18	35	6

PITCHER	W	L	ERA	G	GS	CG	SV	SHO	IP	H	ER	BB	SO
Nick Altrock	1	1	1.00	2	2	2	0	0	18.0	11	2	2	5
Frank Owen	0	0	3.00	1	0	0	0	0	6.0	6	2	3	2
Ed Walsh	2	0	1.20	2	2	1	0	1	15.0	7	2	6	17
Doc White	1	1	1.80	3	2	1	1	0	15.0	12	3	7	4
TOTAL	4	2	1.50	8	6	4	1	1	54.0	36	9	18	28

CHI (N)

PLAYER/POS	AVG	G	AB	R	H	2B	3B	HR	RB	BB	SO	SB
Mordecai Brown, p	.333	3	6	0	2	0	0	0	0	0	4	0
Frank Chance, 1b	.238	6	21	3	5	1	0	0	0	2	1	2
Johnny Evers, 2b	.150	6	20	2	3	1	0	0	1	1	3	2
Doc Gessler, c	.000	2	1	0	0	0	0	0	0	1	0	0
Solly Hofman, of	.304	6	23	3	7	1	0	0	2	3	5	1
Johnny Kling, c	.176	6	17	2	3	1	0	0	0	4	3	0
Pat Moran, ph	.000	2	2	0	0	0	0	0	0	0	0	0
Orval Overall, p	.250	2	4	1	1	1	0	0	0	1	1	0
Jack Pfiester, p	.000	2	2	0	0	0	0	0	0	0	1	0
Ed Reulbach, p	.000	2	3	0	0	0	0	0	1	0	1	0
Frank Schulte, of	.269	6	26	1	7	3	0	0	3	1	3	0
Jimmy Sheckard, of	.000	6	21	0	0	0	0	0	1	2	4	1
Harry Steinfeldt, 3b	.250	6	20	2	5	1	0	0	2	1	0	0
Joe Tinker, ss	.167	6	18	4	3	0	0	0	1	2	2	3
TOTAL	.196		184	18	36	9	0	0	11	18	28	9

PITCHER	W	L	ERA	G	GS	CG	SV	SHO	IP	H	ER	BB	SO
Mordecai Brown	1	2	3.20	3	3	2	0	1	19.2	14	7	4	12
Orval Overall	0	0	2.25	2	0	0	0	0	12.0	10	3	3	8
Jack Pfiester	0	2	6.10	2	1	1	0	0	10.1	7	7	3	11
Ed Reulbach	1	0	2.45	2	2	1	0	0	11.0	6	3	8	4
TOTAL	2	4	3.40	9	6	4	0	1	53.0	37	20	18	35

GAME 1 AT CHI-N OCT 9

CHI-A	000	011	000	2	4	1
CHI-N	000	001	000	1	4	2

Pitchers: ALTROCK vs BROWN
Attendance: 12,693

GAME 2 AT CHI-A OCT 10

CHI-N	031	001	020	7	10	2
CHI-A	000	010	000	1	1	2

Pitchers: REULBACH vs WHITE, Owen (4)
Attendance: 12,595

GAME 3 AT CHI-N OCT 11

CHI-A	000	003	000	3	4	1
CHI-N	000	000	000	0	2	2

Pitchers: WALSH vs PFIESTER
Attendance: 13,667

GAME 4 AT CHI-A OCT 12

CHI-N	000	000	100	1	7	1
CHI-A	000	000	000	0	2	1

Pitchers: BROWN vs ALTROCK
Attendance: 18,385

GAME 5 AT CHI-N OCT 13

CHI-A	102	401	000	8	12	6
CHI-N	300	102	000	6	6	0

Pitchers: WALSH, White (7) vs Reulbach, PFIESTER (3), Overall (4)
Attendance: 23,257

GAME 6 AT CHI-A OCT 14

CHI-N	100	010	001	3	7	0
CHI-A	340	000	01X	8	14	3

Pitchers: BROWN, Overall (2) vs WHITE
Attendance: 19,249

The two-run lead that Detroit took into the bottom of the ninth inning of Game One proved to be its biggest of the Series. And it was short-lived, as Chicago—after Frank Chance's leadoff single—took advantage of a hit batsman, a fumble at third base, and a dropped third strike to even the score. Three scoreless extra innings later, darkness ended the game in a 3–3 tie.

The Tigers pitched well enough in the Series. Wild Bill Donovan and George Mullin, who provided more than 80 percent of Detroit's pitching, allowed only four earned runs each for a combined 1.89 ERA. But Cub pitchers gave up only four earned runs *as a team,* suffocating the Tigers with a team ERA of 0.75. And while Tiger fielders made one less error than the Cubs, their misplays proved more costly, permitting eight unearned runs to the Cubs' two.

Detroit's three-run eighth in the opener provided half of their Series scoring. Nine Tiger hits in Game Two produced only one run, while the Cubs bunched six of their nine hits into two innings for three runs and the Series' first win. In Games Three and Four, while the Tigers were twice again limited to a single run, the Cubs increased their run production to five and six, clustering 40 percent of their hits into two three-run innings, one in each game. Mordecai (Three Finger) Brown wrapped up the Series for Chicago with a shutout, as his Cubs blended a hit in each of the first two innings with three stolen bases and a Tiger error for the game's only two runs.

Detroit's twenty-year-old Ty Cobb, the American League batting, RBI, and stolen base leader in his first full big league season, hit an anemic .200 in the World Series, stealing no bases and driving in no Tiger runs. If there was an offensive hero, it was Cub centerfielder Jimmy Slagle. At age thirty-four, nearing the end of a ten-year major league career, he led both clubs with four RBIs (nearly quadruple his season's per-game output) and six stolen bases.

Chicago Cubs (NL), 4;
Detroit Tigers (AL), 0; tie, 1

CHI (N)

PLAYER/POS	AVG	G	AB	R	H	2B	3B	HR	RB	BB	SO	SB
Mordecai Brown, p	.000	1	3	0	0	0	0	0	0	1	0	0
Frank Chance, 1b	.214	4	14	3	3	1	0	0	0	3	2	3
Johnny Evers, 2b-5,ss-1	.350	5	20	2	7	2	0	0	1	0	1	3
Del Howard, 1b-1	.200	2	5	0	1	0	0	0	0	0	2	1
Johnny Kling, c	.211	5	19	2	4	0	0	0	1	1	4	0
Pat Moran, ph	.000	1	0	0	0	0	0	0	0	0	0	0
Orval Overall, p	.200	2	5	0	1	0	0	0	2	0	1	0
Jack Pfiester, p	.000	1	2	0	0	0	0	0	0	0	1	0
Ed Reulbach, p	.200	2	5	0	1	0	0	0	1	0	0	0
Frank Schulte, of	.250	5	20	3	5	0	0	0	2	1	2	0
Jimmy Sheckard, of	.238	5	21	0	5	2	0	0	2	0	4	1
Jimmy Slagle, of	.273	5	22	3	6	0	0	0	4	2	3	6
Harry Steinfeldt, 3b	.471	5	17	2	8	1	1	0	2	1	2	1
Joe Tinker, ss	.154	5	13	4	2	0	0	0	1	3	3	1
Heinie Zimmerman, 2b	.000	1	1	0	0	0	0	0	0	0	1	0
TOTAL	.257		167	19	43	6	1	0	16	12	26	16

PITCHER	W	L	ERA	G	GS	CG	SV	SHO	IP	H	ER	BB	SO
Mordecai Brown	1	0	0.00	1	1	1	0	1	9.0	7	0	1	4
Orval Overall	1	0	1.00	2	2	1	0	0	18.0	14	2	4	11
Jack Pfiester	1	0	1.00	1	1	1	0	0	9.0	9	1	1	3
Ed Reulbach	1	0	0.75	2	1	1	0	0	12.0	6	1	3	4
TOTAL	4	0	0.75	6	5	4	0	1	48.0	36	4	9	22

DET (A)

PLAYER/POS	AVG	G	AB	R	H	2B	3B	HR	RB	BB	SO	SB
Jimmy Archer, c	.000	1	3	0	0	0	0	0	0	0	1	0
Ty Cobb, of	.200	5	20	1	4	0	1	0	0	0	3	0
Bill Coughlin, 3b	.250	5	20	0	5	0	0	0	0	1	4	1
Sam Crawford, of	.238	5	21	1	5	1	0	0	3	0	3	0
Bill Donovan, p	.000	2	8	0	0	0	0	0	0	0	3	0
Davy Jones, of	.353	5	17	1	6	0	0	0	0	4	0	3
Ed Killian, p	.500	1	2	1	1	0	0	0	0	0	0	0
George Mullin, p	.000	2	6	0	0	0	0	0	0	0	1	0
Charley O'Leary, ss	.059	5	17	0	1	0	0	0	0	1	3	0
Fred Payne, c-1	.250	2	4	0	1	0	0	0	1	0	0	1
Claude Rossman, 1b	.400	5	20	1	8	0	1	0	2	1	0	1
Germany Schaefer, 2b	.143	5	21	1	3	0	0	0	0	0	3	0
Boss Schmidt, c-3	.167	4	12	0	2	0	0	0	0	2	1	0
Ed Siever, p	.000	1	1	0	0	0	0	0	0	0	0	0
TOTAL	.209		172	6	36	1	2	0	6	9	22	6

PITCHER	W	L	ERA	G	GS	CG	SV	SHO	IP	H	ER	BB	SO
Bill Donovan	0	1	1.71	2	2	2	0	0	21.0	17	4	5	16
Ed Killian	0	0	2.25	1	0	0	0	0	4.0	3	1	1	1
George Mullin	0	2	2.12	2	2	2	0	0	17.0	16	4	6	8
Ed Siever	0	1	4.50	1	1	0	0	0	4.0	7	2	0	1
TOTAL	0	4	2.15	6	5	4	0	0	46.0	43	11	12	26

GAME 1 AT CHI OCT 8

DET	000 000 030 000	3	9	3
CHI	000 100 002 000	3	10	5

Pitchers: Donovan vs Overall, Reulbach (10)
Attendance: 24,377

GAME 2 AT CHI OCT 9

DET	010 000 000	1	9	1
CHI	010 200 00X	3	9	1

Pitchers: MULLIN vs PFIESTER
Attendance: 21,901

GAME 3 AT CHI OCT 10

DET	000 001 000	1	6	1
CHI	010 310 00X	5	10	1

Pitchers: SIEVER, Killian (5) vs REULBACH
Attendance: 13,114

GAME 4 AT DET OCT 11

CHI	000 020 301	6	7	2
DET	000 100 000	1	5	2

Pitchers: OVERALL vs DONOVAN
Attendance: 11,306

GAME 5 AT DET OCT 12

CHI	110 000 000	2	7	1
DET	000 000 000	0	7	2

Pitchers: BROWN vs MULLIN
Attendance: 7,370

The Tigers won their final game of the season to take their second straight pennant, and the Cubs won their third pennant in a row by defeating the Giants in a replay of an earlier tie. Ty Cobb and Detroit improved on their 1907 Series performance, as Cobb led his club in batting, hits, and RBIs, and the Tigers won a game. But the Cubs as a team hit 90 percentage points higher than Detroit, and outscored them 24–15, to take the Series with relative ease.

In Game One, the Tigers took advantage of the Cubs' ragged fielding to score two runs in the eighth for a 6–5 lead. But in the top of the ninth, the Cubs erupted for five runs on six consecutive singles and a double steal, to win the game. The next day Chicago's Orval Overall held Detroit to four hits and one ninth-inning run. The Tigers' Wild Bill Donovan pitched even better for seven innings, holding Pittsburgh to a single in the sixth. But in the eighth, Joe Tinker's two-run homer—the first in a World Series since 1903—began an assault that ended only after six Cubs had crossed the plate.

Detroit finally manufactured a Series win, pummeling Jack Pfiester in Game Three for ten hits (six of them in the sixth inning) and an 8–3 victory. But that was their last burst. As the Series moved to Detroit for Games Four and Five, the Tiger offense collapsed. Three Finger Brown, the winner as a reliever in Game One, won Game Four as a starter, shutting out the Tigers on four hits. The Cubs needed only three of their ten hits, combining them with a couple of walks and stolen bases, and a muffed fly ball, to score twice in the third inning and once in the ninth.

Only 6,210 spectators—the smallest World Series crowd of the century—saw Overall strike out four Tigers in the first inning of Game Five (one reached first on a wild pitch) in what became a three-hit shutout. Meanwhile, his Cubs unloaded for ten hits, defeating Donovan a second time, scoring runs in the first and fifth innings. Overall—after yielding a leadoff walk to Cobb in the fifth—retired Cobb on a force play and set down the final 11 men to face him.

Chicago Cubs (NL), 4;
Detroit Tigers (AL), 1

CHI (N)

PLAYER/POS	AVG	G	AB	R	H	2B	3B	HR	RB	BB	SO	SB
Mordecai Brown, p	.000	2	4	0	0	0	0	0	0	0	2	0
Frank Chance, 1b	.421	5	19	4	8	0	0	0	2	3	1	5
Johnny Evers, 2b	.350	5	20	5	7	1	0	0	2	1	2	2
Solly Hofman, of	.316	5	19	2	6	0	1	0	4	1	4	2
Del Howard, ph	.000	1	1	0	0	0	0	0	0	0	0	0
Johnny Kling, c	.250	5	16	2	4	1	0	0	2	2	2	0
Orval Overall, p	.333	3	6	0	2	0	0	0	0	0	1	0
Jack Pfiester, p	.000	1	2	0	0	0	0	0	0	0	2	0
Ed Reulbach, p	.000	2	3	0	0	0	0	0	0	0	1	0
Frank Schulte, of	.389	5	18	4	7	0	1	0	2	2	1	2
Jimmy Sheckard, of	.238	5	21	2	5	2	0	0	1	2	3	1
Harry Steinfeldt, 3b	.250	5	16	3	4	0	0	0	3	2	5	1
Joe Tinker, ss	.263	5	19	2	5	0	0	1	4	0	2	2
TOTAL	.293		164	24	48	4	2	1	20	13	26	15

PITCHER	W	L	ERA	G	GS	CG	SV	SHO	IP	H	ER	BB	SO
Mordecai Brown	2	0	0.00	2	1	1	0	1	11.0	6	0	1	5
Orval Overall	2	0	0.98	3	2	2	0	1	18.1	7	2	7	15
Jack Pfiester	0	1	7.87	1	1	0	0	0	8.0	10	7	3	1
Ed Reulbach	0	0	4.70	2	1	0	0	0	7.2	9	4	1	5
TOTAL	4	1	2.60	8	5	3	0	2	45.0	32	13	12	26

DET (A)

PLAYER/POS	AVG	G	AB	R	H	2B	3B	HR	RB	BB	SO	SB
Ty Cobb, of	.368	5	19	3	7	1	0	0	4	1	2	2
Bill Coughlin, 3b	.125	3	8	0	1	0	0	0	1	0	1	0
Sam Crawford, of	.238	5	21	2	5	1	0	0	1	1	2	0
Bill Donovan, p	.000	2	4	0	0	0	0	0	0	1	1	1
Red Downs, 2b	.167	2	6	1	1	1	0	0	1	1	2	0
Davy Jones, ph	.000	3	2	1	0	0	0	0	0	1	1	0
Ed Killian, p	.000	1	0	0	0	0	0	0	0	0	0	0
Matty Mc Intyre, of	.222	5	18	2	4	1	0	0	0	3	2	1
George Mullin, p	.333	1	3	1	1	0	0	0	1	1	0	0
Charley O'Leary, ss	.158	5	19	2	3	0	0	0	0	0	3	0
Claude Rossman, 1b	.211	5	19	3	4	0	0	0	3	1	4	1
Germany Schaefer, 2b-3,3b-2	.125	5	16	0	2	0	0	0	0	1	4	1
Boss Schmidt, c	.071	4	14	0	1	0	0	0	1	0	2	0
Ed Summers, p	.200	2	5	0	1	0	0	0	1	0	2	0
Ira Thomas, c-1	.500	2	4	0	2	1	0	0	1	1	0	0
George Winter, p-1	.000	2	0	0	0	0	0	0	0	0	0	0
TOTAL	.203		158	15	32	5	0	0	14	12	26	6

PITCHER	W	L	ERA	G	GS	CG	SV	SHO	IP	H	ER	BB	SO
Bill Donovan	0	2	4.24	2	2	2	0	0	17.0	17	8	4	10
Ed Killian	0	0	11.57	1	1	0	0	0	2.1	5	3	3	1
George Mullin	1	0	0.00	1	1	1	0	0	9.0	7	0	1	8
Ed Summers	0	2	4.30	2	1	0	0	0	14.2	18	7	4	7
George Winter	0	0	0.00	1	0	0	0	0	1.0	1	0	1	0
TOTAL	1	4	3.68	7	5	3	0	0	44.0	48	18	13	26

GAME 1 AT DET OCT 10

CHI	004 000 105	10	14	2
DET	100 000 320	6	10	4

Pitchers: Reulbach, Overall (7), BROWN (8) vs Killian, SUMMERS (3)
Attendance: 10,812

GAME 2 AT CHI OCT 11

DET	000 000 001	1	4	1
CHI	000 000 06X	6	7	1

Pitchers: DONOVAN vs OVERALL
Home Runs: Tinker-CHI
Attendance: 17,760

GAME 3 AT CHI OCT 12

DET	100 005 020	8	11	4
CHI	000 300 000	3	7	2

Pitchers: MULLIN vs PFIESTER, Reulbach (9)
Attendance: 14,543

GAME 4 AT DET OCT 13

CHI	002 000 001	3	10	0
DET	000 000 000	0	4	1

Pitchers: BROWN vs SUMMERS, Winter (9)
Attendance: 12,907

GAME 5 AT DET OCT 14

CHI	100 010 000	2	10	0
DET	000 000 000	0	3	0

Pitchers: OVERALL vs DONOVAN
Attendance: 6,210

Babe Adams, a twenty-seven-year-old rookie pitcher, was only the fifth biggest winner on the Pittsburgh staff. But his fine 12–3 record was supported by a team-best 1.11 ERA, and manager Fred Clarke started him in the Series opener against Detroit's ace George Mullin (who had led the American League with a career-high 29 wins). Mullin pitched well, giving up only one earned run—manager/outfielder Clarke's homer in the fourth inning. But four Tiger errors led to three Pirate runs in the fifth and sixth. Meanwhile, Adams, after yielding a run in the first, pitched shutout ball the rest of the way for the win.

Detroit came back in Game Two with seven runs (including Ty Cobb's theft of home) as Wild Bill Donovan held the Pirates to two runs on five hits. In Game Three the Pirates took an early lead, which Detroit, despite rallies in the seventh and ninth innings, was unable to overcome. Errors determined most of the scoring, as only one of Detroit's six runs and two of Pittsburgh's eight were earned.

Mullin shut out the Pirates on five hits in Game Four, striking out ten men as Detroit scored five runs (all earned, despite Pittsburgh's six errors) to drive out starter Lefty Leifield after four innings. The seesaw Series continued in Game Five, with Babe Adams winning his second game behind his Pirates' ten-hit, eight-run attack. Adams gave up leadoff homers to Davy Jones in the first and Sam Crawford in the eighth. But Pittsburgh's Clarke more than countered these with his three-run shot in the seventh. (All three homers were hit into temporary seats in center field.)

Back in Detroit for Game Six, the Tigers evened the Series for the third time, Mullin winning his second game in a close contest that saw Pittsburgh pull within a run of tying the game in the ninth before a runner thrown out at home and a game-ending double play cut their rally dead.

In the finale it was Babe Adams once again, scattering six Tiger hits for an easy 8–0 win, his third of the Series. Detroit had done better than ever, but still lost their third World Series in three consecutive attempts. A quarter century would pass before they would have a chance to try again.

Pittsburgh Pirates (NL), 4; Detroit Tigers (AL), 3

PIT (N)

PLAYER/POS	AVG	G	AB	R	H	2B	3B	HR	RB	BB	SO	SB
Ed Abbaticchio, ph	.000	1	1	0	0	0	0	0	0	0	0	0
Bill Abstein, 1b	.231	7	26	3	6	2	0	0	2	3	10	1
Babe Adams, p	.000	3	9	0	0	0	0	0	0	0	1	0
Bobby Byrne, 3b	.250	7	24	5	6	1	0	0	0	1	4	1
Howie Camnitz, p	.000	2	1	0	0	0	0	0	0	0	0	0
Fred Clarke, of	.211	7	19	7	4	0	0	2	7	5	3	3
George Gibson, c	.240	7	25	2	6	2	0	0	2	1	1	2
Ham Hyatt, of-1	.000	2	4	1	0	0	0	0	1	1	0	0
Tommy Leach, of-7,3b-1	.360	7	25	8	9	4	0	0	2	2	1	1
Lefty Leifield, p	.000	1	1	0	0	0	0	0	0	0	1	0
Nick Maddox, p	.000	1	4	0	0	0	0	0	0	0	1	0
Dots Miller, 2b	.250	7	28	2	7	1	0	0	4	2	5	3
Paddy O'Connor, ph	.000	1	1	0	0	0	0	0	0	0	1	0
Deacon Phillippe, p	.000	2	1	0	0	0	0	0	0	0	1	0
Honus Wagner, ss	.333	7	24	4	8	2	1	0	6	4	2	6
Vic Willis, p	.000	2	4	0	0	0	0	0	0	0	1	0
Chief Wilson, of	.154	7	26	2	4	1	0	0	1	0	2	1
TOTAL	.224		223	34	50	13	1	2	25	20	34	18

PITCHER	W	L	ERA	G	GS	CG	SV	SHO	IP	H	ER	BB	SO
Babe Adams	3	0	1.33	3	3	3	0	1	27.0	18	4	6	11
Howie Camnitz	0	1	9.82	2	1	0	0	0	3.2	8	4	2	2
Lefty Leifield	0	1	11.25	1	1	0	0	0	4.0	7	5	1	0
Nick Maddox	1	0	1.00	1	1	1	0	0	9.0	10	1	2	4
Deacon Phillippe	0	0	0.00	2	0	0	0	0	6.0	2	0	1	2
Vic Willis	0	1	3.97	2	1	0	0	0	11.1	10	5	8	3
TOTAL	4	3	2.80	11	7	4	0	1	61.0	55	19	20	22

DET (A)

PLAYER/POS	AVG	G	AB	R	H	2B	3B	HR	RB	BB	SO	SB
Donie Bush, ss	.261	7	23	5	6	1	0	0	3	5	3	1
Ty Cobb, of	.231	7	26	3	6	3	0	0	5	2	2	2
Sam Crawford, of-7,1b-1	.250	7	28	4	7	3	0	1	4	1	1	1
Jim Delahanty, 2b	.346	7	26	2	9	4	0	0	4	2	5	0
Bill Donovan, p	.000	2	4	0	0	0	0	0	0	0	1	0
Davy Jones, of	.233	7	30	6	7	0	0	1	1	2	1	1
Tom Jones, 1b	.250	7	24	3	6	1	0	0	2	2	0	1
Matty Mc Intyre, of-1	.000	4	3	0	0	0	0	0	0	0	1	0
George Moriarty, 3b	.273	7	22	4	6	1	0	0	1	3	1	0
George Mullin, p-4	.188	6	16	1	3	1	0	0	0	1	3	0
Charley O'Leary, 3b	.000	1	3	0	0	0	0	0	0	0	0	0
Boss Schmidt, c	.222	6	18	0	4	2	0	0	4	2	0	0
Oscar Stanage, c	.200	2	5	0	1	0	0	0	2	0	2	0
Ed Summers, p	.000	2	3	0	0	0	0	0	0	0	2	0
Ed Willett, p	.000	2	2	0	0	0	0	0	0	0	0	0
Ralph Works, p	.000	1	0	0	0	0	0	0	0	0	0	0
TOTAL	.236		233	28	55	16	0	2	26	20	22	6

PITCHER	W	L	ERA	G	GS	CG	SV	SHO	IP	H	ER	BB	SO
Bill Donovan	1	1	3.00	2	2	1	0	0	12.0	7	4	8	7
George Mullin	2	1	2.25	4	3	3	0	1	32.0	23	8	8	20
Ed Summers	0	2	8.59	2	2	0	0	0	7.1	13	7	4	4
Ed Willett	0	0	0.00	2	0	0	0	0	7.2	3	0	0	1
Ralph Works	0	0	9.00	1	0	0	0	0	2.0	4	2	0	2
TOTAL	3	4	3.10	11	7	4	0	1	61.0	50	21	20	34

GAME 1 AT PIT OCT 8

```
DET   100 000 000   1 6 4
PIT   000 121 00X   4 5 0
```
Pitchers: MULLIN vs ADAMS
Home Runs: Clarke-PIT
Attendance: 29,264

GAME 2 AT PIT OCT 9

```
DET   023 020 000   7 9 3
PIT   200 000 000   2 5 1
```
Pitchers: DONOVAN vs CAMNITZ, Willis (3)
Attendance: 30,915

GAME 3 AT DET OCT 11

```
PIT   510 000 002   8 10 3
DET   000 000 402   6 10 5
```
Pitchers: MADDOX vs SUMMERS, Willett (1), Works (8)
Attendance: 18,277

GAME 4 AT DET OCT 12

```
PIT   000 000 000   0 5 6
DET   020 300 00X   5 8 0
```
Pitchers: LEIFIELD, Phillippe (5) vs MULLIN
Attendance: 17,036

GAME 5 AT PIT OCT 13

```
DET   100 002 010   4 6 1
PIT   111 000 41X   8 10 2
```
Pitchers: SUMMERS, Willett (8) vs ADAMS
Home Runs: D.Jones-DET, Crawford-DET, Clarke-PIT
Attendance: 21,706

GAME 6 AT DET OCT 14

```
PIT   300 000 001   4 7 3
DET   100 211 00X   5 10 3
```
Pitchers: WILLIS, Camnitz (6), Phillippe (7) vs MULLIN
Attendance: 10,535

GAME 7 AT DET OCT 16

```
PIT   020 203 010   8 7 0
DET   000 000 000   0 6 3
```
Pitchers: ADAMS vs DONOVAN, Mullin (4)
Attendance: 17,562

Pitcher Jack Coombs burst into stardom in 1910, emerging as the ace of a Philadelphia pitching staff which dominated the American League with an ERA of only 1.79. Coombs himself led league pitchers with 31 wins and 13 shutouts, and finished second to Chicago's Ed Walsh with an ERA of 1.30—all career bests. He continued his domination into the World Series, pitching three complete-game victories in the Athletics' surpisingly easy triumph over the Cubs.

The Series' finest pitching performance, though, was turned in by the A's Chief Bender in the opener. Only two batters reached base over the first eight innings—on a single and walk—and both of them were cut down trying to steal second. In the ninth, two Cub singles and two Athletic errors produced an unearned run, but as the A's had scored four runs (Bender himself providing the margin of victory with the game's second RBI in the second inning), the Cubs' run did no damage.

Coombs started Game Two and gave up a Cub run in the top of the first inning. But Athletic bats were hot in the Series (their team .316 batting average stood as a Series record for fifty years), and their 14 hits in this game (including four doubles and six runs in the seventh) sank Three Finger Brown and gave Coombs an easy win. Connie Mack also started Coombs in Game Three, two days later, and again the result was a lopsided win. Coombs himself drove in three of his team's 12 runs, and right fielder Danny Murphy added three more with the Series' only home run.

Bender pitched Game Four and suffered the A's only loss, as the Cubs tied the game at 3–3 with a run in the bottom of the ninth, and won it for reliever Three Finger Brown with a two-out RBI single an inning later.

Coombs faced Brown a second time in Game Five. Both clubs made nine hits, but the A's put four of them together with a walk, a wild pitch, and two stolen bases for five runs in the eighth to sink Brown as they had in Game Two, breaking a tight game wide open for Coombs's third win and the Athletics' first world championship.

Philadelphia Athletics (AL), 4; Chicago Cubs (NL), 1

PHI (A)

PLAYER/POS	AVG	G	AB	R	H	2B	3B	HR	RB	BB	SO	SB
Frank Baker, 3b	.409	5	22	6	9	3	0	0	4	2	1	0
Jack Barry, ss	.235	5	17	3	4	2	0	0	3	1	3	0
Chief Bender, p	.333	2	6	1	2	0	0	0	1	1	1	0
Eddie Collins, 2b	.429	5	21	5	9	4	0	0	3	2	0	4
Jack Coombs, p	.385	3	13	0	5	1	0	0	3	0	3	0
Harry Davis, 1b	.353	5	17	5	6	3	0	0	2	3	4	0
Topsy Hartsel, of	.200	1	5	2	1	0	0	0	0	0	1	2
Jack Lapp, c	.250	1	4	0	1	0	0	0	1	0	2	0
Bris Lord, of	.182	5	22	3	4	2	0	0	1	1	3	0
Danny Murphy, of	.350	5	20	6	7	3	0	1	9	1	0	1
Amos Strunk, of	.278	4	18	2	5	1	1	0	2	2	5	0
Ira Thomas, c	.250	4	12	2	3	0	0	0	1	4	1	0
TOTAL	.316		177	35	56	19	1	1	30	17	24	7

PITCHER	W	L	ERA	G	GS	CG	SV	SHO	IP	H	ER	BB	SO
Chief Bender	1	1	1.93	2	2	2	0	0	18.2	12	4	4	14
Jack Coombs	3	0	3.33	3	3	3	0	0	27.0	23	10	14	17
TOTAL	4	1	2.76	5	5	5	0	0	45.2	35	14	18	31

CHI (N)

PLAYER/POS	AVG	G	AB	R	H	2B	3B	HR	RB	BB	SO	SB
Jimmy Archer, c-2,1b-1	.182	3	11	1	2	1	0	0	0	0	3	0
Ginger Beaumont, ph	.000	3	2	1	0	0	0	0	0	1	1	0
Mordecai Brown, p	.000	3	7	0	0	0	0	0	0	0	1	0
Frank Chance, 1b	.353	5	17	1	6	1	1	0	4	0	3	0
King Cole, p	.000	1	2	0	0	0	0	0	0	0	2	0
Solly Hofman, of	.267	5	15	2	4	0	0	0	2	4	3	0
Johnny Kane, pr	.000	1	0	0	0	0	0	0	0	0	0	0
Johnny Kling, c-3	.077	5	13	0	1	0	0	0	1	1	2	0
Harry Mc Intire, p	.000	2	1	0	0	0	0	0	0	0	1	0
Tom Needham, ph	.000	1	1	0	0	0	0	0	0	0	0	0
Orval Overall, p	.000	1	1	0	0	0	0	0	0	0	0	0
Jack Pfiester, p	.000	1	2	0	0	0	0	0	0	0	1	0
Ed Reulbach, p	.000	1	0	0	0	0	0	0	0	0	0	0
Lew Richie, p	.000	1	0	0	0	0	0	0	0	0	0	0
Frank Schulte, of	.353	5	17	3	6	3	0	0	2	2	3	0
Jimmy Sheckard, of	.286	5	14	5	4	2	0	0	1	7	2	1
Harry Steinfeldt, 3b	.100	5	20	0	2	1	0	0	1	0	4	0
Joe Tinker, ss	.333	5	18	2	6	2	0	0	0	2	2	1
Heinie Zimmerman, 2b	.235	5	17	0	4	1	0	0	2	1	3	1
TOTAL	.222		158	15	35	11	1	0	13	18	31	3

PITCHER	W	L	ERA	G	GS	CG	SV	SHO	IP	H	ER	BB	SO
Mordecai Brown	1	2	5.50	3	2	1	0	0	18.0	23	11	7	14
King Cole	0	0	3.38	1	1	0	0	0	8.0	10	3	3	5
Harry Mc Intire	0	1	6.75	2	0	0	0	0	5.1	4	4	3	3
Orval Overall	0	1	9.00	1	1	0	0	0	3.0	6	3	1	1
Jack Pfiester	0	0	0.00	1	0	0	0	0	6.2	9	0	1	1
Ed Reulbach	0	0	9.00	1	1	0	0	0	2.0	3	2	2	0
Lew Richie	0	0	0.00	1	0	0	0	0	1.0	1	0	0	0
TOTAL	1	4	4.70	10	5	1	0	0	44.0	56	23	17	24

GAME 1 AT PHI OCT 17

CHI	000 000 001	1	3	1
PHI	021 000 01X	4	7	2

Pitchers: OVERALL, McIntire (4) vs BENDER
Attendance: 26,891

GAME 2 AT PHI OCT 18

CHI	100 000 101	3	8	3
PHI	002 010 60X	9	14	4

Pitchers: BROWN, Richie (8) vs COOMBS
Attendance: 24,597

GAME 3 AT CHI OCT 20

PHI	125 000 400	12	15	1
CHI	120 000 020	5	6	5

Pitchers: COOMBS vs Reulbach, McINTIRE (3), Pfiester (3)
Home Runs: Murphy-PHI
Attendance: 26,210

GAME 4 AT CHI OCT 22

PHI	001 200 000 0	3	11	3
CHI	100 100 001 1	4	9	1

Pitchers: BENDER vs Cole, BROWN (9)
Attendance: 19,150

GAME 5 AT CHI OCT 23

PHI	100 010 050	7	9	1
CHI	010 000 010	2	9	2

Pitchers: COOMBS vs BROWN
Attendance: 27,374

Connie Mack's pitching aces out-dueled Christy Mathewson, and Frank Baker hit two crucial home runs to become "Home Run" Baker forever more, as the A's avenged their 1905 Series loss to the Giants. Game One, though, belonged to Matty and New York. Philadelphia scored first, but the Giants tied the game with an unearned run in the fourth inning, and won it with two doubles in the seventh, setting at naught Chief Bender's otherwise splendid 11-strikeout performance.

The A's came back to take three in a row. In Game Two Eddie Plank held the Giants to one run and Baker hit the first of his homers, breaking a tie in the sixth with a two-run blast off Rube Marquard. The next day, the A's and Jack Coombs handed Mathewson his first World Series loss. Both pitchers went the distance in an 11-inning duel that saw Matty hold the A's scoreless through eight, only to give up a game-tying home run to Baker in the ninth, and two unearned runs in the eleventh, meanwhile, pitched two-hit, one-run ball through ten innings. In the last of the eleventh, a third Giant hit and an A's error let in a second Giant run, but the rally died when Beals Becker was cut down for the final out trying to steal second.

After a week of rain, Mathewson and Bender squared off in Game Four. The Giants jumped on Bender for two runs in the first, and held the lead until the fourth. But in the last of the fourth, three successive A's doubles and a run-scoring fly put the A's in front to stay as Bender held New York scoreless over the final 8 innings.

In Game Five, a three-run homer by the A's Rube Oldring off Rube Marquard in the third provided the only scoring through 6½ innings. But the Giants crept back with one run in the seventh, and two more in the last of the ninth tied the score. Plank replaced Coombs for the A's in the tenth and took the loss as Larry Doyle led off with a double, took third on a missed force play, and scored on Fred Merkle's fly to deep right.

After five closely contested games, Game Six was a laugher. It, too, was close at first—tied 1–1 after 3½ innings. But the A's scored four runs in the fourth on singles and errors, once in the sixth, and seven times in the seventh on a barrage of hits, an error, and a two-run wild pitch. Chief Bender, who gave up only four hits and two unearned runs, was the beneficiary of this largesse, taking his second win of the Series and giving the A's their second consecutive world title.

Philadelphia Athletics (AL), 4; New York Giants (NL), 2

PHI (A)

PLAYER/POS	AVG	G	AB	R	H	2B	3B	HR	RB	BB	SO	SB
Frank Baker, 3b	.375	6	24	7	9	2	0	2	5	1	5	0
Jack Barry, ss	.368	6	19	2	7	4	0	0	2	0	2	2
Chief Bender, p	.091	3	11	0	1	0	0	0	0	0	1	0
Eddie Collins, 2b	.286	6	21	4	6	1	0	0	1	2	2	2
Jack Coombs, p	.250	2	8	1	2	0	0	0	0	0	0	0
Harry Davis, 1b	.208	6	24	3	5	1	0	0	5	0	3	0
Jack Lapp, c	.250	2	8	1	2	0	0	0	0	0	1	0
Bris Lord, of	.185	6	27	2	5	2	0	0	1	0	5	0
Stuffy Mc Innis, 1b	.000	1	0	0	0	0	0	0	0	0	0	0
Danny Murphy, of	.304	6	23	4	7	3	0	0	3	0	3	0
Rube Oldring, of	.200	6	25	2	5	2	0	1	3	0	5	0
Eddie Plank, p	.000	2	3	0	0	0	0	0	0	0	2	0
Amos Strunk, pr	.000	1	0	0	0	0	0	0	0	0	0	0
Ira Thomas, c	.083	4	12	1	1	0	0	0	1	1	2	0
TOTAL	.244		205	27	50	15	0	3	21	4	31	4

PITCHER	W	L	ERA	G	GS	CG	SV	SHO	IP	H	ER	BB	SO
Chief Bender	2	1	1.04	3	3	3	0	0	26.0	16	3	8	20
Jack Coombs	1	0	1.35	2	2	1	0	0	20.0	11	3	6	16
Eddie Plank	1	1	1.86	2	1	1	0	0	9.2	6	2	0	8
TOTAL	4	2	1.29	7	6	5	0	0	55.2	33	8	14	44

NY (N)

PLAYER/POS	AVG	G	AB	R	H	2B	3B	HR	RB	BB	SO	SB
Red Ames, p	.500	2	2	0	1	0	0	0	0	0	1	0
Beals Becker, ph	.000	3	3	0	0	0	0	0	0	0	0	0
Doc Crandall, p-2	.500	3	2	1	1	1	0	0	1	2	0	0
Josh Devore, of	.167	6	24	1	4	1	0	0	3	1	8	0
Larry Doyle, 2b	.304	6	23	3	7	3	1	0	1	2	1	2
Art Fletcher, ss	.130	6	23	1	3	1	0	0	1	0	4	0
Buck Herzog, 3b	.190	6	21	3	4	2	0	0	0	2	3	2
Rube Marquard, p	.000	3	2	0	0	0	0	0	0	0	2	0
Christy Mathewson, p	.286	3	7	0	2	0	0	0	0	1	3	0
Fred Merkle, 1b	.150	6	20	1	3	1	0	0	1	2	6	0
Chief Meyers, c	.300	6	20	2	6	2	0	0	2	0	3	0
Red Murray, of	.000	6	21	0	0	0	0	0	0	2	5	0
Fred Snodgrass, of	.105	6	19	1	2	0	0	0	0	1	2	7	0
Art Wilson, c	.000	1	1	0	0	0	0	0	0	0	0	0
Hooks Wiltse, p	.000	2	1	0	0	0	0	0	0	0	1	0
TOTAL	.175		189	13	33	11	1	0	10	14	44	4

PITCHER	W	L	ERA	G	GS	CG	SV	SHO	IP	H	ER	BB	SO
Red Ames	0	1	2.25	2	1	0	0	0	8.0	6	2	1	6
Doc Crandall	1	0	0.00	2	0	0	0	0	4.0	2	0	0	2
Rube Marquard	0	1	1.54	3	2	0	0	0	11.2	9	2	1	8
Christy Mathewson	1	2	2.00	3	3	2	0	0	27.0	25	6	2	13
Hooks Wiltse	0	0	18.90	2	0	0	0	0	3.1	8	7	0	2
TOTAL	2	4	2.83	12	6	2	0	0	54.0	50	17	4	31

GAME 1 AT NY OCT 14

PHI	010	000	000		1	6	2
NY	000	100	10X		2	5	0

Pitchers: BENDER vs MATHEWSON
Attendance: 38,281

GAME 2 AT PHI OCT 16

NY	010	000	000		1	5	3
PHI	100	002	00X		3	4	0

Pitchers: MARQUARD, Crandall (8) vs PLANK
Home Runs: Baker-PHI
Attendance: 26,286

GAME 3 AT NY OCT 17

PHI	000	000	001	02	3	9	2
NY	001	000	000	01	2	3	5

Pitchers: COOMBS vs MATHEWSON
Home Runs: Baker-PHI
Attendance: 37,216

GAME 4 AT PHI OCT 24

NY	200	000	000		2	7	3
PHI	000	310	00X		4	11	1

Pitchers: MATHEWSON, Wiltse (8) vs BENDER
Attendance: 24,355

GAME 5 AT NY OCT 25

PHI	003	000	000	0	3	7	1
NY	000	000	102	1	4	9	2

Pitchers: Coombs, PLANK (10) vs Marquard, Ames (4), CRANDALL (8)
Home Runs: Oldring-PHI
Attendance: 33,228

GAME 6 AT PHI OCT 26

NY	100	000	001		2	4	3
PHI	001	401	70X		13	13	5

Pitchers: AMES, Wiltse (5), Marquard (7) vs BENDER
Attendance: 20,485

The Giants outhit the Red Sox by 50 percentage points, and their pitchers let in one less earned run per game. But this was the Series in which Fred Snodgrass's famous muff of a routine fly to center in the tenth inning of the final game helped turn a slim Giant lead into a Red Sox world championship. In all fairness, it must be admitted that Snodgrass followed his muff with a brilliant catch off the next batter, and indecision by the catcher and first baseman permitted a pop foul to drop, keeping the Sox alive to score the tying and winning runs. For that matter, this final game might not have been needed at all if Snodgrass and Beals Becker hadn't both been cut down trying to steal second in the eleventh inning of Game Two, which ended in a tie because of darkness. If either had gone on to score, the Giants would have won the Series in seven games.

Boston's Smokey Joe Wood followed up his spectacular 34–5 regular season with Series wins in Games One and Four, before being rocked for six runs in the first inning of Game Seven for a loss. Relieving in the eighth inning of the finale, he stopped the Giants for two innings, but gave up what would have been the losing run in the tenth had not the Giants' fielding in the last of the inning turned the game around, giving Wood the win and the Sox the Series.

Although Wood won three games, the best pitching of the Series was turned in by the Giants' Rube Marquard and Boston's Hugh Bedient. Marquard (who in the regular season had tied a major league record with 19 consecutive wins) won two of his club's three victories (Games Three and Six), allowing three runs—only one of them earned. Bedient, in two starts and two relief appearances, matched Marquard's 0.50 earned run average, winning a duel with Christy Mathewson in Game Five, and hurling seven effective innings against Matty in the finale.

Mathewson was the Series' hard-luck pitcher: his one tie and two losses were all decided by unearned runs.

Boston Red Sox (AL), 4;
New York Giants (NL), 3; tie, 1

BOS (A)

PLAYER/POS	AVG	G	AB	R	H	2B	3B	HR	RB	BB	SO	SB
Neal Ball, ph	.000	1	1	0	0	0	0	0	0	0	1	0
Hugh Bedient, p	.000	4	6	0	0	0	0	0	0	0	0	0
Hick Cady, c	.136	7	22	1	3	0	0	0	1	0	3	0
Bill Carrigan, c	.000	2	7	0	0	0	0	0	0	0	0	0
Ray Collins, p	.000	2	5	0	0	0	0	0	0	0	2	0
Clyde Engle, ph	.333	3	3	1	1	1	0	0	2	0	0	0
Larry Gardner, 3b	.179	8	28	4	5	2	1	1	4	2	5	0
Charley Hall, p	.750	2	4	0	3	1	0	0	0	1	0	0
Olaf Henricksen, ph	1.000	2	1	0	1	1	0	0	1	0	0	0
Harry Hooper, of	.290	8	31	3	9	2	1	0	2	4	4	2
Duffy Lewis, of	.156	8	32	4	5	3	0	0	2	2	2	0
Buck O'Brien, p	.000	2	2	0	0	0	0	0	0	0	2	0
Tris Speaker, of	.300	8	30	4	9	1	2	0	2	4	2	1
Jake Stahl, 1b	.281	8	32	3	9	2	0	0	2	0	6	2
Heinie Wagner, ss	.167	8	30	1	5	1	0	0	0	3	6	1
Joe Wood, p	.286	4	7	1	2	0	0	0	1	1	0	0
Steve Yerkes, 2b	.250	8	32	3	8	0	2	0	4	2	3	0
TOTAL	.220		273	25	60	14	6	1	21	19	36	6

PITCHER	W	L	ERA	G	GS	CG	SV	SHO	IP	H	ER	BB	SO
Hugh Bedient	1	0	0.50	4	2	1	0	0	18.0	10	2	7	7
Ray Collins	0	0	1.88	2	1	0	0	0	14.1	14	3	0	6
Charley Hall	0	0	3.38	2	0	0	0	0	10.2	11	4	9	1
Buck O'Brien	0	2	5.00	2	2	0	0	0	9.0	12	5	3	4
Joe Wood	3	1	3.68	4	3	2	0	0	22.0	27	9	3	21
TOTAL	4	3	2.80	14	8	3	0	0	74.0	74	23	22	39

NY (N)

PLAYER/POS	AVG	G	AB	R	H	2B	3B	HR	RB	BB	SO	SB
Red Ames, p	.000	1	0	0	0	0	0	0	0	0	0	0
Beals Becker, of-1	.000	2	4	1	0	0	0	0	0	2	0	0
Doc Crandall, p	.000	1	1	0	0	0	0	0	0	0	1	0
Josh Devore, of	.250	7	24	4	6	0	0	0	0	7	5	4
Larry Doyle, 2b	.242	8	33	5	8	1	0	1	2	3	2	2
Art Fletcher, ss	.179	8	28	1	5	1	0	0	3	1	4	1
Buck Herzog, 3b	.400	8	30	6	12	4	1	0	4	1	3	2
Rube Marquard, p	.000	2	4	0	0	0	0	0	0	1	0	0
Christy Mathewson, p	.167	3	12	0	2	0	0	0	0	0	4	0
Moose Mc Cormick, ph	.250	5	4	0	1	0	0	0	1	0	0	0
Fred Merkle, 1b	.273	8	33	5	9	2	1	0	3	0	7	1
Chief Meyers, c	.357	8	28	2	10	0	1	0	3	2	3	1
Red Murray, of	.323	8	31	5	10	4	1	0	5	2	2	0
Tillie Shafer, ph	.000	3	0	0	0	0	0	0	0	0	0	0
Fred Snodgrass, of	.212	8	33	2	7	2	0	0	2	2	5	1
Jeff Tesreau, p	.375	3	8	0	3	0	0	0	2	1	3	0
Art Wilson, c	1.000	2	1	0	1	0	0	0	0	0	0	0
TOTAL	.270		274	31	74	14	4	1	25	22	39	12

PITCHER	W	L	ERA	G	GS	CG	SV	SHO	IP	H	ER	BB	SO
Red Ames	0	0	4.50	1	0	0	0	0	2.0	3	1	1	0
Doc Crandall	0	0	0.00	1	0	0	0	0	2.0	1	0	0	2
Rube Marquard	2	0	0.50	2	2	2	0	0	18.0	14	1	2	9
Christy Mathewson	0	2	1.26	3	3	3	0	0	28.2	23	4	5	10
Jeff Tesreau	1	2	3.13	3	3	1	0	0	23.0	19	8	11	15
TOTAL	3	4	1.71	10	8	6	0	0	73.2	60	14	19	36

GAME 1 AT NY OCT 8

BOS	000	001	300	4	6	1
NY	002	000	001	3	8	1

Pitchers: WOOD vs TESREAU, Crandall (8)
Attendance: 35,730

GAME 2 AT BOS OCT 9

NY	010	100	030	10	6	11	5
BOS	300	010	010	10	6	10	1

Pitchers: Mathewson vs Collins, Hall (8), Bedient (11)
Attendance: 30,148

GAME 3 AT BOS OCT 10

NY	010	010	000	2	7	1
BOS	000	000	001	1	7	0

Pitchers: MARQUARD vs O'BRIEN, Bedient (9)
Attendance: 34,624

GAME 4 AT NY OCT 11

BOS	010	100	001	3	8	1
NY	000	000	100	1	9	1

Pitchers: WOOD vs TESREAU, Ames (8)
Attendance: 36,502

GAME 5 AT BOS OCT 12

NY	000	000	100	1	3	1
BOS	002	000	00X	2	5	1

Pitchers: MATHEWSON vs BEDIENT
Attendance: 34,683

GAME 6 AT NY OCT 14

BOS	020	000	000	2	7	2
NY	500	000	00X	5	11	2

Pitchers: O'BRIEN, Collins (2) vs MARQUARD
Attendance: 30,622

GAME 7 AT BOS OCT 15

NY	610	002	101	11	16	4
BOS	010	000	210	4	9	3

Pitchers: TESREAU vs WOOD, Hall (2)
Home Runs: Doyle-NY, Gardner-BOS
Attendance: 32,694

GAME 8 AT BOS OCT 16

NY	001	000	000	1	2	9	2
BOS	000	000	100	2	3	8	5

Pitchers: MATHEWSON vs Bedient, WOOD (8)
Attendance: 17,034

Third baseman Frank Baker and catcher Wally Schang drove in more than 60 percent of the Athletics' runs, as Philadelphia dispatched the Giants in five games. Chief Bender led A's pitchers with two wins, and rookie Bullet Joe Bush hurled a nifty five-hitter in Game Three, but the Series highlights were two duels between the A's Eddie Plank and the Giant's Christy Mathewson. The A's heavy hitting made Bender's wins possible and Bush's win easy, but pitching dominated the Plank-Matty games.

Bender yielded 11 hits in the opener, as did the Giants' pitchers. But five of the game's six extra-base hits belonged to the A's—including Baker's two-run homer and triples by Schang and Eddie Collins—and Bender emerged victorious. In Game Two, Plank and Mathewson pitched shutout ball through nine innings, but in the top of the tenth Matty himself singled in the game's first run and scored the second. Taking a 3–0 lead into the bottom of the inning, he set the A's down in order for New York's only Series win.

In Game Three, Schang's solo homer and Collins's three hits (including his second Series triple) and three RBIs led a 12-hit A's attack which, with Bush's fine pitching, put Philadelphia back into the Series lead. Bender won again in Game Four, shutting out the Giants through six innings as his A's scored six runs. But in the seventh, New York's Fred Merkle homered for three runs, and a single, double, and triple in the eighth brought in two more Giant runs. With his lead cut to a single run, Bender bore down in the ninth and retired the side in order.

Plank avenged his earlier loss with a brilliant two-hitter in Game Five, facing the minimum three batters in eight of the nine innings. (His own error in the fifth—a dropped pop-up—led to the Giants' only run.) Mathewson pitched well, too, yielding only six singles. But four of them came in the first and third innings, combining with two sacrifice flies and an error for three runs. Only one Athletic batter reached base in the final six innings, but with Plank pitching as he was, the game and the title were in Philadelphia's pocket.

Philadelphia Athletics (AL), 4;
New York Giants (NL), 1

PHI (A)

PLAYER/POS	AVG	G	AB	R	H	2B	3B	HR	RB	BB	SO	SB
Frank Baker, 3b	.450	5	20	2	9	0	0	1	7	0	2	1
Jack Barry, ss	.300	5	20	3	6	3	0	0	2	0	0	0
Chief Bender, p	.000	2	8	0	0	0	0	0	0	1	0	0
Joe Bush, p	.250	1	4	0	1	0	0	0	0	0	1	0
Eddie Collins, 2b	.421	5	19	5	8	0	2	0	3	1	2	3
Jack Lapp, c	.250	1	4	0	1	0	0	0	0	0	1	0
Stuffy Mc Innis, 1b	.118	5	17	1	2	1	0	0	2	0	2	0
Eddie Murphy, of	.227	5	22	2	5	0	0	0	0	2	0	0
Rube Oldring, of	.273	5	22	5	6	0	1	0	0	0	1	1
Eddie Plank, p	.143	2	7	0	1	0	0	0	0	0	0	0
Wally Schang, c	.357	4	14	2	5	0	1	1	6	2	4	0
Amos Strunk, of	.118	5	17	3	2	0	0	0	0	2	2	0
TOTAL	.264		174	23	46	4	4	2	21	7	16	5

PITCHER	W	L	ERA	G	GS	CG	SV	SHO	IP	H	ER	BB	SO
Chief Bender	2	0	4.00	2	2	2	0	0	18.0	19	8	1	9
Joe Bush	1	0	1.00	1	1	1	0	0	9.0	5	1	4	3
Eddie Plank	1	1	0.95	2	2	2	0	0	19.0	9	2	3	7
TOTAL	4	1	2.15	5	5	5	0	0	46.0	33	11	8	19

NY (N)

PLAYER/POS	AVG	G	AB	R	H	2B	3B	HR	RB	BB	SO	SB
George Burns, of	.158	5	19	2	3	2	0	0	1	1	5	1
Claude Cooper, pr	.000	2	0	0	0	0	0	0	0	0	0	1
Doc Crandall, p-2	.000	4	4	0	0	0	0	0	0	0	0	0
Al Demaree, p	.000	1	0	0	0	0	0	0	0	0	0	0
Larry Doyle, 2b	.150	5	20	1	3	0	0	0	2	0	1	0
Art Fletcher, ss	.278	5	18	1	5	0	0	0	4	1	1	1
Eddie Grant, ph	.000	2	1	1	0	0	0	0	0	0	0	0
Buck Herzog, 3b	.053	5	19	1	1	0	0	0	0	0	1	0
Rube Marquard, p	.000	2	1	0	0	0	0	0	0	0	0	0
Christy Mathewson, p	.600	2	5	1	3	0	0	0	1	1	0	0
Moose Mc Cormick, ph	.500	2	2	1	1	0	0	0	0	0	0	0
Larry Mc Lean, c-4	.500	5	12	0	6	0	0	0	2	0	0	0
Fred Merkle, 1b	.231	4	13	3	3	0	0	1	3	1	2	0
Chief Meyers, c	.000	1	4	0	0	0	0	0	0	0	0	0
Red Murray, of	.250	5	16	2	4	0	0	0	1	2	2	2
Tillie Shafer, of-5,3b-1	.158	5	19	2	3	1	1	0	1	2	3	0
Fred Snodgrass, 1b-1,of-1	.333	2	3	0	1	0	0	0	0	0	0	0
Jeff Tesreau, p	.000	2	2	0	0	0	0	0	0	0	1	0
Art Wilson, c	.000	3	3	0	0	0	0	0	0	0	2	0
Hooks Wiltse, 1b	.000	2	2	0	0	0	0	0	0	0	1	0
TOTAL	.201		164	15	33	3	1	1	15	8	19	5

PITCHER	W	L	ERA	G	GS	CG	SV	SHO	IP	H	ER	BB	SO
Doc Crandall	0	0	3.86	2	0	0	0	0	4.2	4	2	0	2
Al Demaree	0	1	4.50	1	1	0	0	0	4.0	7	2	1	0
Rube Marquard	0	1	7.00	2	1	0	0	0	9.0	10	7	3	3
Christy Mathewson	1	1	0.95	2	2	2	0	1	19.0	14	2	2	7
Jeff Tesreau	0	1	6.48	2	1	0	0	0	8.1	11	6	1	4
TOTAL	1	4	3.80	9	5	2	0	1	45.0	46	19	7	16

GAME 1 AT NY OCT 7

PHI	000	320	010	6	11	1
NY	001	030	000	4	11	0

Pitchers: BENDER vs MARQUARD, Crandall (6), Tesreau (8)
Home Runs: Baker-PHI
Attendance: 36,291

GAME 2 AT PHI OCT 8

NY	000	000	000 3	3	7	2
PHI	000	000	000 0	0	8	2

Pitchers: MATHEWSON vs PLANK
Attendance: 20,563

GAME 3 AT NY OCT 9

PHI	320	000	210	8	12	1
NY	000	010	100	2	5	1

Pitchers: BUSH vs TESREAU, Crandall (7)
Home Runs: Schang-PHI
Attendance: 36,896

GAME 4 AT PHI OCT 10

NY	000	000	320	5	8	2
PHI	010	320	00X	6	9	0

Pitchers: MARQUARD vs BENDER
Home Runs: Merkle-NY
Attendance: 20,568

GAME 5 AT NY OCT 11

PHI	102	000	000	3	6	1
NY	000	010	000	1	2	2

Pitchers: PLANK vs MATHEWSON
Attendance: 36,682

The Athletics, easy winners of their fourth pennant in five years, were clear favorites over Boston. But the "Miracle Braves"—who moved from last place to first between July 18 and August 25 and kept going to take the pennant by 10½ games—had the momentum and swept the Series.

Boston pitcher Dick Rudolph (who won 27 games during the season) limited the A's to five hits and an unearned run, to take the opener behind the Braves' heavy hitting, 7–1. But the rest of the games were not won so easily.

Philadelphia's Eddie Plank held the Braves scoreless through eight innings of Game Two, and gave up only one run in the ninth. But the Braves' Bill James (26–7 during the season) allowed only two hits and no runs at all.

Game Three was a seesaw affair not settled until the twelfth inning. Through ten innings, starters Lefty Tyler of Boston and Joe Bush of the A's traded runs. Philadelphia scored one in the top of the first, but Braves' catcher Hank Gowdy doubled in the tying run in the second. The teams traded runs again in the fourth, but no one else crossed the plate until the tenth, when Frank Baker's bases-loaded single drove in two. For the third time, the Braves came back to tie it up. Gowdy opened the last of the tenth with the Series' only home run, and after a walk and single, a sacrifice fly knotted the score. Bill James came on to pitch no-hit ball through the eleventh and twelfth. Bush remained in for the A's, retiring the side in the eleventh. But an inning later Gowdy opened with his third crucial hit of the game, a double. Les Mann replaced him as runner, and after a walk, bunt, and wild throw to third, Mann scampered home with the winning run.

Two of Connie Mack's most promising young pitchers, Bob Shawkey and Herb Pennock (who would later find stardom as New York Yankees), shared the A's pitching in Game Four, and gave up only six hits between them. But a walk and an error led to a Boston run in the fourth, and although Shawkey himself doubled in the tying run a half inning later, two more Braves scored in the last of the fifth on Johnny Evers's single. Pennock came on to pitch three innings of shutout relief, but Rudolph held the A's hitless over the final four innings to preserve his second win and the Braves' crown.

Boston Braves (NL), 4;
Philadelphia Athletics (AL), 0

BOS (N)

PLAYER/POS	AVG	G	AB	R	H	2B	3B	HR	RB	BB	SO	SB
Ted Cather, of	.000	1	5	0	0	0	0	0	0	0	1	0
Joe Connolly, of	.111	3	9	1	1	0	0	0	1	1	1	0
Charlie Deal, 3b	.125	4	16	1	2	2	0	0	0	0	0	2
Josh Devore, ph	.000	1	1	0	0	0	0	0	0	0	1	0
Johnny Evers, 2b	.438	4	16	2	7	0	0	0	2	2	2	1
Larry Gilbert, ph	.000	1	0	0	0	0	0	0	0	1	0	0
Hank Gowdy, c	.545	4	11	3	6	3	1	1	3	5	1	1
Bill James, p	.000	2	4	0	0	0	0	0	0	0	4	0
Les Mann, of-2	.286	3	7	1	2	0	0	0	1	0	1	0
Rabbit Maranville, ss	.308	4	13	1	4	0	0	0	3	1	1	2
Herbie Moran, of	.077	3	13	2	1	1	0	0	0	1	1	1
Dick Rudolph, p	.333	2	6	1	2	0	0	0	0	1	1	0
Butch Schmidt, 1b	.294	4	17	2	5	0	0	0	2	0	2	1
Lefty Tyler, p	.000	1	3	0	0	0	0	0	0	0	1	0
Possum Whitted, of	.214	4	14	2	3	0	1	0	2	3	1	1
TOTAL	.244		135	16	33	6	2	1	14	15	18	9

PITCHER	W	L	ERA	G	GS	CG	SV	SHO	IP	H	ER	BB	SO
Bill James	2	0	0.00	2	1	1	0	1	11.0	2	0	6	9
Dick Rudolph	2	0	0.50	2	2	2	0	0	18.0	12	1	4	15
Lefty Tyler	0	0	3.60	1	1	0	0	0	10.0	8	4	3	4
TOTAL	4	0	1.15	5	4	3	0	1	39.0	22	5	13	28

PHI (A)

PLAYER/POS	AVG	G	AB	R	H	2B	3B	HR	RB	BB	SO	SB
Frank Baker, 3b	.250	4	16	0	4	2	0	0	2	1	3	0
Jack Barry, ss	.071	4	14	1	1	0	0	0	0	1	3	1
Chief Bender, p	.000	1	2	0	0	0	0	0	0	0	0	0
Joe Bush, p	.000	1	5	0	0	0	0	0	0	0	2	0
Eddie Collins, 2b	.214	4	14	0	3	0	0	0	1	2	1	1
Jack Lapp, c	.000	1	1	0	0	0	0	0	0	0	0	0
Stuffy Mc Innis, 1b	.143	4	14	2	2	1	0	0	3	3	0	0
Eddie Murphy, of	.188	4	16	2	3	2	0	0	0	2	2	0
Rube Oldring, of	.067	4	15	0	1	0	0	0	0	0	5	0
Herb Pennock, p	.000	1	1	0	0	0	0	0	0	0	0	0
Eddie Plank, p	.000	1	2	0	0	0	0	0	0	0	1	0
Wally Schang, c	.167	4	12	1	2	1	0	0	0	1	4	0
Bob Shawkey, p	.500	1	2	0	1	1	0	0	1	0	1	0
Amos Strunk, of	.286	2	7	0	2	0	0	0	0	0	2	0
Jimmy Walsh, of-2	.333	3	6	0	2	1	0	0	1	3	1	0
Weldon Wyckoff, p	1.000	1	1	0	1	1	0	0	0	0	0	0
TOTAL	.172		128	6	22	9	0	0	5	13	28	2

PITCHER	W	L	ERA	G	GS	CG	SV	SHO	IP	H	ER	BB	SO
Chief Bender	0	1	10.13	1	1	0	0	0	5.1	8	6	2	3
Joe Bush	0	1	3.27	1	1	1	0	0	11.0	9	4	4	4
Herb Pennock	0	0	0.00	1	0	0	0	0	3.0	2	0	2	3
Eddie Plank	0	1	1.00	1	1	1	0	0	9.0	7	1	4	6
Bob Shawkey	0	1	3.60	1	1	0	0	0	5.0	4	2	2	0
Weldon Wyckoff	0	0	2.45	1	0	0	0	0	3.2	3	1	1	2
TOTAL	0	4	3.41	6	4	2	0	0	37.0	33	14	15	18

GAME 1 AT PHI OCT 9

BOS	020 013 010	7	11	2
PHI	010 000 000	1	5	0

Pitchers: RUDOLPH vs BENDER, Wyckoff (6)
Attendance: 20,562

GAME 2 AT PHI OCT 10

BOS	000 000 001	1	7	1
PHI	000 000 000	0	2	1

Pitchers: JAMES vs PLANK
Attendance: 20,562

GAME 3 AT BOS OCT 12

PHI	100 100 000 200	4	8	2
BOS	010 100 000 201	5	9	1

Pitchers: BUSH vs Tyler, JAMES (11)
Home Runs: Gowdy-BOS
Attendance: 35,520

GAME 4 AT BOS OCT 13

PHI	000 010 000	1	7	0
BOS	000 120 00X	3	6	0

Pitchers: SHAWKEY, Pennock (6) vs RUDOLPH
Attendance: 34,365

Boston's five runs in Game Five were the most scored by either team in a Series characterized by outstanding pitching. It was also one of the most closely contested Series: the deciding run was not scored until the ninth inning in three of the games, and only in Game One was the margin of victory as much as two runs.

Grover Cleveland Alexander pitched the opener for the Phillies, and while the Red Sox tagged him for eight hits, they were all singles, and not until the eighth inning did one manage to drive a runner home. Boston's Ernie Shore pitched just as well, giving up only five singles and four walks. But two Phillie hits produced a run in the fourth, and an alternating pair of walks and infield hits in the eighth broke the tie with two runs for the Phillies' only win.

The next three games were 2–1 Boston victories. Rube Foster held the Phillies to three hits in Game Two, and led his team at the bat, going 3 for 4, including a double in the fifth. But it was his single in the ninth with a man on second that produced what proved to be the winning run as he retired the side in the bottom of the ninth to preserve his win. Dutch Leonard duplicated Foster's three-hit pitching two days later as the Series moved to Boston's spacious new Braves Field for Game Three. Before a new Series record crowd of 42,300, Leonard defeated the great Alexander, as the Sox' Duffy Lewis—with his third hit of the game—singled over second base to score Harry Hooper from third with two out in the bottom of the ninth.

Ernie Shore returned to the mound for Boston in Game Four, and although he gave up more hits (seven) than he had in Game One, his Sox had scored their two runs before the Phillies put across their one in the eighth.

Rube Foster was not as effective in Game Five as he had been in Game Two, twice giving the Phillies a two-run lead as Phillie first baseman Fred Luderus drove in three runs with a double and a home run. But from the fifth inning on, Foster held Philadelphia scoreless on two hits, while Duffy Lewis evened the score with a two-run homer in the eighth, and Harry Hooper (who had tied the score earlier with a home run in the third) won the game and the Series with a second homer in the top of the ninth.

Boston Red Sox (AL), 4; Philadelphia Phillies (NL), 1

BOS (A)

PLAYER/POS	AVG	G	AB	R	H	2B	3B	HR	RB	BB	SO	SB
Jack Barry, 2b	.176	5	17	1	3	0	0	0	0	1	1	2	0
Hick Cady, c	.333	4	6	0	2	0	0	0	0	1	2	0
Bill Carrigan, c	.000	1	2	0	0	0	0	0	0	1	1	0
Rube Foster, p	.500	2	8	0	4	1	0	0	1	0	2	0
Del Gainer, 1b	.333	1	3	1	1	0	0	0	0	0	0	0
Larry Gardner, 3b	.235	5	17	2	4	0	1	0	0	1	0	0
Olaf Henricksen, ph	.000	2	2	0	0	0	0	0	0	0	0	0
Dick Hoblitzel, 1b	.313	5	16	1	5	0	0	0	1	0	1	1
Harry Hooper, of	.350	5	20	4	7	0	0	2	3	2	4	0
Hal Janvrin, ss	.000	1	1	0	0	0	0	0	0	0	0	0
Dutch Leonard, p	.000	1	3	0	0	0	0	0	0	0	2	0
Duffy Lewis, of	.444	5	18	1	8	1	0	1	5	1	4	0
Babe Ruth, ph	.000	1	1	0	0	0	0	0	0	0	0	0
Everett Scott, ss	.056	5	18	0	1	0	0	0	0	0	3	0
Ernie Shore, p	.200	2	5	0	1	0	0	0	0	0	3	0
Tris Speaker, of	.294	5	17	2	5	0	1	0	0	4	1	0
Pinch Thomas, c	.200	2	5	0	1	0	0	0	0	0	0	0
TOTAL	.264		159	12	42	2	2	3	11	11	25	1

PITCHER	W	L	ERA	G	GS	CG	SV	SHO	IP	H	ER	BB	SO
Rube Foster	2	0	2.00	2	2	2	0	0	18.0	12	4	2	13
Dutch Leonard	1	0	1.00	1	1	1	0	0	9.0	3	1	0	6
Ernie Shore	1	1	2.12	2	2	2	0	0	17.0	12	4	8	6
TOTAL	4	1	1.84	5	5	5	0	0	44.0	27	9	10	25

PHI (N)

PLAYER/POS	AVG	G	AB	R	H	2B	3B	HR	RB	BB	SO	SB
Pete Alexander, p	.200	2	5	0	1	0	0	0	0	0	1	0
Dave Bancroft, ss	.294	5	17	2	5	0	0	0	1	2	2	0
Beals Becker, of	.000	2	0	0	0	0	0	0	0	0	0	0
Ed Burns, c	.188	5	16	1	3	0	0	0	0	1	2	0
Bobby Byrne, ph	.000	1	1	0	0	0	0	0	0	0	0	0
George Chalmers, p	.333	1	3	0	1	0	0	0	0	0	1	0
Gavvy Cravath, of	.125	5	16	2	2	1	1	0	1	2	6	0
Oscar Dugey, pr	.000	2	0	0	0	0	0	0	0	0	0	1
Bill Killefer, ph	.000	1	1	0	0	0	0	0	0	0	0	0
Fred Luderus, 1b	.438	5	16	1	7	2	0	1	6	1	4	0
Erskine Mayer, p	.000	2	4	0	0	0	0	0	0	0	2	0
Bert Niehoff, 2b	.063	5	16	1	1	0	0	0	0	1	5	0
Dode Paskert, of	.158	5	19	2	3	0	0	0	0	1	2	0
Eppa Rixey, p	.500	1	2	0	1	0	0	0	0	0	0	0
Milt Stock, 3b	.118	5	17	1	2	1	0	0	0	1	0	0
Possum Whitted, of-5,1b-1	.067	5	15	0	1	0	0	0	1	1	0	1
TOTAL	.182		148	10	27	4	1	1	9	10	25	2

PITCHER	W	L	ERA	G	GS	CG	SV	SHO	IP	H	ER	BB	SO
Pete Alexander	1	1	1.53	2	2	2	0	0	17.2	14	3	4	10
George Chalmers	0	1	2.25	1	1	1	0	0	8.0	8	2	3	6
Erskine Mayer	0	1	2.38	2	2	1	0	0	11.1	16	3	2	7
Eppa Rixey	0	1	4.05	1	0	0	0	0	6.2	4	3	2	2
TOTAL	1	4	2.27	6	5	4	0	0	43.2	42	11	11	25

GAME 1 AT PHI OCT 8

BOS	000	000	010	1	8	1
PHI	000	100	02X	3	5	1

Pitchers: SHORE vs ALEXANDER
Attendance: 19,343

GAME 2 AT PHI OCT 9

BOS	100	000	001	2	10	0
PHI	000	010	000	1	3	1

Pitchers: FOSTER vs MAYER
Attendance: 20,306

GAME 3 AT BOS OCT 11

PHI	001	000	000	1	3	0
BOS	000	100	001	2	6	1

Pitchers: ALEXANDER vs LEONARD
Attendance: 42,300

GAME 4 AT BOS OCT 12

PHI	000	000	010	1	7	0
BOS	001	001	00X	2	8	1

Pitchers: CHALMERS vs SHORE
Attendance: 41,096

GAME 5 AT PHI OCT 13

BOS	011	000	021	5	10	1
PHI	200	200	000	4	9	1

Pitchers: FOSTER vs Mayer, RIXEY (3)
Home Runs: Hooper-BOS (2),
  Lewis-BOS, Luderus-PHI
Attendance: 20,306

In close pennant races, the Red Sox repeated as league champions and Brooklyn won its first pennant since 1900. The first three games of the Series were tightly contested, and the outcomes were determined by only one run apiece. For 6½ innings in the opener, Brooklyn's Rube Marquard dueled Boston's Ernie Shore about equally. But in the last of the seventh the Sox capitalized on a double, some sloppy Brooklyn fielding, and a couple of sacrifice hits for three runs, adding another off reliever Jeff Pfeffer in the eighth for a 6–1 lead. The Robins fought back in the ninth, driving out Shore and drawing within one run of a tie before reliever Carl Mays retired the final man with the bases loaded.

Game Two was even tighter. Boston starter Babe Ruth gave up a first-inning inside-the-park homer to Hy Myers, but in the third he drove in Everett Scott (who had tripled) to tie the game at 1–1. Then for the next ten innings he and Robin pitcher Sherry Smith shut off all scoring. Ruth continued to blank Brooklyn in the fourteenth, and in the last of the inning a walk, sacrifice, and single over the head of the third baseman gave Boston and Ruth the victory.

Brooklyn veteran Jack Coombs took a 4–0 lead into the sixth inning of Game Three before weakening. But after giving up a third Boston run on Larry Gardner's one-out homer in the seventh, he was relieved by Jeff Pfeffer, who set the Sox down in order the rest of the way. In saving what proved to be Coombs's last World Series appearance (as well as the Robins' only Series win), Pfeffer preserved Coombs's perfect Series won-lost record at 5–0.

Games Four and Five proved anticlimactic. In Game Four, Gardner's second homer of the Series—inside the park for three runs in the second inning—overcame the Robins' two runs in the first. The Sox added a run here and there to increase their lead, while Sox starter Dutch Leonard shut Brooklyn out through the final eight innings for a comfortable 6–2 win. And in what became the Series finale, Ernie Shore held the Robins to three singles and one unearned run as his Sox took advantage of a bad-hop triple in the second and two third-inning errors by Robin shortstop Ivy Olson to take the lead—and their fourth world championship.

Boston Red Sox (AL), 4; Brooklyn Robins (NL), 1

BOS (A)

PLAYER/POS	AVG	G	AB	R	H	2B	3B	HR	RB	BB	SO	SB
Hick Cady, c	.250	2	4	1	1	0	0	0	0	3	0	0
Bill Carrigan, c	.667	1	3	0	2	0	0	0	1	0	1	0
Rube Foster, p	.000	1	1	0	0	0	0	0	0	0	1	0
Del Gainer, ph	1.000	1	1	0	1	0	0	0	1	0	0	0
Larry Gardner, 3b	.176	5	17	2	3	0	2	2	6	0	2	0
Olaf Henricksen, ph	.000	1	0	1	0	0	0	0	0	1	0	0
Dick Hoblitzel, 1b	.235	5	17	3	4	1	1	0	2	6	0	0
Harry Hooper, of	.333	5	21	6	7	1	1	0	1	3	1	0
Hal Janvrin, 2b	.217	5	23	2	5	3	0	0	1	0	6	0
Dutch Leonard, p	.000	1	3	0	0	0	0	0	0	1	3	0
Duffy Lewis, of	.353	5	17	3	6	2	1	0	1	2	1	0
Carl Mays, p	.000	2	1	0	0	0	0	0	0	0	1	0
Mike Mc Nally, pr	.000	1	0	1	0	0	0	0	0	0	0	0
Babe Ruth, p	.000	1	5	0	0	0	0	0	0	1	2	0
Everett Scott, ss	.125	5	16	1	2	0	1	0	1	1	1	0
Ernie Shore, p	.000	2	7	0	0	0	0	0	0	0	2	0
Chick Shorten, of	.571	2	7	0	4	0	0	0	2	0	1	0
Pinch Thomas, c	.143	3	7	0	1	0	1	0	0	0	1	0
Tilly Walker, of	.273	3	11	1	3	0	1	0	1	1	2	0
Jimmy Walsh, of	.000	1	3	0	0	0	0	0	0	0	0	0
TOTAL	.238		164	21	39	7	6	2	18	18	25	1

PITCHER	W	L	ERA	G	GS	CG	SV	SHO	IP	H	ER	BB	SO
Rube Foster	0	0	0.00	1	0	0	0	0	3.0	3	0	0	1
Dutch Leonard	1	0	1.00	1	1	1	0	0	9.0	5	1	4	3
Carl Mays	0	1	5.06	2	1	0	1	0	5.1	8	3	3	2
Babe Ruth	1	0	0.64	1	1	1	0	0	14.0	6	1	3	4
Ernie Shore	2	0	1.53	2	2	1	0	0	17.2	12	3	4	9
TOTAL	4	1	1.47	7	5	3	1	0	49.0	34	8	14	19

BRO (N)

PLAYER/POS	AVG	G	AB	R	H	2B	3B	HR	RB	BB	SO	SB
Larry Cheney, p	.000	1	0	0	0	0	0	0	0	0	0	0
Jack Coombs, p	.333	1	3	0	1	0	0	0	1	0	0	0
George Cutshaw, 2b	.105	5	19	2	2	1	0	0	2	1	1	0
Jake Daubert, 1b	.176	4	17	1	3	0	1	0	0	2	3	0
Wheezer Dell, p	.000	1	0	0	0	0	0	0	0	0	0	0
Gus Getz, ph	.000	1	1	0	0	0	0	0	0	0	0	0
Jimmy Johnston, of-2	.300	3	10	1	3	0	1	0	0	1	0	0
Rube Marquard, p	.000	3	0	0	0	0	0	0	0	0	1	0
Fred Merkle, 1b-1	.250	3	4	0	1	0	0	0	1	2	0	0
Chief Meyers, c	.200	3	10	0	2	0	1	0	0	1	0	0
Otto Miller, c	.125	2	8	0	1	0	0	0	0	0	1	0
Harry Mowery, 3b	.176	5	17	2	3	0	0	0	1	3	2	0
Hy Myers, of	.182	5	22	2	4	0	1	1	3	0	3	0
Ivy Olson, ss	.250	5	16	1	4	0	1	0	2	2	2	0
Ollie O'Mara, ph	.000	1	1	0	0	0	0	0	0	0	1	0
Jeff Pfeffer, p-3	.250	4	4	0	1	0	0	0	0	0	2	0
Nap Rucker, p	.000	1	0	0	0	0	0	0	0	0	0	0
Sherry Smith, p	.200	1	5	0	1	1	0	0	0	0	0	0
Casey Stengel, of-3	.364	4	11	2	4	0	0	0	0	0	1	0
Zack Wheat, of	.211	5	19	2	4	0	1	0	1	2	2	1
TOTAL	.200		170	13	34	2	5	1	11	14	19	1

PITCHER	W	L	ERA	G	GS	CG	SV	SHO	IP	H	ER	BB	SO
Larry Cheney	0	0	3.00	1	0	0	0	0	3.0	4	1	1	5
Jack Coombs	1	0	4.26	1	1	0	0	0	6.1	7	3	1	1
Wheezer Dell	0	0	0.00	1	0	0	0	0	1.0	1	0	0	0
Rube Marquard	0	2	6.55	2	2	0	0	0	11.0	12	8	6	9
Jeff Pfeffer	0	1	1.69	3	1	0	1	0	10.2	7	2	4	5
Nap Rucker	0	0	0.00	1	0	0	0	0	2.0	1	0	0	3
Sherry Smith	0	1	1.35	1	1	1	0	0	13.1	7	2	6	2
TOTAL	1	4	3.04	10	5	1	1	0	47.1	39	16	18	25

GAME 1 AT BOS OCT 7

BRO	000	100	004	5	10	4
BOS	001	010	31X	6	8	1

Pitchers: MARQUARD, Pfeffer (8) vs SHORE, Mays (9)
Attendance: 36,117

GAME 2 AT BOS OCT 9

BRO	100 000 000 000 00	1	6	2
BOS	001 000 000 000 01	2	7	1

Pitchers: SMITH vs RUTH
Home Runs: H.Myers-BRO
Attendance: 41,373

GAME 3 AT BRO OCT 10

BOS	000	002	100	3	7	1
BRO	001	120	00X	4	10	0

Pitchers: MAYS, Foster (6) vs COOMBS, Pfeffer (7)
Home Runs: Gardner-BOS
Attendance: 21,087

GAME 4 AT BRO OCT 11

BOS	030	110	100	6	10	1
BRO	200	000	000	2	5	4

Pitchers: LEONARD vs MARQUARD, Cheney (5), Rucker (8)
Home Runs: Gardner-BOS
Attendance: 21,662

GAME 5 AT BOS OCT 12

BRO	010	000	000	1	3	3
BOS	012	010	00X	4	7	2

Pitchers: PFEFFER, Dell (8) vs SHORE
Attendance: 42,620

Easy winners in their pennant races, the White Sox and Giants traded pairs of victories in the Series before the Sox came up with a second pair to take the title in six games. In the opener, Happy Felsch's solo homer in the fourth inning gave Sox starter Eddie Cicotte the margin he needed to defeat Giant Slim Sallee 2–1, and in Game Two Red Faber went all the way, as his Sox broke a 2–2 tie in the fourth inning with five runs on six singles for Chicago's second win.

The clubs traveled to New York for Games Three and Four, and Giant pitchers rewarded their fans with a pair of shutouts to even the Series. In Game Three, a triple, double, and single against the Sox' Cicotte in the fourth inning produced the only scoring, as Giant Rube Benton blanked the Sox on five hits, walking none. Giant ace Ferdie Schupp (a 21-game winner during the season) did the honors in Game Four, scattering seven hits, as teammate Benny Kauff, with his first Series hit in the fourth inning, homered inside the park to deep center against Red Faber for the deciding run. Two later runs against Faber and two more in the eighth (on Kauff's second homer) against reliever Dave Danforth made Schupp's win easy.

But Faber, the loser in Game Four, came in to pitch two innings of perfect relief two days later in Chicago for his second win, as the Sox rebounded from a 2–5 deficit with three runs in the bottom of the seventh to tie the game and three more an inning later to win it.

After a day of rest and a return to New York, Faber was given his third start. He pitched well enough, but his third win and the Series clincher was really the gift of some infamous Giant fielding. In the fourth inning, the first two Sox batters—Eddie Collins and Joe Jackson—reached on a high throw to first and a dropped fly. Happy Felsch, the third man up, reached on a fielder's choice as Giant third baseman Heinie Zimmerman chased Collins across the plate in a botched rundown. Jackson and Felsch scored the second and third unearned runs as Chick Gandil singled off the hapless Rube Benton. The Giants recovered to score two runs an inning later, but Faber shut them out the rest of the way to give his Sox the Series.

Chicago White Sox (AL), 4; New York Giants (NL), 2

CHI (A)

PLAYER/POS	AVG	G	AB	R	H	2B	3B	HR	RB	BB	SO	SB
Eddie Cicotte, p	.143	3	7	0	1	0	0	0	0	0	1	2	0
Eddie Collins, 2b	.409	6	22	4	9	1	0	0	2	2	3	3
Shano Collins, of	.286	6	21	2	6	1	0	0	0	0	2	0
Dave Danforth, p	.000	1	0	0	0	0	0	0	0	0	0	0
Red Faber, p	.143	4	7	0	1	0	0	0	0	2	3	0
Happy Felsch, of	.273	6	22	4	6	1	0	1	3	1	5	0
Chick Gandil, 1b	.261	6	23	1	6	1	0	0	5	0	2	1
Joe Jackson, of	.304	6	23	4	7	0	0	0	2	1	0	1
Nemo Leibold, of	.400	2	5	1	2	0	0	0	2	1	1	0
Byrd Lynn, ph	.000	1	1	0	0	0	0	0	0	0	1	0
Fred Mc Mullin, 3b	.125	6	24	1	3	1	0	0	2	1	6	0
Swede Risberg, ph	.500	2	2	0	1	0	0	0	1	0	0	0
Reb Russell, p	.000	1	0	0	0	0	0	0	0	0	0	0
Ray Schalk, c	.263	6	19	1	5	0	0	0	0	2	1	1
Buck Weaver, ss	.333	6	21	3	7	1	0	0	1	0	2	0
Lefty Williams, p	.000	1	0	0	0	0	0	0	0	0	0	0
TOTAL	.274		197	21	54	6	0	1	18	11	28	6

PITCHER	W	L	ERA	G	GS	CG	SV	SHO	IP	H	ER	BB	SO
Eddie Cicotte	1	1	1.96	3	2	2	0	0	23.0	23	5	2	13
Dave Danforth	0	0	18.00	1	0	0	0	0	1.0	3	2	0	2
Red Faber	3	1	2.33	4	3	2	0	0	27.0	21	7	3	9
Reb Russell	0	0	INF	1	1	0	0	0	0.0	2	1	1	0
Lefty Williams	0	0	9.00	1	0	0	0	0	1.0	2	1	0	3
TOTAL	4	2	2.77	10	6	4	0	0	52.0	51	16	6	27

NY (N)

PLAYER/POS	AVG	G	AB	R	H	2B	3B	HR	RB	BB	SO	SB
Fred Anderson, p	.000	1	0	0	0	0	0	0	0	0	0	0
Rube Benton, p	.000	2	4	0	0	0	0	0	0	0	3	0
George Burns, of	.227	6	22	3	5	0	0	0	2	2	6	1
Art Fletcher, ss	.200	6	25	2	5	1	0	0	0	0	2	0
Buck Herzog, 2b	.250	6	24	1	6	0	1	0	2	1	4	0
Walter Holke, 1b	.286	6	21	2	6	2	0	0	1	0	6	0
Benny Kauff, of	.160	6	25	2	4	1	0	2	5	0	2	1
Lew Mc Carty, c-2	.400	3	5	1	2	0	1	0	1	0	0	0
Pol Perritt, p	1.000	3	2	0	2	0	0	0	0	0	0	0
Bill Rariden, c	.385	5	13	2	5	0	0	0	2	2	1	0
Dave Robertson, of	.500	6	22	3	11	1	1	0	1	0	0	2
Slim Sallee, p	.167	2	6	0	1	0	0	0	1	0	2	0
Ferdie Schupp, p	.250	2	4	0	1	0	0	0	1	0	1	0
Jeff Tesreau, p	.000	1	0	0	0	0	0	0	0	0	0	0
Jim Thorpe, of	.000	1	0	0	0	0	0	0	0	0	0	0
Joe Wilhoit, ph	.000	2	1	0	0	0	0	0	0	1	0	0
Heinie Zimmerman, 3b	.120	6	25	1	3	0	1	0	0	0	0	0
TOTAL	.256		199	17	51	5	4	2	16	6	27	4

PITCHER	W	L	ERA	G	GS	CG	SV	SHO	IP	H	ER	BB	SO
Fred Anderson	0	1	18.00	1	0	0	0	0	2.0	5	4	0	3
Rube Benton	1	1	0.00	2	2	1	0	1	14.0	9	0	1	8
Pol Perritt	0	0	2.16	3	0	0	0	0	8.1	9	2	3	3
Slim Sallee	0	2	5.28	2	2	1	0	0	15.1	20	9	4	4
Ferdie Schupp	1	0	1.74	2	2	1	0	0	10.1	11	2	2	9
Jeff Tesreau	0	0	0.00	1	0	0	0	0	1.0	0	0	1	1
TOTAL	2	4	3.00	11	6	3	0	2	51.0	54	17	11	28

GAME 1 AT CHI OCT 6

NY	000	010	000	1	7	1
CHI	001	100	00X	2	7	1

Pitchers: SALLEE vs CICOTTE
Home Runs: Felsch-CHI
Attendance: 32,000

GAME 2 AT CHI OCT 7

NY	020	000	000	2	8	1
CHI	020	500	00X	7	14	1

Pitchers: Schupp, ANDERSON (2), Perritt (4), Tesreau (8) vs FABER
Attendance: 32,000

GAME 3 AT NY OCT 10

CHI	000	000	000	0	5	3
NY	000	200	00X	2	8	2

Pitchers: CICOTTE vs BENTON
Attendance: 33,616

GAME 4 AT NY OCT 11

CHI	000	000	000	0	7	0
NY	000	110	12X	5	10	1

Pitchers: FABER, Danforth (8) vs SCHUPP
Home Runs: Kauff-NY (2)
Attendance: 27,746

GAME 5 AT CHI OCT 13

NY	200	200	100	5	12	3
CHI	001	001	33X	8	14	6

Pitchers: SALLEE, Perritt (8) VS Russell, Cicotte (1), Williams (7), FABER (8)
Attendance: 27,323

GAME 6 AT NY OCT 15

CHI	000	300	001	4	7	1
NY	000	020	000	2	6	3

Pitchers: FABER vs BENTON, Perritt (6)
Attendance: 33,969

Although both clubs had lost key players to military service, so had other major league teams, and after a season shortened by a month because of the war, the Red Sox and Cubs found themselves opponents in an early-September World Series.

In the opener, Babe Ruth pushed his string of consecutive scoreless World Series innings to 22, holding the Cubs to six singles as he went the distance. The Cubs' Hippo Vaughn pitched just as well, but two of the five singles he yielded followed a leadoff walk in the fourth and produced the game's only run. Chicago evened the Series in Game Two, bunching four of their seven hits after a walk in the second inning to take a 3–0 lead. Successive triples in Boston's ninth spoiled Lefty Tyler's shutout but not his victory.

Hippo Vaughn lost another close one in Game Three when he gave up two runs in the fourth inning on a hit batsman and a succession of singles. The Cubs got him one run back in the fifth, but the Sox' Carl Mays held Chicago to that one run as he hurled Boston back into the Series lead. Ruth pushed the Sox farther ahead the next day in another squeaker. As he continued his mastery over Cub hitters, he drove Boston into the lead with a two-run triple in the fourth inning (his only Series hit). But in the eighth a run-scoring ground out ended his record setting string of scoreless innings at 29⅔, and a single drove in another run to tie the game. The Sox, though, scored a third run on a Chicago error in the last of the eighth, and reliever Bullet Joe Bush shut down a threat in the ninth to save Ruth's win.

Vaughn, in his third start, finally found what was needed for victory—a shutout, on five hits, as the Cubs added hits to walks from Boston's Sad Sam Jones in the third and eighth to push across their three runs. But in Game Six the Sox scored two unearned runs on a dropped line drive to right in the third inning. It was their only scoring off Lefty Tyler, but Boston's Carl Mays was on his way to a one-run three-hitter that brought the Red Sox their fifth world championship in five tries. To date, although they have tried four more times, they have not won a sixth.

Boston Red Sox (AL), 4;
Chicago Cubs (NL), 2

BOS (A)

PLAYER/POS	AVG	G	AB	R	H	2B	3B	HR	RB	BB	SO	SB
Sam Agnew, c	.000	4	9	0	0	0	0	0	0	0	0	0
Joe Bush, p	.000	2	2	0	0	0	0	0	0	1	0	0
Jean Dubuc, ph	.000	1	1	0	0	0	0	0	0	0	1	0
Harry Hooper, of	.200	6	20	0	4	0	0	0	0	2	2	0
Sam Jones, p	.000	1	1	0	0	0	0	0	0	1	0	0
Carl Mays, p	.200	2	5	1	1	0	0	0	0	1	0	0
Stuffy McInnis, 1b	.250	6	20	2	5	0	0	0	1	1	1	0
Hack Miller, ph	.000	1	1	0	0	0	0	0	0	0	0	0
Babe Ruth, p-2,of-2	.200	3	5	0	1	0	1	0	2	0	2	0
Wally Schang, c	.444	5	9	1	4	0	0	0	1	2	3	1
Everett Scott, ss	.095	6	21	0	2	0	0	0	1	1	1	0
Dave Shean, 2b	.211	6	19	2	4	1	0	0	0	4	3	1
Amos Strunk, of	.174	6	23	1	4	1	1	0	0	0	5	0
Fred Thomas, 3b	.125	6	16	0	2	0	0	0	0	1	2	0
George Whiteman, of	.250	6	20	2	5	0	1	0	1	2	1	1
TOTAL	.186		172	9	32	2	3	0	6	16	21	3

PITCHER	W	L	ERA	G	GS	CG	SV	SHO	IP	H	ER	BB	SO
Joe Bush	0	1	3.00	2	1	1	1	0	9.0	7	3	3	0
Sam Jones	0	1	3.00	1	1	1	0	0	9.0	7	3	5	5
Carl Mays	2	0	1.00	2	2	2	0	0	18.0	10	2	3	5
Babe Ruth	2	0	1.06	2	2	1	0	1	17.0	13	2	7	4
TOTAL	4	2	1.70	7	6	5	1	1	53.0	37	10	18	14

CHI (N)

PLAYER/POS	AVG	G	AB	R	H	2B	3B	HR	RB	BB	SO	SB
Turner Barber, ph	.000	3	2	0	0	0	0	0	0	0	0	0
Charlie Deal, 3b	.176	6	17	0	3	0	0	0	0	0	1	0
Phil Douglas, p	.000	1	0	0	0	0	0	0	0	0	0	0
Max Flack, of	.263	6	19	2	5	0	0	0	0	4	1	1
Claude Hendrix, p-1	1.000	2	1	0	1	0	0	0	0	0	0	0
Charlie Hollocher, ss	.190	6	21	2	4	0	1	0	1	1	1	1
Bill Killefer, c	.118	6	17	2	2	1	0	0	2	2	0	0
Les Mann, of	.227	6	22	0	5	2	0	0	2	0	0	0
Bill McCabe, ph	.000	3	1	0	0	0	0	0	0	0	0	0
Fred Merkle, 1b	.278	6	18	1	5	0	0	0	1	4	3	0
Bob O'Farrell, c-1	.000	3	3	0	0	0	0	0	0	0	0	0
Dode Paskert, of	.190	6	21	0	4	1	0	0	2	2	2	0
Charlie Pick, 2b	.389	6	18	2	7	1	0	0	0	1	1	1
Lefty Tyler, p	.200	3	5	0	1	0	0	0	2	2	0	0
Hippo Vaughn, p	.000	3	10	0	0	0	0	0	0	0	5	0
Chuck Wortman, 2b	.000	1	1	0	0	0	0	0	0	0	0	0
Rollie Zeider, 3b	.000	2	0	0	0	0	0	0	0	2	0	0
TOTAL	.210		176	10	37	5	1	0	10	18	14	3

PITCHER	W	L	ERA	G	GS	CG	SV	SHO	IP	H	ER	BB	SO
Phil Douglas	0	1	0.00	1	0	0	0	0	1.0	1	0	0	0
Claude Hendrix	0	0	0.00	1	0	0	0	0	1.0	0	0	0	0
Lefty Tyler	1	1	1.17	3	3	1	0	0	23.0	14	3	11	4
Hippo Vaughn	1	2	1.00	3	3	3	0	1	27.0	17	3	5	17
TOTAL	2	4	1.04	8	6	4	0	1	52.0	32	6	16	21

GAME 1 AT CHI SEPT 5

BOS	000	100	000	1	5	0
CHI	000	000	000	0	6	0

Pitchers: RUTH vs VAUGHN
Attendance: 19,274

GAME 2 AT CHI SEPT 6

BOS	000	000	001	1	6	1
CHI	030	000	000	3	7	1

Pitchers: BUSH vs TYLER
Attendance: 20,040

GAME 3 AT CHI SEPT 7

BOS	000	200	000	2	7	0
CHI	000	010	000	1	7	1

Pitchers: MAYS vs VAUGHN
Attendance: 27,054

GAME 4 AT BOS SEPT 9

CHI	000	000	020	2	7	1
BOS	000	200	01X	3	4	0

Pitchers: Tyler, DOUGLAS (8) vs RUTH, Bush (9)
Attendance: 22,183

GAME 5 AT BOS SEPT 10

CHI	001	000	002	3	7	0
BOS	000	000	000	0	5	0

Pitchers: VAUGHN vs JONES
Attendance: 24,694

GAME 6 AT BOS SEPT 11

CHI	000	100	000	1	3	2
BOS	002	000	00X	2	5	0

Pitchers: TYLER, Hendrix (8) vs MAYS
Attendance: 15,238

In the bottom of the first inning of Game One, White Sox pitcher Eddie Cicotte hit the first batter to face him, a prearranged signal to gamblers that "the fix was on"—that the Sox would throw the Series. The eight Chicago conspirators—pitching aces Cicotte and Lefty Williams, outfielders Joe Jackson and Happy Felsch, and infielders Chick Gandil, Buck Weaver, Fred McMullin and Swede Risberg—received no more than a fraction of the $100,000 promised them but "honored" their end of the deal. Cicotte (winner of 29 regular-season games, with a 1.82 ERA) gave up seven hits and six runs in the opening innings of Game One en route to a 1–9 loss, and Williams, though he held the Reds to four hits in Game Two, uncharacteristically walked six and fanned only one, a performance bad enough for a 2–4 loss.

Dickie Kerr, Chicago's third-best pitcher and not in on the fix, won Game Three with a three-hit shutout. But although Cicotte pitched well in Game Four, Chicago lost a third time as the Reds' Jimmy Ring hurled a three-hit shutout of his own (all three hits coming, ironically, off the bats of conspirators Jackson, Felsch, and Gandil).

Cincinnati's Hod Eller beat Chicago in Game Five with the Series' third successive three-hit shutout. Loser Lefty Williams once again yielded only four hits, but three came in a four-run sixth inning which also saw a walk and a throwing error by Felsch. (The win, the Reds' fourth, did not decide the Series, which had been expanded to the best five of nine in the exuberance which followed the end of the Great War.)

Chicago exerted itself to win the next two games. In Game Six, Kerr's second win depended on crucial hits by Jackson and Gandil in the tenth inning; and in Game Seven Cicotte held the Reds to one run as Jackson and Felsch drove in all the Sox' four.

But in Game Eight, Williams gave up two singles and two doubles before being pulled with only one away in the first. Jackson homered in the third. And he doubled and Gandil tripled to drive in three Chicago runs in the eighth. But by then the Reds had scored ten runs on their way to an easy win and their tainted world title.

Cincinnati Reds (NL), 5;
Chicago White Sox (AL), 3

CIN (N)

PLAYER/POS	AVG	G	AB	R	H	2B	3B	HR	RB	BB	SO	SB
Jake Daubert, 1b	.241	8	29	4	7	0	1	0	1	1	2	1
Pat Duncan, of	.269	8	26	3	7	2	0	0	8	2	2	0
Hod Eller, p	.286	2	7	2	2	1	0	0	0	0	2	0
Ray Fisher, p	.500	2	2	0	1	0	0	0	0	0	0	0
Heinie Groh, 3b	.172	8	29	6	5	2	0	0	2	6	4	0
Larry Kopf, ss	.222	8	27	3	6	0	2	0	3	3	2	0
Dolf Luque, p	.000	2	1	0	0	0	0	0	0	0	1	0
Sherry Magee, ph	.500	2	2	0	1	0	0	0	0	0	0	0
Greasy Neale, of	.357	8	28	3	10	1	1	0	4	2	5	1
Bill Rariden, c	.211	5	19	0	4	0	0	0	2	0	0	1
Morrie Rath, 2b	.226	8	31	5	7	1	0	0	2	4	1	2
Jimmy Ring, p	.000	2	5	0	0	0	0	0	0	0	2	0
Edd Roush, of	.214	8	28	6	6	2	1	0	7	3	0	2
Dutch Ruether, p-2	.667	3	6	2	4	1	2	0	4	1	0	0
Slim Sallee, p	.000	2	4	0	0	0	0	0	0	0	0	0
Jimmy Smith, pr	.000	1	0	0	0	0	0	0	0	0	0	0
Ivey Wingo, c	.571	3	7	1	4	0	0	0	1	3	1	0
TOTAL	.255		251	35	64	10	7	0	34	25	22	7

PITCHER	W	L	ERA	G	GS	CG	SV	SHO	IP	H	ER	BB	SO
Hod Eller	2	0	2.00	2	2	2	0	1	18.0	13	4	2	15
Ray Fisher	0	1	2.35	2	1	0	0	0	7.2	7	2	2	2
Dolf Luque	0	0	0.00	2	0	0	0	0	5.0	1	0	0	6
Jimmy Ring	1	1	0.64	2	1	1	0	1	14.0	7	1	6	4
Dutch Ruether	1	0	2.57	2	2	1	0	0	14.0	12	4	4	1
Slim Sallee	1	1	1.35	2	2	1	0	0	13.1	19	2	1	2
TOTAL	5	3	1.63	12	8	5	0	2	72.0	59	13	15	30

CHI (A)

PLAYER/POS	AVG	G	AB	R	H	2B	3B	HR	RB	BB	SO	SB
Eddie Cicotte, p	.000	3	8	0	0	0	0	0	0	0	3	0
Eddie Collins, 2b	.226	8	31	2	7	1	0	0	1	1	2	1
Shano Collins, of	.250	4	16	2	4	1	0	0	0	0	0	0
Happy Felsch, of	.192	8	26	2	5	1	0	0	3	1	4	0
Chick Gandil, 1b	.233	8	30	1	7	0	1	0	5	1	3	1
Joe Jackson, of	.375	8	32	5	12	3	0	1	6	1	2	0
Bill James, p	.000	1	2	0	0	0	0	0	0	0	1	0
Dickie Kerr, p	.167	2	6	0	1	0	0	0	0	0	0	0
Nemo Leibold, of	.056	5	18	0	1	0	0	0	0	2	3	1
Grover Lowdermilk, p	.000	1	0	0	0	0	0	0	0	0	0	0
Byrd Lynn, c	.000	1	1	0	0	0	0	0	0	0	0	0
Erskine Mayer, p	.000	1	0	0	0	0	0	0	0	0	0	0
Fred McMullin, ph	.500	2	2	0	1	0	0	0	0	0	0	0
Eddie Murphy, ph	.000	3	2	0	0	0	0	0	0	0	1	0
Swede Risberg, ss	.080	8	25	3	2	0	1	0	0	5	3	1
Ray Schalk, c	.304	8	23	1	7	0	0	0	2	4	2	1
Buck Weaver, 3b	.324	8	34	4	11	4	1	0	0	0	2	0
Roy Wilkinson, p	.000	2	2	0	0	0	0	0	0	0	1	0
Lefty Williams, p	.200	3	5	0	1	0	0	0	0	0	3	0
TOTAL	.224		263	20	59	10	3	1	17	15	30	5

PITCHER	W	L	ERA	G	GS	CG	SV	SHO	IP	H	ER	BB	SO
Eddie Cicotte	1	2	2.91	3	3	2	0	0	21.2	19	7	5	7
Bill James	0	0	5.79	1	0	0	0	0	4.2	8	3	3	2
Dickie Kerr	2	0	1.42	2	2	2	0	1	19.0	14	3	3	6
Grover Lowdermilk	0	0	9.00	1	0	0	0	0	1.0	2	1	1	0
Erskine Mayer	0	0	0.00	1	0	0	0	0	1.0	0	0	1	0
Roy Wilkinson	0	0	1.23	2	0	0	0	0	7.1	9	1	4	3
Lefty Williams	0	3	6.61	3	3	1	0	0	16.1	12	12	8	4
TOTAL	3	5	3.42	13	8	5	0	1	71.0	64	27	25	22

GAME 1 AT CIN OCT 1

CHI 010 000 000   1 6 1
CIN 100 500 21X   9 14 1
Pitchers: CICOTTE, Wilkinson (4), Lowdermilk (8) vs RUETHER
Attendance: 30,511

GAME 2 AT CIN OCT 2

CHI 000 000 200   2 10 1
CIN 000 301 00X   4 4 2
Pitchers: WILLIAMS vs SALLEE
Attendance: 29,690

GAME 3 AT CHI OCT 3

CIN 000 000 000   0 3 1
CHI 020 100 00X   3 7 0
Pitchers: FISHER, Luque (8) vs KERR
Attendance: 29,126

GAME 4 AT CHI OCT 4

CIN 000 020 000   2 5 2
CHI 000 000 000   0 3 2
Pitchers: RING vs CICOTTE
Attendance: 34,363

GAME 5 AT CHI OCT 6

CIN 000 004 001   5 4 0
CHI 000 000 000   0 3 3
Pitchers: ELLER vs WILLIAMS, Mayer (9)
Attendance: 34,379

GAME 6 AT CIN OCT 7

CHI 000 013 000 1   5 10 3
CIN 002 200 000 0   4 11 0
Pitchers: KERR vs Ruether, RING (6)
Attendance: 32,006

GAME 7 AT CIN OCT 8

CHI 101 020 000   4 10 1
CIN 000 001 000   1 7 4
Pitchers: CICOTTE vs SALLEE, Fisher (5), Luque (6)
Attendance: 13,923

GAME 8 AT CHI OCT 9

CIN 410 013 010 10 16 2
CHI 001 000 040   5 10 1
Pitchers: ELLER vs WILLIAMS, James (1), Wilkinson (6)
Home Runs: Jackson-CHI
Attendance: 32,930

The Indians outscored the Robins in the Series, 21 runs to 8. Yet after losing the opener in Brooklyn, the Robins fought back to take the next two, and held the Series lead as the teams traveled to Cleveland for the next four games.

Both clubs garnered five hits in Game One, but an error, walk, single, and double gave the Indians two runs in the second and a lead they never yielded, as Stan Coveleski outlasted Rube Marquard for the win. In Game Two, both clubs increased their hit totals to seven, but the Robins bunched six of theirs into three innings for three runs, while Burleigh Grimes, only once yielding two hits in an inning, shut the Indians out. The two runs Brooklyn scored in the first inning of Game Three were all Sherry Smith needed to give the Robins their second win behind his three-hit pitching. But Brooklyn scored only twice more in the Series as the Indians swept to the championship with four wins in Cleveland.

With the Indians scoring four runs in Game Four before Brooklyn put its one run on the board, Coveleski breezed to his second five-hit Series run. Jim Bagby had it even easier the next day. The Robins tagged him for 13 hits, but not until the ninth inning were they able to put them together for a run. Meanwhile Bagby and his teammates were registering a couple of Series firsts as they moved to an eight-run lead. Right fielder Elmer Smith opened the scoring in the first inning with the first World Series grand slam, and Bagby himself homered for three more in the fourth—the first pitcher to hit a Series home run.

But the 1920 Series is best remembered for second baseman Bill Wambsganss's unassisted triple play in the fifth inning. With runners on first and second going on pitcher Clarence Mitchell's liner, Wambsganss snared the ball for the first out, stepped on second to force one runner, and tagged the runner coming in from first to retire the side.

In Game Six Duster Mails, a late-season addition to the team, shut out Brooklyn on three hits in a 1–0 squeaker over Sherry Smith. Coveleski won the clincher the next day, also via the shutout, with his third five-hitter of the Series and his third Series win.

Cleveland Indians (AL), 5;
Brooklyn Robins (NL), 2

CLE (A)

PLAYER/POS	AVG	G	AB	R	H	2B	3B	HR	RB	BB	SO	SB
Jim Bagby, p	.333	2	6	1	2	0	0	1	3	0	0	0
George Burns, 1b-4	.300	5	10	1	3	1	0	0	2	3	3	0
Ray Caldwell, p	.000	1	0	0	0	0	0	0	0	0	0	0
Stan Coveleski, p	.100	3	10	2	1	0	0	0	0	0	4	0
Joe Evans, of	.308	4	13	0	4	0	0	0	0	1	0	0
Larry Gardner, 3b	.208	7	24	1	5	1	0	0	2	1	1	0
Jack Graney, of-2	.000	3	3	0	0	0	0	0	0	0	2	0
Charlie Jamieson, of-5	.333	6	15	2	5	1	0	0	1	1	0	1
Doc Johnston, 1b	.273	5	11	1	3	0	0	0	0	2	1	1
Harry Lunte, 2b	.000	1	0	0	0	0	0	0	0	0	0	0
Duster Mails, p	.000	2	5	0	0	0	0	0	0	0	1	0
Les Nunamaker, c-1	.500	2	2	0	1	0	0	0	0	0	0	0
Steve O'Neill, c	.333	7	21	1	7	3	0	0	2	4	3	0
Joe Sewell, ss	.174	7	23	0	4	0	0	0	0	2	1	0
Elmer Smith, of	.308	5	13	1	4	0	1	1	5	1	5	0
Tris Speaker, of	.320	7	25	6	8	2	1	0	1	3	1	0
Pinch Thomas, c	.000	1	0	0	0	0	0	0	0	0	0	0
George Uhle, p	.000	2	0	0	0	0	0	0	0	0	0	0
Bill Wambsganss, 2b	.154	7	26	3	4	0	0	0	1	2	1	0
Joe Wood, of	.200	4	10	2	2	1	0	0	0	1	2	0
TOTAL	.244		217	21	53	9	2	2	17	21	21	2

PITCHER	W	L	ERA	G	GS	CG	SV	SHO	IP	H	ER	BB	SO
Jim Bagby	1	1	1.80	2	2	1	0	0	15.0	20	3	1	3
Ray Caldwell	0	1	27.00	1	1	0	0	0	0.1	2	1	1	0
Stan Coveleski	3	0	0.67	3	3	3	0	1	27.0	15	2	2	8
Duster Mails	1	0	0.00	2	1	1	0	1	15.2	6	0	6	6
George Uhle	0	0	0.00	2	0	0	0	0	3.0	1	0	0	3
TOTAL	5	2	0.89	10	7	5	0	2	61.0	44	6	10	20

BRO (N)

PLAYER/POS	AVG	G	AB	R	H	2B	3B	HR	RB	BB	SO	SB
Leon Cadore, p	.000	2	0	0	0	0	0	0	0	0	0	0
Tommy Griffith, of	.190	7	21	1	4	2	0	0	3	0	2	0
Burleigh Grimes, p	.333	3	6	1	2	0	0	0	0	0	0	0
Jimmy Johnston, 3b	.214	4	14	2	3	0	0	0	0	0	2	1
Pete Kilduff, 2b	.095	7	21	0	2	0	0	0	0	1	4	0
Ed Konetchy, 1b	.174	7	23	0	4	0	1	0	2	3	2	0
Ernie Krueger, c-3	.167	4	6	0	1	0	0	0	0	0	0	0
Bill Lamar, ph	.000	3	3	0	0	0	0	0	0	0	0	0
Al Mamaux, p	.000	3	1	0	0	0	0	0	0	0	1	0
Rube Marquard, p	.000	2	1	0	0	0	0	0	0	0	0	0
Bill Mc Cabe, pr	.000	1	0	0	0	0	0	0	0	0	0	0
Otto Miller, c	.143	6	14	0	2	0	0	0	0	1	2	0
Clarence Mitchell, p-1	.333	2	3	0	1	0	0	0	0	0	0	0
Hy Myers, of	.231	7	26	0	6	0	0	0	1	0	1	0
Bernie Neis, of-2	.000	4	5	0	0	0	0	0	0	1	0	0
Ivy Olson, ss	.320	7	25	2	8	1	0	0	0	3	1	0
Jeff Pfeffer, p	.000	1	1	0	0	0	0	0	0	0	0	0
Ray Schmandt, ph	.000	1	1	0	0	0	0	0	0	0	0	0
Jack Sheehan, 3b	.182	3	11	0	2	0	0	0	0	0	1	0
Sherry Smith, p	.000	2	6	0	0	0	0	0	0	0	2	0
Zack Wheat, of	.333	7	27	2	9	2	0	0	2	1	2	0
TOTAL	.205		215	8	44	5	1	0	8	10	20	1

PITCHER	W	L	ERA	G	GS	CG	SV	SHO	IP	H	ER	BB	SO
Leon Cadore	0	1	9.00	2	1	0	0	0	2.0	4	2	1	1
Burleigh Grimes	1	2	4.19	3	3	1	0	1	19.1	23	9	9	4
Al Mamaux	0	0	4.50	3	0	0	0	0	4.0	2	2	0	5
Rube Marquard	0	1	1.00	2	1	0	0	0	9.0	7	1	3	6
Clarence Mitchell	0	0	0.00	1	0	0	0	0	4.2	3	0	3	1
Jeff Pfeffer	0	0	3.00	1	0	0	0	0	3.0	4	1	2	1
Sherry Smith	1	1	0.53	2	2	2	0	0	17.0	10	1	3	3
TOTAL	2	5	2.44	14	7	3	0	1	59.0	53	16	21	21

GAME 1 AT BRO OCT 5

CLE	020	100	000	3	5	0
BRO	000	000	100	1	5	1

Pitchers: COVELESKI vs MARQUARD, Mamaux (7), Cadore (9)
Attendance: 23,753

GAME 2 AT BRO OCT 6

CLE	000	000	000	0	7	1
BRO	101	010	00X	3	7	0

Pitchers: BAGBY, Uhle (7) vs GRIMES
Attendance: 22,559

GAME 3 AT BRO OCT 7

CLE	000	100	000	1	3	1
BRO	200	000	00X	2	6	1

Pitchers: CALDWELL, Mails (1), Uhle (8) vs SMITH
Attendance: 25,088

GAME 4 AT CLE OCT 9

BRO	000	100	000	1	5	1
CLE	202	001	00X	5	12	2

Pitchers: CADORE, Mamaux (2), Marquard (3), Pfeffer (6) vs COVELESKI
Attendance: 25,734

GAME 5 AT CLE OCT 10

BRO	000	000	001	1	13	1
CLE	400	310	00X	8	12	2

Pitchers: GRIMES, Mitchell (4) vs BAGBY
Home Runs: E.Smith-CLE, Bagby-CLE
Attendance: 26,884

GAME 6 AT CLE OCT 11

BRO	000	000	000	0	3	0
CLE	000	001	00X	1	7	3

Pitchers: SMITH vs MAILS
Attendance: 27,194

GAME 7 AT CLE OCT 12

BRO	000	000	000	0	5	2
CLE	000	110	10X	3	7	3

Pitchers: GRIMES, Mamaux (8) vs COVELESKI
Attendance: 27,525

Since both the Giants and Yankees called the Polo Grounds home, all eight games were played there, with the two clubs alternating from game to game as the hometeam. Pitching dominated the first two games—especially Yankee pitching. In Game One, Giant third baseman Frank Frisch went 4 for 4 against Carl Mays. But Mays gave up only one other hit and walked no one, to fashion a shutout. The next day Art Nehf of the Giants allowed the Yankees only three singles. But the Yankees capitalized on two of them, together with one of Nehf's seven walks, a couple of Giant errors, and Bob Meusel's steal of home to score three times, as pitcher Waite Hoyt shut out the Giants on two singles to put the Yanks two up in the Series.

In Game Three the hitters finally came alive. With the score tied 4–4 in the last of the seventh, the Giants unloaded for eight hits which, with two walks and a sacrifice fly, produced eight runs and the first Giant win. They evened the Series the next day, scoring three runs in the eighth to take a 3–1 lead, adding another in the ninth. Babe Ruth's first World Series home run, a solo shot in the bottom of the ninth, thrilled the fans but had no effect on the game's outcome.

The Yankees regained the Series lead in Game Five. Waite Hoyt was not as sharp as he had been in the opener, yielding ten hits. But the only run scored against him came as the result of a first-inning error, a deficit his Yankee teammates overcame for a 3–1 win. In Game Six the Yankees took a quick 3–0 lead in the first. The Giants tied it in the top of the second on home runs by Irish Meusel and Frank Snyder, but Chick Fewster hit a two-run shot a half inning later to restore the Yankee lead. In the fourth inning, though, the Giants parlayed four singles and an error into four runs and a lead that held up for a Series-tying win.

The Yankees scored only one run the rest of the way as the Giants took the final two games on unearned runs. In Game Seven, Mays and the Giants' Phil Douglas dueled into the seventh tied 1–1. But in the last of the seventh, Giant Frank Snyder's double drove in Johnny Rawlings, who had reached on an error, for the game's deciding run. In Game Eight, Hoyt held the Giants to four hits and completed his third game without giving up an earned run. But a Giant runner had scored in the first inning when a grounder shot through the legs of shortstop Roger Peckinpaugh. It turned out to be the game's only run, as Art Nehf and his Giants'

New York Giants (NL), 5;
New York Yankees (AL), 3

NY (N)

PLAYER/POS	AVG	G	AB	R	H	2B	3B	HR	RB	BB	SO	SB
Dave Bancroft, ss	.152	8	33	3	5	1	0	0	3	1	5	0
Jesse Barnes, p	.444	3	9	3	4	0	0	0	0	0	0	0
George Burns, of	.333	8	33	2	11	4	1	0	2	3	5	1
Phil Douglas, p	.000	3	7	0	0	0	0	0	0	0	2	0
Frankie Frisch, 3b	.300	8	30	5	9	0	1	0	1	4	3	3
George Kelly, 1b	.233	8	30	3	7	1	0	0	4	3	10	0
Irish Meusel, of	.345	8	29	4	10	2	1	1	7	2	3	1
Art Nehf, p	.000	3	9	0	0	0	0	0	0	1	3	0
Johnny Rawlings, 2b	.333	8	30	2	10	3	0	0	4	0	3	0
Earl Smith, c-2	.000	3	7	0	0	0	0	0	0	1	0	0
Frank Snyder, c-6	.364	7	22	4	8	1	0	1	3	0	2	0
Fred Toney, p	.000	2	0	0	0	0	0	0	0	0	0	0
Ross Youngs, of	.280	8	25	3	7	1	0	0	4	7	2	2
TOTAL	.269		264	29	71	13	4	2	28	22	38	7

PITCHER	W	L	ERA	G	GS	CG	SV	SHO	IP	H	ER	BB	SO
Jesse Barnes	2	0	1.65	3	0	0	0	0	16.1	10	3	6	18
Phil Douglas	2	1	2.08	3	3	2	0	0	26.0	20	6	5	17
Art Nehf	1	2	1.38	3	3	3	0	1	26.0	13	4	13	8
Fred Toney	0	0	23.63	2	2	0	0	0	2.2	7	7	3	1
TOTAL	5	3	2.54	11	8	5	0	1	71.0	50	20	27	44

NY (A)

PLAYER/POS	AVG	G	AB	R	H	2B	3B	HR	RB	BB	SO	SB
Frank Baker, 3b-2	.250	4	8	0	2	0	0	0	0	1	0	0
Rip Collins, p	.000	1	0	0	0	0	0	0	0	0	0	0
Al De Vormer, c-1	.000	2	1	0	0	0	0	0	0	0	0	0
Chick Fewster, of	.200	4	10	3	2	0	0	1	2	3	3	0
Harry Harper, p	.000	1	0	0	0	0	0	0	0	0	0	0
Waite Hoyt, p	.222	3	9	0	2	0	0	0	1	0	1	0
Carl Mays, p	.111	3	9	0	1	0	0	0	0	0	1	0
Mike McNally, 3b	.200	7	20	3	4	1	0	0	1	1	3	2
Bob Meusel, of	.200	8	30	3	6	2	0	0	3	2	5	1
Elmer Miller, of	.161	8	31	3	5	1	0	0	2	2	5	0
Roger Peckinpaugh, ss	.179	8	28	2	5	1	0	0	0	4	3	0
Bill Piercy, p	.000	1	0	0	0	0	0	0	00		0	0
Wally Pipp, 1b	.154	8	26	1	4	1	0	0	2	2	3	1
Jack Quinn, p	.000	1	2	0	0	0	0	0	0	0	1	0
Tom Rogers, p	.000	1	0	0	0	0	0	0	0	0	0	0
Babe Ruth, of	.313	6	16	3	5	0	0	1	4	5	8	2
Wally Schang, c	.286	8	21	1	6	1	1	0	1	5	4	0
Bob Shawkey, p	.500	2	4	2	2	0	0	0	0	0	1	0
Aaron Ward, 2b	.231	8	26	1	6	0	0	0	4	2	6	0
TOTAL	.207		241	22	50	7	1	2	20	27	44	6

PITCHER	W	L	ERA	G	GS	CG	SV	SHO	IP	H	ER	BB	SO
Rip Collins	0	0	54.00	1	0	0	0	0	0.2	4	4	1	0
Harry Harper	0	0	20.25	1	1	0	0	0	1.1	3	3	2	1
Waite Hoyt	2	1	0.00	3	3	3	0	1	27.0	18	0	11	18
Carl Mays	1	2	1.73	3	3	3	0	1	26.0	20	5	0	9
Bill Piercy	0	0	0.00	1	0	0	0	0	1.0	2	0	0	2
Jack Quinn	0	1	9.82	1	0	0	0	0	3.2	8	4	2	2
Tom Rogers	0	0	6.75	1	0	0	0	0	1.1	3	1	0	1
Bob Shawkey	0	1	7.00	2	1	0	0	0	9.0	13	7	6	5
TOTAL	3	5	3.09	13	8	6	0	2	70.0	71	24	22	38

flawless fielding blanked the Yankees to give manager John McGraw his first world championship since 1905.

GAME 1 AT NY -N OCT 5

NY-A	100	011	000	3	7	0
NY-N	000	000	000	0	5	0

Pitchers: MAYS vs DOUGLAS, Barnes (9)
Attendance: 30,202

GAME 2 AT NY -A OCT 6

NY-N	000	000	000	0	2	3
NY-A	000	100	02X	3	3	0

Pitchers: NEHF vs HOYT
Attendance: 34,939

GAME 3 AT NY -N OCT 7

NY-A	004	000	010	5	8	0
NY-N	004	000	81X	13	20	0

Pitchers: Shawkey, QUINN (3), Collins (7), Rogers (8) vs Toney, BARNES (3)
Attendance: 36,509

GAME 4 AT NY -A OCT 9

NY-N	000	000	031	4	9	1
NY-A	000	010	001	2	7	1

Pitchers: DOUGLAS vs MAYS
Home Runs: Ruth-NY(A)
Attendance: 36,372

GAME 5 AT NY -N OCT 10

NY-A	001	200	000	3	6	1
NY-N	100	000	000	1	10	1

Pitchers: HOYT vs NEHF
Attendance: 35,758

GAME 6 AT NY -A OCT 11

NY-N	030	401	000	8	13	0
NY-A	320	000	000	5	7	2

Pitchers: Toney, BARNES (1) vs Harper, SHAWKEY (2), Piercy (9)
Home Runs: E.Meusel-NY(N), Snyder-NY(N), Fewster-NY(A)
Attendance: 34,283

GAME 7 AT NY -N OCT 12

NY-A	010	000	000	1	8	1
NY-N	000	100	10X	2	6	0

Pitchers: MAYS vs DOUGLAS
Attendance: 36,503

GAME 8 AT NY -A OCT 13

NY-N	100	000	000	1	6	0
NY-A	000	000	000	0	4	1

Pitchers: NEHF vs HOYT
Attendance: 25,410

The Giants didn't quite sweep the Series—a tie in Game Two interrupted their string of victories—but they shut down the Yankee offense, holding Yankee scoring to three runs or less per game, and Babe Ruth to two hits and a .118 BA. This Series restored the best-of-seven-games format after three years of best-of-nine.

The Giants had to come from behind to take Game One. Yankee Bullet Joe Bush and Giant Art Nehf hurled shutout ball through five innings before the Yankees scored single runs in the sixth and seventh innings (Ruth driving in the Series' first run for the second year in a row with his single in the sixth). But in the eighth, Bush gave up four straight singles and two runs before Waite Hoyt relieved him with the score tied and men on first and third. Hoyt set down all three men he faced, but the first out—Ross Youngs's fly to center—drove in what proved to be the Giants' winning run.

The Giants led off Game Two with three first-inning runs on Irish Meusel's home run, but scored no more as Bob Shawkey stopped them for nine innings while his Yankees picked up runs in the first, fourth (on Aaron Ward's homer), and eighth to tie it all up. At the end of the tenth, with forty-five minutes left before sundown, the umpires called the game for darkness and provoked a storm of seat cushions and bottles from the stands.

The Giants resumed their winning ways in Game Three behind Jack Scott's shutout. Scott—picked up by the Giants in midseason—gave up only four Yankee hits, walking one, in the Series' top pitching performance. In Game Four the Yankees scored twice in the first inning, but in the fifth the Giants pounced on Carl Mays for four hits and two runs before the first out was recorded. Before the inning ended, a ground out and another hit had brought two more Giants across the plate, enough to survive Aaron Ward's second Series home run for a 4–3 win.

Game Five, the clincher, showed Nehf the winner by two runs at game's end, but the game went back and forth before the outcome was decided. Nehf gave up only five hits—all singles—but all of them contributed toward scoring Yankee runs in the first, fifth, and seventh innings. The Giants took the lead in the second with a pair of runs, but again fell behind until four hits and a walk in the eighth undid Yankee pitcher Joe Bush's fine effort, giving the Giants three additional runs and John McGraw his third world title.

New York Giants (NL), 4; New York Yankees (AL), 0; tie, 1

NY (N)

PLAYER/POS	AVG	G	AB	R	H	2B	3B	HR	RB	BB	SO	SB
Dave Bancroft, ss	.211	5	19	4	4	0	0	0	2	2	1	0
Jesse Barnes, p	.000	1	4	0	0	0	0	0	0	0	1	0
Bill Cunningham, of	.200	4	10	0	2	0	0	0	2	2	1	0
Frankie Frisch, 2b	.471	5	17	3	8	1	0	0	2	1	0	1
Heinie Groh, 3b	.474	5	19	4	9	0	1	0	0	2	1	0
George Kelly, 1b	.278	5	18	0	5	0	0	0	2	0	3	0
Lee King, of	1.000	2	1	0	1	0	0	0	1	0	0	0
Hugh Mc Quillan, p	.250	1	4	1	1	1	0	0	0	0	1	0
Irish Meusel, of	.250	5	20	3	5	0	0	1	7	0	1	0
Art Nehf, p	.000	2	3	0	0	0	0	0	0	2	0	0
Rosy Ryan, p	.000	1	0	0	0	0	0	0	0	0	0	0
Jack Scott, p	.250	1	4	0	1	0	0	0	0	0	1	0
Earl Smith, c-1	.143	4	7	0	1	0	0	0	0	0	2	0
Frank Snyder, c	.333	4	15	1	5	0	0	0	0	0	1	0
Casey Stengel, of	.400	2	5	0	2	0	0	0	0	0	1	0
Ross Youngs, of	.375	5	16	2	6	0	0	0	2	3	1	0
TOTAL	.309		162	18	50	2	1	1	18	12	15	1

PITCHER	W	L	ERA	G	GS	CG	SV	SHO	IP	H	ER	BB	SO
Jesse Barnes	0	0	1.80	1	1	1	0	0	10.0	8	2	2	6
Hugh Mc Quillan	1	0	3.00	1	1	1	0	0	9.0	8	3	2	4
Art Nehf	1	0	2.25	2	2	1	0	0	16.0	11	4	3	6
Rosy Ryan	1	0	0.00	1	0	0	0	0	2.0	1	0	0	2
Jack Scott	1	0	0.00	1	1	1	0	1	9.0	4	0	1	2
TOTAL	4	0	1.76	6	5	4	0	1	46.0	32	9	8	20

NY (A)

PLAYER/POS	AVG	G	AB	R	H	2B	3B	HR	RB	BB	SO	SB
Frank Baker, ph	.000	1	1	0	0	0	0	0	0	0	0	0
Joe Bush, p	.167	2	6	0	1	0	0	0	1	0	0	0
Joe Dugan, 3b	.250	5	20	4	5	1	0	0	0	0	1	0
Waite Hoyt, p	.500	2	2	0	1	0	0	0	0	0	0	0
Sam Jones, p	.000	2	0	0	0	0	0	0	0	0	0	0
Carl Mays, p	.000	1	2	0	0	0	0	0	0	0	0	0
Norm Mc Millan, of	.000	1	2	0	0	0	0	0	0	0	0	0
Mike Mc Nally, 2b	.000	1	0	0	0	0	0	0	0	0	0	0
Bob Meusel, of	.300	5	20	2	6	1	0	0	2	1	3	1
Wally Pipp, 1b	.286	5	21	0	6	1	0	0	3	0	2	1
Babe Ruth, of	.118	5	17	1	2	1	0	0	1	2	3	0
Wally Schang, c	.188	5	16	0	3	1	0	0	0	0	3	0
Everett Scott, ss	.143	5	14	0	2	0	0	0	1	1	0	0
Bob Shawkey, p	.000	1	4	0	0	0	0	0	0	0	1	0
Elmer Smith, ph	.000	2	2	0	0	0	0	0	0	0	2	0
Aaron Ward, 2b	.154	5	13	3	2	0	0	2	3	3	3	0
Whitey Witt, of	.222	5	18	1	4	1	1	0	0	1	2	0
TOTAL	.203		158	11	32	6	1	2	11	8	20	2

PITCHER	W	L	ERA	G	GS	CG	SV	SHO	IP	H	ER	BB	SO
Joe Bush	0	2	4.80	2	2	1	0	0	15.0	21	8	5	6
Waite Hoyt	0	1	1.13	2	1	0	0	0	8.0	11	1	2	4
Sam Jones	0	0	0.00	2	0	0	0	0	2.0	1	0	1	0
Carl Mays	0	1	4.50	1	1	0	0	0	8.0	9	4	2	1
Bob Shawkey	0	0	2.70	1	1	1	0	0	10.0	8	3	2	4
TOTAL	0	4	3.35	8	5	2	0	0	43.0	50	16	12	15

GAME 1 AT NY -N OCT 4

NY-A	000	001	100	2	7	0
NY-N	000	000	03X	3	11	3

Pitchers: BUSH, Hoyt (8) vs Nehf, RYAN (8)
Attendance: 36,514

GAME 2 AT NY -A OCT 5

NY-N	300	000	000	0	3	8	1
NY-A	100	100	010	0	3	8	0

Pitchers: Barnes vs Shawkey
Home Runs: E.Meusel-NY(N), Ward-NY(A)
Attendance: 37,020

GAME 3 AT NY -N OCT 6

NY-A	000	000	000	0	4	1
NY-N	002	000	10X	3	12	1

Pitchers: HOYT, Jones (8) vs J.SCOTT
Attendance: 37,620

GAME 4 AT NY -A OCT 7

NY-N	000	040	000	4	9	1
NY-A	200	000	100	3	8	0

Pitchers: McQUILLAN vs MAYS, Jones (9)
Home Runs: Ward-NY(A)
Attendance: 36,242

GAME 5 AT NY -N OCT 8

NY-A	100	010	100	3	5	0
NY-N	020	000	03X	5	10	0

Pitchers: BUSH vs NEHF
Attendance: 38,551

After two Series played entirely in the Polo Grounds, the Giants and Yankees in 1923 had Yankee Stadium across the river to play alternate games. Celebrating the opener in the new "house that Ruth built," the Yankees took an early three-run lead. In the third inning, though, the Giants drove out starter Waite Hoyt, emerging with four runs. Yankee reliever Joe Bush prevented further Giant scoring for several innings as the Yankees picked up a tying run in the seventh. But with the game still knotted in the top of the ninth, Giant Casey Stengel legged out an inside-the-park homer to win it.

Babe Ruth gave Herb Pennock his first World Series win with a pair of homers in Game Two. The first, a solo blast over the roof in right, broke a 1–1 tie in the fourth, and the second, an inning later, concluded Yankee scoring in their 4–2 win that evened the Series. Stengel sent the Giants ahead in the seventh inning of Game Three, lifting a home run over the fence this time for the game's only score. The run gave Art Nehf the win in his duel with Sad Sam Jones, and again gave the Giants the Series lead.

Giant Ross Youngs's fourth hit of Game Four, an inside-the-park homer into the Polo Grounds' deep outfield, gave the Giants a fourth run to lead off the bottom of the ninth, but as a rally it fell short; the Yankees, who had already scored eight, took the game to even the Series. In Game Five Joe Bush gave up only three Giant hits—a single, double, and triple to Irish Meusel. Irish scored the only Giant run, but his Yankee brother Bob drove in three runs with his three hits—sharing RBI honors with Joe Dugan, whose four hits included the Series' third inside-the-park home run, a three-run shot in the second inning. Final score: 8–1.

In Game Six, Herb Pennock yielded four Giant runs in his seven innings on the mound and seemed on the edge of defeat. But in the top of the eighth, Art Nehf (who had pitched one-hit ball since Ruth homered for a Yankee run in the first) lost his stuff. With one out, two singles followed by two walks (on eight pitches) forced in a run. Rosy Ryan replaced Nehf and walked in another run. Ruth struck out, but Bob Meusel's single and a wild throw from center cleared the bases to put the Yankees ahead 6–4, where they remained to game's end for the first of their twenty-two world championships.

New York Yankees (AL), 4; New York Giants (NL), 2

NY (A)

PLAYER/POS	AVG	G	AB	R	H	2B	3B	HR	RB	BB	SO	SB
Joe Bush, p-3	.429	4	7	2	3	1	0	0	1	1	1	0
Joe Dugan, 3b	.280	6	25	5	7	2	1	1	5	3	0	0
Hinky Haines, of	.000	2	1	1	0	0	0	0	0	0	0	0
Harvey Hendrick, ph	.000	1	1	0	0	0	0	0	0	0	0	0
Fred Hoffmann, ph	.000	2	1	0	0	0	0	0	0	1	0	0
Waite Hoyt, p	.000	1	1	0	0	0	0	0	0	0	1	0
Ernie Johnson, ss-1	.000	2	0	1	0	0	0	0	0	0	0	0
Sam Jones, p	.000	2	2	0	0	0	0	0	0	0	1	0
Bob Meusel, of	.269	6	26	1	7	1	2	0	8	0	3	0
Herb Pennock, p	.000	3	6	0	0	0	0	0	0	0	2	0
Wally Pipp, 1b	.250	6	20	2	5	0	0	0	2	4	1	0
Babe Ruth, of-6,1b-1	.368	6	19	8	7	1	1	3	3	8	6	0
Wally Schang, c	.318	6	22	3	7	1	0	0	0	1	2	0
Everett Scott, ss	.318	6	22	2	7	0	0	0	3	0	1	0
Bob Shawkey, p	.333	1	3	0	1	0	0	0	1	0	0	0
Aaron Ward, 2b	.417	6	24	4	10	0	0	1	2	1	3	1
Whitey Witt, of	.240	6	25	1	6	2	0	0	4	1	1	0
TOTAL	.293		205	30	60	8	4	5	29	20	22	1

PITCHER	W	L	ERA	G	GS	CG	SV	SHO	IP	H	ER	BB	SO
Joe Bush	1	1	1.08	3	1	1	0	0	16.2	7	2	4	5
Waite Hoyt	0	0	15.43	1	1	0	0	0	2.1	4	4	1	0
Sam Jones	0	1	0.90	2	1	0	1	0	10.0	5	1	2	3
Herb Pennock	2	0	3.63	3	2	1	1	0	17.1	19	7	1	8
Bob Shawkey	1	0	3.52	1	1	0	0	0	7.2	12	3	4	2
TOTAL	4	2	2.83	10	6	2	2	0	54.0	47	17	12	18

NY (N)

PLAYER/POS	AVG	G	AB	R	H	2B	3B	HR	RB	BB	SO	SB
Dave Bancroft, ss	.083	6	24	1	2	0	0	0	1	1	2	1
Virgil Barnes, p	.000	2	1	0	0	0	0	0	0	0	1	0
Jack Bentley, p-2	.600	5	5	0	3	1	0	0	3	0	0	0
Bill Cunningham, of-3	.143	4	7	0	1	0	0	0	1	0	1	0
Frankie Frisch, 2b	.400	6	25	2	10	0	1	0	1	0	0	0
Dinty Gearin, pr	.000	1	0	0	0	0	0	0	0	0	0	0
Hank Gowdy, c-2	.000	3	4	0	0	0	0	0	0	1	0	0
Heinie Groh, 3b	.182	6	22	3	4	0	1	0	2	3	1	0
Travis Jackson, ph	.000	1	1	0	0	0	0	0	0	0	0	0
Claude Jonnard, p	.000	2	0	0	0	0	0	0	0	0	0	0
George Kelly, 1b	.182	6	22	1	4	0	0	0	1	1	2	0
Freddie Maguire, pr	.000	2	0	1	0	0	0	0	0	0	0	0
Hugh Mc Quillan, p	.000	2	3	0	0	0	0	0	0	0	1	0
Irish Meusel, of	.280	6	25	3	7	1	1	1	2	0	2	0
Art Nehf, p	.167	2	6	0	1	0	0	0	0	0	4	0
Jimmy O'Connell, ph	.000	2	1	0	0	0	0	0	0	0	1	0
Rosy Ryan, p	.000	3	2	0	0	0	0	0	0	0	1	0
Jack Scott, p	.000	2	1	0	0	0	0	0	0	0	0	0
Frank Snyder, c	.118	5	17	1	2	0	0	1	2	0	2	0
Casey Stengel, of	.417	6	12	3	5	0	0	2	4	4	0	0
Mule Watson, p	.000	1	0	0	0	0	0	0	0	0	0	0
Ross Youngs, of	.348	6	23	2	8	0	0	1	3	2	0	0
TOTAL	.234		201	17	47	2	3	5	17	12	18	1

PITCHER	W	L	ERA	G	GS	CG	SV	SHO	IP	H	ER	BB	SO
Virgil Barnes	0	0	0.00	2	0	0	0	0	4.2	4	0	0	4
Jack Bentley	0	1	9.45	2	1	0	0	0	6.2	10	7	4	1
Claude Jonnard	0	0	0.00	2	0	0	0	0	2.0	1	0	1	1
Hugh Mc Quillan	0	1	5.00	2	1	0	0	0	9.0	11	5	4	3
Art Nehf	1	1	2.76	2	2	1	0	1	16.1	10	5	6	7
Rosy Ryan	1	0	0.96	3	0	0	0	0	9.1	11	1	3	3
Jack Scott	0	1	12.00	2	1	0	0	0	3.0	9	4	1	2
Mule Watson	0	0	13.50	1	1	0	0	0	2.0	4	3	1	1
TOTAL	2	4	4.25	16	6	1	0	1	53.0	60	25	20	22

GAME 1 AT NY -A OCT 10

NY-N 004 000 001   5 8 0
NY-A 120 000 100   4 12 1
Pitchers: Watson, RYAN (3) vs Hoyt, BUSH (3)
Home Runs: Stengel-NY(N)
Attendance: 55,307

GAME 2 AT NY -N OCT 11

NY-A 010 210 000   4 10 0
NY-N 010 001 000   2 9 2
Pitchers: PENNOCK vs McQUILLAN, Bentley (4)
Home Runs: Ward-NY(A), E.Meusel-NY(N), Ruth-NY(A) (2)
Attendance: 40,402

GAME 3 AT NY -A OCT 12

NY-N 000 000 100   1 4 0
NY-A 000 000 000   0 6 1
Pitchers: NEHF vs JONES, Bush (8)
Home Runs: Stengel-NY(N)
Attendance: 62,430

GAME 4 AT NY -N OCT 13

NY-A 061 100 000   8 13 1
NY-N 000 000 031   4 13 1
Pitchers: SHAWKEY, Pennock (8) vs J.SCOTT, Ryan (2), McQuillan (3), Jonnard (8)
Home Runs: Youngs-NY(N)
Attendance: 46,302

GAME 5 AT NY -A OCT 14

NY-N 010 000 000   1 3 2
NY-A 340 100 00X   8 14 0
Pitchers: BENTLEY, J.Scott (2), Barnes (4), Jonnard (8) vs BUSH
Home Runs: Dugan-NY(A)
Attendance: 62,817

GAME 6 AT NY -N OCT 15

NY-A 100 000 050   6 5 0
NY-N 100 111 000   4 10 1
Pitchers: PENNOCK, Jones (8) vs NEHF, Ryan (8)
Home Runs: Ruth-NY(A), Snyder-NY(N)
Attendance: 34,172

Four of the seven games in this exciting Series were decided by one run—two of them after twelve innings. Pitcher Walter Johnson, in his first World Series after eighteen big-league seasons and 376 victories, opened for Washington against the Giants' Art Nehf. Although fourteen Giants reached base on hits or walks in the first nine innings, only two scored—George Kelly and Bill Terry, both of whom homered. In the bottom of the ninth, the Senators scored their second run to send the game into extra innings. Johnson shut out the Giants for two more frames, but in the top of the twelfth, two walks and three singles put New York ahead by two. Washington came back with a run and had a man on third. But Kelly at second base stopped Goose Goslin's grounder with his bare hand, and Nehf had the Giants' first win.

Goslin and manager/second baseman Bucky Harris homered in Game Two to give the Senators a 3–0 lead through six innings. The Giants scored once in the seventh and drove out starter Tom Zachary with two more in the ninth to tie the game, but in the last of the ninth Senator Roger Peckinpaugh doubled in the tie breaker to even the Series.

The Giants took an early lead in Game Three and held it to retake the Series lead, but Washington (led by Goslin's three-run homer in the third) unleashed a 13-hit, seven-run attack the next day to even the Series once more. In Game Five, though, New York pulled ahead again, defeating Johnson a second time as winning pitcher Jack Bentley put the Giants into the lead for good with a two-run homer in the fifth. In Game Six, Washington's two runs in the fifth inning overcame a first-inning Giant run and gave Tom Zachary all he needed for the Senators' third win, which set the stage for one of the most memorable games in Series history.

Washington scored first in Game Seven on manager Harris's homer in the fourth inning, but the Giants scored three runs in the sixth (two of them on Senator errors) to go ahead 3–1. In the last of the eighth, though, Harris's grounder over the head of rookie Freddie Lindstrom for two more Senator runs and a 3–3 tie. Walter Johnson came in to face the Giants in the ninth, and shut them out through the twelfth, fanning five. Then in the bottom of the twelfth, with one out, Muddy Ruel (given a second chance after Giant catcher Hank Gowdy caught his foot in his mask and missed Ruel's pop foul) doubled to left. Pitcher Johnson then reached first when

shortstop Travis Jackson bobbled what ought to have been a third-out grounder. With men on second and first, Earl McNeely bounced to Lindstrom at third. But again the ball bounded over Lindstrom's head, and Ruel raced home with Johnson's first Series win and Washington's first world championship.

Washington Senators (AL), 4; New York Giants (NL), 3

WAS (A)

PLAYER/POS	AVG	G	AB	R	H	2B	3B	HR	RB	BB	SO	SB
Ossie Bluege, ss-5,3b-4	.192	7	26	2	5	0	0	0	2	3	4	1
Goose Goslin, of	.344	7	32	4	11	1	0	3	7	0	7	0
Bucky Harris, 2b	.333	7	33	5	11	0	0	2	7	1	4	0
Walter Johnson, p	.111	3	9	0	1	0	0	0	0	0	0	0
Joe Judge, 1b	.385	7	26	4	10	1	0	0	0	5	2	0
Nemo Leibold, of-1	.167	3	6	1	1	1	0	0	0	1	0	0
Firpo Marberry, p	.000	4	2	0	0	0	0	0	0	0	0	0
Joe Martina, p	.000	1	0	0	0	0	0	0	0	0	0	0
Earl Mc Neely, of	.222	7	27	4	6	3	0	0	1	4	4	1
Ralph Miller, 3b	.182	4	11	0	2	0	0	0	2	1	0	0
George Mogridge, p	.000	2	5	0	0	0	0	0	0	0	5	0
Curly Ogden, p	.000	1	0	0	0	0	0	0	0	0	0	0
Roger Peckinpaugh, ss	.417	4	12	1	5	2	0	0	2	1	0	1
Sam Rice, of	.207	7	29	2	6	0	0	0	1	3	2	2
Muddy Ruel, c	.095	7	21	2	2	1	0	0	0	6	1	0
Allan Russell, p	.000	1	0	0	0	0	0	0	0	0	0	0
Mule Shirley, ph	.500	3	2	1	1	0	0	0	1	0	0	0
By Speece, p	.000	1	0	0	0	0	0	0	0	0	0	0
Bennie Tate, ph	.000	3	0	0	0	0	0	0	1	3	0	0
Tommy Taylor, 3b	.000	2	3	0	0	0	0	0	0	0	2	0
Tom Zachary, p	.000	2	5	0	0	0	0	0	0	1	3	0
TOTAL	.246		248	26	61	9	0	5	24	29	34	5

PITCHER	W	L	ERA	G	GS	CG	SV	SHO	IP	H	ER	BB	SO
Walter Johnson	1	2	2.25	3	2	2	0	0	24.0	30	6	11	20
Firpo Marberry	0	1	1.13	4	1	0	2	0	8.0	9	1	4	10
Joe Martina	0	0	0.00	1	0	0	0	0	1.0	0	0	0	1
George Mogridge	1	0	2.25	2	1	0	0	0	12.0	7	3	6	5
Curly Ogden	0	0	0.00	1	1	0	0	0	0.1	0	0	1	1
Allan Russell	0	0	3.00	1	0	0	0	0	3.0	4	1	0	0
By Speece	0	0	9.00	1	0	0	0	0	1.0	3	1	0	0
Tom Zachary	2	0	2.04	2	2	1	0	0	17.2	13	4	3	3
TOTAL	4	3	2.15	15	7	3	2	0	67.0	66	16	25	40

NY (N)

PLAYER/POS	AVG	G	AB	R	H	2B	3B	HR	RB	BB	SO	SB
Harry Baldwin, p	.000	1	0	0	0	0	0	0	0	0	0	0
Virgil Barnes, p	.000	2	4	0	0	0	0	0	0	1	2	0
Jack Bentley, p-3	.286	5	7	1	2	0	0	1	2	1	1	0
Wayland Dean, p	.000	1	0	0	0	0	0	0	0	0	0	0
Frankie Frisch, 2b-7,3b-1	.333	7	30	1	10	4	1	0	4	4	1	1
Hank Gowdy, c	.259	4	27	4	7	0	0	0	1	2	2	0
Heinie Groh, ph	1.000	1	1	0	1	0	0	0	0	0	0	0
Travis Jackson, ss	.074	7	27	3	2	0	0	0	1	1	4	1
Claude Jonnard, p	.000	1	0	0	0	0	0	0	0	0	0	0
George Kelly, 1b-4,of-4,2b-1	.290	7	31	7	9	1	0	1	4	1	8	0
Fred Lindstrom, 3b	.333	7	30	1	10	2	0	0	4	3	6	0
Hugh Mc Quillan, p	1.000	3	1	0	1	0	0	0	1	1	0	0
Irish Meusel, of	.154	4	13	0	2	0	0	0	1	2	0	0
Art Nehf, p	.429	3	7	1	3	0	0	0	0	0	0	0
Rosy Ryan, p	.500	2	2	1	1	0	0	1	2	0	0	0
Frank Snyder, ph	.000	1	1	0	0	0	0	0	0	0	0	0
Billy Southworth, of-2	.000	5	1	1	0	0	0	0	0	0	0	0
Bill Terry, 1b-4	.429	5	14	3	6	0	1	1	1	3	1	0
Mule Watson, p	.000	1	0	0	0	0	0	0	0	0	0	0
Hack Wilson, of	.233	7	30	1	7	1	0	0	3	1	9	0
Ross Youngs, of	.185	7	27	3	5	1	0	0	2	5	6	1
TOTAL	.261		253	27	66	9	2	4	22	25	40	3

PITCHER	W	L	ERA	G	GS	CG	SV	SHO	IP	H	ER	BB	SO
Harry Baldwin	0	0	0.00	1	0	0	0	0	2.0	1	0	0	1
Virgil Barnes	0	1	5.68	2	2	0	0	0	12.2	15	8	1	9
Jack Bentley	1	2	3.71	3	2	1	0	0	17.0	18	7	8	10
Wayland Dean	0	0	4.50	1	0	0	0	0	2.0	3	1	0	2
Claude Jonnard	0	0	INF	1	0	0	0	0	0.0	0	0	1	0
Hugh Mc Quillan	0	0	2.57	3	1	0	1	0	7.0	2	2	6	2
Art Nehf	1	1	1.83	3	2	1	0	0	19.2	15	4	9	7
Rosy Ryan	1	0	3.18	2	0	0	0	0	5.2	7	2	4	3
Mule Watson	0	0	0.00	1	0	0	1	0	0.2	0	0	0	0
TOTAL	3	4	3.24	17	7	2	2	0	66.2	61	24	29	34

GAME 1 AT WAS OCT 4

NY	010 100 000 002	4	14	1
WAS	000 001 001 001	3	10	1

Pitchers: NEHF vs JOHNSON
Home Runs: Kelly-NY, Terry-NY
Attendance: 35,760

GAME 2 AT WAS OCT 5

NY	000 000 102	3	6	0
WAS	200 010 001	4	6	1

Pitchers: BENTLEY vs ZACHARY, Marberry (9)
Home Runs: Goslin-WAS, Harris-WAS
Attendance: 35,922

GAME 3 AT NY OCT 6

WAS	000 200 011	4	9	2
NY	021 101 01X	6	12	4

Pitchers: MARBERRY, Russell (4), Martina (7), Speece (8) vs McQUILLAN, RYAN (4), Jonnard (9), Watson (9)
Home Runs: Ryan-NY
Attendance: 47,608

GAME 4 AT NY OCT 7

WAS	003 020 020	7	13	3
NY	100 001 011	4	6	1

Pitchers: MOGRIDGE, Marberry (8) vs BARNES, Baldwin (6), Dean (8)
Home Runs: Goslin-WAS
Attendance: 49,243

GAME 5 AT NY OCT 8

WAS	000 100 010	2	9	1
NY	001 020 03X	6	13	0

Pitchers: JOHNSON vs BENTLEY, McQuillan (8)
Home Runs: Bentley-NY, Goslin-WAS
Attendance: 49,211

GAME 6 AT WAS OCT 9

NY	100 000 000	1	7	1
WAS	000 020 00X	2	4	0

Pitchers: NEHF, Ryan (8) vs ZACHARY
Attendance: 34,254

GAME 7 AT WAS OCT 10

NY	000 003 000 000	3	8	3
WAS	000 100 020 001	4	10	4

Pitchers: Barnes, McQuillan (8), Nehf (10), BENTLEY (11) vs Ogden, Mogridge (1), Marberry (6), JOHNSON (9)
Home Runs: Harris-WAS
Attendance: 31,667

Repeating as pennant winners, the Senators found themselves again locked in a tight Series, this time with the Pirates, who hadn't won a pennant since 1909. Again Walter Johnson pitched the Series opener, winning this time with a strong five-hit, ten-strikeout performance, giving up only one run on Pie Traynor's homer in the fifth. Home runs by Pirates Kiki Cuyler and Glenn Wright and Senator Joe Judge accounted for four of the five runs scored in Game Two, in which Pirate Vic Aldridge dueled Senator Stan Coveleski to a narrow 3–2 win, evening the Series.

Washington took Games Three and Four, though, for a 3–1 Series advantage, Goose Goslin's solo homer in the sixth inning providing the margin of victory in Game Three, and homers by Goslin (for three runs) and Joe Harris the next day providing all the scoring as Johnson shut the Pirates out.

Harris hit his third Series homer in Game Five, but Pirate bats overwhelmed Coveleski as he lost to Aldridge for a second time. And although Goslin's third homer gave the Senators an early lead in Game Six, Pittsburgh's Ray Kremer shut Washington out from the third inning on as his teammates pulled even with two runs in the bottom of the third, and Eddie Moore's homer in the fifth gave him the run he needed for a win that sent the Series into a seventh game.

Both clubs went with their best in the finale as Johnson, winner of Games One and Four, faced Aldridge, victor in Games Two and Five. But Aldridge was wild, issuing three walks and two wild pitches in addition to two hits before being yanked with only one out in the top of the first. Johnson was hardly more effective: although he lasted the whole game, he gave up 15 hits and five earned runs. But if there was a Series goat, it would have to be Senator shortstop Roger Peckinpaugh, the American League MVP. Though he drove in a run in the first and homered for another in the eighth, his dropped pop fly in the seventh and wild throw in the eighth (his seventh and eighth errors of the Series) opened the way to four unearned runs and Pittsburgh's 9–7 triumph.

Pittsburgh Pirates (NL), 4; Washington Senators (AL), 3

PIT (N)

PLAYER/POS	AVG	G	AB	R	H	2B	3B	HR	RB	BB	SO	SB
Babe Adams, p	.000	1	0	0	0	0	0	0	0	0	0	0
Vic Aldridge, p	.000	3	7	0	0	0	0	0	0	0	0	0
Clyde Barnhart, of	.250	7	28	1	7	1	0	0	5	3	5	1
Carson Bigbee, of-1	.333	4	3	1	1	1	0	0	1	0	0	1
Max Carey, of	.458	7	24	6	11	4	0	0	2	2	3	3
Kiki Cuyler, of	.269	7	26	3	7	3	0	1	6	1	4	0
Johnny Gooch, c	.000	3	3	0	0	0	0	0	0	0	0	0
George Grantham, 1b-4	.133	5	15	0	2	0	0	0	0	0	3	1
Ray Kremer, p	.143	3	7	0	1	0	0	0	1	0	5	0
Stuffy Mc Innis, 1b-3	.286	4	14	0	4	0	0	0	1	0	2	0
Lee Meadows, p	.000	1	1	0	0	0	0	0	0	1	1	0
Eddie Moore, 2b	.231	7	26	7	6	1	0	1	2	5	2	0
Johnny Morrison, p	.500	3	2	1	1	0	0	0	0	0	0	0
Red Oldham, p	.000	1	0	0	0	0	0	0	0	0	0	0
Earl Smith, c	.350	6	20	0	7	1	0	0	0	1	2	0
Pie Traynor, 3b	.346	7	26	2	9	0	2	1	4	3	1	1
Glenn Wright, ss	.185	7	27	3	5	1	0	1	3	1	4	0
Emil Yde, p-1	.000	2	1	1	0	0	0	0	0	0	0	0
TOTAL	.265		230	25	61	12	2	4	25	17	32	7

PITCHER	W	L	ERA	G	GS	CG	SV	SHO	IP	H	ER	BB	SO
Babe Adams	0	0	0.00	1	0	0	0	0	1.0	2	0	0	0
Vic Aldridge	2	0	4.42	3	3	2	0	0	18.1	18	9	9	9
Ray Kremer	2	-1	3.00	3	2	2	0	0	21.0	17	7	4	9
Lee Meadows	0	1	3.38	1	0	0	0	0	8.0	8	3	0	4
Johnny Morrison	0	0	2.89	3	1	0	0	0	9.1	11	3	1	7
Red Oldham	0	0	0.00	1	0	0	1	0	1.0	0	0	0	2
Emil Yde	0	1	11.57	1	1	0	0	0	2.1	5	3	3	1
TOTAL	4	1	3.69	13	7	4	1	0	61.0	59	25	17	32

WAS (A)

PLAYER/POS	AVG	G	AB	R	H	2B	3B	HR	RB	BB	SO	SB
Spencer Adams, 2b-1	.000	2	1	0	0	0	0	0	0	0	0	0
Win Ballou, p	.000	2	0	0	0	0	0	0	0	0	0	0
Ossie Bluege, 3b	.278	5	18	2	5	1	0	0	2	1	4	0
Stan Coveleski, p	.000	2	3	0	0	0	0	0	0	0	2	0
Alex Ferguson, p	.000	2	4	0	0	0	0	0	0	0	3	0
Goose Goslin, of	.308	7	26	6	8	1	0	3	6	3	3	0
Joe Harris, of	.440	7	25	5	11	2	0	3	6	3	4	0
Bucky Harris, 2b	.087	7	23	2	2	0	0	0	0	1	3	0
Walter Johnson, p	.091	3	11	0	1	0	0	0	0	0	3	0
Joe Judge, 1b	.174	7	23	2	4	1	0	1	3	3	2	0
Nemo Leibold, ph	.500	3	2	1	1	1	0	0	0	1	0	0
Firpo Marberry, p	.000	2	0	0	0	0	0	0	0	0	0	0
Earl Mc Neely, of-2	.000	4	0	2	0	0	0	0	0	0	0	1
Buddy Myer, 3b	.250	3	8	0	2	0	0	0	0	1	2	0
Roger Peckinpaugh, ss	.250	7	24	1	6	1	0	1	3	1	2	1
Sam Rice, of	.364	7	33	5	12	0	0	0	3	0	1	0
Muddy Ruel, c	.316	7	19	0	6	1	0	0	1	3	2	0
Dutch Ruether, ph	.000	1	1	0	0	0	0	0	0	0	1	0
Hank Severeid, c	.333	1	3	0	1	0	0	0	0	0	0	0
Bobby Veach, ph	.000	2	1	0	0	0	0	0	1	0	0	0
Tom Zachary, p	.000	1	0	0	0	0	0	0	0	0	0	0
TOTAL	.262		225	26	59	8	0	8	25	17	32	2

PITCHER	W	L	ERA	G	GS	CG	SV	SHO	IP	H	ER	BB	SO
Win Ballou	0	0	0.00	2	0	0	0	0	1.2	0	0	1	1
Stan Coveleski	0	2	3.77	2	2	1	0	0	14.1	16	6	5	3
Alex Ferguson	1	1	3.21	2	2	1	0	0	14.0	13	5	6	11
Walter Johnson	2	1	2.08	3	3	3	0	1	26.0	26	6	4	15
Firpo Marberry	0	0	0.00	2	0	0	1	0	2.1	3	0	0	2
Tom Zachary	0	0	10.80	1	0	0	0	0	1.2	3	2	1	0
TOTAL	3	4	2.85	12	7	5	1	1	60.0	61	19	17	32

GAME 1 AT PIT OCT 7

WAS	010 020 001	4	8	1
PIT	000 010 000	1	5	0

Pitchers: JOHNSON vs MEADOWS, Morrison (9)
Home Runs: J.Harris-WAS, Traynor-PIT
Attendance: 41,723

GAME 2 AT PIT OCT 8

WAS	010 000 001	2	8	2
PIT	000 100 02X	3	7	0

Pitchers: COVELESKI vs ALDRIDGE
Home Runs: Judge-WAS, Wright-PIT, Cuyler-PIT
Attendance: 43,364

GAME 3 AT WAS OCT 10

PIT	010 101 000	3	8	3
WAS	001 001 20X	4	10	1

Pitchers: KREMER vs FERGUSON, Marberry (8)
Home Runs: Goslin-WAS
Attendance: 36,495

GAME 4 AT WAS OCT 11

PIT	000 000 000	0	6	1
WAS	004 000 00X	4	12	0

Pitchers: YDE, Morrison (3), Adams (8) vs JOHNSON
Home Runs: Goslin-WAS, J.Harris-WAS
Attendance: 38,701

GAME 5 AT WAS OCT 12

PIT	002 000 211	6	13	0
WAS	100 100 100	3	8	1

Pitchers: ALDRIDGE vs COVELESKI, Ballou (7), Zachary (8), Marberry (9)
Home Runs: J.Harris-WAS
Attendance: 35,899

GAME 6 AT PIT OCT 13

WAS	110 000 000	2	6	2
PIT	002 010 00X	3	7	1

Pitchers: FERGUSON, Ballou (8) vs KREMER
Home Runs: Goslin-WAS, Moore-PIT
Attendance: 43,810

GAME 7 AT PIT OCT 15

WAS	400 200 010	7	7	7
PIT	003 010 23X	9	15	2

Pitchers: JOHNSON vs Aldridge, Morrison (1), KREMER (5), Oldham (9)
Home Runs: Peckinpaugh-WAS
Attendance: 42,856

The Yankees, returning to the World Series after a two-year absence, faced the Cardinals, who had won their first pennant since joining the National League in 1892. Both clubs led their league in slugging and runs scored; this power erupted occasionally in the Series, but over all, pitching dominated as each staff bettered its regular-season earned run average by nearly a run per game.

Herb Pennock of the Yankees pitched a splendid three-hitter in the opener. After yielding two hits and a run in the first inning, he shut out the Cards the rest of the way, holding them hitless until the ninth. Cardinal starter Bill Sherdel also pitched effectively, but three walks in the first and a hit-sacrifice-hit sandwich in the sixth brought in enough runs to beat him.

In Game Two, the veteran Grover Cleveland Alexander evened the Series, striking out ten and holding the Yankees to four singles (three of them in the two-run second) as Billy Southworth and Tommy Thevenow homered for four of St. Louis's six runs. Two days later Jesse Haines put the Cards into the lead, winning the game both ways with a five-hit shutout and a two-run homer.

New York's big bats finally awoke in Game Four. Five Yankees doubled, and Babe Ruth hit three home runs (a World Series record) in a 14-hit, 10-run assault on half the Cardinal pitching staff. Yankee pitcher Waite Hoyt also gave up 14 hits, but 12 were singles and only four runs scored. In contrast, Game Five was a pitchers' duel. Pennock and Sherdel again faced each other and held the opposition to two runs apiece through nine innings. But in the tenth, rookie Tony Lazzeri's sacrifice fly gave New York a 3–2 lead, which Pennock held in the last of the tenth for his second win.

With St. Louis down three games to two, the Series moved to hostile New York for the final games. This didn't seem to trouble the Cardinals, who erupted in Game Six for their own ten-run game, four of them driven in by Les Bell's first-inning single and seventh-inning home run. Alexander pitched a complete game for his second Series win, and came back the next day to relieve Haines in the seventh with a 3–2 lead and the bases full. He struck out Lazzeri to end the inning and kept the Yankees off the bases until he issued Babe Ruth his eleventh Series walk with two away in the ninth. But Ruth, trying to steal second, was caught, and the Cards were world champions.

St. Louis Cardinals (NL), 4; New York Yankees (AL), 3

STL (N)

PLAYER/POS	AVG	G	AB	R	H	2B	3B	HR	RB	BB	SO	SB
Pete Alexander, p	.000	3	7	1	0	0	0	0	0	0	2	0
Hi Bell, p	.000	1	0	0	0	0	0	0	0	0	0	0
Les Bell, 3b	.259	7	27	4	7	1	0	1	6	2	5	0
Jim Bottomley, 1b	.345	7	29	4	10	3	0	0	5	1	2	0
Taylor Douthit, of	.267	4	15	3	4	2	0	0	1	3	2	0
Jake Flowers, ph	.000	3	3	0	0	0	0	0	0	0	1	0
Chick Hafey, of	.185	7	27	2	5	2	0	0	0	0	7	0
Jesse Haines, p	.600	3	5	1	3	0	0	1	2	0	1	0
Bill Hallahan, p	.000	1	0	0	0	0	0	0	0	0	0	0
Wattie Holm, of-4	.125	5	16	1	2	0	0	0	1	1	2	0
Rogers Hornsby, 2b	.250	7	28	2	7	1	0	0	4	2	2	1
Vic Keen, p	.000	1	0	0	0	0	0	0	0	0	0	0
Bob O'Farrell, c	.304	7	23	2	7	1	0	0	2	2	2	0
Art Reinhart, p	.000	1	0	0	0	0	0	0	0	0	0	0
Flint Rhem, p	.000	1	1	0	0	0	0	0	0	0	1	0
Bill Sherdel, p	.000	2	5	0	0	0	0	0	0	0	2	0
Billy Southworth, of	.345	7	29	6	10	1	1	1	4	0	0	1
Tommy Thevenow, ss	.417	7	24	5	10	1	0	1	4	0	1	0
Specs Toporcer, ph	.000	1	0	0	0	0	0	0	1	0	0	0
TOTAL	.272		239	31	65	12	1	4	30	11	30	2

PITCHER	W	L	ERA	G	GS	CG	SV	SHO	IP	H	ER	BB	SO
Pete Alexander	2	0	1.33	3	2	2	1	0	20.1	12	3	4	17
Hi Bell	0	0	9.00	1	0	0	0	0	2.0	4	2	1	1
Jesse Haines	2	0	1.08	3	2	1	0	1	16.2	13	2	9	5
Bill Hallahan	0	0	4.50	1	0	0	0	0	2.0	2	1	3	1
Vic Keen	0	0	0.00	1	0	0	0	0	1.0	0	0	0	0
Art Reinhart	0	1	INF	1	0	0	0	0	0.0	1	4	4	0
Flint Rhem	0	0	6.75	1	1	0	0	0	4.0	7	3	2	4
Bill Sherdel	0	2	2.12	2	2	1	0	0	17.0	15	4	8	3
TOTAL	4	3	2.71	13	7	4	1	1	63.0	54	19	31	31

NY (A)

PLAYER/POS	AVG	G	AB	R	H	2B	3B	HR	RB	BB	SO	SB
Spencer Adams, ph	.000	2	0	0	0	0	0	0	0	0	0	0
Pat Collins, c	.000	3	2	0	0	0	0	0	0	0	1	0
Earle Combs, of	.357	7	28	3	10	2	0	0	2	5	2	0
Joe Dugan, 3b	.333	7	24	2	8	1	0	0	2	1	1	0
Mike Gazella, 3b	.000	1	0	0	0	0	0	0	0	0	0	0
Lou Gehrig, 1b	.348	7	23	1	8	2	0	0	4	5	4	0
Waite Hoyt, p	.000	2	6	0	0	0	0	0	0	0	1	0
Sam Jones, p	.000	1	0	0	0	0	0	0	0	0	0	0
Mark Koenig, ss	.125	7	32	2	4	1	0	0	2	0	6	0
Tony Lazzeri, 2b	.192	7	26	2	5	1	0	0	3	1	6	0
Bob Meusel, of	.238	7	21	3	5	1	1	0	0	6	1	0
Ben Paschal, ph	.250	5	4	0	1	0	0	0	1	1	2	0
Herb Pennock, p	.143	3	7	1	1	1	0	0	0	0	0	0
Dutch Ruether, p-1	.000	3	4	0	0	0	0	0	0	0	0	0
Babe Ruth, of	.300	7	20	6	6	0	0	4	5	11	2	1
Hank Severeid, c	.273	7	22	1	6	1	0	0	1	1	2	0
Bob Shawkey, p	.000	3	2	0	0	0	0	0	0	0	1	0
Urban Shocker, p	.000	2	2	0	0	0	0	0	0	0	2	0
Myles Thomas, p	.000	2	0	0	0	0	0	0	0	0	0	0
TOTAL	.242		223	21	54	10	1	4	20	31	31	1

PITCHER	W	L	ERA	G	GS	CG	SV	SHO	IP	H	ER	BB	SO
Waite Hoyt	1	1	1.20	2	2	1	0	0	15.0	19	2	1	10
Sam Jones	0	0	9.00	1	0	0	0	0	1.0	2	1	2	1
Herb Pennock	2	0	1.23	3	2	2	0	0	22.0	13	3	4	8
Dutch Ruether	0	1	4.15	1	1	0	0	0	4.1	7	2	2	1
Bob Shawkey	0	1	5.40	3	1	0	0	0	10.0	8	6	2	7
Urban Shocker	0	1	5.87	2	1	0	0	0	7.2	13	5	0	3
Myles Thomas	0	0	3.00	2	0	0	0	0	3.0	3	1	0	0
TOTAL	3	4	2.86	14	7	3	0	0	63.0	65	20	11	30

GAME 1 AT NY OCT 2

STL	100 000 000	1	3	1
NY	100 001 00X	2	6	0

Pitchers: SHERDEL, Haines (8) vs PENNOCK
Attendance: 61,658

GAME 2 AT NY OCT 3

STL	002 000 301	6	12	1
NY	020 000 000	2	4	0

Pitchers: ALEXANDER vs SHOCKER, Shawkey (8), Jones (9)
Home Runs: Southworth-STL, Thevenow-STL
Attendance: 63,600

GAME 3 AT STL OCT 5

NY	000 000 000	0	5	1
STL	000 310 00X	4	8	0

Pitchers: RUETHER, Shawkey (5), Thomas (8) vs HAINES
Home Runs: Haines-STL
Attendance: 37,708

GAME 4 AT STL OCT 6

NY	101 142 100	10	14	1
STL	100 300 001	5	14	0

Pitchers: HOYT vs Rhem, REINHART (5), H.Bell (5), Hallahan (7), Keen (9)
Home Runs: Ruth-NY (3)
Attendance: 38,825

GAME 5 AT STL OCT 7

NY	000 001 001 1	3	9	1
STL	000 100 100 0	2	7	1

Pitchers: PENNOCK vs SHERDEL
Attendance: 39,552

GAME 6 AT NY OCT 9

STL	300 010 501	10	13	2
NY	000 100 100	2	8	1

Pitchers: ALEXANDER vs SHAWKEY, Shocker (7), Thomas (8)
Home Runs: L.Bell-STL
Attendance: 48,615

GAME 7 AT NY OCT 10

STL	000 300 000	3	8	0
NY	001 001 000	2	8	3

Pitchers: HAINES, Alexander (7) vs HOYT, Pennock (7)
Home Runs: Ruth-NY
Attendance: 38,093

The Pirates, who struggled to a narrow pennant win in a four-team race, were no slouches at the bat. Their team BA of .305 led the National League, and in the Waner brothers—Paul and Lloyd—and Pie Traynor they had three of the league's five top hitters. But in the World Series they came up against a Yankee team that is still widely regarded as the game's greatest ever. With 110 season victories and a 19-game margin over second-place Philadelphia, the Yankees led the American League in nearly every offensive category. Three Yankees—Earle Combs, Lou Gehrig, and Babe Ruth—hit over .350, and divided among them league crowns in runs, hits, doubles, triples, home runs (Ruth's 60), RBIs, and slugging average. The Yankees not only hit: their pitching staff boasted the league's lowest earned run average.

In the Series, though, it was Pittsburgh's erratic play that brought about the first American League sweep. The Pirates scored four times off Yankee starter Waite Hoyt in Game One, and might have won the game. But Paul Waner misplayed a Gehrig fly for a run-scoring triple in the first, and in the third, two Pirate errors led to three more Yankee runs. A final run in the fifth was all New York needed to win, 5–4.

The Yankees won the next two games more convincingly, with strong pitching and timely hitting. George Pipgras held Pittsburgh to two runs in Game Two as his Yankees bunched seven of their 11 hits into the third and eighth innings (also taking advantage of two walks and a hit batsman in the eighth) for their six runs. And in Game Three—as Herb Pennock pitched perfectly into the eighth inning before yielding two hits and a run—Yankee batters again bunched most of their hits into two innings, scoring two runs on Gehrig's first-inning triple and six more in the seventh, climaxed by Ruth's three-run homer.

Pittsburgh took advantage of two Yankee errors in the seventh inning of Game Four to score two runs and tie the game at three-all. But in the last of the ninth, after the Pirates' Johnny Miljus had struck out Gehrig and Bob Meusel with the bases loaded, his second wild pitch of the inning undid him—Combs scored from third with the Series' winning run.

New York Yankees (AL), 4; Pittsburgh Pirates (NL), 0

NY (A)

PLAYER/POS	AVG	G	AB	R	H	2B	3B	HR	RB	BB	SO	SB
Benny Bengough, c	.000	2	4	1	0	0	0	0	0	1	0	0
Pat Collins, c	.600	2	5	0	3	1	0	0	0	3	0	0
Earle Combs, of	.313	4	16	6	5	0	0	0	2	1	2	0
Joe Dugan, 3b	.200	4	15	2	3	0	0	0	0	0	0	0
Cedric Durst, ph	.000	1	1	0	0	0	0	0	0	0	0	0
Lou Gehrig, 1b	.308	4	13	2	4	2	2	0	4	3	3	0
Johnny Grabowski, c	.000	1	2	0	0	0	0	0	0	0	0	0
Waite Hoyt, p	.000	1	3	0	0	0	0	0	0	0	0	0
Mark Koenig, ss	.500	4	18	5	9	2	0	0	2	0	2	0
Tony Lazzeri, 2b	.267	4	15	1	4	1	0	0	2	1	4	0
Bob Meusel, of	.118	4	17	1	2	0	0	0	1	1	7	1
Wilcy Moore, p	.200	2	5	0	1	0	0	0	0	0	3	0
Herb Pennock, p	.000	1	4	1	0	0	0	0	1	0	0	0
George Pipgras, p	.333	1	3	0	1	0	0	0	0	1	1	0
Babe Ruth, of	.400	4	15	4	6	0	0	2	7	2	2	1
TOTAL	.279		136	23	38	6	2	2	19	13	25	2

PITCHER	W	L	ERA	G	GS	CG	SV	SHO	IP	H	ER	BB	SO
Waite Hoyt	1	0	4.91	1	1	0	0	0	7.1	8	4	1	2
Wilcy Moore	1	0	0.84	2	1	1	1	0	10.2	11	1	2	2
Herb Pennock	1	0	1.00	1	1	1	0	0	9.0	3	1	0	1
George Pipgras	1	0	2.00	1	1	1	0	0	9.0	7	2	1	2
TOTAL	4	0	2.00	5	4	3	1	0	36.0	29	8	4	7

PIT (N)

PLAYER/POS	AVG	G	AB	R	H	2B	3B	HR	RB	BB	SO	SB
Vic Aldridge, p	.000	1	2	0	0	0	0	0	0	0	0	0
Clyde Barnhart, of	.313	4	16	0	5	1	0	0	4	0	0	0
Fred Brickell, ph	.000	2	2	1	0	0	0	0	0	0	0	0
Mike Cvengros, p	.000	2	0	0	0	0	0	0	0	0	0	0
Joe Dawson, p	.000	1	0	0	0	0	0	0	0	0	0	0
Johnny Gooch, c	.000	3	5	0	0	0	0	0	0	1	1	0
George Grantham, 2b	.364	3	11	0	4	1	0	0	0	1	1	0
Heinie Groh, ph	.000	1	1	0	0	0	0	0	0	0	0	0
Joe Harris, 1b	.200	4	15	0	3	0	0	0	1	0	0	0
Carmen Hill, p	.000	1	1	0	0	0	0	0	0	1	1	0
Ray Kremer, p	.500	1	2	1	1	1	0	0	0	0	1	0
Lee Meadows, p	.000	1	2	0	0	0	0	0	0	0	0	0
Johnny Miljus, p	.000	2	2	0	0	0	0	0	0	0	2	0
Hal Rhyne, 2b	.000	1	4	0	0	0	0	0	0	0	0	0
Earl Smith, c-2	.000	3	8	0	0	0	0	0	0	0	0	0
Roy Spencer, c	.000	1	1	0	0	0	0	0	0	0	0	0
Pie Traynor, 3b	.200	4	15	1	3	1	0	0	0	0	1	0
Lloyd Waner, of	.400	4	15	5	6	1	1	0	0	1	0	0
Paul Waner, of	.333	4	15	0	5	1	0	0	3	0	1	0
Glenn Wright, ss	.154	4	13	1	2	0	0	0	2	0	0	0
Emil Yde, pr	.000	1	0	1	0	0	0	0	0	0	0	0
TOTAL	.223		130	10	29	6	1	0	10	4	7	0

PITCHER	W	L	ERA	G	GS	CG	SV	SHO	IP	H	ER	BB	SO
Vic Aldridge	0	1	7.36	1	1	0	0	0	7.1	10	6	4	4
Mike Cvengros	0	0	3.86	2	0	0	0	0	2.1	3	1	0	2
Joe Dawson	0	0	0.00	1	0	0	0	0	1.0	0	0	0	0
Carmen Hill	0	0	4.50	1	1	0	0	0	6.0	9	3	1	6
Ray Kremer	0	1	3.60	1	1	0	0	0	5.0	5	2	3	1
Lee Meadows	0	1	9.95	1	1	0	0	0	6.1	7	7	1	6
Johnny Miljus	0	1	1.35	2	0	0	0	0	6.2	4	1	4	6
TOTAL	0	4	5.19	9	4	0	0	0	34.2	38	20	13	25

GAME 1 AT PIT OCT 5

NY	103 010 000	5 6 1
PIT	101 010 010	4 9 2

Pitchers: HOYT, Moore (8) vs KREMER, Miljus (6)
Attendance: 41,467

GAME 2 AT PIT OCT 6

NY	003 000 030	6 11 0
PIT	100 000 010	2 7 2

Pitchers: PIPGRAS vs ALDRIDGE, Cvengros (8), Dawson (9)
Attendance: 41,634

GAME 3 AT NY OCT 7

PIT	000 000 010	1 3 1
NY	200 000 60X	8 9 0

Pitchers: MEADOWS, Cvengros (7) vs PENNOCK
Home Runs: Ruth-NY
Attendance: 60,695

GAME 4 AT NY OCT 8

PIT	100 000 200	3 10 1
NY	100 020 001	4 12 2

Pitchers: Hill, MILJUS (7) vs MOORE
Home Runs: Ruth-NY
Attendance: 57,909

After squandering a 13½-game lead and falling briefly behind the Athletics in early September, the Yankees recovered to meet the Cardinals—winners of another tight National League race—in the Series. With Herb Pennock lost to arm trouble, the Yankees made do with just three pitchers in extending their Series win streak to eight games.

The four games offered little suspense, but for Yankee fans there were thrills aplenty. The Bronx Bombers' nine home runs (including four by Lou Gehrig and three by Babe Ruth) nearly equalled St. Louis's total scoring (ten runs), and Gehrig himself drove in as many runs (nine) as the entire Cardinal offense. Ruth and Gehrig started things off with successive doubles and a run in the first inning of the opener, and when Bob Meusel followed Ruth's second double with a home run in the fourth, the Yanks had more than they would need to support Waite Hoyt's three-hitter. The Cardinals' Jim Bottomley homered off Hoyt in the seventh, but successive singles by Mark Koenig, Ruth, and Gehrig produced a fourth Yankee run and concluded the scoring.

Gehrig homered in the first inning of Game Two to get New York off to a 3–0 lead against forty-one-year-old Grover Cleveland Alexander. The Cards snapped back to tie the game, but the Yankees retook the lead with a run in the last of the second and put together four hits, two walks, and a hit batsman for four more in the third. A final Yankee run in the seventh capped a 9–3 four-hit win for pitcher George Pipgras.

Jim Bottomley gave St. Louis its first lead of the Series with a two-run triple in the first inning of Game Three. But Yankee Tom Zachary gave up only one more run, taking the third Yankee win as Gehrig drove in three runs with homers in the second and fourth, and his teammates scored three more in the sixth (thanks in large part to two Cardinal errors and Meusel's steal of home) and a final (unearned) run an inning later.

New York completed its second straight Series sweep with another 7–3 win two days later. Waite Hoyt gained his second victory, mostly on the strength of five solo Yankee homers, including three by Babe Ruth.

New York Yankees (AL), 4;
St. Louis Cardinals (NL), 0

NY (A)

PLAYER/POS	AVG	G	AB	R	H	2B	3B	HR	RB	BB	SO	SB
Benny Bengough, c	.231	4	13	1	3	0	0	0	1	1	1	0
Pat Collins, c	1.000	1	1	0	1	1	0	0	0	0	0	0
Earle Combs, ph	.000	1	0	0	0	0	0	0	1	0	0	0
Joe Dugan, 3b	.167	3	6	0	1	0	0	0	1	0	0	0
Leo Durocher, 2b	.000	4	2	0	0	0	0	0	0	0	1	0
Cedric Durst, of	.375	4	8	3	3	0	0	1	2	0	1	0
Lou Gehrig, 1b	.545	4	11	5	6	1	0	4	9	6	0	0
Waite Hoyt, p	.143	2	7	0	1	0	0	0	0	0	0	0
Mark Koenig, ss	.158	4	19	1	3	0	0	0	0	0	1	0
Tony Lazzeri, 2b	.250	4	12	2	3	1	0	0	0	1	0	2
Bob Meusel, of	.200	4	15	5	3	1	0	1	3	2	5	2
Ben Paschal, of	.200	3	10	0	2	0	0	0	1	1	0	0
George Pipgras, p	.000	1	2	0	0	0	0	0	1	0	0	0
Gene Robertson, 3b	.125	3	8	1	1	0	0	0	2	1	0	0
Babe Ruth, of	.625	4	16	9	10	3	0	3	4	1	2	0
Tom Zachary, p	.000	1	4	0	0	0	0	0	0	0	1	0
TOTAL	.276		134	27	37	7	0	9	25	13	12	4

PITCHER	W	L	ERA	G	GS	CG	SV	SHO	IP	H	ER	BB	SO
Waite Hoyt	2	0	1.50	2	2	2	0	0	18.0	14	3	6	14
George Pipgras	1	0	2.00	1	1	1	0	0	9.0	4	2	4	8
Tom Zachary	1	0	3.00	1	1	1	0	0	9.0	9	3	1	7
TOTAL	4	0	2.00	4	4	4	0	0	36.0	27	8	11	29

STL (N)

PLAYER/POS	AVG	G	AB	R	H	2B	3B	HR	RB	BB	SO	SB
Pete Alexander, p	.000	2	1	0	0	0	0	0	1	0	0	0
Ray Blades, ph	.000	1	1	0	0	0	0	0	0	0	1	0
Jim Bottomley, 1b	.214	4	14	1	3	0	1	1	3	2	6	0
Taylor Douthit, of	.091	3	11	1	1	0	0	0	1	1	1	0
Frankie Frisch, 2b	.231	4	13	1	3	0	0	0	1	2	2	2
Chick Hafey, of	.200	4	15	0	3	0	0	0	0	1	4	0
Jesse Haines, p	.000	1	2	0	0	0	0	0	0	0	0	0
George Harper, of	.111	3	9	1	1	0	0	0	0	2	2	0
Andy High, 3b	.294	4	17	1	5	2	0	0	1	1	3	0
Wattie Holm, of-1	.167	3	6	0	1	0	0	0	1	0	1	0
Syl Johnson, p	.000	2	0	0	0	0	0	0	0	0	0	0
Rabbit Maranville, ss	.308	4	13	2	4	1	0	0	0	1	1	1
Pepper Martin, pr	.000	1	0	1	0	0	0	0	0	0	0	0
Clarence Mitchell, p	.000	1	2	0	0	0	0	0	0	0	0	0
Ernie Orsatti, of-1	.286	4	7	1	2	1	0	0	0	1	3	0
Flint Rhem, p	.000	1	0	0	0	0	0	0	0	0	0	0
Bill Sherdel, p	.000	2	5	0	0	0	0	0	0	0	2	0
Earl Smith, c	.750	1	4	0	3	0	0	0	0	0	0	0
Tommy Thevenow, ss	.000	1	0	0	0	0	0	0	0	0	0	0
Jimmie Wilson, c	.091	3	11	1	1	1	0	0	1	0	3	0
TOTAL	.206		131	10	27	5	1	1	9	11	29	3

PITCHER	W	L	ERA	G	GS	CG	SV	SHO	IP	H	ER	BB	SO
Pete Alexander	0	1	19.80	2	1	0	0	0	5.0	10	11	4	2
Jesse Haines	0	1	4.50	1	1	0	0	0	6.0	6	3	3	3
Syl Johnson	0	0	4.50	2	0	0	0	0	2.0	4	1	1	1
Clarence Mitchell	0	0	1.59	1	0	0	0	0	5.2	2	1	2	2
Flint Rhem	0	0	0.00	1	0	0	0	0	2.0	0	0	0	1
Bill Sherdel	0	2	4.72	2	2	0	0	0	13.1	15	7	3	3
TOTAL	0	4	6.09	9	4	0	0	0	34.0	37	23	13	12

GAME 1 AT NY OCT 4

STL	000	000	100	1	3	1
NY	100	200	01X	4	7	0

Pitchers: SHERDEL, Johnson (8) vs HOYT
Home Runs: Meusel-NY, Bottomley-STL
Attendance: 61,425

GAME 2 AT NY OCT 5

STL	030	000	000	3	4	1
NY	314	000	10X	9	8	2

Pitchers: ALEXANDER, Mitchell (3) vs PIPGRAS
Home Runs: Gehrig-NY
Attendance: 60,714

GAME 3 AT STL OCT 7

NY	010	203	100	7	7	2
STL	200	010	000	3	9	3

Pitchers: ZACHARY vs HAINES, Johnson (7), Rhem (8)
Home Runs: Gehrig-NY (2)
Attendance: 39,602

GAME 4 AT STL OCT 9

NY	000	100	420	7	15	2
STL	001	100	001	3	11	0

Pitchers: HOYT vs SHERDEL, Alexander (7)
Home Runs: Ruth-NY (3), Durst-NY, Gehrig-NY
Attendance: 37,331

The surprising success of a surprise starter and the ultimate in big innings highlighted the return of the Athletics to World Series play after a gap of fifteen years. In the opener, A's manager Connie Mack passed over the aces of his pitching staff in favor of Howard Ehmke, an aging journeyman who that season had started only eight times and pitched under 55 innings. But Ehmke, who (per Mack's instructions) had studied the Cubs' hitters in a series of late-season games, held the Cubs scoreless through the first eight innings of Game One (yielding an unearned run in the last of the ninth) while fanning 13 batters for a new Series record. Chicago's Charlie Root also pitched effectively until Jimmie Foxx's solo homer in the seventh gave the A's the game's first score. A pair of errors by Cub shortstop Woody English in the ninth set up two unearned runs against reliever Guy Bush and gave Ehmke and the A's all the lead they needed.

Home runs by Foxx and Al Simmons drove in five of the A's nine runs in Game Two as Philadelphia took a 2–0 Series lead. But Guy Bush held Mack's sluggers to nine singles and one run in Game Three as his Cubs scored three runs in the sixth to take their first win.

The Cubs seemed well on their way to tying the Series in Game Four as they entered the last of the seventh with an 8–0 lead. But Simmons led off with a homer to erase Charlie Root's shutout, and five of the next six batters singled. Art Nehf relieved Root, but the first batter to face him—Mule Haas—lofted a fly to center which Hack Wilson lost in the sun for a three-run inside-the-park homer, and the score was 8–7. After walking Mickey Cochrane, Nehf was replaced by Sheriff Blake, who gave up two singles and saw the tying run come home before Pat Malone took the mound with two men still on base and only one away. Malone struck out two in a row to end the inning—but not until he first hit a batter and gave up a double by Jimmy Dykes for the two runs that gave the A's a 10–8 win and a 3–1 Series advantage.

Game Five, although inevitably anticlimactic, was not decided until the final at-bat. Chicago scored twice off Ehmke in the fourth as Malone shut out the A's with only two hits through eight. But in the last of the ninth a single and Haas's home run tied the score, and—with two men out—Simmons doubled, Foxx was walked intentionally, Bing Miller doubled, and the Series was history.

Philadelphia Athletics (AL), 4;
Chicago Cubs (NL), 1

PHI (A)

PLAYER/POS	AVG	G	AB	R	H	2B	3B	HR	RB	BB	SO	SB
Max Bishop, 2b	.190	5	21	2	4	0	0	0	1	2	3	0
Joe Boley, ss	.235	5	17	1	4	0	0	0	1	0	3	0
George Burns, ph	.000	1	2	0	0	0	0	0	0	0	1	0
Mickey Cochrane, c	.400	5	15	5	6	1	0	0	0	7	0	0
Jimmy Dykes, 3b	.421	5	19	2	8	1	0	0	4	1	1	0
George Earnshaw, p	.000	2	5	1	0	0	0	0	0	0	4	0
Howard Ehmke, p	.200	2	5	0	1	0	0	0	0	0	0	0
Jimmie Foxx, 1b	.350	5	20	5	7	1	0	2	5	1	1	0
Walter French, ph	.000	1	1	0	0	0	0	0	0	0	1	0
Lefty Grove, p	.000	2	2	0	0	0	0	0	0	0	1	0
Mule Haas, of	.238	5	21	3	5	0	0	2	6	1	3	0
Bing Miller, of	.368	5	19	1	7	1	0	0	4	0	2	0
Jack Quinn, p	.000	1	2	0	0	0	0	0	0	0	2	0
Eddie Rommel, p	.000	1	0	0	0	0	0	0	0	0	0	0
Al Simmons, of	.300	5	20	6	6	1	0	2	5	1	4	0
Homer Summa, ph	.000	1	1	0	0	0	0	0	0	0	1	0
Rube Walberg, p	.000	2	1	0	0	0	0	0	0	0	0	0
TOTAL	.281		171	26	48	5	0	6	26	13	27	0

PITCHER	W	L	ERA	G	GS	CG	SV	SHO	IP	H	ER	BB	SO
George Earnshaw	1	1	2.63	2	2	1	0	0	13.2	14	4	6	17
Howard Ehmke	1	0	1.42	2	2	1	0	0	12.2	14	2	3	13
Lefty Grove	0	0	0.00	2	0	0	2	0	6.1	3	0	1	10
Jack Quinn	0	0	9.00	1	1	0	0	0	5.0	7	5	2	2
Eddie Rommel	1	0	9.00	1	0	0	0	0	1.0	2	1	1	0
Rube Walberg	1	0	0.00	2	0	0	0	0	6.1	3	0	0	8
TOTAL	4	1	2.40	10	5	2	2	0	45.0	43	12	13	50

CHI (N)

PLAYER/POS	AVG	G	AB	R	H	2B	3B	HR	RB	BB	SO	SB
Footsie Blair, ph	.000	1	1	0	0	0	0	0	0	0	0	0
Sheriff Blake, p	1.000	2	1	0	1	0	0	0	0	0	0	0
Guy Bush, p	.000	2	3	1	0	0	0	0	0	1	3	0
Hal Carlson, p	.000	2	0	0	0	0	0	0	0	0	0	0
Kiki Cuyler, of	.300	5	20	4	6	1	0	0	4	1	7	0
Woody English, ss	.190	5	21	1	4	2	0	0	0	1	6	0
Mike Gonzalez, c-1	.000	2	1	0	0	0	0	0	0	0	1	0
Charlie Grimm, 1b	.389	5	18	2	7	0	0	1	4	1	2	0
Gabby Hartnett, ph	.000	3	3	0	0	0	0	0	0	0	3	0
Cliff Heathcote, ph	.000	2	1	0	0	0	0	0	0	0	0	0
Rogers Hornsby, 2b	.238	5	21	4	5	1	1	0	1	1	8	0
Pat Malone, p	.250	3	4	0	1	1	0	0	0	0	2	0
Norm Mc Millan, 3b	.100	5	20	0	2	0	0	0	0	2	6	1
Art Nehf, p	.000	2	0	0	0	0	0	0	0	0	0	0
Charlie Root, p	.000	2	5	0	0	0	0	0	0	0	3	0
Riggs Stephenson, of	.316	5	19	3	6	1	0	0	3	2	2	0
Zack Taylor, c	.176	5	17	0	3	0	0	0	3	0	3	0
Chick Tolson, ph	.000	1	1	0	0	0	0	0	0	0	1	0
Hack Wilson, of	.471	5	17	2	8	0	1	0	0	4	3	0
TOTAL	.249		173	17	43	6	2	1	15	13	50	1

PITCHER	W	L	ERA	G	GS	CG	SV	SHO	IP	H	ER	BB	SO
Sheriff Blake	0	1	13.50	2	0	0	0	0	1.1	4	2	0	1
Guy Bush	1	0	0.82	2	1	1	0	0	11.0	12	1	2	4
Hal Carlson	0	0	6.75	2	0	0	0	0	4.0	7	3	1	3
Pat Malone	0	2	4.15	3	2	1	0	0	13.0	12	6	7	11
Art Nehf	0	0	18.00	2	0	0	0	0	1.0	1	2	1	0
Charlie Root	0	1	4.72	2	2	0	0	0	13.1	12	7	2	8
TOTAL	1	4	4.33	13	5	2	0	0	43.2	48	21	13	27

GAME 1 AT CHI OCT 8

PHI	000 000 102	3	6	1
CHI	000 000 001	1	8	2

Pitchers: EHMKE vs ROOT, Bush (8)
Home Runs: Foxx-PHI
Attendance: 50,740

GAME 2 AT CHI OCT 9

PHI	003 300 120	9	12	0
CHI	000 030 000	3	11	1

Pitchers: EARNSHAW, Grove (5) vs MALONE, Blake (4), Carlson (6), Nehf (9)
Home Runs: Simmons-PHI, Foxx-PHI
Attendance: 49,987

GAME 3 AT PHI OCT 11

CHI	000 003 000	3	6	1
PHI	000 010 000	1	9	1

Pitchers: BUSH vs EARNSHAW
Attendance: 29,921

GAME 4 AT PHI OCT 12

CHI	000 205 100	8	10	2
PHI	000 000 100 X	10	15	2

Pitchers: Root, Nehf (7), BLAKE (7), Malone (7), Carlson (8) vs Quinn, Walberg (6), ROMMEL (7), Grove (8)
Home Runs: Grimm-CHI, Haas-PHI, Simmons-PHI
Attendance: 29,921

GAME 5 AT PHI OCT 14

CHI	002 000 000	2	8	1
PHI	000 000 003	3	6	0

Pitchers: MALONE vs Ehmke, WALBERG (4)
Home Runs: Haas-PHI
Attendance: 29,921

Pitching 85 percent of the Series with a combined ERA of 1.02, Philadelphia aces George Earnshaw and Lefty Grove chilled the hot Cardinals, who had hit .314 and averaged 6½ runs per game during the season. The A's hit only .197 themselves in the Series, but more than half their hits went for extra bases as they outscored St. Louis 21–12 and took their second consecutive world championship in six games.

Grove faced Cardinal spitballer Burleigh Grimes in the opener, giving up nine hits, including four singles in the Cards' two-run third. The Athletics, for their part, touched Grimes for only five hits, all in separate innings. But every hit—a double, two triples, and home runs by Al Simmons and Mike Cochrane—resulted in a run, and Grove and the A's emerged 5–2 victors. In the first inning of Game Two, Cochrane again homered, sending Earnshaw on his way to Philadelphia's second win, 6–1.

When the Series moved to St. Louis, though, the Cards came alive. Wild Bill Hallahan (their leading winner during the season, with 15) spaced seven hits for a shutout. Taylor Douthit's fourth-inning home run off Rube Walberg was the first Cardinal hit, but the Cards knocked out nine more for four more runs before they were finished. A pair of unearned runs evened the Series the next day when A's third baseman Jimmy Dykes's wild throw to first in the fourth inning let in a tie-breaking second Cardinal run and led to a third against the ultimate loser Lefty Grove. Meanwhile, Cardinal veteran Jesse Haines, after yielding three Philadelphia hits and a run in the first inning, shut out the A's on one hit the rest of the way.

Earnshaw and Grove combined to restore the Series lead to the Athletics in Game Five with a three-hit shutout. Grove, who took over when Earnshaw left for a pinch hitter in the eighth, garnered his second Series win as Jimmie Foxx homered off Grimes in the top of the ninth for the game's only runs. After a travel day to Philadelphia, Earnshaw pitched again for the A's in Game Six, and pushed the Cardinals' scoreless streak to 21 innings before allowing them a token run in the ninth. But by then seven A's had crossed the plate and the Series was theirs.

Philadelphia Athletics (AL), 4; St. Louis Cardinals (NL), 2

PHI (A)

PLAYER/POS	AVG	G	AB	R	H	2B	3B	HR	RB	BB	SO	SB
Max Bishop, 2b	.222	6	18	5	4	0	0	0	0	7	3	0
Joe Boley, ss	.095	6	21	1	2	0	0	0	1	0	1	0
Mickey Cochrane, c	.222	6	18	5	4	1	0	2	4	5	2	0
Jimmy Dykes, 3b	.222	6	18	2	4	3	0	1	5	5	3	0
George Earnshaw, p	.000	3	9	0	0	0	0	0	0	0	5	0
Jimmie Foxx, 1b	.333	6	21	3	7	2	1	1	3	2	4	0
Lefty Grove, p	.000	3	6	0	0	0	0	0	0	0	3	0
Mule Haas, of	.111	6	18	1	2	0	1	0	1	1	3	0
Eric Mc Nair, ph	.000	1	1	0	0	0	0	0	0	0	0	0
Bing Miller, of	.143	6	21	0	3	2	0	0	3	0	4	0
Jim Moore, of-1	.333	3	3	0	1	0	0	0	0	1	1	0
Jack Quinn, p	.000	1	0	0	0	0	0	0	0	0	0	0
Bill Shores, p	.000	1	0	0	0	0	0	0	0	1	0	0
Al Simmons, of	.364	6	22	4	8	2	0	2	4	2	2	0
Rube Walberg, p	.000	1	2	0	0	0	0	0	0	0	0	0
TOTAL	.197		178	21	35	10	2	6	21	24	32	0

PITCHER	W	L	ERA	G	GS	CG	SV	SHO	IP	H	ER	BB	SO
George Earnshaw	2	0	0.72	3	3	2	0	0	25.0	13	2	7	19
Lefty Grove	2	1	1.42	3	2	2	0	0	19.0	15	3	3	10
Jack Quinn	0	0	4.50	1	0	0	0	0	2.0	3	1	0	1
Bill Shores	0	0	13.50	1	0	0	0	0	1.1	3	2	0	0
Rube Walberg	0	1	3.86	1	1	0	0	0	4.2	4	2	1	3
TOTAL	4	2	1.73	9	6	4	0	0	52.0	38	10	11	33

STL (N)

PLAYER/POS	AVG	G	AB	R	H	2B	3B	HR	RB	BB	SO	SB
Sparky Adams, 3b	.143	6	21	0	3	0	0	0	1	0	4	0
Hi Bell, p	.000	1	0	0	0	0	0	0	0	0	0	0
Ray Blades, of-3	.111	5	9	2	1	0	0	0	0	2	2	0
Jim Bottomley, 1b	.045	6	22	1	1	1	0	0	0	2	9	0
Taylor Douthit, of	.083	6	24	1	2	0	0	1	2	0	2	0
George Fisher, ph	.500	2	2	0	1	1	0	0	0	0	1	0
Frankie Frisch, 2b	.208	6	24	5	5	2	0	0	0	0	0	1
Charlie Gelbert, ss	.353	6	17	2	6	0	1	0	2	3	3	0
Burleigh Grimes, p	.400	2	5	0	2	0	0	0	0	0	1	0
Chick Hafey, of	.273	6	22	2	6	5	0	0	2	1	3	0
Jesse Haines, p	.500	1	2	0	1	0	0	0	1	0	0	0
Bill Hallahan, p	.000	2	2	0	0	0	0	0	0	1	1	0
Andy High, 3b	.500	1	2	1	1	0	0	0	0	0	0	0
Syl Johnson, p	.000	2	0	0	0	0	0	0	0	0	0	0
Jim Lindsey, p	1.000	2	1	0	1	0	0	0	0	0	0	0
Gus Mancuso, c	.286	2	7	1	2	0	0	0	0	1	2	0
Ernie Orsatti, ph	.000	1	1	0	0	0	0	0	0	0	0	0
George Puccinelli, ph	.000	1	1	0	0	0	0	0	0	0	1	0
Flint Rhem, p	.000	1	1	0	0	0	0	0	0	0	1	0
George Watkins, of	.167	4	12	2	2	0	0	1	1	1	3	0
Jimmie Wilson, c	.267	4	15	0	4	1	0	0	2	0	1	0
TOTAL	.200		190	12	38	10	1	2	11	11	33	1

PITCHER	W	L	ERA	G	GS	CG	SV	SHO	IP	H	ER	BB	SO
Hi Bell	0	0	0.00	1	0	0	0	0	1.0	0	0	0	0
Burleigh Grimes	0	2	3.71	2	2	2	0	0	17.0	10	7	6	13
Jesse Haines	1	0	1.00	1	1	1	0	0	9.0	4	1	4	2
Bill Hallahan	1	1	1.64	2	2	1	0	1	11.0	9	2	8	8
Syl Johnson	0	0	7.20	2	0	0	0	0	5.0	4	4	3	4
Jim Lindsey	0	0	1.93	2	0	0	0	0	4.2	1	1	1	2
Flint Rhem	0	1	10.80	1	1	0	0	0	3.1	7	4	2	3
TOTAL	2	4	3.35	11	6	4	0	1	51.0	35	19	24	32

GAME 1 AT PHI OCT 1

STL	002	000	000	2	9	0
PHI	010	101	11X	5	5	0

Pitchers: GRIMES vs GROVE
Home Runs: Cochrane-PHI, Simmons-PHI
Attendance: 32,295

GAME 2 AT PHI OCT 2

STL	010	000	000	1	6	2
PHI	202	200	00X	6	7	2

Pitchers: RHEM, Lindsey (4), Johnson (7) vs EARNSHAW
Home Runs: Cochrane-PHI, Watkins-STL
Attendance: 32,295

GAME 3 AT STL OCT 4

PHI	000	000	000	0	7	0
STL	000	110	21X	5	10	0

Pitchers: WALBERG, Shores (5), Quinn (7) vs HALLAHAN
Home Runs: Douthit-STL
Attendance: 36,944

GAME 4 AT STL OCT 5

PHI	100	000	000	1	4	1
STL	001	200	00X	3	5	1

Pitchers: GROVE vs HAINES
Attendance: 39,946

GAME 5 AT STL OCT 6

PHI	000	000	002	2	5	0
STL	000	000	000	0	3	1

Pitchers: Earnshaw, GROVE (8) vs GRIMES
Home Runs: Foxx-PHI
Attendance: 38,844

GAME 6 AT PHI OCT 8

STL	000	000	001	1	5	1
PHI	201	211	00X	7	7	0

Pitchers: HALLAHAN, Johnson (3), Lindsey (6), Bell (8) vs EARNSHAW
Home Runs: Dykes-PHI, Simmons-PHI
Attendance: 32,295

For the second year in a row, the A's met the Cardinals in the Series, and once again pitchers Lefty Grove and George Earnshaw provided more than 80 percent of the Athletics' pitching, performing splendidly and winning three games between them. But this time Cardinal pitchers Wild Bill Hallahan and Burleigh Grimes outshone them, winning two games apiece to bring St. Louis the world championship.

Grove gave up four hits and two runs in the first inning of the opener, but shut out the Cards the rest of the way as the A's scored six off Paul Derringer to take the Series lead. Earnshaw also held St. Louis to two runs the next day—both manufactured by Pepper Martin's daring baserunning. But they were more than enough for Hallahan, who shut out the A's on three singles.

The Cardinals took their first Series lead in Game Three, scoring five times off Grove and reliever Roy Mahaffey while Grimes held the A's hitless through seven innings and scoreless through eight before giving up a harmless two-run homer to Al Simmons in the bottom of the ninth. But the A's came back to even the Series the next day on Earnshaw's two-hit shutout.

Pepper Martin, the Cardinal hero of Game Two, homered for two runs in Game Five, and drove in two more of St. Louis's five runs with a sacrifice fly and a single. Meanwhile pitcher Hallahan held Philadelphia to a lone run, returning the Series lead to the Cardinals with his second win.

Game Six pitted Grove and Derringer against each other again as in the opener, and again Grove emerged the victor, holding the Cardinals to one run and five hits. The Athletics scored four unearned runs in the fifth off the unfortunate Derringer who, after an error put a runner on base to open the inning, gave up two singles and walked four, including two with the bases full, before leaving the game. Four more Philadelphia runs in the seventh (two of them scoring on a dropped fly ball) gave the A's the Series' only lopsided win.

In the finale, Grimes once again held the A's scoreless through eight before giving up two runs in the ninth. And once again the runs proved harmless against an early Cardinal lead, as Hallahan came on to retire Max Bishop for the final out.

St. Louis Cardinals (NL), 4; Philadelphia Athletics (AL), 3

STL (N)

PLAYER/POS	AVG	G	AB	R	H	2B	3B	HR	RB	BB	SO	SB
Sparky Adams, 3b	.250	2	4	0	1	0	0	0	0	0	1	0
Ray Blades, ph	.000	2	2	0	0	0	0	0	0	0	2	0
Jim Bottomley, 1b	.160	7	25	2	4	1	0	0	2	2	5	0
Ripper Collins, ph	.000	2	2	0	0	0	0	0	0	0	1	0
Paul Derringer, p	.000	3	2	0	0	0	0	0	0	0	1	0
Jake Flowers, 3b-4	.091	5	11	1	1	1	0	0	0	1	0	0
Frankie Frisch, 2b	.259	7	27	2	7	2	0	0	1	1	2	1
Charlie Gelbert, ss	.261	7	23	0	6	1	0	0	3	0	4	0
Burleigh Grimes, p	.286	2	7	0	2	0	0	0	2	0	2	0
Chick Hafey, of	.167	6	24	1	4	0	0	0	0	0	5	1
Bill Hallahan, p	.000	3	6	0	0	0	0	0	0	0	3	0
Andy High, 3b	.267	4	15	3	4	0	0	0	0	0	2	0
Syl Johnson, p	.000	3	2	0	0	0	0	0	0	0	2	0
Jim Lindsey, p	.000	2	0	0	0	0	0	0	0	0	0	0
Gus Mancuso, c-1	.000	2	1	0	0	0	0	0	0	0	0	.0
Pepper Martin, of	.500	7	24	5	12	4	0	1	5	2	3	5
Ernie Orsatti, of	.000	1	3	0	0	0	0	0	0	0	3	0
Flint Rhem, p	.000	1	0	0	0	0	0	0	0	0	0	0
Wally Roettger, of	.286	3	14	1	4	1	0	0	0	0	3	0
George Watkins, of	.286	5	14	4	4	1	0	1	2	2	1	1
Jimmie Wilson, c	.217	7	23	0	5	0	0	0	2	1	1	0
TOTAL	.236		229	19	54	11	0	2	17	9	41	8

PITCHER	W	L	ERA	G	GS	CG	SV	SHO	IP	H	ER	BB	SO
Paul Derringer	0	2	4.26	3	2	0	0	0	12.2	14	6	7	14
Burleigh Grimes	2	0	2.04	2	2	1	0	0	17.2	9	4	9	11
Bill Hallahan	2	0	0.49	3	2	2	1	1	18.1	12	1	8	12
Syl Johnson	0	1	3.00	3	1	0	0	0	9.0	10	3	1	6
Jim Lindsey	0	0	5.40	2	0	0	0	0	3.1	4	2	3	2
Flint Rhem	0	0	0.00	1	0	0	0	0	1.0	1	0	0	1
TOTAL	4	3	2.32	14	7	3	1	1	62.0	50	16	28	46

PHI (A)

PLAYER/POS	AVG	G	AB	R	H	2B	3B	HR	RB	BB	SO	SB
Max Bishop, 2b	.148	7	27	4	4	0	0	0	0	3	5	0
Joe Boley, ph	.000	1	1	0	0	0	0	0	0	0	1	0
Mickey Cochrane, c	.160	7	25	2	4	0	0	0	1	5	2	0
Doc Cramer, ph	.500	2	2	0	1	0	0	0	2	0	0	0
Jimmy Dykes, 3b	.227	7	22	2	5	0	0	0	2	5	1	0
George Earnshaw, p	.000	3	8	0	0	0	0	0	0	0	2	0
Jimmie Foxx, 1b	.348	7	23	3	8	0	0	1	3	6	5	0
Lefty Grove, p	.000	3	10	0	0	0	0	0	0	0	7	0
Mule Haas, of	.130	7	23	1	3	1	0	0	2	3	5	0
Johnnie Heving, ph	.000	1	1	0	0	0	0	0	0	0	0	0
Waite Hoyt, p	.000	1	2	0	0	0	0	0	0	0	0	0
Roy Mahaffey, p	.000	1	0	0	0	0	0	0	0	0	0	0
Eric Mc Nair, 2b-1	.000	2	2	1	0	0	0	0	0	0	1	0
Bing Miller, of	.269	7	26	3	7	1	0	0	1	0	4	0
Jim Moore, of-1	.333	2	3	0	1	0	0	0	0	0	1	0
Eddie Rommel, p	.000	1	0	0	0	0	0	0	0	0	0	0
Al Simmons, of	.333	7	27	4	9	2	0	2	8	3	3	0
Phil Todt, ph	.000	1	0	0	0	0	0	0	0	1	0	0
Rube Walberg, p	.000	2	0	0	0	0	0	0	0	0	0	0
Dib Williams, ss	.320	7	25	2	8	1	0	0	1	2	9	0
TOTAL	.220		227	22	50	5	0	3	20	28	46	0

PITCHER	W	L	ERA	G	GS	CG	SV	SHO	IP	H	ER	BB	SO
George Earnshaw	1	2	1.88	3	3	2	0	1	24.0	12	5	4	20
Lefty Grove	2	1	2.42	3	3	2	0	0	26.0	28	7	2	16
Waite Hoyt	0	1	4.50	1	1	0	0	0	6.0	7	3	0	1
Roy Mahaffey	0	0	9.00	1	0	0	0	0	1.0	1	1	1	0
Eddie Rommel	0	0	9.00	1	0	0	0	0	1.0	3	1	0	0
Rube Walberg	0	0	3.00	2	0	0	0	0	3.0	3	1	2	4
TOTAL	3	4	2.66	11	7	4	0	1	61.0	54	18	9	41

GAME 1 AT STL OCT 1

PHI	004	000	200	6	11	0
STL	200	000	000	2	12	0

Pitchers: GROVE vs DERRINGER, Johnson (8)
Home Runs: Simmons-PHI
Attendance: 38,529

GAME 2 AT STL OCT 2

PHI	000	000	000	0	3	0
STL	010	000	10X	2	6	1

Pitchers: EARNSHAW vs HALLAHAN
Attendance: 35,947

GAME 3 AT PHI OCT 5

STL	020	200	001	5	12	0
PHI	000	000	002	2	2	0

Pitchers: GRIMES vs GROVE, Mahaffey (9)
Home Runs: Simmons-PHI
Attendance: 32,295

GAME 4 AT PHI OCT 6

STL	000	000	000	0	2	1
PHI	100	002	00X	3	10	0

Pitchers: JOHNSON, Lindsey (6) vs EARNSHAW
Home Runs: Foxx-PHI
Attendance: 32,295

GAME 5 AT PHI OCT 7

STL	100	002	011	5	12	0
PHI	000	000	100	1	9	0

Pitchers: HALLAHAN vs HOYT, Walberg (7), Rommel (9)
Home Runs: Martin-STL, Watkins-STL
Attendance: 32,295

GAME 6 AT STL OCT 9

PHI	000	040	400	8	8	1
STL	000	001	000	1	5	2

Pitchers: GROVE vs DERRINGER, Johnson (5), Lindsey (7), Rhem (9)
Attendance: 39,401

GAME 7 AT STL OCT 10

PHI	000	000	002	2	7	1
STL	202	000	00X	4	5	0

Pitchers: EARNSHAW, Walberg (8) vs GRIMES, Hallahan (9)
Attendance: 20,805

Lou Gehrig, who hit .529 and scored nearly a quarter of New York's runs, led both clubs in batting, slugging, hits, runs, and RBIs as the Yankees crushed the Cubs in four games. But the Series is best remembered for Babe Ruth's "called" shot in Game Three, when he pointed his bat atp itcher Charlie Root in the fifth inning and broke the game's 4–4 tie a moment later with a massive home run into the center field bleachers. Debate has raged ever since about whether Ruth intended his gesture as a home run prediction. Whether intended or not, it erased from public memory Gehrig's home run that followed Ruth's (and the homers both men had hit earlier in the game), and made memorable an otherwise undistinguished Series.

Chicago scored in the first inning of each game, taking early leads in three of the four, but held no lead beyond the sixth inning. In Game One, the Cubs connected for ten hits to the Yankees' eight, but managed to score only half as many runs as the New Yorkers, who put what had been a close game out of reach with five runs in the sixth (on four walks, two singles, and a ground out) and three more in the seventh (a walk, two singles, a hit batsman, a sacrifice fly, and a wild pitch).

Chicago's Lon Warneke walked four batters in Game Two, and three of them went on to score as the Yankees countered single Cub runs in the first and third with pairs of their own on two walks and two singles in each frame. (A fifth Yankee run—on two singles without bases on balls—concluded the scoring for the game.)

Game Three featured not only the two homers each by Ruth and Gehrig, but home runs by the Cubs' Kiki Cuyler and Gabby Hartnett. Hartnett's solo shot in the last of the ninth brought Chicago to within two runs of New York for the Series' closest finish.

Four first-inning singles, Frank Demaree's three-run homer, and a Yankee error gave the Cubs a 4–1 advantage early in Game Four—their biggest lead of the Series. But by game's end, 19 Yankee hits (including two home runs by Tony Lazzeri and one by Earle Combs) had created 13 Yankee runs, and the world title was theirs.

New York Yankees (AL), 4; Chicago Cubs (NL), 0

NY (A)

PLAYER/POS	AVG	G	AB	R	H	2B	3B	HR	RB	BB	SO	SB
Johnny Allen, p	.000	1	0	0	0	0	0	0	0	0	0	0
Sammy Byrd, of	.000	1	0	0	0	0	0	0	0	0	0	0
Ben Chapman, of	.294	4	17	1	5	2	0	0	6	2	4	0
Earle Combs, of	.375	4	16	8	6	1	0	1	4	4	3	0
Frankie Crosetti, ss	.133	4	15	2	2	1	0	0	0	2	3	0
Bill Dickey, c	.438	4	16	2	7	0	0	0	4	2	1	0
Lou Gehrig, 1b	.529	4	17	9	9	1	0	3	8	2	1	0
Lefty Gomez, p	.000	1	3	0	0	0	0	0	0	0	2	0
Myril Hoag, pr	.000	1	0	1	0	0	0	0	0	0	0	0
Tony Lazzeri, 2b	.294	4	17	4	5	0	0	2	5	2	1	0
Wilcy Moore, p	.333	3	0	1	0	0	0	0	0	0	2	0
Herb Pennock, p	.000	2	1	0	0	0	0	0	0	0	0	0
George Pipgras, p	.000	1	5	0	0	0	0	0	0	0	5	0
Red Ruffing, p-1	.000	2	4	0	0	0	0	0	0	0	1	0
Babe Ruth, of	.333	4	15	6	5	0	0	2	6	4	3	0
Joe Sewell, 3b	.333	4	15	4	5	1	0	0	3	4	0	0
TOTAL	.313		144	37	45	6	0	8	36	23	26	0

PITCHER	W	L	ERA	G	GS	CG	SV	SHO	IP	H	ER	BB	SO
Johnny Allen	0	0	40.50	1	1	0	0	0	0.2	5	3	0	0
Lefty Gomez	1	0	1.00	1	1	1	0	0	9.0	9	1	1	8
Wilcy Moore	1	0	0.00	1	0	0	0	0	5.1	2	0	0	1
Herb Pennock	0	0	2.25	2	0	0	2	0	4.0	2	1	1	4
George Pipgras	1	0	4.50	1	1	0	0	0	8.0	9	4	3	1
Red Ruffing	1	0	4.00	1	1	1	0	0	9.0	10	4	6	10
TOTAL	4	0	3.25	7	4	2	2	0	36.0	37	13	11	24

CHI (N)

PLAYER/POS	AVG	G	AB	R	H	2B	3B	HR	RB	BB	SO	SB
Guy Bush, p	.000	2	1	0	0	0	0	0	0	1	0	0
Kiki Cuyler, of	.278	4	18	2	5	1	1	1	2	0	3	1
Frank Demaree, of	.286	2	7	1	2	0	0	1	4	1	0	0
Woody English, 3b	.176	4	17	2	3	0	0	0	1	2	2	0
Burleigh Grimes, p	.000	2	1	0	0	0	0	0	0	0	1	0
Charlie Grimm, 1b	.333	4	15	2	5	2	0	0	1	2	2	0
Marv Gudat, ph	.000	2	2	0	0	0	0	0	0	0	1	0
Stan Hack, ph	.000	1	0	0	0	0	0	0	0	0	0	0
Gabby Hartnett, c	.313	4	16	2	5	2	0	1	1	1	3	0
Rollie Hemsley, c-1	.000	3	3	0	0	0	0	0	0	0	3	0
Billy Herman, 2b	.222	4	18	5	4	1	0	0	1	1	3	0
Billy Jurges, ss	.364	3	11	1	4	1	0	0	1	0	1	2
Mark Koenig, ss-1	.250	2	4	1	1	0	1	0	1	1	0	0
Pat Malone, p	.000	1	0	0	0	0	0	0	0	0	0	0
Jakie May, p	.000	2	2	0	0	0	0	0	0	0	0	0
Johnny Moore, of	.000	2	7	0	0	0	0	0	0	2	1	0
Charlie Root, p	.000	2	2	0	0	0	0	0	0	0	1	0
Bob Smith, p	.000	1	0	0	0	0	0	0	0	0	0	0
Riggs Stephenson, of	.444	4	18	2	8	1	0	0	4	0	0	0
Bud Tinning, p	.000	2	0	0	0	0	0	0	0	0	0	0
Lon Warneke, p	.000	2	4	0	0	0	0	0	0	0	3	0
TOTAL	.253		146	19	37	8	2	3	16	11	24	3

PITCHER	W	L	ERA	G	GS	CG	SV	SHO	IP	H	ER	BB	SO
Guy Bush	0	1	14.29	2	2	0	0	0	5.2	5	9	6	2
Burleigh Grimes	0	0	23.63	2	0	0	0	0	2.2	7	7	2	0
Pat Malone	0	0	0.00	1	0	0	0	0	2.2	1	0	4	4
Jakie May	0	1	11.57	2	0	0	0	0	4.2	9	6	3	4
Charlie Root	0	1	10.38	1	1	0	0	0	4.1	6	5	3	4
Bob Smith	0	0	9.00	1	0	0	0	0	1.0	2	1	0	1
Bud Tinning	0	0	0.00	2	0	0	0	0	2.1	0	0	0	3
Lon Warneke	0	1	5.91	2	1	1	0	0	10.2	15	7	5	8
TOTAL	0	4	9.26	13	4	1	0	0	34.0	45	35	23	26

GAME 1 AT NY SEPT 28

CHI	200	000	220	6	10	1
NY	000	305	31X	12	8	2

Pitchers: BUSH, Grimes (6), Smith (8) vs RUFFING
Home Runs: Gehrig-NY
Attendance: 41,459

GAME 2 AT NY SEPT 29

CHI	101	000	000	2	9	0
NY	202	010	00X	5	10	1

Pitchers: WARNEKE vs GOMEZ
Attendance: 50,709

GAME 3 AT CHI OCT 1

NY	301	020	001	7	8	1
CHI	102	100	001	5	9	4

Pitchers: PIPGRAS, Pennock (9) vs ROOT, Malone (5), May (7), Tinning (9)
Home Runs: Ruth-NY (2), Gehrig-NY (2), Cuyler-CHI, Hartnett-CHI
Attendance: 49,986

GAME 4 AT CHI OCT 2

NY	102	002	404	13	19	4
CHI	400	001	001	6	9	1

Pitchers: Allen, MOORE (1), Pennock (7) vs Bush, Warneke (1), MAY (4), Tinning (7), Grimes (9)
Home Runs: Demaree-CHI, Lazzeri-NY (2), Combs-NY
Attendance: 49,844

Although John McGraw had retired from managing the Giants in 1932, he continued to regard them as "his" team. Led now by first baseman Bill Terry, the Giants faced a club also led by an active player, shortstop Joe Cronin in his rookie managerial season.

Giant ace Carl Hubbell dominated the first game, striking out ten while limiting the Senators to five singles and a pair of unearned runs. Mel Ott set the tone for New York with a two-out two-run homer in the first inning, and singled home a third Giant run in the third to build a lead Washington would not overcome. The next day the Senators scored first, on Goose Goslin's solo homer in the third. But that was the only run scored off Giant pitcher Hal Schumacher, and when the Giants drove out Senator starter Alvin Crowder with six runs in the sixth they had their second win well in hand.

The Senators revived when the Series moved to Washington for Game Three. Each of second baseman Buddy Myer's three hits scored or drove in a run, providing a growing cushion for pitcher Earl Whitehill, who recorded the Series' only shutout.

Games Four and Five went to New York, but not without a struggle. In the fourth game, manager Terry's home run broke the ice in the fourth inning, but Giant pitcher Hubbell muffed a bunt in the seventh which led to the tying run. Hubbell and Senator starter Monty Weaver dueled without further scoring until shortstop Blondy Ryan's single in the top of the eleventh put New York up by one. Hubbell let men reach second and third with one out in the last of the eleventh, but an intentional walk set up the hoped-for double play to end the game.

New York had built a three-run lead in Game Five when Senator Fred Schulte evened the score in the last of the sixth with a three-run homer. Relievers Jack Russell and Dolf Luque then dueled scorelessly into the tenth, when Giant Mel Ott (whose homer had begun the Series' scoring in the first inning of Game One) homered once again for what proved the Series' final run. Luque shut down the Senators in their half of the tenth, and "McGraw's Giants" were for the fourth time the world's finest. But before the advent of another spring, McGraw was dead.

New York Giants (NL), 4; Washington Senators (AL), 1

NY (N)

PLAYER/POS	AVG	G	AB	R	H	2B	3B	HR	RB	BB	SO	SB
Hi Bell, p	.000	1	0	0	0	0	0	0	0	0	0	0
Hughie Critz, 2b	.136	5	22	2	3	0	0	0	0	1	0	0
Kiddo Davis, of	.368	5	19	1	7	1	0	0	0	0	3	0
Freddie Fitzsimmons, p	.500	1	2	0	1	0	0	0	0	0	0	0
Carl Hubbell, p	.286	2	7	0	2	0	0	0	0	0	0	0
Dolf Luque, p	1.000	1	1	0	1	0	0	0	0	0	0	0
Gus Mancuso, c	.118	5	17	2	2	1	0	0	2	3	0	0
Jo-Jo Moore, of	.227	5	22	1	5	1	0	0	1	1	3	0
Lefty O'Doul, ph	1.000	1	1	1	1	0	0	0	2	0	0	0
Mel Ott, of	.389	5	18	3	7	0	0	2	4	4	4	0
Homer Peel, of-1	.500	2	2	0	1	0	0	0	0	0	0	0
Blondy Ryan, ss	.278	5	18	0	5	0	0	0	1	1	5	0
Hal Schumacher, p	.286	2	7	0	2	0	0	0	3	0	3	0
Bill Terry, 1b	.273	5	22	3	6	1	0	1	1	0	0	0
TOTAL	.267		176	16	47	5	0	3	16	11	21	0

PITCHER	W	L	ERA	G	GS	CG	SV	SHO	IP	H	ER	BB	SO
Hi Bell	0	0	0.00	1	0	0	0	0	1.0	0	0	0	0
Freddie Fitzsimmons	0	1	5.14	1	1	0	0	0	7.0	9	4	0	2
Carl Hubbell	2	0	0.00	2	2	2	0	0	20.0	13	0	6	15
Dolf Luque	1	0	0.00	1	0	0	0	0	4.1	2	0	2	5
Hal Schumacher	1	0	2.45	2	2	1	0	0	14.2	13	4	5	3
TOTAL	4	1	1.53	7	5	3	0	0	47.0	37	8	13	25

WAS (A)

PLAYER/POS	AVG	G	AB	R	H	2B	3B	HR	RB	BB	SO	SB
Ossie Bluege, 3b	.125	5	16	1	2	1	0	0	0	1	6	0
Cliff Bolton, ph	.000	2	2	0	0	0	0	0	0	0	0	0
Joe Cronin, ss	.318	5	22	1	7	0	0	0	2	0	2	0
General Crowder, p	.250	2	4	0	1	0	0	0	0	0	0	0
Goose Goslin, of	.250	5	20	2	5	1	0	1	1	1	3	0
Dave Harris, of-1	.000	3	2	0	0	0	0	0	0	2	0	0
John Kerr, pr	.000	1	0	0	0	0	0	0	0	0	0	0
Joe Kuhel, 1b	.150	5	20	1	3	0	0	0	1	1	4	0
Heinie Manush, of	.111	5	18	2	2	0	0	0	0	2	1	0
Alex Mc Coll, p	.000	1	0	0	0	0	0	0	0	0	0	0
Buddy Myer, 2b	.300	5	20	2	6	1	0	0	2	2	3	0
Sam Rice, ph	1.000	1	1	0	1	0	0	0	0	0	0	0
Jack Russell, p	.000	3	2	0	0	0	0	0	0	1	2	0
Fred Schulte, of	.333	5	21	1	7	1	0	1	4	1	1	0
Luke Sewell, c	.176	5	17	1	3	0	0	0	1	2	0	1
Lefty Stewart, p	.000	1	1	0	0	0	0	0	0	0	1	0
Tommy Thomas, p	.000	2	0	0	0	0	0	0	0	0	0	0
Monte Weaver, p	.000	1	4	0	0	0	0	0	0	0	2	0
Earl Whitehill, p	.000	1	3	0	0	0	0	0	0	0	0	0
TOTAL	.214		173	11	37	4	0	2	11	13	25	1

PITCHER	W	L	ERA	G	GS	CG	SV	SHO	IP	H	ER	BB	SO
General Crowder	0	1	7.36	2	2	0	0	0	11.0	16	9	5	7
Alex Mc Coll	0	0	0.00	1	0	0	0	0	2.0	0	0	0	0
Jack Russell	0	1	0.87	3	0	0	0	0	10.1	8	1	0	7
Lefty Stewart	0	1	9.00	1	1	0	0	0	2.0	6	2	0	0
Tommy Thomas	0	0	0.00	2	0	0	0	0	1.1	1	0	0	2
Monte Weaver	0	1	1.74	1	1	0	0	0	10.1	11	2	4	3
Earl Whitehill	1	0	0.00	1	1	1	0	1	9.0	5	0	2	2
TOTAL	1	4	2.74	11	5	1	0	1	46.0	47	14	11	21

GAME 1 AT NY OCT 3

WAS	000	100	001	2	5	3
NY	202	000	00X	4	10	2

Pitchers: STEWART, Russell (3), Thomas (8) vs HUBBELL
Home Runs: Ott-NY
Attendance: 46,672

GAME 2 AT NY OCT 4

WAS	001	000	000	1	5	0
NY	000	006	00X	6	10	0

Pitchers: CROWDER, Thomas (6), McColl (7) vs SCHUMACHER
Home Runs: Goslin-WAS
Attendance: 35,461

GAME 3 AT WAS OCT 5

NY	000	000	000	0	5	0
WAS	210	000	10X	4	9	1

Pitchers: FITZSIMMONS, Bell (8) vs WHITEHILL
Attendance: 25,727

GAME 4 AT WAS OCT 6

NY	000	100	000	01	2	11	1
WAS	000	000	100	00	1	8	0

Pitchers: HUBBELL vs WEAVER, Russell (11)
Home Runs: Terry-NY
Attendance: 26,762

GAME 5 AT WAS OCT 7

NY	020	001	000	1	4	11	1
WAS	000	003	000	0	3	10	1

Pitchers: Schumacher, LUQUE (6) vs Crowder, RUSSELL (6)
Home Runs: Schulte-WAS, Ott-NY
Attendance: 28,454

Pitching brothers Dizzy and Paul Dean won seven games in ten days to give the Cardinals the pennant on the final day of the season. In the Series they continued their winning ways, chalking up all four Cardinal victories. Dizzy pitched the opener in Detroit. Given a 3–0 lead, thanks to five Tiger errors in the first three innings, he breezed to an 8–3 win.

Detroit's Schoolboy Rowe brought the Tigers back with a pitching masterpiece in Game Two. After giving up single runs in the second and third innings, he allowed only one runner to reach base over the next nine as his Tigers tied the score in the ninth, and won it on two walks and a single in the twelfth.

Paul Dean nearly pitched a shutout in Game Three, yielding a harmless run with two out in the ninth after the Cards had built him a 4–0 lead. Brother Diz figured in a curious and painful play in Game Four. Pinch-running in the fourth inning, he was beaned by a would-be double-play throw as he ran to second. The tying run scored from third on the play, but Detroit's pitcher Eldon Auker shut out the Cards through the final five innings, and his teammates scored six more runs to bury St. Louis 10–4, evening the Series at two apiece. Diz was rushed to the hospital, but as no damage was found he started Game Five the next day. He pitched well enough, but Detroit's Tommy Bridges pitched better, giving the Cardinals only one run to the Tigers' three.

Paul Dean evened the Series again with a win against Rowe in a closely contested sixth game. A grounder through Dean's legs allowed the Tigers to tie the game in the sixth inning, but Paul redeemed his error in the seventh when he singled in the tie-breaking—and as it turned out, winning—run. Dizzy came back after only a day's rest to hurl a six-hit shutout in the finale. He also scored the game's first run and drove in the sixth with a double and single in his team's seven-run third. Three innings later, frustrated Tiger fans, angered by Cardinal Joe Medwick's rough slide into their third baseman, pelted Medwick with food and bottles, halting the game for twenty minutes until Commissioner Landis ordered Medwick from the game. The delay only forestalled Detroit's defeat, as the Cards took the title game 11–0.

St. Louis Cardinals (NL), 4; Detroit Tigers (AL), 3

STL (N)

PLAYER/POS	AVG	G	AB	R	H	2B	3B	HR	RB	BB	SO	SB
Tex Carleton, p	.000	2	1	0	0	0	0	0	0	0	0	0
Ripper Collins, 1b	.367	7	30	4	11	1	0	0	3	1	2	0
Pat Crawford, ph	.000	2	2	0	0	0	0	0	0	0	0	0
Spud Davis, ph	1.000	2	2	0	2	0	0	0	1	0	0	0
Dizzy Dean, p-3	.250	4	12	3	3	2	0	0	1	0	3	0
Paul Dean, p	.167	2	6	0	1	0	0	0	2	0	1	0
Bill De Lancey, c	.172	7	29	3	5	3	0	1	4	2	8	0
Leo Durocher, ss	.259	7	27	4	7	1	1	0	0	0	0	0
Frankie Frisch, 2b	.194	7	31	2	6	1	0	0	4	0	1	0
Chick Fullis, of	.400	3	5	0	2	0	0	0	0	0	0	0
Jesse Haines, p	.000	1	0	0	0	0	0	0	0	0	0	0
Bill Hallahan, p	.000	1	3	0	0	0	0	0	0	0	1	0
Pepper Martin, 3b	.355	7	31	8	11	3	1	0	4	3	3	2
Joe Medwick, of	.379	7	29	4	11	0	1	1	5	1	7	0
Jim Mooney, p	.000	1	0	0	0	0	0	0	0	0	0	0
Ernie Orsatti, of	.318	7	22	3	7	0	1	0	2	3	1	0
Jack Rothrock, of	.233	7	30	3	7	3	1	0	6	1	2	0
Dazzy Vance, p	.000	1	0	0	0	0	0	0	0	0	0	0
Bill Walker, p	.000	2	2	0	0	0	0	0	0	0	2	0
Burgess Whitehead, ss	.000	1	0	0	0	0	0	0	0	0	0	0
TOTAL	.279		262	34	73	14	5	2	32	11	31	2

PITCHER	W	L	ERA	G	GS	CG	SV	SHO	IP	H	ER	BB	SO
Tex Carleton	0	0	7.36	2	1	0	0	0	3.2	5	3	2	2
Dizzy Dean	2	1	1.73	3	3	2	0	1	26.0	20	5	5	17
Paul Dean	2	0	1.00	2	2	2	0	0	18.0	15	2	7	11
Jesse Haines	0	0	0.00	1	0	0	0	0	0.2	1	0	0	2
Bill Hallahan	0	0	2.16	1	1	0	0	0	8.1	6	2	4	6
Jim Mooney	0	0	0.00	1	0	0	0	0	1.0	1	0	0	0
Dazzy Vance	0	0	0.00	1	0	0	0	0	1.1	2	0	1	3
Bill Walker	0	2	7.11	2	0	0	0	0	6.1	6	5	6	2
TOTAL	4	3	2.34	13	7	4	0	1	65.1	56	17	25	43

DET (A)

PLAYER/POS	AVG	G	AB	R	H	2B	3B	HR	RB	BB	SO	SB
Eldon Auker, p	.000	2	4	0	0	0	0	0	0	0	2	0
Tommy Bridges, p	.143	3	7	0	1	0	0	0	0	1	4	0
Mickey Cochrane, c	.214	7	28	2	6	1	0	0	1	4	3	0
General Crowder, p	.000	2	1	0	0	0	0	0	0	0	0	0
Frank Doljack, of-1	.000	2	2	0	0	0	0	0	0	0	0	0
Pete Fox, of	.286	7	28	1	8	6	0	0	2	1	4	0
Charlie Gehringer, 2b	.379	7	29	5	11	1	0	1	2	3	0	1
Goose Goslin, of	.241	7	29	2	7	1	0	0	2	3	1	0
Hank Greenberg, 1b	.321	7	28	4	9	2	1	1	7	4	9	1
Ray Hayworth, c	.000	1	0	0	0	0	0	0	0	0	0	0
Chief Hogsett, p	.000	3	0	0	0	0	0	0	0	0	1	0
Firpo Marberry, p	.000	2	0	0	0	0	0	0	0	0	0	0
Marv Owen, 3b	.069	7	29	0	2	0	0	0	1	0	5	1
Billy Rogell, ss	.276	7	29	3	8	1	0	0	4	1	4	1
Schoolboy Rowe, p	.000	3	7	0	0	0	0	0	0	0	5	0
Gee Walker, ph	.333	3	3	0	1	0	0	0	1	0	1	0
Jo-Jo White, of	.130	7	23	6	3	0	0	0	0	8	4	1
TOTAL	.224		250	23	56	12	1	2	20	25	43	5

PITCHER	W	L	ERA	G	GS	CG	SV	SHO	IP	H	ER	BB	SO
Eldon Auker	1	1	5.56	2	2	1	0	0	11.1	16	7	5	2
Tommy Bridges	1	1	3.63	3	2	1	0	0	17.1	21	7	1	12
General Crowder	0	1	1.50	2	1	0	0	0	6.0	6	1	1	2
Chief Hogsett	0	0	1.23	3	0	0	0	0	7.1	6	1	3	3
Firpo Marberry	0	0	21.60	2	0	0	0	0	1.2	5	4	1	0
Schoolboy Rowe	1	1	2.95	3	2	2	0	0	21.1	19	7	0	12
TOTAL	3	4	3.74	15	7	4	0	0	65.0	73	27	11	31

With a 21-game September winning streak, the Cubs vaulted over the Giants and Cardinals to face Detroit in the Series, and for a moment it seemed as if their momentum might carry them past the Tigers as well. Chicago scored two runs off Schoolboy Rowe in the top of the first in the opener, and right fielder Frank Demaree homered to open the ninth as Lon Warneke blanked the Tigers on four hits. But Detroit retaliated quickly in Game Two, driving out starter Charlie Root in the first inning with four runs (including Hank Greenberg's two-run homer) before Root had had a chance to record even one out. Tiger pitcher Rocky Bridges gained an easy 8–3 win, but Greenberg broke a wrist and was finished for the Series.

In Game Three the Cubs scored three times before Detroit countered with their first run in the sixth. But a walk and four Tiger hits in the eighth put the Bengals ahead 4–3, and Billy Rogell's baserunning as he turned a foiled steal into a rundown permitted a fifth Tiger to cross the plate. Two Cub runs in the last of the ninth tied the score, but Detroit pulled out the victory in the eleventh as a pair of singles sandwiched Fred Lindstrom's error at third to give them an unearned run.

Detroit's Alvin "General" Crowder followed up the Tigers' advantage the next day with a neat five-hit 2–1 win. Once again the Cubs bobbled away the game, this time with two sixth-inning errors that enabled Detroit to score the winning run without a hit. Chuck Klein's two-run homer saved Chicago from elimination in Game Five as Lon Warneke and Bill Lee shut out the Tigers through eight before letting in a harmless run in the ninth.

Chicago's Larry French and Tiger Rocky Bridges yielded 12 hits apiece in Game Six. Cub second baseman Billy Herman singled in a run in the third to tie the score, and homered for two more runs in the fifth to put the Cubs ahead. But the Tigers tied it up an inning later, and took their first world title ever when Goose Goslin singled in Mickey Cochrane with two out in the bottom of the ninth.

Detroit Tigers (AL), 4; Chicago Cubs (NL), 2

DET (A)

PLAYER/POS	AVG	G	AB	R	H	2B	3B	HR	RB	BB	SO	SB
Eldon Auker, p	.000	1	2	0	0	0	0	0	0	0	1	0
Tommy Bridges, p	.125	2	8	1	1	0	0	0	1	0	3	0
Flea Clifton, 3b	.000	4	16	1	0	0	0	0	0	2	4	0
Mickey Cochrane, c	.292	6	24	3	7	1	0	0	1	4	1	0
General Crowder, p	.333	1	3	1	1	0	0	0	0	1	0	0
Pete Fox, of	.385	6	26	1	10	3	1	0	4	0	1	0
Charlie Gehringer, 2b	.375	6	24	4	9	3	0	0	4	2	1	1
Goose Goslin, of	.273	6	22	2	6	1	0	0	3	5	0	0
Hank Greenberg, 1b	.167	2	6	1	1	0	0	1	2	1	0	0
Chief Hogsett, p	.000	1	0	0	0	0	0	0	0	0	0	0
Marv Owen, 1b-4,3b-2	.050	6	20	2	1	0	0	0	1	2	3	0
Billy Rogell, ss	.292	6	24	1	7	2	0	0	1	2	5	0
Schoolboy Rowe, p	.250	3	8	0	2	1	0	0	0	0	1	0
Gee Walker, of-1	.250	3	4	1	1	0	0	0	0	0	1	0
Jo-Jo White, of	.263	5	19	3	5	0	0	0	1	5	7	0
TOTAL	.248		206	21	51	11	1	1	18	25	27	1

PITCHER	W	L	ERA	G	GS	CG	SV	SHO	IP	H	ER	BB	SO
Eldon Auker	0	0	3.00	1	1	0	0	0	6.0	6	2	2	1
Tommy Bridges	2	0	2.50	2	2	2	0	0	18.0	18	5	4	9
General Crowder	1	0	1.00	1	1	1	0	0	9.0	5	1	3	5
Chief Hogsett	0	0	0.00	1	0	0	0	0	1.0	0	0	1	0
Schoolboy Rowe	1	2	2.57	3	2	2	0	0	21.0	19	6	1	14
TOTAL	4	2	2.29	8	6	5	0	0	55.0	48	14	11	29

CHI (N)

PLAYER/POS	AVG	G	AB	R	H	2B	3B	HR	RB	BB	SO	SB
Tex Carleton, p	.000	1	1	0	0	0	0	0	0	1	1	0
Phil Cavaretta, 1b	.125	6	24	1	3	0	0	0	0	0	5	0
Frank Demaree, of	.250	6	24	2	6	1	0	2	2	1	4	0
Larry French, p	.250	2	4	1	1	0	0	0	0	0	2	0
Augie Galan, of	.160	6	25	2	4	1	0	0	2	2	2	0
Stan Hack, 3b-6,ss-1	.227	6	22	2	5	1	1	0	0	2	2	1
Gabby Hartnett, c	.292	6	24	1	7	0	0	1	2	0	3	0
Roy Henshaw, p	.000	1	1	0	0	0	0	0	0	0	0	0
Billy Herman, 2b	.333	6	24	3	8	2	1	1	6	0	2	0
Billy Jurges, ss	.250	6	16	3	4	0	0	0	1	4	4	0
Chuck Klein, of-3	.333	5	12	2	4	0	0	1	2	0	2	0
Fabian Kowalik, p	.500	1	2	1	1	0	0	0	0	0	0	0
Bill Lee, p	.000	2	1	0	0	0	0	0	1	0	0	0
Fred Lindstrom, of-4,3b-1	.200	4	15	0	3	1	0	0	0	1	1	0
Ken O'Dea, ph	1.000	1	1	0	1	0	0	0	1	0	0	0
Charlie Root, p	.000	2	0	0	0	0	0	0	0	0	0	0
Walter Stephenson, ph	.000	1	1	0	0	0	0	0	0	0	1	0
Lon Warneke, p	.200	3	5	0	1	0	0	0	0	0	0	0
TOTAL	.238		202	18	48	6	2	5	17	11	29	1

PITCHER	W	L	ERA	G	GS	CG	SV	SHO	IP	H	ER	BB	SO
Tex Carleton	0	1	1.29	1	1	0	0	0	7.0	6	1	7	4
Larry French	0	2	3.38	2	1	1	0	0	10.2	15	4	2	8
Roy Henshaw	0	0	7.36	1	0	0	0	0	3.2	2	3	5	2
Fabian Kowalik	0	0	2.08	1	0	0	0	0	4.1	3	1	1	1
Bill Lee	0	0	3.48	2	1	0	1	0	10.1	11	4	5	5
Charlie Root	0	1	18.00	2	1	0	0	0	2.0	5	4	1	2
Lon Warneke	2	0	0.54	3	2	1	0	1	16.2	9	1	4	5
TOTAL	2	4	2.96	12	6	2	1	1	54.2	51	18	25	27

GAME 1 AT DET OCT 2

CHI	200	000	001	3	7	0
DET	000	000	000	0	4	3

Pitchers: WARNEKE vs ROWE
Home Runs: Demaree-CHI
Attendance: 47,391

GAME 2 AT DET OCT 3

CHI	000	010	200	3	6	1
DET	400	300	10X	8	9	2

Pitchers: ROOT, Henshaw (1), Kowalik (4) vs BRIDGES
Home Runs: Greenberg-DET
Attendance: 46,742

GAME 3 AT CHI OCT 4

DET	000 001 040 01	6	12	2
CHI	020 010 002 00	5	10	3

Pitchers: Auker, Hogsett (7), ROWE (8) vs Lee, Warneke (8), FRENCH (10)
Home Runs: Demaree-CHI
Attendance: 45,532

GAME 4 AT CHI OCT 5

DET	001	001	000	2	7	0
CHI	010	000	000	1	5	2

Pitchers: CROWDER vs CARLETON, Root (8)
Home Runs: Hartnett-CHI
Attendance: 49,350

GAME 5 AT CHI OCT 6

DET	000	000	001	1	7	1
CHI	002	000	10X	3	8	0

Pitchers: ROWE vs WARNEKE, Lee (7)
Home Runs: Klein-CHI
Attendance: 49,237

GAME 6 AT DET OCT 7

CHI	001	020	000	3	12	0
DET	100	101	001	4	12	1

Pitchers: FRENCH vs BRIDGES
Home Runs: Herman-CHI
Attendance: 48,420

The Giants managed to win two games, but this first Series between the cross-river rivals in thirteen years was really no contest. Babe Ruth was gone, but Lou Gehrig was still there, and Joe DiMaggio had arrived. The Yankees outhit the Giants by 56 percentage points and outscored them by 20 runs.

Giant ace Carl Hubbell, who had won his final 16 decisions of the regular season, continued his streak in the Series opener. The Yankees scored first on George Selkirk's third-inning homer, but Giant shortstop Dick Bartell homered to even things in the fifth. Hubbell held the Yankees to that one run, but the Giants roughed up Red Ruffing for five more runs, to give the Polo Grounders a brief Series advantage.

Game Two was a Yankee blowout, as the Yankees hammered five Giant pitchers for 18 runs—four of them on Tony Lazzeri's grand slam in the third—to give Lefty Gomez an easy win. By contrast, Game Three was a pitchers' duel. Although the Giants touched Bump Hadley and Pat Malone for 11 hits, only Jimmy Ripple's fifth-inning homer produced a run. Giant Freddie Fitzsimmons was much more stingy with hits, yielding only four. But one was Gehrig's home run in the second inning, and another was Frank Crosetti's game-winning RBI single in the eighth.

Gehrig homered again in the third inning of Game Four to give the Yankees an insurmountable lead—and Hubbell his first loss in months. Down three games to one, the Giants struggled back in Game Five. They took a first-inning 3–0 lead, but the Yankees clawed their way back, and by the end of six the score was 4–4. There it stayed until the tenth, when a double, sacrifice, and fly to center put the Giants ahead by a run. Hal Schumacher, who had pitched the whole game, held the Yankees scoreless one more time for the win.

Fitzsimmons, who had pitched so well in his third-game loss, didn't last four innings in Game Six. Though the Giants scored first, Yankee Jake Powell (who led all Series hitters at .455) tied the game with a two-run homer in the top of the second. Two more runs in the fourth drove out Fitzsimmons, but the game stayed close until the top of the ninth, when five Yankee singles and three walks produced seven runs and a Series-ending 13–5 rout.

New York Yankees (AL), 4; New York Giants (NL), 2

NY (A)

PLAYER/POS	AVG	G	AB	R	H	2B	3B	HR	RB	BB	SO	SB
Frankie Crosetti, ss	.269	6	26	5	7	2	0	0	3	3	5	0
Bill Dickey, c	.120	6	25	5	3	0	0	1	5	3	4	0
Joe DiMaggio, of	.346	6	26	3	9	3	0	0	3	1	3	0
Lou Gehrig, 1b	.292	6	24	5	7	1	0	2	7	3	2	0
Lefty Gomez, p	.250	2	8	1	2	0	0	0	3	0	3	0
Bump Hadley, p	.000	1	2	0	0	0	0	0	0	0	1	0
Roy Johnson, ph	.000	2	1	0	0	0	0	0	0	0	1	0
Tony Lazzeri, 2b	.250	6	20	4	5	0	0	1	7	4	4	0
Pat Malone, p	1.000	2	1	0	1	0	0	0	0	0	0	0
Johnny Murphy, p	.500	1	2	1	1	0	0	0	1	0	1	0
Monte Pearson, p	.500	1	4	0	2	1	0	0	0	0	0	0
Jake Powell, of	.455	6	22	8	10	1	0	1	5	4	4	1
Red Rolfe, 3b	.400	6	25	5	10	0	0	0	4	3	1	0
Red Ruffing, p-2	.000	3	5	0	0	0	0	0	0	1	2	0
Bob Seeds, pr	.000	1	0	0	0	0	0	0	0	0	0	0
George Selkirk, of	.333	6	24	6	8	0	1	2	3	4	4	0
TOTAL	.302		215	43	65	8	1	7	41	26	35	1

PITCHER	W	L	ERA	G	GS	CG	SV	SHO	IP	H	ER	BB	SO
Lefty Gomez	2	0	4.70	2	2	1	0	0	15.1	14	8	11	9
Bump Hadley	1	0	1.13	1	1	0	0	0	8.0	10	1	1	2
Pat Malone	0	1	1.80	2	0	0	1	0	5.0	2	1	1	2
Johnny Murphy	0	0	3.38	1	0	0	1	0	2.2	1	1	1	1
Monte Pearson	1	0	2.00	1	1	1	0	0	9.0	7	2	2	7
Red Ruffing	0	1	4.50	2	2	0	0	0	14.0	16	7	5	12
TOTAL	4	2	3.33	9	6	2	2	0	54.0	50	20	21	33

NY (N)

PLAYER/POS	AVG	G	AB	R	H	2B	3B	HR	RB	BB	SO	SB
Dick Bartell, ss	.381	6	21	5	8	3	0	1	3	4	4	0
Slick Castleman, p	.500	1	2	0	1	0	0	0	0	0	0	0
Dick Coffman, p	.000	2	0	0	0	0	0	0	0	0	0	0
Harry Danning, c-1	.000	2	2	0	0	0	0	0	0	0	1	0
Kiddo Davis, ph	.500	4	2	2	1	0	0	0	0	0	0	0
Freddie Fitzsimmons, p	.500	2	4	0	2	0	0	0	0	0	1	0
Frank Gabler, p	.000	2	0	0	0	0	0	0	0	1	0	0
Harry Gumbert, p	.000	2	0	0	0	0	0	0	0	0	0	0
Carl Hubbell, p	.333	2	6	0	2	0	0	0	1	0	0	0
Travis Jackson, 3b	.190	6	21	1	4	0	0	0	1	1	3	0
Mark Koenig, 2b-1	.333	3	3	0	1	0	0	0	0	1	1	0
Hank Leiber, of	.000	2	6	0	0	0	0	0	0	2	2	0
Sam Leslie, ph	.667	3	3	0	2	0	0	0	0	0	0	0
Gus Mancuso, c	.263	6	19	3	5	2	0	0	1	3	3	0
Eddie Mayo, 3b	.000	1	1	0	0	0	0	0	0	0	0	0
Jo-Jo Moore, of	.214	6	28	4	6	2	0	1	1	1	4	0
Mel Ott, of	.304	6	23	4	7	2	0	1	3	3	1	0
Jimmy Ripple, of	.333	5	12	2	4	0	0	1	3	3	3	0
Hal Schumacher, p	.000	2	4	0	0	0	0	0	0	1	3	0
Al Smith, p	.000	1	0	0	0	0	0	0	0	0	0	0
Bill Terry, 1b	.240	6	25	1	6	0	0	0	5	1	4	0
Burgess Whitehead, 2b	.048	6	21	1	1	0	0	0	0	2	3	0
TOTAL	.246		203	23	50	9	0	4	20	21	33	0

PITCHER	W	L	ERA	G	GS	CG	SV	SHO	IP	H	ER	BB	SO
Slick Castleman	0	0	2.08	1	0	0	0	0	4.1	3	1	2	5
Dick Coffman	0	0	32.40	2	0	0	0	0	1.2	5	6	1	1
Freddie Fitzsimmons	0	2	5.40	2	2	1	0	0	11.2	13	7	2	6
Frank Gabler	0	0	7.20	2	0	0	0	0	5.0	7	4	4	0
Harry Gumbert	0	0	36.00	2	0	0	0	0	2.0	7	8	4	2
Carl Hubbell	1	1	2.25	2	2	1	0	0	16.0	15	4	2	10
Hal Schumacher	1	1	5.25	2	2	1	0	0	12.0	13	7	10	11
Al Smith	0	0	81.00	1	0	0	0	0	0.1	2	3	1	0
TOTAL	2	4	6.79	14	6	3	0	0	53.0	65	40	26	35

GAME 1 AT NY -N SEPT 30

NY-A	001	000	000	1	7	2
NY-N	000	011	04X	6	9	1

Pitchers: RUFFING vs HUBBELL
Home Runs: Bartell-NY(N), Selkirk-NY(A)
Attendance: 39,419

GAME 2 AT NY -N OCT 2

NY-A	207	001	206	18	17	0
NY-N	010	300	000	4	6	1

Pitchers: GOMEZ vs SCHUMACHER, Smith (3), Coffman (3), Gabler (5), Gumbert (9)
Home Runs: Dickey-NY(A), Lazzeri-NY(A)
Attendance: 43,543

GAME 3 AT NY -A OCT 3

NY-N	000	010	000	1	11	0
NY-A	010	000	01X	2	4	0

Pitchers: FITZSIMMONS vs HADLEY, Malone (9)
Home Runs: Gerhig-NY(A), Ripple-NY(N)
Attendance: 64,842

GAME 4 AT NY -A OCT 4

NY-N	000	100	010	2	7	1
NY-A	013	000	01X	5	10	1

Pitchers: HUBBELL, Gabler (8) vs PEARSON
Home Runs: Gehrig-NY(A)
Attendance: 66,669

GAME 5 AT NY -A OCT 5

NY-N	300	001	000 1	5	8	3
NY-A	011	002	000 0	4	10	1

Pitchers: SCHUMACHER vs Ruffing, MALONE (7)
Home Runs: Selkirk-NY(A)
Attendance: 50,024

GAME 6 AT NY -N OCT 6

NY-A	021	200	017	13	17	2
NY-N	200	010	110	5	9	1

Pitchers: GOMEZ, Murphy (7) vs FITZSIMMONS, Castleman (4), Coffman (9), Gumbert (9)
Home Runs: Moore-NY(N), Ott-NY(N), Powell-NY(A)
Attendance: 38,427

For the second year in a row, the Yankees overwhelmed the Giants, this time in just five games. Giant ace Carl Hubbell, who took the opener in 1936, was unable to repeat this year. For five innings he held the Yankees to one hit. But in the sixth everything fell apart. Before Hubbell was taken out, two walks, five singles, and a Giant error had let in five runs. And the two runners Hubbell left on base scored later on a second Giant error and two walks by reliever Dick Coffman. The Yankees' Lefty Gomez also yielded six hits, but wider spacing and better field support held the Giants to one run in the fifth. Tony Lazzeri's homer in the eighth made the final score 8–1.

The Yankees spread their runs a bit more evenly in Game Two. For the second time the Giants gained a 1–0 lead. Rookie phenom Cliff Melton held the Yankees scoreless through four, but four straight hits for two runs at the start of the fifth drove him out. Reliever Ad Gumbert stopped the Yankees in the rest of the inning but gave up four more hits—and four more runs—in the sixth before Coffman stepped in to stop the assault. But Coffman gave up two final Yankee runs in the seventh, to complete a second straight 8–1 Yankee win, as Red Ruffing held the Giants scoreless through the final eight innings.

The Yankees had scored five times off Hal Schumacher in Game Three before the Giants got their one run in the seventh. But Yankee starter Monte Pearson made the game tighter as he yielded a single and two walks to load the bases in the ninth before Johnny Murphy came on to record the final out.

Giant bats finally came alive in the second inning of Game Four. Seven singles, plus a walk and a missed play at the plate gave the club a 6–1 lead, which starter Hubbell protected for the only Giant win of the Series.

Solo homers by Myril Hoag in the second and Joe DiMaggio in the third gave the Yankees a 2–0 lead early in Game Five, but Giant Mel Ott tied it up with a two-run shot off Lefty Gomez in the last of the third. But Gomez shut the Giants down the rest of the way, and singled in Lazzeri in the fifth with what proved the game winner (scoring himself on Lou Gehrig's double for the final run of the Series).

New York Yankees (AL), 4;
New York Giants (NL), 1

NY (A)

PLAYER/POS	AVG	G	AB	R	H	2B	3B	HR	RB	BB	SO	SB
Ivy Andrews, p	.000	1	2	0	0	0	0	0	0	0	1	0
Frankie Crosetti, ss	.048	5	21	2	1	0	0	0	0	3	2	0
Bill Dickey, c	.211	5	19	3	4	0	1	0	3	2	2	0
Joe DiMaggio, of	.273	5	22	2	6	0	0	1	4	0	3	0
Lou Gehrig, 1b	.294	5	17	4	5	1	1	1	3	5	4	0
Lefty Gomez, p	.167	2	6	2	1	0	0	0	1	2	1	0
Bump Hadley, p	.000	1	0	0	0	0	0	0	0	0	0	0
Myril Hoag, of	.300	5	20	4	6	1	0	1	2	0	1	0
Tony Lazzeri, 2b	.400	5	15	3	6	0	1	1	2	3	3	0
Johnny Murphy, p	.000	1	0	0	0	0	0	0	0	0	0	0
Monte Pearson, p	.000	1	3	0	0	0	0	0	0	1	1	0
Jake Powell, ph	.000	1	1	0	0	0	0	0	0	0	1	0
Red Rolfe, 3b	.300	5	20	3	6	2	1	0	1	3	2	0
Red Ruffing, p	.500	1	4	0	2	1	0	0	3	0	0	0
George Selkirk, of	.263	5	19	5	5	1	0	0	6	2	0	0
Kemp Wicker, p	.000	1	0	0	0	0	0	0	0	0	0	0
TOTAL	.249		169	28	42	6	4	4	25	21	21	0

PITCHER	W	L	ERA	G	GS	CG	SV	SHO	IP	H	ER	BB	SO
Ivy Andrews	0	0	3.18	1	0	0	0	0	5.2	6	2	4	1
Lefty Gomez	2	0	1.50	2	2	2	0	0	18.0	16	3	2	8
Bump Hadley	0	1	33.75	1	1	0	0	0	1.1	6	5	0	0
Johnny Murphy	0	0	0.00	1	0	0	1	0	0.1	0	0	0	0
Monte Pearson	1	0	1.04	1	1	0	0	0	8.2	5	1	2	4
Red Ruffing	1	0	1.00	1	1	1	0	0	9.0	7	1	3	8
Kemp Wicker	0	0	0.00	1	0	0	0	0	1.0	0	0	0	0
TOTAL	4	1	2.45	8	5	3	1	0	44.0	40	12	11	21

NY (N)

PLAYER/POS	AVG	G	AB	R	H	2B	3B	HR	RB	BB	SO	SB
Dick Bartell, ss	.238	5	21	3	5	1	0	0	1	0	3	0
Wally Berger, ph	.000	3	3	0	0	0	0	0	0	0	1	0
Don Brennan, p	.000	2	0	0	0	0	0	0	0	0	0	0
Lou Chiozza, of	.286	2	7	0	2	0	0	0	0	1	1	0
Dick Coffman, p	.000	2	1	0	0	0	0	0	0	0	1	0
Harry Danning, c	.250	3	12	0	3	1	0	0	2	0	2	0
Harry Gumbert, p	.000	2	0	0	0	0	0	0	0	0	0	0
Carl Hubbell, p	.000	2	6	1	0	0	0	0	1	0	0	0
Hank Leiber, of	.364	3	11	2	4	0	0	0	2	1	1	0
Sam Leslie, ph	.000	2	1	0	0	0	0	0	0	1	0	0
Gus Mancuso, c-2	.000	3	8	0	0	0	0	0	1	0	1	0
Johnny Mc Carthy, 1b	.211	5	19	1	4	1	0	0	1	1	2	0
Cliff Melton, p	.000	3	2	0	0	0	0	0	0	1	1	0
Jo-Jo Moore, of	.391	5	23	1	9	1	0	0	1	0	1	0
Mel Ott, 3b	.200	5	20	1	4	0	0	1	3	1	4	0
Jimmy Ripple, of	.294	5	17	2	5	0	0	0	0	3	1	0
Blondy Ryan, ph	.000	1	1	0	0	0	0	0	0	0	1	0
Hal Schumacher, p	.000	1	1	0	0	0	0	0	0	0	1	0
Al Smith, p	.000	2	0	0	0	0	0	0	0	0	0	0
Burgess Whitehead, 2b	.250	5	16	1	4	2	0	0	0	2	0	1
TOTAL	.237		169	12	40	6	0	1	12	11	21	1

PITCHER	W	L	ERA	G	GS	CG	SV	SHO	IP	H	ER	BB	SO
Don Brennan	0	0	0.00	2	0	0	0	0	3.0	1	0	1	1
Dick Coffman	0	0	4.15	2	0	0	0	0	4.1	2	2	5	1
Harry Gumbert	0	0	27.00	2	0	0	0	0	1.1	4	4	1	1
Carl Hubbell	1	1	3.77	2	2	1	0	0	14.1	12	6	4	7
Cliff Melton	0	2	4.91	3	2	0	0	0	11.0	12	6	6	7
Hal Schumacher	0	1	6.00	1	1	0	0	0	6.0	9	4	4	3
Al Smith	0	0	3.00	2	0	0	0	0	3.0	2	1	0	1
TOTAL	1	4	4.81	14	5	1	0	0	43.0	42	23	21	21

GAME 1 AT NY -A OCT 6

NY-N	000	010	000	1	6	2
NY-A	000	007	01X	8	7	0

Pitchers: HUBBELL, Gumbert (6), Coffman (6), Smith (8) vs GOMEZ
Home Runs: Lazzeri-NY(A)
Attendance: 60,573

GAME 2 AT NY -A OCT 7

NY-N	100	000	000	1	7	0
NY-A	000	024	20X	8	12	0

Pitchers: MELTON, Gumbert (5), Coffman (6) vs RUFFING
Attendance: 57,675

GAME 3 AT NY -N OCT 8

NY-A	012	110	000	5	9	0
NY-N	000	000	100	1	5	4

Pitchers: PEARSON, Murphy (9) vs SCHUMACHER, Melton (7), Brennan (9)
Attendance: 37,385

GAME 4 AT NY -N OCT 9

NY-A	101	000	001	3	6	0
NY-N	060	000	00X	7	12	3

Pitchers: HADLEY, Andrews (2), Wicker (8) vs HUBBELL
Home Runs: Gehrig-NY(A)
Attendance: 44,293

GAME 5 AT NY -N OCT 10

NY-A	011	020	000	4	8	0
NY-N	002	000	000	2	10	0

Pitchers: GOMEZ vs MELTON, Smith (6), Brennan (8)
Home Runs: DiMaggio-NY(A), Hoag-NY(A), Ott-NY(N)
Attendance: 38,216

As they had six years earlier, the Cubs faced the Yankees in the World Series, and as they had six years earlier, New York swept the Series in four games. Although Cub batters made nearly as many hits as the Yankees, they did much less damage, driving in 13 fewer runs. In Game One, Yankee ace Red Ruffing scattered nine Cub hits, holding Chicago to a single run. The Cubs' Bill Lee was nearly as effective in scattering hits, but a base on balls in the second (the game's only walk) followed by a pair of singles sandwiched around an error accounted for two runs—all the Yankees would need for the win (though they scored once more in the sixth).

In Game Two the Cubs outhit the Yankees 11 to 7, but scored only half as many runs as the New Yorkers. Chicago's Dizzy Dean, pitching on craft and guile with his fastball gone, managed to keep the game close until the final innings. With a 3–2 lead going into the eighth, though, he gave up a two-run homer to Frank Crosetti, and the same to Joe DiMaggio in the ninth before being relieved. Yankee fireman Johnny Murphy, meanwhile, held Chicago scoreless over the final two innings to preserve Lefty Gomez's win.

Utility outfielder Joe Marty drove in both Chicago runs in Game Three with a grounder to third in the fifth and a homer in the eighth. (His .500 BA was tops for both teams, and he drove in five of the Cubs' nine Series runs.) But again the Cubs fell short, as Yankee rookie second baseman Joe Gordon homered to tie the score in the bottom of the fifth with the first of what would be five Yankee runs by the time Bill Dickey's homer in the eighth ended the scoring for the day.

Cub second baseman Billy Herman's wild throw with two out in the second inning of Game Four led to three unearned runs, and a Yankee lead they would not relinquish. Though their lead was cut to one run (4–3) when Chicago scored twice in the top of the eighth, the Yankees took advantage of two wild pitches and two walks to turn their four hits into four runs that crushed Cub hopes and gave the New Yorkers a record third consecutive world championship.

New York Yankees (AL), 4;
Chicago Cubs (NL), 0

NY (A)

PLAYER/POS	AVG	G	AB	R	H	2B	3B	HR	RB	BB	SO	SB
Frankie Crosetti, ss	.250	4	16	1	4	2	1	1	6	2	4	0
Bill Dickey, c	.400	4	15	2	6	0	0	1	2	1	0	1
Joe DiMaggio, of	.267	4	15	4	4	0	0	1	2	1	1	0
Lou Gehrig, 1b	.286	4	14	4	4	0	0	0	0	2	3	0
Lefty Gomez, p	.000	1	2	0	0	0	0	0	0	0	0	0
Joe Gordon, 2b	.400	4	15	3	6	2	0	1	6	1	3	1
Tommy Henrich, of	.250	4	16	3	4	1	0	1	1	0	1	0
Myril Hoag, of-1	.400	2	5	3	2	1	0	0	1	0	0	0
Johnny Murphy, p	.000	1	0	0	0	0	0	0	0	0	0	0
Monte Pearson, p	.333	1	3	1	1	0	0	0	0	1	0	0
Jake Powell, of	.000	1	0	0	0	0	0	0	0	0	0	0
Red Rolfe, 3b	.167	4	18	0	3	0	0	0	1	0	3	1
Red Ruffing, p	.167	2	6	1	1	0	0	0	1	1	0	0
George Selkirk, of	.200	3	10	0	2	0	0	0	1	2	1	0
TOTAL	.274		135	22	37	6	1	5	21	11	16	3

PITCHER	W	L	ERA	G	GS	CG	SV	SHO	IP	H	ER	BB	SO
Lefty Gomez	1	0	3.86	1	1	0	0	0	7.0	9	3	1	5
Johnny Murphy	0	0	0.00	1	0	0	1	0	2.0	2	0	1	1
Monte Pearson	1	0	1.00	1	1	1	0	0	9.0	5	1	2	9
Red Ruffing	2	0	1.50	2	2	2	0	0	18.0	17	3	2	11
TOTAL	4	0	1.75	5	4	3	1	0	36.0	33	7	6	26

CHI (N)

PLAYER/POS	AVG	G	AB	R	H	2B	3B	HR	RB	BB	SO	SB
Clay Bryant, p	.000	1	2	0	0	0	0	0	0	0	1	0
Tex Carleton, p	.000	1	0	0	0	0	0	0	0	0	0	0
Phil Cavaretta, of-3	.462	4	13	1	6	1	0	0	0	0	1	0
Ripper Collins, 1b	.133	4	15	1	2	0	0	0	0	0	3	0
Dizzy Dean, p	.667	2	3	0	2	0	0	0	0	0	0	0
Frank Demaree, of	.100	3	10	1	1	0	0	0	0	1	2	0
Larry French, p	.000	3	0	0	0	0	0	0	0	0	0	0
Augie Galan, ph	.000	2	2	0	0	0	0	0	0	0	1	0
Stan Hack, 3b	.471	4	17	3	8	1	0	0	1	1	2	0
Gabby Hartnett, c	.091	3	11	0	1	0	1	0	0	0	2	0
Billy Herman, 2b	.188	4	16	1	3	0	0	0	0	1	4	0
Billy Jurges, ss	.231	4	13	0	3	1	0	0	0	1	3	0
Tony Lazzeri, ph	.000	2	2	0	0	0	0	0	0	0	1	0
Bill Lee, p	.000	2	3	0	0	0	0	0	0	0	1	0
Joe Marty, of	.500	3	12	1	6	1	0	1	5	0	2	0
Ken O'Dea, c-1	.200	3	5	1	1	0	0	1	2	1	0	0
Vance Page, p	.000	1	0	0	0	0	0	0	0	0	0	0
Carl Reynolds, of-3	.000	4	12	0	0	0	0	0	0	1	3	0
Charlie Root, p	.000	1	0	0	0	0	0	0	0	0	0	0
Jack Russell, p	.000	2	0	0	0	0	0	0	0	0	0	0
TOTAL	.243		136	9	33	4	1	2	8	6	26	0

PITCHER	W	L	ERA	G	GS	CG	SV	SHO	IP	H	ER	BB	SO
Clay Bryant	0	1	6.75	1	1	0	0	0	5.1	6	4	5	3
Tex Carleton	0	0	INF	1	0	0	0	0	0.0	1	2	2	0
Dizzy Dean	0	1	6.48	2	1	0	0	0	8.1	8	6	1	2
Larry French	0	0	2.70	3	0	0	0	0	3.1	1	1	1	2
Bill Lee	0	2	2.45	2	2	0	0	0	11.0	15	3	1	8
Vance Page	0	0	13.50	1	0	0	0	0	1.1	2	2	0	0
Charlie Root	0	0	3.00	1	0	0	0	0	3.0	3	1	0	1
Jack Russell	0	0	0.00	2	0	0	0	0	1.2	1	0	1	0
TOTAL	0	4	5.03	13	4	0	0	0	34.0	37	19	11	16

GAME 1 AT CHI OCT 5

NY	020	000	100	3	12	1
CHI	001	000	000	1	9	1

Pitchers: RUFFING vs LEE, Russell (9)
Attendance: 43,642

GAME 2 AT CHI OCT 6

NY	020	000	022	6	7	2
CHI	102	000	000	3	11	0

Pitchers: GOMEZ, Murphy (8) vs J.DEAN, French (9)
Home Runs: Crosetti-NY, DiMaggio-NY
Attendance: 42,108

GAME 3 AT NY OCT 8

CHI	000	010	010	2	5	1
NY	000	022	01X	5	7	2

Pitchers: BRYANT, Russell (6), French (7) vs PEARSON
Home Runs: Dickey-NY, Gordon-NY, Marty-CHI
Attendance: 55,236

GAME 4 AT NY OCT 9

CHI	000	100	020	3	8	1
NY	030	001	04X	8	11	1

Pitchers: LEE, Root (4), Page (7), French (8), Carleton (8), J.Dean (8) vs RUFFING
Home Runs: Henrich-NY, O'Dea-CHI
Attendance: 59,847

The Yankees won their fourth consecutive World Series with their second sweep in a row. This time the victim was Cincinnati, in the Series for the first time since their tainted triumph over the Black Sox two decades earlier. New York had lost the power of Lou Gehrig (whose illness forced his retirement early in the season), but in the Series rookie outfielder Charlie Keller took up the slack. He led both clubs in batting, slugging, home runs, RBIs, hits, and runs, and hit one of the Series' two triples. His eight runs scored equalled those of the whole Cincinnati team.

The Yankees' Red Ruffing and Cincinnati's Paul Derringer hurled matching four-hitters through eight innings of Game One. With the score tied 1–1, Ruffing set the Reds down in order in the ninth. But in the bottom of the ninth Keller tripled off Derringer with one away, and scored the deciding run on catcher Bill Dickey's single.

Babe Dahlgren, Gehrig's replacement at first base, doubled in the third and later scored the Yankees' first run in Game Two, and homered in the next inning for New York's fourth and final run of the game. Red starter Bucky Walters stopped the Yankees after that, but they had more than enough runs for the win, as Monte Pearson held the Reds hitless through seven and wound up with a two-hit shutout.

Keller provided the margin of victory with a pair of two-run homers in the first and fifth innings of Game Three. Joe DiMaggio's two-run homer in the third and Bill Dickey's solo shot that followed Keller's homer in the fifth accounted for the rest of New York's runs in their 7–3 win.

No one scored through six innings of Game Four. Keller and Dickey then homered in the top of the seventh, but Red Rolfe's error at third in the last of the inning opened the way for the Reds to go ahead with three unearned runs. They earned a fourth run an inning later, but the Yankees tied it up with two in the ninth (one unearned) and took the lead in the tenth with three more runs (two unearned) on a walk, a single, and three more Red errors. Reliever Johnny Murphy held off a Red threat in the last of the tenth and the Series was over.

New York Yankees (AL), 4;
Cincinnati Reds (NL), 0

NY (A)

PLAYER/POS	AVG	G	AB	R	H	2B	3B	HR	RB	BB	SO	SB
Frankie Crosetti, ss	.063	4	16	2	1	0	0	0	1	2	2	0
Babe Dahlgren, 1b	.214	4	14	2	3	2	0	1	2	0	4	0
Bill Dickey, c	.267	4	15	2	4	0	0	2	5	1	2	0
Joe DiMaggio, of	.313	4	16	3	5	0	0	1	3	1	1	0
Lefty Gomez, p	.000	1	1	0	0	0	0	0	0	0	1	0
Joe Gordon, 2b	.143	4	14	1	2	0	0	0	1	0	2	0
Bump Hadley, p	.000	1	3	0	0	0	0	0	0	0	0	0
Oral Hildebrand, p	.000	1	1	0	0	0	0	0	0	0	1	0
Charlie Keller, of	.438	4	16	8	7	1	1	3	6	1	2	0
Johnny Murphy, p	.000	1	2	0	0	0	0	0	0	0	1	0
Monte Pearson, p	.000	1	2	0	0	0	0	0	0	0	1	0
Red Rolfe, 3b	.125	4	16	2	2	0	0	0	0	0	0	0
Red Ruffing, p	.333	1	3	0	1	0	0	0	0	0	1	0
George Selkirk, of	.167	4	12	0	2	1	0	0	0	3	2	0
Steve Sundra, p	.000	1	0	0	0	0	0	0	0	1	0	0
TOTAL	.206		131	20	27	4	1	7	18	9	20	0

PITCHER	W	L	ERA	G	GS	CG	SV	SHO	IP	H	ER	BB	SO
Lefty Gomez	0	0	9.00	1	1	0	0	0	1.0	3	1	0	1
Bump Hadley	1	0	2.25	1	0	0	0	0	8.0	7	2	3	2
Oral Hildebrand	0	0	0.00	1	1	0	0	0	4.0	2	0	0	3
Johnny Murphy	1	0	2.70	1	0	0	0	0	3.1	5	1	0	2
Monte Pearson	1	0	0.00	1	1	1	0	1	9.0	2	0	1	8
Red Ruffing	1	0	1.00	1	1	1	0	0	9.0	4	1	1	4
Steve Sundra	0	0	0.00	1	0	0	0	0	2.2	4	0	1	2
TOTAL	4	0	1.22	7	4	2	0	1	37.0	27	5	6	22

CIN (N)

PLAYER/POS	AVG	G	AB	R	H	2B	3B	HR	RB	BB	SO	SB
Wally Berger, of	.000	4	15	0	0	0	0	0	1	0	4	0
Nino Bongiovanni, ph	.000	1	1	0	0	0	0	0	0	0	0	0
Frenchy Bordagaray, pr	.000	2	0	0	0	0	0	0	0	0	0	0
Harry Craft, of	.091	4	11	0	1	0	0	0	0	0	6	0
Paul Derringer, p	.200	2	5	0	1	0	0	0	0	0	0	0
Lonny Frey, 2b	.000	4	17	0	0	0	0	0	0	1	4	0
Lee Gamble, ph	.000	1	1	0	0	0	0	0	0	0	1	0
Ival Goodman, of	.333	4	15	3	5	1	0	0	1	1	2	1
Lee Grissom, p	.000	1	0	0	0	0	0	0	0	0	0	0
Willard Hershberger, c-2	.500	3	2	0	1	0	0	0	1	0	0	0
Ernie Lombardi, c	.214	4	14	0	3	0	0	0	2	0	1	0
Frank Mc Cormick, 1b	.400	4	15	1	6	1	0	0	1	0	1	0
Whitey Moore, p	.000	1	1	0	0	0	0	0	0	0	0	0
Billy Myers, ss	.333	4	12	2	4	0	1	0	0	2	3	0
Al Simmons, of	.250	1	4	1	1	1	0	0	0	0	0	0
Junior Thompson, p	1.000	1	1	0	1	0	0	0	0	0	0	0
Bucky Walters, p	.000	2	3	0	0	0	0	0	0	0	0	0
Billy Werber, 3b	.250	4	16	1	4	0	0	0	2	2	0	0
TOTAL	.203		133	8	27	3	1	0	8	6	22	1

PITCHER	W	L	ERA	G	GS	CG	SV	SHO	IP	H	ER	BB	SO
Paul Derringer	0	1	2.35	2	2	1	0	0	15.1	9	4	3	9
Lee Grissom	0	0	0.00	1	0	0	0	0	1.1	0	0	1	0
Whitey Moore	0	0	0.00	1	0	0	0	0	3.0	0	0	0	2
Junior Thompson	0	1	13.50	1	1	0	0	0	4.2	5	7	4	3
Bucky Walters	0	2	4.91	2	2	1	0	0	11.0	13	6	1	6
TOTAL	0	4	4.33	7	4	2	0	0	35.1	27	17	9	20

GAME 1 AT NY OCT 4

CIN	000	100	000	1	4	0
NY	000	010	001	2	6	0

Pitchers: DERRINGER vs RUFFING
Attendance: 58,541

GAME 2 AT NY OCT 5

CIN	000	000	000	0	2	0
NY	003	100	00X	4	9	0

Pitchers: WALTERS vs PEARSON
Home Runs: Dalhgren-NY
Attendance: 59,791

GAME 3 AT CIN OCT 7

NY	202	030	000	7	5	1
CIN	120	000	000	3	10	4

Pitchers: Gomez, HADLEY (2) vs THOMPSON, Grissom (5), Moore (7)
Home Runs: Keller-NY (2), DiMaggio-NY, Dickey-NY
Attendance: 32,723

GAME 4 AT CIN OCT 8

NY	000	000	202	3	7	1
CIN	000	000	310	0	4	11	4

Pitchers: Hildebrand, Sundra (5), MURPHY (7) vs Derringer, WALTERS (8)
Home Runs: Keller-NY, Dickey-NY
Attendance: 32,794

The Tigers outpitched and out-slugged the Reds, and scored six more runs than the Reds did. What they failed to do was win the Series.

Tiger ace Bobo Newsom, who had enjoyed what would be his finest season in a long career, carried his mastery into the Series opener. Detroit gave him an early lead, driving out Red starter Paul Derringer with five runs in the second inning, and added a pair of runs in the fifth on Bruce Campbell's home run. Newsom, meanwhile, held the Reds to single runs in the fourth and eighth.

Cincinnati's Bucky Walters walked the first two Tigers he faced in Game Two, and both scored. But two Red runs in the second tied the game, Jimmy Ripple's two-run homer an inning later gave them the lead, and pitcher Walters scored an insurance run in the fourth after doubling. Another Tiger walk in the sixth led to their third run, but Walters retired the remaining Tigers in order.

The Series moved to Detroit and the lead to the Tigers in Game Three. Detroit's Rocky Bridges yielded ten hits and four runs, but his teammates responded with 13 hits and seven runs, including a pair of two-run homers by Rudy York and Pinky Higgins in the seventh. Cincinnati again evened the Series the next day, though, with five runs to support Derringer's five-hit, two-run pitching. Although Newsom's father had suffered a fatal heart attack the day after seeing his son win the opener, the son pitched Game Five, and improved on his previous performance with a three-hit shutout. Hank Greenberg's homer in the third inning accounted for the first three of the Tigers' eight runs in their lopsided win.

The Reds returned home needing to win the final two games. Like Newsom, Bucky Walters bettered his earlier win with a shutout in Game Six, and drove in two of the Reds' four runs, one with a solo homer in the eighth. In the Series finale, Newsom and Derringer found themselves evenly matched. The Tigers scored a run in the third, while Newsom held Cincinnati scoreless through six. But in the seventh, leadoff doubles by Frank McCormick and Jimmy Ripple, plus a successful bunt and a fly to deep center, gave the Reds two runs—all they needed as Derringer stopped the Tigers through the final six innings for the victory.

Cincinnati Reds (NL), 4;
Detroit Tigers (AL), 3

CIN (N)

PLAYER/POS	AVG	G	AB	R	H	2B	3B	HR	RB	BB	SO	SB
Morrie Arnovich, of	.000	1	1	0	0	0	0	0	0	0	0	0
Bill Baker, c	.250	3	4	1	1	0	0	0	0	0	1	0
Joe Beggs, p	.000	1	0	0	0	0	0	0	0	0	0	0
Harry Craft, ph	.000	1	1	0	0	0	0	0	0	0	0	0
Paul Derringer, p	.000	3	7	0	0	0	0	0	0	0	1	0
Lonny Frey, ph	.000	3	2	0	0	0	0	0	0	0	0	0
Ival Goodman, of	.276	7	29	5	8	2	0	0	5	0	3	0
Johnny Hutchings, p	.000	1	0	0	0	0	0	0	0	0	0	0
Eddie Joost, 2b	.200	7	25	0	5	0	0	0	2	1	2	0
Ernie Lombardi, c-1	.333	2	3	0	1	1	0	0	0	1	0	0
Frank Mc Cormick, 1b	.214	7	28	2	6	1	0	0	0	1	1	0
Mike Mc Cormick, of	.310	7	29	1	9	3	0	0	2	1	6	0
Whitey Moore, p	.000	3	2	0	0	0	0	0	0	0	1	0
Billy Myers, ss	.130	7	23	0	3	0	0	0	2	2	5	0
Elmer Riddle, p	.000	1	0	0	0	0	0	0	0	0	0	0
Lew Riggs, ph	.000	3	3	1	0	0	0	0	0	0	2	0
Jimmy Ripple, of	.333	7	21	3	7	2	0	1	6	4	2	0
Junior Thompson, p	.000	1	1	0	0	0	0	0	0	0	1	0
Jim Turner, p	.000	1	2	0	0	0	0	0	0	0	0	0
Johnny Vander Meer, p	.000	1	0	0	0	0	0	0	0	0	0	0
Bucky Walters, p	.286	2	7	2	2	1	0	1	2	0	1	0
Billy Werber, 3b	.370	7	27	5	10	4	0	0	2	4	2	0
Jimmie Wilson, c	.353	6	17	2	6	0	0	0	1	2	1	1
TOTAL	.250		232	22	58	14	0	2	21	15	30	1

PITCHER	W	L	ERA	G	GS	CG	SV	SHO	IP	H	ER	BB	SO
Joe Beggs	0	0	9.00	1	0	0	0	0	1.0	3	1	0	1
Paul Derringer	2	1	2.79	3	3	2	0	0	19.1	17	6	10	6
Johnny Hutchings	0	0	9.00	1	0	0	0	0	1.0	2	1	1	0
Whitey Moore	0	0	3.24	3	0	0	0	0	8.1	8	3	6	7
Elmer Riddle	0	0	0.00	1	0	0	0	0	1.0	0	0	0	2
Junior Thompson	0	1	16.20	1	1	0	0	0	3.1	8	6	4	2
Jim Turner	0	1	7.50	1	1	0	0	0	6.0	8	5	0	4
Johnny Vander Meer	0	0	0.00	1	0	0	0	0	3.0	2	0	3	2
Bucky Walters	2	0	1.50	2	2	2	0	1	18.0	8	3	6	6
TOTAL	4	3	3.69	14	7	4	0	1	61.0	56	25	30	30

DET (A)

PLAYER/POS	AVG	G	AB	R	H	2B	3B	HR	RB	BB	SO	SB
Earl Averill, ph	.000	3	3	0	0	0	0	0	0	0	0	0
Dick Bartell, ss	.269	7	26	2	7	2	0	0	3	3	3	0
Tommy Bridges, p	.000	1	3	0	0	0	0	0	0	0	1	0
Bruce Campbell, of	.360	7	25	4	9	1	0	1	5	4	4	0
Frank Croucher, ss	.000	1	0	0	0	0	0	0	0	0	0	0
Pete Fox, ph	.000	1	1	0	0	0	0	0	0	0	0	0
Charlie Gehringer, 2b	.214	7	28	3	6	0	0	0	1	2	0	0
Johnny Gorsica, p	.000	2	4	0	0	0	0	0	0	0	2	0
Hank Greenberg, of	.357	7	28	5	10	2	1	1	6	2	5	0
Pinky Higgins, 3b	.333	7	24	2	8	3	1	1	6	3	3	0
Fred Hutchinson, p	.000	1	0	0	0	0	0	0	0	0	0	0
Barney Mc Cosky, of	.304	7	23	5	7	1	0	0	1	7	0	0
Archie Mc Kain, p	.000	1	0	0	0	0	0	0	0	0	0	0
Bobo Newsom, p	.100	3	10	1	1	0	0	0	0	0	1	0
Schoolboy Rowe, p	.000	2	1	0	0	0	0	0	0	0	1	0
Clay Smith, p	.000	1	1	0	0	0	0	0	0	0	1	0
Billy Sullivan, c-4	.154	5	13	3	2	0	0	0	0	5	2	0
Birdie Tebbetts, c-3	.000	4	11	0	0	0	0	0	0	0	0	0
Dizzy Trout, p	.000	1	1	0	0	0	0	0	0	0	0	0
Rudy York, 1b	.231	7	26	3	6	0	1	1	2	4	7	0
TOTAL	.246		228	28	56	9	3	4	24	30	30	0

PITCHER	W	L	ERA	G	GS	CG	SV	SHO	IP	H	ER	BB	SO
Tommy Bridges	1	0	3.00	1	1	1	0	0	9.0	10	3	1	5
Johnny Gorsica	0	0	0.79	2	0	0	0	0	11.1	6	1	4	4
Fred Hutchinson	0	0	9.00	1	0	0	0	0	1.0	1	1	1	1
Archie Mc Kain	0	0	3.00	1	0	0	0	0	3.0	4	1	0	0
Bobo Newsom	2	1	1.38	3	3	3	0	1	26.0	18	4	4	17
Schoolboy Rowe	0	2	17.18	2	2	0	0	0	3.2	12	7	1	1
Clay Smith	0	0	2.25	1	0	0	0	0	4.0	1	1	3	1
Dizzy Trout	0	1	9.00	1	1	0	0	0	2.0	6	2	1	1
TOTAL	3	4	3.00	12	7	4	0	1	60.0	58	20	15	30

GAME 1 AT CIN OCT 2

DET	050	020	000	7	10	1
CIN	000	100	010	2	8	3

Pitchers: NEWSOM vs DERRINGER, Moore (2), Riddle (9)
Home Runs: Campbell-DET
Attendance: 31,793

GAME 2 AT CIN OCT 3

DET	200	001	000	3	3	1
CIN	022	100	00X	5	9	0

Pitchers: ROWE, Gorsica (4) vs WALTERS
Home Runs: Ripple-CIN
Attendance: 30,640

GAME 3 AT DET OCT 4

CIN	100	000	012	4	10	1
DET	000	100	42X	7	13	1

Pitchers: TURNER, Moore (7), Beggs (8) vs BRIDGES
Home Runs: York-DET, Higgins-DET
Attendance: 52,877

GAME 4 AT DET OCT 5

CIN	201	100	010	5	11	1
DET	001	001	000	2	5	1

Pitchers: DERRINGER vs TROUT, Smith (3), McKain (7)
Attendance: 54,093

GAME 5 AT DET OCT 6

CIN	000	000	000	0	3	0
DET	003	400	01X	8	13	0

Pitchers: THOMPSON, Moore (4), Vander Meer (5), Hutchings (8) vs NEWSOM
Home Runs: Greenberg-DET
Attendance: 55,189

GAME 6 AT CIN OCT 7

DET	000	000	000	0	5	0
CIN	200	001	01X	4	10	2

Pitchers: ROWE, Gorsica (1), Hutchinson (8) vs WALTERS
Home Runs: Walters-CIN
Attendance: 30,481

GAME 7 AT CIN OCT 8

DET	001	000	000	1	7	0
CIN	000	000	20X	2	7	1

Pitchers: NEWSOM vs DERRINGER
Attendance: 26,854

Dodger catcher Mickey Owen's dropped third strike in Game Four was the Series' memorable boner, but it was not the chief cause of Brooklyn's downfall. Yankee pitching was. Three Yankee starters hurled complete-game wins, with each giving the Dodgers only one earned run. And relief ace Johnny Murphy hurled two-hit shutout ball in six innings over two games, winning one.

Yankee Joe Gordon opened the Series scoring with a solo homer in the second inning of Game One, and the Yankees added runs in the fourth and sixth. Owen tripled in the Dodgers' first run in the fifth, and pinch hitter Lew Riggs singled in an unearned run in the seventh. But Yankee starter Red Ruffing held on to his slim lead through the final two innings for the win.

Dodger ace Whitlow Wyatt gave the Yankees single runs in the second and third innings of Game Two, but held them scoreless the rest of the way. Meanwhile, the Dodgers tied the game in the fifth, and scored an unearned run in the sixth to finish the scoring and give Brooklyn its only win of the Series.

Freddie Fitzsimmons, with the Dodgers' best pitching of the Series, dueled Yankee Marius Russo through seven scoreless innings in Game Three. But Fitzsimmons's final out of the seventh—a line drive by Russo that bounced off Fitzsimmons's leg into the glove of shortstop Pee Wee Reese—broke his kneecap. Hugh Casey, who replaced Fitzsimmons in the eighth, retired the first batter, but then gave up four straight singles for two runs before being removed. The Yankees scored no more, and Brooklyn came up with a run in the last of the eighth. But Russo stopped the Dodgers in order in the ninth to preserve his lead for the Yankees' second win.

In Game Four, for the first time in the Series, the margin of victory was more than one run, thanks to catcher Owen's famous boner. Brooklyn held the lead 4–3 with two out in the top of the ninth. Dodger reliever Casey, who had shut out the Yankees since coming on in the fifth inning, then struck out Tommy Henrich for what should have been the game-ending out. But Owen let the ball get by him, and before the third out was recorded Casey had given up a single, two doubles, and two walks—and four runs, for Brooklyn's third loss.

The Yankees scored twice off Wyatt in the second inning of Game Five, and once more in the fifth (on Henrich's home run), as Tiny Bonham held Brooklyn to four hits and a single run to clinch the ninth Yankee world title.

New York Yankees (AL), 4; Brooklyn Dodgers (NL), 1

NY (A)

PLAYER/POS	AVG	G	AB	R	H	2B	3B	HR	RB	BB	SO	SB
Tiny Bonham, p	.000	1	4	0	0	0	0	0	0	0	4	0
Frenchy Bordagaray, pr	.000	1	0	0	0	0	0	0	0	0	0	0
Marv Breuer, p	.000	1	1	0	0	0	0	0	0	0	0	0
Spud Chandler, p	.500	1	2	0	1	0	0	0	1	0	0	0
Bill Dickey, c	.167	5	18	3	3	1	0	0	1	3	1	0
Joe DiMaggio, of	.263	5	19	1	5	0	0	0	1	2	2	0
Atley Donald, p	.000	1	2	0	0	0	0	0	0	0	1	0
Joe Gordon, 2b	.500	5	14	2	7	1	1	1	5	7	0	0
Tommy Henrich, of	.167	5	18	4	3	1	0	1	1	3	3	0
Charlie Keller, of	.389	5	18	5	7	2	0	0	5	3	1	0
Johnny Murphy, p	.000	2	2	0	0	0	0	0	0	0	1	0
Phil Rizzuto, ss	.111	5	18	0	2	0	0	0	0	3	1	1
Red Rolfe, 3b	.300	5	20	2	6	0	0	0	0	2	1	0
Buddy Rosar, c	.000	1	0	0	0	0	0	0	0	0	0	0
Red Ruffing, p	.000	1	3	0	0	0	0	0	0	0	0	0
Marius Russo, p	.000	1	4	0	0	0	0	0	0	0	1	0
George Selkirk, ph	.500	2	2	0	1	0	0	0	0	0	0	0
Johnny Sturm, 1b	.286	5	21	0	6	0	0	0	2	0	2	1
TOTAL	.247		166	17	41	5	1	2	16	23	18	2

PITCHER	W	L	ERA	G	GS	CG	SV	SHO	IP	H	ER	BB	SO
Tiny Bonham	1	0	1.00	1	1	1	0	0	9.0	4	1	2	2
Marv Breuer	0	0	0.00	1	0	0	0	0	3.0	3	0	1	2
Spud Chandler	0	1	3.60	1	1	0	0	0	5.0	4	2	2	2
Atley Donald	0	0	9.00	1	1	0	0	0	4.0	6	4	3	2
Johnny Murphy	1	0	0.00	2	0	0	0	0	6.0	2	0	1	3
Red Ruffing	1	0	1.00	1	1	1	0	0	9.0	6	1	3	5
Marius Russo	1	0	1.00	1	1	1	0	0	9.0	4	1	2	5
TOTAL	4	1	1.80	8	5	3	0	0	45.0	29	9	14	21

BRO (N)

PLAYER/POS	AVG	G	AB	R	H	2B	3B	HR	RB	BB	SO	SB
Johnny Allen, p	.000	3	0	0	0	0	0	0	0	0	0	0
Dolph Camilli, 1b	.167	5	18	1	3	1	0	0	1	1	6	0
Hugh Casey, p	.500	3	2	0	1	0	0	0	0	0	1	0
Pete Coscarart, 2b	.000	3	7	1	0	0	0	0	0	1	2	0
Curt Davis, p	.000	1	2	0	0	0	0	0	0	0	0	0
Freddie Fitzsimmons, p	.000	1	2	0	0	0	0	0	0	0	0	0
Herman Franks, c	.000	1	1	0	0	0	0	0	0	0	0	0
Larry French, p	.000	2	0	0	0	0	0	0	0	0	0	0
Augie Galan, ph	.000	2	2	0	0	0	0	0	0	0	1	0
Billy Herman, 2b	.125	4	8	0	1	0	0	0	0	2	0	0
Kirby Higbe, p	1.000	1	1	0	1	0	0	0	0	0	0	0
Cookie Lavagetto, 3b	.100	3	10	1	1	0	0	0	0	2	0	0
Joe Medwick, of	.235	5	17	1	4	1	0	0	0	1	2	0
Mickey Owen, c	.167	5	12	1	2	0	1	0	2	3	0	0
Pee Wee Reese, ss	.200	5	20	1	4	0	0	0	2	0	0	0
Pete Reiser, of	.200	5	20	1	4	1	1	1	3	1	6	0
Lew Riggs, 3b-2	.250	3	8	0	2	0	0	0	1	1	1	0
Dixie Walker, of	.222	5	18	3	4	2	0	0	0	2	1	0
Jimmy Wasdell, of-1	.200	3	5	0	1	1	0	0	2	0	0	0
Whit Wyatt, p	.167	2	6	1	1	1	0	0	0	0	1	0
TOTAL	.182		159	11	29	7	2	1	11	14	21	0

PITCHER	W	L	ERA	G	GS	CG	SV	SHO	IP	H	ER	BB	SO
Johnny Allen	0	0	0.00	3	0	0	0	0	3.2	1	0	3	0
Hugh Casey	0	2	3.38	3	0	0	0	0	5.1	9	2	2	1
Curt Davis	0	1	5.06	1	1	0	0	0	5.1	6	3	3	1
Freddie Fitzsimmons	0	0	0.00	1	1	0	0	0	7.0	4	0	3	1
Larry French	0	0	0.00	2	0	0	0	0	1.0	0	0	0	0
Kirby Higbe	0	0	7.36	1	1	0	0	0	3.2	6	3	2	1
Whit Wyatt	1	1	2.50	2	2	2	0	0	18.0	15	5	10	14
TOTAL	1	4	2.66	13	5	2	0	0	44.0	41	13	23	18

GAME 1 AT NY OCT 1

BRO	000	010	100	2	6	0
NY	010	101	00X	3	6	1

Pitchers: DAVIS, Casey (6), Allen (7) vs RUFFING
Home Runs: Gordon-NY
Attendance: 68,540

GAME 2 AT NY OCT 2

BRO	000	021	000	3	6	2
NY	011	000	000	2	9	1

Pitchers: WYATT vs CHANDLER, Murphy (6)
Attendance: 66,248

GAME 3 AT BRO OCT 4

NY	000	000	020	2	8	0
BRO	000	000	010	1	4	0

Pitchers: RUSSO vs Fitzsimmons, CASEY (8), French (8), Allen (9)
Attendance: 33,100

GAME 4 AT BRO OCT 5

NY	100	200	004	7	12	0
BRO	000	220	000	4	9	1

Pitchers: Donald, Breuer (5), MURPHY (8) VS Higbe, French (4), Allen (5), CASEY (5)
Home Runs: Reiser-BRO
Attendance: 33,813

GAME 5 AT BRO OCT 6

NY	020	010	000	3	6	0
BRO	001	000	000	1	4	1

Pitchers: BONHAM vs WYATT
Home Runs: Henrich-NY
Attendance: 34,072

Cardinal rookies Stan Musial and Whitey Kurowski drove in game-winning runs for rookie-pitcher Johnny Beazley in Games Two and Five as the major leagues' youngest team upset the Yankees. New York won only the opener, building a seven-run lead for starter Red Ruffing, who shut out St. Louis on one hit through 8⅓ innings before giving up four hits and four harmless runs in the last of the ninth.

The Cardinals scored first in Game Two on catcher Walker Cooper's two-run double in the first inning. Kurowski tripled in a third Cardinal run in the seventh, but pitcher Beazley, after holding the Yankees scoreless through seven innings, gave up three runs in the eighth on two singles and Charlie Keller's two-run homer. St. Louis regained the lead a half inning later when Musial singled home Enos Slaughter (who had doubled), and stifled a threat in the ninth as Slaughter's great throw from right field nailed a Yankee runner at third.

Second-year Cardinal pitcher Ernie White turned in the Series' top mound performance with a six-single, no-walk shutout in Game Three (aided by outfielders Musial and Slaughter, who hauled in a pair of potential home run blasts in the seventh inning). The Cards managed only five singles themselves, but they combined one with a walk, sacrifice, and ground out for a run in the third, and sandwiched a Yankee error with two hits in the ninth for an unearned insurance run.

Game Four saw the Series' heaviest hitting. New York scored once in the first, but the Cards exploded in the fourth for six runs on six hits and two walks. The Yankees tied it up two innings later, with Keller's three-run homer the feature of the five-run inning. St. Louis took the lead for good with two runs in the seventh, and added a ninth run in the ninth.

Beazley and Ruffing tangled in Game Five. Phil Rizzuto's solo homer put New York ahead in the first inning. Slaughter's fourth-inning home run tied the score, but the Yankees regained the lead with a run later in the inning. The Cards retied the game in the sixth, and took the final lead when Kurowski homered for two runs in the top of the ninth. The Yankees threatened in the last of the ninth, putting their first two men on with a single and error. But catcher Cooper picked a runner off second, second baseman Jimmy Brown redeemed his earlier error with a sparkling catch, then fielded a routine grounder for the final out and the Cardinal triumph.

St. Louis Cardinals (NL), 4; New York Yankees (AL), 1

STL (N)

PLAYER/POS	AVG	G	AB	R	H	2B	3B	HR	RB	BB	SO	SB
Johnny Beazley, p	.143	2	7	0	1	0	0	0	0	0	5	0
Jimmy Brown, 2b	.300	5	20	2	6	0	0	0	1	0	0	0
Mort Cooper, p	.200	2	5	1	1	0	0	0	2	0	1	0
Walker Cooper, c	.286	5	21	3	6	1	0	0	4	0	1	0
Creepy Crespi, pr	.000	1	0	1	0	0	0	0	0	0	0	0
Harry Gumbert, p	.000	2	0	0	0	0	0	0	0	0	0	0
Johnny Hopp, 1b	.176	5	17	3	3	0	0	0	0	1	1	0
Whitey Kurowski, 3b	.267	5	15	3	4	0	1	1	5	2	3	0
Max Lanier, p	1.000	2	1	0	1	0	0	0	1	0	0	0
Marty Marion, ss	.111	5	18	2	2	0	1	0	3	1	2	0
Terry Moore, of	.294	5	17	2	5	1	0	0	2	2	3	0
Stan Musial, of	.222	5	18	2	4	1	0	0	2	4	0	0
Ken O'Dea, ph	1.000	1	1	0	1	0	0	0	1	0	0	0
Howie Pollet, p	.000	1	0	0	0	0	0	0	0	0	0	0
Ray Sanders, ph	.000	2	1	1	0	0	0	0	0	1	0	0
Enos Slaughter, of	.263	5	19	3	5	1	0	1	2	3	2	0
Harry Walker, ph	.000	1	1	0	0	0	0	0	0	0	1	0
Ernie White, p	.000	1	2	0	0	0	0	0	0	0	0	0
TOTAL	.239		163	23	39	4	2	2	23	17	19	0

PITCHER	W	L	ERA	G	GS	CG	SV	SHO	IP	H	ER	BB	SO
Johnny Beazley	2	0	2.50	2	2	2	0	0	18.0	17	5	3	6
Mort Cooper	0	1	5.54	2	2	0	0	0	13.0	17	8	4	9
Harry Gumbert	0	0	0.00	2	0	0	0	0	0.2	1	0	0	0
Max Lanier	1	0	0.00	2	0	0	0	0	4.0	3	0	1	1
Howie Pollet	0	0	0.00	1	0	0	0	0	0.1	0	0	0	0
Ernie White	1	0	0.00	1	1	1	0	1	9.0	6	0	0	6
TOTAL	4	1	2.60	10	5	3	0	1	45.0	44	13	8	22

NY (A)

PLAYER/POS	AVG	G	AB	R	H	2B	3B	HR	RB	BB	SO	SB
Tiny Bonham, p	.000	2	2	0	0	0	0	0	0	0	1	0
Hank Borowy, p	.000	1	1	0	0	0	0	0	0	0	1	0
Marv Breuer, p	.000	1	0	0	0	0	0	0	0	0	0	0
Spud Chandler, p	.000	2	2	0	0	0	0	0	0	0	1	0
Frankie Crosetti, 3b	.000	1	3	0	0	0	0	0	0	0	1	0
Roy Cullenbine, of	.263	5	19	3	5	1	0	0	2	1	2	1
Bill Dickey, c	.263	5	19	1	5	0	0	0	0	1	0	0
Joe DiMaggio, of	.333	5	21	3	7	0	0	0	3	0	1	0
Atley Donald, p	.000	1	2	0	0	0	0	0	0	0	0	0
Joe Gordon, 2b	.095	5	21	1	2	1	0	0	0	0	7	0
Buddy Hassett, 1b	.333	3	9	1	3	1	0	0	2	0	1	0
Charlie Keller, of	.200	5	20	2	4	0	0	2	5	1	3	0
Jerry Priddy, 1b-3,3b-1	.100	3	10	0	1	1	0	0	1	1	0	0
Phil Rizzuto, ss	.381	5	21	2	8	0	0	1	1	2	1	2
Red Rolfe, 3b	.353	4	17	5	6	2	0	0	0	1	2	0
Buddy Rosar, ph	1.000	1	1	0	1	0	0	0	0	0	0	0
Red Ruffing, p-2	.222	4	9	0	2	0	0	0	0	0	2	0
George Selkirk, ph	.000	1	1	0	0	0	0	0	0	0	0	0
Tuck Stainback, pr	.000	2	0	0	0	0	0	0	0	0	0	0
Jim Turner, p	.000	1	0	0	0	0	0	0	0	0	0	0
TOTAL	.247		178	18	44	6	0	3	14	8	22	3

PITCHER	W	L	ERA	G	GS	CG	SV	SHO	IP	H	ER	BB	SO
Tiny Bonham	0	1	4.09	2	1	1	0	0	11.0	9	5	3	3
Hank Borowy	0	0	18.00	1	1	0	0	0	3.0	6	6	3	1
Marv Breuer	0	0	INF	1	0	0	0	0	0.0	2	0	0	0
Spud Chandler	0	1	1.08	2	1	0	1	0	8.1	5	1	1	3
Atley Donald	0	1	6.00	1	0	0	0	0	3.0	3	2	2	1
Red Ruffing	1	1	4.08	2	2	1	0	0	17.2	14	8	7	11
Jim Turner	0	0	0.00	1	0	0	0	0	1.0	0	0	1	0
TOTAL	1	4	4.50	10	5	2	1	0	44.0	39	22	17	19

GAME 1 AT STL SEPT 30

NY	000 110 032	7 11 0
STL	000 000 004	4 7 4

Pitchers: RUFFING, Chandler (9) vs M.COOPER, Gumbert (8), Lanier (9)
Attendance: 34,769

GAME 2 AT STL OCT 1

NY	000 000 030	3 10 2
STL	200 000 110	4 6 0

Pitchers: BONHAM vs BEAZLEY
Home Runs: Keller-NY
Attendance: 34,255

GAME 3 AT NY OCT 2

STL	001 000 001	2 5 1
NY	000 000 000	0 6 1

Pitchers: WHITE vs CHANDLER, Breuer (9), Turner (9)
Attendance: 69,123

GAME 4 AT NY OCT 4

STL	000 600 201	9 12 1
NY	100 004 000	6 10 1

Pitchers: M.Cooper, Gumbert (6), Pollet (6), LANIER (7) vs Borowy, DONALD (4), Bonham (7)
Home Runs: Keller-NY
Attendance: 69,902

GAME 5 AT NY OCT 5

STL	000 101 002	4 9 4
NY	100 100 000	2 7 1

Pitchers: BEAZLEY vs RUFFING
Home Runs: Rizzuto-NY, Slaughter-STL, Kurowski-STL
Attendance: 69,052

Although both clubs had lost players to military service since the previous World Series, history seemed to be repeating itself. The Cardinals lost to the Yankees in the opener and won the second game, as they had the previous year. But this year it was the Yankees who took the next three games and the Series, as fine Cardinal pitching gave way to even finer Yankee mound work.

Yankee pitcher Spurgeon (Spud) Chandler, coming off his finest season (20–4, 1.64 ERA), continued to overwhelm the opposition in the Series. He held the Cards to two runs (only one earned) in Game One, and the Yankees took advantage of a wild pitch to score two runs of their own in the sixth inning, breaking a 2–2 tie for a 4–2 win. Cardinal shortstop Marty Marion homered in the third inning for the first Cardinal run the next day, and first baseman Ray Sanders homered for two more runs in a three-run fourth. Cardinal ace Mort Cooper held New York to one run on four hits through eight innings, but he weakened in the last of the ninth, giving up a double and triple to the first two batters. But only two runs scored as he retired the next three men for St. Louis's only victory.

The Cardinals carried a 2–1 lead into the last of the eighth inning of Game Three, when a pair of errors, two walks, and five Yankee hits (including Billy Johnson's three-run triple) undid them. Yankee fireman Johnny Murphy retired the Cards in order in the ninth to save Hank Borowy's win. Max Lanier and Harry Brecheen held New York to just two runs (and six hits) in Game Four, but Yankee pitcher Marius Russo gave up only one run—and that was scored only because of two Yankee errors in the seventh inning.

In the fifth and (as it turned out) final game, St. Louis couldn't score even an unearned run, although they knocked Spud Chandler for ten hits. But they were all singles and were spaced harmlessly over eight of the nine innings. Three St. Louis pitchers held the Yankees to just seven hits, six of them singles. But in the sixth inning Bill Dickey followed one of the Yankee singles with the game's only extra-base hit—a home run—to produce the game's only scoring, and bring the Yankees yet another world championship, their tenth.

New York Yankees (AL), 4;
St. Louis Cardinals (NL), 1

NY (A)

PLAYER/POS	AVG	G	AB	R	H	2B	3B	HR	RB	BB	SO	SB
Tiny Bonham, p	.000	1	2	0	0	0	0	0	0	0	0	0
Hank Borowy, p	.500	1	2	1	1	1	0	0	0	0	1	0
Spud Chandler, p	.167	2	6	0	1	0	0	0	0	0	2	0
Frankie Crosetti, ss	.278	5	18	4	5	0	0	0	1	2	3	1
Bill Dickey, c	.278	5	18	1	5	0	0	1	4	2	2	0
Nick Etten, 1b	.105	5	19	0	2	0	0	0	2	1	2	0
Joe Gordon, 2b	.235	5	17	2	4	1	0	1	2	3	3	0
Billy Johnson, 3b	.300	5	20	3	6	1	1	0	3	0	3	0
Charlie Keller, of	.222	5	18	3	4	0	1	0	2	2	5	1
Johnny Lindell, of	.111	4	9	1	1	0	0	0	0	1	4	0
Bud Metheny, of	.125	2	8	0	1	0	0	0	0	0	2	0
Johnny Murphy, p	.000	2	0	0	0	0	0	0	0	0	0	0
Marius Russo, p	.667	1	3	1	2	2	0	0	0	1	1	0
Tuck Stainback, of	.176	5	17	0	3	0	0	0	0	0	2	0
Snuffy Stirnweiss, ph	.000	1	1	1	0	0	0	0	0	0	0	0
Roy Weatherly, ph	.000	1	1	0	0	0	0	0	0	0	0	0
TOTAL	.220		159	17	35	5	2	2	14	12	30	2

PITCHER	W	L	ERA	G	GS	CG	SV	SHO	IP	H	ER	BB	SO
Tiny Bonham	0	1	4.50	1	1	0	0	0	8.0	6	4	3	9
Hank Borowy	1	0	2.25	1	1	0	0	0	8.0	6	2	3	4
Spud Chandler	2	0	0.50	2	2	2	0	1	18.0	17	1	3	10
Johnny Murphy	0	0	0.00	2	0	0	1	0	2.0	1	0	1	1
Marius Russo	1	0	0.00	1	1	1	0	0	9.0	7	0	1	2
TOTAL	4	1	1.40	7	5	3	1	1	45.0	37	7	11	26

STL (N)

PLAYER/POS	AVG	G	AB	R	H	2B	3B	HR	RB	BB	SO	SB
Al Brazle, p	.000	1	3	0	0	0	0	0	0	0	1	0
Harry Brecheen, p	.000	3	0	0	0	0	0	0	0	0	0	0
Mort Cooper, p	.000	2	5	0	0	0	0	0	0	0	3	0
Walker Cooper, c	.294	5	17	1	5	0	0	0	0	0	1	0
Frank Demaree, ph	.000	1	1	0	0	0	0	0	0	0	0	0
Murry Dickson, p	.000	1	0	0	0	0	0	0	0	0	0	0
Debs Garms, of-1	.000	2	5	0	0	0	0	0	0	0	2	0
Johnny Hopp, of	.000	1	4	0	0	0	0	0	0	0	1	0
Lou Klein, 2b	.136	5	22	0	3	0	0	0	0	1	2	0
Howie Krist, p	.000	1	0	0	0	0	0	0	0	0	0	0
Whitey Kurowski, 3b	.222	5	18	2	4	1	0	0	1	0	3	0
Max Lanier, p	.250	3	4	0	1	0	0	0	1	0	0	0
Danny Litwhiler, of-4	.267	5	15	0	4	1	0	0	2	2	4	0
Marty Marion, ss	.357	5	14	1	5	2	0	1	2	3	1	1
Stan Musial, of	.278	5	18	2	5	0	0	0	0	2	2	0
Sam Narron, ph	.000	1	1	0	0	0	0	0	0	0	0	0
Ken O'Dea, c-1	.667	2	3	0	2	0	0	0	0	0	0	0
Ray Sanders, 1b	.294	5	17	3	5	0	0	1	2	3	4	0
Harry Walker, of	.167	5	18	0	3	1	0	0	0	0	2	0
Ernie White, pr	.000	1	0	0	0	0	0	0	0	0	0	0
TOTAL	.224		165	9	37	5	0	2	8	11	26	1

PITCHER	W	L	ERA	G	GS	CG	SV	SHO	IP	H	ER	BB	SO
Al Brazle	0	1	3.68	1	1	0	0	0	7.1	5	3	2	4
Harry Brecheen	0	1	2.45	3	0	0	0	0	3.2	5	1	3	3
Mort Cooper	1	1	2.81	2	2	1	0	0	16.0	11	5	3	10
Murry Dickson	0	0	0.00	1	0	0	0	0	0.2	0	0	1	0
Howie Krist	0	0	INF	1	0	0	0	0	0.0	1	0	0	0
Max Lanier	0	1	1.76	3	2	0	0	0	15.1	13	3	3	13
TOTAL	1	4	2.51	11	5	1	0	0	43.0	35	12	12	30

GAME 1 AT NY OCT 5

STL   010 010 000   2 7 2
NY   000 202 00X   4 8 2

Pitchers: LANIER vs CHANDLER
Home Runs: Gordon-NY
Attendance: 68,676

GAME 2 AT NY OCT 6

STL   001 300 000   4 7 2
NY   000 100 002   3 6 0

Pitchers: M.COOPER vs BONHAM, Murphy (9)
Home Runs: Marion-STL, Sanders-STL
Attendance: 68,578

GAME 3 AT NY OCT 7

STL   000 200 000   2 6 4
NY   000 001 05X   6 8 0

Pitchers: BRAZLE, Krist (8), Brecheen (8) VS BOROWY, Murphy (9)
Attendance: 69,990

GAME 4 AT STL OCT 10

NY   000 100 010   2 6 2
STL   000 000 100   1 7 1

Pitchers: RUSSO vs Lanier, BRECHEEN (8)
Attendance: 36,196

GAME 5 AT STL OCT 11

NY   000 002 000   2 7 1
STL   000 000 000   0 10 1

Pitchers: CHANDLER vs M.COOPER, Lanier (8), Dickson (9)
Home Runs: Dickey-NY
Attendance: 33,872

The Cardinals—a much stronger team in the regular season—entered the World Series against their landlord Browns (who owned Sportsman's Park, where both teams played) as clear favorites. They won the Series in six games, but if the Browns' fielding had been as good as their pitching the outcome might have been different.

The Browns won the opener on Denny Galehouse's strong pitching. Galehouse gave up seven hits and four walks, but held the Cards scoreless for 8⅔ innings before yielding a run in the ninth. Cardinal ace Mort Cooper also pitched well in six of his seven innings. He allowed the Browns only two hits, but they came back to back in the fourth inning—a single followed by George McQuinn's home run—to give the Browns all the scoring they needed.

Brown pitcher Nelson Potter's two errors (a fumble and a wild throw) on a bunt in the third inning of Game Two led to an unearned run, and third baseman Mark Christman's fumble an inning later set up a second unearned run. The Browns tied the score with a pair of runs on three two-out hits in the seventh—enough to have won an error-free game—but lost when the Cardinals singled a run across in the last of the eleventh.

Two Brown errors led to a pair of unearned runs in Game Three, but Jack Kramer held the Cards scoreless apart from that, striking out ten. Meanwhile, Brown hitters tied together five singles with two out in the third inning for three runs, adding a fourth run on a wild pitch before the inning ended. In the seventh the Browns tacked on two more runs for a comfortable win and a 2–1 Series advantage.

The Cardinals came back to earn victory in Games Four and Five, knocking three Brown pitchers for 12 hits in Game Four (including Stan Musial's two-run homer in the first) and a 5–1 win for pitcher Harry Brecheen, then rapping Denny Galehouse for two solo homers in Game Five (by Danny Litwhiler and Ray Sanders) for the game's only scoring as Mort Cooper fanned 12 Browns while shutting them out.

Two of the Cardinals' three runs in the fourth inning of Game Six were made possible by Brown shortstop Vern Stephens's throwing error. They provided the margin of victory, as Cardinal pitchers Max Lanier and Ted Wilks held the Browns to three hits and a single run, and brought the Cards their second world title in three years.

St. Louis Cardinals (NL), 4; St. Louis Browns (AL), 2

STL (N)

PLAYER/POS	AVG	G	AB	R	H	2B	3B	HR	RB	BB	SO	SB
Augie Bergamo, of-2	.000	3	6	0	0	0	0	0	1	2	3	0
Harry Brecheen, p	.000	1	4	0	0	0	0	0	0	0	1	0
Bud Byerly, p	.000	1	0	0	0	0	0	0	0	0	0	0
Mort Cooper, p	.000	2	4	0	0	0	0	0	0	0	2	0
Walker Cooper, c	.318	6	22	1	7	2	1	0	2	3	2	0
Blix Donnelly, p	.000	2	1	0	0	0	0	0	0	0	1	0
George Fallon, 2b	.000	2	2	0	0	0	0	0	0	0	1	0
Debs Garms, ph	.000	2	2	0	0	0	0	0	0	0	0	0
Johnny Hopp, of	.185	6	27	2	5	0	0	0	0	0	8	0
Al Jurisich, p	.000	1	0	0	0	0	0	0	0	0	0	0
Whitey Kurowski, 3b	.217	6	23	2	5	1	0	0	1	1	4	0
Max Lanier, p	.500	2	4	0	2	0	0	0	1	0	0	0
Danny Litwhiler, of	.200	5	20	2	4	1	0	1	1	2	7	0
Marty Marion, ss	.227	6	22	1	5	3	0	0	2	2	3	0
Stan Musial, of	.304	6	23	2	7	2	0	1	2	2	0	0
Ken O'Dea, ph	.333	3	3	0	1	0	0	0	2	0	0	0
Ray Sanders, 1b	.286	6	21	5	6	0	0	1	1	5	8	0
Freddy Schmidt, p	.000	1	1	0	0	0	0	0	0	0	1	0
Emil Verban, 2b	.412	6	17	1	7	0	0	0	2	2	0	0
Ted Wilks, p	.000	2	2	0	0	0	0	0	0	0	2	0
TOTAL	.240		204	16	49	9	1	3	15	19	43	0

PITCHER	W	L	ERA	G	GS	CG	SV	SHO	IP	H	ER	BB	SO
Harry Brecheen	1	0	1.00	1	1	1	0	0	9.0	9	1	4	4
Bud Byerly	0	0	0.00	1	0	0	0	0	1.1	0	0	0	1
Mort Cooper	1	1	1.13	2	2	1	0	1	16.0	9	2	5	16
Blix Donnelly	1	0	0.00	2	0	0	0	0	6.0	2	0	1	9
Al Jurisich	0	0	27.00	1	0	0	0	0	0.2	2	2	1	0
Max Lanier	1	0	2.19	2	2	0	0	0	12.1	8	3	8	11
Freddy Schmidt	0	0	0.00	1	0	0	0	0	3.1	1	0	1	1
Ted Wilks	0	1	5.68	2	1	0	1	0	6.1	5	4	3	7
TOTAL	4	2	1.96	12	6	2	1	1	55.0	36	12	23	49

STL (A)

PLAYER/POS	AVG	G	AB	R	H	2B	3B	HR	RB	BB	SO	SB
Floyd Baker, 2b	.000	2	2	0	0	0	0	0	0	0	2	0
Milt Byrnes, ph	.000	3	2	0	0	0	0	0	0	1	2	0
Mike Chartak, ph	.000	2	2	0	0	0	0	0	0	0	2	0
Mark Christman, 3b	.091	6	22	0	2	0	0	0	1	0	6	0
Ellis Clary, ph	.000	1	1	0	0	0	0	0	0	0	0	0
Denny Galehouse, p	.200	2	5	0	1	0	0	0	0	1	1	0
Don Gutteridge, 2b	.143	6	21	1	3	1	0	0	0	3	5	0
Red Hayworth, c	.118	6	17	1	2	1	0	0	1	3	1	0
Al Hollingsworth, p	.000	1	1	0	0	0	0	0	0	0	0	0
Sig Jakucki, p	.000	1	0	0	0	0	0	0	0	0	0	0
Jack Kramer, p	.000	2	4	0	0	0	0	0	0	0	2	0
Mike Kreevich, of	.231	6	26	0	6	3	0	0	0	0	5	0
Chet Laabs, of-4	.200	5	15	1	3	1	1	0	0	2	6	0
Frank Mancuso, c-1	.667	2	3	0	2	0	0	0	1	0	0	0
George McQuinn, 1b	.438	6	16	2	7	2	0	1	5	7	2	0
Gene Moore, of	.182	6	22	4	4	0	0	0	0	3	6	0
Bob Muncrief, p	.000	2	1	0	0	0	0	0	0	0	1	0
Nelson Potter, p	.000	2	4	0	0	0	0	0	0	0	1	0
Tex Shirley, p	.000	2	0	0	0	0	0	0	0	0	0	0
Vern Stephens, ss	.227	6	22	2	5	1	0	0	3	3	3	0
Tom Turner, ph	.000	1	1	0	0	0	0	0	0	0	0	0
Al Zarilla, of-3	.100	4	10	1	1	0	0	0	1	0	4	0
TOTAL	.183		197	12	36	9	1	1	9	23	49	0

PITCHER	W	L	ERA	G	GS	CG	SV	SHO	IP	H	ER	BB	SO
Denny Galehouse	1	1	1.50	2	2	2	0	0	18.0	13	3	5	15
Al Hollingsworth	0	0	2.25	1	0	0	0	0	4.0	5	1	2	1
Sig Jakucki	0	1	9.00	1	1	0	0	0	3.0	5	3	0	4
Jack Kramer	1	0	0.00	2	1	1	0	0	11.0	9	0	4	12
Bob Muncrief	0	1	1.35	2	0	0	0	0	6.2	5	1	4	4
Nelson Potter	0	1	0.93	2	2	0	0	0	9.2	10	1	3	6
Tex Shirley	0	0	0.00	2	0	0	0	0	2.0	2	0	1	1
TOTAL	2	4	1.49	12	6	3	0	0	54.1	49	9	19	43

GAME 1 AT STL-N OCT 4

STL-A	000 200 000	2	2	0
STL-N	000 000 001	1	7	0

Pitchers: GALEHOUSE vs M.COOPER, Donnelly (8)
Home Runs: McQuinn-STL(A)
Attendance: 33,242

GAME 2 AT STL-N OCT 5

STL-A	000 002 000 0	2	7	4
STL-N	001 100 000 1	3	7	0

Pitchers: Potter, MUNCRIEF (7) vs Lanier, DONNELLY (8)
Attendance: 35,076

GAME 3 AT STL-A OCT 6

STL-N	100 000 100	2	7	0
STL-A	004 000 20X	6	8	2

Pitchers: WILKS, Schmidt (3), Jurisich (7), Byerly (7) vs KRAMER
Attendance: 34,737

GAME 4 AT STL-A OCT 7

STL-N	202 001 000	5	12	0
STL-A	000 000 010	1	9	1

Pitchers: BRECHEEN vs JAKUCKI, Hollingsworth (4), Shirley (8)
Home Runs: Musial-STL(N)
Attendance: 35,455

GAME 5 AT STL-A OCT 8

STL-N	000 001 010	2	6	1
STL-A	000 000 000	0	7	1

Pitchers: M.COOPER vs GALEHOUSE
Home Runs: Sanders-STL(N), Litwhiler-STL(N)
Attendance: 36,568

GAME 6 AT STL-N OCT 9

STL-A	010 000 000	1	3	2
STL-N	000 300 00X	3	10	0

Pitchers: POTTER, Muncrief (4), Kramer (7) vs LANIER, Wilks (6)
Attendance: 31,630

As World War Two ended during the summer, military major leaguers began returning to their clubs. Hank Greenberg's return in July provided the spark needed for Detroit's narrow pennant victory, and his three-run homer in Game Two of the World Series proved to be the decisive blow in the Tigers' successful struggle for the world title.

Chicago started strong as Cub ace Hank Borowy shut out the Tigers on six singles while his teammates drove out Tiger ace Hal Newhouser with seven runs in the first three innings, to win 9–0. Chicago continued its assault the next day with a run in the top of the fourth, but in the fifth inning Tiger Doc Cramer—with two out and two on—singled in the tying run, and Greenberg followed with his tie-breaking homer for three additional runs. Detroit pitcher Virgil Trucks (who had returned from the Navy in time to pitch in the regular-season finale) held the Cubs scoreless after the fourth inning for the Tiger win.

Chicago's Claude Passeau moved the Cubs back into the Series lead with a one-hit shutout in Game Three, but Tiger Dizzy Trout's five-hitter in Game Four again evened the Series. The Tigers bunched four of their seven hits in the fourth inning for all four of their runs.

Detroit took the Series lead for the first time with an 8–4 win in Game Five. Borowy and Newhouser faced each other as they had in the opener, but this time Borowy was hit hard. Driven out when four Tigers opened the sixth inning with safe hits, he took the loss as Newhouser went the distance for the win.

In Game Six, Chicago concluded the seventh inning of a heavy-hitting game leading 7–3. Detroit tied the score with four runs in the top of the eighth (capped by Greenberg's home run), but in the last of the twelfth the Cubs' Stan Hack doubled home the winning run to keep Chicago's hopes alive.

Two days later in the finale, Cub manager Charlie Grimm started Borowy, who had relieved for four shutout innings to win Game Six. But this third appearance in four days proved too much. Removed after the first three batters to face him singled, he took the loss, as the Tigers went on to score nine runs to the Cubs' three.

Detroit Tigers (AL), 4; Chicago Cubs (NL), 3

DET (A)

PLAYER/POS	AVG	G	AB	R	H	2B	3B	HR	RB	BB	SO	SB
Al Benton, p	.000	3	0	0	0	0	0	0	0	0	0	0
Red Borom, ph	.000	2	1	0	0	0	0	0	0	0	0	0
Tommy Bridges, p	.000	1	0	0	0	0	0	0	0	0	0	0
George Caster, p	.000	1	0	0	0	0	0	0	0	0	0	0
Doc Cramer, of	.379	7	29	7	11	0	0	0	4	1	0	1
Roy Cullenbine, of	.227	7	22	5	5	2	0	0	4	8	2	1
Zeb Eaton, ph	.000	1	1	0	0	0	0	0	0	0	1	0
Hank Greenberg, of	.304	7	23	7	7	3	0	2	7	6	5	0
Joe Hoover, ss	.333	1	3	1	1	0	0	0	1	0	0	0
Chuck Hostetler, ph	.000	3	3	0	0	0	0	0	0	0	0	0
Bob Maier, ph	1.000	1	1	0	1	0	0	0	0	0	0	0
Eddie Mayo, 2b	.250	7	28	4	7	1	0	0	2	2	2	0
John Mc Hale, ph	.000	3	3	0	0	0	0	0	0	0	1	0
Ed Mierkowicz, of	.000	1	0	0	0	0	0	0	0	0	0	0
Les Mueller, p	.000	1	0	0	0	0	0	0	0	0	0	0
Hal Newhouser, p	.000	3	8	0	0	0	0	0	0	1	1	0
Jimmy Outlaw, 3b	.179	7	28	1	5	0	0	0	3	2	1	1
Stubby Overmire, p	.000	1	1	0	0	0	0	0	0	0	0	0
Paul Richards, c	.211	7	19	0	4	2	0	0	6	4	3	0
Bob Swift, c	.250	3	4	1	1	0	0	0	0	2	0	0
Jim Tobin, p	.000	1	1	0	0	0	0	0	0	0	0	0
Dizzy Trout, p	.167	2	6	0	1	0	0	0	0	0	0	0
Virgil Trucks, p	.000	2	4	0	0	0	0	0	0	1	1	0
Hub Walker, ph	.500	2	2	1	1	0	0	0	0	0	0	0
Skeeter Webb, ss	.185	7	27	4	5	0	0	0	1	3	1	0
Rudy York, 1b	.179	7	28	1	5	1	0	0	3	3	4	0
TOTAL	.223		242	32	54	10	0	2	32	33	22	3

PITCHER	W	L	ERA	G	GS	CG	SV	SHO	IP	H	ER	BB	SO
Al Benton	0	0	1.93	3	0	0	0	0	4.2	6	1	0	5
Tommy Bridges	0	0	16.20	1	0	0	0	0	1.2	3	3	3	1
George Caster	0	0	0.00	1	0	0	0	0	0.2	0	0	0	1
Les Mueller	0	0	0.00	1	0	0	0	0	2.0	0	0	1	1
Hal Newhouser	2	1	6.10	3	3	2	0	0	20.2	25	14	4	22
Stubby Overmire	0	1	3.00	1	1	0	0	0	6.0	4	2	2	2
Jim Tobin	0	0	6.00	1	0	0	0	0	3.0	4	2	1	0
Dizzy Trout	1	1	0.66	2	1	1	0	0	13.2	9	1	3	9
Virgil Trucks	1	0	3.38	2	2	1	0	0	13.1	14	5	5	7
TOTAL	4	3	3.84	15	7	4	0	0	65.2	65	28	19	48

CHI (N)

PLAYER/POS	AVG	G	AB	R	H	2B	3B	HR	RB	BB	SO	SB
Heinz Becker, ph	.500	3	2	0	1	0	0	0	0	1	1	0
Cy Block, pr	.000	1	0	0	0	0	0	0	0	0	0	0
Hank Borowy, p	.167	4	6	1	1	1	0	0	0	0	3	0
Phil Cavaretta, 1b	.423	7	26	7	11	2	0	1	5	4	3	0
Bob Chipman, p	.000	1	0	0	0	0	0	0	0	0	0	0
Paul Derringer, p	.000	3	0	0	0	0	0	0	0	0	0	0
Paul Erickson, p	.000	4	0	0	0	0	0	0	0	0	0	0
Paul Gillespie, c-1	.000	3	6	0	0	0	0	0	0	0	0	0
Stan Hack, 3b	.367	7	30	1	11	3	0	0	4	4	2	0
Roy Hughes, ss	.294	6	17	1	5	1	0	0	3	4	5	0
Don Johnson, 2b	.172	7	29	4	5	2	1	0	0	0	8	1
Mickey Livingston, c	.364	6	22	3	8	3	0	0	4	1	1	0
Peanuts Lowrey, of	.310	7	29	4	9	1	0	0	0	1	2	0
Clyde Mc Cullough, ph	.000	1	1	0	0	0	0	0	0	0	1	0
Lennie Merullo, ss	.000	3	2	0	0	0	0	0	0	0	1	0
Bill Nicholson, of	.214	7	28	1	6	1	1	0	8	2	5	0
Andy Pafko, of	.214	7	28	5	6	2	1	0	2	2	5	1
Claude Passeau, p	.000	3	7	1	0	0	0	0	1	0	4	0
Ray Prim, p	.000	2	0	0	0	0	0	0	0	0	0	0
Ed Sauer, ph	.000	2	2	0	0	0	0	0	0	0	2	0
Bill Schuster, ss-1	.000	2	1	1	0	0	0	0	0	0	0	0
Frank Secory, ph	.200	5	5	0	1	0	0	0	1	0	2	0
Hy Vandenberg, p	.000	3	1	0	0	0	0	0	0	0	0	0
Dewey Williams, c-1	.000	2	2	0	0	0	0	0	0	0	1	0
Hank Wyse, p	.000	3	3	0	0	0	0	0	0	0	2	0
TOTAL	.259		247	29	64	16	3	1	27	19	48	2

PITCHER	W	L	ERA	G	GS	CG	SV	SHO	IP	H	ER	BB	SO
Hank Borowy	2	2	4.00	4	3	1	0	1	18.0	21	8	6	8
Bob Chipman	0	0	0.00	1	0	0	0	0	0.1	0	0	1	0
Paul Derringer	0	0	6.75	3	0	0	0	0	5.1	5	4	7	1
Paul Erickson	0	0	3.86	4	0	0	0	0	7.0	8	3	3	5
Claude Passeau	1	0	2.70	3	2	1	0	1	16.2	7	5	8	3
Ray Prim	0	1	9.00	2	1	0	0	0	4.0	4	4	1	1
Hy Vandenberg	0	0	0.00	3	0	0	0	0	6.0	1	0	3	3
Hank Wyse	0	1	7.04	3	1	0	0	0	7.2	8	6	4	1
TOTAL	3	4	4.15	23	7	2	0	2	65.0	54	30	33	22

GAME 1 AT DET OCT 3

CHI	403 000 200	9	13	0
DET	000 000 000	0	6	0

Pitchers: BOROWY vs NEWHOUSER, Benton (3), Tobin (5), Mueller (8)
Home Runs: Cavaretta-CHI
Attendance: 54,637

GAME 2 AT DET OCT 4

CHI	000 100 000	1	7	0
DET	000 040 00X	4	7	0

Pitchers: WYSE, Erickson (7) vs TRUCKS
Home Runs: Greenberg-DET
Attendance: 53,636

GAME 3 AT DET OCT 5

CHI	000 200 100	3	8	0
DET	000 000 000	0	1	2

Pitchers: PASSEAU vs OVERMIRE, Benton (7)
Attendance: 55,500

GAME 4 AT CHI OCT 6

DET	000 400 000	4	7	1
CHI	000 001 000	1	5	1

Pitchers: TROUT vs PRIM, Derringer (4), Vandenberg (6), Erickson (8)
Attendance: 42,923

GAME 5 AT CHI OCT 7

DET	001 004 102	8	11	0
CHI	001 000 201	4	7	2

Pitchers: NEWHOUSER vs BOROWY, Vandenberg (6), Chipman (6), Derringer (7), Erickson (9)
Attendance: 43,463

GAME 6 AT CHI OCT 8

DET	010 000 240 000	7	13	1
CHI	000 041 200 001	8	15	3

Pitchers: Trucks, Caster (5), Bridges (6), Benton (7), TROUT (8) vs Passeau, Wyse (7), Prim (8), BOROWY (9)
Home Runs: Greenberg-DET
Attendance: 41,708

GAME 7 AT CHI OCT 10

DET	510 000 120	9	9	1
CHI	100 100 010	3	10	0

Pitchers: NEWHOUSER vs BOROWY, Derringer (1), Vandenberg (2), Erickson (6), Passeau (8), Wyse (9)
Attendance: 41,590

With World War Two over, the majors were at full strength for the first time in five years. Boston's big bats were back, and the Sox ran away with the American League pennant. St. Louis had Stan Musial back, but they struggled to their pennant, finishing the regular schedule tied with Brooklyn, and defeating them in the first major league tie-breaker playoff, two games to none.

Favored Boston edged St. Louis in the opener, but it took a home run by Rudy York in the top of the tenth to spoil Cardinal ace Howie Pollet's strong showing. Harry Brecheen brought the Cards back the next day with the first of his three Series wins—a four-hit shutout.

Boston regained the lead in Game Three. Sox ace Dave Ferriss spaced six hits and a walk, one per inning, in shutting out the Cardinals, and Rudy York hit his second game-winning homer, this time a three-run shot in the first inning. The next day, though, St. Louis exploded for a record-tying 20 hits—four apiece by Enos Slaughter, Joe Garagiola and Whitey Kurowski—to give Cardinal pitcher George Munger (who had completed only two of his seven regular-season starts) an easy complete-game 12–3 victory.

For the third time the Red Sox took the Series lead, winning Game Five 6–3 behind Joe Dobson's four-hit pitching (the Cards' three runs were unearned), but St. Louis tied the Series for the third time with a win in Game Six. Brecheen, in his second start, again pitched splendidly, holding Boston to a single run in the seventh inning, long after the Cards had driven out Sox starter Mickey Harris with three runs in the third.

The final game, like the Series itself, was a seesaw battle. Boston scored the first run in the top of the first, but St. Louis tied the score an inning later. The Cards took a two-run lead on three hits in the fifth, but the Sox came back in the eighth to tie it up as Dom DiMaggio doubled off reliever Brecheen to drive in a pair of pinch hitters who had singled and doubled off starter Murry Dickson. The Series' final run came a half inning later. Slaughter opened with a single, but moved no farther as the next two batters were retired. Then Harry Walker hit a liner over short. Slaughter, off with the crack of the bat, never paused and beat the relay to the plate with what proved the winning run, as Brecheen held the Sox in the ninth for his third win of the Series and the Cardinals' seventh world title.

St. Louis Cardinals (NL), 4; Boston Red Sox (AL), 3

STL (N)

PLAYER/POS	AVG	G	AB	R	H	2B	3B	HR	RB	BB	SO	SB
Johnny Beazley, p	.000	1	0	0	0	0	0	0	0	0	0	0
Al Brazle, p	.000	1	2	0	0	0	0	0	0	0	0	0
Harry Brecheen, p	.125	3	8	2	1	0	0	0	1	0	1	0
Murry Dickson, p	.400	2	5	1	2	2	0	0	1	0	1	0
Erv Dusak, of	.250	4	4	0	1	1	0	0	0	2	2	0
Joe Garagiola, c	.316	5	19	2	6	2	0	0	4	0	3	0
Nippy Jones, ph	.000	1	1	0	0	0	0	0	0	0	1	0
Whitey Kurowski, 3b	.296	7	27	5	8	3	0	0	2	0	3	0
Marty Marion, ss	.250	7	24	1	6	2	0	0	4	1	1	0
Terry Moore, of	.148	7	27	1	4	0	0	0	2	2	6	0
Red Munger, p	.250	1	4	0	1	0	0	0	0	0	0	0
Stan Musial, 1b	.222	7	27	3	6	4	1	0	4	4	2	1
Howie Pollet, p	.000	2	4	0	0	0	0	0	0	0	1	0
Del Rice, c	.500	3	6	2	3	1	0	0	0	2	0	0
Red Schoendienst, 2b	.233	7	30	3	7	1	0	0	1	0	2	1
Dick Sisler, ph	.000	2	2	0	0	0	0	0	0	0	0	0
Enos Slaughter, of	.320	7	25	5	8	1	1	1	2	4	3	1
Harry Walker, of	.412	7	17	3	7	2	0	0	6	4	2	0
Ted Wilks, p	.000	1	0	0	0	0	0	0	0	0	0	0
TOTAL	.259		232	28	60	19	2	1	27	19	30	3

PITCHER	W	L	ERA	G	GS	CG	SV	SHO	IP	H	ER	BB	SO
Johnny Beazley	0	0	0.00	1	0	0	0	0	1.0	1	0	0	1
Al Brazle	0	1	5.40	1	0	0	0	0	6.2	7	4	6	4
Harry Brecheen	3	0	0.45	3	2	2	0	1	20.0	14	1	5	11
Murry Dickson	0	1	3.86	2	2	0	0	0	14.0	11	6	4	7
Red Munger	1	0	1.00	1	1	1	0	0	9.0	9	1	3	2
Howie Pollet	0	1	3.48	2	2	1	0	0	10.1	12	4	4	3
Ted Wilks	0	0	0.00	1	0	0	0	0	1.0	2	0	0	0
TOTAL	4	3	2.32	11	7	4	0	1	62.0	56	16	22	28

BOS (A)

PLAYER/POS	AVG	G	AB	R	H	2B	3B	HR	RB	BB	SO	SB
Jim Bagby, p	.000	1	1	0	0	0	0	0	0	0	0	0
Mace Brown, p	.000	1	0	0	0	0	0	0	0	0	0	0
Paul Campbell, pr	.000	1	0	0	0	0	0	0	0	0	0	0
Leon Culberson, of-3	.222	5	9	1	2	0	0	1	1	1	2	1
Dom DiMaggio, of	.259	7	27	2	7	3	0	0	3	2	2	0
Joe Dobson, p	.000	3	3	0	0	0	0	0	0	0	2	0
Bobby Doerr, 2b	.409	6	22	1	9	1	0	1	3	2	2	0
Clem Dreisewerd, p	.000	1	0	0	0	0	0	0	0	0	0	0
Dave Ferriss, p	.000	2	6	0	0	0	0	0	0	0	1	0
Don Gutteridge, 2b-2	.400	3	5	1	2	0	0	0	1	0	0	0
Mickey Harris, p	.333	2	3	0	1	0	0	0	0	0	1	0
Pinky Higgins, 3b	.208	7	24	1	5	1	0	0	2	2	0	0
Tex Hughson, p	.333	3	3	0	1	0	0	0	0	1	0	0
Earl Johnson, p	.000	3	1	0	0	0	0	0	0	0	0	0
Bob Klinger, p	.000	1	0	0	0	0	0	0	0	0	0	0
Tom Mc Bride, of-2	.167	5	12	0	2	0	0	0	1	0	1	0
Catfish Metkovich, ph	.500	2	2	1	1	1	0	0	0	0	0	0
Wally Moses, of	.417	4	12	1	5	0	0	0	0	1	2	0
Roy Partee, c	.100	5	10	1	1	0	0	0	1	1	2	0
Johnny Pesky, ss	.233	7	30	2	7	0	0	0	0	1	3	1
Rip Russell, 3b-1	1.000	2	2	1	2	0	0	0	0	0	0	0
Mike Ryba, p	.000	1	0	0	0	0	0	0	0	0	0	0
Hal Wagner, c	.000	5	13	0	0	0	0	0	0	0	1	0
Ted Williams, of	.200	7	25	2	5	0	0	0	1	5	5	0
Rudy York, 1b	.261	7	23	6	6	1	1	2	5	6	4	0
Bill Zuber, p	.000	1	0	0	0	0	0	0	0	0	0	0
TOTAL	.240		233	20	56	7	1	4	18	22	28	2

PITCHER	W	L	ERA	G	GS	CG	SV	SHO	IP	H	ER	BB	SO
Jim Bagby	0	0	3.00	1	0	0	0	0	3.0	6	1	1	1
Mace Brown	0	0	27.00	1	0	0	0	0	1.0	4	3	1	0
Joe Dobson	1	0	0.00	3	1	1	0	0	12.2	4	0	3	10
Clem Dreisewerd	0	0	0.00	1	0	0	0	0	0.1	0	0	0	0
Dave Ferriss	1	0	2.03	2	2	1	0	1	13.1	13	3	2	4
Mickey Harris	0	2	3.72	2	2	0	0	0	9.2	11	4	4	5
Tex Hughson	0	1	3.14	3	2	0	0	0	14.1	14	5	3	8
Earl Johnson	1	0	2.70	3	0	0	0	0	3.1	1	1	2	1
Bob Klinger	0	1	13.50	1	0	0	0	0	0.2	2	1	0	0
Mike Ryba	0	0	13.50	1	0	0	0	0	0.2	1	1	0	0
Bill Zuber	0	0	4.50	1	0	0	0	0	2.0	3	1	1	1
TOTAL	3	4	2.95	19	7	2	0	1	61.0	60	20	19	30

GAME 1 AT STL OCT 6

BOS	010 000 001 1	3	9	2
STL	000 001 010 0	2	7	0

Pitchers: Hughson, JOHNSON (9) vs POLLET
Home Runs: York-BOS
Attendance: 36,218

GAME 2 AT STL OCT 7

BOS	000 000 000	0	4	1
STL	001 020 00X	3	6	0

Pitchers: HARRIS, Dobson (8) vs BRECHEEN
Attendance: 35,815

GAME 3 AT BOS OCT 9

STL	000 000 000	0	6	1
BOS	300 000 01X	4	8	0

Pitchers: DICKSON, Wilks (8) vs FERRISS
Home Runs: York-BOS
Attendance: 34,500

GAME 4 AT BOS OCT 10

STL	033 010 104	12	20	1
BOS	000 100 020	3	9	4

Pitchers: MUNGER vs HUGHSON, Bagby (3), Zuber (6), Brown (8), Ryba (9), Dreisewerd (9)
Home Runs: Slaughter-STL, Doerr-BOS
Attendance: 35,645

GAME 5 AT BOS OCT 11

STL	010 000 002	3	4	1
BOS	110 001 30X	6	11	3

Pitchers: Pollet, BRAZLE (1), Beazley (8) vs DOBSON
Home Runs: Culberson-BOS
Attendance: 35,982

GAME 6 AT STL OCT 13

BOS	000 000 100	1	7	0
STL	003 000 01X	4	8	0

Pitchers: HARRIS, Hughson (3), Johnson (8) vs BRECHEEN
Attendance: 35,768

GAME 7 AT STL OCT 15

BOS	100 000 020	3	8	0
STL	010 020 01X	4	9	1

Pitchers: Ferriss, Dobson (5), KLINGER (8), Johnson (8) vs Dickson, BRECHEEN (8)
Attendance: 36,143

Two of the most memorable plays in World Series history brought Brooklyn victory in Games Four and Six, but when the Series had ended the Yankees were world champions for the eleventh time. Dodger ace Ralph Branca set New York down in order through the first four innings of Game One. But the first five batters to face him in the fifth inning reached base. Branca was lifted, but before the inning was over five Yankees had crossed the plate—more than enough for their first win.

The Yankees went two-up the next day, rocking four Brooklyn pitchers for 15 hits and an easy 10–3 win. Brooklyn finally made its presence felt in Game Three, another heavy-hitting affair, scoring six times in the second inning to establish a lead the Yankees could not overcome. Both teams recorded 13 hits, but Dodger fireman Hugh Casey extinguished the last Yankee flame in the seventh inning, and preserved a narrow 9–8 Dodger lead the rest of the way.

Shortstop Pee Wee Reese's error and a bases-loaded walk gave the Yankees an unearned run in the first inning of Game Four, and they earned a second run in the fourth. Meanwhile, Yankee pitcher Bill Bevens, although he averaged a walk an inning, had allowed no Dodger hits and only one run as the game entered the last of the ninth. Bevens retired two in the ninth, but walked his ninth and tenth batters (one intentionally), then lost both his no-hitter and the game as Dodger pinch hitter Cookie Lavagetto doubled home the two baserunners to even the Series at two-all.

Yankee Spec Shea (the winning pitcher in Game One) held Brooklyn to four hits and one run in Game Five. Joe DiMaggio homered in the fifth inning for New York's second run, enough to put the Yankees back in the Series lead. The Dodgers rebounded in Game Six to build an early 4–0 lead. But the Yankees tied the score in the last of the third and took a lead in the fourth. Brooklyn regained the lead in the sixth with four runs, but when DiMaggio hit a long fly to left with two on in the Yankee half of the inning, it looked as if the score would be tied. But substitute left fielder Al Gionfriddo (in what turned out to be his last big league game) raced to the bullpen fence 415 feet out to rob DiMag of the home run. New York scored a run in the ninth, but thanks to Gionfriddo's catch it was not enough to win the game.

Brooklyn scored first in the finale with a pair of second-inning runs, but Yankee relievers Bill

New York Yankees (AL), 4; Brooklyn Dodgers (NL), 3

NY (A)

PLAYER/POS	AVG	G	AB	R	H	2B	3B	HR	RB	BB	SO	SB
Yogi Berra, c-4,of-2	.158	6	19	2	3	0	0	1	2	1	2	0
Bill Bevens, p	.000	2	4	0	0	0	0	0	0	0	2	0
Bobby Brown, ph	1.000	4	3	2	3	2	0	0	3	1	0	0
Spud Chandler, p	.000	1	0	0	0	0	0	0	0	0	0	0
Allie Clark, of-1	.500	3	2	1	1	0	0	0	1	1	0	0
Joe DiMaggio, of	.231	7	26	4	6	0	0	2	5	6	2	0
Karl Drews, p	.000	2	2	0	0	0	0	0	0	0	2	0
Lonny Frey, ph	.000	1	1	0	0	0	0	0	0	1	0	0
Tommy Henrich, of	.323	7	31	2	10	2	0	1	5	2	3	0
Ralph Houk, ph	1.000	1	1	0	1	0	0	0	0	0	0	0
Billy Johnson, 3b	.269	7	26	8	7	0	3	0	2	3	4	0
Johnny Lindell, of	.500	6	18	3	9	3	1	0	7	5	2	0
Sherm Lollar, c	.750	2	4	3	3	2	0	0	1	0	0	0
George Mc Quinn, 1b	.130	7	23	3	3	0	0	0	1	5	8	0
Bobo Newsom, p	.000	2	0	0	0	0	0	0	0	0	0	0
Joe Page, p	.000	4	4	0	0	0	0	0	0	0	1	0
Jack Phillips, 1b-1	.000	2	2	0	0	0	0	0	0	0	0	0
Vic Raschi, p	.000	2	0	0	0	0	0	0	0	0	0	0
Allie Reynolds, p	.500	2	4	2	2	0	0	0	1	0	0	0
Phil Rizzuto, ss	.308	7	26	3	8	1	0	0	2	4	0	2
Aaron Robinson, c	.200	3	10	2	2	0	0	0	1	2	1	0
Spec Shea, p	.400	3	5	0	2	1	0	0	1	0	2	0
Snuffy Stirnweiss, 2b	.259	7	27	3	7	0	1	0	3	8	8	0
Butch Wensloff, p	.000	1	0	0	0	0	0	0	0	0	0	0
TOTAL	.282		238	38	67	11	5	4	36	38	37	2

PITCHER	W	L	ERA	G	GS	CG	SV	SHO	IP	H	ER	BB	SO
Bill Bevens	0	1	2.38	2	1	1	0	0	11.1	3	3	11	7
Spud Chandler	0	0	9.00	1	0	0	0	0	2.0	2	2	3	1
Karl Drews	0	0	3.00	2	0	0	0	0	3.0	2	1	1	0
Bobo Newsom	0	1	19.29	2	1	0	0	0	2.1	6	5	2	0
Joe Page	1	1	4.15	4	0	0	1	0	13.0	12	6	2	7
Vic Raschi	0	0	6.75	2	0	0	0	0	1.1	2	1	0	1
Allie Reynolds	1	0	4.76	2	2	1	0	0	11.1	15	6	3	6
Spec Shea	2	0	2.35	3	3	1	0	0	15.1	10	4	8	10
Butch Wensloff	0	0	0.00	1	0	0	0	0	2.0	0	0	0	0
TOTAL	4	3	4.09	19	7	3	1	0	61.2	52	28	30	32

BRO (N)

PLAYER/POS	AVG	G	AB	R	H	2B	3B	HR	RB	BB	SO	SB
Dan Bankhead, pr	.000	1	0	1	0	0	0	0	0	0	0	0
Rex Barney, p	.000	3	1	0	0	0	0	0	0	0	0	0
Hank Behrman, p	.000	5	0	0	0	0	0	0	0	0	0	0
Bobby Bragan, ph	1.000	1	1	0	1	1	0	0	1	0	0	0
Ralph Branca, p	.000	3	4	0	0	0	0	0	0	0	1	0
Hugh Casey, p	.000	6	1	0	0	0	0	0	0	0	1	0
Bruce Edwards, c	.222	7	27	3	6	1	0	0	2	2	7	0
Carl Furillo, of	.353	6	17	2	6	2	0	0	3	3	0	0
Al Gionfriddo, of-1	.000	4	3	2	0	0	0	0	0	1	0	1
Hal Gregg, p	.000	3	3	0	0	0	0	0	0	1	1	0
Joe Hatten, p	.333	4	3	1	1	0	0	0	0	0	0	0
Gene Hermanski, of	.158	7	19	4	3	0	0	1	0	1	3	0
Gil Hodges, ph	.000	1	1	0	0	0	0	0	0	0	1	0
Spider Jorgensen, 3b	.200	7	20	1	4	2	0	0	3	2	4	0
Cookie Lavagetto, 3b-3	.143	5	7	0	1	1	0	0	3	0	2	0
Vic Lombardi, p-2	.000	3	3	0	0	0	0	0	0	0	0	0
Eddie Miksis, 2b-1,of-1	.250	5	4	1	1	0	0	0	0	0	1	0
Pee Wee Reese, ss	.304	7	23	5	7	1	0	0	4	6	3	3
Pete Reiser, of-3	.250	5	8	1	2	0	0	0	0	3	1	0
Jackie Robinson, 1b	.259	7	27	3	7	2	0	0	3	2	4	2
Eddie Stanky, 2b	.240	7	25	4	6	1	0	0	2	3	2	0
Harry Taylor, p	.000	1	0	0	0	0	0	0	0	0	0	0
Arky Vaughan, ph	.500	3	2	0	1	1	0	0	0	1	0	0
Dixie Walker, of	.222	7	27	1	6	1	0	1	4	3	1	1
TOTAL	.230		226	29	52	13	1	1	26	30	32	7

PITCHER	W	L	ERA	G	GS	CG	SV	SHO	IP	H	ER	BB	SO
Rex Barney	0	1	2.70	3	1	0	0	0	6.2	4	2	10	3
Hank Behrman	0	0	7.11	5	0	0	0	0	6.1	9	5	5	3
Ralph Branca	1	1	8.64	3	1	0	0	0	8.1	12	8	5	8
Hugh Casey	2	0	0.87	6	0	0	1	0	10.1	5	1	1	3
Hal Gregg	0	1	3.55	3	1	0	0	0	12.2	9	5	8	10
Joe Hatten	0	0	7.00	4	1	0	0	0	9.0	12	7	7	5
Vic Lombardi	0	1	12.15	2	2	0	0	0	6.2	14	9	1	5
Harry Taylor	0	0	INF	1	1	0	0	0	0.0	2	0	1	0
TOTAL	3	4	5.55	27	7	0	1	0	60.0	67	37	38	37

Bevens and Joe Page shut them out through the final seven innings as their teammates gradually built a Series-clinching 5–2 victory.

GAME 1 AT NY SEPT 30

BRO	100 001 100	3	6	0
NY	000 050 00X	5	4	0

Pitchers: BRANCA, Behrman (5), Casey (7) vs SHEA, Page (6)
Attendance: 73,365

GAME 2 AT NY OCT 1

BRO	001 100 001	3	9	2
NY	101 121 40X	10	15	1

Pitchers: LOMBARDI, Gregg (5), Behrman (7), Barney (7) vs REYNOLDS
Home Runs: Walker-BRO, Henrich-NY
Attendance: 69,865

GAME 3 AT BRO OCT 2

NY	002 221 100	8	13	0
BRO	061 200 00X	9	13	1

Pitchers: NEWSOM, Raschi (2), Drews (3), Chandler (4), Page (6) vs Hatten, Branca (5), CASEY (7)
Home Runs: DiMaggio-NY, Berra-NY
Attendance: 33,098

GAME 4 AT BRO OCT 3

NY	100 100 000	2	8	1
BRO	000 010 002	3	1	3

Pitchers: BEVENS vs Taylor, Gregg (1), Behrman (8), CASEY (9)
Attendance: 33,443

GAME 5 AT BRO OCT 4

NY	000 110 000	2	5	0
BRO	000 001 000	1	4	1

Pitchers: SHEA vs BARNEY, Hatten (5), Behrman (7), Casey (8)
Home Runs: DiMaggio-NY
Attendance: 34,379

GAME 6 AT NY OCT 5

BRO	202 004 000	8	12	1
NY	004 100 001	6	15	2

Pitchers: Lombardi, BRANCA, Hatten (6), Casey (9) vs Reynolds, Drews (3), PAGE (5), Newsom (6), Raschi (7), Wensloff (8)
Attendance: 74,065

GAME 7 AT NY OCT 6

BRO	020 000 000	2	7	0
NY	010 201 10X	5	7	0

Pitchers: GREGG, Behrman (4), Hatten (6), Barney (6), Casey (7) vs Shea, Bevens (2), PAGE (5)
Attendance: 71,548

Boston outpitched and outhit Cleveland, and the clubs tied in runs scored. But the Braves scored most of their runs in one game, and the Indians, spreading theirs more evenly, took the Series. Boston ace Johnny Sain dueled Bob Feller in the opener. Feller gave up only two singles, but one of them followed a walk and a sacrifice (and a controversial pickoff play at second, in which the Boston runner was ruled safe although photos later showed him clearly out) and drove in the game's only run. Both teams registered eight hits in Game Two, but Cleveland's led to four runs, while Indian hurler Bob Lemon held Boston to just one—and that was unearned.

Cleveland's rookie sensation Gene Bearden shut out the Braves on five hits in Game Three as the Series moved to Cleveland's huge Municipal Stadium. Bearden himself, after doubling in the third, scored on a Boston error what proved to be the winning run. A record 81,897 fans saw Sain face Steve Gromek in Game Four. Only five Indians hit Sain safely, but a first-inning single and double put Cleveland on the board, and Larry Doby's home run two innings later made the score 2–0. Boston's Marv Rickert homered in the seventh to narrow Cleveland's lead, but that ended the scoring.

Another attendance record was set at Game Five as 86,288 fans gathered to watch Bob Feller sew up the title for Cleveland. They went home disappointed. In a game that featured five of the Series' eight home runs, Boston jumped ahead on Bob Elliott's three-run blast in the first. Dale Mitchell opened Cleveland's half of the inning with a home run, but Elliott neutralized it in the third with his second homer. The Indians drove out Boston starter Nelson Potter with four runs in the fourth inning (three coming on Jim Hegan's homer). But Warren Spahn (who had lost Game Two) hurled one-hit shutout relief over the final five frames as his Braves tied the game on Bill Salkeld's homer in the sixth, and blew out Feller and two relievers with six runs in the seventh. The fourth Indian pitcher, Satchel Paige (in his only World Series appearance), retired two batters to end the inning, but the damage had been done.

A day later though, back in Boston, Cleveland edged the Braves 4–3 for the title. Gene Bearden's relief pitching allowed two inherited baserunners to score in the eighth, but halted Boston's rally one run short of a tie.

Cleveland Indians (AL), 4; Boston Braves (NL), 2

CLE (A)

PLAYER/POS	AVG	G	AB	R	H	2B	3B	HR	RB	BB	SO	SB
Gene Bearden, p	.500	2	4	1	2	1	0	0	0	0	1	0
Ray Boone, ph	.000	1	1	0	0	0	0	0	0	0	1	0
Lou Boudreau, ss	.273	6	22	1	6	4	0	0	3	1	1	0
Russ Christopher, p	.000	1	0	0	0	0	0	0	0	0	0	0
Allie Clark, of	.000	1	3	0	0	0	0	0	0	0	1	0
Larry Doby, of	.318	6	22	1	7	1	0	1	2	2	4	0
Bob Feller, p	.000	2	4	0	0	0	0	0	0	0	2	0
Joe Gordon, 2b	.182	6	22	3	4	0	0	1	2	1	2	1
Steve Gromek, p	.000	1	3	0	0	0	0	0	0	0	1	0
Jim Hegan, c	.211	6	19	2	4	0	0	1	5	1	4	1
Wally Judnich, of	.077	4	13	1	1	0	0	0	1	1	4	0
Ken Keltner, 3b	.095	6	21	3	2	0	0	0	0	2	3	0
Bob Kennedy, of	.500	3	2	0	1	0	0	0	1	0	1	0
Ed Klieman, p	.000	1	0	0	0	0	0	0	0	0	0	0
Bob Lemon, p	.000	2	7	0	0	0	0	0	0	0	0	0
Dale Mitchell, of	.174	6	23	4	4	1	0	1	1	2	0	0
Bob Muncrief, p	.000	1	0	0	0	0	0	0	0	0	0	0
Satchel Paige, p	.000	1	0	0	0	0	0	0	0	0	0	0
Hal Peck, of	.000	1	0	0	0	0	0	0	0	0	0	0
Eddie Robinson, 1b	.300	6	20	0	6	0	0	0	1	1	0	0
Al Rosen, ph	.000	1	1	0	0	0	0	0	0	0	0	0
Joe Tipton, ph	.000	1	1	0	0	0	0	0	0	0	1	0
Thurman Tucker, of	.333	1	3	1	1	0	0	0	0	0	1	0
TOTAL	.199		191	17	38	7	0	4	16	12	26	2

PITCHER	W	L	ERA	G	GS	CG	SV	SHO	IP	H	ER	BB	SO
Gene Bearden	1	0	0.00	2	1	1	1	1	10.2	6	0	1	4
Russ Christopher	0	0	INF	1	0	0	0	0	0.0	2	1	0	0
Bob Feller	0	2	5.02	2	2	1	0	0	14.1	10	8	5	7
Steve Gromek	1	0	1.00	1	1	1	0	0	9.0	7	1	1	2
Ed Klieman	0	0	INF	1	0	0	0	0	0.0	1	3	2	0
Bob Lemon	2	0	1.65	2	2	1	0	0	16.1	16	3	7	6
Bob Muncrief	0	0	0.00	1	0	0	0	0	2.0	1	0	0	0
Satchel Paige	0	0	0.00	1	0	0	0	0	0.2	0	0	0	0
TOTAL	4	2	2.72	11	6	4	1	1	53.0	43	16	16	19

BOS (N)

PLAYER/POS	AVG	G	AB	R	H	2B	3B	HR	RB	BB	SO	SB
Red Barrett, p	.000	2	0	0	0	0	0	0	0	0	0	0
Vern Bickford, p	.000	1	0	0	0	0	0	0	0	0	0	0
Clint Conatser, of	.000	2	4	0	0	0	0	0	1	0	0	0
Alvin Dark, ss	.167	6	24	2	4	1	0	0	0	0	2	0
Bob Elliott, 3b	.333	6	21	4	7	0	0	2	5	2	2	0
Tommy Holmes, of	.192	6	26	3	5	0	0	0	1	0	0	0
Phil Masi, c	.125	5	8	1	1	1	0	0	1	0	0	0
Frank Mc Cormick, 1b-1	.200	3	5	0	1	0	0	0	0	0	2	0
Mike Mc Cormick, of	.261	6	23	1	6	0	0	0	2	0	4	0
Nelson Potter, p	.500	2	2	0	1	0	0	0	0	0	1	0
Marv Rickert, of	.211	5	19	2	4	0	0	1	2	0	4	0
Connie Ryan, ph	.000	2	1	0	0	0	0	0	0	0	1	0
Johnny Sain, p	.200	2	5	0	1	0	0	0	0	0	0	0
Bill Salkeld, c	.222	5	9	2	2	0	0	1	1	5	1	0
Ray Sanders, ph	.000	1	1	0	0	0	0	0	0	0	0	0
Sibby Sisti, 2b	.000	2	1	0	0	0	0	0	0	0	0	0
Warren Spahn, p	.000	3	4	0	0	0	0	0	1	0	0	0
Eddie Stanky, 2b	.286	6	14	0	4	1	0	0	1	7	1	0
Earl Torgeson, 1b	.389	5	18	2	7	3	0	0	1	2	1	1
Bill Voiselle, p	.000	2	2	0	0	0	0	0	0	0	0	0
TOTAL	.230		187	17	43	6	0	4	16	16	19	1

PITCHER	W	L	ERA	G	GS	CG	SV	SHO	IP	H	ER	BB	SO
Red Barrett	0	0	0.00	2	0	0	0	0	3.2	1	0	0	1
Vern Bickford	0	1	2.70	1	1	0	0	0	3.1	4	1	5	1
Nelson Potter	0	0	8.44	2	1	0	0	0	5.1	6	5	2	1
Johnny Sain	1	1	1.06	2	2	2	0	1	17.0	9	2	0	9
Warren Spahn	1	1	3.00	3	1	0	0	0	12.0	10	4	3	12
Bill Voiselle	0	1	2.53	2	1	0	0	0	10.2	8	3	2	2
TOTAL	2	4	2.60	12	6	2	0	1	52.0	38	15	12	26

GAME 1 AT BOS OCT 6

CLE	000	000	000	0	4	0
BOS	000	000	01X	1	2	2

Pitchers: FELLER vs SAIN
Attendance: 40,135

GAME 2 AT BOS OCT 7

CLE	000	210	001	4	8	1
BOS	100	000	000	1	8	3

Pitchers: LEMON vs SPAHN, Barrett (5), Potter (8)
Attendance: 39,633

GAME 3 AT CLE OCT 8

BOS	000	000	000	0	5	1
CLE	001	100	00X	2	5	0

Pitchers: BICKFORD, Voiselle (4), Barrett (8) vs BEARDEN
Attendance: 70,306

GAME 4 AT CLE OCT 9

BOS	000	000	100	1	7	0
CLE	101	000	00X	2	5	0

Pitchers: SAIN vs GROMEK
Home Runs: Doby-CLE, Rickert-BOS
Attendance: 81,897

GAME 5 AT CLE OCT 10

BOS	301	001	600	11	12	0
CLE	100	400	000	5	6	2

Pitchers: Potter, SPAHN (4) vs FELLER, Klieman (7), Christopher (7), Paige (7), Muncrief (8)
Home Runs: Elliott-BOS (2), Mitchell-CLE, Hegan-CLE, Salkeld-BOS
Attendance: 86,288

GAME 6 AT BOS OCT 11

CLE	001	002	010	4	10	0
BOS	000	100	020	3	9	0

Pitchers: LEMON, Bearden (8) vs VOISELLE, Spahn (8)
Home Runs: Gordon-CLE
Attendance: 40,103

Casey Stengel, in the first of his twelve years as Yankee manager, edged his team past the Boston Red Sox for his first of ten American League pennants, then past the Dodgers for his first of seven world championships. New York and Brooklyn traded 1–0 wins to begin the Series. In Game One Yankee Allie Reynolds dueled Dodger rookie Don Newcombe scorelessly through 8½ innings—until Tommy Henrich led off the last of the ninth with a Yankee home run. Dodger Jackie Robinson scored after doubling off Vic Raschi in the second inning of Game Two for that game's only score, while Dodger ace Preacher Roe permitted the Yankees just six scattered hits—never more than one per inning.

The teams entered the ninth inning of Game Three tied 1–1. But in the top of the ninth, Dodger starter Ralph Branca, after loading the bases on two walks and a single, gave up another single to pinch hitter Johnny Mize for two runs. Jerry Coleman's single off reliever Jack Banta drove in another run before the third out was made. In the last of the ninth, Yankee fireman Joe Page (who had held Brooklyn scoreless since coming on with the bases loaded in the fourth) finally weakened. But after yielding solo homers to Luis Olmo and Roy Campanella, he struck out pinch hitter Bruce Edwards for New York's second win.

The Yankees' victory in Game Four came a little easier. They scored first, driving out starter Don Newcombe with three runs in the fourth, and rapping reliever Joe Hatten for three more runs an inning later. Brooklyn retaliated in the sixth, sending Yankee starter Ed Lopat to the showers with seven singles for four runs. But Allie Reynolds came on for 3⅓ innings of no-hit relief to preserve the Yankees lead—and his Series 0.00 earned run average.

After four closely contested games, the Yankees erupted in Game Five for ten runs in the first six innings as Brooklyn was held to just two. In the last of the seventh, the Dodgers came back, driving out starter Vic Raschi with a four-run rally, capped by Gil Hodges's three-run homer. But Joe Page came on to get the final out of the seventh, and held the Dodgers scoreless over the final two innings to bring the Yankees' world titles to an even dozen.

New York Yankees (AL), 4; Brooklyn Dodgers (NL), 1

NY (A)

PLAYER/POS	AVG	G	AB	R	H	2B	3B	HR	RB	BB	SO	SB
Hank Bauer, of	.167	3	6	0	1	0	0	0	0	0	0	0
Yogi Berra, c	.063	4	16	2	1	0	0	0	1	1	3	0
Bobby Brown, 3b-3	.500	4	12	4	6	1	2	0	5	2	2	0
Tommy Byrne, p	1.000	1	1	0	1	0	0	0	0	0	0	0
Gerry Coleman, 2b	.250	5	20	0	5	3	0	0	4	0	4	0
Joe DiMaggio, of	.111	5	18	2	2	0	0	1	2	3	5	0
Tommy Henrich, 1b	.263	5	19	4	5	0	0	1	1	3	0	0
Billy Johnson, 3b	.143	2	7	0	1	0	0	0	0	0	2	1
Johnny Lindell, of	.143	2	7	0	1	0	0	0	0	0	2	0
Ed Lopat, p	.333	1	3	0	1	1	0	0	1	0	0	0
Cliff Mapes, of	.100	4	10	3	1	1	0	0	2	2	4	0
Johnny Mize, ph	1.000	2	2	0	2	0	0	0	2	0	0	0
Gus Niarhos, c	.000	1	0	0	0	0	0	0	0	0	0	0
Joe Page, p	.000	3	4	0	0	0	0	0	0	0	2	0
Vic Raschi, p	.200	2	5	0	1	0	0	0	1	1	1	0
Allie Reynolds, p	.500	2	4	0	2	1	0	0	0	0	1	0
Phil Rizzuto, ss	.167	5	18	2	3	0	0	0	1	3	1	1
Charlie Silvera, c	.000	1	2	0	0	0	0	0	0	0	0	0
Snuffy Stirnweiss, ph	.000	1	0	0	0	0	0	0	0	0	0	0
Gene Woodling, of	.400	3	10	4	4	3	0	0	0	3	0	0
TOTAL	.226		164	21	37	10	2	2	20	18	27	2

PITCHER	W	L	ERA	G	GS	CG	SV	SHO	IP	H	ER	BB	SO
Tommy Byrne	0	0	2.70	1	1	0	0	0	3.1	2	1	2	1
Ed Lopat	1	0	6.35	1	1	0	0	0	5.2	9	4	1	4
Joe Page	1	0	2.00	3	0	0	1	0	9.0	6	2	3	8
Vic Raschi	1	1	4.30	2	2	0	0	0	14.2	15	7	5	11
Allie Reynolds	1	0	0.00	2	1	1	1	1	12.1	2	0	4	14
TOTAL	4	1	2.80	9	5	1	2	1	45.0	34	14	15	38

BRO (N)

PLAYER/POS	AVG	G	AB	R	H	2B	3B	HR	RB	BB	SO	SB
Jack Banta, p	.000	3	1	0	0	0	0	0	0	0	0	0
Rex Barney, p	.000	1	0	0	0	0	0	0	0	0	0	0
Ralph Branca, p	.000	1	3	0	0	0	0	0	0	0	3	0
Tommy Brown, ph	.000	2	2	0	0	0	0	0	0	0	1	0
Roy Campanella, c	.267	5	15	2	4	1	0	1	2	3	1	0
Billy Cox, 3b-1	.333	2	3	0	1	0	0	0	0	0	0	0
Bruce Edwards, ph	.500	2	2	0	1	0	0	0	0	0	1	0
Carl Erskine, p	.000	2	0	0	0	0	0	0	0	0	0	0
Carl Furillo, of-2	.125	3	8	0	1	0	0	0	0	1	0	0
Joe Hatten, p	.000	2	0	0	0	0	0	0	0	0	0	0
Gene Hermanski, of	.308	4	13	1	4	0	1	0	2	3	3	0
Gil Hodges, 1b	.235	5	17	2	4	0	0	1	4	1	4	0
Spider Jorgensen, 3b-3	.182	4	11	1	2	2	0	0	0	2	2	0
Mike Mc Cormick, ph	.000	1	0	0	0	0	0	0	0	0	0	0
Eddie Miksis, 3b-2	.286	3	7	0	2	1	0	0	0	0	1	0
Paul Minner, p	.000	1	0	0	0	0	0	0	0	0	0	0
Don Newcombe, p	.000	2	4	0	0	0	0	0	0	0	3	0
Luis Olmo, of	.273	4	11	2	3	0	0	1	2	0	2	0
Erv Palica, p	.000	1	0	0	0	0	0	0	0	0	0	0
Marv Rackley, of	.000	2	5	0	0	0	0	0	0	0	2	0
Pee Wee Reese, ss	.316	5	19	2	6	1	0	1	2	1	0	1
Jackie Robinson, 2b	.188	5	16	2	3	1	0	0	2	4	2	0
Preacher Roe, p	.000	1	3	0	0	0	0	0	0	0	3	0
Duke Snider, of	.143	5	21	2	3	1	0	0	0	0	8	0
Dick Whitman, ph	.000	1	1	0	0	0	0	0	0	0	1	0
TOTAL	.210		162	14	34	7	1	4	14	15	38	1

PITCHER	W	L	ERA	G	GS	CG	SV	SHO	IP	H	ER	BB	SO
Jack Banta	0	0	3.18	3	0	0	0	0	5.2	5	2	1	4
Rex Barney	0	1	16.88	1	1	0	0	0	2.2	3	5	6	2
Ralph Branca	0	1	4.15	1	1	0	0	0	8.2	4	4	4	6
Carl Erskine	0	0	16.20	2	0	0	0	0	1.2	3	3	1	0
Joe Hatten	0	0	16.20	2	0	0	0	0	1.2	4	3	2	0
Paul Minner	0	0	0.00	1	0	0	0	0	1.0	1	0	0	0
Don Newcombe	0	2	3.09	2	2	1	0	0	11.2	10	4	3	11
Erv Palica	0	0	0.00	1	0	0	0	0	2.0	1	0	1	1
Preacher Roe	1	0	0.00	1	1	1	0	1	9.0	6	0	0	3
TOTAL	1	4	4.30	14	5	2	0	1	44.0	37	21	18	27

GAME 1 AT NY OCT 5

BRO	000	000	000	0	2	0
NY	000	000	001	1	5	1

Pitchers: NEWCOMBE vs REYNOLDS
Home Runs: Henrich-NY
Attendance: 66,224

GAME 2 AT NY OCT 6

BRO	010	000	000	1	7	2
NY	000	000	000	0	6	1

Pitchers: ROE vs RASCHI
Attendance: 70,053

GAME 3 AT BRO OCT 7

NY	001	000	003	4	5	0
BRO	000	100	002	3	5	0

Pitchers: Byrne, PAGE (4) vs BRANCA, Banta (9)
Home Runs: Reese-BRO, Olmo-BRO, Campanella-BRO
Attendance: 32,788

GAME 4 AT BRO OCT 8

NY	000	330	000	6	10	0
BRO	000	004	000	4	9	1

Pitchers: LOPAT, Reynolds (6) VS NEWCOMBE, Hatten (4), Erskine (6), Banta (7)
Attendance: 33,934

GAME 5 AT BRO OCT 9

NY	203	113	000	10	11	1
BRO	001	001	400	6	11	2

Pitchers: RASCHI, Page (7) vs BARNEY, Banta (3), Erskine (6), Hatten (6), Palica (7), Minner (9)
Home Runs: DiMaggio-NY, Hodges-BRO
Attendance: 33,711

Philadelphia's Whiz Kids, who had capped an exciting pennant race with the Phillies' first flag in thirty-five years, carried the excitement into the World Series but couldn't quite catch up with the Yankees. New York scored only one run in the opener; Philadelphia didn't score any. The Phillies did score a run in the second game, but the Yankees scored two. In Game Three the Phillies scored two runs, the Yankees three.

Jim Konstanty, the National League's ace reliever (and MVP), started his first major league game in four years to lead off the Series, and held the Yankees to just four hits in eight innings of work. But Bobby Brown's double in the fourth was followed by two long flies which moved Brown around to the plate—all the scoring New York needed as Vic Raschi held the Phillies to two singles and a walk.

Robin Roberts and Allie Reynolds dueled in Game Two. New York scored first with a run on a walk and two singles in the second inning, but two Phillie singles and a fly to left tied the game in the last of the fifth. There matters stood until the top of the tenth, when Joe DiMaggio led off with a home run to the upper deck in left. Reynolds held the Phillies in the bottom of the tenth for the second Yankee win.

The Phillies took a lead for the only time in the Series when they broke a 1–1 tie with a run in the seventh inning of Game Three. But New York scored on a Phillie error to tie the game again in the eighth, and in the last of the ninth—with two outs—Yankees Gene Woodling, Phil Rizzuto, and Jerry Coleman singled to produce the winning run.

Rookie sensation Whitey Ford started Game Four and held Philadelphia scoreless into the ninth inning as his Yankees scored twice in the first and three more times in the sixth. He was taken out with two away in the ninth after two singles, a hit batsman, and a Yankee error had permitted two Phillies to score. But reliever Allie Reynolds struck out the final batter to secure for the Yankees a Series sweep.

New York Yankees (AL), 4; Philadelphia Phillies (NL), 0

NY (A)

PLAYER/POS	AVG	G	AB	R	H	2B	3B	HR	RB	BB	SO	SB
Hank Bauer, of	.133	4	15	0	2	0	0	0	0	1	0	0
Yogi Berra, c	.200	4	15	2	3	0	0	1	2	2	1	0
Bobby Brown, 3b	.333	4	12	2	4	1	1	0	1	0	0	0
Gerry Coleman, 2b	.286	4	14	2	4	1	0	0	3	2	0	0
Joe Collins, 1b	.000	1	0	0	0	0	0	0	0	0	0	0
Joe Di Maggio, of	.308	4	13	2	4	1	0	1	2	3	1	0
Tom Ferrick, p	.000	1	0	0	0	0	0	0	0	0	0	0
Whitey Ford, p	.000	1	3	0	0	0	0	0	0	0	2	0
Johnny Hopp, 1b	.000	3	2	0	0	0	0	0	0	0	0	0
Jackie Jensen, pr	.000	1	0	0	0	0	0	0	0	0	0	0
Billy Johnson, 3b	.000	4	6	0	0	0	0	0	0	0	3	0
Ed Lopat, p	.500	1	2	0	1	0	0	0	0	0	1	0
Cliff Mapes, of	.000	1	4	0	0	0	0	0	0	0	1	0
Johnny Mize, 1b	.133	4	15	0	2	0	0	0	0	0	1	0
Vic Raschi, p	.333	1	3	0	1	0	0	0	0	0	0	0
Allie Reynolds, p	.333	2	3	0	1	0	0	0	0	1	2	0
Phil Rizzuto, ss	.143	4	14	1	2	0	0	0	0	3	0	1
Gene Woodling, of	.429	4	14	2	6	0	0	0	1	2	0	0
TOTAL	.222		135	11	30	3	1	2	10	13	12	1

PITCHER	W	L	ERA	G	GS	CG	SV	SHO	IP	H	ER	BB	SO
Tom Ferrick	1	0	0.00	1	0	0	0	0	1.0	1	0	1	0
Whitey Ford	1	0	0.00	1	1	0	0	0	8.2	7	0	1	7
Ed Lopat	0	0	2.25	1	1	0	0	0	8.0	9	2	0	5
Vic Raschi	1	0	0.00	1	1	1	0	1	9.0	2	0	1	5
Allie Reynolds	1	0	0.87	2	1	1	1	0	10.1	7	1	4	7
TOTAL	4	0	0.73	6	4	2	1	1	37.0	26	3	7	24

PHI (N)

PLAYER/POS	AVG	G	AB	R	H	2B	3B	HR	RB	BB	SO	SB
Richie Ashburn, of	.176	4	17	0	3	1	0	0	1	0	4	0
Jimmy Bloodworth, 2b	.000	1	0	0	0	0	0	0	0	0	0	0
Putsy Caballero, ph	.000	3	1	0	0	0	0	0	0	0	1	0
Del Ennis, of	.143	4	14	1	2	1	0	0	0	0	1	0
Mike Goliat, 2b	.214	4	14	1	3	0	0	0	1	1	2	0
Granny Hamner, ss	.429	4	14	1	6	2	1	0	0	1	2	1
Ken Heintzelman, p	.000	1	2	0	0	0	0	0	0	0	0	0
Ken Johnson, pr	.000	1	0	1	0	0	0	0	0	0	0	0
Willie Jones, 3b	.286	4	14	1	4	1	0	0	0	0	3	0
Jim Konstanty, p	.250	3	4	0	1	0	0	0	0	0	1	0
Stan Lopata, c-1	.000	2	1	0	0	0	0	0	0	0	1	0
Jackie Mayo, of-1	.000	3	0	0	0	0	0	0	0	1	0	0
Russ Meyer, p	.000	2	0	0	0	0	0	0	0	0	0	0
Bob Miller, p	.000	1	0	0	0	0	0	0	0	0	0	0
Robin Roberts, p	.000	2	2	0	0	0	0	0	0	0	1	0
Andy Seminick, c	.182	4	11	0	2	0	0	0	0	1	3	0
Ken Silvestri, c	.000	1	0	0	0	0	0	0	0	0	0	0
Dick Sisler, of	.059	4	17	0	1	0	0	0	1	0	5	0
Eddie Waitkus, 1b	.267	4	15	0	4	1	0	0	0	2	0	0
Dick Whitman, ph	.000	3	2	0	0	0	0	0	0	1	0	0
TOTAL	.203		128	5	26	6	1	0	3	7	24	1

PITCHER	W	L	ERA	G	GS	CG	SV	SHO	IP	H	ER	BB	SO
Ken Heintzelman	0	0	1.17	1	1	0	0	0	7.2	4	1	6	3
Jim Konstanty	0	1	2.40	3	1	0	0	0	15.0	9	4	4	3
Russ Meyer	0	1	5.40	2	0	0	0	0	1.2	4	1	0	1
Bob Miller	0	1	27.00	1	1	0	0	0	0.1	2	1	0	0
Robin Roberts	0	1	1.64	2	1	1	0	0	11.0	11	2	3	5
TOTAL	0	4	2.27	9	4	1	0	0	35.2	30	9	13	12

GAME 1 AT PHI OCT 4

NY	000 100 000	1 5 0
PHI	000 000 000	0 2 1

Pitchers: RASCHI vs KONSTANTY, Meyer (9)
Attendance: 30,746

GAME 2 AT PHI OCT 5

NY	010 000 000 1	2 10 0
PHI	000 010 000 0	1 7 0

Pitchers: REYNOLDS vs ROBERTS
Home Runs: DiMaggio-NY
Attendance: 32,660

GAME 3 AT NY OCT 6

PHI	000 001 100	2 10 2
NY	001 000 011	3 7 0

Pitchers: Heintzelman, Konstanty (8), MEYER (9) vs Lopat, FERRICK (9)
Attendance: 64,505

GAME 4 AT NY OCT 7

PHI	000 000 002	2 7 1
NY	200 003 00X	5 8 2

Pitchers: MILLER, Konstanty (1), Roberts (8) vs FORD, Reynolds (9)
Home Runs: Berra-NY
Attendance: 68,098

The Giants—who caught Brooklyn with a tremendous late-season drive, then defeated them for the pennant on Bobby Thomson's ninth-inning home run in Game Three of the tie-breaker playoff series—carried their momentum through Game Three of the World Series before bowing to the Yankees. Dave Koslo (the only Giant starter not to see action in the playoff) pitched the Series opener and held the Yankees to one run. Monte Irvin's steal of home for the Giants' second run in the top of the first was enough for the win, but Al Dark made Koslo's lead more secure with a three-run homer in the sixth.

The Yankees evened the Series in Game Two, scoring two early runs (one of them Joe Collins's home run) off Larry Jansen, and holding on for the win behind Ed Lopat's five-hit pitching. But the Giants regained the lead in Game Three with five unearned runs (three of them on Whitey Lockman's homer) in a fifth inning prolonged by two Yankee errors, as pitchers Jim Hearn and Sheldon Jones combined to hold the Bronx Bombers to five hits and a pair of runs (though Hearn issued eight walks).

But that was the end of the Giants' drive. Although they scored first in games Four and Five with first-inning runs, they couldn't hold the lead either time. In Game Four Allie Reynolds held the Giants to two runs as his Yankees scored six—including a two-run homer by Joe DiMaggio in the fifth inning that proved to be the last home run of his career. DiMag drove in three more Yankee runs in Game Five, as did Phil Rizzuto, and rookie infielder Gil McDougald contributed a grand slam as the Bombers earned their nickname in obliterating Giant pitching with 13 runs. Ed Lopat, meanwhile, hurled his second five-hitter of the Series for his second win.

Yankee Hank Bauer tripled with the bases full in the sixth inning of Game Six to break a tie and give the Yankees a 4–1 lead. The Giants loaded the bases with three straight singles to open the top of the ninth, and scored two runners on successive flies to left, to come within one run of a tie. But pinch hitter Sal Yvars (in his only Series at-bat) lined out to right and the Yankees had their fourteenth world title.

New York Yankees (AL), 4;
New York Giants (NL), 2

NY (A)

PLAYER/POS	AVG	G	AB	R	H	2B	3B	HR	RB	BB	SO	SB
Hank Bauer, of	.167	6	18	0	3	0	1	0	3	1	1	0
Yogi Berra, c	.261	6	23	4	6	1	0	0	0	2	1	0
Bobby Brown, 3b-4	.357	5	14	1	5	1	0	0	0	2	1	0
Gerry Coleman, 2b	.250	5	8	2	2	0	0	0	0	1	2	0
Joe Collins, 1b-6,of-1	.222	6	18	2	4	0	0	1	3	2	1	0
Joe Di Maggio, of	.261	6	23	3	6	2	0	1	5	2	4	0
Bobby Hogue, p	.000	2	0	0	0	0	0	0	0	0	0	0
Johnny Hopp, ph	.000	1	0	0	0	0	0	0	0	1	0	0
Bob Kuzava, p	.000	1	0	0	0	0	0	0	0	0	0	0
Ed Lopat, p	.125	2	8	0	1	0	0	0	0	1	0	2	0
Mickey Mantle, of	.200	2	5	1	1	0	0	0	0	2	1	0
Billy Martin, pr	.000	1	0	1	0	0	0	0	0	0	0	0
Gil Mc Dougald, 3b-5,2b-4	.261	6	23	2	6	1	0	1	7	2	2	0
Johnny Mize, 1b-2	.286	4	7	2	2	1	0	0	1	2	0	0
Tom Morgan, p	.000	1	0	0	0	0	0	0	0	0	0	0
Joe Ostrowski, p	.000	1	0	0	0	0	0	0	0	0	0	0
Vic Raschi, p	.000	2	2	0	0	0	0	0	0	0	2	0
Allie Reynolds, p	.333	2	6	0	2	0	0	0	0	1	0	1	0
Phil Rizzuto, ss	.320	6	25	5	8	0	0	1	3	2	3	0
Johnny Sain, p	.000	1	1	0	0	0	0	0	0	0	0	0
Gene Woodling, of-5	.167	6	18	6	3	1	1	1	1	1	5	0
TOTAL	.246		199	29	49	7	2	5	25	26	23	0

PITCHER	W	L	ERA	G	GS	CG	SV	SHO	IP	H	ER	BB	SO
Bobby Hogue	0	0	0.00	2	0	0	0	0	2.2	1	0	0	0
Bob Kuzava	0	0	0.00	1	0	0	1	0	1.0	0	0	0	0
Ed Lopat	2	0	0.50	2	2	2	0	0	18.0	10	1	3	4
Tom Morgan	0	0	0.00	1	0	0	0	0	2.0	2	0	1	3
Joe Ostrowski	0	0	0.00	1	0	0	0	0	2.0	1	0	0	1
Vic Raschi	1	1	0.87	2	2	0	0	0	10.1	12	1	8	4
Allie Reynolds	1	1	4.20	2	2	1	0	0	15.0	16	7	11	8
Johnny Sain	0	0	9.00	1	0	0	0	0	2.0	4	2	2	2
TOTAL	4	2	1.87	12	6	3	1	0	53.0	46	11	25	22

NY (N)

PLAYER/POS	AVG	G	AB	R	H	2B	3B	HR	RB	BB	SO	SB
Al Corwin, p	.000	1	0	0	0	0	0	0	0	0	0	0
Alvin Dark, ss	.417	6	24	5	10	3	0	1	4	2	3	0
Clint Hartung, of	.000	2	4	0	0	0	0	0	0	0	0	0
Jim Hearn, p	.000	2	3	0	0	0	0	0	0	0	1	0
Monte Irvin, of	.458	6	24	3	11	0	1	0	2	2	1	2
Larry Jansen, p	.000	3	2	0	0	0	0	0	0	0	0	0
Sheldon Jones, p	.000	2	0	0	0	0	0	0	0	0	0	0
Monte Kennedy, p	.000	2	0	0	0	0	0	0	0	0	0	0
Alex Konikowski, p	.000	1	0	0	0	0	0	0	0	0	0	0
Dave Koslo, p	.000	2	5	0	0	0	0	0	0	0	2	0
Whitey Lockman, 1b	.240	6	25	1	6	2	0	1	4	1	2	0
Jack Lohrke, ph	.000	2	2	0	0	0	0	0	0	0	1	0
Sal Maglie, p	.000	1	1	0	0	0	0	0	0	0	1	0
Willie Mays, of	.182	6	22	1	4	0	0	0	1	2	2	0
Ray Noble, c	.000	2	2	0	0	0	0	0	0	0	1	0
Bill Rigney, ph	.250	4	4	0	1	0	0	0	0	1	0	1	0
Hank Schenz, pr	.000	1	0	0	0	0	0	0	0	0	0	0
George Spencer, p	.000	2	0	0	0	0	0	0	0	0	0	0
Eddie Stanky, 2b	.136	6	22	3	3	0	0	0	1	3	2	0
Hank Thompson, of	.143	5	14	3	2	0	0	0	0	5	2	0
Bobby Thomson, 3b	.238	6	21	1	5	1	0	0	2	5	0	0
Wes Westrum, c	.235	6	17	1	4	1	0	0	0	5	3	0
Davey Williams, ph	.000	2	1	0	0	0	0	0	0	0	0	0
Sal Yvars, ph	.000	1	1	0	0	0	0	0	0	0	0	0
TOTAL	.237		194	18	46	7	1	2	15	25	22	2

PITCHER	W	L	ERA	G	GS	CG	SV	SHO	IP	H	ER	BB	SO
Al Corwin	0	0	0.00	1	0	0	0	0	1.2	1	0	0	1
Jim Hearn	1	0	1.04	2	1	0	0	0	8.2	5	1	8	1
Larry Jansen	0	2	6.30	3	2	0	0	0	10.0	8	7	4	6
Sheldon Jones	0	0	2.08	2	0	0	1	0	4.1	5	1	1	2
Monte Kennedy	0	0	6.00	2	0	0	0	0	3.0	3	2	1	4
Alex Konikowski	0	0	0.00	1	0	0	0	0	1.0	1	0	0	0
Dave Koslo	1	1	3.00	2	2	1	0	0	15.0	12	5	7	6
Sal Maglie	0	1	7.20	1	1	0	0	0	5.0	8	4	2	3
George Spencer	0	0	18.90	2	0	0	0	0	3.1	6	7	3	0
TOTAL	2	4	4.67	16	6	1	1	0	52.0	49	27	26	23

GAME 1 AT NY-A OCT 4

NY-N	200	003	000	5 10 1
NY-A	010	000	000	1 7 1

Pitchers: KOSLO vs REYNOLDS, Hogue (7), Morgan (8)
Home Runs: Dark-NY(N)
Attendance: 65,673

GAME 2 AT NY-A OCT 5

NY-N	000	000	100	1 5 1
NY-A	110	000	01X	3 6 0

Pitchers: JANSEN, Spencer (7) vs LOPAT
Home Runs: Collins-NY(A)
Attendance: 66,018

GAME 3 AT NY-N OCT 6

NY-A	000	000	011	2 5 2
NY-N	010	050	00X	6 7 2

Pitchers: RASCHI, Hogue (5), Ostrowski (7) vs HEARN, Jones (8)
Home Runs: Lockman-NY(N), Woodling-NY(A)
Attendance: 52,035

GAME 4 AT NY-N OCT 8

NY-A	010	120	200	6 12 0
NY-N	100	010	000	2 8 2

Pitchers: REYNOLDS vs MAGLIE, Jones (6), Kennedy (9)
Home Runs: DiMaggio-NY(A)
Attendance: 49,010

GAME 5 AT NY-N OCT 9

NY-A	005	202	400	13 12 1
NY-N	100	000	000	1 5 3

Pitchers: LOPAT vs JANSEN, Kennedy (4), Spencer (6), Corwin (7), Konikowski (9)
Home Runs: McDougald-NY(A), Rizzuto-NY(A)
Attendance: 47,530

GAME 6 AT NY-A OCT 10

NY-N	000	010	002	3 11 1
NY-A	100	003	00X	4 7 0

Pitchers: KOSLO, Hearn (7), Jansen (8) vs RASCHI, Sain (7), Kuzava (9)
Attendance: 61,711

In four of the seven games, home runs provided the margin of victory. Homers accounted for five of the six runs scored in the opener, with Duke Snider's two-run blast in the sixth putting Brooklyn ahead to stay. Star Dodger reliever Joe Black, in only his third start of the year, held New York to six hits and two runs in defeating Yankee ace Allie Reynolds.

Four home runs enlivened the next three games but did not govern the outcomes. Billy Martin's three-run shot was the centerpiece of the Yankee assault in Game Two, but New York would have won without it behind Vic Raschi's one-run three-hitter. Brooklyn needed no homers to regain the Series advantage in Game Three. In the top of the ninth, with the Dodgers leading by a run, Pee Wee Reese and Jackie Robinson singled (driving out starter Ed Lopat) and pulled a double steal. Both then scored on a passed ball. Yankee pinch hitter Johnny Mize homered in the last of the ninth, but Preacher Roe escaped without further scoring for a complete-game 5–3 win.

Black opposed Reynolds again in Game Four and bettered his earlier performance, holding New York to three hits and one run (a Mize homer) in seven innings. But Reynolds improved even more, fanning ten as he shut the Dodgers out.

Snider hit his second homer of the Series and Mize his third in the fifth inning of Game Five. Mize's shot put New York ahead, but Brooklyn tied the game in the seventh and took a 6–5 lead when Snider doubled home a run in the eleventh. Dodger right fielder Carl Furillo's leaping catch in the last of the eleventh robbed Mize of another home run, and starter Carl Erskine held on for the win, giving Brooklyn a 3–2 Series lead.

Snider's home run in the last of the sixth ended Vic Raschi's shutout in Game Six, but Yogi Berra, the first Yankee up in the seventh, tied the game and spoiled Billy Loes's shutout with his home run, and pitcher Raschi singled home the go-ahead run two outs later. Yankee sophomore Mickey Mantle's blast in the eighth (the first of his record 18 World Series home runs) made the score 3–1. Snider's fourth homer of the Series gave the Dodgers a second run in the eighth, but Allie Reynolds relieved Raschi and prevented further scoring, sending the Series to a seventh game.

Joe Black traded three shutout innings with Yankee Ed Lopat in the finale before both clubs scored single runs in the fourth and fifth innings. Mantle homered off Black in the sixth for a third Yankee run that proved the Series

New York Yankees (AL), 4; Brooklyn Dodgers (NL), 3

NY (A)

PLAYER/POS	AVG	G	AB	R	H	2B	3B	HR	RB	BB	SO	SB
Hank Bauer, of	.056	7	18	2	1	0	0	0	1	4	3	0
Yogi Berra, c	.214	7	28	2	6	1	0	2	3	2	4	0
Ewell Blackwell, p	.000	1	1	0	0	0	0	0	0	0	0	0
Joe Collins, 1b	.000	6	12	1	0	0	0	0	0	1	3	0
Tom Gorman, p	.000	1	0	0	0	0	0	0	0	0	0	0
Ralph Houk, ph	.000	1	1	0	0	0	0	0	0	0	0	0
Bob Kuzava, p	.000	1	1	0	0	0	0	0	0	0	0	0
Ed Lopat, p	.333	2	3	0	1	0	0	0	1	1	1	0
Mickey Mantle, of	.345	7	29	5	10	1	1	2	3	3	4	0
Billy Martin, 2b	.217	7	23	2	5	0	0	1	4	2	2	0
Gil Mc Dougald, 3b	.200	7	25	5	5	0	0	1	3	5	2	1
Johnny Mize, 1b-4	.400	5	15	3	6	1	0	3	6	3	1	0
Irv Noren, of-3	.300	4	10	0	3	0	0	0	1	1	3	0
Vic Raschi, p	.167	3	6	0	1	0	0	0	1	1	2	0
Allie Reynolds, p	.000	4	7	0	0	0	0	0	0	0	2	0
Phil Rizzuto, ss	.148	7	27	2	4	1	0	0	0	5	2	0
Johnny Sain, p-1	.000	2	3	0	0	0	0	0	0	0	0	0
Ray Scarborough, p	.000	1	0	0	0	0	0	0	0	0	0	0
Gene Woodling, of-6	.348	7	23	4	8	1	1	1	1	3	3	0
TOTAL	.216		232	26	50	5	2	10	24	31	32	1

PITCHER	W	L	ERA	G	GS	CG	SV	SHO	IP	H	ER	BB	SO
Ewell Blackwell	0	0	7.20	1	1	0	0	0	5.0	4	4	3	4
Tom Gorman	0	0	0.00	1	0	0	0	0	0.2	1	0	0	0
Bob Kuzava	0	0	0.00	1	0	0	1	0	2.2	0	0	0	2
Ed Lopat	0	1	4.76	2	2	0	0	0	11.1	14	6	4	3
Vic Raschi	2	0	1.59	3	2	1	0	0	17.0	12	3	8	18
Allie Reynolds	2	1	1.77	4	2	1	1	1	20.1	12	4	6	18
Johnny Sain	0	1	3.00	2	1	0	0	0	6.0	6	2	3	3
Ray Scarborough	0	0	9.00	1	0	0	0	0	1.0	1	1	0	1
TOTAL	4	3	2.81	14	7	2	2	1	64.0	50	20	24	49

BRO (N)

PLAYER/POS	AVG	G	AB	R	H	2B	3B	HR	RB	BB	SO	SB
Sandy Amoros, ph	.000	1	0	0	0	0	0	0	0	0	0	0
Joe Black, p	.000	3	6	0	0	0	0	0	0	1	6	0
Roy Campanella, c	.214	7	28	0	6	0	0	0	1	1	6	0
Billy Cox, 3b	.296	7	27	4	8	2	0	0	0	3	4	0
Carl Erskine, p	.000	3	6	1	0	0	0	0	0	0	1	0
Carl Furillo, of	.174	7	23	1	4	2	0	0	0	3	3	0
Gil Hodges, 1b	.000	7	21	1	0	0	0	0	1	5	6	0
Tommy Holmes, of	.000	3	1	0	0	0	0	0	0	0	0	0
Ken Lehman, p	.000	1	0	0	0	0	0	0	0	0	0	0
Billy Loes, p	.333	2	3	0	1	0	0	0	0	0	1	1
Bobby Morgan, 3b	.000	2	1	0	0	0	0	0	0	0	0	0
Rocky Nelson, ph	.000	4	3	0	0	0	0	0	0	1	2	0
Andy Pafko, of-5	.190	7	21	0	4	0	0	0	2	0	4	0
Pee Wee Reese, ss	.345	7	29	4	10	0	0	1	4	2	2	1
Jackie Robinson, 2b	.174	7	23	4	4	0	0	1	2	7	5	2
Preacher Roe, p	.000	3	2	0	0	0	0	0	0	0	0	0
Johnny Rutherford, p	.000	1	0	0	0	0	0	0	0	0	0	0
George Shuba, of-3	.300	4	10	0	3	1	0	0	0	0	4	0
Duke Snider, of	.345	7	29	5	10	2	0	4	8	1	5	1
TOTAL	.215		233	20	50	7	0	6	18	24	49	5

PITCHER	W	L	ERA	G	GS	CG	SV	SHO	IP	H	ER	BB	SO
Joe Black	1	2	2.53	3	3	1	0	0	21.1	15	6	8	9
Carl Erskine	1	1	4.50	3	2	1	0	0	18.0	12	9	10	10
Ken Lehman	0	0	0.00	1	0	0	0	0	2.0	2	0	1	0
Billy Loes	0	1	4.35	2	1	0	0	0	10.1	11	5	5	5
Preacher Roe	1	0	3.18	3	1	1	0	0	11.1	9	4	6	7
Johnny Rutherford	0	0	9.00	1	0	0	0	0	1.0	1	1	1	1
TOTAL	3	4	3.52	13	7	3	0	0	64.0	50	25	31	32

winner, as three Yankee relievers held Brooklyn scoreless through the final four frames.

GAME 1 AT BRO OCT 1

```
NY    010 000 010    2 6 2
BRO   010 002 01X    4 6 0
```
Pitchers: REYNOLDS, Scarborough (8) vs BLACK
Home Runs: Robinson-BRO, Snider-BRO, Reese-BRO, McDougald-NY
Attendance: 34,861

GAME 2 AT BRO OCT 2

```
NY    000 115 000    7 10 0
BRO   001 000 000    1 3 1
```
Pitchers: RASCHI vs ERSKINE, Loes (6), Lehman (8)
Home Runs: Martin-NY
Attendance: 33,792

GAME 3 AT NY OCT 3

```
BRO   001 010 012    5 11 0
NY    010 000 011    3 6 2
```
Pitchers: ROE vs LOPAT, Gorman (9)
Home Runs: Berra-NY, Mize-NY
Attendance: 66,698

GAME 4 AT NY OCT 4

```
BRO   000 000 000    0 4 1
NY    000 100 01X    2 4 1
```
Pitchers: BLACK, Rutherford (8) VS REYNOLDS
Home Runs: Mize-NY
Attendance: 71,787

GAME 5 AT NY OCT 5

```
BRO   010 030 100 01    6 10 0
NY    000 050 000 00    5 5 1
```
Pitchers: ERSKINE vs Blackwell, SAIN (6)
Home Runs: Snider-BRO, Mize-NY
Attendance: 70,536

GAME 6 AT BRO OCT 6

```
NY    000 000 210    3 9 0
BRO   000 001 010    2 8 1
```
Pitchers: RASCHI, Reynolds (8) vs LOES, Roe (9)
Home Runs: Snider-BRO (2), Berra-NY, Mantle-NY
Attendance: 30,037

GAME 7 AT BRO OCT 7

```
NY    000 111 100    4 10 4
BRO   000 110 000    2 8 1
```
Pitchers: Lopat, REYNOLDS (4), Raschi (7), Kuzava (7) vs BLACK, Roe (6), Erskine (8)
Home Runs: Woodling-NY, Mantle-NY
Attendance: 33,195

Although the Yankees easily won the American League pennant, the Dodgers seemed even more overwhelming, with a team batting average of .285 and a club-record 105 season wins. But when the Series was over, the Yankees had added a record fifth straight world championship to their record fifth straight pennant.

Dodger ace Carl Erskine lasted only one inning of the Series opener, giving up three walks and two triples for four Yankee runs. By the middle of the seventh inning, the Dodgers had tied the score at 5–5. But Yankee Joe Collins homered to break the tie in the last of the seventh, and reliever Johnny Sain ensured his own win with a two-run double an inning later. The Dodgers outhit New York in Game Two, and held a 2–1 lead entering the bottom of the seventh. But Billy Martin (who hit .500 and slugged .958 in the Series) tied the game with a leadoff homer in the seventh, and Mickey Mantle won it with a two-run blast in the eighth.

Down 0–2, Brooklyn evened the Series at home with victories in Games Three and Four. Erskine redeemed his poor start in Game One with a record-setting 14-strikeout performance in Game Three. But it was a narrow win, settled only when Roy Campanella homered in the last of the eighth to break a 2–2 tie. In Game Four, Duke Snider made Billy Loes's three-run pitching a winning performance, driving in four of the Dodgers' seven runs with two doubles and a homer.

But Brooklyn never even took the lead in the final two games. Four Yankee home runs (including a Mantle grand slam) rocked Dodger pitching in Game Five as the Bombers built a lead which Dodger home runs in the eighth and ninth were unable to overcome. In Game Six the Yankees built a 3–0 lead over Erskine in the first two innings. Brooklyn fought back with a run in the sixth, and tied the game on Carl Furillo's two-run homer in the top of the ninth. But with men on first and second in the last of the ninth, Yankee Billy Martin singled in the game-ending, Series-winning run. It was Martin's twelfth hit, a new record for a six-game Series.

New York Yankees (AL), 4; Brooklyn Dodgers (NL), 2

NY (A)

PLAYER/POS	AVG	G	AB	R	H	2B	3B	HR	RB	BB	SO	SB
Hank Bauer, of	.261	6	23	6	6	0	1	0	1	2	4	0
Yogi Berra, c	.429	6	21	3	9	1	0	1	4	3	3	0
Don Bollweg, 1b-1	.000	3	2	0	0	0	0	0	0	0	2	0
Joe Collins, 1b	.167	6	24	4	4	1	0	1	2	3	8	0
Whitey Ford, p	.333	2	3	0	1	0	0	0	0	0	0	0
Tom Gorman, p	.000	1	1	0	0	0	0	0	0	0	1	0
Bob Kuzava, p	.000	1	1	0	0	0	0	0	0	0	1	0
Ed Lopat, p	.000	1	3	0	0	0	0	0	0	0	0	0
Mickey Mantle, of	.208	6	24	3	5	0	0	2	7	3	8	0
Billy Martin, 2b	.500	6	24	5	12	1	2	2	8	1	2	1
Jim Mc Donald, p	.500	1	2	0	1	1	0	0	1	1	1	0
Gil Mc Dougald, 3b	.167	6	24	2	4	0	1	2	4	1	3	0
Johnny Mize, ph	.000	3	3	0	0	0	0	0	0	0	1	0
Irv Noren, ph	.000	2	1	0	0	0	0	0	0	1	0	0
Vic Raschi, p	.000	1	2	0	0	0	0	0	0	0	1	0
Allie Reynolds, p	.500	3	2	0	1	0	0	0	0	1	1	0
Phil Rizzuto, ss	.316	6	19	4	6	1	0	0	0	3	2	1
Johnny Sain, p	.500	2	2	1	1	1	0	0	2	0	1	0
Art Schallock, p	.000	1	0	0	0	0	0	0	0	0	0	0
Gene Woodling, of	.300	6	20	5	6	0	0	1	3	6	2	0
TOTAL	.279		201	33	56	6	4	9	32	25	43	2

PITCHER	W	L	ERA	G	GS	CG	SV	SHO	IP	H	ER	BB	SO
Whitey Ford	0	1	4.50	2	2	0	0	0	8.0	9	4	2	7
Tom Gorman	0	0	3.00	1	0	0	0	0	3.0	4	1	0	1
Bob Kuzava	0	0	13.50	1	0	0	0	0	0.2	2	1	0	1
Ed Lopat	1	0	2.00	1	1	1	0	0	9.0	9	2	4	3
Jim Mc Donald	1	0	5.87	1	1	0	0	0	7.2	12	5	0	3
Vic Raschi	0	1	3.38	1	1	1	0	0	8.0	9	3	3	4
Allie Reynolds	1	0	6.75	3	1	0	1	0	8.0	9	6	4	9
Johnny Sain	1	0	4.76	2	0	0	0	0	5.2	8	3	1	1
Art Schallock	0	0	4.50	1	0	0	0	0	2.0	2	1	1	1
TOTAL	4	2	4.50	13	6	2	1	0	52.0	64	26	15	30

BRO (N)

PLAYER/POS	AVG	G	AB	R	H	2B	3B	HR	RB	BB	SO	SB
Wayne Belardi, ph	.000	2	2	0	0	0	0	0	0	0	1	0
Joe Black, p	.000	1	0	0	0	0	0	0	0	0	0	0
Roy Campanella, c	.273	6	22	6	6	0	0	1	2	2	3	0
Billy Cox, 3b	.304	6	23	3	7	3	0	1	6	1	4	0
Carl Erskine, p	.250	3	4	0	1	0	0	0	0	0	1	0
Carl Furillo, of	.333	6	24	4	8	2	0	1	4	1	3	0
Jim Gilliam, 2b	.296	6	27	4	8	3	0	2	4	0	2	0
Gil Hodges, 1b	.364	6	22	3	8	0	0	1	1	3	3	1
Jim Hughes, p	.000	1	1	0	0	0	0	0	0	0	1	0
Clem Labine, p	.000	3	2	0	0	0	0	0	0	0	1	0
Billy Loes, p	.667	1	3	0	2	0	0	0	0	0	0	0
Russ Meyer, p	.000	1	1	0	0	0	0	0	0	0	1	0
Bob Milliken, p	.000	1	0	0	0	0	0	0	0	0	0	0
Bobby Morgan, ph	.000	1	1	0	0	0	0	0	0	0	0	0
Johnny Podres, p	1.000	1	1	0	1	0	0	0	0	0	0	0
Pee Wee Reese, ss	.208	6	24	0	5	0	1	0	4	4	1	0
Jackie Robinson, of	.320	6	25	3	8	2	0	0	2	1	0	1
Preacher Roe, p	.000	1	3	0	0	0	0	0	0	0	2	0
George Shuba, ph	1.000	2	1	1	1	0	0	1	2	0	0	0
Duke Snider, of	.320	6	25	3	8	3	0	1	5	2	6	0
Don Thompson, of	.000	2	0	0	0	0	0	0	0	0	0	0
Ben Wade, p	.000	2	0	0	0	0	0	0	0	0	0	0
Dick Williams, ph	.500	3	2	0	1	0	0	0	0	1	1	0
TOTAL	.300		213	27	64	13	1	8	26	15	30	2

PITCHER	W	L	ERA	G	GS	CG	SV	SHO	IP	H	ER	BB	SO
Joe Black	0	0	9.00	1	0	0	0	0	1.0	1	1	0	2
Carl Erskine	1	0	5.79	3	3	1	0	0	14.0	14	9	9	16
Jim Hughes	0	0	2.25	1	0	0	0	0	4.0	3	1	1	3
Clem Labine	0	2	3.60	3	0	0	1	0	5.0	10	2	1	3
Billy Loes	1	0	3.38	1	1	0	0	0	8.0	8	3	2	8
Russ Meyer	0	0	6.23	1	1	0	0	0	4.1	8	3	4	5
Bob Milliken	0	0	0.00	1	0	0	0	0	2.0	2	0	1	0
Johnny Podres	0	1	3.38	1	1	0	0	0	2.2	1	1	2	0
Preacher Roe	0	1	4.50	1	1	1	0	0	8.0	5	4	4	4
Ben Wade	0	0	15.43	2	0	0	0	0	2.1	4	4	1	2
TOTAL	2	4	4.91	15	6	2	1	0	51.1	56	28	25	43

GAME 1 AT NY SEPT 30

BRO	000	013	100	5	12 2
NY	400	010	13X	9	12 0

Pitchers: Erskine, Hughes (2), LABINE (6), Wade (8) vs Reynolds, SAIN (6)
Home Runs: Gilliam-BRO, Hodges-BRO, Shuba-BRO, Berra-NY, Collins-NY
Attendance: 69,374

GAME 2 AT NY OCT 1

BRO	000	200	000	2	9 1
NY	100	000	12X	4	5 0

Pitchers: ROE vs LOPAT
Home Runs: Martin-NY, Mantle-NY
Attendance: 66,786

GAME 3 AT BRO OCT 2

NY	000	010	010	2	6 0
BRO	000	011	01X	3	9 0

Pitchers: RASCHI vs ERSKINE
Home Runs: Campanella-BRO
Attendance: 35,270

GAME 4 AT BRO OCT 3

NY	000	020	001	3	9 0
BRO	300	102	10X	7	12 0

Pitchers: FORD, Gorman (2), Sain (5), Schallock (7) vs LOES, Labine (9)
Home Runs: McDougald-NY, Snider-BRO
Attendance: 36,775

GAME 5 AT BRO OCT 4

NY	105	000	311	11	11 1
BRO	010	010	041	7	14 1

Pitchers: McDONALD, Kuzava (8), Reynolds (9) vs PODRES, Meyer (3), Wade (8), Black (9)
Home Runs: Woodling-NY, Mantle-NY, Martin-NY, McDougald-NY, Cox-BRO, Gilliam-BRO
Attendance: 36,775

GAME 6 AT NY OCT 5

BRO	000	001	002	3	8 3
NY	210	000	001	4	13 0

Pitchers: Erskine, Milliken (5), LABINE (7) vs Ford, REYNOLDS (8)
Home Runs: Furillo-BRO
Attendance: 62,370

The Indians, who had won a league-record 111 games to break the American League domination of the New York Yankees, entered the World Series as strong favorites to humble the Giants. It was not to be.

Cleveland would have won the opener had it not been played in New York's Polo Grounds, with their short foul lines and deep center field. Most of the game was a pitchers' duel. Vic Wertz (the only Indian to hit safely in all four games) tripled off Sal Maglie to give Cleveland a two-run lead in the top of the first, but three Giant singles and a walk in the third off Bob Lemon tied the score. Lemon then settled down to hold New York scoreless through the ninth. Cleveland threatened in the eighth when the first two batters reached base, bringing Wertz to the plate. As he had already hit Maglie safely three times, Don Liddle was brought in to pitch to him. Wertz responded with a fly to deep center that would have been a home run in Cleveland, but in New York turned into the most famous catch in World Series history as Willie Mays raced out and tracked down the ball about 425 feet from the plate. Marv Grissom replaced Liddle on the mound and issued a walk to load the bases, but he retired the next two batters and (despite Wertz's double in the top of the tenth) held Cleveland scoreless the rest of the way. In the last of the tenth, Lemon retired the first batter, but Mays walked and stole second, and Hank Thompson was walked intentionally to set up the double play. Pinch hitter Dusty Rhodes then entered the hall of heroes with a short fly to right that—though it would have been an out in Cleveland—fell into the Polo Grounds stands for three runs and a Giant victory.

The rest of the Series was anticlimax. In the second game Rhodes, with half the Giants' four hits, drove in two runs on a single and another homer, providing the margin of victory for Giant ace Johnny Antonelli, who allowed only one of Cleveland's 14 baserunners to score. Game Three was no contest. New York had scored all six of its runs before the Indians managed to come up with single runs in both the seventh and eighth. Pinch hitter Hank Majeski's three-run homer put Cleveland on the board in the fifth inning of Game Four. But as New York had already scored seven times, even a fourth Cleveland run in the seventh proved too little to prevent a Giant sweep.

New York Giants (NL), 4; Cleveland Indians (AL), 0

NY (N)

PLAYER/POS	AVG	G	AB	R	H	2B	3B	HR	RB	BB	SO	SB
Johnny Antonelli, p	.000	2	3	0	0	0	0	0	0	1	0	0
Alvin Dark, ss	.412	4	17	2	7	0	0	0	0	1	1	0
Ruben Gomez, p	.000	1	4	0	0	0	0	0	0	0	2	0
Marv Grissom, p	.000	1	1	0	0	0	0	0	0	0	1	0
Monte Irvin, of	.222	4	9	1	2	1	0	0	2	0	3	0
Don Liddle, p	.000	2	3	0	0	0	0	0	0	0	2	0
Whitey Lockman, 1b	.111	4	18	2	2	0	0	0	0	1	2	0
Sal Maglie, p	.000	1	3	0	0	0	0	0	0	0	2	0
Willie Mays, of	.286	4	14	4	4	1	0	0	3	4	1	1
Don Mueller, of	.389	4	18	4	7	0	0	0	1	0	1	0
Dusty Rhodes, of-2	.667	3	6	2	4	0	0	2	7	1	2	0
Hank Thompson, 3b	.364	4	11	6	4	1	0	0	2	7	1	0
Wes Westrum, c	.273	4	11	0	3	0	0	0	3	1	3	0
Hoyt Wilhelm, p	.000	2	1	0	0	0	0	0	0	0	1	0
Davey Williams, 2b	.000	4	11	0	0	0	0	0	1	2	2	0
TOTAL	.254		130	21	33	3	0	2	20	17	24	1

PITCHER	W	L	ERA	G	GS	CG	SV	SHO	IP	H	ER	BB	SO
Johnny Antonelli	1	0	0.84	2	1	1	1	0	10.2	8	1	7	12
Ruben Gomez	1	0	2.45	1	1	0	0	0	7.1	4	2	3	2
Marv Grissom	1	0	0.00	1	0	0	0	0	2.2	1	0	3	2
Don Liddle	1	0	1.29	2	1	0	0	0	7.0	5	1	1	2
Sal Maglie	0	0	2.57	1	1	0	0	0	7.0	7	2	2	2
Hoyt Wilhelm	0	0	0.00	2	0	0	1	0	2.1	1	0	0	3
TOTAL	4	0	1.46	9	4	1	2	0	37.0	26	6	16	23

CLE (A)

PLAYER/POS	AVG	G	AB	R	H	2B	3B	HR	RB	BB	SO	SB
Bobby Avila, 2b	.133	4	15	1	2	0	0	0	0	2	1	0
Sam Dente, ss	.000	3	3	1	0	0	0	0	0	1	0	0
Larry Doby, of	.125	4	16	0	2	0	0	0	0	2	4	0
Mike Garcia, p	.000	2	0	0	0	0	0	0	0	0	0	0
Bill Glynn, 1b-1	.500	2	2	1	1	1	0	0	0	0	1	0
Mickey Grasso, c	.000	1	0	0	0	0	0	0	0	0	0	0
Jim Hegan, c	.154	4	13	1	2	1	0	0	0	1	1	0
Art Houtteman, p	.000	1	0	0	0	0	0	0	0	0	0	0
Bob Lemon, p-2	.000	3	6	0	0	0	0	0	0	1	1	0
Hank Majeski, 3b-1	.167	4	6	1	1	0	0	1	3	0	1	0
Dale Mitchell, ph	.000	3	2	0	0	0	0	0	0	1	0	0
Don Mossi, p	.000	3	0	0	0	0	0	0	0	0	0	0
Hal Naragon, c	.000	1	0	0	0	0	0	0	0	0	0	0
Ray Narleski, p	.000	2	0	0	0	0	0	0	0	0	0	0
Hal Newhouser, p	.000	1	0	0	0	0	0	0	0	0	0	0
Dave Philley, of-2	.125	4	8	0	1	0	0	0	0	1	3	0
Dave Pope, of-2	.000	3	3	0	0	0	0	0	0	1	1	0
Rudy Regalado, 3b-1	.333	4	3	0	1	0	0	0	1	0	0	0
Al Rosen, 3b	.250	3	12	0	3	0	0	0	0	1	0	0
Al Smith, of	.214	4	14	2	3	0	0	1	2	2	2	0
George Strickland, ss	.000	3	9	0	0	0	0	0	0	0	2	0
Vic Wertz, 1b	.500	4	16	2	8	2	1	1	3	2	2	0
Wally Westlake, of	.143	2	7	0	1	0	0	0	0	1	3	0
Early Wynn, p	.500	1	2	0	1	1	0	0	0	0	1	0
TOTAL	.190		137	9	26	5	1	3	9	16	23	0

PITCHER	W	L	ERA	G	GS	CG	SV	SHO	IP	H	ER	BB	SO
Mike Garcia	0	1	5.40	2	1	0	0	0	5.0	6	3	4	4
Art Houtteman	0	0	4.50	1	0	0	0	0	2.0	2	1	1	1
Bob Lemon	0	2	6.75	2	2	1	0	0	13.1	16	10	8	11
Don Mossi	0	0	0.00	3	0	0	0	0	4.0	3	0	0	1
Ray Narleski	0	0	2.25	2	0	0	0	0	4.0	1	1	1	2
Hal Newhouser	0	0	INF	1	0	0	0	0	0.0	1	1	1	0
Early Wynn	0	1	3.86	1	1	0	0	0	7.0	4	3	2	5
TOTAL	0	4	4.84	12	4	1	0	0	35.1	33	19	17	24

GAME 1 AT NY SEPT 29

```
CLE  200 000 000 0   2  8  0
NY   002 000 000 3   5  9  3
```
Pitchers: LEMON vs Maglie, Liddle (8), GRISSOM (8)
Home Runs: Rhodes-NY
Attendance: 52,751

GAME 2 AT NY SEPT 30

```
CLE  100 000 000   1  8  0
NY   000 020 10X   3  4  0
```
Pitchers: WYNN, Mossi (8) vs ANTONELLI
Home Runs: Smith-CLE, Rhodes-NY
Attendance: 49,099

GAME 3 AT CLE OCT 1

```
NY   103 011 000   6 10  1
CLE  000 000 110   2  4  2
```
Pitchers: GOMEZ, Wilhelm (7) vs GARCIA, Houtteman (4), Narleski (6), Mossi (9)
Home Runs: Wertz-CLE
Attendance: 71,555

GAME 4 AT CLE OCT 2

```
NY   021 040 000   7 10  3
CLE  000 030 100   4  6  2
```
Pitchers: LIDDLE, Wilhelm (7), Antonelli (8) vs LEMON, Newhouser (5), Narleski (5), Mossi (6), Garcia (8)
Home Runs: Majeski-CLE
Attendance: 78,102

The Dodgers and Yankees, after a year's absence, faced each other again in the World Series—their sixth Series confrontation in fifteen years. And after Brooklyn had lost the first two games it began to look as though 1955 might also mark the Yankees' sixth Series triumph over the Dodgers. But this was Brooklyn's year.

The opener was a hitters' game, but closely contested. Both teams scored twice in the second inning and once in the third, but Yankee first baseman Joe Collins's leadoff homer in the last of the fourth gave New York its first lead of the game, and his two-run blast in the sixth made the score 6–3. Brooklyn clawed back in the eighth for two runs—including Jackie Robinson's steal of home—to pull within one run of a tie, but they came no closer. In Game Two, Yankee pitcher Tommy Byrne held the Dodgers to five hits and two runs, and won his own game at the bat with a two-run single that capped the Yankees' four-run fourth.

The Series turned around as the Dodgers captured the next three games in Brooklyn. Roy Campanella's two-run homer in the first inning of Game Three gave Brooklyn a quick lead. New York tied the game with a pair of runs in the second (one of them a homer by Mickey Mantle, who appeared in only three Series games because of a leg injury). But two more Dodger runs in the last of the second drove out Yankee starter Bob Turley and put them ahead to stay as Dodger hurler Johnny Podres held the Yankees to three runs. Home runs by Campanella, Gil Hodges, and Duke Snider accounted for six of Brooklyn's eight runs in Game Four as the Dodgers evened the Series at two-all. Sandy Amoros's second-inning homer initiated the scoring in Game Five, and Snider's blasts in the third and fifth (which made him the first player to hit four home runs in two different Series) gave Brooklyn a 4–1 lead, which even late-inning Yankee homers by Bob Cerv and Yogi Berra could not overcome.

New York bounced back in Game Six, scoring all five of their runs in the first inning (including three on Bill Skowron's homer) to give Whitey Ford a comfortable lead, which he held with a one-run four-hitter. But in the finale, Gil Hodges drove in two Brooklyn runs with a single in the fourth and a sacrifice fly in the sixth. They were all Brooklyn got, but they proved more than enough to carry the Dodgers to their first world title in fifty-five years, as left fielder Sandy Amoros stifled New York's only real scoring

Brooklyn Dodgers (NL), 4;
New York Yankees (AL), 3

BRO (N)

PLAYER/POS	AVG	G	AB	R	H	2B	3B	HR	RB	BB	SO	SB
Sandy Amoros, of	.333	5	12	3	4	0	0	1	3	4	4	0
Don Bessent, p	.000	3	1	0	0	0	0	0	0	0	1	0
Roy Campanella, c	.259	7	27	4	7	3	0	2	4	3	3	0
Roger Craig, p	.000	1	0	0	0	0	0	0	0	1	0	0
Carl Erskine, p	.000	1	1	0	0	0	0	0	0	0	0	0
Carl Furillo, of	.296	7	27	4	8	1	0	1	3	3	5	0
Jim Gilliam, 2b-5,of-4	.292	7	24	2	7	1	0	0	3	8	1	1
Don Hoak, 3b-1	.333	3	3	0	1	0	0	0	0	2	0	0
Gil Hodges, 1b	.292	7	24	2	7	0	0	1	5	3	2	0
Frank Kellert, ph	.333	3	3	0	1	0	0	0	0	0	0	0
Clem Labine, p	.000	4	4	0	0	0	0	0	0	0	3	0
Billy Loes, p	.000	1	1	0	0	0	0	0	0	0	0	0
Russ Meyer, p	.000	1	2	0	0	0	0	0	0	0	1	0
Don Newcombe, p	.000	1	3	0	0	0	0	0	0	0	0	0
Johnny Podres, p	.143	2	7	1	1	0	0	0	0	0	1	0
Pee Wee Reese, ss	.296	7	27	5	8	1	0	0	2	3	5	0
Jackie Robinson, 3b	.182	6	22	5	4	1	1	0	1	2	1	1
Ed Roebuck, p	.000	1	0	0	0	0	0	0	0	0	0	0
George Shuba, ph	.000	1	1	0	0	0	0	0	0	0	0	0
Duke Snider, of	.320	7	25	5	8	1	0	4	7	2	6	0
Karl Spooner, p	.000	2	0	0	0	0	0	0	0	0	0	0
Don Zimmer, 2b	.222	4	9	0	2	0	0	0	0	2	2	5
TOTAL	.260		223	31	58	8	1	9	30	33	38	2

PITCHER	W	L	ERA	G	GS	CG	SV	SHO	IP	H	ER	BB	SO
Don Bessent	0	0	0.00	3	0	0	0	0	3.1	3	0	1	1
Roger Craig	1	0	3.00	1	1	0	0	0	6.0	4	2	5	4
Carl Erskine	0	0	9.00	1	1	0	0	0	3.0	3	3	2	3
Clem Labine	1	0	2.89	4	0	0	1	0	9.1	6	3	2	2
Billy Loes	0	1	9.82	1	1	0	0	0	3.2	7	4	1	5
Russ Meyer	0	0	0.00	1	0	0	0	0	5.2	4	0	2	4
Don Newcombe	0	1	9.53	1	1	0	0	0	5.2	8	6	2	4
Johnny Podres	2	0	1.00	2	2	2	0	1	18.0	15	2	4	10
Ed Roebuck	0	0	0.00	1	0	0	0	0	2.0	1	0	0	0
Karl Spooner	0	1	13.50	2	1	0	0	0	3.1	4	5	3	6
TOTAL	4	3	3.75	17	7	2	1	1	60.0	55	25	22	39

NY (A)

PLAYER/POS	AVG	G	AB	R	H	2B	3B	HR	RB	BB	SO	SB
Hank Bauer, of-5	.429	6	14	1	6	0	0	0	1	0	1	0
Yogi Berra, c	.417	7	24	5	10	1	0	1	2	3	1	0
Tommy Byrne, p-2	.167	3	6	0	1	0	0	0	2	0	2	0
Andy Carey, ph	.500	2	2	0	1	0	1	0	1	0	0	0
Tom Carroll, pr	.000	2	0	0	0	0	0	0	0	0	0	0
Bob Cerv, of-4	.125	5	16	1	2	0	0	1	1	0	4	0
Gerry Coleman, ss	.000	3	3	0	0	0	0	0	0	0	1	0
Rip Coleman, p	.000	1	0	0	0	0	0	0	0	0	0	0
Joe Collins, 1b-5,of-1	.167	5	12	6	2	0	0	2	3	6	4	1
Whitey Ford, p	.000	2	6	1	0	0	0	0	0	1	1	0
Bob Grim, p	.000	3	2	0	0	0	0	0	0	0	0	0
Elston Howard, of	.192	7	26	3	5	0	0	1	3	1	8	0
Johnny Kucks, p	.000	2	0	0	0	0	0	0	0	0	0	0
Don Larsen, p	.000	1	2	0	0	0	0	0	0	0	0	0
Mickey Mantle, of-2	.200	3	10	1	2	0	0	1	1	0	2	0
Billy Martin, 2b	.320	7	25	2	8	1	1	0	4	1	5	0
Gil Mc Dougald, 3b	.259	7	27	2	7	0	0	1	1	2	6	0
Tom Morgan, p	.000	2	0	0	0	0	0	0	0	0	0	0
Irv Noren, of	.063	5	16	0	1	0	0	0	0	1	1	0
Phil Rizzuto, ss	.267	7	15	2	4	0	0	0	1	5	1	2
Eddie Robinson, 1b-1	.667	4	3	0	2	0	0	0	1	2	1	0
Bill Skowron, 1b-3	.333	5	12	2	4	2	0	1	3	0	1	0
Tom Sturdivant, p	.000	2	0	0	0	0	0	0	0	0	0	0
Bob Turley, p	.000	3	1	0	0	0	0	0	0	0	0	0
TOTAL	.248		222	26	55	4	2	8	25	22	39	3

PITCHER	W	L	ERA	G	GS	CG	SV	SHO	IP	H	ER	BB	SO
Tommy Byrne	1	1	1.88	2	2	1	0	0	14.1	8	3	8	8
Rip Coleman	0	0	9.00	1	0	0	0	0	1.0	5	1	0	1
Whitey Ford	2	0	2.12	2	2	1	0	0	17.0	13	4	8	10
Bob Grim	0	1	4.15	3	1	0	1	0	8.2	8	4	5	8
Johnny Kucks	0	0	6.00	2	0	0	0	0	3.0	4	2	1	1
Don Larsen	0	1	11.25	1	1	0	0	0	4.0	5	5	2	2
Tom Morgan	0	0	4.91	2	0	0	0	0	3.2	3	2	3	1
Tom Sturdivant	0	0	6.00	2	0	0	0	0	3.0	5	2	2	0
Bob Turley	0	1	8.44	3	1	0	0	0	5.1	7	5	4	7
TOTAL	3	4	4.20	18	7	2	1	0	60.0	58	28	33	38

threat with a spectacular running catch in the sixth that started a double play and preserved Johnny Podres's second Series win.

GAME 1 AT NY SEPT 28

BRO	021	000	020	5	10	0
NY	021	102	00X	6	9	1

Pitchers: NEWCOMBE, Bessent (6), Labine (8) vs FORD, Grim (9)
Home Runs: Furillo-BRO, Snider-BRO, Howard-NY, Collins-NY (2)
Attendance: 63,869

GAME 2 AT NY SEPT 29

BRO	000	110	000	2	5	2
NY	000	400	00X	4	8	0

Pitchers: LOES, Bessent (4), Spooner (5), Labine (8) vs BYRNE
Attendance: 64,707

GAME 3 AT BRO SEPT 30

NY	020	000	100	3	7	0
BRO	220	200	02X	8	11	1

Pitchers: TURLEY, Morgan (2), Kucks (5), Sturdivant (7) vs PODRES
Home Runs: Campanella-BRO, Mantle-NY
Attendance: 34,209

GAME 4 AT BRO OCT 1

NY	110	102	000	5	9	0
BRO	001	330	10X	8	14	0

Pitchers: LARSEN, Kucks (5), R.Coleman (6), Morgan (7), Sturdivant (8) VS Erskine, Bessent (4), LABINE (5)
Home Runs: McDougald-NY, Campanella-BRO, Hodges-BRO, Snider-BRO
Attendance: 36,242

GAME 5 AT BRO OCT 2

NY	000	100	110	3	6	0
BRO	021	010	01X	5	9	2

Pitchers: GRIM, Turley (7) vs CRAIG, Labine (7)
Home Runs: Cerv-NY, Berra-NY, Amoros-BRO, Snider-BRO (2)
Attendance: 36,796

GAME 6 AT NY OCT 3

BRO	000	100	000	1	4	1
NY	500	000	00X	5	8	0

Pitchers: SPOONER, Meyer (1), Roebuck (7) vs FORD
Home Runs: Skowron-NY
Attendance: 64,022

GAME 7 AT NY OCT 4

BRO	000	101	000	2	5	0
NY	000	000	000	0	8	1

Pitchers: PODRES vs BYRNE, Grim (6), Turley (8)
Attendance: 62,465

The 1956 Series was a mirror image of 1955. With both teams repeaters as league champions, the Yankees this year followed Brooklyn's winning pattern of the previous Series: losing the first two games, winning the next three, then splitting the final pair.

Sal Maglie outlasted Yankee ace Whitey Ford in the opener. Maglie gave up nine hits and three runs (on homers by Mickey Mantle and Billy Martin), but struck out ten and took the win as Jackie Robinson and Gil Hodges contributed homers for four of Brooklyn's six runs. Dodger ace Don Newcombe was blown out by six Yankee runs (capped by Yogi Berra's grand slam) in the first two innings of Game Two. But Brooklyn came back with six unearned runs in their half of the second (three of them on Duke Snider's homer) and proceeded to run through seven Yankee pitchers for a 13–8 win and a two-game Series edge.

Whitey Ford tried again in Game Three, and this time held on for a complete-game 5–3 win, supported by Billy Martin's game-tying solo homer in the second and forty-year-old Enos Slaughter's go-ahead three-run shot in the sixth. Tom Sturdivant duplicated Ford's effectiveness and success the next day with a six-hit 6–2 win to even the Series.

Sal Maglie pitched Game Five for Brooklyn and improved on his winning performance of Game One, yielding only two runs and holding New York hitless until Mantle's two-out homer in the fourth inning. But no one was a match for Yankee pitcher Don Larsen that day. There was a close out on a deflected Dodger liner in the second inning, and center fielder Mantle made a fine running catch to prevent a hit in the fifth. But Larsen retired the rest routinely, and when Dale Mitchell fanned in the ninth Larsen had his perfect game—a feat still unique in World Series history.

Brooklyn reliever Clem Labine was started in Game Six against Yankee fastballer Bob Turley. No runner scored for either side until the last of the tenth inning when, with two out, Jackie Robinson lined a Turley pitch over the head of the left fielder, scoring Jim Gilliam from second and forcing New York into a seventh game.

The finale proved an anticlimactic disaster for Brooklyn. Once again Dodger starter Newcombe was driven out—this time by Yogi Berra's two two-run homers and Elston Howard's solo shot. By the time it was over, Bill Skowron had increased the Yankee run total to nine with a grand slam, and Yankee starter Johnny Kucks had shut Brooklyn out on three

singles. For New York it was world title number seventeen.

New York Yankees (AL), 4; Brooklyn Dodgers (NL), 3

NY (A)

PLAYER/POS	AVG	G	AB	R	H	2B	3B	HR	RB	BB	SO	SB
Hank Bauer, of	.281	7	32	3	9	0	0	1	3	0	5	1
Yogi Berra, c	.360	7	25	5	9	2	0	3	10	4	1	0
Tommy Byrne, p-1	.000	2	1	0	0	0	0	0	0	0	0	0
Andy Carey, 3b	.158	7	19	2	3	0	0	0	0	1	6	0
Bob Cerv, ph	1.000	1	1	0	1	0	0	0	0	0	0	0
Gerry Coleman, 2b	.000	2	2	0	0	0	0	0	0	0	0	0
Joe Collins, 1b-5	.238	6	21	2	5	2	0	0	2	2	3	0
Whitey Ford, p	.000	2	4	0	0	0	0	0	0	0	3	0
Elston Howard, of	.400	1	5	1	2	1	0	1	1	0	0	0
Johnny Kucks, p	.000	3	3	0	0	0	0	0	0	0	1	0
Don Larsen, p	.333	2	3	1	1	0	0	0	1	0	1	0
Mickey Mantle, of	.250	7	24	6	6	1	0	3	4	6	5	1
Billy Martin, 2b-7,3b-1	.296	7	27	5	8	0	0	2	3	1	6	0
Maury Mc Dermott, p	1.000	1	1	0	1	0	0	0	0	0	0	0
Gil Mc Dougald, ss	.143	7	21	0	3	0	0	0	1	3	6	0
Tom Morgan, p	1.000	2	1	1	1	0	0	0	0	0	0	0
Norm Siebern, ph	.000	1	1	0	0	0	0	0	0	0	0	0
Bill Skowron, 1b-2	.100	3	10	1	1	0	0	1	4	0	3	0
Enos Slaughter, of	.350	6	20	6	7	0	0	1	4	4	0	0
Tom Sturdivant, p	.333	2	3	0	1	0	0	0	0	0	1	0
Bob Turley, p	.000	3	4	0	0	0	0	0	0	0	1	0
George Wilson, ph	.000	1	1	0	0	0	0	0	0	0	1	0
TOTAL	.253		229	33	58	6	0	12	33	21	43	2

PITCHER	W	L	ERA	G	GS	CG	SV	SHO	IP	H	ER	BB	SO
Tommy Byrne	0	0	0.00	1	0	0	0	0	0.1	1	0	0	1
Whitey Ford	1	1	5.25	2	2	1	0	0	12.0	14	7	2	8
Johnny Kucks	1	0	0.82	3	1	1	0	1	11.0	6	1	3	2
Don Larsen	1	0	0.00	2	2	1	0	1	10.2	1	0	4	7
Maury Mc Dermott	0	0	3.00	1	0	0	0	0	3.0	2	1	3	3
Tom Morgan	0	1	9.00	2	0	0	0	0	4.0	6	4	4	3
Tom Sturdivant	1	0	2.79	2	1	1	0	0	9.2	8	3	8	9
Bob Turley	0	1	0.82	3	1	1	0	0	11.0	4	1	8	14
TOTAL	4	3	2.48	16	7	5	0	2	61.2	42	17	32	47

BRO (N)

PLAYER/POS	AVG	G	AB	R	H	2B	3B	HR	RB	BB	SO	SB
Sandy Amoros, of	.053	6	19	1	1	0	0	0	1	2	4	0
Don Bessent, p	.500	2	2	0	1	0	0	0	1	1	1	0
Roy Campanella, c	.182	7	22	2	4	1	0	0	3	3	7	0
Gino Cimoli, of	.000	1	0	0	0	0	0	0	0	0	0	0
Roger Craig, p	.500	2	2	0	1	0	0	0	0	0	0	0
Don Drysdale, p	.000	1	0	0	0	0	0	0	0	0	0	0
Carl Erskine, p	.000	2	1	0	0	0	0	0	0	0	1	0
Carl Furillo, of	.240	7	25	2	6	2	0	0	1	2	3	0
Jim Gilliam, 2b-6,of-1	.083	7	24	2	2	0	0	0	2	7	3	1
Gil Hodges, 1b	.304	7	23	5	7	2	0	1	8	4	4	0
Ransom Jackson, ph	.000	3	3	0	0	0	0	0	0	0	2	0
Clem Labine, p	.250	2	4	0	1	1	0	0	0	0	2	0
Sal Maglie, p	.000	2	5	0	0	0	0	0	0	0	2	0
Dale Mitchell, ph	.000	4	4	0	0	0	0	0	0	0	1	0
Charlie Neal, 2b	.000	1	4	0	0	0	0	0	0	0	1	0
Don Newcombe, p	.000	2	1	0	0	0	0	0	0	0	0	0
Pee Wee Reese, ss	.222	7	27	3	6	0	1	0	2	2	6	0
Jackie Robinson, 3b	.250	7	24	5	6	1	0	1	2	5	2	0
Ed Roebuck, p	.000	3	0	0	0	0	0	0	0	0	0	0
Duke Snider, of	.304	7	23	5	7	1	0	1	4	6	8	0
Rube Walker, ph	.000	2	2	0	0	0	0	0	0	0	0	0
TOTAL	.195		215	25	42	8	1	3	24	32	47	1

PITCHER	W	L	ERA	G	GS	CG	SV	SHO	IP	H	ER	BB	SO
Don Bessent	1	0	1.80	2	0	0	0	0	10.0	8	2	3	5
Roger Craig	0	1	12.00	2	1	0	0	0	6.0	10	8	3	4
Don Drysdale	0	0	9.00	1	0	0	0	0	2.0	2	2	1	1
Carl Erskine	0	1	5.40	2	1	0	0	0	5.0	4	3	2	2
Clem Labine	1	0	0.00	2	1	1	0	1	12.0	8	0	3	7
Sal Maglie	1	1	2.65	2	2	2	0	0	17.0	14	5	6	15
Don Newcombe	0	1	21.21	2	2	0	0	0	4.2	11	11	3	4
Ed Roebuck	0	0	2.08	3	0	0	0	0	4.1	1	1	0	5
TOTAL	3	4	4.72	16	7	3	0	1	61.0	58	32	21	43

Overall, the Yankees pitched better, hit oftener, and scored more runs than the Braves. But the Braves had Lew Burdette, and with him they won the Series.

The opener pitted the Braves' established great Warren Spahn against New York's emerging great Whitey Ford. Ford prevailed, with a five-hit 3–1 win as Spahn was chased in the sixth. Burdette, winner of 17 regular-season games, started Game Two against veteran Bobby Shantz, the American League ERA leader. After a scoreless first inning, both pitchers gave up a run in the second and another in the third. Two go-ahead runs in the top of the fourth ended the Braves' scoring, but they were enough, as Burdette blanked New York through the final six innings to even the Series. Before he was finished, Burdette would stretch his consecutive scoreless innings to 24.

The Yankees exploded in Game Three, in Milwaukee, running through six Brave pitchers for a 12–3 rout. Braves fans even ended up cheering Yankee second baseman Tony Kubek—a Milwaukee native—who opened the scoring with a solo homer in the first, scored again after singling in the fourth (on Mickey Mantle's home run), and concluded the Yankee scoring in the seventh with his second homer, with two aboard.

Warren Spahn carried a 4–1 Braves lead into the ninth inning of Game Four, but after retiring the first two batters in the ninth, he gave up singles to Yogi Berra and Gil McDougald, and a game-tying home run to Elston Howard. In the top of the tenth, Hank Bauer tripled in a go-ahead Yankee run, but Milwaukee's Johnny Logan doubled to tie it up in the last of the tenth, and Eddie Mathews homered to give Spahn a shaky victory.

Burdette faced Ford in Game Five. In the sixth inning the Braves put half their hits—three singles—back to back for a run. It was all they needed as Burdette spaced seven singles for the shutout. Back in New York the next day, all the scoring came on home runs. Each club hit a pair, but Berra's in the third was the only one with a man aboard. Brave blasts in the fifth (Frank Torre) and seventh (Hank Aaron) tied the score, but Bauer answered Aaron's homer in the last of the seventh with what proved the winning shot. Bob Turley, who yielded just four hits while fanning eight (the Series high) claimed the Yankee victory.

In the finale, Burdette, with only two days' rest, scattered four hits over the first eight innings as the Braves gave him a 5–0 lead. In the bottom of the ninth, though, three Yankee singles loaded the bases with two out. But third baseman Eddie Mathews snared Bil Skowron's sharp grounder and stepped on the bag for a force out that preserved Burdette's second shutout and gave Milwaukee its first world championship.

Milwaukee Braves (NL), 4; New York Yankees (AL), 3

MIL (N)

PLAYER/POS	AVG	G	AB	R	H	2B	3B	HR	RB	BB	SO	SB
Hank Aaron, of	.393	7	28	5	11	0	1	3	7	1	6	0
Joe Adcock, 1b	.200	5	15	1	3	0	0	0	2	0	2	0
Bob Buhl, p	.000	2	1	0	0	0	0	0	0	0	1	0
Lew Burdette, p	.000	3	8	0	0	0	0	0	0	1	2	0
Gene Conley, p	.000	1	0	0	0	0	0	0	0	0	0	0
Wes Covington, of	.208	7	24	1	5	1	0	0	1	2	6	1
Del Crandall, c	.211	6	19	1	4	0	0	1	1	1	1	0
John De Merit, pr	.000	1	0	0	0	0	0	0	0	0	0	0
Bob Hazle, of	.154	4	13	2	2	0	0	0	0	1	2	0
Ernie Johnson, p	.000	3	1	0	0	0	0	0	0	0	1	0
Nippy Jones, ph	.000	3	2	0	0	0	0	0	0	0	0	0
Johnny Logan, ss	.185	7	27	5	5	1	0	1	2	3	6	0
Felix Mantilla, 2b-3	.000	4	10	1	0	0	0	0	0	1	0	0
Eddie Mathews, 3b	.227	7	22	4	5	3	0	1	4	8	5	0
Don Mc Mahon, p	.000	3	0	0	0	0	0	0	0	0	0	0
Andy Pafko, of-5	.214	6	14	1	3	0	0	0	0	0	1	0
Juan Pizarro, p	.000	1	1	0	0	0	0	0	0	0	0	0
Del Rice, c	.167	2	6	0	1	0	0	0	0	1	2	0
Carl Sawatski, ph	.000	2	2	0	0	0	0	0	0	0	2	0
Red Schoendienst, 2b	.278	5	18	0	5	1	0	0	2	0	1	0
Warren Spahn, p	.000	2	4	0	0	0	0	0	0	1	2	0
Frank Torre, 1b	.300	7	10	2	3	0	0	2	3	2	0	0
Bob Trowbridge, p	.000	1	0	0	0	0	0	0	0	0	0	0
TOTAL	.209		225	23	47	6	1	8	22	22	40	1

PITCHER	W	L	ERA	G	GS	CG	SV	SHO	IP	H	ER	BB	SO
Bob Buhl	0	1	10.80	2	2	0	0	0	3.1	6	4	6	4
Lew Burdette	3	0	0.67	3	3	3	0	2	27.0	21	2	4	13
Gene Conley	0	0	10.80	1	0	0	0	0	1.2	2	2	1	0
Ernie Johnson	0	1	1.29	3	0	0	0	0	7.0	2	1	1	8
Don Mc Mahon	0	0	0.00	3	0	0	0	0	5.0	3	0	3	5
Juan Pizarro	0	0	10.80	1	0	0	0	0	1.2	3	2	2	1
Warren Spahn	1	1	4.70	2	2	1	0	0	15.1	18	8	2	2
Bob Trowbridge	0	0	45.00	1	0	0	0	0	1.0	2	5	3	1
TOTAL	4	3	3.48	16	7	4	0	2	62.0	57	24	22	34

NY (A)

PLAYER/POS	AVG	G	AB	R	H	2B	3B	HR	RB	BB	SO	SB
Hank Bauer, of	.258	7	31	3	8	2	1	2	6	1	6	0
Yogi Berra, c	.320	7	25	5	8	1	0	1	2	4	0	0
Tommy Byrne, p	.500	2	2	0	1	0	0	0	0	0	1	0
Andy Carey, 3b	.286	2	7	0	2	1	0	0	1	1	0	0
Gerry Coleman, 2b	.364	7	22	2	8	2	0	0	2	3	1	0
Joe Collins, 1b-5	.000	6	5	0	0	0	0	0	0	0	3	0
Art Ditmar, p	.000	2	1	0	0	0	0	0	0	0	1	0
Whitey Ford, p	.000	2	5	0	0	0	0	0	0	0	1	0
Bob Grim, p	.000	2	0	0	0	0	0	0	0	0	0	0
Elston Howard, 1b-3	.273	6	11	2	3	0	0	1	3	1	3	0
Tony Kubek, of-5,3b-2	.286	7	28	4	8	0	0	2	4	0	4	0
Johnny Kucks, p	.000	1	0	0	0	0	0	0	0	0	0	0
Don Larsen, p	.000	2	2	1	0	0	0	0	0	0	2	0
Jerry Lumpe, 3b-3	.286	6	14	0	4	0	0	0	2	1	1	0
Mickey Mantle, of-5	.263	6	19	3	5	0	0	1	2	3	1	0
Gil Mc Dougald, ss	.250	7	24	3	6	0	0	0	2	3	3	1
Bobby Richardson, 2b-1	.000	2	0	0	0	0	0	0	0	0	0	0
Bobby Shantz, p	.000	3	1	0	0	0	0	0	0	0	0	0
Harry Simpson, 1b-4	.083	5	12	0	1	0	0	0	1	0	4	0
Bill Skowron, 1b	.000	2	4	0	0	0	0	0	0	0	0	0
Enos Slaughter, of	.250	5	12	2	3	1	0	0	0	3	2	0
Tom Sturdivant, p	.000	2	1	0	0	0	0	0	0	0	1	0
Bob Turley, p	.000	3	4	0	0	0	0	0	0	0	2	0
TOTAL	.248		230	25	57	7	1	7	25	22	34	1

PITCHER	W	L	ERA	G	GS	CG	SV	SHO	IP	H	ER	BB	SO
Tommy Byrne	0	0	5.40	2	0	0	0	0	3.1	1	2	2	1
Art Ditmar	0	0	0.00	2	0	0	0	0	6.0	2	0	0	2
Whitey Ford	1	1	1.13	2	2	1	0	0	16.0	11	2	5	7
Bob Grim	0	1	7.71	2	0	0	0	0	2.1	3	2	0	2
Johnny Kucks	0	0	0.00	1	0	0	0	0	0.2	0	0	1	1
Don Larsen	1	1	3.72	2	1	0	0	0	9.2	8	4	5	6
Bobby Shantz	0	1	4.05	3	1	0	0	0	6.2	8	3	2	7
Tom Sturdivant	0	0	6.00	2	1	0	0	0	6.0	6	4	1	2
Bob Turley	1	0	2.31	3	2	1	0	0	11.2	7	3	6	12
TOTAL	3	4	2.89	19	7	2	0	0	62.1	47	20	22	40

GAME 1 AT NY OCT 2

MIL	000 000 100	1	5	0
NY	000 012 00X	3	9	1

Pitchers: SPAHN, Johnson (6), McMahon (7) vs FORD
Attendance: 69,476

GAME 2 AT NY OCT 3

MIL	011 200 000	4	8	0
NY	011 000 000	2	7	2

Pitchers: BURDETTE vs SHANTZ, Ditmar (4), Grim (8)
Home Runs: Logan-MIL, Bauer-NY
Attendance: 65,202

GAME 3 AT MIL OCT 5

NY	302 200 500	12	9	0
MIL	010 020 000	3	8	1

Pitchers: Turley, LARSEN (2) vs BUHL, Pizarro (1), Conley (3), Johnson (5), Trowbridge (7), McMahon (8)
Home Runs: Kubek (2), Mantle-NY, Aaron-MIL
Attendance: 45,804

GAME 4 AT MIL OCT 6

NY	100 000 003 1	5	11	0
MIL	000 400 000 3	7	7	0

Pitchers: Sturdivant, Shantz (5), Kucks (8), Byrne (8), GRIM (10) vs SPAHN
Home Runs: Aaron-MIL, Torre-MIL, Howard-NY, Mathews-MIL
Attendance: 45,804

GAME 5 AT MIL OCT 7

NY	000 000 000	0	7	0
MIL	000 001 00X	1	6	1

Pitchers: FORD, Turley (8) vs BURDETTE
Attendance: 45,811

GAME 6 AT NY OCT 9

MIL	000 010 100	2	4	0
NY	002 000 10X	3	7	0

Pitchers: Buhl, JOHNSON (3), McMahon (8) vs TURLEY
Home Runs: Berra-NY, Torre-MIL, Aaron-MIL, Bauer-NY
Attendance: 61,408

GAME 7 AT NY OCT 10

MIL	004 000 010	5	9	1
NY	000 000 000	0	7	3

Pitchers: BURDETTE vs LARSEN, Shantz (3), Ditmar (4), Sturdivant (6), Byrne (8)
Home Runs: Crandall-MIL
Attendance: 61,207

After four games, Milwaukee held a 3–1 Series advantage, but New York rebounded to take the final three games and avenge their loss to the Braves the year before. As in the previous series, Warren Spahn faced Whitey Ford in the opener. The durable Spahn emerged the victor when Bill Bruton singled home the Braves' winning run off reliever Ryne Duren in the last of the tenth. In Game Two, home runs by Bruton and pitcher Lew Burdette (for three runs) helped put the Braves ahead 7–1 in the first inning. Milwaukee scored off five Yankee hurlers in their eventual 13–5 win.

Don Larsen and Ryne Duren combined for a shutout in Game Three to give New York its first victory. Hank Bauer drove in all four Yankee runs with a two-run single in the fifth and his third home run in three games in the seventh. Warren Spahn held Bauer hitless in Game Four, blanking New York on two hits to defeat Whitey Ford and bring Milwaukee within a win of the championship.

Yankee Bob Turley came up with a shutout of his own the next day, though, fanning ten men along the way. Gil McDougald's solo homer in the third inning was all the offense Turley needed, but as insurance the Yankees bunched six of their ten hits into the sixth inning for six more runs.

Spahn and Ford, with only two days' rest, confronted each other a third time in Game Six. Ford lasted less than two innings, but Spahn (despite Hank Bauer's fourth Series home run in the first inning) endured into extra innings, when McDougald put New York ahead with a leadoff homer in the tenth. Two outs and two hits later, Spahn was removed, and Bill Skowron's single off reliever Don McMahon drove home another Yankee run. Milwaukee scored once in the last of the tenth and threatened further damage with men on first and third. But Bob Turley came on to retire the final batter and send the Series to a seventh game.

In the sixth inning of the finale, the Braves' Del Crandall homered against Turley (who had relieved Don Larsen in the third) to tie the game 2–2. But four Yankee runs off starter Lew Burdette in the top of the eighth (including Skowron's three-run homer) made the score 6–2, where it remained, as Turley held on to bring Casey Stengel his seventh (and last) Series triumph—and the Yankees their eighteenth.

New York Yankees (AL), 4; Milwaukee Braves (NL), 3

NY (A)

PLAYER/POS	AVG	G	AB	R	H	2B	3B	HR	RB	BB	SO	SB
Hank Bauer, of	.323	7	31	6	10	0	0	4	8	0	5	0
Yogi Berra, c	.222	7	27	3	6	3	0	0	2	1	0	0
Andy Carey, 3b	.083	5	12	1	1	0	0	0	0	0	3	0
Murry Dickson, p	.000	2	0	0	0	0	0	0	0	0	0	0
Art Ditmar, p	.000	1	1	0	0	0	0	0	0	0	0	0
Ryne Duren, p	.000	3	3	0	0	0	0	0	0	0	2	0
Whitey Ford, p	.000	3	4	1	0	0	0	0	0	2	2	0
Elston Howard, of	.222	6	18	4	4	0	0	0	2	1	4	1
Tony Kubek, ss	.048	7	21	0	1	0	0	0	1	1	7	0
Johnny Kucks, p	1.000	2	1	0	1	0	0	0	0	0	0	0
Don Larsen, p	.000	2	2	0	0	0	0	0	0	1	0	0
Jerry Lumpe, 3b-3,ss-2	.167	6	12	0	2	0	0	0	0	1	2	0
Duke Maas, p	.000	1	0	0	0	0	0	0	0	0	0	0
Mickey Mantle, of	.250	7	24	4	6	0	1	2	3	7	4	0
Gil Mc Dougald, 2b	.321	7	28	5	9	2	0	2	4	2	4	0
Zach Monroe, p	.000	1	0	0	0	0	0	0	0	0	0	0
Bobby Richardson, 3b	.000	4	5	0	0	0	0	0	0	0	0	0
Norm Siebern, of	.125	3	8	1	1	0	0	0	0	3	2	0
Bill Skowron, 1b	.259	7	27	3	7	0	0	2	7	1	4	0
Enos Slaughter, ph	.000	4	3	1	0	0	0	0	0	1	1	0
Marv Throneberry, ph	.000	1	1	0	0	0	0	0	0	1	0	0
Bob Turley, p	.200	4	5	0	1	0	0	0	2	0	1	0
TOTAL	.210		233	29	49	5	1	10	29	21	42	1

PITCHER	W	L	ERA	G	GS	CG	SV	SHO	IP	H	ER	BB	SO
Murry Dickson	0	0	4.50	2	0	0	0	0	4.0	4	2	0	1
Art Ditmar	0	0	0.00	1	0	0	0	0	3.2	2	0	0	2
Ryne Duren	1	1	1.93	3	0	0	1	0	9.1	7	2	6	14
Whitey Ford	0	1	4.11	3	3	0	0	0	15.1	19	7	5	16
Johnny Kucks	0	0	2.08	2	0	0	0	0	4.1	4	1	1	0
Don Larsen	1	0	0.96	2	2	0	0	0	9.1	9	1	6	9
Duke Maas	0	0	81.00	1	0	0	0	0	0.1	2	3	1	0
Zach Monroe	0	0	27.00	1	0	0	0	0	1.0	3	3	1	1
Bob Turley	2	1	2.76	4	2	1	1	1	16.1	10	5	7	13
TOTAL	4	3	3.39	19	7	1	2	1	63.2	60	24	27	56

MIL (N)

PLAYER/POS	AVG	G	AB	R	H	2B	3B	HR	RB	BB	SO	SB
Hank Aaron, of	.333	7	27	3	9	2	0	0	2	4	6	0
Joe Adcock, 1b	.308	4	13	1	4	0	0	0	0	1	3	0
Billy Bruton, of	.412	7	17	2	7	0	0	1	2	5	5	0
Lew Burdette, p	.111	3	9	1	1	0	0	1	3	0	3	0
Wes Covington, of	.269	7	26	2	7	0	0	0	4	2	4	0
Del Crandall, c	.240	7	25	4	6	0	0	1	3	3	10	0
Harry Hanebrink, ph	.000	2	2	0	0	0	0	0	0	0	0	0
Johnny Logan, ss	.120	7	25	3	3	2	0	0	2	2	4	0
Felix Mantilla, ss-1	.000	4	0	1	0	0	0	0	0	0	0	0
Eddie Mathews, 3b	.160	7	25	3	4	2	0	0	3	6	11	1
Don Mc Mahon, p	.000	3	0	0	0	0	0	0	0	0	0	0
Andy Pafko, of	.333	4	9	0	3	1	0	0	1	0	0	0
Juan Pizarro, p	.000	1	0	0	0	0	0	0	0	0	0	0
Bob Rush, p	.000	1	2	0	0	0	0	0	0	0	2	0
Red Schoendienst, 2b	.300	7	30	5	9	3	1	0	0	2	1	0
Warren Spahn, p	.333	3	12	0	4	0	0	0	3	0	6	0
Frank Torre, 1b	.176	7	17	0	3	0	0	0	1	2	0	0
Carl Willey, p	.000	1	0	0	0	0	0	0	0	0	0	0
Casey Wise, ph	.000	2	1	0	0	0	0	0	0	0	1	0
TOTAL	.250		240	25	60	10	1	3	24	27	56	1

PITCHER	W	L	ERA	G	GS	CG	SV	SHO	IP	H	ER	BB	SO
Lew Burdette	1	2	5.64	3	3	1	0	0	22.1	22	14	4	12
Don Mc Mahon	0	0	5.40	3	0	0	0	0	3.1	3	2	3	5
Juan Pizarro	0	0	5.40	1	0	0	0	0	1.2	2	1	1	3
Bob Rush	0	1	3.00	1	1	0	0	0	6.0	3	2	5	2
Warren Spahn	2	1	2.20	3	3	2	0	1	28.2	19	7	8	18
Carl Willey	0	0	0.00	1	0	0	0	0	1.0	0	0	0	2
TOTAL	3	4	3.71	12	7	3	0	1	63.0	49	26	21	42

GAME 1 AT MIL OCT 1

NY	000 120 000 0	3	8	1
MIL	000 200 010 1	4	10	0

Pitchers: Ford, DUREN (8) vs SPAHN
Home Runs: Skowron-NY, Bauer-NY
Attendance: 46,367

GAME 2 AT MIL OCT 2

NY	100 100 003	5	7	0
MIL	710 000 23X	13	15	1

Pitchers: TURLEY, Maas (1), Kucks (1), Dickson (5), Monroe (8) vs BURDETTE
Home Runs: Bruton-MIL, Burdette-MIL, Mantle-NY (2), Bauer-NY
Attendance: 46,367

GAME 3 AT NY OCT 4

MIL	000 000 000	0	6	0
NY	000 020 20X	4	4	0

Pitchers: RUSH, McMahon (7) vs LARSEN, Duren (8)
Home Runs: Bauer-NY
Attendance: 71,599

GAME 4 AT NY OCT 5

MIL	000 001 110	3	9	0
NY	000 000 000	0	2	1

Pitchers: SPAHN vs FORD, Kucks (8), Dickson (9)
Attendance: 71,563

GAME 5 AT NY OCT 6

MIL	000 000 000	0	5	0
NY	001 006 00X	7	10	0

Pitchers: BURDETTE, Pizarro (6), Willey (8) vs TURLEY
Home Runs: McDougald-NY
Attendance: 65,279

GAME 6 AT MIL OCT 8

NY	100 001 000 2	4	10	1
MIL	110 000 000 1	3	10	4

Pitchers: Ford, Ditmar (2), DUREN (6), Turley (10) vs SPAHN, McMahon (10)
Home Runs: Bauer-NY, McDougald-NY
Attendance: 46,367

GAME 7 AT MIL OCT 9

NY	020 000 040	6	8	0
MIL	100 001 000	2	5	2

Pitchers: Larsen, TURLEY (3) vs BURDETTE, McMahon (8)
Home Runs: Crandall-MIL, Skowron-NY
Attendance: 46,367

It took a nosedive from first to third by San Francisco and a Dodger playoff victory over Milwaukee (who had finished the season tied with the Dodgers), to bring Los Angeles the city's first major league pennant. But once they had made it to the Series, the Dodgers dispatched the White Sox in six games.

The opener, though, belonged to Chicago. In their first World Series in forty years, the White Sox overwhelmed Los Angeles with 11 runs in the first four innings as pitchers Early Wynn and Gerry Staley combined to blank the Dodgers. Chicago's big gun was veteran slugger Ted Kluszewski (acquired from Pittsburgh in late August), whose single and two homers drove in five runs. Chicago scored twice in the first inning the next day, but Dodger starter Johnny Podres settled down to blank the Sox over the next five innings as home runs by Charlie Neal in the fifth and pinch hitter Chuck Essegian and Neal (again) in the seventh put the Dodgers ahead by two. Rookie reliever Larry Sherry gave up a third Chicago run in the eighth on Al Smith's double, but a second runner was nailed at the plate, and Sherry set down the side in the ninth to save Podres's win.

When the Series moved to Los Angeles' cavernous Coliseum for the West Coast's first World Series games ever, fans turned out in record numbers, setting a new Series mark in each of the next three games. Dodger starter Don Drysdale yielded 11 hits and four walks in Game Three, but the only run scored against him came on a double-play after Larry Sherry had relieved him with two men on in the eighth. As Los Angeles had already scored twice, and added a third run in their half of the eighth, Drysdale emerged with the win and Sherry with his second save. In Game Four, the Sox's Sherm Lollar's three-run homer had tied the score by the time Sherry relieved Dodger starter Roger Craig in the eighth, so Gil Hodges's solo homer in the last of the eighth gave Sherry the win this time—and Los Angeles a 3–1 Series advantage.

Chicago's Bob Shaw dueled Dodger Sandy Koufax through seven innings of Game Five before 92,706 spectators (still a Series high). The Sox scored only once off Koufax, but one run was enough for their second win as a pair of Sox relievers continued Shaw's shutout through the final two innings.

Back in Chicago for Game Six, the Dodgers unloaded on Early Wynn and Dick Donovan for eight runs in the third and fourth innings. Ted Kluszewski's three-run homer in the last of the fourth led to Larry Sherry's fourth relief appearance—and his second Series win, as he held the Sox scoreless the rest of the game to bring the world championship to the West Coast for the first time.

Los Angeles Dodgers (NL), 4; Chicago White Sox (AL), 2

LA (N)

PLAYER/POS	AVG	G	AB	R	H	2B	3B	HR	RB	BB	SO	SB
Chuck Churn, p	.000	1	0	0	0	0	0	0	0	0	0	0
Roger Craig, p	.000	2	3	0	0	0	0	0	0	0	2	0
Don Demeter, of	.250	6	12	2	3	0	0	0	0	1	3	0
Don Drysdale, p	.000	1	2	0	0	0	0	0	0	0	2	0
Chuck Essegian, ph	.667	4	3	2	2	0	0	2	2	1	1	0
Ron Fairly, of-4	.000	6	3	0	0	0	0	0	0	0	1	0
Carl Furillo, of-1	.250	4	4	0	1	0	0	0	2	0	1	0
Jim Gilliam, 3b	.240	6	25	2	6	0	0	0	0	2	2	2
Gil Hodges, 1b	.391	6	23	2	9	0	1	1	2	1	2	0
Johnny Klippstein, p	.000	1	0	0	0	0	0	0	0	0	0	0
Sandy Koufax, p	.000	2	2	0	0	0	0	0	0	0	1	0
Clem Labine, p	.000	1	0	0	0	0	0	0	0	0	0	0
Norm Larker, of	.188	6	16	2	3	0	0	0	0	2	3	0
Wally Moon, of	.261	6	23	3	6	0	0	1	2	2	2	1
Charlie Neal, 2b	.370	6	27	4	10	2	0	2	6	0	1	1
Joe Pignatano, c	.000	1	0	0	0	0	0	0	0	0	0	0
Johnny Podres, p-2	.500	3	4	1	2	1	0	0	1	0	0	0
Rip Repulski, of	.000	1	0	0	0	0	0	0	0	1	0	0
Johnny Roseboro, c	.095	6	21	0	2	0	0	0	1	0	2	0
Larry Sherry, p-4	.500	5	4	0	2	0	0	0	0	0	1	0
Duke Snider, of-3	.200	4	10	1	2	0	0	1	2	2	0	0
Stan Williams, p	.000	1	0	0	0	0	0	0	0	0	0	0
Maury Wills, ss	.250	6	20	2	5	0	0	0	1	0	3	1
Don Zimmer, ss	.000	1	1	0	0	0	0	0	0	0	0	0
TOTAL	.261		203	21	53	3	1	7	19	12	27	5

PITCHER	W	L	ERA	G	GS	CG	SV	SHO	IP	H	ER	BB	SO
Chuck Churn	0	0	27.00	1	0	0	0	0	0.2	5	2	0	0
Roger Craig	0	1	8.68	2	2	0	0	0	9.1	15	9	5	8
Don Drysdale	1	0	1.29	1	1	0	0	0	7.0	11	1	4	5
Johnny Klippstein	0	0	0.00	1	0	0	0	0	2.0	1	0	0	2
Sandy Koufax	0	1	1.00	2	1	0	0	0	9.0	5	1	1	7
Clem Labine	0	0	0.00	1	0	0	0	0	1.0	0	0	0	1
Johnny Podres	1	0	4.82	2	2	0	0	0	9.1	7	5	6	4
Larry Sherry	2	0	0.71	4	0	0	2	0	12.2	8	1	2	5
Stan Williams	0	0	0.00	1	0	0	0	0	2.0	0	0	2	1
TOTAL	4	2	3.23	15	6	0	2	0	53.0	52	19	20	33

CHI (A)

PLAYER/POS	AVG	G	AB	R	H	2B	3B	HR	RB	BB	SO	SB
Luis Aparicio, ss	.308	6	26	1	8	1	0	0	0	2	3	1
Norm Cash, ph	.000	4	4	0	0	0	0	0	0	0	2	0
Dick Donovan, p	.333	3	3	0	1	0	0	0	0	0	1	0
Sammy Esposito, 3b	.000	2	2	0	0	0	0	0	0	0	1	0
Nellie Fox, 2b	.375	6	24	4	9	3	0	0	0	4	1	0
Billy Goodman, 3b	.231	5	13	1	3	0	0	0	1	0	5	0
Ted Kluszewski, 1b	.391	6	23	5	9	1	0	3	10	2	0	0
Jim Landis, of	.292	6	24	6	7	0	0	0	1	1	7	1
Sherm Lollar, c	.227	6	22	3	5	0	0	1	5	1	3	0
Turk Lown, p	.000	3	0	0	0	0	0	0	0	0	0	0
Jim Mc Anany, of	.000	3	5	0	0	0	0	0	0	1	0	0
Ray Moore, p	.000	1	0	0	0	0	0	0	0	0	0	0
Bubba Phillips, 3b-3,of-1	.300	3	10	0	3	1	0	0	0	0	0	0
Billy Pierce, p	.000	3	0	0	0	0	0	0	0	0	0	0
Jim Rivera, of	.000	5	11	1	0	0	0	0	0	3	1	0
Johnny Romano, ph	.000	1	1	0	0	0	0	0	0	0	0	0
Bob Shaw, p	.250	2	4	0	1	0	0	0	0	0	2	0
Al Smith, of	.250	6	20	1	5	3	0	0	1	4	4	0
Gerry Staley, p	.000	4	1	0	0	0	0	0	0	0	1	0
Earl Torgeson, 1b-1	.000	3	1	1	0	0	0	0	0	1	0	0
Early Wynn, p	.200	3	5	0	1	1	0	0	1	0	2	0
TOTAL	.261		199	23	52	10	0	4	19	20	33	2

PITCHER	W	L	ERA	G	GS	CG	SV	SHO	IP	H	ER	BB	SO
Dick Donovan	0	1	5.40	3	1	0	1	0	8.1	4	5	3	5
Turk Lown	0	0	0.00	3	0	0	0	0	3.1	2	0	1	3
Ray Moore	0	0	9.00	1	0	0	0	0	1.0	1	1	0	1
Billy Pierce	0	0	0.00	3	0	0	0	0	4.0	2	0	2	3
Bob Shaw	1	1	2.57	2	2	0	0	0	14.0	17	4	2	2
Gerry Staley	0	1	2.16	4	0	0	1	0	8.1	8	2	0	3
Early Wynn	1	1	5.54	3	3	0	0	0	13.0	19	8	4	10
TOTAL	2	4	3.46	19	6	0	2	0	52.0	53	20	12	27

GAME 1 AT CHI OCT 1

LA	000 000 000	0 8 3
CHI	207 200 00X	11 11 0

Pitchers: CRAIG, Churn (3), Labine (4), Koufax (5), Klippstein (7) vs WYNN, Staley (8)
Home Runs: Kluszewski-CHI (2)
Attendance: 48,013

GAME 2 AT CHI OCT 2

LA	000 010 300	4 9 1
CHI	200 000 010	3 8 0

Pitchers: PODRES, Sherry (7) vs SHAW, Lown (7)
Home Runs: Neal-LA (2), Essegian-LA
Attendance: 47,368

GAME 3 AT LA OCT 4

CHI	000 000 010	1 12 0
LA	000 000 21X	3 5 0

Pitchers: DONOVAN, Staley (7) vs DRYSDALE, Sherry (8)
Attendance: 92,394

GAME 4 AT LA OCT 5

CHI	000 000 400	4 10 3
LA	004 000 01X	5 9 0

Pitchers: Wynn, Lown (3), Pierce (4), STALEY (7) vs Craig, SHERRY (8)
Home Runs: Lollar-CHI, Hodges-LA
Attendance: 92,650

GAME 5 AT LA OCT 6

CHI	000 100 000	1 5 0
LA	000 000 000	0 9 0

Pitchers: SHAW, Pierce (7), Donovan (8) VS KOUFAX, Williams (8)
Attendance: 92,706

GAME 6 AT CHI OCT 8

LA	002 600 001	9 13 0
CHI	000 300 000	3 6 1

Pitchers: Podres, SHERRY (4) vs WYNN, Donovan (4), Staley (5), Pierce (8), Moore (9)
Home Runs: Snider-LA, Moon-LA, Kluszewski-CHI, Essegian-LA
Attendance: 47,653

Through six games and 8½ innings of the seventh, the Yankees had outscored the Pirates by 29 runs. But as Pirate second baseman Bill Mazeroski stepped to the plate to open the last of the ninth, the Series was even at three games apiece, and Game Seven was tied 9–9. The stage was set for Mazeroski to fulfill that ultimate baseball fantasy, and he did, on pitcher Ralph Terry's second pitch.

Yankee Roger Maris opened the Series scoring with a solo homer in the first inning of Game One, and Elston Howard added two more Yankee runs with a homer in the ninth. But between the home runs New York scored only one run to the Pirates' six (including a two-run homer by Mazeroski in the fourth).

The Yankees avenged their first-game loss with a blowout in Game Two—their first of three. Pittsburgh hit safely 13 times, but scored only three runs. New York, though, turned 19 hits (and a Pirate error) into 16 runs—five of them driven in by Mickey Mantle's two home runs. Continuing their assault in New York the next day, the Bronx Bombers scored six runs in the first inning and four in the fourth as Whitey Ford blanked the Pirates on four hits. Mantle homered again, and second baseman Bobby Richardson drove in a Series single-game record six runs with a grand slam and a single.

Pirate ace Vernon Law—the winner of Game One—started Game Four and, with relief help once again from Roy Face, held the Yankees to two runs to even the Series. Law's bat proved crucial, too, as he doubled in Pittsburgh's first run and scored the third in a three-run fifth that provided all the Pirate scoring. In Game Five, the Pirates' Mazeroski doubled in what proved the two decisive runs in a three-run second as Harvey Haddix and Roy Face (who recorded his third save of the Series) duplicated the previous day's achievement of limiting New York to two runs.

But once again the Yankees came back. Bobby Richardson drove in three of New York's 12 runs with two triples to establish a new Series record of 12 RBIs as the Yankees, behind Whitey Ford's second shutout, sent the Series into a seventh game.

Home runs dominated the finale. Rocky Nelson's two-run shot in the first opened the scoring, and Yankee homers by Bill Skowron in the fifth and Yogi Berra in the sixth contributed four of the five runs that put New York ahead 5–4. Pirate Hal Smith's three-run homer in the bottom of the eighth restored the lead to Pittsburgh, 9–7, and after the Yankees had

tied the game in the top of the ninth (on three singles and a ground out), Mazeroski's immortal shot over the wall in left gave Pittsburgh its first world championship in thirty-five years.

Pittsburgh Pirates (NL), 4;
New York Yankees (AL), 3

PIT (N)

PLAYER/POS	AVG	G	AB	R	H	2B	3B	HR	RB	BB	SO	SB
Gene Baker, ph	.000	3	3	0	0	0	0	0	0	0	1	0
Smoky Burgess, c	.333	5	18	2	6	1	0	0	0	2	1	0
Tom Cheney, p	.000	3	0	0	0	0	0	0	0	0	0	0
Joe Christopher, ph	.000	3	0	2	0	0	0	0	0	0	0	0
Gino Cimoli, of-6	.250	7	20	4	5	0	0	0	1	2	4	0
Roberto Clemente, of	.310	7	29	1	9	0	0	0	3	0	4	0
Roy Face, p	.000	4	3	0	0	0	0	0	0	0	2	0
Bob Friend, p	.000	3	1	0	0	0	0	0	0	0	0	0
Joe Gibbon, p	.000	2	0	0	0	0	0	0	0	0	0	0
Fred Green, p	.000	3	1	0	0	0	0	0	0	0	0	0
Dick Groat, ss	.214	7	28	3	6	2	0	0	2	0	1	0
Harvey Haddix, p	.333	2	3	0	1	0	0	0	0	0	1	0
Don Hoak, 3b	.217	7	23	3	5	2	0	0	3	4	1	0
Clem Labine, p	.000	3	0	0	0	0	0	0	0	0	0	0
Vern Law, p	.333	3	6	1	2	1	0	0	1	0	1	0
Bill Mazeroski, 2b	.320	7	25	4	8	2	0	2	5	0	3	0
Vinegar Bend Mizell, p	.000	2	0	0	0	0	0	0	0	0	0	0
Rocky Nelson, 1b-3	.333	4	9	2	3	0	0	1	2	1	1	0
Bob Oldis, c	.000	3	0	0	0	0	0	0	0	0	0	0
Dick Schofield, ss-2	.333	3	3	0	1	0	0	0	0	1	0	0
Bob Skinner, of	.200	2	5	2	1	0	0	0	1	1	0	1
Hal Smith, c	.375	3	8	1	3	0	0	1	3	0	0	0
Dick Stuart, 1b	.150	5	20	0	3	0	0	0	0	0	3	0
Bill Virdon, of	.241	7	29	2	7	3	0	0	5	1	3	1
George Witt, p	.000	3	0	0	0	0	0	0	0	0	0	0
TOTAL	.256		234	27	60	11	0	4	26	12	26	2

PITCHER	W	L	ERA	G	GS	CG	SV	SHO	IP	H	ER	BB	SO
Tom Cheney	0	0	4.50	3	0	0	0	0	4.0	4	2	1	6
Roy Face	0	0	5.23	4	0	0	3	0	10.1	9	6	2	4
Bob Friend	0	2	13.50	3	2	0	0	0	6.0	13	9	3	7
Joe Gibbon	0	0	9.00	2	0	0	0	0	3.0	4	3	1	2
Fred Green	0	0	22.50	3	0	0	0	0	4.0	11	10	1	3
Harvey Haddix	2	0	2.45	2	1	0	0	0	7.1	6	2	2	6
Clem Labine	0	0	13.50	3	0	0	0	0	4.0	13	6	1	2
Vern Law	2	0	3.44	3	3	0	0	0	18.1	22	7	3	8
Vinegar Bend Mizell	0	1	15.43	2	1	0	0	0	2.1	4	4	2	1
George Witt	0	0	0.00	3	0	0	0	0	2.2	5	0	2	1
TOTAL	4	3	7.11	28	7	0	3	0	62.0	91	49	18	40

NY (A)

PLAYER/POS	AVG	G	AB	R	H	2B	3B	HR	RB	BB	SO	SB
Luis Arroyo, p	.000	1	1	0	0	0	0	0	0	0	0	0
Yogi Berra, of-4,c-3	.318	7	22	6	7	0	0	1	8	2	0	0
Johnny Blanchard, c-2	.455	5	11	2	5	2	0	0	2	0	0	0
Clete Boyer, 3b-4,ss-1	.250	4	12	1	3	2	1	0	1	0	1	0
Bob Cerv, of-3	.357	4	14	1	5	0	0	0	0	0	3	0
Jim Coates, p	.000	3	1	0	0	0	0	0	0	0	1	0
Joe De Maestri, ss-3	.500	4	2	1	1	0	0	0	0	0	1	0
Art Ditmar, p	.000	2	0	0	0	0	0	0	0	0	0	0
Ryne Duren, p	.000	2	0	0	0	0	0	0	0	0	0	0
Whitey Ford, p	.250	2	8	1	2	0	0	0	0	2	0	0
Eli Grba, pr	.000	1	0	0	0	0	0	0	0	0	0	0
Elston Howard, c-4	.462	5	13	4	6	1	1	1	4	1	4	0
Tony Kubek, ss-7,of-2	.333	7	30	6	10	1	0	0	3	2	2	0
Dale Long, ph	.333	3	3	0	1	0	0	0	0	0	0	0
Hector Lopez, of-1	.429	3	7	0	3	0	0	0	0	0	0	0
Duke Maas, p	.000	1	0	0	0	0	0	0	0	0	0	0
Mickey Mantle, of	.400	7	25	8	10	1	0	3	11	8	9	0
Roger Maris, of	.267	7	30	6	8	1	0	2	2	2	4	0
Gil McDougald, 3b	.278	6	18	4	5	1	0	0	2	2	3	0
Bobby Richardson, 2b	.367	7	30	8	11	2	2	1	12	1	1	0
Bobby Shantz, p	.333	3	3	0	1	0	0	0	0	0	0	0
Bill Skowron, 1b	.375	7	32	7	12	2	0	2	6	0	6	0
Bill Stafford, p	.000	2	1	0	0	0	0	0	0	0	1	0
Ralph Terry, p	.000	2	2	0	0	0	0	0	0	0	1	0
Bob Turley, p	.250	2	4	0	1	0	0	0	1	0	1	0
TOTAL	.338		269	55	91	13	4	10	54	18	40	0

PITCHER	W	L	ERA	G	GS	CG	SV	SHO	IP	H	ER	BB	SO
Luis Arroyo	0	0	13.50	1	0	0	0	0	0.2	2	1	0	1
Jim Coates	0	0	5.68	3	0	0	0	0	6.1	6	4	1	3
Art Ditmar	0	2	21.60	2	2	0	0	0	1.2	6	4	1	0
Ryne Duren	0	0	2.25	2	0	0	0	0	4.0	2	1	1	5
Whitey Ford	2	0	0.00	2	2	2	0	2	18.0	11	0	2	8
Duke Maas	0	0	4.50	1	0	0	0	0	2.0	2	1	0	1
Bobby Shantz	0	0	4.26	3	0	0	1	0	6.1	4	3	1	1
Bill Stafford	0	0	1.50	2	0	0	0	0	6.0	5	1	1	2
Ralph Terry	0	2	5.40	2	1	0	0	0	6.2	7	4	1	5
Bob Turley	1	0	4.82	2	2	0	0	0	9.1	15	5	4	0
TOTAL	3	4	3.54	20	7	2	1	2	61.0	60	24	12	26

Slugger Mickey Mantle sat out most of the Series with a thigh infection, but rookie manager Ralph Houk enjoyed an otherwise splendid finish to a splendid season as his Yankees mauled the Reds, 27 runs to 13. Yankee ace Whitey Ford, coming off one of his finest seasons (25–4), carried his mound mastery into the Series opener, holding Cincinnati to two singles and a walk as he hurled his third straight World Series shutout. New York recorded only six hits, but two of them were home runs by Elston Howard and Bill Skowron.

Gordy Coleman's two-run homer the next day in the top of the fourth inning broke Cincinnati's scoring drought and gave the Reds a 2–0 lead. Yogi Berra tied the score half an inning later with a two-run blast for New York, but that was all they would get. Red starter Joey Jay blanked the Yankees the rest of the way as his teammates put across four more runs to even the Series. Bob Purkey pitched for the Reds in Game Three and blanked New York on one hit through the first six innings, taking a 1–0 lead into the top of the seventh. A pair of Yankee singles sandwiched around a passed ball evened the score, but the Reds regained the lead with a run in the last of the seventh. But Yankee pinch hitter Johnny Blanchard homered to retie the game in the eighth and—while Yankee relief ace Luis Arroyo stopped the Reds through the final two innings—Roger Maris hit his sixty-second home run of the year to win the game and regain the Series lead for New York.

Cincinnati never again threatened. In Game Four, Whitey Ford held the Reds to four harmless singles until he was removed in the sixth because of an ankle injury. (In the third inning he passed Babe Ruth's World Series record of 29⅔ consecutive scoreless innings.) Reliever Jim Coates continued Ford's shutout as the Yankees scored seven runs for the decisive win. The fifth and final game also was no contest. Cincinnati did score five runs—three on Frank Robinson's third-inning home run and two on Wally Post's shot in the fifth. But the Yankees ran through eight Red pitchers, scoring 13 times. Seven of their 15 hits went for extra bases, including Johnny Blanchard's second home run of the Series, and a triple and homer by utility outfielder Hector Lopez.

New York Yankees (AL), 4; Cincinnati Reds (NL), 1

NY (A)

PLAYER/POS	AVG	G	AB	R	H	2B	3B	HR	RB	BB	SO	SB
Luis Arroyo, p	.000	2	0	0	0	0	0	0	0	0	0	0
Yogi Berra, of	.273	4	11	2	3	0	0	1	3	5	1	0
Johnny Blanchard, of-2	.400	4	10	4	4	1	0	2	3	2	0	0
Clete Boyer, 3b	.267	5	15	0	4	2	0	0	3	4	0	0
Jim Coates, p	.000	1	1	0	0	0	0	0	0	0	1	0
Buddy Daley, p	.000	2	1	0	0	0	0	0	1	0	0	0
Whitey Ford, p	.000	2	5	1	0	0	0	0	0	1	0	0
Billy Gardner, ph	.000	1	1	0	0	0	0	0	0	0	0	0
Elston Howard, c	.250	5	20	5	5	3	0	1	1	2	3	0
Tony Kubek, ss	.227	5	22	3	5	0	0	0	1	1	4	0
Hector Lopez, of-3	.333	4	9	3	3	0	1	1	7	2	3	0
Mickey Mantle, of	.167	2	6	0	1	0	0	0	0	0	2	0
Roger Maris, of	.105	5	19	4	2	1	0	1	2	4	6	0
Jack Reed, of	.000	3	0	0	0	0	0	0	0	0	0	0
Bobby Richardson, 2b	.391	5	23	2	9	1	0	0	0	0	0	1
Bill Skowron, 1b	.353	5	17	3	6	0	0	1	5	3	4	0
Bill Stafford, p	.000	1	2	0	0	0	0	0	0	0	0	0
Ralph Terry, p	.000	2	3	0	0	0	0	0	0	0	1	0
TOTAL	.255		165	27	42	8	1	7	26	24	25	1

PITCHER	W	L	ERA	G	GS	CG	SV	SHO	IP	H	ER	BB	SO
Luis Arroyo	1	0	2.25	2	0	0	0	0	4.0	4	1	2	3
Jim Coates	0	0	0.00	1	0	0	1	0	4.0	1	0	1	2
Buddy Daley	1	0	0.00	2	0	0	0	0	7.0	5	0	0	3
Whitey Ford	2	0	0.00	2	2	1	0	1	14.0	6	0	1	7
Bill Stafford	0	0	2.70	1	1	0	0	0	6.2	7	2	2	5
Ralph Terry	0	1	4.82	2	2	0	0	0	9.1	12	5	2	7
TOTAL	4	1	1.60	10	5	1	1	1	45.0	35	8	8	27

CIN (N)

PLAYER/POS	AVG	G	AB	R	H	2B	3B	HR	RB	BB	SO	SB
Gus Bell, ph	.000	3	3	0	0	0	0	0	0	0	0	0
Don Blasingame, 2b	.143	3	7	1	1	0	0	0	0	0	3	0
Jim Brosnan, p	.000	3	0	0	0	0	0	0	0	0	0	0
Leo Cardenas, ph	.333	3	3	0	1	1	0	0	0	0	1	0
Elio Chacon, 2b-3	.250	4	12	2	3	0	0	0	0	1	2	0
Gordie Coleman, 1b	.250	5	20	2	5	0	0	1	2	0	1	0
Johnny Edwards, c	.364	3	11	1	4	2	0	0	2	0	0	0
Gene Freese, 3b	.063	5	16	0	1	1	0	0	0	3	4	0
Dick Gernert, ph	.000	4	4	0	0	0	0	0	0	0	1	0
Bill Henry, p	.000	2	0	0	0	0	0	0	0	0	0	0
Ken Hunt, p	.000	1	0	0	0	0	0	0	0	0	0	0
Joey Jay, p	.000	2	4	0	0	0	0	0	0	0	2	0
Darrell Johnson, c	.500	2	4	0	2	0	0	0	0	0	0	0
Ken Johnson, p	.000	1	0	0	0	0	0	0	0	0	0	0
Sherman Jones, p	.000	1	0	0	0	0	0	0	0	0	0	0
Eddie Kasko, ss	.318	5	22	1	7	0	0	0	1	0	2	0
Jerry Lynch, ph	.000	4	3	0	0	0	0	0	0	1	1	0
Jim Maloney, p	.000	1	0	0	0	0	0	0	0	0	0	0
Jim O'Toole, p	.000	2	3	0	0	0	0	0	0	0	1	0
Vada Pinson, of	.091	5	22	0	2	1	0	0	0	0	1	0
Wally Post, of	.333	5	18	3	6	1	0	1	2	0	1	0
Bob Purkey, p	.000	2	3	0	0	0	0	0	0	0	3	0
Frank Robinson, of	.200	5	15	3	3	2	0	1	4	3	4	0
Jerry Zimmerman, c	.000	2	0	0	0	0	0	0	0	0	0	0
TOTAL	.206		170	13	35	8	0	3	11	8	27	0

PITCHER	W	L	ERA	G	GS	CG	SV	SHO	IP	H	ER	BB	SO
Jim Brosnan	0	0	7.50	3	0	0	0	0	6.0	9	5	4	5
Bill Henry	0	0	19.29	2	0	0	0	0	2.1	4	5	2	3
Ken Hunt	0	0	0.00	1	0	0	0	0	1.0	0	0	1	1
Joey Jay	1	1	5.59	2	2	1	0	0	9.2	8	6	6	6
Ken Johnson	0	0	0.00	1	0	0	0	0	0.2	0	0	0	0
Sherman Jones	0	0	0.00	1	0	0	0	0	0.2	0	0	0	0
Jim Maloney	0	0	27.00	1	0	0	0	0	0.2	4	2	1	1
Jim O'Toole	0	2	3.00	2	2	0	0	0	12.0	11	4	7	4
Bob Purkey	0	1	1.64	2	1	1	0	0	11.0	6	2	3	5
TOTAL	1	4	4.91	15	5	2	0	0	44.0	42	24	24	25

GAME 1 AT NY OCT 4

CIN	000	000	000	0	2	0
NY	000	101	00X	2	6	0

Pitchers: O'TOOLE, Brosnan (8) vs FORD
Home Runs: Howard-NY, Skowron-NY
Attendance: 62,397

GAME 2 AT NY OCT 5

CIN	000	211	020	6	9	0
NY	000	200	000	2	4	3

Pitchers: JAY vs TERRY, Arroyo (8)
Home Runs: Coleman-CIN, Berra-NY
Attendance: 63,083

GAME 3 AT CIN OCT 7

NY	000	000	111	3	6	1
CIN	001	000	100	2	8	0

Pitchers: Stafford, Daley (7), ARROYO (8) vs PURKEY
Home Runs: Blanchard-NY, Maris-NY
Attendance: 32,589

GAME 4 AT CIN OCT 8

NY	000	112	300	7	11	0
CIN	000	000	000	0	5	1

Pitchers: FORD, Coates (6) vs O'TOOLE, Brosnan (6), Henry (9)
Attendance: 32,589

GAME 5 AT CIN OCT 9

NY	510	502	000	13	15	1
CIN	003	020	000	5	11	3

Pitchers: Terry, DALEY (3) vs JAY, Maloney (1), K.Johnson (2), Henry (3), Jones (4), Purkey (5), Brosnan (7), Hunt (9)
Home Runs: Blanchard-NY, Robinson-CIN, Lopez-NY, Post-CIN
Attendance: 32,589

After edging Los Angeles for the pennant in a three-game playoff to break a regular-season tie, San Francisco battled to the final out of Game Seven before falling to New York in the World Series. The teams alternated wins throughout the Series. In the opener Roger Maris doubled two runs home for a quick Yankee lead. Whitey Ford gave up a run in the second (ending his record streak for consecutive scoreless World Series innings pitched at 33⅔) and a tying run an inning later. But he blanked the Giants after that, and won the game on Clete Boyer's homer in the seventh.

Giant Jack Sanford blanked the Yankees on three hits in Game Two, but in Game Three Yankee Bill Stafford restored the Series edge to New York with a four-hit 3–2 win (a shutout until Giant Ed Bailey's ninth-inning home run). Both clubs hit safely nine times in Game Four. But one of the Giants' hits was Chuck Hiller's tie-breaking grand slam in the seventh— more than enough for a Giant win and another Series tie. In Game Five Sanford brought a three-hit 2–2 tie into the last of the eighth. But after he had notched his tenth strikeout, two singles and Tom Tresh's home run drove him out and gave Yankee pitcher Ralph Terry all the margin he needed to avenge his second-game loss to Sanford, and put the Yankees ahead in the Series for the third time.

When play resumed in San Francisco after several days of rain, Billy Pierce held New York to just three hits. One was Roger Maris's solo homer in the fifth, but Pierce's Giants unloaded on Whitey Ford for five runs, driving Ford out and keeping Giant hopes alive.

The finale pitted Terry against Sanford for the third time. Both pitched effectively, but Terry carried a 1–0 lead into the last of the ninth. Pinch hitter Matty Alou led off with a bunt single, but Terry fanned the next two batters. Then Willie Mays doubled to right, but Roger Maris's slick fielding stopped Alou at third. As Terry faced Willie McCovey (who had homered off him in Game Two), he pondered the home run he had given up to Bill Mazeroski two years earlier to lose the 1960 World Series to Pittsburgh. McCovey lined Terry's third pitch toward right—but right at second baseman Bobby Richardson, who grabbed it for the Yankees' twentieth world title. It would be fifteen years before they saw another.

New York Yankees (AL), 4;
San Francisco Giants (NL) 3

NY (A)

PLAYER/POS	AVG	G	AB	R	H	2B	3B	HR	RB	BB	SO	SB
Yogi Berra, c-1	.000	2	2	0	0	0	0	0	0	2	0	0
Johnny Blanchard, ph	.000	1	1	0	0	0	0	0	0	0	1	0
Clete Boyer, 3b	.318	7	22	2	7	1	0	1	4	1	3	0
Marshall Bridges, p	.000	2	0	0	0	0	0	0	0	0	0	0
Jim Coates, p	.000	2	0	0	0	0	0	0	0	0	0	0
Buddy Daley, p	.000	1	0	0	0	0	0	0	0	0	0	0
Whitey Ford, p	.000	3	7	0	0	0	0	0	0	0	1	3	0
Elston Howard, c	.143	6	21	1	3	1	0	0	1	1	4	0
Tony Kubek, ss	.276	7	29	2	8	1	0	0	1	1	3	0
Dale Long, 1b	.200	2	5	0	1	0	0	0	1	0	1	0
Hector Lopez, ph	.000	2	2	0	0	0	0	0	0	0	0	0
Mickey Mantle, of	.120	7	25	2	3	1	0	0	0	4	5	2
Roger Maris, of	.174	7	23	4	4	1	0	1	5	5	2	0
Bobby Richardson, 2b	.148	7	27	3	4	0	0	0	0	3	1	0
Bill Skowron, 1b	.222	6	18	1	4	0	1	0	1	1	5	0
Bill Stafford, p	.000	1	3	0	0	0	0	0	0	0	1	0
Ralph Terry, p	.125	3	8	0	1	0	0	0	0	1	6	0
Tom Tresh, of	.321	7	28	5	9	1	0	1	4	1	4	2
TOTAL	.199		221	20	44	6	1	3	17	21	39	4

PITCHER	W	L	ERA	G	GS	CG	SV	SHO	IP	H	ER	BB	SO
Marshall Bridges	0	0	4.91	2	0	0	0	0	3.2	4	2	2	3
Jim Coates	0	1	6.75	2	0	0	0	0	2.2	1	2	1	3
Buddy Daley	0	0	0.00	1	0	0	0	0	1.0	1	0	1	0
Whitey Ford	1	1	4.12	3	3	1	0	0	19.2	24	9	4	12
Bill Stafford	1	0	2.00	1	1	1	0	0	9.0	4	2	2	5
Ralph Terry	2	1	1.80	3	3	2	0	1	25.0	17	5	2	16
TOTAL	4	3	2.95	12	7	4	0	1	61.0	51	20	12	39

SF (N)

PLAYER/POS	AVG	G	AB	R	H	2B	3B	HR	RB	BB	SO	SB
Felipe Alou, of	.269	7	26	2	7	1	1	0	1	1	4	0
Matty Alou, of-4	.333	6	12	2	4	1	0	0	1	0	1	0
Ed Bailey, c-3	.071	6	14	1	1	0	0	1	2	0	3	0
Bobby Bolin, p	.000	2	0	0	0	0	0	0	0	0	0	0
Ernie Bowman, ss-1	.000	2	1	1	0	0	0	0	0	0	0	0
Orlando Cepeda, 1b	.158	5	19	1	3	1	0	0	2	0	4	0
Jim Davenport, 3b	.136	7	22	1	3	1	0	0	1	4	7	0
Tom Haller, c	.286	4	14	1	4	1	0	1	3	0	2	0
Chuck Hiller, 2b	.269	7	26	4	7	3	0	1	5	3	4	0
Harvey Kuenn, of	.083	4	12	1	1	0	0	0	0	1	1	0
Don Larsen, p	.000	3	0	0	0	0	0	0	0	0	0	0
Juan Marichal, p	.000	1	2	0	0	0	0	0	0	0	1	0
Willie Mays, of	.250	7	28	3	7	2	0	0	1	1	5	1
Willie Mc Covey, 1b-2,of-2	.200	4	15	2	3	0	1	1	1	1	3	0
Stu Miller, p	.000	2	0	0	0	0	0	0	0	0	0	0
Bob Nieman, ph	.000	1	0	0	0	0	0	0	0	1	0	0
Billy O'Dell, p	.333	3	3	0	1	0	0	0	0	0	0	0
John Orsino, c	.000	1	1	0	0	0	0	0	0	0	0	0
Jose Pagan, ss	.368	7	19	2	7	0	0	1	2	0	1	0
Billy Pierce, p	.000	2	5	0	0	0	0	0	0	0	1	0
Jack Sanford, p	.429	3	7	0	3	0	0	0	0	0	2	0
TOTAL	.226		226	21	51	10	2	5	19	12	39	1

PITCHER	W	L	ERA	G	GS	CG	SV	SHO	IP	H	ER	BB	SO
Bobby Bolin	0	0	6.75	2	0	0	0	0	2.2	4	2	2	2
Don Larsen	1	0	3.86	3	0	0	0	0	2.1	1	1	2	0
Juan Marichal	0	0	0.00	1	1	0	0	0	4.0	2	0	2	4
Stu Miller	0	0	0.00	2	0	0	0	0	1.1	1	0	2	0
Billy O'Dell	0	1	4.38	3	1	0	1	0	12.1	12	6	3	9
Billy Pierce	1	1	2.40	2	2	1	0	0	15.0	8	4	2	5
Jack Sanford	1	2	1.93	3	3	1	0	1	23.1	16	5	8	19
TOTAL	3	4	2.66	16	7	2	1	1	61.0	44	18	21	39

GAME 1 AT SF OCT 4

NY	200 000 121	6	11	0
SF	011 000 000	2	10	0

Pitchers: FORD vs O'DELL, Larsen (7), Miller (9)
Home Runs: Boyer-NY
Attendance: 43,852

GAME 2 AT SF OCT 5

NY	000 000 000	0	3	1
SF	100 000 10X	2	6	0

Pitchers: TERRY, Daley (8) vs SANFORD
Home Runs: McCovey-SF
Attendance: 43,910

GAME 3 AT NY OCT 7

SF	000 000 002	2	4	3
NY	000 000 30X	3	5	1

Pitchers: PIERCE, Larsen (7), Bolin (8) vs STAFFORD
Home Runs: Bailey-SF
Attendance: 71,434

GAME 4 AT NY OCT 8

SF	020 000 401	7	9	1
NY	000 002 001	3	9	1

Pitchers: Marichal, Bolin (5), LARSEN (6), O'Dell (7) vs Ford, COATES (7), Bridges (7)
Home Runs: Haller-SF, Hiller-SF
Attendance: 66,607

GAME 5 AT NY OCT 10

SF	001 010 001	3	8	2
NY	000 101 03X	5	6	0

Pitchers: SANFORD, Miller (8) vs TERRY
Home Runs: Pagan-SF, Tresh-NY
Attendance: 63,165

GAME 6 AT SF OCT 15

NY	000 010 010	2	3	2
SF	000 320 00X	5	10	1

Pitchers: FORD, Coates (5), Bridges (8) vs PIERCE
Home Runs: Maris-NY
Attendance: 43,948

GAME 7 AT SF OCT 16

NY	000 100 000	1	7	0
SF	000 000 000	0	4	1

Pitchers: TERRY vs SANFORD, O'Dell (8)
Attendance: 43,948

The Yankees won the American League pennant by 10½ games, but in the Series they were overwhelmed by Dodger pitching. The opener pitted two all-time greats against each other: Yankee Whitey Ford (24–7 that season) and Sandy Koufax (25–5). For an inning it was close. Ford fanned two of the first three batters to face him, and Koufax struck out the side. But in the top of the second the Dodgers' Frank Howard doubled with one out, and before Ford could record the second out, two singles and John Roseboro's home run had put four Dodger runs across. Koufax ran his consecutive Ks to five and had tied the Series single-game record of 14 by the time Tom Tresh tagged him for a two-run homer in the eighth. That was New York's only scoring, and Koufax ended the game with a new-record fifteenth strikeout an inning later.

Veteran Johnny Podres pitched shutout ball through 8⅓ innings of Game Two as his Dodgers built him a four-run lead (one of the runs a homer by ex-Yankee Bill Skowron). New York scored a run in the last of the ninth, but it was not enough to keep the Dodgers from returning to Los Angeles with a 2–0 Series advantage.

A first-inning walk, a wild pitch, and a single moved Dodger Jim Gilliam around the bases for the only scoring in Game Three as Yankee Jim Bouton hooked up in a duel with Don Drysdale. Bouton left after seven innings for Yankee relief ace Hal Reniff, who held Los Angeles hitless through the final frames. When Drysdale completed his shutout, only three singles had been hit against him, and he had struck out nine.

Ford and Koufax tangled again in the fourth game. Ford pitched much more impressively than he had in the opener, walking just one and yielding only two hits in seven innings. One of the Dodger hits was Frank Howard's solo homer in the fifth inning, but Mickey Mantle evened the score with a home run off Koufax in the seventh. But in the last of the seventh, Yankee first baseman Joe Pepitone lost sight of a throw from the third baseman for an error that sent batter Jim Gilliam all the way to third, and Willie Davis followed with a fly to center that scored Gilliam with the go-ahead run. No one else scored against Ford (or Reniff, who relieved him in the eighth), but no other Yankee scored against Koufax either, and the Dodgers, with just two hits, captured the game and the Series.

Los Angeles Dodgers (NL), 4;
New York Yankees (AL), 0

LA (N)

PLAYER/POS	AVG	G	AB	R	H	2B	3B	HR	RB	BB	SO	SB
Tommy Davis, of	.400	4	15	0	6	0	2	0	2	0	2	1
Willie Davis, of	.167	4	12	2	2	2	0	0	3	0	6	0
Don Drysdale, p	.000	1	1	0	0	0	0	0	0	2	0	0
Ron Fairly, of	.000	4	1	0	0	0	0	0	0	3	0	0
Jim Gilliam, 3b	.154	4	13	3	2	0	0	0	0	3	1	0
Frank Howard, of	.300	3	10	2	3	1	0	1	1	0	2	0
Sandy Koufax, p	.000	2	6	0	0	0	0	0	0	0	2	0
Ron Perranoski, p	.000	1	0	0	0	0	0	0	0	0	0	0
Johnny Podres, p	.250	1	4	0	1	0	0	0	0	0	0	0
Johnny Roseboro, c	.143	4	14	1	2	0	0	1	3	0	4	0
Bill Skowron, 1b	.385	4	13	2	5	0	0	1	3	1	3	0
Dick Tracewski, 2b	.154	4	13	1	2	0	0	0	0	1	2	0
Maury Wills, ss	.133	4	15	1	2	0	0	0	0	1	3	1
TOTAL	.214		117	12	25	3	2	3	12	11	25	2

PITCHER	W	L	ERA	G	GS	CG	SV	SHO	IP	H	ER	BB	SO
Don Drysdale	1	0	0.00	1	1	1	0	1	9.0	3	0	1	9
Sandy Koufax	2	0	1.50	2	2	2	0	0	18.0	12	3	3	23
Ron Perranoski	0	0	0.00	1	0	0	1	0	0.2	1	0	0	1
Johnny Podres	1	0	1.08	1	1	0	0	0	8.1	6	1	1	4
TOTAL	4	0	1.00	5	4	3	1	1	36.0	22	4	5	37

NY (A)

PLAYER/POS	AVG	G	AB	R	H	2B	3B	HR	RB	BB	SO	SB
Yogi Berra, ph	.000	1	1	0	0	0	0	0	0	0	0	0
Johnny Blanchard, of-1	.000	1	3	0	0	0	0	0	0	0	0	0
Jim Bouton, p	.000	1	2	0	0	0	0	0	0	0	2	0
Clete Boyer, 3b	.077	4	13	0	1	0	0	0	0	1	6	0
Harry Bright, ph	.000	2	2	0	0	0	0	0	0	0	2	0
Al Downing, p	.000	1	1	0	0	0	0	0	0	0	1	0
Whitey Ford, p	.000	2	3	0	0	0	0	0	0	0	1	0
Steve Hamilton, p	.000	1	0	0	0	0	0	0	0	0	0	0
Elston Howard, c	.333	4	15	0	5	0	0	0	1	0	3	0
Tony Kubek, ss	.188	4	16	1	3	0	0	0	0	0	3	0
Phil Linz, ph	.333	3	3	0	1	0	0	0	0	0	1	0
Hector Lopez, of-2	.250	3	8	1	2	2	0	0	0	0	1	0
Mickey Mantle, of	.133	4	15	1	2	0	0	1	1	1	5	0
Roger Maris, of	.000	2	5	0	0	0	0	0	0	0	1	0
Joe Pepitone, 1b	.154	4	13	0	2	0	0	0	0	1	3	0
Hal Reniff, p	.000	3	0	0	0	0	0	0	0	0	0	0
Bobby Richardson, 2b	.214	4	14	0	3	1	0	0	0	1	3	0
Ralph Terry, p	.000	1	0	0	0	0	0	0	0	0	0	0
Tom Tresh, of	.200	4	15	1	3	0	0	1	2	1	6	0
Stan Williams, p	.000	1	0	0	0	0	0	0	0	0	0	0
TOTAL	.171		129	4	22	3	0	2	4	5	37	0

PITCHER	W	L	ERA	G	GS	CG	SV	SHO	IP	H	ER	BB	SO
Jim Bouton	0	1	1.29	1	1	0	0	0	7.0	4	1	5	4
Al Downing	0	1	5.40	1	1	0	0	0	5.0	7	3	1	6
Whitey Ford	0	2	4.50	2	2	0	0	0	12.0	10	6	3	8
Steve Hamilton	0	0	0.00	1	0	0	0	0	1.0	0	0	0	1
Hal Reniff	0	0	0.00	3	0	0	0	0	3.0	0	0	1	1
Ralph Terry	0	0	3.00	1	0	0	0	0	3.0	3	1	1	0
Stan Williams	0	0	0.00	1	0	0	0	0	3.0	1	0	0	5
TOTAL	0	4	2.91	10	4	0	0	0	34.0	25	11	11	25

GAME 1 AT NY OCT 2

LA	041 000 000	5	9	0
NY	000 000 020	2	6	0

Pitchers: KOUFAX vs FORD, Williams (6), Hamilton (9)
Home Runs: Roseboro-LA, Tresh-NY
Attendance: 69,000

GAME 2 AT NY OCT 3

LA	200 100 010	4	10	1
NY	000 000 001	1	7	0

Pitchers: PODRES, Perranoski (9) vs DOWNING, Terry (6), Reniff (9)
Home Runs: Skowron-LA
Attendance: 66,455

GAME 3 AT LA OCT 5

NY	000 000 000	0	3	0
LA	100 000 00X	1	4	1

Pitchers: BOUTON, Reniff (8) vs DRYSDALE
Attendance: 55,912

GAME 4 AT LA OCT 6

NY	000 000 100	1	6	1
LA	000 010 10X	2	2	1

Pitchers: FORD, Reniff (8) vs KOUFAX
Home Runs: F.Howard-LA, Mantle-NY
Attendance: 55,912

With late-season spurts the Cardinals edged the Reds and Phillies for their first pennant in eighteen years and the Yankees overtook the White Sox and Orioles for their fifteenth in eighteen years and their twenty-ninth over all. But when the Series was over, the long era of Yankee dominance had come to an end.

St. Louis won the opener, a 24-hit slugfest in which Curt Flood's RBI triple in the sixth proved the decisive blow. But New York came back to take the next two games. Rookie Mel Stottlemyre won Game Two, holding the Cards to three runs as his Yankees scored eight. (Loser Bob Gibson struck out nine Yankees, though, on his way to a new Series record of 31.) Game Three, by contrast, featured a pitchers' duel between Jim Bouton and Cardinal veteran Curt Simmons. Cardinal reliever Barney Schultz, who replaced Simmons for the last of the ninth with the score 1–1, lost the game on his first pitch when Mickey Mantle homered to deep right (his sixteenth World Series home run, which moved him ahead of Babe Ruth into the all-time Series lead).

Cardinal Ray Sadecki (the winner in Game One) left with one out in the first inning of Game Four after four Yankee batters hit safely, but relievers Roger Craig and Ron Taylor stopped New York on just two singles the rest of the way. The Cards were also held to six hits, but one was Ken Boyer's grand slam in the sixth, which erased a 3–0 Yankee lead and gave St. Louis runs enough to even the Series at two games apiece.

Gibson and Stottlemyre faced off a second time in Game Five. Gibson carried a 2–0 lead into the last of the ninth, when with two out Tom Tresh tagged him for a game-tying home run. In the top of the tenth, though, the Cards regained the lead on Tim McCarver's three-run homer and held on for the win as Gibson notched his thirteenth K of the game.

Bouton and Simmons tangled again in Game Five. Another 1–1 duel was shattered this time in the top of the sixth when Roger Maris and Mantle tagged Simmons for back-to-back home runs. New York put the game away in the eighth with five runs off Cardinal relievers—four of them on Joe Pepitone's grand slam.

With the series tied 3–3, Gibson and Stottlemyre were called upon to settle the title. Gibson pitched the whole game, striking out nine. Mantle touched him for a three-run homer in the sixth inning, and Clete Boyer and Phil Linz hit solo shots in the ninth.

St. Louis Cardinals (NL), 4; New York Yankees (AL), 3

STL (N)

PLAYER/POS	AVG	G	AB	R	H	2B	3B	HR	RB	BB	SO	SB
Ken Boyer, 3b	.222	7	27	5	6	1	0	2	6	1	5	0
Lou Brock, of	.300	7	30	2	9	2	0	1	5	0	3	0
Gerry Buchek, 2b	1.000	4	1	1	1	0	0	0	0	0	0	0
Roger Craig, p	.000	2	1	0	0	0	0	0	0	0	0	0
Curt Flood, of	.200	7	30	5	6	0	1	0	3	3	1	0
Bob Gibson, p	.222	3	9	1	2	0	0	0	0	0	3	0
Dick Groat, ss	.192	7	26	3	5	1	1	0	1	4	3	0
Bob Humphreys, p	.000	1	0	0	0	0	0	0	0	0	0	0
Charlie James, ph	.000	3	3	0	0	0	0	0	0	0	1	0
Julian Javier, 2b	.000	1	0	1	0	0	0	0	0	0	0	0
Dal Maxvill, 2b	.200	7	20	0	4	1	0	0	1	4	4	0
Tim McCarver, c	.478	7	23	4	11	1	1	1	5	5	1	1
Gordie Richardson, p	.000	2	0	0	0	0	0	0	0	0	0	0
Ray Sadecki, p	.500	2	2	0	1	0	0	0	0	1	0	1
Barney Schultz, p	.000	4	1	0	0	0	0	0	0	0	0	0
Mike Shannon, of	.214	7	28	6	6	0	0	1	2	0	9	1
Curt Simmons, p	.500	2	4	0	2	0	0	0	1	0	1	0
Bob Skinner, ph	.667	4	3	0	2	1	0	0	1	1	0	0
Ron Taylor, p	.000	2	1	0	0	0	0	0	0	0	1	0
Carl Warwick, ph	.750	5	4	2	3	0	0	0	1	1	0	0
Bill White, 1b	.111	7	27	2	3	1	0	0	2	2	6	1
TOTAL	.254		240	32	61	8	3	5	29	18	39	3

PITCHER	W	L	ERA	G	GS	CG	SV	SHO	IP	H	ER	BB	SO
Roger Craig	1	0	0.00	2	0	0	0	0	5.0	2	0	3	9
Bob Gibson	2	1	3.00	3	3	2	0	0	27.0	23	9	8	31
Bob Humphreys	0	0	0.00	1	0	0	0	0	1.0	0	0	0	1
Gordie Richardson	0	0	40.50	2	0	0	0	0	0.2	3	3	2	0
Ray Sadecki	1	0	8.53	2	2	0	0	0	6.1	12	6	5	2
Barney Schultz	0	1	18.00	4	0	0	1	0	4.0	9	8	3	1
Curt Simmons	0	1	2.51	2	2	0	0	0	14.1	11	4	3	8
Ron Taylor	0	0	0.00	2	0	0	1	0	4.2	0	0	1	2
TOTAL	4	3	4.29	18	7	2	2	0	63.0	60	30	25	54

NY (A)

PLAYER/POS	AVG	G	AB	R	H	2B	3B	HR	RB	BB	SO	SB
Johnny Blanchard, ph	.250	4	4	0	1	1	0	0	0	0	1	0
Jim Bouton, p	.143	2	7	0	1	0	0	0	1	0	2	0
Clete Boyer, 3b	.208	7	24	2	5	1	0	1	3	1	5	1
Al Downing, p	.000	3	2	0	0	0	0	0	0	0	2	0
Whitey Ford, p	1.000	1	1	0	1	0	0	0	1	2	0	0
Pedro Gonzalez, 3b	.000	1	1	0	0	0	0	0	0	0	0	0
Steve Hamilton, p	.000	2	0	0	0	0	0	0	0	0	0	0
Mike Hegan, ph	.000	3	1	1	0	0	0	0	0	1	1	0
Elston Howard, c	.292	7	24	5	7	1	0	0	2	4	6	0
Phil Linz, ss	.226	7	31	5	7	1	0	2	2	2	5	0
Hector Lopez, of-1	.000	3	2	0	0	0	0	0	0	0	2	0
Mickey Mantle, of	.333	7	24	8	8	2	0	3	8	6	8	0
Roger Maris, of	.200	7	30	4	6	0	0	1	1	1	4	0
Pete Mikkelsen, p	.000	4	0	0	0	0	0	0	0	0	0	0
Joe Pepitone, 1b	.154	7	26	1	4	1	0	1	5	2	3	0
Hal Reniff, p	.000	1	0	0	0	0	0	0	0	0	0	0
Bobby Richardson, 2b	.406	7	32	3	13	2	0	0	3	0	2	1
Rollie Sheldon, p	.000	2	0	0	0	0	0	0	0	0	0	0
Mel Stottlemyre, p	.125	3	8	0	1	0	0	0	0	0	6	0
Ralph Terry, p	.000	1	0	0	0	0	0	0	0	0	0	0
Tom Tresh, of	.273	7	22	4	6	2	0	2	7	6	7	0
TOTAL	.251		239	33	60	11	0	10	33	25	54	2

PITCHER	W	L	ERA	G	GS	CG	SV	SHO	IP	H	ER	BB	SO
Jim Bouton	2	0	1.56	2	2	1	0	0	17.1	15	3	5	7
Al Downing	0	1	8.22	3	1	0	0	0	7.2	9	7	2	5
Whitey Ford	0	1	8.44	1	1	0	0	0	5.1	8	5	1	4
Steve Hamilton	0	0	4.50	2	0	0	1	0	2.0	3	1	0	2
Pete Mikkelsen	0	1	5.79	4	0	0	0	0	4.2	4	3	2	4
Hal Reniff	0	0	0.00	1	0	0	0	0	0.1	2	0	0	0
Rollie Sheldon	0	0	0.00	2	0	0	0	0	2.2	0	0	2	2
Mel Stottlemyre	1	1	3.15	3	3	1	0	0	20.0	18	7	6	12
Ralph Terry	0	0	0.00	1	0	0	0	0	2.0	2	0	3	3
TOTAL	3	4	3.77	19	7	2	1	0	62.0	61	26	18	39

But as St. Louis had scored six times off Stottlemyre and his replacement Al Downing before the Yankees scored their first runs, the game ended with the Cards victors and world champions. Yogi Berra, New York's rookie manager, was fired the next day. The following season the Yankees finished sixth.

GAME 1 AT STL OCT 7

NY	030 010 010	5	12	2
STL	110 004 03X	9	12	0

Pitchers: FORD, Downing (6), Sheldon (8), Mikkelsen (9) vs SADECKI, Schultz (7)
Home Runs: Tresh-NY, Shannon-STL
Attendance: 30,805

GAME 2 AT STL OCT 8

NY	000 101 204	8	12	0
STL	001 000 011	3	7	0

Pitchers: STOTTLEMYRE vs GIBSON, Schultz (9), Craig (9)
Home Runs: Linz-NY
Attendance: 30,805

GAME 3 AT NY OCT 10

STL	000 010 000	1	6	0
NY	010 000 001	2	5	2

Pitchers: Simmons, SCHULTZ (9) vs BOUTON
Home Runs: Mantle-NY
Attendance: 67,101

GAME 4 AT NY OCT 11

STL	000 004 000	4	6	1
NY	300 000 000	3	6	1

Pitchers: Sadecki, CRAIG (1), Taylor (6) vs DOWNING, Mikkelsen (7), Terry (8)
Home Runs: K.Boyer-STL
Attendance: 66,312

GAME 5 AT NY OCT 12

STL	000 020 000 3	5	10	1
NY	000 000 002 0	2	6	2

Pitchers: GIBSON vs Stottlemyre, Reniff (8), MIKKELSEN (8)
Home Runs: Tresh-NY, McCarver-STL
Attendance: 65,633

GAME 6 AT STL OCT 14

NY	000 012 050	8	10	0
STL	100 000 011	3	10	1

Pitchers: BOUTON, Hamilton (9) VS SIMMONS, Taylor (7), Schultz (8), Richardson (8), Humphreys (9)
Home Runs: Maris-NY, Mantle-NY, Pepitone-NY
Attendance: 30,805

GAME 7 AT STL OCT 15

NY	000 003 002	5	9	2
STL	000 330 10X	7	10	1

Pitchers: STOTTLEMYRE, Downing (5), Sheldon (5), Hamilton (7), Mikkelsen (8) vs GIBSON
Home Runs: Brock-STL, Mantle-NY, K.Boyer-STL, C.Boyer-NY, Linz-NY
Attendance: 30,346

The Twins (bringing the World Series to Minnesota for the first time ever) featured heavy hitting, while Dodger hopes rested on great pitching and speed on the bases. For a while it looked as if batting power would triumph as the Twins took the first two games at home. They drove out Dodger starter Don Drysdale with seven runs in the first three innings of the opener—including home runs by Don Mincher and Zoilo Versalles—on the way to a convincing 8–2 win, and followed up with a 5–1 triumph the next day over Dodger ace Sandy Koufax (who had declined to pitch Game One on Yom Kippur, the holiest day of the Jewish year) and star reliever Ron Perranoski, who was tagged for three of the Twins' runs.

But when the Series moved to Los Angeles, Dodger pitching began to assert itself. Claude Osteen held Minnesota to five hits and no runs, while Los Angeles bunched seven of their ten hits in the middle three innings for four runs. Drysdale evened the Series in Game Four, avenging his first-game pounding with a second Dodger five-hitter. Twins Harmon Killebrew and Tony Oliva tagged him for a pair of solo homers, but that was Minnesota's only scoring—more than balanced by seven Dodger runs, including homers by Wes Parker and Lou Johnson. In Game Five the next day, Koufax avenged his earlier loss, carrying Los Angeles to its first Series lead with a shutout in which he allowed only four singles and a walk, while fanning ten Twins. Speedster Willie Davis stole three bases and Maury Wills stole another as the Dodgers parlayed fourteen hits into a 7–0 victory.

Back in Minnesota for Game Six, the Twins rallied, using the long ball to even the Series again with a 5–1 win. Bob Allison opened the scoring with a two-run shot off Dodger starter Claude Osteen in the fourth, and Minnesota pitcher Mudcat Grant insured his own win with a three-run blast two innings later.

In the finale, though, the visiting team won for the only time in the Series. Koufax again struck out ten men, stopping the Twins on three hits for his second shutout. Lou Johnson's second Series homer (a fourth-inning solo shot to left off Twin starter Jim Kaat that was barely fair) was all the Dodgers needed for their fifth world championship, but Ron Fairly followed Johnson with a double and Wes Parker singled home an insurance run that drove Kaat out and concluded the Series scoring.

Los Angeles Dodgers (NL), 4; Minnesota Twins (AL) 3

LA (N)

PLAYER/POS	AVG	G	AB	R	H	2B	3B	HR	RB	BB	SO	SB
Jim Brewer, p	.000	1	0	0	0	0	0	0	0	0	0	0
Willie Crawford, ph	.500	2	2	0	1	0	0	0	0	0	1	0
Willie Davis, of	.231	7	26	3	6	0	0	0	0	0	2	3
Don Drysdale, p-2	.000	3	5	0	0	0	0	0	0	0	4	0
Ron Fairly, of	.379	7	29	7	11	3	0	2	6	0	1	0
Jim Gilliam, 3b	.214	7	28	2	6	1	0	0	2	1	0	0
Lou Johnson, of	.296	7	27	3	8	2	0	2	4	1	3	0
John Kennedy, 3b	.000	4	1	0	0	0	0	0	0	0	0	0
Sandy Koufax, p	.111	3	9	0	1	0	0	0	0	1	5	0
Jim Lefebvre, 2b	.400	3	10	2	4	0	0	0	0	0	0	0
Don Le John, ph	.000	1	1	0	0	0	0	0	0	0	1	0
Bob Miller, p	.000	2	0	0	0	0	0	0	0	0	0	0
Wally Moon, ph	.000	2	2	0	0	0	0	0	0	0	0	0
Claude Osteen, p	.333	2	3	0	1	0	0	0	0	0	0	0
Wes Parker, 1b	.304	7	23	3	7	0	1	1	2	3	3	2
Ron Perranoski, p	.000	2	0	0	0	0	0	0	0	0	0	0
Howie Reed, p	.000	2	0	0	0	0	0	0	0	0	0	0
Johnny Roseboro, c	.286	7	21	1	6	1	0	0	3	5	3	1
Dick Tracewski, 2b	.118	6	17	0	2	0	0	0	0	1	5	0
Maury Wills, ss	.367	7	30	3	11	3	0	0	3	1	3	3
TOTAL	.274		234	24	64	10	1	5	21	13	31	9

PITCHER	W	L	ERA	G	GS	CG	SV	SHO	IP	H	ER	BB	SO
Jim Brewer	0	0	4.50	1	0	0	0	0	2.0	3	1	0	1
Don Drysdale	1	1	3.86	2	2	1	0	0	11.2	12	5	3	15
Sandy Koufax	2	1	0.38	3	3	2	0	2	24.0	13	1	5	29
Bob Miller	0	0	0.00	2	0	0	0	0	1.1	0	0	0	0
Claude Osteen	1	1	0.64	2	2	1	0	1	14.0	9	1	5	4
Ron Perranoski	0	0	7.36	2	0	0	0	0	3.2	3	3	4	1
Howie Reed	0	0	8.10	2	0	0	0	0	3.1	2	3	2	4
TOTAL	4	3	2.10	14	7	4	0	3	60.0	42	14	19	54

MIN (A)

PLAYER/POS	AVG	G	AB	R	H	2B	3B	HR	RB	BB	SO	SB
Bob Allison, of	.125	5	16	3	2	1	0	1	2	2	9	1
Earl Battey, c	.120	7	25	1	3	0	1	0	2	0	5	0
Dave Boswell, p	.000	0	0	0	0	0	0	0	0	0	0	0
Mudcat Grant, p	.250	3	8	3	2	1	0	1	3	0	1	0
Jimmie Hall, of	.143	2	7	0	1	0	0	0	0	1	5	0
Jim Kaat, p	.167	3	6	0	1	0	0	0	0	2	5	0
Harmon Killebrew, 3b	.286	7	21	2	6	0	0	1	2	6	4	0
Johnny Klippstein, p	.000	2	0	0	0	0	0	0	0	0	0	0
Jim Merritt, p	.000	2	0	0	0	0	0	0	0	0	0	0
Don Mincher, 1b	.130	7	23	3	3	0	0	1	1	2	7	0
Joe Nossek, of-5	.200	6	20	0	4	0	0	0	0	0	1	0
Tony Oliva, of	.192	7	26	2	5	1	0	1	2	1	6	0
Camilo Pascual, p	.000	1	1	0	0	0	0	0	0	0	0	0
Jim Perry, p	.000	2	0	0	0	0	0	0	0	0	0	0
Bill Pleis, p	.000	1	0	0	0	0	0	0	0	0	0	0
Frank Quilici, 2b	.200	7	20	2	4	2	0	0	1	4	3	0
Rich Rollins, ph	.000	3	2	0	0	0	0	0	0	1	0	0
Sandy Valdespino, of-2	.273	5	11	1	3	1	0	0	0	0	1	0
Zoilo Versalles, ss	.286	7	28	3	8	1	1	1	4	2	7	1
Al Worthington, p	.000	2	0	0	0	0	0	0	0	0	0	0
Jerry Zimmerman, c	.000	2	1	0	0	0	0	0	0	0	0	0
TOTAL	.195		215	20	42	7	2	6	19	19	54	2

PITCHER	W	L	ERA	G	GS	CG	SV	SHO	IP	H	ER	BB	SO
Dave Boswell	0	0	3.38	1	0	0	0	0	2.2	3	1	2	3
Mudcat Grant	2	1	2.74	3	3	2	0	0	23.0	22	7	2	12
Jim Kaat	1	2	3.77	3	3	1	0	0	14.1	18	6	2	6
Johnny Klippstein	0	0	0.00	2	0	0	0	0	2.2	2	0	2	3
Jim Merritt	0	0	2.70	2	0	0	0	0	3.1	2	1	0	1
Camilo Pascual	0	1	5.40	1	1	0	0	0	5.0	8	3	1	0
Jim Perry	0	0	4.50	2	0	0	0	0	4.0	5	2	2	4
Bill Pleis	0	0	9.00	1	0	0	0	0	1.0	2	1	0	0
Al Worthington	0	0	0.00	2	0	0	0	0	4.0	2	0	2	2
TOTAL	3	4	3.15	17	7	3	0	0	60.0	64	21	13	31

GAME 1 AT MIN OCT 6

LA	010	000	001	2	10 1
MIN	016	001	00X	8	10 0

Pitchers: DRYSDALE, Reed (3), Brewer (5), Perranoski (7) vs GRANT
Home Runs: Fairly-LA, Mincher-MIN, Versalles-MIN
Attendance: 47,797

GAME 2 AT MIN OCT 7

LA	000	000	100	1	7 3
MIN	000	002	12X	5	9 0

Pitchers: KOUFAX, Perranoski (7), Miller (8) vs KAAT
Attendance: 48,700

GAME 3 AT LA OCT 9

MIN	000	000	000	0	5 0
LA	000	211	00X	4	10 1

Pitchers: PASCUAL, Merritt (6), Klippstein (8) vs OSTEEN
Attendance: 55,934

GAME 4 AT LA OCT 10

MIN	000	101	000	2	5 2
LA	110	103	01X	7	10 0

Pitchers: GRANT, Worthington (6), Pleis (8) vs DRYSDALE
Home Runs: Killebrew-MIN, Parker-LA, Oliva-MIN, Johnson-LA
Attendance: 55,920

GAME 5 AT LA OCT 11

MIN	000	000	000	0	4 1
LA	202	100	20X	7	14 0

Pitchers: KAAT, Boswell (3), Perry (6) vs KOUFAX
Attendance: 55,801

GAME 6 AT MIN OCT 13

LA	000	000	100	1	6 1
MIN	000	203	00X	5	6 1

Pitchers: OSTEEN, Reed (6), Miller (8) vs GRANT
Home Runs: Allison-MIN, Grant-MIN, Fairly-LA
Attendance: 49,578

GAME 7 AT MIN OCT 14

LA	000	200	000	2	7 0
MIN	000	000	000	0	3 1

Pitchers: KOUFAX vs KAAT, Worthington (4), Klippstein (6), Merritt (7), Perry (9)
Home Runs: Johnson-LA
Attendance: 50,596

The Orioles, with their first pennant since moving from St. Louis in 1954, won the franchise's first World Series ever, crushing Series repeater Los Angeles in four games. Back-to-back home runs by Frank and Brooks Robinson in the top of the first inning of the opener gave Baltimore a quick three-run lead, and the O's added a fourth run an inning later before the Dodgers attempted to come back with single runs in the second and third innings. But by then Oriole reliever Moe Drabowsky had come on to pitch, and he stopped the Dodgers on one hit the rest of the way, striking out eleven (including six in a row in the fourth and fifth innings). The Dodgers would not score again in the Series.

Sophomore Jim Palmer (a week shy of his twenty-first birthday) hurled a four-hit shutout at Los Angeles in Game Two, defeating the great—but critically sore-armed—Sandy Koufax, who, though only thirty years old himself, was pitching the final game of his career. Three errors by center fielder Willie Davis in the fifth (including a pair of flies lost in the sun) led to three unearned runs—the first scoring against Koufax. Frank Robinson's leadoff triple in the sixth and Boog Powell's single gave the Orioles an earned run before a double play ended the inning. Koufax was replaced after the inning by a succession of Dodger relievers as Baltimore went on to win 6–0.

Wally Bunker did the honors for the Orioles in Game Three, emerging the victor of a pitching duel with Dodger Claude Osteen on the strength of a fifth-inning home run by Paul Blair, a tremendous 430-foot shot to left. Osteen yielded only two other Orioles hits—both singles—in his seven innings, and Dodger reliever Phil Regan retired the side in the eighth. But one run was all Bunker needed for his shutout win.

Dave McNally, who had given up the Dodgers' only Series runs in Game One, mended his ways with a four-hit shutout in Game Four. He needed the shutout for the Oriole sweep, for Dodger Don Drysdale was also in top form. Drysdale, too, gave up only four hits. But one of them was Frank Robinson's second home run of the Series, a fourth-inning solo shot to left for the game's only scoring.

Baltimore Orioles (AL), 4; Los Angeles Dodgers (NL) 0

BAL (A)

PLAYER/POS	AVG	G	AB	R	H	2B	3B	HR	RB	BB	SO	SB
Luis Aparicio, ss	.250	4	16	0	4	1	0	0	0	2	0	0
Paul Blair, of	.167	4	6	2	1	0	0	1	1	1	0	0
Curt Blefary, of	.077	4	13	0	1	0	0	0	0	2	3	0
Wally Bunker, p	.000	1	2	0	0	0	0	0	0	0	1	0
Moe Drabowsky, p	.000	1	2	0	0	0	0	0	0	1	1	0
Andy Etchebarren, c	.083	4	12	2	1	0	0	0	0	2	4	0
Davy Johnson, 2b	.286	4	14	1	4	1	0	0	1	0	1	0
Dave Mc Nally, p	.000	2	3	0	0	0	0	0	0	0	1	0
Jim Palmer, p	.000	1	4	0	0	0	0	0	0	0	2	0
Boog Powell, 1b	.357	4	14	1	5	1	0	0	1	0	1	0
Brooks Robinson, 3b	.214	4	14	2	3	0	0	1	1	1	0	0
Frank Robinson, of	.286	4	14	4	4	0	1	2	3	2	3	0
Russ Snyder, of	.167	3	6	1	1	0	0	0	1	2	0	0
TOTAL	.200		120	13	24	3	1	4	10	11	17	0

PITCHER	W	L	ERA	G	GS	CG	SV	SHO	IP	H	ER	BB	SO
Wally Bunker	1	0	0.00	1	1	1	0	1	9.0	6	0	1	6
Moe Drabowsky	1	0	0.00	1	0	0	0	0	6.2	1	0	2	11
Dave Mc Nally	1	0	1.59	2	2	1	0	1	11.1	6	2	7	5
Jim Palmer	1	0	0.00	1	1	1	0	1	9.0	4	0	3	6
TOTAL	4	0	0.50	5	4	3	0	3	36.0	17	2	13	28

LA (N)

PLAYER/POS	AVG	G	AB	R	H	2B	3B	HR	RB	BB	SO	SB
Jim Barbieri, ph	.000	1	1	0	0	0	0	0	0	0	1	0
Jim Brewer, p	.000	1	0	0	0	0	0	0	0	0	0	0
Wes Covington, ph	.000	1	1	0	0	0	0	0	0	0	1	0
Tommy Davis, of-3	.250	4	8	0	2	0	0	0	0	1	1	0
Willie Davis, of	.063	4	16	0	1	0	0	0	0	0	4	0
Don Drysdale, p	.000	2	2	0	0	0	0	0	0	0	1	0
Ron Fairly, of-2,1b-1	.143	3	7	0	1	0	0	0	0	2	4	0
Al Ferrara, ph	1.000	1	1	0	1	0	0	0	0	0	0	0
Jim Gilliam, 3b	.000	2	6	0	0	0	0	0	0	1	2	0
Lou Johnson, of	.267	4	15	1	4	1	0	0	0	1	1	0
John Kennedy, 3b	.200	2	5	0	1	0	0	0	0	0	0	0
Sandy Koufax, p	.000	1	2	0	0	0	0	0	0	0	0	0
Jim Lefebvre, 2b	.167	4	12	1	2	0	0	1	1	3	4	0
Bob Miller, p	.000	1	0	0	0	0	0	0	0	0	0	0
Joe Moeller, p	.000	1	0	0	0	0	0	0	0	0	0	0
Nate Oliver, pr	.000	1	0	0	0	0	0	0	0	0	0	0
Claude Osteen, p	.000	1	2	0	0	0	0	0	0	0	1	0
Wes Parker, 1b	.231	4	13	0	3	2	0	0	0	1	3	0
Ron Perranoski, p	.000	2	0	0	0	0	0	0	0	0	0	0
Phil Regan, p	.000	2	0	0	0	0	0	0	0	0	0	0
Johnny Roseboro, c	.071	4	14	0	1	0	0	0	0	0	3	0
Dick Stuart, ph	.000	2	2	0	0	0	0	0	0	0	1	0
Maury Wills, ss	.077	4	13	0	1	0	0	0	0	3	3	1
TOTAL	.142		120	2	17	3	0	1	2	13	28	1

PITCHER	W	L	ERA	G	GS	CG	SV	SHO	IP	H	ER	BB	SO
Jim Brewer	0	0	0.00	1	0	0	0	0	1.0	0	0	0	1
Don Drysdale	0	2	4.50	2	2	1	0	0	10.0	8	5	3	6
Sandy Koufax	0	1	1.50	1	1	0	0	0	6.0	6	1	2	2
Bob Miller	0	0	0.00	1	0	0	0	0	3.0	2	0	2	1
Joe Moeller	0	0	4.50	1	0	0	0	0	2.0	1	1	1	0
Claude Osteen	0	1	1.29	1	1	0	0	0	7.0	3	1	1	3
Ron Perranoski	0	0	5.40	2	0	0	0	0	3.1	4	2	1	2
Phil Regan	0	0	0.00	2	0	0	0	0	1.2	0	0	1	2
TOTAL	0	4	2.65	11	4	1	0	0	34.0	24	10	11	17

GAME 1 AT LA OCT 5

BAL	310	100	000	5	9	0
LA	011	000	000	2	3	0

Pitchers: McNally, DRABOWSKY (3) vs DRYSDALE, Moeller (3), Miller (5), Perranoski (8)
Home Runs: F.Robinson-BAL, B.Robinson-BAL, Lefebvre-LA
Attendance: 55,941

GAME 2 AT LA OCT 6

BAL	000	031	020	6	8	0
LA	000	000	000	0	4	6

Pitchers: PALMER vs KOUFAX, Perranoski (7), Regan (8), Brewer (9)
Attendance: 55,947

GAME 3 AT BAL OCT 8

LA	000	000	000	0	6	0
BAL	000	010	000	1	3	0

Pitchers: OSTEEN, Regan (8) vs BUNKER
Home Runs: Blair-BAL
Attendance: 54,445

GAME 4 AT BAL OCT 9

LA	000	000	000	0	4	0
BAL	000	100	000	1	4	0

Pitchers: DRYSDALE vs McNALLY
Home Runs: F.Robinson-BAL
Attendance: 54,458

The Cardinals cruised into the Series leading by 10½ games, whereas the Red Sox eked out their pennant over Minnesota and Detroit only by a dramatic win at season's end. The Sox continued to claw their way through six games of the Series before finally falling to superior pitching and hitting in the seventh game. Cardinal hurler Bob Gibson (who had missed a third of the season with a broken leg) edged Boston in the opener 2–1 with a six-hitter that included ten strikeouts. The only run against him came on a solo homer by opposing pitcher Jose Santiago in the third that tied the game. But Santiago was undone when Cardinal Lou Brock singled off him to open the seventh, then stole second, and moved around to score on a pair of ground outs.

Boston ace Jim Lonborg evened the Series the next day with a brilliant one-hit shutout. Sox Triple Crown winner Carl Yastrzemski accounted for four of Boston's five runs with homers in the fourth and seventh innings. Cardinal Nelson Briles outlasted a succession of Boston pitchers for a go-ahead 5–2 win in Game Three, and Gibson, with a five-hit shutout in Game Four, put St. Louis up three games to one.

But Boston's Lonborg kept Red Sox hopes alive with another pitching gem—a three-hitter in which the only extra-base hit was Roger Maris's harmless home run in the last of the ninth, after the Sox had already scored three runs (two of them unearned). Boston's bats came alive as the Series moved to Boston for Game Six, and the Sox evened the Series with an 8–4 win. The Cards used eight pitchers in a futile effort to hold off the Boston assault. Boston's score would have been greater had not all four Boston homers (including three in the fourth inning by Yastrzemski, Reggie Smith, and Rico Petrocelli—his second of the game) been solo shots.

With the Series tied at three-all, the Series' two-game winners, Gibson and Lonborg, faced off in the finale. It turned out to be no contest. Lonborg gave up ten hits and seven runs (including a homer by pitcher Gibson in the fifth and a three-run blast by Julian Javier an inning later) in six innings. Four Boston relievers held the Cards scoreless the rest of the game, but it was too late. Gibson's three-hitter included ten strikeouts and yielded only two Boston runs.

St. Louis Cardinals (NL), 4; Boston Red Sox (AL) 3

STL (N)

PLAYER/POS	AVG	G	AB	R	H	2B	3B	HR	RB	BB	SO	SB
Eddie Bressoud, ss	.000	2	0	0	0	0	0	0	0	0	0	0
Nelson Briles, p	.000	2	3	0	0	0	0	0	0	0	0	0
Lou Brock, of	.414	7	29	8	12	2	1	1	3	2	3	7
Steve Carlton, p	.000	1	1	0	0	0	0	0	0	0	0	0
Orlando Cepeda, 1b	.103	7	29	1	3	2	0	0	1	0	4	0
Curt Flood, of	.179	7	28	2	5	1	0	0	3	3	3	0
Phil Gagliano, ph	.000	1	1	0	0	0	0	0	0	0	0	0
Bob Gibson, p	.091	3	11	1	1	0	0	1	1	1	2	0
Joe Hoerner, p	.000	2	0	0	0	0	0	0	0	0	0	0
Dick Hughes, p	.000	2	3	0	0	0	0	0	0	0	3	0
Larry Jaster, p	.000	1	0	0	0	0	0	0	0	0	0	0
Julian Javier, 2b	.360	7	25	2	9	3	0	1	4	0	6	0
Jack Lamabe, p	.000	3	0	0	0	0	0	0	0	0	0	0
Roger Maris, of	.385	7	26	3	10	1	0	1	7	3	1	0
Dal Maxvill, ss	.158	7	19	1	3	0	1	0	1	4	1	0
Tim Mc Carver, c	.125	7	24	3	3	1	0	0	2	2	2	0
Dave Ricketts, ph	.000	3	3	0	0	0	0	0	0	0	0	0
Mike Shannon, 3b	.208	7	24	3	5	1	0	1	2	1	4	0
Ed Spiezio, ph	.000	1	1	0	0	0	0	0	0	0	0	0
Bobby Tolan, ph	.000	3	2	1	0	0	0	0	0	1	1	0
Ray Washburn, p	.000	2	0	0	0	0	0	0	0	0	0	0
Ron Willis, p	.000	3	0	0	0	0	0	0	0	0	0	0
Hal Woodeshick, p	.000	1	0	0	0	0	0	0	0	0	0	0
TOTAL	.223		229	25	51	11	2	5	24	17	30	7

PITCHER	W	L	ERA	G	GS	CG	SV	SHO	IP	H	ER	BB	SO
Nelson Briles	1	0	1.64	2	1	1	0	0	11.0	7	2	1	4
Steve Carlton	0	1	0.00	1	1	0	0	0	6.0	3	0	2	5
Bob Gibson	3	0	1.00	3	3	3	0	1	27.0	14	3	5	26
Joe Hoerner	0	0	40.50	2	0	0	0	0	0.2	4	3	1	0
Dick Hughes	0	1	5.00	2	2	0	0	0	9.0	9	5	3	7
Larry Jaster	0	0	0.00	1	0	0	0	0	0.1	2	0	0	0
Jack Lamabe	0	1	6.75	3	0	0	0	0	2.2	5	2	0	4
Ray Washburn	0	0	0.00	2	0	0	0	0	2.1	1	0	1	2
Ron Willis	0	0	27.00	3	0	0	0	0	1.0	2	3	4	1
Hal Woodeshick	0	0	0.00	1	0	0	0	0	1.0	1	0	0	0
TOTAL	4	3	2.66	20	7	4	0	1	61.0	48	18	17	49

BOS (A)

PLAYER/POS	AVG	G	AB	R	H	2B	3B	HR	RB	BB	SO	SB
Jerry Adair, 2b-4	.125	5	16	0	2	0	0	0	1	0	3	1
Mike Andrews, 2b-3	.308	5	13	2	4	0	0	0	1	0	1	0
Gary Bell, p	.000	3	0	0	0	0	0	0	0	0	0	0
Ken Brett, p	.000	2	0	0	0	0	0	0	0	0	0	0
Joe Foy, 3b-3	.133	6	15	2	2	1	0	0	1	1	5	0
Russ Gibson, c	.000	2	2	0	0	0	0	0	0	0	2	0
Ken Harrelson, of	.077	4	13	0	1	0	0	0	1	1	3	0
Elston Howard, c	.111	7	18	0	2	0	0	0	1	1	2	0
Dalton Jones, 3b-4	.389	6	18	2	7	0	0	0	1	1	3	0
Jim Lonborg, p	.000	3	9	0	0	0	0	0	0	0	7	0
Dave Morehead, p	.000	2	0	0	0	0	0	0	0	0	0	0
Dan Osinski, p	.000	2	0	0	0	0	0	0	0	0	0	0
Rico Petrocelli, ss	.200	7	20	3	4	1	0	2	3	3	8	0
Mike Ryan, c	.000	1	2	0	0	0	0	0	0	0	1	0
Jose Santiago, p	.500	3	2	1	1	0	0	1	1	0	1	0
George Scott, 1b	.231	7	26	3	6	1	1	0	0	3	6	0
Norm Siebern, of-1	.333	3	3	1	1	0	0	0	1	0	0	0
Reggie Smith, of	.250	7	24	3	6	1	0	2	3	2	2	0
Lee Stange, p	.000	1	0	0	0	0	0	0	0	0	0	0
Jerry Stephenson, p	.000	1	0	0	0	0	0	0	0	0	0	0
Jose Tartabull, of-6	.154	7	13	1	2	0	0	0	0	1	2	0
George Thomas, of-1	.000	2	2	0	0	0	0	0	0	0	1	0
Gary Waslewski, p	.000	2	1	0	0	0	0	0	0	0	1	0
John Wyatt, p	.000	2	0	0	0	0	0	0	0	0	0	0
Carl Yastrzemski, of	.400	7	25	4	10	2	0	3	5	4	1	0
TOTAL	.216		222	21	48	6	1	8	19	17	49	1

PITCHER	W	L	ERA	G	GS	CG	SV	SHO	IP	H	ER	BB	SO
Gary Bell	0	1	5.06	3	1	0	1	0	5.1	8	3	1	1
Ken Brett	0	0	0.00	2	0	0	0	0	1.1	0	0	1	1
Jim Lonborg	2	1	2.63	3	3	2	0	1	24.0	14	7	2	11
Dave Morehead	0	0	0.00	2	0	0	0	0	3.1	0	0	4	3
Dan Osinski	0	0	6.75	2	0	0	0	0	1.1	2	1	0	0
Jose Santiago	0	2	5.59	3	2	0	0	0	9.2	16	6	3	6
Lee Stange	0	0	0.00	1	0	0	0	0	2.0	3	0	0	0
Jerry Stephenson	0	0	9.00	1	0	0	0	0	2.0	3	2	1	0
Gary Waslewski	0	0	2.16	2	1	0	0	0	8.1	4	2	2	7
John Wyatt	1	0	4.91	2	0	0	0	0	3.2	1	2	3	1
TOTAL	3	4	3.39	21	7	2	1	1	61.0	51	23	17	30

GAME 1 AT BOS OCT 4

STL	001	000	100	2	10	0
BOS	001	000	000	1	6	0

Pitchers: GIBSON vs SANTIAGO, Wyatt (8)
Home Runs: Santiago-BOS
Attendance: 34,796

GAME 2 AT BOS OCT 5

STL	000	000	000	0	1	1
BOS	000	101	30X	5	9	0

Pitchers: HUGHES, Willis (6), Hoerner (7), Lamabe (7) vs LONBORG
Home Runs: Yastrzemski-BOS (2)
Attendance: 35,188

GAME 3 AT STL OCT 7

BOS	000	001	100	2	7	1
STL	120	001	01X	5	10	0

Pitchers: BELL, Waslewski (3), Stange (6), Osinski (8) vs BRILES
Home Runs: Shannon-STL, Smith-BOS
Attendance: 54,575

GAME 4 AT STL OCT 8

BOS	000	000	000	0	5	0
STL	402	000	00X	6	9	0

Pitchers: SANTIAGO, Bell (1), Stephenson (3), Morehead (5), Brett (8) vs GIBSON
Attendance: 54,575

GAME 5 AT STL OCT 9

BOS	001	000	002	3	6	1
STL	000	000	001	1	3	2

Pitchers: LONBORG vs CARLTON, Washburn (7), Willis (9), Lamabe (9)
Home Runs: Maris-STL
Attendance: 54,575

GAME 6 AT BOS OCT 11

STL	002	000	200	4	8	0
BOS	010	300	40X	8	12	1

Pitchers: Hughes, Willis (4), Briles (5), LAMABE (7), Hoerner (7), Jaster (7), Washburn (7), Woodeshick (8) vs Waslewski, Wyatt (6), Bell (8)
Home Runs: Petrocelli-BOS (2), Yastrzemski-BOS, Smith-BOS, Brock-STL
Attendance: 35,188

GAME 7 AT BOS OCT 12

STL	002	023	000	7	10	1
BOS	000	010	010	2	3	1

Pitchers: GIBSON vs LONBORG, Santiago (7), Morehead (9), Osinski (9), Brett (9)
Home Runs: Gibson-STL, Javier-STL
Attendance: 35,188

In this "year of the pitcher," Tiger Denny McLain's 31 wins were the most for a major leaguer in thirty-seven years. Cardinal Bob Gibson's 1.12 ERA was the majors' best since Dutch Leonard's 1.01 in 1914, and his 13 season shutouts tied for third best of all time. In the Series, though, it was Detroit's second-best pitcher—Mickey Lolich—who emerged as the hero.

McLain came off second-best against Gibson in the opener. He yielded only three hits in his five innings, but two Cardinal singles in the fourth combined with a pair of walks and a Tiger error for three runs. Gibson, meanwhile, was in the process of striking out a Series-record 17 batters on the way to a five-hit shutout. But Lolich brought Detroit back in Game Two. He struck out nine, and his third-inning home run (the only one of his major league career) for the second Tiger run provided all the scoring needed for a Detroit victory, although the Tigers kept putting runs across for an eventual 8–1 win.

Home runs accounted for most of the scoring in Game Three. Veteran Al Kaline's two-run shot in the third opened the scoring, but Cardinal Tim McCarver's three-run blast in the fifth put St. Louis ahead. Tiger Dick McAuliffe's solo shot later in the inning brought Detroit within one run of a tie, but the Cardinals put the game away on Orlando Cepeda's three-run homer in the seventh.

McLain faced Gibson again in Game Four, and again came off second-best. Cardinal Lou Brock led off the game with a home run, and before the end of the third inning McLain was gone. Gibson gave up a solo homer to Tiger Jim Northrup in the fourth, but that was the only Detroit run he allowed. Gibson homered himself and struck out ten in an easy 10–1 win.

Down three games to one, the Tigers were saved from elimination by Lolich's arm. Although three Cardinal hits in the top of the first (including Orlando Cepeda's second homer of the Series) gave St. Louis a quick three runs, Lolich held the Cards scoreless the rest of the game as his Tigers fought back with two runs in the fourth and three more in the seventh (with a rally started by Lolich's single). McLain finally came through in Game Six, evening the Series with an easy 13–1 victory, in which Jim Northrup's grand slam provided the big blow of a ten-run third inning.

Lolich and Gibson—both 2–0 in the Series—faced off in the finale. Gibson broke his own World Series strikeout record in the third inning (finishing with 8 for the

game and 35 for the Series), and both pitchers hurled shutout ball through six innings. But four two-out Tiger hits in the top of the seventh—including a misplayed fly ball in center field—put three runs on the board, and another run in the ninth made the score 4–0. In the last of the ninth, Mike Shannon's solo homer spoiled Lolich's shutout, but not his third Series win—or the Tigers' comeback world title.

Detroit Tigers (AL), 4; St. Louis Cardinals (NL) 3

DET (A)

PLAYER/POS	AVG	G	AB	R	H	2B	3B	HR	RB	BB	SO	SB
Gates Brown, ph	.000	1	1	0	0	0	0	0	0	0	0	0
Norm Cash, 1b	.385	7	26	5	10	0	0	1	5	3	5	0
Wayne Comer, ph	1.000	1	1	0	1	0	0	0	0	0	0	0
Pat Dobson, p	.000	3	0	0	0	0	0	0	0	0	0	0
Bill Freehan, c	.083	7	24	0	2	1	0	0	2	4	8	0
John Hiller, p	.000	2	0	0	0	0	0	0	0	0	0	0
Willie Horton, of	.304	7	23	6	7	1	1	1	3	5	6	0
Al Kaline, of	.379	7	29	6	11	2	0	2	8	0	7	0
Fred Lasher, p	.000	1	0	0	0	0	0	0	0	0	0	0
Mickey Lolich, p	.250	3	12	2	3	0	0	1	2	1	5	0
Tom Matchick, ph	.000	3	3	0	0	0	0	0	0	0	1	0
Eddie Mathews, 3b-1	.333	2	3	0	1	0	0	0	0	1	1	0
Dick Mc Auliffe, 2b	.222	7	27	5	6	0	0	1	3	4	6	0
Denny Mc Lain, p	.000	3	6	0	0	0	0	0	0	0	4	0
Don Mc Mahon, p	.000	2	0	0	0	0	0	0	0	0	0	0
Jim Northrup, of	.250	7	28	4	7	0	1	2	8	1	5	0
Ray Oyler, ss	.000	4	0	0	0	0	0	0	0	0	0	0
Daryl Patterson, p	.000	2	0	0	0	0	0	0	0	0	0	0
Jim Price, ph	.000	2	2	0	0	0	0	0	0	0	1	0
Joe Sparma, p	.000	1	0	0	0	0	0	0	0	0	0	0
Mickey Stanley, ss-7,of-4	.214	7	28	4	6	0	1	0	0	2	4	0
Dick Tracewski, 3b-1	.000	2	0	1	0	0	0	0	0	0	0	0
Don Wert, 3b	.118	6	17	1	2	0	0	0	2	6	5	0
Earl Wilson, p	.000	1	1	0	0	0	0	0	0	0	1	0
TOTAL	.242		231	34	56	4	3	8	33	27	59	0

PITCHER	W	L	ERA	G	GS	CG	SV	SHO	IP	H	ER	BB	SO
Pat Dobson	0	0	3.86	3	0	0	0	0	4.2	5	2	1	0
John Hiller	0	0	13.50	2	0	0	0	0	2.0	6	3	3	1
Fred Lasher	0	0	0.00	1	0	0	0	0	2.0	1	0	0	1
Mickey Lolich	3	0	1.67	3	3	3	0	0	27.0	20	5	6	21
Denny Mc Lain	1	2	3.24	3	3	1	0	0	16.2	18	6	4	13
Don Mc Mahon	0	0	13.50	2	0	0	0	0	2.0	4	3	0	1
Daryl Patterson	0	0	0.00	2	0	0	0	0	3.0	1	0	1	0
Joe Sparma	0	0	54.00	1	0	0	0	0	0.1	2	2	0	0
Earl Wilson	0	1	6.23	1	1	0	0	0	4.1	4	3	6	3
TOTAL	4	3	3.48	18	7	4	0	0	62.0	61	24	21	40

STL (N)

PLAYER/POS	AVG	G	AB	R	H	2B	3B	HR	RB	BB	SO	SB
Nelson Briles, p	.000	2	4	0	0	0	0	0	0	0	4	0
Lou Brock, of	.464	7	28	6	13	3	1	2	5	3	4	7
Steve Carlton, p	.000	2	0	0	0	0	0	0	0	0	0	0
Orlando Cepeda, 1b	.250	7	28	2	7	0	0	2	6	2	3	0
Ron Davis, of	.000	2	7	0	0	0	0	0	0	0	2	0
Johnny Edwards, ph	.000	1	1	0	0	0	0	0	0	0	1	0
Curt Flood, of	.286	7	28	4	8	1	0	0	2	2	2	3
Phil Gagliano, ph	.000	3	3	0	0	0	0	0	0	0	0	0
Bob Gibson, p	.125	3	8	2	1	0	0	1	2	1	2	0
Wayne Granger, p	.000	1	0	0	0	0	0	0	0	0	0	0
Joe Hoerner, p	.500	3	2	0	1	0	0	0	0	0	1	0
Dick Hughes, p	.000	1	0	0	0	0	0	0	0	0	0	0
Larry Jaster, p	.000	1	0	0	0	0	0	0	0	0	0	0
Julian Javier, 2b	.333	7	27	1	9	1	0	0	3	3	4	1
Roger Maris, of-5	.158	6	19	5	3	1	0	0	1	3	3	0
Dal Maxvill, ss	.000	7	22	1	0	0	0	0	0	3	5	0
Tim Mc Carver, c	.333	7	27	3	9	0	2	1	4	3	2	0
Mel Nelson, p	.000	1	0	0	0	0	0	0	0	0	0	0
Dave Ricketts, ph	1.000	1	1	0	1	0	0	0	0	0	0	0
Dick Schofield, ss-1	.000	2	0	0	0	0	0	0	0	0	0	0
Mike Shannon, 3b	.276	7	29	3	8	1	0	1	4	1	5	0
Ed Spiezio, ph	1.000	1	1	0	1	0	0	0	0	0	0	0
Bobby Tolan, ph	.000	1	1	0	0	0	0	0	0	0	1	0
Ray Washburn, p	.000	2	0	0	0	0	0	0	0	0	0	0
Ron Willis, p	.000	3	0	0	0	0	0	0	0	0	0	0
TOTAL	.255		239	27	61	7	3	7	27	21	40	11

PITCHER	W	L	ERA	G	GS	CG	SV	SHO	IP	H	ER	BB	SO
Nelson Briles	0	1	5.56	2	2	0	0	0	11.1	13	7	4	7
Steve Carlton	0	0	6.75	2	0	0	0	0	4.0	7	3	1	3
Bob Gibson	2	1	1.67	3	3	3	0	1	27.0	18	5	4	35
Wayne Granger	0	0	0.00	1	0	0	0	0	2.0	0	0	1	1
Joe Hoerner	0	1	3.86	3	0	0	1	0	4.2	5	2	5	3
Dick Hughes	0	0	0.00	1	0	0	0	0	0.1	2	0	0	0
Larry Jaster	0	0	INF	1	0	0	0	0	0.0	2	3	1	0
Mel Nelson	0	0	0.00	1	0	0	0	0	1.0	0	0	0	1
Ray Washburn	1	1	9.82	2	2	0	0	0	7.1	7	8	7	6
Ron Willis	0	0	8.31	3	0	0	0	0	4.1	4	4	4	3
TOTAL	3	4	4.65	19	7	3	1	1	62.0	56	32	27	59

GAME 1 AT STL OCT 2

DET	000 000 000	0	5	3
STL	000 300 10X	4	6	0

Pitchers: McLAIN, Dobson (6), McMahon (8) vs GIBSON
Home Runs: Brock-STL
Attendance: 54,692

GAME 2 AT STL OCT 3

DET	011 003 102	8	13	1
STL	000 001 000	1	6	1

Pitchers: LOLICH vs BRILES, Carlton (6), Willis (7), Hoerner (9)
Home Runs: Horton-DET, Lolich-DET, Cash-DET
Attendance: 54,692

GAME 3 AT DET OCT 5

STL	000 040 300	7	13	0
DET	002 010 000	3	4	0

Pitchers: WASHBURN, Hoerner (6) vs WILSON, Dobson (5), McMahon (6), Patterson (7), Hiller (8)
Home Runs: Kaline-DET, McCarver-STL, McAuliffe-DET, Cepeda-STL
Attendance: 53,634

GAME 4 AT DET OCT 6

STL	202 200 040	10	13	0
DET	000 100 000	1	5	4

Pitchers: GIBSON vs McLAIN, Sparma (3), Patterson (4), Lasher (6), Hiller (8), Dobson (8)
Home Runs: Brock-STL, Gibson-STL, Northrup-DET
Attendance: 53,634

GAME 5 AT DET OCT 7

STL	300 000 000	3	9	0
DET	000 200 30X	5	9	1

Pitchers: Briles, HOERNER (7), Willis (7) vs LOLICH
Home Runs: Cepeda-STL
Attendance: 53,634

GAME 6 AT STL OCT 9

DET	0 210 010 000	13	12	1
STL	00 0 000 001	1	9	1

Pitchers: McLAIN vs WASHBURN, Jaster (3), Willis (3), Hughes (3), Carlton (4), Granger (7), Nelson (9)
Home Runs: Northrup-DET, Kaline-DET
Attendance: 54,692

GAME 7 AT STL OCT 10

DET	000 000 301	4	8	1
STL	000 000 001	1	5	0

Pitchers: LOLICH vs GIBSON
Home Runs: Shannon-STL
Attendance: 54,692

Atlanta's Hank Aaron homered in each game and drove in a series-high seven runs. But the "Miracle Mets" as a team outhomered the Braves six to five, outhit them by seventy-two percentage points, and scored nearly twice as many runs.

Twice in the first game the Braves came from behind to lead by a run, but in the top of the eighth, five New York hits and poor Atlanta fielding buried starter Phil Niekro under five runs. In Game Two, home runs by Tommie Agee and Ken Boswell helped New York take an early 8–0 lead that even Aaron's three-run homer in the fifth couldn't damage.

In the third game the lead changed hands three times on home runs. Aaron began the barrage with a two-run shot in the first inning. Agee's homer in the third followed by Boswell's for two runs in the fourth put the Mets ahead—until Orlando Cepeda's two-run homer in the fifth gave Atlanta another lead. But in the bottom of the fifth, Met rookie Wayne Garrett's two-run blast reversed the lead one last time and, after four final shutout innings by twenty-two-year-old reliever Nolan Ryan, the Mets had swept to their first pennant.

New York Mets (East), 3; Atlanta Braves (West) 0

NY (E)

PLAYER/POS	AVG	G	AB	R	H	2B	3B	HR	RB	BB	SO	SB
Tommie Agee, of	.357	3	14	4	5	1	0	2	4	2	5	2
Ken Boswell, 2b	.333	3	12	4	4	0	0	2	5	1	2	0
Wayne Garrett, 3b	.385	3	13	3	5	2	0	1	3	2	2	1
Rod Gaspar, of	.000	3	0	0	0	0	0	0	0	0	0	0
Gary Gentry, p	.000	1	0	0	0	0	0	0	0	0	0	0
Jerry Grote, c	.167	3	12	3	2	1	0	0	1	1	4	0
Bud Harrelson, ss	.182	3	11	2	2	1	1	0	3	1	2	0
Cleon Jones, of	.429	3	14	4	6	2	0	1	4	1	2	2
Jerry Koosman, p	.000	1	2	1	0	0	0	0	0	1	2	0
Ed Kranepool, 1b	.250	3	12	2	3	1	0	0	1	1	2	0
J. C. Martin, ph	.500	2	2	0	1	0	0	0	2	0	0	0
Tug Mc Graw, p	.000	1	0	0	0	0	0	0	0	0	0	0
Nolan Ryan, p	.500	1	4	1	2	0	0	0	0	0	1	0
Tom Seaver, p	.000	1	3	0	0	0	0	0	0	0	0	0
Art Shamsky, of	.538	3	13	3	7	0	0	0	1	0	3	0
Ron Taylor, p	.000	2	0	0	0	0	0	0	0	0	0	0
Al Weis, 2b	.000	3	1	0	0	0	0	0	0	0	0	0
TOTAL	.327		113	27	37	8	1	6	24	10	25	5

PITCHER	W	L	ERA	G	GS	CG	SV	SHO	IP	H	ER	BB	SO
Gary Gentry	0	0	9.00	1	1	0	0	0	2.0	5	2	1	1
Jerry Koosman	0	0	11.57	1	1	0	0	0	4.2	7	6	4	5
Tug Mc Graw	0	0	0.00	1	0	0	1	0	3.0	1	0	1	1
Nolan Ryan	1	0	2.57	1	0	0	0	0	7.0	3	2	2	7
Tom Seaver	1	0	6.43	1	1	0	0	0	7.0	8	5	3	2
Ron Taylor	1	0	0.00	2	0	0	1	0	3.1	3	0	0	4
TOTAL	3	0	5.00	7	3	0	2	0	27.0	27	15	11	20

ATL (W)

PLAYER/POS	AVG	G	AB	R	H	2B	3B	HR	RB	BB	SO	SB
Hank Aaron, of	.357	3	14	3	5	2	0	3	7	0	1	0
Tommie Aaron, ph	.000	1	1	0	0	0	0	0	0	0	0	0
Felipe Alou, ph	.000	1	1	0	0	0	0	0	0	0	0	0
Bob Aspromonte, ph	.000	3	3	0	0	0	0	0	0	0	0	0
Clete Boyer, 3b	.111	3	9	0	1	0	0	0	3	2	3	0
Jim Britton, p	.000	1	0	0	0	0	0	0	0	0	0	0
Rico Carty, of	.300	3	10	4	3	2	0	0	0	3	1	0
Orlando Cepeda, 1b	.455	3	11	2	5	2	0	1	3	1	2	1
Bob Didier, c	.000	3	11	0	0	0	0	0	0	0	2	0
Paul Doyle, p	.000	1	0	0	0	0	0	0	0	0	0	0
Gil Garrido, ss	.200	3	10	0	2	0	0	0	0	1	1	0
Tony Gonzalez, of	.357	3	14	4	5	1	0	1	2	1	4	0
Sonny Jackson, ss	.000	1	0	0	0	0	0	0	0	0	0	0
Pat Jarvis, p	.000	1	2	0	0	0	0	0	0	0	2	0
Mike Lum, of-1	1.000	2	2	0	2	1	0	0	0	0	0	0
Felix Millan, 2b	.333	3	12	2	4	1	0	0	0	3	0	0
Gary Neibauer, p	.000	1	0	0	0	0	0	0	0	0	0	0
Phil Niekro, p	.000	1	3	0	0	0	0	0	0	0	1	0
Milt Pappas, p	.000	1	1	0	0	0	0	0	0	0	1	0
Ron Reed, p	.000	1	0	0	0	0	0	0	0	0	0	0
George Stone, p	.000	1	0	0	0	0	0	0	0	0	1	0
Bob Tillman, c	.000	1	0	0	0	0	0	0	0	0	0	0
Cecil Upshaw, p	.000	3	1	0	0	0	0	0	0	0	1	0
TOTAL	.255		106	15	27	9	0	5	15	11	20	1

PITCHER	W	L	ERA	G	GS	CG	SV	SHO	IP	H	ER	BB	SO
Jim Britton	0	0	0.00	1	0	0	0	0	0.1	0	0	1	0
Paul Doyle	0	0	0.00	1	0	0	0	0	1.0	2	0	1	3
Pat Jarvis	0	1	12.46	1	1	0	0	0	4.1	10	6	0	6
Gary Neibauer	0	0	0.00	1	0	0	0	0	1.0	0	0	0	1
Phil Niekro	0	1	4.50	1	1	0	0	0	8.0	9	4	4	4
Milt Pappas	0	0	11.57	1	0	0	0	0	2.1	4	3	0	4
Ron Reed	0	1	21.60	1	1	0	0	0	1.2	5	4	3	3
George Stone	0	0	9.00	1	0	0	0	0	1.0	2	1	0	0
Cecil Upshaw	0	0	2.84	3	0	0	0	0	6.1	5	2	1	4
TOTAL	0	3	6.92	11	3	0	0	0	26.0	37	20	10	25

GAME 1 AT ATL OCT 4

NY	020	200	050	9	10	1
ATL	012	010	100	5	10	2

Pitchers: SEAVER, Taylor (8) vs NIEKRO, Upshaw (9)
Home Runs: Gonzalez-ATL, H.Aaron-ATL
Attendance: 50,122

GAME 2 AT ATL OCT 5

NY	132	210	200	11	13	1
ATL	000	150	000	6	9	3

Pitchers: Koosman, TAYLOR (5), McGraw (7) VS REED, Doyle (2), Pappas (3), Britton (6), Upshaw (6), Neibauer (9)
Home Runs: Agee-NY, Boswell-NY, H.Aaron-ATL, Jones-NY
Attendance: 50,270

GAME 3 AT NY OCT 6

ATL	200	020	000	4	8	1
NY	001	231	00X	7	14	0

Pitchers: JARVIS, Stone (5), Upshaw (6) VS Gentry, RYAN (3)
Home Runs: H.Aaron-ATL, Agee-NY, Boswell-NY, Cepeda-ATL, Garrett-NY
Attendance: 53,195

Minnesota led the league in batting, Baltimore in pitching. In the LCS, pitching prevailed as the Twins were held to a series batting average 113 points below their season mark.

Still, Minnesota nearly won the first game with three runs on only four hits. But the Orioles tied the score on Boog Powell's homer in the bottom of the ninth and won the game three innings later on Paul Blair's suicide squeeze bunt with two away. In Game Two, Minnesota's Dave Boswell scattered seven Baltimore hits over 10⅔ scoreless innings before giving way to Ron Perranoski in the eleventh. But Oriole pitcher Dave McNally was more than a match for Boswell. He gave up only three Twin hits—none in the final 7⅔ innings of the 11 he pitched—and took the win when Baltimore pinch hitter Curt Motton lined a single off Perranoski to score Powell from second with the game's only run.

In the third game, the Twins fell apart as the Orioles battered seven Minnesota pitchers for eighteen hits. Baltimore's Jim Palmer gave up more than a hit an inning himself, but coasted to the pennant 11–2.

Baltimore Orioles (East), 3; Minnesota Twins (West) 0

BAL (E)

PLAYER/POS	AVG	G	AB	R	H	2B	3B	HR	RB	BB	SO	SB
Mark Belanger, ss	.267	3	15	4	4	0	1	1	1	0	0	0
Paul Blair, of	.400	3	15	1	6	2	0	1	6	2	2	0
Don Buford, of	.286	3	14	3	4	1	0	0	1	3	0	0
Mike Cuellar, p	.000	1	2	0	0	0	0	0	0	0	1	0
Andy Etchebarren, c	.000	2	4	0	0	0	0	0	0	0	0	0
Dick Hall, p	.000	1	0	0	0	0	0	0	0	0	0	0
Elrod Hendricks, c	.250	3	8	2	2	2	0	0	3	1	2	0
Davy Johnson, 2b	.231	3	13	2	3	0	0	0	0	2	1	0
Marcelino Lopez, p	.000	1	0	0	0	0	0	0	0	0	0	0
Dave May, ph	.000	1	1	0	0	0	0	0	0	0	0	0
Dave Nc Nally, p	.000	1	4	0	0	0	0	0	0	0	2	0
Curt Motton, ph	.500	2	2	0	1	0	0	0	1	0	0	0
Jim Palmer, p	.000	1	5	0	0	0	0	0	0	0	3	0
Boog Powell, 1b	.385	3	13	2	5	0	0	1	1	2	0	0
Merv Rettenmund, ph	.000	1	0	0	0	0	0	0	0	0	0	0
Pete Richert, p	.000	1	0	0	0	0	0	0	0	0	0	0
Brooks Robinson, 3b	.500	3	14	1	7	1	0	0	0	0	0	0
Frank Robinson, of	.333	3	12	1	4	2	0	1	2	3	3	0
Chico Salmon, ph	.000	1	1	0	0	0	0	0	0	0	0	0
Eddie Watt, p	.000	1	0	0	0	0	0	0	0	0	0	0
TOTAL	.293		123	16	36	8	1	4	15	13	14	0

PITCHER	W	L	ERA	G	GS	CG	SV	SHO	IP	H	ER	BB	SO
Mike Cuellar	0	0	2.25	1	1	0	0	0	8.0	3	2	1	7
Dick Hall	1	0	0.00	1	0	0	0	0	0.2	0	0	0	1
Marcelino Lopez	0	0	0.00	1	0	0	0	0	0.1	1	0	2	0
Dave Nc Nally	1	0	0.00	1	1	1	0	1	11.0	3	0	5	11
Jim Palmer	1	0	2.00	1	1	1	0	0	9.0	10	2	2	4
Pete Richert	0	0	0.00	1	0	0	0	0	1.0	0	0	2	2
Eddie Watt	0	0	0.00	1	0	0	0	0	2.0	0	0	0	2
TOTAL	3	0	1.13	7	3	2	0	1	32.0	17	4	12	27

MIN (W)

PLAYER/POS	AVG	G	AB	R	H	2B	3B	HR	RB	BB	SO	SB
Bob Allison, of	.000	2	8	0	0	0	0	0	1	0	0	0
Dave Boswell, p	.000	1	4	0	0	0	0	0	0	0	4	0
Leo Cardenas, ss	.154	3	13	0	2	0	1	0	0	0	7	0
Rod Carew, 2b	.071	3	14	0	1	0	0	0	0	1	4	0
Dean Chance, p	.000	1	0	0	0	0	0	0	0	0	0	0
Joe Grzenda, p	.000	1	0	0	0	0	0	0	0	0	0	0
Tom Hall, p	.000	1	0	0	0	0	0	0	0	0	0	0
Harmon Killebrew, 3b	.125	3	8	2	1	1	0	0	0	6	2	0
Chuck Manuel, ph	.000	1	0	0	0	0	0	0	0	1	0	0
Bob Miller, p	.000	1	0	0	0	0	0	0	0	0	0	0
George Mitterwald, c	.143	2	7	0	1	0	0	0	0	1	3	0
Graig Nettles, ph	1.000	1	1	0	1	0	0	0	0	0	0	0
Tony Oliva, of	.385	3	13	3	5	2	0	1	2	1	3	1
Ron Perranoski, p	.000	3	1	0	0	0	0	0	0	0	1	0
Jim Perry, p	.000	1	3	0	0	0	0	0	0	0	0	0
Rich Reese, 1b	.167	3	12	0	2	0	0	0	2	1	1	0
Rich Renick, ph	.000	1	1	0	0	0	0	0	0	0	0	0
John Roseboro, c	.200	2	5	0	1	0	0	0	0	0	0	0
Cesar Tovar, of	.077	3	13	0	1	0	0	0	0	1	2	1
Ted Uhlaender, of	.167	2	6	0	1	0	0	0	0	0	0	0
Dick Woodson, p	1.000	1	1	0	1	0	0	0	0	0	0	0
Al Worthington, p	.000	1	0	0	0	0	0	0	0	0	0	0
TOTAL	.155		110	5	17	3	1	1	5	12	27	2

PITCHER	W	L	ERA	G	GS	CG	SV	SHO	IP	H	ER	BB	SO
Dave Boswell	0	1	0.84	1	1	0	0	0	10.2	7	1	7	4
Dean Chance	0	0	13.50	1	0	0	0	0	2.0	4	3	0	2
Joe Grzenda	0	0	0.00	1	0	0	0	0	0.2	0	0	0	2
Tom Hall	0	0	0.00	1	0	0	0	0	0.2	0	0	0	0
Bob Miller	0	1	5.40	1	1	0	0	0	1.2	5	1	0	0
Ron Perranoski	0	1	5.79	3	0	0	0	0	4.2	8	3	0	2
Jim Perry	0	0	3.38	1	1	0	0	0	8.0	6	3	3	3
Dick Woodson	0	0	10.80	1	0	0	0	0	1.2	3	2	3	2
Al Worthington	0	0	6.75	1	0	0	0	0	1.1	3	1	0	1
TOTAL	0	3	4.02	11	3	0	0	0	31.1	36	14	13	14

The heavy-hitting, slick-fielding Orioles, who also boasted the majors' top pitching staff, entered the Series clear favorites against the upstart Mets. But the "Miracle Mets," after losing the opener, polished off Baltimore with four straight wins.

The clubs' big winners, Met Tom Seaver (25–7) and Mike Cuellar (23–11) faced each other in the opener. Baltimore's leadoff batter, Don Buford, greeted Seaver with a home run, and a three-run Oriole rally with two out in the fourth made the score 4–0 before the Mets scored their first Series run in the seventh. Cuellar held New York to that one run for the victory.

No one scored for three innings of Game Two off Oriole Dave McNally or even hit Met Jerry Koosman safely. But Met Donn Clendenon led off the fourth with a home run as Koosman continued to no-hit Baltimore for three more innings. In the seventh, though, Baltimore's Paul Blair spoiled Koosman's no-hitter with a leadoff single, and after stealing second, scored the tying run on Brooks Robinson's single. But those were the only hits the O's would get, and in the top of the ninth three successive two-out Met singles produced what proved to be the winning run.

Met pitchers Gary Gentry and Nolan Ryan (with the assist of two spectacular catches by center fielder Tommie Agee that saved a total of five runs) combined for a shutout in Game Three. Agee's leadoff homer against Jim Palmer in the first was all the scoring the Mets would need, but they added four more runs before the game ended. Game Four was the Series' tightest. Seaver went the distance for the win, holding a 1–0 lead until a sacrifice fly scored the tying Baltimore run in the top of the ninth. In the bottom of the tenth, the Mets finally won it as a bunt thrown to first hit the runner and bounded away, allowing pinch runner Rod Gaspar to score all the way from second.

Dave McNally and Jerry Koosman tangled a second time in Game Five, and again Koosman and the Mets emerged victorious. McNally's two-run homer in the third gave him a lead which Frank Robinson expanded with a solo shot. But in an eerie sixth inning reprise of Game Four of the 1957 World Series featuring Nippy Jones, the Mets' Cleon Jones was struck by a pitch on the foot and awarded first base after inspection by the home plate umpire revealed tell-tale shoe polish on the ball. Each Jones produced a key run, Cleon coming home on Donn Clendenon's home run which followed immediately. Al Weis

New York Mets (NL), 4; Baltimore Orioles (AL) 1

NY (N)

PLAYER/POS	AVG	G	AB	R	H	2B	3B	HR	RB	BB	SO	SB
Tommie Agee, of	.167	5	18	1	3	0	0	1	1	1	2	5	1
Ken Boswell, 2b	.333	1	3	1	1	0	0	0	0	0	0	0
Don Cardwell, p	.000	1	0	0	0	0	0	0	0	0	0	0
Ed Charles, 3b	.133	4	15	1	2	1	0	0	0	0	2	0
Donn Clendenon, 1b	.357	4	14	4	5	1	0	3	4	2	6	0
Duffy Dyer, ph	.000	1	1	0	0	0	0	0	0	0	0	0
Wayne Garrett, 3b	.000	2	1	0	0	0	0	0	0	2	1	0
Rod Gaspar, of-1	.000	3	2	1	0	0	0	0	0	0	0	0
Gary Gentry, p	.333	1	3	0	1	1	0	0	2	0	2	0
Jerry Grote, c	.211	5	19	1	4	2	0	0	1	1	3	0
Bud Harrelson, ss	.176	5	17	1	3	0	0	0	0	3	4	0
Cleon Jones, of	.158	5	19	2	3	1	0	0	0	0	1	0
Jerry Koosman, p	.143	2	7	0	1	1	0	0	0	0	4	0
Ed Kranepool, 1b	.250	2	4	1	1	0	0	1	1	0	0	0
J.C. Martin, ph	.000	1	0	0	0	0	0	0	0	0	0	0
Nolan Ryan, p	.000	1	0	0	0	0	0	0	0	0	0	0
Tom Seaver, p	.000	2	4	0	0	0	0	0	0	0	2	0
Art Shamsky, of-1	.000	3	6	0	0	0	0	0	0	0	0	0
Ron Swoboda, of	.400	4	15	1	6	1	0	0	1	1	3	0
Ron Taylor, p	.000	2	0	0	0	0	0	0	0	0	0	0
Al Weis, 2b	.455	5	11	1	5	0	0	1	3	4	2	0
TOTAL	.220		159	15	35	8	0	6	13	15	35	1

PITCHER	W	L	ERA	G	GS	CG	SV	SHO	IP	H	ER	BB	SO
Don Cardwell	0	0	0.00	1	0	0	0	0	1.0	0	0	0	0
Gary Gentry	1	0	0.00	1	1	0	0	0	6.2	3	0	5	4
Jerry Koosman	2	0	2.04	2	2	1	0	0	17.2	7	4	4	9
Nolan Ryan	0	0	0.00	1	0	0	1	0	2.1	1	0	2	3
Tom Seaver	1	1	3.00	2	2	1	0	0	15.0	12	5	3	9
Ron Taylor	0	0	0.00	2	0	0	1	0	2.1	0	0	1	3
TOTAL	4	1	1.80	9	5	2	2	0	45.0	23	9	15	28

BAL (A)

PLAYER/POS	AVG	G	AB	R	H	2B	3B	HR	RB	BB	SO	SB
Mark Belanger, ss	.200	5	15	2	3	0	0	0	1	2	1	0
Paul Blair, of	.100	5	20	1	2	0	0	0	0	2	5	1
Don Buford, of	.100	5	20	1	2	1	0	1	2	2	4	0
Mike Cuellar, p	.400	2	5	0	2	0	0	0	1	0	3	0
Clay Dalrymple, ph	1.000	2	2	0	2	0	0	0	0	0	0	0
Andy Etchebarren, c	.000	2	6	0	0	0	0	0	0	0	1	0
Dick Hall, p	.000	1	0	0	0	0	0	0	0	0	0	0
Elrod Hendricks, c	.100	3	10	1	1	0	0	0	0	1	0	0
Davy Johnson, 2b	.063	5	16	1	1	0	0	0	0	2	1	0
Dave Leonhard, p	.000	1	0	0	0	0	0	0	0	0	0	0
Dave May, ph	.000	2	1	0	0	0	0	0	0	1	1	0
Dave Mc Nally, p	.200	2	5	1	1	0	0	1	2	0	2	0
Curt Motton, ph	.000	1	1	0	0	0	0	0	0	0	0	0
Jim Palmer, p	.000	1	2	0	0	0	0	0	0	0	0	0
Boog Powell, 1b	.263	5	19	0	5	0	0	0	0	1	4	0
Merv Rettenmund, pr	.000	1	0	0	0	0	0	0	0	0	0	0
Pete Richert, p	.000	1	0	0	0	0	0	0	0	0	0	0
Brooks Robinson, 3b	.053	5	19	0	1	0	0	0	2	0	3	0
Frank Robinson, of	.188	5	16	2	3	0	0	1	1	4	3	0
Chico Salmon, pr	.000	2	0	0	0	0	0	0	0	0	0	0
Eddie Watt, p	.000	2	0	0	0	0	0	0	0	0	0	0
TOTAL	.146		157	9	23	1	0	3	9	15	28	1

PITCHER	W	L	ERA	G	GS	CG	SV	SHO	IP	H	ER	BB	SO
Mike Cuellar	1	0	1.13	2	2	1	0	0	16.0	13	2	4	13
Dick Hall	0	1	INF	1	0	0	0	0	0.0	1	0	1	0
Dave Leonhard	0	0	4.50	1	0	0	0	0	2.0	1	1	1	1
Dave Mc Nally	0	1	2.81	2	2	1	0	0	16.0	11	5	5	13
Jim Palmer	0	1	6.00	1	1	0	0	0	6.0	5	4	4	5
Pete Richert	0	0	INF	1	0	0	0	0	0.0	0	0	0	0
Eddie Watt	0	1	3.00	2	0	0	0	0	3.0	4	1	0	3
TOTAL	1	4	2.72	10	5	2	0	0	43.0	35	13	15	35

homered in the seventh for a 3–3 tie. With McNally now gone, two doubles off Eddie Watt in the eighth brought in the go-ahead Met run, and a pair of errors let in a run for insurance. Koosman held Baltimore scoreless in the ninth and the Met miracle was complete.

GAME 1 AT BAL OCT 11

NY	000 000 100	1	6	1
BAL	100 300 00X	4	6	0

Pitchers: SEAVER, Cardwell (6), Taylor (7) vs CUELLAR
Home Runs: Buford-BAL
Attendance: 50,429

GAME 2 AT BAL OCT 12

NY	000 100 001	2	6	0
BAL	000 000 100	1	2	0

Pitchers: KOOSMAN, Taylor (9) vs McNALLY
Home Runs: Clendenon-NY
Attendance: 50,850

GAME 3 AT NY OCT 14

BAL	000 000 000	0	4	1
NY	120 001 01X	5	6	0

Pitchers: PALMER, Leonhard (7) VS GENTRY, Ryan (7)
Home Runs: Agee-NY, Kranepool-NY
Attendance: 56,335

GAME 4 AT NY OCT 15

BAL	000 000 001 0	1	6	1
NY	010 000 000 1	2	10	1

Pitchers: Cuellar, Watt (8), HALL (10), Richert (10) vs SEAVER
Home Runs: Clendenon-NY
Attendance: 57,367

GAME 5 AT NY OCT 16

BAL	003 000 000	3	5	2
NY	000 002 12X	5	7	0

Pitchers: McNally, WATT (8) vs KOOSMAN
Home Runs: McNally-BAL, F.Robinson-BAL, Clendenon-NY, Weis-NY
Attendance: 57,397

Pitching was the game and three the magic number, as Cincinnati swept Pittsburgh, scoring three runs in each game while holding the Pirates to just three runs for the whole series.

Pirate pitcher Dock Ellis matched the Reds' Gary Nolan for nine scoreless innings in Game One before a pinch-hit triple, a single, and a double undid him for three runs in the top of the tenth. In Game Two Pittsburgh scored its first series run, but Red center fielder Bobby Tolan scored three for Baltimore—including a home run—to give Cincinnati its second win.

The Pirates took a lead for the only time in the series with a run in the top of the first inning of Game Three. But Tony Perez and Johnny Bench homered in the bottom of the inning to put the Reds up 2–1. The Pirates tied the score in the fifth, but three Red relievers combined to shut them out over the final four innings, while Tolan sank the Pirate ship with his second game-winner in two days: a single in the eighth that drove in Cincinnati's third—and final—run.

Cincinnati Reds (West), 3;
Pittsburgh Pirates (East) 0

CIN (W)

PLAYER/POS	AVG	G	AB	R	H	2B	3B	HR	RB	BB	SO	SB
Johnny Bench, c	.222	3	9	2	2	0	0	1	1	3	1	0
Angel Bravo, ph	.000	1	1	0	0	0	0	0	0	0	0	0
Bernie Carbo, of	.000	2	6	0	0	0	0	0	0	0	3	0
Clay Carroll, p	.000	2	0	0	0	0	0	0	0	0	0	0
Ty Cline, of-1	1.000	2	1	2	1	0	1	0	0	1	0	0
Tony Cloninger, p	.000	1	1	0	0	0	0	0	0	1	0	0
Dave Concepcion, ss	.000	3	0	0	0	0	0	0	0	0	0	0
Wayne Granger, p	.000	1	0	0	0	0	0	0	0	0	0	0
Don Gullett, p	.000	2	1	0	0	0	0	0	0	0	0	0
Tommy Helms, 2b	.273	3	11	0	3	0	0	0	0	0	1	0
Lee May, 1b	.167	3	12	0	2	1	0	0	2	0	2	0
Hal Mc Rae, of-1	.000	2	4	0	0	0	0	0	0	0	1	0
Jim Merritt, p	.000	1	2	0	0	0	0	0	0	0	2	0
Gary Nolan, p	.333	1	3	0	1	0	0	0	0	0	0	0
Tony Perez, 3b-3,1b-1	.333	3	12	1	4	2	0	1	2	1	1	0
Pete Rose, of	.231	3	13	1	3	0	0	0	1	0	0	0
Jimmy Stewart, of	.000	1	2	0	0	0	0	0	0	0	0	0
Bobby Tolan, of	.417	3	12	3	5	0	0	1	2	1	1	1
Milt Wilcox, p	.000	1	0	0	0	0	0	0	0	0	0	0
Woody Woodward, ss-3,3b-3	.100	3	10	0	1	0	0	0	0	1	0	0
TOTAL	.220		100	9	22	3	1	3	8	8	12	1

PITCHER	W	L	ERA	G	GS	CG	SV	SHO	IP	H	ER	BB	SO
Clay Carroll	0	0	0.00	2	0	0	1	0	1.1	2	0	0	2
Tony Cloninger	0	0	5.40	1	1	0	0	0	5.0	7	3	4	1
Wayne Granger	0	0	0.00	1	0	0	0	0	0.2	1	0	0	0
Don Gullett	0	0	0.00	2	0	0	2	0	3.2	1	0	2	3
Jim Merritt	1	0	1.69	1	1	0	0	0	5.1	3	1	0	2
Gary Nolan	1	0	0.00	1	1	0	0	0	9.0	8	0	4	6
Milt Wilcox	1	0	0.00	1	0	0	0	0	3.0	1	0	2	5
TOTAL	3	0	1.29	9	3	0	3	0	28.0	23	4	12	19

PIT (E)

PLAYER/POS	AVG	G	AB	R	H	2B	3B	HR	RB	BB	SO	SB
Gene Alley, ss	.000	2	7	0	0	0	0	0	0	1	2	0
Matty Alou, of	.250	3	12	1	3	1	0	0	0	2	1	0
Dave Cash, 2b	.125	2	8	1	1	1	0	0	0	1	1	0
Roberto Clemente, of	.214	3	14	1	3	0	0	0	1	0	4	0
Dock Ellis, p	.000	1	2	0	0	0	0	0	0	0	1	0
Joe Gibbon, p	.000	2	0	0	0	0	0	0	0	0	0	0
Dave Giusti, p	.000	2	0	0	0	0	0	0	0	0	0	0
Richie Hebner, 3b	.667	2	6	0	4	2	0	0	0	2	1	0
Johnny Jeter, of-1	.000	3	2	0	0	0	0	0	0	0	2	0
Bill Mazeroski, 2b	.000	1	2	0	0	0	0	0	0	2	0	0
Bob Moose, p	.000	1	4	0	0	0	0	0	0	0	1	0
Al Oliver, 1b	.250	2	8	0	2	0	0	0	1	1	0	0
Jose Pagan, 3b	.333	1	3	0	1	0	0	0	0	1	1	0
Freddie Patek, ss	.000	1	3	0	0	0	0	0	0	1	2	0
Bob Robertson, 1b-1	.200	2	5	0	1	1	0	0	0	0	0	0
Manny Sanguillen, c	.167	3	12	0	2	0	0	0	0	0	1	0
Willie Stargell, of	.500	3	12	0	6	1	0	0	1	1	1	0
Luke Walker, p	.000	1	2	0	0	0	0	0	0	0	1	0
TOTAL	.225		102	3	23	6	0	0	3	12	19	0

PITCHER	W	L	ERA	G	GS	CG	SV	SHO	IP	H	ER	BB	SO
Dock Ellis	0	1	2.79	1	1	0	0	0	9.2	9	3	4	1
Joe Gibbon	0	0	0.00	2	0	0	0	0	0.1	1	0	0	1
Dave Giusti	0	0	3.86	2	0	0	0	0	2.1	3	1	1	1
Bob Moose	0	1	3.52	1	1	0	0	0	7.2	4	3	2	4
Luke Walker	0	1	1.29	1	1	0	0	0	7.0	5	1	1	5
TOTAL	0	3	2.67	7	3	0	0	0	27.0	22	8	8	12

GAME 1 AT PIT OCT 3

CIN	000	000	000	3	3	9	0
PIT	000	000	000	0	0	8	0

Pitchers: NOLAN, Carroll (10) vs ELLIS, Gibbon (10)
Attendance: 33,088

GAME 2 AT PIT OCT 4

CIN	001	010	010	3	8	1
PIT	000	001	000	1	5	2

Pitchers: MERRITT, Carroll (6), Gullett (6) vs WALKER, Giusti (8)
Home Runs: Tolan-CIN
Attendance: 39,317

GAME 3 AT CIN OCT 5

PIT	100	010	000	2	10	0
CIN	200	000	01X	3	5	0

Pitchers: MOOSE, Gibbon (8), Giusti (8) VS CLONINGER, WILCOX (6), Granger (9), Gullett (9)
Home Runs: Perez-CIN, Bench-CIN
Attendance: 40,538

For the second year in a row, Baltimore swept Minnesota in the LCS. In the first two games the Orioles' attack featured the big inning. The score was tied 2–2 in the first game as the Orioles came to bat in the top of the fourth. But by the time the Twins came to bat in the inning, they were seven runs behind—thanks in part to a grand slam by Baltimore pitcher Mike Cuellar. Harmon Killebrew's two-run homer in the fifth helped bring the Twins within three, but they came no closer.

Except for home runs to Killebrew and Tony Oliva in the fourth inning, Oriole pitcher Dave McNally stopped the Twins in Game Two, and Baltimore held a close 4–3 lead after eight. If they had been playing at home, they wouldn't have needed to bat at all in the ninth. But they did come to bat in the top of the ninth, and they once again buried Minnesota under a seven-run inning.

In the third game, for the second year in a row, Oriole pitcher Jim Palmer breezed through the series clincher. Baltimore scored five runs for him in the first three innings, and another in the eighth—four more than he needed to carry his club to another pennant.

Baltimore Orioles (East), 3; Minnesota Twins (West) 0

BAL (E)

PLAYER/POS	AVG	G	AB	R	H	2B	3B	HR	RB	BB	SO	SB
Mark Belanger, ss	.333	3	12	5	4	0	0	0	1	1	0	0
Paul Blair, of	.077	3	13	0	1	0	0	0	0	1	4	0
Don Buford, of	.429	2	7	2	3	1	0	1	3	2	0	0
Mike Cuellar, p	.500	1	2	1	1	0	0	1	4	0	1	0
Andy Etchebarren, c	.111	2	9	1	1	0	0	0	0	0	3	0
Dick Hall, p	.500	1	2	0	1	0	0	0	0	0	1	0
Elrod Hendricks, c	.400	1	5	2	2	0	0	0	0	0	1	0
Davy Johnson, 2b	.364	3	11	4	4	0	0	2	4	1	1	0
Dave Nc Nally, p	.400	1	5	1	2	1	0	0	1	0	1	0
Jim Palmer, p	.250	1	4	1	1	1	0	0	1	0	0	0
Boog Powell, 1b	.429	3	14	2	6	2	0	1	6	0	3	0
Merv Rettenmund, of	.333	1	3	1	1	0	0	0	1	2	1	1
Brooks Robinson, 3b	.583	3	12	4	7	2	0	0	1	0	1	0
Frank Robinson, of	.200	3	10	3	2	0	0	1	2	5	2	0
TOTAL	.330		109	27	36	7	0	6	24	12	19	1

PITCHER	W	L	ERA	G	GS	CG	SV	SHO	IP	H	ER	BB	SO
Mike Cuellar	0	0	12.46	1	1	0	0	0	4.1	10	6	1	2
Dick Hall	1	0	0.00	1	0	0	0	0	4.2	1	0	0	3
Dave Nc Nally	1	0	3.00	1	1	1	0	0	9.0	6	3	5	5
Jim Palmer	1	0	1.00	1	1	1	0	0	9.0	7	1	3	12
TOTAL	3	0	3.33	4	3	2	0	0	27.0	24	10	9	22

MIN (W)

PLAYER/POS	AVG	G	AB	R	H	2B	3B	HR	RB	BB	SO	SB
Bob Allison, ph	.000	3	2	0	0	0	0	0	0	1	1	0
Brant Alyea, of-2	.000	3	7	1	0	0	0	0	0	2	3	0
Bert Blyleven, p	.000	1	0	0	0	0	0	0	0	0	0	0
Leo Cardenas, ss	.182	3	11	1	2	0	0	0	1	1	1	0
Rod Carew, ph	.000	2	2	0	0	0	0	0	0	0	1	0
Tom Hall, p	.000	2	1	0	0	0	0	0	0	0	1	0
Jim Holt, of	.000	3	5	0	0	0	0	0	0	0	2	0
Jim Kaat, p	.000	1	1	0	0	0	0	0	0	0	0	0
Harmon Killebrew, 3b-2,1b-1	.273	3	11	2	3	0	0	2	4	2	4	0
Chuck Manuel, ph	.000	1	1	0	0	0	0	0	0	0	1	0
George Mitterwald, c	.500	2	8	2	4	1	0	0	2	0	2	0
Tony Oliva, of	.500	3	12	2	6	2	0	1	1	0	1	0
Ron Perranoski, p	.000	2	0	0	0	0	0	0	0	0	0	0
Jim Perry, p	.000	2	1	0	0	0	0	0	1	0	1	0
Frank Quilici, 2b-2	.000	3	2	0	0	0	0	0	0	0	1	0
Paul Ratliff, c	.250	1	4	0	1	0	0	0	0	0	1	0
Rich Reese, 1b	.143	2	7	0	1	0	0	0	0	1	1	0
Rich Renick, 3b-1	.200	2	5	0	1	0	0	0	0	0	1	0
Danny Thompson, 2b	.125	3	8	0	1	1	0	0	0	1	0	0
Luis Tiant, p	.000	1	0	0	0	0	0	0	0	0	0	0
Cesar Tovar, of-3,2b-1	.385	3	13	2	5	0	1	0	1	0	0	0
Stan Williams, p	.000	2	0	0	0	0	0	0	0	1	0	0
Dick Woodson, p	.000	1	0	0	0	0	0	0	0	0	0	0
Bill Zepp, p	.000	2	0	0	0	0	0	0	0	0	0	0
TOTAL	.238		101	10	24	4	1	3	10	9	22	0

PITCHER	W	L	ERA	G	GS	CG	SV	SHO	IP	H	ER	BB	SO
Bert Blyleven	0	0	0.00	1	0	0	0	0	2.0	2	0	0	2
Tom Hall	0	1	6.75	2	0	0	0	0	5.1	6	4	4	6
Jim Kaat	0	1	9.00	1	1	0	0	0	2.0	6	2	2	1
Ron Perranoski	0	0	19.29	2	0	0	0	0	2.1	5	5	1	3
Jim Perry	0	1	13.50	2	1	0	0	0	5.1	10	8	1	3
Luis Tiant	0	0	13.50	1	0	0	0	0	0.2	1	1	0	0
Stan Williams	0	0	0.00	2	0	0	0	0	6.0	2	0	1	2
Dick Woodson	0	0	9.00	1	0	0	0	0	1.0	2	1	1	0
Bill Zepp	0	0	6.75	2	0	0	0	0	1.1	2	1	2	2
TOTAL	0	3	7.62	14	3	0	0	0	26.0	36	22	12	19

GAME 1 AT MIN OCT 3

BAL	020	701	000	10	13	0
MIN	110	130	000	6	11	2

Pitchers: Cuellar, HALL (5) vs PERRY, Zepp (4), Woodson (5), Williams (6), Perranoski (9)
Home Runs: Cuellar-BAL, Buford-BAL, Powell-BAL, Killebrew-MIN
Attendance: 26,847

GAME 2 AT MIN OCT 4

BAL	102	100	007	11	13	0
MIN	000	300	000	3	6	2

Pitchers: McNALLY vs HALL, Zepp (4), Williams (5), Perranoski (8), Tiant (9)
Home Runs: F.Robinson-BAL, Killebrew-MIN, Oliva-MIN, Johnson-BAL
Attendance: 27,490

GAME 3 AT BAL OCT 5

MIN	000	010	000	1	7	2
BAL	113	000	10X	6	10	0

Pitchers: KAAT, Blyleven (3), Hall (5), Perry (7) vs PALMER
Home Runs: Johnson-BAL
Attendance: 27,608

With a near-sweep of Cincinnati, the Orioles helped Baltimore fans forget their 1969 Series humiliation by the New York Mets. Baltimore's first two wins, though, were closely contested. In the opener in Cincinnati (the first World Series game played on artificial grass), a Red run in the first inning and Lee May's third-inning two-run homer off Oriole starter Jim Palmer gave Cincinnati a 3–0 lead. But Orioles Boog Powell and Elrod Hendricks tagged Red starter Gary Nolan for home runs in the fourth and fifth that evened the score, and Brooks Robinson—whose otherworldly defense at third gave Reds righthanded hitters nightmares throughout the Series—homered in the seventh for a one-run Baltimore lead that held up as Palmer settled down to pitch one-hit ball from the fourth inning until he was relieved for the final out of the ninth.

Game Two was just as close. The Reds scored four runs in the first three innings, but Baltimore came back with six in the fourth and fifth. Johnny Bench's leadoff homer in the last of the sixth brought the Reds within one, but that was the end of the scoring for either side. In Game Three Oriole Dave McNally gave up nine hits and three runs. But he himself hit a grand slam in the sixth inning to cement what became a 9–3 victory.

On the verge of a Series sweep, the Orioles scored three runs in the last of the third inning of Game Four to take a 4–2 lead. But the Reds' Pete Rose homered in the fifth, and although Baltimore got the run back in the sixth, Lee May's three-run blast in the eighth overcame the Oriole lead and gave the Reds a narrow 6–5 win as Red reliever Clay Carroll permitted only one Oriole to hit safely over the final 3⅔ innings.

Mike Cuellar, driven out of Game Two in the third inning, hurled the complete game for Baltimore in Game Five, even though Cincinnati hammered him for four hits (three of them doubles) and three runs in the top of the first inning. But as Oriole home runs by Frank Robinson and Merv Rettenmund highlighted a Baltimore onslaught that produced fifteen hits and nine runs, Cuellar settled down, holding Cincinnati to a walk and a pair of harmless singles over the final eight innings to bring Baltimore its second world title in five years.

Baltimore Orioles (AL), 4; Cincinnati Reds (NL) 1

BAL (A)

PLAYER/POS	AVG	G	AB	R	H	2B	3B	HR	RB	BB	SO	SB
Mark Belanger, ss	.105	5	19	0	2	0	0	0	1	1	2	0
Paul Blair, of	.474	5	19	5	9	1	0	0	3	2	4	0
Don Buford, of	.267	4	15	3	4	0	0	1	1	3	2	0
Terry Crowley, ph	.000	1	1	0	0	0	0	0	0	0	0	0
Mike Cuellar, p	.000	2	4	0	0	0	0	0	0	0	2	0
Moe Drabowsky, p	.000	2	1	0	0	0	0	0	0	0	1	0
Andy Etchebarren, c	.143	2	7	1	1	0	0	0	0	2	3	0
Dick Hall, p	.000	1	1	0	0	0	0	0	0	0	1	0
Elrod Hendricks, c	.364	3	11	1	4	1	0	1	4	1	2	0
Davy Johnson, 2b	.313	5	16	2	5	2	0	0	2	5	2	0
Marcelino Lopez, p	.000	1	0	0	0	0	0	0	0	0	0	0
Dave Mc Nally, p	.250	1	4	1	1	0	0	1	4	0	2	0
Jim Palmer, p	.143	2	7	1	1	0	0	0	0	0	3	0
Tom Phoebus, p	.000	1	0	0	0	0	0	0	0	0	0	0
Boog Powell, 1b	.294	5	17	6	5	1	0	2	5	5	2	0
Merv Rettenmund, of-1	.400	2	5	2	2	0	0	1	2	1	0	0
Pete Richert, p	.000	1	0	0	0	0	0	0	0	0	0	0
Brooks Robinson, 3b	.429	5	21	5	9	2	0	2	6	0	2	0
Frank Robinson, of	.273	5	22	5	6	0	0	2	4	0	5	0
Chico Salmon, ph	1.000	1	1	1	1	0	0	0	0	0	0	0
Eddie Watt, p	.000	1	0	0	0	0	0	0	0	0	0	0
TOTAL	.292		171	33	50	7	0	10	32	20	33	0

PITCHER	W	L	ERA	G	GS	CG	SV	SHO	IP	H	ER	BB	SO
Mike Cuellar	1	0	3.18	2	2	1	0	0	11.1	10	4	2	5
Moe Drabowsky	0	0	2.70	2	0	0	0	0	3.1	2	1	1	1
Dick Hall	0	0	0.00	1	0	0	1	0	2.1	0	0	0	0
Marcelino Lopez	0	0	0.00	1	0	0	0	0	0.1	0	0	0	0
Dave Mc Nally	1	0	3.00	1	1	1	0	0	9.0	9	3	2	5
Jim Palmer	1	0	4.60	2	2	0	0	0	15.2	11	8	9	9
Tom Phoebus	1	0	0.00	1	0	0	0	0	1.2	1	0	0	0
Pete Richert	0	0	0.00	1	0	0	1	0	0.1	0	0	0	0
Eddie Watt	0	1	9.00	1	0	0	0	0	1.0	2	1	1	3
TOTAL	4	1	3.40	12	5	2	2	0	45.0	35	17	15	23

CIN (N)

PLAYER/POS	AVG	G	AB	R	H	2B	3B	HR	RB	BB	SO	SB
Johnny Bench, c	.211	5	19	3	4	0	0	1	3	1	2	0
Angel Bravo, ph	.000	4	2	0	0	0	0	0	0	1	1	0
Bernie Carbo, of-2	.000	4	8	0	0	0	0	0	0	2	3	0
Clay Carroll, p	.000	4	1	0	0	0	0	0	0	0	1	0
Darrel Chaney, ss	.000	3	1	0	0	0	0	0	0	0	1	0
Ty Cline, ph	.333	3	3	0	1	0	0	0	0	0	0	0
Tony Cloninger, p	.000	2	2	0	0	0	0	0	0	0	1	0
Dave Concepcion, ss	.333	3	9	0	3	0	1	0	3	0	0	0
Pat Corrales, ph	.000	1	1	0	0	0	0	0	0	0	0	0
Wayne Granger, p	.000	2	0	0	0	0	0	0	0	0	0	0
Don Gullett, p	.000	3	1	0	0	0	0	0	0	0	1	0
Tommy Helms, 2b	.222	5	18	1	4	0	0	0	0	1	1	0
Lee May, 1b	.389	5	18	6	7	2	0	2	8	2	2	0
Jim Mc Glothlin, p	.000	1	2	0	0	0	0	0	0	0	1	0
Hal Mc Rae, of	.455	3	11	1	5	2	0	0	3	0	1	0
Jim Merritt, p	.000	1	1	0	0	0	0	0	0	0	1	0
Gary Nolan, p	.000	2	3	0	0	0	0	0	0	0	0	0
Tony Perez, 3b	.056	5	18	2	1	0	0	0	0	3	4	0
Pete Rose, of	.250	5	20	2	5	1	0	1	2	2	0	0
Jimmy Stewart, ph	.000	2	2	0	0	0	0	0	0	0	1	0
Bobby Tolan, of	.211	5	19	5	4	1	0	1	1	3	2	1
Ray Washburn, p	.000	1	0	0	0	0	0	0	0	0	0	0
Milt Wilcox, p	.000	2	0	0	0	0	0	0	0	0	0	0
Woody Woodward, ss-3	.200	4	5	0	1	0	0	0	0	0	0	0
TOTAL	.213		164	20	35	6	1	5	20	15	23	1

PITCHER	W	L	ERA	G	GS	CG	SV	SHO	IP	H	ER	BB	SO
Clay Carroll	1	0	0.00	4	0	0	0	0	9.0	5	0	2	11
Tony Cloninger	0	1	7.36	2	1	0	0	0	7.1	10	6	5	4
Wayne Granger	0	0	33.75	2	0	0	0	0	1.1	7	5	1	1
Don Gullett	0	0	1.35	3	0	0	0	0	6.2	5	1	4	4
Jim Mc Glothlin	0	0	8.31	1	1	0	0	0	4.1	6	4	2	2
Jim Merritt	0	1	21.60	1	1	0	0	0	1.2	3	4	1	0
Gary Nolan	0	1	7.71	2	2	0	0	0	9.1	9	8	3	9
Ray Washburn	0	0	13.50	1	0	0	0	0	1.1	2	2	2	0
Milt Wilcox	0	1	9.00	2	0	0	0	0	2.0	3	2	0	2
TOTAL	1	4	6.70	18	5	0	0	0	43.0	50	32	20	33

GAME 1 AT CIN OCT 10

BAL	000 210 100	4	7	2
CIN	102 000 000	3	5	0

Pitchers: PALMER, Richert (9) vs NOLAN, Carroll (7)
Home Runs: May-CIN, Powell-BAL, Hendricks-BAL, B.Robinson-BAL
Attendance: 51,531

GAME 2 AT CIN OCT 11

BAL	000 150 000	6	10	2
CIN	301 001 000	5	7	0

Pitchers: Cuellar, PHOEBUS (3), Drabowsky (5), Lopez (7), Hall (7) VS McGlothlin, WILCOX (5), Carroll (5), Gullett (8)
Home Runs: Tolan-CIN, Powell-BAL, Bench-CIN
Attendance: 51,531

GAME 3 AT BAL OCT 13

CIN	010 000 200	3	9	0
BAL	201 014 10X	9	10	1

Pitchers: CLONINGER, Granger (6), Gullett (7) vs McNALLY
Home Runs: F.Robinson-BAL, Buford-BAL, McNally-BAL
Attendance: 51,773

GAME 4 AT BAL OCT 14

CIN	011 010 030	6	8	3
BAL	013 001 000	5	8	0

Pitchers: Nolan, Gullett (3), CARROLL (6) VS Palmer, WATT (8), Drabowsky (9)
Home Runs: B.Robinson-BAL, Rose-CIN, May-CIN
Attendance: 53,007

GAME 5 AT BAL OCT 15

CIN	300 000 000	3	6	0
BAL	222 010 02X	9	15	0

Pitchers: MERRITT, Granger (2), Wilcox (3), Cloninger (5), Washburn (7), Carroll (8) vs CUELLAR
Home Runs: F.Robinson-BAL, Rettenmund-BAL
Attendance: 45,341

For the first time, an LCS went more than the minimum three games, as Pittsburgh rebounded from a loss in the opener to take the next three from San Francisco.

The Pirates scored first, with two runs in the third inning of Game One, but the Giants came back with a run in the bottom of the inning and put the game away in the fifth as Tito Fuentes and Willie McCovey both hit two-out two-run homers. Pirate first baseman Bob Robertson avenged his club's opening-game defeat the next day, battering four of the Giants' six pitchers for three home runs and a double—and five RBIs—in the Pirates' 9-1 win. Robertson continued his assault in Game Three, homering off Juan Marichal in the second. The Giants came back with a run in the sixth, but third baseman Richie Hebner put the game away with a second Pirate home run off Marichal in the eighth.

Both clubs scored five times in the first two innings of Game Four. But Pirate relievers Bruce Kison and Dave Giusti then pinned the Giants down for the final seven innings, while Roberto Clemente and Al Oliver combined for four RBIs in the sixth to capture the flag.

Pittsburgh Pirates (East), 3; San Francisco Giants (West), 1

PIT (E)

PLAYER/POS	AVG	G	AB	R	H	2B	3B	HR	RB	BB	SO	SB
Gene Alley, ss	.500	1	2	1	1	0	0	0	0	0	0	0
Steve Blass, p	.000	2	1	0	0	0	0	0	0	0	1	0
Dave Cash, 2b	.421	4	19	5	8	2	0	0	1	0	1	1
Roberto Clemente, of	.333	4	18	2	6	0	0	0	4	1	6	0
Gene Clines, of	.333	1	3	1	1	0	0	1	1	0	1	0
Vic Davalillo, ph	.000	2	2	0	0	0	0	0	0	0	1	0
Dock Ellis, p	.000	1	3	0	0	0	0	0	0	0	2	0
Dave Giusti, p	.000	4	1	0	0	0	0	0	0	0	0	0
Richie Hebner, 3b	.294	4	17	3	5	1	0	2	4	0	4	0
Jackie Hernandez, ss	.231	4	13	2	3	0	0	0	1	0	4	0
Bob Johnson, p	.000	1	2	0	0	0	0	0	0	0	1	0
Bruce Kison, p	.000	1	2	0	0	0	0	0	0	0	0	0
Milt May, p	.000	1	1	0	0	0	0	0	0	0	0	0
Bill Mazeroski, ph	1.000	1	1	1	1	0	0	0	0	0	0	0
Bob Miller, p	.000	1	1	0	0	0	0	0	0	0	0	0
Bob Moose, p	.000	1	0	0	0	0	0	0	0	0	0	0
Al Oliver, of	.250	4	12	2	3	0	0	1	5	1	3	0
Jose Pagan, 3b	.000	1	1	0	0	0	0	0	0	0	0	0
Bob Robertson, 1b	.438	4	16	5	7	1	0	4	6	0	2	0
Manny Sanguillen, c	.267	4	15	1	4	0	0	0	1	1	1	1
Willie Stargell, of	.000	4	14	1	0	0	0	0	0	2	6	0
TOTAL	.271		144	24	39	4	0	8	23	5	33	2

PITCHER	W	L	ERA	G	GS	CG	SV	SHO	IP	H	ER	BB	SO
Steve Blass	0	1	11.57	2	2	0	0	0	7.0	14	9	2	11
Dock Ellis	1	0	3.60	1	1	0	0	0	5.0	6	2	4	1
Dave Giusti	0	0	0.00	4	0	0	3	0	5.1	1	0	2	3
Bob Johnson	1	0	0.00	1	1	0	0	0	8.0	5	0	3	7
Bruce Kison	1	0	0.00	1	0	0	0	0	4.2	2	0	2	3
Bob Miller	0	0	6.00	1	0	0	0	0	3.0	3	2	3	3
Bob Moose	0	0	0.00	1	0	0	0	0	2.0	0	0	0	0
TOTAL	3	1	3.34	11	4	0	3	0	35.0	31	13	16	28

SF (W)

PLAYER/POS	AVG	G	AB	R	H	2B	3B	HR	RB	BB	SO	SB
Jim Barr, p	.000	1	1	0	0	0	0	0	0	0	0	0
Bobby Bonds, of	.250	3	8	0	2	0	0	0	0	2	4	0
Ron Bryant, p	.000	1	0	0	0	0	0	0	0	0	0	0
Don Carrithers, p	.000	1	0	0	0	0	0	0	0	0	0	0
John Cumberland, p	.000	1	0	0	0	0	0	0	0	0	0	0
Dick Dietz, c	.067	4	15	0	1	0	0	0	0	2	5	0
Frank Duffy, ph	.000	1	1	0	0	0	0	0	0	0	1	0
Tito Fuentes, 2b	.313	4	16	4	5	1	0	1	2	1	3	0
Alan Gallagher, 3b	.100	4	10	0	1	0	0	0	0	0	2	0
Steve Hamilton, p	.000	1	0	0	0	0	0	0	0	0	0	0
Jim Ray Hart, 3b-1	.000	3	5	0	0	0	0	0	0	0	2	0
Ken Henderson, of	.313	4	16	3	5	1	0	0	2	2	1	1
Jerry Johnson, p	.000	1	0	0	0	0	0	0	0	0	0	0
Dave Kingman, of-2	.111	4	9	0	1	0	0	0	0	1	3	0
Hal Lanier, 3b	.000	1	1	0	0	0	0	0	0	0	0	0
Juan Marichal, p	.000	1	3	0	0	0	0	0	0	0	1	0
Willie Mays, of	.267	4	15	2	4	2	0	1	3	3	3	1
Willie Mc Covey, 1b	.429	4	14	2	6	0	0	2	6	4	2	0
Don Mc Mahon, p	.000	2	0	0	0	0	0	0	0	0	0	0
Gaylord Perry, p	.250	2	4	0	1	0	0	0	0	0	0	0
Jimmy Rosario, pr	.000	1	0	0	0	0	0	0	0	0	0	0
Chris Speier, ss	.357	4	14	4	5	1	0	1	1	1	1	0
TOTAL	.235		132	15	31	5	0	5	14	16	28	2

PITCHER	W	L	ERA	G	GS	CG	SV	SHO	IP	H	ER	BB	SO
Jim Barr	0	0	9.00	1	0	0	0	0	1.0	3	1	0	2
Ron Bryant	0	0	4.50	1	0	0	0	0	2.0	1	1	1	2
Don Carrithers	0	0	INF	1	0	0	0	0	0.0	3	3	0	0
John Cumberland	0	1	9.00	1	1	0	0	0	3.0	7	3	0	4
Steve Hamilton	0	0	9.00	1	0	0	0	0	1.0	1	1	0	3
Jerry Johnson	0	0	13.50	1	0	0	0	0	1.1	1	2	1	2
Juan Marichal	0	1	2.25	1	1	1	0	0	8.0	4	2	0	6
Don Mc Mahon	0	0	0.00	2	0	0	0	0	3.0	0	0	0	3
Gaylord Perry	1	1	6.14	2	2	1	0	0	14.2	19	10	3	11
TOTAL	1	3	6.09	11	4	2	0	0	34.0	39	23	5	33

Baltimore, dividing its fifteen runs evenly among the three games, swept the ALCS for the third year in a row.

Oakland's Vida Blue took a 3–1 lead into the seventh inning of Game One, but with two away and men on first and third, an Oriole single and two doubles pushed across four runs to beat him 5–3, as Oriole starter Dave McNally and reliever Eddie Watt held the A's scoreless from the fifth inning on. In the second game Oakland managed only one run off Mike Cuellar, while the Orioles hammered Catfish Hunter for five runs on four homers—two of them by Boog Powell, including one in the eighth with a man aboard.

Reggie Jackson retaliated for the A's in Game Three with two home runs off Jim Palmer, and Sal Bando added a third. But Palmer permitted no other A's to score, and—supported by a Baltimore run in the first and two each in the fifth and seventh—preserved an Oriole lead throughout the game, for the third year in a row clinching the pennant for Baltimore with a complete-game victory.

Baltimore Orioles (East), 3;
Oakland A's (West) 0

BAL (E)

PLAYER/POS	AVG	G	AB	R	H	2B	3B	HR	RB	BB	SO	SB
Mark Belanger, ss	.250	3	8	1	2	0	0	0	1	3	2	0
Paul Blair, of	.333	3	9	1	3	1	0	0	2	0	3	0
Don Buford, of	.429	2	7	1	3	0	1	0	0	2	1	0
Mike Cuellar, p	.333	1	3	0	1	0	0	0	0	0	2	0
Andy Etchebarren, c	.000	2	5	0	0	0	0	0	0	0	0	0
Elrod Hendricks, c	.500	2	4	1	2	0	0	1	2	1	1	0
Davy Johnson, 2b	.300	3	10	2	3	2	0	0	0	3	1	0
Dave Nc Nally, p	.000	1	2	0	0	0	0	0	0	0	0	0
Curt Motton, ph	1.000	1	1	0	1	1	0	0	1	0	0	0
Jim Palmer, p-1	.200	2	5	1	1	0	0	0	0	0	1	0
Boog Powell, 1b	.300	3	10	4	3	0	0	2	3	3	3	0
Merv Rettenmund, of	.250	3	8	0	2	1	0	0	1	0	3	0
Brooks Robinson, 3b	.364	3	11	2	4	1	0	1	3	0	1	0
Frank Robinson, of	.083	3	12	2	1	1	0	0	1	1	4	0
Eddie Watt, p	.000	1	0	0	0	0	0	0	0	0	0	0
TOTAL	.274		95	15	26	7	1	4	14	13	22	0

PITCHER	W	L	ERA	G	GS	CG	SV	SHO	IP	H	ER	BB	SO
Mike Cuellar	1	0	1.00	1	1	1	0	0	9.0	6	1	1	2
Dave Nc Nally	1	0	3.86	1	1	0	0	0	7.0	7	3	1	5
Jim Palmer	1	0	3.00	1	1	1	0	0	9.0	7	3	3	8
Eddie Watt	0	0	0.00	1	0	0	1	0	2.0	2	0	0	1
TOTAL	3	0	2.33	4	3	2	1	0	27.0	22	7	5	16

OAK (W)

PLAYER/POS	AVG	G	AB	R	H	2B	3B	HR	RB	BB	SO	SB
Sal Bando, 3b	.364	3	11	3	4	2	0	1	1	1	0	0
Curt Blefary, ph	.000	1	1	0	0	0	0	0	0	0	1	0
Vida Blue, p	.000	1	3	0	0	0	0	0	0	0	3	0
Bert Campaneris, ss	.167	3	12	0	2	1	0	0	0	0	1	0
Tommy Davis, 1b-2	.375	3	8	1	3	1	0	0	0	0	0	0
Dave Duncan, c	.500	2	6	0	3	1	0	0	2	0	0	0
Mike Epstein, 1b-1	.200	2	5	0	1	0	0	0	0	0	3	0
Rollie Fingers, p	.000	2	0	0	0	0	0	0	0	0	0	0
Mudcat Grant, p	.000	1	0	0	0	0	0	0	0	0	0	0
Dick Green, 2b	.286	3	7	0	2	0	0	0	0	1	1	0
Mike Hegan, ph	.000	1	1	0	0	0	0	0	0	0	1	0
Catfish Hunter, p	.000	1	3	0	0	0	0	0	0	0	1	0
Reggie Jackson, of	.333	3	12	2	4	1	0	2	2	0	1	0
Darold Knowles, p	.000	1	0	0	0	0	0	0	0	0	0	0
Bob Locker, p	.000	1	0	0	0	0	0	0	0	0	0	0
Angel Mangual, of	.167	3	12	1	2	1	1	0	2	0	1	0
Rick Monday, of	.000	1	3	0	0	0	0	0	0	1	2	0
Joe Rudi, of	.143	2	7	0	1	1	0	0	0	1	0	0
Diego Segui, p	.000	1	2	0	0	0	0	0	0	0	0	0
Gene Tenace, c	.000	1	3	0	0	0	0	0	0	1	1	0
TOTAL	.229		96	7	22	8	1	3	7	5	16	0

PITCHER	W	L	ERA	G	GS	CG	SV	SHO	IP	H	ER	BB	SO
Vida Blue	0	1	6.43	1	1	0	0	0	7.0	7	5	2	8
Rollie Fingers	0	0	7.71	2	0	0	0	0	2.1	2	2	1	2
Mudcat Grant	0	0	0.00	1	0	0	0	0	2.0	3	0	0	2
Catfish Hunter	0	1	5.63	1	1	1	0	0	8.0	7	5	2	6
Darold Knowles	0	0	0.00	1	0	0	0	0	0.1	1	0	0	0
Bob Locker	0	0	0.00	1	0	0	0	0	0.2	0	0	2	0
Diego Segui	0	1	5.79	1	1	0	0	0	4.2	6	3	6	4
TOTAL	0	3	5.40	8	3	1	0	0	25.0	26	15	13	22

GAME 1 AT BAL OCT 3

OAK	020	100	000	3	9 0
BAL	000	100	40X	5	7 1

Pitchers: BLUE, Fingers (8) vs McNALLY, Watt (8)
Attendance: 42,621

GAME 2 AT BAL OCT 4

OAK	000	100	000	1	6 0
BAL	011	000	12X	5	7 0

Pitchers: HUNTER vs CUELLAR
Home Runs: B.Robinson-BAL, Powell-BAL (2), Hendricks-BAL
Attendance: 35,003

GAME 3 AT OAK OCT 5

BAL	100	020	200	5	12 0
OAK	001	001	010	3	7 0

Pitchers: PALMER vs SEGUI, Fingers (5), Knowles (7), Locker (7), Grant (8)
Home Runs: Jackson-OAK (2), Bando-OAK
Attendance: 33,176

In its third successive Series, Baltimore faced its third different opponent and beat the Pirates in the first two games. A walk, a wild pitch, two Baltimore errors, and a single in the second inning of the opener gave Pittsburgh an early 3–0 lead. But Oriole pitcher Dave McNally shut out the Pirates on two hits the rest of the game as Frank Robinson, Merv Rettenmund and Don Buford homered to give Baltimore a 5–3 victory. Jim Palmer took the win in Game Two as Baltimore hammered Pirate pitching for fourteen hits and eleven runs before Palmer issued Richie Hebner a three-run homer—Pittsburgh's only scoring—in the eighth.

The Pirates overtook the Orioles when the Series moved to Pittsburgh. Steve Blass pitched a three-hitter in Game Three, and while Frank Robinson's solo homer in the seventh ended Blass's shutout, a three-run shot by Pirate Bob Robertson in the last of the inning cemented a 5–1 Pittsburgh win. The next evening (in the first World Series night game ever), Baltimore scored three times in the top of the first inning, but two Pirate runs later in the inning and another run in the third tied the game. It remained tied until Pirate pinch hitter Milt May singled home the game winner with two away in the seventh.

With the Series now even at two wins apiece, Pittsburgh's Nelson Briles stopped the Orioles in Game Five on a pair of singles. Bob Robertson's leadoff homer in the second proved all the Pirates needed for the win, but Briles himself drove in an insurance run later in the inning and Pittsburgh went on to win 4–0.

The Pirates tried to win it all in Game Six, scoring single runs against the O's Jim Palmer in the second inning and the third (Roberto Clemente's home run). But Pirate starter Bob Moose was replaced after giving up a solo homer to Don Buford in the sixth, and a tying Baltimore run came home an inning later. A ninth-inning pinch hitter for Palmer produced nothing, but Baltimore won in the last of the tenth, when Frank Robinson scored on Brooks Robinson's sacrifice fly to shallow center.

Steve Blass, who had defeated Oriole Mike Cuellar in Game Three, faced him again in the finale and again emerged the victor of a pitching duel. Clemente's two-out homer in the fourth inning provided the game's only run until the eighth, when both teams scored single runs. Blass retired Baltimore in order in the ninth and the Pirates were world champions.

Pittsburgh Pirates (NL), 4; Baltimore Orioles (AL) 3

PIT (N)

PLAYER/POS	AVG	G	AB	R	H	2B	3B	HR	RB	BB	SO	SB
Gene Alley, ss	.000	2	2	0	0	0	0	0	0	1	0	0
Steve Blass, p	.000	2	7	0	0	0	0	0	0	0	1	0
Nelson Briles, p	.500	1	2	0	1	0	0	0	1	0	1	0
Dave Cash, 2b	.133	7	30	2	4	1	0	0	1	3	1	1
Roberto Clemente, of	.414	7	29	3	12	2	1	2	4	2	2	0
Gene Clines, of	.091	3	11	2	1	0	1	0	0	1	1	1
Vic Davalillo, of-2	.333	3	3	1	1	0	0	0	0	0	0	0
Dock Ellis, p	.000	1	1	0	0	0	0	0	0	0	1	0
Dave Giusti, p	.000	3	0	0	0	0	0	0	0	0	0	0
Richie Hebner, 3b	.167	3	12	2	2	0	0	1	3	3	3	0
Jackie Hernandez, ss	.222	7	18	2	4	0	0	0	1	2	5	1
Bob Johnson, p	.000	2	3	0	0	0	0	0	0	0	2	0
Bruce Kison, p	.000	2	2	0	0	0	0	0	0	1	2	0
Milt May, ph	.500	2	2	0	1	0	0	0	1	0	0	0
Bill Mazeroski, ph	.000	1	1	0	0	0	0	0	0	0	0	0
Bob Miller, p	.000	3	0	0	0	0	0	0	0	0	0	0
Bob Moose, p	.000	2	2	0	0	0	0	0	0	0	1	0
Al Oliver, of-4	.211	5	19	1	4	2	0	0	2	2	5	0
Jose Pagan, 3b	.267	4	15	0	4	2	0	0	2	0	1	0
Bob Robertson, 1b	.240	7	25	4	6	0	0	2	5	4	8	0
Charlie Sands, ph	.000	1	1	0	0	0	0	0	0	0	1	0
Manny Sanguillen, c	.379	7	29	3	11	1	0	0	0	0	3	2
Willie Stargell, of	.208	7	24	3	5	1	0	0	1	7	9	0
Bob Veale, p	.000	1	0	0	0	0	0	0	0	0	0	0
Luke Walker, p	.000	1	0	0	0	0	0	0	0	0	0	0
TOTAL	.235		238	23	56	9	2	5	21	26	47	5

PITCHER	W	L	ERA	G	GS	CG	SV	SHO	IP	H	ER	BB	SO
Steve Blass	2	0	1.00	2	2	2	0	0	18.0	7	2	4	13
Nelson Briles	1	0	0.00	1	1	1	0	1	9.0	2	0	2	2
Dock Ellis	0	1	15.43	1	1	0	0	0	2.1	4	4	1	1
Dave Giusti	0	0	0.00	3	0	0	1	0	5.1	3	0	2	4
Bob Johnson	0	1	9.00	2	1	0	0	0	5.0	5	5	3	3
Bruce Kison	1	0	0.00	2	0	0	0	0	6.1	1	0	2	3
Bob Miller	0	1	3.86	3	0	0	0	0	4.2	7	2	1	2
Bob Moose	0	0	6.52	3	1	0	0	0	9.2	12	7	2	7
Bob Veale	0	0	13.50	1	0	0	0	0	0.2	1	1	2	0
Luke Walker	0	0	40.50	1	1	0	0	0	0.2	3	3	1	0
TOTAL	4	3	3.50	19	7	3	1	1	61.2	45	24	20	35

BAL (A)

PLAYER/POS	AVG	G	AB	R	H	2B	3B	HR	RB	BB	SO	SB
Mark Belanger, ss	.238	7	21	4	5	0	1	0	0	5	2	1
Paul Blair, of-3	.333	4	9	2	3	1	0	0	0	0	1	0
Don Buford, of	.261	6	23	3	6	1	0	2	4	3	3	0
Mike Cuellar, p	.000	2	3	0	0	0	0	0	0	1	2	0
Pat Dobson, p	.000	3	2	0	0	0	0	0	0	0	2	0
Tom Dukes, p	.000	2	0	0	0	0	0	0	0	0	0	0
Andy Etchebarren, c	.000	1	2	0	0	0	0	0	0	0	0	0
Dick Hall, p	.000	1	0	0	0	0	0	0	0	0	0	0
Elrod Hendricks, c	.263	6	19	3	5	1	0	0	1	3	3	0
Grant Jackson, p	.000	1	0	0	0	0	0	0	0	0	0	0
Davy Johnson, 2b	.148	7	27	1	4	0	0	0	3	0	1	0
Dave Leonhard, p	.000	1	0	0	0	0	0	0	0	0	0	0
Dave Mc Nally, p	.000	4	4	0	0	0	0	0	0	0	3	0
Jim Palmer, p	.000	2	4	0	0	0	0	0	2	2	2	0
Boog Powell, 1b	.111	7	27	1	3	0	0	0	1	1	3	0
Merv Rettenmund, of-6	.185	7	27	3	5	0	0	1	4	0	4	0
Pete Richert, p	.000	1	0	0	0	0	0	0	0	0	0	0
Brooks Robinson, 3b	.318	7	22	2	7	0	0	0	5	3	1	0
Frank Robinson, of	.280	7	25	5	7	0	0	2	2	2	8	0
Tom Shopay, ph	.000	5	4	0	0	0	0	0	0	0	0	0
Eddie Watt, p	.000	2	0	0	0	0	0	0	0	0	0	0
TOTAL	.205		219	24	45	3	1	5	22	20	35	1

PITCHER	W	L	ERA	G	GS	CG	SV	SHO	IP	H	ER	BB	SO
Mike Cuellar	0	2	3.86	2	2	0	0	0	14.0	11	6	6	10
Pat Dobson	0	0	4.05	3	1	0	0	0	6.2	13	3	4	6
Tom Dukes	0	0	0.00	2	0	0	0	0	4.0	2	0	0	1
Dick Hall	0	0	0.00	1	0	0	1	0	1.0	1	0	0	0
Grant Jackson	0	0	0.00	1	0	0	0	0	0.2	0	0	1	0
Dave Leonhard	0	0	0.00	1	0	0	0	0	1.0	0	0	1	0
Dave Mc Nally	2	1	1.98	4	2	1	0	0	13.2	10	3	5	12
Jim Palmer	1	0	2.65	2	2	0	0	0	17.0	15	5	9	15
Pete Richert	0	0	0.00	1	0	0	0	0	0.2	0	0	0	1
Eddie Watt	0	1	3.86	2	0	0	0	0	2.1	4	1	0	2
TOTAL	3	4	2.66	19	7	1	1	0	61.0	56	18	26	47

GAME 1 AT BAL OCT 9

PIT	030 000 000	3	3	0
BAL	013 010 00X	5	10	3

Pitchers: ELLIS, Moose (3), Miller (7) VS McNALLY
Home Runs: F.Robinson-BAL, Rettenmund-BAL, Buford-BAL
Attendance: 53,229

GAME 2 AT BAL OCT 11

PIT	000 000 030	3	8	1
BAL	010 361 00X	11	14	1

Pitchers: R.JOHNSON, Kison (4), Moose (4), Veale (5), Miller (6), Giusti (8) vs PALMER, Hall (9)
Home Runs: Hebner-PIT
Attendance: 53,239

GAME 3 AT PIT OCT 12

BAL	000 000 100	1	3	3
PIT	100 001 30X	5	7	0

Pitchers: CUELLAR, Dukes (7), Watt (8) VS BLASS
Home Runs: F.Robinson-BAL, Robertson-PIT
Attendance: 50,403

GAME 4 AT PIT OCT 13

BAL	300 000 000	3	4	1
PIT	201 000 10X	4	14	0

Pitchers: Dobson, Jackson (6), WATT (7), Richert (8) vs Walker, KISON (1), Giusti (8)
Attendance: 51,378

GAME 5 AT PIT OCT 14

BAL	000 000 000	0	2	1
PIT	021 010 00X	4	9	0

Pitchers: McNALLY, Leonhard (5), Dukes (6) vs BRILES
Home Runs: Robertson-PIT
Attendance: 51,377

GAME 6 AT BAL OCT 16

PIT	011 000 000 0	2	9	1
BAL	000 001 100 1	3	8	0

Pitchers: Moose, R.Johnson (6), Giusti (7), MILLER (10) vs Palmer, Dobson (10), McNALLY (10)
Home Runs: Clemente-PIT, Buford-BAL
Attendance: 44,174

GAME 7 AT BAL OCT 17

PIT	000 100 010	2	6	1
BAL	000 000 010	1	4	0

Pitchers: BLASS vs CUELLAR, Dobson (9), McNally (9)
Home Runs: Clemente-PIT
Attendance: 47,291

Pittsburgh traded wins with Cincinnati through the first four games—winning the first and third—and took a lead into the ninth inning of the fifth game before a home run and a wild pitch undid them.

Cincinnati got eight hits in each of the first two games. In the first game, though, only Joe Morgan's first-inning homer produced a run, and the Reds lost 1–5. But the next day, five first-inning hits gave the Reds four runs and a lead the Pirates could not overcome.

Pirate catcher Manny Sanguillen brought Pittsburgh back in Game Three with a home run in the fifth and the game-winning RBI in the eighth. But Reds pitcher Ross Grimsley evened the series for Cincinnati the next day with a two-hitter, in the series' only complete-game performance.

Game Five was Pittsburgh's for 8½ innings. The Pirates scored first, and held the lead into the bottom of the ninth. But Johnny Bench opened the Reds' half of the ninth with a game-tying home run, and Tony Perez and Denis Menke followed him with singles. Bob Moose came in and retired the next two men, though George Foster (running for Perez) took third on a fly to right. Moose then threw away the pennant with a run-scoring, series-ending wild pitch.

Cincinnati Reds (West), 3; Pittsburgh Pirates (East) 2

CIN (W)

PLAYER/POS	AVG	G	AB	R	H	2B	3B	HR	RB	BB	SO	SB
Johnny Bench, c	.333	5	18	3	6	1	1	1	2	1	3	2
Jack Billingham, p	.000	1	2	0	0	0	0	0	0	0	1	0
Pedro Borbon, p	.000	3	0	0	0	0	0	0	0	0	0	0
Clay Carroll, p	.000	2	0	0	0	0	0	0	0	0	0	0
Darrel Chaney, ss	.188	5	16	3	3	0	0	0	1	1	1	1
Dave Concepcion, ss-1	.000	3	2	0	0	0	0	0	0	0	0	0
George Foster, pr	.000	1	0	1	0	0	0	0	0	0	0	0
Cesar Geronimo, of	.100	5	20	2	2	0	0	1	1	0	2	0
Ross Grimsley, p	.500	1	4	0	2	1	0	0	1	0	1	0
Don Gullett, p	.500	2	2	0	1	0	0	0	0	0	0	0
Joe Hague, ph	.000	3	1	0	0	0	0	0	0	2	1	0
Tom Hall, p	.000	2	1	0	0	0	0	0	0	0	0	0
Jim Mc Glothlin, p	.000	1	0	0	0	0	0	0	0	0	0	0
Hal Mc Rae, ph	.000	1	0	0	0	0	0	0	0	0	0	0
Denis Menke, 3b	.250	5	16	1	4	1	0	0	0	4	3	0
Joe Morgan, 2b	.263	5	19	5	5	0	0	2	3	1	2	1
Gary Nolan, p	.000	1	2	0	0	0	0	0	0	0	1	0
Tony Perez, 1b	.200	5	20	0	4	1	0	0	2	0	7	0
Pete Rose, of	.450	5	20	1	9	4	0	0	2	1	2	0
Bobby Tolan, of	.238	5	21	3	5	1	1	0	4	0	4	0
Ted Uhlaender, ph	.500	2	2	0	1	0	0	0	0	0	0	0
TOTAL	.253		166	19	42	9	2	4	16	10	28	4

PITCHER	W	L	ERA	G	GS	CG	SV	SHO	IP	H	ER	BB	SO
Jack Billingham	0	0	3.86	1	1	0	0	0	4.2	5	2	2	4
Pedro Borbon	0	0	2.08	3	0	0	0	0	4.1	2	1	0	1
Clay Carroll	1	1	3.38	2	0	0	0	0	2.2	2	1	3	0
Ross Grimsley	1	0	1.00	1	1	1	0	0	9.0	2	1	0	5
Don Gullett	0	1	8.00	2	2	0	0	0	9.0	12	8	0	5
Tom Hall	1	0	1.23	2	0	0	0	0	7.1	3	1	3	8
Jim Mc Glothlin	0	0	0.00	1	0	0	0	0	1.0	0	0	0	0
Gary Nolan	0	0	1.50	1	1	0	0	0	6.0	4	1	1	4
TOTAL	3	2	3.07	13	5	1	0	0	44.0	30	15	9	27

PIT (E)

PLAYER/POS	AVG	G	AB	R	H	2B	3B	HR	RB	BB	SO	SB
Gene Alley, ss	.000	5	16	1	0	0	0	0	0	0	3	0
Steve Blass, p	.000	2	6	0	0	0	0	0	0	0	3	0
Nelson Briles, p	.000	1	2	0	0	0	0	0	0	0	1	0
Dave Cash, 2b	.211	5	19	0	4	0	0	0	3	0	0	0
Roberto Clemente, of	.235	5	17	1	4	1	0	1	2	3	5	0
Gene Clines, ph	.000	3	2	1	0	0	0	0	0	0	1	0
Vic Davalillo, ph	.000	1	0	0	0	0	0	0	0	1	0	0
Dock Ellis, p-1	.000	2	1	0	0	0	0	0	0	0	0	0
Dave Giusti, p	.000	3	1	0	0	0	0	0	0	0	0	0
Richie Hebner, 3b	.188	5	16	2	3	1	0	0	1	1	3	0
Ramon Hernandez, p	.000	3	0	0	0	0	0	0	0	0	0	0
Bob Johnson, p	.000	2	1	0	0	0	0	0	0	0	1	0
Bruce Kison, p	.000	2	0	0	0	0	0	0	0	0	0	0
Milt May, c	.500	1	2	0	1	0	0	0	1	0	0	0
Bill Mazeroski, ph	.500	2	2	0	1	0	0	0	0	0	1	0
Bob Miller, p	.000	1	0	0	0	0	0	0	0	0	0	0
Bob Moose, p	.000	2	0	0	0	0	0	0	0	0	0	0
Al Oliver, of	.250	5	20	3	5	2	1	1	3	0	4	0
Bob Robertson, 1b	.000	4	0	0	0	0	0	0	0	1	0	0
Manny Sanguillen, c	.313	5	16	4	5	1	0	1	2	0	0	0
Willie Stargell, 1b-5,of-1	.063	5	16	1	1	1	0	0	1	2	5	0
Rennie Stennett, of-5,2b-1	.286	5	21	2	6	0	0	0	1	1	0	0
Luke Walker, p	.000	1	0	0	0	0	0	0	0	0	0	0
TOTAL	.190		158	15	30	6	1	3	14	9	27	0

PITCHER	W	L	ERA	G	GS	CG	SV	SHO	IP	H	ER	BB	SO
Steve Blass	1	0	1.72	2	2	0	0	0	15.2	12	3	6	5
Nelson Briles	0	0	3.00	1	1	0	0	0	6.0	6	2	1	3
Dock Ellis	0	1	0.00	1	1	0	0	0	5.0	5	0	1	3
Dave Giusti	0	1	6.75	3	0	0	1	0	2.2	5	2	0	3
Ramon Hernandez	0	0	2.70	3	0	0	1	0	3.1	1	1	0	3
Bob Johnson	0	0	3.00	2	0	0	0	0	6.0	4	2	2	7
Bruce Kison	1	0	0.00	2	0	0	0	0	2.1	1	0	0	3
Bob Miller	0	0	0.00	1	0	0	0	0	1.0	0	0	0	1
Bob Moose	0	1	54.00	2	1	0	0	0	0.2	5	4	0	0
Luke Walker	0	0	18.00	1	0	0	0	0	1.0	3	2	0	0
TOTAL	2	3	3.30	18	5	0	2	0	43.2	42	16	10	28

Oakland turned back the Tigers in the first two games, but Detroit evened the series before succumbing in the fifth game.

In Game One, Tiger Al Kaline homered off Rollie Fingers in the eleventh to give starter Mickey Lolich a 2–1 lead. But in the last of the inning, pinch hitter Gonzalo Marquez singled off Tiger reliever Chuck Seelbach with two on to drive in the tying run, and Gene Tenace scored to win it on the same play as right fielder Kaline threw the ball away. Blue Moon Odom increased the A's series lead with a three-hit shutout in Game Two, but Detroit's Joe Coleman retaliated with 14 strikeouts and a shutout of his own to save the Tigers from elimination in Game Three.

In Game Four the A's pulled out of a 1–1 tie with two runs in the top of the tenth. But Detroit in its half of the inning went through three Oakland relievers for three runs and the win. In the finale, after Odom, the A's starter, had given Detroit a run and a brief lead in the first, he and Vida Blue divided eight shutout innings between them as the A's scored twice to capture their first pennant since Connie Mack won his last in Philadelphia forty-one years earlier.

Oakland A's (West), 3; Detroit Tigers (East) 2

OAK (W)

PLAYER/POS	AVG	G	AB	R	H	2B	3B	HR	RB	BB	SO	SB
Matty Alou, of	.381	5	21	2	8	4	0	0	2	0	2	1
Sal Bando, 3b	.200	5	20	0	4	0	0	0	0	0	3	0
Vida Blue, p	.000	4	1	0	0	0	0	0	0	0	0	0
Bert Campaneris, ss	.429	2	7	3	3	0	0	0	0	1	0	2
Tim Cullen, ss	.000	2	1	0	0	0	0	0	0	0	0	0
Dave Duncan, c	.000	2	2	0	0	0	0	0	0	1	1	0
Mike Epstein, 1b	.188	5	16	1	3	0	0	1	1	4	5	1
Rollie Fingers, p	.000	3	1	0	0	0	0	0	0	0	0	0
Dick Green, 2b	.125	5	8	0	1	1	0	0	0	0	0	0
Dave Hamilton, p	.000	1	0	0	0	0	0	0	0	0	0	0
Mike Hegan, 1b-1	.000	3	1	1	0	0	0	0	0	0	0	0
George Hendrick, of-1	.143	5	7	2	1	0	0	0	0	0	1	0
Ken Holtzman, p	.000	1	1	0	0	0	0	0	0	0	1	0
Joe Horlen, p	.000	1	0	0	0	0	0	0	0	0	0	0
Catfish Hunter, p	.167	2	6	0	1	0	0	0	0	0	2	0
Reggie Jackson, of	.278	5	18	1	5	1	0	0	2	1	6	2
Ted Kubiak, 2b-3,ss-1	.500	4	4	0	2	0	0	0	1	0	0	0
Bob Locker, p	.000	2	0	0	0	0	0	0	0	0	0	0
Angel Mangual, ph	.000	3	3	0	0	0	0	0	0	0	1	0
Gonzalo Marquez, ph	.667	3	3	1	2	0	0	0	1	0	0	0
Dal Maxvill, ss-4,2b-1	.125	3	8	0	1	0	0	0	0	1	2	1
Don Mincher, ph	.000	1	1	0	0	0	0	0	0	0	1	0
Blue Moon Odom, p-2	.250	3	4	0	1	1	0	0	0	0	1	0
Joe Rudi, of	.250	5	20	1	5	1	0	0	2	1	4	0
Gene Tenace, c-5,2b-2	.059	5	17	1	1	0	0	0	1	3	5	0
TOTAL	.224		170	13	38	8	0	1	10	12	35	7

PITCHER	W	L	ERA	G	GS	CG	SV	SHO	IP	H	ER	BB	SO
Vida Blue	0	0	0.00	4	0	0	1	0	5.1	4	0	1	5
Rollie Fingers	1	0	1.69	3	0	0	0	0	5.1	4	1	1	3
Dave Hamilton	0	0	INF	1	0	0	0	0	0.0	1	0	1	0
Ken Holtzman	0	1	4.50	1	1	0	0	0	4.0	4	2	2	2
Joe Horlen	0	1	INF	1	0	0	0	0	0.0	0	1	1	0
Catfish Hunter	0	0	1.17	2	2	0	0	0	15.1	10	2	5	9
Bob Locker	0	0	13.50	2	0	0	0	0	2.0	4	3	0	1
Blue Moon Odom	2	0	0.00	2	2	1	0	1	14.0	5	0	2	5
TOTAL	3	2	1.76	16	5	1	1	1	46.0	32	9	13	25

DET (E)

PLAYER/POS	AVG	G	AB	R	H	2B	3B	HR	RB	BB	SO	SB
Ed Brinkman, ss	.250	1	4	0	1	1	0	0	0	0	0	0
Ike Brown, 1b	.500	1	2	0	1	0	0	0	2	0	1	0
Gates Brown, ph	.000	3	2	1	0	0	0	0	0	1	0	0
Norm Cash, 1b	.267	5	15	1	4	0	0	1	2	2	3	0
Joe Coleman, p	.500	1	2	0	1	0	0	0	0	1	0	0
Bill Freehan, c	.250	3	12	2	3	1	0	1	3	0	1	0
Woody Fryman, p	.000	2	3	0	0	0	0	0	0	0	0	0
Tom Haller, ph	.000	1	1	0	0	0	0	0	0	0	0	0
John Hiller, p	.000	3	0	0	0	0	0	0	0	0	0	0
Willie Horton, of-3	.100	5	10	0	1	0	0	0	0	1	3	0
Al Kaline, of	.263	5	19	3	5	0	0	1	1	2	2	0
John Knox, pr	.000	1	0	0	0	0	0	0	0	0	0	0
Lerrin La Grow, p	.000	1	0	0	0	0	0	0	0	0	0	0
Mickey Lolich, p	.000	2	7	0	0	0	0	0	0	0	2	0
Dick Mc Auliffe, ss-4,2b-1	.200	5	20	3	4	0	0	1	1	1	4	0
Jim Northrup, of	.357	5	14	0	5	0	0	0	1	2	3	0
Aurelio Rodriguez, 3b	.000	5	16	0	0	0	0	0	0	2	2	0
Fred Scherman, p	.000	1	0	0	0	0	0	0	0	0	0	0
Chuck Seelbach, p	.000	2	0	0	0	0	0	0	0	0	0	0
Duke Sims, c-2,of-2	.214	4	14	0	3	2	1	0	0	1	2	0
Mickey Stanley, of-3	.333	4	6	0	2	0	0	0	0	0	0	0
Tony Taylor, 2b	.133	4	15	0	2	2	0	0	0	0	2	0
Chris Zachary, p	.000	1	0	0	0	0	0	0	0	0	0	0
TOTAL	.198		162	10	32	6	1	4	10	13	25	0

PITCHER	W	L	ERA	G	GS	CG	SV	SHO	IP	H	ER	BB	SO
Joe Coleman	1	0	0.00	1	1	1	0	1	9.0	7	0	3	14
Woody Fryman	0	2	3.65	2	2	0	0	0	12.1	11	5	2	8
John Hiller	1	0	0.00	3	0	0	0	0	3.1	1	0	1	1
Lerrin La Grow	0	0	0.00	1	0	0	0	0	1.0	0	0	0	1
Mickey Lolich	0	1	1.42	2	2	0	0	0	19.0	14	3	5	10
Fred Scherman	0	0	0.00	1	0	0	0	0	0.2	1	0	0	1
Chuck Seelbach	0	0	18.00	2	0	0	0	0	1.0	4	2	0	0
Chris Zachary	0	0	INF	1	0	0	0	0	0.0	0	1	1	0
TOTAL	2	3	2.14	13	5	1	0	1	46.1	38	11	12	35

GAME 1 AT OAK OCT 7

DET	010 000 000 01	2	6	2
OAK	001 000 000 02	3	10	1

Pitchers: LOLICH, Seelbach (11) VS Hunter, Blue (9), FINGERS (9)
Home Runs: Cash-DET, Kaline-DET
Attendance: 29,536

GAME 2 AT OAK OCT 8

DET	000 000 000	0	3	1
OAK	100 040 00X	5	8	0

Pitchers: FRYMAN, Zachary (5), Scherman (5), LaGrow (6), Hiller (7) VS ODOM
Attendance: 31,088

GAME 3 AT DET OCT 10

OAK	000 000 000	0	7	0
DET	000 200 01X	3	8	1

Pitchers: HOLTZMAN, Fingers (5), Blue (6), Locker (7) vs COLEMAN
Home Runs: Freehan-DET
Attendance: 41,156

GAME 4 AT DET OCT 11

OAK	000 000 100 2	3	9	2
DET	001 000 000 3	4	10	1

Pitchers: Hunter, Fingers (8), Blue (9), Locker (10), HORLEN (10), Hamilton (10) VS Lolich, Seelbach (10), HILLER (10)
Home Runs: McAuliffe-DET, Epstein-OAK
Attendance: 37,615

GAME 5 AT DET OCT 12

OAK	010 100 000	2	4	0
DET	100 000 000	1	5	2

Pitchers: ODOM, Blue (6) vs FRYMAN, Hiller (9)
Attendance: 50,276

Oakland slugger Reggie Jackson missed the Series with a pulled hamstring, but Gene Tenace (the A's backup catcher during the season) took up the slack, hitting four of the club's five homers and driving in nine of their sixteen runs.

Six of the seven games were decided by a single run. Oakland won the first two in Cincinnati, 3–2 and 2–1. Tenace made the difference in the opener, driving in all the A's runs with a two-run homer in the second inning and a solo shot in the fifth. In the second game, A's starting pitcher Catfish Hunter singled in a run in the second inning which proved the margin of his victory. His 8⅔-inning performance was the longest mound outing in a Series which saw the two clubs together use nearly seven pitchers per game.

Cincinnati took the first game in Oakland, 1–0. The A's' Blue Moon Odom dueled the Reds' Jack Billingham scorelessly on one hit through six innings before giving up the game's only run on a single-sacrifice-single in the seventh. Billingham, too, yielded only three hits in eight-plus innings before yielding to ace reliever Clay Carroll, who retired the side in the ninth.

Oakland won Game Four, 3–2. Tenace opened the scoring with a solo homer in the fifth. The Reds' Bobby Tolan doubled in a pair in the eighth to put Cincinnati ahead, but in the last of the ninth four successive A's singles scored two runs, with Tenace scoring the game winner on pinch hitter Angel Mangual's hit. Tenace homered again in Game Five for three runs, but it wasn't enough as the Reds tied the score in the eighth and won on Pete Rose's RBI single in the ninth.

The Reds produced the Series' only blowout with five runs in the seventh inning of Game Six to make the score 8–1, where it remained. The finale saw Tenace drive in a run in the top of the first for a narrow Oakland lead which held until the Reds tied the game in the fifth. In the sixth the A's scored twice—Tenace doubling in the go-ahead run. Cincinnati scored once more in the eighth as a runner inherited by A's reliever Rollie Fingers came home on a sacrifice fly. But Fingers permitted no other runs to score, and the A's took the crown with their fourth one-run victory.

Oakland Athletics (AL), 4;
Cincinnati Reds (NL) 3

OAK (A)

PLAYER/POS	AVG	G	AB	R	H	2B	3B	HR	RB	BB	SO	SB
Matty Alou, of	.042	7	24	0	1	0	0	0	0	3	0	1
Sal Bando, 3b	.269	7	26	2	7	1	0	0	1	2	5	0
Vida Blue, p	.000	4	1	0	0	0	0	0	0	2	1	0
Bert Campaneris, ss	.179	7	28	1	5	0	0	0	0	1	4	0
Dave Duncan, c-1	.200	3	5	0	1	0	0	0	0	1	3	0
Mike Epstein, 1b	.000	6	16	1	0	0	0	0	0	5	3	0
Rollie Fingers, p	.000	6	1	0	0	0	0	0	0	0	0	0
Dick Green, 2b	.333	7	18	0	6	2	0	0	1	0	4	0
Dave Hamilton, p	.000	2	0	0	0	0	0	0	0	0	0	0
Mike Hegan, 1b-5	.200	6	5	0	1	0	0	0	0	0	2	0
George Hendrick, of	.133	5	15	3	2	0	0	0	0	1	2	0
Ken Holtzman, p	.000	3	5	0	0	0	0	0	0	0	0	0
Joe Horlen, p	.000	1	0	0	0	0	0	0	0	0	0	0
Catfish Hunter, p	.200	3	5	0	1	0	0	0	1	2	1	0
Ted Kubiak, 2b	.333	4	3	0	1	0	0	0	0	0	0	0
Allan Lewis, pr	.000	6	0	2	0	0	0	0	0	0	0	0
Bob Locker, p	.000	1	0	0	0	0	0	0	0	0	0	0
Angel Mangual, of-2	.300	4	10	1	3	0	0	0	1	0	0	0
Gonzalo Marquez, ph	.600	5	5	0	3	0	0	0	1	0	0	0
Don Mincher, ph	1.000	3	1	0	1	0	0	0	1	0	0	0
Blue Moon Odom, p-2	.000	4	4	0	0	0	0	0	0	0	3	0
Joe Rudi, of	.240	7	25	1	6	0	0	1	1	2	5	0
Gene Tenace, c-6,1b-1	.348	7	23	5	8	1	0	4	9	2	4	0
TOTAL	.209		220	16	46	4	0	5	16	21	37	1

PITCHER	W	L	ERA	G	GS	CG	SV	SHO	IP	H	ER	BB	SO
Vida Blue	0	1	4.15	4	1	0	1	0	8.2	8	4	5	5
Rollie Fingers	1	1	1.74	6	0	0	2	0	10.1	4	2	4	11
Dave Hamilton	0	0	6.75	2	0	0	0	0	1.1	2	1	2	1
Ken Holtzman	1	0	2.13	3	2	0	0	0	12.2	11	3	3	4
Joe Horlen	0	0	27.00	1	0	0	0	0	1.1	3	4	1	1
Catfish Hunter	2	0	2.81	3	2	0	0	0	16.0	12	5	6	11
Bob Locker	0	0	0.00	1	0	0	0	0	0.1	1	0	0	0
Blue Moon Odom	0	1	1.59	2	2	0	0	0	11.1	5	2	6	13
TOTAL	4	3	3.05	22	7	0	3	0	62.0	46	21	27	46

CIN (N)

PLAYER/POS	AVG	G	AB	R	H	2B	3B	HR	RB	BB	SO	SB
Johnny Bench, c	.261	7	23	4	6	1	0	1	1	5	5	2
Jack Billingham, p	.000	3	5	0	0	0	0	0	0	0	4	0
Pedro Borbon, p	.000	6	0	0	0	0	0	0	0	0	0	0
Clay Carroll, p	.000	5	0	0	0	0	0	0	0	0	0	0
Darrel Chaney, ss-3	.000	4	7	0	0	0	0	0	0	2	2	0
Dave Concepcion, ss-5	.308	6	13	2	4	0	1	0	2	2	2	1
George Foster, of-1	.000	2	0	0	0	0	0	0	0	0	0	0
Cesar Geronimo, of	.158	7	19	1	3	0	0	0	3	1	4	1
Ross Grimsley, p	.000	4	2	0	0	0	0	0	0	0	2	0
Don Gullett, p	.000	1	2	0	0	0	0	0	0	0	0	0
Joe Hague, of-1	.000	3	3	0	0	0	0	0	0	0	0	0
Tom Hall, p	.000	4	2	0	0	0	0	0	0	0	1	0
Julian Javier, ph	.000	4	2	0	0	0	0	0	0	0	0	0
Jim Mc Glothlin, p	.000	1	1	0	0	0	0	0	0	0	0	0
Hal Mc Rae, of-2	.444	5	9	1	4	1	0	0	2	0	1	0
Denis Menke, 3b	.083	7	24	1	2	0	0	1	2	2	6	0
Joe Morgan, 2b	.125	7	24	4	3	2	0	0	1	6	3	2
Gary Nolan, p	.000	2	3	0	0	0	0	0	0	0	3	0
Tony Perez, 1b	.435	7	23	3	10	2	0	0	2	4	4	0
Pete Rose, of	.214	7	28	3	6	0	0	1	2	4	4	1
Bobby Tolan, of	.269	7	26	2	7	1	0	0	6	1	4	5
Ted Uhlaender, ph	.250	4	4	0	1	1	0	0	0	0	1	0
TOTAL	.209		220	21	46	8	1	3	21	27	46	12

PITCHER	W	L	ERA	G	GS	CG	SV	SHO	IP	H	ER	BB	SO
Jack Billingham	1	0	0.00	3	2	0	1	0	13.2	6	0	4	11
Pedro Borbon	0	-1	3.86	6	0	0	0	0	7.0	7	3	2	4
Clay Carroll	0	1	1.59	5	0	0	1	0	5.2	6	1	4	3
Ross Grimsley	2	1	2.57	4	1	0	0	0	7.0	7	2	3	2
Don Gullett	0	0	1.29	1	1	0	0	0	7.0	5	1	2	4
Tom Hall	0	0	0.00	4	0	0	1	0	8.1	6	0	2	7
Jim Mc Glothlin	0	0	12.00	1	1	0	0	0	3.0	2	4	2	3
Gary Nolan	0	1	3.38	2	2	0	0	0	10.2	7	4	2	3
TOTAL	3	2	2.17	26	7	0	3	0	62.1	46	15	21	37

GAME 1 AT CIN OCT 14

OAK	020 010 000	3	4	0
CIN	010 100 000	2	7	0

Pitchers: HOLTZMAN, Fingers (6), Blue (7) VS NOLAN, Borbon (7), Carroll (8)
Home Runs: Tenace-OAK (2)
Attendance: 52,918

GAME 2 AT CIN OCT 15

OAK	011 000 000	2	9	2
CIN	000 000 001	1	6	0

Pitchers: HUNTER, Fingers (9) VS GRIMSLEY, Borbon (6), Hall (8)
Home Runs: Rudi-OAK
Attendance: 53,224

GAME 3 AT OAK OCT 18

CIN	000 000 100	1	4	2
OAK	000 000 000	0	3	2

Pitchers: BILLINGHAM, Carroll (9) VS ODOM, Blue (8), Fingers (8)
Attendance: 49,410

GAME 4 AT OAK OCT 19

CIN	000 000 020	2	7	1
OAK	000 010 002	3	10	1

Pitchers: Gullett, Borbon (8), CARROLL (9) vs Holtzman, Blue (8), FINGERS (9)
Home Runs: Tenace-OAK
Attendance: 49,410

GAME 5 AT OAK OCT 20

CIN	100 110 011	5	8	0
OAK	030 100 000	4	7	2

Pitchers: McGlothlin, Borbon (4), Hall (5), Carroll (7), GRIMSLEY (8), Billingham (9) vs Hunter, FINGERS (9), Hamilton (9)
Home Runs: Rose-CIN, Tenace-OAK, Menke-CIN
Attendance: 49,410

GAME 6 AT CIN OCT 21

OAK	000 010 000	1	7	1
CIN	000 111 50X	8	10	0

Pitchers: BLUE, Locker (6), Hamilton (7), Horlen (7) vs Nolan, GRIMSLEY (5), Borbon (6), Hall (7)
Home Runs: Bench-CIN
Attendance: 52,737

GAME 7 AT CIN OCT 22

OAK	100 002 000	3	6	1
CIN	000 010 010	2	4	2

Pitchers: Odom, HUNTER (5), Holtzman (8), Fingers (8) vs Billingham, BORBON (6), Carroll (6), Grimsley (7), Hall (8)
Attendance: 56,040

The Mets received strong pitching throughout the series, and their offense came through just often enough to defeat Cincinnati in five games.

Though three Reds pitchers held New York to three hits in Game One, the single Met run in the second seemed for a time enough for a win. But Tom Seaver gave up a home run to Pete Rose in the eighth and lost the game in the ninth when Johnny Bench homered. Not wanting another last-inning loss in Game Two, the Mets unloaded for four runs in the top of the ninth to add to their one in the fourth. But this time one would have been enough as Jon Matlack blanked the Reds on two hits.

The Mets made it easy for Jerry Koosman in Game Three in New York, scoring nine times in the first four innings. Things were more difficult for shortstop Bud Harrelson, who exchanged blows with Pete Rose following Rose's hard slide in the fifth inning. A bench-clearing melee ensued, and fans in the left field stands showered Rose with debris until a delegation of Tom Seaver, Willie Mays and Rusty Staub visited the area to calm nerves and eliminate the threat of a forfeit. In Game Four, though, Met bats were stifled once again as four Reds pitchers combined for a 12-inning three-hitter. The Reds won the game and tied the series on Rose's sweetly vengeful twelfth-inning homer.

In the finale the Mets took a quick two-run lead. Cincinnati tied the game in the top of the fifth, but New York retaliated with four more in the bottom of the inning. Seaver—and Tug Mc-Graw in the ninth—held the Reds scoreless the rest of the way.

New York Mets (East), 3; Cincinnati Reds (West) 2

NY (E)

PLAYER/POS	AVG	G	AB	R	H	2B	3B	HR	RB	BB	SO	SB
Ken Boswell, ph	.000	1	1	0	0	0	0	0	0	0	0	0
Wayne Garrett, 3b	.087	5	23	1	2	1	0	0	1	0	5	0
Jerry Grote, c	.211	5	19	2	4	0	0	0	2	1	3	0
Don Hahn, of	.235	5	17	2	4	0	0	0	1	2	4	0
Bud Harrelson, ss	.167	5	18	1	3	0	0	0	2	1	1	0
Cleon Jones, of	.300	5	20	3	6	2	0	0	3	2	4	0
Jerry Koosman, p	.500	1	4	1	2	0	0	0	1	0	0	0
Ed Kranepool, of	.500	1	2	0	1	0	0	0	2	0	0	0
Jon Matlack, p	.000	1	2	0	0	0	0	0	0	1	2	0
Willie Mays, of	.333	1	3	1	1	0	0	0	1	0	0	0
Tug Mc Graw, p	.000	2	1	0	0	0	0	0	0	0	1	0
Felix Millan, 2b	.316	5	19	5	6	0	0	0	2	2	1	0
John Milner, 1b	.176	5	17	2	3	0	0	0	1	5	3	0
Harry Parker, p	.000	1	0	0	0	0	0	0	0	0	0	0
Tom Seaver, p	.333	2	6	1	2	2	0	0	1	1	1	0
Rusty Staub, of	.200	4	15	4	3	0	0	3	5	3	2	0
George Stone, p	.000	1	1	0	0	0	0	0	0	0	1	0
TOTAL	.220		168	23	37	5	0	3	22	19	28	0

PITCHER	W	L	ERA	G	GS	CG	SV	SHO	IP	H	ER	BB	SO
Jerry Koosman	1	0	2.00	1	1	1	0	0	9.0	8	2	0	9
Jon Matlack	1	0	0.00	1	1	1	0	1	9.0	2	0	3	9
Tug Mc Graw	0	0	0.00	2	0	0	1	0	5.0	4	0	3	3
Harry Parker	0	1	9.00	1	0	0	0	0	1.0	1	1	1	0
Tom Seaver	1	1	1.62	2	2	1	0	0	16.2	13	3	5	17
George Stone	0	0	1.35	1	1	0	0	0	6.2	3	1	2	4
TOTAL	3	2	1.33	8	5	3	1	1	47.1	31	7	13	42

CIN (W)

PLAYER/POS	AVG	G	AB	R	H	2B	3B	HR	RB	BB	SO	SB
Ed Armbrister, of-1	.167	3	6	0	1	0	0	0	0	0	5	0
Johnny Bench, c	.263	5	19	1	5	2	0	1	1	2	2	0
Jack Billingham, p	.000	2	3	0	0	0	0	0	0	0	1	0
Pedro Borbon, p	.000	4	0	0	0	0	0	0	0	0	0	0
Clay Carroll, p	.000	3	0	0	0	0	0	0	0	0	0	0
Darrel Chaney, ph	.000	5	9	0	0	0	0	0	0	3	4	0
Ed Crosby, ss	.500	2	2	0	1	0	0	0	0	0	1	0
Dan Driessen, 3b	.167	4	12	0	2	1	0	0	1	0	2	0
Phil Gagliano, ph	.000	3	3	0	0	0	0	0	0	0	2	0
Cesar Geronimo, of	.067	4	15	0	1	0	0	0	0	0	7	0
Ken Griffey, of-2	.143	3	7	0	1	1	0	0	0	0	1	0
Ross Grimsley, p	.000	2	0	0	0	0	0	0	0	0	0	0
Don Gullett, p	.000	3	1	0	0	0	0	0	0	0	0	0
Tom Hall, p	.000	3	0	0	0	0	0	0	0	0	0	0
Hal King, ph	.500	3	2	0	1	0	0	0	0	1	1	0
Andy Kosco, of	.300	3	10	0	3	0	0	0	0	2	3	0
Denis Menke, ss-2,3b-2	.222	3	9	1	2	0	0	1	1	1	2	0
Joe Morgan, 2b	.100	5	20	1	2	1	0	0	1	2	2	0
Roger Nelson, p	.000	1	1	0	0	0	0	0	0	0	1	0
Fred Norman, p	.000	1	1	0	0	0	0	0	0	0	1	0
Tony Perez, 1b	.091	5	22	1	2	0	0	1	2	0	4	0
Pete Rose, of	.381	5	21	3	8	1	0	2	2	2	2	0
Larry Stahl, ph	.500	4	4	1	2	0	0	0	0	0	1	0
Dave Tomlin, p	.000	1	0	0	0	0	0	0	0	0	0	0
TOTAL	.186		167	8	31	6	0	5	8	13	42	0

PITCHER	W	L	ERA	G	GS	CG	SV	SHO	IP	H	ER	BB	SO
Jack Billingham	0	1	4.50	2	2	0	0	0	12.0	9	6	4	9
Pedro Borbon	1	0	0.00	4	0	0	1	0	4.2	3	0	0	3
Clay Carroll	1	0	1.29	3	0	0	0	0	7.0	5	1	1	2
Ross Grimsley	0	1	12.27	2	1	0	0	0	3.2	7	5	2	3
Don Gullett	0	1	2.00	3	1	0	0	0	9.0	4	2	3	6
Tom Hall	0	0	67.50	3	0	0	0	0	0.2	3	5	4	1
Roger Nelson	0	0	0.00	1	0	0	0	0	2.1	0	0	1	0
Fred Norman	0	0	1.80	1	1	0	0	0	5.0	1	1	3	3
Dave Tomlin	0	0	16.20	1	0	0	0	0	1.2	5	3	1	1
TOTAL	2	3	4.50	20	5	0	1	0	46.0	37	23	19	28

GAME 1 AT CIN OCT 6

NY	010	000	000	1	3	0
CIN	000	000	011	2	6	0

Pitchers: SEAVER vs Billingham, Hall (9), BORBON (9)
Home Runs: Rose-CIN, Bench-CIN
Attendance: 53,431

GAME 2 AT CIN OCT 7

NY	000	100	004	5	7	0
CIN	000	000	000	0	2	0

Pitchers: MATLACK vs GULLETT, Carroll (6), Hall (9), Borbon (9)
Home Runs: Staub-NY
Attendance: 54,041

GAME 3 AT NY OCT 8

CIN	002	000	000	2	8	1
NY	151	200	00X	9	11	1

Pitchers: GRIMSLEY, Hall (2), Tomlin (3), Nelson (4), Borbon (7) vs KOOSMAN
Home Runs: Staub-NY (2), Menke-CIN
Attendance: 53,967

GAME 4 AT NY OCT 9

CIN	000	000	100	001	2	8	0
NY	001	000	000	000	1	3	2

Pitchers: Norman, Gullett (6), CARROLL (10), Borbon (12) vs Stone, McGraw (7), PARKER (12)
Home Runs: Perez-CIN, Rose-CIN
Attendance: 50,786

GAME 5 AT NY OCT 10

CIN	001	010	000	2	7	1
NY	200	041	00X	7	13	1

Pitchers: BILLINGHAM, Gullett (5), Carroll (5), Grimsley (7) vs SEAVER, McGraw (9)
Attendance: 50,323

The Orioles finally met their match in an LCS as Oakland took its second consecutive pennant. Baltimore started strong, chasing A's starter Vida Blue with four runs in the first inning as Jim Palmer—pitching the series opener for a change—blanked the A's on five hits. But Oakland snapped back in Game Two, with five of their six runs coming on homers by Sal Bando (two, for three runs), Joe Rudi, and Bert Campaneris.

Oriole Mike Cuellar and the A's Ken Holtzman cut down opposing batters for 10½ innings in Game Three before Oakland's Campaneris broke the 1–1 tie in the bottom of the eleventh with a leadoff home run. The next day Jim Palmer was driven out in the second inning by two Oakland runs, and the A's added to their lead with another run in the sixth. But Andy Etchebarren led a four-run Oriole comeback in the seventh with a three-run homer, and Bobby Grich's solo shot in the next inning gave the Orioles the margin they needed to win the game and tie the series.

The A's took it all in the finale, though, needing only one of their three runs as Catfish Hunter stopped Oakland cold on five scattered hits.

Oakland A's (West), 3; Baltimore Orioles (East) 2

OAK (W)

PLAYER/POS	AVG	G	AB	R	H	2B	3B	HR	RB	BB	SO	SB
Jesus Alou, dh-1	.333	4	6	0	2	0	0	0	1	0	1	0
Mike Andrews, 1b-1,dh-1	.000	2	1	0	0	0	0	0	0	0	0	0
Sal Bando, 3b	.167	5	18	2	3	0	0	2	3	3	6	0
Vida Blue, p	.000	2	0	0	0	0	0	0	0	0	0	0
Pat Bourque, dh	.000	2	1	0	0	0	0	0	0	1	1	0
Bert Campaneris, ss	.333	5	21	3	7	1	0	2	3	2	2	3
Billy Conigliaro, of	.000	1	4	0	0	0	0	0	0	0	2	0
Vic Davalillo, 1b-2,of-2	.625	4	8	2	5	1	1	0	1	1	0	0
Rollie Fingers, p	.000	3	0	0	0	0	0	0	0	0	0	0
Ray Fosse, c	.091	5	11	2	1	1	0	0	3	2	2	0
Dick Green, 2b	.077	5	13	0	1	1	0	0	1	1	4	0
Ken Holtzman, p	.000	1	0	0	0	0	0	0	0	0	0	0
Catfish Hunter, p	.000	2	0	0	0	0	0	0	0	0	0	0
Reggie Jackson, of	.143	5	21	0	3	0	0	0	0	0	6	0
Deron Johnson, dh	.100	4	10	0	1	0	0	0	0	2	6	0
Ted Kubiak, 2b	.000	3	2	0	0	0	0	0	0	0	1	0
Allan Lewis, pr	.000	2	0	1	0	0	0	0	0	0	0	0
Angel Mangual, of	.111	3	9	1	1	0	0	0	0	0	3	0
Blue Moon Odom, p-2	.000	1	0	0	0	0	0	0	0	0	0	0
Horacio Pina, p	.000	1	0	0	0	0	0	0	0	0	0	0
Joe Rudi, of	.222	5	18	1	4	0	0	1	3	3	1	0
Gene Tenace, 1b-5,c-3	.235	5	17	3	4	1	0	0	2	2	4	0
TOTAL	.200		160	15	32	5	1	5	15	17	39	3

PITCHER	W	L	ERA	G	GS	CG	SV	SHO	IP	H	ER	BB	SO
Vida Blue	0	1	10.29	2	2	0	0	0	7.0	8	8	5	3
Rollie Fingers	0	1	1.93	3	0	0	1	0	4.2	4	1	2	4
Ken Holtzman	1	0	0.82	1	1	1	0	0	11.0	3	1	1	7
Catfish Hunter	2	0	1.65	2	2	1	0	0	16.1	12	3	5	6
Blue Moon Odom	0	0	1.80	2	0	0	0	0	5.0	6	1	2	4
Horacio Pina	0	0	0.00	1	0	0	0	0	2.0	3	0	1	1
TOTAL	3	2	2.74	11	5	2	1	0	46.0	36	14	16	25

BAL (E)

PLAYER/POS	AVG	G	AB	R	H	2B	3B	HR	RB	BB	SO	SB
Doyle Alexander, p	.000	1	0	0	0	0	0	0	0	0	0	0
Frank Baker, ss	.000	2	0	0	0	0	0	0	0	0	0	0
Don Baylor, of-3	.273	4	11	3	3	0	0	0	1	3	5	0
Mark Belanger, ss	.125	5	16	0	2	0	0	0	1	1	1	0
Paul Blair, of	.167	5	18	2	3	0	0	0	0	1	5	0
Larry Brown, 3b	.000	1	0	0	0	0	0	0	0	0	0	0
Al Bumbry, of	.000	2	7	1	0	0	0	0	0	2	2	1
Rich Coggins, of	.444	2	9	1	4	1	0	0	0	0	0	0
Terry Crowley, of-1	.000	2	2	0	0	0	0	0	0	0	0	0
Mike Cuellar, p	.000	1	0	0	0	0	0	0	0	0	0	0
Tommy Davis, dh	.286	5	21	1	6	1	0	0	2	1	0	0
Andy Etchebarren, c	.357	4	14	1	5	1	0	1	4	0	1	0
Bobby Grich, 2b	.100	5	20	1	2	0	0	1	1	2	5	0
Grant Jackson, p	.000	2	0	0	0	0	0	0	0	0	0	0
Dave Nc Nally, p	.000	1	0	0	0	0	0	0	0	0	0	0
Jim Palmer, p	.000	3	0	0	0	0	0	0	0	0	0	0
Boog Powell, 1b	.000	1	4	1	0	0	0	0	0	0	1	0
Merv Rettenmund, of	.091	3	11	1	1	0	0	0	0	3	2	0
Bob Reynolds, p	.000	2	0	0	0	0	0	0	0	0	0	0
Brooks Robinson, 3b	.250	5	20	1	5	2	0	0	2	1	1	0
Eddie Watt, p	.000	1	0	0	0	0	0	0	0	0	0	0
Earl Williams, 1b-4,c-1	.278	5	18	2	5	2	0	1	4	2	2	0
TOTAL	.211		171	15	36	7	0	3	15	16	25	1

PITCHER	W	L	ERA	G	GS	CG	SV	SHO	IP	H	ER	BB	SO
Doyle Alexander	0	1	4.91	1	1	0	0	0	3.2	5	2	0	1
Mike Cuellar	0	1	1.80	1	1	1	0	0	10.0	4	2	3	11
Grant Jackson	1	0	0.00	2	0	0	0	0	3.0	0	0	1	0
Dave Nc Nally	0	1	5.87	1	1	0	0	0	7.2	7	5	2	7
Jim Palmer	1	0	1.84	3	2	1	0	1	14.2	11	3	8	15
Bob Reynolds	0	0	3.18	2	0	0	0	0	5.2	5	2	3	5
Eddie Watt	0	0	0.00	1	0	0	0	0	0.1	0	0	0	0
TOTAL	2	3	2.80	11	5	2	0	1	45.0	32	14	17	39

GAME 1 AT BAL OCT 6

OAK	000 000 000	0	5	1
BAL	400 000 11X	6	12	0

Pitchers: BLUE, Pina (1), Odom (3), Fingers (8) vs PALMER
Attendance: 41,279

GAME 2 AT BAL OCT 7

OAK	100 002 021	6	9	0
BAL	100 001 010	3	8	0

Pitchers: HUNTER, Fingers (8) VS McNALLY, Reynolds (8), G.Jackson (9)
Home Runs: Campaneris-OAK, Rudi-OAK, Bando-OAK (2)
Attendance: 48,425

GAME 3 AT OAK OCT 9

BAL	010 000 000 00	1	3	0
OAK	000 000 010 01	2	4	3

Pitchers: CUELLAR vs HOLTZMAN
Home Runs: Williams-BAL, Campaneris-OAK
Attendance: 34,367

GAME 4 AT OAK OCT 10

BAL	000 000 410	5	8	0
OAK	030 001 000	4	7	0

Pitchers: Palmer, Reynolds (2), Watt (7), G.JACKSON (7) vs Blue, FINGERS (7)
Home Runs: Etchebarren-BAL, Grich-BAL
Attendance: 27,497

GAME 5 AT OAK OCT 11

BAL	000 000 000	0	5	2
OAK	001 200 00X	3	7	0

Pitchers: ALEXANDER, Palmer (4) vs HUNTER
Attendance: 24,265

For the second year in a row, the A's were outpitched and outscored by their Series opposition, and this time they were outhit as well. But again, when the dust of Game Seven had risen, they still wore the crown. A's starter Ken Holtzman, who because of the American League's new designated hitter rule had not batted all season, doubled for the A's first hit in the third inning of Game One and scored the first Oakland run on a Met error. The A's scored again in the inning, enough for the win as Holtzman and two relievers held New York to a single run.

The Mets evened things in a Game Two that lasted a record 4 hours 13 minutes, scoring four runs with two out in the top of the twelfth inning for a lead the A's were not able to overcome. (Three of the runs scored on a pair of errors by second-baseman Mike Andrews, prompting a flap that rocked the baseball world as A's owner Charlie Finley tried—unsuccessfully—to "fire" Andrews by declaring him injured.) Final score of the slugfest: 10–7.

In a somewhat more normal third game, the Mets grabbed an early lead on Wayne Garrett's leadoff homer in the bottom of the first and scored a second run on two singles and wild pitch for a 2–0 lead that held up until Oakland tied the game in the eighth. In the eleventh, the A's Ted Kubiak worked his way around the bases on a walk, passed ball, and single for a lead that reliever Rollie Fingers held in the bottom of the inning.

New York evened the Series on Rusty Staub's three-run homer in the first inning of Game Four (scoring three more times later for a 6–1 win). The Mets moved in front on a sparkling 2–0 three-hitter by Jerry Koosman and Tug McGraw in Game Five, but lost their edge as the Series returned to Oakland for Game Six, losing when Reggie Jackson's doubles in the first and third drove in two runs to give the A's a lead New York was unable to overtake.

Oakland made the finale look easy. Bert Campaneris and Jackson both hit two-run homers in the third inning, and Campaneris scored a fifth run two innings later before New York finally got on the board in the sixth. In the ninth inning the Mets scored a second run with two outs, but reliever Darold Knowles came on for a record seventh pitching appearance and retired the final batter for his second Series save.

Oakland Athletics (AL), 4;
New York Mets (NL) 3

OAK (A)

PLAYER/POS	AVG	G	AB	R	H	2B	3B	HR	RB	BB	SO	SB
Jesus Alou, of-6	.158	7	19	0	3	1	0	0	0	3	0	0
Mike Andrews, 2b-1	.000	2	3	0	0	0	0	0	0	0	1	0
Sal Bando, 3b	.231	7	26	5	6	1	1	0	1	4	7	0
Vida Blue, p	.000	2	4	0	0	0	0	0	0	0	4	0
Pat Bourque, 1b	.500	2	2	0	1	0	0	0	0	0	0	0
Bert Campaneris, ss	.290	7	31	6	9	0	1	1	3	1	7	3
Billy Conigliaro, ph	.000	3	3	0	0	0	0	0	0	0	1	0
Vic Davalillo, of-4,1b-1	.091	6	11	0	1	0	0	0	0	2	1	0
Rollie Fingers, p	.333	6	3	0	1	0	0	0	0	0	1	0
Ray Fosse, c	.158	7	19	0	3	1	0	0	0	1	4	0
Dick Green, 2b	.063	7	16	0	1	0	0	0	0	1	6	0
Ken Holtzman, p	.667	3	3	2	2	2	0	0	0	0	0	0
Catfish Hunter, p	.000	2	5	0	0	0	0	0	0	0	3	0
Reggie Jackson, of	.310	7	29	3	9	3	1	1	6	2	7	0
Deron Johnson, 1b-2	.300	6	10	0	3	1	0	0	0	1	4	0
Darold Knowles, p	.000	7	0	0	0	0	0	0	0	0	0	0
Ted Kubiak, 2b	.000	4	3	1	0	0	0	0	0	0	1	0
Allan Lewis, pr	.000	3	0	1	0	0	0	0	0	0	0	0
Paul Lindblad, p	.000	3	1	0	0	0	0	0	0	0	0	0
Angel Mangual, of-1	.000	5	6	0	0	0	0	0	0	0	3	0
Blue Moon Odom, p-2	.000	3	1	0	0	0	0	0	0	0	1	0
Horacio Pina, p	.000	2	0	0	0	0	0	0	0	0	0	0
Joe Rudi, of	.333	7	27	3	9	2	0	0	4	3	4	0
Gene Tenace, 1b-7,c-3	.158	7	19	0	3	1	0	0	3	11	7	0
TOTAL	.212		241	21	51	12	3	2	20	28	62	3

PITCHER	W	L	ERA	G	GS	CG	SV	SHO	IP	H	ER	BB	SO
Vida Blue	0	1	4.91	2	2	0	0	0	11.0	10	6	3	8
Rollie Fingers	0	1	0.66	6	0	0	2	0	13.2	13	1	4	8
Ken Holtzman	2	1	4.22	3	3	0	0	0	10.2	13	5	5	6
Catfish Hunter	1	0	2.03	2	2	0	0	0	13.1	11	3	4	6
Darold Knowles	0	0	0.00	7	0	0	2	0	6.1	4	0	5	5
Paul Lindblad	1	0	0.00	3	0	0	0	0	3.1	4	0	1	1
Blue Moon Odom	0	0	3.86	2	0	0	0	0	4.2	5	2	2	2
Horacio Pina	0	0	0.00	2	0	0	0	0	3.0	6	0	2	0
TOTAL	4	3	2.32	27	7	0	4	0	66.0	66	17	26	36

NY (N)

PLAYER/POS	AVG	G	AB	R	H	2B	3B	HR	RB	BB	SO	SB
Jim Beauchamp, ph	.000	4	4	0	0	0	0	0	0	0	1	0
Ken Boswell, ph	1.000	3	3	1	3	0	0	0	0	0	0	0
Wayne Garrett, 3b	.167	7	30	4	5	0	0	2	2	5	11	0
Jerry Grote, c	.267	7	30	2	8	0	0	0	0	0	1	0
Don Hahn, of	.241	7	29	2	7	1	1	0	2	1	6	0
Bud Harrelson, ss	.250	7	24	2	6	1	0	0	1	5	3	0
Ron Hodges, ph	.000	1	0	0	0	0	0	0	0	1	0	0
Cleon Jones, of	.286	7	28	5	8	2	0	1	1	4	2	0
Jerry Koosman, p	.000	2	4	0	0	0	0	0	0	0	3	0
Ed Kranepool, ph	.000	4	3	0	0	0	0	0	0	0	0	0
Ted Martinez, pr	.000	2	0	0	0	0	0	0	0	0	0	0
Jon Matlack, p	.250	3	4	0	1	0	0	0	0	2	1	0
Willie Mays, of-2	.286	3	7	1	2	0	0	0	1	0	1	0
Tug Mc Graw, p	.333	5	3	1	1	0	0	0	0	0	1	0
Felix Millan, 2b	.188	7	32	3	6	1	1	0	1	1	1	0
John Milner, 1b	.296	7	27	2	8	0	0	0	2	5	1	0
Harry Parker, p	.000	3	0	0	0	0	0	0	0	0	0	0
Ray Sadecki, p	.000	4	0	0	0	0	0	0	0	0	0	0
Tom Seaver, p	.000	2	5	0	0	0	0	0	0	0	2	0
Rusty Staub, of	.423	7	26	1	11	2	0	1	6	2	2	0
George Stone, p	.000	2	0	0	0	0	0	0	0	0	0	0
George Theodore, of-1	.000	2	2	0	0	0	0	0	0	0	0	0
TOTAL	.253		261	24	66	7	2	4	16	26	36	0

PITCHER	W	L	ERA	G	GS	CG	SV	SHO	IP	H	ER	BB	SO
Jerry Koosman	1	0	3.12	2	2	0	0	0	8.2	9	3	7	8
Jon Matlack	1	2	2.16	3	3	0	0	0	16.2	10	4	5	11
Tug Mc Graw	1	0	2.63	5	0	0	1	0	13.2	8	4	9	14
Harry Parker	0	1	0.00	3	0	0	0	0	3.1	2	0	2	2
Ray Sadecki	0	0	1.93	4	0	0	1	0	4.2	5	1	1	6
Tom Seaver	0	1	2.40	2	2	0	0	0	15.0	13	4	3	18
George Stone	0	0	0.00	2	0	0	1	0	3.0	4	0	1	3
TOTAL	3	4	2.22	21	7	0	3	0	65.0	51	16	28	62

GAME 1 AT OAK OCT 13

NY	000	100	000	1	7	2
OAK	002	000	00X	2	4	0

Pitchers: MATLACK, McGraw (7) VS HOLTZMAN, Fingers (6), Knowles (9)
Attendance: 46,021

GAME 2 AT OAK OCT 14

NY	011	004	000	004	10	15	1
OAK	210	000	102	001	7	13	5

Pitchers: Koosman, Sadecki (3), Parker (5), McGRAW (6), Stone (12) VS Blue, Pina (6), Knowles (6), Odom (8), FINGERS (10), Linblad (12)
Home Runs: Jones-NY, Garrett-NY
Attendance: 49,151

GAME 3 AT NY OCT 16

OAK	000	001	010	01	3	10	1
NY	200	000	000	00	2	10	2

Pitchers: Hunter, Knowles (7), LINDBLAD (9), Fingers (11) vs Seaver, Sadecki (9), McGraw (9), PARKER (11)
Home Runs: Garrett-NY
Attendance: 54,817

GAME 4 AT NY OCT 17

OAK	000	100	000	1	5	1
NY	300	300	00X	6	13	1

Pitchers: HOLTZMAN, Odom (1), Knowles (4), Pina (5), Linblad (8) VS MATLACK, Sadecki (9)
Home Runs: Staub-NY
Attendance: 54,817

GAME 5 AT NY OCT 18

OAK	000	000	000	0	3	1
NY	010	001	00X	2	7	1

Pitchers: BLUE, Knowles (6), Fingers (7) VS KOOSMAN, McGraw (7)
Attendance: 54,817

GAME 6 AT OAK OCT 20

NY	000	000	010	1	6	2
OAK	101	000	01X	3	7	0

Pitchers: SEAVER, McGraw (8) vs HUNTER, Knowles (8), Fingers (8)
Attendance: 49,333

GAME 7 AT OAK OCT 21

NY	000	001	001	2	8	1
OAK	004	010	00X	5	9	1

Pitchers: MATLACK, Parker (3), Sadecki (5), Stone (7) vs HOLTZMAN, Fingers (6), Knowles (9)
Home Runs: Campaneris-OAK, Jackson-OAK
Attendance: 49,333

Dodger pitcher Don Sutton—who had brought his won-lost record from 10–9 to 19–9 with a nine-game winning streak in the regular season—continued his winning ways in the LCS, surrendering only seven hits and one run in seventeen innings and taking both the opener and clincher of the four-game series. Los Angeles's Andy Messersmith followed up Sutton's opening-game shutout with six shutout innings of his own in Game Two before Pittsburgh scored its first two runs of the series in the seventh. They tied the score, but the Dodgers countered with three more in the top of the eighth to assure their second win.

The Pirates captured their only victory in Game Three, as Richie Hebner and Willie Stargell homered for five of the Bucs' seven runs, while Bruce Kison and Ramon Hernandez shut out the Dodgers on four hits.

Pittsburgh finally got to Sutton for a run when Stargell homered in the seventh inning of Game Four. But it was too little, and too late to stem a twelve-run Dodger attack led by Steve Garvey's four hits (two of them home runs) and four RBIs.

Los Angeles Dodgers (West), 3; Pittsburgh Pirates (East) 1

LA (W)

PLAYER/POS	AVG	G	AB	R	H	2B	3B	HR	RB	BB	SO	SB
Rick Auerbach, ph	1.000	1	1	0	1	1	0	0	0	0	0	0
Bill Buckner, of	.167	4	18	0	3	1	0	0	0	0	2	0
Ron Cey, 3b	.313	4	16	2	5	3	0	1	1	3	2	0
Willie Crawford, of	.250	2	4	1	1	0	0	0	1	1	1	0
Al Downing, p	.000	1	1	0	0	0	0	0	0	0	0	0
Joe Ferguson, of-3,c-2	.231	4	13	3	3	0	0	0	2	5	1	0
Steve Garvey, 1b	.389	4	18	4	7	1	0	2	5	1	1	0
Charley Hough, p	.000	1	0	0	0	0	0	0	0	0	0	0
Von Joshua, ph	.000	1	0	0	0	0	0	0	0	1	0	0
Lee Lacy, pr	.000	1	0	0	0	0	0	0	0	0	0	0
Davey Lopes, 2b	.267	4	15	4	4	0	1	0	3	5	1	3
Mike Marshall, p	.000	2	0	0	0	0	0	0	0	0	0	0
Ken Mc Mullen, ph	.000	1	1	0	0	0	0	0	0	0	1	0
Andy Messersmith, p	.000	1	3	0	0	0	0	0	0	0	1	0
Manny Mota, of-1	.333	3	3	0	1	0	0	0	1	0	0	0
Tom Paciorek, of	1.000	1	1	0	1	0	0	0	0	0	0	0
Doug Rau, p	.000	1	0	0	0	0	0	0	0	0	0	0
Bill Russell, ss	.389	4	18	1	7	0	0	0	3	1	0	0
Eddie Solomon, p	.000	1	0	0	0	0	0	0	0	0	0	0
Don Sutton, p	.286	2	7	0	2	0	0	0	1	1	2	0
Jimmy Wynn, of	.200	4	10	4	2	2	0	0	2	9	1	1
Steve Yeager, c	.000	3	9	1	0	0	0	0	0	3	3	1
TOTAL	.268		138	20	37	8	1	3	19	30	16	5

PITCHER	W	L	ERA	G	GS	CG	SV	SHO	IP	H	ER	BB	SO
Al Downing	0	0	0.00	1	0	0	0	0	4.0	1	0	1	0
Charley Hough	0	0	7.71	1	0	0	0	0	2.1	4	2	0	2
Mike Marshall	0	0	0.00	2	0	0	0	0	3.0	0	0	0	1
Andy Messersmith	1	0	2.57	1	1	0	0	0	7.0	8	2	3	0
Doug Rau	0	1	40.50	1	1	0	0	0	0.2	3	3	1	0
Eddie Solomon	0	0	0.00	1	0	0	0	0	2.0	2	0	1	1
Don Sutton	2	0	0.53	2	2	1	0	1	17.0	7	1	2	13
TOTAL	3	1	2.00	9	4	1	0	1	36.0	25	8	8	17

PIT (E)

PLAYER/POS	AVG	G	AB	R	H	2B	3B	HR	RB	BB	SO	SB
Ken Brett, p	.000	1	1	0	0	0	0	0	0	0	1	0
Gene Clines, of	.000	2	1	1	0	0	0	0	0	0	0	0
Larry Demery, p	.000	2	0	0	0	0	0	0	0	0	0	0
Dave Giusti, p	.000	3	0	0	0	0	0	0	0	0	0	0
Richie Hebner, 3b	.231	4	13	1	3	0	0	1	4	1	4	0
Ramon Hernandez, p	.000	2	0	0	0	0	0	0	0	0	1	0
Art Howe, ph	.000	1	1	0	0	0	0	0	0	0	0	0
Ed Kirkpatrick, 1b	.000	3	9	0	0	0	0	0	0	2	0	0
Bruce Kison, p	.000	1	3	0	0	0	0	0	0	0	2	0
Mario Mendoza, ss	.200	3	5	0	1	0	0	0	1	1	0	0
Al Oliver, of	.143	4	14	1	2	0	0	0	1	2	2	0
Dave Parker, of-2	.125	3	8	0	1	0	0	0	0	0	1	0
Juan Pizarro, p	.000	1	0	0	0	0	0	0	0	0	0	0
Paul Popovich, ss	.600	3	5	1	3	0	0	0	0	0	0	0
Jerry Reuss, p	.000	2	2	0	0	0	0	0	0	0	0	0
Bob Robertson, 1b	.000	1	5	1	0	0	0	0	0	0	0	0
Jim Rooker, p	.500	1	2	0	1	0	0	0	0	0	0	0
Manny Sanguillen, c	.250	4	16	0	4	1	0	0	0	0	0	0
Willie Stargell, of	.400	4	15	3	6	0	0	2	4	1	2	0
Rennie Stennett, 2b	.063	4	16	1	1	0	0	0	0	1	1	0
Frank Taveras, ss	.000	2	2	0	0	0	0	0	0	0	0	1
Richie Zisk, of-2	.300	3	10	1	3	0	0	0	0	0	3	0
TOTAL	.194		129	10	25	1	0	3	10	8	17	1

PITCHER	W	L	ERA	G	GS	CG	SV	SHO	IP	H	ER	BB	SO
Ken Brett	0	0	7.71	1	0	0	0	0	2.1	3	2	2	1
Larry Demery	0	0	27.00	2	0	0	0	0	1.0	3	3	2	0
Dave Giusti	0	1	21.60	3	0	0	0	0	3.1	13	8	5	1
Ramon Hernandez	0	0	0.00	2	0	0	0	0	4.1	3	0	1	2
Bruce Kison	1	0	0.00	1	1	0	0	0	6.2	2	0	6	5
Juan Pizarro	0	0	0.00	1	0	0	0	0	0.2	0	0	1	0
Jerry Reuss	0	2	3.72	2	2	0	0	0	9.2	7	4	8	3
Jim Rooker	0	0	2.57	1	1	0	0	0	7.0	6	2	5	4
TOTAL	1	3	4.89	13	4	0	0	0	35.0	37	19	30	16

GAME 1 AT PIT OCT 5

LA	010	000	002	3	9 2
PIT	000	000	000	0	4 0

Pitchers: SUTTON vs REUSS, Giusti (8)
Attendance: 40,638

GAME 2 AT PIT OCT 6

LA	100	100	030	5	12 0
PIT	000	000	200	2	8 3

Pitchers: MESSERSMITH, Marshall (8) VS Rooker, GIUSTI (8), Demery (8), Hernandez (8)
Home Runs: Cey-LA
Attendance: 49,247

GAME 3 AT LA OCT 8

PIT	502	000	000	7	10 0
LA	000	000	000	0	4 5

Pitchers: KISON, Hernandez (7) vs RAU, Hough (1), Downing (4), Solomon (8)
Home Runs: Stargell-PIT, Hebner-PIT
Attendance: 55,953

GAME 4 AT LA OCT 9

PIT	000	000	100	1	3 1
LA	102	022	23X	12	12 0

Pitchers: REUSS, Brett (3), Demery (6), Giusti (7), Pizarro (8) vs SUTTON, Marshall (9)
Home Runs: Garvey-LA (2), Stargell-PIT
Attendance: 54,424

After spotting Baltimore a win in the opener, Oakland took the next three games and their third consecutive pennant. Although the A's got nine hits in Game One—their series high—the Orioles hit harder, burying Oakland under home runs by Paul Blair, Brooks Robinson, and Bobby Grich. In Game Two, though, Ken Holtzman shut out Baltimore on five hits as Sal Bando and Ray Fosse homered. Bando homered again in the third game for the only Oakland run as Jim Palmer limited the A's to four hits. But one run was enough to defeat Baltimore, for Vida Blue shut them out on a masterly two-hitter.

Oriole starter Mike Cuellar walked nine men in 4⅔ innings of Game Four, including four in the fifth to force in Oakland's first run. Two innings later Reggie Jackson's double (the only Oakland hit of the game) off reliever Ross Grimsley drove in Oakland's second run, while starter Catfish Hunter was blanking the O's through seven-plus innings. After failing to score for thirty consecutive innings, the Orioles got to reliever Rollie Fingers for a run with two out in the bottom of the ninth. But Fingers then struck out Don Baylor, and the A's had their pennant.

Oakland A's (West), 3; Baltimore Orioles (East) 1

OAK (W)

PLAYER/POS	AVG	G	AB	R	H	2B	3B	HR	RB	BB	SO	SB
Jesus Alou, ph	1.000	1	1	0	1	0	0	0	0	0	0	0
Sal Bando, 3b	.231	4	13	4	3	0	0	2	2	4	0	0
Vida Blue, p	.000	1	0	0	0	0	0	0	0	0	0	0
Bert Campaneris, ss	.176	4	17	0	3	0	0	0	3	0	3	1
Rollie Fingers, p	.000	2	0	0	0	0	0	0	0	0	0	0
Ray Fosse, c	.333	4	12	1	4	1	0	1	3	1	2	0
Dick Green, 2b	.222	4	9	0	2	0	0	0	0	0	2	0
Jim Holt, 1b-1	.000	2	0	0	0	0	0	0	0	1	0	0
Ken Holtzman, p	.000	1	0	0	0	0	0	0	0	0	0	0
Catfish Hunter, p	.000	2	0	0	0	0	0	0	0	0	0	0
Reggie Jackson, dh-3,of-1	.167	4	12	0	2	1	0	0	1	5	2	0
Angel Mangual, dh	.250	1	4	0	1	0	0	0	0	0	0	0
Dal Maxvill, 2b	.000	1	1	0	0	0	0	0	0	0	1	0
Billy North, of	.063	4	16	3	1	1	0	0	0	2	1	1
Blue Moon Odom, p-1	.000	3	0	0	0	0	0	0	0	0	0	0
Joe Rudi, of	.154	4	13	0	2	0	1	0	1	3	2	0
Gene Tenace, 1b	.000	4	11	1	0	0	0	0	1	4	4	1
Manny Trillo, pr	.000	1	0	1	0	0	0	0	0	0	0	0
Claudell Washington, of-3	.273	4	11	1	3	1	0	0	0	0	0	0
Herb Washington, pr	.000	2	0	0	0	0	0	0	0	0	0	0
TOTAL	.183		120	11	22	4	1	3	11	22	16	3

PITCHER	W	L	ERA	G	GS	CG	SV	SHO	IP	H	ER	BB	SO
Vida Blue	1	0	0.00	1	1	1	0	1	9.0	2	0	0	7
Rollie Fingers	0	0	3.00	2	0	0	1	0	3.0	3	1	1	3
Ken Holtzman	1	0	0.00	1	1	1	0	1	9.0	5	0	2	3
Catfish Hunter	1	1	4.63	2	2	0	0	0	11.2	11	6	2	6
Blue Moon Odom	0	0	0.00	1	0	0	0	0	3.1	1	0	0	1
TOTAL	3	1	1.75	7	4	2	1	2	36.0	22	7	5	20

BAL (E)

PLAYER/POS	AVG	G	AB	R	H	2B	3B	HR	RB	BB	SO	SB
Frank Baker, ss	.000	2	0	0	0	0	0	0	0	0	0	0
Don Baylor, of	.267	4	15	0	4	0	0	0	0	0	2	0
Mark Belanger, ss	.000	4	9	0	0	0	0	0	0	1	3	0
Paul Blair, of	.286	4	14	3	4	0	0	1	2	2	2	0
Al Bumbry, ph	.000	2	1	0	0	0	0	0	0	0	1	0
Enos Cabell, of-1	.250	3	4	0	1	0	0	0	0	0	2	0
Rich Coggins, of	.000	3	11	0	0	0	0	0	0	0	3	0
Mike Cuellar, p	.000	2	0	0	0	0	0	0	0	0	0	0
Tommy Davis, dh	.267	4	15	0	4	0	0	0	1	0	1	0
Andy Etchebarren, c	.333	2	6	0	2	0	0	0	0	0	0	0
Wayne Garland, p	.000	1	0	0	0	0	0	0	0	0	0	0
Bobby Grich, 2b	.250	4	16	2	4	1	0	1	2	0	1	0
Ross Grimsley, p	.000	2	0	0	0	0	0	0	0	0	0	0
Elrod Hendricks, c	.167	3	6	1	1	0	0	0	0	1	3	0
Grant Jackson, p	.000	1	0	0	0	0	0	0	0	0	0	0
Dave Nc Nally, p	.000	1	0	0	0	0	0	0	0	0	0	0
Curt Motton, ph	.000	1	1	0	0	0	0	0	0	0	0	0
Jim Palmer, p-1	.000	2	0	0	0	0	0	0	0	0	0	0
Boog Powell, 1b	.125	2	8	0	1	0	0	0	1	0	0	0
Bob Reynolds, p	.000	1	0	0	0	0	0	0	0	0	0	0
Brooks Robinson, 3b	.083	4	12	1	1	0	0	1	1	1	0	0
Earl Williams, 1b	.000	2	6	0	0	0	0	0	0	0	2	0
TOTAL	.177		124	7	22	1	0	3	7	5	20	0

PITCHER	W	L	ERA	G	GS	CG	SV	SHO	IP	H	ER	BB	SO
Mike Cuellar	1	1	2.84	2	2	0	0	0	12.2	9	4	13	6
Wayne Garland	0	0	0.00	1	0	0	0	0	0.2	1	0	1	0
Ross Grimsley	0	0	1.69	2	0	0	0	0	5.1	1	1	2	2
Grant Jackson	0	0	0.00	1	0	0	0	0	0.1	1	0	0	1
Dave Nc Nally	0	1	1.59	1	1	0	0	0	5.2	6	1	2	2
Jim Palmer	0	1	1.00	1	1	1	0	0	9.0	4	1	1	4
Bob Reynolds	0	0	0.00	1	0	0	0	0	1.1	0	0	3	1
TOTAL	1	3	1.80	9	4	1	0	0	35.0	22	7	22	16

GAME 1 AT OAK OCT 5

BAL	100	140	000	6	10	0
OAK	001	010	001	3	9	0

Pitchers: CUELLAR, Grimsley (9) vs HUNTER, Odom (5), Fingers (9)
Home Runs: Blair-BAL, Robinson-BAL, Grich-BAL
Attendance: 41,609

GAME 2 AT OAK OCT 6

BAL	000	000	000	0	5	2
OAK	000	101	03X	5	8	0

Pitchers: McNALLY, Garland (6), Reynolds (7), G.Jackson (8) vs HOLTZMAN
Home Runs: Bando-OAK, Fosse-OAK
Attendance: 42,810

GAME 3 AT BAL OCT 8

OAK	000	100	000	1	4	2
BAL	000	000	000	0	2	1

Pitchers: BLUE vs PALMER
Home Runs: Bando-OAK
Attendance: 32,060

GAME 4 AT BAL OCT 9

OAK	000	010	100	2	1	0
BAL	000	000	001	1	5	1

Pitchers: HUNTER, Fingers (8) vs CUELLAR, Grimsley (5)
Attendance: 28,136

Although the A's were in a turmoil of dislike for owner Charlie Finley—and for each other—they played well enough together to take their third consecutive world championship in just five games. Still, victory didn't come easily, as three of Oakland's wins came by identical 3–2 scores (as did the Dodgers' one victory), and their biggest winning margin was three runs in Game Four. It was the first World Series held entirely on the West Coast.

The A's and Dodgers split the first two games in Los Angeles. Oakland won the opener on the strength of Reggie Jackson's home run in the second inning, pitcher Ken Holtzman's double in the fifth (he moved around on a wild pitch and squeeze bunt), and a Dodger throwing error in the eighth. The Dodgers evened the Series on Joe Ferguson's two-run homer in the sixth inning of the second game, which gave Los Angeles a 3–0 lead that an Oakland rally in the ninth failed to catch.

Los Angeles outhit Oakland in Game Three, but two of the A's runs were unearned, coming after Dodger catcher Ferguson bobbled what should have been a third-out play in the third inning.

Pitcher Ken Holtzman, who had now gone two regular seasons without a time at bat, produced in Game Four his second hit of the Series, this one a homer in the third inning for the game's first run. The Dodgers' Bill Russell tripled off him for two runs a half inning later, but in the last of the sixth inning Oakland regained the lead on three walks interspersed with a pair of singles and an RBI grounder to short. Four runs scored—more in this one inning than either team scored in any of the other four games.

Oakland took an early 2–0 lead in Game Five, with single runs in the first and second innings (the latter a Ray Fosse home run). The Dodgers put together a pinch-hit double, a walk, a pair of sacrifices (bunt and fly), and a single to tie the score in the sixth. But Joe Rudi hit the first pitch of Oakland's half of the seventh into the stands in left for the run that decided the game and the Series.

Oakland Athletics (AL), 4;
Los Angeles Dodgers (NL) 1

OAK (A)

PLAYER/POS	AVG	G	AB	R	H	2B	3B	HR	RB	BB	SO	SB
Jesus Alou, ph	.000	1	1	0	0	0	0	0	0	0	1	0
Sal Bando, 3b	.063	5	16	3	1	0	0	0	2	2	5	0
Vida Blue, p	.000	2	4	0	0	0	0	0	0	0	4	0
Bert Campaneris, ss	.353	5	17	1	6	2	0	0	2	0	2	1
Rollie Fingers, p	.000	4	2	0	0	0	0	0	0	0	1	0
Ray Fosse, c	.143	5	14	1	2	0	0	1	1	1	5	0
Dick Green, 2b	.000	5	13	1	0	0	0	0	1	1	4	0
Larry Haney, c	.000	2	0	0	0	0	0	0	0	0	0	0
Jim Holt, 1b-1	.667	4	3	0	2	0	0	0	2	0	0	0
Ken Holtzman, p	.500	2	4	2	2	1	0	1	1	1	1	0
Catfish Hunter, p	.000	2	2	0	0	0	0	0	0	0	2	0
Reggie Jackson, of	.286	5	14	3	4	1	0	1	1	5	3	1
Angel Mangual, ph	.000	1	1	0	0	0	0	0	0	0	1	0
Dal Maxvill, 2b	.000	2	0	0	0	0	0	0	0	0	0	0
Billy North, of	.059	5	17	3	1	0	0	0	0	2	5	1
Blue Moon Odom, p	.000	2	0	0	0	0	0	0	0	0	0	0
Joe Rudi, of-5,1b-2	.333	5	18	1	6	0	0	1	4	0	3	0
Gene Tenace, 1b	.222	5	9	0	2	0	0	0	0	3	4	0
Claudell Washington, of	.571	5	7	1	4	0	0	0	0	1	1	0
Herb Washington, pr	.000	3	0	0	0	0	0	0	0	0	0	0
TOTAL	.211		142	16	30	4	0	4	14	16	42	3

PITCHER	W	L	ERA	G	GS	CG	SV	SHO	IP	H	ER	BB	SO
Vida Blue	0	1	3.29	2	2	0	0	0	13.2	10	5	7	9
Rollie Fingers	1	0	1.93	4	0	0	2	0	9.1	8	2	2	6
Ken Holtzman	1	0	1.50	2	2	0	0	0	12.0	13	2	4	10
Catfish Hunter	1	0	1.17	2	1	0	1	0	7.2	5	1	2	5
Blue Moon Odom	1	0	0.00	2	0	0	0	0	1.1	0	0	1	2
TOTAL	4	1	2.05	12	5	0	3	0	44.0	36	10	16	32

LA (N)

PLAYER/POS	AVG	G	AB	R	H	2B	3B	HR	RB	BB	SO	SB
Rick Auerbach, pr	.000	1	0	0	0	0	0	0	0	0	0	0
Jim Brewer, p	.000	1	0	0	0	0	0	0	0	0	0	0
Bill Buckner, of	.250	5	20	1	5	1	0	1	1	0	1	0
Ron Cey, 3b	.176	5	17	1	3	0	0	0	0	3	3	0
Willie Crawford, of-2	.333	3	6	1	2	0	0	1	1	0	0	0
Al Downing, p	.000	1	1	0	0	0	0	0	0	0	0	0
Joe Ferguson, of-4,c-2	.125	5	16	2	2	0	0	1	2	4	6	1
Steve Garvey, 1b	.381	5	21	2	8	0	0	0	1	0	3	0
Charley Hough, p	.000	1	0	0	0	0	0	0	0	0	0	0
Von Joshua, ph	.000	4	4	0	0	0	0	0	0	0	0	0
Lee Lacy, ph	.000	1	1	0	0	0	0	0	0	0	1	0
Davey Lopes, 2b	.111	5	18	2	2	0	0	0	0	3	4	2
Mike Marshall, p	.000	5	0	0	0	0	0	0	0	1	0	0
Andy Messersmith, p	.500	2	4	0	2	0	0	0	0	0	2	0
Tom Paciorek, ph	.500	3	2	1	1	1	0	0	0	0	0	0
Bill Russell, ss	.222	5	18	0	4	0	1	0	2	0	2	0
Don Sutton, p	.000	2	3	0	0	0	0	0	0	0	2	0
Jimmy Wynn, of	.188	5	16	1	3	1	0	1	2	4	4	0
Steve Yeager, c	.364	4	11	0	4	1	0	0	1	1	4	0
TOTAL	.228		158	11	36	4	1	4	10	16	32	3

PITCHER	W	L	ERA	G	GS	CG	SV	SHO	IP	H	ER	BB	SO
Jim Brewer	0	0	0.00	1	0	0	0	0	0.1	0	0	0	1
Al Downing	0	1	2.45	1	1	0	0	0	3.2	4	1	4	3
Charley Hough	0	0	0.00	1	0	0	0	0	2.0	0	0	1	4
Mike Marshall	0	1	1.00	5	0	0	1	0	9.0	6	1	1	10
Andy Messersmith	0	2	4.50	2	2	0	0	0	14.0	11	7	7	12
Don Sutton	1	0	2.77	2	2	0	0	0	13.0	9	4	3	12
TOTAL	1	4	2.79	12	5	0	1	0	42.0	30	13	16	42

GAME 1 AT LA OCT 12

OAK	010	010	010	3	6	2
LA	000	010	001	2	11	1

Pitchers: Holtzman, FINGERS (5), Hunter (9) vs MESSERSMITH, Marshall (9)
Home Runs: Jackson-OAK, Wynn-LA
Attendance: 55,974

GAME 2 AT LA OCT 13

OAK	000	000	002	2	6	0
LA	010	002	00X	3	6	1

Pitchers: BLUE, Odom (8) vs SUTTON, Marshall (9)
Home Runs: Ferguson-LA
Attendance: 55,989

GAME 3 AT OAK OCT 15

LA	000	000	011	2	7	2
OAK	002	100	00X	3	5	2

Pitchers: DOWNING, Brewer (4), Hough (5), Marshall (7) vs HUNTER, Fingers (8)
Home Runs: Buckner-LA, Crawford-LA
Attendance: 49,347

GAME 4 AT OAK OCT 16

LA	000	200	000	2	7	1
OAK	001	004	00X	5	7	0

Pitchers: MESSERSMITH, Marshall (7) VS HOLTZMAN, Fingers (8)
Home Runs: Holtzman-OAK
Attendance: 49,347

GAME 5 AT OAK OCT 17

LA	000	002	000	2	5	1
OAK	110	000	10X	3	6	1

Pitchers: Sutton, MARSHALL (6) vs Blue, ODOM (7), Fingers (8)
Home Runs: Fosse-OAK, Rudi-OAK
Attendance: 49,347

The Reds, who had steamrolled the National League during the season, continued their roll in the LCS. Red pitcher Don Gullett gave up three Pirate runs in the first game, but he drove in three himself with a home run and a single. Pitching the series' only complete game, he won easily behind his club's twelve-hit, eight-run attack. The Reds won just as handily in Game Two, with Fred Norman and reliever Rawley Eastwick holding the Pirates to one run as Tony Perez drove in half the Reds' six runs—two of them with a first-inning homer.

In Game Three the Pirates struggled gamely against elimination. Cincinnati scored first in the second, but in the sixth Al Oliver put Pittsburgh ahead with a two-run homer. In the eighth, though, Pete Rose restored the Reds' lead (and nullified rookie John Candelaria's fourteen-strikeout effort over 7⅔ innings) with his two-run shot. The Pirates were granted a brief reprieve when Red reliever Eastwick walked in the tying run in the bottom of the ninth. But in the tenth the Reds scored twice on three hits, and when Eastwick's replacement Pedro Borbon shut the Pirates down in the bottom of the tenth, Cincinnati had its series sweep.

Cincinnati Reds (West), 3;
Pittsburgh Pirates (East) 0

CIN (W)

PLAYER/POS	AVG	G	AB	R	H	2B	3B	HR	RB	BB	SO	SB
Ed Armbrister, ph	.000	2	0	0	0	0	0	0	1	0	0	0
Johnny Bench, c	.077	3	13	1	1	0	0	0	0	1	6	1
Pedro Borbon, p	.000	1	0	0	0	0	0	0	0	0	0	0
Clay Carroll, p	.000	1	0	0	0	0	0	0	0	0	0	0
Dave Concepcion, ss	.455	3	11	2	5	0	0	1	1	1	2	2
Terry Crowley, ph	.000	1	0	0	0	0	0	0	0	0	0	0
Rawly Eastwick, p	.000	2	0	0	0	0	0	0	0	0	0	0
George Foster, of	.364	3	11	3	4	0	0	0	0	1	2	1
Cesar Geronimo, of	.000	3	10	0	0	0	0	0	1	1	7	0
Ken Griffey, of	.333	3	12	4	4	1	0	0	4	0	3	3
Don Gullett, p	.500	1	4	1	2	0	0	1	3	0	0	0
Will Mc Enaney, p	.000	1	0	0	0	0	0	0	0	0	0	0
Joe Morgan, 2b	.273	3	11	2	3	3	0	0	1	3	2	4
Gary Nolan, p	.000	1	2	0	0	0	0	0	0	0	2	0
Fred Norman, p	.000	1	1	0	0	0	0	0	0	1	0	0
Tony Perez, 1b	.417	3	12	3	5	0	0	1	4	1	2	0
Merv Rettenmund, ph	.000	2	1	0	0	0	0	0	0	1	0	0
Pete Rose, 3b	.357	3	14	3	5	0	0	1	2	0	2	0
TOTAL	.284		102	19	29	4	0	4	18	9	28	11

PITCHER	W	L	ERA	G	GS	CG	SV	SHO	IP	H	ER	BB	SO
Pedro Borbon	0	0	0.00	1	0	0	1	0	1.0	0	0	0	1
Clay Carroll	0	0	0.00	1	0	0	0	0	1.0	0	0	1	1
Rawly Eastwick	1	0	0.00	2	0	0	1	0	3.2	2	0	2	1
Don Gullett	1	0	3.00	1	1	1	0	0	9.0	8	3	2	5
Will Mc Enaney	0	0	6.75	1	0	0	0	0	1.1	1	1	0	1
Gary Nolan	0	0	3.00	1	1	0	0	0	6.0	5	2	0	5
Fred Norman	1	0	1.50	1	1	0	0	0	6.0	4	1	5	4
TOTAL	3	0	2.25	8	3	1	2	0	28.0	20	7	10	18

PIT (E)

PLAYER/POS	AVG	G	AB	R	H	2B	3B	HR	RB	BB	SO	SB
Ken Brett, p	.000	2	0	0	0	0	0	0	0	0	0	0
John Candelaria, p	.000	1	3	0	0	0	0	0	0	0	3	0
Larry Demery, p	.000	1	0	0	0	0	0	0	0	0	0	0
Duffy Dyer, ph	.000	1	0	0	0	0	0	0	1	1	0	0
Dock Ellis, p	.000	1	0	0	0	0	0	0	0	0	0	0
Dave Giusti, p	.000	1	0	0	0	0	0	0	0	0	0	0
Richie Hebner, 3b	.333	3	12	2	4	1	0	0	2	1	1	0
Ramon Hernandez, p	.000	1	0	0	0	0	0	0	0	0	0	0
Ed Kirkpatrick, ph	.000	2	2	0	0	0	0	0	0	0	0	0
Bruce Kison, p	.000	1	0	0	0	0	0	0	0	0	0	0
Al Oliver, of	.182	3	11	1	2	0	0	1	2	2	0	0
Dave Parker, of	.000	3	10	2	0	0	0	0	0	1	3	0
Willie Randolph, 2b-1	.000	2	2	1	0	0	0	0	0	0	1	0
Jerry Reuss, p	.000	1	1	0	0	0	0	0	0	0	0	0
Craig Reynolds, ss-1	.000	2	0	0	0	0	0	0	0	0	0	0
Bob Robertson, 1b-1	.500	3	2	0	1	0	0	0	1	1	0	0
Bill Robinson, ph	.000	2	2	0	0	0	0	0	0	0	1	0
Jim Rooker, p	.000	1	1	0	0	0	0	0	0	0	1	0
Manny Sanguillen, c	.167	3	12	0	2	0	0	0	0	0	0	0
Willie Stargell, 1b	.182	3	11	1	2	1	0	0	0	1	3	0
Rennie Stennett, 2b-3,ss-1	.214	3	14	0	3	0	0	0	0	0	1	0
Frank Taveras, ss	.143	3	7	0	1	0	0	0	1	1	2	0
Kent Tekulve, p	.000	2	0	0	0	0	0	0	0	0	0	0
Richie Zisk, of	.500	3	10	0	5	1	0	0	0	2	2	0
TOTAL	.198		101	7	20	3	0	1	7	10	18	0

PITCHER	W	L	ERA	G	GS	CG	SV	SHO	IP	H	ER	BB	SO
Ken Brett	0	0	0.00	2	0	0	0	0	2.1	1	0	0	1
John Candelaria	0	0	3.52	1	1	0	0	0	7.2	3	3	2	14
Larry Demery	0	0	18.00	1	0	0	0	0	2.0	4	4	1	1
Dock Ellis	0	0	0.00	1	0	0	0	0	2.0	2	0	0	2
Dave Giusti	0	0	0.00	1	0	0	0	0	1.1	0	0	0	1
Ramon Hernandez	0	1	27.00	1	0	0	0	0	0.2	3	2	0	0
Bruce Kison	0	0	4.50	1	0	0	0	0	2.0	2	1	1	1
Jerry Reuss	0	1	13.50	1	1	0	0	0	2.2	4	4	4	1
Jim Rooker	0	1	9.00	1	1	0	0	0	4.0	7	4	0	5
Kent Tekulve	0	0	6.75	2	0	0	0	0	1.1	3	1	1	2
TOTAL	0	3	6.58	12	3	0	0	0	26.0	29	19	9	28

GAME 1 AT CIN OCT 4

PIT	020	000	001	3	8	0
CIN	013	040	00X	8	11	0

Pitchers: REUSS, Brett (3), Demery (5), Ellis (7) vs GULLETT
Home Runs: Gullett-CIN
Attendance: 54,633

GAME 2 AT CIN OCT 5

PIT	000	100	000	1	5	0
CIN	200	201	10X	6	12	1

Pitchers: ROOKER, Tekulve (5), Brett (6), Kison (7) vs NORMAN, Eastwick (7)
Home Runs: Perez-CIN
Attendance: 54,752

GAME 3 AT PIT OCT 7

CIN	010	000	020 2	5	6	0
PIT	000	002	001 0	3	7	2

Pitchers: NOLAN, C.Carroll (7), McEnaney (9), Borbon (10) VS Candelaria, Giusti (8), HERNANDEZ (10), Tekulve (10)
Home Runs: Concepcion-CIN, Oliver-PIT, Rose-CIN
Attendance: 46,355

The Oakland A's ran their domination of the American League West to five years, but an aroused Boston team stifled their try for a fourth straight pennant.

In the first game Luis Tiant held Oakland to three hits as his teammates—aided by four Oakland errors—scored seven times before giving the A's an unearned run in the eighth. Oakland scored first in Game Two on Reggie Jackson's two-run homer in the first inning and added a run in the fourth. But Carl Yastrzemski's two-run shot in the last of the fourth, followed by a Carlton Fisk double and a Fred Lynn single, drove out A's starter Vida Blue, and the tying run scored on a double play. Single Boston runs in the sixth, seventh, and eighth put the game away.

The A's started Ken Holtzman for the second time in Game Three, after only two days of rest. He held the Sox scoreless for three innings, but was driven from the game in the fifth. Boston scored four times before Oakland put a run on the board, and retained the lead to the game's conclusion.

Boston Red Sox (East), 3; Oakland A's (West) 0

BOS (E)

PLAYER/POS	AVG	G	AB	R	H	2B	3B	HR	RB	BB	SO	SB
Juan Beniquez, dh	.250	3	12	2	3	0	0	0	1	0	1	2
Rick Burleson, ss	.444	3	9	2	4	2	0	0	1	1	0	0
Reggie Cleveland, p	.000	1	0	0	0	0	0	0	0	0	0	0
Cecil Cooper, 1b	.400	3	10	0	4	2	0	0	1	0	2	0
Denny Doyle, 2b	.273	3	11	3	3	0	0	0	1	0	1	0
Dick Drago, p	.000	2	0	0	0	0	0	0	0	0	0	0
Dwight Evans, of	.100	3	10	1	1	1	0	0	1	1	2	0
Carlton Fisk, c	.417	3	12	4	5	1	0	0	2	0	2	1
Fred Lynn, of	.364	3	11	1	4	1	0	0	3	0	0	0
Roger Moret, p	.000	1	0	0	0	0	0	0	0	0	0	0
Rico Petrocelli, 3b	.167	3	12	1	2	0	0	1	2	0	3	0
Luis Tiant, p	.000	1	0	0	0	0	0	0	0	0	0	0
Rick Wise, p	.000	1	0	0	0	0	0	0	0	0	0	0
Carl Yastrzemski, of	.455	3	11	4	5	1	0	1	2	1	1	0
TOTAL	.316		98	18	31	8	0	2	14	3	12	3

PITCHER	W	L	ERA	G	GS	CG	SV	SHO	IP	H	ER	BB	SO
Reggie Cleveland	0	0	5.40	1	1	0	0	0	5.0	7	3	1	2
Dick Drago	0	0	0.00	2	0	0	2	0	4.2	2	0	1	2
Roger Moret	1	0	0.00	1	0	0	0	0	1.0	1	0	1	0
Luis Tiant	1	0	0.00	1	1	1	0	0	9.0	3	0	3	8
Rick Wise	1	0	2.45	1	1	0	0	0	7.1	6	2	3	2
TOTAL	3	0	1.67	6	3	1	2	0	27.0	19	5	9	14

OAK (W)

PLAYER/POS	AVG	G	AB	R	H	2B	3B	HR	RB	BB	SO	SB
Glenn Abbott, p	.000	1	0	0	0	0	0	0	0	0	0	0
Sal Bando, 3b	.500	3	12	1	6	2	0	0	2	0	3	0
Vida Blue, p	.000	1	0	0	0	0	0	0	0	0	0	0
Dick Bosman, p	.000	1	0	0	0	0	0	0	0	0	0	0
Bert Campaneris, ss	.000	3	11	1	0	0	0	0	0	1	1	0
Rollie Fingers, p	.000	1	0	0	0	0	0	0	0	0	0	0
Ray Fosse, c	.000	1	2	0	0	0	0	0	0	0	1	0
Phil Garner, 2b	.000	3	5	0	0	0	0	0	0	0	1	0
Tommy Harper, ph	.000	1	0	0	0	0	0	0	0	1	0	0
Jim Holt, 1b-1	.333	3	3	0	1	1	0	0	0	0	0	0
Ken Holtzman, p	.000	2	0	0	0	0	0	0	0	0	0	0
Don Hopkins, dh	.000	1	0	0	0	0	0	0	0	0	0	0
Reggie Jackson, of	.417	3	12	1	5	0	0	1	3	0	2	0
Paul Lindblad, p	.000	2	0	0	0	0	0	0	0	0	0	0
Ted Martinez, 2b	.000	3	0	0	0	0	0	0	0	0	0	0
Billy North, of	.000	3	10	0	0	0	0	0	0	1	2	0
Joe Rudi, 1b-2,of-1	.250	3	12	1	3	2	0	0	0	0	1	0
Gene Tenace, c-3,1b-1	.000	3	9	0	0	0	0	0	0	3	2	0
Jim Todd, p	.000	3	0	0	0	0	0	0	0	0	0	0
Cesar Tovar, 2b-1	.500	2	2	2	1	0	0	0	0	1	0	0
Claudell Washington, of-2,dh-1	.250	3	12	1	3	1	0	0	1	0	2	0
Billy Williams, dh-2	.000	3	8	0	0	0	0	0	0	1	1	0
TOTAL	.194		98	7	19	6	0	1	7	9	14	0

PITCHER	W	L	ERA	G	GS	CG	SV	SHO	IP	H	ER	BB	SO
Glenn Abbott	0	0	0.00	1	0	0	0	0	1.0	0	0	0	0
Vida Blue	0	0	9.00	1	1	0	0	0	3.0	6	3	0	2
Dick Bosman	0	0	0.00	1	0	0	0	0	0.1	0	0	0	0
Rollie Fingers	0	1	6.75	1	0	0	0	0	4.0	5	3	1	3
Ken Holtzman	0	2	4.09	2	2	0	0	0	11.0	12	5	1	7
Paul Lindblad	0	0	0.00	2	0	0	0	0	4.2	5	0	1	0
Jim Todd	0	0	9.00	3	0	0	0	0	1.0	3	1	0	0
TOTAL	0	3	4.32	11	3	0	0	0	25.0	31	12	3	12

GAME 1 AT BOS OCT 4

OAK	000	000	010	1	3	4
BOS	200	000	50X	7	8	3

Pitchers: HOLTZMAN, Todd (7), Lindblad (7), Bosman (7), Abbott (8) vs TIANT
Attendance: 35,578

GAME 2 AT BOS OCT 5

OAK	200	100	000	3	10	0
BOS	000	301	11X	6	12	0

Pitchers: Blue, Todd (4), FINGERS (5) VS Cleveland, MORET (6), Drago (7)
Home Runs: Jackson-OAK, Yastrzemski-BOS, Petrocelli-BOS
Attendance: 35,578

GAME 3 AT OAK OCT 7

BOS	000	130	010	5	11	1
OAK	000	001	020	3	6	2

Pitchers: WISE, Drago (8) vs HOLTZMAN, Todd (5), Lindblad (5)
Attendance: 49,358

The Red Sox entered the Series as underdogs to the mighty Reds, who had won 108 regular-season games. In the opening game, though, the Reds were surprised by veteran Sox starter Luis Tiant, who shut them out on five hits with the Series' first complete-game pitching effort in four years. Tiant also opened the Boston seventh with a single, starting a rally that ended only when he fouled out to end the inning after six runs had scored.

Boston took a 2–1 lead into the ninth inning of Game Two before Johnny Bench doubled to drive out starter Bill Lee, and Dave Concepcion and Ken Griffey drove in runs off reliever Dick Drago to turn the tide for Cincinnati. The Reds moved ahead in the Series with a tenth-inning victory in Game Three, a slugfest in which each club hit three home runs and used five pitchers. Boston tied the score on Dwight Evans's two-run homer in the ninth, but in the last of the tenth, the Reds' Joe Morgan drove one over the center fielder's head with the bases full to end the game.

Tiant pitched Game Four for Boston. Four of the nine hits against him went for extra bases, and each drove in a run. But the Sox bunched six of their eleven hits in the fourth inning for five runs—their only scoring, but enough for the win. Tiant himself scored the fifth run after singling. The Reds moved nearer the title in Game Five, though, as Tony Perez homered twice for four runs in a 6–2 win for a 3–2 Series advantage.

A day of travel to Boston and three days of rain between Games Five and Six brought Tiant back to the mound for a third time. Rookie standout Fred Lynn gave Tiant a three-run lead with a first-inning homer, but Ken Griffey's triple and Johnny Bench's long single drove in the tying Red runs in the fifth. Two more Red runs in the seventh and Cesar Geronimo's leadoff homer in the eighth drove out Tiant, but Boston pinch hitter Bernie Carbo homered to center in the last of the eighth for three runs that tied the score again. After a trio of Boston relievers had held Cincinnati in check through the top of the twelfth inning, the Sox leadoff hitter in the last of the twelfth, Carlton Fisk, ended the game dramatically with a home run to left on the first pitch that came within inches of being foul.

After the pyrotechnics of Game Six (ranked by some as the greatest World Series game ever), the seventh game, close as it was, came as an anticlimax. Boston scored three runs in the third inning, but the Reds began their

comeback with Tony Perez's two-run homer in the sixth, tied the game an inning later, and took a 4–3 lead on Joe Morgan's bloop RBI single in the ninth. Red reliever Will McEnaney came on to set the Sox down in order in the last of the ninth, and the Reds went home with their first world title in thirty-five years.

Cincinnati Reds (NL), 4; Boston Red Sox (AL) 3

CIN (N)

PLAYER/POS	AVG	G	AB	R	H	2B	3B	HR	RB	BB	SO	SB
Ed Armbrister, ph	.000	4	1	1	0	0	0	0	0	0	2	0
Johnny Bench, c	.207	7	29	5	6	2	0	1	4	2	4	0
Jack Billingham, p	.000	3	2	0	0	0	0	0	0	0	0	0
Pedro Borbon, p	.000	3	1	0	0	0	0	0	0	0	0	0
Clay Carroll, p	.000	5	0	0	0	0	0	0	0	0	0	0
Darrel Chaney, ph	.000	2	2	0	0	0	0	0	0	0	1	0
Dave Concepcion, ss	.179	7	28	3	5	1	0	1	4	0	1	3
Terry Crowley, ph	.500	2	2	0	1	0	0	0	0	0	1	0
Pat Darcy, p	.000	2	1	0	0	0	0	0	0	0	1	0
Dan Driessen, ph	.000	2	2	0	0	0	0	0	0	0	0	0
Rawly Eastwick, p	.000	5	1	0	0	0	0	0	0	0	0	0
George Foster, of	.276	7	29	1	8	1	0	0	2	1	1	1
Cesar Geronimo, of	.280	7	25	3	7	0	1	2	3	3	5	0
Ken Griffey, of	.269	7	26	4	7	3	1	0	4	4	2	0
Don Gullett, p	.286	3	7	1	2	0	0	0	0	0	2	0
Will Mc Enaney, p	1.000	5	1	0	1	0	0	0	0	0	0	0
Joe Morgan, 2b	.259	7	27	4	7	1	0	0	3	5	1	2
Gary Nolan, p	.000	2	1	0	0	0	0	0	0	0	0	0
Fred Norman, p	.000	2	1	0	0	0	0	0	0	0	0	0
Tony Perez, 1b	.179	7	28	4	5	0	0	3	7	3	9	1
Merv Rettenmund, ph	.000	3	3	0	0	0	0	0	0	0	1	0
Pete Rose, 3b	.370	7	27	3	10	1	1	0	2	5	1	0
TOTAL	.242		244	29	59	9	3	7	29	25	30	9

PITCHER	W	L	ERA	G	GS	CG	SV	SHO	IP	H	ER	BB	SO
Jack Billingham	0	0	1.00	3	1	0	0	0	9.0	8	1	5	7
Pedro Borbon	0	0	6.00	3	0	0	0	0	3.0	3	2	2	1
Clay Carroll	1	0	3.18	5	0	0	0	0	5.2	4	2	2	3
Pat Darcy	0	1	4.50	2	0	0	0	0	4.0	3	2	2	1
Rawly Eastwick	2	0	2.25	5	0	0	1	0	8.0	6	2	3	4
Don Gullett	1	1	4.34	3	3	0	0	0	18.2	19	9	10	15
Will Mc Enaney	0	0	2.70	5	0	0	1	0	6.2	3	2	2	5
Gary Nolan	0	0	6.00	2	2	0	0	0	6.0	6	4	1	2
Fred Norman	0	1	9.00	2	1	0	0	0	4.0	8	4	3	2
TOTAL	4	3	3.88	30	7	0	2	0	65.0	60	28	30	40

BOS (A)

PLAYER/POS	AVG	G	AB	R	H	2B	3B	HR	RB	BB	SO	SB
Juan Beniquez, of-2	.125	3	8	0	1	0	0	0	1	1	1	0
Rick Burleson, ss	.292	7	24	1	7	1	0	0	2	4	2	0
Jim Burton, p	.000	2	0	0	0	0	0	0	0	0	0	0
Bernie Carbo, of-2	.429	4	7	3	3	1	0	2	4	1	1	0
Reggie Cleveland, p	.000	3	2	0	0	0	0	0	0	0	2	0
Cecil Cooper, 1b	.053	5	19	0	1	1	0	0	1	0	3	0
Denny Doyle, 2b	.267	7	30	3	8	1	1	0	0	2	1	0
Dick Drago, p	.000	2	0	0	0	0	0	0	0	0	0	0
Dwight Evans, of	.292	7	24	3	7	1	1	1	5	3	4	0
Carlton Fisk, c	.240	7	25	5	6	0	0	2	4	7	7	0
Doug Griffin, ph	.000	1	1	0	0	0	0	0	0	0	0	0
Bill Lee, p	.167	2	6	0	1	0	0	0	0	0	3	0
Fred Lynn, of	.280	7	25	3	7	1	0	1	5	3	5	0
Rick Miller, of-2	.000	3	2	0	0	0	0	0	0	0	0	0
Bob Montgomery, ph	.000	1	1	0	0	0	0	0	0	0	0	0
Roger Moret, p	.000	3	0	0	0	0	0	0	0	0	0	0
Rico Petrocelli, 3b	.308	7	26	3	8	1	0	0	4	3	6	0
Dick Pole, p	.000	1	0	0	0	0	0	0	0	0	0	0
Diego Segui, p	.000	1	0	0	0	0	0	0	0	0	0	0
Luis Tiant, p	.250	3	8	2	2	0	0	0	0	2	4	0
Jim Willoughby, p	.000	3	0	0	0	0	0	0	0	0	0	0
Rick Wise, p	.000	2	2	0	0	0	0	0	0	0	0	0
Carl Yastrzemski, 1b-4,of-4	.310	7	29	7	9	0	0	0	4	4	1	0
TOTAL	.251		239	30	60	7	2	6	30	30	40	0

PITCHER	W	L	ERA	G	GS	CG	SV	SHO	IP	H	ER	BB	SO
Jim Burton	0	1	9.00	2	0	0	0	0	1.0	1	1	3	0
Reggie Cleveland	0	1	6.75	3	1	0	0	0	6.2	7	5	3	5
Dick Drago	0	1	2.25	2	0	0	0	0	4.0	3	1	1	1
Bill Lee	0	0	3.14	2	2	0	0	0	14.1	12	5	3	7
Roger Moret	0	0	0.00	3	0	0	0	0	1.2	2	0	3	1
Dick Pole	0	0	INF	1	0	0	0	0	0.0	0	1	2	0
Diego Segui	0	0	0.00	1	0	0	0	0	1.0	0	0	0	0
Luis Tiant	2	0	3.60	3	3	2	0	1	25.0	25	10	8	12
Jim Willoughby	0	1	0.00	3	0	0	0	0	6.1	3	0	0	2
Rick Wise	1	0	8.44	2	1	0	0	0	5.1	6	5	2	2
TOTAL	3	4	3.86	22	7	2	0	1	65.1	59	28	25	30

GAME 1 AT BOS OCT 11

CIN	000 000 000	0	5	0
BOS	000 000 60X	6	12	0

Pitchers: GULLETT, Carroll (7), McEnaney (7) vs TIANT
Attendance: 35,205

GAME 2 AT BOS OCT 12

CIN	000 100 002	3	7	1
BOS	100 001 000	2	7	0

Pitchers: Billingham, Borbon (6), McEnaney (7), EASTWICK (8) vs Lee, Drago (9)
Attendance: 35,205

GAME 3 AT CIN OCT 14

BOS	010 001 102 0	5	10	2
CIN	000 230 000 1	6	7	0

Pitchers: Wise, Burton (5), Cleveland (5), WILLOUGHBY (7), Moret (10) VS Nolan, Darcy (5), Carroll (7), McEnaney (7), EASTWICK (9)
Home Runs: Fisk-BOS, Bench-CIN, Concepcion-CIN, Geronimo-CIN, Carbo-BOS, Evans-BOS
Attendance: 55,392

GAME 4 AT CIN OCT 15

BOS	000 500 000	5	11	1
CIN	200 200 000	4	9	1

Pitchers: TIANT vs NORMAN, Borbon (4), Carroll (5), Eastwick (7)
Attendance: 55,667

GAME 5 AT CIN OCT 16

BOS	100 000 001	2	5	0
CIN	000 113 01X	6	8	0

Pitchers: CLEVELAND, Willoughby (6), Pole (8), Segui (8) vs GULLETT, Eastwick (9)
Home Runs: Perez-CIN (2)
Attendance: 56,393

GAME 6 AT BOS OCT 21

CIN	000 030 210 000	6	14	0
BOS	300 000 030 001	7	10	1

Pitchers: Nolan, Norman (3), Billingham (3), Carroll (5), Borbon (6), Eastwick (8), McEnaney (9), DARCY (10) VS Tiant, Moret (8), Drago (9), WISE (12)
Home Runs: Lynn-BOS, Geronimo-CIN, Carbo-BOS, Fisk-BOS
Attendance: 35,205

GAME 7 AT BOS OCT 22

CIN	000 002 101	4	9	0
BOS	003 000 000	3	5	2

Pitchers: Gullett, Billingham (5), CARROLL (7), McEnaney (9) vs Lee, Moret (7), Willoughby (7), BURTON (9), Cleveland (9)
Home Runs: Perez-CIN
Attendance: 35,205

Philadelphia outhit Cincinnati in two of the three games, but couldn't turn enough hits into runs, as the Reds for the second year in a row swept the LCS. The Phillies scored first in Game One with a run in the first inning. But pitcher Don Gullett held them scoreless for the next seven innings as his Reds caught up in the third, moved ahead in the sixth, and took a five-run lead into the last of the ninth. The Phillies scored twice in their half of the inning, but the rally fell short.

In the second game the Phillies outhit the Reds ten to six, scoring the game's first two runs while their starter Jim Lonborg threw a no-hitter for five innings. But in the sixth a walk and two singles drove Lonborg out and set the Reds off on a two-inning six-run spree for their second win.

Again in Game Three the Phillies outhit the Reds, this time going into the last of the ninth ahead by two runs. But George Foster and Johnny Bench hit back-to-back homers off Ron Reed to tie the score, and two relievers (and a single and two walks) later, the Reds brought home another pennant as Ken Griffey's high-bouncing chop glanced off first baseman Bobby Tolan's outstretched glove.

Cincinnati Reds (West), 3; Philadelphia Phillies (East) 0

CIN (W)

PLAYER/POS	AVG	G	AB	R	H	2B	3B	HR	RB	BB	SO	SB
Ed Armbrister, ph	.000	1	0	0	0	0	0	0	0	0	0	0
Johnny Bench, c	.333	3	12	3	4	1	0	1	1	1	2	1
Pedro Borbon, p	.000	2	2	1	0	0	0	0	0	0	2	0
Dave Concepcion, ss	.200	3	10	4	2	1	0	0	0	2	1	0
Dan Driessen, ph	.000	1	1	0	0	0	0	0	0	0	0	0
Rawly Eastwick, p	.000	2	0	0	0	0	0	0	0	0	0	0
Doug Flynn, 2b	.000	1	0	0	0	0	0	0	0	0	0	0
George Foster, of	.167	3	12	2	2	0	0	2	4	0	4	0
Cesar Geronimo, of	.182	3	11	0	2	0	1	0	2	1	3	0
Ken Griffey, of	.385	3	13	2	5	0	1	0	2	2	1	2
Don Gullett, p	.500	1	4	1	2	1	0	0	3	0	0	0
Mike Lum, ph	.000	1	1	0	0	0	0	0	0	0	0	0
Joe Morgan, 2b	.000	3	7	2	0	0	0	0	0	6	1	2
Gary Nolan, p	.000	1	0	0	0	0	0	0	0	1	0	0
Tony Perez, 1b	.200	3	10	1	2	0	0	0	3	1	2	0
Pete Rose, 3b	.429	3	14	3	6	2	1	0	2	1	0	0
Manny Sarmiento, p	.000	1	1	0	0	0	0	0	0	0	0	0
Pat Zachry, p	.000	1	1	0	0	0	0	0	0	0	0	0
TOTAL	.253		99	19	25	5	3	3	17	15	16	5

PITCHER	W	L	ERA	G	GS	CG	SV	SHO	IP	H	ER	BB	SO
Pedro Borbon	0	0	0.00	2	0	0	1	0	4.1	4	0	1	0
Rawly Eastwick	1	0	12.00	2	0	0	0	0	3.0	7	4	2	1
Don Gullett	1	0	1.13	1	1	0	0	0	8.0	2	1	3	4
Gary Nolan	0	0	1.59	1	1	0	0	0	5.2	6	1	2	1
Manny Sarmiento	0	0	18.00	1	0	0	0	0	1.0	2	2	1	0
Pat Zachry	1	0	3.60	1	1	0	0	0	5.0	6	2	3	3
TOTAL	3	0	3.33	8	3	0	1	0	27.0	27	10	12	9

PHI (E)

PLAYER/POS	AVG	G	AB	R	H	2B	3B	HR	RB	BB	SO	SB
Richie Allen, 1b	.222	3	9	1	2	0	0	0	0	3	2	0
Bob Boone, c	.286	3	7	0	2	0	0	0	1	1	0	0
Larry Bowa, ss	.125	3	8	1	1	1	0	0	1	3	0	0
Ollie Brown, of	.000	1	2	0	0	0	0	0	0	1	1	0
Steve Carlton, p	.000	1	2	0	0	0	0	0	0	0	0	0
Dave Cash, 2b	.308	3	13	1	4	1	0	0	1	0	0	0
Gene Garber, p	.000	2	0	0	0	0	0	0	0	0	0	0
Terry Harmon, pr	.000	1	0	1	0	0	0	0	0	0	0	0
Tom Hutton, ph	.000	1	1	0	0	0	0	0	0	0	0	0
Jay Johnstone, of-2	.778	3	9	1	7	1	1	0	2	1	0	0
Jim Kaat, p	.500	1	2	0	1	0	0	0	0	0	0	0
Jim Lonborg, p	.000	1	1	0	0	0	0	0	0	0	0	0
Greg Luzinski, of	.273	3	11	2	3	2	0	1	2	1	4	0
Garry Maddox, of	.231	3	13	2	3	1	0	0	2	2	0	0
Jerry Martin, of	.000	1	1	1	0	0	0	0	0	0	0	0
Tim Mc Carver, c-1	.000	2	4	0	0	0	0	0	0	0	1	0
Tug Mc Graw, p	.000	2	0	0	0	0	0	0	0	0	0	0
Johnny Oates, c	.000	1	1	0	0	0	0	0	0	0	0	0
Ron Reed, p	.000	2	1	0	0	0	0	0	0	0	0	0
Mike Schmidt, 3b	.308	3	13	1	4	2	0	0	2	0	1	0
Bobby Tolan, 1b-1,of-1	.000	3	2	0	0	0	0	0	0	0	0	0
Tom Underwood, p	.000	1	0	0	0	0	0	0	0	0	0	0
TOTAL	.270		100	11	27	8	1	1	11	12	9	0

PITCHER	W	L	ERA	G	GS	CG	SV	SHO	IP	H	ER	BB	SO
Steve Carlton	0	1	3.86	1	1	0	0	0	7.0	8	3	5	6
Gene Garber	0	1	40.50	2	0	0	0	0	0.2	2	3	1	0
Jim Kaat	0	0	3.00	1	1	0	0	0	6.0	2	2	2	1
Jim Lonborg	0	1	1.69	1	1	0	0	0	5.1	2	1	2	2
Tug Mc Graw	0	0	11.57	2	0	0	0	0	2.1	4	3	1	5
Ron Reed	0	0	7.71	2	0	0	0	0	4.2	6	4	2	2
Tom Underwood	0	0	0.00	1	0	0	0	0	0.1	1	0	2	0
TOTAL	0	3	5.47	10	3	0	0	0	26.1	25	16	15	16

GAME 1 AT PHI OCT 9

CIN	001 002 030	6	10	0
PHI	100 000 002	3	6	1

Pitchers: GULLETT, Eastwick (9) VS CARLTON, McGraw (8)
Home Runs: Foster-CIN
Attendance: 62,640

GAME 2 AT PHI OCT 10

CIN	000 004 200	6	6	0
PHI	010 010 000	2	10	1

Pitchers: ZACHRY, Borbon (6) vs LONBORG, Garber (6), McGraw (7), Reed (7)
Home Runs: Luzinski-PHI
Attendance: 62,651

GAME 3 AT CIN OCT 12

PHI	000 100 221	6	11	0
CIN	000 000 403	7	9	2

Pitchers: Kaat, Reed (7), GARBER (9), Underwood (9) vs Nolan, Sarmiento (6), Borbon (7), EASTWICK (8)
Home Runs: Foster-CIN, Bench-CIN
Attendance: 55,047

Returning to postseason play after a dozen years' absence, the Yankees found themselves evenly matched with the first-time-champion Royals. They didn't really need their two ninth-inning runs in the first game: the two they scored in the first inning proved cushion enough for Catfish Hunter's one-run five-hitter. But Kansas City came back the next day, scoring first, losing the lead in the third, then regaining it for good in the sixth.

The Royals again took a first-inning lead in Game Three, but this time the Yankees, once they went ahead in the sixth, didn't let go. Kansas City held on to its early lead in Game Four, building on it throughout the game for a second win, despite Yankee Graig Nettles' two home runs.

But Game Five—like the series itself—was a seesaw affair. For the fourth time the Royals scored first, with a pair in the first on John Mayberry's home run. But the Yankees tied the game when they came to bat, and K.C. retook the lead in the second. New York went ahead again in the third and increased its lead to 6–3 in the sixth. But in the top of the eighth, George Brett's three-run homer tied the score once again, setting the stage for Chris Chambliss to win for the Yankees their thirtieth American League pennant with his first-pitch home run in the bottom of the ninth.

New York Yankees (East), 3; Kansas City Royals (West) 2

NY (E)

PLAYER/POS	AVG	G	AB	R	H	2B	3B	HR	RB	BB	SO	SB
Sandy Alomar, dh-1	.000	2	1	0	0	0	0	0	0	0	0	0
Chris Chambliss, 1b	.524	5	21	5	11	1	1	2	8	0	1	2
Dock Ellis, p	.000	1	0	0	0	0	0	0	0	0	0	0
Ed Figueroa, p	.000	2	0	0	0	0	0	0	0	0	0	0
Oscar Gamble, of	.250	3	8	1	2	1	0	0	1	1	1	0
Ron Guidry, pr	.000	1	0	0	0	0	0	0	0	0	0	0
Elrod Hendricks, ph	1.000	1	1	0	1	0	0	0	0	0	0	0
Catfish Hunter, p	.000	2	0	0	0	0	0	0	0	0	0	0
Grant Jackson, p	.000	2	0	0	0	0	0	0	0	0	0	0
Sparky Lyle, p	.000	1	0	0	0	0	0	0	0	0	0	0
Elliott Maddox, of	.222	3	9	0	2	1	0	0	1	0	1	0
Jim Mason, ss	.000	2	0	0	0	0	0	0	0	0	0	0
Carlos May, dh	.200	3	10	1	2	1	0	0	0	1	4	0
Thurman Munson, c	.435	5	23	3	10	2	0	0	3	0	1	0
Graig Nettles, 3b	.235	5	17	2	4	1	0	2	4	3	3	0
Lou Piniella, dh-3	.273	4	11	1	3	1	0	0	0	0	1	0
Willie Randolph, 2b	.118	5	17	0	2	0	0	0	1	3	1	1
Mickey Rivers, of	.348	5	23	5	8	0	1	0	0	1	1	0
Fred Stanley, ss	.333	5	15	1	5	2	0	0	0	2	0	0
Dick Tidrow, p	.000	3	0	0	0	0	0	0	0	0	0	0
Otto Velez, ph	.000	1	1	0	0	0	0	0	0	0	0	0
Roy White, of	.294	5	17	4	5	3	0	0	3	5	1	1
TOTAL	.316		174	23	55	13	2	4	21	16	15	4

PITCHER	W	L	ERA	G	GS	CG	SV	SHO	IP	H	ER	BB	SO
Dock Ellis	1	0	3.38	1	1	0	0	0	8.0	6	3	2	5
Ed Figueroa	0	1	5.84	2	2	0	0	0	12.1	14	8	2	5
Catfish Hunter	1	1	4.50	2	2	1	0	0	12.0	10	6	1	5
Grant Jackson	0	0	8.10	2	0	0	0	0	3.1	4	3	1	3
Sparky Lyle	0	0	0.00	1	0	0	1	0	1.0	0	0	1	0
Dick Tidrow	1	0	3.68	3	0	0	0	0	7.1	6	3	4	0
TOTAL	3	2	4.70	11	5	1	1	0	44.0	40	23	11	18

KC (W)

PLAYER/POS	AVG	G	AB	R	H	2B	3B	HR	RB	BB	SO	SB
Doug Bird, p	.000	1	0	0	0	0	0	0	0	0	0	0
George Brett, 3b	.444	5	18	4	8	1	1	1	5	2	1	0
Al Cowens, of	.190	5	21	3	4	0	1	0	0	1	1	2
Larry Gura, p	.000	2	0	0	0	0	0	0	0	0	0	0
Tom Hall, p	.000	1	0	0	0	0	0	0	0	0	0	0
Andy Hassler, p	.000	2	0	0	0	0	0	0	0	0	0	0
Dennis Leonard, p	.000	2	0	0	0	0	0	0	0	0	0	0
Mark Littell, p	.000	3	0	0	0	0	0	0	0	0	0	0
Buck Martinez, c	.333	5	15	0	5	0	0	0	4	1	3	0
John Mayberry, 1b	.222	5	18	4	4	0	0	1	3	1	0	0
Hal Mc Rae, dh-3,of-2	.118	5	17	2	2	1	1	0	1	1	4	0
Steve Mingori, p	.000	3	0	0	0	0	0	0	0	0	0	0
Dave Nelson, dh-1	.000	2	2	0	0	0	0	0	0	0	1	0
Amos Otis, of	.000	1	1	0	0	0	0	0	0	0	0	0
Freddie Patek, ss	.389	5	18	2	7	2	0	0	4	0	1	0
Marty Pattin, p	.000	2	0	0	0	0	0	0	0	0	0	0
Tom Poquette, of	.188	5	16	1	3	2	0	0	4	2	3	0
Jamie Quirk, dh-2	.143	4	7	1	1	0	1	0	2	0	2	0
Cookie Rojas, 2b	.333	4	9	2	3	0	0	0	1	0	0	1
Paul Splittorff, p	.000	2	0	0	0	0	0	0	0	0	0	0
Bob Stinson, c-1	.000	2	1	0	0	0	0	0	0	0	0	0
John Wathan, c	.000	1	0	0	0	0	0	0	0	0	0	0
Frank White, 2b	.125	4	8	2	1	0	0	0	0	0	1	0
Jim Wohlford, of	.182	5	11	3	2	0	0	0	0	3	1	2
TOTAL	.247		162	24	40	6	4	2	24	11	18	5

PITCHER	W	L	ERA	G	GS	CG	SV	SHO	IP	H	ER	BB	SO
Doug Bird	1	0	1.93	1	0	0	0	0	4.2	4	1	0	1
Larry Gura	0	1	4.22	2	2	0	0	0	10.2	18	5	1	4
Tom Hall	0	0	0.00	1	0	0	0	0	0.1	1	0	0	0
Andy Hassler	0	1	6.14	2	1	0	0	0	7.1	8	5	6	4
Dennis Leonard	0	0	19.29	2	2	0	0	0	2.1	9	5	2	0
Mark Littell	0	1	1.93	3	0	0	0	0	4.2	4	1	1	3
Steve Mingori	0	0	2.70	3	0	0	1	0	3.⅓	4	1	0	1
Marty Pattin	0	0	27.00	2	0	0	0	0	0.1	0	1	1	0
Paul Splittorff	1	0	1.93	2	0	0	0	0	9.1	7	2	5	2
TOTAL	2	3	4.40	18	5	0	1	0	43.0	55	21	16	15

GAME 1 AT KC OCT 9

| NY | 200 000 002 | 4 12 0 |
| KC | 000 000 010 | 1 5 2 |

Pitchers: HUNTER vs GURA, Littell (9)
Attendance: 41,077

GAME 2 AT KC OCT 10

| NY | 012 000 000 | 3 12 5 |
| KC | 200 002 03X | 7 9 0 |

Pitchers: FIGUEROA, Tidrow (6) vs Leonard, SPLITTORFF (3), Mingori (9)
Attendance: 41,091

GAME 3 AT NY OCT 12

| KC | 300 000 000 | 3 6 0 |
| NY | 000 203 00X | 5 9 0 |

Pitchers: HASSLER, Pattin (6), Hall (6), Mingori (6), Littell (6) vs ELLIS, Lyle (9)
Home Runs: Chambliss-NY
Attendance: 56,808

GAME 4 AT NY OCT 13

| KC | 030 201 010 | 7 9 1 |
| NY | 020 000 101 | 4 11 0 |

Pitchers: Gura, BIRD (3), Mingori (7) vs HUNTER, Tidrow (4), Jackson (7)
Home Runs: Nettles-NY (2)
Attendance: 56,355

GAME 5 AT NY OCT 14

| KC | 210 000 030 | 6 11 1 |
| NY | 202 000 001 | 7 11 1 |

Pitchers: Leonard, Splittorff (1), Pattin (4), Hassler (5), LITTELL (7) vs Figueroa, Jackson (8), TIDROW (9)
Home Runs: Mayberry-KC, Brett-KC, Chambliss-NY
Attendance: 56,821

The Reds led the National League in virtually every offensive category and in fielding as well. In the Series (which, incidentally, was the first to employ the designated hitter), the Big Red Machine continued its roll over the Yankees to become the first National League club in fifty-four years to repeat as world champions, as well as the first team to sweep both a League Championship and World Series. Red catcher Johnny Bench led the attack with eight hits, half of them for extra bases, for a batting average of .533 and a 1.133 average in slugging.

Joe Morgan's home run for Cincinnati in the first inning of Game One was the first hit of the Series, but New York pushed across a tying run half an inning later on a sacrifice fly. Red pitchers Don Gullett and Pedro Borbon held the Yankees scoreless after that as the Reds regained the lead with a run in the third and extended it in the sixth and seventh for a 5–1 win.

Game Two turned out to be the Reds' only narrow victory. They scored first, with three runs in the second inning. In the fourth the Yankees scored their first run, and they tied the score with two more runs in the seventh. But with two men out in the last of the ninth, a throwing error by Yankee shortstop Fred Stanley allowed the Reds' batter Ken Griffey to reach second, from where he scored the winning run on Tony Perez's line single to left.

In Game Three, four hits and a pair of stolen bases put Cincinnati ahead 3–0 in the second inning, and Dan Driessen homered in the fourth to make it 4–0 before the Yankees scored their first run. Another quartet of hits in the eighth gave the Reds two more runs and a 6–2 win.

New York took the lead for the only time in the Series when Chris Chambliss doubled in Thurman Munson in the first inning of Game Four. (Munson had singled with the third of what became six straight hits.) But the Reds' George Foster drove in a tying run in the fourth, and Johnny Bench followed him with a two-run homer. New York scored again an inning later to come close, but Bench's second home run, a three-run blast in the ninth, put the game out of reach, and a pair of ground-rule doubles touched by New York fans nailed the final run in the Yankee coffin.

Cincinnati Reds (NL), 4;
New York Yankees (AL) 0

CIN (N)

PLAYER/POS	AVG	G	AB	R	H	2B	3B	HR	RB	BB	SO	SB
Johnny Bench, c	.533	4	15	4	8	1	1	2	6	0	1	0
Jack Billingham, p	.000	1	0	0	0	0	0	0	0	0	0	0
Pedro Borbon, p	.000	1	0	0	0	0	0	0	0	0	0	0
Dave Concepcion, ss	.357	4	14	1	5	1	1	0	3	1	3	1
Dan Driessen, dh	.357	4	14	4	5	2	0	1	1	2	0	1
George Foster, of	.429	4	14	3	6	1	0	0	4	2	3	0
Cesar Geronimo, of	.308	4	13	3	4	2	0	0	1	2	2	2
Ken Griffey, of	.059	4	17	2	1	0	0	0	1	0	1	1
Don Gullett, p	.000	1	0	0	0	0	0	0	0	0	0	0
Will Mc Enaney, p	.000	2	0	0	0	0	0	0	0	0	0	0
Joe Morgan, 2b	.333	4	15	3	5	1	1	1	2	2	2	2
Gary Nolan, p	.000	1	0	0	0	0	0	0	0	0	0	0
Fred Norman, p	.000	1	0	0	0	0	0	0	0	0	0	0
Tony Perez, 1b	.313	4	16	1	5	1	0	0	2	1	2	0
Pete Rose, 3b	.188	4	16	1	3	1	0	0	1	2	2	0
Pat Zachry, p	.000	1	0	0	0	0	0	0	0	0	0	0
TOTAL	.313		134	22	42	10	3	4	21	12	16	7

PITCHER	W	L	ERA	G	GS	CG	SV	SHO	IP	H	ER	BB	SO
Jack Billingham	1	0	0.00	1	0	0	0	0	2.2	0	0	0	1
Pedro Borbon	0	0	0.00	1	0	0	0	0	1.2	0	0	0	0
Don Gullett	1	0	1.23	1	1	0	0	0	7.1	5	1	3	4
Will Mc Enaney	0	0	0.00	2	0	0	2	0	4.2	2	0	1	2
Gary Nolan	1	0	2.70	1	1	0	0	0	6.2	8	2	1	1
Fred Norman	0	0	4.26	1	1	0	0	0	6.1	9	3	2	2
Pat Zachry	1	0	2.70	1	1	0	0	0	6.2	6	2	5	6
TOTAL	4	0	2.00	8	4	0	2	0	36.0	30	8	12	16

NY (A)

PLAYER/POS	AVG	G	AB	R	H	2B	3B	HR	RB	BB	SO	SB
Doyle Alexander, p	.000	1	0	0	0	0	0	0	0	0	0	0
Chris Chambliss, 1b	.313	4	16	1	5	1	0	0	1	0	2	0
Dock Ellis, p	.000	1	0	0	0	0	0	0	0	0	0	0
Ed Figueroa, p	.000	1	0	0	0	0	0	0	0	0	0	0
Oscar Gamble, of-2	.125	3	8	0	1	0	0	0	1	0	0	0
Elrod Hendricks, ph	.000	2	2	0	0	0	0	0	0	0	0	0
Catfish Hunter, p	.000	1	0	0	0	0	0	0	0	0	0	0
Grant Jackson, p	.000	1	0	0	0	0	0	0	0	0	0	0
Sparky Lyle, p	.000	2	0	0	0	0	0	0	0	0	0	0
Elliott Maddox, of-1,dh-1	.200	2	5	0	1	0	1	0	0	1	2	0
Jim Mason, ss	1.000	3	1	1	1	0	0	1	1	0	0	0
Carlos May, dh	.000	4	9	0	0	0	0	0	0	0	1	0
Thurman Munson, c	.529	4	17	2	9	0	0	0	2	0	1	0
Graig Nettles, 3b	.250	4	12	0	3	0	0	0	2	3	1	0
Lou Piniella, of-2,dh-2	.333	4	9	1	3	1	0	0	0	0	0	0
Willie Randolph, 2b	.071	4	14	1	1	0	0	0	0	1	3	0
Mickey Rivers, of	.167	4	18	1	3	0	0	0	0	1	2	1
Fred Stanley, ss	.167	4	6	1	1	1	0	0	1	3	1	0
Dick Tidrow, p	.000	2	0	0	0	0	0	0	0	0	0	0
Otto Velez, ph	.000	3	3	0	0	0	0	0	0	0	0	0
Roy White, of	.133	4	15	0	2	0	0	0	0	3	0	0
TOTAL	.222		135	8	30	3	1	1	8	12	16	1

PITCHER	W	L	ERA	G	GS	CG	SV	SHO	IP	H	ER	BB	SO
Doyle Alexander	0	1	7.50	1	1	0	0	0	6.0	9	5	2	1
Dock Ellis	0	1	10.80	1	1	0	0	0	3.1	7	4	0	1
Ed Figueroa	0	1	5.63	1	1	0	0	0	8.0	6	5	5	2
Catfish Hunter	0	1	3.12	1	1	1	0	0	8.2	10	3	4	5
Grant Jackson	0	0	4.91	1	0	0	0	0	3.2	4	2	0	3
Sparky Lyle	0	0	0.00	2	0	0	0	0	2.2	1	0	0	3
Dick Tidrow	0	0	7.71	2	0	0	0	0	2.1	5	2	1	1
TOTAL	0	4	5.45	9	4	1	0	0	34.2	42	21	12	16

GAME 1 AT CIN OCT 16

NY	010 000 000	1	5	1
CIN	101 001 20X	5	10	1

Pitchers: ALEXANDER, Lyle (7) vs GULLETT, Borbon (8)
Home Runs: Morgan-CIN
Attendance: 54,826

GAME 2 AT CIN OCT 17

NY	000 100 200	3	9	1
CIN	030 000 001	4	10	0

Pitchers: HUNTER vs Norman, BILLINGHAM (7)
Attendance: 54,816

GAME 3 AT NY OCT 19

CIN	030 100 020	6	13	2
NY	000 100 100	2	8	0

Pitchers: ZACHRY, McEnaney (7) vs ELLIS, Jackson (4), Tidrow (8)
Home Runs: Driessen-CIN, Mason-NY
Attendance: 56,667

GAME 4 AT NY OCT 21

CIN	000 300 004	7	9	2
NY	100 010 000	2	8	0

Pitchers: NOLAN, McEnaney (7) vs FIGUEROA, Tidrow (9), Lyle (9)
Home Runs: Bench-CIN (2)
Attendance: 56,700

The Phillies took the first game, but the Dodgers proved better over all at turning hits into runs and swept the next three. Philadelphia jumped ahead in the first inning of Game One, and had built a 5–1 lead by the seventh, when Ron Cey tied the score with a Dodger grand slam. But the Phillies came back with two runs on three singles in the top of the ninth and held on for the win. As in Game One, both clubs again got nine hits apiece in Game Two, but this time Dodger pitcher Don Sutton scattered the Phillies' hits for a single run over nine innings, while Phillie starter Jim Lonborg—in the four innings he pitched—yielded five runs, including a grand slam to Dusty Baker.

In Game Three Los Angeles outhit the Phillies, but the Dodgers were nearly undone when starter Burt Hooton walked in three Philadelphia runs in the second inning. The Phillies took a two-run lead into the ninth, but after two men were out the Dodgers rebounded, thanks largely to a couple of old pros. Pinch hitter Vic Davalillo, age 38, beat out a drag bunt on a disputed call, and 39-year-old Manny Mota doubled to deep left. Two more Dodger singles scored three runs that proved enough for the win.

The Dodgers didn't even need all of their five hits to take the final game behind Tommy John's one-run seven-hitter, for one of those hits was another Dusty Baker home run with a man aboard.

Los Angeles Dodgers (West), 3;
Philadelphia Phillies (East) 1

LA (W)

PLAYER/POS	AVG	G	AB	R	H	2B	3B	HR	RB	BB	SO	SB
Dusty Baker, of	.357	4	14	4	5	1	0	2	8	2	3	0
Glenn Burke, of	.000	4	7	0	0	0	0	0	0	0	3	0
Ron Cey, 3b	.308	4	13	4	4	1	0	1	4	2	4	1
Vic Davalillo, ph	1.000	1	1	1	1	0	0	0	0	0	0	0
Mike Garman, p	.000	2	0	0	0	0	0	0	0	0	0	0
Steve Garvey, 1b	.308	4	13	2	4	0	0	0	0	2	1	1
Ed Goodson, ph	.000	1	1	0	0	0	0	0	0	0	0	0
Jerry Grote, c-1	.000	2	0	0	0	0	0	0	0	1	0	0
Burt Hooton, p	1.000	1	1	0	1	1	0	0	0	0	0	0
Charley Hough, p	.000	1	0	0	0	0	0	0	0	0	0	0
Tommy John, p	.200	2	5	0	1	0	0	0	0	0	2	0
Lee Lacy, ph	1.000	1	1	1	1	0	0	0	0	0	0	0
Davey Lopes, 2b	.235	4	17	2	4	0	0	0	3	2	0	0
Rick Monday, of	.286	3	7	1	2	1	0	0	0	2	1	0
Manny Mota, ph	1.000	1	1	1	1	1	0	0	0	0	0	0
Doug Rau, p	.000	1	0	0	0	0	0	0	0	0	0	0
Lance Rautzhan, p	.000	1	0	0	0	0	0	0	0	0	0	0
Rick Rhoden, p	.000	1	1	0	0	0	0	0	0	0	0	0
Bill Russell, ss	.278	4	18	3	5	1	0	0	2	0	0	0
Reggie Smith, of	.188	4	16	2	3	0	1	0	1	2	5	1
Elias Sosa, p	.000	2	1	0	0	0	0	0	0	0	0	0
Don Sutton, p	.000	1	3	0	0	0	0	0	0	0	0	0
Steve Yeager, c	.231	4	13	1	3	0	0	0	2	1	3	0
TOTAL	.263		133	22	35	6	1	3	20	14	22	3

PITCHER	W	L	ERA	G	GS	CG	SV	SHO	IP	H	ER	BB	SO
Mike Garman	0	0	0.00	2	0	0	1	0	1.1	0	0	0	1
Burt Hooton	0	0	16.20	1	1	0	0	0	1.2	3	4	4	1
Charley Hough	0	0	4.50	1	0	0	0	0	2.0	2	1	0	3
Tommy John	1	0	0.66	2	2	1	0	0	13.2	11	1	5	11
Doug Rau	0	0	0.00	1	0	0	0	0	1.0	0	0	0	1
Lance Rautzhan	1	0	0.00	1	0	0	0	0	0.1	0	0	0	0
Rick Rhoden	0	0	0.00	1	0	0	0	0	4.1	2	0	2	0
Elias Sosa	0	1	10.13	2	0	0	0	0	2.2	5	3	0	0
Don Sutton	1	0	1.00	1	1	1	0	0	9.0	9	1	0	4
TOTAL	3	1	2.25	12	4	2	1	0	36.0	31	9	11	21

PHI (E)

PLAYER/POS	AVG	G	AB	R	H	2B	3B	HR	RB	BB	SO	SB
Bob Boone, c	.400	4	10	1	4	0	0	0	0	0	0	0
Larry Bowa, ss	.118	4	17	2	2	0	0	0	1	1	0	0
Ollie Brown, ph	.000	2	2	0	0	0	0	0	0	0	1	0
Warren Brusstar, p	.000	2	0	0	0	0	0	0	0	0	0	0
Steve Carlton, p	.500	2	4	0	2	0	0	0	1	0	2	0
Larry Christenson, p	.000	1	0	0	0	0	0	0	1	1	0	0
Gene Garber, p	.000	3	0	0	0	0	0	0	0	0	0	0
Richie Hebner, 1b-3	.357	4	14	2	5	2	0	0	0	0	1	0
Tom Hutton, 1b-1	.000	3	3	0	0	0	0	0	0	0	0	0
Davy Johnson, 1b	.250	1	4	0	1	0	0	0	2	0	1	0
Jay Johnstone, of	.200	2	5	0	1	0	0	0	0	0	1	0
Jim Lonborg, p	.000	1	1	0	0	0	0	0	0	0	1	0
Greg Luzinski, of	.286	4	14	2	4	1	0	1	2	3	3	1
Garry Maddox, of	.429	2	7	1	3	0	0	0	2	0	1	0
Jerry Martin, of-1	.000	3	4	0	0	0	0	0	0	0	2	0
Bake Mc Bride, of	.222	4	18	2	4	0	0	1	2	1	2	0
Tim Mc Carver, c-2	.167	3	6	1	1	0	0	0	0	1	3	0
Tug Mc Graw, p	.000	2	0	0	0	0	0	0	0	0	0	0
Ron Reed, p	.000	3	0	0	0	0	0	0	0	0	0	0
Mike Schmidt, 3b	.063	4	16	2	1	0	0	0	1	2	3	0
Ted Sizemore, 2b	.231	4	13	1	3	0	0	0	0	2	0	0
TOTAL	.225		138	14	31	3	0	2	12	11	21	1

PITCHER	W	L	ERA	G	GS	CG	SV	SHO	IP	H	ER	BB	SO
Warren Brusstar	0	0	3.38	2	0	0	0	0	2.2	2	1	1	2
Steve Carlton	0	1	6.94	2	2	0	0	0	11.2	13	9	8	6
Larry Christenson	0	0	8.10	1	1	0	0	0	3.1	7	3	0	2
Gene Garber	1	1	3.38	3	0	0	0	0	5.1	4	2	0	3
Jim Lonborg	0	1	11.25	1	1	0	0	0	4.0	5	5	1	1
Tug Mc Graw	0	0	0.00	2	0	0	1	0	3.0	1	0	2	3
Ron Reed	0	0	1.80	3	0	0	0	0	5.0	3	1	2	5
TOTAL	1	3	5.40	14	4	0	1	0	35.0	35	21	14	22

GAME 1 AT LA OCT 4

PHI	200	021	002	7	9 0
LA	000	010	400	5	9 2

Pitchers: Carlton, GARBER (7), McGraw (9) vs John, Garman (5), Hough (6), SOSA (8)
Home Runs: Luzinski-PHI, Cey-LA
Attendance: 55,968

GAME 2 AT LA OCT 5

PHI	001	000	000	1	9 1
LA	001	401	10X	7	9 1

Pitchers: LONBORG, Reed (5), Brusstar (7) vs SUTTON
Home Runs: McBride-PHI, Baker-LA
Attendance: 55,973

GAME 3 AT PHI OCT 7

LA	020	100	003	6	12 2
PHI	030	000	020	5	6 2

Pitchers: Hooton, Rhoden (2), Rau (7), Sosa (8), RAUTZHAN (8), Garman (9) vs Christenson, Brusstar (4), Reed (5), GARBER (7)
Attendance: 63,719

GAME 4 AT PHI OCT 8

LA	020	020	000	4	5 0
PHI	000	100	000	1	7 0

Pitchers: JOHN vs CARLTON, Reed (6), McGraw (7), Garber (9)
Home Runs: Baker-LA
Attendance: 64,924

As in 1976, the Royals met the Yankees in the LCS, and as in 1976 the series went five games, with the Royals outscoring New York by a single run. But this time Kansas City won the first game, and as the teams traded victories through the first four games and K.C. took a lead into the ninth inning of Game Five, it began to look as though this year the Royals might take the pennant.

Royal hitters began things with a bang, scoring six of their seven runs in Game One in the first three innings for an insurmountable lead. New York came back to take the second game 6–2 behind Ron Guidry's three-hitter, but the Royals reversed the score the next day as Dennis Leonard limited the Yankees to four hits. Yankee reliever Sparky Lyle shut K.C. down over the final five innings of Game Four after the Royals had drawn within a run of New York in the fourth inning, and the series was tied.

In the finale, Kansas City drew first blood with two runs in the bottom of the first and led by one run after eight. But with the pennant in sight, the Royals gave up three Yankee runs in the top of the ninth, scoring nothing themselves as reliever Lyle held them off to give the Yankees their thirty-first flag.

New York Yankees (East), 3; Kansas City Royals (West) 2

NY (E)

PLAYER/POS	AVG	G	AB	R	H	2B	3B	HR	RB	BB	SO	SB
Paul Blair, of	.400	3	5	1	2	0	0	0	0	0	0	0
Chris Chambliss, 1b	.059	5	17	0	1	0	0	0	0	3	4	0
Bucky Dent, ss	.214	5	14	1	3	1	0	0	2	1	0	0
Ed Figueroa, p	.000	1	0	0	0	0	0	0	0	0	0	0
Ron Guidry, p	.000	2	0	0	0	0	0	0	0	0	0	0
Don Gullett, p	.000	1	0	0	0	0	0	0	0	0	0	0
Reggie Jackson, of-4,dh-1	.125	5	16	1	2	0	0	0	1	2	2	1
Cliff Johnson, dh-4	.400	5	15	2	6	2	0	1	2	1	2	0
Sparky Lyle, p	.000	4	0	0	0	0	0	0	0	0	0	0
Thurman Munson, c	.286	5	21	3	6	1	0	1	5	0	2	0
Graig Nettles, 3b	.150	5	20	1	3	0	0	0	1	0	3	0
Lou Piniella, of-4,dh-1	.333	5	21	1	7	3	0	0	2	0	1	0
Willie Randolph, 2b	.278	5	18	4	5	1	0	0	2	1	0	0
Mickey Rivers, of	.391	5	23	5	9	2	0	0	2	0	2	1
Fred Stanley, ss	.000	2	0	0	0	0	0	0	0	0	0	0
Dick Tidrow, p	.000	2	0	0	0	0	0	0	0	0	0	0
Mike Torrez, p	.000	2	0	0	0	0	0	0	0	0	0	0
Roy White, of-1,dh-1	.400	4	5	2	2	2	0	0	0	1	0	0
TOTAL	.263		175	21	46	12	0	2	17	9	16	2

PITCHER	W	L	ERA	G	GS	CG	SV	SHO	IP	H	ER	BB	SO
Ed Figueroa	0	0	10.80	1	1	0	0	0	3.1	5	4	2	3
Ron Guidry	1	0	3.97	2	2	1	0	0	11.1	9	5	3	8
Don Gullett	0	1	18.00	1	1	0	0	0	2.0	4	4	2	0
Sparky Lyle	2	0	0.96	4	0	0	0	0	9.1	7	1	0	3
Dick Tidrow	0	0	3.86	2	0	0	0	0	7.0	6	3	3	3
Mike Torrez	0	1	4.09	2	1	0	0	0	11.0	11	5	5	5
TOTAL	3	2	4.50	12	5	1	0	0	44.0	42	22	15	22

KC (W)

PLAYER/POS	AVG	G	AB	R	H	2B	3B	HR	RB	BB	SO	SB
Doug Bird, p	.000	3	0	0	0	0	0	0	0	0	0	0
George Brett, 3b	.300	5	20	2	6	0	2	0	2	1	0	0
Al Cowens, of	.263	5	19	2	5	0	0	1	5	1	3	0
Larry Gura, p	.000	2	0	0	0	0	0	0	0	0	0	0
Andy Hassler, p	.000	1	0	0	0	0	0	0	0	0	0	0
Pete La Cock, 1b	.000	1	1	0	0	0	0	0	0	1	1	0
Joe Lahoud, dh	.000	1	1	2	0	0	0	0	0	2	0	0
Dennis Leonard, p	.000	2	0	0	0	0	0	0	0	0	0	0
Mark Littell, p	.000	2	0	0	0	0	0	0	0	0	0	0
John Mayberry, 1b	.167	4	12	1	2	1	0	1	3	1	2	0
Hal Mc Rae, dh-3,of-2	.444	5	18	6	8	3	0	1	2	3	1	0
Steve Mingori, p	.000	3	0	0	0	0	0	0	0	0	0	0
Amos Otis, of	.125	5	16	1	2	1	0	0	2	2	3	2
Freddie Patek, ss	.389	5	18	4	7	3	1	0	5	1	2	0
Marty Pattin, p	.000	1	0	0	0	0	0	0	0	0	0	0
Tom Poquette, of	.167	2	6	0	1	0	0	0	0	0	0	0
Darrell Porter, c	.333	5	15	3	5	0	0	0	0	3	0	0
Cookie Rojas, dh	.250	1	4	0	1	0	0	0	0	0	1	1
Paul Splittorff, p	.000	2	0	0	0	0	0	0	0	0	0	0
John Wathan, 1b-2,c-1,dh-1	.000	4	6	0	0	0	0	0	0	0	3	0
Frank White, 2b	.278	5	18	1	5	1	0	0	2	0	4	1
Joe Zdeb, of	.000	4	9	0	0	0	0	0	0	0	2	1
TOTAL	.258		163	22	42	9	3	3	21	15	22	5

PITCHER	W	L	ERA	G	GS	CG	SV	SHO	IP	H	ER	BB	SO
Doug Bird	0	0	0.00	3	0	0	0	0	2.0	4	0	0	1
Larry Gura	0	1	18.00	2	1	0	0	0	2.0	7	4	1	2
Andy Hassler	0	1	4.76	1	1	0	0	0	5.2	5	3	0	3
Dennis Leonard	1	1	3.00	2	1	1	0	0	9.0	5	3	2	4
Mark Littell	0	0	3.00	2	0	0	0	0	3.0	5	1	3	1
Steve Mingori	0	0	0.00	3	0	0	0	0	1.1	0	0	0	1
Marty Pattin	0	0	1.50	1	0	0	0	0	6.0	6	1	0	0
Paul Splittorff	1	0	2.40	2	2	0	0	0	15.0	14	4	3	4
TOTAL	2	3	3.27	16	5	1	0	0	44.0	46	16	9	16

GAME 1 AT NY OCT 5

KC	222	000	010	7	9	0
NY	002	000	000	2	9	0

Pitchers: SPLITTORFF, Bird (9) vs GULLETT. Tidrow (3), Lyle (9)
Home Runs: McRae-KC, Mayberry-KC, Munson-NY, Cowens-KC
Attendance: 54,930

GAME 2 AT NY OCT 6

KC	001	001	000	2	3	1
NY	000	023	01X	6	10	1

Pitchers: HASSLER, Littell (6), Mingori (8) vs GUIDRY
Home Runs: Johnson-NY
Attendance: 56,230

GAME 3 AT KC OCT 7

NY	000	010	001	2	4	1
KC	011	012	10X	6	12	1

Pitchers: TORREZ. Lyle (6) vs LEONARD
Attendance: 41,285

GAME 4 AT KC OCT 8

NY	121	100	001	6	13	0
KC	002	200	000	4	8	2

Pitchers: Figueroa, Tidrow (4), LYLE (4) vs GURA, Pattin (3), Mingori (9), Bird (9)
Attendance: 41,135

GAME 5 AT KC OCT 9

NY	001	000	013	5	10	0
KC	201	000	000	3	10	1

Pitchers: Guidry, Torrez (3), LYLE (8) vs Splittorff, Bird (8), Mingori (8), LEONARD (9), Gura (9), Littell (9)
Attendance: 41,133

This was the Series in which Yankee Reggie Jackson established his reputation as "Mr. October" with a record five home runs, including three in successive at-bats in the final game, and the Yankees showed that after a decade or so of decline they were once again the world's best. Los Angeles scored first in the opening game with a pair of first-inning runs. But New York gained back half the ground in the bottom of the first and tied the game on Willie Randolph's leadoff homer in the sixth. The clubs traded runs in the eighth and ninth to take the game into extra innings. The impasse was not breached until the last of the twelfth, when Randolph doubled and Paul Blair singled him home.

Game Two, by contrast, was a runaway Dodger victory. Home runs in the first three innings by Ron Cey, Steve Yeager, and Reggie Smith made the score 5–0 before New York scored its lone run in the fourth. Burt Hooton hurled the Dodger win, a five-hitter. And for good measure, Dodger Steve Garvey homered in the ninth inning. The Yankees returned to form two days later in Los Angeles, though, scoring three runs in the top of the first on pairs of doubles and singles (and a Dodger error). Dodger Dusty Baker's three-run homer tied the game in the third, but single Yankee runs in the next two innings provided pitcher Mike Torrez with runs enough for the win.

Two of the four hits yielded by emerging Yankee ace Ron Guidry in Game Four were pitcher Rick Rhoden's double followed by Davey Lopes's home run in the third inning. But the Yankees had already scored three times in the second, and Reggie Jackson homered in the sixth as Guidry held Los Angeles scoreless after the third for a 4–2 win. A Yankee assault against Dodger pitcher Don Sutton in Game Five included back-to-back home runs by Thurman Munson and Jackson in the eighth inning. But Los Angeles rocked Yankee pitching even harder, with homers by Steve Yeager and Reggie Smith producing five of the Dodgers' ten runs as the club evaded elimination with its second win.

The Dodgers scored first in the sixth game when Steve Garvey's first-inning triple drove in two runners. Yankee Chris Chambliss matched that an inning later with a two-run homer. Smith restored the lead to Los Angeles with a solo shot in the third inning, but Jackson put the Yankees back in front with the first of his three home runs, a two-run blast in the fourth. By the time he had homered again for two in the fifth and for the third time in the eighth, the

New York Yankees (AL), 4; Los Angeles Dodgers (NL) 2

NY (A)

PLAYER/POS	AVG	G	AB	R	H	2B	3B	HR	RB	BB	SO	SB
Paul Blair, of-3	.250	4	4	0	1	0	0	0	1	0	0	0
Chris Chambliss, 1b	.292	6	24	4	7	2	0	1	4	0	2	0
Ken Clay, p	.000	2	0	0	0	0	0	0	0	0	0	0
Bucky Dent, ss	.263	6	19	0	5	0	0	0	2	2	1	0
Ron Guidry, p	.000	1	2	0	0	0	0	0	0	0	1	0
Don Gullett, p	.000	2	2	0	0	0	0	0	0	0	2	0
Catfish Hunter, p	.000	2	0	0	0	0	0	0	0	0	0	0
Reggie Jackson, of	.450	6	20	10	9	1	0	5	8	3	4	0
Cliff Johnson, c-1	.000	2	1	0	0	0	0	0	0	0	0	0
Sparky Lyle, p	.000	2	2	0	0	0	0	0	0	0	2	0
Thurman Munson, c	.320	6	25	4	8	2	0	1	3	2	8	0
Graig Nettles, 3b	.190	6	21	1	4	1	0	0	2	2	3	0
Lou Piniella, of	.273	6	22	1	6	0	0	0	3	0	3	0
Willie Randolph, 2b	.160	6	25	5	4	2	0	1	1	1	2	0
Mickey Rivers, of	.222	6	27	1	6	2	0	0	1	0	2	1
Fred Stanley, ss	.000	1	0	0	0	0	0	0	0	0	0	0
Dick Tidrow, p	.000	2	1	0	0	0	0	0	0	0	1	0
Mike Torrez, p	.000	2	6	0	0	0	0	0	0	0	4	0
Roy White, ph	.000	2	2	0	0	0	0	0	0	0	0	0
George Zeber, ph	.000	2	2	0	0	0	0	0	0	0	2	0
TOTAL	.244		205	26	50	10	0	8	25	11	37	1

PITCHER	W	L	ERA	G	GS	CG	SV	SHO	IP	H	ER	BB	SO
Ken Clay	0	0	2.45	2	0	0	0	0	3.2	2	1	1	0
Ron Guidry	1	0	2.00	1	1	1	0	0	9.0	4	2	3	7
Don Gullett	0	1	6.39	2	2	0	0	0	12.2	13	9	7	10
Catfish Hunter	0	1	10.38	2	1	0	0	0	4.1	6	5	0	1
Sparky Lyle	1	0	1.93	2	0	0	0	0	4.2	2	1	0	2
Dick Tidrow	0	0	4.91	2	0	0	0	0	3.2	5	2	0	1
Mike Torrez	2	0	2.50	2	2	2	0	0	18.0	16	5	5	15
TOTAL	4	2	4.02	13	6	3	0	0	56.0	48	25	16	36

LA (N)

PLAYER/POS	AVG	G	AB	R	H	2B	3B	HR	RB	BB	SO	SB
Dusty Baker, of	.292	6	24	4	7	0	0	1	5	0	2	0
Glenn Burke, of	.200	3	5	0	1	0	0	0	0	0	1	0
Ron Cey, 3b	.190	6	21	2	4	1	0	1	3	3	5	0
Vic Davalillo, ph	.333	3	3	0	1	0	0	0	1	0	0	0
Mike Garman, p	.000	2	0	0	0	0	0	0	0	0	0	0
Steve Garvey, 1b	.375	6	24	5	9	1	1	1	3	1	4	0
Ed Goodson, ph	.000	1	1	0	0	0	0	0	0	0	1	0
Jerry Grote, c	.000	1	1	0	0	0	0	0	0	0	0	0
Burt Hooton, p	.000	2	5	0	0	0	0	0	0	0	2	0
Charley Hough, p	.000	2	0	0	0	0	0	0	0	0	0	0
Tommy John, p	.000	1	2	0	0	0	0	0	0	0	2	0
Lee Lacy, of-2	.429	4	7	1	3	0	0	0	2	1	1	0
Rafael Landestoy, pr	.000	1	0	0	0	0	0	0	0	0	0	0
Davey Lopes, 2b	.167	6	24	3	4	0	1	1	2	4	3	2
Rick Monday, of	.167	4	12	0	2	0	0	0	0	0	3	0
Manny Mota, ph	.000	3	3	0	0	0	0	0	0	0	1	0
Johnny Oates, c	.000	1	1	0	0	0	0	0	0	0	0	0
Doug Rau, p	.000	2	0	0	0	0	0	0	0	0	0	0
Lance Rautzhan, p	.000	1	0	0	0	0	0	0	0	0	0	0
Rick Rhoden, p	.500	2	2	1	1	1	0	0	0	0	0	0
Bill Russell, ss	.154	6	26	3	4	0	1	0	2	1	3	0
Reggie Smith, of	.273	6	22	7	6	1	0	3	5	4	3	0
Elias Sosa, p	.000	2	0	0	0	0	0	0	0	0	0	0
Don Sutton, p	.000	2	6	0	0	0	0	0	0	0	1	0
Steve Yeager, c	.316	6	19	2	6	1	0	2	5	1	1	0
TOTAL	.231		208	28	48	5	3	9	28	16	36	2

PITCHER	W	L	ERA	G	GS	CG	SV	SHO	IP	H	ER	BB	SO
Mike Garman	0	0	0.00	2	0	0	0	0	4.0	2	0	1	3
Burt Hooton	1	1	3.75	2	2	1	0	0	12.0	8	5	2	9
Charley Hough	0	0	1.80	2	0	0	0	0	5.0	3	1	0	5
Tommy John	0	1	6.00	1	1	0	0	0	6.0	9	4	3	7
Doug Rau	0	1	11.57	2	1	0	0	0	2.1	4	3	0	1
Lance Rautzhan	0	0	0.00	1	0	0	0	0	0.1	0	0	2	0
Rick Rhoden	0	1	2.57	2	0	0	0	0	7.0	4	2	1	5
Elias Sosa	0	0	11.57	2	0	0	0	0	2.1	3	3	1	1
Don Sutton	1	0	3.94	2	2	1	0	0	16.0	17	7	7	3
TOTAL	2	4	4.09	16	6	2	0	0	55.0	50	25	17	34

Yankees' twenty-first world title was well in hand.

GAME 1 AT NY OCT 11

LA	200 000 001 000	3	6	0
NY	100 001 010 001	4	11	0

Pitchers: Sutton, Rautzhan (8), Sosa (8), Garman (9), RHODEN (12) vs Gullett, LYLE (9)
Home Runs: Randolph-NY
Attendance: 56,668

GAME 2 AT NY OCT 12

LA	212 000 001	6	9	0
NY	000 100 000	1	5	0

Pitchers: HOOTON vs HUNTER, Tidrow (3), Clay (6), Lyle (9)
Home Runs: Cey-LA, Yeager-LA, Smith-LA, Garvey-LA
Attendance: 56,691

GAME 3 AT LA OCT 14

NY	300 110 000	5	10	0
LA	003 000 000	3	7	1

Pitchers: TORREZ vs JOHN, Hough (7)
Home Runs: Baker-LA
Attendance: 55,992

GAME 4 AT LA OCT 15

NY	030 001 000	4	7	0
LA	002 000 000	2	4	0

Pitchers: GUIDRY vs RAU, Rhoden (2), Garman (9)
Home Runs: Lopes-LA, Jackson-NY
Attendance: 55,995

GAME 5 AT LA OCT 16

NY	000 000 220	4	9	2
LA	100 432 00X	10	13	0

Pitchers: GULLETT, Clay (5), Tidrow (6), Hunter (7) vs SUTTON
Home Runs: Yeager-LA, Smith-LA, Munson-NY, Jackson-NY
Attendance: 55,955

GAME 6 AT NY OCT 18

LA	201 000 001	4	9	0
NY	020 320 01X	8	8	1

Pitchers: HOOTON, Sosa (4), Rau (5), Hough (7) vs TORREZ
Home Runs: Chambliss-NY, Smith-LA, Jackson-NY (3)
Attendance: 56,407

Steve Garvey hit half the Dodgers' eight home runs and Tommy John hurled the first LCS shutout in four years as Los Angeles, for the second year in a row, defeated the Phillies for the pennant in four games. Philadelphia's five runs in Game One would have been enough to win any of the other games, but not this one as the Dodgers outhomered the Phillies four to one (including two by Garvey) and scored nine times. Dodger Davey Lopes hit the game's only home run the next day (with a man aboard), but it was more than enough support for John's four-hit shutout.

The series' most decisive win went to the Phillies in Game Three. Steve Carlton allowed four Dodger runs to score, but he made up for it by driving in his own four runs on a homer and sacrifice fly. His teammates added five more, rendering futile Garvey's third series home run.

But Garvey's fourth homer, in Game Four, helped carry the Dodgers into the tenth inning, when Bill Russell—capitalizing on Gary Maddox's muff of Ron Cey's fly to center—singled home Cey with the Dodgers' unearned pennant winner.

Los Angeles Dodgers (West), 3; Philadelphia Phillies (East), 1

LA (W)

PLAYER/POS	AVG	G	AB	R	H	2B	3B	HR	RB	BB	SO	SB
Dusty Baker, of	.467	4	15	1	7	2	0	0	1	3	0	0
Ron Cey, 3b	.313	4	16	4	5	1	0	1	3	2	4	0
Joe Ferguson, ph	.000	2	2	0	0	0	0	0	0	0	1	0
Terry Forster, p	.000	1	0	0	0	0	0	0	0	0	0	0
Steve Garvey, 1b	.389	4	18	6	7	1	1	4	7	0	1	0
Jerry Grote, c	.000	1	0	0	0	0	0	0	0	0	0	0
Burt Hooton, p	.000	1	2	0	0	0	0	0	0	0	1	0
Charley Hough, p	.000	1	0	0	0	0	0	0	0	0	0	0
Tommy John, p	.000	1	3	0	0	0	0	0	0	0	0	0
Lee Lacy, ph	.000	2	2	0	0	0	0	0	0	0	0	0
Davey Lopes, 2b	.389	4	18	3	7	1	1	2	5	0	1	1
Rick Monday, of	.200	3	10	2	2	0	1	0	0	1	5	0
Manny Mota, ph	1.000	2	1	0	1	1	0	0	0	0	0	0
Billy North, of	.000	4	8	0	0	0	0	0	0	0	1	0
Doug Rau, p	.000	1	1	0	0	0	0	0	0	0	0	0
Lance Rautzhan, p	.000	1	0	0	0	0	0	0	0	0	0	0
Rick Rhoden, p	.000	1	1	0	0	0	0	0	0	0	0	0
Bill Russell, ss	.412	4	17	1	7	1	0	0	2	1	1	0
Reggie Smith, of	.188	4	16	2	3	1	0	0	1	0	2	0
Don Sutton, p	.000	1	2	0	0	0	0	0	0	0	2	0
Bob Welch, p	.000	1	2	0	0	0	0	0	0	0	1	0
Steve Yeager, c	.231	4	13	2	3	0	0	1	2	2	2	1
TOTAL	.286		147	21	42	8	3	8	21	9	22	2

PITCHER	W	L	ERA	G	GS	CG	SV	SHO	IP	H	ER	BB	SO
Terry Forster	1	0	0.00	1	0	0	0	0	1.0	1	0	0	2
Burt Hooton	0	0	7.71	1	1	0	0	0	4.2	10	4	0	5
Charley Hough	0	0	4.50	1	0	0	0	0	2.0	1	1	0	1
Tommy John	1	0	0.00	1	1	1	0	1	9.0	4	0	2	4
Doug Rau	0	0	3.60	1	1	0	0	0	5.0	5	2	2	1
Lance Rautzhan	0	0	6.75	1	0	0	0	0	1.1	3	1	2	0
Rick Rhoden	0	0	2.25	1	0	0	0	0	4.0	2	1	1	3
Don Sutton	0	1	6.35	1	1	0	0	0	5.2	7	4	2	0
Bob Welch	1	0	2.08	1	0	0	0	0	4.1	2	1	0	5
TOTAL	3	1	3.41	9	4	1	0	1	37.0	35	14	9	21

PHI (E)

PLAYER/POS	AVG	G	AB	R	H	2B	3B	HR	RB	BB	SO	SB
Bob Boone, c	.182	3	11	0	2	0	0	0	0	0	1	0
Larry Bowa, ss	.333	4	18	2	6	0	0	0	0	1	2	0
Warren Brusstar, p	.000	3	0	0	0	0	0	0	0	0	0	0
Jose Cardenal, 1b	.167	2	6	0	1	0	0	0	0	1	1	0
Steve Carlton, p	.500	1	4	2	2	0	0	1	4	0	0	0
Larry Christenson, p	.000	1	1	0	0	0	0	0	0	0	1	0
Rawly Eastwick, p	.000	1	0	0	0	0	0	0	0	0	0	0
Barry Foote, ph	.000	1	1	0	0	0	0	0	0	0	1	0
Orlando Gonzalez, ph	.000	1	1	0	0	0	0	0	0	0	1	0
Richie Hebner, 1b-2	.111	3	9	0	1	0	0	0	1	0	0	0
Randy Lerch, p	.000	1	2	0	0	0	0	0	0	0	0	0
Greg Luzinski, of	.375	4	16	3	6	0	1	2	3	1	2	0
Garry Maddox, of	.263	4	19	1	5	0	0	0	2	0	3	0
Jerry Martin, of-3	.222	4	9	1	2	1	0	1	2	1	3	0
Bake Mc Bride, of-2	.222	3	9	2	2	0	0	1	1	0	2	0
Tim Mc Carver, c-1	.000	2	4	2	0	0	0	0	1	2	0	0
Tug Mc Graw, p	.000	3	0	0	0	0	0	0	0	0	0	0
Jim Morrison, ph	.000	1	1	0	0	0	0	0	0	0	1	0
Ron Reed, p	.000	2	0	0	0	0	0	0	0	0	0	0
Dick Ruthven, p	.000	1	1	0	0	0	0	0	0	0	1	0
Mike Schmidt, 3b	.200	4	15	1	3	2	0	0	1	2	2	0
Ted Sizemore, 2b	.385	4	13	3	5	0	1	0	1	1	0	0
TOTAL	.250		140	17	35	3	2	5	16	9	21	0

PITCHER	W	L	ERA	G	GS	CG	SV	SHO	IP	H	ER	BB	SO
Warren Brusstar	0	0	0.00	3	0	0	0	0	2.2	2	0	1	0
Steve Carlton	1	0	4.00	1	1	1	0	0	9.0	8	4	2	8
Larry Christenson	0	1	12.46	1	1	0	0	0	4.1	7	6	1	3
Rawly Eastwick	0	0	9.00	1	0	0	0	0	1.0	3	1	0	1
Randy Lerch	0	0	5.06	1	1	0	0	0	5.1	7	3	0	0
Tug Mc Graw	0	1	1.59	3	0	0	0	0	5.2	3	1	5	5
Ron Reed	0	0	2.25	2	0	0	0	0	4.0	6	1	0	2
Dick Ruthven	0	1	5.79	1	1	0	0	0	4.2	6	3	0	3
TOTAL	1	3	4.66	13	4	1	0	0	36.2	42	19	9	22

GAME 1 AT PHI OCT 4

LA	004 211 001	9 13 1
PHI	010 030 001	5 12 1

Pitchers: Hooton, WELCH (5) vs CHRISTENSEN, Brusstar (5), Eastwick (6), McGraw (7)
Home Runs: Garvey-LA (2), Lopes-LA, Yeager-LA, Martin-PHI
Attendance: 63,460

GAME 2 AT PHI OCT 5

LA	000 120 100	4 8 0
PHI	000 000 000	0 4 0

Pitchers: JOHN vs RUTHVEN, Brusstar (5), Reed (7), McGraw (9)
Home Runs: Lopes-LA
Attendance: 60,642

GAME 3 AT LA OCT 6

PHI	040 003 101	9 11 1
LA	012 000 010	4 8 2

Pitchers: CARLTON vs SUTTON, Rautzhan (6), Hough (8)
Home Runs: Carlton-PHI, Luzinski-PHI, Garvey-LA
Attendance: 55,043

GAME 4 AT LA OCT 7

PHI	002 000 100 0	3 8 2
LA	010 101 000 1	4 13 0

Pitchers: Lerch, Brusstar (6), Reed (7), McGRAW (9) vs Rau, Rhoden (6), FORSTER (10)
Home Runs: Luzinski-PHI, Cey-LA, Garvey-LA, McBride-PHI
Attendance: 55,124

It took Bucky Dent's pop-fly home run against Boston in an Eastern Division tiebreaker to carry the Yankees into the LCS. But once there they took the pennant, downing the Royals for the third year in a row. Reggie Jackson's three-run homer in the eighth inning of Game One capped a sixteen-hit, seven-run Yankee attack, as pitchers Jim Beattie and Ken Clay combined to limit Kansas City to two hits and a single run. The Royals, though, made it look just as easy the next day as their own sixteen hits and ten runs evened the series.

Twice in Game Three George Brett gave the Royals a lead with a home run, and he tied the game with a third homer in the fifth. But Jackson's two-run homer in the fourth brought the Yankees back, and Thurman Munson's two-run shot in the eighth gave New York a close win. Game Four was just as close, but more of a pitcher's duel. Dennis Leonard, who went the distance, gave up only four hits, but two of them were home runs to Graig Nettles and Roy White. Yankee starter Ron Guidry allowed a run in the first, but shut out the Royals for the next seven innings. Goose Gossage preserved Guidry's good work—and the pennant—in the ninth.

New York Yankees (East), 3; Kansas City Royals (West), 1

NY (E)

PLAYER/POS	AVG	G	AB	R	H	2B	3B	HR	RB	BB	SO	SB
Jim Beattie, p	.000	1	0	0	0	0	0	0	0	0	0	0
Paul Blair, of-3,2b-1	.000	4	6	1	0	0	0	0	0	0	1	0
Chris Chambliss, 1b	.400	4	15	1	6	0	0	0	2	0	4	0
Ken Clay, p	.000	1	0	0	0	0	0	0	0	0	0	0
Bucky Dent, ss	.200	4	15	0	3	0	0	0	4	0	0	0
Brian Doyle, 2b	.286	3	7	0	2	0	0	0	1	1	1	0
Ed Figueroa, p	.000	1	0	0	0	0	0	0	0	0	0	0
Rich Gossage, p	.000	2	0	0	0	0	0	0	0	0	0	0
Ron Guidry, p	.000	1	0	0	0	0	0	0	0	0	0	0
Catfish Hunter, p	.000	1	0	0	0	0	0	0	0	0	0	0
Reggie Jackson, dh-3,of-1	.462	4	13	5	6	1	0	2	6	3	4	0
Cliff Johnson, ph	.000	1	1	0	0	0	0	0	0	0	0	0
Sparky Lyle, p	.000	1	0	0	0	0	0	0	0	0	0	0
Thurman Munson, c	.278	4	18	2	5	1	0	1	2	0	0	0
Graig Nettles, 3b	.333	4	15	3	5	0	1	1	2	0	1	0
Lou Piniella, of	.235	4	17	2	4	0	0	0	0	0	3	0
Mickey Rivers, of	.455	4	11	0	5	0	0	0	0	2	0	0
Fred Stanley, 2b	.200	2	5	0	1	0	0	0	0	0	2	0
Gary Thomasson, of	.000	3	1	0	0	0	0	0	0	0	0	0
Dick Tidrow, p	.000	1	0	0	0	0	0	0	0	0	0	0
Roy White, of-3,dh-1	.313	4	16	5	5	1	0	1	1	1	2	0
TOTAL	.300		140	19	42	3	1	5	18	7	18	0

PITCHER	W	L	ERA	G	GS	CG	SV	SHO	IP	H	ER	BB	SO
Jim Beattie	1	0	1.69	1	1	0	0	0	5.1	2	1	5	3
Ken Clay	0	0	0.00	1	0	0	1	0	3.2	0	0	3	2
Ed Figueroa	0	1	27.00	1	1	0	0	0	1.0	5	3	0	0
Rich Gossage	1	0	4.50	2	0	0	1	0	4.0	3	2	0	3
Ron Guidry	1	0	1.13	1	1	0	0	0	8.0	7	1	1	7
Catfish Hunter	0	0	4.50	1	1	0	0	0	6.0	7	3	3	5
Sparky Lyle	0	0	13.50	1	0	0	0	0	1.1	3	2	0	0
Dick Tidrow	0	0	4.76	1	0	0	0	0	5.2	8	3	2	1
TOTAL	3	1	3.86	9	4	0	2	0	35.0	35	15	14	21

KC (W)

PLAYER/POS	AVG	G	AB	R	H	2B	3B	HR	RB	BB	SO	SB
Doug Bird, p	.000	2	0	0	0	0	0	0	0	0	0	0
Steve Braun, of-1	.000	2	5	0	0	0	0	0	0	1	1	0
George Brett, 3b	.389	4	18	7	7	1	1	3	3	0	1	0
Al Cowens, of	.133	4	15	2	2	0	0	0	1	0	2	0
Larry Gura, p	.000	1	0	0	0	0	0	0	0	0	0	0
Al Hrabosky, p	.000	3	0	0	0	0	0	0	0	0	0	0
Clint Hurdle, of-2	.375	4	8	1	3	0	1	0	1	2	3	0
Pete La Cock, 1b-3	.364	4	11	1	4	2	1	0	1	3	1	1
Dennis Leonard, p	.000	2	0	0	0	0	0	0	0	0	0	0
Hal Mc Rae, dh	.214	4	14	0	3	0	0	0	2	2	2	1
Steve Mingori, p	.000	1	0	0	0	0	0	0	0	0	0	0
Amos Otis, of	.429	4	14	2	6	2	0	0	1	3	5	4
Freddie Patek, ss	.077	4	13	2	1	0	0	1	2	1	4	0
Marty Pattin, p	.000	1	0	0	0	0	0	0	0	0	0	0
Tom Poquette, ph	.000	1	1	0	0	0	0	0	0	0	0	0
Darrell Porter, c	.357	4	14	1	5	1	0	0	3	2	0	0
Paul Splittorff, p	.000	1	0	0	0	0	0	0	0	0	0	0
John Wathan, 1b	.000	1	3	0	0	0	0	0	0	0	0	0
Frank White, 2b	.231	4	13	1	3	0	0	0	2	0	0	0
Willie Wilson, of	.250	3	4	0	1	0	0	0	0	0	2	0
TOTAL	.263		133	17	35	6	3	4	16	14	21	6

PITCHER	W	L	ERA	G	GS	CG	SV	SHO	IP	H	ER	BB	SO
Doug Bird	0	1	9.00	2	0	0	0	0	1.0	2	1	0	1
Larry Gura	1	0	2.84	1	1	0	0	0	6.1	8	2	2	2
Al Hrabosky	0	0	3.00	3	0	0	0	0	3.0	3	1	0	2
Dennis Leonard	0	2	3.75	2	2	1	0	0	12.0	13	5	2	11
Steve Mingori	0	0	7.36	1	0	0	0	0	3.2	5	3	3	0
Marty Pattin	0	0	27.00	1	0	0	0	0	0.2	2	2	0	0
Paul Splittorff	0	0	4.91	1	1	0	0	0	7.1	9	4	0	2
TOTAL	1	3	4.76	11	4	1	0	0	34.0	42	18	7	18

GAME 1 AT KC OCT 3

NY	011 020 030	7	16	0
KC	000 001 000	1	2	2

Pitchers: BEATTIE, Clay (6) vs LEONARD, Mingori (5), Hrabosky (8), Bird (9)
Home Runs: Jackson-NY
Attendance: 41,143

GAME 2 AT KC OCT 4

NY	000 000 220	4	12	1
KC	140 000 32X	10	16	1

Pitchers: FIGUEROA, Tidrow (2), Lyle (7) vs GURA, Pattin (7), Hrabosky (8)
Home Runs: Patek-KC
Attendance: 41,158

GAME 3 AT NY OCT 6

KC	101 010 020	5	10	1
NY	010 201 02X	6	10	0

Pitchers: Splittorff, BIRD (8), Hrabosky (8) vs Hunter, GOSSAGE (7)
Home Runs: Brett-KC (3), Jackson-NY, Munson-NY
Attendance: 55,535

GAME 4 AT NY OCT 7

KC	100 000 000	1	7	0
NY	010 001 00X	2	4	0

Pitchers: LEONARD vs GUIDRY, Gossage (9)
Home Runs: Nettles-NY, R.White-NY
Attendance: 56,356

The outcome was the same as in 1977: the Yankees over the Dodgers in six games. But this year New York overcame a two-game deficit by sweeping the next four, a feat never before achieved in a World Series.

Los Angeles overwhelmed New York in the opener. Home runs in the second and fourth innings by Dusty Baker and Davey Lopes (two, for five RBIs), and another run in the fifth, gave the Dodgers a 7–0 lead before Reggie Jackson's leadoff homer in the seventh gave New York its first score. The Yankees scored four more times, but so did the Dodgers for an 11–5 win. Game Two was closer. The Yankees scored first and held a lead through the top of the sixth, but Ron Cey's three-run homer in the bottom of the inning gave Los Angeles the runs they needed to win 4–3.

Yankee Ron Guidry, coming off a spectacular 25–3 regular season, pitched Game Three as the Series moved to New York. He gave up eight hits and issued seven walks. But only one baserunner scored, thanks in large part to several memorable stops and throws by third baseman Graig Nettles. Meanwhile, Roy White's home run in the first inning began Yankee scoring in what would become a 5–1 win.

It took ten innings for New York to win Game Four. Starters Tommy John and Ed Figueroa hurled shutout ball until Dodger Reggie Smith tagged Figueroa for a three-run homer in the top of the fifth. The Yankees clawed back in the sixth. Reggie Jackson singled in one run, then—in a play that stirred great controversy—got in the way (the Dodgers claimed intentionally) of a throw from second on an attempted double play, deflecting the ball to the outfield and permitting a second run to score. In the eighth, Thurman Munson doubled home the tying Yankee run, and in the last of the tenth Lou Piniella's two-out drive to center scored baserunner Roy White with the game winner.

Game Five was a Yankee blowout. No one hit home runs, but the Yankees hit sixteen singles (a Series record) and two doubles for twelve runs (five of them driven in by Munson's three hits) to give Yankee pitcher Jim Beattie (nine hits, two runs) an easy win. Back in Los Angeles for the sixth game, the Yankees won the crown on the hitting of two men at the bottom of the batting order: Denny Doyle and Bucky Dent. With three hits each, they combined for five RBIs in the 7–2 win. For good measure, Reggie Jackson concluded the Series scoring with a mighty two-run in the seventh.

New York Yankees (AL), 4; Los Angeles Dodgers (NL), 2

NY (A)

PLAYER/POS	AVG	G	AB	R	H	2B	3B	HR	RB	BB	SO	SB
Jim Beattie, p	.000	1	0	0	0	0	0	0	0	0	0	0
Paul Blair, of	.375	6	8	2	3	1	0	0	0	1	4	0
Chris Chambliss, 1b	.182	3	11	1	2	0	0	0	0	1	1	0
Ken Clay, p	.000	1	0	0	0	0	0	0	0	0	0	0
Bucky Dent, ss	.417	6	24	3	10	1	0	0	7	1	2	0
Brian Doyle, 2b	.438	6	16	4	7	1	0	0	2	0	0	0
Ed Figueroa, p	.000	2	0	0	0	0	0	0	0	0	0	0
Rich Gossage, p	.000	3	0	0	0	0	0	0	0	0	0	0
Ron Guidry, p	.000	1	0	0	0	0	0	0	0	0	0	0
Mike Heath, c	.000	1	0	0	0	0	0	0	0	0	0	0
Catfish Hunter, p	.000	2	0	0	0	0	0	0	0	0	0	0
Reggie Jackson, dh	.391	6	23	2	9	1	0	2	8	3	7	0
Cliff Johnson, ph	.000	2	2	0	0	0	0	0	0	0	1	0
Jay Johnstone, of	.000	2	0	0	0	0	0	0	0	0	0	0
Paul Lindblad, p	.000	1	0	0	0	0	0	0	0	0	0	0
Thurman Munson, c	.320	6	25	5	8	3	0	0	7	3	7	1
Graig Nettles, 3b	.160	6	25	2	4	0	0	0	1	0	6	0
Lou Piniella, of	.280	6	25	3	7	0	0	0	4	0	0	1
Mickey Rivers, of-4	.333	5	18	2	6	0	0	0	1	0	2	1
Jim Spencer, 1b-3	.167	4	12	3	2	0	0	0	0	2	4	0
Fred Stanley, 2b	.200	3	5	0	1	1	0	0	0	1	0	0
Gary Thomasson, of	.250	3	4	0	1	0	0	0	0	0	1	0
Dick Tidrow, p	.000	2	0	0	0	0	0	0	0	0	0	0
Roy White, of	.333	6	24	9	8	0	0	1	4	4	5	2
TOTAL	.306		222	36	68	8	0	3	34	16	40	5

PITCHER	W	L	ERA	G	GS	CG	SV	SHO	IP	H	ER	BB	SO
Jim Beattie	1	0	2.00	1	1	1	0	0	9.0	9	2	4	8
Ken Clay	0	0	11.57	1	0	0	0	0	2.1	4	3	2	2
Ed Figueroa	0	1	8.10	2	2	0	0	0	6.2	9	6	5	2
Rich Gossage	1	0	0.00	3	0	0	0	0	6.0	1	0	1	4
Ron Guidry	1	0	1.00	1	1	1	0	0	9.0	8	1	7	4
Catfish Hunter	1	1	4.15	2	2	0	0	0	13.0	13	6	1	5
Paul Lindblad	0	0	11.57	1	0	0	0	0	2.1	4	3	0	1
Dick Tidrow	0	0	1.93	2	0	0	0	0	4.2	4	1	0	5
TOTAL	4	2	3.74	13	6	2	0	0	53.0	52	22	20	31

LA (N)

PLAYER/POS	AVG	G	AB	R	H	2B	3B	HR	RB	BB	SO	SB
Dusty Baker, of	.238	6	21	2	5	0	0	1	1	1	3	0
Ron Cey, 3b	.286	6	21	2	6	0	0	1	4	3	3	0
Vic Davalillo, dh-1	.333	2	3	0	1	0	0	0	0	0	0	0
Joe Ferguson, c	.500	2	4	1	2	2	0	0	0	0	1	0
Terry Forster, p	.000	3	0	0	0	0	0	0	0	0	0	0
Steve Garvey, 1b	.208	6	24	1	5	1	0	0	0	1	7	1
Jerry Grote, c	.000	2	0	0	0	0	0	0	0	0	0	0
Burt Hooton, p	.000	2	0	0	0	0	0	0	0	0	0	0
Charley Hough, p	.000	2	0	0	0	0	0	0	0	0	0	0
Tommy John, p	.000	2	0	0	0	0	0	0	0	0	0	0
Lee Lacy, dh	.143	4	14	0	2	0	0	0	1	1	3	0
Davey Lopes, 2b	.308	6	26	7	8	0	0	3	7	2	1	2
Rick Monday, of-4,dh-1	.154	5	13	2	2	1	0	0	0	4	3	0
Manny Mota, ph	.000	1	0	0	0	0	0	0	0	0	0	0
Billy North, of	.125	4	8	2	1	1	0	0	0	2	1	1
Johnny Oates, c	1.000	1	1	0	1	0	0	0	0	1	0	0
Doug Rau, p	.000	1	0	0	0	0	0	0	0	0	0	0
Lance Rautzhan, p	.000	2	0	0	0	0	0	0	0	0	0	0
Bill Russell, ss	.423	6	26	1	11	2	0	0	2	2	2	1
Reggie Smith, of	.200	6	25	3	5	0	0	1	5	2	6	0
Don Sutton, p	.000	2	0	0	0	0	0	0	0	0	0	0
Bob Welch, p	.000	3	0	0	0	0	0	0	0	0	0	0
Steve Yeager, c	.231	5	13	2	3	1	0	0	0	1	2	0
TOTAL	.261		199	23	52	8	0	6	22	20	31	5

PITCHER	W	L	ERA	G	GS	CG	SV	SHO	IP	H	ER	BB	SO
Terry Forster	0	0	0.00	3	0	0	0	0	4.0	5	0	1	6
Burt Hooton	1	1	6.48	2	2	0	0	0	8.1	13	6	3	6
Charley Hough	0	0	8.44	2	0	0	0	0	5.1	10	5	2	5
Tommy John	1	0	3.07	2	2	0	0	0	14.2	14	5	4	6
Doug Rau	0	0	0.00	1	0	0	0	0	2.0	1	0	0	3
Lance Rautzhan	0	0	13.50	2	0	0	0	0	2.0	4	3	0	0
Don Sutton	0	2	7.50	2	2	0	0	0	12.0	17	10	4	8
Bob Welch	0	1	6.23	3	0	0	1	0	4.1	4	3	2	6
TOTAL	2	4	5.47	17	6	0	1	0	52.2	68	32	16	40

GAME 1 AT LA OCT 10

NY	000	000	320	5	9	1
LA	030	310	31X	11	15	2

Pitchers: FIGUEROA, Clay (2), Lindblad (5), Tidrow (7) vs JOHN, Forster (8)
Home Runs: Baker-LA, Lopes-LA (2), Jackson-NY
Attendance: 55,997

GAME 2 AT LA OCT 11

NY	002	000	100	3	11	0
LA	000	103	00X	4	7	0

Pitchers: HUNTER, Gossage (7) vs HOOTON, Forster (7), Welch (9)
Home Runs: Cey-LA
Attendance: 55,982

GAME 3 AT NY OCT 13

LA	001	000	000	1	8	0
NY	110	000	30X	5	10	1

Pitchers: SUTTON, Rautzhan (7), Hough (8) vs GUIDRY
Home Runs: White-NY
Attendance: 56,447

GAME 4 AT NY OCT 14

LA	000	030	000	0	3	6	1
NY	000	002	010	1	4	9	0

Pitchers: John, Forster (8), WELCH (8) vs Figueroa, Tidrow (6), GOSSAGE (9)
Home Runs: Smith-LA
Attendance: 56,445

GAME 5 AT NY OCT 15

LA	101	000	000	2	9	3
NY	004	300	41X	12	18	0

Pitchers: HOOTON, Rautzhan (3), Hough (4) vs BEATTIE
Attendance: 56,448

GAME 6 AT LA OCT 17

NY	030	002	200	7	11	0
LA	101	000	000	2	7	1

Pitchers: HUNTER, Gossage (8) vs SUTTON, Welch (7), Rau (8)
Home Runs: Lopes-LA, Jackson-NY
Attendance: 55,985

The Pirates—with a better season's record than Cincinnati and stronger hitting and pitching—proved their superiority in the LCS as well, dominating the statistics and sweeping the series. Yet the games were closer than the stats alone would suggest. Pittsburgh won the first game by three runs—but they didn't come until Willie Stargell's homer in the eleventh inning broke a 2–2 tie.

In Game Two, Cincinnati scored first. The Pirates tied the game with a run in the fourth and took a narrow lead with another in the fifth. But the Reds came back on a game-tying pair of doubles in the ninth, and it wasn't until the tenth that Pittsburgh eked out its victory with a run on two singles and Don Robinson's shutout relief.

Only in the third game did the Pirates take a commanding lead, with six runs in the first four innings (two of them on home runs by Stargell and Bill Madlock). The Reds outhit Pittsburgh eight to seven, but only Johnny Bench's homer brought them a run, as Bert Blyleven overcame them in the series' only complete-game pitching performance.

Pittsburgh Pirates (East), 3; Cincinnati Reds (West), 0

PIT (E)

PLAYER/POS	AVG	G	AB	R	H	2B	3B	HR	RB	BB	SO	SB
Matt Alexander, pr	.000	1	0	1	0	0	0	0	0	0	0	0
Jim Bibby, p	.000	1	0	0	0	0	0	0	0	1	0	0
Bert Blyleven, p	.333	1	3	1	1	0	0	0	0	0	1	0
John Candelaria, p	.000	1	3	0	0	0	0	0	0	0	2	0
Mike Easler, ph	.000	1	1	0	0	0	0	0	0	0	0	0
Tim Foli, ss	.333	3	12	1	4	1	0	0	3	0	0	0
Phil Garner, 2b-3,ss-1	.417	3	12	4	5	0	1	1	1	1	0	0
Grant Jackson, p	.000	2	1	0	0	0	0	0	0	0	0	0
Bill Madlock, 3b	.250	3	12	1	3	0	0	1	2	2	0	2
John Milner, of	.000	3	9	0	0	0	0	0	0	2	0	0
Omar Moreno, of	.250	3	12	3	3	0	1	0	0	2	2	1
Ed Ott, c	.231	3	13	0	3	0	0	0	0	0	2	0
Dave Parker, of	.333	3	12	2	4	0	0	0	2	2	3	1
Dave Roberts, p	.000	1	0	0	0	0	0	0	0	0	0	0
Don Robinson, p	.000	2	0	0	0	0	0	0	0	0	0	0
Bill Robinson, of	.000	3	3	0	0	0	0	0	0	0	0	0
Enrique Romo, p	.000	2	0	0	0	0	0	0	0	0	0	0
Willie Stargell, 1b	.455	3	11	2	5	2	0	2	6	3	2	0
Rennie Stennett, 2b	.000	1	0	0	0	0	0	0	0	0	0	0
Kent Tekulve, p	.000	2	1	0	0	0	0	0	0	0	1	0
TOTAL	.267		105	15	28	3	2	4	14	13	13	4

PITCHER	W	L	ERA	G	GS	CG	SV	SHO	IP	H	ER	BB	SO
Jim Bibby	0	0	1.29	1	1	0	0	0	7.0	4	1	4	5
Bert Blyleven	1	0	1.00	1	1	1	0	0	9.0	8	1	0	9
John Candelaria	0	0	2.57	1	1	0	0	0	7.0	5	2	1	4
Grant Jackson	0	0	0.00	2	0	0	0	0	2.0	1	0	1	2
Dave Roberts	0	0	INF	1	0	0	0	0	0.0	0	0	1	0
Don Robinson	1	0	0.00	2	0	0	1	0	2.0	0	0	1	3
Enrique Romo	0	0	0.00	2	0	0	0	0	0.1	3	0	1	1
Kent Tekulve	0	0	3.00	2	0	0	0	0	3.0	2	1	2	2
TOTAL	3	0	1.48	12	3	1	1	0	30.1	23	5	11	26

CIN (W)

PLAYER/POS	AVG	G	AB	R	H	2B	3B	HR	RB	BB	SO	SB
Rick Auerbach, ph	.000	2	2	0	0	0	0	0	0	0	1	0
Doug Bair, p	.000	1	0	0	0	0	0	0	0	0	0	0
Johnny Bench, c	.250	3	12	1	3	0	1	1	1	2	2	0
Dave Collins, of	.357	3	14	0	5	1	0	0	1	0	2	2
Dave Concepcion, ss	.429	3	14	1	6	1	0	0	0	0	3	0
Hector Cruz, of-1	.200	2	5	1	1	1	0	0	0	0	1	0
Dan Driessen, 1b	.083	3	12	1	1	0	0	0	0	1	3	0
George Foster, of	.200	3	10	1	2	0	0	1	2	4	3	0
Cesar Geronimo, of	.143	2	7	0	1	0	0	0	0	0	5	0
Tom Hume, p	.000	3	1	0	0	0	0	0	0	0	1	0
Ray Knight, 3b	.286	3	14	0	4	1	0	0	0	0	2	1
Mike La Coss, p	.000	1	0	0	0	0	0	0	0	0	0	0
Charlie Leibrandt, p	.000	1	0	0	0	0	0	0	0	0	0	0
Joe Morgan, 2b	.000	3	11	0	0	0	0	0	0	3	1	1
Fred Norman, p	.000	1	1	0	0	0	0	0	0	0	1	0
Frank Pastore, p	.000	1	0	0	0	0	0	0	0	1	0	0
Tom Seaver, p	.000	1	2	0	0	0	0	0	0	0	1	0
Mario Soto, p	.000	1	0	0	0	0	0	0	0	0	0	0
Harry Spilman, ph	.000	2	2	0	0	0	0	0	0	0	0	0
Dave Tomlin, p	.000	3	0	0	0	0	0	0	0	0	0	0
TOTAL	.215		107	5	23	4	1	2	5	11	26	4

PITCHER	W	L	ERA	G	GS	CG	SV	SHO	IP	H	ER	BB	SO
Doug Bair	0	1	9.00	1	0	0	0	0	1.0	2	1	1	0
Tom Hume	0	1	6.75	3	0	0	0	0	4.0	6	3	0	2
Mike La Coss	0	1	10.80	1	1	0	0	0	1.2	1	2	4	0
Charlie Leibrandt	0	0	0.00	1	0	0	0	0	0.1	0	0	0	0
Fred Norman	0	0	18.00	1	0	0	0	0	2.0	4	4	1	1
Frank Pastore	0	0	2.57	1	1	0	0	0	7.0	7	2	3	1
Tom Seaver	0	0	2.25	1	1	0	0	0	8.0	5	2	2	5
Mario Soto	0	0	0.00	1	0	0	0	0	2.0	0	0	1	1
Dave Tomlin	0	0	0.00	3	0	0	0	0	3.0	3	0	2	3
TOTAL	0	3	4.34	13	3	0	0	0	29.0	28	14	13	13

GAME 1 AT CIN OCT 2

PIT	002 000 000 03	5 10 0
CIN	000 200 000 00	2 7 0

Pitchers: Candelaria, Romo (8), Tekulve (8), JACKSON (10), D.Robinson (11) vs Seaver, HUME (9), Tomlin (11)
Home Runs: Garner-PIT, Foster-CIN, Stargell-PIT
Attendance: 55,006

GAME 2 AT CIN OCT 3

PIT	000 110 000 1	3 11 0
CIN	010 000 001 0	2 8 0

Pitchers: Bibby, Jackson (8), Romo (8), Tekulve (8), Roberts (9), D.ROBINSON (9) vs Pastore, Tomlin (8), Hume (8), BAIR (10)
Attendance: 55,000

GAME 3 AT PIT OCT 5

CIN	000 001 000	1 8 1
PIT	112 200 01X	7 7 0

Pitchers: LaCOSS, Norman (2), Leibrandt (4), Soto (5), Tomlin (7), Hume (8) vs BLYLEVEN
Home Runs: Stargell-PIT, Madlock-PIT, Bench-CIN
Attendance: 42,240

Baltimore, returning to post-season play after a four-year absence, struggled with first-timer California through three games before blowing them away in the fourth. Game One went into the last of the tenth, tied 3–3, when Oriole pinch hitter John Lowenstein, up with two men on, ended it with a two-out, two-strike shot that just cleared the left field wall.

Game Two looked like a blowout for Baltimore. Eddie Murray drove in four runs, and the rest of the team added five more to give the O's a 9–1 lead by the end of three. But California chipped away at the lead in the latter half of the game and drew within one in the ninth, before Brian Downing hit into a forceout with the bases full to end their scoring.

The Angels' late rally in Game Three was more successful. Down by a run in the bottom of the ninth, they scored twice, on a walk, a dropped outfield fly, and Larry Harlow's game-winning double. The final game, though, was all Baltimore's, as Scott McGregor—pitching the series' only complete game—blanked the Angels on six hits. The Orioles scored two in the third and another in the fourth, before Pat Kelly put Angel pennant hopes out of reach with a three-run homer in the O's five-run seventh.

Baltimore Orioles (East), 3; California Angels (West), 1

BAL (E)

PLAYER/POS	AVG	G	AB	R	H	2B	3B	HR	RB	BB	SO	SB
Mark Belanger, ss	.200	3	5	0	1	0	0	0	1	0	2	0
Al Bumbry, of	.250	4	16	5	4	0	1	0	0	4	3	2
Terry Crowley, ph	.500	2	2	0	1	0	0	0	1	0	0	0
Rich Dauer, 2b	.182	4	11	0	2	0	0	0	0	0	1	0
Doug De Cinces, 3b	.308	4	13	4	4	1	0	0	3	1	1	0
Rick Dempsey, c	.400	3	10	3	4	2	0	0	2	1	0	1
Mike Flanagan, p	.000	1	0	0	0	0	0	0	0	0	0	0
Kiko Garcia, ss	.273	3	11	1	3	0	0	0	2	2	4	0
Pat Kelly, dh-2,of-1	.364	3	11	3	4	0	0	1	4	1	3	2
John Lowenstein, of-3	.167	4	6	2	1	0	0	1	3	2	2	0
Dennis Martinez, p	.000	1	0	0	0	0	0	0	0	0	0	0
Lee May, dh	.143	2	7	0	1	0	0	0	1	1	3	0
Scott Mc Gregor, p	.000	1	0	0	0	0	0	0	0	0	0	0
Eddie Murray, 1b	.417	4	12	3	5	0	0	1	5	5	2	0
Jim Palmer, p	.000	1	0	0	0	0	0	0	0	0	0	0
Gary Roenicke, of	.200	2	5	1	1	0	0	0	1	0	0	0
Ken Singleton, of	.375	4	16	4	6	2	0	0	2	1	2	0
Dave Skaggs, c	.000	1	4	0	0	0	0	0	0	0	0	0
Billy Smith, 2b	.000	1	4	0	0	0	0	0	0	0	1	0
Don Stanhouse, p	.000	3	0	0	0	0	0	0	0	0	0	0
TOTAL	.278		133	26	37	5	1	3	25	18	24	5

PITCHER	W	L	ERA	G	GS	CG	SV	SHO	IP	H	ER	BB	SO
Mike Flanagan	1	0	5.14	1	1	0	0	0	7.0	6	4	1	2
Dennis Martinez	0	0	3.24	1	1	0	0	0	8.1	8	3	0	4
Scott Mc Gregor	1	0	0.00	1	1	1	0	1	9.0	6	0	1	4
Jim Palmer	0	0	3.00	1	1	0	0	0	9.0	7	3	2	3
Don Stanhouse	1	1	6.00	3	0	0	0	0	3.0	5	2	3	0
TOTAL	3	1	2.97	7	4	1	0	1	36.1	32	12	7	13

CAL (W)

PLAYER/POS	AVG	G	AB	R	H	2B	3B	HR	RB	BB	SO	SB
Don Aase, p	.000	2	0	0	0	0	0	0	0	0	0	0
Jim Anderson, ss	.091	4	11	0	1	0	0	0	0	0	1	0
Mike Barlow, p	.000	1	0	0	0	0	0	0	0	0	0	0
Don Baylor, dh-3,of-1	.188	4	16	2	3	0	0	1	2	1	2	0
Bert Campaneris, ss	.000	1	0	0	0	0	0	0	0	0	0	0
Rod Carew, 1b	.412	4	17	4	7	3	0	0	1	0	0	1
Bobby Clark, of	.000	1	3	0	0	0	0	0	0	0	2	0
Mark Clear, p	.000	1	0	0	0	0	0	0	0	0	0	0
Willie Davis, ph	.500	2	2	1	1	1	0	0	0	0	0	0
Brian Downing, c	.200	4	15	1	3	0	0	0	1	1	1	0
Dan Ford, of	.294	4	17	2	5	1	0	2	4	0	0	0
Dave Frost, p	.000	2	0	0	0	0	0	0	0	0	0	0
Bobby Grich, 2b	.154	4	13	0	2	1	0	0	2	1	1	0
Larry Harlow, of-2	.125	3	8	0	1	1	0	0	1	1	2	0
Chris Knapp, p	.000	1	0	0	0	0	0	0	0	0	0	0
Carney Lansford, 3b	.294	4	17	2	5	0	0	0	3	1	2	1
Dave La Roche, p	.000	1	0	0	0	0	0	0	0	0	0	0
Rick Miller, of	.250	4	16	2	4	0	0	0	0	0	1	0
John Montague, p	.000	2	0	0	0	0	0	0	0	0	0	0
Merv Rettenmund, dh	.000	2	2	0	0	0	0	0	0	2	1	0
Nolan Ryan, p	.000	1	0	0	0	0	0	0	0	0	0	0
Frank Tanana, p	.000	1	0	0	0	0	0	0	0	0	0	0
Dickie Thon, ss	.000	1	0	1	0	0	0	0	0	0	0	0
TOTAL	.234		137	15	32	7	0	3	14	7	13	2

PITCHER	W	L	ERA	G	GS	CG	SV	SHO	IP	H	ER	BB	SO
Don Aase	1	0	1.80	2	0	0	0	0	5.0	4	1	2	6
Mike Barlow	0	0	0.00	1	0	0	0	0	1.0	0	0	0	0
Mark Clear	0	0	4.76	1	0	0	0	0	5.2	4	3	2	3
Dave Frost	0	1	18.69	2	1	0	0	0	4.1	8	9	5	1
Chris Knapp	0	1	7.71	1	1	0	0	0	2.1	5	2	1	0
Dave La Roche	0	0	6.75	1	0	0	0	0	1.1	2	1	1	1
John Montague	0	1	9.00	2	0	0	0	0	4.0	4	4	2	2
Nolan Ryan	0	0	1.29	1	1	0	0	0	7.0	4	1	3	8
Frank Tanana	0	0	3.60	1	1	0	0	0	5.0	6	2	2	3
TOTAL	1	3	5.80	12	4	0	0	0	35.2	37	23	18	24

GAME 1 AT BAL OCT 3

CAL	101 001 000 0	3	7	1
BAL	002 100 000 3	6	6	0

Pitchers: Ryan, MONTAGUE (8) vs Palmer, STANHOUSE (10)
Home Runs: Ford-CAL, Lowenstein-BAL
Attendance: 52,787

GAME 2 AT BAL OCT 4

CAL	100 001 132	8	10	1
BAL	441 000 00X	9	11	1

Pitchers: FROST, Clear (2), Aase (8) vs FLANAGAN, Stanhouse (8)
Home Runs: Ford-CAL, Murray-BAL
Attendance: 52,108

GAME 3 AT CAL OCT 5

BAL	000 101 100	3	8	3
CAL	100 100 002	4	9	0

Pitchers: D.Martinez, STANHOUSE (9) vs Tanana, AASE (6)
Home Runs: Baylor-CAL
Attendance: 43,199

GAME 4 AT CAL OCT 6

BAL	002 100 500	8	12	1
CAL	000 000 000	0	6	0

Pitchers: McGREGOR vs KNAPP, LaRoche (3), Frost (4), Montague (7), Barlow (9)
Home Runs: Kelly-BAL
Attendance: 43,199

Veteran Willie Stargell was "Pops," and in the Series he showed his Pirate "family" the way. Seven of his twelve hits went for extra bases, and he drove in a Series-high seven runs. What Stargell began, submarine reliever Kent Tekulve finished, appearing in five of the seven games and recording a record-tying three saves.

Stargell drove in a pair of runs in the opener—one of them with an eighth-inning homer—but Pittsburgh's four runs fell short of the five Baltimore had scored in the first inning. The only extra-base hits in Game Two came from the bat of Eddie Murray, who homered and doubled to drive in both Baltimore runs. But three singles and a sacrifice fly had already given Pittsburgh two runs in the second inning, and two more Pirate singles and a walk in the top of the ninth made the score 3–2. Tekulve came on in the last of the ninth to preserve the lead, fanning two as he retired the side in order.

Baltimore bounced back, though, to take the next two games in convincing fashion. The score favored the Orioles 8–4 when Tekulve came on to set the birds down in order over the final two innings. But Baltimore starter Scott McGregor had by then settled into his groove, retiring the final eleven Pirates with relative ease to preserve his lead and the Oriole win. It took four Orioles pitchers to hold the Pirates in Game Four. Stargell led the Bucs' seventeen-hit attack with a homer, double, and single, and the Pirates led 6–3 entering the eighth inning. But Baltimore loaded the bases in the top of the eighth, prompting Pirate manager Chuck Tanner to bring Tekulve in again. This one time the strategy failed, as Tekulve saw six runs score before he retired his first batter.

Down three games to one, the Pirates rebounded in Game Five, scoring seven in the final three innings for a 7–1 victory. Baltimore starter Jim Palmer matched John Candelaria's shutout pitching through six innings of Game Six before the Pirates tagged him for pairs of runs in the seventh and eighth. Tekulve, meanwhile, continued Candelaria's shutout through the final three innings, retiring the last seven men in order, four by strikeout. Baltimore scored first in the finale on Rich Dauer's leadoff home run in the third inning, but Stargell put the Pirates ahead with a two-run homer in the sixth. Tekulve came in with two Orioles on base in the eighth to stifle the threat, and (after the Pirates had scored a pair of insurance runs in the top of the ninth) set Baltimore

Pittsburgh Pirates (NL), 4;
Baltimore Orioles (AL), 3

PIT (N)

PLAYER/POS	AVG	G	AB	R	H	2B	3B	HR	RB	BB	SO	SB
Matt Alexander, of	.000	1	0	0	0	0	0	0	0	0	0	0
Jim Bibby, p	.000	2	4	0	0	0	0	0	0	0	1	0
Bert Blyleven, p	.000	2	3	0	0	0	0	0	0	0	0	0
John Candelaria, p	.333	2	3	0	1	0	0	0	0	0	2	0
Mike Easler, ph	.000	2	1	0	0	0	0	0	0	1	0	0
Tim Foli, ss	.333	7	30	6	10	1	1	0	3	2	0	0
Phil Garner, 2b	.500	7	24	4	12	4	0	0	5	3	1	0
Grant Jackson, p	.000	4	1	0	0	0	0	0	0	0	0	0
Bruce Kison, p	.000	1	0	0	0	0	0	0	0	0	0	0
Lee Lacy, ph	.250	4	4	0	1	0	0	0	0	0	1	0
Bill Madlock, 3b	.375	7	24	2	9	1	0	0	3	5	1	0
John Milner, of	.333	3	9	2	3	1	0	0	1	2	0	0
Omar Moreno, of	.333	7	33	4	11	2	0	0	3	1	7	0
Steve Nicosia, c	.063	4	16	1	1	0	0	0	0	0	2	0
Ed Ott, c	.333	3	12	2	4	1	0	0	3	0	2	0
Dave Parker, of	.345	7	29	2	10	3	0	0	4	2	7	0
Don Robinson, p	.000	4	0	0	0	0	0	0	0	0	0	0
Bill Robinson, of-6	.263	7	19	2	5	1	0	0	2	0	4	0
Enrique Romo, p	.000	2	1	0	0	0	0	0	0	0	0	0
Jim Rooker, p	.000	2	2	0	0	0	0	0	0	0	1	0
Manny Sanguillen, ph	.333	3	3	0	1	0	0	0	0	1	0	0
Willie Stargell, 1b	.400	7	30	7	12	4	0	3	7	0	6	0
Rennie Stennett, ph	1.000	1	1	0	1	0	0	0	0	0	0	0
Kent Tekulve, p	.000	5	2	0	0	0	0	0	0	0	0	0
TOTAL	.323		251	32	81	18	1	3	32	16	35	0

PITCHER	W	L	ERA	G	GS	CG	SV	SHO	IP	H	ER	BB	SO
Jim Bibby	0	0	2.61	2	2	0	0	0	10.1	10	3	2	10
Bert Blyleven	1	0	1.80	2	1	0	0	0	10.0	8	2	3	4
John Candelaria	1	1	5.00	2	2	0	0	0	9.0	14	5	2	4
Grant Jackson	1	0	0.00	4	0	0	0	0	4.2	1	0	2	2
Bruce Kison	0	1	108.00	1	1	0	0	0	0.1	3	4	2	0
Don Robinson	1	0	5.40	4	0	0	0	0	5.0	4	3	6	3
Enrique Romo	0	0	3.86	2	0	0	0	0	4.2	5	2	3	4
Jim Rooker	0	0	1.04	2	1	0	0	0	8.2	5	1	3	4
Kent Tekulve	0	1	2.89	5	0	0	3	0	9.1	4	3	3	10
TOTAL	4	3	3.34	24	7	0	3	0	62.0	54	23	26	41

BAL (A)

PLAYER/POS	AVG	G	AB	R	H	2B	3B	HR	RB	BB	SO	SB
Benny Ayala, of-3	.333	4	6	1	2	0	0	1	2	1	0	0
Mark Belanger, ss-4	.000	5	6	1	0	0	0	0	0	1	1	0
Al Bumbry, of	.143	7	21	3	3	0	0	0	1	2	1	0
Terry Crowley, ph	.250	5	4	0	1	1	0	0	2	1	0	0
Rich Dauer, 2b-5	.294	6	17	2	5	1	0	1	1	0	1	0
Doug De Cinces, 3b	.200	7	25	2	5	0	0	1	3	5	5	1
Rick Dempsey, c-6	.286	7	21	3	6	2	0	0	1	3	0	0
Mike Flanagan, p	.000	3	5	0	0	0	0	0	0	1	2	0
Kiko Garcia, ss	.400	6	20	4	8	2	1	0	6	1	3	0
Pat Kelly, ph	.250	5	4	0	1	0	0	0	0	1	1	0
John Lowenstein, of-3	.231	6	13	2	3	1	0	0	3	1	3	0
Tippy Martinez, p	.000	3	0	0	0	0	0	0	0	0	0	0
Dennis Martinez, p	.000	2	0	0	0	0	0	0	0	0	0	0
Lee May, ph	.000	2	1	0	0	0	0	0	0	0	1	0
Scott Mc Gregor, p	.000	2	4	1	0	0	0	0	0	0	2	0
Eddie Murray, 1b	.154	7	26	3	4	1	0	1	2	4	4	1
Jim Palmer, p	.000	2	4	0	0	0	0	0	0	0	3	0
Gary Roenicke, of-5	.125	6	16	1	2	1	0	0	0	0	6	0
Ken Singleton, of	.357	7	28	1	10	1	0	0	2	2	5	0
Dave Skaggs, c	.333	1	3	1	1	0	0	0	0	0	0	0
Billy Smith, 2b-2	.286	4	7	1	2	0	0	0	0	0	2	0
Don Stanhouse, p	.000	3	0	0	0	0	0	0	0	0	0	0
Sammy Stewart, p	.000	1	1	0	0	0	0	0	0	0	1	0
Tim Stoddard, p	1.000	4	1	0	1	0	0	0	0	1	0	0
Steve Stone, p	.000	1	0	0	0	0	0	0	0	0	0	0
TOTAL	.232		233	26	54	10	1	4	23	26	41	2

PITCHER	W	L	ERA	G	GS	CG	SV	SHO	IP	H	ER	BB	SO
Mike Flanagan	1	1	3.00	3	2	1	0	0	15.0	18	5	2	13
Tippy Martinez	0	0	6.75	3	0	0	0	0	1.1	3	1	0	1
Dennis Martinez	0	0	18.00	2	1	0	0	0	2.0	6	4	0	0
Scott Mc Gregor	1	1	3.18	2	2	1	0	0	17.0	16	6	2	8
Jim Palmer	0	1	3.60	2	2	0	0	0	15.0	18	6	5	8
Don Stanhouse	0	1	13.50	3	0	0	0	0	2.0	6	3	3	0
Sammy Stewart	0	0	0.00	1	0	0	0	0	2.2	4	0	1	0
Tim Stoddard	1	0	5.40	4	0	0	0	0	5.0	6	3	1	3
Steve Stone	0	0	9.00	1	0	0	0	0	2.0	4	2	2	2
TOTAL	3	4	4.35	21	7	2	0	0	62.0	81	30	16	35

down in order to complete the Pirate comeback.

GAME 1 AT BAL OCT 10

PIT	000	102	010	4	11 3
BAL	500	000	000	5	6 3

Pitchers: KISON, Rooker (1), Romo (5), D.Robinson (6), Jackson (8) vs FLANAGAN
Home Runs: Stargell-PIT, DeCinces-BAL
Attendance: 53,735

GAME 2 AT BAL OCT 11

PIT	020	000	001	3	11 2
BAL	010	001	000	2	6 1

Pitchers: BLYLEVEN, D.Robinson (7), Tekulve (9) vs PALMER, Stanhouse (8), T.Martinez (9)
Home Runs: Muuray-BAL
Attendance: 53,739

GAME 3 AT PIT OCT 12

BAL	002	500	100	8	13 0
PIT	120	001	000	4	9 2

Pitchers: McGREGOR vs CANDELARIA, Romo (4), Jackson (7), Tekulve (8)
Home Runs: Ayala-BAL
Attendance: 50,848

GAME 4 AT PIT OCT 13

BAL	003	000	060	9	12 0
PIT	040	011	000	6	17 1

Pitchers: D.MARTINEZ, Stewart (2), Stone (5), Stoddard (7) vs BIBBY, Jackson (6), D.Robinson (8), Tekulve (8)
Home Runs: Stargell-PIT
Attendance: 50,883

GAME 5 AT PIT OCT 14

BAL	000	010	000	1	6 2
PIT	000	002	23X	7	13 1

Pitchers: FLANAGAN, Stoddard (7), T.Martinez (7), Stanhouse (8) vs ROOKER, Blyleven (6)
Attendance: 50,920

GAME 6 AT BAL OCT 16

PIT	000	000	220	4	10 0
BAL	000	000	000	0	7 1

Pitchers: CANDELARIA, Tekluve (7) vs PALMER, Stoddard (9)
Attendance: 53,739

GAME 7 AT BAL OCT 17

PIT	000	002	002	4	10 0
BAL	001	000	000	1	4 2

Pitchers: BIBBY, D.Robinson (5), Jackson (5), Tekulve (8) vs McGREGOR, Stoddard (9), Flanagan (9), T.Martinez (9), D.Martinez (9)
Home Runs: Stargell-PIT, Dauer-BAL
Attendance: 53,733

In the tightest LCS yet, the Phillies took the opener 3–1 on the series' only home run—Greg Luzinski's two-run blast in the sixth inning. It was the only game not to go into extra innings.

The Astros evened the series in Game Two—demolishing a 3–3 tie with four runs in the tenth—and took the series lead in a Game Three pitchers' duel that saw Astro Joe Niekro hurl ten scoreless innings. Reliever Dave Smith continued the shutout and took the win as Joe Morgan's triple and Denny Walling's sacrifice fly off ace Phillie reliever Tug McGraw scored the game's only run in the bottom of the eleventh.

The Phillies rebounded, though, with their own set of extra-inning victories. In Game Four, a single and two doubles pushed across two go-ahead runs in the top of the tenth, and McGraw preserved the edge for his second series save. And in the finale—which saw the lead change hands three times—after Del Unser scored on Gary Maddox's tenth-inning double, Dick Ruthven held off Houston to bring the Phillies their first pennant in thirty years.

Philadelphia Phillies (East), 3; Houston Astros (West), 2

PHI (E)

PLAYER/POS	AVG	G	AB	R	H	2B	3B	HR	RB	BB	SO	SB
Ramon Aviles, pr	.000	1	0	1	0	0	0	0	0	0	0	0
Bob Boone, c	.222	5	18	1	4	0	0	0	2	1	2	0
Larry Bowa, ss	.316	5	19	2	6	0	0	0	0	3	3	1
Warren Brusstar, p	.000	2	1	0	0	0	0	0	0	0	1	0
Marty Bystrom, p	.000	1	2	0	0	0	0	0	0	0	1	0
Steve Carlton, p	.000	2	4	0	0	0	0	0	0	0	1	0
Larry Christenson, p	.000	1	2	0	0	0	0	0	0	0	1	0
Greg Gross, of-1	.750	4	4	2	3	0	0	0	1	0	0	0
Greg Luzinski, of	.294	5	17	3	5	2	0	1	4	0	6	0
Garry Maddox, of	.300	5	20	2	6	2	0	0	3	2	2	2
Bake Mc Bride, of	.238	5	21	0	5	0	0	0	0	1	5	2
Tug Mc Graw, p	.000	5	1	0	0	0	0	0	0	0	0	0
Keith Moreland, c-1	.000	2	1	0	0	0	0	0	1	0	0	0
Dickie Noles, p	.000	2	0	0	0	0	0	0	0	0	0	0
Ron Reed, p	.000	3	0	0	0	0	0	0	0	0	0	0
Pete Rose, 1b	.400	5	20	3	8	0	0	0	2	5	3	0
Dick Ruthven, p	.000	2	2	0	0	0	0	0	0	0	2	0
Kevin Saucier, p	.000	2	0	0	0	0	0	0	0	0	0	0
Mike Schmidt, 3b	.208	5	24	1	5	1	0	0	1	1	6	1
Lonnie Smith, of-2	.600	3	5	2	3	0	0	0	0	0	0	1
Manny Trillo, 2b	.381	5	21	1	8	2	1	0	4	0	2	0
Del Unser, of-2	.400	5	5	2	2	1	0	0	1	0	2	0
George Vukovich, of-1	.000	4	3	0	0	0	0	0	0	0	0	0
TOTAL	.289		190	20	55	8	1	1	19	13	37	7

PITCHER	W	L	ERA	G	GS	CG	SV	SHO	IP	H	ER	BB	SO
Warren Brusstar	1	0	3.38	2	0	0	0	0	2.2	1	1	1	0
Marty Bystrom	0	0	1.69	1	1	0	0	0	5.1	7	1	2	1
Steve Carlton	1	0	2.19	2	2	0	0	0	12.1	11	3	8	6
Larry Christenson	0	0	4.05	1	1	0	0	0	6.2	5	3	5	2
Tug Mc Graw	0	1	4.50	5	0	0	2	0	8.0	8	4	4	5
Dickie Noles	0	0	0.00	2	0	0	0	0	2.2	1	0	3	0
Ron Reed	0	1	18.00	3	0	0	0	0	2.0	3	4	1	1
Dick Ruthven	1	0	2.00	2	1	0	0	0	9.0	3	2	5	4
Kevin Saucier	0	0	0.00	2	0	0	0	0	0.2	1	0	2	0
TOTAL	3	2	3.28	20	5	0	2	0	49.1	40	18	31	19

HOU (W)

PLAYER/POS	AVG	G	AB	R	H	2B	3B	HR	RB	BB	SO	SB
Joaquin Andujar, p	.000	1	0	0	0	0	0	0	0	0	0	0
Alan Ashby, c	.125	2	8	0	1	0	0	0	1	0	0	0
Dave Bergman, 1b	.333	4	3	0	1	0	1	0	2	0	0	0
Bruce Bochy, c	.000	1	1	0	0	0	0	0	0	0	0	0
Enos Cabell, 3b	.238	5	21	1	5	1	0	0	0	1	3	0
Cesar Cedeno, of	.182	3	11	1	2	0	0	0	1	1	0	0
Jose Cruz, of	.400	5	15	3	6	1	1	0	4	8	1	0
Ken Forsch, p	1.000	2	2	0	2	0	0	0	0	0	0	0
Danny Heep, ph	.000	1	1	0	0	0	0	0	0	0	0	0
Art Howe, 1b-4	.200	5	15	0	3	1	1	0	2	2	2	0
Frank La Corte, p	.000	2	1	0	0	0	0	0	0	0	0	0
Rafael Landestoy, 2b-3,ss-1	.222	5	9	3	2	0	0	0	2	1	0	1
Jeffrey Leonard, of-1	.000	3	3	0	0	0	0	0	0	0	2	0
Joe Morgan, 2b	.154	4	13	1	2	1	1	0	0	6	1	0
Joe Niekro, p	.000	1	3	0	0	0	0	0	0	0	1	0
Terry Puhl, of-4	.526	5	19	4	10	2	0	0	3	3	2	2
Luis Pujols, c	.100	4	10	1	1	0	1	0	0	3	0	0
Craig Reynolds, ss	.154	4	13	2	2	1	0	0	0	3	1	0
Vern Ruhle, p	.000	1	3	0	0	0	0	0	0	0	1	0
Nolan Ryan, p	.000	2	4	1	0	0	0	0	0	1	2	0
Joe Sambito, p	.000	3	0	0	0	0	0	0	0	0	0	0
Dave Smith, p	.000	3	0	0	0	0	0	0	0	0	0	0
Denny Walling, of-2,1b-1	.111	3	9	2	1	0	0	0	2	1	0	0
Gary Woods, of-3	.250	4	8	0	2	0	0	0	1	1	3	1
TOTAL	.233		172	19	40	7	5	0	18	31	19	4

PITCHER	W	L	ERA	G	GS	CG	SV	SHO	IP	H	ER	BB	SO
Joaquin Andujar	0	0	0.00	1	0	0	1	0	1.0	0	0	1	0
Ken Forsch	0	1	4.15	2	1	1	0	0	8.2	10	4	1	6
Frank La Corte	1	1	3.00	2	0	0	0	0	3.0	7	1	2	2
Joe Niekro	0	0	0.00	1	1	0	0	0	10.0	6	0	1	2
Vern Ruhle	0	0	3.86	1	1	0	0	0	7.0	8	3	1	3
Nolan Ryan	0	0	5.40	2	2	0	0	0	13.1	16	8	3	14
Joe Sambito	0	1	4.91	3	0	0	0	0	3.2	4	2	2	6
Dave Smith	1	0	3.86	3	0	0	0	0	2.1	4	1	2	4
TOTAL	2	3	3.49	15	5	1	1	0	49.0	55	19	13	37

GAME 1 AT PHI OCT 7

HOU	001 000 000	1	7	0
PHI	000 002 10X	3	8	1

Pitchers: FORSCH vs CARLTON, McGraw (8)
Home Runs: Luzinski-PHI
Attendance: 65,277

GAME 2 AT PHI OCT 8

HOU	001 000 110 4	7	8	1
PHI	200 000 010 1	4	14	2

Pitchers: Ryan, Sambito (7), D.Smith (7), LaCORTE (9), Andujar (10) vs Ruthven, McGraw (8), REED (9), Saucier (10)
Attendance: 65,476

GAME 3 AT HOU OCT 10

PHI	000 000 000 00	0	7	1
HOU	000 000 000 01	1	6	1

Pitchers: Christensen, Noles (7), McGRAW (8) vs Niekro, D.SMITH (11)
Attendance: 44,443

GAME 4 AT HOU OCT 11

PHI	000 000 030 2	5	13	0
HOU	000 110 001 0	3	5	1

Pitchers: Carlton, Noles (6), Saucier (7), Reed (7), BRUSSTAR (8), McGraw (10) vs Ruhle, D.Smith (8), SAMBITO (8)
Attendance: 44,952

GAME 5 AT HOU OCT 12

PHI	020 000 050 1	8	13	2
HOU	100 001 320 0	7	14	0

Pitchers: Bystrom, Brusstar (6), Christensen (7), Reed (7), McGraw (8), RUTHVEN (9) vs Ryan, Sambito (8), Forsch (8), LaCORTE (9)
Attendance: 44,802

Kansas City and New York met for the fourth time in the LCS, and this time the Royals swept to their first pennant. In the first game the Yankees scored first, with second-inning home runs by Rick Cerone and Lou Piniella, but the Royals' Frank White doubled in a pair later in the inning to tie it, and Willie Aikens's hit in the third gave K.C. the lead. They held it to the end as Larry Gura shut out New York the rest of the way.

The Royals scored three runs in the third inning of Game Two, on Willie Wilson's two-run triple and an RBI double by U. L. Washington. Yankee starter Rudy May stopped K.C. after that, but the Royals already had enough for the win as Dennis Leonard in eight innings held New York to two runs, and Dan Quisenberry kept the lid on in the ninth.

Game Three was decided by home runs. White scored first for the Royals with a solo shot in the fifth. New York took the lead briefly with a two-run sixth, but lost it—and the pennant—in the top of the seventh when Goose Gossage, relieving starter Tommy John with two out and a man on, gave up an infield single to Washington and a home run to George Brett.

Kansas City Royals (West), 3; New York Yankees (East), 0

KC (W)

PLAYER/POS	AVG	G	AB	R	H	2B	3B	HR	RB	BB	SO	SB
Willie Aikens, 1b	.364	3	11	0	4	0	0	0	2	0	1	0
George Brett, 3b	.273	3	11	3	3	1	0	2	4	1	0	0
Larry Gura, p	.000	1	0	0	0	0	0	0	0	0	0	0
Clint Hurdle, of	.000	3	2	0	0	0	0	0	0	0	1	0
Pete La Cock, 1b	.000	1	0	0	0	0	0	0	0	0	0	0
Dennis Leonard, p	.000	1	0	0	0	0	0	0	0	0	0	0
Hal Mc Rae, dh	.200	3	10	0	2	0	0	0	0	1	3	0
Amos Otis, of	.333	3	12	2	4	1	0	0	0	0	3	2
Darrell Porter, c	.100	3	10	2	1	0	0	0	0	1	0	0
Dan Quisenberry, p	.000	2	0	0	0	0	0	0	0	0	0	0
Paul Splittorff, p	.000	1	0	0	0	0	0	0	0	0	0	0
U. L. Washington, ss	.364	3	11	1	4	1	0	0	1	2	3	0
John Wathan, of	.000	3	6	1	0	0	0	0	0	3	1	0
Frank White, 2b	.545	3	11	3	6	1	0	1	3	0	1	1
Willie Wilson, of	.308	3	13	1	4	1	1	0	4	1	2	0
TOTAL	.289		97	14	28	6	1	3	14	9	15	3

PITCHER	W	L	ERA	G	GS	CG	SV	SHO	IP	H	ER	BB	SO
Larry Gura	1	0	2.00	1	1	1	0	0	9.0	10	2	1	4
Dennis Leonard	1	0	2.25	1	1	0	0	0	8.0	7	2	1	8
Dan Quisenberry	1	0	0.00	2	0	0	1	0	4.2	4	0	2	1
Paul Splittorff	0	0	1.69	1	1	0	0	0	5.1	5	1	2	3
TOTAL	3	0	1.67	5	3	1	1	0	27.0	26	5	6	16

NY (E)

PLAYER/POS	AVG	G	AB	R	H	2B	3B	HR	RB	BB	SO	SB
Bobby Brown, of	.000	3	10	1	0	0	0	0	0	1	2	0
Rick Cerone, c	.333	3	12	1	4	0	0	1	2	0	1	0
Ron Davis, p	.000	1	0	0	0	0	0	0	0	0	0	0
Bucky Dent, ss	.182	3	11	0	2	0	0	0	0	0	1	0
Oscar Gamble, of-1,dh-1	.200	2	5	1	1	0	0	0	0	1	1	0
Rich Gossage, p	.000	1	0	0	0	0	0	0	0	0	0	0
Ron Guidry, p	.000	1	0	0	0	0	0	0	0	0	0	0
Reggie Jackson, of	.273	3	11	1	3	1	0	0	0	1	4	0
Tommy John, p	.000	1	0	0	0	0	0	0	0	0	0	0
Joe Lefebvre, of	.000	1	0	0	0	0	0	0	0	0	0	0
Rudy May, p	.000	1	0	0	0	0	0	0	0	0	0	0
Bobby Murcer, dh	.000	1	4	0	0	0	0	0	0	0	2	0
Graig Nettles, 3b	.167	2	6	1	1	0	0	1	1	0	1	0
Lou Piniella, of	.200	2	5	1	1	0	0	1	1	2	1	0
Willie Randolph, 2b	.385	3	13	0	5	2	0	0	1	1	3	0
Aurelio Rodriguez, 3b	.333	2	6	0	2	1	0	0	0	0	0	0
Eric Soderholm, dh	.167	2	6	0	1	0	0	0	0	0	0	0
Jim Spencer, ph	.000	1	1	0	0	0	0	0	0	0	0	0
Tom Underwood, p	.000	2	0	0	0	0	0	0	0	0	0	0
Bob Watson, 1b	.500	3	12	0	6	3	1	0	0	0	0	0
TOTAL	.255		102	6	26	7	1	3	5	6	16	0

PITCHER	W	L	ERA	G	GS	CG	SV	SHO	IP	H	ER	BB	SO
Ron Davis	0	0	2.25	1	0	0	0	0	4.0	3	1	1	3
Rich Gossage	0	1	54.00	1	0	0	0	0	0.1	3	2	0	0
Ron Guidry	0	1	12.00	1	1	0	0	0	3.0	5	4	4	2
Tommy John	0	0	2.70	1	1	0	0	0	6.2	8	2	1	3
Rudy May	0	1	3.38	1	1	1	0	0	8.0	6	3	3	4
Tom Underwood	0	0	0.00	2	0	0	0	0	3.0	3	0	0	3
TOTAL	0	3	4.32	7	3	1	0	0	25.0	28	12	9	15

GAME 1 AT KC OCT 8

NY	020	000	000	2	10	1
KC	022	000	12X	7	10	0

Pitchers: GUIDRY, Davis (4), Underwood (8) vs GURA
Home Runs: Cerone-NY, Piniella-NY, G.Brett-KC
Attendance: 42,598

GAME 2 AT KC OCT 9

NY	000	020	000	2	8	0
KC	003	000	00X	3	6	0

Pitchers: MAY vs LEONARD, Quisenberry (9)
Home Runs: Nettles-NY
Attendance: 42,633

GAME 3 AT NY OCT 10

KC	000	010	300	4	12	1
NY	000	002	000	2	8	0

Pitchers: Splittorff, QUISENBERRY (6) vs John, GOSSAGE (7), Underwood (8)
Home Runs: White-KC, G.Brett-KC
Attendance: 56,588

Both clubs had won divisional titles three years in a row—1976–1978—only to lose the League Championship Series. But both overcame the jinx in 1980 to face off in the World Series—the Phillies for the first time in thirty years, the Royals for the first time ever. Kansas City began with a rush in the opener, scoring two runs on Amos Otis's homer in the second inning and two more on Willie Aikens's blast an inning later. But the Phillies came back to take the lead in their half of the third with a five-run rally capped by Bake McBride's three-run homer. Single Phillie runs in each of the next two innings kept them out of reach of Aikens's second two-run shot in the eighth for a narrow 7–6 win. The Phillies extended their Series advantage with a 6–4 win in the second game, rebounding from a two-run deficit with four runs in the eighth inning.

The two clubs traded single runs throughout Game Three. Royal George Brett's first-inning homer began the scoring. The Phillies got the run back in the second inning, the Royals took the lead back in the fourth, Phillie Mike Schmidt homered to tie it again in the fifth, Amos Otis countered with a homer in the seventh, and Pete Rose singled in another tying Phillie run in the eighth. Phillie reliever Tug McGraw (who had a save in the opening game) came on to pitch the last of the tenth inning, but couldn't hold the tie, though two men were out before Willie Aikens singled in the Royals' winning run. The Royals evened the Series with their second victory the next day, scoring four times in the first inning and once in the second (with Willie Aikens for the second time in the Series hitting two home runs in a game), then holding on for a 5–3 win.

But the Phillies recovered to win the next two, and their first world crown. Mike Schmidt's fourth-inning two-run homer began the Phillies' scoring in Game Five. The Royals replied with one run in the fifth, and Amos Otis's home run an inning later tied the game. A second K.C. run in the inning put the Royals ahead until the top of the ninth, when pinch hitter Del Unser doubled home Schmidt to tie the game, and Manny Trillo drove home Unser with the go-ahead run. Tug McGraw, who had held K.C. scoreless through two innings of relief, loaded the bases in the last of the ninth with three walks, but at last fanned Jose Cardenal for the final out. In Game Six, with the Phillies ahead 4–0 in the eighth inning, McGraw relieved starter Steve Carlton with two men on, and

loaded the bases with a walk. One Royal scored on a sacrifice fly before McGraw got his third out. In the ninth, another McGraw walk and two singles again loaded the bases with only one away, but Frank White popped out foul, the ball bouncing off Bob Boone's catcher's mitt into Pete Rose's hand, and Willie Wilson struck out for the twelfth time to end the Series.

Philadelphia Phillies (NL), 4; Kansas City Royals (AL), 2

PHI (N)

PLAYER/POS	AVG	G	AB	R	H	2B	3B	HR	RB	BB	SO	SB
Bob Boone, c	.412	6	17	3	7	2	0	0	4	4	0	0
Larry Bowa, ss	.375	6	24	3	9	1	0	0	2	0	0	3
Warren Brusstar, p	.000	1	0	0	0	0	0	0	0	0	0	0
Marty Bystrom, p	.000	1	0	0	0	0	0	0	0	0	0	0
Steve Carlton, p	.000	2	0	0	0	0	0	0	0	0	0	0
Larry Christenson, p	.000	1	0	0	0	0	0	0	0	0	0	0
Greg Gross, of-3	.000	4	2	0	0	0	0	0	0	0	0	0
Greg Luzinski, dh-2,of-1	.000	3	9	0	0	0	0	0	0	1	5	0
Garry Maddox, of	.227	6	22	1	5	2	0	0	1	1	3	0
Bake Mc Bride, of	.304	6	23	3	7	1	0	1	5	2	1	0
Tug Mc Graw, p	.000	4	0	0	0	0	0	0	0	0	0	0
Keith Moreland, dh	.333	3	12	1	4	0	0	0	1	0	1	0
Dickie Noles, p	.000	1	0	0	0	0	0	0	0	0	0	0
Ron Reed, p	.000	2	0	0	0	0	0	0	0	0	0	0
Pete Rose, 1b	.261	6	23	2	6	1	0	0	1	2	2	0
Dick Ruthven, p	.000	1	0	0	0	0	0	0	0	0	0	0
Kevin Saucier, p	.000	1	0	0	0	0	0	0	0	0	0	0
Mike Schmidt, 3b	.381	6	21	6	8	1	0	2	7	4	3	0
Lonnie Smith, of-5,dh-1	.263	6	19	2	5	1	0	0	1	1	1	0
Manny Trillo, 2b	.217	6	23	4	5	2	0	0	2	0	0	0
Del Unser, of	.500	3	6	2	3	2	0	0	2	0	1	0
Bob Walk, p	.000	1	0	0	0	0	0	0	0	0	0	0
TOTAL	.294		201	27	59	13	0	3	26	15	17	3

PITCHER	W	L	ERA	G	GS	CG	SV	SHO	IP	H	ER	BB	SO
Warren Brusstar	0	0	0.00	1	0	0	0	0	2.1	0	0	1	0
Marty Bystrom	0	0	5.40	1	1	0	0	0	5.0	10	3	1	4
Steve Carlton	2	0	2.40	2	2	0	0	0	15.0	14	4	9	17
Larry Christenson	0	1	108.00	1	1	0	0	0	0.1	5	4	1	0
Tug Mc Graw	1	1	1.17	4	0	0	2	0	7.2	7	1	8	10
Dickie Noles	0	0	1.93	1	0	0	0	0	4.2	5	1	2	6
Ron Reed	0	0	0.00	2	0	0	1	0	2.0	2	0	0	2
Dick Ruthven	0	0	3.00	1	1	0	0	0	9.0	9	3	0	7
Kevin Saucier	0	0	0.00	1	0	0	0	0	0.2	0	0	2	0
Bob Walk	1	0	7.71	1	1	0	0	0	7.0	8	6	3	3
TOTAL	4	2	3.69	15	6	0	3	0	53.2	60	22	27	49

KC (A)

PLAYER/POS	AVG	G	AB	R	H	2B	3B	HR	RB	BB	SO	SB
Willie Aikens, 1b	.400	6	20	5	8	0	1	4	8	6	8	0
George Brett, 3b	.375	6	24	3	9	2	1	1	3	2	4	1
Jose Cardenal, of	.200	4	10	0	2	0	0	0	0	0	3	0
Dave Chalk, 3b	.000	1	0	1	0	0	0	0	0	1	0	1
Onix Concepcion, pr	.000	3	0	0	0	0	0	0	0	0	0	0
Rich Gale, p	.000	2	0	0	0	0	0	0	0	0	0	0
Larry Gura, p	.000	2	0	0	0	0	0	0	0	0	0	0
Clint Hurdle, of	.417	4	12	1	5	1	0	0	0	2	1	1
Pete La Cock, 1b	.000	1	0	0	0	0	0	0	0	0	0	0
Dennis Leonard, p	.000	2	0	0	0	0	0	0	0	0	0	0
Renie Martin, p	.000	3	0	0	0	0	0	0	0	0	0	0
Hal Mc Rae, dh	.375	6	24	3	9	3	0	0	1	2	2	0
Amos Otis, of	.478	6	23	4	11	2	0	3	7	3	3	0
Marty Pattin, p	.000	1	0	0	0	0	0	0	0	0	0	0
Darrell Porter, c-4	.143	5	14	1	2	0	0	0	0	3	4	0
Dan Quisenberry, p	.000	6	0	0	0	0	0	0	0	0	0	0
Paul Splittorff, p	.000	1	0	0	0	0	0	0	0	0	0	0
U L Washington, ss	.273	6	22	1	6	0	0	0	2	0	6	0
John Wathan, c-2,of-1	.286	3	7	1	2	0	0	0	1	2	1	0
Frank White, 2b	.080	6	25	2	2	0	0	0	0	1	5	1
Willie Wilson, of	.154	6	26	3	4	1	0	0	0	4	12	2
TOTAL	.290		207	23	60	9	2	8	22	26	49	6

PITCHER	W	L	ERA	G	GS	CG	SV	SHO	IP	H	ER	BB	SO
Rich Gale	0	1	4.26	2	2	0	0	0	6.1	11	3	4	4
Larry Gura	0	0	2.19	2	2	0	0	0	12.1	8	3	3	4
Dennis Leonard	1	1	6.75	2	2	0	0	0	10.2	15	8	2	5
Renie Martin	0	0	2.79	3	0	0	0	0	9.2	11	3	3	2
Marty Pattin	0	0	0.00	1	0	0	0	0	1.0	0	0	0	2
Dan Quisenberry	1	2	5.23	6	0	0	1	0	10.1	10	6	3	0
Paul Splittorff	0	0	5.40	1	0	0	0	0	1.2	4	1	0	0
TOTAL	2	4	4.15	17	6	0	1	0	52.0	59	24	15	17

GAME 1 AT PHI OCT 14

KC	022 000 020	6	9	1
PHI	005 110 00X	7	11	0

Pitchers: LEONARD, Martin (4), Quisenberry (8) vs WALK, McGraw (8)
Home Runs: Otis-KC, Aikens-KC (2), McBride-PHI
Attendance: 65,791

GAME 2 AT PHI OCT 15

KC	000 001 300	4	11	0
PHI	000 020 04X	6	8	1

Pitchers: Gura, QUISENBERRY (7) vs CARLTON, Reed (9)
Attendance: 65,775

GAME 3 AT KC OCT 17

PHI	010 010 010 0	3	14	0
KC	100 100 100 1	4	11	0

Pitchers: Ruthven, McGRAW (10) vs Gale, Martin (5), QUISENBERRY (8)
Home Runs: Schmidt-PHI, G.Brett-KC, Otis-KC
Attendance: 42,380

GAME 4 AT KC OCT 18

PHI	010 000 110	3	10	1
KC	410 000 00X	5	10	2

Pitchers: CHRISTENSEN, Noles (1), Saucier (6), Brusstar vs LEONARD, Quisenberry (8)
Home Runs: Aikens-KC (2)
Attendance: 42,363

GAME 5 AT KC OCT 19

PHI	000 200 002	4	7	0
KC	000 012 000	3	12	2

Pitchers: Bystrom, Reed (6), McGRAW (7) vs Gura, QUISENBERRY (7)
Home Runs: Schmidt-PHI, Otis-KC
Attendance: 42,369

GAME 6 AT PHI OCT 21

KC	000 000 010	1	7	2
PHI	002 011 00X	4	9	0

Pitchers: GALE (3), Martin (3), Splittorff (5), Pattin (7), Quisenberry (8) vs CARLTON, McGraw (8)
Attendance: 65,838

The Expos, who triumphed over the NL East in the second half of the season, won the first two playoff games at home by identical 3–1 scores over the first-half champion Phillies. The Phillies rapped Expo ace Steve Rogers for ten hits in Game One, but Keith Moreland's solo home run in the second was the only hit to produce a run. The homer tied the score briefly, but the Expos regained the lead in the last of the second inning on Chris Speier's double and increased it to 3–1, two innings later. The Expos scored their three runs early in Game Two on Speier's second-inning single and Gary Carter's two-run homer an inning later. Expo starter Bill Gullickson blanked the Phillies on three hits through 7⅔ innings, but three two-out hits in the eighth scored a Phillie run and brought on reliever Jeff Reardon, who ended the threat for his second save in as many days.

When the Series moved to Philadelphia, the Phillies recovered to even things up with a pair of wins. After an easy 13-hit 6–2 victory in Game Three, they took a 4–0 lead into the fourth inning of Game Four. Montreal fought back to tie the game, fell behind again, then re-tied the score at 5–5 in the top of the seventh. The final innings featured a duel between relievers Tug McGraw and Jeff Reardon. McGraw stopped the Expos on one hit through three innings, and took the win when Reardon, after retiring eight Phillies in a row, gave up a leadoff homer to pinch hitter George Vukovich in the bottom of the tenth.

Steve Rogers won the division title for Montreal in the finale, hurling a six-hit shutout against the Phillies and driving in the first two of the Expos' three runs with a bases-loaded single through the box in the fifth inning.

Montreal Expos, 3; Philadelphia Phillies, 2

MON (E)

PLAYER/POS	AVG	G	AB	R	H	2B	3B	HR	RB	BB	SO	SB
Stan Bahnsen, p	.000	1	0	0	0	0	0	0	0	0	0	0
Ray Burris, p	.000	1	2	0	0	0	0	0	0	0	2	0
Gary Carter, c	.421	5	19	3	8	3	0	2	6	1	1	0
Warren Cromartie, 1b	.227	5	22	1	5	2	0	0	1	0	9	0
Andre Dawson, of	.300	5	20	1	6	0	1	0	0	1	6	2
Terry Francona, of	.333	5	12	0	4	0	0	0	0	2	2	2
Woody Fryman, p	.000	1	0	0	0	0	0	0	0	0	0	0
Bill Gullickson, p	.000	1	3	0	0	0	0	0	0	0	1	0
Wallace Johnson, ph	.500	2	2	0	1	0	0	0	1	0	0	0
Bill Lee, p	.000	1	0	0	0	0	0	0	0	0	0	0
Jerry Manuel, 2b	.071	5	14	0	1	0	0	0	0	2	5	0
Brad Mills, ph	.000	1	0	0	0	0	0	0	0	1	0	0
John Milner, ph	.500	2	2	0	1	0	0	0	1	0	0	0
Larry Parrish, 3b	.150	5	20	3	3	1	0	0	1	1	3	0
Mike Phillips, 2b	.000	1	1	0	0	0	0	0	0	0	0	0
Jeff Reardon, p	.000	3	1	0	0	0	0	0	0	0	1	0
Steve Rogers, p	.400	2	5	0	2	0	0	0	2	0	1	0
Scott Sanderson, p	.000	1	1	0	0	0	0	0	0	0	1	0
Elias Sosa, p	.000	2	0	0	0	0	0	0	0	0	0	0
Chris Speier, ss	.400	5	15	4	6	2	0	0	3	4	2	0
Tim Wallach, of-3	.250	4	4	1	1	1	0	0	0	4	0	0
Jerry White, of	.167	5	18	3	3	1	0	0	1	2	2	3
TOTAL	.255		161	16	41	10	1	2	16	18	36	7

PITCHER	W	L	ERA	G	GS	CG	SV	SHO	IP	H	ER	BB	SO
Stan Bahnsen	0	0	0.00	1	0	0	0	0	1.1	1	0	1	1
Ray Burris	0	1	5.06	1	1	0	0	0	5.1	7	3	4	4
Woody Fryman	0	0	6.75	1	0	0	0	0	1.1	3	1	1	0
Bill Gullickson	1	0	1.17	1	1	0	0	0	7.2	6	1	1	3
Bill Lee	0	0	0.00	1	0	0	0	0	0.2	2	0	0	1
Jeff Reardon	0	1	2.08	3	0	0	2	0	4.1	1	1	1	2
Steve Rogers	2	0	0.51	2	2	1	0	1	17.2	16	1	3	5
Scott Sanderson	0	0	6.75	1	1	0	0	0	2.2	4	2	2	2
Elias Sosa	0	0	3.00	2	0	0	0	0	3.0	4	1	0	1
TOTAL	3	2	2.05	13	5	1	2	1	44.0	44	10	13	19

PHI (E)

PLAYER/POS	AVG	G	AB	R	H	2B	3B	HR	RB	BB	SO	SB
Luis Aguayo, pr	.000	2	0	1	0	0	0	0	0	0	0	0
Ramon Aviles, ph	.000	1	0	0	0	0	0	0	0	1	0	0
Bob Boone, c	.000	3	5	0	0	0	0	0	0	0	0	0
Larry Bowa, ss	.176	5	17	0	3	1	0	0	1	0	0	0
Warren Brusstar, p	.000	2	0	0	0	0	0	0	0	0	0	0
Steve Carlton, p	.250	2	4	0	1	0	0	0	0	0	0	0
Larry Christensen, p	.000	1	2	0	0	0	0	0	0	0	1	0
Dick Davis, of	.000	1	2	0	0	0	0	0	0	0	1	0
Greg Gross, of-2	.000	4	4	0	0	0	0	0	0	0	0	0
Sparky Lyle, p	.000	3	0	0	0	0	0	0	0	0	0	0
Garry Maddox, of	.333	2	3	0	1	1	0	0	0	0	0	0
Gary Matthews, of	.400	5	20	3	8	0	1	1	1	0	2	0
Bake Mc Bride, of	.200	4	15	1	3	1	0	0	0	0	5	0
Tug Mc Graw, p	.000	2	0	0	0	0	0	0	0	0	0	0
Keith Moreland, c	.462	4	13	2	6	0	0	1	3	1	1	0
Dickie Noles, p	.000	1	0	0	0	0	0	0	0	1	0	0
Ron Reed, p	.000	4	0	0	0	0	0	0	0	0	0	0
Pete Rose, 1b	.300	5	20	1	6	1	0	0	2	2	0	0
Dick Ruthven, p	.000	1	1	0	0	0	0	0	0	0	0	0
Mike Schmidt, 3b	.250	5	16	3	4	1	0	1	2	4	2	0
Lonnie Smith, of	.263	5	19	1	5	1	0	0	0	0	4	0
Manny Trillo, 2b	.188	5	16	1	3	0	0	0	1	4	0	0
George Vukovich, of-3	.444	5	9	1	4	0	0	1	2	0	3	0
TOTAL	.265		166	14	44	6	1	4	12	13	19	0

PITCHER	W	L	ERA	G	GS	CG	SV	SHO	IP	H	ER	BB	SO
Warren Brusstar	0	0	4.91	2	0	0	0	0	3.2	5	2	1	3
Steve Carlton	0	2	3.86	2	2	0	0	0	14.0	14	6	8	13
Larry Christensen	1	0	1.50	1	1	0	0	0	6.0	4	1	1	8
Sparky Lyle	0	0	0.00	3	0	0	0	0	2.1	4	0	2	1
Tug Mc Graw	1	0	0.00	2	0	0	0	0	4.0	2	0	0	2
Dickie Noles	0	0	4.50	1	1	0	0	0	4.0	4	2	2	5
Ron Reed	0	0	3.00	4	0	0	0	0	6.0	5	2	3	4
Dick Ruthven	0	1	4.50	1	1	0	0	0	4.0	3	2	1	0
TOTAL	2	3	3.07	16	5	0	0	0	44.0	41	15	18	36

Cincinnati, with the league's best overall season record, failed to win either half season in the NL West, and watched from the sidelines as first-half winner Los Angeles, down 0–2, recovered to win the final three games—and the division title—from second-half victor Houston. In the opener, Astro Alan Ashby's two-run homer in the last of the ninth broke a 1–1 tie and gave Nolan Ryan a two-hit victory. The next day, Astro Denny Walling's two-out bases-loaded single in the last of the eleventh scored Phil Garner with the game's only run.

When the clubs shifted to Los Angeles for the remainder of the series, the Dodgers came alive. In Game Three, a first-inning double by Dusty Baker and home run by Steve Garvey drove in three Dodger runs. Pitcher Burt Hooton and two relievers held Houston to three hits in what became a 6–1 Dodger victory. The next day, Dodger Fernando Valenzuela and Astro Vern Ruhle hurled matching four-hitters. But Pedro Guerrero's home run in the fifth inning and a pair of Dodger singles sandwiched around a sacrifice and intentional walk in the seventh gave Los Angeles two runs, while Valenzuela held Houston to a single run in the ninth. In the finale, Jerry Reuss blanked the Astros on five hits while his Dodgers blended three of their seven hits with a walk and Astro error for three runs in the sixth. Two more hits produced a final run an inning later.

Los Angeles Dodgers, 3; Houston Astros, 2

LA (W)

PLAYER/POS	AVG	G	AB	R	H	2B	3B	HR	RB	BB	SO	SB
Dusty Baker, of	.167	5	18	2	3	1	0	0	1	2	0	0
Terry Forster, p	.000	1	0	0	0	0	0	0	0	0	0	0
Steve Garvey, 1b	.368	5	19	4	7	0	1	2	4	0	2	0
Pedro Guerrero, 3b	.176	5	17	1	3	1	0	1	1	2	4	1
Burt Hooton, p	.000	1	3	0	0	0	0	0	0	0	0	0
Steve Howe, p	.000	2	0	0	0	0	0	0	0	0	0	0
Jay Johnstone, ph	.000	1	1	0	0	0	0	0	0	0	0	0
Ken Landreaux, of	.200	5	20	1	4	1	0	0	1	0	1	0
Davey Lopes, 2b	.200	5	20	1	4	1	0	0	0	3	7	1
Mike Marshall, ph	.000	1	1	0	0	0	0	0	0	0	1	0
Rick Monday, of	.214	5	14	1	3	0	0	0	1	2	4	0
Tom Niedenfuer, p	.000	1	0	0	0	0	0	0	0	0	0	0
Jerry Reuss, p	.000	2	8	0	0	0	0	0	0	0	8	0
Bill Russell, ss	.250	5	16	1	4	1	0	0	2	3	1	0
Steve Sax, 2b	.000	1	0	0	0	0	0	0	0	0	0	0
Mike Scioscia, c	.154	4	13	0	2	0	0	0	1	1	2	0
Reggie Smith, ph	.000	2	1	0	0	0	0	0	1	0	1	0
Dave Stewart, p	.000	2	0	0	0	0	0	0	0	0	0	0
Derrel Thomas, of	.000	4	2	1	0	0	0	0	0	0	1	0
Fernando Valenzuela, p	.000	2	4	0	0	0	0	0	0	0	1	0
Bob Welch, p	.000	1	0	0	0	0	0	0	0	0	0	0
Steve Yeager, c	.400	2	5	1	2	1	0	0	0	0	1	0
TOTAL	.198		162	13	32	6	1	3	12	13	34	2

PITCHER	W	L	ERA	G	GS	CG	SV	SHO	IP	H	ER	BB	SO
Terry Forster	0	0	0.00	1	0	0	0	0	0.1	0	0	0	0
Burt Hooton	1	0	1.29	1	1	0	0	0	7.0	3	1	3	2
Steve Howe	0	0	0.00	2	0	0	0	0	2.0	1	0	0	2
Tom Niedenfuer	0	0	0.00	1	0	0	0	0	0.1	1	0	1	1
Jerry Reuss	1	0	0.00	2	2	1	0	1	18.0	10	0	5	7
Dave Stewart	0	2	40.50	2	0	0	0	0	0.2	4	3	0	1
Fernando Valenzuela	1	0	1.06	2	2	1	0	0	17.0	10	2	3	10
Bob Welch	0	0	0.00	1	0	0	0	0	1.0	0	0	1	1
TOTAL	3	2	1.17	12	5	2	0	1	46.1	29	6	13	24

HOU (W)

PLAYER/POS	AVG	G	AB	R	H	2B	3B	HR	RB	BB	SO	SB
Alan Ashby, c	.111	3	9	1	1	0	0	1	2	2	0	0
Cesar Cedeno, 1b	.231	4	13	0	3	1	0	0	0	2	2	2
Jose Cruz, of	.300	5	20	0	6	1	0	0	0	1	3	1
Kiko Garcia, ss-1	.000	2	4	0	0	0	0	0	0	0	1	0
Phil Garner, 2b	.111	5	18	1	2	0	0	0	0	3	3	0
Art Howe, 3b	.235	5	17	1	4	0	0	1	1	2	1	0
Bob Knepper, p	.000	1	1	0	0	0	0	0	0	0	0	0
Frank La Corte, p	.000	2	0	0	0	0	0	0	0	0	0	0
Joe Niekro, p	.000	1	2	0	0	0	0	0	0	0	0	0
Joe Pittman, ph	.000	2	2	0	0	0	0	0	0	0	0	0
Terry Puhl, of	.190	5	21	2	4	1	0	0	0	0	1	1
Luis Pujols, c	.000	2	6	0	0	0	0	0	0	0	1	0
Craig Reynolds, ss-1	.333	2	3	1	1	0	0	0	0	0	1	0
Dave Roberts, ph	.000	1	1	0	0	0	0	0	0	0	1	0
Vern Ruhle, p	.000	1	1	0	0	0	0	0	0	0	1	0
Nolan Ryan, p	.250	2	4	0	1	0	0	0	0	1	1	0
Joe Sambito, p	.000	2	0	0	0	0	0	0	0	0	0	0
Tony Scott, of	.150	5	20	0	3	0	0	0	2	1	6	0
Billy Smith, p	.000	1	0	0	0	0	0	0	0	0	0	0
Dave Smith, p	.000	2	0	0	0	0	0	0	0	0	0	0
Harry Spilman, ph	.000	1	1	0	0	0	0	0	0	0	0	0
Dickie Thon, ss	.182	4	11	0	2	0	0	0	0	1	0	0
Denny Walling, 1b-2	.333	3	6	0	2	0	0	0	1	0	1	0
Gary Woods, ph	.000	2	2	0	0	0	0	0	0	0	1	0
TOTAL	.179		162	6	29	3	0	2	6	13	24	4

PITCHER	W	L	ERA	G	GS	CG	SV	SHO	IP	H	ER	BB	SO
Bob Knepper	0	1	5.40	1	1	0	0	0	5.0	6	3	2	4
Frank La Corte	0	0	0.00	2	0	0	0	0	3.2	2	0	1	5
Joe Niekro	0	0	0.00	1	1	0	0	0	8.0	7	0	3	4
Vern Ruhle	0	1	2.25	1	1	1	0	0	8.0	4	2	2	1
Nolan Ryan	1	1	1.80	2	2	1	0	0	15.0	6	3	3	14
Joe Sambito	1	0	16.20	2	0	0	0	0	1.2	5	3	2	2
Billy Smith	0	0	0.00	1	0	0	0	0	0.1	0	0	0	0
Dave Smith	0	0	3.86	2	0	0	0	0	2.1	2	1	0	4
TOTAL	2	3	2.45	12	5	2	0	0	44.0	32	12	13	34

GAME 1 AT HOU OCT 6

LA	000	000	100	1	2	0
HOU	000	001	002	3	8	0

Pitchers: Valenzuela, STEWART (9) vs RYAN
Home Runs: Garvey-LA, Ashby-HOU
Attendance: 44,836

GAME 2 AT HOU OCT 7

LA	000	000	000 00	0	9	1
HOU	000	000	000 01	1	9	0

Pitchers: Reuss, S.Howe (10), STEWART (11), Forster (11), Niedenfuer (11) vs Niekro, D.Smith (9), SAMBITO (11)
Attendance: 42,398

GAME 3 AT LA OCT 9

HOU	001	000	000	1	3	2
LA	300	000	03X	6	10	0

Pitchers: KNEPPER, LaCorte (6), Sambito (8), B.Smith (8) vs HOOTON, S.Howe (8), Welch (9)
Home Runs: Garvey-LA, A.Howe-HOU
Attendance: 46,820

GAME 4 AT LA OCT 10

HOU	000	000	001	1	4	0
LA	000	010	10X	2	4	0

Pitchers: RUHLE vs VALENZUELA
Home Runs: Guerrero-LA
Attendance: 55,983

GAME 5 AT LA OCT 11

HOU	000	000	000	0	5	3
LA	000	003	10X	4	7	2

Pitchers: RYAN, D.Smith (7), LaCorte (7) vs REUSS
Attendance: 55,979

Fine pitching characterized the series, with the losing team held to one run in four of the five games. In the exception Expo Ray Burris hurled a shutout.

Montreal put men on base in each inning of the opener. But the pitching of Burt Hooton and Bob Welch—plus some fine Dodger fielding—kept the Expos from scoring until the ninth, when their one run was too little to overcome the Dodger lead. Burris's shutout evened the series in Game Two as the Expos scored three times against rookie sensation Fernando Valenzuela. The Expos took the series lead in Game Three, overcoming a 0–1 deficit with a two-out four-run burst in the sixth (capped by Jerry White's three-run homer).

In the end, though, the Dodgers prevailed. Through seven innings of Game Four, Hooton and the Expos' Bill Gullickson dueled at 1–1. But in the top of the eighth, Steve Garvey homered with a man aboard, and four more Dodger runs in the ninth put the game away. The finale—Burris vs. Valenzuela again—featured another 1–1 duel, this one reaching into the top of the ninth when, with two out, Dodger Rick Monday homered off reliever Steve Rogers. In the bottom of the ninth, Valenzuela walked two batters after retiring two, but Welch came on to save the game and the pennant.

Los Angeles Dodgers (West), 3;
Montreal Expos (East), 2

LA (W)

PLAYER/POS	AVG	G	AB	R	H	2B	3B	HR	RB	BB	SO	SB
Dusty Baker, of	.316	5	19	3	6	1	0	0	3	1	0	0
Bobby Castillo, p	.000	1	0	0	0	0	0	0	0	0	0	0
Ron Cey, 3b	.278	5	18	1	5	1	0	0	3	3	2	0
Terry Forster, p	.000	1	0	0	0	0	0	0	0	0	0	0
Steve Garvey, 1b	.286	5	21	2	6	0	0	1	2	0	4	0
Pedro Guerrero, of	.105	5	19	1	2	0	0	1	2	1	4	0
Burt Hooton, p	.000	2	5	0	0	0	0	0	0	0	2	0
Steve Howe, p	.000	2	0	0	0	0	0	0	0	0	0	0
Jay Johnstone, ph	.000	2	2	0	0	0	0	0	0	0	0	0
Ken Landreaux, of-3	.100	5	10	0	1	1	0	0	0	3	2	0
Davey Lopes, 2b	.278	5	18	0	5	0	0	0	0	1	3	5
Rick Monday, of-2	.333	3	9	2	3	0	0	1	1	0	4	0
Tom Niedenfuer, p	.000	1	0	0	0	0	0	0	0	0	0	0
Alejandro Pena, p	.000	2	0	0	0	0	0	0	0	0	0	0
Jerry Reuss, p	.000	1	2	0	0	0	0	0	0	0	0	0
Bill Russell, ss	.313	5	16	2	5	0	1	0	1	1	1	0
Steve Sax, 2b	.000	1	0	0	0	0	0	0	0	0	0	0
Mike Scioscia, c	.133	5	15	1	2	0	0	1	1	2	1	0
Reggie Smith, ph	1.000	1	1	0	1	0	0	0	1	0	0	0
Derrel Thomas, 3b-1,of-1	1.000	2	1	2	1	0	0	0	0	0	0	0
Fernando Valenzuela, p	.000	2	5	0	0	0	0	0	1	0	0	0
Bob Welch, p	.000	3	0	0	0	0	0	0	0	0	0	0
Steve Yeager, c	.500	1	2	1	1	0	0	0	0	0	0	0
TOTAL	.233		163	15	38	3	1	4	15	12	23	5

PITCHER	W	L	ERA	G	GS	CG	SV	SHO	IP	H	ER	BB	SO
Bobby Castillo	0	0	0.00	1	0	0	0	0	1.0	0	0	0	1
Terry Forster	0	0	0.00	1	0	0	0	0	0.1	0	0	0	1
Burt Hooton	2	0	0.00	2	2	0	0	0	14.2	11	0	6	7
Steve Howe	0	0	0.00	2	0	0	0	0	2.0	1	0	0	2
Tom Niedenfuer	0	0	0.00	1	0	0	0	0	0.1	2	0	0	0
Alejandro Pena	0	0	0.00	2	0	0	0	0	2.1	1	0	0	0
Jerry Reuss	0	1	5.14	1	1	0	0	0	7.0	7	4	1	2
Fernando Valenzuela	1	1	2.45	2	2	0	0	0	14.2	10	4	5	10
Bob Welch	0	0	5.40	3	0	0	1	0	1.2	2	1	0	2
TOTAL	3	2	1.84	15	5	0	1	0	44.0	34	9	12	25

MON (E)

PLAYER/POS	AVG	G	AB	R	H	2B	3B	HR	RB	BB	SO	SB
Ray Burris, p	.000	2	6	0	0	0	0	0	0	0	4	0
Gary Carter, c	.438	5	16	3	7	1	0	0	0	4	2	0
Warren Cromartie, 1b	.167	5	18	0	3	1	0	0	2	0	2	0
Andre Dawson, of	.150	5	20	2	3	0	0	0	0	0	4	0
Terry Francona, of-1	.000	2	1	0	0	0	0	0	0	0	1	0
Woody Fryman, p	.000	1	0	0	0	0	0	0	0	0	0	0
Bill Gullickson, p	.000	2	3	0	0	0	0	0	0	1	2	0
Bill Lee, p	.000	1	0	0	0	0	0	0	0	0	0	0
Jerry Manuel, pr	.000	1	0	0	0	0	0	0	0	0	0	0
John Milner, ph	.000	1	1	0	0	0	0	0	0	0	1	0
Larry Parrish, 3b	.263	5	19	2	5	2	0	0	2	1	1	0
Tim Raines, of	.238	5	21	1	5	2	0	0	1	0	3	0
Jeff Reardon, p	.000	1	0	0	0	0	0	0	0	0	0	0
Steve Rogers, p	.000	2	2	0	0	0	0	0	0	0	1	0
Rodney Scott, 2b	.167	5	18	0	3	0	0	0	0	1	3	1
Elias Sosa, p	.000	1	0	0	0	0	0	0	0	0	0	0
Chris Speier, ss	.188	5	16	0	3	0	0	0	0	2	0	0
Tim Wallach, ph	.000	1	1	0	0	0	0	0	0	0	0	0
Jerry White, of	.313	5	16	2	5	1	0	1	3	3	1	1
TOTAL	.215		158	10	34	7	0	1	8	12	25	2

PITCHER	W	L	ERA	G	GS	CG	SV	SHO	IP	H	ER	BB	SO
Ray Burris	1	0	0.53	2	2	1	0	1	17.0	10	1	3	4
Woody Fryman	0	0	36.00	1	0	0	0	0	1.0	3	4	1	1
Bill Gullickson	0	2	2.51	2	2	0	0	0	14.1	12	4	6	12
Bill Lee	0	0	0.00	1	0	0	0	0	0.1	1	0	0	0
Jeff Reardon	0	0	27.00	1	0	0	0	0	1.0	3	3	0	0
Steve Rogers	1	1	1.80	2	1	1	0	0	10.0	8	2	1	6
Elias Sosa	0	0	0.00	1	0	0	0	0	0.1	1	0	1	0
TOTAL	2	3	2.86	10	5	2	0	1	44.0	38	14	12	23

GAME 1 AT LA OCT 13

MON	000	000	001	1	9	0
LA	020	000	03X	5	8	0

Pitchers: GULLICKSON, Reardon (8) vs HOOTON, Welch (8), Howe (9)
Home Runs: Guerrero-LA, Scioscia-LA
Attendance: 51,273

GAME 2 AT LA OCT 14

MON	020	001	000	3	10	1
LA	000	000	000	0	5	1

Pitchers: BURRIS vs VALENZUELA, Niedenfuer (7), Forster (7), Pena (7), Castillo (9)
Attendance: 53,463

GAME 3 AT MON OCT 16

LA	000	100	000	1	7	0
MON	000	004	00X	4	7	1

Pitchers: REUSS, Pena (8) vs ROGERS
Home Runs: White-MON
Attendance: 54,372

GAME 4 AT MON OCT 17

LA	001	000	024	7	12	1
MON	000	100	000	1	5	1

Pitchers: HOOTON, Welch (8), Howe (9) vs GULLICKSON, Fryman (8), Sosa (9), Lee (9)
Home Runs: Garvey-LA
Attendance: 54,499

GAME 5 AT MON OCT 19

LA	000	010	001	2	6	0
MON	100	000	000	1	3	1

Pitchers: VALENZUELA, Welch (9) vs Burris, ROGERS (9)
Home Runs: Monday-LA
Attendance: 36,491

The home field didn't seem to offer any advantage. First-half winner New York captured both games played in Milwaukee, but when the Series moved to Yankee Stadium for the final three games, the second-half champion Brewers evened the series.

Milwaukee took a 2–0 lead early in the opener, but New York erupted for four runs in the fourth on Oscar Gamble's two-run homer and Rick Cerone's double, and held on to win 5–3. In Game Two, rookie starter Dave Righetti fanned ten Brewers in his six innings, and Goose Gossage's brilliant relief earned him his second save in two days as the Yankees took a 3–0 win on homers by Lou Piniella and Reggie Jackson.

Milwaukee, struggling against elimination, took the lead in the seventh inning of Game Three on Ted Simmons' two-run homer. New York tied the score at 3–3 in their half of the inning, but Paul Molitor broke the tie in the eighth with a solo homer. Simmons doubled home an insurance run later in the inning for a 5–3 Brewer win. The Brewers tagged Yankee pitching for only four hits in Game Four, but three of them came in the fourth inning and combined with a sacrifice fly to produce the Brewers' two runs. New York scored once in the sixth, but baserunning errors an inning later ended their only other scoring threat.

In the finale Milwaukee scored two early runs, but the Yankees (as they had done in the opener) took the lead with a four-run fourth—this time on home runs by Reggie Jackson and Oscar Gamble, and Rick Cerone's single. Cerone later hit an insurance homer, as the home team finally won a game—and captured the division crown.

New York Yankees, 3; Milwaukee Brewers, 2

NY (E)

PLAYER/POS	AVG	G	AB	R	H	2B	3B	HR	RB	BB	SO	SB
Bobby Brown, pr	.000	1	0	0	0	0	0	0	0	0	0	0
Rick Cerone, c	.333	5	18	1	6	2	0	1	5	0	2	0
Ron Davis, p	.000	3	0	0	0	0	0	0	0	0	0	0
Barry Foote, ph	.000	1	0	0	0	0	0	0	0	0	0	0
Oscar Gamble, dh	.556	4	9	2	5	1	0	2	3	1	2	0
Rich Gossage, p	.000	3	0	0	0	0	0	0	0	0	0	0
Ron Guidry, p	.000	2	0	0	0	0	0	0	0	0	0	0
Reggie Jackson, of	.300	5	20	4	6	0	0	2	4	1	5	0
Tommy John, p	.000	1	0	0	0	0	0	0	0	0	0	0
Rudy May, p	.000	1	0	0	0	0	0	0	0	0	0	0
Larry Milbourne, ss	.316	5	19	4	6	1	0	0	0	0	1	0
Jerry Mumphrey, of	.095	5	21	2	2	0	0	0	0	0	1	1
Bobby Murcer, ph	.000	2	1	0	0	0	0	0	0	1	0	0
Graig Nettles, 3b	.059	5	17	1	1	0	0	0	1	3	1	0
Lou Piniella, dh	.200	4	10	1	2	1	0	1	3	0	0	0
Willie Randolph, 2b	.200	5	20	0	4	0	0	0	1	1	4	0
Rick Reuschel, p	.000	1	0	0	0	0	0	0	0	0	0	0
Dave Revering, 1b	.000	2	0	0	0	0	0	0	0	0	0	0
Dave Righetti, p	.000	2	0	0	0	0	0	0	0	0	0	0
Bob Watson, 1b	.438	5	16	2	7	0	0	0	1	1	1	0
Dave Winfield, of	.350	5	20	2	7	3	0	0	0	1	5	0
TOTAL	.269		171	19	46	8	0	6	18	9	22	1

PITCHER	W	L	ERA	G	GS	CG	SV	SHO	IP	H	ER	BB	SO
Ron Davis	1	0	0.00	3	0	0	0	0	6.0	1	0	2	6
Rich Gossage	0	0	0.00	3	0	0	3	0	6.2	3	0	2	8
Ron Guidry	0	0	5.40	2	2	0	0	0	8.1	11	5	3	8
Tommy John	0	1	6.43	1	1	0	0	0	7.0	8	5	2	0
Rudy May	0	0	0.00	1	0	0	0	0	2.0	1	0	0	1
Rick Reuschel	0	1	3.00	1	1	0	0	0	6.0	4	2	1	3
Dave Righetti	2	0	1.00	2	1	0	0	0	9.0	8	1	3	13
TOTAL	3	2	2.60	13	5	0	3	0	45.0	36	13	13	39

MIL (E)

PLAYER/POS	AVG	G	AB	R	H	2B	3B	HR	RB	BB	SO	SB
Sal Bando, 3b	.294	5	17	1	5	3	0	0	1	2	3	0
Dwight Bernard, p	.000	2	0	0	0	0	0	0	0	0	0	0
Thad Bosley, ph	.000	1	0	0	0	0	0	0	0	0	0	0
Mike Caldwell, p	.000	2	0	0	0	0	0	0	0	0	0	0
Cecil Cooper, 1b	.222	5	18	1	4	0	0	0	3	1	3	0
Jamie Easterly, p	.000	2	0	0	0	0	0	0	0	0	0	0
Marshall Edwards, of	.000	2	1	0	0	0	0	0	0	0	1	0
Rollie Fingers, p	.000	3	0	0	0	0	0	0	0	0	0	0
Jim Gantner, 2b	.143	4	14	1	2	1	0	0	0	0	2	0
Moose Haas, p	.000	2	0	0	0	0	0	0	0	0	0	0
Roy Howell, dh-3	.400	4	5	0	2	0	0	0	0	2	2	0
Randy Lerch, p	.000	1	0	0	0	0	0	0	0	0	0	0
Bob Mc Clure, p	.000	3	0	0	0	0	0	0	0	0	0	0
Paul Molitor, of	.250	5	20	2	5	0	0	1	1	2	5	0
Don Money, 2b-1,dh-1	.000	2	3	0	0	0	0	0	0	0	0	0
Charlie Moore, of-2,dh-2	.222	4	9	0	2	0	0	0	1	1	2	0
Ben Oglivie, of	.167	5	18	0	3	1	0	0	1	0	7	0
Ed Romero, 2b	.500	1	2	1	1	0	0	0	0	0	1	0
Ted Simmons, c	.211	5	19	1	4	1	0	1	4	2	2	0
Jim Slaton, p	.000	4	0	0	0	0	0	0	0	0	0	0
Gorman Thomas, of-3,dh-2	.118	5	17	2	2	0	0	1	1	1	9	0
Pete Vuckovich, p	.000	2	0	0	0	0	0	0	0	0	0	0
Robin Yount, ss	.316	5	19	4	6	0	1	0	1	2	2	1
TOTAL	.222		162	13	36	6	1	3	13	13	39	1

PITCHER	W	L	ERA	G	GS	CG	SV	SHO	IP	H	ER	BB	SO
Dwight Bernard	0	0	0.00	2	0	0	0	0	2.1	0	0	0	0
Mike Caldwell	0	1	4.32	2	1	0	0	0	8.1	9	4	0	4
Jamie Easterly	0	0	6.75	2	0	0	0	0	1.1	2	1	0	1
Rollie Fingers	1	0	3.86	3	0	0	1	0	4.2	7	2	1	5
Moose Haas	0	2	9.45	2	2	0	0	0	6.2	13	7	1	1
Randy Lerch	0	0	1.50	1	1	0	0	0	6.0	3	1	4	3
Bob Mc Clure	0	0	0.00	3	0	0	0	0	3.1	4	0	0	2
Jim Slaton	0	0	3.00	4	0	0	0	0	6.0	6	2	0	2
Pete Vuckovich	1	0	0.00	2	1	0	0	0	5.1	2	0	3	4
TOTAL	2	3	3.48	21	5	0	1	0	44.0	46	17	9	22

First-half winner Oakland, with the league's best win-loss record over the full season, swept the division title from second-half champ Kansas City (who, with a full-season record of 50–53, had become the only club in major-league history to qualify for postseason play with a losing record). Twice in the opener the Royals loaded the bases against Mike Norris with fewer than two outs, but both times failed to score. Meanwhile, after a Royal error had prolonged the A's fourth inning, Wayne Gross homered for three unearned Oakland runs. Dwayne Murphy's eighth-inning solo shot gave the A's a fourth run. The game ended with Norris possessor of a four-hit shutout.

Game Two was closer. Oakland's Tony Armas doubled in a run in the top of the first, and doubled home another in the eighth (his fourth hit of the game) to break a 1–1 tie and provide the margin needed for pitcher Steve McCatty's six-hit win. The A's Rick Langford yielded ten hits in Game Three (including Kansas City's only extra-base hit of the series, a double), but only one Royal scored, meanwhile the A's were sending four runs across the plate—three of them by Rickey Henderson, who reached base four times on pairs of hits and walks.

Oakland Athletics, 3;
Kansas City Royals, 0

KC (W)

PLAYER/POS	AVG	G	AB	R	H	2B	3B	HR	RB	BB	SO	SB
Willie Aikens, 1b	.333	3	9	0	3	0	0	0	0	3	2	0
George Brett, 3b	.167	3	12	0	2	0	0	0	0	0	0	0
Cesar Geronimo, pr	.000	1	0	0	0	0	0	0	0	0	0	0
Larry Gura, p	.000	1	0	0	0	0	0	0	0	0	0	0
Clint Hurdle, of	.273	3	11	0	3	0	0	0	0	1	1	0
Mike Jones, p	.000	1	0	0	0	0	0	0	0	0	0	0
Dennis Leonard, p	.000	1	0	0	0	0	0	0	0	0	0	0
Renie Martin, p	.000	2	0	0	0	0	0	0	0	0	0	0
Lee May, 1b	.000	1	0	0	0	0	0	0	0	0	0	0
Hal Mc Rae, dh	.091	3	11	0	1	1	0	0	0	1	1	0
Amos Otis, of	.000	3	12	0	0	0	0	0	1	0	4	0
Dan Quisenberry, p	.000	1	0	0	0	0	0	0	0	0	0	0
U. L. Washington, ss	.222	3	9	0	2	0	0	0	0	0	1	0
John Wathan, c	.300	3	10	1	3	0	0	0	0	1	1	0
Frank White, 2b	.182	3	11	1	2	0	0	0	0	1	1	0
Willie Wilson, of	.308	3	13	0	4	0	0	0	1	0	0	0
TOTAL	.204		98	2	20	1	0	0	2	7	11	0

PITCHER	W	L	ERA	G	GS	CG	SV	SHO	IP	H	ER	BB	SO
Larry Gura	0	1	7.36	1	1	0	0	0	3.2	7	3	3	3
Mike Jones	0	1	2.25	1	1	0	0	0	8.0	9	2	0	2
Dennis Leonard	0	1	1.13	1	1	0	0	0	8.0	7	1	1	3
Renie Martin	0	0	0.00	2	0	0	0	0	5.1	1	0	2	2
Dan Quisenberry	0	0	0.00	1	0	0	0	0	1.0	1	0	0	0
TOTAL	0	3	2.08	6	3	0	0	0	26.0	25	6	6	10

OAK (W)

PLAYER/POS	AVG	G	AB	R	H	2B	3B	HR	RB	BB	SO	SB
Tony Armas, of	.545	3	11	1	6	2	0	0	3	1	1	0
Dave Beard, p	.000	1	0	0	0	0	0	0	0	0	0	0
Rick Bosetti, of	.000	1	0	0	0	0	0	0	0	0	0	0
Keith Drumright, dh	.250	1	4	0	1	0	0	0	0	0	0	0
Wayne Gross, 3b-1	.400	2	5	1	2	0	0	1	3	0	0	0
Mike Heath, c	.000	2	8	0	0	0	0	0	0	0	1	0
Rickey Henderson, of	.182	3	11	3	2	0	0	0	0	2	0	2
Cliff Johnson, dh	.286	2	7	0	2	1	0	0	0	0	1	0
Mickey Klutts, 3b	.143	2	7	0	1	0	0	0	0	0	1	0
Rick Langford, p	.000	1	0	0	0	0	0	0	0	0	0	0
Steve Mc Catty, p	.000	1	0	0	0	0	0	0	0	0	0	0
Dave Mc Kay, 2b	.273	3	11	1	3	0	0	1	1	1	1	0
Kelvin Moore, 1b	.000	2	8	0	0	0	0	0	0	0	2	0
Dwayne Murphy, of	.545	3	11	4	6	1	0	1	2	1	1	0
Jeff Newman, c	.000	1	3	0	0	0	0	0	0	0	1	0
Mike Norris, p	.000	1	0	0	0	0	0	0	0	0	0	0
Rob Picciolo, ss	.333	1	3	0	1	0	0	0	0	0	0	0
Jim Spencer, 1b	.250	1	4	0	1	1	0	0	0	0	0	0
Fred Stanley, ss	.000	3	6	0	0	0	0	0	0	1	1	0
Tom Underwood, p	.000	1	0	0	0	0	0	0	0	0	0	0
TOTAL	.253		99	10	25	5	0	3	9	6	10	2

PITCHER	W	L	ERA	G	GS	CG	SV	SHO	IP	H	ER	BB	SO
Dave Beard	0	0	0.00	1	0	0	1	0	1.1	0	0	0	2
Rick Langford	1	0	1.23	1	1	0	0	0	7.1	10	1	0	3
Steve Mc Catty	1	0	1.00	1	1	1	0	0	9.0	6	1	4	3
Mike Norris	1	0	0.00	1	1	1	0	1	9.0	4	0	3	2
Tom Underwood	0	0	0.00	1	0	0	0	0	0.1	0	0	0	1
TOTAL	3	0	0.67	5	3	2	1	1	27.0	20	2	7	11

GAME 1 AT KC OCT 6

OAK	000 300 010	4 8 2
KC	000 000 000	0 4 1

Pitchers: NORRIS vs LEONARD, Martin (9)
Home Runs: Gross-OAK, Murphy-OAK
Attendance: 40,592

GAME 2 AT KC OCT 7

OAK	100 000 010	2 10 1
KC	000 010 000	1 6 0

Pitchers: McCATTY vs JONES, Quisenberry (9)
Attendance: 40,274

GAME 3 AT OAK OCT 9

KC	000 100 000	1 10 3
OAK	101 200 00X	4 7 0

Pitchers: GURA, Martin (4) vs LANGFORD, Underwood (8), Beard (8)
Home Runs: McKay-OAK
Attendance: 40,002

The A's scored only four runs to their opponents' twenty as the Yankees swept the series. And only two of the six Yankee pitchers permitted an Oakland runner to score, while not one of Oakland's eight pitchers held New York scoreless. Even so, two of the three games were closely contested.

Oakland's Mike Norris gave up a bases-loaded double to Graig Nettles in the first inning of Game One before settling down to pitch shutout ball. But the three runs Nettles drove in were more than enough, as Tommy John and two relievers held the A's to a single run.

Game Two was the series' only blowout, and even it remained close for three innings. But, led by a pair of three-run homers from Nettles and Lou Piniella, the Yankees parlayed nineteen hits into thirteen runs as Yankee reliever George Frazier held the A's scoreless over the final five frames.

Game Three remained tight until the ninth. Through eight innings the only run came on Yankee Willie Randolph's homer off Oakland starter Matt Keough. But in the top of the ninth, Graig Nettles tagged reliever Tom Underwood for his second bases-clearing double of the series. The three runs weren't really needed, as Dave Righetti, Ron Davis, and Goose Gossage combined to shut out the A's for the full nine.

New York Yankees (East), 3; Oakland A's (West), 0

NY (E)

PLAYER/POS	AVG	G	AB	R	H	2B	3B	HR	RB	BB	SO	SB
Bobby Brown, of-2	1.000	3	1	2	1	0	0	0	0	0	0	0
Rick Cerone, c	.100	3	10	1	1	0	0	0	0	0	0	0
Ron Davis, p	.000	2	0	0	0	0	0	0	0	0	0	0
Barry Foote, c-1	1.000	2	1	0	1	0	0	0	0	0	0	0
George Frazier, p	.000	1	0	0	0	0	0	0	0	0	0	0
Oscar Gamble, dh-2,of-1	.167	3	6	2	1	0	0	0	1	5	3	0
Rich Gossage, p	.000	2	0	0	0	0	0	0	0	0	0	0
Reggie Jackson, of	.000	2	4	1	0	0	0	0	1	1	0	1
Tommy John, p	.000	1	0	0	0	0	0	0	0	0	0	0
Rudy May, p	.000	1	0	0	0	0	0	0	0	0	0	0
Larry Milbourne, ss	.462	3	13	4	6	0	0	0	1	0	0	0
Jerry Mumphrey, of	.500	3	12	2	6	1	0	0	0	3	2	0
Bobby Murcer, dh	.333	1	3	0	1	0	0	0	0	1	1	0
Graig Nettles, 3b	.500	3	12	2	6	2	0	1	9	1	0	0
Lou Piniella, dh-2,of-1	.600	3	5	2	3	0	0	1	3	0	0	0
Willie Randolph, 2b	.333	3	12	2	4	0	0	1	2	0	1	0
Dave Revering, 1b	.500	2	2	0	1	0	0	0	0	0	0	0
Dave Righetti, p	.000	1	0	0	0	0	0	0	0	0	0	0
Andre Robertson, ss	.000	1	1	0	0	0	0	0	0	0	0	0
Aurelio Rodriguez, 3b	.000	1	0	0	0	0	0	0	0	0	0	0
Bob Watson, 1b	.250	3	12	0	3	0	0	0	1	0	1	0
Dave Winfield, of	.154	3	13	2	2	1	0	0	2	2	2	1
TOTAL	.336		107	20	36	4	0	3	20	13	10	2

PITCHER	W	L	ERA	G	GS	CG	SV	SHO	IP	H	ER	BB	SO
Ron Davis	0	0	0.00	2	0	0	0	0	3.1	0	0	2	4
George Frazier	1	0	0.00	1	0	0	0	0	5.2	5	0	1	5
Rich Gossage	0	0	0.00	2	0	0	1	0	2.2	1	0	0	2
Tommy John	1	0	1.50	1	1	0	0	0	6.0	6	1	1	3
Rudy May	0	0	8.10	1	0	0	0	0	3.1	6	3	0	5
Dave Righetti	1	0	0.00	1	1	0	0	0	6.0	4	0	2	4
TOTAL	3	0	1.33	8	2	0	1	0	27.0	22	4	6	23

OAK (W)

PLAYER/POS	AVG	G	AB	R	H	2B	3B	HR	RB	BB	SO	SB
Tony Armas, of	.167	3	12	0	2	0	0	0	0	0	5	0
Dave Beard, p	.000	1	0	0	0	0	0	0	0	0	0	0
Rick Bosetti, of-1,dh-1	.250	2	4	1	1	1	0	0	0	0	1	0
Mike Davis, ph	1.000	1	1	0	1	0	0	0	0	0	0	0
Keith Drumright, dh-1	.000	3	4	0	0	0	0	0	0	1	0	0
Wayne Gross, 3b	.000	3	5	0	0	0	0	0	0	0	0	0
Mike Heath, c-2,of-1	.333	3	6	1	2	0	0	0	0	0	1	0
Rickey Henderson, of	.364	3	11	0	4	2	1	0	1	1	2	2
Cliff Johnson, dh	.000	2	6	0	0	0	0	0	0	2	2	0
Jeff Jones, p	.000	1	0	0	0	0	0	0	0	0	0	0
Matt Keough, p	.000	1	0	0	0	0	0	0	0	0	0	0
Brian Kingman, p	.000	1	0	0	0	0	0	0	0	0	0	0
Mickey Klutts, 3b	.429	3	7	1	3	0	0	0	0	0	1	0
Steve Mc Catty, p	.000	1	0	0	0	0	0	0	0	0	0	0
Dave Mc Kay, 2b	.273	3	11	0	3	0	0	0	1	0	2	0
Kelvin Moore, 1b	.222	3	9	0	2	0	0	0	0	0	1	0
Dwayne Murphy, of	.250	3	8	0	2	1	0	0	1	2	3	0
Jeff Newman, c	.000	2	5	0	0	0	0	0	0	0	2	0
Mike Norris, p	.000	1	0	0	0	0	0	0	0	0	0	0
Bob Owchinko, p	.000	1	0	0	0	0	0	0	0	0	0	0
Rob Picciolo, ss	.200	2	5	1	1	0	0	0	0	0	2	0
Jim Spencer, 1b	.000	2	2	0	0	0	0	0	0	0	0	0
Fred Stanley, ss	.333	2	3	0	1	0	0	0	0	1	0	1
Tom Underwood, p	.000	2	0	0	0	0	0	0	0	0	0	0
TOTAL	.222		99	4	22	4	1	0	4	6	23	2

PITCHER	W	L	ERA	G	GS	CG	SV	SHO	IP	H	ER	BB	SO
Dave Beard	0	0	40.50	1	0	0	0	0	0.2	5	3	0	0
Jeff Jones	0	0	4.50	1	0	0	0	0	2.0	2	1	1	0
Matt Keough	0	1	1.08	1	1	0	0	0	8.1	7	1	6	2
Brian Kingman	0	0	81.00	1	0	0	0	0	0.1	3	3	0	0
Steve Mc Catty	0	1	13.50	1	1	0	0	0	3.1	6	5	2	2
Mike Norris	0	1	3.68	1	1	0	0	0	7.1	6	3	2	4
Bob Owchinko	0	0	5.40	1	0	0	0	0	1.2	3	1	0	0
Tom Underwood	0	0	13.50	2	0	0	0	0	1.1	4	2	2	2
TOTAL	0	3	6.84	9	3	0	0	0	25.0	36	19	13	10

GAME 1 AT NY OCT 13

OAK	000	010	000	1	6	1
NY	300	000	00X	3	7	1

Pitchers: NORRIS, Underwood (8) vs JOHN, Davis (7), Gossage (8)
Attendance: 55,740

GAME 2 AT NY OCT 14

OAK	001	200	000	3	11	1
NY	100	701	40X	13	19	0

Pitchers: McCATTY, Beard (4), Jones (5), Kingman (7), Owchinko (7) vs May, FRAZIER (4)
Home Runs: Piniella-NY, Nettles-NY
Attendance: 48,497

GAME 3 AT OAK OCT 15

NY	000	001	003	4	10	0
OAK	000	000	000	0	5	2

Pitchers: RIGHETTI, Davis (7), Gossage (9) vs KEOUGH, Underwood (9)
Home Runs: Randolph-NY
Attendance: 47,302

What the Yankees had done to the Dodgers three years earlier, the Dodgers now did to the Yankees in this, their eleventh meeting in the Series: they took the crown with four straight wins after losing the first two games. In the opener Bob Watson's first-inning three-run homer gave New York an insurmountable lead. Yankee starter Ron Guidry pitched seven strong innings, yielding just one run on a Steve Yeager homer, but two eighth-inning Dodger runs charged to reliever Ron Davis made things exciting until Yankee third baseman Graig Nettles dampened the rally with a splendid diving catch of Steve Garvey's line drive. In Game Two, Tommy John (now a Yankee) shut out his old teammates on three hits for seven innings. Reliever Goose Gossage completed the shutout, earning his second save in two days in the 3–0 Yankee victory.

But as the Series moved to Los Angeles, the Dodgers took the upper hand. Rookie ace Fernando Valenzuela experienced rocky going in the early innings of Game Three, yielding six hits (including home runs to Bob Watson and Rick Cerone) and four runs in the second and third innings. But Ron Cey's first-inning home run had given Los Angeles three early runs, and Dodger hitters added two more in the fifth as Valenzuela settled down to blank New York on three hits over the final six innings. The next day the Dodgers evened the Series with another close win. New York scored four times before the Dodgers got their first runs, but L.A. tied the game at 6–6 in the sixth and took an 8–6 lead an inning later. Reggie Jackson homered in the eighth to bring New York within one run of a tie, but they came no closer.

In Game Five, for the third day in a row, the Dodgers ovecame a Yankee lead to claim a one-run victory. Dodger pitcher Jerry Reuss gave the Yankees a run on two hits in the second inning, but shut them out on just three additional hits the rest of the way. Yankee starter Ron Guidry, meanwhile, stopped the Dodgers on two hits through the first six innings, but then gave up back-to-back homers to Pedro Guerrero and Steve Yeager in the seventh—runs enough for a 2–1 Dodger win. The final game was close for four innings, but in the fifth and sixth the Dodgers broke it open with seven runs and coasted in on Steve Howe's 3⅔ innings of shutout relief to a 9–2 win and, including 1900, their sixth world championship.

Los Angeles Dodgers (NL), 4; New York Yankees (AL), 2

LA (N)

PLAYER/POS	AVG	G	AB	R	H	2B	3B	HR	RB	BB	SO	SB
Dusty Baker, of	.167	6	24	3	4	0	0	0	1	1	6	0
Bobby Castillo, p	.000	1	0	0	0	0	0	0	0	0	0	0
Ron Cey, 3b	.350	6	20	3	7	0	0	1	6	3	3	0
Terry Forster, p	.000	2	0	0	0	0	0	0	0	0	0	0
Steve Garvey, 1b	.417	6	24	3	10	1	0	0	0	2	5	0
Dave Goltz, p	.000	2	0	0	0	0	0	0	0	0	0	0
Pedro Guerrero, of	.333	6	21	2	7	1	1	2	7	2	6	0
Burt Hooton, p	.000	2	4	1	0	0	0	0	0	1	3	0
Steve Howe, p	.000	3	2	0	0	0	0	0	0	0	2	0
Jay Johnstone, ph	.667	3	3	1	2	0	0	1	3	0	0	0
Ken Landreaux, of-3	.167	5	6	1	1	1	0	0	0	0	2	1
Davey Lopes, 2b	.227	6	22	6	5	1	0	0	2	4	3	4
Rick Monday, of-4	.231	5	13	1	3	1	0	0	0	3	6	0
Tom Niedenfuer, p	.000	2	0	0	0	0	0	0	0	0	0	0
Jerry Reuss, p	.000	2	3	0	0	0	0	0	0	0	1	0
Bill Russell, ss	.240	6	25	1	6	0	0	0	2	0	1	1
Steve Sax, 2b-1	.000	2	1	0	0	0	0	0	0	0	0	0
Mike Scioscia, c	.250	3	4	1	1	0	0	0	0	1	0	0
Reggie Smith, ph	.500	2	2	0	1	0	0	0	0	0	1	0
Dave Stewart, p	.000	2	0	0	0	0	0	0	0	0	0	0
Derrel Thomas, of-3,3b-2,ss-1	.000	5	7	2	0	0	0	0	1	1	2	0
Fernando Valenzuela, p	.000	1	3	0	0	0	0	0	0	1	0	0
Bob Welch, p	.000	1	0	0	0	0	0	0	0	0	0	0
Steve Yeager, c	.286	6	14	2	4	1	0	2	4	0	2	0
TOTAL	.258		198	27	51	6	1	6	26	20	44	6

PITCHER	W	L	ERA	G	GS	CG	SV	SHO	IP	H	ER	BB	SO
Bobby Castillo	0	0	9.00	1	0	0	0	0	1.0	0	1	5	0
Terry Forster	0	0	0.00	2	0	0	0	0	2.0	1	0	3	0
Dave Goltz	0	0	5.40	2	0	0	0	0	3.1	4	2	1	2
Burt Hooton	1	1	1.59	2	2	0	0	0	11.1	8	2	9	3
Steve Howe	1	0	3.86	3	0	0	1	0	7.0	7	3	1	4
Tom Niedenfuer	0	0	0.00	2	0	0	0	0	5.0	3	0	1	0
Jerry Reuss	1	1	3.86	2	2	1	0	0	11.2	10	5	3	8
Dave Stewart	0	0	0.00	2	0	0	0	0	1.2	1	0	2	1
Fernando Valenzuela	1	0	4.00	1	1	1	0	0	9.0	9	4	7	6
Bob Welch	0	0	INF	1	1	0	0	0	0.0	3	2	1	0
TOTAL	4	2	3.29	18	6	2	1	0	52.0	46	19	33	24

NY (A)

PLAYER/POS	AVG	G	AB	R	H	2B	3B	HR	RB	BB	SO	SB
Bobby Brown, of-2	.000	4	1	1	0	0	0	0	0	0	1	0
Rick Cerone, c	.190	6	21	2	4	1	0	1	3	4	2	0
Ron Davis, p	.000	4	0	0	0	0	0	0	0	0	0	0
Barry Foote, ph	.000	1	1	0	0	0	0	0	0	0	1	0
George Frazier, p	.000	3	2	0	0	0	0	0	0	0	0	0
Oscar Gamble, of-2	.333	3	6	1	2	0	0	0	1	1	0	0
Rich Gossage, p	.000	3	1	0	0	0	0	0	0	0	1	0
Ron Guidry, p	.000	3	5	0	0	0	0	0	0	0	3	0
Reggie Jackson, of	.333	3	12	3	4	1	0	1	1	2	3	0
Tommy John, p	.000	3	2	0	0	0	0	0	0	0	0	0
Dave La Roche, p	.000	1	0	0	0	0	0	0	0	0	0	0
Rudy May, p	.000	3	1	0	0	0	0	0	0	0	0	0
Larry Milbourne, ss	.250	6	20	2	5	2	0	0	3	4	0	0
Jerry Mumphrey, of	.200	5	15	2	3	0	0	0	0	3	2	1
Bobby Murcer, ph	.000	4	3	0	0	0	0	0	0	0	0	0
Graig Nettles, 3b	.400	3	10	1	4	1	0	0	1	0	1	0
Lou Piniella, of-3	.438	6	16	2	7	1	0	0	3	0	1	1
Willie Randolph, 2b	.222	6	18	5	4	1	1	2	3	9	0	1
Rick Reuschel, p	.000	2	2	0	0	0	0	0	0	0	0	0
Dave Righetti, p	.000	1	1	0	0	0	0	0	0	0	1	0
Andre Robertson, pr	.000	1	0	0	0	0	0	0	0	0	0	0
Aurelio Rodriguez, 3b-3	.417	4	12	1	5	0	0	0	0	1	2	0
Bob Watson, 1b	.318	6	22	2	7	1	0	2	7	3	0	0
Dave Winfield, of	.045	6	22	0	1	0	0	0	1	5	4	1
TOTAL	.238		193	22	46	8	1	6	22	33	24	4

PITCHER	W	L	ERA	G	GS	CG	SV	SHO	IP	H	ER	BB	SO
Ron Davis	0	0	23.14	4	0	0	0	0	2.1	4	6	5	4
George Frazier	0	3	17.18	3	0	0	0	0	3.2	9	7	3	2
Rich Gossage	0	0	0.00	3	0	0	2	0	5.0	2	0	2	5
Ron Guidry	1	1	1.93	2	2	0	0	0	14.0	8	3	4	15
Tommy John	1	0	0.69	3	2	0	0	0	13.0	11	1	0	8
Dave La Roche	0	0	0.00	1	0	0	0	0	1.0	0	0	0	2
Rudy May	0	0	2.84	3	0	0	0	0	6.1	5	2	1	5
Rick Reuschel	0	0	4.91	2	1	0	0	0	3.2	7	2	3	2
Dave Righetti	0	0	13.50	1	1	0	0	0	2.0	5	3	2	1
TOTAL	2	4	4.24	22	6	0	2	0	51.0	51	24	20	44

GAME 1 AT NY OCT 20

LA	000 010 020	3	5	0
NY	301 100 00X	5	6	0

Pitchers: REUSS, Castillo (3), Goltz (4), Niedenfuer (5), Stewart (8) vs GUIDRY, Davis (8), Gossage (8)
Home Runs: Watson-NY, Yeager-LA
Attendance: 56,470

GAME 2 AT NY OCT 21

LA	000 000 000	0	4	2
NY	000 010 02X	3	6	1

Pitchers: HOOTON, Forster (7), Howe (8), Stewart (8) vs JOHN, Gossage (8)
Attendance: 56,505

GAME 3 AT LA OCT 23

NY	022 000 000	4	9	0
LA	300 020 00X	5	11	1

Pitchers: Righetti, FRAZIER (3), May (5), Davis (8) vs VALENZUELA
Home Runs: Cey-LA, Watson-NY, Cerone-NY
Attendance: 56,236

GAME 4 AT LA OCT 24

NY	211 002 010	7	13	1
LA	002 013 20X	8	14	2

Pitchers: Reuschel, May (4), Davis (5), FRAZIER (5), John (7) vs Welch, Goltz (1), Forster (4), Niedenfuer (5), HOWE (7)
Home Runs: Johnstone-LA, Randolph-NY, Jackson-NY
Attendance: 56,242

GAME 5 AT LA OCT 25

NY	010 000 000	1	5	0
LA	000 000 20X	2	4	3

Pitchers: GUIDRY, Gossage (8) vs REUSS
Home Runs: Guerrero-LA, Yeager-LA
Attendance: 56,115

GAME 6 AT NY OCT 28

LA	000 134 010	9	13	1
NY	001 001 000	2	7	2

Pitchers: HOOTON, Howe (6) vs John, FRAZIER (5), Davis (6), Reuschel (6), May (7), LaRoche (9)
Home Runs: Guerrero-LA, Randolph-NY
Attendance: 56,513

The official records show Atlanta ahead and threatening only once in a three-game series swept by the Cardinals. But in the original Game One, Phil Niekro held a slim 1–0 Atlanta lead in the fifth inning when rain wiped out the game just before it could become official.

In the first official game, the Braves scored nothing at all as Bob Forsch held them to three hits. Atlanta's Pascual Perez gave up only one run through the first five innings, but the Cardinals exploded for five runs in the sixth to put the game away. Following another rainout, Niekro tried again in Game Two. He gave up a run in the first, but Atlanta came back with three before he yielded a second run in the sixth. Gene Garber, who relieved Niekro, gave up the tying run in the eighth and lost the game in the bottom of the ninth on Ken Oberkfell's RBI liner over the center fielder's head.

Joaquin Andujar shut out the Braves through six innings of Game Three before giving up two runs in the seventh. But by then St. Louis had scored five times. Bruce Sutter retired the last seven Braves in relief of Andujar, and the Cardinals had their pennant.

St. Louis Cardinals (East), 3; Atlanta Braves (West), 0

STL (E)

PLAYER/POS	AVG	G	AB	R	H	2B	3B	HR	RB	BB	SO	SB
Joaquin Andujar, p	.000	1	1	0	0	0	0	0	0	0	1	0
Doug Bair, p	.000	1	0	0	0	0	0	0	0	0	0	0
Steve Braun, ph	.000	1	1	0	0	0	0	0	0	0	0	0
Bob Forsch, p	.667	1	3	1	2	0	0	0	1	0	0	0
David Green, of	1.000	2	1	1	1	0	0	0	0	0	0	0
George Hendrick, of	.308	3	13	2	4	0	0	0	2	1	2	0
Keith Hernandez, 1b	.333	3	12	3	4	0	0	0	1	2	3	0
Tommy Herr, 2b	.231	3	13	1	3	1	0	0	0	1	2	0
Willie Mc Gee, of	.308	3	13	4	4	0	2	1	5	0	5	0
Ken Oberkfell, 3b	.200	3	15	1	3	0	0	0	2	0	0	0
Darrell Porter, c	.556	3	9	3	5	3	0	0	1	5	2	0
Lonnie Smith, of	.273	3	11	1	3	0	0	0	1	0	1	0
Ozzie Smith, ss	.556	3	9	0	5	0	0	0	3	3	0	1
John Stuper, p	.000	1	1	0	0	0	0	0	0	0	0	0
Bruce Sutter, p	.000	2	1	0	0	0	0	0	0	0	0	0
TOTAL	.330		103	17	34	4	2	1	16	12	16	1

PITCHER	W	L	ERA	G	GS	CG	SV	SHO	IP	H	ER	BB	SO
Joaquin Andujar	1	0	2.70	1	1	0	0	0	6.2	6	2	2	4
Doug Bair	0	0	0.00	1	0	0	0	0	1.0	2	0	3	0
Bob Forsch	1	0	0.00	1	1	1	0	1	9.0	3	0	0	6
John Stuper	0	0	3.00	1	1	0	0	0	6.0	4	2	1	4
Bruce Sutter	1	0	0.00	2	0	0	1	0	4.1	0	0	0	1
TOTAL	3	0	1.33	6	3	1	1	1	27.0	15	4	6	15

ATL (W)

PLAYER/POS	AVG	G	AB	R	H	2B	3B	HR	RB	BB	SO	SB
Steve Bedrosian, p	.000	2	0	0	0	0	0	0	0	0	0	0
Bruce Benedict, c	.250	3	8	1	2	1	0	0	0	2	1	0
Brett Butler, of-1	.000	2	1	0	0	0	0	0	0	0	0	0
Rick Camp, p	.000	1	0	0	0	0	0	0	0	0	0	0
Chris Chambliss, 1b	.000	3	10	0	0	0	0	0	0	1	0	0
Gene Garber, p	.000	2	1	0	0	0	0	0	0	0	0	0
Terry Harper, of	.000	1	1	0	0	0	0	0	0	0	0	0
Bob Horner, 3b	.091	3	11	0	1	0	0	0	0	0	2	0
Glenn Hubbard, 2b	.222	3	9	1	2	0	0	0	1	0	3	0
Rick Mahler, p	.000	1	0	0	0	0	0	0	0	0	0	0
Donnie Moore, p	.000	2	0	0	0	0	0	0	0	0	0	0
Dale Murphy, of	.273	3	11	1	3	0	0	0	0	0	2	1
Phil Niekro, p	.000	1	0	0	0	0	0	0	1	0	0	0
Pascual Perez, p	.000	2	3	0	0	0	0	0	0	0	1	0
Biff Pocoroba, ph	.000	1	1	0	0	0	0	0	0	0	0	0
Rafael Ramirez, ss	.182	3	11	1	2	0	0	0	1	1	1	0
Jerry Royster, of-3,3b-1	.182	3	11	0	2	0	0	0	0	0	2	0
Bob Walk, p	.000	1	0	0	0	0	0	0	0	0	0	0
Claudell Washington, of	.333	3	9	0	3	0	0	0	0	2	2	0
Larry Whisenton, ph	.000	2	2	0	0	0	0	0	0	0	0	0
TOTAL	.169		89	5	15	1	0	0	3	6	15	1

PITCHER	W	L	ERA	G	GS	CG	SV	SHO	IP	H	ER	BB	SO
Steve Bedrosian	0	0	18.00	2	0	0	0	0	1.0	3	2	1	2
Rick Camp	0	1	36.00	1	1	0	0	0	1.0	4	4	1	0
Gene Garber	0	1	8.10	2	0	0	0	0	3.1	4	3	1	3
Rick Mahler	0	0	0.00	1	0	0	0	0	1.2	3	0	2	0
Donnie Moore	0	0	0.00	2	0	0	0	0	2.2	2	0	0	1
Phil Niekro	0	0	3.00	1	1	0	0	0	6.0	6	2	4	5
Pascual Perez	0	1	5.19	2	1	0	0	0	8.2	10	5	2	4
Bob Walk	0	0	9.00	1	0	0	0	0	1.0	2	1	1	1
TOTAL	0	3	6.04	12	3	0	0	0	25.1	34	17	12	16

GAME 1 AT STL OCT 7

ATL	000 000 000	0	3	0
STL	001 005 01X	7	13	1

Pitchers: PEREZ, Bedrosian (6), Moore (6), Walk (8) vs FORSCH
Attendance: 53,008

GAME 2 AT STL OCT 9

ATL	002 010 000	3	6	0
STL	100 001 011	4	9	1

Pitchers: Niekro, GARBER (7) vs Stuper, Bair (7), SUTTER (8)
Attendance: 53,408

GAME 3 AT ATL OCT 10

STL	040 010 001	6	12	0
ATL	000 000 200	2	6	1

Pitchers: ANDUJAR, Sutter (7) vs CAMP, Perez (2), Moore (5), Mahler (7), Bedrosian (8), Garber (9)
Home Runs: McGee-STL
Attendance: 52,173

For the first time in LCS play, a club won the first two games but lost the series. The Angels overcame a 1–3 deficit to take Game One, with four runs in the third and three more later, while starter Tommy John settled down to stop the Brewers through the final six innings. In Game Two Bruce Kison prevailed, as the Angels built a 4–0 lead over Milwaukee and Pete Vuckovich before Kison gave up what proved to be a harmless two-run homer to Paul Molitor in the fifth.

With three chances to clinch the pennant, California three times fell short. In the third game, their three eighth-inning runs couldn't catch the Brewers, who already had five. In Game Four, Don Baylor's eighth-inning grand slam completed Angel scoring at five runs, but Milwaukee had already scored seven, and they added two more. In the finale, Kison held a 3–2 lead when he was relieved after five innings. But Cecil Cooper singled off Luis Sanchez in the seventh (with two out and the bases loaded) for two runs and a Brewer lead. Bob McClure and Pete Ladd held off the Angels through the final two innings, and the Brewers were on their way to their first World Series.

Milwaukee Brewers (East), 3; California Angels (West), 2

MIL (E)

PLAYER/POS	AVG	G	AB	R	H	2B	3B	HR	RB	BB	SO	SB
Dwight Bernard, p	.000	1	0	0	0	0	0	0	0	0	0	0
Mark Brouhard, of	.750	1	4	4	3	1	0	1	3	0	0	0
Mike Caldwell, p	.000	1	0	0	0	0	0	0	0	0	0	0
Cecil Cooper, 1b	.150	5	20	1	3	2	0	0	4	0	6	0
Marshall Edwards, dh-2,of-1	.000	3	1	2	0	0	0	0	0	0	0	1
Jim Gantner, 2b	.188	5	16	1	3	0	0	0	2	1	1	0
Moose Haas, p	.000	1	0	0	0	0	0	0	0	0	0	0
Roy Howell, dh	.000	1	3	0	0	0	0	0	0	0	1	0
Pete Ladd, p	.000	3	0	0	0	0	0	0	0	0	0	0
Bob Mc Clure, p	.000	1	0	0	0	0	0	0	0	0	0	0
Paul Molitor, 3b	.316	5	19	4	6	1	0	2	5	2	3	1
Don Money, dh	.182	4	11	2	2	0	0	0	1	3	1	0
Charlie Moore, of	.462	5	13	3	6	0	0	0	0	1	2	0
Ben Oglivie, of	.133	4	15	1	2	0	0	1	1	0	3	0
Ted Simmons, c	.167	5	18	3	3	0	0	0	1	1	4	0
Jim Slaton, p	.000	2	0	0	0	0	0	0	0	0	0	0
Don Sutton, p	.000	1	0	0	0	0	0	0	0	0	0	0
Gorman Thomas, of	.067	5	15	1	1	0	0	1	3	2	7	0
Pete Vuckovich, p	.000	2	0	0	0	0	0	0	0	0	0	0
Robin Yount, ss	.250	5	16	1	4	0	0	0	0	5	0	0
TOTAL	.219		151	23	33	4	0	5	20	15	28	2

PITCHER	W	L	ERA	G	GS	CG	SV	SHO	IP	H	ER	BB	SO
Dwight Bernard	0	0	0.00	1	0	0	0	0	1.0	0	0	0	0
Mike Caldwell	0	1	15.00	1	1	0	0	0	3.0	7	5	1	2
Moose Haas	1	0	4.91	1	1	0	0	0	7.1	5	4	5	7
Pete Ladd	0	0	0.00	3	0	0	2	0	3.1	0	0	0	5
Bob Mc Clure	1	0	0.00	1	0	0	0	0	1.2	2	0	0	0
Jim Slaton	0	0	1.93	2	0	0	1	0	4.2	3	1	1	3
Don Sutton	1	0	3.52	1	1	0	0	0	7.2	8	3	2	9
Pete Vuckovich	0	1	4.40	2	2	1	0	0	14.1	15	7	7	8
TOTAL	3	2	4.19	12	5	1	3	0	43.0	40	20	16	34

CAL (W)

PLAYER/POS	AVG	G	AB	R	H	2B	3B	HR	RB	BB	SO	SB
Don Baylor, dh	.294	5	17	2	5	1	1	1	10	2	0	0
Juan Beniquez, of	.000	2	0	0	0	0	0	0	0	0	0	0
Bob Boone, c	.250	5	16	3	4	0	0	1	4	0	2	0
Rod Carew, 1b	.176	5	17	2	3	1	0	0	0	4	4	1
Bobby Clark, of	.000	2	0	0	0	0	0	0	0	0	0	0
Doug De Cinces, 3b	.316	5	19	5	6	2	0	0	0	1	5	0
Brian Downing, of	.158	5	19	4	3	1	0	0	0	3	2	0
Tim Foli, ss	.125	5	16	0	2	0	0	0	1	0	3	0
Dave Goltz, p	.000	1	0	0	0	0	0	0	0	0	0	0
Bobby Grich, 2b	.200	5	15	1	3	1	0	0	1	2	7	0
Andy Hassler, p	.000	2	0	0	0	0	0	0	0	0	0	0
Reggie Jackson, of	.111	5	18	2	2	0	0	1	2	2	7	0
Ron Jackson, ph	1.000	1	1	0	1	0	0	0	0	0	0	0
Tommy John, p	.000	2	0	0	0	0	0	0	0	0	0	0
Bruce Kison, p	.000	2	0	0	0	0	0	0	0	0	0	0
Fred Lynn, of	.611	5	18	4	11	2	0	1	5	2	3	0
Luis Sanchez, p	.000	2	0	0	0	0	0	0	0	0	0	0
Rob Wilfong, ph	.000	2	1	0	0	0	0	0	0	0	1	0
Mike Witt, p	.000	1	0	0	0	0	0	0	0	0	0	0
Geoff Zahn, p	.000	1	0	0	0	0	0	0	0	0	0	0
TOTAL	.255		157	23	40	8	1	4	23	16	34	1

PITCHER	W	L	ERA	G	GS	CG	SV	SHO	IP	H	ER	BB	SO
Dave Goltz	0	0	7.36	1	0	0	0	0	3.2	4	3	2	2
Andy Hassler	0	0	0.00	2	0	0	0	0	2.2	0	0	0	2
Tommy John	1	1	5.11	2	2	1	0	0	12.1	11	7	6	6
Bruce Kison	1	0	1.93	2	2	1	0	0	14.0	8	3	3	12
Luis Sanchez	0	1	6.75	2	0	0	0	0	2.2	4	2	1	1
Mike Witt	0	0	6.00	1	0	0	0	0	3.0	2	2	2	3
Geoff Zahn	0	1	7.36	1	1	0	0	0	3.2	4	3	1	2
TOTAL	2	3	4.29	11	5	2	0	0	42.0	33	20	15	28

GAME 1 AT CAL OCT 5

MIL	021 000 000	3 7 2
CAL	104 210 00X	8 10 0

Pitchers: CALDWELL, Slaton (4), Ladd (7), Bernard (8) vs JOHN
Home Runs: Thomas-MIL, Lynn-CAL
Attendance: 64,406

GAME 2 AT CAL OCT 6

MIL	000 020 000	2 5 0
CAL	021 100 00X	4 6 0

Pitchers: VUCKOVICH vs KISON
Home Runs: Re.Jackson-CAL, Molitor-MIL
Attendance: 64,179

GAME 3 AT MIL OCT 8

CAL	000 000 030	3 8 0
MIL	000 300 20X	5 6 0

Pitchers: ZAHN, Witt (4), Hassler (7) vs SUTTON, Ladd (8)
Home Runs: Molitor-MIL, Boone-CAL
Attendance: 50,135

GAME 4 AT MIL OCT 9

CAL	000 001 040	5 5 3
MIL	030 301 02X	9 9 2

Pitchers: JOHN, Goltz (4), Sanchez (8) vs HAAS, Slaton (8)
Home Runs: Baylor-CAL, Brouhard-MIL
Attendance: 51,003

GAME 5 AT MIL OCT 10

CAL	101 100 000	3 11 1
MIL	100 100 20X	4 6 4

Pitchers: Kison, SANCHEZ (6), Hassler (7) vs Vuckovich, McCLURE (7), Ladd (9)
Home Runs: Oglivie-MIL
Attendance: 54,968

The Series was anticipated as a matchup of Cardinal speed and Brewer power. In the event, though, St. Louis outslugged the Brewers and wound up with their tenth world championship.

The Brewers, in their first World Series, looked unstoppable in the opening game. Hammering four Cardinal pitchers for seventeen hits (including a record five for Paul Molitor), they scored ten runs while pitcher Mike Caldwell was shutting out the Cards on three hits. In the second game Milwaukee continued the onslaught, building an early 3–0 lead. But St. Louis finally got on the scoreboard with two runs in the last of the third, and tied the game at 4–4 in the sixth on Darrell Porter's two-RBI double. And the Cards won the game on a bases-loaded walk in the eighth as relievers Doug Bair and Bruce Sutter held the Brewers scoreless over the final four innings.

St. Louis pushed into the Series lead in Game Three, thanks mostly to the 6⅓ shutout innings of starter Joaquin Andujar and the fielding and batting of center fielder Willie McGee. McGee drove in four of the six Cardinal runs with a pair of homers and prevented an extra-base hit and a two-run Brewer homer with leaping catches in the first and final innings. The Cards pressed their advantage in Game Four with four early runs. But in the last of the seventh (with the score now 5–1), an error by Cardinal pitcher Dave La Point opened the way for Milwaukee to win the game with six two-out runs on a barrage of hits (and the added assistance of a pair of walks and a wild pitch).

Brewer pitcher Mike Caldwell wasn't as effective in Game Five as he had been in the opener, yielding fourteen hits and four runs in 8⅓ innings of work. But he was never behind in the game as his teammates, with eleven hits of their own (four of them by Robin Yount, including a home run) and several fielding gems put Milwaukee ahead again in the Series with a 6–4 win.

The Cards had their backs to the wall as the Series moved to St. Louis for the final games. But in Game Six the Cards responded to their opening-game humiliation with a laugher of their own, 13–1, on John Stuper's four-hitter. And in the finale they rocked Brewer ace Pete Vuckovich and three relievers for fifteen hits and a 6–3 victory that gave starter Joaquin Andujar his second Series win and reliever Bruce Sutter his second save.

St. Louis Cardinals (NL), 4; Milwaukee Brewers (AL), 3

STL (N)

PLAYER/POS	AVG	G	AB	R	H	2B	3B	HR	RB	BB	SO	SB
Joaquin Andujar, p	.000	2	0	0	0	0	0	0	0	0	0	0
Doug Bair, p	.000	3	0	0	0	0	0	0	0	0	0	0
Steve Braun, dh	.500	2	2	0	1	0	0	0	2	1	0	0
Glenn Brummer, c	.000	1	0	0	0	0	0	0	0	0	0	0
Bob Forsch, p	.000	2	0	0	0	0	0	0	0	0	0	0
David Green, of-4,dh-3	.200	7	10	3	2	1	1	0	0	1	3	0
George Hendrick, of	.321	7	28	5	9	0	0	0	5	2	2	0
Keith Hernandez, 1b	.259	7	27	4	7	2	0	1	8	4	2	0
Tommy Herr, 2b	.160	7	25	2	4	2	0	0	5	3	3	0
Dane Iorg, dh	.529	5	17	4	9	4	1	0	1	0	0	0
Jim Kaat, p	.000	4	0	0	0	0	0	0	0	0	0	0
Jeff Lahti, p	.000	2	0	0	0	0	0	0	0	0	0	0
Dave La Point, p	.000	2	0	0	0	0	0	0	0	0	0	0
Willie Mc Gee, of	.240	6	25	6	6	0	0	2	5	1	3	2
Ken Oberkfell, 3b	.292	7	24	4	7	1	0	0	1	2	1	2
Darrell Porter, c	.286	7	28	1	8	2	0	1	5	1	4	0
Mike Ramsey, 3b-2	.000	3	1	1	0	0	0	0	0	0	1	0
Lonnie Smith, of-6,dh-1	.321	7	28	6	9	4	1	0	1	1	5	2
Ozzie Smith, ss	.208	7	24	3	5	0	0	0	1	3	0	1
John Stuper, p	.000	2	0	0	0	0	0	0	0	0	0	0
Bruce Sutter, p	.000	4	0	0	0	0	0	0	0	0	0	0
Gene Tenace, dh-1	.000	5	6	0	0	0	0	0	0	1	2	0
TOTAL	.273		245	39	67	16	3	4	34	20	26	7

PITCHER	W	L	ERA	G	GS	CG	SV	SHO	IP	H	ER	BB	SO
Joaquin Andujar	2	0	1.35	2	2	0	0	0	13.1	10	2	1	4
Doug Bair	0	1	9.00	3	0	0	0	0	2.0	2	2	2	3
Bob Forsch	0	2	4.97	2	2	0	0	0	12.2	18	7	3	4
Jim Kaat	0	0	3.86	4	0	0	0	0	2.1	4	1	2	2
Jeff Lahti	0	0	10.80	2	0	0	0	0	1.2	4	2	1	1
Dave La Point	0	0	3.24	2	1	0	0	0	8.1	10	3	2	3
John Stuper	1	0	3.46	2	2	1	0	0	13.0	10	5	5	5
Bruce Sutter	1	0	4.70	4	0	0	2	0	7.2	6	4	3	6
TOTAL	4	3	3.84	21	7	1	2	0	61.0	64	26	19	28

MIL (A)

PLAYER/POS	AVG	G	AB	R	H	2B	3B	HR	RB	BB	SO	SB
Dwight Bernard, p	.000	1	0	0	0	0	0	0	0	0	0	0
Mike Caldwell, p	.000	3	0	0	0	0	0	0	0	0	0	0
Cecil Cooper, 1b	.286	7	28	3	8	1	0	1	6	1	1	0
Marshall Edwards, of	.000	1	0	0	0	0	0	0	0	0	0	0
Jim Gantner, 2b	.333	7	24	5	8	4	1	0	4	1	1	0
Moose Haas, p	.000	2	0	0	0	0	0	0	0	0	0	0
Roy Howell, dh	.000	4	11	1	0	0	0	0	0	0	3	0
Pete Ladd, p	.000	1	0	0	0	0	0	0	0	0	0	0
Bob Mc Clure, p	.000	5	0	0	0	0	0	0	0	0	0	0
Doc Medich, p	.000	1	0	0	0	0	0	0	0	0	0	0
Paul Molitor, 3b	.355	7	31	5	11	0	0	0	3	2	4	1
Don Money, dh-4	.231	5	13	4	3	1	0	0	1	2	3	0
Charlie Moore, of	.346	7	26	3	9	3	0	0	2	1	0	0
Ben Oglivie, of	.222	7	27	4	6	0	1	1	1	2	4	0
Ted Simmons, c	.174	7	23	2	4	0	0	2	3	5	3	0
Jim Slaton, p	.000	2	0	0	0	0	0	0	0	0	0	0
Don Sutton, p	.000	2	0	0	0	0	0	0	0	0	0	0
Gorman Thomas, of	.115	7	26	0	3	0	0	0	3	2	7	0
Pete Vuckovich, p	.000	2	0	0	0	0	0	0	0	0	0	0
Ned Yost, c	.000	1	0	0	0	0	0	0	0	1	0	0
Robin Yount, ss	.414	7	29	6	12	3	0	1	6	2	2	0
TOTAL	.269		238	33	64	12	2	5	29	19	28	1

PITCHER	W	L	ERA	G	GS	CG	SV	SHO	IP	H	ER	BB	SO
Dwight Bernard	0	0	0.00	1	0	0	0	0	1.0	0	0	0	1
Mike Caldwell	2	0	2.04	3	2	1	0	1	17.2	19	4	3	6
Moose Haas	0	0	7.36	2	1	0	0	0	7.1	8	6	3	4
Pete Ladd	0	0	0.00	1	0	0	0	0	0.2	1	0	2	0
Bob Mc Clure	0	2	4.15	5	0	0	2	0	4.1	5	2	3	5
Doc Medich	0	0	18.00	1	0	0	0	0	2.0	5	4	1	0
Jim Slaton	1	0	0.00	2	0	0	0	0	2.2	1	0	2	1
Don Sutton	0	1	7.84	2	2	0	0	0	10.1	12	9	1	5
Pete Vuckovich	0	1	4.50	2	2	0	0	0	14.0	16	7	5	4
TOTAL	3	4	4.80	19	7	1	2	1	60.0	67	32	20	26

GAME 1 AT STL OCT 12

MIL	200 112 004	10	17	0
STL	000 000 000	0	3	1

Pitchers: CALDWELL vs FORSCH, Kaat (6), LaPoint (8), Lahti (9)
Home Runs: Simmoms-MIL
Attendance: 53,723

GAME 2 AT STL OCT 13

MIL	012 010 000	4	10	1
STL	002 002 01X	5	8	0

Pitchers: Sutton, McCLURE (7), Ladd (8) vs Stuper, Kaat (5), Bair (5), SUTTER (7)
Home Runs: Simmons-MIL
Attendance: 53,723

GAME 3 AT MIL OCT 15

STL	000 030 201	6	6	1
MIL	000 000 020	2	5	3

Pitchers: ANDUJAR, Kaat (7), Bair (7), Sutter (7) vs VUCKOVICH, McClure (9)
Home Runs: McGee-STL (2), Cooper-MIL
Attendance: 56,556

GAME 4 AT MIL OCT 16

STL	130 001 000	5	8	1
MIL	000 010 60X	7	10	2

Pitchers: LaPoint, BAIR (7), Kaat (7), Lahti (7) vs Haas, SLATON (6), McClure (8)
Attendance: 56,560

GAME 5 AT MIL OCT 17

STL	001 000 102	4	15	2
MIL	101 010 12X	6	11	1

Pitchers: FORSCH, Sutter (8) vs CALDWELL, McClure (9)
Home Runs: Yount-MIL
Attendance: 56,562

GAME 6 AT STL OCT 19

MIL	000 000 001	1	4	4
STL	020 326 00X	13	12	1

Pitchers: SUTTON, Slaton (5), Medich (6), Bernard (8) vs STUPER
Home Runs: Porter-STL, Hernandez-STL
Attendance: 53,723

GAME 7 AT STL OCT 20

MIL	000 012 000	3	7	0
STL	000 103 02X	6	15	1

Pitchers: Vuckovich, McCLURE (6), Haas (6), Caldwell (8) vs ANDUJAR, Sutter (8)
Home Runs: Oglivie-MIL
Attendance: 53,723

The Dodgers earned only four runs off Philadelphia pitching, and even though they doubled their run total to eight on unearned runs, the Phillies scored twice that number to take the pennant in four games.

Mike Schmidt homered off Jerry Reuss in the first inning of the opener for the game's only run. Phillie starter Steve Carlton loaded the bases in the eighth, but Al Holland came on to get the third out and preserve the shutout. The Phillies also scored only one run in the second game, on Gary Matthews's homer off Fernando Valenzuela in the second. But this time the run only tied the score, and in the fifth Pedro Guerrero tripled in two unearned runs to give Valenzuela the Dodgers' only win.

The Phillies' Charlie Hudson hurled the series' only complete game—a four-hitter—to win Game Three. Gary Matthews's four hits in Game Three and Four included his second and third series homers, and drove in half the Phillies' fourteen runs as they took the two games by identical 7–2 scores.

Philadelphia Phillies (East), 3;
Los Angeles Dodgers (West), 1

PHI (E)

PLAYER/POS	AVG	G	AB	R	H	2B	3B	HR	RB	BB	SO	SB
Steve Carlton, p	.200	2	5	0	1	0	0	0	0	0	3	0
Ivan De Jesus, ss	.250	4	12	0	3	0	0	0	1	3	3	0
John Denny, p	.000	1	1	0	0	0	0	0	0	0	0	0
Bob Dernier, of	.000	1	0	0	0	0	0	0	0	0	0	0
Bo Diaz, c	.154	4	13	0	2	1	0	0	0	2	1	0
Greg Gross, of-3	.000	4	5	1	0	0	0	0	0	2	2	0
Von Hayes, of-1	.000	2	2	0	0	0	0	0	0	0	0	0
Al Holland, p	.000	2	0	0	0	0	0	0	0	0	0	0
Charles Hudson, p	.000	1	4	0	0	0	0	0	0	0	3	0
Joe Lefebvre, of-1	.000	2	2	0	0	0	0	0	1	0	1	0
Sixto Lezcano, of	.308	4	13	2	4	0	0	1	2	1	1	0
Garry Maddox, of	.273	3	11	0	3	1	0	0	1	0	1	0
Gary Matthews, of	.429	4	14	4	6	0	0	3	8	2	1	1
Joe Morgan, 2b	.067	4	15	1	1	0	0	0	0	2	1	0
Tony Perez, ph	1.000	1	1	0	1	0	0	0	0	0	0	0
Ron Reed, p	.000	2	0	0	0	0	0	0	0	0	0	0
Pete Rose, 1b	.375	4	16	3	6	0	0	0	0	1	1	1
Juan Samuel, pr	.000	1	0	0	0	0	0	0	0	0	0	0
Mike Schmidt, 3b	.467	4	15	5	7	2	0	1	2	2	3	0
Ossie Virgil, ph	.000	1	1	0	0	0	0	0	0	0	1	0
TOTAL	.262		130	16	34	4	0	5	15	15	22	2

PITCHER	W	L	ERA	G	GS	CG	SV	SHO	IP	H	ER	BB	SO
Steve Carlton	2	0	0.66	2	2	0	0	0	13.2	13	1	5	13
John Denny	0	1	0.00	1	1	0	0	0	6.0	5	0	3	3
Al Holland	0	0	0.00	2	0	0	1	0	3.0	1	0	0	3
Charles Hudson	1	0	2.00	1	1	1	0	0	9.0	4	2	2	9
Ron Reed	0	0	2.70	2	0	0	0	0	3.1	4	1	1	3
TOTAL	3	1	1.03	8	4	1	1	0	35.0	27	4	11	31

LA (W)

PLAYER/POS	AVG	G	AB	R	H	2B	3B	HR	RB	BB	SO	SB
Dusty Baker, of	.357	4	14	4	5	1	0	1	1	2	0	0
Joe Beckwith, p	.000	2	0	0	0	0	0	0	0	0	0	0
Greg Brock, 1b	.000	3	9	1	0	0	0	0	0	0	3	0
Jack Fimple, c	.143	3	7	0	1	0	0	0	1	0	3	0
Pedro Guerrero, 3b	.250	4	12	1	3	1	1	0	2	3	3	0
Rick Honeycutt, p	.000	2	0	0	0	0	0	0	0	0	0	0
Rafael Landestoy, ph	.000	2	2	0	0	0	0	0	0	0	1	0
Ken Landreaux, of	.143	4	14	0	2	0	0	0	1	1	3	0
Candy Maldonado, ph	.000	2	2	0	0	0	0	0	0	0	1	0
Mike Marshall, 1b-3,of-2	.133	4	15	1	2	1	0	1	2	1	6	0
Rick Monday, ph	.000	1	0	0	0	0	0	0	0	0	0	0
Jose Morales, ph	.000	2	2	0	0	0	0	0	0	0	1	0
Tom Niedenfuer, p	.000	2	0	0	0	0	0	0	0	0	0	0
Alejandro Pena, p	1.000	1	1	0	1	0	0	0	0	0	0	0
Jerry Reuss, p	.000	2	3	0	0	0	0	0	0	0	3	0
Bill Russell, ss	.286	4	14	1	4	0	0	0	0	2	4	1
Steve Sax, 2b	.250	4	16	0	4	0	0	0	0	1	0	1
Derrel Thomas, of	.444	4	9	0	4	1	0	0	0	0	3	1
Fernando Valenzuela, p	.000	1	3	0	0	0	0	0	0	1	0	0
Bob Welch, p	.000	1	0	0	0	0	0	0	0	0	0	0
Steve Yeager, c	.167	2	6	0	1	1	0	0	0	0	0	0
Pat Zachry, p	.000	2	0	0	0	0	0	0	0	0	0	0
TOTAL	.209		129	8	27	5	1	2	7	11	31	3

PITCHER	W	L	ERA	G	GS	CG	SV	SHO	IP	H	ER	BB	SO
Joe Beckwith	0	0	0.00	2	0	0	0	0	2.1	1	0	2	3
Rick Honeycutt	0	0	21.60	2	0	0	0	0	1.2	4	4	0	2
Tom Niedenfuer	0	0	0.00	2	0	0	1	0	2.0	0	0	1	3
Alejandro Pena	0	0	6.75	2	1	0	0	0	2.2	4	2	1	3
Jerry Reuss	0	2	4.50	2	2	0	0	0	12.0	14	6	3	4
Fernando Valenzuela	1	0	1.13	1	1	0	0	0	8.0	7	1	4	5
Bob Welch	0	1	6.75	1	1	0	0	0	1.1	0	1	2	0
Pat Zachry	0	0	2.25	2	0	0	0	0	4.0	4	1	2	2
TOTAL	1	3	3.97	13	4	0	1	0	34.0	34	15	15	22

GAME 1 AT LA OCT 4

PHI	100 000 000	1	5	1
LA	000 000 000	0	7	0

Pitchers: CARLTON, Holland (8) vs REUSS, Niedenfuer (9)
Home Runs: Schmidt-PHI
Attendance: 49,963

GAME 2 AT LA OCT 5

PHI	010 000 000	1	7	2
LA	100 020 01X	4	6	1

Pitchers: DENNY, Reed (7) vs VALENZUELA, Niedenfuer (9)
Home Runs: Matthews-PHI
Attendance: 55,967

GAME 3 AT PHI OCT 7

LA	000 200 000	2	4	0
PHI	021 120 10X	7	9	1

Pitchers: WELCH, Pena (2), Honeycutt (5), Beckwith (5), Zachry (7) vs HUDSON
Home Runs: Marshall-LA, Matthews-PHI
Attendance: 53,490

GAME 4 AT PHI OCT 8

LA	000 100 010	2	10	0
PHI	300 022 00X	7	13	1

Pitchers: REUSS, Beckwith (5), Honeycutt (5), Zachry (7) vs CARLTON, Reed (7), Holland (8)
Home Runs: Matthews-PHI, Baker-LA, Lezcano-PHI
Attendance: 64,494

The White Sox and Orioles entered the LCS evenly matched, with similar season's records and stats. But in the LCS, Baltimore all but shut down Chicago's run production. Both teams had 28 hits, but the Sox, held to four for extra bases, found themselves outslugged by 116 percentage points and outscored by 16 runs.

Chicago won the first game, scoring two of their three series runs as LaMarr Hoyt shut Baltimore out for eight innings before letting in a run in the ninth. But the White Sox had concluded their effective scoring. In Game Two, Oriole rookie Mike Boddicker shut them out on five hits, striking out fourteen. In Game Three the Sox scored their final run. The Orioles got only two more hits than Chicago, but blended them with nine walks, a hit batsman, and a Sox error to score eleven runs. In the fourth game, Oriole pitchers Storm Davis and Tippy Martinez saw that ten Chicago hits scored no runs. Britt Burns held Baltimore scoreless, too, through nine innings. But Tito Landrum's solo homer in the top of the tenth drove Burns out, and two more Oriole runs provided more than enough scoring to win Baltimore the flag.

Baltimore Orioles (East), 3; Chicago White Sox (West), 1

BAL (E)

PLAYER/POS	AVG	G	AB	R	H	2B	3B	HR	RB	BB	SO	SB
Benny Ayala, dh	.000	1	0	0	0	0	0	0	0	1	0	0
Mike Boddicker, p	.000	1	0	0	0	0	0	0	0	0	0	0
Al Bumbry, of	.125	3	8	0	1	1	0	0	1	0	2	0
Todd Cruz, 3b	.133	4	15	0	2	0	0	0	1	0	5	0
Rich Dauer, 2b	.000	4	14	0	0	0	0	0	0	1	0	0
Storm Davis, p	.000	1	0	0	0	0	0	0	0	0	0	0
Rick Dempsey, c	.167	4	12	1	2	0	0	0	0	1	1	0
Jim Dwyer, of-1	.250	2	4	1	1	1	0	0	0	1	0	0
Mike Flanagan, p	.000	1	0	0	0	0	0	0	0	0	0	0
Dan Ford, of-1	.200	2	5	0	1	1	0	0	0	0	1	0
Tito Landrum, of-3	.200	4	10	2	2	0	0	1	1	0	2	0
John Lowenstein, of	.167	2	6	0	1	1	0	0	2	1	2	0
Tippy Martinez, p	.000	2	0	0	0	0	0	0	0	0	0	0
Scott Mc Gregor, p	.000	1	0	0	0	0	0	0	0	0	0	0
Eddie Murray, 1b	.267	4	15	5	4	0	0	1	3	3	3	1
Joe Nolan, ph	.000	1	0	0	0	0	0	0	1	0	0	0
Jim Palmer, pr	.000	1	0	0	0	0	0	0	0	0	0	0
Cal Ripken, ss	.400	4	15	5	6	2	0	0	1	2	3	0
Gary Roenicke, of	.750	3	4	4	3	1	0	1	4	5	0	0
John Shelby, of-2	.222	3	9	1	2	0	0	0	0	1	3	1
Ken Singleton, dh	.250	4	12	0	3	2	0	0	1	2	2	0
Sammy Stewart, p	.000	2	0	0	0	0	0	0	0	0	0	0
TOTAL	.217		129	19	28	9	0	3	17	16	24	2

PITCHER	W	L	ERA	G	GS	CG	SV	SHO	IP	H	ER	BB	SO
Mike Boddicker	1	0	0.00	1	1	1	0	1	9.0	5	0	3	14
Storm Davis	0	0	0.00	1	1	0	0	0	6.0	5	0	2	2
Mike Flanagan	1	0	1.80	1	1	0	0	0	5.0	5	1	0	1
Tippy Martinez	1	0	0.00	2	0	0	0	0	6.0	5	0	3	5
Scott Mc Gregor	0	1	1.35	1	1	0	0	0	6.2	6	1	3	2
Sammy Stewart	0	0	0.00	2	0	0	1	0	4.1	2	0	1	2
TOTAL	3	1	0.49	8	4	1	1	1	37.0	28	2	12	26

CHI (W)

PLAYER/POS	AVG	G	AB	R	H	2B	3B	HR	RB	BB	SO	SB
Juan Agosto, p	.000	1	0	0	0	0	0	0	0	0	0	0
Harold Baines, of	.125	4	16	0	2	0	0	0	0	1	3	0
Floyd Bannister, p	.000	1	0	0	0	0	0	0	0	0	0	0
Salome Barojas, p	.000	2	0	0	0	0	0	0	0	0	0	0
Britt Burns, p	.000	1	0	0	0	0	0	0	0	0	0	0
Julio Cruz, 2b	.333	4	12	0	4	0	0	0	0	3	4	2
Richard Dotson, p	.000	1	0	0	0	0	0	0	0	0	0	0
Jerry Dybzinski, ss	.250	2	4	0	1	0	0	0	0	0	0	0
Carlton Fisk, c	.176	4	17	0	3	1	0	0	0	1	3	0
Scott Fletcher, ss	.000	3	7	0	0	0	0	0	0	1	0	0
Jerry Hairston, of	.000	2	3	0	0	0	0	0	0	1	1	0
La Marr Hoyt, p	.000	1	0	0	0	0	0	0	0	0	0	0
Ron Kittle, of	.286	3	7	1	2	1	0	0	0	1	2	0
Jerry Koosman, p	.000	1	0	0	0	0	0	0	0	0	0	0
Dennis Lamp, p	.000	3	0	0	0	0	0	0	0	0	0	0
Rudy Law, of	.389	4	18	0	7	1	0	0	0	0	1	2
Vance Law, 3b	.182	4	11	0	2	0	0	0	1	1	3	0
Greg Luzinski, dh	.133	4	15	0	2	1	0	0	0	1	5	0
Tom Paciorek, 1b-3,of-2	.250	4	16	1	4	0	0	0	1	1	2	0
Aurelio Rodriguez, 3b	.000	2	0	0	0	0	0	0	0	0	0	0
Mike Squires, 1b-3	.000	4	4	0	0	0	0	0	0	0	0	0
Dick Tidrow, p	.000	1	0	0	0	0	0	0	0	0	0	0
Greg Walker, 1b-1	.333	2	3	0	1	0	0	0	0	1	2	0
TOTAL	.211		133	3	28	4	0	0	2	12	26	4

PITCHER	W	L	ERA	G	GS	CG	SV	SHO	IP	H	ER	BB	SO
Juan Agosto	0	0	0.00	1	0	0	0	0	0.1	0	0	0	0
Floyd Bannister	0	1	4.50	1	1	0	0	0	6.0	5	3	1	5
Salome Barojas	0	0	18.00	2	0	0	0	0	1.0	4	2	0	0
Britt Burns	0	1	0.96	1	1	0	0	0	9.1	6	1	5	8
Richard Dotson	0	1	10.80	1	1	0	0	0	5.0	6	6	3	3
La Marr Hoyt	1	0	1.00	1	1	1	0	0	9.0	5	1	0	4
Jerry Koosman	0	0	54.00	1	0	0	0	0	0.1	1	2	2	0
Dennis Lamp	0	0	0.00	3	0	0	0	0	2.0	0	0	2	1
Dick Tidrow	0	0	3.00	1	0	0	0	0	3.0	1	1	3	3
TOTAL	1	3	4.00	12	4	1	0	0	36.0	28	16	16	24

GAME 1 AT BAL OCT 5

CHI	001	001	000	2	7	0
BAL	000	000	001	1	5	1

Pitchers: HOYT vs McGREGOR, Stewart (7), T.Martinez (8)
Attendance: 51,289

GAME 2 AT BAL OCT 6

CHI	000	000	000	0	5	2
BAL	010	102	00X	4	6	0

Pitchers: BANNISTER, Barojas (7), Lamp (8) vs BODDICKER
Home Runs: Roenicke-BAL
Attendance: 52,347

GAME 3 AT CHI OCT 7

BAL	310	020	014	11	8	1
CHI	010	000	000	1	6	1

Pitchers: FLANAGAN, Stewart (6) vs DOTSON, Tidrow (6), Koosman (9), Lamp (9)
Home Runs: Murray-BAL
Attendance: 46,635

GAME 4 AT CHI OCT 8

BAL	000	000	000	3	3	9	0
CHI	000	000	000	0	0	10	0

Pitchers: Davis, T.MARTINEZ (7) vs BURNS, Barojas (10), Agosto (10), Lamp (10)
Home Runs: Landrum-BAL
Attendance: 45,477

Near neighbors Baltimore and Philadelphia met in a World Series for the first time. Both clubs were led by new managers: Baltimore by Joe Altobelli, who inherited a team built under longtime Oriole manager Earl Weaver; and the Phillies by general manager Paul Owens, who replaced Pat Corrales with himself in midseason. Both started their top game winners in the opener, and the result was a pitchers' duel, with all three runs scored on solo homers. Phillie John Denny gave up the first home run to Jim Dwyer in the first inning, but after that (with late-inning help from Al Holland) he blanked the Orioles, while Baltimore's Scott McGregor, after 5⅔ scoreless innings gave up home runs to Joe Morgan and (the game-loser two innings later) to Garry Maddox.

The Orioles swept the next four games. In Game Two, Mike Boddicker yielded just three singles (and no walks) to Phillie batters. Though one of the singles led to a run in the fourth inning, giving the Phillies a 1–0 lead, Oriole John Lowenstein tied the score with a home run in the fifth. Three more Oriole hits in the inning and a sacrifice fly made the score 3–1, and three two-out singles in the seventh inning brought in a fourth Baltimore run.

Philadelphia again scored first in Game Three, on leadoff home runs in the second and third innings by Gary Matthews and Joe Morgan. But the Orioles finally got to veteran starter Steve Carlton in the sixth for one run and drove him out after a second run scored an inning later. Carlton suffered the loss when the baserunner he left scored the tie-breaking run from second on an error by shortstop Ivan DeJesus.

The Phillies also lost Game Four by a single run. Baltimore scored first with two runs in the top of the fourth, but Philadelphia recovered with one run in the fourth and two an inning later. They would not lead again in the Series. Baltimore scored twice in the sixth to go ahead again, and once more in the seventh. The Phillies scored once more with two down in the last of the ninth to draw within one run of a tie, but Joe Morgan lined out to second to end the game.

Home runs by Rick Dempsey and Eddie Murray (who hit two) accounted for four of Baltimore's five runs in the final game—more than enough to support Scott McGregor's five-hit shutout pitching.

Baltimore Orioles (AL), 4; Philadelphia Phillies (NL), 1

BAL (A)

PLAYER/POS	AVG	G	AB	R	H	2B	3B	HR	RB	BB	SO	SB
Benny Ayala, ph	1.000	1	1	1	1	0	0	0	1	0	0	0
Mike Boddicker, p	.000	1	3	0	0	0	0	0	1	0	1	0
Al Bumbry, of	.091	4	11	0	1	1	0	0	1	0	1	0
Todd Cruz, 3b	.125	6	16	1	2	0	0	0	0	1	3	0
Rich Dauer, 2b	.211	5	19	2	4	1	0	0	3	0	3	0
Storm Davis, p	.000	1	2	0	0	0	0	0	0	0	2	0
Rick Dempsey, c	.385	5	13	3	5	4	0	1	2	2	2	0
Jim Dwyer, of	.375	2	8	3	3	1	0	1	1	0	0	0
Mike Flanagan, p	.000	1	1	0	0	0	0	0	0	0	1	0
Dan Ford, of-4	.167	5	12	1	2	0	0	1	1	1	5	0
Tito Landrum, of	.000	3	0	0	0	0	0	0	0	0	0	1
John Lowenstein, of	.385	4	13	2	5	1	0	1	1	0	3	0
Tippy Martinez, p	.000	3	0	0	0	0	0	0	0	0	0	0
Scott Mc Gregor, p	.000	2	5	0	0	0	0	0	0	0	0	0
Eddie Murray, 1b	.250	5	20	2	5	0	0	2	3	1	4	0
Joe Nolan, c	.000	2	2	0	0	0	0	0	0	1	0	0
Jim Palmer, p	.000	1	0	0	0	0	0	0	0	0	0	0
Cal Ripken, ss	.167	5	18	2	3	0	0	0	1	3	4	0
Gary Roenicke, of-2	.000	3	7	0	0	0	0	0	0	0	2	0
Len Sakata, 2b	.000	1	1	0	0	0	0	0	0	0	0	0
John Shelby, of	.444	5	9	1	4	0	0	0	1	0	4	0
Ken Singleton, ph	.000	2	1	0	0	0	0	0	0	1	1	0
Sammy Stewart, p	.000	3	2	0	0	0	0	0	0	0	1	0
TOTAL	.213		164	18	35	8	0	6	17	10	37	1

PITCHER	W	L	ERA	G	GS	CG	SV	SHO	IP	H	ER	BB	SO
Mike Boddicker	1	0	0.00	1	1	1	0	0	9.0	3	0	0	6
Storm Davis	1	0	5.40	1	1	0	0	0	5.0	6	3	1	3
Mike Flanagan	0	0	4.50	1	1	0	0	0	4.0	6	2	1	1
Tippy Martinez	0	0	3.00	3	0	0	2	0	3.0	3	1	0	0
Scott Mc Gregor	1	1	1.06	2	2	1	0	1	17.0	9	2	2	12
Jim Palmer	1	0	0.00	1	0	0	0	0	2.0	2	0	1	1
Sammy Stewart	0	0	0.00	3	0	0	0	0	5.0	2	0	2	6
TOTAL	4	1	1.60	12	5	2	2		45.0	31	8	7	29

PHI (N)

PLAYER/POS	AVG	G	AB	R	H	2B	3B	HR	RB	BB	SO	SB
Larry Andersen, p	.000	2	0	0	0	0	0	0	0	0	0	0
Marty Bystrom, p	.000	1	0	0	0	0	0	0	0	0	0	0
Steve Carlton, p	.000	1	3	0	0	0	0	0	0	0	1	0
Ivan De Jesus, ss	.125	5	16	0	2	0	0	0	0	1	2	0
John Denny, p	.200	2	5	1	1	0	0	0	1	0	1	0
Bob Dernier, pr	.000	1	0	1	0	0	0	0	0	0	0	0
Bo Diaz, c	.333	5	15	1	5	1	0	0	0	1	2	0
Greg Gross, of	.000	2	6	0	0	0	0	0	0	0	0	0
Von Hayes, of-1	.000	4	3	0	0	0	0	0	0	0	1	0
Willie Hernandez, p	.000	3	0	0	0	0	0	0	0	0	0	0
Al Holland, p	.000	2	0	0	0	0	0	0	0	0	0	0
Charles Hudson, p	.000	2	2	0	0	0	0	0	0	0	1	0
Joe Lefebvre, of-2	.200	3	5	0	1	1	0	0	2	0	1	0
Sixto Lezcano, of-3	.125	4	8	0	1	0	0	0	0	0	2	0
Garry Maddox, of-3	.250	4	12	1	3	1	0	1	1	0	2	0
Gary Matthews, of	.250	5	16	1	4	0	0	1	1	2	2	0
Joe Morgan, 2b	.263	5	19	3	5	0	1	2	2	2	3	1
Tony Perez, 1b-2	.200	4	10	0	2	0	0	0	0	0	2	0
Ron Reed, p	.000	3	0	0	0	0	0	0	0	0	0	0
Pete Rose, 1b-3,of-1	.313	5	16	1	5	1	0	0	1	1	3	0
Juan Samuel, ph	.000	3	1	0	0	0	0	0	0	0	0	0
Mike Schmidt, 3b	.050	5	20	0	1	0	0	0	0	0	6	0
Ossie Virgil, c-1	.500	3	2	0	1	0	0	0	1	0	0	0
TOTAL	.195		159	9	31	4	1	4	9	7	29	1

PITCHER	W	L	ERA	G	GS	CG	SV	SHO	IP	H	ER	BB	SO
Larry Andersen	0	0	2.25	2	0	0	0	0	4.0	4	1	0	1
Marty Bystrom	0	0	0.00	1	0	0	0	0	1.0	0	0	0	1
Steve Carlton	0	1	2.70	1	1	0	0	0	6.2	5	2	3	7
John Denny	1	1	3.46	2	2	0	0	0	13.0	12	5	3	9
Willie Hernandez	0	0	0.00	3	0	0	0	0	4.0	0	0	1	4
Al Holland	0	0	0.00	2	0	0	1	0	3.2	1	0	0	5
Charles Hudson	0	2	8.64	2	2	0	0	0	8.1	9	8	1	6
Ron Reed	0	0	2.70	3	0	0	0	0	3.1	4	1	2	4
TOTAL	1	4	3.48	16	5	0	1	0	44.0	35	17	10	37

GAME 1 AT BAL OCT 11

PHI	000	001	010	2	5	0
BAL	100	000	000	1	5	1

Pitchers: DENNY, Holland (8) vs McGREGOR, Stewart (9), T.Martinez (9)
Home Runs: Morgan-PHI, Maddox-PHI, Dwyer-BAL
Attendance: 52,204

GAME 2 AT BAL OCT 12

PHI	000	100	000	1	3	0
BAL	000	030	10X	4	9	1

Pitchers: HUDSON, Hernandez (5), Andersen (6), Reed (8) vs BODDICKER
Home Runs: Lowenstein-BAL
Attendance: 52,132

GAME 3 AT PHI OCT 14

BAL	000	001	200	3	6	1
PHI	011	000	000	2	8	2

Pitchers: Flanagan, PALMER (5), Stewart (7), T.Martinez (9) vs CARLTON, Holland (7)
Home Runs: Matthews-PHI, Morgan-PHI, Ford-BAL
Attendance: 65,792

GAME 4 AT PHI OCT 15

BAL	000	202	100	5	10	1
PHI	000	120	001	4	10	0

Pitchers: DAVIS, Stewart (6), T.Martinez (8) vs DENNY, Hernandez (6), Reed (6), Andersen (8)
Attendance: 66,947

GAME 5 AT PHI OCT 16

BAL	011	210	000	5	5	0
PHI	000	000	000	0	5	1

Pitchers: McGREGOR vs HUDSON, Bystrom (5), Hernandez (6), Reed (9)
Home Runs: Murray-BAL (2), Dempsey-BAL
Attendance: 67,064

After two games in Chicago, the Cubs appeared headed for their first pennant in thirty-nine years. Rick Sutcliffe and Warren Brusstar shut out the Padres 13–0 in an opener enlivened by five Cub home runs. In a quieter second game, the Cubs built a 4–1 lead over the first four innings and held on for the win.

When the series moved to San Diego, though, the Padres came to life. In the fifth and sixth innings of Game Three, they obliterated a 1–0 Cub lead with seven runs, as Ed Whitson and Goose Gossage held the Cubs scoreless after the second inning for what turned into an easy Padres win.

Game Four was not so easy. San Diego scored first in the third inning, lost their lead in the fourth, tied in the fifth, went ahead in the seventh, and fell back into a 5–5 tie in the eighth. But in the bottom of the ninth, Padre Steve Garvey's two-run homer sent the series into a fifth game.

Leon Durham put the Cubs ahead with a two-run homer in the first inning of the finale, and Jody Davis added to the lead with a solo shot in the second. Rick Sutcliffe, meanwhile, was setting down Padres as he added five shutout innings to his seven from Game One. But he gave up two runs in the sixth, and after first baseman Durham saw a grounder go through his legs to let in the tying run in the seventh, the Cubs watched the pennant slip away as Tony Gwynn's double and Garvey's single drove in the game's three final runs.

San Diego Padres (West), 3;
Chicago Cubs (East), 2

SD (W)

PLAYER/POS	AVG	G	AB	R	H	2B	3B	HR	RB	BB	SO	SB
Kurt Bevacqua, ph	.000	2	2	0	0	0	0	0	0	0	0	0
Greg Booker, p	.000	1	0	0	0	0	0	0	0	0	0	0
Bobby Brown, of	.000	3	4	1	0	0	0	0	0	1	2	1
Dave Dravecky, p	.000	3	0	0	0	0	0	0	0	0	0	0
Tim Flannery, ph	.500	3	2	2	1	0	0	0	0	0	0	0
Steve Garvey, 1b	.400	5	20	1	8	1	0	1	7	1	2	0
Rich Gossage, p	.000	3	0	0	0	0	0	0	0	0	0	0
Tony Gwynn, of	.368	5	19	6	7	3	0	0	3	1	2	0
Greg Harris, p	.000	1	0	0	0	0	0	0	0	0	0	0
Andy Hawkins, p	.000	3	0	0	0	0	0	0	0	0	0	0
Terry Kennedy, c	.222	5	18	2	4	0	0	0	1	1	3	0
Craig Lefferts, p	.000	3	0	0	0	0	0	0	0	0	0	0
Tim Lollar, p	.000	1	1	0	0	0	0	0	0	0	1	0
Carmelo Martinez, of	.176	5	17	1	3	0	0	0	0	2	4	0
Kevin Mc Reynolds, of	.300	4	10	2	3	0	0	1	4	3	1	0
Graig Nettles, 3b	.143	4	14	1	2	0	0	0	2	1	1	0
Mario Ramirez, ph	.000	2	2	0	0	0	0	0	0	0	0	0
Luis Salazar, of-2,3b-1	.200	3	5	0	1	0	1	0	0	0	1	0
Eric Show, p	.000	2	1	0	0	0	0	0	0	0	1	0
Champ Summers, ph	.000	2	2	0	0	0	0	0	0	0	1	0
Garry Templeton, ss	.333	5	15	2	5	1	0	0	2	2	0	1
Mark Thurmond, p	1.000	1	1	0	1	0	0	0	0	0	0	0
Ed Whitson, p	.000	1	3	0	0	0	0	0	0	0	1	0
Alan Wiggins, 2b	.316	5	19	4	6	0	0	0	1	2	2	0
TOTAL	.265		155	22	41	5	1	2	20	14	22	2

PITCHER	W	L	ERA	G	GS	CG	SV	SHO	IP	H	ER	BB	SO
Greg Booker	0	0	0.00	1	0	0	0	0	2.0	2	0	1	2
Dave Dravecky	0	0	0.00	3	0	0	0	0	6.0	2	0	0	5
Rich Gossage	0	0	4.50	3	0	0	1	0	4.0	5	2	1	5
Greg Harris	0	0	31.50	1	0	0	0	0	2.0	9	7	3	2
Andy Hawkins	0	0	0.00	3	0	0	0	0	3.2	0	0	2	1
Craig Lefferts	2	0	0.00	3	0	0	0	0	4.0	1	0	1	1
Tim Lollar	0	0	6.23	1	1	0	0	0	4.1	3	3	4	3
Eric Show	0	1	13.50	2	2	0	0	0	5.1	8	8	4	2
Mark Thurmond	0	1	9.82	1	1	0	0	0	3.2	7	4	2	1
Ed Whitson	1	0	1.13	1	1	0	0	0	8.0	5	1	2	6
TOTAL	3	2	5.23	19	5	0	1	0	43.0	42	25	20	28

CHI (E)

PLAYER/POS	AVG	G	AB	R	H	2B	3B	HR	RB	BB	SO	SB
Thad Bosley, ph	.000	2	2	0	0	0	0	0	0	0	2	0
Larry Bowa, ss	.200	5	15	1	3	1	0	0	1	1	0	0
Warren Brusstar, p	.000	3	1	0	0	0	0	0	0	0	0	0
Ron Cey, 3b	.158	5	19	3	3	1	0	1	3	3	3	0
Henry Cotto, of	1.000	3	1	1	1	0	0	0	0	0	0	0
Jody Davis, c	.389	5	18	3	7	2	0	2	6	0	3	0
Bob Dernier, of	.235	5	17	5	4	2	0	1	1	5	4	2
Leon Durham, 1b	.150	5	20	2	3	0	0	2	4	1	4	0
Dennis Eckersley, p	.000	1	2	0	0	0	0	0	0	0	1	0
George Frazier, p	.000	1	0	0	0	0	0	0	0	0	0	0
Richie Hebner, ph	.000	2	1	0	0	0	0	0	0	0	0	0
Steve Lake, c	1.000	1	1	0	1	1	0	0	0	0	0	0
Davey Lopes, of-1	.000	2	1	0	0	0	0	0	0	0	0	0
Gary Matthews, of	.200	5	15	4	3	0	0	2	5	6	4	1
Keith Moreland, of	.333	5	18	3	6	2	0	0	2	1	1	0
Ryne Sandberg, 2b	.368	5	19	3	7	2	0	0	2	3	2	3
Scott Sanderson, p	.000	1	2	0	0	0	0	0	0	0	1	0
Lee Smith, p	.000	2	0	0	0	0	0	0	0	0	0	0
Tim Stoddard, p	.000	2	0	0	0	0	0	0	0	0	0	0
Rick Sutcliffe, p	.500	2	6	1	3	0	0	1	1	0	2	0
Steve Trout, p	.500	2	2	0	1	0	0	0	0	0	0	0
Tom Veryzer, ss-2,3b-1	.000	3	1	0	0	0	0	0	0	0	0	0
Gary Woods, of	.000	1	1	0	0	0	0	0	0	0	1	0
TOTAL	.259		162	26	42	11	0	9	25	20	28	6

PITCHER	W	L	ERA	G	GS	CG	SV	SHO	IP	H	ER	BB	SO
Warren Brusstar	0	0	0.00	3	0	0	0	0	4.1	6	0	0	1
Dennis Eckersley	0	1	8.44	1	1	0	0	0	5.1	9	5	0	0
George Frazier	0	0	10.80	1	0	0	0	0	1.2	2	2	0	1
Scott Sanderson	0	0	5.79	1	1	0	0	0	4.2	6	3	1	2
Lee Smith	0	1	9.00	2	0	0	1	0	2.0	3	2	0	3
Tim Stoddard	0	0	4.50	2	0	0	0	0	2.0	1	1	2	2
Rick Sutcliffe	1	1	3.38	2	2	0	0	0	13.1	9	5	8	10
Steve Trout	1	0	2.00	2	1	0	0	0	9.0	5	2	3	3
TOTAL	2	3	4.25	14	5	0	1	0	42.1	41	20	14	22

GAME 1 AT CHI OCT 2

SD	000	000	000	0	6	1
CHI	203	062	00X	13	16	0

Pitchers: SHOW, Harris (5), Booker (7) vs SUTCLIFFE, Brusstar (8)
Home Runs: Dernier-CHI, Matthews-CHI (2), Sutcliffe-CHI, Cey-CHI
Attendance: 36,282

GAME 2 AT CHI OCT 3

SD	000	101	000	2	5	0
CHI	102	100	00X	4	8	1

Pitchers: THURMOND, Hawkins (4), Dravecky (6), Lefferts (8) vs TROUT, Smith (9)
Attendance: 36,282

GAME 3 AT SD OCT 4

CHI	010	000	000	1	5	0
SD	000	034	00X	7	11	0

Pitchers: ECKERSLEY, Frazier (6), Stoddard (8) vs WHITSON, Gossage (9)
Home Runs: McReynolds-SD
Attendance: 58,346

GAME 4 AT SD OCT 6

CHI	000	300	020	5	8	1
SD	002	010	202	7	11	0

Pitchers: Sanderson, Brusstar (5), Stoddard (7), SMITH (8) vs Lollar, Hawkins (5), Dravecky (6), Gossage (8), LEFFERTS (9)
Home Runs: Davis-CHI, Durham-CHI, Garvey-SD
Attendance: 58,354

GAME 5 AT SD OCT 7

CHI	210	000	000	3	5	1
SD	000	002	40X	6	8	0

Pitchers: SUTCLIFFE, Trout (7), Brusstar (8) vs Show, Hawkins (2), Dravecky (4), LEFFERTS (6), Gossage (8)
Home Runs: Durham-CHI, Davis-CHI
Attendance: 58,359

The heavily favored Tigers swept the series, but not without difficulty, despite a fourteen-hit, three-homer, 8–1 romp in the opener.

Games Two and Three were much tighter. In the second game, after Detroit had built a 3–0 lead over the first three innings, Royal rookie starter Bret Saberhagen settled down and blanked the Tigers for the next five innings as K.C. inched its way to a tie with runs in the fourth, seventh, and eighth. Through the ninth and tenth innings, Tiger reliever Aurelio Lopez and Royal Dan Quisenberry dueled scorelessly, but in the top of the eleventh Johnny Grubb doubled home two Tiger runs. Lopez struggled but held the Royals scoreless in the last of the eleventh for the win.

In Game Three, the Royals' Charlie Leibrandt and Tigers' Milt Wilcox and Willie Hernandez hurled matching three-hitters. But the Tigers secured the game—and the pennant—when Chet Lemon scored on a broken double play in the second inning for the game's only run.

Detroit Tigers (East), 3;
Kansas City Royals (West), 0

DET (E)

PLAYER/POS	AVG	G	AB	R	H	2B	3B	HR	RB	BB	SO	SB
Doug Baker, ss	.000	1	0	0	0	0	0	0	0	0	0	0
Dave Bergman, 1b-1	1.000	2	1	1	1	0	0	0	0	0	0	1
Tom Brookens, 2b-1,3b-1	.000	2	2	0	0	0	0	0	0	0	1	0
Marty Castillo, 3b	.250	3	8	0	2	0	0	0	2	0	3	1
Darrell Evans, 1b-3,3b-1	.300	3	10	1	3	1	0	0	1	1	0	1
Barbaro Garbey, dh-2	.333	3	9	1	3	0	0	0	0	0	1	0
Kirk Gibson, of	.417	3	12	2	5	1	0	1	2	2	1	1
Johnny Grubb, dh	.250	1	4	0	1	1	0	0	2	0	0	0
Willie Hernandez, p	.000	3	0	0	0	0	0	0	0	0	0	0
Larry Herndon, of	.200	2	5	1	1	0	0	1	1	1	2	0
Ruppert Jones, of	.000	2	5	1	0	0	0	0	0	1	1	0
Rusty Kuntz, of	.000	1	1	0	0	0	0	0	0	0	0	0
Chet Lemon, of	.000	3	13	1	0	0	0	0	0	0	1	0
Aurelio Lopez, p	.000	1	0	0	0	0	0	0	0	0	0	0
Jack Morris, p	.000	1	0	0	0	0	0	0	0	0	0	0
Lance Parrish, c	.250	3	12	1	3	1	0	1	3	0	3	0
Dan Petry, p	.000	1	0	0	0	0	0	0	0	0	0	0
Alan Trammell, ss	.364	3	11	2	4	0	1	1	3	3	1	0
Lou Whitaker, 2b	.143	3	14	3	2	0	0	0	0	0	3	0
Milt Wilcox, p	.000	1	0	0	0	0	0	0	0	0	0	0
TOTAL	.234		107	14	25	4	1	4	14	8	17	4

PITCHER	W	L	ERA	G	GS	CG	SV	SHO	IP	H	ER	BB	SO
Willie Hernandez	0	0	2.25	3	0	0	1	0	4.0	3	1	1	3
Aurelio Lopez	1	0	0.00	1	0	0	0	0	3.0	4	0	1	0
Jack Morris	1	0	1.29	1	1	0	0	0	7.0	5	1	1	4
Dan Petry	0	0	2.57	1	1	0	0	0	7.0	4	2	1	4
Milt Wilcox	1	0	0.00	1	1	0	0	0	8.0	2	0	2	8
TOTAL	3	0	1.24	7	3	0	1	0	29.0	18	4	6	21

KC (W)

PLAYER/POS	AVG	G	AB	R	H	2B	3B	HR	RB	BB	SO	SB
Steve Balboni, 1b	.100	3	10	0	1	0	0	0	0	1	4	0
Buddy Biancalana, ss	.000	2	1	0	0	0	0	0	0	0	1	0
Bud Black, p	.000	1	0	0	0	0	0	0	0	0	0	0
George Brett, 3b	.231	3	13	0	3	0	0	0	0	0	2	0
Onix Concepcion, ss	.000	3	7	0	0	0	0	0	0	0	0	0
Mark Huismann, p	.000	1	0	0	0	0	0	0	0	0	0	0
Dane Iorg, ph	.500	2	2	0	1	0	0	0	1	0	0	0
Lynn Jones, of-2	.200	3	5	1	1	0	0	0	0	0	0	0
Mike Jones, p	.000	1	0	0	0	0	0	0	0	0	0	0
Charlie Leibrandt, p	.000	1	0	0	0	0	0	0	0	0	0	0
Hal Mc Rae, ph	1.000	2	2	0	2	1	0	0	1	0	0	0
Darryl Motley, of	.167	3	12	0	2	0	0	0	1	1	3	0
Jorge Orta, dh	.100	3	10	1	1	0	1	0	1	0	2	0
Greg Pryor, 3b	.000	1	0	0	0	0	0	0	0	0	0	0
Dan Quisenberry, p	.000	1	0	0	0	0	0	0	0	0	0	0
Bret Saberhagen, p	.000	1	0	0	0	0	0	0	0	0	0	0
Pat Sheridan, of	.000	3	6	1	0	0	0	0	0	3	3	0
Don Slaught, c	.364	3	11	0	4	0	0	0	0	0	0	0
U. L. Washington, ph	.000	2	1	0	0	0	0	0	0	0	1	0
John Wathan, dh	.000	1	1	0	0	0	0	0	0	0	0	0
Frank White, 2b	.083	3	12	1	1	0	0	0	0	0	3	0
Willie Wilson, of	.154	3	13	0	2	0	0	0	0	1	2	0
TOTAL	.170		106	4	18	1	1	0	4	6	21	0

PITCHER	W	L	ERA	G	GS	CG	SV	SHO	IP	H	ER	BB	SO
Bud Black	0	1	5.40	1	1	0	0	0	5.0	7	3	1	3
Mark Huismann	0	0	10.13	1	0	0	0	0	2.2	6	3	1	2
Mike Jones	0	0	6.75	1	0	0	0	0	1.1	1	1	0	0
Charlie Leibrandt	0	1	1.13	1	1	1	0	0	8.0	3	1	4	6
Dan Quisenberry	0	1	3.00	1	0	0	0	0	3.0	2	1	1	1
Bret Saberhagen	0	0	2.25	1	1	0	0	0	8.0	6	2	1	5
TOTAL	0	3	3.54	6	3	1	0	0	28.0	25	11	8	17

GAME 1 AT KC OCT 2

DET	200 110 121	8 14 0
KC	000 000 100	1 5 1

Pitchers: MORRIS, Hernandez (8) vs BLACK, Huismann (6), M.Jones (8)
Home Runs: Herndon-DET, Trammell-DET, Parrish-DET
Attendance: 41,973

GAME 2 AT KC OCT 3

DET	201 000 000 02	5 8 1
KC	000 100 110 00	3 10 3

Pitchers: Petry, Hernandez (8), LOPEZ (9) vs Saberhagen, QUISENBERRY (9)
Home Runs: Gibson-DET
Attendance: 42,019

GAME 3 AT DET OCT 5

KC	000 000 000	0 3 3
DET	010 000 00X	1 3 0

Pitchers: LEIBRANDT vs WILCOX, Hernandez (9)
Attendance: 52,168

Few objective observers expected the Padres (playing in their first World Series) to best the mighty Tigers—and they didn't. Detroit's first two batters in Game One hit safely to produce the Series' first scoring before an out had been recorded. San Diego countered with three two-out hits in their half of the first to go ahead 2–1. But Detroit starter Jack Morris settled down to shut out the Padres over the final eight innings, and his Tigers scored the tying and winning runs in the fifth on Larry Herndon's two-run homer. The Tigers scored again in Game Two before the first out was recorded and drove out Padre starter Ed Whitson with three first-inning runs on five singles. But this time Detroit was shut out (by relievers Andy Hawkins and Craig Lefferts) over the final eight, while San Diego scored single runs in the first and fourth and the winning runs in the fifth on a three-run homer by the normally light-hitting Kurt Bevacqua.

The Tigers won Game Three on walks—a Series-record eleven—as the Series moved to Detroit. After scoring their first two runs in the second on a single and Marty Castillo's home run, they continued on to put across two more in the inning on a pair of hits alternated with three walks (the last with the bases full). Three more walks an inning later, followed by a hit batsman, gave Detroit its final run in what became a 5–2 win.

Alan Trammell's two-run homer in the first inning of Game Four put the Tigers ahead to stay. Tiger pitcher Jack Morris gave up a solo home run to Terry Kennedy in the second, but Trammell swatted a second two-run shot an inning later for a 4–1 lead. Morris let a second Padre runner score on a wild pitch in the ninth, but then retired Kennedy for the third out and his second Series win. Kirk Gibson's two home runs framed Tiger scoring in the final game. His two-run shot in the first inning opened the game's scoring. San Diego tied it up with runs in the third and fourth, but Detroit took a 5–3 lead with runs in the fifth and seventh (the latter on Lance Parrish's homer). The unlikely Kurt Bevacqua brought the Padres within a run of tying the game with his second Series homer in the eighth (doubling his regular-season total), but Gibson ended the scoring—and Padre hopes—with a three-run blast half an inning later.

Detroit Tigers (AL), 4;
San Diego Padres (NL), 1

DET (A)

PLAYER/POS	AVG	G	AB	R	H	2B	3B	HR	RB	BB	SO	SB
Doug Bair, p	.000	1	0	0	0	0	0	0	0	0	0	0
Dave Bergman, 1b	.000	5	5	0	0	0	0	0	0	0	1	0
Tom Brookens, 3b	.000	3	3	0	0	0	0	0	0	0	1	0
Marty Castillo, 3b	.333	3	9	2	3	0	0	1	2	2	1	0
Darrell Evans, 1b-4,3b-2	.067	5	15	1	1	0	0	0	1	4	4	0
Barbaro Garbey, dh-3	.000	4	12	0	0	0	0	0	0	0	2	0
Kirk Gibson, of	.333	5	18	4	6	0	0	2	7	4	4	3
Johnny Grubb, dh-2	.333	4	3	0	1	0	0	0	0	0	0	0
Willie Hernandez, p	.000	3	0	0	0	0	0	0	0	0	0	0
Larry Herndon, of	.333	5	15	1	5	0	0	1	3	3	2	0
Howard Johnson, ph	.000	1	1	0	0	0	0	0	0	0	0	0
Ruppert Jones, of	.000	2	3	0	0	0	0	0	0	0	1	0
Rusty Kuntz, ph	.000	2	1	0	0	0	0	0	0	1	0	1
Chet Lemon, of	.294	5	17	1	5	0	0	0	1	2	2	2
Jack Morris, p	.000	2	0	0	0	0	0	0	0	0	0	0
Lance Parrish, c	.278	5	18	3	5	1	0	1	2	3	2	1
Dan Petry, p	.000	2	0	0	0	0	0	0	0	0	0	0
Bill Scherrer, p	.000	3	0	0	0	0	0	0	0	0	0	0
Alan Trammell, ss	.450	5	20	5	9	1	0	2	6	2	2	1
Lou Whitaker, 2b	.278	5	18	6	5	2	0	0	0	4	4	0
Milt Wilcox, p	.000	1	0	0	0	0	0	0	0	0	0	0
TOTAL	.253		158	23	40	4	0	7	23	24	27	7

PITCHER	W	L	ERA	G	GS	CG	SV	SHO	IP	H	ER	BB	SO
Doug Bair	0	0	0.00	1	0	0	0	0	0.2	0	0	0	1
Willie Hernandez	0	0	1.69	3	0	0	2	0	5.1	4	1	0	0
Aurelio Lopez	1	0	0.00	2	0	0	0	0	3.0	1	0	1	4
Jack Morris	2	0	2.00	2	2	2	0	0	18.0	13	4	3	13
Dan Petry	0	1	9.00	2	2	0	0	0	8.0	14	8	5	4
Bill Scherrer	0	0	3.00	3	0	0	0	0	3.0	5	1	0	0
Milt Wilcox	1	0	1.50	1	1	0	0	0	6.0	7	1	2	4
TOTAL	4	1	3.07	14	5	2	2	0	44.0	44	15	11	26

SD (N)

PLAYER/POS	AVG	G	AB	R	H	2B	3B	HR	RB	BB	SO	SB
Kurt Bevacqua, dh	.412	5	17	4	7	2	0	2	4	1	2	0
Bruce Bochy, ph	1.000	1	1	0	1	0	0	0	0	0	0	0
Greg Booker, p	.000	1	0	0	0	0	0	0	0	0	0	0
Bobby Brown, of	.067	5	15	1	1	0	0	0	2	0	4	0
Dave Dravecky, p	.000	2	0	0	0	0	0	0	0	0	0	0
Tim Flannery, 2b	1.000	1	1	0	1	0	0	0	0	0	0	0
Steve Garvey, 1b	.200	5	20	2	4	2	0	0	2	0	2	0
Rich Gossage, p	.000	2	0	0	0	0	0	0	0	0	0	0
Tony Gwynn, of	.263	5	19	1	5	0	0	0	0	3	2	1
Greg Harris, p	.000	1	0	0	0	0	0	0	0	0	0	0
Andy Hawkins, p	.000	3	0	0	0	0	0	0	0	0	0	0
Terry Kennedy, c	.211	5	19	2	4	1	0	1	3	1	1	0
Craig Lefferts, p	.000	3	0	0	0	0	0	0	0	0	0	0
Tim Lollar, p	.000	1	0	0	0	0	0	0	0	0	0	0
Carmelo Martinez, of	.176	5	17	0	3	0	0	0	0	1	9	0
Graig Nettles, 3b	.250	5	12	2	3	0	0	0	2	5	0	0
Ron Roenicke, of-1	.000	2	0	0	0	0	0	0	0	0	0	0
Luis Salazar, of-2,3b-1	.333	4	3	0	1	0	0	0	0	0	0	0
Eric Show, p	.000	1	0	0	0	0	0	0	0	0	0	0
Champ Summers, ph	.000	1	1	0	0	0	0	0	0	0	1	0
Garry Templeton, ss	.316	5	19	1	6	1	0	0	0	0	3	0
Mark Thurmond, p	.000	2	0	0	0	0	0	0	0	0	0	0
Ed Whitson, p	.000	1	0	0	0	0	0	0	0	0	0	0
Alan Wiggins, 2b	.364	5	22	2	8	1	0	0	1	0	2	1
TOTAL	.265		166	15	44	7	0	3	14	11	26	2

PITCHER	W	L	ERA	G	GS	CG	SV	SHO	IP	H	ER	BB	SO
Greg Booker	0	0	9.00	1	0	0	0	0	1.0	0	1	4	0
Dave Dravecky	0	0	0.00	2	0	0	0	0	4.2	3	0	1	5
Rich Gossage	0	0	13.50	2	0	0	0	0	2.2	3	4	1	2
Greg Harris	0	0	0.00	1	0	0	0	0	5.1	3	0	3	5
Andy Hawkins	1	1	0.75	3	0	0	0	0	12.0	4	1	6	4
Craig Lefferts	0	0	0.00	3	0	0	1	0	6.0	2	0	1	7
Tim Lollar	0	1	21.60	1	1	0	0	0	1.2	4	4	4	0
Eric Show	0	1	10.13	1	1	0	0	0	2.2	4	3	1	2
Mark Thurmond	0	1	10.13	2	2	0	0	0	5.1	12	6	3	2
Ed Whitson	0	0	40.50	1	1	0	0	0	0.2	5	3	0	0
TOTAL	1	4	4.71	17	5	0	1	0	42.0	40	22	24	27

GAME 1 AT SD OCT 9

DET	100	020	000	3	8	0
SD	200	000	000	2	8	1

Pitchers: MORRIS vs THURMOND, Hawkins (6), Dravecky (8)
Home Runs: Herndon-DET
Attendance: 57,908

GAME 2 AT SD OCT 10

DET	300	000	000	3	7	3
SD	100	130	00X	5	11	0

Pitchers: PETRY, Lopez (5), Scherrer (6), Bair (7), Hernandez (8) vs Whitson, HAWKINS (1), Lefferts)7)
Home Runs: Bevacqua-SD
Attendance: 57,911

GAME 3 AT DET OCT 12

SD	001	000	100	2	5	0
DET	041	000	00X	5	7	0

Pitchers: LOLLAR, Booker (2), Harris (3) vs WILCOX, Scherrer (7), Hernandez (7)
Home Runs: Castillo-DET
Attendance: 51,970

GAME 4 AT DET OCT 13

SD	010	000	001	2	10	2
DET	202	000	00X	4	7	0

Pitchers: SHOW, Dravecky (3), Lefferts (7), Gossage (8) vs MORRIS
Home Runs: Trammell-DET (2), Kennedy-SD
Attendance: 52,130

GAME 5 AT DET OCT 14

SD	001	200	010	4	10	1
DET	300	010	13X	8	11	1

Pitchers: Thurmond, HAWKINS (1), Lefferts (5), Gossage (8) vs Petry, Scherrer (4), LOPEZ (5), Hernandez (8)
Home Runs: Gibson-DET (2), Parrish-DET, Bevacqua-SD
Attendance: 51,901

The Dodgers' league-leading pitchers held St. Louis to three runs over the first two games, even though the Cardinals recorded eight hits per game. But the Cards' league-leading hitters put their blows to better advantage in the next four games of the expanded LCS, scoring twenty-six times for four wins and the pennant.

Fernando Valenzuela captured Game One for the Dodgers, thanks in part to some ragged fielding by the usually sharp Cardinal infield. And as Orel Hershiser was holding St. Louis to two runs in Game Two, an errant Cardinal pickoff throw and heavy Dodger hitting gave him an increasingly comfortable lead.

When the series shifted to St. Louis for Game Three, the Cardinals revived, scoring twice in each of the first two innings for a quick lead, which they held for their first win. In Game Four they unloaded for nine runs in the second inning, and in Game Five—with the game and series tied in the bottom of the ninth—Ozzie Smith hit his first lefthanded home run ever to give St. Louis the series lead.

Back in Los Angeles, the Dodgers scored first in Game Six, and held a 4–1 lead after six innings. But three Cardinals scored on four hits in the seventh, and though Dodger Mike Marshall's eighth-inning home run restored the lead to Los Angeles, Cardinal Jack Clark settled things with a three-run homer in the ninth.

St. Louis Cardinals (East), 4; Los Angeles Dodgers (West), 2

STL (E)

PLAYER/POS	AVG	G	AB	R	H	2B	3B	HR	RB	BB	SO	SB
Joaquin Andujar, p	.250	2	4	1	1	1	0	0	0	0	1	0
Steve Braun, ph	.000	2	2	0	0	0	0	0	0	0	0	0
Bill Campbell, p	.000	3	0	0	0	0	0	0	0	0	0	0
Cesar Cedeno, of-4	.167	5	12	2	2	1	0	0	0	2	3	0
Jack Clark, 1b	.381	6	21	4	8	0	0	1	4	5	5	0
Vince Coleman, of	.286	3	14	2	4	0	0	0	1	0	2	1
Danny Cox, p	.000	1	2	0	0	0	0	0	0	1	1	0
Ken Dayley, p	.500	5	2	0	1	0	0	0	0	0	0	0
Bob Forsch, p	.000	1	0	0	0	0	0	0	0	0	0	0
Brian Harper, ph	.000	1	1	0	0	0	0	0	0	0	0	0
Tommy Herr, 2b	.333	6	21	2	7	4	0	1	6	5	2	1
Rick Horton, p	.000	3	0	0	0	0	0	0	0	0	0	0
Mike Jorgensen, ph	.000	2	2	0	0	0	0	0	0	0	1	0
Jeff Lahti, p	.000	2	0	0	0	0	0	0	0	0	0	0
Tito Landrum, of-4	.429	5	14	2	6	0	0	0	4	1	1	1
Willie Mc Gee, of	.269	6	26	6	7	1	0	0	3	3	6	2
Tom Nieto, c	.000	1	3	1	0	0	0	0	0	1	2	0
Terry Pendleton, 3b	.208	6	24	2	5	1	0	0	4	1	3	0
Darrell Porter, c	.267	5	15	1	4	1	0	0	0	5	4	0
Ozzie Smith, ss	.435	6	23	4	10	1	1	1	3	3	1	1
John Tudor, p	.000	2	4	1	0	0	0	0	0	1	1	0
Andy Van Slyke, of	.091	5	11	1	1	0	0	0	0	1	2	0
Todd Worrell, p	.000	4	0	0	0	0	0	0	0	0	0	0
TOTAL	.279		201	29	56	10	1	3	26	30	34	6

PITCHER	W	L	ERA	G	GS	CG	SV	SHO	IP	H	ER	BB	SO
Joaquin Andujar	0	1	6.97	2	2	0	0	0	10.1	14	8	4	9
Bill Campbell	0	0	0.00	3	0	0	0	0	2.1	3	0	0	2
Danny Cox	1	0	3.00	1	1	0	0	0	6.0	4	2	5	4
Ken Dayley	0	0	0.00	5	0	0	2	0	6.0	2	0	1	3
Bob Forsch	0	0	5.40	1	1	0	0	0	3.1	3	2	2	0
Rick Horton	0	0	9.00	3	0	0	0	0	3.0	4	3	2	1
Jeff Lahti	1	0	0.00	2	0	0	0	0	2.0	2	0	0	1
John Tudor	1	1	2.84	2	2	0	0	0	12.2	10	4	3	8
Todd Worrell	1	0	1.42	4	0	0	0	0	6.1	4	1	2	3
TOTAL	4	2	3.46	23	6	0	2	0	52.0	46	20	19	31

LA (W)

PLAYER/POS	AVG	G	AB	R	H	2B	3B	HR	RB	BB	SO	SB
Dave Anderson, ss-3,3b-1	.000	4	5	1	0	0	0	0	0	3	1	0
Bob Bailor, 3b	.000	2	1	0	0	0	0	0	0	0	0	0
Greg Brock, 1b-4	.083	5	12	2	1	0	0	1	2	2	2	0
Enos Cabell, 1b-3	.077	5	13	1	1	0	0	0	0	0	3	0
Bobby Castillo, p	.000	1	2	0	0	0	0	0	0	0	1	0
Carlos Diaz, p	.000	2	0	0	0	0	0	0	0	0	0	0
Mariano Duncan, ss	.222	5	18	2	4	2	1	0	1	1	3	1
Pedro Guerrero, of	.250	6	20	2	5	1	0	0	4	5	2	2
Orel Hershiser, p	.286	2	7	1	2	0	0	0	1	0	2	0
Rick Honeycutt, p	.000	2	0	0	0	0	0	0	0	0	0	0
Ken Howell, p	.000	1	0	0	0	0	0	0	0	0	0	0
Jay Johnstone, ph	.000	1	1	0	0	0	0	0	0	0	0	0
Ken Landreaux, of	.389	5	18	4	7	3	0	0	2	1	1	0
Bill Madlock, 3b	.333	6	24	5	8	1	0	3	7	0	2	1
Candy Maldonado, of-3	.143	4	7	0	1	0	0	0	0	1	3	0
Mike Marshall, of	.217	6	23	1	5	2	0	1	3	1	3	0
Len Matuszek, 1b-1,of-1	1.000	3	1	1	1	0	0	0	0	0	0	0
Tom Niedenfuer, p	.000	3	1	0	0	0	0	0	0	0	1	0
Jerry Reuss, p	.000	1	0	0	0	0	0	0	0	0	0	0
Steve Sax, 2b	.300	6	20	1	6	3	0	0	1	1	5	0
Mike Scioscia, c	.250	6	16	2	4	0	0	0	1	4	0	0
Fernando Valenzuela, p	.200	2	5	0	1	0	0	0	0	0	0	0
Bob Welch, p	.000	1	1	0	0	0	0	0	0	0	1	0
Terry Whitfield, ph	.000	1	0	0	0	0	0	0	0	0	0	0
Steve Yeager, c	.000	1	2	0	0	0	0	0	0	1	1	0
TOTAL	.234		197	23	46	12	1	5	23	19	31	4

PITCHER	W	L	ERA	G	GS	CG	SV	SHO	IP	H	ER	BB	SO
Bobby Castillo	0	0	3.38	1	0	0	0	0	5.1	4	2	2	4
Carlos Diaz	0	0	3.00	2	0	0	0	0	3.0	5	1	1	2
Orel Hershiser	1	0	3.52	2	2	1	0	0	15.1	17	6	6	5
Rick Honeycutt	0	0	13.50	2	0	0	0	0	1.1	4	2	2	1
Ken Howell	0	0	0.00	1	0	0	0	0	2.0	0	0	0	2
Tom Niedenfuer	0	2	6.35	3	0	0	1	0	5.2	5	4	2	5
Jerry Reuss	0	1	10.80	1	1	0	0	0	1.2	5	2	1	0
F. Valenzuela	1	0	1.88	2	2	0	0	0	14.1	11	3	10	13
Bob Welch	0	1	6.75	1	1	0	0	0	2.2	5	2	6	2
TOTAL	2	4	3.86	15	6	1	1	0	51.1	56	22	30	34

GAME 1 AT LA OCT 9

STL	000	000	100	1	8	1
LA	000	103	00X	4	8	0

Pitchers: TUDOR, Dayley (6), Campbell (7), Worrell (8) vs VALENZUELA, Niedenfuer (7)
Attendance: 55,270

GAME 2 AT LA OCT 10

STL	001	000	001	2	8	1
LA	003	212	00X	8	13	1

Pitchers: ANDUJAR, Horton (5), Campbell (6), Dayley (7), Lahti (8) vs HERSHISER
Home Runs: Brock-LA
Attendance: 55,222

GAME 3 AT STL OCT 12

LA	000	100	100	2	7	2
STL	220	000	00X	4	8	0

Pitchers: WELCH, Honeycutt (3), Diaz (5), Howell (7) vs COX, Horton (7), Worrell (7), Dayley (9)
Home Runs: Herr-STL
Attendance: 53,708

GAME 4 AT STL OCT 13

LA	000	000	110	2	5	2
STL	090	110	01X	12	15	0

Pitchers: REUSS, Honeycutt (2), Castillo (2), Diaz (8) vs TUDOR, Horton (8), Campbell (9)
Home Runs: Madlock-LA
Attendance: 53,708

GAME 5 AT STL OCT 14

LA	000	200	000	2	5	1
STL	200	000	001	3	5	1

Pitchers: Valenzuela, NIEDENFUER (9) vs Forsch, Dayley (4), Worrell (7), LAHTI (9)
Home Runs: Madlock-LA, Smith-STL
Attendance: 53,708

GAME 6 AT LA OCT 16

STL	001	000	303	7	12	1
LA	110	020	010	5	8	0

Pitchers: Andujar, WORRELL (7), Dayley (9) vs Hershiser, NIEDENFUER (7)
Home Runs: Madlock-LA, Marshall-LA, Clark-STL
Attendance: 55,208

Were it not for the expansion of the LCS to a best-of-seven series, the Blue Jays would have won the pennant. But after winning three of the first four games, the Jays lost their steam and K.C. swept to their second pennant.

The pitching of Toronto ace Dave Stieb proved a key to the club's fortunes. Three times he started for the Jays. In the opener he threw eight shutout innings as the Jays won easily. In Game Four he continued to dominate batters, though three walks in the sixth helped the Royals score a go-ahead run before Toronto pulled it out (for reliever Tom Henke) with a three-run ninth. Had the series ended there, Stieb would have been a hero. But it didn't, and he was called upon again for Game Seven—perhaps with inadequate rest. This time he faltered. After giving up single runs in the second and fourth innings, he loaded the bases in the sixth with two walks and a hit batsman. Jim Sundberg unloaded them with a wind-blown triple, later scoring himself, and the Royals were on the road to victory.

George Brett keyed Kansas City's triumph. His four hits in Game Three (including two home runs) gave the club its first victory, and his RBI ground out in Game Five and go-ahead homer in Game Six proved game-winners in contests the Royals had to win.

Kansas City Royals (West), 4;
Toronto Blue Jays (East), 3

KC (W)

PLAYER/POS	AVG	G	AB	R	H	2B	3B	HR	RB	BB	SO	SB
Steve Balboni, 1b	.120	7	25	1	3	0	0	0	1	2	8	0
Buddy Biancalana, ss	.222	7	18	2	4	1	0	0	1	1	6	0
Bud Black, p	.000	3	0	0	0	0	0	0	0	0	0	0
George Brett, 3b	.348	7	23	6	8	2	0	3	5	7	5	0
Onix Concepcion, ss	.000	4	1	0	0	0	0	0	0	0	0	0
Steve Farr, p	.000	2	0	0	0	0	0	0	0	0	0	0
Mark Gubicza, p	.000	2	0	0	0	0	0	0	0	0	0	0
Dane Iorg, ph	.500	4	2	0	1	1	0	0	0	2	0	0
Danny Jackson, p	.000	2	0	0	0	0	0	0	0	0	0	0
Lynn Jones, of	.000	5	0	0	0	0	0	0	0	0	0	0
Charlie Leibrandt, p	.000	3	0	0	0	0	0	0	0	0	0	0
Hal Mc Rae, dh	.261	6	23	1	6	2	0	0	3	1	6	0
Darryl Motley, of	.333	2	3	1	1	0	0	0	1	1	2	0
Jorge Orta, dh-1	.000	2	5	0	0	0	0	0	0	0	1	0
Jamie Quirk, ph	.000	1	1	0	0	0	0	0	0	0	0	0
Dan Quisenberry, p	.000	4	0	0	0	0	0	0	0	0	0	0
Bret Saberhagen, p	.000	2	0	0	0	0	0	0	0	0	0	0
Pat Sheridan, of	.150	7	20	4	3	0	0	2	3	2	3	0
Lonnie Smith, of	.250	7	28	2	7	2	0	0	1	3	6	1
Jim Sundberg, c	.167	7	24	3	4	1	1	1	6	1	7	0
Frank White, 2b	.200	7	25	1	5	0	0	0	3	1	2	0
Willie Wilson, of	.310	7	29	5	9	0	0	1	2	1	5	1
TOTAL	.225		227	26	51	9	1	7	26	22	51	2

PITCHER	W	L	ERA	G	GS	CG	SV	SHO	IP	H	ER	BB	SO
Bud Black	0	0	1.69	3	1	0	0	0	10.2	11	2	4	8
Steve Farr	1	0	1.42	2	0	0	0	0	6.1	4	1	1	3
Mark Gubicza	1	0	3.24	2	1	0	0	0	8.1	4	3	4	4
Danny Jackson	1	0	0.00	2	1	1	0	1	10.0	10	0	1	7
Charlie Leibrandt	1	2	5.28	3	2	0	0	0	15.1	17	9	4	6
Dan Quisenberry	0	1	3.86	4	0	0	1	0	4.2	7	2	0	3
Bret Saberhagen	0	0	6.14	2	2	0	0	0	7.1	12	5	2	6
TOTAL	4	3	3.16	18	7	1	1	1	62.2	65	22	16	37

TOR (E)

PLAYER/POS	AVG	G	AB	R	H	2B	3B	HR	RB	BB	SO	SB
Jim Acker, p	.000	2	0	0	0	0	0	0	0	0	0	0
Doyle Alexander, p	.000	2	0	0	0	0	0	0	0	0	0	0
Jesse Barfield, of	.280	7	25	3	7	1	0	1	4	3	7	1
George Bell, of	.321	7	28	4	9	3	0	0	1	0	4	0
Jeff Burroughs, ph	.000	1	1	0	0	0	0	0	0	0	0	0
Jim Clancy, p	.000	1	0	0	0	0	0	0	0	0	0	0
Tony Fernandez, ss	.333	7	24	2	8	2	0	0	2	1	2	0
Cecil Fielder, ph	.333	3	3	0	1	1	0	0	0	0	1	0
Damaso Garcia, 2b	.233	7	30	4	7	4	0	0	1	3	3	0
Jeff Hearron, c	.000	2	0	0	0	0	0	0	0	0	0	0
Tom Henke, p	.000	3	0	0	0	0	0	0	0	0	0	0
Garth Iorg, 3b	.133	6	15	1	2	0	0	0	0	1	3	0
Cliff Johnson, dh	.368	7	19	1	7	2	0	0	2	1	4	0
Jimmy Key, p	.000	2	0	0	0	0	0	0	0	0	0	0
Dennis Lamp, p	.000	3	0	0	0	0	0	0	0	0	0	0
Gary Lavelle, p	.000	1	0	0	0	0	0	0	0	0	0	0
Manny Lee, 2b	.000	1	0	0	0	0	0	0	0	0	0	0
Lloyd Moseby, of	.226	7	31	5	7	1	0	0	4	2	3	1
Rance Mulliniks, 3b	.364	5	11	1	4	1	0	1	3	2	2	0
Al Oliver, dh	.375	5	8	0	3	1	0	0	3	0	0	0
Dave Stieb, p	.000	3	0	0	0	0	0	0	0	0	0	0
Lou Thornton, pr	.000	2	0	1	0	0	0	0	0	0	0	0
Willie Upshaw, 1b	.231	7	26	2	6	2	0	0	1	1	4	0
Ernie Whitt, c	.190	7	21	1	4	1	0	0	2	2	4	0
TOTAL	.269		242	25	65	19	0	2	23	16	37	2

PITCHER	W	L	ERA	G	GS	CG	SV	SHO	IP	H	ER	BB	SO
Jim Acker	0	0	0.00	2	0	0	0	0	6.0	2	0	0	5
Doyle Alexander	0	1	8.71	2	2	0	0	0	10.1	14	10	3	9
Jim Clancy	0	1	9.00	1	0	0	0	0	1.0	2	1	1	0
Tom Henke	2	0	4.26	3	0	0	0	0	6.1	5	3	4	4
Jimmy Key	0	1	5.19	2	2	0	0	0	8.2	15	5	2	5
Dennis Lamp	0	0	0.00	3	0	0	0	0	9.1	2	0	1	10
Gary Lavelle	0	0	INF	1	0	0	0	0	0.0	0	0	1	0
Dave Stieb	1	1	3.10	3	3	0	0	0	20.1	11	7	10	18
TOTAL	3	4	3.77	17	7	0	0	0	62.0	51	26	22	51

GAME 1 AT TOR OCT 8

KC	000	000	001	1	5	1
TOR	023	100	00X	6	11	0

Pitchers: LEIBRANDT, Farr (3), Gubicza (5), Jackson (8) vs STIEB, Henke (9)
Attendance: 39,115

GAME 2 AT TOR OCT 9

KC	002	100	001	1	5	10	3
TOR	000	102	010	2	6	10	0

Pitchers: Black, QUISENBERRY (8) vs Key, Lamp (4), Lavelle (8), HENKE (8)
Home Runs: Wilson-KC, Sheridan-KC
Attendance: 34,029

GAME 3 AT KC OCT 11

TOR	000	050	000	5	13	1
KC	100	124	00X	6	10	1

Pitchers: Alexander, Lamp (6), CLANCY (8) vs Saberhagen, Black (5), FARR (5)
Home Runs: Brett-KC (2), Barfield-TOR, Mulliniks-TOR, Sundberg-KC
Attendance: 40,224

GAME 4 AT KC OCT 12

TOR	000	000	003	3	7	0
KC	000	001	000	1	2	0

Pitchers: Stieb, HENKE (7) vs LEIBRANDT, Quisenberry (9)
Attendance: 41,112

GAME 5 AT KC OCT 13

TOR	000	000	000	0	8	0
KC	110	000	00X	2	8	0

Pitchers: KEY, Acker (6) vs JACKSON
Attendance: 40,046

GAME 6 AT TOR OCT 15

KC	101	012	000	5	8	1
TOR	101	001	000	3	8	2

Pitchers: GUBICZA, Black (6), Quisenberry (9) vs ALEXANDER, Lamp (6)
Home Runs: Brett-KC
Attendance: 37,557

GAME 7 AT TOR OCT 16

KC	010	104	000	6	8	0
TOR	000	010	001	2	8	1

Pitchers: Saberhagen, LEIBRANDT (4), Quisenberry (9) vs STIEB, Acker (6)
Home Runs: Sheridan-KC
Attendance: 32,084

The underdog Royals surprised St. Louis with superior hitting and pitching, and even outstole the speedy Cards six bases to two. Still, had an umpire not muffed a call at first base in Game Six, St. Louis might have emerged from the fray wearing the world crown.

The Cardinals broke a 1–1 tie in the fourth inning of the opener with back-to-back doubles off Royal starter Danny Jackson, and held on behind the strong pitching of John Tudor and reliever Todd Worrell for a 3–1 win. In Game Two, except for the fourth inning, when he yielded a single and two doubles (for two runs) before retiring his first batter, Cardinal starter Danny Cox held the Royals in check. Royal starter Charlie Leibrandt hurled even more effectively, holding St. Louis to two hits—until the ninth inning, when four Cardinal hits (three of them doubles) produced four runs and a second Card victory.

Kansas City finally demonstrated its punch in Game Three. Frank White hit a two-run homer in the fifth, and the Royals scored four more times to win behind the six-hit hurling of sophomore sensation Bret Saberhagen. The next day, though, Royal bats died again against John Tudor, who shut them out on five hits. Three Royal pitchers yielded only six hits to Cardinal batters, but two were home runs to Tito Landrum and Willie McGee, and one was a triple to Terry Pendleton, who scored on a sacrifice squeeze.

Down three games to one, the Royals hammered eleven hits in Game Five for six runs to win behind Danny Jackson's five-hitter. Seven Royal hits in the first eight innings of Game Six, though, scored no runs against Cardinal starter Danny Cox and reliever Ken Dayley. But in the last of the ninth, with the Cards ahead 1–0 and Todd Worrell now pitching, Royal pinch hitter Jorge Orta was ruled safe at first on what the cameras showed clearly as an out. This miscall, followed by a pop foul that first baseman Jack Clark should have caught but didn't, opened the door to Cardinal disintegration. A single and passed ball put Royals at second and third, and after an intentional walk to set up the double play, pinch hitter Dane Iorg singled home the tying and winning Royal runs.

The Cardinals threw seven pitchers at Kansas City in the finale in a vain attempt to halt the Royals' fourteen-hit, eleven-run attack, while Bret Saberhagen stopped the Cards cold on five hits to bring the Royals their first world title.

Kansas City Royals (AL), 4;
St. Louis Cardinals (NL), 3

KC (A)

PLAYER/POS	AVG	G	AB	R	H	2B	3B	HR	RB	BB	SO	SB
Steve Balboni, 1b	.320	7	25	2	8	0	0	0	3	5	4	0
Joe Beckwith, p	.000	1	0	0	0	0	0	0	0	0	0	0
Buddy Biancalana, ss	.278	7	18	2	5	0	0	0	2	5	4	0
Bud Black, p	.000	2	1	0	0	0	0	0	0	0	1	0
George Brett, 3b	.370	7	27	5	10	1	0	0	1	4	7	1
Onix Concepcion, ss-2	.000	3	0	1	0	0	0	0	0	0	0	0
Dane Iorg, ph	.500	2	2	0	1	0	0	0	2	0	0	0
Danny Jackson, p	.000	2	6	0	0	0	0	0	0	0	5	0
Lynn Jones, of-4	.667	6	3	0	2	1	1	0	0	0	0	0
Charlie Leibrandt, p	.000	2	4	0	0	0	0	0	0	0	2	0
Hal Mc Rae, ph	.000	3	1	0	0	0	0	0	0	1	0	0
Darryl Motley, of-4	.364	5	11	1	4	0	0	1	3	0	1	0
Jorge Orta, ph	.333	3	3	0	1	0	0	0	0	0	0	0
Greg Pryor, 3b	.000	1	0	0	0	0	0	0	0	0	0	0
Dan Quisenberry, p	.000	4	0	0	0	0	0	0	0	0	0	0
Bret Saberhagen, p	.000	2	7	1	0	0	0	0	0	0	4	0
Pat Sheridan, of-4	.222	5	18	0	4	2	0	0	1	0	7	0
Lonnie Smith, of	.333	7	27	4	9	3	0	0	4	3	8	2
Jim Sundberg, c	.250	7	24	6	6	2	0	0	1	6	4	0
John Wathan, ph	.000	2	1	0	0	0	0	0	0	0	1	0
Frank White, 2b	.250	7	28	4	7	3	0	1	6	3	4	0
Willie Wilson, of	.367	7	30	2	11	0	1	0	3	1	4	3
TOTAL	.288		236	28	68	12	2	2	26	28	56	6

PITCHER	W	L	ERA	G	GS	CG	SV	SHO	IP	H	ER	BB	SO
Joe Beckwith	0	0	0.00	1	0	0	0	0	2.0	1	0	0	3
Bud Black	0	1	5.06	2	1	0	0	0	5.1	4	3	5	4
Danny Jackson	1	1	1.69	2	2	1	0	0	16.0	9	3	5	12
Charlie Leibrandt	0	1	2.76	2	2	0	0	0	16.1	10	5	4	10
Dan Quisenberry	1	0	2.08	4	0	0	0	0	4.1	5	1	3	3
Bret Saberhagen	2	0	0.50	2	2	2	0	1	18.0	11	1	1	10
TOTAL	4	3	1.89	13	7	3	0	1	62.0	40	13	18	42

STL (N)

PLAYER/POS	AVG	G	AB	R	H	2B	3B	HR	RB	BB	SO	SB
Joaquin Andujar, p	.000	2	1	0	0	0	0	0	0	0	1	0
Steve Braun, ph	.000	1	1	0	0	0	0	0	0	0	0	0
Bill Campbell, p	.000	3	0	0	0	0	0	0	0	0	0	0
Cesar Cedeno, of	.133	5	15	1	2	1	0	0	1	2	2	0
Jack Clark, 1b	.240	7	25	1	6	2	0	0	4	3	9	0
Danny Cox, p	.000	2	4	0	0	0	0	0	0	0	2	0
Ken Dayley, p	.000	4	0	0	0	0	0	0	0	0	0	0
Ivan De Jesus, ph	.000	1	1	0	0	0	0	0	0	0	0	0
Bob Forsch, p	.000	2	0	0	0	0	0	0	0	0	0	0
Brian Harper, ph	.250	4	4	0	1	0	0	0	1	0	1	0
Tommy Herr, 2b	.154	7	26	2	4	2	0	0	0	2	2	0
Rick Horton, p	.000	3	1	0	0	0	0	0	0	0	1	0
Mike Jorgensen, of-1	.000	2	3	0	0	0	0	0	0	0	0	0
Jeff Lahti, p	.000	3	0	0	0	0	0	0	0	0	0	0
Tito Landrum, of	.360	7	25	3	9	2	0	1	1	0	2	0
Tom Lawless, pr	.000	1	0	0	0	0	0	0	0	0	0	0
Willie Mc Gee, of	.259	7	27	2	7	2	0	1	2	1	3	1
Tom Nieto, c	.000	2	5	0	0	0	0	0	1	1	2	0
Terry Pendleton, 3b	.261	7	23	3	6	1	1	0	3	3	2	0
Darrell Porter, c	.133	5	15	0	2	0	0	0	0	2	5	0
Ozzie Smith, ss	.087	7	23	1	2	0	0	0	0	4	0	1
John Tudor, p	.000	3	5	0	0	0	0	0	0	0	4	0
Andy Van Slyke, of	.091	6	11	0	1	0	0	0	0	0	5	0
Todd Worrell, p	.000	3	1	0	0	0	0	0	0	0	1	0
TOTAL	.185		216	13	40	10	1	2	13	18	42	2

PITCHER	W	L	ERA	G	GS	CG	SV	SHO	IP	H	ER	BB	SO
Joaquin Andujar	0	1	9.00	2	1	0	0	0	4.0	10	4	4	3
Bill Campbell	0	0	2.25	3	0	0	0	0	4.0	4	1	2	5
Danny Cox	0	0	1.29	2	2	0	0	0	14.0	14	2	4	13
Ken Dayley	1	0	0.00	4	0	0	0	0	6.0	1	0	3	5
Bob Forsch	0	1	12.00	2	1	0	0	0	3.0	6	4	1	3
Rick Horton	0	0	6.75	3	0	0	0	0	4.0	4	3	5	5
Jeff Lahti	0	0	12.27	3	0	0	0	1	3.2	10	5	0	2
John Tudor	2	1	3.00	3	3	1	0	1	18.0	15	6	7	14
Todd Worrell	0	1	3.86	3	0	0	1	0	4.2	4	2	2	6
TOTAL	3	4	3.96	25	7	1	2	1	61.1	68	27	28	56

GAME 1 AT KC OCT 19

STL	001 100 001	3	7	1
KC	010 000 000	1	8	0

Pitchers: TUDOR, Worrell (7) vs JACKSON, Quisenberry (8), Black (9)
Attendance: 41,650

GAME 2 AT KC OCT 20

STL	000 000 004	4	6	0
KC	000 200 000	2	9	0

Pitchers: Cox, DAYLEY (8), Lahti (9) vs LEIBRANDT, Quisenberry (9)
Attendance: 41,656

GAME 3 AT STL OCT 22

KC	000 220 200	6	11	0
STL	000 000 001	1	6	0

Pitchers: SABERHAGEN vs ANDUJAR, Campbell (5), Horton (6), Dayley (8)
Home Runs: White-KC
Attendance: 53,634

GAME 4 AT STL OCT 23

KC	000 000 000	0	5	1
STL	011 010 00X	3	6	0

Pitchers: BLACK, Beckwith (6), Quisenberry (8) vs TUDOR
Home Runs: Landrum-STL, McGee-STL
Attendance: 53,634

GAME 5 AT STL OCT 24

KC	130 000 011	6	11	2
STL	100 000 000	1	5	1

Pitchers: JACKSON vs FORSCH, Horton (2), Campbell (4), Worrell (6), Lahti (8)
Attendance: 53,634

GAME 6 AT KC OCT 26

STL	000 000 010	1	5	0
KC	000 000 002	2	10	0

Pitchers: Cox, Dayley (8), WORRELL (9) vs Leibrandt, QUISENBERRY (8)
Attendance: 41,628

GAME 7 AT KC OCT 27

STL	000 000 000	0	5	0
KC	023 060 00X	11	14	0

Pitchers: TUDOR, Campbell (3), Lahti (5), Horton (5), Andujar (5), Forsch (5), Dayley (7) vs SABERHAGEN
Home Runs: Motley-KC
Attendance: 41,658

Houston pitcher Mike Scott overwhelmed the Mets in Games One and Four, and would have faced them a third time in Game Seven if the Astros had won Game Six. They tried, scoring three runs in the first as Bob Knepper shut out the Mets on two hits through eight innings. But in the top of the ninth New York tied the game and held on into extra innings. No one scored again until the Mets put a run across in the fourteenth. Astro Billy Hatcher tied it up again later in the fourteenth with a home run just inside the left field foul pole. Two innings later the Mets (aided by a pair of wild pitches) scored three runs. Again the Astros came back, scoring twice, but fell just short as Jesse Orosco struck out Kevin Bass with two men on base to win his third game of the series and give New York the pennant.

In the series opener Houston scored just one run off Dwight Gooden, but it was enough, as Mike Scott, fanning fourteen, shut out the Mets on five hits. New York came back with five runs in Game Two to win behind Bob Ojeda, who gave up ten hits but only one run. In Game Three the Astros held the lead into the last of the sixth, when New York tied the score with four runs. Houston retook the lead in the seventh with a run, but Met Len Dykstra won it for New York with a two-run homer in the bottom of the ninth.

The Astros' win in Game Four evened the series. Houston had scored three runs by the time Scott (on his way to a three-hitter) gave the Mets their only run in the eighth. Houston's Nolan Ryan gave up only two hits in the first nine innings of Game Five (one of them Darryl Strawberry's game-tying solo homer in the fifth), striking out twelve. But New York's Gooden also yielded only one run in ten innings of work. Astro Charlie Kerfeld shut out the Mets in the tenth and eleventh, and the Mets' Orosco stopped Houston in the eleventh and twelfth. But in the last of the twelfth, Met catcher Gary Carter singled home a run off Kerfeld to end the game (and his series-long batting slump)—setting the stage for the sixteen-inning marathon the next day.

New York Mets (East), 4; Houston Astros (West), 2

NY (E)

PLAYER/POS	AVG	G	AB	R	H	2B	3B	HR	RB	BB	SO	SB
Rick Aguilera, p	.000	2	0	0	0	0	0	0	0	0	0	0
Wally Backman, 2b	.238	6	21	5	5	0	0	0	2	2	4	1
Gary Carter, c	.148	6	27	1	4	1	0	0	2	2	5	0
Ron Darling, p	.000	1	1	0	0	0	0	0	0	0	0	0
Lenny Dykstra, of	.304	6	23	3	7	1	1	1	3	2	4	1
Kevin Elster, ss	.000	4	3	0	0	0	0	0	0	0	1	0
Sid Fernandez, p	.000	1	1	0	0	0	0	0	0	0	0	0
Dwight Gooden, p	.000	2	5	0	0	0	0	0	0	0	2	0
Danny Heep, of-1	.250	5	4	0	1	0	0	0	1	0	2	0
Keith Hernandez, 1b	.269	6	26	3	7	1	1	0	3	3	6	0
Howard Johnson, ph	.000	2	2	0	0	0	0	0	0	0	0	0
Ray Knight, 3b	.167	6	24	1	4	0	0	0	2	1	5	0
Lee Mazzilli, ph	.200	5	5	0	1	0	0	0	0	0	3	0
Roger Mc Dowell, p	.000	2	1	0	0	0	0	0	0	0	0	0
Kevin Mitchell, of	.250	2	8	1	2	0	0	0	0	0	1	0
Bob Ojeda, p	.000	2	5	1	0	0	0	0	0	0	2	0
Jesse Orosco, p	.000	4	0	0	0	0	0	0	0	0	0	0
Rafael Santana, ss	.176	6	17	0	3	0	0	0	0	0	3	0
Doug Sisk, p	.000	1	0	0	0	0	0	0	0	0	0	0
Darryl Strawberry, of	.227	6	22	4	5	1	0	2	5	3	12	1
Tim Teufel, 2b	.167	2	6	0	1	0	0	0	0	0	0	0
Mookie Wilson, of	.115	6	26	2	3	0	0	0	1	1	7	1
TOTAL	.189		227	21	43	4	2	3	19	14	57	4

PITCHER	W	L	ERA	G	GS	CG	SV	SHO	IP	H	ER	BB	SO
Rick Aguilera	0	0	0.00	2	0	0	0	0	5.0	2	0	2	2
Ron Darling	0	0	7.20	1	1	0	0	0	5.0	6	4	2	5
Sid Fernandez	0	1	4.50	1	1	0	0	0	6.0	3	3	1	5
Dwight Gooden	0	1	1.06	2	2	0	0	0	17.0	16	2	5	9
Roger Mc Dowell	0	0	0.00	2	0	0	0	0	7.0	1	0	0	3
Bob Ojeda	1	0	2.57	2	2	1	0	0	14.0	15	4	4	6
Jesse Orosco	3	0	3.38	4	0	0	0	0	8.0	5	3	2	10
Doug Sisk	0	0	0.00	1	0	0	0	0	1.0	1	0	1	0
TOTAL	4	2	2.29	15	6	1	0	0	63.0	49	16	17	40

HOU (W)

PLAYER/POS	AVG	G	AB	R	H	2B	3B	HR	RB	BB	SO	SB
Larry Andersen, p	.000	2	0	0	0	0	0	0	0	0	0	0
Alan Ashby, c	.130	6	23	2	3	1	0	1	2	2	1	0
Kevin Bass, of	.292	6	24	0	7	2	0	0	4	4	4	2
Jeff Calhoun, p	.000	1	0	0	0	0	0	0	0	0	0	0
Jose Cruz, of	.192	6	26	0	5	0	0	0	2	1	8	0
Glenn Davis, 1b	.269	6	26	3	7	1	0	1	3	1	3	0
Bill Doran, 2b	.222	6	27	3	6	0	0	1	3	2	2	2
Phil Garner, 3b	.222	3	9	1	2	1	0	0	2	1	2	0
Billy Hatcher, of	.280	6	25	4	7	0	0	1	2	3	2	3
Charlie Kerfeld, p	.000	3	0	0	0	0	0	0	0	0	0	0
Bob Knepper, p	.000	2	5	0	0	0	0	0	0	1	2	0
Davey Lopes, ph	.000	3	2	1	0	0	0	0	0	1	0	0
Aurelio Lopez, p	.000	2	0	0	0	0	0	0	0	0	0	0
Jim Pankovits, ph	.000	2	2	0	0	0	0	0	0	0	1	0
Terry Puhl, ph	.667	3	3	0	2	0	0	0	0	0	0	1
Craig Reynolds, ss	.333	4	12	1	4	0	0	0	0	1	3	0
Nolan Ryan, p	.000	2	4	0	0	0	0	0	0	0	2	0
Mike Scott, p	.000	2	6	0	0	0	0	0	0	0	5	0
Dave Smith, p	.000	2	0	0	0	0	0	0	0	0	0	0
Dickie Thon, ss	.250	6	12	1	3	0	0	1	1	0	1	0
Denny Walling, 3b	.158	5	19	1	3	1	0	0	2	0	4	0
TOTAL	.218		225	17	49	6	0	5	17	17	40	8

PITCHER	W	L	ERA	G	GS	CG	SV	SHO	IP	H	ER	BB	SO
Larry Andersen	0	0	0.00	2	0	0	0	0	5.0	1	0	2	3
Jeff Calhoun	0	0	9.00	1	0	0	0	0	1.0	1	1	1	0
Charlie Kerfeld	0	1	2.25	3	0	0	0	0	4.0	2	1	1	4
Bob Knepper	0	0	3.52	2	2	0	0	0	15.1	13	6	1	9
Aurelio Lopez	0	1	8.10	2	0	0	0	0	3.1	7	3	4	3
Nolan Ryan	0	1	3.86	2	2	0	0	0	14.0	9	6	1	17
Mike Scott	2	0	0.50	2	2	2	0	1	18.0	8	1	1	19
Dave Smith	0	1	9.00	2	0	0	0	0	2.0	2	2	3	2
TOTAL	2	4	2.87	16	6	2	0	1	62.2	43	20	14	57

GAME 1 AT HOU OCT 8

NY	000	000	000	0	5	0
HOU	010	000	00X	1	7	1

Pitchers: GOODEN, Orosco (8) vs SCOTT
Home Runs: Davis-HOU
Attendance: 44,131

GAME 2 AT HOU OCT 9

NY	000	230	000	5	10	0
HOU	000	000	100	1	10	2

Pitchers: OJEDA vs RYAN, Andersen, Lopez (8), Kerfeld (9)
Attendance: 44,391

GAME 3 AT NY OCT 11

HOU	220	000	100	5	8	1
NY	000	004	002	6	10	1

Pitchers: Knepper, Kerfeld (8), SMITH (9) vs Darling, Aguilera (6), OROSCO (8)
Home Runs: Doran-HOU, Strawberry-NY, Dykstra-NY
Attendance: 55,052

GAME 4 AT NY OCT 12

HOU	020	010	000	3	4	1
NY	000	000	010	1	3	0

Pitchers: SCOTT vs FERNANDEZ, McDowell (7), Sisk (9)
Home Runs: Ashby-HOU, Thon-HOU
Attendance: 55,038

GAME 5 AT NY OCT 14

HOU	000	010	000	000	1	9	1
NY	000	010	000	001	2	4	0

Pitchers: Ryan, KERFELD (10) vs Gooden, OROSCO (11)
Home Runs: Strawberry-NY
Attendance: 54,986

GAME 6 AT HOU OCT 15

NY	000 000 003 000 010	3	7	11	0
HOU	300 000 000 000 010	2	6	11	1

Pitchers: Ojeda, Aguilera (6), McDowell (9), OROSCO (14) vs Knepper, Smith (9), Andersen (11), LOPEZ (14), Calhoun (16)
Home Runs: Hatcher-HOU
Attendance: 45,718

For the second time in the two years of the expanded LCS, a club that would have been eliminated in a five-game series came back to take the pennant in seven games. The first two games were one-sided. California scored five early runs off Roger Clemens and breezed to an easy 8–1 win in the opener. Boston retaliated in Game Two with nine runs, breaking the game open with six unanswered runs in the seventh and eighth innings.

Game Three was close until the Angels homered twice for three runs with two out in the seventh to break a 1–1 tie. In Game Four, the Angels were handed a tie in the last of the ninth when Boston reliever Calvin Schiraldi hit a batter with the bases loaded and won in the eleventh on Bobby Grich's RBI single.

The Red Sox, down three games to one, were on the brink of elimination in Game Five, with two out in the ninth, when Dave Henderson, after fouling off one third-strike pitch, hit the next for a two-run homer that gave Boston a one-run lead. The Angels tied the game in the last of the ninth, but Henderson's sacrifice fly in the eleventh put the Sox ahead for good.

Boston needed two more wins and got them with surprising ease, 10–4 and 8–1, as Oil Can Boyd and Clemens redeemed their earlier losses.

Boston Red Sox (East), 4; California Angels (West), 3

BOS (E)

PLAYER/POS	AVG	G	AB	R	H	2B	3B	HR	RB	BB	SO	SB
Tony Armas, of	.125	5	16	1	2	1	0	0	0	0	2	0
Marty Barrett, 2b	.367	7	30	4	11	2	0	0	5	2	2	0
Don Baylor, dh	.346	7	26	6	9	3	0	1	2	4	5	0
Wade Boggs, 3b	.233	7	30	3	7	1	1	0	2	4	1	0
Oil Can Boyd, p	.000	2	0	0	0	0	0	0	0	0	0	0
Bill Buckner, 1b	.214	7	28	3	6	1	0	0	3	0	2	0
Roger Clemens, p	.000	3	0	0	0	0	0	0	0	0	0	0
Steve Crawford, p	.000	1	0	0	0	0	0	0	0	0	0	0
Dwight Evans, of	.214	7	28	2	6	1	0	1	4	3	3	0
Rich Gedman, c	.357	7	28	4	10	1	0	1	6	0	4	0
Mike Greenwell, ph	.500	2	2	0	1	0	0	0	0	0	0	0
Dave Henderson, of	.111	5	9	3	1	0	0	1	4	2	2	0
Bruce Hurst, p	.000	2	0	0	0	0	0	0	0	0	0	0
Spike Owen, ss	.429	7	21	5	9	0	1	0	3	2	2	1
Jim Rice, of	.161	7	31	8	5	1	0	2	6	1	8	0
Ed Romero, ss	.000	1	2	0	0	0	0	0	0	0	0	0
Joe Sambito, p	.000	3	0	0	0	0	0	0	0	0	0	0
Calvin Schiraldi, p	.000	4	0	0	0	0	0	0	0	0	0	0
Bob Stanley, p	.000	3	0	0	0	0	0	0	0	0	0	0
Dave Stapleton, 1b	.667	4	3	2	2	0	0	0	0	1	0	0
TOTAL	.272		254	41	69	11	2	6	35	19	31	1

PITCHER	W	L	ERA	G	GS	CG	SV	SHO	IP	H	ER	BB	SO
Oil Can Boyd	1	1	4.61	2	2	0	0	0	13.2	17	7	3	8
Roger Clemens	1	1	4.37	3	3	0	0	0	22.2	22	11	7	17
Steve Crawford	1	0	0.00	1	0	0	0	0	1.2	1	0	2	1
Bruce Hurst	1	0	2.40	2	2	1	0	0	15.0	18	4	1	8
Joe Sambito	0	0	13.50	3	0	0	0	0	0.2	1	1	1	2
Calvin Schiraldi	0	1	1.50	4	0	0	1	0	6.0	5	1	3	9
Bob Stanley	0	0	3.18	3	0	0	0	0	5.2	7	2	3	1
TOTAL	4	3	3.58	18	7	1	1	0	65.1	71	26	20	44

CAL (W)

PLAYER/POS	AVG	G	AB	R	H	2B	3B	HR	RB	BB	SO	SB
Bob Boone, c	.455	7	22	4	10	0	0	1	2	1	3	0
Rick Burleson, 2b-2,dh-1	.273	4	11	0	3	0	0	0	0	0	0	0
John Candelaria, p	.000	2	0	0	0	0	0	0	0	0	0	0
Doug Corbett, p	.000	3	0	0	0	0	0	0	0	0	0	0
Doug De Cinces, 3b	.281	7	32	2	9	3	0	1	3	0	2	0
Brian Downing, of	.222	7	27	2	6	0	0	1	7	4	5	0
Chuck Finley, p	.000	3	0	0	0	0	0	0	0	0	0	0
Bobby Grich, 2b-3,1b-3	.208	6	24	1	5	0	0	1	3	0	8	0
George Hendrick, of-2,1b-1	.083	3	12	0	1	0	0	0	0	0	2	0
Jack Howell, ph	.000	2	1	0	0	0	0	0	0	1	1	0
Reggie Jackson, dh	.192	6	26	2	5	2	0	0	2	2	7	0
Ruppert Jones, of-5	.176	6	17	4	3	1	0	0	2	5	2	0
Wally Joyner, 1b	.455	3	11	3	5	2	0	1	2	2	0	0
Gary Lucas, p	.000	4	0	0	0	0	0	0	0	0	0	0
Kirk Mc Caskill, p	.000	2	0	0	0	0	0	0	0	0	0	0
Donnie Moore, p	.000	3	0	0	0	0	0	0	0	0	0	0
Jerry Narron, c-3	.500	4	2	1	1	0	0	0	0	1	1	0
Gary Pettis, of	.346	7	26	4	9	1	0	1	4	3	5	0
Vern Ruhle, p	.000	1	0	0	0	0	0	0	0	0	0	0
Dick Schofield, ss	.300	7	30	4	9	1	0	1	2	1	5	1
Don Sutton, p	.000	2	0	0	0	0	0	0	0	0	0	0
Devon White, of-3	.500	4	2	2	1	0	0	0	0	0	1	0
Rob Wilfong, 2b	.308	4	13	1	4	1	0	0	2	0	2	0
Mike Witt, p	.000	2	0	0	0	0	0	0	0	0	0	0
TOTAL	.277		256	30	71	11	0	7	29	20	44	1

PITCHER	W	L	ERA	G	GS	CG	SV	SHO	IP	H	ER	BB	SO
John Candelaria	1	1	0.84	2	2	0	0	0	10.2	11	1	6	7
Doug Corbett	1	0	5.40	3	0	0	0	0	6.2	9	4	2	2
Chuck Finley	0	0	0.00	3	0	0	0	0	2.0	1	0	0	1
Gary Lucas	0	0	11.57	4	0	0	0	0	2.1	3	3	1	2
Kirk Mc Caskill	0	2	7.71	2	2	0	0	0	9.1	16	8	5	7
Donnie Moore	0	1	7.20	3	0	0	1	0	5.0	8	4	2	0
Vern Ruhle	0	0	13.50	1	0	0	0	0	0.2	2	1	0	0
Don Sutton	0	0	1.86	2	2	0	0	0	9.2	6	2	1	4
Mike Witt	1	0	2.55	2	2	1	0	0	17.2	13	5	2	8
TOTAL	3	4	3.94	22	7	1	1	0	64.0	69	28	19	31

GAME 1 AT BOS OCT 7

CAL	041	000	030	8	11	0
BOS	000	001	000	1	5	1

Pitchers: WITT vs CLEMENS, Sambito (8), Stanley (8)
Attendance: 32,993

GAME 2 AT BOS OCT 8

CAL	000	110	000	2	11	3
BOS	110	010	33X	9	13	2

Pitchers: McCASKILL, Lucas (8), Corbett (8) vs HURST
Home Runs: Joyner-CAL, Rice-BOS
Attendance: 32,786

GAME 3 AT CAL OCT 10

BOS	010	000	020	3	9	1
CAL	000	001	31X	5	8	0

Pitchers: BOYD, Sambito (7), Schiraldi (8) vs CANDELARIA, Moore (8)
Home Runs: Schofield-CAL, Pettis-CAL
Attendance: 64,206

GAME 4 AT CAL OCT 11

BOS	000	001	020 00	3	6	1
CAL	000	000	003 01	4	11	2

Pitchers: Clemens, SCHIRALDI (9) vs Sutton, Lucas (7), Ruhle (7), Finley (8), CORBETT (8)
Home Runs: DeCinces-CAL
Attendance: 64,223

GAME 5 AT CAL OCT 12

BOS	020	000	004 01	7	12	0
CAL	001	002	201 00	6	13	0

Pitchers: Hurst, Stanley (7), Sambito (9), CRAWFORD (9), Schiraldi (11) vs Witt, Lucas (9), MOORE (9), Finley (11)
Home Runs: Gedman-BOS, Boone-CAL, Grich-CAL, Baylor-BOS, Henderson-BOS
Attendance: 64,223

GAME 6 AT BOS OCT 14

CAL	200	000	110	4	11	1
BOS	205	010	20X	10	16	1

Pitchers: McCASKILL, Lucas (3), Corbett (4), Finley (7) vs BOYD, Stanley (8)
Home Runs: Downing-CAL
Attendance: 32,998

GAME 7 AT BOS OCT 15

CAL	000	000	010	1	6	2
BOS	030	400	10X	8	8	1

Pitchers: CANDELARIA, Sutton (4), Moore (8) vs CLEMENS, Schiraldi (8)
Home Runs: Rice-BOS, Evans-BOS
Attendance: 33,001

In their three most recent Series appearances—1946, 1967, and 1975—the Red Sox had battled to a seventh game, only to lose. This time they came within one strike of winning the crown in the sixth game—but wound up losing again in Game Seven.

Boston surprised the favored Mets by taking the first two games in New York. Bruce Hurst (with relief from Calvin Schiradli in the ninth) pitched a four-hitter. New York's Ron Darling hurled just as well but lost when a seventh-inning walk, a wild pitch, and an error by second baseman Tim Teufel moved Jim Rice around the bases with the game's only run. Game Two, close for three innings, turned into a 9–3 Boston blowout as the Sox racked four of the five Met pitchers for eighteen hits, including home runs by Dave Henderson and Dwight Evans.

When the Series moved to Boston, though, the Mets revived to rap Sox starter Oil Can Boyd and two relievers for thirteen hits and seven runs (starting with Len Dykstra's leadoff home run in the first inning) as former Sox pitcher Bob Ojeda subdued his old teammates, giving up just one run on five hits in his seven innings of work. The next day Ron Darling redeemed his first-game loss with seven shutout innings as his teammates built him a 6–0 lead (five of the runs scoring on homers by Dykstra and a pair by Gary Carter). The game ended at 6–2, with the Series even at two wins apiece.

Boston recovered in its final home appearance, taking a 4–0 lead and holding it until Teufel spoiled Bruce Hurst's try for a second shutout by homering in the eighth inning. Hurst yielded a second run in the ninth with two out, but struck out Len Dykstra on three pitches to seal his second win.

The ninth inning of Game Six ended with the score tied 3–3. Boston's Dave Henderson led off the tenth with a home run and two more Sox hits made the score 5–3. Boston reliever Calvin Schiraldi retired the first two Mets in the last of the tenth on long flies, but then three Mets singled, driving in one run and driving out Schiraldi. Bob Stanley, his replacement, had two strikes on Mookie Wilson when a wild pitch let in the tying run, and then Wilson's grounder went through first baseman Bill Buckner's legs as the winning Met bounded across the plate.

The Red Sox nearly recovered in Game Seven. Second-inning home runs by Dwight Evans and Rich Gedman, a walk, sacrifice, and single gave Boston a 3–0 lead which they held into the sixth inning. But then starter Bruce

Hurst lost his touch: four hits and a walk later the score was tied. A succession of five Sox relievers tried to hold the line, but the Mets scored five runs to Boston's two in the final innings for an 8–5 triumph.

New York Mets (NL), 4;
Boston Red Sox (AL), 3

NY (N)

PLAYER/POS	AVG	G	AB	R	H	2B	3B	HR	RB	BB	SO	SB
Rick Aguilera, p	.000	1	0	0	0	0	0	0	0	0	0	0
Wally Backman, 2b	.333	6	18	4	6	0	0	0	1	3	2	1
Gary Carter, c	.276	7	29	4	8	2	0	2	9	0	4	0
Ron Darling, p	.000	3	3	0	0	0	0	0	0	0	1	0
Lenny Dykstra, of	.296	7	27	4	8	0	0	2	3	2	7	0
Kevin Elster, ss	.000	1	1	0	0	0	0	0	0	0	0	0
Sid Fernandez, p	.000	3	0	0	0	0	0	0	0	0	0	0
Dwight Gooden, p	.500	2	2	1	1	0	0	0	0	0	0	0
Danny Heep, dh-2,of-1	.091	5	11	0	1	0	0	0	2	1	1	0
Keith Hernandez, 1b	.231	7	26	1	6	0	0	0	4	5	1	0
Howard Johnson, 3b-1,ss-1	.000	2	5	0	0	0	0	0	0	0	2	0
Ray Knight, 3b	.391	6	23	4	9	1	0	1	5	2	2	0
Lee Mazzilli, of-1	.400	4	5	2	2	0	0	0	0	0	0	0
Roger Mc Dowell, p	.000	5	0	0	0	0	0	0	0	0	0	0
Kevin Mitchell, of-2,dh-1	.250	5	8	1	2	0	0	0	0	0	3	0
Bob Ojeda, p	.000	2	2	0	0	0	0	0	0	0	1	0
Jesse Orosco, p	1.000	4	1	0	1	0	0	0	0	1	0	0
Rafael Santana, ss	.250	7	20	3	5	0	0	0	2	2	5	0
Doug Sisk, p	.000	1	0	0	0	0	0	0	0	0	0	0
Darryl Strawberry, of	.208	7	24	4	5	1	0	1	1	4	6	3
Tim Teufel, 2b	.444	3	9	1	4	1	0	1	1	1	2	0
Mookie Wilson, of	.269	7	26	3	7	1	0	0	0	1	6	3
TOTAL	.271		240	32	65	6	0	7	29	21	43	7

PITCHER	W	L	ERA	G	GS	CG	SV	SHO	IP	H	ER	BB	SO
Rick Aguilera	1	0	12.00	1	0	0	0	0	3.0	8	4	1	4
Ron Darling	1	1	1.53	3	3	0	0	0	17.2	13	3	10	12
Sid Fernandez	0	0	1.35	3	0	0	0	0	6.2	6	1	1	10
Dwight Gooden	0	2	8.00	2	2	0	0	0	9.0	17	8	4	9
Roger Mc Dowell	1	0	4.91	5	0	0	0	0	7.1	10	4	6	2
Bob Ojeda	1	0	2.08	2	2	0	0	0	13.0	13	3	5	9
Jesse Orosco	0	0	0.00	4	0	0	2	0	5.2	2	0	0	6
Doug Sisk	0	0	0.00	1	0	0	0	0	0.2	0	0	1	1
TOTAL	4	3	3.29	21	7	0	2	0	63.0	69	23	28	53

BOS (A)

PLAYER/POS	AVG	G	AB	R	H	2B	3B	HR	RB	BB	SO	SB
Tony Armas, ph	.000	1	1	0	0	0	0	0	0	0	1	0
Marty Barrett, 2b	.433	7	30	1	13	2	0	0	4	5	2	0
Don Baylor, dh-3	.182	4	11	1	2	1	0	0	1	1	3	0
Wade Boggs, 3b	.290	7	31	3	9	3	0	0	3	4	2	0
Oil Can Boyd, p	.000	1	0	0	0	0	0	0	0	0	0	0
Bill Buckner, 1b	.188	7	32	2	6	0	0	0	0	1	3	0
Roger Clemens, p	.000	2	4	1	0	0	0	0	0	0	1	0
Steve Crawford, p	.000	3	1	0	0	0	0	0	0	0	0	0
Dwight Evans, of	.308	7	26	4	8	2	0	2	9	4	3	0
Rich Gedman, c	.200	7	30	1	6	1	0	1	1	0	10	0
Mike Greenwell, ph	.000	4	3	0	0	0	0	0	0	1	2	0
Dave Henderson, of	.667	7	15	6	10	1	1	2	5	2	6	0
Bruce Hurst, p	.000	3	3	0	0	0	0	0	0	0	3	0
Al Nipper, p	.000	2	0	0	0	0	0	0	0	0	0	0
Spike Owen, ss	.300	7	20	2	6	0	0	0	2	5	6	0
Jim Rice, of	.333	7	27	6	9	1	1	0	0	6	9	0
Ed Romero, ss	.000	3	1	0	0	0	0	0	0	0	0	0
Joe Sambito, p	.000	2	0	0	0	0	0	0	0	0	0	0
Calvin Schiraldi, p	.000	3	1	0	0	0	0	0	0	0	1	0
Bob Stanley, p	.000	5	1	0	0	0	0	0	0	0	1	0
Dave Stapleton, 1b	.000	3	1	0	0	0	0	0	0	0	0	0
TOTAL	.290		238	27	69	11	2	5	26	28	53	0

PITCHER	W	L	ERA	G	GS	CG	SV	SHO	IP	H	ER	BB	SO
Oil Can Boyd	0	1	7.71	1	1	0	0	0	7.0	9	6	1	3
Roger Clemens	0	0	3.18	2	2	0	0	0	11.1	9	4	6	11
Steve Crawford	1	0	6.23	3	0	0	0	0	4.1	5	3	0	4
Bruce Hurst	2	0	1.96	3	3	1	0	0	23.0	18	5	6	17
Al Nipper	0	1	7.11	2	1	0	0	0	6.1	10	5	2	2
Joe Sambito	0	0	27.00	2	0	0	0	0	0.1	2	1	2	0
Calvin Schiraldi	0	2	13.50	3	0	0	1	0	4.0	7	6	3	2
Bob Stanley	0	0	0.00	5	0	0	1	0	6.1	5	0	1	4
TOTAL	3	4	4.31	21	7	1	2	0	62.2	65	30	21	43

GAME 1 AT NY OCT 18

BOS	000 000 100	1 5 0
NY	000 000 000	0 4 1

Pitchers: HURST, Schiradli (9) vs DARLING, McDowell (8)
Attendance: 55,076

GAME 2 AT NY OCT 19

BOS	003 120 201	9 18 0
NY	002 010 000	3 8 1

Pitchers: Clemens, CARWFORD (5), Stanley (7) vs GOODEN, Aguilera (6), Orosco (7), Fernandez (9), Sisk (9)
Home Runs: Henderson-BOS, Evans-BOS
Attendance: 55,063

GAME 3 AT BOS OCT 21

NY	400 000 210	7 13 0
BOS	001 000 000	1 5 0

Pitchers: OJEDA, McDowell (8) vs BOYD, Sambito (8), Stanley (8)
Home Runs: Dykstra-NY
Attendance: 33,595

GAME 4 AT BOS OCT 22

NY	000 300 210	6 12 0
BOS	000 000 020	2 7 1

Pitchers: DARLING, McDowell (7), Orosco (7) vs NIPPER, Crawford (7), Stanley (9)
Home Runs: Dykstra-NY, Carter-NY (2)
Attendance: 33,920

GAME 5 AT BOS OCT 23

NY	000 000 011	2 10 1
BOS	011 020 00X	4 12 0

Pitchers: GOODEN, Fernandez (5) vs HURST
Home Runs: Teufel-NY
Attendance: 34,010

GAME 6 AT NY OCT 25

BOS	110 000 100 2	5 13 3
NY	000 020 010 3	6 8 2

Pitchers: Clemens, SCHIRALDI (8), Stanley (10) vs Ojeda, McDowell (7), Orosco (8), AGUILERA (9)
Home Runs: Henderson-BOS
Attendance: 55,078

GAME 7 AT NY OCT 27

BOS	030 000 020	5 9 0
NY	000 003 32X	8 10 0

Pitchers: Hurst, SCHIRALDI (7), Sambito (7), Stanley (7), Nipper (8), Crawford (8) vs Darling, Fernandez (4), McDOWELL (8), Orosco (9)
Home Runs: Evans-BOS, Gedman-BOS, Knight-NY, Strawberry-NY
Attendance: 55,032

The Giants scored four times in the fourth inning of Game Five, winning the game and taking a 3–2 series advantage. But Cardinal pitchers shut them out the rest of the series (an NLCS record 22 innings) to capture the flag.

St. Louis won the opener 5–3, with pitcher Greg Mathews's two-run single in the sixth providing his margin of victory. The Giants came back in Game Two, supporting Dave Dravecky's two-hit shutout with home runs by Will Clark and Jeffrey Leonard. But the Cards retook the series lead in Game Three, overcoming a 0–4 deficit with two runs on Jim Lindeman's homer in the sixth and four more in the seventh (capped by Lindeman's sacrifice fly) for an eventual 6–5 win.

The Giants snapped back with a pair of wins, scoring four runs on three homers in Game Four (including Leonard's fourth in successive games—an LCS record), and six runs in Game Five. But Dravecky and the Giants lost a heartbreaker in Game Six when right fielder Candy Maldonado lost Tony Pena's fly in the lights for a triple. Pena scored on a sacrifice fly for the game's only run, as John Tudor and two late-inning relievers blanked the Giants. Danny Cox pitched an easier shutout in the finale as his Cardinals hammered seven Giant pitchers for twelve hits and six runs.

St. Louis Cardinals (East), 4; San Francisco Giants (West) 3

STL (E)

PLAYER/POS	AVG	G	AB	R	H	2B	3B	HR	RB	BB	SO	SB
Jack Clark, ph	.000	1	1	0	0	0	0	0	0	0	1	0
Vince Coleman, of	.269	7	26	3	7	1	0	0	4	4	6	1
Danny Cox, p	.333	2	6	0	2	0	0	0	1	0	2	0
Ken Dayley, p	.000	3	0	0	0	0	0	0	0	0	0	0
Dan Driessen, 1b-4	.250	5	12	1	3	2	0	0	1	1	1	0
Curt Ford, of	.333	4	9	2	3	0	0	0	0	1	1	0
Bob Forsch, p	.000	3	0	0	0	0	0	0	0	0	0	0
Tommy Herr, 2b	.222	7	27	0	6	0	0	0	3	0	1	1
Rick Horton, p	.000	1	0	0	0	0	0	0	0	0	0	0
Lance Johnson, pr	.000	1	0	1	0	0	0	0	0	0	0	1
Tom Lawless, 3b-2,of-1	.333	3	6	0	2	0	0	0	0	1	1	0
Jim Lindeman, 1b	.308	5	13	1	4	0	0	1	3	0	3	0
Joe Magrane, p	.000	1	1	0	0	0	0	0	0	0	0	0
Greg Mathews, p	1.000	2	2	0	2	0	0	0	2	0	0	0
Willie Mc Gee, of	.308	7	26	2	8	1	1	0	2	0	5	0
John Morris, of	.000	2	3	0	0	0	0	0	0	0	0	0
Jose Oquendo, of-5,3b-1	.167	5	12	3	2	0	0	1	4	3	2	0
Tom Pagnozzi, ph	.000	1	1	0	0	0	0	0	0	0	0	0
Tony Pena, c	.381	7	21	5	8	0	1	0	0	3	4	1
Terry Pendleton, 3b	.211	6	19	3	4	0	1	0	1	0	6	0
Ozzie Smith, ss	.200	7	25	2	5	0	1	0	1	3	4	0
John Tudor, p	.000	2	4	0	0	0	0	0	0	0	4	0
Todd Worrell, p-3,of-1	.000	3	1	0	0	0	0	0	0	0	1	0
TOTAL	.260		215	23	56	4	4	2	22	16	42	4

PITCHER	W	L	ERA	G	GS	CG	SV	SHO	IP	H	ER	BB	SO
Danny Cox	1	1	2.12	2	2	2	0	1	17.0	17	4	3	11
Ken Dayley	0	0	0.00	3	0	0	2	0	4.0	1	0	2	4
Bob Forsch	1	1	12.00	3	0	0	0	0	3.0	4	4	1	3
Rick Horton	0	0	0.00	1	0	0	0	0	3.0	2	0	0	2
Joe Magrane	0	0	9.00	1	1	0	0	0	4.0	4	4	2	3
Greg Mathews	1	0	3.48	2	2	0	0	0	10.1	6	4	3	10
John Tudor	1	1	1.76	2	2	0	0	0	15.1	16	3	5	12
Todd Worrell	0	0	2.08	3	0	0	1	0	4.1	4	1	1	6
TOTAL	4	3	2.95	17	7	2	3	1	61.0	54	20	17	51

SF (W)

PLAYER/POS	AVG	G	AB	R	H	2B	3B	HR	RB	BB	SO	SB
Mike Aldrete, of-3	.100	5	10	0	1	0	0	0	1	0	2	0
Bob Brenly, c	.235	6	17	3	4	1	0	1	2	3	7	0
Will Clark, 1b	.360	7	25	3	9	2	0	1	3	3	6	1
Chili Davis, of	.150	6	20	2	3	1	0	0	0	1	4	0
Kelly Downs, p	.000	1	0	0	0	0	0	0	0	0	0	0
Dave Dravecky, p	.167	2	6	0	1	0	0	0	0	0	1	0
Scott Garrelts, p	.000	2	0	0	0	0	0	0	0	0	0	0
Atlee Hammaker, p	.000	2	3	0	0	0	0	0	0	0	2	0
Mike Krukow, p	.000	1	2	0	0	0	0	0	0	0	1	0
Mike La Coss, p	.000	2	0	0	0	0	0	0	0	0	0	0
Craig Lefferts, p	.000	3	0	0	0	0	0	0	0	0	0	0
Jeffrey Leonard, of	.417	7	24	5	10	0	0	4	5	3	4	0
Candy Maldonado, of	.211	5	19	2	4	1	0	0	2	0	3	0
Bob Melvin, c-2	.429	3	7	0	3	0	0	0	0	1	1	0
Eddie Milner, of-4	.143	6	7	0	1	0	0	0	0	0	3	0
Kevin Mitchell, 3b	.267	7	30	2	8	1	0	1	2	0	3	1
Joe Price, p	.000	2	1	0	0	0	0	0	0	0	1	0
Rick Reuschel, p	.000	2	2	0	0	0	0	0	0	0	1	0
Don Robinson, p	.000	3	0	0	0	0	0	0	0	0	0	0
Chris Speier, 2b-1	.000	3	5	0	0	0	0	0	0	0	2	0
Harry Spilman, ph	.500	3	2	1	1	0	0	1	1	0	0	0
Rob Thompson, 2b-6	.100	7	20	4	2	0	1	1	1	2	5	2
Jose Uribe, ss	.269	7	26	1	7	1	0	0	2	0	4	1
TOTAL	.239		226	23	54	7	1	9	20	17	51	5

PITCHER	W	L	ERA	G	GS	CG	SV	SHO	IP	H	ER	BB	SO
Kelly Downs	0	0	0.00	1	0	0	0	0	1.1	1	0	0	0
Dave Dravecky	1	1	0.60	2	2	1	0	1	15.0	7	1	4	14
Scott Garrelts	0	0	6.75	2	0	0	0	0	2.2	2	2	4	4
Atlee Hammaker	0	1	7.87	2	2	0	0	0	8.0	12	7	0	7
Mike Krukow	1	0	2.00	1	1	1	0	0	9.0	9	2	1	3
Mike La Coss	0	0	0.00	2	0	0	0	0	3.1	1	0	3	2
Craig Lefferts	0	0	0.00	3	0	0	0	0	2.0	3	0	1	0
Joe Price	1	0	0.00	2	0	0	0	0	5.2	3	0	1	7
Rick Reuschel	0	1	6.30	2	2	0	0	0	10.0	15	7	2	2
Don Robinson	0	1	9.00	3	0	0	0	0	3.0	3	3	0	3
TOTAL	3	4	3.30	20	7	2	0	1	60.0	56	22	16	42

GAME 1 AT STL OCT 6

SF	100	100	010	3 7 1
STL	001	103	00X	5 10 1

Pitchers: REUSCHEL, Lefferts (7), Garrelts (8) vs MATHEWS, Worrell (8), Dayley (8)
Home Runs: Leonard-SF
Attendance: 55,331

GAME 2 AT STL OCT 7

SF	020	100	020	5 10 0
STL	000	000	000	0 2 1

Pitchers: DRAVECKY vs TUDOR, Forsch (9)
Home Runs: Clark-SF, Leonard-SF
Attendance: 55,331

GAME 3 AT SF OCT 9

STL	000	002	400	6 11 1
SF	031	000	001	5 7 1

Pitchers: Magrane, FORSCH (5), Worrell (7) vs D.ROBINSON (7), Lefferts (7), LaCoss (8)
Home Runs: Lindeman-STL, Leonard-SF, Spilman-SF
Attendance: 57,913

GAME 4 AT SF OCT 10

STL	020	000	000	2 9 0
SF	000	100	03X	4 9 2

Pitchers: COX vs KRUKOW
Home Runs: Thompson-SF, Leonard-SF, Brenly-SF
Attendance: 57,997

GAME 5 AT SF OCT 11

STL	101	100	000	3 7 0
SF	101	400	00X	6 7 1

Pitchers: Mathews, FORSCH (4), Horton (4), Dayley (7) vs Reuschel, PRICE (5)
Home Runs: Mitchell-SF
Attendance: 59,363

GAME 6 AT STL OCT 13

SF	000	000	000	0 6 0
STL	010	000	00X	1 5 0

Pitchers: DRAVECKY, D.Robinson (7) vs TUDOR, Worrell (8), Dayley (9)
Attendance: 55,331

GAME 7 AT STL OCT 14

SF	000	000	000	0 8 1
STL	040	002	00X	6 12 0

Pitchers: HAMMAKER, Price (3), Downs (3), Garrelts (5), Lefferts (6), LaCoss (6), D.Robinson (8) vs COX
Home Runs: Oquendo-STL
Attendance: 55,331

The Tigers, with the best over-all won-lost record in the majors, were favored to defeat the ninth-ranked Twins, although Minnesota held the home field advantage and the major leagues' best record at home. Tiger pitcher Doyle Alexander—he had been 9–0 since joining Detroit in mid-August—took a 5–4 lead into the last of the eighth in Game One. But a single and double drove him out, and before the inning was over three more Twins had scored to sew up their first win. Detroit scored twice in the second inning the next day, but the Twins responded later in the inning with three runs, two on Tim Laudner's double off Tiger ace Jack Morris, and increased their lead in the fourth and fifth to seal Morris's first loss in Minnesota after eleven wins.

The Tigers won a game after the series moved to Detroit, when Pat Sheridan's two-run homer in the eighth inning of Game Three restored a lead they had squandered in the middle innings. But that was it for Detroit, as the Twins surprised everyone by subduing the Tigers in their den. In Game Four they took the lead for good on Greg Gagne's fourth-inning home run. And in Game Five, after initiating the scoring with four runs in the second, Minnesota pushed on to a 9–5 win and their first pennant in twenty-two years.

Minnesota Twins (West) 4;
Detroit Tigers (East), 1

MIN (W)

PLAYER/POS	AVG	G	AB	R	H	2B	3B	HR	RB	BB	SO	SB
Keith Atherton, p	.000	1	0	0	0	0	0	0	0	0	0	0
Don Baylor, dh	.400	2	5	0	2	0	0	0	1	0	0	0
Juan Berenguer, p	.000	4	0	0	0	0	0	0	0	0	0	0
Bert Blyleven, p	.000	2	0	0	0	0	0	0	0	0	0	0
Tom Brunansky, of	.412	5	17	5	7	4	0	2	9	4	3	0
Randy Bush, dh	.250	4	12	4	3	0	1	0	2	3	2	3
Sal Butera, c	.667	1	3	0	2	0	0	0	0	0	0	0
Mark Davidson, pr	.000	1	0	0	0	0	0	0	0	0	0	0
Gary Gaetti, 3b	.300	5	20	5	6	1	0	2	5	1	3	0
Greg Gagne, ss	.278	5	18	5	5	3	0	2	3	3	4	0
Dan Gladden, of	.350	5	20	5	7	2	0	0	5	2	1	0
Kent Hrbek, 1b	.150	5	20	4	3	0	0	1	1	3	0	0
Gene Larkin, ph	1.000	1	1	0	1	1	0	0	1	0	0	0
Tim Laudner, c	.071	5	14	1	1	1	0	0	2	2	5	0
Steve Lombardozzi, 2b	.267	5	15	2	4	0	0	0	1	2	2	0
Al Newman, 2b	.000	1	2	0	0	0	0	0	0	0	0	0
Kirby Puckett, of	.208	5	24	3	5	1	0	1	3	0	5	1
Jeff Reardon, p	.000	4	0	0	0	0	0	0	0	0	0	0
Dan Schatzeder, p	.000	2	0	0	0	0	0	0	0	0	0	0
Les Straker, p	.000	1	0	0	0	0	0	0	0	0	0	0
Frank Viola, p	.000	2	0	0	0	0	0	0	0	0	0	0
TOTAL	.269		171	34	46	13	1	8	33	20	25	4

PITCHER	W	L	ERA	G	GS	CG	SV	SHO	IP	H	ER	BB	SO
Keith Atherton	0	0	0.00	1	0	0	0	0	0.1	1	0	0	0
Juan Berenguer	0	0	1.50	4	0	0	1	0	6.0	1	1	3	6
Bert Blyleven	2	0	4.05	2	2	0	0	0	13.1	12	6	3	9
Jeff Reardon	1	1	5.06	4	0	0	2	0	5.1	7	3	3	5
Dan Schatzeder	0	0	0.00	2	0	0	0	0	4.1	2	0	0	5
Les Straker	0	0	16.88	1	1	0	0	0	2.2	3	5	4	1
Frank Viola	1	0	5.25	2	2	0	0	0	12.0	14	7	5	9
TOTAL	4	1	4.50	16	5	0	3	0	44.0	40	22	18	35

DET (E)

PLAYER/POS	AVG	G	AB	R	H	2B	3B	HR	RB	BB	SO	SB
Doyle Alexander, p	.000	2	0	0	0	0	0	0	0	0	0	0
Dave Bergman, 1b-1,dh-1	.250	4	4	0	1	0	0	0	2	0	1	0
Tom Brookens, 3b	.000	5	13	0	0	0	0	0	0	0	3	0
Darrell Evans, 1b-5,3b-1	.294	5	17	0	5	0	0	0	4	2	0	0
Kirk Gibson, of	.286	5	21	4	6	1	0	1	4	3	8	3
Johnny Grubb, dh-1	.571	4	7	0	4	0	0	0	0	0	1	0
Mike Heath, c	.286	3	7	1	2	0	0	1	2	0	0	0
Mike Henneman, p	.000	3	0	0	0	0	0	0	0	0	0	0
Willie Hernandez, p	.000	1	0	0	0	0	0	0	0	0	0	0
Larry Herndon, of-2,dh-1	.333	3	9	1	3	1	0	0	2	1	1	0
Eric King, p	.000	2	0	0	0	0	0	0	0	0	0	0
Chet Lemon, of	.278	5	18	4	5	0	0	2	4	1	4	0
Bill Madlock, dh	.000	1	5	0	0	0	0	0	0	0	3	0
Jack Morris, p-1,dh-1	.000	2	0	1	0	0	0	0	0	0	0	0
Jim Morrison, 3b-1,dh-1	.400	2	5	1	2	0	0	0	0	0	1	0
Matt Nokes, c-3,dh-2	.143	5	14	2	2	0	0	1	2	1	4	0
Dan Petry, p	.000	1	0	0	0	0	0	0	0	0	0	0
Jeff Robinson, p	.000	1	0	0	0	0	0	0	0	0	0	0
Pat Sheridan, of-4	.300	5	10	2	3	1	0	1	2	0	2	1
Frank Tanana, p	.000	1	0	0	0	0	0	0	0	0	0	0
Walt Terrell, p	.000	1	0	0	0	0	0	0	0	0	0	0
Mark Thurmond, p	.000	1	0	0	0	0	0	0	0	0	0	0
Alan Trammell, ss	.200	5	20	3	4	1	0	0	2	1	2	0
Lou Whitaker, 2b	.176	5	17	4	3	0	0	1	1	7	3	1
TOTAL	.240		167	23	40	4	0	7	21	18	35	5

PITCHER	W	L	ERA	G	GS	CG	SV	SHO	IP	H	ER	BB	SO
Doyle Alexander	0	2	10.00	2	2	0	0	0	9.0	14	10	1	5
Mike Henneman	1	0	10.80	3	0	0	0	0	5.0	6	6	6	3
Willie Hernandez	0	0	0.00	1	0	0	0	0	0.1	2	0	0	0
Eric King	0	0	1.69	2	0	0	0	0	5.1	3	1	2	4
Jack Morris	0	1	6.75	1	1	1	0	0	8.0	6	6	3	7
Dan Petry	0	0	0.00	1	0	0	0	0	3.1	1	0	0	1
Jeff Robinson	0	0	0.00	1	0	0	0	0	0.1	1	0	0	0
Frank Tanana	0	1	5.06	1	1	0	0	0	5.1	6	3	4	1
Walt Terrell	0	0	9.00	1	1	0	0	0	6.0	7	6	4	4
Mark Thurmond	0	0	0.00	1	0	0	0	0	0.1	0	0	0	0
TOTAL	1	4	6.70	14	5	1	0	0	43.0	46	32	20	25

GAME 1 AT MIN OCT 7

DET	001	001	120	5	10 0
MIN	010	030	04X	8	10 0

Pitchers: ALEXANDER, Henneman (8), Hernandez (8), King (8) vs Viola, REARDON (8)
Home Runs: Heath-DET, Gibson-DET, Gaetti-MIN (2)
Attendance: 53,269

GAME 2 AT MIN OCT 8

DET	020	000	010	3	7 1
MIN	030	210	00X	6	6 0

Pitchers: MORRIS vs BLYLEVEN, Berenguer (8)
Home Runs: Lemon-DET, Whitaker-DET, Hrbek-MIN
Attendance: 55,245

GAME 3 AT DET OCT 10

MIN	000	202	200	6	8 1
DET	005	000	02X	7	7 0

Pitchers: Straker, Schatzeder (3), Berenguer (7), REARDON (8) vs Terrell, HENNEMAN (7)
Home Runs: Gagne-MIN, Brunansky-MIN, Sheridan-DET
Attendance: 49,730

GAME 4 AT DET OCT 11

MIN	001	111	010	5	7 1
DET	100	011	000	3	7 3

Pitchers: VIOLA, Atherton (6), Berenguer (6), Reardon (9) vs TANANA, Petry (6), Thurmond (9)
Home Runs: Puckett-MIN, Gagne-MIN
Attendance: 51,939

GAME 5 AT DET OCT 12

MIN	040	000	113	9	15 1
DET	000	300	011	5	9 1

Pitchers: BLYLEVEN, Schatzeder (7), Berenguer (8), Reardon (8) vs ALEXANDER, King (2), Henneman (7), Robinson (9)
Home Runs: Brunansky-MIN, Nokes-DET, Lemon-DET
Attendance: 47,448

Although the Twins compiled a dismal record on the road during the season (29–52), their play at home (56–25) topped the majors. In postseason play they won all six games played in their Metrodome, including the four that won them the world championship. They overwhelmed St. Louis in the Series opener, the first World Series game ever played indoors. The Cardinals scored first, in the second inning, but Twin ace Frank Viola (with relief from Keith Atherton in the ninth) stopped them after that as his teammates unloaded for seven runs in the fourth inning (capped by Dan Gladden's grand slam) on their way to a 10–1 win. The Cardinals scored four runs in Game Two, but again the Twins enjoyed a big fourth inning—bunching six of their ten hits together for six runs—and scored two other runs on homers by Gary Gaetti and Tim Laudner.

When the Series moved to St. Louis, the Cardinals grabbed the home advantage to post their three wins. In Game Three, Cardinal pitchers John Tudor and Todd Worrell combined for a five-hitter as the Cards came from behind with a three-run seventh to win 3–1. The next day St. Louis broke a 1–1 tie with their own fourth-inning explosion, for six runs. The big blow was a three-run homer by utility infielder Tom Lawless—only the second home run of his big league career. Final score: 7–2. After five scoreless innings in Game Five, St. Louis moved out to a 4–0 lead in the sixth and seventh innings. Gaetti's eighth-inning triple put two Minnesota runs across, but the Cards held on for a 4–2 win.

Back in Minneapolis, St. Louis built up a 5–2 lead in Game Six before the Twins retaliated with four runs in the fifth inning (with Don Baylor's three-run homer providing the tying runs) and four more an inning later on Kent Hrbek's grand slam. A final Twins run in the eighth ended the scoring at 11–5.

The Cardinals scored first in Game Seven, with a pair of runs in the second inning, but the Twins edged their way to a tie with single runs in the second and fifth, and an inning later took the lead on three walks and an infield single. As Twin starter Frank Viola held St. Louis scoreless on two hits after the second inning, Minnesota made the score 4–2 with a final run in the eighth, and ace reliever Jeff Reardon retired the Cards in order in the ninth to bring Minnesota its first world championship.

Minnesota Twins (AL) 4;
St. Louis Cardinals (NL), 3

MIN (A)

PLAYER/POS	AVG	G	AB	R	H	2B	3B	HR	RB	BB	SO	SB
Keith Atherton, p	.000	2	0	0	0	0	0	0	0	0	0	0
Don Baylor, dh-3	.385	5	13	3	5	0	0	1	3	1	1	0
Juan Berenguer, p	.000	3	0	0	0	0	0	0	0	0	0	0
Bert Blyleven, p	.000	2	1	0	0	0	0	0	0	0	1	0
Tom Brunansky, of	.200	7	25	5	5	0	0	0	2	4	4	1
Randy Bush, dh-2	.167	4	6	1	1	1	0	0	2	0	1	0
Sal Butera, c	.000	1	0	0	0	0	0	0	0	0	0	0
Mark Davidson, of-1	.000	2	1	0	0	0	0	0	0	0	0	0
George Frazier, p	.000	1	0	0	0	0	0	0	0	0	0	0
Gary Gaetti, 3b	.259	7	27	4	7	2	1	1	4	2	5	2
Greg Gagne, ss	.200	7	30	5	6	1	0	1	3	1	6	0
Dan Gladden, of	.290	7	31	3	9	2	1	1	7	3	4	2
Kent Hrbek, 1b	.208	7	24	4	5	0	0	1	6	5	3	0
Gene Larkin, 1b-1,dh-1	.000	5	3	1	0	0	0	0	0	1	0	0
Tim Laudner, c	.318	7	22	4	7	1	0	1	4	5	3	0
Steve Lombardozzi, 2b	.412	6	17	3	7	1	0	1	4	2	3	0
Al Newman, 2b-3	.200	4	5	0	1	0	0	0	0	1	1	0
Joe Niekro, p	.000	1	0	0	0	0	0	0	0	0	0	0
Kirby Puckett, of	.357	7	28	5	10	1	1	0	3	2	1	1
Jeff Reardon, p	.000	4	0	0	0	0	0	0	0	0	0	0
Dan Schatzeder, p	.000	3	0	0	0	0	0	0	0	0	0	0
Roy Smalley, ph	.500	4	2	0	1	1	0	0	0	2	0	0
Les Straker, p	.000	2	2	0	0	0	0	0	0	0	2	0
Frank Viola, p	.000	3	1	0	0	0	0	0	0	0	1	0
TOTAL	.269		238	38	64	10	3	7	38	29	36	6

PITCHER	W	L	ERA	G	GS	CG	SV	SHO	IP	H	ER	BB	SO
Keith Atherton	0	0	6.75	2	0	0	0	0	1.1	0	1	1	0
Juan Berenguer	0	1	10.38	3	0	0	0	0	4.1	10	5	0	1
Bert Blyleven	1	1	2.77	2	2	0	0	0	13.0	13	4	2	12
George Frazier	0	0	0.00	1	0	0	0	0	2.0	1	0	0	2
Joe Niekro	0	0	0.00	1	0	0	0	0	2.0	1	0	1	1
Jeff Reardon	0	0	0.00	4	0	0	1	0	4.2	5	0	0	3
Dan Schatzeder	1	0	6.23	3	0	0	0	0	4.1	4	3	3	3
Les Straker	0	0	4.00	2	2	0	0	0	9.0	9	4	3	6
Frank Viola	2	1	3.72	3	3	0	0	0	19.1	17	8	3	16
TOTAL	4	3	3.75	21	7	0	1	0	60.0	60	25	13	44

STL (N)

PLAYER/POS	AVG	G	AB	R	H	2B	3B	HR	RB	BB	SO	SB
Vince Coleman, of	.143	7	28	5	4	2	0	0	2	2	10	6
Danny Cox, p	.000	3	2	0	0	0	0	0	0	0	1	0
Ken Dayley, p	.000	4	1	0	0	0	0	0	0	0	1	0
Dan Driessen, 1b	.231	4	13	3	3	2	0	0	1	1	1	0
Curt Ford, of-4	.308	5	13	1	4	0	0	0	2	1	1	0
Bob Forsch, p	.000	3	2	0	0	0	0	0	0	0	0	0
Tommy Herr, 2b	.250	7	28	2	7	0	0	1	1	2	2	0
Rick Horton, p	.000	2	0	0	0	0	0	0	0	0	0	0
Lance Johnson, pr	.000	1	0	0	0	0	0	0	0	0	0	1
Steve Lake, c	.333	2	3	0	1	0	0	0	1	0	0	0
Tom Lawless, 3b	.100	3	10	1	1	0	0	1	3	0	4	0
Jim Lindeman, 1b-6,of-1	.333	6	15	3	5	1	0	0	2	0	3	0
Joe Magrane, p	.000	2	0	0	0	0	0	0	0	0	0	0
Greg Mathews, p	.000	1	1	0	0	0	0	0	0	0	0	0
Willie Mc Gee, of	.370	7	27	2	10	2	0	0	4	0	9	0
John Morris, of	.000	1	2	0	0	0	0	0	0	0	0	0
Jose Oquendo, 3b-4,of-3	.250	7	24	2	6	0	0	0	2	1	4	0
Tom Pagnozzi, dh-1	.250	2	4	0	1	0	0	0	0	0	0	0
Tony Pena, c-6,dh-1	.409	7	22	2	9	1	0	0	4	3	2	1
Terry Pendleton, dh-2	.429	3	7	2	3	0	0	0	1	1	1	2
Ozzie Smith, ss	.214	7	28	3	6	0	0	0	2	2	3	2
John Tudor, p	.000	2	2	0	0	0	0	0	0	0	2	0
Lee Tunnell, p	.000	2	0	0	0	0	0	0	0	0	0	0
Todd Worrell, p	.000	4	0	0	0	0	0	0	0	0	0	0
TOTAL	.259		232	26	60	8	0	2	25	13	44	12

PITCHER	W	L	ERA	G	GS	CG	SV	SHO	IP	H	ER	BB	SO
Danny Cox	1	2	7.71	3	2	0	0	0	11.2	13	10	8	9
Ken Dayley	0	0	1.93	4	0	0	1	0	4.2	2	1	0	3
Bob Forsch	1	0	9.95	3	0	0	0	0	6.1	8	7	5	3
Rick Horton	0	0	6.00	2	0	0	0	0	3.0	5	2	0	1
Joe Magrane	0	1	8.59	2	2	0	0	0	7.1	9	7	5	5
Greg Mathews	0	0	2.45	1	1	0	0	0	3.2	2	1	2	3
John Tudor	1	1	5.73	2	2	0	0	0	11.0	15	7	3	8
Lee Tunnell	0	0	2.08	2	0	0	0	0	4.1	4	1	2	1
Todd Worrell	0	0	1.29	4	0	0	2	0	7.0	6	1	4	3
TOTAL	3	4	5.64	23	7	0	3	0	59.0	64	37	29	36

GAME 1 AT MIN OCT 17

STL	010	000	000	1	5	1
MIN	000	720	10X	10	11	0

Pitchers: MAGRANE, Forsch (4), Horton (9) vs VIOLA, Atherton (9)
Home Runs: Gladden-MIN, Lombardozzi-MIN
Attendance: 55,171

GAME 2 AT MIN OCT 18

STL	000	010	120	4	9	0
MIN	010	601	00X	8	10	0

Pitchers: COX, Tunnell (4), Dayley (7), Worrell (8) vs BLYLEVEN, Berenguer (8), Reardon (9)
Home Runs: Gaetti-MIN, Laudner-MIN
Attendance: 55,257

GAME 3 AT STL OCT 20

MIN	000	001	000	1	5	1
STL	000	000	30X	3	9	1

Pitchers: Straker, BERENGUER (7), Schatzeder (7) vs TUDOR, Worrell (8)
Attendance: 55,347

GAME 4 AT STL OCT 21

MIN	001	010	000	2	7	1
STL	001	600	00X	7	10	1

Pitchers: VIOLA, Schatzeder (4), Niekro (5), Frazier (7) vs Mathews, FORSCH (4), Dayley (7)
Home Runs: Gagne-MIN, Lawless-STL
Attendance: 55,347

GAME 5 AT STL OCT 22

MIN	000	000	020	2	6	1
STL	000	003	10X	4	10	0

Pitchers: BLYLEVEN, Atherton (7), Reardon (7) vs COX, Dayley (8), Worrell (8)
Attendance: 55,347

GAME 6 AT MIN OCT 24

STL	110	210	000	5	11	2
MIN	200	044	01X	11	15	0

Pitchers: TUDOR, Horton (5), Forsch (6), Dayley (6), Tunnell (7) vs Straker, SCHATZEDER (4), Berenguer (6), Reardon (9)
Home Runs: Herr-STL, Baylor-MIN, Hrbek-MIN
Attendance: 55,293

GAME 7 AT MIN OCT 25

STL	020	000	000	2	6	1
MIN	010	011	01X	4	10	0

Pitchers: Magrane, COX (5), Worrell (6) vs VIOLA, Reardon (9)
Attendance: 55,376

The Mets had defeated the Dodgers in 10 of 11 regular season games, but in the LCS the pitching of Dodger ace Orel Hershiser and rookie Tim Belcher, and the timely hitting of Mike Scioscia and Kirk Gibson, propelled L.A. to the pennant. The Dodgers scored a first-inning run in the opener and carried a 2–0 lead into the ninth. But three Met runs in the top of the ninth (the final two scoring with two outs on a fly to short center that bounced off the glove of a diving John Shelby) gave New York the victory.

Dodger pitcher Tim Belcher singled with two away in the second inning of Game Two to start a four-run rally—the margin of victory in Belcher's 6–3 win. In Game Three (played in a steady downpour after a rainout the night before), the Mets overcame a 3–4 deficit, rapping four Dodger pitchers for five runs in the last of the eighth to take the series lead.

Kirk Gibson's twelfth-inning solo homer the next night put the Dodgers ahead 5–4, after Mike Scioscia's ninth-inning home run had pulled them into a tie. In the last of the twelfth, Orel Hershiser (who had pitched seven innings to no decision in the previous game) took the mound with two out and the bases full, and saved the game as center fielder Shelby, on the run, snared Kevin McReynolds' looping fly.

Gibson homered again in Game Four—for three runs that provided the winning margin in a 7–4 Dodger victory. One game from the pennant, as the series moved back to Los Angeles, the Dodgers for the first time failed to score first and saw the series evened a third time as David Cone held them to five hits and one run while the Mets scored five. But in the finale, the Dodgers unloaded on Ron Darling for six runs in the first two innings and Hershiser blanked the Mets on five hits.

Los Angeles Dodgers (West), 4; New York Mets (East), 3

LA (W)

PLAYER/POS	AVG	G	AB	R	H	2B	3B	HR	RB	BB	SO	SB
Tim Belcher, p	.125	2	8	1	1	0	0	0	0	0	3	0
Mike Davis, ph	.000	4	2	0	0	0	0	0	0	1	0	0
Rick Dempsey, c-3	.400	4	5	1	2	2	0	0	2	1	0	0
Kirk Gibson, of	.154	7	26	2	4	0	0	2	6	3	6	2
Jose Gonzalez, of-3	.000	4	0	2	0	0	0	0	0	0	0	0
Alfredo Griffin, ss	.160	7	25	1	4	1	0	0	3	0	5	0
Jeff Hamilton, 3b	.217	7	23	2	5	0	0	0	1	3	4	0
Mickey Hatcher, 1b-6,of-1	.238	6	21	4	5	2	0	0	3	3	0	0
Danny Heep, ph	.000	3	1	0	0	0	0	0	0	1	1	0
Orel Hershiser, p	.000	4	9	1	0	0	0	0	0	1	2	0
Brian Holton, p	1.000	3	1	1	1	0	0	0	0	0	0	0
Rick Horton, p	.000	4	0	0	0	0	0	0	0	0	0	0
Jay Howell, p	.000	2	0	0	0	0	0	0	0	0	0	0
Tim Leary, p	.000	2	1	0	0	0	0	0	0	0	0	0
Mike Marshall, of	.233	7	30	3	7	1	1	0	5	2	9	0
Jesse Orosco, p	.000	4	0	0	0	0	0	0	0	0	0	0
Alejandro Pena, p	.000	3	0	0	0	0	0	0	0	0	0	0
Steve Sax, 2b	.267	7	30	7	8	0	0	0	3	3	3	5
Mike Scioscia, c	.364	7	22	3	8	1	0	1	2	1	2	0
Mike Sharperson, ss-1,3b-1	.000	2	1	0	0	0	0	0	1	1	0	0
John Shelby, of	.167	7	24	3	4	0	0	0	3	5	12	2
Franklin Stubbs, 1b-3	.250	4	8	0	2	0	0	0	0	0	4	0
John Tudor, p	.000	1	2	0	0	0	0	0	0	0	2	0
Tracy Woodson, 1b	.250	3	4	0	1	0	0	0	0	0	1	0
TOTAL	.214		243	31	52	7	1	3	30	25	54	9

PITCHER	W	L	ERA	G	GS	CG	SV	SHO	IP	H	ER	BB	SO
Tim Belcher	2	0	4.11	2	2	0	0	0	15.1	12	7	4	16
Orel Hershiser	1	0	1.09	4	3	1	1	1	24.2	18	3	7	15
Brian Holton	0	0	2.25	3	0	0	1	0	4.0	2	1	1	2
Rick Horton	0	0	4.15	4	0	0	0	0	4.1	4	2	3	3
Jay Howell	0	1	27.00	2	0	0	0	0	0.2	1	2	2	1
Tim Leary	0	1	6.23	2	1	0	0	0	4.1	8	3	3	3
Jesse Orosco	0	0	7.71	4	0	0	0	0	2.1	4	2	3	0
Alejandro Pena	1	1	4.15	3	0	0	1	0	4.1	1	2	5	1
John Tudor	0	0	7.20	1	1	0	0	0	5.0	8	4	1	4
TOTAL	4	3	3.32	25	7	1	3	1	65.0	58	24	28	42

NY (E)

PLAYER/POS	AVG	G	AB	R	H	2B	3B	HR	RB	BB	SO	SB
Rick Aguilera, p	.000	3	1	0	0	0	0	0	0	0	1	0
Wally Backman, 2b	.273	7	22	2	6	1	0	0	2	2	5	1
Gary Carter, c	.222	7	27	0	6	1	1	0	4	1	3	0
David Cone, p	.000	3	4	0	0	0	0	0	0	0	0	0
Ron Darling, p-2	.000	2	3	0	0	0	0	0	0	0	2	0
Lennie Dykstra, of	.429	7	14	6	6	3	0	1	3	4	0	0
Kevin Elster, ss	.250	5	8	1	2	1	0	0	1	3	0	0
Sid Fernandez, p	.000	1	1	0	0	0	0	0	0	0	0	0
Dwight Gooden, p	.200	3	5	0	1	0	0	0	0	0	2	0
Keith Hernandez, 1b	.269	7	26	2	7	0	0	1	5	6	7	1
Gregg Jefferies, 3b	.333	7	27	2	9	2	0	0	1	4	0	0
Howard Johnson, ss-5,3b-1	.056	6	18	3	1	0	0	0	0	1	6	1
Terry Leach, p	.000	3	0	0	0	0	0	0	0	0	0	0
Dave Magadan, ph	.000	3	3	0	0	0	0	0	0	0	2	0
Lee Mazzilli, ph	.500	3	2	0	1	0	0	0	0	0	0	1
Roger Mc Dowell, p	.000	4	0	0	0	0	0	0	0	0	0	0
Kevin Mc Reynolds, of	.250	7	28	4	7	2	0	2	4	3	5	2
Randy Myers, p	.000	3	0	0	0	0	0	0	0	0	0	0
Mackey Sasser, c-1	.200	4	5	0	1	0	0	0	0	0	1	0
Darryl Strawberry, of	.300	7	30	5	9	2	0	1	6	2	5	0
Tim Teufel, 2b	.000	1	3	0	0	0	0	0	0	0	1	0
Mookie Wilson, of-3	.154	4	13	2	2	0	0	0	1	2	2	0
TOTAL	.242		240	27	58	12	1	5	27	28	42	6

PITCHER	W	L	ERA	G	GS	CG	SV	SHO	IP	H	ER	BB	SO
Rick Aguilera	0	0	1.29	3	0	0	0	0	7.0	3	1	2	4
David Cone	1	1	4.50	3	2	1	0	0	12.0	10	6	5	9
Ron Darling	0	1	7.71	2	2	0	0	0	7.0	11	6	4	7
Sid Fernandez	0	1	13.50	1	1	0	0	0	4.0	7	6	1	5
Dwight Gooden	0	0	2.95	3	2	0	0	0	18.1	10	6	8	20
Terry Leach	0	0	0.00	3	0	0	0	0	5.0	4	0	1	4
Roger Mc Dowell	0	1	4.50	4	0	0	0	0	6.0	6	3	2	5
Randy Myers	2	0	0.00	3	0	0	0	0	4.2	1	0	2	0
TOTAL	3	4	3.94	22	7	1	0	0	64.0	52	28	25	54

GAME 1 AT LA OCT 4

NY	000	000	003	3	8	1
LA	100	000	100	2	4	0

Pitchers: Gooden, MYERS (8) vs Hershiser, J.HOWELL (9)
Attendance: 55,582

GAME 2 AT LA OCT 5

NY	000	200	001	3	6	0
LA	140	010	00X	6	7	0

Pitchers: CONE, Aguilera (3), Leach (6), McDowell (8) vs BELCHER, Orosco (9), Pena (9)
Home Runs: Hernandez-NY
Attendance: 55,780

GAME 3 AT NY OCT 8

LA	021	000	010	4	7	2
NY	001	002	05X	8	9	2

Pitchers: Hershiser, J.Howell (8), PENA (8), Orosco (8), Horton (8) vs Darling, McDowell (7), MYERS (8), Cone (9)
Attendance: 44,672

GAME 4 AT NY OCT 9

LA	200	000	002	001	5	7	1
NY	000	301	000	000	4	10	2

Pitchers: Tudor, Holton (6), Horton (7), PENA (9), Leary (12), Orosco (12), Hershiser (12) vs Gooden, Myers (9), McDOWELL (12)
Home Runs: Strawberry-NY, McReynolds-NY, Scioscia-LA, Gibson-LA
Attendance: 54,014

GAME 5 AT NY OCT 10

LA	000	330	001	7	12	0
NY	000	030	010	4	9	1

Pitchers: BELCHER, Horton (8), Holton (8) vs FERNANDEZ, Leach (5), Aguilera (5), McDowell (8)
Home Runs: Gibson-LA, Dykstra-NY
Attendance: 52,069

GAME 6 AT LA OCT 11

NY	101	021	000	5	11	0
LA	000	010	000	1	5	2

Pitchers: CONE vs LEARY, Holton (5), Horton (6), Orosco (8)
Home Runs: McReynolds-NY
Attendance: 55,885

GAME 7 AT LA OCT 12

NY	000	000	000	0	5	2
LA	150	000	00X	6	10	0

Pitchers: DARLING, Gooden (2), Leach (5), Aguilera (7) vs HERSHISER
Attendance: 55,693

Jose Canseco's three home runs and Dennis Eckersley's sparkling relief pitching highlighted Oakland's sweep to the pennant. In his six shutout innings, Eckersley gave up just one hit and a pair of walks while fanning five, to record an LCS record four saves.

Canseco's fourth-inning solo shot off the Sox's Bruce Hurst put the A's out in front in Game One. Boston tied it up in the seventh, but two former Boston players—Carney Lansford, who doubled, and Dave Henderson, who singled him home—put Oakland back in front in the eighth, and Eckersley (also an ex-Bostonian) held the Sox through the final two innings.

Oakland's Storm Davis and Boston's Roger Clemens dueled scorelessly through five innings of Game Two. The Sox took advantage of an Oakland error to score twice in the sixth, but four Oakland hits in the seventh (including a two-run homer by Canseco), a balk, and a wild pitch put the A's up 3–2. Rich Gedman's home run for Boston in the last of the seventh tied the score, but in the ninth Oakland's rookie shortstop Walt Weiss singled home what proved the game winner off Sox ace reliever Lee Smith.

Boston unloaded for five runs in the first two innings of Game Three. But Weiss's double and home runs by Mark McGwire and Carney Lansford in the last of the second brought the A's within one run of a tie, and Ron Hassey's two-run homer an inning later gave the A's a lead that they held to the end. Dave Henderson's two-run blast in the eighth capped the A's 10–6 victory.

Canseco's first-inning homer in Game Four put the A's ahead to stay, as starter Dave Stewart and relievers Rick Honeycutt and Eckersley combined for a four-hit, 4–1 pennant clincher.

Oakland Athletics (West), 4;
Boston Red Sox (East), 0

OAK (W)

PLAYER/POS	AVG	G	AB	R	H	2B	3B	HR	RB	BB	SO	SB
Don Baylor, dh	.000	2	6	0	0	0	0	0	1	1	2	0
Greg Cadaret, p	.000	1	0	0	0	0	0	0	0	0	0	0
Jose Canseco, of	.313	4	16	4	5	1	0	3	4	1	2	1
Storm Davis, p	.000	1	0	0	0	0	0	0	0	0	0	0
Dennis Eckersley, p	.000	4	0	0	0	0	0	0	0	0	0	0
Mike Gallego, 2b	.083	4	12	1	1	0	0	0	0	0	3	0
Ron Hassey, c	.500	4	8	2	4	1	0	1	3	1	1	0
Dave Henderson, of	.375	4	16	2	6	1	0	1	4	1	7	0
Rick Honeycutt, p	.000	3	0	0	0	0	0	0	0	0	0	0
Stan Javier, of	.500	2	4	0	2	0	0	0	1	1	0	0
Carney Lansford, 3b	.294	4	17	4	5	1	0	1	2	0	2	0
Mark Mc Gwire, 1b	.333	4	15	4	5	0	0	1	3	1	5	0
Gene Nelson, p	.000	2	0	0	0	0	0	0	0	0	0	0
Dave Parker, dh-2,of-1	.250	4	12	1	3	1	0	0	0	0	4	0
Tony Phillips, of-2,2b-1	.286	2	7	0	2	1	0	0	0	1	4	0
Eric Plunk, p	.000	1	0	0	0	0	0	0	0	0	0	0
Luis Polonia, of-1	.400	3	5	0	2	0	0	0	0	1	1	0
Terry Steinbach, c	.250	2	4	0	1	0	0	0	0	0	2	0
Dave Stewart, p	.000	2	0	0	0	0	0	0	0	0	0	0
Walt Weiss, ss	.333	4	15	2	5	2	0	0	2	0	4	0
Bob Welch, p	.000	1	0	0	0	0	0	0	0	0	0	0
Curt Young, p	.000	1	0	0	0	0	0	0	0	0	0	0
TOTAL	.299		137	20	41	8	0	7	20	10	35	1

PITCHER	W	L	ERA	G	GS	CG	SV	SHO	IP	H	ER	BB	SO
Greg Cadaret	0	0	27.00	1	0	0	0	0	0.1	1	1	0	0
Storm Davis	0	0	0.00	1	1	0	0	0	6.1	2	0	5	4
Dennis Eckersley	0	0	0.00	4	0	0	4	0	6.0	1	0	2	5
Rick Honeycutt	1	0	0.00	3	0	0	0	0	2.0	0	0	2	0
Gene Nelson	2	0	0.00	2	0	0	0	0	4.2	5	0	1	0
Eric Plunk	0	0	0.00	1	0	0	0	0	0.1	1	0	1	1
Dave Stewart	1	0	1.35	2	2	0	0	0	13.1	9	2	6	11
Bob Welch	0	0	27.00	1	1	0	0	0	1.2	6	5	2	0
Curt Young	0	0	0.00	1	0	0	0	0	1.1	1	0	0	2
TOTAL	4	0	2.00	16	4	0	4	0	36.0	26	8	18	23

BOS (E)

PLAYER/POS	AVG	G	AB	R	H	2B	3B	HR	RB	BB	SO	SB
Marty Barrett, 2b	.067	4	15	2	1	0	0	0	0	1	0	0
Todd Benzinger, 1b-3	.091	4	11	0	1	0	0	0	0	1	3	0
Mike Boddicker, p	.000	1	0	0	0	0	0	0	0	0	0	0
Wade Boggs, 3b	.385	4	13	2	5	0	0	0	3	3	4	0
Ellis Burks, of	.235	4	17	2	4	1	0	0	1	0	3	0
Roger Clemens, p	.000	1	0	0	0	0	0	0	0	0	0	0
Dwight Evans, of	.167	4	12	1	2	1	0	0	1	3	5	0
Wes Gardner, p	.000	1	0	0	0	0	0	0	0	0	0	0
Rich Gedman, c	.357	4	14	1	5	0	0	1	1	2	1	0
Mike Greenwell, of	.214	4	14	2	3	1	0	1	3	3	0	0
Bruce Hurst, p	.000	2	0	0	0	0	0	0	0	0	0	0
Spike Owen, dh	.000	1	0	0	0	0	0	0	0	1	0	0
Larry Parrish, 1b-2	.000	4	6	0	0	0	0	0	0	0	2	0
Jody Reed, ss	.273	4	11	0	3	1	0	0	0	2	1	0
Jim Rice, dh	.154	4	13	0	2	0	0	0	1	2	4	0
Ed Romero, pr	.000	1	0	0	0	0	0	0	0	0	0	0
Kevin Romine, pr	.000	2	0	1	0	0	0	0	0	0	0	0
Lee Smith, p	.000	2	0	0	0	0	0	0	0	0	0	0
Mike Smithson, p	.000	1	0	0	0	0	0	0	0	0	0	0
Bob Stanley, p	.000	2	0	0	0	0	0	0	0	0	0	0
TOTAL	.206		126	11	26	4	0	2	10	18	23	0

PITCHER	W	L	ERA	G	GS	CG	SV	SHO	IP	H	ER	BB	SO
Mike Boddicker	0	1	20.25	1	1	0	0	0	2.2	8	6	1	2
Roger Clemens	0	0	3.86	1	1	0	0	0	7.0	6	3	0	8
Wes Gardner	0	0	5.79	1	0	0	0	0	4.2	6	3	2	8
Bruce Hurst	0	2	2.77	2	2	1	0	0	13.0	10	4	5	12
Lee Smith	0	1	8.10	2	0	0	0	0	3.1	6	3	1	4
Mike Smithson	0	0	0.00	1	0	0	0	0	2.1	3	0	0	1
Bob Stanley	0	0	9.00	2	0	0	0	0	1.0	2	1	1	0
TOTAL	0	4	5.29	10	4	1	0	0	34.0	41	20	10	35

GAME 1 AT BOS OCT 5

OAK	000 100 010	2	6	0
BOS	000 000 100	1	6	0

Pitchers: Stewart, HONEYCUTT (7), Eckersley (8) vs HURST
Home Runs: Canseco-OAK
Attendance: 34,104

GAME 2 AT BOS OCT 6

OAK	000 000 301	4	10	1
BOS	000 002 100	3	4	1

Pitchers: Davis, Cadaret (7), NELSON (7), Eckersley (9) vs Clemens, Stanley (8), SMITH (8)
Home Runs: Canseco-OAK, Gedman-BOS
Attendance: 34,605

GAME 3 AT OAK OCT 8

BOS	320 000 100	6	12	0
OAK	042 010 12X	10	15	1

Pitchers: BODDICKER, Gardner (3), Stanley (8) vs Welch, NELSON (2), Young (6), Plunk (7), Honeycutt (7), Eckersley (8)
Home Runs: Greenwell-BOS, McGwire-OAK, Lansford-OAK, Hassey-OAK, Henderson-OAK
Attendance: 49,261

GAME 4 AT OAK OCT 9

BOS	000 001 000	1	4	0
OAK	101 000 02X	4	10	1

Pitchers: HURST, Smithson (5), Smith (7) vs STEWART, Honeycutt (8), Eckersley (9)
Home Runs: Canseco-OAK
Attendance: 49,406

Mickey Hatcher's home run in the first inning of Game One set the tone for the Dodgers' surprising triumph over Oakland's mighty A's. Hatcher, who homered only once during the season, initiated the Series scoring with a two-run blast to left center. Half an inning later the A's Jose Canseco—baseball's leading slugger, with 42 season homers—erased the Dodger lead with his first career grand slam. But while Hatcher went on to hit safely six more times in the Series—including another home run—Canseco's first hit was also his last, as he went 0 for 19 the rest of the way. The Dodgers scored once in the sixth inning to draw within one run of a tie, but remained behind until the last of the ninth when, with two out and one on, Kirk Gibson pinch hit for pitcher Alejandro Peña. Gibson, the Dodgers' top source of power during the season, was so hobbled by leg injuries that he had, till that moment, sat out the game in the training room. But with two strikes on him he belted a home run off baseball's premier reliever, Dennis Eckersley, to win the game. It was Gibson's only Series appearance.

Dodger ace Orel Hershiser blanked the A's on three hits in Game Two and led the offense with three hits of his own. His single in the third inning began a five-run Dodger rally (capped by Mike Marshall's three-run homer), and his fourth-inning double drove in the Dodgers' sixth and final run.

When the Series moved to Oakland, the A's recovered for a dramatic win in Game Three, as Mark McGwire (who had homered 32 times during the season) broke a 1–1 tie with his only Series hit, a solo homer in the last of the ninth. In Game Four, Dodger reliever Jay Howell, who had yielded the losing home run the day before, got McGwire to pop up with the bases full to end the seventh inning, and blanked the A's the rest of the way to preserve a narrow 4–3 Dodger victory.

Hershiser returned to pitch Game Five. He allowed two runs in his four-hitter, but Mickey Hatcher had given the Dodgers the lead with a two-run homer in the first inning, and Mike Davis (who had homered just twice during the season) drove a 3–0 pitch into the stands for two more runs in the fourth. Veteran catcher Rick Dempsey (substituting for injured first-stringer Mike Scioscia) doubled home a fifth Los Angeles run in the sixth, and the Dodgers were on their way to a seventh world title.

Los Angeles Dodgers (NL), 4;
Oakland Athletics (AL), 1

LA (N)

PLAYER/POS	AVG	G	AB	R	H	2B	3B	HR	RBI	BB	SO	SB
Dave Anderson, dh	.000	1	1	0	0	0	0	0	0	0	1	0
Tim Belcher, p	.000	2	0	0	0	0	0	0	0	0	0	0
Mike Davis, dh-2,of-1	.143	4	7	3	1	0	0	1	2	4	0	2
Rick Dempsey, c	.200	2	5	0	1	1	0	0	1	1	2	0
Kirk Gibson, ph	1.000	1	1	1	1	0	0	1	2	0	0	0
Jose Gonzalez, of-3	.000	4	2	0	0	0	0	0	0	0	2	0
Alfredo Griffin, ss	.188	5	16	2	3	0	0	0	0	2	4	0
Jeff Hamilton, 3b	.105	5	19	1	2	0	0	0	0	1	4	0
Mickey Hatcher, of	.368	5	19	5	7	1	0	2	5	1	3	0
Danny Heep, of-1,dh-1	.250	3	8	0	2	1	0	0	0	0	2	0
Orel Hershiser, p	1.000	2	3	1	3	2	0	0	1	0	0	0
Brian Holton, p	.000	1	0	0	0	0	0	0	0	0	0	0
Jay Howell, p	.000	2	0	0	0	0	0	0	0	0	0	0
Tim Leary, p	.000	2	0	0	0	0	0	0	0	0	0	0
Mike Marshall, of	.231	5	13	2	3	0	0	1	3	0	5	0
Alejandro Pena, p	.000	2	0	0	0	0	0	0	0	0	0	0
Steve Sax, 2b	.300	5	20	3	6	0	0	0	0	1	1	1
Mike Scioscia, c	.214	4	14	0	3	0	0	0	1	0	2	0
John Shelby, of	.222	5	18	0	4	1	0	0	1	2	7	1
Franklin Stubbs, 1b	.294	5	17	3	5	2	0	0	2	1	3	0
John Tudor, p	.000	1	0	0	0	0	0	0	0	0	0	0
Tracy Woodson, 1b-3	.000	4	4	0	0	0	0	0	1	0	0	0
TOTAL	.246		167	21	41	8	1	5	19	13	36	4

PITCHER	W	L	ERA	G	GS	CG	SV	SHO	IP	H	ER	BB	SO
Tim Belcher	1	0	6.23	2	2	0	0	0	8.2	10	6	6	10
Orel Hershiser	2	0	1.00	2	2	2	0	1	18.0	7	2	6	17
Brian Holton	0	0	0.00	1	0	0	0	0	2.0	0	0	0	0
Jay Howell	0	1	3.38	2	0	0	1	0	2.2	3	1	1	2
Tim Leary	0	0	1.35	2	0	0	0	0	6.2	6	1	2	4
Alejandro Pena	1	0	0.00	2	0	0	0	0	5.0	2	0	1	7
John Tudor	0	0	0.00	1	1	0	0	0	1.1	0	0	0	1
TOTAL	4	1	2.03	12	5	2	1	1	44.1	28	10	17	41

OAK (A)

PLAYER/POS	AVG	G	AB	R	H	2B	3B	HR	RBI	BB	SO	SB
Don Baylor, ph	.000	1	1	0	0	0	0	0	0	0	1	0
Todd Burns, p	.000	1	0	0	0	0	0	0	0	0	0	0
Greg Cadaret, p	.000	3	0	0	0	0	0	0	0	0	0	0
Jose Canseco, of	.053	5	19	1	1	0	0	1	5	2	5	1
Storm Davis, p	.000	2	1	0	0	0	0	0	0	0	1	0
Dennis Eckersley, p	.000	2	0	0	0	0	0	0	0	0	0	0
Mike Gallego, 2b	.000	1	0	0	0	0	0	0	0	0	0	0
Ron Hassey, c-4	.250	5	8	0	2	0	0	0	1	3	3	0
Dave Henderson, of	.300	5	20	1	6	2	0	0	1	2	7	0
Rick Honeycutt, p	.000	3	0	0	0	0	0	0	0	0	0	0
Glenn Hubbard, 2b	.250	4	12	2	3	0	0	0	0	1	2	1
Stan Javier, of-2	.500	3	4	0	2	0	0	0	2	0	1	0
Carney Lansford, 3b	.167	5	18	2	3	0	0	0	1	2	2	0
Mark Mc Gwire, 1b	.059	5	17	1	1	0	0	1	1	3	4	0
Gene Nelson, p	.000	3	0	0	0	0	0	0	0	0	0	0
Dave Parker, of-2,dh-2	.200	4	15	0	3	0	0	0	0	2	4	0
Tony Phillips, 2b-1,of-1	.250	2	4	1	1	0	0	0	0	1	2	0
Eric Plunk, p	.000	2	0	0	0	0	0	0	0	0	0	0
Luis Polonia, of-2	.111	3	9	1	1	0	0	0	0	0	2	0
Terry Steinbach, c-2,dh-1	.364	3	11	0	4	1	0	0	0	0	2	0
Dave Stewart, p	.000	2	3	1	0	0	0	0	0	1	3	0
Walt Weiss, ss	.063	5	16	1	1	0	0	0	0	0	2	1
Bob Welch, p	.000	1	0	0	0	0	0	0	0	0	0	0
Curt Young, p	.000	1	0	0	0	0	0	0	0	0	0	0
TOTAL	.177		158	11	28	3	0	2	11	17	41	3

PITCHER	W	L	ERA	G	GS	CG	SV	SHO	IP	H	ER	BB	SO
Todd Burns	0	0	0.00	1	0	0	0	0	0.1	0	0	0	0
Greg Cadaret	0	0	0.00	3	0	0	0	0	2.0	2	0	0	3
Storm Davis	0	2	11.25	2	2	0	0	0	8.0	14	10	1	7
Dennis Eckersley	0	1	10.80	2	0	0	0	0	1.2	2	2	1	2
Rick Honeycutt	1	0	0.00	3	0	0	0	0	3.1	0	0	0	5
Gene Nelson	0	0	1.42	3	0	0	0	0	6.1	4	1	3	3
Eric Plunk	0	0	0.00	2	0	0	0	0	1.2	0	0	0	3
Dave Stewart	0	1	3.14	2	2	0	0	0	14.1	12	5	5	5
Bob Welch	0	0	1.80	1	1	0	0	0	5.0	6	1	3	8
Curt Young	0	0	0.00	1	1	0	0	0	1.0	1	0	0	0
TOTAL	1	4	3.92	20	5	0	0	0	43.2	41	19	13	36

GAME 1 AT LA OCT 15

OAK	040 000 000	4	7	0
LA	200 001 002	5	7	0

Pitchers: Stewart, ECKERSLEY (9) vs Belcher, Leary (3), Holton (6), PENA (8) Home Runs: Hatcher-LA, Canseco-OAK, Gibson-LA
Attendance: 55,983

GAME 2 AT LA OCT 16

OAK	000 000 000	0	3	0
LA	005 100 00X	6	10	1

Pitchers: DAVIS, Nelson (4), Young (6), Plunk (7), Honeycutt (8) vs HERSHISER
Home Runs: Marshall-LA
Attendance: 56,051

GAME 3 AT OAK OCT 18

LA	000 010 000	1	8	1
OAK	001 000 001	2	5	0

Pitchers: Tudor, Leary (2), Pena (6), J.HOWELL (9) vs Welch, Cadaret (6), Nelson (6), HONEYCUTT (8)
Home Runs: McGwire-OAK
Attendance: 49,316

GAME 4 AT OAK OCT 19

LA	201 000 100	4	8	1
OAK	100 001 100	3	9	2

Pitchers: BELCHER, J.Howell (7) vs STEWART, Cadaret (7), Eckersley (9)
Attendance: 49,317

GAME 5 AT OAK OCT 20

LA	200 201 000	5	8	0
OAK	001 000 010	2	4	0

Pitchers: HERSHISER vs DAVIS, Cadaret (5), Nelson (6), Honeycutt (8), Plunk (9), Burns (9)
Home Runs: Hatcher-LA, Davis-LA
Attendance: 49,317

From the first inning of Game 1 when they drove in their teams' first runs, first basemen Will Clark of the Giants and Mark Grace of the Cubs dominated the offense, finishing with eight RBIs apiece and LCS record-shattering BAs of .650 and .647. Although Grace homered for two Chicago runs in the opener, the game belonged to Clark, whose four hits—two of them home runs, one a grand slam—drove in six of the eleven Giant runs.

Grace led the Cubs' retaliation the next day with his second three-hit game, driving in four of Chicago's nine runs with doubles in the first and sixth innings. Kevin Mitchell, Matt Williams, and Rob Thompson—runners-up to Clark for Giant offensive honors in the series—all homered in the losing cause.

Chicago scored first in the next three games but narrowly lost them all. Thompson's two-run homer in the last of the seventh put the Giants ahead for good in Game 3. The next day, Williams's two-run single in the third inning overcame Chicago's lead, and his two-run homer in the fifth broke a 4–4 tie to conclude the scoring.

Cub starter Mike Bielecki stopped San Francisco on a pair of singles through six innings of Game 5, and carried a 1–0 lead into the seventh, when Clark's triple and Mitchell's sacrifice fly tied the score. An inning later, after Bielecki loaded the bases with three two-out walks, relief ace Mitch Williams was called on to face Clark and got two strikes on him. But after fouling off a slider and fastball, Clark lined a single up the middle for two go-ahead Giant runs. San Francisco closer Steve Bedrosian yielded Chicago a second run in the ninth on a trio of two-out singles, but Ryne Sandberg (until then batting .421 in the series) grounded out, and the Giants owned their first pennant in twenty-seven years.

San Francisco Giants (West), 4; Chicago Cubs (East), 1

SF (W)

PLAYER/POS	AVG	G	AB	R	H	2B	3B	HR	RB	BB	SO	SB
Bill Bathe, ph	.000	2	1	0	0	0	0	0	0	0	1	0
Steve Bedrosian, p	.000	4	0	0	0	0	0	0	0	0	0	0
Jeff Brantley, p	.000	3	0	0	0	0	0	0	0	1	0	0
Brett Butler, of	.211	5	19	6	4	0	0	0	0	3	3	0
Will Clark, 1b	.650	5	20	8	13	3	1	2	8	2	2	0
Kelly Downs, p	.000	2	3	0	0	0	0	0	0	0	1	0
Scott Garrelts, p	.000	2	4	0	0	0	0	0	0	1	1	0
Atlee Hammaker, p	.000	1	0	0	0	0	0	0	0	0	0	0
Terry Kennedy, c	.188	5	16	0	3	1	0	0	0	1	4	0
Mike La Coss, p	.000	1	1	0	0	0	0	0	0	0	0	0
Craig Lefferts, p	.000	2	0	0	0	0	0	0	0	0	0	0
Greg Litton, 3b	1.000	1	1	0	1	0	0	0	0	0	0	0
Candy Maldonado, of	.000	3	3	1	0	0	0	0	1	2	0	0
Kirt Manwaring, c	.000	3	2	0	0	0	0	0	0	0	0	0
Kevin Mitchell, of	.353	5	17	5	6	0	0	2	7	3	3	0
Donell Nixon, of-2	.000	3	3	0	0	0	0	0	0	0	1	1
Ken Oberkfell, 3b-1	.000	3	4	0	0	0	0	0	0	0	0	0
Rick Reuschel, p	.000	2	2	0	0	0	0	0	0	0	0	0
Ernie Riles, ph	.000	1	1	0	0	0	0	0	0	0	0	0
Don Robinson, p	.000	1	0	0	0	0	0	0	0	0	0	0
Pat Sheridan, of	.154	5	13	1	2	0	1	0	0	0	4	0
Robby Thompson, 2b	.278	5	18	5	5	0	0	2	3	3	2	0
Jose Uribe, ss	.235	5	17	2	4	1	0	0	1	1	5	1
Matt Williams, 3b-5,ss-1	.300	5	20	2	6	1	0	2	9	0	2	0
TOTAL	.267		165	30	44	6	2	8	29	17	29	2

PITCHER	W	L	ERA	G	GS	CG	SV	SHO	IP	H	ER	BB	SO
Steve Bedrosian	0	0	2.70	4	0	0	3	0	3.1	4	1	2	2
Jeff Brantley	0	0	0.00	3	0	0	0	0	5.0	1	0	2	3
Kelly Downs	1	0	3.12	2	0	0	0	0	8.2	8	3	6	6
Scott Garrelts	1	0	5.40	2	2	0	0	0	11.2	16	7	2	8
Atlee Hammaker	0	0	0.00	1	0	0	0	0	1.0	1	0	0	0
Mike La Coss	0	0	9.00	1	1	0	0	0	3.0	7	3	0	2
Craig Lefferts	0	0	9.00	2	0	0	0	0	1.0	1	1	2	1
Rick Reuschel	1	1	5.19	2	2	9	0	0	8.2	12	5	2	5
Don Robinson	1	0	0.00	1	0	0	0	0	1.2	3	0	0	0
TOTAL	4	1	4.09	18	5	9	3	0	44.0	53	20	16	27

CHI (E)

PLAYER/POS	AVG	G	AB	R	H	2B	3B	HR	RB	BB	SO	SB
Paul Assenmacher, p	.000	2	0	0	0	0	0	0	0	0	0	0
Mike Bielecki, p	.200	2	5	0	1	0	0	0	2	0	2	0
Andre Dawson, of	.105	5	19	0	2	1	0	0	3	2	6	0
Shawon Dunston, ss	.316	5	19	2	6	0	0	0	0	1	1	1
Joe Girardi, c	.100	4	10	1	1	0	0	0	0	1	2	0
Mark Grace, 1b	.647	5	17	3	11	3	1	1	8	4	1	1
Paul Kilgus, p	.000	1	0	0	0	0	0	0	0	0	0	0
Lester Lancaster, p	.000	3	1	0	0	0	0	0	0	0	1	0
Vance Law, 3b-1	.000	2	3	0	0	0	0	0	0	0	3	0
Greg Maddux, p-2	.000	3	3	1	0	0	0	0	0	0	0	0
L. McClendon, c-2,of-1	.667	3	3	0	2	0	0	0	0	1	0	0
Domingo Ramos, ph	.000	1	1	0	0	0	0	0	0	0	0	0
Luis Salazar, 3b	.368	5	19	2	7	0	1	1	2	0	0	0
Ryne Sandberg, 2b	.400	5	20	6	8	3	1	1	4	3	4	0
Scott Sanderson, p	.000	1	0	0	0	0	0	0	0	0	0	0
Dwight Smith, of	.200	4	15	2	3	1	0	0	0	2	2	1
Rick Sutcliffe, p	.500	1	2	0	1	1	0	0	0	0	0	0
Jerome Walton, of	.364	5	22	4	8	0	0	0	2	2	2	0
Mitch Webster, of-2	.333	3	3	0	1	0	0	0	0	0	0	0
Curtis Wilkerson, 3b-1	.500	2	2	1	1	0	0	0	0	0	0	0
Mitch Williams, p	.000	2	0	0	0	0	0	0	0	0	0	0
Steve Wilson, p	.000	2	0	0	0	0	0	0	0	0	0	0
Rick Wrona, c	.000	2	5	0	0	0	0	0	0	0	3	0
Marvell Wynne, of-2	.167	4	6	0	1	0	0	0	0	0	0	0
TOTAL	.303		175	22	53	9	3	3	21	16	27	3

PITCHER	W	L	ERA	G	GS	CG	SV	SHO	IP	H	ER	BB	SO
P. Assenmacher	0	0	13.50	2	0	0	0	0	0.2	3	1	0	0
Mike Bielecki	0	1	3.65	2	2	0	0	0	12.1	7	5	6	11
Paul Kilgus	0	0	0.00	1	0	0	0	0	3.0	4	0	1	1
Lester Lancaster	1	1	6.00	3	0	0	0	0	6.0	6	4	1	3
Greg Maddux	0	1	13.50	2	2	0	0	0	7.1	13	11	4	5
Scott Sanderson	0	0	0.00	1	0	0	0	0	2.0	2	0	0	1
Rick Sutcliffe	0	1	4.50	1	1	0	0	0	6.0	5	3	4	2
Mitch Williams	0	0	0.00	2	0	0	0	0	1.0	1	0	0	2
Steve Wilson	0	0	4.91	2	0	0	0	0	3.2	3	2	1	4
TOTAL	1	4	5.57	16	5	0	0	0	42.0	44	26	17	29

GAME 1 AT CHI OCT 4

SF	301	400	030	11	13	0
CHI	201	000	000	3	10	1

Pitchers: GARRELTS, Brantley (8), Hammaker (9) vs MADDUX, Kilgus (5), Wilson (8)
Home Runs: Grace-CHI, Clark-SF (2), Sandberg-CHI, Mitchell-SF
Attendance: 39,195

GAME 2 AT CHI OCT 5

SF	000	200	021	5	10	0
CHI	600	003	00X	9	11	0

Pitchers: REUSCHEL, Downs (1), Lefferts (6), Brantley (7), Bedrosian (8) vs Bielecki, Assenmacher (5), LANCASTER (6)
Home Runs: Mitchell-SF, Williams-SF, Thompson-SF
Attendance: 39,195

GAME 3 AT SF OCT 7

CHI	200	100	100	4	10	0
SF	300	000	20X	5	8	3

Pitchers: Sutcliffe, Assenmacher (7), LANCASTER (7) vs LaCoss, Brantley (4), Robinson (7), Lefferts (8), Bedrosian (9)
Home Runs: Thompson-SF
Attendance: 62,065

GAME 4 AT SF OCT 8

CHI	110	020	000	4	12	1
SF	102	120	00X	6	9	1

Pitchers: Maddux, WILSON (4), Sanderson (6), Williams (8) vs Garrelts, DOWNS (5), Bedrosian (9)
Home Runs: Salazar-CHI, Williams-SF
Attendance: 62,078

GAME 5 AT SF OCT 9

CHI	001	000	001	2	10	1
SF	000	000	12X	3	4	1

Pitchers: BIELECKI, Williams (8), Lancaster (8) vs REUSCHEL, Bedrosian (9)
Attendance: 62,084

The awesome A's produced their share of heroes. Jose Canseco powered a truly heroic home run into the top deck of Toronto's SkyDome in Game 4; Dave Parker, in his seventh postseason series, at last hit his first post-season homer (and later his second); closer Dennis Eckersley added three saves to his four from 1988 to establish a new LCS record; and Carney Lansford was batting .455, with four RBIs, when a hamstring pull in Game 3 ended his series play. But the hero of heroes was leadoff batter Rickey Henderson.

Oakland might have won the opener without Henderson, even though his hard slide into second in the sixth inning broke up a double play and forced a wide throw that gave the A's two runs and their first lead of the game. And the A's might also have won the next day even if Henderson had not rattled Toronto with four stolen bases. The A's suffered their loss in Game 3 despite an early 2–0 lead with Henderson scoring both runs—the first after walking, the second after a double and stolen base.

But in the final two games, Rickey Henderson's contribution made the difference between defeat and victory. A pair of two-run Henderson homers (together with Canseco's memorable blast and later RBI single) gave the A's their 6–5 win in Game 4. And in the first inning of Game 5, Henderson, after walking, stole his eighth base—a postseason series record—before Canseco singled him home with the A's first run. Two innings later Henderson tripled home the second Oakland run. The A's scored twice more in the seventh, but Toronto had narrowed Oakland's lead to one run when Eckersley fanned a final Blue Jay to secure the second straight Oakland pennant. Rickey Henderson was the unanimous choice for series MVP.

Oakland Athletics (West), 4; Toronto Blue Jays (East), 1

OAK (W)

PLAYER/POS	AVG	G	AB	R	H	2B	3B	HR	RB	BB	SO	SB
Lance Blankenship, 2b	.000	1	0	0	0	0	0	0	0	0	0	0
Jose Canseco, of	.294	5	17	1	5	0	0	1	3	3	7	0
Storm Davis, p	.000	1	0	0	0	0	0	0	0	0	0	0
Dennis Eckersley, p	.000	4	0	0	0	0	0	0	0	0	0	0
Mike Gallego, 2b-2,ss-2	.273	4	11	3	3	1	0	0	1	0	2	0
Ron Hassey, c	.167	2	6	0	1	0	0	0	1	1	2	0
Dave Henderson, of	.263	5	19	4	5	3	0	1	1	2	5	0
Rickey Henderson, of	.400	5	15	8	6	1	1	2	5	7	0	8
Rick Honeycutt, p	.000	3	0	0	0	0	0	0	0	0	0	0
Stan Javier, of	.000	1	2	0	0	0	0	0	0	0	1	0
Carney Lansford, 3b	.455	3	11	2	5	0	0	0	4	2	1	2
Mark McGwire, 1b	.389	5	18	3	7	1	0	1	3	1	4	0
Mike Moore, p	.000	1	0	0	0	0	0	0	0	0	0	0
Gene Nelson, p	.000	1	0	0	0	0	0	0	0	0	0	0
Dave Parker, dh	.188	4	16	2	3	0	0	2	3	0	0	0
Ken Phelps, ph	1.000	1	1	0	1	1	0	0	0	0	0	0
Tony Phillips, 2b-3,3b	.167	5	18	1	3	1	0	0	1	2	4	2
Terry Steinbach, c-3,dh-1	.200	4	15	0	3	0	0	0	1	1	5	0
Dave Stewart, p	.000	2	0	0	0	0	0	0	0	0	0	0
Walt Weiss, ss	.111	4	9	2	1	1	0	0	0	1	1	1
Bob Welch, p	.000	1	0	0	0	0	0	0	0	0	0	0
Matt Young, p	.000	1	0	0	0	0	0	0	0	0	0	0
TOTAL	.272		158	26	43	9	1	7	23	20	32	13

PITCHER	W	L	ERA	G	GS	CG	SV	SHO	IP	H	ER	BB	SO
Storm Davis	0	1	7.11	1	1	0	0	0	6.1	5	5	2	3
Dennis Eckersley	0	0	1.59	4	0	0	3	0	5.2	4	1	0	2
Rick Honeycutt	0	0	32.40	3	0	0	0	0	1.2	6	6	5	1
Mike Moore	1	0	0.00	1	1	0	0	0	7.0	3	0	2	3
Gene Nelson	0	0	0.00	1	0	0	0	0	1.1	1	0	0	2
Dave Stewart	2	0	2.81	2	2	0	0	0	16.0	13	5	3	9
Bob Welch	1	0	3.18	1	1	0	0	0	5.2	8	2	1	4
Matt Young	0	0	0.00	1	0	0	0	0	0.1	0	0	2	0
TOTAL	4	1	3.89	14	5	0	3	0	44.0	40	19	15	24

TOR (E)

PLAYER/POS	AVG	G	AB	R	H	2B	3B	HR	RB	BB	SO	SB
Jim Acker, p	.000	5	0	0	0	0	0	0	0	0	0	0
George Bell, dh-3,of-2	.200	5	20	2	4	0	0	1	2	0	3	0
Pat Borders, c	1.000	1	1	0	1	0	0	0	1	0	0	0
John Cerutti, p	.000	2	0	0	0	0	0	0	0	0	0	0
Junior Felix, of	.273	3	11	0	3	1	0	0	3	0	2	0
Tony Fernandez, ss	.350	5	20	6	7	3	0	0	1	1	2	5
Mike Flanagan, p	.000	1	0	0	0	0	0	0	0	0	0	0
Kelly Gruber, 3b	.294	5	17	2	5	1	0	0	1	3	2	1
Tom Henke, p	.000	3	0	0	0	0	0	0	0	0	0	0
Jimmy Key, p	.000	1	0	0	0	0	0	0	0	0	0	0
Manny Lee, 2b	.250	2	8	2	2	0	0	0	0	0	1	0
Lee Mazzilli, dh-2	.000	3	8	0	0	0	0	0	0	0	2	0
Nelson Liriano, 2b	.429	3	7	1	3	0	0	0	1	2	0	3
Fred McGriff, 1b	.143	5	21	1	3	0	0	0	3	0	4	0
Lloyd Moseby, of	.313	5	16	4	5	0	0	1	2	5	2	1
Rance Mulliniks, ph	.000	1	1	0	0	0	0	0	0	0	1	0
Dave Stieb, p	.000	2	0	0	0	0	0	0	0	0	0	0
Todd Stottlemyre, p	.000	1	0	0	0	0	0	0	0	0	0	0
Duane Ward, p	.000	2	0	0	0	0	0	0	0	0	0	0
David Wells, p	.000	1	0	0	0	0	0	0	0	0	0	0
Ernie Whitt, c	.125	5	16	1	2	0	0	1	3	2	3	0
Mookie Wilson, of	.263	5	19	2	5	0	0	0	2	2	2	1
TOTAL	.242		165	21	40	5	0	3	19	15	24	11

PITCHER	W	L	ERA	G	GS	CG	SV	SHO	IP	H	ER	BB	SO
Jim Acker	0	0	1.42	5	0	0	0	0	6.1	4	1	1	4
John Cerutti	0	0	0.00	2	0	0	0	0	2.2	0	0	3	1
Mike Flanagan	0	1	10.38	1	1	0	0	0	4.1	7	5	1	3
Tom Henke	0	0	0.00	3	0	0	0	0	2.2	0	0	0	3
Jimmy Key	1	0	4.50	1	1	0	0	0	6.0	7	3	2	2
Dave Stieb	0	2	6.35	2	2	0	0	0	11.1	12	8	6	10
Todd Stottlemyre	0	1	7.20	1	1	0	0	0	5.0	7	4	2	3
Duane Ward	0	0	7.36	2	0	0	0	0	3.2	6	3	3	5
David Wells	0	0	0.00	1	0	0	0	0	1.0	0	0	2	1
TOTAL	1	4	5.02	18	5	0	0	0	43.0	43	24	20	32

GAME 1 AT OAK OCT 3

```
TOR   020 100 000    3  5  1
OAK   010 013 02X    7 11  0
```
Pitchers: STIEB, Acker (6), Ward (8) vs STEWART, Eckersley (9)
Home Runs: D.Henderson-OAK, Whitt-TOR, McGwire-OAK
Attendance: 49,435

GAME 2 AT OAK OCT 4

```
TOR   001 000 020    3  5  1
OAK   000 203 10X    6  9  1
```
Pitchers: STOTTLEMYRE, Acker (6), Wells (6), Henke (7), Cerutti (8) vs MOORE, Honeycutt (8), Eckersley (8)
Home Runs: Parker-OAK
Attendance: 49,444

GAME 3 AT TOR OCT 6

```
OAK   101 100 000    3  8  1
TOR   000 400 00X    7  8  0
```
Pitchers: DAVIS, Honeycutt (7), Nelson (7), M.Young (8) vs KEY, Acker (7), Henke (9)
Home Runs: Parker-OAK
Attendance: 50,268

GAME 4 AT TOR OCT 7

```
OAK   003 020 100    6 11  1
TOR   000 101 120    5 13  0
```
Pitchers: WELCH, Honeycutt (6), Eckersley (8) vs STIEB, Ward (5), Cerutti (8), Acker (9)
Home Runs: R.Henderson-OAK (2), Canseco-OAK
Attendance: 50,076

GAME 5 AT TOR OCT 8

```
OAK   101 000 200    4  4  0
TOR   000 000 012    3  9  0
```
Pitchers: STEWART, Eckersley (9) vs STIEB, Acker (7), Henke (9)
Home Runs: Moseby-TOR, Bell-TOR
Attendance: 50,024

Not even the devastating earthquake that blindsided baseball's first San Francisco Bay World Series could halt the Oakland juggernaut. The A's scored first in every game and, except for 1½ innings of Game 2 in which the score stood at 1–1, held their lead to the finish.

Athletic ace Dave Stewart shut out the Giants on five hits in the opener. Three second-inning Oakland runs initiated the Series scoring, and Dave Parker and Walt Weiss expanded Stewart's margin of comfort with solo homers in the third and fourth. In Game 2, doubles by Carney Lansford in the first inning and Parker in the fourth drove home the two runs the A's would need for victory; Terry Steinbach's three-run blast later in the fourth added frosting to Oakland's cake. A's starter Mike Moore yielded a pair of singles and the first Giant run of the Series in the third inning but held the Giants to just two more singles in his seven-plus innings of work. Relievers Rick Honeycutt and Dennis Eckersley hurled perfect ball in the eighth and ninth.

After a day off, the Series shifted eleven miles across the Bay to San Francisco for Game 3. But just as fans were settling into their seats, the earthquake struck, knocking out power to Candlestick Park and (as gradually became known) killing 67 people in scattered pockets of destruction throughout the Bay Area. The fans were sent home, but despite the pleas of a few Eastern reporters that the rest of the Series be cancelled, the overwhelming desire of Bay Area residents prevailed, and Game 3 came off at last, ten days late. Starter Dave Stewart gave up three Giant runs in seven innings, but by the time he was relieved, his A's had sent nine men across the plate. Four more runs in the eighth completed the Oakland scoring. The Giants put together their first big inning of the Series, scoring four runs in the last of the ninth. Although the Giants' effort fell far short of what was needed, pinch hitter Bill Bathe's home run—the game's seventh, including five by the A's—set a new World Series record.

Game 4 began as yet another Giant humiliation. Oakland's Rickey Henderson led off the game with a home run, and by the time Giant Kevin Mitchell homered in his team's first pair of runs in the sixth inning, the A's had scored eight times. The Giants struggled back, though, scoring four times in the seventh on a walk and a cycle of hits—home run, triple, double, and single—to draw within two runs of a tie. But

Oakland Athletics (AL), 4; San Francisco Giants (NL), 0

OAK (A)

PLAYER/POS	AVG	G	AB	R	H	2B	3B	HR	RB	BB	SO	SB
Lance Blankenship, 2b	.500	1	2	1	1	0	0	0	0	0	0	0
Todd Burns, p	.000	2	0	0	0	0	0	0	0	0	0	0
Jose Canseco, of	.357	4	14	5	5	0	0	1	3	4	3	1
Dennis Eckersley, p	.000	2	0	0	0	0	0	0	0	0	0	0
Mike Gallego, 2b-1,3b-1	.000	2	1	0	0	0	0	0	0	0	0	0
Dave Henderson, of	.308	4	13	6	4	2	0	2	4	4	3	0
Rickey Henderson, of	.474	4	19	4	9	1	2	1	3	2	2	3
Rick Honeycutt, p	.000	3	0	0	0	0	0	0	0	0	0	0
Stan Javier, of	.000	1	0	0	0	0	0	0	0	0	0	0
Carney Lansford, 3b	.438	4	16	5	7	1	0	1	4	3	1	0
Mark McGwire, 1b	.294	4	17	0	5	1	0	0	1	1	3	0
Mike Moore, p	.333	2	3	1	1	1	0	0	2	0	1	0
Gene Nelson, p	.000	2	0	0	0	0	0	0	0	0	0	0
Dave Parker, dh-2	.222	3	9	2	2	1	0	1	2	0	2	0
Ken Phelps, ph	.000	1	1	0	0	0	0	0	0	0	0	0
	.235		4	17	2	4	1	0	1	3	0	3	0
Terry Steinbach, c	.250	4	16	3	4	0	1	1	7	2	1	0
Dave Stewart, p	.000	2	3	0	0	0	0	0	0	0	1	0
Walt Weiss, ss	.133	4	15	3	2	0	0	1	1	2	2	0
TOTAL	.301		146	32	44	8	3	9	30	18	22	4

PITCHER	W	L	ERA	G	GS	CG	SV	SHO	IP	H	ER	BB	SO
Todd Burns	0	0	0.00	2	0	0	0	0	1.2	1	0	1	0
Dennis Eckersley	0	0	0.00	2	0	0	1	0	1.2	0	0	0	0
Rick Honeycutt	0	0	6.75	3	0	0	0	0	2.2	4	2	0	2
Mike Moore	2	0	2.08	2	2	0	0	0	13.0	9	3	3	10
Gene Nelson	0	0	54.00	2	0	0	0	0	1.0	4	6	2	1
Dave Stewart	2	0	1.69	2	2	1	0	1	16.0	10	3	2	14
TOTAL	4	0	3.50	13	4	1	1	1	36.0	28	14	8	27

SF (N)

PLAYER/POS	AVG	G	AB	R	H	2B	3B	HR	RB	BB	SO	SB
Bill Bathe, ph	.500	2	2	1	1	0	0	1	3	0	0	0
Steve Bedrosian, p	.000	2	0	0	0	0	0	0	0	0	0	0
Jeff Brantley, p	.000	3	0	0	0	0	0	0	0	0	0	0
Brett Butler, of	.286	4	14	1	4	1	0	0	1	2	1	2
Will Clark, 1b	.250	4	16	2	4	1	0	0	0	1	3	0
Kelly Downs, p	.000	3	0	0	0	0	0	0	0	0	0	0
Scott Garrelts, p	.000	2	1	0	0	0	0	0	0	0	1	0
Atlee Hammaker, p	.000	2	0	0	0	0	0	0	0	0	0	0
Terry Kennedy, c	.167	4	12	1	2	0	0	0	2	1	3	0
Mike La Coss, p	.000	2	1	0	0	0	0	0	0	0	0	0
Craig Lefferts, p	.000	3	0	0	0	0	0	0	0	0	0	0
Greg Litton, 2b-2,3b-1	.500	2	6	1	3	1	0	1	3	0	0	0
Candy Maldonado, of-3	.091	4	11	1	1	0	1	0	0	0	4	0
Kirt Manwaring, c	1.000	1	1	1	1	1	0	0	0	0	0	0
Kevin Mitchell, of	.294	4	17	2	5	0	0	1	2	0	3	0
Donell Nixon, of	.200	2	5	1	1	0	0	0	0	1	1	0
Ken Oberkfell, 3b	.333	4	6	1	2	0	0	0	0	3	0	0
Rick Reuschel, p	.000	1	0	0	0	0	0	0	0	0	0	0
Ernie Riles, dh-2	.000	3	8	0	0	0	0	0	0	0	1	0
Don Robinson, p	.000	1	0	0	0	0	0	0	0	0	0	0
Pat Sheridan, of	.000	1	2	0	0	0	0	0	0	0	0	0
Robby Thompson, 2b	.091	4	11	0	1	0	0	0	0	2	4	0
Jose Uribe, ss	.200	3	5	1	1	0	0	0	0	0	0	0
Matt Williams, ss-4,ss-3	.125	4	16	1	2	0	0	1	1	0	6	0
TOTAL	.209		134	14	28	4	1	4	14	8	27	2

PITCHER	W	L	ERA	G	GS	CG	SV	SHO	IP	H	ER	BB	SO
Steve Bedrosian	0	0	0.00	2	0	0	0	0	2.2	0	0	2	2
Jeff Brantley	0	0	4.15	3	0	0	0	0	4.1	5	2	3	1
Kelly Downs	0	0	7.71	3	0	0	0	0	4.2	3	4	2	4
Scott Garrelts	0	2	9.82	2	2	0	0	0	7.1	13	8	1	8
Atlee Hammaker	0	0	15.43	2	0	0	0	0	2.1	8	4	0	2
Mike La Coss	0	0	6.23	2	0	0	0	0	4.1	4	3	3	2
Craig Lefferts	0	0	3.38	3	0	0	0	0	2.2	2	1	2	1
Rick Reuschel	0	1	11.25	1	1	0	0	0	4.0	5	5	4	2
Don Robinson	0	1	21.60	1	1	0	0	0	1.2	4	4	1	0
TOTAL	0	4	8.21	19	4	0	0	0	34.0	44	31	18	22

they came no closer. Oakland scored a ninth run an inning later, and Todd Burns and Dennis Eckersley hurled the Series to its conclusion with 2⅓ innings of perfect relief.

GAME 1 AT OAK OCT 14

SF	000 000 000	0	5	1
OAK	031 100 00X	5	11	1

Pitchers: GARRELTS, Hammaker (5), Brantley (6), LaCoss (8) vs STEWART
Home Runs: Parker-OAK, Weiss-OAK
Attendance: 49,385

GAME 2 AT OAK OCT 15

SF	001 000 000	1	4	0
OAK	100 400 00X	5	7	0

Pitchers: REUSCHEL, Downs (5), Lefferts (7), Bedrosian (8) vs MOORE, Honeycutt (8), Eckersley (9)
Home Runs: Steinbach-OAK
Attendance: 49,388

GAME 3 AT SF OCT 27

OAK	200 241 040	13	14	0
SF	010 200 004	7	10	3

Pitchers: STEWART, Honeycutt (8), Nelson (9), Burns (9) vs GARRELTS, Downs (4), Brantley (5), Hammaker (8), Lefferts (9)
Home Runs: Williams-SF, D.Henderson-OAK (2), Phillips-OAK, Canseco-OAK, Lansford-OAK, Bathe-SF
Attendance: 62,038

GAME 4 AT SF OCT 28

OAK	130 031 010	9	12	0
SF	000 002 400	6	9	0

Pitchers: MOORE, Nelson (7), Honeycutt (7), Burns (7), Eckersley (9) vs ROBINSON, LaCoss (2), Brantley (6), Downs (6), Lefferts (8), Bedrosian (8)
Home Runs: R.Henderson-OAK, Mitchell-SF, Litton-SF
Attendance: 62,032

Fielding plays and misplays provided some of the most crucial moments of the series. After the Pirates had overcome a three-run deficit to tie the score in Game 1, for example, they won the game when Eric Davis misplayed Andy Van Slyke's fly to left field for a run-scoring double. Cincinnati right fielder Paul O'Neill evened the series in Game 2 by singling home the game's first run in the first inning, then (with the game tied 1–1 in the fifth) doubling in the go-ahead—and final—run on a fly Pirate left fielder Barry Bonds lost in the late afternoon sun. Finally, O'Neill gunned down Pittsburgh's potential tying run at third base when Van Slyke attempted to move up after Bonds's fly-out to right.

Two- and three-run homers by Reds Billy Hatcher and Mariano Duncan gave Cincinnati the series advantage in Game 3, and Chris Sabo's sacrifice fly and two-run blast proved the decisive blows a day later as the Reds pushed their series lead to 3–1. In that game left fielder Eric Davis, backing up Bobby Bonilla, prevented what would have become a game-tying run when, with a perfect throw to third, he nailed Bonilla trying for a triple.

The Pirates staved off elimination with a narrow 3–2 win in Game 5, a win preserved by a spectacular bases-loaded game-ending double play. But in Game 6, Pittsburgh's uncertain fielding in the first inning gave the Reds their first and, as it turned out, decisive run. In the ninth inning, with the Reds ahead 2–1, Reds right fielder Glen Braggs snared a deep fly with a leaping catch that prevented at least one, and perhaps two, Pirate runs from scoring. One strikeout later the Reds had snared the National League pennant.

Cincinnati Reds (West), 4; Pittsburgh Pirates (East), 2

CIN (W)

PLAYER/POS	AVG	G	AB	R	H	2B	3B	HR	RB	BB	SO	SB
Billy Bates, pr	.000	2	0	1	0	0	0	0	0	0	0	0
Todd Benzinger, 1b-2	.333	5	9	0	3	0	0	0	0	2	0	0
Glenn Braggs, of	.200	2	5	0	1	0	0	0	0	0	1	0
Tom Browning, p	.000	2	3	0	0	0	0	0	0	0	1	0
Norm Charlton, p	.000	4	0	0	0	0	0	0	0	0	0	0
Eric Davis, of	.174	6	23	2	4	1	0	0	2	1	9	0
Rob Dibble, p	.000	4	2	0	0	0	0	0	0	0	1	0
Mariano Duncan, 2b	.300	6	20	1	6	0	0	1	4	0	8	0
Billy Hatcher, of	.333	4	15	2	5	1	0	1	2	0	2	0
Danny Jackson, p	.000	2	3	0	0	0	0	0	0	0	2	0
Barry Larkin, ss	.261	6	23	5	6	2	0	0	1	3	1	3
Rick Mahler, p	.000	1	0	0	0	0	0	0	0	0	0	0
Hal Morris, 1b-4	.417	5	12	3	5	1	0	0	1	1	0	0
Randy Myers, p	.000	4	0	0	0	0	0	0	0	0	0	0
Ron Oester, 2b-2	.333	3	3	1	1	0	0	0	0	0	1	0
Joe Oliver, c	.143	5	14	1	2	0	0	0	0	0	2	0
Paul O'Neill, of	.471	5	17	1	8	3	0	1	4	1	1	1
Luis Quinones, ph	.500	3	2	1	1	0	0	0	2	0	0	1
Jeff Reed, c	.000	4	7	0	0	0	0	0	0	0	2	0
Jose Rijo, p	.000	2	5	0	0	0	0	0	0	0	1	0
Chris Sabo, 3b	.227	6	22	1	5	0	0	1	3	1	4	0
Scott Scudder, p	.000	1	0	0	0	0	0	0	0	0	0	0
Herm Winningham, of-2	.286	3	7	1	2	1	0	0	1	1	1	1
TOTAL	.255		192	20	49	9	0	4	20	10	37	6

PITCHER	W	L	ERA	G	GS	CG	SV	SHO	IP	H	ER	BB	SO
Tom Browning	1	1	3.27	2	2	0	0	0	11.0	9	4	6	5
Norm Charlton	1	1	1.80	4	0	0	0	0	5.0	4	1	3	3
Rob Dibble	0	0	0.00	4	0	0	1	0	5.0	0	0	1	10
Danny Jackson	1	0	2.38	2	2	0	0	0	11.1	8	3	7	8
Rick Mahler	0	0	0.00	1	0	0	0	0	1.2	2	0	0	0
Randy Myers	0	0	0.00	4	0	0	3	0	5.2	2	0	3	7
Jose Rijo	1	0	4.38	2	2	0	0	0	12.1	10	6	7	15
Scott Scudder	0	0	0.00	1	0	0	0	0	1.0	1	0	0	1
TOTAL	4	2	2.38	20	6	0	4	0	53.0	36	14	27	49

PIT (E)

PLAYER/POS	AVG	G	AB	R	H	2B	3B	HR	RB	BB	SO	SB
Wally Backman, 3b-2	.143	3	7	1	1	1	0	0	0	1	3	1
Stan Belinda, p	.000	3	0	0	0	0	0	0	0	0	0	0
Jay Bell, ss	.250	6	20	3	5	1	0	1	1	4	3	0
Barry Bonds, of	.167	6	18	4	3	0	0	0	1	6	6	2
Bobby Bonilla, of-5,3b-3	.190	6	21	0	4	1	0	0	1	3	1	0
Sid Bream, 1b	.500	4	8	1	4	1	0	1	3	2	3	0
Doug Drabeck, p	.167	2	6	0	1	0	0	0	0	0	2	0
Jeff King, 3b-4	.100	5	10	0	1	0	0	0	0	1	5	0
Bill Landrum, p	.000	2	0	0	0	0	0	0	0	0	0	0
Mike La Valliere, c	.000	3	6	1	0	0	0	0	0	3	1	0
Jose Lind, 2b	.238	6	21	1	5	1	1	1	2	1	4	0
Carmelo Martinez, 1b	.250	2	8	0	2	2	0	0	2	0	1	0
Bob Patterson, p	.000	2	0	0	0	0	0	0	0	0	0	0
Ted Power, p	.000	2	1	0	0	0	0	0	0	0	1	0
Gary Redus, 1b-2	.250	5	8	1	2	0	0	0	0	1	3	1
R. J. Reynolds, of-3	.200	6	10	0	2	0	0	0	0	2	2	1
Don Slaught, c	.091	4	11	0	1	1	0	0	1	2	3	0
John Smiley, p	.000	1	0	0	0	0	0	0	0	0	0	0
Zane Smith, p	.000	2	3	0	0	0	0	0	0	0	1	0
Andy Van Slyke, of	.208	6	24	3	5	1	1	0	3	1	6	1
Bob Walk, p	.000	2	4	0	0	0	0	0	0	0	4	0
TOTAL	.194		186	15	36	9	2	3	14	27	49	6

PITCHER	W	L	ERA	G	GS	CG	SV	SHO	IP	H	ER	BB	SO
Stan Belinda	0	0	2.45	3	0	0	0	0	3.2	3	1	0	4
Doug Drabeck	1	1	1.65	2	2	1	0	0	16.1	12	3	3	13
Bill Landrum	0	0	0.00	2	0	0	0	0	2.0	0	0	0	1
Bob Patterson	0	0	0.00	2	0	0	1	0	1.0	1	0	2	0
Ted Power	0	0	3.60	2	1	0	1	0	5.0	6	2	2	3
John Smiley	0	0	0.00	1	0	0	0	0	2.0	2	0	0	0
Zane Smith	0	2	6.00	2	1	0	0	0	9.0	14	6	1	8
Bob Walk	1	1	4.85	2	2	0	0	0	13.0	11	7	2	8
TOTAL	2	4	3.29	16	6	1	2	0	52.0	49	19	10	37

GAME 1 AT CIN OCT 4

PIT	001	200	100	4	7	1
CIN	300	000	000	3	5	0

Pitchers: WALK, Belinda (7), Patterson (9), Power (9) vs Rijo, CHARLTON (6), Dibble (9)
Home Runs: Bream-PIT
Attendance: 55,700

GAME 2 AT CIN OCT 5

PIT	000	010	000	1	6	0
CIN	100	010	00X	2	5	0

Pitchers: DRABEK vs BROWNING, Dibble (7), Myers (8)
Home Runs: Lind-PIT
Attendance: 54,456

GAME 3 AT PIT OCT 8

CIN	020	030	001	6	13	1
PIT	000	200	010	3	8	0

Pitchers: JACKSON, Dibble (6), Charlton (8), Myers (9) vs SMITH, Landrum (6), Smiley (7), Belinda (9)
Home Runs: Duncan-CIN, Hatcher-CIN
Attendance: 45,611

GAME 4 AT PIT OCT 9

CIN	000	200	201	5	10	1
PIT	100	100	010	3	8	0

Pitchers: RIJO, Myers (8), Dibble (9) vs WALK, Power (8)
Home Runs: O'Neill-CIN, Sabo-CIN, Bell-PIT
Attendance: 50,461

GAME 5 AT PIT OCT 10

CIN	100	000	010	2	7	0
PIT	200	100	00X	3	6	1

Pitchers: BROWNING, Mahler (6), Charlton (7), Scudder (8) vs DRABEK, Patterson (9)
Attendance: 48,221

GAME 6 AT CIN OCT 12

PIT	000	010	000	1	1	3
CIN	100	000	10X	2	9	0

Pitchers: Power, SMITH (3), Belinda (7), Landrum (8) vs Jackson, CHARLTON (7), Myers (8)
Attendance: 56,079

The ejection of Boston ace Roger Clemens from Game 4 for mouthing off to an umpire provided a moment of raucous counterpoint to the surgical precision with which Oakland dismembered the Red Sox. While the A's pitchers anesthetized Boston's hitters, parceling out just one run per game, their batters sliced up the Sox with singles, steals, and sacrifices.

In the fourth inning of Game 1, Boston's Wade Boggs interrupted a pitchers' duel between Clemens and Oakland's Dave Stewart with the series' only home run. But in the top of the seventh—after a tiring Clemens had been relieved—the A's evened the score with a walk, single, and sacrifice fly, took the lead an inning later with a pair of singles sandwiched around a bunt and stolen base, then buried the Sox with seven runs in the ninth. DH Harold Baines provided Oakland's most productive offense in the second game, singling home the tying run in the fourth inning, driving in the tiebreaker with a groundout in the seventh, and doubling home a third run in the ninth. In Game 3, a double steal by Baines and Jose Canseco set up the A's tying and tiebreaking runs, which scored on a sacrifice fly and a single.

The A's scored first for the only time in the series in Game 4, on a pair of singles and a grounder to short in the second inning. Following the shouting match between the Sox and umpires that erupted when pitcher Clemens was thrown out for disputing a walk to the next batter, Mike Gallego doubled home two more Oakland runs. A trio of Boston relievers stopped the Athletics the rest of the way, and a pair of Red Sox hits in the ninth ended Dave Stewart's shutout bid. But Rick Honeycutt came on to preserve Stewart's second win of the series and sew up Oakland's third successive American League championship.

Oakland Athletics (West), 4;
Boston Red Sox (East), 0

OAK (W)

PLAYER/POS	AVG	G	AB	R	H	2B	3B	HR	RB	BB	SO	SB
Harold Baines, dh	.357	4	14	2	5	1	0	0	3	2	1	1
Lance Blankenship, dh	.000	3	0	1	0	0	0	0	0	0	0	1
Jose Canseco, of	.182	4	11	3	2	0	0	0	1	5	5	2
Dennis Eckersley, p	.000	3	0	0	0	0	0	0	0	0	0	0
Mike Gallego, ss-3,2b-2	.400	4	10	1	4	1	0	0	2	1	1	0
Ron Hassey, c-1,dh-1	.333	2	3	0	1	0	0	0	0	2	0	0
Dave Henderson, of	.167	2	6	0	1	0	0	0	1	0	2	1
Rickey Henderson, of	.294	4	17	1	5	0	0	0	3	1	2	2
Rick Honeycutt, p	.000	3	0	0	0	0	0	0	0	0	0	0
Doug Jennings, of	.000	1	1	0	0	0	0	0	0	0	0	0
Carney Lansford, 3b	.438	4	16	2	7	1	0	0	2	0	1	0
Willie McGee, of-2,dh-1	.222	3	9	3	2	1	0	0	0	1	2	2
Mark McGwire, 1b	.154	4	13	2	2	0	0	0	2	3	3	0
Mike Moore, p	.000	1	0	0	0	0	0	0	0	0	0	0
Gene Nelson, p	.000	1	0	0	0	0	0	0	0	0	0	0
Jamie Quirk, ph	1.000	1	1	0	1	0	0	0	0	0	0	0
Willie Randolph, 2b	.375	4	8	1	3	0	0	0	3	1	0	0
Terry Steinbach, c	.455	3	11	2	5	0	0	0	1	1	2	0
Dave Stewart, p	.000	2	0	0	0	0	0	0	0	0	0	0
Walt Weiss, ss	.000	2	7	2	0	0	0	0	0	2	2	0
Bob Welch, p	.000	1	0	0	0	0	0	0	0	0	0	0
TOTAL	.299		127	20	38	4	0	0	18	19	21	9

PITCHER	W	L	ERA	G	GS	CG	SV	SHO	IP	H	ER	BB	SO
Dennis Eckersley	0	0	0.00	3	0	0	2	0	3.1	2	0	0	3
Rick Honeycutt	0	0	0.00	3	0	0	1	0	1.2	0	0	0	0
Mike Moore	1	0	1.50	1	1	0	0	0	6.0	4	1	1	5
Gene Nelson	0	0	0.00	1	0	0	0	0	1.2	3	0	0	0
Dave Stewart	2	0	1.13	2	2	0	0	0	16.0	8	2	2	4
Bob Welch	1	0	1.23	1	1	0	0	0	7.1	6	1	3	4
TOTAL	4	0	1.00	11	4	0	3	0	36.0	23	4	6	16

BOS (E)

PLAYER/POS	AVG	G	AB	R	H	2B	3B	HR	RB	BB	SO	SB
Larry Andersen, p	.000	3	0	0	0	0	0	0	0	0	0	0
Marty Barrett, 2b	.000	3	0	0	0	0	0	0	0	0	0	0
Mike Boddicker, p	.000	1	0	0	0	0	0	0	0	0	0	0
Wade Boggs, 3b	.438	4	16	1	7	1	0	1	1	0	3	0
Tom Bolton, p	.000	2	0	0	0	0	0	0	0	0	0	0
Tom Brunansky, of	.083	4	12	0	1	0	0	0	1	1	3	0
Ellis Burks, of	.267	4	15	1	4	2	0	0	0	1	1	1
Roger Clemens, p	.000	2	0	0	0	0	0	0	0	0	0	0
Dwight Evans, dh	.231	4	13	0	3	1	0	0	0	1	3	0
Jeff Gray, p	.000	2	0	0	0	0	0	0	0	0	0	0
Mike Greenwell, of	.000	4	14	1	0	0	0	0	0	2	2	0
Greg Harris, p	.000	1	0	0	0	0	0	0	0	0	0	0
Danny Heep, ph	.000	2	2	0	0	0	0	0	0	0	0	0
Dana Kiecker, p	.000	1	0	0	0	0	0	0	0	0	0	0
Randy Kutcher, pr	.000	2	0	0	0	0	0	0	0	0	0	0
Dennis Lamp, p	.000	1	0	0	0	0	0	0	0	0	0	0
Mike Marshall, ph	.333	3	3	0	1	0	0	0	0	0	0	0
Rob Murphy, p	.000	1	0	0	0	0	0	0	0	0	0	0
Tony Pena, c	.214	4	14	0	3	0	0	0	0	0	0	0
Carlos Quintana, 1b	.000	4	13	0	0	0	0	0	1	1	0	0
Jeff Reardon, p	.000	1	0	0	0	0	0	0	0	0	0	0
Jody Reed, 2b-4,ss-3	.133	4	15	0	2	0	0	0	1	0	2	0
Luis Rivera, ss	.222	4	9	1	2	1	0	0	0	0	2	0
TOTAL	.183		126	4	23	5	0	1	4	6	16	1

PITCHER	W	L	ERA	G	GS	CG	SV	SHO	IP	H	ER	BB	SO
Larry Andersen	0	1	6.00	3	0	0	0	0	3.0	3	2	3	3
Mike Boddicker	0	1	2.25	1	1	1	0	0	8.0	6	2	3	7
Tom Bolton	0	0	0.00	2	0	0	0	0	3.0	2	0	2	3
Roger Clemens	0	1	3.52	2	2	0	0	0	7.2	7	3	5	4
Jeff Gray	0	0	2.70	2	0	0	0	0	3.1	4	1	1	2
Greg Harris	0	1	27.00	1	0	0	0	0	0.1	3	1	0	0
Dana Kiecker	0	0	1.59	1	1	0	0	0	5.2	6	1	1	2
Dennis Lamp	0	0	108.00	1	0	0	0	0	0.1	2	4	2	0
Rob Murphy	0	0	13.50	1	0	0	0	0	0.2	2	1	1	0
Jeff Reardon	0	0	9.00	1	0	0	0	0	2.0	3	2	1	0
TOTAL	0	4	4.50	15	4	1	0	0	34.0	38	17	19	21

GAME 1 AT BOS OCT 6

OAK	000	000	117	9	13	0
BOS	000	100	000	1	5	1

Pitchers: STEWART, Eckersley (9) vs Clemens, ANDERSEN (7), Bolton (8), Gray (8), Lamp (9), Murphy (9)
Home Runs: Boggs-BOS
Attendance: 35,192

GAME 2 AT BOS OCT 7

OAK	000	100	102	4	13	1
BOS	001	000	000	1	6	0

Pitchers: WELCH, Honeycutt (8), Eckersley (8) vs Kiecker, HARRIS (6), Andersen (7), Reardon (8)
Attendance: 35,070

GAME 3 AT OAK OCT 9

BOS	010	000	000	1	8	3
OAK	000	202	00X	4	6	0

Pitchers: BODDICKER vs MOORE, Nelson (7), Honeycutt (8), Eckersley (9)
Attendance: 49,026

GAME 4 AT OAK OCT 10

BOS	000	000	001	1	4	1
OAK	030	000	00X	3	6	0

Pitchers: CLEMENS, Bolton (2), Gray (5), Andersen (8) vs STEWART, Honeycutt (9)
Attendance: 49,052

In the most stunning World Series sweep since 1954, Cincinnati's fired-up Reds roasted the team many were proclaiming baseball's newest dynasty. Reds left fielder Eric Davis, playing despite shoulder and knee injuries, provided the A's their first hint of what was to come when—on the first pitch thrown to him in the first inning—he homered over the center field wall for two runs. Billy Hatcher, on base with a walk, scored ahead of Davis, the first of his Series-high six runs. Hatcher would not be retired at the plate until Game 3. Final score: 7–0. For Oakland starter Dave Stewart, the loss ended a personal postseason six-game win streak. For the club, the loss ended a streak of ten postseason wins.

The A's put up their best fight of the Series in Game 2, scoring first, then overcoming a 1–2 deficit in the third inning with three more runs for a 4–2 lead. Cincinnati narrowed the gap with a run in the fourth and tied the score in the eighth when Hatcher tripled—setting a World Series record with his seventh straight hit—and came home on a grounder to short. The A's held on until the tenth inning, when ace reliever Dennis Eckersley gave up three straight hits to lose the game.

Game 3 was another Cincinnati blowout, an 8–3 contest in which all eleven runs were scored in the second and third innings. Chris Sabo led the Reds assault with two home runs, and handled a Series-record ten chances at third base.

For seven innings of Game 4 the tide of battle seemed to be turning in Oakland's favor. Billy Hatcher—who was batting .750—left the game after a pitch hit his hand in the first inning. Later in the inning Eric Davis tore a kidney diving for a Willie McGee shot that went for a double. McGee went on to score, and Davis departed for the hospital. A renewed Dave Stewart, supported by sharp fielding, seemed capable of sustaining his 1–0 lead to the finish. But in the eighth the Reds, with just one solid hit, eked out the two runs they would need for victory. After loading the bases with a leadoff single, a third-strike bunt that went for a hit, and a sacrifice bunt that Stewart misplayed for an error, the Reds drove home the tying run with a grounder to short and took the lead on a sacrifice fly. Meanwhile Reds starter Jose Rijo held the A's hitless after the first inning, leveling twenty men in order from the second into the ninth, when ace closer Randy Myers relieved him for the final two outs of the splendid sweep.

Cincinnati Reds (NL), 4; Oakland Athletics (AL), 0

CIN (N)

PLAYER/POS	AVG	G	AB	R	H	2B	3B	HR	RB	BB	SO	SB
Jack Armstrong, p	.000	1	0	0	0	0	0	0	0	0	0	0
Billy Bates, ph	1.000	1	1	1	1	0	0	0	0	0	0	0
Todd Benzinger, 1b-3	.182	4	11	1	2	0	0	0	0	0	0	0
Glenn Braggs, of-1	.000	2	4	0	0	0	0	0	2	1	0	0
Tom Browning, p	.000	1	0	0	0	0	0	0	0	0	0	0
Norm Charlton, p	.000	1	0	0	0	0	0	0	0	0	0	0
Eric Davis, of	.286	4	14	3	4	0	0	1	5	0	0	0
Rob Dibble, p	.000	3	0	0	0	0	0	0	0	0	0	0
Mariano Duncan, 2b	.143	4	14	1	2	0	0	0	1	2	2	1
Billy Hatcher, of	.750	4	12	6	9	4	1	0	2	2	0	0
Danny Jackson, p	.000	1	0	0	0	0	0	0	0	0	1	0
Barry Larkin, ss	.353	4	17	3	6	1	1	0	1	2	0	0
Hal Morris, 1b-2,dh-2	.071	4	14	0	1	0	0	0	2	1	1	0
Randy Myers, p	.000	3	0	0	0	0	0	0	0	0	0	0
Ron Oester, ph	1.000	1	1	0	1	0	0	0	1	0	0	0
Joe Oliver, c	.333	4	18	2	6	3	0	0	2	0	1	0
Paul O'Neill, of	.083	4	12	2	1	0	0	0	1	5	2	1
Jose Rijo, p	.333	2	3	0	1	0	0	0	0	0	0	0
Chris Sabo, 3b	.563	4	16	2	9	1	0	2	5	2	2	0
Scott Scudder, p	.000	1	0	0	0	0	0	0	0	0	0	0
Herm Winningham, of-1	.500	2	4	1	2	0	0	0	0	0	0	0
TOTAL	.317		142	22	45	9	2	3	22	15	9	2

PITCHER	W	L	ERA	G	GS	CG	SV	SHO	IP	H	ER	BB	SO
Jack Armstrong	0	0	0.00	1	0	0	0	0	3.0	1	0	0	3
Tom Browning	1	0	4.50	1	1	0	0	0	6.0	6	3	2	2
Norm Charlton	0	0	0.00	1	0	0	0	0	1.0	1	0	0	0
Rob Dibble	1	0	0.00	3	0	0	0	0	4.2	3	0	1	4
Danny Jackson	0	0	10.13	1	1	0	0	0	2.2	6	3	2	0
Randy Myers	0	0	0.00	3	0	0	0	1	3.0	2	0	0	3
Jose Rijo	2	0	0.59	2	2	0	0	0	15.1	9	1	5	14
Scott Scudder	0	0	0.00	1	0	0	0	0	1.1	0	0	2	2
TOTAL	4	0	1.70	13	4	0	1	0	37.0	28	7	12	28

OAK (A)

PLAYER/POS	AVG	G	AB	R	H	2B	3B	HR	RB	BB	SO	SB
Harold Baines, dh-2	.143	3	7	1	1	0	0	1	2	1	2	0
Lance Blankenship, ph	.000	1	1	0	0	0	0	0	0	0	1	0
Mike Bordick, ss	.000	3	0	0	0	0	0	0	0	0	0	0
Todd Burns, p	.000	2	0	0	0	0	0	0	0	0	0	0
Jose Canseco, of-3,dh-1	.083	4	12	1	1	0	0	1	2	2	3	0
Dennis Eckersley, p	.000	2	0	0	0	0	0	0	0	0	0	0
Mike Gallego, ss	.091	4	11	0	1	0	0	0	1	1	3	1
Ron Hassey, c-1	.333	3	6	0	2	0	0	0	1	0	0	0
Dave Henderson, of-3	.231	4	13	2	3	1	0	0	0	1	3	0
Rickey Henderson, of	.333	4	15	2	5	2	0	1	1	3	4	3
Rick Honeycutt, p	.000	1	0	0	0	0	0	0	0	0	0	0
Doug Jennings, ph	1.000	1	1	0	1	0	0	0	0	0	0	0
Joe Klink, p	.000	1	0	0	0	0	0	0	0	0	0	0
Carney Lansford, 3b	.267	4	15	0	4	0	0	0	1	1	0	1
Willie McGee, of-3	.200	4	10	1	2	1	0	0	0	0	2	1
Mark McGwire, 1b	.214	4	14	1	3	0	0	0	0	2	4	0
Mike Moore, p	.000	1	0	0	0	0	0	0	0	0	0	0
Gene Nelson, p	.000	2	0	0	0	0	0	0	0	0	0	0
Jamie Quirk, c	.000	1	3	0	0	0	0	0	0	0	2	0
Willie Randolph, 2b	.267	4	15	4	4	0	0	0	0	1	0	1
Scott Sanderson, p	.000	2	0	0	0	0	0	0	0	0	0	0
Terry Steinbach, c	.125	3	8	0	1	0	0	0	0	0	1	0
Dave Stewart, p	.000	2	1	0	0	0	0	0	0	0	1	0
Bob Welch, p	.000	1	3	0	0	0	0	0	0	0	2	0
Curt Young, p	.000	1	0	0	0	0	0	0	0	0	0	0
TOTAL	.207		135	8	28	4	0	3	8	12	28	7

PITCHER	W	L	ERA	G	GS	CG	SV	SHO	IP	H	ER	BB	SO
Todd Burns	0	0	16.20	2	0	0	0	0	1.2	5	3	2	0
Dennis Eckersley	0	1	6.75	2	0	0	0	0	1.1	3	1	0	1
Rick Honeycutt	0	0	0.00	1	0	0	0	0	1.2	2	0	1	0
Joe Klink	0	0	INF	1	0	0	0	0	0.0	0	0	1	0
Mike Moore	0	1	6.75	1	1	0	0	0	2.2	8	2	0	1
Gene Nelson	0	0	0.00	2	0	0	0	0	5.0	3	0	2	0
Scott Sanderson	0	0	10.80	2	0	0	0	0	1.2	4	2	1	0
Dave Stewart	0	2	3.46	2	2	1	0	0	13.0	10	5	6	5
Bob Welch	0	0	4.91	1	1	0	0	0	7.1	9	4	2	2
Curt Young	0	0	0.00	1	0	0	0	0	1.0	1	0	0	0
TOTAL	0	4	4.33	15	4	1	0	0	35.1	45	17	15	9

GAME 1 AT CIN OCT 16

OAK	000	000	000	0	9 1
CIN	202	030	00X	7	10 0

Pitchers: STEWART, Burns (5), Nelson (5), Sanderson (7), Eckersley (8) vs RIJO, Dibble (8), Myers (9)
Home Runs: Davis-CIN
Attendance: 55,830

GAME 2 AT CIN OCT 17

OAK	103	000	000	0	4 10
CIN	200	100	010	1	5 14

Pitchers: Welch, Honeycutt (8), ECKERSLEY (10) vs Jackson, Scudder (3), Armstrong (5), Charlton (8), DIBBLE (9)
Home Runs: Canseco-OAK
Attendance: 55,832

GAME 3 AT OAK OCT 19

CIN	017	000	000	8 14 1
OAK	021	000	000	3 7 1

Pitchers: BROWNING, Dibble (7), Myers (8) vs MOORE, Sanderson (3), Klink (4), Nelson (4), Burns (8), Young (9)
Home Runs: Sabo-CIN (2), Baines-OAK, R.Henderson-OAK
Attendance: 48,269

GAME 4 AT OAK OCT 20

CIN	000	000	020	2 7 1
OAK	100	000	000	1 2 1

Pitchers: RIJO, Myers (9) vs STEWART
Attendance: 48,613

The All-Star Game

Frederick Ivor-Campbell

Although the tradition of All-Star Games in baseball dates back to an 1858 series between teams of stars from Brooklyn and New York (they were called "picked nines" in those days), the current All-Star series began when Arch Ward, sports editor of the *Chicago Tribune*, persuaded hesitant league owners to go along with his proposal for a game between stars from the American and National leagues, to be played in Chicago during that city's Century of Progress Exposition in 1933.

All-Star managers (who, except for the first game, have been the pilots of the previous year's pennant winners) shared with fans the selection of players for the first two games. From 1935 through 1946 the manager selected his whole squad. Since 1947, he has chosen his pitchers and all other players except the eight members of the starting lineup. The fans chose the starters in 1947–1957; after an incident of ballot-box stuffing by Cincinnati partisans in 1957, the major league players, coaches, and managers made the choice in 1958–1969; in 1970 the selection of starting lineups was returned to the fans.

The American League dominated the early years of the series, winning the first three games, and extending their winning margin to eight games (12–4) by 1949. The National League cut the lead in half with four straight wins, and by 1964 had drawn even in the series (17–17–1). From 1965 through 1985 the National Leaguers continued their drive, winning 19 All-Star Games while losing only two, to build a commanding 36–19 lead in the series. In recent years, though, the American Leaguers have begun to come back, winning in 1990 their fourth game in five years, and their third in a row. But even if they were to continue winning every year, it would take them until 2004 to catch up.

GAME 1
Comiskey Park, Chicago
July 6, 1933
AL, 4-2

NL	000 002 000	2	8	0
AL	012 001 00X	4	9	1

Pitchers: HALLAHAN, Warneke (3), Hubbell (7) vs GOMEZ, Crowder (4), Grove (7)
Home Runs: Ruth-A, Frisch-N
Attendance: 49,200

Baseball's two grand old managers—Connie Mack and John McGraw—were chosen to lead the American and National League squads in the first All-Star Game, and American starting pitcher Lefty Gomez of the Yankees took home honors both as the first All-Star winning pitcher and as the first player to drive in an All-Star run (singling in Jimmie Dykes in the second inning). But it was another "grand old man"—Babe Ruth—who made the game's headlines. At thirty-eight, in his next-to-last season as a Yankee, he lined a two-run homer in the third to make the score 3-0, and as right fielder in the eighth he robbed Chick Hafey of a hit with a remarkable running catch of Hafey's line drive.

Frank Frisch homered for the Nationals, following up Pepper Martin's RBI with a solo shot in the National League's two-run sixth. But the American stars countered with an insurance run in the bottom of the sixth, as Earl Averill singled in Joe Cronin to end the scoring. Carl Hubbell for the Nationals and Lefty Grove for the Americans blanked the opposition through the final innings.

GAME 2
Polo Grounds, New York
July 10, 1934
AL, 9-7

AL	000 261 000	9	14	1
NL	103 030 000	7	8	1

Pitchers: Gomez, Ruffing (4), HARDER (5) vs Hubbell, Warneke (4), MUNGO (5), J.Dean (6), Frankhouse (9)
Home Runs: Frisch-N, Medwick-N
Attendance: 48,363

This was the game in which Carl Hubbell struck out Babe Ruth, Lou Gehrig, Jimmie Foxx, Al Simmons, and Joe Cronin in order in the first two innings. Hubbell also walked two and gave up two hits in his three innings of work, but allowed no run to score as his Nationals took a 4-0 lead on homers by Frank Frisch in the first and Joe Medwick (for three runs) in the third off American starter (and first-game winner) Lefty Gomez.

But with Hubbell gone, the Americans pounced on Lon Warneke and Van Lingle Mungo for four runs each in the fourth and fifth innings. The Nationals battled back for three off Red Ruffing in their half of the fifth, to come within a run of tying the game. But Mel Harder relieved Ruffing with none out and put out the fire, one-hitting the National stars over the final five innings. The Americans picked up an insurance run in the sixth off Dizzy Dean before Dean and Fred Frankhouse shut them down, too, through the final three frames.

GAME 3
Municipal Stadium, Cleveland
July 8, 1935
AL, 4-1

NL	000 100 000	1	4	1
AL	210 010 00X	4	8	0

Pitchers: WALKER, Schumacher (3), Derringer (7), J.Dean (8) vs GOMEZ, Harder (7)
Home Runs: Foxx-A
Attendance: 69,812

Lefty Gomez started his third All-Star Game, and pitched a record six innings to pick up his second All-Star win. For three innings he shut out the Nationals as the Americans built a lead behind him on Jimmie Foxx's two-run homer in the first, and Rollie Hemsley's triple and Joe Cronin's run-scoring fly in the second.

The National Leaguers tried to catch up in the fourth, when they put together two of their three hits off Gomez—a double by Arky Vaughan and a single by Bill Terry—and scored a run. But an inning later Foxx nullified the National run, singling Joe Vosmik home for his third RBI.

Gomez blanked the National stars through two more innings before yielding to Mel Harder, who came in to close his second All-Star Game. Harder had created an All-Star record the previous year with his five consecutive scoreless innings pitched, and extended the record to eight, with three more shutout innings to end the game.

GAME 4
Braves Field, Boston
July 7, 1936
NL, 4-3

AL	000 000 300	3	7	1
NL	020 020 00X	4	9	0

Pitchers: GROVE, Rowe (4), Harder (7) vs J.DEAN, Hubbell (4), C.Davis (7), Warneke (7)
Home Runs: Galan-N, Gehrig-A
Attendance: 25,534

The National League, which had not yet won an All-Star Game, scored first in the second when Gabby Hartnett tripled in a run off Lefty Grove—rookie Joe DiMaggio missing his try for a shoe-top catch of Hartnett's drive to right field. Pinky Whitney then singled in Hartnett. Augie Galan homered off Schoolboy Rowe (and the right field foul pole) in the fifth, and DiMaggio's bobble of Billy Herman's single a batter later put Herman in position to score an unearned fourth run, on Joe Medwick's single, that proved to be the margin of victory.

The Americans, shut out through six by Dizzy Dean and Carl Hubbell, nearly tied the game in the seventh off Curt Davis as Lou Gehrig homered and Luke Appling singled in two more. But Lon Warneke took over and, after loading the bases with a walk, escaped disaster as shortstop Leo Durocher snared DiMaggio's vicious line drive to his right for the third out. Warneke shut the Americans out over the final two innings to preserve the one-run lead and the National League's first All-Star win.

GAME 5
Griffith Stadium, Washington
July 7, 1937
AL, 8-3

NL	000 111 000	3	13	0
AL	002 312 00X	8	13	2

Pitchers: J.DEAN, Hubbell (4), Blanton (4), Grissom (5), Mungo (6), Walters (8) vs GOMEZ, Bridges (4), Harder (7)
Home Runs: Gehrig-A
Attendance: 31,391

President Franklin Roosevelt attended the game. Lou Gehrig homered and doubled to drive in half the American League's eight runs in an easy American win. Lefty Gomez started his fourth All-Star Game in five years, winning his third. And American reliever Mel Harder pitched the final innings for the fourth All-Star Game in a row, pushing his record for consecutive All-Star shutout innings to 13. But the game is remembered not for any of these things, but for Earl Averill's line drive in the third inning which fractured Dizzy Dean's toe and led to the premature end of his spectacular career. (Dean recovered from the broken toe, but tried to resume his pitching too soon. In favoring the toe, he changed his delivery and irreparably injured his pitching arm.)

The Americans began their scoring when Gehrig, who preceded Averill in the batting order, homered off Dean in the third, with one aboard. They added to their score in each of the next three innings, so that although the Nationals countered with single runs in the three middle innings, they only fell farther behind.

GAME 6
Crosley Field, Cincinnati
July 6, 1938
NL, 4-1

AL	000 000 001	1	7	4
NL	100 100 20X	4	8	0

Pitchers: GOMEZ, Allen (4), Grove (7) vs VANDER MEER, Lee (4), Brown (7)
Attendance: 27,607

For the fifth (and final) time, Lefty Gomez started for the American League, and although he gave up only two hits and no earned runs in his three innings, he was saddled with the loss when an error by shortstop Joe Cronin paved the way for a National League run in the first.

The Nationals scored their only earned run in the fourth when Mel Ott tripled and Ernie Lombardi singled him home. But in the seventh they recorded two more unearned runs when Leo Durocher bunted to move Frank McCormick to second. Both McCormick and Durocher scored as third baseman Jimmie Foxx threw wildly to first and right fielder Joe DiMaggio (who chased the ball down) missed home plate with his throw.

In the ninth DiMaggio singled and Cronin doubled him home in partial atonement for their errors. But as Johnny Vander Meer and Big Bill Lee had each blanked the American stars on one hit in their three-inning stints, and some fine outfield catches had kept them from scoring more than this one run off Mace Brown, the Americans' errors cost them the game.

GAME 7
Yankee Stadium, New York
July 11, 1939
AL, 3-1

NL	001 000 000	1	7	1
AL	000 210 00X	3	6	1

Pitchers: Derringer, LEE (4), Fette (7) vs Ruffing, BRIDGES (4), Feller (6)
Home Runs: J.DiMaggio-A
Attendance: 62,892

Six Yankees started for the American League, and one of them—Joe DiMaggio—hit the game's only home run. But it was a young Cleveland pitcher—twenty-year-old Bob Feller, playing in his first All-Star Game—who turned in the most memorable performance.

The Nationals scored first, with a run in the third on three hits off the American League starter, Red Ruffing. But the Americans came back with two runs in the fourth on a walk, two singles, and a bobbled grounder by shortstop Arky Vaughan. DiMaggio hit his insurance homer an inning later.

In the top of the sixth, after two singles and an error had loaded the bases with National stars, with only one out, Feller replaced Tommy Bridges to face Vaughan (who had earlier singled and scored his team's only run). One pitch got Feller out of the inning as Vaughan grounded into a 4-6-3 double play. Feller shut out the National stars over the final three innings, striking out Johnny Mize and Stan Hack in the ninth to end the game and give the Americans their fifth All-Star victory.

GAME 8
Sportsman's Park, St. Louis
July 9, 1940
NL, 4-0

AL	000 000 000	0	3	1
NL	300 000 01X	4	7	0

Pitchers: RUFFING, Newsom (4), Feller (7) vs DERRINGER, Walters (3), Wyatt (5), French (7), Hubbell (9)
Home Runs: West-N
Attendance: 32,373

The National Leaguers made short work of the Americans, scoring three times in the first inning and holding the opposing stars to three hits for the All-Star Game's first shutout. Before American League starter Red Ruffing retired a single National batter in the bottom of the first inning, three of the game's four runs had been scored, on singles by Arky Vaughan and Billy Herman and Max West's home run to right center.

Ruffing then settled down, and he and Buck Newsom held the Nationals to just three additional hits through the seventh. Bob Feller gave up the Nationals' fourth run in the eighth, on a walk, a sacrifice, and Harry Danning's single.

Five National League pitchers combined for the shutout, permitting only five batters to reach base while striking out seven. Starter Paul Derringer, who struck out three men in his two innings, was awarded the win.

GAME 9
Briggs Stadium, Detroit
July 8, 1941
AL, 7–5

```
NL   000 001 220     5 10 2
AL   000 101 014     7 11 3
```

Pitchers: Wyatt, Derringer (3), Walters (5), PASSEAU (7) vs Feller, Lee (4), Hudson (7), SMITH (8)
Home Runs: Vaughn-N (2), Williams-A
Attendance: 54,674

The National Leaguers entered the last of the ninth with a 5–3 lead and hopes of nailing down their first back-to-back All-Star victories. The American stars had scored their first run in the fourth. The Nationals tied the score in the top of the sixth, but the Americans countered with a run later in the inning. The Nationals' Arky Vaughan then made a bid to be the game's hero, homering in the seventh off Sid Hudson with a man aboard to restore the National lead, and homering again an inning later off Edgar Smith for two more runs.

A double and single by the DiMaggio brothers Joe and Dom brought the Americans a run closer in the eighth, but they still needed two to tie as they faced Claude Passeau in the bottom of the ninth. Two one-out singles and a walk loaded the bases, and a force play at second (that just missed being a game-ending double play) scored Ken Keltner from third. With two men now out and the Americans still down a run, Ted Williams homered on a letter-high fastball against the upper parapet in right for three more runs and another American League victory.

GAME 10
Polo Grounds, New York
July 6, 1942
AL, 3–1

```
AL   300 000 000     3 7 0
NL   000 000 010     1 6 1
```

Pitchers: CHANDLER, Benton (5) vs M.COOPER, Vander Meer (4), Passeau (7), Walters (9)
Home Runs: Boudreau-A, York-A, Owen-N
Attendance: 33,694

Home runs accounted for all the scoring as the American League, in something of a reverse of the 1940 game, scored three times in the top of the first to defeat the Nationals. Lou Boudreau, leading off, hit the game winner off Mort Cooper's second pitch, into the upper deck in left field. A double and two outs later, Rudy York put one over the fence near the short right field foul line for two more runs.

The Americans hit safely only four more times, and scored no more runs, but they already had more than enough, as Spud Chandler and Al Benton combined to shut out the National League stars for seven innings, until Mickey Owen, pinch-hitting for pitcher Claude Passeau in the eighth, hit his only home run of the summer.

This was the second All-Star Game played in the Polo Grounds. It had been Brooklyn's turn to host the game at Ebbets Field, but because the proceeds were destined for the war effort, the site was shifted to the larger stadium. The game might as well have been held in Brooklyn, though, as a pregame rain held attendance to well below the Polo Grounds' capacity.

GAME 11
Shibe Park, Philadelphia
July 13, 1943
AL, 5–3

```
NL   100 000 101     3 10 3
AL   031 010 00X     5 8 1
```

Pitchers: M.COOPER, Vander Meer (3), SeweLL (6), Javery (7) vs LEONARD, Newhouser (4), Hughson (7)
Home Runs: Doerr-A, V.DiMaggio-N
Attendance: 31,938

For the first time, the All-Star Game was played at night. And for the only time in All-Star history, no Yankee played—although six had been named to the American League squad. But Yankee Joe McCarthy (serving for the sixth time as American manager) was piqued by criticism that he favored his own players, and retaliated by keeping them all on the bench.

The only DiMaggio in this wartime game was Pittsburgh's Vince, and he provided most of the National League power—batting 3 for 3, with eight total bases and two of his team's three runs. But after the Nationals had jumped to a one-run lead in the first, Bobby Doerr of the Americans homered off Mort Cooper with two aboard in the second to put the American stars ahead. They added to their lead with a run in the third and another in the fifth. DiMaggio scored in the seventh after tripling off Tex Hughson and added a homer against Hughson in the ninth, but his heroics were not enough to overcome the American League's march to its third win in a row, and its eighth in eleven tries.

GAME 12
Forbes Field, Pittsburgh
July 11, 1944
NL, 7–1

```
AL   010 000 000     1 6 3
NL   000 040 21X     7 12 1
```

Pitchers: Borowy, HUGHSON (4), Muncrief (5), Newhouser (7), Newsom (8) vs Walters, RAFFENSBERGER (4), Sewell (6), Tobin (9)
Attendance: 29,589

For the second time the game was played at night, and for the seventh time Joe McCarthy managed the American League team. But this time—unlike Game 11—he let his Yankees play. He started Yankee pitcher Hank Borowy, who not only shut out the Nationals in his three innings but drove in a run in the second to give his team the lead.

But that was all the American stars got. For the first four innings it was enough, but in the fifth a double, four singles, a walk, an error, and a stolen base brought in four National League runs. In the seventh, Whitey Kurowski doubled in two more National runs, and in the eighth a missed third strike, two walks, and a fly ball produced a seventh and final tally.

No home runs were hit in the game, only the second time that had happened in All-Star play. But Phil Cavarretta of the Nationals tripled—and reached base four additional times on a single and three walks for a new All-Star on-base record.

GAME 13
Fenway Park, Boston
July 9, 1946
AL, 12-0

```
NL  000 000 000   0  3  0
AL  200 130 24X  12 14  1
```
Pitchers: PASSEAU, Higbe (4),
  Blackwell (5), Sewell (8) vs FELLER,
  Newhouser (4), Kramer (7)
Home Runs: Keller-A, Williams-A (2)
Attendance: 34,906

No All-Star Game was played in 1945 because of restrictions on wartime travel, but when the classic resumed in 1946 the American stars avenged their 1944 loss with the most decisive All-Star victory to date: 12–0. American pitchers Bob Feller, Hal Newhouser, and Jack Kramer combined to hold the National stars to three singles and a walk, as their teammates pounded National pitching for 14 hits, including two doubles and three home runs.

But the game belonged to Ted Williams. Back after three years at war, and playing before his hometown fans, he equaled Phil Cavarretta's 1944 on-base record in spectacular fashion, with one walk, two singles, and two home runs: one a drive into the center field bleachers and the other the first homer ever hit off Rip Sewell's looping "eephus" pitch. He scored the game's first run in the first inning as Charlie Keller followed his walk with a homer, and went on to break an All-Star record by scoring three more times, while driving in a record five runs.

GAME 14
Wrigley Field, Chicago
July 8, 1947
AL, 2-1

```
AL  000 001 100   2  8  0
NL  000 100 000   1  5  1
```
Pitchers: Newhouser, SHEA (4),
  Masterson (7), Page (8) vs
  Blackwell, Brecheen (4), SAIN (7),
  Spahn (8)
Home Runs: Mize-N
Attendance: 41,123

Johnny Mize homered for the National League off rookie Spec Shea in the fourth inning for the game's first run, after three one-hit innings by the two lanky starters, Ewell Blackwell of the Nationals and Hal Newhouser of the Americans. Mize's run remained the only score until the sixth inning, when the American Leaguers tied the game on two singles and a double-play grounder.

Sharp baserunning by Bobby Doerr—plus a little luck—led to the Americans' second run an inning later. Doerr singled, then stole second. He took third when pitcher Johnny Sain's pickoff throw bounced off Doerr's back into the outfield. Pinch hitter Stan Spence then singled Doerr home with what proved to be the game's final—and winning—run. The Nationals put men on first and third in the eighth, but shortstop Lou Boudreau's spectacular stop of a hot grounder and sharp throw to first retired the side and ended the threat.

GAME 15
Sportsman's Park, St. Louis
July 13, 1948
AL, 5-2

```
NL  200 000 000   2  8  0
AL  011 300 00X   5  6  0
```
Pitchers: Branca, SCHMITZ (4),
  Sain (4), Blackwell (6) vs
  Masterson, RASCHI (4),
  Coleman (7)
Home Runs: Musial-N, Evers-A
Attendance: 34,009

Vic Raschi pitched three shutout innings for the American stars and drove in two go-ahead runs with a fourth-inning single as the American League—for the third time since the All-Star Game originated in 1933—won its third classic in a row. The Nationals scored first on Stan Musial's two-run homer in the top of the first. But that was all they got, as starter Walt Masterson settled down and shut out the Nationals through the second and third innings. Raschi then came on for his shutout stint, and Joe Coleman stopped the Nationals without even a hit over the final three innings.

Meanwhile, the Americans scored a run in the second on Hoot Evers's homer, and tied the game with another run in the third on two walks, a double steal, and an outfield fly. Then in the fourth, when two walks and a single had loaded the bases, pitcher Raschi singled in the third and fourth American runs. Joe DiMaggio's pinch-hit fly scored a fifth run. Johnny Sain and Ewell Blackwell shut out the Americans the rest of the way, but the damage had been done.

GAME 16
Ebbets Field, Brooklyn
July 12, 1949
AL, 11-7

```
AL  400 202 300  11 13  1
NL  212 002 000   7 12  5
```
Pitchers: Parnell, TRUCKS (2),
  Brissie (4), Raschi (7) vs Spahn,
  NEWCOMBE (2), Munger (5),
  Bickford (6), Pollet (7), Blackwell (8),
  Roe (9)
Home Runs: Musial-N, Kiner-N
Attendance: 32,577

Each team scored seven earned runs in this game which saw a total of 25 hits, including seven doubles and two home runs. But two first-inning National League errors let in four unearned American runs to provide the margin for the American League's fourth consecutive All-Star win. Stan Musial and Ralph Kiner each drove in two National runs with homers, but Eddie Joost singled in two runs for the Americans and Joe DiMaggio singled and doubled in three more to lead the American attack. For the second year in a row, Vic Raschi shut out the National stars for three innings, this time holding the American lead over the final third of the game.

The game was notable as the first to include black players: three Dodgers (Jackie Robinson, Roy Campanella, and Don Newcombe) for the National League, and Larry Doby for the American. With the Americans now ahead 12–4, it also marked the farthest extent of American League domination of the midsummer classic.

GAME 17
Comiskey Park, Chicago
July 11, 1950
NL, 4–3

```
NL   020 000 001 000 01   4 10 0
AL   001 020 000 000 00   3  8 1
```

Pitchers: Roberts, Newcombe (4), Konstanty (6), Jansen (7), BLACKWELL (12) vs Raschi, Lemon (4), Houtteman (7), Reynolds (10), GRAY (13), Feller (14)
Home Runs: Kiner-N, Schoendienst-N
Attendance: 46,127

For the first time, the All-Star Game went into extra innings, and for the first time the National League won a game as the visiting team. Three pitchers each hurled three innings of shutout ball: Bob Lemon and Allie Reynolds for the American League and Ewell Blackwell (who finished the game and got the win) for the Nationals. But top pitching honors were earned by National Leaguer Larry Jansen, who struck out six and gave up only one hit over *five* shutout innings (7–11).

The National stars scored first with two runs in the second. The Americans came back with one in the third, and tied and took the lead in the fifth on George Kell's run-scoring fly and an RBI single by Ted Williams (who, it was later learned, had broken his left elbow making an off-the-wall catch in the first inning). But in the top of the ninth, Ralph Kiner of the Nationals hit a game-tying homer, and 4½ scoreless innings later Red Schoendienst—on the first pitch of the fourteenth inning—homered off American Ted Gray with what proved to be the game winner.

GAME 18
Briggs Stadium, Detroit
July 10, 1951
NL, 8–3

```
NL   100 302 110   8 12 1
AL   010 110 000   3 10 2
```

Pitchers: Roberts, MAGLIE (3), Newcombe (6), Blackwell (9) vs Garver, LOPAT (4), Hutchinson (5), Parnell (8), Lemon (9)
Home Runs: Musial-N, Elliott-N, Wertz-A, Kell-A, Hodges-N, Kiner-N
Attendance: 52,075

In a game moved from Philadelphia to help Detroit celebrate its 250th birthday, hometowners Vic Wertz and George Kell of the Tigers hit solo homers in the fourth and fifth innings to bring the American stars within a run of the Nationals. But they came no closer, as the National Leaguers pulled away for a convincing 8–3 victory.

The Nationals, aided by six innings of shutout pitching (including three by Don Newcombe), produced four home runs of their own to drive in six of their eight runs. With the score tied 1–1 going into the fourth inning, Stan Musial greeted Ed Lopat's first pitch with a shot to the right field upper deck, and Bob Elliott added two more runs later in the inning with a homer to left. Gil Hodges increased the National League lead to 6–3 with a two-run homer in the sixth, and Ralph Kiner concluded the Nationals' scoring with a solo upper-deck shot to left center in the eighth. For the first time in All-Star play, the National League had won two games in a row.

GAME 19
Shibe Park, Philadelphia
July 8, 1952
NL, 3–2

```
AL   000 20   2 5 0
NL   100 20   3 3 0
```

Pitchers: Raschi, LEMON (3), Shantz (5) vs Simmons, RUSH (4)
Home Runs: J.Robinson-N, Sauer-N
Attendance: 32,785

No sun shone for this rain-shortened game, but two hometown pitchers did. Curt Simmons of the Phillies held the American stars to one hit as he shut them out over the first three innings. And the Athletics' Bobby Shantz—in the midst of an MVP season—struck out the side in the fifth for the Americans.

But home runs and rain determined the final outcome. Jackie Robinson opened the scoring with a homer off Vic Raschi in the bottom of the first to give the Nationals a 1–0 lead. In the fourth the Americans came back to take the lead briefly with two runs on a double, a walk, and two singles off eventual winner Bob Rush. But in the bottom of the inning, Hank Sauer's home run off Bob Lemon with one aboard returned the lead to the National League. And there it stayed through a scoreless fifth, when the rain, which had fallen throughout the game, at last brought the soggy festivities to the All-Star series' first premature conclusion.

GAME 20
Crosley Field, Cincinnati
July 14, 1953
NL, 5–1

```
AL   000 000 001   1  5 0
NL   000 020 12X   5 10 0
```

Pitchers: Pierce, REYNOLDS (4), Garcia (6) Paige (8) vs Roberts, SPAHN (4), Simmons (6), Dickson (8)
Attendance: 30,846

For the first 4½ innings, pitchers for both sides held the opposition scoreless, with one hit each. Then the National Leaguers got to Allie Reynolds for two runs in the bottom of the fifth on a hit batsman, a walk, and two singles.

This proved margin enough for the National League's fourth consecutive victory, as four National pitchers held the Americans to just two hits through eight innings before three singles in the ninth gave the American Leaguers their only run. For good measure, though, the National stars added a run in the seventh, and two more in the eighth (with three singles and a walk off Satchel Paige in his only All-Star appearance).

Enos Slaughter of the Nationals provided much of the game's excitement. With two singles, a walk, and a stolen base, he drove in one run and scored two others, and defensively made a spectacular diving catch in right field. Pee Wee Reese's double in the seventh (scoring Slaughter) was the game's only extra-base hit.

GAME 21
Municipal Stadium,
Cleveland
July 13, 1954
AL, 11–9

```
NL   000 520 020    9 14 0
AL   004 121 03X   11 17 1
```

Pitchers: Roberts, Antonelli (4),
Spahn (6), Grissom (6),
CONLEY (8), Erskine (8) vs Ford,
Consuegra (4), Lemon (4),
Porterfield (5), Keegan (8),
STONE (8), Trucks (9)
Home Runs: Rosen-A (2), Boone-A,
Kluszewski-N, Bell-N, Doby-A
Attendance: 68,751

American starter Whitey Ford
gave up only one hit in three
shutout innings, and National
starter Robin Roberts shut out
the American stars through two.
But in the bottom of the third Al
Rosen tagged Roberts for a
three-run homer, and Ray Boone
followed with a solo shot. By the
end of the game new All-Star
records had been set for hits (31),
runs (20), and pitchers used (13),
and the record of 6 home runs
had been equaled.

The Nationals topped the
American four-run third with five
straight hits off Sandy Consuegra
in the fourth, for five runs. The
Americans tied the game with a
run in their half of the fourth, but
Ted Kluszewski homered in the
fifth for two more National
League runs. In the bottom of the
fifth, Rosen homered again, for
two, to bring the Americans even
again.

A run in the sixth put the
Americans ahead, but Gus Bell's
two-run blast in the eighth returned the Nationals to the top by
one. They were threatening to
lengthen that lead when Dean
Stone entered the contest in relief
of Bob Keegan with two out and
Red Schoendienst on third. Before Stone's first delivery,
Schoendienst broke for home and
was tagged out, setting the stage
for Stone to become the winning
pitcher without making a pitch.
American Larry Doby tied it up
again later in the eighth with a
home run, and Nellie Fox drove
in the game's final two runs a few
batters later with a bases-loaded
single.

In the ninth, the Nationals'
Stan Musial blasted two over the
fence—both foul—with a man
aboard. But Virgil Trucks retired
him and Gil Hodges, who followed, to preserve the American
League's first victory in five
games.

GAME 22
County Stadium, Milwaukee
July 12, 1955
NL, 6–5

```
AL   400 001 000 000   5 10 2
NL   000 000 230 001   6 13 1
```

Pitchers: Pierce, Wynn (4), Ford (7),
SULLIVAN (8) vs Roberts,
Haddix (4), Newcombe (7),
Jones (8), Nuxhall (8), CONLEY (12)
Home Runs: Mantle-A, Musial-N
Attendance: 45,314

Down 0–5 in the seventh inning,
the National Leaguers came
back to tie the game and send it
into extra innings. The Americans attacked early, scoring four
runs off Robin Roberts (three of
them on Mickey Mantle's home
run to center) before the game's
first out had been recorded. They
added a fifth run in the sixth inning. Meanwhile, pitchers Billy
Pierce and Early Wynn were
shutting the Nationals down on
four hits.

In the seventh, though, two singles, a walk, and an American error gave the Nationals two runs,
and in the eighth, four two-out
singles and another error tied the
game. Joe Nuxhall for the Nationals and the Americans' Frank
Sullivan prevented further scoring through the eleventh. In the
top of the twelfth, Gene Conley
replaced Nuxhall and struck out
the side: Al Kaline, Mickey
Vernon, and Al Rosen. Sullivan
returned for the Americans to
face Stan Musial in the bottom of
the twelfth. Musial hit the first
pitch—a fastball—over the
screen in right and the game was
over.

GAME 23
Griffith Stadium, Washington
July 10, 1956
NL, 7–3

```
NL   001 211 200   7 11 0
AL   000 003 000   3 11 0
```

Pitchers: FRIEND, Spahn (4),
Antonelli (6) vs PIERCE, Ford (4),
Wilson (5), Brewer (6), Score (8),
Wynn (9)
Home Runs: Mays-N, Williams-A,
Mantle-A, Musial-N
Attendance: 28,843

Four of the game's greatest sluggers—Willie Mays, Stan Musial,
Ted Williams, and Mickey Mantle—hit home runs, three of them
off two of the game's greatest
pitchers—Whitey Ford and Warren Spahn. But the star of the
game was National League third
baseman Ken Boyer, who went 3
for 5, scoring one run and driving
in another, while making three
spectacular diving and leaping
plays in the field.

The National stars scored five
times—including twice in the
fourth on Mays's homer off
Ford—before the Americans put
a run on the board. But in the
bottom of the sixth, Williams
homered for two runs off Spahn,
and Mantle followed him with another homer to bring the Americans within two. But that was the
end of their scoring, as Johnny
Antonelli relieved Spahn to stop
the American stars the rest of the
way. The Nationals scored twice
more in the seventh—one of the
runs coming on Musial's homer—
ensuring them a comfortable 7–3
victory.

GAME 24
Busch Stadium, St. Louis
July 9, 1957
AL, 6–5

```
AL   020 001 003   6 10 0
NL   000 000 203   5  9 1
```

Pitchers: BUNNING, Loes (4),
Wynn (7), Pierce (7), Mossi (9),
Grim (9) vs SIMMONS, Burdette (2),
Sanford (6), Jackson (7), Labine (9)
Attendance: 30,693

Cincinnati fans stuffed the ballot
boxes and elected Reds to start
everywhere but first base. Commissioner Ford Frick removed
two elected starters, but left five
Reds in the lineup. They could
not bring the National League
the victory, though.

The Americans scored twice in
the second on singles and walks to
take a lead they held to the finish.
Although reliever Lew Burdette—after walking in the second run—stopped the American
stars through the fifth, Jim Bunning and Billy Loes were combining to keep the Nationals from
scoring through the first six innings. The Americans, meanwhile, added a third run in the top
of the sixth on a double, a wild
pitch, and a single.

The Nationals scored their first
two in the seventh, on two singles
and a double, to draw within a
run of a tie. But in the top of the
ninth the Americans combined
two singles, an error, a sacrifice
bunt, and Minnie Minoso's pinch
double for three more runs. They
needed them all, for the Nationals responded in their half of the
ninth with three runs of their own
on a blend of walks, hits (including Willie Mays's triple), and a
wild pitch. With two out and a
runner at second, Gil Hodges
lined one deep to left center. But
Minoso, now in left field, snared
the drive on the run to end the
game.

GAME 25
Memorial Stadium, Baltimore
July 8, 1958
AL, 4–3

```
NL   210 000 000    3 4 2
AL   110 011 00X    4 9 2
```
Pitchers: Spahn, FRIEND (4), Jackson (6), Farrell (7) vs Turley, Narleski (2), WYNN (6), O'Dell (7)
Attendance: 48,829

Although American League pitchers held the National Leaguers to only four hits (all singles), the Nationals took a quick lead, and held it for half the game before they were overtaken. Willie Mays and Stan Musial singled in the top of the first, both scoring as American starter Bob Turley proceeded to give up a sacrifice fly, hit a batter, walk a man, and unload a wild pitch.

The Americans came back with one run in their half of the first, but the Nationals drove Turley out with their third run as Mays (who had reached on a fielder's choice) worked his way around the bases on a steal, an error, and Bob Skinner's single. Once again the Americans answered with a run, but they didn't tie the game until Mickey Vernon scored on a bases-loaded ground out in the fifth. An inning later they took the lead when pinch hitter Gil McDougald singled home Frank Malzone.

Billy O'Dell set down the Nationals in order over the final three innings to preserve the lead and give the American Leaguers their second consecutive victory.

GAME 26
Forbes Field, Pittsburgh
July 7, 1959
NL, 5–4

```
AL   000 100 030    4 8 0
NL   100 000 22X    5 9 1
```
Pitchers: Wynn, Duren (4), Bunning (7), FORD (8), Daley (8) vs Drysdale, Burdette (4), Face (7), ANTONELLI (8), Elston (9)
Home Runs: Mathews-N, Kaline-A
Attendance: 35,277

For the third year in a row, the game was decided by one run, with the National League celebrating the city of Pittsburgh's bicentennial by breaking the American League's win streak at two.

Eddie Mathews homered for the Nationals in the bottom of the first for the only run in the first three innings, as Don Drysdale stopped the Americans without a hit or walk, fanning four. Al Kaline tied the game in the top of the fourth with an American home run for the only score of the middle three innings, as Ryne Duren one-hit the Nationals, like Drysdale striking out four.

In the last of the seventh, though, a double and two singles off Jim Bunning put the Nationals ahead by two runs. The NL lead lasted only briefly, however, as the Americans moved back into the lead with three runs in the eighth off Roy Face, with two singles, a walk, and a double after Face had retired the first two men. But in their half of the eighth the Nationals hit on Whitey Ford, tying the game with a single-sacrifice-single, and scoring the game winner on Willie Mays's triple to center.

GAME 27
Memorial Coliseum, Los Angeles
August 3, 1959
AL, 5–3

```
AL   012 000 110    5 6 0
NL   100 010 100    3 6 3
```
Pitchers: WALKER, Wynn (4), Wilhelm, (6), O'Dell (7), McLish (8) vs DRYSDALE, Conley (4), Jones (6), Face (8)
Home Runs: Malzone-A, Berra-A, F. Robinson-N, Gilliam-N, Colavito-A
Attendance: 55,105

To raise extra money for the players' pension fund and other causes, a second All-Star Game was scheduled for 1959, the first ever to be played in August, and the first on the West Coast. The American stars avenged their earlier defeat with a 5–3 win, out-homering the Nationals three to two.

The National Leaguers scored first on a first-inning double and sacrifice fly, but Frank Malzone tied the score with the game's first home run. Yogi Berra homered an inning later with one on for a 3–1 American lead, but Frank Robinson brought the Nationals back to within one with his homer in the fifth. The Americans replaced that run in the top of the seventh on a walk, two errors, and a single, but Junior Gilliam countered with a home run in the last of the inning. Rocky Colavito scored the game's final run for the Americans in the eighth with the game's final homer.

Don Drysdale, the pitching standout of the July game, struck out five this time, but also walked three and gave up three runs on homers to take the loss.

GAME 28
Municipal Stadium, Kansas City
July 11, 1960
NL, 5–3

```
NL   311 000 000    5 12 4
AL   000 001 020    3  6 1
```
Pitchers: FRIEND, McCormick (4), Face (6), Buhl (8), Law (9) vs MONBOUQUETTE, Estrada (3), Coates (4), Bell (6), Lary (8), Daley (9)
Home Runs: Banks-N, Crandall-N, Kaline-A
Attendance: 30,619

The day was hot—the temperature broke 100—and so were the National League bats. Willie Mays went 3 for 4, including a leadoff triple and a double; Ernie Banks homered and doubled; Del Crandall homered and singled; and Joe Adcock doubled and singled for three-fourths of the Nationals' 12 hits as the National League scored five unanswered runs in the first three innings to take an unbeatable lead. Starter Bob Friend, meanwhile, blanked the Americans on one hit through three innings and Mike McCormick held them scoreless for two more before yielding the first American run in the sixth on Nellie Fox's bases-loaded single. Roy Face then came on to douse the fire, getting Luis Aparicio to ground into a double play.

Four American League pitchers stopped the National stars after the third inning, and Al Kaline homered for two more American runs in the eighth. In the ninth the Americans put men on first and second with one away. But their comeback fell short, as Vern Law came on to retire Brooks Robinson and Harvey Kuenn and preserve the National victory.

GAME 29
Yankee Stadium, New York
July 13, 1960
NL, 6–0

| NL | 021 000 102 | 6 10 0 |
| AL | 000 000 000 | 0 8 0 |

Pitchers: LAW, Podres (3),
S.Williams (5), Jackson (7),
Henry (8), McDaniel (9) vs FORD,
Wynn (4), Staley (6), Lary (8), Bell (9)
Home Runs: Mathews-N, Mays-N,
Musial-N, Boyer-N
Attendance: 38,362

Only two days after the first All-Star Game, the squads met a second time before fewer than 39,000 fans in capacious Yankee Stadium. It was no contest. Vern Law, who had completed and saved the first game, started and won this one. His two shutout innings set the pace for the five National pitchers who followed him to fashion the first National League shutout in twenty years. The American stars got only two fewer hits than the Nationals (8 to 10), but only one was for extra bases, whereas four of the National League hits were home runs.

Eddie Mathews began the scoring with a two-run homer in the second, and Willie Mays (on his way to a second straight 3-for-4 game) homered for the third National run an inning later. No one scored through the three middle innings, but in the seventh Stan Musial broke his own record with his sixth All-Star homer—a mighty shot three tiers up in right—and in the ninth Ken Boyer completed the rout with a two-run shot to left.

GAME 30
Candlestick Park, San Francisco
July 11, 1961
NL, 5–4

| AL | 000 001 002 1 | 4 4 2 |
| NL | 010 100 010 2 | 5 11 5 |

Pitchers: Ford, Lary (4), Donovan (4),
Bunning (6), Fornieles (8),
WILHELM (8) vs Spahn, Purkey (4),
McCormick (6), Face (9), Koufax (9),
MILLER (9)
Home Runs: Killebrew-A, Altman-N
Attendance: 44,115

National League pitchers began the game where they had left off the year before. For five innings Warren Spahn and Bob Purkey shut out the American stars without a hit or base on balls. In the sixth, Harmon Killebrew homered off Mike McCormick to end the American drought, but it was the only hit McCormick yielded through the eighth.

Meanwhile, the Nationals had taken a 3–1 lead with runs in the second and fourth innings and George Altman's homer in the eighth. But in the top of the ninth, Candlestick's notorious winds helped put the Americans back in the game. Their second and third hits of the game brought in one run, and their fourth (and last) hit put another man on base. The tying run came in when the wind first of all blew pitcher Stu Miller off the mound for a balk to advance the runners, and then twisted a grounder out of third baseman Ken Boyer's grasp for a run-scoring error. In the tenth, the wind may have contributed to the Americans' go-ahead run as Boyer's throw to first sailed into the outfield, allowing Nellie Fox (who had walked) to score from first.

But in the last of the tenth the wind finally came to the aid of the Nationals, rendering useless the famous knuckleball of American reliever Hoyt Wilhelm, who gave up the tying run on hits by Hank Aaron and Willie Mays and lost the game when Roberto Clemente singled in Mays from second.

GAME 31
Fenway Park, Boston
July 31, 1961
Tie, 1–1

| NL | 000 001 000 | 1 5 1 |
| AL | 100 000 000 | 1 4 0 |

Pitchers: Purkey, Mahaffey (3),
Koufax (5), Miller (7) vs Bunning,
Schwall (4), Pascual (7)
Home Runs: Colavito-A
Attendance: 31,851

In the second All-Star Game of 1961, the weather again played a crucial role, as heavy rain at the end of the ninth inning forced the first (and, so far, only) All-Star tie.

Rocky Colavito's home run for the Americans in the first inning turned out to be his squad's only run, as four National League pitchers combined to shut out the American stars on only three singles the rest of the way. The American League pitching was just as effective, with starter Jim Bunning and finisher Camilo Pascual each pitching three no-hit innings. Don Schwall, who pitched the middle three innings, gave up all five National League hits and the Nationals' one run. But even that might have been prevented.

In the sixth, with two on and two out, American shortstop Luis Aparicio waited for a slow grounder, failing to get the ball in time to throw the batter out and end the inning. The Nationals scored on the next play, Bill White's hot ground single up the middle, which Aparicio stopped brilliantly to prevent more than one run from scoring, but which did drive in the game's tying—and final—run.

GAME 32
D.C. Stadium, Washington
July 10, 1962
NL, 3–1

| NL | 000 002 010 | 3 8 0 |
| AL | 000 001 000 | 1 4 0 |

Pitchers: Drysdale, MARICHAL (4),
Purkey (6), Shaw (8) vs Bunning,
PASCUAL (4), Donovan (7),
Pappas (9)
Attendance: 45,480

The stadium was new, President Kennedy threw out the first ball, and starters Don Drysdale of the Nationals and Jim Bunning of the Americans both pitched three innings of one-hit shutout ball. But Maury Wills stole the show. Entering the game in the sixth inning to run for forty-one-year-old Stan Musial, who had singled, Wills stole second, then scored on Dick Groat's single up the middle for the game's first run. Another single, a long fly out, and a ground out scored Groat with the second (and, as it turned out, winning) run.

Two singles and a fly out by Roger Maris brought in an American run in the bottom of the sixth off Bob Purkey. But that was all they got, as Purkey and Bob Shaw one-hit the American stars through the final three innings.

In the eighth inning Wills manufactured an insurance run for the Nationals. On first with a leadoff single, he somehow reached third on Jim Davenport's single to short left, racing from second to third as left fielder Rocky Colavito threw in to second. He scored after tagging on a foul out to right.

GAME 33
Wrigley Field, Chicago
July 30, 1962
AL, 9–4

```
AL   001 201 302    9 10  0
NL   010 000 111    4 10  4
```
Pitchers: Stenhouse, HERBERT (3),
  Aguirre (6), Pappas (9) vs Podres,
  MAHAFFEY (3), Gibson (5),
  Farrell (7), Marichal (8)
Home Runs: Runnels-A, Wagner-A.
  Colavito-A, Roseboro-N
Attendance: 38,359

With this second game of 1962,
the leagues ended their four-year
experiment of playing two
All-Star games a year. The Americans out-homered the Nationals
to spoil the National League's attempt to even the series at 16
wins apiece. But no matter—the
American stars would win only
once again in the next twenty
years.

The National stars scored first
on a double and single in the second, but Pete Runnels evened the
score in the third with a solo
homer, and Leon Wagner put the
Americans ahead with a two-run
shot an inning later. After Tom
Tresh doubled home a fourth
American run in the sixth, Rocky
Colavito put the game out of
reach with a three-run blast in the
seventh.

The Nationals tried to come
back with runs in the seventh and
eighth, but the Americans neutralized them with two more of
their own in the ninth (on two errors, two Juan Marichal wild
pitches, a double, and a long fly
out). With the score now 9–3,
John Roseboro's solo homer in
the last of the ninth put the Nationals in the home-run column,
but that was all.

GAME 34
Municipal Stadium,
Cleveland
July 9, 1963
NL, 5–3

```
NL   012 010 010    5  6  0
AL   012 000 000    3 11  1
```
Pitchers: O'Toole, JACKSON (3),
  Culp (5), Woodeshick (6),
  Drysdale (8) vs McBride,
  BUNNING (4), Bouton (6),
  Pizarro (7), Radatz (8)
Attendance: 44,160

Willie Mays sparked the National League to victory with his
baserunning and timely hitting.
Although he had only one hit—a
single—he scored two runs and
drove in two others in the Nationals' 5–3 win.

The National stars scored first
when Mays walked in the second
inning, stole second, and came in
on a single by Dick Groat. The
Americans tied the game in the
last of the second, but in the top
of the third Mays singled in one
run, stole second again, and
scored his second run on Ed Bailey's single.

Once again the Americans
came back in the bottom of the
third to tie the game on Albie
Pearson's double, followed by two
singles sandwiched around an infield out. But these were their last
runs, as four National pitchers
shut them out on four singles the
rest of the way. Meanwhile, Mays
drove in what proved to be the
winning run with a ground out in
the fifth. In the eighth the Nationals scored a final run when
Ron Santo singled home Bill
White, who had singled and stolen second.

GAME 35
Shea Stadium, New York
July 7, 1964
NL, 7–4

```
AL   100 002 100    4  9  1
NL   000 210 004    7  8  0
```
Pitchers: Chance, Wyatt (4),
  Pascual (5), RADATZ (7) vs
  Drysdale, Bunning (4), Short (6),
  Farrell (7), MARICHAL (9)
Home Runs: B.Williams-N, Boyer-N,
  Callison-N
Attendance: 50,850

A new stadium in the midst of a
World's Fair was the venue for
this game in which the National
League at last drew even with the
American at 17 wins apiece.

The American stars jumped
into the lead with an unearned
run in the first, but the Nationals
(after Dean Chance had shut
them out through three innings)
overtook the Americans in the
fourth, on home runs by Billy
Williams and Ken Boyer, and
Dick Groat doubled in a third run
in the fifth. In the top of the sixth
the Americans tied the score
when Brooks Robinson tripled in
a pair, and took the lead again an
inning later on a sacrifice fly that
barely scored Elston Howard
ahead of Willie Mays's throw
from center.

The Americans held their slim
lead into the bottom of the ninth.
But Mays walked (after fouling
off five third strikes), stole second, and scored the tying run on a
single to short right and an errant
throw home. One intentional
walk and two outs later, Johnny
Callison hit Dick Radatz's 1–2
fastball over the fence in right to
win the game.

GAME 36
Metropolitan Stadium,
Bloomington, Minnesota
July 13, 1965
NL, 6–5

```
NL   320 000 100    6 11  0
AL   000 140 000    5  8  0
```
Pitchers: Marichal, Maloney (4),
  Drysdale (5), KOUFAX (6),
  Farrell (7), Gibson (8) vs Pappas,
  Grant (2), Richert (4),
  McDOWELL (6), Fisher (8)
Home Runs: Mays-N, Torre-N,
  Stargell-N, McAuliffe-A, Killebrew-A
Attendance: 46,706

For a while it looked as though
the Nationals would run away
with the game. Willie Mays led
off with a home run in the first,
and Joe Torre added two runs
with a homer later in the inning.
In the second Willie Stargell
homered for two more runs to
make the score 5–0. National
starter Juan Marichal stopped
the Americans on one hit through
three innings.

But the American stars battled
back. A single, a walk, and another single off Marichal's replacement, Jim Maloney,
brought in one run in the fourth.
Maloney retired the first two men
in the fifth, but then he gave up a
walk followed by a home run to
Dick McAuliffe, and a scratch
single followed by a Harmon Killebrew homer—and the score was
tied at 5–5.

Only one more run was scored.
In the seventh, Willie Mays, who
had walked and gone to third on
Hank Aaron's single, scored on
Ron Santo's infield hit to short.
The Nationals held off American
threats in the eighth and ninth to
take the All-Star series lead for
the first time.

GAME 37
Busch Memorial Stadium,
St. Louis
July 12, 1966
NL, 2-1

AL	010 000 000 0	1	6	0
NL	000 100 000 1	2	6	0

Pitchers: McLain, Kaat (4),
Stottlemyre (6), Siebert (8),
RICHERT (10) vs Koufax,
Bunning (4), Marichal (6),
G.PERRY (9)
Attendance: 49,936

The celebration of another new stadium and the city's bicentennial—and a temperature of 106°F—greeted participants in the 1966 classic. Pitching dominated: seven pitchers hurled two innings or more each of shutout ball. American starter Denny McLain threw three perfect innings, but the National League's Sandy Koufax gave the Americans a run in the second when he let loose a wild pitch after Brooks Robinson had tripled.

The Nationals tied the score in the fourth with three singles off Jim Kaat, but that ended the scoring for both sides through the regulation nine innings. In the top of the tenth, Gaylord Perry stopped the American stars. But in the last half of the inning, National Leaguer Tim McCarver singled off Pete Richert, was sacrificed to second, and came across with the winning run on Maury Wills's single to right.

GAME 38
Anaheim Stadium,
Anaheim, California
July 11, 1967
NL, 2-1

NL	010 000 000 000 001	2	9	0
AL	000 001 000 000 000	1	8	0

Pitchers: Marichal, Jenkins (4),
Gibson (7), Short (9), Cuellar (11),
DRYSDALE (13), Seaver (15) vs
Chance, McGlothlin (4), Peters (6),
Downing (9), HUNTER (11)
Home Runs: Allen-N, B.Robinson-A,
Perez-N
Attendance: 46,309

This was a game of strikeouts, home runs, and extra innings. Every one of the twelve pitchers used in the game struck out at least one batter. American Leaguers Gary Peters (who pitched three perfect middle innings) and Catfish Hunter struck out four apiece, while Ferguson Jenkins of the Nationals tied the All-Star record with six. The game total of 30 strikeouts shattered the previous record of 20 set in 1955.

Apart from the splendid pitching, three home runs provided the only excitement—and the only scoring—in this longest All-Star Game. Richie Allen of the Nationals scored first, homering to center off Dean Chance in the second inning. The Americans' Brooks Robinson tied the score in the sixth with a shot off Jenkins. And 8½ innings later, in the top of the fifteenth, National Leaguer Tony Perez homered off Hunter for the game's third and final run. Tom Seaver set down the Americans in the bottom of the fifteenth, and the game—after a record 3 hours and 41 minutes—was history.

GAME 39
Astrodome, Houston
July 9, 1968
NL, 1-0

AL	000 000 000	0	3	1
NL	100 000 00X	1	5	0

Pitchers: TIANT, Odom (3), McLain (5),
McDowell (7), Stottlemyre (8),
John (8) vs DRYSDALE,
Marichal (4), Carlton (6), Seaver (7),
Reed (9), Koosman (9)
Attendance: 48,321

This game could be described by what was missing: fresh air and real grass (it was the first All-Star Game held indoors), hitting (the eight hits were a new low for a nine-inning All-Star Game), and earned runs (the game's only run came with the help of an error). In fact, if it weren't for thirty-seven-year-old Willie Mays, the game might not have had any runs at all. Starting only because of an injury to Pete Rose, National Leaguer Mays led off the bottom of the first with a single, and took second when first baseman Harmon Killebrew mishandled pitcher Luis Tiant's pickoff throw for an error. Mays took third as the rattled Tiant threw a wild pitch to walk Curt Flood, and scored when Willie McCovey grounded into a double play.

The pitching on both sides was superb, but the National Leaguers shone especially bright. Tom Seaver gave up two of the Americans' three hits (all of which were doubles), but struck out five in his two innings. Juan Marichal hurled two perfect innings, fanning three. And none of the six National pitchers walked a man. One American, Killebrew, couldn't walk. Stretching for a throw at first, the slugger tore a hamstring and missed the next two months, the most serious All-Star Game casualty since Ted Williams's broken elbow 18 years earlier.

GAME 40
R.F.K. Memorial Stadium,
Washington, D.C.
July 23, 1969
NL, 9-3

NL	125 100 000	9	11	0
AL	011 100 000	3	6	2

Pitchers: CARLTON, Gibson (4),
Singer (5), Koosman (7), Dierker (8),
P.Niekro (9) vs STOTTLEMYRE,
Odom (3), Knowles (3), McLain (4),
McNally (5), McDowell (7), Culp (9)
Home Runs: Bench-N, Howard-A,
McCovey-N (2), Freehan-A
Attendance: 45,259

After four one-run victories in a row, the National Leaguers finally broke loose, massing 10 of their 11 hits in the first four innings for nine runs and a crushing win. Scoring an unearned run in the first on a dropped outfield fly, and two in the second on Johnny Bench's home run, the Nationals erupted in the third for five runs off Blue Moon Odom before two outs had been recorded. Willie McCovey's two-run homer began the third-inning scoring, and an error, single, and two doubles added three more runs before Odom was mercifully relieved. McCovey homered again in the fourth for the Nationals' final tally.

The American bats were not wholly silent, but the solo homers by Frank Howard and Bill Freehan in the second and third, and a third run in the fourth, couldn't counter the Nationals' attack.

The final five innings of the game were as quiet as the opening four had been noisy. No runs scored, and the two teams together managed only three hits.

GAME 41
Riverfront Stadium, Cincinnati
July 14, 1970
NL, 5-4

```
AL  000 001 120 000   4 12 0
NL  000 000 103 001   5 10 0
```

Pitchers: Palmer, McDowell (4),
  J.Perry (7), Hunter (9), Peterson (9),
  Stottlemyre (9), WRIGHT (11) vs
  Seaver, Merritt (4), G.Perry (6),
  Gibson (8), OSTEEN (10)
Home Runs: Dietz-N
Attendance: 51,838

In a new stadium, opened only
two weeks earlier, no one scored
for the first five innings, as Jim
Palmer and Sam McDowell of
the Americans and Tom Seaver
and Jim Merritt of the Nationals
held the opposition to two hits per
team. The Americans finally
scored a run in the sixth, and another in the seventh. The Nationals got one back in the last of the
seventh, but the Americans increased their lead to 4-1 in the
eighth when Brooks Robinson
tripled home two baserunners.

Fans had already begun to
leave the park when the Nationals' Dick Dietz homered off Catfish Hunter to lead off the last of
the ninth. Two pitchers, three singles, and a sacrifice fly later, the
game was tied and headed for extra innings. Claude Osteen held
the Americans scoreless from the
tenth through the twelfth, and
the Nationals also failed to score
in the tenth and eleventh. But in
the last of the twelfth, with two
out, Pete Rose, Billy Grabarkewitz, and Jim Hickman singled. Hometowner Rose, racing
home from second on Hickman's
hit, crashed into catcher Ray
Fosse with a force that injured
both players and still provokes
controversy—but which also
gave the National League its
eighth straight victory.

GAME 42
Tiger Stadium, Detroit
July 13, 1971
AL, 6-4

```
NL  021 000 010   4 5 0
AL  004 002 00X   6 7 0
```

Pitchers: ELLIS, Marichal (4),
  Jenkins (6), Wilson (7) vs BLUE,
  Palmer (4), Cuellar (6), Lolich (8)
Home Runs: Bench-N, Aaron-N,
  Jackson-A, F.Robinson-A,
  Killebrew-A, Clemente-N
Attendance: 53,559

With an assist from a favorable
wind, six all-time greats homered
to account for all the scoring as
the American League broke its
eight-game All-Star drought with
a 6-4 victory. Johnny Bench put
the Nationals in front with a
two-run homer in the second inning off Vida Blue, and Hank
Aaron—with his first All-Star
home run—added a third run off
Blue an inning later. But the
Americans, shut out by Dock Ellis through the first two innings,
rocked him in the bottom of the
third as Reggie Jackson and
Frank Robinson wrested the lead
from the Nationals with a pair of
two-run homers. (Robinson's
made him the first player to hit an
All-Star home run for both
leagues.)

Ferguson Jenkins yielded the
game's fifth homer, Harmon Killebrew's two-run shot for the
Americans in the sixth. Roberto
Clemente brought the Nationals
a run closer with his solo homer
off Mickey Lolich in the eighth,
but that ended the team's scoring,
and (for a year, anyway) the
National League's All-Star
stranglehold.

GAME 43
Atlanta Stadium, Atlanta
July 25, 1972
NL, 4-3

```
AL  001 000 020 0   3 6 0
NL  000 000 011     4 8 0
```

Pitchers: Palmer, Lolich (4),
  G.Perry (6), Wood (8),
  McNALLY (10) vs Gibson, Blass (3),
  Sutton (4), Carlton (6),
  Stoneman (7), McGRAW (9)
Home Runs: Aaron-N, Rojas-A
Attendance: 53,107

The American Leaguers tried to
extend their All-Star win streak
to two games, and for a time it
looked as though they might do
it. In the third, they scored the
only run of the first half of the
game as Jim Palmer and Mickey
Lolich held the Nationals to two
hits through the first five innings.
In the sixth Hank Aaron thrilled
the hometown crowd with a
two-run homer deep to left to
shift the lead to the National
League. But Cookie Rojas restored the American lead with his
own two-run shot in the eighth.

The Americans held their lead
into the bottom of the ninth, but
after two singles and a force out,
the score was tied. Tug McGraw
set down the American stars in
order in the tenth, but American
reliever Dave McNally was not so
fortunate. He walked leadoff batter Nate Colbert, who was sacrificed to second. Joe Morgan then
sent the American Leaguers back
into the ranks of losers with a
sharp RBI single to right center.
His single also gave the Nationals
their seventh win in seven extra-inning games.

GAME 44
Royals Stadium, Kansas City
July 24, 1973
NL, 7-1

```
NL  002 122 000   7 10 0
AL  010 000 000   1  5 0
```

Pitchers: WISE, Osteen (3), Sutton (5),
  Twitchell (6), Giusti (7), Seaver (8),
  Brewer (9) vs Hunter, Holtzman (2),
  BLYLEVEN (3), Singer (4), Ryan (6),
  Lyle (8), Fingers (9)
Home Runs: Bench-N, Bonds-N,
  W.Davis-N
Attendance: 40,849

Once again a new stadium was
chosen to host the All-Star Game,
and once again the National
League emerged victorious. The
Americans scored first, with a run
in the second when Reggie Jackson scored from second on a single after doubling off the center
field wall. But that was the beginning and end of their offense, as
six National pitchers shut them
out on three hits the rest of the
way.

Meanwhile the National
League hitters came to life, producing seven runs in four innings.
Two walks and two singles in the
third brought in two runs, and
Johnny Bench's homer in the
fourth made the score 3-1. In the
fifth, Bobby Bonds—in the midst
of his finest season—homered for
two more National runs. And in
the sixth, Willie Davis's home run
completed the game's scoring,
bringing in the Nationals' sixth
and seventh runs.

The final third of the game was
anticlimactic, as only two hits
were made after the sixth inning.
But Bonds brought the crowd to
life briefly in the seventh, stretching one of those hits into a double
with some audacious baserunning
(ensuring his selection as the
game's MVP).

GAME 45
Three Rivers Stadium, Pittsburgh
July 23, 1974
NL, 7-2

AL	002	000	000		2 4 1	
NL	010	210	12X		7 10 1	

Pitchers: G.Perry, TIANT (4), Hunter (6), Fingers (8) vs Messersmith, BRETT (4), Matlack (6), McGlothen (7), Marshall (8)
Home Runs: R.Smith-N
Attendance: 50,706

Steve Garvey, who was elected to the National League starting lineup on write-in votes (his name was omitted from the fans' All-Star ballot), sparked the Nationals to yet another convincing win over the hapless American stars. After singling in the second inning, he scored the game's first run on Ron Cey's double.

The Americans took the lead with two runs in the top of the third, capitalizing on two walks and an error sandwiched between Thurman Munson's leadoff double and Dick Allen's single. They might have scored more had not Garvey snared Bobby Murcer's hot grounder for an assist on the third out.

Garvey doubled in the tying run in the fourth, and Cey's RBI ground out restored the Nationals' lead. Lou Brock added a run in the fifth with a single and some inspired baserunning, and Reggie Smith homered for another in the seventh. Don Kessinger's triple and a wild pitch by Rollie Fingers in the eighth contributed to two final National League runs.

GAME 46
County Stadium, Milwaukee
July 15, 1975
NL, 6-3

NL	021	000	003		6 13 1	
AL	000	003	000		3 10 1	

Pitchers: Reuss, Sutton (4), Seaver (6), MATLACK (7), R.Jones (9) vs Blue, Busby (3), Kaat (5), HUNTER (7), Gossage (9)
Home Runs: Garvey-N, Wynn-N, Yastrzemski-A
Attendance: 51,480

When National stars Steve Garvey and Jim Wynn led off the second with back-to-back homers and their teammates added another run in the third, it looked as if the National League might be on its way to another easy win. But the American pitchers shut down the National League offense for the next five innings, and Carl Yastrzemski made a contest of it with a three-run homer in the sixth off Tom Seaver to tie the score.

In the top of the ninth, though, the Americans all but gave the game away. Left fielder Claudell Washington dropped a fly on the run (it was scored a hit) and misplayed a line drive that went for a double. Goose Gossage came in to relieve Catfish Hunter on the mound and hit the next batter to load the bases. Bill Madlock then drove in two of the baserunners with a single through the drawn-in infield, and Pete Rose knocked in the third run of the inning with a sacrifice fly.

Randy Jones set the Americans down in order in the bottom of the ninth, and—voilà!—the National League had won again.

GAME 47
Veterans Stadium, Philadelphia
July 13, 1976
NL, 7-1

AL	000	100	000		1 5 0	
NL	202	000	03X		7 10 0	

Pitchers: FIDRYCH, Hunter (3), Tiant (5), Tanana (7) vs R.JONES, Seaver (4), Montefusco (6), Rhoden (8), K.Forsch (9)
Home Runs: Foster-N, Lynn-A, Cedeno-N
Attendance: 63,974

Tom Seaver gave up a home run to Fred Lynn in the fourth inning, but that was the Americans' only score as the Nationals held the American stars to five hits while celebrating the nation's bicentennial with ten hits and seven runs.

Rookie standout Mark Fidrych was chosen to start for the Americans and was promptly rapped for two runs. Pete Rose led off with a single and was tripled home by Steve Garvey, who scored himself on a ground out. The Nationals doubled their score in the third inning as George Foster tagged Catfish Hunter for two runs with a mighty home run to left center, and capped their assault with three more in the eighth off Frank Tanana, including a two-run homer by Cesar Cedeno.

The fans had elected five members of Cincinnati's "big red machine" to the National League starting lineup, and Sparky Anderson, the Reds' and National squad's manager, added two more. They provided the bulk of the Nationals' offense, with seven hits, four RBIs, and four runs scored.

GAME 48
Yankee Stadium, New York
July 19, 1977
NL, 7-5

NL	401	000	020		7 9 1	
AL	000	002	102		5 8 0	

Pitchers: SUTTON, Lavelle (4), Seaver (6), R.Reuschel (8), Gossage (9) vs PALMER, Kern (3), Eckersley (4), LaRoche (6), Campbell (7), Lyle (8)
Home Runs: Morgan-N, Luzinski-N, Garvey-N, Scott-A
Attendance: 56,683

The Nationals' Joe Morgan homered off Jim Palmer to open the game, and before Palmer escaped the first inning three more National Leaguers had crossed the plate on a single, double, and Greg Luzinski's homer. Palmer got through the second inning without further damage, but before he was relieved in the third Steve Garvey had homered to give the Nationals a 5–0 lead.

The Americans fought back against Tom Seaver in the sixth and seventh. Seaver retired two in the sixth, but then gave up two singles, and two runs as Richie Zisk doubled the runners home. Two more singles in the seventh produced a third American run.

But the Nationals—assisted by pitcher Sparky Lyle's wild pitch and hit batsman—put a sixth and seventh run on the board in the eighth with a double and single. The Americans added two final runs of their own in the bottom of the ninth on George Scott's homer off Goose Gossage, but fell short of victory once again.

GAME 49
San Diego Stadium,
July 11, 1978
NL, 7-3

```
AL    201 000 000    3  8  1
NL    003 000 04X    7 10  0
```

Pitchers: Palmer, Keough (3),
  Sorensen (4), Kern (7), Guidry (7),
  GOSSAGE (8) vs Blue, Rogers (4),
  Fingers (6), SUTTER (8),
  P.Niekro (9)
Attendance: 51,549

Rod Carew led off both the first and third innings with triples—an All-Star record— scoring both times as the Americans took a 3–0 lead in the bottom of the third. But then Jim Palmer, who had shut the Nationals out on one hit through the first two innings, lost his touch. After yielding a leadoff single, he retired two batters, but then issued three walks to force in a run, and when Steve Garvey singled past the shortstop two more runs scored to tie the game.

No one scored through the next 4½ innings, with Larry Sorensen turning in the game's top pitching performance as he shut the Nationals out on one hit through the three middle innings. But in the last of the eighth, Gosse Gossage (the National League closer the previous year) took the mound this year for the Americans. Garvey greeted him with a leadoff triple and scored what proved to be the winning run on a wild pitch. A walk and three singles added three insurance runs before the inning ended. Bruce Sutter and Phil Niekro blanked the Americans in the ninth, and the Nationals has extended their current win streak to seven.

GAME 50
Kingdome, Seattle
July 17, 1979
NL, 7-6

```
NL    211 001 011    7 10  0
AL    302 001 000    6 10  0
```

Pitchers: Carlton, Andujar (2),
  Rogers (4), G.Perry (6), Sambito (6),
  LaCoss (6), SUTTER (8) vs Ryan,
  Stanley (3), Clear (5), KERN (7),
  Guidry (9)
Home Runs: Lynn-A, Mazzilli-N
Attendance: 58,905

Mike Schmidt tripled and George Foster doubled to drive in the game's first runs as the Nationals began their scoring in the top of the first. The Americans fought back to take the lead later in the inning as Don Baylor doubled home one run and Fred Lynn homered for two more. The Nationals tied the score with a run in the second and went ahead again in the third when Schmidt scored after doubling. But the Americans recaptured the lead in the bottom of the third, scoring twice on a single, wild pitch, ground out, hit batsman, single, and error.

Three innings later the Nationals again tied the game, but the Americans went ahead for the third time with a run in their half of the sixth. Outstanding throws by right fielder Dave Parker, who notched two assists, helped to keep the Americans from pulling away. In the eighth the Nationals' Lee Mazzilli homered for yet another tie, and an inning later Ron Guidry walked Mazzilli with the bases loaded to force in the Nationals' go-ahead seventh run. When Bruce Sutter kept the Americans from scoring in the bottom of the ninth, the National Leaguers had for the second time defeated the Americans eight years in a row.

GAME 51
Dodger Stadium,
Los Angeles
July 8, 1980
NL, 4-2

```
AL    000 020 000    2  7  1
NL    000 012 10X    4  7  0
```

Pitchers: Stone, JOHN (4), Farmer (6),
  Stieb (7), Gossage (8) vs Richard,
  Welch (3), REUSS (6), Bibby (7),
  Sutter (8)
Home Runs: Lynn-A, Griffey-N
Attendance: 56,088

For 4⅔ innings J.R. Richard and Bob Welch held the American stars scoreless. But then Rod Carew singled and Fred Lynn drove in the game's first runs with his third All-Star homer.

The Americans' Steve Stone and Tommy John pitched even better, setting the Nationals down in order through four innings. John continued the perfect streak through the first two outs of the fifth, but then Ken Griffey homered, and the Americans' spell on the National Leaguers was broken.

While three National pitchers limited the Americans to a single and a walk over the final four innings, three singles and an error sent the Nationals into the lead in the sixth. A passed ball surrounded by two wild pitches moved Dave Concepcion around the bases in the seventh (he had reached on a fielder's choice) for the Nationals' fourth run. They didn't really need it, though, as Bruce Sutter—the winning pitcher in the two previous All-Star games—saved this one with two final innings of no-hit ball for the Nationals' ninth successive win.

GAME 52
Municipal Stadium,
Cleveland
August 9, 1981
NL, 5-4

```
NL    000 011 120    5  9  1
AL    010 003 000    4 11  1
```

Pitchers: Valenzuela, Seaver (2),
  Knepper (3), Hooton (5),
  Ruthven (6), BLUE (7), Ryan (8),
  Sutter (9) vs Morris, Barker (3),
  K.Forsch (5), Norris (6), Davis (7),
  FINGERS (8), Stieb (8)
Home Runs: Singleton-A, Carter-N
  (2), Parker-N, Schmidt-N
Attendance: 72,086

The game, delayed until August by the midseason players' strike, drew an All-Star record crowd of more than 72,000 fans, and the managers set a new record by using 56 players. But the game itself followed a familiar pattern.

The Americans scored first in the second inning on Ken Singleton's home run off Tom Seaver, and held their slim lead into the fifth on Len Barker's two innings of perfect pitching. But Ken Forsch replaced Barker in the fifth and Gary Carter homered off his first pitch to tie the score. Dave Parker's homer off Mike Norris an inning later put the Nationals ahead for the first time, but the Americans came right back in the bottom of the inning, putting together four singles and a sacrifice fly for three runs and a two-run advantage.

Gary Carter's second home run of the game—this time off Ron Davis's first pitch—brought the Nationals within one in the seventh, and Mike Schmidt's two-run blast off Rollie Fingers in the eighth restored their lead. Three National pitchers shut out the Americans without a hit over the final three innings as closer Bruce Sutter picked up his second consecutive All-Star save and the National Leaguers their tenth consecutive victory.

GAME 53
Olympic Stadium, Montreal
July 13, 1982
NL, 4-1

```
AL   100 000 000     1  8  2
NL   021 001 00X     4  8  1
```

Pitchers: ECKERSLEY, Clancy (4), Bannister (5), Quisenberry (6), Fingers (8) vs ROGERS, Carlton (4), Soto (6), Valenzuela (8), Minton (8), Howe (9), Hume (9)
Home Runs: Concepcion-N
Attendance: 59,057

In the first All-Star Game held outside the United States, the American League for the third year in a row put the first run on the board, but for the eleventh year in a row the final score showed the National League the winner. Two singles, a wild pitch, and a sacrifice fly gave the Americans a run in the top of the first. But starter Steve Rogers of the host Expos held the Americans scoreless for the remainder of his three innings while the Nationals struck back for two runs in the second on Dave Concepcion's home run, and added another in the third when Ruppert Jones—who had tripled to open the inning—scored on a sacrifice fly.

Six National League pitchers (and shortstop Ozzie Smith's spectacular stop and throw to first with two on in the eighth) joined Rogers in holding the American stars scoreless after the first inning. Two hometowners put together the Nationals' final run in the sixth. Al Oliver, leading off, doubled down the line in left and took third as the ball got by left fielder Rickey Henderson. Two outs later Gary Carter lined a pitch to center, scoring Oliver as Willie Wilson's dive for the ball came up short.

GAME 54
Comiskey Park, Chicago
July 6, 1983
AL, 13-3

```
NL   100 110 000     3  8  3
AL   117 000 22X    13 15  2
```

Pitchers: SOTO, Hammaker (3), Dawley (3), Dravecky (5), Perez (7), Orosco (7), L.Smith (8) vs STIEB, Honeycutt (4), Stanley (6), Young (8), Quisenberry (9)
Home Runs: Rice-A, Lynn-A
Attendance: 43,801

The game returned to the park where it had originated fifty years earlier, and the American League, after eleven years of All-Star losses, unleashed its pent-up fury to produce the greatest margin of victory in thirty-seven years. The game began, though, as an embarrassment of errors. American starter Dave Stieb struck out the side in the first, but along the way two errors (one of them Stieb's) let in a run. An unearned run in the bottom of the first tied the score and another in the second put the American League ahead for good (making a loser out of the unfortunate National starter Mario Soto).

The hitting began in earnest in the last of the third as the Americans scored seven times for a new one-inning record. Among their six hits (also a record for an All-Star inning) were a homer by Jim Rice, a triple by George Brett, and a bases-loaded blast by Fred Lynn—his fourth All-Star home run and the first grand slam in All-Star history. With the score now 9–1, the National League's single runs in the fourth and fifth were exercises in futility, and the Americans' two each in the seventh and eighth served chiefly to boost the winning total to 13—another All-Star high.

GAME 55
Candlestick Park,
San Francisco
July 10, 1984
NL, 3-1

```
AL   010 000 000     1  7  2
NL   110 000 01X     3  8  0
```

Pitchers: STIEB, Morris (3), Dotson (5), Caudill (7), Hernandez (8) vs LEA, Valenzuela (3), Gooden (5), Soto (7), Gossage (9)
Home Runs: Brett-A, Carter-N, Murphy-N
Attendance: 57,756

Only four times in the previous fifty-four All-Star Games had a pitcher struck out the side in order. In this game, three more pitchers did it. And, on this fiftieth anniversary of Carl Hubbell's five consecutive strikeouts, two of those pitchers combined to break Hubbell's record with six back-to-back whiffs. Hubbell, who threw out the first ball, also saw an All-Star nine-inning record set with 21 total Ks (11 by National League pitchers, 10 by American).

In the fourth inning, National star Fernando Valenzuela mowed down three of the game's premier sluggers: Dave Winfield, Reggie Jackson, and George Brett. If the three men Dwight Gooden retired on strikes an inning later (Lance Parrish, Chet Lemon, and rookie Alvin Davis) were slightly less formidable, still, it was an impressive performance for a nineteen-year-old rookie (the youngest player in All-Star history). The three that American Leaguer Bill Caudill struck out in the seventh were no slouches either: Tim Raines, Ryne Sandberg (in the midst of an MVP season), and Keith Hernandez.

Three of the four runs scored in the game were homers. The National League's run in the first was unearned, but the Americans' George Brett homered to center to tie the game in the second, and the Nationals' go-ahead run later in the inning came on Gary Carter's blast to left. In the eighth, National Leaguer Dale Murphy also put one over the left field fence to end the scoring.

GAME 56
H. Humphrey Metrodome,
Minneapolis
July 16, 1985
NL, 6-1

```
NL   011 020 002     6  9  1
AL   100 000 000     1  5  0
```

Pitchers: HOYT, Ryan (4), Valenzuela (7), Reardon (8), Gossage (9) vs MORRIS, Key (3), Blyleven (4), Stieb (6), Moore (7), Petry (9), Hernandez (9)
Attendance: 54,960

The American Leaguers scored first, as Rickey Henderson led off the bottom of the first with a single and circled the bases on a steal, error, and sacrifice fly. But the five National pitchers blanked the Americans the rest of the way on only four more singles.

Meanwhile, the National stars methodically dismantled the Americans for their thirty-sixth All-Star victory. In the top of the second, after Darryl Strawberry singled and stole second, Terry Kennedy, whose error had led to the American League run, redeemed himself by singling Strawberry home. An inning later, with two out, Tom Herr doubled and scored the go-ahead (and winning) run on Steve Garvey's single.

In the fifth the Nationals scored two more runs on a hit batsman, Tim Wallach's ground-rule double, and Ozzie Virgil's single, and finished their scoring in the ninth with another pair on three walks and Willie McGee's double—another ground-rule bounce out of play off the lively Metrodome surface. Goose Gossage struck out the final two American batters in the bottom of the ninth, and the Nationals had increased their winning margin in the series to a new high of seventeen games.

GAME 57
Astrodome, Houston
July 15, 1986
AL, 3–2

AL	020	000	100	3	5	0
NL	000	000	020	2	5	1

Pitchers: CLEMENS, Higuera (4), Hough (7), Righetti (8), Aase (9) vs GOODEN, Valenzuela (4), Scott (7), Fernandez (8), Krukow (9)
Home Runs: Whitaker-A, White-A
Attendance: 45,774

National League pitchers struck out 12 Americans, led by Fernando Valenzuela's five in a row, which matched the mark set by Carl Hubbell in 1934. (Two years earlier Valenzuela had helped set a multipitcher All-Star record of six consecutive strikeouts.) In the eighth inning Sid Fernandez, after walking two, struck out the next three.

Though the American Leaguers struck out fewer men, their pitching was more effective over all. Starter Roger Clemens hurled three perfect innings (3 balls and 21 strikes), and Teddy Higuera one-hit the Nationals over the next three. Charlie Hough struck out three in the eighth after yielding the Nationals' only extra-base hit (a double) to Chris Brown. But catcher Rich Gedman couldn't handle Hough's knuckleball, and Brown advanced to third on the first strikeout (ruled a wild pitch) and scored on the second, a passed ball which also enabled batter Hubie Brooks to reach first safely. Brooks moved up on a balk and scored the Nationals' second run on Steve Sax's single.

But home runs had already undone the Nationals. With two gone in the second, Dave Winfield doubled off starter Dwight Gooden, and Lou Whitaker clubbed an 0–2 pitch over the fence in right. And in the seventh, Frank White (hitting for Whitaker) knocked Mike Scott's 0–2 pitch over the fence in left center for what proved the margin of American League victory.

GAME 58
Oakland-Alameda County
Stadium, Oakland
July 14, 1987
NL, 2–0

NL	000	000	000	000 2	2	8	2
AL	000	000	000	000 0	0	6	1

Pitchers: Scott, Sutcliffe (3), Hershiser (5), R.Reuschel (7), Franco (8), Bedrosian (9), L.SMITH (10), S. Fernandez (13) vs Saberhagen, Morris (4), Langston (6), Plesac (8), Righetti (9), Henke (9), J.HOWELL (12)
Attendance: 49,671

None of the previous fifty-seven All-Star Games had gone more than five innings without at least one run crossing the plate. But this game went more than twice that before National Leaguer Tim Raines tripled in two runs in the top of the thirteenth for the game's only scoring. It was the National League's eighth win in eight extra-inning All-Star games.

Both teams missed scoring opportunities in the ninth inning. Raines singled for the Nationals with only one out, and became the game's first runner to reach third when a throw from first on his attempted steal went into center field. But a fly to short right and a foul left him stranded. In the bottom of the ninth, the Americans came close to winning the game as Dave Winfield headed for home from second on a missed 4–6–1 double play. But National pitcher Steve Bedrosian, covering first, snared the off-center throw from short and fired it home to catch Winfield for the third out.

The Americans again reached third in the eleventh as Larry Parrish singled and moved around on a sacrifice and ground out. But pitcher Lee Smith (whose three shutout innings earned him the win) struck out Tony Fernandez to end the threat.

GAME 59
Riverfront Stadium,
Cincinnati
July 12, 1988
AL, 2–1

AL	001	100	000	2	6	2
NL	000	100	000	1	5	0

Pitchers: VIOLA, Clemens (3), Gubicza (4), Stieb (6), Russell (7), Jones (8), Plesac (8), Eckersley (9) vs GOODEN, Knepper (4), Cone (5), Gross (6), Davis (7), Walk (7), Hershiser (8), Worrell (9)
Home Run: Steinbach-A
Attendance: 55,837

Oakland's Terry Steinbach was not among the ten top American League catchers in batting; because of time lost to injuries, he was not even his club's leading catcher in games played. But the fans voted him to start in the All-Star Game, and he won it for the American Leaguers with a home run in his first trip to the plate and a sacrifice fly his next time up. Steinbach's homer—a drive off Dwight Gooden that led off the third inning—caromed off the glove of a leaping Darryl Strawberry over the wall in right for the game's first score. His sacrifice fly—high and deep to left in the fourth inning—scored Dave Winfield (aboard with his record seventh All-Star double) to put the Americans ahead 2–0.

Steinbach also contributed negatively to the National League run later in the fourth. His throwing error on Vince Coleman's steal of second enabled Coleman to advance to third, whence he scored on a wild pitch by Mark Gubicza.

American starter Frank Viola, the midseason league leader in wins, was awarded the victory for his two perfect innings pitched. Dennis Eckersley, the majors' top reliever, preserved the win for the Americans with a perfect ninth inning.

GAME 60
Anaheim Stadium,
Anaheim, California
July 11, 1989
AL, 5–3

NL	200	000	010	3	9	1
AL	212	000	00X	5	12	0

Pitchers: Reuschel, SMOLTZ (2), Sutcliffe (3), Burke (4), M. Davis (6), Howell (7), Williams (8) vs Stewart, RYAN (2), Gubicza (4), Moore (5), Swindell (6), Russell (7), Plesac (8), Jones (8)
Home Runs: Jackson-A, Boggs-A
Attendance: 64,036

The National stars struck early with a pair of two-out runs in the top of the first inning, and a double steal put two more runners in scoring position. But left fielder Bo Jackson stifled the assault with a fine running catch, then opened the American half of the first with a massive home run to center field off Rick Reuschel. Wade Boggs, the next man up, added insult to the forty-year-old Reuschel's first All-Star start, tying the game with another homer.

In the second inning Jackson drove in the American League's go-ahead run with a slow grounder off young John Smoltz, and an inning later four American singles produced two more runs. A quartet of National League pitchers held the Americans scoreless on just three hits over the final six innings, and their teammates rallied for a third National run in the eighth. But Doug Jones (the majors' top reliever in 1989) came on to get the final out of the eighth, and in the ninth preserved the American lead to give the American Leaguers their first repeat All-Star victory in thirty-one years.

National League hurler Smoltz, at age twenty-two the youngest player in the lineup, took the loss. Nolan Ryan, back in the American League after nine National League seasons, earned the win with two shutout innings. Not only was he the oldest player on either side, at forty-two he was the oldest All-Star winning pitcher ever.

GAME 61
Wrigley Field, Chicago
July 10, 1990
AL, 2-0

AL   000 000 200   2 7 0
NL   000 000 000   0 2 1

Pitchers: Welch, Stieb (3),
    SABERHAGEN (5), Thigpen (7),
    Finley (8), Eckersley (9) vs
    Armstrong, R. Martinez (3), D.
    Martinez (4), Viola (5), D. Smith (6),
    BRANTLEY (6), Dibble (7),
    Myers (8), Franco (9)
Attendance: 39,071

Back-to-back American League
singles off Jeff Brantley had put
men on third and first and
brought Julio Franco to the plate
in the seventh inning, when heavy
rain halted the game for more
than an hour. During the delay
Brantley's side stiffened, so when
Franco finally got his turn at bat
he faced a new National pitcher,
Rob Dibble. Franco lined Dibble's third pitch into the gap in
right center for a double—the
only extra-base hit of the game—
driving in what proved to be the
game's only runs.

Damp air and a stiff breeze in
from left field helped tame the
offense. American League batters managed to accumulate
seven hits, but the Nationals were
held to two—an All-Star all-time
low. No runner advanced as far as
third base until the sixth inning,
when American stars Kelly Gruber and Jose Canseco pulled off a
double steal. No National
Leaguer reached that far, and if it
weren't for Barry Larkin's
third-inning steal, no National
runner would even have stood on
second base.

American hurler Bret
Saberhagen's two perfect middle
innings earned him the win, and
Dennis Eckersley, after yielding a
leadoff hit in the ninth, retired
the final three batters to record
his second All-Star save in three
years. The victory was the third
in a row for the American Leaguers, the first time they had put
together such a string of triumphs
in forty-one years.

Ballparks

Philip J. Lowry

What follows are the vital statistics of each of the current twenty-six major league baseball stadiums and a selection of the storied parks of the past. My book, *Green Cathedrals,* from which much of this section is taken, encompassed the whole of major league history, from 1871 to the present, including the extraordinary variety of early playing sites, from cricket grounds and polo fields to agricultural fairgrounds and cow pastures. That book also covered Negro League ballparks in a depth beyond the scope possible here, including the vast array of barnstorming sites, even for official league games, that was characteristic of impoverished ballclubs looking to maximize their gate receipts in any way possible. All the same, despite the space constraints imposed upon this entry, the primary Negro League parks will be covered, as well as classic shrines such as Ebbets Field, Griffith Stadium, Forbes Field, and others.

The focus here is on ballpark geometry and the oddities in play that resulted from the unique configuration of the park. Dimensional changes are catalogued and dated, particularly in outfield fence distances and heights. This subject is crucial to an understanding of the statistical history of baseball, whether or not one is a devotee of the park-adusted figures on display in this volume.

The following leagues are covered by this study. The accompanying abbreviations may be employed for the twentieth century's principal leagues:

NL	National League, 1876–
AL	American League, 1901–
FL	Federal League, 1914–1915
NNL	Negro National League, 1920–1931, 1933–1948
ECL	Eastern Colored League, 1923–1928
NAL	Negro American League, 1929, 1937–1950
NSL	Negro Southern League, 1932
NEWL	Negro East-West League, 1932

Before 1900, most parks were small wooden grandstands hastily constructed around recreation fields that often were not even enclosed by outfield fences. Beginning with the erection of Shibe park and Forbes Field in 1909, however, concrete-and-steel ballparks became the rule. These palaces signaled the growing prominence of baseball and constituted to my mind the best in ballpark design; the term I have applied to this type of park is "Major League Classic." In the 1950s a transitional type of park—one that retained the beauty of the older parks while affording some of the conveniences of the new— became the home of the Braves, transplanted from Boston to Milwaukee, and the Orioles, who flew into Baltimore from St. Louis, where they had been the Browns.

Using the Outlines

"Style" defines the structural design of the park as designated in the introduction.

"A.K.A." (Also Known As) lists alternate names and nicknames used for the ballpark.

"Occupant" lists teams using the park in chronological order. Inclusive dates of play within the league follow.

"Event" contains postseason contests and All-Star Games.

"Location" lists the surrounding streets. When possible, fields and bases are associated with the streets. Geographical directions, (N) for North, (S) for South, (E) for East, and (W) for West, are provided when available.

Because all older stadiums had grass "surfaces," information concerning carpet or grass is included only for modern ballparks.

Under "Dimensions" the distance is given in feet from home plate to the fences, and to the backstop. Dates, in parentheses, denote the *first* month and/or year when the boundaries stood at the stated distance.

"Fences" lists the heights of the outfield fences in feet. Dates denote the *first* time the fences stood at the stated height.

"Former Use" describes how the site was utilized before stadium construction. Similarly, "Current Use" chronicles the development of the site after a ballpark was demolished or abandoned.

"Phenomena" is a more general category for historical data. Included here will be special features of the park's physical plant, important changes over the years, and events of note throughout the years of operation.

ANAHEIM, CALIFORNIA

ANAHEIM STADIUM
STYLE Superstructure with natural surface
A.K.A. Big A 1966, Bigger A 1981
OCCUPANT AL Angels April 19, 1966 to date
EVENT All Star Game 1967, 1989
LOCATION *Left Field (N)* Katella Avenue; *3rd Base (W)* 2000 State College Boulevard and Interstate 5; *1st Base (S)* Orangewood Freeway, then Santa Ana River; *Center Field (NE)* Amtrak Railroad Station
SURFACE Bluegrass

DIMENSIONS *Foul Lines:* 333; *Bullpens:* 362; *Power Alleys:* 375 (1966), 369 (1973), 370 (1974); *Deep Alleys:* 386; *Center Field:* 406 (1966), 402 (1973), 404 (1974); *Backstop:* 55 (1966), 60.5 (1973)
FENCES *Majority of the Fence:* 10 (wire 1966), 7.86 (wire 1973), 7.86 (padded 1981); *Corners Between Foul Poles and Bullpens:* 4.75 (steel 1966); *Left-center Between 386 and 404 Marks:* 7.5 (padded 1981); *Padded Posts at the Left Sides of Both Left and Right Field; Bullpen Gates:* 9 (padded 1981); *Bullpen Gates:* 9.95 (wire 1966)
FORMER USE Four farms—Camille Allec's 39 acres of orange and eucalyptus trees, Roland Reynolds' 70 acres of alfalfa, John Knutgen's 20 acres of corn, Bill Ross and George Lenney's 19 acres of corn
PHENOMENA
• Power hitter's park, the ball carries well.
• Huge 230-foot-high letter "A" stood behind the fence in left as a scoreboard support until 1980, then it was moved to the parking lot. The letter has a gold halo at its top.
• Sections 69 and 70 in center covered by green-canvas batters' background.
• Two thin black TV cables run in fair territory on the warning track from the left field corner bullpen gate to the foul pole, and then along the wall in foul territory about 50 feet toward third base, then into the stands.
• Outfield enclosed and tripledecked in 1980.
• 6 doors on ivy-covered wall in deep left-center behind outfield fence labeled: "warning track," "skin material," "screen clay mounds," "raw clay," "sand," "equipment."

ATLANTA, GEORGIA

ATLANTA-FULTON COUNTY STADIUM
STYLE Superstructure with natural surface
A.K.A. Atlanta Stadium 1966-74, Launching Pad
OCCUPANT NL Braves April 12, 1966 to date
EVENT All Star Game 1972
LOCATION *Left Field (NE)* Pullman Street and Interstate 20; *3rd Base (NW)* Washington Street and Interstate 75/85 and Georgia Avenue; *1st Base (SW)* 521 Capitol Avenue; *Right Field (SE)* Fulton Street
SURFACE 419 Bermuda grass
DIMENSIONS *Foul Lines:* 325 (1966), 330 (1967); *Power Alleys:* 385 (1966), 375 (1969), 385 (1973); *Center Field:* 402 (1966), 400 (1969), 402 (1973); Back Stop: 59.92 (1973); *Foul Territory:* Large (1966), Medium (1977)
FENCES 6 (wire 1966), 10 (4 plexiglass above 6 wire 1983), 10 (plexiglass 1985)
PHENOMENA
• Three statues outside the stadium honor Ty Cobb, Hank Aaron, and Phil Niekro.
• Used by 1965 Triple A IL Crackers.
• Big Victor, a large totem-pole-styled figure, stood in the stadium in 1966. The huge head tilted and the eyes rolled whenever a Brave hit a home run.
• With an altitude of more than 1,000 feet above sea level, it is the highest park in the majors, which results in many homers and the nickname "the Launching Pad."
• Chief Noc-A-Homa's Wigwam replaced Big Victor in 1967. From 1967 to 1971 the teepee stood on a 20-foot-

square platform behind the left field fence. In 1972 the teepee was moved to right field. From 1973 to 1977 it returned to left field. From 1978 to August 1982 the teepee was moved to left-center, occupying 235 seats between aisles 128 and 130, rows 18-30. From August to early September, 1982, it was removed in anticipation of additional revenue in the playoffs, "causing" a disastrous tailspin for the first-place Braves. Its replacement coincided with the Braves' comeback to win the division crown in 1982. The teepee's removal on August 11, 1983, saw another losing streak which could not be overcome by its return on September 16. It stands today, a permanent outfield installation.
• 22-foot outfield wall never in play.
• 80-year-old calliope organ installed 1971.

BALTIMORE, MARYLAND

MEMORIAL STADIUM
STYLE 1950s Transitional
OCCUPANT AL Orioles April 15, 1954 to date
EVENT All Star Game 1958
LOCATION *Center Field (N)* East 36th Street; *3rd Base (W)* Ellerslie Avenue; *Home Plate (S)* 1000 East 33rd Street, section of 33rd Street near ballpark is known as Babe Ruth Plaza; *1st Base (E)* Ednor Road
SURFACE Bluegrass
DIMENSIONS *Foul Lines:* 309; where the 7-foot fence meets the 14-foot wall, 360; Power Alleys: 446 (1954), 447 (1955), 405 (1956), 380 (1958), 370 (1962), 385 (1970), 375 (1976), 378 (1977), 376 (1980), 378 (1990); *Center Field:* 445 (1954), 450 (1955), 425 (1956), 410 (1958), 400 (1976), 405 (1977), 410 (1978), 405 (1980); *Backstop:* 78 (1954), 58 (1961), 54 (1980); *Foul Territory:* Large
FENCES *Foul Line Corners:* 11.33 (concrete 1954), 14 (11 concrete below 3 plywood 1959); these walls bounce balls toward center, reducing triples; *Left-Center to Right-Center:* 10 (hedges April and May, 1954), 8 (wire June 1954), 7 (wire 1955), 6 (wire 1958), 14 (wire 1961), 6 (wire 1963), 7 (canvas 1977)
FORMER USE Venable Stadium
PHENOMENA
• Beautiful trees on an embankment beyond the fence in center.
• Oriole Landing was a picnic area in the upper deck in the 1960s.
• At the beginning of the 1954 season, hedges served as the center field fence. In June 1954 a wire fence was erected which stood right in front of a row of high hedges. The top 6 feet of the fence were covered with canvas padding in 1958 after Harvey Kuenn cut his face trying to catch a home run ball by climbing the fence. The walls in the left and right field corners were also padded after Curt Blefary injured his hip chasing a Max Alvis fly.
• Fans yell "O" (for Orioles) in unison when "The Star-Spangled Banner" reaches "O say does that star-spangled banner yet wave . . ."
• Wind usually helps lefthanded hitters.
• Venable Stadium, a football stadium also used for baseball after the July 4, 1944 fire destroyed Oriole Park (V), was torn down to make way for Memorial Stadium. Home

plate was moved from where it had been in the north to its current location in the south.

• Home of the best crabcakes in baseball; crab races in the bottom of the sixth on the scoreboard between Wee Willie in orange, Paco in blue, and Mugsy in yellow.

• To be replaced by new baseball-only park in Camden Yards, near the Inner Harbor, by 1991.

• Inscribed into the concrete facade: "Dedicated as a memorial to all who so valiantly fought in the world wars with eternal gratitude to those who made the supreme sacrifice to preserve equality and freedom throughout the world—time will not dim the glory of their deeds."

BOSTON, MASSACHUSETTS

FENWAY PARK

STYLE Major League Classic
OCCUPANT AL Red Sox April 20, 1912 to date
EVENT NL Braves vs. New York April 19, May 30, 1913; August 1 and 8, September 7 to 29, 1914; 1914 World Series; April 14 to July 26, 1915; All Star Game 1946, 1961
LOCATION *Left Field (N)* Lansdowne Street, Boston & Albany Railroad tracks, and Mass. Turnpike/Interstate 90; *3rd Base (W)* Brookline Avenue and 24 Jersey Street, renamed 24 Yawkey Way in 1976, also bowling alley building attached to park; *1st Base (S)* Van Ness Street (built after park was done); *Right Field (E)* Ipswich Street and Fenway Garage building
SURFACE Bluegrass
DIMENSIONS *Left Field:* 321 (1921), 320.5 (1926), 320 (1930), 318 (1931), 320 (1933), 312 (1934), 315 (1936); *Left-Center:* 379 (1934); *Deep Left-Center at Flagpole:* 388 (1934); *Flagpole Removed from Field of Play in 1970; Centerfield:* 488 (1922), 468 (1930), 388.67 (1934), 389.67 (1954); *Deepest Corner, Just Right of Center:* 550 (1922), 593 (1931), 420 (1934) [Note: 593 is cited in 1931-33 Bluebooks; this could be a misprint.] *Right-Center, Just Right of Deepest Corner Where the Bullpen Begins:* 380 (1938), 383 (1955); *Right of Right Center:* 405 (1939), 382 (1940), 381 (1942), 380 (1943); *Right Field:* 313.5 (1921), 358.5 (1926), 358 (1930), 325 (1931) 358 (1933), 334 (1934), 332 (1936), 322 (1938), 332 (1939), 304 (1940), 302 (1942); *Backstop:* 68 (1912), 60 (1934); *Foul Territory:* Very small, smallest in the majors
FENCES *Left Field:* 25 (wood 1912), 37.17 (tin over wood over concrete lower section 1934), 37.17 (hard plastic 1976); *Left Field Wall to Center Bleacher Wall Behind Flagpole:* 18 sloping to 17 (concrete 1934), (padding 1976) crash pad added from 18 inches to 6 feet on left and center field walls (1976); *Center Field to Bullpen Fence:* 8.75 (wood 1940); *Right-Center Bullpen Fence:* 5.25 (wood 1940); *Right Field Wall and Railing:* Bullpen 3.42 sloping to 5.37 at foul pole (steel 1940); *Right Field Belly:* the low railing and wall curve out sharply from the 302 marker at the right field foul pole into deep right field—many a right fielder has run toward the foul line and watched helplessly as a 310-foot pop fly falls over the railing for a home run.
PHENOMENA
• Seats made of oak.

• 1976 electronic scoreboard significantly altered the wind currents.

• 43 private 28-seat rooftop boxes added 1984.

• Duffy's Cliff was a 10-foot-high mound which formed an incline in front of the left field wall from 1912 to 1933, extending from the left field foul pole to the flag pole in center—named after Red Sox left fielder Duffy Lewis, who was the acknowledged master of defensive play on the cliff. It was greatly reduced but not completely eliminated in 1934.

• The Green Monster Wall in left completely dominates the field of play—now all green, it used to be covered with advertisements.

• Ladder starts near upper-left corner of scoreboard, 13 feet above ground, and rises to top of the Green Monster to allow groundskeeper to remove batting practice home run balls from the netting above the Wall.

• Scoreboard numbers—runs and hits: 16 inches by 16 inches, 3 pounds; errors, innings, pitcher's numbers: 12 inches by 16 inches, 2 pounds.

• Bleachers in foul territory down the left field line burned down in 1926. The charred remains were removed, increasing the size of foul territory there.

• No ball has ever been hit over the right field roof.

• Balls that hit uprights above the Wall, and should have been homers, were declared in play by the umpires.

• Wooden bleachers stood down the left field line in foul territory in the 1910s and 1920s, but burned down on May 8, 1926, and were not replaced. Wooden bleachers were completed in center and right-center by the 1912 World Series.

• Infield grass was transplanted from Huntington Avenue Baseball Grounds to Fenway in 1912.

• During the winter of 1933-34, all the wooden grandstands were replaced with concrete and steel. A big fire on January 5, 1934, destroyed much of what had already been built, but all was finished for the 1934 season opener on April 17.

• In 1935, a 23.33-foot net was placed atop the wall in left to protect windows on Landsdowne Street.

• Wind usually helps the batters. New pressbox built in late 1980s above home plate causes wind swirl which pushes foul balls back into fair territory. This is the park with the tiniest foul territory in the majors.

• When tin covered the two-by-fours on the Wall, balls hitting the tin over two-by-fours had a live bounce, but balls hitting between the two-by-fours were dead and just dropped straight down.

• In 1940, in an effort to help Ted Williams hit home runs, the Red Sox added the right field bullpens, called Williamsburg, which reduced the distance to the fence by 23 feet.

• In 1947 all advertisements were removed from the left field wall, which was painted green.

• Tom A. Yawkey's and his wife Jean R. Yawkey's initials, TAY and JRY, appear in Morse code in two vertical stripes on the scoreboard in left. The 1946 roof boxes were replaced in 1982.

• The screen behind home plate, designed to protect fans and allow foul balls to roll back down onto the field of play, was the first of its kind in the majors.

• Left field scoreboard installed on the Wall in 1934, moved 20 feet to the right in 1976.

• The low concrete base of the left and center field walls was padded after the 1975 World Series, during which Fred Lynn crashed into the concrete wall in center.
• The left field foul line was measured by Art Keefe and George Sullivan, authors of *The Picture History of the Boston Red Sox,* in October 1975 as 309 feet 5 inches. On October 19, 1975, the Boston *Globe* used aerial photography and measured it at 304.779 feet. Osborn Engineering Co. blueprints document the distance at 308 feet.
• Fenway—"where you can sit for hours and feel a security that does not exist anywhere else in the world."

CHICAGO, ILLINOIS

COMISKEY PARK
STYLE Major League Classic
A.K.A. White Sox Park (II) 1910 to 1912, Charles A. Comiskey's Baseball Palace 1910, White Sox Park(III) May 1962 to 1975
OCCUPANT AL White Sox July 1, 1910 through 1990; NL Cubs 1918 World Series; NAL American Giants 1941 to 1950
EVENT All Negro League East-West All Star games, 1933 to 1950; Negro League World Series, eighth through tenth games, 1926; third game, 1943; fifth game, 1946; fourth game, 1947
LOCATION *Left Field (N)* West 34th; *3rd Base (W)* Portland Avenue, later called South Shield's Avenue; *1st Base (S)* 324 West 35th Street; *Right Field (E)* South Wentworth Avenue, later Dan Ryan Expressway/I-94
SURFACE *Outfield:* Grass; *Infield:* Grass (1910), Carpet (1969), Grass (1976)
DIMENSIONS *Foul Lines:* 363 (1910), 362 (1911), 365 (1927), 362 (1930), 342 (1934), 353 (1935), 340 (1936), 352 (1937), 332 (April 22, 1949), 352 (May 5, 1949), 335 (1969), 352 (marked 1971), 349 (actual 1971), 341 (1983), 347 (1986); *Power Alleys:* 382 (1910), 375 (1927), 370 (1934), 382 (1942), 362 (April 22, 1949), 375 (May 5, 1949), 382 (1954), 365 (1955), 375 (1956), 365 (1959), 375 (1968), 370 (1969), 375 (marked 1971), 382 (actual 1971), 374 (1983), 382 (1986); *Center Field:* 420 (1910), 450 (1926), 455 (1927), 450 (1930), 436 (1934), 422 (1936), 440 (1937), 420 (April 22, 1949), 415 (May 5, 1949), 410 (1951), 415 (1952), 400 (1969), 440 (1976), 445 (1977), 402 (marked 1981), 409 (actual 1981), 401 (1983), 409 (1986); *Backstop:* 98 (1910), 71 (1933), 85 (1934), 86 (1955); *Foul Territory:* Large
FENCES *Foul Lines and Power Alleys:* 12 (concrete 1955), 9.83 (concrete 1959), 5 (wire 1969), 9.83 (concrete 1971); *Center Field:* 15 (1927), 30 (1948), 17 (1976), 18 (1980); *Left-Center to Right-Center Inner Fences:* 5 (canvas 1949), 6.5 (24-foot section in front of bullpens 1969), 9 (1974), 7 (canvas 1981), 7.5 (1982), 11 (1984), 7.5 (1986)
FORMER USE A truck garden owned by Signor Scavado, and/or a city dump. South Side Park (II) was almost on the same site, across Wentworth Avenue.
PHENOMENA
• Foul lines are old water hoses, painted white and squished flat.
• In 1910, there were bleachers in left and right, but not in center.

• In the winter of 1926-27, wooden bleachers were replaced with concrete and steel, and the pavilions from left around home plate to right were doubledecked. The scoreboard was moved from right center to two locations on the left field and right field walls.
• Center field bleachers were eliminated in 1947 to improve batter's visibility.
• Section of grandstand collapsed May 17, 1913.
• Special elevator for Lou Comiskey, in use from 1931 to 1982, had an inlaid tile floor.
• In 1950 the bullpens were moved from foul territory down the lines to behind the center field fence.
• In 1960 Bill Veeck installed the first exploding scoreboard in the majors, high above the bleachers in center. In 1982, when the Diamond Vision Board replaced the original, the pinwheels were retained.
• Green cornerstone laid on St. Patrick's Day in 1910 stayed green until 1960 when the exterior was painted all white by Bill Veeck.
• Scene of many masterful groundskeeping tricks by Roger, Gene, and Emil Bossard: (a) Camp Swampy in 1967 referred to the area in front of the plate, dug up and soaked with water when White Sox sinkerball pitchers were on the mound, but mixed with clay and gasoline and burned to provide hard soil if a sinkerballer was pitching for the visiting team. (b) Opposing team bullpen mounds were lowered or raised from the standard 10-inch height to upset visiting pitchers' rhythm. (c) Under Eddie Stanky's managerial tenure, the grass in front of shortstop was cut long because the Sox shortstop had limited range, but at second the grass was cut short because the Sox second sacker had very good range. (d) When the Sox had a lousy defensive outfield, the grass was cut long to turn triples into doubles. (e) When the Sox had speedy line drive hitters, the outfield grass was cut long to turn singles into doubles. (f) When the Sox had good bunters, more paint was added to the foul line in order to tilt the ball back fair.
• Nine speaker horns on the center field bleacher wall.
• Clock on wall in center to left of flag pole.
• Picnic areas, including Bullring in left and Bullpens I and II in right and right-center, Bavarian and Mexican restaurants and beer halls under the stands behind the plate.
• New park, across the street to the south, ready 1991.
• Showers in the bleachers in center.
• Foul poles bend back slightly to join the top of the roof.
• 540 center field listing in 1931-33 *Baseball Guides* is a misprint.
• Organist Nancy Faust plays "Na-na-na-na, hey-hey, Good bye."
• Open arches between first and second decks.

WRIGLEY FIELD
STYLE Major League Classic
A.K.A. North Side Ball Park, 1914; Weeghman Park, 1914-15; Cubs' Park, 1916-26; Whales Park, 1915; Eddie Dorr's House
OCCUPANT FL Whales April 23, 1914 to October 3, 1915; NL Cubs April 20, 1916 to date
EVENT All Star Game 1947, 1962, 1990
LOCATION *Left Field (N)* West Waveland Avenue; *3rd Base (W)* Seminary Avenue; *Home Plate (SW)* North Clark Street; *1st Base (S)* 1060 West Addison Street;

Right Field (E) North Sheffield Avenue
SURFACE Grass, mixture of Merion Bluegrass and clover
DIMENSIONS *Left Field:* 345 (April 1914), 310 (May 1914), 327 (June 1914), 343 (1921), 325 (1923), 348 (1926), 364 (1928), 355 (1938); *Left-Center Deepest:* 357 (1938); *Power Alleys:* 364 (1914), 368 (1938); *Center Field:* 440 (1914), 447 (1923), 436 (1928), 400 (1938); *Right-Center Deepest:* 363 (1938); *Right Field:* 356 (April 1914), 345 (June 1914), 321 (1915), 298 (1921), 399 (1922), 318 (1923), 321 (1928), 353 (1938); *Backstop:* 62.42 (1930), 60.5 (1957), 62.42 (1982); *Foul Territory:* Very small
FENCES *Left Field Corner:* 15.92 (11.33 brick with Boston and Bittersweet Ivy, below 4.59 plywood), 3 wire basket in front 1985 (does not change height of fence); *Transition Between Left Field Corner and Bleachers:* 12.5 (screen and yellow railing on top of brick wall); *Left-Center to Right-Center:* 8 (screen 1914), 11.33 (brick with ivy 1938); in front is wire basket (May 1970); *Left Field Scoreboard:* 40 (wood July 9 to September 3, 1937); *Center Field Screen:* 1933 (8 wire above 11.33 brick June 18, 1963 to October 1964); *Right Center Triangle:* 17.5 in front of catwalk steps sloping down to 15.5 (screen 1928, plywood 1979, removed 1985); *Right Field Corner:* 15.5 (11.33 brick with ivy, below 4.17 plywood), wire basket in front (1985)
PHENOMENA
• IBM Home Run Distance calculation appears on center field scoreboard after a home run.
• The only remaining Federal League ballpark.
• Beautiful ivy vines on the outfield wall.
• After the game, a blue flag with a white W flying from the center field flag pole signifies a Cub win, a white flag with a blue L a Cub loss.
• Sea breeze off the lake favors pitchers.
• 452 seats added July 1985 to catwalks near foul pole, in fair territory.
• The center field 400 sign is slightly right of straight-away center.
• The only park where it's more difficult to hit a homer down the foul line than to hit one 50 or so feet out in fair territory because the bleachers protrude into the outfield.
• In 1923, the foul lines were shifted slightly amidst park renovations.
• During the 1930s Bobby Dorr, the groundskeeper, lived in a 6 room apartment at the ballpark, adjacent to the left field corner gate; the apartment is still there.
• Eight-foot-high batter's background wire fence, 64 feet wide, stood on top of the center field wall from June 18, 1963 through the end of the 1964 season. Called the Whitlow fence because Cub Athletic Director Robert Whitlow put it up. The screen prevented 10 homers, 4 by Cubs and 6 by visitors, 1 each by 500+ homer hitters Ernie Banks and Willie McCovey.
• Current green Astroturf cover on center field seats used for batters' background and debuted on May 18, 1967.
• In the winter of 1926-27, the left field bleachers were removed, the grandstand was doubledecked, and the playing area was lowered several feet.
• For World Series in 1929, 1932, and 1935, extra bleachers were built on the street on Waveland and Sheffield.
• The park was located so it would be easy for fans to get

there on the Milwaukee Road train.
• The 27-foot-high, 75-foot-wide scoreboard was built in 1937 by Bill Veeck. Its top is 85 feet above the field. The 10 foot diameter clock was added in 1941.
• In 1937, the bleacher stairstep was created to allow potted plants and eight huge Chinese elm trees to grow, complementing the ivy. The trees eventually died.
• Ivy planted on the outfield walls in 1937 by Bill Veeck. Originally 350 Japanese bittersweet plants and 200 Boston ivy plants.
• During the 1937 season, new outfield bleachers were built, and the six gates in the brick wall were emplaced. They were red, repainted blue in 1981.
• The bleachers were expanded to their present state in the 1940s; famous Bleacher Bums formed here in 1966 by 10 bleacher fans.
• Lights were inside the park in the early 1940s ready to be installed, but Mr. Wrigley donated them to the war effort instead on December 8, 1941, thus allowing Wrigley Field to remain dark at night until 1988.
• The right field wall was remodeled in 1950-51.
• On April 14, 1976, Met Dave "King Kong" Kingman hit a homer 550 feet over Waveland and against a frame house 3 doors down on the east side of Kenmore Avenue. If the ball had carried 3 feet higher, it would have crashed through a window and smashed a TV screen on which Ms. Naomi Martinez was watching Mr. Kingman round the bases.
• Park is affected by wind conditions more than any other major league park, with the possible exception of Candlestick.
• More home runs than normal are caused by high altitude of over 600 feet above sea level, and by the heat involved in playing so many daylight games.
• Water fountain moved to the Cub Hall of Fame under the first base stands, near the Friendly Confines cafe.
• Arched dormers on the roof.
• Outfield wall distances before 1981 were marked on plywood markers screwed into the brick. Since then they have been painted directly on the brick.
• Foul pole screens have distances marked on plywood vertically "355" and "353."
• The most distant current outfield measurement sign is at Wrigley Field. On the roof of a house across Sheffield Avenue in right-center, the sign says "495."
• Winds blowing toward the lake take homers with them.

CINCINNATI, OHIO

RIVERFRONT STADIUM

STYLE Superstructure with artificial surface
OCCUPANT NL Reds June 30, 1970 to date
EVENT All Star Game 1970
LOCATION *Left Field (E)* Riverfront Coliseum, Central Bridge and Broadway; *3rd Base (N)* 201 East Second Street, renamed Pete Rose Way on September 10, 1985; *1st Base (W)* Interstate 71 Suspension Bridge Approach Ramp; *Right Field (S)* Mehring Way, railroad tracks, and Ohio River
SURFACE Astroturf—hard, balls bounce high off it
DIMENSIONS *Foul Lines:* 330; *Power Alleys:* 375; *Center Field:* 404; *Backstop:* 51; *Foul Territory:* Small

FENCES   12 (wood, 1970); 8 (wood, 1984)
PHENOMENA
• First to paint metric distances on outfield walls: 100.58 down the lines, 114.30 to the alleys, 123.13 to center.
• Uses Crosley Field's home plate.
• Parking garage beneath stadium.
• 4,192 circle in left center commemorates Pete Rose's 4,192nd hit here on 9/10/85 vs. the Padres.
• Reds and Pirates played slowest game ever here 8/30/78—80.6 minutes per inning, called off after 3½ innings and 3½ hours of rain delays at 12:47 A.M.
• Winds help righthanded hitters.

CLEVELAND, OHIO

CLEVELAND STADIUM
STYLE   Summer Olympics Stadium
A.K.A.   Lakefront Stadium 1930s, Cleveland Public Municipal Stadium 1930s, Municipal Stadium 1940s and 1950s
OCCUPANT   AL Indians July 31, 1932 to September 24, 1933; August 2, 1936 vs. New York; AL Indians May 30 to September 6, 1937 Sundays and holidays only between Memorial Day and Labor Day; April 1938 to June 1939 Sundays, holidays and selected important games only; AL Indians June 27, 1939 to September 1947 nights, Sundays, holidays, and selected important games (this was a majority of home games in 1940, 1942-46); AL Indians April 15, 1947 to date all games
EVENT   All Star Game 1935, 1954, 1963, 1981
LOCATION   *Center Field (NE)* East Ninth Street; *3rd Base (NW)* Erieside Avenue and Donald Gray Lakefront Gardens Port Authority Dock 28 and Lake Erie; *Home Plate (SW)* West Third Street; *1st Base (SE)* Cleveland Memorial Shoreway, Amtrak/Conrail railroad tracks; Boudreau Boulevard encircles the park
SURFACE   Bluegrass
DIMENSIONS   *Foul Lines:* 322 (1932), 320 (1933), 321 (1948), 320 (1953); *Corners Where Inner Fence Meets Stadium Walls:* 362 (1947), 360 (1980); *Power Alleys:* 435 (1932), 365 (1947), 362 (1948), 385 (1949), 380 (1954), 400 (1965), 390 (1967), 395 (1968), 385 (1970); *Left Center:* 377 (1980); *Right-Center:* 385 (1980); *Deep Left-Center:* 387 (1980); *Deep Right Center:* 395 (1980); *Bleacher Corners:* 463 (1932); *Grandstand Corners:* 435 (1932); *Center Field:* 470 (1932), 467 (1938), 450 (1939), 410 (April 27, 1947), 408 (1966), 407 (1967), 410 (1968), 400 (1970); *Backstop:* 60; *Foul Territory:* Large
FENCES   *Left and Right Field:* 5.25 (concrete 1932), 5.5 (wire April 27, 1947), 5.25 (concrete June 6, 1947), 6 (1955), 9 (1976), 8 (1977), 8 (canvas 1984)
PHENOMENA
• Architectural style has been called "stripped classicism," and has been compared to later Memorial and County Stadiums in Baltimore and Milwaukee.
• Groundskeepers' tools kept in foul territory in 1930s and 1940s.
• Before the inner fences were installed on April 27 after the first two weeks of the 1947 season, there was an incline in front of the center field bleacher wall; strange shape in power alleys caused by the end of the doubledecked grandstand, where the fence jumped abruptly deeper to the bleacher wall in center. The April 27 inner fence curved all the way to the foul poles. On June 6, 1947, it was changed so the inner fence just stretched across center field, hitting the permanent wall at 362 mark.
• Teepees erected in 1946 in center.
• Foul poles are 32 feet 8 inches high, 27 inches wide, and the screen on them is 22 inches wide.
• No one has ever hit a ball into the center field bleachers.
• Music bandstand in center field between fence and bleachers set up in 1953.
• Wind usually blows out toward the lake.
• Center field standing-room area was a garden in 1957.
• Field was lowered 2 feet in 1976.
• Cleveland Stadium/League Park ratio of home games from 1936 to 1946—1/77, 15/63, 18/58, 30/47, 49/33, 32/45, 46/34, 48/29, 44/34, 46/31, 41/36.
• Featured in 2 movies—*The Kid from Cleveland* in 1949, *Fortune Cookie* in mid-1960s.
• Opened formally on July 1, 1931—13 months before the Indians' first home game on July 31, 1932.

DALLAS, TEXAS

ARLINGTON STADIUM
STYLE   Expanded Minor League
A.K.A.   Turnpike Stadium, 1965 to 1971
OCCUPANT   AL Rangers April 21, 1972 to date
LOCATION   Arlington, Texas—between Dallas and Fort Worth; *Left Field (E)* Stadium Drive East and Six Flags Over Texas Amusement Park; *3rd Base (N)* 1500 South Copeland Road; *1st Base (W)* Stadium Drive West; *Right Field (S)* Randol Mill Road
SURFACE   419 Bermuda grass
DIMENSIONS   *Foul Lines:* 330; *Power Alleys:* 380 (1972), 370 (1974), 383 (1981), 380 (1982); *Center Field:* 400; *Backstop:* 60; *Foul Territory:* Small
FENCES   11 (1972), 12 (1981), 11 (1986)
FORMER USE   Minor league ballpark from 1965 to 1971 called Turnpike Stadium
PHENOMENA
• Built in 1965 as Turnpike Stadium.
• Huge Texas-shaped scoreboard behind the bleachers in left center runs from section E to section K.
• Like Dodger Stadium, the field is below the surrounding parking lots. Before 1978, when the upper deck was added, fans would walk in at the top of the stadium.
• Wind blows in directly from the outfield.
• Hottest park in the majors, which increases the number of home runs hit here since the warm humid air is not as dense as cooler drier air elsewhere and therefore does not offer as much resistance to the ball in flight.
• More advertising signs than any other major league park.
• The Lone Ranger on Diamond Vision scoreboard roots for the Rangers.

DETROIT, MICHIGAN

TIGER STADIUM
STYLE   Major League Classic

A.K.A. Navin Field 1912 to 1937, Briggs Stadium 1938 to 1960

OCCUPANT AL Tigers April 20, 1912 to date

EVENT All Star Game 1941, 1951, 1971

LOCATION *Left Field (NW)* Cherry Street, later Kaline Drive, and Interstate 75; *3rd Base (SW)* National Avenue, later Cochrane Avenue; *1st Base (SE)* Michigan Avenue; *Right Field (NE)* 2121 Trumbull Avenue, same site as Bennett park but turned around 90 degrees, in the Corktown neighborhood

SURFACE Bluegrass

DIMENSIONS *Left Field:* 345 (1921), 340.58 (1926), 339 (1930), 367 (1931), 339 (1934), 340 (1938), 342 (1939), 340 (1942); *Left Center:* 365 (1942); *Center Field:* 467 (1927), 455 (1930), 464 (1931), 459 (1936), 450 (1937), 440 (1938), 450 (1939), 420 (1942), 440 (1944); *Right Center:* 370 (1942), 375 (1982); *Right Field:* 370 (1921), 370.91 (1926), 372 (1930), 367 (1931), 325 (1936), 315 (1939), 325 (1942), 302 (1954), 325 (1955); *Backstop:* 54.35 (1954), 66 (1955); *Foul Territory:* Small

FENCES *All Fences:* 5 concrete topped by screen; *Left Field:* 20 (1935), 30 (1937), 10 (1938), 12 (1940), 15 (1946), 12 (1953), 14 (1954), 12 (1955), 11 (1958), 9 (1962); *Center Field:* 9 (1940), 15 (1946), 11 (1950), 9 (1953), 14 (1954), 9 (1955); *Right of Flag Pole:* 7 (1946); *Right Field:* 8 (1940), 30 (1944), 10 (1945), 20 (1950), 8 (1953), 9 (1958), 30 (1961), 9 (1962); *Flag Pole:* 125 in play (5 feet in front of fence in center field, just left of dead center)

PHENOMENA

• First named for Frank Navin, a Tiger president.

• Right field second deck overhangs the lower deck by 10 feet. Screen in right in 1944 and in 1961 required balls to be hit into the second deck to be home runs.

• Only doubledecked bleachers in the majors—upper deck from left-center to center, lower deck from center to right-center.

• 125-foot-high flag pole in play in deep center, just to the left of the 440 mark—highest outfield obstacle ever in play in baseball history. The scoreboard now on the left field fence was orignally placed at the 440 mark in dead center in 1961 but was moved when Norm Cash, Al Kaline, and Charlie Maxwell complained that it hindered the batters' view of the pitch.

• There is a string of spotlights mounted under the overhang to illuminate the right field warning track which is shadowed from the normal light standards.

• Cobb's Lake—area in front of plate which was always soaked with water by the groundskeepers to slow down Ty Cobb's bunts.

• When slugging teams came to visit, manager Ty Cobb had the groundskeepers put in temporary bleachers in the outfield, so that long drives would be just ground-rule doubles.

• Sign above entrance to visitors' clubhouse: "Visitors' Clubhouse—No Visitors Allowed."

• Doubledecked in winter of 1923-24 from first to third base.

• Capacity increased in winter of 1935-36 by doubledecking the right field stands, and in the winter of 1937-38 by doubledecking both the left field stands and the center field bleachers.

• In the 1930s and 1940s, there was a 315 marker on the second deck in right field.

• In 1942 and 1943, the center field distance was only 420. The notches just left and right of dead center were closer than 420, at 405.

• Next-to-last classic old ballyard to put in lights, in 1948.

• Saved in 1974 when owner John Fetzer told the Pontiac Silverdome committee, "This franchise belongs to the inner city of Detroit; I'm just the caretaker." Now that mantle of caretaker has been forfeited by owner Tom Monaghan to the Tiger Stadium Fan Club and the Cochrane Plan, an architectural plan to preserve the ballpark.

• First homer at Navin Field, on May 5, 1912, came on a fluke bounce which hopped through the side door of the left-center scoreboard.

• Home plate and batters' boxes oriented towards right-center rather than straight out to the mound. This tends to give righthanded pitchers more outside corner strike calls and can disorient visiting batters.

HOUSTON, TEXAS

ASTRODOME

STYLE Dome

A.K.A. Harris County Domed Stadium 1965, Eighth Wonder of the World 1960s

OCCUPANT NL Astros April 12, 1965 to date

EVENT All Star Game 1968, 1986

LOCATION *Center Field (E)* Fannin Street; *3rd Base (N)* Old Spanish Trail; *Home Plate (W)* Kirby Drive; *1st Base (S)* South Loop Freeway/Interstate 610; *Above:* Domed roof of 4796 Lucite panels and steel girders

SURFACE *Infield:* Grass (1965) Tifway 419 Bermuda grass specially selected for indoor play—died; Astroturf, fast (April 1966 to date); *Outfield:* Grass (April 12, 1965 to July 19, 1966)—died too; Astroturf, fast (July 19, 1966 to date)

DIMENSIONS *Foul Lines:* 340 (1965), 330 (1972), 340 (1977), 330 (1985); *Power Alleys:* 375 (1965), 390 (1966), 378 (1972), 390 (1977), 378 (1985); *Center Field:* 406 (1965), 400 (1972), 406 (1977), 400 (1985); *Apex of Dome:* 208; *Backstop:* 60.5

FENCES *Left and Right Field:* 16 (9 concrete below 3 wire, 2 concrete, and 2 wire plus railing, 1965), 12 (concrete, 1969), 10 (concrete, 1977); *Center Field:* 12 (concrete, 1965), 10 (concrete, 1977)

PHENOMENA

• The second major league covered stadium, the first being the field under the Queensboro 59th Street Bridge in New York City used by the New York Cubans.

• Maximum height of the dome is 208 feet, just beyond second base.

• The roof had 4,796 clear panes of glass originally, but they caused a glare which prevented fielders from seeing the ball, thus two of the eight roof sections were painted white. This killed the grass and unfortunately introduced the world to Astroturf.

• Excepting Yankee Stadium's Death Valley, the most distant power alleys in the majors at 390 feet, until changed in 1985.

• Too much yellow, orange, and red.

• Hard to see through the screen from behind the plate.

• In its inaugural season of 1965, the Astrodome was the scene of a unique groundskeeping argument. The New York Mets claimed that the groundskeepers were roof-keeping as well by manipulating the air conditioning system so that the air currents helped Astro long balls and hindered visitors' long balls.

• The first game on a carpet was versus the Dodgers on April 8, 1966.

• Shoeshine stands behind home plate in lower deck.

• On April 28, 1965, Met announcer Lindsey Nelson broadcast a game from a gondola suspended from the apex of the dome.

• On June 10, 1974, Phillie Mike Schmidt hit the public address speaker 117 feet up and 329 feet from home—what would have been a 500-plus-foot homer ended up as a single as the ball dropped in center field.

• On June 15, 1976, a game was rained out because of flooding in the streets.

• The old location of Colt Stadium (now rebuilt in Toncon, Mexico) is just northwest of the Astrodome; Astrohall and Astroarena are just south of the Astrodome.

KANSAS CITY, MISSOURI

ROYALS STADIUM

STYLE Traditional Baseball Only
A.K.A. Harry S. Truman Sports Complex
OCCUPANT AL Royals April 10, 1973 to date
EVENT All Star Game 1973
LOCATION *Center Field (N)* Spectacular Drive, then Interstate 70; *3rd Base (W)* Lancer Lane, then Dutton Brookfield Drive; *Home Plate (S)* Royal Way, then Chiefs Way, Arrowhead Stadium, Raytown Road, and CRI&P Railroad tracks; *1st Base (E)* Red Coat Drive, then Blue Ridge Cut-Off; Stadium Drive encircles the park
SURFACE Astroturf—very fast
DIMENSIONS *Foul Lines:* 330; *Power Alleys:* 385; *Center Field:* 410; *Backstop:* 60; *Foul Territory:* Small
FENCES 12 (canvas)
PHENOMENA

• Waterfalls and fountains run for 322 feet on the embankment overlooking right-center.

• Best visibility for hitters in the majors.

• Homers few here because alleys are deep and the fence cuts away sharply from the 330 foul poles.

• Kenny Pippin, in his frogman suit, cleans the pond periodically in right-center.

• Royals 1985 World Series cup and other trophies are on display through the sixth inning of each game at Section 107.

• Upper deck fans near foul poles are in relative darkness.

• Best groundskeeper in baseball has the ironic job of maintaining an ugly plastic carpet. He keeps busy maintaining the Runway and the Boja, the grassy running area and the 125-tree forest beyond the left-center fence.

LOS ANGELES, CALIFORNIA

DODGER STADIUM

STYLE Traditional Baseball Only
A.K.A. Chavez Ravine during AL use 1962 to 1965 by Angels, Taj O'Malley, O'Malley's Golden Gulch
OCCUPANT NL Dodgers April 10, 1962 to date; AL Angels April 17, 1962 to September 22, 1965
EVENT All Star Game 1980
LOCATION *Left Field (NW)* Glendale Boulevard; *3rd Base (SW)* Sunset Boulevard; *Home Plate (S)* 1000 Elysian Park Avenue; *1st Base (SE)* Pasadena Freeway; *Right Field (NE)* Los Angeles Police Academy, Elysian Park, and Golden State Freeway/Interstate; Stadium Way encircles the park; in Chavez Ravine, on a hill overlooking downtown Los Angeles
SURFACE Santa Ana Bermuda grass
DIMENSIONS *Foul Lines:* 330; *Power Alleys:* 380 (1962), 370 (1969), 385 (1983); *Center Field:* 410 (1962), 400 (1969); *Back Stop:* 65 (1962), 68.19 (1963), 75 (1969); *Foul Territory:* Large
FENCES *Left-Center to Right-Center:* 10 (wood 1962), 8 (1973); *Foul Poles to Bullpens in Left and Right Field Corners:* 3.75 (steel 1962), 3.83 (1969); *The Dip:* (where low corner steel wall and screen bullpen fence meet) 3.42 (1962), 3.5 (1969)
FORMER USE Used by squatters and goats.
PHENOMENA

• A classic pitcher's park.

• Cleanest ballpark, bar none.

• Designed by architect Emil Praeger to be expandable to 85,000 seats.

• Along with the modernized Yankee Stadium, Dodger Stadium is a modern stadium that has retained the classical character of the old ballparks and avoided the "concrete ashtray" appearance of most modern-era stadia.

• Infield dirt and outfield warning track made of 70 percent crushed red building brick and 30 percent mountain clay and calcium chlorate. Palm trees beyond the fence down the foul lines.

• See-through windows in bullpen fence installed in 1974.

• Although the center field 400 sign came down in 1980, the distance is still 400 to center; the two 395 signs are left and right of dead center.

• No drinking-water fountains when first built. Original design had a huge fountain in center field, like that in right-center at Royals Stadium.

• When foul poles were installed in 1962, discovered that they were positioned completely foul. Special dispensation was received from National League so they were recognized as fair, but the next year plate was moved so that poles are now actually fair.

MILWAUKEE, WISCONSIN

COUNTY STADIUM

STYLE 1950s transitional
OCCUPANT NL Braves April 14, 1953 to September 22, 1965; AL White Sox for nine 1968 games and and eleven in 1969; games from May 15, 1968 to September 26, 1969; AL Brewers April 7, 1970 to date
EVENT All Star Game 1955, 1975
LOCATION *Left Field (E)* Menominee River and South 44th Street, later US-41 Stadium Freeway; *3rd Base (N)* Story Parkway and Interstate 94; *1st Base (W)* General Mitchell Boulevard; *Right Field (S)* West National Avenue and the National Soldiers Home

SURFACE　Bluegrass
DIMENSIONS　*Left Field:* 320 (1953), 315 (1975); *Power Alleys:* 355 (1953), 362 (1962); *Deep Alleys:* 397 (1953), 392 (1955); *Center Field:* 404 (1953), 410 (1954), 402 (1955); *Right Field:* 320 (1953), 315.37 (1954); *Backstop:* 60
FENCES　*Left Field:* 4 (1953), 8 (1955), 8.33 (1959), 10 (1985); *Center Field:* 4 (1953), 8 (1955), 8.33 (1959), 10 (1985); *Right Field:* 4 (1953), 10 (1955)
FORMER USE　Story Quarry
PHENOMENA
• Surveyor's mark on right field foul pole: "315.37."
• Before the park was expanded from 1953 to 1973, hospital patients at the National Soldiers Home V.A. Hospital sat outside their rooms on Mockingbird Hill overlooking right field and watched the game for free.
• Perini's Woods, spruce and fir trees behind center field fence, planted in 1954, replaced by bleachers in 1961.
• Braves Reservation, a picnic area down the left field line, was inaugurated in 1961.
• Bernie Brewer slides into a huge beer stein in right-center whenever a Brewer hits a homer.
• Only homer ever hit over left field roof was hit by Jose Canseco.
• Scene of Midwest League minor league game on August 27, 1966 between Fox Cities and Wisconsin Rapids.
• Braves hosted both the Reds and the Cards on September 24, 1954. The first game was the finish of a game two days earlier whose conclusion on a disputed double play was successfully protested by the Reds. The Reds tied the game after the protested game's resumption, but the Braves won 4-3 in the bottom of the ninth, and then beat the Cards 4-2.

MINNEAPOLIS, MINNESOTA

HUBERT H. HUMPHREY METRODOME
STYLE　Dome
A.K.A.　Minnedome, Bounce Dome, Hump Dome, Homer Dome, Hubie Dome, Sweat Box (before June 28, 1983, when air conditioning arrived), Domed Stadium, Thunderdome
OCCUPANT　AL Twins April 6, 1982 to date
EVENT　All Star Game 1985
LOCATION　*Left Field (SW)* Fourth Street South; *3rd Base (NW)* 501 Chicago Avenue South; *1st Base (NE)* Sixth Street South; *Right Field (SE)* Tenth Avenue South; *Above:* Domed roof
SURFACE　SporTurf (1982 to 1986—liveliest bounce ever), Astroturf (1987 to date)
DIMENSIONS　*Apex of Dome:* 186; *Left Field:* 344 (1982), 343 (1983); *Left-Center:* 385; *Center Field:* 407 (1982), 408 (1983); *Right Center:* 367; *Right Field:* 327; *Backstop:* 60; *Foul Territory:* Small
FENCES　*Left Field:* 7 (canvas 1982), 13 (6 plexiglass above 7 canvas 1983); *Center Field:* 7 (canvas 1982); *Right Field:* 7 (canvas 1982), 13 (canvas 1983), 23 (canvas 1985)
PHENOMENA
• A power hitter's park.
• Right field wall called Hefty Bag.
• Almost an exact duplicate of the domed stadiums in

Seattle, Pontiac, and Vancouver. All four were built by the same engineering firm.
• Game on April 27, 1986 delayed as violent rainstorm knocked out the lights and had the scoreboard and roof swaying.
• The white air-supported fabric Teflon roof makes it difficult to see the ball when hit high in the air.
• Playoffs and World Series of 1987 set new decibel records for sound in the Thunderdome.
• Sections 107 to 113 are football seats which in baseball season are tilted up and back to create a 40-foot wall behind the right field fence.
• The roof collapsed in the fall of 1982 but was repaired quickly.
• Twin batter Randy Bush hit a ball off the roof in 1983. The ball was caught foul for an out by Blue Jays catcher Buck Martinez.
• On May 4, 1984, in the top of the fourth inning, A's batter Dave Kingman hit a ball through the roof. It should have been a homer, but Kingman got only a double.
• Balls bounced very high off the carpet used from 1982 to 1986.
• More home runs tend to be hit when the air conditioning is turned off.
• Curvature of wall behind plate causes wild pitches and passed balls to bounce directly toward first base.

MONTREAL, QUEBEC

STADE OLYMPIQUE
STYLE　Summer Olympics Stadium/Dome
A.K.A.　Olympic Stadium, Big O, Big Owe
OCCUPANT　NL Expos April 15, 1977 to date
EVENT　All Star Game 1982
LOCATION　*Left Field (NW)* rue Sherbrooke; *3rd Base (SW)* boulevard Pie-IX; *1st Base (SE)* 4549, avenue Pierre-de-Coubertin; *Right Field (NE)* boulevard Viau
SURFACE　Astroturf
DIMENSIONS　*Foul Lines:* 325 (1977), 330 (1981), 325 (1983); *Power Alleys:* 375; *Center Field:* 404 (1977), 405 (1979), 404 (1980), 400 (1981), 404 (1983); *Apex of Dome:* 171; *Backstop:* 62 (1977), 65 (1983), 53 (1989); *Foul Territory:* Large
FENCES　12 (wood 1977), 12 (foam 1989)
PHENOMENA
• Labatt's Noise-Meter high above right field is baseball's answer to the NBA Sacramento Kings' Arco Arena Noise-Meter.
• Roof improves offense by keeping out extreme cold.
• Built for 1976 Olympics.
• Plaque inside and statue of Jackie Robinson at main entrance. Robinson starred at the Delorimier Downs for the IL Montreal Royals in 1946. Huge 623-foot-high umbrella tower in center field from section 766 in left-center to section 767 in right-center stood half finished from 1976 to 1987. Became a covered-dome stadium in 1989. The retractable dome is silver on top, and orange on the bottom, with 26 white cones which link the roof to the tower. It consists of 60,696 square feet of Kevlar, weighing 50 tons. Retractable roof not actually retractable until 1988 due to generator problems.

NEW YORK, NEW YORK

YANKEE STADIUM

STYLE Major League Classic
A.K.A. House That Ruth Built
OCCUPANT AL Yankees April 18, 1923 to September 30, 1973; NEWL Black Yankees 1932; NNL Black Yankees 1946 to 1948; Negro League World Series 3rd game, 1942; 1st game 1947; AL Yankees April 15, 1976 to date
EVENT All Star Game 1939, 1960, 1977
LOCATION *Left Field (NE)* East 161st Street; *3rd Base (NW)* Doughty Street, later Ruppert Place; *Home Plate (W)* Major Degan Expressway/Interstate 87 and Harlem River; *1st Base (SW)* East 157th Street; *Right Field (SE)* River Avenue and IRT elevated tracks; In the southwest Bronx
SURFACE Grass—Merion Bluegrass
DIMENSIONS *Left Field:* 280.58 (1923), 301 (1928), 312 (1976), 318 (1988); *Left Side of Bullpen Gate in Short Left-Center:* 395 (1923), 402 (1928), 387 (1976), 379 (1985); *Right Side of Bullpen Gate:* 415 (1937); *Deepest Left-Center:* 500 (1923), 490 (1924), 457 (1937), 430 (1976), 411 (1985), 399 (1988); *Left Side of Center Field Screen:* 466 (1937); *Center Field:* 487 (1923), 461 (1937), 463 (1967), 417 (1976), 410 (1985), 408 (1988); *Deepest Right Center:* 429 (1923), 407 (1937), 385 (1976); *Left Side of Bullpen Gate in Short Right Center:* 350 (1923), 367 (1937), 353 (1976); *Right Side of Bullpen Gate:* 344 (1937); *Right Field:* 294.75 (1923), 295 (1930), 296 (1939), 310 (1976), 314 (1988); *Backstop:* 82 (1942), 80 (1953), 84 (1976); *Foul Territory:* Large for the catcher behind home plate, but small for fielders down the foul lines
FENCES *Left Field–Foul Line:* 3.92 (3 wire above .92 concrete 1923), 8 (canvas 1976); *Left Center–Left of Visitors' Bullpen:* 3.58 (3 wire above .58 concrete); *Right of Visitors' Bullpen:* 7.83 (3 wire above 4.83 concrete), 7 (canvas 1976); *Center Field-Left Screen When Up for Hitters' Background:* 20 (1953), 22.25 (1959), 22.42 (1954); *Screen When Down:* 13.83,7 (canvas 1976); *Right Center-Right of Screen:* 14.5 (3 wire above 11.5 concrete 1923); *Left of Home Bullpen:* 7.83 (3 wire above 4.83 concrete 1923); *Right of Home Bullpen:* 3.58 (3 wire above .58 concrete 1923), 8 (canvas 1976), 9 (canvas 1979); *Right Field-Foul Line:* 3.75 (3 wire above .75 concrete 1923), 10 (canvas 1976)
PHENOMENA
• Left-center field monuments and plaques: Yankee Stadium (I) Monuments in fair territory, Lou Gehrig on the left, Miller Huggins in the middle, Babe Ruth on the right; Yankee Stadium (II) Monuments beyond the fence; same as Yankee Stadium I. Plaques beyond the fence, Ed Barnow, Jacob Ruppert, Joe DiMaggio, Mickey Mantle, Casey Stengel, Joe McCarthy, Pope Paul VI, Thurman Munson, Pope John Paul II, Billy Martin.
• A ball hitting the foul pole in the 1930s was in play, not a homer.
• "Death Valley" in left-center.
• Green curtain in center sometimes raised and lowered like a window shade to force visiting batters to face a background of white-shirted bleacher fans but allow Yankee hitters to face a dark green background. Removed in World Series to sell more seats.
• Bleachers in right-center often called Ruthville and Gehrigville.
• Warning track red cinders; later on, red brick dust.
• Extra grass kept near monuments in center, in play.
• Underneath second base in Yankee Stadium (I), there was a 15-foot-deep brick-lined vault with electrical, telephone, and telegraphic connections for boxing events.
• As originally constructed, from May 5, 1922, to April 18, 1923, three concrete decks extended from behind home plate to each corner, with a single deck in left-center, and wooden bleachers around the rest of the outfield.
• In the winter of 1927-28, second and third decks were added to left-center, and several rows of box seats were removed in left, extending the foul pole from 281 to 301.
• During the 1936 season, the winter of 1936-37, and continuing through the 1937 season, the wooden bleachers were replaced with concrete ones. During the 1937 season, second and third decks were added in right-center. The bleacher changes shortened straightaway center from 490 to 461 and reduced seating capacity from the 80,000s to the 70,000s.
• As the outfield bench seats were gradually replaced with chair seats, in the 1930s and 1940s, the seating capacity gradually dropped from over 70,000 to about 67,000.
• Bloody Angle—between bleachers and RF foul line in 1923 season was very asymmetric and caused crazy bounces. Eliminating this in 1924 caused the plate to be moved 13 feet, and the deepest left center corner to change from 500 to 490.
• Auxiliary scoreboards were built in the late 1940s, which covered up the 367 right-center sign and the 415 left-center sign.
• Minor modifications were made in the winter of 1966-67. During this work, a new 463 sign and a 433 sign appeared in the power alleys, and the exterior was painted blue and white.
• During 1974-75 renovation, iron third deck distinctive facade was removed, and a portion was placed in the bleachers.

SHEA STADIUM

STYLE Superstructure with natural surface
A.K.A. Flushing Meadow Park, William A. Shea Municipal Stadium
OCCUPANT NL Mets April 17, 1964 to date; AL Yankees, April 6, 1974 to September 28, 1975
EVENT All Star Game 1964
LOCATION *Centerfield (E)* 126th Street; *3rd Base (N)* Whitestone Expressway/Interstate 678, and Flushing Bay; *Home Plate (W)* Grand Central Parkway; *1st Base (S)* Roosevelt Avenue; In Queens, near Flushing Meadow Park, site of 1939 and 1964 World's Fairs, just southeast of La Guardia Airport
SURFACE Bluegrass
DIMENSIONS *Foul Line:* 330 (marked 1964), 341 (actual 1964), 341 (1965), 338 (1979); *Power Alleys:* 371; *Center Field:* 410; *Backstop:* 80 (1964); *Foul Territory:* Very large
FENCES *Foul Lines:* 16.33 (4 wire and railing above 12.33 brick 1964), 12.33 (brick 1965), 8 (wood 1979);

Power Alleys: 8 (wood); *Center Field:* Small section 8.75 (wood), most 8 (wood)

PHENOMENA

• Designed to be expandable to 90,000 seats.

• Noisiest outdoor ballpark; frequent La Guardia Airport air traffic noise overhead.

• Named for attorney William Shea, who obtained the Mets franchise for New York by organizing the Continental League.

• Right-center scoreboard is largest in majors, 86 feet high with Bulova clock on top, about 25 feet behind the outfield fence, and 175 feet long.

• Practice facilities under the right field stands.

• Behind fence in center, just to the right of the 410 mark, is a Mets Magic Top Hat. When a Met hits a homer, a red Big Apple rises out of the black top hat, which actually looks more like a big kettle.

• Foul lines from 1965 to 1978 had an orange home run line painted at the top of the 12-foot, 4-inch brick wall. Above this was a 4-foot wire screen and railing. A ball was a homer if it hit above the line. Like a similar ground rule at Crosley Field in center field, this caused many controversies, so in 1979 an inner 8-foot wooden fence was installed.

• Worst visibility for hitters in the majors.

• Churchlike spire beyond center field fence with "Serval Zippers" sign.

• Outfield fences also marked as 358 and 396. From 1973 to 1979, there were also distance markers, outside the field of play, on the rear bullpen walls at 428, base of left-center light tower at 442, bottom edge of right-center scoreboard at 405 on right field end and 420 on center field end.

• 1964 Mets Banner Day—"Mongolia Loves The Mets" (in Mongolian) banner carried by the author; other banners included "E=mc2" (or Errors = Mets times customers squared),"Eamus Metropoli" (Let's go Mets in Latin).

• Christened April 16, 1964 with Dodger Holy Water from the Gowanus Canal in Brooklyn and Giant Holy Water from the Harlem River at the exact location where it passed the old Polo Grounds.

OAKLAND, CALIFORNIA

OAKLAND-ALAMEDA COUNTY COLISEUM

STYLE   Superstructure with natural surface

A.K.A.   Oakland Coliseum Complex, Oakland Mausoleum

OCCUPANT   AL Athletics April 17, 1968 to date

EVENT   All Star Game 1987

LOCATION   *Center Field (NE)* San Leandro Street and Southern Pacific Railroad tracks; *3rd Base (NW)* 66th Avenue; *Home Plate (SW)* Oakland-Alameda County Coliseum Arena, Nimitz Freeway, and San Leandro Bay; *1st Base (SE)* Hegenberger Drive

SURFACE   Bluegrass

DIMENSIONS   *Foul Lines:* 330; *Power Alleys:* 378 (1968), 375 (1969), 372 (1981); *Center Field:* 410 (1968), 400 (1969), 396 (1981), 397 (1982), 400 (1990); *Backstop:* 90 (1968), 60 (1969); *Foul Territory:* Huge, largest in the majors

FENCES   8 (plywood 1968), 10 (canvas over plywood

and plexiglass 1981), 8 (1986)

PHENOMENA

• Surrounded by beautiful green ivy slope.

• Backstop is a notch cut in stands.

• Possible to watch game for free from concourse behind the field seats by peering between wooden slats on cyclone fence.

• Steel shell of pitcher's mound was exposed on Opening Day April 17, 1968 and had to keep being covered between innings.

• Right field scoreboard installed June 1968.

• Finley Fun Board put in for 1969 season—24 feet high and 126 feet long.

• Named the Mausoleum in the 1970s when the scoreboard didn't work, the entire stadium was gray concrete in color, and the A's were terrible.

• Huge foul territory area reduces batting average by roughly 5 to 7 points, making this the best pitcher's park in the AL.

• Fun picnic atmosphere is the very best in the majors of all new concrete circular ugly ashtray stadia.

• Best food in baseball.

• Winds favor lefthanded batters.

• Next door to Jewel Box, home of the NBA Golden State Warriors.

• Scoreboard shows upcoming home stands, with A's annihilating the opposition.

• Fans sitting at the foul poles can catch home run fair balls by reaching in front of the foul pole screens.

• Hand-operated scoreboard showing major league line scores installed in 1986.

PHILADELPHIA, PENNSYLVANIA

VETERANS STADIUM

STYLE   Superstructure with artificial surface

A.K.A.   Vet

OCCUPANT   April 10, 1971 to date

EVENT   All Star Game 1976

LOCATION   *Left Field (NE)* Packer Street and Interstate 76; *3rd Base (NW)* Broad Street and Philadelphia Naval Hospital; *1st Base (SW)* Pattison Avenue, Spectrum, and JFK Stadium; *Right Field (SE)* Tenth Street

SURFACE   Astroturf—fast, but slower since 1977

DIMENSIONS   *Foul Lines:* 330; *Power Alleys:* 371; *Center Field:* 408; *Backstop:* 60; *Foul Territory:* Large

FENCES   6 (wood April 1972); 8 (wood June 1971); 12 (6 plexiglass above 6 wood 1972)

PHENOMENA

• The park's rounded rectangular shape is called an octorad by the architects.

• Connie Mack Stadium's home plate was transplanted here.

• Plastic tarp covered unfinished right field wall in April 1971.

• "Liberty Bell" used to hang from center field roof in fourth level—hit only by Greg Luzinski on May 16, 1972.

• First ball dropped from a helicopter on April 10, 1971.

• Smallest hot dogs and loudest boos in baseball.

• Statues of Connie Mack and a sliding runner outside the park.

PITTSBURGH, PENNSYLVANIA

THREE RIVERS STADIUM
STYLE Superstructure with artificial surface
A.K.A. House That Clemente Built
OCCUPANT NL Pirates July 16, 1970 to date
EVENT All Star Game 1974
LOCATION *Left Field (E)* Interstate 279 Fort Duquesne Bridge approach ramp; *3rd Base (N)* Reedsdale Street; *1st Base (W)* Allegheny Avenue, Ohio River, and the original point where the Monongahela River joins the Allegheny River to form the Ohio River; *Right Field (S)* North Shore Avenue, Roberto Clemente Memorial Park, Allegheny River; Stadium Circle encircles the park
SURFACE Carpet—Tartanturf 1970 to 1982; Astroturf 1983 to date
DIMENSIONS *Foul Lines:* 340 (1970), 335 (1975); *Power Alleys:* 385 (1970), 375 (1975); *Center Field:* 410 (1970), 400 (1975); *Backstop:* 60; *Foul Territory:* Large
FENCES 10 (wood)
PHENOMENA
• On a site that was an island during the French and Indian Wars. It had been an Indian burial ground, a fact discovered when the Big Flood of 1763 uncovered many graves. Named Kilbuck Island after a friendly Delaware Indian chief. Back channels filled with silt, and it was no longer an island in 1852.
• Numbers painted on seats in right field upper deck where Willie Stargell's homers landed.
• Without the inner fence, the outfield would be 342 down the lines and 434 to center.
• The Honus Wagner statue, which used to stand outside of Forbes Field, now stands outside of Three Rivers Stadium.
• An 8- by 12-foot area of the 406 marker section of the Forbes Field brick wall, 12 Romanesque window frames, and the Babe Ruth plaque showing where his 714th home run landed are in the Allegheny Club at Three Rivers.
• Original design by Erik Sirko was for a "Stadium Over the Monongahela," with stadium above two parking lot levels, all sitting above the Monongahela River with plenty of room for boats to pass beneath on the river.

ST. LOUIS, MISSOURI

BUSCH STADIUM (II)
STYLE Superstructure with artificial surface
A.K.A. Civic Center Stadium 1966, Busch Memorial Stadium 1966 to 1983
OCCUPANT NL Cardinals May 12, 1966 to date
EVENT All Star Game 1966
LOCATION *Left Field (E)* Broadway, Interstate 70, Gateway Arch and Mississippi River; *3rd Base (N)* Walnut Street; *1st Base (W)* Seventh Street and 300 Stadium Plaza; *Right Field (S)* Spruce Street; Stadium Plaza surrounds the park
SURFACE Grass 1966 to 1969. Carpet—very fast—1970 to date. From 1970 to 1976, the entire field was carpeted except for the part of the infield that is normally dirt on a grass field. In 1977, this was carpeted except for the sliding pits. This is one of only two instances where there was a full dirt infield, with an otherwise fully

carpeted field, the other being Candlestick in 1971.
DIMENSIONS *Foul Lines:* 330; *Power Alleys:* 386 (1966), 376 (1973), 386 (1977), 383 (July 1983); *Center Field:* 414 (1966), 410 (1971), 414 (1972), 404 (1973), 414 (1977); *Backstop:* 64 (Vin Scully's unofficial measurement during 1985 World Series showed this to be 50 rather than 64); *Foul Territory:* Large
FENCES *Left and Right Fields:* 10.5 (padded concrete); *Center Field:* 10.5 (padded concrete 1966), 8 (wood 1973), 10.5 (padded concrete 1977)
PHENOMENA
• A line drive park because of the deep alleys and deep center field and the quick turf.
• Open arches surround the field just below the roof.
• From 1966 to 1982 right field scoreboard lights showed a cardinal in flight when a Cardinal hit a home run; same show was put on each time Lou Brock set a new base-stealing record.
• Home plate transplanted from old Busch Stadium at opener on May 12, 1966.
• Next to the Gateway Arch and the Mississippi River; you can see the Arch from the top deck in right field.
• Statue of "Stan the Man" Musial outside the stadium was unveiled in 1968.
• Small sections of bleachers in the outfield.
• Chicken wire basket (à la Wrigley Field in Chicago), installed in front of left-center and right-center bleacher sections in July 1983, is 2 feet high and reduces distance to fence by 3 feet (386 to 383 in power alleys). It does not raise the height of the 10½ foot wall. No basket in center field bleacher section since it is used only for football.
• At league direction, the site designated for any Cubs playoffs or World Series home games from 1986 until 1988, when Wrigley Field got lights.
• Most fans at the stadium seem to be wearing Cardinal red.
• Seventh inning brings the Clydesdale horses to the scoreboard.
• Only ballpark where the seventh-inning stretch does not bring on "Take Me Out to the Ballgame." Instead, here they play the "King of Beers" theme song on the organ.

SAN DIEGO, CALIFORNIA

SAN DIEGO JACK MURPHY STADIUM
STYLE Superstructure with natural surface
A.K.A. San Diego Stadium 1969 to 1980, Jack Murphy Stadium thereafter
OCCUPANT NL Padres April 8, 1969 to date
EVENT All Star Game 1978
LOCATION *Left Field (N)* 9449 Friars Road; *3rd Base (W)* Stadium Way and a quarry; *1st Base (S)* San Diego River, Camino del Rio North, and Interstate 8; *Right Field (E)* Interstate 15
SURFACE Santa Ana Bermuda grass
DIMENSIONS *Foul Lines:* 330 (1969), fence 327 (1982), foul poles 329 (1982); *Power Alleys:* 375 (1969), 370 (1982); *Center Field:* 420 (1969), 410 (1973), 420 (1978), 405 (1982); *Backstop:* 80 (1969), 75 (1982)
FENCES *Left and Right Fields:* 17.5 (concrete 1969), 9 (line painted on concrete 1973), 18 (concrete 1974), 8.5 (canvas 1982); *Center Field:* 17.5 (concrete 1969), 10

(wood 1973), 18 (concrete 1978), 8.5 (canvas 1982), one section in right center 9 (canvas 1982)

FORMER USE San Diego River ran through the area, which was then a marshy swampland.

PHENOMENA

• Named for sports editor who campaigned to bring major league baseball to San Diego.

• Noticeable lack of Spanish-speaking fans and Spanish language advertisements in the only major league ballpark on the Mexican border.

• The stadium is circular but open in right.

• Foul poles sit two feet behind the fence, and one foot in front of the wall.

• The right-center scoreboard sits directly behind the right center seats, and is so hot that fans there feel the heat on their backs.

• Only park where bullpen dirt area touches the foul lines.

• Only park where a foul ball can be caught out of sight of all umpires and most players. Location is in either bullpen near the foul poles.

• After 1981 season, the plate was moved 5 feet back toward the backstop.

• Expanded during 1983 football season by adding seats in right and right-center.

• Ivy put on center field fence in 1980.

• 20-foot-wide black batter's eye section on both center field wall and fence July-October 1982.

SAN FRANCISCO, CALIFORNIA

CANDLESTICK PARK

STYLE Superstructure with natural surface

A.K.A. NL Giants April 12, 1960 to date

EVENT All Star Game 1961, 1984

LOCATION *Left Field (NW)* Giants Drive; *3rd Base (SW)* Jamestown Avenue and Bay View Hill; *1st Base (SE)* Jamestown Avenue, Candlestick Point and San Francisco; *Right Field (NE)* Hunters Point Expressway and San Francisco Bay; Candlestick Point, with its rock outcroppings, was leveled to fill in the water for the parking lots.

SURFACE Grass (1960), Carpet (1971), Bluegrass (1979)

DIMENSIONS *Left Field:* 330 (1960), 335 (1968); *Left-Center:* 397 (1960), 365 (1961); *Center Field:* 420 (1960), 410 (1961), 400 (1982); *Right-Center:* 397 (1960), 330 (1970), 335 (1981); *Backstop:* 73 (1960), 70 (1961), 55 (1975), 65 (1982), 66 (1985); *Foul Territory:* Very large

FENCES 10 (wire 1960); 8 (wire 1972); 12 (6 canvas below 6 plexiglass 1975); 9 (6 canvas below 3 plexiglass 1982); 9 (wire 1984), 9.5 (fence posts 1984)

PHENOMENA

• Named for jagged rocks and trees which rise from the tidelands like giant candlesticks.

• Bay View Hill overlooks the park from behind 3rd base.

• Many fans arrived by boat in 1960s.

• Only hot-water-heated open-air stadium in the majors.

• Before the bleachers were enclosed, so many fans would stream out of the bleachers in right-center when Mays and McCovey batted and crowd up against the flimsy

cyclone fence, that a white line was painted on the asphalt 20 feet behind the fence. Fans had to stand behind this line.

• Fifty-nine posts every 20 feet or so on the outfield fence can cause strange bounces—their tips extend 6 inches above the 9 foot wire fence.

• Wind, wind, and more wind! Before the stadium was enclosed, wind blew in from left-center and out toward right-center. Now that it is enclosed, the wind is a swirling monster, just as strong as before.

• Six Giants retired numbers on white baseballs on the right field fence.

• Maury's Lake—the basepath between first and second was drenched before the game to make it more difficult for Dodger Maury Wills to steal second.

• Umps protested location of foul poles completely in fair territory in third inning of opening game on April 12, 1960.

• Stu Miller was blown off the mound by the wind in the 1961 All-Star Game.

• The stadium was enlarged and fully enclosed in the winter of 1971-72 to house the 49ers.

• Architect John Bolles' boomerang-shaped concrete shell baffle behind the upper tier's last row of seats was intended to protect the park from wind; it didn't work.

• In the winter of 1978-79, the Giants ripped up their carpet and replaced it with grass.

• Coldest park in the majors, resulting in less home runs.

• Croix de Candlestick pin awarded to fans in 1982 and 1984 at conclusion of night extra-inning games.

SEATTLE, WASHINGTON

KINGDOME

STYLE Dome

A.K.A. King County Stadium, Tomb (1980s), Puget Puke (1980s)

OCCUPANT AL Mariners April 6, 1977 to date

EVENT All Star Game 1979

LOCATION *Left Field (N)* 201 South King Street; *3rd Base (W)* 589 Occidental Avenue South; *1st Base (S)* South Royal Brougham Way; *Right Field (E)* Fourth Avenue South and Burlington Northern Railroad tracks; *Above:* Domed roof

DIMENSIONS *Left Field:* 315 (1977), 316 (marked 1978), 314 (actual 1978), 324 (1990); *Left Center:* 375 (1977), 365 (1978), 357 (1981), 362 (1990); *Deep Left-Center:* 385 (1990); *Center Field:* 405 (1977), 410 (1978), 405 (1981), 410 (1986); *Deep Right Center:* 375 (1990); *Right Center:* 375 (1977), 365 (1978), 357 (1981), 352 (1990); *Right Field:* 315 (1977), 316 (1978), 314 (1990); *Speakers in Left (3), Left Center, and Center:* 110 (1977), 133.5 (1981); 11 other speakers 130; *Backstop:* 63; *Apex of Dome:* 250; *Foul Territory:* Large

FENCES *Left Field:* 11.5 (wood 1977), 17.5 (6 plexiglass over wood); *Center Field:* 11.5 (wood 1977); *Right Field:* 11.5 (wood 1977), 23.25 (wood 1982), 11.5 (wood 1988)

PHENOMENA

• Large American flag flies above the concrete dome.

• 23-foot Mini-Green Monster in right and right-center is called the Walla Walla.

- Carpet is rolled out by the Rhinoceros machine, and smoothed by the Grasshopper machine after it has been zipped together.
- Baby-changing areas in aisles 111, 113, 201, 203.
- Domed roof looks from below like it's made of thousands of bricks.
- Sick's Stadium home plate on display in Royal Brougham trophy case.
- In the winter of 1980-81, the three speakers above left, left-center, and center were raised from 102 to 133.5 feet to reduce the chance of their being hit again.
- Two foul balls have gone up but never come down: August 4, 1979—Ruppert Jones of Mariners hit a foul ball that stuck in the speaker above the first base dugout, thus disproving the old adage of physics that what goes up must come down. On May 20, 1983, Brewer Ricky Nelson did the same. By some arcane logic, both fly balls were ruled strikes.
- Four foul balls have bounced off speakers and been caught for outs: August 3, 1979, caught by A's pitcher Matt Keough; September 3, 1979, caught by Mariners' first baseman; May 19, 1980, caught by Mariners' first baseman; April 25, 1985, caught by Mariners' pitcher Mark Langston.
- Other foul balls have bounced off the Seattle Supersonics basketball speakers above first base and the basketball scoreboard above and behind home plate, without being caught.
- One fair ball bounced off a roof support wire and remained in play on April 11, 1985—a ball hit by Dave Kingman of A's was caught for an out in deep left: it would have been a home run. One fair ball has struck the right field speaker—Ken Phelps of the Mariners hit a tape-measure homer on August 13, 1987—the ball landed foul.
- Seven fair balls have bounced off speakers and remained in play.
- Called the Tomb by visiting sportswriters because it's sickeningly gray concrete and quiet.
- Roof's hanging red, white, and blue streamers can tangle up an infield fly and deflect it from the pitcher's mound to behind second base.
- U.S.S. *Mariner*—a huge yellow sailing ship behind the center-field fence which fires a cannon after every Mariner homer.
- 42 air-conditioning units, 16 in fair territory, 26 in foul territory, 8 ducts in each unit. These blow air in toward the field which means less home runs in what would normally be a "Homer Dome" because of the short 357 foot power alleys.
- Outfield distances marked on fences in both feet and fathoms 1977-80 (1 fathom = 6 feet).
- Third deck highest at third base and in right field. AL East and AL West standings posted on right field third deck facade.
- Plate moved 10 feet toward first base dugout in 1990 in a change that altered outfield distances.
- New classic "in-play" 123-feet by 11½-foot scoreboard placed on right field wall in 1990 in dramatic facelift.
- Scene of Funny Nose-Eye Glasses night.

TORONTO, ONTARIO

SKYDOME

STYLE Dome
OCCUPANT AL Blue Jays June 5, 1989 to date
LOCATION *Center Field (N)* Front Street West; *3rd Base (W)* Spadina Avenue; *Home Plate (S)* Gardiner Expressway; *1st Base (E)* John Street and CN Tower, the world's largest free-standing structure
SURFACE Astroturf
DIMENSIONS *Foul Lines:* 328; *Power Alleys:* 375; *Center Field:* 400
FENCES 12
FORMER USE Water supply pumping station where second base is now
PHENOMENA
- Designed by Roderick Robbie, who prior to designing the park had never been to a baseball game. It shows.

Storied Parks of the Past

BROOKLYN, NEW YORK

EBBETS FIELD

STYLE Major League Classic
OCCUPANT NL Dodgers April 9, 1913 to September 24, 1957, NNL Eagles 1935
EVENT All Star Game 1942
LOCATION *Left Field (NE)* Montgomery Street; *3rd Base (NW)* Franklin Avenue, later Cedar Place, later McKeever Place; *1st Base (SW)* 55 Sullivan Place; *Right Field (SE)* Bedford Avenue; in the Pigtown/Crown Heights district of Flatbush, near the Gowanus Canal.
DIMENSIONS *Left Field:* 419 (1913), 410 (1914), 418.75 (1921), 383.67 (1926), 382.83 (1930), 384 (1931), 353 (1932), 356.33 (1934), 365 (1938), 357 (1939), 365 (1940), 356 (1942), 357 (1947), 343 (1948), 348 (1953), 343 (1955), 348 (1957). There is some confusion about distances because the left field foul line and grandstand wall were the same near the corner between the 343 and 357 markers. *Left-Center:* 365 (1932), 351 (1948); *Deep Left-Center at Bend in Wall:* 407 (1932), 393 (1948), 395 (1954); *Center Field:* 450 (1914), 466 (1930), 460.79 (early 1931), 447 (late 1931), 399.42 (1932), 399 (1936), 402 (1938), 400 (1939), 399 (1947), 384 (1948), 393 (1955); *Right Side of Center Field Grandstand:* 390 (1932), 376 (1948); *Right-Center's Deepest Corner:* 500 (1913), 476.75 (1926), 415 (1932), 403 (1948), 405 (1950), 403 (1955); *Right Side of Right-Center Field Exit Gate:* 399 (1932); *Right-Center:* 352; *Scoreboard:* left side 344, right side 318; *Right Field:* 301 (1913), 300 (1914), 296.17 (1921), 292 (1922), 301 (1926), 296.08 (1930), 295.92 (1931), 296.5 (1934), 297 (1938); *Backstop:* 64 (1942), 70.5 (1954), 72 (1957)
FENCES *Left Field to Left-Center:* 20 (1913), 3 (wood 1920), 9.87 (concrete 1931); *Center Field:* 20 (1913), 393 marker: 9.87 (concrete 1931) sloping upward; 376 marker: 15 (concrete 1931); *Right-Center:* 9 (concrete 1913), from 376 point to screen: 15 sloping upward to 19, then down to 13; *Right-Center to Right Field:* 38 (top 19 screen, bottom 19 concave concrete wall, bent at 9.5 mid-

point, vertical top half, concave angled bottom half); *Screen in Center Field:* 20 (screen above sloping concrete 1920s); *Right Field Before the Screen:* 9 (concrete 1913)

FORMER USE   The Pigtown garbage dump

CURRENT USE   Scoreboard clock now sits on top of right field scoreboard at McCormick Field, Asheville, North Carolina. Ebbets Field Apartments housing development built in 1963 and the I.S. 320 Intermediate School is across the road. Apartments renamed Jackie Robinson Apartments at Ebbets Field in 1972; renamed Ebbets Field Apartments in mid-1970s. Jackie Robinson School, previously known as Crown Heights, houses the Brooklyn Dodger Hall of Fame.

PHENOMENA

• Rotunda was 80-foot circle enclosed in Italian marble with floor tiled with stitches of a baseball, a chandelier with 12 baseball-bat arms holding 12 globes shaped like baseballs. There were 12 turnstiles and 12 gilded ticket windows. The domed ceiling was 27 feet high at its center.

• Little kids watched the game through a gap under the metal gate in right-center.

• Cobblestoned Bedford Avenue was a hill, climbing from a low point in right field to higher ground in center field.

• Right field wall and scoreboard had approximately 289 different angles—the scoreboard jutted out 5 feet from the wall at a 45-degree angle. Overhang of the center field second deck hung out over the field. Scoreboard built after 1930.

• Schaefer Beer sign on the top of the right-center scoreboard notified fans of official scorer's decision—the "H" in Schaefer lit up for a hit, an "E" for an error—the sign was erected after World War II.

• Abe Stark sign offered a free suit at 1514 Pitkin Avenue to any batter hitting the 3-foot-by-30-foot sign.

• Opened on April 5, 1914 for an exhibition game vs. the Yankees; it was discovered that the flag, a press box, and the keys to the bleachers had been forgotten. A press box was finally added in 1929.

• In the winter of 1931-32, the double deck was extended from 3rd base to the left field corner and across to center field.

• According to Roger Kahn, the park was "a narrow cockpit of iron and concrete along a steep cobblestone slope."

• In the winter of 1937-38, box seats were added in center field.

• In the winter of 1947-48, more seats were added to left and center.

• Demolition began on February 23, 1960. Same wrecking ball used 4 years later to demolish Polo Grounds. Eight light towers were moved to Downing Stadium on Randall's Island.

• George Cutshaw of Dodgers hit groundball home run in 1916 which bounced crazily up the concave wall in right and over the fence, to the amazement of Phillies rightfielder Gavvy Cravath.

LOS ANGELES, CALIFORNIA

LOS ANGELES MEMORIAL COLISEUM

STYLE   Summer Olympics Stadium

A.K.A.   O'Malley's Chinese Theatre, O'Malley's Alley

OCCUPANT   NL Dodgers April 18, 1958 to September 20, 1961

EVENT   All Star Game 1959

LOCATION   *Left Field (N)* Exposition Boulevard and museums; *3rd Base (W)* Merlo Avenue and Los Angeles Olympic Swimming Stadium; *1st Base (S)* Santa Barbara Avenue, now Martin Luther King, Jr. Drive; *Right Field (E)* 3911 South Figueroa Street and Los Angeles Memorial Sports Arena

DIMENSIONS   *Left Field:* 250 (1958), 251.6 (1959); *Left-Center:* 320 at end of screen rectangle; *Left-Center Where Fence Met Wall:* 425 (1958), 417 (1959); *Center Field:* 425 (1958), 420 (1959); *Right-Center:* 440 (1958), 375 (1959), 394 (1960), 380 (1961); *Right Field Where Fence Met Wall:* 390 (1958), 333 (1959), 340 (1960); *Right Field:* 301 (1958), 300 (1959); *Back-stop:* 60 (1958), 66 (1959); *Foul Territory:* Large; tremendous area on 3rd base line, but almost none on 1st base line

FENCES   *Left Field:* 40 (screen 1958), 42 (screen 1959); 60 (2 support towers for screen 1958); *Left Center:* 40 (fence (1958); from foul pole 140 feet into left center, 42 sloping to ground at 30 degree angle from 320 mark to 348 mark for a distance of 24 feet (1959 to 1960); 4 steps down from 42 to 8: 1st step left corner 42 sloping to 41, 2nd step 31, 3rd step 20, 4th step 12 (1961); *Right of Screen in Left-Center:* 8 (wire); *Center Field to Right Field Corner:* 6 (wire); *Right Field Corner:* 4 (concrete)

FORMER USE   Agriculture Park in 1890s—fairs, livestock shows, amusement park booths, horse-racing track and barns, saloons. Exposition Park—armory, museum, gardens from 1908 to 1921 along with gravel pit

PHENOMENA

• Wall in left-center jutted out twice, going from chest to thigh level, jutting out to ankle level, jutting out to thigh level, then back again to chest level.

• Concrete wall in the right field corner was the wall surrounding the football field. It sloped sharply away, creating a Fenway-like belly, and allowing a situation where a long drive near the right field foul line would be an out but a short fly down the line would be a home run.

• Huge tunnel behind home plate.

• First used for baseball by USC Trojans, who worked out here before the Dodgers opened the 1958 season.

• O'Malley considered using the Rose Bowl in Pasadena for the first years after the move from Brooklyn and before the Dodgers' Stadium opened. It would have been laid out differently from the Coliseum. Ten rows would have been removed in right and left to deepen the foul lines to 300 feet, and center field would have been 460. The field would have been symmetrical, because home plate would have been in one endzone and center field in the other endzone. Box seats were to have been added behind the plate and between 1st and 3rd.

• The 42-foot screen in left placed to prevent 251 foot popups from becoming homers.

• Commissioner Ford Frick attempted to order the Dodgers to construct a second screen in left, in the seats at 333 feet. A ball clearing both screens would be a home run, but a ball clearing just the shorter screen would be a double. The California Earthquake Law made construction of such a screen illegal.

• 79 rows of seats.

- 700 feet to furthest seats under peristylum.
- Two stones are on exhibit under the peristylum atop the bleachers in right-center at one end of the oval—the one on the left from Altis, Olympia, Greece, and the one on the right from the Colosseum, Rome, Italy.
- Rim of stadium 110 feet above ground level, field 33 feet below ground level.
- Cable and towers and wires above screen in play.
- Small green light pole in field of play in right field.
- 74,000 seats built from 1921 to 1923, expanded to 105,000 seats for the 1932 Olympic games.
- The right-center fence was shortened in 1959 after 182 homers were hit to left but only 3 to center and 8 to right. In 1959, there were 132 homers to left, 1 to center, 39 to right. In 1960, 155 to left, 3 to center, 28 to right. In 1961, 147 to left, 7 to center, 38 to right.

NEW YORK, NEW YORK

POLO GROUNDS (IV)

STYLE Major League Classic

A.K.A. Brush Stadium 1911 to 1919, Coogan's Bluff, Coogan's Hollow, Matty Schwab's House, Harlem Meadow

OCCUPANT NL Giants June 18, 1911 to September 29, 1957; AL Yankees May 30, 1912 (morning game); April 17, 1913 to October 8, 1922; NL Mets April 13, 1962 to September 18, 1962

EVENT Negro League World Series first game, 1946; All Star Game 1934, 1949

LOCATION *Center Field (SE)* Eighth Avenue, then IRT elevated tracks, Harlem River and Harlem River Drive; *3rd Base (NE)* West 159th Street and IRT Rail Yards; *Home Plate (NW)* Bridge Park, then Harlem River Speedway, Coogan's Bluff, and Croton Aqueduct; *1st Base (SW)* West 157th Street trace; Same site as Polo Grounds (III); In Coogan's Hollow, 115 feet below Coogan's Bluff, the last remaining portion of a farm granted to Mr. John Lion Gardiner by the King of England in the seventeenth century

DIMENSIONS *Left Field:* 277 (1911), 286.67 (1921), 279.67 (1923), 279 (1930), 280 (1943), 279 (1955); *Left Field, Second Deck:* 250; *Left Center, Left of Bullpen:* 447; *Left-Center, Right of Bullpen:* 455; *Front Clubhouse Steps:* 460; *Center Field:* 433 (1911), 483 (1923), 484.75 (1927), 505 (1930), 430 (1931), 480 (1934), 430 (1938), 505 (1940), 490 (1943), 505 (1944), 480 (1945), 490 (1946), 484 (1947), 505 (1949), 483 (1952), 480 (1953), 483 (1954), 480 (1955), 475 (1962), 483 (1963); *Bleacher Corners:* 475; *Right-Center, Left of Bullpen:* 449; *Right-Center, Right of Bullpen:* 440; *Right Field:* 256.25 (1921), 257.67 (1923), 257.5 (1931), 257.67 (1942), 259 (1943), 257.67 (1944); *Right Field Photographers Perch:* 249; *Backstop:* 65 (1942), 70 (1943), 65 (1944), 70 (1946), 74 (1949), 65 (1954), 74 (1955), 65 (1962); *Foul Territory:* Very large. There's a lot of confusion here. During the Giants' stay it was 483 to the front of the clubhouse, and probably 505 to the rear clubhouse wall above the overhang. Why the 483 marker sometimes was changed to 480 or 475, is not known but it could have been due to remeasurements or a slight shift of home plate's location. Or it could have been a measurement to

the base of the Eddie Grant Memorial. In the Giants' time, reading from left to right, the markers read 315, 360, 414, 447, 455, 483, 455, 449, 395, 338, 294. In the Mets' time, they read 306, 405, 475, 405, 281. The foul lines were never marked. One possibility is that it was 433 feet to the front of the bleachers, 475 to the beginning of the clubhouse overhang, 483 to the rear wall under the overhang, and 505 to the front of the high wall. The 21-foot overhang of the second deck in left reduced the distance to the second deck from 279 to 250, not 258, because of the angle involved.

FENCES—1911-22 *Left to Center:* 10 (concrete); *Center:* 20 (tarp); *Right-Center:* 10 (concrete); *Right Field:* 12 sloping to 11 at pole (concrete)

FENCES—1923-63 *Left Field:* 16.81 (concrete); *Left-Center:* 18 (concrete); *Where Left-Center Wall Ended at Bleachers:* 12 (concrete); *Center Field Bleachers Wall:* 8.5 (4.25 wire on top of 4.25 concrete) on both sides of clubhouse runway; *Center Field Hitters' Background:* 16.5 on both sides of clubhouse runway; *Center Field Clubhouse:* 60 high and 60 wide—50 high in 1963; *Center Field Top of Longines Clock:* 80; *Center Field Top of Right Side of Scoreboard:* 71; *Center Field Top of Left Side of Scoreboard:* 68; *Center Field Top of Middle of Scoreboard:* 64; *Center Field Top of 5 Right Scoreboard Windows:* 57; *Center Field Top of 4 Left Scoreboard Windows:* 55; *Center Field Bottom of 5 Right Scoreboard Windows:* 53; *Center Field Bottom of 4 Left Scoreboard Windows:* 48; *Center Field Bottom of Clubhouse Scoreboard:* 31; *Center Field Top of Rear Clubhouse Wall:* 28; *Center Field Top of Front Clubhouse Wall:* 19; *Center Field Top of 14 Lower Clubhouse Windows:* 16; *Center Field Bottom of 14 Lower Clubhouse Windows:* 11; *Center Field Clubhouse floor Overhang:* 8; *Center Field Top of Eddie Grant Memorial:* 5; *Center Field Width of Little Office on Top of Lower Clubhouse:* 10; *Right Center:* 12 (concrete); *Right Field:* 10.64 (concrete)

FORMER USE Underneath the Harlem River until filled in with dirt in the late 1870s.

CURRENT USE Polo Grounds Towers—four 30-story apartment buildings. Willie Mays Field—an asphalt playground with 6 basketball backboards where center field used to be, a brass historical marker in place.

PHENOMENA

- Originally named for owner John T. Brush.
- Second deck in right had 9-foot photographer's perch overhang 60 feet from foul pole out into right-center.
- Bullpens in fair territory in left-center and right-center.
- There was no line on the 60-foot-high center field clubhouse above which a ball would be a home run.
- The outfield was slightly sunken. A manager, standing in his dugout, could see only the top half of his outfielders. At the wall, the field was 8 feet below the infield.
- The left field second deck overhang meant that a homer to left was easier than a homer to right, even though the wall in left was 279 and the wall in right was 258. The overhang was 21 feet, but it effectively shortened the distance required for a pop-fly homer to the second deck in left to 250 feet because of the angle involved.
- The overhangs here and at Tiger Stadium and Shibe Park have more significance than one might suspect, according to research published by the professional society

for physicists, the American Physical Society. The batted ball's trajectory consists of two component vectors, horizontal and vertical. The vertical deceleration is constant over time due to gravity, but the horizontal deceleration increases over time due to wind resistance and atmospheric drag. Near the end of its flight, the ball is coming down sharply, rather than arcing down as it arched up, as would occur in a vacuum. So many outfielders have watched helplessly as a ball they could catch dropped into the 2nd deck.
• Hitter's background extended beyond the end of the bleacher wall, several feet into the clubhouse gap.
• The field sloped in a "turtle back" just beyond the infield dirt. It sloped down 1.5 feet to drains about 20 feet into the outfield, then back up again.
• Right-center wall sloped gradually from 11 feet at pole to 12 feet at the bleachers.
• Left-center wall sloped from 16 feet 9.75 inches at the pole to 18 feet in left center, then abruptly fell to 16 feet and then to 14 feet and sloped gradually to 12 feet at the bleachers. When ad signs were removed in the 1940s, the abrupt changes in height in left-center disappeared.
• After the all-wooden Polo Grounds (III) burned down April 14, 1911, Polo Grounds (IV) was built with temporary stands for 1911. The infield stands were rebuilt with concrete for 1912, and the outfield concrete double deck was finished in 1922. The bleachers in left-center and center were wood remaining from before the fire.
• In 1914, there were 2 bends in the wall in right-center.
• In 1917, the fans exited from the field through gates under the center field bleachers.
• Morris James Mansion sat up on Coogan's Bluff, overlooking the ballpark.
• Brush Stairway led down from Coogan's Bluff to the Speedway and the ticket booths behind home plate.
• Coats of arms of all the teams in the National League on the top of the grandstand. Removed in the 1920s.
• Dedicated on May 30, 1921, to a former Giant killed in World War I, the Eddie Grant Memorial stood in center at the base of the clubhouse wall. It was 5 feet high. The Memorial reads:

In Memory of
Capt. Edward Leslie Grant
307th Infantry - 77th Division
A.E.F.
Soldier - Scholar - Athlete
Killed in action
Argonne Forest
October 5, 1918
Philadelphia Nationals
1907-1908-1909-1910
Cincinnati Reds
1911-1912-1913
New York Giants
1913-1914-1915
Erected by friends in Baseball,
Journalism, and the Service.

• In the winter of 1922-23, the concrete double decks were extended all the way to either side of the new concrete bleachers in center, housing the clubhouse. Unfortunately, the Roman Colosseum facade frescoes were removed during that winter also.
• Bleachers in center remodeled in 1923.

• In 1929, the first attempt was made to wire the umpires for sound and reconnect them into the PA system. It didn't work too well.
• Speaker placed above Grant Memorial in 1931.
• Field raised 4½ feet in 1949 to help with drainage. In 1609 and 1874 maps, the location is shown to be underneath the Harlem River. The water table was only 2-6 feet below the playing surface, and drainage was complicated by rainwater cascading off the 115-foot-high Coogan's Bluff down onto the site.
• During the 1950s, groundskeeper Matty Schwab and his family lived in an apartment under Section 3 of the left field stands built for him by Horace Stoneham. The apartment was the main bait in Mr. Stoneham's successful offer to grab Mr. Schwab away from the hated Dodgers in 1950.
• A two-foot-square section of sod from center field was removed and taken to San Francisco in the fall of 1957.
• Home plate was moved out toward center several feet by the Mets in the winter of 1961-62.
• During the Mets' stay in 1962 and 1963, Johnny McCarthy and his crew of groundskeepers painted Schwab's four rooms pink, installed a shower and plywood on the floor and lockers, and called it their Pink Room.
• In 1962 and 1963, the Howard Clothes sign on the outfield wall promised a boat to any player hitting it.
• Demolition started on April 10, 1964, with same wrecking ball that demolished Ebbets Field.

PHILADELPHIA, PENNSYLVANIA

BAKER BOWL
STYLE Major League Classic
A.K.A. Huntingdon Street Baseball Grounds 1895 to July 1913, National League Park (III) 1895 to 1938, Hump, Cigar Box, Band Box, Philadelphia Park
OCCUPANT NL Phillies April 14, 1904 to May 14, 1927; NL Phillies June 24, 1927 to June 20, 1938; also neutral use by NL Cleveland versus Baltimore July 29, July 30, and August 11, 1898; and versus Washington August 5, 6, and 8, 1898
EVENT Negro League World Series first and second games 1924, fifth and sixth games 1925, fourth and fifth games 1926
LOCATION *Left Field (N)* West Lehigh Avenue; *3rd Base (W)* North 15th Street; *1st Base (S)* West Huntingdon Street; *Right Field (E)* North Broad Street; *Beneath* Philadelphia and Reading Railroad tracks in a tunnel
DIMENSIONS *Left Field:* 335 (1921), 341.5 (1926), 341 (1930), 341.5 (1931); *Center Field:* 408; *Right-Center:* 300; *Right Field:* 272 (1921), 279.5 (1924), 280.5 (1925)
FENCES *Left Field:* 4 (1895), 12 July (1929); *Left-Center Field Clubhouse to Right-Center:* 35 (1895), 47 (with 12 screen on top 1915); *Right Field:* 40 (tin over brick 1895), 60 (40 tin over brick, topped by 20 screen 1915)
CURRENT USE Parking lot and car wash in right-center, gas station in center, bus garage from home down right field foul line
PHENOMENA
• Named after Phillie owner William F. Baker.

• Named the Hump because it was on an elevated piece of ground that had a railroad tunnel underneath the outfield.

• Swimming pool in the basement of the center field clubhouse prior to World War I.

• Coke and "Health Soap Stops B.O." Lifebuoy signs on the high right field wall.

• Extra seats added in front of the fence in center for the 1915 World Series led directly to the Phillies losing the Series' last game.

• During Prohibition, the outfield wall liquor ads were boarded over with dirty grimy blank boards.

• Home plate moved back a foot in 1925, making the right field foul pole 280.5 rather than 279.5.

• Torn down in 1950.

SHIBE PARK

STYLE Major League Classic

A.K.A. Connie Mack Stadium 1953 to 1970

OCCUPANT AL Athletics April 12, 1909 to September 19, 1954; NL Phillies May 16 to May 28, 1927; NL Phillies July 4, 1938 to October 1, 1970

EVENT Negro League World Series fifth game 1942; fourth game 1945; third game 1947; All Star Game 1943, 1952

LOCATION *Left Field (N)* West Somerset Street; *3rd Base (W)* North 21st Street; *1st Base (S)* West Lehigh Avenue; *Right Field (E)* North 20th Street

DIMENSIONS *Left Field:* 360 (1909), 378 (late 1909), 380 (1921), 334 (1922), 312 (1926), 334 (1930); *Left Center:* 515 (1909), 502 (late 1909), 468 (1922), 448 (1950), 440 (1951), 460 (1953), 468 (1954), 447 (1956), 410 (1969); *Right Center:* 393 (1909), 390 (1969); *Right Center, Left of Scoreboard:* 400 (1942); *Right Field:* 360 (1909), 340 (late 1909), 380 (1921), 307 (1926), 331 (1931), 331 (to lower 1934), 329 (to upper iron fence 1934); *Backstop:* 90 (1942), 86 (1943), 78 (1956), 64 (1960)

FENCES *Left Field to Left Center:* 12 (4 screen above 8 concrete 1949); *Center Field, Small Section:* 20 (1955), 8 (wood 1956), 3 (canvas 1969); *Right-Center Scoreboard:* 50 (top of black scoreboard 1956), 60 (top of Ballantine Beer sign 1956); *Right Field:* 12 (concrete 1909), 34 (22 corrugated iron above 12 concrete 1935), 30 (1943), 50 (1949), 40 (1953), 30 (1954), 40 (1955), 32 (1956)

FORMER USE City dog pound, also a brickyard in the Swampoodle neighborhood nearby

CURRENT USE Vacant site. Several hundred of the seats are being used now in Duncan Park, home of the Sally League Phillies in Spartanburg, South Carolina, and in War Memorial Stadium, Greensboro, North Carolina

PHENOMENA

• The first concrete and steel stadium in the majors.

• Named for Ben Shibe, an A's stockholder and baseball manufacturer.

• French Renaissance churchlike dome on exterior roof behind the plate which housed Connie Mack's office.

• Sod transplanted here from Columbia Park.

• Highest pitcher's mound—20 inches high.

• Batting cage sat behind short fence in center when the measurement was only 447.

• Corrugated iron fence in right—balls bounced at crazy angles off it—top 22 feet of 34-foot fence—2-foot-deep frame—was 329 to front of frame, 231 to rear of frame where iron sheets were.

• Conduit on right field wall was in play.

• Slopes in front of the outfield fences in early years.

• Ladder in front of left field scoreboard, 1909—went all the way to the top.

• Doubledecked in 1925; also in that year left field stands added.

• Mezzanine added in 1929.

• Right field wall reinforcement in 1934 reduced distance to front of the frame from 331 to 329, but sign wasn't changed until 1956.

• Before 1935, 20th Street residents could sit in their front bedroom or on their roof and see the game free over the 12-foot right-field fence. Fans could see the lines of laundry on the roof of 20th Street houses. Connie Mack lost a suit to prevent this, so he built the high right-field fence.

• 1948 plans to add 18,000 seats in right field and reduce foul line to 315 feet never materialized.

• In 1956, the old Yankee Stadium scoreboard was installed in front of the right-center wall; later a clock was added—balls hitting the clock were homers—top of clock was 75 feet high; top of Ballantine Beer sign, 60 feet high.

• In 1956 the normal screen was replaced by see-through plexiglass—protected the fans behind the plate from foul balls.

• Home plate moved to Veterans Stadium in 1971.

• Fire damaged it on August 20, 1971.

• Last game on October 1, 1970.

• Torn down in June 1976.

PITTSBURGH, PENNSYLVANIA

FORBES FIELD

STYLE Major League Classic

A.K.A. Oakland Orchard, Dreyfuss Folly

OCCUPANT NL Pirates June 30, 1909 to June 28, 1970; NNL Grays 1939 to 1948

EVENT Negro League World Series second game 1942; fourth and fifth games 1944; second game in 1945; All Star Game 1944, 1959

LOCATION *Left Field (NE)* Schenley Park, then Bigelow Boulevard; *3rd Base (NW)* Sennott (also spelled "Sonnett" at times) Street, then Cathedral of Learning; *1st Base (SW)* Boquet (also spelled "Bouquet" at times) Street; *Right Field (SE)* Joncaire Street, Pierre Ravine, Junction Hollow, Junction Railroad tracks

DIMENSIONS *Left Field:* 360 (1909), 356.5 (1921), 356 (1922), 360 (1926), 365 (1930), 335 (1947), 406 (1954); *Deepest Corner, Left of Straightaway Center, at the Flag Pole:* 462 (1909), 457 (1930); *Center Field:* 442 (1926), 435 (1930); *Right-Center, Right Side of Exit Gate:* 416 (1955); *Right-Center:* 408 (1942); *Bend at Left End of Screen:* 375; *Right Field:* 376 (1909), 376.5 (1921), 376 (1922), 300 (1925); *Backstop:* 110 (1909), 84 (1938), 80 (1947), 84 (1953), 75 (1959)

FENCES *Left Field Front Fence:* 8 (5 screen above 3 wood 1947), 12 (9 screen on top of 3 wood 1949), 14

(screen 1950); *Left Field Wall:* 12 (1909), 12 (brick and ivy 1946); *Left Field Scoreboard:* 25.42 (steel left and right sides), 27 (middle); *Wooden Marine Sergeant at Parade Rest to Right of Scoreboard:* 32 (June 26, 1943 to end of season); *Side Wall Angling Back to Meet Brick Wall in Left-Center:* 12 (wood, when front fence was up); *Cages Around Light Tower Just Right of Scoreboard and in Power Alleys:* 16.5; *Center Field:* 12 (wood 1909), 12 (brick and ivy 1946); *Right-Center:* 9.5 (concrete 1925); *Screen—Left Side at 375 Mark:* 24 (14.5 wire above 9.5 concrete 1932); *Screen—Right Side at Flag Pole:* 27.67 (18.17 wire above 9.5 concrete 1932)

FORMER USE   Part of Schenley Farms, a hothouse and livery stable. Land for grazing cows. Ravine where right field would be. Football site for University of Pennsylvania vs. Carnegie Tech October 31, 1908, game. Penn won on the rocky field.

CURRENT USE   Mervis Hall, out in right field, and the University of Pittsburgh's Forbes Quadrangle in the infield. The center field and right-center brick walls still stand, along with the base of the flag pole. Mazeroski Field, a Little League diamond beyond the left field brick wall, still remains. Roberto Clemente Drive now bisects the site, and runs about 10 feet under what used to be the playing surface of the infield.

PHENOMENA

• 1st base by a misspelled street: Boquet Street was named for General Henry Bouquet, a Swiss soldier who fought for the British in the French and Indian War's decisive battle at Fort Duquesne.

• Named for General John Forbes, a British general in the French and Indian War who captured Fort Duquesne and renamed it Fort Pitt in 1758.

• Ivy-covered brick wall in left and left-center.

• The 14-foot Longines clock with speaker horns on top of the left field scoreboard were out of play—a drive hitting it was a home run.

• Fans in the upper left corner of the left field bleachers could not see the plate because of the third base grandstand, which stood between them and the plate. Right field roof was 86 feet high.

• During World War II, the right field screen could not be replaced due to the priority given to the war effort. It deteriorated badly.

• No no-hitter was ever pitched here.

• Home plate remains in almost its exact original location, only now it is encased in glass on the first-floor walkway of the University of Pittsburgh's Forbes Quadrangle.

• The bottoms of the light-tower cages in left-center, center, and right-center were in play, as was the bottom of the center field flag pole.

• Just to the left of the flag pole stood the batting cage, also in play. Before being placed in left-center, it stood behind home plate.

• Very hard infield surface—ask Tony Kubek!

• Back in the 1910s, there was a small scoreboard on the center field wall.

• In 1920s, cars and trucks were repaired and sold beneath the left field bleachers.

• Right field stands built in 1925, reducing distance to right field foul pole by 76.5 feet. Right field screen added in 1932. It was taken down for a short period once, then put back up.

• Barney Dreyfuss Monument was just to the left of the exit gate in right-center where fans exited the ballpark into Schenley Park after a game. It was installed on June 30, 1934, on the park's 25th anniversary, and was made of granite with a bronze tablet.

• Greenberg Gardens, also called Kiner's Korner: the area between the scoreboard and a chicken coop wire short fence in left put there to increase home run production from 1947 to 1953—called Greenberg Gardens 1947, Kiner's Korner 1948 to 1953.

• When Greenberg Gardens were in place, a Western Union clock stood on top of the scoreboard, to the right of the familiar Gruen Clock. Torn down in 1972 and 1973.

• In 1938, with the Buccos apparently on their way to the World Series, they built a third deck of seats behind the plate called the Crow's Nest, which had the major leagues' first elevator. Bucs finally made the Series 22 years later.

• During World War II, from June 26 through the end of the 1943 season, a huge U.S. Marine made of wood stood against the left field wall, just to the right of the scoreboard. Standing at parade rest, the Marine sergeant was 32 feet high, 15 feet wide across his feet, and in play.

• Honus Wagner statue in Schenley Park erected 1955—18 feet high, 1,800 pounds—moved to Three Rivers with Bucs in 1970.

• A plaque today marks the spot where Bill Mazeroski's World Series-winning homer left the park in 1960 and flew into the trees above Yogi Berra's head.

• Green foam rubber crash pads placed on concrete wall in right and right-center, first in majors. Wooden walls installed in left and center in 1909, replaced with brick and ivy in 1946.

• Street deadending into Sennott Street by 3rd base was called at various times Pennant Place and Forbes Field Avenue.

• Fires damaged park December 24, 1970, and July 17, 1971. Destruction began July 28, 1971.

ST. LOUIS, MISSOURI

SPORTSMAN'S PARK (IV)

STYLE   Major League Classic

A.K.A.   Busch Stadium (I) 1953 to 1966, Bill Veeck's House

OCCUPANT   AL Browns April 14, 1909 to September 27, 1953; NL Cardinals July 1, 1920 to May 8, 1966; NAL New Orleans–St. Louis Stars one game 1941

EVENT   All Star Game 1940, 1948, 1957

LOCATION   *Left Field (NE)* Sullivan Avenue; *3rd Base (NW)* North Spring Avenue; *1st Base (SW)* 3623 Dodier Street; *Right Field (SE)* 2911 North Grand Avenue, later North Grand Boulevard. Same as earlier Sportsman's Parks, but turned around so that home plate was in the west-southwest corner

DIMENSIONS   *Left Field:* 368 (1909), 340 (1921), 356 (1923), 355 (1926), 360 (1930), 351.1 (1931); *Left Center:* 379; *Center Field:* 430 (1926), 450 (1930), 445 (1931), 420 (1938), 422 (1939); *Deepest Corner Just Left of Dead Center:* 426 (1938); *Deepest Corner Just Right of Dead Center:* 422 (1938); *Right Center:* 354 (1942); *Right Field:* 335 (1909), 315 (1921), 320 (1926), 310

(1931), 332 (1938), 309.5 (1939); *Backstop:* 75 (1942), 67 (1953)

FENCES *Left to Center:* 11.5 (concrete); *354 Mark in Right-Center to Right:* 11.5 (1909), 33 (11.5 concrete below 21.5 wire July 5, 1929), 11.5 (1955), 36.67 (11.5 concrete below 25.17 wire 1956)

CURRENT USE Herbert Hoover Boys' Club, with a baseball diamond where the major league one used to be

PHENOMENA

• The local newspaper, the *Globe-Democrat*, had an ad on the right-center wall which showed the star of the previous game. Just to the right of this ad, the league standings for both leagues were listed.

• The Busch eagle would flap its wings after a Cardinal home run. It sat on top of the left-center scoreboard. During World War II, there was a War Chest sign there.

• Cards office was at 3623 Dodier, Browns office was at 2911 North Grand.

• Pavilion seats in the power alley in right center.

• Second deck from first to third added in 1909.

• Second deck expanded to foul poles in 1925.

• Bleachers were added to parts of outfield in 1926.

• Beginning in the 1940s, the outfield signs were 351, 358, 379, 400, 426, 425, 422, 422, 405, 354, 322, and 310. In the mid 1950s, the 426 and the right 422 signs that marked the corners just left and right of straightaway center were removed.

• Flag pole in fair territory until removed in the 1950s.

• Bill Veeck's family lived in an apartment under the stands in the 1950s.

• When he bought the stadium from the Browns in 1953, Card owner Gussie Busch almost named it Budweiser Stadium, but was prevented by league pressure.

• The wire screen in front of the right field pavilion was removed for the entire 1955 season. It had been installed on July 5, 1929.

• A helicopter carried home plate to Busch Memorial Stadium after the last game on May 8, 1966.

• The old 1902–8 grandstand behind home plate became the left field pavilion in this park from 1909 to 1925 when it was replaced.

SAN FRANCISCO, CALIFORNIA

SEALS STADIUM

STYLE Minor League

A.K.A. Home Plate Mine

OCCUPANT NL Giants April 15, 1958 to September 20, 1959

LOCATION *Left Field (E)* Potrero Avenue; *3rd Base (N)* Alameda Street; *1st Base (W)* Bryant Street; *Right Field (S)* 16th Street and Franklin Square Park

DIMENSIONS *Left Field:* 365 (1958), 361 (1959); *Left Center:* 375 (1958), 364 (1959); *Just Left of Straightaway Center in the Corner:* 404; *Center Field:* 410 (1958), 400 (1959); *Just Right of Straightaway Center in the Corner:* 415; *Just Right of the 415 Mark Where the Seats Jutted Out:* 397; *Right Field:* 355 (1958), 350 (1959); *Back Stop:* 55.42

FENCES *Left Field:* 15 (5 concrete below 10 wire); *Center Field Scoreboard:* 30.5; *Right Field:* 16 (5 concrete below 11 wire)

CURRENT USE San Francisco Auto Center

PHENOMENA

• Opened April 7, 1931.

• The original deed for the land under the park was listed as "Home Plate Mine."

• No warning track.

• Wind blew from right to left.

• Nearby Hamms Brewery still standing.

WASHINGTON, D.C.

GRIFFITH STADIUM

STYLE Major League Classic

A.K.A. National Park (III) 1911 to 1921, Clark Griffith Park 1922

OCCUPANT AL Senators (I) April 12, 1911 to October 2, 1960; ECL Potomacs 1924; NEWL Pilots 1932; NNL Elite Giants 1936 to 1937; NNL Washington-Homestead Grays half of their home games 1937 to 1948; NNL Black Senators 1938; AL Senators (II) April 10 to September 21, 1961; Negro League World Series first game 1942, first and second games 1943; third game 1945

EVENT All Star Game 1937, 1956

LOCATION *Left Field (E)* Larch Street, later Fifth Street NW; *3rd Base (N)* Howard University, then W Street NW; *1st Base (W)* J. Frank Kelley Lumber and Mill Works, then Georgia Avenue NW, also called Seventh Street NW; *Right Field (S)* Spruce Street, later U Street NW

DIMENSIONS *Left Field:* 407 (1911), 424 (1921), 358 (1926), 407 (1931), 402 (1936), 405 (1942), 375 (Opening Day 1947), 405 (remainder 1947), 402 (1948), 386 (1950), 408 (1951), 405 (1952), 388 (1954), 386 (1956), 350 (1957), 388 (1961); *Left of Left-Center at Corner:* 383 (1931), 366 (1954), 360 (1956); *Right of Left-Center at Bend in Bleachers:* 409 (1942), 398 (1954), 383 (1955), 380 (1956); *Left- Center:* 391 (1911), 372 (1950); *Center Field:* 421; *Center Field Corner to Left of Building Protection Wall:* 423 (1926), 441 (1930), 422 (1931), 426 (1936), 420 (1942), 426 (1948), 420 (1950), 394 (1951), 420 (1952) 421 (1953), 426 (1954), 421 (1955), 426 (1961); *Inner Tip of Building Protection Wall:* 409 (1943), 408 (1953); *Deepest Corner—Right End of Building Protection Wall; Right Center:* 378 (1954), 372 (1955), 373 (1956); *Right Field:* 328 (1909), 326 (1921), 328 (marked 1926), 320 (actual 1926), 320 (1956); *Backstop:* 61

FENCES *Left Field:* 11.25 (foul pole to 408 mark concrete 1953), 12 (from 410 corner near left field foul pole to 408 mark just right of dead center 1954), 8 to 10 (wood in the corner in front of the bullpen at the foul pole 1955), 6.5 (wire and plywood in front of bullpen 1956); *Center Field:* 30 (concrete 408 mark to 457 mark 1953), 31 (concrete 408 mark to 457 mark 1954), 6 (wire and plywood 1956); *Right-Center:* to the left of the scoreboard in front of the bullpen: 4 (wood from 457 mark to 435 mark 1953), 10 (wood 1955), 4 (wood 1959); *Right Center Scoreboard:* 41 (1946); *National Bohemian Beer Bottle:* 56 (1946); *Right Field:* 30 (concrete 1953), 31 (concrete 1954)

CURRENT USE Howard University Medical Center and Howard University College of Dentistry, 909 seats

now in use at Tinker Field in Orlando, Florida
PHENOMENA
• Loudspeaker horn high on the wall in center.
• The center field wall detoured around 5 houses and a huge tree in center, jutting into the field of play.
• Right field foul line was the grandstand wall for the last 15 or so feet in front of the foul pole, so there was no way to catch a foul ball there.
• It was downhill from the plate to first base, supposedly to help save a step for slow Washington batters.
• Right field clock out of play.
• Ball rolling between top of scoreboard and bottom of the clock was in play: if it didn't come out, it was a homer; if it did, the outfielder could throw it back into play.
• U.S. presidents traditionally opened each season here by throwing out the first ball.
• Memorials honoring Walter Johnson and Clark Griffith stood outside the main entrance to the first base grandstand. The former now stands at Walter Johnson High School in Bethesda, Maryland; the latter at RFK Stadium.
• Height of National Bohemian Beer Bottle, above right-center scoreboard, approximately 50 feet.
• Park rebuilt after March 17, 1911 fire; completed on July 24, 1911.
• Doubledecked in 1920 from the bases down to the foul poles with a roof higher than the original second deck roof behind the plate.
• Temporary seats placed in front of left field bleachers for the 1924 World Series.
• In 1954, the visitor's bullpen was enclosed behind a screen fence in the left field corner in fair territory.
• Clark Calvin Griffith Memorial, dedicated by Vice President Nixon on August 8, 1956, was later moved to D.C. Stadium.
• In 1956, all the distances to the outfield fences were remeasured, and it was discovered that right field had lost 8 feet over the years!
• Also in 1956, 10 rows of temporary seats were added in front of the left field bleacher section.
• Park demolished from January 26 to August 14, 1965.

Negro League and Auxilliary Major League Baseball Sites

ATLANTA, GEORGIA

PONCE DE LEON PARK
STYLE   Minor League
A.K.A.   Spiller Park 1924 to 1932, Poncey
OCCUPANT   NSL Black Crackers 1932; NAL Black Crackers 1938
LOCATION   *Left Field (N)* Parking lot; *3rd Base (W)* North Boulevard; *1st Base (S)* 650 Ponce de Leon Boulevard; *Right Field (E) Southern Railroad tracks*
DIMENSIONS   *Left Field: 365 (1932), 330 (1949); Left-Center, Left Side of Scoreboard: 525; Center Field: 462 (1932), 448 (1938), 410 (1949); Right Field: 321 (1932), 324 (1938)*
FENCES   *Left Field:*2 (hedge, April 1949), 4 (cyclone fence, May 1949); *Left-Center:* 25 (scoreboard); *Center*

Field: 6; *Right-Center:* Magnolia Tree halfway up very steep embankment, no fence; *Right Field:* 15
CURRENT USE   Parking lot opposite Sears department store since being torn down in 1967
PHENOMENA
• First Ponce de Leon Park, built in 1907, burned down September 9, 1923.
• A 2-foot-high hedge formed the outfield fence from the left field line to the right side of the left-center scoreboard in 1949. It reduced the foul line from 365 to 330 and caused numerous arguments because a left fielder had to stay within the hedge. If he fell over it, the hit was a homer.

BROOKLYN, NEW YORK

DEXTER PARK
STYLE   Negro League
A.K.A.   Sterling Oval
OCCUPANT   ECL Royal Giants 1923 to 1927
LOCATION   Woodhaven, Long Island *Left (N)* Simpson Street, now called Park Lane South; *3rd Base (NW)* Cypress Hills Cemetery; *1st Base (W)* Elderta Lane and 75th Street; *Center Field (E)* Lott Avenue, now called 76th Street
PHENOMENA
• Had probably the most creative outfield wall billboard ever. An optician's ad read: "Don't Kill the Umpire— Maybe It's Your Eyes."
• Owners Max and Milt Rosner operated the semipro Brooklyn Bushwicks.
• Huge incline in right field caused by horse buried under the grass.

CHICAGO, ILLINOIS

SOUTH SIDE PARK (III)
STYLE   Cricket Ground
A.K.A.   39th Street Grounds (II), White Stocking Park (III) 1901 to 1903, Chicago Cricket Club, White Sox Park (I) 1904 to 1910, American Giants Field 1911 to 1940, Schorling's Park 1920 to 1940
OCCUPANT   AL White Sox April 24, 1901 to June 27, 1910; NNL Giants 1920; NNL American Giants 1920 to 1931, 1933 to 1935; NSL American Giants 1932; NAL American Giants 1937 to 1940; Neutral site use by NNL Cleveland Tigers 1928, by NNL Kansas City Monarchs in 1920s, by NNL Cuban Stars West in 1920s
LOCATION   *Left Field (N) West 38th Street; 3rd Base (W)* South Princeton Avenue; *1st Base (S)* West 39th Street, now West Pershing Road; *Right Field (E)* Wentworth Avenue
DIMENSIONS   *Left Field:* 355; *Left Center:* 400; *Center Field:* 450
FORMER USE   Home of Wanderers cricket team
CURRENT USE   Housing project three blocks from Comiskey Park
PHENOMENA
• Opened in 1900.
• Overhanging roof added in 1902.
• Fence cut back sharply around J. F. Kidwell Green-

house buildings in right center, making right-center relatively short compared to center and right.

• Used as a dog racing track during the summer of 1933, forcing the NNL American Giants to move all their home games from May 28 through the end of the 1933 season to Indianapolis.

• Burned down Christmas Day 1940.

EAST ORANGE, NEW JERSEY

GROVE STREET OVAL

STYLE Negro League

A.K.A. Grove Street Senior Ball Diamond, Monte Irvin Field, East Orange Oval

OCCUPANT NNL Cubans 1940 to 1948; NAL Cubans 1949 to 1950; also neutral site used by NNL Newark Bears 1936 to 1948

LOCATION East Orange, New Jersey *Left Field (E)* Greenwood Avenue; *3rd Base (N)* Grove Place; *1st Base (W)* Grove Street North; *Right Field (S)* Eaton Place;

DIMENSIONS *Left Field:* 240; *Center Field:* 360 to the water fountain; *Right Field:* 280

FENCES *Left Field:* 25 (garage walls); *Center Field:* 4 (water fountain); *Right Field:* None

CURRENT USE Still used as a community ball diamond

PHENOMENA

• No fence in center field where there were some hedges.

• Water fountain in play in deepest center field.

• Trees in right, as well as tennis courts beyond.

• Scoreboard in left, as well as poplar trees.

• Clubhouse down right field line in foul territory.

• "Bujum" Jud Wilson hit longest ball ever hit over water fountain in center.

• Property purchased by city in October 1907 and park dedicated Labor Day 1908 in a game between the New Jersey State Senate and the New Jersey State General Assembly.

• Fire destroyed the first grandstand at 4 AM, May 3, 1925; new grandstand dedicated May 1, 1926.

• Renamed Monte Irvin Field at June 6, 1986 ceremony in culmination of 4 years effort initiated by this author and the SABR Negro Leagues Committee, who designed the plaque marking the site.

JERSEY CITY, NEW JERSEY

ROOSEVELT STADIUM

STYLE Minor League

OCCUPANT NL Dodgers for seven 1956 games and eight 1957 games from April 19, 1956 to September 3, 1957; some NNL New York Black Yankees games in 1940s

LOCATION *Left Field (NE)* Hackensack River; *3rd Base (NW)* Newark Bay; *1st Base (SW)* Danforth Avenue; *Right Field (SE)* State Highway 440; at Droyers Point

DIMENSIONS *Foul lines:* 330; *Power Alleys:* 397; *Center Field:* 411; *Backstop:* 60

FENCES *Foul Line Corners:* 11; *Left Field to Center Field:* 4; *Right-Center to Right Field:* 7

FORMER USE A landfill for dirt excavated from Holland Tunnel

PHENOMENA

• Built as a WPA project in 1937 and named for FDR.

• Newark Bay mist brought mosquitoes and mist into the outfield.

• Thanksgiving morning football games between St. Peter's and Dickinson were always sold out in the 1940s.

• Torn down in 1984.

NASHVILLE, TENNESSEE

SULPHUR DELL (II)

STYLE Minor League

A.K.A. Sulphur Springs Bottom, Sulphur Dell Park, Athletic Park, Dump, Suffer Hell

OCCUPANT NNL Elite Giants 1933 to 1934

LOCATION *Left Field (N)* Jackson Street; *3rd Base (W)* Summer Street, later 900 Fifth Avenue North; *1st Base (S)* Tennessee Central Railroad tracks; *Right Field (E)* Cherry Street, later Fourth Avenue North

DIMENSIONS *Left Field:* 334; *Center Field:* 421; *Right Field:* 262 (235 when fans sat behind ropes on the bank)

FENCES *All Around:* 16 (wood 1927); *Left and Center:* 16 (wood 1931); *Right Field:* 38.5 to 46 (16 wood below 22.5 to 30 screen to a point 186 feet from the right field foul line)

PHENOMENA

• Only one-quarter mile from the Cumberland River, the park was often flooded.

• Nicknamed "the Dump" in honor of the exceptional fragrance that drifted over from the nearby smoldering city dump and lent a unique character to Sulphur Dell hot dogs!

• Sulphur Dell had the craziest right field in history. Right fielders were called mountain goats because they had to go up and down the irregular hills in right-center and right. The incline in right rose 25 feet, beginning gradually behind first, then rising sharply at a 45-degree angle, then leveling off at a 10-foot-wide shelf one-third of the way up the incline, and then continuing at a 45-degree angle to the fence.

• Fielders used to play on the shelf, 235 feet from the plate. When overflow crowds were attracted to a game, a rope was extended in front of the shelf, and fans sat on the upper two thirds of the incline, reducing right field to 235 rather than 262.

• The stands were very close to the pancake-shaped diamond. First base was 42 feet from the seats; third base was 26 feet from the seats.

• Embankments began in left at 301 and in right at 224.

• Casey Stengel once joked that he hit a bunt home run down the 1st base line.

NEW YORK, NEW YORK

DYCKMAN OVAL

STYLE Negro League

OCCUPANT NNL Cuban Stars 1922; ECL Cuban Stars East 1923 to 1928; ECL Bachrach Giants many

games 1923 to 1928; NAL Cuban Stars East 1929; NNL Cuban House of David 1931; NEWL Cuban Stars 1932
LOCATION *Left Field (NE)* West 204th Street; *3rd Base (NW)* Nagle Avenue; *1st Base (SW)* Academy Street; *Right Field (SE)* Tenth Avenue. In Upper Manhattan, 8 blocks east of the Henry Hudson Parkway, 5 blocks east of Inwood Hill Park, south of the Harlem Ship Canal, 4 blocks north of Dyckman Street, in Dyckman section
PHENOMENA
• The first major league park in New York to have lights for evening games. They were installed in 1930 by Cuban Stars owner Alex Pompez.

CAPITAL TEXTURE
STYLE Negro League
OCCUPANT ECL Lincoln Giants 1928; NAL Lincoln Giants 1929
LOCATION *(N)* East 138th Street; *(W)* Fifth Avenue; *(S)* East 135th Street; *(E)* Madison Avenue
CURRENT USE Riverton Apartments

CATHOLIC PROTECTORY OVAL
STYLE Amateur
OCCUPANT ECL Lincoln Giants 1923 to 1926; NNL Cubans 1935 to 1936
LOCATION *Left Field (E)* Hoguet Avenue; *3rd Base (N)* East Tremont Avenue; *1st Base (W)* White Plains Road; *Right Field (S)* McGraw Avenue. Bronx, 5 miles northeast of Yankee Stadium
CURRENT USE Parkchester Apartments, built by the Metropolitan Life Insurance Company—Unionport Road now crosses the site from home plate to center field; Metropolitan Avenue now runs from right field in to second base and then curves out to left field.
PHENOMENA
• The Protectory was a Catholic home and school for impoverished boys whose 50-piece marching band was much in demand. One of the students, Hank Greenberg, is now in the Hall of Fame.
• No grass in the infield.
• Leveled in 1939 so that Parkchester Apartments could be built.

TRIBOROUGH STADIUM
STYLE Football Stadium
A.K.A. Randall's Island Stadium, J. J. Downing Memorial Stadium
OCCUPANT NNL Black Yankees 1938
LOCATION *(N)* Bronx Kills and Harlem River, Eastern Parkway and Triborough Bridge; *(W)* House of Refuge, Vesta Avenue; *(S)* Little Hell Gate, East River, and Ward's Island, Sutter Avenue; *(E)* Sunken Meadow, Powell Street, Triborough Bridge
CURRENT USE Still standing, was used for WFL Stars football games in 1974 and NASL Cosmos soccer games in 1975
PHENOMENA
• A U-shaped stadium, open at the southwest end.

• Eight Ebbets Field light towers were moved here in 1939 when Ebbets had new lights installed.

PATERSON, NEW JERSEY

HINCHCLIFFE STADIUM
STYLE Football Stadium
OCCUPANT NNL Black Yankees 1936 to 1937, 1939 to 1945
LOCATION Paterson, New Jersey *Center Field (SE)* Passaic River; *3rd Base (NE)* Redwood Avenue; *Home Plate (NW)* Liberty Street; *1st Base (SW)* Maple Street
CURRENT USE Community baseball, still standing, opened 1932

PHILADELPHIA, PENNSYLVANIA

HILLDALE PARK
STYLE High School
A.K.A. Darby Catholic School Stadium
OCCUPANT ECL Hilldales 1923 to 1927; NAL Hilldales 1929; NEWL Hilldales 1932
LOCATION Yeadon, Pennsylvania *Left Field (N)* Bunting Lane, later MacDade Boulevard; *3rd Base (W)* Greenhouses and Cedar Avenue; *1st Base (S)* Chester Avenue; *Right Field (E)* Yeadon School In the suburbs of Philadelphia at a Catholic school on the Darby-Yeadon borderline
DIMENSIONS *Left Field:* 315; *Right Center:* 400; *Right Field:* 370
CURRENT USE Acme Super Saver supermarket and drive-in bank
PHENOMENA
• A huge tree sat beyond the fence in right-center; branches hung over the fence and were in play.

PITTSBURGH, PENNSYLVANIA

GUS GREENLEE FIELD
STYLE Negro League
OCCUPANT NEWL Grays 1932; NEWL Crawfords 1932; NNL Grays 1933, 1935 to 1938; NNL Crawfords 1933 to 1938
LOCATION In the Hill District *Left Field (N)* Ridgeway Street; *3rd Base (W)* Junilla Street; *1st Base (S)* 2500 Bedford Avenue; *Right Field (E)* Municipal Hospital and Francis Street
FORMER USE Entress Brick Company factory
CURRENT USE Pittsburgh Housing Authority projects
PHENOMENA
• Opened on April 29, 1932.
• Tin fence in outfield.
• Left field foul line was longer than at Forbes Field, where it was 365.
• The structure was torn down on December 10, 1938.

The Players

Lives of the Players

John B. Holway and Bob Carroll

On the following pages you'll find biographical sketches of 400 men, all in one way or another connected to baseball. Two questions naturally arise. First, why 400? And second, why *these* 400?

To deal with the easier question first, we were limited by space. If we were going to say anything worthwhile, we had to forget about doing 13,000-plus baseballers and concentrate our attention somewhere in the 350–500 range. We also knew that we would include a number of men for reasons other than how well they played. For example, Earl Weaver never made the majors as a second baseman and Judge Landis played a punk shortstop, but we knew they belonged on our list. When we counted up the "nonplayers," we had about fifty-five. A couple were waffley: was Clark Griffith a pitcher, a manager, or an executive?

Why not 396 or 413? Look, we had to draw a line somewhere. If we drew it at 407, we'd have no earthly reason for excluding player 408.

Once we settled on 400 total, we were ready for the hard part. Who?

We had to have the 200 members of the Hall of Fame. Most of them would have been included under any reasonable criteria anyway. The few arguable enshrinees belong in our 400 just because they *are* enshrinees, sort of a self-fulfilling immortality.

A few individuals not yet in the Hall of Fame made the cut as managers or contributors. We were ruthless here and probably a little hard on managers. Well, they're used to rejection.

Four other factors weighed heavily in our choices of players.

We wanted a strong sampling of players from all nine positions—nine and a half counting DH's. Pitching may be 75 percent of baseball, as Connie Mack used to say, but we weren't about to present 300 pitchers and 100 position players. Neither did we want 112 slugging left fielders and 8 catchers. We decided that we'd include roughly 30 players at each position. Those who will say they can name a dozen shortstops more valuable than our last couple of second basemen may be right; they'll also be irrelevant. We ended up being hoisted a little by our own petard; we kept grieving over terrific pitchers we'd left out, but we already had included over 100 hurlers.

Obviously we had to consider quality. Everyone has an opinion, but most of us could agree on the greatest-of-the-great —maybe even on the great. It was the "darned good's" that gave us trouble. Example: no one would leave out Ted Williams and few would skip Billy Williams. But what about Cy, Dick, Earl, or Ken?

Pete Palmer, Bill James, and a few others have done a lot of valuable work using statistical analysis in ranking players from different eras of baseball history. We used their various rankings as a starting point, but we couldn't follow them slavishly. They do not always agree in their rankings. Furthermore, many nineteenth-century players and the great black players of the pre-Jackie Robinson days are not subject to the same statistical analysis. And finally there are players we felt we must include for reasons other than pure competency.

Which brings us to our third consideration—fame. Quite often, as we made our final cuts, we were faced with two or three or more players who seemed virtually interchangeable. When we could find no statistical reason to include one and not the others, we made a judgment as to which player was the best known to a modern reader. If our estimate was correct, we included the one you would most like to read about.

Two large groups of players were helped by our including fame in our calculations: nineteenth-century players and players from the Negro Leagues. Both groups are at a disadvantage in that their statistical records are incomplete and those that exist do not always relate well to modern major league baseball's numbers. Was a 30-game winner in 1880 the equivalent of a 15-game winner today? What does a .350 batting average in the Negro National League of 1935 really mean? We must depend on contemporary accounts to rank these players. Of course, those accounts are highly subjective. We know we'll be hearing, "How can you leave out so-and-so and include whoozis?"

Our fourth and final consideration applied to only a few players. These were borderline candidates. They could have been in or out. If one player had a more interesting story than another of apparently equal worthiness, we told the more entertaining tale.

We have to say something about why a few men were not included. Fame was a consideration but not when all other factors said no. Smead Jolley was famous but overrated as a hitter, and in the field he was unsafe at any speed. Jose Canseco is famous, but he needs a few more years of excellent play to be included. All of the Black Sox were notorious; we included Eddie Cicotte and Joe Jackson, with some misgivings, because their records prior to their shame were too good to ignore.

We passed on players who had supreme moments of accomplishment but failed to measure up over the long haul. Johnny Vander Meer and Bobby Thomson came awfully close anyway. Bobo Holloman and Pat Seerey didn't.

We did not use any absolute statistical cutoffs. Dave Kingman hit 442 home runs, Riggs Stephenson hit .336, and Tony Mullane won 285 games. We thought some other players were better.

In preparing the biographical sketches, we wanted to show first of all why we included each man in our 400. Much of this involves repeating numbers. For the most part, we tried to rely on traditional categories that nearly everyone understands: batting average, ERA, RBIs, strikeouts, etc. There are often more meaningful statistics, pioneered by Palmer, James, and others, but this does not seem like the proper forum to explain them. We refer you to the Introduction to the statistical portion of this book.

We tried to avoid speculation of the if-he-hadn't-been-struck-by-lightning-he-would-have-hit-a-hundred-homers kind. We don't pretend to know what might have happened if there'd been no war, if the fences had been moved in, if Herb Score had ducked, if Cap Anson had played for the 1927 Yankees. We have our hands full with what did happen; let others worry about might have been.

The notorious "park factor" is part of this. By now, everyone must know that it's easier to hit in Wrigley Field than in the Astrodome—and on and on. We mentioned park factors in a few sketches when it seemed unavoidable, but to harp on it for every player affected would have put us all to sleep.

A few purists may find a note of levity in some of the sketches. Does that mean we do not view the annual pennant struggles as being on a par with, say, the struggle for world peace? Golly, we hope so. We can certainly be accused of enjoying our subjects. When baseball isn't fun anymore, we're *all* going to be in trouble.

HANK AARON
Outfielder, Mil (N) 1954–65, Atl (NL) 1966–74, Mil (A) 1975–76
If charisma were a baseball stat, Aaron would have been benched. No question he was great, but was he *box office*? Yearly, while lesser lights adorned magazine covers, the unassuming Alabaman quietly went his Hall of Fame way, winning baseball games with his quick feet, strong arm, and powerful bat. No Rodney Dangerfield, he always got respect; he *deserved* adulation.

His numbers were terrific: four times he led the league in home runs, four times in RBIs, thrice he scored the most runs, twice he had the most hits, and twice he topped all National Leaguers in batting average. In 1957, when his Braves were world champs, he was MVP, but most fans recognized him as a great player quicker than they'd have recognized him on the street. He made a more exciting stat line than an interview. It didn't help that he played in Milwaukee and Atlanta, places New York-based media *still* have to look up before they can point to them on a map. Worst of all, he was pleasant, modest, hard-working, and uncontroversial.

Then, as he neared the end of his career, this unpretentious superstar was thrust into the full glare of media hype as he fought the battle of his life—taking on Babe Ruth's ghost. "Hammerin' Hank" finished the 1973 season with 713 career home runs, only one less than Ruth's lifetime 714. After enduring a whole winter of "experts" speculating when he would, whether he could, and even *if* he

should break the record, Aaron tied it in his first at-bat of 1974. A few days later, on April 8, at 9:07 EST, before 53,775 Atlanta fans, he elevated Al Downing's pitch into the record books as number 715. Before retiring in 1976, Aaron brought his record total up to 755.

More than a decade later, the "greatest home run hitter" ruckus remains unsettled. Aaronites like to point out that Hank faced some un-Ruthian obstacles in playing most of his career in a "pitcher's park," facing more "good" pitchers and batting under lights. Ah, yes, say the pro-Ruthians, but the Babe had charisma!

Although he was never spectacular, on the basis of consistency Aaron was awesome. Among all players, he ranks third in games and hits, second in at-bats, runs, and total runs (runs plus RBIs), and first in home runs and RBIs—and grounding into double plays. His average season over twenty-three years was .305, 33 home runs, 100 RBIs. He hit 40 home runs or better eight times, the last when he was thirty-nine years old. Just running out his homers covered over fifty-one miles. He was named to the Hall of Fame in 1982.

When Reggie Jackson hit his 400th homer, he was asked if he could catch Aaron's 755. Reggie shook his head. Aaron, he said, was still an entire career away.

CHARLES "BABE" ADAMS
Pitcher, StL (N) 1906, Pit (N) 1907–26
The 1909 World Series had Detroit's Ty Cobb and Pittsburgh's Honus Wagner, but the star of the classic was Adams, a twenty-seven-year-old Pirate rookie. The quiet righthander from Indiana—a creditable 12–3 in 1909 but hardly the Buc ace — might not have pitched at all had star hurler Howie Camnitz not come down with an attack of quinsy. Pittsburgh manager Fred Clarke had been tipped that Adams threw with the "same style but faster" than AL pitcher Dolly Gray, who'd stumped Detroit batters during the season. Playing the hunch, Clarke sent the boy to do a man's job in the Series opener. Adams responded with a six-hitter, then six-hit the Tigers again in the fifth and seventh games to make the Pirates world champs.

Babe's best pitches were a good fastball (which earned him his nickname as a kid) but especially a curveball that could freeze batters in their tracks. His real talent, however, was his control. It took him to 194 Pirate wins over eighteen seasons, including 22–12 in 1911 and 21–10 in 1913. In 1914, he pitched a twenty-one-inning game without allowing a single walk. He averaged just 1.29 walks per nine innings over his career, with a pinpoint 0.62 record in 1920 (18 walks in 263 innings), tying with Christy Mathewson (1913) for best of all time.

GROVER CLEVELAND "PETE" ALEXANDER
Pitcher, Phi (N) 1911–17, 1930, Chi (N) 1918–26, StL (N) 1926–29
When Grover Cleveland Alexander retired in 1930, he saw his name at the top of the "Games Won" column in the National League record book. A recount eventually added one more win to Christy Mathewson's lifetime total to leave them tied at 373 (Matty has now lost a win after all, returning him to 372), which was kind of fitting because one or the other was certainly the best NL right-hander of the first half of the twentieth century.

Alexander went into the Hall of Fame in 1938, two years after Mathewson. Military service in World War One cost Alex one-plus years after three straight 30-win seasons, and a shell that burst in his ear may have triggered the epilepsy and led to the alcoholism that plagued him for the rest of his days; a gas attack in a training drill eventually cost Mathewson his life. Matty's out pitch was his fadeaway; Alex had a good fastball and better curve, all delivered with an easy, just-tossin' motion. Both had the kind of control that could carve a roast. Alex won two of the three games in which they faced each other.

Not even Matty ever had a moment like Alex's in the 1926 World Series. The grizzled veteran, nearing forty, won his second Series game for the Cardinals in Game Six and then allegedly went out to save St. Louis from alcohol by drinking it all himself. The next day, more hung over than the Gardens of Babylon, he was summoned to the mound in the seventh inning of the final game. The Cards led 3–2, but the Yankees had slugger Tony Lazzeri up with two outs and the bases loaded. Alex worked the count to 1-and-2, including a heart-stopping foul down the left field line, then whooshed strike three past Lazzeri's bat. After two more shutout innings, the Cards were champs and Alexander was a legend. The incident served as the climax of the movie *The Winning Team*, with Ronald Reagan portraying Alexander.

The Lazzeri strikeout crowned a career that glittered with three 30-win seasons and six 20-win seasons. His 90 career shutouts are second only to Walter Johnson's 110. His lifetime ERA of 2.56 included seasons of 1.22, 1.55, 1.72, and 1.73.

Alexander's 227 strikeouts in 1911 was the rookie record until Dwight Gooden broke it. But his 28 wins still stand as the freshman mark. Four of his wins were consecutive shutouts. In 1915 he led the Phillies to a pennant, winning 31 and clinching the flag with a one-hitter. He won one more in the Series against Boston—the last Series win for the Phils until 1980.

All this was doubly impressive because he pitched his home games from 1911 to 1917 in little Baker Bowl, with a right field wall just off the second baseman's hip, and from 1918 to 1925 at hitter-friendly Wrigley Field. In 1916 Alexander tied a forty-year-old mark with 16 shutouts—and nine of these were registered at Baker Bowl.

As his career closed, Alex's alcoholism was so bad he couldn't shake hands without taking three stabs at it, and his wife hid her perfume so he wouldn't drink that. He ended up re-enacting the Lazzeri strikeout with a flea circus on Broadway. In 1950, he died alone in a rented room.

DICK ALLEN
Third Baseman/First Baseman, Phi (N) 1963–69,
1975–76, StL (N) 1970, LA (N) 1971, Chi (A) 1972–74,
Oak (A) 1977
Dick ("Don't call me Richie!") Allen had baseball talent and opera-star temperament. When his mood was right, he was a one-man offense who could carry a team for a week or a month. When his mood was wrong, he could pout or even disappear for an equal length of time. He found spring training a waste of time and avoided as much of it as possible. He drove enemy pitchers and friendly managers crazy with equal nonchalance.

He came to the Phillies a professed third baseman in 1963, led the league in errors a couple of times, and from 1969 until he retired in 1977 was more or less a first baseman. Allen lived by his bat: seven seasons over .300, ten seasons with 20 or more homers, and six seasons of 90-plus RBIs.

In 1970 the Phillies traded him to the Cardinals, who kept him a year and then passed him on to the Dodgers. In both cases, the teams improved their records, but decided Allen would never win the Employee of the Month award. In 1972 he was sent to the White Sox and patient manager Chuck Tanner (a.k.a. Job). Allen responded with an MVP year, hitting .308 and leading the AL in homers (37) and RBIs (113). After that, he got bored or sulky or whatever. By 1974, even Tanner was miffed over such Allen foibles as taking the last month of the season off to go tend his prize horses. Always his own man but often his worst enemy (despite heated competition among former teammates), Allen was ever an enigma.

WALTER ALSTON
Manager, Bkn (N) 1954–57, LA (N) 1958–76.
First base, StL (N) 1936
For twenty-three years—all on one-year contracts — Alston managed the Dodgers, overseeing their migration from Brooklyn to Los Angeles and presiding as they became baseball's most financially successful franchise. The Dodgers topped two million in attendance seven times with Walter in the dugout, their prosperity based on consistent wins. Alston brought them to four world championships, seven pennants, and eight second-place finishes. Only John McGraw, who managed thirty-one years, won more National League games or pennants.

Alston's entire major league playing career consisted of one at bat. Lon Warneke struck him out. But twenty years of playing and managing in the minors taught him to handle a team with patience and straightforward honesty. He was managing Nashua in the Dodgers' system in 1946, when the presence of black players was a hot potato. He volunteered to be the first white manager for a couple of talented black prospects and sent Roy Campanella and Don Newcombe on to stardom.

His Dodger teams had many stars but were renowned for their pitchers. Sandy Koufax and Don Drysdale are Hall of Famers, and countless others starred while hurling in the Dodger blue. Some of the credit goes to Alston and his patient handling. Named Major League Manager of the Year by *The Sporting News* in 1955, 1959, and 1963, Alston was elected to the Baseball Hall of Fame in 1983.

GEORGE "SPARKY" ANDERSON
Manager, Cin (N) 1970–78, Det (A) 1979–90.
Second base, Phi (N) 1959
To paraphrase Will Rogers, Anderson never met a man he didn't talk to death. If he could have hit as well as he talks, he'd have been an All-Star player. Instead he batted a mute .218 in his only major league season as a player. Despite his own lack of prowess, the loquacious leader has become one of baseball's great managers. Employing a slow fuse with problem players, a quick hook for pitchers, and an outlook more upbeat than a Basie riff, Anderson is the only man to win a World Series in both leagues, to win 100 games in both leagues, and to be Manager of the Year

in both leagues. In 1970, his first year at the helm, he guided Cincinnati's Big Red Machine to a pennant, then followed with more in 1972, 1973, 1975, and 1976; the latter two years also produced World Championships. It was the first time since John McGraw's New York Giants in 1921–1922 that a National League team had won back-to-back championships. In 1984 he led the Tigers to a world title. All told, he's guided his teams to seven first-place finishes and five seconds. His postseason record, 34–21 and .619, is the best of any manager.

ADRIAN "CAP" ANSON

First Baseman/Third Baseman, Rock (NA) 1871, Phil (NA) 1872-75, Chi (N) 1876–97. Manager, Chi (N) 1879–1897, NY (N) 1898

Anson was the biggest star of the nineteenth century, one of the men who popularized baseball. During his twenty-seven-season career (1871–1897), he became the first man to make over 3,000 hits, even though nineteenth-century teams played fewer games per season than to-day's clubs. Twenty-four times he went over .300; three times he topped .380. He had good power for the dead-ball days. In 1884 he slugged five homers in two games, a feat that would not be matched until 1925.

He wasn't much of a fielder, though. His 58 errors in 1884 is still a record for first basemen. Even fielding with bare hands, that's a ton.

Cap managed Chicago's NL team (then called the "White Stockings") to five pennants between 1880 and 1886. He was a pioneer in the use of the hit-and-run, signals, platoons, a pitching rotation, and spring training. A big man—six-two, 220 pounds—he was a stiff-backed martinet who marched his men onto the field in military formation and used his fists to enforce his rules, the least popular being his no-drinking edict. Once he threw Chicago team owner A. G. Spalding off the field for challenging one of his decisions.

When he was finally let go by Chicago, his fans raised $50,000 for him. He turned it down.

LUIS APARICIO

Shortstop, Chi (A) 1956–62, 1968–70, Bal (A) 1963–67, Bos (A)1971–73

"Little Looie" played 2,581 games, more than any other shortstop, led the American League in stolen bases nine times (in a row), topped AL shortstops in fielding average eight times, and in 1984 became the first Venezuelan voted into the Hall of Fame. But he wasn't the be-all and end-all of short fielders. His lifetime batting average of .262 embraces *nada* power, and his .308 on-base average is embarrassing for a guy who was almost always used to lead off. Small wonder he never scored 100 runs and rarely led even his own team. What he did on offense was steal bases—506 of them. On the other hand, he was thrown out over 100 times.

He was smooth defensively—he won nine Gold Gloves. After being among the league leaders in total chances early in his career, his putouts and assists declined as his fielding average went up, indicating sure hands but the loss of the kind of range that wins extra ballgames. But no shortstop was ever more durable, and the amiable Aparicio helped win flags for the White Sox in 1959 and for the Orioles in 1966. He was arguably the best player in

the AL in 1960 when Roger Maris was named the MVP. That year Luis hit only .277 but stole 51 bases, led all shortstops in assists and fielding average, and knocked in 62 runs as a leadoff man.

LUKE APPLING

Shortstop, Chi (A) 1930–50. Manager, KC (A) 1967

Shortstops who can hit are as rare as Chicago pennants. Luke Appling could hit, and he spent twenty years wearing a White Sox uniform while other teams popped champagne corks at seasons' end. Although he never got into a World Series, he played in seven All-Star Games and averaged .444 there. He led the AL in batting in 1936, hitting .388, still the highest average by a shortstop in this century. He copped another crown in 1943, with .328. His are the only batting crowns won by a Sox hitter in spacious Comiskey Park. His career average of .310 came on 2,749 hits, and while he was never a power hitter (45 homers), he both scored and batted in over 1,000 runs. In 1964, he was elected to the Hall of Fame.

His specialty was fouling off pitches until he got one he wanted. According to legend, he once fouled twelve straight into the stands when the hard-strapped White Sox management refused him a dozen souvenir balls for friends. According to another version, it was fourteen straight after being turned down for two passes.

Originally a poor fielder, he led AL shortstops in errors six times. But he improved greatly over his career and finished with a record seven years leading in assists.

Nicknamed "Old Aches and Pains" because he led the league in hypochondria every year, he somehow survived aching ankles, pink eye, perpetual flu, a permanently sore back, headaches, inflamed throats, chills, vertigo, a real broken finger, and a fractured leg to play twenty years and usually top the Sox in games played. Among AL short-stops, only Aparicio put in more time at the position. At age seventy-five, he was healthy enough to slug a home run in the first Cracker Jack Old-Timers' Game in Washington, in 1984.

RICHIE ASHBURN

Outfielder, Phi (N) 1948–59, Chi (N) 1960–61, NY (N) 1962

Ashburn was one of the three best defensive center fielders ever. From 1948 through 1958 he led National League outfielders in chances per game every year but 1955 (when he finished second by 0.1). Sure, the other Phillie outfielders never won any dash medals, and ace Robin Roberts threw fly balls like they'd been ordered C.O.D., but Ashburn's gift for covering center made it all work. Willie Mays got the Gold Gloves; Ashburn got the outs — about 50 more each season. According to Pete Palmer's analytical stats, only Tris Speaker and Max Carey rank ahead of Richie as fly chasers, and then by a margin so small you'd get a recount in most states.

Ashburn's arm never got him a blue ribbon, but it got the Phillies a pennant in 1950, when he gunned down the Dodgers' Cal Abrams at the plate to preserve a tie in the season's final game. The Phillies won the game and the flag in the tenth.

Richie broke in with the Phillies in 1948, topping the NL in steals and hitting in 23 straight games, the rookie record until Santiago passed it in 1987. He led the league in batting in 1955 and 1958. He hit over .300 in nine of his fifteen seasons. He was a leadoff man who homered only slightly more often than swallows visit Capistrano, but he led the NL in hits three times and bases on balls four times. His career on-base average was near .400.

He closed out with .306 for the expansion Mets, providing some respectability to an otherwise comical outfit. He has since gone on to become one of the top broadcasters in the game for the Phillies.

EARL AVERILL
Outfielder, Cle (A) 1929–39, Det (A) 1939–40, Bos (N) 1941

After three excellent seasons with San Francisco of the PCL, Averill was purchased by the Indians in 1929 for $50,000. In his first major league at bat, he homered. He stood only five-nine and weighed just 172, but he generated home run power. For a half dozen years in the 1930s, he was one of the most feared batters in baseball. A back injury and a malformed spine affected his swing in 1937, left him as just an ordinary hitter, and prematurely shortened his career.

When Averill joined the Hall of Fame in 1975, he complained that he had had to wait thirty-four years. "Stats alone are enough," he said. His numbers were impressive, all right: .318 career batting average, 238 home runs, 1,164 RBIs, and 1,224 runs scored. During his ten best seasons, he averaged 23 home runs, 12 triples. 108 RBIs and 115 runs scored. He also led all outfielders in putouts twice. But hitting stats were inflated by an animated baseball during the time Averill was at his peak. Probably a better gauge of his ability is that he was the only outfielder selected to the first six All-Star Games.

The most famous incident in his career came in the 1937 All-Star Game, when a line drive off his bat broke pitcher Dizzy Dean's toe. Dean tried to come back from the injury too soon, altered his pitching motion, and ruined his arm. Ironically it was during that same 1937 season that Averill's back problem began to cut into his career.

FRANK "HOME RUN" BAKER
Third Baseman, Phi (A) 1908–14, NY (A) 1916–19, 1921–22

Although he led the American League in homers four straight years (1911–1914) with his fifty-two-ounce bat, Baker's season high was an un-Ruthian 12 in 1913. He spent most of his career in the dead-ball era, when the baseball was as lively as an octogenarian's libido. His "Home Run" nickname stemmed from two timely shots off Christy Mathewson and Rube Marquard to win a pair of games in the 1911 World Series.

Later third basemen punched more round-trippers with a bouncier baseball, but few could match Baker's all-around play. Named to the Hall of Fame in 1955, his career Relative Batting Average (batting average adjusted to the league average) of .307 is surpassed only by Wade Boggs and George Brett among hot corner practitioners. He was anchor man of the Philadelphia's "$100,000 infield" (with first baseman Stuffy McInnis, second baseman Eddie Collins, and shortstop Jack Barry), a quartet so adept that the A's won four flags in five years. In World Series play, Baker hit .409 in 1910,

.375 in 1911, and .450 in 1913. When he slipped to .250 in 1914, the A's lost the Series four straight.

Baker sat out the 1915 season in a salary dispute. (He also missed the 1920 season due to the death of his wife.) Connie Mack began selling off his stars, and Baker was sold to the Yankees in 1916 for a then-tidy $37,500. He was New York's biggest drawing card until Babe Ruth arrived in 1920 and redefined the job description for "home run hitter."

DAVE "BEAUTY" BANCROFT
Shortstop, Phi (N) 1915–19, NY (N) 1920–23, Bos (N) 1924–27, Bkn (N) 1928–29, NY (N) 1930. Manager, Bos (N) 1924–27

Bancroft is less famous than some, but he's one of the three top fielding shortstops ever, along with Ozzie Smith and Art Fletcher. No shortstop has ever handled more chances than Bancroft did in 1922—984 (Smith's busiest season was 933 in 1980). Of course strikeouts were fewer in Beauty's day than in Ozzie's, meaning more opportunities for fielders, and the ball is more lively today. But gloves were much smaller in 1922, which explains why three times Bancroft committed 60 errors or more.

Beauty, who was named to the Hall of Fame in 1971, was a winner. Manager Pat Moran gave him credit for sparking the Phils from sixth place to the pennant as a rookie in 1915. Traded to New York in 1920, Bancroft was made captain right away, and the next year the Giants won their first of four straight flags. He teamed with Frankie Frisch on the double play, and with George Kelly at first base and Heinie Groh at third, to form one of the game's top infields. Bancroft got his nickname from his habit of yelling "Beauty!" whenever his pitcher made a good pitch.

A switch-hitting leadoff man who crowded the plate, Bancroft coaxed plenty of walks but was a light hitter until the lively ball appeared in 1920. That year he hit .299 and followed it up with three consecutive .300 seasons, skipped a year, and then hit .300 twice more.

Bancroft was a sparkplug on the field, a fiery team leader with great instincts for the game who also managed during his four seasons in Boston. When he first joined the Giants, they asked if he wanted to go over their signs. "I don't have to," Beauty said, "I know them already."

ERNIE BANKS
Shortstop/First Baseman, Chi (N) 1953–71

Likable, popular Ernie hit more home runs than any other shortstop, 47 in 1958. He's also the first National Leaguer to win back-to-back MVPs (Yogi Berra did it in the AL).

A slim man for a slugger, Ernie had fast wrists and swung a light, thirty-one-ounce bat, producing a powerful buggy-whip action. His 44 home runs in 1955 included a record 5 grand slams. He led the NL with his 47 homers in 1958 and again with 41 in 1960, to complete ℵ 'r straight years of 40-plus homers. But his homer totals are slightly inflated because he played in "the friendly confines of Wrigley Field" (his words)—Ernie hit 290 at home, 222 away.

Banks's batting average was modest, and he was a disaster on base. He was thrown out more than he stole, 53–50. Although he was a solid fielder and set an NL season record for shortstops in fielding average with .985

(only 12 errors) in 1959, Banks did not win many games with his glove. And he could never lead the Cubs to a pennant—they finished fifth in both his MVP years. Banks was at first base, where he had moved in 1962, when the Cubs collapsed in 1969 and lost the pennant to the Mets. But at age thirty-eight, Ernie still contributed 23 home runs and 106 runs batted in and led NL first basemen in fielding percentage.

His sunny disposition and his chirpy "Let's play two!" made him "Mr. Cub," a favorite of Wrigley's bleacher bums. In 1977 he was elected to the Hall of Fame.

AL BARLICK
Umpire 1940–43, 1946–1955, 1958–71
When a labor strike shut down the coal mine where he worked in Springfield, Illinois, young Al Barlick turned to umpiring local sandlot games for a dollar each. Soon he entered the minor leagues, and in 1940, when famed ump Bill Klem was sidelined with an injury, Al was brought up to the majors. He stayed for thirty-one years, with time out for military service during World War II and two years off after suffering a heart attack in the mid-1950s.

Barlick worked a record seven All-Star Games and seven World Series. He was universally regarded as strict but fair—unyielding in his demand for respect. Fellow man-in-blue Ed Vargo called him " an umpire's umpire."

In 1990 he became only the sixth umpire to be named to the Hall of Fame.

EDWARD BARROW
Executive, Bos (AL) 1917–20, NY (A) 1921–45.
Manager, Det (A) 1903–04, Boston (A) 1918–20
The beetle-browed Barrow discovered Honus Wagner, switched Babe Ruth to the outfield, developed the Yankees' farm system, and masterminded them to fourteen flags and ten world championships.

This former bare-knuckle fighter and hotelman also pioneered night ball (at Paterson, New Jersey, in 1896), sanctioned the only woman to pitch in organized baseball (Lizzie Arlington, Eastern League, in 1897), was the first man to paint distances on outfield fences (Yankees, 1923), and to put large numbers on players' uniforms (Yanks, 1929).

After starting as a concession manager in 1894, he managed, operated, and part-owned several minor league teams, including Wheeling, West Virginia, where author Zane Grey played outfield. Barrow also was a fight promoter, and he sometimes hired heavyweight champs John L. Sullivan, James Corbett, and Jim Jeffries as umpires.

In 1917 Barrow became manager of the Red Sox. He led them to the world championship in 1918, when he began the transition of Ruth from pitcher to everyday player. Sox owner Harry Frazee sold Ruth to New York in 1920, and Barrow followed in 1921 as general manager.

Upon his arrival he told Yankee owner Colonel Jacob Ruppert, "If you ran your brewery the way you run this club, you'd go broke." Babe's 54 homers in 1920 had not been enough to move New York out of third place, but the next year, Barrow's first, the Yanks finally won their first flag. As he and assistant George Weiss built up a farm system, the Yankees would win six pennants in Barrow's first eight years, another in 1932, and another four between 1936 and 1939.

Barrow became president of the Yankees after the death of Ruppert in 1939 and held that position until the team was sold in 1945. He is memorialized with plaques in Cooperstown and one in center field of Yankee Stadium, the park he did so much to build.

DICK BARTELL
Shortstop, Pit (N) 1927–30, Phi (N) 1931–34, NY (N) 1935–38, Chi (N) 1939, Det (A) 1940–41, NY (N) 1941–43, 1946
In his autobiography, *Rowdy Richard*, Bartell modestly argued that he ought to be in the Hall of Fame. He found few backers outside his immediate family, but the old battler has a better case for the Hall than if he were running for Mr. Congeniality. In Palmer's Linear Weights System, Bartell's 27 Games Won put him ahead of five shortstops now in the Hall—Ernie Banks, Travis Jackson, Joe Tinker, Pee Wee Reese, and Luis Aparicio.

A pepperpot who usually batted first or second in the order, he hit over .300 six times in his career. In 1933, he tied a record with four doubles in one game. Dick was at the top of his game in 1936 and 1937. In the former year he hit .298 for the Giants and led all shortstops in assists, double plays, and total chances per game. His teammate, Carl Hubbell, was the MVP with 26 victories, but Bartell played every day and may have had more total value. In the World Series Dick hammered Yankee pitchers at a .381 clip in a losing cause. The Giants won the NL pennant again in 1937, as Dick hit .306 and again led in total chances per game.

In 1940 Bartell was traded to Detroit in the AL. He hit only .233, but the Tigers won nine games more than they had the year before without him and rose all the way from fifth to first. Dick was the World Series goat, though, when, with the Tigers leading the seventh game 1–0, he took a throw from the outfield with his back to the plate and let the Reds' Frank McCormick score the tying run. Detroit eventually lost 2–1.

Bartell was sent back to the Giants the next year, after a slow start in which he saw little action. He batted .303 for New York over the rest of the season. The Tigers fell back to fifth.

For all his participation on pennant winners, the image that remains (and the one Bartell himself perpetuates in his autobiography) is one of a hot-headed scrapper who enjoyed fighting and baseball in that order.

DON BAYLOR
Designated Hitter/Outfielder, Bal (N) 1970–75, Oak (A) 1976, Cal (A) 1977–82, NY (A) 1983–85, Bos (A) 1986–87, Min (A) 1987, Oak (A) 1988
Look up DH in the baseball dictionary and you'll see a picture of Baylor. He was one of the most effective at that ersatz position of all the American Leaguers who've tried it. He was even the AL MVP in 1979 when he decorated his .296 batting average with 36 homers and league highs in RBIs (139) and runs scored (120). Actually he was in the outfield in 97 and DH'd in only 65 that year, but who's counting? Baylor's defensive limitations made him somewhat of a designated hitter even when he had a glove on.

All told, Baylor officially DH'd in nearly 1,300 of his more than 2,200 games. Except for six seasons in California, he was pretty much of a have-bat/will-travel around the AL. It moved him into rarefied sluggers' air: more than 300 homers and nearly 1,300 RBIs. Although he was hired for his bat, he also had an admirable reputation as a team leader and steadying influence in the clubhouse. While such things are not subject to statistical evaluation, most of the teams he hit for were winners.

JAKE "EAGLE EYE" BECKLEY

First Baseman, Pit (N) 1888–89, 1891–96, Pit (P) 1890, NY (N) 1896–97, Cin (N) 1897–1903, StL (N) 1904–07
One of the last of the handlebar-mustache players and a big star at the turn of the century, Beckley played more games than any first baseman in history, 2,377—Gehrig was more than 200 behind. Jake rapped out 2,930 hits, paving the way to his Hall of Fame election in 1971. He batted over .300 thirteen times, and hit three home runs in one game in 1897, a feat that would not be repeated for twenty-five years (by Ken Williams in 1922).

It was hard to hit homers then. Not only were the baseballs deader than Saturday night in Des Moines, but the fences were deeper because they built ballparks to the shapes of city blocks. The center field fence could be some 550 feet away with an area in front roped off for carriages. Players could sooner mail the ball to the fence than hit it there. Triples were a better indicator of power. Jake hit 243, more than anyone in his day, and fourth best all time, behind Ty Cobb, Sam Crawford, and Honus Wagner. Twice he hit three in one game.

When the players revolted against management in 1890 and formed the short-lived Players League, Beckley was one of the many stars who jumped with them. "I'm only in this game for the money," he said candidly.

But he played with verve too. Sometimes he turned the bat around and bunted with the handle. His favorite stunt was a cute hidden ball trick. Jake liked to hide the ball under first base, and then pull it out and shock the runner who'd just seen him barehanded. Somehow the naive runners never caught on.

JOHN BECKWITH

Shortstop/Catcher, Negro Leagues, 1919–38: Chicago Giants, Chicago American Giants, Baltimore Black Sox, Homestead Grays, Harrisburg Giants, Lincoln Giants, Bacharach Giants, New York Black Yankees, Newark Dodgers, Brooklyn Royal Giants
Beckwith was only nineteen when he knocked the first ball ever hit over the left field fence at Redland Field, Cincinnati, in 1920. A righthanded pull hitter, he went on to rank as one of the great long-ball sluggers in the black leagues, clouting a reported 72 and 54 home runs in two of his seasons in Chicago. After he moved East in the late 1920s, he topped all hitters there, including Josh Gibson, in home runs in 1930 and 1931.

John could also hit for average, belting black and white big leaguers equally well—.323 in the black majors and .311 in twenty-nine games against top white big leaguers. His two best seasons were 1924, when he led all hitters with a .452 average, and 1930, when he posted an amazing .546.

A big man at 230 pounds, Beckwith could play any position on the field and would even pitch occasionally. He was a moody, antisocial man whose personality may have kept him on the move from team to team. But it also

helped enhance his reputation as one of the most fearsome sluggers of his day.

DAVID "BUDDY" BELL

Third Baseman, Cle (A) 1972–78, Tex (A) 1979–85, 1989 Cin (N) 1986–87, Hou (N) 1988
Buddy never made it to a World Series or even to the playoffs, so he never got much national publicity. But he was among the top four defensive third basemen, according to Palmer's linear weights. His hard-nosed, give-all-for-the-team style of play made him a crowd favorite at each of his stops and won him six consecutive Gold Gloves. Bell was a sixteenth-round Cleveland draft pick as an outfielder and wasn't moved to third until his second year with the Indians.

A consistent .280-.290 hitter throughout his career, Bell's best season was 1979, his first in Texas. He played in every game, led the league in at-bats, and hit .299, with 200 hits, 42 doubles, 18 home runs, and 101 RBIs. He gave the Rangers two more .290 seasons and two .300 years before being packed off to Cincinnati, where he had his first 20-home run season. Bell left holding the Ranger records for doubles, RBIs, extra-base hits, and total bases.

Over his career, Buddy amassed more than 2,500 hits, and his 201 homers, when added to his father Gus's 206, give the Bells second place in the father-son home run derby.

JAMES "COOL PAPA" BELL

Outfielder, Negro Leagues, 1922–46; St. Louis Stars, Pittsburgh Crawfords, Detroit Wolves, Kansas City Monarchs, Chicago American Giants, Memphis Red Sox, Homestead Grays
That Bell could switch off the light and jump into bed before the room got dark, as Satchel Paige always claimed, may be a slight exaggeration. (Bell says he did it but admits that the light switch had a short in it.) But he *was* fast enough to score from second on a fly, which he did against Dizzy Dean in Yankee Stadium in 1935, and to score from first on a sacrifice, which he did against Bob Lemon in 1948, when Bell was forty-five years old. According to legend at least, Cool Papa was the fastest man in spikes.

Like Ruth, George Sisler, and Stan Musial, Bell started as a pitcher at age nineteen with the St. Louis Stars. He threw a knuckleball and won his first three games, calmly sleeping before a big game against Rube Foster's American Giants to win his nickname, "Cool Papa."

Bell, who stood over six feet, could also hit the long ball righthanded. His manager, Big Bill Gatewood, who taught Satchel Paige the hesitation pitch, converted the rookie Bell into a switch-hitting outfielder and told him to hit the ball on the ground. Infielders like Judy Johnson admit that if the ball took two hops, you might as well put it in your pocket.

Eventually Bell joined two of the most famous teams in blackball annals, the Crawfords (with Paige, Josh Gibson, Johnson, and Oscar Charleston), and the Grays (with Gibson and Buck Leonard).

Bell's lifetime batting average, though records are still incomplete, is tenth on the Negro League list. Surprisingly he is ninth among home run hitters. In games against white big leaguers Bell hit .392.

Although he never had a chance at the white majors himself, Cool Papa helped some others. He was hitting .411 in 1946, but he sat out the final doubleheader so the batting title would go to young Monte Irvin and help boost him into integrated ball. Bell also counseled Jackie Robinson to give up playing shortstop and concentrate on second, the position he settled on with the Dodgers. He said his greatest thrill was the day Jackie made good in the majors.

In 1974 Cool Papa was named to the Baseball Hall of Fame.

JOHNNY BENCH
Catcher, Cin (N) 1967–83
Bench was all but elected to Cooperstown in 1970 at the age of twenty-two when he slugged 45 home runs with 148 RBIs and was named MVP. It was a bit of an overreaction. He proved to be an outstanding player and a certain Hall of Famer during the rest of his career, but he never quite matched that 1970 season. His second best season came two years later in 1972, when he hit 40 home runs and won his second MVP.

With eleven seasons of 20-plus home runs, Bench demolished the home run record for catchers with 325 (to Yogi Berra's 313). But his batting average was unimpressive, and even his high RBI totals were dependent on the wealth of opportunities offered anyone batting mid-lineup for Cincinnati's Big Red Machine.

Johnny had a splendid Series in 1976, hitting .529 in his direct competition with Yankee Thurman Munson, the AL's top catcher. Bench's two homers and five RBIs was the *coup de grace* in Game Four of the Reds' sweep.

No one, including Bench, could live up to Bench's reputation as a catcher. In his first year, 1968, he led in both assists and passed balls. As esteem for his throwing arm grew, runners tested it less, and his caught-stealing numbers declined. Whether he was the best came second to whether everyone *thought* he was the best.

He called the pitches as Cincinnati's Big Red Machine rolled to six division titles, four NL pennants, and two World Series. But he handled only one 20-game winner, and the Reds' pitching usually had the same relationship to the team as his heel had to Achilles. In 1989, he was elected to the Hall of Fame.

ALBERT "CHIEF" BENDER
Pitcher, Phi (A) 1903–14, Bal (F) 1915, Phi (N) 1916–17, Chi (A) 1925
This half-Chippewa Indian from the White Earth reservation in Minnesota was the money pitcher on Connie Mack's champion A's of the 1905–14 era, the man Connie said he'd pick if he had one game he had to win. Connie never spoke with a forked tongue, yet oddly Bender pitched only one must-win game in his life, the final game of the 1905 World Series, and lost it 2–0. Altogether the Chief won six out of ten Series games for Philadelphia. In 1910 Eddie Plank was hurt, and Bender and Jack Coombs pitched the entire Series, winning 4–1. In 1913, when Coombs was hurt, Mack asked Bender to pitch out of turn and promised to pay the Chief's mortgage of $2,500 if he would do it. Said Connie: "I knew then the Giants were done for." Bender won both his starts.

A product of the Carlisle Indian School, Bender never

pitched in the minors and won the first big league game he pitched, a four-hitter, when he was nineteen. He was a big man (six-two), who pitched with a high kick and an overhand delivery. His out pitch, in those days before doctoring was illegal, was the "talcum ball," which he rubbed with talcum powder to make it smooth. He claimed it gave the ball a sharp drop.

Although he won 212 games in his sixteen seasons, the Chief won 20 games only twice (in 1910 and 1913). But he had some terrific ERA years. Four times he went under 2.00. Even in the dead-ball era, that wasn't chopped liver. No one sold off his Hall of Fame stock when he was elected in 1953. If he was no superstar, he was a very good pitcher with a great team—one that included Eddie Collins and Home Run Baker—behind him.

LAWRENCE "YOGI" BERRA
Catcher, NY (A) 1946–63, NY (N) 1965. Manager NY (A) 1964,1984–85, NY (N) 1972–75
Yogi just might have been the best catcher the game has ever seen. Certainly he's the most *seen* catcher, having appeared on TV in a record 14 World Series, ten of them as a member of the world champs. He holds the records for most Series games (75) and most hits (71). Yogi is also the only catcher ever to call a perfect World Series game.

After shuttling between catching and the outfield, Berra was handed the first-string catcher's job by new manager Casey Stengel in 1949, and the Yankees won the first of five straight pennants. The two facts are not a coincidence. Yogi was "the man who holds us together," Stengel said in 1955, when Yogi won his third MVP.

One of the game's great bad-ball hitters, Berra hit only .285, but Oriole manager Paul Richards called him the most dangerous hitter in baseball after the seventh inning. He totaled 358 homers, and his 313 as a catcher are more than any backstop except Bench. Yogi could field, too, once going 148 straight games and 950 chances without an error, both records for catchers. His handling of pitchers always earned good reviews, and the Yankee staff numbers indicate the kudos were deserved.

Berra's best year was 1950, when he hit .322 with 124 RBIs but saw the MVP go to teammate Phil Rizzuto. Berra did win the award in 1951, 1954, and 1955. In 1972, he was elected to the Hall of Fame.

Though an intelligent student of baseball (and an intelligent person), Berra was considered a buffoon by people who think reading the headlines on the sports page makes them experts. Yogi's favorite reading was comic books, he finished out of the money in the Mark Harmon Look-alike Contest, and his natural shyness sometimes makes him seem slow on the uptake. His malaprops have made him the most quoted person in baseball history, although it's getting harder every year to know what he said and what they *said* he said. Either way, he's moving up fast on Bill Shakespeare in Bartlett's. Some Yogi-isms: "He was a big clog in their machine." "It gets late early there [left field]." "Nobody goes there anymore, it's too crowded." "Take it with a grin of salt." Or the immortal "It's never over till it's over." When Yogi was given a benefit on his retirement, he graciously thanked "all those who made this day necessary."

Thus it came as a surprise when Berra was named to manage the Yankees in 1964. Despite injuries to Mantle,

Whitey Ford, and others, they came from six games back to win. But Yogi lost the Series to Johnny Keane's Cards, then was summarily replaced by Keane. He went cross-town to coach the Mets and managed them to a pennant in 1973. His winning percentage as a manager is an impressive .522.

MAX BISHOP
Second Baseman, Phi (A) 1924–33, Bos (A) 1934–35
Bishop was called "Camera Eye" for the way he looked over pitches. He led the AL second basemen in fielding in 1926 and 1928, but his range was only ordinary. He seldom stole a base and had little power at bat. Although he hit .316 in 1928, he was more comfortable at .270 and often a good deal lower.

What made Bishop valuable was his ability to draw walks. The Philadelphia A's of 1929–1931 had plenty of people who could hit a ton; Bishop gave them someone to drive home. Only 165 pounds, he never played in more than 130 games in a season, but in seven of the eight years when he played in at least 114 games, he walked over 100 times. From 1928 through 1931, he scored over 100 runs each season.

An extreme example of his unique talent came in 1929. He played in 129 games and made only 110 hits for a poor .232 batting average. But he walked a league-leading 128 times, nearly one a game, and scored 102 runs. His on-base percentage was .395!

BERT BLYLEVEN
Pitcher, Min (A) 1970–76, Tex (A) 1976–77, Pit (N) 1978–80, Cle (A) 1981–85, Min (A) 1985–88, Cal 1989–
One of six foreign-born pitchers to win over 200 games, handsome Bert Blyleven was born in Holland. Had he stayed there, he might have wasted his long fingers plugging dikes instead of throwing the most wicked curves since the Burma Road. Bert's roundhouse was voted best in the league by AL managers, but the hitters knew it before the ballots were passed out. He didn't get to number three on the all-time strikeout list by throwing tulips.

Blyleven is a control pitcher. When his hook isn't hooking, he spends a lot of time watching the ball sail into the seats. He surrendered an amazing 50 home runs in 1986, although pitching in the Metrodome surely had something to do with that.

He has been one of the top AL pitchers of his generation. Unfortunately he had some of his best years for teams ranging from bad to mediocre, making his more than 250 wins all the more impressive. In 1973 Bert was 20–17 for third-place Minnesota, his only 20-win season. Eleven years later, he almost made it at 19–7 for the tail-end Indians.

In one of his rare sojourns with a strong team, he was 12–5 for the 1979 Pirates and won a playoff game and a World Series tilt. His complaints the next year that he was being underused and overrelieved by manager Chuck Tanner did not endear him to Pirate fans but won him a ticket back to the American League. His subsequent record would tend to support his argument. He helped the Twins to the AL pennant in 1987 with a pair of LCS wins and added another in the World Series victory over the Cardinals.

WADE BOGGS
Third Baseman, Bos (N) 1982-
If Boggs were to be run over in an elephant stampede tomorrow, he would still be remembered as one of the best hitters of the 1980s—perhaps *the* best. Certainly his batting averages put him in the lead. As a rookie in 1982, he batted a terrific .349. It turned out to be an "off" year. Every year from 1983 to 1988, he topped .350 except for 1984, when he slumped to .325. Three times he's been over .360. All this has added up to five AL batting crowns in his first seven seasons. He is probably the only player in baseball who could lead his league in hitting and see his career average go *down*.

Criticized for shoddy defense when he first arrived in Boston, he's worked hard to improve that. He also showed surprising power in 1987, when he hit 24 home runs. Nevertheless his job in the Red Sox scheme is to get on base and be driven in. He's done that so well that for seven straight seasons (1983–89) he scored 100 or more runs.

According to published reports, Boggs eats chicken before every game as a sort of charm. Perhaps it wards off krypton.

BOBBY BONDS
Outfield, SF (N) 1968–74, NY (A) 1975, Cal (A) 1976–77, Chi (A) 1978, Tex (A) 1978, Cle (A) 1979, StL (N) 1980, Chi (N) 1981
Bonds combined power and speed like no player before him. In 1969 he became only the fourth player to hit 30 home runs and steal 30 bases in a season, and then he went on to repeat that feat four more times, to take permanent possession. He was also the first man to 30–30 in both leagues.

Bobby stole 461 bases and hit 332 homers, 35 of them as leadoff man, 11 of those in one season, both records at the time. He is one of two men to hit a grand slam in his first big league game, and the first to do it since 1898.

Twice he led the league in runs scored and once in total bases, but where he was a real pacesetter was in strikeouts. That was Bonds' weakness. He set the major league record when he whiffed 187 times in 1979 and then broke it with 189 in 1970. He averaged one K in every four at-bats and ranks number six on the all-time strikeout list.

After seven seasons with the Giants, Bonds became a nomad, spending the next seven years with seven teams, all of them looking for his instant offense. In 1979, at age thirty-three, he hit 25 home runs and stole 34 bases for Cleveland, missing a sixth 30–30 season.

His son Barry has hit 117 home runs in his first five seasons in Pittsburgh, putting the Bondses at the top of the all-time father-son home run championship.

BOB BOONE
Catcher, Phi (A) 1972–81, Cal (A) 1982-88, KC 1989-
Boone has caught more games than any other man in big league history, passing Hall of Famer Al Lopez (1,918 games) in 1987.

As a defensive catcher, Boone has been one of the best. He led league catchers in assists in 1973 and 1984. His 89 assists in 1973 were the most for a rookie since Johnny Bench had 108 in 1968. With California from 1982 to 1988, he threw out better than 45 percent of runners attempting to steal, including 58 percent in his first yea꘠ with the Angels. He won his first Gold Glove in 1978 with a .991 fielding average, breaking Bench's ten-year streak. Since then he's earned four more.

Boone's record as a handler of pitchers has been a mixed bag. The ERAs of both the Phillies and Angels went up after he joined them, and when he left the Phils, the club ERA went down. Nevertheless on his arrival in California, the Angels immediately rose from fifth to first. In all, he's guided his staffs to six division flags. And although Tim McCarver was Steve Carlton's personal catcher in Philadelphia in the late 1970s, Steve's wins went up from 18 to 24 when Boone took over in 1980.

Not much of a hitter during the regular season, Boone has had a splendid postseason record at bat—.311, including .400 for the Phils in the 1977 LCS and .455 for the Angels in the 1986 championship series. He appeared in one World Series, with Philadelphia in 1980, and batted .412.

Bob and father Ray, a longtime infielder for Cleveland and Detroit, are the second father and son after the Bells to each have 100 career home runs.

"SUNNY JIM" BOTTOMLEY
First Baseman, StL (N) 1922–32, Cin (N) 1933–35, StL (A) 1936–37. Manager StL (A) 1937
Swaggering, popular, his hat cocked rakishly on the side of his head, Sunny Jim is in the record books for batting in 12 runs in one game. He did it in 1924 on two homers, a double, and three singles. That game, more than his career record, got him elected to the Hall of Fame in 1974.

In his sixteen major league seasons, Bottomley batted .300 eight times and batted in 100 or more runs six years in a row. Certainly not a wimp record but less impressive than it would be if it had occurred at any time in history other than the hit-happy 1920s and 1930s. In those days .300 hitters were as common as hip flasks at a hop. Bottomley was not particularly adept defensively, leading NL first basemen in errors four times.

Jim helped the Cardinals win four flags, in 1926, 1928, 1930, and 1931. He was named MVP in 1928 after leading the league in RBIs and triples and tying for homers with Hack Wilson.

In 1931 Jim figured in the closest batting race in history. Though injured, he hit .3482, losing to Bill Terry with .3486, and to his own roommate, Chick Hafey, who had .3489. If batting averages had been adjusted according to difficulty of the home ballpark, the Giants' Terry, playing in the cavernous Polo Grounds, would have won fair and square.

LOU BOUDREAU
Shortstop, Cle (A) 1938–50, Bos (A) 1951–52. Manager, Cle (A) 1942–50, Bos (A) 1952–54, KC (A) 1955–57, Chi (N) 1960
Boudreau got a lot of ink by pulling the "Boudreau Shift" against Ted Williams in 1946, bunching six of his Cleveland players on the right side of second base and daring Williams to take a shot. Actually Boudreau's manager Roger Peckinpaugh had first used the shift against Ted in 1941. But the maneuver earned Lou a reputation as a creative strategist, a fame unsupported by his record, which, except for one unforgettable year, was a losing one.

Lou Boudreau's greatest asset as a manager was that he could write the name *Lou Boudreau* in at shortstop every day. His hitting and his fielding combined to make him one of the half dozen best shortstops in this century.

A fine fielder, he led AL shortstops in fielding average a record-tying eight times, in double plays five times, and in putouts four. His 134 double plays in 1943 was a record, as was his .982 fielding average in 1947. His arm was only so-so, and others had more flat-out range, but Boudreau's knowledge of hitters allowed him to compensate by positioning himself where the action was.

In 1942, at the age of twenty-four, Lou applied for the Cleveland manager's job and got it, becoming the youngest man to manage a full season. The Indians finished fourth, the same spot they had held under Peckinpaugh. The Tribe moved up to third in 1943, then slipped to fifth in 1944, although Boudreau won the batting title with .327.

By 1947, when the Indians finished a ho-hum fourth, new owner Bill Veeck tried to trade Boudreau to the St. Louis Browns, a fate considered only slightly more humane than the guillotine. Angry Cleveland fans cast a newspaper vote 90 percent in favor of keeping Lou and trading Veeck. The owner decided to stick with Lou for one more year.

What a year! "Lou was determined to prove I was a jerk," Bill wrote. "And he did." In that magical 1948 Boudreau had the kind of season Frank Merriwell used to dream about. He hit .355, with 18 homers and 106 RBIs. He was always—or seemed always —to be at the center of a rally. One day he sat out with a slight injury, then came off the bench to pinch-hit for a win. More, he inspired his team; several players had career years. A furious four-way pennant race ended with the Indians and Red Sox tied. In the playoff at Boston, Boudreau daringly named a rookie lefty, Gene Bearden, to start. He himself smacked two home runs to destroy the Sox 8–3. The Indians then bested the Braves in the Series. Lou was AL MVP with more than 100 votes to spare.

Everything after that was an anticlimax. Lou managed four teams, finishing between third and eighth, before becoming a broadcaster for the Cubs and the father-in-law of Denny McLain.

In 1970 he was elected to the Hall of Fame.

KEN BOYER
Third Baseman, StL (N) 1955–65, NY (N) 1966–67, Chi (A) 1967–68, LA (N) 1968–69. Manager, StL 1978–80
The best of six brothers who all played professional ball, Ken was a third baseman in the Brooks Robinson mold, diving into the hole to snare hard grounders or running them down backhand behind the bag. Pie Traynor called him the best he ever saw.

Five times Ken led NL third basemen in double plays. Six times he won Gold Gloves. He even played center field one season, 1957, and led all NL outfielders in fielding average. His kid brother Clete, a Yankees' third baseman, was perhaps even better afield, but lacked Ken's bat. Ken hit over .300 five times and drove in 90 runs or better seven years in a row.

He sparked the Cards to the flag in 1964, hitting .295 with 24 home runs and a league-leading 119 RBIs, and won the MVP. It was to be his last big season before a bad back slowed him down.

In the Series that year Ken beat Clete's Yanks in Game Four with a grand slam to even the Series. Then he helped win the seventh with a homer and three runs scored. It was the only time brothers hit homers in the same Series game.

HARRY BRECHEEN
Pitcher, StL (N) 1940–52, StL (A) 1953
Brecheen was the Cardinal pitcher in 1946 when Enos Slaughter raced home from first to beat the Red Sox in the seventh game of the World Series. It gave Harry his third win of the Series, making him the first man to notch three since Stan Coveleski twenty-six years earlier and the only lefthander until Mickey Lolich twenty-two years later. The moment was a teensy tainted: pitching in relief, Brecheen had just allowed two inherited runners to score, blowing the lead he'd been sent in to hold. He nailed the win by shutting out the Sox in the ninth.

Two years later, 1948, Brecheen posted a 20–7 mark and the NL's lowest ERA. He won 14 games or better six years in a row for the Cardinals and pitched in three World Series, winning four and losing one. After eleven seasons with the proud Cardinals, he moved over to the humble Browns and discovered where their humility came from. He went 5–13 despite a decent 3.07 ERA. The next year the Browns moved to Baltimore and Harry became the pitching coach.

Nicknamed "the Cat" for the way he would pounce off the mound to field his position, Harry's World Series ERA of 0.83 is the second-best ever.

ROGER BRESNAHAN
Catcher, Was (N) 1897, Chi (N) 1900, Bal (A) 1901–02, NY (N) 1902–08, StL (N) 1909–12, Chi (N) 1913–15.
Manager, StL (N) 1090–12, Chi (N) 1915
Bresnahan is best known as the man who introduced shin guards for catchers in 1907, though some insist they had been worn earlier by black infielders. Some white catchers also reportedly wore protection under their socks. But Roger was the first white big leaguer to wear them openly, which brought jeering from fans and other players. He is said to have borrowed the idea from cricket. He also pioneered a crude leather batting helmet as early as 1908, after nearly being killed by a beaning.

Bresnahan caught Christy Mathewson and Joe McGinnity for the Giants. He, McGinnity, and manager John McGraw had arrived from Baltimore, picked up a last-place club, made a 32-game winner out of McGinnity and a 29-game winner out of Matty, and raised the team to second in 1903 and first in 1904 and 1905. In 1905 Roger achieved a feat that may never be duplicated—he caught four World Series shutouts, three of them by Matty. He also batted .313.

At bat, Bresnahan favored the thick-handled bats popular then. His best season was 1903, when he batted .350 with 42 extra-base hits and 34 stolen bases. He was unusually fast for a catcher, enough to bat first or second in the lineup. He had started out as a pitcher and then played center field, not becoming a regular catcher until 1905. He was a natural leader and, like his boss, McGraw, a fiery umpire baiter with frequent suspensions.

In 1945 Bresnahan became the first catcher elected to Cooperstown, two years ahead of Mickey Cochrane, who was a much better hitter and arguably better defensively and as a handler of pitchers.

Roger said he was born in Tralee, Ireland, so he was nicknamed "The Duke of Tralee." Actually, he was born (and died) in Toledo, Ohio.

GEORGE BRETT
Third Baseman/First Baseman KC (A) 1973-
A curly-haired heart throb, Brett was the jewel in batting coach Charlie Lau's crown. He'd never gotten to .300 in the minor leagues, yet hitting off his front foot with the distinctive one-hand followthrough Lau taught, the left-handed hitter went on to win three American League batting titles, the last one in 1990 to become the first to win batting crowns in three decades.

His .390 in 1980 came within a point of John Mc-Graw's 1899 mark for highest batting average by a third baseman and was the closest assault on .400 since Ted Williams's .406 in 1941. Also in 1980, Brett knocked in 118 runs in 117 games to become the first player since Joe DiMaggio in 1948 to drive in over one run per game played.

Three times (in 1975, 1976, and 1979) George has led the AL in both hits and triples during the same season, a feat matched only by Ty Cobb. In 1979 he became one of only five players to slug 20 doubles, triples, and home runs in the same season.

Brett has thrived in postseason play, leading Kansas City to the playoffs six times, 1976–1985, and hitting .349 in playoff and Series competition. His nine homers—three in one 1976 game—are a record in the playoffs. One of his homers, a three-run shot off the Yanks' Goose Gossage, won the 1980 playoff, ending three years of consecutive playoff losses to New York.

Ironically George may be remembered longest for one at-bat at Yankee Stadium in 1985 and the homer he did-didn't-did hit. In the ninth inning, Brett put the ball in the stands to give Kansas City the lead. But Yankee manager Billy Martin convinced the umpire to take a homer away from him because there was too much pine tar on the bat handle. The usually calm Brett blew up like the Hindenburg. His frenzied, screaming protest is still among the most popular and amusing TV replays. A couple of days later, AL President Lee McPhail overruled his umpires and restored the homer on the grounds that they should have called the bat for excess pine tar *before* Brett batted.

TOMMY BRIDGES
Pitcher, Det (A) 1930–46
In his first major league appearance, Bridges entered the game in relief against the Yankees, got Babe Ruth to ground out, and struck out Lou Gehrig. He went on from there to carve out an outstanding career with the Tigers. The slightly built righthander's trademark was a hard-breaking, heart-breaking curve that skittered sharply down and away. It helped make him one of the top AL pitchers of the 1930s, a milieu that included Lefty Grove, Ted Lyons, Red Ruffing, and Lefty Gomez—Hall of Famers all.

Tommy won 20 games three years in a row, 1934–1936, and helped pitch the Tigers to pennants in the first two. He also led the league in strikeouts in 1935 and 1936. But Bridges was also prone to control problems; he wal___ over 100 batters six times and averaged 3.79 walks per nine innings pitched. Nevertheless his career ERA of 3.57 wasn't bad at all in an era when the league averaged well above four. Bridges missed perfect-game immortality in 1932, when he gave up a single to pinch hitter Dave Harris (.327) with two out in the ninth.

He pitched in four World Series, winning four games and losing one. The win they all remember came in the 1935 Series, when, leading 4-3 in the ninth inning of Game Six, he gave up a leadoff triple to Stan Hack of the Cubs. Tom slammed the door with a strikeout, a grounder, and a fly to make the Tigers champs.

LOU BROCK
Outfielder, Chi (N) 1961-64, StL (N) 1964-79
According to traditionalists, the trade that sent Brock from the Cubs to the Cardinals in 1964 for pitcher Ernie Broglio was the greatest steal since Brinks. "Steal," of course, is a significant word when discussing Brock—he once held the season record for stolen bases with his 118 in 1974. Actually the Cards also got a couple of guys named Jack Spring and Paul Toth, and the Cubs received Bobby Shantz and Doug Clemens, but Shantz was near the end of the line and the others never had one to begin with. So when Broglio won only seven games for Chicago in three years before disappearing into a trivia question and Brock played in the Cardinal outfield for sixteen years, made over 3,000 hits, and led the Cards to three pennants, the deal looked pretty darn good for the Redbirds.

But wait! According to some revisionist statisticians, Brock wasn't the bargain he was cracked up to be. They point out that Lou didn't walk enough for a leadoff man, so that his 3,023 career hits and .293 batting average become only a .341 on-base percentage. They also murmur seductively that he struck out way too often—1,730 times. And even though Brock finished up as the all-time base-stealing champ with 938 and led the NL eight times, revisionists ho-hum. They weigh the rally-killing effect of a caught-stealing against the marginal value of a successful theft, and downgrade the whole maneuver as something that just keeps 'em happy in the cheap seats. Finally revisionists point out that Brock was barely adequate in left field and had an arm you could stuff in a Christmas stocking.

Against all that evidence, the traditionalists can only mumble that Lou led the league in runs scored twice and wound up with 1,610. That he hit 149 homers and batted in 900, both above par for leadoff batters. That he hit .300 in one World Series, .400-plus in two, and twice stole seven bases in a Series, for an all-time record of fourteen. He also scored sixteen runs in twenty-one Series games and knocked in thirteen. And, the traditionalists quibble, for all those seasons he played in St. Louis, opponents *thought* he was doing things that beat them and had the losses to show for it.

In 1985, the first chance they got, the baseball writers elected Brock to the Hall of Fame. Shows whose side they're on.

DENNIS "DAN" BROUTHERS
First Baseman, Troy (N) 1879-80, Buf (N) 1881-85, Det (N) 1886-88, Bos (N) 1889, Bos (P) 1890, Bos (AA)
1891, Bkn (N) 1892-93, Bal (N) 1894-95, Lou (N) 1895, Phi (N) 1896
Brouthers (pronounced "Broothers") was the Mickey Mantle of the 1880s. He hit only 106 home runs—no one hit many in those days—but many of Dan's were tape-measure blows. In 1886 one knocked the fans out of a tower *behind* the park in Boston. He led the National League in home runs twice (1881 and 1886), not counting a career-high 14 in 1884.

A big man for his era (six-two, 220 pounds), Brouthers possessed a great batting eye and rarely struck out. He is said to have originated the phrase "Keep your eye on the ball." And that he did. His lifetime batting average of .342 is ninth-best all-time. He was the first man to win back-to-back batting titles, in 1882 and 1883; he won five overall. He drove in 100 or more runs five times and led in slugging average six straight seasons (1881–1886); his .519 lifetime slugging average was by far the best in the nineteenth century.

With Buffalo in the early 1880s, Brouthers played lead assassin in baseball's first Murderers' Row: "the Big Four" that also included Hardy Richardson, Jack Rowe, and Deacon White. All four were sold to Detroit after the 1885 season for a then princely $7,500. They won the pennant in 1887 and beat American Association champ St. Louis in a challenge Series, ten games to five. "We slugged 'em to death," Dan said.

Dan moved up to Boston in 1889, where he played in three leagues in three years. His Players League and AA teams won pennants. Finally, at Baltimore in 1894 he teamed with John McGraw to help the Orioles win their first flag.

Brouthers ended as a night watchman at the Polo Grounds. He died in 1932 and was inducted into the Hall of Fame in 1945.

MORDECAI "THREE FINGER" BROWN
Pitcher, StL (N) 1903, Chi (N) 1904-12, 1916, Cin (N) 1913, StL (F) 1914, Bkn (F) 1914, Chi (F) 1915.
Manager StL (F) 1914
When Brown was seven, he stuck his right hand in his uncle's corn shredder, cutting off the top two joints of his index finger and paralyzing his little finger. The accident probably put him in the Hall of Fame. The damaged fingers gave Mordecai a natural knuckler, and he used it to star for the Cubs in their great years, 1905–1910. The shredder became a tourist attraction.

His biggest win was one of the most famous games ever played, the 1908 makeup of the Cubs-Giants game suspended when Fred Merkle failed to touch second base. Merkle's "boner" nullified a Giant win and left the teams tied at season's end. The makeup game was in New York in a park loaded with partisan fans, who thought they had been cheated out of victory. Brown and other Cubs received fistfuls of "black hand letters"—death threats—before they took the field. When Chicago starter Jack Pfeister got in trouble in the first inning, manager Frank Chance quickly called in Brown, who walked to the mound amid savage catcalls while a policeman stood guard. Brown was 29-9 in 1908 with a 1.47 ERA, while his mound opponent, Christy Mathewson, was 37-11, 1.43, but Brown had the edge that day, winning 4-2.

It was one of nine straight victories Mordecai scored

over Matty going back to 1905. Their lifetime record versus each other: 13–11, Brown.

From 1904 through 1910, Brown had ERAs of 1.87, 2.17, 1.04, 1.39, 1.47, 1.31, and 1.86. That 1.04 is the record and the only time he led the NL. Low ERAs were the norm during those dead-ball days, but such consistency was scary. Speaking of consistency, he won 20 or more for six straight seasons from 1906 through 1911. Brown totaled a tidy 239 career wins, with a .648 winning percentage. In addition, he recorded 49 saves. By the modern definition of saves, he led the league four years in a row, topped by 13 in 1910. Of course, he had a first-rate team — the Tinker-to-Evers-to-Chance Cubs—playing behind him. Or maybe they had a great pitcher out front. He three-fingered Chicago to pennants in 1906, 1907, 1908, and 1910, and then took the Chicago Feds to the flag in 1915 with 17–8, 2.10.

LOUIS "PETE" BROWNING
Outfielder, Lou (AA) 1882–89, Cle (P) 1890, Pit (N) 1891, Cin (N) 1891–92, Lou (N) 1892–93, StL (N) 1894, Bkn (N) 1894
The original Louisville Slugger, Browning hit a career .341 back in the 1880s, mostly for Louisville of the AA. Pete, who lived and died in the city by the Ohio River, was the first man to have his bats made to order for him, by John Hillerich, who went on to found the famous bat-making firm.

Although he led the American Association in batting twice and the Players League once, Pete's best year was 1887, when he finished second. He hit .471 under that year's rule which counted walks as hits. With the walks factored out, he dropped to "only" .402. His worst year was .256 in 1889. He blamed it on too much "German tea," swore off the stuff, and hit .373 the next season.

A pure hitter, Browning was pollution in the field with a lifetime .882 fielding average.

MORGAN G. BULKELEY
Executive
Ever since Bulkeley was elected to the Hall of Fame in 1937, Cooperstown apologists have been hard-pressed to explain the error. They point out that old Bulks was a successful businessman and banker, head of Aetna Life Insurance for years, governor of Connecticut (1889–1893), U.S. senator (1905–1911), and a distinguished citizen of many public and personal virtues all his long life—all of which should get him into the Hall of Fame about as much as wearing a tutu should get you into the Marines.

As to what he did for baseball: well, he was president of the Hartford Dark Blues baseball club in 1874–1875. Remember them? Then, because they needed a figurehead, he let them make him President of the brand-new National League in 1876. He doesn't seem to have done anything during his year in office, but that's pretty much what the real power in the league—founder William Hulbert—wanted. When he didn't show up at the 1877 meeting, the club presidents elected Hulbert president since he'd been doing Bulkeley's job anyway. About thirty years later, Bulkeley's name was on the report of the committee that decided Abner Doubleday invented baseball, but Bulkeley doesn't appear to have been any more active in

that than he'd been as NL prexy. At least *that's* in his favor. We are also told that he remained "close" to the game all his life. Define "close."

In point of fact, Bulkeley was a fine person who got into the Hall of Fame because the selectors of 1937 didn't know beans about baseball's history and figured the first NL president *must* have been a pioneer. They were wrong.

JIM BUNNING
Pitcher, Det (A) 1955–63, Phi (N) 1964–67, 1970–71, Pit (N) 1968–69, LA (N) 1969
Bunning not only won 100 games in each league, he pitched a no-hitter in each. His NL effort was a perfect game, one of only thirteen in the history of the game, thrown against the last-place Mets on Father's Day in 1964. Jim won 20 only once, 20–8 with the fourth-place Tigers in 1957, but he won 19 in 1962 for the Tigers and three straight times for the Phillies (1964–66).

At six-three, Bunning was an intimidating power pitcher. He led the AL twice in strikeouts and the NL once. When he retired, he had 2,855 strikeouts, then second only to Walter Johnson.

With a degree in economics and nine children to support, Jim went into Republican politics in his home state of Kentucky when he left baseball. He lost a bid to become governor, but later won a seat in the U.S. Congress.

SELVA "LEW" BURDETTE
Pitcher, NY (A) 1950, Bos (N) 1951–52, Mil (N) 1953–63, StL (N) 1963–64, Chi (N) 1964–65, Phi (N) 1965, Cal (N) 1966–67
Burdette was born in Nitro, West Virginia, and media types liked to refer to him as "Nitro Lew" during his career because it gave their accounts an excitingly explosive ambience. Burdette's temper could go off occasionally. And his curve—especially his wet curve—could drop like a bomb. But his career was anything but rocketlike.

He was twenty-seven before he became a journeyman starter with the Braves in 1953, playing a righthanded second banana to Warren Spahn's lefthanded lead. He was thirty when he became a very good pitcher in 1956, winning 19 and leading the NL in ERA. He was nearing thirty-two the next year when, after 17 regular-season wins, he became a great pitcher in the World Series. In that fall of 1957, he defeated the Yankees three times, throwing three complete-game seven-hitters. Two of them —including the seventh game—were shutouts. His Series ERA was 0.67.

Having hit his peak, he stayed for a while, winning 60 games in the next three seasons, including a 1–0 no-hit win in 1960. Then came a slow decline into spot starter and reliever, until he closed up shop with 203 career victories in 1967. The media types missed the proper metaphor. Nitro is in coal country, and West Virginia coal burns slow but gives off excellent heat.

JESSE BURKETT
Outfield, NY (N) 1890, Cle (N) 1891–98, StL (N) 1899–1901, StL (A) 1902–04, Bos (A) 1905
Burkett was known as the "Crab." He was argumentative, surly, and unpopular with both opponents and teammates. He once punched a rival manager in the nose and another

time left a game under police guard for fomenting a riot. When he wasn't fighting, he was complaining. He griped *almost* as often as he cracked out base hits.

Burkett hit .400 twice. He hit .409 in 1895, and .410 in 1896. Those two marks led the NL, but his 1899 .396 left him second to Big Ed Delahanty's .410. How he must have grumbled about that! Two years later, the Crab got his third NL batting title with a solid .376. Those were hitters' years. The pitcher's mound had been moved back to its present position of sixty feet, six inches from home plate in 1894, and the batters were able to tee off on those longer throws. It would take several years for the pitchers to catch up.

But Jesse would have hit, anyway. With the kind of speed that enabled him to steal 389 bases in his career and beat out many infield hits, Jesse boasted he could *bunt* .300. He bunted so well, in fact, that he could foul off third strikes indefinitely. His prowess inspired the creation of the present rule calling a bunted foul with two strikes an out.

Jesse started out as a pitcher for the Giants, but promptly proved a much better hitter and was moved to the outfield by the Cleveland Spiders. But he never seemed to get the hang of the outfield and, also hampered by the small gloves of the day, was perennially among the league leaders in errors. His .338 lifetime batting average made up for his bobbles and made his personality almost tolerable.

ROY CAMPANELLA
Catcher, Negro Leagues, 1937–45, Baltimore Elite Giants, Bkn (N) 1948–57
For a decade with the Brooklyn Dodgers (1948–1957), Campanella was one of the two best catchers in baseball. His only serious rival was the Yankees' Yogi Berra. The Dodgers and Yankees dominated their leagues during that period, and each catcher received three MVP awards. An auto accident in 1958 left Campy substantially paralyzed and ended his career. In 1969 he was elected to the Hall of Fame.

The squat, powerful Campanella began playing in the Negro Leagues with the Baltimore Elite Giants while still a teenager. He played in All-Star Games in 1941, 1944, and 1945. He was the second black player (after Jackie Robinson) signed by the Dodgers, and he joined Nashua in the Brooklyn farm system in 1946.

In 1948, a month into the season, he was called up to the Dodgers and quickly established himself as the NL's top catcher. Campanella was excellent defensively, an acknowledged master in handling pitchers, and durable. His rookie year was the only one of his ten in the majors in which he didn't catch in over 100 games.

Campy's Dodgers won NL pennants in 1949, 1952, 1953, 1955 and 1956. The 1955 crew defeated the Yankees in the World Series to become the first Brooklyn world champs in this century. Although he was always steady as Gibraltar behind the plate, Campanella's hitting fluctuated wildly. But in his best seasons he was a terror. In 1951 he hit .325 with 33 home runs and 108 RBIs to win his first MVP Award. Two years later, in 1953, he won his second MVP with .312, 41 homers, and a league-leading 142 RBIs. At the time, both the home run and RBI marks were records for catchers. He slipped to

his poorest season in 1954, batting only .207. But in the championship year of 1955 he bounced back with .318, 32, and 107 to gain his third MVP. His career totals were .276, 242, 856, with the home run total being the most ever hit by a catcher up to that time.

Campanella's autobiography, *It's Good to Be Alive*, told the story of his courageous struggle to overcome the effects of his auto accident. It was later made into a movie for television.

ROD CAREW
Second Baseman/First Baseman, Min (A) 1967–78, Cal (A) 1979–85
Only Ty Cobb won more batting championships than Carew, the moody Panamanian who sprayed 3,053 hits where they ain't. He won seven AL titles for Minnesota, including four in a row from 1972 through 1975. In 1969, when Rod won his first batting crown with .332, he stole home 7 times, tying a mark set by Brooklyn's Pete Reiser. In 1972 Rod hit a league-leading .318 without a single homer, the only batting champ ever to do that. Fifteen of his hits were bunts. Carew's high mark was .388 in 1977, like Ted Williams' mark of 1957 the second highest batting average in the majors since 1941. That year he also led in runs scored (128) and triples (16). He was named MVP.

Carew spent his last seven years with the Angels in a poor park for hitters. Although he won no more batting championships in California, he was over .300 in his first five seasons there. He retired with a .328 career average.

The main raps against Carew related to his defense. He played second base through 1975, but critics carped that his arm was too weak for the job. Shifted to first base for his remaining ten seasons, he caught flack as a single-hitter in a power position.

MAX CAREY
Outfielder, Pit (N) 1910–26, Bkn (N) 1926–29.
Manager, Bkn (N) 1932–33
Pittsburgh's Max Carey was probably the best center fielder National League batters ever cursed. The only thing that covered more grass at Forbes Field was smoke from the steel mills. In Palmer's Linear Weights, only Tris Speaker ranks with Max as an outfield bandit.

Born Maximillian Carnerius, the former divinity student led the league in putouts nine times and retired with an NL record of 6,363, a mark later broken by Willie Mays in a longer career. Carey's 339 assists are still the twentieth-century NL record.

A good-but-not-great hitter, Carey averaged .285 and led the league twice in triples, more on speed than power. He was a great baserunner—fifth on the all-time stolen base list with 738. He led the league in thefts ten times, and once, in 1922, he stole 51 bases in 53 attempts.

In 1925, his final full year with Pittsburgh, at age thirty-five, he stole second, third, and home in the same inning on two different days in August. Playing in the World Series that year with a broken rib, he batted .458, stole three bases, and in the seventh game clipped Walter Johnson for four hits and scored three times to help win the world championship 9–7.

In 1961 Carey was elected to the Hall of Fame.

STEVE CARLTON

Pitcher, StL (N) 1965–71, Phi (N) 1972–86, SF (N) 1986, Chi (A) 1986, Cle (A) 1987, Min (A) 1987–88

For most of his career Carlton answered a short "——" to questions from the press and refused to grant interviews. He let his pitching do his talking, but as a consequence his training methods remained a mystery. One report had him preparing for a game with meditation while floating weightless in total darkness. However he prepared, it worked.

With Spahn and Koufax, Carlton was one of the three best NL lefthanders of all time. He won 329 games, second only to Spahn among lefties. He had 4,131 strikeouts—19 in one game – more than anyone except Nolan Ryan. (He's also second to Ryan in walks with 1,828.) He won four Cy Youngs, one of them unanimous.

He's the only man to win a Cy Young with a last-place team. That was in 1972, after he'd been swapped from the Cardinals. Steve was an amazing 27–10 with the Phils, who won only 32 without him that year. He was Triple Crown winner—wins, ERA, and strikeouts (27, 1.97, 310). It earned him a record salary from the Phillies the following year—$167,000, a figure that is laughable today. Carlton took special delight during 1972 in whipping his old team, the Cards, who had refused to give him a raise after his 20–9 season helped them take second place in 1971. He beat the Birds four times, allowing a total of only two runs. One of the wins was his 100th. He also got his 300th victory, over St. Louis Cardinals.

Steve had four more 20-win seasons as the Phillies moved from being "phutile" in the early 1970s to contenders, finally becoming world champions in 1980. He won two games in the 1980 World Series, including the Game Six clincher.

Using a fastball, curve, and legendary slider, the six-four lefty was a workhorse, leading the NL in innings pitched five times. When he suffered a strained shoulder in 1985, he went on the disabled list for the first time in his career.

GARY CARTER

Catcher, Mon (N) 1974–84, NY (N) 1985-89, SF 1990–

Although cynics admit Carter ranks as the top catcher of the 1980s, they criticize his personality. After all, the guy is friendly, open, cooperative, thoughtful, enthusiastic, and has never been involved in a scandal. *What's he hiding*?

Granting for the moment that he just might be what he seems as a person, the next question might be: is he what he seems to be as a catcher? Long regarded as the best-throwing backstop in the NL, he has slipped a bit in the past few years. He makes up for his aging arm in part with good footwork and a quick release. He is widely admired as a handler of pitchers, but since coming to the Mets in 1985 he's had more to work with than most NL catchers. He is given much of the credit for the development of young Dwight Gooden into a star. In summary, for all his virtues behind the plate, Carter would not be a virtual shoo-in for the Hall of Fame were it not for his bat.

His career batting average is in the middling range, but his power stats are excellent: more than 300 career home runs, with a high of 32 in 1985; four seasons with over 100 RBIs, including a league-leading 106 in 1984.

In the strike-shortened 1981 season, Gary hit only .251 for the Expos but slugged .421 in the divisional series to help get them into the playoff and .438 there, as they lost to the Dodgers. In the 1986 World Series he hit two key home runs in the third-game win and ignited the tenth-inning rally in Game Six that culminated in Bill Buckner's fatal error.

ALEXANDER JOY CARTWRIGHT

Founder

The first man to formulate baseball's rules, Cartwright may have "invented" baseball in 1845 when he organized the New York Knickerbockers, who played their first match game in Hoboken, New Jersey, on the nineteenth day of June in the following year (and lost 23–1).

The Knicks were a company of volunteer firemen, and Cartwright a bank teller, when the historic marriage was made. It was a game for gentlemen, and Cartwright once fined a Knick sixpence for swearing. The rules for the "New York Game" included three strikes per out, and three outs per inning. But balls hit over the fence were fouls, a ball caught on one bounce was an out, and the first team to score 21 runs ("aces") was declared the winner. A committee later provided formally for nine-men teams, for nine innings to the game, and for ninety feet between bases.

Then he went west to California where he found the '49ers in the big Gold Rush, spreading his new game, like Johnny Appleseed, at every village he stopped, and carrying with him the ball of that historic first game. He eventually reached Honolulu, where he found business success and became a respected civic leader. He died in 1892, but the publicity surrounding the Abner Doubleday legend with the foundation of the Hall of Fame at Cooperstown led to an investigation of Cartwright's role in the origin of the game. He was enshrined in the Hall in 1938.

BOB CARUTHERS

Pitcher, StL (AA) 1884–87, Bkn (AA) 1888–89, 1890–91, StL (N) 1892

Twice a 40-game winner, 138-pound Bob Caruthers retired with a 218–99 record for an amazing .688 percentage, the highest of any pitcher with a significant number of decisions. In a nine-year career Caruthers pitched for five championship teams and one runner-up. His only losing team was sixth place Brooklyn in 1891, but he was still 18–14.

As a twenty-one-year old rookie with the old St Louis Browns, Bob led the American Association in wins, percentage, and ERA (40–13, .755, 2.07). The next year he was 30–14. In the postseason series against Cap Anson's NL White Stockings, he won a one-hit shutout over Jim McCormick. When he tried to come back the next day, he was blasted for twelve hits. But he won the sixth and final game, 4–3, over Hall of Famer John Clarkson in ten innings. Parisian Bob—so named for his off-season trip to France— was 29–9 in 1887, as the Browns won their third straight flag.

After a 29–15 season with second-place Brooklyn, he had his best year in 1889, 40–11, as the Brooks won the AA pennant.

As the rules governing pitching tightened and the number of balls needed for a base on balls fell, Caruthers's walks increased. His wins dropped to 23, then 18. After starting 1892 at 2–10 for St. Louis, he called it a career.

NORM CASH
First Baseman, Chi (A) 1958–59, Det (A) 1960–74
Cash hit .300 only once, and it was a big one—.361 in 1961, his second year as the Tigers' first baseman. He also slugged 41 HRs and knocked in 132.

The next year Norm fell 118 points to .263, a record fall for a batting champ. He never approached 100 RBIs again or hit higher than .283, but he remained a dangerous batter. He had more RBIs per official at-bats than his roommate, Al Kaline, in part because he drew 1,043 walks. He finished with 1,046 runs scored, 1,103 RBIs, and 377 homers. Four times he cleared the roof at Tiger Stadium.

The popular and personable first sacker was somewhat immobile in the field, but he had sure hands and twice led AL first basemen in fielding. He hit .385 in the 1968 World Series to help the Tigers win in seven.

A good football player at Sul Ross State, Cash had been a thirteenth-round draft choice of the NFL Chicago Bears, but he chose to play baseball.

CESAR CEDENO
Outfielder, Hou (N) 1970–81, Cin (N) 1982–85, StL (N) 1985, LA (N) 1986
Leo Durocher once called Cedeno another Willie Mays. Then, in his third and fourth seasons, the young Dominican made the mistake of compiling back-to-back .320 years. From there on, he staggered through the remainder of his career under that back-breaking tonnage of *potential*. Cedeno might have come closer to imitating Mays if he'd played anywhere but Houston, where his long drives were outs. It didn't help that he got into only two postseason series with Houston and didn't do well in either.

For one brief period he was the player everyone predicted he'd be. In 1985 the Cardinals picked him up in late season. In 28 games, he hit .434 to help St. Louis to the division title. Again he slumped in postseason play, hitting only .167 in the LCS and .133 in the Series.

His career totals of 2,087 hits for a .285 average, 976 RBIs, and 199 home runs would look a lot better if so much hadn't been expected of him. His 550 stolen bases put him in ninth place all-time when he retired.

ORLANDO CEPEDA
First Baseman, SF (N) 1958–66, StL (N) 1966–68, Atl (N) 1969–72, Oak (A) 1972, Bos (A) 1973, KC (A) 1974
Cepeda's first big league home run was also the first major league homer ever hit on the West Coast. It came in 1958 against Los Angeles. Orlando hit 24 more to win the Rookie of the Year and helped pull the Giants from sixth to third. He was only twenty years old. His father, Perucho, a shortstop, had been hailed as the greatest player in Puerto Rico. Orlando's first seven seasons gave rise to predictions that he would become the greatest Latin player. In those seven seasons, he topped .300 six times, had at least 96 RBIs each year, and totaled 222 home runs. His 46 homers and 142 RBIs led the NL in 1961. Despite his success in San Francisco, his stay was stormy as he fought managers and fans who tagged him as lazy.

A bad knee had begun to limit his play, and surgery in 1965 cost him most of the season. The Cards took a chance on him, and he was named Comeback of the Year in 1966 with 20 homers and 73 RBIs. The next year, as the Cardinals won the pennant, he was a unanimous choice for MVP. He hit a career high .325, with 25 home runs and a league-high 111 RBIs. Cepeda hit a disappointing .103 in the World Series.

Further knee problems pulled down the rest of his career, although he showed occasional flashes of his old power. His career totals of .297, 379 homers, and 1,365 RBI put him in rarefied atmosphere. However, a post-career, ten-month prison sentence for marijuana possession has thus far weighed more heavily with Cooperstown selectors.

HENRY CHADWICK
Pioneer
Having played cricket and rounders in his native England, Chadwick came to America with his family in 1837 at age thirteen. He first played baseball in 1847 and pronounced it a descendant of the earlier English games. When nearly a decade later he first saw games between skilled players, he recognized baseball's potential to become America's national game. His writings and influence helped make that potential a fact.

In the late 1850s, he began covering baseball games as a reporter for several newspapers, most notably the *New York Clipper* and the *Brooklyn Eagle*. In connection with this, he developed the box score and devised a system of scoring that is little changed today.

Chadwick continued to write and comment on baseball for more than fifty years. He originated the first guide, *Beadle's Dime Baseball Player*, in 1860, edited *DeWitt's Guide* through the 1870s and *Spalding's Base Ball Guide* from 1881 to 1908. His *The Game of Base Ball* (1868) was the first hardcover book published on the subject.

Widely influential for his writings, he also had a direct influence in shaping the game by serving on various rules committees, beginning in 1858. He opposed gambling, drunkenness, and rowdiness among players, sometimes to no avail. Chadwick considered himself one of "the intelligent majority" who preferred scientific hitting over slugging and fielding prowess.

Among the honors he received during his lifetime were an honorary membership in the National League in 1894 (though the $600-a-year pension the league granted two years later had more practical value) and a medal awarded at the St. Louis World's Fair.

The "Father of Baseball," as he was called, died from pneumonia in 1908 after attending Opening Day in Brooklyn. Flags around the league flew at half-staff in his honor. In 1938 he was named to the Hall of Fame.

FRANK "HUSK" CHANCE
First Baseman, Chi (N) 1898–1912, NY (A) 1913–14. Manager, Chi (N) 1905–12, NY (A) 1913–14, Bos (A) 1923
Because of the popularity of F. P. Adams' poem bemoaning that his favorites, the Giants, were often victims of double plays by the Cubs' Tinker-to-Evers-to-Chance, there is a tendency to view the trio's election to Cooperstown in 1946 as some sort of P.R. fluke. In point of fact, a

strong case can be made for Tinker's and Evers's enshrinements as players. Chance, however, had too short a career as a regular to rank with the game's foremost first basemen. Nevertheless he's the most deserving Hall of Famer of the three. He was called "The Peerless Leader" for good reason.

Chance never played in the minors. He broke in as a catcher before winning the first base job in 1903. By 1904 he was captain of the team, and in 1905 at age twenty-seven he succeeded Frank Selee as manager.

As the Cubs manager he led the Chicago to glory in 1906–1910, when they won four flags in five years. They also won two World Series under Chance, which is two more than they've won since. In his first full year at the helm, the Cubbies won 116 games, a record that still stands, despite the fact that modern teams play more games. They *averaged* 106 wins in the five-year span. Of course, he had good players, but so did John McGraw in New York and Fred Clarke in Pittsburgh.

Even counting two seventh-place years with the New York Highlanders (1913–14) and one last-place finish with the Red Sox (1923), Frank's winning percentage of .593 is sixth best ever.

And he wasn't a bad first baseman, big for his day and very powerful. He played only six full years. The victim of frequent beanings, Frank played his last full season in 1908. He hit .272 and slammed three hits against Mathewson in the unforgettable playoff that gave the Cubs the flag. In the World Series victory over Detroit, he hit .421. He averaged .310 in Series play overall, and his ten Series stolen bases are topped only by Eddie Collins and Lou Brock. His career batting average was a strong .296 during the most inert days of the dead-ball era. He usually batted himself cleanup, just another indication that he knew what to do with a good player when he had one.

A. B. "HAPPY" CHANDLER
Commissioner
The popular, outgoing Kentucky U.S. senator (and former governor) was a surprise choice to become commissioner of baseball in 1945, filling the office held by Judge Kenesaw Mountain Landis until his death in 1944. Chandler was the choice of the Yankees' Leland "Larry" Mac-Phail. Other candidates had included Ford Frick, Jim Farley, J. Edgar Hoover, and Tom Dewey.

As commissioner, Chandler proved well liked by fans, press, and even most players. Undoubtedly many of his decisions worked to the benefit of baseball. His downfall was that he *made* decisions when most baseball owners would have preferred a figurehead.

Early in his tenure, he was confronted with the decision of the Dodgers' Branch Rickey to sign Jackie Robinson and other black players. Chandler was already on record as favoring black entrance to the heretofore all-white major leagues. Over the objections of the other fifteen owners, the commissioner stood behind Rickey, making baseball open to all.

Early in 1946, Chandler faced another crisis when eighteen major league players jumped to the Mexican League for promises of higher salaries. Chandler banned the players from major league baseball for five years. Many believe that this decision more than any other eventually led to his downfall as commissioner because it left

baseball's reserve clause open to the courts. The player ban was lifted in 1950, and most of the players returned to their former clubs—some, such as pitcher Sal Maglie, to outstanding success. However, a suit filed by outfielder Danny Gardella shook baseball to its foundations.

One of Chandler's more controversial decisions was a suspension handed out to popular manager Leo Durocher for the 1947 season. The action was apparently precipitated by Durocher's being seen in the company of known gamblers. Chandler was criticized at the time for not taking action against some owners, including MacPhail, who also numbered gamblers among their acquaintances. His defense was that Durocher's suspension was the culmination of a long string of controversial incidents.

In 1951 he received only nine of sixteen owner votes for his re-election. A two-thirds endorsement was necessary. Chandler resigned and returned to Kentucky, where he was again elected governor. In 1982 he was named to the Baseball Hall of Fame.

RAY CHAPMAN
Shortstop, Cle (A) 1912–20
Chapman was the only major leaguer ever killed in a game. On August 16, 1920, as his Indians fought toward their first pennant, he froze on a Carl Mays pitch. The ball fractured his skull and he died the next day. He was only twenty-nine years old.

At the time Chapman was the AL's leading shortstop. He had hit .300 in three of his last four seasons and was among the leaders each year in stolen bases. A clever hit-and-run man, he led in walks in 1918. In the field he had the best range in the league.

In the furor after his death, most "trick" pitches were banned, among them the spitball. Ironically Mays's pitch had been a fastball. More important, the leagues mandated more frequent disposal of discolored or bruised baseballs; this produced conditions that were safer for batters. This step may also have done more to usher in the prodigious batting boom of the 1920s than even the injection of rabbit hormones into the ball.

OSCAR CHARLESTON
Outfielder, Negro Leagues, 1915–50, Indianapolis ABCs, Lincoln Stars, Chicago American Giants, St. Louis Giants, Harrisburg Giants, Hilldale, Homestead Grays, Pittsburgh Crawfords, Toledo Crawfords, Indianapolis Crawfords, Philadelphia Stars, Brooklyn Brown Dodgers
Charleston is often cited as the greatest player of the Negro Leagues. Contemporaries lauded him as "the black Tris Speaker" for his center field play, "the black Ty Cobb" for his base running, and "the black Babe Ruth" for his hitting. While such analogies are useful in showing the range of Charleston's abilities, they have a counterfeit aura that is unfair to a unique performer. His combination of speed and strength places him among the foremost players, black or white, of all time. New York Giants' manager John McGraw said Charleston was the best player, period. Then he sighed: "If only I could calcimine him."

As a center fielder, Charleston was able to play unusually shallow because his great speed and judgment allowed him to get back for deep fly balls. He ranged far to his left and right, enabling the other outfielders to play closer to the foul lines. His arm has been reported as "weak", but all sources agree on its accuracy.

Charleston ran bases with speed (he was clocked at 23 seconds for the 220-yard dash) and savagery. He was quick-tempered and possessed legendary strength. Many who saw him remark on his "mean streak," indicating he preferred running over an opponent or spiking him than sliding around him to avoid a tag. On the other hand, some of the same observers indicate that Charleston picked his victims judiciously, always choosing those he knew he could physically bully.

He hit with great power and consistency. While statistics are incomplete, it is known that he batted .366 in the Negro National League in 1920 and followed that with .434 in 1921. He is unofficially credited with a lifetime league average of .353, and he batted .318 with 11 home runs in fifty-three barnstorming games against white major leaguers. He led the NNL in home runs several times, and many of his homers were of the tape-measure variety.

He started in 1915, became a player-manager in the late 1920s, and was active as a manager until his death in 1954. When Branch Rickey decided to break white baseball's color line, he had Charleston scout the Negro Leagues. Among his recommendations were Jackie Robinson and Roy Campanella.

Charleston was elected to the Hall of Fame in 1976.

JACK CHESBRO
Pitcher, Pit (N) 1899–1902, NY (A) 1903–09, Bos (A) 1909

Until Ralph Branca threw the "Shot Heard 'Round the World" to Bobby Thomson in 1951, Chesbro was notorious for tossing the most infamous pitch in history. It was probably a spitter, and it definitely sailed over the head of New York Highlander catcher Red Kleinow, and, according to baseball lore, it absolutely cost New York the 1904 pennant.

It was the final day of the season at old Hilltop Park (now the site of the New York Medical Center). The Highlanders were a game and a half behind Boston but could have won the pennant by sweeping a doubleheader against the Red Sox (then called the Puritans). Chesbro pitched the first game for New York. The score was 1–1 with two out in the Boston ninth. Boston's Lou Criger was on third and the count was 2–0. Then Chesbro threw *the pitch*. Jack, and later Mrs. Chesbro, always maintained that Kleinow should have caught the ball, but neither was a disinterested observer and there was no instant replay. New York won the second game of the doubleheader (though by then Boston couldn't have cared less).

The New York press elected Chesbro goat and never let him forget it for the rest of his life. No one ever seemed to notice that the team could have won by rallying in its half of the ninth (or by scoring two more runs in any of the earlier innings). It was like pulling teeth to get anyone in New York to admit that the Highlanders wouldn't have had a sniff at the pennant had it not been for Chesbro. He'd earlier earned the nickname "Happy Jack" for his pleasant disposition while working in the state mental hospital in Middletown, New York. To smile after that pitch no doubt required steel facial muscles.

Ironically, up to that awful pitch the stocky righthander

was enjoying one of the best seasons of any pitcher in the twentieth century: it would end up 41–12, with a 1.82 ERA. He started 51 games, completed 48, pitched 455 innings, and whiffed 239—still the Yankee record.

Chesbro won 21 and 28 with Pittsburgh in 1901–02, then jumped to New York. He won 21 in his first year there, but missed pitching in the 1903 World Series with the Pirates. He won 19 in 1905 and 23 in 1906, but people kept asking, "Yeah, but what about that pitch in 1904?"

Chesbro was named to the Hall of Fame in 1946 for what he did on all his *other* pitches.

EDDIE "KNUCKLES" CICOTTE
Pitcher, Det (A) 1905, Bos (A) 1908–12, Chi (A) 1912–20

Cicotte was a key conspirator in the infamous "Black Sox" scandal over the 1919 World Series. He tearfully confessed: "I did it for the wife and kiddies." Although neither he nor any of the other seven Soiled Sox were ever convicted of their misdeeds in a court of law—the evidence mysteriously disappeared before the trial—they were banned from baseball for life.

Until the revelations of the scandal, Cicotte was one of the AL's most successful pitchers, using trick pitches such as the knuckleball, shine ball, emery ball, and spitball. From 1908 through 1916, he won between 10 and 18 games each season. In 1917, when the Sox won the AL pennant, he was 28–12, leading the league in wins, innings pitched and ERA. After an off-year, he bounced back with his best season in 1919: he led in both wins and percentage with a 29–7 mark. In spite of Cicotte's success, White Sox owner Charles Comiskey paid him considerably less than several lesser pitchers in the league received. Apparently this left him open to entreaties by gamblers that he help throw the 1919 World Series to underdog Cincinnati.

He lost two Series games to the Reds, both under circumstances that appeared more suspicious when the fix conspiracy became public. That did not occur until near the end of the 1920 season, one in which Cicotte had a 21–10 record.

After he was barred from baseball, Cicotte lived in Detroit, using a pseudonym to protect the family for whom he claimed to have entered the conspiracy.

FRED CLARKE
Outfielder, Lou (N) 1894–99, Pit (N) 1900–1915.
Manager, Lou (N) 1897–99, Pit (N) 1900–15

Clarke was a sure-handed, speedy outfielder and an excellent hitter with surprising power for a 160-pounder. He hit .390 in 1897, topped .300 eleven times, and finished with a career .312 average. He totaled 2,672 hits, scored 1,619 runs, batted in 1,015, and stole 506 bases.

But he was an even better manager. He won four pennants at Pittsburgh and finished second five times. He came to Pittsburgh from Louisville in 1900 when the NL pared down from twelve to eight teams. Honus Wagner, Tommy Leach, Deacon Phillippe, and Claude Ritchey were among the other former Louisville players who joined the Pirates. In his first year as Pirate skipper, 1900, Fred and the other Louisville imports lifted the Pirates from seventh to the thick of the pennant fight—and they eventually finished second.

He brought the Buccos in first the next three years, 1901–1903. In 1903 he took them to the first World Series, losing to Boston only after eight hard-fought games.

In 1909 the Pirates won 110, a total exceeded only by the 1906 Cubs and 1954 Indians. In the World Series, Fred's three-run homer in the seventh inning of Game Five broke open a 3–3 tie, as Pittsburgh went on to defeat Ty Cobb's Tigers. Clarke drove in seven runs in the Series.

He was elected to the Hall of Fame in 1951.

JOHN CLARKSON
Pitcher, Wor (N) 1882, Chi (N) 1884–87, Bos (N) 1890–92, Cle (N) 1892–94
One of the greatest pitchers of the nineteenth century, Clarkson combined a curve and cunning to win 327 games, but his manager in Chicago insisted that he "pitched on praise" and needed continuous ego boosting to be effective. If scolded, the handsome, high-strung righthander would lose all confidence and sulk. The temperamental pitcher ended his years confined in an insane asylum.

Clarkson joined Chicago in 1884 and the next year led the NL in victories while compiling a 53–16 record. He won 36 in 1886 and 38 in 1887, again leading in victories in the latter year.

By the 1888 season he and outfielder/catcher King Kelly had been sold to Boston for $10,000 each, an incredible sum at that time. Clarkson justified the price by continuing his outstanding pitching, winning 33 in 1889, 49 in 1890 (when he also led the NL in winning percentage and ERA), 25 in 1891, and 33 in 1892.

In 1963 he was named to the Hall of Fame.

ROBERTO CLEMENTE
Outfielder, Pit (N) 1955–72
The first Hispanic to be elected to the Hall of Fame and the second ballplayer to be honored on a U.S. stamp, Clemente won four batting titles.

A proud, even vain, man, Clemente was sensitive to prejudice against Latin players and quick to speak out against real or imagined slights. He believed he deserved more MVP Awards than the one that he won in 1966. Whether that was true or not, Roberto was handicapped by playing his entire career in Pittsburgh instead of New York or Los Angeles. Critics also pointed out that he missed many games and labeled him a hypochondriac. Clemente's physical ills were real, the worst being a chronic bad back stemming from a 1956 auto accident. He played in over 100 games in each of his eighteen major league seasons, but the criticism remained.

Clemente finished with a .317 career batting average, an even 3,000 base hits, 1,416 runs scored, and 1,305 RBIs. Standing deep in the righthand batter's box, he put all of his body into an all-or-nothing swing, but though he cracked 240 homers, he was not really a home run hitter. His forte was the line drive, often lashing pitches to the opposite field for extra-base hits.

His arm became legendary. He set the NL record by leading in assists five times. His season high was 27 in 1961. He won 12 straight Gold Gloves.

Roberto led the Pirates to two world championships, hitting .362 in the World Series. His great showcase was in 1971, when he hit .414 and played with an inspiring

recklessness in leading the Pirates to a seven-game victory over the Baltimore Orioles. Only then did some of his severest critics admit his greatness.

He died in a plane crash on New Year's Eve, 1972, on a mercy flight carrying supplies to earthquake victims in Nicaragua. The usual five-year waiting period was waived, and he was named to the Hall of Fame in 1973.

HARLOND CLIFT
Third Baseman, StL (A) 1934–43, Was (A) 1943–45
Clift was an outstanding player whose competent light was hidden beneath bushels of ineptitude provided by his St. Louis Browns teammates. It was difficult for fans in the 1930s to think of anyone with the laughing-stock Browns as a serious talent. Of course, the Browns' attendance was so low in the 1930s—in only two seasons did they draw over 200,000—that there were few in the stands to admire Clift or chuckle at his teammates.

An exceptional fielder, he was the first third baseman to start 50 double plays in a season. And while that record was in part due to a penchant that Brownies' pitchers had for putting runners on base, the rest of Clift's fielding stats support the idea that he had range and reliability beyond most AL third sackers.

He was certainly the most productive hitter among the league's third basemen. He hit .300 a couple of times, but his career batting average was an unexceptional .272. But he walked a lot, going over the 100 mark seven times in eight seasons. And he hit with more power than any third baseman ever had. In 1937 he set a record for third basemen with 29 homers. The next year he upped that to 34. In both years he drove in more than 100 runs.

TY COBB
Outfielder, Det (A) 1905–26, Phi (A) 1927–28. Manager, Det (A) 1921–26
In 1936 Cobb was the first man elected to Cooperstown, mostly by voters who grew up in his era. Babe Ruth was second. The majority of today's critics would reverse the order and maybe drop Cobb a few more pegs besides. The reason, of course, is that the modern game, with its emphasis on home runs, has evolved in a Ruthian rather than a Cobbian direction.

Cobb's strengths were his ability to reach first, steal a base or two, and then score. After all these years, he's still first in batting average (.366), second in hits (4,190), second in steals (892), and first in runs scored (2,245). He collected ten AL batting titles, hit over .400 three times, led in steals six times and in runs scored five. In other words, he was the best at the things he tried to be best *at*.

He was no home run hitter, managing only 118 in twenty-four seasons. But for most of those seasons, going for homers against the dead ball was a losing proposition. He *did* lead in slugging average eight times, proving he wasn't just a powder-puff hitter with extra puffs. The ball was invigorated during the last third of Cobb's career, but that was a little late to ask the old dog to learn a new trick. Still, in 1925 he hit three homers in one game, just showing off.

Admittedly, for all his heavy hitting his Tigers won only three pennants and no World Series. In nineteen of his twenty-two seasons in Detroit, the Tabbies missed the brass ring. The fault, dear Brutus, was not in their star; it was on their pitcher's mound. Cobb was the best player of his time—or at least the first two-thirds of his time.

Considering all that, it's a bit disconcerting to find a few modernists working overtime to chisel Cobb down to a so-so level. Essentially, the argument is that modern players are bigger, faster, better trained, and face more difficult challenges. None of the old-timers could make it big today, they say. Cobb might hit .260.

Well, games and times change, all right. Fifty years from now, our grandchildren will be looking at a different game and some of them will be wondering what we ever saw in Mike Schmidt or Hank Aaron. The problem with that kind of thinking is that it keeps the player from the past anchored in his time while giving any benefits of a later age to the moderns. One critic snickered at Cobb's batting stance; he held his hands apart and then choked up or swung from the end, according to the pitch. Tyrus, the critic insisted, would be tied up by Dwight Gooden or Nolan Ryan. The critic apparently credits Cobb with the IQ of an ashtray. It would take him about half of one at-bat to figure out what he had to do to adjust. Moreover, our "modern" Cobb would have the same advantages in diet, training, and baseball experiences the other moderns have. He'd be bigger, faster, and better trained. He might not hit .366—though we shouldn't bet against it—but he'd be right up there showing other moderns his heels.

Relative comparisons from one era to another work better when they have some statistical reality—like Bill Terry's .401 in 1930, when just about everybody else hit .300, being adjusted down (but we still leave him at the top for that year!). Given Cobb's situation, he excelled all others in batting average.

Now, if the critics want to stomp on Cobb, they can put their clodhoppers on his personality. "The Georgia Peach" was no peach. He was mean, vindictive, selfish, vain, a bully, a racist, paranoid, cruel, and hot-tempered. He spiked infielders just for the hell of it, fought—that is, physically attacked—anyone who crossed him, would do literally anything to be first in literally anything.

But it was just because of those nasty attributes that Cobb would have found a way to win in any age. The Cobb persona made him a great player, gave him a shipload of records, and put him into the Hall of Fame first. And when he died, three baseball people showed up at the funeral, probably only because they were expecting free eats afterward.

"We may never see his like again," Connie Mack once said of him. Indeed we won't.

GORDON "MICKEY" COCHRANE
Catcher, Phi (A) 1925–33, Det (A) 1934–37. Manager, Det (A) 1934–38
They used to argue who was the greatest catcher ever, Cochrane or Bill Dickey. Modern statistical techniques have moved Gabby Hartnett into the discussion. Josh Gibson has his backers. And later ages shout the praises of Yogi Berra and Johnny Bench. But the final cut usually comes down to "Cochrane or —."

When Mickey gets the edge, it's usually on "leadership," which is measured as easily as the distance to Oz. Nevertheless, Cochrane played on five AL pennant winners in a seven-year stretch, and that's at least tertiary evidence that he was officer material. As a matter of fact,

he managed two of those teams (Detroit in 1934–1935) while taking his regular turn behind the plate.

If Mickey had a fault, it was that his fire burned too bright. He was such an intense, take-charge competitor that he used himself up some seasons. Connie Mack called him the biggest factor in the Athletics' three straight pennants (1929–1931), but there must have been times when nobody wanted to be in the same room with Cochrane.

He was considered an exceptional defender once he underwent intensive instruction from old pro Cy Perkins. So it shocked everyone when Pepper Martin, the "Wild Horse of the Osage," stole five bases on him in the 1931 World Series—"ran wild" is the way it's usually put. Most people blamed the Philadelphia pitchers.

Cochrane got high marks in his day for handling pitchers, and there's not much doubt that he did it well. Of course, having guys like Lefty Grove, George Earnshaw, and Tommy Bridges to work with gave him a leg up.

We can measure what he did at the plate better than what he did behind it. From the time Mack purchased his contract for $50,000 in 1925, through his sale to the Tigers for $100,000 in 1934, until a Bump Hadley pitch ended his career and nearly killed him in 1937, Black Mike averaged .320, the best career mark for any catcher. He had good speed for a catcher (64 stolen bases) and usually batted second. He scored 1,041 runs—four times over 100. He was a line drive hitter, but in 1932, when he drove in 112 runs, he also knocked 23 homers. He won Most Valuable Player Awards in 1928 and 1934, although neither year was his best with a bat.

He was named to the Hall of Fame in 1947.

ROCCO "ROCKY" COLAVITO
Outfielder, Cle (A) 1955–59, 1965–67, Det (A) 1960–63, KC (A) 1964, Chi (A) 1967, LA (N) 1968, NY (A) 1968
Colavito hit with power—374 career homers, three seasons over 40—and threw like a cannon. He hit four home runs in a row in a 1959 game against Baltimore. And though he was as slow as a tax refund, he was sure-handed. He played in 234 straight games in 1964–1966 before anybody said "E, Colavito." He only led the league in assists once, but that was because runners knew enough not to challenge him. There ought to be a stat for runners who don't tag up and score on a fly; Rocky was responsible for a lot of those.

In 1959, when he led the AL in homers with 42, he was the most adored player in Cleveland, maybe the most popular person. So naturally, the Indians' braintrust traded him to Detroit for singles hitter Harvey Kuenn. And right then and there a lot of Cleveland baseball fans started looking for another kind of summer entertainment. Some of them haven't forgiven the Indians yet.

EDDIE "COCKY" COLLINS
Second Baseman, Phi (A) 1906–14, 1927–30, Chi (A) 1915–26. Manager, Chi (A) 1925–26
Photos of Collins in his prime show a wimpy-looking guy, thin but hippy, with come-fly-with-me ears, a generous nose, and a chin that barely clears his neck. He wasn't a hunk, but he was a real beauty at second base. For twenty-five years, 1906–1930, Collins suited up for major league games, and for nineteen of those he was the regular at a

position that lends itself to injuries. He was the pivot man in the A's $100,000 infield that helped win four pennants from 1910 through 1914. Then he did the same job for the world champion White Sox of 1917 and the 1919 club, a hose of a different color.

Batting lefthanded, he cracked out 3,310 hits for a .333 career batting average. He was a perfect leadoff or number two hitter, drawing five walks for every strikeout, but for much of his career he batted third, where his lack of home run power limited his RBIs. He ended with 1,299, which puts him behind a lot of sluggers. Once on base, though, he got around, scoring 1,819 runs, including seven seasons of 100-plus. He led the American League three years in a row (1912–14).

He stole more bases than anyone but Lou Brock and Ty Cobb. And he is the only man since 1900 to steal six bases in one game. He did it on September 11, 1912. Eleven days later he did it again. He set the mark for most World Series steals, with 14, later tied by Brock. However, his stolen base percentage was only a break-even 65 percent.

No second baseman has accepted more chances than Collins, nor led the league in fielding as many times— nine.

Connie Mack, who managed both Collins and Nap Lajoie, called Eddie the best second baseman he ever saw. Even so, Collins went into the Hall of Fame in 1939, two years after Lajoie.

JIMMY COLLINS
Third Baseman, Lou (N) 1895, Bos (N) 1895–1900, Bos (A) 1901–07, Phi (A) 1907–08. Manager, Bos (A) 1901–06

Back at the turn of the century, Collins revolutionized third base play. Before his time, most third sackers anchored themselves on the basepath. Collins was one of the first men to play in or back depending upon the situation. It allowed him to range over more ground than any other third baseman of his time.

As a brash rookie in 1895, he dared the greatest bunters of a bunting era—Keeler, McGraw, Jennings, Burkett, Hamilton — to test him. When they did, he charged in to bare-hand the ball and whip it to first, S.O.P. for third basemen now but a real marvel in his day.

In 1898 Jimmy played the hot corner on the Boston Beaneaters' great infield of Fred Tenney, Bobby Lowe, and Herman Long, which led Boston to the pennant. He hit .328 with a National League–leading 15 homers. His best year afield was 1900; he handled 601 putouts and assists, which is still the record.

In 1901 Jim jumped to the new Boston Americans, as player/manager, hit .332, and brought the club in second. In 1903 he led them to the pennant and that fall became the first manager to win a World Series. Collins' club had no chance to defend its honors against the NL in 1904; no Series was played that year, but his Bostons won a second consecutive AL pennant.

He was elected to the Hall of Fame in 1945.

EARLE COMBS
Outfielder, NY (A) 1924–35

Combs (it rhymes with "tombs") was the whippet-fast leadoff man for the Ruth-Gehrig Yankees. Possessing a warm and generous personality, he seemed unruffled that the Yankee sluggers got the spotlight; his job was to get on and get home. From 1925 through 1932 he scored at least 100 runs each season. In 1927, when the Babe hit 60 homers, Combs batted .356, scored 137 runs, and led the AL in hits (231) and triples (23). When Gehrig drove in 184 runs in 1931, Combs scored 120. The next year he touched home 143 times. He had a career batting average of .325, led the AL three times in three-base hits, and scored 1,186 runs.

He was at his best in three World Series (1926, 1927, and 1932), hitting a cumulative .350 and scoring 17 runs in fifteen games. A broken finger limited him to a single pinch-hitting appearance in the 1928 Series; he drove in a run in the final-game win with a sacrifice fly.

His arm didn't intimidate anyone. Speed was his trademark in center field. He used it well, leading AL outfielders in putouts a couple times. He suffered a fractured skull when he crashed into an outfield fence in 1934 and retired after one more year.

He was named to the Hall of Fame in 1970.

CHARLES COMISKEY
First Baseman, StL (AA) 1882–89, 1891, Chi (P) 1890, Cin (N) 1892–94. Manager, StL (AA) 1883–89, Chi (P) 1890, StL (AA) 1891, Cin (N) 1892–94

Comiskey helped Ban Johnson create the American League and was one of its strongest voices until his death in 1931. He founded the White Sox and owned the AL team for its first thirty-one years. He gave Chicago two world champions, four pennants, and the ballpark that bears his name. He was called the "Old Roman" because of his handsome, Barrymore profile, and wavy, silver hair.

He was also, to put it charitably, a cheapskate. An example of Comiskey's miserliness: pitcher Dickie Kerr, one of the honest Sox in the 1919 World Series, won twice against the Reds and half his own team, then won 2l in 1920 and 19 in 1921. Comiskey paid him $4,500 and refused to give him a raise. Kerr quit. He could make $5,000 playing semipro!

The fact that Comiskey paid some of his greatest players coolie wages has been used by some revisionist historians to justify the action of the eight Black Sox players in selling the 1919 World Series down the river. Whether Commie "deserved" what he got, America's baseball fans didn't.

Before owning the White Sox, Comiskey played first base for the old St. Louis Browns of the American Association. He wasn't much as a hitter—lifetime .264—but he's credited with revolutionizing the position by letting the pitcher cover on grounders wide of the bag. As captain and manager, beginning at age twenty-five, he pioneered moving his fielders around for different hitters. He led the Browns to four straight AA flags, 1885–1888.

Some have found it curious that Comiskey could treat his White Sox players like indentured servants yet was one of the players who supported the Players League in 1890.

DAVEY CONCEPCION
Shortstop, Cin (N) 1970–88

Among major league shortstops from Venezuela, Concepcion ranks second in reputation only to Luis Aparicio. Luis may have had a little more range at his best, but

Davey popularized the technique of bouncing long throws from the hole to first to get runners who would have beaten high-arc tosses. With career batting averages in the .260s, neither set any hitting records. Davey had more power—he surprised with 16 homers in 1979— but Luis stole a couple hundred more bases.

Although Concepcion topped .300 only twice (and never in a championship year), he got hot in the October playoffs and Series. He averaged over .400 in the 1975 and 1979 playoffs and over .300 in the 1970, 1972, and 1976 Series. In the 1975 classic, Concepcion came up in the ninth inning of Game Two, with the Reds losing 2–1, two out, and Johnny Bench on second. He slapped a single to tie the score, stole second, and scored on Ken Griffey's double to win the game.

JOHN "JOCKO" CONLAN
Umpire
A long-time minor league outfielder with two brief shots at the White Sox, Conlan got into umpiring by accident in 1935 in Chicago. One of the regular umpires was overcome by the heat. Jocko, who was on the bench, was rushed in to pinch-ump and did well.

In Conlan's first year as a real umpire, 1941, he ejected twenty-six men. His favorite target was Leo Durocher. He gradually mellowed, learned to use psychology and snappy retorts instead of his thumb to keep order. His trademarks were a polka-dot bow tie and a quick grin.

He spent twenty-seven seasons as an NL umpire, worked six World Series, six All-Star Games, and four pennant-deciding playoffs. In 1974, he was elected to the Hall of Fame.

TOM CONNOLLY
Umpire
Connolly was born in England and came to the U.S. with his family at age fifteen in 1885. Enamored of baseball, he studied the rule book assiduously and became an NL umpire in 1898. He quit in 1900 because the weak league president wouldn't support his rulings. Hired by the AL, he umpired the first league game, Chicago versus Cleveland, on April 24, 1901. He was also chosen to umpire the first World Series in 1903.

In those days umpires worked alone, one to a game (two in the Series), and took the taunts of both players and fans. Connally once rowed out of Boston at midnight under threat from irate fans. Pitcher Joe McGinnity reportedly spit in his face, was fined and suspended, and jumped to the NL. But even the irascible Ty Cobb learned to back off when Tom's neck turned red. Eventually, Connolly was able to go ten years straight without ejecting a dissenter.

After thirty-three years behind the mask, Tom became chief of AL umpires for twenty-three more, calling it quits in 1954 at the age of eighty-three. He lived to be ninety-one. In 1953, he was named to the Hall of Fame along with Bill Klem, the first two umpires so honored.

ROGER CONNOR
First Baseman, Tro (N) 1880–82, NY (N) 1883–89, 1891, 1893–94, NY (P) 1890, Phi (N) 1892, StL (N) 1894–97. Manager, StL (N) 1896
Whose career home run record did Babe Ruth break?

Connor's, of course. Roger hit 137 (some sources say 132) of the old dead balls for four bases. The mark stood until 1921, when Babe broke it on his way to 59.

Oddly, Connor only once led his league in homers (13 in the 1890 Players League), but he got as high as 17 in 1887. Triples were his specialty—he was tops in that department twice, in double figures twelve times, and cracked a personal high of 25 in 1894. He hit 233 altogether, and only four men have topped that— Crawford, Cobb, Wagner, and Beckley.

At six-two and 210 pounds, Connor was a big man for his day. He was one of the men New York manager Jim Mutrie meant when he called his team "giants," a name that stuck in the imagination longer than the team stuck in New York. In 1888 and 1889, Connor helped the Giants to two pennants. He was named to the Hall of Fame in 1976.

WALKER COOPER
Catcher, StL (N) 1940–45, 1956–57, NY (N) 1946–49, Cin (N) 1949–50, Bos (N) 1950–52, Mil (N) 1953, Pit (N) 1954, Chi (N) 1954–55
Lon Warneke, who pitched to him and against him and umpired behind him, called Cooper a better catcher than Bill Dickey or Gabby Hartnett. That tells us never to buy real estate from Mr. Warneke. Still, the six-three Coop gave the Cardinals, Giants, Braves, and nearly every other team in the NL solid catching for years and years. He hit .300 several times and ended with a .285 career average. In three World Series, he averaged .300. When he got too old to do the job behind the plate, he remained an effective pinch-hitter.

The Giants wanted him so badly in 1946 they paid the Cardinals $175,000 for him while he was still in the Navy. In 1947 he hit 35 home runs for New York, but that was uncharacteristic. His next highest season total was 20.

He wasn't Dickey or Hartnett, but he was a darn sight better than most.

STAN COVELESKI
Pitcher, Phi (A) 1912, Cle (A) 1916–24, Was (A) 1925–27, NY (A) 1928
Baseball got Coveleski out of the Pennsylvania coal mines (five cents an hour, seventy-two hours a week). "I only saw the sun on Sundays," he cracked. "I would have been great in night baseball." And the spitter got him into the majors with Cleveland in 1916 at the age of twenty-seven. In his first year, the introverted righthander was 15–13 with a sixth-place club. Over the next few years, the Indians moved up in the standings. Coveleski followed a 19-win sophomore season with four straight 20-plus-win years (22, 24, 24, and 23). In 1920, when the Indians won the pennant, Jim Bagby led the staff with 31 wins to Coveleski's 24. But in the World Series against Brooklyn, Coveleski ran up the best performance since Mathewson's three shutouts in the 1905 classic, winning 3–1, 5–1, and 3–0 for an 0.67 ERA.

Only of average build, Covie was a workhorse, three times hurling 300 innings. One reason was the spitter, which is easy on arms. The other was Stan's philosophy: let them hit the first pitch. They seldom hit it far. Stan allowed only 1 home run per 46 innings, even in tiny League Park with its 290-foot right field fence. He had superb control of the spitter. Supposedly, he once went seven straight innings without throwing a called ball.

After Covie won 23 in 1921, Cleveland slipped in the standings and his victory totals declined. He led the AL in ERA in 1923 but won only 13. Traded to Washington in 1925, he responded with another league-leading ERA and a 20–5 record, as the Senators won the pennant. He'd lost his World Series magic, however, and lost twice to the world champion Pirates.

Stan's older brother Harry was known as the "Giant Killer" when, as a rookie with the Phils in 1908, he beat the Giants three times down the stretch. More than Fred Merkle's "boner," Harry's efforts knocked New York out of pennant contention.

CLIFFORD "GAVVY" CRAVATH
Outfielder, Bos (A) 1908, Chi (A) 1909, Was (A) 1909, Phi (N) 1912–20. Manager, Phi (N) 1919–20
Born a generation too soon, Cravath was the home run king in the dead-ball years immediately preceding the Babe Ruth Revolution. In a seven-year span—1913–1919—the Phillies' outfielder led the NL in homers five times and tied once. A short right field target in Philadelphia's Baker Bowl helped quite a bit, but Gavvy, a righthanded batter deserves credit for knowing what to do with it.

He flunked two earlier trials in the AL and didn't get to the Phillies until 1912, when he was thirty-one. A genial practical joker, he kept his teammates loose with his jokes and pitchers up tight with his bat. In 1915 he helped Philadelphia to a pennant with a league-high 115 RBIs and a then twentieth-century record of 24 homers.

SAM CRAWFORD
Outfielder, Cin (N) 1899–1902, Det (A) 1903–17
Wahoo Sam (he was born in Wahoo, Nebraska) played right field beside Ty Cobb on the Tigers, hit behind him—and once even pinch-hit for him—but was overshadowed by him, much as Gehrig was overshadowed by Ruth.

Cobb disliked Crawford. Supposedly Tyrus Rex was convinced the modest right fielder was jealous of his accomplishments. More likely he resented Crawford for already being a star when Cobb arrived in Detroit. Another possibility was that Cobb envied Crawford for being both a great player and a likable person.

Nevertheless Cobb campaigned for years to get Crawford into the Hall of Fame. It was an uncharacteristic act on Cobb's part, but perhaps moved his eventual destination out one ring. Crawford shouldn't have needed any campaign. He was elected to the Hall of Fame in 1957 and deservedly so.

Sam was the greatest triples hitter in history, with 309 to Ty's 297. Only two other men, Honus Wagner and Tris Speaker, are even over 200, and no modern player has hit half as many. Crawford lashed 26 of them in 1914 for an AL record (tied by Joe Jackson), and led the league six times. It's a given, today, to assume that Crawford would have hit tons of home runs with a livelier ball. He *did* lead the NL in homers with 16 in 1901 and the AL with 7 in 1908, but mostly he hit screaming line drives that might have bounced off (or punctured) modern fences.

Sam had six 100-plus-RBI seasons and led the American League three times. Many of Cobb's record 2,245

runs scored were batted in by Sam.

He left the majors after 1917, just 39 hits shy of 3,000. The figure was no big deal then, or he might have hung around and picked them up. Two years later he could still hit .360 in the Pacific Coast League.

JOE CRONIN
Shortstop/Manager, Pit (N) 1926–27, Was (A) 1928–34, Bos (A) 1935–45
Cronin spent fifty years in baseball, rising from All-Star shortstop to pennant-winning manager, to general manager, and finally to AL president. He was even nominated for commissioner. Horatio Alger should have written his bio.

Born in San Francisco just after the 1906 earthquake, Joe joined the Washington Senators in 1928 and was a full-fledged star by 1930, when he hit .346 and drove in 126. He was the AL's MVP. In all, he had eight seasons with over 100 RBIs, ten full seasons over .300, and 170 homers. Only seven shortstops have ever scored 100 runs and batted in 100 in the same season. Honus Wagner did it three times, Cronin four. He sure didn't hit like a shortstop. He didn't field like one either, at least not like the best. He wasn't embarrassing, but he would never have made the mythical AL All-Star team seven times with his glove.

In 1933, a near-beardless youth of twenty-six, he was named manager of the Senators. Darned if he didn't win the pennant that year, and no Senator manager ever won another. The next year he married the boss's niece in September. And in October the boss sold him to the Red Sox for $225,000.

He continued as player/manager for the Bosox, although he mainly pinch-hit after 1941. In 1943 he pinch-hit five homers, an AL record. In 1946, after he'd become strictly a bench manager, his Red Sox won the pennant. Two years later he moved upstairs to become the Boston general manager, and in 1959 he was elected AL prexy, serving until 1973. He was the AL's chairman of the board until his death in 1984.

A hearty, affable man, modest to a fault, Cronin was a great player, an adequate manager (albeit with a tendency to chew up his pitching staff), and a popular executive. He was named to the Hall of Fame in 1956.

ARTHUR "CANDY" CUMMINGS
Pitcher, NY (NA) 1872, Bal (NA) 1873, Phi (NA) 1874, Hartford (NA) 1875, Hartford (NL) 1876, Cin (NL) 1877
Cummings was elected to the Hall of Fame in 1939 as the inventor of the curveball, and historians have been perplexed ever since. Well, he said he came up with the curve in 1866 after seeing a spinning clamshell curve as it was skipped across the water. Clamshell spinning and curveball tossing are unrelated throwing techniques, but let that pass. Cummings apparently used his clam-curve against Harvard the next year, and the scholars were baffled. So was President Andrew Johnson, another early observer. (Johnson was baffled by just about everything while he was in the White House.)

Cummings was a pitcher for the Excelsiors of Brooklyn when the revolutionary discovery was made. Back then pitchers had to throw underhand with both feet on the ground, but they were only forty-five feet away from the batter. Cummings discovered that he could make the ball curve with the wind in his face but not with it at his back.

Anyway, the curve brought Cummings success, and in 1870 Henry Chadwick, the most knowledgeable authority of the day, said that he was the best pitcher in the land. Chadwick sometimes agreed with Cummings's clam-curve-creation claims, but at other times talked about seeing curves in the 1850s.

Between 1872 and 1875, Cummings won 124 games in the National Association, the league that preceded the NL. He also picked up his nickname—"candy" meant "best" in nineteenth-century slang. But he was just a little wisp of a thing, barely 120 pounds, and the overwork caught up with him. By 1878 he was done.

Many others disputed Cummings's claim to being the first curveball pitcher. Among them were Alphonse Martin, Bobby Mathews, Fred Goldsmith, and Joseph Mann. Most likely it was invented independently by many different pitchers over a couple of decades.

HAZEN "KIKI" CUYLER
Outfielder, Pit (N) 1921–27, Chi (N) 1928–35, Cin (N) 1935–37, Bkn (N) 1938

Cuyler broke in with Pittsburgh in 1924, hitting .354, and he was hailed as "another Cobb." The next year he made the prophets look good as he hit .357, with 17 homers, 26 triples, and 45 doubles. He drove in 102 runs and scored 144. He even stole 41 bases. In one span, he had ten consecutive hits. The Pirates won the pennant. That October, Cuyler homered to win the second Series game against Washington. He came up in the seventh game with the bases loaded against Walter Johnson, crossed himself, and doubled in two for the victory.

After a .321 season in 1926, when he led the NL in runs scored and stolen bases, he ran into *l'affaire de Bush* in 1927. Manager Donie Bush wanted Cuyler to bat second (which was a little strange because Cuyler was the best home run threat on the club). Kiki was superstitious about the slot, insisting he couldn't and wouldn't hit second. Bush benched Cuyler, accused him of not hustling, and put a lesser player in Cuyler's position. The Pirates still won the pennant but lost the Series four straight. Around Pittsburgh there are fans to this day who'll swear the Bucs, with Cuyler, would have wiped up those 1927 Yankees. After the season, Cuyler was shipped to the Cubs for no one very useful. The Pirates took thirty-three years to win another pennant.

Meanwhile, Cuyler hit .360 for the Cub pennant winners of 1929. In 1930 he slumped to .355. But he had 228 hits, 155 runs scored, and 134 RBIs. In all, he hit .300 ten times. He was still around in 1932 to hit a solid .291 when the Cubs won again.

He never became "another Cobb" but, except for that silliness about batting second, it's hard to fault him. He ended with a .321 batting average, scored 1,305 runs, batted in 1,065. He hit line drives, so his homer total was a modest 127, but he had 394 doubles and 157 triples. He led the league in stolen bases four times, used his speed well in the outfield, and had a good arm. He was quiet, never drank or smoked, and only Donie Bush ever accused him of malingering. He was named to the Hall of Fame in 1968.

Some people want to pronounce his nickname "Kee-Kee," as if he was a belly dancer. Actually he got it when other outfielders called for him to take fly balls: "Cuy! Cuy!"

RAY DANDRIDGE
Third Baseman, Negro Leagues, 1933–48, Detroit Stars, Newark Dodgers, Newark Eagles, New York Cubans

Dandridge, old-timers from the Negro Leagues say, could field like Brooks Robinson and hit like Pie Traynor and George Kell. Even allowing for hyperbole, Dandridge was a terrific third baseman—perhaps the best never to play in the white major leagues.

Ray was so bowlegged that "You could drive a freight train through there," Monte Irvin says, "but not a base-ball." He was a marvelous fielder, cat-quick, with a power-ful arm.

Not a power hitter, Dandridge concentrated on hitting the ball where it was pitched. He hit .347 against white big league pitching in barnstorming exhibitions. His best mark in the Negro National League was .370 in 1944.

Much of Ray's career was spent in the Mexican League and in the Cuban winter league. He spurned an offer from Cleveland in 1948 because it didn't carry a bonus. The next year he signed with the New York Giants, who sent him to the Minneapolis Millers of the American Association. He said he was twenty-nine; in actuality, he was past thirty-six.

He was AA Rookie of the Year in '49 and the league's MVP the next year when he hit .311 for the champion Millers. The Giants brought other players with lesser records to the majors but— perhaps because of his age— kept Dandridge in the minors, a great disappointment to him. He retired after the 1955 season.

In 1987 he was named to the Baseball Hall of Fame.

ANDRE DAWSON
Outfielder, Mon (N) 1976–86, Chi (N) 1987-

Rookie of the Year in 1977, Dawson played ten full seasons in Montreal. He earned a reputation as an excellent fielder and dangerous hitter. In the early 1980s major league players voted him the best all-around player in the NL. He also earned bad knees and several operations on Expo Stadium's artificial surface. When he became a free agent in 1987, he sought out the Chicago Cubs, signed a blank contract, and told them to fill in the figure. Despite his uncertain knees, he could have signed with other teams for considerably more money. But Wrigley Field had real grass, reachable walls, and Dawson had hit .346 in Chicago over the preceding ten years. The Cubs acquired a bargain. Dawson hit only .287, but smashed 49 homers and drove in 137 runs, both NL highs in '87. He was voted the MVP Award and signed a new (much more lucrative) contract for 1988.

LEON DAY
Pitcher, Negro Leagues, 1934–50, Bacharach Giants, Brooklyn Eagles, Newark Eagles, Baltimore Elite Giants

The five-seven 140-pound Day was an all-around performer who pitched and played second base and center field. Although many statistics are missing, it is known that he hit over .300 in nearly every season. But his fame rests on his pitching. Day holds the Negro League record with 18 strikeouts in one game in 1940—one of his victims was Roy Campanella (who fanned three times). Day won three of four games he pitched against the legendary Satchel Paige, including victories in the East-West (All-Star) Game and the 1942 Negro World Series.

Day's career was interrupted by World War Two service in Europe. In 1945 he defeated Ewell Blackwell for the European Service Championship before 50,000 G.I.'s in Nuremburg. In his first game back home in 1946, he tossed a no-hit game with 17 strikeouts.

JAY HANNA "DIZZY" DEAN
Pitcher, StL (N) 1930–37, Chi (N) 1938–41, StL (A) 1947

After winning 20 games for the 1933 Cardinals, Dizzy was joined on the St. Louis staff by his younger brother. "Me and Paul will probably win 40 games," Dizzy predicted for 1934. He was wrong. They won 49, with Diz winning 30 to lead the Cards to the pennant. "It ain't braggin' if yuh can do it," explained Diz. In the World Series, each brother won two games. Always the headline maker, Dizzy broke up a double play while pinch-running in Game Four by blocking the relay with his forehead. It was feared he might be lost for the remainder of the Series until the next day's headline reported: X-RAY OF DEAN'S HEAD REVEALS NOTHING. At least, that's the way they tell the story, and if it isn't true, it should be.

Dizzy clowned, bragged, and pitched his way to immortality. Even his marvelous work on the mound was sometimes overshadowed by colorful "Dean stories." Supposedly, one day he was interviewed by three different reporters, one after the other. He told each a new "story of Dizzy's life" with different birthdates, birthplaces, and even gave himself three different Christian names. "All those felluhs wanted a exclusive," he explained.

In 1935 Dean won 28 and followed with 24 in 1936. He was in the midst of another fine year in 1937 when a line drive off Earl Averill's bat in the All-Star Game broke his toe. He tried to come back too soon, altered his motion to favor the toe, and ruined his arm. He was twenty-six and had won 134 games.

Traded to the Cubs in 1938, he used a "nuffin' ball" to sore-arm his way to a 7–1 record for the pennant winners. In a courageous World Series appearance, he held the mighty Yankees at bay for seven innings before the roof fell in. It was his last hurrah.

After retiring, Diz became a colorful national play-by-play announcer who enriched the English language with exciting new grammar, such as "He slud into third." Brief though his career was, it was so brilliant at its height and Dean himself brought so much more to baseball than his pitching talent, that he was elected to the Hall of Fame in 1953.

ED DELAHANTY
Outfielder, Phi (N) 1888–89, 1891–01, Cle (P) 1890, Was (A) 1902–03

The Phillies had the trio of Delahanty, Billy Hamilton, and Sam Thompson in the same outfield from 1891 to 1895. They all were magnificent hitters and all three are

in the Hall of Fame. Did the Phillies destroy the rest of the league? They did not; they finished fourth four times and third in '95. Makes you wonder about the rest of the team, doesn't it?

"Big Ed" Delahanty weighed only about 170 pounds, but he went up a couple tons when he had a bat in his hands. He is the only man to lead both major leagues in batting, topping the NL with .410 in 1899 and the AL with .376 in 1902. His lifetime .346 is the fourth-best of all time. From 1894 to 1896, he hit .407, .404, and .397. That .407 was only fourth-best in the league, and it was a period of high batting averages, still . . .

Oldest of four ball-playing brothers, Ed hit with power and speed; his 19 homers in 1893 was one of the highest totals of the nineteenth century. In 1896 he became the second man to hit four home runs in one game.

A notorious bad-ball hitter, Ed "often" stepped across the plate to smash a fat pitch, according to legend.

And try this one. He once reputedly knocked a baseball in half. They sure don't build 'em the way they used to!

Tall tales aside, Delahanty was a magnificent hitter who went into the Hall of Fame in 1945.

Unfortunately, he was also a drunk. Beset by drinking, debts, and divorce, he was suspended by his team in the summer of 1903. He caught a train from Chicago for New York, got boisterously loaded, and was kicked off the team train at Niagara Falls. Still drunk, he staggered onto a bridge, fell into the river, and was swept over the falls. He was thirty-five years old.

BILL DICKEY
Catcher, NY (A) 1928–43, 1946. Manager, NY (A) 1946

Dickey's reputation appears to have slipped of late, but it's a trick of perception. He was a great catcher, but there have been several great catchers since, and new statistical techniques indicate some of Dickey's contemporaries (and some of those who followed) may have been better than anyone realized at the time. So the question that used to be so popular—who's the greatest catcher, Dickey or Cochrane?—has a few more multiple choices.

Then, too, there's the out-of-sight, out-of-mind philosophy. Dickey caught his last game in 1946. The people who watched him half a century ago figured they were looking at something special in catchers. They could cite several facts to prove their eyes weren't playing tricks.

Dickey caught 100 games or more for thirteen straight years, a record. His .362 batting average in 1936 was a record for a catcher. He had a career average of .313, with 202 home runs and 1,209 RBIs. He was on eleven AL All-Star teams, and the first game wasn't played until his fifth year as a regular. He played in eight World Series, hit 5 homers, and his 24 World Series RBIs are the eighth-highest total ever. Dickey knew how to make 'em count. He had several clutch World Series hits. His ninth-inning single won the Opening Game in 1939. And his two-run homer won the Game Five in 1943.

Defensive prowess is hard to prove—next to impossible with a catcher —but Dickey got raves when he played and was called in later to show Yogi Berra the way to do it.

Dickey wasn't the rah-rah type. He led quietly, but the point is, *he led*. One day in 1932 he took exception to the way a runner slid in at home, so he flattened the guy and broke his jaw. It was out of character for Dickey and got him fined and suspended, but it probably made the next fellow sliding home against the Yankees think twice about how he did it.

If there's an argument against him, it's that Dickey played on so many winning teams that he was bound to look good. How's that for a Catch-22? It's kind of like the Yogi-ism that "Nobody goes there 'cause it's too crowded." Would the Yankees have been good with another catcher? Sure. Would they have been as good? Hah!

Dickey was named to the Hall of Fame in 1954.

MARTIN DIHIGO
Pitcher/Outfielder, Negro Leagues, 1923–45, Cuban
Stars (East), New York Cubans, Homestead Grays,
Hilldale, Darby Daisies
Dihigo was one of the most versatile athletes in the history of baseball. In a career that lasted from 1923 to 1950, he starred as a pitcher, as a hitter, as an outfielder, and occasionally as an infielder.

As a pitcher, counting several seasons in Mexico, Venezuela, and the Dominican Republic, Dihigo was 256–136. His stock in trade was a blazing fastball.

As a batter, he hit over .400 three times in Cuba and the States. He led the Eastern Colored League in homers in 1926 and the American Negro League in batting with .386 in 1929. Reportedly, his longest home run came in Pittsburgh in 1936, a 500-foot shot that landed on a hospital roof.

In the outfield, he had exceptional range, and his throwing arm was claimed to be among the best ever. Supposedly, a contest was once held in Cuba wherein a *jai alai* player, using his basketlike *cesto*, slung a ball from home plate against the center field wall on one bounce. Dihigo threw the ball over the wall.

As a manager, he led the New York Cubans to the Negro National League playoff in 1935 and starred both on the mound and at the plate.

Dihigo was a big man (six-three, 220 pounds), but he was amazingly agile. Friendly, extremely popular, and with a great sense of humor, in 1977 he became the first Cuban ever to be elected to the Baseball Hall of Fame.

DOM DIMAGGIO
Outfielder, Bos (A) 1940–42, 1946–53
Red Sox fans used to sing: "He's better than his brother Joe—Dominick DiMaaaggiiiooooh!" Well, he wasn't. Dom was five-nine and 168 pounds, about 90 percent Joe's size and he was about 90 percent the player Joe was. But 90 percent of Joe DiMaggio is better than 100 percent of most of the guys who've ever drawn major league salaries. Dom wore glasses and because not very many players wore them he was called "The Little Professor," which is a better moniker than "Joe's Kid Brother."

Okay, comparisons are inevitable. Dom didn't have Joe's home run power; he was in double figures for homers only twice (in Fenway!) in his career. Nor did he hit as often; Joe's .325 is 27 points better than Dom's .298. But Dom was a leadoff man, and he did that very well. He led the AL in runs scored in 1950 and '51. He was more likely to walk than Joe, pulling his .380 OBA to within 14 points of his big brother's. Surprisingly, Dom was more likely to strike out than Joe. He had 571 strikeouts (to Joe's 369) in a lot fewer at-bats. Proving that Joe was a better hitter is

kind of like proving that beans give gas—everybody but Boston already knows it.

They were both good center fielders. We can give Dom an edge there. He led AL center fielders in chances per game three times when one of the other AL center fielders was Joe. Some would argue that Dom got less help from his left and right fielders and *had* to accept more chances. The point is, he did it.

In the final game of the 1946 World Series, Dom twisted an ankle while tying the game with a double in the top of the eighth. Enos Slaughter made his famous dash all the way home from first in the bottom of the inning to win the game, but said later he wouldn't have tried it if Dom had still been in center.

JOE DIMAGGIO
Outfielder, NY (A) 1936–42, 1946–51
Jolting Joe, the "Yankee Clipper," sells coffee makers, married Marilyn Monroe, hit in 56 straight games, and was voted baseball's greatest living player. (Extensive research has failed to uncover anyone who ever wanted to be known as baseball's greatest dead player.)

Revisionists blame the New York media for the DiMaggio mystique. Like everyone outside the Big Apple thought he was just another ballplayer! Actually, in some cities around the AL where Yankee-hating was a religious test, DiMag received a special dispensation. Fans who would have kicked Tommy Henrich's dog still cheered for DiMaggio.

The revisionists miss the point. Declaring anyone the "greatest" anything may be pretty silly, but when it's done it comes from the heart, not from the stats. DiMaggio warmed more baseball fans' chests than hot-dog heartburn. He was adored, idealized, lionized. The symbol.

As a symbol, he was handsome, quiet, a little aloof. They would have called him a Greek god but he was an Italian. Even that worked because he was a symbol for loyal Italian-Americans at a time when Mussolini's fascists stood for a lot of nasty things.

And—oh boy!—did he ever look good on the field! Graceful out there in center, he wasn't slow but it always seemed as if the film had been slowed down a bit so you could catch the nuances. At the plate, he stood with his feet planted wide apart and his bat ready but straight-up, motionless. And when you saw him swing, you never forgot it—no matter where the ball went.

Joe's stats were terrific, maybe not the best ever, but close enough to support the emotions of his fans. He lost three years to the service, but still ended with 2,214 hits, 361 home runs, 1,390 runs scored, 1,537 RBIs, and a .325 career batting average. He led the league in homers twice, RBIs twice, batting average twice. When he batted in 155 runs in 1948, he had more RBIs than games. Only one hitter has done that since. He played 13 years and was named to 13 AL All-Star teams. He was the AL MVP three times, including the 1941 season, in which he hit in a record 565 consecutive games.

Joltin' Joe went into the Hall of Fame in 1955, just a year after he was eligible. Incredible!

LARRY DOBY
Outfielder, Cle (A) 1947–55, 1958, Chi (A) 1956–57,
1959, Det (A) 1959. Manager, Chi (A) 1978

Doby was the first black to play in the AL, joining Cleveland in 1947 as a second baseman. He was switched to center field the next season, after extensive tutelage by Tris Speaker, and helped the Indians win their first pennant since Speaker played center in 1920. Doby hit .301 for the season; his home run off Johnny Sain won Game Four of the World Series that year.

Although Doby became an outstanding center fielder, he was more feared for his bat. He is one of the few men to drive one over the distant center field wall at Griffith Stadium in Washington (Ruth, Williams, and Mantle are the others). Larry was the first black player to lead either major league in home runs with his 32 in 1952. He led again with the same total in 1954 and also topped the AL in RBIs with 126, as the Indians won the pennant with an AL record win total of 111. He ended his career with 242 homers, 969 RBIs, and a .283 batting average.

In addition to power, speed, and consistency, Larry had a temper that sometimes brought criticism but in the long run probably earned respect for blacks. With the black Newark Eagles, Larry teamed with Monte Irvin in 1946 to win the black world championship over Satchel Paige's Kansas City Monarchs.

Doby had a brief stint as interim manager of the Chicago White Sox in 1978.

BOBBY DOERR
Second Baseman, Bos (A) 1937–44, 1946–51
The Red Sox of the late 1940s won more games than any team in baseball, but kept coming up just short of a pennant—except in 1946 when they blew the World Series. No one in his right mind ever blamed Doerr for the shortfalls that gave Bosox fans short falls. From the day he took over Boston's second base in 1937 until a chronic bad back forced him to hang up his glove at thirty-three in 1951, he was a rock—so reliable in the field they should have checked his glove for a 23-jewel movement. In 1948, smack in the middle of a pennant race, Bobby went almost three months—414 chances— without an error. Doerr didn't make spectacular plays. He didn't have to. He anticipated and was already in position. He's still in the all-time top ten second basemen in putouts and assists, surrounded by guys who played longer.

Bobby was no slouch with a bat either. He adjusted to Fenway's Green Monster early, so that his numbers in Boston are way better than on the road, but that's a way of life for righthanded Red Soxers. Averaging it out, he hit a solid .288, with 223 home runs and 1,247 RBIs. In 1944—admittedly a war year—he got his average up to .325 and led the AL in slugging average. Doerr was named MVP that season. During his career, he played in nine All-Star Games.

Doerr had a knack for the clutch, though it sometimes was wasted. He hit .409 in the 1946 Series. In the do-or-die ninth inning of the seventh game, with the Sox down, 4–3, he singled the tying run into scoring position. The next three men made outs. In 1949, in the final game against the Yankees, with the pennant on the line, he slugged a three-run triple against Vic Raschi. The Sox lost anyway.

In 1986 the Veterans Committee put him in the Hall of Fame at Cooperstown.

DON DRYSDALE
Pitcher, Bkn (N) 1956–57, LA (N) 1958–69
When Drysdale pitched for the Dodgers, the *batters* had to be dodgers. The big righthander could have written *Winning Through Intimidation*. At six-five, he delivered his 90-plus m.p.h. fastball with a big sidearm motion—"all spikes, elbows, and fingernails"—that made righthanded batters think they were under a rocket attack from third base. They say that, halfway through some of his games the groundskeeper had to come out and sprinkle sand in the batter's box. Batter's fears were justified. Big Don hit 154 batters, about 1 every 22 innings. It's the all-time record. Off the field, Drysdale was always a considerate gentleman; but when he walked onto the field he was Freddy on Elm Street. He broke one batter's hand and was suspended for throwing beanballs. He threatened to sue and was reinstated. Adding to the terror, Don had a temper and everyone knew it. After giving up one home run, he threw the ball into the stands. He claimed that it "slipped."

Through the 1960s, Drysdale and Sandy Koufax were the Dodgers' one-two mound punch. One year they negotiated their contracts as an entry. Together, they put Los Angeles in three World Series during the decade.

Don compiled a 209–166 record over his fourteen-year career. His ERA was 2.95 and he totaled 2,486 strikeouts, three times leading the NL. He won the Cy Young Award in 1962 with a 25–9 mark. In 1968 he threw six straight shutouts on his way to a record of 58 consecutive scoreless innings which stood until Orel Hershiser surpassed it in 1988.

He was named to the Baseball Hall of Fame in 1984.

HUGH DUFFY
Outfielder, Chi (N) 1888–89, Chi (P) 1890, Bos (AA) 1891, Bos (N) 1892–1900, Mil (A) 1901, Phi (N) 1904–06. Manager, Mil (A) 1901, Phi (N) 1904–06, Chi (A) 1910–11, Bos (A) 1921–22
Pint-sized Duffy had the biggest batting average ever, .440 (originally thought to be .438) in 1894, the hottest-hitting year ever, when the entire *league* batted .309. Hugh hit 41 percent better than average, which isn't the record, but is pretty darned good. He also tied for the home run lead with 18 and led in RBIs with 145. It helped put him in the Hall of Fame in 1945.

Rejected by the White Sox in 1889 as too small ("We've got a batboy," Cap Anson said), Duffy was signed by the Bostons in 1892. There he joined another New England Irishman now in Cooperstown, Tommy McCarthy, to form the best defensive duo of the era. Boston fans called them the "Heavenly Twins." Frustrated batters called them less printable things.

Duffy ended his seventeen-year career with a .324 batting average, 1,553 runs scored, 1,299 RBIs, and 574 stolen bases.

FRED "SURE SHOT" DUNLAP
Second Baseman, Cle (N) 1880–83, StL (U) 1884, StL (N) 1885–86, Det (N) 1886–87, Pit (N) 1888–90, NY (P) 1890, Was (AA) 1891. Manager, Pit (N) 1889
Dunlap was the biggest star of the one-year Union Association, which is sort of like being the most coveted Cracker Jacks prize. Labeled the "King of Second Basemen" in

the 1880s, he was a noble hitter and fielder, but what set him above infield commoners was a powerful arm, which earned him the nickname "Sure Shot." Reportedly, he didn't so much throw the ball as sling it. He was an established NL star who'd twice hit .300 for Cleveland when Union Association dollars persuaded him to move to that ill-fated league and made him the highest-paid player in baseball.

Dunlap hit .412 in 1884 and led the Union Association in almost everything—batting average, slugging average, hits, runs, home runs, and every second base fielding category but errors —as his St Louis team won the only ever UA flag.

When the UA folded the next year, Fred folded as a slugger. Back in the NL, his batting average plunged 100 points. He never hit .300 again, but he continued his reign at second for several more seasons.

LEO "THE LIP" DUROCHER
Manager, Bkn (N) 1939–46, 1948, NY (N) 1948–55, Chi (N) 1966–72, Hou (N) 1972–3 Shortstop, NY (A) 1925, 1928–29, Cin (N) 1930–33, StL (N) 1933–37, Bkn (N) 1938–41, 1943, 1945
Loud-mouthed, pugnacious Leo was the Billy Martin of the 1940s. He baited umpires, picked fights, won more games than Stengel, and made his lifelong credo—"Nice guys finish last"—a part of the American language.

He broke in with the 1928 Yankees as a scrappy good-field-no-hit infielder, who delighted in getting Babe Ruth's goat. His gung-ho attitude and gone-south bat earned him the moniker "The All-American Out." By 1934 he was with the Cards, regarded as the best-fielding shortstop in the NL. He reportedly gave them their Gas House Gang nickname and helped spark them to the 1934 pennant.

In 1939 Brooklyn boss Larry MacPhail, a firebrand himself, tapped Durocher to lead the Dodgers. Lippy punched a golf caddy, fought with MacPhail, gambled, was fired, rehired, and raised the Bums from sixth to third, to second, and finally to first in 1941.

In 1946 Leo feuded with MacPhail, then owner of the Yanks, consorted with gangster Bugsy Siegel, married movie star Larraine Day upon her divorce, and finally was suspended for 1947 by Baseball Commissioner Happy Chandler.

Leo returned to the Dodger helm in 1948 but was let go in midseason. He shocked his fans by moving over to the hated Giants. He had his greatest success in New York. In 1951 he nurtured young Willie Mays through a horrendous career-opening slump and won one of the most thrilling pennant races in history, as Bobby Thomson sank the Dodgers with his "shot heard 'round the world."

Three years later Leo won his third flag, his first World Series— and his third Manager of the Year Award. After the 1955 season, he worked for several years in television.

In 1966 Leo returned to the dugout as manager of the Cubs, where he served until late in the 1972 season. Although he brought the Cubbies into contention, he was unable to get them over the hump. Then he managed Houston at the end of 1972 and all of '73.

Many have written that Durocher was no more than an ordinary manager with a poor or noncontending team, but that he could ride a winner down a hot pennant race better than any other skipper.

Leo's 2,010 victories rank him sixth all-time among managers. His 1,710 losses are seventh.

JIMMY DYKES
Manager, Chi (A) 1934–46, Phi (A) 1951–53, Bal (A) 1954, Cin (N) 1958, Det (A) 1959–60, Cle (A) 1960–61. Third Baseman, Phi (A) 1918–32, Chi (A) 1933–39
Dykes managed for twenty-one years in the major leagues and never won a pennant. His teams finished in the first division only eight times and never higher than third. Yet he was regarded as an outstanding manager who got more out of his often-talentless teams than could reasonably be expected. Patient, humorous, knowledgeable, he lost 1,538 games—ninth all-time—but won a creditable 1,407. A quotable, nonstop talker, he said that winning without good players was like trying to steal first base. His best-known statement was to label Yankees' skipper Joe McCarthy a "push-button manager," meaning that McCarthy had only to push the right button to trot out another .300 hitter or quality pitcher. Dykes, of course, had few buttons.

Dykes was an infielder with the Philadelphia A's throughout the 1920s and played on the championship teams of 1929–31. A good and versatile fielder, he performed mostly at third base, but played extensively at second and occasionally at short and first. Initially a poor hitter, he developed into a reliable batsman and finished his career with a .280 batting average, 2,256 hits, and 1,071 RBIs.

BILLY EVANS
Umpire
Evans began as a sportswriter and umpired his first minor league game only because the assigned man didn't show up. In 1906 his ability got him promoted all the way from a Class C minor league to the AL. He was only twenty-two.

Billy umpired back when it took guts to wear a blue suit. He once had his skull fractured by a bottle during a riot in a ballpark. Another time he tangled with Ty Cobb under the stands and was nearly choked to death. But Evans learned to substitute diplomacy for belligerence and became one of the great umpires. A friendly, fastidious man, he helped gain respect for all umps.

In Game Two of the 1909 World Series, Evans and Bill Klem had to ask the bleacherites whether a ball had landed fair or foul because temporary seats jutted out onto the field and hid the deep foul line. The next day four umpires worked the game, a practice that was eventually adopted for all major league games.

After 1927 Evans left umpiring to become the general manager for the Cleveland Indians. He also wrote a sports column, and later served as vice-president of the Detroit Tigers.

In 1973 Evans was elected to the Baseball Hall of Fame.

DARRELL EVANS
Third Baseman/First Baseman, Atl (N) 1969–76, 1989, SF (N) 1976–83, Det (A) 1983–1988, Atl (N) 1989
Evans combined a home run bat and an ability to draw walks into a twenty-one-year major league career. His career batting average hovered around .250.

Evans says his career turned around when he saw a UFO while sitting on his porch in California in 1976. He'd just been traded from Atlanta, where he'd been hitting .173, to San Francisco. He took the sighting as a good omen and began hitting with renewed energy.

In 1985, in friendly Tiger Stadium, Darrell led the AL with 40 homers at the age of thirty-eight, the oldest HR champ ever and the only man to hit 40 in both leagues. Two years later he slugged 34, the oldest man to reach that height.

DWIGHT EVANS
Outfielder, Bos (A) 1972-

In his first years with the Red Sox, Evans was regarded as a good defensive outfielder but a poor hitter. Slowly he won respect for his bat. His strength was not his batting average, although he finally cracked .300 in his eighteenth AL season. Evans learned to draw walks, leading the league three times, and at the same time turned into one of the AL's better home run hitters. His 22 in the strike-shortened 1981 season tied for first in the league, but he has also had three seasons with more than 30 homers. Whether making circus World Series catches or driving long shots over or against the Fenway Wall, Evans became a darling of Boston fans.

His leaping one-handed catch of Joe Morgan's home run bid in the eleventh inning of the Sixth Game in the 1975 World Series was one of the most heart-stopping ever seen. He then threw to the infield to double off Ken Griffey for the third out, setting the stage for Carlton Fisk's game-winning homer in the twelfth.

JOHNNY EVERS
Second Baseman, Chi (N) 1902–13, Bos (N) 1914–17, 1929, Phi (N) 1917, Chi (A) 1922. Manager, Chi (N) 1913, 1921; Chi (A) 1924

Rumor to the contrary, Evers did not earn his way into Cooperstown in 1946 by being the middle word in the refrain of F. P. Adams's poem about "Tinker to Evers to Chance." However, like a bowl of chicken soup, it didn't hurt. Except for an un-Evers-like .341 in 1912, his batting averages look sad beside those of AL contemporaries Nap Lajoie and Eddie Collins. Still, at the time Johnny played, what with the dead ball, there weren't many players at any position who hit with Lajoie or Collins. Evers's batting averages were consistently above the league average. Little Johnny was undeniably the top NL second baseman of the twentieth century's first two decades.

The Cubbie double-play combination that set F. P. Adams's pen in motion never led the league in twin killings—and small wonder. The Chicago pitchers kept baserunners to a minimum. What made "T to E to C" exceptional was their timing; on those rare occasions when a DP was crucial, they were the best in the business.

They were the main men in Chicago's four pennants between 1906 and 1910. Of the three, the 140-pound Evers was probably the most valuable player both in the field and at the plate. The hardest to get along with, too. His nickname was "The Crab." Even Tinker didn't like him; except for obligatory *You take its* and *I got its*, they didn't speak for years. Grouchy as he was, little Johnny was also skilled, pugnacious, and ingenious.

Evers was the culprit who called for the ball and tagged second base, putting out poor Fred Merkle and throwing the 1908 race into a tie. It worked in part because he'd warned the umpire that he would do it if the occasion arose. When Merkle made a beeline for the clubhouse instead of touching second and Johnny put the ball on the bag, the umpire had no choice but to call Fred out.

Sold to Boston in 1914, Evers joined shortstop Rabbit Maranville and sparked the miracle come-from-behind flag. He was voted MVP. Johnny was usually hot in the Series; he hit .350 in both 1908 and '09. He hit .438 in this one, and his single drove in the winning run in the fourth and final game.

WILLIAM "BUCK" EWING
Catcher, Tro (N) 1880–82, NY (N) 1883–89, 1891–92, NY (P) 1890, Cle (N) 1893–94, Cin (N) 1895–97.
Manager, NY (P) 1890, Cin (N) 1895–99, NY (N) 1900

Ewing was the subject of an early lithograph dramatizing the day he stole second and third, then announced, "And now I'm going to steal home"—and did. In 1919, twenty-five years after he stepped down as a regular, no less authority than the *Reach Guide* linked him with Ty Cobb and Honus Wagner as the three top stars of all time. Very likely, Buck was the greatest all-around player of the nineteenth century.

He wasn't the greatest with the bat, but he was a strong hitter, averaging .303 over eighteen seasons. He led the NL with 10 home runs in 1883 and hit 20 triples the next year. And, as the lithograph showed, he was a daring and dangerous baserunner.

In the field, Ewing was just about as good as it got. He could and did play every position, but he was most famous as a catcher, the most demanding defensive slot. He was quick and had an exceptional arm. In fact, his arm was so strong that he regularly threw out runners without rising from his catcher's crouch, a feat unheard of before his time.

A field leader *par excellence*, Ewing captained New York's NL champions of 1888–1889. After he retired as a player, he managed for several years, compiling a 489–395 mark. He was named to the Baseball Hall of Fame in 1939.

Connie Mack, a catcher himself, called Ewing the greatest ever. Buck's teammate, Mickey Welch, called him the greatest *player*, period. Buck was the first catcher to throw from the crouch and one of the first to use the big mitt.

His biggest rival was "King" Kelly of Chi, though Kelly played the outfield, too. Both were consistent—.303 for Ewing, .308 for Kelly. Ewing had power (a league-leading 10 homers in 1883) but Kelly had more (with 13 in '84).

Buck was fast enough to lead off, often stealing over 50 bases a year; but, then again, so did Kelly.

In 1893 Ewing played all nine positions. But Kelly played all but pitcher.

Kelly and Ewing—what little there was to choose between them was in their handling of pitchers, and in this Ewing had no peer.

URBAN "RED" FABER
Pitcher, Chi (A) 1914–33

The last of the AL's "legal" spitball pitchers, Faber spent his entire career with the White Sox. In 1921 he scored one of the finest pitching feats ever. Playing for the seventh-place White Sox, he was 25–15, with a league-leading ERA of 2.48. To prove it was no fluke, he went 21–17 the next year and again led in ERA, as the White Sox climbed to fifth.

Faber had won 20 earlier with strong teams behind him, but 1921 was the beginning of the post-Black Sox era, when Chicago plunged into the second division for almost two decades. In fifteen of Red's twenty seasons, Chicago finished in the second division. Yet, he had only six losing years and finished with 254 victories.

Disdaining strikeouts, Faber wanted batters to hit his pitch— his spitter—right into the dirt. He once pitched a nine-inning game with 67 pitches, or less than 3 pitches per out.

In the 1917 World Series, Red won 3 games and lost 1. He sat out the 1919 Black Sox Series with an injury, watching eight of his teammates lose on purpose.

In 1964 he was elected to the Baseball Hall of Fame.

ELROY FACE
Pitcher, Pit (N) 1953, 1955–68, Det (A) 1968, Mon (N) 1969
In 1959 Face and his newfangled forkball set an amazing record, 18–1, in relief for the fourth-place Pirates. Because the practice today is to bring in the "closer" almost exclusively to protect a lead, relief pitchers now accumulate more saves than ever before, but wins are rare. Face often relieved with the score tied or the Pirates a run or two behind. Of course, he "vultured" a few, also—blowing the lead, then getting the victory when the Pirates came from behind to win.

When Pittsburgh reached the World Series the next year, Face saved the first 3 games, as the Pirates beat the Yankees in 7 games on Bill Mazeroski's homer. With the different utilization of relief pitchers in his day, Face saved 193 games in his sixteen-year career. He won 96 games in relief and 8 more as a starter. His "out" pitch was the forkball, which he threw as an off-speed pitch. Now it is better known as the split-fingered fastball.

FERRIS FAIN
First Baseman, Phi (A) 1947–52, Chi (A) 1953–54, Det (A) 1955, Cle (A) 1955
Fain was a singles hitter in a HR position. He won two batting crowns, hitting .344 in 1951 and .327 in 1952, but had only one other .300 year. His OBP, however, was consistently high, as he drew at least 94 walks in seven of his nine seasons. In fact, his lifetime OBP of .425 is the eighth best of all players.

Although he led AL first basemen in errors five times, he was considered an exceptional fielder, with unusual range. He led in assists four times.

Fain became a star in the Pacific Coast League and complained that he had to take a pay cut when he came to the majors.

BOB FELLER
Pitcher, Cle (N) 1936–41, 1945–56
Feller came out of Iowa as a phenom—a schoolboy with a legendary fastball. Unlike so many prodigies, Feller made good on his promise. He just may have been the best pitcher ever. Many veterans say Bob was the fastest they ever saw, but Feller had a dangerous curve as well. He set the standard as the strikeout pitcher of his time.

As a seventeen-year-old kid, just off the farm, in 1936, Bobby whiffed 8 Cardinals in three innings in his first big league exhibition. In Bob's AL debut he fanned 15. At the age of nineteen in '38 Feller set a record with 18 strikeouts. That year Bob led the league in both strikeouts (240) and walks (208).

In 1939, at the age of twenty, Bob had his first big year—24–9, for the third-place Indians. Again he led in Ks and BBs. At twenty-one Bob hurled the only Opening Day no-hitter, went on to a 27–11 mark, fanned a league-high 261, and won *The Sporting News*' vote as Player of the Year. His no-hitter was the first of three. He also had a record 12 one-hitters, seven of them spoiled by the scratchiest of hits. Crowds flocked to see him duel Williams or DiMaggio. "It's just me against them," he exulted, "man to man."

Bob was 25–13 in 1941, as the Indians almost won the flag. Then, with his mountaintop years just ahead, he volunteered for combat duty as a naval gunner in the Pacific. He would go on to win eight battle stars. The war took almost four full years out of the very peak of Bob's career, ages twenty-three through twenty-six. His own estimate, probably conservative, is that it cost him 1,000 strikeouts and 100 wins, enough to give him over 3,500 whiffs and 360 victories.

Instead he ended with 2,581 Ks (once third on the all-time list, now farther down) and 266 wins. Bob also had a then-record 1,764 walks. In his first full season back, in 1946, Feller added a slider and struck out 348, one short of an AL record set by Rube Waddell in 1904. Feller had three more 20-win seasons in the postwar years.

Feller often pitched relief between starts and saved 21 games in addition to his 266 wins.

Bob never won a World Series game. In 1948 he lost an opening-game two-hitter, 1–0, when the Braves' Phil Masi was called safe on a pickoff play. Films clearly showed Masi was out, but Masi scored the only run of the game.

Feller was elected to the Baseball Hall of Fame in 1962.

RICK FERRELL
Catcher, StL (A) 1929–33, 1941–43, Bos (A) 1933–37, Was (A) 1937–41, 1944–45, 1947
Ferrell was the catcher for the AL in the first All-Star Game and caught all nine innings. Durability was one of his virtues. He held the AL record for most games caught with 1,805 until Carlton Fisk surpassed it in 1988. A fine defensive catcher with a strong arm, he was considered one of the best handlers of pitchers around. Ferrell was a fair hitter, who topped .300 four times, but had little home run power. His brother Wes, a pitcher, hit 10 more career homers, but Rick seldom struck out and drew more than his share of walks.

From 1934 into 1938, Rick caught his kid brother Wes, one of the more successful brother batteries in history. They were so in tune, it was said, that Rick could catch a whole game without signs. When they were on opposite sides, Rick did well against Wes, once homering off him.

Rick had a rare knack for handling knuckleball pitchers. In 1945 he caught for Washington, a team with four knuckleballers as starters.

He was elected to the Baseball Hall of Fame in 1984.

WES FERRELL
Pitcher, Cle (A) 1927–33, Bos (A) 1934–37, Was (A) 1937–38, NY (A) 1939, Bkn (N) 1940, Bos (N) 1941
Ferrell won 20 or more games for the Indians in each of his first four full years, starting in 1929. Possessed of a blazing fastball and a blazing temper, the handsome righthander was a little wild on the mound. In two of those seasons, his walks outnumbered his strikeouts.

A sore arm in 1933 cost him his fastball and he was traded to Boston the next year, where he joined his catcher brother Rick. Wes became a junkball pitcher and twice won 20 for the Bosox. He had his best season in 1935 when he was 25–14 with the fourth-place Red Sox and led the AL in wins, complete games, and innings pitched. He finished his career with a 193–128 record and .601 percentage. His 4.04 career ERA looks better in the context of his time than it does when compared with earlier and later eras.

Ferrell may have been the best-hitting-pitcher of all. He had a career batting average of .280 and his 38 home runs are the most by any pitcher. Wes's best home run year was 1931 with 9. That year he also tossed a no-hitter, a rare feat in the high-hitting 1930s.

An amateur astrologer, Wes guided his career by the stars and said they accurately predicted his ups and downs.

ROLLIE FINGERS
Pitcher, Oak (A) 1968–76, SD (N) 1977–80, Mil (A) 1981–82, 1984–85
In his seventeen-year career, Fingers saved 341 games. That's more preserving than Grandma used to do at canning time and it's also the all-time record for relief pitchers. His 107 relief wins are third on the list.

Rollie was the main man out of the Oakland bullpen in the early 1970s when the A's won five division titles, three pennants, and three World Championships. In the 1974 World Series, his 1 win and 2 saves earned him the MVP nod. His 6 saves in three Series is a record.

Fingers pitched for San Diego from 1977 to 1980 and had his two top save seasons there, with 35 in 1977 and 37 the next year. Both marks led the NL. He was named Relief Man of the Year by Rolaids and Fireman of the Year by *The Sporting News* in both seasons.

Returning to the AL with Milwaukee in 1981, he led the AL in saves with 28 in a strike-shortened season. He was named both MVP and Cy Young winner. An arm injury in 1982 kept him out of the World Series and caused him to miss the 1983 season.

Famous for his handlebar mustache, the spare, six-foot-four righthander relied on good control of his fastball. Later in his career, Fingers added a slider.

CHARLES O. FINLEY
Owner, KC (A) 1961–67, Oak (A) 1968–80
Only George Steinbrenner, among ballclub owners, has been more controversial than Finley, an insurance tycoon who bought the old Kansas City A's and moved them to Oakland. He feuded with his players, with fans, and with Commissioner Bowie Kuhn. He also built a dynasty around Reggie Jackson, Catfish Hunter, Sal Bando, Rollie Fingers, Vida Blue, and others. His Athletics won five straight division titles from 1971 to 1975, and three consecutive World Championships.

Free agency eventually did Finley's A's in. Unwilling to pay the ever-increasing salaries, Finley tried to sell off a few of his stars before they became free agents, but the deals were blocked by the commissioner. Finley went to court but lost. And then he lost the players. Ironically, it was some of his controversial labor relations with players that inadvertently helped hasten free agency.

Finley hired and fired managers at a pace that seemed breakneck in those pre-Steinbrenner days. He also drew fans with sometimes outrageous promotions. He put a jackass in his bullpen and named it "Charley O." He burst with ideas—many of which were originally laughed at but many of which have also come to pass. He favored night World Series games, colorful uniforms, and designated hitters. He also advocated interleague play and *orange* baseballs.

Stubborn and volatile, Finley changed baseball in his twenty years with the A's. For the worse, his critics said. For the better, time seems to be saying.

CARLTON FISK
Catcher, Bos (A) 1969–80, Chi (A) 1981-
The image of Fisk using body English to coax his game-winning homer to stay fair in the twelfth inning of Game Six in the 1975 World Series is locked in the minds of millions of baseball fans who saw it on television. But Fisk was more than a one-hit hero.

He won the Rookie of the Year Award with the Red Sox in 1972, hitting .293 with 22 home runs. Although he's topped .300 twice, his batting average has normally been well below that of his first year. However, he's maintained his long-ball power. In 1985, at age thirty-seven, he hit 37 homers. In 1987 he surpassed 300 career home runs. And in 1988 he established a new mark for games caught in the AL.

Durable, strong-armed, and an outstanding handler of pitchers, Fisk ranks among the best catchers in the history of the game. In 1981 he left Boston via free agency and signed with the White Sox.

FREDDIE FITZSIMMONS
Pitcher, NY (N) 1925–37, Bkn (N) 1937–43. Manager, Phi (N) 1943–45
Fitzsimmons combined with southpaw Carl Hubbell to give the Giants an excellent righty-lefty one-two punch in the late 1920s and early 1930s. Although Hubbell was the Giants' "Meal Ticket," the team also fed on a steady diet of wins by "Fat Freddie." Fitzsimmons combined a wide assortment of pitches, excellent control, and an odd windup involving a turn toward second base (à la Luis Tiant) to go 20–9 in 1928 and 19–7 in 1930. Twice he won 18.

Traded to Brooklyn in 1937, he was used as a spot starter with great success. His 16–2 mark in 1940 led the NL in winning percentage. In 1941, at the age of forty, Fitzsimmons started Game Three of the World Series to become the oldest starter in Series history. For seven innings he shut out the mighty Yankees, but a drive off the bat of his mound opponent, Marius Russo, hit him flush on the knee and put him out of the game. The Yankees scored twice in the next inning to win, 2–1.

Fitzsimmons finished his career at 217–146.

ELMER FLICK

Outfielder, Phi (N) 1898–1902; Cle (A) 1902–10

Although he's chiefly famous for winning the 1905 AL batting crown with an average of just .308, Flick was actually one of the top hitters at the turn of the century. In 1905 the league batting average was only .241; Willie Keeler, another pretty good hitter, was the only other regular in the league to get above .300. Elmer's best mark, .367 in 1900, almost won the NL title; he lost to Honus Wagner's .381 on the final day.

For three years straight, 1905 to 1907, Flick led the AL in triples. His career batting average was .313.

Flick was so good, in fact, that when he hit .302 for Cleveland in 1907, Detroit offered to swap their young star outfielder for Elmer even up. Cleveland preferred to stick with Flick and so passed up the offer of Ty Cobb. Unfortunately, injuries all but ended Elmer's career the next year; he played in only 99 more games.

He was named to the Baseball Hall of Fame in 1963.

CURT FLOOD

Outfielder, Cin (N) 1956–57, StL (N) 1958–69, Was (A) 1971

Flood was one of the most important and influential players in the history of baseball, though his significance was unrelated to his undeniable talent. During the 1960s Flood helped the Cardinals to three pennants as their center fielder. A good hitter (career average .293), Curt excelled in the outfield. He was voted Gold Gloves from 1963 through 1969.

However, when the Cardinals attempted to trade him to the Phillies after the '69 season, he refused. "I do not feel I am a piece of property to be bought and sold irrespective of my wishes," he wrote to Commissioner Bowie Kuhn. He turned down a $100,000 contract with the Phillies to challenge baseball's reserve clause in federal court. The case went all the way to the U.S. Supreme Court, where his plea was rejected, 5–3. Nevertheless, the narrowness of the ruling forced baseball's owners to agree to an arbitration system, which eventually ended the reserve clause.

Flood, a serious, introspective man, briefly attempted a comeback in 1971 and then retired. Though he received none of the benefits of baseball's current free agency, he—more than any other player—is responsible for it.

ED "WHITEY" FORD

Pitcher, NY (A) 1950, 1953–67

The "Chairman of the Board," Ford ranks as one of the greatest lefthanded pitchers of all time. His 236–106 career record yields a winning percentage of .690, third all-time and the best of any 200-game winner in this century. He led the AL in victories three times, ERA and shutouts twice. He won the 1961 Cy Young Award at a time when only one was given to cover both leagues.

But Whitey's fame rests primarily on his ability as a "money pitcher," and pitching for eleven Yankee pennant winners gave him ample opportunity to earn his reputation. His World Series performances alone were enough. He started the most games (22), pitched the most innings (146), gave up the most hits (134), struck out the most batters (94), walked the most (34), and won the most (10). He also ranks first in losses (8), but his 2.71 ERA speaks

better for the quality of his efforts.

A fun-loving native New Yorker, Whitey first pitched for the Yankees in 1950, when he went 9–1 and added his first Series win after a midseason call-up. He then entered the service for two years, but upon his return, picked up where he'd left off. Yankees Manager Casey Stengel used him judiciously throughout the 1950s; in only 1955 did Ford start more than 30 games, limiting the number of wins (and losses) he could earn in a given season. After Stengel was replaced in 1961, the number of Whitey's starts per year increased sharply. He won 25 games in 1961 and 24 in 1963.

Ford pitched with his head more than his arm. He was the master of a variety of pitches, including a few frowned upon in the rulebook. He was moderately wild in his early years, but developed into one of the best control artists in the league.

In 1974 Ford was elected to the Baseball Hall of Fame.

BILL FOSTER

Pitcher, Negro Leagues, 1923–37, Memphis Red Sox, Chicago American Giants, Homestead Grays, Kansas City Monarchs, Cole's American Giants

Big Bill, Rube Foster's younger half-brother, was considered one of the two best lefthanded pitchers in the black leagues. He ranks first in wins and his 18 victories in 1927 are the third-highest season total.

Foster's two most famous wins came for the Chicago American Giants over "Bullet Joe" Rogan, ace of the rival Kansas City Monarchs, in the 1926 championship play-off. Bill's team was down 3 games to 2, when he beat Rogan 2–0 and 5–0 in a double-header to clinch the pennant.

Foster's best seasons were 1927 (18–3) and '32 (14–6).

ANDREW "RUBE" FOSTER

League President/Owner/Manager/Pitcher, Negro Leagues, 1902–26, Chicago Union Giants, Cuban-X Giants, Philadelphia Giants, Leland Giants, Chicago American Giants

"The Father of Black Baseball," Foster first attracted attention with his pitching. In 1902, he won four of the Philadelphia Cuban-X Giants' five wins against the Philadelphia Giants in a playoff billed as for the "Colored Championship of the World." The next year he switched to the Giants and led them to the title.

In 1910, in partnership with the son-in-law of Charles Comiskey, he formed the Chicago American Giants to play at the White Sox's old South Side Park. Although there was no league, Foster's Giants were generally recognized as the leading black team throughout the decade. As their manager, Foster built his teams on speed and pitching, insisted on disciplined play and initiated several strategies that became standard.

Black baseball was generally in a chaotic state when Foster and the owners of six Midwestern teams formed the Negro National League. Foster was named president and his Giants won the first three pennants. The NNL raised standards for players, drew fans with pennant races, and, according to many, saved black baseball. As president, Foster worked fifteen-hour days but drew no regular salary. He did receive a percentage of league-game attendance, but contributed part of that to the league. He preached that if blacks maintained a high level of play, when the whites were ready to open the doors, the blacks would be ready to walk through.

In 1926 Foster suffered a nervous breakdown from overwork. He died four years later, but black baseball had been put on a solid footing.

In 1981 Foster was named to the Baseball Hall of Fame.

GEORGE FOSTER
Outfielder, SF (N) 1969–71, Cin (N) 1971–81, NY (N) 1982–86, Chi (A) 1986

Foster earned the nickname "The Destroyer" as well as the NL's 1977 MVP Award for his heavy hitting with Cincinnati's Big Red Machine in the 1970s. A quiet, introspective man with deep religious convictions, he conversely presented one of baseball's most menacing presences when standing at the plate with his black bat and glowering expression. From 1976–78 he led the NL in RBIs, with 121, 149, and 120. He also was home run leader in 1977–1978, with 52 and 40.

Traded to the Mets in 1982, he found himself playing half his games in a poor hitter's park and without the flock of teammates clogging the bases, waiting to be driven home, that he had known in Cincinnati. Although he twice drove in 90 runs, he could never regain the slugging level he'd attained with the Reds, and his fielding—never good—became a major liability.

He completed his career with 348 home runs and 1,239 RBIs.

NELLIE FOX
Second Baseman, Phi (A) 1947–49, Chi (A) 1950–63, Hou (N) 1964–65

Little Nellie (five-ten, 160 pounds) was a plucky second baseman, known for his choke-up batting grip and huge wad of tobacco. He was the heart of the Go-Go White Sox of the 1950s, teaming first with Chico Carrasquel and then with Luis Aparicio as the AL's premier keystone combo. He led the league's second basemen five times in turning double plays.

Considered a poor hitter when he first arrived in the majors, Fox learned to punch out short drives and led the AL seven straight years (1954–1960) in singles and four years in total hits. He batted .300 or better six times and finished with a .288 career batting average. He struck out about as often as Chicago has an honest election, and ranks as the third-hardest batter to whiff in history.

But more than for his stats, Nellie was known for his all-out hustling play and infectious spirit. When the White Sox won their first pennant in forty years in 1959, Fox was named Most Valuable Player, though several other players had better statistics.

JIMMIE FOXX
First Baseman, Phi (A) 1925–35, Bos (A) 1936–42, Chi (N) 1942, 1944–45

Foxx, the Maryland strongman discovered appropriately by Home Run Baker, ranks with the greatest sluggers of all time. When he retired, his 534 homers ranked second to Babe Ruth and only Ruth and Roger Maris hit more in one season than Jimmie's 58 in 1932.

"Double X" loved to show off his bulging biceps by cutting the sleeves off his shirts. "Even his hair has muscles," winced Lefty Gomez, who threw a pitch that Jimmie walloped into the farthest corner of the third deck in Yankee Stadium. "It took forty-five minutes to walk up there," Lefty said.

Originally a catcher, Foxx found that way blocked with the A's by Mickey Cochrane. He switched to first base and became one of the key players in Philadelphia's 1929–1931 dynasty. In those three seasons he hit 100 home runs and drove in 343.

In 1932 the good-natured, moon-faced Foxx launched an assault on Babe Ruth's five-year-old mark of 60 homers. Although he fell short with 58, fans noted he had 2 home runs washed out by rainouts. His homers, 169 RBIs, and .364 batting average won him the MVP award. He won again in 1933 with a Triple Crown year: 48 home runs, 163 RBIs, and a .356 batting average.

Traded to the Red Sox after tying for the home run crown with 36 in 1935, he took advantage of Fenway Park's short left field fence to produce several fine years. In 1938 his league-leading 175 RBIs and .349 batting average earned him his third Most Valuable Player award. Curiously, his 50 homers did not lead the league, but his more modest 35 the next year did.

"The Beast," as he was affectionately known, finished his career with 1,921 RBIs (sixth all-time) and a .325 batting average. His lifetime .609 slugging average ranks fourth behind only Ruth, Williams, and Gehrig.

In 1951 Foxx was elected to the Baseball Hall of Fame.

BILL FREEHAN
Catcher, Det (A) 1961, 1963–76

Signed for a $100,000 bonus by the Tigers, Freehan turned out to be an excellent investment. He solved their catching problems for thirteen seasons (1963–1975). Freehan was a terrific catcher who won five Gold Gloves and holds the AL record for career fielding percentage (.993) for catchers. He hit an even .300 in 1964, but most of his batting marks were considerably lower, and he ended with a .262 career average. That was offset by his 200 career home runs. He got high marks as a team leader and helped the Tigers to a World Championship in 1968 and an American League East pennant in 1972.

LARRY FRENCH
Pitcher, Pit (N) 1929–34, Chi (N) 1935–41, Bkn (N) 1942

Four men have broken into the majors with one-hitters. French is the only man who went out with one. He tossed it for the Dodgers in September of 1942 at the age of thirty-four. Then he marched into the Navy for the next twenty-seven years, emerging as a four-stripe captain. His career mark of 197–171 left him only 3 victories shy of becoming the first pitcher to win 200 without a 20-win season.

A lefthanded knuckleballer, French spent the first half of his career with the lowly Pirates, then joined the Cubs in 1935 in time to help them to the pennant with a 17–10 mark.

Chicago won again in 1938, but Larry had his worst season to become the only man ever to lose 19 games with a pennant winner.

FORD FRICK

Commissioner/League President

Starting as a sportswriter (and Ruth's "ghost"), Frick spent forty-three years in baseball. As NL president (1934–1951), he was pivotal in the Jackie Robinson Revolution. When the Cardinals threatened to strike rather than play against Robinson in 1947, Frick told them bluntly: "I don't care if half the league strikes. Those who do will . . . be suspended, and I do not care if it wrecks the NL for five years. This is the United States of America, and one citizen has as much right to play as another."

He was also one of the forces behind the establishment of a Hall of Fame; in 1970 he was elected to the Hall himself.

As Baseball Commissioner (1951–1968), Frick presided over expansion to Milwaukee, Los Angeles, San Francisco, Minneapolis-St. Paul, Houston, Baltimore, Oakland, and Atlanta. He negotiated a $13-million TV package with NBC, and oversaw the end of the reserve clause and the birth of the free agent draft.

His most controversial ruling was probably his decision that an asterisk be placed beside Roger Maris's 61-homer record, an edict that was never enforced.

FRANKIE FRISCH

Second Baseman, NY (N) 1919–26, StL (N) 1927–37.
Manager, StL (N) 1933–38, Pit (N) 1940–46, Chi (N) 1949–51

"The Fordham Flash" stepped straight from the Rams' campus into the major leagues with the Giants in 1919. He was a key man on New York's four straight pennant winners from 1921 through 1924. A slashing switch-hitter, he "never hit a home run when a single would win the game" but cracked plenty of singles, doubles, and triples. He led the NL with 223 hits in 1923, had thirteen seasons of batting over .300, scored over 100 seven times, and batted in over 100 three times. His career marks included 1,532 runs scored, 1,244 RBIs, and a .316 batting average.

For several years he was considered the likely heir to John McGraw as manager of the Giants, but the feisty Frisch rebelled at McGraw's dictatorial methods. In 1927 he was traded to St. Louis in exchange for Rogers Hornsby, a swap that shocked and angered Cardinal fans.

Though never the hitter that Hornsby was, Frisch was a better fielder and his equal as a team leader. He played on Cardinal pennant winners in 1928, 1930–1931, and after becoming player-manager, in 1934. All told, he played on eight pennant winners and six runners-up. He was named NL MVP in 1931, but he is probably better known as the scrappy leader of the Cardinal "Gashouse Gang" that won the 1934 world championship.

In sixteen years as a manager, and despite being saddled with weak teams in Chicago during his final seasons, he compiled a .513 winning percentage.

He was elected to the Hall of Fame in 1947.

JIM "PUD" GALVIN

Pitcher, StL (NA) 1875, Buf (N) 1879–85, Pit (AA) 1885–86, Pit (N) 1887–89, 1891–92, Pit (P) 1890, StL (N) 1892. Manager, Buf (N) 1885

Supposedly Galvin picked up the nickname "Pud" for making "pudding" out of batters. On the other hand, the five-eight pitcher checked in at 190 pounds at his lightest and once ballooned to 320. When he ran, what did he jiggle like a bowl of?

He was the greatest fat pitcher, and the hardest-working. In the early 1880s, when pound-for-pound Galvin was as good as any pitcher around, slabmen threw underhand from a shorter distance. Usually two pitchers worked every other game, and regulars always had high numbers. But Galvin was ridiculous.

One year he pitched 656 innings, the next year 636. He had one 593-inning season and six more over 400. He was effective, too. Although his teams ran from fair to rotten, he had two seasons with 46 wins, one with 37, and seven years with from 20 to 29. He pitched 2 no-hitters and 57 shutouts. He walked almost no one—1.13 per nine innings. And he had the greatest pick-off move of his day— once nailing three baserunners in the same inning!

In fourteen seasons, he won 361 games to rank sixth all-time. His 307 losses are the second-most ever. He's also second all-time in innings pitched (5,941) and complete games (639).

A placid, gentle man, Galvin opened a saloon in Pittsburgh after he retired from baseball. Reportedly the place was always packed, but he went broke anyway. Then the nine bartenders he'd hired each opened a bar.

In 1965 he was named to the Hall of Fame.

LOU GEHRIG

First Baseman, NY (A) 1923–39

Gehrig played in the shadow of Ruth and, later, DiMaggio. He played in an era of great first basemen—Foxx, Mize, Greenberg, and Terry. He also played a record 2,130 straight games, and became in his quiet way perhaps the best first baseman ever. They called him "The Iron Horse"; he hauled the Yankees to seven pennants.

"I'm not a headline guy," Lou said. When he hit .545 in the 1928 World Series, Ruth hit .625. When Gehrig hit a home run in the 1932 Series, Ruth had just hit his "called shot" homer ahead of him. When Lou slugged 4 home runs in one game, John McGraw retired the same day to steal the headlines.

When Gehrig was voted MVP in 1927, he was paid $6,000. Ruth got $80,000. That was the year Babe hit 60 homers to 47 for Lou.

But Lou set some marks even Babe couldn't touch— 184 RBIs in 1931. That year Lou produced 301 runs (runs scored plus RBIs, minus home runs), the all-time record. His 23 grand slams are also a record. In the 1932 World Series, Lou was truly Ruthian. In four games he hit 3 home runs, batted .529, and knocked in a four-game record eight runs.

Before Lou's death at the age of thirty-seven, he had hit 493 homers, then the third-highest ever, behind Ruth and Foxx. Some old-timers say Gehrig hit the ball as hard as they did, but he hit it on a line with overspin; they lifted it into the air for greater distance.

Gehrig had 1,991 RBIs, third behind Ruth and Aaron. Of course, Babe was on base to score a lot of those runs. On the other hand, Gehrig often came up with the bases empty after Babe had cleared them. Yankee Stadium didn't help him—he actually hit better on the road. He led the AL in RBIs five times.

Gehrig won the Triple Crown in 1934 (.363, 49 homers, 165 RBIs) but finished only fifth in the MVP voting. He won the award in 1936 with 49 home runs, 167 runs scored, and 152 RBIs.

In 1939 Gehrig finally took himself out of the lineup. With death approaching, he told sixty-one thousand fans in Yankee Stadium, "I consider myself the luckiest man on the face of the earth."

The normal waiting period was waived and he was elected to the Baseball Hall of Fame in 1939.

CHARLIE GEHRINGER
Second Baseman, Det (A) 1924–42
A lefthanded hitter, Gehringer slapped hits to all fields. He made 2,839 base hits over nineteen years, including 184 home runs, 146 triples, and—tenth all-time—574 doubles. He topped .300 in thirteen of his sixteen full seasons, led the AL with a .371 mark in 1937 to earn MVP honors, drove in 100-plus runs seven times and 1,427 for his career.

In the field his hallmarks were grace and efficiency. He made even the hardest plays look easy. Seven times he led AL second basemen in assists, nine times in fielding average.

He was tough in World Series play. His home run in the fifth game in 1934 beat Dizzy Dean of the Cardinals. A year later he singled in the ninth against the Cubs and scored the winning run that gave Detroit the championship.

But he hardly ever showed emotion or said anything about *anything*. Reporters liked to quote him—". . ." They called him the "Mechanical Man." He was as colorful as a glass of water.

He was elected to the Baseball Hall of Fame in 1949.

BOB "HOOT" GIBSON
Pitcher, StL (N) 1959–75
In 1968 Gibson registered the lowest ERA in NL history, 1.12; hurled 13 shutouts, second-best in NL annals; went 22–9; and then fanned a record 35 in the World Series, including 17 in one game to shut out the Tigers and 31-game winner Denny McLain. It was a pitcher's year, but *wow!*

A fire-breathing, flame-throwing competitor, Bob was the best righthanded pitcher of the power-pitching 1960s. He won two Cy Youngs and one MVP.

In three World Series Bob was 7–2, had a 1.89 ERA, and struck out 92 men in 81 innings. In his first Series, against the Yanks in 1964, he lost the second game, then came back to win games Five and Seven. Three years later, 1967, Gibson broke his leg in midseason but threw away his crutches to win 3 against Boston that fall, a six-hitter, a five-hitter, and a three-hitter, in that order.

The broken leg in 1967 came after two 20-win seasons and before three more 20-win years. He also won 19 twice. In 1971 he threw a no-hitter against Pittsburgh, the world champions that year. When Gibson retired, he was the winningest pitcher in St Louis history (251–174) and second all-time in strikeouts (3,117).

Immensely intimidating on the mound, Bob put every ounce of power into his pitches—primarily a fastball and slider. He had a reputation as a headhunter, but insists he "hardly ever threw at a batter." Nevertheless, he has been heard to admit, "When I did, I hit 'em."

He was elected to the Baseball Hall of Fame in 1981.

JOSH GIBSON
Catcher, Negro Leagues, 1930–46, Homestead Grays, Pittsburgh Crawfords
"There is a catcher," said Walter Johnson, the Hall of Fame pitcher, "that any big league club would like to buy for $200,000. His name is Gibson. He can do everything. He hits the ball a mile, catches so easily he might as well be in a rocking chair, throws like a bullet. Bill Dickey isn't as good a catcher. Too bad this Gibson is a colored fellow."

Because black players were barred from the white major leagues during Gibson's time, there is no way to know for certain that he was the best catcher of all time. He may have been only one of the half dozen best. No lower ranking seems possible for the man they called "the Black Babe Ruth."

Actually accounts of his catching skills vary. Some say he was a little weak on pop fouls, but everyone agrees he had a good arm.

There's no dispute about his hitting. It was magnificent. The barrel-chested, 215-pound slugger hit home runs of tremendous length. One was measured with a tape at 575 feet, but it may not have been his longest. He also hit them often. One estimate, including barnstorming, Mexican League, Caribbean, and semipro games, puts his total at about 950. In Negro League and semi-pro games he was credited with 75 homers in 1931 and 69 in 1934. His batting average for seventeen years with the Homestead Grays and Pittsburgh Crawfords was over .350. He topped .400 at least twice. Combining with Buck Leonard in a "Ruth-Gehrig" tandem, Gibson led the Grays to nine straight pennants (1937–1945).

A warm, fun-loving man, Gibson was popular everywhere he played and, next to Satchel Paige, the Negro Leagues' greatest drawing card. For a time, he and Paige were battery mates.

Gibson was thirty-three years old when Jackie Robinson signed to play for the Dodgers. Reportedly he was bitter at having been passed over. Many believe he would have been signed by a white major league team in 1947, but he died of a brain hemorrhage in January of that year.

In 1972 he became the second Negro League player elected to the Hall of Fame.

WARREN GILES
National League President, 1951–69
Wounded as a lieutenant in World War One, Giles was elected president of the Moline (Illinois) team in the Three-I League in 1919, to start a baseball career that spanned fifty years. He helped Branch Rickey build the Cardinals' farm system into baseball's best. In 1937 he took over as general manager of the last-place Cincinnati Reds. Two years later he had them in the World Series. In 1940 they were world champions.

As NL president, Giles oversaw league expansion to the West Coast, the attendance boom that followed the Vietnam War, and the battles with the players' union.

He was elected to the Hall of Fame in 1979.

VERNON "LEFTY" GOMEZ
Pitcher, NY (A) 1930–42, Was (A) 1943

"Goofy" Gomez, inventor of the revolving goldfish bowl for tired goldfish, is one of the wittiest men ever to pitch a baseball. He entertained his teammates with his antics and one-liners. And sometimes—when he wasn't pitching—drew a smile from the opposition. His credo was "I'd rather be lucky than good." Actually he was both.

He was lucky to pitch for powerful Yankees' teams of the 1930s. They gave him baseball's most consistent support with their bats and gloves and enabled him to pitch in five World Series. And he was lucky to pitch half the time in Yankee Stadium, where "Death Valley" in the left field power alley swallowed up long drives from righthanded hitters.

But he was good too—one of the best lefthanders of the century. He won 20 games four times, including a sensational 26–5 year in 1934. He led the AL in strikeouts three times, with a top mark of 194 in 1938. He won 189 and lost 102. And in five World Series, he won six without a single loss.

He took his pitching seriously, but he had the ability to laugh at himself. He said the secret of his success was "clean living and a fast outfield—I'm the guy who made Joe DiMaggio famous."

Gomez was elected to the Hall of Fame in 1972.

JOE GORDON
Second Baseman, NY (A) 1938–43, 1946, Cle (A) 1947–50. Manager, Cle (A) 1958–60, Det (A) 1960, KC (A) 1961, 1969
Anyone with Gordon's surname is likely to be nicknamed "Flash," but Joe lived up to the label with his acrobatic defensive skills. He ranged over the Yankee infield, making plays that other second basemen dream about. One game he made eleven assists. He was at the head of AL second sackers in assists four times. Of course, the flip side was that in getting to balls others couldn't, he sometimes fumbled them. He led or tied in errors four times too. It was worth the price. In the first six years he cavorted at second base for the Yankees, they went to five World Series.

He seldom hit for average, but he had home run power. The one year he topped .300—.322 in 1942—he was named AL MVP. After he returned from military service, he struggled though a .210 season, and the Yankees, figuring he was washed up, dealt him to Cleveland. There he combined with Lou Boudreau to form what many still consider the most deadly double-play combination ever.

In 1948 he had his greatest season, batting .280, with 32 homers and 124 RBIs, as the Indians won the world championship. He completed his career with 253 home runs and 975 RBIs.

LEON "GOOSE" GOSLIN
Outfield, Was (A) 1921–30, 1933, 1938, StL (A) 1930–32, Det (A) 1934–37
Except for the years Ted Williams managed the team, Goslin was the best hitter ever to wear a Washington uniform. He was with the Senators for all of the 1920s and looked in on them twice in the 1930s, slumming. The Senators were a pretty terrible team through most of their stay in the AL. Everybody knows the line: "Washington: first in war, first in peace, and last in the American League." But actually they weren't so awful when Goslin

was with them; they won three pennants, the only ones they'd ever win.

Goslin showed up at the end of the 1921 season, and by the next year he was a fixture in left field. "Fixture" is a little harsh. He was neither the worst nor the slowest outfielder in the AL, just sort of lumbering.

But when he had the lumber in his hands, he was a star. He hit .300 or over in his first seven full years as a Senator. In 1924 he led the AL in RBIs with 129, hit .344 and knocked 12 homers, which was a fair number for anyone playing half his games in cavernous Griffith Stadium. The Senators won their first pennant and only World Series, as Goslin at one point set a record with 6 consecutive hits. The next year the Senators won their second pennant, as Goslin led the AL in triples, while hitting .334 with 18 homers and 113 RBIs. He hit .354 and .334 in the next two seasons, then topped the AL in 1928 with a .379 mark in the closest batting race in AL history; Goose singled in his last at-bat of the season to edge Heinie Manush by .001.

He hurt his arm horsing around in 1929, and for a time it looked like curtains. The Senators dealt him to the Browns ("St. Louis: gateway to the West and to the bottom of the American League") and his arm came back. After a couple of good years in St. Louis (the Brownies even finished fifth in 1931), he was sent back to Washington with thanks in 1933. And darned if the Senators didn't win their third and last-ever pennant that year!

Next, it was off to Detroit for Goose and pennants in 1934 and 1935, something they hadn't seen in Detroit since 1909.

Goslin finished up with a career batting average of .316 and 248 home runs, but his best thing was batting in runs—1,609.

He was elected to the Hall of Fame in 1968.

RICH "GOOSE" GOSSAGE
Pitcher, Chi (A) 1972–76, Pit (N) 1977, NY (A) 1978–83, 1989, SD (N) 1984–87, Chi (N) 1988, SF (N) 1989
In his heyday, 1975–86, the big, mustachioed Goose glowered at the hitters, then blew his fastball by them. He didn't have a whole lot more than heat and intimidation, but for an inning or two he was devastating. He led the AL in saves with the fifth-place White Sox in 1975. The next year, desperate for starters, the Sox put him into the rotation. He struggled to 9–17 and was traded to Pittsburgh. Returned to his natural habitat, the bullpen, he saved 26, won 11, and set an NL record for relievers with 151 strikeouts.

In 1978 Goose signed with the Yankees as a free agent. He led the AL with 27 saves and won 10 as New York caught Boston on the last day of the season and then won the pennant in a playoff. Gossage spent six seasons in New York, earning a reputation as one of the top relievers in the game. In 1984 he moved again as a free agent, this time to San Diego, where he helped the Padres to their first pennant.

HANK GOWDY
Catcher, NY (N) 1910–11, 1923–25, Bos (N) 1911–17, 1919–23, 1929–30
A quality catcher and fair hitter. Gowdy was the first

major league player to enter military service in World War One. He was the regular receiver for the "Miracle Braves" of 1914. In the four-game World Series sweep over the A's, he hit .545, with three doubles, a triple, and a home run.

Ten years later, catching for the Giants in the 1924 Series, he was a goat in the final game. Hank tripped over his face mask on an easy pop foul by Muddy Ruel, who then doubled and scored the winning run.

HANK GREENBERG
First Baseman, Det (A) 1930, 1933–41, 1945–46, Pit (N) 1947

One of the most fearsome home run hitters of all time, Greenberg played only nine full seasons, yet amassed 331 homers and 1,276 RBIs. Although he was an impressive six-four and 210 pounds, his success stemmed more from hard work than natural gifts. Thought too tall and awkward to play baseball, he applied himself with diligence and made himself into an adequate defensive first baseman. In 1940, when the Tigers wanted to get Rudy York's bat into the lineup, Hank went to left field, and did the job well enough that the Tigers won the pennant.

In 1934 he led the Tigers to the World Series with 26 homers, 139 RBIs, and a league-leading 63 doubles. In 1935 he was even better, winning his first MVP Award with 36 home runs and 170 RBIs, both leading the AL. The Tigers were world champions,

The following year a broken wrist limited him to 12 games, but in 1937 he came back with 40 home runs and 183 RBIs, the third-highest RBI total ever. Perhaps his 1938 season is his most famous. That year he chased Babe Ruth's record down to the wire, finishing with 58 home runs. No righthanded hitter has ever exceeded that total. He had a knack for hitting more than one in a game, accomplishing that eleven times during the year. Two years later, as the Tigers' new left fielder, he won his second MVP on 41 homers and 150 RBIs, and the Tigers again won the pennant.

Then in 1941, only 19 games into the season, Greenberg was inducted into the Army. He was thirty-one. He did not return to the Tigers until midway through 1945. Fittingly his ninth-inning grand slam on the final day of the season won Detroit another pennant. After once more leading the AL in homers (with 44) and RBIs (with 127) in 1946, he was sold to Pittsburgh before the 1947 season for $75,000. The Pirates shortened the distant left field fence at Forbes Field in his honor by erecting a bullpen, quickly labeled "Greenberg Gardens." Hank hit 25 homers in 1947, then retired, but the Pirates' young slugger, Ralph Kiner, who'd been Greenberg's roommate on the Pirates, credited Greenberg's instruction and example with much of his subsequent success as a home run hitter.

Greenberg was elected to the Hall of Fame in 1956.

GUS GREENLEE
Owner, Negro League

The flamboyant Greenlee, cigar-chomping Pittsburgh racketeer and numbers lord, never would have passed Judge Landis's scrutiny as a white owner. But he may have saved black baseball in the dreary days of the Depression.

Gus owned the Pittsburgh Crawfords, acclaimed by many as the best black team of all time, with Satchel Paige, Josh Gibson, Oscar Charleston, Cool Papa Bell, Judy Johnson, and other greats of black baseball. He waged a spirited war against Homestead Grays' owner Cum Posey for supremacy in Pittsburgh. Cum got his own racketeer to bankroll him, and the two fought both in the park and out.

Greenlee signed Paige from Birmingham and promoted him into the greatest drawing card in black ball. He also publicized Pepper Bassett, who caught Satch sitting in a rocking chair.

In 1933 Gus helped revive the Negro National League after the Depression had put it out for a year. He served as league president from 1933 to 1937. He also provided the inspiration for the East-West or All-Star Game, played in Comiskey Park a month after the first white All-Star Game there. It proved a financial life-saver, with upwards of 50,000 fans some years. The only profit many black clubs made all year was their share of receipts from that one game.

Gus also owned a stable of boxers, including world light-heavyweight champ John Henry Lewis. Like the ball team, the hobby lost money but was a cover for his numbers activities.

In 1937 Dominican dictator Rafael Trujillo bought Gus's stars out from under him, the Pittsburgh police finally raided his numbers store, and Gus at last was on the ropes.

BOBBY GRICH
Second Baseman, Bal (A) 1970–76, Cal (A) 1977–86

One of the most underrated players in the game, Grich was an outstanding all-around player who was generally thought of as only a glove man. His fielding, of course, *was* exceptional. In 1985 he made only two errors all season, to set a new standard for second basemen with a .997 fielding average. In 1973 he had a .995 mark. His career percentage of .984 is also the record. He won four Gold Gloves.

What was often overlooked was his hitting. He hit .304 in 1981 and got into the .290s a couple of times, but he was more comfortable at .250-.260. Nevertheless his ability to draw walks—twice over 100—kept him on base and allowed him to score 1,033 runs. He had good home run power with 224 career round-trippers. In the strike-shortened 1981 season he tied for the AL homer title with 22. Two years earlier he blasted 30 and drove in 101 runs.

Part of Grich's image problem was his postseason play. With Baltimore and California he appeared in five LCS's, always on the losing side. And in 24 LCS games he hit only .182.

CLARK GRIFFITH
Pitcher, StL (AA) 1891, Bos (AA) 1891, Chi (N) 1893–1900, Chi (A) 1901–02, NY (A) 1903–07, Cin (N) 1909–10, Was (A) 1912-14. Manager, Chi (A) 1901–02, NY (A) 1903–08, Cin (N) 1909–11, Was (A) 1912-20

"The Old Fox," Griffith was elected to the Hall of Fame in 1946 as one of the game's pioneers. He could just as easily have gone in for his pitching. And he wasn't a bad manager either. Clark was born in a Missouri log cabin. His father was shot and killed when Clark was two. The boy held Jesse James's horse, was a trapper, cowpuncher, faro dealer, and singer in frontier saloons before taking up baseball.

Only five-eight, he learned to use guile from Old Hoss Radbourn, another great little man. He got the hitters out with brains, a primitive slider (Cy Young called it a "dinky-dinky pitch")— and a little scuffing of the ball. He won 20 or more games for Chicago six straight years, from 1894 through 1899. Jumping to the AL in 1901, Griff pitched (24–7) and managed the White Sox to the first flag in the new league's history. He took over as the Yankees (then known as the Highlanders) first manager when the club moved to New York in 1903. It was his last season as a full-time pitcher. His career mark was a sparkling 240–141.

Although the Highlanders nearly won the 1904 American League pennant, and finished second again in 1906, Griff was let go in mid-1908. He always felt he'd been mistreated by the New York owners, fans, and press. It led to his life-long loathing of the Yankees.

After managing Cincinnati for three years, AL president Ban Johnson prevailed upon him to help rescue the failing Washington franchise in 1912. Griffith became manager and mortgaged his ranch to buy 10 percent of the stock. With Walter Johnson pitching and Griffith managing, the Senators finished second two years in a row, then began a slow drift toward the second division as financial problems continued to beset the team.

In 1920 Griffith purchased controlling interest in the Senators, resigned as field manager, and took over as president. Although the team won a world championship in 1924 and pennants in 1925 and 1933, it was always financially strapped. Unable to compete with the richer AL clubs, Griffith was often forced to sell his better players to keep operating. In 1934 he even had to sell his manager-shortstop and son-in-law, Joe Cronin, for $225,000. Griffith was a leader in popularizing night games, the use of on-field entertainers such as Al Schacht, and in the signing of Latin players—all dictated by the constant financial woes of the Senators. Perhaps his greatest achievement was keeping baseball in the nation's capital during his lifetime. He should receive accolades for his off-field friendships with James A. Farley, Postmaster-General, and President Franklin D. Roosevelt; these friendships were responsible for the famous "Green Light" to wartime baseball.

BURLEIGH GRIMES
Pitcher, Pit (N) 1916–17, 1928–29, 1934, Bkn (N) 1918–26, NY (N) 1927, Bos (N) 1930, StL (N) 1930–31, 1933–34, Chi (N) 1932–33, NY (A) 1934. Manager, Bkn (N) 1937–38

Grimes threw the last legal spitball in 1934. But "Old Stubblebeard"—a nickname derived from his habit of not shaving on days he pitched —won games as much on willpower as "wetpower." Pitching for the Cardinals in the 1931 World Series, he threw a two-hitter in Game Three to beat Lefty Grove. Came the final game, he had an inflamed appendix. The trainer put ice packs on his stomach between innings while Grimes shut out Philadelphia for eight innings. He weakened in the ninth, but still got two outs before a reliever nailed down the win.

"Boiley," as they called him in Brooklyn, was a workhorse who led the NL in innings pitched three times and topped 300 innings in five different seasons. A gruff, hard-bitten type he was only too willing to knock down any batter with the temerity to dig in at the plate.

His greatest seasons were with Brooklyn, where he four times won 20 games between 1918 and 1926. In 1920 he helped the Dodgers to a pennant with a 23–11 mark.

In the World Series that year, he shut out Cleveland on seven hits in Game Two, but Game Five is the one everyone remembers. Cleveland loaded the bases in the first inning; the scouting report said to throw the Indians' outfielder Elmer Smith spitballs. Grimes did and Smith took issue with the scouting report by hitting the first grand-slam home run in Series history. In the fourth inning Grimes gave up the first Series home run by a pitcher, to Cleveland's Jim Bagby. The weirdness wasn't over. Grimes was replaced by Clarence Mitchell, who then batted in the fifth inning and lined the ball to Tribe second baseman Bill Wambsganss, who turned it into an unassisted triple play!

After leaving Brooklyn, Grimes was 19–8 for the Giants in 1927 and 25-14 for Pittsburgh in 1928. He got to St. Louis in 1930 and helped them win two straight pennants.

One of the small group identified as spitballers and allowed to keep throwing the pitch after it was outlawed in 1920, Grimes both lasted longer than the rest and won more games. He finished up in 1934 with a 270–212 mark. His career ERA of 3.53 was acquired in an age of heavy hitting, when any season mark under 4.00 was hot pitching.

He was elected to the Hall of Fame in 1964.

HENRY "HEINIE" GROH
Third Baseman, NY (N) 1912–13, 1922–26, Cin (N) 1913–21, Pit (N) 1927. Manager, Cin (N) 1918

Only five-eight, Heinie was famous for his bat, shaped like a big milk bottle. Its handle ballooned into a thick barrel, which he held high over his right shoulder. He looked sort of like a cartoon. But don't laugh. In the 1922 World Series, he used it to hit .474. The next year Heinie reportedly drove around with license plate #474.

The Giants picked up Groh in 1922 from Cincinnati, where he'd been an outstanding third baseman for years, and he helped them win pennants for three straight years. A good fielder and dangerous hitter (.292 lifetime), he believed his odd bat gave him better control on bunts.

ROBERT "LEFTY" GROVE
Pitcher, Phi (A) 1925–33, Bos (A) 1934–41

Grove boggles the mind, to say nothing of how he boggled AL batters. The consensus pick as best lefthander in history, Lefty might also have been the best pitcher, period. Some hitters insist he was faster than Johnson or Feller. His ball didn't have a hop at all—but still they couldn't hit it.

He was terrific from the day in 1920 when he first began pitching for Jack Dunn's Baltimore Orioles of the International League. But Dunn wasn't about to sell him to a major league team until he got his price—and the price went up every year. By the close of the 1924 season, Grove had won 108 games for Dunn and had yet to pitch in the majors. Connie Mack finally came up with $100,600, a new record. Grove was twenty-five when he pitched his first game for the A's.

Although it took him a couple of years to begin rolling up big victory totals, Lefty led the AL in strikeouts as a rookie. In walks, too—earning a reputation for wildness that was unmerited after that first season. He was, however, wild after a loss. He set new records for clubhouse tantrums, but it was noted he always punched lockers with his right hand. His theory on kicking water buckets was "Always be sure the bucket is empty."

After leading the league in ERA and strikeouts in 1926, he really got rolling. In the next seven seasons, he won 20 or more seven times, led in wins four times, led in winning percentage four times, in ERA four, in strikeouts five, and in shutouts twice. Death and taxes are less consistent. His 31–4 record in 1931 is his gaudiest season and earned him the MVP.

The A's won pennants from 1929 through 1931, but by 1934 the Depression was killing attendance and Connie Mack needed money. He sold Grove to the Red Sox for $125,000 (a $24,400 capital gain). Lefty's fabled fastball was a memory, and it took him an 8–8 season to change over to a "curves and control" pitcher. Then he won 20 for the eighth time and followed with a couple of 17-win seasons. He also took four more ERA titles. On July 25, 1941, he became the sixth modern pitcher to win 300 games. At 300–141 his .680 career percentage ranks fourth all-time but doesn't include his 55 saves. His lifetime ERA of 3.06, when normalized to the league average and adjusted for home park, was the best ever—even topping Walter Johnson's.

In 1947 he was named to the Hall of Fame.

RON GUIDRY
Pitcher, NY (A) 1975–88

In 1978 Guidry had one of the most effective years of any pitcher any time any place. The slightly built Louisiana lefthander was 25–3, to lead the AL in both wins and percentage. Also tops were his 1.74 ERA and 9 shutouts. In 273 innings, he allowed a skimpy 187 hits. He struck out 248 but walked only 72. Led by Guidry, the Yankees moved from 10 1/2 games back on July 24 to tie the fading Red Sox on the last day of the season, then won the playoff on Bucky Dent's homer. Naturally it had to be Ron, on short rest, who started and won the playoff victory. He added two more wins in the postseason.

He won the Cy Young Award hands down and finished second in the MVP voting.

"Louisiana Lightning" was never quite the same world-beater again, though he had several fine seasons, including 21–9 in 1983 and 22–6 in 1985.

STAN HACK
Third Baseman, Chi (N) 1932–47. Manager, Chi (N) 1954–56, StL (N) 1958

"Smiling Stan" played on four Cubs pennant winners and hit .348 in the Series (.471 in 1938), though the Cubs lost all four. *The Sporting News* chose him as its all-star third baseman three years in a row, 1940–1942.

A lifetime .301 hitter, he cracked out 2,193 hits in sixteen years. He also drew 1,092 walks and scored 1,239 runs. He seldom hit with much power, but he was consistent.

Hack's most famous hit came in the sixth game of the 1935 Series against the Tigers. Down three games to two, and tied in this game 3–3, Stan led off the ninth inning and smote one of Tommy Bridges' curves over the Tiger center fielder's head for a triple. A sacrifice fly ball would give the Cubs the lead. But Billy Jurges struck out, Larry French bounced out, and when Augie Galan finally got the fly, it was too late. A half inning later the Tigers won the game and the Series.

CHARLES "CHICK" HAFEY
Outfielder, StL (N) 1924–31, Cin (N) 1932–35, 1937

Hafey had everything you could ask for in a ballplayer except good health. He hit for a good average with fair power. He was fast. He could field. And he had the best throwing arm of any NL outfielder during his time.

The quiet, modest slugger was at the same time known for playing practical jokes on his teammates. He first became a regular with the Cardinals in 1926, as the team fought toward its first pennant. He was beaned several times during the season, affecting his sight. He was advised to wear glasses, a rarity among players of his day. His sight fluctuated so that he actually used three different pairs, depending on the state of his eyes.

From 1927 through 1931 he hit above .300 each season for the Cards, who won pennants in 1928, 1930, and 1931. He drove in over 100 runs in three of those seasons, and had a career-high 29 home runs in 1929—this despite a chronic sinus infection that required several operations.

In 1931 Hafey won the closest batting race in NL history, nosing out Bill Terry by .0003. Terry hit .3486 to Hafey's .3489. Chick had been a holdout several times before; when he asked for a raise to $17,000 after winning the batting championship, St. Louis traded him to Cincinnati. He had several good seasons with the Reds before retiring in 1935. A comeback attempt in 1937 was unsuccessful.

Hafey was elected to the Hall of Fame in 1971.

JESSE "POP" HAINES
Pitcher, Cin (N) 1918, StL (N) 1920–37

Haines was a temperamental workhorse who relied on a good fastball and tricky knuckleball to win 210 games, all with the St. Louis Cardinals. Until Bob Gibson surpassed his mark, he was the Cards' all-time winner. He didn't join the team until he was twenty-six years old but stayed until he was forty-five—hence his nickname "Pop."

He won 20 or more three times and pitched a no-hitter in 1924. During his time with the Redbirds, they won five pennants and three world championships. Haines was 3–1 in World Series play.

Haines was 13–4 in 1926, as the Cards won their first pennant. In the Series he shut out the Yanks, the last time that would happen for sixteen years.

Oddly Haines was most famous for being relieved in a ball game. In the seventh game of the 1926 Series, he was leading 3–2 when he developed a blister from throwing the knuckler and loaded the bases in the seventh inning with two out and Tony Lazzeri up. Manager Rogers Hornsby waved in Grover Alexander from the bullpen. Alexander's strikeout of Lazzeri is one of the most famous events in baseball history.

Haines was elected to the Hall of Fame in 1970.

BILLY HAMILTON
Outfielder, KC (AA) 1888–89, Phi (N) 1890–95, Bos (N) 1896–1901
"Sliding Billy" epitomized the jackrabbit era of the 1890s. Only five-six, he stole 912 bases—111 in 1889, 102 in 1890, and 111 in 1891—and led his league in steals in seven of his fourteen seasons. The 111 steals was a record until Lou Brock broke it eighty-five years later. Of course they were not all what we call stolen bases today. Going from first to third on a single was counted as a "steal."

Hamilton was the most efficient leadoff man ever. He had more runs scored than games played—a record—1,690 runs in 1,591 games. He also holds the all-time record for runs scored in a single season with 192 in 1894. He led the league four times. He was able to accomplish these things for several reasons in addition to his undeniable speed. In the first place, he was an exceptional hitter, leading the NL twice—.340 in 1891 and .380 in 1893. His career average was .344, eighth best of all time. Second, he walked a lot. He topped the NL in bases on balls five times. Third, he was followed in the batting order through most of his career by other outstanding hitters.

In 1894, his record year for scoring runs, he played center field for the Phillies and hit .404. Left fielder Ed Delahanty hit .407, and right fielder Sam Thompson hit .407. And substitute outfielder Tuck Turner hit .416 in 80 games! Even so, the Phillies finished fourth.

In 1896 the Phillies traded him to Boston for veteran third baseman Billy Nash. He joined Hall of Famer Hugh Duffy in the Beaneaters' outfield and helped his new team win pennants in 1897–1898.

Hamilton was elected to the Hall of Fame in 1961.

NED HANLON
Outfielder, Cle (N) 1880, Det (N) 1881–1888, Pit (N) 1889, 1891, Pit (P) 1890, Bal (N) 1892. Manager, Pit (N) 1889, 1891, Pit (P) 1890, Bal (N) 1892–98, Bkn (N) 1899–1905, Cin (N) 1906–07
Ned Hanlon was the original dirty tricks manager with the old Baltimore Orioles and Brooklyn Superbas of the Gay Nineties. With Willie Keeler, John McGraw, Joe Kelley, Hughie Jennings, and the rest, Hanlon's teams bunted and hit-and-ran their way to five flags.

They also reportedly:
- raised the foul lines so bunts would stay fair
- grabbed runners' belts as they rounded third base
- hid extra balls in the outfield grass to throw in on long hits
- flashed mirrors in the faces of the other teams' batters and fielders
- rolled on the ground and pinched their arms to fake being hit by pitches
- buried cement in front of home plate, then beat balls down on it so they'd bounce high enough to beat out—the famous "Baltimore Chop."

After a dozen years as a good field/no hit outfielder, Hanlon took over the Orioles in 1892, when they finished twelfth. He picked on young McGraw mercilessly until John offered to "punch his big head"—exactly the reaction Ned wanted.

The next year he had the O's up to eighth, and by 1894 to first. They won three straight flags, then finished second twice. Moving to Brooklyn, he won flags his first two

years, 1899–1900, then began a descent to last. But Ned still ended with a .530 winning percentage.

After baseball he went into real estate and made a fortune.

MEL HARDER
Pitcher, Cle (A) 1928–47
Harder won over 223 games in twenty years of pitching for Cleveland, including 20-win seasons in 1934–1935. Only Bob Feller won more for the Tribe. He had the honor of pitching the opening game in Municipal Stadium against Lefty Grove before 82,000 fans. He lost 1–0. In the 1934 All-Star Game, he hurled five scoreless innings.

After retiring from the mound, Mel coached the Indian pitchers in 1949 through 1963, the glory years of their magnificent pitching staffs. He was credited with helping Feller, Bob Lemon, Early Wynn, Mike Garcia, Herb Score, and others. It was said that "he had a camera in his head" because of his uncanny ability to spot pitching flaws.

MIKE HARGROVE
First Baseman, Tex (A) 1974–78, SD (N) 1979, Cle (A) 1979–85
Hargrove was called "the Human Rain Delay" because of his long, involved ritual before taking his stance in the batter's box. He'd walk up near the plate and take exactly three deliberate practice swings. Then he would step into the box and meticulously dig in his left foot. Next he'd adjust his helmet. Arrange his uniform. Tug his belt. At last, he was ready. But after the first pitch, he'd go through it all again. He drove pitchers crazy. But it worked. He hit .290 for his twelve seasons, led his league in walks twice, and had four seasons of over 100 walks. His lifetime OBP of .401, when normalized to the league average and adjusted for home park, is among the top twenty of this century.

WILL HARRIDGE
American League President, 1931–59
Harridge worked for the Wabash Railroad handling travel arrangements for AL teams and umpires. He had never seen a major league game until he became private secretary to AL President Ban Johnson in 1911. Twenty years later the efficient but colorless, conservative Harridge was promoted to chief and served twenty-eight years, 1931–1959.

He preferred to stay in the background, but he never hesitated to enforce league rules and decorum. In 1931, shortly after taking office and in the middle of a heated pennant race, he suspended Yankee catcher Bill Dickey for a month for slugging another player. Harridge was a strong advocate of the All-Star Game. He opposed night baseball until he saw that such games made baseball more available to families. He hated gimmicks and showboating, and was not amused when Bill Veeck used a midget as a pinch hitter.

He fined Boston's Ted Williams for spitting at fans. But when Ted won the 1941 All-Star Game with a ninth-inning homer, Harridge lost his reserve. He almost kissed Ted, he said, and would have "if there weren't so many people around."

Harridge was named to the Hall of Fame in 1972.

STANLEY "BUCKY" HARRIS

Second Baseman, Was (A) 1919–28, Det (A) 1929, 1931.
Manager, Was (A) 1924–28, Det (A) 1929–33, Bos (A)
1934, Was (A) 1935–42, Phi (N) 1943, NY (A) 1947–48,
Was (A) 1950–54, Det (A) 1955–56

Harris broke in as a regular second baseman with the Senators in 1920, hitting .300 for the only time in his career. In 1924 "the Boy Manager" became the Senators' skipper at age twenty-seven. He took the team to its first pennant and a World Series victory over the Giants. With Washington down three games to two, Harris knocked in both runs to win Game Six 2–1 and tie the Series. The next day Bucky drove in three runs to pull his team to a 3–3 tie after nine innings. They won in the twelfth on the famous hit that bounced over third baseman Fred Lindstrom's head. Harris hit .333 for the Series, with seven RBIs, and two homers—he hit only nine other home runs in his career.

Though the Senators repeated as pennant winners in 1925, they lost the Series to the Pirates. In 1929 Harris moved to Detroit as player-manager and began a career as the "Available Man." All told, he managed for twenty-nine years. He had two more sessions in Washington (1935–1942 and 1950–1954), two in Detroit (1929–1933 and 1955–1956), one year in Boston (1934), two-thirds of a season with the Phillies (1943), and two years with the Yankees (1947–1948). Most of the time he was saddled with teams that had little chance to win; twenty of them finished in the second division. But Harris was respected as a manager who got the most out of his limited material.

He won his last pennant and world championship with the Yankees in 1947 but lost a three-way race to Boston and Cleveland in 1948. The Yanks promptly fired Harris and hired Casey Stengel.

Bucky ranks third all-time in managerial wins with 2,159 and second in losses with 2,219. He was elected to the Hall of Fame in 1975.

CHARLES "GABBY" HARTNETT

Catcher, Chi (N) 1922–40, NY (N) 1941. Manager, Chi (N) 1938–40

While AL fans argued the merits of Cochrane and Dickey, NL fans had no problem identifying their circuit's best catcher. Hartnett was the cream of the NL, and to some the best of all. Although he was often described as a "beefy man with a tomato face who talked a lot," his nickname was actually hung on him ironically when as a Cubs rookie in 1922 he said virtually nothing. He developed his communication skills, of course, but for twenty seasons his batting and catching skills spoke louder.

An excellent defensive catcher with a powerful arm and a take-charge handler of pitchers, he caught 1,790 games. In twelve seasons, he played in over 100 games. He led National League catchers in fielding six times.

His lifetime batting average was .297, and at one time he held the record for home runs by a catcher, with 236. He drove in 1,179 runs, with a personal high of 122 in 1930. While he was with them, the Cubs won four pennants. He appeared in five All-Star Games and was NL MVP in 1935.

He was behind the plate in the 1932 World Series when Babe Ruth hit his "called shot" off Charley Root. Gabby always insisted the Babe didn't point.

In 1934 he caught Carl Hubbell's great All-Star Game feat of striking out Ruth, Gehrig, Foxx, Simmons, and Cronin. "Just throw them what you throw me," he told Hub, "I can't hit it, and neither will they."

But Hartnett's greatest moment—perhaps the greatest in Chicago baseball history—was his "homer in the gloaming" against Pittsburgh as darkness fell on Wrigley Field, September 28, 1938. Gabby had become Cubs manager in midseason and led the club from 6½ games behind to 1½ behind the Pirates. The teams met in Chicago for a series that would decide the pennant. In the leadoff game, the score was tied after eight innings, and the umps warned that the ninth would be the last. There were two out in the bottom of the ninth, 34,465 crazed fans in the stands, and Mace Brown had an 0–2 count against Gabby. Hartnett hit the next ball into the bleachers and the Cubs went on to the flag.

Gabby was named to the Hall of Fame in 1955.

GUY HECKER

Pitcher/First Baseman/Manager, Lou (AA) 1882–89, Pit (N) 1890. Manager, Pit (N) 1890

In 1884 Hecker led the old American Association with a 52–20 mark and 1.80 ERA. Two years later he led the league in batting with .342. Guy was surely the best hitting pitcher until Ferrell. He averaged .283 for his career and even stole 48 bases in 1887. On August 15, 1886, he allowed Baltimore four hits in a complete-game victory while registering six hits himself, including three homers and two doubles. He also scored a record of seven runs.

Hecker's pitching was his forte, however. In four years 1883–1886, he *averaged* 34–22 for a team that finished third, fourth, fifth, and fifth. In his big year, 1884, he also led in complete games, innings pitched, and strikeouts.

JIM HEGAN

Catcher, Cle (A) 1941–42, 1946–57, Det (A) 1958, Phi (N) 1958–59, SF (N) 1959, Chi (N) 1960

The top defensive catcher in the AL in the post-World War Two period, Hegan holds a record that may never be broken—he handled eighteen 20-game winners with the Indians, 1946–1957. The glory years of Cleveland pitching coincided with the tenure of Jim (and pitching coach Mel Harder). Three of Hegan's stars—Bob Feller, Bob Lemon, and Early Wynn—are in the Hall of Fame. Two of them—Feller and Wynn—call him the best receiver ever.

In 1946, in his first season as a regular, Hegan handled Feller's 348-strikeout season. That year the Indians were 45–43 with him, 21–43 without. In 1954 his pitchers won 111 games, the most ever in the AL. In between he caught three no-hitters, by Feller, Lemon, and Don Black.

A poor hitter with a career .228 batting average, Hegan had his best offensive season in the Indians' world championship season of 1948. He batted .248, hit 14 homers, and drove in 61 runs.

HARRY "SLUG" HEILMANN

Outfielder, Det (A) 1914, 1916–29, Cin (N) 1930, 1932

Heilmann was a good hitter who became a great hitter when the lively ball was introduced in 1920. Line drives that fielders had previously reached began whizzing by their gloves before they could react. Harry was a line drive machine. His homer totals were only average; his biggest year was 21 in 1923. But he hit plenty of gappers for doubles and triples. For much of his career he batted behind Ty Cobb, helping him to his all-time record in runs scored. Harry had 1,538 RBIs and topped 100 in eight seasons.

"Slug" didn't help his team in the outfield. He was slow and awkward. For two years the Tigers tried to put him at first base. He led AL first basemen in errors both years, so they sent him back to the outfield, where he had fewer opportunities to be slow and awkward.

But with a bat in his hand, Heilmann rivaled the NL's Rogers Hornsby as the greatest righthanded hitter of the time. He led the AL in hitting four times, oddly—in alternating odd years. In 1921, he led with .394; in 1923 it was .403; in 1925, .393; and in 1927, .398. In his "off-years" between titles, he bided his time with .356, .346, and .367. His career average was .342.

Heilmann was a low-key, articulate man, who told droll stories of his playing days. After retiring, he put those talents to work as a popular play-by-play radio broadcaster for the Tigers.

He was named to the Hall of Fame in 1952.

RICKEY HENDERSON
Outfielder, Oak (A) 1979–84, 1989– NY (A) 1985–89
The greatest thief since Willie Sutton, Henderson demolished the single-season stolen base record in 1982, when he swiped 130 for Oakland. Three times he has gone over 100, and he's led the AL in steals ten times. After only twelve years in the majors, he ranks second all-time in stolen bases, standing just two behind Lou Brock.

An ideal leadoff man, Rickey usually bats in the .290-.310 range, draws plenty of walks (he's twice led the American League), and scores and scores and scores; he's averaged over 100 runs scored per season for his career.

Henderson also hits with occasional power, setting the record for leadoff home runs.

TOMMY HENRICH
Outfielder, NY (A) 1937–42, 1946–50
"Old Reliable" Henrich played right field on eight Yankee champions in eleven years. Yankee fans like to say that the Keller-DiMaggio-Henrich outfield was the best ever, but Yankee fans are like that. Tommy was a first-rate player, but his .282 batting average and 183 homers do not quite put him in "best" circles. On the other hand, DiMaggio called him the smartest player in the majors, and nobody gave tests to prove otherwise.

One thing, Tommy was always in the middle of the action.

In the 1941 Series, he was at bat when Mickey Owen dropped that third strike. Henrich alertly raced to first, igniting the game-winning rally in Game Four.

He got the game-winning hits in three of the four Yankee victories in the 1947 Series, including the deciding seventh game.

He played hurt most of 1949 but was such a clutch hitter in the 115 games he limped into that he finished sixth in the MVP voting. He finished the season with a flourish, whipping the home run that beat Boston on the

final day to clinch the flag, the first of Casey Stengel's record-breaking five straight pennants. Then, in the opening game of the World Series, Tommy slugged a homer off Newcombe in the bottom of the ninth to beat the Dodgers, 1–0.

BILLY HERMAN
Second Baseman, Chi (N) 1931–41, Bkn (N) 1941–43, 1946, Bos (N) 1946, Pit (N) 1947. Manager, Pit (N) 1947, Bos (A) 1964–66
Herman was a great hit-and-run man and smart second baseman, who played on four NL champs with the Cubs and Dodgers, winning every third year—1932, 1935, 1938, and 1941.

Billy succeeded Rogers Hornsby at second base for the Cubs in 1932, hit .314, improved the defense, and helped the team move up from third to the flag. He set an NL record by handling over 900 chances at second for five straight years. For his first seven seasons in Chicago, Billy teamed with shortstop Billy Jurges in a double-play combination that had even old-time Cubs fans asking "Who-to-who-to-Chance?" Herman's best year was 1935, when he hit .341, cracked 227 hits to lead the NL, and scored 113 runs. His career batting average was .304.

Early in the 1941 season, Billy was sent off to Brooklyn. "I just bought a pennant," Dodger owner Larry MacPhail crowed. He was right. Billy and his new partner young Pee Wee Reese meshed beautifully and the Dodgers won their first flag in twenty-one years.

Herman was elected to the Hall of Fame in 1975.

FLOYD "BABE" HERMAN
Outfielder, Bkn (N) 1926–31, 1945, Cin (N) 1932, 1935–36, Chi (N) 1933–34, Pit (N) 1935, Det (A) 1937
Poor Babe is remembered as the man who hit .393 and couldn't win the batting crown, and as the daffy Dodger who got hit on the head with a fly ball and somehow tripled into a triple play.

True on the first count. Libel on the other two.

Babe hit .393 in 1930, when players were benched for hitting .290 and optioned to Topeka for hitting .280. Bill Terry won the batting championship with .401, the last time a National Leaguer topped the .400 mark.

In 1935 he hit the first night-game home run in big league history. Even after he left Brooklyn, someone was always willing to hire him for his hitting and look the other way while he tried to play the outfield. For his thirteen major league seasons, he averaged .324 with his bat and slightly higher with his glove.

Herman was not the naive simpleton that the writers and historians created. He was a thoughtful, intelligent man, and he did not triple into a triple play. He doubled into a double play. It happened like this: With the bases loaded at Ebbets Field, Herman slammed a drive off the wall, and the ball bounced all the way back to second base. One run scored, and someone yelled to throw home. Dazzy Vance, halfway home, turned and scrambled back to third base, where Chick Fewster had already arrived from first base. Herman, running full out but head down, heard the yell and thought Fewster must be scoring, so he raced for third. He slid in safely—even stylishly—to find the other two already there. They called Fewster and

Herman out and gave him credit for a double. Ever after, when the Dodgers put three men on base, some wag was sure to ask, "Which base?"

As for getting hit on the head with a fly, Herman stoutly denied it. "How about the shoulder, Babe?" someone asked. "No," he said, "the shoulder don't count."

KEITH HERNANDEZ

First Baseman, StL (N) 1974–83, NY (N) 1983–89, Cle (A) 1990–

If Hernandez ever melts down his Gold Gloves, he can fill every cavity in New York. As of 1990, he's won eleven and may be good for a few more before he's done. He is easily the premier fielding first baseman of today. The only argument is whether he is the best of all time. The fact that he already holds the record for career assists by a first baseman (but is not in the top ten of games played) supports the "Aye" vote.

A consistent .300 hitter with line-drive power, Keith led the NL with a .344 batting average in 1979 and was voted co-MVP with Willie Stargell. In 1982 he hit .299 and drove in 94 runs, as the Cardinals won the world championship. His surprise trade to the Mets the next season is still a sore point with Cardinals' fans. Mets fans think of it as akin to Christmas morning.

Hernandez played on his second world champion team with New York in 1986 and a divisional championship in 1988. The handsome lefthanded hitter is considered a leader in the clubhouse and on the field.

DORREL "WHITEY" HERZOG

Manager, Tex (A) 1973, KC (A) 1975–79, StL (N) 1980–90. Outfielder, Was (A) 1956–58, KC (A) 1958–60, Bal (A) 1961–62, Det (A) 1963

Herzog's playing career was eight years of undistinguished outfielding. His managing career ranks as one of the best and brightest.

He took over at Kansas City in mid-1975 and brought them home second. Three consecutive division titles followed, but the Royals lost the LCS all three times. When Kansas City finished second in 1979, he was fired.

He crossed the state to St. Louis, where he had his greatest success. His Cardinals won the world championship in 1982 and pennants in 1985 and 1987. In none of those years was St. Louis favored in preseason appraisals.

Whitey's best Series may have been 1987. Playing without his top hitter, Jack Clark, and with substitutes in several positions, he still took the Series to seven games against Minnesota.

"Whitey-ball" in the 1980s was tailored to Busch Stadium, with its artificial surface and deep power alleys. Typically his lineup was mostly made up of speedy, good-fielding, line-drive hitters, with at least one strong power hitter to bat cleanup. His pitching staff normally hosted more than the usual number of lefthanders.

GIL HODGES

First Baseman, Bkn (N) 1943, 1947–57, LA (N) 1958–61, NY (N) 1962–63. Manager, Was (A) 1963–67, NY (N) 1968–71

Gil was one of the top guns in the Dodgers' Murderers' Row, 1948–1959. He slugged 370 homers during an eighteen-year career, drove in 1,274, and was considered a top

fielder among National League first basemen. He played on seven Dodger pennant winners, six in Brooklyn and the last in 1959 for Los Angeles.

Hodges was an even-tempered gentleman of immense strength, both in physique and character. His inner strength helped him persevere during the extended batting slumps that he was prone to as a player. Most fans know Hodges's frustrating 1952 Series when he went 0-for-21. Dodger fans were sending him batting tips and lighting candles in church for him. Fewer recall that he hit .364 the next year in the Series or that he drove in both runs of the final game in 1955, as the Dodgers won their first world championship.

As manager of the dreadful Washington Senators (1963–1967), he needed every ounce of his patience. When he brought the team up to sixth in 1967, people said his next project would be parting the Red Sea.

Actually he undertook something more difficult—he became manager of the Mets. Throughout the 1960s the Mets had always been good for a laugh but rarely good for a win. They didn't disappoint the stand-up comics in 1968, Hodges's first year at the helm, finishing ninth. Then, in 1969, with Hodges platooning a lineup of mostly retreads and with a young pitching staff boasting Tom Seaver, Jerry Koosman, and Tug McGraw, the team became the Amazing Mets. They won the NL East, brushed aside Atlanta in the LCS, and humbled Baltimore in a five-game World Series—"The Miracle of Flushing Meadows."

HARRY HOOPER

Outfielder, Bos (A) 1909–20, Chi (A) 1921–25

Hooper was an excellent rightfielder with a legendary throwing arm. He played with Tris Speaker and Duffy Lewis in what old-timers called the best outfield ever. There have been several "best-ever" outfields since, but the trio brought the Red Sox two world titles—in 1912 and 1915. Speaker was the star, of course, but after Spoke moved on to Cleveland, Lewis and Hooper helped the Sox win another World Series in 1916. And *then*, when Duffy wasn't around in 1918, Hooper was still there for a fourth championship. If you get the idea that Harry was a winner, you're probably running on all cylinders.

In the final game of the 1912 World Series, he went back as far as he could, then leaped, speared Larry Doyle's drive barehanded, and fell backward into the stands. His robbery kept the Sox alive to win in the tenth.

In 1915, after hitting only two home runs all season, he hit two in the final game of the World Series with the last one providing the margin of victory. In the 1916 Series, he hit .333 and scored six runs in five days.

Harry was a leadoff hitter with a modest .281 lifetime batting average, but he drew a lot of walks, which allowed him to score 1,429 runs in his career.

Hooper was elected to the Hall of Fame in 1971.

ROGERS HORNSBY

Second Baseman, StL (N) 1915–26, 1933, NY (N) 1927, Bos (N) 1928, Chi (N) 1929–32, StL (A) 1933–37. Manager, StL (N) 1925–26, Bos (N) 1927, Chi (N) 1930–32, StL (A) 1933–37, 1952, Cin (N) 1952–53

Hornsby always said he could have made it to the majors on his fielding even if he'd only been an ordinary hitter.

Well, maybe. The question is, how long would he have stayed there? Using his chances-handled-per-game as a gauge, he started out with pretty good range but slowed down fast. By 1920, when he first showed himself to be a great hitter, he was average at best in the field. And throughout the 1920s just about every good team in the NL had a second baseman covering more ground than the Rajah.

Of course, none of them hit as well. Hornsby never had to make a living with his glove; he was a magnificent hitter. Many call him the greatest righthanded hitter of all time. Proving that takes all sorts of adjustments as you try to relate one era to another, so there might have been a righthander to rank ahead of Hornsby, but he has to be in the top handful. Take a deep breath and listen:

His career batting average of .358 is second only to Ty Cobb, who batted southpaw. Hornsby is the only right-handed batter to hit .400 three times, and his .424 in 1924 is a record for this century. He won six straight batting titles from 1920 to 1925 and added a seventh in 1928. He made 250 hits in 1922, led the league four times, and cracked over 200 seven times. He led the NL in home runs twice, led in triples once and tied once, led in doubles four times. He led or tied in runs five times and in RBIs four times. He won two Triple Crowns and two MVPs. Whew!

In the feet-of-clay department, the Rajah had a royal disdain for the opinions and feelings of everybody he ever met. He was brusque, blunt, hypercritical, dictatorial, moody, and argumentative. He alienated almost everyone sooner or later. St. Louis traded him right after he'd player-managed them to a world championship in 1926. The Giants traded him in 1927 after he hit .361. He predicted he'd lead the league again in 1928. He did, and the Braves immediately traded him to the Cubs for 1929.

Except for that 1926 pennant in his second year as skipper, he had no success as a major league manager. He never had any other Hornsbys playing for him, and he was satisfied with nothing less.

His only vice—outside of a personality that could sand wood—was betting on horses. He was bad at it. What he was, was a hitter. He never drank, smoked, read, or went to movies because he wanted to protect his batting eye.

Hornsby was elected to the Hall of Fame in 1942.

FRANK HOWARD
Outfielder, LA (N) 1958–64, Was (A) 1965–71, Tex (A) 1972, Det (A) 1972–73. Manager, SD (N) 1981, NY (N) 1983

When six-seven, 255-pound Howard came up to bat, the pitcher must have figured someone had moved the mound closer to the plate. "Hondo" was intimidating and he could deliver. He hit some of the mightiest blasts ever seen and left painted seats in the upper decks all over both leagues as mementoes of his homers. Even Ted Williams, his manager at Washington, shook his head in admiration.

Of course Howard struck out a lot too, flailing at low outside curves. But when he connected, the balls flew. Playing for the Dodgers, he walloped a long home run in the 1963 World Series to beat Whitey Ford, 2–1, and complete a four-game sweep of the Yankees. With Washington, he hit 136 home runs from 1968 through 1970. In 1968, the Year of the Pitcher, Howard had a streak of ten homers in twenty at-bats. Number ten, against Lolich, hit the roof of Tiger Stadium.

He was a bit clumsy in the outfield but was no Babe Herman. And he played hard, was always hustling. He finished with 382 career homers and everyone's respect.

WAITE HOYT
Pitcher, NY (N) 1918, 1932, Bos (A) 1919–20, NY (A) 1921–30, Det (A) 1930–31, Phi (A) 1931, Bkn (N) 1932, 1937–38, Pit (N) 1933–37

"The secret of success," Hoyt once said, "is to pitch for the New York Yankees." This Broadway playboy, vaude-ville singer, part-time undertaker, and baseball broadcaster won 237 games, mostly for the great Yankees of Ruth and Gehrig.

Signed by John McGraw when he was only fifteen, Hoyt pitched only one inning for the Giants before he was sent to the Boston Red Sox in 1919. His record was mediocre over two seasons, except for one brilliant eleven-inning perfecto stint sandwiched between hits in a thirteen-inning game against the Yankees. Impressed, New York acquired him in 1921 and made him a regular starter. Hoyt won 19 as the Yankees won their first pennant. He was sensational in the World Series that fall, pitching three complete games without allowing an earned run. Nevertheless, an error cost him the final game of the Series, 1–0.

He was the ace of the Yankees' staff throughout the 1920s, with his top seasons coming in 1927, when he was 22–7 and led the AL in ERA, and in 1928, when he went 23–7. After leaving the Yankees in 1930, he pitched for many teams with only occasional success as a starter. He was, however, an effective relief pitcher for four seasons with the Pirates in the mid-1930s.

Hoyt, who was elected to the Hall of Fame in 1969, was a popular play-by-play man for Cincinnati for twenty-four years.

CAL HUBBARD
Umpire, 1936–50

Hubbard is the only man in the baseball, college football, and pro football Halls of Fame. A 250-pound behemoth when most football linemen were 200–210 pounds, Big Cal played end and tackle at both Centenary and Geneva Colleges in the mid-1920s, then went on to an all-pro career with the New York Giants and Green Bay Packers of the NFL. A devastating defensive player and road-clearing blocker, he starred on four championship teams.

Cal had taken up umpiring in the summers while still a football player and moved smoothly into his new career. He became an AL umpire in 1936 and served for fifteen years. He was known for his intimate knowledge of the rules and for the efficient and authoritative way he ran a game. A hunting accident prematurely ended his active career, but he continued as supervisor of umpires for the AL for another fifteen years.

CARL HUBBELL
Pitcher, NY (N) 1928–43

In one of baseball's small ironies, the intelligent, level-headed Hubbell will forever be known as a "screwball" pitcher. The adjective refers, of course, to what he threw, not what he was. The pitch, thrown with a clockwise snap of his left wrist, left Carl with a left arm so twisted that the palm of his hand faces out! It also made him the NL's premier lefthander of the 1930s.

Reportedly, when he was a Tiger farmhand, Detroit manager Ty Cobb discouraged him from throwing "that thing." Fortunately, Carl continued to toss what is, in effect, a reverse curve, and when the Giants bought his contract, he got the chance to use it against major league batters. They hated it!

He had five straight winning seasons under his belt, twice posting 18 wins, when he suddenly blossomed into "Super Pitcher" in 1933. Carl considered his greatest game to be a 1933 18-inning shutout without giving up a base on balls. In July, he went 46 straight innings without allowing a run. He pitched ten shutouts in all that year, had a 23–12 mark for the champion Giants, with the unbelievably low (for those years) ERA of 1.66. He won the MVP.

In the Series that fall, Hub beat Washington in the opener, giving up two unearned runs. In Game Four he went eleven innings, giving up another unearned run. In the eleventh he loaded the bases on a single, a walk, and a bunt that didn't roll foul. Then he calmly ended the game on a double play to win 2–1. His ERA for the Series was 0.00.

In 1934 he went 21–12, with a league-leading 2.30 ERA. In the All-Star Game that year he struck out Babe Ruth, Lou Gehrig, Jimmie Foxx, Al Simmons, and Joe Cronin in succession.

After a 23–12 year in 1935, "King Carl," the Giants' "Meal Ticket," took them to another pennant in 1936 with his second MVP year, a 26–6 gem that saw him again lead the NL in ERA. That year Hubbell began a 24-game regular-season winning streak that extended into 1937. His 22–8 mark in 1937 gave him five straight 20-win seasons and gave New York one more flag.

Carl became a spot starter for his final six seasons, with his only losing mark being 11–12 in 1940. He finished with a 253–154 career record, and was elected to the Hall of Fame in 1947. Not bad for a screwball!

MILLER HUGGINS

Second Baseman, Cin (N) 1904–09, StL (N) 1910–16.
Manager, StL (N) 1913–17, NY (A) 1918–29
Huggins wasn't a bad little second baseman for thirteen years in the NL, but his main claim to fame is as manager of the Yankees' "Murderers' Row" of the 1920s.

He began as the Cardinals' manager in 1913. The Redbirds had never won a pennant up till then, and Hug didn't change the *status quo.* He did, however, twice get them as high as third. That earned him a chance with the Yankees in 1918. New York was another team that had never won a pennant but had some prospects for improvement. Hug got them up to fourth and then third in 1919.

The Yankees bought Babe Ruth in 1920, and when they finished third went out and bought more talent. By 1921 they were ready. Almost as interesting as the yearly pennant races was the relationship between the five-four, 140-pound Huggins and his overgrown Peck's Bad Boy, Ruth. Hug fought with him, fined him, suspended him, was hung over the rear platform of trains by him, and above all won pennants with him—six of them in eight years, 1921–1928, including three world championships. In

1925 Babe was making $52,000 and hitting .246, when he stayed out three nights in a row. Hug called Babe and all the players into the dugout and slapped a $5,000 fine on him, ten times the previous record. Ruth complained to owner Jacob Ruppert, who backed Hug. The fine stuck. The Babe apologized.

Many consider Hug's 1927 Yankees the greatest team of all time. Both his 1927 and 1928 teams swept the World Series in four straight games.

The little guy died suddenly of blood poisoning in 1929. Even Ruth cried at the news. Their monuments now stand side by side in Yankee Stadium's center field. In 1964 Huggins joined Ruth in the Hall of Fame.

WILLIAM HULBERT

National League Founder, President 1877–82
Hulbert's Hall of Fame plaque is incorrectly identified as "Morgan Bulkeley." The real Bulkeley was a figurehead president in the NL's first year; Hulbert founded the National League. What they did in Cooperstown was sort of like citing that dog that used to listen to "his master's voice" as the inventor of the phonograph.

From 1871 to 1875, the loose, rowdy, gambler-ridden National Association made a stab at being a league. Hulbert, the Chicago team owner, thought it might be nice to have a league with enforced rules, regular schedules, civilized behavior, and scores that weren't known on the mornings of the games. In 1876 he called together some like-minded owners, convinced them there was hope for the future, and formed the National League. The only mistake he made was to get Bulkeley from Hartford to pretend to be president as a sop to the eastern teams. Hulbert had a problem with the east; he'd just lured four of Boston's best players to Chicago.

Well, the next year—after Chicago had won the first NL pennant—Bulkeley didn't show up at the league meeting, so there was nothing to do but elect Hulbert as president. He did things like kick New York and Philadelphia out of the league for failing to fulfill their schedules, ban four players for life for fixing games, come down hard on drunks and rowdies, and generally run things with a firm hand until his death in 1882.

In the 1800s, he was referred to as the "Savior of the Game," which is a bit much but beats "What's-his-name-from-Hartford" hands down.

JIM "CATFISH" HUNTER

Pitcher, KC (A) 1965–67, Oak (A) 1968–74, NY (A) 1975–79
Hunter was the ace of the A's great teams in the first half of the 1970s and helped the Yankees win three straight pennants in the second half of the decade. And he started as a batting practice pitcher!

In 1964 A's owner Charles O. Finley signed Hunter to a $50,000 bonus contract. And because Finley thought "Jim Hunter" lacked oomph and because his bonus baby liked to hunt and fish, the owner hung the nickname "Catfish" on him. Considering the possibilities in the animal kingdom, it could have been worse.

In his first season, the eighteen-year-old righthander pitched only batting practice for the A's. At one point, Finley had a publicity photo taken with Hunter sitting on the lap of Satchel Paige, who was sitting in a rocker.

Maybe you had to be there to appreciate the joke.

In 1965 the nineteen-year-old Hunter became a regular starter for the A's and went 8–8. The next year he was named to the AL All-Star team; his record was 9–11 with the seventh-place A's. He pitched a perfect game in 1968 but didn't have his first winning season until 1970, when he was 18–14. By then Finley had moved the A's to Oakland, and his young players were becoming stars.

Starting in 1971, Hunter was 21–11, 21–7, and 21–5, and he won the Cy Young Award in 1974 with a 25–12 mark and a league-leading 2.49 ERA. The A's won pennants and world championships from 1972 to 1974. But all was not happy in A's-ville. Hunter sued Finley for breach of contract and ended up winning a bigger award than the Cy Young: he was declared a free agent and signed a five-year contract with the Yankees for an estimated $3.75 million.

His best year in New York was his first, 25–14, his fifth straight 20-win season. He slumped after that, but was still a useful starter in the three pennant-winning seasons (1976–1978). After the 1979 season, he retired. His career totals were 224–166. In 1987 he was elected to the Hall of Fame.

MONFORD "MONTE" IRVIN
Outfielder, Negro Leagues, 1938–48, Newark Eagles, NY (N) 1949–55, Chi (N) 1956
Irvin got to the New York Giants after a fine career in the Negro Leagues, where he was credited with two batting titles with the Newark Eagles, .396 in 1941 and .398 in 1946. In the latter year, Irvin played shortstop for Newark, and he and second baseman Larry Doby helped bring the Eagles the black world championship of 1946 over Satchel Paige's Kansas City Monarchs.

Irvin signed with the New York Giants in 1949 and played briefly with the team that year. He was thirty years old, and all agree that his skills had diminished from the level he had shown in the Negro Leagues. The "diminished" Irvin hit .299 in 1950. In 1951 he upped that to .312, led the NL in RBIs with 121, and knocked out 24 homers. Down the stretch, as the Giants chased the Dodgers to a playoff and ultimate victory, he hit over .400. In the World Series, he hit .458 and even stole home in the opening game.

A broken leg in 1952 almost ended Irvin's career, but he bounced back with .323 in 1953. In eight years but only five full seasons, his NL batting average was .293, with 99 homers.

In 1968 Irvin joined the Commissioner's Office as a public relations expert. Irvin represented Commissioner Kuhn at Atlanta when Henry Aaron broke Babe Ruth's home run record.

Irvin was elected to the Hall of Fame in 1973.

JOE JACKSON
Outfielder, Phi (A) 1908–09, Cle (A) 1910–15, Chi (A) 1915–20
One of the great natural hitters, Shoeless Joe threw his career and his honor away for thirty pieces of silver. Joe averaged .356 for his career, the third best ever, using his favorite bat, "Black Betsy," and a swing so pretty it would make Will Clark weep. Babe Ruth said he copied Joe's swing. Ironically it was Ruth's popularity that helped fans

forget the shame that Jackson and his coconspirators brought to baseball.

An illiterate millhand, Joe hit .408 as a Cleveland rookie in 1911. He finished second to Ty Cobb's .420. The next year Joe hit .395 and finished second again to Cobb (.410). Except for ten games in 1908–1909, Joe always hit .300. But a trade to the White Sox in 1915 threw him in with the proverbial bad company.

The White Sox were building a great team, but it was a team split. Joe resented the Sox' educated second baseman Eddie Collins and his cadre of followers. The other side, the ones who griped about the admittedly low salaries owner Charles Comiskey paid, the ones who figured baseball was a stick and they had the wrong end, the ones who hung with the sharpies who looked for an edge, *that* side accepted Joe. They were his friends. They didn't laugh at his naiveté, snicker at his lack of sophistication, or make fun of his southern drawl.

Despite the division on the team, it won the 1917 pennant and World Series. Because 1918 was a war year, Joe took a shipyard job and played only in 17 games. Others were missing. When everyone returned in 1919, the Sox paraded to another pennant and were installed as heavy favorites over Cincinnati in the World Series. But the chiselers on the team had a different idea. They conspired with gamblers to throw the Series for a promised $20,000. In Jackson, who was grossly underpaid at $8,000, the sharpies found a willing conspirator.

The story broke late in the 1920 season, while Jackson was hitting .382. Eight players were indicted in Chicago. Jackson admitted his guilt, but none of the players were convicted in court. There was no doubt of what they'd done, but the carefully assembled evidence suddenly and mysteriously disappeared. No matter, Judge Landis, the baseball commissioner, banned the "Black Sox" from the game for life. Jackson, as well as others in the group of "eight men out," played outlaw ball under an assumed name. Even fat and out of shape he never lost that great swing.

LARRY JACKSON
Pitcher, StL (N) 1955–62, Chi (N) 1963–66, Phi (N) 1966–68
Jackson won 184 games for the Cardinals and Cubs in the 1950s and 1960s. Although in double figures twelve of his fourteen seasons, Larry had only one 20-game season. In 1964 he was 24–11 for the eighth-place Cubs, finishing second in the Cy Young voting.

He didn't get much help from his teams, so Larry helped himself in the field, leading all pitchers in chances accepted and fielding average several seasons.

REGGIE JACKSON
Outfielder. KC (A) 1967, Oak (A) 1968–75, 1987, Bal (A) 1976, NY (A) 1977–81, Cal (A) 1982–86
"Mr. October," Jackson was perhaps the most electrifying hitter of the 1970s. "I'd like to be able to light the fire a little bit," he said. And he did.

Reggie was at his best in the World Series, hitting .357, ninth best ever. His Series slugging average of .755 is tops all time. He's probably most famous for driving three home runs on three pitches in the final game of the 1977 Series to sink the Dodgers. Reggie was a winner. In twelve years, 1971–1982, his teams—the A's, Yanks, and Angels—won ten division crowns and five world championships. Jackson won the MVP in 1973, when he led the league with 32 homers and 117 RBIs for Oakland's champs. Perhaps Reggie's longest homer was walloped in the 1971 All-Star Game. It hit a light tower above the roof of Tiger Stadium like a rifle shot.

Jackson is sixth on the all-time home run list with 563. He won four home run crowns and drove in 1,702 runs. He also struck out more than any other man in history, 2,597 times—once in every four at-bats. But he considered the strikeouts a bargain price for the homers.

Intelligent, outspoken, egomaniacal, Reggie fought with his team owners, Charles Finley and George Steinbrenner, and with his managers, especially Billy Martin, who benched him once for loafing.

Jackson wanted to be "the straw that stirs the drink," the highest-paid star, with his own eponymous candy bar. If there were an Ego Hall of Fame, Jackson would be the first one in. But the doors of Cooperstown will open for him too.

TRAVIS JACKSON
Shortstop, NY (N) 1922–36
Jackson was a member of the Giants' "Hall of Fame Infield" of 1925–27. While Jackson played short and Fred Lindstrom third, they were joined by George Kelly, Bill Terry, Frankie Frisch, and Rogers Hornsby.

However, Jackson and the others had many better years. Travis played on New York pennant winners in 1923, 1924, 1933, and 1936, his final season. He was a reliable shortstop with good range, and inevitably was given the nickname "Stonewall." (Like, you couldn't hit a ball through him. Get it?) He led NL shortstops in assists four times, total chances three times, and fielding average twice. Defensively his strongest feature was his powerful throwing arm.

If Jackson had an edge over a half dozen good-fielding shortstops of his day, it was that he hit better. He topped .300 six times and finished with a career mark of .291. That wasn't sensational for the hit-happy time he played in, but it was excellent for a shortstop. He even learned to jerk the ball down the Polo Grounds' short foul lines. One year he hit 21 homers. His 929 RBIs are also high for someone playing his position.

FERGUSON JENKINS
Pitcher, Phi (N) 1965–66, Chi (N) 1966–73, 1982–83, Tex (A) 1974–75, 1978–81, Bos (A) 1976–77
Pitching in the hitters' haven, Wrigley Field, Jenkins strung six consecutive 20-win seasons together. In 1971 he was the NL's Cy Young winner with a 24–13 mark and 2.77 ERA. He pitched 325 innings that season, one of the five years he topped 300.

Jenkins combined excellent control with a good fastball and curve. Traded to Texas in 1974, he responded with a 25–12 season, leading the AL in wins. In a nineteen-season career, he never pitched for a pennant winner, yet he compiled a 284–226 mark.

HUGHIE JENNINGS
Shortstop, Lou (AA) 1891, Lou (N) 1892–93, Bal (N) 1893–99, Bkn (N) 1899–1900, 1903, Phi (N) 1901–02,

Det (A) 1907, 1909, 1912, 1918. Manager, Det (A) 1907–20
A law school graduate, Jennings played on the famous rip 'n' run Baltimore Orioles of the Gay Nineties. He was their shortstop and captain, and they won the pennant his first three years, 1894–1896, plus the Temple Cup playoffs the next year. Hugh helped with averages of .335, .386, .401, .355, and .328—the best years he ever had, thanks in part to the new, longer pitching distance, which was inflating everyone's batting stats. In 1895 Hughie scored 159 runs and knocked in 125 more, with only four home runs.

Jennings's specialty was getting hit with the pitch, which he did 49 times in 1896, the record until Ron Hunt broke it in 1971. The Orioles weren't above faking it a bit, by taking a close pitch, then rolling around in supposed pain, while raising a welt by pinching themselves. However, Jennings had his skull fractured by an Amos Rusie pitch in 1897. That one was almost certainly legitimate.

Hughie took over as Detroit manager in 1907 and won pennants in his first three seasons. Only Ralph Houk of the Yankees matched that. In eleven more years of trying, Jennings never won again, but he finished in the first division seven times. His greatest player was, of course, Ty Cobb, whom he disliked but coddled. His other players were treated sternly, often sarcastically.

Jennings's nickname was "Eeyah," because he used to shout it from the coaching box. He said it was Hawaiian for "Watch out!"

He was elected to the Hall of Fame in 1945.

TOMMY JOHN
Pitcher, Cle (A) 1963–64, Chi (A) 1965–71, LA (N) 1972–74, (injured 1975) 1976–78, NY (A) 1979–82, 1986–89, Cal (A) 1982–85, Oak (A) 1985
John is the bionic man, with two arms and two careers. In July of 1974 he had only a fair 124–106 lifetime mark, but was coming off his best season, a career high of 16 wins for the Dodgers. He was 13–3 for 1974, and seemed headed for a great year when he tore a ligament in his elbow.

Dr. Frank Jobe sewed a new one back in. It was history's first ligament transplant. Tommy said he asked Dr. Jobe to give him Koufax's arm but said he got Mrs. Koufax's by mistake. He could throw again, but he had no fastball—he didn't even have a medium ball. Still, he could throw curves and get them over the plate. And he knew how to pitch.

In 1976 he was 10–10 for the Dodgers and was named the Comeback Player of the Year. That was nice, but he was just beginning his second career. In 1977, he was 20–7. After joining the New York Yankees as a free agent in 1979, he won 21 and 22. And he pitched on and on: 1989 was his twenty-sixth season.

BANCROFT "BAN" JOHNSON
American League President, 1901–27
A former sportswriter, Johnson built the AL from the old Western League, a minor loop which he and Charles Comiskey took over in 1893. In 1900 they changed its name and in 1901 proclaimed it a major league. They raided the NL for star players and managers and built the league into what they claimed it to be.

By 1903 Johnson had forced the NL to make peace, leading to the first modern World Series—won by Ban's AL Boston boys over Pittsburgh. In fact, the AL would win fourteen of the first twenty-four Series.

Johnson ran his league with tunnel vision. A humorless workaholic, his word was law among the original AL team owners. He banned liquor from his ballparks and fined for profanity and rowdyism. He backed his umpires, raising their status. Although nominally the president of the AL, he was called the "Czar of Baseball" because he dominated the three-man commission that governed the game until 1920.

But his power slipped as new owners who resented his dictatorial ways entered the AL. Even his old ally, Comiskey, turned against him. When the Black Sox scandal broke in 1920, Johnson demanded a full investigation, causing a final break with Comiskey, who owned the Sox. One result was that the commission was replaced by one czar, Judge Landis. Ban fought his loss of power for six years before resigning.

He was elected to the Hall of Fame in 1937.

"INDIAN BOB" JOHNSON
Outfielder, Phi (A) 1933–42, Was (A) 1943, Bos (A) 1944–45
The lesson of Johnson's career was "Play for a contender or they'll never remember." It was his misfortune to join the Philadelphia A's in 1933, just when Connie Mack was selling off his high-priced stars and the team was heading for the bottom of the AL like a lead submarine. So for ten years with the awful A's and three more with a couple of other *nolo contenderes*, Johnson played the outfield, hit a ton, and today is too obscure for a good trivia question.

Even when he'd do things like go 6-for-6 (in 1934) or bat in six runs in one inning (1937), the A's were so far out of contention that their contests were carried on sports pages after "In other games . . ." Of course, fans knew about him then—he was elected to seven All-Star Games—they just forgot quickly because none of his hits ever meant anything in a pennant race.

What hitting? Five seasons over .300 and a .296 career mark; three years with 30 or better homers among a total of 288; seven straight 100-RBI years (eight altogether) for teams that considered each baserunner a moral victory.

Now, just for a second, close your eyes and picture that record in Yankee pinstripes.

WILLIAM "JUDY" JOHNSON
Third Baseman, Negro League, 1921–38, Hilldale, Homestead Grays, Darby Daisies, Pittsburgh Cranfords
Johnson was one of the three best third baseman during the 1920s and 1930s. A steady defensive player, he was dependable rather than flashy. At bat he was an intelligent, scientific hitter who consistently exceeded .300 and was acclaimed for his ability to come through in the clutch. Known for his quiet, down-to-business manner, Johnson was considered a steadying influence on younger players.

He played on the famous Philadelphia Hilldales (1921–1929), hitting .364 in the 1924 black World Series. His inside-the-park grand slam won Game Four. In 1929 he hit .383 with 22 stolen bases. The next year he joined

the Homestead Grays as player-manager. Judy also played on the 1935 Pittsburgh Crawfords, perhaps the best black team of all time, with Satchel Paige, Cool Papa Bell, Oscar Charleston, and Josh Gibson.

In later years, Johnson scouted first for the Philadelphia A's and later found Dick Allen for the Phillies. He was named to the Hall of Fame in 1975.

WALTER JOHNSON
Pitcher, Was (A) 1907–27. Manager, Was (A) 1929–32, Cle (A) 1933–35
Johnson is high up on everyone's list of nominees as the greatest pitcher of all time. His statistics alone are staggering. Working for a Washington team that finished in the second division in ten of his twenty-one seasons, he nevertheless won 417 games (second only to Cy Young), pitched in 5,925 innings (third most of all time), threw an all-time record 110 shutouts, and compiled a 2.17 ERA, the seventh-best career mark. For years his 3,506 strikeouts was considered an unbreakable record, but a later, more free-swinging age has changed that; even though he has been surpassed by Nolan Ryan, Steve Carlton, and Don Sutton, he still may be the greatest strikeout artist ever.

He won more than 30 games in two seasons, more than 20 in ten other years. He led the AL in wins six times, in ERA five times, and in strikeouts twelve!

He did nearly all of this with a fabled fastball, thrown with an easy side-arm motion. It came in straight as string, but the hitters couldn't get around on it. Only late in his career did Johnson bother to develop a curve. He had good control, and for all his innings pitched only in one season did he walk more than 100 batters.

He won more more 1–0 games—and lost more—than any other man. In 1908, Johnson's first full year in the league, he won three shutouts in four days, giving up twelve hits in the three games, yet he had to settle for a 14–14 record for a last-place club. In 1913 he battled for fifteen innings to win 1–0; in 1918 he struggled twenty innings for a 1–0 win, giving up only one walk the whole game.

Of all his great seasons, 1913 was no doubt the acme. He was 36–7, to lead in wins and percentage. His ERA was 1.14. In a league-leading 346 innings he gave up only 232 hits, an average of less than six per nine innings. He struck out 243 to lead the league and walked—now get this—only 38! Oh, yes, he pitched eleven shutouts and had 55⅔ straight shutout innings, a mark which stood until 1968. He even set the record for fielding that year, with no errors in 103 chances. Naturally he was MVP.

Even with a sore arm in 1921 (when he had an 8–10 record), he could still pitch a no-hitter. It was his only one; strangely, he never pitched one in spacious Griffith Stadium.

Johnson finally made it to the World Series in 1924 at the age of thirty-six. The old man was 23–7 and led the league in his usual categories: wins, ERA, strikeouts, and shutouts. The writers gave him another MVP.

As much as batters hated to bat against him, everybody liked "the Big Train." Open, honest, modest, soft-spoken, considerate, shy, he never drank or smoked but didn't condemn those who did. A big evening for him was going to a movie or just talking baseball. If he wasn't the greatest pitcher ever, you'd want him to be. In 1936 he was one of the first five players elected to the Hall of Fame.

ADRIAN "ADDIE" JOSS
Pitcher, Cle (A) 1902–10
Joss's death at age thirty-one cut off one of baseball's most brilliant pitching careers. He was the hardest man in history to reach base against, just 8.7 runners per nine innings; only 1.4 of them were walks. At six-three, 185 pounds, the long-armed Joss pitched with an exaggerated pinwheel motion that earned him the nickname of "the Human Hairpin." Addie pivoted away from the hitter before the pitch, then came side-armed with a "jump" ball that—the batters swore—dipped, leveled off, and dipped again, something like Frank Merriwell's fictional curve that broke both ways on the way to the plate. It earned him a lifetime 1.89 ERA, second best ever to Ed Walsh's 1.82.

Joss broke in with Cleveland in 1902. He fanned four of the first six men he faced and ended with a one-hitter, a single by Jesse Burkett. A few days later Addie just missed another no-hitter; with one out in the ninth, an error and two singles spoiled it.

As a rookie, he was 17–13 with fifth-place Cleveland and 18–13 the next year, as the club rose to third. In two years Addie started 60 games and completed 59. For his career he finished 234 out of 260.

He won 20 or more each year from 1905 through 1908, with a high of 27 in 1907.

Joss's best year came in 1908, when Cleveland made a run for the pennant against Ed Walsh's White Sox and Ty Cobb's Tigers. Addie won seven of his club's first eleven games. The three teams were neck and neck (and neck) on October 2, when Joss faced Walsh. Big Ed was 40–14 at that point. Ed pitched a four-hitter; Addie topped him 1–0 with a perfect game. Though Cleveland lost to Detroit by ½ game, Joss was 24–11 with a 1.16 ERA.

Addie was a fine barbershop singer and often harmonized on the sidelines with Walsh.

Joss threw another no-hitter in 1910 but hurt his elbow and ended the season early with a 5–5 record. The next spring he fainted on the trip north; eleven days later he was dead of tubercular meningitis.

Although he played only nine years, his record was so outstanding that the usual ten-year requirement was waived when he was elected to the Hall of Fame in 1978.

JIM KAAT
Pitcher, Was (A) 1959–60, Min (A) 1961–73, Chi (A) 1973–75, Phi (N) 1976–79, NY (A) 1979–80, StL (N) 1980–83
"I've never craved center stage," Kaat said, but only Warren Spahn, Eddie Plank, Steve Carlton, Lefty Grove, and Tommy John won more among lefties than Jim's 283. Three times a 20-game winner, he used a good fastball, guile, and a brutal conditioning program to pitch for a record twenty-five seasons. His best year was 1966 with Minnesota, when he led the league with 25 wins and won the *Sporting News*'s Pitcher of the Year Award. His other 20-win seasons came with the White Sox in 1974–1975.

Not only did Kaat put in a lot of years, he put in some workhorse seasons, going over 300 innings twice and over 200 twelve other times, in spite of several serious injuries.

Kaat helped himself in ways other than with his arm. His .185 career batting average was fair for a pitcher and his 134 career sacrifices is the record for hurlers. He may have been the best-fielding pitcher ever, winning sixteen straight Golden Gloves.

AL KALINE
Outfielder, Det (A) 1953–74
Kaline accepted a $30,000 bonus to sign with Detroit in 1953. Two years later, without having spent a day in the minors, the twenty-year-old Kaline won the 1955 AL batting title with .340, the youngest champ ever. Al never hit that high again, but for twenty-two years he was an outstanding player for Detroit. Though never again spectacular with a bat, he was steady, accumulating 1,622 runs scored and 1,583 RBIs. Kaline finished with 3,007 hits, a .297 batting average, and 399 home runs. He played in eighteen All-Star Games.

Kaline was a sensational defensive outfielder, with a powerful, accurate arm. He won eleven Gold Gloves. In 1971 he went through 133 games without an error.

Although Al battled injuries his whole career—he broke his cheek bone, collar bone, rib, foot, finger, and arm at various times—he set an AL record with twenty years of 100 games or more.

He played in only one World Series. In 1968 he hit .379 with eight RBIs to lead the Tigers to a victory in seven games over the Cardinals.

He was elected to the Hall of Fame in 1980.

WILLIE KAMM
Third Baseman, Chi (A) 1923–31, Cle (A) 1931–35
The White Sox bought Kamm from San Francisco of the Pacific Coast League in 1923 for the then sensational price of $100,000 to try to plug the hole at third left by banned Black Soxer Buck Weaver. In a career trapped in the second division, Willie earned a reputation as one of the best-fielding third basemen ever. He led the AL at his position eight times in fielding average and was consistently among the leaders in all fielding categories except errors. Although he had no home run power, he was a good contact hitter, with a .281 career batting average. His .308 in 1928 was his single-season best.

TIM KEEFE
Pitcher, Troy (N) 1880–82, NY (AA) 1883–84, NY (N) 1885–89, 1891, NY (P) 1890, Phi (N) 1891–93
Keefe was one of the first great changeup artists. For six straight years, 1883–1888, the unassuming righthand⌐ combined a fair fastball and curve with his cha⌐ win 32 games or more. Twice he went over⌐ his career with 342 victories.

In 1888 he won 19 straight. i⌐ effort. That's the year ⌐ Welch pitched the ⌐ wins, percenta⌐ championship s⌐ St. Louis Browns⌐ York's victories.

Tim's finest day ⌐ July 4 doubleheader⌐ two-hitter in the aftern⌐

He was named to the

WILLIE KEELER
Outfielder, NY (N) 1892–93, 1910, Bkn (N) 1893, 1899–1902, Bal (N) 1894–98, NY (A) 1903–09
At 5'4½" and 140 pounds, "Wee Willie" looked like the batboy. He choked up a foot on his thirty-inch bat, the lightest in the league, stood stiff-legged, leaning over the plate, and chopped down on the ball, the famous "Baltimore Chop." The ball bounced into the air, and before it came down, Willie was safe at first. Or if the infielders charged in, he'd bounce it over their heads. His "I hit 'em where they ain't" has been quoted more often than the Gettysburg Address.

He hit .424 in 1897, second best ever, to lead the NL, and followed with a league-topping .385 in 1898. He had four other seasons over .370. His .341 career average ranks him thirteenth all-time. He had over 200 hits eight years in a row. The ultimate singles hitter, 2,511 of his 2,932 hits were for one base.

Keeler hit in 44 straight games in 1897. No one kept such records then, but in all the years since, only Rose has tied it and only DiMaggio has surpassed it.

A brilliant bunter, he is one of the men responsible for the modern foul-strike rule. He could bunt fouls by the hour until they changed the rule and began calling them outs after two strikes.

Known as an outstanding right fielder, he played his first major league games as a lefthanded-throwing third baseman. A practical joker in moments of leisure, Keeler was deadly serious on the field. He was elected to the Hall of Fame in 1939.

GEORGE KELL
Third Baseman, Phi (A) 1943–46, Det (A) 1946–52, Bos (A) 1952–54, Chi (A) 1954–56, Bal (A) 1956–57
Kell gave the Tigers and several other AL clubs some steady fielding and .300 hitting after World War Two. He led the league in batting average in 1949, just inching out Ted Williams by .0002 with a .3429 mark. Kell was safely in front of Williams as he approached his last at-bat of the season. Teammates urged him to let a pinch hitter bat in his place since an out would lose him the title. He refused and took his place in the on-deck circle, but before he could bat a teammate ended the inning and the season by hitting into a double play. In nine seasons, Kell batted over .300. Never a power hitter, Kell is one of the few modern hitters to have over 100 RBIs with fewer than 10 home runs, a feat he achieved in 1950.

Kell had an excellent throwing arm and was surehanded. He led AL third basemen in fielding average seven times, in assists four times, and in putouts and double plays twice.

In 1983 he was named to the Hall of Fame.

CHARLIE KELLER
er, NY (A) 1939–43, 1945–49, 1952, Det (A)
genital back problem forced him to the side-eemed destined to take his place as one of all the Yankees' hitters. "King Kong" DiMaggio and Tommy Henrich in the at helped win four flags in five years, the New York short porch to propel uns and averaged 98 RBIs a year.

Though Keller hit .300 only three times, pitchers respected him and regularly gave him 100 walks. He was a hard man to double up.

Charlie was a great October hitter. In 1939 he hit .438 in the World Series; his two homers and four RBIs won the third game, 7–3, and it was he who barreled into the Reds' Ernie Lombardi to score the deciding run in the tenth inning of the final game. In the 1941 Series, Keller hit .389. In the fourth game, after Henrich reached first on Mickey Owen's passed ball, Charlie doubled in the two runs that won the game. Then he scored the run that won the fifth and final game. In 1942 his two-run homer in the second game tied the score in the eighth, though the Cardinals went on to win the game and the Series.

Following another pennant winner in 1943, he went into the Navy. He returned in 1945 and played until 1951, but the back problem limited him to only one more season of more than 83 games. He retired to raise horses on his Maryland farm, Yankeeland.

JOE KELLEY
Outfielder, Bos (N) 1891, 1908, Pit (N) 1891–92, Bal (N) 1892–98, Bkn (N) 1899–01, Bal (A) 1902, Cin (N) 1902–06. Manager, Cin (N) 1902–05, Bos (N) 1908
Kelley was the heavy-hitting left fielder for the famous Baltimore Orioles of the 1890s. Joe played on six pennant winners in seven years, 1894–1900. The final two were with the Brooklyn Superbas, whom he captained.

He hit over .300 for eleven consecutive seasons. In 1894, when he hit .393, he went 9-for-9 in a doubleheader, still the record. Two years later he hit .364. His lifetime average was .317.

Kelley was a speedy outfielder with a powerful arm. He used to come to the park at nine in the morning to practice his bunting and running. A handsome if vain man, he kept a mirror under his cap and liked to sneak looks at himself in the outfield.

He was elected to the Hall of Fame in 1971.

GEORGE "HIGHPOCKETS" KELLY
First Baseman, NY (N) 1915–17, 1919–26, Pit (N) 1917, Cin (N) 1927–30, Chi (N) 1930, Bkn (N) 1932
Kelly was the slick-fielding, clutch-hitting first baseman for a Giants team that won four straight NL pennants, 1921–1924. John McGraw, the New York manager, said that Kelly made "more important hits" for him than any player he ever had. He led the NL in RBIs with 94 in 1920, then knocked home over 100 in each of the pennant-winning seasons. In 1924 he led the league again with 136.

A good home run hitter, he led the NL in 1921 with 23 and set a record in 1924 with 7 homers in 6 games.

The lanky "Highpockets" had one of the most powerful arms in the league. His on-the-money throw across the infield completed a brilliant double play to end the 1921 World Series. He consistently ranked high in assists and holds the NL records for most putouts and most chances in a season.

He was named to the Hall of Fame in 1973.

MIKE "KING" KELLY
Outfielder/Catcher/Manager, Cin (N) 1878–79, Chi (N) 1880–86, Bos (N) 1887–89, 1891–92, Bos (P) 1890, Cin-Mil (AA) 1891, Bos (AA) 1891, NY (N) 1893

With his dark hair, black mustache, and flashing white smile, the King was a matinee idol and the subject of a popular song, "Slide, Kelly, Slide." ("If your batting doesn't fail ya, they will take ya to Australia / Slide, Kelly, on your belly, slide, slide, slide.")

Mike rode to the park in a silk hat, ascot, and patent leather shoes, in a carriage pulled by two white horses (and sometimes by his "cranks," or fans). He was one of the best-dressed men in America. He went on the stage reciting "Casey at the Bat" and made $3,000 for the use of his picture on advertisements. He was a big gambler and was often seen at the races.

Mike was one of the first hitters to perfect the hit-and-run, one of the first catchers to give finger signals, and one of the first outfielders to play close to back up infield plays. And despite the song, he was one of the first runners to use the hook slide. His most famous slide knocked the ball out of George Wright's hand to clinch the 1882 flag.

He also liked to catch the ump asleep (they had only one then) and cut from first base to third base without going near second. He'd take a similar shortcut from second base to home.

In all, Kelly sparked Anson's White Stockings to five flags in seven years, 1880–1886. He led the NL in hitting with .354 in 1884 and .388 in 1886.

In 1887 Boston bought him for a record price, and he became "the $10,000 Beauty." He reputedly kept $5,000 of his purchase price for the use of his likeness for promotional purposes. Mike hit .322 his first year with them and stole 84 bases.

Kelly also managed and batted the Bostons to the Players League flag in 1890.

Mike played all nine positions. Once, while sitting on the bench, a foul fly came back. "Kelly now catching," he shouted and made the catch. They changed the substitute rule after that.

Anson always said, "Mike's only enemy is himself." He died of pneumonia at the age of thirty-six, penniless after giving his only suit of clothes to a tramp while on a boat to Boston to recite "Casey" one more time. The city gave him a grand funeral send-off.

He was named to the Hall of Fame in 1945.

KEN KELTNER
Third Baseman, Cle (A) 1937–44, 1946–49, Bos (A) 1950
Keltner was the AL's top-fielding third baseman in the 1940s. He led AL third sackers in fielding average three times, assists four times, and double plays five times. With Keltner on third and Lou Boudreau at short, Cleveland fans saw some of the best fielding of the decade. Ken's habit of taking a quick look at the ball in his hand before he gunned it to first was imitated by Cleveland schoolboys. Keltner is best known for the two fine plays he made to stop Joe DiMaggio's hit streak at 56.

A fair hitter with some long-ball power, his best year was 1948, when he hit 31 homers, knocked in 119 runs, and hit .297, as the Indians won a tight race and the Series.

BILL KILLEFER
Catcher, StL (A) 1909–10, Phi (N) 1911–17, Chi (N) 1918–21. Manager, Chi (N) 1921–25, StL (A) 1930–33

Killefer was a typical catcher of the dead-ball era—a good handler of pitchers, strong-armed, reliable on defense, and a rotten hitter. He averaged .238 over thirteen seasons and crushed a grand career total of 4 home runs.

His primary claim to fame is that he was Grover Alexander's favorite catcher. They first hooked up in 1911, Alex's rookie year with the Phillies. Their partnership continued when they were traded in tandem to the Cubs after the 1917 season and lasted until Killefer took over as the Cubs' manager and retired as a player in 1921.

There seems little doubt that he was an intelligent player whose handling helped Alexander be one of baseball's greatest pitchers. There's no way of knowing how many games Alex might have won with a catcher who had less brains and more RBIs.

HARMON KILLEBREW
First Baseman/Third Baseman/Outfielder, Was (A) 1954–60, Min (A) 1961–74, KC (A) 1975
A few eyebrows went up among the Old School observers when Killebrew was elected to the Hall of Fame in 1984. The Killer didn't fit the traditional mold of so many enshrined in Cooperstown. He didn't hit for breathtaking batting averages; not once in his career did he bat above .288 for a full season, and his career average was a mere .256. Shortstops do better. He was no jackrabbit on the bases; he stole 19 in twenty-two seasons. Catchers do better. He didn't dazzle anyone with his glove; he played three positions without ever winning even a Pyrite Glove, much less real gold. He wasn't even a colorful character, just a modest, nice guy who came to work, did his job, and went home to his wife and children.

Killebrew was a one-dimensional player.

Of course, that one dimension—smashing home runs in gargantuan quantities—produced more runs for his team than all the singles of a half dozen "good" hitters. And unless there's been a sudden and secret change in the rules, the object of hitting is to score runs.

Killebrew lifted 573 lordly blasts over the fences. Only one AL player hit more—Babe Ruth. In home run frequency, Harmon is third behind only Ruth and Ralph Kiner. Such slugging helped win the Killer spots on *The Sporting News*'s All-Star teams at three different positions—3B, 1B, and OF. Eight times he went over 40 homers; six times he led or tied for the league lead. Harmon was MVP in 1969, when he led the league with 49 homers and 140 RBIs. He had 1,584 RBIs for his career.

And while that .256 batting average draws no raves, he drew 1,559 walks, which puts his on-base percentage up over .375.

RALPH KINER
Outfielder, Pit (N) 1946–53, Chi (N) 1953–54, Cle (A) 1955
Kiner never said, "Home run hitters drive Cadillacs"; Fritz Ostermueller did. But he was talking about Ralph.

Kiner was like Killebrew a "one-dimensional ballplayer," who was worth more than most two- or three-dimensional players who ever lived. Such is the structure of baseball that blasting one three-run home run will help a team more than a leaping one-handed catch, or two or three steals of second. Moaned Warren Spahn: "Kiner can wipe out your lead with one swing."

No one except Babe Ruth ever dominated home run hitting the way Kiner did from 1946 to 1952, as he led or tied for the NL leadership in his first seven major league seasons. Aaron, Mays, Killebrew, Jackson, Foxx, and others hit more, but Ralph averaged 40 every 550 at-bats; only Babe did better. In 1947 he hit 51; in 1949 he raised that to 54, the second-highest total in NL history.

Like the Babe, Ralph got a lot of walks, going over 100 six times. He was usually found on *The Sporting News*'s All-Star team, and by 1951 Ralph was the highest-paid player in the league.

But the big difference between them was that the Yankees, with a strong supporting cast, won pennants on Babe's homers; the Pirates were usually last in spite of Ralph's.

Kiner, who was elected to the Hall of Fame in 1975, became a TV commentator for the Mets in the year of their inception, 1962, and remains behind the mike as one of the hardiest of all baseball's voices.

CHUCK KLEIN
Outfielder, Phi (N) 1928–33, 1937–44, Chi (N) 1934–36, Pit (N) 1939
Philadelphia's Baker Bowl, the Phillies' home through the 1930s, had a short right field that was batter-friendly, to say the least. No player ever took better advantage of the situation than Klein, a powerful lefthanded hitter whose pokes against and over the Bowl's cozy wall helped him produce a startling five-year record.

In 1929, his first full season, he led the NL with 43 home runs, while hitting .356 and driving in 145 runs. He beat Mel Ott by one for the homer crown when Phillie pitchers walked Mel five straight times on the final day, including once with the bases full.

The next year he was awesome: .386, 40 homers, 170 RBIs—but did not lead the league in any of those categories in that hit-happy year. He continued his assault in 1931: .337, 31 home runs, and 121 RBIs, the last two figures leading the league.

He was named MVP in 1932, when he led again in homers with 38, while driving in 137 and hitting .348. In 1933 he climaxed his five years of excellence with a Triple Crown: .368, 28, 120.

Traded to the Cubs in 1934, he continued to be a productive hitter, but without his best friend, the wall, his great days were over. He finished his career with an even 300 homers and a .320 batting average.

The wall even helped Klein to a defensive record. In 1930 he threw out 44 runners from his up-close and personal right field spot.

Other players had the same wall to shoot for in the era; nobody used it better.

He was named to the Hall of Fame in 1980.

BILL KLEM
Umpire, 1905–40
In a career that stretched from 1905 through 1940, Bill Klem was considered the greatest umpire of all time. He's credited by some with being the first umpire to use hand signals and the first to use the smaller chest protector.

Klem officiated in eighteen World Series, a record.

When Bill broke in, there was only one ump per game,

and he literally dodged bottles from angry fans. When a player advanced on Klem to argue, he drew a line in the dirt with his shoe and called it "the Rio Grande." One step over, and the player was out.

Bill kind of resembled a catfish, but saying so to his face was another cause for automatic ejection. He once slugged it out with outfielder Goose Goslin in a hotel elevator.

Baseball was "more than a game, it's a religion," Klem said. "I never missed one," he always said of his calls. But after he retired, he would add, "in here," tapping his heart.

Klem was elected to the Hall of Fame in 1953.

JOHNNY KLING
Catcher, Chi (N) 1900–08, 1910–11, Bos (N) 1911–12, Cin (N) 1913. Manager, Bos (N) 1912
Kling was the peppery catcher for the great Tinker-to-Evers-to-Chance Cub teams of the century's first decade. A good defensive catcher, he pulled his weight as a hitter with a career average of .271. That was a little unusual in those days, when backstops were catchers first and hitters only if convenient. He was also rated as one of the best handlers of pitchers in the game. Certainly the record of the Cubs' moundmen during that period did nothing to tarnish that reputation.

The Cubs, with "Noisy" Kling behind the plate, won three straight pennants, 1906–1908. He sat out 1909, and they finished second. When he returned in 1910, they won another flag.

CASIMIR "JIM" KONSTANTY
Pitcher, Cin (N) 1944, Bos (N) 1946, Phi (N) 1948–54, NY (A) 1954–56, StL (N) 1956
Big, bespectacled Jim was one of the early relief chiefs, and like so many, he had one truly great year. In 1950 he led the NL with 22 saves and 16 relief wins for the Whiz Kid Phils, who just nipped the Dodgers for the pennant on the last day of the 1950 season. He was named MVP.

He was the surprise starter in the World Series against New York, when Phillie ace Robin Roberts needed rest after pitching the season finale. He dueled Vic Raschi for eight innings, gave up just one run on a double and two flies, and lost 1–0.

JERRY KOOSMAN
Pitcher, NY (N) 1967–78, Min (A) 1979–81, Chi (A) 1981–83, Phi (N) 1984–85
Quietly Koosman emerged as a solid 222-game winner trapped mostly with inferior teams. As a rookie in 1968, Jerry was 19–12, with a 2.08 ERA, setting a rookie record with 7 shutouts. (His other record was striking out 62 times in 1968 as a batter.)

Koosman had a sore arm in 1969 but still posted a 17–9 record to join Seaver in sparking the Mets to their dramatic World Series win. Kooz's contribution: a two-hit shutout of the Orioles in Game Two, a 5–3 victory in Game Five, and an overall Series ERA of 2.04.

Jerry added another win in the 1973 Series. He won 21 games for the 1976 Mets and 20 for the 1979 Twins. In 1983 he went 11–7 to help the White Sox reach the playoffs.

SANFORD "SANDY" KOUFAX
Pitcher, Bkn (N) 1955–57, LA (N) 1958–66

For five fabulous years, 1962–1966, Sandy Koufax did things with a baseball that no other lefty has done: five ERA titles, four no-hitters, three Cy Youngs, and one MVP.

And much of it was achieved pitching while in excruciating pain.

Wild as a youngster, Koufax labored for six years to compile a 36–40 record. Then he found his groove and became a star.

In 1965 Koo struck out 382, breaking Waddell's season record of 349. He also threw a perfect game.

In 1966 he won more games, 27, and pitched more shutouts, 11, than any NL lefty in one year in this century.

Then his arm went bad, and he walked away at the age of thirty "while I could still comb my hair."

Koufax won only 165 games, but no man who won twice that many ever reached the same heights. In 1972, at thirty-six, he was the youngest man ever elected to Cooperstown.

As a fastball hurler, Koufax ranked with Ryan, Johnson, Feller, Grove, and Gooden. Unlike Grove and Johnson, Sandy had a dandy curve too. He whiffed 18 men in one game twice, in 1959 and 1962.

His World Series ERA was 0.95, although his won-lost record was only 4–3. Four of the ten runs against him were unearned.

BOWIE KUHN
Commissioner, 1969–84

A Princeton lawyer, Bowie Kuhn replaced "the unknown soldier," General William Eckert, as commissioner for three controversial terms. Considered the owners' commissioner—as indeed every commissioner is—Kuhn resisted players' demands for more money, saying greedy players would bankrupt the teams. Player-negotiator Marvin Miller called it Kuhn's "annual poor-mouth speech."

Ironically many owners also opposed Kuhn, and he was bypassed in the negotiations with Miller. Charles Finley of Oakland led the "dump Bowie" movement, which almost succeeded until two owners changed their votes. Kuhn would later void Finley's sales of $3.5 million worth of stars, which helped to drive the combative Finley out of the game.

One of Kuhn's moves was to sanction playing the World Series at night. He appeared at the first night game on a cold October evening wearing no top coat to dramatize how "mild" the weather was. But he was wearing thermal skivvies underneath.

NAPOLEON "LARRY" LAJOIE
Second Baseman, Phi (N) 1896–1900, Phi (A) 1901–02, 1915–16, Cle (A) 1902–14. Manager, Cle (A) 1905–09.

One of the best second basemen of all time and, by all accounts, the most graceful, Lajoie was also one of the most successful righthanded hitters. An established star with the NL Phillies, where he'd hit .378 in 1899, he jumped to Connie Mack's AL Philadelphia A's in 1901. The presence of Lajoie, Cy Young, and a few others helped legitimize the AL as a major league. Lajoie's .426 in the league's first year is still the highest batting average

ever achieved in the American League.

The following year an injunction by the Phillies forced AL president Ban Johnson to shift Lajoie to Cleveland, where he spent the bulk of his career. In 1903, 1904, and 1910, he led the AL in batting with averages of .344, .376, and .384.

Lajoie's status was such that the team was named after him during his tenure—the Cleveland Naps. He managed the club from 1905 to part of 1909 and got them as high as second in 1908. Late in the 1909 campaign, he gave up the reins because he felt the cares of managing were hurting his play.

Lajoie was a powerful line-drive hitter who pulled the ball. In 1910 the popular second baseman was locked in a tight batting race with Ty Cobb, despised by nearly everyone in the AL. The winner of the race was to receive a gift of a new Chalmers automobile. On the final day of the season the St. Louis Browns' manager ordered his young third baseman to play extremely deep on Lajoie during a doubleheader, ostensibly because of Larry's ability to smash the ball. Lajoie went 8 for 8, with seven of the hits being bunts, but lost the title to Cobb by .0007. He was given the auto anyway. In 1981 Paul MacFarlane of *The Sporting News* discovered that Ty got credit for an extra hit that year and Lajoie should have won the title. Commissioner Kuhn ruled that, damn the facts, the records remain as they had been.

Lajoie hit over .300 in sixteen of his twenty-one seasons and finished with 3,242 hits for a .338 average. He accumulated 1,599 RBIs and scored 1,502. He led AL second basemen in fielding six times.

In 1937 he was named to the Hall of Fame.

KENESAW MOUNTAIN LANDIS
Commissioner, 1920–44

Baseball's first commissioner and only true czar, Landis demanded and got autocratic power to clean up the Black Sox scandal ruthlessly. By doing so, he restored public confidence in the integrity of baseball. He went on to rule the game with a power never wielded since. Historian David Q. Voigt calls him one of the five most influential men in baseball history.

A shock of white hair, a thin, unsmiling mouth, and a crushed fedora hat—this was the image of Landis, who restored integrity to the game and ruled it for more than two decades.

As a federal judge, Landis had won fame by fining John D. Rockefeller's Standard Oil trust $29 million and for jailing ninety-four Socialist Labor Party leaders during World War One. But he refused to rule in the Federal League's suit against the NL and AL, saying it "would be a blow against a national institution." It won him the job as commissioner.

Landis banned the Black Sox for life, though no court had convicted them. He banned several other players for less publicized fixing charges. He suspended Babe Ruth for barnstorming without permission.

On the other hand, he was zealous in defending player rights. He opposed the farm system, and though he could not stop it, he released two hundred Tiger and Cardinal farm hands into free agency on the grounds that they were being "covered up" by the teams.

Team owners bridled under his iron rule and never

again granted a commissioner such powers. He was elected to the Hall of Fame in 1944, a month after his death.

TONY LAZZERI
Second Baseman, NY (A) 1926–37, Chi (N) 1938, Bkn (N) 1939, NY (N) 1939
Poor Lazzeri. As a twenty-two-year-old Yankee rookie, he was the victim of the most famous strikeout in history. He whiffed with the bases loaded against a hung-over Grover Alexander in the 1926 World Series. But with a tiny change of wind, Tony could have been the hero; before striking out he hit a long drive to left that faded foul by a few inches. "A few feet more," said Alex, "and he'd have been the hero and I'd have been the bum."

Like his nemesis Alexander, Lazzeri was a victim of epilepsy. And like Alex, he overcame it to have an outstanding career.

Ironically Lazzeri hit a World Series grand slam ten years later in 1936.

Overall he played second base for six Yankee pennant winners and helped the Cubs to a flag in 1938. He drove in over 100 runs in seven different seasons and finished with a .292 career batting average.

Tony also had one of the greatest minor league years ever—202 runs, 222 RBIs, and 60 HRs for San Francisco of the Pacific Coast League in 1925 (of course, they played a 197-game season).

BOB LEMON
Pitcher, Cle (A) 1941–42, 1946–58. Manager, KC (A) 1970–72, Chi (A) 1977–78, NY (A) 1978–82
Lemon was the ace of perhaps the finest pitching staff in AL history—the Indians of 1948–1956, with Bob Feller, Early Wynn, Mike Garcia, Herb Score, and others. Lem won 207 games for Cleveland, yet didn't become a pitcher until he was nearly twenty-six years old.

As a third baseman, he played ten games with the Tribe before going into military service for World War Two. He demonstrated that he was not a good enough hitter to replace Ken Keltner at third for the Indians. Moreover, his arm was erratic. He seemed unable to throw a ball straight.

When he returned to the Tribe in 1946, the decision was made to turn his liability into a virtue by making him a pitcher. He showed promise in 1947 when he won 11. By 1948 he was a star. As the Indians won their first pennant in 28 years, he pitched a no-hitter, 10 shutouts, and won 20 games. He added two more wins in the World Series.

He had seven 20-win seasons from 1948 to 1956. Three times he led the AL in victories, including 1955, when he won "only" 18.

Lem helped himself with his glove and bat. Often used as a pinch hitter, his 37 home runs are second all-time among pitchers.

In 1978 Lem took over as manager of the Yankees when they were 10½ games behind the Red Sox and split with dissension. With patient handling—plus a raft of Red Sox injuries—Bob achieved one of the unforgettable modern miracles by bringing the Yankees back to a last-day tie with Boston and a playoff victory.

Lemon was elected to the Hall of Fame in 1976.

WALTER "BUCK" LEONARD
First Baseman, Negro League, 1933–50, Brooklyn Royal Giants, Homestead Grays
They called Leonard "the black Gehrig." Like Lou, Buck was a durable first baseman with plenty of lefthanded power. He teamed with Josh Gibson to give the Homestead Grays a mighty one-two home run punch as the Grays won nine straight Negro National League flags, 1937–1945. When Gibson left the club, 1940–1941, for Mexico, the Grays won on Buck's power alone.

In 1939 Leonard led all black batters with .492. He also slugged 7 homers in the short season, hitting them at a rate of 66/550 at-bats. Runner-up Gibson hit 6 (a rate of 59/550). Buck's entire career has not yet been compiled, but one estimate of his Negro League record puts his batting average at .336. He was also one of black baseball's most popular players.

He was elected to the Hall of Fame in 1972.

FREDDIE LINDSTROM
Third Baseman/Outfielder, NY (N) 1924–32, Pit (N) 1933–34, Chi (N) 1935–36
Lindstrom was a victim of pebbles. It was his bad luck that when he was an eighteen-year-old Giants rookie in the seventh game of the 1924 Series, not one but two balls hit pebbles and bounced over his head. The first, in the eighth inning, let in the tying run. The second, in the twelfth, lost the game for the Giants.

Ironically Lindstrom went on to be considered one of the NL's best-fielding third basemen until a foot injury in 1931 forced him to the outfield.

When he became a Giants regular in 1925 and began showing his hitting ability, New York fans called him "the Boy Wonder." A consistent .300 hitter, his top seasons were 1928, when he led the NL with 231 hits and batted .358, and 1930, when he hit .379 and swatted 22 home runs.

In 1935 he helped the Cubs to a pennant as an outfielder.

He was elected to the Hall of Fame in 1976.

JOHN HENRY "POP" LLOYD
Shortstop, Negro League, 1905–31, Macon Acmes, Cuban-X Giants, Philadelphia Giants, Leland Giants, Lincoln Giants, Chicago American Giants, Brooklyn Royal Giants, Columbus Buckeyes, Bacharach Giants, Hilldale, New York Black Yankees
"You could put Wagner and Lloyd in a bag together," Connie Mack once said, "and whichever you pulled out, you wouldn't go wrong." They called Lloyd "the black Wagner," and Honus said he considered it an honor.

Starting in 1905, Lloyd established himself as the finest shortstop in black baseball and one of the finest ever. He played for independent black teams and in Cuba, where he was adored. They called him *Cuchara*, which means "scoop" or "shovel." Much like Wagner, he would scoop up a grounder and fire it to first in a hail of dust and pebbles that he'd also shoveled up with the ball.

His finest hour came in 1909 against Ty Cobb and the Tigers in five exhibition games in Havana. Cobb did not steal a base, as Lloyd tagged him out three times. Lloyd hit .500 against the Tiger pitchers; Cobb hit .369 against the Cubans. The Georgia Peach was so angry and embarrassed he stomped off the field, vowing never to play blacks again.

At bat, Lloyd was a scientific hitter, spraying line drives where the ball was pitched. Although he was in his mid-thirties when the Negro National League was formed, Lloyd played for a dozen years and compiled a league average of .342. His best season was 1928 when he hit .564 and led the league in home runs at the age of 44.

More than a great shortstop and hitter, Lloyd was the model gentleman of black ball, as Mathewson was the paragon role model of the white game. "Gosh bob it!" was his strongest oath.

In 1977 he was elected to the Hall of Fame.

SHERM LOLLAR
Catcher, Cle (A) 1946, NY (A) 1947–48, StL (A)
1949–51, Chi (A) 1952–63
Lollar put the Stop-Stop in the Go-Go White Sox of the 1950s. The underrated catcher anchored the Sox, a team built on speed, defense, and pitching. On the base paths, Sherm literally anchored the Sox' running attack as he brought out various allusions to snails, molasses, and Ernie Lombardi. Nevertheless, as one of the few Sox with punch in his bat, he earned his keep on offense. In their pennant year of 1959, he socked 22 homers.

He excelled in defense. He was a rock behind the plate and an excellent handler of pitchers, absolutely crucial in the Sox scheme. And when the opposition tried a little go-going of its own, it was usually gone. In 1954 Sherm played for five months straight without permitting a single stolen base.

ERNIE LOMBARDI
Catcher, Bkn (N) 1931, Cin (N) 1932–41, Bos (N) 1942,
NY (N) 1943–47
Lombardi was the slowest runner in the Hall of Fame, including executives, pioneers, and exhibits. "Schnozz" was a big, muscular guy, with a banana nose, an easygoing manner, and feet of pure lead. His lack of foot speed was legendary. Infielders played shallow in the outfield and could still throw him out. It was said he had to hit .400 to bat .300. He was a cinch double play anytime they got the runner at second; if they couldn't trust the infielder's arm, he could carry it to first.

Nonetheless, Lombardi was one of baseball's greatest catchers. He is the only catcher to ever lead his league in hitting while amassing 400 or more at bats. In 1938, he hit .342 and was voted the MVP. His career average was .306. He hit with tremendous power—he had to because he never got a "leg" hit— but on a line. His home run totals were modest: a high of 20 in 1939 and 190 for his career.

He was considered barely adequate as a defensive catcher in his day, whenever he let a pitch get even a few steps away from him, it was a passed ball for sure. He was on the receiving end of Johnny Vander Meer's two no-hitters and one of the keys to Cincinnati's two straight pennants in 1939–1940.

Lombardi was criticized unfairly for his famous "snooze" in the fourth and final game of the 1939 World Series. What actually happened is this:

With Yankee runners at the corners and the score tied in the tenth, Joe DiMaggio singled the go-ahead run home. The right fielder misplayed the ball and Charlie

Keller, running from first, came charging homeward. He hit Lombardi where the chest protector doesn't cover, and while Ernie fell to the ground in agony, DiMaggio scored. The play didn't lose the Series, but it probably kept Ernie out of Cooperstown until 1986, nine years after his death.

DAVEY LOPES
Second Baseman, LA (N) 1972–81, Oak (A) 1982–84,
Chi (N) 1984–86, Hou (N) 1986–87
Lopes was the kind of player who earns a reputation as "pesty." Translated, that means he won a lot of games for his team without piling up big statistics. He was okay in the field, but no world beater. He never led NL second basemen in fielding, but he did top them a couple of times in errors. He had a .263 career batting average and hit 28 homers in 1979, but it was the only time he socked more than 17. He *did* steal bases, leading the league in 1975–1976 and totaling 557. What made that part of his game significant was that he was almost never caught. He had one string of 38 straight successes.

Davey was a member of the Dodger infield with Steve Garvey, Bill Russell, and Ron Cey, a group that played together from 1973 to 1980. By doing all the little things, Lopes played in four World Series.

AL LOPEZ
Catcher, Bkn (N) 1928, 1930–35, Bos (N) 1936–40, Pit
(N) 1940–46, Cle (A) 1947. Manager, Cle (A) 1951–56,
Chi (A) 1957–65, 1968–69
Until Bob Boone broke it in 1987, Lopez had the record for most games caught. A good take-charge backstop, he played for nineteen seasons, mostly with second division clubs, and hit a decent .261. He learned a lot of baseball and a lot more patience. Both helped him become one of baseball's greatest managers.

Taking over the helm at Cleveland in 1951, he chased the Yankees to three straight second-place finishes. The ex-catcher's Tribe teams were built on great pitching, with Bob Feller, Bob Lemon, Early Wynn, and Mike Garcia, and home runs. Unfortunately for Cleveland, the Yankees always seemed to have enough pitching and more of everything else. But in 1954 the *Señor*'s Indians won 111 games, the AL record, to win the pennant.

Al moved to the White Sox in 1957 and won his second flag two years later. He did it with mirrors, since the Sox had almost no power. Owner Bill Veeck said a typical rally was two bloopers, an error, a passed ball, and two walks. A hit batsman would be "the final crusher." Thirty-five of their wins were by one run.

Lopez was a popular leader. If he had any fault, said Veeck, it was that "he was too decent." From 1949 to 1964 Lopez was the only manager other than a Yankee to win an AL pennant. He also brought his clubs in second ten times.

In 1977 he was elected to the Hall of Fame.

DICK LUNDY
Shortstop, Negro League, 1916–48, Bacharach Giants,
Lincoln Giants, Hilldale, Baltimore Black Sox,
Philadelphia Stars, Newark Dodgers, New York
Cubans, Newark Eagles, Jacksonville Eagles
"King Richard" was one of the top shortstops of blackball history, possessing a strong arm, sure hands, and excep-

tional range. Although batting records are incomplete, the clever switch-hitter hit in the .330 range over his long career. He hit .400 four times between 1921 and 1930 in the United States and Cuba.

Big, graceful, and a natural leader, Lundy played on several championship teams. In 1925, when he and "Pop" Lloyd, the nonpareil of black shortstops, were both members of the Atlantic City Bacharach Giants, Lloyd moved over to second base because of the younger man's then-superior range. Lundy replaced Lloyd as manager of the Bacharachs and led them from fourth to two straight pennants, while hitting .329 and .306. In 1933–1934 he was a starting shortstop in the first two black All-Star Games.

ADOLFO "DOLF" LUQUE
Pitcher, Bos (N) 1914–15, Cin (N) 1918–29, Bkn (N) 1930–31, NY (N) 1932–35
One of Cuba's first major league pitching stars, Luque was the leading pitcher in the NL in 1923. He was 27–8 for the second-place Reds, with a league-leading 1.93 ERA. Two years later, he led the NL in ERA again with a 2.63 mark. In twenty years of pitching, twelve with the Reds, he won 193 games.

The pride of Havana even found a new career at age 43. He became the bullpen stopper of the New York Giants and led the NL in relief wins with 8.

Always hot-tempered, he reportedly stomped into the opposing team's dugout one day in response to some unkind words and popped Casey Stengel on the nose.

ALBERT "SPARKY" LYLE
Pitcher, Bos (A) 1967–71, NY (A) 1972–78, Tex (A) 1979–80, Phi (N) 1980–82, Chi (A) 1982
Lyle won 99 games in relief and saved 238. Every one of his 899 pitching appearances was in relief. The durable lefthander was a big factor in getting the Yankees into the 1976 and 1977 World Series, with 23 saves the first year and 26 the next, when he also won 13 and earned the Cy Young Award.

Sparky used his slider to write a fine postseason record in 1977. With New York losing the LCS two games to one, Lyle pitched 5⅔ shutout innings to beat Kansas City and even the series. The next day he went 1⅓ more scoreless innings as the Yanks rallied to win. Two days later he pitched 3⅓ more innings of one-hit ball to beat the Dodgers in the World Series opener.

Then in 1978 his world was shattered when the Yanks paid millions to sign free agent Goose Gossage. Goose pushed Sparky right off the bullpen bench, and he spent the season in mop-up roles. He told of it in his book, *The Bronx Zoo.*

A flake and clubhouse cutup, Sparky once leaped nude onto a birthday cake, only to learn later that it was intended for Yankee manager Ralph Houk.

FRED LYNN
Outfielder, Bos (A) 1974–80, Cal (A) 1981–84, Bal (A) 1985–88, Det (A) 1988–89, SD (N) 1990–
Lynn had one of baseball's most remarkable rookie years in 1975—he is the only man to win the MVP his first year in the majors. The Red Sox won the pennant as Lynn, their center fielder, hit .331, led the league in doubles and

runs, cracked 21 homers, and batted in 105 runs.

Fred continued to hit with good power, getting up to 39 home runs in 1979, when he won the batting title with .333. In 1982 Lynn helped California win the division title, then walloped .611 in the LCS. He's won four Gold Gloves.

Yet Fred's career has been a disappointment in view of its brilliant beginning. His batting average has fallen through the 1980s, as have his RBIs. Many of his problems stem from frequent injuries—too frequent, say his critics.

TED LYONS
Pitcher, Chi (A) 1923–42, 1946. Manager, Chi (A) 1946–48
Lyons pitched twenty-one seasons for the White Sox. During those years, the Sox finished in the second division sixteen times. Fans in other cities celebrated pennants; in Chicago they celebrated Ted Lyons. Possibly the most popular player ever to take the mound in the Windy City, he earned fans' devotion with his upbeat personality, indomitable spirit, and by being one of the greatest pitchers of all time.

He came straight out of Baylor University, skipped the minors, and relieved in the first major league game he ever saw. By the next year he was a regular starter. Using a good fastball, curve, and knuckler, he won 20-plus three times with the second-division White Sox: in 1925, 1927, and for the last time in 1930.

In 1931 a sore arm cost him his fastball and nearly his career. Although he was no longer the dominating pitcher he had been in the 1920s, he used control and guile to remain the Sox stopper through the 1930s. Near the end of the decade, he became a "Sunday" pitcher, always pitching on that day because the biggest crowds showed up then.

Lyons won 260 games for the Sox, many fewer than he might have won for stronger teams, but he never complained. In 1955 he was named to the Hall of Fame.

CONNIE MACK (CORNELIUS McGILLICUDDY)
Catcher, Was (N) 1886–89, Buf (P), 1890, Pit (N) 1891–96. Manager, Pit (N) 1894–96, Phi (A) 1901–50.
For fifty years Mack managed the Philadelphia A's, building and destroying two dynasties. He had some of the greatest and some of the worst teams in history—his 1916 A's lost 117 games. Mack finished first nine times and last sixteen times. His lifetime 3,731–3,948 record is first among all managers in both wins and losses.

A lean, sweet-faced man in derby hat and stiff collar, even in the dugout, he was known to everyone as "Mr. Mack." To some he was a skinflint. But lack of money was his lifelong problem. With a modest fortune behind him, he might have dominated the AL, as the Yankees did in the 1920s and 1930s.

Born during the American Civil War, he quit school in the sixth grade to work in a cotton mill. He was a weak-hitting (.245) catcher for a while in the 1880s before sinking his life savings in Buffalo of the Players League. When the league folded after one year, Mack was wiped out.

After three years of managing lackluster Pittsburgh in the 1890s, and a four-year stint with Milwaukee of the

Western League, he was given the Philadelphia franchise in the new AL in 1901, with backing from Ben Shibe. Some said the team would be a "White Elephant," a symbol of wasted capital, but Mack brought the A's in first in 1902. The White Elephant became the team's symbol. He developed stars such as Rube Waddell, Eddie Plank, Chief Bender, Eddie Collins, and Home Run Baker and won five flags in ten years, 1905–1914.

John McGraw's Giants beat him in the 1905 World Series, but Mack got revenge in 1911 and 1913.

But the Miracle Braves of 1914 shocked him in four straight; the Federal League was raiding his stars and bidding salaries up. Mack began selling his stars, plunged to the bottom in 1915, and stumbled in last for seven years in a row. Anyone else would have been canned, but Connie was, after all, a stockholder.

Patiently Mack founded another dynasty with Foxx, Simmons, and Cochrane, and even shelled out a record $100,600 for Lefty Grove. They brought him three more flags, 1929–1931, before the Depression broke, and he sold his stars to pay the rent.

He was elected to the Hall of Fame in 1937. He was still managing in 1950 at eighty-seven, still looking for that third dynasty. New York gave him a tickertape parade. He died in 1956 at the age of ninety-three, after his heirs had sold the club to a corporation in Kansas City.

RALEIGH "BIZ" MACKEY
Catcher, Negro League, 1918–47, San Antonio Giants,
Indianapolis ABCs, Hilldale, Darby Daisies,
Philadelphia Stars, Washington Elite Giants, Baltimore
Elite Giants, Newark Eagles

Mackey is usually named as the finest defensive catcher of the Negro Leagues. Josh Gibson hit with much more power, but Mackey was his superior with a glove. "He was the master of defense," his protégé, Roy Campanella, would say. "For real catching skills, I don't think Cochrane was the master that Mackey was."

Pitchers loved to throw to Biz. He built up their confidence, called their game, "stole" borderline strikes for them. A jolly, bubbly man, he "jived" the hitters to take their mind off the game. Infielders loved to cover bases for him. "You didn't have to move your glove six inches," Judy Johnson said. The ball reached second light as a feather.

And he could hit, from either side—.364 in 1923, .363 in 1924, .317 lifetime.

In 1935 Biz met fifteen-year-old Campanella and shaped him into a Hall of Famer. "You saw Campy catch, you saw Mackey," oldsters say. In 1941 Biz could still outpoll Campy in the balloting for the black All-Star Game by 30,000 votes.

Biz retired as a forklift operator in Los Angeles. When the Dodgers gave Campy a "night" in 1959 before 93,000 fans at the Coliseum, Roy called on Biz to stand and take their applause. He died soon afterwards.

LARRY MacPHAIL
Executive, Owner

Night ball, radio broadcasts, batting helmets, air travel, old-timers' day, fireworks, three championship dynasties, loud feuds with his managers—the chances are that anything that Bill Veeck, Charles Finley, or George Stein-

brenner thought up, Larry MacPhail had already done.

Wounded and gassed in World War One, the fiery redhead had even tried to kidnap the German Kaiser in a daring adventure. (All he got was the Kaiser's ashtray.)

Back home Larry took over the Cardinals' Columbus farm team and pioneered in the advent of night games and air travel by baseball clubs. He also slugged a cop in a hotel lobby and was fired by St. Louis.

As general manager of Cincinnati in 1935, MacPhail brought the first lights to a major league park ("Every night will be a Sunday") and laid the groundwork for the Reds' champs of 1939–1940.

Moving to the moribund Dodgers in 1938, Larry brought Red Barber in to broadcast home games, hired manager Leo Durocher, and built a winner in 1941.

After another tour in the Army as a colonel, MacPhail bought a one-third interest in the Yankees. He installed lights in Yankee Stadium and brought the Yanks to a pennant and world championship in 1947. During the victory celebration, he engaged in a loud public brawl. The next day his partners terminated his contract as club administrator and bought him out.

He was elected to the Hall of Fame in 1978. His legacy lived on in his son Lee, president of the AL (1974–1983), and grandson, Andy, general manager of the Minnesota Twins.

BILL MADLOCK
Third Baseman, Tex (A) 1973, Chi (N) 1974–76, SF (N)
1977–79, Pit (N) 1979–85, LA (N) 1985–87, Det (N)
1987

Madlock won four batting titles to put him in rarefied company. The first two came with the Cubs in 1975–1976. Then after a disappointing two and a half seasons in San Francisco, he was traded in mid-1979 to the Pirates and hit .328 down the stretch to help them win the pennant. In the World Series that year, he hit .375.

Although he won batting titles for the Pirates in 1981 and 1983, the team slipped lower in the standings. Many Pittsburgh fans placed some of the blame on Madlock— unfairly it would seem. He had never been a power hitter or an outstanding fielder, but these failings became increasingly criticized as the Pirates slumped. He played with injuries, but when he sat out games, he was accused of malingering. Much of the criticism actually stemmed from his habit of speaking his mind honestly about a deteriorating situation with the ball club. Pirate fans, not liking the message, wanted to shoot the messenger.

He later helped Los Angeles and Detroit win division titles.

SHERRY MAGEE
Outfielder, Phi (N) 1904–14, Bos (N) 1915–17, Cin (N)
1917–19

Magee was an excellent hitter in the dead-ball era. He stole a lot of bases (441), hit a lot of doubles (425), and led the league three times in RBIs, twice in slugging average, and once in batting. He finished his career in 1919 with a .291 career average and 1,182 RBIs. His reputation would be higher today except for two quirks of fate. First, after eleven seasons with the Phillies, he was traded to the Braves in 1915, just before the Phils' first pennant and just after the "Miracle Braves" pennant, thus depriving him of a World Series showcase. Second, and worse, he is often confused with Lee Magee, a contemporary who was banned from baseball on fixing charges.

SAL MAGLIE
Pitcher, NY (N) 1945, 1950–55, Cle (A) 1955–56, Bkn (N) 1956–57, NY (A) 1957–58, StL (N) 1958
Maglie was one of the jumpers who signed with the Mexican League in 1946. It cost him a four-year suspension from the majors. When he returned in 1950 at age thirty-three, he was 18–4.

He had a 23–6 mark in 1951, the year of the Miracle of Coogan's Bluff. It was Sal who kept the Giants in the race the first half before their other hurlers caught fire.

In 1956 the thirty-nine-year-old Maglie stunned New York by moving to the Dodgers, where he went 13–5. Sal pitched one crucial September game against fifth-place Philadelphia, when a loss would have put Brooklyn out of the race. He responded with a no-hitter, and the Bums captured the flag.

They called him "the Barber" because he shaved the hitters close with inside pitches (and because he had a permanent five o'clock shadow himself). As a coach, he passed on his philosophy to Jim Bouton: "If you're 2–0 on a guy, go ahead and flatten his ass."

JIM MALONEY
Pitcher, Cin (N) 1960–70, Cal (A) 1971
Before a sore arm ended his career at age thirty-one, Maloney pitched three no-hitters and five one-hitters. Some say he was faster than Koufax.

In 1963 he struck out eight straight Braves—Eddie Mathews was eighth—before Hank Aaron grounded out. Jim was 23–7 that year for the fifth-place Reds. (He also led in wild pitches, keeping the hitters honest.)

Two years later he was 20–9, as Cincy finished fourth. Two of his wins were no-hitters; the first went ten innings against the last-place Mets before two hits in the eleventh beat him 1–0.

MICKEY MANTLE
Outfielder, NY (A) 1951–68
The most powerful switch-hitter ever, Mantle was a magnificent talent who was beset throughout his entire career by injuries. A high school football injury left him with a chronic bone infection in his legs. He had a shoulder operation, a broken foot, a torn hamstring. He taped his legs every day he played; even so, he sometimes took to the field in pants soaked with blood. He compounded his injury problems by refusing to follow exercise programs and partying into the wee hours with his Yankee buddies. His attitude was "live now"; no male member of his family had lived past forty.

Joining the Yankees in 1951 as the designated successor to Joe DiMaggio, Mantle had a difficult rookie year, was farmed out, and considered quitting baseball. A visit from his terminally ill father, who had named him Mickey after Mickey Cochrane, convinced the young slugger to go on. He returned to the Yankees but injured a knee in the second game of the World Series that year.

In 1952 he began to show his awesome talent, hitting .311. He quickly became known for his tape measure home runs. Among others during his career, he walloped one to the facade on Yankee Stadium's roof, estimated at 600 feet, hit a 565-footer in Washington, and blasted one in Chicago, which, Yankee Manager Casey Stengel said left seats "flyin' around for five minutes."

In eighteen seasons he twice topped 50 homers, led the AL in home runs four times, and finished with a total of 536. He scored a Triple Crown in 1956, played in twenty All-Star Games, and earned three MVP Awards (in 1956, 1957, and 1962).

Mantle played in twelve World Series. He hit the most Series homers (18), scored the most runs (42), and batted in the most (40).

He was named to the Hall of Fame in 1974.

HEINIE MANUSH
Outfielder, Det (A) 1923–27, StL (A) 1928–30, Was (A) 1930–35, Bos (A) 1936, Bkn (N) 1937–38, Pit (N) 1938–39
Manush was an outstanding hitter during the 1920s and 1930s with several AL teams. He compiled a lifetime batting average of .330. A line drive hitter, he knocked out more triples (160) than home runs (110). As a Detroit rookie in 1923, Heinie played beside Harry Heilmann and Ty Cobb, who gave him batting tips. Three years later he dueled Babe Ruth for the batting title. He went 6 for 9 in the final doubleheader to hit .378 and beat the Babe by six points.

In 1928 he cracked out 241 base hits to again hit .378 but lost the batting crown to Goose Goslin by one point. Two years later the two men would be traded for each other.

WALTER "RABBIT" MARANVILLE
Shortstop, Bos (N) 1912–20, 1929–35, Pit (N) 1921–24, Chi (N) 1925, Bkn (N) 1926, StL (N) 1927–28.
Manager, Chi (N) 1925
The real miracle behind the 1914 "Miracle Braves" was a hoppity little five-five shortstop named Maranville (accent on the "an"). He hit only .246, but he put on a *nonpareil* show at shortstop.

Sporting a "vest pocket catch" and a better range than General Electric, Rabbit handled more chances than any shortstop ever had before and teamed with Evers to lead the league in double plays (far more than Evers had ever made with Tinker and Chance).

Maranville was sick for the first few weeks in 1914, as the Braves stumbled in the cellar. Then after July 14 he, and they, stormed to the pennant. In the World Series he even hit .308 as the Braves swept the mighty A's in four straight.

Braves' manager George Stallings hailed Maranville as another Cobb, but the only way he might have had Cobb's bat would have been to swipe it from the rack. His career average was .258. An incorrigible prankster, he was famous for his mischief. A free spirit, he was sometimes free with spirits; "there's a lot less alcohol consumed since 1926," he once said, "because that's when I stopped drinking."

He played for twenty-three seasons and was considered a top gloveman to the end. He was elected to the Hall of Fame in 1954.

FRED "FIRPO" MARBERRY
Pitcher, Was (A) 1923–32, 1936, Det (A) 1933–35, NY (N) 1936

One of the earliest relief artists, Marberry was the forerunner of the great relief pitchers of today. Nicknamed for the Argentine fighter Luis Firpo, Marberry had a similar, powerful physique. He both started and relieved, but his reputation was built on relieving as he led the AL in saves five times. He helped Washington to two flags (1924–1925) and Detroit to one (1934).

Marberry had 15 saves in 1924, plus 2 in the World Series, 15 more in 1925 as the Senators won again, and 22 in 1926. He was 15–5 with 3 saves for Detroit in 1934 to help them to their first flag in a quarter century, and he ended with a 148–88 won-lost mark and 101 saves.

JUAN MARICHAL
Pitcher, SF (N) 1960–73, Bos (A) 1974, LA (N) 1975

Facing Marichal was like facing a dozen different pitchers. His high leg kick was his trademark, but once the leg came down, the ball could zip toward the batter from any angle—sidearm, three-quarters, over the top—as he delivered fastballs, curves, and sliders in a multiplicity of speeds, yet always with marvelous control. From 1963 through 1969, the brilliant righthander from the Dominican Republic was the major league's winningest pitcher.

After winning 18 for the Giants in 1962, Marichal won 20 or more in six of the next seven seasons. He was 25–8 in 1963, including a no-hitter, to lead the NL in wins and 25–6 in 1966 to lead in percentage. In 1968 he was back on top in wins: 26–9. And the next season he led in ERA. He completed 244 of his 457 starts; manager Al Dark said, "Put your club a run ahead in the late innings, and Marichal is the greatest pitcher I ever saw."

He did not have a losing season until 1972. He averaged nearly 6 strikeouts per nine innings while walking less than 2.

Usually easy-going, with a ready, impish grin, Marichal's reputation was tarnished by one out-of-character moment. In 1965, during a game with the Dodgers, he was brushed back by the pitch. Then the return throw from Dodger catcher John Roseboro whizzed close by his ear. Suddenly getting it from in front and behind, Marichal turned and clubbed Roseboro on the head with his bat. He was fined $1,750, an NL record at the time, and suspended for nine days.

In 1983 Marichal was named to the Hall of Fame.

ROGER MARIS
Outfielder, Cle (A) 1957–58, KC (A) 1958–59, NY (A) 1960–66, StL (N) 1967–68

Maris may never be forgiven. He broke the Babe's sacrosanct record of 60 home runs in a season. How dare he! When Hank Aaron passed Ruth's career total, there was anger among the unreasoning, but the 714 never had the magic of 60. And Aaron roared past and added 30 more after he broke it. Maris topped 60 by only one in a season eight games longer than the Babe's. And Aaron was a great player. Maris wasn't.

"I don't want to be Babe Ruth," Maris protested. He needn't have said it. There were too many others anxious to prove that he wasn't. So Maris struck more home runs than any other major league batter had ever hit in a single season and spent the rest of his life hearing what a bum he was. Commissioner Ford Frick even ordered an asterisk placed beside Roger's 61, though he might have preferred a scarlet letter.

Maris was no bum. He was an intelligent, likable man, a bit reserved—a private sort of person—totally unprepared to turn the media blitz that drowned him to his advantage. He was a talented player. All right, not a great player, but a good one. He was sure in the outfield, with a fine arm. He never hit for much of an average, and he ended his twelve-year career with only a .260 mark, but he had good home run power. In eleven *other* seasons he totaled 214 homers.

He was AL MVP the year *before* his 61-homer season, with 39 home runs and a league-leading 112 RBIs. In 1961, besides the homers, he led in runs (132) and RBIs (142), so his second MVP wasn't just for breaking Ruth's record. In 1962, he had 33 homers and 100 RBIs. He had some injuries after that, and the numbers fell off, but he was the regular right fielder when healthy for five straight Yankees pennant winners (1960–1964). He finished up in 1967–1968, as a regular for two Cardinals teams that won flags.

If he'd hit 59, he'd have been a hero.

RICHARD "RUBE" MARQUARD
Pitcher, NY (N) 1908–15, Bkn (N) 1915–20, Cin (N) 1921, Bos (N) 1922–25

The Giants bought Marquard from Indianapolis for a record $11,000 in 1908 and rushed him into the pennant race before he was ready. The result was an "$11,000 Lemon" until careful nurturing by coach Wilbert Robinson turned him into a "beauty" in 1911. Rube was 24–7 to help win the flag. It was the first of three 20-victory years for the lefthander and three straight flags for the Giants. In the 1911 Series he had a 1.54 ERA but lost his only decision.

In 1912, when he was 26–11, Marquard won his first 19 games to tie Tim Keefe's record. He actually won 20 if modern scoring rules are applied; one "win" was scored a save. In the World Series that year, he had an 0.50 ERA and won two of the Giants' three victories.

In 1913 he was 23–10, giving him 73 victories in three years.

Those were his three best years. He had a brief comeback with Brooklyn under Robinson in 1916. He was 13–6, and the Dodgers won the flag. He upped that to 19–12 the next year, but led the NL in losses in 1918. He helped the Dodgers to another pennant with a 10–7 mark in 1920.

Although nicknamed after another star lefthander, Rube Waddell, Marquard was no Rube. He was sophisticated, a flashy dresser, no drinker (unlike Waddell), and married a Broadway actress.

He was elected to the Hall of Fame in 1971.

MIKE MARSHALL
Pitcher, Det (A) 1967, Sea (A) 1969, Hou (N) 1970, Mon (N) 1970–73, LA (N) 1974–76, Atl (N) 1976–77, Tex (A) 1977, Min (A) 1978–80, NY (N) 1981

A doctor of physiology, Marshall jogged four miles a day and set a record pitching in 106 games in 1974. That year he was 15–12 with 21 saves for the Dodgers, all tops in the

NL for relievers that year. That performance earned him the Cy Young Award, the first ever won by a reliever. Two other times (1973 and 1979) he went over 90 games.

Mike designed his own conditioning program, but his education intimidated coaches and managers. He fought with Mayo Smith, Sal Maglie, and Harry Walker, with little success, until he joined Montreal under Gene Mauch, who let him do what he wanted. Marshall's saves shot up to 23 in 1971 and 31 in 1973.

In Minnesota in 1979 he used his screwball to save 32 games, his all-time high.

He ended his fourteen-season career with 92 relief wins and 188 saves.

BILLY MARTIN

Second Base, NY (A) 1950–57, KC (A) 1957, Det (A) 1958, Cle (A) 1959, Cin (N) 1960, Mil (N) 1961, Min (A) 1961. Manager, Min (A) 1969, Det (A) 1971–73, Tex (A) 1974–75, NY (A) 1975–78, 1979, 1983, 1985, 1988, Oak (A) 1980–83

"Everybody looks up to Billy Martin," one player said. "That's because he probably just knocked them down."

As a Yankee second baseman in the 1950s, he earned a reputation for light-hitting, heads-up play, and ready fists. He'd once considered becoming a middleweight boxer, and he was only too anxious to demonstrate his prowess. A brawl in the Copacabana night club in 1957 led to a trade to Kansas City and four final nomadic seasons.

He became a major league manager with the Twins in 1969, and the Martin pattern emerged. His clubs invariably improved their record from the previous year—the Twins jumped to the division title. Then Martin would be involved in a well-publicized fight, usually involving alcohol, and would be fired. One season in Minnesota, three in Detroit, two in Texas, and three in Oakland.

His saddest moments came with the Yankees, where he was hired and fired five times. Hired first in 1975, he took them to the pennant in 1976 and a world championship in 1977, only to be fired after 94 games in 1978. He was rehired in 1979 for the final two-thirds of the season, then fired again. After his three years in Oakland, he was back with the Yankees for all of 1983, most of 1985, and part of 1988.

Martin, when sober and with his temper under control, was a bright, articulate man. He had many friends who were intensely loyal, and he showed himself to be a talented manager. Unfortunately his destructive side had one enduring victim—himself. He died on Christmas Day, 1989.

EDDIE MATHEWS

Third Baseman, Bos (N) 1952, Mil (N) 1953–65, Atl (N) 1966, Hou (N) 1967, Det (A) 1967–68. Manager, Atl (N) 1972–74

Lefthanded hitting Mathews was the greatest home run hitter among third basemen until Mike Schmidt. Mathews's 512 homers made him only the seventh man to hit 500, and he had four seasons with over 40, including league-leading marks of 47 in 1953 and 46 in 1959. Although he hit over .300 three times, his career average was only .271; however, he supplemented his 2,315 hits with 1,444 walks, leading the NL four times.

He played fifteen of his seventeen seasons in a Braves uniform, beginning with the team's last season in Boston and ending with its first year in Atlanta. In between were thirteen seasons in Milwaukee. He combined with Hank Aaron to form perhaps the best one-two punch of all time. Their total of 863 home runs while together ranks ahead of Mays-McCovey (800) and Ruth-Gehrig (772). Mathews usually batted third ahead of Aaron to take advantage of his ability to draw walks. He scored 1,509 runs, often being plated by Aaron. Eddie drove in 1,453 runs himself.

Curiously, with all his outstanding seasons in Milwaukee, two of the most ordinary were the pennant winning years of 1957–1958.

The handsome slugger was elected to the Hall of Fame in 1978.

DON MATTINGLY

First Baseman, NY (A) 1982–

Mattingly won the AL batting title with a .343 mark in 1984, his first full major league season, and he has been one of the most consistent hitters in baseball since, although back injuries limited him to just 102 games and a .256 average in 1990. Perhaps no hitter in baseball today has combined high average with home run power to the same extent. He's topped 200 hits three times, 30 homers three times, and 100 RBIs five times. His 145 RBIs in 1985 led the AL. He led in doubles in 1984–1986. The 1985 MVP, he has been voted the top player in baseball in more than one poll.

Mattingly made headlines in 1988 with his criticism of the atmosphere Yankees' owner George Steinbrenner produced on the ballclub.

CHRISTY MATHEWSON

Pitcher, NY (N) 1900–16, Cin (N) 1916. Manager, Cin (N) 1916–18

One of the first five men elected to Cooperstown in 1936, Matty was handsome, intelligent, clean-cut, clean-living, the most popular pitcher of his day and possibly the best. They called Matty "Big Six," after New York's most famous fire engine. In an era of roughnecks, Matty was a college man who sang in the Bucknell glee club, belonged to the literary society, was president of his class, and could beat twelve foes at checkers at the same time. He refused to pitch on Sunday. The childless John McGraw virtually made him his son. Matty was the model for the Frank Merriwell of Yale books and the "Baseball Joe" stories that molded young boys' characters when Great Grandpa was a kid. Christy's own book, *Pitching in a Pinch*, is still a delight to read.

Connie Mack once compared Mathewson with Walter Johnson, who was also one of the first five in the Hall of Fame. "With Johnson, it was brute force," Mack said. "With Mathewson, it was knowledge and judgment, perfect control, and form."

Mathewson was famous for his "fadeaway," a screwball. With it, Matty won 30 three years in a row (1903–1905). He won 37 in 1908 and had nine other seasons with 20 or more wins. He brought the Giants five pennants. Matty's 78 shutouts are surpassed only by Walter Johnson and Grover Alexander. In the 1905 World Series, Matty pitched three shutouts in six days, giving up just 14 hits—and only one walk!

Mathewson had great control. In 1908 he had 391 innings pitched, 259 strikeouts, and only 42 walks. In 1913 he averaged only 0.6 walks per nine innings; he went 68 straight innings without a walk. He once won a game with 67 pitches.

Yet he wasn't out for records and always held something in reserve in those pre-relief days.

Before the Perrys and Niekros, Christy and his brother Henry held the record for wins by brothers—372 by Christy, none by Henry, whose big league career produced only one decision. Christy joined the Army in World War One and was the victim of poison gas. He suffered pulminary tuberculosis brought on by the gas, and died in 1925 at the age of forty-five.

CARL MAYS

Pitcher, Bos (A) 1915–19, NY (A) 1919–23, Cin (N) 1924–28, NY (N) 1929

Mays, of course, is the man whose submarine pitch killed Cleveland shortstop Ray Chapman in 1920. That tragic incident has obscured the fact that he was one of the best pitchers of his day.

Mays had a reputation for throwing at batters—and once he threw at a fan—but he denied intent to hit Chapman, and the game situation—leadoff batter, start of the inning—argues strongly that it was an accident. Actually, Mays hit only seven batters that year, far from the league high. Still, at least two teams threatened not to play against him after that. But Carl calmly won his next start 8–0. He was 26–11 for the Yankees that year, and 27–9 the next season when the Yanks won their first pennant.

A morose loner, Mays was unpopular with teammates and extremely so with fans after the Chapman tragedy. Mays "has no friends and doesn't want any," one player said of him. Mays's response: That's what made him a great pitcher. In addition to his two great Yankee years, he earlier won 21 and 22 with the Red Sox, and in the mid-1920s won 20 and 19 for the Reds. He played on six pennant winners at Boston and New York.

WILLIE MAYS

Outfielder, Negro League, 1948–50, Birmingham Black Barons, NY (N) 1951–52, 1954–57, SF (N) 1958–72, NY (N) 1972–73

The most exciting player of the 1960s, Mays hit 660 home runs, raced around the bases or into deepest center field, his hat flying off behind him. "The only man who could have caught that ball," one announcer said, "just hit it."

His catch off Vic Wertz in the 1954 World Series is sometimes cited as the greatest ever—a long sprint, an over-the-shoulder catch near the wall 460 feet away, a spin, and a bullet throw back to the infield. The hat flew off, of course—Willie later admitted he wore hats a size too small to make them do that.

New Yorkers gloried in their three great center fielders, "Willie, Mickey, and the Duke." The most ebullient—and to many the best—Willie was the "Say Hey Kid" who played stickball with the kids in Harlem and hardball in the Polo Grounds at night.

He won eleven straight Gold Gloves and set the record for career putouts by an outfielder and the NL record for total chances.

He also stole 337 bases, led the league four times, and

was the first man in the 300/300 club—300 steals, 300 homers. He was one of the few stolen-base kings who wasn't spinning his wheels, with a 77 percent success ratio (anything below 66 percent is a net negative).

Willie came up to the Giants in 1951. He started by going 0 for 22. But manager Leo Durocher stuck with him, pepped him up, and both Willie and the Giants caught fire. The team came from 13½ games behind to catch the Dodgers and win the playoff on Bobby Thomson's home run. "The only reason I pitched to Thomson," Dodger manager Chuck Dressen said, "was because Willie was the next hitter."

After military service in 1953, Mays returned to lead the Giants to the 1954 pennant with an NL-high .345 and 41 homers. He was named MVP. "If he could cook," said Leo, "I'd marry him."

Willie led the league in homers four times, topping 50 twice.

Moving to San Francisco in 1958 hurt his home run totals (as Aaron's move to Atlanta helped his). Still, Willie slugged four in one game in 1961. In 1962 he hit 49 with 141 RBIs to lead the Giants to a playoff victory over Los Angeles.

In 1965 he slugged 52 homers, 17 of them in August, to pass 500 and win his second MVP. *The Sporting News* named him the Player of the 1960s.

In 1979 he was elected to the Hall of Fame.

BILL MAZEROSKI

Second Baseman, Pit (N) 1956–72

Possibly the greatest-fielding second baseman who ever lived, Maz's 1,706 double plays is the all-time record for second-sackers. Around Pittsburgh, they called him "no-hands"—the ball seemed to go from the shortstop's shovel pass and ricochet to first with him hardly touching it. He led the league in assists nine times, double plays eight, putouts five, and fielding average three.

Bill also hit the most dramatic World Series homer ever struck, a *sayonara* blow in the ninth to win the seventh game of the 1960 Series and make the Pirates world champions.

Generally he wasn't too bad at bat, and in a friendlier park he would have been even better. He had a respectable .260 career batting average, with fair home run power. His Series-ending homer in 1960 was his second round-tripper of the Series: his two-run blast provided the margin of victory in Game One.

JOE McCARTHY

Manager, Chi (N) 1926–30, NY (A) 1931–46, Bos (A) 1948–50

If McCarthy was a "push-button manager," as rival skipper Jimmy Dykes once said, no manager ever pushed them more effectively. In twenty-four years as a major league manager, his teams won seven world championships, nine pennants, and never finished out of the first division. His .614 winning percentage for nearly 3,500 games is the record, as is his .698 for nine World Series.

A minor league second baseman who never played a game in the majors, McCarthy won American Association pennants at Louisville and was hired by the Cubs in 1926. He instituted discipline on the free-spirited club and in 1929 led them to the NL pennant. They lost the

World Series to the A's. The following year McCarthy resigned in September with the Cubs in second place.

The Yankees hired him for the 1931 season expressly to bring the team back to the heights it had enjoyed in the 1920s. Despite some resentment by some of the older Yankee players, including Babe Ruth, who had expected to be named manager, McCarthy brought the team home second in his first season and won the pennant and his first world championship in 1932.

He kept them in second place for the next three years while retooling the team. By 1936, with the arrival of rookie Joe DiMaggio, he had a dynasty. His Yankees won four straight world championships, slipped to third in 1940, then rebounded for three more pennants and two World Series wins. He resigned in 1945 because of ill health and a personality clash with new Yankee owner Larry MacPhail.

McCarthy accepted the job as manager of the Red Sox in 1948. The team had an awesome lineup of hitters but lacked pitching. Nevertheless he finished second two years in a row, losing the pennant in a playoff in 1948 and on the last day of the season in 1949. He retired during the 1950 season for health reasons.

Nicknamed "Marse Joe," McCarthy was a strict disciplinarian as a manager, but a warm, friendly man in his off-field moments.

He was elected to the Hall of Fame in 1957.

TOMMY McCARTHY
Outfielder, Bos (U) 1884, Bos (N) 1885, 1892–95, Phi (N) 1886–87, StL (AA) 1888–91, Bkn (N) 1896.
Manager, StL (AA) 1890

McCarthy broke in with the Union Association in 1884, but did not really establish himself until he joined the American Association's St. Louis Browns in 1888. He helped the Browns win the '88 pennant and gained a reputation as an outstanding defensive player. He stole 93 bases in 1888 and led the AA in stolen bases in 1890.

His greatest years were with Boston's pennant-winning teams of the early 1890s. He and Hugh Duffy became known as the "Heavenly Twins" for their defensive plays in the outfield. Although McCarthy hit .346 in 1893 and .349 the following year, he was not a great hitter; he averaged .292 for his career. His strengths were his speed, his powerful throwing arm, and his scientific approach. He was an excellent bunter, and he and Duffy were brilliant hit-and-run artists and deadly on the double steal. McCarthy also popularized the practice of trapping fly balls and throwing runners out at second, sometimes starting double plays.

He was named to the Hall of Fame in 1946.

JIM McCORMICK
Pitcher, Ind (N) 1878, Cle (N) 1879–84, Cin (U) 1884, Prov (N) 1885, Chi (N) 1885–87. Manager, Cle (N) 1879–80

Way back in 1880, husky, mustachioed McCormick was probably the MVP of the young NL. He won 45, tops in the league, hurled 658 innings, held hitters to a 1.85 ERA—and managed Cleveland to a third-place finish. He was twenty-four years old.

For much of his career, 1878–1887, Jim suffered with losing clubs—he lost 40 games for sixth-place Cleveland

in 1879. Still, he was ERA king twice. Not until 1885–1886 did he land with a flag winner, Anson's White Sox. He rewarded them with seasons of 21–7 and 31–11.

His totals for his ten-year career were 265–214, 2.43 ERA.

WILLIE McCOVEY
First Baseman, SF (N) 1959–73, 1977–80, SD (N) 1974–76, Oak (A) 1976

McCovey slugged 18 grand slams, an NL record, and led the league in homers three times, but according to Willie "the hardest ball I ever hit" was an out. The Giants were losing 1–0 in the ninth inning of the seventh game of the 1962 World Series, but they had the tying run on third and the winning run at second. Willie lined a bullet at Yankees' second baseman Bobby Richardson for the final out. A foot either way and the Giants would have been champs.

In the second game of the Series, McCovey had blasted one against a Candlestick Park light tower off the same pitcher, Ralph Terry.

Although extremely shy in his first years, Willie became a friendly, gregarious team leader. He hit 521 homers and batted in 1,555 runs during his twenty-two seasons.

Willie broke in 1959 with a perfect 4 for 4 against Robin Roberts. He hit .354 that year to win the Rookie of the Year Award.

Ten years later he was MVP with 45 homers and 126 RBIs, both league-leading totals, and a .320 batting average.

He was named to the Hall of Fame in 1986.

JOE "IRON MAN" McGINNITY
Pitcher, Bal (N) 1899, Bkn (N) 1900, Bal (A) 1901–02, NY (N) 1902–08

McGinnity got his nickname from working in an iron foundry in his youth, but it just as easily could have come from winning seven games in six days in the minors in 1896, or from pitching five doubleheaders in the majors. Joe also pitched a two-year record for this century of 434 innings in 1903 and 408 the next year, and he was still hurling minor league ball at the age of fifty-four.

Three of those doubleheader victories came in one month—August 1, 8, and 31, 1903. Joe won a league-leading 31 games for the second-place Giants that year. He pitched 44 complete games.

McGinnity threw an underhand curveball, with a motion so low his hand almost touched the ground. The fastball broke down, and the curve appeared to break up. Joe called it "Old Sal," and it may have put less strain on his arm than an overhand curve would have. He pitched for twenty-six years, though only ten in the majors. After leaving the Giants, Joe could still win 29 and 30 in the International League. He won 246 in the majors, but his total wins, majors and minors, came to 471.

McGinnity won 28 games as a rookie with Baltimore in 1899, but his greatest seasons were with the Giants (1902–08), for whom he won 31 in 1903 and 35 in 1904.

McGinnity had a reputation for throwing at hitters. He scored one hit batsman for every 19 men he faced—a record.

He was named to the Hall of Fame in 1946.

JOHN McGRAW

Third Baseman, Bal (AA) 1891, Bal (N) 1892–99, StL (N) 1900, Bal (A) 1901–02, NY (N) 1902–06. Manager, Bal (N) 1899, Bal (A) 1901–02, NY (N) 1902–32

A brawling, brilliant bully, McGraw and his Giants won ten pennants in twenty-one years, 1904–24. He dominated the NL for three decades as the Giants' manager after nearly a decade as a scrappy third baseman for the old Orioles of the 1890s.

As a manager, his strategic cleverness and his determination to control every aspect of his team won him the title "Little Napoleon." In 1892 McGraw joined the Baltimore Orioles of Keeler, Jennings, Hanlon *et al.* Mac could trip and spike with the rest of them, and he and Keeler are among those who are credited with inventing the hit-and-run. The O's won the flag in 1894–1896, with McGraw hitting .325 or better each year, the first of nine straight years he would hit .300. The O's won the Temple Cup playoffs in 1896–1897.

In 1899 Mac served as player-manager and hit .391; most of the star players had been sent to Brooklyn and the O's team finished fourth. Of all nineteenth-century players, no one had a higher on-base percentage than McGraw's .460.

He led Baltimore in the new AL 1901–1902, finishing fifth and seventh. John also fought with umpires and when league president Ban Johnson backed the umps, Mac jumped to New York in the NL, taking fellow Irishmen Joe McGinnity and Roger Bresnahan with him.

The Giants finished last in 1902, but leaped all the way to second in 1903 and first in 1904. McGraw haughtily refused to play a World Series against Johnson's AL. Mac won again in 1905, and this time he played the Series and demolished the AL Athletics in five games.

He lost a pennant narrowly in 1908 after the Merkle "boner," but stoutly defended the young first baseman from criticism.

A master psychologist, McGraw played on superstition and in 1911 put a Kansas lunatic, Charlie Faust, in uniform as a good luck mascot; the team charged from third place to the flag, the first of three straight.

By 1911 McGraw was already recognized as a managerial genius, he drove his players hard, called pitches from the bench, and was one of the first managers to grasp the concept of relief pitching, using Claude Elliott, George Ferguson, and Doc Crandall in that role in the first decade of the century. He won another pennant in 1917, though the Giants were upended in the World Series.

McGraw captured an unprecedented four straight pennants in 1921–1924, a record that would stand until Casey Stengel broke it in 1953. But though the Giants stayed in the first division through most of his remaining years, he had won his last flag. Players began to rebel against his vicious, profane tongue lashings. In 1932 the Giants dived to eighth and he resigned after thirty-three seasons as a manager. His 2,784 career victories rank second only to Connie Mack.

He was named to the Hall of Fame in 1937.

BILL McKECHNIE

Third Baseman, Pit (N) 1907, 1910–12, 1918, 1920, Bos (N) 1913, NY (A) 1913, Ind (F) 1914, Nwk (F) 1915, NY (N) 1916, Cin (N) 1916–17. Manager, Nwk (F) 1915, Pit (N) 1922–26, StL (N) 1928–29, Bos (N) 1930–37, Cin (N) 1938–46

A light-hitting infielder during his playing career, McKechnie became one of baseball's most respected managers, winning pennants with three different NL teams. Known as "the Deacon" because of his years singing in a church choir and his cadaverous "parson" looks, his virtues as a skipper were his deep knowledge of baseball, his likable personality, and his infinite patience.

His first manager's job was with Newark in the short-lived Federal League. In 1922 he took over in Pittsburgh and brought them from the second division to a pennant and World Championship in 1925. When the team slipped to third in 1926, he was fired.

He was hired by the Cardinals in 1928 and immediately won the pennant. However, the team lost the World Series in four games. Midway through 1929 he was fired again.

In 1930 he was hired as skipper of the Boston Braves and stayed for eight years. Although Boston was the only NL team he managed that did not win a pennant, he earned wide respect for his efforts in sometimes making "silk purses" out of the material at hand. When he led them to fifth place in 1937, he was named Manager of the Year.

McKechnie moved to Cincinnati in 1938, the scene of his greatest teams. He won pennants in 1939 and 1940 and the World Series in the latter year.

McKechnie was elected to the Hall of Fame in 1962.

JOHN "BID" McPHEE

Second Baseman, Cin (AA) 1882–89, Cin (N) 1890–99. Manager, Cin (N) 1901–02

McPhee was utterly boring. He played eighteen seasons before 1900, every one at the same position, second base; every one for the same team, Cincinnati (the team changed leagues in 1890 or McPhee would have stayed in the same one). He played hard but clean. In all of his eighteen seasons he was never fined. He was never even thrown out of a game! At a time when rough and rowdy baseballers were providing a wealth of wicked anecdotes, McPhee showed up every day in shape, stayed sober, did his job, and went home to a good night's sleep. The only thing remotely interesting about him was that he refused to wear a glove until 1897, more than a decade after they'd become common.

Oh yes, he was an excellent leadoff man, walked a lot, and scored 1,678 runs on his .271 batting average. He led the AA in triples in 1887 and totaled 188 for his career. But except for an obvious ability to score runs and an assumption that such an ability might lead to a number of victories, he really wasn't anything special with a bat. See? Boring.

He was at his most monotonous at second base. Game after game, season after season, batters would knock balls his way, and he just kept plucking them from the ground or the air and putting the batters out. He did this with such tedious regularity that he led his league's second basemen in fielding ten times, finished second four seasons, and was never lower than fourth. He was the leader in double plays eleven years, in putouts eight, and in assists six. He set the record for fielding average with .978 in 1896, the year before he started wearing a glove. That might be slightly interesting except that someone broke his record after a mere twenty-three years. True, in more than one hundred years, no second baseman has exceeded his 1886 total of 529 putouts. And true, he also holds the career mark in putouts with 6,545, ranks fourth in assists with 6,905, and second in total chances with 14,241. But what are those things compared to stories of droll nights on the town or a few hundred home runs? What a yawn! No wonder he's not in the Hall of Fame.

HAL McRAE
DH/Outfielder, Cin (N) 1968, 1970–72, KC (A) 1973–87
McRae became a star with the Kansas City Royals as a designated hitter. He was named the top DH in the AL five times. Perhaps only Don Baylor rivals him at that job. McRae, a disciple of the Charlie Lau school of hitting, managed to combine good home run power (191 career homers) with a good batting average (.290 lifetime). His 133 RBIs in 1982 were the most ever by a DH and won him the nickname of "Mr. Ribbie" among teammates.

He hit a career-high .332 in 1976 but was narrowly nosed out for the batting title by teammate George Brett. An inside-the-park home run gave Brett the title; McRae later asserted that the ball might have been caught and suggested that Brett had received favorable treatment through the season to keep the batting title in white hands. He was offered the manager's job at Kansas City in midseason of 1987 but declined because there was no assurance that he would be rehired for a full season.

JOE MEDWICK
Outfielder, StL (N) 1932–40, 1947–48, Bkn (N) 1940–43, 1946, NY (N) 1943–45, Bos (N) 1945
A rough-house, tough guy from the Cardinals' Gashouse Gang, Medwick was one of the top sluggers of the 1930s. A notorious bad-ball hitter, he led the NL in RBIs three straight years, 1936–38, and won the batting Triple Crown in 1937 (.374, 31, 154). He was named MVP that year.

He picked up the odd nickname "Ducky Wucky" in the minors because of his unusual waddle.

In the seventh game of the 1934 World Series, he slid hard into the Tigers' third baseman—too hard, thought Tiger fans, who pelted him with garbage until Commissioner Landis ordered him out of the game.

Sold to the Dodgers for $125,000 in 1940, he helped them win the 1941 pennant but suffered a near-fatal beaning by former teammate Bob Bowman. Though he recovered and played until 1948, he was never the same hitter he had been.

His career totals include a .324 batting average, 202 home runs, and 1,383 RBIs.

In 1968 he was elected to the Hall of Fame.

JOSE MENDEZ
Pitcher, Negro League, 1908–26, Cuban Stars, Stars of Cuba, All Nations, Los Angeles White Sox, Chicago American Giants, Detroit Stars, Kansas City Monarchs
Baseball's troubadour of the tropics, Mendez was an outstanding Cuban pitcher in the early twentieth century. His success against touring major league clubs made him a national hero. Among others, he won games against Eddie Plank in 1910 and Christy Mathewson in 1911. In

1908 he beat the Cincinnati Reds three times, without allowing a run in twenty-five innings. In the summers, Mendez played with the U.S. multiracial All Nations club, the forerunner of the Kansas City Monarchs. Late in his career, as manager of the Monarchs, he put himself in to pitch the final game of the 1924 Black World Series and won, 5–0. Musically talented, Mendez played the cornet for dances after games and later traveled the Caribbean, playing the guitar and teaching baseball.

ANDY MESSERSMITH
Pitcher, Cal (A) 1968–72, LA (N) 1973–75, 1979, Atl (N) 1976–77, NY (A) 1978
Every player today should say a prayer of thanks to Messersmith. It was he, along with Dave McNally, who overturned the sacrosanct reserve clause, leading to the present six-year re-entry draft that has made millionaires of .240 hitters.

He was an excellent pitcher when healthy, winning 20 games for the Angels in 1971. He was traded to the Dodgers after the 1972 season and had a brilliant 20–6 mark in 1974. It was then that he and McNally challenged the reserve clause in their contracts that forced them to re-sign the next year with the same team. Five years earlier Curt Flood had filed suit in an attempt to overturn the clause but had lost in the Supreme Court by a narrow vote. This time the players won on a split decision. The ruling was that by playing the 1975 season without signing contracts, they had fulfilled their "option year." Although McNally chose to retire, Messersmith signed with Atlanta in 1976 for a huge salary increase. Unfortunately a sore arm limited his effectiveness with the Braves, but he had opened the door to free agentry for all players.

MARVIN MILLER
Labor Negotiator
Miller, "the players' commissioner," was the enemy of the owners and the real commissioner, but fewer than half a dozen men have turned the baseball world upside down as he did. In 1981 he led the first extended players' strike in history, ushering in a new era in baseball negotiations. A labor economist with the steelworkers' union, Miller was chosen by the players to head their union in 1966, in the most serious challenge to the owners' control since the Players League in 1890.

Miller negotiated five labor contracts with the owners. In the first the owners increased their contribution to the pension fund, increased the minimum major league salary, and agreed to reconsider the reserve clause. The second recognized the Major League Players Association as the official bargaining agent for players (except with regard to salaries), allowed players to be represented by agents when negotiating salaries, and permitted arbitration in disputes that could not be otherwise settled.

In 1972 Miller led a brief strike to force the negotiation of a third contract. This one extended arbitration and resulted in a further increase in salaries.

In 1975, when Andy Messersmith and Dave McNally were declared free agents by a federal court (by having played out the option years of their contracts), the reserve clause was dead. Miller's fourth contract compromised by limiting free agency to six-year veterans, who would become available through re-entry drafts.

Again salaries soared. Owners demanded compensation for players lost to free agency, and this led to the 1981 strike of fifty days. Again Miller reached a compromise; owners were to receive some compensation in the form of established players from a general pool, but the union had proved its strength. Miller retired in 1984.

MINNIE MINOSO
Thirdbase, Negro League, 1946–48, New York Cubans, outfielder, Cle (A) 1949–51, 1958–59, Chi (A) 1951–57, 1960–61, 1964, 1976, 1980, StL (N) 1962, Was (A) 1963
Minoso didn't have a full season in the majors until he was twenty-eight, but when he burst on the scene with the Go-Go White Sox in 1951, he immediately became one of the most exciting players in the AL. He led in stolen bases, 1951–53, in triples three times, in doubles once, and once in hits. He compiled a career batting average of .298, lashed out 1,963 hits, and had 1,023 RBIs, most of it crammed into eleven exciting seasons.

Of the seventeen seasons he is credited with playing, one was a nine-game "cup of coffee" in 1949, two were fan-pleasing, end-of-season returns in 1976 and 1980, and three were as a reserve in the early 1960s, when he was over forty years old.

JOHNNY MIZE
First Baseman, StL (N) 1936–41, NY (N) 1942, 1946–49, NY (A) 1949–53
Mize won four home run crowns, three RBI titles, a batting championship, and finished among the top three in various offensive categories a total of fifty-four times. His 51 homers with the Giants in 1947 are an NL record for lefthanded hitters. The burly first baseman slugged 359 career home runs, hitting three in a game six different times. His .312 batting average and 1,337 RBIs mark him as one of baseball's great sluggers.

In both 1939 and 1940 he finished second in the voting for the NL MVP. In 1939 he led in homers (28) and batting average (.349); the next year he topped in homers (43) and RBIs (137).

After a long career with the Cardinals and Giants, "the Big Cat" joined the Yankees in mid-1949 as a part-time first baseman and full-time pinch hitter. In 1952 he became the second man in World Series history to pinch-hit a home run. For the entire Series he batted .400, with 3 homers and a slugging average of 1.067.

Mize was named to the Hall of Fame in 1981.

JOE MORGAN
Second Baseman, Hou (N) 1963–71, 1980, Cin (N) 1972–79, SF (N) 1981–82, Phi (N) 1983, Oak (A) 1984
Little Joe stood only five-seven but he played more games at second base than any man but Eddie Collins and won back-to-back MVPs in 1975–1976.

Morgan began his career with Houston, where he twice scored over 100 runs and developed an ability to draw walks. Traded to Cincinnati in 1972, he came into his own as an offensive star with the Big Red Machine. In 1975 he won his first MVP with a .327 batting average, 17 homers, 107 runs scored, 94 RBIs, and 67 stolen bases. The next year he hit .320, with 27 homers, 113 runs scored, 111 RBIs, and 60 stolen bases.

For his career, he hit 268 home runs, scored 1,651 runs, and batted in 1,134. He stole 689 bases and is third all-time in walks with 1,865.

In the field, Morgan won five Gold Gloves, and in 1977–1978 put together a string of 91 straight games without an error. Still, the stubborn fact is that Joe was not a great fielder. Apparently the writers went on form and not substance in voting him those Gold Gloves. For instance, he led the league in assists only once, a sign that he didn't cover a great deal of ground.

But above all, Morgan was a winner. He led the Reds to five division titles and three World Series. After signing with Houston in 1980, he took them to a division title. And in 1983 he was one of several veterans (they were called "the Wheeze Kids") who brought the Phillies a pennant.

Morgan was named to the Hall of Fame in 1990.

JACK MORRIS
Pitcher, Det (A) 1977–
Jack was the workhorse of two Tiger champions, 1984 and 1987. Always near the top in innings pitched, he won 20 games twice—20–13 in 1983 and 21–8 in 1986. He also led the AL in victories in the strike-shortened 1981 season, going 14–7. In the 1980s, no AL pitcher won more games.

Morris's ERAs were not spectacular, but he was a master at preventing unearned runs, especially in the postseason.

A convert to the split-fingered fastball, Morris had a no-hitter going into the ninth inning in Chicago in 1984. A fan tried to jinx him by yelling about the no-hitter. "I know, I'm working on it," Jack shot back, "and I'm going to get it too." And he did.

THURMAN MUNSON
Catcher, NY (A) 1969–79
A fiery plane crash on August 2, 1979, cut short Munson's career after slightly less than ten full seasons and knocked the bottom out of the Yankees' team. The Yankees' captain was an outstanding catcher in the tradition of Bill Dickey, Yogi Berra, and Elston Howard.

He led New York to three straight pennants, 1976–1978, and was voted the AL MVP in 1976, when he batted .302, hit 17 homers, and drove in 105 runs.

A basketball star in college, Munson was fast enough to bat second in the lineup. He packed a home run punch in his bat, but was primarily a line drive hitter.

Munson hit .302 and was AL Rookie of the Year in 1970. He was named to the AL All-Star team in 1971 and then every year from 1973 to '78. A durable backstop, he played at least 125 games a year from his rookie season until his death; his total of 1,423 games exceeds those of several excellent catchers who played far longer. His career batting average was .292.

At the close of the memorable pennant race of 1978, in the playoff versus Kansas City, he trumped Brett's three homers with a two-run shot of his own in the eighth to win the third game.

In the World Series a year earlier, Munson had nearly matched Bench's .533 with a .529 of his own in a battle of super catchers.

He was a proud man with a venomous tongue, and he

bridled in 1977, when Reggie Jackson joined the team at a higher salary. The angry energy that flared between the two men nevertheless spurred the dissension-ridden Yanks to two flags.

DALE MURPHY
Outfielder, Atl (N) 1976–90, Phi (N) 1990–
Nice guys may not always finish last, but Murphy, one of baseball's nicest people, has had little luck in NL pennant races. In eleven seasons as a Braves' regular, the best his team has done is one appearance in the 1982 League Championship Series. No one has blamed Murph.

The righthanded slugger came to the Braves as a catcher but was switched to first base in 1978, his first season as a regular. Two years later he was moved again, this time to center field, where he became one of the best.

His strong suit is his powerful bat. He won back-to-back MVP Awards in 1982–1983, leading the NL in RBIs and slugging average both years. In 1984–1985, he led in homers. He's paid the price for his more than 370 homers, striking out over 100 times in ten different seasons.

EDDIE MURRAY
First Baseman, Bal (A) 1977-88, LA (N) 1989-
One of the better power hitters of the 1980s, Murray averaged over 100 RBIs per season for his first eleven seasons, yet led the AL only once—in the strike-shortened 1981 season. He also tied for the lead in homers that season with 22. Probably the most powerful switch-hitter since Mickey Mantle, Murray was the model of consistency for Baltimore until injuries cut into his homer and RBI titles. Fans who had cheered him on with cries of "Ed-dee, Ed-dee!" turned against him and booed. Murray demanded a trade, and generally handled the situation poorly. After a difficult first season in the NL, Murray rebounded to lead the Dodgers with a .330 average in 1990.

Though he played in only two World Series (1979, 1983), he had the Orioles in the thick of six pennant races. His batting average in those Septembers was .318, says *Sports Illustrated*'s Peter Gammons.

Murray, who commands a multimillion dollar salary, donates a generous portion of it to provide summer camps for city kids in memory of his mother.

STAN "THE MAN" MUSIAL
Outfielder/First Baseman, StL (N) 1941–44, 1946–63
At one time Musial held almost every NL batting record except homers, and he was close to that too—some fifty major league and NL marks. His 3,630 career hits were second only to Cobb. Now Rose, Aaron, Mays, and others have passed most of them.

Popular with fans and writers alike, Stan was three times MVP, four times coming in second. He used an odd, "peek-a-boo" batting stance—lefthanded, curled up, almost as if he was looking around a corner, his bat barrel held back and straight up. It worked for him. Stan led the NL seven times in batting.

Son of a Polish immigrant miner, Stan started as a minor league pitcher until he hurt his arm and switched to the outfield.

After playing twelve end-of-season games for the Cardinals in 1941, he led them to the world championship in 1942. He specialized in doubles and triples, and won two batting championships in his first four years (not counting Navy service in 1945). The Cards were NL champs all four of those seasons and world champs three of them.

In 1948 Stan suddenly blossomed as a home run threat. His batting average, doubles, and triples stayed high too. He was slugging average champion three times before the change and three times after it.

Musial won his last batting title in 1957 at the age of thirty-six (.351).

As a forty-one-year-old grandfather in 1962, he could still hit .330, third best in the league.

Stan once hit five homers in a doubleheader. His most famous home run won the 1955 All-Star Game in the twelfth inning. "I'll get you out of here in a hurry," he told Yogi Berra, the AL catcher, then whacked the first pitch over the wall.

His career totals: .331, 475 home runs, 725 doubles, 177 triples, 1,949 runs, and 1,951 RBIs.

He was elected to the Hall of Fame in 1969.

GRAIG NETTLES
Third Baseman, Min (A) 1967–69, Cle (A) 1970–72, NY (A) 1973–83, SD (N) 1984–86, Atl (N) 1987, Mon (N) 1988–
One of the best glove men to play third base, Nettles finally began winning Gold Gloves when Brooks Robinson retired, although he'd been an acknowledged master for several years. His eye-popping stops in the 1978 World Series were a big factor in the Yankee victory. And Series watchers saw him pull his spectacular act again in 1981. Only Robinson played more games at third or accepted more fielding chances.

Although his lifetime batting average is below .250, Graig hit with power. His nearly 400 homers put him third among third basemen, after Mike Schmidt and Eddie Mathews. He led the AL in homers with 32 in 1976 and followed with a career-high 37 the next season.

DON NEWCOMBE
Pitcher, Negro League, 1944–45, Newark Eagles; Bkn (N) 1949–51, 1954–57, LA (N) 1958, Cin (N) 1958–60, Cle (A) 1960
Big Don was Rookie of the Year with the Dodgers in 1949, with a 17–8 mark and an NL-leading five shutouts. He jumped to 19–11 in 1950 and 20–9 in '51. Then he lost two years to the Army. It took the 1954 season to get him back to where he'd been, but in the next two seasons, he was brilliant: 20–5 and 27–7 to win the first Cy Young Award.

Suddenly, in 1957, he struggled. The next year he slipped further and was traded to Cincinnati. After a brief comeback to 13–8 with the sixth-place Reds in 1959, he fell off the charts.

After his brilliant beginning, Newk finished his career with a disappointing 149–90 record.

The problem was alcohol. It ruined his career and nearly his life. But, heroically, he pulled himself back and now counsels other baseball alcoholics as a member of the Dodgers' front office.

HAL NEWHOUSER
Pitcher, Det (A) 1939–53, Cle (A) 1954–55
Wrongly stigmatized as a wartime phenom, Newhouser was actually the AL's top lefthander for the 1940s. Ted Williams called him one of the three best hurlers he ever faced. Other stars played part or all of the war years without having their records denigrated. But Newhouser was so dominant in 1944–1945 that it's sometimes forgotten he had two 20-win years and won more than half of his 207 career victories after the war.

In 1944 he overcame the wildness that had plagued him in his first seasons with the Tigers. He was voted AL MVP for his 29–9 record and 2.22 ERA. The next year he was 25–9 and led the AL in shutouts (8) and ERA (1.81). The Tigers won the AL pennant in 1945, and though he didn't pitch well in the World Series win over the Cubs, he was still credited with 2 victories. In both 1944 and 1945 he led the AL in strikeouts.

The stars were all back in 1946, but Newhouser sailed on. He had the most wins of any pitcher at 26–9 and again led the league in ERA with 1.94. He had his greatest strikeout year at 275, but finished second to Bob Feller's 348. "Prince Hal" was the AL's top winner again in 1948, with 21.

CHARLES "KID" NICHOLS
Pitcher, Bos (N) 1890–1901, StL (N) 1904–05, Phi (N) 1905–06. Manager, StL (N) 1904–05
Perhaps the best of the pre-1900 pitching greats, Nichols' seven seasons of 30 or more wins is topped by no one. He won 20 or more games for ten straight seasons and had twelve 20-win seasons altogether.

Pitching without a windup, "Kid" had control and speed but no curve. He took over as ace of the Bostons in 1890 at the age of twenty and pitched them to five pennants, 1891–93 and 1897–98.

His best year was 1892 (35–16). He won 3 complete game victories in three days in September, then in the Temple Cup playoff against second-place Cleveland, he dueled Cleveland ace Cy Young (36–11) for eleven scoreless innings before darkness forced a stoppage of play.

Nichols was 30–14 for a fourth-place team in 1896. The next year he beat the Orioles two out of three in September to clinch a flag.

Sixth all-time in wins, with a 362–207 record, the Kid also notched 533 complete games for fourth on the all-time list. In 502 starts with Boston, he was relieved only 25 times.

PHIL NIEKRO
Pitcher, Mil (N) 1964–65, Atl (N) 1966–83, 1987, NY (A) 1984–85, Cle (A) 1986–87, Tor (A) 1987
For twenty-four years, to the age of forty-eight, Niekro tossed his knuckler, most of the time for weak Atlanta teams in a notorious hitters' park. When he approached win number 300, some experts were surprised; they'd never thought of him as a star. But he was. Hitters knew it long before the writers suspected. Bobby Murcer said hitting Niekro's knuckler was like "eating jelly with chopsticks."

For his 300th win, Phil decided not to throw a single knuckler—until the last batter, when he struck Jeff Burroughs out with three of them.

Not only did Phil win 318, he saved 30 others, a rarity for modern starters. Among his 274 losses were 47 shutouts—only Johnson and Young had more.

Niekro wandered seven years in the minors and didn't become a regular starter with the Braves until 1967 when he was twenty-eight. He led the NL with a 1.87 ERA that season and was 11–9 with seventh-place Atlanta.

Niekro's club—the Braves—held him down. Atlanta finished last six times with him, and he led the league in defeats four times, a record. He somehow managed to win 20 three times. In 1979 he led the NL in both wins and losses with a 21–20 mark.

Phil's home park also hurt. It was part of the reason he led the league four times in throwing gopher pitches.

Phil was 23–13 in 1969 to lead Atlanta to the division title.

He holds the record for most wins after the age of forty—121. He's the second-oldest man (forty-three and a half) to hit a homer.

When he retired in 1987 he had 3,342 strikeouts and was third all-time in bases on balls, fourth in innings pitched, and first in wild pitches, 200. He once threw 6 wild ones in one game—four in one inning.

PEDRO "TONY" OLIVA
Outfielder, Min (A) 1962–76
There's no telling what the Oliva's batting marks might have been if he'd had a healthy knee. Instead, he had five operations, each one slowing him down a little more. As a Minnesota rookie in 1964, he lined out 217 hits, the AL rookie record. He also tied the rookie mark for total bases and, incidentally, led in batting, .323. Naturally, he was Rookie of the Year.

Tony led the league in batting the next year too, as the Twins won the flag and almost won the Series. He tied Johnny Pesky's mark of leading the league in hits each of his first two seasons.

And then he hurt his knee. Two subpar seasons followed, but by 1969 he was back over .300.

In 1971 Oliva was having his best year ever, .375, when he fell and hurt his knee again. His average dropped to .337, and though he hung on to win his third batting title, he was through as an outfielder and as a great hitter. He became exclusively a DH until he finally retired in 1976 with a career average of .304 and 220 home runs.

Incidentally, he was born Pedro Oliva and became Tony when he used his brother's passport to get out of Cuba. A third brother, Juan Carlos, stayed in Havana and became one of Cuba's top pitchers.

JAMES "ORATOR JIM" O'ROURKE
Outfielder, Middletown (NA) 1872, Bos (NA) 1873–75, Bos (N) 1876–78, 1880, Prov (N) 1879, Buf (N) 1881–84, NY (N) 1885–89, 1891–92, 1904, NY (P) 1890, Was (N) 1893. Manager, Buf (N) 1881–84, Was (N) 1893
O'Rourke reportedly had only average speed and a weak arm, but he was a star in the National Association for four seasons before the National League was formed, averaging .317. He helped the Boston Red Stockings to five pennants (three in the National Association), then switched to Providence and helped them win a flag in 1879. Ten years later he was the regular left fielder for the

New York Giants champions of 1888–89. In between, he spent four seasons as player-manager of Buffalo's NL club.

From 1876 on, he hit over .300 in eleven major league seasons, averaging .310. After retiring he managed and umpired, and at the age of 52 caught a nine-inning game for the Giants, their pennant clincher in 1904. He even got his 2,304th major league hit and scored his 1,446th run.

And *then* he became president of a minor league.

His nickname stemmed from his Yale Law School background and his flowery, bombastic speech.

In 1945 he was named to the Baseball Hall of Fame.

AMOS OTIS
Outfielder, NY (N) 1967, 1969, KC (A) 1970–83, Pit (N) 1984
Otis is another underrated player. He helped Kansas City win four division titles and one World Series between 1976 and 1980. He hit a strong .277, with 193 home runs and 1,008 RBIs. He hit .429 in the 1978 League Championship Series in a futile effort to upset the Yanks.

Two years later Amos hit .333, as the Royals won the LCS. He then hit .478 in the World Series against Philadelphia, including a home run in Game Five to bring Kansas City to within one run of victory.

Otis was one of the best baserunners of his day. When he led the AL in stolen bases in 1971 with 52, he was caught only eight times. The year before that he had done even better with 33 out of 34—the only time they caught him was on a steal of home.

He was a fine fielder too. In his first two years, 1970–71, he went 165 straight games without an error. He led the league's outfielders in putouts, double plays, and total chances both years.

MEL OTT
Outfielder, NY (N) 1926–47. Manager, NY (N) 1942–48
With his quick, distinctive leg kick as he stepped into the ball, Ott used to golf high flies into the chummy upper deck of the Polo Grounds, 256 feet away. He hit almost two thirds of his homers at home. When he retired after twenty-two seasons, he had 511 homers, the third highest total at the time, and a .304 career average. He set new NL career records for runs (1,859), RBIs (1,860), and walks (1,708). The run and RBI marks were first broken by Stan Musial; the walks by Joe Morgan.

Ott's famous leg kick helped him compensate for his lack of size; he weighed only 165–170 pounds. It was a graceful kick, unlike that of Sadaharu Oh, who lifted his front knee and pulled his foot back with his bat cocked forward. Mel lifted his front foot high, his weight perfectly balanced on the fulcrum of his bat handle at his belt. Babe Ruth, Ducky Medwick, Rudy York, and other big men used modified versions of it.

Ott arrived in New York with a straw suitcase at the age of sixteen and adopted Manager John McGraw as a father. He stayed to become one of the Giants' all-time most popular players and six-time home run champ.

Six times Mel led the league in walks and ten times drew 100 or more. Four times he drew 5 walks in one game; the first time was on the final day of the 1929 season, when Phillies pitchers gave him five intentional walks, one with the bases loaded, so he couldn't tie Philadelphia's Chuck Klein for the homer title.

Mel hit .389 in the 1933 World Series and won the deciding game with a home run in the tenth inning. It was his eighth season on the Giants, though he was only twenty-five years old.

Ott became player-manager of the Giants in 1942. It was in reference to Ott that Leo Durocher made his famous pronouncement that "Nice guys finish last."

He was elected to the Baseball Hall of Fame in 1951.

LEROY "SATCHEL" PAIGE
Pitcher, Negro League, 1926–50, Chattanooga Black Lookouts, Birmingham Black Barons, Cleveland Cubs, Pittsburgh Crawfords, Kansas City Monarchs, New York Black Yankees, Satchel Paige's All-Stars, Philadelphia Stars, Cle (A) 1948–50, StL (A) 1951–53, KC (A) 1965
If Satch wasn't the greatest black pitcher of all time (and many say he was), he was by far the most famous. He began pitching semipro in 1924, and made his professional debut in 1926, age twenty-two; he was 9–6 the next year, and pitched the Birmingham Black Barons into the playoffs. His white major league debut was in 1948 with Cleveland, age forty-two; he was 6–1, set attendance records, and helped the Indians to the pennant. When they said he should be Rookie of the Year, he asked what year they meant.

Satch got his name from toting bags at the Mobile railroad station at the age of seven. He got his hesitation pitch from throwing rocks at other kids, fooling them into ducking too soon. After a stretch in reform school for stealing toys, Satchel learned his control from Black Baron vets who taught him to throw over a Coke bottle cap until he could "nip frosting off a cake." Satch called it his "be ball," " 'cause it be where I want it to be." He got his fastball from the Lord.

Joining the Pittsburgh Crawfords in 1931, Paige teamed with Josh Gibson in one of the greatest batteries of all time. In 1934 he led all Negro League pitchers with a 16–2 mark and threw a 17-strikeout no-hitter against the Homestead Grays. Barnstorming in the offseason, he dueled many a game against Dizzy Dean and later Bob Feller. Much of his pitching was on tour, traveling packed into a car, knees against chin, to prairie towns, where, "if I didn't pitch, they didn't want the team—in *town*, let alone the park." From there he sailed to Latin America, where his fabled bronze arm went dead.

The Kansas City Monarchs took a chance on him, and Paige miraculously pitched his arm back into shape. He usually pitched two or three innings a night to draw a crowd. One of his great moments came when he deliberately walked the bases "drunk" to face his old buddy Gibson, then whiffed Josh. In the 1942 Series against the Grays, he and Hilton Smith held Josh to a .125 average and swept all 4 games.

Satch loved fast cars and fast women. He was always dallying, then racing to the park, police sirens screaming either in escort or pursuit. Fined twenty-five dollars for speeding, he peeled off fifty dollars and told the judge, "Here. I'm comin' back tomorrow."

When Satch signed with Cleveland for the 1948 pennant stretch, *The Sporting News* called it a publicity stunt. "Everybody told me he was through," said the Indians' boss, Bill Veeck. "That was understandable. They thought he was human." Satch pitched a shutout in his second start, drew two hundred thousand fans to his first three starts, plus thousands more who couldn't get in.

In 1951 Veeck took Satch to the Browns, where he had his own rocking chair in the bullpen and could still win 12 games and save 10. Finally, in 1965, aged fifty-nine, Paige pitched three innings for the Kansas City Athletics to draw a bonus, the oldest man ever to pitch in the majors. He allowed one hit.

Satch's wit has entered the language. His most famous saying is "Never look back. Something may be gaining on you."

JIM PALMER
Pitcher, Bal (A) 1965–67, 1969–84
Winner of three Cy Youngs, Palmer won 20 games eight times and helped the Orioles win six flags. The handsome righthander is the greatest jockey shorts salesman in baseball history, and his seminude posters advertising underwear are almost as famous in Europe and Asia as they are in the United States.

Jim won 268 games despite suffering a sore arm after shutting out the Dodgers as a twenty-year-old in the 1966 Series. The injury kept him out of the majors for virtually two years.

When he got back, Palmer won 20 or more four straight seasons, from 1970 to 1973. After an off-year, he put together another four-straight, 20-plus streak, 1975–78. He won three Cy Young awards, 1973, 1975, and 1976. He led the AL in ERA in 1973 and '75.

Throughout his career, Jim shared a stormy, symbiotic relationship with Manager Earl Weaver. They yelled at each other but respected each other and, in the end, helped each other achieve greatness.

As a high fastball pitcher, Palmer gave up a lot of home runs—but never a grand slam.

He was also excellent in preventing unearned runs, a neglected side of pitching. He modestly says that's because he gave up few ground balls to make errors on. But his World Series record shows that, even when his mates did kick a ball, Jim slammed the door.

Palmer was elected to the Hall of Fame in 1990.

DAVE PARKER
Outfielder, Pit (N) 1973–83, Cin (N) 1984–87, Oak (A) 1988–89, Mil (A) 1990–
Parker's career divides into three distinct stages.

First, 1975–1979: the superstar. Starting with his first full year, Parker was a .300 hitter, with back-to-back NL batting championships in 1977 and 1978, 30 home runs in 1978, MVP in the 1979 All-Star Game, a leader of the 1979 World Championship team, and a reputation as a hustling "complete" player, with speed and the best right field arm in baseball.

Second, 1980–1983: the disappointment. After signing a five-year $5-million contract to become the highest-paid player in baseball, his batting average and power fell off alarmingly, as did his availability. He was constantly injured and obviously overweight. He reacted to criticism by Pittsburgh fans by criticizing the fans. He became arguably the most unpopular player ever to wear a Pirate

uniform. One day he was nearly skulled by a battery thrown from the stands. Only later was it learned that he had become deeply involved in drug abuse.

Third, 1984–?: the aging slugger: Parker signed with Cincinnati as a free agent. Given a new start, he apparently conquered his addiction and produced excellent power stats for the Reds, twice topping 30 homers and leading the NL in RBIs in 1985. No longer an all-around player, he was traded to Oakland for 1988 and became an outstanding DH, a role he continued to play with Milwaukee beginning in 1990.

ROGER PECKINPAUGH
Shortstop, Cle (A) 1910–13, NY (A) 1913–21, Was (A) 1922–26, Chi (A) 1927. Manager, NY (A) 1914, Cle (A) 1928–33, 1941
Peckinpaugh was a fine-fielding shortstop with bad luck. In the eight years he played for the Yankees he led AL shortstops in assists three times. In any later age, that sort of range would have had him canonized by the New York media, but Roger did his work in those years when the Giants were *the* team in New York and the Yankees were a distant "other." The Yanks won the pennant in 1921, his last season with them, but the Giants beat them in the World Series, as Peckinpaugh's error let in the winning run in the final game.

Traded to Washington, he helped the Senators win a pennant and World Series in 1924, but his contributions were overshadowed by those of the "Boy Manager," Bucky Harris, and Walter Johnson, who finally had the chance to pitch for a winner after years with poor teams.

Peckinpaugh was a liability at bat early in his career, but gradually improved to ordinary. He actually hit .305 in 1919. In 1925 he hit a sprightly .294 and fielded brilliantly all season to lead the Senators to another pennant. This time he was named AL MVP just before the World Series.

But the 1925 Series was a nightmare for Roger. By the eighth inning of the final game, he had made 7 errors. Suddenly, in the top of the eighth, he became a hero—he hit a home run to put the Senators in the lead. Alas! In the bottom of the eighth, the Pirates tied the game, and poor Roger made error number 8—a Series record for any position that still stands—to keep the inning going. The Pirates scored twice more to become champions. In Peckinpaugh's greatest season, he became the World Series' greatest goat.

HERB PENNOCK
Pitcher, Phi (A) 1912–15, Bos (A) 1915–17, 1918–22, 1934, NY (A) 1923–33
Pennock was a smooth lefthander whose effortless style took him to a 240–162 career. Anything but overpowering, he blended curves and excellent control with the excellent bat support he usually received. Although he threw 35 shutouts over his twenty-two seasons, he was the kind of pitcher who pitched just well enough to win. In World Series competition, he was 5–0.

He came to the big leagues right out of high school, joining the Athletics and winning 11 games for the 1914 team at age twenty. When Connie Mack dismantled his team after the loss to the Braves in the 1914 World Series, Pennock was sold to the Red Sox, another strong team. By

1920 the Sox owner began selling his stars. In 1923 Pennock was passed on to the Yankees, with whom he had his best seasons. He was 21–9 in 1924 and 23–11 in 1926, and had two other seasons with 19 wins.

At 160 pounds, Pennock was seldom a staff workhorse. He led the AL with 277 innings pitched in 1925, but he usually threw 50–60 fewer innings. He nearly always gave up more hits than innings, although his low number of walks somewhat compensated for that. He once pitched an 11-hit shutout. His career ERA of 3.61 isn't spectacular. But, while the spectacular pitchers came and went, Pennock and his soft curves prevailed.

In 1948 he was elected to the Baseball Hall of Fame.

ATANACIO "TONY" PEREZ
*First Baseman/Third Baseman, Cin (N) 1964–76,
1984–86, Mon (N) 1977–79, Bos (A) 1980–82, Phi (N)
1983*

One of the biggest cogs in the Big Red Machine of the 1970s, Perez helped put the Reds in four World Series. He knocked in 90 or more runs eleven straight seasons, 1967–1977. His career totals read 1,652 RBIs and 1,272 runs scored. He hit 379 homers, with a high of 40 in 1970. He hit .300 a couple of times and finished with a respectable .279 for twenty-three seasons. Yet, amazingly, he never led his league in a single important offensive statistic.

But he was consistent. He was also a good enough glove man to play third base for five seasons for Cincinnati so slugger Lee May could play first.

He hit .435 in the 1972 World Series. In the 1975 Series, Tony went 0 for 15, then exploded with 2 homers and 4 RBIs to win the fifth game, 6–2. He added another homer and 2 RBIs in the final game to key a 4–3 win.

GAYLORD PERRY
*Pitcher, SF (N) 1962–71, Cle (A) 1972–75, Tex (A)
1976–77, 1980, SD (N) 1978–79, NY (A) 1980, Atl (N)
1981, Sea (A) 1982–83, KC (A) 1983*

The only man to win a Cy Young Award in both leagues, Perry had as much fun outwitting the umpires with his spitter as he did fooling the hitters with it. He even wrote a hilarious book about it, revealing for instance that KY Jelly and Preparation H work as well as the old standbys: spit, sweat, and Vaseline. The trick was to lubricate the fingers enough to squirt the ball out without spin, like squirting a watermelon seed. The ball then behaves like a knuckleball but is easier to control. Perry was still winning games at the age of forty-three.

Perry won 20-plus twice for the Giants in the 1960s before he was traded to the AL after the 1971 season. NL umps were glad to see Perry go. Umpire Chris Pelekoudas gave him a giant jar of Vaseline as a going-away present.

His first year in the AL, Perry was 24–16 with the fifth-place Indians. He was the first man to top 20 in both leagues in nearly fifty years.

By 1978 he was back in the NL, where his 21–6 mark for San Diego earned him his second Cy Young. It was his fifth 20-win season.

In twenty-two years Perry played on only one division champ. With support like that, a guy needs a little extra edge to win 314 games.

CHARLES "DEACON" PHILLIPPE
Pitcher, Lou (N) 1899, Pit (N) 1900–11

Phillippe was the best control pitcher in the twentieth century, giving up a stingy 1.25 walks per nine innings.

The Deacon's best year was 25–9 in 1903, his fifth 20-victory year in five years in the league. In the first World Series that fall, Phillippe pitched 5 complete games in thirteen days (a total of 44 innings pitched) and gave up only 3 walks. He won his first 3 starts in a period of six days. But he lost Game Six on ground rule triples into the crowd. The next day he pitched his fifth complete game in eleven days and was shut out, 3–0, as Boston took the Series.

The Deacon was still around to pitch 6 innings in the 1909 Series without allowing an earned run.

BILLY PIERCE
*Pitcher, Det (A) 1945, 1948, Chi (A) 1949–61, SF (N)
1962–64*

Pierce was the epitome of "stylish lefty," the kind who looks good even when he loses. But Billy didn't lose that often. The White Sox got him and $10,000 from the Tigers in 1949 for an aging catcher. It was the kind of deal that should have got the Sox four-to-seven at Joliet.

Billy stepped in immediately as the Sox ace; that wasn't any great honor in 1949, but after Chicago added such as Nellie Fox, Minnie Minoso, and Chico Carrasquel for a few broken bats or bubble gum cards or some other trade imbalance, the White Sox became a consistent first-division team. Billy led the AL in ERA in 1955, won 20 games in 1956 and '57, and totaled 186 wins for his thirteen years with the Sox. In 1959 he helped them win their first pennant in forty years.

In 1962 he joined the Giants and led them to a flag with a record of 16–6 that included a 12–0 record at Candlestick Park.

EDDIE PLANK
*Pitcher, Phi (A) 1901–14, StL (F) 1915, StL (A)
1916–17*

Plank came out of Gettysburg College to win 327 games. He held the record for most wins by a lefthander until Warren Spahn surpassed that mark in 1963, forty-six years after Eddie retired. He won 20 or more games eight times, seven with the Philadelphia A's and one with St. Louis of the Federal League. He pitched for six AL championship teams with the A's. He was only 2–5 in World Series games, but 4 of his losses were shutouts. His Series ERA was 1.32. He threw a lot of shutouts himself—69—the most for a lefty and fifth-best of all time.

Plank drove batters crazy *before* he threw the ball. He'd fuss around the mound, fidgeting with his uniform, talking to the ball ("Only nine more to go," etc.), shaking off signs. By the time he threw the ball, the batter was ready to swing at anything.

Of course, Plank didn't throw just anything. He had a good fastball and curve, which he delivered sidearm with good control. He struck out 2,246 batters and walked fewer than half that many. Despite all his good years, he never led the league in wins, strikeouts, or ERA.

He was named to the Baseball Hall of Fame in 1946.

CUMBERLAND "CUM" POSEY
Outfielder, Owner, Negro League, Homestead Grays,
Detroit Wolves

Posey's Homestead Grays wrote a record never approached by any other U.S. pro team in any sport—they won nine straight pennants from 1937 to 1945 with Josh Gibson, Buck Leonard, and Cool Papa Bell generating the power. Only the Tokyo Giants, with nine straight Japanese championships, can match them. Yet they may not have been the greatest Grays teams of all.

The 1926 club, starring Joe Williams, won 43 straight (mostly against white semipro teams). The 1930 Grays, with Williams, Gibson, and Charleston, won 11 out of 12 from the western champion Monarchs. And the 1931 club boasted a record of 136–17, again mostly against semipros. They even challenged the white major league Pirates to a winner-take-all series, but Pittsburgh simply refused.

Posey's father was a wealthy barge captain, his mother the first black to graduate from Ohio State. At various times Cum attended Penn State, Pitt, and Duquesne universities, but failed to graduate from any of them. He was considered the best colored basketball player in America in 1913 and also managed the Murdock Grays, a steel mill team. Eventually he founded the Loendi Big Five, which claimed the U.S. basketball championship of 1919. He gained control of the Homestead Grays in the early 1920s, played for the team until 1928, and managed it until 1935.

But when the Depression struck, Posey lost his stars to racketeer Gus Greenlee's well-bankrolled Pittsburgh Crawfords. Cum got his own racketeer, Sonnyman Jackson, and fought back, eventually driving Greenlee out of the league.

In 1937 Cum bought Gibson back for $2,500, and the team went 152–11 to embark on their pennant streak.

The Grays shuttled between Pittsburgh and Washington by bus, playing two or three games a day, league and semi-pro. Rain could wipe out all profit for the week, until World War II brought prosperity at last. In 1945 Posey's Grays sometimes drew thirty thousand fans to Griffith Stadium hours after the AL Senators had played before three thousand in the same park.

But when baseball was at last integrated after the war, the raids of major league clubs soon destroyed Cum's life investment. Luke Easter was snatched up by the Indians for only $10,000. Posey moaned, "It's like coming into a man's store and stealing the merchandise right off the shelves."

JOHN "BOOG" POWELL
First Baseman, Bal (A) 1961–74, Cle (A) 1975–76, LA
(N) 1977

Powell drove some long blasts out of parks—469 feet in Baltimore in 1962, over the roof of Tiger Stadium in 1969. He and Frank Robinson provided the power that brought the Orioles four pennants and two world titles between 1966 and 1971. Big Boog (six-four, 230 pounds) crushed 339 home runs, with a high of 39 in 1964.

Boog hit .357 in the 1966 World Series as Baltimore swept the Dodgers in four straight. In 1969 he hit .385 to help sweep Minnesota in the LCS and .429 to key the sweep again a year later. In the 1970 Series his home runs

won the first two games to get the O's off to a five-game victory over the Big Red Machine.

DEL PRATT
Second Baseman, StL (A) 1912–17, NY (A) 1918–20,
Bos (A) 1921–22, Det (A) 1923–24

Pratt had a knack for picking losers. He went from the 1912 Browns to the 1918 Yanks, 1921 Red Sox, and 1923 Tigers, spending most of his thirteen-year career in the second division.

Del was a fair singles hitter with a high of .324 in 1921. Curiously, he hit .302 as a Browns' rookie, then missed that level for seven straight seasons. But in 1920, with the livelier ball, he suddenly remembered how to do it and hit over .300 in each of his last five seasons, bowing out with .303 in 1924. Another oddity about Pratt was that he played over 100 games in each of his seasons. He quit with 1,996 hits; if he'd been keeping track, he might have tried to hang around for one more year.

He was a good glove man, although he slowed down rapidly near the end. He led AL second basemen in putouts five times.

He was somewhat of a clubhouse lawyer and was traded away from the Yankees following the 1920 season after a dispute over the division of New York's World Series money for finishing in third place in the AL. The Yankees won the pennant in 1921 and Pratt's new team, Boston, finished fifth, reducing his bonus to nothing. Well, penny wise and pound foolish . . .

The way Pratt got to the Yankees was that he and a teammate sued the Browns' owner for calling them "lazy" and intimating they lost games purposely. The players settled out of court and then—surprise!—were traded.

JOHN PICUS "JACK" QUINN
Pitcher, NY (A) 1909–12, 1919–21, Bos (N) 1913, Bal
(F) 1914–15, Chi (A) 1918, Bos (A) 1922–25, Phi (A)
1925–30, Bkn (N) 1931–32, Cin (N) 1933

An old spitballer, Quinn pitched almost 1,000 pro games in almost thirty years, 1907–1935. He hit his last home run in the majors at the age of forty-six and won his last game when he was forty-seven. Or maybe forty-seven and forty-eight—there's a disagreement as to when he was born. Anyway, he was old! Spitballers, like knuckleballers, tend to have long careers.

Trapped in a coal mine fire as a youth, Jack had a checkered baseball career. He bounced around the Yanks (Highlanders) when they were down, 1909–1912, the minors, the Federal League, the Yanks again when they were rebuilding, 1919–1921, the Red Sox when they were down, 1922–1924, then caught the A's on the upswing, 1925–1930. He hurled two Series games in 1930 at the age of forty-six (or thereabouts)—the oldest man to do so.

During all that time, he kept his spitball low and usually over the plate. His only 20-win season was with the Feds in 1914, which makes it a bit suspect, but he won 18 three times in the AL. Well, no one ever said he was great, just good for a long, long time.

DAN QUISENBERRY
Pitcher, KC (A) 1979–88, StL (N) 1988–89, SF (N) 1990

The submarine baller Quisenberry was baseball's premier reliever of the 1980s, leading the AL in saves five years out of six, 1980–1985. He was Fireman of the Year four times and was one of the top reasons Kansas City got into four playoffs in that period.

Calling himself "just a garbage man," Quiz saved 45 in 1983, a record since topped by Dave Righetti (46) in 1986, and Dennis Eckersley (48) and Bobby Thigpen (57) in 1990.

Dan has a dry sense of humor. "I have seen the future," he was fond of saying. "It is much like the present, only longer." As for his underhand style, he shrugged. "I found a delivery in my flaw."

DICK RADATZ
Pitcher, Bos (A) 1962–66, Cle (A) 1966–67, Chi (N) 1967, Det (A) 1969, Mon (N) 1969
For nearly four years, 1962–1965, Fenway Park's leftfield wall was only the second-most-fearsome "Monster" in Red Sox land. Number one was the six-six, 250-pound fastballer who stomped in from the bullpen and turned batters to mush. Radatz won two Fireman of the Year Awards for the Red Sox, 1962 and 1964, when he led the AL in saves. He led in relief wins three straight years, 1962–1964. His 16 relief wins in 1964 set an AL record (since broken).

The Monster intimidated hitters, averaging more than a strikeout an inning, and after every win he'd shove his fist triumphantly into the air. And just when they didn't think he could get any better, he lost it. As soon as he lost a foot off his fastball, he was done. He didn't have anything else to throw. His final figures: 52–43 and 122 saves—100 in four years.

CHARLES "OL' HOSS" RADBOURN
Pitcher, Buf (N) 1880, Pro (N) 1881–85, Bos (N) 1886–89, Bos (P) 1890, Cin (N) 1891
Radbourn was hardly a "hoss." He stood only five-nine and weighed 168. But he earned his name by winning 60 games in one year, 1884—that's 679 innings, 441 strikeouts, and a 1.38 ERA. He won the NL pennant for Providence. By season's end he was pitching every day until he could barely lift his arm to comb his hair. Then he won three more against the AA champs in the freezing cold in the championship series.

Hoss had a great curveball. He also had an "in-shoot," or screwball. He delivered both underhand, although overhand pitching had been legalized that year. The pitching distance was only fifty feet, but batters could ask for a high or low ball, in effect cutting the strike zone in half.

Charlie had already won 33 in 1882 and 48 in 1883 when the historic 1884 season with Providence began.

The temperamental Radbourn resented young Charlie Sweeney trying to push him out as ace. He was suspended for loafing, but when Sweeney got drunk and jumped the club, they begged Rad to come back. The only pitcher on the roster, he pitched nearly every game until Providence clinched the flag. He pitched 30 of 32 remaining games, won 26 of them—18 in a row, including 5 shutouts and 4 one-run games. His winning streak was broken when he lost, 2–0.

Rad had several more good years to bring his career record to 310–195. Then he bought a bar and retired. In 1894 he shot himself hunting, losing one eye and half his face. He ended his days in the back of a pool hall, refusing to come out. He died at the age of forty-two. Sweeney died five years later, reportedly in San Quentin on a murder rap.

Radbourn was elected to the Baseball Hall of Fame in 1939.

TIM RAINES
Outfielder, Mon (N) 1979–
Raines may be the top player in the NL in the 1980s. A compact switch-hitter, his main weapon is blinding speed, but he also hits with occasional power. As a rookie in 1981, he stole 71 bases in only 88 games. He led the NL in steals in his first four seasons, with a high of 90 in 1983. Entering the 1988 season, he had the best base-stealing percentage in history for players with 300 or more steals: 511 out of 585 for 87 percent. He led the league in runs scored in 1983 and 1987. In 1986, he topped the NL with a .334 batting average. He opted for free agency in 1987, but no team made a legitimate offer, an absurd situation that was later ruled to have resulted from collusion on the part of owners. They couldn't have been more obvious if they'd held a meeting on "60 Minutes." Raines eventually re-signed with Montreal, but he missed spring training and the first month of the season. When he hit .330, he set a lot of people wondering about the need for spring training.

WILLIE RANDOLPH
Second Baseman, Pit (N) 1975, NY (A) 1976–88, LA (N) 1989–1990, Oak (A) 1990
Randolph was one of the sparkplugs who drove the Yankees to five titles in six years, 1976–1981. Solid defensively and excellent on double plays, he enjoyed his best year at bat in 1980 (.294). His worst was 1981 (.232, two HRs); however, his homer in the League Championship Series won the third game to clinch the pennant. Although held back by injuries the last few years, he hit a career-high .305 in 1987. One of his strengths has been that he walks about twice as often as he strikes out.

DICK REDDING
Pitcher, Negro League, 1911–38, Lincoln Giants, Lincoln Stars, Indianapolis ABCs, Chicago American Giants, Brooklyn Royal Giants, Bacharach Giants
Cannonball Dick could knock the bat out of a man's hand back in the pre-World War One era. He is credited with twelve no-hitters, though this is unverified and probably mostly against semipro foes.

From 1912 to 1914 Dick teamed with Joe Williams on the Lincoln Giants to form perhaps black baseball's strongest one-two pitching punch ever. Real old-timers insist the two were both faster than the younger and more famous Satchel Paige.

Thereafter Dick and Joe became fierce rivals. In 1920 Redding beat Joe with a no-hitter at Ebbets Field in probably the finest game he ever pitched.

An illiterate Georgian, he was credited with 17 straight wins as a rookie in 1911. In 1915 he reportedly won 20 straight. He pitched the Indianapolis ABC's to a championship in 1917, then spent 1918 seeing combat service in France.

No stats were kept until the Eastern League was

formed in 1923, when Dick was over the hill and managing the Brook Royals, one of the weakest clubs. He was a losing pitcher then.

He often faced Ruth and Gehrig in exhibitions; his job was to groove soft pitches to them to please the customers.

HAROLD "PEE WEE" REESE
Shortstop, Bkn (N) 1940–42, 1946–57, LA (N) 1958
Reese was shortstop on seven pennant-winning Dodger teams, from 1941 to 1956. An average hitter, he nevertheless led the NL in runs scored in 1949 with 132 and totaled 1,338 for his career. A good baserunner, he played during a time when base stealing was not stressed. His 30 steals led the league in 1952, and his career total of 232 stolen bases is one of the better marks for the era. He was at his best in the field and in providing leadership as captain of the team. Reese once faked a splinter in his eye to give his reliever more time to warm up. The performance was so convincing that the hurler dropped the ball and came over to see if he could help. A Southerner, one of Pee Wee's greatest accomplishments was winning Jackie Robinson's acceptance on the team.

His nickname stemmed not from his lack of size (five-ten, 160), but from the fact he was a marbles champion as a lad.

Although he hit .300 only once and never amassed exceptional stats, he finished in the top ten in MVP voting in eight of his sixteen seasons.

Reese was elected to the Baseball Hall of Fame in 1984.

ED REULBACH
Pitcher, Chi (N) 1905–13, Bkn (N) 1913–14, Nwk (F) 1915, Bos (N) 1916–17
Reulbach is the only man ever to pitch a doubleheader shutout, which he did in the stretch of the 1908 pennant race, won by the Cubs in a playoff of the Merkle game. When the Cubs' other starters came out of the hectic Giant series (that included the Merkle game) in September, exhausted, Ed agreed to pitch the doubleheader against the seventh-place Dodgers, whom he had already beaten seven times. He shut them out for eighteen innings, and the Cubs went on to win in a playoff.

Ed had pitched marathons before—in 1905 he had won an eighteen-inning game, then went twenty innings to win another.

For three years, 1906–08, Reulbach had a remarkable record—60–15. He led the league in winning percentage all three seasons (only Lefty Grove has matched that)—as the Cubs swept three pennants. In the 1906 Series against the Hitless Wonder White Sox, Ed pitched a one-hitter in Game Two.

Reulbach died July 17, 1961, the same day as Ty Cobb.

RICK REUSCHEL
Pitcher, Chi (N) 1972–81, 1983–84, NY (A) 1981, Pit (N) 1985–87, SF (N) 1987–
Reuschel was an outstanding starter for the Cubs' throughout the 1970s, winning 20 in 1977 and 18 in 1979 for so-so teams. Traded to the Yankees in 1981, he was expected to thrive with the Yankees' bats behind him. Instead, his career was nearly ended by a sore arm. He tried a comeback with the Cubs and finally signed a minor

league contract with the Pirates in 1985.

He made a remarkable comeback with the Bucs, 14–8. Traded to the Giants in 1987, he help win their division and continued with an outstandi. son in 1988, winning 19 and contending for Cy Yu honors.

"Big Daddy"—he's a well-upholstered six foot three—throws with a deceptively easy motion; he almost seems to be lobbing the ball. But he has surprising velocity, good movement, changes speeds well, and has fine control.

JIM RICE
Outfielder, Bos (A) 1974–89
Rice was made for Fenway Park and took advantage of it. He and Fred Lynn enjoyed splendid rookie seasons in 1975 to lift the Red Sox from ninth to the flag. An injury kept Rice out of the World Series, which Boston lost to the Reds in seven games.

Jim's best season was the thrilling 1978 pennant race with New York, won by the Yankees in a playoff. Rice led the league in homers (46), RBIs (139), triples (15), and hits (213), with a .315 batting average. He was voted MVP over New York's Ron Guidry in a hotly debated vote.

Rice led in home runs three times and RBIs twice. On the downside, he was also among the all-time leaders in hitting into double plays. But you know who the leader is? Hank Aaron. Not bad company to be in.

EDGAR "SAM" RICE
Outfielder, Was (A) 1915–33, Cle (A) 1934
Rice stopped only 13 hits short of 3,000, hit .322, topped .300 fourteen times, stole 351 bases, had good range in the outfield and a strong arm, and played on all three Washington pennant winners. He rarely struck out; in 1929 Sam came to bat 616 times and whiffed only 9 of them. He had no power; he once hit 182 singles in one season; most batters don't get that many hits.

A victim of a tragic killer tornado that killed most of his family, Sam wandered aimlessly, joining a shipping concern. As a sailor in Mexico, he began to play baseball. Rice joined the Senators as a pitcher in 1915. When Detroit hurler Hooks Dauss tripled off him, Sam cut his toe plate off forever.

In 1924 Rice put together a thirty-one-game hit streak, led the AL with 216 hits, and batted .334 as the Senators won their first pennant.

In 1925 he hit .350 and cracked 227 hits to lead the Senators into the World Series, then slapped 12 hits in the Series, a record (later broken by Bobby Richardson of the Yankees). In Game Three he made the most famous play of his life; he chased down Pirate Earl Smith's drive but fell into the stands as he reached the ball. An out or a home run? Rice would never answer directly. "The ump called him out." He would smile mysteriously. He left a letter to be opened at his death. In it, he at last answered the question. He caught the ball.

Rice was elected to the Baseball Hall of Fame in 1963.

BRANCH RICKEY
Executive. Manager, StL (A) 1913–15, StL (N) 1919–25
Rickey invented the farm system and integrated the game. One would have been enough to put him among the

ve most influential men in baseball history. Rickey's decision to sign Jackie Robinson to a Dodger contract took great courage. His motives were not completely pure. Robinson, Roy Campanella, and Don Newcombe, and other black stars helped win seven pennants for the Dodgers.

Rickey had powerful fundamentalist religious scruples against playing ball on Sunday. As a player and manager, he was not available on Sundays. He wasn't missed that much as a player. He was a catcher, but he hit only .239 in 120 major league games and once was victimized for 13 stolen bases in a game. He was however a brilliant teacher and innovator. After a period as both field manager and business manager of the Browns, he joined the Cardinals as president of the club in 1916. After 1925 he concentrated on his front office job.

In 1919 Branch conceived the farm system. Unable to outbid the rich clubs for players, he decided to grow his own, and his minor league chain was one reason for the Cardinals' five flags in nine years, 1926–1934. Eventually he had eight hundred players under contract on fifty teams.

Rickey had taken over a team $175,000 in debt and made it a champ. He also instituted ladies' day, the Knothole Gang to get kids interested in the game, the batting cage, and the sliding pit.

After the season in 1942, he moved to the Dodgers and laid the groundwork for the champions of 1947 to 1955. He eventually sold his stock in the club for a cool million.

He moved on to Pittsburgh in 1951. There Rickey left a legacy that produced a flag in 1960 after he had gone. His trial balloon of a Continental League pushed baseball to expand in the 1960s.

He was elected to the Baseball Hall of Fame in 1967.

EPPA RIXEY
Pitcher, Phi (N) 1912–17, 1919–20, Cin (N) 1921–33
The winningest National League lefthander until Warren Spahn—and still the losingest—Rixey was a control artist who seldom walked anyone and seldom whiffed anyone. If Spahn hadn't broken his record, he said, nobody would have known about him. That's an exaggeration, but he seldom pitched for teams that were likely to make him a household name at World Series time.

Straight off the University of Virginia campus, Rixey began on the 1912 Phillies in the shadow of Pete Alexander. He was 11–12 on the 1915 champs and lost his only World Series game.

He was 22–10 for the second-place Phils in 1916, lost 21 for them in 1917, then went into the Army for a year in France. He lost 22 in 1920 as the Phillies finished last.

Switching to the sixth-place Reds, Rixey won 20-plus three times, including a league-leading 25–13 in 1922, when they rose to second. The six-five stringbean with a big sweeping motion was voted the Reds' all-time lefthander in a 1969 fan vote. He pitched for twenty-one years, amassing a career record of 266–251. His home run ratio, one per forty-eight innings, was the best in the Ruthian era.

He was named to the Baseball Hall of Fame in 1963.

CAL RIPKEN, JR.
Shortstop, Bal (A) 1981–

Ripken is the best power-hitting shortstop since Ernie Banks. Originally a third baseman, he was switched to short in 1982, his first full year with the Orioles. When he slugged 28 home runs and batted in 93 runs, he was named Rookie of the Year. His second season was even better. He led the AL in hits (211), doubles (47), and runs (121), while hitting .318, with 27 homers and 102 RBIs. The Orioles were World Champions and Ripkin was named MVP.

Although he's been chosen on the AL All-Star team each year since 1983, his batting average and RBIs have slipped, mirroring the Orioles' slippage in the standings. Extremely durable, Ripken's consecutive-game streak of over 1,200 games was second only to Lou Gehrig's after the 1990 season.

PHIL "SCOOTER" RIZZUTO
Shortstop, NY (A) 1941–42, 1946–56
Rizzuto played on ten Yankee pennant winners and in nine World Series. A superior fielder, he led AL shortstops in fielding in 1949 and 1950. Those were his best offensive years, too, as he scored over 100 runs each season. His 1950 season won him the MVP, as he hit .324, fifty-one points above his career average.

A Yankee broadcaster, the five-foot-six Rizzuto has remained highly visible in New York, and his "Holy cow!" has become his trademark.

As a rookie in 1941, he was called to the mound by Lefty Gomez. "Kid, is your mother in the stands?" Lefty asked. "Yes, sir, Mr. Gomez," Phil replied. "Well, stay here and talk to me a little; she'll think you're giving advice to the great Lefty Gomez." That day Phil hit his first home run and circled the bases with his face wreathed in smiles.

ROBIN ROBERTS
Pitcher, Phi (N) 1948–61, Bal (A) 1962–65, Hou (N) 1965–66, Chi (N) 1966
Roberts had great control and a fastball. He came close to a rare 30 wins with 28 in 1952, and came within 14 of winning 300 games.

His moment supreme came in October 1950, when he hurled the Whiz Kids to their first flag in thirty-five years. After pitcher Curt Simmons was drafted, the Phils lost their comfortable lead and went into the final game—against the Dodgers—only one game ahead. Robin, taking up the slack, was making his third start in five days. He battled Don Newcombe into the tenth inning, 1–1, before Dick Sisler's home run finally won it for Robin.

In the Series a weary Roberts started Game Two, but this time he was the loser, 2–1, in the tenth on a home run by Joe DiMaggio. It was his only World Series. Though he won 20-plus for six years in a row and led the league in five of them, the Phils never got closer than third again.

He was voted MVP in 1952, when he was 28–7 with a fourth-place team. He was 6–0 against the champion Dodgers.

Roberts had excellent control—1.7 walks per game lifetime. In 1953–1954 he had the least walks and most strikeouts per game in the NL. But he gave up more than 500 home runs, including a then-record 46 in 1956, as hitters knew they could dig in on him.

Roberts was a workhorse, leading the league in complete games and innings pitched five times each. It finally cost him the snap in his fastball. Roberts was 10–22 in 1957, 1–10 in 1961. But he learned to pitch with finesse, went to the AL, and won another 52 games.

In 1976 he was named to the Baseball Hall of Fame.

BROOKS ROBINSON
Third Baseman, Bal (A) 1955–77
Robbie led AL third basemen in fielding average a record ten times, he won sixteen straight Gold Gloves, and he set the existing career records in assists, putouts, double plays, and fielding average. And he made some postseason plays that brought millions of viewers to their feet, cheering.

His best year at bat was 1964, when he hit .317 and led in RBIs and all the fielding categories for his position. The BBWA named him MVP. In twenty-three seasons, he had 268 homers, 1,357 RBIs, and a .267 batting average.

The postseason brought out the best in Brooks at bat as well. He hit .429 in the 1970 Series, sparkled in the field, and was named Series MVP. The next year he hit .364 in the ALCS and .318 in the Series.

Personable and extremely popular with Oriole fans, he could have been elected King of Baltimore during his playing days. He was elected to the Baseball Hall of Fame in 1983.

FRANK ROBINSON
Outfielder, Cin (N) 1956–65, Bal (A) 1966–71, LA (N) 1972, Cal (A) 1973–74, Cle (A) 1974–76. Manager, Cle (A) 1975–77, SF (N) 1981–84, Bal (A) 1988–
From 1956, when he blasted 38 home runs to tie the rookie record, until 1976, when he hit his last, Robbie was one of the best-hitting outfielders of all time. His career marks include 586 homers, 1,812 RBIs, 1,829 runs, 2,943 hits, and a .294 batting average. In 1970 he hit two grand slams in a single game.

Frank is also the Jackie Robinson of managing, the first black man to lead a white big league team. He managed the Indians to two fourth-place finishes and a fifth from 1975 to 1977, and later managed San Francisco and Baltimore.

An aggressive, intelligent leader, he's the first man to win MVPs in each league—1961 with the Reds and 1966 with the Orioles. He led them both to pennants, and in the latter year, his first in the AL, won the Triple Crown as well. The two Robinsons, Frank and Brooks, provided the punch for four Oriole champions: 1966, 1969, 1970, and 1971.

In 1982 he was named to the Baseball Hall of Fame.

JACKIE ROBINSON
Infield, Negro League, 1945, Kansas City Monarchs, Bkn (N) 1947–56
Aggressive, exciting, driven with an inner fire, Robinson battled his opponents, history, and himself. He made integration succeed, and in doing so helped the Dodgers win six flags. Historian David Q. Voigt calls him one of the five most pivotal men in baseball history—and he ranks right up there in American history as well.

He could drop a bunt, line a homer, or steal a base—whatever was needed to win. "If it wasn't for him," the Cards' Red Schoendienst once remarked, "the Dodgers would be in the second division."

Jack's story is familiar: football star at UCLA, an Army court martial (and acquittal) for refusing to sit in the back of the bus, a year with the Kansas City Monarchs (hitting .345), the surprise announcement that he would be the first black to sign in the white majors, the promise to Branch Rickey to turn the other cheek to insults, the jockeying, the knockdown pitches, the threat of a strike, and the triumphant rookie year of 1947.

Robinson was not the best black prospect, Negro Leaguers agree. But he was college-educated and had played with whites, two intangibles that Rickey sought above sheer talent.

Jackie was twenty-eight before he reached the white majors, his athletic peak behind him. Yet he revolutionized the game with his running, dancing off base to rattle the pitcher, and 19 steals of home—5 in one year. It was a new brand of ball, and blacks who followed Robinson's footsteps perfected it.

Jack's best season was 1949. He led the league in batting and stolen bases, knocked in 124 runs, and won the MVP, as the Dodgers won the pennant by a single game.

In 1951 the Dodgers were fighting to stave off the Giants' amazing drive. On the final day, against the Phils, with the bases loaded, Jack made a spectacular catch of Eddie Waitkus's drive up the middle to preserve the tie. In the fourteenth he walloped a homer to win it and end the season all tied up. The Giants, however, won the three-game playoff for the pennant, somewhat obscuring one of Robinson's greatest seasons.

Robinson played for only ten years. He finished with a .311 career batting average, but more important, he led his team to six pennants.

After retiring, Robinson became active in politics and spoke out militantly on civil rights. He was one of the first to denounce the game for not hiring black managers. At last, the tensions took their toll, the fires burned out, and he died at the age of fifty-three, leaving the game unalterably changed.

He was named to the Baseball Hall of Fame in 1962.

WILBERT ROBINSON
Catcher, Phi (AA) 1886–90, Bro-Bal (AA) 1890, Bal (AA) 1891, Bal (N) 1892–99, StL (N) 1900, Bal (A) 1901–02. Manager, Bal (A) 1902, Bkn (N) 1914–31
Uncle Wilbert was chubby and cherubic, a former catching star with the great Orioles, later the lovable manager of Brooklyn's Daffiness Boys and winner of two pennants.

He's one of only two men to get seven hits in a nine-inning game—he drove in 11 runs that same day in 1892. A lifetime .273 hitter, Robbie had three .330-plus years with the Orioles.

In 1911 he joined his old teammate and friend John McGraw as Giant coach. His patient handling helped make an $11,000 beauty out of the former "$11,000 lemon," Rube Marquard.

But the friendship with McGraw broke up in an argument over a missed sign in the 1913 World Series, and Robbie went to manage the crosstown Dodgers. He raised attendance, started a Bonehead Club for stupid plays, and became its first member when he handed the wrong lineup card to the umpire. He agreed to catch a baseball dropped from a plane; the ball turned out to be a grapefruit and splattered all over his chest, and thinking the wet was blood Robbie though he'd been killed. He once benched a player because he couldn't spell his name for the lineup card.

Incredibly lax as a disciplinarian, Robbie nevertheless had a knack for developing pitchers.

Robbie won Brooklyn's first twentieth-century flag in 1916. He finished fifth in 1919, hired hunchbacked Eddie Bennett as batboy, and finished first in 1920. He left Bennett home and lost the last four games of the World Series in Cleveland. He fired Eddie and fell back to fifth in 1921. He almost won again in 1924 but lost to McGraw by one and a half games.

He was elected to the Baseball Hall of Fame in 1945.

WILBUR "BULLET JOE" ROGAN
Pitcher, Negro League, 1917–46, Los Angeles White Sox, Kansas City Monarchs
Little (five-six) Rogan pitched for the Kansas City Monarchs a decade before Satchel Paige, and most black vets who saw them both believe that Joe was the better. Monarch second baseman Newt Allen said, "Satchel had the stuff, but Rogan had the brains."

Joe's 109 wins are second best for the black leagues. Satch is fourth with 100, though several of Paige's seasons have not yet been compiled, and he won 63 more in the white majors and minors. On the other hand, Rogan did not begin pitching in the big time until he was thirty.

Satch was languid and loose, Bullet Joe stocky and dour. Paige threw his fastball in a cup, Rogan threw a farago of curves, sliders, and palm balls all over the plate. Satchel was a comedian at bat, Joe hit cleanup on one of the greatest murderers' rows in blackball annals.

Casey Stengel also called Rogan "one of the best, if not the best, pitchers that ever lived." He discovered Rogan in the Arizona desert with a black cavalry team on the Mexican border in 1918. Stengel, a Kansas City native, tipped off the Monarch owner, and Joe's pro career was launched at the age of thirty.

He pitched and batted the Monarchs to three straight flags, 1923–1925, hitting .426, .450, and .355. On the mound he was 12–9, 19–10, and 12–2 in the 100-game Negro League seasons. He was probably the MVP in 1924 or 1925—if not both. His postseason record was .421 at bat, 8–4 on the mound.

In fifteen games against white big leaguers, Joe hit .389. In one 1929 game, Al Simmons went 0 for 5 against Joe, and struck out three times.

EDDIE ROMMEL
Pitcher, Phi (A) 1920–32
In 1922 Rommel had one of the finest seasons of all time— 27–13 for the seventh-place A's (they were a last-place team without him), a feat almost as amazing as Carlton's 27–10 with the last-place Phils of 1972.

The next year he led the league in losses, 18–19 with the sixth-place A's. In five roller coaster years, 1921–1925, Ed and his knuckler led the league in victories two times and in losses twice.

By the time the A's dynasty blossomed, Ed was past his prime. Nevertheless, he was 28–11 during the pennant-winning seasons of 1929 to 1931.

He later became an outstanding AL umpire.

PETE "CHARLIE HUSTLE" ROSE
Outfielder/First Baseman/Third Baseman/Second Baseman, Cin (N) 1963–78, 1984–86, Phi (N) 1979–83, Mon (N) 1984. Manager, Cin (N) 1984–89
The most exciting player of his age, Charlie Hustle monopolized center stage with his unsuccessful pursuit of Joe DiMaggio's hit streak in 1978 and his successful pursuit of Ty Cobb's lifetime hit record in 1985.

Rose played more games than any other man (3,562), batted more times (14,053), made more hits (4,256), stands second in doubles (746), and fourth in runs (2,165). He had fourteen .300 years and ten 200-hit seasons (Cobb had only nine), won three batting titles, and made the NL All-Star team in seventeen seasons at five positions. He was Rookie of the Year in 1963, MVP in 1973, and played in his last World Series in 1983.

He was a hell-for-leather baserunner who wasn't very fast. He was a great hitter who lacked home run power. On any given day in his career there were probably a couple of hundred players in the majors with more talent. None made as much out of his talent as Rose. He didn't drink or smoke and kept himself in perfect shape. He worked and he hustled. In an exhibition game with the lordly Yankees in the early 1960s, he ran out a walk. "Charlie Hustle," they sneered. Rose turned the putdown into a compliment.

He played hard every day. He played wherever he was needed. And he loved every inning. Long after some of those Yankees who sneered had retired, in part because they disdained conditioning as much as Pete's gung-ho style, Rose was winning games with head-first dives and key hits.

Above all, Rose was a winner. Pete played on four pennant winners in Cincinnati during the 1970s, then he signed a lucrative contract with the Phillies in 1979 and helped them to two more pennants in the 1980s. *The Sporting News* voted him Player of the 1970s, then Man of the Year in 1985.

"There are a lot of players better than me," Rose said, "but I do the same thing day in and day out, year in and year out."

Rose's post-playing career has been marked by disappointment, controversy and personal tragedy. In his first five years as Cincinnati manager, he was unable to lift his team above second place. But there was worse to come. In 1989, Commissioner Bart Giamatti suspended him from baseball for life, after investigating accusations that Rose had bet on baseball games, including those involving the Reds.

And 1990 brought more ugly headlines, as Rose was sentenced to five months in prison for tax evasion. A hot talk-show topic was whether Rose—in spite of his playing record—should be denied entrance into the Hall of Fame.

AL ROSEN
Third Baseman, Cle (A) 1947–56
For a few years, Al Rosen was one of the most feared hitters in the American League. He played thirty-five games for the Indians from 1947 to 1949, but couldn't move Ken Keltner off third base until 1950. That year his 37 homers set an AL rookie record not broken until 1987. In 1953 he was AL MVP, narrowly missing the Triple Crown with a .336 batting average, while leading the

league with 43 homers (still the record for AL third basemen) and 145 RBIs.

In 1954 he was on his way to an equally impressive season when he suffered a broken finger. The injury permanently affected his grip on the bat. He returned to the lineup and helped the Indians set the AL record with 111 victories in winning the pennant, but his batting stats fell off badly. He retired two years later. From 1950 to 1954, he averaged .298, 31 home runs, and 114 RBIs.

EDD ROUSH
Outfielder, Chi (A) 1913, Ind (F) 1914, Nwk (F) 1915, NY (N) 1916, 1927–29, Cin (N) 1916–26, 1931
Roush was the Tris Speaker of the NL. He made circus catches and won batting titles—.341 in 1917, his first year as a Cincinnati regular, and .321 in 1919. He just missed the one in between, losing by two points to Brooklyn's Zach Wheat.

Edd's 1919 title helped the Reds win the flag, but he hit only .214 in the Series. Not that it mattered; that was the year the Black Sox decided to lose the Series.

Roush swung the heaviest bat in the league, a 48-ounce club, but he wasn't a home run hitter; only 67 of his 2,376 career hits went the distance. He was a singles hitter, but darned consistent. In both 1921 and 1922 he hit .352; then in 1923 he slumped to .351.

Roush was an independent cuss who held out year after year just so he could miss spring training. When he *really* got into a money dispute in 1930, he held out the entire season.

He was named to the Baseball Hall of Fame in 1962.

CHARLES "RED" RUFFING
Pitcher, Bos (A) 1924–30, NY (A) 1930–42, 1945–46, Chi (A) 1947
Mired with the bottom-of-the-barrel Red Sox of the late 1920s, Ruffing seemed to go with the flow, compiling a 39–96 record with appropriate sky-high ERAs. In 1928 he was 10–25; the next year 9–22.

Traded to the Yankees in 1930, he became the new improved version. Buoyed by better defense and far more hitting, Ruffing's pitching "became much better," as though a weight had been lifted. His victories shot up as his ERA dropped. Four straight years (1936–1939), he won 20, and he had eight other seasons of at least 14 wins. His total Yankee record was 231-124. In six World Series he was 7–2, with a 2.63 ERA.

The burly redhead was primarily a fastball pitcher, but though he was often lauded for his "pinpoint" control, he walked more than 100 in three different seasons and finished his career with a total of 1,541 free passes.

Ruffing had hoped for a career as an outfielder, but a childhood accident cost him four toes on his left foot. No longer able to run, he became a pitcher. However, he remained an excellent hitter for a pitcher, averaging .269 with 36 career home runs. He was often used as a pinch-hitter.

He was named to the Baseball Hall of Fame in 1967.

AMOS RUSIE
Pitcher, Ind (N) 1889, NY (N) 1890–95, 1897–98, Cin (N) 1901
Rusie helped revolutionize the game. The Hoosier Thunderbolt was the fastest pitcher of the 1890s. In 1893 they moved the pitching distance back five feet (and six inches) to its present distance because of him and a few others. At the old fifty-foot distance (measured from the front of the box, not the back), Rusie had struck out 341, 337, and 288 from 1890 to 1892. After they moved it back, his whiffs dropped to 208—and everyone's batting average jumped up.

Rusie was as wild as he was fast. He whiffed 1,934 batters and walked 1,704. His 289 walks (in 549 innings) in 1890 is the record. In four seasons he led the league in both walks and strikeouts. Amos was a workhorse, often going over 300 innings pitched and twice over 500.

In the eight years he pitched for the Giants, Rusie won 20 or more in each of those eight years. His top year was 1894, 36-13, plus 2 more wins in the Temple Cup playoff over Baltimore. His ERA that year of 2.78 was awesome compared to the NL average of 5.32.

In 1895 he was 23–23, as the Giants finished twelfth. He sat out 1896 in a dispute with his owner, who tried to subtract a fine he had levied from the pitcher's salary for the coming year. Rusie went to court, and the other owners paid the fine and Rusie's 1896 salary rather than see the reserve clause tested.

As the league's top box-office draw he returned in 1897 and went 28–10, as he lifted the Giants from seventh to second.

His wins fell to 20 in 1898, and he blamed it on the wear on his arm. When the club tried to cut his pay again, from $3,000 to $2,000, Rusie sat out for two years. In 1901 he was traded to Cincinnati, but his arm was gone and he retired after three games. The Giants did better on their end of the trade, picking up a kid pitcher named Christy Mathewson.

Rusie, who compiled a 245–174 mark in only nine full seasons, was named to the Baseball Hall of Fame in 1977.

BABE RUTH
Outfielder, Bos (A) 1914–19, NY (A) 1920–34, Bos (N) 1935
There has never been another figure in American sports like the Babe. Gargantuan—nay, Rabelaisian—in his appetites, prodigious in his production, he is the most famous athlete this nation has ever produced. Maris and Aaron topped some of his records, but they can never top him in American mythology.

Ruth revolutionized the game. Authorities disagree whether his home runs gave birth to the lively ball or vice versa. They also disagree on whether Babe created attendance records with his homers or whether the postwar Roaring Twenties prosperity created them. But Babe gave the game a lift after the Black Sox scandal and personified his time as no other American has.

No one has dominated the game as the Babe did.

He began as a lefthanded pitcher with the Red Sox. He went 18–8 in his first full season, 23–12 as a sophomore, and 24–13 in 1917, his third year. He led the AL in ERA in 1916. Yet his hitting was so impressive that he became a part-time outfielder in 1918 and won his first home run crown, with 11 in ninety-five games. In 1919, still batting against the dead ball, he crushed 29 homers, breaking a record that had stood for thirty-five years.

In 1920 he was sold to the Yankees for an announced

figure of $100,000 (in truth it was far more). He arrived in New York the same year the lively ball arrived in baseball. *They* hit a new record 54 homers (in only 458 at bats!), batted .376, and led in RBIs with 137. The next year the Babe had arguably the greatest season any batter ever had: 59 home runs, 171 RBIs, 177 runs, a .378 batting average, and an otherworldly slugging percentage of .846. Only one batter was able to top his 59 homers during the next forty years—the Babe with 60 in 1927.

All told, he led in home runs twelve times, in RBIs six, in runs scored eight, in walks eleven, in slugging percentage thirteen times, and in batting average only once (in 1924 with .378).

His career totals: 714 homers, 2,209 RBIs, 2,174 runs, a record 2,056 walks, a record .690 slugging average, and a .342 batting average.

Equally important to the Ruthian Mystique was the Public Ruth, the hefty child-man the fans loved. The Private Ruth ate too much, drank too deeply, partied too long, womanized too indiscriminately, cursed like a wounded Marine, held petty grudges, and sometimes bullied lesser mortals. The Public Ruth signed autographs, was naughty but nice, hit home runs for hospitalized boys, grinned on cue, and even "called his shot" before a home run in the 1932 World Series. The "called shot" illustrates how pervasive was the Ruthian Mystique; any other batter would have been merely pointing and yelling at the Cubs' pitcher, as the Chicago players always insisted he did. But the public chose to believe The Ruth had pointed to the center field bleachers moments before hitting his fifteenth and final World Series home run out there. The fans believed he could do anything, so they let him.

In 1936, a year after he retired, he was named to the Baseball Hall of Fame.

NOLAN RYAN
Pitcher, NY (N) 1966, 1968–71, Cal (A) 1972–79, Hou (N) 1980–88, Tex (A) 1989–
There's no way to know if Ryan threw faster than any of the great fastballers of the past, but no one has ever thrown so fast for *so long* as Ryan. In his twenty-fourth major league season, at the age of forty-three, he can still strike out batters with heat. As a sheer athlete, he is the greatest pitcher who ever lived. No one else has pitched six no-hitters. His 383 strikeouts in one year (1973) stands as the record—and that was accomplished in the first year of the DH, so he had no patsies in his opposing lineups. His total K's are over 4,700, more than 600 past his nearest rival. His 300-plus wins were accomplished with mostly average or less support. "My job is to give my team a chance to win," he said. "I have no control over how many runs they score."

Actually, Ryan's control was for many years the only flaw in his pitching. He led his league eight times in walks. In 1977 he walked 204 in 299 innings (he also struck out 341). His career total of walks will probably stand as the record as long as his strikeout total—perhaps well past the time this page has turned to dust. But, as his fastball has slowed—relatively—his control has improved.

Surprisingly, he's never won a Cy Young Award. But consider his 1974 season: most innings pitched, 333; fewest hits per nine innings, 5.97; most strikeouts per nine innings, 9.92; and a 22-16 record with a *last-place team.*

RYNE SANDBERG
Second Baseman, Phi (N) 1981; Chi (N) 1982–
Sandberg has been the top NL second baseman of the 1980s and may be rated one of the best ever by the time he's done. He played third base in 1982, his first season in Cubland, but since has settled in at second to make it his own. He could probably play any field position. He has an above-average range and arm, and if he lacks the flash of some more acrobatic second-sackers, he's a whole lot steadier. In 1990 he set the second base records for consecutive games and chances without an error. He hustles all the time—not always the easiest thing to do in Chicago where they lose a lot of 10–2 games. He's got home run power—40 in 1990—and a steady bat.

In 1984, when the Cubs won their division (yes, Virginia, there is a first place!), Sandberg hit .314, with 19 homers and 19 triples! He led the league in three-baggers and in runs scored (114). He was a runaway MVP.

RON SANTO
Third Baseman, Chi (N) 1960–73, Chi (A) 1974
The Brooks Robinson of the NL, Santo gave the Cubs some fine third base play in the 1960s. If he wasn't quite the fielder Brooks was, he outhit, outhomered, and out-RBI'ed Robby. Santo, Billy Williams, and Ernie Banks provided a tremendous power trio for Chicago.

Ron is the fourth highest home run hitter among third basemen, with 342, behind Mike Schmidt, Eddie Mathews, and Graig Nettles. He had ten seasons of 90 or more RBIs. In his best year, 1969, he drove in 129, as the Cubs made their strongest bid for a flag.

The pitchers feared him; he led in walks four times.

In the field Ron was double-play champ five times, putout king six times straight, and assist leader seven straight. Among NL third basemen, only Schmidt rivals him in total chances.

RAY SCHALK
Catcher, Chi (A) 1912–28, NY (A) 1929.
Manager, Chi (A) 1927–28
Schalk was small for a catcher (five-nine, 165 pounds), and his nickname "Cracker" reportedly referred to his view from behind, which was said to resemble a cracker box. At any rate he was a cracker jack catcher. He caught 100 or more games in twelve seasons, including eleven in a row. He led AL catchers in fielding eight times.

In 1920 Schalk caught four 20-game winners (Red Faber, Ed Cicotte, Lefty Williams, and Dickie Kerr), a feat matched only by Baltimore's Elrod Hendricks. Over the years Ray caught four no-hitters (Jim Scott, Joe Benz, Cicotte, and Charlie Robertson), a feat matched by no one. The last one was a perfect game. Until his death in 1970 Schalk sent telegrams of congratulation to every no-hit catcher.

Schalk caught spitters, shine balls, emery balls, and knucklers. It earned him a fistful of broken fingers. Fast enough to steal 30 bases in 1916, a record for catchers, Schalk was the first catcher to back up first and third bases. He could make putouts at all four bases and did.

Ray had a strong arm, and he holds the AL record for career assists by a catcher. He had a good record against Cobb especially.

Offensively he wasn't an asset. His career batting average was only .253, and he had no power. He lived by his glove, wits, durability, and honesty. With the White Sox of 1919, that last quality was important, as eight of Schalk's teammates conspired to lose the World Series that year.

Schalk was named to the Hall of Fame in 1955.

WALLY SCHANG
Catcher, Phi (A) 1913–17, 1930, Bos (A) 1918–20,
NY (A) 1921–25, StL (A) 1926–29, Det (A) 1931
Wally Schang just had a knack for showing up at the right time.

In 1913, his rookie year, the Philadelphia A's won the pennant and World Series. They followed with another pennant in his sophomore season. Traded to Boston in 1918, he arrived just in time to enjoy the Red Sox' last world championship. Three years later, he was dealt to the Yankees, who had never finished first. But Wally's luck held, and they took the flag in his first three seasons in pinstripes. They even won the world championship in 1923. In 1926 he was traded again—to the St. Louis Browns. Not even Wally and a world of rabbits' feet could help the Brownies, but he did get himself traded back to Philadelphia in 1930. The A's were already world champs from 1929, but with Schang backing up Mickey Cochrane, they repeated.

All in all, Schang played on seven pennant winners in his nineteen years, but it wasn't all serendipity.

Schang was an excellent defensive catcher with a deadly arm; in a 1920 game he threw out six runners. He also had a nice sting in his bat. He is the first switch-hitter to hit home runs both lefthanded and righthanded in a single game. He hit over .300 six times and had a career .284 average. On days he wasn't catching, he was sometimes put in the outfield or at third base to keep his bat in the lineup.

MIKE SCHMIDT
Third Baseman, Phi (N) 1972–89
Schmidt is not only the greatest hitter to play third base—everyone knows that—he is also arguably the greatest fielder. His homers are famous; less well known is his 404 assists in 1974, the most ever by an NL third baseman. Three years later his 396 assists were the *second* highest total in NL history. He won eight Gold Gloves in a row.

Mike also won eight home run crowns, four RBI titles, and three MVPs. His home run to at-bat ratio ranks in the top ten all-time, and he is one of only 14 major leaguers to hit over 500 home runs.

He paid a high price—nearly one strikeout every four at-bats, or about three for every home run. But it was indisputably worth it. He put the Phillies into the playoffs six times.

He was amazingly durable. Until his season-ending rotator tear in 1988, he had never been sidelined for an extended period.

RED SCHOENDIENST
Second Baseman, StL (N) 1945–56, 1961–63, NY (N)
1956–57, Mil (N) 1957–60. Manager, StL (N) 1965–76,
1980, 1989
Schoendienst has spent nearly half a century in a baseball

uniform, mostly that of the St. Louis Cardinals. He arrived in St. Louis in 1945 as a wartime leftfielder, leading the NL in stolen bases with 26 as a rookie. An arm injury caused his switch to second base the next year, as the Cardinals won the World Championship.

A smooth fielder—he led league second basemen in fielding seven times—Red was chosen to ten All-Star Games. His best seasons were 1952–54, when the red-haired, freckle-faced switch-hitter batted .303, .342, and .315. Redbird fans were shocked when he was traded to the New York Giants in mid-1956. Another trade a year later took him to Milwaukee, where he helped the Braves win two pennants and one world title.

In 1959, he was stricken with tuberculosis and played only five games, but he made a remarkable comeback at age thirty-seven in 1960 to win back his job with the Braves. Schoendienst put in three final seasons as a reserve infielder and pinch-hitter with the Cardinals.

Schoendienst was the Cardinals' manager for a dozen seasons, 1965–76, winning a World Championship in 1967 and a second pennant in 1968. A Card coach since 1979, he's twice served as interim manager.

In 1989 he was named to the Hall of Fame.

TOM SEAVER
Pitcher, NY (N) 1967–77, 1983, Cin (N) 1977–82,
Chi (A) 1984–86, Bos (A) 1986
Of all the great pitchers since World War Two, Seaver may have been the best. He won 311 games, struck out 3,640 batters, compiled a career ERA of 2.86, but most important he seemed able to win with both good and losing teams. As Rookie of the Year in 1967, he was 16–13 with the seventh-place Mets, and he just kept doing that sort of thing. In twenty years of pitching, his winning percentage exceeded his team's in sixteen seasons.

On the other hand, he could ride a winning team. He was 25–7 for the "Amazin' Mets" world champs in 1969, when he won his first Cy Young Award. The second came for his 19–10 mark and NL-leading ERA with the 1973 pennant winners. Two years later he was 22–9 with an ERA of 2.38 and won his third Cy Young.

Although he led the NL in strikeouts five times, had ten seasons with over 200 strikeouts, and still holds the NL record with 19 whiffs in a nine-inning game, he was never a "thrower." He exhibited excellent control and pitch selection from the start. He just happened to be a heady control pitcher who also threw a ninety-eight-mile-per-hour fastball throughout most of his career. His power came from tremendous lower body strength and a low pitching motion designed to take full advantage of his leg muscles. When he was throwing correctly, his right knee would drag on the ground with each pitch.

Tom resembled Christy Mathewson—clean-cut, handsome, intelligent, a student of pitching, and a devotee of the *New York Times* crossword puzzle. Ironically, when all votes are in, it may be a toss-up as to who was the best righthander a New York NL team ever had.

FRANK SELEE
Manager, Bos (N) 1890–1901, Chi (N) 1902–05
Selee was the number one dynasty builder of the 1890s. Only a so-so minor league outfielder, he turned to managing in the mid-1880s and it was immediately Eureka time.

He quickly earned a brace of minor league pennants and a reputation as a judge of talent who could "tell a ball player in his street clothes." In 1890 the Boston Beaneaters brought him in fron Omaha along with star pitcher Kid Nichols. It took Selee only a year to get all the pieces in place. His Beaneaters won pennants in 1891-92-93 and then tacked on two more in 1897-98. The Baltimore Orioles are the team most modern fans remember, but Selee's Bostons won more flags. Among his stars: Nichols, Hugh Duffy, Tommy McCarthy, Jimmy Collins, Billy Hamilton, Herman Long, and Bobby Lowe.

When he went three years without a pennant, Boston decided the magic was gone and cut him loose. Sixth-place Chicago snapped him up quicker than you could say Tinker to Evers to Chance—to name only three of the players he discovered and installed as Cub regulars. Chicago zoomed up in the standings, reaching second by 1904. In mid-1905, tuberculosis forced Selee to take an indefinite leave of absence, which became definite at his death in 1909. Frank Chance, the "Peerless Leader," won four pennants with the team Selee built.

Mild mannered and courteous, Selee never had a team finish lower than fifth. Over sixteen years, he won at a .598 clip by identifying talent and putting it on the field where it belonged. Among his most successful moves were to turn catchers Chance and Fred Teney into first basemen and to shift third baseman Joe Tinker to shortstop.

JOE SEWELL
Shortstop, Cle (A) 1920–30, NY (A) 1931–33
Sewell was rushed into the Cleveland infield when shortstop Ray Chapman was killed during the 1920 pennant race. He hit .329 in the stretch to help rally the club back from the tragedy and win a three-way race.

Overshadowed by teammates such as Tris Speaker, and later by Ruth and Gehrig, little Joe quietly made a place among the top shortstops of all time. A good defensive player, he had a career batting average of .312 and both scored and batted in over 1,000 runs.

With his forty-ounce bat, Joe punched the ball where they ain't. Nine times he hit over .300, playing in a hitter's dream era. In 1923 he reached .353 and knocked in 109 runs. In 1925 he hit .336, cracked 204 hits, and batted in 98 runs with only one HR.

Sewell is famous for not striking out—only 114 times in 7,132 at-bats. In 1925 he whiffed an incredible four times in 608 at-bats.

He also ran up a streak of 1,103 consecutive games.

His brother Luke caught for many years. The two were teammates on the Indians.

Joe was named to the Hall of Fame in 1977.

JAMES "CY" SEYMOUR
Outfielder, NY (N) 1896–1900, 1906–10,
Bal (A) 1901–02, Cin (N) 1902–06, Bos (N) 1913
Seymour won 25 games for the Giants of 1898. He was fast but wild as a starving wolf, leading the league three times in walks. Meanwhile, his hitting was improving every year, and when it topped .300 it was suggested that he do the rest of his throwing from the outfield.

He was with Cincinnati in 1905, when he had one heckuva year. He led the NL in—get this—hits, doubles, triples, RBI, batting average and slugging average. But

he only finished second with his eight home runs because his teammate, one Fred Odwell, hit nine. Mr. Odwell is perhaps the most obscure and unusual home run champ of all time, having hit exactly one homer before 1905 and never hitting another after that one year when he deprived his fellow Red of a triple crown.

URBAN SHOCKER
Pitcher, NY (A) 1916–17, 1925–28, StL (A) 1918–24
The spitballer Shocker won 20 four years in a row for the Browns in 1920–1923, as St. Louis finished fourth, third, second, and fifth. In 1921 he led the league in wins, going 27–12 with a third-place club. In 1922 he led in strikeouts and went 24–17, almost pitching the Brownies to the pennant over the Yankees. Shocker would be remembered much better today if he had spent his prime years with the Yankees. His first two seasons (1916–1917) were in New York, and he was traded back to them in 1925. That was the year Babe Ruth got his famous bellyache and the team fell to seventh; Shocker would have been better off staying with the Browns. He won 19 and 18 the next two years, as the Yankees won pennants, but heart disease took his life in 1928 at the age of thirty-seven.

AL SIMMONS
Outfielder, Phi (A) 1924–32, 1940–41, 1944,
Chi (A) 1933–35, Det (A) 1936, Was (A) 1937–38,
Bos (N) 1939, Cin (A) 1939, Bos (A) 1943
In 1930, when Bucketfoot Al was at his best, Connie Mack said he wished he had nine players named Simmons. Actually he didn't even have one; Al's real name was Alois Szymanski.

When he first joined the A's in 1924, everybody hooted. He had a classic "foot-in-the-bucket" batting stance with his left foot pointing at third base, just the way kids are taught *not* to do it from the time they pick up a bat. Critics said he'd better change or he'd be back in Milwaukee double quick. He hit .308 as a rookie, but really convinced them the next year when he went to .384 and pounded out 253 hits, the second highest total in AL history and the most ever by a righthanded batter. After that, when he stood there like he was going to kill ants on the foul line, the critics just said, "Nice stance, Mr. Simmons."

Al hit .392 in 1927, but his top years were the three A's pennant seasons of 1929–31. In 1929 he led in RBIs, with 34 homers and a .365 batting average; *The Sporting News* named him the AL MVP. In 1930 he led in batting with .381, and had 36 homers and 165 RBIs. Then in 1931 he upped his average to .390 and led the league again.

Mack started selling his stars as the Depression hurt him pretty hard. Simmons was sent to Chicago in 1933, and though he had a few more good years, the great ones were over. He finished with 2,927 hits, 307 home runs, 1,827 RBIs, and a .334 batting average.

In Game Four of the 1929 World Series, he ignited the famous ten-run seventh inning rally, when the A's came from an 8–0 deficit. Al led off with a blast over the roof against the Cubs' Charlie Root. Before the inning ended, Simmons had not only singled to set up the ninth run but also scored number ten himself.

He was named to the Hall of Fame in 1953.

TED SIMMONS

Catcher, StL (N) 1968–80, Mil (A) 1981–85,
Atl (N) 1986–88

Simmons was an outstanding hitter for a catcher. Unfortunately he wasn't an outstanding *catcher* for a catcher. His receiving, pitcher handling, and throwing were adequate at best. In 1973 he led NL catchers in assists, but much of that may reflect the liberties runners were taking. Ted always seemed like a first baseman waiting to happen.

At bat rather than behind it, he was one of the best, hitting over .300 seven times in his sixteen seasons as a regular. Five times he had 20 or more homers, and he had eight seasons of 90 or more RBIs.

GEORGE SISLER

First Baseman, StL (A) 1915–22, 1924–27, Was (A)
1928, Bos (N) 1928–30. Manager, StL (A) 1924–26

The original "Gorgeous George," Sisler was the best first baseman who ever lived until 1923. He was one of the best *players* ever—until 1923.

Consider: from 1916 to 1919, when the dead ball was still the order of the day, he hit .338 for the Browns. There was another hitter in St. Louis at the time, a fellow named Hornsby. Sisler outhit him. Sisler only hit 38 home runs, but no one was hitting many then. He did steal 45 bases in 1918 to lead the AL. And he also was already regarded as the equal of Hal Chase with a glove, which would make him the best-fielding honest first baseman up till then.

So in 1920 they brought in the lively ball, and everyone's batting average went up—but nobody's more than Sisler's. From 1920 through 1922 he hit .407, .371, and .420. His hit totals were 257 (the all-time record), 216, and 246. He hit 19 homers in 1920, led in stolen bases in 1921 and 1922, batted in over 100 runs, and scored over 125 each season. And all the time he kept fielding up a storm. Ty Cobb, who handed out compliments as often as he handed out hundred-dollar bills, said Sisler was "the nearest thing to a perfect ballplayer."

And then came 1923. Sisler missed the whole year with a sinus infection that caused double vision. And when he came back in 1924, he was just a very good ballplayer. He played seven more years, but he never regained the magic.

He was elected to the Hall of Fame in 1939.

ENOS "COUNTRY" SLAUGHTER

Outfielder, StL (N) 1938–42, 1946–53,
NY (A) 1954–59, KC (A) 1955–56, Mil (N) 1959

In ten dramatic seconds in the 1946 World Series, Slaughter dashed all the way from first base to immortality. His mad race to score the winning run for the Cardinals in the final game was the greatest highlight of his career, but it was certainly not the only highlight.

He had ten seasons hitting .300 or better, finishing with a career mark right at an even .300. He led the NL in RBIs in 1946, and though he wasn't a big home run hitter (169 in nineteen seasons), he led the league in triples twice. He was a fine fielder with a good arm. He played on two world championship teams with the Cardinals in 1942 and 1946; then in the 1950s he helped the Yankees win three pennants.

And until Pete Rose came along, Slaughter was known as the epitome of hustle. When people said "a player like Slaughter," they didn't mean a .300 hitter or a strong-armed outfielder; they meant a smart, aggressive player who never walked anywhere on a ballfield when he could run and who'd cut your throat to win a game.

He was named to the Hall of Fame in 1985.

OSBOURNE "OZZIE" SMITH

Shortstop, SD (N) 1978–81, StL (N) 1982–

The acrobatic Wizard of Oz may be the best defensive shortstop of all time. "He's changed fielding for shortstops," admits Hall of Fame shortstop Lou Boudreau. Smith's famous back flip when he runs to his position at the start of a game is for show, but it illustrates the kind of defensive plays he can make. His range is exceptional, and while his arm is not, his ability to make accurate, off-balance throws makes up for any lack of strength. No shortstop has ever made more assists than Oz in 1980 (621). He helped take the Cards to three World Series, in 1982, 1985, and 1987.

Originally a good field/no hit player, Smith has turned himself into a valuable offensive performer. He's become adept at drawing walks, held his strikeout totals low, and moved his batting average up. He hit .303 in 1987. Although he has no home run power, his ability to steal bases somewhat makes up for that. When he hit a rare home run in the 1985 LCS, he explained, "I was trying to hit the top half of the ball and hit the bottom by mistake."

At a salary of $2 million a year, Ozzie is also changing the old dictum that singles hitters drive Fords.

REGGIE SMITH

Outfielder, Bos (A) 1966–73, StL (N) 1974–76,
LA (N) 1976–81, SF (N) 1982

Until injuries wore him down, Smith was one of the best all-around players in baseball. He was also generally unrecognized as such. He joined the Red Sox in 1967, played a mean center field, contributed 15 homers, and helped the team to the pennant. He got one vote for Rookie of the Year.

Over the next six seasons, he hit .300 three times for the Sox and cracked as many as 30 home runs, yet never finished in the top twenty in MVP voting.

Traded to the NL, he got a little more recognition. With the Cardinals in 1974, he hit .309 and drove in 100 runs. In 1977 he led the Dodgers to a pennant with 32 homers and a .307 batting average. He was fourth in the MVP voting, the only time he ever made the top ten.

Though he may have been overlooked when he played, his career totals mark him as a star: 314 home runs, 2,020 hits, 1,092 RBIs, and a .287 batting average.

EDWIN "DUKE" SNIDER

Outfielder, Bkn (N) 1947–57, LA (N) 1958–62,
NY (N) 1963, SF (N) 1964

"Willie, Mickey, and the Duke" gave New Yorkers the game's three hardest hitting center fielders from 1951 to 1957. For the last four of those years the most consistent home run hitter of the three was Snider. He hit 40 or more homers five years in a row, an NL record tied only by Ralph Kiner. He was helped by often being the only lefthanded batter in the Dodgers' lineup, and Ebbets Field's cozy confines didn't hurt.

Snider was a smooth-fielding center fielder for six Dodger pennant winners. He was usually at his best in the World Series. His lifetime 11 Series home runs and 26 RBIs are the best marks for any National Leaguer. He hit four homers in both the 1952 Series and in the 1955 Series, when the Dodgers finally defeated the Yankees for the world championship.

The popular, articulate Duke is the all-time Dodger home run leader. His career totals are 407 homers, 1,333 RBIs, 1,259 runs scored, and a .295 batting average.

He was named to the Hall of Fame in 1980.

WARREN SPAHN
Pitcher, Bos (N) 1942, 1946–52, Mil (N) 1953–64,
NY (N) 1965, SF (N) 1965
The winningest lefthander of all time, Spahn won 20 or more games 13 times, tying Christy Mathewson's NL record. He needed only 11 more wins to top Grover Alexander's 373 lifetime victories. Yet he didn't win his first major league game until he was twenty-five years old.

He seemed to get better as he got older. His good control became great; his fastball slipped a little, but he added a screwball and slider to his curve and change-up; and, of course, he got smarter and smarter. His ability to place his pitches and vary the speeds kept batters always off-stride.

He led the NL in strikeouts four straight years (1949–1952), in ERA twice, and in victories eight times, including five straight (1957–61). His 63 shutouts are the most by an NL lefty.

Spahn had his first 20-win season in 1947; then, curiously, he fell to 15 wins in 1948 when the Boston Braves won the pennant. Nevertheless the Braves' shallow pitching staff was described as "Spahn, [Johnny] Sain, and pray for rain." He was still at the top of his game in 1957–1958, when the Milwaukee Braves won pennants. In 1957 he was voted the Cy Young Award.

In 1960, at the age of thirty-nine, he pitched his first no-hitter. The next year, five days past his fortieth birthday, he pitched his second.

Spahn was elected to the Hall of Fame in 1973. He would have been elected earlier, but he found it so hard to hang up the spikes that he kept on pitching in the minors in 1966–67, delaying the onset of his eligibility for the Hall.

AL SPALDING
Pitcher, Boston (NA) 1871–75, Chi (N) 1876–78.
Manager, Chi (N) 1876–77. Executive
Spalding might have won 300 if we knew how many he pitched as a teenager in top independent ball. His wins are unknown, but they included one as a seventeen-year-old in 1867 over George Wright's Washingtons, 29–23.

Al's official record starts when the National Association was founded in 1871. Playing for Boston, his totals were 20–10, 37–8, 41–15, and 52–18. In 1875 he posted an amazing 57–5, including 24 in a row, pitching in every game his team played. He also hit .300 each of the last four years, as the Bostons won four straight flags.

Lured to Chicago with the formation of the National League in 1876, Spalding helped write the new league's constitution. He was that first year's biggest winner at 47–12, as Chicago won the flag.

Then his arm finally gave out. He left behind a lifetime W-L percentage of .789. Of course it's the record.

Al opened a sporting goods business and issued the first Spalding Baseball Guide in 1877.

In 1882 he took over as president of the champion Chicagos with stars such as Cap Anson, George Gore, Larry Corcoran, and Fred Goldsmith.

He led a world tour of teams in 1888 and was instrumental in the NL's successful war with the Players League in 1890. He helped plan the Chicago World's Fair of 1893. In 1905 he organized a commission to determine where baseball was born: Chadwick had said England; Spalding chauvinistically said America, supporting the Abner Doubleday legend, a claim he repeated in 1911 in his history of baseball, *America's National Game*.

Spalding ran for the U.S. Senate in 1910 and lost. He died in 1915, but his name remained an essential part of the game, on every official NL ball used until the year 1976.

He was named to the Hall of Fame in 1939.

TRIS SPEAKER
Outfielder, Bos (A) 1907–15, Cle (A) 1916–26,
Was (A) 1927, Phi (A) 1928. Manager, Cle (A) 1919–26
Speaker revolutionized center field play, taking advantage of the dead ball to play behind second base almost as a fifth infielder. He made unassisted double plays on short flies (the only man to do it in a World Series), was the pivot man on 4–8–3 plays, and even took pickoff throws from the pitcher. Yet he could still go back to get flies over his head. He is second in lifetime putouts and total chances in the outfield and first in assists—35 of them as a rookie in 1909. He may have been the first outfielder to test the wind by throwing grass in the air.

Tris won only one batting title, but he topped .375 six times and had a lifetime mark of .344. In 1916 he broke Ty Cobb's streak of five straight batting crowns. His 793 doubles are first on the all-time list, and his 223 triples are sixth. "Spoke's" 3,514 hits knocked in 1,528 runs and he scored 1,881 times. He almost never struck out. He stole 433 bases.

And he did it all after breaking his right arm as a kid in Texas and learning to throw and hit lefty instead.

Speaker broke in with the Red Sox in 1909 and soon formed, with Harry Hooper and Duffy Lewis, perhaps the best defensive outfield ever. He was MVP in 1912 as the Sox won pennants that year and in 1915. Traded to Cleveland in 1916, he became player-manager in 1919 and led the Indians to their first pennant in 1920. He hit .388.

He was named to the Hall of Fame in 1937.

WILLIE STARGELL
Outfielder/First Baseman, Pit (N) 1962–82
The only man to hit a ball clear out of Dodger Stadium, a feat he accomplished twice, Stargell is also the only man to hit four into the upper deck of Three Rivers Stadium. He hit seven over the roof of old Forbes Field (only nine others have done it even once).

Forbes was tough on Willie. In one stretch, 1965–1966, he hit only 19 home runs at home, 41 on the road. His totals took a jump after the Pirates moved to Three Rivers, though even that is a pitchers' park. Willie led the league in homers in 1971 and 1973.

In 1979 Stargell won three MVPs—in the regular season (tying Keith Hernandez), the playoffs, and the World Series.

In the World Series versus the Orioles, Willie came up in the seventh game with Pittsburgh losing 1–0 in the sixth. He crashed his third home run of the Series, to give the Pirates the championship.

In twenty-one years, he thumped 475 homers, batted in 1,540 runs, and compiled a .282 batting average. He paid a high price for his homers, striking out once every four at-bats.

Not included in Willie's numbers are "intangibles." Much of his 1979 MVP Award was for leadership. As captain of the Pirates, he led with a combination of quiet example and symbols. He passed out "Stargell Star" decals for outstanding plays and invented (and exemplified) the "We are family" slogan which tied the team together.

He was elected to the Hall of Fame in 1988.

DANIEL "RUSTY" STAUB
Outfielder/First Baseman, Hou (N) 1963–68,
Mon (N) 1969–71, 1979, NY (N) 1972–75, 1981–85,
Det (A) 1976–79, Tex (A) 1980
"*Le grand orange*" (the big redhead), as Montreal fans called him, Staub played well for some undistinguished teams (the Astros, Expos, Mets, and Tigers), usually flirting with .300 and 100 RBIs.

His best year, 1967, he hit .333 in the Hitters' Horror, the Astrodome. He led the league with 44 doubles.

Rusty finally found a winner with the Mets in 1973. He hit only .269 during the season but shone in the World Series, hitting .423. His five RBIs won Game 4 6–1.

After he got too "grand" to play the outfield, he became an outstanding DH for the Tigers, twice batting in over 100 runs. Then he finished as a deadly pinch hitter for the Mets. In his final season, he became the eleventh man to register 100 career pinch hits.

GEORGE STEINBRENNER
Owner
The Yankees' controversial owner was often more newsworthy than his team. He took over the team in the early 1970s when the once lordly Yankees had wallowed in the depths of the AL for nearly a decade. His stated intention was to return the Yankees to their former glory. He made the moves that brought four pennants to New York, 1976–1978 and 1981, and the club was competitive in most years.

Steinbrenner showed an admirable willingness to spend huge amounts of money in pursuit of excellence. He signed such free agents as Catfish Hunter, Reggie Jackson, Goose Gossage, Dave Winfield, and Jack Clark. His employees were well paid for their efforts.

On the other hand, his constant switching of managers—nineteen changes after Steinbrenner bought the team—became a national joke. Billy Martin was hired and fired five times. His verbal battles with his own players, his public second-guessing, and his interference in the daily operation of the team opened him to criticism from those who believed his influence was counterproductive.

He brought back to the Yankees many fans who had switched allegiance to the Mets. At the same time, he sent a large number of former Yankee fans scurrying to Shea Stadium. Volatile, yet often charming, he was forced by the commissioner to give up running the Yankees in 1990 for conduct not in the best interests of baseball.

CHARLES "CASEY" STENGEL
Outfielder, Bkn (N) 1912–17, Pit (N) 1918–19,
Phi (N) 1920–21, NY (N) 1921–23, Bos (N) 1924–25.
Manager, Bkn (N) 1934–36, Bos (N) 1938–43,
NY (N) 1949–60, NY (N) 1962–65
Stengel won ten pennants in twelve years, hid a bird under his hat, and doubled up a Senate hearing with the funniest monologue in the history of the *Congressional Record*, which, as Will Rogers said, "is goin' some."

Casey put in fourteen seasons as a useful NL outfielder, compiling a .284 batting average and a reputation as a prankster. The bird, for example, he had captured in the outfield, then let escape when he strode to the plate and doffed his cap to the fans.

Stengel embarked on a managerial career in the minors and low majors, frequently getting a pink slip. ("I say fired," he said, "because there is no doubt I had to leave.")

Leading the lowly Dodgers in 1934, he achieved brief fame when Giant manager Bill Terry sneered, "Is Brooklyn still in the league?" The insulted Bums knocked New York out of the pennant.

With the old Boston Braves, 1938–1943, Casey finished seventh four times in a row. When he was hit by a Boston cab and broke his leg, the city voted the cabbie MVP.

Case went back to the minors, won a flag at Milwaukee and another at Oakland in the Pacific Coast League.

Then fate struck with a surprise call from the Yankees. In Stengel's first year, 1949, the club was hit with a record number of injuries. All summer he juggled his lineup and platooned players, a strategy that would become his trademark. On the last day of the season, the Yankees caught the Red Sox for the pennant. They beat the Dodgers in the World Series to begin an amazing string of five straight world championships, 1949–1953.

In 1954 he won 103 games—and finished second to Cleveland's 111. His Yanks won four pennants in a row (1955–1958) and two more world championships, missed a year, then won Casey's final pennant in 1960. His ten pennants and seven world titles in twelve years is considered by some the greatest managerial accomplishment of all time.

The Yankees fired him as too old, but he took on the new challenge of wet-nursing the perfectly awful Mets through their first four seasons. Though the team finished a well-deserved last each year, they did show improvement each season.

Casey's warmth, his pixie sense of humor, and his unique, rambling, ungrammatical, nonstop monologues made him perhaps baseball's most loved figure since Babe Ruth.

He was named to the Hall of Fame in 1966.

NORMAN "TURKEY" STEARNES
Outfielder, Negro leagues, 1921–41: Montgomery Grey
Sox, Detroit Stars, New York Lincoln Giants, Kansas
City Monarchs, Cole's American Giants, Chicago
American Giants, Philadelphia Stars, Detroit Black
Sox
Stearnes is the all-time HR champ of the Negro leagues,

beating the more famous Gibson 171–137. (Josh, it is true, had more HR/AB.) Turkey led or tied the league seven times from 1923–1932; Josh, six. He averaged 30 every 550 at bats. Stearnes led the league in BA once, with .430 in 1935. His lifetime mark was .341. Against white big leaguers, he hit .313. His fellow Detroiter, Hank Greenberg, heard the stories and asked Cool Papa Bell if they were true. Bell assured him that they were.

Turkey weighed only 168 and swung from an odd left-handed stance, choking up on the bat, with his right toe pointing up. Yet he smashed some long blows, including a 450-footer into the upper deck of Comiskey Park. He played an excellent center field and was fast enough to lead off, which he often did with a home run. In 1935 he and Mule Suttles played together on the western league champion Chicago American Giants, Stearnes batting lead-off and Suttles clean-up.

Stearnes played his best in the postseason, hitting .474 in nine games, including four HRs. In the 1929 playoff against St. Louis—and Mule Suttles, the black leagues' number-two man in homers—Turkey hit .481 with 11 RBIs and the first homer ever hit over the 450' wall at Hamtramck Stadium.

"If they don't put him in the Hall of Fame," says Bell, "they shouldn't put *anybody* in."

HARRY STOVEY
Outfielder/First Baseman, Wor (N) 1880–82, Phi (AA) 1883–89, Bos (P) 1890, Bos (N) 1891–92, Bal (N) 1892–93, Bkn (N) 1893

Stovey hit .326 for the old Philadelphia AA club in 1884 while leading the league in triples and runs. Of course it was an expansion year, with three leagues and thirty-three teams.

A husky righthanded hitter, renowned for his gentlemanly conduct, he topped his league in homers five times, with a high of 19 in 1889. He retired in 1893 with 121 career home runs, the record at the time. It was later broken by Roger Connor in 1895 and by many more since.

Despite stealing as many as 97 bases in a season and scoring more than one run per game over his career, Stovey finished with only a .288 batting average. His strengths were his strong arm, power, and speed. He reportedly once circled the bases in fourteen seconds.

BRUCE SUTTER
Pitcher, Chi (N) 1976–80, StL (N) 1981–84, Atl (N) 1985–88

Sutter was one of the most effective relief pitchers in history. His split-finger fastball baffled NL hitters and sent other NL pitchers to learning how to throw it.

He came to the NL with the Cubs in 1976 and in his second season saved 31 games. His 6 wins and league-leading 37 saves earned him the Cy Young Award for 1979.

Traded to the Cardinals in 1981, he continued to star. His 36 saves in 1982 helped the team to the world championship in 1982. In 1984 he had a career-high 45 saves, to lead the NL for the fifth time.

He signed with Atlanta as a free agent for 1985, but after a disappointing season, he underwent elbow surgery. He pitched in only 16 games in 1986 and missed all of the 1987 season.

Sutter pitched with occasional success in 1988 before retiring at the end of the season.

DON SUTTON
Pitcher, LA (N) 1966–80, 1988, Hou (N) 1981–82, Mil (A) 1982–83, Oak (A) 1985, Cal (A) 1985–87

Sutton won 20 games only once, but he kept plugging away to become one of the big winners of all time. He was probably both hurt and helped by the five-day rotation, which cuts about five starts out of each season but might mean longer careers: Sutton pitched for twenty-three seasons.

Don was 21–10 for the 1976 Dodgers for his only 20-win year, but he had eleven other seasons with 15 wins or more. One of his best years was 1980. He was only 13–5, but he led the NL in ERA.

Sutton never pitched a no-hitter, but he has five one-hitters, tying the NL record.

He was accused of throwing "doctored" pitches, but his long career is evidence of either his legality or his legerdemain.

JESSE TANNEHILL
Pitcher, Cin (N) 1894, 1911, Pit (N) 1897–1902, NY (A) 1903, Bos (A) 1904–08, Was (A) 1908–09

A great control pitcher, lefthander Tannehill won 20 games six times from 1898 to 1905 and had a 197–116 career record. He averaged only 1.6 walks per nine innings. He helped pitch the Pirates to the 1901 and 1902 NL pennants. He won the 1901 ERA title with a 2.18 mark.

The Pirates won the 1903 pennant without Tannehill; he and Happy Jack Chesbro jumped to the AL New York Highlanders (Yankees) that year. It cost him a chance to appear in the first World Series.

He was a disappointing 15–15 in New York and was traded to Boston, the winner of the 1903 Series. His 21–11 season helped Boston win the 1904 pennant, but again he lost his World Series chance when the NL's Giants refused to meet the AL champs.

With Cy Young, Bill Dineen, and Tannehill doing most of the pitching, Boston set a team record low of 1.5 walks per nine innings in 1904.

JACK TAYLOR
Pitcher, Chi (N) 1898–1903, 1906–07, StL (N) 1904–06

Taylor won 20 games four times and 152 during his career, but his claim to fame is an uncanny ability to finish what he started. On June 20, 1901, he pitched a complete game. Through his next 186 starts—more than five years' worth—he would pitch a complete game every time he started. One game went nineteen innings; another went eighteen. He finished them both. On another occasion, he pitched both ends of a doubleheader. Fifteen times he relieved other, less stouthearted hurlers, and each time finished the game. Taylor wasn't a particularly imposing physical specimen. At five-ten and 170 pounds, he was average or a little less for a pitcher of his day. Finally, on August 9, 1906, he was relieved in a game.

Although he pitched only ten years in the NL, two of them partial seasons, Taylor had six seasons of over 300 innings and completed 278 of his 286 starts.

GENE TENACE

Catcher, Oak (A) 1969–76, SD (N) 1977–80,
StL (N) 1981–82, Pit (N) 1983

Tenace was the steady catcher for the Oakland A's dynasty that won three World Series, 1972–74. A decent enough defensive catcher, he was actually very dangerous with the bat, despite a dreary .241 batting average. Over his career, he was nearly as likely to get a walk as to get a hit—984 walks to 1,060 hits. He led the AL twice in bases on balls and had a .380 on-base average.

When he did get a hit, the odds were five-to-one it would go out of the park. Nearly 20 percent of his hits were homers—201.

Tenace first showed he could be something out of the ordinary in the 1972 World Series. He'd just limped through a .225 season with 5 homers, followed by an .059 LCS. He looked like a soft touch to the Reds. So in his first two Series at bats he homered, not only setting a record but also providing the A's with all the runs they needed in a 3–2 win. For the Series he hit .348 and had 4 homers and 9 RBIs.

BILL TERRY

First Baseman, NY (N) 1923–36. Manager, NY (N)
1932–41

Terry was the last NL batter to hit .400, but it doesn't impress some modern commentators, who point out that when Memphis Bill hit .401 in 1930, the whole blessed league hit .303. Still, anyone who knocks out 254 hits as Terry did in 1930 deserves respect. And it wasn't that he was a one-year wonder. He played fourteen seasons and topped .300 eleven times. Besides his .400 year, he had averages of .372, .354, .350, .349, and .341—the last mark also being his career average.

He wasn't Lou Gehrig, of course. His 154 career homers don't look all that great against Gehrig or Foxx, two AL first basemen of the period. There are two answers to that. The first is obvious: Terry wasn't the home run hitter that either of those brawny gentlemen were. He was a line drive hitter who hit to all fields. And that's part of the second answer: he played his home games in the Polo Grounds, which had wonderfully short foul lines for dead pull hitters and horrifyingly deep power alleys for anyone who wasn't. Terry made the decision to go with the percentages, which was considered smart baseball in his day. One tipoff is that in five of the six years from 1927 through 1932, he averaged 20 homers a year. The sixth year was 1930 when he hit only 9. That looks suspiciously as though he cut his swing just a little when he saw a chance to hit .400.

Some oldtime sportswriters are kind of happy to see Terry low-rated. He was the kind of player who, if he thought you were a jerk, said so. Some call that "refreshing honesty"; others call it "arrogance." Whatever. Once the reputation was set, he couldn't say anything to please some writers. One day in 1934, after he'd become manager of the Giants, a writer asked him what he thought of the Dodgers, at a time when everyone knew the Dodgers were pretty awful. Terry, trying to be one of the guys, made a little joke. "Is Brooklyn still in the league?" he asked. Naturally it got blown all out of proportion, especially when the Dodgers beat the Giants a couple of times at the end of the season to knock them out of the pennant.

One thing about Terry: he was a much better fielder than the home run-hitting first sackers of his time. And he also became a better manager, winning three pennants and a world title in 1933 when he was a player-manager.

SAM THOMPSON

Outfielder, Det (N) 1885–88, Phi (N) 1889–98, Det (A)
1906

Big Sam played in two Hall of Fame outfields. In the early 1890s, he, Billy Hamilton, and Ed Delahanty made a heavy-lumber trio for the Phillies. In 1894 Hamilton hit .404, Delahanty .407, and Thompson .407. The second Hall of Fame outfield was in 1906, when the Detroit Tigers had suffered so many injuries that they asked Sam out of retirement. For the final eight games of the season, he lined up with Ty Cobb and Sam Crawford. He hit a mere .226, but he was forty-six years old at the time.

Thompson started with the old NL Detroit Wolverines in 1885. At first they didn't have a uniform to fit his six-two, 220-pound frame, and he squeezed into what was available. Running out a double, he split his pants right up the middle.

The modest, good-humored slugger became the most popular player in Detroit. In 1887, when they won the NL pennant, he led the NL with a .372 batting average and 166 RBIs.

Thompson compiled a .331 career batting average. One of the best home run hitters of the nineteenth century, he led the NL with 20 in 1889 and 18 in 1895. His 127 career homers rank him second only to Roger Connor for the era. And Thompson's ratio of RBIs to games played is the best of *all* time.

An outstanding fielder, he was renowned for his powerful arm. Reportedly he popularized throwing all the way from the outfield to the catcher on one bounce.

In 1974 he was named to the Hall of Fame.

LUIS TIANT

Pitcher, Cle (A) 1964–69, Min (A) 1970, Bos (A)
1971–78, NY (A) 1979–80, Pit (N) 1981, Cal (A) 1982

The herky-jerky Cuban dervish Tiant won 20 games four times and finished with a 229–172 record in a career that looked to be over in the middle. After four merely good years with Cleveland, he was suddenly great in 1968 with a 21–9 mark and a league-leading 1.60 ERA. But the next year he led the AL in losses at 9–20. Traded to Minnesota, he appeared washed up with no arm left.

Boston took a chance on him, but he struggled to 1–7 in 1971. But the next year he was the Comeback of the Year with 15–6 and his second ERA title (1.91). He won 20 games three times for the Red Sox but was at his best in 1975, when his season's record was 18–14. The Sox won the division; then Luis started them on a three-game sweep in the LCS with a three-hitter over Oakland. He opened the World Series against the powerful Reds with another shutout, threw a 163-pitch, complete game victory in Game Four, and went seven innings in Game Six before weakening.

After games Luis would entertain writers, puffing his long Cuban cigar and telling stories. Some say he took the cigar with him into the shower.

Tiant's father, Luis Sr., had been a skinny lefthanded junk pitcher in the Negro Leagues. Neither had seen the other pitch until the older man got a visa to leave Havana and was given an emotional welcome to Fenway Park.

JOE TINKER
Shortstop, Chi (N) 1902–12, 1916, Cin (N) 1913, Chi (F) 1914–15. Manager, Cin (N) 1913, Chi (F) (1914–15, Chi (N) 1916.

Sometimes the whole is more than the sum of its parts, and that sort of rep seems to forever follow Tinker, Evers, and Chance. Bound together in F. P. Adams's famous bit of doggerel and in their simultaneous election to the Hall of Fame in 1946, the impression persists that they were three ordinary guys who somehow made magic only as a trio. The impression is unfair. Each was an excellent player, and no doubt they could have proved their worth as individuals.

Manager Chance's Cubs depended on pitching, speed, and defense. They won four pennants and two world championships from 1906 to 1910 using that recipe. None of the Cubbies hit much in those dead-ball days; the 1907 world champs didn't have a .300 hitter, their RBI leader had 70, and the Cubs' best home run man had 2. Of course, most other NL teams were similar.

In that context, Tinker was a pretty decent hitter for his time. His .262 average ranks right up there with those of shortstops of later, better-hitting eras. He usually knocked in 60–70 runs a season, and he hit 6 homers in 1908. He was practically a slugger! For some reason, Lord knows why, he always hit Christy Mathewson well, and since the Giants were always trying to nudge the Cubs out of first place, that was a very valuable talent. Once on base, Joe also had the required speed, stealing 336 bases over his career.

But Joe was paid to field. And that he did very well, leading NL shortstops five times in average, in assists twice, and in putouts twice. He even led once in double plays. Only once, you ask? Isn't that the maneuver T-to-E-to-C were supposedly such whizzes at? Well, they were—everyone who saw them agrees—but the Cubs' pitchers just didn't give them as many chances to get two as some other combinations had. In the case of double plays, it looks like the sum wasn't equal to the parts.

JOE TORRE
Catcher/First Baseman/Third Baseman, Mil (N) 1960–65, Atl (N) 1966-68, StL (N) 1969–74, NY (N) 1975–77. Manager, NY (N) 1977–81, Atl (N) 1982–84, StL (N) 1990–

Torre started out with the Braves as a catcher because he kept getting fat. The idea was that catchers don't have to run much, something fat guys hate to do. Everything went well for a while. Joe didn't have the best arm in the world, but it wasn't embarrassing. He did all the other catching chores okay, and he was a terrific hitter. They selected him for the NL All-Star team from 1963 through 1967. The only thing was that catchers need rest every couple of days. In Joe's case, he usually spent his day of rest at first base so they could keep his bat in the lineup.

In 1969 he was traded to the Cardinals, who put him at first base full-time. Along about then, Joe figured he'd better get serious about a diet. It wasn't quite as quick as with the frog who turned into a prince, but in 1971, slim, trim Torre emerged as a third baseman and had the sea-

son of his life. He led the NL in batting (.363), hits (230), and RBIs (137). He was named MVP.

Although he never got back to that level, Torre had a lot of good seasons in his eighteen years. He finished with a .297 career average, 252 homers, and 1,185 RBIs.

CRISTOBAL TORRIENTE
Outfielder, Negro League, 1914–32, Cuban Stars, Chicago American Giants, Kansas City Monarchs, Detroit Stars, Gilkerson's Union Giants, Atlanta Black Crackers, Cleveland Cubs

Many authorities pick the big Cuban on the all-time All-Negro League outfield. In 1919 Torriente, Oscar Charleston, and speedster Jimmy Lyons patrolled the outfield for the Chicago American Giants, making perhaps the best trio ever among black teams.

Torriente was called the Ruth of Cuba, and in 1920 the two faced each other in Havana, one on one. Torri got three homers, two off first baseman Highpockets Kelly and one off Ruth himself. The Babe went 0-for-4 against Cuban hurling. Two home runs were usually good enough to lead the league for an entire season in the cavernous parks down there, making Torri's feat the more remarkable.

Cris wore bracelets, which he shook before going to bat, and a red bandana around his neck, for his Cuban club, the *Rojos*, or Reds.

He was Cuban batting champion three times, stolen base champ four times, and triple and home run champ five times each. In 1919–1920 he led in every batting department.

Torriente's highest averages were .401 in Cuba, 1915–1916, and .402 in the States in 1920. He led the Negro League in 1923 with .389.

Torri pitched occasionally and even played a left-handed second base. He was also a notorious playboy, and he died an alcoholic at an early age.

ALAN TRAMMELL
Shortstop, Det (A) 1977–

Trammell is a good glove in the process of becoming an outstanding bat. He and second baseman Lou Whitaker have held down the keystone positions for the Tigers for thirteen seasons. A four-time Gold Glove winner, Trammell's home runs climbed from 2 in 1978, his first full season, to 14 in 1983, to 28 in 1987. His batting average, though its climb has not been so steady, began in the .260s and peaked with .343 in 1987, as the Tigers won the Eastern Division.

In 1984, when the Tigers won the World Series, Trammell was named Series MVP for his .450 average, including two homers and six RBIs in five games.

HAROLD "PIE" TRAYNOR
Third Baseman, Pit (N) 1920–37. Manager, Pit (N) 1934–39

Traynor used to be figured as the best-ever third baseman, but his halo has tarnished a little of late, as sluggers like Eddie Mathews, Brooks Robinson, Graig Nettles, and Mike Schmidt have appeared. There even seems to be some effort to show that he wasn't even the best when he was playing, but that's a little harder to swallow.

Traynor, who usually batted fifth for the Pirates, was no

home run hitter; he knocked a mere 58 in his 1,941 games. Of course, half those games were in Forbes Field, where any righthanded batter who swung for the distant left field fence would have been considered a little goofy. Traynor doubled and tripled at a pretty good clip.

He seems to have driven runs home pretty well too, with seven seasons of 100-plus RBIs, but some critics worry that he didn't walk a whole lot. They also point out that batting averages were at an all-time high in the twenty years between the World Wars, making his .320 less impressive. However, it *does* happen to be the best for any of the third basemen who played during that period.

Traynor was regarded as the top-fielding third baseman of his day. A Pittsburgh sportswriter once wrote: "He doubled down the left field foul line, but Traynor threw him out." He led NL third sackers in putouts seven times, assists three times, and, surprisingly, only once in fielding average. There's no way to really rank him against modern third basemen. His career and single-season marks have been far surpassed by post-World War Two players, perhaps because more business comes to the hot corner now that most players try to pull the ball. Fielding stats being what they are, they neither prove nor disprove that he was the best gloveman playing third during his time. Most of the fans, teammates, and opponents thought he was, but they could be wrong.

Maybe they gave him extra for personality; Traynor was a genial, articulate man, with more friends than bookkeepers have decimal points. *The Sporting News* named him to its All-Star Major League team seven times between 1925 and 1933. He finished in the top ten in NL MVP voting six times through the same period. Let's put it this way, the people who looked at third basemen when Pie was playing thought he was Pie à la mode. Some moderns disagree. Of course, there are also people around today who can prove that Elvis lives, nobody ever walked on the moon, and fast food is good for you.

Traynor was named to the Hall of Fame in 1948.

PAUL "DIZZY" TROUT
Pitcher, Det (A) 1939–52, Bos (A) 1952, Bal (A) 1957
It was a wartime year, but in 1944 Trout was 27–14 and led the AL in ERA, complete games, innings pitched, and shutouts. Dizzy's teammate Hal Newhouser got the headlines with 29–9, but Trout may have been even better. He finished second to Hal in the MVP voting, 232 to 236.

In 1945 Diz was only 18–15 (while Newhouser was 25–9), but in the stretch, he pitched six games in nine days and won four of them, as the Tigers won the pennant on the final day. In the Series he had an 0.64 ERA but had to split his two decisions. He won the fourth game 4–1 and lost the sixth game in relief in the twelfth inning.

After the war, Trout's record slipped more than Newhouser's, but for two years they were terrific.

Trout's son Steve is a current major league pitcher, and their total of more than 250 wins makes them the winningest father-son combo.

GEORGE UHLE
Pitcher, Cle (A) 1919–28, 1936, Det (A) 1929–33, NY (N) 1933, NY (A) 1933–34
One of the best hitting pitchers ever, with a .288 career batting average, Uhle (pronounced "Yoo-lee") was also

one of the first to throw a slider, two decades before it became widespread in the 1940s. He was 26–16 for third-place Cleveland in 1923 and 27–11 for the second-place Tribe in 1926, leading in wins, complete games, and innings pitched each year. He was also first in putting men on base the latter year, with 300 hits and 118 walks, or a dangerous 11.8 per nine innings. George pitched a 20-inning game in 1929. He finished his seventeen-year career with exactly 200 wins.

ARTHUR "DAZZY" VANCE
Pitcher, Pit (N) 1915, NY (A) 1915, 1918, Bkn (N) 1922–32, 1935, StL (N) 1933–34, Cin (N) 1934
One of the Dodgers' Daffiness Boys, Dazzy didn't win his first big league game until he was thirty-one in 1922. Vance had pitched five complete games in seven days in the minors, causing a chronic sore arm which almost ended his career. He bounced around the minors for ten years until manager Wilbert Robinson of the Dodgers tried starting him every fifth day, instead of every fourth, the common practice.

Vance responded magnificently. His high-kick windup and extremely long arms (he had an eighty-three-inch reach) gave him a roaring fastball. Pitching with a tattered sleeve to confuse the hitters, he led the NL in strikeouts seven straight years, a record, in ERA three years, and in wins two.

Dazzy was the best pitcher in the league in 1924, with 28–6, as the Bums almost beat the Giants for the pennant. He won the MVP, even though Rogers Hornsby hit a mere .424 that year.

In 1925 the Bums fell to seventh, but Vance led in wins again, with 22–8. One was a one-hitter, and another, five days later, a rare 1920s no-hitter (against the Phils). In 1928 the Dodgers were sixth, but Vance was 22–10.

Vance was as famous for clowning as for pitching. He liked to party, often staying out until the detectives in the lobby yawned and went to bed. Then he would slip in unnoticed.

He was the key man in the famous play when Babe Herman doubled into a double play. Vance was on second base, but instead of scoring on Herman's drive, he rounded third and then went back to find Herman and one other runner sliding in from the opposite direction.

Vance was named to the Hall of Fame in 1955.

FLOYD "ARKY" VAUGHAN
Shortstop, Pit (N) 1932–41, Bkn (N) 1942–43, 1947–48
Next to Honus Wagner, Vaughan may have been the best-hitting shortstop ever, hitting over .300 twelve times, including his first ten years in the NL. His .385 in 1935 is the twentieth-century record for shortstops. In fourteen seasons he averaged .318 and led the league in runs scored three times. Vaughan had a good eye and rarely whiffed; from 1934 to 1936 he was the top NL hitter in drawing walks.

Though he was not a power hitter, Arky hit 19 homers one season and led the league in triples three different years. He slugged two home runs in the 1941 All-Star Game, the first man to do so.

He fielded his position well and led NL shortstops in putouts and assists three times each.

Vaughan was respected around the league for his honesty and integrity. In 1943, believing Brooklyn manager Leo Durocher had unfairly suspended another player and then lied about him to reporters, he handed in his uniform, threatening to leave the team until Durocher backed down. He retired at the end of the season and didn't return to the Dodgers until 1947, when Durocher was suspended for the season.

Vaughan was named to the Hall of Fame in 1985.

JAMES "HIPPO" VAUGHN
Pitcher, NY (A) 1908, 1910–12, Was (A) 1912, Chi (N) 1913–21

Like Harvey Haddix, lefthander Vaughn is remembered for one outstanding game, somewhat obscuring the fact that he pitched a number of excellent games. Indeed he was one of the best pitchers around during the World War One period. He didn't really settle in until he was twenty-six years old in 1914. But in seven years with the Cubs, he won 20 or more games five times, 10 once, and 17 once.

In 1918 he was 22–10 to lead the NL in wins, tops in ERA at 1.74, and led in strikeouts and innings pitched. In the World Series that year, he pitched three complete games and gave up only three earned runs, yet he was only 1–2.

Now about *The* game. On May 2 in Chicago, he hurled nine no-hit innings against Cincinnati. What made this no-hitter really special was that Fred Toney, pitching for the Reds, also tossed a no-hitter. So they went into the top of the tenth and Hard Luck Hippo gave up a single to light-hitting Larry Kopf. An outfield error followed, putting the runner on third. The next batter, Jim Thorpe, topped a little roller down the third base line. Vaughn was called Hippo because he ran like one, but he was on the ball quickly and shoveled it to the catcher. Too late. The runner slid in with the run. In the bottom of the tenth, Toney retired the Cubs hitless again.

BILL VEECK
Owner, Cle (A), StL (A), Chi (A)

Veeck sent a midget to bat, integrated the AL, invented the exploding scoreboard, put players' names on their uniforms, and gave baseball its first two-million-attendance team, the 1948 Indians. He even tried to field an integrated Phillies club in 1943 until Judge Landis shot down his quest for ownership.

With his open collar, his wooden leg (a souvenir of the Marines), and his extroverted twinkle, Bill was a fans' owner who lounged in the bleachers, chain-drinking beer and listening to gripes. He owned three different AL teams at various times.

He learned the game at the hotdog stand in Wrigley Field, where his father was general manager for the Cubs. Later, Bill himself became general manager of the minor league Milwaukee Brewers.

After the war Veeck brought Cleveland a pennant in 1948. His promotions brought in fans and he brought in the players, including Larry Doby, the AL's first black player and forty-two-year-old Satchel Paige. In the early 1950s, Veeck tried to save the Browns. Some of his gimmicks were outrageous, such as sending midget Eddie Gaedel to pinch-hit (he walked) and having the fans manage a game by holding up decision cards. As White Sox owner, he gave the team its first flag in forty years in 1959.

His iconoclastic ways alienated the other owners but enchanted the fans. He wrote about his adventures entertainingly in *Veeck as in Wreck*. He even wrote about his sabbatical as a race track owner in a book entitled *30 Tons a Day*. Veeck died in 1986.

GEORGE "RUBE" WADDELL
Pitcher, Lou (N) 1897, 1899, Pit (N) 1900–1901, Chi (N) 1901, Phi (A) 1902–07, StL (N) 1908–10

Lefthander Waddell had a terrific fastball, a biting curve, and exceptional control of his pitches. His life was fast, veered wildly, and had no control whatsoever. He is usually called eccentric, or erratic, or flaky, or unstable, or capricious. He was nutty. Completely uneducated, he fits the old line "If he had a brain, he would be dangerous."

He missed games because he was fishing, or helping the local firemen, or playing marbles, or drunk, or because he just forgot. He missed a World Series because he hurt his arm wrestling. He once dived into a river to save a drowning man—who turned out to be a log.

Everybody liked Rube, even all the managers who fired him, because they never knew if he'd show up or what he'd do if he got there. He *was* likable—a big, overgrown six-year-old.

People told all kinds of stories about him. He was so fast he poured ice water on his arm to slow himself down; he hit birds on the wing by throwing stones; he told his fielders to sit down while he struck out the side; and he did cartwheels off the mound after whipping Cy Young in a twenty-inning showdown. Actually, he did beat Young, 4–2, in twenty innings, and he may have done the outfield stunt a couple of times in exhibition games.

The only manager ever to have the patience to put up with him for an extended period was Connie Mack, who would have probably called the Mad Hatter "a little odd." Especially if he could pitch.

In truth, Waddell was a heckuva pitcher for Mack for four seasons, and a good pitcher for a couple more years after that. He led in strikeouts for six straight seasons, with 349 in 1904, a record that would stand until 1973. He won 97 games from 1902 through 1905 (but he lost 52 and the A's had strong teams). He got his ERA down to 1.48 in 1905 (but five other pitchers were under 2.00).

Finally, even Mack couldn't take it any longer, and he traded Waddell to the Browns in 1908. The fact that Waddell's pitching was slipping probably made it a little easier. Yet in his first game against the A's, Waddell struck out sixteen batters.

By 1910 Rube was back in the minors. A year or so after that, he was visiting in Kentucky when a flood hit. In an act that recalls how he used to help firemen, Waddell stood for hours armpit deep in freezing water, passing sandbags to repair a dike. He contracted tuberculosis and died in 1914.

He was elected to the Hall of Fame in 1946.

JOHN "HONUS" WAGNER
Shortstop, Lou (N) 1897–99, Pit (N) 1900–17. Manager, Pit (N) 1917

Some say Wagner was the best player of all time. He was voted into Cooperstown in 1936 right behind Cobb and ahead of Ruth. The argument goes that a great shortstop is inherently more valuable than a great outfielder. Certainly that's true in the field. What might be more to the point is to rank Wagner against Cobb and Ruth as a hitter. Even allowing for the differences in liveliness of the baseballs each batted against in his prime, Cobb and Ruth were probably more dangerous at bat.

Nevertheless Honus hit .300 seventeen years in a row and won eight batting titles in twelve years, 1900–1911. He had a career mark of .327, with 3,415 hits, 640 doubles, 252 triples (third best all-time), 101 homers, 1,736 runs, and 1,732 RBIs. He led the NL in stolen bases five times. He finished with 722, fifth best all-time. He reputedly stole second, third, and home three times in his career.

In Wagner's only showdown against Cobb, in the 1909 World Series, Ty called to him from first base, "Watch out, Krauthead, I'm coming down." The two-hundred-pound Honus knocked Ty's teeth loose with the tag. Wagner batted .333 to Cobb's .200, and stole six bases to Ty's two, as Pittsburgh beat Detroit in seven. (Wagner's stolen base mark stood until Lou Brock broke it in 1967.)

Wagner was so long-armed and bowlegged, they said he could tie his shoes without bending down. His batting stance, says writer Bob Broeg, resembled a man sitting on a bar stool. He used the hands-apart grip and swung at anything near the plate.

Whether Wagner was the best-*fielding* shortstop of all time, which you hear sometimes, or just one of the best of his day is hard to tell from fielding stats. He didn't become a full-time shortstop until his seventh NL season. He seems to have been a little rough at first, but he had great range. After he'd been at it for a few years, he led NL shortstops a couple of times in fielding average.

They say that when he fielded a grounder, his big hands scooped up dirt, ball, and all, and that he'd let everything fly, showering the first baseman in pebbles. Honus, who could embroider a story like Aunt Tillie could a seat cushion, said a dog once ran onto the field and snatched the ball; he said he threw both dog and ball to first for the out.

If his stories were incredible, at least you could tell them to your mother, he said. One estimate puts him as the most beloved man in baseball during the time between King Kelly and Babe Ruth. If so, he deserved the adoration. He always had time for a friend; he helped rookies; he had a drink now and then, but he was never a drunk; he was brighter than most but suffered fools with patience; and he never, *never*, acted the star. He also refused to let a cigarette company put his picture in their packs because he didn't want to encourage kids to smoke. He made them stop distributing one print, making the few in circulation the most valuable baseball cards in the world.

BOBBY WALLACE

Shortstop, Cle (N) 1894–98, StL (N) 1899–1901,
1917–18, StL (A) 1902–16. Manager, StL (A) 1911–12,
Cin (N) 1937

When Bobby Wallace was elected to the Hall of Fame in 1953, a lot of people asked who-in-hell he was. More than thirty-five years later, when fans file past his plaque at Cooperstown, most of them ask the same question.

To answer: Wallace was the first AL shortstop in the Hall, beating Joe Cronin by three years. He played in the majors for twenty-five years, although you could only count him as a regular for about fifteen. He hit .300 twice, but most years he was down around .250 and a couple of years he was lower yet.

He started as a pitcher with the old Cleveland Spiders of the NL, then moved to third base for a couple of seasons. In 1899 he became a St. Louis Cardinal and switched to shortstop. By 1902 he was so highly regarded that the St. Louis Browns of the new AL paid him a $6,500 advance and signed him to a five-year contract for $32,500, thus making him the highest-paid player in baseball. In sum, he was the Ozzie Smith of his day.

He was generally accepted as the best AL shortstop from 1902 until about 1910, which is a pretty good run. The ranking was based almost entirely on his glove. As usual, fielding statistics don't prove a whole lot. Wallace led in fielding percentage and assists three times each. Big deal! His most significant fielding figure is that he averaged 6.1 chances per game; only four shortstops have ever done better.

Naturally, playing for the Browns meant no World Series appearances and mostly losing teams. It's to Wallace's credit that somebody remembered him forty years later, and it's to the Hall of Fame's credit that they elected a shortstop (in 1953) just because he could field. They've only done that once or twice.

ED WALSH

Pitcher, Chi (A) 1904–16, Bos (N) 1917

The greatest spitballer, Walsh compiled the lowest lifetime ERA in history, 1.82. He was also one of the great ironmen of all time, four times leading the league in innings pitched, with an AL record of 464 in 1908. That's the year he won 40 games and almost pitched his "Hitless Wonder" White Sox to the flag. From 1907 through 1910, Walsh's ERAs were 1.60, 1.42, 1.41, and 1.26. That last one came in 1910, when he lost 20 games for a sixth-place club that hit .211 with seven home runs—for the whole team! He's the only man to lead the league in both ERA and losses at the same time.

A muscular product of the coal mines, Big Ed was square-shouldered and handsome. And he knew it. "He could strut sitting down," someone said.

In 1906 he was 17–13 with a team that hit .230. Ten of his wins were shutouts. In the World Series against the rival Cubs, Ed whiffed a then-record 12 men to win the third game on a two-hitter.

Walsh's finest season was 1908, when Chicago, Cleveland, and Detroit raced down to the wire. His team hit only 3 homers all year, one of them by Ed himself. He started 49 games and relieved in 17 more. He threw 11 shutouts, and won 40 games while losing only 15. He also saved 6.

Ed pitched seven games in the last nine days, including a doubleheader win over Boston, in which he gave one run, one walk, and seven hits. He threw fifteen runners out himself! The next day he pitched another nine innings, his third complete game in two days. In a head-to-head showdown against Cleveland ace Addie Joss, Ed fanned 15 and gave up only four hits—but Joss trumped him with a perfect game.

The next day Walsh was called in to relieve with the bases loaded, two out in the ninth, and Nap Lajoie at bat. He fooled Larry with a fastball instead of a spitter and got him on a called strike three. He would call it the greatest thrill of his career.

Walsh continued to work hard—370 innings in 1910, 369 in 1911, 393 in 1912. He won 27 games in each of the last two years, including a no-hitter. His arm gave out in 1913 and several comeback tries failed. He finished with 195 wins, 57 of them shutouts.

He was named to the Hall of Fame in 1946.

WILLIAM "BUCKY" WALTERS
Pitcher, Bos (N) 1931–34, 1950, Phi (N) 1934–38, Cin (N) 1938–48. Manager, Cin (N) 1948–49
For two magnificent years, 1939–1940, Walters was the premier pitcher in baseball. With Paul Derringer, he led the Reds to their first flags since 1919 after two decades of frustration.

In 1939 Bucky, 27–11, led in wins, ERA, complete games, and strikeouts, easily winning the MVP. In 1940 he led in wins again (22–10), plus ERA and complete games. Walters added two wins in the World Series, holding the Tigers to a 1.50 ERA.

In 1944 Walters had a 23–8 mark for the third-place Reds. He lost a perfect game on a two-out single in the eighth. When the 1948 season began, Bucky needed only two more wins to reach 200 and looked like a dead-bang cinch. But he'd also been named as the Reds' manager that year. He only got around to pitching in seven games and won none of them. Nevertheless, his 198–160 record isn't bad for a fellow who began as a third baseman and never pitched a game until he was in his fifth major league season.

LLOYD WANER
Outfielder, Pit (N) 1927–41, 1944–45, Bos (N) 1941, Cin (N) 1941, Phi (N) 1942, Bkn (N) 1944
A good singles hitter, Lloyd rode to Cooperstown on the coattails of his big brother Paul. The two played next to each other for Pittsburgh from 1927 through 1940.

Lloyd was a steady .300 hitter in an era of steady .300 hitters. As a rookie in 1927, he made 223 hits, a rookie record; 198 of them were singles, still a record for anyone. He led the NL with 133 runs scored. He hit .355, plus .400 in the World Series, as the Yankees crushed the Pirates in four straight.

He made 221 hits in 1928 and 234 in 1929, when he led the league with 20 triples. An illness cost him most of the 1930 season, but he came back to lead the league with 214 hits in 1931.

Lloyd rarely struck out—only 173 times, an average of once in every 45 at-bats. In 1941 he played in 77 games without a single strikeout. The bad news was that he didn't walk very often either, not nearly often enough for a lifetime leadoff man.

His greatest attribute was his speed. It made him an excellent center fielder. Lloyd led the league in putouts four times.

Lloyd was known as "Little Poison" and Paul as "Big Poison," which is Dodger-fan talk for "little person" and "big person." Lloyd didn't drink; Paul was a toper. The two had started out as roomies but later split up.

Lloyd "rejoined" Paul in the Hall of Fame in 1967, two years after Paul's death. Certainly the fact that they formed a duo for so many years must have had some

influence on the voters, but Lloyd's 2,459 hits, .316 batting average, and excellence in the outfield give him some good credentials on his own.

PAUL WANER
Outfield, Pit (N) 1926–40, Bkn (N) 1941, 1943–44, Bos (N) 1941–42, NY (A) 1944–45
"Big Poison" wasn't a big man, at five-eight, 153 pounds, but he was a big talent. Paul hit over .300 twelve straight years. He collected 200 hits eight times, tying Willie Keeler's record.

Waner won three batting titles in 1927, 1934, and 1936. His .380 in 1927 won him the NL MVP Award.

Paul learned to hit swinging at corncobs in Oklahoma. He stood deep in the box, feet together, and aimed at the top of the ball, swinging down as in a golf shot, a theory he later taught as coach. A line drive hitter, he led in doubles and triples twice each.

He wasn't a home run threat, although he hit 15 in 1929. He recognized that approach as a losing game in spacious Forbes Field and became adept at lining the ball down either foul line. The worst that could happen was a foul ball. If the ball hit fair, he had extra bases. In twenty years, Paul had 3,152 hits, including 603 doubles and 190 triples. His batting average was .333, and he scored 1,626 runs and drove in 1,309.

In his prime he was a fine defensive outfielder with the arm to play right field at Forbes.

Paul was notorious for his drinking. One year manager Pie Traynor convinced him to lay off the sauce. When Paul's batting average dropped to .240, Traynor took him out and bought him a drink.

But despite humorous stories about Paul's hungover hitting, the boozing probably kept him from a couple of batting titles and left him only an ordinary player in his last few years.

The story is that Paul beat out a grounder off an infielder's glove one day in 1942 for what could have been his 3,000th hit. However, he signaled the scorer to call it an error, preferring to wait for a clean blow for the big one. The infielder's comment has not survived.

Waner was named to the Hall of Fame in 1952.

JOHN MONTGOMERY WARD
Pitcher/Shortstop, Prov (N) 1878–82, NY (N) 1883–89, 1893–94, Bkn (P) 1890, Bkn (N) 1891–92. Manager, NY (N) 1884, 1893–94, Bkn (P) 1890, Bkn (N) 1891–92
When Monte Ward was named to the Hall of Fame in 1964, the only question was whether he should go in as a pitcher, a shortstop, or as an executive. One of the most remarkable figures in baseball history, he excelled at nearly everything he did.

He broke in as an eighteen-year-old pitcher with Providence in 1878 and led the NL in ERA. The next year he pitched his team to a pennant with a 47–19 mark. In 1880 he pitched the second perfect game in NL history and finished with a 39–24 record. An arm injury ended his pitching career after he'd won 164 games. In 1883 he played center field despite his lame arm—throwing lefthanded!

Undaunted, he became the league's top shortstop, hitting .300 three times, and glueing the infield as captain of the 1888–1889 league champion New York Giants. He led the NL twice in stolen bases and finished with 2,105 career hits and 1,408 runs scored.

A handsome society lion, married to an actress, Ward studied law at night at Columbia, graduating with honors. In 1886 he led the formation of the Players' Brotherhood, the first attempt to improve players' rights. When the Brotherhood got no satisfaction, they formed their own league, the Players League, in 1890. One hundred players jumped their teams in support. Ward played for and managed the Brooklyn club in the league. When the owners sought an injunction against the players, Ward argued the case in court and won.

He won the battles but not the war. Even though the new league drew better than the NL or American Association, the financial backers of the Players League teams became nervous and many pulled out. Ward's league folded after one year, and the players meekly signed new reserve contracts with their old owners.

Ward returned to the Giants, and as player-manager took them to a Temple Cup victory in 1894.

LON WARNEKE
Pitcher, Chi (N) 1930–36, 1942–45, StL (N) 1937–42
"The Arkansas Hummingbird," Warneke was one of the top righthanders of the 1930s, winning 20 games three times and helping the Cubs to two pennants. In 1932 he topped the NL in wins and percentage with a 22–6 mark. He also led in ERA and shutouts. The Cubs won the pennant but lost the World Series to the Yankees. In 1935, when the Cubs won the flag again, Lon went 20–13 and won twice in the World Series.

Although the modest Warneke was one of Chicago's most popular players, he was traded to the Cardinals in 1937. He helped them win the 1942 pennant—after he had been traded back to Chicago. He beat Brooklyn in a crucial September game to give the Cards a slim lead. "Now hold it," he told his old mates, and they did.

Warneke, who finished with a 193–121 career mark, later was a National League umpire from 1949 to 1955.

EARL WEAVER
Manager, Bal (A) 1968–82, 1985–86
Weaver presided over the Orioles' dynasty of the 1970s, leading them to six division titles, four pennants, and one world championship. His winning percentage of .583 ranks in the top ten all-time. Although it was said his teams relied on "pitching and the three-run homer" to win, and the formula has been copied by several teams in the 1980s, Weaver was actually a highly innovative manager. He schooled his players in fundamentals, pioneered the use of computer charts, extended the use of platooning, and even wrote a training manual used by the entire Orioles' organization. Always open to new ideas, his motto became the title of his autobiography: *It's What You Learn After You Know It All That Counts.*

A minor league second baseman who never got beyond Double-A, his success once he turned to managing won him promotion to the Orioles in 1968. Although one of his hurlers cracked, "The only thing Earl knows about pitching is that he couldn't hit it," he and coach George Bamberger produced twenty-two 20-game winners and six Cy Young winners. Several pitchers, including Mike Cueller, Steve Stone, and Mike Torrez came from other organiza-

tions to achieve their best seasons with the Orioles.

Weaver was known for his rages against umpires. He was ejected from ninety-one games during his career. Once he was booted from both ends of a doubleheader. However, Weaver was so respected as a psychologist that some believe that many of his tantrums were staged to arouse his team.

GEORGE WEISS
Executive
"The last of the empire builders," Weiss, more than any other man, was responsible for the unprecedented success of the New York Yankees from the mid-1930s until the mid-1960s: twenty-two pennants and seventeen world championships.

He began with the Eastern League New Haven franchise in 1919 and advanced to become general manager of Baltimore of the International League in 1929. In 1932 he was made farm director of the Yankees and kept an overpowering fountain of talent flowing to the majors for the next fifteen years. Many of the greatest players ever to wear Yankee pinstripes came up through Weiss's farms.

In 1948 he became general manager of the Yankees. One of his first moves was to hire Casey Stengel as manager, despite Stengel's reputation as a clown. With Weiss supplying the players and Stengel managing them, the Yankees won ten pennants between 1949 and 1960.

Both he and Stengel were let go as "too old" after the 1960 season. Weiss became president of the expansion Mets in 1961, hired Stengel as manager, and together they laid the groundwork for the future success of that team. In the meantime, the Yankees that Weiss had built continued to win pennants through 1964, and then collapsed into the poorest Yankees' decade since before World War One.

Weiss was named to the Hall of Fame in 1971.

MICKEY WELCH
Pitcher, Troy (N) 1880–82, NY (N) 1883–92
"Smiling Mickey" was able to grin 307 times as the winning pitcher in games played between 1880 and 1892. He was the third pitcher to win 300 games, preceded only by Pud Galvin and teammate Tim Keefe. Although Welch was not noted for his speed, he was effective with changes of speed on his curveball and screwball.

Welch led the NL in walks for three straight years, 1884–1886, but averaged over 500 innings pitched for each of those years. In 1885 he won 44 games (including a streak of seventeen victories in a row) for the Giants. He finally had a clause written into his contract that he would only pitch every two days.

He and Keefe combined as a one-two pitching punch for the Giants in the late 1880s, helping the team to pennants in 1888 and 1889.

Welch was elected to the Hall of Fame in 1973.

WILLIE "DEVIL" WELLS
Shortstop, Negro League, 1925–49, St. Louis Stars, Detroit Wolves, Kansas City Monarchs, Chicago American Giants, Cole's American Giants, Newark Eagles, Memphis Red Sox, New York Black Yankees, Baltimore Elite Giants
Wells is among the top six Negro League home run hitters

of all time. Though not considered a slugger, Wells owns the all-time Negro League home run record, with 27 in 1927, aided by a short left field fence in his St. Louis home park.

In 1930 Willie led the Negro National League with .404.

Wells's batting average in the black big leagues was .332. Against white big leaguers, he was even better: .369, with 6 homers in 31 games.

At shortstop, Wells had sure hands but did not have a strong arm. He compensated with an uncanny ability to play the hitters. He is usually considered the top shortstop in black baseball during the latter 1920s and 1930s. He was chosen to play in the East-West All-Star Game eight times.

A notorious target of beanball pitches, Wells created an early batting helmet by taking a miner's hardhat and knocking off the gas jet.

He began managing in 1936 with the Newark Eagles and is ranked as one of the finest skippers in Negro League history. His Eagles won the NNL pennant in 1946. Among his players were Ernie Banks, Don Newcombe, Larry Doby, and Monte Irvin.

ZACK WHEAT
Outfielder, Bkn (N) 1909–26, Phi (A) 1927
Wheat was a graceful fielder with an amazingly accurate arm and a reliable line drive hitter. For years there was a sign on the Ebbets Field wall: "Zack Wheat caught 345 flies last year; Tanglefoot fly paper caught 10 million." The only thing that had to be repainted from season to season was the appropriate number of putouts by Wheat; he was the Brooklyn left fielder for eighteen years.

Although he led the NL in hitting only once—.335 in 1918—Wheat topped .300 fourteen times and finished with a .317 career average. He cracked 2,884 hits, scored 1,289 runs, and batted in 1,261. His line drives were usually smoked. Once the lively ball was introduced, drives that had been catchable zoomed past the fielders. Wheat's best batting marks came when he was in his late thirties. In 1924 at the age of thirty-eight, he hit .375, with 14 homers and 97 RBIs. The next year he drove in 103 runs, while hitting .359. Noted for his ability to hit curveballs, Wheat had no weaknesses at bat or in the field, but he did have thin, weak ankles that were often injured.

Although he played on Dodger pennant winners in 1916 and 1920, Wheat always maintained that his favorite game was the twenty-six-inning, 1–1 tie between Brooklyn and Boston in 1920.

He was elected to the Hall of Fame in 1959.

JAMES "DEACON" WHITE
Third Baseman/Catcher, Cle (NA) 1871–72, Bos (NA) 1873–75, Chi (N) 1876, Bos (N) 1877, Cin (N) 1878–80, Buf (N) 1881–85, Det (N) 1886–88, Pit (N) 1889, Buf (P) 1890. Manager Cin (N) 1879
White was one of the most remarkable players of the nineteenth century. His career was long, productive, and filled with firsts. For example, on May 4, 1871, when the Cleveland Forest Citys played the Fort Wayne Kekiongas in the *first* game of the spanking new National Association, who strode up to the plate to become the *first* batter ever in a recognized professional league? White. And a

few moments later, who doubled to make the *first* hit and the *first* extra-base hit? White. And a short while after that, who became the *first* to be put out on a double play? White.

After the 1872 campaign, he left Cleveland for the Boston Red Stockings, who then became the *first* team to win two consecutive pennants, then three consecutive, and then four. And speaking of four, White, Al Spalding, Ross Barnes, and Cal McVey, among Boston's best players, were called "the Big Four" (historically, the *first* "Big Four") when they deserted for Chicago in 1876. The resulting ruckus brought about the formation of the National League, and Chicago won the NL's *first* pennant, as White became its *first* RBI leader.

Back to Boston in 1877, White became Beantown's *first* batting champion (.387) as the Red Stockings won their *first* NL pennant. Deacon next formed the catching half of baseball's *first* brother battery with pitcher Will White, the *first* player to wear glasses on the field.

In the early 1880s at Buffalo, White became part of the *second* "Big Four," along with Dan Brouthers, Hardy Richardson, and Jack Rowe. In 1885 all four were sold to Detroit in the *first* big player deal. And in 1887 they led Detroit to its *first* (and last) NL pennant. White hit .303 at the age of forty.

White's nickname suited him; he never drank, smoked, or cursed, and he carried his Bible with him when the team was on the road.

FRANK WHITE
Second Baseman, KC (A) 1973–
An often unsung hero, White has been an outstanding second baseman for all of the Royals' better teams. At first used as a utility man, he settled in as the regular at second in 1976, the year the Royals won their first-division championship. Although he's only led AL second basemen twice in fielding average, his range factor has been excellent. He has won eight Gold Gloves, symbolic of the best fielder. His career fielding average is in the top ten all-time.

His career batting average is .255, but he has shown home run power. In both 1985 and 1986 he hit 22 homers.

SOL WHITE
Second Baseman, Executive, Negro League, 1887–1926, Pittsburgh Keystones, Washington Capital Citys, Wheeling (O.B.), New York Gorhams, York Monarchs (O.B.), Cuban Giants, Genuine Cuban Giants, Fort Wayne (O.B.), Page Fence Giants, Cuban X-Giants, Columbia Giants, Philadelphia Giants, Lincoln Giants, Quaker Giants, Cleveland Browns, Newark Stars
If Rube Foster was the "father of black baseball," White was the grandfather. Born in 1868, he was nineteen when major league baseball's bars clanged shut on blacks in 1887, and he lived to see the end of sixty years of baseball *apartheid* in 1947. White played with white minor league teams in the 1880s (once playing against Ban Johnson); then after *apartheid*, he played for the Cuban Giants, the Page Fence Giants, and the Philadelphia Giants. Finally he joined the Cuban X-Giants, along with black pioneers Charley "Tokahoma" Grant, Rube Foster, Home Run Johnson, Frank Grant, Pop Lloyd, etc.

White managed the 1903 Philadelphia Giants, who

beat Newark of the International League four straight but lost the first black World Series to Foster's X-Giants two games to three. He hired Foster and got revenge the following year two-to-one.

In his *History of Colored Baseball*, White wrote of the financial pressures on black teams in 1906 and of walking around towns for hours looking for hotels which would accept them. The average white big leaguer made $2,000 a year, he wrote; the average black, $466.

White took Pop Lloyd, Dick Redding, Louis Santop, and Spotswood Poles to the New York Lincoln Giants in 1911. The Lincolns were perhaps the strongest black team in pre-World War One days.

After retiring, White coached at Wilberforce College and wrote a sports column. In his *History* he had urged blacks to keep up their skills so they would be ready when the doors were opened again. He was seventy-nine in 1947 when his prophecy came true in Brooklyn.

HOYT WILHELM
Pitcher, NY (N) 1952–56, StL (N) 1957, Cle (A) 1957–58, Bal (A) 1958-62, Chi (A) 1963–68, Cal (A) 1969, Atl (N) 1969–71, Chi (N) 1970, LA (N) 1971–72
The first relief pitcher honored by Cooperstown, Hoyt used his knuckler to pitch until he was forty-eight. Hoyt's 1,070 games are a record for pitchers. Although he saved 227 games, he never in any season led in saves. He did lead in relief wins twice, and his 123 relief victories are the all-time record.

The way a staff's stopper is used has changed since Wilhelm's day. When he pitched, a top reliever was often brought in when a game was close, no matter which team was leading, a system that led to many wins but reduced the chance for saves. The most common modern practice is to bring in a club's closer primarily in save situations with the team ahead. Although saves have increased greatly, a relief win now often means that the reliever must first lose the lead he was sent in to protect.

Wilhelm's top save total was 27 in 1964 with the White Sox. He also had 12 relief wins that year. Yet the only category he led in was relief losses with 9.

An infantryman in World War Two, Hoyt was wounded and received the Purple Heart during the Battle of the Bulge. He was twenty-eight before he reached the majors and slugged a home run in his first at-bat. He never hit another. (His lifetime batting average was .088.)

Although many pitchers had used the knuckleball before Wilhelm, perhaps no pitcher had ever used it so much to the exclusion of other pitches. Certainly no pitcher popularized it so.

Hoyt baffled the batters—and catchers—with his knuckler. Five of his receivers set records for the most passed balls in an inning, and he gave up a whopping total of unearned runs.

As a rookie with the New York Giants in 1952, Wilhelm led the NL in appearances (71), ERA (2.43), and winning percentage with a 15–3 mark.

In late 1958 he was given an infrequent start by the Orioles and responded with a no-hitter over the Yankees. The next year he was used primarily as a starter; he was 15–11 and led the AL in ERA. But after a few starts in 1960, he was returned to the bullpen.

Wilhelm was elected to the Hall of Fame in 1985.

J. L. WILKINSON
Executive, owner, Negro League, 1909–48, All Nations, Kansas City Monarchs
The white owner of the famous Kansas City Monarchs, Wilkinson was one of the pioneers of night baseball who gave Satchel Paige his second chance and Jackie Robinson his first. His lights saved Negro baseball in the Depression and helped to save the white minor league as well.

Wilkinson's first club, the All Nations—a multiracial team of blacks, whites, and orientals, plus a woman—barnstormed the prairies before World War One. He was one of the founders of the Negro NL in 1920. His Monarchs were black world champs in 1924, league champs in 1925, and reached the playoffs in 1926.

When the Depression struck, Wilkie bought portable lights, playing his first night game in Enid, Oklahoma, two weeks before Des Moines opened with its lights and the same night that Independence, Kansas, played organized baseball's first night game. Wilkinson took his lights to St. Louis, Detroit, Pittsburgh, and elsewhere, helping spread the idea to countless cities.

In 1937, when Paige's career seemed dead because of a sore arm, Wilkie took a chance on him and the arm magically healed. Satch helped win pennants in 1937, 1939–1942, and 1946, and brought in much needed dollars. Satch got 15 percent off the top.

In 1945 Wilkinson also gave a job to a rookie shortstop named Robinson.

When the white big league raids decimated the black leagues, no club lost more than the Monarchs. Wilkinson sold out his interest in 1948.

BILLY WILLIAMS
Outfield, Chi (N) 1959–74, Oak (A) 1975–76
Williams played in 1,117 straight games, the NL record.

The NL Rookie of the Year in 1961, Williams established himself in left field for the Cubs and remained for fourteen seasons. His final two years were spent as a DH with Oakland.

Nicknamed "Sweet Swinging" because of his batting swing, the popular Williams slugged 426 home runs and drove in 1,475 runs, while fashioning a .290 career batting average. He, Ernie Banks, and Ron Santo gave the Cubs a terrific power trio throughout the 1960s, but the Cubbies were never quite able to win a pennant.

Billy usually hit around 25–30 homers a year, reaching his peak, 42, in 1970. Two years later *The Sporting News* named him Player of the Year, when he led the NL in batting and slugging with .333 and .606.

He was named to the NL All-Star team six times. In 1987 he was elected to the Hall of Fame.

SMOKEY JOE WILLIAMS
Pitcher, Negro League, 1897–1932, San Antonio Bronchos, Leland Giants, Chicago Giants, Lincoln Giants, Chicago American Giants, Bacharach Giants, Brooklyn Royal Giants, Homestead Grays
In a 1952 poll conducted by the *Pittsburgh Courier* a panel of black veterans and sportswriters picked Williams as the best black pitcher of all time. He defeated Satchel Paige by a single vote. He was considered faster than Paige.

A big half-black, half-Commanche, Joe resembled Walter Johnson in age, build, and style—both threw blazing fastballs and little else. In their one head-to-head confrontation, Joe won 1–0.

It was one of 19 wins (and 7 losses) Joe recorded against white big leaguers in exhibition games. He defeated seven Hall of Famers—Johnson, Grover Alexander, Chief Bender, Rube Marquard (twice), Waite Hoyt, and Satchel Paige. Two of his losses came after the age of forty; two more were 1–0 decisions.

Joe's best game was a ten-inning, 20-strikeout no-hitter against John McGraw's NL champion Giants in 1917. He lost it 1–0 on an error. Reportedly he gained his nickname after the game when Ross Youngs remarked, "That was a hell of a game, Smokey." Until then Williams had been called Cyclone Joe. In 1930 he fanned twenty-seven Kansas City Monarchs in a twelve-inning night game. The primitive lights and tobacco juice on the ball didn't hurt.

Williams and Paige faced each other twice in the early 1930s. They split the two games. "Smokey Joe could throw harder than all of them," Paige declared.

Joe's rival was Cannonball Redding. They started as teammates on the 1911–1914 New York Lincolns, forming one of the best one-two pitching punches in baseball history.

KEN WILLIAMS
Outfield, Cin (N) 1915–16, StL (A) 1918–27, Bos (A) 1928–29

Overshadowed by Babe Ruth and by his own teammate, George Sisler, Williams was a good hitter who in his best season almost batted the Browns to a pennant in 1922. They lost to the Yankees by a single game, and might have won had Sisler not injured his shoulder just before a crucial head-to-head series in the stretch. Ken knocked in 155 runs and won the home run crown with 39. (It should be noted that Ruth missed a quarter of the season that year.) Williams hit thirty-two of his homers in Sportsman's Park.

Ken played in a fine outfield alongside Jack Tobin and Baby Doll Jacobson. All of them were later picked as outfielders on various Browns all-time teams.

Although he never matched his 1922 numbers, the tall lefthanded hitter finished second in the AL in homers in 1921, 1923, and 1925.

TED WILLIAMS
Outfielder, 1939–42, 1946–60. Manager, Was (A) 1969–71, Tex (A) 1972

Either Williams or Babe Ruth was the greatest hitter of all time, and you could probably cover the difference with an ant's umbrella. Despite losing nearly five seasons in various wars, Williams put together a statistical record that would stand against anyone's. Whether that makes Williams one-two as the greatest *player* of all time is another question altogether.

First the career figures: .344 career batting average, 521 home runs, 1,798 runs, 1,839 RBIs, 2,019 walks, and a .634 slugging average.

And what about individual seasons? He won six AL batting championships, including the famous .406 of 1941; four home run titles, including a personal high of 43 in 1949; six times leading in runs scored; four times in

RBIs; eight times in walks; and nine times in slugging average.

And how about the clutch? Remember Williams's home run with two out in the ninth to win the 1941 All-Star Game? Or the 1946 All-Star homer off Rip Sewell's blooper pitch? Or that he could have sat down the final day in 1941 and finished with a rounded-off .400 (.3995) but insisted on playing and lifted his average to .406? Or that he homered in his last major league at-bat?

And remember he won two MVPs, in 1946 and 1949, and his fans never stopped complaining about the ones he didn't win. And remember *The Sporting News* named him Player of the Decade for the 1950s, which raised a few eyebrows among the fans of Musial, Mays, and Mantle, to name only the M's.

One thing seems certain: Williams will get better every year in our memories as we look at his statistical record. There was never a question that he was the best hitter when he was playing. He was criticized for other things and we tend to forget those. They said he was no better than adequate in the field with a so-so arm, with the footnote that he played Fenway's left field wall very well. They complained that the Red Sox won only a single pennant in all the Williams years, with the footnote that there were some serious pitching problems nearly every year in Boston. They grumbled that he was sometimes boorish, with the footnote that he was often charming.

Most of the gripes were about intangible things. If you were playing a computer baseball game and could pick your roster from players from any era, you'd probably start with Williams if Ruth was already taken.

Williams was elected to the Hall of Fame in 1966.

VIC WILLIS
Pitcher, Bos (N) 1898–1905, Pit (N) 1906–09, StL (N) 1910

Willis holds the NL record for complete games in this century, with 45 in 1902, as well as for losses, with 29 in 1905 for the seventh-place Bostonians. But the curveballer won 20 or more eight times, including four of his first five years, 1898–1902. He finished with a hefty 247–204 record.

As a twenty-two-year-old rookie in 1898, Vic helped pitch Boston to the flag with a 25–13 record. In 1899 he was 27–8 with a no-hitter.

After an off-year in 1900, Willis came back in 1901 to go 18–17 for a fifth-place team. The next year he was 27–19, led in innings pitched and strikeouts, and set a modern record with 45 complete games.

Vic had two big losing years in 1904–1905, when he was 18–25 and 12–29 as Boston stumbled in next-to-last. But a trade to third-place Pittsburgh in 1906 brought him back to a 22–13 record, the first of four straight 20-win years. In the last one, 1909, Willis was 22–11 to lead the Pirates to the world championship.

Willis's 247 victories appear to be some sort of Hall of Fame dividing line. With the exception of a couple of recent retirees, every eligible pitcher with a career predominantly in the twentieth century who won more than Willis has been elected to the Hall.

MAURY WILLS
Shortstop, LA (N) 1959–66, 1969–72, Pit (N) 1967–68,

Mon (N) 1969. Manager, Sea (A) 1980–81
Wills brought the stolen base back into baseball. No NL player had stolen 50 bases since Max Carey in 1923 when Wills grabbed that many in 1960. Two years later he shattered Ty Cobb's 1915 record of 96 and became the first man to break 100 in this century. (Nineteenth-century rules counted extra bases taken on others' hits as steals.) Maury's 104 steals lit the way for the Brocks, Hendersons, and Colemans and changed the nature of the game.

Wills was the shortstop for Los Angeles, a team long on pitching and short on power. His steals were of more value to the Dodgers than they might have been to a team of greater batting proficiency. He led the NL in stolen bases six straight years, 1960–1965, and he finished his fourteen-year career with 586. In addition to the 104 in 1962, which won him the MVP Award, he stole 94 in 1965.

Wills spent eight years in the minors before finally being given a chance with the Dodgers midway through the 1959 season. Although he had no home run power, Wills was more than a one-dimensional player. He had a career batting average of .281, and he twice won Gold Gloves as a shortstop. With Wills at short, the Dodgers won four pennants.

His son Bump Wills played six years (1977–1982) in the majors and was also an excellent base stealer.

LEWIS "HACK" WILSON
Outfield, NY (N) 1923–25, Chi (N) 1926–31, Bkn (N) 1932–34, Phi (N) 1934
It was often said of Wilson that "he was a lowball hitter and a highball drinker." The line could still get a chuckle after his career went down the tube at age thirty-four but lost its mirth when he died at forty-eight. For five years he was the most fearsome slugger in the NL; then, almost overnight, he became a has-been.

He was one of the strangest-looking men ever to play in the majors. He stood only five-six but weighed around 210. He had an eighteen-inch neck and wore a size-six shoe. Because someone thought he resembled the famous strongman George Hackenschmidt, Wilson was tagged "Hack," but that probably didn't do him justice. What he really looked like was Barney Rubble with Wilma Flintstone's feet.

After he'd played a couple of years for the Giants and been found wanting, the Cubs picked him up for a song— a little ditty called $5,000—in 1926. Right away he started hitting homers and driving in runs. From 1926 through 1930 he led the NL in homers four times, drove in over 100 runs each year, and hit over .300. The really big seasons were 1929, when he hit .345 and had 159 RBIs to help the Cubs to the pennant, and 1930, which made everything else look like a preamble. In 1930 he hit .356, he scored 146 runs, he hammered out 56 homers— still the NL record— and he drove in a grand total of (drum roll) 191 runs!

Hack was thirty years old and it was "top-of-the-world-ma"! And if you remember what happened next in the Cagney movie, just about the same thing happened to Hack in 1931. His boozing was at the base. Manager Rogers Hornsby got on his case about the cases he was consuming. Hack sulked and drank more. And when he hit .261, with 13 homers and 61 RBIs, they exiled him to

Brooklyn. By 1934, he was done hitting lowballs.

He was elected to the Hall of Fame in 1979.

DAVE WINFIELD
Outfield, SD (N) 1973–80, NY (A) 1981–88, 1990, Cal (A) 1990–
Probably the best all-around athlete in the majors in the last quarter century, the six-six, 220-pound Winfield was drafted to play both pro football and pro basketball but opted instead to step directly from the University of Minnesota into a regular job in the San Diego outfield in 1973. Although the San Diego park was a poor one for right-handed power hitters and the Padres team was annually awful, he established himself as one of the NL's best players, hitting .300 twice, leading in RBIs in 1979, and earning two Gold Gloves.

Frustrated at playing for a losing team, he signed an estimated $25-million contract as a free agent with the Yankees in 1981. He has seldom been out of the news since. Discounting 1981, the strike year, he batted in at least 100 runs every year as a Yankee except 1987, when he drove home 97. His home run totals have been as high as 37 and as low as 19 (in 1984, when he batted .340). He has brightened innumerable highlight films with leaping outfield catches. He has been a team leader and has conducted himself as a model citizen, and his Winfield Foundation is known for its charitable work with underprivileged youth.

There's a downside. He has also been involved in numerous verbal skirmishes and even a lawsuit with Yankee owner George Steinbrenner. The Yankees played in only one World Series (1981) during his tenure in New York, and he hit only .045 there. And the seagulls of Toronto will never forgive him for his mighty outfield toss that nailed one of their number. Winfield missed the entire 1989 season with a back injury and was traded to California early in 1990.

GEORGE WRIGHT
Shortstop, Bos (NA), 1871–75, Bos (N) 1876–78, 1880–81, Prov (N) 1879, 1882. Manager, Prov (N) 1879
Baseball's Wright brothers weren't related to the airplane inventors, but they got professional baseball off the ground in 1869 with the first completely pro team. George starred at shortstop for older brother Harry's pioneer pro club, the Cincinnati Red Stockings, which went unbeaten that year while playing all comers from east coast to west. George hit .629, with 49 homers in the Reds' 57 counted games.

George had been named shortstop on pioneer baseball writer Henry Chadwick's first All-Star team in 1868. He was the first shortstop to play out beyond the baselines, thereby increasing his range. He was valued even more for his fielding than his hitting. And small wonder! The Red Stockings won games by scores of 85–7, 40–0, and 103–8. Who needed another hitter?

The Wrights moved to Boston of the new National Association following the 1870 campaign and won four straight flags, 1872–1875. George's batting average ranged from .409 to .336.

When the NL was founded in 1876, George was the first man to come to bat. He hit a grounder to shortstop.

His batting began dropping off, however, and with the

advent of sidearm and curveball pitching in 1877, it was down to .276, but Boston won the flag and repeated in 1878. In 1879 he moved to Providence as player-manager and beat Harry's Bostonians for the flag, giving him eight pennants in nine years.

George founded a sporting goods company in Boston. When he took on a partner in 1879, the company became Wright & Ditson. An all-around athlete, George had starred at cricket before turning full-time to baseball. After retiring from the diamond, he returned to cricket. He introduced golf to the Boston area and was instrumental in introducing hockey to the United States. He also supported tennis, and his two sons won national championships.

George was named to the Hall of Fame in 1937.

WILLIAM "HARRY" WRIGHT

Outfielder/Pitcher, Bos (NA) 1871–75, Bos (N) 1876–77. Manager, Bos (NA) 1871–75, Bos (N) 1876–81, Pro (N) 1882–83, Phi (N) 1884–93

Henry Chadwick, "the father of baseball," called Wright the "father of pro baseball."

Harry organized the game's first completely professional team, the Cincinnati Red Stockings, paving the way for the first pro league, the National Association. He designed the basic uniform that is still worn today, knee-length knickers instead of pantaloons. And he patented the first scorecard.

A professional cricket player, in 1858 Harry decided to try the new American game of baseball. He joined the New York Knickerbockers as an outfielder. He occasionally pitched in relief, throwing a change-up he called a "dew drop."

In 1867 Harry joined the Cincinnati Red Stockings as a pitcher. Since 1865 he had been a paid bowler for the Cincinnati Union Cricket Club. By 1868, with several pros on the team, the Red Stockings were Midwest champions. The next year his younger brother George, a star shortstop, joined the team, and the Red Stockings took the field as the first fully professional baseball team. The Red Stockings toured the country and won every game in 1869. The winning streak continued until June 14, 1870, when they were finally bested by the Atlantics of Brooklyn in an extra-inning thriller. The publicity the Reds generated stirred public interest in professional baseball and led to the establishment of the National Association, the first pro baseball league, in 1871.

With the formation of the National Association, Harry became manager of the Boston team, called the Red Stockings since the Cincinnati team had disbanded, with George as shortstop. They won four pennants, in 1872–1875. The Red Stockings joined the newly formed National League in 1876, its first year. Harry won pennants in 1877 and 1878.

Harry continued as a manager in the NL until 1893. Although he won no more pennants, several of his teams come close. He was universally respected for his integrity and innovative ideas.

Among the changes he reportedly advocated that were later instituted: the fifty-foot and then the fifty-five-foot pitching distance, six balls for a walk instead of nine, pre-game practice, a livelier ball with a cork center, and overhand pitching.

One idea that was tried out but did not prevail: a flat bat.

Harry Wright was named to the Hall of Fame in 1953.

EARLY WYNN

Pitcher, Was (A) 1939, 1941–44, 1946–48, Cle (A) 1949–57, 1963, Chi (A) 1958–62

Wynn pitched his first major league game at age nineteen, but he didn't get any (ahem) early wins. Throwing for the Senators in the 1940s, he was erratic—a burly batch of talent with no clear idea of what to do. He was 18–12 in 1943 and 8–17 the next year, 17–15 in 1947 and 8–19 in 1948, with a 5.82 ERA. The Senators finally said the heck with him and shipped him to Cleveland.

Indians' pitching coach Mel Harder taught him the fine art of pitching, sharpened his pitches, and by 1950, the new, improved model was 18–8 with the AL's best ERA. Cleveland had the best pitching in the world in the 1950s, with Bob Feller, Bob Lemon, Mike Garcia, and their equal—sometimes better—Wynn. As an Indian, he won 20 games four times, 18 once, 17 twice.

In a sense, Wynn was a throwback, a 1950s pitcher with the attitude of an old 1890s Oriole. The plate was *his*. Any batter with the audacity to dig in could expect the next pitch to be aimed at his sinuses. They said Wynn would have brushed back his grandmother. "Only if she dug in," said Early. He didn't so much win games as wrestle for them, earning victory by intimidation, force of will, anger, and downright cussedness.

He walked scads and struck out a ton, eventually leading the AL twice in both departments. In all, he walked 1,775, yet he wasn't really wild; he just refused to give a batter a good pitch.

In 1958, Al Lopez, his former Indians' manager, acquired him for the White Sox. His 22–10 record in 1959 helped the Sox win their first pennant in forty years and earned the thirty-nine-year-old Wynn the Cy Young Award.

By 1960 Early needed 29 more victories for 300. He developed a gouty elbow. It took him four years and a lot of pain, but on July 13, 1963, he became baseball's fourteenth 300-game winner.

In 1972 he was elected to the Hall of Fame.

JIM WYNN

Outfielder, Hou (N) 1963–73, LA (N) 1974–75, Atl (N) 1976, NY (A) 1977, Mil (A) 1977

Wynn, at five-ten and 160 pounds, was called "the Toy Cannon" because he generated so much power for his size. For most of his career, he played half his games in the Astrodome, the second worst park to hit a ball out of (the first worst is Yellowstone). Nevertheless, he popped 37 homers in 1967 and 33 in 1969. Joe Morgan, a pretty fair hitter, finished second on the team both years with 10 and 15.

Playing for the Astros in the 1960s had other disadvantages. There usually weren't a lot of runners for Jimmy to knock in; he topped 100 RBIs once for Houston but was over 80 three other years. And there was seldom anyone to knock Wynn home when he got on; Wynn walked over 100 times in seven different seasons, four as an Astro. His 148 free passes in 1969 tied the NL record.

In 1974 Wynn was traded to the Dodgers. Chavez

Ravine is no hitter's paradise, but finally he was with a winner. He hit 32 homers, scored 108 runs, and batted in 104, to help the Dodgers to a pennant. Wynn finished fifth in the MVP voting, and everyone wondered where he'd been all these years.

The answer was he'd been hiding at Loop 610, Kirby and Fannin Streets, Houston, Texas.

CARL YASTRZEMSKI
Outfielder/First Baseman, Bos (A) 1961–83
For one month—September 1967—Ted Williams said, Yaz was the greatest player who ever lived. Almost single-handedly the Boston left fielder lifted the Red Sox from ninth in 1966 to the flag. In a final doubleheader victory over pursuing Minnesota, Carl got 7-for-8 to sink the Twins. He won the Triple Crown and played a sensational left field with his glove and arm. Naturally he was MVP. He hit .400 in the World Series against St. Louis, with three homers.

Yaz won three batting titles, including .301 in 1968, the lowest ever to win. But that was the Year of the Pitcher, when the *average* American Leaguer hit .230. In a normal year Carl would have hit .331; in the 1930 NL, .388.

Carl began as a line drive hitter. Then at age twenty-seven he began lifting weights and came out slugging in 1967, the "Impossible Dream" season, with 44 homers. He had two more 40-homer seasons and finished with 452. His career .285 batting average is more impressive in light of his 1,844 RBIs, 1,816 runs scored, and 1,845 walks.

He led the league in assists six times, more than any other outfielder in AL history, and he got 190 intentional walks, more than any other AL hitter since such records were kept starting in 1955. Yaz was elected to the Hall of Fame in 1989.

TOM YAWKEY
Owner, Bos (A) 1933–77
A wealthy lumberman and mine owner, Yawkey was the adopted son of onetime Detroit owner William Yawkey. He bought the moribund Red Sox in 1933 and set out to buy a pennant by acquiring star players such as Joe Cronin, Lefty Grove, Jimmie Foxx, and Wes Ferrell. It didn't work, mostly because the Yankees were in the league, but he did revive fan interest that had all but disappeared in the years that the Sox spent scraping the bottom of the AL. Yawkey finally won pennants in 1946, 1967, and 1975. He never saw them win a World Series though—they lost in seven games every time.

Generous and popular with his players, Yawkey often worked out with them before games and was interested in their affairs. Critics said that he overpaid and pampered his stars, thus diminishing their desire to win. He was also accused of bucking racial integration; the Sox were the last team to have a black player, and that was not until 1959.

He served as AL vice president in 1956–1973.

Yawkey was elected to the Hall of Fame in 1980.

RUDY YORK
First Baseman, Det (A) 1934, 1937–45, Bos (A) 1946–47, Chi (A) 1947, Phi (A) 1948. Manager, Bos (A) 1959

As a rookie catcher in 1937, the scarfaced part-Cherokee smashed 18 home runs for Detroit in August alone, the record for one month. In all, he slugged 35 in only 375 at-bats.

In 1940, with the Tigers well-stocked with catchers and needing York's big bat in the lineup, slugger Hank Greenberg was moved to left field and York was installed at first base. The change did nothing for the Tiger defense ("Rudy York is part Indian and part first baseman" was a popular line), but it gave them a pennant-winning attack. Greenberg was named MVP; York hit 33 homers, drove in 134 runs, and batted .316.

He led the AL in homers and RBIs in 1943, and helped the Tigers win another flag in 1945. Traded to the Red Sox in 1946, he again found himself on a pennant winner. In thirteen seasons, York hit 277 home runs and had 1,152 RBIs.

DENTON "CY" YOUNG
Pitcher, Cle (N) 1890–98, StL (N) 1899–1900, Bos (A) 1901–08, Cle (A) 1909–11, Bos (N) 1911. Manager, Bos (A) 1907
Young's career record looks like a misprint: 511–313. Surely there must be a couple of decimal points missing! If nothing else, it prepares you to gosh-and-golly through some of the other high points: Young was number one in innings pitched with 7,357 and in complete games with 749. He had 15 seasons of 20 or more wins, five seasons of winning 30 or more; 76 shutouts; a 2.63 career ERA; three no-hitters, with the one in 1904 a perfect game. Ridiculous!

They called him Cy either because he threw baseballs against a fence until it looked like a cyclone had hit it or because he showed up at the Cleveland Spiders' park in 1890 carrying a cardboard suitcase, wearing a cheap, too-small suit, and looking like what you'd get if you mail-ordered for a hick. But from his first pitch, he was the Spiders' best pitcher, and he continued being the staff ace for whatever team he played for during the next twenty years. His last two seasons he slipped, but there was nothing wrong with his arm; he just got too fat to field bunts.

Young's arm was a wonder. He never had a sore arm, even though he pitched over 400 innings five times and over 300 eleven other seasons. He'd go home to his Ohio farm in October, do chores all winter, and show up ready for another 400 innings the next spring.

Cy threw twelve pitches before each game and was ready to go. On the mound he wheeled away from the hitter to hide the ball, then uncorked one of four deliveries, including an overhand curve, a sidearm curve, and a "tobacco ball." Young was a great control pitcher, averaging 1.5 walks per game. He once went twenty innings in a game without giving a walk. Eleven times he led the league in fewest walks and most strikeouts.

If they'd had a Cy Young Award when he pitched, he probably would have won only a couple at most. There was usually somebody having a more phenomenal individual season—Kid Nichols, Amos Rusie, Joe McGinnity, Christy Mathewson, Three-Finger Brown, Addie Joss, or Ed Walsh. A few pitchers in history have been terrific for enough seasons that they might actually rank ahead of Young on the all-time scale. Maybe Lefty Grove, Walter

Johnson, Bob Feller, Tom Seaver, Matty, or Alexander. Cy had some advantages over most of them. He was almost always on winning teams. He didn't have to fret a lively ball. In its first years, the AL he jumped to in 1901 was definitely weaker than the NL. If you could choose any pitcher who has ever played to pitch for you in a big game, you probably wouldn't pick Young. But if your opponent picked him, he might beat you. After all, Cy was the winning pitcher 511 times.

He was elected to the Hall of Fame in 1937.

ROSS YOUNGS
Outfielder, NY (N) 1917–26

Virtually John McGraw's "son"—Mac called him "the greatest outfielder I ever had"—Youngs played on the Giants' four straight pennant winners in 1921 through 1924. When he hit .375 in the 1922 Series to Ruth's .118, Mac said he wouldn't trade him for the Babe. It got a big laugh over at the Yankee office. Hyperbole aside, Youngs was a splendid right fielder—a fast runner, fearless, with excellent judgment and a fine arm. A smart baserunner, too. At bat, the stocky lefthanded hitter had double and triple power and hit .300 from the moment he first came to bat in the Polo Grounds.

In 1924 he hit .356. If he wasn't Ruth, he was definitely one of the best players in the NL. Then, in 1925, something was wrong. He struggled at bat all season and fin-ished at .264. In the off-season, he was diagnosed as suffering from Bright's Disease. He played through 1926 on guts, teaching young Mel Ott everything he knew about playing right field. By will alone he hit .302. By 1927 he was bedridden, and in October he died at the age of thirty.

He was elected to the Hall of Fame in 1972.

ROBIN YOUNT
Shortstop/Outfielder, Mil (A) 1974–

Yount became the Brewers' regular shortstop in 1974 at age eighteen and held the job with his glove for a few years until his bat caught up. By the 1980s he was hitting for average and power.

The tousle-headed Yount was the best player in the AL in 1982. Robin smacked two home runs off Jim Palmer to clinch the flag for Milwaukee on the final day, to end with 29 homers, .331, and the best slugging average in the league. He won the MVP by a landslide. Yount stayed hot in the World Series, hitting .414 with a record-setting two four-hit games, as the Brewers lost to the Cardinals in seven games.

After 1,479 games at shortstop, a shoulder injury in 1984 finally sent Yount to center field, where he has continued to rank among the AL's best players. A .318 average and 103 RBIs led Yount to a second MVP in 1989, although that was followed by a subpar 1990 season.

Phantom Ballplayers

Clifford S. Kachline

arbage in, garbage out is an expression that gained currency with the advent of the computer age. The logic behind the catch phrase, however, prevailed long before the electronic marvels came into being. Baseball, in fact, has had its own version of the maxim almost since the game's earliest days, largely as a consequence of recordkeepers who sometimes unwittingly entered erroneous data into the record books.

Numerous examples of the *garbage in, garbage out* principle have been discovered in baseball's statistical archives through the years. But statistics aren't the only area where the phenomenon has shown up. Another involves what researchers of the sport refer to as "phantoms"—players credited with having performed in the major leagues but who in reality never did appear in a big league game.

Phantoms are hardly a recent phenomenon. They have existed almost as long as boxscores have been published. Some were the product of misunderstandings by—or misinformation given to—official scorers or the parties who compiled the boxscores. A few of these crept into the leagues' official records. Others were created by mistakes on the part of telegraph operators or by typographical errors and appeared only in newspaper boxscores.

Little if any attention was paid to the situation until the 1950s. The original edition of *The Official Encyclopedia of Baseball,* published by A. S. Barnes and Co. in 1951, provided fans for the first time with a supposedly complete alphabetical tabulation of every man who ever played in the majors, together with his basic yearly big league stats. The publication stimulated the interest of the sport's researchers. When editors Hy Turkin and S. C. Thompson deleted the names of some players—most of whom were previously shown as having a one-game career—from subsequent revised editions, the matter of phantoms started to become a source of fascination.

Who really were the "impostors" that were listed in earlier editions? What had prompted the editors to include them in the first place? And what evidence had been found to prove conclusively that they never played in the big leagues?

The introduction of *The Baseball Encyclopedia* by the Macmillan Publishing Company in 1969 focused additional attention on the subject. In compiling data for that publication, David Neft and his crew of Information Concepts, Inc. researchers continued the process of purging phantoms from the records. Since then, further investigation by Neft, Pete Palmer, Bill Haber, Al Kermisch, and others has led to the expunging of several more players.

In many instances confirming the status of a phantom was a complicated chore. The task sometimes was made more difficult because the player's name was included in the official league statistics. In other cases, especially those involving nineteenth-century performers, the fact that official league records no longer exist compounded the problem because it made it impossible to determine who was credited by the official scorer and/or league statistician with appearing in the game or games in question. (The American League's official game-by-game player sheets of 1901–1904 reportedly were destroyed by fire decades ago, while the official National League data also vanished for the pre-1902 period except for the 1899 season.)

An example of a phantom who appears in the league records is Albert W. Olsen. For thirty-five years he was carried in the *Encyclopedias* and shown as participating in one game—as a pinch hitter—for the Boston Red Sox in 1943. Olsen did train with the Red Sox that spring, but he was shipped to San Diego of the Pacific Coast League before opening day and spent the entire season in the minors. In addition, it was his exploits as a lefthanded pitcher, not as a hitter, that originally attracted the Red Sox.

Nevertheless, American League records list Olsen as playing for Boston in a game in Chicago on May 16, 1943. Newspaper boxscores credited him with drawing a walk while batting for pitcher Dick Newsome and subsequently stealing a base. However, research has confirmed that the Red Sox pinch-hitter on that occasion definitely was not Olsen. Instead, it may have been outfielder Leon Culberson, who had just been called up from Louisville of the American Association, or possibly another Boston rookie outfielder, Johnny Lazor.

And why is there still uncertainty as to who the pinch-hitter really was? How could this mistake have occurred? First off, the exchange of roster data among major league teams during that period was quite limited. Consequently scorecards often contained the same player names and uniform numbers for the visiting team, especially early in the season, as the team listed in spring training. For example, the scorecard for a Red Sox–Senators game in Washington approximately a week before the incident in question showed Olsen on Boston's roster with uniform number 14, even though he was pitching for San Diego. Second, it's unlikely there were phone lines from the pressbox to the dugouts in those days, and in the absence of being able to call down to check on the identity of a player, the media and official scorers relied on outdated roster information.

Several years ago researchers felt they had cleared up the Olsen mystery upon discovering that one Boston newspaper identified the pinch-hitter as "Culbeson." This seemed to settle the matter. After all, Culberson had joined the team that day and was installed as the Red Sox' leadoff batter in the second half of the afternoon doubleheader, collecting a single and triple in five at-bats. But the mystery was revived when Ed Walton, a Red Sox historian, discussed the situation with Culberson at a Red Sox Old Timers affair in 1986. According to Walton, Culberson contended he did not pinch-hit in the twin-bill opener, but rather made his debut in the second game. He added that manager Joe Cronin said he wanted the young newcomer to sit beside him (Cronin) through the first game to get a feel of the big leagues. However, the records reveal Cronin played third base during the entire first game. All of which raises the questions: Was Culberson's memory playing tricks on him and was he indeed the pinch-hitter listed as Olsen? Or was it Lazor, who is shown as wearing uniform number 14 later in the year but who was batting a mere .136 (3 for 22) at the time? Because the passage of time makes memories hazy and also because the incident was of no particular significance, the mystery may never be solved.

A manager's pique led to a phantom known as J. A. Costello getting into the early *Encyclopedias*. Curiously, the incident also took place in Chicago and likewise involved a player's big league debut. It occurred in the morning half of a holiday bill between Cleveland and the White Sox on July 4, 1912. Late in the contest, Indians' Manager Harry Davis, still burning over an umpire's decision, sent the newcomer into the game to replace center fielder Joe Birmingham and instructed him to announce himself to umpire Gene Hart as "Costello."

In reality, the player was Kenneth Nash, who had only recently joined Cleveland from Boston University law school. He subsequently appeared in ten additional games with Cleveland that season under his correct surname, mostly as a shortstop, and then played with the St. Louis Cardinals for part of 1914. Nash later became a prominent state representative, state senator, and judge in his home state of Massachusetts.

The 1903 official National League records contain a phantom who long baffled researchers. Among the Pittsburgh player sheets is one headed "George Gray" with entries for two games as an outfielder—on May 28 and May 31. Four years earlier the Pirates had a pitcher named George "Chummy" Gray, and it's possible the scorer or league statistician remembered him while filling in the player's first name. When the first *Official Encyclopedia* appeared in 1951, the player was identified as William (rather than George) Gray, a native of Pittsburgh.

It turns out that the two George (or William) Gray entries properly belonged to not one, but two different players. The Pirates' left fielder in the May 28 game really was Romer Carl "Reddy" Grey, younger brother of novelist Zane Grey. He had been obtained on loan from the Worcester club of the Eastern League to fill in that afternoon in the final game of a series in Boston.

On the other hand, while boxscores in Cincinnati newspapers listed the Pittsburgh left fielder for the May 31 game in Cincinnati as "Gray," the player actually was Ernest Diehl, a Cincinnati sandlotter who had been re-

cruited by the injury-riddled Pirates. The game represented Diehl's first appearance in the major leagues and his only game that season, but he played 12 more games with Pittsburgh the following year. It should be noted that ever since the original Turkin/Thompson tome, the *Encyclopedias* have credited Diehl with playing one game with Pittsburgh in 1903, but until recent years they also carried William Gray with two games.

A majority of baseball's phantoms were the product of typographical errors—instances where a linotypist or a typesetter mistakenly included one or more incorrect letters in a name, or where a printer inserted a correction line in the wrong place. In compiling data for the *Encyclopedias*, the authors/researchers relied not only on the so-called official league records but also combed boxscores published in *The Sporting News, Sporting Life, The New York Clipper*, and various local newspapers. In the process they occasionally came upon what appeared to be a previously unlisted "new" player who, in the final analysis, proved to be someone else. Even today, misspellings of this type in newspapers can cause great befuddlement.

A classic illustration of a phantom who was created by a typographical error is the player carried in the early *Encyclopedias* as John P. Morgan. He was listed as appearing in one game as a third baseman with the Philadelphia Athletics in 1916. A study of A's boxscores for the season disclosed the source of the mix-up: It was *The Sporting News*'s boxscore of the August 3 game at Cleveland. (*Sporting Life* had dropped boxscores by this time.) The Philadelphia half of *TSN*'s box has "Morgan, 2b," while on the same line in Cleveland's half is "Gandil, 1b."

Careful examination reveals the Morgan/Gandil type slug was a correction line that the printer inserted in the wrong place. It was intended for the Washington-at-Cleveland boxscore of the previous day (August 2) in which the Senators' second baseman, Harry Morgan, appeared on the same line as Chick Gandil and contained the identical AB-H-PO-A-E figures given for each player in the misaligned August 2 line.

This explanation may well leave you, the reader, with several questions, to wit: (1) Who did play third for the A's that day, and was he properly credited in the official records? (2) Why did the *Encyclopedia* compilers show Morgan as a third baseman instead of a second baseman? (3) How did they come up with "John P." for the impostor's name?

The answers are: (1) Lee McElwee and, yes, he was credited with this game; (2) because veteran Nap Lajoie played the entire game at his usual second base position for the A's, the researcher who made this "discovery" apparently assumed it should have read "Morgan, 3b" rather than "2b"; (3) an infielder named John P. Morgan was active in the minor leagues that season, and the *Encyclopedia* editors probably figured the A's had given him a trial. Numerous other phantoms were similarly tagged with the first names of then-current minor leaguers.

Typos involving misspelled names led to a number of one-game phantoms. Two examples will serve to demonstrate the point. They are John H. Carlock (1912, Cleveland) and a player listed simply as Deniens (no first name given) with the 1914 Chicago Federals. *Sporting Life* had "Carlock, ph" for Cleveland in an August 24, 1912, game at Boston, but Cleveland newspapers and *The Sporting News* reported the pinch-hitter was Fred Carisch, a reserve catcher with the Indians. Official AL records also credit Carisch with that appearance. "Deniens, c" turned out to be Clem Clemens, a catcher in 13 games with the 1914 ChiFeds. One can readily visualize how handwritten names "Carisch" and "Clemens" could have been misinterpreted by a telegrapher or linotypist for "Carlock" and "Deniens."

The origins of some other phantoms are more mysterious. Take the case of Lou Proctor. The *Encyclopedias* credited him with one appearance with the 1912 St. Louis Browns. *The Sporting News* and *Sporting Life,* which may have obtained their boxscores from the same source, show "Proctor, ph" and "Procter, pi," respectively, in a May 13 game at Boston. However, a Boston newspaper referred to the pinch hitter as Albert "Pete" Compton, a catcher with the Browns that season (whose real first name was, of all things, Anna). While AL records contain no reference to Proctor, they unfortunately also fail to include the May 13 appearance among Compton's 100 games. Rumor has it that Proctor was a prankish Western Union telegrapher who inserted his own name as a pinch hitter.

The presence on one team of two players with the same or an almost similar surname can lead to problems. The Washington Senators figured in three such mixups. Ironically, in one instance research by Kermisch has established that a player long labeled a phantom was, in fact, the real McCoy. The player in question was Charles C. Conway. In 1911 the Senators had both Conway, a rookie outfielder up from Youngstown (Ohio-Pennsylvania), and William "Wid" Conroy, veteran infielder-outfielder, on their spring roster. When the season began, Conroy was idled by a stone bruise of the foot. Meantime, Conway appeared in two games during opening week, finishing up in right field on April 15 and starting at that position three days later, before the Senators returned him to Youngstown. Unfortunately, *Sporting Life* and *The Sporting News* each showed "Conroy" as the replacement in the first contest, but both had "Conway, rf" in their April 18 boxscore. Although the early *Encyclopedias* listed Conway and credited him with playing two games, the Macmillan compilers dropped his name 20 years ago on the erroneous premise that it was the veteran Conroy who participated in the April 15-18 games. Actually, Conway didn't make the first of his 106 appearances that year until April 27.

An equally confusing puzzle centered on a 1914 Washington pitcher known as Barron or Barton. The early *Encyclopedias* carried both John J. Barron (later changed to Frank John Barron) and Carroll R. "Buck" Barton and credited each with pitching in one game for the '14 Senators. Actually only one pitcher was involved (and just one appearance), but which pitcher was it? Player contract data of the period reveal that Washington signed Carroll R. Barton in 1913 and retained rights to him while he pitched for Newport News (Virginia League) that season and again in 1914. During the same two years John J. Barron was pitching in the New England League. To complicate matters further, Washington signed Frank J. Barron in 1914 and shipped him to Newport News, where he became a teammate of Barton. While Barron posted a

dismal 1-3 record, Barton was a 16-game winner that year.

So who was the 1914 Washington pitcher? The American League player records contain an entry headed "Barron" with data for an August 18 game, and boxscores of the contest likewise have "Barron" pitching one inning—the ninth—for the Senators against the visiting St. Louis Browns. The player's correct identity was confirmed when, shortly before his death in 1964, Frank Barron disclosed in an interview that while still studying for his law degree at West Virginia University he was signed by Clark Griffith in 1914, was assigned to Newport News and later pitched one inning for Washington before resuming his law studies.

The third Washington mix-up relates to a 1944 player identified in the *Encyclopedias* as Armando Viera Valdes. Official AL records contain a sheet for Armand (without the final "o") Valdes and note that he made a pinch-hitting appearance for the Senators in a May 3 game at Boston, but Richard Topp's research has disclosed that the pinch hitter was Rogelio "Roy" Valdes, a fellow Cuban but no relative of Armando.

With many major leaguers lost to military service in 1944, scout Joe Cambria lined up several Cubans to fill voids on the Senators' roster. Early in the year he signed an outfielder who was listed in the 1944 *American League Red Book* as Armand (without the "o") Valdes. Several weeks thereafter—too late for inclusion in the *Red Book*—Cambria signed Rogelio Valdes, a catcher. Both spent the early weeks of the season with Washington (each was later optioned to Williamsport of the Eastern League), and presumably the official scorer and/or league statistician picked up the incorrect first name from the Senator roster in the *AL Red Book*.

As in the case of Charles Conway, another player once regarded as a phantom has turned out to be a legitimate athlete after all. The Turkin-Thompson tomes listed him as William Krouse, a second baseman in one game with Cincinnati in 1901. Compilers of the Macmillan encyclopedia decided he was an imposter and dropped him, crediting his appearance to Bill Fox, the Reds' regular keystoner. However, research has revealed that the "Krouse, 2b" for Cincinnati in the July 27, 1901 game at Chicago was a recently-released minor leaguer whose correct name was Charles "Famous" Krause. Krause, who was on his way home to Detroit at the time, was given a chance with the Reds because Fox was sidelined with a split finger, but the newcomer performed so poorly that he was dumped after that one appearance.

The accompanying table lists the phantoms who have been eliminated from the all-time roster of major league players since the first Turkin/Thompson *Official Encyclopedia* of 1951. In the absence of an official clearinghouse for such data, no claim is made that the list is complete. Where it is available, brief information on the reason for the deletion of the player is given. Unfortunately, documentation by Turkin/Thompson and the ICI group that compiled the 1969 *Encyclopedia* disappeared years ago.

With today's sophisticated technology and record-keeping procedures, the margin for error in the identification of players—and in the official statistics—has been reduced considerably. Still, a slipup that occurred in the 1984 official American League averages (Alvaro Espinoza was omitted completely, even though he appeared in one game with Minnesota) emphasizes that mistakes still are possible.

A factor that poses the potential for error is the frequency of teams having two players with the same—or nearly identical—surname. In 1987, for instance, the Atlanta Braves' pitching staff at one time or another included two Smiths (Zane and Pete) as well as a Cary (Chuck) and Clary (Marty), while the St. Louis Cardinals had two relief specialists named Dayley (Ken) and Dawley (Bill) and also a Perry (Pat) and a Terry (Scott), two pitchers who coincidentally were traded for each other during the season. Meanwhile, Seattle's lineup often included both Phil Bradley and Scott Bradley, while Craig Reynolds and Ronn Reynolds occasionally appeared in the same lineup for Houston, and Baltimore, of course, had the brothers Ripken. Other examples—such as Sandberg (Ryne) and Sundberg (Jim) of the Cubs and infielders Jeltz (Steve) and Jelks (Greg) of the Phillies—could be cited, but the duo that could cause the greatest difficulty for researchers circa 2000 consists of pitchers Don Robinson and Jeff Robinson, both of whom pitched for San Francisco and Pittsburgh in 1987.

Couple this with the typographical errors that still show up in newspaper boxscores, and you can see that the days of *garbage in, garbage out* are likely to continue.

Tabulation of Phantoms

Baldwin,——. 1907 Boston NL, 1 game as C. One of James C. Ball's 10 games.

Barton, Carroll R. 1914 Washington AL, 1 game as P. Same as game credited to Frank J. Barron.

Bigler, Ivan E. 1917 St. Louis AL, 1 game as 1B. Typographical error; one of George H. Sisler's 135 games.

Boylan,——. 1887 Philadelphia NL, 1 game as 2B. One of Charles J. Bastian's 60 games.

Carlock, John H. 1912 Cleveland AL, 1 game as PH. Typographical error; one of Frederick B. Carisch's 26 games.

Christman, H. B. 1888 Kansas City AA, 1 game as C. Documentation behind deletion no longer available.

Collins, Frank. 1892 St. Louis NL, 1 game as OF. Documentation behind deletion no longer available.

Costello, J. A. 1912 Cleveland AL, 1 game as OF. One of 11 games played by Kenneth L. Nash, who used pseudonym in debut.

Davis, Thomas J. 1890 Cleveland NL, 1 game as OF. One of George Stacey Davis' 136 games.

Davis, ——. 1903 Chicago NL, 1 game as OF. Documentation behind deletion no longer available.

Deniens,——. 1914 Chicago FL, 1 game as C. Typographical error; one of Clement L. Clemens' 13 games.

Drennan, K. John. 1904 Detroit AL, 1 game as 1B. Typographical error; one of William "Wild Bill" Donovan's 46 games.

Dresser, Edward. 1898 Brooklyn NL, 1 game as SS. Typographical error; one of Jack Dunn's 51 games.

Dugan, E. 1884 Kansas City UA, 3 games as OF. Same player as William H. Dugan, who played 9 games with Richmond AA the same year.

Gray, William. 1903 Pittsburgh NL, 2 games as OF. One

game belongs to Romer C. Grey; other game belongs to Ernest G. Diehl.

King, Frederick. 1901 Milwaukee AL, 1 game as C. Game belongs to John A. Butler, later with St. Louis and Brooklyn NL, who used pseudonym in debut.

Lane,——. 1901 Boston NL, 1 game as 3B. Typographical error; one of Bobby Lowe's 129 games.

Leonard,——. 1892 St. Louis NL, 1 game as OF. Documentation behind deletion no longer available.

Mares,——. 1894 Louisville NL, 1 games as OF. Documentation behind deletion no longer available.

McCauley, William. 1884 St. Louis AA, 1 game as C. Game belongs to James A. McCauley, who also played in 1885–1886.

Meddlebrook,——. 1884 Baltimore UA, 1 game as OF. Documentation behind deletion no longer available.

Merson,——. 1914 Brooklyn FL, 1 game as PH. Typographical error; one of George J. Anderson's 98 games.

Miller, Bert. 1897 Philadelphia NL, 3 games as 2B. Games belong to Frank A. Miller, formerly listed as Frederick Miller, who also played one game each with Washington NL and St. Louis NL in 1892.

Miller, Henry D. 1892 Chicago NL, 4 games as P. Games belong to Harry DeMiller, who was erroneously listed for 1 game as 3B with 1892 St. Louis NL.

Moore, Guy W. 1922 St. Louis NL, 1 game as OF. Documentation behind deletion no longer available.

Morgan, John P. 1916 Philadelphia AL, 1 game as 3B. Typographical error; one of Leland S. McElwee's 54 games.

Olsen, Albert W. 1943 Boston AL, 1 game as PH. Appearance apparently belongs to either Leon Culberson or Johnny Lazor.

Pratt, Thomas J. 1884 Baltimore AA, 1 game as OF. Documentation behind deletion no longer available.

Proctor, Lou. 1912 St. Louis AL, 1 game as PH. Game belongs to Anna S. "Pete" Compton, who played in 101 games that season.

Ritchie,——. 1910 St. Louis NL, 1 game as PH. Documentation behind deletion no longer available.

Schauer,——. 1890 Columbus AA, 1 game as 1B. Documentation behind deletion no longer available.

Seymour, Thomas. 1882 Pittsburgh AA, 1 game as P. Player's correct name was Jacob Semer.

Sheehan, Timothy. 1884 Washington UA, 1 game as OF. One of John A. Ryan's seven games.

Smith, Charles H. "Pacer." 1877 Chicago/Cincinnati NL, 34 games as 2B-OF-C. Record belongs to Harry W. Smith, who also played 1 game with 1889 Louisville AA.

Smith, E. J. 1890 Buffalo PL, 1 game as 1B. One of John Irwin's 77 games.

Strands, Lewis. 1915 Chicago FL, 1 game as 2B. One of John J. Farrell's 70 games.

Thayer, Edward L. 1876 New York NL, 1 game as 2B. Player's correct name was George T. Fair.

Turbot,——. 1902 St. Louis NL, 1 game as OF. Documentation behind deletion no longer available.

Valdes, Armando V. 1944 Washington AL, 1 game as PH. Game belongs to a different player, Rogelio "Roy" Valdes.

Young, David. 1895 St. Louis NL, 1 game as 3B. Documentation behind deletion no longer available.

CHAPTER 8

Baseball Families

Larry Amman

Just as the Wright brothers were first in flight, so were Wright brothers first in baseball. In the National Association's inaugural season of 1871, the Boston team featured Harry Wright as manager and reserve outfielder, and George at shortstop. Brother Sam joined them on the bench for the 1876 season, after an apprenticeship in New Haven the year before.

Since then there have been 330 brother combinations in the majors. The only season in which there was not at least one such pair was 1899. There were three new ones in both 1989 and 1990.

The first thing that strikes the eye as one reads the list is the large number who were teammates, however briefly—more than 25 percent.

Another observation one must make is how one-sided the big league performance was between so many of the combinations. For example, there are twenty-five members of the Hall of Fame who had brothers in the majors. Yet how many baseball fans have ever heard of the brothers of Bill Dickey, Christy Mathewson, or Honus Wagner? As another example, how many people remember the brothers of Steve Sax, Eddie Murray, Graig Nettles, and Robin Yount? All four of these current big names have brothers who played in the majors briefly.

Of course, being the brother of a major leaguer never guarantees success, nor even a shot at the big leagues. The five Delahantys, the three Boyers, and the two Ferrells all had other brothers who played minor league ball only.

Because the combinations in which more than one brother excelled are so rare, we can focus on the more outstanding ones.

In terms of balanced, outstanding achievement no group of three or more brothers can match the DiMaggios. The enduring folk hero status of Joe DiMaggio unfortunately has not done anything to keep alive the memory of his brothers, Vince and Dom. All three were gifted outfielders, good hitters, and fine all-around athletes. Vince, the oldest of these sons of a San Francisco fisherman, played for five different National League teams. In 1941 he had 21 homers and 100 RBIs for Pittsburgh. Four years later he hit four grand slams for the Phillies.

Dom DiMaggio was the youngest and smallest of the three brothers. Although lacking any of the power of the other two, he was the fastest on the bases and yielded nothing to his two brothers in the grace and skill he exhibited in the outfield. His lifetime batting average was just under .300.

In the 1941 All-Star Game, Dom went to right field as a late-inning substitute to play alongside Joe in center. This was a first in the mid-summer classic. In the eighth inning, Joe doubled and Dom singled him home. In the 1949 All-Star Game, Joe drove in Dom with what proved to be the margin of victory for the junior circuit.

Dominic, or the "Little Professor" as he was called, started four different All-Star games, including the 1946 contest. That year he was voted to start in center field ahead of his brother. On the season, Dom outhit Joe by 26 points (.316 to .290).

In the 1943 All-Star Game, Vince went 3 for 3, including a ninth-inning home run. While Joe and Dom were away in the military, Vince was ". . . maintaining the family tradition of excellence in All-Star Games."

The first time two brothers played against each other in an All-Star Game was in 1969. Carlos May of the White Sox came to bat as a pinch-hitter with brother Lee of the Reds playing first base. In the 1990 mid-summer classic, television cameras showed Sandy Alomar, Jr., at bat while Roberto Alomar set himself at second base, ready to field anything his brother might have hit his way.

For the title of the best brother pitching combination, the competition is very close between the Niekros of Ohio and the Perrys of Williamston, North Carolina. In 1987 the ancient knuckleballing duo of Phil and Joe Niekro passed Jim and Gaylord Perry in wins. The two families remain very close in most statistical categories.

The Perry brothers had one full season as teammates—1974 with Cleveland, when the two combined for 39 victories, almost half of the team total. A year earlier, when Jim was with Detroit, the two made their only start against each other. Gaylord took the loss for Cleveland. Jim got a no-decision. In the 1970 All-Star Game, the National League pitcher in the sixth and seventh innings was Gaylord Perry of the Giants. On the mound for the American League in the seventh and eighth innings was Jim Perry of the Twins. This is the only time two brothers were rival pitchers in the mid-summer classic. Both have also won the Cy Young Award.

For Joe and Phil Niekro, pitching against each other was not that uncommon. It happened nine different times. The most noteworthy occasion came on September 26, 1978, in Atlanta. Before this, his last start of the season, Phil was 19–17 for the Braves; Joe was 12–14 for the Astros. Houston won 2–0, much to the dismay of victor Joe. He loathed the idea of pitching against his brother in these circumstances.

Harry and Stan Coveleski of the coal-mining country in Pennsylvania were brother hurlers who refused to start games against each other. Stan, the younger, was in his first full season in the majors in 1916 at Cleveland while Harry was winning 20 for the third consecutive year at Detroit. Harry developed arm trouble and did not pitch another full season, but Stan went on to five 20-win seasons and a niche in the Hall of Fame.

Virtually every baseball fan has heard of the game on September 15, 1963, in which Felipe, Matty, and Jesus Alou formed the San Francisco outfield for one inning. A better story about this Dominican family, however, is the race for the 1966 National League batting title.

Going into the season, Felipe, with the Atlanta Braves, had established himself as a hitter of high average and respectable power. Younger brother Matty's career so far had been disappointing. With no power, his lifetime batting average was .260. In the off-season the Giants had traded him to Pittsburgh.

With the Bucs, Matty came under the special tutelage of manager Harry Walker. "Harry the Hat" taught his pupil to chop down on the ball and to hit to left field instead of trying to pull. This, plus over 20 bunt and 30 infield singles, propelled Matty to the top of the league batting race. Second or third to him almost all year was Atlanta leadoff man and first baseman Felipe Alou. Matty won the crown with a .342 average, while Felipe finished second at .327. The elder brother, however, led the circuit in runs, hits, and total bases.

It was only fitting that Harry Walker was the cause of the enormous jump in Matty's batting average. In 1947 Harry Walker the outfielder was traded from the Cardinals to the Phillies early in the season. There he won the batting title with an average 100 points higher than the year before. This was the second batting title in the family. In 1944 older brother Dixie had led the senior circuit with a .357 mark at Brooklyn.

Brother rivalries and brother teammates come into very sharp focus under the media glare of the World Series. The fall classics from 1921 to 1932 featured Bob Meusel of the Yankees versus older brother Emil or "Irish" of the Giants. These two California outfielders were very similar in physical appearance and in capabilities.

Before the 1921 Series one writer summed up the pair: *Bob hits harder than Emil though he is not as consistent in garnering his hits. Bob also excels Emil as a thrower, but Emil is the more finished fielder. Bob is a left field hitter, and Emil often hits to right, so the play of "Meusel flied to Meusel" may be repeated frequently during the Series.*

Indeed, it was so in all three series. In Game Three of the 1923 fall classic, each brother robbed the other of an extra-base hit. Over all, Irish emerged superior to Bob in every category—even in extra-base hits. Bob, however, had the last laugh, driving in the go-ahead run in Game Six of 1923 to give the Yankees their first world title.

For their entire careers, the Meusels startle the observer with the closeness of all their statistics. Irish averaged .310 to Bob's .309, both for 11 seasons. Bob leads in all other categories, but not by much. If Irish's totals were increased by prorating them based on his 100 fewer games, the two would look like clones. Each man led his league in RBIs one time.

Two brothers whose lifetime batting averages are identical are Bob and Roy Johnson. Both of these Oklahoma

Indians hit .296 as American League outfielders in the 1930s. Bob amassed 2,000 hits and almost 300 home runs, playing mostly for Connie Mack. Elder brother Roy was a speedy singles and doubles hitter. He exceeded his brother only in stolen bases in his considerably shorter career.

The 1927 World Series featured Lloyd Waner leading off and playing center field for Pittsburgh while older brother Paul hit third and patrolled right field. In just his second season, Paul had won the batting title. Rookie Lloyd finished second in hits and third in batting average. The two combined for 460 hits during the season and were 11 for 30 in the World Series as the Yankees swept the Pirates in four games.

The Waners played parts of 16 seasons together, much longer than any other pair. Paul hit 17 points higher in batting and almost 70 points higher in slugging. However, "Big Poison" was actually shorter than Lloyd. Paul's moniker came from all the doubles and triples he delivered.

In 1934 Dizzy and Paul Dean had the greatest year any pitching brothers have ever enjoyed. "Me 'n' Paul" together won 49 games during the regular season and all four of the games the Cardinals won from the Tigers in the World Series. In 1935 their combined victory total was only two less. These two 19-win seasons were Paul's only full years in the majors.

An even more memorable year in St. Louis Cardinal history was 1942. In the last week of August, the Red Birds were five games behind the defending champion Brooklyn Dodgers. Five weeks later the Cardinals clinched first place with a record September rush. Winning five games in the last month for a total of 22 on the season was Mort Cooper. Catching him was younger brother Walker, in his first season as a regular. Mort won his September games with great flair. He was called the "fashion plate" for wearing the number on his back which equaled the victory he was seeking that day. The Cardinals beat the Yankees in a five-game World Series to shock all of baseball. Walker Cooper contributed several timely hits to the Series upset.

Mort also won 20 for the 1943 and 1944 pennant winners and had a victory in each of the World Series. Both brothers were named to *The Sporting News* All-Star team in 1944. Walker hit an even .300 for three Fall Classics.

The Coopers may have been the best of the 15 brother battery combinations, but Wes and Rick Ferrell have to be a close second. Rick caught his younger brother for five straight seasons. Wes won 20 the first two years together.

The next great brother act in the World Series was in 1964, when Ken and Clete Boyer were the opposing third basemen. Elder brother Ken was the National League's Most Valuable Player with a league-leading 119 RBIs for St. Louis. Clete had hit an anemic .219 for the Yankees. Still, this was his chance to show the baseball world he was Ken's equal in the field.

Although neither hit for a high average in the seven games, both did well with the glove. Ken gave his team all its runs in Game Four with a grand-slam homer. St. Louis won that contest 4–3. In the seventh game, Ken scored the first run and later homered. Brother Clete helped make the finish exciting as he hit one of the two solo home runs off Bob Gibson in the ninth inning. Like the Coopers, the Boyers were born and raised in the "Show Me" state.

Both parents were in the stands maintaining their strict neutrality and feeling great pride.

The integrity of play when brothers square off against each other has been taken for granted for many years. This wasn't always the case. In 1933 Joe Sewell, playing third base for the Yankees, and Luke Sewell, catching for Washington, found themselves on opposite sides of a hot pennant race. They had been teammates at Cleveland for a number of years.

Reporting on a crucial game in the 1933 American League race, Shirley Povich of the *Washington Post* wrote:

It was brother versus brother in the seventh when Joe Sewell made a whale of a stop and throw to cut down Luke. It's things like that help prove the honesty of baseball.

The shadow of the Black Sox Scandal still hung over the game.

Now for a trivia windup: There have been five brother shortstop–second base combinations in big league history: Granny and Garvin Hamner of the 1945 Phillies, Lou and Dino Chiozza of the 1935 Phillies, Milt and Frank Bolling of the 1958 Tigers, Eddie and Johnny O'Brien of the

Pirates in the mid-1950s, and Cal and Bill Ripken of the 1987 Orioles. The O'Briens were one of seven sets of twins in the majors.

Josh Clarke with Louisville in the National League in 1898 and George "White Wings" Tebeau of Cleveland in 1894–1895 must have felt some sense of constraint in criticizing their managers. In both cases it was a brother: Fred Clarke and Patsy Tebeau. Both pilots were regular players those seasons as well. Ed Hengle, who never played in the majors, managed his brother Moxie in the Union Association for the entry that began the season in Chicago. By the end of the campaign, both Mengels were gone, and the club had moved to Pittsburgh.

Wes and Rick Ferrell have something in common with Jesse and Lee Tannehill. In each case the pitching brother—Wes and Jesse—had a higher career batting average and more home runs than the brother who played every day.

No, Henry and Tommie Aaron were not the first "soul-brother" brother combination in major-league baseball. The game's first black siblings were Fleet and Welday Walker, who both played for Toledo of the American Association in 1884. That circuit was then considered a major league.

Brothers' Combined Totals

Seasons		Games		Hits		Doubles		Triples	
Alou	47	Alou	5,129	Waner	5,611	DiMaggio	906	Waner	308
Niekro	46	Waner	4,541	Alou	5,094	Waner	884	Delahanty	280
Delahanty	41	DiMaggio	4,245	DiMaggio	4,853	Delahanty	769	Wagner	256
Perry	39	Boyer	3,872	Delahanty	4,211	Alou	765	Clarke	233
Waner	38	Aaron	3,735	Aaron	3,987	Sewell	709	Connor	225
Boyer	36	Delahanty	3,595	Sewell	3,619	Johnson	671	DiMaggio	212
Sewell	35	Sewell	3,532	Boyer	3,559	Aaron	666	Meusel	187
DiMaggio	34	May	3,236	Wagner	3,489	Wagner	658	Johnson	178
Ferrell	33	Cruz	3,077	Johnson	3,343	Meusel	618	Ewing	178
Forsch	32	Johnson	3,016	Meusel	3,214	*Brett	577	Wheat	177
*Brett	32								

Home Runs		Runs		RBI's		Batting Average (10 seasons)		Steals	
Aaron	768	DiMaggio	2,927	DiMaggio	2,739	Manush	.329	Wagner	726
DiMaggio	573	Waner	2,827	Aaron	2,391	Wagner	.326	Delahanty	685
Boyer	444	Delahanty	2,309	Delahanty	2,153	*Gwynn	.326	Clarke	557
May	444	Aaron	2,276	Waner	1,907	Waner	.325	Milan	501
Nettles	406	Alou	2,213	Meusel	1,887	Connor	.314	Cruz	322
Allen	358	Johnson	1,956	Johnson	1,839	Delahanty	.311	Alou	294
*Murray	383	Sewell	1,794	Boyer	1,803	*Brett	.310	Meusel	253
Johnson	346	Wagner	1,762	May	1,780	Meusel	.309	Moriarty	250
*Brett	291	Boyer	1,761	Wagner	1,750	Wheat	.309	Aaron	249
Bando	269	Clarke	1,744	Sewell	1,747	Clarke	.308	*Yount	241
						O'Rourke	.308		

Brother Pitching Totals

Games		Innings		Wins		Losses		Strikeouts		Shutouts		Complete Games	
Niekro	1,566	Niekro	8,690	Niekro	538	Niekro	478	Perry	5,110	Perry	85	Clarkson	571
Perry	1,407	Perry	8,637	Perry	529	Perry	439	Niekro	5,089	Niekro	74	Radbourn	491
Forsch	1,019	Clarkson	5,616	Clarkson	383	Forsch	249	Mathewson	2,504	Coveleski	51	Weyhing	455
McDaniel	1,006	Forsch	4,921	Radbourn	309	Weyhing	239	Clarkson	2,326	Clarkson	43	Mathewson	436
Reuschel	751	Mathewson	4,793	Coveleski	296	Clarkson	232	Forsch	2,180	Forsch	37	Perry	412
*Still active		Reuschel	3,854	Forsch	282							Niekro	352
												Coveleski	308

Fathers and Sons

Shortly after breaking into the majors, Dale Berra was asked about similarities between himself and his famous father, Yogi. The younger Berra replied, "Our similarities are different."

Like the many malapropisms of Yogi Berra, this one by his son may appear foolish on the surface, but it contains quite a bit of underlying wisdom. In fact, it can serve as a metaphor for father-son combinations in major league baseball.

Of the 120 combinations, only thirty-seven feature both

generations at the same position. There are eighteen father-son pitcher combinations, five cases where both father and son caught, one where both played first, two where both played shortstop, and eleven where both father and son were outfielders. Very few fathers and sons at any position have career totals that are at all close.

Another important generalization is the great increase in father-son combinations since World War Two, especially in the last twenty years. The first son of a former big leaguer to break into the majors was Jack Doscher in 1903 as a pitcher for the Chicago Cubs—one of the three teams with whom his father, Herm, had toiled as a utility player twenty years earlier. By 1945 the number of father-son combinations was 36. In 1965 the total was 66. That means almost 40 percent of today's number has been added in the last two decades.

Is the son of a big league ballplayer more apt to develop into a major leaguer than the average boy? Some people think not. In the 1950s, Hall of Famer George Sisler was asked this very question. The two-time .400 hitter shook his head over how two of his offspring had made the majors. He pointed out that baseball players are absentee fathers. They don't have much opportunity to teach their boys the fundamentals of the game or to practice with them.

If not their fathers, perhaps other well-qualified professionals have instructed the second generation. A worthwhile study could be conducted to determine how many second-generation players who have broken in during the last two decades attended baseball camps as boys. If the number is significant, this could explain the big increase during this period.

Certainly, the Sisler family deserves special attention. Father George broke into the majors just before World War One as a pitcher for the St. Louis Browns. After being switched to first base, he spent fifteen years as one of the greatest performers ever at that position. Accordingly, it is only fitting that he should have one son, Dick, who was a good hitter and another son, Dave, who pitched in the majors briefly. Dick's home run on the last day of the 1950 season, which gave the Philadelphia Whiz Kids the pennant, has given him an identity independent of his father. Also, these two men both managed in the majors for a short time. Currently they are the only father-son combination in this category.

Baseball families fall into one of three categories: famous fathers only, famous sons only, and equals.

Let us consider the famous son category first. Another way of describing these men would be to call them "fathers of . . ." Two families stand out in this category. They are the Muellers and the Walkers.

Walter Mueller was a reserve outfielder for the Pirates for four seasons in the 1920s. His son, Don, hit .296 in twelve seasons as a National League outfielder. In 1954 Mueller and teammate Willie Mays battled all season for the batting title on the pennant-winning Giants. Mays finished first in hitting by three points, but Mueller led the league in hits with 212.

Dixie Walker was a pitcher for the Washington team from 1909 through 1912. His lifetime record was 24–30. Both his sons, Fred (or "Dixie") and Harry, won batting titles.

These two are the only clear cases of a son of All-Star

quality who had a father whose career in the majors was forgettable. Other families with "fathers of . . ." are Coleman, Grimsley, and Smalley.

In contrast, the list of "sons of . . ." is a long one. There are seven baseball fathers in the Hall of Fame. Averill, Berra, Collins, Lindstrom, Mack, and Walsh had offspring who fit this category. Four more families—Bagby, Camilli, Trosky, and Wood—had fathers of All-Star quality and sons who are footnotes to their careers. Hegan, Wills, and Trout are families where the sons had respectable careers and characteristics similar to those of the fathers, but the older generation was clearly superior.

We must consider first whether some of the "sons of . . ." got to the majors, or second, stayed longer than they merited, because of the family name. I would cite Collins, Walsh, and Wood to prove the former proposition, and Dale Berra and Marc Sullivan as support for the latter.

The younger Berra and Sullivan not only had the temerity to go into their father's business, but, like Bill and Cal Ripken, Jr., of Baltimore, they had dad for their boss. The Ripkens (in 1988) and Dale Berra (in 1985) saw their fathers dismissed as managers early in the season. Cal Ripken, Sr., was not only the first father to manage two sons at once, but the first without major league playing experience to manage his sons.

Sullivan, whose father owned part of the Red Sox, traded his son to the Houston Astros organization before the 1988 season, where he could commiserate with the Berras on the difficulties of combining a baseball career with family obligations.

By far the most interesting category is that of the fathers and sons whose careers parallel or equal each other.

The two Billy Sullivans caught for both the White Sox and the Tigers. Both played other positions as well as caught in one World Series. Sullivan Senior caught the older Ed Walsh; Junior caught the younger Ed Walsh—both at Chicago. Junior hit for what appears a much higher average, but we must remember that Senior played in the Dead-Ball Era, and Junior in the high-hitting 1930s.

Jim and Mike Hegan were a father-son combination well known for defensive ability. Father Jim was a great handler of pitchers for Cleveland. Mike played first base and the outfield for several American League teams. Both appeared in two World Series. Mike broke into the majors just four seasons after his father's finale.

The father-son pitching combinations have few parallels. Both Thornton Lee and son Don gave up homers to Ted Williams. The two Jim Bagbys are the only father and son who both pitched in a World Series.

Joe Schultz, Junior, received some unwanted publicity in Jim Bouton's book *Ball Four,* for being Bouton's manager. Schultz and his father, Joe Senior, each spent almost a decade in the majors as reserve players. Senior was 46 for 170 as a pinch-hitter. Junior went 43 for 160 in that same role.

It is only fitting that Buddy Bell spent a portion of his fine career with the Cincinnati Reds, the team on which his father Gus spent his best years. The two ended their careers with nearly identical batting averages and home run totals.

Five father-son combinations have played in All-Star Games. Prior to 1990 only the Bell and Boone families could have made that boast. Then Barry Bonds, Ken Griffey, Jr., and both Alomar sons made their debuts in the mid-summer classic. The Bells and Boones have similar statistics. Gus was 2 for 6, hitting a home run his first time up; Buddy was 1 for 7, hitting a triple in his first plate appearance. Ray Boone went 1 for 5 in All-Star games with a homer; Bob is 2 for 5 in three games.

In Game One of the 1984 World Series, a two-run double by San Diego catcher Terry Kennedy was noted by the television announcers as something significant. This was the first time in the history of the fall classic that both a father and son had a World Series RBI. Terry's father, Bob, knocked in a run for Cleveland as an outfielder in the 1948 Series. There have been seven families in which the father and son both played in a World Series. Five have been mentioned already; there is also Ernie and Don Johnson. The father was a substitute infielder for the Yankees in the 1923 Series. Don was the regular second baseman for the Cubs in the 1945 fall classic. Stan Javier

in 1988 and 1989 with Oakland makes seven; his father, Julian, played in four World Series.

An interesting father-son parallel to watch for in the future is that between Bobby and Barry Bonds. The son, an outfielder for Pittsburgh, has his father's penchant for home runs, stolen bases, and strikeouts.

The Bondses are not the first black father-son combination. That honor goes to the Hairstons. Father Sam caught two games for the White Sox in 1951. Son Jerry was a respected pinch-hitter for that team for over a decade.

Now that Ken Griffey, Sr., and Ken Griffey, Jr., have combined to give the Seattle Mariners a public-relations bonanza, what does the future hold for baseball fathers and sons? Will Bob Boone be the first son of a big leaguer to be voted into the Hall of Fame? Will the Treshes or the Boones provide the first father-son-grandson combination in the majors? We can be sure there will be many more combinations and more interesting parallels.

Father-Son Hitters

	Years	Games	Runs	Hits	Homers	RBIs	BA	Steals		Years	Games	Runs	Hits	Homers	RBIs	BA	Steals
AVERILL									**KENNEDY**								
Earl, Sr.	13	1,669	1,224	2,020	238	1,165	.318	69	Bob	16	1,483	514	1,176	63	514	.254	45
Earl, Jr.	9	449	137	249	44	159	.242	3	Terry	13	1,422	462	1,273	110	615	.265	6
BELL									**SCHOFIELD**								
Gus	15	1,741	865	1,823	206	942	.281	30	Ducky	19	1,321	394	699	21	211	.227	12
Buddy	18	2,405	1,150	2,514	201	1,106	.279	55	Dick	8	926	356	692	48	247	.233	89
BERRA									**SISLER**								
Yogi	19	2,120	1,175	2,150	358	1,430	.285	30	George	15	2,055	1,283	2,812	99	1,175	.340	375
Dale	11	853	236	603	49	278	.236	32	Dick	8	799	302	720	55	360	.276	6
BONDS									**SMALLEY**								
Bobby	14	1,849	1,258	1,886	332	1,024	.268	461	Roy, Jr.	11	872	277	601	61	305	.227	4
Barry	5	717	468	688	117	337	.265	169	Roy, III	13	1,653	745	1,454	163	694	.257	27
BOONE									**SULLIVAN**								
Ray	13	1,373	645	1,260	151	737	.275	21	Billy, Sr.	16	1,146	363	777	20	378	.212	98
Bob	19	2,264	679	1,838	105	826	.254	38	Billy, Jr.	12	962	347	820	29	388	.289	30
CAMILLI									**TRESH**								
Dolf	12	1,490	936	1,482	239	950	.277	60	Mike	12	1,027	326	788	2	297	.249	19
Doug	9	313	56	153	18	80	.199	0	Tom	9	1,192	595	1,041	153	530	.245	45
HEGAN									**WILLS**								
Jim	17	1,666	550	1,087	92	525	.228	15	Maury	14	1,942	1,067	2,134	20	458	.281	586
Mike	12	965	281	504	53	229	.242	28	Bump	6	831	472	807	36	302	.266	196

Father-Son Pitchers

	Years	Games	W-L	SO	CG	ERA		Years	Games	W-L	SO	CG	ERA
BAGBY							**QUEEN**						
Jim, Sr.	9	316	127–89	450	132	3.10	Mel, Sr.	8	146	27–40	328	15	5.09
Jim, Jr.	10	303	97–96	431	84	3.96	Mel, Jr.	9	140	20–17	302	6	3.14
COLEMAN							**SISLER**						
Joe, Sr.	10	223	52–76	444	60	4.38	George	7	24	5–6	63	9	2.35
Joe, Jr.	15	484	142–135	1728	94	3.69	Dave	7	247	38–44	355	12	4.33
KRAUSSE							**TROUT**						
Lew, Sr.	2	23	5–1	17	3	4.48	Paul	15	521	170–161	1,256	158	3.23
Lew, Jr.	12	321	68–91	721	21	4.00	Steve	12	301	88–92	656	32	4.18
LEE							**WALSH**						
Thornton	16	374	117–124	937	155	3.56	Ed, Sr.	14	430	195–126	2,346	250	1.82
Don	9	244	40–44	467	13	3.61	Ed, Jr.	4	79	11–24	107	15	5.57
PILLETTE													
Herman	4	107	34–32	148	33	3.45							
Duane	8	188	38–66	305	34	4.40							

Baseball Families

KEY

tm teammates
F-S father-son

BROTHERS
AARON   Henry & Tommie *tm*
ACOSTA   Jose & Merito
ADAMS   Bobby & Dick *F-S also*
ALLEN   Dick, Hank & Ron *tm*
ALLISON   Art & Doug *tm*
ALOMAR   Roberto & Sandy Jr.
ALOU   Felipe, Matty & Jesus *tm*
ANDERSON   Kent & Mike
ANDREWS   Rob & Mike
ASPROMONTE   Bob & Ken

BAILEY   Ed & Jim *tm*
BAKER   Dave & Doug
BANDO   Chris & Sal
BANNON   Jimmy & Tom
BARNES   Jesse & Virgil
BARRETT   Marty & Tom
BAXES   Jim & Mike
BELL   Charlie & Frank
BELL   George & Juan
BENNETT   Dave & Dennis *tm*
BERGEN   Bill & Marty
BIGBEE   Carson & Lyle *tm*
BLANKENSHIP   Homer & Ted *tm*
BLUEGE   Ossie & Otto
BOLLING   Frank & Milt *tm*
BOONE   Danny & Ike
BOYER   Clete, Ken & Cloyd *tm*
BOYLE   Buzz & Jim
BOYLE   Eddie & Jack
BRADY   Steve & Tom
BRASHEAR   Kitty & Roy
BREEDEN   Danny & Hal *tm*
BRETT   George & Ken
BREWER   Mike & Tony
BRINKMAN   Chuck & Ed
BROWN   Dick & Larry
BROWN   Jackie & Paul
BROWN   Oscar & Ollie

CAMNITZ   Harry & Howie *tm*
CAMP   Kid & Llewellan *tm*
CAMPBELL   Hugh & Mat *tm*
CANSECO   Jose & Ozzie
CANTWELL   Mike & Tom
CARLYLE   Cleo & Roy
CASEY   Dan & Dennis *tm*
CHIOZZA   Dino & Lou *tm*
CHRISTOPHER   Lloyd & Russ
CLAPP   Aaron & John
CLARKE   Fred & Josh *tm*
CLARKE   Sumpter & Rufe
CLARKSON   Dad, John &
   Walter *tm*
CLIBURN   Stan & Stew
COFFMAN   Dick & Slick
COHEN   Andy & Syd
CONIGLIARO   Billy & Tony
CONNELL   Gene & Joe
CONNOR   Joe & Roger
CONWAY   Jim & Pete
CONWAY   Bill & Dick
COONEY   Jimmy & Johnny *tm F-S*
   also
COOPER   Mort & Walker *tm*
CORCORAN   Larry & Mike *tm*
COSCARART   Joe & Pete
COVELESKI   Harry & Stan
COVINGTON   Sam & Tex
CROSS   Amos, Frank & Lave *tm*
CRUZ   Hector, Jose & Tommy *tm*
CUCCINELLO   Al & Tony

DAILY   Con & Ed
DALY   Joe & Tom
DANNING   Harry & Ike
DARINGER   Cliff & Rolla
DAVALILLO   Vic & Yo-Yo
DAVENPORT   Claude & Dave
DEAN   Dizzy & Paul *tm*
DEASLEY   Jim & Pat
DELAHANTY   Ed, Frank, Jim,
   Joe & Tom *tm*
DEMONTREVILLE   Gene & Lee
DICKEY   Bill & George

DILLON   Packy & Joe *tm*
DIMAGGIO   Vince, Joe & Dom
DONAHUE   Jiggs & Pat
DONNELLY   Pete & John
DONOVAN   Jerry & Tom
DORGAN   Jerry & Mike
DOWNS   Kelly & Dave
DOYLE   Brian & Doyle
DRAKE   Sammy & Solly
DUGAN   Bill & Ed *tm*

EDWARDS   Dave, Marshall &
   Mike (twins)
ENS   Jewel & Mutz
ERAUTT   Eddie & Joe
EVERS   Joe & Johnny
EWING   Buck & John *tm*

FALK   Bibb & Chet
FERRELL   Rick & Wes *tm*
FERRY   Cy & Jack
FINNEY   Hal & Lou
FISHER   Bob & Newt
FISHER   Chauncey & Tom
FOGARTY   Jim & Joe
FORD   Gene & Russ
FOREMAN   Brownie & Frank *tm*
FORSCH   Bob & Ken
FOUTZ   Dave & Frank
FOWLER   Art & Jesse
FREESE   Gene & George
FRIEL   Bill & Pat
FULLER   Harry & Shorty
FULMER   Chick & Washington

GAGLIANO   Phil & Ralph
GANZEL   Charlie & John *F-S also*
GARBARK   Bob & Mike
GARDELLA   Al & Danny *tm*
GARRETT   Adrian & Wayne
GASTON   Alex & Milt *tm*
GEISS   Bill & Emil
GENTRY   Harvey & Rufe
GILBERT   Harry & John *tm*
GILBERT   Charlie & Tookie *F-S*
   also
GLEASON   Bill & Jack *tm*
GLEASON   Harry & Kid
GRABOWSKI   Al & Reggie
GRAVES   Joe & Sid
GREGG   Dave & Vean
GRIMES   Ray & Roy (twins) *F-*
   S also
GRISSOM   Lee & Marv
GROH   Heine & Lew
GUMBERT   Ad & Billy
GWYNN   Chris & Tony

HACKETT   Mert & Walter *tm*
HAFEY   Bud & Tom
HAIRSTON   Jerry & John *F-S also*
HAMNER   Garvin & Granny *tm*
HANDLEY   Gene & Lee
HARGRAVE   Bubbles & Pinky
HATFIELD   Gil & John
HAYWORTH   Ray & Red
HEMPHILL   Charlie & Frank
HENGLE   Emery (Moxie) & Ed *tm*
HEVING   Joe & Johnnie
HIGH   Andy, Charlie & Hugh
HILL   Hugh & Still Bill
HINCHMAN   Bill & Harry *tm*
HITCHCOCK   Billy & Jim
HOGAN   George & Happy
HOVLIK   Hick & Joe
HOWARD   Del & Ivon
HUGHES   Jim & Mickey
HUGHES   Ed & Tom
HUNTER   Bill & George

IORG   Dane & Garth
IRWIN   Arthur & John

JEFFCOAT   George & Hal
JIMENEZ   Elvio & Manny
JONES   Darryl & Lynn
JONES   Gary & Steve
JOHNSON   Bob & Roy
JOHNSON   Chet & Earl
JOHNSTON   Doc & Jimmy

JONNARD   Bubber & Claude
   (twins)
JORGENS   Arndt & Orville

KAPPEL   Heinie & Joe
KELL   George & Skeeter
KELLER   Charlie & Hal
KELLNER   Alex & Walt *tm*
KELLY   George & Ren
KENNEDY   Jim & Junior
KEOUGH   Marty & Joe *F-S also*
KILLEFER   Bill & Red
KILROY   Matt & Mike *tm*
KLAUS   Billy & Bobby
KLING   Bill & Johnny
KNODE   Mike & Ray
KNOTHE   Fritz & George
KOPF   Larry & Wally
KRSNICH   Mike & Rocky

LACHEMANN   Marcel & Rene
LANNING   Johnny & Tom
LANSFORD   Carney & Joe
LARY   Al & Frank
LEITER   Al & Mark
LELIVELT   Bill & Jack
LILLARD   Bill & Gene *tm*
LOBERT   Frank & Hans
LOOK   Bruce & Dean
LOWDERMILK   Grover & Lou *tm*
LUSH   Billy & Ernie

MACHA   Ken & Mike
MADDUX   Greg & Mike
MAHLER   Mickey & Rick *tm*
MAISEL   Fritz & George
MANCUSO   Frank & Gus
MANGUAL   Angel & Pepe
MANSELL   John, Mike & Tom *tm*
MANUSH   Frank & Heine
MARION   Marty & Red
MASKREY   Harry & Leech *tm*
MATHEWSON   Christy & Henry *tm*
MATTOX   Cloy & Jim
MAY   Carlos & Lee
MAYER   Erskine & Sam
MCDANIEL   Lindy & Von *tm*
MCFARLAN   Alex & Dan
MCFARLAND   Lamont & Charles
MCGEEHAN   Connie & Dan
MCLAUGHLIN   Barney & Frank *tm*
MEUSEL   Bob & Irish
MILAN   Clyde & Horace *tm*
MILLER   Jake & Russ
MILLER   Bing & Ralph *tm*
MITCHELL   John & Charlie
MOFFETT   Joe & Sam
MORIARTY   Bill & George
MORRISON   Johnny & Phil *tm*
MORRISSEY   John & Tom
MUELLER   Clarence & Walter
   F-S also
MURRAY   George & Rich
MYERS   Billy & Lynn

NETTLES   Graig & Jim
NEWKIRK   Floyd & Joel
NIEKRO   Joe & Phil *tm*
NIXON   Otis & Donnell
NYMAN   Chris & Nyls

O'BRIEN   Eddie & Johnny
   (twins) *tm*
OGDEN   Curley & Jack
OLIVO   Chi Chi & Diomedes
O'NEILL   Jack, Jim, Mike &
   Steve *tm*
ONSLOW   Eddie & Jack
O'ROURKE   Jim & John *F-S also*
ORTIZ   Baby & Roberto *tm*
O'TOOLE   Denny & Jim
OWEN   Dave & Spike

PACIOREK   John, Tom & Jim
PARKER   Jay & Doc
PARROTT   Jiggs & Tom *tm*
PASCUAL   Camilo & Carlos
PATTERSON   Ham & Pat
PEITZ   Heine & Joe *tm*
PENA   Ramon & Tony

PEPLOSKI   Henry & Pepper
PERRY   Gaylord & Jim *tm*
PEREZ   Pascual & Melido
PFEFFER   Big Jeff & Jeff
PIERSON   Dave & Dick
PIKE   Jay & Lip
PIPGRAS   Ed & George
POTTER   Dykes & Squire

RADBOURN   George & Old Hoss
RAJSICH   Dave & Gary
REACH   Al & Bob
RECCIUS   John & Phil (twins) *tm*
REUSCHEL   Paul & Rick *tm*
REYNOLDS   Hal & Don
RICKETTS   Dick & Dave
RIDDLE   Elmer & Johnny *tm*
RIPKEN   Cal & Billy   *tm F-S also*
ROBINSON   Bruce & Dave
ROBINSON   Fred & Wilbert
ROENICKE   Gary & Ron
ROETTGER   Oscar & Wally
ROMO   Vicente & Romero Enrique
ROOF   Gene & Phil
ROSENBERG   Harry & Lou
ROTH   Braggo & Frank
ROWE   Dave & Jack
ROY   Charlie & Luther
RUSSELL   Allan & Lefty

SADOWSKI   Bob, Eddie & Ted
SAUER   Ed & Hank
SAX   Dave & Steve *tm*
SAY   Jimmie & Lou *tm*
SCANLAN   Doc & Frank
SCHANG   Bobby & Wally
SCHAREIN   Art & George
SCHMIDT   Boss & Walt
SCHULTE   Herman & Leonard
SEWELL   Luke, Joe & Tommie *tm*
SHAFFER   Orator & Taylor *tm*
SHANNON   Joe & Red *tm*
SHANTZ   Billy & Bobby *tm*
SHERLOCK   Monk & Vince
SHERRY   Larry & Norm *tm*
SISLER   Dave & Dick *F-S also*
SMITH   Charlie & Fred
SOWDERS   Bill, John & Len
STAFFORD   John & Jim
STANICEK   Steve & Pete
STANLEY   Buck & Joe
STOTTLEMYRE   Mel, Jr. & Todd
STOVALL   George & Jessie
SURHOFF   Bill & Rich
SUTHERLAND   Darrell & Gary

TANNEHILL   Jesse & Lee
TEBEAU   Patsy & White Wings *tm*
THIELMAN   Henry & Jake
THOMAS   Bill & Roy *tm*
THOMPSON   Homer & Tommy *tm*
THRONEBERRY   Faye & Marv
TOBIN   Jim & Johnny
TORRE   Frank & Joe *tm*
TRAFFLEY   Bill & John
TREACEY   Fred & Pete *tm*
TREVINO   Alex & Bobby
TWOMBLY   Babe & George
TYLER   Fred & Lefty *tm*
TYRONE   Jim & Wayne

UNDERWOOD   Pat & Tom
UPTON   Bill & Tom

VAN CUYK   Chris & Johnny

WADE   Ben & Jake
WAGNER   Butts & Honus
WALKER   Dixie Sr. & Ernie *F-S*
   also
WALKER   Dixie Jr. & Harry
WALKER   Gee & Hub *tm*
WALKER   Fleet & Welday *tm*
WANER   Lloyd & Paul *tm*
WATT   Al & Frank
WEILAND   Bob & Ed
WESTLAKE   Jim & Wally
WEYHING   Gus & John
WHEAT   Mack & Zack
WHITE   Deacon & Will *tm*

WHITNEY   Art & Frank
WILLIAMS   Gus & Harry
WILTSE   Hooks & Snake
WINGO   Al & Ivy
WOOD   Fred & Pete *tm*
WRIGHT   George, Harry &
    Sam *tm*
YOCHIM   Len & Ray
YOUNT   Larry & Robin

FATHERS-SONS

ADAMS   Bobby-Mike
ALOMAR   Sandy-Roberto &
  Sandy Jr.
ALOU   Felipe-Moises
ARAGON   Angel-Jack
AVERILL   Earl-Earl

BAGBY   Jim Sr. & Jr.
BARNHART   Clyde-Vic
BEAMON   Charlie-Charlie
BELL   Gus-Buddy
BERRA   Yogi-Dale
BERRY   Charlie-Charlie
BERRY   Joe-Joe
BONDS   Bobby-Barry
BOONE   Ray-Bob
BRICKELL   Fred-Fritzie
BRUCKER   Earle Sr. & Jr.
BRUMLEY   Mike-Tony

CAMILLI   Dolf-Doug
CAMPANIS   Alex-Jim
CARREON   Camilo-Mark
COLEMAN   Joe-Joe
COLLINS   Ed Sr. & Jr.
CONNOLLY   Ed Sr. & Jr.
COONEY   Jimmy-Jimmy & John
CORRIDEN   Red-John
CROUCH   Bill-Wilmer

DOSCHER   Herm-Jack

ELLSWORTH   Dick-Steve
ESCHEN   Jim-Larry

FRANCONA   Tito-Terry

GABRIELSON   Len-Len
GANZEL   Charlie-Babe
GILBERT   Larry-Charlie & Tookie
GRAHAM   Peaches-Jack
GREEN   Fred-Gary
GRIFFEY   Ken Sr. & Jr. *tm*
GRIMES   Ray-Oscar
GRIMSLEY   Ross-Ross

HAIRSTON   Sam-Jerry & John
HEGAN   Jim-Mike
HEINTZELMAN   Ken-Tom
HOOD   Wally Sr. & Jr.
HUNDLEY   Randy-Todd

JAVIER   Julian-Stan
JOHNSON   Adam-Adam
JOHNSON   Ernie-Don

KENNEDY   Bob-Terry
KEOUGH   Marty-Matty
KRAUSE   Lew Sr. & Jr.
KUNKEL   Bill-Jeff

LANDRUM   Joe-Bill
LANIER   Max-Hal
LAW   Vern-Vance
LEE   Thornton-Don
LERCHEN   Dutch-George
LIEBHARDT   Glenn-Glenn
LINDSTROM   Fred-Charlie
LIVELY   Jack-Bud

MACK   Connie-Earle
MAGGERT   Harl-Harl
MALAY   Charlie-Joe
MARTIN   Barney-Jerry

MATTICK   Wally-Bobby
MAY   Dave-Derrick
MAY   Pinky-Milt
MCKNIGHT   Jim-Jeff
MCRAE   Hal-Brian
MEINKE   Frank-Bob
MILLS   Willie-Art
MONTEAGUDO   Rene-Aurelio
MOORE   Eugene Sr. & Jr.
MORTON   Guy Sr. & Jr.
MUELLER   Walter-Don

NARLESKI   Bill-Ray
NAVARRO   Julio-Jaime
NICHOLS   Chet Sr. & Jr.
NORTHEY   Ron-Scott

OKRIE   Frank-Len
OLIVARES   Ed-Omar
OLIVO   Diomedes-Gilbert Rondon
O'ROURKE   Patsy-Joe
O'ROURKE   Jim-Queenie
OSBORNE   Tiny-Bobo

PARTENHEIMER   Steve-Stan
PILLETTE   Herman-Duane

QUEEN   Mel-Mel

RIPLEY   Walt-Allen

SAVIDGE   Ralph-Don
SCHOFIELD   Ducky-Dick
SCHULTZ   Joe Sr. & Jr.
SEGUI   Diego-David
SHEELY   Earl-Bub
SIEBERT   Dick-Paul
SISLER   George-Dick & Dave
SKINNER   Bob-Joel
SMALLEY   Roy Jr.-Roy III
ST. CLAIRE   Ebba-Randy
STENHOUSE   Dave-Mike

STEPHENSON   Joe-Jerry
STILLWELL   Ron-Kurt
STOTTLEMYRE   Mel-Todd &
    Mel Jr.
SULLIVAN   Billy Sr.-Jr.
SULLIVAN   Haywood-Marc
SUSCE   George-George

TANNER   Chuck-Bruce
TARTABULL   Jose-Danny
TORRES   Ricardo-Gil
TRESH   Mike-Tom
TROSKY   Hal Sr. & Jr.
TROUT   Paul-Steve

UNSER   Al-Del

VIRGIL   Ozzie Sr. & Jr.

WAKEFIELD   Howard-Dick
WALKER   Dixie-Dixie & Harry
WALSH   Ed-Ed
WHITE   JoJo-Mike
WILLS   Maury-Bump
WINE   Bobby-Robbie
WOOD   Joe-Joe

YOUNG   Del-Del

**GREAT GRANDFATHER-GREAT
GRANDSON**

Jim Bluejacket & Bill Wilkinson

GRANDFATHER-GRANDSON

George Rooks-Lou Possehl
Shano Collins-Bob Gallagher
Bill Brubaker-Dennis Rasmussen
Marty & Ed Herrmann
Lloyd & Jim Spencer
Lennie & Matt Merullo

No Minor League Experience

Cappy Gagnon

If a group of baseball experts were asked to pick the all-time greatest players, a handful of names would be on everyone's list: Ruth, Williams, Gehrig, Cobb, Musial, Mays, Aaron, etc. Great players, all of them, but none of them made it to the big leagues without first prepping in the minors. In fact, among the more than 13,000 men who've appeared in the big show, only a very small number were able to complete a ten-year career without first spending some time in the bushes.

Without the ten-year requirement, many more players would qualify, but this would not be a true indicator of talent, because the list would include players like the Detroit Tigers "fill-ins" of 1912, the midget Eddie Gaedel, and the mascot Charles "Victory" Faust, among others. In addition, many players particularly batter-ymen, were recruited off sandlots or campuses to replace injured players, or to get a cup-of-coffee tryout.

Two other types of players went straight to the big leagues, frequently with disastrous results. The first were the 1950s bonus babies. According to the rules at that time, a player signing for more than a $4,000 bonus was required to stay in the majors for at least two years after signing. Most of these players were not ready for big league competition, but because they could not be sent down, they were unable to receive the minor league seasoning which lower-rated prospects were getting.

Among American League players adversely affected by this rule during the 1955 season were Kenny Kuhn of the Indians, Tommy Carroll of the Yankees, and Jim Small and "Diamond Jim" Brady of the Tigers. Kuhn was a schoolboy star from Louisville; Small, a speedster from Portland; Carroll and Brady were signed off the campus of the University of Notre Dame. At the time of signing, most of these bonus babies were faced with the choice of college or the majors. For those like Carroll and Jim Brady, Ph.D., who had both, there was a fallback position if their major-league careers ended without the anticipated stardom. But many other players found a lot of disappointment in their mid-twenties when they found themselves without a baseball career or a college education.

The other type of player who was rushed to the majors was the high school or college "phenom." To paraphrase a comment at the time, most of these phenoms did not "phenominate." The most famous example of this type was David Clyde. In 1973 the Texas Rangers ended the season with the worst record in the major leagues (57–105), costing the manager (Whitey Herzog) his job. The ballclub was in deep financial trouble, and drastic measures were called for. A Texas high-schooler, just eighteen, Clyde was the obvious choice for a quick fix.

Barely out of high school, Clyde pitched his first big league game with all the attendant hype. The game was an artistic and financial success. The year's biggest crowd saw him win. Unfortunately, the bubble burst soon thereafter. He developed a sore arm and a taste for drinking and nightlife that his new manager (Billy Martin) was unable to control, for reasons which are well known now. Eddie Bane, of Arizona State, was the collegiate equivalent of Clyde, at least on the field.

Various factors play a role in determining how quickly a player will advance to the majors. In the long-ago, a small number of "bird dogs"—injured and retired players mostly—scoured the country for fresh talent. Playing and living conditions were harsh in the big leagues, and there was little coaching to polish a player's skills. The minors, or occasionally the colleges, were the crucible to teach fundamentals and "inside play." In those pre-expansion, pre-TV days, minor league teams would locate, sign, teach and develop their own players until they could get a good price from a higher league or the majors. This practice continued into the 1950s.

Bonus baby rules from 1947 until the establishment of the combined draft in the 1960s altered this system. Although many players arrived in the majors straight out of high school or college, their lack of experience doomed most of them to a trip to the minors after their enforced bench sitting was over. For Kuhn, Brady, Carroll, and Small, their careers never lived up to their schoolboy promise. Harmon Killebrew was one of the few bonus babies who was able later to make it big after a stretch in the minors.

Some players, however, have had the right combination of polished talent and maturity, or have managed to be selected by a team with a spot on the roster at the right position, or have had a manager who was willing to give a young player a trial or have simply been lucky. It was then up to the player to avoid slumps and injuries.

At least forty men have skipped the minors and completed ten or more seasons without being farmed out. Seven of them played for only one team. Six jumped directly from high school. Fifteen reached the Hall of Fame, with at least one more likely to make it (Dave Winfield). The group would make a pretty good All-Star squad, except that there are no full-time catchers (Fred Tenney made his mark as a first baseman).

There are some asterisks to attach to the players on this list. For example, although Walter Johnson did not play in organized baseball before he signed with the Senators, he did play nearly a full season with a Weiser (Idaho) semipro team in 1907. Similarly, Red Murray played a few years of semipro ball in Elmira (N.Y.) while in his first college (Lock Haven Normal School in Pennsylvania).

Bob Horner is a more complicated case. He successfully fought the Atlanta Braves' management during the 1980 season when they tried to send him down to the minors, but when he could find no takers in the free-agent market after the 1986 season, he spent 1987 playing in Japan. Since this was in their "major" league and he returned to the American majors for the 1988 season, I have listed him. Horner was a slugging shortstop for the Arizona State Sun Devils when he was signed by the Braves.

Ernie Banks and Larry Doby are more troublesome variations of the Horner problem. Gentleman Ernie played for the Negro League Kansas City Monarchs for three years prior to joining the Cubs in 1953; Doby played five years with the Newark Eagles, as a second baseman, before joining the Indians in 1947. Doby's composite career may someday gain him Hall of Fame admission. Only the cruel color line of organized baseball prevented many deserving players from reaching the majors. Some Negro League researchers believe that major league status should be conferred on the Negro Leagues.

Most of the players on this list went to college before being picked for the majors. They should probably rate a special category, since colleges have served as the equivalent of a big league farm system for many years. Among the collegians on this list are three who later had their colleges attached to their names: the Fordham Flash (Frisch), Gettysburg Eddie (Plank), and Colby Jack (Coombs). The rough-and-tumble players of the early game often ridiculed collegians.

Some of the collegians on this list were, for a time, better known on campus as basketball players (Koufax, Groat, Yost, Chapman, and Winfield). After setting scoring records at Duke, Groat also played a year of NBA basketball with the Fort Wayne Pistons.

Charles Albert "Chief" Bender jumped to the majors directly from the Carlisle Indian School. He was the first of five players on this list to be brought to the big leagues by Connie Mack. The others were Barry, Coombs, Plank, and Dugan. Connie liked smart players with good personal habits and seemed to favor collegians.

Barry's development as a shortstop moved Stuffy McInnis to first base and gave the $100,000 infield defensive wizards at all four spots. Barry later became one of the college game's most successful coaches, at Holy Cross, which sent many other players to the Athletics, including Dugan.

Coombs wrote one of the bestselling and most popular texts on baseball play while coaching Duke University. He is also a little tainted to be on this list, having played in the outlaw Vermont League in 1905. Plank, like Bender, was a Hall of Famer.

Ethan Allen also wrote a fine text on baseball and created All-Star Baseball, a terrific table game. Like Koufax, Allen was a product of the University of Cincinnati. Dave Winfield is another author from this list. Although his book angered his employer, Winfield has enjoyed a reputation as a thoughtful man. His athletic ability and tremendous physique were very impressive. Winfield was drafted by all three major pro sports. Cy

Williams was also an all-around athlete; at Notre Dame, Cy and Knute Rockne were backup ends on the 1910 football team. Cy also lettered in track as a hurdler. He made the most of his education, graduating as an architect and gaining as much prominence in his postplaying career as when he won four home run titles in the National League.

Most of the men on this list possessed a high degree of intelligence along with their ability to hit, run, and throw. This may be a result of the high percentage of collegians, or it may have been the quality which kept them in the majors without minor league preparation.

Ted Lyons (Baylor) and Eppa Rixey (Virginia) won 526 games between them during twenty-one-year careers. Pete Donohue and Wild Bill Donovan won 320 games, led their leagues in eleven pitching categories, and had five 20-win seasons. Sisler was such an all-around player that he was both a pitcher and a first baseman in the majors. Brought to the majors by the St. Louis Browns, he played for his former college coach at Michigan, the immortal Branch Rickey. Pitcher George Uhle hit .302 in his brief rookie year, foreshadowing that he would become the greatest hitting pitcher in the history of the game.

An interesting aspect of the first-year accomplishments of these players is that except for three of the pitchers (Bender, Plank, and Powell) they broke in with modest production. Few were regulars. Most came up to teams with second-division records and a hole to fill, although Connie Mack brought up Coombs and Bender to pennant-winning teams and Barry to a second-place finisher. Milt Gaston also came up to a defending league champ when he joined the 1924 Yankees.

Bibb Falk also came up to a defending league champ, but since the 1920 White Sox were decimated by the Black Sox Scandal, there was a lot of room for new blood. Falk later became a prominent college coach at Texas, the school which has produced the second-most current major league players and which is among the top three all-time.

Carl Scheib, Eddie Yost, and Johnny Antonelli were sixteen, seventeen, and eighteen, respectively, when they first appeared in a big league game, during the forties. The first two were helped by the wartime depletion of talent. Johnny Antonelli was one of the biggest bonus babies of the forties, signing for a reported $65,000 during the Braves' 1948 pennant-winning season. Yost needed federal government intervention to stay on this list.

"The Walking Man" grew up in Brooklyn. He attended NYU in the fall of 1944, playing basketball. He skipped college baseball, playing semipro ball in New Jersey on weekends. While Senator scout Joe Cambria was on a rare scouting mission (rare because it was not in a Spanish-speaking country), he spotted Yost. It is alleged that Yost was signed on the spot. He went to the majors right away, playing in a few games at the end of the 1944 season.

Yost spent all of 1945 and much of 1946 in the Navy. When the 1947 season began, Clark Griffith decided that Eddie should serve a little time in Chattanooga. The Senators' manager, Ossie Bluege, the former great Nat third sacker, agreed with this assessment. Eddie also agreed, but there was a congressional act that protected jobs for ex-servicemen. This law said that Eddie had to be retained until July 15. Yost would likely have languished on the bench until he could be sent down, except that veteran Cecil Travis slumped badly and, on May 21, Eddie got a chance to play third as a temporary regular. He lasted fourteen years with the Senators.

Among this precocious group, three players stand above the others for the uniqueness of their accomplishment: Bob Feller, Al Kaline, and Mel Ott. They each went directly from high school to the majors, without the benefit of college or semipro experience, and completed Hall of Fame careers without ever changing teams. Except for the years taken from Feller during the war, all of these players have had more than twenty years of big league service. In effect, they wore only one uniform after high school! They could be the subject of a story, "From High School to Cooperstown, with Only One Stop in Between."

The chart that follows summarizes the accomplishment of the players referred to in this chapter:

KEY: YRS = Seasons in the majors; POS = Primary Position(s) played during rookie season; TMS = Number of teams on during career; AGE = Years and month of age during April of Rookie year; OPPORTUNITY = Finish of team during season prior to rookie year; player's rookie year; RESULT = Won-lost record (pitchers) or batting average (others) during the rookie year.

NAME	YRS	POS	TEAMS	AGE	OPPORTUNITY	RESULT
Allen, Ethan	13	OF	6	22/3	3, 1926	.308
Antonelli, Johnny	12	P	3	18/0	3, 1948	0–0
Banks, Ernie	19	SS	1	22/3	5, 1953	.314
Barry, Jack	11	2B-SS	2	21/0	2, 1908	.222
Bender, Chief	16	P	4	20/1	1, 1902	17–15
Chapman, Sam	11	OF	2	22/0	7, 1938	.259
Coombs, Jack	15	P	3	23/5	1, 1906	10–10
Doby, Larry	13	OF	3	22/5	6, 1947	.156
Donohue, Pete	12	P	4	20/5	3, 1921	7–6
Donovan, Wild Bill	18	P	4	21/6	7, 1898	1–6
Dugan, Joe	14	SS	5	19/11	8, 1917	.194
Falk, Bibb	12	OF	2	21/3	1, 1920	.294
Feller, Bob	18	P	1	17/5	3, 1936	5–3
Frisch, Frank	20	2B-3B	2	20/7	2, 1919	.226
Gaston, Milton	11	P	5	28/3	1, 1924	5–3
Groat, Dick	14	SS	4	21/5	7, 1952	.284
Horner, Bob	11	3B	3	20/8	6, 1978	.266
Hunter, Catfish	15	P	2	20/0	10, 1965	8–8
Johnson, Walter	21	P	1	19/5	7, 1907	5–9
Kaline, Al	23	OF	1	18/4	8, 1953	.250
Koufax, Sandy	13	P	1	19/4	2, 1955	2–2
Lyons, Ted	21	P	1	22/4	5, 1923	2–1
MacFayden, Danny	17	P	6	20/10	8, 1926	0–1
Magee, Sherry	16	OF	3	18/8	7, 1904	.277
Murray, Red	11	OF	3	22/1	6, 1905	.257
O'Dell, Digger	13	P	5	21/2	8, 1954	1–1
Ott, Mel	22	OF	1	17/1	2, 1926	.383
Plank, Eddie	17	P	3	25/8	0*, 1901	17–11
Powell, Jack	11	P	3	22/9	2, 1897	15–9
Rixey, Eppa	21	P	2	21/11	4, 1912	10–10
Scheib, Carl	11	P	2	16/3	8, 1943	0–1
Sisler, George	16	1B-OF-P	3	22/1	6, 1915	.285,4–4
Tenney, Fred	17	C	2	22/5	1, 1894	.388
Uhle, George	17	P	4	20/7	2, 1919	10–5
Wallace, Bobby	25	SS	3	19/5	3, 1894	.154
Williams, Cy	19	OF	2	24/4	2, 1912	.242
Winfield, Dave	16	OF	2	21/6	6, 1973	.277
Yost, Eddie	18	3B	3	17/6	2, 1944	.143
Zachary, Tom	19	P	7	22/1	5, 1918	2–0

*Eddie Plank's rookie year was also the rookie year of his team (Philadelphia) and league (the AL).

CHAPTER 10

Scandals and Controversies

Stephen S. Hall

Scandal is in the eye of the beholder. The biggest scandal of baseball's 1876 season was the failure of the New York Mutuals and Philadelphia Athletics to fulfill their obligatory season-ending western road trip, resulting in their expulsion from the National League. Yet when black players were virtually excluded from the first eight decades of organized ball, few saw it as a long-running institutional scandal. When the likable but wayward Babe Ruth cut a broad swath through most notions of civilized behavior, the Sultan of Swat's charmed, forgiving public responded with winks and nods. But when Walter O'Malley, in a business decision calculated to maximize profits (surely one of baseball's most enduring and honored traditions), moved his Dodgers to Los Angeles after the 1957 season, he traumatized an entire generation of Brooklyn fans. Which was more scandalous behavior?

From its earliest days, baseball has indulged gamblers, fixers, drunkards, brawlers, disreputable moguls, bad actors, felons, homicidal maniacs, crooked umpires, vindictive owners, pyromaniacal fans, and at least one ax murderer. Just as a Dickens novel reflects all the voices and vices of Victorian London, baseball hears from all precincts of the American experience, including the seedy.

Gambling, Bribery, and Game-Fixing

Baseball's greatest scandal is unquestionably the fixing of the 1919 World Series, but the Black Sox scandal merely climaxed more than five decades of dubious collusion between players and gamblers. Half a century before the World Series fix, in 1872, the *New York Times* harumphed editorially that the aim of baseball was "to employ professional players to perspire in public for the benefit of gamblers . . ." Many small scandals lit the way to the disgrace of 1919.

Baseball began as a gentlemanly avocation, but any disputatious athletic event quickly caught the attention of gamblers. As early as 1857, crowds at Elysian Fields in Hoboken, New Jersey, one of amateur baseball's most hallowed venues, came to bet on games. It was but a short step from gambling to influencing the outcome of games. Soon word drifted eastward that gamblers on the West Coast were not averse to firing their guns into the air at crucial moments to disrupt the concentration of fielders—and, of course, to protect their investments.

A slang term, "hippodroming," soon emerged to indicate a game played with the illusion of spontaneity when, in fact, the outcome had already been fixed. Gamblers reportedly harassed members of the Brooklyn Excelsiors in an 1860 game with the Brooklyn Atlantics—after which the Excelsiors refused to play the Atlantics again. Another team, the Haymakers of Troy, New York, was suspected of hippodroming, largely because its owners included renowned New York gamblers like John Morrissey. Rumors of fixed games so dogged baseball in its early years that a Buffalo writer once suggested, "Any professional base ball club will 'throw' a game if there is money in it. A horse race is a pretty safe thing to speculate on, in comparison with an average ball match."

Gamblers freely circulated in baseball parks, occasioning such warnings as the BETTING POSITIVELY PROHIBITED sign that graced the wall of the Washington Nationals' ballpark in 1867. A forerunner of bookmaking, called pool selling, sprung up in conjunction with baseball, and by the 1870s as much as $70,000 might be riding on a single game. With all the betting, it was inevitable that gamblers would approach players with bribes—even during the "amateur" era. Players of that era—ill educated, often immigrants—were particularly susceptible; the under-the-table payments they received as amateurs did little to instill moral probity. Indeed, patronage jobs were often offered in lieu of outright salaries by such well-connected owners as Boss Tweed, part owner of the New York Mutuals. A lot of baseball players found well-paying jobs in such unlikely spots as the U.S. Treasury Department in Washington and the coroner's office in New York.

Indeed, a scant six years after the formation of the amateur National Association, organized baseball confronted its first gambling scandal. On September 28, 1865, the heavily favored New York Mutuals lost to the Brooklyn Eckfords, 28–11. It later developed that two Mutuals players, Ed Duffy and William Wansley, offered money to Mutuals shortstop Thomas Devyr to throw the game. For their role in the conspiracy, which was investigated by the Judicial Committee of the National Association, Duffy and Wansley were banned from match play; the Mutuals, in desperate need of a shortstop, helped to have charges against Devyr dismissed. By 1870, all three players had won reinstatement—a prophetic indication that organized baseball was not yet prepared to take a firm stand against gambling.

A little-known footnote to the amazing 60–0 season of the 1869 Cincinnati Red Stockings, baseball's first avowedly professional team, is that the lone blemish in their record came as the result of a tie with the hippodroming Haymakers of Troy, who walked off the field in the sixth inning of a 17–17 game on some reportedly dubious pretext to save their gambling bosses from a probable loss.

Five years into the professional era, the legendary base-ball writer Henry Chadwick felt compelled to charge in print that players were in cahoots with gamblers and had staged "rather questionable" games during the 1874 campaign. The charges remained just that—accusations—until the Louisville Grays scandal of 1877. It was, according to historian J. E. Findling, "the first documented case of player crookedness after the founding of the National League."

The senior circuit was barely a year old when Chadwick's worst fears came true. The National League had been organized in February of 1876, at least in part as a response to growing public disenchantment with baseball's wayward ways—the influence of gamblers, the appearance of fixed games, the drunken, salacious antics of players. In August of 1877 the league-leading Louisville Grays embarked on a long eastern road trip. After a disastrous stretch of seven losses and a tie, in part facilitated by suspiciously inept play, the team returned home. Sportswriters openly hinted that Louisville had dumped its games and deliberately blown the pennant.

Since a Louisville newspaper magnate served as club president, the *Courier-Journal* ran speculative articles intended to smoke out the suspected fixers. The ploy worked when one of the players confessed. On October 30, 1877, the Louisville directors expelled four players—Jim "Terror" Devlin, George "Gentleman George" Hall, Bill "Butcher" Craver, and Al "Slippery Elm" Nichols—for life. Nichols, a utility player, had befriended a "pool seller" named James McCloud, who paid Devlin and Hall $100 to throw a game. An examination of Western Union telegrams conclusively established links between the gambler and the players. Craver refused to sign a loyalty oath, thus earning his expulsion, but Devlin, Hall, and Nichols were accused of selling games and "tampering with players." In their defense, they claimed that the Louisville management had failed to pay their salaries as promised—not an unlikely charge, given the parlous finances of the nineteenth-century clubs. All four were banned for life, and the Louisville Grays were disbanded before the start of the 1878 season. The *Louisville Courier-Journal* attributed the dissolution to "the rascality of last year's players and the general conviction that dishonest players on other clubs were more the rule than the exception . . ."

Umpires were not immune to the emoluments of gamblers either. As a player for the Chicago White Stockings, Richard Higham's desultory attitude and outright ineptitude had aroused suspicion. As umpire, Higham handled many games involving the Detroit Wolverines at the outset of the 1882 season, and a number of observers—including Wolverine owner William Thompson—believed that many of the close calls went against Detroit. Thompson, who also happened to be mayor of Detroit, assigned a private detective to investigate Higham. The detective ultimately uncovered the scam: Higham placed bets by telegram with a well-known gambler on the very games he was scheduled to umpire, then made calls favoring the team he'd bet on. Baseball officials confronted Higham with the evidence and banished him from the game. It represented no midlife crisis for Higham, however—he promptly became a bookie based in Chicago. This expulsion marks the only documented case of dishonesty by an umpire in the history of major league baseball.

The influence—or at least suspicion—of gambling did not subside after the Louisville Grays and Higham scandals. Contemporary commentators speak of "a little odor" hovering over the pennant races of 1891 and 1892, but no details ever emerged. Then, at the turn of the century, baseball took a two-decade running start toward the scandal that would forever blacken its name.

The lassitude with which baseball viewed the gambling establishment by 1900 affected every part of the game. Players openly associated with gamblers; and, indeed, in some cases that was a politic thing to do, for those gamblers happened to be team owners. The original bankrollers of the New York Highlanders, Frank Farrell and William "Big Bill" Devery, typified the unhealthy cross-pollination of sports and gaming. Devery went unbowed by his reputation as New York's most corrupt police commissioner, and Farrell's notorious gambling habits placed him many chits above the middling pool seller. One of their favorite pals was the player known as "Prince Hal": Hal Chase, probably the most corrupt ballplayer ever.

Chase began his career with the Highlanders in 1905 and was an extraordinarily gifted fielder at first base. He was also a well-known gambler who thought nothing of betting on his own team, and sometimes even against it. Many of his managers—including George Stallings of the Highlanders, Frank Chance of the Yankees (as the Highlanders came to be called), and Christy Mathewson in Cincinnati—suggested at one time or another that he threw games. It is typical of the *laissez-faire* days before the Black Sox scandal that when Stallings publicly complained about Chase, American League President Ban Johnson did not investigate the alleged game fixing, but rather dressed down Chase's manager for smearing the reputation of a big gate attraction. By 1918, when he was suspended by the Reds for gambling and attempting to bribe an opposing pitcher, Chase's appearance on the field was sometimes greeted with cynical cries of "What are the odds?"

At least once, and probably on many occasions, Chase offered bribes to teammates and opposing players to give substandard performances. He concluded his malodorous career with the 1919 New York Giants; true to form, he was blacklisted from the game in February 1920. It later emerged that Chase and third baseman Heinie Zimmerman, who was indefinitely suspended by the Giants in September 1919, offered an $800 bribe to Giant pitcher Rube Benton to throw a game; bribes were also offered to Benny Kauff, Lee Magee, Fred Toney, and Jean Dubuc. Despite no public explanation, Giants manager John McGraw later suggested that Chase and Zimmerman's questionable play against Cincinnati helped the Reds win the pennant—lending, if true, a rarely noted but fitting symmetry to that year's corrupt World Series. Prince Hal's crowning achievement in this record of deceit was to bring gamblers and fixers together to throw the 1919 World Series.

Hal Chase's machinations were merely the most obvious symptoms of pervasive corruption in the period 1900–1920, according to baseball historian David Quentin Voight. There was a reported attempt to bribe players in the first two World Series, in 1903 and 1905; in the former year, Boston catcher Lou Criger was offered a bribe to "lay down," while in the latter year, Philadelphia pitcher Rube Waddell did not play due to an injury, when he had allegedly received a $17,000 offer not to play. It was widely believed that gamblers tried to fix the 1908 season. In 1916, the New York Giants were rumored to have helped the Dodgers beat out the Phillies in the pennant race, and the 1918 World Series may have been tampered with as well. There was even the bizarre attempt, on the last day of the 1910 season, to bribe an official scorer, so that Cleveland's popular Nap Lajoie could beat out the detested Ty Cobb for the batting crown. The unsuccessful attempt—to change an error into a hit for Lajoie—resulted in dismissal for St. Louis Browns coach Harry Howell; St. Louis manager Jack O'Connor, too, got fired for ordering his third baseman to play so deep that Lajoie got seven bunt singles in the season-ending doubleheader. Yet these transgressions were more of degree than nature. Since at least the 1890s, it was commonplace for teams to reward opposition players with clothes, cigars, even money for a good performance against rivals; it no doubt took but a short step to rewarding bad performances as well.

All the corruption came home to roost in 1919. Even before the very first pitch had been thrown in what became Cincinnati's "improbable" World Series victory over the Chicago White Sox, rumors swirled that the fix was on. It took a year for the rumors to come true. The initial reaction was to dismiss the allegations, including reports that gamblers had offered Cincinnati pitcher Hod Eller a $5,000 bribe which he turned down.

But the 1920 season was a cauldron of renewed rumors of bribery and game fixing. No less than seven clubs—the Giants, Cubs, Yankees, Braves, Red Sox, Indians, and White Sox—were suspected of throwing games that season. Cub players Lee Magee and Claude Hendrix were blacklisted, Hendrix toward the end of the 1920 season for trying to fix a game with the Phillies. Finally, in September 1920, a Chicago grand jury convened to investigate charges about the 1919 World Series. Meanwhile, an article appeared on September 27, 1920, in the *Philadelphia North American* in which local gambler Bill Maharg went beyond innuendo and blew open the scandal. Maharg described how White Sox pitcher Eddie Cicotte volunteered to fix the Series; how Maharg and his partner, former major leaguer Billy Burns, promised to pay $100,000 to eight White Sox players; how the gamblers double-crossed the players by paying them only $10,000 at first; how the players double-crossed the gamblers by winning a game they were supposed to lose; and how Burns and Maharg got double-crossed by a rival fixer, New York gambler (and former boxing champion) Abe Attell, who *also* was bribing the players. The following day, Cicotte agreed to testify to the grand jury and named the names ever after branded the "Black Sox": pitchers Cicotte and Claude Williams, batting star Joe Jackson, infielders Buck Weaver (who had "guilty knowledge" of the fix but refused to take part in it), Swede Risberg, and Chick Gandil, outfielder Oscar "Happy" Felsch, and even a utility man, Fred McMullin. Not only did they throw the 1919 World Series to the Reds, but, in a disreputable postscript to their season of infamy, they dumped the 1920 pennant race to the Indians, too.

In grand jury testimony, Gandil emerged as the ringleader, pocketing $35,000. Cicotte received $10,000; Jackson got $5,000 (he was earning about $6,000 a year from the tight-fisted White Sox owner Charles Comiskey). Arnold Rothstein, the notorious gangster, reputedly masterminded the fix, although his role was never legally proven and he was never charged with a crime. The scandal left no one untainted. Joe Jackson wrote a letter to Comiskey shortly after the calamitous Series, stating that the Series outcome was questionable and volunteering to meet with the owner to provide details, but Comiskey—said to be concerned about the effect of such revelations on attendance and profits, not to mention his equity in the franchise—never followed up on Jackson's offer.

Following the mysterious disappearance of their confessions and other legal skullduggery, the "eight" Black Sox won acquittal during their June 1921 conspiracy trial; none of the big-fish gamblers and fixers went to trial. But the newly appointed baseball commissioner, Kenesaw Mountain Landis, in an extraordinarily usurptive move aimed at restoring public confidence in the game, suspended all eight players for life. The sentence was particularly brutal for Weaver, who had not participated in the scam, and Jackson. "Shoeless Joe," in throwing the series, batted .375, and it was his apparently accurate throw to the plate in the tense fourth game, inexplicably cut off by pitcher Cicotte, which convinced cognoscenti in the stands beyond a doubt that the White Sox were deliberately tossing the games. In the roundelay of accusations that later emerged, Rube Benton charged that Hal Chase made $40,000 betting on the Reds; others charged that Benton knew of the fix and had made $3,200; and St. Louis infielder Joe Gedeon won $600 following a tip from Swede Risberg.

Bill James, in his *Historical Baseball Abstract,* estimates that a total of thirty-eight major league ballplayers were implicated in scandals during the period 1917–1927, and that nineteen were formally banned or effectively blacklisted (James's list includes several players, however, who were suspended not for corruption, but for such offenses as contract jumping). In addition to the Chase and Black Sox scandals, James cites the allegations of Jimmy O'Connell, who claimed to have offered $500 to Philadelphia player Heinie Sand to fix a game in 1924; O'Connell and Giants coach Cozy Dolan were banned for life, but Frankie Frisch denied he'd known about the fix.

Under Landis's stern tutelage, baseball took a far less tolerant view of gamblers, though tales of the corrupt teens continued to trickle out. In 1926, player-managers Ty Cobb of the Tigers and Tris Speaker of the Indians both resigned under a cloud; the public later learned that ex-pitcher Dutch Leonard alleged that they had conspired to fix the last game of the 1919 season so that Detroit could win third-place money and that Smoky Joe Wood allegedly placed bets for Cobb and Speaker. And in 1927, "Black Sox" Swede Risberg publicly charged that some fifty players had known of a four-game series in 1917 that the Tigers threw to the White Sox.

Compared to the tormented twenties, the Depression and war years seemed peaceably upright. But never entirely so. In 1943, for example, Phillies owner William D. Cox received a swift and permanent suspension from Landis for betting on Philadelphia games. It would be perhaps naive to think that Landis's crowd-pleasing gestures totally eliminated gambling from the game, but they certainly sent a message to players and administrators alike that, if caught, the price would be steep. The antigambling fervor carried over into the commissionership of A. B. "Happy" Chandler, who in the spring of 1947 suspended Brooklyn manager Leo Durocher for one year for "conduct detrimental to baseball." Personality clashes and baseball politics apparently influenced Chandler's decision, but he had previously warned Durocher against associating with gamblers and other "unsavory" characters, including actor George Raft. Durocher, not heeding the warning, had actually been living in Raft's home the previous fall.

Commissioner Bowie Kuhn prided himself on an aggressive Landis-style stance against even the *appearance* of association with gamblers, and so in 1969 presented an ultimatum to four prominent baseball people, including Oakland owner Charles O. Finley and Atlanta Brave directors Bill Bartholomay, John Louis, and Del Coleman. All four had interests in the Parvin-Dohrmann Co., which owned and operated the Fremont, Stardust, and Aladdin casinos in Las Vegas. Faced with choosing baseball or gaming, Finley sold his stock, and all but Coleman resigned their directorships. Somewhat more controversial (and problematic) was Kuhn's insistence that players or coaches employed by baseball teams could not accept public relations work at casinos. Thus Mets batting instructor Willie Mays (in 1979) and Yankee spring training instructor Mickey Mantle (in 1983) were forced to give up their baseball jobs in order to serve as greeters at Atlantic City casinos. Shortly after Kuhn left office, incoming Commissioner Peter Ueberroth revoked the orders.

Baseball's next great gambling scandal unwittingly reaffirmed the old Graig Nettles adage about going from Cy Young to Sayonara. Detroit pitcher Denny McLain made the trip in four years, winning the prestigious award outright in 1968 with a 31–6 record and sharing it again in 1969, only to bounce out of the majors by 1972. Around the beginning of 1970, word circulated that a Detroit grand jury had begun investigating McLain. Against a backdrop of personal financial difficulties, McLain's rumored involvement with gamblers prompted a meeting with Bowie Kuhn, at which the pitcher admitted investing $5,700 in a bookmaking operation at a bar he frequented in Flint, Michigan. The confession preceded by several days a *Sports Illustrated* article on February 17, 1970, which described McLain's involvement in the bookmaking operation. The article went on to suggest that when McLain failed to pay out $46,600 on a winning bet in 1967, organized crime enforcer Tony Giacalone allegedly stomped on the pitcher's foot, dislocating several toes and causing him to miss at least two September starts during Detroit's heated pennant race with Boston. The article further alleged that Detroit mobster Billy Giacalone, brother of Tony, bet heavily on Boston to win the pennant, and also against Detroit in their final game of the season, which McLain started and the Tigers lost; in all, McLain lost his last three decisions of the 1967 season. The bookie connection and the allegations earned an indefinite suspension from Kuhn, although the commissioner later stated there was no proof of McLain's having bet on baseball games.

Unindicted but never clear of the clouds over his head, McLain returned to the Tigers in July. He received two more suspensions that season amid increasingly bizarre behavior: threatening a parking lot attendant, dumping a bucket of ice water on two sportswriters, and violating federal law by carrying a gun on a commercial airliner. McLain was traded to the Senators, and tried comebacks with Oakland and Atlanta before bouncing entirely out of baseball in 1972. In 1985, he was found guilty in a Florida trial and sentenced to twenty-three years in jail on charges of racketeering, loan sharking, extortion, and possession of cocaine with intent to distribute. After serving nearly thirty months, McLain won his appeal and regained freedom. (Late in 1988, however, he pled guilty to several of the charges and once again faced a jail term.) In allegedly dabbling both in gambling and drugs, McLain bridged the gap between baseball's more traditional vices and the modern fascination with controlled substances.

Even McLain's peccadilloes pale compared to those of Pete Rose. It is difficult to choose one aspect of the Rose scandal that is richer with outrage or pathos than another: that the greatest hitter the game has seen would be forced to peddle, reportedly because of gambling debts, the bat with which he broke Ty Cobb's seemingly unassailable hit record; that "Charlie Hustle," the quintessential gamer, was banned for life from the game; that the rough-hewn moptop who played with such boyish abandon would end up in jail with the most hardened of men. But all the career hits (4,256), all the career games (3,562), all twelve major league records provided no immunity when Peter Edward Rose was permanently banned from baseball on August 24, 1989. It represented baseball's darkest moment since the Black Sox scandal of 1919.

No one knows when Rose's gambling problems got out of control; his legal problems with baseball began to surface in February 1989, when then-commissioner Peter Ueberroth called him to a meeting in New York—a meeting, it was soon reported, to discuss allegations of gambling. Press reports began to appear soon thereafter describing Rose's predilection for dog races and horse tracks, and then the commissioner's office confirmed that a special investigation was underway. In selecting John Dowd to head the probe, baseball entrusted its inquiry to a man who had successfully investigated a sitting FBI director (Clarence Kelley, ultimately dismissed for improprieties) and a sitting congressman (Rep. Daniel Flood, ultimately convicted of illegal campaign contributions). Dowd would not submit the results of his investigation until May 9, but in the course of its preparation, he interviewed and deposed more than half a dozen figures who professed knowledge of Rose's gambling activities.

On March 21, *Sports Illustrated* published a well-documented investigative article reporting that Rose bet on baseball games—a violation of baseball rule 21(d), which states that any player who bets on a game "shall be declared ineligible for one year" and any player who bets on his own team "shall be declared permanently ineligible." These public allegations of improprieties mirrored the charges privately being assembled by Dowd. But on April 18, 1989, the new commissioner, A. Bartlett Giamatti, committed a legal blunder that provided Rose's lawyers with the maneuvering room that allowed them to keep the issue churning in court, and on the front pages, all summer. In a letter to a federal judge in charge of sentencing one of Dowd's sources, an Ohio bookmaker named Ron Peters, Giamatti wrote that Peters had been "candid, forthright and truthful . . ." That last word, "truthful," with its implication that Giamatti accepted the veracity of Peters' allegation before hearing Rose's side of the story, allowed Rose and his lawyers to claim that Giamatti had prejudged the case. Indeed, when Giamatti requested Rose to appear at a May 25 hearing, Rose's lawyers asked for a thirty-day postponement and laid the grounds for an epic lawsuit that would challenge the very authority of the commissioner's office to rule on his—and, by implication, any player's—fate. The battle thus joined, it overshadowed the season for the next four months.

It was a classic battle pitting two considerable antagonists. Giamatti was erudite but tough, well spoken, as blue blood as the son of an immigrant could get, a Renaissance scholar conversant with the sense as well as the syntax of Macchiavelli, a man with an almost poetic love of the game; Rose was the diehard, in-your-face burr-headed hustler, blue-collar and rough-edged, not terribly conversant with the kings's English, but willing to do anything to win. For all that, Rose's lawyers sought an early settlement in April, but discussions broke down and they filed suit against baseball on June 19, 1989, challenging Giamatti's ability to be fair and requesting a temporary restraining order barring the commissioner from holding his scheduled June 26 hearing with Rose. In granting the request on June 26, Hamilton County Common Pleas Court Judge Norbert A. Nadel ruled that Giamatti had prejudged the case. The stunning decision, widely criticized at the time, nonetheless raised the stakes considerably. Rose's suit, in effect, challenged the right of the baseball commissioner to adjudicate internal matters—threatened, in short, to chisel away at the bedrock on which the authority of baseball rests, and of which the sport, understandably, is most loathe to entertain the slightest erosion.

The Nadel ruling triggered a furious round of legal thrusts and parries by both sides that lasted nearly two months. As is often the case, broad issues took a back seat to nuts-and-bolts skirmishes over jurisdiction. Organized baseball methodically won these skirmishes. Baseball's lawyers got Rose's suit against Giamatti assigned to a federal court, and U.S. District Court Judge John Holschuh scheduled a hearing for August 28 on Rose's request. Once the case moved to federal court, historically sympathetic to baseball's arguments of self-administration, Rose faced a difficult legal battle, at enormous cost, to pursue the issue, and it is believed that this contributed to his decision to reach a settlement.

With the distraction of court arguments and rulings and reassignments, it was easy to forget that the Rose case was ultimately about gambling, not the authority of the commissioner. One day after his June 26 ruling, Judge Nadel was compelled to make public—against both his and baseball's wishes—the report compiled by John Dowd. This 225-page report, and seven supporting volumes of evidence, provided a comprehensive and devastating portrait of Rose the Gambler in the years 1985–87.

The Dowd report revealed that Rose routinely bet not only on baseball games (typically $2,000 per game), but that he bet on Cincinnati games—a violation of baseball rules that would automatically draw a permanent expulsion from the game. In the first three months of the 1987 season alone, for example, gambling records indicated that Rose bet on the Reds to win fifty-two times, winning twenty-nine times (there was no evidence that Rose bet against his own team). He typically used intermediaries named Thomas Gioiosa or Paul Janszen, both convicted felons and both destined to join the names Abe Attell and Bill Maharg in the tainted pantheon of baseball low-lifes; these gambling gofers would then place Rose's bets either with Ohio bookie Ron Peters or an unnamed bookmaker in Staten Island, N.Y. Baseball investigators obtained dated betting slips in Rose's handwriting—and, according to an FBI analysis cited in the New York Times, with Rose's fingerprints—to document his gambling activities.

Rose's gambling habits were certainly out of control by 1985. Gambling debts in fall 1985 forced Rose to borrow $47,000 from Michael Fry, who authorities allege was involved in a cocaine ring operating between Florida and southwest Ohio; Rose reportedly came under investigation for involvement in the drug ring, though no charges were ever filed. Among the nine individuals making allegations against Rose, however, his principal accusers—Gioiosa, Peters, Janszen, and Fry—all faced legal difficulties and had reason to seek the leniency of the courts. Their testimony was never challenged by Rose's representatives in a hearing.

Through it all, Rose—firm of jaw, defiant as ever—steadfastly denied he had ever bet on baseball. But behind the scenes, with damaging evidence and legal costs mounting, Rose's lawyers once again approached the commissioner's office in mid-July with a proposed settlement. The sticking point was Rose's refusal to admit he bet on baseball games. Only after Rose's lawsuit was headed for federal court did a settlement get ironed out. On August 24, 1989, a grim and infamous Thursday in baseball history, A. Barlett Giamatti announced "the sad end of a sorry episode" by declaring Pete Rose "permanently ineligible" for employment in baseball—the most prolific hitter in the game, banned for life.

As part of the settlement, the language of the agreement did not explicitly accuse Rose of betting on baseball games, only of "conduct not to be in the best interests of Baseball." In exchange for that legalistic blurring of culpability, Rose agreed to drop all litigation against Giamatti, acknowledged that the commissioner had acted in good faith and had sole and exclusive authority to decide the issue. Rose neither denied nor admitted he bet on baseball (not since Spiro Agnew had nolo contendere boasted such a celebrated practitioner). Then Giamatti went and undid all the legal tiptoeing, in reply to a question at the ensuing press conference, by saying yes, his personal opinion was that Rose bet on baseball, Reds games included. Rose, stung, felt he'd been betrayed. Under the rules of baseball, Rose was eligible to apply for reinstatement after one year. "The burden to show a redirected, reconfigured, or rehabilitated life," Giamatti told reporters, "is entirely Pete Rose's." Three months later, Rose publicly admitted he had a gambling problem.

The settlement was widely viewed as a complete capitulation by Rose. But not everyone viewed Rose's lawsuit as frivolous. In the view of Los Angeles Times columnist

Jim Murray, for example, "Baseball commissioner Giamatti just wanted to get the matter out of the courts. Baseball fears the courts the way safecrackers do." Was a deal struck? Giamatti emphatically denied it at the time. At least three newspapers—the *Los Angeles Times*, *Chicago Tribune*, and *Dayton Daily News*—quoted sources on the eve of the August 24 announcement saying that Rose agreed to a settlement only when the commissioner agreed that the expulsion would not be permanent. In the unlikely event that a deal was struck, Giamatti may well have taken the secret with him to the grave, for he died of a heart attack little more than a week after the decision was rendered.

Will Pete Rose make it back into baseball's graces? Precedent suggests not. Of the fourteen people previously booted out of the game, none has ever won reinstatement. Circumstances suggest not. One of the negotiators who represented baseball and worked on the Rose settlement reportedly took the position that Rose shouldn't even be allowed to *apply* for reinstatement for seven years; that negotiator was Francis (Fay) Vincent, who succeeded Giamatti as commissioner. And Rose's subsequent problems suggest not. In April 1990 Rose pled guilty in federal court to two counts of filing false income tax returns, dating back to 1985 and 1987, and in July he received a sentence of five months in the federal minimum security Correctional Institution Camp in Marion, Illinois. He also faced three months in a halfway house, fines of $50,000, and obligations to perform 1,000 hours of community service. Baseball's career hit leader reported to jail on August 10.

Rose has consistently referred to baseball's judgment as a "suspension," and he remarked at the time of the August 24 settlement that "to think that I'll be out of baseball for a very short time hurts." This seeming belief in the ban's temporary nature may simply reflect the same fierce denial that fueled Rose in his battle against the game. Whatever the decision, the hurt it causes Pete Rose can be inferred from a remark Charlie Hustle made earlier in his career. "I'd go through hell in a gasoline suit," he said, "to play baseball." Who could have imagined that the suit came with prison stripes and that Rose would be doing time in civilization's closest approximation of hell? Any place outside of baseball is hell for Pete Rose, and that is where he will live for the foreseeable future.

Alcohol and Controlled Substances

John Barleycorn's name has never been entered into a major league scorecard, but alcohol has undoubtedly affected the outcome of games and certainly determined the length of careers. Two anecdotes a century apart suggest just how endemic drink—and drunks—have been to the game. When the Philadelphia Athletics won the pennant in 1871 (and in those days, it was a *real* pennant), the flag flew not from a stadium flagpole, nor did someone hoist it up in the clubhouse. No, it was promptly hung in a Philadelphia saloon. In 1974, after both Whitey Ford and Mickey Mantle won election to the Hall of Fame, restauranteur Toots Shor remarked, "It shows what you can accomplish if you stay up all night drinking whiskey all the time." In the 1970s and 1980s, drug use by the players became pervasive, leading to baseball's worst scandal since the days of the Black Sox.

Nineteenth-century ballplayers were inordinately fond of what they called "German tea," and "lushers" were common on every team. In 1880, in a dispute as political as it was moral, the Cincinnati ball club was expelled from the National League for selling liquor at the stadium (as well as for playing on Sunday). Shortly before his death in 1882, National League president William A. Hulbert issued lifetime suspensions to the "ten chronic lushers" in the league. "Drinking, late hours, and wenching were more common in the early decades of professionalism than they are now," historian Harold Seymour wrote in 1963, "or at least more regularly publicized in the newspapers."

Drinking by ballplayers had become so bad that it had attracted the notice and interest of temperance groups, as well as self-ordained protectors of the game's image. Thus in the 1880s, *The Sporting News* attacked such popular gate attractions as Mike "King" Kelly, Jim McCormick, Pete Browning, and Curt Welch for their notorious drinking. The most flagrant violator was probably Welch. An outfielder for St. Louis, Welch could be seen out in the field sneaking sips of beer, which he hid behind the billboards of Sportsman's Park. This may in part explain why he was known for his circus catches.

In 1886, Chicago White Stockings owner A. G. Spalding went on the warpath against his boozing players. He dangled $350 bonuses in front of two of his stars, Kelly and McCormick, if they would curtail their heavy drinking. They did not. Prior to their departure for spring training that year, the White Stockings even gathered en masse in Spalding's sporting goods store in Chicago to take public vows of temperence, with Chicago manager Adrian "Cap" Anson administering the oaths. Spalding then packed them off to the thermal waters of Hot Springs, Arkansas; the express purpose, according to one writer, was "to boil out the alcoholic microbes." Lushing being a league-wide problem, many teams added Hot Springs to their February itineraries.

Many outstanding players have achieved notoriety with their drinking escapades. Chicago manager Anson got into a drunken fistfight in a saloon and was arrested on one occasion; Rube Waddell, the turn-of-the-century left-hander, often disappeared after long benders. The most tragic victim of drinking may well have been Ed Delahanty. Suspended by the Washington Senators for disciplinary problems in Detroit in July of 1903, Big Ed headed back east by train, got drunk and abusive on board, and had to be put off in Canada, just north of the Niagara River. He started to walk across the railroad bridge that led to the U.S., got into a tussle with the night watchman, and tumbled into the Niagara River; eight days later, his body washed up below Niagara Falls, some eleven miles downstream from the bridge.

In the era of prohibition, Babe Ruth was a walking advertisement for the ease with which alcohol could be obtained. That fine Yankee tradition was upheld by Mantle and Ford, aided and abetted by their drinking partner Billy Martin. But alcoholism unquestionably shortened the career of Cub outfielder Hack Wilson, and drinking problems came to be associated with such players as Paul Waner, Jimmie Foxx, Don Newcombe, Ryne Duren, and Dennis Martinez, to mention but a few. For many decades, during which sportswriting shared more with hagiography than journalism, incidents of alcohol abuse never reached the public. It could be argued that only upon the publication of *Ball Four* by Jim Bouton in 1970 did the hangover earn its rightful spot in the locker room.

While baseball clubs naturally condemned alcohol and drug use, teams continued to sell beer in the stands, of course. This hypocritical policy reached a sodden apotheosis on June 4, 1974, in Cleveland's Municipal Stadium, when the Indians sponsored a 10¢ beer night. Increasingly rowdy as the game progressed, drunken Cleveland fans spilled out onto the field and pelted the visiting Texas Rangers with firecrackers. By the bottom of the ninth inning of a 5–5 game, dozens of fans streamed onto the field, threatened Texas players, and ignited a riot requiring police action to quell. Cleveland lost the game on a forfeit.

Alcohol abuse continued to be a problem into the 1980s. In 1980, Dodger pitcher Bob Welch publicly acknowledged a drinking problem that occasioned a five-week stay in The Meadows, which would become a popular substance-abuse treatment center. That same year, Kansas City catcher Darrell Porter checked in for drug and alcohol counseling.

Baseball players reflected general social trends with their increasing experimentation with drugs during the 1960s and 1970s, although a lot of disposable income and free time contributed to crash courses in recreational pharmacology. Access to drugs was easy. Many players routinely used "greenies," amphetamine-barbiturate combos, that allegedly gave them a lift before games. In some cases, the pills were distributed by club physicians, and the problem had become sufficiently widespread that in 1971 Commissioner Bowie Kuhn instituted baseball's first Drug Education and Prevention Program. Its effectiveness was questionable: in 1980, the team physician for the Phillies' Reading farm team was arrested for illegally writing prescriptions for amphetamines. The charges were later dismissed, but the doctor, Patrick A. Mazza, testified that he prescribed the pep pills at the request of seven Philadelphia players.

Baseball formally entered the era of mind-altering drugs on August 25, 1980, when Texas pitcher Ferguson Jenkins was arrested at the Toronto airport for possession of two ounces of marijuana, two grams of hashish, and four grams of cocaine; he was later found guilty of cocaine possession. Unofficially, baseball had tipped its hand during the previous decade. Pitcher Bill Lee, then of Montreal, had openly admitted use of marijuana. More startlingly, Pittsburg pitcher Dock Ellis, reportedly suffering a hangover on a day he didn't expect to pitch, flung a no-hitter (with eight walks) against the San Diego Padres on June 12, 1970. Ellis later denied that he was working on a hangover; he was working, rather, on a tab of LSD.

By the 1980s, the list of baseball's drug abusers began to read like a crime wave in a "good neighborhood." July 1982—San Diego infielder Alan Wiggins was arrested for cocaine possession. November 1982—Dodger relief pitcher Steve Howe began the first of three treatment regimens for drug abuse, which culminated with his suspension for the entire 1984 season. October 1983—four Kansas City Royal players (Willie Aikens, Vida Blue, Jerry Martin, and Willie Wilson) pled guilty to charges of

attempting to possess cocaine and later served time in prison. January 1984—Atlanta pitcher Pasquel Perez was arrested in the Dominican Republic with half of a gram of cocaine; found guilty, he paid about $400 in fines. May 1984—Anthony J. Peters, a former ice cream salesman in Milwaukee, received twenty-two years in jail for selling cocaine; at least ten players on the Milwaukee Brewers, Chicago White Sox, and Cleveland Indians were customers, and players Dick Davis, Paul Molitor, and Claudell Washington all reportedly admitted cocaine use during interviews with federal agents. In 1985 San Francisco outfielder Chili Davis publicly admitted using cocaine in 1983, but stopped when the Federal Bureau of Investigation reportedly questioned him about it.

These incidents were symptomatic of the widespread drug use that became a matter of record in the celebrated drug trials of 1985. In the spring of that year, a federal grand jury in Pittsburg heard testimony from eleven active major league players, resulting in a May 31, 1985, indictment of seven drug dealers who associated with players from December 1979 to January 1985. The dealers had access to the clubhouse and team flights of the Pittsburgh Pirates, and in one of the more bizarre twists on baseball's already bizarre modern-day marketing, FBI agents wired the Pittsburgh mascot, the Pirate Parrot, to obtain evidence used in the indictments.

During the trials in September, seven active or former players testified under grants of immunity: Dale Berra (Yankees), Enos Cabell (L.A. Dodgers), Keith Hernandez (Mets), Jeff Leonard (S.F. Giants), John Milner (ex-Pirate), Dave Parker (Reds), and Lonnie Smith (Cardinals). All confessed to extensive drug use, and several implicated peers during their testimony. Milner, for example, indicated that former Pittsburgh teammates Parker, Berra, Lee Lacy, and Rod Scurry used cocaine during the 1981 and 1982 seasons. Parker and Berra testified that Pirate stars Bill Madlock and Willie Stargell distributed amphetamines to team players (a charge denied by the two, who were never prosecuted); Parker also said he had arranged sales of cocaine to Dusty Baker, Steve Howe, and Derrell Thomas of the Dodgers as well as Cabell and J. R. Richard of the Astros. Smith and Hernandez implicated their former Cardinal teammate Joaquin Andujar. In gripping testimony, Hernandez described cocaine as "the devil on this earth" and shocked observers by estimating that by 1980 40 percent of all major league baseball players used cocaine.

Not a single player went on trial, however. Pittsburgh juries separately convicted part-time caterer Curtis Strong of Philadelphia and Robert McCue of drug-trafficking charges. Free-lance photographer Dale Shiffman of Pittsburgh and Philadelphia salesman Shelby Greer pled guilty and received sentences of twelve years, and three other Pittsburgh men entered guilty pleas.

In a 1985 interview with the *New York Times,* Montreal President John McHale flatly stated that cocaine use by eight of his players cost the Expos the National League Eastern Division race in 1982. Drug use was so widespread and casual, according to Lonnie Smith, that opposing players sometimes exchanged information on drug availability when they met at midfield during pregame warmup sprints. The extent of the involvement became pathetically clear when Montreal outfielder Tim Raines, the National League's leading base stealer, admitted that he often slid headfirst into second base during a steal so as to protect the gram bottle of cocaine he kept in his back pocket.

And still the roll call continued. Two former Cy Young winners, LaMarr Hoyt of San Diego and Dwight Gooden of the New York Mets, became involved in drug use. Gooden underwent treatment for cocaine and missed the first six weeks of the 1987 season. Hoyt served time for drug trafficking following his release by the Padres in 1987. Dale Berra, Yogi's son and one of the "Pittsburgh Seven," faced renewed difficulties when he was arrested at his New Jersey home for possession of cocaine with intent to sell in April 1990.

Brawlers, Perverts, Felons and Fellow Travelers

From the origins of baseball until well into the 1890s, baseball players were regarded mainly as roughnecks, quick to anger, quicker to fight. Fans were rowdy, and brawls between players and the public were not unusual (a doozy occurred in Louisville in 1896, when the bellicose Cleveland Spiders, protesting the umpire's decision to call the game, sparked a riot that required police intervention—and landed all the Spiders in jail). In 1904, during a spring training exhibition game in Mobile, Alabama, the New York Giants became so enraged by the calls of a hometown umpire that they finally attacked the man and beat him unconscious. John McGraw hustled his team out of town, even as warrants were being sworn for the players' arrest.

Sometimes the violence has been more serious. In 1883, former National League pitcher Terry Larkin shot his wife Catherine after she complained about his drinking. In the game's goriest story, Marty Bergen, became baseball's first and only ax murderer in January of 1900, when he killed his wife and two children in North Brookfield, Massachusetts, before committing suicide. In 1917, in a crime with racial overtones, Milwaukee (of the American Association) manager Danny Shay shot and killed a black waiter in an Indianapolis hotel during an argument over the amount of sugar in a sugar bowl; Shay was later acquitted.

Debt, the impending end of his career, and an unfortunate pitch that he couldn't take back apparently pushed former Angels relief pitcher Donnie Moore, thirty-five, over the brink in July 1989. Moore shot his wife of sixteen years, Tonya, three times with a pistol during an argument at their suburban Anaheim home, then shot himself in the head in front of his three children and died instantly (his wife survived). Beset with financial difficulties and marital problems, Moore never recovered from surrendering a two-out, two-strike home run to Dave Henderson in the 1986 American League Championship Series, which allowed Boston to tie a game they later won in extra innings. Moore blamed himself too harshly, though, because the Red Sox had to win two more games (which they did) to go on to the World Series. "I think insanity set in," David Pinter, Moore's agent, later told the press. "He could not live with himself after Henderson hit the home run. He kept blaming himself."

In perhaps the most celebrated shooting in baseball history, a "disturbed" nineteen-year-old woman, said to be a "fan," shot Phillie first baseman Eddie Waitkus in a Chicago hotel on June 15, 1949. Waitkus missed the rest of the 1949 season and had to undergo four operations, but he returned to play six more seasons—and to serve as a model for a similar incident in Bernard Malamud's baseball novel, *The Natural*. Cesar Cedeno of the Houston Astros was implicated in a more lethal incident. On December 11, 1973, the twenty-two-year-old outfielder was charged with voluntary manslaughter in the Dominican Republic when the body of a nineteen-year-old woman, shot to death, was found in his motel room. The charges were later changed—without much explanation—to involuntary manslaughter; Cedeno paid a small fine (about $100) and court costs. There have been no shootings between teammates, but not for lack of paranoia: Ty Cobb got along so poorly with his Detriot teammates during his early years that he retired to his railroad berth at night with a loaded pistol. Possibly the closest thing to an on-the-field homicide occurred in 1965, when San Francisco Giant pitcher Juan Marichal assaulted Los Angeles Dodger catcher John Roseboro with a bat.

The Mets' Darryl Strawberry enlivened the 1990 off-season when, in January, blood tests proved definitively he was the father in a paternity suit brought by a St. Louis woman. Two days later he was arrested by police in Encino, California, for threatening his wife Lisa with a loaded semiautomatic pistol. According to police, Strawberry slapped his wife during an argument (he had previously broken her nose in a tiff during the 1986 World Series); when she responded by striking him several times with a fire poker, he reached into a closet and produced the gun. Strawberry originally faced charges of assault with a deadly weapon, but the charges were later dropped. Within a week of the incident, the Mets slugger checked into New York's Smithers Clinic for alcohol rehabilitation.

In the old days, it was not uncommon for players to duke it out with their managers. One of the most savage beatings was administered in 1929 by White Sox player Art "Whattaman" Shires, a notorious drunkard and self-styled boxer. Shires cornered Chicago manager Lena Blackburne and the team's traveling secretary in a hotel room and thrashed both; it took four men, including two hotel detectives, to drag Shires off. He beat up his manager three times in one year. More recently, in 1977, Texas infielder Lenny Randle landed several punches on the face of manager Frank Lucchesi, shattering his cheekbone and requiring plastic surgery. The Rangers suspended Randle, fined him $10,000 and then released him; in court, Randle plea-bargained a felony charge down to simple battery and paid a $1,000 fine, along with medical expenses.

Umpires have not escaped controversy. In September 1988, National League umpire Dave Pallone—one of the original "scab" umpires hired during the 1979 season—took a leave of absence after news reports incorrectly linked him to an investigation of sex crimes against teenage boys in Saratoga Springs, New York. Pallone, who later admitted he was homosexual, was never charged with any crime, but headlines like "Ump Tied to Sex Ring" (New York *Daily News*) helped turn the leave into a permanent resignation. National League ump Bob Engel, meanwhile, resigned from baseball in July 1990 after pleading no contest to a shoplifting charge. The previous April he had been arrested for stealing less than $200 worth of merchandise from a convenience store in Bakersfield, California. The merchandise? Baseball cards.

In the twentieth century, three figures stand out for their combativeness as well as their ability to arouse controversy over the long haul: Ty Cobb, Babe Ruth, and Billy Martin.

Ty Cobb is generally considered the meanest player ever to don spikes. Cobb had to leave his first major league spring training camp, in 1906, to attend the trial of his mother, Amanda Cobb, who was acquitted of voluntary manslaughter charges in the death of Ty's father; she had shot him in 1905, believing him to be a prowler. Cobb seemed to carry a chip on his shoulder throughout his career. Thin-skinned, bigoted, a nasty street fighter, Cobb forever blemished his reputation in 1912 when he dove into the stands in New York to silence a heckler, kicking and spiking the man. The spectator turned out to be a man with no hands. Cobb's response was "I don't care if he has no feet"; American League president Ban Johnson's response was to suspend Cobb for ten days. (His Tiger teammates, in sympathy with Cobb, launched a strike that lasted one game.) During his career, Cobb engaged in drawn-out, knock-down fights with umpires, teammates, opposing players, fans, even a hotel watchman (the latter resulted in an indictment in Cleveland in 1909 for felonious assault). A racist with a broad palette, Cobb tarred all races with his brush: he liked to refer to Honus Wagner as "Kraut-head" and once refused to room with Babe Ruth, believing Ruth's dark complexion suggested black ancestry.

Ruth, on the other hand, enjoyed the reputation of a good-hearted, if adolescently rambunctious, personality; although he often indulged in scandalous behavior, he never amounted to a scandal. A man of immense and uncontrollable appetites, Ruth set new standards for eating, drinking, and whoring off the field just as he set long-ball standards on it. Particularly in the early days of his career, Ruth had little control of his temper. In 1917, as a Boston pitcher, he attacked umpire Brick Owens, and once went into the stands with a bat to chase a heckler; in the 1922 season alone, he was suspended five times, usually for swearing at umpires. He drank whiskey and ginger ale for breakfast, spent countless hours and dollars at the racetrack, partied past curfews in any time zone, frequented illegal breweries, and never wanted for liquor during Prohibition. A legendary philanderer, Ruth once bragged that he had slept with every girl in a St. Louis whorehouse, and even when his first wife Helen accompanied him on road trips, teammates facilitated Ruth's infidelities by making their rooms available for the Babe's liaisons. For all his energetic rutting, Ruth apparently contracted venereal disease more than once. A $50,000 paternity suit filed against Ruth by a Long Island woman accelerated the demise of his marriage, which was also undermined by Ruth's open affair with Claire Merritt Hodgson (she later became his second wife). Ruth's behavior struck many as reckless and often infantile, but it was rarely malicious and often perversely innocent, which is why he never lost the admiration and love of the public. That strange brew of raging hormones and American innocence is perfectly summed up by an incident during a

barnstorming trip to the Orient in the 1930s: brought to a geisha house, Ruth mistook it for a bordello and promptly started to undress.

Innocence seems lamentably absent from the adventures of infielder Billy Martin, who gave new, darker meaning to the word "scrappy." He was involved in at least five major fights on the field. He beat up one of his own pitchers, Dave Boswell, while managing the Twins in 1969 (Boswell required twenty stitches in the face); had punched out reporters (Nevada State Journal writer Ray Hagar in 1978) and marshmallow sales man (Joseph Cooper in 1979); got into a vicious fight with another member of his pitching staff while managing the Yankees (Ed Whitson in 1985); and brawled in a Texas strip joint (1988). He earned his reputation as "King of the Sucker Punch" in 1960 when, playing for the Reds, he suckerpunched Cub pitcher Jim Brewer after an inside pitch, shattering Brewer's cheekbone and landing him in the hospital for two weeks. No crass gesture has been too small or juvenile to be excluded from the Martin oeuvre: for his 1972 baseball card, as manager of the Detroit Tigers, Martin reverted to the classic junior high school prank of extending his middle finger in an unmistakably vulgar gesture while leaning on a bat.

The Billy Martin story came, inevitably, to a tragic end on an ice-slick country road near his home outside Binghamton, New York. On Christmas Day 1989, Martin's pickup truck skidded off the road and tumbled down an embankment; Martin died of massive internal injuries. William Reedy, a Detroit saloon owner and long-time Martin drinking companion, was charged with driving while intoxicated. Press reports indicated that the two men had been drinking for several hours, and Martin, too, was apparently drunk at the time of his death. Martin's widow Jill filed a lawsuit in July 1990, charging that Reedy's reckless driving caused Martin's death.

Although often suspected of prevarication, Martin spoke the absolute truth when he once referred to his boss as a "convicted felon." Indeed, Yankee principal owner George Steinbrenner had the dubious distinction of dragging baseball down into the Watergate scandal. In 1974, a federal grand jury in Cleveland indicted Steinbrenner on fourteen felony counts for illegal corporate contributions (by his American Shipbuilding Company) to the reelection campaign of Richard Nixon as well as for obstruction of justice. Represented by famed criminal attorney Edward Bennet Williams, Steinbrenner struck a deal with Watergate special prosecutor Leon Jaworski and pled guilty to a single felony charge.

Some observers considered Steinbrenner's light sentence (a $15,000 fine; no jail term) puzzling, since the Yankee owner admitted in court to such grave offenses as causing his employees to lie to the FBI and give false testimony to a federal grand jury. Williams literally saved Steinbrenner's baseball career; Commissioner Kuhn later admitted he would have expelled Steinbrenner for life had he received a jail sentence. Instead, Kuhn suspended Steinbrenner for two years, later reduced to one season. To the bewilderment of lawyers who prosecuted the case, Ronald Regan pardoned Steinbrenner in 1989. Steinbrenner, incidentally, was not the first owner to commit a felonious offense. In 1953, St. Louis owner Fred Saigh was forced to divest his control of the Cardinals when he began a fifteen-month sentence for tax evasion; that paved the way for Saigh's sale of the team to Anheuser-Busch.

Steinbrenner ran permanently afoul of the baseball establishment in 1990, when commissioner Fay Vincent ordered him to resign as general partner of the Yankees and, in effect, banned him from any active management of the club's baseball affairs. The decision culminated Steinbrenner's most tumultuous year in baseball. There was the usual nonfelonious bullying and double-talk; the usual revolving-door style of management (at final count, nineteen managerial changes in eighteen seasons); the usual odor of suspicious hijinx, as in the probe of former team official Syd Thrift for "scouting improprieties" (an investigation, it turns out, triggered by Steinbrenner himself and which yielded naught); and the usual good sportsmanship historically associated with the Yankees, as in allegations that Steinbrenner's famous "baseball people" spent part of their evenings sneaking into the visitors' locker room at Yankee Stadium, at the boss's orders, to search for corked bats (*et tu*, George Brett?). In July baseball fined Steinbrenner $25,000 and ordered him to pay the Angels $200,000 for tampering with Dave Winfield following his trade to California. His shipbuilding company faced mounting losses. And to add insult to the usual injury, a poll conducted in summer 1990 by the *New York Times* revealed that Met fans outnumbered Yankee fans in New York by three to one, and that only one in ten Yankee fans gave Steinbrenner a "favorable" rating.

A cloud of considerably darker and more ominous nature dogged Steinbrenner beginning in spring 1990. On March 18, 1990, the New York *Daily News* reported that Steinbrenner had paid $40,000 to an admitted small-time gambler named Howard Spira, allegedly in exchange for damaging information about Dave Winfield. Claiming Steinbrenner had reneged on the promise of a job, Spira demanded an additional $110,000, at which point Steinbrenner filed a complaint of extortion; Spira was later indicted by a federal grand jury in Tampa. Just another day at the office in the Bronx.

According to press accounts, Spira first contacted Steinbrenner on December 17, 1986, with an offer to provide negative information about Winfield, with whom Steinbrenner had feuded for nearly a decade. Winfield, it will be recalled, locked horns with the Yankee owner over the latter's contributions to the outfielder's nonprofit Winfield Foundation, and relations further deteriorated when Winfield vetoed several trades. The prevailing theory was that Steinbrenner sought negative information about Winfield as a bargaining chip to get the player to accept a trade.

Whatever the merit of the charges and countercharges, they got a full airing in the national press. The *New York Times* published excerpts from taped telephone conversations in which Steinbrenner told Spira, "I'm anxious to hear what you want to tell me, what you have to say . . ." Spira reportedly dished the following dirt: He claimed that Winfield and his agent, the late Al Frohman, concocted phony death threats against Winfield during the 1981 World Series to distract attention from the player's poor on-field performance, that Winfield Foundation funds were misused and misappropriated, and that Winfield had once held a gun to Spira's head and threatened to kill him if he didn't pay back a loan of $15,000. What-

ever the substance of these allegations (denied by Winfield), there was nothing casual about the contacts between Spira and Yankee representatives. Spira conversed primarily with Philip McNiff, a former FBI agent who served as a vice president at Steinbrenner's American Shipbuilding Company in Tampa. Records show that Spira called McNiff at least 426 times between December 1986 and December 1989. According to the *New York Times*, McNiff sent Spira a card on his thirtieth birthday with the inscription, "Howie, may all your dreams come true."

Spira, to the contrary, became Steinbrenner's worst nightmare. The Yankee owner acknowledged paying Spira $40,000 as the first press reports came out, but said he did it "out of the goodness of my heart." Even George conceded the inherent implausibility of that explanation, for he soon changed his story and said the payoff was to prevent Spira from disclosing embarrassing information about former Yankee employees. Steinbrenner changed his story once again while pleading his case in a private meeting with commissioner Fay Vincent—the transcript of which was leaked almost immediately and appeared first in *The National*. This time Steinbrenner claimed he paid Spira because he feared for the safety of his family and himself; dragging more names into the widening scandal, Steinbrenner also said Spira threatened to go public with information about Lou Piniella's gambling habits (an understandably touchy topic in Cincinnati, where Piniella replaced an admitted gambler as manager) and misappropriation of funds by two other Yankee employees. Vincent attached no merit to either charge.

Vincent had already enlisted John Dowd, head of the Rose investigation, to check out the Spira affair. Steinbrenner hired two high-powered criminal lawyers to represent his side of the story, and for the second time in two summers, it appeared that baseball was headed for a confrontation in court. But after an eleven-hour meeting with Steinbrenner on July 30, 1990, Vincent met with the press to announce his severe decision. Citing Steinbrenner's bad judgment, questioning his "candor and contrition," and expressing puzzlement over "a pattern of behavior that borders on the bizarre," Vincent said Steinbrenner's actions had not been in the best interests of baseball and ordered him to reduce his ownership in the Yankees to less than 50 percent by August 20, 1991. In booting Steinbrenner out of baseball, Vincent faulted Steinbrenner for paying a gambler money in "a furtive fashion" and for initiating an investigation of a player with the help of Spira without notifying the commissioner, he dismissed Steinbrenner's claims of extortion as "not credible," and he charged Steinbrenner with an attempt to cover up the Spira payment. As to the accusation that he had been unfair, Vincent wrote in the ruling, "In my view, Mr. Steinbrenner's dilemma is not with the procedures I have utilized, but with his inability to rewrite history." Ronald Reagan acceded to this revisionism; Vincent did not.

According to the guidelines established by Vincent, Steinbrenner could no longer participate in baseball decisions involving the Yankees and would even have to obtain permission in writing from the commissioner in order to attend games. Vincent did not rule out the possibility that Steinbrenner's son Hank might assume day-to-day management of the team; however, the commissioner's assertion that severe restrictions would apply seemed, short of wiretaps and full-time surveillance, virtually impossible to enforce. Within twenty-four hours, Steinbrenner—who pronounced himself "very happy" with Vincent's ruling—tabbed his son to take over the club as general partner. As if Vincent's decision was not enough of a bombshell, the commissioner later revealed that he had planned only to suspend Steinbrenner for two years; it was Steinbrenner who pushed for a second decision that amounted to a permanent ban. "From where I sit," Vincent later said, "the second proposal [penalty] was stronger. I don't understand why he took it."

When word of Vincent's decision reached Yankee Stadium on the night of July 30, fans cheered the news with a ninety-second standing ovation. "Christmas in July" is how one fan characterized the end of Steinbrenner's reign of terror in New York baseball.

One of Steinbrenner's old nemeses made news during this period as well. Former commissioner Bowie Kuhn, that balding paragon of probity, received a bad haircut in the press in early 1990 when, as a *New York Times* headline had it, "Bowie Kuhn Is Said to Be in Hiding." Bowie's bad luck began the previous year, when his law firm Myerson & Kuhn overbilled a client and was ordered to pay back $1 million. By December 1989, the law firm had filed for bankruptcy protection, but one of the creditors, Marine Midland Bank, sued Kuhn to recover $3.1 million in loans. In court papers, the bank charged that Kuhn had sold his New Jersey home and fled to Florida, where state laws exempt residences from being seized in bankruptcy proceedings. Kuhn told the *Florida Times-Union* that he and his wife Luisa had simply moved to Florida for a change of pace.

No Sex, Please; We're Heroes

As baseball became popular, so too did public interest in its practitioners extend beyond the field to the home, and sometimes right on through the bedroom door. Within the bounds of Victorian society, one of baseball's earliest sex "scandals" involved the hard-fighting Walter "Arlie" Latham, third baseman of the St. Louis Browns. Around 1885, his second wife filed for divorce on the grounds of assault, desertion, infidelity, and perversion.

Sports pages in the 1880s also carried accounts of Sam Crane, infielder for the Metropolitans and later a prominent sportswriter, who was arrested for running off with $1,500 belonging to a Scranton fruit dealer named Travenfelter—*and* with his wife Hattie. Edwin "Ned" Bligh was among the earliest of players named in a paternity suit; Bligh just missed more serious charges, since his accuser was seventeen-year-old Zella Coleman. By the end of the century, domestic problems—such as the divorces of popular players like John Montgomery Ward, Amos Rusie, and Tony Mullane—became fodder for reporters.

Probably the most tragic scandal involved minor league pitcher Edgar McNabb, who made it to the majors for one season with Baltimore in 1893. McNabb had been carrying on an affair with actress Louise Kellogg, wife of Seattle businessman R. E. Rockwell. The idyll came to an end on February 28, 1894, in a room at the Hotel Eiffel in Pittsburgh. For reasons that remain a mystery to this day, McNabb shot Kellogg twice (paralyzing her but not killing her), then turned the gun on himself and showed better control. In another romance-related suicide, Red Sox manager Chick Stahl took his life in 1907 after facing pressure from a woman who'd become pregnant by him.

On the whole, though, twentieth century sex scandals in baseball have been more elliptical than explicit. Apart from Ruth's legendary wenching, there was little to arouse prurient interest, except perhaps the vicarious experience of Joe DiMaggio's marriage to Marilyn Monroe or perhaps Bo Belinsky's dalliance with Mamie Van Doren. In 1988, Dave Winfield's bout with Ruth Roper, mother-in-law of Mike Tyson, brought VD into the courts. But in terms of vague but suggestive explanations, nothing beats the adventure of Brooklyn pitcher Van Lingle Mungo during spring training in 1941 in Havana. Authors Gene Karst and Martin J. Jones, Jr., note that the Dodger player had to be hustled hastily back to the mainland after he "became involved with a former bullfighter and his girlfriend." No further explanations offered.

Amidst the usual paternity suits (Darryl Strawberry, Pascual Perez), wife beatings, and even the rare case of mother beating (Jim Presley of Atlanta), Margo Adams provided an unusually juicy sex scandal in June 1988 when she filed a $6 million palimony suit against Boston third baseman Wade Boggs. The perennial AL All-Star and batting champ admitted he'd had a four-year affair with the California woman. When Adams's lawyer sought to depose nine other players, tensions rose on the Red Sox, including reports of an ugly confrontation between Boggs and teammate Dwight Evans. Boggs won the suit, Adams landed a pictorial in *Penthouse*, and none of the pictures Boggs allegedly took showing Red Sox teammates in compromising positions—so they wouldn't talk about his affair with Adams, it was said—ever saw the light of day. Everything you need to know about the baseball ethic in this arena of activity, however, can be inferred from a remark Boggs made at the end of the controversy: *One-night stands are acceptable,* he said, *but two-year affairs are not.*

Boggs's mantle passed the following season to former Dodger and Padre first baseman Steve Garvey. Baseball's former "Mr. Clean" managed to impregnate two women while pursuing and marrying a third, occasioning the appearance of two young children in the world and bumper stickers in Southern California that read: "Steve Garvey is not *my* Padre." Garvey's woes were complicated by a nasty child-custody suit with ex-wife Cyndi and his postbaseball career suffered a further setback in 1990, when he was fired by a San Diego radio station because of poor ratings for his talk show.

Back in the junior circuit, so to speak, Yankee outfielder Luis Polonia spent October 1989 in a Milwaukee jail, serving a sixty-day sentence (later reduced to thirty days) for having had sexual intercourse with a minor when the Yankees visited the Brewers in August. Polonia claimed he was set up by the fifteen-year-old girl; the judge remained unconvinced, imposing fines and contributions totaling $11,500. The incident may have encouraged the Yankees to trade Polonia in 1990, but probably didn't influence Polonia's bizarre assessment of the transaction. "They only had one thing on their mind,"

Polonia charged, "and I don't know what it is."

But hardly a sex scandal in any field quite measures up to a wife-swapping scheme that became public in March 1973. New York Yankee pitchers Fritz Peterson and Mike Kekich pulled off one of the most daring trades in baseball history: they exchanged wives and children. In a straight-up deal, Peterson received Susanne Kekich, her two young daughters, and the Kekich family dog, in exchange for Marilyn "Chip" Peterson, her two young sons, and the Peterson family pet. If, as is often said, you cannot judge the value of a trade until five years have passed, it must be stated that neither side came out ahead on this one. Marilyn Peterson left Kekich and both pitchers were out of baseball by 1980.

Tragedies and Shortened Careers

Joseph M. Overfield

If, of all words of tongue and pen,
The saddest are, "It might have been,"
More sad are these we daily see:
"It is, but hadn't ought to be."
—Bret Harte

In the eleventh century in the reign of William the Conqueror, detailed information about the landowners of England and their assets was gathered and then recorded in what were called *Domesday Books.* Much of what is known of the demographics of early England is derived from these books.

Baseball also has its *Domesday Books,* but they are called *Encyclopedias.* They list the name, vital statistics, and records of every player who ever appeared in a major league game, beginning with the formation of the National Association in 1871. So assiduously have baseball's *Domesday Books* been corrected, refined, and updated, it is safe to say that detailed information is more readily available about ballplayers, even the most obscure, than it is for statesmen, authors, artists, poets, or captains of industry.

Informative as they are, the *Encyclopedias* still leave much unsaid. For example, why did Bert Shepard play but a single game, while Jim McGuire played for twenty-six seasons? Short careers, like Shepard's, usually mean a lack of ability or, perhaps, the failure to receive a fair opportunity; but often they are short for other reasons—death, illness, injury, accident, suicide, or even murder. It is with such tragically shortened careers that this chapter will deal. Although the subject was carefully researched, no assertion of 100 percent completeness is proffered.

Since baseball's *Domesday Books* are limited to major league players and managers, no listing will be found there for James P. Creighton of the preprofessional era, nor for minor leaguers like Bill Thomas of the 1906 Buffalo Bisons or Ralph Worrell of the 1918 Baltimore Orioles.

James Creighton was the star pitcher of the Excelsior Club, a famous Brooklyn amateur nine of the 1850s and 1860s. Before Creighton's day, it was customary for pitchers to toss the ball gently to the plate. Creighton changed all this by developing a snap throw that gave speed and spin to the ball. In addition, he was one of the most powerful hitters of his day. It is said that he completed one entire season without being put out. On October 14, 1862, the Excelsiors were playing the Union Club of Morrisania in their final match of the season. Creighton, at bat for the Excelsiors, swung mightily and sent the ball beyond the reach of the outfielders. As he crossed first base, he collapsed, obviously in great pain. Legend has it that he staggered around the bases for a home run. He was immediately taken home by his teammates. Four days later, the twenty-one-year-old pitcher was dead. According to an account in the *Brooklyn Eagle,* headlined "Obsequies of a Celebrated Ballplayer," Creighton had ruptured his bladder with the force of his final swing and died from internal bleeding.

A. G. Spalding, in his book *Baseball, America's National Game,* devoted two pages to Creighton, with his picture and a view of the towering granite monument his teammates erected in his memory on Tulip Hill in Brooklyn's Greenwood Cemetery. The monument is embossed with crossed bats, a cap, a base, and a scorebook.

The circumstances of the death of Bill Thomas, a twenty-five-year-old Buffalo pitcher, in April 1906, are still a mystery. Thomas had been a big winner in the Pacific Coast League, and manager George Stallings of Buffalo had brought him east to test his mettle in the stronger Eastern League. He was successful in his first start at Baltimore. The Bisons then finished a series at Providence and took a train to New Bedford, Massachusetts, from which point they boarded the night boat *Richard Peck,* en route to New York City. Thomas had left word with the porter and with his roommate, pitcher Joe Galaski, that he wanted an early call so he could see the New York skyline at sunrise. In the morning, when the porter came into the stateroom, the Thomas bunk, which had been slept in, was empty. Thomas was never seen again.

In 1918 Ralph Worrell, only nineteen, won 25 games for Jack Dunn's Baltimore Orioles, but he never pitched again. Instead of becoming another Lefty Grove (also a Jack Dunn discovery), Worrell failed to survive the winter, dying in the terrible World War One flu epidemic.

The deaths of young, healthy, vigorous athletes like Creighton, Thomas, and Worrell are sad and decidedly against the odds, but in the muster rolls of major league players in baseball's *Domesday Books,* such cases are far from rare.

Fatal Illnesses of Players and Managers

Elmer White was long thought to be a brother of James "Deacon" White and Will White. The early encyclopedias listed him as playing 15 games for the Forest Cities of Cleveland in 1872, but nothing more. A trip by the writer to the village of Caton in New York's southern tier and to the cemetery behind the Methodist Church there resulted in the finding of Elmer White's grave. The inscription on the tombstone, which showed he was Jim's and Will's cousin, not a brother, told with great economy of words the story of a short life and a short baseball career: "Born December 7, 1850. Died March 17, 1873."

Of all the deaths of active major leaguers to be recounted here, significantly, only one—that of Ray Chapman, who was killed by a Carl Mays pitch—resulted directly from activity on the diamond. Many of the deaths, especially those in the first fifty years, were from illnesses routinely controlled today. Typhoid fever, for example, killed first baseman Alex McKinnon of Pittsburgh (NL) on July 24, 1887. He played in the July 4 game, complained of not feeling well, and was taken home. He died twenty days later at the age of thirty. Less than a year later, on April 29, 1888, Charlie Ferguson, an outstanding young pitcher who had won 21, 26, 30, and 22 games for Philadelphia (NL) from 1884 through 1887 and was a strong hitter as well (.288 in four seasons), died from the same disease, twelve days after his twenty-fifth birthday.

Edward "Sy" Sutcliffe, a catcher for most of his career, had shifted to first base for Baltimore (NL) in 1892 and had done quite well, batting .279 in 66 games. In the off-season, the twenty-nine-year-old native of Wheaton, Illinois, developed Bright's disease. He died February 13, 1893.

Joe Cassidy, an infielder for the Washington Senators in 1904 and 1905, was a third victim of the deadly typhoid. He was only twenty-three when he died at his home in Chester, Pennsylvania, March 25, 1906. Just a year and four days later, March 29, 1907, Patrick Henry "Cozy" Dolan, a nine-year outfielder in the majors, most recently with Boston (NL), also died of typhoid. He took ill during Boston's spring training trip, and died in a Louisville hospital, at age thirty-four. News of his death was overshadowed in the Boston papers by the extensive coverage given to the sensational suicide of manager Chick Stahl of the other Boston club, the day before in West Baden, Indiana.

Mike Powers, who caught in the majors from 1898 to 1909, mainly with the Philadelphia Athletics, was an anomaly in those hard-bitten days of the game's history, in that he held a degree from Holy Cross College and had also attended Notre Dame Medical School. Powers, incidentally, recruited the legendary Louis "Chief" Sockalexis for both of his alma maters, as shall be seen later. Powers was not a strong hitter (.216 lifetime), but he was considered a fine defensive catcher. He was behind the plate in an early season game in 1909, when he complained of nausea and asked to be taken to a hospital. He underwent three stomach operations, and then gangrene set in. He died April 26, 1909, at the age of thirty-eight.

Alan Storke was an infielder for Pittsburgh and St. Louis (NL) from 1906 through 1909. He never made it to spring training in 1910. He was a mere twenty-five when he died in Newton, Massachusetts, March 18, 1910, following a lung operation. Less than two years later, February 1, 1912, another National League infielder, thirty-year-old Jimmy Doyle, who had batted .282 for the Cubs in 1911, died in Syracuse, New York, after an appendicitis operation.

Addie Joss pitched in the majors only eight seasons and part of a ninth, but his record was so extraordinary that he was elected to the Hall of Fame (in 1978), despite his short tenure. With Cleveland from 1902 to 1910, he won 160 games, lost 97, and compiled an ERA of 1.88 (second on the all-time list). He pitched a perfect game on October 2, 1908, defeating Big Ed Walsh, 1–0, with first place on the line. Joss had another no-hitter on April 20, 1910, also against the White Sox, just before his health began to fail.

Joss made only 13 appearances in 1910, and still felt weak when he went south in 1911. He collapsed on the bench during an exhibition game at Chattanooga, Tennessee, then became ill again when the team reached Cincinnati. Doctors said it was pleurisy and sent him home to Toledo. On April 14, 1911, two days after his team had opened the season in St. Louis, he died at the age of thirty-one. The cause of his death was given as tubercular meningitis. Famed ballplayer-preacher Billy Sunday presided at his funeral, said to have been the biggest ever seen in Toledo.

Leonard "King" Cole, a righthanded pitcher who had won 20 games for the Cubs in 1910 and 18 the following season, was, like Charlie Ferguson, to have a brilliant career nipped in the bud by a fatal illness. During the 1915 season, when Cole was with the Yankees, it was discovered that he had been suffering from tuberculosis. He returned to his home in Bay City, Michigan, where he died on January 6, 1916, at twenty-nine. He left a splendid 56–27 (.675) won–lost record.

Joe Leonard, a twenty-five-year-old infielder who began with Pittsburgh in 1914 and played for Washington in 1916, 1917, and 1919, appeared in only one game for the Senators in 1920, became ill, and was taken to George Washington Hospital. He died there on May 1, following an appendicitis operation.

In 1922, the St. Louis Cardinals lost two young ballplayers within nine months. First to go was William "Pickles" Dillhoefer, who had caught in the majors since 1917, usually in a backup role. He was twenty-seven when he died in a St. Louis hospital, February 22, 1922, of that old bugaboo, typhoid fever. Outfielder Austin McHenry had started with the Cardinals in 1918, but had not really blossomed until 1921, when he batted .350 and hit 37 doubles, 8 triples, and 17 home runs. The following year he began to have difficulties in judging fly balls. Manager Branch Rickey sent him to a doctor, who diagnosed his problem as a brain tumor. An operation proved unsuccessful, and he died at Jefferson Township, Ohio, November 27, 1922. He was twenty-seven, the same age as Dillhoefer.

The 1924 season saw the deaths of two veterans of the Cincinnati Reds within eight months. Pat Moran was a catcher in the majors from 1901 to 1914 and then a highly successful manager, first with the Phillies and then with the Reds. In nine managerial seasons, he compiled a record of 748–586 and won a pennant with each team. His 1915 Phillies lost the World Series to Boston, in five games, while his 1919 Reds won the tainted 1919 Series from the White Sox, 5–3. Moran was forty-eight when he died of Bright's disease at Orlando, Florida, March 7, 1924, while at spring training with the Reds. The second Red to die that year was Jake Daubert, a fancy-fielding first baseman who could hit (.303 in fifteen years with the Dodgers and the Reds). Although forty years old, he played 102 games for the Reds in 1924, batted .281 and fielded .990. He became ill in October and was taken to Good Samaritan Hospital in Cincinnati, where he died on October 9 following an appendicitis operation, just as Jimmy Doyle and Joe Leonard had before him.

Legendary New York Giants outfielder and future Hall of Famer Ross Youngs was at the height of his career when he was struck down by Bright's disease, diagnosed during spring training in 1926. Despite his illness, he played 95 games and batted .306. All through the season, he was accompanied by a male nurse hired by manager John McGraw. Youngs was bedridden for the entire 1927 season and died on October 22 at the age of thirty. Despite his relatively short career, nine seasons and part of another, his record was impressive enough to earn him election to the Hall of Fame in 1972. McGraw said he was the greatest outfielder he had ever seen.

Urban Shocker was an outstanding pitcher for the great Yankee teams of the 1925–1927 period. His record was 18–6 for the 1927 Yankees, but illness kept him out of the World Series. His thirteen-year record with the St. Louis Browns and the Yankees is in Hall of Fame country—187–117 (.615)—and he never had a losing season. His health continued to fail in 1928, and he appeared in only one game before being released. On September 9, 1928, in Denver, he died of heart disease and pneumonia. He was thirty-eight.

Shocker's manager, Miller Huggins, was to survive him little more than a year. On September 20, 1929, Huggins, who had managed the Yankees since 1918 and had won six pennants and three world's championships, asked coach Art Fletcher to take over for him, so that he could check into a hospital. Five days later, he was dead of erysipelas, a streptococcal skin infection. Huggins, who was of Munchkin size at 5'6" and 140 pounds, had been in the majors since 1904, batting a career .265, and winning 1,413 games and losing 1,134 as a manager. His showdowns with his rambunctious slugger, Babe Ruth, are part of baseball lore. Huggins was elected to the Hall of Fame in 1964.

On May 28, 1930, Hal Carlson, thirty-eight-year-old righthanded pitcher of the Chicago Cubs, and a fourteen-year veteran of the National League, called several of his teammates to his apartment in a Chicago hotel, saying that he was in severe pain. Shortly after the team physician arrived, Carlson was dead from what was described as "an internal hemorrhage." He left a three-year-old son and his wife, who was expecting another child.

Twenty-nine-year-old infielder Mickey Finn, who had played for the Dodgers from 1930 to 1932 and then for the Phillies, became ill midway through the 1933 season. Owner Gerry Nugent of the Phillies summoned his brother-in-law, Dr. H. P. Boyle, who diagnosed Finn's trouble as a duodenal ulcer. Surgery was performed in an Allentown, Pennsylvania, hospital. He seemed on the road to recovery, but unforeseen medical problems arose, leading to his death on July 7, 1933.

On August 28, 1949, Ernie Bonham, who had pitched seven seasons for the Yankees and appeared in three World Series, but who was now with the Pirates, pitched his team to an 8–2 win over the Phillies. He had complained of some discomfort during the game, and as a precaution was taken to a Pittsburgh hospital, where appendicitis was diagnosed. The normally routine operation

extended for three hours when complications developed. He was very weak when manager Billy Meyer visited him a few days later. "Billy, they are hitting me all over the field, and I can't get anybody out," he mumbled. On September 15, minutes before Meyer and coach Goldie Holt arrived for another visit, he passed away. Bonham, who was thirty-six, left an impressive 103–72 record.

Perhaps the closest parallel to the death of James Creighton in the preprofessional era was the shocking and tragic passing of first baseman Harry Agganis of the Boston Red Sox, on June 27, 1955 at the age of twenty-five. Like Creighton, Agganis was young and talented, with a glorious career seemingly assured.

At 6'2", 200 pounds, and lefthanded, Agganis was a drawing-board first baseman. "The Golden Greek," as he was called, was the most publicized athlete to come out of Boston University since Mickey Cochrane in 1923. Such were Agganis's skills as a quarterback that he was a first-round draft pick of the Cleveland Browns, who offered him $25,000 to sign. When the Boston Red Sox upped this figure by $10,000, he chose baseball. After the 1953 season at Louisville (American Association), where he batted .281, had 23 home runs, 108 RBIs, and played in 155 games, he took over at first base for the parent club in 1954. He batted only .251 his first season. In the early going in 1955, he was over .300 when he developed pneumonia and was hospitalized for ten days. He returned to the lineup, but became ill again in Kansas City. He flew back to Boston and checked into Sancta Maria Hospital in nearby Cambridge. He was thought to be recovering nicely, when suddenly on June 27, he died. The cause of his death was given as a massive pulmonary embolism.

Agganis's body lay in state at St. George's Greek Orthodox Church in his home town of Lynn, Massachusetts. On the day before the funeral, ten thousand mourners passed the bier.

Righthanded pitcher Jim Umbricht of Houston underwent a cancer operation on March 8, 1963. By May 9 he was back in uniform, and he finished the year with a 4–3 record and an ERA of 2.61 in 35 appearances. He did not make it into the next season. The malignancy spread, and he died on April 8, 1964, at age thirty-three.

According to present information, two active major leaguers succumbed to leukemia. Both were twenty-nine when they died and both at one time played with Minnesota. The first was giant 6'7" Walter Bond, who started with Cleveland in 1960, moved to Houston in 1964 and then to Minnesota in 1967, when illness forced him to quit. He died in Houston, September 14, 1967.

The second, infielder Danny Thompson, who broke in with Minnesota in 1970, had played for three years in the majors when he learned he had leukemia. He continued to play, however, and on June 1, 1976, he was involved in one of the big trades of the year, when he was bundled wtih pitcher Bert Blyleven and shipped to Texas for Roy Smalley, Bill Singer, Mike Cubbage, Jim Gideon, and $250,000. Thompson finished the season with Texas, but it was to be his last. Baseball's Most Courageous Performer (he was so voted in 1974) was only twenty-nine when he died December 10, 1976, at Rochester, Minnesota.

In a single year, 1966, the Detroit Tigers lost two managers to illness and subsequent death, a tragic sequence not duplicated in major league history. On May 16 Charley Dressen, who had managed in the majors for sixteen seasons, suffered a heart attack and was succeeded by coach Bob Swift. Dressen died three months later at the age of sixty-seven. Swift himself became ill in July and was hospitalized, with another coach, Frank Skaff, taking over. It was found that Swift had an advanced case of lung cancer. He died October 16 at the age of fifty-one.

Quiet, efficient, and soft-spoken Dick Howser was an American League infielder from 1961 to 1968 with Kansas City, Cleveland, and New York. He became manager of the Yankees in 1980 and led them to 103 wins and a division title. After the Yankees lost the league championship series to Kansas City, 0–3, owner George Steinbrenner made things so uncomfortable for Howser that he resigned. He moved to Kansas City in 1981, winning a division title in 1984, then a pennant and a world's championship in 1985.

Early in the 1986 season, Howser began to suffer from headaches and to experience visual and memory problems. On July 18, he learned he had a malignant brain tumor. Operations followed, and he recovered sufficiently to return to uniform in 1987. But his health continued to deteriorate and he was forced to give up his managerial duties. He was fifty years old when he died, June 17, 1987.

Suicides and Other Violent Deaths

According to present information, five active major leaguers and one league president ended their lives by their own hands. Two others, Dan McGann and Benny Frey, killed themselves in the year after they had been sent to the minors. An eighth, Johnny Mostil, attempted suicide but recovered. There is also some intimation that the violent deaths of Len Koenecke and Ed Delahanty might have been "death wish" situations.

On February 28, 1894, Edgar McNabb, a pitcher who had won eight games for the Baltimore Orioles in 1893, checked in at the Eiffel Hotel on Smithfield Street in Pittsburgh. He told the clerk that his wife had gone to Braddock to visit her ailing parents and that he should give her the room key when she returned. Earlier that day, the McNabbs had run into a friend, one Louis Gillen, and the three had agreed to attend the theater that evening.

When the agreed time for the meeting passed, Gillen became concerned and went to the McNabbs' room. As he stood outside the door, he heard a woman's screams. He called for help, and when the room clerk opened the door, the two were shocked and sickened by the bloody and grisly scene before them. Mrs. McNabb lay on the floor, bleeding horribly from bullet holes in her neck and head, but still breathing. Lying beside her, dead, with bullet holes in the head, was Edgar McNabb. A pistol was still in his hand.

As the story unfolded, it became more than a tragic domestic confrontation. The dying woman was not Mrs. McNabb at all. She was Mrs. E. E. Rockwell, wife of a prominent Seattle businessman who had once been president of the Pacific Northwest Baseball League. She was an actress by profession and used the stage name of Louise Kellogg.

It appeared that Miss Kellogg, who had just finished a theatrical engagement in New York, had asked McNabb to meet her in Pittsburgh. According to a newspaper account, she was planning to break off her relationship with the ballplayer. Letters found in the room indicated that she had been sending him money to tide him over the winter, and further that there had been recent disagreements between them. In the judgment of the police who investigated, an argument had developed, culminating in McNabb's shooting of Miss Kellogg and then turning the gun on himself.

Among McNabb's possessions on the scene was a copy of a message which read: IN GREAT TROUBLE, TELEGRAPH $100 IMMEDIATELY. SEE YOU IN TWO WEEKS. It was probably this message that led Edgar McNabb and Louise Kellogg to their fateful rendezvous at the Eiffel Hotel.

Even more shocking than the McNabb affair was the sad denouement of Marty Bergen, first-string catcher for Frank Selee's Boston (NL) club from 1896 to 1899.

On the morning of January 19, 1900, Marty's father, Michael Bergen, who was staying at the house of a neighbor, walked to his son's property, which was called "Snowball Farm," to get some milk. Seeing no activity around the house, he left. He returned at noon and still saw no signs of life. He walked through the unlocked kitchen door, only to be confronted by a scene of unspeakable horror. On the kitchen floor, lay the body of his six-year-old granddaughter Florence. In the adjoining room, he found the body of his daughter-in-law Harriet Bergen and next to her that of her three-year-old son Joseph. Mrs. Bergen's hands were raised as though in supplication or as though trying to ward off a blow. A bloody ax, the apparent murder weapon, was found on the scene. Bergen himself had committed suicide with a straight razor, almost severing his head from his body.

Dr. W. E. Norwood, the medical examiner, made an almost on-the-spot judgment, ruling that the crime had been committed "in a fit of insanity," and that no autopsies would be necessary. According to the account in *The Sporting Life*, the funeral service at St. Joseph's Church in North Brookfield was somber and brief, and "only a few words suitable to the occasion were spoken." The only prominent baseball people present were Connie Mack of the Milwaukee club and Billy Hamilton, a Bergen teammate.

What triggered the carnage at Snowball Farm will never be known. Bergen's manager, Frank Selee, said that he seemed, at times, to act irrationally and to be pursued by hallucinations. It was also revealed that he had sought help from his pastor and his doctor, and that on one occasion he had accused the latter of trying to kill him. Bergen was not a drinker and apparently had no pressing money problems. He was buying the farm on the installment plan and had $2,000 in cash.

On January 12, 1903, not quite three years after the Bergen murder-suicide, the baseball world was stunned by the self-inflicted death of another prominent player. George Barclay "Win" Mercer was a versatile performer who had played every position but catcher in nine years in the majors, winning 131 games as a pitcher and batting .285. He was manager-designate for Detroit, where he had played in 1902.

Mercer was on the West Coast for a series of exhibition games between teams from the American and National leagues. A small man with striking good looks, he had a weakness for fast women and slow horses, a deadly combination that apparently was to do him in. On the fatal day, he did not appear when expected in the dining room of the San Francisco hotel where the players were staying. When the door of his room was opened, Mercer's body was found. A rubber hose was connected to a gas jet. He had died of self-inflicted asphyxiation.

Mercer left a suicide note in which he warned of the evils of women and gambling. He also left a note for his mother and one for his fiancée in East Liverpool, Ohio. Another letter was addressed to Tip O'Neill, manager of the ballplayer troupe, for which Mercer was in charge of finances. Even though Mercer had recently incurred heavy gambling losses, it was reported that his baseball accounts were in order.

Charles "Chick" Stahl had batted .307 in ten major league seasons and was considered one of the game's premier defensive outfielders. Stahl, a Marty Bergen teammate at Boston (NL) from 1897 to 1899, had been named manager of the Boston Puritans (AL) late in the 1906 season, succeeding his friend and roommate Jimmy Collins. Stahl was handsome, popular, well paid for his era, and recently married. Despite his oft-expressed distaste for managing and a recent attempt to resign, it seemed he had almost every reason to be on top of the world; but on March 28, 1907, in his room at the West Baden Hotel in West Baden, Indiana, he ingested a lethal dose of carbolic acid. As he staggered toward his bed, roommate Collins went to his assistance, just in time to hear him gasp: "Boys, I couldn't help it; it drove me to it."

For years, baseball historians pondered Stahl's cryptic words, then usually concluded it was the pressure of managing that forced him to swallow the poison. Dissenting was Harold Seymour, who, in his *Baseball, The Early Years,* strongly hints at the real reason: *cherchez la femme.* In the May 1986 issue of *Boston Magazine,* author Glenn Stout dug out the rest of the Stahl story and wrote it.

Stahl, according to Stout, although in love with a young lady named Julia Harmon of Roxbury, Massachusetts, was also attracted to other young ladies, the groupies of his day. Furthermore, according to Stout, one of his admirers, a Lulu Ortman, demanded that Stahl marry her. When he spurned her, she twice tried to shoot him but missed. Meanwhile, on November 14, 1906, Stahl had married Miss Harmon at St. Francis de Sales Church in Roxbury. It seems that he had also been involved, late in the 1906 season, with another woman, who now claimed to be pregnant by him. She pressured Stahl to marry her on pain of exposure. He told her that marriage was impossible, since he was already married. She persisted that spring, and it was this pressure, concludes Stout, not the pressure of managing, that led to his suicide.

A sad postscript to the Stahl suicide was the fate of his wife, Julia. Shortly after his death, she attempted suicide herself, but survived. On November 15, 1908, she was found dead in the doorway of a house in South Boston, after a night on the town. An autopsy showed that she had died of edema of the brain.

Little more than two years after the Stahl tragedy, another suicide rocked the game, but it had none of the nasty characteristics of the McNabb, Bergen, or Stahl cases.

Richard Cory, in Edwin Arlington Robinson's poem of the same name, was young, elegant, and well thought of, but one summer night he "went home and put a bullet through his head." Harry Clay Pulliam, president of the National League, was baseball's Richard Cory. On June 28, 1909, Pulliam went to his room in the New York Athletic Club and fired a shot through his head. He died the next morning. The forty-year-old bachelor left no suicide note. Presumably it was a combination of poor health (he had been on leave of absence for health reasons) and the burdens of his job that caused him to do it.

On December 13, 1910, Dennis "Dan" McGann, former captain of the New York Giants and a premier first baseman for thirteen seasons, but most recently a member of the Milwaukee club of the American Association, was found dead in a Louisville hotel room, a bullet hole in his heart and a revolver in his hand. He had been seen around the hotel during the day and had appeared to be in good spirits. One explanation was that he was depressed over the suicide of a brother the past summer.

On March 28, 1927, at the Youree Hotel in Shreveport, Louisiana, spring training headquarters of the Chicago White Sox, Johnny Mostil, the team's star center fielder, slashed both wrists and wounded himself in the chest, throat, and legs with a razor blade and a knife. Early reports, giving him little chance to survive, were wrong. He did recover, played later that same season, and two more seasons thereafter, followed by a long career in the game as a scout. The only explanation for his act seems to have been his hypochondriacal nature. He constantly worried and brooded over his health, although a physical examination that spring had revealed no serious problems.

In eight major league seasons, Cincinnati righthander Benny Frey had struggled to a 57–82 record. At the end of the 1936 season, the best of his career (he was 10–8), he was sent to Nashville to work an ailing arm back into shape. Apparently despondent over the failure of his arm to recover, Frey, on November 1, 1937, at Jackson, Michigan, sat in his car with the motor running and a rubber hose attached to the exhaust pipe. When police found the thirty-one-year-old pitcher, he was dead from carbon monoxide poisoning.

It was August 3, 1940, and the Cincinnati Reds were in Boston. Pleading illness, catcher Willard Hershberger told his roommate, Bill Baker (some accounts say it was Lew Riggs), that he would not be able to come to the ballpark until later. When he did not appear and his telephone was not answered, manager Bill McKechnie sent Dan Cohen, Hershberger's close friend, to the hotel to get him. When the room was entered, Hershberger's body was found in the bathroom, his jugular vein severed by a razor.

Hershberger was young (just thirty), successful, and single, and there seemed no apparent reason for his act. As in the McGann case, there had been a previous suicide in the family. Hershberger's father had shot himself to death in 1928. It has been theorized that the catcher was depressed over his recent failures on the diamond. He had gone hitless in a crucial game, and on another occasion had supposedly called a wrong pitch to Harry Danning of the Giants, who then had hit a home run to beat the Reds in the ninth inning. On the other hand, it was no secret that he had been contemplating suicide. He had told manager McKechnie as much in recent weeks. Also, he had recently purchased a $500 bond, placed it in the hotel safe, and asked that it be given to his mother "if anything happens to me."

With all the obvious planning, it is curious that no suicide note was found. Suicidal tendencies notwithstanding, a hitless game and the call of a wrong pitch hardly seem sufficient to have provoked the deed. It took almost eighty years for the truth to be revealed about the Stahl suicide. Someday, perhaps, more light will be shed on the Hershberger story.

Over the years, ballplayers have died violently, other than by suicide. The bizarre death of Hall of Famer Ed Delahanty is a case in point. In 1903 he was with Washington of the American League, but wanted to be with the Giants in New York, where he felt he could earn more money. He dealt with his unhappiness by consuming generous doses of alcohol, starting with a drinking spree in Cleveland. Later, in Detroit, where he took out an accident policy in favor of his daughter, he was heard to threaten to take his own life.

On July 2, 1903, Delahanty boarded a Michigan Central train at Detroit with a ticket to Buffalo, from where, it is believed, he planned to catch another train to Washington to meet his wife. The conductor said Delahanty was "under the weather" when he got on at Detroit and that he had downed at least five shots of whiskey along the way. Not only was he boisterous, but he also threatened some passengers with a razor. At Bridgeburg, Ontario, just across the Niagara River from Buffalo, the conductor ejected him from the train. Delahanty, in the darkness, began to walk across the International Bridge, a railroad bridge connecting Bridgeburg and Buffalo. Bridge watchman Sam Kingston had just escorted a freight across the bridge and, lantern in hand, was walking back to the Canadian side when he confronted Delahanty. Words were exchanged and a scuffle ensued. It is not clear (Kingston told conflicting stories) if Delahanty fell, jumped, or was pushed into the river. Eight days later, his body was found at Niagara Falls, below the Horseshoe Falls.

Subsequently, Delahanty's widow filed suit in the Ontario courts against the Michigan Central Railroad, seeking $20,000 damages for the wrongful death of her husband. She was awarded $3,000, and her daughter received $2,000.

When Walter "Big Ed" Morris won 19 games for the last-place Boston Red Sox in 1928 and then came back with 14 wins for another cellar Boston club in 1929, he became one of the most sought-after pitchers in the league. One story had the Red Sox turning down a $100,000 offer. A sore arm slowed Morris in 1930 and 1931, and his record retrogressed to 4–9 and 5–7. Confident that his arm had regained its strength, he prepared to go to spring training in 1932. As a going-away present, some of his buddies arranged a party for him at a tavern in Century, Florida, just across the state line from Morris's hometown of Flomaton, Alabama. Unfortunately, the party began to get out of hand, and soon the guest of honor was involved in a fight with Joe White, a gas station attendant from Brewton, Alabama. When Morris slipped to the floor, White pulled a knife and stabbed him twice, fatally. Morris was thirty-one and left a widow and two children.

Len Koenecke was an impressive-looking athlete—broad of shoulder, slim of waist, and ruggedly handsome. He was said to have been the last player personally scouted by John McGraw, who arranged for his purchase from Indianapolis (American Association) in 1931 for players valued at $75,000. The young outfielder failed to live up to his minor league billings and was farmed to Jersey City in 1932 and to Buffalo in 1933. An outstanding season for the Bisons in 1933 led to his sale to Brooklyn, where in 1934 he batted .320 and fielded a league-leading .994. But he slumped in 1935, and late that year manager Casey Stengel sent Koenecke and two other players home from St. Louis so that he could try out some young prospects.

On the flight from St. Louis to Detroit, Koenecke, who had been drinking, created a disturbance, and when the airport was reached he was ordered off the plane. Although it was late in the evening, he decided to charter a private plane and fly to Buffalo, where he had friends. The plane he chartered had an interesting past. It had once been owned by Smith Reynolds of the tobacco family and his wife, torch singer Libby Holman, who were principals in one of the most sensational murder cases of the 1930s. When Reynolds was shot to death at the family estate in Winston-Salem, North Carolina, his wife was charged with the crime but was later exonerated.

While the plane was still over Canada, Koenecke tried to take over the controls from pilot William Mulqueeny. Irwin Davis, the copilot, attempted to restrain the husky ballplayer but was pushed to the floor. Mulqueeny, while trying to guide the plane with one hand, picked up a fire extinguisher with the other and bludgeoned Koenecke until he was dead. Mulqueeny had no idea where he was until he spotted the lights of Toronto. Seeing a racetrack on the outskirts of the city, he decided to use the backstretch as an airport and brought the plane safely down. Then, to cap their night of terror, the two men were attacked by watch dogs as they left the plane. The dogs eventually backed off, and they were able to summon help.

After two hearings in Canadian courts, Mulqueeny and Davis were absolved of all blame in Koenecke's death. Blood tests had shown that the dead ballplayer was drunk. At one of the hearings, Edward J. Murphy, attorney for the pilots, alleged that Koenecke was trying to commit suicide and to do it "in a grand and glorious manner."

In the early hours of January 5, 1975, Don Wilson, star righthanded pitcher of the Houston Astros, who had won 104 games in nine major league seasons and pitched two no-hitters, drove his luxury car into the garage of his suburban Houston home and left the motor running. At one P.M. his lifeless body was found slumped in the passenger seat. The ignition was on, the battery was dead, the gas tank was empty, and there were exhaust-fume stains on the garage floor. In the room above the garage, his five-year-old son Alexander was dead from the fumes. His wife, Bernice, and his daughter, Denise, were taken to the hospital in serious condition. Bernice Wilson also had a badly bruised jaw, which was never explained, but which could have been caused by a fall.

Mrs. Wilson and her daughter both recovered. Tests on the twenty-nine-year-old Don Wilson revealed a blood-alcohol content of .167. On February 5, 1975, the medical examiner ruled the deaths were accidental.

Mickey Fuentes, a righthanded pitcher who was 1–3 for Seattle in 1969, never made it to spring training in 1970. He was shot to death in a tavern brawl in his native Loiza Aldea, Puerto Rico, January 29, 1970, He was only twenty years old.

With Lyman Bostock, who had starred for Minnesota (in 1975–1977) and then had signed a lucrative free-agent contract with California, it was a case of being in the wrong place at the wrong time. On September 23, 1978, in Gary, Indiana, he was in a car being driven by his uncle when he was shot by a man named Leonard Smith, whose apparent target was Smith's estranged wife, seated next to Bostock in the back seat. Three hours after the assault, the twenty-seven-year-old Bostock was dead. There was whispering that something was going on between Bostock and Mrs. Smith. Actually they had met only twenty minutes before and were heading for different destinations.

Leonard Smith was twice tried for murder. The first trial, in which insanity was pleaded, ended in a hung jury. In the second trial, he was found not guilty by reason of insanity, spent six months in a mental hospital, and then was a free man. Outrage over the outcome of the two trials resulted in a change in the Indiana law, whereby an accused can now be judged both insane and guilty of a crime.

Planes, Cars, Trucks, and a Dune Buggy

When superstars Roberto Clemente and Thurman Munson lost their lives in air crashes, it was front-page news all over the country. In Clemente's case, the coverage was international in scope because of the mercy mission in which he was involved.

Clemente and Munson were not the first active major leaguers to perish in airplane accidents. There were at least six prior air fatalities—seven if Koenecke is included. Marvin Goodwin, a righthanded spitball pitcher who saw action with the Senators, Cardinals, and Reds from 1916 through 1925, was the first. In 1925, nearing the end of his career, he was pitcher-manager of Houston of the Texas League, on assignment from the Cardinals. He did so well at Houston (21–9) that Cincinnati purchased him conditionally late in the season, with the understanding that final payment on the deal would be made only if he lasted thirty days into the 1926 season. He made four September appearances for the Reds with no wins and no losses.

Goodwin had been a flying instructor in World War One and was still a lieutenant in the reserve. On October 18, 1925, he took off on a practice flight from Ellington Field, near Houston, with a mechanic on board. The engine failed at 200 feet, and the plane crashed. The mechanic miraculously survived, but Goodwin, who suffered two broken legs and internal injuries, died four days later. The fatality had a ghoulish aftermath. The following year, the Cardinals demanded full payment for Goodwin's contract. The Reds refused on the grounds that he was not on their roster thirty days into the 1926 season. The case was referred to the commissioner's office. Judge Landis, citing the terms of the contract, ruled in favor of the Reds.

Elmer Joseph Gedeon played in the outfield for the Washington Senators in 1939. He had been a track star at the University of Michigan and had given up a chance to run in the Olympic Games to go into baseball. But then World War Two came along, and Gedeon gave up baseball to become an early volunteer in the Air Corps. He died April 15, 1944, when his plane was shot down over France. (Two others who played in the majors in 1939 also died in battle. Bob Neighbors, a shortstop for seven games with the St. Louis Browns, died in North Korea in 1952, and Harry O'Neill, who caught one game for the Philadelphia Athletics, perished in the assault on Iwo Jima in 1945.)

After his graduation from Boston University in 1955, catcher Tom Gastall pocketed a $40,000 bonus from the Baltimore Orioles. He was used sparingly, playing 20 games in 1955 and 32 in 1956. On September 20, 1956, he took off in a light plane from Harbor Field, near Baltimore. He landed at Easton, from where he later took off for the return flight over the Chesapeake Bay. Five days later, his body and the wreckage of the plane were found in the water off Riviera Beach. Gastall was just twenty-four.

A little over two months later, on November 27, 1956, outfielder Charlie Peete, who had played 23 games for the St. Louis Cardinals that summer, died in a plane crash in the mountains of Venezuela, near Caracas, while en route to play winter ball. His wife and three children also perished in the crash.

Another victim of a Venezuelan air disaster was twenty-one-year-old Nestor Chavez, a San Francisco Giant farmhand who played in two games for the Giants in 1967. On March 16, 1969, the young pitcher was on his way to join the Giants' Phoenix farm club when his plane crashed, killing 155 passengers. It was one of the worst accidents in aviation history.

Ken Hubbs, playing 160 games for the Chicago Cubs in 1962, handled 148 consecutive chances without an error and was Rookie of the Year. He tailed off in 1963 but was still rated one of the game's rising young stars. At the end of the 1963 season, he began to take flying lessons. In early February 1964, shortly after he had received his license, Hubbs, who lived in Colton, California, flew to Provo, Utah, with a friend, Dennis Doyle, to visit Doyle's in-laws. On February 15, Hubbs and Doyle took off in a snowstorm for their return trip to California. Only five miles from Provo, the plane crashed into Utah Lake, killing Hubbs and Doyle.

After investigation, the Civil Aeronautics Board reported the probable cause as "Hubbs's attempt to continue visual flight into an area of adverse weather." The twenty-two-year-old Hubbs, who was not licensed for instrument flying, left a log book which showed he had flown just 71 hours, 16 minutes.

On September 30, 1972, Roberto Clemente, who had batted .317 in eighteen seasons with Pittsburgh, touched Jon Matlack of the Mets for a base hit. It was Clemente's 3,000th and last hit. On December 31, 1972, Clemente and four others were killed when a plane carrying food, clothing, and medical supplies to earthquake-stricken Nicaragua crashed moments after takeoff from San Juan, Puerto Rico.

Clemente's career had all the elements of a Horatio Alger tale. Born August 18, 1934, in Carolina, Puerto Rico, the son of a sugar plantation foreman, he was signed by Al Campanis of the Dodgers as a teenager. The Dodgers tried to cover him up on the Montreal (International League) roster, but Pittsburgh general manager Branch Rickey, who knew all about him from his days with the Dodgers, drafted him for a piddling $4,000. It was one of the greatest bargains in baseball history. Clemente immediately became a regular and won all manner of plaudits for his hitting, fielding, and magnificent throwing arm. He was Most Valuable Player in 1966, batted .310 and .414 in two World Series (1960, 1971), and was *Sporting News*'s Gold Glove outfielder twelve times. Twice he hit three home runs in one game, and five times he led National League outfielders in assists.

Clemente was voted into the Baseball Hall of Fame in 1973 in a special election, with the usual five-year waiting period waived by a change of the voting rules.

Thurman Munson was the only New York Yankee to win both Rookie of the Year (1970) and Most Valuable Player (1976) awards. He was the regular Yankee catcher from 1970, averaging more than 140 games a year, despite aching knees, a beaning, and a foul ball in the throat. He was one of the league's top clutch hitters, with 701 RBIs and a .292 average over eleven seasons. His clashes with Reggie Jackson over which of them was the straw that stirred the Yankee drink drew national attention.

On August 2, 1979, an off-day, Munson flew his new Cessna Citation jet from New York to Canton, Ohio, to visit his family. Late in the afternoon, he was practicing takeoffs and landings at the Akron-Canton Airport when the plane crashed a thousand feet short of the runway. Munson's flying companions, David Hall and Jerry Anderson, survived and at great danger to themselves, attempted to pull Munson from the flaming wreckage. But there was no chance. Munson, who was thirty-two, left his wife, Diane, and three children, not to mention millions of mourning baseball fans. On August 6 of that year, 51,000 fans at Yankee Stadium participated in an impressive nine-minute salute to the Yankee captain, who, with a few more years under his belt, could well have been a good bet for the Hall of Fame.

As far as is known, the first active major leaguer to die in a vehicular accident was Norman Boeckel, a .298 hitter for the 1923 Boston Braves. The thirty-one-year-old third baseman died February 16, 1924, in a San Diego hospital, from pelvic injuries sustained the day before in a collision between his car and a truck. Earlier, Boeckel had played a fringe role in another piece of baseball history. He had submitted an affidavit to National League President John Heydler, attesting that he had heard pitcher Rube Benton boast of winning $3,200 on the 1919 World Series on a tip from Hal Chase. Benton was thrown out of baseball, but was later reinstated by Judge Landis.

The year 1929 saw the deaths of two major leaguers in vehicular accidents. Denny Williams, a twenty-nine-year-old outfielder, who had played with the Reds in 1921 and the Red Sox in 1924, 1925 and 1928, was killed in Los Angeles, March 21. Seven months later, on October 22, Walter "Peck" Lerian, regular catcher for the Phillies in 1928 and 1929, died in a Baltimore hospital, after being hit by a truck that vaulted over a curb and pinned him against the wall of a building.

Catcher Al Montgomery was only twenty years old when he appeared in 42 games for the Boston Braves in 1941. While returning from spring training on April 26, 1942, having been assigned to Hartford of the Eastern League, he was involved in a car accident near Waverly, Virginia, and killed.

While Paul Edmondson, a twenty-seven-year-old pitcher who had been 1–6 with the 1969 White Sox, was en route to spring training, he was involved in a fatal auto accident February 13, 1970, near Santa Barbara, California. Another victim of a California crash was Chico Ruiz, who had been in the majors for eight years, first with Cincinnati and most recently with California. He was killed in San Diego February 9, 1972.

The pitching career of Bob Moose was a series of highs and lows. In ten years with the Pirates, he won 76 games and lost 71. One of his wins was a no-hitter against the New York Mets on September 20, 1969. On the other side of the coin is the wild pitch he uncorked in the final game of the 1972 league championship series that permitted Cincinnati to defeat Pittsburgh. He also made three appearances in the 1971 World Series, but had no decisions. On October 9, 1976, at Martin's Ferry, Ohio, he suffered fatal injuries in an automobile accident. It was his twenty-ninth birthday.

Righthanded pitcher Danny Frisella, who in ten years in the majors saw action with the Mets, Braves, Padres, Cardinals, and Brewers (34–40), took a dune buggy out in the desert near Phoenix on New Year's Day, 1977. When the buggy overturned, he was killed instantly.

Just six days later, on January 6, Mike Miley, a twenty-three-year-old shortstop with California in 1975 and 1976, was killed in a car crash at Baton Rouge.

On Friday night, December 19, 1986, Honolulu native Joe DeSa hit four doubles to help his Ponce Lions defeat the Mayaguez Indians, 11–8, in a Puerto Rico winter league game. At four A.M. on December 20, DeSa was killed in a head-on crash on the Las Americas Expressway. DeSa, who had played for Buffalo (American Association) in 1985 and 1986 and was the team's most valuable player in the latter year, had signed with Kansas City and was due to report in the spring for his third hitch in the majors.

The two known deaths of active players by drowning are separated by almost one hundred years. The first was England-born Al Thake, second baseman for the Brooklyn Atlantics. He drowned off Fort Hamilton, New York, while fishing, September 1, 1872. Almost a century later, on December 14, 1970, Herman Hill, twenty-five-year-old outfielder with Minnesota in 1969 and 1970, was in Venezuela for winter ball when he drowned off Valencia.

Bean Balls

Every time a batter steps to the plate, it is an act of courage. With pitches hurtling toward him at 90 miles per hour, he has but a fraction of a second to decide if he should swing, take, or bail out. Modern helmets with ear flaps have removed much of the peril, but not all. Prior to the 1950s, batters had no head protection at all; and before 1893 the risk was even greater, since the pitching distance was only 50 feet.

Considering the danger involved, it is somewhat of a miracle that only one batter has been killed by a pitched ball in the long history of major league baseball. No definitive statistics are available, but it is known that many have been killed at the amateur level and at least five in minor league play.

Major league baseball's only bean ball fatality, and its only diamond fatality for any reason, occurred on August 16, 1920, at the Polo Grounds, New York, in a game between the New York Yankees and the Cleveland Indians. It was the first half of the fifth inning, and shortstop Ray Chapman of the Indians was at bat, faced by Yankee submarine-baller Carl Mays. Chapman liked to crowd the plate and crouch over it. Mays, who had a mean streak, was not averse to throwing at any batter who encroached on his territory. Mays's first pitch was a strike, his second a ball, as Chapman seemed to edge even closer to the plate. Predictably the third pitch was high and inside. There was an ominous crack that was heard all over the Polo Grounds. Mays, thinking his pitch had hit Chapman's bat, fielded the ball and started to throw to Wally Pipp at first base, but then he saw Chapman slumped in the arms of catcher Muddy Ruel and he knew the batter had been hit. A doctor was summoned from the stands and Chapman was temporarily revived. Assisted by two of his teammates, he began the long walk to the clubhouse in center field, but he soon collapsed and was carried the rest of the way.

When a preliminary examination in the clubhouse showed the injury was extremely serious, he was taken to nearby St. Lawrence Hospital, where an operation was performed. He was still under ether when he died at five A.M. the following day, August 17.

The repercussions were immediate and furious. Mays, a surly sort and never popular among his peers, was strongly criticized. Detroit and Boston players demanded that he be barred for life, while those on the Washington and St. Louis clubs threatened to strike if Mays was allowed to pitch again. But Mays did have his defenders. Cleveland pitcher Ray Caldwell, a former Yankee, said it seemed to him that Chapman had turned his head right into the ball. Connie Mack, venerable skipper of the Philadelphia Athletics, while deploring the fatal accident, pleaded for sympathy for Mays. Catcher Muddy Ruel, who caught Chapman when he fell, said in later years that the pitch could have been a strike.

Mays appeared before the district attorney and, after a deposition, was cleared of any criminal charges. He said he was not trying to hit Chapman, only to pitch him tight. That spring, Mays pointed out, he had seen Yankee infielder Chick Fewster nearly killed by a pitch delivered by Jeff Pfeffer of the Dodgers, and from that time on he had been reluctant even to throw inside pitches, let alone throw at batters. He then suggested the fatality might have been averted had plate umpire Tom Connolly not refused to remove from play the scuffed ball that hit Chapman. This drew a sharp rejoinder from American League umpires Billy Evans and Bill Dinneen, who charged that Mays was one of the league's most notorious scuffers. They said further that club owners had complained to Ban Johnson, league president, that too many balls were being thrown out, and that Johnson had responded by sending out a directive, instructing umpires to keep balls in play, "except those which are dangerous."

In the *New York Times* of August 19, there was an impassioned plea for the development and use of batting helmets, but it was to be more than thirty years before this advice would be heeded.

At least five minor leaguers have been killed by pitched balls. On August 9, 1906, Joe Yaeger of Fall River of the New England League hit Tom Burke of Lynn in the head with a pitch. Two days later, Burke was dead. Two days after attending Burke's funeral, Yaeger took his turn on the mound, only to be arrested by Lynn police on a manslaughter charge. Shortly thereafter, the charges were dropped. Jaeger, who had pitched for six years in the majors with Brooklyn and Detroit, completed the season with a 15–19 record.

In the second game of a Central League doubleheader, played in gathering darkness at Dayton, September 14, 1909, Charles "Cupid" Pickney, twenty-year-old Dayton second baseman, was beaned by Casey Hageman of Grand Rapids. At first, it was thought he would recover, but his condition deteriorated, and he died following an operation. Pinkney's father, who had traveled from Cleveland to watch his son play, was at his side when he died.

On June 18, 1916, Johnny Dodge, infielder for Mobile of the Southern Association, was hit on the head by Tom "Shotgun" Rogers of Nashville and died the next day of a fractured skull. It is believed that Dodge was thrown at in retaliation for the beaning of a Nashville player the previous day. By the strangest of coincidences, Rogers and Carl Mays were to be teammates briefly on the 1921 Yankees.

On July 4, 1933, at Omaha, Jesse Batterson, nineteen-year-old third baseman for Springfield of the Western League, suffered a fractured skull when hit by a pitch thrown by Omaha's Floyd "Swede" Carlson. He was able to get to his feet and walk to the clubhouse, but then collapsed and was taken to a hospital. He died there following an operation, with pitcher Carlson at his bedside.

A fifth fatality occurred in the Alabama-Florida League on June 2, 1951. Lefty Jack Clifton of Headland hit Ottis Johnson of the Dothan Browns on the head and killed him. In his next start, Clifton, who had already hit twelve batters that season, pitched a no-hit, no-run game against Panama City. According to Ken Brooks in his book *The Last Rebel Yell,* every Panama City batter had one foot in the dugout.

In major league history there have been countless beanings. In most cases, the batters came back, but often were not the same hitters as before. Lowell

Reidenbaugh, in his *Cooperstown*, writes that Hughie Jennings survived three skull fractures. His most serious injury was from a pitch delivered by Amos Rusie of New York, said to have been the swiftest pitcher of his day. The blow left Jennings near death and unconscious for four days. Some historians say it was Rusie's speed and the fear that he might kill someone that brought about the lengthening of the pitching distance in 1893 to the present 60 feet, 6 inches.

On May 25, 1937, future Hall of Famer Mickey Cochrane, player-manager of the Detroit Tigers, lost sight of a pitch by Bump Hadley of the Yankees. It hit him in the right temple and fractured his skull. He lay unconscious for ten days but eventually recovered, although he never played again. He did, however, resume his managerial duties and also served with distinction in the Navy in World War Two.

Tony Conigliaro of the Boston Red Sox, who hit 166 home runs in six full seasons and parts of two others (all with the Red Sox, except for 74 games and 4 home runs for California in 1971), surely would have racked up more impressive numbers had he not been hit in the face and nearly killed by a Jack Hamilton (of California) pitch on August 18, 1967. He was out of the game for a year and a half, but then came back to hit 20 home runs in 1969 and 36 in 1970. On October 11, 1970, in a most controversial deal, he was traded to California, where he was to see only limited duty. He returned to Boston for 21 games in 1975 and then was out of baseball. He died February 24, 1990.

Dickie Thon was the All-Star National League shortstop for Houston in 1983 and also led the league in game-winning hits. In the fifth game of the 1984 season, he was hit in the eye by a Mike Torrez (Mets) fastball. Despite permament damage to his eye, he was able to return to action, and through the 1990 season was playing effectively for the Philadelphia Phillies.

Don Zimmer, 1988 manager of the Chicago Cubs, suffered two serious beanings and still carries a metal plate in his head from the injuries. Paul Blair, center field magician of the Baltimore Orioles, Minnie Minoso of the White Sox, and Wayne Terwilliger, utility player for several clubs, were others whose careers were interrupted or affected by bean balls.

Sore Arms, Illnesses, Injuries, and Accidents

Up to this point, the subject has been (with a few exceptions) deaths off or on the diamond. But fatalities are only part of the story. Many a baseball career has aborted for reasons not resulting in death, at least, not at once.

In the old days, sore arms were usually rested. If there was any treatment at all, it was by the likes of John D. "Bonesetter" Reese, a self-trained muscle manipulator of Youngstown, Ohio. Nobody ever heard of the rotator cuff or even dreamed of such sophisticated operations as those which prolonged the careers of Tommy John, Ken Dayley, and others.

Charles "Lady" Baldwin was one old-timer who could have used a Tommy John bionic arm. In 1886 he won 42 games for Detroit (NL) and pitched 487 innings. He then developed arm trouble and dropped to 13 wins in 1887 and to 3 each in 1888 and 1890, after which he retired for

good to his Michigan farm. Hall of Famer Christy Mathewson's arm went dead in 1916, but by then he was thirty-eight, had won 373 games, and had achieved immortality. Smoky Joe Wood was another sore arm victim, but he did beat the rap in a way. After winning 23 games for the Red Sox in 1911 and then 34 in 1912, including 16 in a row, he developed a sore arm the following spring. His days as an intimidating fireballer were over, although he did win 35 games for the Sox over the next three seasons. Realizing he could no longer pitch, he decided to become a sore-armed outfielder, and played that position with fair success for Cleveland through the 1922 season. Altogether he played in fourteen major league seasons and left a 116–57 pitching record and a career batting mark of .283.

Undocumented are the names of countless other pitchers of the game's early years who dropped out prematurely because of so-called dead arms. More is known of modern pitchers, like Dave Ferris and Karl Spooner. Ferris joined the Boston Red Sox in 1945, having been mustered out of the Army because of asthma. He raised plenty of eyebrows with a 21–10 record in the last year of wartime baseball, but then made believers out of everyone by winning 25 and losing just 6 in 1946. But in a night game in Cleveland in June of 1947, he suffered a shoulder injury, from which he never fully recovered although he did hang on until 1950. His career log shows 65–30 for a phenomenal .684 percentage. No pitcher ever made a more dazzling entrance or faded as fast as Karl Spooner.

The twenty-three-year-old lefthander was called up by Brooklyn from Fort Worth (Texas), late in the 1954 season. He pitched shutouts against New York and Pittsburgh in his first two starts, allowing just 7 hits and striking out 27. Hampered by a sore arm, he struggled to an 8–6 record in 1955, made two appearances in the World Series (0–1), then never pitched again.

In 1966 another Dodger lefthander, Hall of Famer Sandy Koufax was 27–9, with 5 shutouts and an ERA of 1.73 in 323 innings of work. Talk about going out on top! No pitcher in major league history ever matched that in a final season. He pitched against Baltimore in the 1966 World Series (0–1), but at the age of thirty his career was over. Traumatic arthritis in the left elbow, triggered by a fall on his left arm when attempting a pickoff during the 1964 season, made it impossible for him to continue. Had Koufax been able to pitch as long as, say Warren Spahn, there is no telling what his record might have been. As it was, he left an imposing mark of 165–87 (.655) and an ERA of 2.76.

Mark Fidrych, the colorful Detroit pitcher known as "the Bird," was 19–9 in 1976 and was the starting pitcher in the All-Star game. But plagued by arm trouble, he faded to a combined 10–11 record over the next four seasons. He was only twenty-six when he pitched his final big league game in 1980. Twice he tried comebacks in the minors, but failed.

Lefty Don Gullett, the only man to pitch the opening game in successive World Series for two different teams (Cincinnati Reds, 1976; and New York Yankees, 1977), was just twenty-seven when his career ended with a bad arm after the 1978 season. He had been one of the first free agents signed by the Yankees, and was certainly one of their most expensive, costing them $2 million for his 18 wins in two seasons.

Righthander Wayne Garland of the Indians was operated on for a rotator cuff tear on May 5, 1978. He had won 33 games the two previous seasons. After the operation, he came back, hanging on until 1981, but he was never the same pitcher. And like Gullett, he was working on a lucrative long-term contract.

The previous pages have told of the surprising number of active major leaguers who succumbed to illness. Many others became ill and were forced to give up the game or see their baseball livelihoods interrupted. An early example was Jimmy Wood, who played for Chicago, Brooklyn, and Philadelphia in the National Association from 1871 to 1873. In 1873 he developed a leg abscess which he attempted to lance with a penknife. A severe infection developed, resulting in the loss of his leg. His playing days, of course, were over, but he did return as a manager in 1874 and 1875.

In 1890 first baseman Dave Orr of Brooklyn (in the Players' League) batted .373, hit 32 doubles, 13 triples, and 6 home runs, while striking out only 11 times. For a nonpitcher, this was the ultimate in final seasons. In the off-season, the thirty-one-year-old Orr suffered a stroke and never played again. He died in Brooklyn on June 3, 1915. He had been caretaker of Ebbets Field for many years.

Hall of Famer Amos Rusie won 243 games in nine seasons and part of a tenth, but saw his career shrouded by misfortune, some of his own making. The so-called "Hoosier Thunderbolt," who almost killed Hughie Jennings with a bean ball, himself took a line drive to the head which permanently damaged his hearing. He threw out his arm in 1898 and was out of the game for two years. He compounded his other problems with heavy drinking. Although he tried to come back in 1901, he failed. At the age of thirty he was through.

The aforementioned Jennings, another Hall of Famer, had a baseball life replete with illness and adversity. In addition to the almost fatal beaning by Rusie, he suffered a nervous breakdown in 1925, after taking over as manager of the New York Giants when John McGraw became ill. Jennings died of spinal meningitis in 1928 at the age of fifty-eight.

Often documented is the tragic accident that terminated the career of catcher Charley Bennett, who played in the majors from 1878 to 1893 (except for 1879). In January of 1894, while on a hunting trip, he tried to catch and board a moving train at Wellsville, Kansas, but lost his grip and fell under the wheels, losing both legs.

Shortstop Charlie Hollocher, who played for the Cubs from 1918 to 1924, was constantly bedeviled by illness, real and imaginary, blunting what some observers feel could have been a Hall of Fame–level career. His tormented life came to an end on August 14, 1940, when he parked his car on a quiet Clayton, Missouri, street, then tore his throat apart with a blast from a sixteen-gauge shotgun.

Jackie Hayes, outstanding second baseman and shortstop for the Senators and the White Sox (1927–1940), was 3 for 3 in a 1940 Sox spring game; then in the shower room he noticed a cloudiness in one eye. He played 18 games that year, but by August he had lost his sight in the clouded eye. In a matter of three years, he had lost his sight in the other. Similarly, George "Specs" Toporcer, a former major league infielder, had lost his sight while managing Buffalo (International League) in 1951. Both men learned to live with their blindness and went on to lead productive lives, Hayes as the tax collector of Chilton County, Alabama, and Toporcer as a writer and lecturer.

Righthanded pitcher Monty Stratton (15–5 and 15–9 for the Chicago White Sox in 1937 and 1938) was hunting rabbits near his mother's home in Greenville, Texas, after the 1938 season, when he accidentally discharged a .22-caliber pistol. The slug lodged in his right knee, severing the main artery and necessitating amputation of the leg. Stratton did not pitch again in the majors, but he was a White Sox coach for three seasons. In 1946 he pitched for Sherman in the Class C East Texas League, where, remarkably, he won 18 games. Hollywood thought it saw a story in the courageous way he had faced his tragedy and made a much-acclaimed movie of his life, *The Stratton Story*, starring Jimmy Stewart.

A third victim of a leg injury was Joe Cronin, Hall of Fame shortstop who played twenty years for Washington and Boston, and probably would have played a few more had he not fractured his leg three games into the 1945 season. He never played again, but continued in the game for many years as a manager, front office executive, and as American League president.

He looked so indestructible that they called him "The Iron Horse." Henry Louis Gehrig, in seventeen years at first base for the New York Yankees, averaged .340, hit 535 doubles, 162 triples, and 493 home runs. He scored 1,888 runs, had 1,990 RBIs, and posted a slugging percentage of .632. His incredible record of playing in 2,130 consecutive games remains unchallenged. On May 2, 1939, Gehrig approached manager Joe McCarthy, told him he was not feeling well. Gehrig thought he was hurting the team, and he asked to be taken from the lineup. McCarthy, of course, complied, and so for the first time since the famous Wally Pipp headache of June 2, 1925, Gehrig missed a Yankee game. He was never to play another.

A few months later the bad news came from the Mayo Clinic. The indestructible one, "The Iron Horse," had been stricken with amyotrophic lateral sclerosis, a disease of the central nervous system for which no cure was known. On July 4, 1939, 61,000 gathered at Yankee Stadium for a gigantic Gehrig tribute. There he spoke his memorable words: "I consider myself the luckiest man on the face of the earth."

In the short time left to him, Gehrig devoted himself to public service. On June 2, 1941, exactly sixteen years from the day he replaced Pipp at first base, he died. He was thirty-seven years old. The malady that killed him is now generally referred to as Lou Gehrig's disease. Unfortunately it is almost as much a medical mystery today as it was fifty years ago when it struck him.

Catcher Bill DeLancey was a product of the St. Louis Cardinal farm system. After playing eight games for the parent club in 1932 and then spending a year at Columbus (American Association), he became a regular member of the "Gas House Gang" in 1934. In 1935 he found that he had tuberculosis and faced a long recovery period. It was not until 1940 that he made it back, and then it was just for 15 games. By then, he knew it was no use. His career was over. He died November 28, 1946, on his forty-fifth birthday.

When Don Black went to the mound for the Cleveland Indians against the St. Louis Browns on September 13, 1948, he could have looked back on an undistinguished six-year record with the Athletics and Indians (34–55). But there were two victories—one off the diamond—that he could recall with pride. The first was against the bottle; the second was a no-hit, no-run game against the Philadelphia Athletics on July 10, 1947.

In the late-season game against the Browns, upon retiring the Browns in the first two innings, Black came to bat against Bill Kennedy. After swinging mightily at the first pitch and fouling it back, he began to stagger and finally sank to his knees. Umpire Bill Summers bent over to assist Black and heard him whisper, "That last pitch to [Ed] Pellagrini did it." (He had struck out the Browns' shortstop with a curve ball to end the top of the second.) Apparently, that pitch plus the force of his swing had caused an aneurism to rupture, sending blood to his brain and spinal cord. (Shades of James Creighton, who had injured himself fatally while batting on August 14, 1862.) An eminent neurosurgeon was summoned. He ruled out surgery as too risky, but said Black had just a 50-50 chance of surviving. But Black did survive and on September 22 he was recipient of a large purse from a benefit game against the Red Sox that attracted a crowd of 76,772.

The Indians went on to win the pennant and then defeated the Boston Braves in the World Series, but without Black, who never pitched again. He died April 21, 1959 at the age of 42.

Baseball's *Domesday Books* credit lefthanded pitcher Bert Shepard with one major league appearance. What the books do not say is that this game was pitched by a one-legged man. When Shepard's call to World War Two service came, he was a promising young pitcher. The fortunes of war took him to the European front, where he was downed over Germany on his thirty-fifth mission and taken prisoner. Doctors removed his shattered right leg, after which a fellow prisoner of war fashioned him a wooden leg. After his recapture and return to the States, he was signed by the Washington Senators as a batting practice pitcher. In his one appearance in a regular game, he allowed one run in 5⅓ innings for an ERA of 1.69.

Lou Brissie, like Bert Shepard, was a victim of World War Two combat. Brissie, who joined the Army in 1942 as a teenager, was badly wounded on the Italian front and forced to undergo twenty-three operations. Despite the handicap of a steel leg brace and a leather guard, he never gave up his dream of becoming a major league pitcher. In 1947, for Savannah of the Sally League, he won 23 games and earned a late-season call-up from the Philadelphia Athletics. From 1947 to 1953, he won 44 games for the A's and the Indians, to whom he was traded in 1951. His best year was 1949, when he won 16 games and pitched in the All-Star Game. He was only twenty-nine when his career came to a close. He then became national director of the American Legion baseball program.

Herb Score was a third American League lefty to see his career abbreviated by injury. In 1955, Score won 16 games for Cleveland and struck out 245; then in 1956 he improved to 20 wins and 263 strikeouts. Along the banks of Lake Erie, he was hailed as a lefthanded Bob Feller. But it was not to be. On May 7, 1957, at Municipal Stadium in Cleveland, he was hit in the eye by a torrid line drive off the bat of Gil McDougald of the New York Yankees and seriously injured.

His recovery was slow, and he did not return to the Indians until 1958 and then only for 12 games. On April 18, 1960, he was traded to the White Sox for Barry Latman. After three seasons of limited duty for the Sox, he called it a day. He remains in baseball as the play-by-play announcer for the Indians.

Brooklyn catcher Roy Campanella was thirty-six and in the twilight of a remarkable career that had seen him win three Most Valuable Player awards, when disaster struck on a January night in 1958. He was driving to his Long Island home in the early hours of the morning when his borrowed car skidded on a slippery spot in the road and slammed into a utility pole. The two broken vertebrae he suffered doomed him to a long and excruciatingly painful period of recovery and rehabilitation, not to mention lifelong confinement to a wheelchair.

On May 7, 1959, before a crowd of 93,103 fans at the Los Angeles Coliseum, the Dodgers and the Yankees met in a mammoth benefit for the paralyzed Campanella. It was an emotional affair, rivaling similar tributes to Yankee greats Gehrig and Ruth at Yankee Stadium.

The courage Campanella displayed in his rehabilitation was an inspiration to many others who suffered severe spinal injuries. He received baseball's highest honor in 1969—election to the Hall of Fame.

Mike Pazik, a lefthander from Lynn, Mass., who appeared briefly for Minnesota in 1975, 1976, and 1977, saw his pitching career terminated when he suffered multiple fractures of both legs in a 1977 autombile accident. He returned to the game in 1980 as a coach for the White Sox. Later, he served four years as a roving pitching instructor for the Milwaukee Brewers, and then in late 1987 he was named pitching coach for Charlotte of the Double-A Southern League.

Houston righthander J. R. Richard, at 6'8" and 222 pounds, was an intimidating figure on the mound. From 1976 through 1979, his strikeout log showed 214, 214, 303, and 313, respectively, while his victories totaled 74. In 1980, even though slowed by arm and shoulder injuries, he was chosen to start for the National League in the All-Star Game at Los Angeles. But, as fate would have it, he was to pitch just two more innings for the Astros before being laid low by a stroke. The rehabilitation was painfully slow, but there always seemed to be hope that his career could be salvaged, but such hopes proved to be futile. Twice (in 1982 and 1983) he tried to pitch in the lower minors, but the illness had taken too great a toll.

Careers cut short for psychological reasons are not common, but there have been a few. Steve Blass, hero of the 1971 Pittsburgh World Series victory over Baltimore and winner of 19 games in 1972, suddenly could not throw strikes. So severe was the mental block that his baseball life ended in 1972 when he was only thirty-two. Kevin Saucier, a lefthanded relief pitcher for Detroit, had 13 saves and 4 wins in 1981; then, inexplicably, he developed the Steve Blass syndrome and could not throw strikes. In his case it was a fear of hitting and injuring a batter. He could not overcome the problem, and at twenty-six he was out of baseball. Joe Cowley, who pitched for the Braves, Yankees, White Sox, and Phillies, and who has a no-hit game to his credit, simply could not throw strikes and was sent to the minors by the Phillies in 1987. He could not throw strikes there either and finally was sent home.

At least one career came to a premature end because of a fear of flying. Jackie Jensen, who hit 199 home runs in eleven seasons with the Yankees, Senators, and Red Sox, retired first in 1959, tried again in 1961, but then quit for good at the age of thirty-four.

Alcohol and Drugs

It is impossible to put a number on the baseball careers shortened or adversely affected by the excessive use of alcohol. In at least four cases (Delahanty, Koenecke, Morris, and Wilson), dealt with elsewhere in this chapter, fatalities resulted. Countless players of the game's early years were lushes. Liquor was readily available to them, often on the house, and there was plenty of time for carousing, especially when on the road. Some of the worst offenders were quielty blacklisted and faded from the game. Others who were heavy drinkers continued in uniform, because they were star players and the owners winked at their alcoholic escapades. Future Hall of Famer Michael "King" Kelly, for example, drank as hard as he played; yet in 1887 Boston paid an unheard of $10,000 to Chicago for his contract. Toward the end of his career, he opened a saloon in New York, which was like putting the fox in charge of the chicken coop. His performance level deteriorated rapidly, and by 1894 he was in the minors. That fall he developed pneumonia, and on November 8 he died at the age of thirty-six.

Terry Larkin, who won 29 games for Hartford in 1877, and 29 and 31, respectively, for Chicago in 1878 and 1879, was another nineteenth-century player whose career self-destructed from the ravages of strong drink. In 1883, while drunk, he shot his wife (she recovered) and then tried to commit suicide in jail. In 1886, while employed as a bartender in Brooklyn, he showed up for work with two pistols and challenged his employer to a duel. Police ware called and he was thrown into jail until he sobered up. He died in Brooklyn in 1894.

Equally melancholy is the story of James (The Troy Terrier) Egan, who pitched, caught and played the outfield for Troy (NL) in 1882 and then was blacklisted for drunkenness. Supposedly rehabilitated, he was given a chance with Brooklyn (AA) in 1884, but before he played a game he was arrested for theft and jailed. He died of what was described as "brain fever" in a New Haven, Connecticut, jail, September 26, 1884.

Few players have come to the majors with more raw talent than Louis Sockalexis, a Penobscot Indian from Old Towne, Maine. He played college baseball at both Holy Cross and Notre Dame. While at the latter school in 1897, he and a companion broke up an establishment run by a certain "Popcorn Jennie" and threw the furniture out the windows. When the good fathers who ran Notre Dame read about this caper in the *South Bend Tribune,* they promptly threw him out. Future major league catcher Mike Powers, who had been instrumental in getting Sockalexis into both Holy Cross and Notre Dame, wired the Cleveland Club, with whom the Indian had signed a con-

tract to take effect at the end of the school year, and suggested it send someone to South Bend to bail him out. Manager Patsy Tebeau caught the next train west, and in a few days Sockalexis was in a Cleveland uniform. He impressed with his strength, speed, and magnificent arm. In later years, both John McGraw and Hughie Jennings said he was the greatest natural talent they had ever seen. Even allowing for the hyperbole that often accompanies such reminiscence, it is apparent that he was a player of exceptional ability. But just as exceptional was his appetite for strong drink. Frequently interrupted by binges and injuries (once he jumped from a second-floor window and severely injured an ankle), his major league career was limited to 94 games in three seasons.

Sockalexis died in Burlington, Maine, on December 24, 1913, at the age of forty-two. His baseball monument is not his .313 batting average but the Cleveland Indians baseball club, which was nicknamed after him.

Hall of Famer Rube Waddell gained almost as much notoriety for his drinking as he did recognition for his pitching. Lowell Reidenbaugh, in his *Cooperstown,* tells how Waddell would come into a bar, penniless, and whisper to the bartender, "Give me a drink, and I will give you the ball I used to defeat Cy Young in twenty innings." According to Reidenbaugh, hundreds of bartenders "displayed what they considered to be the historic souvenir."

Despite the abuse he gave his body, the Rube lasted for thirteen major league seasons and won 191 games. But his indiscretions led to tuberculosis and he died in San Antonio, Texas, on April 1, 1914, at the age of thirty-seven.

The problem of alcoholism continues in the modern game, but added to it is an affliction even more virulent— the use of illegal drugs. Careers are being shortened or interrupted by excessive drinking or the ingestion of drugs, or by a combination of both. In the old days, when a player drank too much, he was either shunted aside or his problem was swept under the rug. Now, the usual pattern is a confession of the problem, or exposure, followed by treatment, rehabilitation, sometimes suspension, but then a return to the game.

In 1983 the baseball world was rocked by the news that four players on the Kansas City Royals—Willie Wilson, Willie Aikens, Jerry Martin, and Vida Blue (no longer with the team)—had been involved with illegal drugs. All were suspended for one year by Commissioner Bowie Kuhn, although later an arbitrator reduced the suspensions, except for Blue's. Meanwhile, indictments were handed down and all were convicted and sentenced to one year in jail, with the last nine months suspended. Eventually Wilson returned to the Royals. Aikens was traded to Toronto but then went to the minors. Martin and Blue are out of baseball.

Pitcher Steve Howe of the Los Angeles Dodgers was suspended for the 1984 season for alleged drug use and did not challenge it. After at least two relapses, he was signed by the Texas Rangers and appeared for them late in the 1987 season. Atlanta pitcher Pascual Perez spent three months in a Dominican Republic jail on drug charges during the 1983–1984 off-season and was also suspended by Commissioner Kuhn. Arbitrator Richard I. Bloch, who had also ruled in the Willie Wilson et al. cases, subsequently threw out the Perez suspension because of lack of evidence.

Also in 1983, pitcher Dickie Noles of the Cubs spent time in jail after a drunken brawl in Cincinnati. Outfielder Ron LeFlore was arrested on drug and weapons charges in 1982 while with the White Sox. Although found not guilty, he was released by the Sox in April 1983.

Bob Welch, talented righthanded pitcher of the Dodgers, best remembered for his classic confrontation with Reggie Jackson of the Yankees in the 1978 World Series, revealed that he had been an alcoholic for many years. After rehabilitation and relegation to the minors, he returned to the Dodgers in 1986 and Oakland two years later. He has written a book about his experiences, *Five O'Clock Comes Early*.

A much-publicized drug trial that began in Pittsburgh on September 5, 1985, exposed the drug involvement of numerous players, including Keith Hernandez of the Mets (formerly with the Cardinals) and Dave Parker of the Reds (formerly with the Pirates). After the trial, Commissioner Peter Ueberroth meted out penalties to twenty-one players, ranging from heavy fines to be paid to drug prevention programs, orders to participate in random drug testing, and the performance of drug-related community service.

The shocking disclosures of widespread drug use that came out of the 1985 trial and the severe penalties that followed seemed to have a favorable impact on the drug problem, but did not eliminate it entirely. In 1986 San Diego pitcher LaMarr Hoyt, a Cy Young Award winner in 1983 when he was with the White Sox, was arrested three times on drug-related charges, and after the third was sentenced to forty-five days in federal prison. Hoyt's suspension from baseball was later overturned, and he was ordered reinstated with back pay, much to the dismay of the baseball hierarchy.

Hoyt then signed with his old club, the Chicago White Sox, but his troubles were far from over. He tested positive for cocaine three times in October 1987, and then on December 4 he was arrested in his Columbia, S.C., apart-ment and charged with intent to distribute cocaine and marijuana. He was convicted the following year and sentenced to one year in prison.

The list has been a long one, and sad. It has included paragons and playboys, teetotalers and tosspots, the great, the near-great, and the never-were; some who self-destructed and many more who were simply the victims of the cruelest of bad luck. However classified, for each player the hypothetical question remains: Had his tragedy not occurred, what might have been?

Careers Shortened by Blacklisting or Expulsion

Listed below, but not discussed in this chapter, are players blacklisted or expelled from baseball for gambling, dishonest play (or knowledge of same), criminal activity, or, in one case—that of Ray Fisher—violation of a contract. The players involved in the 1877 Louisville and 1919 Chicago White Sox scandals, all of whom were barred for life, are grouped; the others are listed alphabetically:

1877 Louisville players   Bill Craver, Jim Devlin, George Hall, Al Nichols.

1919 Chicago White Sox players   Eddie Cicotte, Oscar Felsch, Chick Gandil, Joe Jackson, Fred McMullin, Swede Risberg, Buck Weaver, Claude Williams.

Others   George Bechtel, Rube Benton (who was later reinstated and returned to the majors), Paul Carter, Hal Chase, Cozy Dolan, Phil Douglas, Jean Dubuc (who returned as a coach with Detroit in 1931), Ray Fisher, Joe Gedeon, Claude Hendrix, Richard Higham (umpire), Benny Kauff, Hubert Leonard, Lee Magee, Jimmy O'Connell, Eugene Paulette, Heinie Zimmerman. [Former major leaguers banned from baseball for their activities in the minor leagues include Babe Borton, Gene Dale, Jess Levan, Harl Maggert, Tom Seaton and Joe Tipton.]

The Pinch Hitters

L. Robert Davids

It was approximately 100 years ago, in 1891, when baseball rules were amended to allow substitute batters for other than emergency conditions. There apparently were a few occasions earlier when a batter was substituted because of an injury to a regular player. In fact, historian Al Kermisch has documented such an occurrence as early as 1876, the first year of the National League, but the batter did not make a hit. There might have been others who did hit safely, but the narrative reporting of the time was usually quite limited, and it was fairly typical for substitutes to be omitted from the box score.

For many years it was believed that the first successful pinch hit occurred June 7, 1892, when Jack Doyle of Cleveland batted for pitcher George Davies and delivered a ninth-inning single against Brooklyn. However, there were two earlier pinch hits achieved that season. On April 29, 1892, Philadelphia was playing in Chicago and losing in the ninth, 4–2. Manager Harry Wright called on Charles Reilly, a switch hitter, to bat in place of pitcher Kid Carsey. He singled sharply to center off Wild Bill Hutchison, but the game ended two outs later.

A more dramatic pinch hit was achieved about two weeks later with Brooklyn playing at Boston. The Boston *Journal* described the May 14 circumstance as follows:

Boston could do nothing in the ninth. Ward [Brooklyn manager John M. Ward] meant business in his turn at bat and instead of sending Collins [the left fielder] to bat he substituted Tom Daly. Hardly had the spectators recognized the newcomer when he lifted one of Clarkson's slow balls over the left field fence and the game was tied.

That description is quoted to confirm that Hub Collins, who was not feeling well, was replaced at bat in the ninth rather than in the field one-half inning earlier. There was a tragic footnote to this first pinch home run as it was soon learned that Collins had typhoid fever. He never returned to the lineup and died a week later.

In spite of three successful pinch hits in the first six weeks of the 1892 season, there was very limited use of substitute batsmen in that period. In fact, in the middle of the 1892 season, roster sizes would be reduced from 15 to 13. With a roster that small, most of the extra players had to be pitchers. Consequently, those pitchers who could also fill in as outfielders were the most available and most used in the early years. The first player to collect two pinch hits in a season was Kid Gleason in 1894. He was then a hurler with St. Louis and Baltimore. Jack Stivetts of Boston was the second player to hit a pinch homer, on

June 28, 1894, and probably was the first to hit a pinch triple on August 15, 1895. We will include a separate section later in this chapter on the contributions of pitchers as pinch hitters.

Catchers also made an early contribution to pinch hitting. They were very vulnerable to injury in those days and it was always necessary to have available a second backstop. One or the other then could be used as a substitute batter. Jack Clements, best known as the lefthanded catcher of the Phillies, hit baseball's third pinch home run on May 5, 1896. However, he did poorly off the bench after that, collecting only 1 hit in 12 at bats in 1898. Duke Farrell of New York and Washington had much better success, going 10–4, 14–8, and 10–5 in 1896–97–98, and winding up with a 59–23 (.389) career mark in 1904.

In spite of Farrell's good record, there were still some low spots in pinch hitting after 1900. In 1904, for example, which was the first year of the 154-game schedule in this century, the AL leader in pinch hits had only two for the season. There were seven tied with that number, and you had to give the nod to catcher Jim McGuire, who was 2 for 2. The Deacon didn't do particularly well as a substitute batter until he became forty years old. From 1904 through 1908 he was 9–6. While managing Boston in 1907, he inserted himself as a pinch hitter against Detroit on July 27. He made quite a hit with Boston fans by slamming a home run in the ninth to tie the game at 2–2. It was only the second pinch homer hit in the American League. More significantly, McGuire, at age 43 years and 8 months, was the oldest ever to hit a pinch homer.

There was a significant change in the level of pinch hitter activity in 1908, when the St. Louis Browns acquired a big pitcher-first baseman named Dode Criss. He did not pitch very well and his fielding was of the same caliber, but he did bat .341 that first year as a substitute. He set new records for pinch-hit at bats with 41 and hits with 12, and he led the AL in both categories for the next three years as well. Since he pinch-hit in about 70 percent of his major league games, he logically could be described as the first professional pinch hitter.

The regular use of Criss as a substitute batter opened the doors for several other "have bat, will travel" types. They included Moose McCormick, Ted Easterly, Ham Hyatt, Doc Miller, and Bill Rumler. McCormick of the Giants wasn't really the pioneer pinch hitter of this era as later described by New York writers. Most of the stories on this subject stated that John McGraw popularized pinch hitting by his use of McCormick. McCormick did not make much impression until 1912, when he collected 11 hits in 30 at bats. Criss, who played on a second-division team, had left the majors by that time. McCormick played on pennant winners and gained additional publicity when he pinch-hit in the 1912 and 1913 World Series. In seven appearances, he hit two singles and a sacrifice fly, and knocked in one run. More about World Series pinch hitters later.

Ted Easterly was a catcher who came up with Cleveland in 1909. In 1912 he set a new mark for hits when he collected 13 in 30 at bats (.433). He also established career records with 152 at bats and 45 hits by 1915. That was good for a pinch-hit average of .296, outstanding for the Dead Ball Era.

Doc Miller, a Canadian-born outfielder, did practically no pinch hitting in his first two years with the Boston Braves in 1910–11, but when he was traded to the Phillies in 1912, he was called on frequently. In fact, in 1913 he set new marks for at bats with 56 and hits with 20 (.357). In 1917, catcher Bill Rumler of the Browns, one of the few righthanded pinch-hit specialists in this era, upped the at bats to 71 and slapped out 16 hits along the way. The seventh-place Browns, still trying to get their act together, used a record 14 different pinch batters and averaged at least one appearance per game for the 154-game schedule.

Ham Hyatt, a well-built outfielder-first baseman and a recognized hitter in the minors, made his mark in the majors as a power hitter in the pinch. He broke in with the Pirates in 1909 and his 9 pinch hits that year included 3 triples. This was a season record, since tied, and he also shares the career mark with 5. In 1913 he became the first to hit three pinch homers in a season and he was the first to hit four in a career. He also was the first to reach the 50 level in hits. He closed out his major league career with the Yankees in 1918 with 57 hits in 240 at bats.

Hyatt's successor as career pinch-hit leader was even more sturdy in appearance. In fact, at 5-10 and 230 pounds, he was *fat*. Bob (Fatty) Fothergill also had fun poked at him by Catholic teammates because of his last name. There was no kidding around, however, when the Detroit outfielder was at bat as he compiled a career batting average (1923–33) of .326. In the pinch he was at an even .300, based on 76 hits in 253 at bats.

In 1933, while Fothergill was still an active player, he suffered the embarrassment of being passed on the pinch-hit list by a National Leaguer, and a pitcher at that. It was Charles "Red" Lucas, a dumpy-looking righthander who pitched for the second-division Cincinnati Reds. But on the mound he was a master craftsman with offspeed pitches and pinpoint control, and at the plate he swung with confidence from the left side. In the five years from 1929 to 1933, he averaged 13 pinch hits a season. Traded to Pittsburgh, he was used less as a pinch batter but went on to push the pinch-hit record seemingly out of reach by 1937, at which time he had 114 career pinch hits.

Lucas's hit record lasted almost thirty years; in fact, no one came close in the next quarter century. Sam Leslie, Bill Terry's backup first baseman with the Giants, had a big season in 1932, when he banged out 22 hits in 72 trips. Both were new season marks, but Leslie wound up in 1938 with only 59 career hits. The colorful and unpredictable Frenchy Bordagaray had one of the great pinch-hit seasons with the Cardinals in 1938, when he produced 20 hits in 43 at bats for a lofty .452 mark. However, when he finished his career with the Dodgers in 1945 he had accumulated only 54 pinch hits.

Pinch hitting expanded in general after World War II, a process enhanced in part by Casey Stengel's success at platooning players. Peanuts Lowrey of the Cardinals had two of the best back-to-back seasons when he had 14 hits in 28 at bats (.500) in 1952, and 21 hits in 59 at bats the next season. This righthanded batter closed out in 1955 with 62 career hits. Switch hitters also began to be used more in the pinch. Dave Philley of the Phillies was a primary example. In 1958 he had 18 hits in 44 at bats (.409), and this included eight in a row at the end of the season. In 1961 with the Orioles, he established a new pinch-hit record with 24 in 72 at bats. When he retired the next year, he had 93 career pinch-hits, the closest to Lucas's 114. Red Schoendienst was another good switch hitter of this period. In 1962, he almost duplicated Philley's great 1961 season with 22 hits in 72 at bats.

Another leading pinch hitter of the post–World War II period was Elmer Valo, a native of Czechoslovakia. Actually he was the leading "pinch walker." He summed up his role in terms of "There are times when all a pinch hitter has to do is to get a pass. In that sort of situation, the trick is to walk and forget your temptation to go for a long hit." In 1960 with the Senators and Yankees, he was on base 33 times with 18 walks, 14 hits, and 1 hit-by-pitch. Over his career, he received a record 91 walks while collecting 90 pinch hits. Research on this anomaly reveals that Harry McCurdy of the 1933 Phillies had 16 walks to go with 15 hits, and Dom Dallessandro of the 1946 Cubs had 15 walks and only 6 pinch hits. Dom's diminutive stature (5 feet, 6 inches) might have been a contributing factor. More recently, Merv Rettenmund of the 1977 Padres had 16 walks and 21 hits in 86 appearances. No pinch hitter has been on base more often.

The major assault on Lucas's long-standing pinch-hit record of 114 came in the mid-1960s. Catcher Smoky Burgess and outfielder Jerry Lynch both reached the century level in 1965, and Smoky had enough momentum from a 20-hit season to pass Lucas with his last hit of the year. Lynch finished his career in 1966 with 116 hits—only two beyond Lucas. Since all of his career was spent in the NL, he at least held that record. Burgess, on the other hand, didn't look back. Essentially a full-time pinch hitter with the White Sox, he had 21 hits in 1966 and 8 in 1967, and wound up his career with 145.

Just as Lucas's pinch-hit total seemed secure at 114—and it was for 28 years—so did Smoky's grand total of 145. However, the man to break his record was already hitting well for the Pirates. It was Manny Mota of the Dominican Republic, one of the growing number of Latin Americans entering the major leagues. Unlike most other players, who did their pinch hitting in their later years, Mota was a substitute batter some 20–30 times a season in the first part of his long career, slacked off somewhat in the middle, and pushed for a record in the later years. He pinch-hit in every one of his 20 seasons, passing Burgess's mark in 1979 and winding up with a round 150 in 1980. It looked like Greg Gross might challenge his career mark, but the latter was released after the 1989 season with 143 hits in a record 588 at bats. Ironically, not one of Gross's 143 hits went for a home run. On the other hand, not one of Burgess's 145 hits went for a triple.

Pinch Home Runs

Home runs, the most dramatic and productive of pinch hits, have played an important role ever since the first pinch home run was hit by Tom Daly on May 14, 1892. National League pinch hitters had slammed ten homers by the time the AL entered the majors in 1901, and had hit six more by the time Germany Schaefer of Detroit hit the Junior Circuit's first on June 25, 1906, in Chicago. Doc White, who had hit a pinch homer for the Phillies in 1902, was on the mound for the White Sox and leading 2–1 in the ninth. With a Tiger on base, Schaefer hit a long drive which skipped around in the outfield long enough for both to circle the bases for a 3–2 win.

In 1910, Beals Becker of the Giants was the first to hit 2 pinch homers in a season, one coming with the bases loaded. Ham Hyatt was the first to hit 3 with Pittsburgh in 1913. Cliff Cravath of Philadelphia hit 2 that season, the second off Christy Mathewson on July 4. The NL exploded for 11 pinch four-baggers in all. Cravath again showed up the Giants on April 20, 1920, when, as manager of the Phillies, he inserted himself as a pinch batter in a scoreless game and hit a 3-run game-winner. It was his last in the majors and his sixth in the pinch, a record that lasted until an old Phillies teammate, Cy Williams, connected for his seventh on April 16, 1928. That round-tripper also came against the Giants, when a young and not-so-fat Freddie Fitzsimmons served up a knuckleball with two on base. Williams hit 3 pinch home runs that season and 2 in 1929, to close out his career with 11. That mark was expected to last for years and did.

Johnny Frederick of Brooklyn had a good crack at it, but his six-year career was too short. He concentrated most of his pinch-hit prowess in the 1932 season, when he collected 9 pinch hits in 29 at bats. However, a spectacular 6 of those hits went the distance. When Ford Sawyer, an early authority on pinch hitting, had this story published in *The Sporting News* in October 1932, the bold headline read: FREDERICK'S SIX PINCH-HIT HOME RUNS EPOCHAL ACHIEVEMENT OF MAJOR HISTORY. That might have sounded a bit exaggerated, but the standing record after forty years of pinch hitting was only 3 pinch homers. And even now, almost sixty years later, no one else has hit more than five. Frederick, who went "downtown" off such notable hurlers as Burleigh Grimes, Carl Hubbell, Lon Warneke, and Pat Malone, also hit 2 pinch doubles, giving him 29 total bases in 29 pinch at bats for a 1.000 slugging mark. His short career ended with 8 pinch-hit homers.

Red Sox manager Joe Cronin had an exceptionally productive year in 1943, when he batted .429 (43–18), hit 4 doubles and 5 homers, and batted in a record 25 runs, since tied. Six of the RBIs came in a June 17 twinbill, when he blasted a 3-run homer in each game. Ironically those 5 pinch homers became his career total as well. Hal Breeden of Montreal was the only other to duplicate this doubleheader feat. He apparently was not affected by superstition because his twin blasts came on Friday the thirteenth of July, 1973, and resulted in a split with Atlanta.

Cy Williams's record of 11 career pinch homers remained on the books for 31 years until George Crowe swept it away with a four-homer flourish in 1960 that raised his total to 14. Jerry Lynch then took over, not with

four in a season, but one each season for 1963–64–65–66. His total of 18 was passed by Cliff Johnson, who was primarily a designated hitter, in 1985. Johnson's record of 20 pinch homers in 277 at bats gives him a frequency factor of 1 per 13.9 at bats. Among players with ten or more pinch homers, only Joe Adcock's 12.8 (153–12) and Cy Williams's 12.9 (142–11) rank ahead of him.

What about that ultimate dream hit, the pinch grand slam? It happens anywhere from two to seven times a year now but was very rare in the early days. More than 200 pinch slams have been hit, all in this century. Ironically, the first was hit by a pitcher, Mike O'Neill of the Cardinals, in a victory over the Boston NL team on June 3, 1902. Mike's brother Jack, one of four O'Neills who played in the majors, caught this game and also rode home on Mike's blast, which was inside the park in Boston. The second pinch slam occurred just two months later, hit by catcher Pat Moral of Boston, but then it was eight years before Beals Becker connected for the Giants. The first AL pinch slam did not take place until September 24, 1916, when Marty Kavanagh, a utility infielder for Cleveland, hit a hard liner off Hub Leonard of the Red Sox. The ball rolled through a hole in the fence and everyone scored.

Two playing managers looked good by inserting themselves in the box and belting the ball. Rogers Hornsby hit a pinch slam for his Cubs in the eleventh inning against the Braves on September 13, 1931. Phil Cavarretta also hit one for the Cubs shortly after taking over the helm on July 29, 1951. His came off Robin Roberts when the latter was a leading hurler. Pitcher Early Wynn hit one for Washington on September 15, 1946. He was the only player to experience both the ecstasy and the agony as he also served one up to Bob Cerv on May 28, 1961.

Jimmie Foxx was the first player to experience the emotional impact of hitting two pinch grand slams. The first was for the Athletics on September 21, 1931. His memory had faded by the time he hit the next one, which was for the Phillies on May 18, 1945, his last season. Ron Northey was the first to hit the jackpot three times—for the Cardinals in 1947 and 1948, and with the Cubs in 1950. Later Rich Reese did it three times for the Twins and Willie McCovey connected twice for the San Francisco Giants and once for the Padres. Chuck Klein is believed to have been the only player to hit two pinch-hit triples with the bases loaded. He delivered for the Phillies on May 8, 1939, and September 14, 1940.

Pitchers as Pinch Hitters

Pitcher Don Robinson's pinch home run for the Giants on June 19, 1990, the first hit by a hurler in nineteen years, serves as a reminder that special mention should be made of their contribution as substitute batters. They were among the first used in 1891, when pinch hitters were officially allowed. Bob Caruthers and Jack Stivetts made their initial efforts that season. On June 28, 1894, when Stivetts was with Boston, he went to the plate for Kid Nichols in the ninth with Boston trailing St. Louis 10–7. The Boston Strong Boy belted a home run with two on to tie the game. He then went in to pitch, and the Beantowners won in the tenth, 11–10. He hit two more before closing out his career in 1899.

Pitchers used most frequently as pinch hitters at the turn of the century were Jim Callahan, Win Mercer, Mike O'Neill, Jesse Tannehill, Al Orth, Frank Kitson, and George Mullin. There was one game on July 17, 1901, when Vic Willis was hurling for the Boston NL team, where two other Beantown hurlers were called off the bench to pinch hit in the ninth. Kid Nichols hit a triple and Bill Dinneen scored him with a single.

A memorable highlight for pinch-hitting pitchers came on June 10–11, 1915, when Ray Caldwell of the Yankees hit pinch homers in consecutive games against the White Sox. The second was a three-run shot against Red Faber. This was the first time this feat was achieved by any pinch batter and was not duplicated for twenty-eight years.

Over the years, several hurlers led all substitute batsmen in season pinch-hit average. Examples included Frank Lange in 1911, who had 8 hits in 19 trips; Clarence Mitchell, 6 for 18 in 1920; Jack Bentley, 10 for 20 in 1923; George Uhle, 11 for 26 in 1924; Ervin Brame, 10 for 21 in 1930; Red Ruffing, 8 for 18 in 1935; and Chubby Dean, 10 for 26 in 1939.

The major pinch-hitting role of Red Lucas has already been discussed. However, there was another red-headed hurler over in the AL who made his contribution. Red Ruffing was not as active as Red Lucas, but he had a longer career. He banged out 58 hits as a substitute swinger. Teammates he batted for included Joe Sewell, Bill Dickey, and Tommy Henrich. Red faced Lefty Grove 15 times and hit him safely 5 times. He got his last pinch hit on August 8, 1947, when he was 43 years old. It was an RBI single off Hal Newhouser, then at the top of his form. Ruffing was proud of his pinch-hitting prowess; in fact, he wanted to be paid a little extra for that work and held out for a while in the spring of 1937.

Ranking after Lucas and Ruffing in pitcher pinch hits were George Uhle with 44, Ray Caldwell 36, Dutch Ruether 34, Wes Ferrell 31, and Chubby Dean and Bob Lemon with 30. Gary Peters was the hurler hitting the most pinch home runs with 4, followed by Lynn Nelson with 3. Peters had only 16 career pinch hits to his credit, but he made them count. His first homer, on July 19, 1964, came in the thirteenth inning and gave the White Sox a 3–2 win over Kansas City. His fourth pinch homer came on September 4, 1971, and was the last one until Don Robinson's recent clout.

Effects of the Designated-Hitter Rule

The introduction of the designated hitter in the AL in 1973 not only sharply reduced hitting by pitchers, but disrupted a fairly balanced pinch-hitter competition between the two leagues since 1901. Over that period, the level of activity was about the same in each circuit, as were the pinch-hit batting averages. The NL did show surprising superiority in pinch homers, even in the AL power era of 1920–40. Apparently those sluggers like Ruth, Gehrig, Foxx, and Greenberg were hitting all those home runs as regular players. For whatever the reason, NL pinch batters hit 1,123 home runs from 1901 through 1972, and their AL counterparts hit 991.

A review of pinch-hit stats in the two leagues in the four years (1969–72) prior to the DH, and the four years after its introductory season (1974–77), show that AL pinch-

hitter activity was cut almost in half. The reason, of course, is that the clubs' best substitute batters were already in the batting order. In prior years, most pinch batters entered the game to bat for the pitcher, but that role was usurped by the DH. It is true that sometimes when opposing pitchers are changed, a new DH may be inserted, and the first time he bats he is a pinch hitter. But that hasn't changed the sharply reduced use of pinch batters in the AL. This disparity has continued through 1989. In the latter year, for example, the fourteen-team AL had 1,674 pinch-hit at bats and 378 hits (.226) while the twelve-team NL had 2,879 at bats and 625 hits (.219). The AL is making up the difference with more home runs per hit, belting 29 to 36 for the NL. In 1985 the AL actually surpassed the NL in pinch homers, 47 to 41.

One Season Pinch-Hit Analysis

The ultimate success of a pinch batter is measured by his ability to knock in the winning run in a close game. This should make him a hero in the eyes of his manager, at least until the next game. The late John Tattersall, who was an authority on pinch hitting as well as home runs, analyzed the 1962 season to determine how many games were won by pinch hitters who came through in the clutch. He found there were 33 such dramatic victories during the year, 17 in the AL and 16 in the NL. All but 5 would be one-run victories, but 12 would be come-from-behind triumphs. Ten of the 33 would be wins in extra innings. Pinch singles won 17 games, doubles 2, and homers 12. A sacrifice fly and a bases-loaded walk won 2 other contests. A brief discussion of some of these games might flavor the analysis.

Jim Lemon of the Minnesota Twins was the first to wear the halo on April 25, 1962, when he was sent in to hit in the ninth against Baltimore with the score tied 1–1. He homered with a man on for a 3–1 victory.

At the Polo Grounds on May 5, Cal Koonce of the Cubs walked Mets pinch batter Hobie Landrith in the thirteenth with the bases full. Landrith got the 6–5 game-winning RBI.

Three games were won by 1–0 scores. On June 6, a sacrifice fly by Tom Burgess of the Angels with the bases full in the ninth drove in the only run against the White Sox. At Baltimore on June 26, Charlie Lau, who would later teach players how to hit, demonstrated with a pinch single off Johnny Buzhardt of the White Sox in the ninth to give the Orioles the 1–0 win. At Cleveland on Independence Day, Gene Green burned Hank Aguirre of the Tigers with a single in the tenth to give Jim Perry a 1–0 squeaker.

Canada's Pete Ward had an auspicious debut with Baltimore on September 21. With the Orioles trailing the Twins 2–1 in the seventh, he drove in two Birds with a sharp single off Camilo Pascual to win the game 3–2.

On August 11, Don Drysdale of the Dodgers had the Giants beaten 4–2 in the sixth when Willie McCovey belted a 3-run homer for a 5–4 win. McCovey would hit 12 of his career homers off Drysdale. The bases were loaded with Cardinals on September 9 when Carl Sawatski swatted a homer in the ninth for a 5–3 come-from-behind triumph over the Reds.

The New York Mets won only 40 games and lost 120 in

1962, but Marv Throneberry won the nickname of "Marvelous Marv" with his energetic exploits. He delivered a 2-run homer on July 7, and a 3-run homer on August 21, each time in the ninth inning, to win come-from-behind games from the Cardinals and Pirates. In the AL, Vic Wertz of the Tigers also won 2 games with pinch blows. On May 1, he hit a tenth-inning single which drove in 2 runs to beat the Athletics 3–2. His July 6 contribution was a ninth-inning homer off Hoyt Wilhelm to beat Baltimore 5–4.

Pinch Hitters in the World Series

There have been some outstanding game or single Series exploits by pinch hitters, but nothing very significant has been compiled by substitute batsmen on a "career" basis. In fact, in the long history of World Series play, no player has collected more than 3 pinch hits. Four players did that, two from the Yankees. Bobby Brown had 7 pinch hit appearances in four World Series but concentrated almost all his production in the 1947 classic. He had a single, 2 doubles, a walk, and 3 RBIs. Johnny Blanchard had 10 at bats in 5 World Series between 1960 and 1964 and collected 3 singles. Nothing outstanding there. Ken O'Dea, backup catcher for the Cubs and Cardinals in 5 World Series between 1935 and 1944, never had more than one pinch hit in a Series but knocked in 4 runs.

Although Chuck Essegian hit 2 pinch homers for the Los Angeles Dodgers in the 1959 World Series, both were solo shots and neither won a game. Bernie Carbo of the Red Sox also hit two round-trippers for the Red Sox in the 1975 Series, one being a solo circling of the bases and the other a 3-run homer which temporarily tied the game with the Reds.

No pinch hitter dominated a World Series more than Dusty Rhodes with the New York Giants in 1954. In the Fall Classic with Cleveland, which had won a record 111 games during the season, he led the New Yorkers to a dramatic 5–2 opening-game victory on September 29 with a 3-run home run in the tenth. In the second game he singled in the tying run (and then homered after going into the lineup). Ironically, Rhodes, a .253 lifetime hitter, batted for future Hall of Famer Monte Irvin in his first two appearances. In the third game he knocked in 2 runs with a single. He didn't even have to get off the bench as the Giants swept the fourth game and the Series. He had knocked in 6 runs with his 3 pinch hits, not only a record for one Series but for all Series.

For individual one-game dramatics, Kirk Gibson of the 1988 Dodgers probably takes the cake. In the first game of the 1988 Series against the powerful Oakland A's on October 15, the Dodgers were down 4–3 with two down in the last of the ninth. With Mike Davis on base with a walk, Gibson, unable to play in the regular lineup because of a leg injury, was called in to bat for pitcher Alejandro Pena. On a 3-2 pitch from relief ace Dennis Eckersley, he drove the ball into the right field bleachers for a 5–4 Los Angeles victory. It was his only appearance in the Series, which was won by the Dodgers in 5 games.

Season Pinch Hitting Records

At Bats	Rusty Staub, Mets, 1983	81	
Hits	Jose Morales, Expos, 1976	25	
Doubles	Vic Davalillo, Cards, 1970	8	
Triples	Ham Hyatt, Pirates, 1909	3	
	Gene Robertson, Browns, 1926	3	
	Vic Davalillo, Cards, 1970	3	
Homers	John Frederick, Dodgers, 1932	6	
Walks	Elmer Valo, Yanks-Senators, 1960	18	
RBIs	Joe Cronin, Red Sox, 1943	25	
	Jerry Lynch, Reds, 1961	25	
	Rusty Staub, Mets, 1983	25	
High BA	Bruce Boisclair, Mets, 1976	.571	(21–12)
	Peanuts Lowrey, Cards, 1952	.500	(28–14)
	Ed Kranepool, Mets, 1974	.486	(35–17)
	Frenchy Bordagaray, Cards, 1938	.465	(43–20)

Career Pinch Hitting Records

At Bats	Greg Gross (1973–89)	588	
Hits	Manny Mota (1962–82)	150	
Doubles	Smoky Burgess (1949–67)	27	
Triples	Ham Hyatt (1909–18)	5	
	Gates Brown (1963–75)	5	
Homers	Cliff Johnson (1972–86)	20	
Walks	Elmer Valo (1940–61)	91	
RBIs	Smoky Burgess (1949–67)	142	
High BA	Gordon Coleman (1959–67)	.333	(120–40)
	Tommy Davis (1959–76)	.320	(197–63)
	Bob Fothergill (1922–33)	.300	(253–76)
	Dave Philley (1941–62)	.299	(311–95)
	Manny Mota (1962–82)	.297	(505–150)

First Players to Collect 50 (or More) Pinch Hits

50	**60**	**70**	**80**	**90**
1915 Ham Hyatt	1932 Bob Fothergill	1933 Red Lucas	1933 Red Lucas	1935 Red Lucas
1930 Bob Fothergill	1932 Red Lucas	1933 Bob Fothergill	1961 Elmer Valo	1962 Dave Philley
1931 Red Lucas	1947 Ernie Lombardi	1958 Enos Slaughter	1961 Dave Philley	1962 Elmer Valo
1934 Harvey Hendrick	1954 Peanuts Lowrey	1959 George Crowe	1961 Smoky Burgess	1963 Jerry Lynch
1937 Sam Leslie	1958 Enos Slaughter	1960 Elmer Valo	1962 Jerry Lynch	1964 Smoky Burgess
1941 Red Ruffing	1958 Smoky Burgess	1960 Smoky Burgess	1970 Tito Francona	1974 Gates Brown
1941 Billy Sullivan	1959 Dave Philley	1961 Dave Philley	1971 Gates Brown	1975 Manny Mota
1945 Frenchy	1959 George Crowe	1961 Jerry Lynch	1972 Dalton Jones	1979 Vic Davallilo
Bordagaray	1960 Dave Philley	1970 Tito Francona	1974 Manny Mota	1979 Ed Kranepool
1945 Debs Garms	1961 Julio Becquer	1970 Gates Brown	1978 Vic Davallilo	1980 Mike Lum
1945 Ernie Lombardi				

100	**110**	**120**	**130**	**140**
1936 Red Lucas	1937 Red Lucas	1966 Smoky Burgess	1966 Smoky Burgess	1967 Smoky Burgess
1965 Smoky Burgess	1965 Smoky Burgess	1977 Manny Mota	1978 Manny Mota	1979 Manny Mota
1965 Jerry Lynch	1966 Jerry Lynch	1983 Jose Morales	1988 Greg Gross	1989 Greg Gross
1974 Gates Brown	1977 Manny Mota	1987 Greg Gross		
1976 Manny Mota	1983 Jose Morales			
1981 Mike Lum	1985 Steve Braun			**150**
1982 Jose Morales	1987 Greg Gross			1980 Manny Mota
1982 Terry Crowley				
1984 Steve Braun				
1985 Rusty Staub				

Evolution of Pinch Home Runs

Seven	**Eight**	**Nine**	**Ten**	**Eleven**
Cy Williams 1928	Cy Williams 1928	Cy Williams 1929	Cy Williams 1929	Cy Williams 1929
Johnny Frederick ...1932	Johnny Frederick ...1934	Bobby Hofman 1955	Smoky Burgess.....1959	George Crowe......1960
Ernie Lombardi 1946	Ernie Lombardi 1947	Ron Northey 1957	Gus Zernial 1959	Smoky Burgess.....1960
Bill Nicholson.......1952	Bobby Hofman 1955	Gus Zernial 1958	George Crowe......1959	Bob Cerv 1961
Johnny Mize 1953	Ron Northey 1956	Smoky Burgess.....1959	Jerry Lynch 1961	Jerry Lynch 1962
Bobby Hofman 1955	Gus Zernial 1958	George Crowe......1959	Bob Cerv 1961	Joe Adcock 1966
Ron Northey 1956	Smoky Burgess.....1958	Jerry Lynch 1961	Wally Post 1962	Fred Whitfield 1967
Ted Williams.......1957	George Crowe......1959	Bob Cerv 1960	Joe Adcock 1966	Gates Brown 1971
Gus Zernial 1958	Bob Cerv 1960	Yogi Berra 1962	Fred Whitfield 1967	Willie McCovey 1975
Smoky Burgess.....1958	Jerry Lynch 1961	Wally Post 1962	Gates Brown 1971	Cliff Johnson 1978

Twelve	**Thirteen**	**Fourteen**	**Fifteen**	**Sixteen**
George Crowe......1960	George Crowe......1960	George Crowe......1960	Jerry Lynch 1963	Jerry Lynch 1964
Bob Cerv 1961	Jerry Lynch 1963	Jerry Lynch 1963	Smoky Burgess.....1967	Smoky Burgess.....1967
Jerry Lynch 1963	Smoky Burgess.....1965	Smoky Burgess.....1965	Gates Brown 1974	Gates Brown 1975
Smoky Burgess....1964	Gates Brown 1974	Gates Brown 1974	Willie McCovey 1979	Willie McCovey 1979
Joe Adcock 1966	Will McCovey.......1977	Willie McCovey 1978	Cliff Johnson 1980	Cliff Johnson 1981
Gates Brown 1972	Cliff Johnson 1980	Cliff Johnson 1980		
Willie McCovey 1976				
Cliff Johnson 1979				
Jose Morales.......1983				
Graig Nettles 1988				

Seventeen	**Eighteen**	**Nineteen**	**Twenty**
Jerry Lynch 1965	Jerry Lynch 1966	Cliff Johnson 1985	Cliff Johnson 1986
Cliff Johnson 1983	Cliff Johnson 1984		

Multiple Pinch Grand Slams	
Jimmie Foxx	1931, 1945
Ron Northey	1947, 1948, 1950
Bill Skowron	1954, 1957
Vic Wertz	1958, 1960
Ed Bailey	1962, 1963
Willie McCovey	1960, 1965, 1975
Rick Reese	1969, 1970, 1972
Reggie Jackson	1970, 1976
Dave Johnson	1978, 1978
Mike Ivie	1978, 1978

Career Pinch Home Run Leader		
Jack Stivetts	3	1898
Ham Hyatt	4	1914
Cliff Cravath	5	1919
Cliff Cravath	6	1920
Cy Williams	7	1928
Cy Williams	8	1928
Cy Williams	9	1929
Cy Williams	10	1929
Cy Williams	11	1929
George Crowe	12	1960
George Crowe	13	1960
George Crowe	14	1960
Jerry Lynch	15	1963
Jerry Lynch	16	1964
Jerry Lynch	17	1965
Jerry Lynch	18	1966
Cliff Johnson	19	1985
Cliff Johnson	20	1986

Two-Sport Stars

Stan Grosshandler

There was a time when the first pitch of Opening Day was in early April and the last out of the World Series occurred during the first week of October. The NFL kicked off the second week of September and finished their Championship Game shortly after Thanksgiving. Basketball was just something to occupy the time until Opening Day came again.

It was relatively easy for a gifted athlete to exchange his steel baseball spikes for the long, hard rubber cleats used in football; therefore early in this century the two-sport star was not unusual, and most of these are found in the first four decades of this century.

Professional baseball has always been well defined, dating back to the National Association of 1871; however, prior to the formation of the American Professional Football League in 1920, it is difficult to determine what football teams were truly professional.

It is the opinion of knowledgeable sports historians that several teams that played in western Pennsylvania and central Ohio at the turn of the century were indeed professional teams. These clubs recruited the best athletes available, therefore the majority of two-sport players played for cities like Latrobe and Greensburg, Pennsylvania, and the Ohio cities of Canton and Massillon.

Ed "Batty" Abbattichio was the first and one of the most successful of the two-sport players. The husky 5'11", 170-pound native of Latrobe was a slick-fielding second sacker for Philadelphia, Boston, and Pittsburgh of the National League from 1897 through 1910 and a hard-running and -punting fullback for Latrobe from 1895 to the turn of the century.

The most famous of all early two-sport athletes was Christy Mathewson, the legendary Giants pitcher who between 1900 and 1916 won 373 games. He was a member of the first group of players voted into the Cooperstown Hall of Fame. Christy had played football at Bucknell, where he was a star fullback and punter. He played the 1900 season with the Pittsburgh Stars, winning several games with his punting.

In 1900 a team with the unusual name of the Homestead Library and Athletic Club did a fine job of recruiting, signing two great Brown halfbacks, Fred Crolius and John Gammons, plus David Fultz of Dartmouth. All three proved to be among the top football players of the day; but they also played major league baseball.

All three were outfielders: Fred Crolius played a total of 58 games in 1901 for the Boston Braves and for the 1902 Pittsburgh Pirates. John Gammons was a teammate of Crolius on the 1901 Braves, getting into only 28 games.

David Fultz, who spent one season as a player-coach with the Athletic Club, enjoyed success between 1898 and 1905 with Philadelphia and Baltimore of the NL and with Philadelphia and New York of the AL. His career average was .271. He also earned a law degree at N.Y.U. and was to become an early-day advocate for the rights of players.

In 1912 he organized the Players Fraternity, challenging the treatment of players and the reserve clause. Prior to the 1916 season he threatened a strike which never materialized. Baseball was not quite ready for a union, and David eventually became president of the International League.

In 1902 Philadelphia Athletic manager Connie Mack and owner Ben Shibe were convinced to organize a football team to take advantage of the many rivalries within the state. Connie put together a team and included Rube Waddell, allegedly to keep track of the eccentric southpaw pitcher during the off-season. Though Rube was supposed to have gotten into a few games briefly as a lineman, there is no real documentation that he ever played pro football.

Charles Moran, who had two cups of coffee with the Cardinals, one in 1903 as a pitcher and a second in 1908 as a catcher, played halfback for the powerful 1905 Massillon Tigers.

"Uncle Charley," as he came to be known, gained considerable fame as a football coach. His Centre College team was nationally known as the "Praying Colonels," as a result of Charley's asking them to have a prayer session prior to each game. Moran then went on to a second career, umpiring in the National League from 1917 through 1939.

The lives of Jim Thorpe and Earle "Greasy" Neale seem to intertwine on both the diamond and gridiron.

After his great triumph in the 1912 Olympic Games, Jim Thorpe joined the New York Giants as an outfielder. His great power and speed made him very attractive as a baseball player; however, pitchers soon found out that "the world's greatest athlete" could not hit a curve. Jim's lackadaisical approach to the game did not go well with the tough Giant manager John McGraw; yet Jim played for the Giants intermittently from 1913 through 1919.

In April 1917 Jim was sold to the Cincinnati Reds. On May 2, 1917, he was playing right field when Fred Toney of the Reds opposed Jim "Hippo" Vaughn of the Cubs. Each pitched hitless ball until the top of the tenth, when with runners on second and third and two out Thorpe, who had struck out twice, hit the ball on the handle, resulting in a high hopper to Vaughn. The pitcher realized he could not throw the fleet Thorpe out at first, so he threw home late and the only run of the game scored. Jim was given credit for a single and the RBI that broke up the only double no-hitter ever played.

In August he was sold back to the Giants and played in one game of the World Series. In his final season with both the Giants and Braves, Jim hit .327 over 62 games.

Jim Thorpe was a member of the Canton Bulldogs from 1915 until they became part of the new professional league in 1920. Thorpe was actually elected president of the league, an obvious figurehead position. He went on to play for several NFL clubs, retiring in 1929 at age forty-two.

Hitting ahead of Thorpe and playing center field the day of the double no-hitter was Earle "Greasy" Neale. A sharp lefthanded hitter, Greasy was a Red from 1916 through '24, had a career .259 average, with his best season in 1917 when he batted .294. Neale's zenith on the diamond came in the 1919 World Series. His .357 was the best on the club as the Reds won the Series.

Greasy Neale was coaching at West Virginia Wesleyan when he played end for the 1917 Canton Bulldogs under the name of Foster. Thorpe was running the team, and he asked Greasy to play several backfield positions during the year due to many injuries. In 1917 he played backfield and coached the Dayton Triangles.

It is as a coach that Greasy Neale gained his highest accolades. He took an underdog Washington and Jefferson team to the Rose Bowl in 1921 and tied a powerful California team. After several successful college coaching jobs, he took over the Philadelphia Eagles in 1941, and before he retired after the 1950 season, he had built the club into an NFL power, winning three divisional and two league titles. He is in both the college and pro Halls of Fame for his coaching ability.

The star of the 1919 Rose Bowl, George Halas joined the New York Yankees that spring. A switch-hitting outfielder, Halas injured his hip sliding into third at Cleveland. After 12 games and an .091 average, his diamond career was over.

George then turned his attention to pro football, organizing the Decatur Staleys, who were to become the Chicago Bears. Halas played end, coached, and owned this franchise, developing it into one of the all-time greatest sports franchises.

On the 1920 Decatur Staleys were a 5'6", 145-pound quarterback and a 5'8", 155-pound halfback. The quarterback, Chuck Dressen, played third base seven years for the Reds and one for the Giants, compiling a career .272 mark. He then spent sixteen years as a manager, leading the Cincinnati Reds, Brooklyn Dodgers, Washington Senators, Milwaukee Braves, and Detroit Tigers. His Dodger teams were defeated in the 1952 and '53 World Series.

The halfback, Paddy Driscoll, played in only 13 games for the 1917 Chicago Cubs. He was to have a Hall of Fame career as an NFL player and coach.

On April 22, 1922, Ty Cobb injured his ankle and rookie Johnny Mohardt took his place on the bases. Mohardt had played football at Notre Dame in the same backfield as George Gipp and was now trying to win a spot in the Tiger outfield.

Mohardt only played in 5 games, batted just once (he got a hit, so his career average was 1.000), and then left baseball. Mohardt played for five seasons in the NFL, financing his medical training. He eventually became a distinguished surgeon and the Assistant Medical Director of the Veterans Administration.

Hinkey Haines appeared in 14 regular and 2 World Series games for the 1923 World Champion Yankees, his only season of major league baseball. He was also a member of the 1927 New York Giants, the NFL champs, making Hinkey the only man to be a member of two major league championship teams in different sports.

Hinkey had played college football at Penn State, where his coach was Hugo Bezdek.

"He was a tough guy," recalled Hinkey, "but we all felt he was very fair. He had emigrated from Czechoslovakia and learned his football with Stagg at Chicago. [Bezdek] is the only man to take three different schools to the Rose Bowl, manage a big league baseball team (the Pittsburgh Pirates), and coach an NFL team (the Cleveland Rams)."

Charlie Berry, a Walter Camp All-American end at Lafayette College in 1924, joined the 1925 Philadelphia Athletics as a catcher. On the A's he found outfielder Walter French, who had starred at West Point, and Mickey Cochrane, a former Boston College football player. Unfortunately for Charlie, Cochrane was one of the greatest catchers the game has ever seen, so Berry only played in 10 games that year.

In the fall he and French played for the Pottstown Maroons, an NFL power at the time. Exhibiting great pass-catching and field goal-kicking ability, Berry was the top scorer in the league with 72 points, while French averaged 5.4 yards per carry.

Both Berry and French soon gave up the gridiron. Berry caught for eleven years with the Red Sox, White Sox, and A's, while French was a gifted pinch hitter and a career .303 batter for six seasons as an A.

When Berry graduated from Lafayette, his place at end was taken by Frank Grube, who caught for seven seasons in the AL, was a teammate of Berry's on the Chisox, and also played in the NFL.

After finishing his active career, Berry remained with Connie Mack as a coach until 1940. He officiated in the NFL from 1941 to 1961 and was also an American League ump from 1942 to 1962. In 1958 Charlie Berry had the unique experience of officiating the World Series and the NFL Championship Game, the sudden-death game, one of sports' all-time great events.

Whether it was Connie Mack's brief football experience back in 1902 or the fact that he liked college-educated men on his teams, he seemed to have a proclivity for hiring football stars. Besides Cochrane and French, he signed All-Americans Berry, Ace Parker, Sam Chapman, and Eric Tipton (though the latter two never played pro football).

Ace Parker was a highly acclaimed Duke athlete when he joined the A's in 1937. On April 30 of that year, he made his initial appearance at bat as a pinch hitter and hit a home run. This was the first time an American League rookie had ever hit a homer in his first at bat as a pinch hitter.

That fall Parker wanted to join the Brooklyn Dodgers of the NFL, but Connie Mack would not grant permission; however, by November the old gentleman relented and Ace entered the NFL, where he became a Hall of

Famer. His baseball career ended after his second season.

Other dual-sport players on the A's were Lyle Bigbee, Jim Castiglia, Bruno Haas, Bert Kuczynski, and Ernie Orwell.

Perhaps because they were always desperate for talent, the St. Louis Browns usually had a two-sport man on the team. By far the most notable was Ernie Nevers, a terrific all-round athlete from Stanford.

"When I finished in college in 1926, I was offered a $25,000 bonus by the Browns and another $25,000 bonus by the Duluth Eskimos of the NFL," Ernie recalled several years before his death. "I took both."

"My greatest thrill in baseball was just pitching to those famous players like Ruth [he gave up Babe's eighth and forty-first homers in 1927], Foxx, and others. My fondest recollection was one of the first times I faced Walter Johnson. I never saw his first two pitches. Johnson then called time and motioned the catcher out. When he got back, he told me Walter was going to groove it. When I uttered my disbelief, he replied that Walter always means what he says.

"Well, I started swinging as he wound up and hit the ball to the wall for a double. When I got to second, he was smiling for he had let a raw rookie look good."

In three years for the Browns, Nevers posted only a 6–12 record due to a sore arm. He then devoted his time to the gridiron. His biggest day in football was Thanksgiving Day of 1929. Playing for the Chicago Cardinals against the Bears, he scored 6 touchdowns and kicked 4 extra points, a total of 40 points, a record that has never been surpassed.

Though he had a brief NFL career as both a player and coach, his impact was such that he is a member of the Pro Football Hall of Fame.

Other Brownies who performed on the gridiron were outfielder Red Badgro, now in the Pro Football Hall of Fame; outfielder-third baseman Larry Bettencourt, now in the College Football Hall of Fame; catcher Russ Young; shortstop Jim Levey; and outfielder Pete Layden.

The most prominent dual-sport stars of the 1950s were Vic Janowicz, who won the 1950 Heisman Award as a junior at Ohio State, and Carroll Hardy from Colorado.

Janowicz caught for the 1953 Pirates with little success and switched to third the next season, again without success. That fall he joined the Washington Redskins and gave up the diamond sport. A terrific runner, passer, and kicker, he was the number-two scorer in the NFL the next season; however, a postseason accident finished his great sports career.

Carroll Hardy had been a defensive back and punter at Colorado when he joined the '49ers in 1955.

"I was picked as a defensive back and punter," Carroll recalls. "However, they had an unusual amount of injuries and I ended up playing in the offensive backfield with Y. A. Tittle, Hugh McElhenny, Joe Perry, and John Henry Johnson—all of whom made the Pro Football Hall of Fame."

"I had a pretty good season, caught 12 passes for 4 TDs, one of which was a 79-yarder from Tittle. Hank Greenberg, G.M. of the Indians, convinced me to concentrate on baseball."

Hardy then joined the Cleveland Indians for the 1958 season and later played until 1968 with the Boston Red Sox, Houston Astros, and Minnesota Twins.

"I am probably the only man to pinch-hit for Ted Williams, Roger Maris, and Carl Yastrzemski. On September 30, 1960, Ted was hitting against Hector Brown of the Orioles in the first inning when he fouled a ball off his leg and just walked off the field. Manager Pinky Higgins yelled at me to get up there and I promptly lined into a double play. I later found out I was the only man who had ever pinch-hit for Ted Williams.

"I hit for Roger while we were with the Indians as Billy Pierce, a lefty, was pitching. There were two men on in the eleventh, and I hit a ball I was positive was foul, but the ump called it fair and we won."

One of the last to try both sports until the present day was Tom Brown, a lefthanded, switch-hitting first sacker. Tom opened the 1963 season with the Senators but was soon back in the minors. He then opted for football, joined the Green Bay Packers in time to enjoy their most successful period, and is the only man to play in the Super Bowl and major league baseball. It would be twenty-four years until another athlete attempted both baseball and football.

Bo Jackson won the Heisman Award in 1985 but opted to play for the Kansas City Royals. After two seasons in the Royal outfield, he also became a running back for the Los Angeles Raiders and has successfully competed in both sports simultaneously.

Deion Sanders was the first-round draft choice of the Atlanta Falcons in 1989. During the same season he played outfield for the Yankees and defensive back for the Falcons, becoming one of a small group to hit a home run and score a touchdown in the same year.

Umpires have also been two-sport stars. Cal Hubbard, an American League arbitrator for twenty-five years, was such a fine football player that he has been elected to both the College and Professional Halls of Fame.

Hank Soar is a three-sport man. An AL man in blue for twenty-four years, he was also a star halfback for the Giants and briefly coached Providence in the BAA.

"My greatest baseball thrill," Hank stated, "was the day I was at first and Don Larsen pitched his perfect game. My only close call was on Jackie Robinson in the second and nobody complained. One of my best football days was the 1938 Championship Game, when I caught the winning TD pass. The basketball job was a fluke. I worked for the team and was the only one they could get to coach it that season."

With Soar on the 1943 and '44 Giants was guard Frank Umont, who called balls and strikes in the AL for nineteen years.

Bill Stewart is best remembered in sports as the ump who missed the Feller-Masi pickoff play in the 1948 Series, but Bill deserves better. An NL umpire for twenty-two years, he was the first American-born referee in the NHL, where he officiated for fourteen years. In 1937–38 he became coach of the Chicago Black Hawks. The team won but 14 games; however, they captured the Stanley Cup. The next season Bill was fired halfway into the schedule.

Because of the length of a baseball season and the physical demands of football, it takes a very talented man with exceptional endurance to play both in the same year. One of the most unusual groups to participate in both sports are the six who hit a home run and scored a touch-down the same year. This elite club includes Pid Purdy, Red Badgro, Ace Parker, Steve Filipowicz, Bo Jackson, and Deion Sanders.

Professional basketball has a history very similar to pro football. At the turn of the century several professional teams appeared, mostly on the East Coast. Eventually leagues appeared that were considered major leagues by some historians and minor leagues by others. The first professional basketball league to be considered a major league by most historians is the ABL, which existed from 1925 to 1931.

As the schedules of major league baseball and basketball were somewhat compatible, it is not surprising to find diamond stars playing the court sport for extra money and to stay in condition.

Perhaps the most successful of all the dual athletes was Gene Conley, who starred in both major league baseball and the NBA.

The 6'8" Conley joined the 1952 Boston Braves as a pitcher and the Celtics the same year as a C-F. For the next several years Gene concentrated on baseball with the Milwaukee Braves, pitching in one World Series and three All-Star Games. In 1969 he returned to the Celtics and proved a perfect backup man for the super stars of that team as they won three straight titles.

"There is no doubt my greatest thrill in sports came in the 1955 All-Star Game. I was the losing pitcher the previous year, and as this game was in Milwaukee, I really wanted to pitch. I finally got to in the twelfth inning and struck out Al Kaline, Mickey Vernon, and Al Rosen. We won on a Stan Musial home run in the bottom of the inning.

"One day I was sitting in front of my locker," Gene continued, "when coach Red Auerbach walked up and asked me if I realized I was the only man to have a World Series and NBA Championship ring. Until Red mentioned it, I was unaware of the fact."

The only member of the Baseball Hall of Fame who played major league basketball is shortstop Lou Boudreau.

Lou joined Cleveland in late 1938 and then played guard for the Hammond Ciesar All-Americans, where his fellow guard was John Wooden, who became one of the game's greatest coaches. The next season Boudreau was briefly a nonplaying coach.

A career .295 hitter, Lou hit over .300 four times in his career, leading the league in hitting in 1944 and batting a tremendous .355 in 1948, when he captured the MVP Award.

The Indians realized that twenty-four-year-old Boudreau was a natural leader and appointed him as manager in 1942. He won the World Series in 1948 and managed through 1950. He then spent six seasons managing the Red Sox and one with the Cubs.

Dick Groat led the nation's college basketball players in scoring as a junior at Duke. In 1952 he went directly from the campus to the Pittsburgh Pirates, becoming one of thirty-nine men to go directly to the big leagues and never play minor league ball.

"The Pirates were not going anywhere," Dick said, "so they had nothing to lose by putting me at short. That fall I played with Fort Wayne. I had returned to Duke to finish

my studies, and the owner of the team sent his private plane to take me to games. I then was called into the service, and when I got out, Branch Rickey of the Pirates convinced me the hard gym floor would ruin my legs for baseball, so I never returned to basketball, though it was my favorite game."

A fourteen-year player in the National League, Dick was captain of the World Champion 1960 Pirates, leading the league in hitting and winning the MVP Award. Dick played in a second Series with the Cards in 1964. A career .286 hitter, he surpassed the .300 mark four times.

Frank Baumholtz played the outfield for ten years in the senior circuit. In 1952 he finished second to Stan Musial in the batting race and posted a lifetime .290 mark. Frankie, a star at Ohio U., played for Youngstown of the NBL in 1946–47 and Cleveland of the BBA in 1947–48; he was a top scorer both years.

Dave DeBusschere and Ron Reed were forwards on the 1965–66 Detroit Pistons, where Dave was the player-coach. Both were aspiring major league pitchers whose careers took different turns. Dave's fame was made on the basketball court, while Ron made it on the diamonds of the National League.

DeBusschere's baseball career consisted of two undistinguished years on the mound for the White Sox; however, he had twelve brilliant seasons in the NBA. After six seasons with the Pistons, two as a player-coach, he joined the great Knicks of the early 1970s and enjoyed their championship seasons. He later served briefly as Commissioner of the ABA. His career scoring average was 16.1 per game.

Reed spent nineteen years playing for several NL teams. As a starter for Atlanta, his best season was an 18–10 mark in 1969. When he joined the Phillies, he became a relief artist and in 1979 led the league in relief wins. Ron appeared in five World Series games for the Phillies and posted a career record of 146–140, with 103 saves and an ERA of 3.46.

Steve Hamilton played for the 1958–59 Minneapolis Lakers, but, like Reed, he found his talents were more successful in baseball. A southpaw, he pitched for twelve years in both leagues and, upon joining the Yankees, became an outstanding bullpen man, appearing in three games of the 1963 and '64 World Series, recording one save. Steve's career ERA was a very respectable 3.05.

Several major league players who had brief pro basketball careers were George Crowe, a top National League pinch hitter for ten years; Irv Noren, who played the outfield in both leagues for twelve seasons; and Del Rice, a longtime catcher.

Howie Schultz, of whom great slugging feats were expected when he joined the Dodgers in 1943, found greater success as a scorer in the NBL and NBA. In 1950 he was a player-coach for Anderson of the NBL. Another NBL coach was Red Rolfe, the great third baseman of the Bronx Bombers of the 1930s, who led Toronto of the NBL for a single season.

The only dual-sport player to pitch a no-hitter was Bill McCahan, who joined the Philadelphia Athletics after his military duty. In 1947 he threw a no-hit game against the Washington Senators.

Chuck Connors, who had brief careers in both professional baseball and basketball, found his real calling in

T.V. series and the movies, gaining genuine stardom in those fields.

The latest man to try both sports was Danny Ainge, who after three seasons with the Toronto Blue Jays joined the Boston Celtics, where his great athletic ability became more apparent.

Key

The following are keys for abbreviations used in Two-Sport Stars.

The name of the player will be followed by his position and then the college he attended, if any. CHF after the player's name indicates that he has been inducted into the College Football Hall of Fame. PHF indicates induction into the Professional Football Hall of Fame and BHF indicates induction into the Baseball Hall of Fame.

There have been several professional football leagues since 1920. Prior to that professional teams did not play in any organized leagues. The leagues are:

AAFC	All-American Football Conference	1946–49
AFL	American Football League	1926
		1936–37
		1940–41
		1960–69
APFL	American Professional Football League	1920–21
CFL	Canadian Football League	1958–present
NFL	National Football League	1922–present
WFL	World Football League	1974–75

Major league basketball has had a multitude of professional leagues since the 1890s. Many of these leagues were in existence for only a few years before folding. New leagues later appeared and often adopted the name of a former league. The leagues and their life spans are:

ABA	American Basketball Association	1967–76
ABL	American Basketball League	1903–04
		1925–31
		1933–46
		1961–63
BAA	Basketball Association of America	1947–49
CBL	Central Basketball League	1906–12

CSL	Connecticut State League	1917–18
		1920–21
EBL	Eastern Basketball League	1909–18
		1919–23
		1931–33
EL	Eastern League	1909–18
		1919–23
		1931–33
IL	Interstate League (New York Area)	1915–17
		1919–20
MBC	Midwest Basketball Conference	1935–37
MBL	Metropolitan Basketball League	1921–28
		1931–33
NBA	National Basketball Association	1949–present
NBL	National Basketball League	1898–1904
		1926–27
		1929–30
		1932–33
		1937–49
		1950–51
NYSL	New York State League	1911–15
		1916–17
		1919–23
PBLA	Professional Basketball League of America	1947–48
PSL	Pennsylvania State League	1914–18
		1919–21
WBT	World Basketball Tournament	1938–48
WMBL	Western Massachusetts Basketball League	1903–04

The only professional hockey major league mentioned in this table is the National Hockey League (NHL), which has been in existence since 1917.

BASEBALL—FOOTBALL

Ed Abbaticchio
Fullback, Mt. St. Mary's
1895–1900, Latrobe.

Cliff Aberson
Halfback
1946, Green Bay, NFL.

Red Badgro (PFH)
End, Southern California
1927–28, New York Yankees, NFL; 1930–35, New York Giants, NFL; 1936, Brooklyn, NFL.

George Barclay
Halfback, Bucknell, Lafayette
1896–98, Greensburg.

Norman Bass
Defensive Halfback, University of the Pacific
1964, Denver, AFL.

Jim Bedford
End, Southern Methodist University
1925, Rochester, NFL; 1926, Hammond, NFL.

Dutch Bergman
Head Coach, Notre Dame
1943, Washington, NFL.

Charles Berry (CHF)
End/Linesman, Lafayette
1925–26, Pottsville, NFL; 1940–60, NFL head linesman.

Joe Berry
Halfback, Pennsylvania, Muhlenberg
1921, Rochester, NFL.

Larry Bettencourt (CHF)
Center, St. Mary's
1933, Green Bay, NFL.

Hugo Bezdek (CHF)
Coach, Chicago
1937–38, Cleveland, NFL.

Lyle Bigbee
End, Oregon
1922, Milwaukee.

Tom Brown
Defensive Halfback, Maryland
1964–68, Green Bay, NFL; 1969, Washington, NFL.

Garyland Buckeye
Guard
1920, Chicago Tigers, NFL; 1921–24, Chicago Cardinals; 1926, Chicago, AFL.

Bruce Caldwell
Halfback, Brown, Yale
1928, New York Giants.

Ralph Capron
Halfback, Minnesota
1920, Chicago Tigers, NFL.

Jim Castiglia
Halfback, Georgetown
1941, 1945–46, Philadelphia; 1947, Baltimore, AAFC; 1947–48, Washington.

Chuck Corgan
Halfback, Arkansas
1924–26, Kansas City, NFL; 1926, Hartford; 1927, New York Giants.

Fred Corlius
Halfback, Brown
1900–01, Homestead; 1902, Pittsburgh.

Paul Desjardien (CHF)
Guard, Chicago University
1920, Chicago Tigers, NFL; 1922, Minneapolis.

Charles Dressen
Quarterback
1920, Decatur; 1922–23, Racine.

Paddy Driscoll (PHF, CHF)
Quarterback, Northwestern
1919, Hammond; 1920, Decatur, APFL; 1920–25, Chicago Cardinals; 1926–29, Chicago Bears; 1942–45, 1956–57, Chicago Bears, head coach.

Oscar Eckhardt
Halfback, Texas
1928, New York Giants.

Steve Filipowicz
Quarterback, Fordham
1945–46, New York Giants.

Paul Florence
End, Loyola
1920, Chicago Cardinals.

Walter French
Halfback, Army
1922, Rochester; 1925, Pottsville.

David Fultz
Halfback, Brown
1900–01, Homestead.

John Gammons
Halfback, Brown
1898–99, Duquesne; 1900–01, Homestead; 1902, Pittsburgh.

Walter Gilbert
Halfback, Valparaiso
1923–26, Duluth.

Norman Glockson
Guard
1922, Racine.

Frank Grube
End, Lafayette
1928, New York Yankees.

Bruno Haas
Halfback, Worcester
1921, Cleveland; 1921, Akron; 1922, Dayton.

Hinky Haines
Halfback, Penn State
1925–28, New York Giants; 1929, 1931, Staten Island.

George Halas (PHF)
End, Coach, Owner, Illinois
1919, Hammond; 1920, Decatur, APFL; 1921, Chicago, APFL; 1922–83, Chicago, NFL.

Carroll Hardy
Halfback, Colorado
1955, SF, NFL.

Cal Hubbard (BHF, PHF, CHF)
Tackle, Centenary, Geneva
1927–28, 1936, New York Giants; 1929–33, Green Bay; 1936, Pittsburgh.

Bo Jackson
Halfback, Auburn
1987– , LA Raiders, NFL.

Vic Janowicz (CHF)
Halfback, Ohio State
1954–55, Washington.

Rex Johnston
Halfback, Southern California
1960, Pittsburgh.

Matt Kinzer
Punter, Purdue
1987, Detroit.

Bert Kuczynski
End, Pennsylvania
1943, Detroit; 1946, Philadelphia.

Pete Layden
Halfback, Texas
1948–49, New York, AAFC; 1950, New York
Yankees.

Jim Levey
Halfback
1934–36, Pittsburgh.

Dean Lok
Quarterback, Michigan State
1962, New York, AFL.

Wally MacPhee
Halfback, Princeton
1926, Providence.

Howard Maple
Halfback, Oregon State
1930, Chicago Cardinals.

Walter Masters
Halfback, Pennsylvania
1936, Philadelphia; 1943, Cardinals; 1944,
Cardinals–Pittsburgh.

Christy Mathewson (BHF)
Fullback, Bucknell
1902, Pittsburgh Stars.

Jim McKean
Quarterback,
1964–65, Montreal, CFL.

John Mohardt
Halfback, Notre Dame
1922–23, Chicago Cardinals; 1924, Racine; 1925,
Chicago Bears; 1926, Chicago, AFL.

Charles Moran
Halfback, Tennessee
1905–06, Massillon.

Earle Neale (PHF, CHF)
Halfback, West Virginia Wesleyan
1916–17, Canton; 1918, Dayton; 1941–50, Philadelphia, coach.

Ernie Nevers (PHF, CHF)
Fullback, Stanford
1926–27, Duluth; 1929–31, Chicago Cardinals;
1939, Cardinals, head coach.

Ossie Orwell
Halfback, Luther
1926, Milwaukee.

Ace Parker (PHF, CHF)
Halfback, Duke
1937–41, Brooklyn, NFL; 1945, Boston; 1946,
New York, AAFC.

John Perrin
Halfback, Michigan
1926, Hartford.

Al Pierotti
C/G/T, Washington & Lee
1920, Akron, NFL; 1920, Cleveland; 1921, New
York; 1923–24, Milwaukee; 1923, Racine; 1926,
Boston, AFL; 1927, Providence; 1929, Boston.

Pid Purdy
Halfback, Beloit
1926–27, Green Bay.

Dick Reichle
End, Illinois
1923, Milwaukee.

Deion Sanders
Defensive Halfback, Florida State
1989– , Atlanta.

John Scalzi
Halfback, Georgetown
1931, Brooklyn.

John Singleton
Halfback
1929, Dayton.

Red Smith
Halfback, Notre Dame
1927, 1929, Green Bay; 1928, 1931, New York
Giants; 1928, New York Yankees; 1930, Newark.

Hank Soar
Halfback, Providence
1936, Boston, AFL; 1937–44, 1946, New York
Giants.

Evar Swanson
End, Lombard
1924, Milwaukee; 1925, Rock Isle; 1925–27,
Chicago Cardinals.

Jim Thorpe (PHF, CHF)
Halfback, Carlisle
1915–19, Canton; 1920, Canton, APFA; 1921,
Cleveland, NFL; 1922–23, Oorang; 1924, Rock
Isle; 1925, New York Giants; 1926, Canton; 1928,
Chicago Cardinals.

Andy Tomasic
Halfback, Temple
1942, 1946, Pittsburgh.

Frank Umont
Guard
1943–45, New York Giants.

Louis Urban
End, Boston College
1921–23, Buffalo.

Joe Vance
Halfback, Southwest Texas
1931, Brooklyn.

Ernie Vick (CHF)
Center, Michigan
1925, 1928, Detroit; 1927–28, Chicago Bears.

Tom Whalen
End/Center, Georgetown, Notre Dame
1920, Canton; 1921, Cleveland.

Mike Wilson
End, Lehigh
1923–24, Rock Isle.

Hoge Workman
Halfback, Ohio State
1924, 1931, Cleveland; 1932, New York Giants.

Ab Wright
Halfback, Oklahoma A&M
1930, Frank.

Tom Yewcic
Quarterback, Michigan State
1961–66, Boston, AFL.

Russ Young
Halfback
1925, Dayton.

BASEBALL—BASKETBALL

Danny Ainge
Guard, Brigham Young
1981–89, Boston; 1989– , Sacramento.

Ernie Andres
Guard/Forward, Indiana
1939–40, 1945–48, Indianapolis, NBL.

Babe Barna
Forward, West Virginia
1939–40, Clarksburg, WBT.

Rex Barney
Guard
1947–48, Omaha, PBLA.

Bill Barrett
Guard/Forward
1921–22, Worcester, IL.

Frank Baumholtz
Guard, Ohio University
1945–46, Youngstown, NBL; 1946–47, Cleveland,
BAA.

Bozie Berger
Forward, Maryland
1938–39, Washington, ABL.

Hank Biasetti
Guard, Assumption (Canada)
1946–47, Toronto, NBL.

Lou Boudreau (BHF)
Guard/Forward, Illinois
1938–39, Hammond, NBL; 1939–40, Hammond,
coach, NBL.

Art Bramhall
Guard/Forward
1929–31, Chicago, ABL.

Frank Bruggy
Forward
1909–10, Elizabeth, EL; 1913–14, Gloversville,
NYSL; 1914–15, South Philadelphia, EL, Gloversville, NYSL; 1915–16, Kingston, Elizabeth, North
Hudson, IL; 1916–17, Paterson, IL; 1917–18, An-
sonia, CSL; Providence–Scranton, PSL;
1919–20, Germantown, EL, Scranton, PSL
(coach), Jersey City, IL; 1920–21, Scranton, PSL
(coach), Germantown, EL, Easthamp-
ton–Springfield, IL; 1921–22, Brooklyn, MBL,
Scranton-Wilkes-Barre, EL; 1922–23, Elizabeth,
MBL (coach), Atlantic City, EL; 1924–25, Paterson, MBL.

Frank Carswell
Guard, Rice
1947–48, Houston, PBLA, Flint, NBL.

Gene Conley
Forward, Washington State
1952–53, 1958–61, Boston; 1962–64, New York,
NBA.

Chuck Connors
Center/Forward, Seton Hall
1945–46, Rochester, NBL; 1946–48, Boston,
BAA.

Jerry Conway
Guard/Forward, St. Anselm
1919–20, Turners Falls, IL; 1920–21, Holyoke, IL;
1921–22, Holyoke, IL, Glens Falls; 1922–23, Holyoke, IL, Albany, NYSL; 1925–26, Washington,
ABL; 1927–28, Albany, MBL.

Bill Crouch
Forward/Guard, Michigan, Eastern Michigan
1935–26, Windsor, MBC.

George Crowe
Forward/Center, Indiana Central
1946–48, New York, WBT; 1948–49, Dayton,
NBL.

Snake Deal
Center/Forward
1898–99, Germantown, Philadelphia, NBL;
1899–1900, Chester, Camden, NBL; 1900–01,
Philadelphia, NBL; 1901–03, Camden, NBL;
1903–04, Pittsfield–Chicopee–Springfield,
WMBL; 1905–06, East Falls, PBL; 1906–08, East
Liverpool, CBL; 1908–10, Johnstown, CBL;
1914–15, Tamaqua, PSL.

Dave DeBusschere
Forward, Detroit University
1962–69, Detroit; 1968–74, New York; 1975–76, commissioner, ABA.

Brooks Dowd
Forward, Lehigh, Springfield
1916–17, Mohawk, NYSL; 1919–20, Springfield, IL, Mohawk, NYSL; 1920–21, Springfield (coach), IL, Mohawk, NYSL; 1921–22, Mohawk, NYSL, Springfield, IL; 1922–23, Springfield, IL; 1925–26, Boston, ABL; 1926–27, Baltimore, ABL.

Grant Dunlap
Forward
College of the Pacific, Occidental
1947–48, Birmingham, PBLA; 1950–51, Anderson, NBL.

Joe Evers
Forward
1913–14, Troy, NYSL; 1915–16, Carbondale, PSL; 1916–17, Hudson, NYSL, Nanticoke, PSL; 1919–20, Troy, NYSL; 1920–21, Cohoes, NYSL; 1921–22, Gloversville–Troy, NYSL; 1922–23, Troy–Schenectady, NYSL; 1927–28, Troy (coach), MBL.

Frankie Frisch (BHF)
Guard/Forward, Fordham
1919–20, New York, IL.

Les Fuchs
Referee, John Marshall
1938–46, ABL.

Johnny Gee
Center/Forward, Michigan
1946–47, Syracuse, NBL.

Tom Gorman
Forward
1944–45, New York, ABL; 1945–46, Trenton, ABL.

Don Grate
Forward/Guard, Ohio State
1947–48, Indiana, NBL; 1949–50, Sheboygan.

Hank Greenberg (BHF)
Center/Forward, New York University
1931–32, Brooklyn Jewish Center, MBL; 1932–33, Brooklyn Jewels, MBL.

Dick Groat
Guard, Duke
1952–53, Fort Wayne, NBA.

Steve Hamilton
Forward/Center, Morehead State
1959–60, Minnesota, NBA.

Walter Hammond
Forward, Colgate
1919–20, Amsterdam, NYSL; 1920–21, Westfield, IL; 1920–21, 1922–23, Amsterdam, NYSL.

Bucky Harris (BHF)
Guard
1915–18, Pittston, PSL; 1917–18, Bridgeport, Jersey City, CSL; 1919–20, Pittston, PSL; 1919–20, Paterson, Brooklyn, IL; 1920–21, Pittston, PSL; 1923–24, Glens Falls, NYSL.

Doug Harvey
Referee, San Diego State
1967–69, ABA.

Buddy Hassett
Guard, Manhattan
1933–34, Union City, ABL; 1934–35, Jersey, ABL.

Rick Herrscher
Guard, Southern Methodist University
1961–62, Hawaii, ABL.

Orel Hildebrand
Forward, Butler
1935–36, Indianapolis, MBC.

Waite Hoyt (BHF)
Forward, Middlebury
1925–26, Brooklyn, ABL.

Carl Husta
Forward/Guard
1925–30, Cleveland; 1930–31, Cleveland, Fort Wayne, ABL.

Ted Kearns
Guard/Forward
1925–26, Washington; 1926–27, Baltimore–Washington; 1927–28, Philadelphia; 1928–29, Trenton; 1929–30, Syracuse, ABL.

Al Kellett
Center, Penn State
1926–28, Philadelphia; 1928–29, Trenton–Chicago; 1929–30, Chicago; 1930–31, Brooklyn, ABL.

Fritz Knothe
Forward, Pennsylvania
1925–26, Passaic, MBL; 1926–27, Baltimore, ABL, Kingston, MBL; 1927–28, Rochester, ABL, Kingston, MBL; 1928–29, Paterson, ABL.

Pip Koehler
Guard, Penn State
1927–28, Fort Wayne; 1929–31, Toledo, ABL.

Stan Landes
Referee
1953–54, NBA

Bert Lewis
Forward
1925–26, Buffalo, ABL.

Jerry Loeber
Referee, Rhode Island
1969–76, NBA.

Bill McCahan
Forward/Guard, Duke
1928–49, Syracuse, NBL; 1943–44, 1945–46, Wilmington, ABL.

Mel McGaha
Guard, Arkansas
1948–49, New York, NBL.

Ralph Miller
Guard
1925–30, Fort Wayne; 1930–31, Fort Wayne, Chicago, ABL.

Cotton Nash
Forward/Center, Kentucky
1964–65, Los Angeles, San Francisco; 1967–68, Kentucky, ABA.

Irv Noren
Forward, Pasadena College
1946–47, Chicago, NBL.

Ron Reed
Forward, Notre Dame
1966–67, Detroit, NBA.

Del Rice
Forward
1943–44, Rochester, WBT; 1945–46, Rochester, NBL.

Dick Ricketts
Forward, Duquesne
1955–56, St. Louis; 1955–57, Rochester; 1957–58, Cincinnati, NBA.

Harry Riconda
Forward
1926–27, Philadelphia; 1928–29, Paterson; 1929–30, New York, ABL.

Red Rolfe
Coach, Dartmouth
1946–47, Toronto, NBL.

Rusty Saunders
Forward
1925–26, Brooklyn, Washington; 1926–27, Washington; 1927–28, Brooklyn, Fort Wayne; 1928–31, Fort Wayne, ABL; 1940–41, Detroit; 1945–46, Indianapolis, NBL.

John Scalzi
Referee, Georgetown
1948–49, BAA; 1949–51, NBA.

Howie Schultz
Center/Forward, Hamline
1947–49, Anderson, NBL; 1949–50, PC; 1949–50, Fort Wayne, NBA; 1952–53, Minnesota.

Danny Silva
Forward
1921–22, Worcester, IL.

John Simmons
Guard, New York University
1946–47, Boston, BAA.

Hank Soar
Head Coach, Providence
1947–48, Providence, BAA.

Keith Thomas
Guard/Referee, Kansas State
1947–48, Kansas City, PBLA; 1961–62, referee, ABL.

Bucky Walters
Center
1931–32, Philadelphia Moose, EBL; 1932–33, Philadelphia Broadcasters, EBL.

Ed Wineapple
Forward Providence
1929–30, Syracuse, ABL.

BASEBALL—HOCKEY

Bill Stewart
Referee/Coach
1928–37, 1940–44, NHL referee; 1937–38, Chicago, NHL, coach.

Managers and Coaches

Fred Stein

The job [managing] then, on the face of it, seems virtually impossible to perform. Not only must a man be a strategist and tactician with sophisticated knowledge of a highly detailed game and have the capability of making snap decisions in critical moments, bt he must also maintain harmony on a squad of twenty-five men of diverse social, economic, cultural, ethnic, and racial backgrounds during seven months of continuous traveling and constant pressures from within and without. He must be the soother of the delicate ego and the builder of the broken self-confidence. He must disguise his despair and disappointment, temper his elation, and maintain his optimism. He must deal daily with an inquiring press, be polite to countless strangers, and reassure his employers, who have placed the heart of a multimillion-dollar franchise in his care. He schemes and scrambles to keep it all going, to somehow get more spring into a man's legs and snap into his swing. And if he is a realist—and they all are—he knows that one day the general manager will call him into the office or appear suddenly at the hotel in the middle of a road trip and tell him that "for the best interests of the club we have decided. . . ."

from *The Man in the Dugout*, by Donald Honig

The Baseball Manager

Baseball as we know it was established as a "gentleman's sport" by the 1840s and had attained a degree of commercial success by the end of the 1860s. Sometime within this transition from a participatory, upper-class social game to an organized professional, spectator sport for mass consumption, there developed a need for accountability. Someone had to be responsible for the team's success, both as a sporting endeavor and as a money-making enterprise.

Harry Wright was the first important baseball manager, and the functions thrust upon him in the 1860s were typical of the workload carried by many of the managers of that period. A former professional cricket player, Wright saw his first baseball game at age twenty-two, and it was love at first sight. A decade later, he helped organize the famous Cincinnati Red Stockings, the first all-salaried team, which won 84 consecutive games in 1869–1870. Wright's duties at the time included the following: field manager, center fielder, relief pitcher, team trainer, tracker of team baseballs and field equipment, disciplinarian, scheduler of games and travel arrangements, checker of gate receipts, and bursar.

Wright continued his managing career with the advent of "organized baseball" in 1871, winning four straight pennants with the Boston Red Stockings from 1872 through 1875. He managed the National League entry at Boston through 1881, then managed Providence for two seasons, and Philadelphia from 1884 through 1893. The highly moral, immensely popular Wright is credited with playing the dominant role in establishing the integrity of professional baseball in its critical, formative years.

It bothered Wright to hear that other managers felt they could do as well as he had done with his players. He felt that managing a team effectively involved handling players with proper recognition of their human frailties as well as capitalization of their physical skills. To a young hopeful, writing to ask what he had to do to become a professional player, Wright could be fatherly and helpful. He suggested to one young man that he develop the necessary skills—become a "sure catch," a good "thrower," a reliable batter, and a good runner—all by devoted practice. Wright added a wonderfully homespun touch, admonishing the young man to ". . . eat hearty. Roast beef rare will aid, live regularly, keep good hours, and abstain from intoxicating drinks and tobacco."

The baseball manager's role became more clearly defined in the 1870–1900 period, as increased revenues permitted clubs to hire people—"managers" akin to today's general managers—to handle such administrative functions as monitoring gate receipts, paying salaries, and supervising equipment and stadium operations. But these business managers, twenty-eight of whom have been carried in the Macmillan *Encyclopedia* as managers, never filled out a lineup card or accompanied the team on a road trip. The research of Rich Topp and Bob Tiemann has set the matter straight in this volume. Scheduling of games became the function of league offices, relieving the manager of this responsibility. Still, for economic reasons, the on-field manager (or "captain," as he was often designated) usually was expected to perform double duty—serving as a player as well as the field boss. He was also responsible for disciplining players, keeping them in condition, and, depending on circumstances, handling player transactions. The 1890s in particular featured increased emphasis on scientific baseball, and the strategies employed by managers became a matter of increased interest and importance.

Adrian "Cap" Anson was the most prominent manager and player of the 1880s and '90s. The massive (for the time) first baseman hit .334 over twenty-two National League seasons and .336 for his full twenty-seven-year career, and was the first National League player with more than 3,000 career hits. A gruff, no-nonsense type, Anson ranked high on the all-time managers list with a .578 won-and-lost percentage over twenty-one seasons as a manager. He directed Chicago to five pennants in his first eight seasons as a manager.

The outspoken, mustachioed Iowa native was a stern taskmaster who ruled his club with an iron hand. He was an innovative manager—he utilized spring training for conditioning purposes, encouraged base stealing, rotated pitchers with contrasting styles, used signals, and employed the hit-and-run play. On the down side, the extremely conservative Anson played an important role in barring black players from organized baseball. The rough-hewn Anson had little of the philosophical concern for the game which characterized the gentle, high-minded Harry Wright. Yet Anson, not Wright, became the principal hero to the crowds of the era.

Ned Hanlon was an important manager in the 1890s, a prime exponent of the rough-and-ready, anything-to-win approach which was typical of the play of that decade. Hanlon's famed Baltimore Orioles won three successive pennants in 1894–1896, then finished in second place twice before Hanlon moved to the Brooklyn club, which he led to pennant wins in 1899 and 1900. The bookish-appearing Hanlon headed a Baltimore cast which included such legendary players as John McGraw, Wee Willie Keller, Wilbert Robinson, Joe Kelley, and Hugh Jennings. Even allowing for hyperbole, the club was noted for its "inside baseball" execution and rowdy antics reminiscent of the Katzenjammer Kids. Baseball scholars differ as to who invented strategies like the squeeze play, the "Baltimore chop," and judicious doctoring of the baseball diamond, but there is little doubt that the Orioles, under Hanlon's direction, perfected these techniques.

The managerial role in the 1900–1920 period was marked by continuing emphasis on scientific baseball, scratching out runs in a dead-ball era when runs were hard to come by. During these two decades, the game reached new heights of popularity, and some managers, along with star players, became national heroes.

Connie Mack and John McGraw were the towering managerial figures of the period. Mack (his name mercifully shortened from Cornelius McGillicuddy) was a journeyman catcher whose managing career began with Pittsburgh of the National League in 1894. After three seasons, he managed Milwaukee of the Western League until 1901, when he and Benjamin Shibe were awarded the Philadelphia franchise in the new American League.

Nicknamed "The Tall Tactician," Mack put together, and then took apart, two dominating teams in two different eras. Between 1910 and 1914, his Athletics won four pennants before, feeling the need for financial retrenchment, he began shedding such high-priced stars as second baseman Eddie Collins and pitchers Jack Coombs, Eddie Plank, and Chief Bender. As a result, the A's finished dead last from 1915 through 1921.

Beginning in the mid-1920s, Mack gathered several future Hall of Famers—Mickey Cochrane, Al Simmons, Jimmie Foxx, and Lefty Grove—and the A's won three straight pennants starting in 1929. However, with the Depression deepening and attendance dropping drastically, Mack again was forced to sell his stars. The rest was all downhill for the cash-poor Mack as the A's finished in the second division from 1934 through 1950, his last year as manager.

During Mack's incredible fifty-three-year managerial career, he won and lost more games (3,731 and 3,948) than any other major league pilot. In addition to his records, he is remembered for managing from the bench in street clothes and for deploying his fielders (usually with remarkable precision) with a wave of his ever-present scorecard. Many fans felt that the canny Irishman remained at the helm for too long, simply because he couldn't be fired. They pointed to the Athletics' ineffectual showing over the last seventeen years of his tenure, and his tendency in later years to nod off on the bench. Regardless, baseball men respected his shrewd judgment of player talent, his ability to manage unlettered eccentrics and college men with equal effectiveness, his skill in building great teams in both the dead- and live-ball eras, and his entrepreneurial skill in keeping his team afloat on a financial shoestring. Mack's players revered the dignified, erect, spindly old man with the pronounced New England accent—a link between them and the years when baseball was barely beyond its infancy.

John McGraw shared Connie Mack's Irish background and his managerial acumen, but they were direct opposites in most other respects. "The Little Napoleon" was a scrappy little third baseman whose .334 lifetime batting average, fielding skill, and driving aggressiveness would have justified Hall of Fame recognition if his managing career had not done so. McGraw was the field ringleader of Ned Hanlon's Baltimore Orioles of the 1890s. After moving to St. Louis of the National League in 1900, he went to the new American League, accepting Ban Johnson's offer to manage the Baltimore club in 1901.

Unable to get along with Johnson, McGraw jumped at the chance to manage the New York Giants in July 1902. The Giants became the most successful National League team for the next thirty years, with McGraw engendering high excitement and emotions. As famed sportswriter Grantland Rice wrote, "His very walk across the field in a hostile town is a challenge to the multitude." McGraw is credited with stimulating the growth of baseball during the 1900–1920 period, just before the advent of the lively-ball era.

Most experts consider McGraw the greatest manager ever. He ranks second only to Mack in major league games managed (4,845) and in games won (2,816). His teams captured ten National League pennants in thirty years with only two second-division finishes. McGraw's managerial genius produced strategic and tactical innovations, and attracted and developed many superb players. His career evoked continuous arguments, fistfights, and controversies with league presidents, owners, umpires, opposing managers and players, and off-the-field acquaintances. However, this bon vivant, raconteur, and man of varied nonbaseball interests was also famous for helping downtrodden former players.

Clark Griffith, Fred Clarke, and Frank Chance were three other prominent managers of the 1900-1920 period. Griffith had pitching credentials (240–141) which would have justified his election to the Hall of Fame as a player as well as a manager. The pocket-sized righthander, nicknamed "The Old Fox," relied upon control, guile, and uncanny skill at nicking or otherwise doctoring the ball to fool the hitters. He won at least 21 games a year from 1894 through 1899, then went 24–7 while managing the Chicago club of the new American League to the pennant in 1901.

At the request of American League President Ban Johnson, Griffith managed the New York Highlanders from 1903 through 1908. He managed Cincinnati in 1909–1911 before purchasing a 10 percent interest in the Washington Senators. During his managerial tenure with the Senators from 1912 to 1920, Griffith operated with little capital, as evidenced by only two first-division finishes during the period, both largely attributable to the superhuman efforts of speedballing Walter Johnson. Griffith gained controlling interest in the Senators in 1920 and vacated the manager's slot to become club president.

Fred Clarke, another outstanding player, was a field manager in nineteen of his twenty-one major league seasons. The compact outfielder had a .315 batting average while collecting 2,708 hits. He hit a career high .406 in 1897, stole over 30 bases in seven seasons, and was a superb left fielder.

Clarke managed Louisville from 1897 to 1899 and Pittsburgh for the next sixteen years, ranking among the top managers with 1,602 wins and a .576 winning percentage. Led by Clarke himself, all-time great shortstop Honus Wagner, and center fielder Ginger Beaumont, the Pirates won consecutive pennants in 1901–1903, then won the World Championship in 1909. The hallmarks of the energetic Clarke's teams were their excellent physical condition and tight discipline, both on and off the field.

Clubs managed by Frank Chance, along with McGraw and Clarke, won every National League pennant from 1901 through 1913. Chance is best remembered as the first baseman of the famous "Tinker to Evers to Chance" double-play combination of the Chicago Cubs, as the Cubs won three straight pennants in 1906–1908 and added another in 1910.

Chance, a smart, natural leader, took over the Cubs in midseason of 1905 from Frank Selee, himself a great but little-remembered pilot, and remained as manager through the 1912 season. During his 7½-year tenure, the "Peerless Leader's" clubs won 753 games and lost only 379, for a remarkable .665 winning percentage. Handicapped by recurring headaches attributable to several beanings, Chance withdrew from active play and later managed the New York Highlanders in 1913–1914 and the Boston Red Sox in 1923, but with none of his earlier success.

The lively ball changed major league baseball and managerial strategy after 1920. Such offensive baseball tactics as the stolen base, the sacrifice bunt in early innings, and the squeeze play were virtually ignored as the long ball came into vogue. "Big bang" baseball became the rule rather than the exception, with only occasional aberrations such as the deadened ball used by the National League in the early 1930s and the inferior baseball offensive talent during World War Two. Big-inning baseball strategies had largely replaced those of the dead-ball era, and baseball managers were forced to adapt to the changes.

Connie Mack successfully shifted his managerial focus to the new offensive game, and the Athletics won pennants in 1929–1931. John McGraw won four successive pennants in the early twenties, largely on the strength of strong, well-balanced teams rather than offensive powerhouses. After 1924 McGraw's failure to adapt to the power game prevented him from winning any more pennants before he left the game in 1932.

The powerful Yankees of the twenties, thirties, and early forties were famed for their power hitting complemented by exemplary pitching and fielding. Yankee managers Miller Huggins and Joe McCarthy were the beneficiaries of crushing offenses led by Babe Ruth, Lou Gehrig, Bob Meusel, Earle Combs, Tony Lazzeri, and Bill Dickey, then later by Joe DiMaggio, Tom Henrich, Joe Gordon and Charlie Keller.

Miller Huggins was a tiny second baseman, considered an excellent fielder but a weak hitter (.265 lifetime average with little extra-base power), whose offensive forte was drawing walks and stealing bases. The bright "Mighty Mite," a Cincinnati native and law school graduate, managed the St. Louis Cardinals in 1913–1917 with modest success. He was then hired by Yankee owner Col. Jacob Ruppert against the wishes of co-owner Col. Tillinghast Huston, who was overseas in World War One action at the time.

Huggins's masterstroke was in convincing the Yankees to purchase Babe Ruth from the financially troubled Boston Red Sox. Ruth's powerful hitting was largely responsible for the Yankees' developing dynasty, which brought Huggins six pennant wins in twelve seasons with New York. Ruth was important to Huggins in another respect: maintaining player discipline. Ruth regularly broke club rules until Huggins fined him $5,000 (a lot of money in 1925) and suspended him. The Yankees' management strongly supported Huggins, and Ruth and his fellow recalcitrants bowed to the diminutive Huggins's authority.

Huggins died unexpectedly at fifty while managing the Yankees in 1929, and Joe McCarthy took over as the Yankees' manager a year later. Another weak-hitting infielder, "Marse Joe" never made it to the major leagues as a player. After gaining recognition as one of the leading minor league managers, McCarthy managed the Chicago Cubs from 1926 to 1930, winning the National League pennant in 1929. McCarthy went on to win eight pennants and seven World Championships in fifteen full seasons as the Yankees' manager, with only one finish as low as fourth place. Under McCarthy the Yankees did not merely outshine the competition, they annihilated them, winning the 1936 flag by a record 19½ games and winning the 1932, 1938, and 1939 World Series in four games straight.

McCarthy's teams were noted for their attention to detail and their teamwork, as well as their overpowering talent. McCarthy was a strict, if undemonstrative, disciplinarian (ties and jackets were compulsory, and even pipe smoking was discouraged) and was adept at maintaining the defensive excellence which undergirded his teams' successes. McCarthy ranks first among all managers with a .614 winning percentage.

Charles Dillon "Casey" Stengel was the third in a line of great Yankee managers. He was a sometimes comic journeyman outfielder (.284 career batting average) whose playing career is best remembered for his sparkling hitting in the 1923 World Series, when he won two games for the Giants against the Yankees with home runs.

The lovable "Old Perfessor" with the great sense of humor, total recall of past game situations, and singular gift of gab (he specialized in long-winded non sequiturs) began his fabled major league managerial career with Brooklyn in 1934. After three mediocre seasons with the Dodgers and one season (1937) when he was paid *not* to manage the Dodgers, Stengel spent six seasons managing the Boston Braves, still unable to rise above the second-division level.

After managing in the high minors from 1944 to 1948, Stengel signed with the Yankees for 1949. He managed the club to an unprecedented five consecutive pennants, finished in second place in 1954 (despite 103 wins), then won four more consecutive pennants before falling to third place in 1959. He closed out his stint with the Yankees with another pennant win in 1960, making it a phenomenal total of ten pennants and seven World Championships in twelve seasons. Dismissed by the Yankees as "too old," Stengel managed the fledgling New York Mets from 1962 to 1965, finishing in last place each season, before retiring two-thirds into the 1965 season. Stengel had a won–lost percentage of .508 for twenty-five seasons, ranking fourth in games managed and seventh in games won.

Huggins and McCarthy were essentially orthodox, conservative managers who consistently turned out magnificent teams with magnificent players. Stengel, also gifted with great players—DiMaggio, Yogi Berra, Phil Rizzuto, Whitey Ford, Mickey Mantle—added another dimension to managing. He rose above crushing injuries to his stars and obtained high levels of performance from unexpected sources. Even more remarkable, he played the percentages and played *against* the percentages with outstanding success. In addition, he had unparalleled rapport with baseball writers, thereby helping the Yankees in the press as well as on the field. Stengel was, in his own word, "amazin'!"

Leo Durocher was another interesting, if more controversial, manager. The brash, street-smart "Lippy Leo" was a weak-hitting but great-fielding shortstop for the Yankees, Reds, "Gas House Gang" Cardinals, and Dodgers. Durocher became the Dodgers' player-manager in 1939, just as the frenetic, high-spending efforts of President Larry MacPhail were beginning to raise the club from its long-standing doldrums. In 1941, the Dodgers, with the help of such stars as Dolf Camilli, Pee Wee Reese, Pete Reiser, Billy Herman, Dixie Walker, Joe Medwick, and Whitlow Wyatt, won Brooklyn's first pennant in twenty-one years. Durocher's club just barely lost out to St. Louis in 1942 and 1946. Sparked by rookie Jackie Robinson, the Dodgers won the pennant in 1947, but Durocher was not on hand—he had been suspended for "conduct detrimental to baseball" for the entire 1947 season. Lippy Leo returned in 1948, but with the Dodgers doing poorly, he was moved in midseason across town to the New York Giants. It was a shocking deal for Giants' fans—their idolized Mel Ott replaced by the hated Durocher.

Durocher's revamped Giants, 13½ games off the pace in August 1951, came back to beat the Dodgers on Bobby Thomson's "Miracle at Coogan's Bluff" home run. In many respects this was Durocher's finest season, as he maneuvered the Giants to the pennant. Although

Durocher's club went on to win both the pennant and the World Championship in 1954, the Polo Grounders slipped, and Durocher, never completely accepted by Giants' fans, was let out after the 1955 season. He returned to manage the Chicago Cubs from 1966 through mid-season 1972 but was unable to win a pennant. His managerial career ended after he piloted Houston unsuccessfully through the 1973 season.

Durocher was recognized as a knowledgeable, aggressive manager who could inspire a team with winning potential but seemed to lose interest with lesser teams. Leo tended to find himself in unsavory company, the basic reason for his suspension in 1947. Although he was respected as a strategist and competitor, he was disliked intensely by many baseball men who resented his beanball orders and by umpires and fans offended by his rowdy tactics. Over his twenty-four-year managerial career, Durocher ranks fifth in games managed and sixth in wins.

Walter "Smokey" Alston was the antithesis of Durocher—a quiet, unassuming, stable man who at first won with power-packed teams, then with speedy clubs. A hard-hitting first baseman in the minors, the Ohio strongman had only one sip of a cup of coffee in the majors—in 1936 he struck out in his only major league at-bat. He was installed as the manager of the then-Brooklyn Dodgers in 1954 after they fired pennant-winning pilot Charlie Dressen, who wanted a multiyear contract. Alston, who never received more than a single-year contract in his twenty-three Dodger seasons, responded with seven pennants and four World Championships. He led the famous "Boys of Summer" Dodgers—Pee Wee Reese, Gil Hodges, Jackie Robinson, Roy Campanella, Carl Furillo, Duke Snider, Carl Erskine—to pennant wins in 1955–1956. His 1965–1966 pennant winners were sparked by the herculean pitching of Sandy Koufax and the base-stealing heroics of Maury Wills. Only two men, Connie Mack and John McGraw, managed the same team for a longer period than Alston. He ranks fifth in games won with a .558 winning percentage.

The role (some would say the importance) of the manager has changed significantly over the past two decades, in terms of both strategy and the maintenance of discipline. The designated hitter rule has changed the game drastically, giving the manager either more or fewer options, depending on the viewpoint. Pitching strategy has shifted to a decreased emphasis on the starting pitcher going the route and an increased emphasis on a dominant relief pitcher to finish off the opposition. Play on artificial turf requires different strategies and playing styles from play on natural grass. Greater emphasis on base stealing has changed strategies. Platooning players, which has been around for at least seventy years, has been refined to an exquisite art.

Maintaining player discipline has become much more difficult over the years. Until the 1960s, the manager ruled completely. But today most players are paid more than managers, implying that a higher-paid star is more valuable to the team than the manager. As a result, fining highly paid players is a relatively ineffective disciplinary tactic. Today air travel has telescoped travel time, and players spend more time during the season away from their teammates. The resulting reduced team discipline and togetherness have made it more difficult for managers to weld their players into cohesive units.

Drug abuse presents an extremely difficult managerial problem. Excessive drinking has been a common difficulty from the early days of professional baseball. But drinking and its impact upon a player's performance are usually readily determined. However, the use of drugs is extremely difficult to detect, and its impact on performance is long term and virtually impossible to judge.

Managers have been laid off, sacrifices on the altars of second-division finishes or general fan or owner discontent, since the game began. But over the last two decades there is evidence that managers have become an increasingly endangered species. From 1970 through 1981, for example, National League managers enjoyed a mere 2.4-year average tenure, while their American League counterparts lasted only 1.9 years on the average.

On the positive side, today's manager has a multitude of helpers, a sufficient number to give his job a chairman-of-the-board aura. He now has available hitting instructors, base-stealing coaches, specialists in playing each position, pitching coaches, conditioning specialists, motivation experts, and, yes, someone to check on the inventory of baseballs. Shades of Harry Wright!

Several managers have been especially adept at dealing with these emerging changes. Some of the more prominent include Sparky Anderson, Earl Weaver, Dick Williams, and Billy Martin.

George Lee "Sparky" Anderson fits the classic pattern of the successful major league manager—a brainy, hustling, good-field–no-hit infielder. After hitting .218 for the Phillies in his only major league season and playing several additional minor league seasons, Anderson managed in the minors from 1964 to 1968, then coached for the fledgling San Diego Padres in 1969.

Appointed to manage the Cincinnati Reds in 1970, Anderson was an immediate success, winning the pennant by 14½ games. Anderson's clubs won pennants again in 1972, 1975, and 1976, powered by catcher Johnny Bench, first baseman Tony Perez, left fielder Pete Rose, and second baseman Joe Morgan. Many experts rate his 1976 powerhouse with the great Yankee teams of 1927, 1936, and 1961. Despite Anderson's brilliant tenure at Cincinnati (four pennants and two World Championships in nine years), the Reds released him after a second-place finish in 1978. The Detroit Tigers hired him immediately, and he improved the club steadily, guiding them to a World Championship in 1984.

The garrulous Anderson is one of the most popular men in the game, frequently selected to broadcast postseason games despite his lamentable diction. Nicknamed "Captain Hook" because of his crisp yanking of struggling pitchers, Anderson is highly respected for his diligence, his ready availability to the press, and his fairness and loyalty to his players.

The inimitable Earl Weaver has been considered by many experts the top manager of the last twenty years. Another ex–minor league infielder who never made it to the major leagues as a player, Weaver managed in the minors from 1956 through 1967, then took over the managership of the Baltimore Orioles in midseason of 1968. He led the Orioles through the 1982 season, then stepped down voluntarily for the 1983–1984 campaigns. Sum-

moned back as the Orioles faltered in 1985, Weaver managed through the 1986 season before retiring to pursue the good life in Florida.

Weaver ranks among the ten best managers statistically, with a .583 winning percentage. During his seventeen seasons, he won four pennants and one World Championship, but was remarkably consistent, finishing out of the first division only once.

Weaver's managerial style combined those of John McGraw and Casey Stengel. He was the most frequently ejected major league manager of his era, with ninety-one dismissals from games and four suspensions. The picture of his explosive debates with umpires (many precipitated by Weaver for his own strategic purposes) is unforgettable—the stocky little manager cheek to cheek with the umpire, his cap turned around to prevent contact, and his violent outbursts punctuated by vigorous hand slaps against his ever-present rule book.

The innovative Weaver set up an instruction plan in the early 1960s which is still used throughout the Orioles organization, permitting a future Eddie Murray or a Cal Ripken, Jr., to move from the lowest farm club in the system to the parent club with a minimum of adjustment. Weaver made unprecedented use of charts and computers, although he never abandoned his fundamental reliance upon three-run homers (he called them "a visit from Dr. Longball"), a relatively walk-free pitching staff, and a tight, well-disciplined defense.

Weaver was a complete realist in recognizing his players' capabilities and limitations. Accordingly he was a master in using his entire roster to maximize player strengths and minimize weaknesses. He accomplished this by extensive analysis of scouting reports and past performances of Oriole players against individual opponents. Earl Weaver was unquestionably the supreme strategist of his time.

Dick Williams has been one of the most successful managers since the late 1960s. He was a journeyman outfielder-infielder with Brooklyn, Baltimore, Kansas City, Cleveland and Boston, hitting .260 over his injury-plagued thirteen-year playing career. After managing the Red Sox's Triple-A Toronto farm team in 1965–1966, Williams led the parent club to a pennant in 1967. Released after failing to repeat in 1968–1969, Williams was hired by Oakland owner Charles Finley to manage the Athletics in 1971.

Williams won two straight pennants and World Championships in three boisterous seasons in Oakland. He had an imposing aggregation of young players led by outfielders Reggie Jackson and Joe Rudi, third baseman Sal Bando, and pitchers Catfish Hunter, Vida Blue, and Rollie Fingers, as well as the unpredictable—and unignorable—Finley as his boss. Tiring of the meddling Finley, Williams quit after winning his second straight World Championship in 1973. He managed the California Angels in 1974–1976, but with little success, then managed the Montreal Expos from 1977 to 1981 without winning a pennant. Williams piloted the San Diego Padres from 1982 to 1985, winning the 1984 flag. He left the Padres before the 1986 season to take over the youthful Seattle Mariners.

Especially effective with younger players, Williams runs a no-nonsense, well-disciplined ship—no simple task in the game today. Among active managers, he trails only Sparky Anderson and Gene Mauch in career wins, going into the 1988 season.

Billy Martin was the most combative figure in the game from the time he joined the Yankees as a twenty-two-year-old second baseman in 1950 until his death in 1989. A fair fielder and an average hitter for a middle infielder (.257 lifetime average) who enhanced his value by his razor-sharp baseball instincts and aggressiveness, Martin was best known for his many brawls with other players, club officials, and miscellaneous bystanders. He attributed much of his bellicosity to a rough childhood in Berkeley, California, where, as he put it, "I awoke every morning figuring there was a damn good chance I'd be in a fistfight before the day was over."

Martin's managerial career produced winning teams everywhere he managed, but off-field troubles with owners and other incidents resulted in his string of firings and resignations. He began managing at Denver in 1968 and in the majors with Minnesota in 1969, where his club won the American League's Western Division. Fired "for ignoring Twins policies," Martin was hired to manage Detroit in 1971. After a second-place finish, he led the Tigers to the Eastern Division title in 1972. He left the Tigers near the end of the 1973 season and finished out the season managing the Texas Rangers. Martin was fired by the Rangers on July 21, 1975, then took over as Yankees manager on August 2, 1975. Hired by Yankees owner George Steinbrenner to restore the Yankees to their former glory, Martin produced a pennant win in 1976. Reggie Jackson joined the Yankees in 1977, contributing to a World Championship in a tumultuous season remembered for a highly publicized feud (and a nationally televised dugout confrontation and near fight) between Jackson and Martin.

In 1978 Steinbrenner fired Martin in midseason. Then, in a dramatic announcement preceding the Yankees' Old-Timers' Game in July 1978, Steinbrenner promised to rehire Martin. Billy returned in 1979 but was fired again in midseason because of an off-field incident. Martin managed Oakland in 1980 and, with the last-place club of the previous year playing spirited "Billy Ball," he lifted the Athletics to second place in 1980 and a division title in 1981. The A's deteriorated in 1982 and Martin was dismissed at the end of the season.

In a familiar scenario, Martin returned to manage the Yankees in 1983 but was replaced after finishing in third place. Incredibly he was rehired for a fourth time in 1985, but, after committing the crime of not winning the pennant, was dismissed at season's end and replaced by Lou Piniella. He had a career winning percentage of .552, five divisional championships, two pennants, and a World Championship.

Martin served the Yankees in the broadcasting booth and other capacities in 1986–1987. Then, as Steinbrenner's opinion of Piniella's managing soured (while others were recommending him as a candidate for Manager of the Year!), the by-now-monotonous announcement came over the wires: Martin would manage the Yankees again in 1988. The other shoe dropped to the floor in the early summer, as Martin was let go in favor of Piniella.

Similar to his mentor Casey Stengel, Martin's success in large part stemmed from his intense concentration on the game and his ability to motivate players of average talent. However, unlike Stengel, Martin's greatest problem was handling young players. He also had difficulties with established players, especially stars such as Reggie Jackson and Don Baylor, who made no bones of their intense dislike for Martin. He had tremendous success in attaining immediate improvement in team performance. However, he tended to wear out his welcome with owners within a short time, and he was thought to have a tendency to burn out his starting pitchers, particularly evident during his tenure at Oakland.

Baseball historian David Voigt presented a masterful analysis of the role of expansion-era managers in the premiere issue of *The National Pastime*. Voigt wrote:

The role of the modern manager is that of supervisor, disciplinarian, and strategist. As supervisors, managers now delegate authority to coaches who conduct practices and instruct players; each coach contributes his bit of expertise and the manager is charged with coordinating these activities. As a disciplinarian, the manager retains enough authority to compel players to follow rules and do their duty. Indeed, some managerial discipline codes yet resemble those of closed institutions like police forces and mental asylums . . . As strategists, which is still the essence of the managerial mystique, pilots still rely on time-honored devices such as flashing signals to third-base coaches, devising defensive alignments to thwart hitters, and most important, setting a pitching rotation and knowing when to change pitchers.

In the final analysis, however, it may be that the manager's main function is to serve as scapegoat and thus preserve the jobs of others . . . [He] is answerable for a multitude of sins, few of his direct commission . . .

And with an owner like Steinbrenner intervening incessantly, going so far as to order special fundamental drills, one can only expect continuing pressure on managers. Indeed, the best relief for these besieged foremen seems to have been hit upon by Whitey Herzog. By functioning both as manager and GM, he seems to be pointing the way toward a protective adaptation for an otherwise highly endangered species. And if he can find a way to buy his club—well, how do you think Connie Mack lasted fifty years?

Managerial Styles

As John McGraw—with simple directness—put it, "The idea [in managing] is to win." No argument there, but it is interesting to consider the widely different approaches major league managers have brought to the task.

First, there are the autocrats, the "you'll do it my way or else" types. Some prime examples are Cap Anson, John McGraw, Rogers Hornsby, Leo Durocher, Charlie Dressen, Earl Weaver, Gene Mauch, Dick Williams, and Billy Martin.

Cap Anson was a strong disciplinarian, a manager who did not allow his players to smoke cigarettes or cigars (apparently chewing tobacco was permitted) or to drink alcoholic beverages in a notably heavy-drinking era. Anson was the largest player on his team and was known to exert brute strength to carry out his edicts. On one occasion during a card game, Anson and his third baseman, Ed Williamson, got into a scuffle. It seems that Williamson, holding four aces, won a sizable pot from Anson, who had four queens. Anson accused Williamson of cheating, and Williamson responded by grabbing a water pitcher, prepared to part Anson's skull before cooler heads broke up the scrap. Williamson, probably aware that he had been spared a bloody beating by the huge player-manager, commented colloquially, "Cap, you're okay as a player, but you don't count for cornstalks as a man."

McGraw was the most notorious autocrat of them all. He demanded that his players submit to his will unconditionally. This included strict curfews and long hours of sliding, fielding, hitting, and bunting practice. In his rediscovered book, *Pitching in a Pinch,* Christy Mathewson told of games during which McGraw called every pitch. Mathewson wrote, ". . . McGraw . . . plans every move, most of the hitters going to the plate with definite instructions from him as to what to try to do. In order to make this system efficient, absolute discipline must be assured. If a player has other ideas than McGraw, . . . the invariable answer to him is 'You do what I tell you, and I'll take the responsibility if we lose.' "

McGraw's insistence on strict adherence to his instructions was illustrated one day in Pittsburgh. Giants' outfielder Red Murray came to bat in the ninth inning of a tied game with none out and a runner on second. He acknowledged McGraw's signal to bunt the runner to third base, then to McGraw's consternation drilled the next pitch for a game-winning home run. Flushed with success, Murray met with the outraged Little Napoleon after the game. "Murray, what did I tell you to do?" McGraw asked him. Murray responded, "You told me to bunt, but the pitch came in right in my gut, so I whacked it." McGraw snapped, "Well, I'm fining you one hundred dollars, and you can try putting that in your gut."

McGraw's unending signals and commands from the bench were a constant source of irritation to his players. One story tells of the spring training exhibition game where McGraw sat sunning himself in the center field bleachers instead of his usual place on the bench. Mrs. McGraw, seated in a box near the dugout, was uncertain whether her husband was going to stay for the full game. So at the end of one inning she called to Giant center fielder Fred Lindstrom to have him ask McGraw what he intended to do. Lindstrom didn't hear her, and one of the reporters seated near by yelled to get his attention, indicating that Mrs. McGraw wanted to speak to him. When Lindstrom came over to the box, she said, in mock severity, "Freddy! Why don't you pay attention?" Lindstrom's eyes widened. "Good God!" he exclaimed. "Are you giving signals, too?"

The success of the stifling McGraw approach continued as long as players followed his orders without question during the first twenty of his thirty years at the Giants' helm. But Fred Lindstrom described its effect on the club in McGraw's later years. Lindstrom said, "With the advent of fellows like Bill Terry, Mel Ott, Carl Hubbell, Travis Jackson, and me, we were a different breed. We didn't need someone hitting us over the head to keep us in shape. In fact, we wouldn't take it—at least Terry and I wouldn't. I don't think McGraw was able to adapt his methods of handling . . . the more modern-style players.

And after 1924 he never won another pennant."

While McGraw's players merely chafed restlessly at their boss's domineering style, manager Harry "the Hat" Walker's 1971 Houston Astros broadcast their defiance to the world. It seems that Walker was having extreme difficulty in preventing his players from drinking and chasing women. Walker's rebellious charges mocked his lectures and fines and openly parodied his moral stance by loudly singing a satirical clubhouse refrain with the following lyrics:

> *Now Harry Walker is the one*
>   *that manages this crew;*
> *He doesn't like it when we drink*
>   *and fight and smoke and screw;*
> *But when we win our game each day,*
> *Then what the fuck can Harry say?*
> *It makes a fellow proud to be an Astro.*

McGraw's postgame "meetings," which the entire team was required to sit through before showering, were noted for their length (sometimes as long as three hours) and for McGraw's vicious harangues. (Pete Reiser reported that Leo Durocher, another absolute ruler, forbade his Brooklyn Dodger players from taking off their uniforms after losing a game until the Lippy One gave his permission.)

Rogers Hornsby, a blunt, humorless man, was another imperious manager. Hall of Famer Billy Herman, who joined the Chicago Cubs as a rookie at the end of the 1931 season, later described Hornsby as follows:

He was a hard-nosed guy. He ran the clubhouse like a gestapo camp. You couldn't smoke, drink a soft drink, eat a sandwich. Couldn't read a paper. When you walked in the clubhouse, you put your uniform on and got ready to play . . . no more kidding around, no joking, no laughing . . . When you would *hear from him is if you made a play he didn't think was quite up to his standards. It still burns me up just a little bit to remember some of his sarcastic remarks.*

Billy Martin, at least in his earlier managerial years, acted like a Marine drill sergeant. Graig Nettles played for Martin in 1968 at Denver. In his book *Balls,* Nettles reports that Martin would scream from the dugout at an errant player as the player came in from the field. Martin held his players in contempt, thought they had not "scuffled around." So Martin put his players through "boot camp" to toughen them up. He taught them that things had to be done his way. Nettles concluded gamely that "on a Billy Martin team, there is only one boss: Billy Martin. And if you do it his way, you'll win."

Then there are the managers who downplay their own importance in deference to their players. They have been likened to school guidance counselors. Typical members of this group include Connie Mack, Wilbert Robinson, Bill McKechnie, Miller Huggins, Bucky Harris, Eddie Sawyer, Walter Alston, Danny Murtaugh, Ralph Houk, Tom Lasorda, and Sparky Anderson.

Connie Mack, despite his historic importance as a baseball figure, was an unobtrusive figure who never upstaged his players. He preferred not to wear a uniform and, therefore, was forbidden from stepping onto the field. As a result, he did not project himself into the public eye during a game. According to Jimmy Dykes, who was associated with Mack for many years, nothing ever seemed to bother the equable Mack, who was perfectly content to yield the spotlight to his players. He was the same placid man sitting on the bench, whether his Athletics were in last place or playing a World Series game. To Dykes's knowledge, Mack never fined a player, although he was known to express his displeasure when a player violated the midnight curfew without permission.

The saintly Mack never used profanity; Dykes said that if Mack used the word "damn," he was deeply disturbed. There was one occasion, though, when Mack showed anger—using another four-letter word. His great pitcher, Robert "Lefty" Grove, had a rare off-day against the Yankees of the "Murderers' Row" game. When the dour, short-tempered Grove returned to the dugout after a difficult inning, Mack called out a quiet suggestion as to how to deal with Ruth, Gehrig, Dickey, et al. Grove looked angrily across the dugout at the patriarchal Mack, who was sitting there with his customary high, starched collar despite the 95-degree heat. "Oh, go take a shit," gritted Grove out of the side of his mouth. No one *ever* spoke that way to "Mr. Mack" (as his players called him). A visibly angered Mack put his scorecard down deliberately and walked stiff-legged the length of the dugout to where Grove was sitting. Moving in front of the surprised Lefty, Mack stood motionless for a moment, then delivered a curt, "*You* go take a shit, Robert." Then, while the entire team fought back giggles, the dignified Mack returned to his seat, picked up his scorecard, and focused on the game.

Eddie Sawyer was the perfect manager for the pennant-winning 1950 Philadelphia Phillies "Whiz Kids," a group of youngsters more in need of friendly encouragement and understanding than of a domineering boss. The unassuming, fatherly Sawyer made it a point to involve himself in the personal problems of his players. He played his father-confessor role to the hilt during one season when nine of his players were expectant fathers.

The low-key Sawyer had an unusual approach in getting his players to observe regular hours. Since Harry Wright's day, managers have applied an evening curfew—that is, they have required players to be in their rooms by a specified evening hour. Sawyer, in effect, applied a reverse curfew. There was no check-in time at night, but he would rout his players out unexpectedly for early-morning workouts. He deliberately refrained from telling his players when to go to sleep, feeling that they would get to bed at reasonable hours in order to make it through the strenuous early-morning exertions, whenever they occurred.

John McGraw's old Baltimore Orioles teammate, Wilbert Robinson, had a much more relaxed approach to managing than the intense McGraw. One day while managing Brooklyn, "Uncle Robby" flashed the bunt sign to slugging future Hall of Fame outfielder Zack Wheat. But Wheat missed the sign and clubbed the next pitch out of the park, putting Brooklyn ahead. As Wheat trotted around past Robinson, who was coaching at third base, the jovial Robinson shouted out gleefully, "Way to go, Zack." Robby was not about to pull a McGraw and bawl out an erring player who was in the process of winning the game for his club.

His players loved Robinson for his down-to-earth approach to baseball and his reluctance to exaggerate his own considerable store of baseball knowledge. Hall of Fame pitcher Burleigh Grimes claimed that Robby was the man who made him a successful pitcher. Nobody had been interested in Grimes after two miserable seasons with Pittsburgh. Robinson, a recognized expert on pitching, picked up Grimes, and the tough spitballer surprised everyone with a 19–9 season. When Robby was asked what he had done, he responded, "Hell, all I did was just give him the ball." As Grimes described it, "Some managers would have filled a billboard telling all they had done for me, but not Robby. He told the truth; he just gave me the ball."

Again unlike McGraw, the lovable if not overly educated, Robinson was relaxed even when it came to making out his lineups. He had difficulty remembering names and, if he could remember them, he often was handcuffed by their proper spelling. One day he told rarely used outfielder Oscar Roettger that he was to play first base. But when it came to writing out the lineup card, the thought of dealing with a name like Roettger was too much for Robby. "Never mind," he said weakly, "[Babe] Herman will play first."

Walter Alston, a strong, silent man, had a simple philosophy of managing. "Be your own self. To me that's probably the most important part of it, more so than the strategy part. If you know yourself, you'll know your players—how to handle them, . . . which ones to pat on the back, which ones to give a kick in the ass now and then . . . the winning of the ballgame and the good of the team come first." With that simple credo, Alston lasted through twenty-three seasons as the Dodgers' manager, the classic "faceless" manager whose records did the talking for him.

Then there's the "I'm just one of the boys" managing school. This includes managers who wear their authority lightly, often treating their players as equals. Some who come readily to mind are Pie Traynor, Rabbit Maranville, Charlie Grimm, Mel Ott, Yogi Berra, Billy Herman, and Harvey Kuenn. Unfortunately, with some exceptions, this group tends to be comprised of "nice guys" who have been known to finish last.

By his own admission, Billy Herman was not a good manager in his rookie season as field boss of the Pittsburgh Pirates in 1946. As he put it, "I could run the game as well as anybody. But I was terrible with the men. I was too easy with them, letting them have too much latitude . . . I wanted to treat my men the way I'd always wanted to be treated, and it didn't work . . . For years you were friendly with everybody and one of the boys . . . I was determined not to change, and that's where I was wrong." The Pirates finished tied for last and Herman was fired.

Mel Ott, who managed the New York Giants with indifferent success in the 1940s, was the subject of Leo Durocher's tough-guy contribution to the American idiom: "Nice guys finish last." Similar to that of Herman, Ott's appointment as the Giants' manager was accompanied by admonitions to the little southern gentleman that he prevent his players from taking advantage of him. In response, Ott acted out of character during his first few years as manager. Self-conscious of his reputation for being easygoing, he overcompensated, notably in 1945 when he fined pitcher Bill Voiselle $500 for grooving an 0-and-2 pitch that resulted in a game-losing hit.

But Ott relaxed after that and became one of the boys. Giants' catcher Walker Cooper pulled a practical joke on Ott which showed how relaxed Master Melvin's relationship with his players had become. Time and again, with Ott deep in thought on the bench, Cooper slipped a lighted cigarette in the boss's hip pocket, seconds before Ott would reach into his pocket to draw out his lineup card. One day Ott pulled out his hip pockets for protection, but Cooper was ahead of him, having snipped off the pocket linings. When Ott stuck the batting-order cards in his pocket, they dropped down farther into his pants. For some time later, Giants players imitated an embarrassed Ott standing at the plate before 40,000 at the Polo Grounds, trying to fish down the inside of his uniform pants for the lineup cards.

Yet there have been pleasant, relaxed "one of the boys" managers who have done well. Laid-back Harvey Kuenn was the perfect leader for the pennant-winning Milwaukee Brewers in 1982, and relaxed Joe Altobelli replaced overwrought Earl Weaver in 1983 and led the Baltimore Orioles to the World Championship. Charlie Grimm was one of the most successful of the easygoing managers. "Jolly Cholly" replaced the forbidding Rogers Hornsby as manager of the Chicago Cubs in midseason of 1932 and managed the Cubs to the pennant. Grimm permitted his players to do things their own way, with no rules or curfews. He ran the club on the field, but he was a happy-go-lucky man off the field, singing and dancing in the clubhouse and playing his banjo after the games.

And then there was vest-pocket-sized Walter "Rabbit" Maranville, renowned for his basket catch and his world-class carousing. Informed of his appointment to manage the Cubs in midseason of 1925 while on a train with his teammates, the well-oiled Rabbit celebrated by waking up all hands and shouting at the top of his lungs, "There will be no sleeping on this train under Maranville management." Not surprisingly, the Maranville regime ended only fifty-three games after it started, with the Cubs resolutely on their way to a last-place finish.

Pitcher-author Jim Brosnan has identified another category of managers—those whose central goal is to weld their players into tightly knit communities. Adherents of this managerial style tend to insist on conformity to team standards and to unload nonconformists and troublemakers. Of the great managers, Brosnan lumps Joe McCarthy, Casey Stengel, and Al Lopez in this category. Bill Terry and Whitey Herzog, among others, can also be included in this group.

Joe McCarthy's skills as a builder of unified teams, well developed during his pre–New York Yankees managerial years, were honed to perfection during the 1931–1934 seasons, when he had to deal with a fractious, aging Babe Ruth. The Bambino made no bones about his goal: he wanted to replace McCarthy without even managing in the minor leagues (Ruth had turned down Colonel Jake Ruppert's offer of the managership of the Yankees' crack farm team at Triple-A Newark). McCarthy managed to keep his club in the running, and the team from splitting into pro- and anti-Ruth factions, until the disillusioned Babe left the Bronx Bombers after the 1934 season.

McCarthy, a quiet but strict disciplinarian, attained tight control over his players by requiring model behavior both on and off the field. He traded two established regulars, righthander Johnny Allen and outfielder Ben Chapman, whose hot tempers did not fit the classic Yankee mold. McCarthy's demands that his players dress formally led baseball men to anticipate a confrontation between McCarthy and Ted Williams when Marse Joe took over as Boston Red Sox manager in 1948. Williams was the embodiment of the nonconformist, as witness his refusal to wear a necktie. The first morning of spring training, Williams appeared at breakfast with an open-neck sport shirt. Said the surprisingly flexible Marse Joe, "Any manager who can't get along with a .400 hitter is out of his mind."

Bill Terry's New York Giants of the 1930s built their success on close teamwork and a tight defense, as Terry scratched for runs in the best early-1900s style. He frequently had Mel Ott, the club's only authentic home run threat, bunt runners along as early as the first inning of a game. Ken Smith, formerly the director of the Baseball Hall of Fame and before that a sportswriter for the (New York) *Daily Mirror,* told a story which illustrated Memphis Bill's emphasis on defense. The Giants took a tough 2–1 loss one day, and Smith and Terry were discussing it after the game. The amiable Smith, trying to comfort Terry, said, "Just another timely hit, Bill, and you'd have won it." Terry responded soberly, "Kenny, they shouldn't have scored two runs."

Terry was on good terms with the veteran Smith, but he had little use for most of the other writers, whom he referred to scornfully as "a bunch of twenty-five-dollar-a-week clerks." Terry refused to talk with them on his own time, and he discouraged his players from talking to writers, probably feeling that these contacts could well break down the tight unity among the Giant players. So there was a continuing feud between Terry and the writers. The (New York) *World-Telegram*'s Tom Meany, a sharp man with a one-liner, crossed verbal swords constantly with Terry. An example of the sarcastic dialogue: After learning that Terry, a shrewd businessman, had begun breeding cattle on his farm, Meany cracked, "I'll bet Terry is breeding white-faced cattle—that way he can count them at night!"

Whitey Herzog resembles Terry in mental toughness, the *esprit de corps* he engenders in his players, and in his reliance on defensive strength to keep his team competitive. Herzog's executive capacity and competence are also reminiscent of Terry in that both men served simultaneously and successfully as general manager and field manager. But they differ in two other respects: unlike Memphis Bill, Whitey talks to the media willingly; and there's the matter of playing ability—Herzog hit .293 in his best season with a journeyman .257 career average, while Hall of Famer Terry's best was .401 in 1930 en route to a resplendent .341 career average.

Managing a ballclub is a crazy business, mainly because the human element is so unpredictable. Many years ago, when Casey Stengel was managing in the minors, he walked into a hotel lobby with a writer and saw his star pitcher sprawled out fast asleep on a divan, mouth open and a silly, moronic look on his face. "This is what drives managers nuts," Casey growled. "As a manager, you work hard, analyze the game, study your players, learn the weaknesses of every team in the league, and think and sweat all day long. And once every four or five days you have to trust your job and reputation to a lunkhead like that."

The Coaches

The first major league coaches were managers and players assigned to direct traffic on the base paths and to pass along signs, not the nonplaying, full-time coaches as we know them today. Another of the primary functions of the pre-1910 coaches was to distract the opposing pitcher. This was frequently accomplished by running up and down the baselines to divert his attention, a practice which was curtailed in 1887 with the establishment of coaching boxes in foul territory off first and third bases.

Many of the early-day coaches were especially adept at heckling pitchers to reduce their effectiveness. Often this was a matter of screaming obscenities or insults at the pitcher. Hall of Fame outfielder Mike "King" Kelly, coaching at third base for the Boston Beaneaters in the late 1880s, threw in a new variation. With Boston and Pittsburgh tied in the ninth inning and two Beaneaters on base, Kelly called authoritatively to the rookie Pittsburgh pitcher, "Let's see the ball, son." The young pitcher obliged guilelessly, tossing the ball to Kelly. Mike stepped aside to let the ball bounce past him, and the game-winning run scored.

Arlie Latham was the first full-time coach. John McGraw hired Latham in 1909, presumably without any illusions that Latham would be a character builder. Latham was a favorite of the more hardboiled fans, recognized as a relentless heckler who could stir opponents' ire; not for nothing was he known as "The Freshest Man Alive." A former infielder, he had been a troublemaker to his managers during his seventeen-year major league career. Moreover, Latham's private life was a disaster. His first wife had attempted suicide, and his second wife divorced him, charging "perversion, assault, desertion, and infidelity."

The employment of the mercurial Latham as a coach notwithstanding, coaching was becoming a more serious, reputable aspect of the game by the early 1900s. The Giants' great pitcher Christy Mathewson wrote in 1912 in his *Pitching in a Pinch:*

With the development of baseball, coaching has advanced until it is now an exact science. For many years the two men who stood at first and third bases were stationed there merely to bullyrag and abuse the pitchers, often using language that was a disgrace to a ballfield. When they were not busy with this part of their art, they handed helpful hints to the runners as to where the ball was . . . while the pitcher pretended to prepare to deliver it. But as rules were made which strictly forbade the use of indecent language to a pitcher, and as the old school of clowns passed, coaching developed into a science, and the sentries stationed at first and third bases found themselves occupying important jobs.

In 1911 McGraw hired the majors' second full-time coach, Wilbert Robinson. Uncle Robby was the first pitching coach, a man who aided the entire Giant pitching staff, but most particularly lefthander Rube Marquand, whom Robinson converted from a "$11,000 lemon" to a Hall of Fame pitcher. The rotund, jovial Robinson remained with the Giants until 1913, when he left the club after a quarrel with McGraw.

Nick Altrock, hired by the Washington Senators' Clark Griffith, was the best-known coach over the next twenty years. A former major league pitcher, Altrock was a competent coach, but his forte was his talent as a clown. He was a master mimic, imitating the mannerisms of players and umpires, throwing and catching baseballs in impossible positions, and acting out elaborate shadow-boxing routines. In his later years he teamed with Al Schacht, the "Clown Prince of Baseball," to entertain at a number of World Series. Altrock coached for the Senators for forty years.

Altrock was the only full-time nonplaying major league coach from 1914 until 1920, when the Giants hired former second baseman Johnny Evers and the Phillies picked up former lefthander Jesse Tannehill. By the end of the decade, most major league clubs employed at least one nonplaying coach. Just before World War Two, each major league club employed at least one full-time coach, and there were a total of forty major league coaches, an average of 2.5 per team.

The number of coaches increased after World War Two as major league baseball became more complex and increasing attendance and broadcasting revenues made it more economically feasible to hire bigger staffs. Teams routinely began to employ at least three coaches, two to coach the bases and one to oversee the bullpen. In addition, from the 1960s to the present, almost all teams have had a full-time pitching coach. Many clubs have employed batting coaches, rotating them from the parent club to the organization's farm teams.

The third base coach is the quarterback of the team. He relays signs from the manager, and he directs offensive strategy on the field. "Coaching at third base," Al Simmons, the Hall of Famer who was one of the top third base coaches, once remarked, "is the toughest job on the club. The coach on third gets all the blame when things go wrong, and he gets none of the credit when things go right. Yet a good coach can win a dozen or more games a season. A bad coach can lose that many—except, he doesn't last that long."

Two celebrated incidents involving third base coaches illustrate Simmons's point. First there was Enos "Country" Slaughter's famous World Series-winning score from first base in the 1946 fall classic. Slaughter tallied on a routine hit to left center, which was generously scored as a double. Enos, breaking into full stride even before the ball was hit, rounded second and headed for third. Standing in the coaching box, in full view of the charging Slaughter, stood Mike Gonzales. Mike raised both arms in the classic "stop" gesture, all the time screaming, *"No! No! No!"* But Enos ignored Gonzales. He rounded third and slid home with the winning run in one of the most unforgettable plays of Series history. Technically the play should never have been attempted. Gonzales was right, and Slaughter was wrong—except that the determined Enos made it work.

Then there was the Mike Ferraro incident. Ferraro was the hapless Yankee third base coach who, in Game Two of the 1980 American League Championship Series, waved home a Yankee runner on a two-out hit. The runner was thrown out, and the Yankees lost to Kansas City, 3–2. George Steinbrenner, who had been unhappy with Ferraro's coaching before the incident, precipitated an ugly public argument with the late Dick Howser, the Yankees' manager. At Steinbrenner's insistence, Ferraro coached at first base in 1981, constantly bedeviled by taunts from the stands to "Send him home, Mike" when a batter approached first base on a weak hit to the outfield.

The first base coach has less burdensome duties. A runner traveling from second to third cannot see what's happening behind him and has to use the third base traffic cop as his eyes. But the hitter running toward first base has the field spread out in front of him. The responsibility of going for the extra base is his, not the coach's.

The first base coach is responsible for helping the runner avoid a pickoff play and, elementary as it may seem, being sure that the runner touches first base en route to an extra-base hit. When Bobby Thomson hit his pennant-winning home run in the 1951 playoff, the other Giants' players tumbled out of their dugout and danced joyously to home plate to mob Thomson. Even manager Leo Durocher, coaching at third base, went crazy. But first base coach Freddie Fitzsimmons maintained his cool, shouting to the deliriously happy Thomson, "Don't forget to touch all the bases." Fitz watched intently as Thomson touched first and second; then the coach raced for home plate to join the celebration.

The bullpen coach gets the relief pitchers ready to enter the game and sometimes recommends their selection to the manager. Ten minutes before Thomson's historic home run, Dodger manager Charlie Dressen phoned bullpen coach Clyde Sukeforth. "Who's got the best stuff out there, Sukey?" asked Dressen. "[Ralph] Branca," replied Sukeforth. "[Carl] Erskine's bouncing 'em in the dirt." So Dressen brought in Branca, and Thomson ended the game dramatically. When Dressen attempted to place the blame for the defeat on Sukeforth, the angry Sukey understandably quit. It was the manager's decision, not the coach's, and there was no way that Dressen could escape that basic truth.

There have been many well-publicized pitching coaches. Jim Turner was credited for much of the effectiveness of the Yankee pitching staff during the 1949–1959 period. Johnny Sain has been an independent-minded, exemplary pitching coach for six different teams over the last thirty years. Art Fowler, Billy Martin's ever-present alter ego in several major league jobs, has long been accused of teaching Martin's pitchers to throw the spitball. George Bamberger and Ray Miller were given much of the credit for the Baltimore Orioles' pitching excellence over the 1968–1985 period. And Roger Craig has been a highly respected pitching mentor, largely responsible for widespread use of the devastating split-fingered fastball.

Batting coaches have come into vogue over the last twenty years. Wally Moses, one of the first, was the hitting specialist for the Philadelphia Athletics as early as 1952. The late Charlie Lau and Walter Hriniak, both former catchers, have been the most celebrated batting coaches over the last several years. Lau developed a revolutionary style of hitting which has gained wide use throughout baseball—especially with star pupil George Brett and other players Lau has coached. Interestingly, Lau hit a mere .255 over his eleven-year career, and Hriniak hit .253 (without an extra-base hit) in 47 career games. These are two classic examples of "Do as I say, not as I do."

Over the last forty years, there has been a noticeable improvement in the quality of coaching. There was a time when most coaches were thought to be old pensioners or drinking companions of the manager. Or maybe they were, as Casey Stengel once commented, "relatives of the manager's wife." In contrast, today's coaches are primarily teachers with established expertise in specific areas.

There was one circumstance where coaches had a touch of managing. After the Chicago Cubs finished seventh (in an eight-team league) in 1960, Cubs owner Philip K. Wrigley pondered how best to utilize his field supervisory team. He hit upon a novel idea. In 1961 he launched a grand experiment, called the "College of Coaches," in which a staff of coaches shared equally in managing, coaching, and player development. Wrigley hired no less than eight coaches to rotate as the supervisory "manager." The result: the player-poor Cubs finished seventh again in 1961 and did not rise above that level during the following four seasons while the unique arrangement remained in place. Needless to say, there has been no interest since in rotating coaches in the manager's job.

Albert "Cozy" Dolan, a New York Giants' coach from 1922 through 1924, represented the coaching profession at its worst and its best. In September 1924, Dolan left organized baseball in disgrace when Commissioner Kenesaw Mountain Landis barred him for life. Dolan reportedly had urged gullible Giants' outfielder Jimmy O'Connell to offer Philadelphia Phillies' shortstop Heinie Sand a bribe not to "bear down too hard" in an important game against the Giants. But a finer Dolan hour came earlier that season during spring training camp in Sarasota, Florida.

As Frank Graham described it in *McGraw of the Giants:*

This was the spring of 1924 and the Ku Klux Klan wielded a dreaded threat throughout the South. And so, one night, the lights on the main street were extinguished and there was a thin, eerie bugle call in the distance, and hooded Klansmen marched through the town. They marched in silence, and in silence they were watched by the crowd that lined the sidewalks. It was, for a split second, faintly frightening to most of the watchers [including Giant players and accompanying newspapermen]. Then the silence was broken.

"Give me a fungo stick," Cozy Dolan said, very loudly, "and I will lick all the bums by myself."

The ballplayers and the writers howled. The rest of the crowd, taking courage, giggled. The spell was broken. So was the spirit of the marching Klansmen. There was nothing even faintly frightening about them now. They were just a lot of fellows in ridiculous garb tramping along a darkened street.

Perhaps this is the way Cozy Dolan, major league coach, also ought to be remembered.

Umpires

Larry R. Gerlach

Traditionally regarded as villains by fans, adversarial autocrats by players, and invisible men by the press, umpires have been, as Furman Bisher put it, "submerged in the history of baseball like idiot children in a family album." Yet the umpire is baseball's indispensable man, for the arbiter transformed baseball from a recreational activity to a competitive sport and has personified the integrity of the professional game. Since attorney William R. Wheaton officiated the first recorded "modern" game on October 6, 1845, umpires have made important contributions to the National Pastime. Indeed, the history of the umpire mirrors the distinctive eras and developments of the game itself.

From the creation of the modern game in the 1840s through the Civil War, the umpire was the personification of base ball (two words then) as an amateur sport played by gentlemen. According to the September 23, 1845, rules of the Knickerbocker Club of New York, which created modern baseball, the president of the club "shall appoint an Umpire, who shall keep the game in a book provided for that purpose, and note all violations of the Bylaws and Rules." As "match" games between clubs became more frequent, three officials were commonly used—one umpire chosen by each team and a neutral "referee" to decide the often partisan split decisions. In 1858 the National Association of Base Ball Players sanctioned a single umpire, sometimes a spectator or even a player, chosen by the home team with the consent of the rival captain. There was no dress code, but contemporary prints depict the idealized portrait of the gentleman arbiter—a distinguished-looking gentleman resplendent in top hat, Prince Albert coat, and cane, who stood, kneeled, or sat on a stool in foul territory along the first base line. Although the attire became less formal by the Civil War, the volunteer arbiters continued to receive no remuneration for their services other than the "honor" of being chosen "the sole judge of fair and unfair play."

The nationwide popularity of the game after the Civil War led to the professionalization of baseball and, in turn, to professional umpires. In 1871 the newly formed National Association of Professional Base Ball Players continued the tradition of unpaid volunteers by allowing the home team to choose the umpire from a list of five names submitted by the visiting club, but gave the arbiter greater authority by limiting appeals to decisions involving rules interpretation, not judgment. In 1878 the National League of Professional Base Ball Clubs, organized two years earlier, instructed home teams to pay umpires $5 per game, and in 1879 National League president

William A. Hulbert appointed baseball's first umpire staff—a group of twenty men from which teams could chose an arbiter. The approved list and compensation did not free the umpires from the "homer" syndrome (ruling in favor of the home team as a civic gesture) or suspicion of collusion with gamblers. Indeed, in 1882 Richard Higham of Troy, New York, former manager and National League player, was banished from the league for advising gamblers how to bet on games he umpired, thus earning the infamous distinction of being the only umpire ever judged guilty of dishonesty on the field. That same year a new professional circuit, the American Association, pioneered in the creation of an umpiring staff that was hired, paid, and assigned to games by the league itself. Paid $140 a month and $3 per diem for expenses while on the road, American Association umpires were required to wear blue flannel coats and caps while working games. The next year the National League adopted its own permanent paid and uniformed staff, thus completing the professionalization of major league "men in blue."

Despite increased status, umpiring in the major leagues was an uncertain, stressful, and even dangerous occupation through the end of the century. Frequent revisions in the rules and innovations in playing techniques made the umpire's job exceedingly difficult, while the physical and verbal abuse from fans and players alike often made an umpire's life intolerable. Umpires were routinely spiked, kicked, cursed, and spat upon by players, while fans hurled vile epithets and all manner of debris at the arbiters. Mobbings and physical assaults were frequent, so much so that police escorts were familiar and welcome sights to the men in blue. The transformation of the umpire from esteemed arbitrator to despised villain was largely deliberate. As club owners and league officials recognized that umpire baiting boosted gate receipts, they refused to support the umpires's field decisions, dismissed or paid player's fines, did little to curb rowdiness, and even joined sportswriters in depicting umpires as scoundrels and scapegoats. Occasionally umpires retaliated by hurling objects back into the stands or by punching players and reporters—and were summarily punished for so doing. But most found other jobs. In an era when "Kill the umpire!" was not mere rhetoric, there was a high turnover rate in umpires as few men were willing to endure such trials and tribulations for paltry pay and poor working conditions.

Nonetheless, baseball's tumultuous era produced several umpires of historical importance. William B. "Billy" McLean, part-time pugilist from Philadelphia, was the first professional umpire. So great was his ability and reputation for fairness that National League officials in 1876 not only agreed to his demands for the unheard of $5 per game but also sent him on a expense-paid tour of every city in the league. The most famous early exponents of the two basic styles of umpiring were Robert V. Ferguson and John H. Gaffney. Ferguson, known during his playing days as "Robert the Great" and "Death to Flying Things," ruled as an iron-fisted autocrat, while Gaffney, dubbed "The King of the Umpires," controlled the game through tact and diplomacy. Gaffney also popularized the technique of working behind home plate until a player reached base and then moving behind the pitcher. (Before this the umpire worked either behind the batter or behind the pitcher and did not shift.) In 1888 Gaffney was the highest-paid umpire in baseball, earning $2,500 a year, plus expenses on the road. Other umpires of note include John O. "Honest John" Kelly, who appeared in more World Series (five) than any other umpire of the day; fiesty Timothy Hurst, quick and handy with curses, quips, and fists; Benjamin F. Young, killed in a railroad accident en route to a game, who in 1887 drew up a professional code of ethics for umpires as well as a ten-point proposal to improve their status; John F. Sheridan, the prototype of the modern umpire; and John A. Heydler and Thomas J. Lynch, each of whom later became president of the National League.

With the 1903 peace agreement between the National League and the new American League, major league baseball entered the modern era and brought stature and stability for umpires. Byron Bancroft "Ban" Johnson, president of the upstart American League, led in providing the strong support from league officials that was essential to the morale and effectiveness of the umpires. Noted for his backing of umpires when he had been the head of the Western League, Johnson insisted that umpires be respected and backed up his words by supporting their decisions and suspending players who were guilty of flagrant misconduct. In turn, he insisted upon tactfulness in contrast to the combativeness of the previous era. The National League followed suit, especially under ex-umps Lynch and Heydler, and by World War One, major league umpires enjoyed "unprecedented authority, dignity, and security." As umpire, manager, and baseball executive, Clarence "Pants" Rowland later remarked: "All umpires ought to tip their hats whenever Ban Johnson's name is mentioned."

Johnson also took the lead in dealing with the obvious handicaps presented by the single-umpire system. The game had long since become too fast and the players too devious for a lone arbiter to follow the action, let alone control the contest; moreover, in case of illness or injury clubs had to use a player to officiate the game. A three-umpire system, suggested in 1885 and actually used in the World Series that year, was an aberration, but a two-umpire system was much discussed in the 1880s and 1890s. Although the Players League of 1890 employed two umpires and in 1898 the two-umpire system was sanctioned in the rules, club owners continued to resist the expense of a second arbiter. After Johnson added a fifth umpire in 1902, the use of two arbiters became frequent, common, and then standard—an umpire-in-chief to call balls and strikes and a field umpire to make decisions on the bases. Again, the National League followed apace

and in 1912 both leagues had ten-man staffs—two umpires per game and two replacements in reserve.

While front office support and the two-man system contributed greatly to the effectiveness of the umpire on the field, the enhanced stature of umpires was due perhaps as much to the personalities and contributions of the men who served in the first two decades of the twentieth century. That so many of the umpires who loom large in baseball history (and mythology) hail from the early decades of the century is partly the result of the extraordinary skill required to manage the game during the dead-ball era, when the bunt, stolen base, and hit-and-run were primary offensive tactics, and partly because of the media attention lavished on major league baseball at the time.

Ban Johnson, who personally selected his umpires with an exacting eye for ability and character, assembled an imposing staff for the American League. The senior umpire was John F. "Jack" Sheridan, veteran from the nineteenth century, who served as the acknowledged model for the younger men in both leagues and popularized working from a crouch position behind the plate. Another holdover was Franklin O'Loughlin, nicknamed "Silk" as a boy because of his long, curly hair, who successfully matched wits and words with players. College-educated William G. "Billy" Evans, who in 1906 became, at twenty-two, the youngest major league umpire in history, wrote nationally syndicated sports columns while working as an umpire, and went on to be a baseball executive. A fastidious dresser, Evans set the standard for the appearance of umpires on the field. English-born Thomas H. "Tommy" Connolly umpired the American League's first game in 1901 and thirty years later became the Junior Circuit's first umpire-in-chief (1931–54); patient and reserved yet firm, he established the league's tradition of ejecting players only as a last resort and once went ten years without a banishment.

The National League had its own illustrious arbiters. Outstanding were Canadian Bob Emslie, who for years umpired wearing a wig because his frazzled nerves caused premature baldness; hulking Cy Rigler, who while in the minors in 1905 started the tradition of raising his right hand on called strikes; Hank O'Day, stickler for technicalities, whose controversial Merkle decision in 1908 is a staple of baseball lore; and William J. "Lord" Byron, "The Singing Umpire," who periodically announced his decisions in melodious (if not poetical) singsong verse. But it was William G. "Bill" Klem, generally regarded as the greatest umpire in history, who dominated the league staff and set the style for Senior Circuit arbiters. Self-righteous and autocratic, Klem boasted of his scrupulous honesty and encyclopedic knowledge of the rules, intimidated players with threats of fines, and dramatically illustrated his insistence upon discipline and authority during arguments by drawing a mark in the dirt and warning antagonists, "Don't cross the line!" He also popularized the inside chest protector, the over-the-shoulder position for calling balls and strikes, emphatic arm signals for calls, and straddling the lines instead of standing in foul territory. Sharp-tongued and tough-minded, the highly publicized "Old Arbitrator," who for sixteen consecutive years worked every game behind the plate (instead of rotating with the base umpire as had become the norm) and vowed, "I never missed one [call] in my life," was for most of his thirty-six-year career the public's personification of the major league umpire. Upon retiring in 1941, Klem served as the league's first modern chief of umpires until his death in 1951.

Between World Wars One and Two, when baseball dominated the nation's sport consciousness as the National Pastime, umpiring became a career vocation instead of a limited occupational opportunity. Expanded schedules meant seven months of employment, and umpires received better salaries and more recognition. Staff stability became the norm: an umpire who passed muster the first two or three years could look forward to a long career. Umpires continued to be vexed by arguments with players, insults from fans, and occasional flying objects, but the vicious rowdiness declined. The physical abuse was curtailed significantly because of the stiff penalties imposed for fighting and bottle tossing, while the verbal abuse abated as league officials and the press did an about-face after the infamous Black Sox Scandal by proclaiming the umpire the personification the game's integrity. To underscore their role as independent arbitrators, umpires had to make travel arrangements separate from players and patronize different bars, hotels, and restaurants.

Umpiring had become a desirable and respectable vocation, but the odds against a major league career were far greater for umpires than for players. Competition was keen, as normally only one or two of the some two dozen umpiring positions came open each year. And the low pay, primitive working conditions, wearisome travel, and vicious abuse from players and fans that characterized the life of the minor league umpire drove out those who would or could pursue other employment. Moreover, there was no prescribed system of career development. Becoming a professional umpire was a matter of chance opportunity or personal contacts; there was no systematic evaluation or supervision of minor league arbiters; and advancement, even to the major leagues, was sometimes more a matter of politics and personalities than merit or ability. Nonetheless, those who persevered as "men of the cloth" and proved their mettle in the big time enjoyed a secure and esteemed career. Where Tim Hurst justified working as an umpire by saying, "You can't beat the hours," Bill Klem would declare, "Baseball to me is not a game; it is a religion."

Still, major league umpires received far greater recognition than remuneration. The pay scales for umpires were the same in both leagues. In the early 1900s the annual salary for major league umpires ranged from $1,500 to $2,000; by 1910 the top salary in the National League was $3,000, with only four of the seven umpires earning more than $2,000. Umpires who worked the World Series received $400 until Bill Klem demanded and received $650 in 1917; the next year Klem received $1,000 for the Fall Classic, but the pay for all other umpires remained $650. In 1937 salaries ranged from $4,000 for new umpires to $10,000 for the most veteran arbiters; umpires could expect an extra $2,500 from the World Series. Five years later the pay scale rose to $5,000 and $12,000, but compensation for the Series remained the same. Although the salaries for men at the top of the pay scale seem good for a 154-game, seven-month season, umpires had to pay all their expenses except railroad fares

while on the road until 1940, when they received a $750 allowance for travel, a sum that most umpires argued covered only about one-half of their expenses. Moreover, they had to buy and maintain their own clothing and equipment, including ball-strike indicators, masks, and chest protectors. Nonetheless, better pay, working conditions, and status translated into more attractive and thus longer careers; twenty years' service was not uncommon. Consequently, both major leagues established a pension plan for retired umpires, but they were restricted to those who had served more than fifteen years and limited to $100 per year with maximum lifetime benefits of $2,400.

The size of umpiring staffs was also increased. The two-umpire system was the norm during the 1920s, but it became common practice to assign one of the reserve umpires to critical games or series; by 1933 three umpires were assigned routinely to regular-season games. The four-man crew was instituted in 1952. In the World Series the two-man crew, one umpire from each league, was used until 1908, when a pair of two-man teams alternated games. In the third game of the 1909 Series, all four umpires were on the field at the same time, thus establishing the four-umpire tradition that continued through 1946; in 1947 an "alternate" umpire from each league was stationed along a foul line in the outfield, thus creating the current six-umpire crew. Four umpires worked the All-Star Game from 1933 to 1948; the following year it conformed to the World Series format in putting the alternates on the field.

Although major league umpires, save for a few short-lived experiments, wore blue serge suits and officiated according to the same rule book, subtle and not-so-subtle differences in the style and technique of umpiring developed between the two leagues. Inasmuch as league presidents from the beginning hired, assigned, and instructed their umpires, personal preferences were reflected in the umpiring staffs early in the century. Then interleague chauvinism sustained and accentuated the distinctiveness. Under Ban Johnson's leadership, the American League soon boasted an overall staff that was superior to the National League, just as the Junior Circuit had more star players, stronger teams, and more successful managers during the same period. Because Johnson believed that all of his umpires were good enough to work the World Series, the prestigious (and lucrative) assignment was rotated among his staff, whereas postseason honors in the National League went selectively to the best (or most favored) umpires. In return for backing his umpires to the hilt, Johnson demanded reserve and restraint on the field, whereas National League presidents adopted a more laissez-faire attitude toward their umpires.

As a result, arbiters in the Senior Circuit were far more colorful, pugnacious, and individualistic than their American League counterparts, just as National League players and managers were freer and higher spirited than those in the Junior Circuit. It was a volatile mix, and there were many more rhubarbs, fines, and suspensions in the National League, where arbiters had to be courageous in fending off mean-spirited players and managers. And because Johnson liked his umpires to display a strong physical presence, a preference shared by Tommy Connolly, American League umpires were generally "big" men, whereas most National League arbiters, because of the dominant role of the five-foot-seven-inch Bill Klem, were shorter and slight of build.

More important than general differences in style and appearance were the specific differences in technique between the two leagues. At first umpires in both leagues held large inflated chest protectors in front of their bodies when behind the plate. Consequently, they called balls and strikes by crouching directly behind the catcher and looking over his head. The American League continued to use the "balloon" or "mattress" as favored by Tommy Connolly, but it became *de rigueur* in the National League to follow Bill Klem's preference for wearing a more compact chest protector under his coat and calling balls and strikes by viewing the plate from just over the catcher's shoulder nearest the batter. Here, form had great effect: the American League umpires became known for calling more "high" strikes and the National League for calling more "low" strikes.

Not as well known as the flamboyant umpires of the formative years, the men who worked between the World Wars were collectively better umpires and included some of the game's greatest arbiters. Along with Emslie, Klem, O'Day, and Rigler, the National League staff boasted George Barr, Lee Ballanfant, Larry Goetz, George Magerkurth, "Uncle Charley" Moran, Ralph "Babe" Pinelli, Ernie Quigley, and John "Beans" Reardon. Joining Connolly and Bill Dinneen in the American League were such illuminaries as Harry Geisel, Cal Hubbard, George Moriarty, Bill McGowan, Emmett "Red" Ormsby, and Clarence "Brick" Owens. Perhaps the best was McGowan, who for thirty years received universal praise from his peers and ranks as one of the premier umpires in history.

Sociologically, the umpires of the Golden Age represented both change and continuity. Like their predecessors, the majority hailed from the Northeast, the Midwest, and the South; and many were former athletes for whom umpiring was a way of staying in baseball. Some were ex-major leaguers— Charlie Berry, Bill Dinneen, George Hildebrand, Charlie Moran, George Moriarty, Hank O'Day, Al Orth, Babe Pinelli, George Pipgras, and Eddie Rommel. There were, however, important changes. Ethnically, the umpires reflected a pattern of cultural assimilation similar to that evident in the rosters of players. Initially umpires were overwhelmingly English in origin, but then the Irish by the 1890s and Germans by World War One became conspicuous and were followed by Jews in the 1920s and Italians and Slavs in the 1930s. And where collegian Billy Evans was unique among the mostly unlettered arbiters early in the century, college-educated (or graduated) umpires were increasingly common. Essentially, umpires between the wars had become a reasonable cross section of the white working-class American population.

Spurred by war-induced prosperity, continental expansion, and television revenue, baseball led the transformation of professional sport from a commercial business to an entertainment industry. Moreover, baseball, like all organized sport, felt the impact of the social and cultural changes that swept over America. After World War Two umpiring truly became a profession, and by the end of the 1980s major league umpires were not only far better trained and organized than ever before but also a forceful

and independent voice in baseball affairs.

Umpiring, like baseball itself, was enormously popular in the days following World War Two. By 1949 some fifty-nine minor leagues provided extensive on-the-job training for an unprecedented number of aspiring arbiters, but it was the umpire training school that was responsible for postwar umpires being so much better prepared than their predecessors. George Barr of the National League opened the first umpire training school in 1935, and in 1939 Bill McGowan of the American League established a second school. In 1946 Bill McKinley, who attended both the Barr and McGowan schools, became the first graduate of a training school to reach the major leagues. By the mid-1950s training school graduates were common, and by the 1960s it was virtually impossible to become a professional umpire without attending one of several training schools.

The umpire schools had profound effects on umpiring. First, graduates of the training schools were more knowledgeable of rules and more skilled in techniques than the earlier "self-taught" umpires. Second, formal training had the predictable effect of imposing uniformity of style and personality, as students were instructed "by the book" and maverick characters were weeded out. Finally—and most significantly—the umpire school was the catalyst that transformed umpiring from vocation to profession.

The professionalization of umpiring had profound effects. Formalized instruction and systematic career development attracted more middle-class college men, as umpiring was increasingly viewed less as a way of staying in professional sport than as a desirable career choice. And, reflecting the demographic shifts that prompted continental expansion, most umpires, like players, now hailed from the Sun Belt or the Pacific Coast. The lone area in which umpires lagged far behind players in mirroring the social changes of society at large was race. It was not until 1966, twenty years after Jackie Robinson broke the color line, that Emmett Ashford joined the American League and became the first black major league umpire. (He was also the first black professional umpire, breaking in with the Southwestern International League in 1951.) In 1973 Art Williams integrated the National League. Despite the strong presence of Latino players since the 1940s, Armando Rodriguez (1974) and Rich Garcia (1975) were the first Hispanic umpires in the majors.

Umpires also adopted a more professional attitude. They candidly admitted errors and portrayed themselves not as omnipotent enforcers of the law who demanded respect but as impartial judges who deserved respect. That umpires were skilled but fallible men became clearly visible in 1956, when Ed Rommel and Frank Umont broke a long-standing taboo by wearing eyeglasses on the field. But the most important effect of growing professionalization was that umpires increasingly viewed themselves as deserving the pay and perquisites of professionals.

In contrast with the strong support from league headquarters for their actions on the field, umpires historically were unable to protect themselves from monetary and personnel injustices because they negotiated individually instead of collectively with the leagues. Umpires repeatedly were dismissed arbitrarily, and in 1953, for the first time in fifteen years, umpires received a modest salary increase—a salary range of $6,000 to $16,000 and an increase in World Series pay to $3,000. Early efforts at organizing were to no avail, and in 1945 Ernie Stewart of the American League was fired for alleged unionizing activity. But in 1963, led by Augie Donatelli, umpires in the Senior Circuit organized the National League Umpires Association, headed by Chicago labor attorney John J. Reynolds. After Reynolds's success in raising salaries, American League umpires became unionists. When Bill Valentine and Al Salerno were dismissed in 1968, allegedly for incompetence but patently for unionizing activities, an appeal to the National Labor Relations Board resulted in umpires in both leagues being organized into the Major League Umpires Association. A one-day strike of the first game of the championship playoffs on October 3, 1970, the first by umpires in major league history, prompted the league presidents to recognize the Association and negotiate a labor contract that set a minimum salary of $11,000 and raised the average salary to $21,000.

Eight years later the Umpires Association made major advances under the new leadership of Richard G. "Richie" Phillips, a Philadelphia lawyer who also represented National Basketball Association referees. A second umpire's strike on August 25, 1978, lasted only one day, owing to a court injunction against the Association, but a third strike from Opening Day to May 18, 1979, won major concessions for the union, including a salary schedule of $22,000 to $55,000, based on years of service; annual no-cut contracts; $77 per diem while traveling; and two weeks' midseason vacation. The aftermath of the prolonged strike, which demonstrated the power of the Association and the inadequacy of replacement umpires, was marked by ill will between the union umpires and "the Class of '79"—the four "scab" umpires retained on each league's staff. A fourth strike of seven of the eight 1984 playoff games was settled by the intercession of new Commissioner Peter Ueberroth, who granted the umpires a sizable increase for playoff and World Series games as well as providing that the money go into a pool that would be distributed in part to umpires not working postseason contests. A fifth strike was adverted in 1985 when an arbitrator—former President Richard M. Nixon—awarded umpires a 40 percent pay increase for the expanded best-of-seven playoff series. Although most attention has been focused on contract negotiations, umpires have also successfully used the power of the Association to seek from league presidents and the commissioner the impositions of fines and suspensions on players, managers, and even owners for objectionable conduct and comments.

The growth and success of the umpire's union was made possible by two factors. First, with the expansion of franchises from the traditional sixteen (8 in each league) to twenty in 1961-1962, twenty-four in 1969, and twenty-six in 1977, umpires became a numerically significant force. Second—and far more important—was television, which not only brought unprecedented publicity to umpires but also generated the enormous revenue that made it possible for major league baseball to meet the monetary demands of umpires as well as players.

Finances aside, television was a mixed blessing for umpires. If heightened visibility underscored the umpire's skill and central role in the game, it also glaringly exposed errors to millions of viewers. The photographer's camera had occasionally exposed an incorrect call, but television's instant replay both emphasized mistakes and encouraged second-guessing. When slow-motion replays began to be shown on scoreboard screens, one crew in 1975 left the field and refused to return until the practice stopped. Television also affected performance and appearance. It had once been axiomatic for umpires to develop a subdued, even somber appearance, and take pride in anonymity. But in the Age of Television, arbiters began to project themselves into leading roles. From the time televised games became popular in the early 1950s, some umpires played to the camera through flamboyant, demonstrative motions when making calls. While a few like Emmett Ashford and Ron Luciano subsequently developed "showboating" to a fine art, umpires no longer shunned the spotlight of publicity; Luciano even parlayed his popularity for comedic calls on the field into a career in the telecast booth and as a writer.

The physical appearance of umpires was also tailored for the public eye. Increased emphasis was placed on size, as taller and more muscular men were in vogue—perhaps to personify the umpire's authority in an antiauthoritarian age. The American League's adoption of gray slacks in 1968 and maroon blazers in 1971 was part of an effort to project a distinctive "sporty" image, as was the case later when umpires in both leagues began wearing numerals on their sleeves and baseball caps with letters designating league affiliation. Similarly, contact lenses were favored over glasses and in 1988 obese umpires were put on weight-reduction programs.

Aside from the superficialities of cap insignia and jacket color, there was little to distinguish the two umpire staffs in appearance. Training in umpire schools and minor league supervision by the Umpire Development Program had the effect of imposing uniformity of style and technique on umpires and thus on the leagues. Moreover, by the 1970s American League arbiters had adopted the inside chest protector, while the National League mimicked the preference for "big" men. However, a reversal in league images also occurred: just as the players in the Senior Circuit were widely regarded as superior to those in the Junior, National League umpires were similarly perceived as better in the 1960s and 1970s; meanwhile, the American League, with umpires like Ashford and Luciano and fiery managers like Billy Martin and Earl Weaver, became more volatile than the now staid National League.

Despite television exposure, heightened after 1969 by intraleague championship playoffs, umpires as a group were more anonymous than before. Exceptions like Luciano notwithstanding, the individuality of umpires was submerged by the four-member crew, the numerical expansion of staffs, the frequent rotation among cities, the standardization of styles and techniques, the decline in the frequency of rhubarbs, and the attempt to project a more staid professional image. Few umpires stood out as demonstrably superior to their colleagues, partly because systematic training and preparation had increased generally the competence of all arbiters and partly because professional basketball and football now offered competition for outstanding officials. Nonetheless, there were some premier umpires in the postwar era, chief among them Nestor Chylak and John Stevens of the American and Al Barlick and Doug Harvey of the National League.

During the course of a century of major league baseball, the umpire became transformed from a despised, untrained, semiprofessional "necessary evil" to a respected, skilled professional who epitomizes the integrity of the game itself. In the process some arbiters became immortalized in record books for notable achievements and distinctions. J. L. Boake umpired the first professional league game (1871), Billy McLean the first National League game (1876), and Tommy Connolly the first American League game (1901). Hank O'Day and Connolly umpired the first modern World Series (1903), while Bill Dinneen, Bill Klem, Bill McGowan, and Cy Rigler worked the first All-Star Game (1933). Bill Klem holds the record for most seasons in the majors (thirty-seven), most World Series (eighteen) and most World Series games (one hundred-eight). Al Barlick and Bill Summers worked the most All-Star Games (seven). George Hildebrand holds the record for most consecutive games umpired (3,510). (Babe Pinelli has claimed that he did not miss a regulation game in his twenty-two-year career.) Emmett Ashford was the first black professional umpire in both the minor (1951) and major leagues (1966), while Armando Rodriguez (1974) was the first Hispanic umpire in the majors. Bernice Gera was the first female professional umpire (1972). Evans was the youngest (twenty-two) and Klem the oldest (sixty-eight) to umpire a major league game. Six umpires are enshrined in the Baseball Hall of Fame: Jocko Conlan (1974), Tommy Connolly (1953), Bill Klem (1953), Billy Evans (1973), Cal Hubbard (1976), and Al Barlick (1989).

The Highlights
of the Game

Streaks and Feats

Jack Kavanagh

The past of baseball is accented by feats of accomplishment. The heroics of individual players or collective efforts of teams are listed in record books as bare statistics. It is the purpose of this section to clothe these with accounts of how such records were made.

These are the achievements of mortals whom we have made into heroes by giving great value to things they have done. Deeds of baseball players are valued more highly than scholarship, skills in creative crafts, or sustaining a precarious balance of world peace. We can name more Cy Young Award winners than we can list those given the Nobel Peace Prize; we can rattle off batting champions but not name holders of the Pulitzer Prize.

It is axiomatic that all records are made to be broken, yet it is wasteful to throw away old records which have been cherished by generations of fans and only replace them with a newly minted line of agate type. Those who have been on the top of the list, or came close to the peak, have been recognized by relying on lists which sustain enough depth to single out the most noteworthy performances in the many categories which are represented.

As the former mayor of New York City, the dapper, perceptive Jimmy Walker, once admonished Babe Ruth when he had fallen from grace in the eyes of fans, "The cheers of yesterday have a short echo."

The Streaks

Most records are, eventually, displaced by new ones. Some survive because the conditions under which they were made have been altered by changing circumstances in baseball. Some, such as the accumulation of sheer totals, are pushed higher. This is not so much a matter of accomplishment as it is of perseverance and lengthened seasons.

Longest Hitting Streaks

Joe DiMaggio's feat of hitting safely in 56 consecutive games is the type of record which is in jeopardy of being broken when each new baseball season begins. It is in jeopardy because every player has the same chance as DiMaggio to hit safely in every game he plays. Stringing enough of these games together to reach the level DiMaggio did in 1941 tests both a player's skill and his nerve.

The way baseball is played has not altered significantly since 1941. That year DiMaggio batted .357. In 1987 Wade Boggs, a current threat to topple DiMaggio's re-

cord, batted .363. He even temporarily moved into DiMaggio's class as a home run hitter, with 24. In 1941 DiMaggio had hit 30. Boggs was also dropped from batting first or second to hitting third. Players with power have a different approach to collecting base hits than did Willie Keeler, whose nineteenth-century record of 44 consecutive games in which he hit safely was broken by Joe DiMaggio. Those with extra-base power are expected to sacrifice the string-extending single for a game-winning home run when the occasion rises. In setting his record, DiMaggio never once bunted for a base hit.

DiMaggio's streak is mind-boggling in its length, yet temptingly attainable by batters capable of hitting for high averages. And any player might get on a hot streak and sustain it long enough to challenge DiMaggio's total. However, those who have set extended streaks did it while accomplishing a high season's average. The trick is to string those games with base hits together. The more games in which a batter has hit safely, the greater the possibility these will come in succession for long stretches.

Until the New York press, wire services, and broadcast industry made Joe DiMaggio's consecutive-game hitting streak a matter of national awareness and interest, this kind of feat was not noted with a daily fanaticism. Streaks drew comment, but this was mostly reserved to be relished during the winter's Hot Stove League sessions among sport-starved fans.

Although Willie Keeler's consecutive-game string became the target for future attempts to exceed it, it might have been only one of the records made under special circumstances. Keeler's 44 consecutive games might only be unusual in retrospect because the string began on Opening Day, 1897. Had Bad Bill Dahlen not had a most peculiar bad day on August 7, 1894, even Joe DiMaggio's 56-game streak would only be a "modern record" set after 1900. As it is, Bill Dahlen appears high on the list with the 42 games in which he hit safely.

DiMaggio was stopped by stellar infield play. Bill Dahlen was stopped by his own inability to fatten his record in a game in which almost everyone else did. Dahlen's team, the Chicago Colts, had 17 hits, winning a ten-inning game from Cincinnati 1311. Dahlen's blanking was more evident because it was sandwiched between the feats that day of his teammates, Jimmy Ryan and Walter Wilmot. Ryan, the leadoff batter, had five hits, three of them doubles, and Walter Wilmot, who followed Dahlen in the batting order, also had five hits, two of them triples.

Dahlen was at bat a half dozen times, but the Reds' pitchers, Chauncey Fisher and Tom Parrott, found him, uniquely that day, an easy out. Dahlen's feat was obscured. When Willie Keeler, a star of greater national awareness, hit safely in 44 games three years later, the eclipsed record was simply noted but not recounted in the detail which was later paid to the strings which exceeded it. Although appearing in 121 games and batting .362, Dahlen was not a regular shortstop at that time, dividing his games between short and third.

It was Keeler's feat which caught the public fancy, particularly as it began on Opening Day, April 22, 1897, and continued for 44 games into the season. He was eventually stopped on June 18. Until then, it seemed he had found an unending series of opportunities to "hit 'em where they ain't"—his simplistic explanation for his base-hit totals. Keeler's record not only stood the test of time until Joe DiMaggio broke it in 1941, it still stands as the National League record, tied only by Pete Rose in 1978.

It wasn't until 1922 that the feat of hitting successfully in successive games became a real target for seekers of new records. Keeler's streak had been regarded more as evidence of his great ability to rap out base hits than as a model of daily consistency. He was a widely admired player, the leadoff batter for the Baltimore Orioles, three times pennant winners prior to the 1897 season.

When Ty Cobb came along, the fact that he nearly equaled Keeler's mark in 1911, when he set an American League record with 40 successive games in which he got at least one hit, was also taken as a sign of his superiority, not necessarily observed as a model event.

But in 1922 the public and press were ready for new records, and they had popular heroes to set them. In 1922 both George Sisler and Rogers Hornsby created new marks in hitting safely in consecutive games. Sisler broke Cobb's American League record and Hornsby notched 33 games in a row in which he had a base hit. This was hailed as a new record for righthanded batters, at least since 1900. Dahlen's 42 had been made before the turn of the century. While such a demarcation might be a dubious distinction, it serves to create new records. (Eventually those who are insatiable for "new records" will draw a line across some point in the twentieth century and begin proclaiming new records by ignoring those which, like DiMaggio's 56-game streak, seem unbreakable.)

Consider, too, that Ty Cobb, the American League record holder, whose 1911 mark was Sisler's target, was still quite capable of breaking his own record in 1922. Although the hit which raised his final average that year to .401 was argued about, he was still a high-average batter and needed only to string enough games together to set a new mark. Hitting safely in consecutive games was a trademark for Cobb. He hit in 20 or more games in a row seven times during his career.

George Sisler was a very popular player. A college product when the campus was not a direct line to the major leagues, with superlative skills and a gentlemanly manner, he was widely admired. In addition, his team, the St. Louis Browns, was engaged in a hot pennant battle with the New York Yankees.

Sisler began his string on July 27 and continued through August and past Labor Day, getting his base hit in game after game. Then, with his targets in sight— Cobb's American League record and Keeler's major league record, set in the National League—Sisler injured his right shoulder. It was thought at first that not only might he not be able to keep his consecutive string going,

but he might not be able to finish the season.

Ironically Sisler found himself at the threshhold of Cobb's record while playing against the Detroit Tigers, managed by Cobb, who patrolled center field. Sisler notched games 37 and 38 when the Tigers came to Sportsman's Park in St. Louis. On September 11, struggling to keep his streak alive, Sisler tried for game 39, one short of Cobb's record.

Sisler had been granted a streak-extending single by a generous scorer on a fly ball which Bobby Veach had reached but couldn't hold, but in 1922 there were no message boards or public address systems to inform fans of scorer's decisions. So Cobb, playing center field, was too far away from the press box to see the scorer hold up one finger, the traditional sign of a safe hit. He didn't know Veach's muff had been ruled a hit. As far as he knew, Sisler, coming to bat in the bottom of the ninth, with two out, a runner on first, and the score 43 in favor of Detroit, was hitless.

Manager Cobb had a choice. He could order Sisler, the Browns' most dangerous hitter, walked. This would move the tying run into scoring position and put the winning run on base. It would have been bad baseball and worse sportsmanship to order an intentional walk. Cobb might have been tempted to deny his rival what he thought was a last chance, but he didn't. He did take the precaution of removing Bob "Fatty" Fothergill, a slow-footed fielder, and replacing him in right with a better defensive player, Ira Flagstead. Then he signaled Howard Ehmke to pitch. He did, and Sisler lined a triple between Cobb and Flagstead. He scored the game-winning run a moment later on a Marty McManus single. Cobb had lost a game he might have won by passing Sisler, and George had moved to within one game of tying Ty's record.

At this point Sisler's shoulder ached so much he couldn't play the next four games, a series against the last-place Boston Red Sox. It was one of those "might have been" situations. He might have set a new American League record then against the Red Sox. However, it was much more dramatically attained when the Yankees, a half game ahead of the Browns in a torrid pennant race's final stages, came to St. Louis for a crucial three-game series.

Sisler played. His shoulder and right arm were bandaged, and he could only swing his bat with one hand. But, he played and, in a 21 loss, he managed a lone hit off Bob Shawkey to tie Cobb's record. The next day, September 17, the Browns evened the series as Babe Ruth's nemesis, Hub Pruett, stopped the Yankees. Ruth did get a home run, but more importantly Sisler managed another one-handed base hit to break Cobb's record.

The final game of the series was won by the Yankees as Joe Bush gained his twenty-fifth victory and Sisler went hitless in four plate appearances, never making solid contact. The Yankees left town with an increased lead they nursed to a pennant by a one-game margin. With his team still in contention, Sisler was unable to play. He pinch-hit unsuccessfully the next day, as Walter Johnson defeated the Browns, then sat out games until he returned to action with a hit against the Athletics on September 23. He hit safely the next day, and then, in a peculiarity of the 1922 season, the whole league was idle for four days.

When the league resumed for the final Friday, Saturday, and Sunday, the Browns were unable to catch the Yankees, although George Sisler hit safely in the three final games. Leave out the pinch-hit effort against Walter Johnson, a desperate attempt by a player who, if he had been swinging with two hands, would have played the full game. Without an injured shoulder, Sisler arguably might have kept his string alive against Joe Bush. He might not have missed those four games against the pitching-poor Red Sox or the two final games against the Senators. He might have hit safely in all of those games as well as the three he added at the season's end. If he had, he would have finished the season, with no more games to play to extend his streak, with 52 games in which he hit consecutively. Think what a target that would have been for Joe DiMaggio in 1941.

The DiMaggio Streak

Joe DiMaggio was playing poorly when his epochal feat began. He wasn't thinking about hitting in 56 straight games; he was worrying about getting a hit in the game of May 15. In spring training DiMaggio hit safely in every exhibition game, a forecast of the record-setting year ahead. His momentum carried through the first eight games of the 1941 season. Then he was thrown into a slump by a junk-ball pitcher, Lester McCrabbe of the Philadelphia Athletics.

By mid-May DiMaggio was still floundering, hitting below .300 and without his usual authority. On May 15 he managed a scratch single. It was an unimpressive handle hit off Cotton Ed Smith of the Chicago White Sox. However, it began a streak that wouldn't end until another pitcher named Smith, Al Smith, paired with Jim Bagby, Jr., held Joe hitless in a game against the Cleveland Indians.

The well-known DiMaggio batting eye that had produced batting championships the two preceding seasons, grew sharper, although in most games he made only a single hit. There were to be 34 games in which the string was kept alive with a lone hit. Not only was this a precarious way to sustain a batting streak, it did not, in its opening stages, draw attention to the feat that was under way. Fans followed Joe's rising batting average but not his successive daily contributions to it. He was thought to be in a contest with Ted Williams, not with the ghosts of record holders whose feats had been both unchallenged and unnoticed since the 1920s. He never caught Williams, who was enjoying the last season a champion would bat over .400.

As DiMaggio's string lengthened, the days of another Yankee immortal, Lou Gehrig, grew fewer. The Iron Horse, who had set another sort of consecutive streak by appearing in 2,130 games, died on June 2, as DiMaggio's skein reached 19.

As the string stretched into the twenties, reporters began digging into record books. The last time this arcane event excited interest had been in 1922, when George Sisler broke Ty Cobb's American League record but was stopped short of Willie Keeler's total. In 1938 another St. Louis Browns first baseman, George McQuinn, had run off a string of 34 games in which he had hit safely. Since McQuinn was playing in the anonymity of the second division, little attention was paid to his challenge.

Because there are two major leagues, record setters have two targets. DiMaggio was required first to set a league mark at 42 and then proceed to reach 45 and set an all-time mark by breaking Keeler's total set in the past century.

By regarding DiMaggio first as a righthanded batter, he could challenge the closer record of Rogers Hornsby, who had hit in 33 straight games in 1922. No mention was made of Bill Dahlen's record of 1894. Perhaps the reporters assumed it had been made under different playing conditions and shouldn't count. They were wrong; the pitching distance had been established at sixty feet, six inches in 1893, and bunts fouled off counted as strikes from 1894. In any case, Dahlen's 42 games was less than Keeler's total, which became the ultimate target.

When DiMaggio passed Rogers Hornsby's total, the public's attention was heightened. Sisler's American League record was only a week's play away. The hype went into full swing. Les Brown's orchestra hurried a phonograph record onto the market, "Jolting Joe DiMaggio." As banal a tune as ever came from Tin Pan Alley, the song became a pep rally number as the band chanted, "Joe, Joe, DiMaggio, we want you on our side."

Bill "Bojangles" Robinson, who had tap-danced in movies with little Shirley Temple, did routines atop the Yankees dugout while he sprinkled what he called "goofer dust" to enhance DiMaggio's luck.

Despite the distractions of people pressing their attention on the reserved, unemotional DiMaggio, he continued his consistent, game-after-game pursuit of the next milestone, Sisler's league record. At the same time, he was carrying the Yankees toward a pennant. They had lost the title in 1940 after four successive world championships under manager Joe McCarthy. They were out to recapture their league's title.

Interest in Joe DiMaggio's quest went beyond the readers of the sports pages. The wire services carried stories assuring newspaper readers that Joe had extended his string before they gave the account of the game in which he did it. Radio newscasts began with bulletins about Joe's progress.

Cynics and debunkers, who concentrated their suspicions on anything coming out of New York, particularly if it gave credit to the Yankees, watched closely for scoring decisions which would give DiMaggio a favored ruling.

Rival managers juggled pitching rotations to bring their best to the mound when DiMaggio and the Yankees came to town.

Dan Daniel, a prolific and conscientious sportswriter and editor, was the official scorer for games at Yankee Stadium in 1941, and he covered the team on the road for his paper. He has written extensively about DiMaggio's 56-game hitting streak. He saw every game.

The scorer's circumstances at Yankee Stadium, as described by Daniel, placed him in view of rabid Yankee supporters who gathered behind him to demand a base hit no matter how glaring the error which allowed DiMaggio to reach base.

Daniel wrote afterward that he had to have his home phone number changed. He also insisted both he and the other scorers around the league became hyperattentive every time DiMaggio came to bat once his string had become established as a potential record breaker.

Daniel also explained that players on the opposing teams were keyed up when DiMaggio batted, none wanting to contribute to extending the string by loafing on a ball and turning it into a hit. DiMaggio's streak lifted the quality of play, umpiring, and press coverage. Everyone, including DiMaggio, wanted him to earn a new record.

Years afterward, DiMaggio looked back on the 56 games and could only find one where he wished the play had not been as judgmental as it was. It came in the thirtieth game, when he was still short of Hornsby's record. The White Sox came to the Stadium, and Johnny Rigney was the pitcher. He had twice been DiMaggio's victim in earlier games in the streak but on this day had stopped the Yankee Clipper until the seventh inning.

Then DiMaggio hit a routine grounder to Luke Appling. The future Hall of Fame shortstop moved for the ball, but it took a bad bounce, hitting him in the shoulder. In his rush to recover, Appling grabbed at the ball, dropped it, then threw too late. A bad-hop single? Butterfingered retrieval? The official scorer, Dan Daniel, ruled it a hit. Lucky for Joe and fortunate for legend, too, because on his last time up, in the ninth, Taft Wright made a leaping catch to snatch a home run out of the right field stands. Joe would have been blanked.

The next day DiMaggio got another streak-extending break, almost the same way. This time the ball was hard hit and Appling could only knock it down. He couldn't make a throw. Too hard to handle? Scorer Daniel ruled so and the fans relaxed. A few days later Hornsby's record for righthanded batters would be broken and DiMaggio would be headed for Sisler's mark. However, it took another break for DiMaggio to get there.

Eldon Auker, a St. Louis submarine-ball pitcher, held Joe hitless until the eighth inning at Yankee Stadium. Unless one of the first three batters kept the inning alive, Joe, due up fourth, would not bat again. The Yankees were ahead by two runs, and it did not appear as though there would be a bottom of the ninth.

Johnny Sturm popped up, but Red Rolfe drew a walk. Tommy Henrich, the next batter, had a dilemma. He could still deprive Joe of a chance to bat if he hit into a double play. With manager McCarthy's consent, Henrich bunted and moved Rolfe to second base. Now, with first base open, it was Auker who had a dilemma. He could walk DiMaggio, hit him with a pitch (a strategy as underhanded as his delivery), or pitch to him.

DiMaggio stood at the plate, unruffled. Coolly he smashed the first pitch into left field for a double. It was a close call, but now Sisler's record was in reach.

In a Sunday doubleheader with Washington at Yankee Stadium, on June 29, DiMaggio tied Sisler's record in the first game and broke it in the nightcap. The record-tying hit came off knuckleballer Dutch Leonard and was broken with a last-chance single off the unknown Arnold Anderson. DiMaggio was one game short of tying Willie Keeler's 1897 record.

The only mark left for DiMaggio to eclipse was tied in the second game of a July 1 doubleheader with the Boston Red Sox and broken the next day.

The day DiMaggio claimed the American League record was marked by two extremes of luck. It was fortunate his record-tying hit came early in the game because a downpour deluged Yankee Stadium and the game was called after five innings. It was unfortunate that during the rain delay no one kept an eye on the bat rack. A souvenir hunter reached over the dugout and pulled out a bat. He grabbed DiMaggio's favorite club.

Although he was upset, the man who rarely showed emotion quietly borrowed a bat from teammate Tommy Henrich the next day. It was an identical thirty-six-inch, thirty-six-ounce bat, and Joe used it to break Keeler's record. His record-smashing hit was a prodigeous home run off Dick Newsome, a 19-game winner for the Red Sox. It carried high over the head of his rival, Ted Williams, into the left field stands.

Joe DiMaggio did not rest on his laurels. Actually, with the pressure to produce at least one base hit each game lifted, he began pounding out hits in clusters. He passed the 50-game mark and his luck still held. In the fifty-fourth game, he again came up against Johnny Rigney of the White Sox. This time he would have been stopped except for a topped roller. A typical lusty swing sent a dribbler slowly toward third base where Bob Kennedy was playing fearfully deep, a precaution normally taken by rival third baseman against DiMaggio. It worked to Joe's advantage that day as he beat out the slowly hit ball for his only hit. However, it would work to his disadvantage a few days later in Cleveland.

Although Joe DiMaggio said after his streak had ended, "I wish it could have gone on forever," like all good things it had to come to an end. Joe had reached 56 games when the kind of luck which occasionally had sustained him, such as the topped roller against Chicago, turned around. The Yankees came into Cleveland and crowds came, divided between fans' wishes to witness the streak extended and hometeam rooters' hopes that their team could bring the mighty DiMaggio to a halt.

What could only be a matter of time happened. As a minor league star in his native San Francisco, a nineteen-year-old Joe DiMaggio had been stopped after hitting in 61 consecutive games. After the 1941 streak ended, the *San Francisco Chronicle,* which had made daily reports of DiMaggio's record-breaking games, observed that the Pacific Coast League string had been ended by the son of a former major league pitching star, Bob Walsh, whose father, Big Ed Walsh, would be elected to the Hall of Fame. It was pointed out that DiMaggio's major league string was ended, in part, by Jim Bagby, Jr., another son of a successful major leaguer, a 31-game winner for the 1920 world champion Cleveland Indians.

It wasn't so much the pitching of starter Al Smith or reliever Bagby that halted DiMaggio as the glove work on the right side of the Indians' infield. Twice Ken Keltner, playing a very deep third base, took drives down the baseline and turned them into outs. And Joe's last chance found him deserted by luck on a bad bounce. A ball headed up the middle took an erratic hop, and shortstop Lou Boudreau grabbed it and flipped to second to start a double play that closed off DiMaggio's chance to keep safely intact the stretch of games in which he had hit.

Although the DiMaggio streak had been stopped, he was still a hot hitter, and even his favorite bat was back. An embarrassed fan from Newark admitted the theft and returned the bat, and Joe used it to continue his torrid hitting. He kept pounding out hits on a daily basis until he had hit safely in 16 more consecutive games. This meant

Joe DiMaggio's 1941 Hitting Streak

Game No.	Date	Club and Pitcher	AB	R	H
1	5-15	White Sox, Smith	4	0	1
2	5-16	White Sox, Lee	4	2	2
3	5-17	White Sox, Rigney	3	1	1
4	5-18	Browns, Harris, Niggeling	3	3	3
5	5-19	Browns, Galehouse	3	0	1
6	5-20	Browns, Auker	5	1	1
7	5-21	Tigers, Rowe, Benton	5	0	2
8	5-22	Tigers, McKain	4	0	1
9	5-23	Red Sox, Newsome	5	0	1
10	5-24	Red Sox, Johnson	4	2	1
11	5-25	Red Sox, Grove	4	0	1
12	5-27	Senators, Chase, Anderson, Carrasquel	5	3	4
13	5-28	Senators, Hudson	4	1	1
14	5-29	Senators, Sundra	3	1	1
15	5-30	Red Sox, Johnson	2	1	1
16	5-30	Red Sox, Harris	3	0	1
17	6-1	Indians, Milnar	4	1	1
18	6-1	Indians, Harder	4	0	1
19	6-2	Indians, Feller	4	2	2
20	6-3	Tigers, Trout	4	1	1
21	6-5	Tigers, Newhouser	5	1	1
22	6-7	Browns, Muncrief, Allen, Caster	5	2	3
23	6-8	Browns, Auker	4	3	2
24	6-8	Browns, Caster, Kramer	4	1	2
25	6-10	White Sox, Rigney	5	1	1
26	6-12	White Sox, Lee	4	1	2
27	6-14	Indians, Feller	2	0	1
28	6-15	Indians, Bagby	3	1	1
29	6-16	Indians, Milnar	5	0	1
30	6-17	White Sox, Rigney	4	1	1
31	6-18	White Sox, Lee	3	0	1
32	6-19	White Sox, Smith, Ross	3	2	3
33	6-20	Tigers, Newsom, McKain	5	3	4
34	6-21	Tigers, Trout	4	0	1
35	6-22	Tigers, Newhouser, Newsom	5	1	2
36	6-24	Browns, Muncrief	4	1	1
37	6-25	Browns, Galehouse	4	1	1
38	6-26	Browns, Auker	4	0	1
39	6-27	Athletics, Dean	3	1	2
40	6-28	Athletics, Babich, Harris	5	1	2
41	6-29	Senators, Leonard	4	1	1
42	6-29	Senators, Anderson	5	1	1
43	7-1	Red Sox, Harris, Ryba	4	0	2
44	7-1	Red Sox, Wilson	3	1	1
45	7-2	Red Sox, Newsome	5	1	1
46	7-5	Athletics, Marchildon	4	2	1
47	7-6	Athletics, Babich, Hadley	5	2	4
48	7-6	Athletics, Knott	4	0	2
49	7-10	Browns, Niggling	2	0	1
50	7-11	Browns, Harris, Kramer	5	1	4
51	7-12	Browns, Auker, Muncrief	5	1	2
52	7-13	White Sox, Lyons, Hallett	4	2	3
53	7-13	White Sox, Lee	4	0	1
54	7-14	White Sox, Rigney	3	0	1
55	7-15	White Sox, Smith	4	1	2
56	7-16	Indians, Milnar, Krakauskas	4	3	3
Totals			223	55	91

he would have reached an incredible 73 games had not Keltner and Boudreau pulled off outstanding defensive plays after game 56.

As it is, hitting safely in 72 of 73 games is almost unimaginable. Historians had to go back to the over-looked Bad Bill Dahlen to find a comparable feat for DiMaggio to eclipse almost half a century later. Back in 1894, after he had run up a string of 42 games, Dahlen ran off another stretch of 28 games in which he hit safely. He had left a neglected legacy of hitting in 70 of 71 games for DiMaggio to top with 72 in 73.

During his 56-game streak, Joe DiMaggio batted .408. Although he finished the 1941 season with a .357 average, he was second to Ted Williams's league-leading .406. However, DiMaggio had led his team to a championship

and this, with the incredible feat of hitting in 56 straight games, earned him the Most Valuable Player Award by a close margin.

Those whose interest in statistics match, if not exceed, a curiosity about the drama of making them, will want to know that, in hitting .408 during the 56 games, DiMaggio scored 56 runs and batted in 55. He hit 15 home runs, half his season's total, and had 35 extra-base hits among the 91 hits he collected in 223 at-bats. He walked 21 times, was hit by a pitch twice, and struck out only 7 times.

The Yankees went on to defeat the Brooklyn Dodgers in the World Series and, as the Japanese went on to bomb Pearl Harbor and involve the United States in World War Two, Joe was asked to take a $2,500 cut in salary for 1942. He managed to get a $5,000 raise and play the 1942 season before entering military service in possession of a unique feat which still attracts its new challengers.

The Pete Rose Challenge

The year 1978 was a tremendous one for Pete Rose, whose career with the Cincinnati Reds qualified him as a potential challenger for Joe DiMaggio's record of hitting safely in 56 consecutive games. Although he did not hit for the high averages of the other streakers who had held records—Keeler, Sisler, Hornsby, and DiMaggio—Rose batted leadoff and had amassed 10 seasons with 200 or more hits. Even more, he was the kind of player who would rise to any occasion. He loved a challenge.

Longest Hitting Streaks, NL

Player	Team	Year	G
Willie Keeler	BAL	1897	44
Pete Rose	CIN	1978	44
Bill Dahlen	CHI	1894	42
Tommy Holmes	BOS	1945	37
Billy Hamilton	PHI	1894	36
Fred Clarke	LOU	1895	35
Benito Santiago	SD	1987	34
George Davis	NY	1893	33
Rogers Hornsby	STL	1922	32
Ed Delahanty	PHI	1899	31
Willie Davis	LA	1969	31
Rico Carty	ATL	1970	31
Elmer Smith	CIN	1898	30
Stan Musial	STL	1950	30

Longest Hitting Streaks, AL

Player	Team	Year	G
Joe DiMaggio	NY	1941	56
George Sisler	STL	1922	41
Ty Cobb	DET	1911	40
Paul Molitor	MIL	1987	39
Ty Cobb	DET	1917	35
George Sisler	STL	1925	34
John Stone	DET	1930	34
George McQuinn	STL	1938	34
Dom DiMaggio	BOS	1949	34
Heinie Manush	WAS	1933	33
Sam Rice	WAS	1924	31
Ken Landreaux	MIN	1980	31
Tris Speaker	BOS	1912	30
Goose Goslin	DET	1934	30
Ron LeFlore	DET	1976	30
George Brett	KC	1980	30

Pete Rose's 1978 Hitting Streak

Game No.	Date	Club and Pitcher	AB	R	H
1	6-14	Cubs, Roberts	4	1	2
2	6-16	Cardinals, Denny	4	1	2
3	6-17	Cardinals, Yuckovich, Schultz	4	2	2
4	6-18	Cardinals, Martinez	4	1	1
5	6-20	Giants, Montefusco	5	2	2
6	6-21	Giants, Halicki	4	0	1
7	6-22	Giants, Knepper	4	0	1
8	6-23	Dodgers, Hooton	4	0	1
9	6-24	Dodgers, Welch	5	1	4
10	6-25	Dodgers, John	3	1	2
11	6-26	Astros, Lemongello	5	1	1
12	6-27	Astros, Niekro	4	1	1
13	6-28	Astros, Dixon	4	0	1
14	6-29	Astros, Bannister	3	0	1
15	6-30	Dodgers, Rautzhan	4	1	1
16	6-30	Dodgers, Welch, Forster, Hough	5	1	3
17	7-1	Dodgers, Rhoden	5	0	1
18	7-2	Dodgers, Rau	4	1	1
19	7-3	Astros, Bannister, McLaughlin	5	1	3
20	7-4	Astros, Richard	4	1	1
21	7-5	Astros, Niekro	4	0	1
22	7-6	Giants, Blue, Curtis	5	1	3
23	7-7	Giants, Barr	4	0	1
24	7-8	Giants, Montefusco	4	1	1
25	7-9	Giants, Halicki, Knepper	4	1	3
26	7-13	Mets, Koosman, Lockwood	5	0	2
27	7-14	Mets, Zachry	5	0	2
28	7-15	Mets, Swan	2	2	1
29	7-16	Mets, Siebert	5	1	1
30	7-17	Expos, Bahnsen	4	0	1
31	7-18	Expos, Dues	4	0	2
32	7-19	Phillies, Reed	4	1	1
33	7-20	Phillies, Kaat	5	1	1
34	7-21	Expos, Grimsley	3	1	1
35	7-22	Expos, Schatzeder	3	0	1
36	7-23	Expos, Rogers, Knowles	6	0	2
37	7-24	Mets, Zachry, Lockwood	5	2	2
38	7-25	Mets, Swan	4	1	3
39	7-26	Mets, Espinosa	3	0	1
40	7-28	Phillies, Lerch	2	1	1
41	7-28	Phillies, Carlton	4	0	1
42	7-29	Phillies, Lonborg, Kaat	4	1	3
43	7-30	Phillies, Christenson	5	0	2
44	7-31	Braves, Niekro	4	0	1
Totals			182	30	70

Willie Keeler's 1897 Hitting Streak

Game No.	Date	AB	R	H
1	April 22	5	2	2
2	April 23	4	1	2
3	April 24	4	1	2
4	April 26	4	0	1
5	April 27	5	2	2
6	April 28	5	1	3
7	April 29	4	1	2
8	April 20	4	3	3
9	May 3	4	0	1
10	May 4	4	0	2
11	May 5	4	0	1
12	May 6	5	0	3
13	May 7	6	2	1
14	May 8	3	1	1
15	May 10	4	0	1
16	May 11	5	1	2
17	May 12	5	0	3
18	May 14	6	2	2
19	May 15	6	2	2
20	May 16	6	3	3
21	May 17	4	1	2
22	May 18	6	1	1
23	May 19	4	1	1
24	May 20	4	1	3
25	May 21	3	1	2
26	May 22	4	2	2
27	May 25	5	0	1
28	May 26	5	1	2
29	May 27	5	1	3
30	May 29	6	2	2
31	May 30	4	0	1
32	May 31	4	1	1
33	May 31	5	2	1
34	June 2	5	1	4
35	June 5	5	1	1
36	June 7	4	1	1
37	June 9	5	2	2
38	June 10	4	0	2
39	June 11	4	0	2
40	June 12	5	2	2
41	June 14	5	1	2
42	June 15	3	0	1
43	June 16	5	2	1
44	June 18	4	3	3
Totals		201	49	82

Before he got around to taking a swing at DiMaggio's record, Rose had, as his first order of business, the matter of making his 3,000th career base hit. He opened the 1978 season needing 34 hits to reach a plateau only twelve others had gained. On May 5 Rose reached 3,000 with a single off Montreal pitcher Steve Rogers, before a hometown crowd at Riverfront Stadium.

"Charlie Hustle" was having an epoch-making season and, with one landmark reached, he soon found himself en route to another. Consecutive-game hitting streaks begin without signaling their advent. It is only as they grow that they attract attention.

Pete Rose was only batting .267 when he got a pair of hits against the Cubs on June 14. He kept adding hits in the games he played and, eventually, it was decided he had enough in a row to start looking for a record to be broken.

DiMaggio's 56-game streak in 1941 loomed far beyond expectation. However, the record keepers had gerrymandered Willie Keeler, holder of the National League record at 44, out of the books. There was a modern mark of 37, set during the wartime year of 1945, by Tommy Holmes of the Boston Braves.

Pete Rose hustled onward and, as luck would have it, came into Shea Stadium for a series with the Mets on the verge of knocking Holmes out of the record book. The patron saint of hype was on the ball, and a now sixty-one-year-old Tommy Holmes was on hand to root for Rose. Rose. He was there in a dual capacity. Tommy Holmes was also the Mets' community relations director.

There was another reward in having Pete Rose break Holmes's record in front of the Mets' fans. In 1973 Pete had been *persona non grata* when he had wrestled on the ground with skinny shortstop Bud Harrelson in a League Championship Game after a takeout slide by Rose at second base. The Mets fans remembered Rose calling them "animals" as they threatened to avenge the honor of the team by challenging the wives and children of the Reds' players in field boxes behind the Cincinnati dugout. However, hype places a statute of limitations on vengeance in New York. Whipped to a frenzy of impartiality by the Mets' announcers and a record-hungry press, people filled Shea Stadium ready to cheer Rose on while trusting he'd not be so unappreciative as to make his record-extending safety a game-winning hit.

On July 24 Pete Rose equaled the record of Tommy Holmes and to chants of "Go, Pete, Go!" broke it the next night against Craig Swan. An appreciative Holmes, pleased to have been a short-term celebrity, came onto the field to shake the hand of the man who had erased him from the record books. Pete now held the "modern" National League record for hitting safely in consecutive games. In fairness, he would now try to reach Willie Keeler's mark of 44, a feat turned before the century began. Pete continued his quest. He had the skill, the competitive instincts, and the attitude to do it. He was unruffled by press attention, accustomed to it as the consequence of being the game's most colorful player of his time. Would he break DiMaggio's seemingly unreachable mark? If anyone could, Pete Rose could do it. But first he had to lay the ghost of Willie Keeler and his 81-year-old record.

It was a struggle, as the whole streak had been, but Rose reached Keeler's mark on July 31 in Atlanta. His record-equaling hit came off the knuckleball pitching of Phil Niekro, a man whose own feats as a middle-aged ballplayer also merited recognition.

Keeler had been caught. Would he be passed? No. The next night a rookie lefthander, Larry McWilliams, held Pete Rose hitless through most of the game, and reliever Gene Garber provided the final denial. He struck Rose out.

Pete Rose is joined with Willie Keeler, linked now, regardless of the era when the feat was accomplished, as coholders of the National League record for hitting safely in consecutive games.

Consecutive Games Played

On June 1, 1925, no one thought the young substitute pinch-hitting for the New York Yankees was launching the most extraordinary streak of durability the game would ever see. The next day Lou Gehrig took the place of the team's star first baseman, Wally Pipp, and continued his uncertain start toward a goal so distant it was unimaginable.

Gehrig had played for Hartford in the Eastern League after the Yankees signed him off the campus of Columbia University. It was thought he would make the major league grade, but he had not been handed a starting job. Only when Pipp complained of a headache and was given the day off by manager Miller Huggins did Gehrig get a chance to start a game. So uncertain of the rookie's skills was management that two days later Aaron Ward pinch-hit for Gehrig and Pipp finished the game in the field.

Before June ended, Gehrig had been taken out of games three times for pinch hitters, although he continued to start games. On July 5 he wasn't even the starting first baseman. Fred Merkle, who in 1908, as a rookie himself, had failed to run to second on what appeared to be a game-winning single, started the game. Merkle, whose gaffe eventually cost the New York Giants a pennant to the Chicago Cubs, had been forever more labeled Bonehead by unforgiving fans. Gehrig was destined for adulation. This day he made a ninth-inning appearance, an unsuspected extension of a fledgling feat.

Of course at the time there was no suspicion that young Lou Gehrig had launched a string of consecutive-game appearances which wouldn't end until fourteen years later. He began it as a young giant in the prime of his life and ended it a dying man, forced out of the lineup with a rare disease. From start to finish it became a matter of drama as the survival of the string became a compelling goal which Gehrig sustained despite injury, sickness, acci-

dent, and managed to avoid ending inadvertently.

Gehrig is remembered, or known to people who never saw him play, as the gentle giant who was portrayed by actor Gary Cooper in the movie *The Pride of the Yankees*. In reality, particularly in his early years, Gehrig was a hard-nosed, competitive player who would readily leap into argument with umpires and enemy players. He was ejected from a major league game a half dozen times without drawing a suspension which would have ended his string of games.

Durable, yes. Gehrig was well dubbed "the Iron Horse" for his rawboned toughness. However, he never spared himself. A statistic which astonishes fans is that he stole home 15 times, risking crashing into a plate-blocking catcher. He ran the bases with surprising speed and fearless abandon. Babe Ruth and Lou Gehrig are remembered for the home runs they hit; yet they were also daring base runners.

Once Gehrig's penchant for never missing a game was established, just being in the boxscore was the goal. He could have simultaneously set records for consecutive games played at first base, while extending his string of boxscore appearances. However, while in the sixth year of his developing string, in a late-season game, the Yankees promoted a game in which Babe Ruth would pitch while Lou Gehrig took his place in the outfield. Harry Rice, an outfielder who sometimes spelled Gehrig late in one-sided games, played first base.

Gehrig's 2,130-game skein, stretched over fourteen seasons, was not simply a matter of having him go out to first base day after day. For one thing, there were times when he could hardly play. When the Iron Horse was no longer a frisky colt, he developed lumbago, and it hobbled him from time to time. In midseason of 1934, Lou was seized by an attack and, immobilized, had to be helped off the field.

There was a conscious awareness on the part of the Yankees of the consecutive games Gehrig played, and this was kept alive by the sportswriters who covered the team. Everett Scott had astonished baseball with his consecutive-game appearances at shortstop, ending a string of 1,307 in 1925, the season Gehrig, his rookie roommate, began his string. Scott had started his run of games with the Boston Red Sox, and when he was bought by the Yankees in 1923, he carried on the string without interruption. He slowed down drastically early in 1925 and was first benched, then sold to the Senators. Unlike Scott, Lou Gehrig, the Iron Horse, would never be put out to pasture. However, Scott had left a legend behind, and it served to lead Gehrig toward new standards of durability.

The day after Gehrig had been helped off the field, with his string at 1,426, and Scott's record broken, he made a contrived appearance in the lineup. Hardly able to stand, he was in the lineup of the visiting Yankees in Detroit as the leadoff batter, penciled in to play shortstop. Despite his pain, he lined out a single and, with his appearance established in the boxscore, gave way to pinch runner Red Rolfe, who finished the game at short while Gehrig took his aching back to the hotel. Jack Saltzgaver, a utility infielder who, over the years, replaced Gehrig at first base more often than any other player, filled in at first that day.

Gehrig was back in the regular lineup the next day, collecting four hits, three of them doubles. He was on his way to the only batting title he ever won and the Triple Crown for 1934. But it wasn't a pain-free future ahead for Lou. Lumbago continued to be a problem. He left games early because he was feeling ill, and he had a thumb injury in 1938 which he ignored to keep his string going.

It was during 1938 that the perpetual machine began to show signs of wearing out. For the first time he batted below .300; his stats—a .295 average, 29 home runs, and 107 runs batted in—would have pleased most players. But they were substandard for Lou, and so was his general play. Just age catching up, it was thought, just the way it had slowed Everett Scott in 1925 when Gehrig was starting out.

In spring training the next season, it was evident that something was amiss, but manager Joe McCarthy left it to Gehrig to decide when to call it quits. It was on May 2, 1939, after eight feebly played games had brought his string to 2,130, that Gehrig advised McCarthy to replace him.

The longest streak of its kind, seemingly impossible to ever exceed despite the longer seasons, ended. For fourteen years Gehrig had played despite a broken thumb, a broken toe, back spasms, frequent colds, and recurring attacks of lumbago. He had been forced from the lineup by something no one could foresee and almost no one had ever heard about. When the tests at Mayo Clinic proved that he had amyotrophic lateral sclerosis, it was so singular an affliction that it was renamed Lou Gehrig's Disease. It was incurable then and still is. Gehrig was a doomed man. He knew it, as did his wife, Eleanor. They bravely pretended to each other that Lou would regain his strength.

He continued to carry the lineup card to home plate during the 1939 pennant-winning season, as the team captain, but soon he had to surrender even that role. On July 4, 1939, a Lou Gehrig Day was arranged at Yankee Stadium. The scene was repeated in the Gary Cooper movie and is seen often in filmed highlights of baseball history.

Babe Ruth, who had broken relationships with Gehrig during a 1934 postseason tour to the Pacific and Japan, embraced his former teammate, and the occasion came to a climax as Gehrig, a man who knew his life was nearly over, stood at a microphone, surrounded by the Yankees who had been his fellow players. He told a choked-up audience, "Today, I consider myself the luckiest man on the face of the earth." He died on June 2, 1941.

Far in the Distance

Lou Gehrig's legacy of stamina and determination reached such a length that all historians can do about the sturdy players who came after him is measure them for the role of runner-up.

As Gehrig's record was made in the American League, a separate claim can be laid to a National League record. Even so, the next longest string is Everett Scott's 1,307 made in the American League and, for many years, Joe Sewell's 1,103 was third on the list.

While the Gehrig streak was under way, Sewell, a future teammate, piled up most of his seasons of consecu-

tive play with Cleveland during the 1920s. Like Everett Scott, Sewell's daily appearances were to keep his glove available for defense and to make steady contributions at bat. Sewell is best remembered for his avoidance of strikeouts. Twice he fanned only 4 times in a whole season. Once he went 115 games without striking out in 437 times at bat. He set his consecutive-game string with Cleveland, later moving to the Yankees where he played for three years as Lou Gehrig's teammate. He was elected to the Hall of Fame in 1977.

During the 1930s, Gus Suhr, a fine-fielding first baseman for the Pittsburgh Pirates, reached 822 consecutive games played. It was dwarfed, even as he made it, by Gehrig's still intact string, but he far exceeded earlier National League marks.

Gus Suhr's National League record was broken by Stan Musial, who played in 895 straight games, ending in 1957 at age thirty-six. This provided a target for Billy Williams when his career with the Cubs got under way in 1963 and daily appearances were part of his routine. He sailed past Musial to claim the National League record at 1,117. He stopped in 1970, and the occasional rest did him good. He led the National League in batting in 1972 and his career, with Oakland, ended in 1975. He has been elected to the Hall of Fame.

Williams's new National League record provided an attainable goal for the only player since Gehrig to have the remotest expectation of breaking the all-time record. Steve Garvey was not a realistic bet, but he exuded the strength, stamina, and willpower it would take. He just didn't get started soon enough. Gehrig was twenty-two when his streak began; Garvey was twenty-six.

Also, Garvey did not become an everyday regular with the Los Angeles Dodgers until 1975, his sixth season with the team. He had been regarded as erratic at third base but, once moved across the diamond in 1974, he delivered with consistency in the field, at the bat, with power, and refused to budge from the lineup.

He left the Dodgers with his string intact after the 1982 season and took his Iron Man act to San Diego. A hand injury took him out of the lineup on July 29, 1983. He had broken Billy Williams's record the previous season, and all told he played in 1,207 consecutive games.

A special recognition is due to Pete Rose. Had he not paused to catch his breath during the 1978 season, when he was thirty-seven years old, he would be in second place behind Gehrig. In 1978 Rose had more realistic aims than Gehrig's too distant goal. During that season he reached the 3,000-hit mark and set aim on Ty Cobb's all-time total. He also captured the headlines with his assault on Joe DiMaggio's 56-game hitting streak.

The year 1978 was also Rose's last season with the Cincinnati Reds and, in a celebrated case of free agency, he moved to Philadelphia. There he not only resumed his climb toward Cobb's hit totals, but played again on a daily basis. When he sat down for two games in 1978 with the Reds, he snapped a somewhat modest run of 678 games. When he finally left the daily lineup in Philadelphia, in 1983, he had run off an even longer string of 745 games. Add them together and Rose's total is 1,423 games, longer than anyone's stretch except Gehrig's but far, far behind it.

Most Consecutive Games Played

2,130	Lou Gehrig
1,307	Everett Scott
1,250	Cal Ripken (through 1990)
1,207	Steve Garvey
1,117	Billy Williams
1,103	Joe Sewell
895	Stan Musial
829	Eddie Yost
822	Gus Suhr
798	Nellie Fox

Successive Pitching Victories

The 1912 baseball season produced a bumper crop of pitchers winning successive victories. Rube Marquard of the New York Giants topped everyone by running up a total of 19. This tied the record set by Tim Keefe, also of New York. Keefe had won his games in 1888, when the pitching distance was only fifty feet between pitcher and batter, but he had won them in a row and that is the measurement of this feat. The present distance of sixty feet, six inches (actually, this is only about 55 feet from the pitcher's point of release) was set in 1893, Keefe's last season.

Marquard's mark remains unmatched within the confines of a single season. The record for consecutive wins beginning in the midst of one season and extending into the next season is held by Carl Hubbell, whose 24 consecutive victories, starting in 1936 and continuing into 1937, tops the list.

However, 1912 produced more than just Marquard's record. It also produced a new American League record and an immediate challenger to it. Even while Rube Marquard was engaged in his run in the National League, Walter Johnson, almost concurrently, was setting the American League record at 16. And by the time he was stopped, another streak was under way, this one by Smokey Joe Wood of the Boston Red Sox.

No one could ask for a better matchup in 1912 than the one which brought Walter Johnson, the record holder, to the mound at Fenway Park to face Joe Wood the challenger. Johnson was the premier pitcher in the American League and its strikeout king. Wood had dazzled the baseball world while en route to a 34–5 season, with 10 shutouts. He won three more games in the 1912 World Series. Then he injured his arm and never returned to his single-season pinnacle.

Walter Johnson, himself a 32-game winner in 1912, had broken the former American League record of 14 straight, set by Jack Chesbro in 1904. By winning his sixteenth straight game on August 23, he had set a new league mark and had his sights on the brand-new record of Rube Marquard. The New York lefthander had won his 19 by July 3. Johnson never caught Marquard.

Johnson was a victim of both bad luck and a scoring rule which today would not have cost him a loss. He lost a game in relief, taking over in the seventh inning of a tie game. There were two runners on base, and before Johnson could get the side out, one of them scored the winning run. Today the loss would be charged to the starting pitcher, Tom Hughes, who had allowed the runner to get on base. At that time the loss went against whoever was pitching when the winning run scored.

Even so, in 1912 the scorer's decision was denounced by the press and sympathetic fans. However, Ban Johnson, not only president of the American League but its iron-fisted founder, decreed the loss be placed against Walter Johnson's record, and there it remains forever. He had been stopped at 16.

When the 1912 penchant for pitchers winning consecutive victories identified the next challenger as Smokey Joe Wood of the pennant-bound Boston Red Sox, Johnson was called upon to stop him personally. The schedule brought the Washington Senators to Fenway Park to play the Red Sox, and the management was well aware they had a great gate attraction. Johnson was asked to pitch a day sooner so he would face Wood. He was glad to do it.

Whatever the capacity of Fenway Park in 1912, it was far exceeded when, on a weekday, over 30,000 baseball fans crowded the park. The crowd overflowed the stands. In fact, the players could not sit in their dugouts. Instead, they sat on chairs arranged in front of the throngs that stood just outside the baselines. Thousands more people stood in the outfield, behind ropes, reducing the area for the great Red Sox outfield to cover. Tris Speaker, Duffy Lewis, and Harry Hooper would not be able to roam back to catch deep fly balls. These would be automatic doubles if they reached the crowd herded behind the ropes.

Walter Johnson held the American League record, a string of 16 straight victories. Joe Wood had drawn nearer to Johnson's mark in his last start, beating New York on September 2 for his thirteenth win without a loss during the streak. Today he was after his fourteenth straight, Chesbro's old mark, and Walter Johnson didn't want him to get it. Unless Johnson himself stopped Wood, his own record, and possibly Marquard's, were in danger.

The game lived up to expectations. It was a pitcher's battle. Great defensive plays snuffed out rallies, and both pitchers stopped scoring threats with clutch strikeouts. A scoreless tie was broken in the sixth inning, when Tris Speaker hit a fly ball that reached the roped-back crowd for a ground-rule double and Duffy Lewis hit an opposite-field double down the right field foul line. It just eluded the grab of Danny Moeller and Speaker scored. And that was it. The game ended 1–0 as Walter Johnson lost another game in which his team failed to get him any runs. He lost 65 games during his career when his team was shut out.

When Wood pitched next, in Chicago, he was not in top form but held a 5–3 lead going into the bottom of the ninth. When the first two White Sox batters reached base with hits, manager Jake Stahl replaced Wood with reliever Charles "Sea Lion" Hall. A sacrifice fly made the final score 5–4, but Hall retired the White Sox without further damage and Joe Wood was within one game of tying Walter Johnson.

The Red Sox rode on to St. Louis in Pullman cars for a game on September 15, and Joe Wood pitched another strong game, a 2–1 victory in eight innings to tie Johnson's record. Darkness caused the game to be called after Wood himself had scored the go-ahead run in the top of the eighth inning.

It all came to an end on September 20 in Detroit. Wood failed to break Walter Johnson's mark. He went the distance but mostly on the sufferance of manager Jake Stahl. Although two of the Tigers' runs were unearned, the 6–4 final score indicated Joe Wood's fastball lacked its usual smoke that day.

The Marquard Inheritance

When Rube Marquard wrote his way into the record books in 1912, with 19 consecutive victories, he established a benchmark which has been approached but never equaled, or excelled, since that time. Although Walter Johnson's American League mark, itself never beaten, took on extra importance because of the affection and awe he inspired in baseball fans, Marquard set the standard for all others to challenge.

The Johnson-Wood confrontation excited the imagination, and other challenges have created their own temporary focus, but always there stands the record of Marquard. It is the pinnacle toward which others climb and never reach, on a single-season, starting pitcher basis. It has only been exceeded by joining the end of one season to the start of the next.

Perhaps even more than the way Walter Johnson was revered in the American League, Rube Marquard's teammate, Christy Mathewson, overshadowed everyone. Marquard's record was the sort of achievement Matty should have had. Until 1912 all the heroics on the Giants' staff had been his. Rube's emergence took everyone by surprise; he was still living down the onerous nickname "the $11,000 Lemon."

Just a kid pitcher, only eighteen, when the Giants bought him from Indianapolis where he had won 28 games in 1908, Marquard had been a disappointment until the 1912 season. Then he began his streak with his first start of the season and, as he added to it, he began to attract favorable attention for the first time. When he won his sixth game, he exceeded any previous high; when he won the tenth game, he had won more than he had in his first two seasons combined.

Rube Marquard had been dubbed "the $11,000 Lemon" because John McGraw, with an eye to publicity value, had paid that much so it would top the $10,000 paid for Mike "King" Kelly when he was sold by Chicago to Boston in the previous century. In 1912, "the Lemon" turned it all around. He started right in on April 11 and didn't lose a game until July 8.

Actually, under the present scoring rules, Marquard's record would total 20 consecutive victories. In a game at the Polo Grounds, McGraw inserted Rube in the eighth inning of a game against the Brooklyn Dodgers which was tied at 3–3. Marquard inherited a bases-loaded situation but stopped Zach Wheat and Jake Daubert, both to become batting champions, and retired George Cutshaw, without a run being scored. The Giants won the game in the bottom of the ninth, but the rules then gave the victory to the starting pitcher.

The Giants, in 1912, were winning the middle of three successive pennants, and Marquard joined with Christy Mathewson to lead the Giants' staff. He was called "Rube," a nickname often given to lefthanders with a superior fastball. This was a tribute to Rube Waddell and

had no bucolic significance: Marquard was no innocent country boy turned loose on Broadway.

Marquard married a vaudeville headliner, Blossom Seeley, who was even more popular than he was. Her life story was later made into a motion picture which ignored Marquard in favor of Blossom's subsequent husband, song-and-dance man Benny Fields.

However, Rube had held up his end of the vaudeville act, serving as a straight man for the comedienne and added female impersonations, in which he sang and danced as well. This too is a performance unlikely to be duplicated by a modern player.

Streakers Blurred by Time

Although it is convenient to separate the "modern era" of baseball from its ancient past at 1900, the better dividing line would be 1893. That year the pitcher was moved back from fifty feet to the still-prevailing sixty feet, six inches. He had been allowed to throw overhand since 1884.

Until the 1890s, teams rarely used more than two principal pitchers. More open dates existed in the schedules, and two strong-armed men could carry the bulk of the work. A third pitcher, or a general substitute, could help out in doubleheaders. However, the regular duo met most occasions and had many more opportunities to reel off long strings of victories.

When Tim Keefe set the mark at 19 straight, he required only seven weeks to do it. Between June 23 and August 10, 1888, he won all his starts, 17 of them complete games. He alternated on the mound with Mickey Welch, himself the owner of an impressive winning streak. In 1885 Smiling Mickey had run off 17 in a row. That had been one less than the record Hoss Radbourn set in 1884. Pitchers in those years were capable of putting together long winning streaks.

Another contemporary, Jim McCormick of Chicago, won 14 in a row in 1885 and 16 straight the next year. When Keefe set his mark in 1888, the public was impressed but not stunned by its magnitude. After all, it only topped the recent mark of Radbourn's by one.

The New York Giants of 1888 were the toast of the town. They were led by Jim Mutrie, who had dubbed them "my Giants," marveling at the magnitude of the star players. Such stalwarts as Roger Connor, Montgomery Ward, and Buck Ewing—all future Hall of Fame members—were in the lineup. Keefe and Welch, pitching in tandem, were also destined for Cooperstown and immortality. The Giants were easy pennant winners over Cap Anson's Chicago team.

Tim Keefe began his 19-game winning streak on June 23. He had lost his previous start to yet another star pitcher, John Clarkson. Also elected to the Hall of Fame, even before Keefe and Welch, Clarkson had won 13 straight in 1885.

Keefe's first win was a squeaker, 7–6, over Philadelphia. Then he marched along, and when he won his twelfth in a row, his opponent was Clarkson. During the streak Tim Keefe pitched 17 complete games. The two he failed to finish included one in which he was hit on the arm by a line drive while leading 8–3 in the sixth inning. A replacement with a name more domineering than the record he left behind, Cannonball Eddie Crane, held on for a 9–6 victory credited to Keefe.

The other incomplete game would not have been added to his string by today's scoring rules. On July 16, while leading Chicago 9–0, Keefe was excused for the day after two innings. The practices of the time gave him the win.

Tim Keefe's string came to an end on August 14, when his defense betrayed him and two unearned runs were the difference in a 4–2 loss. Gus Krock, of the Chicago White Stockings, was a lefthanded rookie who soon disappeared from the major leagues, but he had the satisfaction of stopping Keefe at 19.

Considering the winning streaks his contemporaries had run off, it was probably thought that Keefe's record was temporary. Had it not been for the victory gained in that two-inning start, it would have been. He would have been tied with Hoss Radbourn at 18 and eclipsed when Rube Marquard reached 19 in 1912. As it is, more than a century after his feat, Tim Keefe stands beside Marquard with a total no one has surpassed.

American League Record Tied

It wasn't until 1931 that the lesser American League record of 16 consecutive pitching victories was challenged. Lefty Grove came very close to setting a new record in the American League and narrowly missed being the pitcher to break Marquard's mark of 19. Grove had a 31–4 season, figures which could have accommodated both record-breaking streaks.

However, the luck even the best must have to sustain a long streak deserted Grove at the critical point. He was luckless in the game which would have moved him past Walter Johnson and Smokey Joe Wood, coholders of the American League mark.

The 1931 Philadelphia Athletics were awesome. Connie Mack's last championship team won its third pennant in a row. Responding to Depression-related financial pressures, Mack would break up the team, selling off its stars, including Grove, who went to the Red Sox. Future Hall of Famers Jimmie Foxx, Mickey Cochrane, Al Simmons, and Grove himself were at the peak of their careers. The members of the supporting cast—Max Bishop, Jimmie Dykes, Mule Haas, Bing Miller, and others—were all excellent role players. This was a team which did not beat itself.

As the season advanced into August, the Athletics were virtually coasting to a pennant. They would win 107 games and distance the runner-up New York Yankees by 13 games. Grove, pitching every fourth game and appearing in relief when needed, was on his personal roll. For the first time in many years, it appeared the American League record for consecutive victories could be broken by a pitcher. It was possible to project that Grove might go on and catch Marquard's record. There was enough time left.

Lefty Grove tied the American League record on August 19 and was expected to break it four days later with his seventeenth straight win. The day the record coheld by Walter Johnson and Joe Wood since 1912 was to fall was Sunday, August 23.

The St. Louis Browns, a second-division team and perennial victim, would provide only token opposition, and the unheralded Dick Coffman would be the sacrificial pitching opponent. Grove pitched with close to his usual brilliance, limiting the Browns to six hits, allowing only one run, and striking out six.

However, Dick Coffman, on that particular day, outpitched Grove and shut out the Athletics with only three hits. Grove's streak came to an end at 16 straight victories. He had only joined Johnson and Wood at the top of the American League's list.

Lefty Grove had never been a gracious, philosophical loser. He refused to accept defeat gracefully. He blamed the loss on the absence of Al Simmons from the lineup. True, Simmons was at home, in Milwaukee, seeing a doctor, and his replacement, Jim Moore, was far from being a sure-handed defensive player. When Moore misjudged a fly ball, which became the game-winning hit, Grove fumed that Simmons would have caught the ball. Further, he complained, Simmons, the league-leading batter, would surely have knocked in a few runs as well as preventing the Browns from scoring a tainted one.

Grove complained every time he was asked about the end of his streak, and the image of Simmons idling away the afternoon, thumbing through *National Geographic*s in a doctor's waiting room, persisted. Actually, Simmons had an infected ankle and had already been out of the lineup for a week.

What made the defeat more bitter in retrospect was that Grove went on to win his next five starts. These victories would have put the record at 21, eclipsing not only the American League record but topping Marquard's all-time total of 19. (Grove won his next two starts, incidentally, with Simmons still missing from the lineup.) He did not lose until the final game of the season, on September 27.

Schoolboy Rowe's Row

It was only a few years later, in 1934, when the next assault was made on the American League record, now held by Lefty Grove as well as by Walter Johnson and Joe Wood. This time it was the colorful Schoolboy Rowe, blessed with a rural candor that the press found refreshing and the public fascinating, who made the run.

Mickey Cochrane, Grove's former battery mate, was a first-term manager, having been sold by the Athletics to Detroit. Still a great player and catcher, Cochrane had his team headed for the pennant and Schoolboy Rowe led the way. Rowe had been a pitcher of promise and Cochrane had brought about its fulfillment. Rowe had made a slow start, splitting his first eight decisions. His inauspicious beginning offered no portent that when, on June 15, he won his fifth victory, it was the start of a record-equaling skein. During the summer months Rowe shared the spotlight with Dizzy Dean of the National League. However, while Dean was garnering the victories which would eventually reach 30 for the season, he did not string them together the way Rowe did.

Rowe won his sixteenth straight game on August 26 but then ran into the barrier which had blocked other American League pitchers at that point. He joined Grove, Johnson, and Wood at the top of the list but also joined them among the frustrated who could not go past that point.

Rowe stumbled from the path toward a new record on

August 29, when the Tigers met the now lowly Philadelphia Athletics in a doubleheader. Gone from Connie Mack's A's were Lefty Grove, Mickey Cochrane, Al Simmons, George Earnshaw, and Rube Walberg. Only Jimmie Foxx remained from the recent championship teams.

It was the second game of an August 29 doubleheader, and Rowe was far off form. He was knocked out in the sixth inning. Unlike the contentious Lefty Grove, Rowe blamed no one but himself, saying without rancor that he'd just had an off-day. He refused the alibi offered by his manager, Mickey Cochrane, who contended that the demands of the press and public on the young pitcher had produced more turmoil than Schoolboy could handle. Rowe scoffed at the idea and went on to finish the season with 24 wins. He didn't face Dizzy Dean in the 1934 World Series, but he split two decisions, as the Cardinals won a seven-game series from Detroit. Another pennant year followed for Detroit, with Rowe winning 19 games. After that a chronic arm problem hindered his career, although he lasted a long while in the major leagues, winning 158 games, with a .610 winning average, over fifteen years.

Carl Hubbell's Fabulous Streak

When one adds the start of one season to the end of the preceding one, one finds a 17-game streak for Cleveland's Johnny Allen in 1936–1937 and another for Baltimore's Dave McNally in 1969–1970. But in this area Carl Hubbell claims all the records.

In the quirky way that records for consecutive victories by pitchers seem to come almost simultaneously, the same two seasons which provided Johnny Allen's 17 straight wins, also produced one of the most fabulous feats of all time. As had been the case with 1912, there was a magic about 1936–1937.

Carl Hubbell, between July 17, 1936, and May 27, 1937, won 24 games in a row. He won his last 16 decisions in 1936 and added 8 more victories before losing a game in 1937.

Carl Hubbell, and the team which would support him in his quest for a record, the New York Giants, were at their best in 1936 and 1937. They were the best in the National League at a time when their crosstown rivals, the Yankees, were dominant in the American League and also in the World Series. They beat the Giants both years despite Hubbell's presence. The Giants won only three World Series games in the two years and Hubbell won two of them.

Carl Hubbell was the ace of the Giants staff and the National League's most valuable player in 1936. He led the league in 1936 with 26 victories, an .813 winning percentage, and a 2.31 ERA. In 1937 he again topped the league in wins with 22 and percentage with .733 and added the strikeout crown with 159, his career high.

It was this kind of consistency that earned Carl Hubbell the nickname "the Meal Ticket." His manager, Bill Terry, knew Hubbell would pitch in rotation and stop any losing streak before it gained momentum.

The Giants were off to a bad start in 1936, although Hubbell was winning two of every three decisions. The day Hubbell's winning streak began, July 17, the Giants were in fifth place, barely over .500 at 42–41 and 10 games behind the defending champion Chicago Cubs. Hubbell had lost his last start, a tough two-hit 1–0 game, to the Cubs' Big Bill Lee. Chicago's run was unearned.

Appropriately Hubbell got the Giants back on a winning track by shutting out Pittsburgh, 6–0. The game contained a streak of another kind. In the first inning Joe Moore, Mel Ott, and Hank Leiber hit successive triples. Before the inning ended, Eddie Mayo, a utility infielder, added another triple. Not only was Hubbell off on a personal winning streak that wouldn't end until the next year, the Giants had found their own victory pace.

Oddly, considering the magnitude of Hubbell's record, the streak-starting shutout was the last one he pitched in 1936. He had a season-opening shutout the next year. However, low-run games predominated, and he produced an ERA of 1.95 for the run of 24 games.

Carl Hubbell's great rival was Dizzy Dean, and duels between the two were matchups between two titans. Hubbell's lefthanded screwball was matched against the fastball of the colorful screwball of the Cardinals. These confrontations were arranged as often as possible for their gate appeal, and Dean tried to head off Hubbell's march toward glory three times during the string.

Twice he failed gloriously and once ingloriously. During the 1936 portion of the skein, Dean lost 2–1 in an extra-inning game and lost another 2–1 game in the regulation nine innings. These were typical Hubbell-Dean matchups, with both pitchers rising to the occasion. Hubbell, over the years, rose higher more often.

Probably in frustration, when the streak reached 22 on May 19, 1937, Dean lost both the game and his temper when umpire George Barr called a balk against Dizzy for the third time. It gave a reprieve to the batter, Dick Bartell, who had flied out. He then hit a line drive which Pepper Martin dropped, and a flurry of runs followed.

Dean's retaliation was to throw beanballs at every Giant batter who dared step to the plate. In this pre-helmet time such tactics were not viewed kindly, and outfielder Jimmy Ripple offered to take Dean on in a one-to-one fistfight. Dean, who spent a career vainly trying to find someone he could lick, accepted the challenge. He was engulfed by Giant bodies, topped by players in Cardinal uniforms, in what turned into one of the best displays of belligerence ever seen on a ballfield. Individual fights ranged all around the diamond. There were no peacemakers among the players. Among the few who chose to be spectators was Carl Hubbell. He had better use for his arm than swinging it at someone. When order was restored, Hubbell finished pitching a one-run, seven-hit game.

Dean protested his subsequent fine and threatened to boycott the upcoming All Star Game. As usual his threat was unfulfilled. It would have been far better for him if he had stayed away. It was in the 1937 All Star Game that Dean was hit on the foot by an Earl Averill line drive. He tried to pitch while favoring a broken toe and ruined a great right arm.

The end of Hubbell's streak came on May 31 at the hands of the team which considered any victory over the Giants as compensation for an otherwise dismal season. The Brooklyn Dodgers invaded the Polo Grounds for a doubleheader which drew the second-largest crowd that had ever crammed into the Giants home field.

The Dodgers had always been a tough team for

Pitchers with 12 or More Straight Victories in Season

<table>
<tr><td colspan="3" align="center">National League (36)</td></tr>
<tr><td>Year</td><td>Pitcher</td><td>Won</td></tr>
<tr><td>1888</td><td>Timothy Keefe, N.Y.</td><td>19</td></tr>
<tr><td>1912</td><td>Richard Marquard, N.Y.</td><td>19</td></tr>
<tr><td>1884</td><td>Charles Radbourn, Provi.</td><td>18</td></tr>
<tr><td>1885</td><td>Michael Welch, N.Y.</td><td>17</td></tr>
<tr><td>1890</td><td>John Luby, Chi.</td><td>17</td></tr>
<tr><td>1959</td><td>El Roy Face, Pitts.</td><td>17</td></tr>
<tr><td>1886</td><td>James McCormick, Chi.</td><td>16</td></tr>
<tr><td>1936</td><td>Carl Hubbell, N.Y.</td><td>16</td></tr>
<tr><td>1947</td><td>Ewell Blackwell, Cinn.</td><td>16</td></tr>
<tr><td>1962</td><td>John Sanford, S.F.</td><td>16</td></tr>
<tr><td>1924</td><td>Arthur Vance, Brook.</td><td>15</td></tr>
<tr><td>1968</td><td>Robert Gibson, St. L.</td><td>15</td></tr>
<tr><td>1972</td><td>Steven Carlton, Phila.</td><td>15</td></tr>
<tr><td>1885</td><td>James McCormick, Chi.</td><td>14</td></tr>
<tr><td>1886</td><td>John Flynn, Chi.</td><td>14</td></tr>
<tr><td>1904</td><td>Joseph McGinnity, N.Y.</td><td>14</td></tr>
<tr><td>1909</td><td>Edward Reulbach, Chi.</td><td>14</td></tr>
<tr><td>1984</td><td>Richard Sutcliffe, Chi.</td><td>14</td></tr>
<tr><td>1985</td><td>Dwight Gooden, N.Y.</td><td>14</td></tr>
<tr><td>1880</td><td>Lawrence Corcoran, Chi.</td><td>13</td></tr>
<tr><td>1884</td><td>Charles Buffinton, Bos.</td><td>13</td></tr>
<tr><td>1892</td><td>Denton Young, Cleve.</td><td>13</td></tr>
<tr><td>1896</td><td>Frank Dwyer, Cin.</td><td>13</td></tr>
<tr><td>1909</td><td>Chris. Mathewson, N.Y.</td><td>13</td></tr>
<tr><td>1910</td><td>Charles Phillippe, Pitts.</td><td>13</td></tr>
<tr><td>1927</td><td>Burleigh Grimes, N.Y.</td><td>13</td></tr>
<tr><td>1956</td><td>Brooks Lawrence, Cin.</td><td>13</td></tr>
<tr><td>1966</td><td>Philip Regan, L.A.</td><td>13</td></tr>
<tr><td>1971</td><td>Dock Ellis, Pitts.</td><td>13</td></tr>
<tr><td>1885</td><td>John Clarkson, Chi.</td><td>13</td></tr>
<tr><td>1886</td><td>Charles Ferguson, Phila.</td><td>12</td></tr>
<tr><td>1902</td><td>John Chesbro, Pitts.</td><td>12</td></tr>
<tr><td>1904</td><td>George Wiltse, N.Y.</td><td>12</td></tr>
<tr><td>1906</td><td>Edward Reulbach, Chi.</td><td>12</td></tr>
<tr><td>1914</td><td>Richard Rudolph, Bos.</td><td>12</td></tr>
<tr><td>1975</td><td>Burt Hooton, L.A.</td><td>12</td></tr>
</table>

<table>
<tr><td colspan="3" align="center">American League (37)</td></tr>
<tr><td>Year</td><td>Pitcher</td><td>Won</td></tr>
<tr><td>1912</td><td>Walter Johnson, Wash.</td><td>16</td></tr>
<tr><td>1912</td><td>Joseph Wood, Bos.</td><td>16</td></tr>
<tr><td>1931</td><td>Robert Grove, Phila.</td><td>16</td></tr>
<tr><td>1934</td><td>Lynwood Rowe, Det.</td><td>16</td></tr>
<tr><td>1932</td><td>Alvin Crowder, Wash.</td><td>15</td></tr>
<tr><td>1937</td><td>John Allen, Cleve.</td><td>15</td></tr>
<tr><td>1969</td><td>David McNally, Balt.</td><td>15</td></tr>
<tr><td>1974</td><td>Gaylord Perry, Cleve.</td><td>15</td></tr>
<tr><td>1904</td><td>John Chesbro, N.Y.</td><td>14</td></tr>
<tr><td>1913</td><td>Walter Johnson, Wash.</td><td>14</td></tr>
<tr><td>1914</td><td>Charles Bender, Phila.</td><td>14</td></tr>
<tr><td>1928</td><td>Robert Grove, Phila.</td><td>14</td></tr>
<tr><td>1961</td><td>Edward Ford, N.Y.</td><td>14</td></tr>
<tr><td>1980</td><td>Steven Stone, Balt.</td><td>14</td></tr>
<tr><td>1986</td><td>W. Roger Clemens, Bos.</td><td>14</td></tr>
<tr><td>1924</td><td>Walter Johnson, Wash.</td><td>13</td></tr>
<tr><td>1925</td><td>Stanley Coveleski, Wash.</td><td>13</td></tr>
<tr><td>1930</td><td>Wesley Ferrell, Cleve.</td><td>13</td></tr>
<tr><td>1940</td><td>Louis Newsom, Det.</td><td>13</td></tr>
<tr><td>1949</td><td>Ellis Kinder, Bos.</td><td>13</td></tr>
<tr><td>1971</td><td>David McNally, Balt.</td><td>13</td></tr>
<tr><td>1973</td><td>James Hunter, Oak.</td><td>13</td></tr>
<tr><td>1978</td><td>Ronald Guidry, N.Y.</td><td>13</td></tr>
<tr><td>1983</td><td>D. LaMarr Hoyt, Chi.</td><td>13</td></tr>
<tr><td>1901</td><td>Denton Young, Bos.</td><td>12</td></tr>
<tr><td>1910</td><td>Russell Ford, N.Y.</td><td>12</td></tr>
<tr><td>1914</td><td>Hubert Leonard, Bos.</td><td>12</td></tr>
<tr><td>1929</td><td>Jonathan Zachary, N.Y.</td><td>12</td></tr>
<tr><td>1931</td><td>George Earnshaw, Phila.</td><td>12</td></tr>
<tr><td>1938</td><td>John Allen, Cleve.</td><td>12</td></tr>
<tr><td>1939</td><td>Atley Donald, N.Y.</td><td>12</td></tr>
<tr><td>1946</td><td>David Ferriss, Bos.</td><td>12</td></tr>
<tr><td>1961</td><td>Luis Arroyo, N.Y.</td><td>12</td></tr>
<tr><td>1963</td><td>Edward Ford, N.Y.</td><td>12</td></tr>
<tr><td>1968</td><td>David McNally, Balt.</td><td>12</td></tr>
<tr><td>1971</td><td>Patrick Dobson, Balt.</td><td>12</td></tr>
<tr><td>1985</td><td>Ronald Guidry, N.Y.</td><td>12</td></tr>
</table>

Hubbell. He had beaten them five times during his 24-game streak, twice in relief, but in the opening game of the doubleheader Brooklyn closed the door on Hubbell's feat.

Carl Hubbell took the long walk from the mound to the clubhouse in center field during the third inning. Five runs had scored. There had been seven hits and three walks. In came Dick Coffman, who had been Lefty Grove's nemesis. It would have been fitting if he had stopped the Dodgers in their tracks and the Giants had rallied to save Hubbell's streak so he could extend it the next time. Neither happened; Brooklyn scored five more runs, the Giants only tallied three runs for the whole game.

Lost in the Crowd

By winning 24 games in a row over two seasons, Carl Hubbell obscured the feat of Roy Face in 1958 and 1959 when the forkballer won 22 consecutive games, all in relief. That stands as the best achievement for a reliever. Also in 1959, Face equaled Johnny Allen's mark of 17 consecutive wins, doing it all in one season.

Roy Face, only five-eight and weighing just 160 pounds, didn't lose his first decision in 1959 until September 11. He had entered the game in relief and gave up the winning run in the ninth inning of a game at Los Angeles when Charlie Neal hit a single. Until then, it appeared that Roy Face was destined to never lose a game. Even when his forkball wasn't working its usual magic, he won.

A modest man, Face would point to six or seven games when the Pirates' hitters bailed him out. The most extreme of these times came in a June 11 game, when the San Francisco Giants played Pittsburgh. Face came in to protect a 7–5 lead in the eighth inning. The Giants had two men on base and Willie Mays came up as a pinch hitter. He homered and the Giants led, 8–7. In the bottom of the inning, the Pirates erupted with five runs and Face had a win instead of a loss.

During his string, Face won eleven of his games in extra innings.

Consecutive Base Hits

The feat of making a dozen consecutive base hits has been accomplished only twice in all the years major league baseball has been played. The record has rested there for thirty-five years and might never see the time when a batter delivers a baker's dozen to provide a new record. The hitter who reaches 13 will cap a slow, gradual climb toward a peak shared by Pinky Higgins and Walt Dropo, both American Leaguers. The National League's record is 10.

The history of consecutive base hits goes back to 1897, when Ed Delahanty, whom you would expect to set such standards, and Jake Gettman, whom you wouldn't, each got ten hits in a row during the season. Delahanty, one of five major-league-playing brothers, batted .377 for Philadelphia in 129 games. Gettman, who only played one season as a regular, got his ten straight while appearing in only 36 games for Washington. He hit .315 overall. The National League record is still 10 consecutive hits, and six others have joined the original pair.

Tris Speaker was the first to top 10, getting 11 straight

hits in 1920. Speaker had eclipsed Doc Johnson's American League total of 9, hit in 1919, the same season Brooklyn's Ed Konetchy had joined Delahanty and Gettman with 10.

The next year, when Speaker moved the major league record up a notch, his feat came amid such epoch record-setting as Babe Ruth's 54 home runs. This had broken Ruth's own mark of 29 set the season before. It dwarfed Speaker's rattling of 11 straight hits. In fact, Speaker's own accomplishment, leading the Cleveland Indians to a World Series victory despite the loss of shortstop Ray

Most Consecutive Hits

American League

Player	Team	Year	H
Pinky Higgins	Bos.	1938	12
Walt Dropo	Det.	1952	12
Tris Speaker	Cleve.	1920	11
Johnny Pesky	Bos.	1946	11
George Sisler	St.L.	1921	10
Harry Heilmann	Det.	1922	10
Harry McCurdy	Chi.	1926	10
Ken Singleton	Balt.	1981	10
Kirby Puckett	Minn.	1987	10
Doc Johnston	Cleve.	1919	9
Ty Cobb	Det.	1925	9
Sam Rice	Wash.	1925	9
Hal Trosky	Cleve.	1936	9
Ted Williams	Bos.	1939	9
Tony Oliva	Minn.	1967	9
Nap Lajoie	Cleve.	1910	8
George Sisler	St.L.	1922	8
	St.L.	1927	8
Buddy Myer	Wash.	1929	8
Oscar Melillo	St.L.	1931	8
Sammy West	St.L.	1933	8
Hank Bauer	N.Y.	1952	8
Johnny Groth	Det.	1950	8
Don Baylor	Cal.	1978	8
Dan Ford	Cal.	1979	8
Jorge Orta	Cleve.	1980	8

National League

Player	Team	Year	H
Ed Delahanty	Phila.	1897	10
Jake Gettman	Wash.	1897	10
Ed Konetchy	Brook.	1919	10
Kiki Cuyler	Pitts.	1925	10
Chick Hafey	St.L.	1929	10
Joe Medwick	St.L.	1936	10
Buddy Hassett	Bos.	1940	10
Woody Williams	Cin.	1943	10
Joe Kelley	Balt.	1894	9
Rogers Hornsby	St.L.	1924	9
Taylor Douthit	St.L.	1926	9
Babe Herman	Brook.	1926	9
Bill Jurges	N.Y.	1941	9
Terry Moore	St.L.	1947	9
Dave Philley	Phila.	1958	9
	Phila.	1959	9
Felipe Alou	S.F.	1962	9
Willie Stargell	Pitts.	1966	9
Rennie Stennett	Pitts.	1975	9
Ron Cey	L.A.	1977	9
Roger Connor	St.L.	1895	8
Sammy Strang	Chi.	1900	8
Jack Fournier	Brook.	1923	8
Jimmy Johnston	Brook.	1923	8
Glenn Wright	Pitts.	1924	8
Chick Hafey	St.L.	1928	8
Lefty O'Doul	N.Y.	1933	8
Kiki Cuyler	Cin.	1936	8
Augie Galan	Brook.	1944	8
Wayne Terwilliger	Chi.	1949	8
Dick Sisler	Phila.	1950	8
Eddie Waitkus	Phila.	1950	8
Sid Gordon	Bos.	1952	8
Lee Walls	Chi.	1958	8
Curt Flood	St.L.	1964	8
Jerry Grote	N.Y.	1970	8
Billy Williams	Chi.	1972	8
Dave Winfield	S.D.	1979	8

Chapman to a fatal beaning during the pennant chase, overshadowed his own batting feats. This included a runner-up .388 to George Sisler's league-leading batting average of .407.

However, Speaker's 11 straight stood the test of time. During the 1920s others made a run at the record but couldn't get beyond 10 straight hits. They included Sisler in 1921 and Harry Heilmann in 1922. Kiki Cuyler in 1925 and Chick Hafey in 1929, all future Hall of Famers, got up to 10 straight in the National League. In 1936 another Hall of Famer to be, Joe Medwick, hit in 10 straight times at bat.

One outsider who edged onto the list with those headed for baseball's Hall of Fame was a reserve catcher, Harry McCurdy. A rookie with the White Sox in 1926, he only played in 33 games, but cracked out 10 straight hits while batting .326. He might have played in more games, but he had a month's vacation in August. He was claimed by the Yankees on waivers, but when New York discovered this included an obligation for the rookie's bonus of $30,000, they refused to complete the deal. The White Sox insisted they were honor-bound. As is usual in baseball, honor lost and McCurdy remained a substitue catcher with Chicago.

Speaker's record finally tumbled in 1938, when Mike "Pinky" Higgins, the Boston Red Sox third baseman, began by going 4 for 4 against the White Sox in Chicago. The next day the team was in Detroit to play a doubleheader with the Tigers. When Higgins went 4 for 4, with a walk, against Roxie Lawson in the first game, and singled his first time up in the second game, Cal Hubbard, umpiring on the bases, observed, "That makes you 5 for 5 for the day."

Higgins told Hubbard he was 9 for 9, counting the previous day in Chicago. It wasn't enough that Higgins put pressure on himself, but after he got his tenth straight hit, the field announcer at Briggs Field, Ty Tyson, made a public-address announcement that Higgins could tie Speaker's record if he got another hit the next time up.

Higgins shook off the hex and got the hit and, with everyone knowing a new record was on the line, ripped a single off Tommy Bridges, the best curveballer in the league, the next time up. It was an unlucky 13, however, as Higgins fanned his last time at bat. The catcher in both games of the doubleheader was Rudy York. It was the year the Tigers tried to find a place for him to play.

Even though he was to be described by Tom Meany as "part Indian, part first baseman," when Hank Greenberg moved to the outfield so York could play where he'd do the least damage, the one season as a catcher had been a disaster. Higgins later confided he had little trouble guessing a fastball was coming as York had become known to avoid complications by refusing to call for curveballs.

In 1952 the slugging first baseman of the Red Sox, Walt Dropo, tied Higgins's record. He had debuted in 1950 with a sensational season, hitting .322, but he never hit above .300 again. Dropo had begun the season with Boston, but in a multiplayer deal in June, he had been traded to Detroit. Going along with Dropo was Johnny Pesky, longtime shortstop for the Red Sox and, in the way of coincidences in record setting, had reached 11 straight hits, one behind Higgins's record, in 1946. Pesky was at shortstop in the games when Dropo tied him first for runner-up, a spot he now shared with Speaker. He watched as Dropo got his twelfth straight.

Like Higgins, Walt Dropo made his run in a doubleheader. He had gone 5 for 5 against the Yankees in a single game on July 14, and the next day, in Griffith Stadium, he had four straight in the first game. All the hits had been singles, but starting off in the first inning of the nightcap, the powerful Dropo hit a triple with the bases loaded.

In the third inning he had his eleventh straight hit, another single, and Mickey Vernon, the Washington first baseman, told him he could tie the record with a hit the next time at bat. He did with a double. And he had another time at bat coming, in the seventh inning. Despite Dropo's hitting, the Tigers trailed, 7–6. He swung from the heels but only lifted a foul fly which catcher Mickey Grasso caught at the edge of the field boxes. The streak was over. Dropo added a single in the ninth inning but had to settle for a shared record which has stood against more recent assaults.

Ken Singleton of Baltimore got 10 in 1981, and Kirby Puckett of Minnesota reached 10 in 1987. No one in the National League has had 10 straight hits since Woody William did it in 1943, with the World War Two Cincinnati Reds.

Team Winning Streaks

The two longest winning streaks by teams had different outcomes. Twice National League clubs won 21 in a row and the pennant. When the Chicago White Stockings did it, under Cap Anson, in 1880, they were simply running away from the pack. They won the pennant by 15 games.

However, when their descendants, the Chicago Cubs, won 21 in a row in 1935, the drive capped a sensational stretch battle that caught and passed their rivals, the St. Louis Cardinals, within a few days of the season's end.

These two 21-game streaks are not the longest on record. The record of 26 games won in a row by the 1916 New York Giants stands as the most perverse record of achievement in baseball. No other team has won so many games so convincingly to such little purpose. The Giants came in fourth, despite having had another win streak the same season of 17 straight. Even more peculiarly, the 26 games in a row were all played at home. Maybe the Giants could only win at the Polo Grounds? No. The 17 straight were all won on the road.

John McGraw did a remarkable thing in 1916. He rebuilt the team well into the season, after they had won 17 in a row. The season had started dismally, and before they hit their stride, they had lost thirteen of the first fifteen games played. When they ran off a streak of wins, it only made up for seriously lost ground. Then they flattened out again. McGraw acted.

He had a flawed infield. Shortstop Art Fletcher was a gem, but the other positions were played by former stars, Fred Merkle at first and Larry Doyle at second. Bill McKechnie, the third baseman, would someday be a Hall of Famer, but as a manager.

John McGraw had a love-hate relationship with Buck Herzog. He loved him as a player, but hated him as an individual. Herzog had been a rookie with the Giants and was traded away to the Braves, then swapped back again to star on three successive pennant winners, in 1911 through 1913. Then he was exiled again.

McGraw coveted Herzog, an unrepentant infielder who could hit and play any place with superb skill. They met privately, agreed that the money and opportunity involved was more important than any blood feud, and McGraw swapped the immortal Christy Mathewson, whose fadeaway pitch had failed, to Cincinnati, where he would become manager. He sent McKechnie along and a young outfielder of promise but little playing time, Edd Roush. The next year and two years later Roush won the batting championships. McGraw never regretted his move. He had laid the groundwork for the 1917 pennant.

Even though the season was well along, McGraw shipped his former captain, Larry Doyle, to Chicago for Heinie Zimmerman. Doyle, who had shouted in boyish enthusiasm, "It's great to be young and a Giant," was no longer young and no longer a Giant.

Fred Merkle, forgiven the blunder of 1908, when he failed to touch second as an apparent winning run scored and cost the Giants a pennant, had also grown old in McGraw's service and was shipped out so a rookie, Walter Holke, could finish the season at first base. When Zimmerman arrived, Herzog was shifted to second, and double plays began to be turned, base hits became infield outs, and the pitchers relished their new-found support. The Giants' drive began as late as September 7, when they were in fourth place, ten games out of third. Ferdie Schupp emerged as a star pitcher and won six games in the string. Pol Perritt won the first game of a doubleheader on September 9 and enjoyed it so much he came back and pitched a shutout in the second game. Regulars won, and rookies debuted and won. The Giants won, but they didn't move up.

The Giants ripped off 12 in a row and then paused for a rain-stopped tie game, 1–1, as Burleigh Grimes, who lost 13 in a row that season, managed a tie game for Pittsburgh. The streak resumed the next day and went on and on, although the Giants had been eliminated from catching Brooklyn in first place. It was the Phillies who were breathing on the necks of the Dodgers, with a chance to tie on the last day.

The Giants' streak was stopped in their last home game of the season, when they lost to the Boston Braves. They crossed the bridge to Brooklyn to close out the season on October 2, and McGraw set off wide speculation in the press by leaving the bench during the game and intimating afterward that the Giants had deliberately lost the game to ensure a Dodger pennant. Brooklyn was managed by Wilbert Robinson, once McGraw's closest crony, his coach and developer of pitchers. Some argument, some twist to the volatile McGraw temper had made them enemies. McGraw, who hated to lose, loathed losing to Brooklyn and Uncle Robbie. Maybe that's all there was to it, just another symptom of McGraw being a sore loser. Yet just ahead was the Black Sox scandal, and playing for the Giants were two non-Chicago players who were to be swept out of baseball when Judge Landis purged its suspect characters—Heinie Zimmerman and Bennie Kauff. McGraw's 1916 Giants finished in fourth place—right where they were when they began their 26-game streak!—and 7 games out of first place.

The 1935 Chicago Cubs, whose 21 straight wins carried them to a pennant, were a streaky team that year and the next year, too. In 1935 they faced a task made tougher by the schedule. The St. Louis Cardinals, the Gas House Gang world champions from 1934, not only led by 2 games, but the indomitable Deans, Dizzy and Paul, headed the staff. Even more comforting for the Cards, the schedule called for the Cubs to play the last five games of the season at Sportsman's Park in St. Louis.

In 1935 the Cubs picked up momentum, and it took them past the Cards in the middle of the streak. They took the lead on September 14 as they won their eleventh game and were three games ahead of the crumbling Cards when they reached St. Louis for the final five games. Lon Warneke beat Paul Dean 1–0 in the opener, and Bill Lee won his twentieth game of the season, beating Dizzy Dean 6–3 to clinch the pennant. It was the first game of a doubleheader, and the Cubs reached 21 straight by taking the nightcap.

They lost the next game, a meaningless one in the pennant race, in extra innings on Joe Medwick's second home run of the game. The Cards won the season's finale, 2–1, but it was the Cubs who went on to the World Series.

The next year was also a season of streaks. Again the Cubs got in gear with an impressive run of victories, taking 15 straight before midseason was reached. It did not lead to a pennant. Another 15-game winning streak, by the New York Giants, brought the championship to the Polo Grounds.

It was a streak that started late in the season and ran, in part, concurrently with Carl Hubbell's own string of 16 wins. While the Giants were racking up 15 straight, Hubbell appeared in ten consecutive games. He never ran out of steam, only games to win. The season ended with Hubbell experiencing a 16-game streak. He extended it by winning his first 8 decisions the next year to reach 24 straight wins over two seasons.

Other very long winning streaks in the National League that added late-season zest to pennant races were those of the 1924 Dodgers and, of course, the 1951 Giants. It was Dazzy Vance against the world in 1924 when he dominated the league and was the MVP. The Dodgers came up short, unable to catch the leading Giants, who added a fourth straight pennant in 1924, when Brooklyn's 15 straight were not enough.

In 1951 the same traditional rivals reversed roles, but not results. It was the Dodgers who were far in front when the Giants, managed by former Dodger skipper Leo Durocher, began a late-season drive. The Giants had started with the wrong kind of a streak. They lost their first 11 games and spent the season trying to catch the fast-flying Dodgers. They were 13 games behind when they won the first of 16 straight decisions on August 12 and began to close the gap the Dodgers had opened.

The Giants slowly edged closer and into a tie with a game to play. When both teams won their final games, the Dodgers on Jackie Robinson's extra-inning heroics in Philadelphia, the stage was set for a playoff series. It was won by Bobby Thomson's dramatic home run in the last of the ninth of the third, and decisive, game.

The American League's consecutive winning streaks have been turned in mostly by powerhouse teams headed for easy pennant triumphs. However, the 1906 American League season produced long strings of wins by two teams locked in a hotly contested pennant race. The Chicago White Sox set a record, since tied by the 1947 Yankees and the 1988 Boston Red Sox, of 19 straight wins.

Dubbed "the Hitless Wonders" because of a .230 team batting average, the White Sox engaged in a dramatic scenario with the New York team, then called the Highlanders.

In early August the White Sox were in fourth place. Ahead of them were Philadelphia, New York, and Cleveland. Day after day the White Sox chipped away at the lead held by the teams ahead of them. They eventually passed Philadelphia and Cleveland.

The Highlanders proved the hardest to catch. They had benefited from a winning streak of their own, 15 in a row. However, in the final surge of the pennant race, it was the White Sox who came home in first place. New York became the only team to win 15 in a row and not win a pennant in the American League. In the National League since 1900, three teams have won at least 15 in a row and not won the pennant. The most glaring example, of course, was the 1916 Giants, winners of 26 and 17 straight. The 1936 Cubs won 15 in a row and finished second to the Giants, also winners of 15 straight. The 1907 Giants had the poorest finish. Despite 17 straight wins, they finished fourth, 25 games out of first place.

In the main, however, if a team wants to ensure winning a pennant, a good way to do it is rack up 15 or more consecutive victories along the way, preferably in the stretch run.

The Feats

What follows is a celebration of three of baseball's most rare and heroic feats: the triple crowns of batting and pitching, and the triple putout by one player, better known as the unassisted triple play. These feats do not rank with the central records of the game: Henry Aaron's 755 homers, Cy Young's 511 wins, Pete Rose's 4,256 hits, Ty Cobb's lifetime batting average of .366. They are not as distant in memory as a .400 hitter or a 40-game winner. But they are remarkable achievements and—unlike those mentioned above—are not evident from a perusal of the leaders tables found later in this book.

Triple Crown Winners—Batting

Baseball's first Triple Crown winner, Paul Hines, waited ninety years to be enthroned. The crown consists of three jewels: the batting, home run, and runs-batted-in titles must be won in a single season. The RBI count was a late starter among baseball stats and had to be reconstructed for earlier seasons. However, it was not for lack of the RBI distinction that Hines, of the Providence Grays, waited for belated recognition. His feat went unacknowledged until researchers turned up information which made him the true 1878 batting champion.

A special Baseball Records Committee met in 1968 and put a stamp of approval on statistics which had been in dispute or unverified from baseball's past. The new information appeared the next year when Macmillan published the first edition of *The Baseball Encyclopedia.*

Abner Dalrymple had gone to his grave in 1939, the year the Baseball Hall of Fame Museum opened in Cooperstown, New York, with one baseball honor to his name. He had won the National League batting championship in 1878. Paul Hines, who died in 1935, was remembered only as the winner of the 1879 title. New data—coming from the two tie games he played and the one for Dalrymple—have revealed that Hines was a repeat batting champion who won both the 1878 and 1879 championships, and Abner Dalrymple has been demoted into relative obscurity.

Paul Hines, who had previously been credited with making an unassisted triple play, then lost that distinction as historians and researchers perused boxscores, gained two others—and eventually will regain his unassisted triple play, but more on that soon.

With his newly acknowledged batting title, the RBI leadership which resulted from reconstructed stats and the small but clearly superior total of 4 home runs, Paul Hines had attained the first Triple Crown. In addition, when he won the batting title again in 1879, again through later research efforts, he became the first to repeat as hitting leader.

Another nineteenth-century player, Hugh Duffy, had—since 1969, when his RBI data first was published—been considered the first to wear the Triple Crown. In 1894 he had won the three necessary titles but had almost obscured his own feat by batting .438, later corrected upward to .440. This remains the highest batting average of all time and has always interested interviewers more than the Triple Crown. Duffy's 18 home runs and 145 runs batted in led the league in these departments in 1894, but the idea of linking them as a diadem had not yet been formed. No one knew Paul Hines had done it and few cared that Hugh Duffy had. Although the RBI was known as a baseball stat as early as 1879, it was not commonly used until the 1910s, and not an official measure until 1920.

Hugh Duffy, a twinkle-eyed New Englander, told about his batting record for the fifty subsequent years that he spent in major league baseball, the last several decades as a coach for the Boston Red Sox. When a rookie named Ted Williams arrived in the big leagues in 1939, Hugh Duffy became his first mentor. Duffy proclaimed Williams as the greatest hitter he ever saw and watched while Williams won two Triple Crowns and missed a third by the closest margin possible.

The player who placed the stamp of the superstar most firmly on the concept of the Triple Crown was Nap Lajoie, who was the dominant player in the game when the American League was formed and ushered in twentieth-century baseball. The great Napoleon Lajoie had become the star of the Philadelphia Phillies as the nineteenth century closed. He was the prize recruit for the new league, remaining in Philadelphia where Connie Mack was establishing a new franchise. Lajoie put the team and the American League on the baseball map in 1901, when he provided the league-leading totals in the three prize categories. He batted .426, hit 14 home runs in the dead-ball era of the time, as later research showed, and, batted in 145 runs. It was the greatest season the immortal would ever have. He would win two more batting titles and again

lead the league in RBIs. However, home runs were not his specialty.

Still, his Triple Crown brought instant respect to the new league and, together with other stars who had switched leagues, forced acceptance that the American League was a full-fledged major league and would be part of the basis of baseball's structure from then on.

Lajoie was succeeded as the American League's superstar by Ty Cobb, who also laid claim to the Triple Crown in 1909. As with Lajoie, hitting home runs was not Cobb's dominant ability, and despite ten batting championships and four RBI titles, he wore the Triple Crown but once. He came close two other times, in 1907 and 1911, finishing second in home runs each of those years.

Cobb's great rival was the National League's Honus Wagner, who never wore the Triple Crown, although he too missed it by a close margin. In 1908 he was second in home runs, the most difficult final jewel for the superstars of the dead-ball era to achieve. Wagner's eight batting titles and four RBI championships were never accompanied by a home run leadership.

While the list of those who have won the Triple Crown is short, it is a quality list. All but two of the twentieth-century members have been elected to the Hall of Fame, and one seems likely, at this writing, to achieve this honor: Carl Yastrzemski.

In 1912 Heinie Zimmerman, one of the best major league third basemen, put together the greatest season he would ever have. Honus Wagner failed to repeat as batting champion, and his 102 RBI total was one less than Zimmerman's, according to the tabulations of Ernie Lanigan. The 14 home runs Zimmerman hit edged teammate Wildfire Schulte, who had led the league in four-baggers the two previous seasons, by one. Only in batting average, where Zimmerman's .372 far distanced the field, did he have a clear superiority, but a Triple Crown by any measure is a rare treasure and it was Heinie's without dispute, that is until the researchers of Information Concepts, Inc., the group that compiled *The Baseball Encyclopedia,* downgraded his RBI total to 99. Later, an editor of *The Baseball Encyclopedia* fudged Zim's RBI count back up to 103 to restore his Triple Crown, but we cannot subscribe to such nonsense.

It was 1922 before the Triple Crown would again rest on a player's head, but when it did, it landed on the brow of the royally nicknamed "Rajah" Hornsby and just eluded Babe Ruth, "the Sultan of Swat."

Hornsby strung together six successive batting titles, from 1920 through 1925, and added another in 1928. Although he had home run power to go with his high averages, the title escaped him in 1921, when George Kelly outhomered him by two. It would have been the first Triple Crown for the Rajah and would have given him an eventual three, a total no one has ever achieved.

Babe Ruth, who got two legs up on the Triple Crown seven times without ever winning one, had many home run titles and frequently topped the league in RBIs. However, the competition for batting championships in the 1920s, when Cobb, Sisler, and Heilmann topped .400 and Heilmann alone accounted for four batting titles, was tough. Ruth managed one hitting title but lost the RBI leg that year, 1924, to Goose Goslin. The Babe won many honors, but the Triple Crown was not among them.

In the 1930s a quartet of superstars and future Hall of Fame members competed for the Triple Crown during most of the decade, and each took a single turn wearing it.

The American League had two great first baseman, Jimmie Foxx and Lou Gehrig. Each was a threat to claim the Crown every year, but when Foxx narrowly failed on two occasions, it was not Gehrig who stymied him. In 1932 Jimmie came frustratingly close. He was edged out of the batting title by the clumsy-fielding Dale Alexander in 1932. Called "Moose," Alexander split the season between Detroit and Boston, the first player to win a batting title while appearing with two teams. Alexander barely qualified for the championship, but his .367 topped the .364 by Foxx. The following year, 1933, Foxx won his lone Triple Crown.

Alexander was long gone back to the minor leagues before Jimmie Foxx had his second near-miss of the Triple Crown in 1938. This time it was the home run lead that eluded him. Although Foxx hit 50 home runs in 1938, while winning the batting and RBI honors, Hank Greenberg hit 58 homers to almost equal Babe Ruth's record of 60.

While Gehrig and Foxx were trying on the Triple Crown for size in the American League, two sluggers in the National League were sharing domination of their league. Chuck Klein was the league's outstanding batter during the early 1930s and Joe Medwick took over for the final half of the decade. Both wore the Triple Crown, Klein getting his in 1933 when Jimmie Foxx was doing likewise. It was the only year that each league produced a Triple Crown winner. Medwick won his in 1937.

The next to claim the Triple Crown was Ted Williams. A brash rookie when he reported to the Boston Red Sox in 1939, he had little to learn from the old guy hitting fungos in practice. Hugh Duffy took one look at Williams's swing and knew the only part he could serve was as a role model. Williams had his eye on hitting .400. When he did it, in 1941, his .406 was far short of Duffy's .440, the all-time record.

Williams was also one leg short of the Triple Crown in 1941. He added the home run title to his batting championship, but his main rival, Joe DiMaggio, had topped the RBI column. DiMaggio had piled up his runs-batted-in totals largely during his 56-game hitting streak that season.

Ted Williams won all three titles for the Triple Crown the next season, 1942, and then went off to serve in World War Two. Several wartime players won two legs of the Triple Crown: Rudy York, with the Detroit Tigers in 1943, and Bill Nicholson, a Chicago Cubs outfielder in 1943 and 1944. Both hit home runs and batted in runs at league-leading levels, but they were far outdistanced for the batting-average honors.

Ted Williams returned from the war in 1946 and finished second in each of the Triple Crown categories. Mickey Vernon beat him out for the batting title, and Hank Greenberg, who had blocked Jimmie Foxx in 1938, had his last hurrah with the Tigers, topping Williams in both home runs and runs batted in.

The next year, with Greenberg gone to the National League, Ted Williams claimed his second Triple Crown. No one was close to him in any of the three prize categories, and despite three prime seasons lost to wartime serv-

ice, the Red Sox star seemed most likely to be the first to wear the Triple Crown three times. He had won in 1942 and 1947.

In 1948 his old nemesis, Joe DiMaggio, who was never to win a Triple Crown, picked off two of the crown jewels, leading the American League in home runs with 39 and in runs batted in with 155. Ted Williams was far ahead of the pack as batting champion with a .369 average.

It was 1949 that proved the greatest disappointment to Williams. DiMaggio was injured much of the season and did not compete for individual honors. However, the pennant race was tightly contested between the Yankees and Red Sox, and more interest was focused on that than on the seemingly assured third Triple Crown to be worn by Ted Williams.

As the season reached the final weekend, Boston came to New York for two games between the Red Sox and Yankees. Boston was a game ahead and needed to win only one to gain the pennant. They lost on Saturday, and the teams were tied when Sunday's game began.

The biggest threat to Ted Williams' third Triple Crown came from teammate Vern Stephens, a slugging shortstop who was tied with Ted for RBIs. Williams held a small but probably secure batting lead over George Kell of the Detroit Tigers.

However, Williams and the Red Sox were in a slump, and it cost both the team and the individual their honors. The final game of the season between the Yankees and Red Sox was one of the most exciting of all time, if you were a Yankee fan. If you were among the generations of faithful Red Sox followers who have seen their team fail in the final situation, one frustrating season after another, it was a bitter end. The Red Sox blew a lead in the bottom of the ninth as the Yankees rose to the heights with a last-ditch rally to win the pennant.

Williams had gone hitless and ended up not only missing a World Series appearance but his third Triple Crown. While Williams had sputtered in the final games, George Kell, who had missed two stretches of games with injuries, got back in the lineup for Detroit's final three games. With only a batting title at stake, Kell had two hits in his final game. When the final statistics were known, George Kell had batted .3429 and Ted Williams .3427. It was the closest any player ever came to a Triple Crown without actually winning it and the closest anyone has come to earning the honor three times.

The year before, in the National League, Stan Musial had narrowly missed his bid for a Triple Crown, when he was one behind Johnny Mize and Ralph Kiner, who tied for the home run title with 40.

In 1953 Al Rosen had a near-miss almost as tight as Ted Williams had had in 1949. Rosen won the home run and RBI titles but was edged out, .337 to .336, for the batting championship by Mickey Vernon, who had blocked Williams's bid in that category in 1946.

Mickey Mantle hit his peak in 1956 when he put the necessary ingredients together to win a Triple Crown. He hit .353 for the only batting title he would win, had top totals in home runs with 52, and piled up 130 runs batted in.

Ten years later, in 1966, Frank Robinson reacted to being traded out of the National League by winning the Triple Crown in the American League. His .316 batting average was one of only two above .300 that year in the American League. He had switched leagues just in time. A .316 average wouldn't have made the top five in the National League in 1966. He won the home run and RBI titles comfortably.

In 1967, the year of the Red Sox "Impossible Dream," the team was driven to a surprise championship by the captain, Carl Yastrzemski, who had an astounding year. Yaz won the only home run title of his career and also the lone RBI championship he would record. He joined these with one of his three batting crowns and ended the season with what was to become an elusive honor, the Triple Crown.

He is the last player to wear the title, although a number of players have gained two legs, including Yaz's teammate, Jim Rice, who has done this twice. In the American League the inability of power hitters to achieve a high batting average has resulted in a parade of sluggers leading in home runs and runs batted in but falling short in base-hit percentage.

Harmon Killebrew, who tied with Yaz for home runs in Yastrzemski's crown-winning season, Frank Howard, Dick Allen, Reggie Jackson, George Scott, Eddie Murray, Tony Armas, and Jose Canseco have won two legs but failed the batting title.

Since Yaz won the last Triple Crown, two National Leaguers have won batting titles and the RBI championship, but failed in home runs. Joe Torre in 1971 and Al Oliver in 1982 earned two legs one way, and Johnny Bench, Willie Stargell, George Foster, Andre Dawson, and Mike Schmidt have done it with the home run and RBI crowns. Foster did it twice and Schmidt four times.

Combining a high batting average with power is a rare characteristic in contemporary baseball. Players such as Rod Carew and Wade Boggs, who have won frequent batting championships without expectation of adding the other elements of the Triple Crown, serve to reduce the likelihood that a pure power hitter will also annex a batting title, especially in the course of the same season.

Carl Yastrzemski might not be just part of a vanishing breed. He might be the last example of a breed that has already vanished.

Triple Crown Winners—Pitching

Tommy Bond, the only nineteenth-century pitcher on the list of Triple Crown Winners who is not in the Hall of Fame, has, at least, the honor of turning the feat first. When the National League was formed in 1876, Bond was an established star in the National Association. The others who eventually won the pitchers' Triple Crown, for the most wins and strikeouts and the lowest ERA in a single season, began their careers in the National League.

Although he was only twenty-one when he won the Triple Crown in 1877, Bond had been pitching for prominent teams since he had been sixteen and joined the Athletics of Brooklyn. He entered the National League with Hartford but moved to Boston for his best seasons. He was Boston's only pitcher during 1877 and 1878 and pitched the great majority of games in 1879. He won 123

Triple Crown Hitters

American League

Player	Team	Year	HR	RBI	BA
Nap Lajoie	Phila.	1901	14	125	.422
Ty Cobb	Det.	1909	9	115	.377
Jimmie Foxx	Phila.	1933	48	163	.356
Lou Gehrig	N.Y.	1934	49	165	.363
Ted Williams	Bos.	1942	36	137	.356
	Bos.	1947	32	114	.343
Mickey Mantle	N.Y.	1956	52	130	.353
Frank Robinson	Bal.	1966	49	122	.316
Carl Yastrzemski	Bos.	1967	44	121	.326

National League

Player	Team	Year	HR	RBI	BA
Paul Hines	Prov.	1878	4	50	.358
Hugh Duffy	Bos.	1894	18	145	.438
Heinie Zimmerman*	Chi.	1912	14	103	.372
Rogers Hornsby	St.L.	1922	42	152	.401
	St.L.	1925	39	143	.403
Chuck Klein	Phila.	1933	28	120	.368
Joe Medwick	St.L.	1937	31	154	.374

*Zimmerman ranked first in RBIs as calculated by Ernie Lanigan, but only third as calculated by ICI research in 1969.

of the 204 games Boston played in those early years of short schedules.

Bond, who later coached baseball at Harvard, was celebrated for his victories and strikeouts. The measurement of earned runs was done retroactively.

As Bond's career lapsed, the next to claim the Triple Crown of pitching emerged. Old Hoss Radbourn reached the peak year that gave him his nickname for durability in 1884. He pitched the Providence Grays to the National League pennant, almost singlehandedly, after Charlie Sweeney's departure had left only Radbourn as the team's pitcher.

His 60 victories is the most ever won by a pitcher in a season. It shines brightest among all such jewels in the Triple Crowns worn by those who came after him. Radbourn won 308 games in his big league career, but the 60 he totaled in his 1884 season—including a streak of 26 wins in 27 decisions—gave him a celebrity which was recognized when he was named to the Hall of Fame in its opening year, 1939.

A Triple Crown is an exacting measurement of a pitcher's superiority at any time. However, because of the circumstance that he started so many games for the league's best team, Radbourn's win totals and strikeout numbers can largely be attributed to sheer volume. However, it is his 1.38 ERA at a time when the league mark was 2.98 that stamps Old Hoss as truly remarkable for his time.

Tim Keefe, the next pitcher to annex a Triple Crown, wore his for a season that has kept his name in the active files of modern baseball writers. Whenever a pitcher runs off a string of victories, this prompts a review of the record book, and Keefe's 19 in a row is remembered as the highest total, shared with Rube Marquard's 1912 season total of 19 straight. In all, Tim Keefe won 35 games for the New York Giants in 1888, just edging out the man who would take the Triple Crown the next year.

John Clarkson pitched Boston to a pennant in 1889, winning the Triple Crown as the workhorse of a staff which included the worn Old Hoss Radbourn. Clarkson won 49 games and Radbourn 20.

Clarkson's career was overlapped by that of Amos

Rusie, the most awesome pitcher of the 1890s. A burly farm boy, "the Hoosier Thunderbolt" was the principal reason the distance of the pitcher's box was pushed back in 1893. Rusie responded the following year by continuing to dominate the league in strikeouts, while topping all pitchers with 36 wins and an ERA of 2.78.

Probably because of the increased pitching distance, the league ERA ballooned to 5.32 and batters averaged .309 in 1894. This was the year Hugh Duffy won the batter's Triple Crown and set a still-unexcelled .440 batting record.

Rusie's career peaked in 1894. The next season one of the most oppressive men to own a big league team, Andrew Freedman, bought the Giants and began a blood feud with Rusie. Rusie sat out the 1896 season, but returned as a reluctant star for two more 20-game-winning seasons. Then he tore his arm muscles and retired. A token appearance in 1901 was the tenth season which qualified him for election to the Hall of Fame.

Just as Nap Lajoie marked the American League's inaugural in 1901 by winning a Triple Crown for batters, another established star, Cy Young, did the same for the pitchers' version. Young, in midcareer as a big league pitcher, won 33 games, a total almost dwarfed among the 511 he won in his career. This latter is a mark certain to stand permanently.

With two major leagues now offering the potential of a Triple Crown winner each year, it took only until 1905 to have both the American and National Leagues produce such winners. Christy Mathewson won the first of the two Triple Crowns he would win for the New York Giants, and the eccentric Rube Waddell had his last great year with the Philadelphia Athletics.

Matty won 31 games, struck out 206, and had an ERA of 1.43. The Rube produced 26 wins, 287 strikeouts, and an ERA of 1.48. The World Series, inaugurated in 1903 but boycotted by the Giants in 1904, was resumed in 1905. It would have provided marvelous theater for the two Triple Crown winners. The confrontation would have been the only one of its kind. Never since have two pennant winners also had pitching's Triple Crown winners. Alas, the colorful Rube Waddell injured his arm while wrestling a teammate just before the Series began.

Without Waddell to oppose him, Christy Mathewson won three games, all shutouts, and the Giants took the Series in five. Matty won the Triple Crown again in 1908 but lost his last start when the Chicago Cubs won the playoff game of a season which had ended in a tie. It was the failure of Fred Merkle to reach second as the winning run scored, resulting in his becoming an inning-ending force out, that deprived Matty of a second opportunity to wear his Triple Crown into a World Series.

Walter Johnson, the next to sport a Triple Crown, won three at widely spaced intervals in his long career. The first came in 1913, the next in 1918, and the last in 1924 when, in his eighteenth season, Johnson once more topped the American League in the three prize categories. This time it also brought a pennant to the Senators, the first in their history. The World Series came close to being a disappointing anticlimax for Johnson. He lost the opener to the New York Giants in extra innings, then lost again, but salvaged glory by winning the deciding seventh game in relief.

Earlier, during Walter Johnson's widely spaced crown jewels, Grover Alexander produced the most impressive reign ever enjoyed by a Triple Crown winner. Pitching for the Philadelphia Phillies, he had three successive seasons with 30 or more victories, starting with the pennant-winning 1915 season; each time he led the NL in ERA and K's as well. What stopped Alexander's run of mastery was World War One. Old Pete swapped his baseball uniform for the khaki of the Army and his Triple Crown honors for a sergeant's stripes.

While Pete was in the Army, another pitcher claimed the Triple Crown. Hippo Vaughn, who in 1917 had achieved immortality by engaging in a double no-hit game, losing in the tenth inning. In 1918, with Alexander away, Vaughn won the Triple Crown pitching for the Cubs.

Ironically Grover Alexander had served his Army hitch as a new member of the Cubs. With his battery mate, Reindeer Bill Killefer, he had been sold to Chicago after winning his third Triple Crown, in 1917. He pitched only three games in 1918 while Vaughn was in the star's role, and in 1919 the two teammates competed for the Triple Crown. Alexander led the league in ERA and Vaughn in strikeouts. Between them they won 37 games, but neither came close to topping the league.

However, in 1920 Grover Alexander again emerged as the Triple Crown winner. It was his fourth, the most ever won by a pitcher. He continued to star, despite personal and physical problems, during the 1920s without again leading in any of the categories which make up the diadem of the Triple Crown.

Next to wear the Triple Crown of pitchers was Dazzy Vance. Like Rusie, Waddell, and Johnson, Vance began with expectation of finishing each season with a league-leading total in strikeouts. In 1924 he won the Most Valuable Player Award, even though the Brooklyn Dodgers as a team could not win the pennant. To his strikeout superiority, the Dazzler added leadership in wins with 24 and an ERA of 2.16. His domination of the league can best be measured by comparing his ERA to a league total of 3.87 as the lively ball bounded off hitters' bats.

Lefty Grove of the Philadelphia Athletics won back to back Triple Crowns in 1930 and 1931, having missed one of the three legs in 1929. The A's won pennants all three of those years, and Grove was their leading pitcher. In 1929 teammate George Earnshaw topped him in wins, 24 to 20, as Grove missed getting decisions in an unusual number of games.

Another southpaw ace, Lefty Gomez, succeeded Lefty Grove as a Triple Crown winner. Like Grove, he wore the title twice, but not consecutively. He won his first Triple Crown, oddly, in a season when his team, the New York Yankees, didn't win a pennant, 1934. His next came in 1937 as the Yankees were in the midst of a run of four straight pennants.

Gomez was only a spot starter in 1939, when the Yankees met the Reds in the World Series, but Cincinnati had a converted third baseman, Bucky Walters heading their staff, the first National Leaguer to win the Triple Crown in fifteen years.

During World War Two, Hal Newhouser emerged as a superlative pitcher who might have been equally impressive against peacetime competition. He missed the Triple

Crown in 1944, winning two legs but coming in second to Detroit Tiger teammate Dizzy Trout for ERA honors. In 1945, the final wartime year, Newhouser topped the American League in the three prize categories, and winning the Triple Crown went into a long hiatus when the 1946 season resumed with the star pitchers back from service.

Despite leading the league in victories six times and in strikeouts seven, Bob Feller never won an official ERA title to match up with the other components of the Triple Crown; although Feller's ERA in 1940 is today regarded as the lowest for that year, at that time Ernie Bonham won the title despite pitching only 99 innings.

Warren Spahn topped the National League in victories eight times, led in strikeouts four times, and even took ERA honors three times, but he could never link them up in a single season.

Robin Roberts, like Feller, never won an ERA title, so despite leading in victories four times and strikeouts twice, the singular honor of the Triple Crown eluded him, as it did all other pitchers once baseball had returned to the normalcy of peacetime play.

Triple Crown Pitchers

American League

Player	Team	Year	W	L	SO	ERA
Cy Young	Bos.	1901	33	10	158	1.62
Rube Waddell	Phila.	1905	26	11	287	1.48
Walter Johnson	Wash.	1913	36	7	303	1.09
	Wash.	1918	23	13	162	1.27
	Wash.	1924	23	7	158	2.72
Lefty Grove	Phila.	1930	28	5	209	2.54
	Phila.	1931	31	4	175	2.06
Lefty Gomez	N.Y.	1934	26	5	158	2.33
	N.Y.	1937	21	11	194	2.33
Hal Newhouser	Det.	1945	25	9	212	1.81

National League

Player	Team	Year	W	L	SO	ERA
Tommy Bond	Bos.	1877	40	17	170	2.11
Old Hoss Radbourn	Prov.	1884	60	12	441	1.38
Tim Keefe................	N.Y.	1888	35	12	333	1.74
John Clarkson	Bos.	1889	49	19	284	2.73
Amos Rusie	N.Y.	1894	36	13	195	2.78
Christy Mathewson	N.Y.	1905	31	8	206	1.27
	N.Y.	1908	37	11	259	1.43
Grover Alexander	Phila.	1915	31	10	241	1.22
	Phila.	1916	33	12	167	1.55
	Phila.	1917	30	13	201	1.86
Hippo Vaughn	Chi.	1918	22	10	148	1.74
Grover Alexander	Chi.	1920	27	14	173	1.91
Dazzy Vance	Brook.	1924	28	6	262	2.16
Bucky Walters	Cin.	1939	27	11	137	2.29
Sandy Koufax	L.A.	1963	25	5	306	1.88
	L.A.	1965	26	8	382	2.04
	L.A.	1966	27	9	317	1.73
Steve Carlton	Phila.	1972	27	10	310	1.97
Dwight Gooden	N.Y.	1985	24	4	268	1.53

It wasn't until Sandy Koufax reached stardom when the Dodgers were transplanted to Los Angeles and notched three Triple Crown titles that the distinction was again achieved. Koufax topped the three needed categories in 1963, 1965, and 1966. Unlike any other winner of the Triple Crown, Koufax retired with the honor. An aching arthritic arm caused his early retirement, leaving a final season of 27 victories, 317 strikeouts, and an ERA of 1.73.

A Triple Crown-winning pitcher has not always meant a pennant for his team, although the two have gone together more often than not. However, in 1972 Steve Carlton took the honor despite pitching for a last-place team. There has never been such a contrast in the success of a team's best pitcher and the rest of its staff. The Phillies won 59 games, and Carlton was responsible for 27 of them. He also led, for the only time, in ERA, with 1.97, and struck out 310.

Again a drought followed, despite the presence of such star pitchers as Tom Seaver, Fergie Jenkins, Juan Marichal, Jim Palmer, Gaylord Perry, and others who led in some of the prize-earning stats. Then in 1985 Dwight Gooden took up the challenge and claimed the Triple Crown with a remarkable record: 24-4, 1.53, and 268 strikeouts. Gooden faltered the next year, but Roger Clemens came forward to just miss the honor by finishing second in strikeouts while winning the other two legs.

The Unassisted Triple Play

On May 30, 1987, family and friends of ninety-three-year-old Jimmy Cooney gathered at his home to celebrate the sixtieth anniversary of his unassisted triple play. Rare? It was the last one made in the National League. Only two have been made since that long ago Memorial Day—one, oddly, the day after Cooney's.

Letters from National League president A. Bartlett Giamatti and Dallas Green, the general manager of the Chicago Cubs, congratulated Jimmy Cooney. He had worn a Chicago Cubs uniform the day fate had decreed he be in the right place at the right time. A much-traveled infielder, he had worn six major league uniforms in seven seasons. It was a happy coincidence that he was Chicago's shortstop when he made his unassisted triple play. His father, the first Jimmy Cooney, had been Chicago's shortstop in 1890, '91, and part of '92.

Jimmy's younger brother John had logged twenty years in the big leagues as a pitcher, and after his arm went lame, he had become an outfielder and first baseman.

Jimmy Cooney was no stranger to unassisted triple plays. Two seasons earlier, when he was shortstop for the St. Louis Cardinals, he was doubled off second by the Pirate shortstop Glenn Wright, who next tagged out Rogers Hornsby coming from first base. Wright had snared a line drive off the bat of Jim Bottomley to start his triple play. He watched from the Pirates' bench the day Cooney emulated his feat in much the same manner.

Paul Waner provided the line drive to make the first out, with Cooney snaring it as he ran toward second base. Clyde Barnhart had broken for second on the pitch, and Lloyd Waner, the runner on second, had dashed for third as his brother, Paul, swung. Lloyd was doubled off second, and Cooney simply tagged the startled Barnhart, who thought the ball had gone into center field for a base hit.

There are certain similarities among eight of the nine unassisted triple plays which have been recorded. These have occurred with runners on first and second, have been made by infielders, and have required the complicity of base runners either attempting a double steal or racing away on a hit-and-run play. The ninth—which is soon to be revealed—was by an outfielder, with runners on second and third.

Even the most celebrated unassisted-triple-play feat had an explanation that almost absolved the victims, the Brooklyn Dodgers, of bonehead base running. This was the only such event to happen in a World Series, and it was turned in by Bill Wambsganss, the Cleveland Indian second baseman in 1920. Those who have examined the boxscore have questioned the tactics of Uncle Wilbert Robinson, the Brooklyn manager whose strategies often were charitably called "unusual." It was the fifth inning, and Brooklyn, behind 7–0, had the first two runners on base. Play it safe? Not Uncle Robbie.

Despite being scoreless, the Dodgers had been hitting the Cleveland pitcher, Jim Bagby, hard. It was a game in which they made thirteen hits and scored a lone run. Bill Wambsganss, who told the story hundreds of times, explained that he chose to play very deep when Clarence Mitchell, a very good-hitting pitcher came to bat in the fifth inning. He didn't think a seven-run lead, so early in the game, was too secure the way the Dodgers had been hitting.

When Mitchell cracked the ball on a line, the batters took off, not thinking that Wamby was where the ball was going. He was and ran over and doubled Kilduff off second and turned and found a dumbfounded Otto Miller standing in the baseline. He tagged him out and, as has been the case after every unassisted triple play, trotted off the field in silence. It always takes the crowd a minute or more to realize what has happened.

In the early years of baseball, outfielder Paul Hines of the Providence Grays, had been credited with making an unassisted triple play. Later-day research indicated Hines had made an unassisted double play but had thrown to a base for the third out. But according to the rules of 1878, Hines did indeed register an unassisted triple play.

In 1928, Providence sportswriter W. D. "Bill" Perrin—who at that time had covered the Providence Grays for nearly half a century—described Hines' actions in the game played on May 8, 1878, in Providence. "The circumstances of this play have afforded more arguments than any other known play. That the play was made is not disputed, but whether Hines made the play unassisted or whether [second baseman Charles] Sweasy completed it by retiring the third man. . . . Here is what happened: [Jim] O'Rourke drew a base on balls and scored when Sweasy threw [Jack] Manning's drive over [Providence first baseman Tim] Murnane's head, Manning going to third on the error. Murnane muffed [Ezra] Sutton's fly, Manning holding third [as Sutton took second]. [Jack] Burdock was next up and dropped the ball just over [shortstop Tom] Carey's head for what looked like a safe hit. . . .

"The story in the *Providence Journal* of the next day thus describes the play: 'Manning and Sutton proceeded to the home plate,' meaning that both rounded third. 'Hines ran in and caught the ball, and kept going to tag third.' The rule then as now requires that when a base runner is forced to retrace his steps he must retouch the bases passed in reverse order. As Hines touched third with the ball in his hand, after making the catch, before either Manning or Sutton could get back, both were out automatically. It is true that Hines then on a signal from Sweasy threw the ball to second, but this was unnecessary as both runners were out at third."

To confirm Perrin's view, let's look at the playing rules for 1878, the year in which Hines made his celebrated play. Rule V, Section 1 reads: "Players running the bases must touch each base in regular order, viz., first, second,

third, and home bases; and when obliged to return to bases they have occupied they must retouch them in reverse order. . . ." And Rule V, Section 15 reads: "Any base-runner failing to touch the base he runs for shall be declared out if the ball be held by a fielder, while touching said base, before the base-runner returns and touches it." Henry Chadwick's gloss on the latter rule stated: ". . . it is only necessary for a fielder to hold the ball on the base, which should have been touched, in order to put the runner out."

Eureka! The controversy of over a century is thus resolved, and in favor of Paul Hines and his unassisted triple play. Rewrite the record books!

Johnny Neun had read in the morning paper of May 31, 1927, about Jimmy Cooney's unassisted triple play in the National League. As first baseman for the Detroit Tigers, known for his fielding and base stealing, Neun was alert to all possibilities when Homer Summa's line drive landed in his glove. Charlie Jamieson was a dead duck, caught off first and easily tagged for the second out. Shortstop Jackie Tavener was jumping up and down at second base calling for the ball. Slow-footed Glen Myatt was lumbering back from third base.

Neun waved his shortstop out of the way and raced toward second base, implausibly shouting, "I'm running into the Hall of Fame."

In a nice touch of journalistic enterprise, *Sports Illustrated,* in 1987, noted that both Jimmy Cooney and Johnny Neun were still alive and arranged for them to talk on the telephone about their unique plays made sixty years earlier. They had been contemporaries but had played in different leagues and had never met.

When each had gone back to the minor leagues, they played against each other in the International League but simply passed each other without fraternal comment, despite having shared such an extremely rare experience. They had a very nice talk, and months later, when Jimmy reached his anniversary a day ahead of Johnny, it was Neun who called to extend congratulations. Jimmy's National League record has not been matched. Johnny Neun's American League record has.

On July 30, 1968, Ron Hansen, playing shortstop for the Washington Senators, made an unassisted triple play, following the process all other shortstops have used. He grabbed a line drive, off the bat of Joe Azcue, stepped on second to retire Dave Nelson, and tagged Russ Snyder coming from first. It was the first time the feat had been pulled since 1927, forty-one years earlier.

It was the most memorable event of Hansen's week, which was an unusual one in other ways as well. Following his play, he struck out six consecutive times, perhaps still stunned by the event. Then he regained his batting eye to hit a grand-slam home run. His unassisted triple play had been made on a road trip. He could expect applause when he came to bat the first time before hometown Washington fans when the team returned home. But he didn't get this. Instead, he was traded to the White Sox.

The first unassisted triple play of the twentieth century was made on July 19, 1909, by a Cleveland shortstop, Neal Ball. Overall Cleveland has been involved in five of the nine unassisted triple plays in the major leagues. Three times the event has taken place there, twice executed by Cleveland players, and in all a Cleveland player has been involved somewhere five times. It all began with Neal Ball, who snagged a liner hit by Boston's Amby McConnell and retired Charley Wagner and Jake Stahl on the basepaths.

George Burns, playing for the Boston Red Sox between stints as a member of the Indians, turned the tables for Boston and made Cleveland the victim in 1923. He caught Frank Brower's liner, tagged Rube Lutzke off first, and ran to second to get Riggs Stephenson before he could return.

Burns made his play on September 14, and on October 6 another unassisted triple play occurred, making the feat which had been so rare appear almost commonplace, for a while. This time Ernie Padgett, a redheaded shortstop for the Boston Braves, turned the trick. Again the play was made in typical fashion—a line drive, a runner doubled off second base, and a surprised baserunner from first being tagged out.

Triple plays are rare enough; some are rapidly executed by quick-throwing infielders, and others are the result of erratic base running and convoluted attempts to advance or retreat by confused baserunners. An unassisted triple play is an event most baseball followers will never see. However, every time there are two runners on base and none out, the potential is there.

Unassisted Triple Plays

Player/Team	Date	Pos.	Opp.	Opp. Batter
Paul Hines, Prov.	May 8, 1878	OF	Bos.	Jack Burdock
Neal Ball, Cleve.	July 19, 1909	SS	Bos.	Amby McConnell
Bill Wambsganss, Cleve.	October 10, 1920	2B	Brook.	Clarence Mitchell
George Burns, Bos.	September 14, 1923	1B	Cleve.	Frank Brower
Ernie Padgett, Bos.	October 6, 1923	SS	Phila.	Walter Holke
Glenn Wright, Pitts.	May 7, 1925	SS	St.L.	Jim Bottomley
Johnny Cooney, Chi.	May 30, 1927	SS	Pitts.	Paul Waner
Johnny Neun, Det.	May 31, 1927	1B	Cleve.	Homer Summa
Ron Hansen, Wash.	July 29, 1968	SS	Cleve.	Joe Azcue

The No-Hitters

What follows is the traditional honor roll of the 200-plus pitchers who have attained the no-hit heights. Also provided is a list of those handful of ugly-duckling no-hitters that didn't go nine innings, and those 32 games in which a pitcher retired 27 or more batters in succession. Concerning the last-named group, only 13 are officially recognized as perfect games—the rest were deprived of perfection by their fielding support, their stars, or like Dick Bosman, simply themselves.

No hit games, nine or more innings.

(Number to left is career total if greater than one)
(Home team is that of pitcher, unless team is in italics)

Joe Borden, Phi vs. Chi NA, 4-0; July 28, 1875.
George Bradley, StL vs. Har NL, 2-0; July 15, 1876.
Lee Richmond, Wor vs. Cle NL, 1-0; June 12, 1880 (perfect game).
Monte Ward, Pro vs. Buf NL, 5-0; June 17, 1880.
Larry Corcoran, Chi vs. Bos NL, 6-0; August 19, 1880.
Jim Galvin, Buf vs. Wor NL, 1-0; August 20, 1880.
Tony Mullane, Lou vs. Cin AA, 2-0; September 19, 1882.
Guy Hecker, Lou vs. Pit AA, 3-1; September 19, 1882
2 Larry Corcoran, Chi vs. Wor NL, 5-0; September 20, 1882

Hoss Radbourn, Pro vs. Cle NL, 8-0; July 25, 1883
Hugh (One Arm). Daily, Cle vs. Phi NL, 1-0; September 13, 1883.
Al Atkisson, Phi vs. Pit AA, 10-1; May 24, 1884.
Ed Morris, Col vs. Pit AA, 5-0; May 29, 1884.
Frank Mountain, Col vs. Was AA, 12-0; June 5, 1884.
3 Larry Corcoran, Chi vs. Pro NL, 6-0; June 27, 1884.
2 Jim Galvin, Buf vs. Det NL, 18-0; August 4, 1884.
Dick Burns, Cin vs. KC UA, 3-1; August 26, 1884.
Ed Cushman, Mil vs. Was UA, 5-0; September 28, 1884.
Sam Kimber, Bro vs. Tol AA, 0-0; October 4, 1884 (10 innings, tie).
John Clarkson, Chi vs. Pro NL, 4-0; July 27, 1885.
Charlie Ferguson, Phi vs. Pro NL, 1-0; August 29, 1885.
2 Al Atkisson, Phi vs. NY AA, 3-2; May 1, 1886.
Adonis Terry, Bro vs. StL AA, 1-0; July 24, 1886.
Matt Kilroy, Bal vs. Pit AA, 6-0; October 6, 1886.
2 Adonis Terry, Bro vs. Lou AA, 4-0; May 27, 1888.
Henry Porter, KC vs. Bal AA, 4-0; June 6, 1888.
Ed Seward, Phi vs. Cin AA, 12-2; July 26, 1888.
Gus Weyhing, Phi vs. KC AA, 4-0; July 31, 1888.
Cannonball Titcomb, Roch vs. Syr AA, 7-0; September 15, 1890.
Tom Lovett, Bro vs. NY NL, 4-0; June 22, 1891.
Amos Rusie, NY vs. Bro NL, 6-0; July 31, 1891.
Ted Breitenstein, StL vs. Lou AA, 8-0; October 4, 1891 (1st game). (first start in the major leagues).
Jack Stivetts, Bos vs. Bro NL, 11-0; August 6, 1892.
Ben Sanders, Lou vs. Bal NL, 6-2; August 22, 1892.
Bumpus Jones, Cin vs. Pit NL, 7-1; October 15, 1892. (first game in the major leagues).
Bill Hawke, Bal vs. Was NL, 5-0; August 16, 1893.
Cy Young, Cle vs. Cin NL, 6-0; September 18, 1897 (1st game).
2 Ted Breitenstein, Cin vs. Pit NL, 11-0; April 22, 1898.
Jim Hughes, Bal vs. Bos NL, 8-0; April 22, 1898.
Red Donahue, Phi vs. Bos NL, 5-0; July 8, 1898.
Walter Thornton, Chi vs. Bro NL, 2-0; August 21, 1898 (2nd game).
Deacon Phillippe, Lou vs. NY NL, 7-0; May 25, 1899.
Vic Willis, Bos vs. Was NL, 7-1; August 7, 1899.
Noodles Hahn, Cin vs. Phi NL, 4-0; July 12, 1900.
Earl Moore, Cle vs. Chi AL, 2-4; May 9, 1901 (lost on two hits in 10th).
Christy Mathewson, NY vs. StL NL, 5-0; July 15, 1901.
Jim Callahan, Chi vs. Det AL, 3-0; September 20, 1902 (1st game).
Chick Fraser, Phi vs. Chi NL, 10-0; September 18, 1903 (2nd game).
2 Cy Young, Bos vs. Phi AL, 3-0; May 5, 1904 (perfect game).
Bob Wicker, Chi vs. NY NL, 1-0; June 11, 1904. (won in 12 innings after allowing one hit in the 10th).
Jesse Tannehill, Bos vs. Chi AL, 6-0; August 17, 1904.
2 Christy Mathewson, NY vs. Chi NL, 1-0; June 13, 1905.
Weldon Henley, Phi vs. StL AL, 6-0; July 22, 1905 (1st game).
Frank Smith, Chi vs. Det AL, 15-0; September 6, 1905 (2nd game).
Bill Dinneen, Bos vs. Chi AL, 2-0; September 27, 1905 (1st game).
Johnny Lush, Phi vs. Bro NL, 6-0; May 1, 1906.
Mal Eason, Bro vs. StL NL, 2-0; July 20, 1906.
Harry McIntyre, Bro vs. Pit NL, 0-1; August 1, 1906. (lost on four hits in 13 innings after allowing first hit in 11th).
Frank (Jeff). Pfeffer, Bos vs. Cin NL, 6-0; May 8, 1907.
Nick Maddox, Pit vs. Bro NL, 2-1; September 20, 1907.
3 Cy Young, Bos vs. NY AL, 8-0; June 30, 1908.
Hooks Wiltse, NY vs. Phi NL, 1-0; July 4, 1908 (first game, ten innings).
Nap Rucker, Bro vs. Bos NL, 6-0; September 5, 1908 (2nd game).
Dusty Rhoades, Cle vs. Bos AL, 2-1; September 18, 1908.
2 Frank Smith, Chi vs. Phi AL, 1-0; September 20, 1908.
Addie Joss, Cle vs. Chi AL, 1-0; October 2, 1908 (perfect game).
Red Ames, NY vs, Bro NL, 0-3; April 15, 1909. (lost on seven hits in 13 innings after allowing first hit in 10th).
2 Addie Joss, Cle vs. Chi AL, 1-0; April 20, 1910.
Chief Bender, Phi vs. Cle AL, 4-0; May 12, 1910.
Tom L. Hughes, NY vs. Cle AL, 0-5; August 30, 1910 (2nd game). (lost on seven hits in 11 innings after allowing first hit in 10th).
Joe Wood, Bos vs StL AL, 5-0; July 29, 1911 (1st game).
Ed Walsh, Chi vs. Bos AL, 5-0; August 27, 1911.
George Mullin, Det vs. StL AL, 7-0; July 4, 1912 (2nd game).
Earl Hamilton, StL vs. Det AL, 5-1; August 30, 1912.
Jeff Tesreau, NY vs. Phi NL, 3-0; September 6, 1912 (1st game).
Jim Scott, Chi vs. Was AL, 0-1; May 14, 1914 (lost on 2 two hits in 10th).
Joe Benz, Chi vs. Cle Al, 6-1; May 31, 1914.
George Davis, Bos vs. Phi NL, 7-0; September 9, 1914 (2nd game).
Ed Lafitte, Bro vs. KC FL, 6-2; September 19, 1914.
Rube Marquard, NY vs. Bro NL, 2-0; April 15, 1915.
Frank Allen, Pit vs. StL FL, 2-0; April 24, 1915
Claude Hendrix, Chi vs. Pit FL, 10-0; May 15, 1915.
Alex Main, KC vs Buf FL, 5-0; August 16, 1915.
Jimmy Lavender, Chi vs. NY NL, 2-0; August 31, 1915 (1st game).
Dave Davenport, StL vs. Chi FL, 3-0; September 7, 1915.
2 Tom L. Hughes, Bos vs. Pit NL, 2-0; June 16, 1916.
Rube Foster, Bos vs. NY AL, 2-0; June 16, 1916.
Joe Bush, Phi vs. Cle AL, 5-0; August 26, 1916.
Hubert (Dutch) Leonard, Bos vs. StL AL, 4-0; August 30, 1916
Eddie Cicotte, Chi vs. StL AL, 11-0; April 14, 1917.
George Mogridge, NY vs. Bos AL, 2-1; April 24, 1917.
Fred Toney, Cin vs. Chi NL, 1-0; May 2, 1917 (10 innings).
Hippo Vaughn, Chi vs. Cin NL, 0-1; May 2, 1917. (lost on two hits in 10th; Toney pitched a no-hitter in this game).
Ernie Koob, StL vs. Chi AL, 1-0; May 5, 1917.
Bob Groom, StL vs. Chi AL, May 6, 1917 (2nd game).

Ernie Shore, Bos vs. Was AL, 3-0; June 23, 1917 (1st game). (perfect game).
(Shore relieved Babe Ruth in the first inning after Ruth had been thrown
out of the game for protesting a walk to the first batter. The runner was
caught stealing and Shore retired the remaining 26 batters in order).
2 Hubert (Dutch). Leonard, Bos vs. Det AL, 5-0; June 3, 1918.
Hod Eller, Cin vs. StL NL, 6-0; May 11, 1919.
Ray Caldwell, Cle vs. NY AL, 3-0; September 10, 1919 (1st game).
Walter Johnson, Was vs. Bos AL, 1-0; July 1, 1920.
Charlie Robertson, Chi vs. Det AL, 2-0; April 30, 1922 (perfect game).
Jesse Barnes, NY vs. Phi NL, 6-0; May 7, 1922.
Sam Jones, NY vs. Phi AL, 2-0; September 4, 1923.
Howard Ehmke, Bos vs. Phi AL, 4-0; September 7, 1923.
Jesse Haines, StL vs Bos NL, 5-0; July 17, 1924.
Dazzy Vance, Bro vs. Phi NL, 10-1; September 13, 1925 (1st game).
led Lyons, Chi vs. Bos AL, 6-0; August 21, 1926.
Carl Hubbell, NY vs. Pit NL, 11-0; May 8, 1929.
Wes Ferrell, Cle vs. StL AL, 9-0; April 29, 1931.
Bobby Burke, Was vs. Bos AL, 5-0; August 8, 1931.
Bobo Newsom, StL vs Bos AL, 1-2; September 18, 1934 (lost on one hit in
10th).
Paul Dean, StL vs. Bro NL, 3-0; September 21, 1934 (2nd game).
Vern Kennedy, Chi vs. Cle AL, 5-0; August 31, 1935.
Bill Dietrich, Chi vs. StL AL, 8-0; June 1, 1937.
Johnny Vander Meer, Cin vs. Bos NL, 3-0; June 11, 1938.
2 Johnny Vander Meer, Cin vs. Bro NL, 6-0; June 15, 1938 (next start after June
11).
Monte Pearson, NY vs. Cle AL, 13-0; August 27, 1938 (2nd game).
Bob Feller, Cle vs. Chi AL, 1-0; April 16, 1940 (opening day).
Tex Carleton, Bro vs. Cin NL, 3-0; April 30, 1940.
Lon Warneke, StL vs. Cin NL, 2-0; August 30, 1941.
Jim Tobin, Bos vs. Bro NL, 2-0; April 27, 1944.
Clyde Shoun, Cin vs. Bos NL, 1-0; May 15, 1944.
Dick Fowler, Phi vs. StL AL, 1-0; September 9, 1945 (2nd game).
Ed Head, Bro vs. Bos NL, 5-0; April 23, 1946.
2 Bob Feller, Cle vs. NY AL, 1-0; April 30, 1946.
Ewell Blackwell, Cin vs. Bos NL, 6-0; June 18, 1947.
Don Black, Cle vs. Phi AL, 3-0; July 10, 1947 (1st game).
Bill McCahan, Phi vs. Was AL, 3-0; September 3, 1947.
Bob Lemon, Cle vs. Det AL, 2-0; June 30, 1948.
Rex Barney, Bro vs. NY NL, 2-0; September 9, 1948.
Vern Bickford, Bos vs. Bro NL, 7-0; August 11, 1950.
Cliff Chambers, Pit vs. Bos NL, 3-0; May 6, 1951 (2nd game).
3 Bob Feller, Cle vs. Det AL, 2-1; July 1, 1951 (1st game).
Allie Reynolds, NY vs. Cle AL, 1-0; July 12, 1951.
2 Allie Reynolds, NY vs. Bos AL, 8-0; September 28, 1951 (1st game).
Virgil Trucks, Det vs. Was AL, 1-0; May 15, 1952
Carl Erskine, Bro vs. Chi NL, 5-0; June 19, 1952.
2 Virgil Trucks, Det vs. NY AL, 1-0; August 25, 1952.
Bobo Holloman, StL vs. Phi AL, 6-0; May 6, 1953 (first start in the major
leagues).
Jim Wilson, Mil vs. Phi NL, 2-0; June 12, 1954.
Sam Jones, Chi vs Pit NL, 4-0; May 12, 1955.
2 Carl Erskine, Bro vs. NY NL, 3-0; May 12, 1956.
Johnny Klippstein (7 innings), Hershell Freeman (1 inning) and Joe Black (3
innings)., Cin vs. Mil NL, 1-2; May 26, 1956. (lost on three hits in 11 innings
after allowing first hit in 10th).
Mel Parnell, Bos vs. Chi AL, 4-0; July 14, 1956.
Sal Maglie, Bro vs. Phi NL, 5-0; September 25, 1956.
Don Larsen, NY AL vs. Bro NL, 2-0; October 8, 1956. (World Series). (perfect
game).
Bob Keegan, Chi vs. Was AL, 6-0; August 20, 1957 (2nd game).
Jim Bunning, Det vs. Bos AL, 3-0; July 20, 1958 (1st game).
Hoyt Wilhelm, Bal vs. NY AL, 1-0; September 20, 1958.
Harvey Haddix, Pit vs. Mil NL, 0-1; May 26, 1959 (lost
on one hit in 13 innings after pitching 12 perfect innings).
Don Cardwell, Chi vs. StL NL, 4-0; May 15, 1960 (2nd game).
Lew Burdette, Mil vs. Phi NL, 1-0; August 18, 1960.
Warren Spahn, Mil vs. Phi NL, 4-0; September 16, 1960.
2 Warren Spahn, Mil vs. SF NL, 1-0; April 28, 1961.
Bo Belinsky, LA vs. Bal AL, 2-0; May 5, 1962.
Earl Wilson, Bos vs. LA Al, 2-0; June 26, 1962.
Sandy Koufax, LA vs. NY NL, 5-0; June 30, 1962.
Bill Monbouquette, Bos vs. Chi AL, 1-0; August 1, 1962.
Jack Kralick, Min vs. KC AL, 1-0; August 26, 1962.
2 Sandy Koufax, LA vs. SF NL, 8-0; May 11, 1963.
Don Nottebart, Hou vs. Phi NL, 4-1; May 17, 1963.
Juan Marichal, SF vs. Hou NL, 1-0; June 15, 1963.
Ken T. Johnson, Hou vs. Cin NL, 0-1; April 23, 1964 (lost game).
3 Sandy Koufax, LA vs. Phi NL, 3-0; June 4, 1964.
2 Jim Bunning, Phi vs. NY NL, 6-0; June 21, 1964 (1st game; perfect game).
Jim Maloney, Cin vs. NY NL, 0-1; June 14, 1965 (lsot on two hits in 11 innings
after pitching 10 hitless innings).
Jim Maloney, Cin vs. Chi NL, 1-0; August 19, 1965 (1st game; 10 innings).
4 Sandy Koufax, LA vs. Chi NL, 1-0; September 9, 1965 (perfect game).
Dave Morehead, Bos vs. Cle AL, 2-0; September 16, 1965.
Sonny Siebert, Cle vs. Was AL, 2-0; June 10, 1966.
Steve D. Barber (8⅔ innings). and Stu Miller (⅓ inning) Bal vs. Det AL, 1-2;
April 30, 1967 (1st game; lost game).
Don Wilson, Hou vs. Atl NL, 2-0; June 18, 1967.
Dean Chance, Min vs. Cle AL, 2-1; August 25, 1967 (2nd game).
Joe Horlen, Chi vs. Det AL, 6-0; September 10, 1967 (1st game).
Tom Phoebus, Bal vs. Bos AL, 6-0; April 27, 1968.
Catfish Hunter, Oak vs. Min AL, 4-0; May 8, 1968 (perfect game).

George Culver, Cin vs. Phi NL, 6-1; July 29, 1968 (2nd game).
Gaylord Perry, SF vs. StL NL, 1-0; Sept. 17, 1968.
Ray Washburn, StL vs. SF NL, 2-0; September 18, 1968.
Bill Stoneman, Mon vs. Phi NL, 7-0; April 17, 1969.
3 Jim Maloney, Cin vs. Hou NL, 10-0; April 30, 1969.
2 Don Wilson, Hou vs. Cin NL, 4-0; May 1, 1969.
Jim Palmer, Bal vs. Oak AL, 8-0; August 13, 1969.
Ken Holtzman, Chi vs. Atl NL, 3-0; August 19, 1969.
Bob Moose, Pit vs. NY NL, 4-0; September 20, 1969.
Dock Ellis, Pit vs. SD NL, 2-0; June 12, 1970 (1st game).
Clyde Wright, Cal vs. Oak AL, 4-0; July 3, 1970.
Bill Singer, LA vs. Phi NL, 5-0; July 20, 1970.
Vida Blue, Oak vs. Min AL, 6-0; September 21, 1970.
2 Ken Holtzman, Chi vs. Cin NL, 1-0; June 3, 1971.
Rick Wise, Phi vs. CinNL, 4-0; June 23, 1971.
Bob Gibson, StL vs. Pit NL, 11-0; August 14, 1971.
Burt Hooton, Chi vs. Phi NL, 4-0; April 16, 1972.
Milt Pappas, Chi vs. SD NL, 8-0; September 2, 1972.
2 Bill Stoneman, Mon vs. NY NL, 7-0; October 2, 1972 (1st game).
Steve Busby, KC vs. Det AL, 3-0; April 27, 1973.
Nolan Ryan, Cal vs. KC AL, 3-0; May 15, 1973.
2 Nolan Ryan, Cal vs. Det AL, 6-0; July 15, 1973.
Jim Bibby, Tex vs. OakAL, 6-0; July 20, 1973.
Phil Niekro, Atl vs. SD NL, 9-0; August 5, 1973.
2 Steve Busby, KC vs. Mil AL, 2-0; June 19, 1974.
Dick Bosman, Cle vs. Oak AL, 4-0; July 19, 1974.
3 Nolan Ryan, Cal vs. Min AL, 4-0; September 28, 1974
4 Nolan Ryan, Cal vs. Bal AL, 1-0; June 1, 1975.
Ed Halicki, SF vs. NY NL, 6-0; August 24, 1975 (2nd game).
Vida Blue (5 innings), Glenn Abbott (1 inning), Paul Lindblad (1 inning), and
Rollie Fingers (2 innings), Oak vs. Cal AL, 5-0; September 28, 1975.
Larry Dierker, Hou vs. Mon NL, 5-0; July 9, 1976.
Blue Moon Odom (5 innings) and Francisco Barrios (4 innings), Chi vs. Oak
AL, 6-0; July 28, 1976.
John Candelaria, Pit vs. LA NL, 2-0; August 9, 1976.
John Montefusco, SF vs. Atl NL, 9-0; September 29, 1976.
Jim Colborn, KC vs. Tex AL, 6-0; May 14, 1977.
Dennis Eckersley, Cle vs. Cal AL, 1-0; May 30, 1977.
Bert Blyleven, Tex vs. Cal AL, 6-0; September 22, 1977.
Bob Forsch, StL vs. Phi NL, 5-0; April 16, 1978.
Tom Seaver, Cin vs. StL NL, 4-0; June 16, 1978.
Ken Forsch, Hou vs. AtL NL, 6-0; April 7, 1979.
Jerry Reuss, LA vs. SF NL, 8-0; June 27, 1980.
Charlie Lea, Mon vs. SF NL, 4-0; May 10, 1981 (2nd game).
Len Barker, Cle vs. Tor AL, 3-0; May 15, 1981 (perfect game).
5 Nolan Ryan, Hou vs. LA NL, 5-0; September 26, 1981.
Dave Righetti, NY vs. Bos AL, 4-0; July 4, 1983.
2 Bob Forsch, StL vs. Mon NL, 3-0; September 26, 1983.
Mike Warren, Oak vs. Chi AL, 3-0; September 29, 1983.
Jack Morris, Det vs. Chi AL, 4-0; April 7, 1984.
Mike Witt, Cal vs. Tex AL, 1-0; September 30, 1984 (perfect game).
Joe Cowley, Chi vs. Cal AL, 7-1; September 19, 1986.
Mike Scott, Hou vs. SF NL, 2-0; September 25, 1986.
Juan Nieves, Mil vs. Bal AL, 7-0; April 15, 1987.
Tom Browning, Cin vs. LA NL, 1-0; September 16, 1988 (perfect game).
Mark Langston (7 innings) and Mike Witt (2 innings), Cal vs Sea AL, 1-0; April
11, 1990.
Randy Johnson, Sea vs Det AL, 2-0; June 2, 1990.
6 Nolan Ryan, Tex at Oak AL, 5-0; June 11, 1990.
Dave Stewart, Oak at Tor AL, 5-0; June 29, 1990.
Fernando Valenzuela, LA vs StL NL, 6-0; June 29, 1990.
Andy Hawkins, NY at Chi AL, 0-4; July 1, 1990 (8 innings, lost the game).
Terry Mulholland, Phi vs SF NL, 6-0; August 15, 1990.
Dave Stieb, Tor at Det AL, 3-0; September 2, 1990.

No hit games, fewer than nine innings

(Home team is that of pitcher, unless team is in italics)

Larry McKeon, six innings, Ind vs. Cin AA, 0-0; May 6, 1884.
Charlie Gagus, eight innings, Was vs. Wil UA, 12-1; August 21, 1884.
Charlie Getzien, six innings, Det vs. Phi NL, 1-0; October 1, 1884.
Charlie Sweeney (3 innings) and Henry Boyle (2 innings), five innings, StL vs.
StP U.A., 0-1; October 5, 1884.
Dupee Shaw, five innings, Pro vs. Buf NL, 4-0; October 7, 1885 (1st game).
George Van Haltren, six innings, Chi vs. Pit NL, 1-0; June 21, 1888.
Cannonball Crane, seven innings, NY vs. Was NL, 3-0; September 27, 1888.
Matt Kilroy, seven innings, Bal vs. StL AA, 0-0; July 29, 1889 (2nd game).
Silver King, eight innings, Chi vs. Bro PL, 0-1; June 21, 1890.
George Nicol, seven innings, StL vs. Phi AA, 21-2; September 23, 1890.
Hank Gastright, eight innings, Col vs. Tol AA, 6-0; October 12, 1890.
Jack Stivetts, five innings, Bos vs. Was NL, 6-0; October 15, 1892 (2nd game).
Icebox Chamberlain, seven innings, Cin vs. Bos NL, 6-0; September 23, 1893
(2nd game).
Ed Stein, six innings, Bro vs. Chi NL, 6-0; June 2, 1894.
Red Ames, five innings, NY vs. StL NL, 5-0; September 14, 1903 (2nd game).
Rube Waddell, five innings, Phi vs. StL AL, 2-0; August 15, 1905.
Jake Weimer, seven innings, Cin vs. Bro NL, 1-0; August 24, 1906 (2nd game).
Jimmy Dygert (3 innings) and Rube Waddell (2 innings), five innings, Phi vs. Chi
AL, 4-3; September 24, 1906.

Stoney McGlynn, seven innings, StL vs. *Bro* NL, 1-1; September 24, 1906 (2nd game).

Lefty Leifield, six innings, Pit vs. *Phi* NL, 8-0; September 26, 1906, (2nd game).

Ed Walsh, five innings, Chi vs. NY AL, 8-1; May 26, 1907.

Ed Karger, seven perfect innings, StL vs. Bos NL, 4-0; August 11, 1907 (2nd game).

Howie Camnitz, five innings, Pit vs. *NY* NL, 1-0; August 23, 1907 (2nd game).

Rube Vickers, five perfect innings, Phi vs. *Was* AL, 4-0; October 5, 1907 (2nd game).

Johnny Lush, six innings, StL vs. *Bro* NL, 2-0; August 6, 1908.

King Cole, seven innings, Chi vs. *StL* NL, 4-0; July 31, 1910 (2nd game).

Jay Cashion, six innings, Was vs. Cle AL, 2-0; August 20, 1910 (2nd game).

Walter Johnson, seven innings, Was vs. StL Al, 2-0; August 25, 1910.

Fred Frankhouse, seven and two-thirds innings, Bro vs. Cin NL, 5-0; August 27, 1937.

John Whitehead, six innings, StL vs. Det AL, 4-0; August 5, 1940 (2nd game).

Jim Tobin, five innings, Bos vs. Phi NL, 7-0; June 22, 1944 (2nd game).

Mike McCormick, five innings, SF vs. *Phi* NL, 3-0; June 12, 1959.

Sam Jones, seven innings, SF vs. *StL* NL, 4-0; September 26, 1959.

Dean Chance, five perfect innings, Min vs. Bos AL, 2-0; August 6, 1967.

Dave Palmer, five perfect innings, Mon vs. *StL* NL, 4-0; April 21, 1984 (2nd game).

Pascual Perez, five innings, Mon vs. *Phi* NL, 1-0; September 24, 1988.

Melido Perez, five innings, rain, Chi at NY AL, 8-0; July 12, 1990.

Perfection Plus

Year	Pitcher	Batters	Opponent	Notes
1959	Harvey Haddix	36	Milwaukee	(12 innings)
1919	Waite Hoyt	34	Yanks	(2nd-13th inning)
1880	Pud Galvin	33	Worcester	(6errors)
1884	Charlie Buffinton	32	Providence	(5 errors)
1971	Rick Wise	32	Chicago	(2nd-12th inning)
1908	Nap Rucker	30	Braves	(3 errors)
1885	John Clarkson	29	Providence	(3 errors, 1 DP)
1970	Bill Singer	29	Philadelphia	(2 errors, both his own)
1883	Hoss Radbourn	28	Cleveland	(1 error)
1884	Pud Galvin	28	Detroit	(1 error)
1905	Christy Mathewson	28	Cubs	(2 errors, one DP)
1910	Tom Hughes	28	Cleveland	(1 error)
1920	Walter Johnson	28	Red Sox	(1 error)
1947	Bill McCahan	28	Washington	(1 error)
1967	Joel Horlen	28	Detroit	(1 error)
1974	Dick Bosman	28	Oakland	(1 error, his own)
1980	Jerry Reuss	28	San Francisco	(1 error)
1880	J. L. Richmond	27	Cleveland	
1880	J. M. Ward	27	Buffalo	
1904	Cy Young	27	Philadelphia	

Year	Pitcher	Batters	Opponent	Notes
1906	Lefty Leifield	27	Cubs	(8 innings, 3 errors)
1908	Addie Joss	27	White Sox	
1922	Charlie Robertson	27	Detroit	
1956	Don Larsen	27	Brooklyn	
1964	Jim Bunning	27	Mets	
1965	Sandy Koufax	27	Cubs	
1968	Catfish Hunter	27	Minnesota	
1981	Len Barker	27	Toronto	
1984	Mike Witt	27	Texas	
1988	Tom Browning	27	Los Angeles	
1954	Robin Roberts	27*	Cincinnati	
1981	Jim Bibby	27*	Atlanta	
1917	Ernie Shore	26	Washington	

*Retired last twenty-seven batters in a row after giving up a hit to leadoff man.

†Starter Babe Ruth walked the first man and promptly slugged the umpire in the jaw and was banished. Ernie Shore rushed in from the bull pen, got the runner on a steal attempt, and retired the next twenty-six.

Note: Hooks Wiltse in 1908 and Lew Burdette in 1960 missed perfection because each hit a batter, with Wiltse hitting the *last* batter—the opposing pitcher—with an 0–2 count.

CHAPTER 17

Awards and Honors

Bill Deane

This chapter presents the history and voting results of baseball's most prestigious awards and honors, including the complete balloting and current constituency of the Baseball Hall of Fame. This material will be of interest to the fan who wonders how a player of the past was viewed by his contemporaries. I have ventured an additional section of "what if" awards: what if the Cy Young Award had been instituted long before its actual inception in 1956, or the Rookie of the Year before its real debut in 1947, and so on. What follows is divided into six sections:

MVP Award: history and balloting.
Rookie of the Year Award: history and balloting.
Cy Young Award: history and balloting.
Hypothetical Awards: explanation and selections.
Gold Glove Award: history, discussion, and list of winners.
Hall of Fame: history of elections and balloting.

Balloting tables and lists of winners include each player's first initial, last name, and club city abbreviation (and point total, if applicable).

Most Valuable Player Award: History

The concept of most valuable player awards dates back more than a century. The first documented MVP-type honor in pro ball was bestowed upon James "Deacon" White of the 1875 Boston Red Stockings in the National Association. Catcher White sparked Boston to a remarkable 71–8 record that year, scoring 77 runs in 80 games and batting .355. An ardent Red Stockings' admirer presented Deacon with a silver tray, water pitcher, and loving cup inscribed with the words: WON BY JIM WHITE AS MOST VALUABLE PLAYER TO BOSTON TEAM, 1875.

The first official MVP honor was initiated some thirty-five years later. Prior to the 1910 season, baseball fan Hugh Chalmers, president and general manager of the Chalmers Motor Company, announced that he would present one of his company's automobiles—a Chalmers "30"—to the major league player who compiled the highest batting average. What appeared to be a harmless promotional gimmick was to soon turn into a public relations disaster.

The rules specified that players must accumulate a specific minimum number of times at bat, depending on position, to qualify for the award. For infielders and outfielders, it was a minimum of 350 at-bats; for catchers, 250 at-bats; and for pitchers, 100 at-bats. Interest in the award was tremendous from the outset. Ty Cobb, who already owned a Chalmers "30" roadster, wrote: "I am glad that something besides medals and trophies is offered for the championship in batting. I think the offer of a Chalmers "30" is simply great and I hope to be lucky enough to own a new Chalmers next fall."

It developed into a two-man race, with Detroit's Cobb and Cleveland's Napoleon Lajoie, both American Leaguers, the only serious challengers for the coveted prize. Throughout the season there were charges and counter-charges of favoritism by scorers in various cities. Furthermore, the general consensus of the press was that Cobb's selfish pursuit of this individual honor had cost his team the pennant. The controversy was capped by scandalous circumstances on the final day of the season.

Through games of September 16, Cobb held a solid lead over Lajoie, .368 to .357 (although, because of the era's sloppy record keeping, few actually knew the official figures at the time). From then through October 8, Cobb batted a torrid .532 (25 for 47) to seemingly lock up the crown with a .383 average. But Lajoie refused to surrender, going 30 for 54 (.556) in that same span to enter the final day, October 9, with a .376 mark. Cobb chose to sit out his final game, while Lajoie played the infamous doubleheader with the St. Louis Browns in which he went 8 for 8, including *seven bunt hits*—remarkable for a slow-footed slugger—to apparently edge out Cobb in the batting race. Browns' manager Jack O'Connor had instructed his rookie third baseman, Red Corriden, to play deep on Lajoie, advice with which Corriden complied. Lajoie took advantage of the strange defensive arrangement with the repeated safe bunts. Although neither Lajoie nor Corriden were implicated, there were charges of a Browns' frame-up to give the coveted batting title (and car) to the respected Lajoie over the disliked Cobb.

O'Connor lost his job due to his role in the alleged fix. Subsequently, AL President Ban Johnson announced that a "discrepancy" had been found in the official records, and that Cobb had actually won the batting crown after all (although this point is challenged by many current researchers, who have evidence that Cobb was credited wrongly for a 2 for 4 game). Meanwhile, Hugh Chalmers, attempting to divorce himself from the controversy, presented autos to both Cobb and Lajoie. It was generally acknowledged that this fiasco doomed the future of individual awards of any kind.

Hoping to salvage some goodwill out of the whole idea, Chalmers came up with a new proposal for the 1911 season. This time he would award an auto to one player in each league who "should prove himself as the most impor-

496

tant and useful player to his club and to the league at large in point of deportment and value of services rendered." The decision for this honor was to be made by a committee of baseball writers, one writer from each club city in each league. Each writer was to make eight selections, with a first-place ballot scoring eight points, on down to an eighth-place vote counting one point. Thus was born the short-lived Chalmers Award, with Ty Cobb and Frank Schulte earning recognition in 1911. Both Cobb and Schulte voluntarily withdrew from the competition in 1912, although the former received seventeen points anyway.

Interest in the award diminished within a few years. By 1914 the public was distracted by baseball's battles with the new Federal League and the escalation of the World War in Europe. The timing was right for the Chalmers Award to quietly disappear; it was noted that Mr. Chalmers had agreed to present vehicles for five years and that the 1914 awards marked the fifth presentations.

On July 15, 1922, the newly formed American League Trophy Committee adopted a set of rules governing the selection of an annual award-winner. The rules specified that "the purpose of the American League Trophy is to honor the baseball player who is of greatest all-round service to his club and credit to the sport during each season; to recognize and reward uncommon skill and ability when exercised by a player for the best interests of his team, and to perpetuate his memory." The rules further instructed voters to seek out the "winning ball player," reminding them that "combined offensive and defensive ability is not always indicated by any system of records."

Eight baseball writers, one from each AL city, were enfranchised, with each required to select exactly one player from each team, for a total of eight selections. Player-managers and previous winners were to be excluded from consideration. Points were distributed the same as in the Chalmers Award: eight for first place, down to one for eighth.

The intention of AL President Ban Johnson was to have a monument to baseball erected in East Potomac Park, Washington, D.C., engraved with the names of winners of the AL Award. This proposal was introduced as a congressional resolution in 1924, and passed in the House of Representatives before dying on the Senate Floor.

The AL voting rules led to growing criticism for several reasons, one of which was the limitation on the number of vote-getters from each team. For example, when the Browns' George Sisler won the first AL Award in 1922, he was named on all eight ballots—thus disqualifying his teammates from receiving any votes. As a result, fellow Brownie Ken Williams, who led the league in home runs (39), RBIs (155), and total bases (367) and became the first player ever to have 30 homers and 30 stolen bases in the same season, was shut out in the League Award voting.

Secondly, the rule prohibiting player-managers from eligibility drew fire. In 1925, when this rule eliminated five solid candidates from consideration, *The New York Times* wrote, "to say that it is impossible or impractical to divorce a man's managerial skill from his talents purely as a player is to reflect on the intelligence of the committee that awards the prize."

The *Times* further editorialized on the fallacy of assuming that no player can be the "most valuable" more than one year: "the purpose, of course, is to pass the honor around, but the effect is to pass an empty honor around." This rule became increasingly ridiculous when it eliminated Babe Ruth (and his 60 home runs) from consideration in 1927; by the following year, both Ruth and teammate Lou Gehrig, who were in the process of finishing one-two in the AL home run derby in five consecutive seasons, were ineligible for the League Award.

In 1924 the National League instituted its own award, with radical differences in the selection method: each writer voted for ten players rather than eight (ten points for first place, and so on); he was not bound to vote for a certain number of players from each team; he was free to select a player-manager; and, later, he was allowed to consider previous winners of the award. Additionally, the NL offered a cash "present" of $1,000 to the award-winner.

At various times between 1925–51, writers were permitted to name "honorable mention" candidates, whose vote totals were listed but not counted in the balloting. Another feature of early voting reports was the listing of "cumulative vote leaders"—a forerunner to Bill James's "award shares"—over a period of years.

A number of factors led to the demise of the AL Award, including the award's loss of credibility due to the previously mentioned shortsighted voting rules. Secondly, Ban Johnson, having failed to secure the erection of his proposed monument, felt the award had fallen short of its aim. Finally, management was concerned with the efforts of award-winners to parlay their honors into substantial pay raises. The AL Award was officially voted out at a special league meeting on May 6, 1929.

The National League followed suit with the AL's decision, but agreed to continue its award through the 1929 season.

In October 1929, the Baseball Writers' Association of America (BBWAA) announced the results of an "unofficial" AL most valuable player poll, whose winner was Lew Fonseca of Cleveland. Two months later, *The Sporting News* (TSN) conducted a poll of the eight writers who had previously voted on the League Award, thereby reporting Al Simmons as the "unofficial" AL Award-winner. Combining the results of these two unofficial polls gives Fonseca 77 points, followed by Heinie Manush (57), Simmons (56), Tony Lazzeri (55) and Charlie Gehringer (44).

The Sporting News announced that, thereafter, they would take it upon themselves to conduct an annual poll to substitute for the defunct league awards. However, they retained the stipulation that each voter must select just one player on each team. In 1930, TSN chose Joe Cronin in the AL and Bill Terry in the NL. Earlier, the Associated Press also had a special committee of writers make an unofficial AL selection for 1930, while the BBWAA did the same for the NL (adding a check for $1,000 for the winner). The respective selections here were Cronin in the AL and Hack Wilson in the NL. Again combining the two sets of polls, the AL leaders were Cronin (100), Al Simmons (85), Lou Gehrig (68), Charlie Gehringer (67), and Ted Lyons (56). The NL pace-setters were Hack Wilson (111), Frankie Frisch (107), Bill Terry (105), Chuck Klein (57), and Floyd "Babe" Herman (52).

In an effort to standardize MVP voting, the BBWAA,

in its annual winter meeting in New York on December 11, 1930, decided to appoint two committees (one in each league) to elect most valuable players, with the association to "award suitable emblems to the players selected." Thus was born what is considered the modern MVP Award, with most of the flaws of its forerunners eliminated.

TSN, however, continued to make its own selections in bitter competition with the BBWAA. Finally, beginning in 1938, TSN agreed to unify the award by abiding with BBWAA balloting, and presenting The Sporting News Trophy to the winner. Among the various prizes awarded to the winners were wristwatches and shotguns.

At a meeting during the 1944 World Series, the BBWAA decided to begin issuing its own trophy, the Kenesaw Mountain Landis Award, in honor of the ailing commissioner. Landis died a month later and the official MVP Award has born his name ever since. A plaque engraved with the names of the winners hangs in the National Baseball Library in Cooperstown, New York.

The Sporting News went back to naming its own MVPs in 1944 and '45. Then, at the request of the new commissioner, Happy Chandler, TSN "withdrew from the field to cooperate in making the Landis Awards, provided by the major leagues, the official designations of the year." In 1948, however, TSN went back to its own awards, selecting a Player of the Year and Pitcher of the Year in each league, as they have done ever since. For some reason, TSN awards have never received the public recognition that the BBWAA honors have.

Two major changes in the MVP voting began in 1938. The BBWAA began polling three writers in each major league city, rather than just one, which remained in effect until it was reduced to two writers per city, starting in 1961. Also in 1938, the process was initiated to award fourteen points for each first-place vote, rather than ten.

"Split votes," which have since infiltrated all the major awards, first appeared in MVP Awards in 1959. The American League MVP race that year, by consensus, was between second baseman Nellie Fox and shortstop Luis Aparicio of the champion Chicago White Sox. Late in the season, the suggestion often arose that the two ought to share the award. When the votes were in, Fox had received fourteen first-place votes, Aparicio had gotten six, and four writers had split their votes between the two. Tickled with the idea of a split vote, one NL writer also resorted to this option, dividing his first-place nomination between Ernie Banks and Ed Mathews. The cop-out vote, having been allowed in '59, has since surfaced in sixteen more MVP Awards, ten Rookie of the Year, and six Cy Young Award elections. The ultimate folly of this practice was best exemplified in 1979. One NL writer split his fourth-place vote between pitching brothers Phil and Joe Niekro, evidently convinced that the two were identical

twins. But the writer was still permitted to make six more selections. That meant that his fifth-, sixth-, and seventh-place selections received more points (six, five and four, respectively) than his fourth-place co-selections, who were credited with just three and a half points apiece!

There has long been debate about the consideration of pitchers for the MVP Award, the theory (by some) that a man who plays every fourth game cannot be as valuable as a man who plays every day. The debate escalated after the inception of the Cy Young Award in 1956, giving pitchers their own exclusive honor, and the increasing practice of five-man rotations in the 1970s, giving starting pitchers even less of a chance to contribute. As far as Jack Lang, executive secretary of the BBWAA, is concerned, there is no room for controversy. "The rules that are sent out to the voters on the [MVP] committee state: 'Keep in mind that all players are eligible. That includes pitchers, starters and relievers,' " says Lang. "Anybody on the committee that feels they cannot vote for a pitcher, we replace them. In my twenty-four years running the elections, only two writers have said that to me." Since 1931, pitchers have won the award ten times in the AL and nine times in the NL.

There have been twelve occasions in which one player received all of the available first-place MVP votes in his league. The AL players so honored are Ty Cobb (1911), Babe Ruth (1923), Hank Greenberg (1935), Al Rosen (1953), Mickey Mantle (1956), Frank Robinson (1966), Denny McLain (1968), Reggie Jackson (1973), and Jose Canseco (1988). The three unanimous NL selections are Carl Hubbell (1936), Orlando Cepeda (1967), and Mike Schmidt (1980). Hubbell's distinction is disputable, as two of the eight writers did not submit ballots that year and were not replaced on the selection committee.

Following are the maximum possible point totals that could have been earned by an individual receiving the first-place nomination of every writer polled:

National League		American League	
1911–14	64	1911–14	64
1924–29	80	1922–28	64
1931–37	80	1931–37	80
1938–60	336	1938–60	336
1961	224	1961–68	280
1962–68	280	1969–76	336
1969–present	336	1977–present	392

There have been numerous cases in which the MVP vote point totals did not add up to the correct figure. Reasons for this include inaccuracies in tabulation, inaccuracies in reporting, and writers who failed to vote or to complete their ballots. However, the total impact of all these errors is a small fraction of 1 percent of the total voting over the years.

Following is a complete tabulation of all the recognized MVP elections since 1911:

MVP Award
Chalmers Award, 1911–14

1911 NATIONAL						
F. Schulte, CHI 29	F. Merkle, NY 19	M. Doolan, PHI 6	B. Sweeney, BOS . . . 3	J. Kling, BOS 1	E. Collins, PHI 32	
C. Mathewson, NY . . 25	R. Marquard, NY . . . 19	B. Harmon, SL 6	O. Knabe, PHI 2	B. Adams, PIT 1	J. Jackson, CLE . . . 28	
L. Doyle, NY 23	J. Daubert, BKN . . . 16	J. Archer, CHI 5	E. Konetchy, SL 2	N. Rucker, BKN 1	W. Johnson, WAS . . 19	
J. Tinker, CHI 11	H. Lobert, PHI 4	D. Hoblitzell, CIN . . . 2		B. Cree, NY 16		
H. Wagner, PIT 23	C. Meyers, NY 11	G. Gibson, PIT 4	J. Walsh, PHI 2	**1911 AMERICAN**	T. Speaker, BOS . . . 16	
G. Alexander, PHI . . 23	J. Sheckard, CHI . . . 9	M. Brown, CHI 4	J. Devore, NY 2	T. Cobb, DET 64	I. Thomas, PHI 12	
M. Huggins, SL 21	M. Mitchell, CIN 9	B. Bescher, CIN 4	F. Luderus, PHI 1	E. Walsh, CHI 35	C. Milan, WAS 10	

V. Gregg, CLE 9	J. Tesreau, NY 6	G. Moriarty, DET . . . 3	B. Adams, PIT 3	C. Bender, PHI 2	**1914 AMERICAN**
F. Baker, PHI 8	R. Murray, NY 5	J. Birmingham, CLE . 2	G. Cutshaw, BKN . . . 3	T. Turner, CLE 2	E. Collins, PHI 63
J. Coombs, PHI 6	M. Huggins, SL 5	D. Moeller, WAS . . . 1	G. Burns, NY 2	S. O'Neill, CLE 1	S. Crawford, DET . . 35
N. Lajoie, CLE 5	A. Marsans, CIN . . . 4	G. McBride, WAS . . . 1	A. Marsans, CIN . . . 2	H. Hooper, BOS 1	D. Bush, DET 17
J. Knight, NY 4	F. Merkle, NY 4	S. McInnis, PHI 1	A. Humphries, CHI . . 2		F. Baker, PHI 17
S. Crawford, DET . . . 4	J. Evers, CHI 2	B. Daniels, NY 1	M. Brown, CIN 1	**1914 NATIONAL**	J. Jackson, CLE . . . 15
B. Lord, PHI 4	C. Hendrix, PIT 2			J. Evers, BOS 50	R. Schalk, CHI 13
D. Bush, DET 4	J. Archer, CHI 1	**1913 NATIONAL**	**1913 AMERICAN**	R. Maranville, BOS. . 44	E. Foster, WAS 11
R. Ford, NY 3	G. Alexander, PHI . . . 1	J. Daubert, BKN . . . 50	W. Johnson, WAS . . 54	B. James, BOS 33	B. Weaver, CHI 11
J. Barry, PHI 3		G. Cravath, PHI 40	J. Jackson, CLE . . . 43	G. Burns, NY 31	S. McInnis, PHI 11
J. Austin, SL 2	**1912 AMERICAN**	R. Maranville, BOS. . 23	E. Collins, PHI 30	J. Miller, SL 18	D. Pratt, SL 10
F. LaPorte, SL 2	T. Speaker, BOS . . . 59	C. Mathewson, NY. . 21	T. Speaker, BOS . . . 26	J. Tesreau, NY 15	W. Schang, PHI 10
S. McInnis, PHI 1	E. Walsh, CHI 30	C. Meyers, NY 20	F. Baker, PHI 21	D. Rudolph, BOS . . . 14	T. Speaker, BOS . . . 9
G. McBride, WAS . . . 1	W. Johnson, WAS . . 28	V. Saier, CHI 15	C. Gandil, WAS 14	S. Magee, PHI 14	T. Walker, SL 9
	C. Milan, WAS 23	L. Cheney, CHI 12	S. McInnis, PHI 12	Z. Wheat, BKN 10	T. Cobb, DET 7
1912 NATIONAL	J. Wood, BOS 22	D. Miller, PIT 11	W. Schang, PHI 11	G. Alexander, PHI . . . 9	E. Scott, BOS 7
L. Doyle, NY 48	E. Collins, PHI 18	H. Wagner, PIT 11	C. Milan, WAS 8	R. Bresnahan, CHI . . 6	J. Barry, PHI 6
H. Wagner, PIT 43	F. Baker, PHI 17	J. Evers, CHI 10	J. Barry, PHI 8	L. Magee, SL 6	D. Leonard, BOS . . . 6
C. Meyers, NY 25	T. Cobb, DET 17	T. Seaton, PHI 9	N. Lajoie, CLE 7	B. Doak, SL 5	E. Plank, PHI 5
J. Tinker, CHI 22	J. Jackson, CLE . . . 16	A. Fletcher, NY 7	D. Bush, DET 6	J. Viox, PIT 5	G. McBride, WAS . . . 5
B. Bescher, CIN 17	H. Wagner, BOS . . . 12	J. Archer, CHI 6	H. Wagner, BOS . . . 6	A. Fletcher, NY 5	D. Lewis, BOS 4
B. Sweeney, BOS . . . 16	C. Gandil, WAS 7	M. Doolan, PHI 6	R. Russell, CHI 5	C. Mathewson, NY . . 4	H. Hooper, BOS 4
H. Zimmerman, CHI 16	B. Shotton, SL 6	B. Sweeney, BOS . . . 6	B. Shotton, SL 5	V. Saier, CHI 4	F. Maisel, NY 3
R. Marquard, NY . . . 13	D. Pratt, SL 5	J. Viox, PIT 6	G. McBride, WAS . . . 5	B. Schmidt, BOS . . . 4	R. Peckinpaugh, NY . 2
O. Wilson, PIT 13	E. Foster, WAS 4	J. Doyle, NY 5	J. Scott, CHI 5	J. Daubert, BKN . . . 3	C. Milan, WAS 2
J. Daubert, BKN . . . 13	L. Gardner, BOS . . . 4	T. Shafer, NY 5	G. Stovall, SL 5	L. McCarty, BKN . . . 3	S. Agnew, SL 2
O. Knabe, PHI 10	S. Crawford, DET . . . 4	R. Murray, NY 4	S. Crawford, DET . . . 5	H. Groh, CIN 2	R. Hartzell, NY 2
E. Konetchy, SL 8	J. Barry, PHI 4	H. Zimmerman, CHI . 4	T. Cobb, DET 3	T. Clark, CIN 1	E. Cicotte, CHI 1
C. Mathewson, NY . . 8	B. Carrigan, BOS . . . 3	O. Knabe, PHI 4	R. Schalk, CHI 3	G. Cravath, PHI 1	G. Moriarty, DET . . . 1
D. Paskert, PHI 6					

(No official awards, 1915–21)

MVP Award
League Awards, 1922-29

1922 AMERICAN	W. Pipp, NY 12	U. Shocker, SL 5	C. Perkins, PHI 1	J. Bassler, DET . . . 17	J. Judge, WAS 4
G. Sisler, SL 59	L. Blue, DET 11	C. Jamieson, CLE . . 4		C. Galloway, PHI . . . 13	M. McManus, SL . . . 4
E. Rommel, PHI 31	C. Galloway, PHI . . . 10	J. Sewell, CLE 4	**1923 AMERICAN**	G. Uhle, CLE 13	K. Williams, SL 4
R. Schalk, CHI 26	H. Heilmann, DET . . 8	G. Burns, BOS 2	B. Ruth, NY 64	G. Burns, BOS 8	J. Harris, BOS 3
L. Bush, NY 19	D. Pratt, BOS 7	J. Dykes, PHI 2	E. Collins, CHI 37	H. Ehmke, BOS . . . 7	B. Harris, WAS 3
E. Collins, CHI 18	W. Schang, NY 7	B. Harris, WAS 2	H. Heilmann, DET . . 31	M. Ruel, WAS 7	J. Hauser, PHI 1
J. Bassler, DET . . . 13	B. Meusel, NY 6	R. Peckinpaugh, WAS 2	W. Gerber, SL 20	R. Peckinpaugh,	W. Johnson, WAS . . . 1
S. O'Neill, CLE 13	E. Scott, NY 6	B. Wambsganss, CLE 2	J. Sewell, CLE 20	WAS 6	C. Perkins, PHI 1
J. Judge, WAS 12	W. Johnson, WAS . . 5	G. Cutshaw, DET . . . 1	C. Jamieson, CLE . . 19	U. Shocker, SL 5	

(No National League awards, 1922-23)

1924 NATIONAL	I. Flagstead, BOS . . . 5	O. Bluege, WAS 8	C. Mays, CIN 4	R. Lucas, CIN 10	P. Todt, BOS 1
D. Vance, BKN 74	W. Gerber, SL 4	M. Cochrane, PHI . . 8	G. Kelly, NY 2	H. Wilson, CHI 9	
R. Hornsby, SL 62	E. Whitehill, DET . . . 4	L. Blue, DET 7	C. Walker, CIN 1	B. Terry, NY 6	**1928 NATIONAL**
F. Frisch, NY 40	L. Blue, DET 3	S. Coveleski, WAS . . 7		J. Bottomley, SL . . . 6	J. Bottomley, SL . . . 76
Z. Wheat, BKN 40	I. Boone, BOS 2	W. Kamm, CHI 7	**1926 AMERICAN**	B. Hargrave, CIN . . . 6	F. Lindstrom, NY . . . 70
R. Youngs, NY 35	J. Harris, BOS 2	E. Rommel, PHI 7	G. Burns, CLE 63	F. May, CIN 6	B. Grimes, PIT 53
G. Kelly, NY 34	C. Galloway, PHI . . . 1	R. Schalk, CHI 7	J. Mostil, CHI 33	C. Williams, PHI . . . 6	L. Benton, NY 37
R. Maranville, PIT . . 33	K. Williams, SL 1	A. Wingo, DET 7	H. Pennock, NY . . . 32	E. Farrell, BOS 6	H. Critz, CIN 37
K. Cuyler, PIT 25		E. Combs, NY 6	S. Rice, WAS 18	B. Grimes, NY 4	P. Traynor, PIT 28
J. Fournier, BKN . . . 21	**1925 NATIONAL**	B. Meusel, NY 5	H. Heilmann, DET . . 16	M. Carey, BKN 4	H. Wilson, CHI 21
E. Roush, CIN 12	R. Hornsby, SL 73	T. Lyons, CHI 5	H. Manush, DET . . . 16	R. Stephenson, CHI 3	S. Hogan, NY 17
G. Wright, PIT 10	K. Cuyler, PIT 61	G. Burns, CLE 4	A. Simmons, PHI . . . 16	G. Alexander, SL . . . 3	T. Jackson, NY 16
A. High, BKN 9	G. Kelly, NY 52	M. McManus, SL . . . 4	L. Grove, PHI 12	C. Hill, PIT 2	R. Maranville, SL . . . 14
B. Pinelli, CIN 7	G. Wright, PIT 43	H. Pennock, NY 4	L. Goslin, WAS 9	J. Petty, BKN 2	D. Vance, BKN 13
R. Bressler, CIN . . . 5	D. Vance, BKN 42	B. Bengough, NY . . . 2	L. Gehrig, NY 7	F. Ulrich, PHI 2	C. Hafey, SL 11
G. Hartnett, CHI 5	D. Bancroft, BOS . . 41	H. Ehmke, BOS 2	T. Lazzeri, NY 7	C. Hafey, SL 1	R. Hornsby, BOS . . . 10
B. Grimes, BKN 5	J. Bottomley, SL . . . 28	L. Gehrig, NY 2	B. Falk, CHI 6		G. Hartnett, CHI . . . 6
J. Bottomley, SL . . . 4	P. Traynor, PIT 27	I. Boone, BOS 1	F. Fothergill, DET . . . 6	**1927 AMERICAN**	P. Waner, PIT 5
J. Johnston, BKN . . . 3	F. Frisch, NY 13	J. Dugan, NY 1	O. Melillo, SL 6	L. Gehrig, NY 56	L. Richbourg, BOS . . 5
M. Carey, PIT 3	E. Roush, CIN 12	P. Todt, BOS 1	H. Rice, SL 6	H. Heilmann, DET . . 35	T. Douthit, SL 5
T. Jackson, NY 3	M. Carey, PIT 11		O. Bluege, WAS . . . 5	T. Lyons, CHI 34	D. Bissonette, BKN . 3
E. Yde, PIT 2	I. Meusel, NY 6	**1926 NATIONAL**	P. Todt, BOS 5	M. Cochrane, PHI . . 18	D. Flowers, BKN . . . 3
C. Williams, PHI 1	D. Luque, CIN 5	B. O'Farrell, SL . . . 79	M. Cochrane, PHI . . 4	A. Simmons, PHI . . . 18	J. Wilson, SL 3
E. Rixey, CIN 1	C. Grimm, CHI 5	H. Critz, CIN 60	J. Judge, WAS 4	L. Goslin, WAS 15	A. Whitney, PHI . . . 3
G. Alexander, CHI . . 1	Z. Wheat, BKN 4	R. Kremer, PIT 32	M. McManus, SL . . . 4	M. Ruel, WAS 15	H. Ford, CIN 2
H. DeBerry, BKN . . . 1	P. Donohue, CIN . . . 4	T. Thevenow, SL . . . 30	B. Meusel, NY 3	J. Dykes, PHI 14	L. Thompson, PHI . . 1
	B. Hargrave, CIN . . . 4	W. Wilson, CHI 25	E. Rigney, BOS 3	L. Sewell, CLE 13	
1924 AMERICAN	G. Harper, PHI 3	L. Bell, SL 24	I. Flagstead, BOS . . 2	J. Sewell, CLE 9	**1928 AMERICAN**
W. Johnson, WAS . . 55	J. Sand, PHI 3	B. Hargrave, CIN . . . 24	W. Gerber, SL 2	T. Lazzeri, NY 8	M. Cochrane, PHI . . 53
E. Collins, CHI 49	W. Gautreau, BOS . . 2	F. Rhem, SL 20	T. Zachary, SL 2	R. Reeves, WAS . . . 7	H. Manush, SL 51
C. Jamieson, CLE . . 25	V. Aldridge, PIT 1	F. Lindstrom, NY . . . 17	W. Jacobson, BOS . . 1	F. O'Rourke, SL . . . 6	J. Judge, WAS 27
H. Pennock, NY . . . 24		D. Bancroft, BOS . . 17		J. Tavener, DET . . . 6	T. Lazzeri, NY 27
J. Bassler, DET . . . 22	**1925 AMERICAN**	H. Carlson, PHI 16	**1927 NATIONAL**	H. Lisenbee, WAS . . 5	W. Kamm, CHI 15
H. Severeid, SL . . . 17	R. Peckinpaugh,	P. Waner, PIT 15	P. Waner, PIT 72	E. Miller, SL 5	G. Goslin, WAS 13
J. Hauser, PHI 13	WAS 45	P. Traynor, PIT 14	F. Frisch, SL 66	A. Metzler, CHI 5	E. Combs, NY 13
W. Jacobson, SL . . . 11	A. Simmons, PHI . . . 41	W. Pipp, CIN 12	R. Hornsby, NY 54	I. Flagstead, BOS . . 3	C. Gehringer, DET . . 12
H. Heilmann, DET . . 9	J. Sewell, CLE 21	E. Brown, BOS 10	C. Root, CHI 46	C. Jamieson, CLE . . 3	C. Myer, BOS 11
J. Sewell, CLE 9	H. Heilmann, DET . . 20	F. Herman, BKN . . . 8	T. Jackson, NY 42	W. Schang, SL 3	W. Hoyt, NY 8
M. Ruel, WAS 7	H. Rice, SL 18	C. Root, CHI 8	L. Waner, PIT 25	F. Schulte, SL 3	J. Foxx, PHI 7
W. Schang, NY 7	E. Sheely, CHI 17	R. Hornsby, SL 7	P. Traynor, PIT 18	W. Hudlin, CLE 2	J. Sewell, CLE 6
A. Simmons, PHI . . . 7	I. Flagstead, BOS . . 10	J. Butler, BKN 5	J. Haines, SL 16	W. Regan, BOS 2	L. Sewell, CLE 6
W. Pipp, NY 6	W. Jacobson, SL . . . 10	B. Southworth, SL. . 5	R. Kremer, PIT 14	J. Rothrock, BOS . . 2	I. Flagstead, BOS . . 5
H. Ehmke, BOS 5	J. Mostil, CHI 10	G. Alexander, SL . . . 5	G. Hartnett, CHI . . . 12	B. Harriss, BOS . . . 1	E. Morris, BOS 4

H. Heilmann, DET . . . 4
C. Lind, CLE 4
W. Cissell, CHI 4
A. Thomas, CHI 4
O. Carroll, DET . . . 3
H. Rice, DET 3
L. Fonseca, CLE 2

T. Lyons, CHI 2
J. Hodapp, CLE 2
A. Metzler, CHI 1
W. Regan, BOS 1

1929 NATIONAL
R. Hornsby, CHI . . . 60

L. O'Doul, PHI 54
B. Terry, NY 48
B. Grimes, PIT 35
L. Waner, PIT 30
R. Lucas, CIN 29
P. Traynor, PIT 27

H. Wilson, CHI 24
F. Herman, BKN 24
G. Bush, CHI 16
C. Klein, PHI 15
M. Ott, NY 15
T. Douthit, SL 14

C. Grimm, CHI 13
T. Jackson, NY 8
R. Maranville, BOS . . 8
H. Critz, CHI 5
B. Friberg, PHI 4
P. Malone, CHI 3

F. Frisch, SL 2
P. Whitney, PHI 2
J. Frederick, BKN . . . 2
R. Stephenson, CHI . 1
Z. Taylor, BOS-CHI . .1

(There were no official selections for the American League in 1929 or for either league in 1930.)

MVP Award
Baseball Writers' Association of America Awards, 1931–Present

1931 NATIONAL
F. Frisch, SL 65
C. Klein, PHI 55
B. Terry, NY 53
W. English, CHI . . . 30
C. Hafey, SL 29
J. Wilson, SL 28
T. Jackson, NY 24
C. Grimm, CHI 21
E. Adams, SL 18
E. Brandt, BOS 15
R. Maranville, BOS . 15
K. Cuyler, CHI 14
P. Traynor, PIT 12
R. Lucas, CIN 10
L. Waner, PIT 8
J. Bottomley, SL 8
J. Elliott, PHI 6
J. Quinn, BKN 6
N. Finn, BKN 5
W. Clark, BKN 5
P. Derringer, SL 3
C. Root, CHI 3
D. Bartell, PHI 2
J. Vergez, NY 2
F. Fitzsimmons, NY . .1
L. O'Doul, BKN 1
G. Wright, BKN 1
T. Cuccinello, CIN . . 1
C. Gelbert, SL 1

1931 AMERICAN
L. Grove, PHI 78
L. Gehrig, NY 59
A. Simmons, PHI . . . 51
E. Averill, CLE 43
B. Ruth, NY 40
E. Webb, BOS 22
J. Cronin, WAS . . . 18
O. Melillo, SL 17
S. West, WAS 16
M. Cochrane, PHI . . 16
G. Earnshaw, PHI . . 12
W. Ferrell, CLE 12
F. Marberry, WAS . . 11
H. Rhyne, BOS 10
B. Chapman, NY 7
J. Stone, DET 6
C. Gehringer, DET . . 4
L. Blue, DET 4
R. Kress, SL 3
C. Reynolds, CHI . . . 2
W. Stewart, SL. 2
G. Goslin, SL 2
D. MacFayden, BOS .2
T. Oliver, BOS 2
J. Foxx, PHI 1

1932 NATIONAL
C. Klein, PHI 78
L. Warneke, CHI . . 68
L. O'Doul, BKN . . . 58
P. Waner, PIT 37
R. Stephenson, CHI 32
B. Terry, NY 25
D. Hurst, PHI 24
P. Traynor, PIT 17
B. Herman, CIN . . . 16
M. Ott, NY 15
R. Brown, BOS 10
F. Herman, CIN 8
L. Waner, PIT 6
W. Berger, BOS 6
H. Wilson, BKN 6
E. Orsatti, SL 6
R. Maranville, BOS . 5
J. Wilson, SL 5
T. Cuccinello, BKN . . 4

J. Dean, SL 4
F. Frisch, SL 3
R. Collins, SL. 3
A. Vaughan, PIT 1
G. Bush, CHI 1

1932 AMERICAN
J. Foxx, PHI 75
L. Gehrig, NY 55
H. Manush, WAS . . . 41
E. Averill, CLE 37
L. Gomez, NY 27
J. Cronin, WAS 26
B. Ruth, NY 26
T. Lazzeri, NY 21
A. Simmons, PHI . . . 13
C. Gehringer, DET . . 13
D. Alexander,
  DET-BOS 10
W. Cissell, CLE 10
R. Ferrell, SL 9
L. Grove, PHI 8
J. Allen, NY 8
B. Dickey, NY 8
G. Goslin, SL 7
M. Weaver, WAS . . . 6
H. Davis, DET 5
D. Harris, WAS 5
W. Ferrell, CLE. 5
J. Levey, SL 5
T. Lyons, CHI 5
B. Sullivan, CHI 3
E. McNair, PHI 3
S. Jolley, BOS 3
G. Crowder, WAS . . . 2
M. McManus, BOS . . 2
G. Walker, DET 1
J. Sewell, NY 1

1933 NATIONAL
C. Hubbell, NY 77
C. Klein, PHI 48
W. Berger, BOS 44
B. Terry, NY 35
P. Martin, SL 31
G. Mancuso, NY . . . 24
J. Dean, SL 23
P. Traynor, PIT 20
B. Ryan, NY 19
A. Lopez, BKN 18
B. Cantwell, BOS . . . 18
H. Schumacher, NY . 11
R. Maranville, BOS . 11
G. Bush, CHI 11
L. French, PIT 10
F. Frisch, SL 7
J. Bottomley, CIN. . . 6
J. Medwick, SL 5
G. Hartnett, CHI . . . 5
L. Warneke, CHI . . . 4
R. Lucas, CIN 3
D. Bartell, PHI 3
A. Vaughan, PIT 2
R. Moore, BOS 2
V. Davis, PHI 1
C. Hafey, CIN 1
D. Luque, NY 1

1933 AMERICAN
J. Foxx, PHI 74
J. Cronin, WAS 62
H. Manush, WAS . . . 54
L. Gehrig, NY 39
L. Grove, PHI 35
C. Gehringer, DET . . 32
G. Crowder, WAS . . 28
A. Simmons, CHI . . 19
E. Whitehill, WAS . . 18

O. Melillo, SL 12
S. West, SL 11
R. Ferrell, BOS 9
B. Dickey, NY 9
T. Lazzeri, NY 6
J. Kuhel, WAS 5
E. Averill, CLE 5
C. Myer, WAS 5
M. Cochrane, PHI . . 5
B. Johnson, PHI . . . 5
B. Chapman, NY . . . 4
M. Bishop, PHI 1
L. Appling, CHI 1
W. Kamm, CLE 1

1934 NATIONAL
J. Dean, SL 78
P. Waner, PIT 50
J. Moore, NY 42
T. Jackson, NY 39
M. Ott, NY 37
J. Collins, SL 32
B. Terry, NY 30
C. Davis, PHI 18
P. Dean, SL 16
H. Schumacher, NY . 16
C. Hubbell, NY 16
W. Berger, BOS . . . 13
L. Warneke, CHI . . . 10
G. Hartnett, CHI 9
G. Slade, CIN 5
K. Cuyler, CHI 4
B. Frey, CIN 4
F. Frankhouse, BOS . 4
R. Boyle, BKN 4
B. Herman, CHI 4
F. Frisch, SL 4
W. Hoyt, PIT 4
A. Lopez, BKN 1
V. Mungo, BKN 1
A. Vaughan, PIT 1

1934 AMERICAN
M. Cochrane, DET . . 67
C. Gehringer, DET . . 65
L. Gomez, NY 60
S. Rowe, DET 59
L. Gehrig, NY 54
H. Greenberg, DET . 29
H. Trosky, CLE 18
W. Ferrell, BOS 16
M. Owen, DET 13
J. Foxx, PHI 11
A. Simmons, CHI . . . 9
W. Werber, BOS . . . 8
R. Johnson, BOS . . . 8
G. Goslin, DET 6
S. West, SL 5
M. Harder, CLE 4
F. Higgins, PHI 3
E. Averill, CLE 3
B. Knickerbocker,
  CLE 2

1935 NATIONAL
G. Hartnett, CHI . . . 75
J. Dean, SL 66
A. Vaughan, PIT . . . 45
B. Herman, CHI . . . 38
J. Medwick, SL 37
C. Hubbell, NY 20
W. Berger, BOS . . . 20
B. Terry, NY 20
A. Galan, CHI 18
P. Martin, SL 16
H. Leiber, NY 11
L. Warneke, CHI 9
E. Lombardi, CIN . . . 8

F. Frisch, SL 7
C. Blanton, PIT 5
J. Moore, PHI 5
E. Allen, PHI 4
G. Mancuso, NY 4
P. Derringer, CIN . . . 4
M. Ott, NY 3
P. Dean, SL 2
R. Collins, SL 2
C. Davis, PHI 2
P. Waner, PIT 1
B. Lee, CHI 1
T. Jackson, NY 1
D. Camilli, PHI 1

1935 AMERICAN
H. Greenberg, DET . 80
W. Ferrell, BOS 62
J. Vosmik, CLE 39
C. Myer, WAS 36
L. Gehrig, NY 29
C. Gehringer, DET . . 26
M. Cochrane, DET . . 24
R. Cramer, PHI 18
J. Solters, SL 16
R. Hemsley, SL 16
J. Foxx, PHI 11
T. Bridges, DET 11
T. Lyons, CHI 10
L. Grove, BOS 8
Z. Bonura, CHI 7
L. Appling, CHI 7
L. Sewell, CHI 7
J. Allen, NY 5
J. Whitehead, CHI . . 4
F. Higgins, PHI 3
J. Marcum, PHI 3
E. Auker, DET 2
M. Harder, CLE 2
L. Lary, SL 1

1936 NATIONAL
C. Hubbell, NY 60
J. Dean, SL 53
B. Herman, CHI . . . 37
J. Medwick, SL 30
P. Waner, PIT 29
M. Ott, NY 28
F. Demaree, CHI . . . 17
G. Mancuso, NY . . . 13
D. MacFayden,
  BOS 12
L. Durocher, SL 8
P. Derringer, CIN . . . 6
G. Hartnett, CHI . . . 6
B. Whitehead, NY . . 6
A. Lopez, BOS 5
V. Mungo, BKN 5
W. Berger, BOS 4
D. Camilli, PHI 4
G. Phelps, BKN 3
D. Bartell, NY 2
E. Lombardi, CIN . . . 1
T. Moore, SL 1

1936 AMERICAN
L. Gehrig, NY 73
L. Appling, CHI 65
E. Averill, CLE 48
C. Gehringer, DET . . 39
B. Dickey, NY 29
V. Kennedy, CHI . . . 27
J. Kuhel, WAS 27
J. DiMaggio, NY . . . 26
T. Bridges, DET 25
H. Trosky, CLE 19
J. Foxx, BOS 16
G. Walker, DET 14

B. Bell, SL 10
W. Moses, PHI 7
L. Grove, BOS 5
J. Dykes, CHI 3
R. Radcliff, CHI 3
S. West, SL 2
Z. Bonura, CHI 1
E. McNair, BOS 1

1937 NATIONAL
J. Medwick, SL 70
G. Hartnett, CHI . . . 68
C. Hubbell, NY 52
J. Turner, BOS 30
L. Fette, BOS 29
D. Bartell, NY 26
M. Ott, NY 24
P. Waner, PIT 21
B. Herman, CHI 19
J. Mize, SL 18
C. Melton, NY 17
C. Root, CHI 15
P. Whitney, PHI 13
H. Danning, NY 10
F. Demaree, CHI 9
L. Warneke, SL 6
B. Jurges, CHI 4
J. Cooney, BKN 4
B. Myers, CIN 2
L. Grissom, CIN 2
H. Manush, BKN . . . 1

1937 AMERICAN
C. Gehringer, DET . . 78
J. DiMaggio, NY . . . 74
H. Greenberg, DET . 48
L. Gehrig, NY 42
L. Sewell, CHI 22
B. Dickey, NY 22
J. Cronin, BOS 19
R. Ruffing, NY 18
L. Gomez, NY 14
M. Kreevich, CHI . . . 13
C. Travis, WAS 12
W. Moses, PHI 12
J. Allen, CLE 11
H. Clift, SL 11
R. Radcliff, CHI 10
B. Lewis, WAS 7
L. Appling, CHI 5
B. Bell, SL 5
E. Averill, CLE 4
L. Lary, CLE 4
R. Lawson, DET 4
G. Walker, DET 3
R. York, DET 1
P. Fox, DET 1

1938 NATIONAL
E. Lombardi, CIN . . 229
B. Lee, CHI 166
A. Vaughan, PIT . . . 163
M. Ott, NY 132
F. McCormick, CIN . 130
J. Rizzo, PIT 96
S. Hack, CHI 87
P. Derringer, CIN . . . 70
M. Brown, PIT 62
G. Hartnett, CHI . . . 61
J. Medwick, SL 55
J. Mize, SL 28
T. Cuccinello, BOS . . 23
P. Young, PIT 19
C. Bryant, CHI 16
H. Danning, NY 13
I. Goodman, CIN . . . 11
J. VanderMeer, CIN . 6
L. Durocher, BKN . . . 6

D. Coffman, NY 6
A. Lopez, BOS 5
L. Waner, PIT 5
D. Garms, BOS 5
D. Camilli, BKN 5
C. Root, CHI 3
J. Moore, NY 3
J. Hudson, BKN 3
H. Mulcahy, PHI . . . 3
L. Handley, PIT 2
L. Warneke, SL 1
F. Fitzsimmons, BKN . 1
H. Martin, PHI 1

1938 AMERICAN
J. Foxx, BOS 305
B. Dickey, NY 196
H. Greenberg,
  DET 162
R. Ruffing, NY 146
B. Newsom, SL 111
J. DiMaggio, NY . . 106
J. Cronin, BOS 92
E. Averill, CLE 34
C. Travis, WAS 33
C. Gehringer, DET . . 27
J. Heath, CLE 24
J. Gordon, NY 23
H. Trosky, CLE 22
K. Keltner, CLE 16
M. Stratton, CHI . . . 15
M. Harder, CLE 14
B. Johnson, PHI . . . 13
H. Clift, SL 11
L. Gehrig, NY 10
P. Fox, DET 9
J. Vosmik, BOS 7
M. McQuinn, SL . . . 7
L. Grove, BOS 7
B. Lewis, WAS 5
R. Rolfe, NY 5
C. Myer, WAS 5
E. Brucker, PHI 5
J. Allen, CLE 3
F. Crosetti, NY 2
L. Gomez, NY 1
D. Cramer, BOS 1

1939 NATIONAL
B. Walters, CIN . . . 303
J. Mize, SL 178
P. Derringer, CIN . . 174
F. McCormick, CIN . 159
C. Davis, SL 106
J. Brown, SL 99
J. Medwick, SL 81
L. Durocher, BKN . . 52
H. Danning, NY . . . 33
L. Hamlin, BKN . . . 32
M. Ott, NY 21
B. Jurges, NY 20
D. Camilli, BKN . . . 20
W. Myers, CIN 18
S. Hack, CHI 17
A. Galan, CHI 15
T. Moore, SL 15
M. Arnovich, PHI . . 10
L. Frey, CIN 8
B. Lee, CHI 8
E. Slaughter, SL . . . 8
W. Werber, CIN 6
M. West, BOS 5
G. Hartnett, CHI . . . 5
I. Goodman, CIN . . . 4
B. Hassett, BOS . . . 4
P. Coscarart, BKN . . 4
E. Fletcher, BOS-PIT . 4
C. Lavagetto, BKN . . 3

R. Bowman, SL 2
E. Miller, BOS 1
B. Herman, CHI 1

1939 AMERICAN
J. DiMaggio, NY . . 280
J. Foxx, BOS 170
B. Feller, CLE 155
T. Williams, BOS . . 126
R. Ruffing, NY 116
B. Dickey, NY 110
E. Leonard, WAS 71
B. Johnson, PHI 52
J. Gordon, NY 43
M. Kreevich, CHI 38
C. Brown, CHI 34
K. Keltner, CLE 26
G. McQuinn, SL 24
C. Gehringer, DET . . . 21
L. Grove, BOS 17
J. Cronin, BOS 15
T. Lyons, CHI 13
H. Greenberg, DET . 12
B. Newsom, DET . . . 11
J. Rigney, CHI 9
J. Kuhel, CHI 8
C. Keller, NY 7
J. Heath, CLE 7
G. Walker, CHI 7
F. Hayes, PHI 7
T. Bridges, DET 7
R. Rolfe, NY 6
B. McCosky, DET . . 6
E. McNair, CHI 5
H. Trosky, CLE 4
G. Case, WAS 3
M. Hoag, SL 3
R. York, DET 1
L. Appling, CHI 1

1940 NATIONAL
F. McCormick, CIN . 274
J. Mize, SL 209
B. Walters, CIN . . 146
P. Derringer, CIN . . 121
F. Fitzsimmons,
BKN 84
D. Walker, BKN 71
H. Danning, NY . . . 64
S. Hack, CHI 61
E. Lombardi, CIN . . 38
W. Werber, CIN 36
J. Cooney, BOS 31
D. Camilli, BKN 30
E. Miller, BOS 28
D. Garms, PIT 28
A. Vaughan, PIT . . . 27
C. Passeau, CHI . . . 26
J. Beggs, CIN 19
T. Moore, SL 18
E. Fletcher, PIT 16
B. Nicholson, CHI . . 12
K. Higbe, PHI 10
C. Rowell, BOS . . . 10
A. Lopez, PIT 9
M. Van Robays, PIT . . 8
R. Sewell, PIT 7
P. Reese, BKN 6
M. West, BOS 6
N. Young, NY 6
W. Wyatt, BKN 3
J. Rizzo, PHI 3
P. May, PHI 3
H. Mulcahy, PHI . . . 3
J. Martin, SL 2
F. Gustine, PIT 1

1940 AMERICAN
H. Greenberg,
DET 292
B. Feller, CLE 222
J. DiMaggio, NY . . 151
B. Newsom, DET . . 120
L. Boudreau, CLE . 119
J. Foxx, BOS 110
L. Rowe, DET 62
R. York, DET 61
R. Radcliff, SL 55
L. Appling, CHI 54
R. Weatherly, CLE . . 34
D. Bartell, DET . . . 26
J. Kuhel, CHI 18
S. Hudson, WAS . . . 16

T. Williams, BOS . . . 16
B. McCosky, DET . . . 11
E. Bonham, NY 8
W. Judnich, SL 6
J. Babich, PHI 5
M. Tresh, CHI 4
F. Hayes, PHI 4
R. Mack, CLE 4
J. Gordon, NY 3
C. Travis, WAS 3
B. Kennedy, CHI . . . 3
C. Gehringer, DET . . 3
R. Hemsley, CLE . . . 2
T. Lyons, CHI 2
L. Finney, BOS 1
E. Auker, SL 1

1941 NATIONAL
D. Camilli, BKN . . . 300
P. Reiser, BKN 183
W. Wyatt, BKN 151
J. Brown, SL 107
E. Riddle, CIN 98
E. White, SL 77
K. Higbe, BKN 64
J. Hopp, SL 61
J. Mize, SL 48
D. Walker, BKN 34
B. Herman, BKN . . . 27
T. Moore, SL 26
S. Hack, CHI 26
E. Fletcher, PIT 22
J. Cooney, BOS 20
B. Nicholson, CHI . . 16
G. Mancuso, SL . . . 14
F. Crespi, SL 13
M. Ott, NY 12
E. Slaughter, SL . . . 12
B. Young, NY 10
V. DiMaggio, PIT . . 10
J. Tobin, BOS 10
A. Lopez, PIT 8
M. Marion, SL 8
M. Cooper, SL 8
L. Warneke, SL 7
N. Etten, PHI 6
B. Walters, CIN 6
B. Dahlgren, CHI . . . 6
W. Werber, CIN 6
E. Crabtree, BKN . . . 5
J. Rucker, NY 4
D. Litwhiler, PHI . . . 3
H. Danning, NY 2
C. Hubbell, NY 2
C. Lavagetto, BKN . . 2
A. Vaughan, PIT . . . 2

1941 AMERICAN
J. DiMaggio, NY . . 291
T. Williams, BOS . . 254
B. Feller, CLE 174
T. Lee, CHI 144
C. Keller, NY 126
C. Travis, WAS . . . 101
J. Gordon, NY 60
J. Heath, CLE 37
H. Newsome, BOS . 32
R. Cullenbine, SL . . 29
J. Cronin, BOS . . . 26
S. Chapman, PHI . . 25
B. Dickey, NY 18
J. Henrich, NY 16
B. McCosky, DET . . 12
T. Lyons, CHI 10
D. Siebert, PHI . . . 10
L. Boudreau, CLE . . 10
A. Benton, DET 8
P. Rizzuto, NY 7
E. Leonard, WAS . . . 7
B. Campbell, DET . . 4
R. York, DET 3
F. Hayes, PHI 3
T. Wright, CHI 2
R. Ruffing, NY 2
E. Auker, SL 1
F. Higgins, DET . . . 1
D. DiMaggio, BOS . . 1

1942 NATIONAL
M. Cooper, SL 263
E. Slaughter, SL . . . 200
M. Ott, NY 190
A. Owen, BKN 103

J. Mize, NY 97
P. Reiser, BKN 91
M. Marion, SL 81
D. Camilli, BKN . . . 42
R. Elliott, PIT 39
C. Passeau, CHI . . . 33
W. Cooper, SL 28
S. Musial, SL 26
E. Lombardi, BOS . . 24
J. Beazley, SL 24
J. Brown, SL 24
W. Wyatt, BKN 22
J. Medwick, BKN . . 20
T. Moore, SL 15
B. Nicholson, CHI . . 14
S. Hack, CHI 11
J. VanderMeer, CIN . 11
T. Hughes, PHI 10
R. Starr, CIN 9
L. French, BKN 7
P. Reese, BKN 6
W. Kurowski, SL . . . 6
R. Lamanno, CIN . . . 4
M. West, BOS 4
L. Frey, CIN 4
F. McCormick, CIN . . 4
A. Javery, BOS 3
E. Miller, BOS 1

1942 AMERICAN
J. Gordon, NY 270
T. Williams, BOS . . 249
J. Pesky, BOS 143
V. Stephens, SL . . . 140
E. Bonham, NY . . . 102
T. Hughson, BOS . . 92
J. DiMaggio, NY . . . 86
S. Spence, WAS . . . 65
P. Marchildon, PHI . . 39
L. Boudreau, CLE . . 34
B. Doerr, BOS 24
T. Lyons, CHI 23
G. Case, WAS 17
K. Keltner, CLE . . . 15
C. Keller, NY 15
W. Judnich, SL . . . 14
B. Dickey, NY 12
D. Gutteridge, SL . . 12
P. Rizzuto, NY 9
C. Laabs, SL 9
R. Ferrell, SL 8
H. Borowy, NY 8
J. Bagby, CLE 6
T. Wright, CHI 6
T. Lupien BOS 4
L. Fleming, CLE . . . 4
S. Chandler, NY . . . 3
R. York, DET 3
B. McCosky, DET . . 1

1943 NATIONAL
S. Musial, SL 267
W. Cooper, SL . . . 192
B. Nicholson, CHI . 181
B. Herman, BKN . . 140
M. Cooper, SL . . . 130
R. Sewell, PIT . . . 127
E. Riddle, CIN 68
R. Elliott, PIT 52
F. McCormick, CIN . 26
C. Shoun, CIN 24
E. Miller, CIN 24
M. Witek, NY 21
M. Marion, SL 20
L. Rowe, PHI 18
W. Wyatt, BKN . . . 15
A. Vaughan, BKN . . 15
R. Mueller, CIN . . . 12
A. Javery, BOS . . . 12
S. Hack, CHI 10
M. Ott, NY 9
E. Fletcher, PIT . . . 7
A. Adams, NY 7
J. Klein, SL 6
A. Galan, BKN 5
D. Walker, BKN . . . 5
J. Tobin, BOS 5
D. Bartell, NY 5
P. Cavaretta, CHI . . 4
T. Holmes, BOS . . . 2
R. Northey, PHI . . . 2
B. Dahlgren, PHI . . 2
H. Bithorn, CHI . . . 1

B. Walters, CIN 1
L. Frey, CIN 1

1943 AMERICAN
S. Chandler, NY . . . 246
L. Appling, CHI . . . 215
R. York, DET 152
W. Johnson, NY . . . 135
B. Johnson, WAS . 116
D. Wakefield, DET . . 72
N. Etten, NY 61
B. Dickey, NY 58
V. Stephens, SL . . . 49
L. Boudreau, CLE . . 40
D. Trout, DET 38
G. Case, WAS 37
C. Keller, NY 31
B. Doerr, BOS 21
A. Smith, CLE 19
G. Priddy, WAS . . . 17
O. Hockett, CLE . . 14
D. Gutteridge, SL . . 13
E. Wynn, WAS . . . 13
J. Bagby, CLE 11
R. Cramer, DET . . . 8
F. Higgins, DET . . . 8
C. Laabs, SL 6
J. Early, WAS 6
J. Gordon, NY 4
R. Wolff, PHI 4
L. Newsome, BOS . . 3
J. Cronin, BOS 3
J. Flores, PHI 3
G. Maltzberger, CHI . 3
F. Crosetti, NY 2
K. Keltner, CLE . . . 2
P. Fox, BOS 1
R. Hodgin, CHI 1
J. Murphy, NY 1
D. Siebert, PHI 1
J. Tabor, BOS 1
H. Wagner, PHI . . . 1

1944 NATIONAL
M. Marion, SL 190
B. Nicholson, CHI . 189
D. Walker, BKN . . . 145
S. Musial, SL 136
B. Walters, CIN . . . 107
B. Voiselle, NY . . . 107
R. Mueller, CIN . . . 85
W. Cooper, SL 72
M. Cooper, SL 63
R. Elliott, PIT 57
R. Sewell, PIT 49
B. Dahlgren, PIT . . 33
F. McCormick, CIN . 32
P. Cavaretta, CHI . . 27
R. Sanders, SL . . . 25
M. Ott, NY 20
J. Tobin, BOS 13
J. Hopp, SL 10
R. Northey, PHI . . . 10
J. Medwick, NY . . . 9
J. Barrett, PIT 8
E. Miller, CIN 7
T. Holmes, BOS . . . 6
T. Wilks, SL 4
T. Lupien, PHI 3
S. Hack, CHI 2
M. Lanier, SL 2
C. Ryan, BOS 2
A. Galan, BKN 1
W. Kurowski, SL . . . 1
J. Russell, PIT 1

1944 AMERICAN
H. Newhouser,
DET 236
D. Trout, DET 232
V. Stephens, SL . . . 193
S. Stirnweiss, NY . . 129
D. Wakefield, DET . 128
L. Boudreau, CLE . . 84
B. Doerr, BOS 75
S. Spence, WAS . . . 56
N. Potter, SL 52
B. Johnson, BOS . . 51
M. Christman, SL . . 27
T. Hughson, BOS . . 22
D. Cramer, DET . . . 14
F. Hayes, PHI 13
P. Fox, BOS 12

J. Kramer, SL 9
J. Lindell, NY 8
P. Richards, DET . . . 8
D. Gutteridge, SL . . . 7
F. Higgins, DET 7
G. McQuinn, SL 7
G. Kell, PHI 6
R. Cullenbine, CLE . . 5
N. Etten, NY 5
R. York, DET 5
R. Hemsley, NY 4
M. Kreevich, SL 4
W. Moses, CHI 4
E. Mayo, DET 3
D. Siebert, PHI 3
H. Borowy, NY 2
F. Crosetti, NY 2
H. Hodgin, CHI 2
B. Muncrief, SL 1

1945 NATIONAL
P. Cavaretta, CHI . . 279
T. Holmes, BOS . . . 175
C. Barrett,
BOS-SL 151
A. Pafko, CHI 131
W. Kurowski, SL . . . 90
H. Borowy, CHI . . . 84
H. Wyse, CHI 72
M. Marion, SL 69
D. Walker, BKN . . . 66
G. Rosen, BKN 56
S. Hack, CHI 42
H. Brecheen, SL . . . 31
M. Ott, NY 22
A. Galan, BKN 18
J. Hopp, SL 17
R. Elliott, PIT 15
L. Olmo, BKN 13
B. Adams, SL 12
C. Passeau, CHI . . . 9
J. Barrett, PIT 8
E. Heusser, CIN . . . 7
D. Johnson, CHI . . . 7
B. Kerr, NY 7
F. McCormick, CIN . . 6
B. Salkeld, PIT 6
P. Lowrey, CHI 5
A. Adams, NY 4
A. Karl, PHI 4
H. Gregg, BKN 2
A. Lopez, PIT 2
P. Masi, BOS 2
E. Miller, CIN 2
V. DiMaggio, PHI . . . 1
E. Stanky, BKN . . . 1

1945 AMERICAN
H. Newhouser,
DET 236
E. Mayo, DET 164
S. Stirnweiss, NY . . 161
B. Ferriss, BOS . . . 148
G. Myatt, WAS 98
V. Stephens, SL . . . 94
R. Wolff, WAS 78
L. Boudreau, CLE . . 70
G. Case, WAS 60
P. Richards, DET . . . 35
M. Tresh, CHI 33
J. Kuhel, WAS 29
R. Cullenbine, DET . 26
H. Greenberg, DET . 25
N. Etten, NY 21
T. Cuccinello, CHI . . 18
D. Trout, DET 17
E. Leonard, WAS . . 16
R. Schalk, CHI 13
J. Heath, CLE 10
G. Binks, WAS 9
B. Muncrief, SL . . . 8
A. Benton, DET . . . 6
R. Ferrell, WAS . . . 6
B. Johnson, BOS . . 6
M. Christman, SL . . 5
B. Estalella, PHI . . . 5
F. Hayes, PHI-CLE . . 5
D. Cramer, DET . . . 4
W. Moses, CHI . . . 4
E. Lake, BOS 2
R. Christopher, PHI . 1
L. Newsome, BOS . . 1
R. York, DET 1

1946 NATIONAL
S. Musial, SL 319
D. Walker, BKN . . . 159
E. Slaughter, SL . . . 144
H. Pollet, SL 116
J. Sain, BOS 95
P. Reese, BKN 79
E. Stanky, BKN . . . 67
D. Ennis, PHI 61
P. Reiser, BKN 58
P. Cavaretta, CHI . . 49
B. Kerr, NY 37
J. Hopp, BOS 34
E. Waitkus, CHI . . . 21
B. Edwards, BKN . . 20
K. Higbe, BKN 18
H. Brecheen, SL . . . 14
J. Mize, NY 14
G. Hatton, CIN 12
T. Holmes, BOS . . . 11
J. Tabor, PHI 10
E. Verban, PHI 10
H. Walker, SL 9
L. Rowe, PHI 8
P. Masi, BOS 7
J. VanderMeer, CIN . 7
R. Schoendienst, SL . 6
B. Cox, PIT 5
F. Gustine, PIT 4
M. Marion, SL 4
R. Kiner, PIT 3
W. Kurowski, SL . . . 3
R. Mueller, CIN . . . 3
J. Schmitz, CHI . . . 3
P. Lowrey, CHI 2
F. McCormick, PHI . . 2
C. Furillo, BKN 1
O. Judd, PHI 1

1946 AMERICAN
T. Williams, BOS . . 224
H. Newhouser,
DET 197
B. Doerr, BOS 158
J. Pesky, BOS 141
M. Vernon, WAS . . 134
B. Feller, CLE 105
B. Ferriss, BOS 94
H. Greenberg, DET . 91
D. DiMaggio, BOS . . 56
L. Boudreau, CLE . . 37
R. York, BOS 28
L. Appling, CHI . . . 26
T. Hughson, BOS . . 19
E. Caldwell, CHI . . . 18
C. Keller, NY 17
G. Kell, DET 12
S. Chandler, NY . . . 12
A. Robinson, NY . . . 12
J. DiMaggio, NY . . . 6
B. Newsom, WAS . . 6
V. Stephens, SL . . . 6
P. Marchildon, PHI . . 5
B. Rosar, PHI 4
S. Spence, WAS . . . 4
J. Berardino, SL . . . 2
T. Henrich, NY 1
H. Wagner, BOS . . . 1

1947 NATIONAL
R. Elliott, BOS 205
E. Blackwell, CIN . . 175
J. Mize, NY 144
B. Edwards, BKN . . 140
J. Robinson, BKN . . 106
R. Kiner, PIT 101
L. Jansen, NY 91
P. Reese, BKN 80
W. Kurowski, SL . . . 45
H. Walker, PHI 45
R. Branca, BKN . . . 40
H. Casey, BKN 37
E. Leonard, PHI . . . 32
E. Stanky, BKN . . . 32
W. Spahn, BOS . . . 26
W. Marshall, NY . . . 20
J. Sain, BOS 20
W. Cooper, NY 19
D. Walker, BKN . . . 14
E. Slaughter, SL . . . 12
S. Musial, SL 12
E. Verban, PHI 9
P. Cavaretta, CHI . . 6

P. Lowrey, CHI 2
E. Miller, CIN 2
A. Pafko, CHI 1

1947 AMERICAN
J. DiMaggio, NY ..202
T. Williams, BOS ..201
L. Boudreau, CLE .168
J. Page, NY 167
G. Kell, DET 132
G. McQuinn, NY 77
J. Gordon, CLE 59
B. Feller, CLE 58
P. Marchildon, PHI ..47
L. Appling, CHI 43
E. Joost, PHI 35
B. McCosky, WAS ...35
T. Henrich, NY 33
F. Shea, NY 23
Y. Berra, NY 18
A. Reynolds, NY ...18
B. Dillinger, SL 13
J. Pesky, BOS 11
F. Fain, PHI 9
W. Johnson, NY....9
S. Spence, WAS 9
F. Hutchison, DET ..8
E. Wynn, WAS 7
B. Doerr, BOS 6
B. Rosar, PHI.......6
M. Christman, WAS ..4
B. McCahan, PHI....4
D. Mitchell, CLE.....4
R. Cullenbine, DET ..3
J. Dobson, BOS 3
J. Heath, SL........1
E. Lopat, CHI.......1
V. Stephens, SL 1
T. Wright, CHI 1

1948 NATIONAL
S. Musial, SL 303
J. Sain, BOS 223
A. Dark, BOS 174
S. Gordon, NY 72
H. Brecheen, SL ...61
P. Reese, BKN 60
R. Kiner, PIT 55
E. Slaughter, SL....55
D. Murtaugh, PIT ...52
S. Rojek, PIT 51
R. Ashburn, PHI ...48
J. Schmitz, CHI 37
R. Elliott, BOS 33
W. Spahn, BOS 31
J. Robinson, BKN ..30
A. Pafko, CHI......25
J. Mize, NY 22
R. Barney, BKN 15
J. VanderMeer, CIN .13
J. Wyrostek, CIN 9
R. Branca, BKN 8
R. Campanella, BKN .8
B. Chesnes, PIT 8
P. Cavaretta, CHI ...6
E. Miller, PHI 4
D. Ennis, PHI 3
G. Hatton, CIN 3
L. Jansen, NY 2
D. Walker, PIT 2
G. Hodges, BKN 1
W. Lockman, NY 1
H. Sauer, CIN 1

1948 AMERICAN
L. Boudreau, CLE .324
J. DiMaggio, NY ..213
T. Williams, BOS ..171
V. Stephens, BOS .121
B. Lemon, CLE ...101
J. Gordon, CLE 63
T. Henrich, NY 63
G. Bearden, CLE ...52
H. Newhouser, DET .48
E. Joost, PHI 39
H. Majeski, PHI 23
B. Tebbetts, BOS ...23
V. Raschi, NY 23
K. Keltner, CLE 18
G. Priddy, SL 16
G. Kell, DET 16
W. Evers, DET 13
A. Zarilla, SL 11

B. Doerr, BOS 10
B. Dillinger, SL 10
J. Hegan, CLE 10
L. Appling, CHI 8
B. Feller, CLE 6
L. Brissie, PHI 5
F. Fain, PHI 5
J. Dobson, BOS 5
B. Goodman, BOS ..4
B. McCosky, PHI ...4
Y. Berra, NY 3
D. DiMaggio, BOS ..3
L. Doby, CLE 3
C. Fannin, SL.......2
P. Mullin, DET 1
P. Rizzuto, NY 1

1949 NATIONAL
J. Robinson, BKN ..264
S. Musial, SL 226
E. Slaughter, SL....181
R. Kiner, PIT 133
P. Reese, BKN 118
C. Furillo, BKN 68
W. Spahn, BOS 60
D. Newcombe, BKN 55
K. Heintzelman, PHI 48
R. Schoendienst, SL 30
G. Hodges, BKN ...29
H. Pollet, SL 29
D. Ennis, PHI 28
B. Thomson, NY ...25
R. Campanella, BKN 22
P. Roe, BKN 21
G. Hamner, PHI 9
W. Lockman, NY 9
R. Meyer, PHI 8
K. Raffensberger, CIN 8
H. Sauer, CHI.......8
T. Wilks, SL 5
R. Ashburn, PHI 6
J. Schmitz, CHI 6
A. Dark, BOS 3
M. Marion, SL 3
W. Jones, PHI 2
W. Marshall, NY 2
E. Torgeson, BOS ...2
S. Gordon, NY 1
D. Sisler, PHI 1

1949 AMERICAN
T. Williams, BOS ..272
P. Rizzuto, NY 175
J. Page, NY 166
M. Parnell, BOS ...151
E. Kinder, BOS ...122
T. Henrich, NY 121
V. Stephens, BOS .100
G. Kell, DET 80
B. Lemon, CLE 57
V. Wertz, DET 51
V. Raschi, NY 19
J. DiMaggio, NY ...18
E. Joost, PHI 11
L. Boudreau, CLE ..10
Y. Berra, NY 9
D. DiMaggio, BOS ...7
B. Doerr, BOS 7
A. Kellner, PHI 6
E. Robinson, WAS ..6
R. Sievers, SL 6
B. Tebbetts, BOS ...6
L. Appling, CHI 3
A. Houtteman, DET ..3
J. Priddy, SL 3
V. Trucks, DET 3
D. Mitchell, CLE 2
A. Reynolds, NY 2

1950 NATIONAL
J. Konstanty, PHI ..286
S. Musial, SL 158
E. Stanky, NY 144
D. Ennis, PHI 104
R. Kiner, PIT 91
G. Hamner, PHI 79
R. Roberts, PHI 68
G. Hodges, BKN ...55

D. Snider, BKN 53
S. Maglie, NY 51
E. Blackwell, CIN ..41
A. Pafko, CHI......38
R. Campanella, BKN 29
A. Seminick, PHI ...25
J. Robinson, BKN ..23
C. Simmons, PHI ...22
P. Roe, BKN 15
T. Kluszewski, CIN ..14
W. Spahn, BOS ...14
D. Newcombe, BKN 14
J. Sain, BOS 12
S. Gordon, BOS ...11
J. Hearn, NY 10
P. Reese, BKN 8
E. Waitkus, PHI 8
R. Elliott, BOS 8
E. Torgeson, BOS ...6
S. Jethroe, BOS 6
H. Sauer, CHI.......5
V. Bickford, BOS ...4
C. Furillo, BKN 4
W. Westrum, NY 4
D. Sisler, PHI 2
H. Thompson, NY ...2
L. Jansen, NY 2
W. Jones, PHI 1

1950 AMERICAN
P. Rizzuto, NY 284
B. Goodman, BOS 180
Y. Berra, NY 146
G. Kell, DET 127
B. Lemon, CLE 102
W. Dropo, BOS 75
V. Raschi, NY 63
L. Doby, CLE 57
J. DiMaggio, NY 54
V. Wertz, DET 50
W. Evers, DET 38
C. Carrasquel, CHI ..21
D. Trout, DET 21
D. DiMaggio, BOS ..17
I. Noren, WAS 16
B. Doerr, BOS 15
J. Mize, NY 11
J. Priddy, DET 11
A. Rosen, CLE 11
E. Yost, WAS 8
M. Parnell, BOS 7
W. Ford, NY 7
T. Williams, BOS 7
N. Garver, SL 6
V. Stephens, BOS ...6
A. Houtteman, DET ..6
S. Lollar, SL 4
E. Lopat, NY 3
K. Wood, SL 2
S. Dente, WAS 1
D. Philley, CHI 1

1951 NATIONAL
R. Campanella, BKN 243
S. Musial, SL 191
M. Irvin, NY 166
S. Maglie, NY 153
P. Roe, BKN 138
J. Robinson, BKN ..92
R. Ashburn, PHI ...69
B. Thomson, NY ...62
M. Dickson, PIT ...59
R. Kiner, PIT 49
W. Spahn, BOS 45
A. Dark, NY 30
R. Roberts, PHI 27
L. Jansen, NY 26
P. Reese, BKN 15
G. Hodges, BKN ...10
S. Gordon, BOS ...10
K. Raffensberger, CIN 8
J. Wyrostek, CIN 6
E. Blackwell, CIN ...6
C. Furillo, BKN 6
D. Newcombe, BKN .3
P. Cavaretta, CHI ...1
H. Sauer, CHI.......1

1951 AMERICAN
Y. Berra, NY 184
N. Garver, SL 157
A. Reynolds, NY ...125
M. Minoso, CHI ...120
B. Feller, CLE 118
F. Fain, PHI 103
E. Kinder, BOS 66
V. Raschi, NY 64
G. McDougald, NY .63
B. Avila, CLE 49
P. Rizzuto, NY 47
E. Lopat, NY 44
T. Williams, BOS ...35
E. Joost, PHI 32
G. Kell, DET 30
E. Wynn, CLE 29
N. Fox, CHI 25
B. Goodman, BOS ..21
D. DiMaggio, BOS .16
G. Zernial, CHI-PHI .15
B. Shantz, PHI 14
M. Garcia, CLE 11
G. Coan, WAS 8
M. Parnell, BOS 7
E. Robinson, CHI....7
G. Woodling, NY ...5
J. Pesky, BOS 5
I. Noren, WAS 4
D. Mitchell, CLE.....4
V. Trucks, DET 2
E. Yost, WAS 2
J. Busby, CHI 2
J. Mize, NY 2

1952 NATIONAL
H. Sauer, CHI.....226
R. Roberts, PHI ...211
J. Black, BKN 208
H. Wilhelm, NY ...133
S. Musial, SL 127
E. Slaughter, SL....92
J. Robinson, BKN ..31
P. Reese, BKN 29
D. Snider, BKN 29
R. Campanella, BKN 25
R. Schoendienst, SL 25
A. Dark, NY 24
M. Dickson, PIT 22
D. Ennis, PHI 18
W. Lockman, NY ...18
B. Thomson, NY ...17
F. Baumholtz, CHI .16
T. Kluszewski, CIN ..16
G. Hodges, BKN ...15
R. McMillan, CIN ...15
M. Mathews, BOS ..13
B. Adams, CIN 9
B. Cox, BKN 8
W. Hacker, CHI 8
R. Kiner, PIT 8
S. Maglie, NY 8
K. Raffensberger, CIN 8
W. Spahn, BOS 8
P. Roe, BKN 7
S. Gordon, BOS 6
G. Hamner, PHI 5
S. Hemus, SL 5
M. Irvin, NY 5
G. Shuba, BKN 5
E. Yuhas, SL 5
A. Brazle, SL 3
J. Logan, BOS 3
T. Atwell, CHI 2
C. Metkovich, PIT ...2
W. Cooper, BOS 1

1952 AMERICAN
B. Shantz, PHI 280
A. Reynolds, NY ...183
M. Mantle, NY 143
Y. Berra, NY 104
E. Wynn, CLE 99
F. Fain, PHI 66
N. Fox, CHI 59
B. Lemon, CLE 58
M. Garcia, CLE 52
A. Rosen, CLE 51
E. Robinson, CHI...47
L. Doby, CLE 46

L. Easter, CLE 40
P. Rizzuto, NY 33
E. Joost, PHI 20
B. Goodman, BOS .18
J. Jensen, NY-WAS .12
S. Paige, SL 12
V. Raschi, NY 12
D. Mitchell, CLE....11
H. Bauer, NY 10
G. Woodling, NY ...10
P. Runnels, WAS 8
C. Courtney, SL 7
D. Gernert, BOS 6
W. Dropo, DET 5
S. Rogovin, CHI.....4
S. White, BOS 4
B. Avila, CLE 3
B. Pierce, CHI 3
J. Sain, NY 3
B. Young, SL 3
J. Collins, NY 2
C. Marrero, WAS 1
B. Porterfield, WAS ..1

1953 NATIONAL
R. Campanella, BKN 297
E. Mathews, MIL ..216
D. Snider, BKN ...157
R. Schoendienst, SL 155
W. Spahn, MIL 120
R. Roberts, PHI ...106
T. Kluszewski, CIN ..69
S. Musial, SL 62
C. Erskine, BKN 54
C. Furillo, BKN 54
P. Reese, BKN 27
J. Robinson, BKN ..19
D. Ennis, PHI 14
G. Hodges, BKN ...13
M. Irvin, NY 11
D. O'Connell, PIT ..10
H. Haddix, SL 9
F. Thomas, PIT 6
R. Ashburn, PHI 5
G. Bell, CIN 3
J. Logan, MIL 3
R. Gomez, NY 2
G. Hamner, PHI 2
D. Crandall, MIL 1
H. Thompson, NY ...1

1953 AMERICAN
A. Rosen, CLE 336
Y. Berra, NY 167
M. Vernon, WAS ..162
M. Minoso, CHI ...100
V. Trucks, CHI 81
P. Rizzuto, NY 76
B. Porterfield, WAS .64
R. Boone, CLE-DET 59
J. Piersall, BOS 56
B. Pierce, CHI 55
E. Kinder, BOS 41
H. Bauer, NY 37
A. Reynolds, NY ...37
M. Parnell, BOS 27
H. Kuenn, DET 23
B. Lemon, CLE 22
E. Lopat, NY 18
G. Zernial, PHI 16
D. Philley, PHI 11
W. Ford, NY 8
B. Goodman, BOS ..5
M. Mantle, NY 4
G. Woodling, NY 3
E. Yost, WAS 3
B. Martin, NY 2
C. Carrasquel, CHI ..1
G. Kell, BOS 1
T. Williams, BOS 1

1954 NATIONAL
W. Mays, NY 283
T. Kluszewski, CIN 217
J. Antonelli, NY ...154
D. Snider, BKN ...135
A. Dark, NY 110
S. Musial, SL 97
R. Roberts, PHI 70

J. Adcock, MIL 60
P. Reese, BKN 53
G. Hodges, BKN ...40
W. Spahn, MIL 38
D. Mueller, NY 30
R. Schoendienst, SL 24
F. Thomas, PIT 24
H. Wilhelm, NY 17
E. Banks, CHI 14
D. Crandall, MIL ...13
J. Logan, MIL 9
E. Mathews, MIL 5
G. Hamner, PHI 5
R. Ashburn, PHI 5
S. Maglie, NY 4
G. Conley, MIL 3
M. Grissom, NY 2
R. McMillan, CIN ...2
D. Rhodes, NY 1
H. Sauer, CHI.......1

1954 AMERICAN
Y. Berra, NY 230
L. Doby, CLE 210
B. Avila, CLE 203
M. Minoso, CHI ...186
B. Lemon, CLE 179
E. Wynn, CLE 72
T. Williams, BOS ...65
H. Kuenn, DET 37
M. Vernon, WAS ...30
N. Fox, CHI 30
B. Grim, NY 25
J. Finigan, PHI 19
V. Trucks, CHI 19
J. Jensen, BOS 17
M. Mantle, NY 16
I. Noren, NY 16
A. Rosen, CLE 16
J. Busby, WAS 7
J. Coleman, BAL 6
B. Goodman, BOS ..6
M. Garcia, CLE 6
J. Hegan, CLE 5
H. Bauer, NY 4
A. Kaline, DET 4
B. Turley, BAL 4
S. Gromek, DET 1
C. Abrams, BAL 1
R. Boone, DET 1
R. Sievers, WAS 1

1955 NATIONAL
R. Campanella, BKN 226
D. Snider, BKN ...221
E. Banks, CHI 195
W. Mays, NY 165
R. Roberts, PHI ...159
T. Kluszewski, CIN 111
D. Newcombe, BKN 89
S. Musial, SL 46
H. Aaron, MIL 36
P. Reese, BKN 36
J. Logan, MIL 24
W. Post, CIN 23
D. Ennis, PHI 21
R. Ashburn, PHI 17
C. Labine, BKN 11
B. Friend, PIT 10
D. Crandall, MIL 8
E. Mathews, MIL 6
D. Long, PIT 3
J. Meyer, PHI 3
G. Baker, CHI 2
C. Furillo, BKN 2
V. Law, PIT 1
F. Thomas, PIT......1

1955 AMERICAN
Y. Berra, NY 218
A. Kaline, DET 201
A. Smith, CLE 200
T. Williams, BOS ..143
M. Mantle, NY 113
R. Narleski, CLE ...90
N. Fox, CHI 84
H. Bauer, NY 64
V. Power, KC 53
J. Jensen, BOS 39

S. Lollar, CHI 37
G. McDougald, NY . 34
B. Klaus, BOS 27
T. Byrne, NY 24
W. Ford, NY 21
R. Boone, DET 16
R. Sievers, WAS . . . 9
H. Kuenn, DET 8
B. Pierce, CHI 8
D. Philley, CLE-BAL . 6
E. Wynn, CLE 6
E. Valo, KC 5
M. Vernon, WAS . . . 4
B. Hoeft, DET 1
D. Mossi, CLE 1
F. Sullivan, BOS 1
G. Triandos, BAL 1
J. Valdivielso, WAS . . 1
S. White, BOS 1

1956 NATIONAL
D. Newcombe,
  BKN 223
S. Maglie, BKN . . . 183
H. Aaron, MIL . . . 146
W. Spahn, MIL . . . 126
J. Gilliam, BKN . . . 103
R. McMillan, CIN . . 96
F. Robinson, CIN . . 79
P. Reese, BKN 71
S. Musial, SL 62
D. Snider, BKN 55
J. Adcock, MIL 54
B. Friend, PIT 38
H. Freeman, CIN . . 25
J. Antonelli, NY . . . 18
T. Kluszewski, CIN . 18
J. Robinson, BKN . . 17
W. Mays, NY 14
E. Bailey, CIN 13
B. Virdon, SL-PIT . . 13
S. Lopata, PHI 11
C. Furillo, BKN . . . 9
L. Burdette, MIL . . . 8
B. Buhl, MIL 7
R. Roberts, PHI . . . 7
B. Lawrence, CIN . . 6
D. Long, PIT 4
W. Moon, SL 3
E. Banks, CHI 2
K. Boyer, SL 2
C. Labine, BKN . . . 1
J. Logan, MIL 1
R. Ashburn, PHI . . . 1

1956 AMERICAN
M. Mantle, NY . . . 336
Y. Berra, NY 186
A. Kaline, DET . . . 142
H. Kuenn, DET . . . 80
B. Pierce, CHI 75
T. Williams, BOS . . 70
B. Nieman,
  CHI-BAL 55
G. McDougald, NY . 55
V. Wertz, CLE 45
B. Lemon, CLE . . . 40
H. Simpson, KC . . . 37
W. Ford, NY 33
E. Wynn, CLE 32
J. Piersall, BOS . . . 28
N. Fox, CHI 28
S. Lollar, CHI 27
F. Lary, DET 24
P. Runnels, WAS . . 24
H. Score, CLE 18
J. Jensen, BOS 15
M. Vernon, BOS . . 14
T. Brewer, BOS . . . 11
H. Bauer, NY 8
C. Maxwell, DET . . 8
L. Aparicio, CHI . . . 7
G. Triandos, BAL . . 6
F. Bolling, DET . . . 3
M. Minoso, CHI . . . 3
V. Power, KC 3
J. Kucks, NY 2
R. Sievers, WAS . . . 1

1957 NATIONAL
H. Aaron, MIL . . . 239
S. Musial, SL 230
R. Schoendienst,

NY-MIL 221
W. Mays, NY 174
W. Spahn, MIL . . . 131
E. Banks, CHI 60
G. Hodges, BKN . . 54
E. Mathews, MIL . . 45
F. Robinson, CIN . . 42
J. Sanford, PHI . . . 39
D. Hoak, CIN 31
D. Blasingame, SL . 26
E. Bouchee, PHI . . 26
B. Buhl, MIL 15
D. Ennis, SL 13
D. Groat, PIT 13
A. Dark, SL 12
D. Snider, BKN . . . 10
F. Thomas, PIT . . . 8
F. Drysdale, BKN . . 6
R. McMillan, CIN . . 6
D. Drott, CHI 6
G. Hamner, PHI . . . 3
L. Burdette, MIL . . 2
J. Logan, MIL 1
H. Anderson, PHI . . 1

1957 AMERICAN
M. Mantle, NY . . . 233
T. Williams, BOS . . 209
R. Sievers, WAS . . 205
N. Fox, CHI 193
G. McDougald,
  NY 165
V. Wertz, CLE 61
F. Malzone, BOS . . 58
M. Minoso, CHI . . 55
J. Bunning, DET . . 46
A. Kaline, DET . . . 40
B. Pierce, CHI 35
B. Gardner, BAL . . 22
D. Donovan, CHI . . 19
Y. Berra, NY 18
G. Woodling, CLE . 13
B. Grim, NY 9
B. Boyd, BAL 9
C. Maxwell, DET . . 5
W. Held, KC 4
W. Ford, NY 4
V. Power, KC 3
J. Piersall, BOS . . . 2
B. Skowron, NY . . 2
H. Kuenn, DET . . . 2
S. Lollar, CHI 2
T. Kubek, NY 1
B. Shantz, NY 1

1958 NATIONAL
E. Banks, CHI . . . 283
W. Mays, SF 185
H. Aaron, MIL . . . 166
F. Thomas, PIT . . . 143
W. Spahn, MIL . . . 108
B. Friend, PIT . . . 98
R. Ashburn, PHI . . 62
B. Mazeroski, PIT . 61
O. Cepeda, SF . . . 57
D. Crandall, MIL . . 48
L. Burdette, MIL . . 47
S. Musial, SL 39
K. Boyer, SL 31
J. Temple, CIN . . . 26
B. Skinner, PIT . . . 18
W. Covington, MIL . 16
E. Face, PIT 8
H. Anderson, PHI . . 5
J. Gilliam, LA 4
B. Purkey, CIN . . . 4
F. Robinson, CIN . . 4
J. Adcock, MIL . . . 2
C. Furillo, LA 1

1958 AMERICAN
J. Jensen, BOS . . . 233
B. Turley, NY 191
R. Colavito, CLE . . 181
B. Cerv, KC 164
M. Mantle, NY . . . 127
R. Sievers, WAS . . 95
T. Williams, BOS . . 89
N. Fox, CHI 88
S. Lollar, CHI 57
P. Runnels, BOS . . 29
G. Triandos, BAL . . 27
D. Hyde, WAS . . . 26

H. Kuenn, DET . . 24
C. McLish, CLE . . 18
V. Power, KC-CLE . 15
F. Bolling, DET . . 10
E. Howard, NY . . . 9
Y. Berra, NY 6
M. Minoso, CLE . . 6
A. Kaline, DET . . . 5
G. McDougald, NY . 5
R. Duren, NY 4
F. Lary, DET 3
J. Harshman, BAL . 2
D. Donovan, CHI . . 1
F. Malzone, BOS . . 1

1959 NATIONAL
E. Banks, CHI . . 232½
E. Mathews,
  MIL 189½
H. Aaron, MIL . . 174
W. Moon, LA . . . 161
S. Jones, SF 130
W. Mays, SF 85
E. Face, PIT 67
C. Neal, LA 64
F. Robinson, CIN . 52
K. Boyer, SL 37
D. Crandall, MIL . . 27
L. Burdette, MIL . . 14
R. Craig, LA 12
J. Cunningham, SL . 12
V. Pinson, CIN . . . 11
J. Temple, CIN . . . 8
D. Hoak, PIT 6
G. Hodges, LA . . . 4
O. Cepeda, SF . . . 3
V. Law, PIT 3
W. Spahn, MIL . . . 3
G. Conley, PHI . . . 1
W. McCovey, SF . . 1
D. Snider, LA 1

1959 AMERICAN
N. Fox, CHI 295
L. Aparicio, CHI . . 255
E. Wynn, CHI . . . 123
R. Colavito, CLE . . 117
T. Francona, CLE . . 102
A. Kaline, DET . . . 84
J. Landis, CHI . . . 66
H. Kuenn, DET . . . 64
S. Lollar, CHI 44
J. Jensen, BOS . . . 40
C. McLish, CLE . . . 35
Y. Berra, NY 26
M. Minoso, CLE . . 26
F. Malzone, BOS . . 24
H. Killebrew, WAS . 21
G. Woodling, BAL . 18
M. Mantle, NY . . . 13
B. Richardson, NY . 11
C. Pascual, WAS . . 9
B. Shaw, CHI 8
G. Triandos, BAL . . 8
B. Daley, KC 7
V. Power, CLE . . . 5
B. Tuttle, KC 5
J. Lemon, WAS . . . 4
P. Runnels, BOS . . 2
T. Williams, BOS . . 2
B. Allison, WAS . . 1
G. Staley, CHI . . . 1

1960 NATIONAL
D. Groat, PIT . . . 276
D. Hoak, PIT . . . 162
W. Mays, SF 155
E. Banks, CHI . . . 100
L. McDaniel, SL . . 95
K. Boyer, SL 80
V. Law, PIT 80
R. Clemente, PIT . . 62
E. Broglio, SL . . . 58
E. Mathews, MIL . . 52
H. Aaron, MIL . . . 49
E. Face, PIT 47
D. Crandall, MIL . . 31
W. Spahn, MIL . . . 27
N. Larker, LA 21
S. Musial, SL 18
M. Wills, LA 7
V. Pinson, CIN . . . 6
J. Adcock, MIL . . . 5

S. Burgess, PIT 2
F. Robinson, CIN . . 2
L. Sherry, LA 2
P. Herrera, PHI 1

1960 AMERICAN
R. Maris, NY 225
M. Mantle, NY . . . 222
B. Robinson, BAL . 211
M. Minoso, CHI . . 141
R. Hansen, BAL . . 110
A. Smith, CHI . . . 73
R. Sievers, CHI . . . 58
E. Battey, WAS . . . 57
B. Skowron, NY . . 56
J. Lemon, WAS . . . 36
T. Kubek, NY 29
C. Estrada, BAL . . 28
T. Williams, BOS . . 25
V. Wertz, BOS . . . 22
Y. Berra, NY 21
J. Gentile, BAL . . . 21
P. Runnels, BOS . . 18
N. Fox, CHI 11
V. Power, CLE . . . 11
S. Barber, BAL . . . 7
L. Aparicio, CHI . . 6
J. Perry, CLE 6
G. Staley, CHI . . . 4
J. Bunning, DET . . 3
G. Woodling, BAL . 3
H. Kuenn, CLE . . . 3
B. Daley, KC 3
M. Fornieles, BOS . 2
C. Maxwell, DET . . 2
J. Piersall, CLE . . . 2

1961 NATIONAL
F. Robinson, CIN . . 219
O. Cepeda, SF . . . 117
V. Pinson, CIN . . . 104
R. Clemente, PIT . . 81
J. Jay, CIN 74
W. Mays, SF 70
K. Boyer, SL 43
H. Aaron, MIL . . . 39
M. Wills, LA 36
J. O'Toole, CIN . . . 31
W. Spahn, MIL . . . 31
S. Miller, SF 26
W. Moon, LA 22
G. Altman, CHI . . . 9
J. Podres, LA 9
R. McMillan, MIL . . 8
E. Mathews, MIL . . 7
S. Koufax, LA 5
J. Roseboro, LA . . . 4
J. Brosnan, CIN . . . 3
J. Torre, MIL 2
L. Jackson, SL . . . 1
J. Lynch, CIN 1
B. Malkmus, PHI . . 1
D. Stuart, PIT 1

1961 AMERICAN
R. Maris, NY 202
M. Mantle, NY . . . 198
J. Gentile, BAL . . . 157
N. Cash, DET . . . 151
W. Ford, NY 102
L. Arroyo, NY 95
F. Lary, DET 53
R. Colavito, DET . . 51
A. Kaline, DET . . . 35
E. Howard, NY . . . 30
H. Killebrew, MIN . 29
L. Aparicio, CHI . . 16
J. Piersall, CLE . . . 10
S. Barber, BAL . . . 7
N. Siebern, KC . . . 7
D. Donovan, WAS . 5
B. Phillips, CLE . . . 5
B. Robinson, BAL . 4
C. Schilling, BOS . . 4
T. Morgan, LA . . . 3
A. Smith, CHI 3
Y. Berra, NY 2
B. Richardson, NY . 1
J. Romano, CLE . . 1
L. Thomas, LA . . . 1
H. Wilhelm, BAL . . 1

1962 NATIONAL
M. Wills, LA 209
W. Mays, SF 202
T. Davis, LA 175
F. Robinson, CIN . . 164
D. Drysdale, LA . . 85
H. Aaron, MIL . . . 72
J. Sanford, SF . . . 62
B. Purkey, CIN . . . 33
F. Howard, LA . . . 32
S. Musial, SL 19
J. Pagan, SF 13
D. Demeter, PHI . . 12
F. Alou, SF 10
B. White, SL 10
O. Cepeda, SF . . . 9
D. Groat, PIT 7
R. Clemente, PIT . . 6
E. Banks, CHI . . . 5
K. Boyer, SL 5
J. Callison, PHI . . . 5
H. Kuenn, SF 5
J. Marichal, SF . . . 4
B. Skinner, PIT . . . 4
J. Davenport, SF . . 3
S. Koufax, LA . . . 3
D. Crandall, MIL . . 2
A. Mahaffey, PHI . . 2
E. Roebuck, LA . . . 2
E. Kasko, CIN . . . 1
E. Mathews, MIL . . 1

1962 AMERICAN
M. Mantle, NY . . . 234
B. Richardson,
  NY 152
H. Killebrew, MIN . 99
L. Wagner, LA . . . 85
D. Donovan, CLE . . 64
A. Kaline, DET . . . 58
N. Siebern, KC . . . 53
R. Rollins, MIN . . . 47
B. Robinson, BAL . 41
F. Robinson, CHI . . 33
L. Thomas, LA . . . 32
T. Tresh, NY 30
B. Moran, LA 28
R. Terry, NY 19
C. Pascual, MIN . . 14
R. Colavito, DET . . 13
H. Aguirre, DET . . 10
J. Cunningham, CHI . 9
P. Runnels, BOS . . 9
C. Yastrzemski,
  BOS 9
V. Power, MIN . . . 8
D. Radatz, BOS . . . 8
J. Bunning, DET . . 8
Z. Versalles, MIN . . 8
J. Lumpe, KC 7
E. Bressoud, BOS . . 6
B. Rodgers, LA . . . 6
W. Ford, NY 6
R. Herbert, CHI . . . 5
C. Hinton, WAS . . . 5
F. Malzone, BOS . . 3
N. Cash, DET 3
A. Smith, CHI 1

1963 NATIONAL
S. Koufax, LA . . . 237
D. Groat, SL 190
H. Aaron, MIL . . . 135
R. Perranoski, LA . 130
W. Mays, SF 102
J. Gilliam, LA . . . 62
B. White, SL 56
T. Davis, LA 41
R. Santo, CHI . . . 41
V. Pinson, CIN . . . 32
J. Marichal, SF . . . 31
W. Spahn, MIL . . . 30
K. Boyer, SL 19
R. Clemente, PIT . . 12
J. Callison, PHI . . . 11
T. Taylor, PHI . . . 10
W. McCovey, SF . . 9
M. Wills, LA 9
D. Ellsworth, CHI . . 7
J. Maloney, CIN . . 7
D. Demeter, PHI . . 3
D. Drysdale, LA . . 3
T. Gonzalez, PHI . . 2

C. Flood, SL 1

1963 AMERICAN
E. Howard, NY . . . 248
A. Kaline, DET . . . 148
W. Ford, NY 125
H. Killebrew, MIN . 85
D. Radatz, BOS . . . 84
C. Yastrzemski,
  BOS 81
E. Battey, MIN . . . 57
G. Peters, CHI . . . 55
P. Ward, CHI 52
B. Richardson, NY . 43
T. Tresh, NY 38
C. Pascual, MIN . . 29
D. Stuart, BOS . . . 25
A. Pearson, LA . . . 22
B. Allison, MIN . . . 15
J. Bouton, NY . . . 11
M. Alvis, CLE 10
J. Pepitone, NY . . . 10
L. Wagner, LA . . . 9
S. Miller, BAL 9
W. Causey, KC . . . 5
R. Rollins, MIN . . . 5
L. Aparicio, BAL . . 3
B. Dailey, MIN . . . 3
J. Fregosi, LA 3
N. Fox, CHI 2
T. Kubek, NY 1
F. Robinson, CHI . . 1
N. Siebern, KC . . . 1

1964 NATIONAL
K. Boyer, SL 243
J. Callison, PHI . . . 187
B. White, SL . . . 106½
F. Robinson, CIN . . 98
J. Torre, MIL 85
W. Mays, SF 66
R. Allen, PHI 63
R. Santo, CHI . . . 59
R. Clemente, PIT . . 56
L. Brock, CHI-SL . . 40
C. Flood, SL 38
L. Jackson, CHI . . 26
J. Bunning, PHI . . 23
H. Aaron, MIL . . . 22
J. Marichal, SF . . . 14
S. Ellis, CIN 13
S. Koufax, LA . . . 7½
V. Pinson, CIN . . . 6
J. Hart, SF 6
B. Williams, CHI . . 6
R. Amaro, PHI . . . 5
T. Davis, LA 4
B. Gibson, SL . . . 2
C. Short, PHI 2
R. Hunt, NY 1
B. Schultz, SL . . . 1

1964 AMERICAN
B. Robinson, BAL . 269
M. Mantle, NY . . . 171
E. Howard, NY . . . 124
T. Oliva, MIN 99
D. Chance, LA . . . 97
P. Ward, CHI . . . 67½
B. Freehan, DET . . 44
G. Peters, CHI . . . 44
D. Radatz, BOS . . . 37
H. Killebrew, MIN . 31
B. Powell, BAL . . . 28
W. Bunker, BAL . . 23
J. Fregosi, LA . . . 21
A. Kaline, DET . . . 17
F. Robinson, CHI . . 14
R. Hansen, CHI . . . 10
B. Richardson, NY . 9
L. Wagner, CLE . . . 9
J. Pizarro, CHI . . . 8
H. Wilhelm, CHI . . 8
J. Horlen, CHI . . . 7
W. Ford, NY 7
B. Allison, MIN . . . 5
R. Colavito, KC . . . 5
M. Stottlemyre, NY . 4
R. Maris, NY 4
W. Causey, KC . . . 4
L. Aparicio, BAL . . 3½
D. Stuart, BOS . . . 3
E. Bressoud, BOS . . 2

C. Osteen, WAS....2
D. Wickersham, DET............2
D. Lock, WAS......1

1965 NATIONAL
W. Mays, SF....224
S. Koufax, LA...177
M. Wills, LA....164
D. Johnson, CIN..108
D. Drysdale, LA...77
P. Rose, CIN....67
H. Aaron, MIL....58
R. Clemente, PIT..56
J. Marichal, SF...26
W. McCovey, SF...25
J. Torre, MIL....23
B. Williams, CHI...21
F. Linzy, SF....16
W. Stargell, PIT....15
C. Flood, SL....13
J. Hart, SF....13
V. Law, PIT....12
F. Robinson, CIN...11
R. Santo, CHI....11
E. Mathews, MIL....8
L. Cardenas, CIN....7
J. Maloney, CIN....7
L. Lefebvre, LA....7
J. Callison, PHI....6
L. Johnson, LA....6
C. Rojas, PHI....5
J. Roseboro, LA....5
R. Allen, PHI....4
T. Cloninger, MIL....4
J. Gilliam, LA....3
J. Morgan, HOU....1

1965 AMERICAN
Z. Versalles, MIN..275
T. Oliva, MIN....174
B. Robinson, BAL..150
E. Fisher, CHI....122
R. Colavito, CLE...89
J. Grant, MIN....74
S. Miller, BAL....45
W. Horton, DET....24
T. Tresh, NY....23
E. Battey, MIN....22
D. Wert, DET....22
C. Yastrzemski, BOS....22
J. Hall, MIN....19
M. Stottlemyre, NY..17
H. Killebrew, MIN...15
A. Kaline, DET....9
J. Adair, BAL....7
R. Hansen, CHI....7
S. McDowell, CLE....7
B. Richardson, NY...6
V. Davalillo, CLE....5
J. Fregosi, CAL....5
F. Whitfield, CLE....5
B. Knoop, CAL....4
D. Buford, CHI....3
M. Mantle, NY....3
P. Richert, WAS....3
F. Robinson, CHI....3
B. Campaneris, KC...2
F. Howard, WAS....2
R. Kline, WAS....2
F. Mantilla, BOS....2
N. Cash, DET....1
T. Conigliaro, BOS...1

1966 NATIONAL
R. Clemente, PIT..218
S. Koufax, LA...208
W. Mays, SF....111
R. Allen, PHI....107
F. Alou, ATL....83
J. Marichal, SF....74
P. Regan, LA....66
H. Aaron, ATL....57
M. Alou, PIT....36
P. Rose, CIN....31
G. Alley, PIT....24
R. Santo, CHI....23
J. Roseboro, LA....22
O. Cepeda, SF-SL..22
W. Stargell, PIT....19
J. Torre, ATL....18
W. McCovey, SF....12

J. Lefebvre, LA....8
G. Perry, SF....8
C. Flood, SL....7
M. Wills, LA....5
R. Staub, HOU....4
B. Mazeroski, PIT....3
G. Beckert, CHI....3
J. Maloney, CIN....3
B. White, PHI....3
L. Brock, SL....2
B. Shaw, SF-NY....1
C. Short, PHI....1
W. Davis, LA....1

1966 AMERICAN
F. Robinson, BAL..280
B. Robinson, BAL..153
B. Powell, BAL....122
H. Killebrew, MIN...96
J. Kaat, MIN....84
T. Oliva, MIN....71
A. Kaline, DET....66
T. Agee, CHI....63
L. Aparicio, BAL...51
B. Campaneris, KC..36
S. Miller, BAL....27
N. Cash, DET....23
J. Aker, KC....22
E. Wilson, BOS-DET.......13
D. McLain, DET....12
B. Freehan, DET....9
A. Etchebarren, BAL..7
B. Knoop, CAL....6
M. Mantle, NY....5
T. Tresh, NY....5
J. Sanford, CAL....4
R. Reichardt, CAL....4
F. Valentine, WAS....4
W. Horton, DET....4
L. Wagner, CLE....4
P. Richert, WAS....3
J. Pepitone, NY....2
T. Conigliaro, BOS...1
S. Siebert, CLE....1
C. Yastrzemski, BOS....1
J. Fregosi, CAL....1

1967 NATIONAL
O. Cepeda, SL....280
T. McCarver, SL....136
R. Clemente, PIT..129
R. Santo, CHI....103
H. Aaron, ATL....79
M. McCormick, SF..73
L. Brock, SL....49
T. Perez, CIN....43
J. Javier, SL....41
P. Rose, CIN....40
J. Wynn, HOU....29
F. Jenkins, CHI....26
C. Flood, SL....24
E. Banks, CHI....22
N. Briles, SL....20
R. Staub, HOU....12
D. Hughes, SL....10
J. Hart, SF....10
R. Allen, PHI....9
T. Abernathy, CIN....7
C. Boyer, ATL....6
B. Gibson, SL....5
R. Hundley, CHI....5
J. Bunning, PHI....5
T. Seaver, NY....5
T. Davis, NY....3
G. Alley, PIT....3
T. Gonzalez, PHI....3
W. McCovey, SF....2

1967 AMERICAN
C. Yastrzemski, BOS..........275
H. Killebrew, MIN...161
B. Freehan, DET...137
J. Horlen, CHI....91
A. Kaline, DET....88
J. Lonborg, BOS...82
C. Tovar, MIN....70
J. Fregosi, CAL....70
G. Peters, CHI....37
G. Scott, BOS....33
F. Robinson, BAL...31

E. Wilson, DET....20
D. Chance, MIN....19
R. Hansen, CHI....13
J. Adair, CHI-BOS...11
P. Blair, BAL....9
R. Petrocelli, BOS...7
E. Howard, NY-BOS..7
T. Oliva, MIN....6
J. Kaat, MIN....4
P. Casanova, WAS...3
D. Mincher, CAL....3
M. Lolich, DET....2
M. Rojas, CAL....1

1968 NATIONAL
B. Gibson, SL....242
P. Rose, CIN....205
W. McCovey, SF...135
C. Flood, SL....116
J. Marichal, SF....93
L. Brock, SL....73
M. Shannon, SL....55
B. Williams, CHI...48
G. Beckert, CHI....40
F. Alou, ATL....33
M. Alou, PIT....32
H. Aaron, ATL....19
W. Mays, SF....14
E. Banks, CHI....14
J. Koosman, NY...14
J. Bench, CIN....11
P. Regan, LA-CHI....7
F. Jenkins, CHI....6
T. Perez, CIN....5
N. Briles, SL....4
D. Maxvill, SL....4
S. Blass, PIT....3
T. Haller, LA....3
R. Santo, CHI....2
C. Carroll, ATL-CIN..1
T. Helms, CIN....1

1968 AMERICAN
D. McLain, DET....280
B. Freehan, DET....161
K. Harrelson, BOS..........103
W. Horton, DET...102
D. McNally, BAL....78
L. Tiant, CLE....78
D. McAuliffe, DET..71
F. Howard, WAS....63
C. Yastrzemski, BOS..........50
M. Stottlemyre, NY..43
B. Campaneris, OAK..........39
R. White, NY....17
J. Northrup, DET....15
L. Aparicio, CHI....13
J. Fregosi, CAL....11
D. Buford, BAL....11
B. Robinson, BAL....8
R. Jackson, OAK....8
T. Oliva, MIN....5
D. Cater, OAK....5
M. Andrews, BOS....4
B. Powell, BAL....4
N. Cash, DET....3
C. Tovar, MIN....3
M. Stanley, DET....2
W. Wood, CHI....2
T. Uhlaender, MIN....1

1969 NATIONAL
W. McCovey, SF...265
T. Seaver, NY....243
H. Aaron, ATL....188
P. Rose, CIN....127
R. Santo, CHI....124
T. Agee, NY....89
C. Jones, NY....82
R. Clemente, PIT...51
P. Niekro, ATL....47
T. Perez, CIN....28
M. Wills, MON-LA..17
E. Banks, CHI....15
R. Carty, ATL....12
J. Bench, CIN....12
D. Kessinger, CHI...8
T. Gonzalez, SD-ATL....8
R. Hunt, SF....8

D. Menke, HOU....8
W. Granger, CIN....8
J. Wynn, HOU....8
W. Davis, LA....7
W. Stargell, PIT....7
J. Marichal, SF....6
B. Williams, CHI....6
J. Koosman, NY....6
J. Torre, SL....6
M. Alou, PIT....6
L. Dierker, HOU....6
T. Haller, LA....3
B. Gibson, SL....2
B. Bonds, SF....2
R. Hundley, CHI....2
L. May, CIN....2
T. Sizemore, LA....2
W. Parker, LA....2
J. Edwards, HOU....1
R. Staub, MON....1
O. Cepeda, ATL....1

1969 AMERICAN
H. Killebrew, MIN..294
B. Powell, BAL....227
F. Robinson, BAL..162
F. Howard, WAS...115
R. Jackson, OAK...110
D. McLain, DET....85
R. Petrocelli, BOS...71
M. Cuellar, BAL....55
J. Perry, MIN....40
R. Carew, MIN....30
P. Blair, BAL....28
L. Cardenas, MIN....27
R. Perranoski, MIN.25
D. McNally, BAL....25
T. Oliva, MIN....21
S. Bando, OAK....18
C. Tovar, MIN....9
M. Stottlemyre, NY..8
C. Yastrzemski, BOS..........8
E. Brinkman, WAS...7
J. Fregosi, CAL....7
R. Smith, BOS....6
D. Unser, WAS....5
B. Robinson, BAL....5
M. Epstein, WAS....4
M. Andrews, BOS....3
D. Bosman, WAS....3
B. Freehan, DET....3
T. Harper, SEA....2
A. Messersmith, CAL............2
R. Reese, MIN....2
K. Tatum, CAL....2
R. White, NY....2
M. Belanger, BAL....2
D. Green, OAK....1
J. Northrup, DET....1
L. Piniella, KC....1

1970 NATIONAL
J. Bench, CIN....326
B. Williams, CHI...218
T. Perez, CIN....149
B. Gibson, SL....110
W. Parker, LA....91
D. Giusti, PIT....72
P. Rose, CIN....54
J. Hickman, CHI...52
W. McCovey, SF....47
R. Carty, ATL....43
M. Sanguillen, PIT...36
R. Clemente, PIT...33
G. Perry, SF....24
W. Stargell, PIT....20
B. Tolan, CIN....17
H. Aaron, ATL....16
J. Torre, SL....15
T. Agee, NY....13
B. Harrelson, NY....10
F. Jenkins, CHI....8
J. Merritt, CIN....8
D. Kessinger, CHI....6
C. Gaston, SD....5
D. Johnson, PHI....4
L. Walker, PIT....4
C. Morton, MON....3
B. Robertson, PIT....3
T. Seaver, NY....2

W. Granger, CIN....1

1970 AMERICAN
B. Powell, BAL....234
T. Oliva, MIN....157
H. Killebrew, MIN..152
C. Yastrzemski, BOS..........136
F. Howard, WAS....91
T. Harper, MIL....78
B. Robinson, BAL...75
A. Johnson, CAL....70
J. Perry, MIN....63
F. Robinson, BAL...60
M. Cuellar, BAL....45
R. Perranoski, MIN.35
J. Fregosi, CAL....35
L. Aparicio, CHI....35
R. White, NY....25
D. McNally, BAL...22
S. McDowell, CLE...22
C. Tovar, MIN....16
T. Munson, NY....15
D. Buford, BAL....12
C. Wright, CAL....8
L. McDaniel, NY....8
R. Fosse, CLE....7
B. Campaneris, OAK............5
J. Palmer, BAL....4
R. Smith, BOS....3
S. Bando, OAK....1
T. Horton, CLE....1
B. Oliver, KC....1

1971 NATIONAL
J. Torre, SL....318
W. Stargell, PIT...222
H. Aaron, ATL....180
B. Bonds, SF....139
R. Clemente, PIT...87
M. Wills, LA....74
F. Jenkins, CHI....71
M. Sanguillen, PIT...49
T. Seaver, NY....46
A. Downing, LA....36
G. Beckert, CHI....35
L. May, CIN....28
L. Brock, SL....20
D. Giusti, PIT....16
W. McCovey, SF...15
T. Simmons, SL....13
W. Davis, LA....13
J. Johnson, SF....12
W. Mays, SF....11
R. Staub, MON....11
B. Williams, CHI....10
B. Harrelson, NY....4
B. Gibson, SL....3
R. Garr, ATL....1
D. Roberts, SD....1
P. Rose, CIN....1

1971 AMERICAN
V. Blue, OAK....268
S. Bando, OAK....182
F. Robinson, BAL..170
B. Robinson, BAL..163
M. Lolich, DET....155
F. Patek, KC....77
B. Murcer, NY....72
A. Otis, KC....67
W. Wood, CHI....54
T. Oliva, MIN....36
D. McNally, BAL....26
N. Cash, DET....21
B. Melton, CHI....18
R. Jackson, OAK....15
C. Rojas, KC....15
K. Sanders, MIL....13
P. Dobson, BAL....9
R. Smith, BOS....9
D. Johnson, BAL....8
M. Rettenmund, BAL............8
H. Killebrew, MIN....5
J. Palmer, BAL....5
L. Cardenas, MIN....5
M. Cuellar, BAL....4
C. Tovar, MIN....4
G. Scott, BOS....3
D. Buford, BAL....2
J. Hunter, OAK....1

G. Nettles, MIN....1

1972 NATIONAL
J. Bench, CIN....263
B. Williams, CHI...211
W. Stargell, PIT...201
J. Morgan, CIN...197
S. Carlton, PHI....124
C. Cedeno, HOU...112
A. Oliver, PIT....52
N. Colbert, SD....45
L. May, HOU....30
T. Simmons, SL....22
M. Marshall, MON...22
P. Rose, CIN....19
R. Clemente, PIT...16
C. Carroll, CIN....16
L. Brock, SL....13
H. Aaron, ATL....12
M. Sanguillen, PIT...12
S. Blass, PIT....9
R. Garr, ATL....7
G. Clines, PIT....6
B. Tolan, CIN....6
D. Baker, ATL....5
A. Mota, LA....3
D. Kingman, SF....3
T. McGraw, NY....2
R. Staub, NY....2
T. Seaver, NY....2
J. Cardenal, CHI....1
F. Jenkins, Chi....1
C. Speier, SF....1

1972 AMERICAN
R. Allen, CHI....321
J. Rudi, OAK....164
S. Lyle, NY....158
C. Fisk, BOS....96
B. Murcer, NY....89
G. Perry, CLE....88
W. Wood, CHI....78
L. Tiant, BOS....70½
E. Brinkman, DET....62
M. Lolich, DET....60
J. Hunter, OAK....57
J. Mayberry, KC....27
J. Palmer, BAL....21
B. Grich, BAL....16
R. Carew, MIN....16
B. Campaneris, OAK............11
M. Epstein, OAK....11
L. Aparicio, BOS..9½
R. Petrocelli, BOS....9
R. Jackson, OAK....9
C. May, CHI....6
G. Scott, MIL....6
D. Thompson, MIN....5
T. Harper, BOS....4
A. Kaline, DET....4
B. Freehan, DET....3
K. McMullen, CAL....3
B. Robinson, BAL....3
R. Smith, BOS....3
S. Bando, OAK....2
N. Ryan, CAL....2
A. Otis, KC....1
L. Piniella, KC....1

1973 NATIONAL
P. Rose, CIN....274
W. Stargell, PIT...250
B. Bonds, SF....174
J. Morgan, CIN...102
M. Marshall, MON..93
L. Brock, SL....65
T. Perez, CIN....59
T. Seaver, NY....57
K. Singleton, MON..52
J. Bench, CIN....41
C. Cedeno, HOU...39
H. Aaron, ATL....35
D. Johnson, ATL....34
T. Simmons, SL....20
T. McGraw, NY....17
F. Millan, NY....12
W. Davis, LA....12
D. Evans, ATL....11
L. May, HOU....9
T. Fuentes, SF....8
B. Watson, HOU....7
J. Ferguson LA....7

J. Cardenal, CHI 6
J. Billingham, CIN . . . 6
A. Oliver, PIT 6
R. Hunt, MON 5
R. Bryant, SF 5
G. Maddox, SF 3
B. Harrelson, NY 2
B. Williams, CHI 2
G. Luzinski, PHI 2
B. Russell, LA 1

1973 AMERICAN
R. Jackson, OAK . . 336
J. Palmer, BAL 172
A. Otis, KC 112
R. Carew, MIN 83
J. Hiller, DET 83
S. Bando, OAK 83
J. Mayberry, KC . . . 76
D. May, MIL 65
B. Murcer, NY 53
T. Davis, BAL 47
J. Hunter, OAK 47
T. Munson, NY 43
T. Harper, BOS . . . 33
G. Scott, MIL 25
O. Cepeda, BOS . . . 21
F. Robinson, CAL . . . 21
N. Ryan, CAL 20
C. Fisk, BOS 16
B. Grich, BAL 9
C. Yastrzemski,
  BOS 9
M. Belanger, BAL . . 8
D. Johnson, OAK . . . 8
J. Briggs, MIL 6
J. Coleman, DET . . . 6
C. Rojas, KC 5
B. Blyleven, MIN . . . 4
G. Perry, CLE 4
B. Campaneris,
  OAK 4
V. Blue, OAK 3
C. May, CHI 3
W. Horton, DET 3
B. North, OAK 3
P. Blair, BAL 2
D. Nelson, TEX 2
R. Allen, CHI 1

1974 NATIONAL
S. Garvey, LA 270
L. Brock, SL 233
M. Marshall, LA . . . 146
J. Bench, CIN 141
J. Wynn, LA 137
M. Schmidt, PHI . . 136
A. Oliver, PIT 87
J. Morgan, CIN 72
R. Zisk, PIT 54
W. Stargell, PIT . . . 43
R. Smith, SL 39
R. Garr, ATL 11
T. Simmons, SL 7
D. Cash, PHI 6
D. Concepcion, CIN . . 5
J. Billingham, CIN . . 4
C. Cedeno, HOU . . . 4
A. Hrabosky, SL . . . 4
A. Messersmith, LA . . 4
B. Capra, ATL 3
L. McGlothen, SL . . . 2
B. McBride, SL 2
R. Hebner, PIT 2
R. Stennett, PIT 2
B. Buckner, LA 1
R. Cey, LA 1

1974 AMERICAN
J. Burroughs, TEX . 248
J. Rudi, OAK . . . 161½
S. Bando, OAK . . 143½
R. Jackson, OAK . . 119
F. Jenkins, TEX . . . 118
J. Hunter, OAK . . . 107
R. Carew, MIN 70
E. Maddox, NY 59
B. Grich, BAL 49
M. Cuellar, BAL . . . 42
L. Tiant, BOS 41
B. Robinson, BAL . . 30
P. Blair, BAL 27
N. Ryan, CAL 24

B. Campaneris,
  OAK 23
R. Fingers, OAK . . 21
G. Perry, CLE 18
C. Yastrzemski,
  BOS 14
K. Henderson, CHI . 12
J. Hiller, DET 11
L. Randle, TEX 10
B. Murcer, NY 10
L. Piniella, NY 8
R. Allen, CHI 8
S. Lyle, NY 7
T. Munson, NY 6
T. Davis, BAL 6
M. Belanger, BAL . . 6
D. Money, MIL 5
T. Murphy, MIL 3
H. McRae, KC 3
S. Busby, KC 3
G. Scott, MIL 2
P. Dobson, NY 1

1975 NATIONAL
J. Morgan, CIN . 321½
G. Luzinski, PHI . . 154
D. Parker, PIT . . . 120
J. Bench, CIN . . . 117
P. Rose, CIN 114
T. Simmons, SL . . 103
W. Stargell, PIT . . 69
A. Hrabosky, SL . . 66
T. Seaver, NY 65
R. Jones, SD 54
S. Garvey, LA 50
B. Madlock, CHI . . 45
D. Cash, PHI 26
R. Staub, NY 20
T. Perez, CIN 18
M. Schmidt, PHI . . 16
M. Sanguillen, PIT . 16
R. Cey, LA 11½
D. Kingman, NY . . . 9
B. Watson, HOU . . . 8
L. Brock, SL 6
L. Bowa, PHI 3
J. Reuss, PIT 2
A. Messersmith, LA . 1
W. Montanez,
  PHI-SF 1

1975 AMERICAN
F. Lynn, BOS 326
J. Mayberry, KC . . 157
J. Rice, BOS 154
R. Fingers, OAK . . 129
R. Jackson, OAK . . 118
J. Palmer, BAL 82
T. Munson, NY 69
G. Scott, MIL . . . 64½
R. Carew, MIN . . 54½
K. Singleton, BAL . . 44
G. Brett, KC 37½
J. Hunter, NY 31
R. Burleson, BOS . . 28
C. Washington,
  OAK 22
T. Harrah, TEX . . . 16
M. Torrez, BAL . . . 12
R. Gossage, CHI . . 11
P. Lindblad, OAK . . . 7
G. Tenace, OAK . . . 7
B. Powell, CLE . . . 6½
D. Baylor, BAL 6
B. Campaneris,
  OAK 6
B. Lee, BOS 5
J. Todd, OAK 5
D. Doyle, BOS 5
R. Wise, BOS 4
J. Rudi, OAK 3
J. Kaat, CHI 2
L. May, BAL 2
B. Bonds, NY 1
C. Yastrzemski,
  BOS 1

1976 NATIONAL
J. Morgan, CIN . . . 311
G. Foster, CIN . . . 221
M. Schmidt, PHI . . 179
P. Rose, CIN 131
G. Maddox, PHI . . . 98

B. Madlock, CHI . . 51
S. Garvey, LA . . . 51
G. Luzinski, PHI . . 49
K. Griffey, CIN . . . 49
R. Jones, SD 48
B. Watson, HOU . . 38
A. Oliver, PIT 30
R. Eastwick, CIN . . 26
J. Koosman, NY . . 20
S. Carlton, PHI . . . 16
D. Cash, PHI 15
J. Richard, HOU . . 12
R. Monday, CHI . . 11
D. Kingman, NY . . 11
D. Parker, PIT . . . 10
B. Robinson, PIT . . 9
D. Sutton, LA 7
R. Cey, LA 6
W. Montanez,
  SF-ATL 4
L. Brock, SL 3
C. Cedeno, HOU . . 3
C. Geronimo, CIN . 3
R. Zisk, PIT 3
L. Bowa, PHI 1

1976 AMERICAN
T. Munson, NY . . . 304
G. Brett, KC 217
M. Rivers, NY . . 179½
H. McRae, KC . . . 99
C. Chambliss,
  NY 71½
R. Carew, MIN . . . 71
A. Otis, KC 58
B. Campbell, MIN . 56
L. May, BAL 51
J. Palmer, BAL . . . 47
M. Fidrych, DET . . 41
J. Rudi, OAK 35
S. Bando, OAK . . . 31
C. Yastrzemski,
  BOS 26
F. Tanana, CAL . . . 19
R. Jackson, BAL . . 17
G. Nettles, NY . . . 17
G. Tenace, OAK . . 13
R. Fingers, OAK . . 12
V. Blue, OAK 10
E. Figueroa, NY . . . 9
S. Lyle, NY 8
R. LeFlore, DET . . . 6
M. Littell, KC 5
R. Carty, CLE 5
R. White, NY 3
L. Tiant, BOS 3
J. Mayberry, KC . . 1
B. Wynegar, MIN . . 1

1977 NATIONAL
G. Foster, CIN . . . 291
G. Luzinski, PHI . . 255
D. Parker, PIT . . . 156
R. Smith, LA 112
S. Carlton, PHI . . . 100
S. Garvey, LA 98
B. Sutter, CHI 68
R. Cey, LA 60
T. Simmons, SL . . . 58
M. Schmidt, PHI . . 48
B. Robinson, PIT . . 34
T. John, LA 33
G. Templeton, SL . . 20
B. Sutter, CHI 17
P. Rose, CIN 15
J. Burroughs, ATL . . 9
A. Oliver, PIT 9
J. Candelaria, PIT . . 8
R. Stennett, PIT . . . 7
W. McCovey, SF . . . 5
J. Bench, CIN 3
R. Reuschel, CHI . . . 3
E. Valentine, MON . . 3
T. McGraw, PHI 2
L. Bowa, PHI 1
T. Seaver, NY-CIN . . 1

1977 AMERICAN
R. Carew, MIN . . . 273
A. Cowens, KC . . . 217
K. Singleton, BAL . 200
J. Rice, BOS 163
G. Nettles, NY . . . 112

S. Lyle, NY 79
T. Munson, NY 70
R. Jackson, NY 67
C. Fisk, BOS 67
B. Campbell, BOS . . 65
M. Rivers, NY 59
L. Hisle, MIN 54
G. Brett, KC 51
R. Zisk, CHI 34
J. Sundberg, TEX . . 30
B. Bonds, CAL 28
C. Yastrzemski,
  BOS 25
R. Guidry, NY 11
J. Palmer, BAL 9
R. LeFlore, DET 7
J. Thompson, DET . . 6
R. Burleson, BOS . . 5
B. Hobson, BOS . . . 4
N. Ryan, CAL 3
G. Scott, BOS 3
H. McRae, KC 3
L. Bostock, MIN . . . 2
T. Johnson, MIN . . . 2
O. Chambliss, NY . . 1
O. Gamble, CHI . . . 1
D. Leonard, KC . . . 1

1978 NATIONAL
D. Parker, PIT . . . 320
S. Garvey, LA . . . 194
L. Bowa, PHI . . . 189
R. Smith, LA 164
J. Clark, SF 107
G. Foster, CIN . . . 104
G. Luzinski, PHI . . 48
G. Perry, SD 45
W. Stargell, PIT . . 39
D. Winfield, SD . . 37
P. Rose, CIN 35
V. Blue, SF 33
K. Tekulve, PIT . . 23
R. Fingers, SD . . . 16
B. Hooton, LA . . . 15
D. Lopes, LA 12
P. Niekro, ATL 8
B. Buckner, CHI . . . 8
J. Burroughs, ATL . . 7
B. Sutter, CHI 5
G. Maddox, PHI . . . 4
E. Cabell, HOU . . . 2
B. Boone, PHI 1

1978 AMERICAN
J. Rice, BOS 352
R. Guidry, NY . . . 291
L. Hisle, MIL 201
A. Otis, KC 90
R. Staub, DET . . . 88
G. Nettles, NY . . . 86
D. Baylor, CAL . . . 51
E. Murray, BAL . . 50
C. Fisk, BOS 49
D. Porter, KC 48
R. Carew, MIN . . . 46
M. Caldwell, MIL . . 41
R. Gossage, NY . . 39
A. Oliver, TEX . . 26½
J. Sundberg, TEX . 24
R. LeFlore, DET . . 21
R. Jackson, NY . . . 18
C. Yastrzemski,
  BOS 17
G. Brett, KC 14
A. Thornton,
  CLE 12½
L. Piniella, NY . . . 11
T. Munson, NY 9
L. Bostock, CAL . . . 8
L. Gura, KC 8
F. Lynn, BOS 6
M. Rivers, NY 6
B. Stanley, BOS . . . 6
D. LaRoche, CAL . . 6
D. Money, MIL 5
W. Randolph, NY . . 5
D. Eckersley, BOS . . 4
H. McRae, KC 4
L. Roberts, SEA . . . 3
R. Gale, KC 2
K. Singleton, BAL . . 2
R. Burleson, BOS . . 1
F. Tanana, CAL . . . 1

1979 NATIONAL
W. Stargell, PIT . . 216
K. Hernandez, SL . 216
D. Winfield, SD . . 155
L. Parrish, MON . . 128
R. Knight, CIN . . . 82
J. Niekro, HOU . . 75½
B. Sutter, CHI . . . 69
K. Tekulve, PIT . . 64
D. Concepcion,
  CIN 63
D. Parker, PIT . . . 56
D. Kingman, CHI . . 53
G. Foster, CIN . . . 34
M. Schmidt, PHI . . 32
S. Garvey, LA . . . 30
O. Moreno, PIT . . 23
P. Rose, PHI 23
G. Carter, MON . . 15
B. Madlock,
  SF-PIT 14
J. Richard, HOU . . 12
P. Niekro, ATL . . 11½
J. Sambito, HOU . . 9
T. Seaver, CIN . . . 9
J. Bench, CIN 7
A. Dawson, MON . . 6
G. Templeton, SL . . 5
G. Matthews, ATL . . 4
D. Collins, CIN . . . 3
B. Horner, ATL . . . 1

1979 AMERICAN
D. Baylor, CAL . . . 347
K. Singleton, BAL . 241
G. Brett, KC 226
F. Lynn, BOS . . . 160½
J. Rice, BOS 124
M. Flanagan, BAL . 100
G. Thomas, MIL . . 87
B. Grich, CAL 58
D. Porter, KC 52
B. Bell, TEX 48
E. Murray, BAL . . 25½
J. Kern, TEX 25
M. Marshall, MIN . . 25
B. Downing, CAL . . 24
S. Lezcano, MIL . . 18
R. Smalley, MIN . . 16
W. Wilson, KC . . . 15
S. Kemp, DET . . . 15
M. Clear, CAL . . . 12
P. Molitor, MIL 8
R. Burleson, BOS . . 7
T. John, NY 5
C. Cooper, MIL . . . 4
R. Jackson, NY . . . 3
W. Horton, SEA . . . 3
D. Ford, CAL 1
R. Guidry, NY 1
M. Hargrove, CLE . . 1

1980 NATIONAL
M. Schmidt, PHI . . 336
G. Carter, MON . . 193
J. Cruz, HOU 166
D. Baker, LA 138
S. Carlton, PHI . . . 134
S. Garvey, LA . . . 131
A. Dawson, MON . . 72
G. Hendrick, SL . . 50
B. Horner, ATL . . . 42
B. McBride, PHI . . 32
K. Hernandez, SL . 29
D. Murphy, ATL . . 23
C. Cedeno, HOU . . 14
J. Bibby, PIT 11
B. Buckner, CHI . . 11
T. McGraw, PHI . . 10
J. Bench, CIN 7
J. Clark, SF 6
J. Niekro, HOU . . . 3
M. Easler, PIT 2
J. Reuss, LA 2
K. Griffey, CIN 1
R. LeFlore, MON . . 1
R. Richards, SD . . . 1
R. Scott, MON . . . 1

1980 AMERICAN
G. Brett, KC 335
R. Jackson, NY . . 234
R. Gossage, NY . . 218

W. Wilson, KC . . . 169
C. Cooper, MIL . . . 160
E. Murray, BAL . . 106
R. Cerone, NY . . . 77
D. Quisenberry,
  KC 76½
S. Stone, BAL . . . 53
R. Henderson,
  OAK 51
A. Oliver, TEX . . 31½
T. Armas, OAK . . 29
A. Bumbry, BAL . . 27
B. Oglivie, MIL . . 27
W. Randolph, NY . 10
M. Norris, OAK . . 10
R. Yount, MIL 8
M. Rivers, TEX . . . 7
B. Bell, TEX 7
A. Trammell, DET . 6
K. Singleton, BAL . 4
T. Perez, BOS . . . 2
M. Dilone, CLE . . 2
F. Lynn, BOS 1
J. Wathan, KC . . . 1

1981 NATIONAL
M. Schmidt, PHI . 321
A. Dawson, MON . 215
G. Foster, CIN . . . 146
D. Concepcion,
  CIN 108
F. Valenzuela, LA . 90
G. Carter, MON . . 77
D. Baker, LA 65
B. Sutter, SL 59
S. Carlton, PHI . . . 41
T. Seaver, CIN . . . 35
P. Rose, PHI 35
B. Buckner, CHI . . 35
G. Matthews, PHI . 31
J. Cruz, HOU 25
G. Hendrick, SL . . 25
N. Ryan, HOU . . . 23
B. Madlock, PIT . . 20
A. Howe, HOU . . . 16
T. Raines, MON . . 15
R. Camp, ATL 9
K. Hernandez, SL . . 9
T. Herr, SL 7
G. Minton, SF 4
W. Cromartie, MON . 3
S. Garvey, LA 1
M. May, SF 1

1981 AMERICAN
R. Fingers, MIL . . 319
R. Henderson,
  OAK 308
D. Evans, BOS . . 140
T. Armas, OAK . . 139
E. Murray, BAL . . 137
C. Lansford, BOS . 109
D. Winfield, NY . . 98
C. Cooper, MIL . . 96
R. Gossage, NY . . 62
T. Paciorek, SEA . 46
D. Murphy, OAK . . 45
K. Gibson, DET . . 40
S. McCatty, OAK . 22
B. Grich, CAL . . . 19
J. Morris, DET . . . 17
A. Oliver, TEX . . . 8
R. Yount, MIL 7
B. Bell, TEX 7
B. Almon, CHI . . . 6
J. Mumphrey, NY . 5
M. Hargrove, CLE . 4
A. Trammell, DET . 4
K. Singleton, BAL . 3
S. Kemp, DET . . . 3
D. Martinez, BAL . 3
G. Luzinski, CHI . . 3
D. Stieb, TOR . . . 1
G. Brett, KC 1

1982 NATIONAL
D. Murphy, ATL . . 283
L. Smith, SL 218
P. Guerrero, LA . . 175
A. Oliver, MON . . 175
B. Sutter, SL 134
M. Schmidt, PHI . . 54
J. Clark, SF 53

G. Minton, SF 44
S. Carlton, PHI 41
B. Buckner, CHI ...38
B. Madlock, PIT 37
G. Carter, MON 35
O. Smith, SL 25
G. Hendrick, SL ...20
T. Kennedy, SD ...20
J. Morgan, SF 17
K. Hernandez, SL ..12
J. Thompson, PIT ..12
G. Garber, ATL......6
J. Andujar, SL......6
F. Valenzuela, LA ...3
A. Dawson, MON ...3
C. Chambliss, ATL ...2
G. Matthews, PHI ..2
R. Knight, HOU 1

1982 AMERICAN
R. Yount, MIL 385
E. Murray, BAL ...228
D. DeCinces, CAL ..178
H. McRae, KC ...175
C. Cooper, MIL ...152
R. Jackson, CAL ...107
D. Evans, BOS 57
G. Thomas, MIL . 44½
D. Quisenberry, KC .39
R. Henderson, OAK 38
D. Winfield, NY ...33
P. Molitor, MIL ...29½
L. Parrish, DET ...26
B. Downing, CAL...22
W. Wilson, KC 16
R. Fingers, MIL 12
B. Boone, CAL 12
P. Vuckovich, MIL ...11
J. Rice, BOS 10
T. Harrah, CLE......9
H. Baines, CHI......9
G. Brett, KC......9
D. Baylor, CAL......8
A. Thornton, CLE ...8
B. Stanley, BOS 6
J. Palmer, BAL......5
D. Garcia, TOR 5
R. Carew, CAL......5
B. Caudill, SEA 4
B. Bell, TEX........3
C. Ripken, BAL 3
C. Lansford, BOS ...1
R. Sutcliffe, CLE 1
G. Ward, MIN.......1

1983 NATIONAL
D. Murphy, ATL ...318
A. Dawson, MON .213
M. Schmidt, PHI ..191
P. Guerrero, LA ..182
T. Raines, MON 83
J. Cruz, HOU 76
D. Thon, HOU 67
B. Madlock, PIT 45
A. Holland, PHI 42
T. Kennedy, SD 37
G. Hendrick, SL 33
T. Pena, PIT 25
J. Denny, PHI 24
M. Soto, CIN 16
D. Evans, SF 16
R. Ramirez, ATL ...15
J. Orosco, NY 14
L. Smith, CHI 8½
A. Oliver, MON 3
J. Leonard, SF......2
L. Smith, SL......1½
J. Davis, CHI 1
K. Hernandez, SL-NY 1
B. Horner, ATL......1

O. Smith, SL 1

1983 AMERICAN
C. Ripken, BAL ...322
E. Murray, BAL ...290
C. Fisk, CHI 209
J. Rice, BOS 150
C. Cooper, MIL ...123
D. Quisenberry, KC 107½
D. Winfield, NY ...85
L. Whitaker, DET ...84
L. Parrish, DET ...66
H. Baines, CHI.....49
W. Upshaw, TOR . 41½
W. Boggs, BOS ...25
L. Hoyt, CHI..... 24½
L. Moseby, TOR ...21
B. Stanley, BOS . 11½
A. Trammell, DET...11
G. Luzinski, CHI ...9
R. Yount, MIL......8
T. Simmons, MIL ...4
R. Dotson, CHI ... 3½
R. Law, CHI 2
N. Guidry, NY......2
J. Morris, DET......2
J. Cruz, SEA-CHI...1
R. Henderson, OAK...1
G. Wright, TEX.....1
T. Martinez, BAL ... ½

1984 NATIONAL
R. Sandberg, CHI .326
K. Hernadez, NY ..195
T. Gwynn, SD.....184
R. Sutcliffe, CHI ..151
G. Matthews, CHI ..70
B. Sutter, SL......67
M. Schmidt, PHI . 55½
J. Cruz, HOU 53
D. Murphy, ATL . 52½
J. Davis, CHI 49
T. Raines, MON 41
L. Durham, CHI ...38
R. Gossage, SD....34
G. Carter, MON ...32
D. Gooden, NY 28
A. Wiggins, SD 14
R. Cey, CHI 6
K. McReynolds, SD ..6
B. Dernier, CHI 6
S. Garvey, SD 5
B. Brenly, SF.......1
J. Samuel, PHI......1
J. Leonard, SF......1

1984 AMERICAN
W. Hernandez, DET 306
K. Hrbek, MIN ...247
D. Quisenberry, KC 235
E. Murray, BAL ...197
D. Mattingly, NY ...113
K. Gibson, DET 96
T. Armas, BOS . 87½
D. Winfield, NY ...83
A. Trammell, DET 76½
W. Wilson, KC 61
D. Evans, BOS 39
A. Davis, SEA 26
J. Rice, BOS 10
H. Baines, CHI.....10
D. Kingman, OAK ..10
L. Parrish, DET 8
W. Upshaw, TOR ...8
B. Downing, CAL...6
S. Balboni, KC 5

A. Thornton, CLE ...5
J. Bell, TOR 5
B. Bell, TEX 4
D. Stieb, TOR 4
L. Moseby, TOR ...4
J. Beniquez, CAL ...2
M. Boddicker, BAL ..2
D. Alexander, TOR...1
C. Ripken, BAL 1

1985 NATIONAL
W. McGee, SL 280
D. Parker, CIN ...220
P. Guerrero, LA ...208
D. Gooden, NY ...162
T. Herr, SL 119
G. Carter, NY 116
D. Murphy, ATL 63
K. Hernandez, NY ..61
J. Tudor, SL 61
J. Clark, SL 20
V. Coleman, SL 16
T. Raines, MON ...15
R. Sandberg, CHI ..14
M. Marshall, LA ...11
H. Brooks, MON ...11
O. Hershiser, LA 9
K. Moreland, CHI...8
O. Smith, SL 5
M. Scioscia, LA 5
J. Reardon, MON ...4
J. Cruz, HOU 2
B. Doran, HOU 2
M. Duncan, LA 1
T. Gwynn, SD......1
F. Valenzuela, LA ...1
G. Wilson, PHI 1

1985 AMERICAN
D. Mattingly, NY ..367
G. Brett, KC 274
R. Henderson, NY .174
W. Boggs, BOS ...159
E. Murray, BAL ...130
D. Moore, CAL 96
J. Barfield, TOR 88
J. Bell, TOR 84
H. Baines, CHI.....49
B. Saberhagen, KC .45
D. Quisenberry, KC .39
D. Winfield, NY ...35
C. Fisk, CHI 29
Dr. Evans, DET 17
R. Guidry, NY......15
P. Bradley, SEA ...12
C. Ripken, BAL 9
K. Gibson, DET 7
S. Balboni, KC......6
T. Henke, TOR 5
D. Lamp, TOR 3
K. Puckett, MIN 3
D. Alexander, TOR...3
D. Garcia, TOR 2
R. Gedman, BOS ...1

1986 NATIONAL
M. Schmidt, PHI . 287
G. Davis, HOU ...231
G. Carter, NY 181
K. Hernandez, NY .179
D. Parker, CIN ...144
T. Raines, MON 99
K. Bass, HOU 73
V. Hayes, PHI......41
T. Gwynn, SD......34
M. Scott, HOU 33
B. Doran, HOU 32
E. Davis, CIN 21
S. Sax, LA 13
R. Knight, NY......9

M. Krukow, SF......8
T. Worrell, SL......7
R. McDowell, NY ...5
D. Smith, HOU 5
F. Valenzuela, LA ...4
L. Dykstra, NY 4
B. Ojeda, NY 2
D. Murphy, ATL 2
C. Maldonado, SF ..2

1986 AMERICAN
R. Clemens, BOS . 339
D. Mattingly, NY ..258
J. Rice, BOS 241
J. Bell, TOR 125
J. Barfield, TOR ...107
K. Puckett, MIN ...105
W. Boggs, BOS 87
W. Joyner, CAL 74
J. Carter, CLE 72
D. Righetti, NY.....71
D. DeCinces, CAL ..56
M. Witt, CAL 34
D. Baylor, BOS 32
T. Fernandez, TOR .17
T. Higuera, MIL 7
G. Gaetti, MIN 6
P. O'Brien, TEX 5
S. Fletcher, TEX 5
M. Barrett, BOS 5
J. Canseco, OAK 3
J. Presley, SEA 2
J. Schofield, CAL ...1

1987 NATIONAL
A. Dawson, CHI...269
O. Smith, SL 193
J. Clark, SL 186
T. Wallach, MON ..165
W. Clark, SF 128
D. Strawberry, NY ..95
T. Raines, MON 80
T. Gwynn, SD......75
E. Davis, CIN 73
H. Johnson, NY 42
D. Murphy, ATL ...34
V. Coleman, SL 20
J. Samuel, PHI.....19
M. Schmidt, PHI ...13
P. Guerrero, LA 12
S. Bedrosian, PHI ...6
M. Thompson, PHI ..4
B. Doran, HOU 1
T. Pendleton, SL 1

1987 AMERICAN
J. Bell, TOR 332
A. Trammell, DET . 311
K. Puckett, MIN ...201
Dw. Evans, BOS ..127
P. Molitor, MIL ...125
M. McGwire, OAK .109
D. Mattingly, NY ...92
T. Fernandez, TOR .79
W. Boggs, BOS 64
G. Gaetti, MIN 47
J. Reardon, MIN ...37
Dr. Evans, DET 21
D. Alexander, DET . 17
T. Henke, TOR 17
W. Joyner, CAL 17
K. Hrbek, MIN 11
D. Tartabull, KC ...10
R. Yount, MIL.......8
R. Clemens, BOS ...7
J. Morris, DET......5
K. Seitzer, KC......5
R. Sierra, TEX......5
J. Canseco, OAK ...4
M. Nokes, DET 1

1988 NATIONAL
K. Gibson, LA ...272
D. Strawberry, NY .236
K. McReynolds, NY 162
A. Van Slyke, PIT ..160
W. Clark, SF 135
O. Hershiser, LA ..111
A. Galarraga, MON 105
G. Davis, HOU 72
D. Jackson, CIN ...41
D. Cone, NY 37
T. Gwynn, SD......29
J. Franco, CIN 23
E. Davis, CIN 14
B. Bonilla, PIT 7
A. Dawson, CHI.....6
R. Myers, NY 3
B. Butler, SF 2
S. Sax, LA 1

1988 AMERICAN
J. Canseco, OAK ..392
M. Greenwell, BOS 242
K. Puckett, MIN ...219
D. Winfield, NY ...164
D. Eckersley, OAK .156
W. Boggs, BOS ...107
A. Trammell, DET ..62
P. Molitor, MIL 50
Dw. Evans, BOS ...49
F. Viola, MIN 39
R. Yount, MIL......34
G. Brett, KC.......29
D. Henderson, OAK .28
B. Hurst, BOS 15
D. Jones, CLE 11
J. Reardon, MIN ...11
F. McGriff, TOR 9
R. Henderson, NY ...8
M. McGwire, OAK ...6
J. Carter, CLE 5
L. Smith, BOS 4
G. Gaetti, MIN 3
D. Plesac, MIL 3
D. Stewart, OAK 3
J. Franco, CLE 2
T. Fernandez, TOR ..1

1989 NATIONAL
K. Mitchell, SF ...314
W. Clark, SF 225
P. Guerrero. SL ...190
R. Sandberg, CHI .157
H. Johnson, NY ...153
M. Davis, SD 76
G. Davis, HOU 64
T. Gwynn, SD......57
E. Davis, CIN 44
M. Williams, CHI ...41
L. Smith, ATL......34
J. Clark, SD 16
J. Walton, CHI 14
M. Grace, CHI 9
M. Scott, HOU 6
B. Bonilla, PIT 5
B. Butler, SF 3
T. Raines, MON 3
M. Thompson, SL ...3
G. Garrelts, SF 2

1989 AMERICAN
R. Yount, MIL.....256
R. Sierra, TEX 228
C. Ripken, BAL ...216
J. Bell, TOR 205
D. Eckersley, OAK .116
F. McGriff, TOR 96

K. Puckett, MIN 84
B. Saberhagen, KC .82
R. Henderson, NY-OAK 67
B. Jackson, KC.....46
D. Parker, OAK 44
G. Olson, BAL 35
B. Blyleven, CAL ...32
D. Stewart, OAK ...30
D. Mattingly, NY ...25
J. Carter, CLE 23
C. Lansford, OAK ..20
N. Esasky, BOS 19
T. Fernandez, TOR ..9
M. Moore, OAK 6
W. Boggs, BOS 3
S. Sax, NY 3
A. Davis, SEA 2
N. Ryan, TEX.......2
C. Davis, CAL 1
M. McGwire, OAK ..1
M. Wilson, TOR 1

1990 NATIONAL
B. Bonds, PIT 331
B. Bonilla, PIT 212
D. Strawberry, NY .167
R. Sandberg, CHI .151
E. Murray, LA 123
M. Williams, SF 95
B. Larkin, CIN 82
D. Drabek, PIT 59
L. Dykstra, PHI 41
T. Wallach, MON ...36
K. Mitchell, SF 20
E. Davis, CIN 12
C. Sabo, CIN 11
R. Gant, ATL 10
D. Gooden, NY 10
R. Martinez, LA 9
J. Carter, SD 7
R. Myers, CIN 7
P. O'Neill, CIN 6
J. Rijo, CIN 6
A. Dawson, CHI.....6
D. Magadan, NY ...4
B. Santiago, SD 3
B. Butler, SF 2
D. Justice, ATL 2
P. Guerrero, SL 2
K. Daniels, LA 1
A. Van Slyke, PIT ...1

1990 AMERICAN
R. Henderson, OAK 317
C. Fielder, DET ...286
R. Clemens, BOS . 212
K. Gruber, TOR ...175
B. Thigpen, CHI...170
D. Eckersley, OAK .112
G. Brett, KC.......60
D. Stewart, OAK ...56
B. Welch, OAK 54
F. McGriff, TOR 30
M. McGwire, OAK ..29
J. Canseco, OAK ...26
E. Burks, BOS 25
R. Palmeiro, TEX ...22
C. Fisk, CHI 16
D. Parker, MIL......11
O. Guillen, CHI.....10
J. Reed, BOS 9
K. Griffey, Jr., SEA ..7
A. Trammell, DET ...7
T. Pena, BOS 6
W. Boggs, BOS 5
D. Jones, CLE 3
C. Ripken, BAL 2
N. Ryan, TEX.......1
D. Stieb, Tor........1

Rookie of the Year Award: History

The Chicago chapter of the Baseball Writers' Association of America (BBWAA) established an award recognizing the major leagues' top rookie following the 1940 season, selecting Lou Boudreau for the honor. This procedure continued for six more years before going national. The subsequent winners of the Chicago chapter's award were Pete Reiser (1941), Johnny Beazley (1942), Bill Johnson (1943), Bill Voiselle (1944), Boo Ferriss (1945), and Eddie Waitkus (1946).

The Sporting News began naming its own Rookie of

the Year in 1946, with the selection of Del Ennis. Their award has competed with that of the BBWAA ever since. In 1949 they began recognizing a winner from each league and in 1957 they started selecting both a rookie player and rookie pitcher of the year for each league.

In 1947 thirty-three baseball writers were asked to name five rookies in order of preference, with votes distributed on a 5–4–3–2–1 basis. Thus, Jackie Robinson became the first nationally recognized winner of the BBWAA Rookie of the Year Award, or the J. Louis Comiskey Memorial Award, as it was called. During the 1987 Hall of Fame induction ceremony, Commissioner Peter Ueberroth announced that, hereafter, the Rookie of the Year Award would be officially known as the Jackie Robinson Award.

In 1948 forty-eight writers took part in the award, this time naming only a single candidate on each ballot. In 1949 the BBWAA began the process of choosing a top rookie in each league. Three writers from each league city, the same men who decided on the MVP Awards, participated in the voting. Voters were free to use their individual judgments as to the eligibility of rookie candidates, which created some problems, especially in 1950 when Al Rosen, and his league-leading 37 homers, was ignored by Rookie of the Year voters. Apparently they felt that Rosen's 58 previous major league at-bats were tantamount to veteran status, while winner Walt Dropo's 41 previous at-bats were not.

In 1957 formal guidelines were finally established for determining rookie status. A player could not have accumulated more than 75 at-bats, 45 innings pitched, or have been on a major league roster between May 15 and September 1 of any previous season. Shortly after, the guidelines were changed to 90 at-bats, 45 innings pitched or 45 days on a major league roster before September 1. Finally, in 1971, the guidelines were set at 130 at-bats, 50 innings, or 45 days on a roster.

There were several instances, especially in the early days of the award, in which some Rookie of the Year voters didn't bother to exercise their franchise. In 1961, as with the MVP Award, the number of voters was reduced from three to two writers from each league city.

Following two tie votes in four years (1976 NL, 1979 AL), the writers adopted the system used in Cy Young Award balloting: naming three rookies on each ballot, in order of preference, with votes distributed on a 5–3–1 basis. This system began in 1980.

The maximum possible point total available to Rookie of the Year candidates was 165 in 1947, 48 in 1948, and 24 in each league in 1949–60. In the National League, it was 16 in 1961, 20 in 1962–68, 24 in 1969–79, and 120 from 1980 to the present. In the American League, it was 20 in 1961–68, 24 in 1969–76, 28 in 1977–79, and 140 from 1980 to the present.

There have been eight unanimous Rookie of the Year selections since 1947: Frank Robinson (NL, 1956), Orlando Cepeda (NL, 1958), Willie McCovey (NL, 1959), Carlton Fisk (AL, 1972), Vince Coleman (NL, 1985), Benito Santiago (NL, 1987), Mark McGwire (AL, 1987), and Sandy Alomar (AL, 1990).

Rookie of the Year Award

1947
J. Robinson, BKN (NL) 129
L. Jansen, NY (NL) 105
F. Shea, NY (AL) 67
F. Fain, PHI (AL) 43
F. Baumholtz, CIN (NL) 42
(Rest of voting unknown)

1948
A. Dark, BOS (NL) . . 27
G. Bearden, CLE (AL) 8
R. Ashburn, PHI (NL) . 7
L. Brissie, PHI (AL) . . 3
B. Goodman, BOS (AL) 3

1949 NATIONAL
D. Newcombe, BKN 21
D. Crandall, BOS 3

1949 AMERICAN
R. Sievers, SL 10
A. Kellner, PHI 5
G. Coleman, NY 4
B. Kuzava, CHI 1
J. Groth, DET 1
M. Garcia, CLE 1

1950 NATIONAL
S. Jethroe, BOS . . . 11
B. Miller, PHI 5
D. O' Connell, PIT . . . 4
E. Church, PHI 2
B. Serena, CHI 1

1950 AMERICAN
W. Dropo, BOS 15

W. Ford, NY 6
C. Carrasquel, CHI . . 2

1951 NATIONAL
W. Mays, NY 18
C. Nichols, BOS 4
C. Labine, BKN 2

1951 AMERICAN
G. McDougald, NY . . 13
M. Minoso, CHI 11

1952 NATIONAL
J. Black, BKN 19
H. Wilhelm, NY 3
D. Groat, PIT 1
E. Mathews, BOS . . . 1

1952 AMERICAN
H. Byrd, PHI 9
C. Courtney, SL 8
S. White, BOS 7

1953 NATIONAL
J. Gilliam, BKN 11
H. Haddix, SL 4
R. Jablonski, SL 3
R. Repulski, SL 2
B. Bruton, MIL 2
F. Baczewski, CIN . . . 1
J. Greengrass, CIN . . 1

1953 AMERICAN
H. Kuenn, DET 23
T. Umphlett, BOS 1

1954 NATIONAL
W. Moon, SL 17
E. Banks, CHI 4
G. Conley, MIL 2
H. Aaron, MIL 1

1954 AMERICAN
B. Grim, NY 15
J. Finigan, PHI 8
A. Kaline, DET 1

1955 NATIONAL
B. Virdon, SL 15
J. Meyer, PHI 7
D. Bessent, BKN 2

1955 AMERICAN
H. Score, CLE 18
B. Klaus, BOS 5
N. Zauchin, BOS 1

1956 NATIONAL
F. Robinson, CIN . . . 24

1956 AMERICAN
L. Aparicio, CHI 22
T. Francona, BAL 1
R. Colavito, CLE 1

1957 NATIONAL
J. Sanford, PHI 16
E. Bouchee, PHI 4
D. Drott, CHI 3
B. Hazle, MIL 1

1957 AMERICAN
T. Kubek, NY 23
F. Malzone, BOS 1

1958 NATIONAL
O. Cepeda, SF 21

1958 AMERICAN
A. Pearson, WAS . . 14
R. Duren, NY 7
G. Bell, CLE 3

1959 NATIONAL
W. McCovey, SF . . 24

1959 AMERICAN
B. Allison, WAS . . . 18
J. Perry, CLE 5
R. Snyder, KC 1

1960 NATIONAL
F. Howard, LA 12
P. Herrera, PHI 4
A. Mahaffey, PHI . . . 3
R. Santo, CHI 2
T. Davis, LA 1

1960 AMERICAN
R. Hansen, BAL . . . 22
C. Estrada, BAL 1
J. Gentile, BAL 1

1961 NATIONAL
B. Williams, CHI . . . 10
J. Torre, MIL 5
J. Curtis, CHI 1

1961 AMERICAN
D. Schwall, BOS . . . 7
D. Howser, KC 6
Fl. Robinson, CHI . . 2
C. Schilling, BOS . . . 2
L. Thomas, LA 2
J. Wood, DET 1

1962 NATIONAL
K. Hubbs, CHI 19
D. Clendenon, PIT . . 1

1962 AMERICAN
T. Tresh, NY 13
B. Rodgers, LA 4
B. Allen, MIN 1
D. Chance, LA 1
D. Radatz, BOS 1

1963 NATIONAL
P. Rose, CIN 17

R. Hunt, NY 2
R. Culp, PHI 1

1963 AMERICAN
G. Peters, CHI 10
P. Ward, CHI 6
J. Hall, MIN 4

1964 NATIONAL
R. Allen, PHI 18
R. Carty, MIL 1
J. Hart, SF 1

1964 AMERICAN
T. Oliva, MIN 19
W. Bunker, BAL 1

1965 NATIONAL
J. Lefebvre, LA 13
J. Morgan, HOU 4
F. Linzy, SF 3

1965 AMERICAN
C. Blefary, BAL 12
M. Lopez, CAL 8

1966 NATIONAL
T. Helms, CIN 12
S. Jackson, HOU . . . 3
T. Fuentes, SF 2
R. Hundley, CHI 1
C. Jones, NY 1
L. Jaster, SL 1

1966 AMERICAN
T. Agee, CHI 16
J. Nash, KC 2
D. Johnson, BAL . . . 1
G. Scott, BOS 1

1967 NATIONAL
T. Seaver, NY 11
D. Hughes, SL 6

G. Nolan, CIN 3

1967 AMERICAN
R. Carew, MIN 19
R. Smith, BOS 1

1968 NATIONAL
J. Bench, CIN . . . 10½
J. Koosman, NY . . 9½

1968 AMERICAN
S. Bahnsen, NY . . . 17
D. Unser, WAS 3

1969 NATIONAL
T. Sizemore, LA . . . 14
C. Laboy, MON 3
A. Oliver, PIT 3
B. Didier, ATL 2
L. Hisle, PHI 2

1969 AMERICAN
L. Piniella, KC 9
M. Nagy, BOS 6
C. May, CHI 5
K. Tatum, CAL 4

1970 NATIONAL
C. Morton, MON . . . 11
B. Carbo, CIN 8
L. Bowa, PHI 3
W. Simpson, CIN . . . 1
C. Cedeno, HOU . . . 1

1970 AMERICAN
T. Munson, NY 23
R. Foster, CLE 1

1971 NATIONAL
E. Williams, ATL . . . 18
W. Montanez, PHI . . 6

1971 AMERICAN
C. Chambliss, CLE .11
B. Parsons, MIL 5
A. Mangual, OAK....4
D. Griffin, BOS.....3
P. Splittorff, KC 1

1972 NATIONAL
J. Matlack, NY 19
Dv. Rader, SF 4
J. Milner, NY 1

1972 AMERICAN
C. Fisk, BOS 24

1973 NATIONAL
G. Matthews, SF ...11
S. Rogers, MON .. 3½
B. Boone, PHI 2
E. Sosa, SF 2
D. Driessen, CIN ..2
R. Cey, LA 1
D. Lopes, LA 1
J. Grubb, SD 1
R. Zisk, PIT .... ½

1973 AMERICAN
A. Bumbry, BAL.. 13½
P. Garcia, MIL 3
D. Porter, MIL 2
S. Busby, KC 2
D. Medich, NY 2
R. Coggins, BAL .. 1½

1974 NATIONAL
B. McBride, SL 16
G. Gross, HOU 7
B. Madlock CHI 1

1974 AMERICAN
M. Hargrove,
  TEX 16½
B. Dent, CHI 3
G. Brett, KC 2
R. Burleson, BOS . 1½
J. Sundberg, TEX ...1

1975 NATIONAL
J. Montefusco, SF .. 12
G. Carter, MON 9
Lr. Parrish, MON 1
R. Eastwick, CIN ...1
M. Trillo, CHI 1

1975 AMERICAN
F. Lynn, BOS 23½

J. Rice, BOS ...... ½

1976 NATIONAL
B. Metzger, SD 11
P. Zachry, CIN 11
H. Cruz, SL 2

1976 AMERICAN
M. Fidrych, DET ...22
B. Wynegar, MIN 2

1977 NATIONAL
A. Dawson, MON ...10
S. Henderson, NY ...9
G. Richards, SD 4
F. Bannister, HOU ...1

1977 AMERICAN
E. Murray, BAL .. 12½
M. Page, OAK 9½
B. Wills, TEX 4
D. Rozema, DET ..2

1978 NATIONAL
B. Horner, ATL... 12½
O. Smith, SD 8½
D. Robinson, PIT 3

1978 AMERICAN
L. Whitaker, DET ...21
P. Molitor, MIL 3
C. Lansford, CAL ..2
R. Gale, KC 1
A. Trammell, DET....1

1979 NATIONAL
R. Sutcliffe, LA 20
J. Leonard, HOU ...3
S. Thompson, CHI...1

1979 AMERICAN
J. Castino, MIN 7
A. Griffin, TOR 7
M. Clear, CAL 5
R. Davis, NY 3
R. Baumgarten, CHI .3
P. Putnam, TEX 3

1980 NATIONAL
S. Howe, LA 80
B. Gullickson,
  MON 53
L. Smith, PHI 49
R. Oester, CIN 16

D. Smith, HOU 13
J. Reardon, NY 2
A. Holland, SF 1
L. Durham, SL 1
B. Walk, PHI 1

1980 AMERICAN
J. Charboneau,
  CLE 102
D. Stapleton, BOS .. 40
D. Corbett, MIN 38
D. Garcia, TOR 35
B. Burns, CHI 33
R. Peters, DET 3
R. Dotson, CHI 1

1981 NATIONAL
F. Valenzuela, LA .. 107
T. Raines, MON 85
H. Brooks, NY 8½
B. Berenyi, CIN 5
J. Bonilla, SD.......5
T. Pena, PIT 4
M. Wilson, NY 1½

1981 AMERICAN
D. Righetti, NY.... 127
R. Gedman, BOS...64
B. Ojeda, BOS.....36
M. Jones, KC 8
D. Engle, MIN 4½
M. Witt, CAL 4
S. Babitt, OAK 4
J. Bell, TOR 2
G. Ward, MIN 1½
B. Havens, MIN 1

1982 NATIONAL
S. Sax, LA 63
J. Ray, PIT 57
W. McGee, SL 39
C. Davis, SF 32
L. DeLeon, SD 10
R. Sandberg, CHI ..9
S. Bedrosian, ATL ..4
D. LaPoint, SL 1
E. Show, SD 1

1982 AMERICAN
C. Ripken, BAL ...132
K. Hrbek, MIN 90
W. Boggs, BOS .. 10½
E. Vande Berg, SEA..9
G. Gaetti, MIN 4

D. Hostetler, TEX ...3
V. Hayes, CLE 2
J. Barfield, TOR ... 1½

1983 NATIONAL
D. Strawberry, NY . 106
C. McMurtry, ATL ..49
M. Hall, CHI 32
G. Redus, CIN 8
B. Doran, HOU 7
F. DiPino, HOU 6
G. Brock, LA 3
J. DeLeon, PIT 3
M. Thurmond, SD ...1
L. Tunnell, PIT 1

1983 AMERICAN
R. Kittle, CHI 104
J. Franco, CLE 78
M. Boddicker, BAL .70

1984 NATIONAL
D. Gooden, NY ...118
J. Samuel, PHI.....67
O. Hershiser, LA ..15
D. Gladden, SF 9
D. Darling, NY 3
C. Martinez, SD 2
J. Stone, PHI 1
T. Pendleton, SL 1

1984 AMERICAN
A. Davis, SEA 134
M. Langston, SEA ..82
K. Puckett, MIN 23
T. Teufel, MIN 5
M. Young, BAL 3
R. Clemens, BOS ...2
M. Gubicza, KC 1
A. Nipper, BOS 1
R. Romanick, CAL...1

1985 NATIONAL
V. Coleman, SL ...120
T. Browning, CIN ..72
M. Duncan, LA 9
C. Brown, SF 7
G. Davis, HOU 3
R. McDowell, NY ...2
J. Orsulak, PIT 2
J. Hesketh, MON 1

1985 AMERICAN
O. Guillen, CHI....101

T. Higuera, MIL 67
E. Riles, MIL 29
O. McDowell, TEX ..25
S. Cliburn, CAL 16
B. Fisher, NY 7
T. Henke, TOR 5
M. Salas, MIN 2

1986 NATIONAL
T. Worrell, SL 118
R. Thompson, SF . 46
K. Mitchell, NY 22
C. Kerfeld, HOU ...17
W. Clark, SF 5
Br. Bonds, PIT 4
J. Deshaies, HOU ...1
B. Larkin, CIN 1
B. Ruffin, PHI 1
J. Kruk, SD 1

1986 AMERICAN
J. Canseco, OAK ..110
W. Joyner, CAL 98
M. Eichhorn, TOR . 23
C. Snyder, CLE 16
D. Tartabull, SEA 4
R. Sierra, TEX 1

1987 NATIONAL
B. Santiago, SD ...120
M. Dunne, PIT 66
J. Magrane, SL 10
C. Candaele, MON ..9
G. Young, HOU 7
C. James, PHI 1
L. Lancaster, CHI....1
G. Mathews, SL.....1
R. Myers, NY 1

1987 AMERICAN
M. McGwire, OAK . 140
K. Seitzer, KC 64
M. Nokes, DET 32
M. Greenwell, BOS ..9
D. White, CAL 5
M. Henneman, DET..1
N. Liriano, TOR 1

1988 NATIONAL
C. Sabo, CIN 79
M. Grace, CHI 61
T. Belcher, LA 35
R. Gant, ATL 22

R. Alomar, SD 11
D. Berryhill, CHI.....3
G. Jefferies, NY 3
R. Jordan, PHI......2

1988 AMERICAN
W. Weiss, OAK ...103
B. Harvey, CAL 49
J. Reed, BOS 48
D. August, MIL 22
D. Gallagher, CHI...18
M. Perez, CHI 9
M. Schooler, SEA ..2
C. Espy, TEX 1

1989 NATIONAL
J. Walton, CHI 116
D. Smith, CHI 68
G. Jeffries, NY 18
D. Lilliquist, ATL 6
A. Benes, SD.......3
C. Hayes, PHI 3
G. Harris, SD 2

1989 AMERICAN
G. Olson, BAL 136
T. Gordon, KC 67
K. Griffey, SEA.....21
C. Worthington, Bal .16
J. Abbott, Cal......10
K. Brown, TEX......2

1990 NATIONAL
D. Justice, ATL ...118
D. DeShields, MON .60
H. Morris, CIN 13
J. Burkett, SF 12
M. Harkey, CHI 7
T. Zeile, SL 4
M. Grissom, MON ...1
L. Walker, MON 1

1990 AMERICAN
S. Alomar, CLE ...140
K. Maas, NY 47
K. Appier, KC 31
J. Olerud, TOR 13
K. Tapani, MIN 9
T. Fryman, DET 5
R. Ventura, CHI 3
B. McDonald, BAL...2
A. Cole, CLE 1
S. Radinsky, CHI 1

Cy Young Award: History

Commissioner Ford Frick, troubled by pitchers' lack of representation in MVP voting, spearheaded the 1956 effort to initiate a "most valuable pitcher" award. Cy Young, baseball's winningest pitcher, who had died the previous November, was the logical choice to name the honor after. At a special meeting on July 9, 1956, the Baseball Writers' Association of America approved, by the slim margin of 14-12, the establishment of the Cy Young Memorial Award, designed to honor the major leagues' outstanding pitcher each year beginning in '56. Ironically, the first winner, Brooklyn's Don Newcombe, also won his league's MVP Award.

One writer from each major league city participated in the balloting. In case of a tie vote, a second balloting was to be taken between the deadlocked pitchers. Hurlers were not to be eligible to win the award more than once, a rule which was evidently scrapped within two years.

Frick was adamantly opposed to the commonly voiced idea to recognize a Cy Young winner in each league but, not long after his December 1965 retirement, the idea became a reality. On March 1, 1967, Frick's successor William Eckert approved the plan for dual awards, with two writers from each league city designated to make selections.

The system of having each writer make only one selection prevailed until 1969, when Detroit's Denny McLain and Baltimore's Mike Cuellar tied for the AL Cy Young Award. Thereafter, writers were instructed to name three pitchers in each league, with 5 points allotted for each first-place vote, 3 for second, and 1 for third.

The maximum number of points available for one pitcher was 16 from 1956–60, 18 in 1961, 20 in 1962–68, 24 in 1969, 120 in 1970–76 (AL) and 1970–present (NL), and 140 in 1977–present (AL). As with every other major award, there have been a few instances in Cy Young voting where at least one writer failed to return a ballot.

Unanimous winners of the Cy Young Award are Sandy Koufax (NL, 1963, '65, and '66), Bob Gibson (NL, 1968), Denny McLain (AL, 1968), Steve Carlton (NL, 1972), Ron Guidry (AL, 1978), Rick Sutcliffe (NL, 1984), Dwight Gooden (NL, 1985), Roger Clemens (AL, 1986), and Orel Hershiser (NL, 1988).

Relief pitchers, once overlooked in Cy Young balloting, have become strong candidates in recent years. Until 1970 only one reliever — Lindy McDaniel in 1960 — had received even a single vote. The new voting system helped open opportunities for bullpen aces and in 1974 the Dodgers' Mike Marshall became the first reliever to win the Cy Young Award. He has been followed in that distinction by Sparky Lyle (AL, 1977), Bruce Sutter (NL, 1979), Rollie Fingers (AL, 1981), Willie Hernández (AL, 1984), Steve Bedrosian (NL, 1987), and Mark Davis (NL, 1989).

Cy Young Award

1956
D. Newcombe, BKN (NL) 10
S. Maglie, BKN (NL) . 4
W. Spahn, MIL (NL) . .1
W. Ford, NY (AL) 1

1957
W. Spahn, MIL (NL) .15
D. Donovan, CHI (AL) 1

1958
B. Turley, NY (AL). . . .5
W. Spahn, MIL (NL) . .4
B. Friend, PIT (NL) . . .3
L. Burdette, MIL (NL) 3

1959
E. Wynn, CHI (AL) . . 13
S. Jones, SF (NL) 2
B. Shaw, CHI (AL) . . .1

1960
V. Law, PIT (NL) 8
W. Spahn, MIL (NL) . .4
E. Broglio, SL (NL). . .1
L. McDaniel, SL (NL) . 1

1961
W. Ford, NY (AL) 9
W. Spahn, MIL (NL) . .6
F. Lary, DET (AL) 2

1962
D. Drysdale, LA (NL) 14
J. Sanford, SF (NL) . .4
B. Purkey, CIN (NL) . .1
B. Pierce, SF (NL) . . .1

1963
S. Koufax, LA (NL). . 20

1964
D. Chance, LA (AL) . 17
L. Jackson, CHI (NL) .2
S. Koufax, LA (NL). . .1

1965
S. Koufax, LA (NL). . 20

1966
S. Koufax, LA (NL). . 20

1967 NATIONAL
M. Mc Cormick, SF . 18
F. Jenkins, CHI 1
J. Bunning, PHI 1

1967 AMERICAN
J. Lonborg, BOS . . . 18
J. Horlen, CHI 2

1968 NATIONAL
B. Gibson, SL 20

1968 AMERICAN
D. McLain, DET 20

1969 NATIONAL
T. Seaver, NY 23
P. Niekro, ATL 1

1969 AMERICAN
M. Cuellar, BAL 10
D. McLain, DET 10
J. Perry, MIN 3
D. McNally, BAL 1

1970 NATIONAL
B. Gibson, SL 118
G. Perry, SF 51

F. Jenkins CHI 16
D. Giusti, PIT 8
J. Merritt, CIN 8
G. Nolan, CIN 5
T. Seaver, NY 4
W. Granger, CIN 3
C. Morton, MON . . . 2
L. Walker, PIT 1

1970 AMERICAN
J. Perry, MIN 55
D. McNally, BAL . . . 47
S. McDowell, CLE . . 45
M. Cuellar, BAL 44
J. Palmer, BAL. 11
C. Wright, CAL 9
R. Perranoski, MIN . .5

1971 NATIONAL
F. Jenkins, CHI 97
T. Seaver, NY 61
A. Downing, LA 40
D. Ellis, PIT 9
B. Gibson, SL 3
J. Johnson, SF 2
D. Roberts, SD 2
J. Marichal, SF 1
B. Stoneman, MON . .1

1971 AMERICAN
V. Blue, OAK 98
M. Lolich, DET 85
W. Wood, CHI 23
D. McNally, BAL 8
D. Drago, KC 1
A. Messersmith, CAL 1

1972 NATIONAL
S. Carlton, PHI . . . 120
S. Blass, PIT 35
F. Jenkins, CHI 23
M. Marshall, MON . .8
G. Nolan, CIN 6
T. Seaver, NY 6
C. Carroll, CIN 6
D. Sutton, LA 6
B. Gibson, SL 3
M. Pappas, CHI 3

1972 AMERICAN
G. Perry, CLE 64
W. Wood, CHI 58
M. Lolich, DET 27
J. Hunter, OAK 26
J. Palmer, BAL 20
L. Tiant, BOS 16
S. Lyle, NY 3
N. Ryan, CAL 2

1973 NATIONAL
T. Seaver, NY 71
M. Marshall, MON . . 54
R. Bryant, SF 50
J. Billingham, CIN . . 30
D. Sutton, LA 7
F. Norman, SD-CIN . .3
D. Giusti, PIT 1

1973 AMERICAN
J. Palmer, BAL 88
N. Ryan, CAL 62
J. Hunter, OAK 52
J. Hiller, DET 6
W. Wood, CHI 3
J. Colborn, MIL 2
V. Blue, OAK 1
B. Blyleven, MIN 1
G. Perry, CLE 1

1974 NATIONAL
M. Marshall, LA 96
A. Messersmith, LA 66

P. Niekro, ATL 15
D. Sutton, LA 12
A. Hrabosky, SL 9
J. Billingham, CIN . . .8
D. Gullett, CIN 5
C. Carroll, CIN 2
D. Giusti, PIT 1
B. Capra, ATL 1
L. McGlothen, SL . . .1

1974 AMERICAN
J. Hunter, OAK 90
F. Jenkins, TEX 75
N. Ryan, CAL 28
G. Perry, CLE 8
L. Tiant, BOS 8
M. Cuellar, BAL 6
J. Hiller, DET 1

1975 NATIONAL
T. Seaver, NY 98
R. Jones, SD 80
A. Hrabosky, SL . . .33
J. Montefusco, SF . . .2
D. Gullett, CIN 1
A. Messersmith, LA . .1
D. Sutton, LA 1

1975 AMERICAN
J. Palmer, BAL 98
J. Hunter, NY 74
R. Fingers, OAK . . . 25
F. Tanana, CAL 7
J. Kaat, CHI 7
V. Blue, OAK 2
R. Gossage, CHI 2
R. Wise, BOS 1

1976 NATIONAL
R. Jones, SD 96
J. Koosman, NY . 69½
D. Sutton, LA 25½
S. Carlton, PHI 11
R. Eastwick, CIN 6
J. Matlack, NY 5
J. Richard, HOU 2
T. Seaver, NY 1

1976 AMERICAN
J. Palmer, BAL 108
M. Fidrych, DET . . . 51
F. Tanana, CAL 18
E. Figueroa, NY . . . 12
L. Tiant, BOS 10
V. Blue, OAK 8
B. Campbell, MIN . . .7
R. Fingers, OAK 1
W. Garland, BAL 1

1977 NATIONAL
S. Carlton, PHI . . . 104
J. John, LA 54
T. Seaver, NY-CIN . . 18
R. Reuschel, CHI . . 18
J. Candelaria, PIT . . 17
B. Sutter, CHI 5

1977 AMERICAN
S. Lyle, NY 56½
J. Palmer, BAL 48
N. Ryan, CAL 46
D. Leonard, KC 45
B. Campbell, BOS 25½
D. Goltz, MIN 19
R. Guidry, NY 5
D. Rozema, DET 4
F. Tanana, CAL. 3

1978 NATIONAL
G. Perry, SD 116
B. Hooton, LA 38
V. Blue, SF 17
J. Richard, HOU . . . 13

K. Tekulve, PIT 12
P. Niekro, ATL 10
R. Grimsley, MON . .7
R. Fingers, SD 1
T. John, LA 1
D. Robinson, PIT . . .1

1978 AMERICAN
R. Guidry, NY 140
M. Caldwell, MIL . . . 76
J. Palmer, BAL 14
D. Eckersley, BOS . . 10
R. Gossage, NY 4
F. Jenkins, TEX 2
E. Figueroa, NY 1
L. Gura, KC 1
D. Leonard, KC 1
M. Marshall, MIN . . .1
P. Splittorff, KC 1
B. Stanley, BOS 1

1979 NATIONAL
B. Sutter, CHI 72
J. Niekro, HOU 66
J. Richard, HOU . . .41
T. Seaver, CIN 20
K. Tekulve, PIT 14
P. Niekro, ATL 3

1979 AMERICAN
M. Flanagan, BAL . 136
T. John, NY 51
R. Guidry, NY 26
J. Kern, TEX 25
M. Marshall, MIN . . .7
J. Koosman, MIN . . .5
D. Eckersley, BOS . . .1
A. Lopez, DET 1

1980 NATIONAL
S. Carlton, PHI . . . 118
J. Reuss, LA 55
J. Bibby, PIT 28
J. Niekro, HOU 11
T. McGraw, PHI 1
S. Rogers, MON 1
J. Sambito, HOU 1
M. Soto, CIN 1

1980 AMERICAN
S. Stone, BAL 100
M. Norris, OAK 91
R. Gossage, NY . . 37½
T. John, NY 14
D. Quisenberry, KC 7½
L. Gura, KC 1
S. McGregor, BAL . .1

1981 NATIONAL
F. Valenzuela, LA . . 70
T. Seaver, CIN 67
S. Carlton, PHI 50
N. Ryan, HOU 28
B. Sutter, SL 1

1981 AMERICAN
R. Fingers, MIL . . . 126
S. McCatty, OAK . 84½
J. Morris, DET 21
P. Vuckovich, MIL . 8½
D. Martinez, BAL . 3½
R. Gossage, NY 3
R. Guidry, NY . . . 2½
B. Burns, CHI 2
L. Gura, KC 1

1982 NATIONAL
S. Carlton, PHI . . . 112
S. Rogers, MON . . . 29
F. Valenzuela, LA . 25½
B. Sutter, SL 25
P. Niekro, ATL 18
G. Minton, SF 4

J. Andujar, SL 1
G. Garber, ATL 1
M. Soto, CIN . . . . . .½

1982 AMERICAN
P. Vuckovich, MIL . .87
J. Palmer, BAL 59
D. Quisenberry, KC .40
D. Stieb, TOR 36
R. Sutcliffe, CLE . . . 14
G. Zahn, CAL 7
B. Stanley, BOS 4
B. Caudill, SEA 4
D. Petry, DET 1

1983 NATIONAL
J. Denny, PHI 103
M. Soto, CIN 61
J. Orosco, NY 19
S. Rogers, MON . . . 15
L. McWilliams, PIT . .7
A. Holland, PHI 4
C. McMurtry, ATL . . .3
B. Welch, LA 2
N. Ryan, HOU 1
L. Smith, CHI 1

1983 AMERICAN
L. Hoyt, CHI 116
D. Quisenberry, KC . 81
J. Morris, DET 38
R. Dotson, CHI 9
R. Guidry, NY 5
S. McGregor, BAL . .3

1984 NATIONAL
R. Sutcliffe, CHI . . . 120
D. Gooden, NY 45
B. Sutter, SL 33½
J. Andujar, SL . . . 12½
R. Gossage, SD 3
M. Soto, CIN 2

1984 AMERICAN
W. Hernandez, DET 88
D. Quisenberry, KC .71
B. Blyleven, CLE . . .45
M. Boddicker, BAL . 41
D. Petry, DET 3
F. Viola, MIN 2
J. Morris, DET 1
D. Stieb, TOR 1

1985 NATIONAL
D. Gooden, NY . . . 120
J. Tudor, SL 65
O. Hershiser, LA . . . 17
J. Andujar, SL 6
F. Valenzuela, LA . . .4
T. Browning, CIN . . .3
J. Reardon, MON . . .1

1985 AMERICAN
B. Saberhagen, KC 127
R. Guidry, NY 88
B. Blyleven, MIN 9
D. Quisenberry, KC . .9
C. Leibrandt, KC . . .7
D. Alexander, TOR . .5
B. Burns, CHI 2
D. Moore, CAL 2
D. Stieb, TOR 2
M. Moore, SEA 1

1986 NATIONAL
M. Scott, HOU 98
F. Valenzuela, LA . . .88
M. Krukow, SF 15
B. Ojeda, NY 9
R. Darling, NY 2
R. Rhoden, PIT 2
D. Gooden, NY 1

S. Fernandez, NY . . .1

1986 AMERICAN
R. Clemens, BOS . 140
T. Higuera, MIL 42
M. Witt, CAL 35
D. Righetti, NY 20
J. Morris, DET 13
M. Eichhorn, TOR . . .2

1987 NATIONAL
S. Bedrosian, PHI . .57
R. Sutcliffe, CHI . . . 55
R. Reuschel, SF . . . 54
O. Hershiser, LA . . .14
D. Gooden, NY 12
N. Ryan, HOU 12
M. Scott, HOU 9
B. Welch, LA 3

1987 AMERICAN
R. Clemens, BOS . 124
J. Key, TOR 64
D. Stewart, OAK . . . 32
D. Alexander, DET . . .8
M. Langston, SEA . . .7
T. Higuera, MIL 5
F. Viola, MIN 5
J. Reardon, MIN 4
J. Morris, DET 3

1988 NATIONAL
O. Hershisher, LA . 120
D. Jackson, CIN . . . 54
D. Cone, NY 42

1988 AMERICAN
F. Viola, MIN 138
D. Eckersley, OAK . . 52
M. Gubicza, KC 26
D. Stewart, OAK . . . 16
B. Hurst, BOS 12
R. Clemens, BOS . . .8

1989 NATIONAL
M. Davis, SD 107
M. Scott, HOU 65
G. Maddux, CHI . . . 17
O. Hershiser, LA . . .7
J. Magrane, SL 7
T. Belcher, LA 4
S. Garrelts, SF 4
R. Reuschel, SF 3
M. Bielecki, CHI 1
M. Williams, CHI 1

1989 AMERICAN
B. Saberhagen, KC 138
D. Stewart, OAK . . . 80
M. Moore, OAK 10
B. Blyleven, CAL 9
N. Ryan, TEX 5
J. Ballard, BAL 3
D. Eckersley, OAK . . .3
G. Olson, BAL 3
J. Russell, TEX 1

1990 NATIONAL
D. Drabek, PIT 118
R. Marinez, LA 70
F. Viola, NY 19
D. Gooden, NY 8
R. Myers, CIN 1

1990 AMERICAN
B. Welch, OAK 107
R. Clemens, BOS . . 77
D. Stewart, OAK . . . 43
B. Thigpen, CHI . . . 20
D. Eckersley, OAK . .2
D. Stieb, TOR 2
C. Finley, CAL 1

Hypothetical Awards

As the "expert" in baseball award-voting, I have been asked to make a set of hypothetical award selections for the years no official honors were given; i.e., pre-1956 Cy Young, pre-1947 Rookie of the Year, and pre-1911 MVP Awards, along with awards for any other "missing" years.

While this assignment gave me unusual freedom, I felt a certain responsibility to make my selections consistent with the perceptions and voting trends of a particular era. For example, although there were better NL players than Cincinnati's Edd Roush in 1919, he did two things which, combined, would have virtually guaranteed him the MVP Award: he won the batting crown, which was *the* individual title in the dead-ball era; and he played on a pennant-winner, which has always been a key factor in MVP voting. Thus, I felt obliged to make Roush my hypothetical selection.

Besides my own opinions and intuitions, several sources were instrumental in my selection process, including:

1. SABR retroactive award surveys, which have been done for pre-1949 Rookie of the Year and pre-1967 Cy Young Awards. SABR (the Society for American Baseball Research) is comprised of more than six thousand hard-core fans, hundreds of whom chose to participate in these surveys. The ballots were tremendously helpful in screening candidates and the voting results were carefully compared to my own choices.

2. Linear Weights, an overall player rating system devised by Pete Palmer, first used in *The Hidden Game of Baseball* (Doubleday, 1984, 1985), and continued in *Total Baseball*.

3. MVP voting results, for comparing Cy Young and Rookie candidates. If rookie "A" receives 75 points in the MVP election, while comparable rookie "B" receives just 10, I am forced to conclude that the on-the-spot observers discerned some important difference that we can't see in the statistics and that "A" is probably the better choice.

(Incidentally, the criteria used to determine rookies was a maximum of 90 at-bats or 45 innings pitched in any previous seasons.)

4. Unofficial awards, including 1940–46 Rookie and 1929–30 MVP selections.

5. Cy Young (1956–66) and Rookie of the Year (1947–48) balloting, for years in which one league had no official winner.

The resulting selections are not necessarily ones the average reader will agree with, nor even that the *writer* agrees with; rather, they are the ones which can be *best justified with the available evidence*. I am prepared to defend any of my choices.

In comparison with the Palmer system, my selections concurred 54 percent with top player selections and 59 percent with top pitcher nominations. In comparison with the SABR surveys, my selections agreed 84 percent in the Rookie of the Year Award and 79 percent in the Cy Young Award.

The big winner in the hypothetical awards is Christy Mathewson, who picks up a Rookie of the Year, two MVPs, and eight Cy Young Awards. Other pitchers capturing at least three Cy Youngs are Walter Johnson (7); Lefty Grove (6, consecutively); Warren Spahn (4, to add to the one he actually did win); Grover Alexander (4); Burleigh Grimes, Carl Hubbell, Bob Feller, Bucky Walters, Bob Lemon, and appropriately, Cy Young himself (3 each).

Notable Rookies of the Year include Grover Alexander, Babe Ruth, Rogers Hornsby, Dizzy Dean, Joe DiMaggio, and Ted Williams.

Honus Wagner cops six MVP Awards, including four in succession. Three-time MVPs are Nap Lajoie, Alexander, Ruth, and Hornsby. Ruth (once) and Hornsby (twice) also won official MVP Awards.

The following pages contain my hypothetical Cy Young (124), Rookie of the Year (97), and MVP (42) selections for this century.

Hypothetical Cy Young Award

American League Pitcher/Club	Year	American League Pitcher/Club	Year	American League Pitcher/Club	Year	National League Pitcher/Club	Year	National League Pitcher/Club	Year	National League Pitcher/Club	Year
C. Young, BOS	1901	W. Johnson, WAS	1924	DET	1945	C. Mathewson, NY	1903	G. Alexander, PHI	1917	B. Lee, CHI	1938
C. Young, BOS	1902	S. Coveleski, WAS	1925	H. Newhouser, DET	1946	J. McGinnity, NY	1904	J. Vaughn, CHI	1918	B. Walters, CIN	1939
C. Young, BOS	1903	G. Uhle, CLE	1926	J. Page, NY	1947	C. Mathewson, NY	1905	J. Vaughn, CHI	1919	B. Walters, CIN	1940
J. Chesbro, NY	1904	W. Moore, NY	1927	B. Lemon, CLE	1948	M. Brown, CHI	1906	G. Alexander, CHI	1920	W. Wyatt, BKN	1941
R. Waddell, PHI	1905	L. Grove, PHI	1928	M. Parnell, BOS	1949	C. Mathewson, NY	1907	B. Grimes, BKN	1921	M. Cooper, SL	1942
O. Hess, CLE	1906	L. Grove, PHI	1929	B. Lemon, CLE	1950	C. Mathewson, NY	1908	W. Cooper, PIT	1922	M. Cooper, SL	1943
E. Walsh, CHI	1907	L. Grove, PHI	1930	N. Garver, SL	1951	C. Mathewson, NY	1909	D. Luque, CIN	1923	B. Walters, CIN	1944
E. Walsh, CHI	1908	L. Grove, PHI	1931	B. Shantz, PHI	1952	C. Mathewson, NY	1910	D. Vance, BKN	1924	H. Wyse, CHI	1945
F. Smith, CHI	1909	L. Grove, PHI	1932	B. Pierce, CHI	1953	C. Mathewson, NY	1911	D. Vance, BKN	1925	H. Pollet, SL	1946
J. Coombs, PHI	1910	L. Grove, PHI	1933	B. Lemon, CLE	1954	R. Marquard, NY	1912	R. Kremer, PIT	1926	E. Blackwell, CIN	1947
W. Johnson, WAS	1911	L. Gomez, NY	1934	R. Narleski, CLE	1955	C. Mathewson, NY	1913	C. Root, CHI	1927	J. Sain, BOS	1948
J. Wood, BOS	1912	W. Ferrell, BOS	1935	B. Pierce, CHI	1956	B. James, BOS	1914	B. Grimes, PIT	1928	W. Spahn, BOS	1949
W. Johnson, WAS	1913	T. Bridges, DET	1936	J. Bunning, DET	1957	G. Alexander, PHI	1915	B. Grimes, PIT	1929	J. Konstanty, PHI	1950
W. Johnson, WAS	1914	L. Gomez, NY	1937	C. Estrada, BAL	1960	G. Alexander, PHI	1916	P. Malone, CHI	1930	S. Maglie, NY	1951
W. Johnson, WAS	1915	B. Feller, CLE	1938	D. Donovan, CLE	1962			E. Brandt, BOS	1931	R. Roberts, PHI	1952
B. Ruth, BOS	1916	B. Feller, CLE	1939	W. Ford, NY	1963			L. Warneke, CHI	1932	W. Spahn, MIL	1953
E. Cicotte, CHI	1917	B. Feller, CLE	1940	E. Fisher, CHI	1965			C. Hubbell, NY	1933	J. Antonelli, NY	1954
W. Johnson, WAS	1918	B. Feller, CLE	1941	J. Kaat, MIN	1966			D. Dean, SL	1934	R. Roberts, PHI	1955
W. Johnson, WAS	1919	T. Hughson, BOS	1942	J. McGinnity, BKN	1900			D. Dean, SL	1935	W. Spahn, MIL	1958
J. Bagby, CLE	1920	S. Chandler, NY	1943	N. Hahn, CIN	1901			C. Hubbell, NY	1936	S. Jones, SF	1959
R. Faber, CHI	1921	D. Trout, DET	1944	J. Taylor, CHI	1902			C. Hubbell, NY	1937	W. Spahn, MIL	1961
E. Rommel, PHI	1922	H. Newhouser,								L. Jackson, CHI	1964
G. Uhle, CLE	1923										

Hypothetical Federal League Awards

	1914	1915
Most Valuable Player	B. Kauff, IND	D. Zwilling, CHI
Cy Young	C. Hendrix, CHI	G. McConnell, CHI
Rookie of the Year	B. Kauff, IND	E. Johnson, SL

Hypothetical Rookie of the Year Award

American League Player/Club	Year	American League Player/Club	Year	American League Player/Club	Year	National League Player/Club	Year	National League Player/Club	Year	National League Player/Club	Year
S. Seybold, PHI	1901	J. Bagby, CLE	1916	J. Allen, NY	1932	E. Scott, CIN	1900	T. Long, SL	1915	W. Berger, BOS	1930
A. Joss, CLE	1902	A. Sothoron, SL	1917	B. Johnson, PHI	1933	C. Mathewson,		R. Hornsby, SL	1916	P. Derringer, SL	1931
C. Bender, PHI	1903	S. Perry, PHI	1918	H. Trosky, CLE	1934	NY	1901	L. Cadore, BKN	1917	D. Dean, SL	1932
F. Glade, SL	1904	D. Kerr, CHI	1919	J. Powell, WAS	1935	H. Smoot, SL	1902	C. Hollocher, CHI	1918	F. Demaree, CHI	1933
G. Stone, SL	1905	B. Meusel, NY	1920	J. DiMaggio, NY	1936	J. Weimer, CHI	1903	O. Tuero, SL	1919	C. Davis, PHI	1934
C. Rossman,		J. Sewell, CLE	1921	R. York, DET	1937	H. Lumley, BKN	1904	J. Haines, SL	1920	C. Blanton, PIT	1935
CLE	1906	H. Pillette, DET	1922	K. Keltner, DET	1938	E. Reulbach, CHI	1905	R. Grimes, CHI	1921	J. Mize, SL	1936
S. Nicholls, PHI	1907	H. Summa, CLE	1923	T. Williams, BOS	1939	J. Pfiester, CHI	1906	H. Miller, CHI	1922	J. Turner, BOS	1937
E. Summers,		A. Simmons, PHI	1924	W. Judnich, SL	1940	N. Rucker, BKN	1907	G. Grantham,		J. Rizzo, PIT	1938
DET	1908	E. Combs, NY	1925	P. Rizzuto, NY	1941	G. McQuillan,		CHI	1923	H. Casey, BKN	1939
F. Baker, PHI	1909	T. Lazzeri, NY	1926	J. Pesky, BOS	1942	PHI	1908	K. Cuyler, PIT	1924	B. Young, NY	1940
R. Ford, NY	1910	W. Moore, NY	1927	B. Johnson, NY	1943	D. Miller, PIT	1909	J. Welsh, BOS	1925	E. Riddle, CIN	1941
V. Gregg, CLE	1911	E. Morris, BOS	1928	J. Berry, PHI	1944	K. Cole, CHI	1910	P. Waner, PIT	1926	J. Beazley, SL	1942
D. Pratt, SL	1912	D. Alexander,		B. Ferriss, BOS	1945	G. Alexander,		L. Waner, PIT	1927	L. Klein, SL	1943
R. Russell, CHI	1913	DET	1929	B. Lemon, CLE	1946	PHI	1911	D. Bissonette,		B. Voiselle, NY	1944
R. Bressler, PHI	1914	S. Jolley, CHI	1930	F. Shea, NY	1947	L. Cheney, CHI	1912	BKN	1928	K. Burkhart, SL	1945
B. Ruth, BOS	1915	J. Vosmik, CLE	1931	G. Bearden, CLE	1948	J. Viox, PIT	1913	J. Frederick,		D. Ennis, PHI	1946
						J. Pfeffer, BKN	1914	BKN	1929		

Hypothetical Most Valuable Player Award

American League Player/Club	Year	American League Player/Club	Year	American League Player/Club	Year	National League Player/Club	Year	National League Player/Club	Year	National League Player/Club	Year
N. Lajoie, PHI	1901	T. Cobb, DET	1907	B. Ruth, BOS	1918	H. Wagner, PIT	1900	H. Wagner, PIT	1907	J. Vaughn, CHI	1918
C. Young, BOS	1902	E. Walsh, CHI	1908	J. Jackson, CHI	1919	H. Wagner, PIT	1901	C. Mathewson,		E. Roush, CIN	1919
N. Lajoie, CLE	1903	T. Cobb, DET	1909	B. Ruth, NY	1920	H. Wagner, PIT	1902	NY	1908	R. Hornsby, SL	1920
J. Chesbro, NY	1904	J. Coombs, PHI	1910	B. Ruth, NY	1921	H. Wagner, PIT	1903	H. Wagner, PIT	1909	R. Hornsby, SL	1921
R. Waddell, PHI	1905	E. Collins, CHI	1915	L. Fonseca, CLE	1929	J. McGinnity, NY	1904	S. Magee, PHI	1910	R. Hornsby, SL	1922
N. Lajoie, CLE	1906	T. Speaker, CLE	1916	J. Cronin, WAS	1930	C. Mathewson,		G. Alexander, PHI	1915	D. Luque, CIN	1923
		E. Cicotte, CHI	1917			NY	1905	G. Alexander, PHI	1916	H. Wilson, CHI	1930
						H. Steinfeldt, CHI	1906	G. Alexander, PHI	1917		

Gold Glove Award: History

In a 1956 spring training survey, Elmer A. Blasco—employed by Rawlings Sporting Goods as advertising, public relations and sales manager—found that 83 percent of the active regular major league players wore Rawlings gloves or mitts. Noting that Hillerich & Bradsby (the major leagues' leading baseball bat supplier) awarded Silver Bats to the leagues' top hitters, Blasco reasoned that Rawlings ought to sponsor some sort of fielding award. After his idea was accepted by Rawlings' management, Blasco contacted the Brown Shoe Company of St. Louis and obtained from them a hide of gold lamé-tanned leather used to make ladies' formal slippers. A glove was crafted from this hide, laced and stamped as a regular fielders glove, and attached to a metal fixture on a walnut base with an appropriate engraved plate.

Thus was born the Gold Glove Award.

The October 2, 1957, edition of *The Sporting News* featured a full-page advertisement/announcement: "Recognizing the importance of superior individual fielding performance to the advancement of baseball as America's national game, Rawlings (Sporting Goods Company) has established Annual Gold Glove Awards beginning with the 1957 season.

"Each of the nine Major League players chosen for *The Sporting News* All-Star Fielding Team will be honored with a Rawlings Gold Glove Award. Selections will be made by a Committee named by *The Sporting News*.

"Awards will be Rawlings custom-built gloves or mitts hand-crafted of special metallic gold-finished leather, each mounted on a suitable hardwood stand bearing an engraved plate."

TSN publisher J. G. Taylor Spink appointed nineteen noted sportswriters for the selection task. They included Shirley Povich, Edgar Munzel, Hy Hurwitz, Earl Lawson, Bob Broeg, Allen Lewis, and Hal Lebowitz. A contest to predict the winners, open to baseball-playing boys, was sponsored by Rawlings.

The first Gold Glove winners were announced with great pomp and circumstance in the December 18, 1957, issue of TSN. "Too long neglected, the magicians of the defense have had no real recognition," the article explained, adding that the selections were made "solely on the basis of their defensive ability."

Rawlings and TSN also joined forces that year in the establishment of the Silver Glove Award, given to the top minor league fielder at each position—based entirely on fielding averages.

In 1958 the Gold Glove selection privilege was turned over to the major league players and an All-Star Fielding Team was selected for each league (as it still is).

In 1961 the method for selecting outfielders was changed. Rather than choosing a left-, center-, and right fielder for each league, each voter was instructed to name three outfielders regardless of position (still the practice today).

In 1965 the managers and coaches of each team took

over the voting responsibility, which they have retained ever since. Voters are not permitted to select players on their own teams. In 1987, 139 different managers and coaches took part in the balloting.

Perhaps because of its originality, the Gold Glove is the one *Sporting News* award that has gained universal acceptance and prestige in the baseball world. However, as with any award, the selections often draw criticism.

One complaint is that too much importance is given to fielding average. Most of us realize that FA is not always a reliable indicator of defensive ability, but how much does it influence the Gold Glove voters?

Of the 366 FA leaders at the various positions between 1957–87 (discounting pitchers and counting only one outfielder per league each year), 118 (32 percent) also won their respective Gold Glove Awards (see Table 1). We can say, then, that if a player leads his league in FA, he has about a one-in-three chance of winning the Gold Glove—not an overwhelming correlation, but about four times better than random chance.

This raises some interesting questions. Since official fielding statistics are not published until months *after* Gold Gloves are voted on, any voter relying on fielding stats would probably have to consult (or remember) the *previous* year's data. Therefore, if FA itself really does impress voters, we should expect to see many players winning a Gold Glove the year *after* they lead in FA. Do they? Well, no (see Table 2). The percentage here is 25 percent or one-in-four—again, considerably better than chance, but less of a factor than leading in FA in the current year.

And what about the influence of Gold Gloves on fielding averages? Is an official scorer less likely to charge an error against a player simply because he won a Gold Glove the previous year? Apparently not (see Table 3). The percentage of Gold Glove recipients leading in FA the following year is 23 percent.

"It is my belief that a lot more is considered than fielding percentage," says *TSN* editor Tom Barnidge, citing "range, throwing arm, the headiness of the ballplayer." Cincinnati's Pete Rose, a two-time Gold Glove winner concurred: "There are a lot of intangibles involved in voting for the Gold Glove. Take an outfielder. The coaches and managers watch these guys all the time. How they play the hitters, how strong their arms are, how often they hit the cutoff man, and all that is taken into consideration—things that do not show up in the statistics."

Another criticism of the Gold Glove is that batting performance plays a role in the selections, contrary to the award's philosophy. As *USA Today* baseball editor Hal Bodley puts it, "A player who is outstanding on defense and respectable on offense has a much better chance of getting a Gold Glove than a counterpart whose forte is fielding alone."

Other factors can be distractions to the voters: flashiness, reputations, and the selection process itself. For insight on some of these and their effects, I consulted an expert on the Gold Glove: Wes Parker, a six-time winner of the award at first base.

Parker, it should be noted, would seem to have no reason to gripe about the award. He grasped the honor from a seven-time winner; he won it even when he batted as low as .239; and he became one of only two nonpitchers (Roberto Clemente is the other) to win the award in his final major league season.

"I would say many, if not most, coaches and managers fail to take their voting responsibility seriously," says Parker. "They don't treat it as a vital act. They are usually much more concerned with their team and the pennant race and, as a result, tend to zip through the ballots (distributed in September). So they wind up voting for the most recognizable names."

Parker brings out another rarely discussed procedural problem: "Since players [when they were voting] and coaches are forbidden to vote for anyone on their own team, they often won't vote for the guy who is contending with their team's leading candidate for the same award. That increases their teammate's chances."

On the subject of reputation, Parker asserts that it "has a lot to do with it, absolutely. In 1966, Bill White won the award (for the seventh consecutive time), although even White admitted that I probably deserved it. It takes a couple of years for your reputation to catch up with you, but that can work to your advantage at the end of your career.

"Flashiness is a factor too," continues Parker. "It puts the player's name in the forefront of the voter's minds." Wes also concurs with the theory that a player's bat can be the difference in winning this 'fielding' award.

"[Four-time Gold Glove winner Steve] Garvey is a good example of someone who won it with his bat and notoriety, a perfect example, in fact," opines Parker. "Garvey was vastly overrated defensively . . . he had no range, no arm, and no aggressiveness. He would hold the ball and allow opposing runners to take extra bases to avoid throwing errors. That's how he compiled his high [fielding] averages at first base. Remember, he was a terrible third baseman, worst I ever saw." (In 1972, Garvey's last season as a third-sacker, he led the NL with 28 errors in just 85 games, posting a woeful .902 percentage.)

"Amazingly, despite these prejudices," Parker concludes, "I think the Gold Glove choices have been excellent. At first base I think they have been perfect, with the exception of Garvey."

TABLE 1 Fielding Average Leaders Winning Gold Glove, 1957-87 (Maximum 61 Each Position).			
POS.	NL	AL	TOT.	PCT.
C	7	7	14	23
1B	13	13	26	43
2B	14	5	19	31
3B	4	15	19	31
SS	14	12	26	43
OF	6	8	14	23
TOT.	58	60	118	32

TABLE 2 Fielding Average Leaders Winning Gold Glove in Following Season, 1956-86 (Maximum 61 Each Position).			
POS.	NL	AL	TOT.	PCT.
C	7	7	14	23
1B	8	11	19	31
2B	9	6	15	25
3B	3	13	16	26
SS	11	9	20	33
OF	2	5	7	11
TOT.	40	51	91	25

TABLE 3 Fielding Average Leaders Who Won Gold Glove in Previous Season, 1958-87 (Maximum 59 Each Position).			
POS.	NL	AL	TOT.	PCT.
C	3	7	10	17
1B	11	8	19	32
2B	8	2	10	17
3B	2	12	14	24
SS	10	9	19	32
OF	6	5	11	19
TOT.	40	43	83	23

While the Gold Glove Award has adequately filled the need for a subjective fielding award, there is still something to be said about fielding statistics. It is fashionable to say that fielding stats are meaningless, but, as analyst Bill James says, "If a baseball statistic is meaningless to you, that is simply because you don't know what it means."

With the understanding of which fielding statistics *are* meaningful for each position, it is possible to make a pretty reliable judgment of a player's defensive skills based on stats alone. In recent years, several analysts have attempted to measure individual fielding performance on the basis of numbers.

One newer method is Linear Weights, Pete Palmer's translation of individual batting, pitching, and fielding statistics into runs gained and thus games won. The fielding portion of the system, Fielding or Defensive Wins, incorporates data (variously weighted according to position) on putouts, assists, errors, and double plays, comparing a player's totals against the league averages.

The formula first determines how many runs a player saves (or costs) his team as compared to an "average" player at the same position. Runs are then translated into wins, based on the league average of runs per win. For example, second baseman Glenn Hubbard was computed to have won about three and a half games for the Braves with his glove in 1986, the top Defensive Wins total in the majors.

Of the sixty players identified by the Palmer system as the best fielders in their leagues between 1957–86, twenty-eight also won their respective Gold Glove Awards.

Palmer has drawn criticism for comparing players with average, rather than replacement-level, players; for overemphasizing the double play; and for the use of arbitrary weighting schemes. It is particularly—and admittedly—inadequate in evaluating catchers.

Bill James has also presented a fielding measurement system, Defensive Won/Lost Percentage (DW/L%), although he hasn't used it since 1984. The formula varies from position to position, using four arbitrarily weighted components at each. These components range from readily available statistics (fielding average, assists per game, and so on) to abstruse estimations and calculations, using some data unavailable to the average researcher. The formula is not designed for cross-era comparisons.

The results of these calculations produce the DW/L%, which in turn is translated into defensive wins and losses, based on still more arbitrary assignments of defensive games at each position (ranging from 3 at first base to 11 at shortstop).

Of the thirty-two players identified by DW/L% as the best at their positions and leagues for the 1983–84 seasons, twelve (38 percent) also won their respective Gold Gloves.

The use of a series of arbitrary values is the glaring flaw of DW/L%. Criticism is also due for the complexity and lack of adaptability of the system(s).

The Elias Sports Bureau has demonstrated a simple and generally effective system for evaluating fielders: comparing the number of runs scored per nine innings while a player is on the field to the number scored when he isn't. For example, Elias calculated that the 1982–86 Cardinals averaged allowing 3.85 runs per nine innings with Ozzie Smith at shortstop, as compared to 4.04 per game with other shortstops.

There is nothing new or brilliant about this concept; the difference is that Elias has the data available to make this type of measurement, right down to thirds of an inning, at least for the last dozen years. Since they generally choose not to share this data with the public, however, it is of no value at present.

So, when all is said and done about modern statistical fielding measurements, a subjective measurement—the Gold Glove—is probably still the best tool we have available to rate fielders.

The following pages list the winners of the Gold Glove at each position since 1957. Complete balloting for Gold Glove elections is, unfortunately, neither available nor researchable.

Gold Glove Award

Pitchers

Year	National League	American League
1957	(No selection)	B. Shantz, NY
1958	H. Haddix, CIN	B. Shantz, NY
1959	H. Haddix, PIT	B. Shantz, NY
1960	H. Haddix, PIT	B. Shantz, NY
1961	B. Shantz, PIT	F. Lary, DET
1962	B. Shantz, SL	J. Kaat, MIN
1963	B. Shantz, SL	J. Kaat, MIN
1964	B. Shantz, PHI	J. Kaat, MIN
1965	B. Gibson, SL	J. Kaat, MIN
1966	B. Gibson, SL	J. Kaat, MIN
1967	B. Gibson, SL	J. Kaat, MIN
1968	B. Gibson, SL	J. Kaat, MIN
1969	B. Gibson, SL	J. Kaat, MIN
1970	B. Gibson, SL	J. Kaat, MIN
1971	B. Gibson, SL	J. Kaat, MIN
1972	B. Gibson, SL	J. Kaat, MIN
1973	B. Gibson, SL	J. Kaat, MIN
1974	A. Messersmith, LA	J. Kaat, CHI
1975	A. Messersmith, LA	J. Kaat, CHI
1976	J. Kaat, PHI	J. Palmer, BAL
1977	J. Kaat, PHI	J. Palmer, BAL
1978	P. Niekro, ATL	J. Palmer, BAL
1979	P. Niekro, ATL	J. Palmer, BAL
1980	P. Niekro, ATL	M. Norris, OAK
1981	S. Carlton, PHI	M. Norris, OAK
1982	P. Niekro, ATL	R. Guidry, NY
1983	P. Niekro, ATL	R. Guidry, NY
1984	J. Andujar, SL	R. Guidry, NY
1985	R. Reuschel, PIT	R. Guidry, NY
1986	F. Valenzuela, LA	R. Guidry, NY
1987	R. Reuschel, SF	M. Langston, SEA
1988	O. Hershiser, LA	M. Langston, SEA
1989	R. Darling, NY	B. Saberhagen, KC
1990	G. Maddux, CHI	M. Boddicker, BOS

Catchers

Year	National League	American League
1957	(No selection)	S. Lollar, CHI
1958	D. Crandall, MIL	S. Lollar, CHI
1959	D. Crandall, MIL	S. Lollar, CHI
1960	D. Crandall, MIL	E. Battey, WAS
1961	J. Roseboro, LA	E. Battey, MIN
1962	D. Crandall, MIL	E. Battey, MIN
1963	J. Edwards, CIN	E. Howard, NY
1964	J. Edwards, CIN	E. Howard, NY
1965	J. Torre, MIL	B. Freehan, DET
1966	J. Roseboro, LA	B. Freehan, DET
1967	R. Hundley, CHI	B. Freehan, DET
1968	J. Bench, CIN	B. Freehan, DET
1969	J. Bench, CIN	B. Freehan, DET
1970	J. Bench, CIN	R. Fosse, CLE
1971	J. Bench, CIN	R. Fosse, CLE
1972	J. Bench, CIN	C. Fisk, BOS
1973	J. Bench, CIN	T. Munson, NY
1974	J. Bench, CIN	T. Munson, NY
1975	J. Bench, CIN	T. Munson, NY
1976	J. Bench, CIN	J. Sundberg, TEX
1977	J. Bench, CIN	J. Sundberg, TEX
1978	B. Boone, PHI	J. Sundberg, TEX
1979	B. Boone, PHI	J. Sundberg, TEX
1980	G. Carter, MON	J. Sundberg, TEX
1981	G. Carter, MON	J. Sundberg, TEX
1982	G. Carter, MON	B. Boone, CAL
1983	T. Pena, PIT	Lc. Parrish, DET
1984	T. Pena, PIT	Lc. Parrish, DET
1985	T. Pena, PIT	Lc. Parrish, DET
1986	J. Davis, CHI	B. Boone, CAL
1987	M. LaValliere, PIT	B. Boone, CAL
1988	B. Santiago, SD	B. Boone, CAL
1989	B. Santiago, SD	B. Boone, CAL
1990	B. Santiago, SD	S. Alomar, CLE

First Baseman

Year	National League	American League
1957	G. Hodges, BKN	(No selection)
1958	G. Hodges, LA	V. Power, CLE
1959	G. Hodges, LA	V. Power, CLE
1960	B. White, SL	V. Power, CLE
1961	B. White, SL	V. Power, CLE
1962	B. White, SL	V. Power, MIN
1963	B. White, SL	V. Power, MIN
1964	B. White, SL	V. Power, LA
1965	B. White, SL	J. Pepitone, NY
1966	B. White, PHI	J. Pepitone, NY
1967	W. Parker, LA	G. Scott, BOS
1968	W. Parker, LA	G. Scott, BOS
1969	W. Parker, LA	J. Pepitone, NY
1970	W. Parker, LA	J. Spencer, CAL
1971	W. Parker, LA	G. Scott, BOS
1972	W. Parker, LA	G. Scott, MIL
1973	M. Jorgenson, MON	G. Scott, MIL
1974	S. Garvey, LA	G. Scott, MIL
1975	S. Garvey, LA	G. Scott, MIL
1976	S. Garvey, LA	G. Scott, MIL
1977	S. Garvey, LA	J. Spencer, CHI
1978	K. Hernandez, SL	C. Chambliss, NY
1979	K. Hernandez, SL	C. Cooper, MIL
1980	K. Hernandez, SL	C. Cooper, MIL
1981	K. Hernandez, SL	M. Squires, CHI
1982	K. Hernandez, SL	E. Murray, BAL
1983	K. Hernandez, SL-NY	E. Murray, BAL
1984	K. Hernandez, NY	E. Murray, BAL
1985	K. Hernandez, NY	D. Mattingly, NY
1986	K. Hernandez, NY	D. Mattingly, NY
1987	K. Hernandez, NY	D. Mattingly, NY
1988	K. Hernandez, NY	D. Mattingly, NY
1989	A. Galarraga, MON	D. Mattingly, NY
1990	A. Galarraga, MON	M. McGwire, OAK

Second Basemen

Year	National League	American League
1957	(No selection)	N. Fox, CHI
1958	B. Mazeroski, PIT	F. Bolling, DET
1959	C. Neal, LA	N. Fox, CHI
1960	B. Mazeroski, PIT	N. Fox, CHI
1961	B. Mazeroski, PIT	B. Richardson, NY
1962	K. Hubbs, CHI	B. Richardson, NY
1963	B. Mazeroski, PIT	B. Richardson, NY
1964	B. Mazeroski, PIT	B. Richardson, NY
1965	B. Mazeroski, PIT	B. Richardson, NY
1966	B. Mazeroski, PIT	B. Knoop, CAL
1967	B. Mazeroski, PIT	B. Knoop, CAL
1968	G. Beckert, CHI	B. Knoop, CAL
1969	F. Millan, ATL	D. Johnson, BAL
1970	T. Helms, CIN	D. Johnson, BAL
1971	T. Helms, CIN	D. Johnson, BAL
1972	F. Millan, ATL	D. Griffin, BOS
1973	J. Morgan, CIN	B. Grich, BAL
1974	J. Morgan, CIN	B. Grich, BAL
1975	J. Morgan, CIN	B. Grich, BAL
1976	J. Morgan, CIN	B. Grich, BAL
1977	J. Morgan, CIN	F. White, KC
1978	D. Lopes, LA	F. White, KC
1979	M. Trillo, PHI	F. White, KC
1980	D. Flynn, NY	F. White, KC
1981	M. Trillo, PHI	F. White, KC
1982	M. Trillo, PHI	F. White, KC
1983	R. Sandberg, CHI	L. Whitaker, DET
1984	R. Sandberg, CHI	L. Whitaker, DET
1985	R. Sandberg, CHI	L. Whitaker, DET
1986	R. Sandberg, CHI	F. White, KC
1987	R. Sandberg, CHI	F. White, KC
1988	R. Sandberg, CHI	H. Reynolds, SEA
1989	R. Sandberg, CHI	H. Reynolds, SEA
1990	R. Sandberg, CHI	H. Reynolds, SEA

Third Basemen

Year	National League	American League
1957	(No selection)	F. Malzone, BOS
1958	K. Boyer, SL	F. Malzone, BOS
1959	K. Boyer, SL	F. Malzone, BOS
1960	K. Boyer, SL	B. Robinson, BAL
1961	K. Boyer, SL	B. Robinson, BAL
1962	J. Davenport, SF	B. Robinson, BAL
1963	K. Boyer, SL	B. Robinson, BAL
1964	R. Santo, CHI	B. Robinson, BAL
1965	R. Santo, CHI	B. Robinson, BAL
1966	R. Santo, CHI	B. Robinson, BAL
1967	R. Santo, CHI	B. Robinson, BAL
1968	R. Santo, CHI	B. Robinson, BAL
1969	C. Boyer, ATL	B. Robinson, BAL
1970	D. Rader, HOU	B. Robinson, BAL
1971	D. Rader, HOU	B. Robinson, BAL
1972	D. Rader, HOU	B. Robinson, BAL
1973	D. Rader, HOU	B. Robinson, BAL
1974	D. Rader, HOU	B. Robinson, BAL
1975	K. Reitz, SL	B. Robinson, BAL
1976	M. Schmidt, PHI	A. Rodriguez, DET
1977	M. Schmidt, PHI	G. Nettles, NY
1978	M. Schmidt, PHI	G. Nettles, NY
1979	M. Schmidt, PHI	B. Bell, TEX
1980	M. Schmidt, PHI	B. Bell, TEX
1981	M. Schmidt, PHI	B. Bell, TEX
1982	M. Schmidt, PHI	B. Bell, TEX
1983	M. Schmidt, PHI	B. Bell, TEX
1984	M. Schmidt, PHI	B. Bell, TEX
1985	T. Wallach, MON	G. Brett, KC
1986	M. Schmidt, PHI	G. Gaetti, MIN
1987	T. Pendleton, SL	G. Gaetti, MIN
1988	T. Wallach, MON	G. Gaetti, MIN
1989	T. Pendleton, SL	G. Gaetti, MIN
1990	T. Wallach, MON	K. Gruber, TOR

Shortstops

Year	National League	American League
1957	R. McMillan, CIN	(No selection)
1958	R. McMillan, CIN	L. Aparicio, CHI
1959	R. McMillan, CIN	L. Aparicio, CHI
1960	E. Banks, CHI	L. Aparicio, CHI
1961	M. Wills, LA	L. Aparicio, CHI
1962	M. Wills, LA	L. Aparicio, CHI
1963	B. Wine, PHI	Z. Versalles, MIN
1964	R. Amaro, PHI	L. Aparicio, BAL
1965	L. Cardenas, CIN	Z. Versalles, MIN
1966	G. Alley, PIT	L. Aparicio, BAL
1967	G. Alley, PIT	J. Fregosi, CAL
1968	D. Maxvill, SL	L. Aparicio, CHI
1969	D. Kessinger, CHI	M. Belanger, BAL
1970	D. Kessinger, CHI	L. Aparicio, CHI
1971	B. Harrelson, NY	M. Belanger, BAL
1972	L. Bowa, PHI	E. Brinkman, DET
1973	R. Metzger, HOU	M. Belanger, BAL
1974	D. Concepcion, CIN	M. Belanger, BAL
1975	D. Concepcion, CIN	M. Belanger, BAL
1976	D. Concepcion, CIN	M. Belanger, BAL
1977	D. Concepcion, CIN	M. Belanger, BAL
1978	L. Bowa, PHI	M. Belanger, BAL
1979	D. Concepcion, CIN	R. Burleson, BOS
1980	O. Smith, SD	A. Trammell, DET
1981	O. Smith, SD	A. Trammell, DET
1982	O. Smith, SL	R. Yount, MIL
1983	O. Smith, SL	A. Trammell, DET
1984	O. Smith, SL	A. Trammell, DET
1985	O. Smith, SL	A. Griffin, OAK
1986	O. Smith, SL	T. Fernandez, TOR
1987	O. Smith, SL	T. Fernandez, TOR
1988	O. Smith, SL	T. Fernandez, TOR
1989	O. Smith, SL	T. Fernandez, TOR
1990	O. Smith, SL	O. Guillen, CHI

National League Outfielders

YEAR	PLAYERS		
1957	W. Mays, NY (CF)	(No other selections)	
1958	F. Robinson, CIN (LF)	W. Mays, SF (CF)	H. Aaron, MIL (RF)
1959	J. Brandt, SF (LF)	W. Mays, SF (CF)	H. Aaron, MIL (RF)
1960	W. Moon, LA (LF)	W. Mays, SF (CF)	H. Aaron, MIL (RF)
1961	W. Mays, SF	R. Clemente, PIT	V. Pinson, CIN
1962	W. Mays, SF	R. Clemente, PIT	B. Virdon, PIT
1963	W. Mays, SF	R. Clemente, PIT	C. Flood, SL
1964	W. Mays, SF	R. Clemente, PIT	C. Flood, SL
1965	W. Mays, SF	R. Clemente, PIT	C. Flood, SL
1966	W. Mays, SF	C. Flood, SL	R. Clemente, PIT
1967	R. Clemente, PIT	C. Flood, SL	W. Mays, SF
1968	W. Mays, SF	R. Clemente, PIT	C. Flood, SL
1969	R. Clemente, PIT	C. Flood, SL	P. Rose, CIN
1970	R. Clemente, PIT	T. Agee, NY	P. Rose, CIN
1971	R. Clemente, PIT	B. Bonds, SF	W. Davis, LA
1972	R. Clemente, PIT	C. Cedeno, HOU	W. Davis, LA
1973	B. Bonds, SF	C. Cedeno, HOU	W. Davis, LA
1974	C. Cedeno, HOU	C. Geronimo, CIN	B. Bonds, SF
1975	C. Cedeno, HOU	C. Geronimo, CIN	G. Maddox, PHI
1976	C. Cedeno, HOU	C. Geronimo, CIN	G. Maddox, PHI
1977	C. Geronimo, CIN	G. Maddox, PHI	D. Parker, PIT
1978	G. Maddox, PHI	D. Parker, PIT	E. Valentine, MON
1979	G. Maddox, PHI	D. Parker, PIT	D. Winfield, SD
1980	A. Dawson, MON	G. Maddox, PHI	D. Winfield, SD
1981	A. Dawson, MON	G. Maddox, PHI	D. Baker, LA
1982	A. Dawson, MON	D. Murphy, ATL	G. Maddox, PHI
1983	A. Dawson, MON	D. Murphy, ATL	W. McGee, SL
1984	D. Murphy, ATL	B. Dernier, CHI	A. Dawson, MON
1985	W. McGee, SL	D. Murphy, ATL	A. Dawson, MON
1986	T. Gwynn, SD	D. Murphy, ATL	W. McGee, SL
1987	E. Davis, CIN	T. Gwynn, SD	A. Dawson, CHI
1988	A. Van Slyke, PIT	E. Davis, CIN	A. Dawson, CHI
1989	A. Van Slyke, PIT	E. Davis, CIN	T. Gwynn, SD
1990	A. Van Slyke, PIT	T. Gwynn, SD	B. Bonds, PIT

American League Outfielders

YEAR	PLAYERS		
1957	M. Minoso, CHI (LF)	A. Kaline, DET (RF)	(No other selection)
1958	N. Siebern, NY (LF)	J. Piersall, BOS (CF)	A. Kaline, DET (RF)
1959	M. Minoso, CLE (LF)	A. Kaline, DET (CF)	J. Jensen, BOS (RF)
1960	M. Minoso, CHI (LF)	J. Landis, CHI (CF)	R. Maris, NY (RF)
1961	A. Kaline, DET	J. Piersall, CLE	J. Landis, CHI
1962	J. Landis, CHI	M. Mantle, NY	A. Kaline, DET
1963	A. Kaline, DET	C. Yastrzemski, BOS	J. Landis, CHI
1964	A. Kaline, DET	J. Landis, CHI	V. Davalillo, CLE
1965	A. Kaline, DET	T. Tresh, NY	C. Yastrzemski, BOS
1966	A. Kaline, DET	T. Agee, CHI	T. Oliva, MIN
1967	C. Yastrzemski, BOS	P. Blair, BAL	A. Kaline, DET
1968	M. Stanley, DET	C. Yastrzemski, BOS	R. Smith, BOS
1969	P. Blair, BAL	M. Stanley, DET	C. Yastrzemski, BOS
1970	M. Stanley, DET	P. Blair, BAL	K. Berry, CHI
1971	P. Blair, BAL	A. Otis, KC	C. Yastrzemski, BOS
1972	P. Blair, BAL	B. Murcer, NY	K. Berry, CAL
1973	P. Blair, BAL	A. Otis, KC	M. Stanley, DET
1974	P. Blair, BAL	A. Otis, KC	J. Rudi, OAK
1975	P. Blair, BAL	J. Rudi, OAK	F. Lynn, BOS
1976	J. Rudi, OAK	Dw. Evans, BOS	R. Manning, CLE
1977	C. Yastrzemski, BOS	Dw. Evans, BOS	A. Cowens, KC
1978	F. Lynn, BOS	Dw. Evans, BOS	R. Miller, CAL
1979	Dw. Evans, BOS	S. Lezcano, MIL	F. Lynn, BOS
1980	F. Lynn, BOS	D. Murphy, OAK	W. Wilson, KC
1981	D. Murphy, OAK	Dw. Evans, BOS	R. Henderson, OAK
1982	Dw. Evans, BOS	D. Winfield, NY	D. Murphy, OAK
1983	Dw. Evans, BOS	D. Winfield, NY	D. Murphy, OAK
1984	Dw. Evans, BOS	D. Winfield, NY	D. Murphy, OAK
1985	G. Pettis, CAL	D. Winfield, NY	Dw. Evans, BOS & D. Murphy, OAK
1986	G. Pettis, CAL	J. Barfield, TOR	K. Puckett, MIN
1987	J. Barfield, TOR	K. Puckett, MIN	D. Winfield, NY
1988	K. Puckett, MIN	D. White, CAL	G. Pettis, DET
1989	D. White, CAL	G. Pettis, DET	K. Puckett, MIN
1990	G. Pettis, TEX	K. Griffey, Jr., SEA	E. Burks, BOS

Hall of Fame Elections: History

In the 1930s plans were being made to celebrate baseball's 100th anniversary, based on the findings of the Mills Commission three decades earlier: "The first scheme for playing baseball, according to the best evidence obtainable to date, was devised by Abner Doubleday at Cooperstown, New York, in 1839." A small-scale baseball museum was established in Cooperstown, and a Centennial Committee composed of six baseball bigwigs ordered the first Hall of Fame election. On January 29, 1936, the results of this election were announced, with five immortals qualifying for enshrinement (although actual induction was delayed until formal opening of the Hall on June 12, 1939).

Actually, there were two elections in 1936: one a poll of 226 members of the Baseball Writers' Association of America (BBWAA), and the other held by a special veterans' committee of 78 designed to choose from among "old-timers." No specific guidelines were set as to who was eligible for consideration (several active players received strong support), nor to which committee would consider whom (resulting in Cy Young's split vote: 49 percent in the writers' election, 41 percent in the veterans'). A 75 percent majority was necessary for election by either committee, a voting feature which has survived a half century of Hall of Fame elections.

Elections were held by both the BBWAA and an old-timers' committee for each of the next three years, resulting in a total of 26 inductees in 1939. After that, BBWAA elections were scheduled at three-year intervals, with only one player elected in 1942 and none in 1945. A decision was made to hold annual elections beginning in 1946. This continued through 1956, when it was decided to hold elections only every other year. Annual elections were resumed a decade later and continue to this day.

A nominating system was installed after the 1945 election, providing for the top twenty vote-getters in a preliminary balloting to be listed alphabetically on a second and final ballot. The preliminary election's vote totals were not to be divulged until after the final balloting (so as not to influence voters), nor would they assure anyone of automatic election. However, this system proved an utter failure in 1946 and was amended in December of that year. Thereafter, anyone receiving 75 percent of the votes on the nominating ballot would be automatically elected, eliminating the runoff election.

No runoff was required until 1949, when Charlie Gehringer was elected on the second ballot. The nominating system was discontinued after that year but revived from 1960 to 1968 (providing for reconsideration of the top thirty vote-getters), being put into practice in 1964 and 1967.

Currently, an eligible candidate must have played at least ten seasons in the majors and been active at some point during a period beginning twenty years and ending five years before a given election. The five-year wait rule was first implemented in 1954 (excepting candidates who had already received 100 or more votes in a previous election); a one-year wait had been in effect from 1946–53, and no wait was specified before then (due to World War II, it was sometimes unclear who was still "active"). At the other end of the span, the twenty-year rule has been in effect since 1962; the cutoff was thirty years from 1956–62, and twenty-five years from 1946–56.

Following Roberto Clemente's tragic death, a rule was passed in 1973 providing for the immediate consideration of an eligible candidate who dies while still active, or before the five-year waiting period has elapsed. Clemente was inducted overwhelmingly (393 of 424 votes) in a special election held that March. A few months later, the new rule was amended to allow consideration at least six months after a player's death (or five years after his retirement, whichever is less).

Ten-year active and honorary members of the BBWAA are eligible to vote in the annual election (the 10-year restriction was installed in 1947). About 400 writers submit ballots each year, voting for up to ten eligible candidates apiece. At various times over the past three decades, it has been suggested that the enfranchisement be limited to a few dozen of the top baseball writers.

A candidate Screening Committee was first employed in 1968, limiting the ballot to forty candidates. Standards were relaxed somewhat after former pitcher Milt Pappas vociferously objected to his elimination by this committee (Pappas was allowed on the ballot in 1979, receiving 5 of 432 votes). Nomination by any of the six members of the Screening Committee now ensures a candidate at least one try on the BBWAA ballot; however, if he receives less than 5 percent of the vote, he is eliminated from future consideration. (Fortunately for many, this rule has not always been existent; more than seventy current Hall of Famers received less than 5 percent of the vote in their first tries!)

The Baseball Hall of Fame Committee on Baseball Veterans was established in July 1953. Previously, special old-timers' committees had elected new members in 1936–39, 1944–46, and 1949.

The new committee was composed of eleven members. This number was increased to twelve in 1960, eighteen in 1979, and twenty in 1987. Elections were held every other year at first, but have been held annually since 1961.

In most years the committee has been limited to naming no more than two new inductees per election. Exceptions occurred in the elections of 1953 (six), 1963 (four), 1964 (six), 1970 (three), 1971 (seven), and 1972–77 (three each). Voting details are not released to the public.

Individuals considered by the Veterans' Committee include managers, umpires, executives, and players no longer eligible through the BBWAA (except members of the committee). For eligibility under the former three groups, a person must have been retired five years, or six months if he has reached the age of sixty-five (a rule tailor-made for Casey Stengel's election in 1966). For players, the minimum wait is twenty-three years; previously, it was twenty-five years (1953–56, 1974–84), thirty years (1957–62), or twenty years (1963–73).

On June 10, 1971, a nine-member Baseball Hall of Fame Committee on Negro Baseball Leagues was established. Candidates were to have totaled at least ten years of service in the pre-1946 Negro Leagues and/or the major leagues, without being eligible for BBWAA election. A rule specified that the "Committee shall serve until it shall dissolve itself of its own motion or until further notice from the Board of Directors" of the Hall of Fame.

At least one new member was inducted by this committee in each year between 1971 and 1977. By 1975 the committee had only 6 remaining members, and by 1979 it had been dissolved and absorbed into the Veterans' Committee. Only two Negro League representatives have been enshrined since 1977.

As far back as 1944, it was suggested that a special "Roll of Honor," distinct from actual Hall of Fame induction, be established for distinguished baseball writers and similar contributors to the baseball world. In 1962 the J. G. Taylor Spink Award was initiated to honor individuals "for meritorious contributions to baseball writing." In 1978 the Ford C. Frick Award was established to dignify broadcasters "for major contributions to the game of Baseball." The awards are presented annually during the Hall of Fame induction ceremonies and the winners' names are engraved on a plaque hanging in the National Baseball Library (explaining references to a writers' or broadcasters' "wing" at the Hall of Fame). Through 1990 there had been forty-one winners of the Spink Award, and fourteen recipients of the Frick trophy.

There have been a total of 200 men inducted into the National Baseball Hall of Fame and Museum through 1988, including 154 major league players, twenty classified as pioneers or executives, eleven Negro Leaguers, ten managers and five umpires (many of the latter four groups also played in the majors or minors); seventy-four individuals have been elected by the BBWAA, 117 by the various veterans' committees, and nine by the Negro Leagues' Committee.

What follows is, first, a roster of the 206 members of the Hall of Fame named between 1936 and 1990; second, an index of every man (661 in all) who ever received so much as a single vote for the Hall of Fame, detailing each man's total for each year he received support; and third, the top ten finishers in the voting for each year of balloting since 1936. Men named to the Hall of Fame by special committee action, such as Alexander Cartwright or Josh Gibson, may not have received votes in an election, but they are included in this index as well. (There have been four such committee groupings: the Centennial Commission of 1937–1938, the Old Timers' Committee of 1939–1949, the Veterans Committee of 1953–present, and the Negro Leagues Committee of 1971–1977.)

Of special interest are some prominent players who were not elected or named to the Hall: Gil Hodges, who received the most votes for the Hall of Fame but remains outside it; Herman Long, who finished among the top ten vote-getters in the Veterans Ballot of 1936, which during later years produced twenty-nine future Hall of Famers; Hank Gowdy and Tony Lazzeri, who in the 1950s experienced a fate similar to Long's; and Marty Marion, and Allie Reynolds, other long-term vote-getters who were not able to bunch their support in a given year. And don't get White Sox fans talking about Nellie Fox and the election of 1985, when, in his final year of eligibility for the Baseball Writers Election, Fox fell only two votes short of the 297 that would have granted him enshrinement—the closest any man has ever come without making it.

The Hall of Fame balloting results were researched and compiled by Pete Palmer.

Hall of Fame Roster

FIRST BASEMEN
Anson, Cap
Beckley, Jake
Bottomley, Jim
Brouthers, Dan
Chance, Frank
Connor, Roger
Foxx, Jimmie
Gehrig, Lou
Greenberg, Hank
Kelly, George
Killebrew, Harmon
McCovey, Willie
Mize, Johnny
Sisler, George
Stargell, Willie
Terry, Bill

SECOND BASEMEN
Collins, Eddie
Doerr, Bobby
Evers, Johnny
Frisch, Frankie
Gehringer, Charlie
Herman, Billy
Hornsby, Rogers
Lajoie, Nap
Morgan, Joe
Robinson, Jackie
Schoendienst, Red

SHORTSTOPS
Aparicio, Luis
Appling, Luke
Bancroft, Dave
Banks, Ernie
Boudreau, Lou
Cronin, Joe
Jackson, Travis
Jennings, Hugh

Maranville, Rabbit
Reese, Pee Wee
Sewell, Joe
Tinker, Joe
Vaughan, Arky
Wagner, Honus
Wallace, Bobby
Ward, Monte

THIRD BASEMEN
Baker, Frank
Collins, Jimmy
Kell, George
Lindstrom, Fred
Mathews, Eddie
Robinson, Brooks
Traynor, Pie

LEFT FIELDERS
Brock, Lou
Burkett, Jesse
Clarke, Fred
Delahanty, Ed
Goslin, Goose
Hafey, Chick
Kelley, Joe
Kiner, Ralph
Manush, Heinie
Medwick, Joe
Musial, Stan
O'Rourke, Jim
Simmons, Al
Wheat, Zack
Williams, Billy
Williams, Ted
Yastrzemski, Carl

CENTER FIELDERS
Averill, Earl

Carey, Max
Cobb, Ty
Combs, Earle
DiMaggio, Joe
Duffy, Hugh
Hamilton, Billy
Mantle, Mickey
Mays, Willie
Roush, Edd
Snider, Duke
Speaker, Tris
Waner, Lloyd
Wilson, Hack

RIGHT FIELDERS
Aaron, Hank
Clemente, Roberto
Crawford, Sam
Cuyler, Kiki
Flick, Elmer
Heilmann, Harry
Hooper, Harry
Kaline, Al
Keeler, Willie
Kelly, King
Klein, Chuck
McCarthy, Tommy
Ott, Mel
Rice, Sam
Robinson, Frank
Ruth, Babe
Slaughter, Enos
Stargell, Willie
Thompson, Sam
Waner, Paul
Youngs, Ross

CATCHERS
Bench, Johnny

Berra, Yogi
Bresnahan, Roger
Campanella, Roy
Cochrane, Mickey
Dickey, Bill
Ewing, Buck
Ferrell, Rick
Hartnett, Gabby
Lombardi, Ernie
Schalk, Ray

PITCHERS
Alexander, Grover
Bender, Chief
Brown, Mordecai
Chesbro, Jack
Clarkson, John
Coveleski, Stan
Dean, Dizzy
Drysdale, Don
Faber, Red
Feller, Bob
Ford, Whitey
Galvin, Pud
Gibson, Bob
Gomez, Lefty
Grimes, Burleigh
Grove, Lefty
Haines, Jess
Hoyt, Waite
Hubbell, Carl
Hunter, Catfish
Johnson, Walter
Joss, Addie
Keefe, Tim
Koufax, Sandy
Lemon, Bob
Lyons, Ted
Marichal, Juan

Marquard, Rube
Mathewson, Christy
McGinnity, Joe
Nichols, Kid
Palmer, Jim
Pennock, Herb
Plank, Eddie
Radbourn, Charles
Rixey, Eppa
Roberts, Robin
Ruffing, Red
Rusie, Amos
Spahn, Warren
Vance, Dazzy
Waddell, Rube
Walsh, Ed
Welch, Mickey
Wilhelm, Hoyt
Wynn, Early
Young, Cy

FROM NEGRO LEAGUES
Bell, Cool Papa
Charleston, Oscar
Dandridge, Ray
Dihigo, Martin
Foster, Rube
Gibson, Josh
Irvin, Monte
Johnson, Judy
Leonard, Buck
Lloyd, John
Paige, Satchel

MANAGERS
Alston, Walter
Harris, Bucky
Huggins, Miller

Lopez, Al
Mack, Connie
McCarthy, Joe
McGraw, John
McKechnie, Bill
Robinson, Wilbert
Stengel, Casey

UMPIRES
Barlick, Al
Conlan, Jocko
Connolly, Tom
Evans, Billy
Hubbard, Cal
Klem, Bill

PIONEERS AND EXECUTIVES
Barrow, Ed
Bulkeley, Morgan
Cartwright, Alexander
Chadwick, Henry
Chandler, Albert
Comiskey, Charles
Cummings, Candy
Frick, Ford
Giles, Warren
Griffith, Clark
Harridge, Will
Johnson, Ban
Landis, Kenesaw
MacPhail, Larry
Rickey, Branch
Spalding, Al
Weiss, George
Wright, George
Wright, Harry
Yawkey, Tom

Hall of Fame Balloting: Vote Totals of All Candidates

Hank Aaron
Inducted in 1982

1982 406

Babe Adams

1937 8
1938 11
1939 11
1942 11
1945 7
1946 NOM 6
1947 22
1948 4
1949 5
1950 6
1951 12
1952 9
1953 17
1954 13
1955 24

Sparky Adams

1958 1
1960 1

Bobby Adams

1966 1

Pete Alexander
Inducted in 1938

1936 55
1937 125
1938 212

Dick Allen

1983 14
1985 28
1986 41
1987 55
1988 52
1989 35
1990 58

Johnny Allen

1955 1

Doug Allison

1936 V 1

Felipe Alou

1980 3

Jay Alou

1985 1

Matty Alou

1980 5

Walt Alston
Inducted in 1983
Manager

1983 . . . . . . Vet. Com.

Nick Altrock

1937 3
1938 7
1939 6
1953 1
1954 2
1958 20
1960 18

Cap Anson
Inducted in 1939

1936 V 40
1939 . . . . . . O/T Com.

Luis Aparicio
Inducted in 1984

1979 120
1980 124
1981 48

1982 174
1983 252
1984 341

Luke Appling
Inducted in 1964

1953 2
1955 3
1956 14
1958 77
1960 72
1962 48
1964 142
1964 RO 189

Jimmy Archer

1937 6
1938 7
1939 3

Richie Ashburn

1968 6
1969 10
1970 11
1971 10
1972 11
1973 25
1974 56
1975 76
1976 85
1977 139
1978 158
1979 130
1980 134
1981 142
1982 126

Jimmy Austin

1958 1

Earl Averill
Inducted in 1975

1949 1
1952 2
1955 2
1956 3
1958 14
1960 11
1962 3
1975 . . . . . . Vet. Com.

Bob Bailey

1984 1

Frank Baker
Inducted in 1955

1936 V 1
1937 13
1938 32
1939 30
1942 39
1945 26
1946 NOM 39
1946 36
1947 49
1948 4
1950 4
1951 8
1955 . . . . . . Vet. Com.

Dave Bancroft
Inducted in 1971

1937 3
1938 2
1939 1
1946 NOM 1
1948 4
1949 5
1950 9
1951 9
1952 11
1953 10
1954 10
1955 19
1956 15

1958 43
1960 30
1971 . . . . . . Vet. Com.

Sal Bando

1987 3

Ernie Banks
Inducted in 1977

1977 321

Al Barlick
Inducted in 1989
Umpire

1989 . . . . . . Vet. Com.

Ross Barnes

1936 V 3

Ed Barrow
Inducted in 1953
Executive

1953 . . . . . . Vet. Com.

Jack Barry

1938 3
1939 1

Dick Bartell

1948 1
1951 1
1958 1
1960 1

Joe Battin

1936 V 1

Hank Bauer

1967 23
1967 RO 9

Ginger Beaumont

1938 1
1942 1
1945 1
1946 NOM 1

Glenn Beckert

1981 1

Jake Beckley
Inducted in 1971

1936 V 1
1942 1
1971 . . . . . . Vet. Com.

Mark Belanger

1988 16

Cool Papa Bell
Inducted in 1974

1974 . . . . . Neg. Com.

Johnny Bench
Inducted in 1989

1989 431

Chief Bender
Inducted in 1953

1936 2
1937 17
1938 33
1939 40
1942 55
1945 40
1946 NOM 39
1946 35
1947 72
1948 5
1949 2
1950 6

1951 35
1952 70
1953 104
1953 . . . . . . Vet. Com.

Charlie Bennett

1936 V 3

Larry Benton

1958 1

Moe Berg

1958 3
1960 5

Marty Bergen

1937 2
1938 1
1939 1

Wally Berger

1956 1
1958 2

Yogi Berra
Inducted in 1972

1971 242
1972 339

Charlie Berry

1955 1
1958 3

Jim Bibby

1990 1

Carson Bigbee

1948 1

Jack Billingham

1986 1

Max Bishop

1955 1
1956 1
1958 4
1960 5

Ewell Blackwell

1968 5
1969 11
1970 14

Ray Blades

1958 1
1960 1

Paul Blair

1986 8

Steve Blass

1980 2

Lu Blue

1954 1

Ossie Bluege

1948 2
1949 1
1954 1
1956 2
1958 2
1960 3

Ping Bodie

1937 2
1949 1

Joe Boley

1942 1

Tommy Bond

1936 V 1

Bobby Bonds

1987 24
1988 27
1989 29
1990 30

Jim Bottomley
Inducted in 1974

1948 4
1949 8
1950 8
1951 6
1952 7
1953 10
1954 16
1955 26
1956 42
1958 57
1960 89
1962 20
1974 . . . . . . Vet. Com.

Lou Boudreau
Inducted in 1970

1956 2
1958 64
1960 35
1962 12
1964 68
1964 RO 43
1966 115
1967 143
1967 RO 68
1968 146
1969 218
1970 232

Jim Bouton

1984 3

Clete Boyer

1978 1
1979 3

Ken Boyer

1975 9
1976 15
1977 14
1978 18
1979 20
1985 68
1986 95
1987 96
1988 109
1989 62
1990 78

Bill Bradley

1936 1
1937 5
1938 2
1939 1
1942 1
1946 NOM 1

Harry Brecheen

1960 7
1968 3
1969 2
1970 3
1971 7
1972 5
1973 3

Ted Breitenstein

1937 1

Roger Bresnahan
Inducted in 1945

1936 47

1937 43
1938 67
1939 67
1942 57
1945 133
1945 . . . . . . O/T Com.

Jim Brewer

1982 2

Tommy Bridges

1956 3
1958 11
1960 4
1962 1
1964 15
1964 RO 1
1966 16

Lou Brock
Inducted in 1985

1985 315

Dan Brouthers
Inducted in 1945

1936 V 2
1945 . . . . . . O/T Com.

Gates Brown

1981 1

Mordecai Brown
Inducted in 1949

1936 6
1937 31
1938 54
1939 54
1942 63
1945 46
1946 NOM 56
1946 48
1949 . . . . . . O/T Com.

Bill Bruton

1971 1

Morgan Bulkeley
Inducted in 1937
Executive

1937 . . . . . . Cen. Com.

Jim Bunning

1977 146
1978 181
1979 147
1980 177
1981 164
1982 138
1983 138
1984 201
1985 214
1986 279
1987 289
1988 317
1989 283
1990 257

Lew Burdette

1973 12
1974 7
1975 11
1976 21
1977 85
1978 76
1979 53
1980 66
1981 48
1982 43
1983 43
1984 97
1985 82
1986 96
1987 96

Smoky Burgess

1973 1
1974 2

Jesse Burkett
Inducted in 1946

1936 V 1
1937 1
1938 2
1942 4
1945 2
1946 NOM 2
1946 . . . . . . O/T Com.

George J. Burns

1937 3
1938 3
1939 1
1949 1
1950 2

Guy Bush

1956 2

Joe Bush

1958 5

Donie Bush

1937 1
1939 2
1942 2
1945 1
1946 NOM 2
1953 1

Leon Cadore

1948 1

Johnny Callison

1979 1

Dolf Camilli

1948 1
1956 1
1958 4
1960 3

Howie Camnitz

1945 1

Roy Campanella
Inducted in 1969

1964 115
1964 RO 138
1966 197
1967 204
1967 RO 170
1968 205
1969 270

Bert Campaneris

1989 14

Jose Cardenal

1986 1

Leo Cardenas

1981 1
1982 1

Max Carey
Inducted in 1961

1937 6
1938 6
1939 7
1945 1
1948 9
1949 12
1950 14
1951 27
1952 36
1953 55
1954 55
1955 119
1956 65
1958 136

1961 . . . . . . Vet. Com.

Chico Carrasquel

1966 1

Bill Carrigan

1937 5
1938 4
1939 2
1945 3

Clay Carroll

1984 1

Rico Carty

1985 1

Alex Cartwright
Inducted in 1938
Pioneer

1938 . . . . . . Cen. Com.

George Case

1958 1
1960 1
1962 1
1964 2

Dave Cash

1986 2

Norm Cash

1980 6

Phil Cavaretta

1962 2
1964 22
1964 RO 1
1966 9
1967 15
1967 RO 4
1968 23
1969 37
1970 51
1971 83
1972 61
1973 73
1974 61
1975 129

Orlando Cepeda

1980 48
1981 77
1982 42
1983 59
1984 124
1985 114
1986 152
1987 179
1988 199
1989 176
1990 211

Henry Chadwick
Inducted in 1938
Pioneer

1938 . . . . . . Cen. Com.

Frank Chance
Inducted in 1946

1936 5
1937 49
1938 133
1939 158
1942 136
1945 179
1946 NOM 144
1946 150
1946 . . . . . . O/T Com.

Happy Chandler
Inducted in 1982
Executive

1982 . . . . . . Vet. Com.

Spud Chandler

1950 2
1951 1
1956 1
1962 2
1964 6

Ben Chapman

1949 1
1952 1

Ray Chapman

1938 1

Sam Chapman

1958 1

Oscar Charleston
Inducted in 1976

1976 . . . . . . Neg. Com.

Hal Chase

1936 11
1937 18

Jack Chesbro
Inducted in 1946

1937 1
1938 2
1939 6
1946 NOM 1
1946 . . . . . . O/T Com.

Bill Cissell

1937 1

Watty Clark

1958 1

Fred Clarke
Inducted in 1945

1936 V 9
1936 1
1937 22
1938 63
1939 59
1942 58
1945 53
1945 . . . . . . O/T Com.

John Clarkson
Inducted in 1963

1936 V 5
1946 NOM 1
1963 . . . . . . Vet. Com.

Roberto Clemente
Inducted in 1973

1973 . . . . Spec. El.

Andy Coakley

1938 1

Ty Cobb
Inducted in 1936

1936 222

Mickey Cochrane
Inducted in 1947

1936 80
1939 28
1942 88
1945 125
1946 NOM 80
1946 65
1947 128

Rocky Colavito

1974 2
1975 1

Eddie Collins
Inducted in 1939

1936 60
1937 115

1938 175
1939 213

Jimmy Collins
Inducted in 1945

1936 V 8
1936 58
1937 66
1938 79
1939 72
1942 68
1945 121
1945 . . . . . . O/T Com.

Shano Collins

1937 1

Earle Combs
Inducted in 1970

1937 4
1938 7
1939 3
1945 1
1948 6
1949 6
1950 3
1952 1
1953 3
1955 1
1956 14
1958 34
1960 43
1962 6
1970 . . . . . Vet. Com.

Charlie Comiskey
Inducted in 1939
Executive

1936 V 6
1939 . . . . . . O/T Com.

Jocko Conlan
Inducted in 1974
Umpire

1974 . . . . . . Vet. Com.

Tommy Connolly
Inducted in 1953
Umpire

1953 . . . . . . Vet. Com.

Roger Connor
Inducted in 1976

1976 . . . . . . Vet. Com.

Wid Conroy

1945 1

Jack Coombs

1937 2
1938 2
1946 NOM 2
1948 2
1951 1

Mort Cooper

1956 2
1958 3
1960 1
1969 3

Walker Cooper

1968 8
1969 5
1970 9
1971 7
1972 8
1973 8
1974 9
1975 13
1976 56
1977 45

Wilbur Cooper

1938 1
1939 1
1948 2

1949 4
1951 1
1952 2
1953 9
1954 7
1955 11

Clint Courtney

1967 1

Stan Coveleski
Inducted in 1969

1938 1
1948 2
1949 3
1950 1
1958 34
1969 . . . . . Vet. Com.

Billy Cox

1962 1

Doc Cramer

1956 4
1958 2
1960 1
1962 1
1964 12

Del Crandall

1976 15
1977 8
1978 6
1979 9

Doc Crandall

1938 1

Gavvy Cravath

1937 2
1938 2
1939 2
1946 NOM 1
1947 2

Sam Crawford
Inducted in 1957

1936 1
1937 5
1938 11
1939 6
1942 2
1945 4
1946 NOM 9
1957 . . . . . . Vet. Com.

Lou Criger

1936 V 1
1936 7
1937 16
1938 11
1939 2
1946 NOM 6

Hughie Critz

1956 2

Joe Cronin
Inducted in 1956

1947 6
1948 25
1949 33
1949 RO 16
1950 33
1951 44
1952 48
1953 69
1954 85
1955 135
1956 152

Frank Crosetti

1950 1
1952 1
1956 1
1958 5
1960 8

1968 15

Lave Cross

1939 1
1942 1

Al Crowder

1958 1
1960 1

Walt Cruise

1938 1

Tony Cuccinello

1956 1
1958 3

Candy Cummings
Inducted in 1939
Pioneer

1939 . . . . . . O/T Com.

Kiki Cuyler
Inducted in 1968

1948 3
1949 4
1950 11
1951 8
1952 10
1953 18
1954 20
1955 35
1956 55
1958 90
1960 72
1962 31
1968 . . . . . . Vet. Com.

Bill Dahlen

1936 V 1
1938 1

Ray Dandridge
Inducted in 1987

1987 . . . . . . Vet. Com.

Harry Danning

1958 1
1960 1

Alvin Dark

1966 17
1967 38
1967 RO 7
1968 36
1969 48
1970 55
1971 54
1972 55
1973 53
1974 54
1975 48
1976 62
1977 66
1978 60
1979 80
1980 43

Jake Daubert

1936 V 1
1937 2
1938 1
1939 1
1951 1
1955 1

Curt Davis

1958 1

Harry Davis

1945 1
1946 NOM 2

Tommy Davis

1982 5

Spud Davis
1948 1
1949 1

Dizzy Dean
Inducted in 1953
1945 17
1946 NOM 40
1946 45
1947 88
1948 40
1949 88
1949 RO 81
1950 85
1951 145
1952 152
1953 209

Ed Delahanty
Inducted in 1945
1936 V 22
1936 17
1937 70
1938 132
1939 145
1942 104
1945 111
1945 . . . . . . O/T Com.

Jerry Denny
1936 V 6

Bucky Dent
1990 3

Paul Derringer
1948 1
1950 1
1951 1
1955 1
1956 12
1958 15
1960 8

Bill Dickey
Inducted in 1954
1945 17
1946 NOM 40
1946 32
1948 39
1949 65
1949 RO 39
1950 78
1951 118
1952 139
1953 179
1954 202

Martin Dihigo
Inducted in 1977
1977 . . . . . . Neg. Com.

Dom DiMaggio
1960 4
1962 2
1964 12
1968 8
1969 13
1970 15
1971 15
1972 36
1973 43

Joe DiMaggio
Inducted in 1955
1945 1
1953 117
1954 175
1955 223

Bill Dinneen
1938 4
1939 7
1942 1
1945 1
1946 NOM 1

Bill Doak
1958 3

Larry Doby
1966 7
1967 10
1967 RO 1

Bobby Doerr
Inducted in 1986
1953 2
1956 5
1958 25
1960 15
1962 10
1964 24
1964 RO 5
1966 30
1967 35
1967 RO 15
1968 48
1969 62
1970 75
1971 78
1986 . . . . Vet. Com.

Mike Donlin
1937 6
1938 5
1939 5
1945 1

Bill Donovan
1937 3
1938 1
1939 2
1945 3
1946 NOM 4

Red Dooin
1937 1
1938 1

Jack Doyle
1936 V 1

Larry Doyle
1937 2
1938 4
1939 1

Walt Dropo
1967 1

Don Drysdale
Inducted in 1984
1975 76
1976 114
1977 197
1978 219
1979 233
1980 238
1981 243
1982 233
1983 242
1984 316

Hugh Duffy
Inducted in 1945
1936 V 4
1937 7
1938 24
1939 34
1942 77
1945 64
1945 . . . . . . O/T Com.

Joe Dugan
1937 1
1938 1
1948 3
1949 2
1956 1
1958 5
1960 8

Fred Dunlap
1936 V 2

Jack Dunn
1942 1
1945 1
1946 NOM 1

Leo Durocher
1948 1
1949 1
1952 1
1956 1
1958 28
1960 10
1962 1
1964 15
1964 RO 2

Eddie Dyer
1947 1

Jimmy Dykes
1948 5
1949 7
1950 2
1951 3
1952 5
1953 5
1955 1
1956 1
1958 26
1960 27
1962 6

George Earnshaw
1948 3
1949 2
1950 2
1955 2
1956 3

Hank Edwards
1960 2

Howard Ehmke
1938 1
1949 1
1951 1
1952 1
1953 3
1954 4
1955 8
1956 8
1958 7
1960 12

Kid Elberfeld
1936 1
1937 1
1938 2
1942 1
1945 2

Jumbo Elliott
1958 1

Bob Elliott
1960 2
1962 1
1964 4

Dock Ellis
1985 1

Del Ennis
1966 3
1967 2

Jewel Ens
1950 1

Carl Erskine
1966 6
1968 9
1969 4

1970 2
1971 3
1972 4
1973 4
1974 11

Billy Evans
Inducted in 1973
Umpire
1973 . . . . . . Vet. Com.

Johnny Evers
Inducted in 1946
1936 6
1937 44
1938 91
1939 107
1942 91
1945 134
1946 NOM 130
1946 110
1946 . . . . O/T Com.

Buck Ewing
Inducted in 1939
1936 V 40
1939 2
1939 . . . . O/T Com.

Red Faber
Inducted in 1964
1937 3
1938 1
1939 3
1942 1
1948 3
1949 6
1950 9
1951 8
1952 9
1953 9
1954 12
1955 27
1956 34
1958 68
1960 83
1962 30
1964 . . . . . . Vet. Com.

Elroy Face
1976 23
1977 33
1978 27
1979 35
1980 21
1981 23
1982 22
1983 32
1984 65
1985 62
1986 74
1987 78
1988 79
1989 47
1990 50

Ron Fairly
1985 3

Cy Falkenberg
1937 1

Bob Feller
Inducted in 1962
1962 150

Rick Ferrell
Inducted in 1984
1956 1
1958 1
1960 1
1984 . . . . . . Vet. Com.

Wes Ferrell
1948 1
1949 1
1956 7
1960 8

1962 1

Fred Fitzsimmons
1948 2
1949 2
1950 1
1956 3
1958 16
1960 13
1962 1

Art Fletcher
1937 2
1938 3
1939 1
1947 3
1948 3
1949 1
1950 1
1951 4

Elmer Flick
Inducted in 1963
1938 1
1963 . . . . . . Vet. Com.

Curt Flood
1977 16
1978 8
1979 14
1985 28
1986 45
1987 50
1988 48
1989 27
1990 35

Lew Fonseca
1948 1
1950 2
1956 2
1958 3
1960 3

Whitey Ford
Inducted in 1974
1973 255
1974 284

Eddie Foster
1938 2

Rube Foster
Inducted in 1981
Manager
1981 . . . . Vet. Com.

Nellie Fox
1971 39
1972 64
1973 73
1974 79
1975 76
1976 174
1977 152
1978 149
1979 174
1980 161
1981 168
1982 127
1983 173
1984 246
1985 295

Jimmie Foxx
Inducted in 1951
1936 21
1946 NOM 26
1947 10
1948 50
1949 85
1949 RO 89
1950 103
1951 179

Curt Fraser
1939 1

Bill Freehan
1982 2

Jim Fregosi
1984 4

Ford Frick
Inducted in 1970
Executive
1970 . . . . . . Vet. Com.

Frankie Frisch
Inducted in 1947
1936 14
1939 26
1942 84
1945 101
1946 NOM 104
1946 67
1947 136

Carl Furillo
1966 2
1967 2
1970 2
1971 5
1972 2

Augie Galan
1968 2
1970 3

Jim Galvin
Inducted in 1965
1965 . . . . . . Vet. Com.

Ned Garver
1967 1

Lou Gehrig
Inducted in 1939
1936 51
1939 . . . . Spec. El.

Charlie Gehringer
Inducted in 1949
1945 10
1946 NOM 43
1946 23
1947 105
1948 52
1949 102
1949 RO 159

Charlie Gelbert
1947 1
1949 2
1950 1
1951 1

Josh Gibson
Inducted in 1972
1972 . . . . . . Neg. Com.

Bob Gibson
Inducted in 1981
1981 337

Warren Giles
Inducted in 1979
Executive
1979 . . . . . . Vet. Com.

Dave Giusti
1983 1

Jack Glasscock
1936 V 2

Kid Gleason
1937 1
1938 1
1939 1
1945 1

Lefty Gomez
Inducted in 1972

1945.............7
1946 NOM........4
1947.............1
1948............16
1949............17
1950............18
1951............23
1952............29
1953............35
1954............38
1955............71
1956............89
1958............76
1960............51
1962............20
1972......Vet. Com.

Mike Gonzales

1950.............1
1952.............1
1953.............1
1958.............3
1960.............2

Joe Gordon

1945.............1
1955.............1
1956.............4
1958............11
1960............11
1962.............4
1964............30
1964 RO..........1
1966............31
1967............66
1967 RO.........13
1968............77
1969............97
1970............79

Goose Goslin
Inducted in 1968

1948.............1
1949.............4
1950.............2
1954.............1
1955.............7
1956............26
1958............26
1960............30
1962............14
1968......Vet. Com.

Hank Gowdy

1937.............2
1938.............8
1939.............4
1942.............8
1945.............3
1947.............1
1948.............3
1949............10
1950.............6
1951............26
1952............34
1953............58
1954............51
1955............90
1956............49
1958............45
1960............38

Eddie Grant

1938.............1
1939.............2
1942.............3
1945.............2
1946 NOM........1

George Grantham

1958.............1

Hank Greenberg
Inducted in 1956

1945.............3
1949............67
1949 RO.........44

1950............64
1951............67
1952............75
1953............80
1954............97
1955...........157
1956...........164

Clark Griffith
Inducted in 1946
Executive

1937.............4
1938............10
1939............20
1942............71
1945...........108
1946 NOM.......73
1946............82
1946......O/T Com.

Burleigh Grimes
Inducted in 1964

1937.............1
1938.............1
1939.............1
1948.............7
1949.............8
1950.............6
1951.............5
1952.............9
1953.............9
1955.............3
1956............25
1958............71
1960............92
1962............43
1964......Vet. Com.

Charlie Grimm

1939.............1
1945.............1
1946 NOM........1
1948.............6
1949............10
1950............13
1951.............9
1952.............6
1953.............9
1958............26
1960............13
1962.............2

Marv Grissom

1966.............2

Dick Groat

1973.............7
1974.............4
1975.............4
1976.............7
1977.............4
1978.............3

Heinie Groh

1937.............1
1938.............3
1945.............1
1948.............1
1950.............2
1954.............1
1955.............5
1960.............1

Steve Gromek

1964.............1

Orval Grove

1958.............5
1960.............7

Lefty Grove
Inducted in 1947

1936............12
1945............28
1946 NOM.......71
1946............61
1947...........123

Frank Gustine

1958.............3

Mule Haas

1955.............1
1956.............1
1958.............1
1960.............1

Stan Hack

1948.............2
1949.............4
1950.............8
1951.............3
1956.............1
1958.............6
1960.............6

Harvey Haddix

1971............10
1972.............9
1973.............1
1974.............8
1975.............8
1976.............8
1977.............7
1978.............7
1979.............8
1985............15

Chick Hafey
Inducted in 1971

1948.............1
1949.............2
1950.............4
1951.............1
1952.............1
1953.............2
1954.............2
1955.............4
1956............16
1958............12
1960............29
1962.............7
1971......Vet. Com.

Noodles Hahn

1939.............1

Jesse Haines
Inducted in 1970

1939.............1
1947.............1
1948.............2
1949.............2
1950............11
1953.............4
1954.............6
1955............10
1956............14
1958............22
1960............20
1962.............3
1970......Vet. Com.

Bill Hallahan

1948.............1
1956.............1
1958.............1
1960.............2

Billy Hamilton
Inducted in 1961

1936 V...........2
1942.............1
1961......Vet. Com.

Mel Harder

1949.............4
1950.............2
1951.............1
1952............10
1953.............8
1958.............6
1960............12
1962.............7
1964............51
1964 RO.........14

1966............34
1967............52
1967 RO.........14

Bubbles Hargrave

1947.............1
1958.............1
1960.............1

Bud Harrelson

1986.............1

Will Harridge
Inducted in 1972
Executive

1972......Vet. Com.

Bucky Harris
Inducted in 1975
Manager

1938.............1
1939.............1
1948.............3
1949............11
1950.............4
1951.............9
1952............12
1953............21
1958............45
1960............31
1975......Vet. Com.

Gabby Hartnett
Inducted in 1955

1945.............2
1946 NOM........2
1947.............2
1948............33
1949............35
1949 RO..........7
1950............54
1951............57
1952............77
1953...........104
1954...........151
1955...........195

Grady Hatton

1966.............4
1967.............1

Jim Hearn

1966.............1
1967.............1

Jim Hegan

1966.............5
1967.............2

Harry Heilmann
Inducted in 1952

1937............10
1938............14
1939.............8
1942.............4
1945.............5
1946 NOM.......23
1947............65
1948............40
1949............59
1949 RO.........52
1950............87
1951...........153
1952...........203

Tommy Helms

1983.............1

Solly Hemus

1966.............1

Tommy Henrich

1952.............4
1953............10
1956.............2
1958............11
1960............10

1962.............3
1964............13
1968............22
1969............50
1970............62

Babe Herman

1942.............1
1948.............2
1949.............5
1950.............2
1951.............1
1952.............3
1953.............2
1954.............1
1955.............5
1956............11
1958............13
1960.............7

Billy Herman
Inducted in 1975

1948.............1
1956.............2
1958.............7
1962.............4
1964............26
1964 RO..........9
1966............28
1967............59
1967 RO.........14
1975......Vet. Com.

Buck Herzog

1938.............1

Jim Hickman

1980.............1

Mike Higgins

1950.............2
1951.............1
1958.............6
1960.............3

John Hiller

1986............11

Bill Hinchman

1937.............1

Gil Hodges

1969............82
1970...........145
1971...........180
1972...........161
1973...........218
1974...........198
1975...........188
1976...........233
1977...........224
1978...........226
1979...........242
1980...........230
1981...........241
1982...........205
1983...........237

Tommy Holmes

1958.............2
1960.............2

Ken Holtzman

1985.............4
1986.............5

Harry Hooper
Inducted in 1971

1937.............6
1938.............4
1939.............5
1948.............2
1950.............2
1951.............3
1971......Vet. Com.

Rogers Hornsby
Inducted in 1942

1936...........105
1937............53
1938............46
1939...........176
1942...........182

Willie Horton

1986.............4

Art Houtteman

1964.............2

Elston Howard

1974............19
1975............23
1976............55
1977............43
1978............41
1979............30
1980............29
1981............83
1982............40
1983............32
1984............45
1985............54
1986............51
1987............44
1988............53

Frank Howard

1979.............6

Waite Hoyt
Inducted in 1969

1939.............1
1942.............1
1946 NOM........1
1948.............7
1949.............7
1950............11
1951............13
1952............12
1953............14
1954............14
1955............33
1956............37
1958............37
1960............29
1962............18
1969......Vet. Com.

Al Hrabosky

1988.............1

Cal Hubbard
Inducted in 1976
Umpire

1976......Vet. Com.

Carl Hubbell
Inducted in 1947

1945............24
1946 NOM......101
1946............75
1947...........140

Miller Huggins
Inducted in 1964
Manager

1937.............5
1938............48
1939............97
1942...........111
1945...........133
1946 NOM......129
1946...........106
1948.............4
1950.............2
1964......Vet. Com.

Catfish Hunter
Inducted in 1987

1985...........212
1986...........289
1987...........315

Fred Hutchinson
1962 1
1964 10

Monte Irvin
Inducted in 1973
1973 . . . . . Neg. Com.

Charlie Irwin
1938 1
1939 1

Joe Jackson
1936 2
1946 NOM 2

Sonny Jackson
1980 1

Travis Jackson
Inducted in 1982
1948 5
1949 6
1950 6
1951 4
1952 1
1953 2
1954 1
1955 5
1956 14
1958 11
1960 11
1962 1
1982 . . . . . . Vet. Com.

Fergie Jenkins
1989 234
1990 296

Hughie Jennings
Inducted in 1945
1936 V 11
1937 4
1938 23
1939 33
1942 64
1945 92
1945 . . . . . . O/T Com.

Jackie Jensen
1967 3
1968 3
1969 1
1970 1
1971 2
1972 1

Ban Johnson,
Inducted in 1937
Executive
1937 . . . . . Cen. Com.

Dave Johnson
1984 3

Judy Johnson
Inducted in 1975
1975 . . . . . Neg. Com.

Bob Johnson
1948 1
1956 1

Walter Johnson
Inducted in 1936
1936 189

Fielder Jones
1946 NOM 1

Sam P. Jones
1939 1
1955 1
1956 1

Tim Jordan
1951 1

Addie Joss
Inducted in 1978
1937 11
1938 18
1939 28
1942 33
1945 23
1946 NOM 14
1960 1
1978 . . . . . . Vet. Com.

Joe Judge
1937 1
1938 2
1949 1
1955 2
1956 2
1958 9
1960 15

Billy Jurges
1949 2
1958 1

Jim Kaat
1989 87
1990 79

Al Kaline
Inducted in 1980
1980 340

Willie Kamm
1958 3
1960 1

Tim Keefe
Inducted in 1964
1936 V 1
1964 . . . . . . Vet. Com.

Willie Keeler
Inducted in 1939
1936 V 33
1936 40
1937 115
1938 177
1939 207

George Kell
Inducted in 1983
1964 33
1964 RO 8
1966 29
1967 40
1967 RO 11
1968 47
1969 60
1970 90
1971 105
1972 115
1973 114
1974 94
1975 114
1976 129
1977 141
1983 . . . . . . Vet. Com.

Charlie Keller
1953 1
1956 2
1958 9
1960 7
1962 1
1964 12
1968 11
1969 14
1970 7
1971 14
1972 24

Joe Kelley
Inducted in 1971
1939 1

Bill Klem
Inducted in 1953
Umpire
1953 . . . . Vet. Com.

Johnny Kling
1936 8
1937 20
1938 26
1939 14
1942 15
1945 12
1946 NOM 20
1948 2
1953 1

Ted Kluszewski
1967 9
1968 14
1969 11
1970 8
1971 9
1972 10
1973 14
1974 28
1975 33
1976 50
1977 55
1978 51
1979 58
1980 50
1981 56

Otto Knabe
1939 1
1946 NOM 1

Sandy Koufax
Inducted in 1972
1972 344

Ray Kremer
1948 1
1958 2

Red Kress
1958 1
1960 3

Harvey Kuenn
1977 57
1978 58
1979 63
1980 83
1981 93
1982 62
1983 77
1984 106
1985 125
1986 144
1987 144
1988 168
1989 115
1990 107

Joe Kuhel
1956 1

Bob Kuzava
1964 1

Nap Lajoie
Inducted in 1937
1936 V 2
1936 146
1937 168

Judge Landis
Inducted in 1944
Executive
1944 . . . . . . O/T Com.

Bill Lange
1936 V 6
1953 1

George Kelly
Inducted in 1973
1947 1
1948 2
1949 1
1956 2
1958 2
1960 5
1962 1
1973 . . . . Vet. Com.

Mike Kelly
Inducted in 1945
1936 V 15
1945 . . . . . . O/T Com.

Ken Keltner
1958 1
1960 1

Dickie Kerr
1937 1
1938 3
1939 5
1942 1
1945 1
1949 1
1951 3
1952 9
1953 13
1954 13
1955 25

Don Kessinger
1985 2

Harmon Killebrew
Inducted in 1984
1981 239
1982 246
1983 269
1984 335

Bill Killefer
1946 NOM 1

Matt Kilroy
1936 V 1

Ellis Kinder
1964 3

Ralph Kiner
Inducted in 1975
1962 5
1964 31
1964 RO 3
1966 74
1967 124
1967 RO 41
1968 118
1969 137
1970 167
1971 212
1972 235
1973 235
1974 215
1975 273

Chuck Klein
Inducted in 1980
1948 3
1949 9
1950 14
1951 15
1952 19
1954 11
1955 25
1956 44
1958 36
1960 37
1962 18
1964 56
1964 RO 18
1980 . . . . . . Vet. Com.

Hal Lanier
1979 1

Don Larsen
1974 29
1975 23
1976 47
1977 39
1978 32
1979 53
1980 31
1981 33
1982 32
1983 22
1984 25
1985 32
1986 33
1987 30
1988 31

Arlie Latham
1936 V 1
1938 1
1942 1

Cookie Lavagetto
1958 4
1960 2

Vern Law
1973 9
1974 5
1975 6
1976 9
1977 5
1978 6
1979 9

Tony Lazzeri
1945 1
1947 1
1948 21
1949 20
1949 RO 6
1950 21
1951 27
1952 29
1953 28
1954 30
1955 66
1956 64
1958 80
1960 59
1962 8

Fred Leach
1958 2
1960 1

Tommy Leach
1937 1
1939 1

Bill Lee
1988 3

Sam Leever
1937 1

Bob Lemon
Inducted in 1976
1964 24
1964 RO 3
1966 21
1967 35
1967 RO 7
1968 47
1969 56
1970 70
1971 90
1972 117
1973 177
1974 190
1975 233
1976 305

Buck Leonard
Inducted in 1972
1972 . . . . . Neg. Com.

Emil Leonard
1960 2
1968 5
1969 4
1970 5
1971 3
1972 5
1973 6

Duffy Lewis
1937 3
1938 5
1939 6
1945 1
1951 2
1952 11
1953 20
1954 20
1955 34

Fred Lindstrom
Inducted in 1976
1949 1
1956 3
1958 5
1960 6
1962 7
1976 . . . . . . Vet. Com.

John Henry Lloyd
Inducted in 1977
1977 . . . . . Neg. Com.

Hans Lobert
1937 2
1938 1
1939 2
1960 1

Whitey Lockman
1966 4

Mickey Lolich
1985 78
1986 86
1987 84
1988 109
1989 47
1990 27

Ernie Lombardi
Inducted in 1986
1950 3
1951 3
1956 8
1958 4
1960 6
1962 5
1964 33
1964 RO 9
1966 34
1967 43
1967 RO 25
1986 . . . . . . Vet. Com.

Jim Lonborg
1985 3
1986 3

Herman Long
1936 V 16
1937 1
1938 1
1939 1
1945 1
1946 NOM 1

Ed Lopat
1968 2
1969 2
1970 1
1971 4
1972 2

Al Lopez
Inducted in 1977
Manager

1949	1
1952	2
1953	2
1956	1
1958	34
1960	26
1962	11
1964	57
1964 RO	34
1966	109
1967	114
1967 RO	50
1977	Vet. Com.

Bobby Lowe

1936 V	2
1942	1
1945	2

Red Lucas

1949	2
1950	1
1958	1

Dolph Luque

1937	1
1938	1
1939	1
1950	1
1952	1
1953	1
1956	1
1958	15
1960	4

Greg Luzinski

1990	1

Sparky Lyle

1988	56
1989	25
1990	25

Ted Lyons
Inducted in 1955

1945	4
1946 NOM	3
1948	15
1949	29
1949 RO	14
1950	42
1951	71
1952	101
1953	139
1954	170
1955	217

Connie Mack
Inducted in 1937
Manager

1936	1
1937	Cen. Com.

Larry MacPhail
Inducted in 1978
Executive

1978	Vet. Com.

Sherry Magee

1937	2
1938	2
1939	1
1942	1
1945	1
1946 NOM	1
1950	1
1951	2

Sal Maglie

1964	13
1968	11

Jim Maloney

1978	2

1979	2

Gus Mancuso

1958	1

Mickey Mantle
Inducted in 1974

1974	322

Heinie Manush
Inducted in 1964

1948	1
1949	1
1956	13
1958	22
1960	20
1962	15
1964	Vet. Com.

Rabbit Maranville
Inducted in 1954

1937	25
1938	73
1939	82
1942	66
1945	51
1946 NOM	50
1946	29
1947	91
1948	38
1949	58
1949 RO	39
1950	66
1951	110
1952	133
1953	164
1954	209

Firpo Marberry

1938	1
1950	1
1958	5
1960	2
1962	2

Juan Marichal
Inducted in 1983

1981	233
1982	305
1983	313

Marty Marion

1956	1
1960	37
1962	16
1964	50
1964 RO	17
1966	86
1967	90
1967 RO	22
1968	89
1969	112
1970	120
1971	123
1972	120
1973	127

Roger Maris

1974	78
1975	70
1976	87
1977	72
1978	83
1979	127
1980	111
1981	94
1982	69
1983	69
1984	107
1985	128
1986	177
1987	176
1988	184

Rube Marquard
Inducted in 1971

1936	1
1937	13
1938	10

1939	4
1946 NOM	6
1947	18
1948	6
1949	4
1951	3
1952	9
1953	19
1954	15
1955	35
1971	Vet. Com.

Mike Marshall

1987	6

Billy Martin

1967	1

Pepper Martin

1942	2
1945	1
1946 NOM	1
1948	7
1949	16
1950	7
1951	19
1952	31
1953	43
1956	7
1958	46
1960	29
1962	6
1964	19
1964 RO	5

Morrie Martin

1966	2

Eddie Mathews
Inducted in 1978

1974	118
1975	148
1976	189
1977	239
1978	301

Christy Mathewson
Inducted in 1936

1936	205

Lee May

1988	2

Carl Mays

1958	6

Willie Mays
Inducted in 1979

1979	409

Bill Mazeroski

1978	23
1979	36
1980	33
1981	38
1982	28
1983	48
1984	74
1985	87
1986	100
1987	125
1988	143
1989	134
1990	131

Jim McAleer

1936 V	1

Joe McCarthy
Inducted in 1957
Manager

1939	3
1947	2
1951	1
1953	1
1958	2
1957	Vet. Com.

Tommy McCarthy
Inducted in 1946

1936 V	1
1946	O/T Com.

Tim McCarver

1986	16

Frank McCormick

1956	3
1962	1
1964	6
1968	3

Willie McCovey
Inducted in 1986

1986	346

Lindy McDaniel

1981	1
1982	3

Gil McDougald

1966	5
1967	4
1968	4
1969	3
1970	1
1971	4
1972	4
1973	2
1974	3

Joe McGinnity
Inducted in 1946

1937	12
1938	36
1939	32
1942	59
1945	44
1946 NOM	53
1946	47
1946	O/T Com.

John McGraw
Inducted in 1937
Manager

1936 V	17
1936	4
1937	35
1937	Cen. Com.

Tug McGraw

1990	6

Stuffy McInnis

1937	1
1938	4
1939	4
1948	5
1949	8
1950	1
1951	3

Bill McKechnie
Inducted in 1962
Manager

1945	2
1946 NOM	2
1950	1
1951	8
1962	Vet. Com.

Denny McLain

1978	1
1979	3
1985	2

Larry McLean

1937	1

Don McMahon

1980	1

Marty McManus

1958	2

1960	2

Roy McMillan

1972	9
1973	5
1974	4

Dave McNally

1981	5
1982	5
1985	7
1986	12

Cal McVey

1936 V	1

Lee Meadows

1958	2

Ducky Medwick
Inducted in 1968

1948	1
1956	31
1958	50
1960	38
1962	34
1964	108
1964 RO	130
1966	187
1967	212
1967 RO	248
1968	240

Andy Messersmith

1985	3
1986	3

Bob Meusel

1937	1
1938	1
1945	1
1948	6
1949	3
1950	2
1952	1
1955	2
1956	1
1958	5
1960	10

Eddie Miksis

1964	1

Clyde Milan

1938	1
1950	1
1951	1
1952	1
1953	1
1954	3
1955	6

Felix Millan

1983	1

Bing Miller

1958	1
1960	6

Dots Miller

1948	1

Hack Miller

1937	1

Minnie Minoso

1969	6
1986	89
1987	82
1988	90
1989	59
1990	51

Johnny Mize
Inducted in 1981

1960	45

1962	14
1964	54
1964 RO	12
1966	81
1967	89
1967 RO	14
1968	103
1969	116
1970	126
1971	157
1972	157
1973	157
1981	Vet. Com.

Rick Monday

1990	2

Don Money

1989	1

Wally Moon

1971	2

Jo-Jo Moore

1950	1

Terry Moore

1950	1
1953	1
1958	12
1960	7
1962	1
1964	14
1967	3
1968	33

Pat Moran

1937	1
1938	1
1939	1
1945	1

Joe Morgan
Inducted in 1990

1990	363

Wally Moses

1958	1
1960	1
1968	4
1969	4
1970	5
1971	7

Johnny Mostil

1956	1
1958	1

Manny Mota

1988	18
1989	9

Hugh Mulcahy

1948	1

Van Mungo

1945	1
1948	1
1958	2
1960	2

Thurman Munson

1981	62
1982	26
1983	18
1984	29
1985	32
1986	35
1987	28
1988	32
1989	31
1990	33

Bobby Murcer

1989	3

Danny Murphy
1937...............1
1945...............1

Red Murray
1937...............1
1938...............1

Stan Musial
Inducted in 1969
1969..........317

Buddy Myer
1949...............1

Art Nehf
1937...............3
1938...............5
1939...............1
1949...............1
1950...............2
1951...............4
1952...............3
1953...............4
1954...............7
1955...............7
1958..............13

Don Newcombe
1966...............7
1967..............18
1967 RO...........2
1968...............9
1969...............3
1970...............5
1971...............8
1972...............7
1973..............11
1974...............7
1975..............11
1976..............21
1977..............43
1978..............48
1979..............52
1980..............59

Hal Newhouser
1962...............4
1964..............26
1964 RO...........3
1966..............32
1967..............62
1967 RO..........13
1968..............67
1969..............82
1970..............80
1971..............94
1972..............92
1973..............79
1974..............73
1975.............155

Bobo Newsom
1960...............6
1962...............3
1964..............17
1964 RO...........1
1966..............25
1967..............19
1967 RO...........6
1968..............22
1969..............32
1970..............12
1971..............17
1972..............31
1973..............33

Kid Nichols
Inducted in 1949
1936 V............3
1938...............3
1939...............7
1942...............5
1945...............5
1946 NOM.........1
1949.......O/T Com.

Bill Nicholson
1960...............1

Ron Northey
1964...............1

Jim Northrup
1981...............1

Lefty O'Doul
1948...............4
1949...............4
1950...............9
1951..............13
1952..............19
1953..............11
1956...............5
1958..............27
1960..............45
1962..............13

Joe Oeschger
1948...............1

Bob O'Farrell
1950...............4
1958...............3
1960...............3

Charlie O'Leary
1953...............1
1958...............1
1960...............1

Tony Oliva
1982..............63
1983..............75
1984.............124
1985.............114
1986.............154
1987.............160
1988.............202
1989.............135
1990.............142

Steve O'Neill
1948...............2
1949...............6
1950...............1
1951...............3
1952..............10
1953..............13
1958..............10

Jim O'Rourke
Inducted in 1945
1945.......O/T Com.

Claude Osteen
1981...............2

Mel Ott
Inducted in 1951
1949..............94
1949 RO.........128
1950.............115
1951.............197

Charlie Pabor
1936 V............1

Andy Pafko
1966...............2
1967...............1

Satchel Paige
Inducted in 1971
1951...............1
1971......Neg. Com.

Jim Palmer
Inducted in 1990
1990.............411

Milt Pappas
1979...............5

Camilo Pascual
1977...............3
1978...............1

Dode Paskert
1937...............1

Monte Pearson
1958...............1

Roger Peckinpaugh
1937...............3
1938...............2
1939...............1
1942...............2
1949...............1
1952...............2
1953...............2
1954...............1
1955...............1

Heinie Peitz
1939...............1

Herb Pennock
Inducted in 1948
1937..............15
1938..............37
1939..............40
1942..............72
1945..............45
1946 NOM........41
1946..............16
1947..............86
1948..............94

Hub Perdue
1938...............1
1939...............1

Cy Perkins
1958...............2

Ron Perranoski
1979...............6

Gaylord Perry
1989.............304
1990.............320

Jim Perry
1981...............6
1983...............7

Johnny Pesky
1960...............1

Rico Petrocelli
1982...............3

Deacon Phillippe
1939...............1
1942...............1
1945...............2
1946 NOM.........1

Billy Pierce
1970...............5
1971...............7
1972...............4
1973...............4
1974...............4

Lip Pike
1936 V............1

Lou Piniella
1990...............2

Vada Pinson
1981..............18

1982...............6
1983..............12
1985..............19
1986..............43
1987..............48
1988..............67
1989..............33
1990..............36

Wally Pipp
1958...............1

Eddie Plank
Inducted in 1946
1937..............23
1938..............38
1939..............28
1942..............63
1945..............33
1946 NOM........34
1946.......O/T Com.

Johnny Podres
1975...............3
1976...............2
1977...............3

Bob Porterfield
1966...............1

Boog Powell
1983...............5

Vic Power
1971...............2
1972...............3

Herb Pruett
1949...............1
1950...............1
1951...............1
1952...............1
1953...............1

Jack Quinn
1948...............2
1958...............9
1960...............2

Charlie Radbourn
Inducted in 1939
1936 V...........16
1939.......O/T Com.

Vic Raschi
1962...............1
1964...............8
1968...............1
1969...............3
1971...............2
1972...............4
1973...............7
1974...............3
1975..............37

Bugs Raymond
1937...............1

Pee Wee Reese
Inducted in 1984
1964..............73
1964 RO..........47
1966..............95
1967..............89
1967 RO..........16
1968..............81
1969..............89
1970..............97
1971.............127
1972.............129
1973.............126
1974.............141
1975.............154
1976.............186
1977.............163
1978.............169
1984......Vet. Com.

Pete Reiser
1958...............6
1960...............8

Jack Remsen
1936 V............1

Jerry Remy
1990...............1

Allie Reynolds
1956...............1
1960..............24
1962..............15
1964..............35
1964 RO...........6
1966..............60
1967..............77
1967 RO..........19
1968..............95
1969..............98
1970..............89
1971.............110
1972.............105
1973..............93
1974.............101

Del Rice
1966...............2

Sam Rice
Inducted in 1963
1938...............1
1948...............1
1949...............3
1950...............1
1951...............1
1952...............1
1953...............3
1954...............9
1955..............28
1956..............45
1958..............90
1960.............143
1962..............81
1963......Vet. Com.

J. R. Richard
1986...............7

Hardy Richardson
1936 V............1

Bobby Richardson
1972...............8
1973...............2
1974...............5

Branch Rickey
Inducted in 1967
Executive
1942...............3
1945...............2
1967......Vet. Com.

Jimmy Ring
1949...............1

Claude Ritchey
1945...............1

Mickey Rivers
1990...............2

Eppa Rixey
Inducted in 1963
1937...............1
1938...............2
1945...............1
1947...............2
1948...............5
1949...............4
1950...............6
1951...............5
1952...............3
1953...............3

1954...............5
1955...............8
1956..............27
1958..............32
1960.............142
1962..............49
1963......Vet. Com.

Phil Rizzuto
1956...............1
1962..............44
1964..............45
1964 RO..........11
1966..............54
1967..............71
1967 RO..........14
1968..............74
1969..............78
1970..............79
1971..............92
1972.............103
1973.............111
1974.............111
1975.............117
1976.............149

Robin Roberts
Inducted in 1976
1973.............213
1974.............224
1975.............263
1976.............337

Dave Robertson
1953...............1

Brooks Robinson
Inducted in 1983
1983.............344

Frank Robinson
Inducted in 1982
1982.............370

Jackie Robinson
Inducted in 1962
1962.............124

Wilbert Robinson
Inducted in 1945
Manager
1936 V............6
1937...............5
1938..............17
1939..............46
1942..............89
1945..............81
1945.......O/T Com.

Preacher Roe
1960...............1
1962...............1
1968...............2
1970...............1
1971...............3
1972...............2

Red Rolfe
1950...............7
1951...............6
1952...............4
1953...............5
1956...............3
1958..............13
1960..............10
1962...............1

Eddie Rommel
1948...............3
1949...............2
1950...............1
1951...............1
1952...............2
1953...............1
1958...............7
1960..............12

Charlie Root

1945	1
1948	3
1949	1
1950	1
1958	6
1960	2

Edd Roush
Inducted in 1962

1936	2
1937	10
1938	9
1939	8
1942	1
1945	5
1946 NOM	11
1947	25
1948	17
1949	14
1950	16
1951	21
1952	24
1953	32
1954	52
1955	97
1956	91
1958	112
1960	146
1962	Vet. Com.

Schoolboy Rowe

1958	12
1960	3
1968	6
1969	17

Nap Rucker

1936	1
1937	11
1938	12
1939	13
1942	15
1945	10
1946 NOM	13

Dick Rudolph

1937	1
1951	1

Muddy Ruel

1946 NOM	1
1950	4
1951	1
1952	1
1953	8
1954	5
1955	11
1956	16
1958	10
1960	9

Red Ruffing
Inducted in 1967

1948	4
1949	22
1949 RO	4
1950	12
1951	9
1952	10
1953	24
1954	29
1955	60
1956	97
1958	99
1960	86
1962	72
1964	141
1964 RO	184
1966	208
1967	212
1967 RO	266

Amos Rusie
Inducted in 1977

1936 V	12
1937	1
1938	8
1939	6

1942	1
1945	1
1977	Vet. Com.

Babe Ruth
Inducted in 1936

1936	215

Ray Sadecki

1983	2

Johnny Sain

1962	1
1964	3
1968	7
1969	8
1970	9
1971	11
1972	21
1973	47
1974	51
1975	123

Manny Sanguillen

1986	2

Ron Santo

1980	15
1985	53
1986	64
1987	78
1988	108
1989	75
1990	96

Hank Sauer

1966	4

Al Schacht

1939	1
1948	2
1951	4
1956	1

Germany Schaefer

1942	1
1953	1

Ray Schalk
Inducted in 1955

1936	4
1937	24
1938	45
1939	35
1942	53
1945	33
1946 NOM	36
1947	50
1948	22
1949	24
1949 RO	17
1950	16
1951	37
1952	44
1953	52
1954	54
1955	113
1955	Vet. Com.

Wally Schang

1948	1
1950	1
1956	1
1958	8
1960	11

Red Schoendienst
Inducted in 1989

1969	65
1970	97
1971	123
1972	104
1973	96
1974	110
1975	94
1976	129
1977	105
1978	130

1979	159
1980	164
1981	166
1982	135
1983	146
1989	Vet. Com.

Ossie Schreck

1937	2
1938	2
1939	2

Frank Schulte

1937	1

Hal Schumacher

1948	1
1955	1
1956	2
1958	1
1960	11
1962	1
1964	10

Everett Scott

1937	2
1938	2
1939	1
1942	1
1947	1
1948	3
1949	3
1950	3
1951	2
1952	4
1953	5
1954	4
1955	8
1956	1

George Scott

1986	1

Jack Scott

1958	1

George Selkirk

1948	1
1949	1
1950	1
1951	2
1952	1
1953	1

Hank Severeid

1948	1

Joe Sewell
Inducted in 1977

1937	1
1948	1
1954	1
1955	1
1956	3
1958	1
1960	23
1977	Vet. Com.

Luke Sewell

1948	1
1958	3
1960	3
1962	1

Rip Sewell

1958	1
1962	1
1964	1

Cy Seymour

1945	1

Bobby Shantz

1970	7
1971	5
1972	9
1973	5

1974	3

Jim Sheckard

1938	1
1945	1
1946 NOM	1

Bill Sherdel

1948	1
1949	1
1950	1
1951	1
1953	1
1955	1
1956	1
1958	2
1960	2

Urban Shocker

1938	1
1939	1
1948	1
1949	2
1958	4

Chris Short

1979	1

Sonny Siebert

1981	1

Roy Sievers

1971	4
1972	3

Al Simmons
Inducted in 1953

1936	4
1946 NOM	1
1947	6
1948	60
1949	89
1949 RO	76
1950	90
1951	116
1952	141
1953	199

Curt Simmons

1973	5
1974	3

George Sisler
Inducted in 1939

1936	77
1937	106
1938	179
1939	235

Sibby Sisti

1960	1

Enos Slaughter
Inducted in 1985

1966	100
1967	123
1967 RO	48
1968	129
1969	128
1970	133
1971	165
1972	149
1973	145
1974	145
1975	177
1976	197
1977	222
1978	261
1979	297
1985	Vet. Com.

Roy Smalley

1964	1

Earl Smith

1948	1
1956	1

Reggie Smith

1988	3

Sherry Smith

1948	1

Duke Snider
Inducted in 1980

1970	51
1971	89
1972	84
1973	101
1974	111
1975	129
1976	159
1977	212
1978	254
1979	308
1980	333

Billy Southworth

1945	1
1946 NOM	1
1949	7
1950	1
1951	4
1952	1
1953	2
1958	18

Warren Spahn
Inducted in 1973

1973	316

Al Spalding
Inducted in 1939
Pioneer

1936 V	4
1939	O/T Com.

Tully Sparks

1946 NOM	1

Tris Speaker
Inducted in 1937

1936	133
1937	165

Jake Stahl

1938	1
1939	1

Eddie Stanky

1960	3

Mickey Stanley

1984	2

Willie Stargell
Inducted in 1988

1988	352

Harry Steinfeldt

1937	1
1939	1
1942	1

Casey Stengel
Inducted in 1966
Manager

1938	2
1939	6
1945	2
1948	1
1949	3
1950	3
1951	8
1952	27
1953	61
1966	Vet. Com.

Riggs Stephenson

1956	2
1958	1
1960	4
1962	1

Mel Stottlemyre

1980	3

Harry Stovey

1936 V	6

Gabby Street

1937	1
1938	1
1953	1

Gus Suhr

1956	1
1958	1
1960	1

Clyde Sukeforth

1958	1

Billy Sullivan

1937	1
1946 NOM	1

Bill Sweeney

1945	1

Jess Tannehill

1946 NOM	1

Birdie Tebbetts

1958	8
1960	1

Gene Tenace

1989	1

Fred Tenney

1936 V	1
1937	5
1938	8
1939	3
1942	1
1946 NOM	1

Bill Terry
Inducted in 1954

1936	9
1938	7
1939	16
1942	36
1945	32
1946 NOM	31
1947	46
1948	52
1949	81
1949 RO	48
1950	105
1951	148
1952	155
1953	191
1954	195

Tommy Thevenow

1950	2

Ira Thomas

1938	1

Sam Thompson
Inducted in 1974

1974	Vet. Com.

Bobby Thomson

1966	12
1967	10
1967 RO	1
1968	13
1969	6
1970	4
1971	1
1972	10
1973	3
1974	6
1975	10
1976	9

1977 10
1978 5
1979 11

Luis Tiant
1988 132
1989 47
1990 42

Joe Tinker
Inducted in 1946
1937 15
1938 16
1939 12
1942 36
1945 49
1946 NOM 55
1946 45
1946 . . . . . . O/T Com.

Jim Tobin
1956 2

Fred Toney
1949 1

Earl Torgeson
1967 2

Joe Torre
1983 20
1984 45
1985 44
1986 60
1987 47
1988 60
1989 40
1990 55

Mike Torrez
1990 1

Pie Traynor
Inducted in 1948
1936 16
1938 3
1939 10
1942 45
1945 81
1946 NOM 65
1946 53
1947 119
1948 93

Dizzy Trout
1964 1

Virgil Trucks
1964 4

Jim Turner
1956 1

Terry Turner
1947 2

George Uhle
1956 1
1958 4
1960 4

Elmer Valo
1967 2

Dazzy Vance
Inducted in 1955
1936 1
1937 10
1938 10
1939 15
1942 37
1945 18
1946 NOM 31
1947 50
1948 23
1949 33

1949 RO 15
1950 52
1951 70
1952 105
1953 150
1954 158
1955 205

Johnny Vander Meer
1945 1
1956 3
1958 35
1960 31
1962 5
1964 51
1964 RO 20
1966 72
1967 87
1967 RO 35
1968 79
1969 95
1970 88
1971 98

George Van Haltren
1936 V 1

Arky Vaughan
Inducted in 1985
1953 1
1954 2
1955 4
1956 9
1958 6
1960 10
1962 6
1964 17
1964 RO 6
1966 36
1967 46
1967 RO 19
1968 82
1985 . . . . Vet. Com.

Bobby Veach
1937 1

Mickey Vernon
1966 20
1967 14
1967 RO 2
1968 22
1969 21
1970 10
1971 12
1972 12
1973 23
1974 27
1975 22
1976 52
1977 52
1978 66
1979 88
1980 96

Bill Virdon
1974 3
1975 1

Rube Waddell
Inducted in 1946
1936 33
1937 67
1938 148
1939 179
1942 126
1945 154
1946 NOM 122
1946 87
1946 . . . . . . O/T Com.

Honus Wagner
Inducted in 1936
1936 V 5
1936 215

Rube Walberg
1958 1
1960 RO 1

Dixie Walker
1962 1
1964 6
1968 6
1969 9

Harry Walker
1958 1

Bobby Wallace
Inducted in 1953
1936 V 1
1937 1
1938 7
1939 5
1942 2
1945 3
1953 . . . . Vet. Com.

Ed Walsh
Inducted in 1946
1936 20
1937 56
1938 110
1939 132
1942 113
1945 137
1946 NOM 115
1946 106
1946 . . . . . . O/T Com.

Bucky Walters
1950 4
1952 3
1953 10
1956 5
1958 33
1960 19
1962 5
1964 35
1964 RO 8
1966 56
1967 65
1967 RO 24
1968 67
1969 20
1970 29

Bill Wambsganss
1942 1
1950 1
1953 1
1954 4
1955 5
1956 1

Lloyd Waner
Inducted in 1967
1949 3
1950 1
1951 1
1952 2
1956 18
1958 39
1960 22
1962 5
1964 47
1964 RO 12
1967 . . . . Vet. Com.

Paul Waner
Inducted in 1952
1946 NOM 4
1948 51
1949 73
1949 RO 63
1950 95
1951 162
1952 195

Monte Ward
Inducted in 1964
1936 V 3
1964 . . . . Vet. Com.

Lon Warneke
1949 2
1958 2

1960 4
1962 2
1964 13

Bob Watson
1990 3

George Weiss
Inducted in 1971
Executive
1971 . . . . Vet. Com.

Mickey Welch
Inducted in 1973
1973 . . . . Vet. Com.

Billy Werber
1949 1
1950 1
1952 1
1958 3

Vic Wertz
1970 2
1971 2
1972 4
1973 2
1974 2
1975 5
1976 5
1977 4
1978 4

Sam West
1948 1

Wes Westrum
1964 2

Zach Wheat
Inducted in 1959
1937 5
1938 7
1939 4
1942 3
1945 2
1946 NOM 6
1947 37
1948 15
1949 15
1950 17
1951 19
1952 30
1953 32
1954 33
1955 51
1956 26
1959 . . . . Vet. Com.

Deacon White
1936 V 1

Will White
1975 7
1976 7
1977 4

Burgess Whitehead
1956 1

Earl Whitehill
1956 1
1958 2
1960 3

Hoyt Wilhelm
Inducted in 1985
1978 158
1979 168
1980 209
1981 238
1982 236
1983 243
1984 290
1985 331

Billy Williams
Inducted in 1987
1982 97
1983 153
1984 202
1985 252
1986 315
1987 354

Fred Williams
1938 1
1945 1
1948 1
1949 2
1950 9
1951 7
1952 4
1953 4
1954 4
1955 3
1956 11
1958 6
1960 11

Ken Williams
1956 1
1958 1

Ted Williams
Inducted in 1966
1966 282

Ned Williamson
1936 V 2

Maury Wills
1978 115
1979 166
1980 146
1981 163
1982 91
1983 77
1984 104
1985 93
1986 124
1987 113
1988 127
1989 95
1990 95

Jimmie Wilson
1948 8
1949 6
1950 4
1951 2
1952 7
1953 10
1954 8
1955 13
1956 17
1958 3
1960 6
1962 4

Jim Wilson
1964 2

Hack Wilson
Inducted in 1979
1937 1
1939 1
1942 1
1948 2
1949 24
1949 RO 12
1950 16
1951 21
1952 21
1953 43
1954 48
1955 81
1956 74
1958 94
1960 72
1962 39
1979 . . . . Vet. Com.

Whitey Witt
1949 1

Joe Wood
1937 13
1938 6
1939 2
1942 1
1946 NOM 5
1947 29
1948 5
1950 1
1951 5

Wilbur Wood
1984 14
1985 16
1986 23
1987 26
1988 30
1989 14

Glenn Wright
1948 2
1949 1
1950 2
1951 1
1952 1
1953 3
1954 1
1955 4
1956 3
1958 8
1960 18
1962 1

George Wright
Inducted in 1937
Pioneer
1936 V 6
1937 . . . . . . Cen. Com.

Harry Wright
Inducted in 1953
Pioneer
1953 . . . . Vet. Com.

Whit Wyatt
1958 1

Early Wynn
Inducted in 1972
1969 95
1970 140
1971 240
1972 301

Tom Yawkey
Inducted in 1980
Executive
1980 . . . . Vet. Com.

Carl Yastrzemski
Inducted in 1989
1989 423

Steve Yerkes
1945 1

Rudy York
1962 1
1964 10

Cy Young
Inducted in 1937
1936 V 32
1936 111
1937 153

Pep Young
1958 1

Ross Youngs
Inducted in 1972
1936 10
1937 16

1938	40
1939	34
1942	44
1945	22
1946 NOM	25
1947	36

1948	19
1949	20
1949 RO	11
1950	17
1951	34

1952	34
1953	31
1954	34
1955	48
1956	19

| 1972 | Vet. Com. |

Tom Zachary

| 1958 | 1 |

| 1960 | 1 |

Chief Zimmer

| 1938 | 1 |

Hall of Fame Balloting: Top Ten Candidates in Each Election

1936 Veterans
Needed to Elect: 59

Cap Anson 40
Buck Ewing 40
Willie Keeler 33
Cy Young 32
Ed Delahanty 22
John McGraw 17
Herman Long 16
Charlie Radbourn . . 16
Mike Kelly 15
Amos Rusie 12

1936
Needed to Elect: 170

Ty Cobb 222
Babe Ruth 215
Honus Wagner . . . 215
Christy Mathewson . . .
. . . . 205
Walter Johnson . . . 189
Nap Lajoie 146
Tris Speaker 133
Cy Young 111
Rogers Hornsby . . 105
Mickey Cochrane . . . 80

1937
Needed to Elect: 151

Nap Lajoie 168
Tris Speaker 165
Cy Young 153
Pete Alexander . . . 125
Eddie Collins 115
Willie Keeler 115
George Sisler 106
Ed Delahanty 70
Rube Waddell 67
Jimmy Collins 66

1938
Needed to Elect: 197

Pete Alexander . . . 212
George Sisler 179
Willie Keeler 177
Eddie Collins 175
Rube Waddell 148
Frank Chance 133
Ed Delahanty 132
Ed Walsh 110
Johnny Evers 91
Jimmy Collins 79

1939
Needed to Elect: 206

George Sisler 235
Eddie Collins 213
Willie Keeler 207
Rube Waddell 179
Rogers Hornsby . . 176
Frank Chance 158
Ed Delahanty 145
Ed Walsh 132
Johnny Evers 107
Miller Huggins 97

1942
Needed to Elect: 175

Rogers Hornsby . . 182
Frank Chance 136
Rube Waddell 126
Ed Walsh 113
Miller Huggins 111
Ed Delahanty 104
Johnny Evers 91

Wilbert Robinson . . 89
Mickey Cochrane . . 88
Frankie Frisch 84

1945
Needed to Elect: 185

Frank Chance 179
Rube Waddell 154
Ed Walsh 137
Johnny Evers 134
Roger Bresnahan . 133
Miller Huggins 133
Mickey Cochrane . . 125
Jimmy Collins 121
Ed Delahanty 111
Clark Griffith 108

1946 Nominating Total Voting: 202

Frank Chance 144
Johnny Evers 130
Miller Huggins 129
Rube Waddell 122
Ed Walsh 115
Frankie Frisch 104
Carl Hubbell 101
Mickey Cochrane . . . 80
Clark Griffith 73
Lefty Grove 71

1946
Needed to Elect: 197

Frank Chance 150
Johnny Evers 110
Miller Huggins 106
Ed Walsh 106
Rube Waddell 87
Clark Griffith 82
Carl Hubbell 75
Frankie Frisch 67
Mickey Cochrane . . 65
Lefty Grove 61

1947
Needed to Elect: 121

Carl Hubbell 140
Frankie Frisch 136
Mickey Cochrane . . 128
Lefty Grove 123
Pie Traynor 119
Charlie Gehringer . . 105
Rabbit Maranville . . 91
Dizzy Dean 88
Herb Pennock 86
Chief Bender 72

1948
Needed to Elect: 91

Herb Pennock 94
Pie Traynor 93
Al Simmons 60
Charlie Gehringer . . 52
Bill Terry 52
Paul Waner 51
Jimmie Foxx 50
Dizzy Dean 40
Harry Heilmann . . . 40
Bill Dickey 39

1949
Needed to Elect: 115

Charlie Gehringer . . 102
Mel Ott 94
Al Simmons 89
Dizzy Dean 88

Jimmie Foxx 85
Bill Terry 81
Paul Waner 73
Hank Greenberg . . 67
Bill Dickey 65
Harry Heilmann . . . 59

1949 Run Off
Needed to Elect: 140
One Player Maximum

Charlie Gehringer . . 159
Mel Ott 128
Jimmie Foxx 89
Dizzy Dean 81
Al Simmons 76
Paul Waner 63
Harry Heilmann . . . 52
Bill Terry 48
Hank Greenberg . . . 44
Bill Dickey 39
Rabbit Maranville . . 39

1950
Needed to Elect: 125

Mel Ott 115
Bill Terry 105
Jimmie Foxx 103
Paul Waner 95
Al Simmons 90
Harry Heilmann . . . 87
Dizzy Dean 85
Bill Dickey 78
Rabbit Maranville . . 66
Hank Greenberg . . 64

1951
Needed to Elect: 170

Mel Ott 197
Jimmie Foxx 179
Paul Waner 162
Harry Heilmann . . . 153
Bill Terry 148
Dizzy Dean 145
Bill Dickey 118
Al Simmons 116
Rabbit Maranville . . 110
Ted Lyons 71

1952
Needed to Elect: 176

Harry Heilmann . . . 203
Paul Waner 195
Bill Terry 155
Dizzy Dean 152
Al Simmons 141
Bill Dickey 139
Rabbit Maranville . . 133
Dazzy Vance 105
Ted Lyons 101
Gabby Hartnett . . . 77

1953
Needed to Elect: 198

Dizzy Dean 209
Al Simmons 199
Bill Terry 191
Bill Dickey 179
Rabbit Maranville . . 164
Dazzy Vance 150
Ted Lyons 139
Joe DiMaggio 117
Chief Bender 104
Gabby Hartnett . . . 104

1954
Needed to Elect: 189

Rabbit Maranville . . 209
Bill Dickey 202
Bill Terry 195
Joe DiMaggio 175
Ted Lyons 170
Dazzy Vance 158
Gabby Hartnett . . . 151
Hank Greenberg . . . 97
Joe Cronin 85
Max Carey 55

1955
Needed to Elect: 188

Joe DiMaggio 223
Ted Lyons 217
Dazzy Vance 205
Gabby Hartnett . . . 195
Hank Greenberg . . 157
Joe Cronin 135
Max Carey 119
Ray Schalk 113
Edd Roush 97
Hank Gowdy 90

1956
Needed to Elect: 145

Hank Greenberg . . 164
Joe Cronin 152
Red Ruffing 97
Edd Roush 91
Lefty Gomez 89
Hack Wilson 74
Max Carey 65
Tony Lazzeri 64
Kiki Cuyler 55
Hank Gowdy 49

1958
Needed to Elect: 200

Max Carey 136
Edd Roush 112
Red Ruffing 99
Hack Wilson 94
Kiki Cuyler 90
Sam Rice 90
Tony Lazzeri 80
Luke Appling 77
Lefty Gomez 76
Burleigh Grimes . . . 71

1960
Needed to Elect: 202

Edd Roush 146
Sam Rice 143
Eppa Rixey 142
Burleigh Grimes . . . 92
Jim Bottomley 89
Red Ruffing 86
Red Faber 83
Luke Appling 72
Kiki Cuyler 72
Hack Wilson 72

1962
Needed to Elect: 120

Bob Feller 150
Jackie Robinson . . 124
Sam Rice 81
Red Ruffing 72
Eppa Rixey 49
Luke Appling 48
Phil Rizzuto 44
Burleigh Grimes . . . 43

Hack Wilson 39
Ducky Medwick 34

1964
Needed to Elect: 151

Luke Appling 142
Red Ruffing 141
Roy Campanella . . 115
Ducky Medwick . . . 108
Pee Wee Reese . . . 73
Lou Boudreau 68
Al Lopez 57
Chuck Klein 56
Johnny Mize 54
Mel Harder 51
Johnny Vander Meer . .
. . . . 51

1964 Run Off
Needed to Elect: 170
One Player Maximum

Luke Appling 189
Red Ruffing 184
Roy Campanella . . 138
Ducky Medwick . . . 130
Pee Wee Reese . . . 47
Lou Boudreau 43
Al Lopez 34
Johnny Vander Meer . .
. . . . 20
Chuck Klein 18
Marty Marion 17

1966
Needed to Elect: 227

Ted Williams 282
Red Ruffing 208
Roy Campanella . . 197
Ducky Medwick . . . 187
Lou Boudreau 115
Al Lopez 109
Enos Slaughter . . . 100
Pee Wee Reese . . . 95
Marty Marion 86
Johnny Mize 81

1967
Needed to Elect: 219

Ducky Medwick . . . 212
Red Ruffing 212
Roy Campanella . . 204
Lou Boudreau 143
Ralph Kiner 124
Enos Slaughter . . . 123
Al Lopez 114
Marty Marion 90
Johnny Mize 89
Pee Wee Reese . . . 89

1967 Run Off
Needed to Elect: 230
One Player Maximum

Red Ruffing 266
Ducky Medwick . . . 248
Roy Campanella . . 170
Lou Boudreau 68
Al Lopez 50
Enos Slaughter . . . 48
Ralph Kiner 41
Johnny Vander Meer . .
. . . . 35
Ernie Lombardi . . . 25
Bucky Walters 24

1968
Needed to Elect: 212

Ducky Medwick . . . 240
Roy Campanella . . 205
Lou Boudreau 146
Enos Slaughter . . . 129
Ralph Kiner 118
Johnny Mize 103
Allie Reynolds 95
Marty Marion 89
Arky Vaughan 82
Pee Wee Reese . . . 81

1969
Needed to Elect: 255

Stan Musial 317
Roy Campanella . . 270
Lou Boudreau 218
Ralph Kiner 137
Enos Slaughter . . . 128
Johnny Mize 116
Marty Marion 112
Allie Reynolds 98
Joe Gordon 97
Johnny Vander Meer . .
. . . . 95
Early Wynn 95

1970
Needed to Elect: 225

Lou Boudreau 232
Ralph Kiner 167
Gil Hodges 145
Early Wynn 140
Enos Slaughter . . . 133
Johnny Mize 126
Marty Marion 120
Pee Wee Reese . . . 97
Red Schoendienst . . 97
George Kell 90

1971
Needed to Elect: 270

Yogi Berra 242
Early Wynn 240
Ralph Kiner 212
Gil Hodges 180
Enos Slaughter . . . 165
Johnny Mize 157
Pee Wee Reese . . . 127
Marty Marion 123
Red Schoendienst . 123
Allie Reynolds 110

1972
Needed to Elect: 297

Sandy Koufax 344
Yogi Berra 339
Early Wynn 301
Ralph Kiner 235
Gil Hodges 161
Johnny Mize 157
Enos Slaughter . . . 149
Pee Wee Reese . . . 129
Marty Marion 120
Bob Lemon 117

1973
Needed to Elect: 285

Warren Spahn 316
Whitey Ford 255
Ralph Kiner 235
Gil Hodges 218
Robin Roberts 213
Bob Lemon 177

Johnny Mize 157
Enos Slaughter . . 145
Marty Marion 127
Pee Wee Reese . . . 126

1974
Needed to Elect: 274

Mickey Mantle 322
Whitey Ford 284
Robin Roberts . . . 224
Ralph Kiner 215
Gil Hodges 198
Bob Lemon 190
Enos Slaughter . . . 145
Pee Wee Reese . . 141
Eddie Mathews . . . 118
Phil Rizzuto 111
Duke Snider 111

1975
Needed to Elect: 272

Ralph Kiner 273
Robin Roberts . . . 263
Bob Lemon 233
Gil Hodges 188
Enos Slaughter . . 177
Hal Newhouser . . 155
Pee Wee Reese . . 154
Eddie Mathews . . 148
Phil Cavaretta . . . 129
Duke Snider 129

1976
Needed to Elect: 291

Robin Roberts . . . 337
Bob Lemon 305
Gil Hodges 233
Enos Slaughter . . 197
Eddie Mathews . . . 189

Pee Wee Reese . . . 186
Nellie Fox 174
Duke Snider 159
Phil Rizzuto 149
George Kell 129
Red Schoendienst . 129

1977
Needed to Elect: 287

Ernie Banks 321
Eddie Mathews . . . 239
Gil Hodges 224
Enos Slaughter . . 222
Duke Snider 212
Don Drysdale 197
Pee Wee Reese . . . 163
Nellie Fox 152
Jim Bunning 146
George Kell 141

1978
Needed to Elect: 284

Eddie Mathews . . . 301
Enos Slaughter . . 261
Duke Snider 254
Gil Hodges 226
Don Drysdale 219
Jim Bunning 181
Pee Wee Reese . . . 169
Richie Ashburn . . 158
Hoyt Wilhelm 158
Nellie Fox 149

1979
Needed to Elect: 324

Willie Mays 409
Duke Snider 308
Enos Slaughter . . 297
Gil Hodges 242

Don Drysdale 233
Nellie Fox 174
Hoyt Wilhelm 168
Maury Wills 166
Red Schoendienst . 159
Jim Bunning 147

1980
Needed to Elect: 289

Al Kaline 340
Duke Snider 333
Don Drysdale 230
Gil Hodges 230
Hoyt Wilhelm 209
Jim Bunning 177
Red Schoendienst . 164
Nellie Fox 161
Maury Wills 146
Richie Ashburn . . . 134

1981
Needed to Elect: 301

Bob Gibson 337
Don Drysdale 243
Gil Hodges 241
Harmon Killebrew . 239
Hoyt Wilhelm 238
Juan Marichal 233
Nellie Fox 168
Red Schoendienst . 166
Jim Bunning 164
Maury Wills 163

1982
Needed to Elect: 311

Hank Aaron 406
Frank Robinson . . . 370
Juan Marichal 305
Harmon Killebrew . 246

Hoyt Wilhelm 236
Don Drysdale 233
Gil Hodges 205
Luis Aparicio 174
Jim Bunning 138
Red Schoendienst . 135

1983
Needed to Elect: 281

Brooks Robinson . . 344
Juan Marichal 313
Harmon Killebrew . 269
Luis Aparicio 252
Hoyt Wilhelm 243
Don Drysdale 242
Gil Hodges 237
Nellie Fox 173
Billy Williams 153
Red Schoendienst . 146

1984
Needed to Elect: 302

Luis Aparicio 341
Harmon Killebrew . 335
Don Drysdale 316
Hoyt Wilhelm 290
Nellie Fox 246
Billy Williams 202
Jim Bunning 201
Orlando Cepeda . . 124
Tony Oliva 124
Roger Maris 107

1985
Needed to Elect: 296

Hoyt Wilhelm 331
Lou Brock 315
Nellie Fox 295

Billy Williams 252
Jim Bunning 214
Catfish Hunter 212
Roger Maris 128
Harvey Kuenn 125
Orlando Cepeda . . 114
Tony Oliva 114

1986
Needed to Elect: 319

Willie McCovey . . . 346
Billy Williams 315
Catfish Hunter 289
Jim Bunning 279
Roger Maris 177
Tony Oliva 154
Orlando Cepeda . . 152
Harvey Kuenn 144
Maury Wills 124
Bill Mazeroski 100

1987
Needed to Elect: 310

Billy Williams 354
Catfish Hunter 315
Jim Bunning 289
Orlando Cepeda . . 179
Roger Maris 176
Tony Oliva 160
Harvey Kuenn 144
Bill Mazeroski 125
Maury Wills 113
Ken Boyer 96
Lew Burdette 96

1988
Needed to Elect: 320

Willie Stargell 352

Jim Bunning 317
Tony Oliva 202
Orlando Cepeda . . 199
Roger Maris 184
Harvey Kuenn 168
Bill Mazeroski 143
Luis Tiant 132
Maury Wills 127
Ken Boyer 109
Mickey Lolich 109

1989
Needed to Elect: 335

Johnny Bench 431
Carl Yastrzemski . . 423
Gaylord Perry 304
Jim Bunning 283
Ferguson Jenkins . 234
Orlando Cepeda . . 176
Tony Oliva 135
Bill Mazeroski 134
Harvey Kuenn 115
Maury Wills 95

1990
Needed to Elect: 333

Jim Palmer 411
Joe Morgan 363
Gaylord Perry 320
Ferguson Jenkins . 296
Jim Bunning 257
Orlando Cepeda . . 211
Tony Oliva 142
Bill Mazeroski 131
Harvey Kuenn 107
Ron Santo 96

Baseball Lore

Eliot Cohen

Throughout this volume you'll find plenty of baseball history, verified down to the slightest nuance and the thousandth decimal place. But there is some history that is as important to the game's life as any pennant race or hitting streak, even though it may or may not be absolutely, positively, guaranteed true. To that end, here's a by no means complete sampling of baseball's lore.

When the Pope came to the United States, a small boy was impressed by the abundant pageantry of the papal motorcade. He stared at the big cars, the robes, the cheering throng lining the sidewalks for miles. After the pontiff had passed, the boy asked his mother, "How'd he get to be Pope?"

"The cardinals selected him," replied the mother.

The boy pondered a moment, then mused, "You think the Giants would do something like that for Willie Mays?"

Classic baseball tales come in several flavors. One variety is passed down through generations, not only in the telling from parent to child, but in character, from Walter Johnson to Nolan Ryan, Babe Herman to Marv Throneberry. The measure of that story may be the number of characters it is (or could be) told about. Other tales revolve around the historic events of the game. A third type grows out of the outstanding personalities in the game. Certain unique figures stand out, but the folklore mirrors the transcendental nature of the game itself. If that prospect can't be the next Hank Aaron or Ty Cobb, maybe he can be the next Mickey Rivers.

"I only have trouble with fly balls."
—Carmelo Martinez, outfielder

It didn't take long for baseball fact to spawn baseball legend. The poem "Casey at the Bat" was written in 1888, and it became an instant classic. Its subtitle, "A Ballad of the Republic," indicates that author Ernest Lawrence Thayer was thinking big. The poem laid the foundation for much of baseball folklore to come, not only because it captured the spirit of the game and its fans, but because Casey failed to get that big hit. In baseball, failure is much more common than success, and some of the best anecdotes and quips are made in response to shortcomings.

Some fail by overreaching, such as erstwhile base stealer Ping Bodie. "He had larceny in his heart, but his feet were honest," observed sportswriter Bugs Baer. Some underachieve, like Commissioner Bowie Kuhn during the 1981 baseball strike. "If Bowie Kuhn were alive today, he'd do something about the strike," wrote Red Smith.

The great Honus Wagner had big hands to go with his bowed legs and didn't always discriminate between ground balls and other loose objects in the infield. He used to tell about when a rabbit ran past him about the same time as a two-hopper. Wagner scooped up both and fired the rabbit to first. "I got the runner by a hare," Wagner confided.

Catcher Bob Uecker took issue with the theory that the knuckler's tough to catch. "You just wait until it stops rolling, then pick it up." The catcher/broadcaster/actor proclaimed that he was proudest of his role in the Cardinals' 1964 pennant drive. His contribution? "I came down with hepatitis." How'd he catch it? "I think the trainer injected me with it."

But few players can joke about their foibles. During the 1910s, Ring Lardner invented a ballplayer named Alibi Ike, honoring a tradition that survives among players. Pitcher Billy Loes once explained missing a grounder by saying, "I lost it in the sun." Loes also cautioned pitchers, "If you win twenty games, they'll want you to do it every year," so he set a personal limit of fourteen. During the 1980s, a member of the Pirates complained, "I wish they wouldn't play that song. Every time they play it, we lose." He was talking about "The Star Spangled Banner." Upon seeing the Astrodome, Gabe Paul's first reaction was "It will revolutionize baseball. It will open a whole new area of alibis for players."

The game has a way of revealing character and exposing flaws.

Leo Durocher told the story (but it could just as well have been Connie Mack or Whitey Herzog) of a horse who asked him for a tryout after a spring training workout. Durocher obliged, sent the nag into the batting cage, and served up a fat pitch. Holding the bat between its teeth, the horse smacked the offering over the fence. The horse hit the curve the other way, got around on the hard stuff, handling the bat better than anyone Durocher had on the club.

So he sent the horse to the outfield and hit it fungoes. The horse caught the ball between its teeth and drop kicked it back to the infield. An impressed Durocher began considering the steed's potential. He called the horse in and said, "Okay, now I want to see you run."

The horse said, "If I could run, would I be here looking for a job?"

Chicago Cubs manager Charlie Grimm told about a kid who approached him at a tryout camp during World War Two, when the military draft had strapped the majors for talent. "I'm 4-F," the aspirant announced, meaning he'd been rejected by the Army, "but I can hit like Ted Williams, throw as fast as Dizzy Dean, and play the outfield like Joe DiMaggio."

"You're nuts," Grimm grumbled.

"Sure. That's why I'm 4-F."

There's a surprising range of ways to fail in baseball. Aside from imparting strategy, signs appear to be designed to give players a chance to make mistakes, judging from all the talk of missed signs throughout history. John McGraw and Wilbert Robinson were friends for three decades, and McGraw hired Robinson as a coach for the Giants. Their relationship ended in acrimony when McGraw accused Robinson of missing a sign and costing the Giants a game. McGraw fined outfielder Red Murray for failing to obey a bunt sign with a runner on second, even though Murray had taken a high and tight serving that would have been nearly impossible to bunt and belted it for a homer.

Durocher once took refuge in the press box after being tossed from a game, then conspired with a sportswriter to give signs. The system worked until the sportswriter wiped his forehead. "What did you do that for?" Durocher blurted. "You just gave the steal sign."

First baseman Rocky Nelson missed a squeeze sign with Pee Wee Reese on third. Nelson swung away and nearly decapitated Reese. The livid shortstop and team captain demanded, "Why'd you swing?"

Nelson replied, "Why do you think they call me Rocky?"

When Frank Howard was with the Dodgers, they used verbal signals. The player's last name signaled a hit and run. So after the big man walked, first base coach Pete Reiser began giving him encouragement, "Okay, *Howard,* be on your toes. Be ready for anything, *Howard.*"

Howard called time and told Reiser, "We're good friends, Pete. Call me Frank."

After the Dodgers infield of Steve Garvey at first, Dave Lopes at second, Bill Russell at short, and Ron Cey at third broke up after an unprecedented run from 1974 through 1981, Tom Lasorda tried to make do with Pedro Guerrero, whose best position is DH, at third base, revolving doors at short and first, and second baseman Steve Sax, who sought help from a hypnotist to overcome a chronic inability to make the throw to first. As only Lasorda can, he cajoled, begged, and badgered Guerrero to make him a better infielder. After one galling loss, Lasorda tried to get inside his star's head. "Okay, Pedro," Lasorda said, "the tying run's on, one out in the ninth. What are you thinking?"

Guerrero answered, "I'm thinking, don't hit the ball to me."

"C'mon, Pete," Lasorda chided, "what else are you thinking?"

"You really want to know?"

"Yes."

"I'm thinking," Guerrero said, "don't hit the ball to Sax either."

Lasorda is generally considered a teddy-bear type manager, but other skippers inspire fear in their players. Playing in Houston before the Astrodome was built, Gene Mauch's fiery temper erupted at the Phillies' constant complaints about the heat. "I'm sick and tired of you guys griping about the climate," Mauch began. "The other guys have to play in it, too. The next guy who complains about the heat gets fined a hundred bucks."

After the Phils' next turn in the field, right fielder Johnny Callison came back to the dugout and fell in a heap on the bench. "God, is it hot out there," he moaned. Then he saw Mauch out of the corner of his eye and, remembering the edict, quickly added, "Good and hot, just the way I like it."

Even the great Lou Gehrig had trouble performing on cue. He was scheduled to do a live radio spot for a cereal called Huskies. The announcer asked the slugger, "To what do you owe your strength and condition?"

"Wheaties," Gehrig told the listeners.

The makers of Huskies insisted that Gehrig's error brought them more publicity than the script would have. But Gehrig found endorsement offers rare after that.

The knuckleball can be equally elusive. Fluttering up to the plate at a half to two-thirds the speed of a fastball, the knuckler is difficult to master, an adventure to catch, and nearly impossible to hit.

After his Brooklyn Dodgers lost on a ninth-inning homer, Casey Stengel asked catcher Babe Phelps why he'd called for a fastball from famed knuckleballer Dutch Leonard. "His knuckler's tough to catch," Phelps explained.

"If his knuckler's tough to catch, don't you think it might be a little tough to hit, too?" Casey asked.

Famed batting coach Charley Lau said, "There are two theories about hitting the knuckleballer. Unfortunately, neither works." Bobby Murcer observed that trying to hit flutterballer Phil Niekro was "like eating Jell-O with chopsticks."

> *"You can't hit what you can't see."*
> —*Joe Tinker reviews Rube Marquard*

Fastball pitchers have been a staple of baseball legends since the overhand delivery was legalized in 1884. Walter Johnson, Lefty Grove, Bob Feller, Sandy Koufax, and Nolan Ryan inherited the mantle of their respective generations as the king of the radio ball—you heard it, but you couldn't see it.

After striking out on three Johnson fastballs, no less an authority than Babe Ruth told the umpire, "You know, I didn't see any of them either, but the last one sounded kind of high to me." Writer Bugs Baer believed that Grove "could throw a lamb chop past a wolf." Manager Bucky Harris offered his Senators these instructions for facing Feller: "Go up and hit what you see. If you don't see it, come on back." Willie Stargell paid lefthander Steve Carlton a high compliment when he admitted, "Sometimes I hit him like I used to hit Koufax, and that's like drinking coffee with a fork." Reggie Jackson labeled Ryan baseball's exorcist because "he scares the devil out of you."

Walter Johnson didn't have the colorful personality to make himself a legend, just his fastball, but that was enough. Ray Chapman walked away from home plate after taking two strikes from Johnson. You've another strike coming, the umpire called. "Keep it. I don't want it," Chapman said and kept on walking.

A figure of grandfatherly kindness even as a rookie,

Johnson was said to lay a fat pitch in for a needy hitter once a game was no longer in doubt. "Ol' Barney" also feared hitting batters, although his career total of 206 hit batsmen tops the all-time list.

Feller, like Koufax and Ryan to follow, was nearly as wild as he was fast. One overcast day, Yankee pitcher Lefty Gomez had to face Feller in the gloaming. Gomez, who earned the nickname Goofy, brought a book of matches to the plate, lit one, and held it over his head as he stepped into the batter's box.

"You think that match is going to help you see Feller's fast one?" the umpire snarled.

"You got it all wrong," Gomez explained. "I just want to make sure he can see me."

Gomez was quicker with this tongue than his fastball. Still, he won nearly 65 percent of his decisions over fourteen seasons and went 6–0 in five World Series, earning his ticket to Cooperstown in 1972, attributing his success to "clean living and swift outfielders." Of the two components, only one can be confirmed.

On occasion, an outfielder, even a great one, might come up short. Rookie Joe DiMaggio, who roomed with Gomez on the road for several seasons, bragged, "I'm going to make 'em forget about Tris Speaker." He crept in to play a shallow center field like the Gray Eagle behind Gomez, and in the late innings, a drive to center outpaced DiMaggio for a triple, allowing the deciding runs to score.

At dinner with teammates after the game, DiMaggio was still saying that he was going to make the fans forget about Speaker. Gomez had had enough. "If you don't back up a little," he told the rookie, "you'll make 'em forget about Gomez."

Facing Jimmie Foxx in a tight game, Gomez shook off catcher Bill Dickey's signs for a fastball, changeup, and curve. So Dickey called time and angrily walked out to the mound. "You tell me what you want to throw," he snarled.

"Well, to tell you truth," Gomez replied, "I don't want to throw the ball at all."

Yankee second baseman Tony Lazzeri had a reputation for heady play. So, in a bases-loaded jam, Gomez snared a comebacker, whirled, and threw to Lazzeri, who was stationed on the edge of the infield grass between first and second. When Lazzeri recovered from the shock, he charged toward Gomez and screamed, "Why in hell did you throw the ball to me?"

"I'd been reading in the papers how smart you are, and how you always know what to do with the ball," Gomez cooed. "Well, I wanted to see what you'd do with that one."

Gomez's antics often infuriated straitlaced Yankee skipper Joe McCarthy. Gomez loved airplanes and would step off the mound to watch any plane passing overhead. After one particularly long break for aerial observation, McCarthy jumped all over Gomez at the end of the inning. "Keep your mind in the game," he scolded. "With you daydreaming like that, I'm surprised they didn't start knocking the ball out of the park."

"Izzatso?" Gomez replied. "I had ahold of the ball all the time I was watching the plane, didn't I? How could they knock it out of the park?" Gomez was always a firm believer in working slowly, "because as long as I have it, they can't hit it." (Fast-working Grover Cleveland Alex-

ander took the opposite approach, reasoning, "What do you want me to do? Let 'em stand up there and think on my time?") When asked if he ever threw the spitball, Gomez demurred, "Not intentionally, but I sweat easily."

McCarthy once saw a bright red biplane doing some death-defying stunts above the ballfield and told Gomez about it over dinner. "You missed a real crackpot flier," he said. "It would have taught you a lesson. I hope you saw it."

"Well, not exactly," Gomez told the skipper. "I was in it."

McCarthy also found fault with Gomez's build, thinking he was too skinny to be a consistent winner. "If you had another fifteen or twenty pounds of meat on you, you'd make them forget every lefthander that ever tossed a ball."

Gomez followed McCarthy's advice and did add twenty pounds, but he had an uncharacteristically bad season on the mound. Near the end of the year, Gomez spoke with his manager. "You told me if I put on some weight, I'd make 'em forget every lefthander that ever pitched. Trouble is, when they start forgetting lefthanders, they're going to start with Gomez."

At the 1934 All-Star Game, catcher Gabby Hartnett reprimanded Gomez, owner of a .147 career batting average. "Are you trying to insult Mister Hubbell," Hartnett asked, "coming up here with a bat?" Gomez bragged that he once broke a bat. "I ran it over in the driveway."

Gomez inherited the flaky lefthander tradition from Rube Waddell, the first oddball player of the twentieth century. Waddell made a show of his trade, pouring water over his arm to cool it off and thus prevent his heat from burning off his catcher's mitt. Waddell liked to fish and chase fire engines, ready to spring off the mound in midgame for either. (Fortunately for his teammates, fish didn't roll past the ballpark with their alarms blaring.) At an Easter Sunday 1900 exhibition game, the lefty was pelted on the head with an egg. In response, he called in his fielders and struck out the side on nine pitches. Waddell wore out a number of managers until he bounced back to the Pacific Coast League in 1902. Connie Mack wanted him for his A's and dispatched two detectives to bring him back.

A pair of Pinkertons were hardly enough to keep Waddell under control in Philadelphia. On days when he wasn't pitching, and on some when he was supposed to be, Waddell could be found at bars, firehouses, playgrounds, the heads of parades, or under the stands shooting marbles with youngsters.

Catcher Ossee Schreckengost was Waddell's roommate and fellow carouser. The two were of similar mind on most issues, but one divisive item nearly ended their friendship. (History is unclear on the offender, but here's the better version of the story.) After a typically successful season, Waddell informed Connie Mack that he wouldn't sign his contract for the upcoming season. Mack, whose creativity had been stretched to the limits, he thought, to accommodate his southpaw, had already offered Waddell time off for fishing if he'd complete both ends of a doubleheader, had allowed him liberal visitation rights to local firehouses, and stood ready with bail money on those not infrequent occasions when the lefty required it.

So what was it Waddell wanted now? Well, in that era,

players often shared beds on the road. Waddell had no problem with splitting the mattress, but objected to Schreckengost's habit of eating crackers on it. So Mack wrote in a contract provision banning the practice, and Waddell was booked for another season.

Otherwise, the battery mates got along famously. The catcher was hovering over Waddell's bandaged body when the pitcher awoke in a hospital after a huge drunk with the boys the night before. "How'd I get here?" Waddell asked.

Schreckengost explained that Waddell insisted he could fly, and when his teammates ridiculed the idea, the pitcher leaped out the second-story window, flapping his arms.

"Why didn't you stop me?" Waddell implored.

"What? And lose the hundred bucks I bet on you?"

Waddell had more success on the ground. While watching an alligator wrestler, Waddell asked for a shot at the reptile. The alligator never had a chance. In 1904, Waddell opened a five-game series against the Red Sox with a one-hitter, allowing a bunt single to the leadoff man, then retiring the next twenty-seven hitters. A cocky Waddell was scheduled to pitch the series finale and warned his opponent, "I'm going to give you the same thing." The opponent was a thirty-seven-year-old veteran named Cy Young, who responded to the challenge by pitching a perfect game. Alligators were simpler foes.

Satchel Paige copied Waddell's stunt of calling in the outfield. But Paige had plenty of stories of his own to tell. The oldest rookie in major league history, Paige claimed he was thirty-nine (he was at least forty-two, probably closer to fifty) when he signed with the Indians in 1948. He challenged the nation to find records of him pitching before 1927. When one of his clippings from 1926 turned up, Paige explained that a billy goat had eaten his birth certificate and asked, "How old would you be if you didn't know how old you was?" Paige also noted, "Age is a question of mind over matter; if you don't mind, it don't matter."

Paige's routines included using a gum wrapper as his home plate, the hesitation pitch, and his be-ball, so named because "it's always where I want it to be." Paige also reminded white fans of his contemporaries in the Negro Leagues. Lists of the greatest fastballers of all time were no longer complete without Bullet Joe Rogan and Smokey Joe Williams. Testimony that Josh Gibson hit a ball out of Yankee Stadium became more credible. Paige was fond of telling about an offering that Gibson hit back between the pitcher's legs that sailed over the fence. That was nothing compared to Cool Papa Bell, who, according to Paige, "hit a line drive by me that hit him on the ass when he was sliding into second."

Paige also offered six rules for staying young, recorded by Richard Donovan in *Collier's* in 1953. Considering that he last appeared in a major league game in 1965, at age fifty-nine or more, they're worth repeating:

- Avoid fried meats which angry up the blood.
- If your stomach disputes you, lie down and pacify it with cool thoughts.
- Keep the juices flowing by jangling around gently as you move.
- Go very light on the vices, such as carrying on in society. The social ramble ain't restful.

- Avoid running at all times.
- Don't look back. Something might be gaining on you.

Dizzy Dean combined devastating stuff, a gift for malapropisms, and a dose of braggadocio when he burst on the scene with the Cardinals in 1931. "The good Lord was good to me," Dean conceded when inducted into the Hall of Fame in 1953. "He gave me a strong body, a good right arm, and a weak mind." In a doubleheader against the Dodgers, Dean pitched a three-hitter in the first game. His brother Paul pitched a no-hitter in the nightcap. "I wished I'd'a known Paul was goin' to pitch a no-hitter," Dizzy said. "I'd'a pitched one, too."

While the Deans were dominating the National League, Dizzy visited Brooklyn Dodgers manager Casey Stengel between games of a doubleheader. Half in jest, Stengel asked, "Are there any more at home like you and Paul?"

"We got another brother, Elmer. He's down in Houston, burning up the league," Dizzy told Casey. "You might get him cheap."

Stengel couldn't contain his enthusiasm, and soon reporters were writing about the third Dean brother bound for Brooklyn. They stopped writing and started laughing when reports from the Texas League filtered back that Elmer was a peanut vendor at the Houston ballpark.

Dean once got caught out after curfew, along with three other Cardinals, in the midst of a pennant race. Manager Frankie Frisch fined all $200, except for Dean, whose fine was $400. When Dean complained to Frisch, the manager replied, "Why, Diz, you're not the same as those guys. You're the great Dizzy Dean. Everything about you has got to be bigger and better than anybody else. And that goes for fines, too." Dean had to agree.

Dean was fond of noting, "It ain't braggin' if you do it." Legend has it that Dean promised at a hospital ward to strike out Bill Terry, then the Giants' heavy hitter, with the bases loaded. So with runners on first and second and two out, Dean walked second baseman Hugh Critz, hardly a threat, to load the bases and bring up Terry. "I hate to do this, Bill," Dean told the slugger, "but I done promised a bunch of kids I'd fan you with the bases loaded." So Dean did, on three pitches.

In the 1934 World Series, Dean won the first and seventh games, and got beaned by a double-play relay throw while pinch-running in the fourth game. He was carried from the field, but was not seriously hurt. "The doctors X-rayed my head and found nothing," Dean proclaimed.

However, Joe Medwick upstaged Dean's antics in the '34 Series. The muscular left fielder was an exception to the happy-go-lucky Gashouse Gang that featured Dean and Pepper Martin. Medwick later became the only man in baseball history to knock out his own relief pitcher when hurler Ed Heusser passed an impertinent remark about Medwick's fielding in the dugout. But in the 1934 Series, Medwick reserved his ire for the Detroit Tigers, batting .379. In the seventh game, he slid into Detroit third baseman Marv Owen with his spikes high, business as usual for Medwick. The triple upped the Cards' advantage of 8–0 and moments later Medwick scored. When he returned to his post in left for the bottom of the sixth, Detroit fans added a barrage of garbage to their torrents of verbal abuse. As the debris rained onto the field, Commissioner Kenesaw Mountain Landis ordered Medwick off the field, the first player ever tossed for his own protection.

Dean understood public relations almost as well as pitching. When riding to the ballpark with a writer, Dean claimed he was puzzled by the science of locating gas stations. "Just how did these fellas know there was gas and oil under there?" he asked. When a reporter challenged him because he told every writer that he was born in a different place, Dean replied indignantly, "Them ain't lies, they's scoops."

A liner off the bat of Earl Averill struck Dean on the toe in the third inning of the 1937 All-Star Game. Billy Herman got the rebound and threw out Averill to end the inning, and Dean retired to the clubhouse with an aching toe. A doctor examined it and said it was fractured. "Fractured, hell," Dean moaned. "The damned thing's broke." The injury caused him to alter his delivery and hurt his arm. After helping the Cubs to a pennant in 1938 with an assortment of junk and hanging on for a couple more years, Dean had to retire when he was just thirty years old.

Dean stayed in the game as a broadcaster, to the exasperation of English teachers. When chided for his ungrammatical calls, Dean reminded his critics, "A lot of people who don't say 'ain't' ain't eating." When the St. Louis Board of Education circulated a petition against Dean's butchery of the language, Dean replied, "You learn 'em English, and I'll learn 'em baseball." With Dean at the mike, batters strode "confidentially" to the plate, players returned to their "respectable" bases, runners "slud," fielders "throwed," and "empires" made the calls. He urged listeners, "Don't fail to miss tomorrow's game."

While Dean was broadcasting for the St. Louis Browns in 1947, a team that lost 95 games, he didn't sugarcoat the Browns' ineptitude. He'd suggested on the radio that he could do better than some of the Brown hurlers. So club president Bill DeWitt offered Dean a chance to start for the Browns, and Dean couldn't resist. On September 28, 1947, more than six years after his last major league action, Dean went to the hill for the Browns against the White Sox. He held the Sox scoreless through four innings, but had to retire, for good, with a pulled leg muscle, suffered when he singled.

After the game, Dean beamed, "I said I could pitch as good as most of these fellows and I can. But I'll be doggoned if I'm ever going to try this stunt again. Talking's my game now, and I'm just glad that the muscle I pulled wasn't in my throat."

Catcher Moe Berg could speak a dozen languages, but couldn't hit in any of them. He went on to stardom with the U.S. intelligence service in World War Two. Dean's success as a broadcaster paved the way for other successful ex-players, some of whom approached his gift for mangling the English language. Jerry Coleman has had pitchers throwing up in the bullpen, outfielders lining up fly balls under the warning track, infielders chasing sun-blown pop-ups, runners sliding into second with stand-up doubles, and this memorable call: "There's a fly ball deep to center. Winfield is going back, back. He hits his head against the wall. It's rolling back toward second base."

Coleman's Yankee double-play partner Phil Rizzuto doesn't pay much attention to the game on the field, but has been known to take a stab at current events. When

Curt Flood was holding out after his trade to Philadelphia, Rizzuto noted that he'd heard the center fielder was in Spain. "Maybe he's a matador," said Bill White, Scooter's partner in the booth. "Or maybe he's a bull-fighter," Rizzuto parried.

Another Yankee teammate of Coleman's was Yogi Berra, who hit the Triple Crown when it came to folklore. He was ugly ("So what? You don't hit with your face."), he was good (a three-time MVP), and he had a gift for self-expression. Berra didn't try to be funny, as when a player's wife complimented him on looking cool on a sweltering afternoon. "Thanks, and you don't look so hot yourself," Yogi replied. When a clubhouse man asked for his cap size in spring training, Yogi shot back, "How should I know? I'm not in shape yet." In appreciation for Yogi Berra Day, he announced, "I want to thank everyone who made this day necessary." When his wife Carmen told him she'd seen (the movie) *Doctor Zhivago,* Berra shrugged, "What's the matter with you now?" When Berra played left field, he explained the shadows by saying, "It gets late early out there." When asked about a hitting slump, Berra asserted, "Slump? What slump? I just ain't hitting." Wary of the press, he warned reporters, "If you ask me something I don't know, I'm not going to answer." Berra contended, "It ain't over till it's over," and you can't argue with that.

Joe McCarthy tried to break Berra's habit of swinging at the first pitch, urging his catcher "to think when you're up there." After taking three strikes, Berra returned to the bench complaining, "How can a guy think and hit at the same time?" Another time, after fanning on three pitches way out of the strike zone, Berra wondered, "How can a pitcher that wild be in the big leagues?"

Some Yogi stories are less likely to be true, but no matter. When asked if he wanted his whole pizza in four or eight pieces, he said, "Better make it four. I don't think I can eat eight." When receiving a "Pay to Bearer" check, Yogi protested, "That's not how you spell my name." Berra was introduced to Ernest Hemingway and told he was a writer. "What paper are you with, Ernie?" Berra asked. Talking about a restaurant, Berra said, "Nobody goes there anymore. It's too crowded." Similarly, he said one of his classmates in high school "was so popular, no one could stand him." Commenting on Mickey Mantle, he said that the switch-hitting slugger had equal power from both sides of the plate. "He's naturally amphibious." After seeing a Steve McQueen movie, Berra reasoned, "He must've made that one before he died."

When Berra visited the Vatican, he was quoted as greeting the Pontiff, "Hello, Pope." That follows the tradition of apocryphal greetings such as Casey Stengel's "Nice to meet you, King," to England's George V, and Babe Ruth's "Hot as hell, ain't it, Prez," to Warren Harding.

Despite his clownish reputation, Berra was a wise investor who made a great deal of money before ballplayers were millionaires. He also had a reputation for stinginess and was an inveterate borrower of locker room toiletries. Trouble came when Berra borrowed deodorant from Whitey Ford's locker after a game. Ford had discovered that a roll-on bottle was the perfect way to store a resin mixture that he used to get his fingers sticky. So when Berra used the roll-on bottle, he cemented his arms to his sides. The trainer had to cut the hair under his arms to free him.

Almost every manager tells the story of going out to the mound after his starter gives up six (give or take a couple) hits to start the game, all on the first pitch. The manager asks the catcher, "How's his stuff?"

"I'm not sure," the catcher replies. "I haven't caught any yet."

(In another version, the manager asks the catcher what pitch the batter hit for a home run. "I don't know," the catcher replies. "I haven't caught it yet.")

Cubs pitcher Bob Muncrief told about facing Ralph Kiner in 1949, when he was the most-feared slugger in the National League. Kiner took Muncrief deep, with a homer off the back wall of the Wrigley Field bleachers. Back in the dugout, manager Frankie Frisch asked what Kiner had hit. "A curveball," Muncrief told him. "He hit a good pitch."

"Well, forget about your curveball and just throw him fastballs next time up," Frisch counseled. "He won't even get a loud foul off you."

So when Kiner batted again with two mates aboard, Muncrief followed Frisch's advice and threw him a fastball. Kiner slugged it over the fence, over the bleachers, and out onto Waveland Avenue. When Muncrief got back to bench, he shouted at Frisch, "Well, brains, he hit yours a whole lot farther than he hit mine."

New York Giants reliever Don Liddle served up Vic Wertz's 460-foot smash to center in the 1954 World Series. Only Willie Mays's unbelievable catch and the Polo Grounds' huge center field dimensions prevented Wertz's clout from breaking the 2–2 tie wide open. Leo Durocher figured Liddle might not have his best stuff, so he summoned Marv Grissom to face the next hitter. As Grissom took the mound, Liddle told him, "Well, I got my guy."

When manager Pat Corrales came to get Jim Kern after a rough outing for the Ranger reliever, Kern complained, "I'm not tired."

"Yeah," Corrales concurred, "but your outfielders are."

Pitchers don't get much sympathy when they run into trouble, not even within their fraternity. In the Seattle Pilots' bullpen during a game, Skip Lockwood called to Jim Bouton to ask, "Bouton, how do you hold your doubles?" When a young pitcher asked manager Lou Boudreau if pitching low to Ted Williams made sense, Boudreau advised, "Yeah, you can pitch him low, but as soon as you throw the ball, run and hide behind second base." Rudy May had his own method for handling George Brett: "The only way to pitch him is inside, so you force him to pull the ball. That way, the line drive won't hit you."

Carl Erskine wasn't shy about revealing his secret for handling Stan Musial. "I just throw him my best stuff, then run over to back up third base."

Sudden Sam McDowell of the Indians warned batters, "Trying to think with me is a mismatch. Hell, most of the time, I don't know where the pitch is going."

Sal "The Barber" Maglie earned his nickname for throwing at hitters he felt were getting a bit too cozy with the plate. "I don't want to get to know the other guys too well," Maglie said. "I might like them, and then I might not want to throw at them." One writer remarked that Maglie would throw at his mother if she crowded the

plate. "You bet," the pitcher replied. "Mother was a hell of a hitter."

Mets pitcher Jerry Hinsley was a twenty-year-old rookie the first time he faced Willie Mays. The veterans advised him to knock down the great man. The right-hander took their advice and decked Mays with his first pitch. Mays dusted himself off and clubbed Hinsley's next offering for a triple. "The problem was," Hinsley said, "they didn't tell me what to throw him on the second pitch."

Don Drysdale was another pitcher who believed in keeping batters loose. "The secret with Drysdale," confided Orlando Cepeda, "is to hit him before he hits you." Drysdale once apologized to Henry Aaron around the batting cage. "I'm sorry I hit you in the back last night, Henry. I meant to hit you in the neck."

Bob Gibson was a lean, mean competitor who worked so fast, it seemed there was a meter on the mound. He hated catchers' interruptions almost as much as he despised opposing batters. When receiver Tim McCarver came out to talk to Gibson in a tight spot, Bullet Bob stormed off the mound toward the catcher. "The only thing you know about pitching is that it's hard to hit!" Gibson screamed. "Now get out of here."

McCarver offered this Yogi-ism in tribute to the Cardinal ace: "That Bob Gibson is the luckiest pitcher ever. Whenever he pitches, the other team doesn't score." He was also the toughest. Gibson suffered a broken leg in 1967 on a drive hit back through the box; he threw the batter out and attempted to continue pitching. After his playing days, Gibson served as a coach under Cardinal teammate Joe Torre, imparting to pitchers his attitude as much as technique. "If there weren't fifteen thousand people watching," he told one staff member during a mound visit, "I'd hit you in the head."

Russ "Mad Monk" Meyer earned his nickname because of a one-in-a-million shot in his first start in Philadelphia after the Phils had traded him to the Brooklyn Dodgers. In the eighth inning of a tie game, Meyer and catcher Roy Campanella thought they'd struck out Richie Ashburn to end the inning. Campanella had rolled the ball to the mound, but umpire Augie Donatelli called the pitch a ball. Meyer went crazy, charging off the mound toward the umpire and calling him a "homer," preceded by several modifiers. So Donatelli gave Meyer the thumb, but Meyer wasn't through. He refused to leave the mound, even after manager Charlie Dressen came out to get him, stomping and shouting. It wasn't until Donatelli threatened to fine him more money that Meyer decided he'd had enough and stalked off the mound, only to discover that he still had the resin bag clenched in his fist. So he whipped the bag into the air and kept stomping toward the dugout. Sure enough, the bag landed right in the middle of Meyer's cap and stuck there. Even Meyer had to laugh.

But by the time he got to the dugout, Meyer was mad all over again and wouldn't leave. He baited Donatelli into coming over to the dugout to get him off the field. As a parting gesture, Meyer grabbed his crotch. He didn't realize that he was a participant in one of the earliest nationally televised games, and his obscene gesture had been beamed to millions of viewers across the country. Commissioner Ford Frick was so disturbed by Meyer's display that he forbid cameras from shooting into the dugout.

When Hank Aguirre was a rookie with the Indians, his first assignment was Ted Williams. Unfamiliarity gave Aguirre an advantage over the Splendid Splinter, and he fanned Williams. After the game, Aguirre brought the strikeout ball into the Red Sox clubhouse and asked Williams to autograph it. Williams was probably too stunned to refuse.

A couple of weeks later, the Indians were facing the Red Sox again, and young Aguirre was called upon to face Williams. This time, the Thumper walloped Aguirre's first offering off the foul pole for a homer. As he rounded the bases, Williams yelled, "Get that ball, and I'll sign it, too."

Aguirre went on to be a pretty fair pitcher for the Tigers and other teams for sixteen years, but he had a career batting average of .085. But every dog has his day, or at least his at-bat, and one afternoon at Yankee Stadium, Aguirre teed off on an offering from Fritz Peterson for a triple. Peterson was beside himself, giving up a hit to a man who went 2 for 72 in 1962, and wasn't paying baserunner Aguirre the slightest mind. So Aguirre walked halfway down the line without drawing a look. On the second pitch, he got another lead unnoticed. Emboldened, Aguirre turned to third base coach Tony Cuccinello and whispered, "Hey, Tony, I think I can steal home."

Cuccinello sighed and told Aguirre, "Hank, you got this far . . . don't screw it up."

Reliever Tug McGraw continued the line of flaky left-handers during his twenty-year career. McGraw is credited with creating the 1973 Mets' battle cry, "You gotta believe." It all started when M. Donald Grant, the Mets' stodgy chairman of the board, came down to the clubhouse to give a speech that included the soon-to-be-famous war cry. Sitting in the back row like any good class clown, McGraw repeated the line, then stood up and did it again. The other players, inspired by this chance to cut Grant short, joined in.

Originally a starter and the owner of the Mets' first victory over Sandy Koufax, McGraw found his niche as a reliever. He had the perfect attitude for the job: "Some days you tame the tiger. And other days the tiger has you for lunch." McGraw, who pitched during an era of unprecedented salary escalation, once commented on a contract, "Ninety percent, I'll spend on good times, women, and Irish whiskey. The rest, I'll probably waste." When asked whether he preferred grass or artificial turf during the more innocent decade of the seventies, McGraw replied, "I don't know, I never smoked Astroturf." (Dick Allen's spin on this question was, "If a horse can't eat it, I don't want to play on it.")

Bill Lee was another flaky lefty. Since the right hemisphere of the brain controls the left side, Lee contended that "lefties are the only ones in their right minds." Lee and a handful of other Red Sox players formed the Loyal Order of Buffalo Heads, dedicated to ridiculing manager Don Zimmer. The name was suggested by Ferguson Jenkins, who believed the buffalo was the dumbest creature on earth.

When Buffalo Head Bernie Carbo was sold to Cleveland for $15,000, Lee walked away from the club for a day. He ripped the phone out of his wall at home, so club president Haywood Sullivan had to summon his left-hander back to the club by telegram. At the meeting, Lee agreed to rejoin the club, but Sullivan said he'd have to dock him a day's pay. Lee asked how much that amounted to, and Sullivan figured about $500. "Great," Lee said, "make it fifteen hundred and I'll take the whole weekend."

Warren Spahn was the winningest lefthander of all time, but he allowed two memorable home runs. In 1951, the Giants promoted a nineteen-year-old center fielder named Willie Mays. After batting .477 in Minneapolis over 35 games, Mays broke in 0 for 12 with the Giants and begged manager Leo Durocher to send him back to the minors. But Mays got a homer off Spahn for his first major league hit. "I'll never forgive myself," Spahn said. "We might have gotten rid of Willie forever if I'd only struck him out."

Thirty years later, Spahn's assignment was Luke Appling in an old-timers' All-Star Game in Washington, D.C. "Old Aches and Pains," who made his reputation with bat control, fouling off boxes of balls to get even with teams that denied free passes for his friends, collected only 45 homers among his 2,749 major league hits. But on that evening in 1981, seventy-four-year old Appling knocked Spahn's offering out of the park. This time, Spahn didn't take it quite so hard.

"I'd have to go with the immoral Babe Ruth."
—shortstop Johnny Logan selecting
the greatest player ever

Babe Ruth's legend was a product of his performances on the field. That's not to say that the Babe didn't go out of his way to foster the myths around him. But his deeds were so awesome as to require neither embellishment nor wit. When he was reported dead in 1925, he didn't say, "Reports of my death are greatly exaggerated." He didn't have to.

Ruth was instantly recognizable and awesomely successful. His singularity and popularity ensured that fables would become attached to him. He shattered home run records in a way no one has before or since. He was purchased for the highest price ever paid for a player and became the highest paid, worth every penny of it. When confronted with the fact that his contract called for more money than the President of the U.S. was making, Ruth retorted, "I had a better year than him."

But the hard facts rendered Ruth legendary, hardly leaving room for invention. Myths that have arisen are mere apocrypha to the actual record. Ruth did spend his formative years chewing tobacco and stealing money from the till at his parents' saloon until they committed their seven-year-old to St. Mary's Industrial School, a combination reform school and vocational institute run by the Xaverian Brothers, where young George learned shirt making and baseball. Ruth really did start as a top-flight pitcher who twice defeated Walter Johnson 1–0 and held the World Series record for consecutive scoreless innings for longer than his home run marks. ("Ruth made a grave mistake when he gave up pitching," Tris Speaker prematurely observed. "Working once a week, he might have lasted a long time and become a great star.") He did hit a ball through a plate-glass window across the street from

Sportsman's Park. He owned a factory that manufactured Babe Ruth cigars with his mug on every wrapper (but the candy bar had already been named for President Grover Cleveland's daughter). He did play ball with kids on a sandlot after a World Series game (on a day he didn't pitch for Boston). He really snacked on a half dozen hot dogs and soda pops, drove fast cars, and signed autographs for children tirelessly. He really broke a slump by staying out all night and hitting two homers the next day. Japanese soldiers in World War Two really did respond to Americans' taunts against the Emperor by screaming, "To hell with Babe Ruth!" Don Mattingly says that before he came to the Yankees, he thought Babe Ruth was a cartoon character. The guy Mattingly heard about couldn't have been human.

One of Ruth's favorite playmates was pitcher Waite Hoyt. When Hoyt checked into a hospital to dry out, the image-conscious ballclub announced that Hoyt was suffering from a case of amnesia. Ruth fired off a telegram to Hoyt: "Read about your case of Amnesia. Must be a new brand." The 1927 Yankees had a thirty-year-old rookie pitcher named Wilcy Moore. Ruth bet him $300 to $100 that Moore wouldn't get three hits in the season. Moore won the bet (he managed five safeties) and invested the money in a pair of mules for his cotton farm in Oklahoma. The appreciative pitcher named the beasts Babe and Ruth.

What really happened to Ruth in 1925 remains a mystery, but his malady became known as the great American bellyache. That he overindulged his passions for food and women is well documented, and some suspect that syphilis was responsible for his illness, which eventually required abdominal surgery. The illness and a suspension after his return to action fed suspicions that Ruth was done at age thirty. His comeback in 1926 and subsequent seasons was nothing short of mythic.

The most famous legend about Babe Ruth involves the alleged called-shot home run in the 1932 World Series versus the Chicago Cubs. Ruth was thirty-seven, two seasons from the end of his career, appearing in his last World Series. The vituperative level of the encounter was heightened by the Cubs' decision to vote only a half share of postseason money to former Yankee Mark Koenig, after the shortstop had been a key contributor in Chicago's pennant drive. On the New York side stood manager Joe McCarthy, who'd been fired by the Cubs after following a pennant in 1929 with a second place finish in 1930.

The Yankees had swept the first two games of the Series in New York. In his first Wrigley Field at-bat, Ruth had smashed a three-run homer. But in the fourth inning, Ruth missed a shoestring catch as the Cubs tied the game at 4–4. As he faced Charlie Root in the fifth inning, the crowd and the Chicago dugout were all over the Bambino. Ruth held up his hand after taking the first pitch for a called strike and again after a second called strike evened the count. Then he pointed with his bat in the direction of the bleachers, but he may have been pointing toward Root, or sweeping the club toward the Cub dugout, or merely indicating that he still had one strike remaining. There was no doubt that Ruth deposited Root's two-two offering into the center field bleachers, giving the Yankees a 5–4 lead. Reporters decided Ruth had called the shot,

but only months after the fact. Ruth bragged of the feat as well, on about the same schedule. Root denied the tale, claiming that he would have knocked Ruth down if he thought the Babe was calling his shot. Lou Gehrig followed with his second homer of the game as the Yankees powered toward a four-game sweep.

The Babe Ruth Story, a movie dismissed as maudlin and excessively melodramatic upon its release, recorded Ruth's promise of a home run to a bedridden boy. There really was a sick boy named Johnny Sylvester who lived in New Jersey, and his father did wire Ruth with the boy's request for an autographed ball during the 1926 World Series. Sylvester did receive autographed balls from the Series rivals before Ruth's three-homer effort in fourth game.

The three-homer game was sensational enough on its own. Each shot traveled farther than the one before, the first two clearing the right field grandstand and the third landing in the center field bleachers at Sportsman's Park. A radio announcer had heard about the sick boy and the baseballs, and embellished the story into a Ruthian promise of a home run, delivered in triplicate. The story grew into legend within weeks (Red Grange sent Sylvester a football), so much so that the Babe was moved to make a surprise visit to little Johnny during a barnstorming tour that fall. Sylvester's tale gave rise to a second story that Ruth told later about a bedridden boy in Tampa who rose to see him parade with the Yankees through town for an exhibition game. True, false, or in between, neither story tops that three-homer game.

The Babe's reputation has outlived him by decades. When Montreal reporters in the late 1970s questioned Dick Williams's unsuccessful strategy of walking Bake McBride to pitch to Mike Schmidt, Williams snarled, "I don't care if Jesus Christ was coming up, I was going to walk Bake McBride."

"What if Babe Ruth was coming up?" asked one of the newsmen.

Williams paused before admitting, "I don't know about Babe Ruth."

Joe DiMaggio wasn't the larger-than-life figure that Babe Ruth was, but he fulfilled a different baseball myth for a different era. Like Ruth, he came from humble beginnings, but DiMaggio wasn't a wild youth from the wrong side of the tracks. His success in the great American game became a parable of assimilation into the American culture. Poppa DiMaggio, the San Francisco fisherman from Sicily, learned to appreciate his son's exploits on the ballfield and the money he earned from them. Lou Gehrig's background fit this mold from the Teutonic side, but like most other things Gehrig did, it was overshadowed. (Don Mattingly, who thought Ruth was a cartoon character, had never heard of Gehrig.) In addition to his success on the diamond, DiMaggio himself ripened from a skinny, hatchet-faced kid, to a dashing figure who married Marilyn Monroe, to a distinguished television pitchman in his golden years. When DiMaggio was named baseball's greatest living player as part of the centennial of professional baseball in 1969, baseball's graceful prince accepted the accolade with modesty. "At my age, I'm just happy to be named the greatest living anything."

Legend says that DiMaggio was discovered peering

through a knothole at Seals Stadium at age seventeen in 1932. Scout Spike Hennessey, the story goes, dropped this pearl of wisdom on the youngster: "Never stand on the outside looking in, unless it's jail." Undoubtedly Hennessey had scouted DiMaggio in the sandlots (brother Vince was already a member of the Seals) and was aware of an offer made by the rival San Francisco Missions for Joe's services. Hennessey hauled DiMaggio to the office of Seals president Charles Graham, who offered the youngster passes to keep him away from the knothole and a tryout after asking, "Does Vince do all the playing in the family?"

In 1933, DiMaggio gained attention with a 61-game hitting streak in the Pacific Coast League. He also had his first brush with reporters, who generally found him aloof; in the prevailing climate, they chose to put him on a pedestal rather than nail him to a cross. But DiMaggio admits, "I can remember a reporter asking me for a quote, and I didn't know what a quote was. I thought it was some kind of soft drink."

But the most famous player in the minor leagues suffered the first of many setbacks in 1934. He injured his left knee getting out of a car on the way to Sunday dinner at his sister's house after a doubleheader. Injuries and recoveries would become a recurring theme in the legend of DiMaggio. The bad knee scared several clubs away, but the Yankees, at their minor league meetings that fall in French Lick, Indiana, decided to risk $25,000 (plus five players for the Seals) for the youngster on the recommendation of scout Bill Essick, a neighbor of the DiMaggio family. An additional year of seasoning in San Francisco, with Lefty O'Doul as his manager, readied Joltin' Joe for the big time in 1936.

The big time was ready for him. Ruth had been released at the end of the 1934 season, and the Yankees had not appeared in the World Series since 1932, their only trip to the fall classic in the last seven seasons. Even before he played in a major league game, Ruth's torch was passed to DiMaggio. He was to be the superstar who'd put the Yankees over the top. A generation later, the torch was passed relatively smoothly to Mickey Mantle. Rooting for the Yankees really was, as Red Smith put it, like rooting for U.S. Steel. Only by recognizing this history can the subsequent failures of Tom Tresh, Bobby Murcer, and others to extend the line of Yankee heroes be fully appreciated.

But even as a rookie, DiMaggio had to overcome an injury. He hurt his left foot sliding into third in an exhibition game, then burned the foot by overdoing heat therapy treatments. He wouldn't make his Yankee debut until May 4, 1936. He led the Yankees to their first pennant in four years and starred in the World Series, batting .346 and making a spectacular catch in front of the clubhouse steps at the Polo Grounds to end the second game. After watching DiMaggio in the Series, Giants manager Bill Terry said, "I've always heard that one player could make the difference between a losing team and a winner, and I never believed it. Now, I know it's true."

The Yankees kept winning with DiMaggio aboard. They won the next three World Series, losing but one postseason game. In the fourth game of the 1939 Series, DiMaggio started the play that would become known as "Schnozz's Snooze." Catcher Ernie "Schnozz" Lombardi

was the slowest man ever to win a batting title, earning two hitting crowns even though he would get thrown out from right field occasionally on apparent singles. But he's better remembered for lying stunned during the tenth inning of the fourth and final game of the Series as DiMaggio crossed the plate with the Yankees' third run of the inning. The Reds had led 4–2 going into the ninth, but shortstop Billy Myers booted Bill Dickey's double-play grounder making the score 4–3. DiMaggio, who was on first before Myers's miscue, raced home from third on a grounder by Joe Gordon, narrowly beating a throw by third baseman Billy Werber to score the tying run.

With runners on first and third and one out in the tenth, DiMaggio laced a tie-breaking single to right. Ival Goodman couldn't handle the drive, allowing Charlie "King Kong" Keller to attempt to score from first. Goodman's one-hop throw hit Lombardi in the groin, and the onrushing Keller leveled the catcher, allowing DiMaggio to score from first. Clearly Lombardi was less at fault than his teammates for the incident, and, if the game had been played at Yankee Stadium instead of Cincinnati, the first run would have ended the contest. Instead, the Yankees had to shut down the Reds, who got their first two men on in the bottom of the tenth before succumbing.

In 1941, DiMaggio established one of the game's great records, a 56-game hitting streak. According to Lefty Gomez, DiMaggio's roommate, the Yankee Clipper remained calm throughout the streak, "But every day after forty-four [the previous record, held by Willie Keeler], I threw up my breakfast."

Myths grew around the streak. One was that Dom DiMaggio made a fantastic catch to rob Joe of a hit, nearly ending the streak at 43 games. Boxscore evidence doesn't support this story. DiMaggio denied rumors that Heinz was prepared to make a big promotional deal with the Yankee Clipper if he could extend the streak to 57, their corporate symbol.

It is true that DiMaggio and Gomez rode to the fateful fifty-seventh game in Cleveland together and their cab driver predicted the streak's end. Versions differ as to whether the cabbie said flatly that the streak would end or if he hedged a bit, saying the streak would end if DiMaggio didn't get a hit his first time up. In any case, Gomez cursed him for giving Joltin' Joe the jinx, but DiMaggio remained calm (although he may not have tipped heavily). DiMaggio went 0-for-3 with a walk in that fifty-seventh game, the first two outs recorded on brilliant plays by third baseman Ken Keltner. DiMaggio could have bunted to extend the streak, since Keltner was playing him in short left field, but DiMaggio's pride said he had to get a legitimate hit. Some historians may pooh-pooh that notion, pointing to several tainted streak-extending hits, but those blots were attributable to the official scorers, not DiMaggio.

Fans who saw him pointed to DiMaggio's effortless grace. His wide stance made his batting stroke fluid, and he rarely seemed to run hard for balls in the outfield, gliding to the spot. There's only one recorded instance of DiMaggio showing emotion on the ballfield. In the sixth game of the 1947 World Series, DiMaggio hit a drive to deep left field, ticketed for the bullpen. The two-on, two-out clout would have tied the game at eight, but Al Gionfriddo went back (" . . . back, back . . . " as called by Red

Barber) to make a one hand stab over the low fence near the 415-foot sign. DiMaggio saw the catch as he approached second base, and kicked at the dirt with his toe to show his disappointment.

The public's other glimpse of DiMaggio's inner self came with his marriage to Marilyn Monroe in 1954. They were divorced later that year, leading raconteur Oscar Levant to remark, "It proves that no man can be a success in two national pastimes." After a trip to entertain troops in the Far East, Monroe returned beaming and told DiMaggio, "Oh, Joe, you've never heard such cheering."

"Yes, I have," DiMaggio answered.

DiMaggio's most fabled comeback from injury was in 1949. The previous November, he underwent surgery to remove bone spurs on his right heel. He was still limping in spring training, missed the Yankees' opener, and was flown to Johns Hopkins Hosptial in Baltimore, where the operation had been performed, for further treatment. Speculation surfaced that the Yankee Clipper's playing days might be at an end. It wasn't until the last week of May that he was able to try out the heel in practice, not until a mid-June exhibition with the Giants that he played in a game. He returned to the regular lineup for a three-game series in Boston beginning June 28, against a hard-driving Red Sox squad that had won ten of its last eleven and was challenging the Yankees for the top spot.

After missing the first sixty-six games of the season, DiMaggio singled in his first at-bat and homered in his second. He broke up a potential double play in the fifth inning and caught Ted Williams's long drive in the ninth for the game's final out in a 5–4 Yankee win. The next day, the Yankees trailed 7–1 early when DiMaggio came up with two aboard. He slugged a three-run shot to make the score 7–4, then broke a 7–7 tie with another homer. In the final game of the series, with the Yankees clinging to a one-run lead, his three-run homer in the seventh brought some welcome insurance. In his first three games of the season, he'd gone five-for-eleven with four homers and nine RBIs. The triumphant return had put the Yankees eight games ahead of the Red Sox.

But the 1949 season wasn't over. The Yankees' rash of injuries continued throughout the summer. With a dozen games to go, a viral infection felled DiMaggio, who'd dropped fifteen pounds and weakened noticeably. The lead over Boston stood at two and a half games when DiMaggio went out. By the time the Red Sox came to New York for the season's final two games, Boston led the Yankees by a game. The opener on October 1 had been scheduled as Joe DiMaggio Day, and 69,551 fans turned out to honor their enervated hero. After the hour-long ceremonies in which he received over $35,000 worth of gifts for himself and his family, DiMaggio told manager Casey Stengel, "I'd like to give it a try." He had two hits in the Yankees' victory that tied them with the Red Sox, and tripled in the second game that brought the Yankees a pennant in their first year under Stengel.

"I had many years when I was not so successful as a ballplayer, as it is a game of skill."—Casey Stengel, testifying before the Senate Subcommittee on Antitrust and Monopoly in 1958.

In 1923, Casey Stengel was immortalized by Damon Runyon's "This is the way old Casey ran running his home run home" report of Stengel's game-winning inside-the-park shot in the World Series opener. Two decades later, Stengel was "The Ol' Perfesser," and two decades after that, still managing, he was able to proclaim, "Most people my age are dead at the present time."

Although he denigrated his skills as a player, Stengel batted .284 in his fourteen-year career as a lefthanded-hitting outfielder. He explained, "I broke in 4 for 4 and folks thought I was the next Ty Cobb. It took them about four days to get over that." Stengel was frequently platooned, a strategy he repopularized as a manager. In three World Series, he hit .393, with a pair of game-winning homers in 1923, the first two fall classic round-trippers hit at Yankee Stadium. As Stengel would say, "You could look it up."

Exactly one month after his second homer, a seventh inning shot that broke a scoreless tie, another Series first, he was traded to the lowly Boston Braves, prompting Stengel to utter, "The paths of glory lead but to the Braves."

Stengel first became noted for his stunts on the field as a player, as well as sharing the name of the character of the famous poem. "He's a dandy ballplayer, but it's all from the neck down," observed one scout. Stengel responded, "Being a clown wasn't safe in the minors. Some of them bush league managers could hit you with a bat at fifty feet." If he somehow missed an opportunity for a prank or quip, his reputation ensured that he'd gain credit for it anyway.

At one of his first spring training camps, Stengel discovered a small hole with a metal cover buried under the lush outfield grass. Stengel could squeeze himself into the hole, which contained utility pipes, and still see the action on the field. When a fly ball came toward his position, teammates wondered where Casey had gone. Suddenly, he popped out of the hole holding the metal cover above his head and made the catch.

Stengel was also involved in another famous spring training episode where the catch wasn't made. In 1917, flying was still a novelty, and at the Dodgers spring training site in Daytona Beach, a pioneer woman aviator named Ruth Law flew a fragile biplane to generate publicity for the area. The Dodger players frequently flew with Law, and one lazy afternoon talk turned to the subject of how fast a ball would travel if dropped from the plane. A few years earlier, Senators catcher Gabby Street had caught a ball dropped from the Washington Monument, but the Dodgers were doubtful that a ball dropped from the airplane could be caught. That was all Dodger manager Wilbert Robinson, the catcher for the great original Orioles teams, needed to hear. "I could catch one," the fifty-one-year-old skipper contended. Egged on by doubting players, and probably fueled by some spirited wagering, it was agreed that Robinson would attempt the stunt the next afternoon.

Robinson strapped on his catcher's mitt and took his position by the mound, prepared to snag the ball dropped from a plane traveling about forty-five miles per hour, five hundred feet above the field. Some place Stengel riding shotgun on the biplane's wing, seated on a kitchen chair, but given the fragile state of aviation, that's not likely. Others say that the designated dropper forgot to bring a baseball into the air. Whatever happened, a sphere of some sort sped earthward with an overweight Robinson circling unsteadily below. The old catcher got a glove on it, but it hit him on the chest, splattered, and the impact knocked him to the ground. The object wasn't a baseball, but a grapefruit.

Feeling the juice, Robinson screamed, "Jesus, I'm killed! I'm dead! My chest's split open! I'm covered in blood!" Then he tasted the glop, realized he'd been had, and immediately blamed Stengel, who eagerly accepted credit, reasoning he'd been singled out because "I had a pretty good arm." Later, lubricated with other juices, Robinson claimed, "If it had been a baseball, I'd have caught it." In a more frank moment, Robinson admitted, "If that had been a baseball, I probably would have been killed." Stengel delighted in telling the story, claiming that he himself was in the biplane.

The true measure of a baseball tale is in its adaptation. George Plimpton used the grapefruit story as the basis for the opening of his 1987 novel, *The Curious Case of Sidd Finch*. To acclimate catcher Ronn Reynolds to handling the 168-mile-per-hour stuff of pitcher Finch, the Mets dropped him baseballs from a blimp at a thousand feet.

After Stengel left the Dodgers as a player, there was no shortage of clowns to take up the slack, although their antics were not necessarily by design. The principal character of Uncle Robbie's Daffiness Boys became Babe Herman, gifted with a thundering bat, a scattershot arm, and hands of steel.

With two on and two out and the Dodgers ahead by a run, the apparent third out of the ninth inning was a line drive toward Herman in right. But the Babe tripped, the ball rolled to the wall, and two runs scored for another Dodger defeat. As the team left the field, Robinson approached Herman and asked compassionately, "What happened?"

"When?" Herman innocently asked.

Fly balls were an adventure, if not a constant danger, for Herman. He denied the story that a fly ball had ever hit him on the head. "If a ball ever hit me on the head, I'd just hang up my spikes and quit," Herman told a reporter.

"What about the shoulder?" asked the reporter.

"Oh, no!" Herman exclaimed, sensing a trap. "The shoulder don't count, only the head."

Herman was wary of newsmen trying to build up his reputation as a character. He was not as careful on the basepaths, once attempting to steal second with the bases loaded. "Why do you guys always harp on me?" Herman complained. "Just because you got to have something to write about every day in the papers, why do you always make me out like a clown? Fun's fun and all that, but I'm a family man, and showing me up like a screwball don't help me in the game, and I gotta make a living same as you guys." With that, Herman reached into his vest pocket and pulled out a cigar.

The reporter, his conscience troubling him, said, "Here, let me give you a light."

"Don't bother," replied Herman, turning away in a puff of smoke. "It's already lit."

To his death, Herman denied the famous story of the three men on third, but this one was too good to have been made up. With the bases loaded, Herman drove a ball off the wall in right. Pitcher Dazzy Vance, the runner at second, turned third, but then retreated. The runner from first, Chick Fewster, made a headfirst dive into third, and Herman, head down, slid into third, meeting his two teammates. The third baseman tagged everyone in sight, and when the dust cleared, Herman had doubled into a double play.

A rookie observing the incident asked Uncle Robbie, "What kind of baseball is that?"

"Leave them be," Robinson replied. "It's the first time they've been together all season."

The incident led to the fable of the Brooklyn cabbie who picked up a fare leaving Ebbets Field before the end of the game and asked how the Dodgers were doing.

"The Dodgers are ahead, and we got three men on base," the spectator said.

"Which base?" asked the cabbie.

Robinson once called on Herman to bunt with a man on first and none out. Herman would have none of it and bunted the first two offerings foul. Then he belted the third delivery into the seats.

Fed up with the goofy antics and mounting losses, Robinson announced that the next dumb stunt would draw a fine, payable to what he called the Bonehead Club. Robinson promptly fattened the club's coffers. At the pregame meeting at home plate, Robinson submitted a laundry slip instead of a lineup card.

Stengel, however, showed that you didn't have to be a Dodger to clown. In spring training with the Phils, he put his uniform on backwards. Manager Gavvy Cravath remarked, "You've done everything else backwards down here. You might as well wear your pants that way, too." As the Phils barnstormed toward opening day, they encountered a heckler who disparaged their abilities until the players challenged him to take the field and see if he could do any better. The heckler was Stengel, disguised in a straw hat, with overalls and a red bandana, who proceeded to smack out loud hits to the astonishment of the crowd.

Many other Stengel stories became standards. Playing for Pittsburgh in 1918, Stengel was having a bad day. He muffed a shoestring catch in right, kicking the ball toward second base but running in pursuit toward the foul line, thinking the ball had gone in that direction. Later, he was tagged out standing up on a play where the few fans in the stands thought he should have slid, and they booed him lustily. So before taking a seat in the dugout, Stengel addressed the crowd. "With the salary I'm getting, I'm so hollow and starving that if I slide, I'm liable to explode like a light bulb." Alibis for not sliding evolved through the years, but none were ever as good. In exhibition contests, Babe Ruth couldn't slide because he was carrying a fountain pen for signing autographs. Several players were accused of avoiding the dirt to preserve hip flasks of liquor. Tim Raines perfected a technique that allowed him to slide while toting vials of cocaine in his socks. Stengel found a way to improve his baseball income in the wartime economy by getting a job in the Brooklyn Navy Yard and arranging games with sailors as soon as their ships docked. "I wanted to play them before they got rid of their sea legs," he confided.

Back with the Pirates after the war, Stengel got into an argument with an umpire over an out call at first, ripped off his own shirt, and offered it to umpire, suggesting,

"Why don't you play for our side for a change?" When the league office informed him of his fine by telegram the next day, Stengel pinned the yellow telegram to his uniform sleeve and wore it for the entire game.

Visiting Brooklyn, where he'd broken in, during 1919, the fans rode Stengel hard as a lefthanded pitcher made him look bad. In addition, Stengel had crashed into the wall in right center while failing to snare a game-breaking double. Between innings, Stengel visited the Brooklyn bullpen to chat with his former teammate Leon Cadore, a like-minded spirit who was a fair amateur magician. That afternoon Cadore's sleight of hand had caught a bird. Stengel knew what to do with it.

Stengel concealed the bird in his cap just before his turn at the plate. When the crowd greeted him with the expected jeers, Stengel turned, bowed, and removed his cap. The sparrow sat on his head for a moment to get its bearings, then flew away. Even the umpire laughed. A year later in Philadelphia, he found another bird in the outfield, caught it in his cap, and returned to his position. After catching a fly ball, he doffed his cap and away flew the bird. Years later, an attempt to re-create the feat a third time fell flat on its beak. The bird was spun by its tail to calm it before being put in his hat. When Stengel took off his cap, the woozy bird dropped to the ground at his feet.

When traded to the Giants in 1921, Stengel learned much of his future managerial skills from John J. Mc-Graw, although Stengel exaggerated his escapades off the field to avoid criticism that he was the manager's pet. Stengel claimed that McGraw assigned one of his detectives to tail him and outfielder Irish Meusel, who had been teammates on the Phils before joining the Giants. After a couple of days, the detective reported that Meusel and Stengel had stopped going out together. McGraw called Stengel into his office to discover the reasons for the friends' falling out. Stengel explained there was no problem between him and Meusel, but he had a beef with McGraw. "I don't want to share a detective," Stengel insisted. "I want one of my own."

Stengel began his managerial career in 1925 with Worcester, an Eastern League farm club of the Boston Braves, serving as player-manager with the added title of club president. At the end of the season, Stengel got an offer to manage the Toledo Mud Hens of the American Association, a more prestigious position. However, Stengel was still contractually obligated to the Braves' organization as a player. So Stengel the club president released Stengel the player, fired Stengel the manager, and then submitted his letter of resignation as president, freeing himself to take the job in Toledo. As a manager, Stengel became better known for his caustic wit, usually directed at players, and his curious rambling discourse known as Stengelese.

Stengel returned to the majors with the Dodgers in 1934, after Giants manager Bill Terry asked, "Is Brooklyn still in the league?" Stengel's Dodgers avenged the crack, knocking the Giants out of the pennant race in the final weekend. But the rest of the season had not been nearly as satisfying, as the Dodgers finished sixth. During a loss at Philadelphia, Stengel went out to get his pitcher, Walter Beck. Beck was earning the nickname "Boom-Boom" as the Phils had been tattooing the tin fence in right, ex-

hausting right fielder Hack Wilson, who was already handicapped by a hangover—gin was his tonic, the pundits said. While Stengel visited the mound, Wilson took the opportunity to lean over, shut his eyes, and rest his aching head. Instead of handing Stengel the ball, Beck heaved it toward right field. The ball struck the fence with a boom, startling Wilson. Properly conditioned by previous shots, Wilson dashed back, retrieved the ball, and made his best throw of the season to second base.

Stengel concocted something called the precision play, a pick-off play to third with a righthanded batter. The pitcher would throw at the hitter, but yell "Look out," clearing the batter out of the box, attempting to freeze the baserunner, and giving the catcher a clear shot to pick him off. "The runner would freeze, but so would my man at third, and my left fielder would wear himself out chasing the overthrows."

Warren Spahn, a member of Stengel's Boston Braves in the 1940s and his Mets in the 1960s, noted, "I played for Stengel before and after he was a genius." Bad ballplayers with flair found their way to Stengel before and after his glory years with the Yankees. The first such character was Frenchy Bordagaray, an outfielder-third baseman who tried to bring back the gay nineties mustache in the thirties. "Go shave it off," Stengel advised, "before someone throws a ball at it and kills you." During pregame drills in the midst of a losing streak, one of Bordagaray's batting practice throws hit Stengel in the head. The Dodgers won that day, so Bordagaray suggested to his manager, "Let me hit you in the head every day." Then there was the time Bordagaray was standing on second base but the umpire called him out. Stengel was eager to argue, but Bordagaray discouraged him. "I was tapping my foot," Bordagaray explained, "and I guess he got me between taps." Stengel listened because Bordagaray wasn't in the habit of agreeing with umpires. He once spit in an arbiter's eye and received a $500 fine and sixty-day suspension. Bordagaray responded, "The penalty is a little more than I expectorated."

Players like him sent Stengel to a postgame shave, instructing the barber, "Don't cut my throat, I may want to do it myself later." Just before the 1943 season, Stengel was hit by a car and suffered a broken leg. Pittsburgh manager Frankie Frisch, a teammate of Stengel's under McGraw, wired, "Your attempt at suicide fully understood. Deepest sympathy you didn't succeed." When Stengel took a Pacific Coast League managing job in Oakland in 1946, he was pleased with the presence of bridges. "Every manager wants to jump off a bridge sooner or later, and it's very nice for an old man to know he doesn't have to walk fifty miles to find one."

On an exhibition tour with the Boston Bees in Mexico, peasants lined the streets to greet the Bees' bus in Monterrey, throwing flowers and cheering wildly. Stengel, who owned a piece of the team, was already counting his club's share of the take from the presumed sellout. "I didn't know you people were so crazy about baseball," he told the guide assigned to the team.

"It's not the team they're cheering," the embarrassed guide replied. "They've never seen a Greyhound bus before."

Many questioned the appointment of this clown who didn't finish out of the second division as manager of the

Yankees in 1949, but Stengel led the Yankees to ten pennants in a dozen seasons. Appreciating the value of having a good team to manage, Stengel summed up his good fortune, "There comes a time in every man's life at least once, and I've had plenty of them." People began to seek his opinions on managing. He suggested that the secret for success as a manager was "to keep the twenty guys who hate you away from the five guys who are undecided." He contended, "Most ballgames are lost, not won." Moreover, Stengel knew why. "Good pitching always stops good hitting. And vice versa."

Stengel found a new audience when he testified before a Senate subcommittee in July 1958 on baseball's antitrust exemption. Stengel gave them nearly an hour of convoluted, hysterical, yet shrewd monologue on the state of the game, the progress it had made, and the need for further improvements. The main feature, however, was Stengelese meandering and quaint phraseology which left the hearing room amused and bewildered. Mickey Mantle followed Stengel to the witness table and told the senators, "My views are just about the same as Casey's."

At the start of the 1960 season, Stengel, sixty-nine years old, was hospitalized for a couple of weeks after complaining of chest pains. Upon release, he offered this medical report: "They examined all my organs. Some of them are quite remarkable and others are not so good. A lot of museums are bidding for them." The remarkable ones held up for the remainder of the season, and Stengel even managed to get in a stunt on the way to his record tenth pennant. In response to Bill Veeck's exploding scoreboard at Comiskey Park, Yankee players stood in front of their dugout and lit sparklers after one of their own homers.

The Yankees lost the 1960 World Series to the Pirates in seven games on Bill Mazeroski's homer leading off the bottom of the ninth in the final game. The Pirates had overcome a three-run Yankee lead in the eighth inning with the help of Bill Virdon's bad-hop grounder that hit Tony Kubek in the throat. But Stengel's managing came under criticism. He didn't start his best pitcher, Whitey Ford, until the third game. Ford threw a pair of shutouts in the third and sixth games, the start of his consecutive scoreless World Series inning streak that overtook Babe Ruth's record, but he wasn't available for a third start or even a relief appearance in the deciding contest. Additionally, Stengel failed to pinch-hit for pitcher Bobby Shantz in the top of the eighth with runners on second and third and two out. A single would have put the game out of reach, and Shantz had already pitched five innings in relief. Less than a week later, the Yankees decided it was time to go with a younger man, to which Stengel responded, "I'll never make the mistake of being seventy again."

A year later, during the 1961 World Series, Stengel accepted the appointment as the first manager of the Mets. The job would require more of his comedic skills than baseball acumen. Stengel showed he was equal to the task when explaining the Mets' first selection in the expansion draft, catcher Hobie Landrith, a veteran of twelve undistinguished years in the National League. "You have to have a catcher or you'll have a lot of passed balls," Stengel explained. A reporter noted that his starting outfield of Gus Bell, Frank Thomas, and Richie

Ashburn had a total of twenty children. "If they produce as well on the field as off the field, we'll win the pennant," Stengel concluded wistfully.

He proclaimed his team "the Amazin' Mets," and the tag stuck. Stengel fully understood what was amazin' about the club: "I been in this game a hundred years, but I see new ways to lose I never knew existed before." At one particularly exasperating juncture in the Mets' 40–120 debut season, the worst record of the twentieth century, Stengel wondered aloud, "Can't anybody play this here game?" He would note after many home losses, "We trimmed the attendance again," meaning that they'd defrauded the public.

Even the rare victories came at a price. After sweeping a Sunday doubleheader from the Braves in Milwaukee, plane trouble and fog conspired to delay the team's arrival in Houston until eight the next morning. On his way to a few hours of sleep before that day's game, the usually voluble Stengel warned, "If any of the writers come looking for me, tell them I'm being embalmed."

On the 1962 Mets, the role of Frenchy Bordagaray was played by first baseman Marv Throneberry, who featured good power, bad hands, and shaky base-running skills. Writer Jimmy Breslin observed, "Having Marv Throneberry play for your team is like having Willie Sutton work for your bank." After clouting an apparent triple, Marvelous Marv was called out on appeal for missing first base. Stengel ran out to argue, but the second base umpire came over, hoping to chill Stengel's anger. "I hate to tell you this, Casey," the arbiter began, "but he missed second base, too." When Throneberry celebrated his twenty-ninth birthday on September 2, Stengel noted that there was no cake. "We was going to get him a birthday cake, but we figured he'd drop it."

Marvelous Marv became a folk hero. One inning, he had a particularly rough time with Frank Thomas, who was playing third base like the outfielder he was. Thomas heaved a throw past Throneberry for an error. Another grounder to Thomas, another poor throw, another error. Getting the idea, a third hitter smacked the ball to third and Thomas heaved it high above Throneberry's head. But Marvelous Marv leaped, spun in midair, and came down with the ball. Following the inning, Throneberry approached Thomas, who expected a well-deserved reproach. "What are you trying to do," Throneberry asked, "take away my fans?"

The Mets had problems up the middle, too. Shortstop Elio Chacon didn't speak English, so he didn't understand center fielder Richie Ashburn when he called, "I got it." After several messed up pop flies, the resourceful Ashburn enlisted the help of a Spanish-speaking teammate and learned to say "Yo la tengo." A couple of days later, a fly ball was lifted into short left center. As Chacon moved back, Ashburn raced in, yelling, "Yo la tengo. Yo la tengo." Sure enough, Chacon moved off. As Ashburn prepared to squeeze the ball, left fielder Frank Thomas ran him over. In the face of this adversity, Ashburn batted .306 and was honored as the team's most valuable player. "MVP on the worst team ever," Ashburn mused. "I wonder exactly what they mean by that."

Behind the plate, the Mets had Choo-Choo Coleman, who called everyone "Bub." In spring training 1963, third baseman Charlie Neal struck up a conversation with

Coleman, who answered, "Yeah, Bub" and "No, Bub." Finally, Neal said, "You don't even know who I am. I was your roommate last season." Coleman considered the statement carefully before replying, "Yeah, Bub. You're number nine."

The Mets were the Siberia of baseball in those days, and some players took unusual routes to get there, none more so than Pumpsie Green, the first black player in the history of the Red Sox. Following a game at Yankee Stadium, the Red Sox bus was stuck in a major-league traffic jam. Green and Gene Conley, a six-foot-eight pitcher who also played basketball for the Boston Celtics, decided they could make better time on foot and left the bus. Some time later, they checked into a hotel without luggage, except for a couple of brown bags acquired at the local liquor store while the Red Sox initiated a search for them. They tired of New York after a couple of days, so Conley suggested they go to Israel. The inspiration for this idea may have been Green's real first name, Elijah. At the airport, some sharp airline employee recognized that this odd couple, traveling without passports or baggage, might be the missing pair of Red Sox. Both were fined, and Green was further punished with a trade to the Mets. He played only 17 games for the Amazin's before he was farmed out for good.

Stengel managed the Mets until the middle of the 1965 season, when a broken hip, suffered in falling off a barstool at an old-timers' celebration, forced his retirement. Many had urged Stengel to quit before that, chiding him for sleeping on the bench and failing to improve the team's dismal record. As the Yankee skipper, Stengel's skill was denigrated by those who felt anyone could have done as well; with the Mets, it was more true that anyone would have finished last, and Stengel never lost sight of how awful his clubs were. At an exhibition at West Point in early 1965, he slipped and broke his wrist. "I got this broken arm watching my team," he moaned. "All they gave me last year was a head cold." Discussing a pair of twenty-year-old prospects one spring morning, he said, "That there's Ed Kranepool. In ten years, he has a chance to be a star in this game. And over there's Greg Goosen. In ten years, he has a chance to be thirty."

After his retirement from the Mets, Stengel continued to make the rounds at spring training, Hall of Fame inductions (his election to Cooperstown in 1966 was a highlight of his life), and other baseball events. He observed, "Old-timers' weekends are like airplane landings. If you can walk away from them, they're successful."

There's a story that ought to be true concerning his final days in 1975. He was in his hospital bed watching a ballgame on television when the national anthem was played. He got out of bed and stood at attention one last time, an imaginary cap over his heart. When he died, his funeral was delayed a week, until an off-day in the playoffs, to allow baseball people to attend, a bit of ironic humor that Stengel would've appreciated.

"The toughest thing about the major leagues is explaining to your wife why she needs a penicillin shot for your kidney infection." —Mike Hegan

Stengel warned his players, "You gotta learn that if you don't get it by midnight, chances are you ain't gonna get it; and if you do, it ain't gonna be worth it." Stengel noted, "Being with a woman all night never hurt no professional baseball player. It's staying up all night looking for a woman that does 'em in."

Jim Bouton revealed a lot of players' tricks in his 1970 book, *Ball Four*, including the obsession with looking as well as touching. Beaver shooting was practiced in ballparks, bullpens, and through pilgrimages under bleacher grandstands and on the roof of the L-shaped Shoreham Hotel in Washington, baseball's greatest loss when the Senators left the nation's capital. Bouton also stated that a favorite player pastime was recording a session with a conquest, then playing it back on the team bus.

Bouton's book told the tale of Jim Gosger, who'd been secreted in a closet by a roommate anticipating a romp with a prime example of the so-called local talent. The thoughtful roommate even provided Gosger with a towel to chew on in the event of laughing. During the session, the woman cried, "I've never done it like that before."

Gosger stuck his head out, opined, "Yeah, sure," and returned to the closet.

As a member of the Yankees last dynasty teams of the early 1960s, Bouton played with Joe Pepitone, a dedicated prankster and victim as well as a highly successful womanizer. Pepitone, a devotee of toupees, is credited with legitimizing the presence of hair dryers in the clubhouse. Players enjoyed filling his dryer with powder so that it spewed all over his head and rug. Pepitone's best gag came at the expense of team trainers. He'd insert a piece of popcorn in his foreskin, then go to the trainer, saying he thought it might be cancer.

Pepitone's antics ran him afoul of many curfews, but avoiding bed checks has always been a part of the game. Even Stengel admitted covering for roommates. When the coach called his name from outside the door, Stengel would respond in his natural voice. If his roommate had gone out, Stengel would answer for him, doing his best to imitate the voice.

Then there's the autographed-ball story that has come down through the ages. Management places a plainclothes security guard in the hotel lobby with a baseball, and the guard asks all the players who arrive after curfew to autograph the ball. The next morning, the signers are fined.

Of course, these tricks haven't stopped the determined carouser. Ping Bodie, an outfielder best known for his quips, bragged that he roomed with Babe Ruth's valises. Pitcher Bob Veale was never bothered by bed checks. "My bed was always there." Many managers have lamented that the problem with bed checks is that "they disturb your best players."

Stengel had strong feelings about drinking. The team's hotel bar was off-limits to players. "That's where I do my drinking," he declared. When Stengel confronted pitcher Mickey McDermott in a freight elevator at four A.M., the manager shook his head in disgust and said, "Drunk again."

The pitcher grinned. "Me too."

Stengel managed Mickey Mantle, Whitey Ford, and Billy Martin, three well-known "whiskey slicks," as the Ol' Perfesser called his drinkers. "Everybody who roomed with Mickey said he took five years off their careers,"

Ford reported. Upon turning forty-six, Mantle declared, "If I'd known I was going to live this long, I'd have taken better care of myself." Stengel believed, "The ones who drink milkshakes don't win many ballgames."

They don't get fooled like Johnny Mize did, either. When the Big Cat went into the shower after a spring workout, Giants trainer Frank Bowman soaked Mize's sweatshirt in alcohol. When Mize came out of the shower, Bowman urged Mize to lay off hard liquor.

"What are you talking about, Frank?" Mize retorted. "I was in at curfew last night, and all I had was a couple of beers."

"Don't try to kid me, John," the trainer said, striking a match and dropping it on the shirt. The shirt burst into flames. "That's alcohol you sweated out."

Mize stamped out the fire and pleaded with Bowman, "Don't say anything about this to anyone."

Cap Anson is credited with starting formal spring training by bringing his players to Hot Springs, Arkansas. Anson's purpose: "To boil out the alcohol microbes." John McGraw once locked pitcher Bugs Raymond in the clubhouse to keep him in shape to start the second game of a doubleheader. So Raymond lowered an empty bucket out of a clubhouse window, and an associate below filled it with beer.

Mike "King" Kelly, the first great star of the game back in the 1880s, continued the tradition of drinking. When asked if he drank during games, Kelly replied, "It depends on the length of the game." After his retirement, he offered advice to the struggling Reds: "When you see three balls, swing at the middle one."

Grover Cleveland Alexander, the only pitcher named for a former President and portrayed in the movies by a future one, was renowned for his drinking. It was assumed that "Ol' Pete" Alexander was badly hung over when he struck out Tony Lazzeri with two on and two out in the seventh inning of the seventh game of the 1926 World Series. After all, Alexander had worked nine innings the day before and presumably celebrated his second complete game victory of the Series hard that night. However, after the game six victory, manager Rogers Hornsby warned Alexander that he might call on him in the finale.

Don Larsen may have been celebrating his perfect game in the 1956 World Series the night before he pitched it. The righthander had a reputation for "mailing letters at three A.M.," as Stengel called it. Unable to find a convenient mailbox on foot during spring training in the retirement haven of St. Petersburg, Florida, Larsen wrapped his car around a telephone pole at five o'clock one morning. Larsen wasn't hurt, but he and the press corps wondered what kind of disciplinary action Stengel would order. The manager ended the mystery by proclaiming, "Anybody who can find something to do in St. Petersburg at five in the morning deserves a medal, not a fine."

"Say it ain't so, Joe."—Young fan to
Shoeless Joe Jackson, who was banned from
baseball for life with seven White Sox teammates
by Commissioner Kenesaw Mountain Landis for
allegedly throwing the 1919 World Series.

The Baltimore Orioles won three straight National

League titles starting in 1894. Manager Ned Hanlon's lineup included Hall of Famers John McGraw, Wee Willie Keeler, Wilbert Robinson, Hugh Jennings, Joe Kelley, and Dan Brouthers. One key to their success was their hustling style of scientific baseball. The original Orioles were credited with inventing the hit-and-run, the relay, and the backing up of throws. Less to their credit, the Orioles also refined techniques such as holding enemy baserunners up by the belt, cutting across the infield to take an extra base, and substituting mushy balls for the more dangerous variety when the opponents batted.

The Orioles' most famous play, one later attributed to Ty Cobb as well, involved spare balls which would be strategically placed in the high outfield grass in case a batted ball eluded the outfielders. The trickery kept a number of startled baserunners from advancing past first on what appeared to be sure extra-base hits. The system worked until one afternoon when a gapper was returned to second base by both the left fielder and center fielder. Upon seeing the two balls, the umpire figured out the gambit and forfeited the game to the Oriole's opponents.

Ty Cobb's father told him, when he left home to play ball, "Don't come home a failure." Cobb stories revolve around his toughness and readiness to beat you with his bat or his spikes or his fists. While Pete Rose was chasing Cobb's all-time hit record, one reporter asked Rose's opinion on what Cobb might be thinking if he was looking down on the chase. "From what I know about him," Rose answered, pointing skyward, "he's probably not up there."

There's hardly a baseball man who hasn't been credited with the "What would Ty Cobb hit today?" story—from Cobb himself to Yogi Berra. The response, no matter who gets the credit, is "Oh, about .350."

"That's not so great," says the surprised questioner. "It might not even lead the league."

"That's true, but you have to take into consideration he'd be seventy-three years old now."

Before an encounter with the Tigers, Red Sox catcher Lou Criger made the mistake of telling a reporter, "This Cobb is one of those ginks with a lot of flash, but he doesn't fool me. Watch him wilt when the going gets tough. I'll cut him down to size." Unfortunately for Criger, Cobb (unlike Rogers Hornsby, who eschewed the printed word and movies as harmful to the batting eye) read the paper. After singling his first time up, Cobb told Criger he'd be running on every pitch. And he did, stealing second, third, and home.

They say you can't steal first base, but Germany Schaefer did it in 1911. With two out in the ninth inning of a tie game between the Senators and White Sox, Schaefer was on first with speedy Clyde Milan on third. With a weak hitter at the dish, Schaefer tried to steal a run for his Senators by dashing toward second base in hopes of drawing a throw that would allow Milan to sneak home. But the White Sox were having none of it, and let Schaefer take second unchallenged. Undaunted, Schaefer had another plan. He took off for first, finishing his dash with a theatrical hook slide. The White Sox protested Schaefer's play, but the rule book didn't cover that situation so the play stood. (A rule was added to keep players from making a "travesty of the game," which prevented Jimmy Piersall from running the bases in reverse order on his hundredth career homer; he had to settle for running backwards.) Schaefer, back on first, lit out for second again. This time, the Sox hoped to end the sham and pegged to second. Schaefer beat the throw, and Milan waltzed home with the winning run.

Schaefer had a number of other stunts. During a wet afternoon, with his team down 5–1 in the top of the fifth, he pleaded for the game to be called, but the umpires let the contest continue. So in the sixth he took his position at second base wearing a raincoat. The umpires let him patrol the keystone in his long coat. Pee Wee Reese recreated the sentiment years later when he carried an open umbrella to the on-deck circle during a misty fifth inning with the Dodgers trailing. Several decades had fouled the temper of arbiters worse than the weather. Reese was tossed, but the game went on.

Reese was also part of another famous stall. A Dodger laugher had suddenly turned tight, and manager Charlie Dressen hastily summoned Clyde King to relieve. When he got to the mound, King said he wasn't warm and asked Reese to buy him some time. So when King completed his allotted warmups, Reese called for time. He put his hand over his eye, in apparent agony, and went over to third baseman Billy Cox to help him get this imaginary speck out of his eye. Reese's act was a little too good; King came over to see if he could help his shortstop.

Managers often put in a rule for their pitching staff: never throw a strike on a no ball–two strike count. As the Giants manager in the forties, Mel Ott was a fervent believer in this rule. He once fined pitcher Bill Voiselle $500 for breaking the rule, and from then on, the rest of the staff toed the line.

A rookie reliever took the hill for the Giants with two runners on and a tough hitter at the plate. He got ahead on the count 0-2 and tried to waste one outside. But the ball curved over the plate, and the umpire rang up strike three. The rookie went into a panic, screaming, "No. That was a ball. What're you tryin' to do, ruin me?"

Players have been raging at umpires from the dawn of the game. Bill Klem was the first great umpire in the game, a small figure who declared, "I never missed one in my heart." He resigned in 1941 after thirty-six years in the majors because he found himself doubting a call he'd made in the game. When he was elected to the Hall of Fame in 1953, he told the crowd in Cooperstown, "To me, baseball was not just a sport; it was a religion." Many of the stories about the men in blue became attached to Klem over the years, just as stories about players stuck to Babe Ruth.

He was a short man with big ears and lips that spit when he made a call. The ballplayers called him "Catfish," but never to his face. He would brook no disrespect. But the Pirates pushed him to the limit in a critical 1913 series against the Giants. Klem threatened to clear the Pirate bench if he heard another peep.

In those days, the umpire announced pinch hitters to the crowd. So when the Pirates sent up a rookie pinch hitter, Klem asked for his name. The rookie mumbled, and Klem asked him for a repeat. "Boo," the rookie said. That was all Klem needed to hear. He threw out the hitter and the rest of the Pirates.

But Pirate manager Fred Clarke approached the red-hot arbiter with an explanation. The rookie wasn't trying to be fresh; his name was Everitt Booe.

A long drive down the line had Klem considering his decision carefully. The anxious batter questioned the Old Arbiter, "Well, was it fair or foul?"

An indignant Klem replied, "It ain't nothing until I call it."

A Klem call once infuriated Frankie Frisch, then manager of the Cardinals, who flew into a white rage and charged the umpire, spewing invective. Suddenly, Frisch collapsed. A crowd gathered around him, and a doctor came on the field to treat him. Klem didn't let sympathy cloud his judgment. "Frisch," he announced, "dead or alive, you're out of this game."

Klem accomplished what many considered impossible when he ejected Pie Traynor from a game. Traynor never cursed and was the most polite player around. There'd been no display of acrimony before the ejection, so a reporter asked Klem why Traynor had been tossed. Klem said he'd ejected Traynor because he wasn't feeling well. The reporter said he didn't see any sign of Traynor's illness.

"That's what he told me," Klem replied. "He came up to me like the perfect gentleman he is and said, 'Mr. Klem, I'm sick and tired of your stupid decisions.'" When a rookie pitcher complained about Klem's ball calls on his first three pitches to Rogers Hornsby, Klem chided the hurler, "Young man, when you pitch a strike, Mr. Hornsby will let you know."

A Klem contemporary, Bill Guthrie, is credited with creating another classic of the umpiring trade. When a batter called out on strikes launched his bat into the air in disgust, Guthrie eyed the bat and calmly announced to the batter, "Son, if that bat comes down, you're out of the game."

Umpire George Moriarty once got taken to the cleaners by a rookie. After taking two called strikes, the batter stepped out and asked, "Just for my information, sir, how do you spell your name?"

Moriarty was so surprised that he spelled out his name.

"That's what I thought, sir," the rookie said as he set himself back in the box. "Moriarty, with only one 'i.'"

Red Ormsby, another umpire during the twenties, was getting heckled from a female fan behind first base. "You blind bum," she shouted, "if you were my husband, I'd give you poison."

Ormsby walked toward the rail, removed his hat, and bowed to the woman, then roared, "If you were my wife, I'd take it."

George Magerkurth, one of the biggest umpires in the National League, got into an argument with Pee Wee Reese, one of league's smallest players. As the disputants went toe to toe, Magerkurth looked down at Reese and threatened, "Get out of here or I'll bite your head off."

"If you do," the shortstop answered, "you'll have more brains in your stomach than in your head."

When huge Frank Howard broke into the majors, umpires joined pitchers in increasing their insurance policies. Although Howard was a gentle giant, at 6'7", 255 pounds, no one wanted to be caught at the limits of his temperament. In his first at-bat with Marty Springstead behind the plate, Howard glowered at the umpire's call of strike one on a pitch around the knees. The next pitch came in at about the same spot. "That's two," Springstead announced.

"Two what?" Howard sneered.

"Too low, Frank, much too low," Springstead replied.

Nestor Chylak complained, "This is the only job in the world where they expect you to be perfect on opening day and improve as the season goes on."

The torrent of abuse hasn't let up on the umpires over the years. Billy Martin (like baseball and malaria, according to Gene Mauch) kept coming back for four decades as a player, coach and especially New York Yankee manager. Martin claimed that Gaylord Perry, the legendary greaseballer, "smelled like a drugstore," and that even his doctored balls had a medicinal air. Bill Kunkel was umpiring when Martin brought him a ball that he thought reeked of tampering. Kunkel deferred, claiming, "I have allergies and a deviated septum."

Martin seethed, "I got an umpire who can't see or smell."

The Mets and Braves played a nineteen-inning game at Atlanta on Independence Day 1985. The contest finished 16–13 in favor of the Mets and lasted until almost four in the morning, followed by fireworks as scheduled. In the seventeenth inning, home plate umpire Terry Tata ejected Darryl Strawberry for arguing a called third strike. "The strike zone changes at three A.M.," Tata told Strawberry.

Tom Gorman was keenly aware that umpires are paid by the game, not by the hour. "Anytime I got those bang-bang plays at first, I called 'em out. It made the game shorter."

In his effort to move the game along, Gorman once called Henry Aaron out on strikes as Bad Henry slugged a home run. There were two strikes on Hammern' Hank when Gorman saw strike three heading for the low, outside corner. He called it, but Aaron's quick wrists smacked the pitch into the seats as Gorman bellowed, "Strike three." As Aaron ran rounded the bases, the catcher asked Gorman what was going on. "Just practicing," Gorman murmured.

Gorman, a former pitcher, may have been partial to his previous craft. When Bob Gibson fanned a record 17 Tigers in the opener of the 1968 World Series, Gorman contended, "Gibson only struck out ten. I struck out seven."

"I won't play for a penny less than fifteen hundred."
—Honus Wagner refusing a $2,000 salary offer.

The advent of professional baseball was no doubt followed closely by the first salary dispute. Until players escaped the reserve clause noose in 1976, management held all the cards.

Branch Rickey was as famous for penny-pinching when it came to players' salaries as anything else he did in the game. Rickey had his share of idiosyncrasies. Religious convictions kept him from attending most Sunday ballgames, but he had no qualms about collecting the Sunday gate. They called him the Mahatma for his canny and sometimes inscrutable ways, but he was years ahead of the baseball establishment in creating the farm system, not only to supply his Cardinals with a fresh stream of talent, but to generate income by selling players to other clubs. Rickey got a piece of the selling price for players in his early days and became a wealthy man. Rickey's also credited with coining the phrase "Baseball is a game of inches." Later, Rickey integrated the game by selecting Jackie Robinson as the first black major leaguer.

If Brooks Robinson played third base as if he came down from a higher league, Rickey was the fellow who negotiated salaries up there. "We were like kids going to war with a popgun," Pee Wee Reese recalled. Eddie Stanky reported, "I got a million dollars worth of advice and a very small increase." Chuck Connors said, "He had the players and the money and just didn't like to see the two of them mix." When Rickey took over Pittsburgh, Rickey told slugger Ralph Kiner, "We could have finished last without you." Rickey announced, "I don't want to sell Ralph, but if something overwhelming comes along, I'm willing to be overwhelmed."

Enos Slaughter said that Rickey "would go into the vault to get change for a nickel." The talk was that Rickey's ideal team would lose a tough battle for the pennant in the final week of the season. That way, the team would draw well for the entire season, but players couldn't seek raises for winning the pennant. "I don't know if that was true," said slugger Johnny Mize, who began his career with Rickey's Cardinals in the 1930s, "but that was the talk."

Preacher Roe went into contract talks with Rickey, and, as usual, the player was demanding a sum that the general manager found unreasonable. After negotiations narrowed the gap a bit, Rickey gave Roe a contract with the Dodgers' final offer. He suggested that Roe think it over at home, and added, "I've got two hunting dogs I'd like you to have. I know how much you like to hunt."

So Roe accepted the dogs and took them home. The dogs turned out to be fine hunters, and they softened Roe's attitude toward Rickey considerably. "So I went back home and signed the contract, and put it in the mail. A few hours later, those two dogs took off across the field, and I haven't seen 'em since."

A player once returned a contract to Hank Greenberg, then general manager of the Indians. Greenberg fired off a telegram, "In your haste to accept the terms, you forgot to sign the contract."

The player wired back, "In your haste to give me a raise, you put in the wrong figure."

Bill Veeck was a great innovator on the public side of the game. Veeck, who planted the ivy in Wrigley Field while his father was president of the Cubs, saw baseball as entertainment, and his clubs always had a carnival element. (Veeck tried to buy the Ringling Brothers circus in the 1950s.) Veeck was a kindly huckster, not unlike the Wizard of Oz. When he staged morning games during World War Two for workers coming off the graveyard shift, Veeck helped serve coffee and doughnuts in the stands. He let fans decide strategy with voting cards.

But Veeck wanted to win, too. He rigged fences so that they could be moved in and out to his team's advantage. His grounds crew would hose down the infield until it was muddy to slow down opposing baserunners. He sold mirrors to fans in the bleachers to shine in enemy batters' eyes. But Veeck's most famous coup was hiring Eddie Gaedel to play for the St. Louis Browns in 1951.

Veeck's stunt came in the second game of a doubleheader between the Browns and Tigers on August 19. Between games, Veeck staged an elaborate fiftieth-anniversary celebration for the American League, attended by Commissioner "Happy" Chandler. The celebration featured acrobats, antique cars, a band made up of Browns players, and for the finale, an anniversary cake. The three-foot-seven-inch Gaedel jumped out of the cake, wearing number ⅛ on a Browns uniform originally made for the son of former owner Bill DeWitt.

Folks thought they'd seen the last of Gaedel, but in the bottom of the first, the midget was announced as a pinch hitter for leadoff batter Frank Saucier. Gaedel came out of the dugout swinging a miniature bat. Gaedel had been signed to a legal contract days before, but Veeck held off mailing the papers to the league office until the Friday before the big day. He wired the league office that morning to add Gaedel to the roster, and St. Louis manager Zack Taylor had copies of both documents to show to stern plate umpire Ed Hurley that Gaedel was a legitimate member of the Browns.

Over the objections of Detroit manager Red Rolfe, Hurley allowed Gaedel to face lefthander Bob Cain. Hurley saw to it that the Tigers held to the letter of the law, forbidding catcher Bob Swift from sitting on the ground to provide a lower target. Gaedel, stationed in the righthanders' box, took a wide stance and crouched, leaving a miniscule strike zone. Hurley called all four of Cain's deliveries high. Before the at-bat, Veeck had warned Gaedel, "I've got a man up in the stands with a high-powered rifle, and if you swing at any pitch, he'll fire." (In James Thurber's story "You Could Look It Up," which Veeck claimed he'd never read, a midget was sent up to walk but, enticed by a fat pitch, grounded out.)

Gaedel trotted to first, where he was replaced by pinch runner Jim Delsing. Gaedel patted his caddy on the rump and trotted to the dugout accompanied by wild applause. "For a minute, I felt like Babe Ruth," Gaedel said in a postgame interview. Although Commissioner Chandler found the incident entertaining, American League president Will Harridge was not amused. He expunged Gaedel's name from the official records, and banned any further appearances by midgets.

"Fine," Veeck wrote back. "Let's establish what a midget is in fact. Is it three-feet-six inches? Eddie's height? Is it four-feet-six? If it's five-feet-six, that's great. We can get rid of Rizzuto."

If any owner could rival Rickey for parsimony and Veeck for showmanship, it was Charles O. Finley, who purchased the Kansas City Athletics in 1960 and held the franchise for two decades. Finley expanded ballpark giveaways, introduced colorful uniforms, installed a mechanical rabbit in a hole behind home plate that popped out to supply the umpire with baseballs, and cajoled his fellow owners into adopting the designated hitter rule and playing World Series games at night. He singlehandedly brought mustaches back into the majors when he offered players $300 to grow them in connection with a promotion. Finley also popularized mascots, hiring a mule that he named "Charlie O." after his favorite owner, and letting the mule defecate all over the press room, preferably on reporters.

But as a businessman, Finley squeezed his players and landlords to get the most out of his franchise. He moved the A's to Oakland in 1968, prompting one Kansas City observer to remark, "Oakland is the luckiest city since Hiroshima." When third baseman Sal Bando escaped from Oakland as a free agent, someone wondered if it was difficult to leave the A's. "Was it hard to leave the *Titanic*?" Bando answered.

Finley probably became best known to the national audience when he attempted to put second baseman Mike Andrews on the disabled list during the 1973 World Series. Andrews had made a pair of errors in the eleventh inning of the second game of the Series to help the Mets to a win over the A's. After the game, Finley arranged for a doctor to examine Andrews and declare him physically unfit to play, allegedly because of a shoulder injury. Finley badgered Andrews into signing the doctor's report, then tried to substitute Manny Trillo, a much better fielder, on the A's roster. The Mets cried foul, and Commissioner Bowie Kuhn ruled that Andrews had to stay on the roster. When the Series moved to New York, Met fans gave Andrews a standing ovation.

"When I was a little boy, I wanted to be a baseball player and join the circus," recalled third baseman Graig Nettles. "With the Yankees, I've accomplished both." The focus of the reenvigorated Yankee franchise of the 1970s was principal owner George Steinbrenner, whose syndicate purchased the team in 1973. In the words of Jim Bouton, "Steinbrenner was born on third base and thinks he hit a triple."

Nettles once observed a fat man waddling past the team bus in spring training and yelled out the window, "Hurry up, George, or we'll leave without you." Nettles added, "There are two things George doesn't know about, baseball and weight control." He figured, "It's a good thing Babe Ruth isn't here. If he was, George would have him bat seventh and tell him he's overweight." When the Yanks got off to a slow start one season, Nettles saw a good side of his boss's trips to observe the club. "The more we lose, the more he flies in. And the more he flies, the better the chance that his plane will crash."

Nettles earned the nickname of "Poof" because he'd instigate trouble in the clubhouse, then, *poof*, he'd disappear. On a team flight, Nettles announced, "We've got a problem. Luis Tiant wants to use the bathroom, and it says 'no foreign objects in the toilet.'" When a flight made an unscheduled stop, Nettles asked, "What are we doing, getting new light bulbs for Bob Lemon's nose?" Lemon got that nose on the way to a successful career as a pitcher and manager. "I never took a tough loss home with me," he said. "I left it at a bar along the way."

Early in his reign, Steinbrenner ordered his troops to get rid of long hair. Lou Piniella objected, saying if long hair was good enough for Jesus Christ, why couldn't Steinbrenner allow it on his ballplayers. So Steinbrenner called Piniella up to his office and pointed off in the distance. "You see that swimming pool, Lou?"

"Yes."

"Well, the day you can go over there and walk across that pool, you can wear your hair any way you like."

Reggie Jackson, signed to a record free agent contract in 1977, made himself unwelcome to his Yankee teammates even before his arrival when he announced, "I'm the straw that stirs the drink." He'd also bragged that if he played in New York they'd name a candy bar after him. Sure enough, the Reggie bar, a clump of chocolate and nuts that bore an unfortunate resemblance to a cow chip, was born. Catfish Hunter thought the bar was unique, "I unwrapped it, and it told me how good it was." Hunter, who played with Jackson in both Oakland and New York, said that Reggie "would give you the shirt off his back. Of course, he'd call a press conference to announce it." Darold Knowles, a reliever with the A's in their glory days, said, "There isn't enough mustard in the world to cover Reggie."

Jackson was a bad outfielder by the time he got to the Yankees, but he made light of it. "Fielding? There are lots of guys who can catch a baseball. I make a million dollars with my bat."

Jackson's Yankee foil was Mickey Rivers, a bizarre character in his own right. Rivers was speedy, but you could time his walk from the on-deck circle to the plate with a sundial. He proclaimed that his goals for one season were "to hit .300, score a hundred runs, and stay injury prone." Rivers once asked, "What was the name of the dog on 'Rin-Tin-Tin'?" He referred to bewildered players as "Lost Mohicans." Rivers said a key to playing center field was sticking his finger in the air "to get the wind-chill factor." While a member of the Texas Rangers, Rivers predicted, "We'll do all right if we can capitalize on our mistakes."

But Rivers knew how to get Jackson's goat. When Jackson bragged that he had an IQ of 160, Rivers asked, "Out of what, a thousand?" Rivers offered this succinct (sanitized) analysis of Reginald Martinez Jackson's personality problem: "No wonder you is messed up. You got a white man's first name, a Spanish middle name, and a black man's last name."

Jackson retorted, "Why do I listen to you? You can't even read or write."

"You better stop reading and start hitting," Rivers warned.

When Rivers was shipped off to Texas, he expected to return to the Yankees someday. "Oh, George understands me," Rivers said of the Yanks' principal owner. "Me and him and Billy, we're two of a kind."

Billy Martin saw it about the same way with Steinbrenner and Jackson. "One's a born liar and the other's convicted," Martin said, referring to Steinbrenner's conviction for making illegal contributions to Richard Nixon's presidential campaign in 1972. That remark got Martin fired from his first of five stints as manager of the New York Yankees.

Steinbrenner was fond of disparaging his players. He fell in love with Jackson, but only after Reggie was gone. When he got Dave Winfield, who suffered through a miserable World Series slump in 1981, Steinbrenner complained, "I got rid of Mr. October and got Mr. May." When Winfield set an American League record for RBIs in April 1988, he told reporters, "Now it's on to May, and you know about me and May."

Steinbrenner didn't confine his barbs to players. He called Chicago White Sox owners Eddie Einhorn and Jerry Reinsdorf, "Abbott and Costello." Reinsdorf retaliated by asking, "How can you tell when George Steinbrenner is lying? You see his lips move."

The antics of Steinbrenner and Finley emboldened other owners. When Ray Kroc bought the San Diego Padres, he took the microphone and announced to his opening day crowd, "The good news is that we've outdrawn the Dodgers. The bad news is that I've never seen such stupid ball playing in my life." Kroc had plenty of blame to distribute in his early days as the Padres' owner. He noted, "I signed Oscar Gamble on advice of my attorney. I no longer have Oscar Gamble, and I no longer have my attorney."

Other Leagues

Black Ball

Jules Tygiel

In 1987, Major League Baseball, amidst much fanfare and publicity, celebrated the 40th anniversary of the finest moment in the history of the national pastime—Jackie Robinson's heroic shattering of the color barrier. But baseball might also have commemorated the centennial of a related, but far less auspicious event—the banishment of blacks from the International League in 1887 which ushered in six disgraceful decades of Jim Crow baseball. During this era, some of America's greatest ballplayers plied their trade on all-black teams, in Negro Leagues, on the playing fields of Latin America, and along the barnstorming frontier of the cities and towns of the United States, but never within the major and minor league realm of "organized baseball." When slowly and grudgingly given their chance in the years after 1947, blacks conclusively proved their competitive abilities on the diamond, but discrimination persisted as baseball executives continued to deny them the opportunity to display their talents in managerial and front office positions.

Scattered evidence exists of blacks playing baseball in the antebellum period, but the first recorded black teams surfaced in Northern cities in the aftermath of the Civil War. In October 1867, the Uniques of Brooklyn hosted the Excelsiors of Philadelphia in a contest billed as the "championship of colored clubs." Before a large crowd of black and white spectators, the Excelsiors marched around the field behind a fife and drum corps before defeating the Uniques, 37–24. Two months later, a second Philadelphia squad, the Pythians, dispatched a representative to the inaugural meetings of the National Association of Base Ball Players, the first organized league. The nominating committee unanimously rejected the Pythian's application, barring "any club which may be composed of one or more colored persons." Using the impeccable logic of a racist society, the committee proclaimed, "If colored clubs were admitted there would be in all probability some division of feeling, whereas, by excluding them no injury could result to anyone." The Philadelphia Pythians, however, continued their quest for interracial competition. In 1869, they became the first black team to face an all-white squad, defeating the cross-town City Items, 27–17.

In 1876, athletic entrepreneurs in the nation's metropolitan centers established the National League which quickly came to represent the pinnacle of the sport. The new entity had no written policy regarding blacks, but precluded them nonetheless through a "gentleman's agreement" among the owners. In the smaller cities and towns of America, however, where under-funded teams

and fragile minor league coalitions quickly appeared and faded, individual blacks found scattered opportunities to pursue baseball careers. During the next decade, at least two dozen black ballplayers sought to earn a living in this erratic professional baseball world.

Bud Fowler ranked among the best and most persistent of these trailblazers. Born John Jackson in upstate New York in 1858 and raised, ironically, in Cooperstown, Fowler first achieved recognition as a 20-year-old pitcher for a local team in Chelsea, Massachusetts. In April 1878, Fowler defeated the National League's Boston club, which included future Hall of Famers George Wright and Jim O' Rourke, 2–1, in an exhibition game, besting 40-game winner Tommy Bond. Later that season, Fowler hurled three games for the Lynn Live Oaks of the International Association, the nation's first minor league, and another for Worcester in the New England League. For the next six years, he toiled for a variety of independent and semi-professional teams in the United States and Canada. Despite a reputation as "one of the best pitchers on the continent," he failed to catch on with any major or minor league squads. In 1884, now appearing regularly as a second baseman, as well as a pitcher, Fowler joined Stillwater, Minnesota, in the Northwestern League. Over the next seven seasons, Fowler played for fourteen teams in nine leagues, seldom batting less than .300 for a season. In 1886, he led the Western League in triples. "He is one of the best general players in the country," reported *Sporting Life* in 1885, "and if he had a white face he would be playing with the best of them. . . Those who know, say there is no better second baseman in the country."

In 1886, however, a better second baseman did appear in the form of Frank Grant, perhaps the greatest black player of the nineteenth century. The light-skinned Grant, described as a "Spaniard" in the *Buffalo Express*, batted .325 for Meridien in the Eastern League. When that squad folded he joined Buffalo in the prestigious International Association and improved his average to .340, third best in the league.

Although not as talented as Fowler and Grant, bare-hand-catcher Moses Fleetwood Walker achieved the highest level of play of blacks of this era. The son of an Ohio physician, Fleet Walker had studied at Oberlin College, where in 1881 he and his younger brother Welday helped launch a varsity baseball team. For the next two years, the elder Walker played for the University of Michigan and in 1883 he appeared in 60 games for the pennant-winning Toledo squad in the Northwestern League. In 1884, Toledo entered the American Association, the

National League's primary rival, and Walker became the first black major leaguer. In an age when many catchers caught barehanded and lacked chest protectors, Walker suffered frequent injuries and played little after a foul tip broke his rib in mid-July. Nonetheless, he batted .263 and pitcher Tony Mullane later called him "the best catcher I ever worked with." In July, Toledo briefly signed Walker's brother, Welday, who appeared in six games batting .182. The following year, Toledo dropped from the league, ending the Walkers' major league careers.

These early black players found limited acceptance among teammates, fans, and opponents. In Ontario, in 1881, Fowler's teammates forced him off the club. Walker found that Mullane and other pitchers preferred not to pitch to him. Although he acknowledged Walker's skills, Mullane confessed, "I disliked a Negro and whenever I had to pitch to him I used anything I wanted without looking at his signals." At Louisville in 1884, insults from Kentucky fans so rattled Walker that he made five errors in a game. In Richmond, after Walker had actually left the team due to injuries, the Toledo manager received a letter from "75 determined men" threatening "to mob Walker" and cause "much bloodshed" if the black catcher appeared. On August 10, 1883, Chicago White Stockings star and manager Cap Anson had threatened to cancel an exhibition game with Toledo if Walker played. The injured catcher had not been slated to start, but Toledo manager Charlie Morton defied Anson and inserted Walker into the lineup. The game proceeded without incident.

In 1887, Walker, Fowler, Grant, Higgins, Stovey, and three other blacks converged on the International League, a newly reorganized circuit in Canada and upstate New York, one notch below the major league level. At the same time, a new six-team entity, the League of Colored Baseball Clubs, won recognition under baseball's National Agreement, a mutual pact to honor player contracts among team owners. Thus, an air of optimism pervaded the start of the season. But 1887 would prove a fateful year for the future of blacks in baseball.

On May 6, the Colored League made its debut in Pittsburgh with "a grand street parade and a brass band concert." Twelve hundred spectators watched the hometown Keystones lose to the Gorhams of New York, 11–8. Within days, however, the new league began to flounder. The Boston franchise disbanded in Louisville on May 8, stranding its players in the Southern city. Three weeks later, league-founder Walter Brown formally announced the demise of the infant circuit.

Meanwhile, in the International League, black players found their numbers growing, but their status increasingly uncertain. Six of the 10 teams fielded blacks, prompting *Sporting Life* to wonder, "How far will this mania for engaging colored players go?" In Newark, fans marveled at the "colored battery" of Fleet Walker, dubbed the "coon catcher" by one Canadian newspaper, and "headstrong" pitcher George Stovey. Stovey, one of the greatest black pitchers of the nineteenth century, won 35 games, still an International League record. Frank Grant, in his second season as the Buffalo second baseman, led the league in both batting average and home runs. Bud Fowler, one of two blacks on the Binghamton squad, compiled a .350 average through early July and stole 23 bases.

These athletes compiled their impressive statistics under the most adverse conditions. "I could not help pitying some of the poor black fellows that played in the International League," reported a white player. "Fowler used to play second base with the lower part of his legs encased in wooden guards. He knew that about every player that came down to second base on a steal had it in for him." Both Fowler and Grant, "would muff balls intentionally, so that [they] would not have to touch runners, fearing that they might injure [them]." In addition, "About half the pitchers try their best to hit these colored players when [they are] at bat." Grant, whose Buffalo teammates had refused to sit with him for a team portrait in 1886, reportedly saved himself from a "drubbing" at their hands in 1887, only by "the effective use of a club." In Toronto, fans chanted, "Kill the Nigger," at Grant, and a local newspaper headline declared, "THE COLORED PLAYERS DISTASTEFUL." In late June, Bud Fowler's Binghamton teammates refused to take the field unless the club removed him from the lineup. Soon after, on July 7, the Binghamton club submitted to these demands, releasing Fowler and a black teammate, a pitcher named Renfroe.

The most dramatic confrontations between black and white players occurred on the Syracuse squad, where a clique of refugees from the Southern League exacerbated racial tensions. In spring training, the club included a catcher named Dick Male, who, rumors had it, was a light-skinned black named Richard Johnson. Male charged "that the man calling him a Negro is himself a black liar," but when released after a poor preseason performance, he returned to his old club, Zanesville in the Ohio State League, and resumed his true identity as Richard Johnson. In May, Syracuse signed 19-year-old black pitcher Robert Higgins, angering the Southern clique. On May 25, Higgins appeared in his first International League game in Toronto. "THE SYRACUSE PLOTTERS," as a *Sporting News* headline called his teammates, undermined his debut. According to one account, they "seemed to want the Toronto team to knock Higgins out of the box, and time and again they fielded so badly that the home team were enabled to secure many hits after the side had been retired." "A disgusting exhibition," admonished *The Toronto World*. "They succeeded in running Male out of the club," reported a Newark paper, "and they will do the same with Higgins." One week later, two Syracuse players refused to pose for a team picture with Higgins. When manager "Ice Water" Joe Simmons suspended pitcher Doug Crothers for this incident, Crothers slugged the manager. Higgins miraculously recovered from his early travails and lack of support to post a 20–7 record.

On July 14, as the directors of the International League discussed the racial situation in Buffalo, the Newark Little Giants planned to send Stovey, their ace, to the mound in an exhibition game against the National League Chicago White Stockings. Once again manager Anson refused to field his squad if either Stovey or Walker appeared. Unlike 1883, Anson's will prevailed. On the same day, team owners, stating that "Many of the best players in the league are anxious to leave on account of the colored element," allowed current black players to remain, but voted by a six-to-four margin to reject all future contracts with blacks. The teams with black players all voted against the measure, but Binghamton, which had just released Fowler and Renfroe, swung the vote in favor of exclusion.

Events in 1887 continued to conspire against black players. On September 11, the St. Louis Browns of the American Association refused to play a scheduled contest against the all-black Cuban Giants. "We are only doing what is right," they proclaimed. In November, the Buffalo and Syracuse teams unsuccessfully attempted to lift the International League ban on blacks. The Ohio State League, which had fielded three black players, also adopted a rule barring additional contracts with blacks, prompting Welday Walker, who had appeared in the league, to protest, "The law is a disgrace to the present age. . . There should be some broader cause—such as lack of ability, behavior and intelligence—for barring a player, rather than his color."

After 1887, only a handful of blacks appeared on integrated squads. Grant and Higgins returned to their original teams in 1888. Walker jumped from Newark to Syracuse. The following year, only Walker remained for one final season, the last black in the International League until 1946. Richard Johnson, the erstwhile Dick Male, reappeared in the Ohio State League in 1888 and in 1889 joined Springfield in the Central Interstate League, where he hit 14 triples, stole 45 bases, and scored 100 runs in 100 games. In 1890, Harrisburg in the Eastern Interstate League fielded two blacks, while Jamestown in the New York Penn League featured another. Bud Fowler and several other black players appeared in the Nebraska State League in 1892. Three years later, Adrian in the Michigan State League signed five blacks, including Fowler and pitcher George Wilson who posted a 29–4 record. Meanwhile Sol White, who later chronicled these events in his 1906 book, *The History of Colored Baseball*, played for Fort Wayne in the Western State League. In 1896, pitcher-outfielder Bert Jones joined Atchison in the Kansas State League where he played for three seasons before being forced out in 1898. Almost 50 years would pass before another black would appear on an interracial club in organized baseball.

While integrated teams grew rare, several leagues allowed entry to all black squads. In 1889, the Middle States League included the New York Gorhams and the Cuban Giants, the most famous black team of the age. The Giants posted a 55–17 record. In 1890, the alliance reorganized as the Eastern Interstate League and again included the Cuban Giants. Giants' star George Williams paced the circuit with a .391 batting average, while teammate Arthur Thomas slugged 26 doubles and 10 triples, both league-leading totals. The Eastern Interstate League folded in midseason, and in 1891 the Giants made one final minor league appearance in the Connecticut State League. When this circuit also disbanded, the brief entry of the Cuban Giants in organized baseball came to an end. In 1898, a team calling itself the Acme Colored Giants affiliated with Pennsylvania's Iron and Oil League, but won only eight of 49 games before dropping out, marking an ignoble conclusion to these early experiments in interracial play.

Overall, at least 70 blacks appeared in organized baseball in the late 19th century. About half played for all-black teams, the remainder for integrated clubs. Few lasted more than one season with the same team. By the 1890s, the pattern for black baseball that would prevail for the next half century had emerged. Blacks were relegated to "colored" teams playing most of their games on the barnstorming circuit, outside of any organized league structure. While exhibition contests allowed them to pit their skills against whites, they remained on the outskirts of baseball's mainstream, unheralded and unknown to most Americans.

As early as the 1880s and 1890s several all-black traveling squads had gained national reputations. The Cuban Giants, formed among the waiters of the Argyle Hotel to entertain guests in 1885, set the pattern and provided the recurrent nickname for these teams. Passing as Cubans, so as not to offend their white clientele, the Giants toured the East in a private railroad car playing amateur and professional opponents. In the 1890s, rivals like the Lincoln Giants from Nebraska, the Page Fence Giants from Michigan, and the Cuban X Giants in New York emerged. From the beginning these teams combined entertainment with their baseball to attract crowds. The Page Fence Giants, founded by Bud Fowler in 1895, would ride through the streets on bicycles to attract attention. In 1899, Fowler organized the All-American Black Tourists, who would arrive in full dress suits with opera hats and silk umbrellas. Their showmanship notwithstanding, the black teams of the 1890s included some of the best players in the nation. The Page Fence Giants won 118 of 154 games in 1895, with two of their losses coming against the major league Cincinnati Reds.

During the early years of the 20th century many blacks still harbored hopes of regaining access to organized baseball. Sol White wrote in 1906 that baseball, "should be taken seriously by the colored player. An honest effort of his great ability will open the avenue in the near future wherein he may walk hand-in-hand with the opposite race in the greatest of all American games—baseball." Rube Foster, the outstanding figure in black baseball from 1910-1926, stressed excellence because "we have to be ready when the time comes for integration."

But even clandestine efforts to bring in blacks met a harsh fate. In 1901, Baltimore Orioles Manager John McGraw attempted to pass second baseman Charlie Grant of the Columbia Giants off as an Indian named Chief Tokohama, until Chicago White Sox President Charles Comiskey exposed the ruse. In 1911, the Cincinnati Reds raised black hopes by signing two light-skinned Cubans, Armando Marsans and Rafael Almeida, prompting the *New York Age* to speculate, "Now that the first shock is over it would not be surprising to see a Cuban a few shades darker. . .breaking into the professional ranks. . .it would then be easier for colored players who are citizens of this country to get into fast company." But the Reds rushed to certify that Marsans and Almeida were "genuine Caucasians," and while light-skinned Cubans became a fixture in the majors, their darker brethren remained unwelcome. Over the years, tales circulated of United States blacks passing as Indians or Cubans, but no documented cases exist.

Although most blacks lived in the South, during the first two decades of the 20th century, the great black teams and players congregated in the metropolises and industrial cities of the North. Chicago emerged as the primary center of black baseball with teams like the Leland Giants and the Chicago American Giants. In New York, the Lincoln Giants, which boasted pitching stars Smokey Joe Williams and Cannonball Dick Redding, shortstop John Henry Lloyd and catcher Louis Santop, reigned supreme. Other top clubs of the era included the Philadelphia Giants, the Hilldale Club (also of Philadelphia), the Indianapolis ABC's and the Bacharach Giants of Atlantic City. Player contracts were nonexistent or nonbinding and stars jumped frequently from team to team. "Wherever the money was," recalled John Henry Lloyd, "that's where I was."

Fans and writers often compared the great black players of this era to their white counterparts. Lloyd, one of the outstanding shortstops and hitters of that or any era, came to be known as "The Black Wagner," after his white contemporary Honus Wagner, who called it an "honor" and a "privilege" to be compared to the gangling black infielder. A St. Louis sportswriter once said when asked who was the best player in baseball history, "If you mean in organized baseball, the answer would be Babe Ruth; but if you mean in all baseball...the answer would have to be a colored man named John Henry Lloyd." Pitcher "Rube" Foster earned his nickname by outpitching future Hall of Famer Rube Waddell, and Cuban Jose Mendez was called "The Black Matty" after Christy Mathewson.

The talents of Foster and Mendez notwithstanding, the greatest black pitcher of the early twentieth century was 6'5" Smokey Joe Williams. Born in 1886, Williams spent a good part of his career pitching in his native Texas, unheralded until he joined the Leland Giants in 1909 at the age of 24. From 1912-1923 he won renown as a strike-out artist for Harlem's Lincoln Giants. Against major league competition Williams won six games, lost 4, and tied two, including a three-hit 1–0 victory over the National League champion Philadelphia Phillies in 1915. In 1925, he signed with the Homestead Grays and although approaching his fortieth birthday, starred for seven more seasons. A 1952 poll to name the outstanding black pitcher of the half-century, placed Williams in first place, ahead of the legendary Satchel Paige.

Oscar Charleston ranks as the greatest outfielder of the 1910s and 1920s. With tremendous speed and a strong, accurate arm, Charleston was the quintessential centerfielder. During his 15-year career starting in 1915, Charleston hit for both power and average and may have been the most popular player of the 1920s. After he retired he managed the Philadelphia Stars, Brooklyn Brown Dodgers, and other clubs.

Several major stars of this era labored outside the usual channels of black baseball. In 1914, white Kansas City promoter J. L. Wilkinson organized the All-Nations team, which included whites, blacks, Indians, Asians, and Latin Americans. Pitchers John Donaldson, Jose Mendez, and Bill Drake and outfielder Cristobel Torriente played for the All-Nations team, described by one observer as "strong enough to give any major league team a nip-and-tuck battle." A black Army team from the 25th Infantry Unit in Nogales, Arizona, featured pitcher Bullet Joe Rogan and shortstop Dobie Moore. In 1920, when Wilkinson formed the famed Kansas City Monarchs, the players from the All-Nations and 25th Infantry teams formed the

nucleus of his club. In 1921, the Monarchs challenged the minor league Kansas City Blues to a tournament for the city championship. The Blues won the series five games to three. In 1922, however, the Monarchs won five of six games to claim boasting honors in Kansas City. One week later, they swept a doubleheader from the touring Babe Ruth All-Stars.

In the years after 1910, Andrew "Rube" Foster emerged as the dominant figure in black baseball. Like many of his white contemporaries, Foster rose through the ranks of the national pastime from star player to field manager to club owner. Born in Texas in 1879, Foster accepted an invitation to pitch for Chicago's Union Giants in 1902. "If you play the best clubs in the land, white clubs as you say," he told owner Frank Leland, "it will be a case of Greek meeting Greek. I fear nobody." By 1903, he was hurling for the Cuban X Giants against the Philadelphia Giants in a series billed as the "Colored Championship of the World." His four victories in a best of nine series clinched the title. The following year, he had switched sides and registered two of three wins for the Philadelphia Giants in a similar matchup, striking out 18 batters in one game and tossing a two-hitter in another. In 1907, he rejoined the Leland Giants and, in 1910, pitched for and managed a reconstituted team of that name to a 123–6 record.

As a pitcher, Foster had ranked among the nation's best; as a manager, his skills achieved legendary proportions. A master strategist and motivator, Foster's teams specialized in the bunt, the steal, and the hit-and-run, which came to characterize black baseball. Fans came to watch him sit on the bench giving signs with a wave of his ever-present pipe. He became the friend and confidant of major league managers like John McGraw. Over the years, Foster trained a generation of black managers, like Dave Malarcher, Biz Mackey, and Oscar Charleston in the subtleties of the game.

In 1911, Foster entered the ownership ranks, uniting with white saloon keeper John Schorling (the son-in-law of White Sox owner Charles Comiskey) to form the Chicago American Giants. With Schorling's financial backing, Foster's managerial acumen, a regular home field in Chicago, and high salaries, the American Giants attracted the best black players in the nation. Throughout the decade, whether barnstorming or hosting opponents in Chicago, the American Giants came to represent the pinnacle of black baseball.

By World War One, Foster dominated black baseball in Chicago and parts of the Midwest. In most other areas, however, white booking agents controlled access to stadiums, and as one newspaperman charged in 1917, "used circus methods to drag a bunch of our best citizens out, only to undergo humiliation . . . while [they sat] back and [grew] rich off a percentage of the proceeds." In the East, Nat Strong, the part owner of the Brooklyn Royal Giants, Philadelphia Giants, Cuban Stars, Cuban Giants, New York Black Yankees, and the renowned white semi-pro team, the Bushwicks, held a stranglehold on black competition. To break this monopoly and place the game more firmly under black control, Foster created the National Association of Professional Baseball Clubs, better known as the Negro National League, in 1920.

Foster's new organization marked the third attempt of

the century to meld black teams into a viable league. In 1906, the International League of Independent Baseball Clubs, which had four black and two white teams, struggled through one season characterized by shifting and collapsing franchises. Four years later, Beauregard Moseley, secretary of Chicago's Leland Giants attempted to form a National Negro Baseball League, but the association folded before a single game had been played.

The new Negro National League, which included the top teams from Chicago, St. Louis, Detroit, and other Midwestern cities, fared far better. At Foster's insistence, all clubs, with the exception of the Kansas City Monarchs, whom Foster reluctantly accepted, were controlled by blacks. J. L. Wilkinson, who owned the Monarchs, a major drawing card, had won the respect of his fellow owners and soon overcame Foster's reservations. He became the league secretary and Foster's trusted ally. Operating under the able guidance of Foster and Wilkinson, the league flourished during its early years. In 1923, it attracted 400,000 fans and accumulated $200,000 in gate receipts.

The success of the Negro National League inspired competitors. In 1923, booking agent Nat Strong formed an Eastern Colored League, with teams in New York, Brooklyn, Baltimore, New Jersey, and Philadelphia. With four of the six teams owned by whites, and Strong controlling an erratic schedule, the league had somewhat less legitimacy than Foster's circuit. Playing in larger population centers, however, the more affluent Eastern clubs successfully raided some of the top players of the Negro National League before the circuits negotiated an uneasy truce in 1924. Throughout the remainder of the decade, however, acrimony rather than harmony characterized interleague relations. A third association emerged in the South, where the stronger independent teams in major cities formed the Southern Negro League. While this group became a breeding ground for top players, the impoverished nature of its clientele, and the inability of clubs to bolster revenues with games against white squads, rendered them unable to prevent their best players from jumping to the higher paying Northern teams.

At their best the Negro Leagues of the 1920s were haphazard affairs. Since most clubs continued to rely on barnstorming for their primary livelihood, scheduling proved difficult. Teams played uneven numbers of games and especially in the Eastern circuit skipped official contests for more lucrative nonleague matchups. Several of the stronger independent teams, like the Homestead Grays, remained unaffiliated. Umpires were often incompetent and lacked authority to control conditions. Finally, players frequently jumped from one franchise to another, peddling their services to the highest bidder. In 1926, Foster grew ill, stripping the Negro National League of his vital leadership. Two years later, the Eastern Colored League disbanded and in 1931, less than a year after Foster's death, the Negro National League departed the scene, once again leaving black baseball with no organized structure.

With the collapse of Foster's Negro National League and the onset of the Great Depression, the always-borderline economics of operating a black baseball club grew more precarious. White booking agents, like Philadelphia's Eddie Gottlieb or Abe Saperstein of the Midwest,

again reigned supreme. In the early 1930s, only the stronger independent clubs like the Homestead Grays or Kansas City Monarchs, novelty acts like the Cincinnati Clowns, or those teams backed by the "numbers kings" of the black ghettos could survive.

The Kansas City Monarchs emerged as the healthiest holdover from the old Negro National League. In 1929, owner Wilkinson had commissioned an Omaha, Nebraska, company to design a portable lighting system for night games. The equipment, consisting of a 250-horsepower motor and a 100-kilowatt generator, which illuminated lights atop telescoping poles 50 feet above the field, took about two hours to assemble. To pay for the innovation, Wilkinson mortgaged everything he owned and took in Kansas City businessman Tom Baird as a partner. But the gamble paid off. The novelty of night baseball allowed the Monarchs to play two and three games a day and made them the most popular touring club in the nation.

Meanwhile, in Pittsburgh, former basketball star Cumberland Posey, Jr. had forged the Homestead Grays into one of the best teams in America. Posey, the son of one of Pittsburgh's wealthiest black businessmen, had joined the Grays, then a sandlot team, as an outfielder in 1911. By the early 1920s he owned the club and began recruiting top national players to supplement local talent. In 1925, he signed 39-year-old Smokey Joe Williams, and the following year he lured Oscar Charleston, whom many consider the top black player of that era. Over the next several seasons Posey recruited Judy Johnson, Martin Dihigo, and Cool Papa Bell. In 1930, he added a catcher from the Pittsburgh sandlots named Josh Gibson, and in 1934 brought in first baseman Buck Leonard from North Carolina. Unwilling to subject himself to outside control, Posey preferred to remain free from league affiliations. Yet for two decades, the Homestead Grays reigned as one of the strongest teams in black baseball.

In the 1930s, Posey faced competition from crosstown rival Gus Greenlee, "Mr. Big" of Pittsburgh's North Side numbers rackets. Greenlee took over the Pittsburgh Crawfords, a local team, in 1930. Greenlee spent $100,000 to build a new stadium, and wooed established ballplayers with lavish salary offers. In 1931, he landed the colorful Satchel Paige, the hottest young pitcher in the land, and the following year raided the Grays, outbidding Posey for the services of Charleston, Johnson, and Gibson. In 1934, James "Cool Papa" Bell jumped the St. Louis Stars and brought his legendary speed to the Crawfords. With five future Hall of Famers, Greenlee had assembled one of the great squads of baseball history.

The emergence of Gus Greenlee marked a new era for black baseball, the reign of the numbers men. In an age of limited opportunities for blacks, many of the most talented northern black entrepreneurs turned to gambling and other illegal operations for their livelihood. Novelist Richard Wright explained, "They would have been steel tycoons, Wall Street brokers, auto moguls, had they been white." Like the political bosses of nineteenth century urban America, numbers operators provided an informal assistance network for needy patrons in the impoverished black communities and represented a major source of capital for black businesses. In city after city, the numbers barons, seeking an element of respectability or an outlet to shield gambling profits from the Internal Revenue Service or merely the thrill of sports ownership, came to dominate black baseball. In Harlem, second-generation Cuban immigrant Alex Pompez, a powerful figure in the Dutch Schultz mob, ran the Cuban Stars, while Ed "Soldier Boy" Semler controlled the Black Yankees. Abe Manley of the Newark Eagles, Ed Bolden of the Philadelphia Stars, and Tom Wilson of the Baltimore Elite Giants all garnered their fortunes from the numbers game. Even Cum Posey, who had no connection with the rackets, had to bring in Homestead numbers banker Rufus "Sonnyman" Jackson as a partner and financier to stave off Greenlee's challenge.

In 1933, Greenlee unified the franchises owned by the numbers kings into a rejuvenated Negro National League. Under his leadership, writes Donn Rogosin, "The Negro National League meetings were enclaves of the most powerful black gangsters in the nation." This "unholy alliance" sustained black baseball in the Northeast through depression and war. Even the collapse of the Crawfords and demolition of Greenlee Stadium in 1939, failed to weaken the league which survived until the onset of integration. In 1937 a second circuit, the Negro American League was formed in the Midwest and South. Dominated by Wilkinson and the Kansas City Monarchs, the Negro American League relied less on numbers brokers, but more on white ownership for their financing.

The formation of the Negro American League encouraged the rejuvenation of an annual World Series, matching the champions of the two leagues. But the Negro League World Series never achieved the prominence of its white counterpart. The fact that league standings were often determined among teams playing uneven numbers of games, diluted the notion of a champion. Furthermore, impoverished urban blacks could not sustain attendance at a prolonged series. As a result, the Negro League World Series always took a back seat to the annual East-West All-Star Game played in Chicago. The East-West Game, originated by Greenlee in 1933, quickly emerged as the centerpiece of black baseball. Fans chose the players in polls conducted by black newspapers. By 1939, leading candidates received as many as 500,000 votes. Large crowds of blacks and whites watched the finest Negro League stars, and the revenues divided among the teams often spelled the difference between profit and loss at the season's end.

By the 1930s and 1940s, black baseball had become an integral part of Northern ghetto life. With hundreds of employees and millions of dollars in revenue, the Negro Leagues, as Donn Rogosin notes, "may rank among the highest achievements of black enterprise during segregation." In addition, baseball provided an economic ripple effect, boosting business in hotels, cafes, restaurants and bars. In Kansas City and other towns, games became social events, as black citizens, recalls manager Buck O'Neil, "wore their finery." The Monarch Booster Club was a leading civic organization and the "Miss Monarch Bathing Beauty" pageant a popular event.

Black baseball also represented a source of pride for the black community. "The Monarchs was Kansas City's team," boasted bartender Jesse Fisher. "They made Kansas City the talk of the town all over the world." In several cities, white politicians routinely appeared at Opening Day games to curry favor with their often neglected black constituents. When Greenlee Field launched its operations in Pittsburgh, the mayor, city council, and county commissioners lined the field boxes. Negro League owners also played a role in the fight against segregation. In Newark, Effa Manley, who ran the Eagles with her husband Abe, served as treasurer of the New Jersey NAACP and belonged to the Citizen's League for Fair Play which fought for black employment opportunities. Manley sponsored a "Stop Lynching" fundraiser at one Eagles home game.

The impact of the Negro Leagues, however, ranged beyond the communities whose names the teams bore. Throughout the age of Jim Crow baseball, even in those years when a substantial league structure existed, official league games accounted for a relatively small part of the black baseball experience. Black teams would typically play over 200 games a year, only a third of which counted in the league standings. The vast majority of contests occurred on the "barnstorming" circuit, pitting black athletes against a broad array of professional and semi-professional competition, white and black, throughout the nation. In the pre-television era, traveling teams brought a higher level of baseball to fans in the towns and cities of America and allowed local talent to test their skills against the professionals. While some all-white teams, like the "House of David" also trod the barnstorming trail, itinerancy was the key to survival for black squads. The capital needed to finance a Negro League team existed primarily in Northern cities, but the overwhelming majority of blacks lived in the South.

"The schedule was a rugged one," recalled Roy Campanella of the Baltimore Elite Giants. "Rarely were we in the same city two days in a row. Mostly we played by day and traveled by night." After the Monarchs introduced night baseball, teams played both day and night appearing in two and sometimes three different ballparks on the same day. Teams traveled in buses—"our home, dressing room, dining room, and hotel"—or sandwiched into touring cars. "We had little time to waste on the road," states Quincy Trouppe, "so it was a rare treat when the cars would stop at times to let us stretch out and exercise for a few minutes." Most major hotels barred black guests, so even when the schedule allowed overnight stays, the athletes found themselves in less than comfortable accommodations. Large cities usually had better black hotels where ballplayers, entertainers, and other members of the black bourgeoisie congregated. On the road, however, Negro Leaguers more frequently were relegated to Jim Crow roadhouses, "continually under attack by bedbugs."

The black baseball experience extended beyond the confines of the United States and into Central America and the Caribbean. Negro Leaguers appeared regularly in the Cuban, Puerto Rican, Venezuelan, and Dominican winter leagues where they competed against black and white Latin stars and major leaguers as well. Some blacks, like Willie Wells and Ray Dandridge, jumped permanently to the Mexican League, where several also became successful managers of interracial teams. As Wells explained, "I am not faced by the racial problem. . . I've found freedom and democracy here, something I never found in the United States. . . In Mexico, I am a man."

In the United States, however, blacks often found themselves in more distasteful roles. To attract crowds throughout the nation and to keep fans interested in the frequently one-sided contests against amateur competition, some black clubs injected elements of clowning and showmanship into their pre-game and competitive performances. As early as the 1880s, comedy had characterized many barnstorming teams. Black baseball, even in its most serious form, tended to be flashier and less formal than white play. Against inferior teams, players often showboated and flaunted their superior skills. Pitcher Satchel Paige would call in his outfielders or guarantee to strike out the first six or nine batters to face him against semi-professional squads. In the late 1930s, Olympic star Jesse Owens traveled with the Monarchs, racing against horses in pre-game exhibitions.

Black teams, like the Tennessee Rats and Zulu Cannibals, thrived on their minstrel show reputations. The most famous of these franchises were the "Ethiopian Clowns." Originating in Miami in the 1930s, the Clowns later operated out of Cincinnati and then Indianapolis. Their antics included a "pepperball and shadowball" performance (later emulated by basketball's Harlem Globetrotters), and mid-game vaudeville routines by comics Spec Bebop, a dwarf, and King Tut. Players like Pepper Bassett, "the Rocking Chair Catcher" and "Goose" Tatum, a talented first baseman and natural comedian, enlivened the festivities. By the 1940s, the Clowns, through the effort of booking agent Syd Pollack, dominated the baseball comedy market. In 1943, their popularity won the Clowns entrance into the Negro Leagues, although other owners demanded they drop the demeaning "Ethiopian" nickname. Although never one of the better black teams, the Clowns greatly bolstered Negro League attendance.

Their popularity notwithstanding, the comedy teams reflected one of the worst elements of black baseball. The Clowns and Zulus perpetuated stereotypes drawn from Stepin Fetchit and Tarzan movies. "Negroes must realize the danger in insisting that ballplayers paint their faces and go through minstrel show revues before each ballgame," protested sportswriter Wendell Smith. Many black players resented the image that all were clowns. "Didn't nobody clown in our league but the Indianapolis Clowns," objected Piper Davis. "We played baseball."

Even without the clowning, black baseball offered a more freewheeling and, in many respects, more exciting brand of baseball than the major leagues. Since the 1920s, when Babe Ruth had revolutionized the game, the majors had pursued power strategies, emphasizing the home run above all else. Although the great sluggers of the Negro Leagues rivaled those in the National and American Leagues, they comprised but one element in the speed-dominated universe of "tricky baseball." Black teams emphasized the bunt, the stolen base, and the hit-and-run. "We played by the 'coonsbury' rules," boasted second baseman Newt Allen. "That's just any way you think you can win, any kind of play you think you could get by on." In games between white and black all-star teams, this style of play often confounded the major leaguers. Centerfielder James "Cool Papa" Bell personified this approach. Bell was so fast, marveled rival third baseman Judy Johnson, "You couldn't play back in your regular position or you'd never throw him out." In one game against a major league All-Star squad, Bell scored from first base on a sacrifice bunt! In center field, his great speed allowed him to lurk in the shallow reaches of the outfield, ranging great distances to make spectacular catches.

Negro League pitching also took on a peculiar caste. "Anything went in the Negro League," reported catcher Roy Campanella, "Spitballs, shineballs, emery balls; pitchers used any and all of them." Since league officials could not afford to replace the balls as frequently as in organized ball, scuffed and nicked baseballs remained in the game, giving pitchers great latitude for creative efforts. "I never knew what the ball would do once it left the pitcher's hand," recalled Campanella.

Since most rosters included only 14 to 18 men, Negro League players demonstrated a wide range of versatility. Each was required to fill in at a variety of positions. Star pitchers often found themselves in the outfield when not on the mound. Some won renown at more than one position. Ted "Double-Duty" Radcliffe often pitched in the first game of a doubleheader and caught in the second. Cuban Martin Dihigo, whom many rank as the greatest player of all time, excelled at every position. In 1938, in the Mexican League he led the league's pitchers with an 18–2 record and the league's hitters with a .387 average.

The manpower shortage offered opportunities for individuals to display their all-around talents, but it also limited the competitiveness of the black teams. While on a given day a Negro League franchise, featuring one of its top pitchers, might defeat a major league squad, most teams lacked the depth to compete on a regular basis. "The big leagues were strong in every position," remarks Radcliffe. "Most of the colored teams had a few stars but they weren't strong in every position."

While black teams may not have matched the top clubs in organized baseball, the individual stars of the 1930s and 1940s clearly ranked among the best of any age. Homestead Gray teammates Josh Gibson and Buck Leonard won renown as the Babe Ruth and Lou Gehrig of the Negro Leagues. The Grays discovered Gibson in 1929 as an 18-year-old catcher on the sandlots of Pittsburgh, where he had already earned a reputation for 500-foot home runs. For 17 years, he launched prodigious blasts off pitchers in the Negro Leagues, on the barnstorming tour, and in Latin America. As talented as any major league star, Gibson died in January 1947, at age 35, just three months before Jackie Robinson joined the Brooklyn Dodgers. Leonard, four-years older than Gibson, starred in both the Negro and Mexican Leagues as a sure-handed, power-hitting first baseman. The Newark Eagles in the early 1940s, boasted the "million dollar infield" of first baseman Mule Suttles, second baseman Dick Seay, shortstop Willie Wells, and third baseman Ray Dandridge. The acrobatic fielding skills of Seay, Wells and Dandridge led Roy Campanella to call this the greatest infield he ever saw.

Amidst the many talented Negro Leaguers of 1930s and 1940s, however, one long, lean figure came to personify black baseball to blacks and whites alike. Leroy "Satchel" Paige began his prolonged athletic odyssey in his hometown in 1924 as a 17-year-old pitcher with the semi-professional Mobile Tigers. He joined the Chattanooga Black Lookouts of the Negro Southern League in

1926. Two years later, the Lookouts sold his contract to the Birmingham Black Barons. By 1930, his explosive fastball, impeccable control, and eccentric mannerisms had made him a legend in the South. In 1932, Gus Greenlee brought Paige to the Pittsburgh Crawfords where the colorful pitcher embellished his reputation by winning 54 games in his first two years. Greenlee also began the practice of hiring out Paige to semi-professional clubs that needed a one-day box office boost.

For seven years Paige feuded with Greenlee, jumping the club when a better offer appeared, being banished "for life," and then returning. In the mid-1930s, in addition to his stints with the Crawfords, Paige won fame by boosting Bismarck, North Dakota, to the national semi-professional championships, hurling for the Dominican Republic at the behest of dictator Rafael Trujillo, in the Mexican League, and especially on the postseason barnstorming trail pitted against Dizzy Dean's Major League All-Stars. "That skinny old Satchel Paige with those long arms is my idea of the pitcher with the greatest stuff I ever saw," claimed the unusually immodest Dean.

Paige's appeal stemmed as much from his unusual persona as his pitching prowess. A born showman, Paige's lanky, lackadaisical presence evoked popular racial stereotypes of the age. "As undependable as a pair of second-hand suspenders," Paige often arrived late or failed to show. His names for his pitches (the "bee ball" which buzzed and all of a sudden, "be there"; the "jump ball"; and the "trouble ball") and his minstrel show one-liners enhanced the image. But on the mound, Paige invariably rose to the occasion against top competition or challenged inferior opponents by calling in the outfield or promising to strike out the side.

In 1938, a sore arm threatened to curtail Paige's career but the Kansas City Monarchs, hoping his reputation alone would draw fans, signed him for their traveling second team. On the road, Paige perfected a repertoire of curves and off-speed pitches, including his famous "hesitation" pitch. When his fastball returned in 1939, he became a better pitcher than ever. Promoted to the main Monarch club, Paige pitched the team to four consecutive Negro American League pennants. From 1941-1947, although officially still a Monarch, Paige spent far more time as an independent performer, hired out by Monarchs' owner J. L. Wilkinson to semi-pro and Negro League clubs. "He kept our league going," recalls Othello Renfroe. "Anytime a team got into trouble, it sent for Satchel to pitch." Paige also continued to hurl against major league All-Star teams. In the 1940s, the example of Satchel Paige, whose legend had spread into the white community, offered the most compelling argument for the desegregation of the National Pastime.

Paige's exploits against white players revealed a fundamental irony about baseball in the Jim Crow era. While organized baseball rigidly enforced its ban on black players within the major and minor leagues, opportunities abounded for black athletes to prove themselves against white competition along the unpoliced boundaries of the national pastime. During the 1930s, Western promoters sponsored tournaments for the best semi-professional teams in the nation. These squads often featured former and future major leaguers as well as top local talent. In 1934, the *Denver Post* tourney, "the little World Series of the West," invited the Kansas City Monarchs to compete for the $7,500 first prize. The Monarchs fought their way into the finals against the House of David team (also owned by J. L. Wilkinson) only to find themselves confronted on the mound by Paige, rented out to pitch this one game. Paige outdueled Monarchs ace, Chet Brewer, 2–1. Black teams became a fixture in the Post series, emerging victorious for several consecutive years.

In 1935, the National Baseball Congress began an annual tournament in Wichita, Kansas. The competition attracted community squads heartily bankrolled by local business leaders. Neil Churchill, an auto dealer from Bismarck, North Dakota, recruited a half-dozen black stars, including Paige and Brewer, to represent the town in the Wichita competition. Bismarck naturally swept the series, and thereafter teams that were either integrated or all black routinely appeared in the National Baseball Congress invitational each year.

In an age in which the major leagues were confined to the East and Midwest, and television had yet to bring baseball into people's homes, postseason tours by big league stars offered yet another opportunity for black players to prove their equality on the diamond. Games pitting blacks against whites were popular features of the barnstorming circuit. Until the late 1920s, when Commissioner Kenesaw Mountain Landis limited postseason play to all-star squads, black teams frequently met and defeated major league clubs in postseason competition. During the next decade, matchups between the Babe Ruth or Dizzy Dean "All-Stars" and black players became frequent. In the autumns of 1934 and 1935, Dean's team traveled the nation accompanied by the "Satchel Paige All-Stars." In one memorable 1934 game, called by baseball executive Bill Veeck, "the greatest pitching battle I have ever seen," Paige bested Dean 1–0. Surviving records of interracial contests during the 1930s reveal that blacks won two-thirds of the games. "That's when we played the hardest," asserted Judy Johnson, "to let them know, and to let the public know, that we had the same talent they did and probably a little better at times."

The rivalries proved particularly keen on the West Coast where Monarchs co-owner Tom Baird organized the California Winter League, which included black teams, white major and minor league stars, and some of Mexico's top players. In 1940, pitcher Chet Brewer formed the Kansas City Royals, which each year fielded one of the best clubs on the coast. One year the Royals defeated the Hollywood Stars, who had won the Pacific Coast League championship, six straight times. In 1945, Brewer's team, including Jackie Robinson and Satchel Paige, regularly defeated major league competition.

The most famous of the interracial barnstorming tours occurred in 1946, when Cleveland Indian pitcher Bob Feller organized a major league All-Star Team, rented two Flying Tiger aircraft and hopped the nation accompanied by the Satchel Paige All-Stars. With Feller and Paige each pitching a few innings a day, the tour proved extremely lucrative for promoters and players alike and gave widespread publicity to the skills of the black athletes.

The World War Two years marked the heyday of the Negro Leagues. With black and white workers flooding into Northern industrial centers, relatively full employment, and a scarcity of available consumer goods, attendance at all sorts of entertainment events increased dramatically. In 1942, three million fans saw Negro League teams play, while the East-West game in 1943 attracted over 51,000 fans. "Even the white folks was coming out big," recalled Satchel Paige.

But World War Two also generated forces which would challenge the foundations of Jim Crow baseball. In the armed forces, baseball teams like the Black Bluejackets of the Great Lakes Naval Station team posted outstanding records against teams featuring white major leaguers. In 1945, a well-publicized tournament of teams in the European theatre featured top black players like Leon Day, Joe Green, and Willard Brown in the championship round. More significantly, the hypocrisy of blacks fighting for their country but unable to participate in the national pastime grew steadily more apparent. As wartime manpower shortages forced major league teams to rely on a 15-year-old pitcher, over-the-hill veterans, and one-armed Pete Gray, their refusal to sign black players seemed increasingly irrational. "How do you think I felt when I saw a one-armed outfielder?" moaned Chet Brewer. Pitcher Nate Moreland protested, "I can play in Mexico, but I have to fight for America where I can't play." Pickets at Yankee Stadium carried placards asking, "If we are able to stop bullets, why not balls?"

Amidst this heightened awareness, organized baseball repeatedly walked to the precipice of integration, but always failed to take the final leap. In 1942, Moreland and All-American football star Jackie Robinson requested a tryout at a White Sox training camp in Pasadena, California. Robinson, in particular, impressed White Sox Jimmy Dykes but nothing came of the event. Brooklyn Dodger manager Leo Durocher publicly stated his willingness to sign blacks, only to receive a stinging rebuke from Commissioner Landis. Landis again short-circuited integration talk the following year. At the annual baseball meetings, black leaders led by actor Paul Robeson gained the opportunity to address major league owners on the issue, but Landis ruled all further discussion out of order.

In 1943, several minor and major league teams were rumored close to signing black players. In California, where winter league play had demonstrated the potential of black players, several clubs considered integration. The Los Angeles Angels of the Pacific Coast League announced tryouts for three black players, but pressure from other league owners doomed the plan. Oakland owner Vince DeVicenzi ordered Manager Johnny Vergez to consider pitcher Chet Brewer, the most popular black player on the West Coast, for the Oaks. Vergez refused and the issue died. Two years later, Bakersfield, a Cleveland Indian farm team in the California League, offered Brewer a position as player-coach, but the parent club vetoed the plan.

At the major league level, Washington Senators owner Clark Griffith called sluggers Josh Gibson and Buck Leonard into his office and asked if they would like to play in the major leagues. They answered affirmatively, but never heard from Griffith again. In Pittsburgh, *Daily Worker* sports editor Nat Low pressured Pirate owner William Benswanger to arrange a tryout for catcher Roy Campanella and pitcher Dave Barnhill. At the last minute, Benswanger canceled the audition, citing "unnamed pressures." The most promising situation occurred in Philadelphia where young Bill Veeck had arranged to buy the Phillies. Veeck planned to stock the team with Negro League stars, whom he felt sure would guarantee Philadelphia the pennant. When Commissioner Landis learned of his plans, however, Veeck suddenly found his purchase blocked.

For more than two decades, the imperial Landis had reigned over baseball as an implacable foe of integration. While hypocritically denying the existence of any "rule, formal or informal, or any understanding—unwritten, subterranean, or sub-anything—against the signing of Negro players," Landis had stringently policed the color line. His death in 1944 removed a major barrier for integration advocates.

In April 1945, with World War Two entering its final months, the integration crusade gained momentum. On April 6, *People's Voice* sportswriter Joe Bostic appeared at the Brooklyn Dodger training camp at Bear Mountain, New York, with two Negro League players, Terris McDuffie and Dave "Showboat" Thomas, and demanded a tryout. An outraged, but outmaneuvered Dodger President Branch Rickey, allowed the pair to work out with the club. One week later, a more serious confrontation occurred in Boston. The Red Sox, under pressure from popular columnist Dave Egan and city councilman Isidore Muchnick, agreed to audition Sam Jethroe, the Negro League's leading hitter in 1944, second baseman Marvin Williams, and Kansas City Monarch shortstop Jackie Robinson, all top prospects in their mid-twenties. The Fenway Park tryout, however, proved little more than a formality and the players never again heard from the Red Sox.

The publicity surrounding these events, however, forced the major leagues to address the issue at its April meetings. At the urging of black sportswriter Sam Lacy, Leslie O'Connor, Landis's interim successor, established a Major League Committee on Baseball Integration in April 1945, to review the problem. In addition, the racial views of newly appointed Commissioner A. B. "Happy" Chandler came under close scrutiny. A former governor of the segregated state of Kentucky, Chandler nonetheless offered at least verbal support to the entry of blacks into organized ball. "If a black boy can make it on Okinawa and Guadalcanal, hell, he can make it in baseball," Chandler told black reporter Rick Roberts. Whether Chandler, however, unlike Landis, would reinforce his rhetoric with positive actions remained uncertain.

Unbeknownst to the integration advocates, baseball officials, and local politicians sand-dancing around the race issue, Branch Rickey, the president of the Brooklyn Dodgers, had already set in motion the events which would lead to the historic breakthrough.

Raised in rural Ohio in a strict Methodist family, Rickey, nicknamed by sportwriters "The Deacon" and "The Mahatma," had financed his way through college and law school playing and coaching baseball. His skills as a catcher merited two years in the major leagues. In 1913, he abandoned a fledgling law career to manage the St. Louis Browns, and in 1917 he began a 25-year relationship with the St. Louis Cardinals. Rickey served as the field manager of the Cardinals from 1919–1925, after which he became the club's vice-president and business manager. In the 1920s and 1930s, Rickey perfected the farm system, whereby a major league team controlled young, undeveloped players through a chain of minor league franchises. This innovation allowed the Cardinals to compete equally with richer teams in larger cities, generating pennants for the "Gas House Gang" and allowing the team to profitably sell off surplus talent.

Although Rickey later claimed that his desire to integrate baseball dated from 1904, when an Indiana hotel had denied lodgings to a black player on his college squad, he gave no indication of any interest in the race issue during his years in St. Louis. Perhaps this stemmed from the fact that St. Louis was a Southern city with firmly entrenched segregationist traditions. Throughout Rickey's reign with the Cardinals, blacks sat in Jim Crow sections at Sportsman's Park, a policy which he never openly challenged.

Nonetheless, in 1942, when Rickey left the Cardinals and assumed control of the Brooklyn Dodgers, he informed the Dodger ownership of his intentions to recruit black players in the near future. Rickey never clearly explained the motivations for this dramatic turnaround. At times Rickey cited moral considerations, stating, "I couldn't face my God much longer knowing that His black creatures are held separate and distinct from His white creatures in the game that has given me all I own." On other occasions, he eschewed the role of "crusader," proclaiming, "My selfish objective is to win baseball games. . .The Negroes will make us winners for years to come." Some observers saw financial reasons behind Rickey's actions, citing the lure of the growing black population in Northern cities and the prospects of increased attendance. Certainly, Brooklyn offered a more congenial atmosphere for integration than St. Louis. In all probability, a combination of these factors—geographic, moral, competitive, and financial—coupled with Rickey's desire for a broader role in history, impelled him to seek black players.

From 1942–1945, Rickey, a conservative, cautious, and conspiratorial man, moved slowly, studying the philosophical and sociological ramifications of integration and taking few people into his confidence. During the spring and summer of 1945, under the guise of creating a new black baseball circuit, the United States League, Rickey's scouts combed the nation and the Caribbean for black players. Rickey sought one player who would spearhead the breakthrough and several other potential stars who would follow in his wake. By August 1945, scouting reports and Rickey's own investigations pointed to one man as the ideal candidate for the struggle ahead—Kansas City Monarch shortstop Jackie Robinson.

In Robinson, Rickey had found a rare combination of athletic ability, competitive fire, intelligence, maturity, and poise. Born in Georgia and raised in Pasadena, California, Robinson had won fame at UCLA as the nation's greatest all-around athlete, earning All-America honors in football, establishing broad-jump records, and leading his basketball conference in scoring, all in addition to his baseball exploits. In 1942, he enlisted in the army where he attended officer's candidate school and became a lieutenant. Two years later, while stationed in Texas, Robinson's refusal to move to the back of a bus resulted in a court martial and ultimate acquittal. This incident demonstrated his commitment to the cause of equal rights. After his discharge from the army, Robinson joined the Monarchs and earned a starting spot in the 1945 East-West All-Star Game. Robinson's college education, experience in interracial athletics, and army career complemented his playing talents. But his fiery pride and temper seemed a potential obstacle to his success.

On August 28, 1945, Robinson met with Rickey at the latter's Brooklyn offices. Rickey revealed his bold plan to integrate organized baseball and challenged Robinson to accept the primary role. The Mahatma flamboyantly playacted, assuming the role of racist players, fans and hotel clerks, impressing upon Robinson the need to "turn the other cheek" in the event of racial confrontations. By the end of the session, Robinson had signed a contract to play for the Montreal Royals in the International League, the top farm team in the Brooklyn system. Rickey promised that if Robinson's performance merited it, he would be promoted to the Dodgers.

Rickey intended to announce the Robinson signing along with that of several other black players, but political pressures stemming from the New York City fall elections forced him to abandon his original plans and, on October 23, 1945, to reveal the signing of Robinson alone. The announcement sent shock waves through the baseball establishment and placed Robinson into a spotlight that he would never relinquish. Numerous sports figures, from players to executives to reporters, predicted the ultimate failure of Rickey's "great experiment."

Robinson's first test came at spring training in Florida in 1946. Thrust into the deep South where Jim Crow reigned supreme, Robinson and black pitcher John Wright, whom Rickey had recruited to room with Robinson, found themselves unable to room with their teammates and barred from playing in Jacksonville and other Florida cities. In addition, a shoulder injury hindered Robinson's performance, raising doubts about his abilities.

On April 18, 1946, at Roosevelt Stadium in Jersey City, Robinson became the first black to appear in modern Organized Baseball (excepting Jimmy Claxton, who passed as white in 1916 for the Oakland Oaks of the Pacific Coast League). In the process he staged one of the most remarkable performances under pressure in the history of the game. In Robinson's second at-bat, he hit a three-run home run. He followed this with three singles and two stolen bases, scoring a total of four runs. As the *New York Times* reported, "This would have been a big day for any man, but under the circumstances, it was a tremendous feat."

In many respects, 1946 proved a nightmare season for Robinson. Fans jeered him in Baltimore, and opposing players tormented him with insults. Pitchers made him a frequent target of brushback pitches and baserunners attempted to spike and maim him at second base. As the season drew to a close, Robinson hovered on the brink of a nervous breakdown. Through it all, however, Robinson remained a dominant force on the field. His .349 batting average and 113 runs-scored led the league and paced the Royals to the International League pennant. His presence inspired new attendance records throughout the circuit. In the Little World Series, which pitted Montreal against the Louisville Colonels of the American Association, Robinson braved the hostility of Kentucky fans and stroked game-winning hits in the final two games to give the Royals the championship.

Rickey's initiative and Robinson's dramatic success failed to inspire other team owners. In August, major league executives debated a controversial report discussing the "Race Question" which argued that integration would "lessen the value of several major league franchises." No other clubs moved to sign black players. Only four blacks, all in the Brooklyn system, joined Robinson in organized baseball in 1946. At Nashua, New Hampshire, in the New England League, the Dodger farm club fielded catcher Roy Campanella and pitcher Don Newcombe. The Nashua Dodgers won the league championship largely due to Campanella's hitting and Newcombe's hurling. In the small town of Trois Rivières in Quebec, pitchers John Wright and Roy Partlow, both of whom had appeared briefly with Robinson at Montreal, led a third Dodger farm team to the Canadian-American league crown. Nonetheless, at the start of the 1947 season, no additional black players appeared on major or minor league rosters.

Although Robinson's performance at Montreal merited promotion to the Dodgers, Robinson remained a Royal when he reported to spring training in 1947. Rickey hoped that the Brooklyn players themselves, when exposed to Robinson's talents, would request his addition to the team. He switched Robinson to first base, a weak spot on the Dodger squad, to make his case more compelling. Robinson compiled a .519 batting average against the major leaguers, but several Dodger players, instead of demanding his promotion, rebelled. Led by "Dixie" Walker, a group of mostly Southern Dodgers circulated a petition against Robinson. Rickey moved quickly to short-circuit the dissension, threatening to trade any athletes who opposed Robinson. In addition, the refusal of Pete Reiser, "Pee Wee" Reese and other Dodger stars to support the protestors, effectively squelched the petition drive. Finally, on April 10, just five days before the start of the 1947 season, Rickey officially announced that Robinson would join the Dodgers.

Throughout the early months of the 1947 campaign Robinson stoically endured crises and challenges. The Philadelphia Phillies, led by manager Ben Chapman, unleashed a barrage of verbal abuse against Robinson which horrified Dodger players and fans. The Benjamin Franklin Hotel in Philadelphia refused lodgings for Robinson and death threats appeared among his voluminous daily mail. In early May, rumors that the St. Louis Cardinals planned to strike rather than compete against Robinson prompted National League President Ford Frick to warn the players, "If you do this you will be suspended from the league." Opposing pitchers targeted Robinson's body at a record setting pace and an early season 0 for 20 batting drought led many to question his qualifications. "But for the fact that he is the first acknowledged Negro in major league history," observed a Cincinnati sportswriter, "he would have been benched a week ago."

Yet, as the season unfolded, Robinson converted doubters and enemies into admirers. By the end of June, a 21-game hitting streak had raised his batting average to .315 and propelled the Dodgers into first place. Robinson's

daring baserunning, typical of Negro League play, evoked images of an "Ebony Ty Cobb." In city after city, record crowds flocked to experience Robinson's charismatic dynamism as five teams set new all-time season attendance marks. While periodic controversies erupted over baserunners who used their spikes "to make a pincushion out of Robinson" at first base, Robinson won the acceptance and respect of teammates and opponents alike. In September, as the Dodgers coasted to the pennant, the *Sporting News* named Robinson the major league Rookie of the Year. To cap his triumphant season, Robinson became the first black player to appear in the World Series.

Robinson's success on the field and at the box office stimulated some movement on the part of other clubs to hire black players. In Cleveland Bill Veeck recruited 23-year-old Larry Doby, who jumped straight from the Negro League Newark Eagles to the Indians in July. Used sparingly, Doby batted a meager .156, casting doubts upon his future. The St. Louis Browns, seeking to boost flagging attendance, signed Willard Brown and Hank Thompson of the Kansas City Monarchs. When the turnstiles failed to respond, the Browns released both Brown and Thompson, although the latter had established himself as a top prospect. In the National League, the Dodgers signed Dan Bankhead to bolster the club's pitching down the stretch. On August 25, Bankhead, the first black pitcher to appear in the major leagues, surrendered eight runs in three innings but also slammed a home run in his initial at bat.

In addition to the five athletes who appeared in the major leagues, a handful of blacks surfaced in the minors. Campanella succeeded Robinson at Montreal, earning accolades as "the best catcher in the business." Newcombe returned to Nashua where he won 19 games. The independent Stamford Bombers of the Colonial League fielded six black players, and two blacks, including future major leaguer Chuck Harmon, played in the Canadian-American League. Veteran Negro League hurler Nate Moreland won 20 games in California's Class C Sunset League. For the most part, however, organized baseball continued to ignore the treasure trove of black talent submerged in the Negro Leagues. A full year would pass before additional major league teams would add black players to their chains.

In 1948, the integration focus shifted from the Dodgers, where Robinson now reigned at second base, to the Cleveland Indians. In spring training, Larry Doby, who had performed so dismally in 1947, unexpectedly won a starting berth in the Cleveland outfield. After an erratic early season stretch in which Doby alternated errors and strikeouts with tape-measure home runs, he batted .301 and became a key performer for the American League champion Indians. In July, Cleveland owner Bill Veeck added the legendary Satchel Paige to the team. Amidst charges that his signing had been a publicity stunt, the 42-year-old Paige won six out of seven decisions, including back-to-back shutouts, and posted a 2.47 earned run average. Standing-room-only crowds greeted him in Washington, Chicago, Boston, and even in Cleveland's mammoth Municipal Stadium. The Indians, after defeating the Boston Red Sox in a pennant playoff, won the World Series in six games with Doby's .318 average leading the club.

In 1947, the Dodgers had integrated and reached the

World Series; in 1948, the Indians had duplicated and surpassed this achievement. Both teams had set all-time attendance records. Remarkably, as the 1948 season drew to a close, no other franchise had followed their lead. In the minor leagues, Roy Campanella became the first black in the American Association, stopping at St. Paul before permanently joining Robinson on the Dodgers. Newcombe and Bankhead each won more than 20 games for Brooklyn affiliates. The Dodgers also added fleet-footed Sam Jethroe to the Montreal roster, where he batted .322. The Indians also began to stockpile black talent, signing future major leaguers Al Smith, Dave Hoskins, and Orestes "Minnie" Minoso to minor league contracts. Several other blacks, including San Diego catcher John Ritchey, who broke the Pacific Coast League color line, played for independent teams.

In the interregnum between the 1948 and 1949 seasons four more teams—the Giants, Yankees, Braves, and Cubs—signed blacks to play in their farm systems, and 1949 would herald the beginning of widespread integration in the minor leagues. Blacks starred in all three Triple A leagues. In the Pacific Coast League, Luke Easter won acclaim as the "greatest natural hitter . . . since Ted Williams," amassing 25 home runs and 92 runs-batted-in in just 80 games before succumbing to a knee injury. Oakland's Artie Wilson led the league in hits, stolen bases, and batting average. In the International League, Jethroe scored 151 runs and stole 89 bases while Montreal teammate Dan Bankhead won 20 games for the second straight year. At Jersey City, Monte Irvin batted .373. The outstanding performer in the American Association was Ray Dandridge. Considered by many the greatest third baseman of all time, the acrobatic Dandridge, now in his late 30s, thrilled Minneapolis fans with his spectacular fielding, batting .364 in the process. Former Negro Leaguers turned in equally stellar performances at lower minor league levels as well.

In the major leagues, the spotlight again returned to Jackie Robinson. For three years, Robinson had honored his pledge to Branch Rickey "to turn the other cheek" and avoid confrontations. With his position in the majors firmly established, Robinson announced, "They better be prepared to be rough this year, because I'm going to be rough on them." The more combative Robinson produced his finest year, batting .342 and earning the Most Valuable Player Award. Complemented by teammates Newcombe and Campanella, Robinson led the Dodgers to another pennant.

By the end of the 1949 season, integration had achieved spectacular success at both the major and minor league level, but most teams moved "with all deliberate speed" in signing black players. The New York Giants joined the interracial ranks in 1949 when they promoted Monte Irvin and Hank Thompson. The following year, the Boston Braves purchased Jethroe from the Dodgers for $100,000 and installed him in the starting lineup. In 1951, the Chicago White Sox acquired Minnie Minoso in a trade with Cleveland, and Bill Veeck, who had acquired the hapless St. Louis Browns, brought back Satchel Paige for another major league stint. Yet, as late as August 1953, out of sixteen major league teams only these six fielded black players. Several teams displayed an interest in signing blacks but bypassed established Negro League stars

who might have jumped directly to the majors, concentrating instead on younger prospects for the minor leagues. Still others like the Red Sox, Phillies, Cardinals, and Tigers continued to pursue a whites-only policy.

This failure to hire and promote blacks occurred amidst a continuing backdrop of outstanding performances by black players. The first generation of players from the Negro Leagues proved an extraordinary group. Jackie Robinson quickly established himself as one of the dominant stars in the national pastime, compiling a .311 batting average over his 10-year career while thrilling fans with his baserunning and clutch-hitting talents. Sportswriters called him, "the most dangerous man in baseball today." Campanella won accolades as the best catcher in the National League and won the Most Valuable Player Award in 1951, 1953, and 1955. Both Campanella and Robinson later won election to the Baseball Hall of Fame. Pitcher Don Newcombe averaged better than 20 wins a season during his first five full years with the Dodgers. In addition, from 1950-1953 Negro League graduates Sam Jethroe, Willie Mays, Joe Black, and Jim Gilliam each won the National League Rookie of the Year Award.

In the American League, where integration proceeded at a slower pace, several players compiled outstanding records. Larry Doby, while never achieving the superstar status many expected, nonetheless became a steady producer, twice leading the league in home runs and five times driving in more than 100 runs. His Cleveland teammate Luke Easter, who reached the majors in his mid-30s, slugged 86 home runs and drove in 300 runs in his brief three-season career. Satchel Paige, after a two-year stint with the Indians, joined the hapless St. Louis Browns from 1951-1953 and became one of the American League's best relief pitchers. On the Chicago White Sox, Minnie Minoso proved himself a consistent .300 hitter. Despite their relatively small numbers, teams with black players in both major leagues regularly finished high in the standings and only in 1950 did both pennant winners field all-white squads. In addition, the more aggressive stance of National League teams in recruiting black players gave that circuit a clear superiority in World Series and All-Star contests for more than two decades.

By the end of the 1953 season, the benefits of integration had grown apparent to all but the most recalcitrant of major league owners. In September, the Chicago Cubs purchased shortstop Ernie Banks from the Kansas City Monarchs and finally elevated longtime minor league standout Gene Baker. Connie Mack's Philadelphia Athletics ended their Jim Crow era by acquiring pitcher Bob Trice. At the start of the 1954 season, the Washington Senators, St. Louis Cardinals, Pittsburgh Pirates, and Cincinnati Reds all joined the interracial ranks. The sudden integration of six more clubs left only the Yankees, Tigers, Phillies, and Red Sox with all-white personnel. In addition, 1954 marked the debut of young Henry Aaron with the Braves and the return of Willie Mays, who had sparkled for the Giants in 1951, from military service.

The desegregation of organized baseball opened the way not only to blacks in the United States but to those in other parts of the Americas as well. Throughout the 20th century, baseball had imposed a curious double standard on Latin players, accepting those with light complexions but rejecting their darker countrymen. With the color barrier down, major league clubs found a wealth of talent in the Carribbean. Minnie Minoso, the "Cuban Comet" who integrated the Chicago White Sox, became the first of the great Latin stars. Over a 15-year career, Minoso compiled a .298 batting average. In 1954, slick-fielding Puerto Rican Vic Power launched his career with the Athletics. The following year, Roberto Clemente, the greatest of the Latin stars, debuted with the Pittsburgh Pirates. The proud Puerto Rican won four batting championships and amassed 3,000 hits en route to a .317 lifetime batting average. In the late 1950s, the San Francisco Giants revealed the previously ignored treasure trove that existed in the Dominican Republic. In 1958, Felipe Alou became the first of three Alou brothers to play for the Giants, and in 1960 the Giants unveiled pitcher Juan Marichal, "the Dominican Dandy," who won 243 games en route to the Hall of Fame.

Among the early Latin players were two sons of stars of the Jim Crow age. Perucho Cepeda, who had won renown as "The Bull" in his native Puerto Rico, had refused to play in the segregated Negro leagues. His son Orlando, dubbed "The Baby Bull," went on to star for the Giants and Cardinals. Luis Tiant, Sr., a standout performer in both Cuba and the Negro Leagues, lived to see Luis, Jr. win over 200 major league games and excel in the 1975 World Series.

As the major leagues moved slowly toward complete desegregation, throughout the nation blacks invaded the minor leagues. In the Northern and Western states, these athletes, a combination of youthful prospects and Negro League veterans, were greeted by a storm of insults, beanballs, and discrimination. "I learned more names than I thought we had," states Piper Davis of his treatment by fans in the Pacific Coast League. At least a half-dozen blacks had to be carried off the field on stretchers after being hit by pitches between 1949 and 1951. In city after city, blacks found hotels and restaurants unwilling to serve them. "At the same time when they signed blacks and Latins," argues John Roseboro about his Dodger employers, "they should have made sure they would be welcome." But neither the Dodgers nor other clubs provided any special assistance for their black farmhands. Despite these conditions, blacks compiled remarkable records in league after league. In the early 1950s, blacks overcame adversity and dominated the lists of batting leaders at the Triple A level and in many of the lower circuits as well.

In 1952, blacks began to appear on minor league clubs in the Jim Crow South. The Dallas Eagles of the Texas League, hoping to boost sagging attendance, signed former Homestead Gray pitcher Dave Hoskins to become the "Jackie Robinson of the Texas League." Hoskins took the Lone Star State by storm, attracting record crowds en route to a 22–10 record. The black pitcher posted a 2.12 earned run average and also finished third in the league in batting with a .328 mark. By 1955, every Texas League club except Shreveport fielded black players.

Hoskins' performance inspired other teams throughout the South to scramble for black players. In 1953, 19-year-old Henry Aaron desegregated the South Atlantic League, which included clubs in Florida, Atlanta, and Georgia, while Bill White appeared in the Carolina League. Playing for Jacksonville (a city which seven years earlier had barred Jackie Robinson), Aaron "led the league in everything but hotel accommodations." By 1954, when the United States Supreme Court issued its historic *Brown* v. *Board of Education* decision ordering school desegregation, blacks had appeared in most Southern minor leagues.

The integration of the South, however, did not proceed without incidents. Black players recall these years as "an ordeal" or a "sentence" and described the South as "enemy country" or a "hellhole." In 1953, the Cotton States League barred brothers Jim and Leander Tugerson from competing. The following year, Nat Peeples broke the color line in the Southern Association, but lasted only two weeks. For the remainder of the decade, the league adhered to a whites-only policy, a strategy which contributed to the collapse of the Southern Association in 1961. As resistance to the civil rights movement mounted in the 1950s, black players found themselves in increasingly hostile territory. Even in the pioneering Texas League, teams visiting Shreveport, Louisiana, in 1956 had to leave their black players at home due to stricter segregation laws.

In the face of these obstacles, young black stars like Aaron, Curt Flood, Frank Robinson, Bill White, and Leon Wagner overcame their frustrations "by taking it out on the ball." "What had started as a chance to test my baseball ability in a professional setting," wrote Curt Flood, "had become an obligation to test myself as a man." Throughout the 1950s, blacks appeared regularly among the league leaders of the Texas, South Atlantic, Carolina, and other circuits, advancing both their own careers and the cause of integration.

As these events unfolded in the South, the major leagues completed their long overdue integration process. In 1955, the Yankees, after denying charges of racism for almost a decade, finally promoted Elston Howard to the parent club. Two more years passed before the Phillies integrated, and not until 1958 did a black player don a Tiger uniform. Thus, at the start of the 1959 season, only the Boston Red Sox, who had yet to hire either black scouts or representatives in the Caribbean, retained their Jim Crow heritage. A storm of protest arose when the Red Sox cut black infielder Elijah "Pumpsie" Green just before Opening Day, but on July 21, 1959, 12 years and 107 days after Jackie Robinson's Dodger debut, Green won promotion to the Boston club, completing the cycle of major league integration.

While integration became a reality in organized baseball, the Negro Leagues gradually faded into oblivion. As early as 1947, Negro League attendance, especially in cities close to National League parks, dropped precipitously. "People wanted to go Brooklynites," recalls Monarch pitcher Hilton Smith. "Even if we were playing here in Kansas City, people wanted to go over to St. Louis to see Jackie." Negro League owners hoped to offset declining attendance by selling players to organized baseball, but major league teams paid what Effa Manley called "bargain basement" prices for all-star talent. In 1948, the Manleys' Newark Eagles and New York Black Yankees disbanded. The Homestead Grays severed all league connections and returned to its roots as a barnstorming unit. Without these teams, the Negro National League collapsed. A reorganized 10-team Negro American League, most of whose franchises were located in minor league cities, vowed to go on, but the spread of integration quickly thinned its ranks. By 1951, the league had dwindled to six teams. Two years later, only the Birmingham Black Barons, Memphis Red Sox, Kansas City Monarchs, and Indianapolis Clowns remained.

For several years in the early 1950s, the Negro Leagues remained a breeding ground for young black talent. The New York Giants plucked Willie Mays from the roster of the Birmingham Black Barons, while the Boston Braves discovered Hank Aaron on the Indianapolis Clowns. The Kansas City Monarchs produced more than two dozen major leaguers, including Robinson, Paige, Banks, and Howard. But for most black players, the demise of the Negro Leagues had disastrous effects. "The livelihoods, the careers, the families of 400 Negro ballplayers are in jeopardy," complained Effa Manley in 1948, "because four players were successful in getting into the major leagues." The slow pace of integration left most in a state of limbo set adrift by their former teams, but still unwelcomed in organized baseball. Some players like Buck Leonard and Cool Papa Bell were too old to be considered, while others like Ray Dandridge and Piper Davis found themselves relegated to the minor leagues, where outstanding records failed to win them promotion.

Throughout the 1950s the Negro American League struggled to survive, recruiting teenagers and second-rate talent for the modest four-team loop. In 1963, Kansas City hosted the 30th and last East-West All-Star Game and the following year the famed Monarchs ceased touring the nation. By 1965, the Indianapolis Clowns remained as a last vestige of Jim Crow baseball. Utilizing white as well as black players, the Clowns continued for another decade. "We are all show now," explained their owner. "We clown, clown, clown."

But the legacy of the Negro Leagues remained. Robinson and other early black players introduced new elements of speed and "tricky baseball" into the major leagues, transforming and improving the quality of play. Since 1947, blacks have led the National League in stolen bases in all but two seasons. In the American League, a black or Latin baserunner has topped the league every year since 1951 with only two exceptions. Nor did this injection of speed come at the expense of power. In the 1950s and 1960s, Hank Aaron, Willie Mays, and Frank Robinson reigned as the greatest power hitters in baseball. Thus, by the 1960s, the national pastime more closely resembled the well-balanced offensive structure of the Negro Leagues than the unidimensional power-oriented attack that had typified the all-white majors.

The demise of the Negro Leagues and the decline of segregation in the majors, however, did not end discrimination. Conditions on and off the field, in spring training and in the executive suites, repeatedly reminded the black athletes of their second-class status. In the early 1950s, all-white teams taunted their black opponents with racial insults. Blacks like Jackie and Frank Robinson, Minnie Minoso and Luke Easter repeatedly appeared among the league leaders in being hit by pitches. While black superstars like Willie Mays had little difficulty ascending to the major leagues, players of only slightly above average talent found themselves buried for years in the minors. Many observers charged that teams had imposed quotas on the number of blacks they would field at one time.

In cities like St. Louis, Washington, D. C., and, later, Baltimore, black ballplayers could not stay at hotels with their teammates. In 1954, they achieved a breakthrough of sorts when the luxury Chase Hotel in St. Louis informed Jackie Robinson and other Dodger players that they could room there, but had to refrain from using the dining room or swimming pool or loitering in the lobby. Ten years later, the hotel had removed these restrictions, but still relegated black players, according to Hank Aaron, to rooms "looking out over some old building or some green pastures or a blank wall, so nobody can see us through a window."

Blacks faced even greater discrimination each year in spring training in Florida. While all spring training sites now accepted blacks, segregation statutes and local traditions forced them to live in all-black boarding houses far from the luxury air-conditioned hotels which accommodated white players. "The whole set-up is wrong," protested Jackie Robinson. "There is no reason why we shouldn't be able to live with our teammates." When teams traveled from place to place, blacks could not join their fellow players in restaurants. Instead they had to wait on the bus until someone brought their food out to them. Some teams attempted to reduce the problems faced by blacks. Several clubs moved to Arizona, where conditions were only moderately improved. The Dodgers built a special spring training camp at Vero Beach where players could live together. Most organizations, however, did very little to assist their black employees.

By the time that Jackie Robinson retired in 1956, conditions had barely improved. "After 10 years of traveling in the South," he charged, " I don't think advances have been fast enough. It's my belief that baseball itself hasn't done all it can to remedy the problems faced by . . . players." Over the next decade, a new generation of black players militantly demanded change. Cardinal stars Bill White, Curt Flood, and Bob Gibson protested against conditions in St. Petersburg, while Aaron and other black Braves demanded changes in Bradenton. In many instances, however, significant changes awaited passage of the Civil Rights Act of 1965 barring segregation in public facilities.

By 1960, Robinson, Campanella, Doby, and the cadre of Negro League veterans who had formed the vanguard of baseball integration had retired. In their wake, a second generation of black players, most of whom had never appeared in the Negro Leagues, made most Americans forget that Jim Crow baseball had ever existed, as they shattered longstanding "unbreakable" records. In 1962, black shortstop Maury Wills stole 104 bases, eclipsing Ty Cobb's 47-year-old stolen base mark. Twelve years later, outfielder Lou Brock stole 118 bases en route to breaking Cobb's career stolen-base record as well. In 1966, Frank Robinson, who had won the National League Most Valuable Player Award in 1961, became the first player to win that honor in both leagues when he led the Baltimore Orioles to the American League pennant. By the end of his career, Robinson had slugged 586 home runs; only Babe Ruth among players of the Jim Crow era had hit more. Both Ernie Banks and Willie McCovey also amassed more than 500 home runs during this era. On the pitcher's mound, the indomitable Bob Gibson proved himself one of the greatest strikeout pitchers in the game's history. Upon retirement, Gibson had amassed more strikeouts than anyone except Walter Johnson. Brock, Frank Robinson, Banks, McCovey, and Gibson all won election to the Hall of Fame in their first year of eligibility.

The greatness of these players notwithstanding, two other black players, Willie Mays and Hank Aaron, both of whom ironically had begun their careers in the Negro Leagues, reigned as the dominant stars of baseball in the 1950s and 1960s. Originally signed by the Birmingham Black Barons of the Negro American League, Mays had joined the New York Giants in midseason 1951, sparking their triumph in the most famous pennant race in history and winning the Rookie of the Year Award. After two years in the military, he returned in 1954 to bat a league-leading .345 and hit 41 home runs. The following year, he pounded 51 homers. A spectacular center fielder, Mays won widespread acclaim as the greatest all-around player in the history of the game. In 1969, he became only the second player in major league history to hit 600 home runs and took aim at Babe Ruth's legendary lifetime total of 714. Over the next four seasons, the aging Mays added 60 more homers before retiring short of Ruth's record.

Unlike Mays, who had begun his career amidst the glare of the New York media, Hank Aaron had spent his career first in Milwaukee and later in Atlanta, far distant from the center of national publicity. Nonetheless, he steadily compiled record-threatening statistics in almost every offensive category. In 1972, at age 38, he surpassed Mays's home run total and set his sights on Ruth. Entering the 1973 season, he needed just 41 home runs to catch the Babe. Performing under tremendous pressure and fanfare, Aaron stroked 40 homers, leaving him just one shy of the record. He tied Ruth's mark with his first swing of the 1974 season. Three days later, on April 8, 1974, a nationwide television audience watched Aaron stroke home run number 715. Babe Ruth's "unreachable" record thus fell to a man whose career had started with the Indianapolis Clowns of the Negro Leagues. When Aaron retired in 1976, he boasted 755 home runs and held major league records for games played, at-bats, runs batted in and extra-base hits. He also ranked second to Ty Cobb in hits and runs scored.

By the 1970s, black players had become an accepted part of the baseball scene and regularly ranked among the most well-known symbols of the sport. Reggie Jackson, Willie Stargell, and Joe Morgan had succeeded Aaron, Mays, and the Robinsons as Hall of Fame caliber superstars. Yet three decades after Jackie Robinson had broken the color barrier, racism and discrimination remained a persistent problem for baseball. Several studies demonstrated that baseball management channeled blacks into positions thought to require less thinking and fewer leadership qualities. In 1968, blacks accounted for more than half of the major league outfielders, but only 20 percent of other position players. Black catchers were rare and fewer than one in 10 pitchers were black. By 1986, the disparity had grown greater. American-born blacks comprised 70 percent of all outfield positions but only 7 percent of all pitcher, second basemen, and third basemen positions. There were no American-born black catchers in the major leagues at the start of the 1986 season.

While superior black players had open access to the major leagues, those of average or slightly above average skills often found their paths blocked. "The Negro player may have to be better qualified than a white player to win the same position," argued Aaron Rosenblatt in 1967. "The undistinguished Negro player is less likely to play in the major leagues than the equally undistinguished white player." Rosenblatt demonstrated that black major leaguers on the whole batted 20 points higher than whites. As batting averages dropped, so did the proportion of blacks. This trend continued into the 1980s. A 1982 study revealed that 70 percent of all black non-pitchers were everyday starters, indicating a substantial bias against blacks who filled utility or pinch-hitting roles. Statistics compiled in 1986 showed a strikingly similar pattern.

The subtle nature of this on-the-field discrimination obscured it from public controversy. The failure of baseball to provide jobs for blacks in managerial and front office positions, however, became an increasing embarrassment. In the early years of integration, baseball executives bypassed the substantial pool of experienced Negro Leaguers from consideration for managerial and coaching positions. A handful of blacks, including Sam Bankhead, Nate Moreland, Marvin Williams, and Chet Brewer managed independent, predominantly all-black teams in the minor leagues. The first generation of black major leaguers fared no better. "We bring dollars into club treasuries when we play," exclaimed Larry Doby, "but when we stop playing, our dollars stop." No major league organization hired a black pilot at any level until 1961 when the Pittsburgh Pirates placed Gene Baker at the helm of their Batavia franchise. By the mid-1960s no blacks had managed in the majors and only two had held full-time major league coaching positions. The first black umpire did not appear in the majors until 1966, when Emmett Ashford appeared in the American League.

In the final years of his life, Jackie Robinson made repeated pleas for baseball to eliminate these lingering vestiges of Jim Crow. "I'd like to live to see a black manager," he stated before a national television audience at the 1972 World Series. Nine days later he died, his dream unfulfilled. In 1975, the Cleveland Indians hired Frank Robinson to be the first black major league manager. This precedent, however, opened few new doors. Robinson lasted two-and-a-half seasons with the Indians, later managed the San Francisco Giants for four years, and in 1988 was made manager of the Baltimore Orioles. Maury Wills and Larry Doby each had brief half-season stints as managers. After four decades of integration, only these three men had received major league managerial opportunities.

A similar situation existed in major league front offices. Only one black man, Bill Lucas of the Atlanta Braves, had served as a general manager. As late as 1982, a survey of 24 clubs (the Yankees and Red Sox refused to provide information) found that of 913 available white-collar baseball jobs, blacks held just 32 positions. Among 568 full-time major league scouts, only 15 were black. While many teams hired former players as announcers, few employed blacks in these roles. Five years later, conditions had not improved. Of the top 879 administrative positions in baseball only 17 were filled by blacks and 15 by Hispanics. Four teams in California—the Dodgers, Giants,

Athletics, and Angels—accounted for almost two-thirds of the minority hiring. Ten out of 14 American League teams, and five of 12 National League franchises had no blacks in management positions.

These shortcomings came to haunt baseball in 1987. Commissioner Peter Ueberroth had dedicated the season to the commemoration of the fortieth anniversary of Jackie Robinson's major league debut. As the celebration began, Los Angeles Dodger general manager Al Campanis, who had played with Robinson at Montreal, appeared on ABC-TV's *Nightline*. When asked about the dearth of black managers, Campanis explained that blacks "may not have some of the necessities to be, let's say, a field manager or general manager." Campanis's statement, which surely reflected the thinking of many baseball executives, evoked a storm of protest, and precipitated his resignation. An embarrassed Ueberroth pledged to take action to bring more blacks into leadership positions and hired University of California sociologist Harry Edwards to facilitate the process. Fifty blacks and Latins with past or present connections to baseball created their own Minority Baseball Network to apprise blacks of employment opportunities and to lobby clubs to recruit more minorities for front office jobs.

When the controversy of 1987 had subsided, few franchises had taken significant steps to increase minority hiring. Several clubs added blacks to administrative positions, but none offered field or general manager positions to nonwhite candidates. In 1988 Frank Robinson received his third chance to manage in the major leagues, this time with the Baltimore Orioles. At midseason 1989 Cito Gaston assumed the reins of the Toronto Blue Jays. When the squads managed by Robinson and Gaston had their initial confrontation, it marked, after 40 years of integration, the first time that two teams managed by black men had competed in a major league game. Fittingly, on the final weekend of the season, the Orioles and Blue Jays met face-to-face in a series to decide the championship of the American League Eastern Division. The spectacle offered a resounding rebuke to the shortsightedness and persistent discrimination that continues to plague the national pastime.

The Minor Leagues

Bob Hoie

The International Association, founded in 1877, is frequently described as the first minor league. For two major reasons it shouldn't be so regarded. First, it was barely a league. Structurally it resembled the old National Association—there was virtually no central authority, no limitation on the number or location of member teams, no set schedule, and haphazard umpire selection. The league was so loosely assembled in fact that some member teams competed at the same time for the championships of other organizations like the New England Association and the League Alliance. Second, the International Association was originally established as a rival to the National League and never officially recognized itself as being subordinate. It was generally acknowledged that several of its teams were as good as or better than some in the National League. Various off-the-field problems, administrative weaknesses, and a lack of solidarity and resolve on the part of the member clubs assured its subordinate status.

A strong case could be made for the 1879 Northwestern League as the first minor league—it had a preset schedule and had no pretensions of rivaling the National League, but the absence of league-appointed umpires led to frequent forfeits due to charges of biased "hometown" umpiring, and the league folded after only two months.

The Eastern Association was founded in 1881, but this was another loose alliance with no set schedule.

The first recognized minor league was another Northwestern League, this one organized on October 27, 1882. At that time they requested of the National League cooperation and reciprocity in protecting player contracts. This was necessary because independent clubs frequently lost their best players during the course of the season to the National League and later to the American Association clubs. In response to this request, the National League, American Association, and Northwestern League signed a "Tripartite Agreement" in March 1883. This agreement bound the clubs to honor the contracts of players on reserve lists, assured mutual recognition of expulsions and suspensions, established territorial rights, and created an arbitration committee to settle disputes. Minimum salaries were established and pegged at a higher level in the National League and American Association than in the Northwestern League or "any other parties to the agreement," thus by implication assigning a "major" and "minor" status to the leagues.

The Interstate Association was established early in 1883 and was quickly accepted as an "alliance" league by the American Association, becoming a junior partner of the Tripartite Agreement. Both the Northwestern and the Interstate opened their seasons on May 1, 1883. Each had a formal league organization, a schedule that was preset before the season opening, and a complement of umpires appointed and paid for by the league. Both leagues recognized and accepted their status as subordinate to the two "majors." In 1884 the Interstate Association reorganized as the Eastern League and became a fourth member of what now became known as the National Agreement.

In October 1885 a new National Agreement was adopted which made the National League and American Association the principal parties and removed from minor league clubs the protection of the reserve clause. Two years later the reserve clause was reinstated for the minors, but the major-minor league distinction had been formalized. Following the collapse of the American Association in 1892, another National Agreement for the first time established minor league classifications and gave major league clubs the right to draft minor league players at fixed prices.

While these events were taking place, organized baseball expanded dramatically, going from two leagues in 1883 to seventeen by 1890. Baseball was played throughout the country, of course, but organized ball was confined to the northeast quadrant of the United States in 1884; it expanded to the South in 1885, to Colorado and the upper Midwest in 1886, California in 1887, Texas in 1888, and the Pacific Northwest in 1890. So in the year that the American frontier was officially declared closed, organized baseball had extended to all corners of the country.

In 1887 an organization called the Negro Baseball League, fearing player raids by the still moderately integrated minors, sought and received protection under the National Agreement. The league was to play in eight cities that also had major league teams, but it folded in less than two weeks. This was unfortunately characteristic of the era. Many teams and leagues were underfinanced and were ultrasensitive to changes in the national or local economy. In addition, being unable or unwilling to pay the required fees for reserving their players, they lost their better ones at the close of the season—and those teams that even managed to finish the season could usually consider themselves lucky. During the nineteenth century, more than one-third of the leagues that started a season failed to finish it. There was, however, a solid core of support for minor league baseball. Regardless of how many leagues started each season—usually about fifteen but sometimes up to nineteen—ten usually finished; the rest failed. The 1890s were not a period of expansion nor of stability as throughout the decade an average of 40 percent of the leagues that started a season failed to finish it. A depression in 1892–1893 and the Spanish-American

War in 1898 were significant factors, but a proliferation of "fly-by-night" operators played a role as well.

At the close of the 1900 season, the still minor American League withdrew from the National Agreement, announcing through that action its intention not to allow its players to be drafted and not to respect the reserve clause or territorial rights any longer.

In September 1901 the National League announced its intention to abrogate the National Agreement, contending that with the American League invading its cities and raiding its players the National League could not be expected to sit back and abide by restrictions which did not hinder its rival. Essentially this meant that the National, like the American, considered the players on minor league rosters "fair game."

In immediate reaction to this, the presidents of seven minor leagues met in Chicago on September 5, 1901, and in an act of self-protection they organized the National Association of Professional Baseball Leagues. On October 25 representatives of nine minor leagues met in New York and adopted a new "National Agreement." This new agreement established league classifications, roster and salary limits, and a draft system; it recognized reserve lists and created a Board of Arbitration which was given the power to suspend players, clubs, or officials for violations of the agreement. By the beginning of the 1902 season, the National Association included fifteen member leagues.

The American and National Leagues ratified a peace agreement early in 1903, and in late August the presidents of the two major leagues and the National Association drafted a National Agreement which was initially rejected by the minors. After some concessions were made by the majors, such as a prohibition on "farming," the plan was adopted in September. The agreement formalized relations between the majors and minors and established a National Commission to serve as a Board of Arbitration.

These agreements were necessary because the majors and minors were mutually dependent on each other. The majors needed the minors as a reliable source of talent, while the minors, many of whom relied on player sales to stay in business, needed assurances from the majors that they would recognize their property rights in players.

Despite this mutual dependence there was a basic buyer-seller conflict. The majors wanted to acquire players as cheaply as possible, while the minors wanted to sell them for as much as possible. This same conflict existed within the minors as well, with the highest-classification clubs wanting to buy cheaply from the lower minors and sell at high prices to the majors. Thus the National Agreement, the major-minor agreement, and the National Association itself were uneasy alliances of clubs and leagues with competing and often conflicting objectives, and the nearly annual revisions in draft rules and prices and limits on optional player assignments were required to maintain the equilibrium necessary to keep the alliance intact.

The majors favored an unlimited draft—i.e., any player on a minor league roster could be purchased for a fixed rate. As early as 1896, when Minneapolis of the Western League was decimated through what were in effect forced sales, it became clear that some limitations were necessary, so by 1905 only one player could be drafted from a

club per year. The draft prices of top-classification minor leaguers went from $750 to $1,000 in 1905 and then to $2,500 in 1911. While these prices were not particularly low for average prospects in that era, they were well below the value of the best prospects in the minors; thus the draft or the threat of it served as an incentive for minor league clubs at all levels to sell their better players to major or higher-classification minor league clubs at competitive market prices. From the players' standpoint, the draft had the positive effect of allowing them eventually to advance to whatever levels their ability would take them. The lower-classification minor league clubs received lower draft prices for their players but seemed relatively satisfied with the system—after all, this was an era when the contracts of Tris Speaker, Rogers Hornsby, and Ty Cobb were sold to major league clubs for $400, $500, and $700 respectively.

On the other hand, many of the higher-classification minor league clubs had never really been satisfied with the draft. As early as 1908, this dissatisfaction nearly caused the two top minor leagues at that time—the American Association and the Eastern League—to go independent. Several of the top minor league clubs drew more fans annually than some major league clubs and represented substantial investments; their owners were understandably not happy with a system that forced the sale of their top players for below-market prices to the majors; in addition to the challenge to club stability and autonomy caused by the draft, the gap between the market value of the top prospects and the draft price widened throughout the 1910s.

Despite the rumblings of discontent, the establishment of the National Association ushered in a period of minor league expansion to a fairly stable core of thirty leagues. While there were still leagues that failed to finish the season, the failure rate was down to 10–15 percent. For some reason, in 1910 the minors reached a level never to be topped until the post–World War Two boom era—fifty-two leagues started the season and forty-six finished it. For the next five years more leagues folded, but each season generally closed with forty leagues operating. Then, for reasons that ranged from the automobile, movies, the war in Europe, and the Federal League War, the bottom started to drop out. Forty-four leagues started in the 1914 season, and by the end of the 1918 season only one was operating (ten leagues had started that year—one folded and eight suspended operations due to the war).

After the 1918 season, with most of the lower minors driven out of business, the National Association, for the first time dominated by the higher minors, adopted a resolution demanding that the majors relinquish the right of the draft and end the practice of "farming out" players. When the majors as expected rejected these demands, the National Association withdrew from the National Agreement. Pending a new major agreement, the majors and minors reached general agreement on property rights in players and territorial rights, and the National Commission ruled that the major league draft would be suspended. In addition the minors would not accept major league players on option, meaning that any players owned or controlled by major league clubs in excess of the active player roster limit would have to be sold or released to minor league clubs.

A. R. Tierney, president of two minor leagues and a leader in the fight to end the draft, said, "This means that the minor leagues will be able to build fences for themselves instead of for the major leagues." He predicted expansion of the minors and higher sale prices for the players. He was correct on both counts. With no players on option, the majors needed to buy more players from the minors, some of whom they had been forced to sell but now had to buy back at higher prices, and without the draft the minor league clubs could virtually name their own price. The minors expanded, as the leagues that had been driven out of business during the war now reentered the fold.

The reappearance of the low minors again shifted the balance of power within the minors. The higher minors had never been happy with the one-league, one-vote system in the National Association. Club owners were wary of having their investments affected by the vote of what they perceived as little more than "fly-by-night" operators, and on occasion they tried to change the arrangement. But just as the majors needed the minors, so the high minors needed the low minors. Thus the high minors always stopped short of enacting measures that might drive their underlings out of the Association.

As noted previously, many of the low minors needed the revenues they received from the draft to survive, and although the minor league draft still existed, it had ceased to be a dependable source of revenue as the combination of numerous prewar minor league failures and returning military veterans yielded more than enough talent to fill the higher minors' rosters. In addition, many of the low-minor clubs did not have the resources to scout for and sign enough players to remain competitive on the field and/or at the box office; thus they were dependent on receiving some players on option.

So while most of the higher minor leagues were prospering as never before under the new independence, by 1920 the low minors were ready to withdraw from the National Association if a new agreement with the majors restoring the draft was not adopted. In addition, some of the higher minor league clubs were upset that the "no-farming" rules were being circumvented by "gentleman's agreements" which enabled the major league clubs to "sell" a player to a minor league club and "buy" him back at the end of the season with little or no money actually changing hands.

On January 10, 1921, a new major-minor league agreement was signed which restored the major league draft with a top price of $5,000 but as a compromise gave individual minor leagues the right to be exempt from the draft; in addition major league clubs could option up to eight players for no more than two consecutive years, and a tax on player sales was instituted to help reduce the fake player transfers. Quickly the top three minors—the International League, Pacific Coast League, and the American Association—together with the Western and Three-I Leagues declared their exemption from the draft; this in turn prohibited them from drafting from the lower minors.

The prices the majors paid for top minor league players nearly doubled between 1919 and 1920, but they skyrocketed during the draft-exemption era. In 1921 the Giants paid $75,000 to San Francisco for Jimmy O'Connell; in 1922 the Giants paid $72,000 to Baltimore for Jack Bentley and the White Sox paid $100,000 to San Francisco for Willie Kamm. The majors clearly were not happy with this situation, and in 1922 they offered to raise the draft price to $7,500, but this failed to lure back the draft-exempt leagues. In early 1923 the majors, after considering but eventually rejecting the idea of a maximum purchase price of $25,000 for any minor league player and/or a boycott of draft-exempt leagues, declared that all players sent to the minors either by sale or option would be subject to the draft and increased the number of players who could be optioned to fifteen. Western League clubs immediately began accepting players on option under these conditions.

The prices for ballplayers remained high in 1923. Baltimore of the International League was reportedly offered $100,000 by Brooklyn for Joe Boley and sold Max Bishop to the Philadelphia A's for $50,000. Salt Lake sold Paul Strand to the A's for a reported $70,000, Louisville sold Earle Combs to the Yankees for $50,000, Toronto sold Red Wingo to the Tigers for $50,000 and Rochester sold Maurice Archdeacon to the White Sox for $50,000, but these were isolated cases. Baltimore, aided by five years of draft exemption, had built a powerhouse, but many of the higher-classification minor league clubs had not been nearly as successful and found that they needed to receive players on option to fill holes and remain competitive. Therefore at the close of the 1923 season all exempt leagues but the International agreed to the modified draft which exempted only those players who had come up through the minors. In 1924, after Baltimore sold Lefty Grove for $100,000 to the A's, the International League also fell into line.

The modified draft did nothing to reduce the prices paid for top minor league stars: Louisville sold Wayland Dean to the Giants for $72,000 in 1924, San Francisco sold Paul Waner and Hal Rhyne to Pittsburgh for $100,000 in 1925, and Baltimore continued selling star players to the majors for big prices—Tommy Thomas to the White Sox in 1925, Joe Boley to the A's in 1926, John Ogden to the Browns and George Earnshaw to the A's in 1927. In 1927 Portland (of the PCL) sold Billy Cissel to the White Sox for a package of cash and players worth over $100,000 and Oakland sold Lyn Lary and Jimmy Reese to the Yankees for $100,000. With prices like these, clubs could afford to lose a Lefty O'Doul or Hack Wilson in the modified draft.

The major-minor agreement expired at the end of the 1927 season, with the National Association members deadlocked on the issue of the draft. The majors and minors were also at an impasse, so the modified draft continued and many of the higher minor league clubs continued to prosper, both through player sales and at the gate. The Los Angeles franchise and ballpark were valued at $2 million, and in 1928 the Oakland club was sold for $500,000. But in the lower minors all was not well through the 1920s. There were generally twenty-five or thirty leagues starting each year, and an average of three or four of these would fold during the season. Leagues were operating that never should have been admitted to the National Association—for example, one of the four leagues that not unexpectedly failed in 1924 was the West Arkansas, which included six towns within a 750-square-mile area with a combined population of 16,000.

In 1929 the rift between the high and low minors widened as the low minors, rebuffed in their efforts to nullify the modified draft agreement, now attempted to impose their own draft exemption—essentially exempting from the draft any player with fewer than two seasons of organized baseball.

Early in 1931 the majors and minors finally adopted a new National Agreement, including a provision which eliminated the modified draft and granted to major league clubs greater control of talent through revised option and draft rules. The higher minors had originally objected, but the majors told them to accept the universal draft or they would no longer have any relations with them—in other words, major league teams would not sell or option players to or buy players from the American Association, the International League, or the Pacific Coast League. While such threats had been taken relatively lightly by the minors in the early days of the draft-exempt leagues, they were now taken seriously enough that in less than a month the three recalcitrant leagues capitulated to the majors' terms. In exchange for all this and largely to secure the support of the low minors, the majors agreed to sign only collegian amateurs, leaving all high-schoolers and sandlotters to the minors. Of course, by this time farm systems had developed to the point that most major league clubs could still sign noncollegian amateurs through their farm clubs.

Milwaukee had sold Fred Schulte to the Browns for a reported $100,000 in 1928, but this was the end of an era. There would be no more $100,000 minor leaguers; in fact there would be few if any minor leaguers sold for as much as $50,000 again. It would be more than fifty years before minor league clubs ever sold for as much as $500,000, and at the 1928 National Association Convention, president Mike Sexton wondered when the majors would own enough clubs to control the National Association. The farm system, an old idea now in the process of being perfected by Branch Rickey, had clearly begun to alter the way the minors operated, and despite the efforts of some—most notably Judge Landis—the trend couldn't be reversed.

The Great Depression caused a contraction of the minors in the early 1930s, but even though a near-record low of fourteen leagues opened the 1933 season, none of them folded. The minors then entered an era of unprecedented growth and stability, reaching forty-four leagues in 1940, with only two leagues failing to finish the season between 1933 and 1941. This can be attributed in part to the substantial involvement of the major leagues through outright ownership or regular infusions of money through working agreements, but there were obviously other factors at work. Judge Bramham, on becoming president of the National Association, instituted a number of reforms, many of which were aimed at getting rid of "fly-by-night" or "shoestring" operators. Minor league baseball was better promoted—they had established a public relations department in 1934—and the advent of night baseball was of incalculable value in generating attendance, which reached 20 million in 1940. Interestingly, that year 54 percent of the minor league clubs were not affiliated with any major league clubs compared to just 37 percent that operated independently in 1936.

World War Two caused the minors to drop to just ten leagues in 1944, but in the first postwar year it was up to forty-three, increasing to an all-time high of fifty-nine in 1949, and during that time no leagues folded. (In 1946 the Mexican National League, set up by organized baseball to compete with the outlaw Mexican League, is listed by the National Association as having folded during the season, but actually it only withdrew from the Association and continued to operate independently.)

According to a general consensus, it was the coming of television that caused the minors to begin to disintegrate. Between 1949 and 1963 the number of minor leagues dropped from fifty-nine to eighteen. Attendance decreased even more sharply, going from 42 million to less than 10 million over the same time period.

By 1963, the minors had become nothing more than a training ground for the majors—90 percent of the clubs were major league affiliates, and most of those that weren't were in the largely autonomous Mexican League. While television was commonly cited as the cause of the minors' contraction, some contended it was a natural response to overexpansion. Gerry Hirn, in an April 1954 *Baseball Digest* article, contended that while the number of minor leagues had dropped from fifty-nine to thirty-six, that was still too many and the minors would be stronger and more efficient if only sixteen to twenty leagues operated. Interestingly, in 1954 three leagues failed to finish the season, the most failures in peacetime since 1932; they remain the last United States–based minor leagues that failed to finish a season (the Inter-American League, which had a team in Miami but was largely based in the Caribbean, failed to finish the 1979 season—the only year it operated).

For reasons that aren't entirely clear, minor league baseball exploded in popularity in the 1980s. Attendance, which had remained stuck at 10–11 million through the 1960s and most of the 1970s, took off in the late 1970s, topping 20 million in 1987 for the first time since 1953. Louisville, which dropped out of organized ball after drawing just 116,000 in 1972, topped a million in 1983. Nashville, which dropped out in 1963 after drawing just 54,000 for the season, drew over half a million in 1980. Buffalo, which drew only 78,000 in 1969 and saw its franchise shifted to Winnipeg the following year, came back to set an all-time minor league attendance record with 1.1 million in 1988. The picture is not all positive: some franchises still draw very poorly, but now there always seems to be a willing buyer when the previous owner gets tired of losing money. The Louisville franchise, which didn't exist in 1981 (what became the Louisville franchise was at that time in Springfield, Illinois, drawing 120,000) sold for more than $4 million in 1987. Minor league franchises that fifteen years ago were given to anyone who would pay the outstanding debts were selling for nearly a million dollars.

The minors have been riding a roller coaster of success and failure over the past century—the Newark franchise which sold for a reported $600,000 during the depths of the Depression didn't even exist twenty years later. Louisville and Nashville have been slipping at the gate the last few years, so it is probably safe to assume the current wave of success won't last forever. Regardless of these fluctuations in popularity and economic viability, the minors have always been, and one can safely assume will continue to be, the primary training ground for major league players.

The Players

Great players have passed through the minors, their careers frequently going in opposite directions and occasionally teaming up or crossing in unlikely locations such as Easton, Maryland, where in 1924 Jimmie Foxx broke into organized baseball as a catcher and the player-manager was Home Run Baker in his last season as an active player. There were many others: Rube Waddell and Red Faber with Minneapolis in 1911, young Waite Hoyt and ancient Jesse Burkett with Hartford in 1916, Dazzy Vance and Roger Bresnahan with Toledo in 1917, Chief Bender and Lefty Grove with Baltimore in 1923, and more recently Enos Slaughter and Billy Williams with Houston in 1960.

Former Negro Leaguers, their careers going in opposite directions, Ray Dandridge and Willie Mays were teammates at Minneapolis in 1951 where another teammate was a seven-year minor league veteran, Hoyt Wilhelm. Wilhelm, a twenty-eight-year-old knuckleballer with a background that included three years in Class D ball and three more in the military service, at that time appeared to be a member of what in that era was a vast army of career minor leaguers, the best of whom held their own with the acknowledged major league greats passing through the minors, but who for a variety of reasons—some good, some not—would themselves spend the bulk of their careers in the minors.

For some of these players who were left behind, the DH rule came fifty years too late, because while they could hit both for average and power, they generally lacked speed or had defensive shortcomings. For others it is less clear what, if any, deficiencies kept them in the minors, but from these groups a few players emerged as true minor league greats whose impact on fans in minor league cities—Buzz Arlett in Oakland, Joe Hauser in Minneapolis, and Bunny Brief in Kansas City, to name a few—was as great as that of more renowned players in major league cities.

The greatest of the minor league players is generally acknowledged to be Buzz Arlett.

Arlett started his career as a right-handed spitball pitcher with the hometown Oakland Oaks in 1918 and went on to win 108 games, twice going over 25 wins in a season. The Detroit Tigers looked at him, but without the spitball, which he wouldn't be able to use in the majors, they did not consider him a prospect. After suffering arm trouble early in 1923, Buzz switched to the outfield. Although he had been nothing more than a fair-hitting pitcher, once becoming a regular he annually averaged nearly .360 with 30 homers and 140 RBIs through the rest of the 1920s, but early in his career as an outfielder a Cardinal scout labeled him "good hit, no field," and it stuck. Finally in 1931 he was purchased by the Phillies. The thirty-two-year-old switch-hitter batted .313 with 18 homers and 73 RBIs in a season when the National League introduced a "dead ball" in reaction to the hitting orgies of 1929–1930. However, at the end of the year Arlett was sent to Baltimore, where in 1932 he hit 4

homers in a game twice within a five-week period and led the league with 54 homers for the season, but he would never return to the majors. He spent another year with Baltimore, when he again won the home run title, a little over a month with Birmingham, and nearly three years with Minneapolis, where he had another home run championship. After a few games with Syracuse in 1937, Arlett's career was over.

In addition to his 108 wins, he hit 432 homers, a minor league record that held up until Hector Espino topped it in 1977. Arlett walked a lot, didn't strike out much, ran pretty well early in his career, had a .341 lifetime batting average—.350 after he became an outfielder—and was the only player to finish in the top five in home runs and slugging percentage in his only season in the majors. In addition, modern statistical analysis, including range factors, suggests he was nowhere near the defensive liability he was portrayed as being. He was big (6-4, 230) and gave the appearance of being lackadaisical, which apparently irritated some of his managers, but the evidence is strong that Arlett, despite nearly two decades spent in the minors, was a major-league-caliber player.

Ike Boone was another player whose hitting feats were not limited to the minors. Boone was a college teammate (at the University of Alabama) of Joe Sewell and Riggs Stephenson; his lifetime major league batting average was .319, and in his only two full seasons in the majors—1924-1925 with the Boston Red Sox—he hit .333 and .330, but due to alleged defensive deficiencies most of his career was spent in the minors. In 1929 with the Missions of San Francisco, Boone probably had the finest season any player has had in the minors. On the all-time minor league list of single-season accomplishments, his 553 total bases that year are first, his 323 hits are second, his 195 runs scored are tied for third, and his 218 RBIs are fourth. On the all-time Pacific Coast League list, his .407 average is second, and his 55 home runs are tied for fourth.

Boone's greatness wasn't confined to a single season; in four of his first eight years in the minors he hit over .400 (he was on his way to perhaps his greatest season in 1930, batting .448 with 22 homers and 96 RBIs when he was sold to Brooklyn in late June). His .402 average with San Antonio in 1923 is the highest in twentieth-century Texas League history; his .389 with New Orleans in 1921 is the fifth highest in the Southern Association; he also led the International League in batting twice. His .370 lifetime average is the minor league record for players with ten or more seasons. He had an exceptional arm, but limited range in the outfield. Although he hit 77 home runs in a season and a half with the Missions, he was not generally regarded as a power hitter. He was, however, a great pure hitter; in eleven of his fourteen seasons in the minors, he hit over .350, and there is no evidence that he couldn't hit major league pitching.

Smead Jolley was an atrocious outfielder. Stories of his defensive lapses are legion, and the statistical evidence suggests those stories are more than isolated anecdotes. Like Boone, Jolley had a powerful arm but no speed; like Arlett, he was big and awkward; and like both, he could hit—majors or minors. In the equivalent of three full major league seasons with the White Sox and Red Sox, he hit .305 and averaged 15 homers and 105 RBIs. He won six minor league batting championships—leading the Pacific Coast League in hitting three times (winning the Triple Crown with San Francisco in 1928) and the International League once. Twice he had over 300 hits in a season, and twice he drove in more than 180 runs. In the thirteen minor league seasons in which he played over 100 games, he had this run: .370, .372, .346, .397, .404, .387, .360, .372, .373, .350, .309, .373, .345. Perhaps because he spent nearly six years in the low minors, the first four as a pitcher, and had a somewhat nomadic career (he was with thirteen minor league teams), he has not always been ranked in the top echelon of minor league greats, yet he may have been the finest hitter of them all.

Minor league stars generally fit two stereotypes: one-dimensional players who could hit but could do nothing else well enough to stay in the majors—justly or not, Arlett, Boone, and Jolley were consigned to this group. Then there are those who excelled in the minors but couldn't produce in the majors. Perhaps the classic example is Bunny Brief.

Brief, born Antonio Bordetski, may have been the most dominant power hitter in the minor leagues. In major league trials with the Browns, White Sox, and Pirates between 1912 and 1917, he was consistently unimpressive—in a combined 569 at-bats, he hit .223 with 5 homers, 59 RBIs, and nearly 100 strikeouts. In the minors, however, it was a different story. Although he hit 40 or more homers only twice and never had more than 42, he had eight league home run championships. Before going up to the majors, he led the Michigan State League twice; later he led the Pacific Coast League once and the American Association five times. He also led the Association in RBIs five times (four in succession), including a league-record 191 in 1921. He had a six-year stretch (1921–1926) with Kansas City and Milwaukee, where he averaged 90 extra-base hits, 151 RBIs, and a .351 average per season. Brief also drew a lot of walks. Early in his career he had excellent speed, and although he played most of his career at first base, he was the best defensive outfielder of the big minor league sluggers, with good range and an excellent arm—yet for reasons that remain unclear, Brief never played in a major league game after his twenty-fifth birthday.

Nick Cullop was another minor league great who never produced in the majors. He, like many of the great minor league sluggers, began his career as a pitcher. In trials with the Yankees, Senators, Indians, Dodgers, and Reds between 1926 and 1931 he totaled 490 at-bats, hit 11 homers, drove in 67 runs, hit .249, and struck out 128 times. He was the first farm-system minor league star, playing 1,450 games in the Cardinal chain from 1932 to 1944. In the minors, he drove in 1,857 runs, the all-time career high, ten times exceeding 100 in a season. He hit 420 home runs, third on the all-time list.

Cullop had good speed early in his career and was a good enough outfielder to play center field into the late 1920s, but he slowed up considerably in the 1930s. While it is not clear why Brief never did well in the majors, Cullop struck out a lot even in the minors and didn't walk much—suggesting that he had holes which could be and were pitched to effectively in the majors.

Ox Eckhardt was a great football star at the University of Texas who signed with both Austin of the Texas Association and the Cleveland Indians after graduation. The resulting dispute delayed his real professional debut until he was twenty-six years old. He made up for lost time, hitting .376 with a league-leading 27 triples for Wichita and Amarillo in the Western League in 1928. That fall he played for the New York Giants of the NFL and then went to spring training with the Detroit Tigers; he didn't make it and was sent to Seattle, where he hit .354 and again led the league in triples. In the spring of 1930, he was back with the Tigers, didn't make the team and was then sent to Beaumont, where he led the Texas League with a .379 average. He was back with the Tigers in the spring of 1931, but again he didn't make the club and was sent to the Missions, where he led the PCL with a .369 average. In the spring of 1932 he was with the Boston Braves—he played 8 games at the start of the season as a pinch hitter and was then sent back to the Missions, where over the next four seasons he hit .371, .414, .378, and .399, winning the batting title three times. He went to the Dodgers in 1936, lasted 16 games batting just .182, and was sent to Indianapolis, where he hit .353 and .341 over the next two years. He hit .321 with Toledo and Beaumont in 1938, .361 with Memphis in 1939, and after hitting .293 with Dallas in 1940, he retired with a minor league career batting average of .367 and the highest career average in organized baseball—.365. (Ty Cobb's minor league record drops his overall average to .3630; Ike Boone's major league record drops his organized-baseball average to .3629.) Eckhardt has the highest single-season and career batting average in the PCL, and ten times he hit over .350.

Unlike many of the minor league stars, Eckhardt did not want for opportunities to play in the majors—counting a trial with the Indians in 1925, he had six shots, but they resulted in his playing in just 24 major league games. The reasons for his failure to make it in the majors are not obscure. Despite being an exceptional athlete with good speed early in his career, he was a poor fielder with a weak arm and no power. Although he was 6-1, 190, the left-handed-hitting Eckhardt sliced or punched almost every hit down the left field line. Reportedly managers tried to get him to pull the ball—an idea that should certainly have advanced his career in Detroit or Brooklyn—but it only served to foul up his swing, which he would rediscover after being returned to the minors.

A few minor league greats don't fit the stereotypes: Jigger Statz was the opposite of most—his strengths were speed and defense. Joe Hauser appeared to be on his way to a successful career in the majors, broke his leg, never regained his past form, and went to the minors, where he became the only player to have two 60-home-run seasons. Hector Espino spent virtually his entire career in Mexico, and while major league scouts believed he could hit in the majors, he apparently had no desire to leave his homeland.

Of the great minor league stars, Statz spent the most time in the majors—683 games—and the most time with one club: all of his eighteen minor league seasons were with Los Angeles. His 3,473 games in organized baseball were a record until broken by Pete Rose in 1983.

Statz was a great fielder; virtually all of his contemporaries considered him the best or one of the best they had seen. Playing very shallow, he reminded many of Tris Speaker. The statistics offer strong support for his claim to greatness. In four full seasons in the majors, he led the league in chances-per-game once and was second the other three years. Between 1922 and 1932 in the majors and minors he had a stretch of ten seasons in which he played in at least 100 games and never finished lower than second in chances-per-game. He had excellent speed, but during most of his career with the Angels they were a hard-hitting club that did not feature the running game, but that changed in the mid-1930s, and in the three seasons following his thirty-sixth birthday he stole 157 bases. His game was not just limited to speed and defense. A classic leadoff man of his era—a good contact hitter, small and fast—he hit .285 in the majors and .315 in the minors, collecting over 2,300 runs, 4,000 hits, 700 doubles, and 500 stolen bases in his organized-baseball career.

On April 7, 1925, the day of Babe Ruth's "big belly-ache," Joe Hauser a twenty-six-year-old first baseman beginning his fourth season with the Athletics, broke his leg in a non-contact play while fielding during a preseason game against the Phillies at Baker Bowl. He had a .304 average for his first three major league seasons and had hit 27 homers with 115 RBIs in 1924. The injury kept him out for the entire 1925 season. In 1926 he tried to come back but hit only .192. After an excellent season with Kansas City, he went back to the majors but didn't do much in stints with the Philadelphia A's and Indians. He went back to the minors and had 4½ remarkable seasons. In 1930 with Baltimore he set a professional record with 63 homers; then he dropped to 31 in 1931 but still led the league. In 1932 he went to Minneapolis, where he led the American Association in homers with 49. In 1933 he broke his own home run record with 69, and he was off to a great start in 1934—33 homers, 88 RBIs in 82 games—when he broke his kneecap, knocking him out for the season. He continued to play until 1942 but never came close to achieving the success he had in the early 1930s.

Hauser did not hit for a high average, and it has been suggested that he took enormous advantage of short right field fences in Baltimore and Minneapolis—no one would argue that point, since 50 of his 69 homers in 1933 came at home—but many greats played in Oriole and Nicollet Parks, and none came close to Hauser's two record-breaking seasons, which remain the two highest home run seasons in the high minors.

Hector Espino holds the minor league career home run record with 484, and all but 3 of those were hit in Mexico. At the end of the 1964 Mexican League season, the twenty-five-year-old first baseman, who had led the league with 46 homers and a .371 batting average, was sold by Monterrey to the St. Louis Cardinals' Jacksonville farm club. He hit .300 with those 3 homers in 100 at-bats and was invited to spring training by the Cards for 1965, but he never reported and was eventually returned to Monterrey. In the late 1960s, the California Angels coveted Espino, who had led the Mexican League in hitting in 1966–1968, but they were never able to consummate a deal. Espino was a legend in Mexico, but it has never been clear why he never tried the majors—he has given conflicting answers. Possibly he enjoyed being a big fish in a small pond—it wasn't the money, since he never made more than $18,000 a year in Mexico. He was notorious for marching to his own drummer, occasionally leaving clubs for a midseason vacation, and perhaps he was unwilling to sacrifice that independence.

Espino could hit for power and average—he led the Mexican League in batting five times and home runs four times—and scouts said he could have done the same in the majors, but like many players he played too long. His power started a sharp decline after his thirty-third birthday, and he was virtually helpless at the plate during his last two or three seasons. Nevertheless he ranks as perhaps the greatest minor league player who never played in the majors.

Great players do not have to be distributed evenly among all positions or across all eras, but the emphasis being on great hitters, the result is a number of outfielder-first baseman-designated hitter types, most of whom played in the high-scoring 1920s and 1930s.

Ray French was perhaps the best middle infielder in the minors. He spent twenty-eight years in the minors, most of it in the Pacific Coast League. He played 2,736 games at shortstop and was a brilliant fielder. In the fourteen seasons that he played more than 100 games at short, he led the league in chances-per-game seven times. He was not an outstanding hitter, but his fielding kept him around long enough for him to collect 3,254 hits—seventh on the all-time minor league list.

The two best nineteenth-century minor leaguers were first baseman Perry Werden and pitcher Willie Mains. Werden had good speed and power. He had several good years in the majors (twice leading the league in triples), won six minor league home run titles, including two seasons when he went over 40, and his .341 lifetime average was exceptionally high for that era.

Mains was the first minor league pitcher to win 300 games, reaching that figure early in 1905. A seven-time twenty-game winner, he was also an excellent hitter in an era when pitchers were frequently expected to take a shift in the outfield. Most of his career was in the New York State League, but in an interesting example of the mobility of players in the game's early years, in 1892–1893 Mains had back-to-back seasons in Portland, Oregon, and Portland, Maine.

A highly productive but not great player who deserves mention is Spencer Harris, a little lefthanded-hitting outfielder who holds the minor league career records for runs, hits, doubles, total bases, and walks. He reached those levels primarily because he kept playing until he was forty-eight years old. He did lead the American Association in homers in 1928 while at Minneapolis, but he was aided enormously by the friendly right field fence at Nicollet Park. (He averaged 17 homers a year in ten seasons with Minneapolis but only 6 a year in his sixteen other minor league seasons.) He was never thought of as the top player on his many minor league clubs—just as a good solid player of the type that formed the backbone of the minors for so many years.

There have been few minor league pitching stars of the magnitude of the great hitters. Perhaps this is because pitching is a one-dimensional skill—no pitchers were kept in the minors because they couldn't hit or field. Many of the outstanding minor league pitchers stayed there because they didn't have great stuff. Bill Thomas, who won 383 games, and Hal Turpin, who won 271 without ever getting shots at the majors, had the same statistical profile—they struck out few, walked even less, and allowed a lot of hits.

Two pitchers that didn't fit that profile, however, were Joe Martina and Dick Barrett. Martina was a power pitcher who spent most of his career with Beaumont and with his hometown New Orleans Pelicans. He held the minor league career strikeout record until ageless George Brunet broke it while toiling in the Mexican League in 1981. Martina was a workhorse, pitching over 250 innings thirteen times and was a seven-time twenty-game winner. He got his first and only big league opportunity at age thirty-five with the world champion Washington Senators in 1924.

Kewpie Dick Barrett didn't really find himself until he joined Seattle of the PCL in 1935, ten years into his professional career. A little lefthander with less than pinpoint control (he holds the minor league record for career bases on balls), he had good stuff and eight 20-win seasons.

Frank Shellenback is most frequently named as the greatest minor league pitcher. The Pacific Coast League career leader in wins with 295, Shellenback won 10 games with the White Sox as a nineteen-year-old rookie spitballer in 1918. After a poor start the following season, he was sent to Minneapolis. In February 1920 the baseball rules committee outlawed the spitball and other trick pitches. Each major league team was allowed to designate two spitball pitchers who would be able to continue using the pitch in the majors. Unfortunately for Shellenbeck, he was on the Vernon roster by this time and at age twenty-one would be consigned forever to pitching in the minors if he couldn't get by without the spitball. Throughout much of his career, articles would be written that usually declared that Shellenback would be a major league star if he was eligible to play there. He did have a great six-year stretch with Hollywood (1928–1933) when he went 142–59. He was a very popular player with the Stars as well as Vernon and a fine hitter with good power, but a review of his record suggests he was never as good as everyone thought he was—he led the PCL in wins twice but never led in another category. He had only five 20-win seasons.

Because of the spitball ban, Shellenback was viewed as a tragic figure, but he wasn't alone. Spitballer Paul Wachtel won 203 games in the Texas League after the ban, including five 20-win seasons. Rube Robinson won 148 games in the Southern Association, including two league-leading 26-win seasons. Wheeler Fuller, who never pitched in the majors, won 156 in the Eastern League after the ban.

Perhaps the greatest minor league pitcher was Tony Freitas, a little lefthander who spent all or part of fifteen seasons with Sacramento. He had great control, could get the strikeout, and had nine 20-win seasons (plus two 19-win seasons). If he hadn't lost three years to the military, he probably would have won 400 games in the minors. Freitas had an impressive major league debut, going 12–5 in less than a full season with the 1932 Philadelphia A's, but that was the last success he would have in the majors.

Four other pitchers worthy of mention are Sam Gibson, George Boehler, Bill Bailey, and George Brunet.

Gibson was an underappreciated pitcher who spent most of his career in the PCL—twelve years with San Francisco. He didn't make his organized-baseball debut until he was twenty-three years old. After two promising seasons with Detroit, he never had much success in the majors, but he was extremely effective in the minors. He had six 20-win seasons (plus three 19-win seasons) and, pitching in a high-scoring era, he had eight seasons where his ERA was below 3.00.

Boehler was a hard-throwing workhorse who spent most of his career in the Western League. Twice he pitched over 400 innings, six times over 300. Unfortunately he was terribly inconsistent: with Tulsa in 1921–1923 his seasonal win totals were 4–38–7. He was consistently ineffective in a number of major league trials.

Bailey had seven league-leading strikeout seasons in four different leagues (International, Texas, Southern, Western) but only three 20-win seasons. After a promising September debut with the Browns in 1907, he pitched over 200 games in the majors with five teams spread over fifteen years with no success.

Brunet pitched in organized ball for thirty-three years (1953-1985), and astonishingly he was a regular-rotation pitcher for all but the last year. When he was forty-eight years old, he had a 1.94 ERA pitching regularly in the Mexican League. He never won more than 17 games in a season, had only two 200-strikeout seasons (they were twenty-one years apart), but he had a credible major league career and holds the minor league career strikeout record.

The Teams

There have been a number of debates about the greatest minor league teams. The 1937 Newark Bears, the 1934 Los Angeles Angels, the 1920-1925 Ft. Worth Panthers, and the 1919-1925 Baltimore Orioles usually draw the most support. All were dominant teams with good players.

The Bears included Charlie Keller, Joe Gordon, George McQuinn, Atley Donald, and five other players who would go to the majors the following year. They won the International League pennant by 25½ games with a 109–41 record. The Angels included Frank Demaree, Jigger Statz, Gene Lillard, and Fay Thomas, and they compiled an astounding 137–50 record. The Panthers (or Cats) won six straight pennants and five Dixie Series. They were led by the home run hitting of Big Boy Kraft and a fine pitching staff that included spitballer Paul Wachtel and Joe Pate.

It is doubtful that any of the three could have competed successfully in the majors. It is occasionally claimed that the 1937 Newark Bears were the Yankee B team and could have finished second in the American League, or at least in the first division. But that ignores the talent that was in the majors. The Red Sox finished fifth in 1937 with a club that included Jimmie Foxx, Joe Cronin, Lefty Grove, Pinky Higgins, Doc Cramer, Ben Chapman, Jack Wilson, and Bobo Newsom, all of whom, it is safe to say, would have started for the Bears. The same is true of the Angels, whose pitching staff chose 1934 to have career years, and of the Cats, who played well as a team but had few players that were even considered minor league standouts.

The Orioles were a different story. Thanks to the draft exemption, Jack Dunn was able to assemble a powerhouse comprised of players ready and capable of playing in the majors. The 1922 team was probably the best minor league club ever assembled. It had Jack Bentley, Max Bishop, Fritz Maisel, and Joe Boley in the infield, and Otis Lawry, Merwyn Jacobson, and Jimmy Walsh in the outfield. The catcher was Lena Styles, and the pitchers were Lefty Grove, John Ogden, Tommy Thomas, Rube Parnham, and Harry Frank with Bentley occasionally seeing action in that capacity.

Grove, Ogden, and Thomas combined for 60 wins and six years later would win a combined 56 games in the majors. Parnham, a free spirit who pitched when he wanted, was around long enough to win 16 (the following year he won 33). Frank won 22, but his career would soon be cut short by illness. Bentley hit .350 and won 13 games; he went to the Giants in 1923 as a pitcher but hit .427. Bishop and Boley, who hit .261 and .343 respectively, went on to become the double-play combo with the 1929-

1930 world champion Philadelphia A's. Styles was just twenty-two years old and hit .315, but that was his peak. Maisel (.306), Walsh (.327), Jacobson (.304), and Lawry (.333) had all played briefly and/or ineffectively in the majors but would all go on to have great careers in the International League. A twenty-year-old rookie utility player on the team was Dick Porter, who hit .279 and would have seven excellent seasons with the Orioles before going on to have several good years with the Indians.

As good as the Orioles were and as good as some of their players became, it is doubtful that even they could have finished in the first division of the American or National Leagues in 1922. Yet the strongest evidence of the attraction of minor league baseball and the hold it has long held on fans who were exposed to it is that those great Oriole, Bear, and Angel teams are far better known and more fondly remembered than hundreds of more talented second-division and higher major league clubs.

Minor Leagues

Year	Leagues Started	Didn't Finish	Year	Leagues Started	Didn't Finish	Year	Leagues Started	Didn't Finish	Year	Leagues Started	Didn't Finish	Year	Leagues Started	Didn't Finish	Year	Leagues Started	Didn't Finish
1883	2		1901	14	3	1919	15	1	1937	37		1955	33		1973	18	
1884	7	2	1902	17	2	1920	22	1	1938	37		1956	28		1974	18	
1885	7	2	1903	20		1921	26		1939	41		1957	28		1975	18	
1886	10	1	1904	24	2	1922	30	2	1940	44	1	1958	24		1976	20	
1887	15	6	1905	31	5	1923	31	3	1941	41		1959	21		1977	19	
1888	17	7	1906	33	3	1924	29	4	1942	31	5	1960	22		1978	18	
1889	15	5	1907	37	4	1925	25	3	1943	10	1	1961	22		1979	18	1
1890	17	7	1908	40	11	1926	30	4	1944	10		1962	20		1980	17	
1891	14	3	1909	35	4	1927	24		1945	11		1963	18		1981	17	
1892	12	3	1910	52	6	1928	31	3	1946	43	1	1964	20		1982	17	
1893	7	4	1911	51	10	1929	26	2	1947	52		1965	19		1983	17	
1894	9	3	1912	47	11	1930	23	2	1948	58		1966	19		1984	17	
1895	18	8	1913	43	4	1931	19	3	1949	59		1967	19		1985	18	
1896	14	7	1914	44	6	1932	19	4	1950	58	1	1968	20		1986	17	
1897	17	7	1915	34	8	1933	14		1951	50	1	1969	21		1987	17	
1898	19	10	1916	27	6	1934	20	1	1952	43		1970	21		1988	18	
1899	14	4	1917	21	9	1935	21		1953	38		1971	20		1989	19	
1900	14	6	1918	10	9	1936	26		1954	36	3	1972	19		1990	19	

Annual Overall Minor League Pitching Percentage Leader (20 or more decisions)

Year	Player	Team (League)	W–L	Pct.	Overall W–L	Overall Pct.
1900	Willie Mains	Rome (N.Y. St.)	27–5	.844		
1901	Henry Allemang	Little Rock (So. Assn.)	20–4	.833		
1902	Louis Bruce	Toronto (Eastern)	18–2	.900		
1903	Ernest Nichols	Spokane (Pac. Nat.)	20–4	.833		
1904	Ed Craig	Springfield (Mo. Valley)	19–4	.826		
1905	Fred Steele	Oskaloosa (Iowa St.)	18–3	.857		
1906	Frank Dick	Marshalltown (Iowa St.)	18–3	.857		
1907	Harley Young	Wichita (West. Assn.)	29–4	.879		
1908	Harry Gaspar	Waterloo (Cent. Assn.)	32–4	.889		
1909	Ray Fisher	Hartford (Conn.)	24–5	.828		
1910	Cyrus Dahlgren	Superior (Minn.-Wis.)	22–3	.880		
1911	Howard Northrop	Reading (Inter.-St.)	27–4	.871		
1912	Larue Kirby	Traverse City (Mich. St.)	18–3	.857		
1913	Ralph Bell	Winona (Northern)	28–6	.824		
1914	Joe Chabek	Harrisburg (Tri-St.)	28–3	.903		
1915	Booth Hopper	Minneapolis (A.A.)	18–3	.857		
1916	Howard Ehmke	Syracuse (N.Y. St.)	31–7	.816		
1917	John Verbout	Wilkes-Barre (N.Y. St.)	26–7	.788		
1918	John Beckvermit	Binghamton (Int.)	17–4	.810		
1919	C. A. (Chief) Bender	Richmond (Va.)	29–2	.935		
1920	George Carmen	London (Mich.,-Ont.)	26–2	.926		
1921	Earl Keiser	Mitchell (Dakota)	20–2			
		Oakland (PCL)	3–0		23–2	.920
1922	Byrd Hodges	Joplin (West. Assn.)	26–3	.897		
1923	Emil Levsen	Cedar Rapids (Miss. Val.)	19–4	.826		
1924	Carl Dunagan	Dyersburg (Kitty)	19–2	.905		
1925	Lloyd Brown	Ardmore-Western Assn.	17–1	.944*		
1926	Frank Tubbs	Port Huron (Mich.-Ont.)	8–1			
		Port Huron (Mich. St.)	8–0			
		Oklahoma City (Western)	9–2		25–3	.893
1927	Ben Cantwell	Jacksonville (So'east.)	25–5	.833		
1928	Paul Fittery	Carrollton (Ga.-Ala.)	21–2	.913		
1929	Andrew Bednar	McCook (Neb. St.)	21–4	.840		
1930	Jim Cameron	McCook (Neb. St.)	19–2	.905		
1931	Lyle (Bud) Tinning	Minneapolis (A.A.)	1–2			
		Des Moines (West. Assn.)	24–2		25–4	.862
1932	Marvin Duke	Erie (Central)	23–4	.852		
1933	Al Piechota	Davenport (Miss. Val.)	19–4	.826		
1934	Fay Thomas	Los Angeles (PCL)	28–4	.875		
1935	Lloyd Sterling	Winnipeg (Northern)	24–2	.923		
1936	Bill Yocke	Akron (Mid. Atl.)	1–2			
		Norfolk (Piedmont)	18–1		19–3	.864
1937	Joe Kohlman	Salisbury (E. Shore)	25–1	.962		
1938	Paige Dennis	Thomasville (N.C. St.)	28–2	.933		
1939	Charles Wensloff	Joplin (West. Assn.)	26–4	.867		
1940	Arthur Cyrolewski	Johnson City (App.)	20–3	.870		
	Mervin Hensley	La Crosse (Wis. St.)	20–3	.870		
1941	Frank Marino	Macon (Sally)	19–1	.950		
1942	Paul Minner	Elizabethton (App.)	18–2			
		Knoxville (So. Assn.)	1–0		19–2	.905
1943	Irvin Stein	Portsmouth (Piedmont)	24–6	.800		
1944	Pete Naktenis	Hartford (Eastern)	18–3	.857		
1945	Lewis Carpenter	Atlanta (So. Assn.)	22–2	.917		
1946	Bill Kennedy	Rocky Mount (C. Plain)	28–3	.903		
1947	Chris VanCuyk	Cambridge (E. Shore)	25–2	.926		
1948	Albert Tefft	Blackstone (Va.)	20–1	.952		
1949	Lynn Southworth	Thomasville (N.C. St.)	21–1	.955		
1950	Mike Hudak	Big Stone Gap (Mt. St.)	19–2	.905		
1951	Anderson Bush	Hagerstown (Int. St.)	22–3	.880		
1952	Russell Harris	Ozark (Ala-Fla.)	27–3	.900		
1953	Steve Kraly	Binghamton (Eastern)	19–2	.905		
1954	Bob Thorpe	Stockton (Calif.)	28–4	875		
1955	Jim Grant	Keokuk (I-I-I)	19–3	.864		
1956	Francisco Ramirez	Mexico City Reds (Mex.)	20–3	.870		
1957	Bob Riesner	Alexandria (Evang.)	20–0			
		New Orleans (So. Assn.)	0–2		20–2	.909
1958	Jerry Walker	Knoxville (Sally)	18–4	.818		
	Art Henriksen	St. Petersburg (Fla. St.)	17–3			
		New Orleans (So. Assn.)	0–1		18–4	.818
1959	Les Bass	Boise (Pioneer)	21–3	.875		
1960	Tom Haake	Grand Forkes (Northern)	0–1			
		Dubuque (Midwest)	19–3		19–4	.826
1961	David Seeman	Selma (Ala.-Fla.)	17–3			
		Burlington (Carolina)	7–0		24–3	.889
1962	Bob Schmidt	Modesto (Calif.)	0–0			
		Jamestown (NYP)	17–3		17–3	.850
1963	Bob Lee	Batavia (NYP)	20–2			
		Asheville (Sally)	1–1		21–3	.875
1964	Ed Watt	Aberdeen (Northern)	14–1			
		Elmira (Eastern)	3–1		17–2	.895**
1965	Billy MacLeod	Pittsfield (Eastern)	18–0	1000†		
1966	Bob Snow	Winston-Salem (Carolina)	20–2	.909		
1967	John Parker	Spartanburg (W. Car.)	17–3	.850		
1968	Pablo Montes De Oca	Campeche (Mex. S.E.)	21–4	.840		
1969	Don Eddy	Appleton (Midwest)	18–3	.857		
1970	Jim Flynn	Albuquerque (Texas)	19–4	.826		
1971	Rich Gossage	Appleton (Midwest)	18–2	.900		
1972	Andres Ayon	Saltillo (Mexican)	22–3	.880		
1973	Silvano Quezada	Tampico (Mexican)	22–2	.917		
1974	Bob Knepper	Fresno (Calif.)	20–5	.800		
1975	Jerry Garvin	Reno (Calif.)	17–5	.773		
1976	Enrique Romo	Mexico City Reds (Mexican)	20–4	.833		
1977	Mike Chris	Lakeland (Fla. St.)	18–5	.783		
1978	Tomas Armas	Saltillo (Mexican)	22–4	.846		
1979	Miguel Solis	Saltillo (Mexican)	25–5	.833		
1980	Gene Nelson	Ft. Lauderdale (Fla. St.)	20–3	.870		
1981	Ted Power	Albuquerque (PCL)	18–3	.857		
1982	Mike Warren	Stockton-Modesto (Calif.)	19–4	.826		
1983	Alfonso Pulido	Mexico City Reds (Mexican)	17–3	.850		
1984	Mike Bielecki	Hawaii (PCL)	19–3	.864		
1985	Eleazar Beltran	Tampico (Mexican)	18–3	.857		
1986	George Ferran	Shreveport (Texas)	16–1	.941‡		
1987	Bob Faron	Springfield (Midwest)	19–2	.905		
1988	Jimmy Rodgers	Myrtle Beach (So. Atl.)	18–4	.818		
1989	Royal Clayton	Albany (Eastern)	16–4	.800		
1989	Mercedes Esquer	Yucatan (Mexican)	16–4	.800		
1989	Walt Trice	Osceola (Fla. St.)	16–4	.800		

*Adding two losses to Brown's record giving him 20 decisions yields a .850 percent, better than John Schmutte, Johnstown Middie Atlantic, 19- 4, .822

**Adding 1 loss to Watt's record, giving him 20 decisions, yields an .850 percentage, better than Dave Leonhard, Aberdeen (Northern), 16-4 .800

†Adding 2 losses to MacLeod's record, giving him 20 decisions, yields a .900 percentage, better than Dave Leonhard, Elmira (Eastern), 20-5 .800

‡Adding 3 losses to Ferran's record, giving him 20 decisions, yields an .800 percentage, better than Kevin Armstrong, Columbia (Sally), 17-5 .773

Annual Overall Minor League Batting Leader (400 or more at-bats)

Year	Player	Team (League)	G	AB	R	H	2B	3B	HR	RBI	SB	AVG.
1900	Kitty Bransfield	Worcester (Eastern)	122	501	115*	186*	30	8	17	—	40	.371*
1901	Frank Huelsman	Shreveport (So. Assn.)	121*	487	98	191*	31	10	9	—	15	.392*
1902	Emil Frisk	Denver (Western)	123	450	89	168	22	22	14*	—	20	.373*
1903	Frank Huelsman	Spokane (Pac. Int.)	98	418	89	160	35	11	6	—	14	.392*
1904	Billy Hamilton	Haverhill (New Eng.)	113	408	113*	168*	32	8	0	—	74*	.412*
1905	Charlie Hemphill	St. Paul (A. A.)	145	560	122	204*	38	12	5	—	40	.364*
1906	Mike Welday	Des Moines (Western)	129	549	93	197	—	—	—	—	31	.359
1907	Ed Householder	Aberdeen (Northwest)	127	499	64	173	30*	19	9	—	19	.347*
1908	Ward Miller	Wausau (Wis.-Ill.)	124	408	91*	156*	—	—	—	—	—	.382*
1909	Harry Welch	Omaha (Western)	151	527	81	196*	41	15	7	—	51	.372*
1910	Dave Callahan	Eau Claire (Minn.-Wis.)	126	460	92*	168*	25	17*	2	—	52	.365*
1911	Frank Huelsman	Great Falls (U.A.)	135	516	117	212	48	15	17*	125*	25	.411*
1912	Charlie Johnson	Trenton (Tri-State)	109	400	86	161	31	5	14	—	22	.403*
1913	Frank Huelsman	Salt Lake City (U.A.)	122	473	123*	200*	36*	20*	22*	126*	16	.423*
1914	Jce Harris	Bay City (So. Michigan)	139	510	135	197*	39	22*	10	—	42	.386*
1915	Big Bill Kay	Binghamton (N.Y. St.)	125	447	98*	169*	22	25*	7	—	35	.378*
1916	Hank Butcher	Denver (Western)	145	541	116	204	31	20*	15	—	32	.377*
1917	Nap Lajoie	Toronto (Int.)	151	581	83	221*	39*	4	5	—	4	.380*
1918	Polly McLarry	Shreveport (Texas)	29	84	12	24	3	1	1	—	6	.286
		Binghamton (Int.)	103	335	51	129	26	7	4	—	15	.385*
											overall	.365
1919	Joe Wilhoit	Seattle (PCL)	17	67	8	11	1	0	0	—	3	.164
		Wichita (Western)	128	526	126*	222*	41	10	7	—	13	.422*
											overall	.393
1920	Merwyn Jacobson	Baltimore (Int.)	154*	581	161*	235*	35	16*	7	—	18	.404*
1921	Jack Lelivelt	Omaha (Western)	166	659	149	274*	70*	9	14	—	24	.416*
1922	Jack Schaefer	London (Mich.-Ont.)	100	407	79	167	27	21	9	—	9	.410*
1923	Moses Solomon	Hutchinson (So'west.)	134	527	143*	222*	40*	15	49*	—	12	.421*
1924	T. P. Osborne	Mt. Pleasant (E. Tex.)	101	396	93	171*	48	3	23	—	46*	.432*¹
1925	Paul Waner	San Francisco (PCL)	174	599	167	280	75*	7	11	130	8	.401*
1926	Bill Diester	Salina (So'west.)	106	428	110*	190*	33*	4	27	—	10	.444*
		Tulsa (Western)	11	44	5	15	4	0	0	—	0	.341
											overall	.434
1927	Elton Langford	Des Moines (Western)	149	611	132	250	47	28*	8	—	31	.409*
1928	Danny Boone	High Point (Piedmont)	128	468	123	196*	40	11	38*	131*	11	.419*
1929	Ed Kallina	Midland(W. Tex.)	94	367	126	159	28	7	44*	—	16	.433*
		Sherman (Lone Star)	17	64	22	22	—	—	6	—	1	.344
											overall	.420
1930	Tony Antista	Bisbee (Arizona St.)	109*	444	127*	191*	36	16*	17	100	18	.430*
1931	Babe Phelps	Youngstown (Mid-Atl.)	115	436	71	178	29	9	15	88	9	.408*
1932	George Puccinelli	Rochester (Int.)	133	478	102	187	34	8	28	115	2	.391*
1933	Ox Eckhardt	Mission (PCL)	189*	760	145	315*	56	16	12	143	15	.414*
1934	Frank Demaree	Los Angeles (PCL)	186	702	190*	269*	51*	4	45*	173*	41	.383*
1935	Ox Eckhardt	Mission (PCL)	172	710	149	283*	40	11	2	114	8	.399*
1936	Cal Lahman	Jamestown (Northern)	127	466	154*	182*	30	9	48*	162*	20	.391*
1937	Earl (Red) Martin	Beckley (Mt. St.)	91	360	80	144	39*	14*	8	96*	7	.400*
		Scranton (NYP)	11	41	7	10	1	0	0	4	1	.244
											overall	.384
1938	Murray Franklin	Beckley (Mt. St.)	94	385	91	169	31	13*	26*	110	13	.439*²
1939	Joe Schmidt	Duluth (Northern)	120	440	114*	194*	29	9	31*	133*	17	.441*
1940	Ed Schweda	Lubbock (W. Tex.-N.M.)	114	469	142	198	39	15	11	118	7	.422*
1941	Lew Flick	Elizabethton (App.)	117	502*	127*	210*	37*	13	5	116*	20	.418*
1942	Don Manno	Welch (Mt. St.)	117	457	136*	174*	32	14*	34*	122*	23	.381*
1943	George Kell	Lancaster (Inter-St.)	138	555	120*	220*	33	23*	5	79	14	.396*
1944	Roland Gladu	Hartford (Eastern)	119	417	92	155	28	14	7	102	8	.372
1945	Arden (Cotton) McCaskey	Bristol (App.)	106	437	72	164*	26*	14*	2	96	5	.375*
1946	Walt Forwood	Carbondale (N. Atl.)	111	419	98	170*	43*	7	3	101	22	.406*
1947	Jim Prince	Midland (Longhorn)	108	415	111	178	31	6	34	141	4	.429*
		Lubbock (W. Tex.-N.M.)	12	37	7	10	3	0	1	12	0	.270
											overall	.416
1948	Hershel Martin	Albuquerque (W. Tex.-N.M.)	132	447	133	190	61*	6	18	128	5	.425*
1949	Bob Montag	Pawtucket (New Eng.)	125	454	139*	192*	36	18*	21*	91	43*	.423*
1950	Oscar Sierra	Hornell (Pony)	93	358	99	151	28	2	21	114	12	.422*
		Newport News (Piedmont)	15	45	5	13	1	0	0	5	0	.289
											overall	.407
1951	D. C. (Pud) Miller	Hickory (N.C. St.)	119	426	115	181	32	1	40*	136*	2	.425*
1952	Don Stafford	Salisbury (N.C. St.)	105	392	99	160	31	3	18	90	1	.408*³
1953	Russ Snyder	McAlester (Sooner St.)	138	556	137	240*	32	16	2	84	74*	.432*
1954	Neal Cobb	Crestview (Ala.-Fla.)	115	435	108	188	27	8	5	124	3	.432*
1955	Tom Jordan	Artesia (Longhorn)	136	543	116	221*	69*	2	28	159*	4	.407*
1956	Len Tucker	Pampa (So'west)	140	565	181*	228	40	13	51	181	47*	.404*
1957	Fran Boniar	Reno (Calif.)	110	443	102	193	33	15	11	138*	4	.436*
		Pueblo (Western)	11	37	5	9	1	0	0	7	3	.243
											overall	.421
1958	Neb Wilson	Ft. Walton Beach-Pensacola (Ala.-Fla.)	119	409	102*	162	38*	3	24*	106*	3	.396*
1959	Tom Hamilton	St. Petersburg (Fla. St.)	125	401	109	155	20	3	20*	96	3	.387*
1960	Al Pinkston	Mexico City Reds (Mexican)	138	567	110	225*	41	11	26	144*	4	.397*
1961	Al Pinkston	Vera Cruz (Mexican)	109	406	79	152	26*	4	13	86	4	.374*
1962	Ramiro Caballero	Guanajuato (Mex. Center)	113	423	123	175*	25	0	59*	170	3	.414*
1963	Vinicio Garcia	Monterrey (Mexican)	122	475	107*	175	36*	5	21	88	3	.368*
1964	Ramiro Caballero	Leon (Mex. Center)	121	460	135*	175*	29	1	35*	145*	3	.380*
1965	Alfonso Peciado	Guanajuato (Mex. Center)	130	529	103	224*	48*	14*	11	147	11	.423*
1966	Heriberto Vargas	Vera Cruz (Mexican)	7	14	0	3	0	0	0	0	0	.214
		Guanajuato (Mex. Center)	127	481	168*	214	33	1	55*	174*	3	.445*
											overall	.438
1967	Hilario Pena	Campeche (Mex. S.E.)	102	404	60	159	61	3	1	49	9	.394*
1968	Jim Hicks	Tulsa (PCL)	117	407	100*	149	32	7	23	85	14	.366*
1969	Bernie Carbo	Indianapolis (A.A.)	111	404	83	145	37	2	21	76	7	.359*

Year	Player	Team (League)	G	AB	R	H	2B	3B	HR	RBI	SB	AVG.
1970	Miguel Suarez	Tampico (Mex. Center)	126	460	105	181*	37*	4	14	101	15	.393*
1971	Téolindo Acosta	Puebla (Mexican)	133	441	75	173	22	11	7	71	17	.392*
1972	Don Anderson	Jalisco (Mexican)	130	445	76	161	31	2	8	68	0	.362*
1973	Hector Espino	Tampico (Mexican)	116	422	82	159	20	2	22	107*	3	.377*
1974	Téolindo Acosta	Puebla (Mexican)	122	464	93*	170*	17	6	2	43	20	.366*
1975	Gene Richards	Reno (Calif.)	134	501*	148*	191*	29	10	12	58	85*	.381*
1976	Pat Putnam	Asheville (W. Car.)	138	538	100	194*	33*	3	24*	142*	8	.361*
1977	Rudy Law	Lodi (California)	122	451	124	174	22	5	9	88	37	.386*
1978	Champ Summers	Indianapolis (A.A.)	132	462	98	170*	25	5	34*	124*	11	.368
1979	Jimmie Collins	Chihuahua (Mexican)	124	470	95	206*	35	10	6	60	33	.438*
1980	Jimmie Collins	Chihuahua (Mex. #1)	91	346	62	131	19	13	4	52	19	.379
		Saltillo (Mex. #2)	39	137	25	52*	8	3*	2	31*	5	.380
											overall	.379
1981	Kent Hrbek	Visalia (Calif.)	121	462	119	175	25	5	27	111	12	.379*
1982	Randy Ready	El Paso (Texas)	132	475	122*	178*	33	5	20	99	13	.375*
1983	Chris Smith	Phoenix (PCL)	123	449	88	170	31	5	21	102	4	.379*
1984	Jimmie Collins	Mexico City Reds-Cordoba (Mexican)	109	403	81	166	35	4	6	59	12	.412*
1985	Oswaldo Olivares	Aguas.-Campeche (Mexican)	110	441	85	175*	22	14*	5	49	20	.397*
1986	Willie Aikens	Puebla (Mexican)	129	445	134	202*	38	3	46	154*	0	.454*
1987	Orlando Sanchez	Puebla (Mexican)	123	439	95	182	34	1	25	115	6	.415*
1988	Nelson Barrera	Mexico City Reds (Mexican)	129	460	90	171	26	0	31	124*	7	.372
1989	Willie Aikens	León (Mexican)	128	423	108*	167	40	1	37	131*	1	.395*
1990	Trench Davis	Saltillo (Mexican)	127	498	84	189*	33	4	5	50	20	.380

*Led league in category

¹If charged with 400 at-bats, Osborne's average would be .428, higher than any player with 400 or more at-bats.
(George Rhinehardt, Greenville (Sally) G: 120, AB: 495, R: 110*, H: 200*, 2B: 45*, 3B: 18, HR: 8, RBI: 92, SB: 32*, AVG: .404*)

²If charged with 400 at-bats, Franklin's average would be .423, higher than any player with 400 or more at-bats.
(Butch Moran, Rogers (Ark.-Mo.) G: 105, AB: 406, R: 107, H: 159, 2B: 43*, 3B: 12, HR: 22*, RBI: 114, SB: 8, AVG: .392*)

³If charged with 400 at-bats, Stafford's average would be .400, higher than any player with 400 or more at-bats.
(Clint McCord, Clinton (Miss. Ohio Val.) G:119, AB: 482, R: 123, H: 189*, 2B: 40, 3B: 15, HR: 15, RBI: 109, SB: 20, AVG: .392*)

Minor League Career Records

Batters	Years	G	AB	R	H	2B	3B	HR	RBI	SB	AVG
Buzz Arlett	1918–37	2390	8001	1610	2726	598	107	432	1786	200	.341
Ike Boone	1920–37	1857	6807	1362	2521	477	128	215	1334	120	.370
Bunny Brief	1910–28	2426	8945	1776	2963	594	152	340	1776	247	.331
Nick Cullop	1920–44	2484	8571	1607	2670	523	147	420	1857	154	.312
Ox Eckhardt	1925–40	1926	7563	1275	2773	455	146	66	1037	140	.367
Hector Espino	1960–84	2500	8605	1597	2898	403	49	484	1678	54	.337
Ray French	1914–41	3278	12174	1769	3254	590	129	46	1029	363	.267
Spencer Harris	1921–48	3258	11377	2287	3617	743	150	258	1769	241	.318
Joe Hauser	1918–42	1854	6426	1430	1923	340	116	399	1353	109	.299
Smead Jolley	1922–41	2231	8298	1455	3037	612	75	334	1593	61	.366
Jigger Statz	1920–42	2790	10657	1996	3356	595	137	66	1044	466	.315
Perry Werden	1884–1908	1539	6233	1214	2124	392	87	169	—	350	.341

Pitchers	Years	G	IP	W	L	H	R	ER	BB	SO	ERA
Bill Bailey	1906–25	578	3730	242	219	3452	1572	612	1565	2375	2.87
Dick Barrett	1925–53	790	4961	325	257	4572	2170	1747	2096	2512	3.34
George Boehler	1911–30	562	3711	248	202	3421	1745	874	1464	2319	3.74
George Brunet	1953–85	668	4041	244	242	3761	1832	1466	1754	3175	3.27
Tony Freitas	1928–53	736	4905	342	238	5090	2073	1694	932	2324	3.11
Sam Gibson	1923–49	661	4469	307	200	4460	1860	1413	1073	2195	3.08
Willie Mains	1887–1906	545	4014	318	179	4399	2417	—	1280	1669	
Joe Martina	1910–31	833	5417	349	277	4950	2307	1355	1868	2770	3.22
Frank Shellenback	1917–38	638	4514	315	192	4922	2110	1775	1021	1742	3.55
Bill Thomas	1926–52	1016	5995	383	347	6721	3098	2211	1230	2204	3.71
Hal Turpin	1927–46	635	4084	271	203	4512	1917	1367	807	1254	3.28

Japanese Baseball

Yoichi Nagata and John B. Holway

Just when baseball arrived in Japan, and who introduced it, is not clear. Horace Wilson, a professor in Tokyo in the 1870s, is one of those credited with being the Abner Doubleday of Japan, teaching baseball to students who ran bases and flagged grounders in *geta,* or wooden clogs. They named it *yakyu* (yok-yoo')—field ball—or *beisu boru.* In 1908, the University of Washington team, the first American college team to visit Japan, won six games but lost four games to Japanese colleges.

In 1913 the Chicago White Sox and New York Giants stopped in Japan on a round-the-world tour, playing three games with Japanese college teams. In 1922 a big league All-Star team, including Casey Stengel, also sailed into Yokohama harbor. And in 1928 Ty Cobb himself went over to teach the Japanese his batting secrets.

By 1930 *yakyu* began to rival *sumo* as the Japanese national pastime. The two games still tug in opposite directions at the nation's sports psyche, the one traditional and native, the other newer and outward-looking, but baseball has far outdistanced *sumo* as the nation's most popular sport.

The game thrived in schools and colleges. In fact, scholastic baseball still has a grip on the fans, like college football in America, high school basketball in Indiana, or the Final Four of the NCAA basketball tourney. Japan's annual national high school tournaments in Osaka every March and August fill huge Koshien Stadium for two weeks and command dawn-to-dusk TV coverage.

Japan's first professional team, the Nihon Undo Kyokai (Japan Athletic Association), was formed in 1920, which was followed by a second club, somewhat like the U.S. Harlem Globetrotters. When the great earthquake of 1923 hit the Tokyo metropolitan area, the NUK was forced to disband. The next year the Hankyu Railway reorganized former NUK players into a third pro club, the Takarazuka Kyokai. However, those teams couldn't survive because of a lack of competition.

In the fall of 1931, Lou Gehrig, Lefty Grove, Frankie Frisch, and Lefty O'Doul arrived for a tour. Several black teams visited Japan in the 1920s and in 1932, with stars such as Bullet Joe Rogan and Biz Mackey, who later became Roy Campanella's mentor.

Japanese baseball reached a watershed in 1934 with the arrival of Babe Ruth, Gehrig, Jimmy Foxx, Al Simmons, Charlie Gehringer, and Lefty Gomez. Matsutaro Shoriki, owner of the Yomiuri newspapers, sponsored the tour and would become the great genius–father figure of professional baseball there. Ruth and the others, soon to receive plaques in Cooperstown, played sixteen games and easily won fifteen of them. Ruth hit thirteen home runs and clowned in right field, holding an umbrella, while Gehrig played first base in galoshes. But they weren't clowning when a high school boy, Eiji Sawamura, almost shut them out, whiffing Gehringer, Ruth, Gehrig, and Foxx in succession before losing 1–0. Sawamura became, and still is, a national hero, especially on his death, at twenty-six, in World War Two.

Shoriki signed a professional, Osamu Mihara (later famous as the "Magic Manager"), to his All-Japan team to oppose Ruth, although the Japanese looked down on professional sports as "unpure." At the end of the year he formed an all-pro team, Dai-Nippon (Greater Japan), with Sawamura, Mihara, the White Russian Vic Starffin, and others. They toured the United States the next year and would become the present-day Yomiuri (Tokyo) Giants (*Kyojin*), a nickname hung on them by O'Doul. Shoriki urged other businesses to form pro teams and by 1936 formed the country's first professional league, the Japan Pro-Baseball League.

World War Two interrupted baseball. American words, such as *out* and *safe*, became *hi-ké* (withdraw) and *yoshi* (good), etc., and Japanese soldiers shouted, "To hell with Beibu Rusu." The league succumbed completely in 1945, and the Giants' proud stadium became an ammo dump.

After the war General MacArthur ordered the stadium cleared and encouraged the rebirth of the game. O'Doul, a veteran of the 1931 and 1934 tours, brought his San Francisco Seals of the PCL in 1949 and won all seven games. He returned with Joe DiMaggio and other big leaguers in 1951.

The big league tours continued every other year or so, and, *mirabile dictu*, in 1953 the Americans even lost one game with two ties. In 1956 the champion Dodgers lost four games, and in 1966 they lost eight and won nine. Of course the players considered the tours as vacations for shopping and partying, but they were learning that unless they played their best, they could no longer waltz to easy victories.

In 1950 the JPBL split into two leagues, which now have six teams apiece. The Central League, dominated by the Giants, is by far the more popular, with the benefit of the nationwide publicity the Yomiuri empire gives its club. The Giants have drawn 3.4 million fans in a 65-game home schedule. That's over 52,000 per game, or 4.2 million for a U.S. schedule of 81 games. Even when they finished last in 1975, they drew 2.8 million. The Pacific League, struggling to break even, in 1973 instituted a split season (since abandoned) and the DH (still in effect). It now averages about 22,000 attendance per game, compared to 31,000 for the Central League. Average pay is $100,000, compared to over $500,000 in the U.S. majors.

Three-time Triple Crown winner Hiromitsu Ochiai is the highest paid, at $1 million, although a few Americans in Japan—former Montreal Expo Warren Cromartie, etc.—make twice that.

Of course every Japanese kid wants to grow up to play for the Giants, leaving the other eleven clubs talent-poor. A draft system, begun in 1966, has helped give the other teams a better chance to compete. Since 1974 the Pacific League has won nine of the sixteen Japan Series.

Every night a Japanese *sarariman* (salaried man, or wage earner) who is *kichigai* (crazy) about *yakyu* can switch on nationwide TV to watch the Giants. Where America has one daily and one weekly sports paper, *The National* and *The Sporting News*, Japan has seven sports *dailies*, which concentrate mostly on baseball.

Most teams are owned by large companies and operated as advertising write-offs. For years Hiroshima was the only club owned by a city, but it is now owned by the Mazda company. Nine of the twelve clubs play in the two metropolitan centers, Tokyo-Yokohama and Osaka-Kobe-Kyoto.

In the early 1950s, it was a shock for Tokyo fans when the American big leaguers arrived, standing a head taller than the Japanese. Today it is a shock for the same fan to visit a U.S. spring training camp and see visiting Japanese dressing at lockers next to the Americans: There isn't that much difference anymore. Sadaharu Oh and Hank Aaron could almost trade uniforms.

The Japanese began talking of a real World Series. Their victory over America in the 1984 Los Angeles Olympics stirred the fantasy even more.

In general, American observers say, Japanese outfielders and catchers don't have the arms of Americans and Latins. But their infielders are among the best in the world, many of their pitchers are outstanding, and their batters are beginning to hit with big league power.

Americans also say the draconian training methods leave the players burned out in the second half of the season. And especially the Japanese attitude that "the future is now" has led to sacrificing many a great young pitcher to brutal overwork until his arm is ruined forever. In 1961 Hiroshi Gondo won 35 games in 429 innings. The next year he won 30 in 362. The next year he was down to 10, then 6, then 1; then he was out. This, however, is changing, as the Japanese are beginning to adopt the American pitching rotation.

About half the teams play on artificial turf, and in 1988 Japan got its first dome, the Tokyo Dome, built on the site of historic Korakuen (Ko-ra'-kwen) Stadium, similar to Minnesota's Metrodome.

Meanwhile Japanese baseball has produced some outstanding heroes and memorable moments.

A Gallery of Stars

Tetsuharu Kawakami "The God of Batting," he has also been called "Japan's Lou Gehrig." Wearing glasses and swinging his famous red bat, Kawakami hit cleanup on the great Tokyo Giant teams of 1938–1958 and hit a high of .377 in 1951. His lifetime .313 is fifth highest in Japanese annals. Against the Dodgers in 1956, he batted .364 with two home runs. His concentration was so intense, he said he could visually "stop" a pitch in midflight.

But Kawakami's hitting paled compared to his managing—11 pennants in fourteen years. He was the man at the helm as the Giants won nine straight Japan Series, a feat accomplished by no other professional team in any sport. The Negro League Homestead Grays won nine straight pennants 1937–1945, but they lost several Black World Series and one playoff.

The Grays had Josh Gibson and Buck Leonard. Kawakami had Sadaharu Oh and Shigeo Nagashima. And he did it without using a single foreign player, desiring to prove the superiority of a "pure" Japanese team with fighting spirit.

Hiroshi Oshita (O'-shta) A three-time batting champ and three-time home run leader, Oshita was the postwar hero who dueled with his blue bat against Kawakami's red bat and helped lift the nation's spirit after World War Two. He was popular with the fans and with visiting Americans, who nicknamed him "Oyster."

With a soft and graceful swing, he lofted balls that left lofty, graceful traces in the sky. His 20 homers in 1946 seem a modest total, but they were 10 percent of all the homers hit in the Japanese majors that year. He hit cleanup on the Lions' "H-Bomb Row" of the 1950s.

Futoshi Nakanishi A Japanese Hack Wilson, in Leo Durocher's phrase, Nakanishi hit the second-longest tape-measure home run in Japanese history—530 feet—as a sophomore in 1953. He led the league in homers five out of the six years 1953–1958 and, with Oshita and pitcher Kazuhisa Inao, helped the Nishitetsu Lions win three successive Japan championships, all over the hated Giants.

Nakanishi helped spark the Lions to an amazing comeback in 1958, beginning from eleven games behind the Hawks. In one September stretch, they won seventeen out of eighteen games, and Nakanishi's homer vanquished the Hawks in their final meeting.

Nakanishi's career was cut short by an injury to his left hand after 244 home runs and a .307 average.

He managed the Lions to the flag in another heroic comeback starting from fourteen games behind. An eight-game winning streak in October finally put them a half game ahead, and American Tony Roig's homer clinched it on the final day.

Katsuya Nomura (Kot'-su-ya) The slugging catcher Nomura was the first home run king Oh had to catch before he could go after Ruth and Aaron. Nomura played in Japan's smallest park, with 280-foot foul lines, but he was a legitimate star, with a high of 52 homers in 150 games in 1963, when he almost batted the Hawks to the pennant over the Lions. Nomura's lifetime homer total, 1954–1980, was 657. He led the Pacific League eight straight times—nine in all.

Nomura was the most enduring catcher of all time. His 2,921 games behind the plate are almost 1,000 more than the U.S. record, by Bob Boone. Six years Nomura played every game on the schedule. Once he caught every inning in 150 games, including 16 doubleheaders. Hard work only made him stronger. He hit a combined .235 in the first games of the doubleheaders, .339 in the second games.

Overshadowed by Oh and Nagashima of the Giants, who enjoyed a tremendous publicity advantage, Nomura called them "sunflowers" and himself "an evening primrose."

Slow afield and afoot (Americans called him "Moose"), Nomura admired Campanella, who taught him how to catch without blocking the ump's view of low pitches and how to give his pitchers more confidence. An intelligent catcher, Nomura played each game in his head, pitch by pitch, the night before. Batters swore he could read their minds.

Nomura made a reliever of strikeout king Enatsu and in 1959 caught Sugiura's magnificent 38–4 season, forming one of the finest batteries of all time.

In 1965 he won the Triple Crown, with a little help from the league's pitchers, who walked American Daryl Spencer to prevent him from winning the home run title.

Shigeo Nagashima (She-gay'-o) The most popular player ever to play in Japan, Nagashima came to the Yomiuri Giants in 1958 and led the league in homers and RBIs his rookie year. He went on to win another HR crown, four more RBI titles, six batting crowns, and five MVPs— pretty good for a man whose main rival for all these honors was Sadaharu Oh.

In fact, Oh joined the team the year after Nagashima, and the two of them gave the Giants the dreaded "O-N Cannons" that propelled them to nine straight Japan championships. With Nagashima hitting cleanup behind Oh, pitchers couldn't pitch around Sadaharu. In the first year of Nagashima's retirement, 1975, Oh lost his HR crown after thirteen straight years as king.

Nagashima was considered the greater clutch hitter. He was nicknamed "Mr. Giant" and "the burning man" for the intensity of his play. His years of greatness coincided with Japan's dramatic economic surge, a period of national pride that he seemed to symbolize.

In 1959 Nagashima won the most famous game ever played in Japan, before the Emperor and Empress, with a ninth-inning homer. Seven years later, in 1966, his majesty attended his second game, against the L.A. Dodgers. Nagashima homered off Alan Foster in the first, singled in the fourth after a brushback pitch, and singled again in the seventh, as the Japanese won 11–3. He was the first baseball player to receive an audience at the Imperial Palace.

At third base, Nagashima was compared to Ron Santo by Americans who saw him. Dodger G.M. Fresco Thompson said Los Angeles could have won two extra pennants with Nagashima on third.

Fans adored him. His every move on the bases, in the field, or at bat, delighted them. Even Oh admitted that Nagashima was the first Japanese to realize that the game belongs to the fans. Early on, Oh realized he would never be able to rival Nagashima in popularity and that he would have to concentrate on setting records instead.

Although the two Giants were not unfriendly, neither were they close friends. Never once, Oh says, did they meet socially off the field or even take a drink together.

Like Gehrig and Ruth, Oh was upstaged by Nagashima. In '64 Oh blasted 55 homers, a Japanese record. But that was the year Nagashima got married— the number one sports story of the year.

When Oh won a then unprecedented second straight Triple Crown in 1974, he again had to take a back seat to Nagashima, whose retirement was the biggest story of the year. In true Ted Williams fashion, Nagashima hit his 444th, and last, home run on his final day, then tearfully toured the field, while his fans wept with him and implored him not to go.

The next year Nagashima succeeded Kawakami as manager. He was officially given the appointment before thousands in Korakuen Stadium in a ceremony which author Robert Whiting called "a coronation."

In his first year at the helm, the Giants came in last, a national shock. Nagashima led the team in a formal bow of apology to the fans on the final day. But they bounced back to first the next two years.

Sadaharu Oh The world home-run king, Oh smashed 868 to pass Ruth and Aaron by more than 100 and put the record out of sight for at least the rest of the twentieth century and probably for several generations into the twenty-first. Clete Boyer, who played and coached for many years in Japan, said Oh had the strength of Aaron and the eyes of Williams. Oh's homers were the result of his samurai dedication, his mastery of the martial arts of *aikido* and *kendo* (swordsmanship), and thousands of hours of work with his devoted coach, Hiroshi Arakawa.

Sadaharu hit .161 as a Yomiuri Giant rookie pitcher (!) in 1959. Then Oh and Arakawa began their search for The Way. Oh gave up late-night drinking bouts on the Ginza and studied with masters of martial arts to attain physical, mental, and spiritual mastery. From the legend of the swordsman Miyamoto Musashi, Oh learned that superior spirit conquers superior technique.

But a hitch in his swing still kept Oh back until Arakawa made him stand on one leg before the pitch. If he hitched, he'd topple over. Thus the famous dog-at-the-hydrant stance, which no one before or since has attempted. (Mel Ott's raised foot was entirely different.) The bat angle, with the barrel pointing toward the pitcher, was an integral part of the balance.

Aikido taught Oh patience at the plate. *Kendo* taught him hip action, a downward swing (the fastest path to the ball), and focusing *ki*, or energy, from the shoulders to the "sweet" part of the bat.

Oh put it together in 1962, and the home runs began to explode. For 14 of the next 15 years he hit 40–55 homers a year. True, Japanese fences are shorter, 300' down the line. But so is the Japanese season—130 games. And Oh saw a lot more junkball pitchers than American hitters do. In addition, they walked him as many as 166 times a year—he never came to bat 500 times in one year in his life. The result: home run totals that ranged up to 67 per 550 at-bats. The 67 came in 1974 with 49 homers in only 385 AB.

Some lifetime comparisons:

	AB	HR	HR/550AB
Aaron	12,364	755	34
Ruth	8,399	714	45
Oh	9,250	868	49

Some other stats on Oh:

- 15 HR titles (13 in a row)—Ruth had 12, Aaron four
- 13 RBI crowns

- 13 straight times leading in runs
- nine MVP's—Ruth and Aaron had one each
- five bat championships—Ruth won one, Aaron two
- two back-to-back Triple Crowns—no American has done it
- nine Gold Gloves (they call them Golden Gloves in Japan).

Early on, Arakawa instilled in Oh the goal of catching Ruth, then Aaron, then going for 800. Aaron and Oh met face to face in 1974 in a home run contest before 50,000 fans in Tokyo. Aaron was still shaking off jet lag when his tenth homer broke a 9–9 tie. Oh was sorry to see Aaron retire—the competition had given him a goal.

Besides becoming a great hitter, Oh also became an excellent pianist. He drinks a secret blend of ginseng tea, the traditional Korean brew for energy. His bats, like Pete Rose's bats and like the sword blades used by samurai warriors, were hand made for him. Oh insisted that his bats be fashioned from a rare tree found only in northern Japan—and only from the branches of female trees.

Isao Harimoto (E′-sow) The only member of Japan's 3,000-hit club, Harimoto set the then Japanese batting record with .383 in 1970, and many thought he could go on to become the country's first .400 hitter. He didn't, partly because he refused to bunt, but he did win two more titles, for a total of seven, slugged 504 home runs, and batted .319, fourth-highest lifetime average in Japan.

A Korean born in Hiroshima, he was being carried by his mother outside the city when the atom bomb went off. She shielded him, but a sister was killed. At the age of four, two fingers on his right hand were severely burned, making it difficult for him to swing a bat. For five years his coach, Kenjiro Matsuki (Maht′-ski), pitched 500 balls a day to him, and Harimoto took 500 one-handed swings a day until suddenly, at the age of twenty-five, he found he could get around even against Yutaka Enatsu, perhaps the fastest pitcher ever in Japan.

Harimoto used a "level-up" swing—the bat was level until it met the ball, then went sharply up on the follow-through. Like Willie Keeler, he hit to all fields, wherever "they ain't."

Harimoto was active in establishing pro ball in Korea.

Shinichi Eto (Shin-i′-chi Et-o) A husky first baseman, Eto hit 367 homers but had the misfortune to come up with the Chunichi Dragons the same year Oh joined the Giants, 1959, and in the same league. It cost Eto several home run crowns.

But he had the pleasure of costing Oh two Triple Crowns, beating him out of the batting titles in 1964 and 1965.

Koichi Tabuchi Big (six-three, 210 pounds), handsome Tabuchi is the man who ended Oh's home run reign in 1975 after thirteen straight titles. Tabuchi slugged 43 that year, in spite of playing in the country's largest park. He had done even better the year before with 45 to Oh's 49. The Japanese call him their Johnny Bench.

Japanese connoisseurs consider Tabuchi's homers even more beautiful than Oh's—long and high, with a lot of "hang time."

Yutaka Fukumoto This fleet little (five-seven) Braves outfielder is the world's stolen base champ—with 1,065 as compared to Lou Brock's 938.

Thirteen straight times, in 1970–1982, Fukumoto led the league in steals. His high, 106 in 122 games in 1972, broke Maury Wills's then record of 104 in 148 games. Brock stole 118 in 1974, but he had many more opportunities:

Player	Year	1B	BB	OB*	SB	SB/OB
Wills	1962	150	59	209	104	.498
Brock	1974	159	61	220	118	.536
Cobb	1915	161	118	279	96	.344
Fukumoto	1972	97	65	163	106	.650

*Times reached first base

Fukumoto stole 95 more in 1973 and 94 in 1974.

In that thirteen-year span, the Braves won six pennants. No wonder they took out a half-million-dollar insurance policy on his legs.

Was he stealing on the weak arms of Japanese receivers? American Don Blasingame, who played for years in Japan, said Fukumoto could have stolen on Bench.

Fukumoto led the league in runs ten times, triples eight times, walks (+ HBP) six times, hits four times, and doubles three times, and won the MVP for his great performance in 1972.

Sachio Kinugasa (Sah′-chio Ke-nu-ga′-sa) Kinugasa passed Lou Gehrig's consecutive-game record in 1987 and topped him in lifetime homers as well, 504–493.

Breaking in with the doormat Hiroshima Carp in 1965, he teamed with college star Koji Yamamoto to lift the Carp to their first pennant in 1975. They won again in 1979 and 1980, the so-called "Red Helmet" era, like Cincinnati's "Big Red Machine"—both teams wore red helmets.

A "GI baby" (his father was black), Kinugasa played in Yamamoto's shadow, often taking practice swings in his hotel room until two A.M. It paid off in 1984, his twentieth season, when he hit .300 for the only time in his life, led in RBI, and won the MVP.

Kinugasa once confided that he would like to find his father someday. "Keep playing like that," a teammate answered, "and your father will find *you*."

Hiromitsu Ochiai (O′-che-aye) With Oh, Nomura, and the other hard hitters of the past retired, Ochiai ranks alone as the top Japanese slugger today and the only man, Japanese or American, to win three Triple Crowns in 1982 and 1985–1986. Nonchalant and outspoken, he doesn't even shrink from predicting his Triple Crowns. As Dizzy Dean said, "If you kin do it, it ain't braggin'." (Ochiai missed the Triple Crown he predicted in 1987, however.)

His 52 homers in 1985 ties him with Nomura for the Pacific League record. He holds Japan's highest lifetime batting average with a .326 mark.

Not a pull hitter, Ochiai has won two other batting titles, in addition to his Triple Crowns. However, he would probably not hit for power in the larger U.S. stadiums.

Pitchers

Eiji Sawamura A true folk hero, in 1934 the eighteen-year-old Sawamura whiffed four of America's greatest

Hall of Famers in a row—Gehringer (.356, 11 home runs), Ruth (.288, 22), Gehrig (.363, 49), and Foxx (.334, 44).

The Americans had been averaging four homers and eight runs per game until they met the schoolboy with the excellent fastball and drop. The kid considered the visitors "gods" but gulped and took the mound against Earl Whitehill (14–11 for the seventh-place Senators).

With the score 0–0 going into the seventh, Ruth grounded out. (The sun got in his eyes, he said.) Next up was Gehrig, who led both majors in both batting and homers that year. Sawamura threw a strike past him. The next pitch was a high curve, which Lou slammed over the right field wall to win the game 1–0.

In the last of the seventh, the Japanese put a man on second with one out, and Shigeru Mizuhara pulled a low line drive down the right field foul line. A diving catch by Bing Miller saved one run and maybe more.

In all, the kid gave seven hits, struck out nine, and walked one. Connie Mack was so impressed, he offered the boy a contract.

The next year Sawamura toured the States with Shoriki's Dai Nippon nine (later tagged the Tokyo Giants by Lefty O'Doul), playing PCL and semipro clubs. American fans crowded around for autographs, and one asked him to sign in English, not Japanese. Sawamura obliged, only to discover later that he had signed a contract! It took some fast talking, and perhaps some yen, to get Sawamura out of the scout's clutches.

Sawamura went on to lead the new pro league in 1936 with a 13–3 record. In the postseason playoff against the Osaka Tigers, he pitched all three games, holding them to a .116 batting average and an 0.19 ERA, as the Giants won, two games to one.

The next year he was 33–10.

In his brief five-year career, he pitched three no-hitters.

Sawamura was called away to military service in 1938–1939, and again in 1942 and 1944. In December 1944 his troop ship was torpedoed by a submarine off Formosa, and he went down with the ship.

Masaichi Kaneda (Masa-ichi Ka-nay'-da) Only Cy Young and Walter Johnson have surpassed Kaneda's 400 victories. Akin to Johnson's experience, he won most of his with one of the weakest teams in Japan, the Kokutetsu Swallows, who finished in the first division only once in his fifteen years with them 1950–1964.

In 1958 the Swallows were last in homers and near last in batting. But Kaneda was 31–14 with a 1.30 ERA. The Swallows were 27–54 without him.

In all, he won 43 percent of the Swallows' victories. He won and lost more 1–0 games than anyone—21 victories, 23 defeats.

The lefthanded Kaneda was the first man to break Walter Johnson's lifetime strikeout record, as well as the first to break his scoreless innings streak. Nolan Ryan broke Kaneda's strikeout mark, 4,490, but no one has touched his mark of 64⅓ straight shutout innings.

Kaneda whiffed the great Nagashima four straight times in Nagashima's big league debut, the only pitcher ever to do that to the great batting star.

Kaneda finally joined the Giants for five years at the end of the line. His 16–5 in 1967 at the age of thirty-four

got them off to the third of their nine straight championships.

Kaneda was also the Wes Ferrell of Japan. His 36 home runs are the Japanese record for pitchers.

A Japanese-born Korean (*kane* is the Japanese equivalent of the Korean name *Kim*), when he retired with bone chips in his elbow, his glove was donated to the U.S. Hall of Fame in Cooperstown.

Takumi Otomo (Ta-ku'-me O'-to-mo) The little submarine-baller beat the New York Giants and Hoyt Wilhelm 2–1 in 1953 in one of the ten greatest games in Japan's history. With Lefty O'Doul urging him to keep the ball high, Otomo stayed ahead in the count, then fed them bad balls until they popped up or rolled out.

He won the MVP that year with a 27–6 record, plus two wins in the Japan Series. His ERA, 1.85, was the highest he posted in a four-year period. The lowest: 1.68 in 1956. In 1955 he was 30–6.

Kazuhisa Inao (Ka-zu-hee'-sa E-now') Until his arm finally weakened from overwork, Inao was one of the world's most amazing pitchers.

His record of pitching six Japan Series games in 1958 and winning the last four of them will probably never be done again by any pitcher in any country. He won 42 games in 1961, 35 in 1957, and 33 in 1958. He was voted best pitcher in the league five times.

A poor fisherman's son, he reported as an unknown rookie to the Nishitetsu Lions' camp, with muscles bulging from rowing his father's boat in rough seas. He threw up to 300 pitches a day, posted a 21–6 record with a 1.06 ERA, and lifted the Lions to the pennant. In 262 innings, he gave up two home runs. He won three more games in the Japan Series.

Nicknamed *"Tetsu Wan"*—Iron Arm—in 1957 Inao won a record 20 straight at the end of the year to lift the Lions from third to another pennant.

In 1961 he tied Vic Starffin's record of 42 wins and lost his bid for his forty-third, 1–0, in the first game of two on the final day. He considered coming back in Game Two and going for the record but at last decided to rest on his laurels.

Inao came back as a relief pitcher in 1966 and led the league in ERA once more, with 1.79.

His final totals: 276–137, 1.98, with 2,574 strikeouts.

Tadashi Sugiura (Su-ghee-u'-ra) One year after Inao won four straight games in the Japan Series, the bespectacled Sugiura won four straight too. But he pitched all four games and won all four!

Nagashima's teammate in college, Sugiura had spurned the Yomiuri Giants after Nankai Hawk manager Kazuto bowed to him and said, "We need you to beat the Giants."

As a rookie Sugiura was 27–12, 2.05 with the second-place Hawks, though Inao (33–10) and the Lions won their third straight flag.

Then in 1959 it was Sugiura's turn. He pitched 371 innings, held enemy hitters to a 1.40 ERA, and posted a 38–4 record. He pitched 29 games in the last eight weeks, or virtually every other day. He was 17–1 after August 1 and won his last 13 in a row. The stretch included 54 straight shutout innings, an ERA of 0.10, 95 strikeouts, and only 4 walks! His final victory clinched the flag.

Then came the Japan Series against the Giants, who had just won their fifth straight flag. The Hawks had never beaten them.

In spite of a painful elbow, Sugiura went eight innings in Game One, gave up nine hits, but won 10–7. The next day Sugiura pitched five innings of relief, gave three hits and one run, and got the victory 6-3.

After travel days Sugiura started Game Three in Tokyo. Midway through, a corn came off his pitching hand, and catcher Nomura suddenly found himself catching a bloody ball. In the samurai spirit, however, Sugiura refused to come out. He lost a 2–1 lead on a homer in the ninth, and the Giants put two more men on second and third with one out. "My God, I'm done for," he says he thought, desperately looking into the dugout for relief. Tsuruoka kept his eyes averted, however, sending a coach out with a good luck amulet instead. Sugiura buckled down and got the last two outs and won in the tenth 3–2. He gave up only one walk.

Rain gave Sugiura a day of rest. Would the Hawks give him another in Game Four? The finger still pained him. "Can you go?" Tsuruoka asked. "I can go," Sugiura answered. He went nine more innings and shut the Giants out on five hits.

Ecstatic Hawk fans rewarded their hero with a new car, license number 38–4.

In his first three years, he had won 96 games:

Year	Rank	G	IP	BB	SO	W–L	ERA	Series	Awards
1958	2	53	299	85	215	27–12	2.05		
1959	1	69	371	46	336	38–4	1.40*	4–0	MVP
1960	2	57	333	49	317	31–11	2.05		

But then the overwork finally told. After an operation on his arm, he fell to 20–9 in 1961. He dropped to 14–15, then 14–16, made a brief comeback in 1964 with 20–15, and then was sent to the bullpen. He was all pitched out.

His final totals: 187–106.

Tetsuya Yoneda (Tet'-su-ya Yo-nay-da)   Like Kaneda or Phil Niekro, Yoneda slaved for a doormat team, the Braves. Yet he posted the second-highest winning total in Japan—350–285, second only to Kaneda's 400 wins.

In 1966 Yoneda led the league with 25–17, while his team finished next to last. His biggest year was 1968, when he went 29–13 as the Braves won the pennant. He was voted the MVP of the league.

Yoneda is second to Kaneda in hitting too, with 33 homers to Kaneda's 36. Yoneda might have passed his rival, but the coming of the DH rule stopped his bid.

He did pass Kaneda, and everyone, including Cy Young, in one department, total games—949.

Keishi Suzuki   For six straight years, 1967–1972—eight years in all—the lefty Suzuki led the Pacific League in strikeouts. As a sophomore lefty in 1967, he was 21–13 for the last-place Kintetsu Buffaloes.

Like Robin Roberts, another fastballing control pitcher, Suzuki gave up a lot of homers—560.

He was a natural righthander, but his father had tied his right hand to force him to pitch as a lefty.

His final figures: 317–238, and 3,061 strikeouts.

Minoru Murayama   In 1959 rookie fastballer Murayama faced Japan's best player, Nagashima, in the greatest game ever played in Japan, a contest before 50,000 fans, including the Emperor himself.

Murayama, as famous for his forkball as his fastball, pitched for the Yomiuri Giants' biggest rivals, the Hanshin Tigers. An Osaka native and boyhood Tiger fan, he spurned a Giant bonus in order to stay home and pitch for the Tigers for half the amount the Giants offered.

The night before the big game, Murayama had come in in the ninth inning against the Giants and struck out the side, Nagashima included.

The next night, before their majesties, Koyama started for the Tigers and they took an early lead. Nagashima ripped a home run to tie the score. The Tigers went back into the lead, and in the seventh Nagashima struck out, but a rookie named Sadaharu Oh pumped a two-run home run to tie it again.

That brought in Murayama, who got the Giants out to end the seventh, then shut them out in the eighth, as the scoreboard clock inched toward nine-thirty, the time when the imperial couple would have to leave. They stayed in their seats, however, to see Nagashima and Murayama duel each other in the last of the ninth.

This was a classic Japanese showdown, or *shobu*. Under the unwritten rule, there could be no nibbling the corners or dirty tricks; it had to be a head-on challenge, strength against strength.

Murayama's first pitch was a forkball, for a ball. Next another forkball, for a strike. Then a fastball, which Nagashima fouled back.

Another fastball was outside, making the count 2–2. Then he uncorked still another fastball on the inside. Nagashima swung and parked it ten rows into the left field stands. To this day Murayama insists it was foul. But Nagashima circled the bases before the royal box, to be mobbed by his teammates waiting at the plate.

Nagashima went on to win the batting championship. Murayama went on to strike out 294 men in 295 innings; he won 18 and lost 10, with a 1.19 ERA, and won the Sawamura Award.

But nothing could erase the memory of that one fateful home run. Nagashima was invited to the palace for an audience. There was no imperial audience for Murayama, however. Ever after, he waited for his revenge.

When he neared the 1,500th strikeout of his career, he announced that he would get it against Nagashima; he did. Then he announced he was saving number 2,000 for Nagashima as well, and he delivered on that promise too.

In 1961 Murayama was 24–13; in 1962, 25–14 with a 1.20 ERA to lift the Tigers to the pennant. It was a partial revenge at least.

That fall Murayama took part of his anger out on the visiting Detroit Tigers. Murayama had been hit hard by the Americans earlier in the tour. But this day his fastball and forkball were snapping.

He struck out the first two hitters, Chico Fernandez (.249) and Bill Bruton (.278). Norm Cash (.243) walked, but Al Kaline (.304) was the third out.

For the next six innings not another Detroiter got on base. "I was keeping every ball down," Murayama said later. "My slider and forkball were working well. I was thinking no-hitter."

Former American League pitcher Tom Ferrick watched the game and repeated what he had said before: Murayama was the best pitcher in Japan; his fastballs were jamming the hitters, and he delivered both the fastball and the forkball with the same deceptive motion. "No major leaguer could have hit Murayama today," Ferrick said.

For seven innings, no major leaguer did. In the eighth Dick McAuliffe (.263) led off with a walk, the first Detroit base runner since the first inning. Murayama retired Bubba Morton (.262) and Steve Boros (.228). Then Mike Roarke (.213) lined one into left field to break up the no-hitter. Lefthanded Bobo Osborne (.230) pinch-hit and popped to second.

Murayama got Fernandez out to open the ninth. Then Bruton dropped a bunt and beat it out for the second—and last—hit. Cash walked again. But Kaline lifted a foul to shortstop, McAuliffe hit a high fly to left, and the Tigers were finished. It was the first shutout a U.S. big league team had ever suffered in Japan.

The Detroiters probably didn't know what hit them, or why. As Murayama said, "I have become what I am because of Nagashima."

His final stats: 222–147, 2.09.

Yutaka Enatsu One of the most amazing athletes in Japanese baseball, in 1968 Enatsu struck out 401 men in 329 innings—that's eleven every nine innings. He was only twenty years old and just two years out of high school.

The lefty was one of the few pitchers who could get Nagashima and Oh out consistently. As a result his pennant-hungry managers worked him like a slave in every series against the Giants. Enatsu pitched the first and third games of a three-game series, and sometimes relieved in the middle game as well.

In 1970 he shut the Giants out twice in three days, then pitched the final game of the season with no rest and lost it 2–1 in ten innings. The Giants won by two games.

In 1971 Enatsu had elbow trouble and won only 15 games—but six of them were against the Giants, including 34 straight scoreless innings. And in the All-Star Game that summer he pitched three innings and struck out all nine men he faced. (In 1984 Suguru Egawa of the Giants almost matched him. He whiffed the first eight men on thirty-seven pitches, or about 4.5 per man, then got two fastball strikes on batter number nine. He shook off a sign for another fastball and instead threw a curve, which the batter hit on the ground for the final out.)

Enatsu was a free spirit who rebelled against the strict samurai-style workouts, saying he wanted to save himself for the season—the way they worked him, he was probably right. To dramatize his revolt one spring, he lay down in the outfield and went to sleep while the other pitchers ran. The Tigers finished last that year. They fired the manager and kept Enatsu.

Another time he was suspended for accepting a watch from a gambler.

In 1973 the Tigers were making a hard run at ending the Giants' pennant streak. On August 30, with one day of rest, Enatsu tossed an eleven-inning no-hitter, winning it himself 1–0 with a home run. In September he pitched a fourteen-inning one-hitter, retiring thirty-three straight batters in a row—the equal of eleven perfect innings—then lost 1–0.

When the Giants arrived for the climactic series, Enatsu faced them with two days rest and lost. As usual manager Murayama put him in to pitch the third game. The exhausted pitcher was leading 3–1 in the seventh, when he loaded the bases on a walk, a single, and a bunt, with Oh at bat. Enatsu got two strikes on Oh, then walked him on four straight pitches. Nagashima followed with a single to win the game and, eventually, the pennant. Enatsu ended with 24–13. It was his last great year as a starter.

He became Japan's greatest relief ace and bounced to the Hawks, Carp, and Lions, fighting with most of his managers. Finally, at the age of thirty-eight, he came to America to try out with the Brewers. It was too late; his arm was gone. Fifteen years earlier, and who knows how he might have done? Red Schoendienst called him one of the greatest lefties he'd ever seen.

Enatsu's final record: 206–158, plus 193 saves. And 2,987 strikeouts.

"East is East, and west is West, and never the twain shall meet."—Rudyard Kipling

Gaijin—*Foreigners*

Next to trade policy, no area of U.S.-Japanese relations contains the seeds of more controversy than baseball. The two games may appear the same from the left field stands, but the two nations actually play two quite different games. The differences can sometimes lead to bitter misunderstanding.

According to U.S. observers, among the differences are:

Japanese managers . . .
- Conduct spring training like marine boot camp.
- Overwork their pitchers.
- Bench players in midgame for one error or one strikeout.
- Overemphasize home runs.
- Resent advice.
- Are too conservative.
- Won't let Americans excel.

Japanese players . . .
- Take half an hour batting practice every day.
- Don't miss signs.
- Don't dive for fly balls.
- Won't break up double plays.
- Don't block the plate.
- Don't backhand grounders.
- Don't chew tobacco.

Japanese pitchers . . .
- Throw sidearm and underhand more than in the States.
- Have good curves but mediocre fastballs.
- Throw brushback pitches to American hard hitters.
- Throw 300–500 pitches a day—just to stay in shape.
- Burn out early.

Japanese fans . . .
- Eat sushi instead of hotdogs at the game.
- Throw foul balls back.

- Never stop cheering with drums and trumpets throughout the game (big noise).

According to the Japanese, among the differences are:
American players . . .
- Are overpaid, stuck up, and out of shape.
- Won't work hard.
- Don't follow orders.
- Play dirty baseball.
- Bait the umpires.
- Are quick to punch opponents.
- Look down on the Japanese.
- Won't learn the language.
- Don't like Japanese food.

Still, like lovers having a quarrel, the two nations can't stay away from each other on the ballfield.

The Japanese have used 400 foreigners—in Japanese, *gaijin*, which means "outside people." There is an ambivalence toward these aliens. On the one hand, teams are tempted to use them to gain a competitive advantage (there's a cap of three per team). On the other hand, the Japanese yearn for the day that an all-Japanese team will win a *real* world series and reign as kings of the baseball world.

Although the Japanese regularly import players, they are paranoid about exporting any to the U.S. majors. America has a very favorable "balance-of-baseball" trade. And the currently devalued dollar means Japan can afford even more American shortstops—more Yanks for the yen.

In 1987 they gave Bob Horner of the Braves $1.4 million dollars. He rewarded them with six homers in his first four games and put an estimated quarter of a million more people in the park. But he spurned a $3 million offer to stay, preferring to go home to the Cards for $1 million rather than play "something like baseball."

The Japanese offered Dave Righetti a reported $8 million for two years and Reggie Jackson $2 million for one. They turned it down. But the Japanese teams landed Bill Madlock for $1 million, Bill Gullickson for $1.1 million, and Doug DeCinces for $1.5 million—this only four years after Japan's commissioner had announced a plan to ban all *gaijin*.

(Gullickson returned from Tokyo after signing his contract to report that he saw only two English words there—Sony and Mitsubishi.) However, 1989 was the most successful year for *gaijin* players, winning MVP and three batting titles of both leagues except the RBI title of the CL.

Here are some of the best—and the worst—foreigners to play in Japan.

Victor Starffin   Now that baseball is an Olympic sport, the Russians have set themselves the goal of winning a gold medal some day. A preview of what the future may hold was big (six-four) Victor Starffin, the White Russian whose parents brought him to Japan fleeing the Bolshevik Revolution. He took to baseball like Khrushchev to vodka and became the greatest Russian baseball player of all time.

Joining the Dai-Nippon team, Starffin towered over the Japanese and opened a rivalry with teammate Sawamura. Vic was 28–11 in 1937, 33–5 in 1938, 42–14 in 1939 (two-thirds of the team's wins), and 38–12 (1.01) in 1940. Those 42 wins remained the record until Inao tied it in 1961.

On the U.S. tour in 1935, Americans assumed he spoke English. He didn't, once telling a waitress, "I am a chicken." (He later learned the language.)

Excused from military service as a stateless person, Starffin served as a Russian translator at the Tokyo war crimes trials. He spent his postwar years with some tailend teams but finished at 303–176, Japan's first 300-game winner.

He was killed soon afterward when he was driving his car home while drunk and hit a train. His plaque in Japan's Hall of Fame is inscribed in both Japanese and Russian.

Henry "Bozo" Wakabayashi (Wa-ka-bah-yah′-shee)   The son of a Japanese immigrant to Hawaii, Wakabayashi first played in Japan in 1928, graduated from one of Tokyo's "Big Six" universities, and pitched for the Osaka Tigers from the beginning of pro ball in 1936. A finesse pitcher, Wakabayashi threw seven different pitches ("seven-color magic pitches"). In 1939 he was 30–7 with a 1.25 ERA. For six years in a row, 1939–1944, he had ERAs of under 1.86; his best was 1.06 in 1943.

Twice MVP, his most famous game came in the first Japan Series in 1950 at the age of forty-two, when he was the surprise starter in Game One against the Robins, who boasted a team batting average of .287. Bozo beat them 3-2.

Wakabayashi retired at 240–141 and 1.99 and remained a baseball ambassador for decades.

Bucky Harris   Bucky Harris, another American (no, not the Senators' manager), was the Japanese home run king in the spring season of 1938 and the first foreigner to win the MVP. A veteran catcher from the American PCL, he had a good throwing arm and repeatedly won exhibitions throwing through a barrel at second base.

He studied hard to learn the language and, given a day of honor at his retirement, replied with a *sayonara* speech in Japanese.

Wally Yonamine (Yo-na′-mi-nay)   The Jackie Robinson of Japan, Yonamine introduced a slashing, running game and blazed the way for American players there. This Hawaiian-born Nisei didn't know a word of Japanese when he left the San Francisco 49ers' backfield to join the Yomiuri Giants in 1951. (He'd played some baseball in the low U.S. minors; Brooklyn's Billy Loes, who pitched against him, said he was the toughest out he ever faced.)

Wally carried a double stigma. Not only was he an American, when the wounds of the war were still fresh, he was a Nisei (son of a Japanese who chooses another country), who was regarded by the Japanese in about the same way as Americans would regard a fellow countryman who had defected to Russia.

The Giants put him in center field and batted him leadoff, and he promptly hit .354. He also ran out sacrifice bunts, which surprised the Japanese, and threw rolling blocks into second basemen on the double play, which horrified them. And he played center like his stateside contemporary, Dom DiMaggio, who also wore glasses.

A Yonamine single, a hit-and-run, and a base hit by Kawakami was the usual Giant formula. They rose from third to first in Wally's first season and won the flag every year he was with them except one. Wally and Kawakami were rivals for hitting honors, and a jealousy arose. Yonamine was much the better fielder and won three batting titles and one MVP, made seven All-Star teams, and ended with a .311 average, one of the highest in Japan. Against the Dodgers in 1956 Wally hit .347. The Japanese hailed him as the greatest leadoff man in their history, and he's probably still the biggest American star to play in Japan.

Another Nisei, Jun Hirota, caught for the Giants. When the New York Giants arrived in 1953, manager Leo Durocher, coaching at first, abandoned signals and merely told his runners to "go down on the next pitch." Hirota calmly threw them out. Leo didn't know Jun was a graduate of the University of Hawaii.

When Kawakami took over as Giant manager, he eased Wally off the team.

Yonamine got his revenge, however. As manager of the Dragons in 1974 he nipped Kawakami's Giants by one game, or .001 points, to end Kawakami's record of nine straight pennants.

Thereafter the U.S.-Japan baseball romance was a rocky one. Some Americans made a big hit. Others were big bombs.

Ugly Americans

Don Newcombe and Larry Doby   The first big-name American stars in Japan, Newcombe and Doby signed with the Chunichi Dragons in 1962. Both were in retirement, and Newk especially arrived overweight and out of shape. He pitched only 4 innings but batted .262 in 81 games in the field. Larry hit .225 with 10 home runs, although some of them were eye-popping 500-footers. The Dragons, who had finished second before they came, finished third with them. The pair were not invited back.

Marshall, Logan, Stuart, Johnson, Howard, Davis   Instead, in 1963 the optimistic Dragons signed Jim Marshall, a reserve first baseman for San Francisco with a .242 big league average, for $40,000, more than either Nagashima or Oh were making. Marshall stayed for three years, averaging .268 and 26 homers a year.

The thirty-seven-year-old Johnny Logan, a former star shortstop for the Milwaukee Braves, joined the Nankai Hawks in 1964. He hit .189 and set a Japanese record by going 38 straight at-bats without a hit.

Dick Stuart came well touted in 1967. He hit 33 homers his first year, but in his second fell to 17 homers and .217. They sent him home, where he signed with the California Angels, the first Japanese reject to return to play in the U.S. majors.

In 1973 Davey Johnson hit 43 homers for Atlanta, a record for big league second basemen. The next year the Tokyo Giants obtained him to replace the great Nagashima and integrate the Giants once again. It was a job no mortal man could fill, and Johnson didn't. He hit .197, as the Giants finished dead last. He did make a comeback the next year, and so did they, hitting .275 with 26 homers, as the Giants won the pennant. But Dave was happy to go home to the Phils, where he hit .321.

Big Frank Howard cost the Lions $80,000 in 1974. He hurt his knee, came to bat twice, and didn't get a hit. His salary came to $40,000 per at-bat.

In mid-season 1988, Dick Davis was arrested for cocaine possession and immediately was dismissed from the Buffaloes.

Joe Pepitone   In 1973 the Yakult Atoms forked over $140,000 to Pepitone, a .258-hitting former Yankee. He arrived with shoulder-length hair, got a headache from bumping his head on low hotel room doors, complained about the food and high prices, played 14 games, hit .163, developed a "bad leg," and refused to play—but discoed into the morning. He finally flew home, leaving his roommate a $2,000 phone bill, and the Japanese with a new noun, *pepitone*, meaning "a goof-off."

The Japanese players' union protested against these high-priced foreigners who were taking jobs away from Japanese and getting paid more for doing less.

Some Handsome Americans

Blasingame, Boyer, Kirkland   Thank goodness Don Blasingame came to Japan in 1967 after hitting .258 for several teams in the States. He hit 20 points better for the Nankai Hawks, learned to speak good Japanese, was cheerful to his teammates, respectful to his manager, and popular with the fans.

When home run champ Katsuya Nomura took over as manager, he appointed "Blaser" as his head coach and *de facto* bench manager, while Nomura concentrated on his play in the field. They got along splendidly and won the pennant in 1973.

Clete Boyer, possibly the greatest fielding third baseman of all time, also won friends and influenced people as a gritty player for the Taiyo Whales in 1972–1975. He also enjoyed the people, spoke their language, ate their food, and showed them the same sensational play he had shown Yankee fans back home.

Willie Kirkland hit .240 with 20 homers a year for the San Francisco Giants and others before he joined the Hanshin Tigers in 1968. He gave them 37 homers his first year, stayed for six years, joked in Japanese with fans in the outfield, and thrilled them with long distance blasts—three in one game against the hated Giants. He hit .246, the same as he had in the States, and averaged 21 homers a year.

Leron and Leon Lee   Leron Lee, a vet of four big league teams (.250), owns the second highest lifetime batting average in Japan, .320, plus 283 homers in 11 seasons, 1977–1987. He almost won the Triple Crown in his rookie year, got an 800 percent raise, and brought his kid brother Leon over.

Leon, who never played in the majors, was almost as good, hitting .309 with 268 homers.

Both were considered "good *gaijin*," on and off the field. Leon learned Japanese well enough to act as Bob Horner's interpreter.

Xenophobia

The Japanese have not been blameless in their handling

of the cross-cultural experiments. Sometimes their bias against *gaijin* is subtle, sometimes blatant.

Daryl Spencer A 33-year-old infielder with fair power and a .244 big league average, Spencer, at six-three, was a "monster" in Japanese eyes. In his first year, 1964, he hit 36 homers, second to Nomura's 41, and lifted the Hankyu Braves from last to second.

The next year Spencer was hitting .300 and leading Nomura by six homers in August, when, he said, his own coaches took him aside and told him to concentrate on the batting title and forget home runs, because Nomura usually finished strong. Spencer refused, so the Japanese pitchers sent their own message—they began walking him. At one stretch he got 16 straight balls. He even stepped into the box holding his bat upside down and still drew a walk. Of course, Nomura's Nankai Hawk pitchers were the most flagrant evaders of Spencer's strike zone. Nomura won the home run crown, 42–38, and took the batting crown too, .320 to .311. (He also won the RBI title for a Triple Crown.) The Braves fell to fourth.

A student of the game, Spencer analyzed every pitch and defensive alignment. One of his ideas: move the left field fence in ten feet to help him hit more homers. Spencer played for seven years. He told Whiting that his manager resented his advice. "I spoke my mind once too many times," Spencer told Whiting, "and I think I'm blackballed." Japanese observers, however, understood that manager Yukio Nishimoto had welcomed Spencer's help.

Other Americans felt a similar sense of discrimination. In 1968 Dave Roberts, a .239-hitting utility man with several big league clubs, hit 40 homers for the Sankei Atoms, to Oh's 49. The next year Roberts was leading for the Triple Crown, when a Giants pitcher ran into him at first base, breaking his shoulder. Dave was out for the rest of the year, and Oh and Nagashima took the three batting titles.

George Altman In 1968 the former National League outfielder (.269, fair power) started a new career in Japan at age thirty-five. He was an immediate success, hitting .320 with 34 homers and 100 RBI. In 1970 he helped pull the Lotte Orions into first place with .319 and 30 homers.

In 1969, George said, he got nothing but balls from the pitchers and nothing but strikes from the umps. He slumped to 21 homers and .269.

In 1971 Altman had his best year—39 homers and 103 RBI, and was in a race for the batting title with his teammate, Shinichi Eto. When Eto came up, he noticed, the infielders suddenly left a big hole between first and second, and Eto punched four hits through it in one game. "That," Altman told Whiting, "is when I figured my chances of winning the title were almost zero."

Randy Bass Big, bewhiskered Randy Bass played a little first base for the Padres and Rangers (batting .212) before joining the Japanese Hanshin Tigers in 1983. In 1985 he burst into stardom, winning the Triple Crown with .350, 134 RBIs, and 54 home runs.

He was just one home run short of tying Oh's Japanese record, with one game left—against the Giants, managed by Oh. The Giant pitchers walked him all four times he came to bat.

But Bass did lead the Tigers to the pennant over the hated Giants, and his home runs won two Japan Series games as the Tigers took the Japanese championship in seven games. He became a media star, his poster advertisements appearing all over Tokyo. He even agreed to shave his beard for a razor blade company.

Some Other Gaijin Stars

Some minor leaguers have done well in Japan.

Jack Bloomfield won two batting titles in 1962 and 1963.

Pitcher Joe Stanka won an MVP, with 26–7 for the Nankai Hawks in 1964.

Gene Bacque (Bock'-ay) won a Sawamura (Cy Young) for pitching the Tigers to the 1964 pennant with a 29–9. However, his brushback pitches appalled the Japanese. When he tried one against the great Oh, the whole Giants team mobbed him. In the melee, Oh says, coach Hiroshi Arakawa, Oh's best friend and an *aikido* black belt, broke Gene's thumb and put him out for the rest of the season.

Clarence Jones won a home run crown in 1974.

Boomer Wells won the Triple Crown and MVP in 1984.

Richard Lancellotti was home run king in 1987 while batting .218.

Japanese in America

Mashi Murakami Many Japanese have played in the U.S. minors and one in the majors.

The big leaguer was Masanori "Mashi" Murakami, who almost caused a complete rupture in U.S.-Japan diamond relations. Murakami was one of three members of the Nankai Hawks sent over to gain experience with the San Francisco Giants' farm teams in Fresno and Magic Valley in 1964. The twenty-year-old did so well (11–7) and was so well liked (bowing to teammates who made good plays behind him) that he was promoted to the Giants. He made his debut against the last-place Mets before 50,000 fans at Shea Stadium and pitched one inning of shutout relief. That year he won one and saved one with a 1.80 ERA. He struck out 15 men in 15 innings and walked only 1.

At this point the Giants invoked the fine print in their contract—the paragraph giving them the right to buy any of the three who made the parent club. The Japanese had never anticipated this development! They said Murakami had only been on loan. Besides, they said, he was homesick and didn't want to go back to the States. The boy dutifully agreed. The Hawks even charged that the contract was a forgery, thus enraging the Giants. Who did they think Murakami was, club president Chub Feeney demanded—Christy Mathewson?

U.S. Commissioner Ford Frick threatened to break relations with Japan if they didn't honor the contract. This could have cut off all further U.S. players going there to play.

At last a compromise broke the impasse. Murakami would play one more year in the States, then would be free to choose his own destiny.

Mashi flew back to San Francisco, won 4 games, lost 1, saved 8, and struck out 85 men in 74 innings. He was a darling of the San Francisco Nisei community.

In 1966 the Hawks enticed him home with a $40,000 contract, twice what the Giants had offered. The Hawks rubbed their hands in anticipation of seeing Murakami obliterate every pitching record in the book. Alas, he never lived up to his promise. He won a total of 9 games his first two years. He had only one good year, 1968, when he was 18–4. He was the first and last Japanese to play in the U.S. majors.

The Young Lions

In a second experiment, the Taiheiyo Lions bought a U.S. minor league team in Lodi, California, and stocked it with nine of their rookies plus a coach, along with U.S. players.

But the Japanese players, like some Americans in Japan, couldn't adjust to the food and the language. After two years the Lions sold their Lodi club and brought their players home.

Undaunted, in 1982 the Seibu Lions (bought by Seibu Railway Co. after the 1978 season) signed a working agreement with the Baltimore Orioles' Class A farm team at San Jose and each year have sent several rookies there for experience. The plan paid off big. The Lions won the pennant five of the next six years, and experts attributed it in part to their San Jose graduates. Most famous of the group was Koji Akiyama, the 1987 Japanese home run king.

In spring 1990, American baseball fans were irritated when a Japanese whiskey company, Suntory, bought the Birmingham Barons (AA).

The "Magic" Manager, Mihara

Two of the greatest managers in Japanese history were Osamu Mihara and Shigeru Mizuhara. Their duels are compared to the legendary duel of the greatest swordsmen of literature, Miyamoto Musashi and Sasaki Kojiro.

Mihara and Mizuhara attended rival high schools on Shikoku Island and went to rival colleges in the highly competitive Tokyo Big Six Conference. In 1931, before 65,000 fans, Mihara stole home against pitcher Mizuhara to lead his school to victory.

In 1934 both played on the All-Japan team against Babe Ruth's Stars. Then Mihara went into military service; Mizuhara toured the States with Dai-Nippon, sparked the Giants to several pennants (he was MVP in 1942), and then was drafted himself.

Mizuhara languished in a Soviet POW camp for four years after the war, while Mihara took over the Giants and rebuilt that once proud club into champs in 1949.

But Mihara's triumph was spoiled when Mizuhara was repatriated that same year. "I am Mizuhara," he announced. "I have returned." Mizuhara was given the manager's job and won eight pennants in ten years, 1950–1959. Mihara was kicked upstairs, where he spent his time playing *go*.

Then Mihara left to manage a new club, the Nishitetsu Lions, in faroff Kyushu. He lived in the dorm with his players, mostly recent high school kids like Nakanishi and slugging shortstop Yasumitsu Toyoda, and built them into

champs in 1954. They won again in 1956 and beat Mizuhara's strutting Yomiuri Giants in the Japan Series. They did it again in 1957 and 1958. In the last year the Giants won the first three games, but the Lions, behind Inao, won the last four.

In 1960 Mihara moved back to the Central League with the Taiyo Whales, who had finished last for six straight years. Shades of the Mets! In Mihara's first year, he whipped the Giants for the pennant by 4½ games, then swept the Japan Series in four straight!

No wonder they called him "the Magician."

A Real World Series

Matsutaro Shoriki died in 1969 with one dream still unfulfilled—a real World Series between his Giants and the winner of the American World Series. It's a goal every Japanese fan keeps before his eyes.

In frequent series against U.S. big league teams, the Japanese have already established one thing: the Americans can still win, but they have to field strong teams and play hard to do it.

In 1966 the Giants played seven games against the NL champion Dodgers and won four of them. Overall, the Dodgers were 9–8–1 in Japan. Of course, Sandy Koufax and Don Drysdale didn't make the trip. But their number three pitcher, Claude Osteen (17–14), did and was bombed out of the box five times.

In 1968 the NL champion Cards (Bob Gibson, Lou Brock, Orlando Cepeda, etc.) arrived fresh from the World Series. Beset by jet lag, they lost two of their first three games but came back to win 12 of their last 15 for a 13–5 record overall. The Japanese might have done better if Nagashima had not missed the series with an injury. Oh hit .356 with six homers.

In 1971, after a 9–6 spring training record against U.S. teams, Kawakami announced that "the Americans have nothing more to teach us." The nation looked confidently forward to the arrival that fall of the AL champ Orioles for what the Japanese were hailing as the long awaited "world series." Bowie Kuhn even threw out the first ball.

The Japanese knocked Jim Palmer (20–9) out three times, but Pat Dobson (20–8) pitched three shutouts, including a no-hitter. The O's held Oh to a .111 average. Nagashima hit .258, and the Orioles won 12 games to two, with four ties. But when the Americans sent subpar teams—the fifth-place Mets in 1974 and the fifth-place Orioles in 1984, the competition was closer.

There is still about a twenty-pound difference between the average U.S. and Japanese big leaguer, which means that today's Japanese player is about as big as a major leaguer of Babe Ruth's day.

Some Japanese doubt that Japan can ever catch up with the U.S. majors. They say the Olympics are a better arena for competition — Japan won the "demonstration" Olympic title in 1984, defeating the United States in the finale.

Will we ever see a *real* World Series? If so, when? In this generation? The next?

Japan's economic miracle, which surprised the world, suggests that one thing is certain—don't bet on anything.

Pennant Winners: Japan Pro-Baseball League

YEAR		TEAM	WON	LOST	PCT.	YEAR		TEAM	WON	LOST	PCT.
1936	FALL	TOKYO GIANTS	18	9	—	1942		TOKYO GIANTS	73	27	.730
1937	SPRING	TOKYO GIANTS	41	13	.759	1943		TOKYO GIANTS	54	27	.667
	FALL	OSAKA TIGERS	39	9	.813	1944		HANSHIN	27	6	.818
1938	SPRING	OSAKA TIGERS	29	6	.829	1945		PLAY SUSPENDED			
	FALL	TOKYO GIANTS	30	9	.769	1946		KINKI GREATRING	65	38	.631
1939		TOKYO GIANTS	66	26	.717	1947		OSAKA TIGERS	79	37	.681
1940		TOKYO GIANTS	76	28	.731	1948		NANKA HAWKSI	87	49	.640
1941		TOKYO GIANTS	62	22	.738	1949		YOMIURI GIANTS	85	48	.639

Pennant Winners: Central League

YEAR	TEAM	WON	LOST	PCT.	YEAR	TEAM	WON	LOST	PCT.
1950	SHOCHIKU ROBINS	98	35	.737	1971	YOMIURI GIANTS	70	52	.574
1951	YOMIURI GIANTS	79	29	.731	1972	YOMIURI GIANTS	74	52	.587
1952	YOMIURI GIANTS	83	37	.692	1973	YOMIURI GIANTS	66	60	.524
1953	YOMIURI GIANTS	87	37	.702	1974	CHUNICHI DRAGONS	70	49	.588
1954	CHUNICHI DRAGONS	86	40	.683	1975	HIROSHIMA CARP	72	47	.605
1955	YOMIURI GIANTS	92	37	.713	1976	YOMIURI GIANTS	76	45	.628
1956	YOMIURI GIANTS	82	44	.646	1977	YOMIURI GIANTS	80	46	.635
1957	YOMIURI GIANTS	74	53	.581	1978	YAKULT SWALLOWS	68	46	.596
1958	YOMIURI GIANTS	77	52	.596	1979	HIROSHIMA CARP	67	50	.573
1959	YOMIURI GIANTS	77	48	.612	1980	HIROSHIMA CARP	73	44	.624
1960	TAYIO WHALES	70	56	.554	1981	YOMIURI GIANTS	73	48	.603
1961	YOMIURI GIANTS	71	53	.569	1982	CHUNICHI DRAGONS	64	47	.577
1962	HANSHIN TIGERS	75	55	.577	1983	YOMIURI GIANTS	72	50	.590
1963	YOMIURI GIANTS	83	55	.601	1984	HIROSHIMA CARP	75	45	.625
1964	HANSHIN TIGERS	80	56	.588	1985	HANSHIN TIGERS	74	49	.602
1965	YOMIURI GIANTS	91	47	.659	1986	HIROSHIMA CARP	73	46	.613
1966	YOMIURI GIANTS	89	41	.685	1987	YOMIURI GIANTS	76	43	.639
1967	YOMIURI GIANTS	84	46	.646	1988	CHUNICHI DRAGONS	79	46	.632
1968	YOMIURI GIANTS	77	53	.592	1989	YOMIURI GIANTS	84	44	.656
1969	YOMIURI GIANTS	73	51	.589	1990	YOMIURI GIANTS	88	42	.677
1970	YOMIURI GIANTS	79	47	.627					

Pennant Winners: Pacific League

YEAR		TEAM	WON	LOST	PCT.	YEAR		TEAM	WON	LOST	PCT.
1950		MAINICHI ORIONS	81	34	.704		2nd HALF	*LOTTE ORIONS	38	23	.623
1951		NANKAI HAWKS	72	24	.750	1975	1st HALF	*HANKYU BRAVES	38	25	.603
1952		NANKAI HAWKS	76	44	.633		2nd HALF	KINTETSU BUFFALOES	40	20	.667
1953		NANKAI HAWKS	71	48	.597	1976	1st HALF	HANKYU BRAVES	42	21	.667
1954		NISHITETSU LIONS	90	47	.657		2nd HALF	HANKYU BRAVES	37	24	.607
1955		NANKAI HAWKS	99	41	.707	1977	1st HALF	*HANKYU BRAVES	35	25	.583
1956		NISHITETSU LIONS	96	51	.646		2nd HALF	LOTTE ORIONS	33	24	.579
1957		NISHITETSU LIONS	83	44	.648	1978	1st HALF	HANKYU BRAVES	44	20	.688
1958		NISHITETSU LIONS	78	47	.619		2nd HALF	HANKYU BRAVES	38	19	.667
1959		NANKAI HAWKS	88	42	.677	1979	1st HALF	*KINTETSU BUFFALOES	39	19	.672
1960		DAIMAI ORIONS	82	48	.631		2nd HALF	HANKYU BRAVES	36	23	.610
1961		NANKAI HAWKS	85	49	.629	1980	1st HALF	LOTTE ORIONS	33	25	.569
1962		TOEI FLYERS	78	52	.600		2nd HALF	*KINTETSU BUFFALOES	35	26	.574
1963		NISHITETSU LIONS	86	60	.589	1981	1st HALF	LOTTE ORIONS	35	26	.574
1964		NANKAI HAWKS	84	63	.571		2nd HALF	*NIPPON HAM FIGHTERS	37	23	.617
1965		NANKAI HAWKS	88	49	.642	1982	1st HALF	*SEIBU LIONS	36	27	.571
1966		NANKAI HAWKS	79	51	.608		2nd HALF	NIPPON HAM FIGHTERS	35	23	.603
1967		HANKYU BRAVES	75	55	.577	1983		SEIBU LIONS	86	40	.683
1968		HANKYU BRAVES	80	50	.615	1984		HANKYU BRAVES	75	45	.625
1969		HANKYU BRAVES	76	50	.603	1985		SEIBU LIONS	79	45	.637
1970		LOTTE ORIONS	80	47	.630	1986		SEIBU LIONS	68	49	.581
1971		HANKYU BRAVES	80	39	.672	1987		SEIBU LIONS	71	45	.612
1972		HANKYU BRAVES	80	48	.625	1988		SEIBU LIONS	73	51	.589
1973	1st HALF	*NANKAI HAWKS	38	26	.594	1989		KINTETSU BUFFALOES	71	54	.568
	2nd HALF	HANKYU BRAVES	43	19	.694	1990		SEIBU LIONS	81	45	.643
1974	1st HALF	HANKYU BRAVES	36	23	.610						

*playoff winner

Japan Series

YEAR	TEAM/LEAGUE	WON	TEAM/LEAGUE	WON		YEAR	TEAM/LEAGUE	WON	TEAM/LEAGUE	WON	
1950	MAINICHI ORIONS, PL	4	SHOCHIKU ROBINS, CL	2		1974	LOTTE ORIONS, PL	4	CHUNICHI DRAGONS, CL	2	
1951	YOMIURI GIANTS, CL	4	NANKAI HAWKS, PL	1							
1952	YOMIURI GIANTS, CL	4	NANKAI HAWKS, PL	2		1975	HANKYU BRAVES, PL	4	HIROSHIMA CARP, CL	0	2 TIES
1953	YOMIURI GIANTS, CL	4	NANKAI HAWKS, PL	2	1 TIE	1976	HANKYU BRAVES, PL	4	YOMIURI GIANTS, CL	3	
1954	CHUNICHI DRAGONS, CL	4	NISHITETSU LIONS, PL	3		1977	HANKYU BRAVES, PL	4	YOMIURI GIANTS, CL	1	
						1978	YAKULT SWALLOWS, CL	4	HANKYU BRAVES, PL	3	
1955	YOMIURI GIANTS, CL	4	NANKAI HAWKS, PL	3		1979	HIROSHIMA CARP, CL	4	KINTETSU BUFFALOES, PL	3	
1956	NISHITETSU LIONS, PL	4	YOMIURI GIANTS, CL	2							
1957	NISHITETSU LIONS, PL	4	YOMIURI GIANTS, CL	0	1 TIE	1980	HIROSHIMA CARP, CL	4	KINTETSU BUFFALOES, PL	3	
1958	NISHITETSU LIONS, PL	4	YOMIURI GIANTS, CL	3							
1959	NANKAI HAWKS, PL	4	YOMIURI GIANTS, CL	0		1981	YOMIURI GIANTS, CL	4	NIPPON HAM FIGHTERS, PL	2	
1960	TAYIO WHALES, CL	4	DAIMAI ORIONS, PL	0							
1961	YOMIURI GIANTS, CL	4	NANKAI HAWKS, PL	2		1982	SEIBU LIONS, PL	4	CHUNICHI DRAGONS, CL	2	
1962	TOEI FLYERS, PL	4	HANSHIN TIGERS, CL	2	1 TIE						
1963	YOMIURI GIANTS, CL	4	NISHITETSU LIONS, PL	3		1983	SEIBU LIONS, PL	4	YOMIURI GIANTS, CL	3	
1964	NANKAI HAWKS, PL	4	HANSHIN TIGERS	3		1984	HIROSHIMA CARP, CL	4	HANYKU BRAVES, PL	3	
1965	YOMIURI GIANTS, CL	4	NANKAI HAWKS, PL	1		1985	HANSHIN TIGERS, CL	4	SEIBU LIONS, PL	2	
1966	YOMIURI GIANTS, CL	4	NANKAI HAWKS, PL	2		1986	SEIBU LIONS, PL	4	HIROSHIMA CARP, CL	3	1 TIE
1967	YOMIURI GIANTS, CL	4	HANKYU BRAVES, PL	2		1987	SEIBU LIONS, PL	4	YOMIURI GIANTS, CL	2	
1968	YOMIURI GIANTS, CL	4	HANKYU BRAVES, PL	2		1988	SEIBU LIONS, PL	4	CHUNICHI DRAGONS, CL	1	
1969	YOMIURI GIANTS, CL	4	HANKYU BRAVES, PL	2							
1970	YOMIURI GIANTS, CL	4	LOTTE ORIONS, PL	1		1989	YOMIURI GIANTS, CL	4	KINTETSU BUFFALOES, PL	3	
1971	YOMIURI GIANTS, CL	4	HANKYU BRAVES, PL	1							
1972	YOMIURI GIANTS, CL	4	HANKYU BRAVES, PL	1		1990	SEIBU LIONS, PL	4	YOMIURI GIANTS, CL	0	
1973	YOMIURI GIANTS, CL	4	NANKAI HAWKS, PL	1							

U.S. Major League Batters in Japan

Name	Yrs		G	HR	BA	Titles Won		Name	Yrs		G	HR	BA	Titles Won
Adair, Jerry	1	1971	90	7	.300			Ewing, Sam	1	1979	119	15	.286	
Adduci, Jim	1	1987	82	13	.268			Fernandez, Chico	1	1965	52	1	.144	
Allen, Kim	2	1982-83	125	5	.265			Fielder, Cecil	1	1989	106	38	.302	
Allen, Rod	1	1989	80	11	.300			Gaines, Joe	1	1969	51	3	.205	
Alou, Matty	3	1974-76	262	14	.283			Gardner, Art	2	1981-82	218	30	.272	
Altman, George	8	1968-75	935	205	.309	68rbi, 71ba		Garrett, Adrian	3	1977-79	384	102	.260	
Andrews, Mike	1	1975-76	123	12	.231			Garrett, Wayne	2	1979-80	192	28	.241	
Arnold, Chris	3	1978-81	330	43	.274			Gentile, Jim	1	1969	65	8	.256	
Aspromonte, Ken	3	1964-66	295	31	.273			Gonzales, Dan	1	1981	9	1	.174	
Ault, Doug	1	1981	102	18	.307			Gonzalez, Tony	1	1972	31	0	.297	
Barbier, Jim	1	1970	93	9	.188			Goodwin, Danny	1	1986	83	8	.231	
Bass, Randy	6	1983-88	614	202	.337	85-86 hr-ba-rbi, 83-84 ba, 85 MVP		Green, David	1	1986	67	10	.270	
								Grunwald, Alfred	1	1962	70	3	.211	
Batista, Rafael	1	1975	48	3	.204			Hadley, Kent	6	1962-67	781	131	.260	
Baumer, Jim	5	1963-67	690	82	.251			Hammond, Steve	1	1987	115	9	.274	
Bernazard, Tony	2	1988-89	233	54	.293			Hampton, Ike	1	1981	72	15	.230	
Bertoia, Reno	1	1964	20	1	.175			Hansen, Jimmy	2	1977-78	232	31	.271	
Blasingame, Don	3	1967-69	366	15	.274			Harlow, Larry	1	1982	42	4	.164	
Boisclair, Bruce	1	1980	80	1	.249			Harper, Terry	1	1988	10	2	.143	
Boles, Carl	6	1966-71	577	117	.265			Harris, Vic	3	1981-83	280	35	.253	
Boyer, Clete	4	1972-75	419	71	.257			Hicks, Jim	2	1973-74	183	33	.247	
Bradford, Buddy	1	1977	56	4	.192			Hilton, Dave	3	1978-80	251	38	.284	
Brant, Marshall	2	1984-85	118	25	.244			Hinshaw, George	1	1989	53	8	.294	
Breedon, Hal	3	1976-78	260	79	.251			Horner, Bob	1	1987	93	31	.327	
Brewer, Tony	3	1986-89	389	82	.310			Hopkins, Gail	3	1975-77	360	69	.282	
Briggs, Dan	2	1982-83	176	18	.258			Hostetler, Dave	2	1986-87	254	42	.270	
Briggs, John	1	1976	47	7	.227			Howard, Frank	1	1974	1	0	.000	
Brouhard, Mark	2	1986-87	140	23	.265			Ireland, Tom	2	1983-84	204	18	.275	
Bryant, Ralph	2	1988-89	203	83	.292	89 hr-MVP		Jackson, Lou	3	1966-68	329	68	.257	
Budaska, Mark	1	1982	86	3	.208			James, Skip	1	1980	111	21	.269	
Buford, Don	4	1973-76	490	65	.270			Jestadt, Garry	2	1975-76	256	27	.239	
Cage, Wayne	2	1981-82	252	62	.235			Johnson, Dave	2	1975-76	199	39	.241	
Chance, Bob	2	1969-70	143	22	.271			Johnson, Frank	1	1972	101	13	.232	
Christian, Bob	2	1971-72	232	27	.263			Johnson, Greg	1	1982	104	10	.256	
Coggins, Frank	1	1973	13	2	.125			Johnson, Randy	2	1987-88	142	9	.306	
Corey, Mark	1	1984	31	3	.215			Johnson, Stan	1	1969	96	5	.242	
Cosey, Ray	1	1981	120	15	.251			Jones, Bobby	2	1979-80	174	20	.284	
Cromartie, Warren	6	1984-89	662	157	.327	89 ba-MVP		Jones, Clarence	8	1970-77	961	246	.239	74, 76 hr
Cruz, Hector	1	1983	58	4	.240			Jones, Ruppert	1	1988	52	8	.254	
Cruz, Tommy	6	1980-85	712	120	.310			Keough, Marty	1	1968	134	17	.231	
Dade, Paul	1	1981	37	1	.219			Kirkland, Willie	6	1968-73	723	126	.246	
Davis, Dick	5	1984-88	461	117	.331			Kostro, Frank	1	1970	37	1	.200	
Davis, Willie	2	1977-78	199	43	.297			Klaus, Billy	1	1963	62	3	.257	
Dayett, Brian	2	1988-89	119	18	.269			Krsnich, Mike	5	1963-67	506	90	.265	
DeCinces, Doug	1	1989	84	19	.244			Lacock, Pete	1	1981	90	10	.269	
Destrade, Orestes	1	1989	83	32	.257			Larker, Norm	2	1965-66	224	14	.267	
Diaz, Mike	1	1989	130	39	.301			Lancellotti, Rich	2	1987-88	200	55	.207	87 hr
Doby, Larry	1	1962	72	10	.225			Lee, Leron	11	1977-87	1315	283	.320	80 ba, 77 hr-rbi
Dodson, Pat	1	1989	6	0	.313			Lefebvre, Jim	4	1973-76	330	60	.263	
Doyle, Jeff	2	1984-85	243	29	.263			Lezcano, Sixto	1	1987	20	3	.217	
Duncan, Taylor	1	1980	64	14	.235			Lind, Jack	1	1977	65	7	.237	
Dupree, Mike	1	1980	127	10	.266			Lis, Joe	1	1978	95	6	.206	
Easler, Mike	2	1988-89	142	26	.302			Llenas, Winston	1	1976	101	6	.227	
Edwards, Mike	1	1983	53	1	.291			Locklear, Gene	1	1978	108	8	.240	
Emery, Calvin	1	1970	94	8	.213			Logan, Johnny	1	1964	96	7	.189	
Essegian, Chuck	1	1964	110	15	.263			Lolich, Ron	3	1974-76	272	56	.238	

Name	Yrs		G	HR	BA	Titles Won
Lopez, Arturo	6	1968-73	750	116	.290	
Loman, Doug	1	1986	126	14	.291	
Lum, Mike	1	1982	117	12	.269	
Lyttle, Jim	7	1977-83	876	166	.285	
Macha, Ken	4	1982-85	473	82	.304	
Madlock, Bill	1	1988	123	19	.263	
Manuel, Charlie	6	1976-81	621	189	.303	79-80 hr, 80 rbi, 79 MVP
Marshall, Jim	3	1963-65	408	78	.268	
Martin, Gene	6	1974-79	746	189	.272	
May, Carlos	4	1978-81	415	70	.309	
McFadden, Leon	1	1972	54	2	.283	
McGuire, Mickey	2	1973-74	207	11	.265	
McManus, Jim	2	1962-63	190	20	.236	
McNulty, Bill	1	1975	64	13	.190	
Mejias, Roman	1	1966	30	0	.288	
Millan, Felix	3	1978-80	325	12	.306	79 ba
Miller, John	3	1970-72	382	79	.245	
Mitchell, Bobby	4	1976-79	474	113	.250	78 hr
Money, Don	1	1984	29	8	.260	
Morton, Bubba	1	1970	48	3	.173	
Muser, Tony	1	1979	65	2	.196	
Nettles, Jim	1	1975	84	3	.234	
Newcombe, Don	1	1962	81	12	.262	
Nieman, Bob	1	1963	110	13	.301	
Nyman, Chris	2	1984-85	246	55	.276	
Oglivie, Ben	2	1987-88	224	46	.306	
Ontiveros, Steve	6	1980-85	686	82	.312	
Ortenzio, Frank	2	1979-80	149	30	.250	
Paciorek, Jim	2	1988-89	248	29	.333	
Parker, Wes	1	1974	127	14	.301	
Parrish, Larry	1	1989	130	42	.268	89 hr
Patterson, Mike	1	1985	88	16	.225	
Palys, Stan	4	1964-67	446	66	.275	
Pepitone, Joe	1	1973	14	1	.163	
Perlozzo, Sam	1	1980	118	15	.281	
Peterson, Carl	3	1961-63	357	58	.272	
Pierce, Jack	1	1977	95	13	.227	
Pointer, Aaron	3	1970-72	302	40	.230	
Ponce, Carlos	4	1986-89	518	119	.299	87 rbi, 88 hr-rbi
Putnam, Pat	2	1986-87	243	37	.266	
Qualls, Jimmy	2	1972-73	162	15	.252	
Raines, Larry	3	1953-55	330	31	.302	54 ba, 53 sb
Rajsich, Gary	3	1986-88	317	76	.283	
Rawdon, Wade	1	1989	123	22	.300	
Reinback, Mike	5	1976-80	565	94	.296	
Repoz, Roger	5	1974-77	526	122	.262	
Rivera, Bombo	2	1985-86	158	37	.240	
Rivera, German	1	1989	123	25	.260	
Roberts, Dave	7	1967-73	814	183	.275	
Robson, Tom	1	1976	37	3	.209	
Rodgers, Andre	1	1969	49	4	.210	
Roig, Tony	6	1963-78	779	126	.255	
Rosario, Jim	2	1975-76	131	5	.215	
Scheinblum, Rich	2	1975-76	239	33	.295	
Scott, John	3	1979-81	279	48	.262	
Shirley, Bart	2	1971-72	246	15	.183	
Sipin, John	9	1972-80	1036	218	.297	
Smith, Chris	2	1984-85	68	5	.202	
Smith, Reggie	2	1983-84	186	45	.271	
Smith, Willie	2	1972-73	170	29	.259	
Solaita, Tony	4	1980-83	510	155	.268	81 hr-rbi
Sorrell, Bill	2	1972-73	183	20	.278	
Spencer, Daryl	7	1964-70	731	152	.275	64, 65 ba
Spikes, Charlie	1	1981	26	1	.122	
Stanton, Leroy	1	1979	121	23	.225	
Stephens, Gene	1	1966	109	5	.224	
Stroughter, Steve	1	1983	28	5	.276	
Stuart, Dick	2	1967-68	208	49	.257	
Tatum, Jarvis	1	1971	31	1	.192	
Taylor, Robert	3	1973-75	358	30	.259	
Testa, Nick	1	1962	57	0	.136	
Thomas, Lee	1	1969	109	12	.263	
Thomasson, Gary	2	1981-82	167	20	.249	
Tolan, Bobby	1	1978	98	6	.267	
Tracy, Jim	2	1983-84	128	20	.301	
Tyrone, Jim	3	1979-82	435	74	.287	
Upshaw, Willie	1	1989	123	33	.255	
Valentine, Fred	1	1970	123	11	.246	
Versalles, Zoilo	1	1972	48	4	.189	
Vidal, Jose	1	1971	39	2	.221	
Vukovich, George	2	1986-87	222	32	.256	
Walls, Lee	1	1965	108	14	.239	
Walton, Danny	1	1978	75	9	.215	
Ward, Jay	1	1966	104	14	.238	
Wells, Greg	7	1983-89	852	224	.328	84 hr-ba-rbi-MVP, 87 rbi, 89 ba-rbi
Werhas, Johnny	1	1971	100	8	.214	
White, Jerry	2	1984-85	218	37	.251	
White, Roy	3	1980-82	362	54	.283	
Whitfield, Terry	3	1981-83	374	85	.289	
Williams, Bernie	6	1975-80	718	96	.258	
Williams, Dallas	1	1988	100	10	.242	
Williams, Walt	2	1976-77	239	44	.277	
Wills, Bump	2	1983-84	203	16	.259	
Wilson, George	2	1963-64	225	27	.258	
Windhorn, Gordon	6	1964-69	641	86	.255	
Wolfe, Larry	1	1982	88	14	.224	
Woods, Ron	2	1975-76	192	19	.263	
Wright, George	1	1988	89	11	.263	
Zimmer, Don	1	1966	87	9	.182	

U.S. Major League Pitchers in Japan*

Name	Yrs		Won-Lost	ERA
Alexander, Bob	1	1959	2-5	4.67
Austin, Rich	1	1974	1-1	2.33
Beene, Andy	1	1985	2-2	7.25
Burnside, Pete	2	1964-65	10-22	3.10
Castillo, Bobby	1	1987	1-1	7.84
Comstock, Keith	2	1985	8-10	4.47
Culver, George	1	1975	1-4	6.50
Davis, Ron	1	1989	4-5	3.97
Eichelberger, Juan	1	1989	0-3	7.04
Foytack, Paul	1	1965	2-3	3.16
Gail, Rich	2	1985-86	18-18	4.42
Gibson, Bob	1	1988	7-11	4.87
Grunwald, Alfred	1	1962	2-8	4.50
Gullickson, Bill	2	1988-89	21-14	3.29
Hoffman, Guy	1	1989	9-6	3.45
Kekich, Mike	1	1974	5-11	4.13
Keough, Matt	3	1987-89	38-35	3.43
Kiely, Leo	1	1953	6-0	1.80
Krueger, Rich	1	1979	2-1	4.66
Kuhaulua, Fred	1	1978	3-4	4.32
Lesley, Brad	2	1986-87	7-5	3.00
Ley, Richard	2	1974-75	5-5	4.09
Mickens, Glenn	5	1959-63	45-51	2.50
Newcombe, Don	1	1962	0-0	4.50
Paine, Phil	1	1953	4-3	1.77
Palmquist, Ed	1	1963	0-1	3.00
Rajsich, David	1	1984	0-1	3.18
Reynolds, Bob	1	1977	0-0	9.00
Sanchez, Luis	2	1986-87	4-4	2.54
Shirley, Steve	2	1983-84	5-7	4.17
Smith, Willie	1	1972	0-1	81.00
Stanka, Joe	7	1960-66	100-72	3.03
Stone, Dean	1	1964	0-0	3.75
Tillotson, Thad	1	1971	3-4	6.40
Wright, Clyde	3	1976-78	22-18	3.97
TOTALS			337-336	

* Lists compiled from Wayne Graczyk, *Americans in Japan 1950-1986,* and Isao Chiba, "Kiroku no Techo (Record Notes)," *Shukan Baseball,* March 28, 1988, and April 4, 1988.

Baseball in the Caribbean

Rob Ruck

Soon after the World Series marks the season's end in the United States, baseball springs back to life in and around the Caribbean. There, to the beat of *salsa* and *merengue* and against a backdrop of palm trees and seasonal labor, some of the best baseball in the world is played each winter. While most of South America follows football and the British West Indies follows cricket, the rest of the Caribbean basin plays baseball—and has for the better part of a century.

Since baseball fever first infected Cuba in the 1870s, the game has infiltrated the sporting psyches of Mexico, Nicaragua, the Dominican Republic, Venezuela, Puerto Rico, Panama, and Colombia. Although tied to major league baseball in four of these countries through a set of winter leagues and as a source of fresh talent, Caribbean baseball is not simply an appendage of the game that is played in the United States. Rather, baseball has acquired an autonomous persona as the peoples of the region have made the game into their own national pastimes.

More than simply recreation or a display of grace and competence, baseball has catalyzed national consciousness and cohesion in the Caribbean basin. A critical part of the fabric of everyday life, the sport has also influenced how these societies have come to define themselves, their relations with each other, and their ties to the United States. "It's more than a game," Dominican winter league general manager Winston Llenas once remarked. "It's our passion. It's almost our way of life."

Pedro Julio Santana stands at his office window in what was once the colonial zone of Santo Domingo. A sportsman at the center of Dominican baseball's evolution earlier this century, he searches for words to describe how the game penetrated his country and the rest of the basin. Glancing below to the hulking walls of the first Catholic cathedral in the western hemisphere, Santana finds his metaphor. "It is much the same as that which happened with Christianity. Jesus could be compared to the North Americans, but the apostles were the ones that spread the faith, and the apostles of baseball were Cubans. Even though the Dominican Republic and Puerto Rico were occupied by the North Americans, the Cubans first brought baseball here, and to Mexico and Venezuela, too."

Caribbean baseball's first epicenter was Cuba, which had fallen into orbit around the United States by the late nineteenth century. Baseball arrived there last century, brought by sailors, students, and businessmen from the United States as well as by Cubans who had traveled north. The U.S. military occupations that followed the 1898 conflict with Spain stimulated baseball's expansion there and across the basin. By the time the Good Neighbor Policy had supplanted the Big Stick in the 1930s, baseball was entrenched. Moreover, Cuban baseball had become the focal point of an international network that stretched from the Caribbean basin through the Negro Leagues.

What was likely the first ballgame in Cuba with local participation occurred in June 1866, when sailors of a U.S. ship taking on sugar invited Cuban longshoremen to play. *El Club Habana* (Havana) began two years later, crushing a team from Matanzas in the first organized contest of two Cuban teams.

Havana's victory over Matanzas featured two of Cuba's sporting pioneers, Esteban Bellan and Emilio Sabourín. Bellan became the first Latino in U.S. organized baseball, playing three seasons in the National Association (1871–1873). Sabourín, the A. G. Spalding of Cuban baseball, was the motivating force behind the *Liga de Beisbol Profesional Cubana,* whose inaugural tournament was won by Sabourín's reconstituted Havana club in 1878. Sabourín proselytized for his sport as well as for the cause of Cuban independence from Spain until his contribution of baseball revenues to the independence movement incurred the wrath of Spanish officials. They imprisoned Sabourín until his death and banned baseball in parts of their colony.

While initially a game of the more affluent and those with contact with the United States, baseball soon spread to all classes of Cuban society, both urban and rural. U.S. military occupations, support by companies and businessmen, and close ties to political elites would shape its subsequent development, much as these forces would elsewhere in the basin.

The game was organized on three overlapping levels in its early years. The first was an ad hoc player-organized, self-directed network of teams. The second involved clubs sponsored by businessmen, companies, and politicians who sought the promotional advantages of such patronage. The third level was that of professional (sometimes semiprofessional) baseball, which organized championships from 1878 until 1961, with a changing cast of teams and format. In some years, no tournaments were held, while in others both a summer and winter season took place. Havana, Almendares, Santa Clara, Cienfuegos, and Marianao were the league's mainstays.

Until the 1959 Cuban Revolution and the ensuing U.S. blockade, Cuba set the standard for Caribbean baseball. It sent the most players to the major and Negro leagues while its winter and summer tournaments featured the highest caliber of Latin ball and attracted players from both the States and the basin. Cuban players, radio broadcasts, and emigrants, in turn, became baseball's emissaries to the rest of the region.

In the Dominican Republic, Cubans who had migrated to escape the turmoil of the Ten Years' War (1868–1878) were the first to form teams. Young Dominicans emulated them and joined with compatriots who had studied in the United States to establish a self-organized matrix of teams and tournaments well in place before the U.S. Marines arrived in 1916 for their eight-year occupation. Santo Domingo's *Licey,* the oldest of the six professional Dominican clubs, formed in 1907, while the forerunners of San Pedro de Macoris's *Estrellas Orientales,* Santiago's *Aguilas Cibaeñas,* and Santo Domingo's other club, *Escogido,* took to the field soon afterward.

While Dominicans refer to these early decades as the romantic epoch of baseball, commercial forces were already at work there and across the basin. Teams occasionally recruited players with the lure of financial reward and soon began importing Cubans and Puerto Ricans for championship tournaments. Moreover, local clubs often induced talented players with payment in cash or work. North American oil companies in Venezuela, rum distilleries and tobacco manufacturers in Cuba, and sugar cane companies in Nicaragua, Puerto Rico, Cuba, and the Dominican Republic sponsored or assisted workplace teams for recreation and community entertainment, but with an industrial agenda, too — winning their workers' hearts and minds.

During these "Yankee years," between 1898 and 1933, when the Marines hit the beaches thirty-four times in ten different basin countries, they found baseball already implanted in Cuba, Puerto Rico, Nicaragua, Mexico, and the Dominican Republic. They never made it to Venezuela, but would have found baseball there, too, as early as the organization of the Caracas club in 1895. The occupations, though, helped to push the sport along. While Nicaraguans had played on their Atlantic coast since 1888, the nation's longest-running pro team, *Boer,* was founded by the U.S. consul in Managua. In the Dominican Republic, U.S. marines and sailors played ball to bolster morale; they were frequently challenged by Dominican teams, for whom these contests were both a test of sporting abilities and national character. Far more baseball was in evidence by the end of the U.S. stay on the island.

While Cubans and some other basin natives had broken into baseball in the States during the first half of the century, the center of gravity for Caribbean baseball remained a regional one. A "Have Glove—Will Travel" mentality soon took hold of basin baseball and its ablest practitioners made the rounds of national tournaments. A core of the finest black players from the States—then barred from major league play by the color line, as were most Latinos—joined them in Cuba, the Dominican Republic, Puerto Rico, Venezuela, and Mexico.

Caribbean baseball's apogee was probably reached in the summer of 1937 in the Dominican Republic during a national championship dedicated to the re-election of the then state-of-the-art dictator Rafael Trujillo. Top Dominican players were joined by the best Cuban, Puerto Rican, and Negro league talent that the Dominican peso could buy to form a three-team league. Santiago boasted the services of Martín Dihigo, Luís Tiant Sr., and Horacio Martínez; San Pedro de Macoris countered with Tetelo Vargas, Ramón Bragaña, and Cocaína García, while the eventual victor, *Ciudad Trujillo* (a merger of *Licey* and *Escogido* that represented the city Trujillo had renamed in his own honor) relied on future Hall of Famers Josh Gibson, Cool Papa Bell, and Satchel Paige, as well as Silvío García, Perucho Cepeda, and Sam Bankhead. Baseball on the island was the equal of that played anywhere that summer. These players barnstormed yearround, and many of them later played together as *Santa Clara* in Cuba and as *La Concordia* in Venezuela.

The proprietary interest taken by caudillos such as Trujillo or Nicaragua's Anastasio Somoza ensured baseball of its most-favored sport status and contributed to the growth of strong regional rivalries. Caribbean participation in the *Mundiales,* the world amateur baseball championships that began in 1938, and later the Caribbean Series of pro circuits, which started in 1949, reinforced the game's hegemony.

Latin ball was an opportunity for North American players to supplement their income and hone their skills in encounters that sometimes surpassed the caliber of major league play. However, it was also a threat to organized baseball in the States. Major league teams had played in Cuba before the turn of the century, and afterward Negro league squads as well as individual black and white pros journeyed south. The 1937 raids on the Negro leagues by Dominican teams destroyed the Pittsburgh Crawfords, and other Negro league squads frequently lost their best players and gate attractions to basin teams. From 1939 until the demise of independent black baseball a decade later, Venezuelan and Mexican franchises vied for Negro leaguers during the summer months, enticing Josh Gibson, Ray Dandridge, and other stars to jump their Negro league teams. They offered better pay and a different atmosphere. "Not only do I get more money playing here, but I live like a king," Willie Wells wrote to *Pittsburgh Courier* sportswriter Wendell Smith in 1939 to explain his switch from the Newark Eagles to Vera Cruz. "I am not faced with the racial problem. . . . I've found freedom and democracy here, something I never found in the United States. . . . Here, in Mexico, I am a man."

The major leagues were less vulnerable to such competition, but even they blanched when Mexican liquor mogul Jorge Pasquel sought major leaguers in addition to Negro leaguers to bolster the six-team summer Mexican League in 1946. Railroad workers from the States taught the game to their Mexican colleagues as early as the 1880s and a strong semipro league formed in the 1920s. In Sonora and Mexico City, the game felt the pull of baseball across the northern border, which Mexican and black teams frequently crossed. In the Yucatan, baseball pointed more toward the Caribbean, especially Cuba. Pasquel, pumping new capital into the league, persuaded Mickey Owens, Sal Maglie, and Max Lanier to desert their major league teams, prompting the latter to ban them. Pasquel also pursued Stan Musial, reportedly placing $50,000 on the bed in his spring training hotel room at a time when the Cardinals' outfielder was making but $13,000 a season. Other basin leagues also lost top players in the Mexican effort to upgrade. Pasquel's challenge, however, was blunted by organized baseball in the States, which tried to limit any competition for its players, and by the Mexican League's own logistical and financial difficulties. The challenge faded after the 1948 season. In the aftermath of the Mexican raids and with integration imminent, major league baseball began to sign accords with professional leagues throughout the basin, formalizing player movement and institutionalizing winter play.

That was especially important, for with the end of the color line in 1947 Latinos soon renewed their assault on major league ball. By the 1970s, the basin would constitute the freshest source of talent in the majors, especially important as the black community turned away from baseball as part of a general shift toward other sports in the United States. But Latin players—black and white—had played pro ball in the United States long before Jackie Robinson's historic debut.

Colombia's Luis Castro broke ground in baseball's modern era, after the creation of the National and American Leagues, but Cubans for the most part led the way. While Castro played only part of the 1902 season, Rafael Almeida and Armando Marsans spearheaded a Cuban invasion in 1911 that left its imprimatur on the game and numbered over thirty players before integration. Another ninety or so Cubans played major league ball after that divide.

The crucial factor controlling the entry of Cubans and other basin players into the major leagues was skin color. Barnstorming their way through black communities from the early century on, Cuban teams had become a mainstay of the Negro leagues that began in 1920. Popular draws, the Cuban Stars and the New York Cubans featured Latinos too dark to pass the color line into the majors. Playing most of their contests on the road, these Caribbean squads injected talent and a tropical allure to the game. Cubans Martín Dihigo, Alejandro Oms, Luís Tiant Sr., Orestes "Minnie" Miñoso, and Silvío García were joined by Dominicans Horacio Martínez and Tetelo Vargas, Puerto Rican Peruchin Cepeda, Panamanian Pat Scantlebury, and sometimes several black North Americans who passed for Cubans, on these pan-Caribbean aggregations. A few Cubans, such as Cristóbal Torriente, a powerful outfielder, and José de la Caridad Méndez, *"El Diamante Negro,"* who took a no-hitter into the ninth inning the first time he faced the barnstorming Cincinnati Reds, became mainstays of other Negro league franchises.

Lighter-skinned Cubans from that predominantly mixed island played on the other side of sport's racial boundary in the States, in the major leagues. Perhaps the greatest pre–Jackie Robinson Cuban major leaguer was Adolfo Luque, a pitcher whose twenty big league seasons were capped by a brilliant 27–8 record in 1923 and a winning relief stint of shutout ball in the seventh game of the 1933 World Series. Following that game, Clark Griffith, whose Washington Senators had lost the Series, decided to back a scouting exhibition to Cuba. He sent Joe Cambria.

"Papa Joe," as many still refer to Cambria, stocked the Senators with Cubans. Among his first signees was Roberto Estalella, from the sugarcane milltown that Hershey Chocolate operated in Cárdenas. The *Cincinnati Enquirer* had greeted the signings of Almeida and Mar-

sans in 1911 with relief, introducing them as "two of the purest bars of Castilian soap to ever wash upon our shores," but the darker-hued Estalella was more controversial. No one challenged this indirect breaching of the color line, although it prompted Red Smith to write his classic column in which he suspected that "there was a Senegambian somewhere in the Cuban batpile where Senatorial lumber was seasoned."

The player regarded in the Caribbean as the best Cuban ever, and arguably the finest ballplayer of all time, never played major league ball. Martín Dihigo displayed his talents in Cuba, the United States, Mexico, Venezuela, and the Dominican Republic, and is enshrined in the Hall of Fame of three of these nations. Dihigo excelled at the plate, on the mound, and as a manager, but integration came too late for him. His bust at Havana's *Estadio Latinoamericano* reads simply, *El Inmortal*.

The contradiction that some Cubans played in the majors and others in the Negro leagues was not lost upon blacks in the States or on Latin ballplayers. As early as Almeida's and Marsans' 1911 debut, the black press began to hope that black ballplayers would soon follow them into baseball's most exclusive league. And while Negro leaguers went south to adulation and greater pay, dark-skinned Latinos who came north encountered prejudice based on both skin color and nationality. As major leaguers such as Ty Cobb, Tris Speaker, and Carl Hubbell traveled south to play in winter ball, black North Americans and Latinos found that they could more than hold their own. These symbolic victories were appreciated both in the States and throughout the basin. North American blacks and the peoples of the region shared each other's athletes and appropriated each other's sporting heroes and symbols. If a proving ground was necessary to show that blacks could compete with whites, that the two could coexist on the same squad, or to dispel any other racial shibboleth, Caribbean baseball was just that.

Following integration, the more farsighted owners began scouring the islands for prospects. Soon a fresh wave of Latinos arrived in the majors, including three future Hall of Famers: Venezuela's Luís Aparicio, Puerto Rico's Roberto Clemente, and the Dominican Republic's Juan Marichal. They signaled, moreover, a shift away from Cuba as the primary spawning waters for Caribbean players.

With the 1959 Cuban Revolution and the subsequent deterioration of relations with the United States, Cuba fell out of organized baseball's system. The Havana Sugar Kings, an International League franchise affiliated with the Reds since 1954, were on their way to winning the Little World Series of the AAA minor leagues in 1959, just months after Fidel Castro came to power. The revolutionary government offered to underwrite the Sugar Kings' debts, and Castro sought to keep the franchise there, "even if I have to pitch," but the International League shipped the club to Jersey City during the 1960 season. Baseball in Cuba was cut off completely from baseball in the United States, and the movement of players and equipment halted. Cuba developed its own sporting goods industry and relied on the repatriated Dihigo, a political exile during the 1950s who had given money to Che Guevara and who now returned to help teach the game. Cuban baseball soon shed its commercial skin and sought instead to advance the social and political aims of the revolution. Cuba has remained *the* powerhouse in world amateur baseball ever since, but the island stopped producing new major leaguers. After the Zoilo Versalles, Tony Oliva, Tony Pérez generations passed out of baseball, the next set of Cubans to reach the majors were those who, while born on the island, had grown up in the United States.

The fulcrum of baseball power, meanwhile, shifted one island to the east, where the Dominican Republic shared Hispaniola with French-speaking, soccer-playing Haiti. After the star-studded 1937 season, pro ball in the Dominican Republic entered a fourteen-year hiatus. While an occasional tournament celebrated an event such as the nation's centennial, Dominican pros Horacio Martínez and Tetelo Vargas plied their trade in Cuba, Venezuela, or the United States. But several forces revitalized Dominican baseball in the 1940s, and after the reappearance of a professional league in 1951, these dynamics propelled over a hundred players to the major leagues.

The first catalyst was the birth of the *Mundial,* an international championship tournament for amateur baseball. After its inauguration in England in 1938, the *Mundial* moved to the Caribbean. Held in the basin throughout the 1940s, with Cuba hosting five consecutive tournaments, the *Mundial* had a decidedly Latin flavor and became the most important sporting competition in which these nations competed on something approximating equal footing, both with each other and with the United States. Basin nations won every championship from 1940 through 1972, with Cuba winning eleven out of eighteen times.

National aspirations and international rivalries sometimes were injected into the *Mundial.* An irate Anastasio Somoza fired the Nicaraguan manager in the midst of one and took to the dugout to direct the team himself. Nicaraguan national honor was restored by a victory over Cuba in the final game of the 1972 series, an event still celebrated as one of the Central American nation's greatest sporting exploits. The Dominican victory in 1948, coming just months after virtually the entire national championship team perished in a plane crash by the Río Verde, captivated the Republic and lent impetus to pro ball's rebirth there.

A second factor in Dominican baseball's rejuvenation was the creation of the *Dirección General de Deportes.* Modeled in part after the comparable Cuban agency, this government body organized regional and then national tournaments for amateur baseball (often with semiprofessional overtones) that gave further purpose to local, company, and armed forces support. Many of the Dominicans that entered the majors from the late 1950s on, including Marichal, Manuel Mota, and the three Rojas Alou brothers, played on these squads.

The final catalysts to Dominican ascendancy were bananas and sugarcane, and the concentrations of baseball fervor and expertise which they fostered. While the sugarcane milltowns of the southeast produce the most prospects today, the banana region along the northwest border with Haiti was instrumental in cultivating the first contingent of pros in the late 1950s. There the Grenada Company, a United Fruit Company subsidiary, began two teams for its workers and their sons in the 1940s. The

squad won three national championships, and Juan Marichal and Guayubín Olivo passed through its ranks to the majors.

Dominican sugarcane milltowns, like those in Cuba, had long spawned ballclubs. The six-month long *tiempo muerto,* or dead season, when the cane required minimal attention and most workers were unemployed, contributed to an intense sporting environment, first for cricket and ultimately for baseball. In the 1920s and '30s, *Central La Romana's Papagayo* team was an amateur powerhouse, and in the 1940s the milltowns in and around San Pedro de Macorís made their play. There the descendants of cricket-playing migrants from the British West Indies brought to cut cane and work in the mills displayed an aptitude for playing baseball and an approach to organizing the game that made San Pedro baseball's Mecca. Since Rico Carty's breakthrough in the 1960s, San Pedro has contributed about one-third of the Dominicans to play in the big leagues. The town currently sends more of its native sons to the majors on a per-capita basis than any town ever has. There is probably no other place on earth where the game is played as well and as widely.

Since the end of the color line, ballplayers from Cuba, the Dominican Republic, Venezuela, Puerto Rico, Panama, Nicaragua, Mexico, Colombia, and even the Bahamas have played major league ball. Although the Dominican Republic leads this basin contingent, substantial numbers of Puerto Ricans and Venezuelans are present, too. Mexico, despite a population that dwarfs the rest of the region combined and its well-developed pro leagues, sends few players to the majors. Unlike the other basin leagues, Mexican teams retain first rights to sign any native amateur. A major league club, therefore, must buy the contract from a player's Mexican club, usually for more than it costs to sign a prospect elsewhere in the region. This relationship, the summer Mexican league, and perhaps cultural factors, too, persuade native ballplayers to remain in Mexico.

Cuba opted out of this network after its revolution, and Nicaragua, whose eleven-year fling with the pro winter leagues ended in 1967, followed suit after its 1979 revolution. Panama and Colombia have also tried winter ball, but financial pressures made play sporadic.

The flow of players continues to run both north and south. Minor and major leaguers from the United States still play in the winter leagues, which presently operate in Venezuela, Puerto Rico, the Dominican Republic, and Mexico. In their heyday during the 1950s and '60s, these winter leagues featured major leaguers like Tommy Lasorda, Whitey Ford, and Willie Stargell. But as major league salaries soared in the 1970s and unfavorable rates of exchanges weakened basin economies, the winter leagues restricted the number of North American imports. Minor leaguers and inexperienced major leaguers have replaced them. For them, these leagues provide the chance to play in the winter months, developing the potential that might allow them to crack a big league roster. They also earn higher pay than they do in the minors, encounter competition from top Latino players, and are treated as demigods by the impassioned *fanáticos* of the winter game.

The winners of the winter leagues have met in a *Serie del Caribe* since 1949. Between 1949 and 1960, the pennant-winning squads of Cuba, Panama, Puerto Rico, and Venezuela played in early February to determine a champion of the Caribbean. Cuba won over half of these tournaments, but after the revolution, the series was discontinued. When it resumed in 1970, Mexico and the Dominican Republic replaced Cuba and Panama. The current round-robin format sends the teams that win their postseason tournaments to the *Serie del Caribe* along with a number of reinforcements, including North Americans, from their defeated opponents. Willie Mays, Monte Irvin, Camilo Pasqual, Rico Carty, and Vic Pellot Power are among those who have starred in these postseason celebrations.

Winter ball has descended from its zenith of the 1950s and '60s largely due to economic dynamics beyond the control of the Caribbean franchises. Rising player and fuel costs, devalued currencies, and underdevelopment pushed many into deficits, with government subsidies often vital to their continuation. Government support, long a feature of basin baseball, helps to keep current the Dominican saying that there will never be political trouble during the baseball season, only afterward. But by the middle of the 1980s, fewer of the established Latin major leaguers suited up for the October-through-January campaign. The demands of the regular season, the threat of injury, and the relatively inconsequential pay of winter ball suggest that this trend will continue. The pattern, however, has given younger Latin ballplayers the chance to play before knowledgeable fans and against competition that is often at a major league level.

While winter ball in the late 1980s was troubled and other sports were making inroads, baseball remains *el rey de deportes* (the king of sports) throughout the basin. From the rocky hillsides and arid plains of northern Mexico through the canefields of the islands to the basin's southernmost flank in the Andes, baseball commands a fascination approaching reverence.

Baseball's significance derives from the role that it has played in the coming together of these societies in the twentieth century. Knitting a common cultural fabric, serving as a vent to social and political tensions, and offering a vehicle not only for individual mobility but collective social affirmation, baseball indeed has been more than a game. It has offered the citizens of the basin a chance to enter a ritual kinship embracing all fans and players. And while reflecting the progressive penetration of the United States in the region, baseball has been more than a cultural transmission belt for North American values. Beating each other and excelling in the major leagues and international competitions at a time when the Caribbean basin has encountered difficulties in asserting either its political or economic autonomy have been tremendous sources of pride. And that symbolic recognition has become a catalyst to national cohesion and consciousness for the region in its troubled evolution this century.

The lights are going out in Santo Domingo, and like so many aspects of this nation's descent into economic chaos, it's affecting baseball. They still play the game, but this year the ballparks are eerily quiet, mute testimony to winter baseball's deepening crisis. And those close to the game are asking what it will take to ensure professional baseball's survival in the 1990s.

The streets outside *Estadio Quisqueya* in Santo Do-

mingo are dark; the players sprawl in clusters on the grass inside. A few take a form of batting practice, hitting balls tossed laterally from a few feet away, into a net. Soon, as darkness becomes nearly complete, they hit off a tee. Then, even that becomes impossible.

Gradually, the Big Dipper becomes visible, standing straight up to form a celestial question mark that might as well be asking if tonight's game will be played.

The question is answered when the generator kicks in with a fireworks-like flourish and bulbs pop on in the light stanchions. At first, nobody moves, then gradually bodies rise stiffly from the grass and walk out onto the field.

This barely averted blackout offers an exaggerated example of winter ball's woes. But the crisis, which has halved attendance here and in Puerto Rico, knocked one franchise out of action, and threatens others, has been brewing for over a decade.

"Dominicans haven't lost their love of the game," Winston Llenas, *Aguilas'* general manager attests. "But this society is in trouble, serious trouble. It's living dangerously now."

Over two years into an economic downturn in which inflation and the exchange rate for the *peso* with the U.S. dollar have soared and living standards have fallen, the Dominican Republic suffers from severe electrical shortages, a lack of potable water, and a transportation system in suspended motion. The ballparks, once a beacon of light in the evening sky, now often remain dark until shortly before game time.

The nation's collapse is part of a continental decline that has seen much of Latin America regress to an economic level last seen during the 1930s.

"Perhaps our biggest problem," Llenas adds, "is the lack of desire on the part of the established Dominican players to play." Indeed, as major league salaries have spiraled upward, the incentive for the better-known Latins to play winter ball has all but disappeared.

Llenas points to the benefits that have accrued to major league baseball from winter ball. "It's been a good partnership. Look at the résumés of players, managers, and even umpires in the United States. You have a saying there, 'What's good for General Motors is good for the USA.' Well, what's good for winter baseball is what's good for the major leagues. They should not let us die. Not when we need their help."

A few nights later in San Pedro de Macoris, La Romana's Jose Offerman goes deep in the hole, spins, and nabs the runner at first in a play that has even a few of San Pedro's players exchanging high fives. In La Romana's dugout, manager Victor Ramirez raises one hand in the air as if to give religious testimony and exclaims, " What a talent!"

Winter ball's lack of established major leaguers means that youths like Offerman are experiencing an accelerated development. By the end of the 1990 season, Offerman will be in the majors, and in coming years, he will attract Dominican fans back to the park. The cycle of regeneration is already at work.

But that process will take a few years—years that are not guaranteed. As the game concludes and a squadron of boys leaps from the top of the dugout onto the field, it seems improbable that such a vibrant institution as winter ball could end in the near future. But it could.

First Major Leaguers from Caribbean Basin Countries

Country	Player	Year	Team
Colombia	Luis "Jud" Castro	1902	Philadelphia Athletics
Cuba	Esteban Bellan	1871	Troy Haymakers
	Rafael Almeida	1911	Cincinnati Reds
	Armando Marsans	1911	Cincinnati Reds
Mexico	Baldomero "Mel" Almada	1933	Boston Red Sox
Venezuela	Alejandro Carrasquel	1939	Washington Senators
Puerto Rico	Hiram Bithorn	1942	Chicago Cubs
Panama	Héctor López	1955	Kansas City Athletics
	Humberto Robinson	1955	Milwaukee Braves
Dominican Republic	Osvaldo Virgil	1956	New York Giants
Nicaragua	Dennis Martínez	1976	Baltimore Orioles
Honduras	Gerald Young	1987	Houston Astros

Serie del Caribe

Series	Year	Site	Winning Team/Country	Series	Year	Site	Winning Team/Country
I	1949	Cuba	Almendares/Cuba	XVII	1974	Mexico	Caguas/Puerto Rico
II	1950	Puerto Rico	Carta Vieja/Panama	XVIII	1975	Puerto Rico	Bayamón/Puerto Rico
III	1951	Venezuela	Santurce/Puerto Rico	XIX	1976	Dominican Republic	Hermosillo/Mexico
IV	1952	Panama	La Habana/Cuba	XX	1977	Venezuela	Licey/Dominican Republic
V	1953	Cuba	Santurce/Puerto Rico	XXI	1978	Mexico	Mayagüez/Puerto Rico
VI	1954	Puerto Rico	Caguas/Puerto Rico	XXII	1979	Puerto Rico	Magallanes/Venezuela
VII	1955	Venezuela	Santurce/Puerto Rico	XXIII	1980	Dominican Republic	Licey/Dominican Republic
VIII	1956	Panama	Cienfuegos/Cuba		1981	Not Held	
IX	1957	Cuba	Marianao/Cuba	XXIV	1982	Mexico	Caracas/Venezuela
X	1958	Puerto Rico	Marianao/Cuba	XXV	1983	Venezuela	Arecibo/Puerto Rico
XI	1959	Venezuela	Almendares/Cuba	XXVI	1984	Puerto Rico	Zulia/Venezuela
XII	1960	Panama	Cienfuegos/Cuba	XXVII	1985	Mexico	Licey/Dominican Republic
	1961–69	Not Held		XXVIII	1986	Venezuela	Mexicali/Mexico
XIII	1970	Venezuela	Magallanes/Venezuela	XXIX	1987	Mexico	Caguas/Venezuela
XIV	1971	Puerto Rico	Licey/Dominican Republic	XXX	1988	Dominican Republic	Escogido/Dominican Republic
XV	1972	Dominican Republic	Ponce/Puerto Rico	XXXI	1989	Mazatlan	Zulia/Venezuela
XVI	1973	Venezuela	Licey/Dominican Republic	XXXII	1990	Miami	Escogido/Dominican Republic

Dominican League Statistics

Year	Champion	BA Leader	HR Leader	Most Games Won
1951	Licey	Luis Villodas .346	Pedro Formental 13	Guayuabín Olivo 10
1952	Aguilas	Luis Olmo .344	Alonzo Perry 11	Terry McDuffie 14
1953	Licey	Tetelo Vargas .355	Alonzo Perry 11	Emilio Cueche 13
1954	Estrellas Orientales	Alonzo Perry .326	Bob Thurman 11	Carrao Bracho G. Olivo 8
1955–56	Escogido*	Bob Wilson .333	Willie Kirkland 9	Fred Waters 11
1956–57	Escogido	Osvaldo Virgil .312	Danny Kravitz 4	Pete Burnside 11
1957–58	Escogido	Alonzo Perry .332	Dick Stuart 14	Fred Kipp 11
1958–59	Licey	Felipe Alou .351	Jim McDaniels 12	Bennie Daniels 12
1959–60	Escogido	Felipe Alou .359	Frank Howard 9	Stan Williams 12
1960–61	Escogido	Manuel Mota .344	Manuel Jiménez J.V. Nicolás Victor Ramirez Felipe Alou N. Saviñón Tied with 4	Danilo Riva 13
1961–62	Incomplete Season			
1962–63	Not Held			
1963–64	Licey	Manuel Mota .379	O. McFarlane 10	G. Olivo Steve Blass 9
1964–65	Aguilas	Manuel Mota .364	O. McFarlane 8	Dick LeMay 8
1965–66	Season not organized by league			
1966–67	Aguilas	Mateo Alou .363	Winston Llenas Bob Robertson 10	Dock Ellis 9
1967–68	Estrellas Orientales	Ricardo Carty .350	Bob Robertson 9	Silvano Quezada 11
1968–69	Escogido	Mateo Alou .390	Nate Colbert 8	Jay Ritchie 9
1969–70	Licey	Ralph Garr .387	Winston Llenas Byron Browne 9	G. Rounsaville 9
1970–71	Licey	Ralph Garr .457	César Cedeño 8	Rollie Fingers 9
1971–72	Aguilas	Ralph Garr .388	Charlie Sands 10	Gene Garber 9
1972–73	Licey	Von Joshua .358	Adrian Garrett 9	Pedro Borbón 9
1973–74	Licey	Dave Parker .345	Ricardo Carty 9	Rick Waits 8
1974–75	Aguilas	Bruce Bochte .352	Rafael Batista Bobby Darwin 8	James Richards 8
1975–76	Aguilas	Wilbur Howard .341	Wilbur Howard John Hale Gary Alexander Larry Parrish G. Thomasson Bill Nahorodny Andre Thornton Tied with 4	Nino Espinosa Tom Dettore 8
1976–77	Licey	Mario Guerrero .365	Pedro Guerrero Ike Hampton 6	Angel Torres 10
1977–78	Aguilas	Omar Moreno .345	Dick Davis 8	Odell Jones Al Holland Mickey Mahler 7
1978–79	Aguilas	Ted Cox .319	Bob Beall Dick Davis 7	Bo McLaughlin Mike Proly 9
1979–80	Licey	Tony Peña .317	A. De Freitas Alberto Lois Leon Durham Samuel Mejía Pedro Guerrero Tied with 3	Jerry Hannahs 9
1980–81	Escogido	Ken Landreaux .394	Tony Peña 7	Mario Soto M. Mahler 7
1981–82	Escogido	Pedro Hernandez .408	Dave Hostetler 9	Pasqual Pérez 10
1982–83	Licey	César Geronimo .341	Howard Johnson 8	Pasqual Pérez 9
1983–84	Licey	Miguel Diloné .343	Reggie Whittemore 12	Orel Hershiser Frank Wills 8
1984–85	Licey	Junior Noboa .327	Ralph Bryant 9	Tom Filer 8
1985–86	Aguilas	Tony Fernández .364	Tony Peña 9	Mickey Mahler 8
1986–87	Aguilas	Stanley Javier .374	Ralph Bryant 13	Gibson Alba José Nuñez Eric Plunk Tied with 5
1987–88	Escogido	Stanley Javier .363	Mark Parent 10	José Bautista 8
1988–89	Licey	Julio Peguero .327	Domingo Michel 9	Melido Perez 8–3
1989–90	Escogido	Angel González .403	Denny González 5	Mel Rojas Jeff Shaw Kevin Wicklander Darren Holmes Tied with 6

* First year held in winter

Cuban League Statistics

Year	Champion	BA Leader	HR Leader	Most Games Won
1878–79	Habana Undefeated			
1879–80	Habana			
1880–81	Not held			
1882	Disputed: Fe and Habana			
1882–83	Habana			
1885	Habana	Pablo Ronquilla .350		
1885–86	Habana Undefeated	Wenceslao Gálvez .345		Adolfo Luján 5–0
1887	Habana	R. Martínez .439		Adolfo Luján 5–0
1888	Fe	Antonio García .448		Francisco Hernández 10–2
1889	Habana	Francisco Salabarria .305		Adolfo Luján 10–3
1889–90	Habana	Antonio García .364		Miguel Prats 11–2
1890–91	Fe	Alfredo Crespo .375		Miguel Prats 9–4
1892	Habana	Antonio García .362		E. Hernández 4–1
1892–93	Matanzas	Antonio García .385		Francisco Hernández 4–1
1893–94	Almendares	Miguel Pratts .394		José Pastoriza 16–7
1894–95	Suspended due to War of Independence	Alfredo Arcaño .430		Enrique García 12–4
1897–98	Not finished			
1898	Habanista	Valentín González .394		José Romero 5–2
1900	San Francisco	Esteban Pratts .333		Luis Padrón 13–4
1901	Habana	Julián Castillo .454		Carlos Royer 12–3

Year	Champion	BA Leader	HR Leader	Most Games Won
1902	Habana Undefeated	Luis Padrón .463		Carlos Royer 17–0
1903	Habana	Julián Castillo .330		Cándido Fontanals 14–6
1904	Habana	Regino García .397		Carlos Royer 13–3
1905	Almendares	Regino García .305		Angel D'Meza 10–4
1905–6	Fe	Regino García .304		José Muñoz 8–1
1907	Almendares	Regino García .324		George Mack 4–2
1908	Almendares	Emilio Palomino .350		José Méndez 9–0
1908–9	Habana	Julián Castillo .315		José Méndez L. Haggerman 15–6
1910	Almendares	Emilio Palomino .408		José Méndez 7–0
1910–11	Almendares	Preston Hill .365		José Méndez 11–2
1912	Habana	Emilio Palomino .440		José Junco 6–1
1913	Fe	Armando Marsans .400		Red Redding 7–2
1913–14	Almendares	Manuel Villa .351		José Méndez 10–0
1914–15	Habana	Cristóbal Torriente .387		José Acosta 5–1
1915–16	Almendares	Eustaquio Pedrosos .413		José Acosta 8–3
1917	Orientales	Adolfo Luque .355		José Acosta 2–1
1918–19	Habana	Manuel Cueto .344		José Acosta 16–10
1919–20	Almendares	Cristóbal Torriente .360		Emilio Palmero 5–1
1920–21	Habana	Pelayo Chacon .344	Cristóbal Torriente M. González B. Jiménez M. Guerra Tied with 1	José "Cheo" Hernández 4–1
1921*	Habana	Bienvenido Jiménez .619	Manuel Cueto 1	Julio Leblanc 2–0
1922–23	Marianao	Bernardo Baró .401	Cristóbal Torriente 4	Lucas Boada 10–4
1923–24	Santa Clara	Oliver Marcells .393	Bienvenido Jiménez 4	Bill Holland 10–2
1924–25	Almendares	Manuel Cueto .364	Esteban Mantalvo 5	José Acosta 4–1
1925–26	Almendares	Johnny Wilson .430	J. H. Lloyd Jud Wilson 3	César Alvarez 10–2
1926–27	Habana	Manuel Cueto .404	J. Hernández 3	Juan Olmo 3–0
1927–28	Habana	Johnny Wilson .424	Oscar Charleston 5	Oscar Levis 7–2
1928–29	Habana	Alejandro Oms .432	Cool Papa Bell 5	Adolfo Luque 9–2
1929–30	Cienfuegos	Alejandro Oms .380	Mule Suttles 7	Heliodoro "Yoyo" Diaz 13–3
1930–31*	Not finished	O. Charleston .373	Ernest Smith José Fernández 3	Martin Dihigo 2–0
1931–32	Almendares	Rámon Cueto .400	Alejandro Oms Ismael Morales 3	Juan Eckelson 5–1
1932–33	Tie: Habana Almendares	M. González .432	R. Estalella 3	Jésus Lorenzo 3–0

Year	Champion	BA Leader	HR Leader	Most Games Won
1933–34	No championship held			
1934–35	Almendares	Lázaro Salazar .407	Eleven tied with 1	Lázaro Salazar 6–1
1935–36	Santa Clara	Martín Dihigo .358	Willie Wells Jacinto Roque 5	Martín Dihigo 11–2
1936–37	Marianao	Harry Williams .349	H. Andrews R. Estalella 5	Raymond Brown 21–4
1937–38	Santa Clara	Sam Bankhead .366	Willie Wells R. Estalella Raymond Brown 4	Raymond Brown 12–5
1938–39	Santa Clara	Tony Castaños .371	Josh Gibson 11	Martín Dihigo 14–2
1939–40	Almendares	Tony Castaños .340	Mule Suttles 4	Rodolfo Fernández 7–4
1940–41	Habana	Lázaro Salazar .316	A. Crespo 3	Gilberto Torres 10–3
1941–42	Almendares	Silvio García .351		Macon Mayor Agapito Mayor 6–2
1942–43	Almendares	A. Crespo .337	Roberto Ortiz Saguita Hernández 2	Cocaina García 10–3
1943–44	Habana	Roberto Ortiz .337	Saguita Hernández 3	Martín Dihigo 8–1
1944–45	Almendares	Claro Duany .340	Claro Duany 3	Oliverio Ortiz 10–4
1945–46	Cienfuegos	L. Davenport .333	Dick Sisler 9	Adrián Zabala 9–3
1946–47	Almendares	Lou Klein .330	Roberto Ortiz 11	Cocaina García 10–3
1947–48	Habana	Harry Kimbro .346	Jesús Chanquilon Díaz 7	C. Marrero 12–2
1948–49	Almendares	A. Crespo .326	Monte Irvin 10	Octavio Rubert 8–1
1949–50	Almendares	P. Formental .336	Roberto Ortiz Don Lenhardt 15	Octavio Rubert 5–1
1950–51	Habana	Silvío García .347	P. Formental, Bert Hass Ed Mierkowitz Charles Grant Tied with 8	Vincente López]7–3
1951–52	Habana	Bert Hass .323	P. Formental James Basso 9	Joe Black 15–6
1952–53	Habana	Edmundo Amorós .373	Louis Klein 16	R. Alexander 10–3
1953–54	Almendares	Rocky Nelson .352	Earl Rapp Rafael Noble 10	Cliff Fanning 13–4
1954–55	Almendares	Angel Scull .370	Rocky Nelson 13	Joe Hatten 13–5
1955–56	Cienfuegos	Forrest Jacobs .321	Ultus Alvarez 10	Pedro Ramos 13–5
1956–57	Marianao	Orestes Miñoso .312	Archie Wilson 11	Camilo Pascual 15–5
1957–58	Marianao	Milton Smith .320	Daniel Morejon Norman Laker B. Robinson Frank Herrera 9	Billy O'Dell 7–2
1958–59	Almendares	Tony Taylor .303	Jim Baxes 9	Orlando Peña 13–5
1959–60	Cienfuegos	Octavio Rojas .322		
1960–61	Cienfuegos			

* Short season

Baseball in Canada

Bruce L. Prentice and Merritt Clifton

Baseball as we know it—with three bases and home, nine players to a side, and three outs to an inning—has been played in Canada at least since 1860, when the existing teams in London, Hamilton, St. Thomas, and Woodstock, Ontario, all accepted the rules of the New York Game popularized by Henry Chadwick. This was the game played on June 19, 1846 between the New York and Knickerbocker clubs on the Elysian Fields of Hoboken, New Jersey.

But a game differing from early baseball mainly in having five bases was played in Beechville, Ontario, as early as June 4, 1838, according to witness Adam Ford, who described it in a letter to *Sporting Life* published on May 5, 1886. The game included at least two "grey-headed men" who "used to play when they were boys."

Thus the Canadian baseball tradition certainly predates Abner Doubleday's apocryphal invention of the game at Cooperstown in 1839, and may go back as far as the U.S. tradition. Indeed, in both nations, ancestors of baseball including cricket and rounders had been played since the early 1700s, and determining exactly where their derivatives ended and baseball began may be well-nigh impossible.

Before the arrival of the New York Game, the southwestern Ontario teams played the Canadian Game, with five bases and eleven fielders. All eleven batters had to be retired to end an inning. Only after the New York rules were adopted did the game spread to the other provinces. By 1865 baseball had become so popular in Montreal that an ordinance was passed forbidding games in city parks as a menace to other users. The Montreal-based Crescents of St. John's claimed the Canadian championship in 1868. The Montreal game was apparently not up to U.S. standards, however, as in 1870 the New York Knickerbockers Lacrosse Club crushed the Montreal Baseball Club, 54–32.

Baseball reached Manitoba no later than 1874, supplanting a local ancestor game called "bat," which had been played around the Red River Settlement as early as the 1840s. A professional three-team Manitoba League failed in 1886, but the game had firmly caught on by 1902, when the Great Northern Railway sponsored a Winnipeg entry in the professional North Dakota League.

Saskatchewan had semiprofessional baseball by 1887, when future provincial prime minister Walter Scott led a Regina team to two successive regional championships. Amateur baseball emerged in Alberta at about the same time, with games recorded as early as 1886.

By 1903 baseball was even played in the Yukon, where games attracted heavy gambling. Professional baseball debuted the same year in British Columbia, as twenty-year-old Hal Chase—"Prince Hal," the slick-fielding first baseman—starred for a Victoria entry in an otherwise Washington-based league.

While major league baseball came late to Canada, Canadian entries in U.S.-based professional leagues won pennants as early as 1877, when the Tecumsehs of London, Ontario, led the International Association. The Tecumsehs reputedly declined a chance to join the two-year-old National League later that year, and disbanded from lack of fan support in early 1878. Ontario acquired another pennant winner in 1887, as Toronto began an only briefly interrupted eighty-year run as a mainstay of the International League, then called the Eastern League. Toronto either finished first during the regular season or won four-team playoffs fifteen times, with back-to-back winners in 1917–1918, 1956–1957, and 1965–1966.

Montreal's first Eastern League entry folded within weeks in 1890. While another Montreal club won the 1898 championship, the by then renamed International League didn't become lastingly situated there until 1928. Even then, Montreal's third entry struggled until it was acquired in 1935 by gas station magnate Charlie Trudeau, father of future Canadian prime minister Pierre Elliot Trudeau. Trudeau anchored the lineup with French-speaking Del Bissonnette and Quebec native Gus Dugas, who hit .327 with 191 homers in thirteen minor league seasons. Under manager Frank Shaughnessy, who became International League president in 1936 and originated the four-club playoff format many experts credit with saving minor league baseball, the Montreal Royals won the 1935 pennant.

Bought by the Brooklyn Dodgers in 1940, the Royals won either pennant or playoffs in ten of the next twenty years. Led by Quebecois Roland Gladu (12 homers, 105 RBIs, .338 batting average) and pitcher Jean Pierre Roy (25–11), the 1945 club was probably Montreal's favorite, but the 1946 Royals are best remembered: with them, second baseman Jackie Robinson (.349) broke the Organized Baseball color line that had prevailed for fifty-five years.

The color line had already been broken in Quebec by .392-hitting pitcher/outfielder Fred Wilson, who joined Granby of the then-outlaw Provincial League for the 1935 stretch run. The Provincial League had included a Montreal-based all-black entry, the Black Panthers, in 1936 and 1937; was all white again in 1940, during a one-year fling at Organized Baseball; and was reintegrated in 1946 by minor league hockey star Manny McIntyre, who signed with Sherbrooke only days after the Dodgers had signed Robinson and optioned him to Montreal.

The Provincial League was the longest-running of numerous native Canadian circuits, many of which owed ancestry to the work of longtime Canadian Pacific Railway sports representative Joseph Page, who helped set up teams and leagues wherever the trains stopped. A former semi-pro teammate of Tip O'Neill, Page was involved with O'Neill in assembling Montreal's 1898 International League pennant winner. He later enlisted former major league pitcher Jean Dubuc to help him organize the Eastern Canada League, a.k.a. the Ontario-Quebec-Vermont League, of 1922–1924. This was an ancestor of three leagues of note, each of which sent over 100 players to the majors—the Provincial, which had already come together for single seasons in 1894 and 1900; the Canadian-American League, which could claim descent from the short lived, Ontario-based Canadian League of 1885; and the outlaw Northern League that flourished in New York and Vermont from 1935 to 1952.

Reorganized a fourth time, the Provincial League grew steadily from 1935 to 1940, was interrupted by World War II, resumed play in 1944, collapsed in 1956 after a disastrous six-year return to Organized Baseball, and struggled on as an outlaw circuit in 1958–1971. Stars were plentiful, from Quebec native Sam LaRoque (1900) to Felix Mantilla (1969), but the zenith came in 1948–1949, as the league attracted: black greats who were hoping to prove themselves against whites, displaced wartime major leaguers, and the so-called Mexican League Jumpers, who were barred from Organized Baseball in 1946–1950 after breaking their major league contracts in an ill-fated stand against the reserve clause. At least twenty-five major leaguers played in the Provincial League during those two years, among them Sal Maglie, Max Lanier, Vic Power, Gladu and Roy, and Negro League stars Dave Pope, Bus Clarkson, and Quincy Trouppe.

The less colorful Can-Am belonged to Organized Baseball from 1936 through 1951. Several of the Ontario teams continued as an outlaw league into the 1960s.

Page also helped promote the Western Canada League, which began play in 1907, continuing with frequent interruptions and occasional name changes into the late 1940s, when Edmonton and Calgary anchored the Big Four League. The Western Canada League's best year was probably 1921, when its stars included Babe Herman and Heinie Manush.

Canadian teams have also been part of the bygone Northern Copper Country League, which later became the Northern League; the Northwestern League and Western International League, which evolved into today's Northwest League; the Pacific Coast League; the American Association; the Eastern League; the New York–Pennsylvania League; and the Pioneer League.

As well as helping return blacks to Organized Baseball, Canada played a part in popularizing baseball in Japan, through the Asahis (Rising Suns), a team of Vancouver teenagers of Japanese descent (Niseis) formed in 1914. In 1921, twelve years after the first visit by a U.S. collegiate team and thirteen years before the first visit by U.S. major leaguers, the Asahis and a touring team from Seattle barnstormed Japan, playing both Japanese clubs and each other. The Asahis remained a power in Vancouver-

area amateur baseball and heroes to the substantial British Columbia Nisei population for over twenty years.

Despite the many major leaguers who have played for Canadian teams, relatively few Canadian natives have made the majors—a reflection of short summers and a paucity of places to play since television killed the old town teams and outlaw leagues in the 1950s. (Only one high school baseball team exists in Quebec; none in several other provinces.)

The Canadian Baseball Hall of Fame has identified a total of 151 Canadian major league players, 4 managers, and 7 umpires. Among them are 86 Ontarians, 18 Quebecois, and 11 New Brunswickers. Of the ten Canadian provinces, only Newfoundland hasn't produced a major leaguer.

Seven players from the late 1800s are listed by most record books as having been born in the U.S., but are believed to have altered their birth records for various reasons, including the 1894 Alien Exemption Act, which barred Canadian athletes from U.S. employment. In addition, several players who were born abroad actually grew up in Canada, e.g., Hank Biasatti and Reno Bertoia, natives of Italy but raised in Windsor, Ontario, and Jimmy Archer, born in Ireland, raised in Toronto, and signed into Organized Baseball from an independent team in Manitoba.

Many of the best Canadian players actually grew up in the U.S., among them infielder Pete Ward, son of former Montreal hockey great Jim Ward, who learned baseball in Oregon; pitcher Dick Lines, born in Montreal but raised in Florida; pitcher Kirk McCaskill, born in Kapuskasing, Ontario, but grew up in Burlington, Vermont; and infielder Sherry Robertson, born in Montreal but raised in Washington, D.C. (as the nephew of Senators and Twins club owner Calvin Griffith, who was also born in Montreal but was brought to Washington in 1921 by Senators owner Clark Griffith, who married Calvin's aunt).

Pitcher Sheldon Burnside reversed that pattern. Born in South Bend, Indiana, Burnside grew up in Toronto.

Not on the Canadian Baseball Hall of Fame list are a number of other special cases. Del Bissonnette and Napoleon Lajoie, for instance, were both born in the U.S., but were conceived in Quebec by Quebecois parents. Bissonnette actually spent more of his life in Quebec than anywhere else. After starring in the Cape Breton Colliery League of New Brunswick, Bissonnette broke into Organized Baseball by hitting .395 for Cap Madeleine, Quebec, of the Eastern Canada League. Years later he ended his playing career with outlaw teams in Quebec City and Iberville. Bissonnette later managed the Toronto Maple Leafs of the International League. Subsequently, as scouts for the Braves, Bissonnette and his protégé Roland Gladu signed half a dozen other Canadian big leaguers. Mel Hall, born at Lyons, New York, has been a winter Montrealer since he married a Quebecois airline stewardess several years ago. Pitcher Lew LaClaire listed his birthplace as Milton, Vermont, but lived in Farnham, Quebec, where he and his family died in the influenza epidemic of 1918.

The first Canadian-born major leaguer was first baseman Bill Phillips, who played for Cleveland, Brooklyn, and Kansas City, from 1879 to 1888. Born in St. John, New Brunswick, Phillips actually grew up in Chicago.

Among the 150 to follow Phillips are 65 pitchers, of whom only McCaskill and Steve Wilson are active, and 34 outfielders, including active players Terry Puhl, Rob Ducey, Larry Walker, and Kevin Reimer. While the number of players by position are roughly proportional to the numbers on major league rosters, pitchers have won the most distinction, perhaps because pitching skills can be developed more readily in short amateur seasons. Bob Emslie of Guelph, Ontario, was the first Canadian pitcher of note, and won more games in a big league season than any other Canadian, posting a 32–17 mark for the 1884 Baltimore Orioles. A poor start in 1885 sent him back to the minors, with a career major league record of just 44–44. Emslie returned to the majors, however, as an umpire, serving thirty-five years before retiring in 1926.

Only George Washington Stovey won more games in a year in Organized Baseball than Emslie. Stovey, probably born in Ontario, was among the top black pitchers of the nineteenth century. A headstrong lefty fireballer, Stovey fanned 22 men in one game with Bridgeport of the Eastern League in 1886, but lost due to poor control. He set an all-time International League record with 35 wins for Newark the next year, 1887, then was ousted from Organized Baseball through the racist efforts of white players including Hall of Famer Cap Anson and slugger Tip O'Neill, whose refusal to play either with or against blacks drew the color line firm by 1890.

O'Neill, born at either Woodstock or Springfield, Ontario, in 1858, was the best Canadian hitter of his time or ever, batting .326 in a big-league career that ran from 1883 to 1892. Breaking into the majors with New York as a pitcher, O'Neill soon switched to the outfield. In 1886 he led the then-major league American Association in hits, doubles, triples, homers, runs scored, batting, and slugging. His batting average, at the time, was actually listed as .492, but 50 walks were counted as hits. Subtracting them, he still hit .435. Though O'Neill fell to .335 in 1887, he repeated as batting champion.

The best Canadian player of all was probably Fergusson Jenkins, a 6′5″ black righthander from Chatham, Ontario, who avenged the injustice done to Stovey with a 284–226 record over nineteen seasons from 1965 to 1983. At his peak, Jenkins won 20 games or more seven times in eight years. Noted for control, Jenkins fanned over three times as many batters as he walked—and led the NL with 273 whiffs in 1969, retiring ninth on the all-time strikeout list. He earned the 1971 NL Cy Young Award by leading the league in wins (24), innings pitched, and, for the third time each, starts and complete games. He also hit 6 homers that year, one behind the NL record for home runs by a pitcher.

Other Canadian pitchers of note include Russ Ford, John Hiller, Reggie Cleveland, Phil Marchildon, Dick Fowler, Claude Raymond, and Ron Taylor. Ford, whose older brother also made the big leagues briefly, won 26 games for the New York Highlanders in 1910, his first full season. Hiller saved a then-record 38 games in 1973 and won an AL record 17 games in relief the next year, but is best known for his comeback from a 1971 heart attack. Marchildon and Fowler were half of the Athletics' rotation during the 1940s. On September 9, 1945, Fowler became the only Canadian to hurl a no-hitter, beating the Browns 1–0 for his only victory that year after coming back from military service. Marchildon peaked with 19 wins in 1947. Raymond is remembered as the first native Quebecois to play for the Expos, but was part of another bit of baseball trivia in 1959, as one of three Quebecois pitchers who helped Louisville to the American Association eastern division pennant. (The others were Georges Maranda and Ron Piche.) Taylor relieved for two World Champions, the 1964 Cardinals and the 1969 Mets, then became team physician for the Toronto Blue Jays.

Other top Canadian hitters were George Selkirk and Jeff Heath. Selkirk, who replaced Babe Ruth in the Yankees' lineup in 1934, hit .290 over nine seasons, topping .300 five times and twice driving in more than 100 runs. He played out the string in the early 1950s as a .300-hitting player-manager for Quebec City of the Provincial League and, following his retirement as a player, served as general manager of the Washington Senators for ten years. Heath, who reputedly never lived up to his potential, averaged .293 over fourteen years, beginning in 1936, with 194 homers. His best years were 1938 (21–112–.343) and 1941 (24–123–.340.) In between he led a player revolt against Indians manager Oscar Vitt. In his final full year, Heath hit .319 with twenty-four homers, pacing the Braves to the 1948 NL pennant, but broke his leg sliding during the last week of the season, missing his only chance at a World Series.

Canadian managers have included Art Irwin, Freddie Lake, Moon Gibson, and Bill Watkins, who led the Detroit Wolverines to the 1887 American Association pennant and had the only winning lifetime record among them.

Catcher Nig Clarke, from Amhurstburg, Ontario, won a spot in the minor league record books on June 15, 1902, hitting eight homers for Corsicana of the Texas League in a 51–3 rout of Texarkana. A Corsicana ordinance against Sunday baseball had forced the teams to play on a youth field at the nearby town of Ennis. Outfielder Jack Graney, of St. Thomas, Ontario, was reputedly the first major leaguer to wear a number, and was also both the first hitter to face Babe Ruth when the latter debuted as a pitcher, and the first ex-player to become a baseball broadcaster. Outfielder Glen Gorbous, of Drumheller, Alberta, made the *Guinness Book of Records* with the longest measured throw on record. Black pitcher Jimmy Claxton, of New Westminster, British Columbia, briefly broke the color line by passing as an alleged Native American with Oakland of the Pacific Coast League in 1916.

Several Canadian women could also claim to have been major leaguers, having played in the All-American Girls' Pro Baseball League organized in 1943 by Branch Rickey and Phil Wrigley. The league, the only women's professional circuit to date, thrived in the Midwest until 1955. First batting champion was Toronto native Gladys Davis. Catcher-manager and off season fashion model Mary "Bonnie" Baker of Regina, Alberta, was the league's best-paid player in 1951 and 1952, earning $1,600 a month—more than many men in the National and American Leagues. Helen Callaghan St. Aubin, of Vancouver, stole 354 bases in 388 games, then became mother of former Expo infielder Casey Candaele. The three followed a tradition of Canadian women players begun by barnstorming star Nellie McClung in the 1880s.

National League baseball finally came to Canada with

the expansion Montreal Expos in 1969. Hoping to get off to a good start, the Expos drafted mainly veterans, including Maury Wills, who became the only player to appear with Montreal in both the majors and the minors. Wills was soon traded for another veteran, Ron Fairly, who had led the University of Edmonton into the 1957 College World Series. A preseason swap of sluggers Donn Clendenon and Rusty Staub had to be rearranged when Clendenon quit rather than join the Astros. Clendenon eventually unretired and was swapped to the Mets. The affair was a landmark in the series of events that led to the overturn of the reserve clause in 1975. Although the Expos won both their first game and their home opener (on a home run by pitcher Dan McGinn), they finished last. No-hitters by Bill Stoneman in 1969 and 1972 were the club high points until 1973. Then, despite a 79–83 record, the Expos were in contention into the final week, paced by Ken Singleton, Ron Hunt, who set an all-time record by getting hit with pitches 50 times, rookie Steve Rogers, and reliever Mike Marshall, who saved 31 games and won 14 in 92 appearances.

Marshall was promptly traded to the Dodgers for Willie Davis, who staged a sit-down strike in center field before moving on. Singleton and pitcher Mike Torrez were sent to the Orioles a year later for former Cy Young Award winner Dave McNally and outfielder Rich Coggins. A thyroid ailment ended Coggins's career at age 25, while McNally played the 1975 season without a contract, then filed one of the two lawsuits that finally broke the reserve clause (Andy Messersmith of the Dodgers filed the other).

The Expos regrouped under new manager Dick Williams to win a club record 95 games in 1979. The arrival of young stars including Rogers, Andre Dawson, Gary Carter, Larry Parrish, Tim Raines, and Tim Wallach led management to bill the Expos as "The Team of the Eighties." The promise seemed real when the Expos won a playoff against the Phillies for the NL East title during the strike-shortened split season of 1981, and were leading the Dodgers 1–0 in the fifth inning of the final game of the NL Championship Series. But Rick Monday singled and scored the tying run, then won the game 2–1 with a two-out ninth inning homer off Rogers, who had come on in relief.

Toronto appeared ready to enter the National League in 1976 by purchasing the San Francisco Giants. When that deal fell through at the last minute, the American League admitted the Blue Jays as an expansion team in 1977. The Blue Jays drafted for the future, enduring six years in the cellar before winning 89 games to place fourth in 1983.

Good trades and a strong farm system loaded the lineup with sluggers George Bell, Jesse Barfield, Lloyd Moseby, and Willie Upshaw, plus hard-hitting infielders Tony Fernandez and Damaso Garcia, and produced a perennially strong pitching staff led by Dave Stieb and Jimmy Key. Ernie Whitt, an expansion draft selection, supplied power behind the plate through 1989. Winning 99 games and the AL East title in 1985, the Jays took a 3–1 lead in the Championship Series against Kansas City, but then dropped three games in a row to lose. Two years later, bolstered by emerging young longball hitters Fred McGriff and Kelly Gruber, the Blue Jays had a three-and-a-half-game lead over the Tigers with a week to play but, after injuries to Fernandez and Whitt, lost their last six games, including three one-run decisions to the Tigers on the final weekend.

The Jays partially redeemed a growing reputation for choking by besting the Orioles in a season-ending series to win the 1989 AL East, but were crushed by the Athletics, four games to one, in the Championship Series. The 1990 club started slowly. Closing fast, however, the Blue Jays overtook the slumping Red Sox with two weeks to play— and lost again, dropping two out of three games to the Bosox in a last-week direct confrontation.

Thus, at least 130 years since the first Canadian game of modern baseball, a World Series game has yet to be played outside the U.S.

[Thanks for research help to Eves Raja; Bill Humber; Donald Guay; and the Brome County Historical Society.]

Honored Members of The Canadian Baseball Hall of Fame

Inducted	Name/Career Facts
1990	Archer, Jimmy: Pit-N 1904, 1918; Det-A 1907; Chi-N 1909-17; Bro-N 1918; Cin-N 1918
1988	Bertoia, Reno Peter: Det-A 1953-58, 1961-62; Was-A 1959-60; Min-A 1961; KC-A 1961
1984	Bilesky, Andy: Little League coach
1988	Bowsfield, Ted: Bos-A 1958-60; Cle-A 1960; LA-A 1961-62; KC-A 1963-64
1984	Bronfman, Charles: executive
1989	Brown, Bob: minor league player, executive and club owner
1985	Bush, Carmen: amateur player, coach, manager, umpire and administrator
1986	Cleveland, Reggie: StL-N 1969-73; Bos-A 1974-78; Tex-A 1978; Mil-A 1979-81
1985	Cooke, Jack Kent: minor league owner and executive
1983	Ducey, John: amateur player, minor league umpire and administrator
1986	Emslie, Bob: Bal-A 1883-85; NL umpire 1891-1924
1987	Ford, Russell William: NY-A 1909-13; Buf-F 1914-15
1985	Fowler, Dick: Phi-A 1941-42, 1945–52
1987	Gibson, George "Moonie": Pit-N 1905-16; NY-N 1917-18
1984	Graney, Jack: Cle-A 1908-22; broadcaster Cle-A 1932-53
1988	Heath, Jeff: Cle-A 1936-45; Was-A 1946; StL-A 1946-47; Bos-N 1948-49
1985	Hiller, John: Det-A 1965-70, 1972-80
1989	Irwin, Arthur: Wor-N 1880-82; Pro-N 1883-85; Phi-N 1886-89, 1894; Was-N 1889; Bos-P 1890; Bos-A 1891
1987	Jenkins, Ferguson: Phi-N 1965-66; Chi-N 1966-73, 1982-83; Tex-A 1974-75, 1978-81; Bos-A 1976-77
1985	Judd, Thomas "Lefty": Bos-A 1941-45; Phi-A 1945-48
1983	Marchildon, Phil: Phi-A 1940-42, 1945-49; Bos-A 1950
1987	Nelson, Glenn "Rocky": StL-N 1949-51, 1956; Tor-IL 1951, 1958, 1962; Pit-N 1951, 1959-61; Chi-A 1951; Bro-N 1952, 1956; Mon-IL 1952-56; Cle-A 1954
1983	O'Neill, James "Tip": NY-N 1883; StL-A 1884-1889; Chi-P 1890; Cin-N 1892
1983	Pearson, Lester B.: (Honorary Inductee) amateur player; former Prime Minister of Canada
1988	Phillips, Bill: Cle-N 1879-84; Bro-A 1885-87; KC-A 1888
1988	Piche, Ron: Mil-A 1960-63; Cal-A 1965; StL-N 1966
1986	Prentice, Bobby: minor league player and scout
1984	Raymond, Claude: Chi-A 1959; Mil-N 1961-63; Hou-N 1964-67; Atl-N 1967-69; Mon-N 1969-71
1984	Rosen, Goody: Bro-N 1937-39, 1944-46; NY-N 1946
1983	Selkirk, George "Twinkletoes": NY-A 1934-42
1983	Shaughnessy, Sr., Frank "Shag": minor league administrator and executive
1985	Taylor, Ron: Cle-A 1962; StL-N 1963-65; Hou-N 1965-66; NY-N 1967-71; SD-N 1972

College Baseball

Cappy Gagnon

Intercollegiate baseball has come a long way since July 1, 1859, when the first match was played between Amherst and Williams Colleges, at Pittsfield, Massachusetts. Amherst won by a 73–32 score, on a playing field unrecognizable today. The pitcher was twenty-five feet closer to the batter, and the diamond was only sixty feet on a side. In keeping more with the academic orientation of the times, the two schools engaged in a chess match on the following day. The baseball game was played under the "Massachusetts rules," which eventually gave way to "New York rules," the forerunner of the game we know today. At the time of this game, Abraham Lincoln was not yet President. After the game there were rumors of some "ringers" being used by each team. This was a problem which haunted college sports for the next six decades.

Early college baseball thus preceded the National League by seventeen years. The colleges also provided one very significant equipment innovation. It was a Harvard man named Fred W. Thayer who invented the catcher's mask. Thayer gave his homemade creation to Harry Thatcher, the Crimson backstop (though several sources credit instead Harvard's star, James Tyng). After overcoming taunts about his "babyish and cowardly" act, Thatcher adjusted to wearing the mask. A short while later, Thayer saw the potential of this invention, and on February 12, 1878, he obtained a patent for it.

From the founding of the National Association in 1871 to the present there has been a collegiate influence on the national pastime. There is little evidence that this influence has raised the level of scholarship in the dugout, but unquestionably college baseball has provided an important feeder system for the majors. Initially, this role was important because major league teams of the pre-Rickey era did not have their own farm systems and competed vigorously with each other for raw playing talent. Colleges were an additional place for youngsters to develop.

The majors became more closely aligned with the campuses beginning in the 1890s, when veteran players began to serve as coaches of college teams. Until about 1910, college teams did not have full-time baseball field coaches. During February and March of each year, teams practiced in gymnasiums until weather permitted outside play. These practices were often supervised by a big leaguer, or other pro, limbering up for his own spring training to follow. He might have been a player from the neighboring area, as when Lou Criger of Elkhart, Indiana, or Harry Arndt of South Bend coached the Notre Dame teams. Or he might have been a recent graduate of the school, as when Jesse Burkett coached Holy Cross.

Such coaches usually retained an entrée with the college when his big league team was looking for prospects. Norwood Gibson and Red Morgan followed Criger to the Red Sox, Red Murray followed Arndt to the Cardinals, and Lou Sockalexis followed Burkett to the Cleveland Spiders.

Once the intercollegiate season began, there would be little or no involvement from university staff in the conduct of play. The team captain, a player, would function as the manager. Another student, a nonplayer, would function as the athletic director, scheduling games with other colleges and with independent and professional teams. George Huff, of Illinois, was probably the first paid full-time "coacher." His knowledge of the game helped make the Illini a "western" power, while at the same time developing future pros. Huff scouted for the Cubs and recruited players from his own teams and neighboring colleges for the Southsiders. In the former group were pitchers Carl Lundgren, Big Jeff Pfeffer, and Fred Beebe. Pitcher Ed Reulbach, of Notre Dame, was an example of the latter.

With a few exceptions in California (notably St. Mary's), college baseball until after World War Two was primarily a northeastern and midwestern sport. Because of travel difficulties and the location of all sixteen major league teams within a handful of eastern and midwestern states, college baseball became dominated by the eastern athletic powers (Harvard, Yale, Princeton, and Brown). "Western" upstarts like Illinois, Michigan, Chicago, and Notre Dame were lightly regarded by them. Because intersectional play did not occur until around 1910, however, there was no way to evaluate the competing claims of superiority.

Early collegians showed their cleverness in choosing pseudonyms. The two great Columbia players were known as "Sullivan" (Eddie Collins) and "Lewis" (Lou Gehrig). John Mohardt of Notre Dame had an interesting story as a result of his baseball alias: Mohardt became "Cavanaugh" when the entire Notre Dame team went to New Hampton, Iowa, for the summer of 1920. Mohardt picked up a girlfriend during that summer. He confided to her what the "ND" on the team caps stood for (his teammates claimed they were from North Dakota), but did not divulge his real name. Later that fall, when she sent a love note to "Johnny Cavanaugh, c/o Notre Dame," it was delivered to the Reverend John Cavanaugh, C.S.C., president of the university, who was not amused.

Early "tramp athletes" went from school to school and played on semipro teams under various aliases. Some "collegiate" players were not even enrolled in the colleges they represented. Bert Daniels was one of a number of itinerant collegians. He played at Villanova, Notre Dame, and Bucknell—all under his own name, while playing minor league ball during the summers, using five different aliases. As "Ayres," at Altoona in 1910, he was called the "next Ty Cobb." Unfortunately, he was already twenty-seven years old and had already played ten years of college and semipro football. All this had taken its toll on his legs. Daniels did make good use of his schooling, however, becoming an engineer.

Big leaguers came from virtually every college, including small and lesser-known colleges. Mathewson of Bucknell, Coombs of Colby, Plank of Gettysburg, Thorpe of Carlisle, and Beaumont of Beloit were good examples of why the majors scouted even the small schools. Although college teams played fewer than thirty games at this time, due to cold weather and travel difficulties and perhaps an occasional class or two, the top collegiate players seemed to get in sufficient playing time to impress big league scouts. Semipro, Industrial League, and town-team leagues were three of the types of ball for which a skilled collegian could pick up a little money for tuition and supporting his family.

The rise of college programs in the South and Far West came much later. The first major leaguer from the University of Southern California was Fay Thomas in 1927. Rod Dedeaux of the 1935 Dodgers was the fourth. Notre Dame had at least forty men reach the big leagues by 1920. Brown had fourteen in the majors by 1900. Georgetown was another early producer of big leaguers.

Once there was full-time college baseball, the relationship between the majors and the colleges became even more pronounced. In 1909 Connie Mack installed Jack Barry, a Holy Cross collegian as the shortstop in his $100,000 infield. During his forty years as coach of the Crusaders (1921–1961), Barry sent at least twenty-three players to the majors, including Gene Desautels and Mike Hegan. Connie Mack sent his son Earle to Niagara and Notre Dame.

According to Ellery Clark in *Red Sox Forever,* the early Bosox team featured many collegians, including two stars from St. Mary's (Duffy Lewis and Harry Hooper) who formed two-thirds of the best outfield of its day and the two best players from Vermont's 1908 team (Ray Collins and Larry Gardner).

One factor which may have encouraged many players to matriculate instead of trying out with the majors was the number of them who were multiple-sports stars. Christy Mathewson played football and basketball; Robin Roberts played basketball at Michigan State; Alvin Dark was a football star at Louisiana State University; Ted Kluszewski and Moose Skowron were football players at Indiana and Purdue respectively; Joe Adcock was a scoring star in basketball at Louisiana State University; Lou Boudreau, Frank Baumholtz, and Dick Groat were All-Americans in basketball at Illinois, Ohio, and Duke; and Jackie Robinson starred in football and track at U.C.L.A.

Many players better known for football were major leaguers too: George Halas, Ernie Nevers, Jim Thorpe, Red Badgro, Ace Parker, etc. Similarly, many collegiate baseball players achieved fame in other professional sports, like NFL quarterbacks Joe Theismann (ND) and John Elway (Stanford). The legendary George Gipp

played a little baseball at Notre Dame. The Cubs allegedly offered him a contract after watching him play semipro baseball with Kiki Cuyler in Michigan.

College men were not always warmly received into the majors. Veteran players had a natural reluctance to accept anyone who was out to win a scarce job, in the days of sixteen teams and eighteen-man rosters. Secondly, the crude, often ill-educated pros were more than a little resentful of the more-cultured and better-educated collegians. Writing just before the turn of the century, sportswriter George E. Stackhouse quoted "a well-known professional catcher . . . [whose manager] . . . was beginning to get the college baseball fever." The player approached a collegian and asked him if he were thinking of becoming a professional. When the collegian said he had no idea of becoming a pro, the catcher replied, "with much warmth: 'Now that's square, old man. You know Greek, Latin, and something about the world. You can make a good living anywhere. Don't interfere with us fellows, because you don't have to.' "

Henry Edwards of the Major League Service Bureau estimated this percentage of collegians in the majors at almost one-third in 1932. This is a big jump from 1909, when only fifty-seven big leaguers—or approximately 14 percent—had college backgrounds.

Because of the harsh conditions they faced, many star baseballers took their schooling seriously and skipped the majors. Another factor is that player salaries, in an era long before Marvin Miller, were often not attractive enough to persuade a bright college man to give up a career in a profession.

According to the 1900 U.S. Census, fewer than 2 percent of twenty-three-year-old men were college graduates. The average annual earnings of a working man from 1900 through World War One ranged from a little more than $400 to a little less than $1,000. A college man stood a much better chance to earn more than his counterpart. Similarly, professional players did not earn much more than average, and their short careers and unpleasant travel conditions made it difficult to develop either a nest egg or a headstart on a post-playing career.

The Notre Dame baseball captain in 1900 was probably as good a player as Peaches O'Neill, Red Morgan, Bob Bescher, Henry Thielman, Norwood Gibson, Bert Keeley, Frank Shaughnessy, and several other of his teammates who went on to the majors. Instead, first baseman Angus MacDonald, a four-letter winner, took his business degree to New York City, where he went to work for the Southern Pacific Railroad, later becoming president of the railroad.

Despite the closer relationship, considerable hostility remained between organized ball and the colleges. An editorial in *The Sporting News* on March 14, 1946, defended major league baseball's plantation treatment of the colleges.

Referring to the case of Gale Bishop of Washington State, who was signed early and made ineligible for further collegiate play, "University authorities have complained about this and similar practices, but few have shown any disposition to give the game an adequate place in their athletic programs, because of the emphasis placed on football and basketball." The fact that Bishop had no major league career to show for the disruption of his college athletics only exacerbated the problem.

On July 2, 1947, *The Sporting News* reported that a foundation was being laid for a truce between organized ball and the colleges. Earlier, Branch Rickey, himself a college man from Ohio Wesleyan and later George Sisler's baseball coach at Michigan when he was the country's top college pitcher, said that he felt the colleges had "dirty skirts" themselves and were in no position to lecture the majors. Rickey said he would continue to scout and sign collegians because he felt that some college teams had relationships with major league teams that were akin to their being farmclubs. And we know that Branch Rickey was not going to be "out-farmclubbed" by anyone.

One of the committee members representing organized baseball in its deliberations with the colleges was Frank "Shag" Shaughnessy, president of the International League. He said, "The player should not be compelled to wait to play professional ball if he needs the money to complete his education."

Shag was a star baseball and football player at Notre Dame who paid for his college education by playing semi-pro (as "Shannon") and professional ball.

Once the minor league teams were no longer able to sign and develop their own players, but were dependent upon "working agreements" with big league teams, long-term player development became a function of college baseball programs. Major league teams could avoid signing hundreds of players and maintaining ten or more minor league affiliates by simply letting the colleges do their work for them. College facilities and coaching were at least as good as the low minors. Players were "signed" to a scholarship and nurtured by the colleges. Big league scouts could watch their playing and learn something about their competitive abilities, injury history, and maturity. After two or three years, the best players would be drafted and sent to Rookie Ball or higher. Some think that a good college program might be the equivalent of Double-A baseball.

From the 1950s on, the major leagues changed their relationship with the minors dramatically, thereby thrusting the college game into an even more prominent role. Schools such as Arizona, Arizona State, and Texas began to produce big leaguers by the gross. When Dedeaux returned to his alma mater as coach, he increased their big league output dramatically while winning ten collegiate championships from 1958 to 1978.

From 1954 through 1980, there were only three years when U.S.C. did not send at least one player to the majors—forty-five players in twenty-seven years. Tom Seaver, Dave Kingman, Fred Lynn, Ron Fairly, and Don Buford were among this invasion. Commissioner Bowie Kuhn estimated in 1978 that more than two-thirds of major leaguers were college men.

There are also advantages for the collegians in this relationship. If an aspiring major leaguer's baseball apprenticeship does not work out, he can concentrate on his studies and find another vocation. He is in an environment where he has more opportunity for enrichment, for overall personal development, than would result from his being thrown into the minors at age seventeen or eighteen, as so often occurred during baseball's early days.

Great collegiate baseball teams can be evaluated in terms of two measures: the number of games won and the number of major league players produced. It is hard to argue with those who regard the University of Southern California as the greatest school on both counts. Since the inception of the Division I NCAA baseball championship in 1947, the U.S.C. Trojans have won eleven times and have finished as runner-up once. Next closest are Arizona State, with five firsts and three seconds; Texas with four firsts and one second; Arizona with three of each; and Minnesota with three titles. Oklahoma State, Cal State at Fullerton, Florida State, Brigham Young, and Miami are other schools with baseball programs that have been very strong during the past decade.

Besides Barry and Dedeaux, former big leaguers coaching these NCAA championship teams have included Bibb Falk (at Texas), Ray Fisher and Don Lund (Michigan), Dick Siebert (Minnesota), and Jerry Kindall (Arizona).

The Trojans, the Longhorns, and the Fighting Irish are the three top schools in terms of total major leaguers produced. The next echelon includes Holy Cross, Illinois, Alabama, Arizona State, Michigan, and Brown.

Texas has provided the majors with Roger Clemens, Greg Swindell, Burt Hooten, Calvin Schiraldi, and Keith Moreland among recent stars. Alabama claims Frank Lary, Riggs Stephenson, Joe Sewell, Del Pratt, and Butch Hobson. Michigan sent Charlie Gehringer, Bill Freehan, and Dick Wakefield. Brigham Young has been strong recently with Jack Morris, Wally Joyner, and Cory Snyder.

In 1973, the California Angels thought so much of the coaching of Bobby Winkles of the Arizona State Sun Devils that they hired him as their manager, the first time the majors had ever hired a college coach with no prior big league experience. Winkles managed two years each with the Angels and the A's. At Arizona State Winkles had coached Rick Monday, Reggie Jackson, and Sal Bando.

The NCAA has selected a championship Series Most Valuable Player since 1949. Winners of this award have included future big leaguers Tom Yewcic (C, Michigan State), Tom Borland (P, Oklahoma State), Cal Emery (P-1B, Penn State), Bob Garibaldi (P, Santa Clara), Sal Bando (3B, Arizona State), Steve Arlin (P, Ohio State), Jerry Tabb (1B, Tulsa), Dave Winfield (P-OF, Minnesota), Bob Horner (3B, Arizona State), Terry Francona (LF, Arizona), and Calvin Schiraldi (P, Texas).

Baseball and the Armed Services

Harrington E. Crissey, Jr.

It is regrettable that the average fan has little or no knowledge of the historical relationship between the military and baseball, considering that the links between the two date back to the beginning of the game's evolution in North America approximately 150 years ago. Perhaps it is because most people associate baseball with pleasure and military service with anything but that; or it may be that those who have never served in the armed forces have no appreciation of the value of baseball in relieving either the stress or boredom of military life, depending on one's circumstances. Whatever the reasons, the connections between the armed services and this truly international pastime are long and storied, and deserve our careful and devoted attention because the military has had a profound impact on the propagation of baseball worldwide and on the development of the game as a social leveler and instrument of international relations.

A story about the origin of baseball was advanced by a committee of the game's elder statesmen in 1907. The committee, led by former player and sporting goods magnate Albert G. Spalding, said that Abner Doubleday had designed the first baseball diamond at Cooperstown, New York, in 1839 while a cadet at the U.S. Military Academy. This version was quickly accepted as official by the baseball moguls and held sway for several decades, but it is now considered a myth by serious baseball historians.

Doubleday fought in the Battle of Monterey during the Mexican War; sighted the first gun in defense of Fort Sumter when it was fired on by Southerners on April 12, 1861, thus starting the Civil War; fought at Second Bull Run and Antietam; distinguished himself at Gettysburg by helping to repel Pickett's Charge, the Confederates' major attack of the battle; and eventually retired from the Army as a general in 1873. He was dead, however, by the time the committee put forth its opinion, so no one could get his views on the matter. There is nothing in his writings which suggests he invented the game, and other early commentators such as Henry Chadwick advanced different theories regarding the origin of the game. Nevertheless, the name of Abner Doubleday, a career soldier, remains inextricably linked to baseball in the popular mind.

To discover the first bona fide influence of the military on baseball, and a tremendous one at that, we must move ahead to the American Civil War (1861–1865). Baseball before the Civil War was almost exclusively a gentleman's game, with the upper classes of society participating and the true amateur spirit and British rules of sportsmanship holding sway. Most of the prominent teams were in the

East, with a few, such as those in Chicago and St. Louis, in the Midwest. During the war, baseball became a sport played by people of all social classes over a wide geographical area. It was played among Union troops during their leisure hours and an unheard-of crowd of 40,000 soldiers watched a game in Hilton Head, South Carolina, on Christmas Day, 1862, between the 165th New York Volunteer Infantry (Duryea's Zouaves) and a team picked from other Union regiments. A. G. Mills, later to become president of the National League, played in that contest.

Baseball was known in the South prior to the Civil War. Soldiers were said to have played baseball during the Mexican War, the game was popular in New Orleans, and many people south of the Mason-Dixon Line subscribed to Northern periodicals which featured baseball news. Nevertheless, the growth of the sport in Dixie was greatly stimulated by Northern prisoners playing the game to relieve boredom or tension in Southern POW camps. Their guards first watched, then decided they wanted to try, and finally organized teams to play against their captives. Southern POWs returned home similarly enlightened about the game. With more than a million men under arms during the conflict, is it any wonder that the game proliferated when the veterans went home to practically every town in the nation?

The Civil War accelerated two trends that were first discernible in the late 1850s: increasingly fierce competition and with it increased commercialism. Diaries written by Union troops in the Army of the Potomac and the Army of Northern Virginia show that as the war went on and baseball became ever more popular and competitive, emphasis on skill was the great consideration. If a player was good, he got to play. Teams in Army units may have been promoted by officers or high-ranking noncoms, but the players on the field were the most skilled. In 1863 and 1864, some outfits had first and second teams based on skill levels. This idea of skill predominating over social or military rank certainly fit the competitive pattern of post–Civil War baseball, as more emphasis on winning led to keen rivalries between cities and the rise of professionalism.

In 1873, eight years after the cessation of hostilities in the United States and twenty years after American ships under Commodore Matthew Perry had succeeded in opening Japan to the West, two American missionaries named Wilson and Maget introduced baseball to the Land of the Rising Sun. The game took root in part because influential Japanese of that time, such as Kido and many former *daimyo* (feudal lords), supported its growth. They originally viewed baseball as an American version of a martial sport like Japanese *judo* or *kendo*. Practicing the sport was in their minds a way of getting at the essence of the American fighting spirit, and thus baseball was played every day, regardless of weather conditions.

As time went on, the game evolved into a high school and college sport. From 1888 until 1902, the top team in Japan was that of First High School, now known as Tokyo University. It sometimes played games against American residents in Yokohama and teams from U.S. Navy battleships. Whenever the battlewagons made port calls in Yokohama, the First High School club would challenge them and usually would win the contests. Judging from a few of the scores, the Japanese students had ample reason to feel good about their progress in the sport: in 1902, they slaughtered the U.S.S. *Kentucky*, 35–1, and the next year clobbered the same ship again, 27–0!

The United States involved itself in war with Spain and its colonial possessions in the Caribbean Sea and Pacific Ocean in 1898. The Spanish-American War was short, lasting roughly the length of the baseball season. The war didn't have a significant impact on the game at home but undoubtedly influenced its spread to Puerto Rico, and other lands which border on the Caribbean, and the Philippine Islands.

Dr. Arlie Pond was pitching for the Baltimore Orioles of the National League when the war started. He had won 16 games for the Orioles in their pennant-winning season of 1896 and followed it up with 18 victories in 1897, but at the start of hostilities he entered the Army, joined a medical unit, and went first to Cuba and then the Philippines. After the war and the Philippine Insurrection, he left active duty but stayed in the Philippines and devoted the rest of his life to combating disease there, except for World War One, when he returned to the States and became assistant surgeon general of the Army with the rank of colonel. Near the end of the war, he went with the U.S. forces to Siberia following the Russian Revolution. In 1919, he returned to the islands after again relinquishing his Army commission and died there in 1930 at the age of fifty-seven.

A year after the war, Dave Wills quit his medical studies at the University of Virginia to play first base for Louisville of the National League. After hitting only .223 in twenty-four games, he decided to join the Marines and wound up staying twenty years in the service. He served as a paymaster in the European Theater with the rank of major in World War One and was buried in Arlington National Cemetery upon his death in 1959. A little more than a decade after the Spanish-American War, Hall of Famer Oscar Charleston, a Negro League great, was first recognized for his baseball ability while serving with the Army (1911–1915) in the Philippines.

World War One began in Europe in August 1914, but the United States didn't enter the conflict until April 1917. Before the Yanks went "over there," Canadian units in the British Army took the lead in teaching many Englishmen and Australians how to play. In the fall of 1917, a series for the championship of the Canadian forces overseas was played in England. One hundred and one teams took part, with several minor league and semipro players dotting the rosters.

By the end of 1917 there were seventy-six American major league players in the service: forty-eight from the American League, including fifteen Boston Red Sox, and twenty-eight from the National League. Forty-two were in the Army, twenty-one in the Navy, and thirteen in other branches of the service.

In May 1918 there occurred the promulgation of a "work or fight" order by the provost marshal of the armed forces, General Enoch Crowder. It was designed to force all men of draft age out of nonessential work and into the Army or war-related employment in order to aid in the prosecution of the war. Baseball players were classified as nonessential while actors, opera singers, and movie stars were deemed essential. This was because the baseball magnates didn't present their case in person, as did representatives of the other specially exempted occupations.

Relatively few players left baseball, however. The great majority remained with their teams. When the July time limit set by the Crowder order was reached, various draft boards issued conflicting orders to the players, some saying their work was essential and others saying it wasn't.

Eventually the Crowder edict was enforced and organized baseball shut down its operation by the beginning of September 1918, although two additional weeks were allotted for the World Series between the Boston Red Sox and the Chicago Cubs. Despite the fact that the Crowder edict applied only to men of draft age, the owners decided not to finish the season with players younger than eighteen or older than thirty-five. The magnates made it clear to the players, however, that the reserve clause was still in effect, that the players weren't free agents, and that they would be bound to their former teams upon resumption of play.

By the end of the war in November 1918, 144 American Leaguers and 103 National Leaguers were in the military. Very few players went into war-related work. Of the 144 American Leaguers serving Uncle Sam, a considerable percentage of them were known to be overseas. At least eighty-three were in the Army and forty-one in the Navy. The Detroit Tigers led the league with twenty-five servicemen, while the team with the fewest was the St. Louis Browns with thirteen, even though the Brownies had won American League prexy Ban Johnson's $500 prize for performing best in military close-order drill (using bats as rifles) in 1917. Among the National Leaguers, the Brooklyn Dodgers and Pittsburgh Pirates tied for the lead in enlistees with eighteen apiece, while the Cincinnati Reds had only six. Boston Brave catcher Hank Gowdy was the first major leaguer to volunteer for military service. He was eventually sent to France, as were other prominent players and executives such as Cincinnati Red manager Christy Mathewson, Detroit Tiger outfielder Ty Cobb, Philadelphia Phillie pitcher Grover Cleveland Alexander, Brooklyn Dodger hurler Sherry Smith, Chicago White Sox catcher Joe Jenkins, Boston Brave executive Percy Haughton, and St. Louis Cardinal executive Branch Rickey. Haughton and Rickey received their commissions as majors and Mathewson was a captain in the Army's gas-and-flame division. Mathewson suffered gas poisoning during his service. It led to tuberculosis and his ultimate demise in 1925. Former major leaguers killed in action were infielder Eddie Grant, who had played for four teams between 1905 and 1915, in the Argonne Forest in October 1918; Robert Troy, who had been born in Germany and pitched and lost one game for the Detroit Tigers in 1912, at the Meuse in October 1918; and Alex Barr, also with one game in the big time as a New York Yankee outfielder in 1914, on his twenty-fifth birthday, November 1, 1918, a mere ten days before the armistice.

Servicemen's baseball was alive and well in Europe in both 1917 and 1918. In addition to the aforementioned Canadian championship series in England in the fall of 1917, an Anglo-American League was formed. It was composed of regular teams of American and Canadian soldiers, and was organized in London by W. E. Booker and former big leaguer Arlie Latham. The league played a regular weekend schedule in London, the English provinces, and Scotland. Every team had four or five professional players. A benefit game between American Army and Navy teams at Chelsea, London, on July 4, 1918, drew more than forty thousand spectators, including the King of England and Allied military notables. The regular season ended on September 7, 1918, but the clubs continued to play Sunday ball until September 29.

Whereas the Canadians had initially taught baseball to the British and Australians, the Americans introduced it to the French. The game was not exactly new in Paris because Americans had occasionally played it there before the war. Once the Yanks began arriving in large numbers, games were played every Sunday in the Bois du Boulogne and other public parks. The YMCA organized an Association League in France, with thirty teams playing a fifteen-game schedule each Sunday up to the middle of September. Shortly before the armistice, French soldiers were under orders to learn baseball! Their primary teacher was erstwhile National League great Johnny Evers, who had been sent to France by the Knights of Columbus for that purpose. Where did all the equipment come from? There were three sources: the aforementioned YMCA, the Knights of Columbus and the Ball and Bat Fund, headed by Clark Griffith, manager of the Washington Senators. The fund disbursed $63,865.29 worth of baseball gear, although the supply ship *Kansan*, with its load of equipment for the American Expeditionary Force, was torpedoed and sunk by a German submarine while en route to Europe.

The top service teams of World War One (1918) included the 342nd Field Artillery, American Expeditionary Force club, which featured Grover Cleveland Alexander and several other major leaguers and beat all comers; the Second Naval District, Newport, Rhode Island, aggregation, with a handful of big leaguers on its roster; the Great Lakes, Illinois, Naval Station club, piloted by White Sox outfielder Phil Chouinard and later Senator shortstop Doc Lavan, which posted a 30–8 won-lost record and had Hall of Fame pitcher Urban "Red" Faber and pro football great George Halas; the 85th Division, Battle Creek, Michigan, nine, which lost only one game, beat the Great Lakes club, and had the Browns' Urban Shocker hurling for them; the Camp Dodge, Iowa, club, which logged 27 wins against 8 setbacks and counted six major leaguers among its players; the San Diego, California, Naval Training Camp team, with a 78–10 record to its credit; and the Kelly Field club in San Antonio, Texas, which won 42 games and lost only 8.

During and immediately after the war, baseball was played in Great Britain, France, Belgium, Italy, and the German Rhineland. There was enthusiastic talk in the *Reach* and *Spalding Baseball Guides* of the period about baseball becoming a major sport in England and France, but such a development failed to take place. Colonel Tillinghast L'Hommedieu Huston, part owner of the New York Yankees, guessed the result correctly. Upon returning to the United States from France after sixteen months in the Army, he commented that if American soldiers had been in Europe for at least another year, baseball might have taken hold, but the soldiers were returning home too fast to make a lasting impression.

The influence of the military during the period between the world wars was negligible, save for the occasional ballplayer who served a hitch in the armed forces. "Barnacle Bill" Posedel joined the Navy in 1925 while still in his teens, put in four years of active duty, later became a pitcher with the Brooklyn Dodgers and Boston Bees on the eve of World War Two, served four more years in the Navy during that conflict, and eventually became a major league pitching coach. Nemo Gaines was a star pitcher for the U.S. Naval Academy, class of 1921. Upon graduation, he received permission to take special leave and pitch for the Washington Senators. After four appearances with the Nats, he went on active duty and served until 1946, when he retired with the rank of captain. Pitcher Sig Jakucki, who was to become an important cog in the St. Louis Browns' drive to their only American League pennant in 1944, was in the Army from 1927 to 1931 and starred for the Schofield Barracks team in Hawaii as an outfielder and occasional hurler. As was customary, American servicemen brought baseball with them wherever they went. On July 29, 1937, sailors from a Navy squadron formed two teams and played a softball game in the sports stadium of the port they were visiting. The locale? Vladivostok in the Soviet Union!

Germany invaded Poland on September 1, 1939, and World War Two was on in Europe. As the war clouds drifted across the Atlantic and became more ominous over America, the United States government instituted a military draft in the autumn of 1940, the first in its history during peacetime. It required the registration of men ages twenty-one to thirty-five. The first major leaguer to get drafted was Philadelphia Phillie pitcher Hugh Mulcahy in March 1941, nine months before Pearl Harbor. The next to go was a star—Detroit Tiger slugger and 1940 American League Most Valuable Player Hank Greenberg. Hammerin' Hank had led the Tigers to the pennant the year before. After hitting two homers in a 7-4 win over the Yankees on May 6, he entered the Army the next day, the same day the Tigers officially raised their 1940 championship flag. Thus began a parade of professional ballplayers into the armed forces, a parade which would continue unabated until the Japanese surrender in August 1945.

Perhaps no other statistic better expresses the extent to which the military put its stamp on professional baseball during World War Two than the one which appeared in the *New York Times* in the spring of 1945: as of January of that year, 5,400 of the 5,800 pro baseball players in the country at the time of Pearl Harbor were in the service. With an impact of that magnitude, it would take a decent-sized book to describe in detail military baseball alone during the war years, not to mention pro and military ball combined, a task which has already been accomplished twice in recent memory. How then should one approach the topic? By emphasizing that the military is ultimately made up of people.

Over fifty professional ballplayers made the supreme sacrifice while serving in the armed forces. The majority of them died in combat. Two were ex–major leaguers who appeared briefly in the American League in 1939. Harry O'Neill, who caught one game for the Philadelphia Athletics, died on Iwo Jima in March 1945. Army Air Corps Captain Elmer Gedeon, an outfielder in 5 games for the Washington Senators in 1939, was shot down over France on April 15, 1944, his twenty-seventh birthday. The first pro player to enlist, minor league outfielder Billy Southworth, Jr., joined the Army Air Corps in December 1940. He was the son of the St. Louis Cardinals' manager and compiled quite a war record as a bomber pilot in Europe before being killed in a crash after takeoff on a routine flight from Long Island to Florida on February 15, 1945. He had attempted an emergency landing at LaGuardia Field but plunged into Flushing Bay after overshooting the runway. His grieving father was not alone among major league pilots. Ex-Tiger skipper Mickey Cochrane and former Cub boss Jimmie Wilson also lost sons in the war.

Several men who played major league ball were wounded in action, among them Army Air Corps fighter pilot Bert Shepard, who was shot down by antiaircraft fire over Germany in May 1944 and had his right leg amputated below the knee. After spending the better part of a year in a German POW camp, he was repatriated in a prisoner-of-war exchange and, with the help of an artificial limb, pitched in one regular-season game and several exhibitions for the Washington Senators in 1945. Others in the category of the wounded included the St. Louis Cardinals' John Grodzicki; the Philadelphia Athletics' Jack Knott, Bob Savage, and Lou Brissie; the Cleveland Indians' Gene Bearden; and the Brooklyn Dodgers' Tommy Warren—all of them pitchers.

Yet another pitcher, Phil Marchildon of the Philadelphia Athletics, spent nine months in a German prison camp while serving in the Royal Canadian Air Force. Cecil Travis, the star Washington shortstop, had his feet frozen at the Battle of the Bulge and lasted only two seasons after the war due to his limited mobility. The major league careers of hurlers Hugh Mulcahy of the Phillies and Charlie Wagner of the Red Sox were effectively curtailed by weight loss brought on by dysentery contracted in the Philippines. Two other pitchers, Johnny Rigney of the White Sox and 1942 rookie sensation Johnny Beazley of the Cardinals, threw their arms out while pitching service exhibitions. Outfielder Elmer "Red" Durrett hooked on with the Dodgers in 1944 after being discharged from the Marine Corps. He had suffered shell shock on Guadalcanal. It took a while for infielder Billy Cox and outfielder Monte Irvin to recover from the emotional effects of their Army experiences before they hit their stride again. Cardinal second baseman Frank Crespi broke his left leg in a game at Fort Riley, Kansas, in 1943. While convalescing at a military hospital, he got into a wheelchair race, slammed into a wall, and broke the leg again, thus ending whatever chance he had of re-

turning to the Redbirds after hostilities had ceased.

There were the great ones—men like Ted Williams, Joe DiMaggio, Bob Feller, and Hank Greenberg—who lost between three and five of their prime years to the service, thus giving rise to a multitude of "what if?" questions regarding their lifetime statistics had there been no war. Then there were the legions of players who didn't stick with their former clubs because of the personnel crunch in the spring of 1946, when the mix of returning veterans and wartime holdovers was so great that many men never had a chance to get back into shape gradually and compete for jobs effectively. Although major league clubs carried thirty men rather than twenty-five on their 1946 rosters in an effort to mitigate the problem, the remedy was hardly adequate to accommodate the flood of returnees. A few players—Tony Lupien, Merrill May, Bob Harris, Bruce Campbell, Steve Sundra, and Al Niemiec— either threatened legal action or undertook it in an effort to protect their reemployment rights under the then-new GI Bill, but most of them settled out of court on the issue of pay, and none stayed with their former teams.

For every sad story, there was a courageous or heartening one. Jack Knott of the Athletics and southpaw Earl Johnson of the Red Sox won battlefield commissions after showing bravery under fire. Former first baseman Zeke Bonura won the Legion of Merit as an Army corporal for organizing and promoting sports programs for service men and women in North Africa. General Dwight D. Eisenhower personally pinned the award on him. The aforementioned Bert Shepard served as an inspiration to all disabled servicemen when he made occasional appearances on the mound for the Senators. The opportunity to gain valuable experience by playing service ball with and against seasoned professionals presented itself to people like outfielder Del Ennis, who jumped from one year in the low minors to the major leagues after discharge. For others, it served to showcase their talents as prior amateurs or semipros. Johnny Groth, an eighteen-year-old wonder fresh out of Chicago Latin High School, proceeded to win a starting berth in centerfield for the 1945 Great Lakes Naval Training Center team with which he hit .341. He was signed to a Detroit organization contract at war's end and went on to have a long and productive major league career despite key injuries along the way. Maurice "Mo" Mozzali was a Louisville area semipro who impressed his teammates while performing for submarine-base teams at Pearl Harbor and New London, Connecticut. He signed a pro contract in 1946 and rose to the level of Triple-A as an All-Star first baseman with Columbus of the American Association.

Several prominent players had triumphant returns to the major leagues after completion of their service hitches. On August 24, 1945, after forty-four months in the Navy, Bob Feller made his first start against the Tigers in Cleveland. His appearance resulted in Cleveland's biggest baseball crowd in three years (46,777 fans). Bullet Bob struck out twelve, gave up only four hits, and won easily, 4–2. In his second game versus Detroit late that summer, he one-hit the Tigers. When he pitched in Yankee Stadium on September 10, a total of 67,816 spectators were present. Hank Greenberg heralded his return to the Tigers on July 1, 1945, by hitting a home run against the Athletics before 48,000 hometown fans. On the final day of the season, his grand slam home run in the rain against the Browns clinched the American League pennant for Detroit. Tiger righthander Virgil Trucks was discharged from the Navy less than a week before the 1945 season ended. He started the Tigers' pennant-winning 6–3 victory over St. Louis and followed that up with a 4–1 complete-game win over the Chicago Cubs in the second game of the World Series.

Navy duty during the war resulted in the beginning of new professions for Max Patkin and Dusty Cooke. Patkin began his long and famous career as a baseball clown while pitching first for Aiea Hospital and then for Aiea Barracks in Hawaii in 1944. Cooke was trained as a pharmacist's mate. This training came in handy after the war. In search of a baseball job, he hooked on with former teammate Ben Chapman and the Philadelphia Phillies as club trainer and later went on to coach and even manage the team for a few days in 1948 between the departure of Chapman and the arrival of Eddie Sawyer.

At times there was an embarrassment of riches on military teams. In the first two years of the war, former heavyweight boxing champion Gene Tunney's eight-week enlisted athletic specialist training course was located at the Norfolk, Virginia Naval Training Station. Thus the Norfolk NTS manager, Gary Bodie, had his pick of the numerous professional athletes who were taking the course. In 1943 he was faced with the difficult yet wonderful prospect of choosing between two of the premier shortstops in baseball, Phil Rizzuto and Pee Wee Reese, for his ballclub. He kept Rizzuto and sent Reese a mile down the road to Norfolk Naval Air Station, where he became part of NTS's opposition.

The Army stockpiled its talent in the Hawaiian Islands at the Seventh Army Air Force, Hickam Field, in 1944. Manager Tom Winsett, a former major league outfielder, had three top-level second basemen—Joe Gordon, Gerry Priddy, and Dario Lodigiani—at his disposal that summer. Priddy and Lodigiani were the first to arrive, with Lodigiani staying at his normal position and Priddy playing shortstop. When Priddy was transferred, Gordon replaced him.

There were also some wacky trades. After the Tunney school was shifted from Norfolk to Bainbridge, Maryland, former St. Louis Browns outfielder Red McQuillen went through the program. Norfolk NTS needed an outfielder and Bainbridge needed a life raft, so the deal was made. The raft turned out to be defective upon receipt in Bainbridge, but the deal wasn't voided and McQuillen went on to bat .367 and lead the Norfolk club in hits and triples in 1944. General William Flood, commanding officer of the aforementioned Seventh Army Air Force at Hickam Field, wanted Eddie Funk, a good pitcher with a little experience in the low minors, for his ballclub. Funk was at another facility on the island of Oahu, and his CO was anxious to keep him; however, the CO had two dogs which he loved, and they were sick. General Flood had the only veterinary service among the military stations in Hawaii, so he made a proposition to Funk's boss: you give me Funk and your two dogs will get well. The deal was consummated, and Funk went on to pitch excellent ball for the Seventh Army Air Force.

It was common for the top service teams to have past or future major leaguers at every position. Both the Army and the Navy had outstanding teams at several of their installations around the country. For instance, Navy outfits at the training centers in Norfolk, Great Lakes, Bainbridge, and Sampson, New York, were superb. The Army aggregations at the Seventh Army Air Force, Fort Riley, Kansas; New Cumberland, Pennsylvania; and the Waco, Texas, Army Flying School distinguished themselves. The Marine Corps had fine clubs at Quantico, Virginia, and Parris Island, South Carolina, and the Coast Guard teams at Curtis Bay, Maryland, and New London, Connecticut, were excellent. There was also a multiplicity of top-notch clubs on the West Coast.

Most of these teams rang up outstanding won–lost records against all types of opposition—for example, the magnificent 48–2 log achieved by the 1944 Great Lakes club. Many exhibitions were played against major and minor league teams, with the majority being won by the service clubs. Some of the scores are legendary, like the 17–4 slaughtering the Great Lakes sailors gave the Cleveland Indians in their 1944 season finale, or the pastings administered to the Boston Red Sox (20–7) and the Cleveland Indians (15–2) by the 1944 Sampson Naval Training Center nine. Were the major leaguers trying? Evidence indicates that they were, although second-line pitchers were often thrown against the service clubs and sometimes the pros played a position other than their normal one. Because big league clubs often took fewer than the normal twenty-five players on road trips during the war, it was not uncommon for players to be platooned at an unfamiliar position—as, for example, a pitcher playing in the outfield.

Service players participated in some great war-benefit games. Perhaps the most famous was the American League All-Stars–Service All-Stars contest at Municipal Stadium in Cleveland on July 7, 1942, when 62,094 fans saw a one-of-a-kind ballgame in which the American Leaguers triumphed, 5–0. The gross receipts from the spectacle totaled $143,571; $100,000 of the net went to the Bat and Ball Fund and the rest to Army and Navy Relief. A month earlier, the Norfolk NTS team had played a group of Army ballplayers in the Polo Grounds in New York. The year 1943 saw the $2 million war-bond game between the Norfolk NTS squad and the Washington Senators, won by Norfolk, 4–3, at Griffith Stadium in Washington, on May 24; the Service All-Stars–Boston Braves contest at Fenway Park, Boston, on July 12, in which the All-Stars, managed by Babe Ruth and featuring Ted Williams, nipped the Braves, 9–8; the July 28 game in Yankee Stadium between North Carolina Pre-Flight (Navy) and a combined team of New York Yankees and Cleveland Indians, called the "Yank-lands" and managed by Babe Ruth, in which North Carolina Pre-Flight triumphed, 11–5, and $30,000 was poured into the Baseball War Relief and Service Fund, Inc.; and the $800 million war-bond game at the Polo Grounds on August 26, when a combined team of Yankees, Dodgers, and Giants beat a group of Army All-Stars, 5–2, before 38,000 people. It is interesting to note that the only picture supposedly taken of Ted Williams and Babe Ruth together in uniform was snapped at that Fenway Park contest in July.

A few takeoffs on the World Series occurred. At the end of the 1943 season, the Norfolk Naval Training Station and Norfolk Naval Air Station clubs engaged in an exciting best-of-seven series, which the Training Station won, four games to three. Following the 1944 baseball campaign in Hawaii, the cream of the crop of Army and Navy ballplayers participated in the famous Service World Series. What started out as a best-of-seven affair limited to Oahu Island wound up as an eleven-game extravaganza, with the final four contests being played on the islands of Maui, Hawaii, and Kauai. The Navy, shored up at the last minute with reinforcements from the continental United States and Australia, won the first six games and finished with an 8–2–1 record for the series, the tie being a fourteen-inning 6–6 humdinger in Hoolulu Park, Hilo, Hawaii. The following fall, the Navy had its own World Series in the Hawaiian Islands, featuring the American League against the National League. The AL squad was favored, but the National Leaguers won, four games to two. As in the previous year, an additional contest was played for the benefit of service men and women, with the Americans beating the Nationals; so the final tally was Nationals four, Americans three.

Baseball was played all over the world during the Second World War. In late February 1945, twenty-eight Navy ballplayers boarded two Marine Corps planes and proceeded to make two tours of the forward areas of the Pacific, with both of them ending on Guam; then the players were dispersed among Guam, Saipan, Tinian, Peleliu, and Ulithi. Shortly afterward, Army Air Corps players did the same thing. Right after the war in Europe ended, many pro players had German and Italian POWs build fields for them and top-flight competition ensued. An Army All-Star team was formed and toured Europe, visiting cities in Germany, France, Italy, and Austria.

Perhaps the most important outgrowth of World War Two military baseball was black-white integration. A full year before Branch Rickey signed Jackie Robinson to a Brooklyn Dodger organization contract, Hal Hairston, a black pitcher formerly with the Homestead Grays of the Negro National League, was hurling for the Army against the Navy in the Service World Series in Hawaii. A year later, Calvin Medley, another black pro, was pitching for the Fleet Marine team on Oahu Island. Two thousand miles away from the U.S. mainland, on a group of islands populated with Hawaiian natives and American, Chinese, and Japanese immigrants, racially integrated baseball could become a reality. Blacks and whites could play together on service teams and black, white, and yellow people could perform as a unit in the Honolulu semipro league. Back in the continental United States, black and white service teams would remain segregated until after the war. Thus the white Great Lakes team won 48 and lost only 2 in 1944, while the black club went 32–10 and won the championship of the Midwest Service League. Larry Doby, star shortstop on the black team and later the first man of his race to play in the American League, could not play with whites in Illinois but was welcome to play softball on Ulithi Atoll a year later with white professionals like Mickey Vernon and Billy Goodman. Negro League stars Leon Day and Willard Brown couldn't as yet crack the color barrier back home, but they could lead a team comprised almost exclusively of white semipro players to victory in Nuremberg's famous stadium, site of the massive Nazi Party rallies of the 1930s. Against the hand-picked professionals of General George Patton's Third Army club, righthanded fireballer Day led the Overseas Invasion Service Expedition (OISE) club to a 2–1 victory for the European Theater of Operations (ETO) championship before a huge crowd.

No description of military baseball during the period would be complete without mention of what transpired in Japan. The Land of the Rising Sun had been on a war footing since the Marco Polo Bridge incident in Beijing, China, on July 7, 1937. Professional ballplayers had been drafted at least from 1938 on, as evidenced by the induction that year of Eiji Sawamura, the country's most famous pitcher. In fact, Sawamura was to be taken into the Army three times: in 1938, 1941, and again in 1944. With the coming of global war following Pearl Harbor, intense Japanese nationalism and militarism manifested themselves in many ways regarding baseball. Team names on uniforms were changed to Japanese characters from Roman letters, and the traditional baseball cap took on a military look. The Tokyo Giants were renamed *Kyojin Gun* or "Giant Troop." Baseball terms imported from the foreign enemy, the United States, were changed to Japanese equivalents. "Strike" became *yoshi* ("good") and "ball" became *dame* ("bad"). "Safe" was transformed into *ikita* ("alive") and "out" to *shinda* ("dead"). A shortstop became a *yugeki* ("free-lancer").

After 1942, many outstanding players, both professionals and collegians, were drafted into the military. The two most famous collegiate baseball clubs, those of Keio and Waseda Universities, had an emotional farewell game before 30,000 students in October 1943. The presidents of both universities had negotiated successfully with the government for this contest to be held, and after it was over tears flowed freely as both players and spectators wondered if they would ever see another game. Their sadness was well founded. Among the three million Japanese, military and civilian, who died on the home islands or in the Pacific, China, and Southeast Asia were a great number of good players, including the best, Sawamura, who was killed on a troop transport in the Taiwan Strait on December 2, 1944. Today the Japanese equivalent of the Cy Young Award, given annually to the best pitcher in each of the American leagues, is named in his memory. Ironically, Japan's number two pitcher, Victor Starffin, was spared because as a child immigrant from the Soviet Union he was exempt from conscription.

By 1944 only six clubs were competing for the professional championship and the season was only thirty-five games long. In 1945, the last year of the war, play was suspended altogether as cities were ravaged by fire bombing, the economy collapsed, and the two atomic bomb detonations hastened Japan's surrender late that summer.

When the last of the American wartime draftees was mustered out of the service and returned home during the 1946 season, it marked the beginning of a temporary halt in the influence of the military on baseball performance but not on fan interest in the United States. The strong desire of many who had been in the service to put rigorous or traumatic wartime experiences aside, to get on with one's life, to get out, relax, and enjoy a ballgame sparked a large increase in attendance at professional games and a rise in the number of minor leagues that was to peak in 1949 before the advent of television took its toll.

In defeated Japan, the victorious Allies, particularly the United States, were calling the shots, and the American military had the fate of Japanese baseball in the palm of its hand. Fortunately the resurrection of the game was in line with the aim of the occupation forces, namely to reform Japanese political, economic, and social institutions so that they would more closely reflect those of the Western democracies.

General Headquarters encouraged the revival of spectator sports, and in November 1945, just three months after the unconditional surrender, the Japanese professional baseball league was reorganized as many players returned from duty in Manchuria, China, and Southeast Asia. There were problems at first because the occupation forces controlled the ballparks, used them for their own entertainment, and made the Japanese professional and college leagues negotiate for their use; but key people in the Allied administration aided the Japanese in their negotiations and smoothed the way for ever-increasing privileges. General Douglas MacArthur, head of the occupation government, personally issued the order to clean up Korakuen Stadium, home of the Tokyo Giants, which had been used as an ammunition dump during the war.

In 1946 Japanese professional play resumed with a total of four hundred and twenty games being contested. By 1948, there were eight teams in the league, and such great progress was made that in 1950 two leagues were formed. There were fifteen teams that year, but the number eventually dropped to twelve, six teams in each league, which is the present setup.

Such was the situation on both sides of the Pacific when on June 25, 1950, North Korean forces invaded the South and the Korean War began. For the second time in a decade, the specter of large-scale military conscription and its inevitable effect on players and pennant races loomed over the American professional baseball scene.

The effect of the war was felt before the 1950 season ended. The Philadelphia Phillies "Whiz Kids" were out in front of the National League pack and aiming for their first pennant in thirty-five years when on September 10, their number two pitcher, Curt Simmons, who had already won 17 games, was called away when his Pennsylvania National Guard unit was mobilized. Simmons's loss, as well as injuries to three other key players, took the steam out of the Phillies, but they managed to hang on and win the pennant on the last day of the season against the Brooklyn Dodgers. Simmons received a furlough to attend the World Series, but Phillie manager Eddie Sawyer decided not to put Curt back on the eligibility list because of his limited baseball activity while away. The Phillies lost the Series to the New York Yankees in four straight games.

The following spring, veteran sportswriters making their predictions about the 1951 pennant races focused in part on the possible effect of the draft. The consensus was that veteran teams like the Boston Red Sox in the American League and the St. Louis Cardinals and Boston Braves in the National League would stand better chances of winning because they would be the least likely to lose players. Comparatively young clubs like the Philadelphia Phillies would be the most vulnerable, while teams like the Brooklyn Dodgers, with a combination of veterans and rookies, might stand the best chance of all. They would do well in the first half of the race with their youngsters, then would come on strong in the second half with their veterans as Selective Service took its toll.

The entire line of reasoning proved almost meaningless because a large-scale call-up never took place. The war was limited. What happened instead was that a handful of individuals got drafted, usually one or two players per team, for a period of two years. This pattern continued throughout the decade of the 1950s, even after the Korean War ended in 1953. The only service that had a general recall of its World War Two veteran ballplayers was the Marine Corps, which took its Reserve aviators. This recall involved only two key players—Red Sox outfielder Ted Williams and Yankee second baseman Jerry Coleman.

Williams's farewell was especially poignant. Shortly after the 1952 season began, on April 30 to be exact, a Wednesday afternoon crowd of 24,764 took part in pregame festivities. The Splendid Splinter was given a Cadillac and a memory book containing 430,000 signatures. The fans held hands and sang "Auld Lang Syne." Williams didn't disappoint them. He hit a two-run homer off Detroit Tiger pitcher Dizzy Trout in the seventh inning in his final at-bat of the game to lead the Red Sox to victory. Given The Thumper's age (thirty-three), many felt they would never see him play again.

Ted's experience as a fighter pilot almost proved their thinking correct. He completed thirty-eight combat missions in Korea, was hit by antiaircraft fire three times, and almost didn't make it back on the second occasion. He was awarded an Air Medal with two Gold Stars in lieu of his second and third Air Medals before being transferred back to the United States for a nagging inner ear and nose ailment that ultimately left him partially deaf in one ear. He was discharged on July 28, 1953. After a little over a week of conditioning, Teddy Ballgame returned to major league play and hit a phenomenal .407 in 37 games, with 13 home runs and a whopping slugging percentage of .901. Seven more years of superb hitting were to follow.

While the Red Sox plunged to sixth place without Williams in 1952, other contending clubs who lost players to the service didn't fare that badly. The Yankees were so deep in talent that they won five straight pennants between 1949 and 1953 despite the loss of ace lefthander Whitey Ford (1951–1952), third baseman Bobby Brown (1952–1953), and infielder Jerry Coleman (1952–1953). They lost to the Cleveland Indians in 1954 without the services of their crack second baseman, Billy Martin, but still managed to win 105 games. Only a tremendous 111-win season by the Indians outdid them; however, Martin returned late in the 1955 campaign, in time to spark the Yankees to the top of the heap again.

The Dodgers won pennants in 1952 and 1953 without their top righthander, Don Newcombe, but lost to the Giants in 1954 when he returned. Newcombe went on to be the bellwether of the Brooklyn staff in the Dodgers' 1955 and 1956 National League championship seasons. The Giants won in a playoff with the Dodgers in 1951, Willie Mays's rookie season, but lost without him in 1952 and 1953. When the Say Hey Kid returned in 1954, they won again.

The Army got practically all of the professional ballplayers who were drafted during the Korean War, and thus it had some outstanding teams, both stateside and overseas. The 1951 Fort Myer, Virginia, club featured pitchers Johnny Antonelli (Braves) and Bob Purkey (Giants), infielder Danny O'Connell (Pirates), and catcher Sam Calderone (Giants). That same year, the Brooke Army Medical Center team in San Antonio, Texas, boasted outfielder Dick Kokos (Browns), second baseman Owen Friend (Browns), pitcher Glenn Mickens (Dodgers), and catcher Gus Triandos (Yankees). In 1953 the All-Army champions at Fort Belvoir, Virginia, had Dick Groat (Pirates) at shortstop and Tom Poholsky (Cardinals) on the mound. Fort Jackson, South Carolina, could call on outfielder Faye Throneberry (Red Sox), catchers Frank House (Tigers) and Haywood Sullivan (Red Sox), and pitcher Joe Landrum (Dodgers).

Several players wound up in the Far East Command, where the real action was. With Japan being used as a staging area for Korea, a few servicemen found themselves playing with or against Japanese professionals. In 1953, Leo Kiely of the Red Sox and Phil Paine of the Braves pitched a few games for the Mainichi Orions and Nishitetsu Lions, respectively. Two years earlier, ex–Pacific Coast League southpaw Ken Lehman of the 40th Infantry Division had been the star performer of the Far East Command, with a 14–1 record on the mound and a .408 average at the plate. Among his accomplishments during the 1951 season was defeating a group of Japanese All-Stars, 1–0, before 32,000 fans at Miyagi Stadium in Sendai. When Lefty O'Doul brought a group of top-flight major leaguers to Japan for an exhibition tour after the American season ended, Lehman was invited to play with them and pitched excellent ball in two games, one a start against the Japanese Central League All-Stars. He later went on to pitch for the Dodgers, Orioles, and Phillies.

Only one ex–big leaguer lost his life in combat during the Korean War: Bob Neighbors, an Air Force major, who died in North Korea in August 1952. He had played in seven games for the St. Louis Browns in 1939 and also served his country in World War Two.

After the cessation of overt hostilities in Korea in 1953, Army baseball continued to feature a smattering of professional players who were two-year draftees; but in 1957 the All-Army championship tournament was discontinued, and the following year the level of competition was reduced to intramurals at the lowest unit level possible. Because the Navy wasn't drafting people and had not been a force to be reckoned with in baseball since the end of the Second World War, the Army's actions effectively spelled the end of top-flight military hardball. Over the last quarter century, softball has been the serviceman's game.

The Vietnam War, like the Korean conflict, was limited in scope. This fact, coupled with the availability of Reserve programs which required only six months of active duty, made the impact of the military on professional baseball slight from 1964, the year the war escalated after the Gulf of Tonkin "incident," to 1973, when the United States began to pull its forces out of Vietnam and terminate the draft.

Most players and executives who were eligible for the draft entered Reserve components of the armed forces, particularly that of the Army. They were obliged to do six months of basic training and spend six years attending one weekend meeting or four weekday meetings each month, and two weeks of active duty for training each fiscal year. The sixth year was basically inactive in the sense of the Reservist not having to attend meetings or do the two-week stint. The active duty obligations were normally performed during the off-season. Monthly attendance at drills became a problem on occasion, and a player might miss a weekend's worth of games here and there, but many Reserve units used the players in public relations roles for recruiting or image-building purposes and, as such, meetings could be staggered to suit the individual.

While pitching the Red Sox to their "Impossible Dream" pennant in 1967, Private First Class Jim Lonborg had to fly down to Atlanta and do his two-week Army Reserve duty. His fortnight began on Sunday, July 30, in the heat of the pennant race, and ended on Saturday, August 12. Fortunately, he was able to work out with the Atlanta Braves and with the aid of passes, didn't miss a start. After being shelled by the Minnesota Twins two days before his departure, he flew back to Boston and worked $5\frac{1}{3}$ innings against the Kansas City Athletics on Tuesday, August 1, giving up three runs and eight hits but gaining his fifteenth win of the season. On Sunday, August 6, he lost to the Twins in Minnesota, 2–0, in a rain-shortened, five-inning contest. His counterpart, Dean Chance, pitched a perfect game. On Wednesday, August 9, he beat the Athletics in Kansas City, 5–1, for win number sixteen, tops in the majors. With his two-week sojourn over, he lost to the California Angels, 3–2, on the West Coast on Sunday, August 13.

While military duty may have caused Lonborg a mild inconvenience, youngsters like Al Bumbry and Garry Maddox were serving in Vietnam. They would go on to make their mark as top-quality major league outfielders in the 1970s. With the demise of the draft, future ballplayers wouldn't have to worry about such unpleasant career interruptions.

If there is another major war ahead of us, modern armaments, particularly nuclear weapons, will probably make it a short one, perhaps a year or less. The influence of the military on baseball should therefore remain minimal and not approach the high-water mark of World War Two, when both the length and the extent of the conflict had a pervasive effect on the game, both at home and abroad. As venerable and fascinating as the link between the military and baseball is, let us hope it remains low-profile in the future.

CHAPTER 26

Women in Baseball

Debra A. Shattuck

Baseball has long been considered a man's game. Traditionally the accepted place for a woman at a baseball stadium has been in the grandstand—not out on the field. This is beginning to change somewhat, as Little League baseball was officially opened up to girls in 1974, but, by and large, many still share the view of the male critic who wrote in *The Reach Official American League Guide, 1911* that the idea of women actually playing baseball was "positively repugnant." It is not surprising in today's open society that girls and women are taking up baseball. What is surprising is how many women actually played baseball at a time when many felt that a woman's place was in the home.

Many of the first female baseball players were college students. The secluded atmosphere of all-girl's schools enabled women to play the game without attracting too much attention. Students at Vassar College organized two baseball clubs as early as 1866. In 1879, according to Vassar alumna Sophia Foster Richardson, the Vassar girls organized at least seven baseball clubs. The private grounds of college campuses did not always protect female players from public criticism, however. In a speech to an alumnae association in 1896, Richardson recalled, "The public, so far as it knew of our playing, was shocked, but in our retired grounds, and protected from observation even in these grounds by sheltering trees, we continued to play in spite of a censorious public." Within a few years, however, the "censorious public" and "disapproving mothers" had succeeded in stifling the game at Vassar. But Vassar was not the only college where women tried their hand at baseball. In a letter to her former classmates at Smith College, Minnie Stephens (class of 1883) reminisced about the baseball clubs they had organized at the school in 1879. Stephens described the enthusiasm of the players and the keen competition at games. She also related how the Victorian-style clothing of the day, generally a hindrance to sporting endeavors, had actually benefited one of the players during a heated contest, "One vicious batter drove a ball directly into the belt line of her opponent, and had it not been for the rigid steel corset clasp worn in those days, she would have been knocked out completely." Like the women at Vassar, baseball players at Smith College faced opposition which eventually forced them to give up the game for a number of years.

Female baseball players were not limited to college campuses. In Springfield, Illinois, three men organized a women's baseball club in 1875. They were confident that the novelty of women playing baseball would attract large crowds and fatten their bankroll. On September 11, 1875, the club's teams, labeled the "Blondes" and "Brunettes," played their first match. Newspapers heralded the event as the "first game of baseball ever played in public for gate money between feminine ball-tossers." The concept evidently caught on, for numerous other male entrepreneurs copied the idea and organized women's baseball teams. One group started the "Young Ladies' Baseball Club" in Philadelphia in 1883. These owners billed their team's games as entertainment spectacles, not serious competition, and they continually stressed the femininity and moral respectability of their players. A newspaper account of one of the club's first games relayed the management's claim that players were "selected with tender solicitude from 200 applicants, variety actresses and ballet girls being positively barred." Furthermore the article noted, "Only three of the lot had ever been on the stage, and they were in the strictly legitimate business."

The Young Ladies Baseball Club played its first game on August 18, 1883, at Pastime Park in Philadelphia. Despite the supposed "200 applicants," only sixteen girls were mustered to form the two teams for the contest; two young men rounded out the rosters. The game was played on a regulation-size diamond, but, as one observer wrote, it was too large for the women. "A ball thrown from pitcher to second base almost invariably fell short and was stopped on the roll. The throw from first to third base was an utter impossibility." Five hundred spectators witnessed the club's debut and were caught up in "uncontrollable laughter" much of the time. From a financial standpoint, however, the venture was a success. More than 1,500 fans turned out for the club's match at the Manhattan Athletic Club on September 23, 1883, where they "laughed themselves hungry and thirsty." Though one observer conceded that "four of the girls had become expert—for girls," it is obvious that "novelty" and not "ability" was the hallmark of women's baseball at the time.

Another novel group of female baseball players was the Bloomer Girls. Actually "Bloomer Girls" was a misnomer, since Bloomer Girls teams were composed of both men and women. Kansas City Bloomer Girls, New York Bloomer Girls, Texas Bloomer Girls, and Boston Bloomer Girls were just a few of the teams traveling from diamond to diamond in the late nineteenth and early twentieth centuries in search of fame and fortune. Despite the number of Bloomer Girl teams, they did not play each other and no formal league was set up. Instead, they journeyed from town to town, challenging men's amateur and semiprofessional teams. The Bloomer Girls teams relied on sideshow style appeal to draw fans and, not surprisingly, the bottom line was money. The manager of the

Texas Bloomer Girls wrote to one prospective promoter in 1913, assuring him that the team's seven girls and four boys, "including the one-armed boy who plays center field," would draw enough fans to ensure the backer "three hundred dollars clear money" each week. A few of the male Bloomer Girls players like "Smoky Joe" Wood and Hall of Famer Rogers Hornsby went on to become successful big league ballplayers, but the future was not as bright for the female players who could not aspire to anything higher in the baseball world.

The Bloomer Girls teams were not the only option available to baseball-playing females around the turn of the century. Women's teams and mixed teams competed occasionally in "pickup" games. One such game took place in Kearsarge, New Hampshire, on August 7, 1903. An article in the *Boston Herald* the following day noted, "The teams were made up of young ladies gowned in white and young men decked out in girls' clothes, all New Englanders, guests at the hotel." On August 31, the newspaper announced an upcoming game at Forest Hills between the "Hickey and Clover clubs," each composed of five women and four men. One year later, in Flat Rock, Indiana, a group of women organized two baseball clubs, one consisting only of married players, the other only of single players.

While some women played on all-female or coed teams, others challenged social constraints of the day by playing on otherwise all-male teams. On June 12, 1903, the *Cincinnati Enquirer* printed an article about the efforts of a local woman, Miss M. E. Phelan, to get a job as center fielder with the all-male Flora Baseball Club of Indiana. Phelan wrote to the club's manager informing him, "I have played with a number of lady ball clubs and am considered the equal of the average country player." Whether the Flora club took Phelan up on her offer to play for them for "$60 per month and expenses" is unknown, but only four years later another Ohioan, Alta Weiss, became an overnight female baseball-playing sensation and, as one article put it, "perhaps the only girl in the United States to obtain [a] college education through skill as a baseball player."

Weiss, a native of Ragersville, Ohio, became a celebrity in the Cleveland area when she made her pitching debut with the all-male, semiprofessional Vermilion Independents on September 2, 1907. More than 1,200 fans attended the game in which Weiss pitched 5 innings, giving up only 4 hits and 1 run. By the time Weiss made her second appearance on September 8, she was already being heralded as the "Girl Wonder" in the press. According to the *Vermilion News,* so many fans wanted to see Weiss play that special trains had to be run to Vermilion from Cleveland and surrounding towns.

Weiss pitched 8 games for the Independents during their 1907 season. More than 13,000 fans saw the games, including a season high of 3,182, who witnessed her debut at Cleveland's League Park on October 2, 1907. At least a dozen newspapers covered her exploits. The following year her father bought a half-interest in a men's semiprofessional team which was known thereafter as the Weiss All-Stars. It was based in Cleveland and, with Alta as a drawing card, played for large crowds throughout Ohio and Kentucky.

Though Weiss was far and away the best-known female

baseball player in northern Ohio at this time, she was not the only one. On June 22, 1908, the *Cleveland Press* introduced fourteen-year-old Carita Masteller to the public. The paper reported that she had been playing baseball for eight or nine years and was as good as Weiss. That same month Weiss pitched against another female pitcher, Irma Gribble. The two dueled again in August. In another unique game, two sisters from Bellevue, Ohio, Irene and Ruth Basford, pitched for opposing men's teams.

Another well-known female baseball player who played on men's teams was Rhode Islander Elizabeth Murphy. "Lizzie," as she liked to be called, played amateur and semiprofessional baseball from about 1915 to 1935 and was known as the "Queen of Baseball" throughout New England and eastern Canada. After playing for a number of amateur teams in Rhode Island, Murphy signed with the semiprofessional Providence Independents in 1918. A few years later she joined Ed Carr's All-Stars of Boston and earned quite a reputation for her skills as a first baseman.

In 1928, while Murphy was still impressing the fans in New England, fourteen-year-old Margaret Gisolo helped her Blanford, Indiana, American Legion men's baseball team win county, district, sectional, and state championships. In seven tournament games she had 9 hits in 21 at-bats. She scored 10 putouts and 28 assists in the field, with no errors charged against her. A protest against her participation filed by opposing teams went all the way to the American Legion's National Americanism Commission, which referred it to the major league baseball commissioner, Judge Kenesaw Mountain Landis. Landis determined that American Legion rules did not specifically ban the participation of women and disallowed the protest.

Landis had to address a similar situation three years later when the "Barnum of Baseball," Chattanooga Lookouts manager Joe Engel, signed seventeen-year-old Jackie Mitchell to a contract with his Class AA minor league team, thus making her the first female professional baseball player. Mitchell had been taught to pitch by major leaguer Dazzy Vance and had once struck out nine men in a row in an amateur game. She became an overnight celebrity on April 2, 1931, when she pitched in an exhibition game against the visiting New York Yankees—and struck out Babe Ruth and Lou Gehrig, back to back. Speculation continues as to whether Ruth and Gehrig were merely putting on a show or really trying to hit Mitchell's pitches. Mitchell contended that it was not a setup and that the only instructions to the Yankee players had been to try not to hit the ball straight through the pitcher's box. A number of Yankee players confirmed her story. Unfortunately Mitchell never had a chance to repeat her performance as a professional baseball player. A few days after her debut, Landis informed Engel that he had disallowed Mitchell's contract on the grounds that life in baseball was too strenuous for women. Organized baseball formalized the ban against women signing professional baseball contracts with men's teams on June 21, 1952; the ruling still stands.

The restriction on women playing professional baseball on men's teams did not prevent the formation of a women's professional baseball league, however. In 1943, with wartime manpower shortages threatening major league baseball, Chicago Cubs' owner Philip K. Wrigley decided to form a women's professional softball league which would play its games in the major league stadiums while the men were away at war. Within a year of its founding, the league modified its rules and the All-American Girls Professional *Baseball* League (AAGPBL) was born. The AAGPBL made its debut in 1943, when four teams—the Rockford [Illinois] Peaches, the South Bend [Indiana] Blue Sox, the Racine [Wisconsin] Belles, and the Kenosha [Wisconsin] Comets—squared off during the League's 108-game schedule. Attendance that year was 176,000 fans, which, according to one contemporary, meant that the League was "drawing a higher percentage of the population [in league cities] than major league baseball ever did in its greatest attendance years." Attendance figures continued to rise year after year, reaching a peak in 1948, when the League's ten teams drew almost 1,000,000 fans. That same year, AAGPBL teams drew more than 100,000 fans for a series of nine games in Puerto Rico.

Unlike women's teams of the past, the AAGPBL relied on players' skills, not their gender, to draw fans to the ballpark. The 500 women who played in the AAGPBL during its eleven-year existence were top-notch athletes. Many were veterans of championship school, community, or industrial softball teams, and a few had even played on boys' or men's baseball teams. In addition, many of the AAGPBL managers were experienced professional baseball players—some, like Bill Wambsganss (the only player ever to achieve an unassisted triple play in a World Series), Max Carey, Jimmie Foxx, and Dave Bancroft, were legends.

By 1954 televised major league baseball games and organizational problems led to the demise of the AAGPBL. But the lack of a formal league has not hindered women who still desire to play baseball. Many girls continue to play the game on an informal basis; a few play on Little League teams, and one women's team even tried to gain admission to the men's Class A Florida State League in 1984. That effort failed, but in June, 1988, baseball enthusiast Darlene Mehrer founded a new women's baseball league in Glenview, Illinois. Time will tell whether the new league will ever achieve the popularity of the AAGPBL. In the meantime, baseball will continue to be considered a "man's" game, but there can be no doubt that female players have enriched baseball's past and are striving to change baseball's future.

The Game Off the Field

The Business of Baseball

Steve Mann and David Pietrusza

Major league baseball, like every other professional sport, is an entertainment business. And the financial success of any top-level entertainment business rests on its ability to attract consistently large audiences. In order to meet that requirement, the business must do two things. It must assemble and maintain a group of the very best performers in their field, and it must provide pleasant accommodations for the spectators. Every other facet of the business is tied to these fundamental necessities.

In professional sports, the top performers are essentially world-class athletes. And, by definition, there is always a relatively scarce supply of such athletes. This scarcity demands constant vigilance on the part of club management in identifying and developing new talent. The task of maintaining an ample supply of highly skilled performers is difficult in any sport for the simple reason that the players have relatively short careers. But it is especially challenging in baseball because the amateur players, no matter how gifted and experienced they are, almost invariably need intensive long-term training to be able to compete at the major league level. To continue producing that level of talent, season after season, the clubs are obliged to invest heavily and continuously in scouting and player development.

Although the association between major league clubs and their towns runs deep, and one therefore tends to think that the clubs belong to their towns, major league baseball is actually a form of private enterprise. It is an industry made up of twenty-six separate, semi-independent franchises, all of which are owned by private individuals, groups, or companies. Each franchise is contractually linked to a half dozen or more minor league clubs through which it develops its big league talent. The network of those two hundred or so clubs is organized under the Office of the Commissioner of Major League Baseball.

Like any other private industry, baseball has had to depend upon income and profits for its existence. In the game's earliest days, nearly all of its revenue came from sales of tickets to spectators. As the sport grew in popularity, and as bigger and more comfortable stadiums were built to accommodate the increasing number of fans, the sale of refreshments, scorecards, pennants and other team paraphernalia became significant new sources of club revenue. The advent of radio broadcasts in the 1920s brought yet another form of income to the game: advertising revenue. Sponsors paid radio stations handsomely for promoting their products during games. And the stations, in turn, paid the clubs for the rights to carry the games. As the

listening audiences grew, the charges for broadcast rights increased. When television was introduced, a generation later, a flood of new advertising money washed over the major leagues. By the mid-1980s, total industry income from radio and television rights, in-stadium advertising and promotions, and club shares of ballpark concessions exceeded gate receipts.

Then, in 1987, baseball commissioner Peter Ueberroth raised several million more dollars for the industry from an entirely new source, the national sponsor. Through this scheme, huge corporations pay large sums for the privilege of becoming the official "mega-sponsors" of baseball. Now, for example, International Business Machines and Chevrolet are the official computer and automobile manufacturers, respectively, of the major leagues.

While all of this new money was being raked in, baseball's resurgent popularity continued to soar. Attendance records were being broken year after year. In 1986, every club exceeded the 1 million mark in home attendance, a major league first. And in 1987, thanks largely to unprecedented competitive parity on the field (fifteen of the twenty-six clubs were still legitimate contenders on September 1), even more fans poured through the turnstiles. At the present time, average annual club revenue exceeds $20 million. Total annual industry income is now, therefore, greater than a half billion dollars.

The baseball business also generates revenue for publishers, sporting goods companies, T-shirt manufacturers, transportation companies, service stations, restaurants, bars, legal and illegal gambling operations, and a variety of other business interests. Consequently a major league franchise is not only a source of pride for its hometown fans but also an economic boon to the city that houses it.

Where all this money comes from, of course, is the fans. It is the fans who pay for the tickets, the fans who purchase the scorecards and yearbooks, the pennants and caps, the hotdogs and sodas that supplement the gate receipts. Furthermore it is the fans who ultimately pay for newspaper, radio, television, and in-stadium advertising, for it is they who absorb the built-in costs of advertising when they buy the sponsors' goods. And for the moment, at least, the fans seem quite willing to pay the increasing costs of their spectatorship.

Given the huge and still growing influx of income to the baseball owners' coffers, one would expect that the clubs are by now embarrassingly profitable. In truth, however, the baseball business is in trouble. The problem is that throughout the revenue bonanza of the 1980s, the rate of increase in the costs of running the clubs has far exceeded the rate of increase in income. The startling rise in costs can be attributed almost entirely to a single category of club expenses—player salaries.

On the surface, the issue is simply money. Ownership claims that it still doesn't have enough of it, and the players seem to behave as though they can't get enough of it either. The sports news media tend to pay only sporadic attention to the dilemma, in part because cries of distress are hard to accept from either party, and in part because there is no base of popular support for either party. The fans are generally unsympathetic toward either camp. In fact, public sentiment on the subject is by and large measured in terms of resentment for one or both sides, with the players lately holding a distinct edge in unpopularity.

The financial situation is quite bleak—major league baseball actually is teetering on the brink of bankruptcy. The primary cause of baseball's paradoxical dilemma is the adversary relationship that has existed between the players and owners since 1879. It was then that the baseball owners first established a limited version of the infamous "reserve clause." This was a provision in certain players' contracts that made them captives, virtual slaves, of their owners. Within six years of its inception, the provision was extended to include all major and minor league players. The ballplayers did not obtain freedom from the reserve clause, and thus did not begin to receive a reasonable share of baseball's income, until the 1977 season.

For today's players, a century-old legacy of financial slavery and the personal animosity and political entrenchment that naturally flow from that condition are neither quickly nor easily erased. In light of the dubious practices of the clubs since the 1985 season, which include collusion in dealing with free agents, the players appear justified in maintaining their basic distrust of management.

For the owners, the eleven years since the players gained their freedom have been a horror show of fiscal ineptitude and mismanagement. They have watched their own club executives drive salaries to unthinkably high levels. In several instances they have themselves added significantly to the escalation. But while many of the baseball moguls privately blame their fellow owners and themselves for allowing the game's financial crisis to develop in the first place, their public anger is directed squarely at the players, their agents, and their union.

So contrary to popular opinion, the current standoff is not merely a case of two greedy opponents using hardball negotiating tactics to force concessions out of each other, all at the fans' expense. Rather it is a clash over rights and principles. And if greed is at all involved in baseball's internal conflict, then it is more as a manifestation of that conflict than a cause of it.

In fact, the history of the business of baseball is the history of the tension between individual rights on the one hand and the priorities and practices of businessmen on the other. Like the game itself, the story is uniquely American. In many respects it runs parallel to the history of labor-management relations in America. The story begins in 1846, with the first match game of the Knickerbocker Base Ball Club, and winds its way through the institution of the reserve clause and the many challenges to it over the years, the breaking of the color bar, transcontinental franchise shifts, rich television contracts, and league expansion. But as these events are detailed else-where in this volume (see the contributions by Voigt, Hailey, Tygiel, Dellinger, Cohen, and Hoie), the present essay will focus on the turbulent years since 1968, when the Players Association and the owners signed the game's first bilateral agreement.

The Storm Before the Calm: 1968–1975

When Ford Frick retired as commissioner in 1965, the owners hired an unheralded Air Force general by the name of William D. Eckert. "Spike," as he was known, was openly pleased to be a ceremonial chief. But he asumed the job just at the time the Players Association was beginning to make bold moves.

To deal with the growing strength of the opposition, owners created a Player Relations Committee in 1967. The PRC, as it is commonly called, was headed by John J. Gaherin, former president of the New York City Newspaper Publishers Association. It included the two major league presidents and three owners from each league and was supported by a legal staff. As its name implied, the Player Relations Committee's sole function was to act as a link between the Players Association and the owners, delivering information to and from both bodies and assisting in the formulation of management policy.

The first big item on the PRC's agenda was a collective-bargaining agreement, something that the association had been angling to get for some time. The purpose of the agreement was to make some inroads into the standard contract. It was not yet time to launch a frontal attack on the reserve clause.

The document which emerged from the negotiations was officially entitled the Basic Agreement. Signed in February 1968, it was the first in a still unbroken series of such accords. It established a formal grievance procedure for the players and provided for subsequent study of the reserve clause by both parties. Probably the most important feature of the first Basic Agreement was that it would take official precedence over the old major league rules wherever they were found to be in conflict. This meant that players were involved in major league policymaking for the first time.

By now the players had racked up a series of important victories, and it was clear that William Eckert's administration was overmatched. During the short period in which Eckert held office, the players hired Marvin Miller, built their Park Avenue office, and successfully negotiated the first Basic Agreement. The war was on, but General Eckert was in the wrong army. The owners fired him in December 1968.

Within three months of Eckert's removal, and with the commissioner's job still vacant, the owners were confronted with a crisis. Management had offered the players a contract package that was a distinct improvement over the previous deal. The Players Association had rejected the offer because they felt they deserved additional increases in health care, life insurance, and pension benefits. Both sides were angry, and neither side would yield an inch of ground. So the players refused to sign contracts and threatened to strike. Spring training was scheduled to begin in a couple of weeks, and it appeared that the players were prepared to delay its start.

The PRC called on one of the National League lawyers, a big pleasant chap named Bowie Kent Kuhn, to see if he could untie the knot. Kuhn, in a style which would become his trademark, devoted most of his time to calming and soothing his irritated management colleagues. Having accomplished that not-so-easy feat, he gave the players everything they had asked for. Six months later, he was rewarded for his efforts with an eight-year term as the commissioner of baseball.

Within seven months after he assumed office, Kuhn was confronted with the Curt Flood case. Flood had been a very fine outfielder with the Cardinals for twelve years when he was informed by a low-level club official after the 1969 season that he would be playing ball with the Phillies in 1970. The Phillies had finished 24 games behind the Cardinals, and Flood apparently didn't much like the town of Philadelphia anyway. So he wrote a letter to the commissioner requesting that he be permitted to "consider offers from other clubs before making any decisions."

Kuhn could not grant the request without simultaneously and singlehandedly overturning the reserve clause. He denied Flood's request. With the Players Association behind him, Curt Flood decided to take the issue to court. The case reached the United States Supreme Court, but, as usual, yet another player went down in defeat.

Why did it always turn out that the lawmakers and judges, many of whom were openly sympathetic to the players' cause, were unwilling to rule in the players' favor? Essentially it was because no less than the relationship between government and private industry was at stake. If Congress or the United States Supreme Court had chosen to modify or overturn the reserve clause, it would have immediately established a fundamentally different and presumably more equal balance of power between the players and the owners, but with unknown results. The uncertainty was the hangup. Whatever the effects of altering the reserve clause might be, the publicity such an action would receive would be enormous. Sports fans and politics watchers, a sizable audience to say the least, would be riveted to the issue. And if major league competition and franchise stability were indeed sacrificed through the removal or modification of the reserve clause, as the owners had been warning would happen since 1885, then the government officials responsible for the decision, either the Supreme Court justices or the members of Congress, would be held accountable. If baseball could not right itself in a reasonable amount of time or, worse, if it were to collapse, this would be especially embarrassing and possibly damaging to nothing less than a branch of the United States government.

Except in the most extreme circumstances, neither Congress nor the Supreme Court is inclined to take a potentially profound step where the outcome of its decisions is so thoroughly unpredictable. Both bodies would much prefer that basic struggles of this sort be brought to a higher level of resolution before they will bring their heavy conclusive weight to bear upon them. Not a single meaningful aspect of the reserve system had been altered yet. The real effects of altering or removing the controversial clause were still basically untested. So it is reasonable to conclude that in the eyes of Washington politicos baseball's eternal adversaries had a long way to go before the federal government would get seriously involved.

Despite the risks involved, the Supreme Court's decision to retain baseball's antitrust exemption in the case of *Flood* v. *Kuhn* was a upheld by a narrow 5–3 margin. Subsequent revelations concerning the justices who ruled on the case suggest that the issue troubled a few of them deeply and that the vote was even closer than the final tally indicated. It could have gone either way. Furthermore public opinion at the time was overwhelmingly on the side of Curt Flood.

These were definite signs that the owners were in a lonelier position than they had ever been in before. Indeed, they were cornered. And Commissoner Kuhn's previous behavior as well as the personal risks his job entailed should have been clear hints to the owners that he would be more inclined to commiserate with them than fight for them when the going got tough.

The Players Association, which had responsibly cautioned Flood against pursuing his case, was nonetheless delighted that he had chosen to disregard their advice. Flood's case would keep the reserve system in full public view.

This was just the first loud shot in what would become an unceasing legal siege on baseball management. Starting with the Flood case, the two sides have engaged in major confrontations roughly once a year ever since. Just during the time that the Flood case was being heard, the association fought a battle over the second Basic Agreement in 1970, which it followed up with a players' strike in 1972, which was in turn followed by a third Basic Agreement in 1973 that gave the players the right to outside, impartial salary arbitration.

Between these big surges, the union maintained a barrage of smaller assaults. And in what was effectively a flanking operation, they directed a flurry of attacks on the renewal clause of the uniform baseball contract. What the renewal provision said, in brief, was that a player who did not sign a new contract for the coming season at a salary set by the club would still be the property of his current club for one year—the renewal year. What it did not say was what would happen after the renewal year. Would a player be free to sell his services to any club at the conclusion of the renewal year? Thus a pivotal legal question remained unanswered, a question that shared its legal border with the reserve clause.

In 1969, pitcher Al Downing of the Yankees made a serious inquiry into the matter. He wanted to play the 1970 season without signing so that he could become a free agent the following year. After being cautioned by Marvin Miller against testing the renewal clause, Downing was told by Yankees management that if he refused to sign his 1970 contract, he might as well not bother to show up at spring training. Downing signed. He was then traded to Oakland before the 1970 season began.

In 1972 St. Louis catcher Ted Simmons came even closer to testing the renewal clause. He played unsigned for half a season before finally agreeing to a two-year contract with the Cardinals. From 1973 to 1975, seventeen more players started seasons without contracts, all of whom threatened to play out their options for a stab at becoming free agents. Two of them, pitchers Dave McNally and Andy Messersmith, carried out the threat—they never did sign.

Meanwhile, association gains were piling up. The 1970 Basic Agreement had given the players the right to arbitrate grievances. The Flood case had led to the inclusion of the "five-and-ten" rule in the 1973 Basic Agreement, by which players with ten or more years of major league service who have played for at least the last five years with one club have the right to approve a trade to another club. Though the rule affected only a very small segment of the major league population, it marked the first time that any group of players had any control over where they would ply their trade. A breach of contract by Oakland A's owner Charles O. Finley had made pitcher Catfish Hunter a free agent in 1974. That decision had been of little direct value to other players, except to grant them protection against illegally drawn contracts. But it had demonstrated the determination and the growing strength of the union.

Next on the agenda was a full test of the renewal clause by Messersmith and McNally in the fall of 1975. Both pitchers had played the entire 1975 season without contracts. The bounds of the Basic Agreement had thus been exceeded, leaving the two pitchers in a legal no-man's-land. Would the parent clubs still own the contracts of the players after the renewal year, or would the players become free agents, thereby allowing them to sell their services to other teams? That was the multimillion-dollar question.

The case was to be heard by a three-man arbitration panel. The panel chairman was Peter Seitz, a man with twenty years of experience as an arbitrator. Marvin Miller and John Gaherin were the other panel members, so naturally their partisan votes on the case would cancel out. This meant that Seitz would, in effect, be making the most important decision in the history of baseball's labor-management relations all by himself.

Although the issue was ostensibly the renewal clause, it was really the reserve clause that was on trial. For if Seitz ruled that the two pitchers were free, then every other player in the major leagues could take the same circuitous route to freedom. It would be a cavernous loophole, but a perfectly legal one.

Seitz tried vigorously to get the two sides to work out the problem through bargaining. Like Congress and the Supreme Court, he felt that the matter was far too important to be adjudicated in any other way. He even went so far as to write a letter to management, explaining that the weight of the case was definitely on the side of the players and warning that he would not shrink from his duty to act, and act quickly, on the case. But the owners stonewalled it. They rejected Seitz's recommendation.

Two days before Christmas 1975, Mr. Seitz placed a nicely wrapped gift under the owners' tree—a sixty-one-page decision in favor of Andy Messersmith and Dave McNally.

The owners' first response was to fire Seitz. Then they sent their attorneys around to all of the courts that would listen, trying desperately to appeal the decision. The courts listened, but did not heed the call. Every appeal was rejected, the last one coming in March 1976. Spring training had not begun. The owners had locked the players out. Another delay in the start of a big league season was looming on the not-too-distant horizon.

Then, suddenly and very uncharacteristically, Bowie Kuhn defied the owners and opened the training camps. Recognizing the unpopularity of their position and having exhausted all of their legal options, the owners entered into negotiations with the Players Association for a new Basic Agreement. By this action, the owners had officially surrendered.

The specter of the Messersmith decision cast a pall over the management negotiators. They knew that they were going to have to yield expensive turf. The only question was how much. This was it, the big face-to-face showdown between baseball management and labor, and the culmination of an ancient quest by ballplayers for a proper share of major league revenue.

On the face of it, the Basic Agreement that emerged from the negotiations in July 1976 did not seem revolutionary. Indeed, to the astonishment of many, it retained nearly all of the elements of the original reserve clause. But there was one historic exception: a provision that any player with six or more years of major league service would now have the right to declare himself a free agent.

Was this what all of the commotion had been about— the freedom to sell one's services after six full major league seasons? The answer was a resounding "Yes!" The new provision gave the players all the freedom they would ever need. In fact, 1976 was a year of unsurpassable celebration for the union members. It marked the two-hundredth birthday of the United States of America, the one-hundredth birthday of major league baseball, and the erection of a fountain of wealth for the men who play the game.

Thus ended the first long chapter in the history of labor-management relations in major league baseball. Nearly a century of internal struggle had been devoted essentially to the revison of a single sentence in the standard player's contract, a single clause that meant the difference between economic slavery and economic freedom. Although the new 1976 version of the reserve clause still restricted that freedom, and although no one could predict what effects limited free agency would ultimately have, the players had finally built a tunnel to the outside from their financial prison. And golden rays of sunshine immediately began to pour into the cells of some of the veteran inmates.

The peculiarities of the baseball industry had produced a strange, even unique form of economic struggle. The last attempt to establish a third baseball league had been crushed sixty years before arbitrator Seitz's ruling. So the baseball players received none of the large and lasting financial boosts that the American Football League, the American Basketball Association, and the World Hockey League had generated for professional football, basketball, and hockey players. And with little more than expressions of positive sentiment on the part of the fans and the politicians, they had had to fight their salary battles in virtual isolation. The transiency of the major league labor force had made it extremely difficult for them to mount a sustained offensive. Furthermore, by paying many of the star players rather handsomely, ownership had bought most of them out of opposition. Given the ease with which the owners could remove ordinary players, who would not be terribly missed by the paying customers anyway, it was next to impossible for the players to get a grassroots movement started. Troublemakers and malcontents generally found themselves tied up in court, or quickly dispatched to the minor leagues, or dispensed with altogether. Besides, it truly was a whole lot better to be turning double plays for a living than turning sod in a field or flapjacks on a grill.

Baseball players had always been a young, hungry, competitive lot, generally unschooled in and intimidated by corporate matters. So most of them were quite content to play ball for a living, regardless of the level of pay. And they tended to look back on their major league experience, their days in the sun, not with rancor, but with understandable pride and satisfaction. What resentment the players did harbor for the barons who owned them generally lasted no longer than their careers.

Under these circumstances, and given the socioeconomic climate of America during baseball's first seventy years, all that the baseball owners had had to do to protect their dictatorial monopoly was play hard-fisted defense. They and their cadre of lawyers and bureaucrats practiced the traditional corporate techniques of stonewalling, name-calling, delaying, and postponing. Furthermore they were an integral part of the business establishment. This had given them unfettered access to and clout with the sports media. Add to those advantages the reluctance of the Congress and the courts to intervene meaningfully on the players' behalf, plus the relative indifference of the fans to the whole matter, and management had been practically invulnerable. Being as ambitious, competitive, and self-interested as they were, management had never even attempted to accommodate the players, in any area, not even when Commissioners Kenesaw M. Landis and A. B. Chandler had advised them to do so.

The owners were The Club. And they had ruled with the club, primitively and uncompromisingly, for one hundred years. The only club the player had had was made of hickory or ash and called a bat. It was the only club he had had, that is, until the star players took up the cause.

The stars were the ones who had attracted the crowds in New York in the 1850s and 1860s and put baseball on the map. It was they who had received the game's first big paychecks and eventually prompted the restrictive methods adopted by the owners, including the oppressive reserve clause. It was the stars upon whom the hapless rival leagues had pinned their takeover attempts. And it was they to whom the established clubs had paid even higher salaries to keep them in the fold.

To the fans the stars were kings, to be envied. To the owners they were pawns, to be played against the other players and the rival leagues in the interest of minimizing salaries and maximizing profits. To the players the stars were the winners in an environment in which it was every man for himself.

Baseball's stars had let their teammates down for seventy-odd years. Ty Cobb's steely disregard for his fellow ballplayers at the Celler Committee hearings in 1952—when he spoke of the necessity for maintaining the reserve clause—was perhaps the most galling example. But in the early 1950s, the stars turned and the rest of the players gradually joined the effort. Perhaps the courage of Jackie Robinson in his fight for integration had inspired them to act. Perhaps Branch Rickey's treatment of Ralph Kiner—paying him far less than his performance warranted, simply because he played for an inferior team

("We could have finished last without you" were Rickey's immortal words)—was the pivotal event in their crusade. Perhaps it was the continuing emergence of the Roosevelt-inspired middle class, or the conclusion of the war. Probably it was all of those things, and more. But whatever their personal reasons, the commitment of stars such as Bob Feller, Allie Reynolds, Ralph Kiner, and Robin Roberts to their fellow players, a commitment that led to the very formation of the Players Association in 1954 and would require their continued attention and devotion to the cause after their own careers were over, was the key to the success of the players' revolt. Others played very significant roles. Marvin Miller, Curt Flood, Andy Messersmith, and Dave McNally are among the most obvious. Dozens of lesser-known participants made important contributions, too. But when the stars finally took action, that is when the scenery really started to change. And by 1976 the stage was set for a new period in major league history—the free-agency era.

The baseball industry had undergone another dramatic change from the late 1950s to the mid-1970s. During that time the mantle of club ownership was being gradually handed over to a new genre of proprietor, the corporate magnate.

Prior to the 1950s, one did not need excessive wealth to become a club owner. Thanks to the reserve clause, operating costs had always been relatively low. And the monopoly status of the sport had served as protection against outside competition, especially after the Federal League incursion had been quashed in 1916. Clubs were generally owned by individuals or small groups of investors. Most franchises were family-run businesses that depended for their survival and success more upon baseball savvy and blood-and-guts determination than upon managerial sophistication or huge cash reserves. The ballclub, in most cases, was the livelihood of the owner. And his fortune normally rose and fell with the standing of his team or the general economic health of the major leagues.

Through the 1950s the motivation to own a ballclub came from the prestige that one automatically acquired, the profits that one stood a very good chance of making, and, perhaps above all, a deep devotion to the game. For without an abiding attachment to baseball, one would have succumbed to the unrelenting, undifferentiated demands of the job. The fact that the game was a cash business practically mandated that management personnel be family members or highly trusted friends. Someone, after all, always had to keep an eye on the till.

In those days, most owners assumed major responsibility for the day-to-day running of their clubs. In nearly all cases, it was they who dictated and negotiated player contracts. This gave the sport a head-to-head, man-to-man character. All were in it together—the owner, his cadre of management personnel, and the players. But the relative intimacy of ballclubs did not promote fair and equitable treatment for club employees. Most of the front-office people and their assistants fared no better than the players.

The fellowship that existed resembled the sort that is found in military organizations. There was a strict top-down chain of command, in which orders were obeyed, rights and privileges were decreed, and nonsense was not tolerated. But along with that stern order came a unity of purpose among all involved and a high level of camaraderie among the troops. Those qualities helped to keep the teams and the sport intact throughout its embattled development.

The quasi-military nature of the sport helped to foster a public perception of team loyalty and stability. That perception grew after the Black Sox scandal and flourished during the Landis regime. In the meantime, the big league clubs had become embedded in their cities. For exactly fifty years, starting in 1903, not one of the sixteen American and National League franchises left its hometown. The music had stopped and the chairs were in place. The sport and each of its teams had become seemingly permanent features of the American cultural landscape.

Then, in 1953, all of that began to change. After having won the National League pennant in 1948 with a record of 91–62, the Boston Braves began to slide. By 1952, they had fallen to seventh place with a 64–89 record. The next year, the franchise moved to Milwaukee. This was the first in a rapid shakeout of two-team cities. Towns like Milwaukee had been aching to obtain major league clubs for years. Since there were as yet no firm plans to expand the major leagues, the obvious takeover targets for the disfranchised towns were the weaker clubs in two-team cities.

The next two teams to move out were both from the American League. The St. Louis Browns became the Baltimore Orioles in 1954, and the Philadelphia A's moved to Kansas City in 1955. Both clubs had been last-place finishers the year before they pulled up stakes. And both had been distinctly weaker, competitively and economically, than their National League counterparts for a long stretch of time. As a result, these first club relocations in a half-century were rather easily accepted by the hometown fans. And the general perception of franchise stability remained unshaken.

During this brief period, the Players Association was being formed, and television had begun to expand the reach and the income of the baseball business. A decade had passed since the end of World War Two, and the jet age was just beginning. It was a new world with new frontiers. And the big leagues could not buck the momentum of change.

After the 1957 season, the baseball industry was thoroughly introduced to the magnitude of that momentum, for it was then that the New York Giants and the Brooklyn Dodgers were moved to San Francisco and Los Angeles, respectively. Both franchises had maintained huge and loyal followings. Thus the decisions by Giants' owner Horace Stoneham and Dodgers' owner Walter O'Malley to go west sent shock waves through the baseball community. It was one thing to sell a wilting franchise to an enthusiastic new owner and a hungry new town. But it was quite a different matter for an owner simply to rip a solid club away from its faithful fans. The Brooklyn fans were particularly enraged. Their team had been one of the very best in baseball for the preceding decade. In their eyes, and in the eyes of many others, mainly from the East, baseball had broken a social contract by allowing the moves to take place.

From the perspective of Stoneham and O'Malley, the uprooting was strictly a sound business decision. Both viewed California as an untapped source of practically boundless opportunity. And despite the strong base of support in New York and Brooklyn, the industrial East was stagnating. Attendance at Giant and Dodger home games, though respectable, did not match the quality of the teams, especially in the case of the Dodgers. Walter O'Malley recognized that baseball was in the midst of a transition to a more demanding, higher profile, and more lucrative entertainment industry.

The Dodgers' first year in Los Angeles was a bust on the field. The club wound up the season in seventh place, 21 games behind the pennant-winning Braves. But the club set its all-time attendance record, reaching nearly 1,850,000. Only twice before had the Dodgers drawn in the 1.8 million range, in the immediate postwar years of 1946 and 1947. And this was only the beginning. After he built his own stadium in 1962 and assumed control of all ballpark concessions, O'Malley's new vision was complete. By putting a solid baseball organization in the booming Los Angeles area and securing ownership of all related property, O'Malley constructed the most successful baseball operation in the history of the sport. For its first sixteen years, club attendance averaged slightly better than 2 million. For the last fifteen years, it has averaged close to 3 million. No other club has remotely approached that degree of success at the turnstiles.

Meanwhile, up the coast, the Giants were trying to win at the same game. The first several years, the years of Willie Mays, Juan Marichal, and Willie McCovey, were magical. Great talent continued to flow into the organization, enabling the club to be a serious contender for most of its first fourteen years in San Francisco, through the 1971 season. But attendance in the city by the bay never reached the dizzying heights attained by the Dodgers. The highest total came in 1960, the year in which the club took up residence at Candlestick Park. The number was an all-time club record 1,795,356. Average attendance held at around 1.5 million through 1967, which was well above the league average of roughly 1 million for the period.

Then, however, the A's moved from Kansas City to Oakland. The Giants' attendance plummeted overnight. By the time the club had lost its edge on the field, in 1972, annual attendance had settled in the 700,000 range, making it one of the weakest draws in the National League. Attendance languished at that level for five more years, during which time the A's were busy winning three World Series and attracting 900,000 fans per year. It was immediately evident that the San Francisco Bay area would have difficulty supporting and sustaining two major league clubs. And Candlestick Park, with its sixtyish temperatures and its erratic, blustery winds, was becoming progressively less acceptable, both to the fans and to the new principal owner of the club, Robert Lurie. Giant attendance has bounced back to the 1.2 million range since 1978. But the club, at this writing, is actively seeking a new home outside California despite the fact that it won the 1987 Western Division championship.

By the mid-1960s, the financial stakes had become higher for the major league baseball business, and the new California teams highlighted some of the opportunities and risks involved.

The most important transformation in the character of

big league club ownership started in the 1960s, when corporate interests began to replace family ownership groups. Overall baseball attendance had ebbed by then, due in part to a severe drop in run production caused by a legislated increase in the size of the strike zone, and due in larger part to the ascendancy of the National Football League. The nation was in a countercultural frenzy at that time, with drugs, sex, rock-and-roll, and the Vietnam War sharing center stage. Under the circumstances, football was hot, baseball was not. There was a growing sense among the members of the major league establishment that the national pastime would have to kick into a higher gear to keep up with the faster pace and more indulgent interests of the society. The first big corporation to get into the act was the Columbia Broadcasting System. CBS purchased the New York Yankees in 1964.

One way to meet the demands of the time was to replace old, typically small, and in some cases dilapidated, baseball parks with large new all-purpose stadiums. Nineteen of the twenty-six stadiums in use today have been built since 1960. Fifteen of those have been constructed since 1966. Yankee Stadium, one of the eight existing parks built before 1960, underwent massive reconstruction in 1974–1975. A few of the seven remaining older parks are soon to be replaced.

The new stadiums reflected the comparatively cold, artificial, plastic, hyped qualities of the new era they were ushering in. They were equipped with massive electronic scoreboards and message boards. Giant sound systems piped advertising jingles through the vast concrete terraces of plastic seats. Spectators were led in cheers, taunts, and songs by computer-graphic instructions flashed on the huge, usually garish message machines. In the Houston Astrodome, touted for its first several years of existence as the eighth manmade wonder of the world, fans were even prompted to applaud by the center field message board, where jerky animated figures of hands would suddenly appear, clapping to the synthesized beat of a high-technology organ.

By way of these innovations, several ballparks became enormous television studios, filled with all of the technical gadgetry and special accommodations needed to put on dazzling spectacles, both for the in-stadium and at-home spectators. Even the playing fields did not escape the reconstruction trend. Artificial grass was developed for the sun-starved floor of the Astrodome in 1966, and it soon spread through the big leagues, as though it was the real thing. Ten stadiums are now paved with plastic turf.

So by the mid-1970s the surface features of baseball had been altered markedly. For the clubs that joined in the reconstruction movement, the immediate and long-term financial costs were high. The new gimmickry, by itself, was very expensive. The cost of building a stadium had become so great by the mid-1960s that practically every one of the newer stadiums was funded by a local bond issue. And even with the local populaces paying for the ballparks, the annual rent charges to the clubs had become quite costly. Club organizations needed to become more diversified to keep up with the increasing complexities of the business. More importantly, to some of the old-style owners the game was turning into a promotion-ridden circus. The days of pure unadulterated baseball entertainment were numbered. As a result, the business was being invaded by public-relations-minded corporate magnates.

And the Messersmith-McNally decision was hanging over the industry, threatening to restructure its century-old financial foundations.

The Free-Agency Era: 1976–1989

The Messersmith-McNally arbitration decision put major league salary matters on hold for a full year while labor and management worked out the details for implementing free agency. Neither side could predict what effects the new arrangement would have, so both sides were inclined to proceed slowly and cautiously in laying it out. As a result, free-agent bidding did not begin until the fall of 1976. The two sides also agreed to suspend the salary arbitration process through the 1977 season.

What emerged from the 1976 bargaining talks was a salary system made up of four basic elements: a guaranteed minimum salary of $19,000, maximum salary cuts of 20 percent in one year and 30 percent over a two-year period, the right for players with at least two years but less than six years of major league service to have their salaries determined through arbitration, and the right for players with six or more years of service to declare free agency and sell their services to any club.

The first two components, the minimum salary and the maximum permissible cuts, were the players' defensive weapons. Both had been in place for many years. Arbitration, which was first adopted after the 1973 season, was designed to allow any player dissatisfied with a club salary offer to have his dispute heard and ruled upon by an impartial arbitrator. It was intended to give the player an opportunity to raise his income to a level commensurate with other players of similar ability and experience and thereby protect him against salary gouging. Free agency was strictly an offensive instrument. It enabled the player to determine his dollar value through free-market bidding by clubs.

In theory, an ordered salary structure would emerge from the new four-part system. There would now be three mutually exclusive "classes" of players.

At the bottom of the salary pyramid would be those players with less than two years of major league service, who would have no explicit rights beyond the major league minimum. Their salaries would be unilaterally determined by management. If such players felt they were underpaid, their only recourse would be to hold out, refusing to play unless and until they received higher pay. Holding out had been the players' only real source of negotiating leverage for one hundred years. Now, just those players with less than two years of service would be forced to rely on such an extreme negotiating measure, and only on rare occasions.

In the middle would be the arbitration eligibles. If they did not want to accept a club's offer, they would be free to take the matter to an arbitrator.

The salary arbitration procedure is essentially simple and straightforward. If, in the course of negotiations, a player has reason to believe that his club will not offer him as much money as he feels he is worth, then he officially files for arbitration by a specified date in early January. If he and the club are still unable to reach an accord as of a second deadline, at the end of January, then both sides are required to submit a salary figure. Within twenty-four hours of the submissions, the player, the club, the Players Association, and the Player Relations Committee are notified of the salary amounts that the two parties have submitted. An arbitration hearing is then scheduled for a specific morning or afternoon between February 1 and February 20, the official arbitration period. If the two parties remain unable to reach a settlement before the appointed hearing, then the case is heard in a four- to six-hour session. The arbitrator then has twenty-four hours to select one of the two submissions. It is an either-or proposition; there is no middle ground. Thus if the player is seeking, say, $350,000 and the club is offering $250,000, the arbitrator must choose one or the other figure. He may not, for example, split the difference and award the player a $300,000 contract.

In its first two years of implementation, in 1974 and 1975, arbitration did not amount to much. Indeed, it could not amount to much because nearly all salaries were relatively low. The average salary was between $40,000 and $45,000; the median was between $30,000 and $35,000. In those years, arbitration battles were generally fought over differences in the $10,000 to $20,000 range.

The top salary class in the new structure would consist of the players eligible to be free agents. They would either receive enough income from their original clubs to stay with those clubs or they would declare themselves free and seek higher pay elsewhere. In either event, there would be pressure on the clubs to pay all players with six or more years of service well enough to secure their services, assuming, of course, that the clubs would uphold the letter and the spirit of the free agency rules by earnestly bidding for players.

The scheme, as a whole, follows the logic of military employment. Like the armed services, the owners would be giving the players training and instruction in the minor leagues in exchange for six years of active duty, at which point the soldiers of summer would be free to remain with their original employers or strike out on their own. Under the circumstances, this seems to have been a surprisingly fair and reasonable resolution of the players' ancient problem. Management had cornered itself, legally, in its dealings with the Players Association and with arbitrator Seitz. So they might well have been backed into a deeper hole by the players. But this final salary arrangement appeared to give the clubs plenty of financial breathing room.

When free agency was set into place in November 1976, it had immediate impact on veteran players. Their salaries took off. In that first year, the average major league salary increased by nearly 50 percent, jumping from $51,501 to $76,066. The median increased by a similar percentage, going from around $40,000 to around $58,000. But the extra $25,000 per player was not distributed evenly. The 1976 minimum salary of $19,000 was retained in 1977, which meant that the younger players had received no boost at the bottom end. So most of the significant raises were going to players with six or more years of major league service behind them. Those veterans represented approximately 40 percent of the player population. Thus what had happened was that the six-

year veterans had realized an average increase of about $50,000, while the players with less than six years of service had, as a group, made only marginal gains. This dichotomy was to have been expected. For not only did the younger players not possess the valuable right of free agency, but they also had no access to arbitration. And even if they had been able to take salary disputes to arbitration, the awards would have been limited by the fact that players of similar skill and experience were not making big salaries either.

Over the next three years, the same principles held. The result was a lopsided three-tiered salary structure, with the youngest players hovering around the minimum, the arbitration eligibles a full notch higher, and the veterans far, far ahead. And the costs of retaining the older players continued to climb steadily and dramatically, widening the gap even further.

The average salary for all players shot up to $113,500 by the end of the 1979 season. Management took on a siege mentality, with owners and executives privately and publicly predicting doom for the baseball business. But the new system created a good deal of interest in baseball's backstage politics. If anything, it contributed to a resurgence in the game's popularity—and in the owners' revenue. The American League's expansion in 1977, from twelve teams to fourteen, and increasing competitive balance on the field in both leagues provided additional boosts to club income. The dollar value of clubs began to skyrocket. More corporate owners bought into the business, and few family-owned and -operated clubs remained. With the stakes now so high, the small owner was simply unable to compete for the better players.

For the players, the last years of the 1970s were an exciting beginning. At long last some of them had started to share in the profits of the entertainment industry that they were the center of. But the huge gap between the arbitration eligibles and the free-agency eligibles kept growing. Even the star players with less than six years of major league service were unable to bridge that gap. What had happened was that the two groups had become segregated. Veterans were being compared with veterans, and younger players were being compared with younger players, due strictly to the difference in service. Consequently middling players with many years of service were generally earning quite a bit more than stars with less than six years of service.

This development kept the rate of salary inflation from getting completely out of control. It was the silver lining in the cloud that had formed over the owners. To the players and their union leaders, it was illogical and unfair that a number of over-the-hill veterans were making hundreds of thousands of dollars more per year than many outstanding young players, such as Eddie Murray, Keith Hernandez, Pete Vuckovich, and Dennis Eckersley. In their view, too much credit was being given for sheer longevity and not enough for quality of play. But under the new salary system, the only way the younger players could move toward the veteran salary range would be through arbitration. The owners certainly weren't going to elevate their salaries out of generosity.

Meanwhile, the arbitration arena was becoming an interesting sideshow feature of the big league circus. Once the combination of free agency and arbitration was permitted to function, after the 1977 season, arbitration began to take on the character of a high stakes pokerfest. The spreads between player demands and club offers were occasionally reaching six figures. Then, after the close of the 1979 season, a major showdown started to take shape. Relief pitcher Bruce Sutter of the Chicago Cubs had completed his fourth year of unsurpassed excellence on the mound. Every big league club would have loved to have Sutter in its bullpen. At the winter meetings in Toronto, in December 1979, several club executives expressed the view that Sutter was among the three or four most valuable players in the game. Some felt that he was the topmost banana in the whole bunch. December trades and purchases of players had dried up considerably as a direct result of the new salary system. As a result, much of the attention of the press and the clubs was given to arbitration, especially to the Sutter matter. The rumors floating around the headquarters hotel suggested that Sutter would be seeking more than a half million dollars for the 1980 season, while the Cubs would not be willing to spend much more than a quarter of a million for his services.

In January the arbitration filing figures came out. The Cubs were offering their relief ace $350,000, a very high amount at that time for a player with barely four years of service, but not much higher than the income he had received the previous year. Sutter's demand was $700,000, a staggering figure that, if granted, would place him near the top of the salary pyramid despite his nonveteran status. In February the case was heard. And to the astonishment of management, Sutter was declared the winner.

This was the first big crack in the wall that separated the free agents from the younger players. The decision implied that a star is a star, regardless of his prior service time, and that he should be paid accordingly. That is to say, he should earn a salary consistent with, though perhaps not quite as high as, that of a veteran with a similar qualitative performance record.

Inside the baseball establishment there was a swirl of controversy surrounding the Cubs' handling of the case. Suggestions were made that Cubs' management committed one or two key tactical blunders. Whether those claims are valid or not, the Sutter case suggested that a few weak links among the clubs with respect to the negotiation and arbitration of salaries could have impact on all other cases and clubs. The case also helped to establish a new high-paid class of player, the relief ace.

The clubs were badly shaken by the Sutter decision. A few of the owners, particularly George Steinbrenner of the Yankees, Ray Kroc of the San Diego Padres, and Brad Corbett of the Texas Rangers, had already sent the salaries of free agents into the stratosphere. Now the clubs felt that they would have to give equal attention to the growing threat of salary arbitration. For even though the Sutter decision was the act of only a single arbitrator, the full precedential impact of which would not be determined for at least a few years, it was a strong signal of danger.

How the clubs responded to their deteriorating position is mystifying. It is also of bottom-line importance to the history of the baseball business, because that response more than anything else is what led the clubs into the

deep and dire financial straits in which they are currently mired. Management's convoluted strategy proceeded more or less along the following lines.

It was obvious to all of the clubs that free agency was costing them dearly. It was equally clear that the big bidders had not reached a plateau, so there was no telling when, where, or if the veterans' spiraling salaries would stop.

By 1980 the $1 million mark had been surpassed by several players. In the meantime, the overarching priority for nearly all of the clubs was still to put the best possible team on the field. That was their business. A handful of less well-off owners refused to enter the fray and simply turned their backs on free agents. But they were too few to buck the inflationary trend. They were on their way out of the industry anyway. For the rest, the problem was not only to decide if and to what extent they would get involved in bidding for free agents. They also had to figure out how they could keep their better young players on their teams once those players reached the sixth year of service and became free agents. Front-office people throughout both leagues dreaded the prospect of having to lose players whom they had selected, trained, and groomed for eight or more years just because some other club would be willing to pay more for them in free-agent bidding. The anxiety was particularly acute among the clubs in the smaller and less profitable media markets. So a defensive contract strategy was needed.

A few clubs responded to the dilemma by entering into long-term contracts with their most prized young players. Such contracts had been virtually nonexistent prior to free agency. The reserve clause had made the player the permanent property of his club, so there had been no good reason for the clubs to guarantee anyone more than the coming year's salary. Now, however, there was a special incentive to sign players for several years at a time. The reasoning went as follows. If a club had an All-Star quality player with four years of service, then by signing that player for, say, five years the club would retain ownership of his contract through the player's ninth year of service. In other words, the club would in effect buy out three years' worth of the player's free agency rights. In practical terms, this meant that the clubs would be willing to risk wheelbarrows full of current dollars on players purely for the purpose of being able to hang on to them for an additional one, two, three years, or more.

The multiyear contract would typically be of great benefit to the player, for no matter what might happen during the term of the contract, most or all of the money would be fully guaranteed. Thus if the player's performance were to fall off, or if he were to become incapacitated through wear and tear or injury, his financial future would be secure.

There were only two risks to the player in agreeing to a multiyear deal. With salaries escalating at a wild rate, no one could know what the future dollar value of a player might be. Consequently a salary of $750,000 in year four of the contract might appear irresistible to the player upon signing, but he could actually be worth much more than that in the major league market by the time that fourth year rolled around. The other risk of entering into a long-term contract was that the player's performance might improve dramatically, again raising his relative dollar value. If both possibilities came to be, then the player might lose hundreds of thousands of dollars, or millions, by taking the multiyear offer. Though there weren't very many of them, future Hall of Famers Johnny Bench and Tom Seaver were among the principal victims of the multiyear contract. Each of them missed out on an income bonanza by agreeing to a long-term deal early in the free agency era, before salaries went through the roof.

Having bitten the multiyear bullet, the question now facing the clubs was how exactly to design these long-term contracts. Since each player belonged to his club through year six, it seemed unnecessary to pay any player more than a fair wage for years three, four, or five. One would have expected, therefore, that the clubs would have granted modest raises prior to a player's sixth year of service, and that they would have built much larger raises into the contract for all subsequent years, raises that would make the player's pay consistent with free agents of similar ability. In fact, what the clubs started to do was to offer free-agent level salaries for each and every year of a multiyear contract.

A hypothetical example will help to illustrate this critical issue. Let's say a club had a better-than-average third baseman who had earned $100,000 in his third year of major league service in 1979. The club wanted to ensure that it would keep the player on the team for as long as reasonably possible. So it decided to offer the player a six-year deal covering the years 1980 through 1985. Comparable third basemen with less than six years of service were making between $150,000 and $250,000. Comparable free agent third basemen, however, were earning between $600,000 and $700,000 per year. With both the player and the club anticipating continued, rampant salary inflation, they might agree that the player would be worth more than $1 million by the beginning of the sixth year of the proposed contract. A fair contract, under these circumstances, might have been constructed as follows:

Calendar Yr.	Yrs. of Service	Contract Yr.	Salary
1979	3	—	$ 100,000
1980	4	1	200,000
1981	5	2	300,000
1982	6	3	700,000
1983	7	4	850,000
1984	8	5	1,000,000
1985	9	6	1,150,000
Tot. Cum. Salary			4,300,000

In the first two contract years, before the player would have reached free agent status, he would have been paid at a rate slightly higher than, but generally consistent with, the pay of other third basemen who had not accrued six years of service. Then his salary would have leaped up to the free-agent level in contract years three through six.

What the clubs in fact did in many such instances was draw up contracts that looked more like the following:

Calendar Yr.	Yrs. of Service	Contract Yr.	Salary
1979	3	—	$ 100,000
1980	4	1	500,000
1981	5	2	650,000
1982	6	3	800,000
1983	7	4	925,000
1984	8	5	1,050,000
1985	9	6	1,175,000
Tot. Cum. Salary			5,200,000

The first two years of this deal, while not quite at the free-agent level, are roughly double what a comparable player would have been worth in normal negotiations or arbitration. And the total value of the second contract is $900,000 greater than the first, more than a 20 percent boost.

Of course, by adopting this approach major league executives cost their clubs both immediate and long-term cash. But, far more important than that, they set into motion a wave of big salary increases via the arbitration process. Why? Because the third baseman from the above example would be used as a basis of comparison by players of similar quality who had also not yet obtained free agency rights. In negotiations, a comparable young player would point to that contract and any others like it, claiming that if the other third baseman were worth $500,000 after just four years in the big leagues, then so, too, was he. And if the club didn't accept the claim, then the player would take the case to an arbitrator. More and more players did indeed take such cases to arbitration.

By the end of the 1983 season, this almost breathtaking act of fiscal self-destruction on the part of club management had become standard policy. Nearly every major league club had a few players with less than six years of service who were reaping very hefty incomes. As a result, the salaries of the arbitration eligibles, as a group, had increased by several hundred percent. Although they were still a clear notch or two behind the veterans in income, they had pulled away from the players with less than two years of service, who had no arbitration rights. Had the clubs not overplayed their new defensive strategy, which they clearly did not have to do, the arbitration eligibles might still have salaries within hailing distance of the major league minimum. It was by this time, of course, too late for the clubs to correct their grave strategic error. And the wall separating the younger players from the veterans had been reduced to an embattled trench.

To make matters worse for management, the Sutter precedent continued to exert its own upward pressure on the salaries of arbitration eligibles. That is, the players were still trying to establish the principle that a star is a star, regardless of his prior experience, and that he should be paid the full wages of a veteran star. The nub of their reasoning was that a young star has at least as much present value as an older star, and certainly greater future value to his club. The clubs continued to insist that service time is the bedrock of the salary structure, just as seniority is in other industries.

The first three years of the free agency era can be regarded as an experimental phase. No one on either side of the table knew precisely what was unfolding or how it would play itself out. As of 1980 it was evident to the clubs that free agency was producing an unchecked inflationary spiral and that arbitration would demand very serious attention.

Help for the clubs in the arbitration arena was already on the way. Talbot M. "Tal" Smith had been the president and general manager of the Houston Astros from 1975 through 1980. He was renowned in management circles as a tough but fair-minded chief executive with extraordinary skills in fiscal management. Smith had also brought the Astros from the depths of mediocrity to a division championship in his relatively brief tenure at Houston. But he and the new Astros owner, John McMullen, did not see eye to eye on a number of internal club matters, particularly the assignment of contracts. So despite his club's 1980 success on the field, Smith was fired almost immediately after the Astros lost the League Championship Series to the Eastern Division champion Phillies, three games to two.

Smith had gotten his feet wet in arbitration prior to his last season at the helm. Although he had lost both cases, his interest in the arbitration process had been piqued by the experience. He genuinely enjoyed the challenge of the specialized competition that arbitration is. So he decided to offer his personal services to a few of his front-office colleagues. The Oakland A's took him up on the offer. The club was headed toward contract battles with two of its best players, outfielder Tony Armas and pitcher Mike Norris. With Tal Smith representing them, the A's prevailed over both players in arbitration.

The victories prompted Smith to set up a business, Tal Smith Enterprises, to extend his salary services to other clubs. At the end of the 1981 season, six major league clubs retained Smith for support in salary negotiations and arbitration. Smith quickly assembled a small group of legal and statistical experts to round out his salary team. He had commented, privately, in his last months as the president of the Astros that backup catchers were now earning more than general managers. He felt strongly that the financial survival of major league baseball was in jeopardy and regarded his new role as a mission, a financial crusade, to save the game. His lament over fiscal conditions was sincere, and it was music to the ears of a lot of club executives.

Prior to the formation of Tal Smith Enterprises, the Player Relations Committee had been solely responsible for providing advice, counsel, and data support to the clubs. The PRC's executive director, Raymond Grebey, was a gruff and rather arrogant veteran of labor-management wars. He had headed the PRC since 1978, but had not scored many victories for the clubs. Instead of allying himself with Smith, Grebey seemed to view Smith as a competitor for Grebey's rightful role as management's protector. He even attempted in various ways to thwart Tal Smith's efforts. This bureaucratic pettiness exemplified management's internal divisions over policies and methods for combating the gains being racked up by the Players Association and its constituents.

Grebey notwithstanding, crusader Smith and his band of Young Turks put on a dazzling display in the 1982 arbitration campaign. Of the eight cases that went to hearings, the Smith team won seven. It was a previously unheard-of margin of victory, and it helped to quell Grebey's noisome opposition. More importantly, it sent a strong message to the players and their agents. They would have a better organized and much more formidable arbitration adversary than they had ever before encountered. A line had been drawn in the arbitration sand, giving the clubs a small but significant beachhead.

As the 1982 salary returns came in, it was plainly evident that the clubs were routinely granting enormous percentage increases to arbitration eligibles and free agents. There was a rising tide of salaries that was lifting nearly all boats. Furthermore, the clubs, inexplicably,

were tendering virtually no salary cuts, even though they were empowered to do so. Equally difficult to explain was the fact that franchise sales were proceeding apace, with prices going up, way up. The last of the family owners was gone, and corporate interests were evidently still anxious to gain membership in the baseball owners' club.

Tal Smith Enterprises' accomplishments the year before led six more clubs to sign up after the 1982 season. Smith had to expand his workforce and computerize his operation to keep up with the demand for his services. The client load increased to thirteen clubs the following year and remained at that level through 1986. Smith was, thus, representing half of the clubs in baseball.

Smith's presence no doubt tempered the submissions of a sizable percentage of players in arbitration, and it helped to slow the pace of inflation in normal negotiations carried out by his client clubs. But the Smith team compiled only a .500 record after its first splashy campaign. Inherent in the arbitration process is a tendency for the arbitrators to split their decisions, for if they come down too heavily on one side they are likely to be permanently removed from the pool of arbitrators by the opposing side. This worked against Smith, perhaps even unduly after his highly publicized rookie campaign. Moreover, even Smith's clients saw their payrolls rise at a bankrupting rate. The past practices of ill-prepared clubs had gone on too long and they were precedential. Those practices had helped to establish the micro-rules of the arbitration game, and there was little that Tal Smith or anyone else could do about it. Besides, of the more than 700 contracts that are signed each year, only 25 or so end up in hearings. And of that total, only about 60 percent, or roughly 15 cases, are handled by Smith. In other words, Smith brought too little, too late. The structural damage had already been done even before he had officially hung up his shingle. To make matters worse, by the end of the 1985 arbitration season many of the club executives and the player agents were complaining that arbitration had become a random process. Decisions were almost totally unpredictable. The term being bandied about was "crapshoot"—arbitration, many were saying, had turned into a crapshoot.

Throughout the first decade of the free agency era, labor-management relations worsened. The clubs' hiring of Smith had put an additional buffer between the players and the clubs, just as the cadre of player agents had done several years earlier. By adding such layers of representation, the ballplayers and their owners became a step more detached and alienated from each other. The more intimate love-hate relationship that had existed between the old family owners and their players, which was more akin to the relationship between troops and their generals, or between sons and their fathers, steadily gave way to an entrenched business relationship after World War Two. Meanwhile, salaries continued to rise. The labor-management war drums were beating, perhaps more loudly than ever before. But now the owners were the Indians.

More bad news greeted the besieged front offices after the 1985 season. Two years earlier, baseball had signed a six-year television contract with ABC and NBC that was worth approximately $8 million per year to each club. The $1.3 billion deal was triple the value of the prior network-TV contract. But now there was open talk that

TV revenues had passed their peak. The networks were initiating an industry-wide reduction in personnel and a streamlining of their corporate structures. Accordingly, they were letting it be known that baseball could fully expect a decline in income when the next contract came up for negotiation in 1989. The clubs also began to see their cable television income level off. And prices for tickets, parking, and concessions had all risen steadily as the players' salaries increased. Those prices were now barely, if at all, increasable. And radio and in-stadium advertising and promotions were rapidly reaching a saturation point.

To demonstrate the gravity of the situation, the owners made the unprecedented and startling decision to open the clubs' financial books in the fall of 1985. The central purposes of this action were to prove management's claims of insolvency and to obtain changes in the Basic Agreement that would reverse, or at least stem, the flow of red ink. By their accounting, the industry was losing roughly $58 million per year, or a bit more than $2 million per club. The Players Association had its own financial analysts review the data. They concluded that the clubs had actually netted $9 million in profits in 1985. According to one highly placed club executive, the financial data were so poorly organized, so incomplete, and so out of date that no one could draw reliable conclusions with respect to club costs or revenues.

Wherever the truth lay, it was clear that no more than two or three clubs were regularly showing profits. The Los Angeles Dodgers were, and still are, in their own special category at the top of the heap. The rest were fighting a losing battle. Nonetheless, between 1982 and 1985 the Detroit, Minnesota, and Cincinnati franchises were purchased—at astronomical prices. And there was talk, encouraged by the game's new commissioner, Peter V. Ueberroth, that the expansion of the major leagues to twenty-eight or thirty teams would take place in the relatively near future.

Given the extremely discouraging financial conditions of the baseball industry in the 1980s, one wonders why anyone, including the high rollers who had replaced their generally less wealthy predecessors, would want to get into the business. By 1985, every big league club was backed by at least one big corporate entity. In name, almost every club was owned by an individual or a group of individuals, but in reality the clubs belonged to large parent companies. The list included a variety of large media corporations, an international brewery, a blue-chip jeans manufacturer, a nationwide pizza franchise, a big-time law firm, a regional car dealership, and two major shipbuilding companies. What distinguished the new breed of owners from the earlier model was that the new baseball moguls were uninvolved in day-to-day club operations. Several owners meddled in important personnel and salary decisions, but club management was now essentially in the hands of front-office executives. This absentee style of ownership was a clear indication of the relative unimportance to the owners of the financial condition of their baseball franchises. It also suggested what the main motivation to own a ballclub had finally become—promotion. For whether or not a club made money, the individuals and the corporate interests that undergirded them would constantly be in the national limelight. Thus the clubs had turned into the promotional, public-relations playthings of their corporate overlords. How else can one explain the appreciation in club values in the midst of the game's financial plunge? Is the alternative view, that so many ultrawealthy parties are just slipshod businesspeople, really credible? After all, if the new owners are so terribly lacking in business acumen, how have they gotten to where they are?

Whatever their individual reasons for buying into the baseball business, the new hands-off owners relied on front-office personnel to oversee their organizations. Within the front offices there had always been a barrier between business and baseball. The baseball people—general managers, player personnel directors, farm system directors, assistants in those areas, scouts, and all the rest—had jealously protected their professional turf and the inside information upon which their jobs rested. They were also a relatively uneducated group, the bulk of whose professional experience was limited to the playing field. The finance people, stadium operations people, ticket office personnel, and so forth minded their own business. This kind of compartmentalization of responsibility and authority was another of the quasi-military aspects of the sport. The new owners in most cases empowered their one or two top baseball executives to hire and supervise the business personnel, thereby keeping the old order intact. As a result, salary matters generally fell to people ill-equipped to deal with salary techniques and strategies.

Salary determination is inherently a blend of performance evaluation and comparative salary analysis, and a rather exacting intellectual exercise. But with the owners basically uninvolved and with the traditional organizational barrier still standing, there were very few club personnel qualified to do a creditable job in the salary arena. The rapid and broad success of Tal Smith stood as proof that the clubs could not adequately manage their own salary matters. And if there was a single area on which the current and future financial health of each franchise depended, it was undeniably the area of salaries. It is for these reasons that free agency and arbitration led to rampant inflation. To put it another way, the Messersmith-McNally decision had freed only the veterans; it was the unsupervised and fiscally deficient baseball executives who had made the rest of the major league players wealthy. In effect, they had given away the store while the owners were fishing.

The first loud signal of ownership's recognition of its managerial shortcomings came when the owners' council selected the business entrepreneur Peter Ueberroth to replace the attorney Bowie Kuhn as baseball's commissioner. Ueberroth had demonstrated his take-charge, no-nonsense, profit-oriented approach to sports when he organized the 1984 Olympic Games held in Los Angeles. The owners' appointment of Ueberroth was nothing less than a reversion to the strong-commissioner strategy that had brought Judge Landis into baseball and saved the game in the aftermath of the Black Sox scandal. It showed that they were deeply concerned about the existing state of affairs. It was also a virtual admission that when the going gets tough, the ever-divided house of owners must seek outside help.

When Ueberroth took office as the commissioner at the

beginning of 1985, baseball was awash in red ink and the tide was still rising. The clubs could not unilaterally rewrite the Basic Agreement. Nor could they control the behavior of arbitrators. They had opened their books, but the players remained unconvinced that they were in trouble. How, the players asked, could the clubs possibly be insolvent and at the same time have a string of anxious buyers waiting in line to pay exorbitant and still escalating prices for those clubs? Management was becoming desperate.

The new commissioner was not the type of administrator who would simply sit back and allow a bad situation to deteriorate further. In late September of 1985, Ueberroth addressed the club owners and their representatives at a regularly scheduled quarterly meeting. After the season ended, he attended two more of management's private meetings. His broad message to the clubs at those gatherings was that they would have to exercise fiscal responsibility in order to keep their industry viable. His more specific advice to them came in the form of a negative statement that he made at the general managers' meeting at Tarpon Springs, Florida, in early November:

"It is not smart to sign long-term contracts."

Shortly after that meeting, sixty-two players filed for free agency. Though the list was long, it was perhaps the least impressive group, talentwise, since free agency was instituted. It was loaded with marginal and soon-to-retire players. One of the few exceptions, however, was All-Star outfielder Kirk Gibson. The twenty-eight-year-old Gibson had been with the Detroit Tigers for his entire professional career, and he was coming off his best season as a major leaguer. Many clubs would normally have had serious interest in obtaining a player of Gibson's caliber. But the deadline for bidding on free agents came and went, and not a single club made an offer to Gibson. In fact, practically all of the free agents had been completely ignored by the clubs. Of the group of sixty-two, only five changed clubs. And all five were players in whom their previous employers had officially indicated no interest by waiving their right to negotiate with them.

To the Players Association, it was obvious that the clubs had entered into a tacit agreement not to pursue any free agents that their most recent employers wished to retain. In their view, that amounted to a conspiracy to violate the terms of the Basic Agreement. The legal term for such behavior is collusion. So the association lodged a grievance against all twenty-six clubs, claiming that they had violated Article XVIII of the agreement, which states that "the Clubs shall not act in concert with the other Clubs" in signing free agents.

Veteran arbitrator Thomas Tuttle Roberts began hearing the case in the summer of 1986. In September the owners attempted to dismiss Roberts from the case. He had just ruled, in a separate case, that the clubs could not insert drug-testing provisions in players' contracts without the consent of the Players Association, and that had angered the owners, or so they claimed. The association felt that this was merely an excuse and that management was engaging, as it had done for more than a century, in delaying tactics. For the longer it would take to resolve the collusion case, the more opportunity the clubs would have to defy free agency and maybe even wreck it.

To the delight of management, the case dragged on through the winter of 1986–1987. This time, however, the free agent pool was one of the best on record. It included perennial All-Stars Tim Raines, Andre Dawson, Jack Morris, and Lance Parrish. But, true to form, the clubs continued the practice of the previous year. They made no bids for free agents whom their previous clubs wanted to keep. And, not surprisingly, the Players Association filed another grievance.

Then the final 1985 salary tallies came in. What those results showed was that management's initial attack on free agency had had little if any effect on salaries. The major league payroll had continued to grow at a bankrupting pace. Management was sweating bullets, and they were looking more and more ready to fight back in other ways.

Some of the provisions of the Basic Agreement had been changed through prior negotiations between the players and the clubs. The changes went into effect after the 1986 season. The most important of them dealt with arbitration rights. Players now would have to complete three full years of major league service instead of just two to become eligible for arbitration. Using the new provision to full advantage, the clubs grossly underpaid some of the game's brightest young stars, including 1986 Cy Young Award winner Roger Clemens of the Boston Red Sox. It was, as it always had been, within the clubs' rights to unilaterally assign contracts to such players. But by recent standards, the salaries tendered to Clemens and a half dozen other outstanding young players were, in each instance, hundreds of thousands of dollars below the established scale. Several of the players threatened to hold out for the 1987 season. Clemens did hold out until shortly after the season began. In addition, the clubs took a firmer stand in arbitration than ever before. They submitted several offers that represented no raise over the previous year's salaries, and they even went so far as to try to cut a few salaries by way of arbitration. Given the almost total absence of holds and cuts in prior arbitration proceedings, these were highly risky actions.

The 1986–1987 arbitration results revealed the chaotic state into which the process had lapsed. At the bottom end of the salary scale, the clubs had cleaned up. Twenty-six players had taken their cases to arbitration and seven of them had returned without salary increases. Four of those had received cuts in pay. But at the high end, Yankee first baseman Don Mattingly received an award of $1,975,000, which was the largest arbitration award ever. Overall, the clubs won sixteen of the twenty-six cases. And the players realized the lowest percentage gain in income in the history of arbitration.

The most interesting case was that of Detroit pitcher Jack Morris. Morris had gone to arbitration four years earlier and had lost. After the 1986 season, he declared himself a free agent. But because the Tigers wanted to keep him, none of the other clubs would bid for his services. His agent, Richard Moss, decided to throw the Tigers a curveball. He advised his client to pursue a new option available to free agents, namely to withdraw his declaration of free agency and subject himself, once again, to arbitration. Detroit management was over a barrel. Morris was one of the best pitchers in the game, and he had plenty of statistical evidence to back up that assessment. So the club knew that if it were to accept the offer, it would stand a pretty good chance of getting clobbered in arbitration. On the other hand, if the club were to turn down the offer to arbitrate, it would not be permitted to negotiate with Morris until May 1, a full month into the 1987 season. The club consented to arbitrate. Jack Morris won this one, and it cost the club a whopping $1,850,000 to retain his services for the 1987 season.

When the final figures for 1987 came in at the end of November, it appeared that the array of extreme measures taken by management had at last reversed the salary inflation trend. In fact, the average major league salary had declined by a few thousand dollars. And Tal Smith Enterprises was still proudly leading the cost-reduction crusade on behalf of the ballclubs.

But it was not yet time for the owners to celebrate, because two months earlier arbitrator Tom Roberts ruled that the major league clubs had indeed operated "in concert" when they shunned the free agents after the 1985 season. In September 1989 that translated into awards of $10,528,086.71 to the 139 players he held had been victims of that first round of collusion. Seven players—including Kirk Gibson and Carlton Fisk—were given "new look" free agency.

In August 1988 arbitrator George Nicolau, after reviewing 8,346 pages of testimony, found owners guilty once more of collusion, this time against seventy-nine free agents following the 1986 season. In October—he had delayed his action to avoid disrupting the pennant races—he granted "new look" free agency to twelve more players, including Bob Boone, Jim Clancy, and Willie Randolph, all of whom signed with new teams.

A "Collusion III" case was filed by the union in January 1989 regarding those who had become free agents after the 1987 campaign. In July 1990 Nicolau again found for labor. Seventy-six players, including such stars as Jack Clark, Gary Gaetti, Jack Morris, Dave Righetti, Mike Witt, and Paul Molitor, were involved in the case, which revolved around management's creation of an "information bank" in the winter of 1986–87. This data bank reported all salary offers made to free agents. Nicolau wrote he found it a "quiet" form of cooperation between supposedly rival clubs endeavoring to keep tabs on what each competitor was offering on the supposedly free market. By the time damages would finally be determined, the union thought, they could reach the $100 million mark.

New Sources of Revenue

Reports of the demise of television's profitability proved grossly exaggerated. Toward the end of Ueberroth's tenure, a series of blockbuster broadcasting deals were negotiated. The biggest was a four-year deal with CBS in December 1988 for $1.06 billion. The network received rights to the All-Star Game, League Championship Series, World Series, and twelve regular-season weekend games. Criticism surrounded the cutback in regular-season broadcasts, but Ueberroth answered with an unprecedented deal with the cable industry. ESPN outbid such rivals as TNT and USA in January 1989 for a four-year, $400-million pact, featuring 175 regular-season games, including groundbreaking Sunday-night cablecasts. No one knew how successful the package would be, but even ESPN officials admitted they would lose money for at least the first two years. At the same time a $50-million, four-year agreement with CBS Radio for the Game of the Week, All-Star Game, and postseason contests was made final.

Not only was Organized Baseball as a whole cashing in; so were the individual clubs. George Steinbrenner obtained a $500-million, twelve-year agreement with Madison Square Garden cable. His colleagues worried that he would again attempt to corner the free-agent market. Big Apple fans, at least what Yankee fans remained, worried over the cost of their cable bills (as did fans nationwide following the ESPN negotiations), but the deal was done.

At the conclusion of Ueberroth's breathtaking round of broadcasting conquests, the commissioner noted baseball's newfound prosperity and respectfully requested owners to hold the line on ticket prices. He was ignored.

Another segment of the business of baseball—and an increasingly lucrative and ugly one—was memorabilia, autographs, and baseball cards. In 1989 it was estimated that these "extras" accounted for $1 billion in business. Its culmination came during a particularly dark day in baseball history. Hours after a disgraced Pete Rose was expelled from the game by Commissioner Giamatti, he appeared on a cable network and peddled $1.2 million in bats, plaques, and balls, taking home $100,000 in pocket money.

While that may have shocked many, it was not the only seaminess marring the trade. Ballplayers peddling autographs at card shows soured stomachs from Fenway to Anaheim. Forgeries and fakes surfaced with regularity. Jose Canseco was sued for his failure to appear at one card show. Two dealers were charged with ripping off an infirm "Cool Papa" Bell of his mementos. A seventy-five-year-old man was killed over memorabilia in the Midwest. By 1990 reports from the New York City area held that the boom was losing steam, that crowds were thinning out at shows, and that overpriced gimcracks were starting to gather dust. Perhaps.

Tying in to this facet of the game was the licensing of logos and related products. Initiated nearly three decades ago by the National Football League, licensed sports marketing now produces over a billion dollars in annual sales in baseball.

The Franchise Game

In 1988 Peter Ueberroth admitted that four years earlier twenty-one out of twenty-six big league clubs suffered financial losses. By 1987 the situation had seen a dramatic turnaround, and twenty-two out of twenty-six clubs either broke even or were profitable. There had always been an interest in ballclubs as rich men's toys, but when it appeared that once again money could be made at the national pastime, bidding went through the roof (dome?) for franchises.

Even the most moribund teams were selling for big bucks. Somewhat understandably the New York Mets changed hands for $100 million, and Baltimore sold for

$70 million, but when the woeful Seattle Mariners were peddled for $77 million (George Argyros had paid $13.1 million for these latter-day St. Louis Browns in 1981), it was clear that the economic balance had been tilted.

Back in the early 1980s Commissioner Ueberroth had announced that the majors would feature two new AL and four new NL clubs by 2000, but calling progress snail-like would have exaggerated its speed. By the late 1980s the game faced increased pressure from a number of sources for expansion. The Players Association wished to open up more jobs for its members. The U.S. Senate formed a fourteen-member panel on the subject. A new league, organized by agent Dick Moss and at one time backed by Donald Trump's ephemeral billions, was another threat in the summer of 1989. Baseball now announced a willingness to add two more NL franchises.

Nothing really happened until the summer of 1990. Slowing up matters, some said, were the recent TV contracts. Established owners were loath to share their new-found riches with any newcomers, and hence expansion would not occur until the current broadcasting contracts expired. Each of the twenty-six teams received $16 million yearly from the national package, but with more dollars going to such stars as Viola, Clark, and Canseco, the owners still felt they needed every last penny.

As a result, a 1993 target for expanding came into view. The National League would announce its two newest members in September 1991. The expansion franchises would draft entry-level minor-league players in late 1991 and actually operate farm systems in 1992. During that season, they will be able to draft college and high school players. Major league expansion drafts will occur after the 1992 World Series. An interesting—and definitely different—aspect of this draft is that the newest senior-circuit clubs may draft personnel (thirty-six for each club) from *both* major leagues, the logic being that if the two newcomers cut into the TV and radio revenues of all clubs, they should draft from all clubs. A corollary of this, of course, is that both the AL and the NL would divvy up the $95 million franchise fee each rookie owner would fork over.

While Organized Baseball is not exactly pooh-poohing those hefty initiation fees, they are not the only factors involved in the initiation process. Such considerations as "substantial financial resources" (obviously) and "long-term commitment" to their local communities were cited. Multipurpose stadiums were deemed passé. Local politicos should be cognizant of "the necessity of the club receiving parking, concession, signage, pay TV, and luxury box revenue."

Frontrunners for the new franchises included Denver (where voters in 1990 approved a new 40,000-seat stadium), St. Petersburg (which nearly hijacked the White Sox in 1988), Miami (assisted by recently retired Mike Schmidt), Buffalo (where the Rich family runs a big-league operation at the AAA level), and Washington (a two-time loser, but a loser with political connections).

The huge franchise fees plus a projected $65 million in start-up costs began to cause several prospective backers to think twice. Nonetheless, barring a massive downturn in either the national or sports economy, there should be no overall shortage of takers.

Major league expansion would trigger minor league expansion, as the new clubs would require farm teams. With such franchises as Oklahoma City going for $4.5 million, the price tag at the AAA level would not be cheap. Most observers estimate it would be $5 million per club (consider that the Mets had cost $1.8 million in 1962 and the Kansas City Royals had cost just $5.55 million in 1969). Even applying for a minor league club required a $5,000 nonrefundable deposit (an unprecedented situation for the bushes), but in September 1990 eighteen groups sent in their checks.

As minor league franchises were being bought and sold for record prices, the major league clubs took notice. Claiming they no longer saw the wisdom of subsidizing such "profitable" ventures (in all too many cases the only profit comes from selling to the next party willing to take operating losses), the big leaguers started to place heavy-handed pressure on their farm clubs in 1990. On a single day in August 1990, sixty-three working agreements were dropped. That was followed by a threat to bring fifty-nine bush-league teams to Florida and Arizona in 1991 for summer versions of complex baseball. Hardball was the name of the game on all negotiating fronts.

The Lockout of 1990

Baseball's Basic Agreement expired on December 31, 1989, and despite the prosperity that both sides now enjoyed, open warfare was imminent. The Players Association was hardly blind to the marvelously round figures Ueberroth had pried out of the networks. Beyond that they were particularly irritated by the year of arbitration they had given away in the last settlement. Club owners, on the other hand, were tired of forking over millions through the arbitration process. The problem for management was not simply the cost of losing specific arbitration cases. Winning could also be costly. In the winter of 1989–90 the ten *losers* in the process received average raises of $477,050. Average salaries doubled for only the second time in the fifteen-year history of the process. First-year arbitration players saw paychecks skyrocket by 166 percent. While the vast majority of disputes were settled before they got to arbitration, they still involved huge increases, such as Teddy Higuera's $2,125,000 stipend and Tom Browning's pact for the same figure. Fred McGriff saw his income rise from $325,000 to $1,450,000 in a prearbitration settlement.

A showdown had to occur.

Negotiations dragged on during the winter of 1989–90, and it was widely believed that the players would collect their checks for a few months and then strike at mid-season, when the owners were gearing up for large crowds and were most vulnerable. To thwart this plan, management struck first, engaging in yet another lockout of spring training camps.

The owners' strategy was to hold firm on the third-year threshold for arbitration. The PRC tendered a number of alternatives to the Players Association, including one granting 48 percent of club profits to players and another offering a cumbersome $4 million bonus-pool scheme to be shared by two-year players.

After thirty-two bitter days, Donald Fehr, the union's combative new representative, and Charles O'Connor, the new PRC negotiator, hammered out a compromise. Seventeen percent of the second-year players would now become eligible for arbitration. The minimum salary would rise from $68,000 to $100,000, the largest percentage increase ever. Management would contribute $55 million to the players' pension fund, up from $39 million. To the casual observer this seemed a victory for labor, but the players had wanted $80 million and the settlement was a giant step back from the traditional one-third of national TV revenues that players had contended was their right. Additionally, it was written into the agreement that baseball would announce its long-stalled expansion plans within ninety days.

It was not a settlement that established any great principles, and most fans were no doubt just as puzzled as ever as to what all the shouting had been about, but it appeared that the process had cooled some tempers. Even the Players Association's Don Fehr, never one to look away from controversy, discerned a "measurably lower degree of hostility" at lockout's conclusion.

What is certain is that the ballplayers and the major league clubs remain deeply entrenched in financial warfare. The chairman of the board, president and chief executive officer of the Philadelphia Phillies, William Y. Giles, has been a baseball executive for more than thirty years. He was one of the principal negotiators in the lucrative six-year pact signed by the television networks. And he is widely regarded as one of the "nicest guys" in the business. When asked recently by a Philadelphia reporter how labor-management relations were faring, Giles said that the animosity between the parties is "at an all-time high."

The Spoils of War

For the better part of a century, major league baseball players fought for a reasonable portion of the proceeds of their entertainment industry. However, with no viable competition from outside the baseball monopoly, the players were forced to accept whatever salaries and conditions their owners saw fit to give them. They eventually made progress, but only after they pulled together as a bargaining unit and slowly and painfully loosened the grip of the reserve clause. In the end, what they obtained was not a specified level of income but rather a system of salary determination. The system contained no financial guarantees beyond the major league minimum salary. How much money the players would ultimately receive through free agency and salary arbitration would rest entirely on the behavior of the clubs.

What the system did was create a form of free-market competition within the monopoly. In a sense, it turned a single business into twenty-six separate businesses and unleashed a self-destructive frenzy of interclub competition. To the players' amazement and joy, they saw their salaries reach heights that they could not have imagined were possible.

To most of the fans and the press, the dizzying escalation in their incomes made the players appear baldly greedy. And when filthy-rich players began to complain that they were being underpaid compared to other individuals or groups of players, the public's growing distaste for them was understandable. But greed really was not the issue. What was at stake for the carping millionaire pitcher or outfielder was not the money but rather his standing as a ballplayer. Money had become the measure of his talent, and every player wanted and still wants his money to match his skills. So when he sees that a player whom he considers himself superior to is earning more than he is, he feels underrated, cheated. That is his value system.

Unfortunately, as long as the salary system remains a chaotic hodgepodge without fixed standards of evaluation, in which the negotiating skills of agents and club executives are often more of a factor in determining the players' worth than their actual on-the-field contributions to their teams are, a good number of players will always feel cheated. And the clubs will continue to be and to feel besieged.

The system is under attack now. Management has chosen to use unethical or illegal methods to achieve its ends, as it has since 1879 when the first version of the reserve clause was introduced. The latest ploy in the owners' bottomless bag of tricks is collusion. Consequently, trust and respect between management and labor are at a low. And whatever hope the clubs might have had of smoothing out their differences with the players and their union has been all but dashed.

The players will continue to earn astounding sums of money and the club owners will continue to bask in the national limelight, thereby getting plenty of public-relations bang for their otherwise poorly managed bucks. And the fans will continue to be the ones who ultimately pay for the follies of both sides. Thus one of the key questions facing the major leagues is how long the fans will go on subsidizing the war of principle between the players and the clubs.

Whether or not the fee-per-game plan is implemented, the recent and steady shift from free over-the-air telecasts to paid-for cable-TV telecasts is continuing. This development is taking viewing opportunities away from those people who either do not have cable access or cannot afford to pay the monthly fee. The problem is already rather acute for New York Yankee fans, because there is no cable television in the Bronx at this time and the majority of Yankee games are broadcast exclusively on MSG, a cable-TV operation.

In the long run, the shift to cable may diminish the size of the baseball viewing audience, which would erode the major league fan population and thereby reduce the future income of the sport.

The shift also raises a fundamental question concerning baseball's exemption from antitrust laws. The matter has been addressed by Charles E. Schumer, a member of the House of Representatives from New York's Tenth Congressional district. In an article for the *New York Times* written in the summer of 1987, he posed the following challenge:

If baseball is simply a "business," then why should it have a special antitrust exemption? On the other hand, if baseball enjoys protection from the nation's laws because it is a national treasure, then Americans have a right to demand reasonable access to it.

Congressman Schumer has introduced legislation which would require that the Yankees and major league baseball choose between two alternatives. They must, in his words, "either act like a business and receive no governmental protection, or behave like a great national pastime by making sure that New Yorkers can see the game on cable or free TV."

There is an eerie quality to the maelstrom in which baseball now finds itself. For none of the central issues that have haunted the game since its inception has really been resolved. The business is still a monopoly. The reserve clause, though drastically altered, remains largely in force, and the owners are trying to resurrect the rest of it by undermining free agency. Many individual players are still dissatisfied because they do not feel that their contracts reflect their relative value as on-the-field performers. Members of Congress are beginning to consider legislation aimed, as before, at removing baseball's antitrust exemption. And baseball's un-merry-go-round, the seamier side of the industry, keeps spinning on its own goofy axis. In the words of Yogi Berra, "It seems like déjà vu all over again."

Nevertheless, the game is bringing in more spectators and more money than ever before. And the irrepressible club owners, though they are now more a clique of promotion-minded high rollers than a league of dyed-in-the-wool baseball men, seem undaunted by the growing financial threats to their industry.

The Future of the Baseball Business

The industry faces two major threats to its well-being, one external and one internal.

The external threat comes from the fans, whose willingness to subsidize the excesses of the clubs and the players is being severely tested. Will the rising costs of attending games and viewing them on television reduce the fan base? Will spectatorship become a privilege available only to those who can afford it?

The internal threat concerns the salary system. By way of collusion, the clubs have discovered that they can beat free agency by simply abstaining from bidding for players. And even though that ploy has been officially ruled illegal, the fact remains that the clubs have learned how to use it. Does this mean that free agency is from this point forward unenforceable? If not, how then can the clubs be made to bid for players? And even if they could somehow be compelled to make bids, how could they be required to offer more money than they wish to offer? Does this mean that free agency is dead? Not if the players can figure out a way to sustain it. Does it mean that arbitration will replace free agency? Not if the owners can help it.

And the drums keep beating, and the music keeps playing, and both sides keep screaming baseball's most familiar war cry:

"Wait till next year!"

Baseball and the Law

Gary D. Hailey

Like many other members of our litigation-happy society, baseball players and team owners have spent their fair share of time in the courtroom. Judges have been asked to decide lawsuits involving everything from a team's liability for fan injuries from foul balls and thrown bats to the legality of the decision to resume the infamous Yankees-Royals "Pine Tar Game" nearly a month after George Brett's home run had been ruled a game-ending out.

But the most significant baseball-related court cases were a series of mostly unsuccessful challenges to organized baseball's attempts to limit competition—especially from rivals like the Players League and the Federal League—for players' services. That litigation has reached the United States Supreme Court three times, and all three times that Court has ruled that baseball is not governed by the antitrust laws. The reasoning behind this holding may have been perfectly logical when the first of those cases was decided in 1922, but it seemed bizarre and irrational when it was reiterated half a century later in *Flood* v. *Kuhn*.

From the game's earliest days, baseball owners have struggled to keep their expenses down and maintain control over the players, who often decide that the grass (and the money) is greener in someone else's ballpark. In 1870 the National Association of Base Ball Players tried to stop "revolving," or contract jumping, by adopting a rule requiring players to give 60 days' notice before leaving one club for another. Tougher controls were agreed to after word leaked that A. G. Spalding and three other Boston Red Stockings stars had signed contracts in the middle of the 1875 season to play for Chicago in 1876. In 1879 the National League secretly agreed to allow each team owner to "reserve" his five best players at the end of the season; other owners were prohibited from bidding for the services of the reserved players. The owners also agreed not to sign any player who refused to play for the team that reserved him.

The reserve rule and blacklist helped protect the National League owners from their fellows, but proved less useful against the newly formed American Association, which declared war on the NL in 1882. One of the biggest names to jump to the rival league was catcher Charles Bennett, who had played for the NL's Pittsburgh club in 1882. In August of that year, he accepted $100 in exchange for his written promise to sign a contract with Pittsburgh for the 1883 season. But before Bennett signed that contract, the Detroit AA team offered him more money. Pittsburgh got wind of what was happening and immediately filed suit in federal court, seeking an injunction ordering Bennett to sign the Pittsburgh contract.

Bennett's lawyers offered a number of legal defenses, some rather narrow and technical. The court ruled in Bennett's favor[1] but did not issue a written opinion, so it is unclear just which of his attorneys' arguments were persuasive. The dismissal may have resulted from the court concluding that the reserve system and blacklist illegally limited Bennett's freedom to earn a living. But the court may have refused to enjoin Bennett's jump to Detroit simply because of the timing of the lawsuit. The Pittsburgh club would have suffered no real harm from Bennett's refusal to sign an 1883 contract until it had to play a game without him in the lineup. Its October 1882 lawsuit was, in a sense, premature because Bennett might have changed his mind and returned to Pittsburgh before the opening day of the 1883 season.

Shortstop Sam Wise did Bennett one better. He signed a contract with the AA's Cincinnati club but then jumped back to Boston when they upped their original offer. Cincinnati got an Ohio court to order Boston not to play Wise, but they were unable to enforce the order in other states. Wise simply stayed at home when the Boston team came to Cleveland to play.

The National League and American Association made peace in 1883 and signed the "National Agreement," which contained a strengthened reserve rule. The promoters of the Union Association hoped to capitalize on the players' resentment of the one-sided terms of their contracts with organized baseball, but the established leagues fought back hard by adopting the "Day Resolution," an agreement to blacklist any reserved player who jumped to a Union club. Star pitcher Tony Mullane, who jumped from the St. Louis Browns to the St. Louis Maroons of the new league, tried to return to the Browns after hearing about the Day Resolution. The Browns refused to welcome their prodigal back because they knew the Maroons would haul them into court if they did. The Toledo AA club wanted Mullane, but the National Agreement did not provide for player trades or sales. The Browns simply released Mullane outright, and Toledo signed him. The Union Association failed to persuade an Ohio federal judge to order Mullane back to the Maroons.[2] After the demise of the upstart league at the end of the 1884 season, Toledo agreed to send Mullane back to the Browns, but the Cincinnati AA club—in flagrant violation of the National Agreement—signed the 35-game winner to a lucrative bonus contract. The Association's powers-that-be ultimately awarded Mullane to Cincinnati, but ordered him to sit out the 1885 season and give back part of his bonus.

Once the Union Association was dead and buried, organized baseball tightened the screws a bit more by trying to establish a maximum annual player salary of $2,000. In response the players formed the National Brotherhood of Professional Base Ball Players under the leadership of John Montgomery Ward, the New York Giants shortstop who attended Columbia University law school in the off-season. Ward claimed that the reserve clause, the black-list, and other intimidating provisions of the standard player contract were legally unenforceable. When the owners refused to scrap the salary cap or to agree not to sell or trade players without their consent, the brotherhood went on to form the Players League, which fielded eight teams in 1890. Over 80 National League players and almost 30 from the American Association— including future Hall of Famers Dan Brouthers, John Clarkson, Hugh Duffy, "Buck" Ewing, "King" Kelly, Connie Mack, and "Old Hoss" Radbourne—signed up with the Players League.

Organized baseball used every weapon at its disposal to strike back at this new rival. The owners told fans that the players were aligned with radical unionists. Boston reportedly gave pitcher Clarkson $10,000—five times the average 1889 salary—to desert the brotherhood, while Spalding offered King Kelly a blank check to play for the White Stockings. When propaganda and bankrolls failed, the established league fielded a team of lawyers at courthouses around the country.

The reserve rule was originally adopted by the parties to the National Agreement as a sort of gentlemen's agreement not to compete for their fellow owners' players. When the National League tried to enforce the reserve clause against the Players League, it got nowhere. A federal court in New York City held that the Giants could not keep catcher Ewing from playing for their brotherhood rival because the reserve provisions in his 1889 contract were "merely a contract to make a contract" for 1890 "if the parties agree."[3] The reserve clause was valuable because it gave the Giants a "prior and exclusive" right to negotiate with Ewing that was enforceable against other clubs in organized baseball. But as a basis for an injunction preventing a player from taking the field for a Players League team, Ewing's contract was held "wholly nugatory" because it did not set forth in detail contract terms and conditions (including salary) for 1890. A party who seeks enforcement of a contract with vague or indefinite terms is really asking the court to fill in the blank spaces in that contract, which is something that courts are reluctant to do.

Other courts objected not only to the indefiniteness of player contracts but also to their one-sidedness, which they referred to as a "lack of mutuality." Owners could release players on ten days' notice, but the reserve clause purported to bind a player to one team for as long as the team wanted him. A New York state court judge expressed disgust at "the spectacle" of the Giants' attempt to enforce "a contract which binds [the player] for a series of years and [the team] for 10 days."[4] The National League spent $15,000 on lawyers' fees in New York alone fighting the Players League, but came away with nothing to show for it.

The Players League won the legal battles, but not the war—in fact, everyone lost money. Both sides agreed to Spalding's suggestion that some Players League teams be merged with existing NL and AA franchises and the rest be dissolved. After a bit of skirmishing over the rights to sign some of the returning Players League stars, the NL and AA merged their sixteen clubs into twelve after the 1891 season, and then signed a new National Agreement with the minor leagues. Players had little choice but to accept the terms offered by the "Baseball Trust," but a few rebelled. Amos Rusie won 22 games in 1895 and led the league in strikeouts, but Giants owner Andrew Freedman rewarded him by withholding $600 in fines from his paycheck. Rusie sat out 1896 and then sued the Giants when they invoked their reserve for 1897 as well. The case was settled before trial, with all the National League owners reportedly kicking in a portion of Rusie's $5,000 claim.

As usual the next baseball war set off a spate of contract jumping and legal skirmishes. Over half of the players who suited up for the American League's first season of play were ex-National Leaguers. The older league went to court to try to wrest back a number of their players, most notably Napoleon Lajoie. Lajoie signed a contract with the Phillies in 1900, but refused to be bound by the reserve clause and jumped to the Athletics before the 1901 season. The Pennsylvania Supreme Court held that the Phillies were entitled to an injunction barring the batting champ from playing for the A's.[5] But that decision turned in part on two unusual factors. First, the Phillies' contract reserved Lajoie for only three years and stated what salary would be paid in each of those three years, so it was not simply "a contract to make a contract." Second, Lajoie was a star of the very highest order. Courts are reluctant to order someone to perform a contract for personal services, although they are not at all reluctant to order the defendant to pay monetary damages equal to the harm caused by his nonperformance. Only when the harm cannot be measured in dollars or the contract involves something unique or irreplaceable are injunctions or other nonmonetary remedies granted by a court. The Phillies may have been able to find equally talented replacements for many of their players, but Lajoie—who led the AL in hits, doubles, home runs, runs, RBIs, batting average, and slugging average in 1901— was a unique talent.

The Phillies' legal victory proved hollow. The A's quickly dealt Lajoie to Cleveland. Whenever Cleveland was scheduled to play in Philadelphia, Lajoie stayed far away. His old team's attempts to obtain an injunction from an Ohio court were not successful.

Other National League efforts to hold on to players also failed. Citing a Supreme Court case holding that a contract that could be abandoned on one year's notice was not enforceable, a federal judge dismissed Brooklyn's suit against veteran catcher Deacon McGuire because the team could terminate his contract on only ten days' notice.[6] The judge also questioned whether McGuire's talents were so "unique and peculiar" that Brooklyn could not replace him. McGuire was a fine player, but he was no Nap Lajoie. A state judge in St. Louis went further in a case involving pitcher Jack Harper. Not only was the standard NL player contract lacking in mutuality, according to the court, but it also unreasonably restrained competition in violation of the Sherman Antitrust Act.[7]

After two years of rivalry, the National League agreed to recognize the American League as an equal. The two major leagues used blacklists and boycotts to bring "outlaw" minor leagues to their knees and keep control of players who had the audacity to hold out for higher salaries. When Ty Cobb refused to accept Detroit's 1913 salary offer, the Tigers suspended him. The impasse was broken only when two Georgia congressmen called for a federal investigation. The threat of government action got Ty Cobb a raise, but the players in general benefited much more from organized baseball's war with the Federal League, which no doubt had the National and American Leagues muttering "Two's company, three's a crowd" when the 1914 season opened.

The established leagues didn't even try to use the courts to stop reserve jumpers from playing for the Federal League, but they did seek injunctions against a number of players who jumped, even though they had signed contracts for the upcoming season. The irrepressible Hal Chase signed a 1914 contract with the White Sox, but then moved on to the new league. Teams could release players they didn't want on ten days' notice, so Chase gave Chicago ten days' warning and shuffled off to the Buffalo Federals. A New York state judge agreed with Chase's reasoning and turned down Chicago's request that he order Chase to return.[8] Not only did the contract lack mutuality, said the judge, but organized baseball placed so many limits on the freedom of players that they were left in a state of "*quasi* peonage" that was "contrary to the spirit of American institutions and . . . contrary to the spirit of the Constitution of the United States." The court's opinion did contain some good news for organized baseball: it ruled that baseball did not involve interstate commerce and, therefore, did not violate the Sherman Act.

The judges who heard cases involving contract jumpers occasionally showed real distaste for the whole nasty business. Phillies catcher Bill Killefer signed with the Chicago Federal League club for a substantial increase in salary, but re-signed with the Phillies only 12 days later when they topped Chicago's offer. When the Federals asked a Michigan federal judge to order Killefer not to play for Philadelphia, they were rudely received. Citing the opinions in the Ewing, Ward, and McGuire cases, Judge Sessions noted that the right of reservation in the Phillies' 1913 contract with Killefer did not bind him for the 1914 season because it was indefinite and lacked mutuality.[9] But he refused to enforce Chicago's contract because it came into court with "unclean hands." Killefer was under a moral, although not a legal obligation to play for Philadelphia in 1914, but Chicago persuaded him to repudiate that obligation. Both teams had "acted wrongfully and in bad faith," and the judge refused to lift a finger to help either one of them. He also let Killefer know what he thought of him, calling him "a person upon whose pledged word little or no reliance can be placed, and who, for gain to himself, neither scruples nor hesitates to disregard and violate his express engagements and agreements." Chicago appealed the decision but was unsuccessful. The Sixth Circuit Court of Appeals agreed with Judge Sessions that none of the parties to these underhanded dealings was deserving of any assistance from the courts.[10]

Knowing that they could not outlast their better-financed rivals, the Federal League owners filed an antitrust suit against organized baseball in Chicago on January 5, 1915. They asked federal Judge Kenesaw Mountain Landis, who had a reputation as a committed trustbuster, to declare the National Agreement's reserve and blacklisting provisions to be unreasonable and illegal restraints on competition. The trial was completed that month, but the Federal League's hopes for a quick verdict in their favor were in vain. The future baseball commissioner pondered the evidence all through the 1915 season, which resulted in another healthy dose of red ink for team owners. After waiting almost a year for Judge Landis to make up his mind, the rival leagues cut a deal. Organized baseball bought some of the Federal League's player contracts and stadiums—in reality, they were buying peace—and the Federals dropped the antitrust suit.

The final deal satisfied everyone except AL president Ban Johnson, who preferred to fight to the death rather than pay his enemies a nickel of tribute, and the Baltimore Federal League club, which wanted to buy an existing major league franchise and move it to Baltimore. Angered by Brooklyn owner Ebbets's scornful description of their city as "one of the worst minor league towns in this country," the Baltimore owners pledged $50,000 to finance a new antitrust suit against organized baseball and the Federal League owners who had sold the league out for a few pieces of silver. When the Department of Justice refused to investigate, Baltimore filed its complaint in federal district court in Washington, D.C., in 1917.

The testimony given at the trial, which didn't begin until March 1919, left little doubt that organized baseball's team owners had agreed to use the reserve clause and blacklisting to maintain tight control over the supply of players and paid the Federal League to go out of business in order to protect their monopoly over professional baseball. The judge's directions to the jury virtually directed a verdict for the plaintiffs. The Baltimore club won $254,000 in damages.

Organized baseball's lawyers immediately appealed the decision. They contended that baseball was not commerce because it involved "personal effort not related to [the] production" of material goods. If baseball did not involve interstate commerce, it was not subject to the Sherman Act or any other federal law. The court of appeals heard oral arguments on October 15, 1920, only three days after the final game of the World Series was played between the Cleveland Indians and the Brooklyn Dodgers. Only a few weeks later, it overturned the lower court's decision in favor of Baltimore.[11] The appellate court first noted that

The transportation in interstate commerce of the players and the paraphernalia used by them was but an incident to the main purpose of the appellants, namely the production of the game. It was for it they were in business— not for the purpose of transferring players, balls, and uniforms . . .

. . . So here, baseball is not commerce, though some of its incidents may be. Suppose a law firm in the city of Washington sends its members to points in different states to try lawsuits; they would travel, and probably carry briefs and records, in interstate commerce. Could it be correctly

said that the firm, in the trial of the lawsuits, was engaged in trade and commerce? Or, take the case of a lecture bureau, which employs persons to deliver lectures before Chautauqua gatherings at points in different states. It would be necessary for the lecturers to travel in interstate commerce, in order that they might fulfill their engagements; but would it not be an unreasonable stretch of the ordinary meaning of the words to say that the bureau was engaged in trade or commerce?

The court of appeals then cited with approval cases holding that those who produce theatrical exhibitions, practice medicine, or launder clothes are not engaged in commerce.

The Baltimore club tried to persuade the United States Supreme Court to reinstate the original verdict in its favor. But Justice Oliver Wendell Holmes, writing for a unanimous Court, upheld the decision of the court of appeals.[12]

[E]xhibitions of base ball . . . are purely state affairs. It is true that, in order to attain for the exhibitions the great popularity that they have achieved, competitions must be arranged between clubs from different cities and States. But the fact that in order to give the exhibitions the League must induce free persons to cross state lines and arrange and pay for their doing so is not enough to change the character of the business . . . [T]he transport is a mere incident, not the essential thing. That to which it is incident, the exhibition, although made for money would not be called trade or commerce in the commonly accepted use of those words. As it is put by the defendants, personal effort, not related to production, is not a subject of commerce. That which in its consummation is not commerce does not become commerce among the States because the transportation that we have mentioned takes place. To repeat the illustrations given by the Court below, a firm of lawyers sending out a member to argue a case, or the Chautauqua lecture bureau sending out lecturers, does not engage in such commerce because the lawyer or lecturer goes to another State.

Only a year later, the Court ruled that a company that presented vaudeville shows in cities around the country was, unlike major league baseball, engaged in interstate commerce.[13] Justice Holmes explained the different outcomes in the two cases by pointing to the difference in "the degree of interstate activity" in baseball games and vaudeville shows, but his reasoning is unconvincing.

The next challenge to organized baseball's hegemony came a quarter century later from Don Jorge Pasqual, the millionaire organizer of the Mexican League, who lured 18 major leaguers south of the border in 1946. In August of that year, the owners amended their Rule 15 to provide that any player who jumped to the new league would be ineligible to return to organized baseball for five years. The Cubs' general manager, who proposed the amendment, said that the prospect of being blacklisted for five years "will do a lot more to discourage Stan Musial from going to Mexico next winter than any suits we may file on the reserve clause."

The Rule 15 blacklist stemmed the southward flow of players. Commissioner A. B. "Happy" Chandler refused to reinstate the players who returned to the states in 1947. Catcher Mickey Owen was reduced to managing a semipro club in Winner, South Dakota, while several other Mexican League refugees signed with Cuban clubs.

When blacklisted outfielder Danny Gardella filed an antitrust complaint against organized baseball, a federal district judge in New York noted the "clear trend toward a broader conception of what constitutes interstate commerce" than had existed when *Federal Baseball Club of Baltimore* was decided over 25 years earlier, but felt bound to follow the Supreme Court's decision in that case.[14] But in February 1949 a federal court of appeals voted 2–1 to reverse the district court's dismissal of Gardella's complaint.[15] Judge Learned Hand distinguished *Federal Baseball* by emphasizing the importance to modern-day baseball of interstate radio and television broadcasts of major league games. Judge Frank's separate opinion strongly condemned the reserve system.

For the "reserve clause," as has been observed, results in something resembling peonage of the baseball player . . . Although many courts have refused to enforce the "reserve" clause, yet severe and practically efficacious extra-legal penalties are imposed for violation. The most extreme of these penalties is the blacklisting of the player so that no club in organized baseball will hire him . . . The violator may perhaps become a . . . bartender or a street-sweeper, but his chances of ever playing baseball are exceedingly slim.

Gardella's victory was not a final one—it simply allowed him the opportunity to prove his allegations in a trial. Former Cardinals Fred Martin, Max Lanier, and Lou Klein filed a separate suit, and all four players asked the district court to order their immediate reinstatement pending the outcome of the trials, but the court declined to do so.[16] Faced with the prospect of spending the 1949 season in a courtroom rather than on a baseball field, the players were receptive to baseball's offer to settle the case. Commissioner Chandler later characterized his reinstatement of the four "good kids" who had "said they were sorry" for jumping their reserves as inspired by his desire to "temper justice with mercy." But the court of appeals decision—and Judge Frank's sentiments in particular—no doubt had an effect too. Gardella, who had been working as a hospital orderly after returning from Mexico, was reportedly given $60,000 to drop his case.

Subsequent litigation and congressional inquiries kept baseball's attorneys busy in the 1950s. Organized baseball was the defendant in eight pending antitrust suits when it sought relief from Congress in 1951. At its behest three separate bills that would have granted all professional sports leagues a complete exemption from the antitrust laws were introduced in the House of Representatives that year. After lengthy hearings, Congressman Emanuel Celler's Subcommittee on the Study of Monopoly Power recommended that the bills not be passed, and none of them were. The Celler Subcommittee did not favor blanket antitrust immunity, but did conclude that professional baseball could not operate successfully without some form of the reserve clause.[17]

After the Gardella decision, organized baseball's lawyers and the Subcommittee assumed that *Federal Base-*

ball was no longer good law. But the Supreme Court surprised them in 1953 in *Toolson* v. *New York Yankees.*[18] When Yankee farmhand George Toolson was placed on the ineligible list for refusing to accept a demotion to a lower-classification team, he sued the Yankees. A California federal judge dismissed the case before trial on the basis of *Federal Baseball.* "If [that] case is, as Judge Frank intimates [in his *Gardella* opinion], an 'impotent zombi,'" the judge wrote, "I feel that it is not my duty to so find but that the Supreme Court should so declare."[19] The Ninth Circuit Court of Appeals agreed,[20] and the Supreme Court reaffirmed *Federal Baseball* in a one-paragraph opinion.

In Federal Baseball . . . *this Court held that . . . professional baseball . . . was not within the scope of the federal antitrust laws. Congress has had the ruling under consideration but has not seen fit to bring such business under these laws by legislation having prospective effect. . . . The present cases ask us to overrule the prior decision, and, with retrospective effect, hold the [antitrust laws] applicable. We think that if there are evils in this field which now warrant application to it of the antitrust laws it should be by legislation. Without re-examination of the underlying issues, the judgments below are affirmed on the authority of* Federal Baseball . . .

The Court's conclusion that "Congress has had the ruling under consideration but has not seen fit to bring [baseball] under [the antitrust] laws by legislation" is questionable. The Celler Subcommittee report concluded that given the *Gardella* decision and cases subsequent to *Federal Baseball,* which took a broader view of what constituted interstate commerce, "it may be seriously doubted whether baseball should now be regarded as exempt from the antitrust laws." If Congress assumed that baseball was subject to the antitrust laws, its failure to act on bills granting an antitrust exemption was evidence that it did not intend baseball to be exempt—which was just the opposite of what the Court said in *Toolson.*

The next few years saw the Supreme Court hold that professional boxing and football did not share baseball's antitrust immunity. In *Radovich* v. *National Football League,*[21] the Court expressly limited the reach of the *Federal Baseball* precedent to baseball. Three justices dissented from this decision "to put baseball in a class by itself."

Another flurry of congressional activity followed. In 1957 the House Antitrust Subcommittee held fifteen days of hearings on seven different bills, some of which would have exempted all professional sports from antitrust liability. Congressman Celler introduced a bill exempting only those acts that were "reasonably necessary" to maintaining competitive balance and the integrity of sports, but the full House voted to give professional sports leagues a broader although not unlimited exemption. A Senate committee held more hearings in 1958—Casey Stengel, Mickey Mantle, Ted Williams, and Stan Musial testified the day after the All-Star Game was played in nearby Baltimore—but the full Senate never considered the bill. In a 1959 report to the membership, the Major League Baseball Players Association's lawyers said, "There does not seem any doubt that Congress will even-

tually pass a law concerning Baseball's right to continue its reserve clause," but Congress never came any closer to passing comprehensive sports antitrust legislation. Bills were introduced year after year—attempts to organize a third major league, franchise moves, and the CBS purchase of the Yankees inspired some of the legislative proposals—but none was enacted.

In 1972 the U.S. Supreme Court upheld *Federal Baseball* once more in *Flood* v. *Kuhn.*[22] When the Cardinals traded Curt Flood to the Phillies after the 1969 season, Flood refused to go. "I am [not] a piece of property to be bought and sold irrespective of my wishes," he wrote to Commissioner Bowie Kuhn. Kuhn refused to declare him a free agent, so Flood hired former Supreme Court Justice and Secretary of Labor Arthur Goldberg and filed suit. The lower court's dismissal of his case was eventually upheld by the Supreme Court. Justice Harry Blackmun's opinion noted that baseball's antitrust immunity was "an anomaly" and "an aberration," but he felt bound by history.

Remedial legislation has been introduced repeatedly in Congress but none has ever been enacted. The Court, accordingly, has concluded that Congress as yet has had no intention to subject baseball's reserve system to the reach of the antitrust statutes . . . If there is any inconsistency or illogic in all this, it is an inconsistency and illogic of long standing that is to be remedied by the Congress and not this Court.

The Court's opinion also noted that state antitrust laws could not apply to baseball. Flood's career had ended by the time the Supreme Court issued its decision. After sitting out the 1970 season, he was traded to the Senators in 1971, but retired after hitting only .200 in 13 games.

It seems unlikely that the Court would reach a different result if a similar antitrust case were presented to it today. But does baseball's antitrust exemption really matter today? The players' union has managed to win free agency, salary arbitration, and limits on trades without a player's consent through collective bargaining or arbitration. After two arbitrators' decisions that the owners violated the collective-bargaining agreement by failing to bid for free agents like Kirk Gibson and Tim Raines after the 1985 and 1986 seasons, the players seem to be in the catbird seat. But what if the baseball owners choose to hang as tough as the football owners did in the 1987 strike? The courts have held that neither labor nor management can be sued under the antitrust laws over provisions in a collective-bargaining agreement, even if those provisions are clearly anticompetitive. The football players are litigating whether the labor exemption applies after a union contract has expired. But even if they win, baseball's unique antitrust exemption might still serve as a shield for the baseball owners if the players ever file a similar suit.

Baseball's exemption might protect it from the players but not from other parties who have less connection to the on-the-field aspects of the business of baseball. For example, an anticompetitive owner conspiracy involving stadium concession or parking revenues might not be exempt.

But what if a maverick owner—say, Ted Turner—tried to move his team to another city without the approval of his peers? Al Davis and Bob Irsay could move the Raiders and Colts to greener pastures because the antitrust laws prevent other NFL owners from agreeing to boycott them or take other punitive action. While there is some authority for the proposition that baseball's antitrust exemption is broad enough to cover that kind of situation, a court that was uncomfortable with the reasoning of *Federal Baseball* and its progeny could justify a different outcome in such a case much more easily than in a case involving free agency or other player-management disputes.

As noted above, the Supreme Court has referred to baseball's antitrust immunity as an "exception," an "anomaly," and an "aberration." According to another federal court, baseball's system of governance—under which the Commissioner has broad authority to prevent or remedy acts that are contrary, in his view, to the best interests of baseball—"is equally an exception, anomaly, and aberration."[23]

The 1921 Major League Agreement, which created the Office of the Commissioner, contained virtually no limits on the Commissioner's authority because Judge Landis refused to accept the job unless he was given carte blanche. The current version of that agreement provides that "[t]he functions of the Commissioner shall be . . . to investigate . . . any act, transaction, or practice . . . not in the best interests of the national game of Baseball" and "to determine . . . what preventive, remedial, or punitive action is appropriate . . . and to take such action."[24] The agreement also states that the club owners agree to be bound by the Commissioner's decisions, and "waive such right of recourse to the courts as would otherwise have existed in their favor."[25]

Perhaps former Oakland A's owner Charles O. Finley should have read that language more carefully before he signed the Major League Agreement. When Finley tried to sell Joe Rudi and Rollie Fingers to the Red Sox and Vida Blue to the Yankees just before the 1976 trading deadline, Commissioner Kuhn quickly nullified the transactions as "inconsistent with the best interests of baseball, the integrity of the game, and the maintenance of public confidence in it." Finley's lawyers tried to persuade a federal judge that Kuhn's action exceeded his authority, but the judge ruled that Kuhn's authority to void player transactions was not limited to cases involving rules violations or moral turpitude, as Finley argued. A federal appeals court later upheld that decision,[26] and also noted that the "waiver of recourse" provision quoted above kept Finley from going to court to challenge Kuhn's ruling unless he could show that the Major League Agreement was inconsistent with state or federal law or that the procedures followed by Kuhn "failed to follow the basic rudiments of due process of law."[27]

Pete Rose's 1989 lawsuit against A. Bartlett Giamatti relied on just that argument—that Rose was being denied the right to a fair hearing by an unbiased decisionmaker. When Rose asked a state court judge to issue an injunction stopping the Commissioner's pending disciplinary proceeding, Giamatti's lawyers filed a motion to remove the case to federal court. In most cases, state courts have jurisdiction if one or both of the parties to the lawsuit are citizens of that state; if the plaintiff and defendant are citizens of different states, federal courts usually have jurisdiction to hear the case. Because Rose was a citizen of Ohio and Giamatti was a citizen of New York, Giamatti was able to remove the case from the Ohio state court—which might favor Ohioans over New Yorkers—to a federal court.[28] After losing that legal skirmish, Rose withdrew his lawsuit and agreed to be suspended indefinitely from baseball, so the court never ruled on the merits of Rose's claim that the Commissioner was not treating him fairly.

[1]*Allegheny Base-ball Club* v. *Bennett,* 14 Fed. 257 (C.C.W.D. Pa., 1882).

[2]*St. Louis Athletic Ass'n* v. *Mullane*, No. 3642 (C.C.S.D. Ohio, May 13, 1884). Reprinted in *Sporting Life*, May 21, 1884, p.2, col.1.

[3]*Metropolitan Exhibition Co.* v. *Ewing*, 42 Fed. 198 (C.C.S.D. N.Y. 1890).

[4]*Metropolitan Exhibition Co.* v. *Ward*, 24 Abb.N.C. 414 (1890).

[5]*Philadelphia Base Ball Club* v. *Lajoie*, 51 Atl. 973 (Pa. S. Ct. 1902).

[6]*Brooklyn Baseball Club* v. *McGuire*, 116 Fed. 783 (C.C.E.D. Pa. 1902).

[7]*American Base Ball & Athletic Exhibition Co. of St. Louis* v. *Harper*, 54 Cent. L.J. 449 (St. Louis Cir. Ct. 1902).

[8]*American League Baseball Club of Chicago* v. *Chase*, 86 Misc. 441, 149 N.Y. Supp. 6 (Sup. Ct. 1914).

[9]*Weeghman* v. *Killefer*, 214 Fed. 168 (W.D. Mich. 1914).

[10]*Weeghman* v. *Killefer*, 215 Fed. 289 (6th Cir. 1914).

[11]*National League of Professional Baseball Clubs* v. *Federal Baseball Club of Baltimore*, 269 Fed. 681 (D.C. Cir. 1921).

[12]*Federal Baseball Club of Baltimore* v. *National League of Professional Baseball Clubs*, 259 U.S. 200 (1922).

[13]*Hart* v. *Keith Vaudeville Exchange*, 262 U.S. 271 (1923).

[14]*Gardella* v. *Chandler*, 79 F.Supp. 260 (S.D.N.Y. 1948).

[15]*Gardella* v. *Chandler*, 172 F.2d 402 (2d Cir. 1949).

[16]*Martin* v. *Chandler*, 174 F.2d 917 (2d. Cir. 1949); *Gardella* v. *Chandler*, 174 F.2d 919 (2d. Cir. 1949).

[17]H.R. Rep. 2002, 82d Cong., 2d Sess. 228–32 (1952).

[18]346 U.S. 356 (1953).

[19]*Toolson* v. *New York Yankees*, 101 F.Supp. 93 (S.D. Cal. 1951).

[20]200 F.2d 198 (9th Cir. 1952).

[21]358 U.S. 445 (1957).

[22]407 U.S. 258 (1972).

[23]*Charles O. Finley & Co., Inc.* v. *Kuhn*, 569 U.S. 527, 537 (1978).

[24]Major League Agreement, Art. I, Sec. 2.

[25]Id. at Art. VII, Sec. 2.

[26]*Finley* v. *Kuhn*, 569 F.2d 527 (1978).

[27]Id. at 544.

[28]*Rose* v. *Giamatti*, 721 F.Supp. 906 (1989).

CHAPTER 29

The Farm System

Bob Hoie

Farm teams are nearly as old as organized baseball. In 1884 the Boston Beaneaters of the National League owned a team called the Boston Reserves in the Massachusetts State Association. The Reserves, also called the Colts, were apparently intended to serve as a source of replacements for disabled members of the major league club. It has also been suggested that the farm team was a device to keep more players under contract and out of the hands of the Union Association that year. Whatever the origins of the idea, during the next decade a number of major league clubs operated such reserve teams, but they usually competed in local semipro leagues rather than in organized baseball and were viewed more as quick sources of replacements rather than as training grounds for players.

With John B. Day's joint ownership of the New York Gothams of the National League and the New York Metropolitans of the American Association as early as 1883 and with the proliferation of interlocking ownerships of major league clubs in the 1890s, it was only natural that some major and minor league clubs would come under joint ownership as well. The first instance of any significance, however, occurred when John T. Brush, owner of Cincinnati in the National League, entered the Indianapolis club in the newly formed Western League in 1894. While this was not the first case of joint major-minor league club ownership, Brush appears to have been the first to grasp the potential of such an arrangement. Indianapolis served as a place to develop talent that was not quite ready for the majors. The team gave Cincinnati an expanded roster as players were frequently shuffled to and from Indianapolis during the season; it also served as a source of profit because Indianapolis drew well at the gate, having become the dominant club in the Western League, with three pennants and two second-place finishes in five seasons (1895–1899). Indianapolis's success was aided in no small part by Brush's practice of drafting players from other Western League clubs and sending them to Indianapolis, thus simultaneously weakening the opposition and strenghtening the Hoosiers. Efforts were made by the other Western League club owners to control "farming" or to modify the draft rules to stop Brush, but none were successful.

Perhaps copying Brush's strategy, in 1896 several National League clubs obtained minor league affiliates: Pittsburgh had Toronto, Boston had Wilkes-Barre, and Cleveland had Ft. Wayne. Philadelphia had a Philadelphia farm club in the Pennsylvania State League, and when that league folded, they shifted the junior club to the Atlantic Association. The New York Giants had the first farm "system," with the New York Mets in the Atlantic Association and Syracuse in the Eastern League.

When the National Agreement was adopted in 1903, it banned the "farming out" of players, but "farming" as defined in the agreement referred only to those efforts by major league clubs to exceed the limits on players who could be optioned through subterfuge—"fake transfers" such as loans or sell/buy-back arrangements with minor league clubs where title to a player was never actually surrendered.

The independent minor league operators saw farming as a curse for two reasons. First, it reduced their autonomy and potential revenue by placing more players under major league ownership, thus reducing the majors' need to buy or draft players from the minors. Second, clubs accepting players from the majors, either openly through options or secretly, might gain an unfair competitive advantage on the field. So while in 1905 the New York Giants' request to establish a working agreement with Bridgeport was validated by the National Commission, most of the legislation was focused on restricting farming, normally by limiting the number of players who could be optioned and the number of times each player could be optioned. For example, in 1904 a rule was adopted which required a player sent out on option to stay with the minor league club for the remainder of that season. In 1907 the rule was relaxed so that a major league club could option a player and recall him, but only once in a season. In 1911 a team could have no more than eight players out on option at one time.

Working agreements became quite common during this period. The major league club furnished the minor league club with its surplus players—youngsters in need of more experience or veterans past their prime who could still strengthen a minor league club—and/or cash. In return the major league club could obtain promising players from the minor league club. During this era the formal working agreement between major and minor league clubs was usually of short duration—a year or two at most—suggesting that major league clubs targeted certain minor league clubs that had two or three players they might be interested in and established a working agreement in order to get first claim on those that developed satisfactorily. There were also informal working agreements, generally based on friendships between major and minor league club operators, and it was usually through such arrangements that the "fake transfers" banned by the National Agreement took place. In the early 1900s, for example, there was substantial traffic in players between the White Sox and Milwaukee of the American

Association and between the Dodgers and Baltimore in the Eastern League. (Brewer manager Joe Cantillon was a long-time friend of Charles Comiskey, and Brooklyn manager Ned Hanlon was also a minority owner of the Orioles.)

The most efficient and only legal method of circumventing the rules relating to major league control of players was through joint ownership of major and minor league clubs. By 1912 Charles W. Somers owned Cleveland and Toledo, and Charles Ebbets owned both Brooklyn and Newark. This enabled the Indians to hold title to sixty players and the Dodgers to sixty-one. In 1913 a National Commission confidential bulletin directed major league clubs to divest their interest in minor league clubs by January 1, 1914, but neither Somers nor Ebbets complied until several years later (in fact, Somers secretly acquired New Orleans in 1913). In 1921 the joint ownership of major and minor league clubs was again permitted, and the New National Agreement, although retaining option limits, dropped the antifarming provisions that had been in it since 1903.

In 1921 the Cardinals, who had already acquired an interest in Ft. Smith of the Western Association and Houston of the Texas League, acquired a half interest in Syracuse of the International League. This was the beginning of Branch Rickey's farm system, but initially it attracted little attention as it didn't appear to represent anything particularly new. Major league clubs had long been signing young talent directly off the sandlots and developing it in the minors. In 1910, for example, Cleveland signed Roger Peckinpaugh out of the Cleveland City League, gave him a brief trial, and then optioned him to New Haven and Portland in successive seasons before recalling him when he was deemed ready for the majors. This practice had developed to the point that Mike Sexton, president of the National Association, in 1921 spoke out against the fact that the majors and higher minors had preempted the low minors' traditional role of discovering and signing young talent.

As we have seen, major league clubs had occasionally owned minor league clubs, primarily to expand the number of players under their control, but these were always higher-classification clubs, where talent was refined rather than developed. Rickey's approach was original because he was the first to assemble a system of teams at various levels or classifications. This enabled him to sign young talent and, through a hierarchy of minor league clubs, to develop and retain continuous title to a large number of players, his theory being that out of quantity comes quality. It didn't take long for the system to begin producing talent—the Cards, who had never finished higher than third in this century, won the World Series in 1926 with a team that included future Hall of Famers Jim Bottomley and Chick Hafey as well as regulars Taylor Douthit, Tommy Thevenow, Les Bell, Ray Blades, Flint Rhem, and Art Reinhardt plus reserves Watty Holm, Jake Flowers, Spec Toporcher, Ernie Vick, and Bill Hallahan—all of whom were products of a farm system that was less than seven years old. In addition, Billy Southworth was acquired from the Giants for Heinie Mueller, another product of the Cardinal farm system.

During those seven years when the Cardinals were discovering, signing, and developing unprecedented quanti-

ties of players at little expense, the other major league clubs were essentially operating as they always had, signing some players out of the amateur ranks, optioning them out for seasoning, and buying top prospects from minor league clubs, even though the new draft rules were driving the prices of such players to unprecedented levels. For example, the Yankee team the Cardinals defeated in the 1926 World Series had just one home-grown player—Lou Gehrig, who was signed out of Columbia University in 1923 and optioned to Hartford until ready. Although this had been an inexpensive acquisition, the Yankees subsequently had purchased, for $50,000 each, Earle Combs from Louisville, Mark Koenig from St. Paul (with whom the Yankees had a working agreement), and Tony Lazzeri from Salt Lake. In 1925, the year the Pirates won the World Series, they acquired Paul Waner and Hal Rhyne from the San Francisco Seals for $100,000 and also signed Joe Cronin off the San Francisco sandlots for little more than train fare to his first assignment—Johnstown, Pennsylvania.

But the escalating prices of players and the success of the Cardinals finally encouraged other clubs to begin acquiring minor league clubs. Shortly after the Cardinals acquired the half interest in Syracuse in 1921, William Wrigley, owner of the Cubs, acquired Los Angeles of the Pacific Coast League, but he treated them virtually as separate investments. By 1927, however, major league acquisition of minor league clubs was causing concern in the minors. The first formal notice came late that year, when the American Association adopted a new Constitution which effectively prohibited major league ownership of its clubs (excluding Columbus, which was already owned by Cincinnati). At the National Association meeting in December 1928, Mike Sexton wondered aloud when the majors would own enough clubs to control the National Association. Early in 1929 major league clubs owned or controlled twenty-seven minor league clubs. At that point Judge Landis, who until then had been remarkably quiet on the issue of farm systems, opened fire. He began granting free agency to minor leaguers "covered up" by various major league organizations. Later in 1929, Landis denounced the farm system, and announced his intention of destroying it. In response, Sam Breadon, owner of the Cardinals, cited letters from seven minor leagues saying the farm system was beneficial to them. Interestingly, in 1921 Landis had said, "The object of organized baseball is to facilitate the development of skill among ball players." No one could seriously argue that this wasn't the purpose of the farm system, but by 1929 Landis was accusing Rickey and Breadon of "raping the minors," robbing smalltown America of its precious heritage of independent minor league baseball.

Through the 1930s Landis tried to make good on his threat to destroy the farm system, but since it was not contrary to baseball law, he had to pick at the edges—by levying fines against teams having an interest in more than one team in a minor league or by granting free agency to players who were "covered up" through violations of the option rules or "secret agreements." Attracting much attention in Landis's crusade was his granting of free agency to seventy-four Cardinal farmhands in 1938, and to ninety-one Detroit minor leaguers in 1940, but these shots were fired after the war was lost.

More important than the fireworks that erupted between Landis and Breadon at the 1929 major league meeting was Yankees owner Jacob Ruppert's declaration at the same meetings that no ball club could afford the prices being paid for minor league players; Ruppert added that he was "going to be forced into owning minor league clubs, and so is every other major league owner in this room." At the time he spoke, the Yankees had already purchased the Chambersburg club of the Class D Blue Ridge League. In November 1931 Ruppert purchased Newark of the International League for a reported $600,000 and soon thereafter hired Baltimore general manager George Weiss to develop a farm system. Thus the farm system, a concept that had been created largely out of necessity by Branch Rickey because the Cardinals didn't have the financial resources to compete with other clubs for top minor league prospects, had in less than a decade been embraced by the wealthiest club in baseball as being the most efficient method of acquiring talent. There would still be an occasional Joe DiMaggio or Ted Williams, signed by a minor league club and sold to the majors, but the major league club that didn't establish a farm system did so at its own peril—it cannot be coincidental that the eight teams which were the slowest to get on the bandwagon and had the thinnest farm systems in the 1930s—the Phillies, Athletics, Senators, White Sox, Giants, Cubs, Braves, and Pirates—were, aside from the Browns, the eight least successful teams in the 1940s. (The Browns and Reds established extensive farm systems in the 1930s, and overall they were the two most improved clubs of the 1940s.)

While several clubs caught on to what the Cardinals were doing, none could catch up as Rickey, taking advantage of the Depression, which had created a large pool of young men with few career options, signed players by the hundreds at tryout camps. Whereas during the 1920s the Cardinal system had only increased from three clubs to five, by 1936 it had expanded to twenty-eight teams—remarkable considering that there were only twenty-six minor leagues that year (the Cardinals had two teams each in the Nebraska State, Georgia-Florida, and Arkansas-Missouri Leagues). The Cardinal system finally topped out with thirty-three clubs in 1937—more than the two next-largest farm systems combined. Rickey's belief that out of quantity comes quality was proven on the field by the 1942 world champion Cardinals. Every player on the active roster, except for second-line pitchers Harry Gumbert and Whitey Moore, was a product of the Cardinal farm system, and Gumbert had been acquired in exchange for Cardinal farm graduate Bill McGee. In addition, the sale of players developed by the Cardinals kept the coffers full—in 1940–1941 alone, Johnny Mize, Joe Medwick, and Mickey Owen were exchanged to other clubs for $240,000 and nine players.

Thus from the perspective of the majors the farm system was a success, and the minors seemed to be flourishing—going from fourteen leagues in 1933 to forty-four by 1940. Sam Breadon, responding to another barrage of attacks by Landis in the late 1930s, claimed that the farm system had brought stability and strength to the minors, but there were other factors at work—the proliferation of night games, better promotion, and an influx of good young talent resulted in a per-club increase in attendance of 40 percent from 1937 to 1940. During that same period the portion of minor league clubs affiliated with the majors actually dropped from 61 to 46 percent. Rickey's theory that out of quantity comes quality might have had practical merit during a depression, or again immediately following World War Two when there was an influx of returning veterans. However, under normal circumstances huge farm systems were not cost-effective. While the minors were still expanding in the late 1930s, the Cardinals began pruning back their farm system of more than thirty teams; again while the minors were expanding in the late 1940s, farm systems were contracting—in 1948 there were six farm systems of twenty or more teams; by 1951 there were none. The portion of minor league teams affiliated with major league teams dropped from 62 percent in 1946 to 47 percent in 1951 as major league farm systems collectively dropped from 280 to 175 clubs and outright major league ownership of minor league clubs dropped from 125 to 75.

In 1950 there were 232 minor league teams not affiliated with the majors. This was the highest number of independent teams in organized baseball since the early teens. Nine of the fifty-eight leagues had no teams with major league affiliations, and more than a dozen others had only one or two affiliates. These leagues operated virtually outside the player-development chain, existing much as a semipro team or league does—to provide entertainment and reflect civic pride. Their only source of revenue was through the turnstiles, and just as forty years earlier automobiles and the movies helped drive out the marginal teams and leagues, now TV did the same. This can be clearly seen as the heavily populated Northeast, the first region to be heavily penetrated by television, suffered the first wave of league failures.

Over the next few years, attendance declined sharply, most of the independent clubs folded, and farm systems continued to contract. In 1956 the majors established a "stabilization fund" of $500,000 to aid clubs and leagues in lower classifications, but the free-fall of leagues, clubs, and attendance continued. In 1959 the majors discontinued the stabilization fund and established a fund of $1 million to finance a player-development and promotional program for the minors. In 1962 the majors and minors adopted the Player Development Plan that, by requiring each major league club to have five farm teams, would guarantee the operation of at least one-hundred minor league teams, which the majors felt was adequate for their player-development purposes. The plan also included the Player Development Contract under the terms of which the parent major league club became responsible for all spring training costs and all or most of the salaries of players, managers, and coaches. After major league expansion in 1969, major league clubs were only required to support four farm clubs each, but their financial support of each was increased. By 1976 there were only 106 minor league teams with major league affiliations, the lowest peacetime total since 1935. American League expansion the following year created the need for additional minor league affiliates, and in subsequent years the major league clubs have expanded their farm systems—all of them back up to a minimum of five clubs by 1984. By 1990 the number of minor league teams with major league affiliations was up to 162.

In 1928 Mike Sexton had asked how long it would be before the majors owned enough minor league clubs to control the National Association. Other than during World War Two, when the minors were severely constricted, major league clubs never have "owned" more than 28 percent of the minor league clubs; however, possibly as early as 1934, probably by 1935, and certainly by 1936, the majors through outright ownership, working agreements, or other interlocking devices "controlled" the National Association, and this situation was generally acknowledged throughout baseball by 1938.

Until about 1960 there was still some room for independent clubs and career minor league players, but since then the minors have existed almost exclusively to develop talent for the majors. While this has dismayed many minor league fans and traditionalists, it should be remembered that the principal role of the minors within organized baseball has always been to develop talent for the majors, and to receive money in exchange. The farm system, which owed its success in no small part to the greed of some minor league operators, was merely a different device by which talent moved to the majors and money moved to the minors.

Major League Farm Systems
1936–1969

	36	37	38	39	40	41	42	43	44	45	46	47	48	49	50	51	52	53	54	55	56	57	58	59	60	61	62	63	64	65	66	67	68	69
Boston, AL	9	10	7	8	6	7	6	3	5	4	12	13	15	11	8	8	6	6	6	6	5	7	7	6	6	6	6	5	5	5	6	5	6	6
Chicago, AL	5	4	10	8	6	5	5	0	0	0	17	12	15	9	8	8	6	6	6	5	6	6	6	6	6	6	5	5	5	6	6	6	6	6
Cleveland, AL	5	7	13	16	8	9	8	3	3	3	11	18	20	20	16	12	10	8	8	9	9	8	8	8	7	5	6	5	4	4	4	4	5	5
Detroit, AL	11	8	12	7	5	11	8	2	3	2	7	11	16	14	9	8	7	7	8	10	9	8	10	7	8	8	6	6	5	5	5	5	6	6
New York, AL	11	15	15	15	14	12	9	5	5	5	15	22	24	22	15	14	10	11	9	10	11	10	10	8	8	7	7	6	5	7	7	7	6	6
Phila.-K.C.-Oakland, AL	5	3	3	3	4	5	3	2	2	4	7	15	10	11	15	9	8	8	6	7	7	9	8	8	8	8	6	5	5	6	6	6	6	5
St. Louis-Baltimore, AL	3	15	16	12	11	11	6	1	3	3	11	15	20	18	13	10	12	10	12	8	9	8	9	7	7	9	6	6	6	7	6	6	6	6
Wash.-Minnesota, AL	1	5	2	8	4	6	3	1	2	2	5	7	12	9	10	6	8	7	8	7	6	8	8	7	6	7	7	7	6	8	8	8	8	8
Milwaukee-Atlanta, NL	4	6	6	6	5	4	4	1	1	2	13	15	15	11	8	8	12	11	10	10	12	15	14	12	10	9	8	7	6	5	6	7	5	4
Brklyn.-Los Angeles, NL	5	14	14	11	18	14	10	4	7	9	21	25	26	26	22	19	17	15	15	16	14	13	12	12	12	11	9	7	8	6	6	6	6	6
Chicago, NL	5	6	5	2	2	9	11	4	6	7	18	23	19	16	15	14	10	9	9	8	8	10	8	6	6	6	5	5	5	5	6	6	5	5
Cincinnati, NL	16	10	10	10	8	8	5	2	1	3	4	8	11	10	7	4	6	7	9	9	9	9	11	11	8	8	6	5	5	5	4	5	5	5
N.Y.-San Francisco, NL	2	11	4	5	6	7	7	3	5	8	16	19	22	19	18	14	13	9	9	10	10	10	12	9	8	9	8	7	7	6	6	6	6	5
Philadelphia, NL	1	2	3	3	8	3	2	1	3	5	9	11	15	14	12	11	11	9	9	8	8	9	9	7	10	8	7	6	6	6	7	7	6	6
Pittsburgh, NL	4	5	7	7	9	8	7	4	4	4	13	14	19	13	13	11	15	11	10	13	13	10	11	9	7	7	7	7	6	6	6	6	6	6
St. Louis, NL	28	33	32	28	29	25	22	6	7	7	18	19	22	20	21	16	15	16	22	18	15	11	14	12	9	8	6	5	5	6	6	7	7	7
L.A.-California, AL																										2	4	6	6	6	5	5	5	5
Washington, AL																										2	4	4	4	4	4	4	5	5
Houston, NL																										2	4	5	5	5	6	6	5	6
New York, NL																										3	4	5	4	4	5	6	6	5
Kansas City, AL																																		7
Seattle, AL																																		4
Montreal, NL																																		3
San Diego, NL																																		4

Minor League Clubs/Major League Affiliations

Year	Minor League Clubs	Affiliated with Majors	Owned by Majors
1936	184	115	38
1937	251	154	39
1938	267	163	48
1939	292	149	47
1940	310	143	60
1941	304	143	61
1942	206	116	46
1943	66	42	23
1944	70	57	21
1945	85	68	33
1946	316	197	79
1947	406	247	103
1948	452	280	125
1949	461	243	116
1950	446	210	99
1951	373	172	75
1952	324	166	65
1953	292	152	50
1954	269	156	49
1955	243	155	40
1956	217	150	33
1957	209	153	32
1958	173	157	34
1959	150	132	30
1960	152	126	18
1961	147	129	21
1962	134	121	22
1963	127	114	22
1964	136	108	19
1965	136	110	28
1966	138	116	32
1967	141	118	36
1968	142	119	39
1969	155	128	46
1970	153	120	39
1971	155	127	45
1972	148	125	49
1973	147	117	38
1974	145	113	27
1975	137	109	26
1976	148	106	24
1977	150	113	23
1978	156	118	24
1979	155	119	
1980	155	125	
1981	152	133	
1982	160	136	
1983	162	139	
1984	164	140	
1985	168	140	
1986	162	143	
1987	168	145	
1988	188	168	
1989	197	177	
1990	202	180	

Baseball Reporting

Jack Lang

If baseball really was invented by Abner Doubleday at Cooperstown, N.Y., in 1839, we have only the findings of the Mills Commission to support the theory. That commission, formed in 1905, relied heavily on the rambling recollections of an old mining engineer named Abner Graves to reach the conclusion that Doubleday indeed "devised the first scheme for playing baseball." Graves's testimonies were later found to be chock full of inaccuracies.

There can be no dispute, however, as to when the art of writing about baseball began. In the mid-1850s William Trotter Porter gave a decided lift to the game with extensive coverage in his publication *Spirit of the Times*. Until Porter's reports began appearing regularly, baseball in America was ignored in most publications.

John Rickards Betts of Tulane University, in his *American Quarterly* paper "Sporting Journalism in Nineteenth-Century America," credits Porter with being the greatest "antebellum sports editor" in America. On December 10, 1831, he published the first copy of *Spirit of the Times*. It was, for a while, the country's leading sports journal. But while it carried great reports on racing, prize fighting, and even cricket, it did not devote space to baseball until the 1850s.

When he did start reporting on baseball, Porter is credited with having given it the title of "the national game" and also with having printed the first box scores (although this claim is questionable) and "dope" stories.

Shortly thereafter, Frank Queen and Harrison Trent founded the New York *Clipper,* which devoted even more space to baseball. One reason was the addition to the staff of Henry Chadwick, who had begun his career as a journalist in 1844 by contributing to the Long Island *Star.* Chadwick, who had played baseball briefly in his youth, was a devotee of the game and wrote of it voluminously.

Alfred H. Spink, in his book *The National Game,* published in 1910, credits William Cauldwell, editor of the New York *Mercury,* as being the first man to write about baseball for a daily newspaper. Spink's authority for this assertion is a gentleman named William M. Rankin, one of the nation's leading reporters on sports in the late 1880s. Rankin, who was the official scorer for the Mutual Club, also wrote extensively for such New York papers as the *Times, Tribune, World, Mail,* and *Express.* He was considered one of the game's leading authorities. According to Rankin, Cauldwell was writing about baseball by 1853. But Cauldwell found the work of editing his newspaper and writing about baseball too exhausting, and he soon hired Chadwick to write on baseball for the *Mercury.* It was not long before Henry Chadwick became the leading baseball authority in America.

If weekly and daily publications were slow to catch on to the popularity of baseball, they caught up in the late 1880s. Magazines like *The Police Gazette* and *Sporting Life* devoted considerable space to the game. Soon editors of daily newspapers recognized the interest in baseball. James Gordon Bennett, one of the world's most respected newspapermen, who was editor of the New York *Tribune,* was one of the first to increase coverage of the game.

In time every newspaper in America devoted a full page to sports . . . focusing on baseball. Charles Dana of the New York *Sun* and Joseph Pulitzer of the New York *World* are recognized as pioneers in the creation of entire sports departments. By the 1890s, most newspapers in America had created a sports staff. It was in the final decade of the nineteenth century that sports writing began to develop as a full-time job on the nation's newspapers.

At the time of his death in 1908, Chadwick was clearly established as the nation's leading baseball authority. Chadwick, who even in his youth had been honored with the nickname "Father Chadwick" for his role in the development of baseball, was such a busy writer that the history of his various affiliations is in conflict. He is credited in some publications as having worked for the Brooklyn *Eagle* in 1856 and the New York *Clipper* in 1857. In others, Chadwick is reported to have written for the *Mercury* before any of the others, or for both at the same time.

Whatever his affiliations, Chadwick was the most prolific of the early-day baseball writers, and eventually he abandoned daily reporting of the game to concentrate on weekly roundups and books about the game.

Chadwick originated what is known today as *The Baseball Guide,* published by *The Sporting News.* He wrote and edited the first baseball guide in 1860, the *Beadle's Dime Base Ball Player.* Later he edited the *DeWitt's Guide* from 1869 to 1880 and, finally, *Spalding's Baseball Guide* from 1881 until his death.

Chadwick's involvement in the game was more than just writing of it. He was instrumental in changing several rules, is credited with having perfected the box score, and was most concerned about drinking, gambling, and rowdyism at ballparks. He led campaigns to clean up the game. Baseball officials of the day heeded his advice.

As early as 1868, Chadwick wrote the first hardcover book in America devoted strictly to baseball. Appropriately, it was titled: *The Game of Base Ball.*

Chadwick's writings on the game led to honors that would be unheard of in the modern era. In 1894, the National League elected Henry an honorary member and two years later voted him a lifetime pension of $600 a year. If a major league today awarded a baseball writer a pension, it would result in an investigation.

Honors continued for Chadwick thirty years after his death. In 1938, one year before the Hall of Fame opened, Chadwick was elected to the Cooperstown shrine as one of the great contributors to the game along with Alexander Cartwright. It was the same year that Grover Cleveland Alexander was elected. Although baseball writers are now honored with the J. G. Taylor Spink Award and scrolls in their honor are mounted in the Hall of Fame Library, Chadwick is the only former baseball writer with a bronze plaque in the main hall, alongside those of Babe Ruth, Ty Cobb, Joe DiMaggio, Cy Young, Mickey Mantle, Ted Williams, and others.

Another early-day baseball writer who earned great respect from the leaders of the game was Timothy H. Murnane, known as the Silver King. When Murnane died in 1917, he was so highly regarded that the American League paid for and erected a huge marble tombstone over his grave in Old Calvary Cemetery in Roslindale, Massachusetts.

The tombstone cites Murnane as a "pioneer of baseball . . . [a] champion of its integrity . . . [a] gifted and fearless writer."

Murnane was a baseball player who turned to writing after his playing days were over. He founded the Boston *Referee* in 1885, and his writings attracted the editors of the Boston *Globe,* who in 1888 hired him as their baseball writer, a job he held until his death. In his thirty years as baseball editor of the *Globe,* he was one of the most influential writers in the country and even found time to serve as president of the New England League for twenty-four years.

Upon his death, it was learned that Murnane left only a small estate to his widow. Immediately, a benefit all-star game was scheduled between great players of the American League and the Boston Red Sox with all proceeds to go to Murnane's widow.

On September 17, 1917, 17,119 Boston fans attended the game which included a pre-game show featuring Ziegfield Follies stars Will Rogers and Fanny Brice. The all-star team included such names as Grover Cleveland Alexander, Walter Johnson, Johnny Evers, Wally Schang, Shoeless Joe Jackson, Buck Weaver, Stuffy McInnis, Eddie Collins, Ty Cobb, and Tris Speaker. Heavyweight boxing champion John L. Sullivan coached first base and Babe Ruth pitched the first six innings for Boston.

All appeared without pay. That was evidence of the esteem in which Murnane was held.

Until the creation of full-time sports staffs in the late 1890s, writing about baseball was, in many cities, a hit-and-miss affair. In many areas, the reports of games were turned in by club secretaries or part-time correspondents. It was often less-than-objective reporting.

With the advent of full-time sports reporters and sports editors in the early 1890s, especially in New York, other major cities suddenly followed suit. This resulted in localized styles of writing and language familiar to the areas. John Rickards Betts describes it in his *American Quarterly* article on nineteenth-century journalism: "The most important developments in sporting journalism outside New York were taking place on the Chicago newspapers.

Charles Seymour of the *Herald,* Finley Peter Dunne of the *News* and a reporter for the *Times* were creators of a novel style among baseball writers, a style based on picturesque jargon, lively humor and grotesque exaggeration."

Hugh Fullerton, who was one of the great turn-of-the-century baseball writers in Chicago, noted that "the style of reporting baseball changed all over the country."

In New York and Boston the style of baseball writing emphasized expert knowledge of the game. In Chicago and other western cities, the style involved more humor and cynicism. Often the final score of the game was secondary. Reporters described games with a great flourish and seemed intent on capturing readers' interest with their individual writing styles. Here is the way one Chicago *Times* writer reported a Chicago Cubs game on September 26, 1888:

"The ninth inning of yesterday's ball game was a marvel of beauty. To describe it one needs a big stretch of canvas, a white-wash brush, a pan of green paint, and an artist's hand. Words are hardly expressive enough . . . Mr. Schoeneck is a large secretion of fat around considerable bone and muscle, and he knocked the ball out of the diamond and puffed down to first base . . . Immediately after which Mr. Buckley bunted the ball and went to first, his fatness moving to second.

"The inning had not been particularly gorgeous up to this moment, but with the hitting of a fly by Mr. Hines it took on a resplendent and glorious aspect, for Mr. Van Altren [Van Haltren] got under the fly, gauged it with his blue eye, and muffed it beautifully. When the ball reached Capt. Anson it had lost much of its virulence and was bounding gently long, smiling the while. But if it had not been for a chunk of lava fresh from the earth it could not have had more fun with Capt. Anson, for it rollicked out of his hands and into them again and all over his person, blithely tapped him in the face, and danced away. Indeed, it was a beautiful error, that one of Anson's—a regular sunset error flushed and radiant with shadings of purple and a mellow border.

"Mr. Van Altren picked it up and looked about irresolutely. He was debating whether he should sacrifice skill to art, and being a young man of no high culture in this respect, he esteemed art as naught, but hurled the ball to the plate to catch Mr. Hines. But art was triumphant for all, for Mr. Van Altren's irresolution had been fatal. The ball came to the plate a second after Mr. Hines crossed safe, and Mr. Raphael, Mr. M. Angelo, and Mr. Turner will have to take a seat near the door."

A reporter describing a game in that manner today would not be assigned to cover the next day's game. But it was in that style that games were recorded around the turn of the century. A baseball writer, covering a game at three o'clock in the afternoon, had until three o'clock in the morning to write his story. This enabled many to write what some journalists later referred to as "fabulous narratives." Writers were bent on influencing the readers with their imaginative use of the language in long, descriptive phrases. Space in newspapers was plentiful, and baseball writers frequently used two and three columns to describe a single game. It gave writers an opportunity to develop their own style in an effort to capture the imagination of the readers.

Nowhere was this more evident than in Chicago, where such writers as Sy Sanborn, Ring Lardner, Hugh Fullerton, and Charles Dryden were winning over readers with their often humorous accounts of baseball games. Lardner came out of South Bend, Indiana, and covered the Chicago Cubs for the *Inter-Ocean,* the *Examiner* and later the *Tribune.* Eventually he abandoned daily baseball writing and made his mark as an author of short stories, many with a baseball theme. *You Know Me Al* and "Alibi Ike" are two of his baseball classics.

Fullerton was considered the most remarkable forecaster of his day, and his predictions on the outcome of games were sought in every major league city. When he died at age seventy-two in 1946, he was hailed in his obituaries as "the game's original dopester." But for all the expertise and humor that he brought to his readers, Fullerton is best remembered in journalistic circles as the writer most responsible for exposing the Chicago White Sox for throwing the 1919 World Series.

Prior to the 1919 Series, the fearless forecaster had predicted an easy victory for the Sox against Cincinnati. But early in the Series Fullerton was convinced that the Sox were not giving it their best effort. In his summary of the Series after Chicago lost, Fullerton suggested as much. But he was not about to let go of it there. Fullerton went to New York, where he followed up leads that tied some of the White Sox to gamblers. The New York *Evening World* published a toned-down version of his theory, and Fullerton was criticized by members of his own craft. But his persistence continued until he convinced American League president Ban Johnson to investigate the matter. Using much of the information Fullerton supplied, Johnson brought the investigation to a head late in the 1920 season. The result was a trial in which eight players were found innocent. But the same eight were later banned from organized baseball for life by Judge Kenesaw Mountain Landis, the newly appointed commissioner of baseball. Fullerton's investigative reporting was responsible for the findings of the commissioner.

Fullerton was a baseball purist, and his Ten Commandments of Sports were widely published. They read:
1. Thou shalt not quit.
2. Thou shalt not alibi.
3. Thou shalt not gloat over winning.
4. Thou shalt not sulk over losing.
5. Thou shalt not take unfair advantage.
6. Thou shalt not ask odds thou art not willing to give.
7. Thou shalt always be willing to give the benefit of doubt.
8. Thou shalt not underestimate an opponent or overestimate thyself.
9. Remember that the game is the thing and he who thinks otherwise is no true sportsman.
10. Honor the game thou playest; he who plays the game straight and hard wins even when he loses.

It was common at the turn of the century for baseball writers to begin their stories with a few lines of verse. Grantland Rice, who came out of Nashville, where he had been sports editor of the *Tennesseean,* to join the staff of the Cleveland *Plain Dealer,* was perhaps the most widely known writer in this style. His poetic jingles were read throughout the American League and many attempted to copy his style.

Rice did not remain long in Cleveland. He longed for the South and returned there. But then he returned North to New York, where his syndicated column appeared throughout the country. Rice actually was better known for his football writing than he was for his baseball work.

Besides Rice, another leading baseball writer of the early twentieth century who frequently began his stories with a few lines of verse was Franklin Pierce Adams, who wrote under the byline of "F.P.A." He wrote what is known as "Baseball's Sad Lexicon" during a New York Giants–Chicago Cubs series in 1908. Quoted to this day, it read in part:

> *Ruthlessly pricking our gonfalon bubble,*
> *Making a Giant hit into a double,*
> *Words that are weighty with nothing but trouble,*
> *Tinker to Evers to Chance.*

That verse, as much as their actual records on the field, is credited with leading to the induction of the Chicago Cubs' infield trio into the Hall of Fame.

Charles Dryden, born in 1857, moved about as much as any baseball writer in the late 1890s and into the 1900s. He covered the California League for the San Francisco *Examiner* and then moved to the New York *American* and on again to Philadelphia with the *North American.* But in 1905 he was offered what was then considered the highest salary paid a baseball writer and moved to the Chicago *Examiner.* The salary was reported to be $100 weekly.

It was in Chicago that Dryden gained fame with his nicknames for the baseball people he wrote about. He called Charles Comiskey, the White Sox owner, "the Old Roman." He termed the light-hitting White Sox the "Hitless Wonders." Chicago Cubs' manager Frank Chance was dubbed "the Peerless Leader." It was also Dryden who coined the phrase about the hapless Washington Senators: "Washington . . . first in war, first in peace and last in the American League."

Dryden was a charter member of the Baseball Writers Association of America (BBWAA), which was formed officially in 1908. It was an association born of necessity when baseball writing in the early years of the twentieth century was attracting some of the nation's outstanding young writers and baseball itself was dominating the sports pages. Only the baseball owners failed to recognize the importance of this feisty band of scribes. They were treated—or mistreated—as a necessary evil.

At the 1908 playoff game between the Chicago Cubs and the New York Giants at New York's Polo Grounds, Hugh Fullerton arrived to find actor Louis Mann in his seat. This was not uncommon. Giants manager John McGraw loved to hobnob with Broadway actors and often told them to sit in the press box. When Fullerton asked Mann to vacate the seat, Mann refused. No Giants official would order him to move. At first Fullerton attempted to write his story sitting on Mann's lap, but eventually he sat on a box in the aisle next to him and covered the entire game from that seat.

Baseball writers continued to suffer mistreatment during the Chicago Cubs–Detroit Tigers World Series that followed. The writers covering the Series were outraged at the treatment accorded them. In Chicago, out-of-town writers were placed in the back row of the grandstand. In Detroit, the writers were compelled to climb a ladder to the roof of the first base pavilion, where they were forced to write in the rain and snow that hampered the Series. Finally, unwilling to endure these conditions another year, the writers decided to organize. At the request of Jack Ryder of Cincinnati and Henry Edwards of Cleveland, Joseph S. Jackson, sports editor of the Detroit *Free Press,* arranged a meeting room in the Hotel Ponchartrain on the morning of the final game. That was October 14, 1908. Present at that first meeting, the founding fathers of the Baseball Writers Association of America, were: Tim Murnane and Paul Shannon, Boston; Charles Hughes, Hugh Keough, Malcolm McLean, Hugh Fullerton, Bill Phelon, and Sy Sanborn, Chicago; Ed Bang and Henry Edwards, Cleveland; Jack Ryder and Charles Zuber, Cincinnati; J. W. McConaughy and Sid Mercer, New York; William Weart, Philadelphia; George Moreland, Pittsburgh; Joseph Jackson and Joseph Smith, Detroit; James Crusinberry, Hal Lanigan, W. G. Murphy, and J. B. Sheridan, St. Louis; and Ed Grillo, Washington.

Joseph Jackson was appointed temporary chairman and Sy Sanborn, secretary. Tim Murnane was appointed treasurer, and he passed the hat to collect $1 dues from each of the founding fathers.

A more formal meeting was held in New York in December 1908 at the annual winter meetings of the two leagues. Fullerton, Edwards, and Weart, who had been appointed in Detroit to draw up a constitution, listed four items as the main objective of the BBWAA. They were:

1. To encourage a square deal in baseball.
2. To simplify the rules in scoring baseball games and promote uniformity in scoring.
3. To secure better facilities for reporting baseball games and better regulation of the scorers' boxes during both championship seasons and World Series at the parks of the American and National League Clubs, hereinafter to be designated the major leagues.
4. To bring together into a closer bond of friendship the writers of baseball throughout the United States and Canada.

The organization was enthusiastically endorsed from the start by both leagues. Promise of full support was received by league presidents, who appointed the local representatives of chapters in each city to serve as custodians of the league press boxes.

Immediately conditions improved throughout baseball. No longer did writers have the problem of outsiders occupying seats in the press box. Interlopers were immediately escorted out by park security men upon orders of the local BBWAA representative. The writers had the backing of the league to police their own work area.

By 1910–11, the baseball writing fraternity was accepting into its ranks some of the bright young writers of that era—men who would go on to greater heights in the field of literature. Covering the Giants in New York that year were men like Grantland Rice, Damon Runyon, Heywood Broun, and Fred Lieb. Rice later became recognized as the dean of America's sportswriters; Runyon became the chronicler of Broadway night life and the characters who inhabited the Great White Way, while Broun went on to the editorial side of newspapers and founded the Newspaper Guild of America. Lieb was a prolific writer who was one of baseball's leading biographers.

Elsewhere in the country, other fine young writers were honing their skills covering baseball. Some of the greats who were regular beat writers in those days were Red Smith, Frank Graham, John Kieran, J. Roy Stockton, Warren Brown, John Carmichael, Shirley Povich, John Drebinger, and Tom Meany.

There was a coterie of writers in that era whose names were synonymous with baseball for the simple reason that they covered baseball from the first day of spring training until the final out of the World Series. A writer assigned to the Tigers or Cardinals or Pirates or any other club stayed with that team the entire season, traveled to the cities in each league, and made every road trip. Writers associated with one club were almost as well known as the players they wrote about.

Baseball coverage did not vary until after World War II. It was standard practice up to then for the writers on morning newspapers to wait until the end of the game and write on who won or lost, and how. The final score might not appear until well down into the story, but the reporter was writing up the details of the game. Writers for afternoon papers also often sat in the press box after the game and wrote their versions, with considerable editorial opinion and second-guessing. Talking to ballplayers after the game was not considered a necessity. Occasionally, but not always, writers did visit the clubhouses after games for some conversation and verification with ballplayers.

The style of writing changed after World War II. The need to know was of primary importance, and reporters for afternoon papers made it a habit to get down to the clubhouse after a game for what was then known as "the second-day angle." The afternoon papers of the next day had to offer the readers something they had not learned in their morning paper.

But starting in 1946 and in the years that followed, a change in the style of covering a baseball game was evident—especially in New York. No longer did the writers on afternoon papers have the ballplayers to themselves after a game. Dick Young was an enterprising young baseball writer for the New York *Daily News,* a morning newspaper. Because of the multiple editions of his newspaper, he had the time to visit the clubhouse and "pick up quotes" or find out why certain plays had occurred.

Young changed the style of baseball reporting with his hustle, and ever since he arrived, the work of the morning newspaper reporter has not been the same. No beat reporter nowadays would dare turn in a story unless it had clubhouse quotes. Editors demand it.

Along with the enterprise of Dick Young came radio and the television age. Fans were now able to listen to and watch games at home. What they wanted in their papers the next day was inside stuff from the players and managers. For reporters working night games with deadlines approaching, the job of writing baseball was no longer the sinecure it had been in the first four decades of the century.

Picture the baseball writer of the 1930s. All games started around 3 PM. There was no need for a pregame story, since most newspapers did not go to press until around midnight. A baseball writer in that era was finished working around 6 or 7 PM and was free again until game time the next day.

Today's baseball writer, what with virtually every game being played at night and early editions at all papers, finds himself working around the clock. The average writer covering baseball today, especially for a morning newspaper, will find himself writing three or four stories in a single day.

Night games and travel have also made it difficult for the modern-day writer. Before plane travel, all clubs moved from city to city by train, and the writers traveled with them. Trains left around midnight and arrived early the next morning in the team's next city. At least there was a night of rest and time to fraternize with the ballplayers. Today, teams fly out right after a game, and writers find it impossible to catch the team plane. They most often travel alone and must handle their own luggage, an added chore the earlier-day writers did not encounter.

The result is that fewer writers remain on the baseball beat for any length of time. The travel, the long hours, and the night games have made it an arduous task. Before the age of television, it was quite common for a writer to remain on the beat for twenty to thirty years. Today, a writer feels "burned out" after just a few years.

The baseball beat writer's job was always considered the glamour assignment on any sports staff. Baseball writers were envied for what was considered an easy lifestyle: spring training in some warm climate around the middle of February and then a ballgame every afternoon for six months followed by the World Series. From mid-October until mid-February, the baseball writer had a relative vacation, covering only signings, trades, and trivial matters.

The job of the baseball writer became even more difficult in the 1960s with the advent of the labor movement that created the Major League Baseball Players Association, the free agency that group won, and the proliferation of baseball players' agents. Whereas baseball was an eight-month-a-year job for writers before the union was formed, it is now a year-round chore.

The job suddenly became more demanding, wearying, and less glamorous. One New York tabloid in the mid-1980s was forced to change beat writers four times in five years. The deadline pressures and arduous travel schedule were too much.

Despite the constant changes, the BBWAA retains the prestige it earned shortly after being founded in 1908. Much of this is due to the organization's annual awards and its responsibility for voting on the Hall of Fame.

The major awards the BBWAA votes on each year are the Most Valuable Player, the Cy Young Award, the Rookie of the Year, the Manager of the Year, and the Hall of Fame, since the Cooperstown shrine's creation in 1936.

The idea of a Most Valuable Player Award was first devised by the Chalmers Motor Company of Detroit in 1911. The company abandoned the award after four years. In 1922 the American League resurrected the award, but it was not until two years later that the National League followed suit. By 1929, however, both leagues had quit their sponsorship.

At the December 11, 1930, meeting of the Baseball Writers Association, the group voted to make the Most

Valuable Player Award their official award. Three writers from each city in both the American and National Leagues were selected to vote. The first "official" winners selected by the BBWAA were announced in the fall of 1931. Since then, the BBWAA has voted on the award every year. In the late 1960s, the BBWAA copyrighted the award. In early years, *The Sporting News* awarded a trophy of sorts to the players selected by the BBWAA. At their 1944 meeting, the writers decided to make the award on their own and renamed the MVP trophy the Kenesaw Mountain Landis Award. The commissioner died one month later, but his name remains on the award to this day.

In 1955, Ford C. Frick, then the baseball commissioner, had the feeling that pitchers were not getting their just recognition—this despite the fact that five American League and six National League pitchers had already won the award. Frick, a former baseball writer himself, suggested that a new award be created honoring the best pitcher in baseball each year. There was to be one award to cover both leagues. Frick suggested it be called the Cy Young Award.

The writers went along with Frick. But in 1956, the first year of the award, Don Newcombe of the Brooklyn Dodgers not only won the Cy Young Award but also was recognized as the National League's Most Valuable Player.

After voting a singular award for eleven years, the BBWAA voted in 1967 to award the Cy Young in each league. Frick had expressed strong objection to the dual awards, but fifteen months after his retirement, it was approved by then-commissioner Will Eckert.

In 1947, after Jackie Robinson broke baseball's color barrier, the BBWAA decided to create a Rookie of the Year Award, naming Robinson as their first choice. The Chicago chapter of BBWAA had its own rookie award from 1940 to 1946 but dropped it when the entire association decided to sponsor an award for freshmen. At first, the writers voted for just one rookie in all of baseball. After Robinson was named in 1947 and Alvin Dark of the Boston Braves in 1948, the writers elected to choose a candidate from each league starting in 1949.

The Manager of the Year Award did not gain sanction from the BBWAA until 1983. Up to then, the Associated Press, the United Press International, and *The Sporting News* all had their own awards for managers. Often, three managers would be named. But the BBWAA Award is now considered the official Manager of the Year Award.

Of all the responsibilities of the Baseball Writers Association, none is taken more seriously than voting for the Hall of Fame. It is, perhaps, because more members participate and because of the honor accorded a player elected to Cooperstown. In the first election in 1936, 226 members voted. More than 450 members now vote in the annual January election.

The idea for a baseball Hall of Fame was first discussed in 1935 to celebrate the hundredth anniversary of baseball in 1939. The National Baseball Centennial Commission was formed. Ford Frick, then the National League president, was the moving force behind the creation of the Hall of Fame and the decision to name Cooperstown as the site for the museum. That same year, the Baseball Writers Association was asked by the Commission to vote for players to be elected to the Hall of Fame and inducted officially when the Hall opened in 1939.

The BBWAA has been charged with that responsibility ever since. Another group, known as the Veterans Committee, also votes on players, former executives, managers, and umpires.

Baseball, especially in recent years, has been the most written-about sport in America. No longer is it a sport covered solely by the beat writers for newspapers. It is a game that captures the imagination of authors, a fact born out by the Hall of Fame Library. By the middle of 1990, the library contained approximately 25,000 books about baseball.

It is a sport that has encouraged political columnists like George Will and Pulitzer Prize–winning authors like James Michener to publish books about the game. Statisticians like Bill James and Pete Palmer publish books annually with their own theories. The Elias Sports Bureau, statisticians for the major leagues, issue their own annual *Elias Baseball Analyst* edited by Seymour Siwoff and the Hirdt brothers, which tells you, among other things, that in 1989, only 29 percent of the fair balls Tony Pena hit to the outfield were pulled.

No sport in America is covered more extensively or comprehensively than baseball. It all begins with the game and the beat writers who cover it. Everyone else just wants to get in on the act.

Baseball on the Air

Paul D. Adomites

The story of broadcast baseball actually begins almost seventy years before the first game was aired. Baseball owners have always been of two minds about any fan interest that wasn't satisfied at the game itself. The common sentiment was "They'll stay home instead of coming to the game." Yet these outside sources generated extra income, and owners are businessmen first of all. As early as the 1860s, it was already clear that baseball sold newspapers, and newspapers sold baseball. Yet some owners feared "giving the game away."

The owners' schizophrenic response also occurred with telegraphy. Even though telegraph operators paid for the privilege of relaying game reports to saloons and poolrooms, a "hot debate" over whether this "free" sport was keeping people away from the parks led some owners to try to ban telegraph machines from their operations.

In 1897, each team received $300 worth of free telegrams on a league-wide contract, and some owners complained that it was hurting attendance. Sixteen years later, Western Union offered each team $17,000 a year for five years for the telegraph rights. It was hard for the owners to say no.

Even the fledgling motion picture industry got into the act, paying baseball $500 in 1910 for the rights to film and show the World Series. American League President Ban Johnson, who saw movies as competition, suggested that baseball ask for ten times as much for rights to film the 1911 Series, figuring that it would frighten the moviemen away. It didn't. However, baseball had to settle for only seven times what it had received the year before.

The point is obvious—baseball was far from being overexposed. Even though he was talking about telegraphy, John R. Tunis in 1923 pointed out the real value of broadcasting baseball. He described the World Series thrilling people in New Orleans, San Francisco, Honolulu, and even "an excited group of Mongolians in Seoul, the capital of Korea." The point is, advanced communications create fans *everywhere*, even thousands of miles from the parks.

Radio Days

The first major league game was broadcast over radio on August 5, 1921, from Pittsburgh, home of the Westinghouse Corporation, over the new Westinghouse station, KDKA. Harold Arlin, a Westinghouse foreman, announced the Pirates-Phillies contest from Forbes Field. Westinghouse was eager to make a name for itself in the new industry. The next day, Arlin broadcast the U.S.

Open tennis tournament, also near Pittsburgh. Two months later he did the first football broadcast.

That same year the first World Series broadcast was aired to a handful of fans on the East Coast. By 1922, the Series was heard "live by 5,000,000 people." Re-creations were heard by fans *on three continents*.

(Many of the early baseball broadcasts, and almost all away-game airings were re-created in a hometown radio studio, with announcers reading pitch-by-pitch information from ticker tapes, and using sound effects and canned crowd noises to simulate live action. In 1950, the Red Sox provided the first live coverage of all their away games. Within five years, major-league re-creations were antiques, as the teams were broadcasting all their games live. At the minor-league level, re-creation continued for away games into the 1960s.)

The first owner to see radio's promise to boost fan interest was the Cubs' boss Philip Wrigley. In 1925 he invited all the Chicago radio stations to carry all the Cubs' games. No charge. Sam Breadon, the Cardinals' owner, followed suit soon thereafter, in the first two attempts to develop regional followings.

In 1926 and 1927 the first great national radio networks began operation: NBC and CBS. This was the beginning of radio's golden era. Sales of radio equipment, a $60 million industry in 1922, were nearly a billion dollars in 1929.

Yet many owners were still wary. By the 1930s, the two-team cities of Boston, Philadelphia, St. Louis, and Chicago had an agreement not to broadcast away games. In other words, if the Braves were at home, you could hear *their* game on the radio, but not the Red Sox. The owners' wail ("they won't come to the park if you give the game away") seemed turned on its logical head under this arrangement, but home radio is where you ballyhoo home-game attendance, which was the concern, anyway.

The New York owners went one step further. In 1932 they agreed to ban all radio, even visitors' re-creations, from their parks.

Larry MacPhail took over the Reds in 1933 and sold a controlling interest in the club to Powel Crosley, owner of two Cincinnati radio stations. It was a match made in economic heaven: MacPhail knew that broadcasting games would promote the team (he hired southerner Red Barber as his announcer), Crosley now could boost his radio ratings. The mutuality was akin to Chris von der Ahe, the St. Louis beer garden magnate, taking over the St. Louis club in the American Association in order to sell more beer.

Then, when MacPhail moved to Brooklyn in 1938, he

brought Red Barber with him, and broke the New York ban. The next year was the first year that all the teams in the major leagues broadcast their games. Prophetically, it was also the year of the first *televised* baseball game.

In 1935, Judge Landis moved in to orchestrate the radio deal to cover the World Series. All three networks were involved, and baseball made $400,000. Landis, as ever, was imperious; he dismissed Ted Husing as announcer of the games, even though with five World Series under his belt, Ted was second only to the ubiquitous Graham MacNamee in Series-announcing experience.

The money for baseball broadcasting was growing. Gillette, the razor blade manufacturer, one of the first companies to realize the power of sports as an advertising vehicle, tried to flex their muscles by offering Red Barber a substantial amount to walk out on his Dodger contract to join Gillette on a new Yankees/Giants network. Barber refused. It's no wonder Gillette felt powerful; in 1946 they were rich enough to sign a ten-year deal for exclusive radio sponsorship of the World Series and All-Star Games, for $14 million.

But the World Series was the exception; otherwise, baseball remained locally dominated. However, in 1950, Gordon McLendon changed all that, when he founded a new radio network, one with daily baseball as its centerpiece: the Liberty Broadcasting System. His announcers re-created a game every day, plus extras on weekends. McLendon charged the stations $10 per game, and enrolled 300 of them. He paid his announcers $27.50 a week, netting himself a weekly profit of over $2,970.

But once again the moguls of baseball feared too much free publicity. A rule banned the Game of the Day from many areas because there were fears that it might conflict with local broadcasts within a 75-mile area.

The paradoxical result, according to Curt Smith, was "If you lived in Butte, Montana, or Amarillo, Texas, you got to hear every club in baseball," as many as ten games a week. But if you lived in a major league town (or near one), you could hear only the locals, and only when the club decided the broadcasts wouldn't "interfere" with attendance. McLendon's gold mine didn't last long: he lost a suit against baseball and folded. Yet the Mutual Broadcasting Network mimicked his strategy and succeeded.

In 1951 Liberty broadcast more than 200 games, almost 600 hours of baseball; Mutual did 145 games. That amount of time was more than quadruple the amount of total network time (via television and radio) that baseball would receive in *1984*. More importantly, the Liberty/Mutual style set a pattern for successful TV coverage years later.

TV or Not TV

Baseball on television began to take hold in the late 1950s. The Yankees were the first team to sell their TV rights (in 1946, for $75,000; in 1987 the Yankees earned 250 times as much for their TV rights). The first televised World Series was the memorable 1947 set. Harry Coyle, the NBC dean of baseball producers, was there. In Chicago, Jack Brickhouse was announcing White Sox telecasts in 1948.

By 1950 the World Series was televised as far west as Omaha; 38 million watched. The next year World Series baseball television reached the West Coast. (Radio still had strengths: the 1953 Brooklyn Dodgers Radio Network linked 117 stations, making the Bums the first "America's Team.")

The era of baseball broadcasting that began in 1953 should have opened the owners' eyes to the future, but it didn't. That year the first televised Game of the Week began (then on ABC). Naturally, it was banned from all major league cities. (Does this sound familiar?) Yet with the irrepressible Dizzy Dean at the microphone, it rolled up incredible ratings anyway: 11.4 percent of all households with sets, 51 percent of all sets in use. That translated to 75 percent of all sets in use not in big league cities.

And there was no doubt that the colorful Diz, with his demented grammar, malapropisms, and ambling yarn-weaving, *was* the program. In 1955, a slick advertising agency move landed the Game of the Week for CBS, and Curt Smith says, "the most transforming baseball series in television's show of shows . . . was born." Two years later a group of Sunday games was added to the schedule. Baseball was on its way to becoming the *truly* national game; the owners just felt they could do it without the help of the fans in the cities where the teams played.

Television was becoming a national mania. By 1955 only three teams didn't televise (the Braves, Pirates, and A's). On the other hand, the Cubs, Dodgers, Yankees, and Giants broadcast every home game, the Indians and Cards every road game. The Reds televised all weekday afternoon home games; the Phillies showed 29 home and 27 road games; Baltimore showed 65 contests; even the Red Sox and Senators had TV on their schedule; six stations in Michigan showed 42 Tigers games; WGN televised every day game from Comiskey Park.

Then came football. The upstart NFL (and their very wise leader Pete Rozelle) realized that TV was the way to *build* fan interest. Baseball's less progressive owners still feared "giving it away," preferring local/regional efforts. As Harold Rosenthal explains, "Football fans were sold as National Football League fans—network television made them that way . . . In Appleton, Wisconsin, a guy would turn on the tube and watch the Giants play the Browns . . . Baseball fans were brought up to follow the Cardinals or Giants or Tigers . . . the local coverage mattered, the local announcer."

When the NFL signed an immense contract with TV in the early 1960s, guaranteeing coverage, with all the NFL teams sharing the wealth, baseball wanted to copy the plan. They asked for millions, but they didn't get it.

What baseball got was the ABC Game of the Week: 28 telecasts a season; each of the clubs receiving $300,000. Curt Smith explains the upshot: "By 1966, instead of watching as many as 123 games on three networks, a majority of American viewers could behold only 28 telecasts on one network." The "common good" policy was a mistake, but baseball couldn't figure this out. They changed networks, to NBC, and we got a new announcer.

"Curt Gowdy emerged for an entire generation of listeners as the national signature of baseball broadcasting. From 1966 through 1975, he called play-by-play for every All-Star Game, every World Series game, and virtually every regular season network game" (Curt Smith). And that list doesn't even include Gowdy's work on seven Super Bowls, seven Olympic Games, twelve NCAA basketball championships, 13 Rose Bowls, the Pan Am Games, and twenty years of "The American Sportsman."

But Curt couldn't bring in the ratings; his highest regular season rating was still two full points below Dizzy Dean's first year (and remember, Dizzy wasn't allowed into any major league markets), and it dropped 15 percent by 1970; Curt's World Series ratings fell by nearly 20 percent, though it was certainly no fault of his own. Solid, professional, and competent, he was just never exciting. People never talked about him as they did about Dizzy or other announcers. And he was definitely overexposed.

Meanwhile football was coming on strong. In 1969 pro football televised three times as many games on network TV as baseball. (Three times!) By 1969 not even all the baseball postseason games were broadcast nationally. The NFL wasn't just growing; they were promoting. Their highlight films featured thrilling action, rich drama, and the golden voice of orator John Facenda.

Baseball, it was clear to everyone in the national press, was losing the battle. "Baseball is dead" was a cliché. A Lou Harris poll showed that football was now Americans' favorite sport. More importantly, another Harris poll showed how baseball's popularity paralleled the degree of its TV coverage. Where the big leagues were most heavily covered, baseball was most popular. Where fans received only network coverage, baseball ranked lowest.

But Commissioner Bowie Kuhn had something to say about the matter; he pushed for World Series night games (the first was in 1971) because they could attract a much larger audience. And while you could cynically dismiss this move as pure economics (bigger viewership means more advertising dollars), it worked.

In 1975 baseball announced a new kind of TV deal: Alternating coverage of the World Series, playoffs and All-Star Games between NBC and ABC. The networks saw the advantages: postseason baseball play was the perfect time to begin promoting the new fall TV season. The alternating feature built in an element of competition without economic overtones: quality of coverage.

Then came October 21, 1975. The Boston Red Sox, unable to win a World Series since 1918, were on their way to a loss in six games to Cincinnati's "Big Red Machine." But a three-run pinch-hit homer by Bernie Carbo tied the game in the eighth, and in the twelfth (by now it was 12:34 A.M.), Carlton Fisk hit a solo shot over the Green Monster to win the game. A total of 62 million people saw it, and television couldn't have planned it better, because as Fisk hit his homer, the camera in the left field scoreboard followed *him*, not the ball, and on replay the audience saw Fisk furiously trying to wave the ball fair: the first-ever home run reaction shot.

The next night, 75,890,000 people watched the seventh game, and baseball was definitely back. In 1976, baseball received revenue from radio and television near $51 million. Lou Harris said in 1977: "For the first time since 1968, more sports fans in the country follow baseball than football." Ten years later baseball received $350 million.

And 1977 is also the year that cable television broadcasts began to have their impact. The situation was analogous to the Liberty/Mutual networks' Game of the Day, or the Dizzy Dean/CBS Game of the Week. Now fans all over the country could see a lot of baseball, every day. By 1982, cable TV was in 35 percent of all American homes; in 1987 it passed the 50 percent mark.

Superstations like Ted Turner's Atlanta TBS, Chicago's WGN, and New York's WWOR and WPIX, along with the all-sports network, ESPN, were giving fans more baseball on a regular basis than they had ever had before. In 1986 Cubs' games were viewed by 20 million fans. For his definitive history, *Voices of the Game,* Curt Smith interviewed Cub fans in Kodiak, Alaska; Costa Rica; and Boise, Idaho—all because of Harry Caray's calls on the Chicago superstation. A Peter Ueberroth–inspired change in the rules to make superstations give the other teams a certain amount of money per viewer passed over Ted Turner's noisy objections. Sports-only premium cable networks have failed in several places, largely due to the availability of the "free" (part of the basic cable charge) coverage.

Even though the superstation teams do not benefit directly, in cash income, from sending their games around the country, (their parent corporations do, of course . . .), they do help to promote interest in baseball as a whole. (For example, every Atlanta Braves game can be seen in 48 percent of U.S. households, yet in 1987 the Braves' broadcast rights earned them the same as the Pittsburgh Pirates, whose five-station network reached as far as Johnstown.) As Harry Caray says, "We've made the Cubs part of their lives; they have to be interested." The point is clear: baseball has not yet reached a saturation point on television. The fears of baseball owners that *too much* would keep people away haven't come true, despite 140 years of worrying.

And neither has the oft-stated fear described by noted historian Harold Seymour in 1971: "Although gate receipts are still the lifeblood of the industry, television receipts have swelled steadily in recent years . . . There are even those who go so far as to predict that eventually television income will supplant gate receipts, and the teams will perform quietly among themselves in deserted stadiums for TV audiences."

By the late '80s, the advertising industry was announcing that the era of megabuck sports TV packages was over; advertisers just didn't have enough money to pay for them. What the ad pundits didn't realize was the value that network TV saw in televising the League Championship series and World Series—prime vehicles for introducing their new fall lineup. When time came to renegotiate a national TV package, NBC (which had carried the Saturday Game of the Week for years) and ABC (which had carried some Monday night games and alternated LCS and Series with NBC) were both outslugged at the bargaining table by third-rated CBS.

CBS's deal for a handful of Saturday games plus all postseason play was for $1.1 billion over four years. ESPN kicked in another $400 million for the same period of time, and each team became instantly richer to the tune of $14 million a year, plus change. The result was felt instantly on the field. Free-agency outrageousness reached new heights, as the $3 Million Man was created, then surpassed. When the owners tried to claim poverty at the 1990 labor negotiations, the players scoffed. And the average player increased his annual wealth by $70,000 overnight.

Baseball Collecting

Barry Halper with Bill Madden

In the early 1970s baseball began to take on a new dimension—one that would transform the hobby of a dedicated few into a national phenomenon and, incidentally, a multimillion dollar industry.

The game's first century did not produce many collectors of baseball memorabilia. Oh, sure, there were a few baseball cards as early as the 1860s and extensive sets by the 1880s; even in the game's infancy there was always that legion of autograph-seekers waiting outside the players' gate at any given ballpark. But the cards were seldom saved (as evidenced by the scarcity today of early cards, even those produced in great quantities in the 1950s) and the autographs were a fancy of one's idol-worshiping days. There were no prices attached to such mementos of youthful infatuation, just as there was no business of collecting.

But then, in 1967, a man by the name of Jefferson Burdick published *The American Card Catalog*—a guide listing the origin, description, and estimated value of every card (baseball or otherwise) ever printed. It was a monumental volume, which took years of painstaking research. What his catalog did was to transform the informal and undocumented hobby of baseball card collecting into the more elevated and established rank of stamp and coin collecting. Prices and values, scarcity and condition—these commercial considerations, once they were applied to cards, quickly moved into just about anything associated with baseball: autographs, bats, balls, uniforms, photos, press pins, chinaware, publications, you name it.

Cards

In the beginning, though, there were the cards, and today they remain at the center of the baseball collecting hobby.

The most extensive early card set (it remains the largest ever issued, with 520 players in one to seventeen variants each!) was the Old Judge Cigarette Brand series of 1887–89, catalogued by Burdick as N172. These insert cards were really photographs mounted on board, in the same manner as the *cartes de visite* that were all the rage in the 1860s. In terms of interest today, however, the most popular early baseball card set was the 1909–11 tobacco issue that Burdick catalogued as the T206. These 523 cards, approximately 2¼ by 1½ inches, were inserted in packages of Sweet Caporal, Piedmont, Sovereign, Cycle, and assorted other cigarette brands of the American Tobacco Company.

Included in that T206 set are two of the most valuable cards in the history of collecting—the Honus Wagner and the Eddie Plank. Both cards are extremely rare for different reasons. According to legend Wagner, a nonsmoker, became incensed when he discovered that his picture on a card was being used to promote smoking. As a result, he ordered that his card be removed from the T206 set. (Evidently, though, he must have had a change of heart years later, as he is depicted in the 1948 Leaf Gum card set with at least two packs of chewing tobacco stuffed in his jaw.) Today, there are believed to be no more than twenty-five or so T206 Wagner cards in existence. The Plank card is believed to be equally as rare—a result of the printing plates for it having been accidentally destroyed back in 1909.

Burdick, acknowledging the scarcity of both cards, lists the Wagner card's value at $50 and the Plank card at $10. The rest of the T206s are listed at ten cents apiece. Today, the common T206 lists at $30 mint, a Plank at $15,000, and the Wagner at $100,000.

Besides the T206s, the most popular early lithographed tobacco cards then and today are the 1887–88 Allen & Ginters (N28, N29, and N43) and the 1911 T3 Turkey Reds. The Allen & Ginters maintain their value and popularity from their sheer beauty. The same size as the T206s, the N28 and N29 series were magnificent watercolor paintings of baseball players, printed on glossy stock. The N28 is generally considered the first of the tobacco card baseball sets and it includes ten players, among them Hall of Famers Cap Anson, John Clarkson, Charles Comiskey, King Kelly, John Montgomery Ward, and Tim Keefe. The N29, or second series, adds six players, among them Hall of Famer Buck Ewing. The Anson card is the most expensive today, listing at $800 mint. Burdick listed the average Allen & Ginter card at ten cents.

The T3s are classified as cabinet cards in that they measured a much larger 5¾ by 8 inches in size and were obtained by sending in coupons found in Turkey Red, Fez, and Old Mill brand cigarettes. They, too, are beautiful cards, depicting players in full-color portraits. All told, there are 100 baseball players in the Turkey Red set of 126 athletes, averaging $150 for commons and considerably more for Hall of Famers (Ty Cobb lists at $2,800). In 1967 Burdick listed the price of T3s at $1 apiece.

In the 1930s the tobacco companies gave way to the gum and confectionery companies as the prime dispensers of baseball cards. The most prominent of those companies was the Goudey Gum Company, which issued significant sets in 1933–41. These cards, like all the gum/confectionery cards of the 1930–50 era, measured 2½ by 3¼ inches.

The most popular of all the Goudey sets is still its initial 1933, effort which was comprised of 240 cards including one of the rarest of all, No. 106, Napoleon Lajoie. For some reason, the Lajoie card was inadvertently omitted from the original 1933 Goudey set, and when collectors inquired about the absence of card No. 106, the company offered it as a premium the following year. As a result, the few Lajoie cards that exist today contain the 1934 Goudey card design. Burdick listed the common R319 1933 Goudeys at twenty cents apiece and the Lajoie at a dollar. Today, the commons list at $33, the numerous Hall of Famers in the set at $100 and upwards, and the Lajoie at $30,000.

In 1939, Gum Inc. of Boston entered the baseball card field, issuing the first of its three Play Ball sets. The 1939 and '40 Play Balls were sepia toned, while the 1941 went to color. The 72-card 1941 Play Ball set is the most popular of the three, listing at $5,000 in mint condition. It also features the first color cards of Joe DiMaggio (mint today $1,000) and Ted Williams ($850).

World War II prompted a shutdown of the baseball card industry, and it did not renew production until 1948, when the Chicago-based Leaf Company issued its 168-card set of colorized photo cards with gum. That Leaf set, which contains a number of less-distributed cards, lists at $13,000 in mint condition today, the DiMaggio and Babe Ruth cards listing at $500 each, and the Satchel Paige, because of its alleged scarcity, at $800.

In 1950 the Bowman Gum Company of Philadelphia displaced Leaf as the number one baseball card manufacturers. They remained atop the field until 1952, when the Topps Gum Company of Brooklyn began making big inroads into this burgeoning industry. Topps, which began modestly with two fifty-two-card sets in 1951, as well as a pair of now extremely valuable premium sets called Connie Mack and Current All Stars, broke historical ground in 1952 when it issued a 407-card set.

The 1952 Topps remains the Holy Grail of modern-day card sets for collectors, if only because of the difficulty in completing it. Cards number 311–407, it seems, were issued late in the year by Topps and reportedly only in the New York area and Canada. As a result, they are considerably harder to find. Burdick listed the 1952 Topps from 1 to 310 at ten cents apiece and 311 to 407 at thirty cents in 1967.

But making that final series even more valuable is the fact that Topps included many of the game's superstars of that year in it, including Mickey Mantle, Jackie Robinson, Pee Wee Reese, Bobby Thomson, Eddie Mathews, and Roy Campanella. All of them list today at over $1,000 mint, and the Mantle card, number 311, at $7,000–$10,000, is considered the *pièce de résistance* of all modern-day baseball cards. The 311–407 commons list at $150 apiece.

When Jefferson Burdick published his *American Card Catalog*, baseball card collecting was limited to just that—collecting. It was not until the mid-'70s, when card values began to be known nationwide, that baseball card shows and flea markets began to crop up across the country. Prior to that, there had been only a small network of what could be considered hard-core baseball card collectors: Frank Nagy of Detroit, Buck Barker of St. Louis, myself, and a few others would trade cards among our-

selves. There was never any selling of cards within that network, although on many occasions the trading would branch into other fields, such as trading an autograph for a suitable card or cards.

All in all, in 1972, there were about ten card dealers who would meet once a month in New York on Friday nights. No money ever changed hands. It was strictly trading.

A couple of years later, however, the hobby began to grow and groups of dealers began putting together once- or twice-a-year baseball card conventions in church basements around New York City and, soon, other large cities. These conventions served to arouse the public interest in baseball cards, rekindling the childhoods of many whose cards had long since been thrown away. As the demand for old cards increased and the prices of them quickly began to rise accordingly, the church basement card shows evolved into much larger productions held in hotels, convention centers, and even ballparks.

As an added attraction for these larger baseball card shows, promoters began bringing in old-time and current ballplayers to sign autographs at a modest price. From that was born the phenomenon that exists today: spectacular baseball card/autograph shows in which as many as ten or twelve Hall of Famers can be found signing autographs at upwards of $10 per item.

Autographs

For the longest time, baseball autographs were something to be personally treasured but not necessarily valued. No one, for instance, put a value on a Babe Ruth autograph even twenty years after the Babe's death. For one thing, a Ruth autograph was still one of the most common of all Hall of Famer autographs, simply because the Babe signed willingly for everyone he came in contact with. A Lou Gehrig, by contrast, was not nearly as common, although until the advent of the autograph-collecting boom—which occurred at the same time the baseball card boom hit in the mid 1970s—collectors paid little notice.

Today Ruth, simply because of who he was and what he is to baseball, remains one of the most sought-after and high-priced baseball autographs. Of the living players, Joe DiMaggio is still commanding top dollar on the autograph circuit, with Mickey Mantle and Willie Mays not far behind. But as autograph collectors will testify, it is the turn-of-the-century Hall of Famers such as Pud Galvin, Tommy McCarthy, King Kelly, John Clarkson, Roger Connor, Candy Cummings, and Cap Anson whose signatures rightfully command the highest prices. These are players who have been dead for well over sixty years and whose autographs are far more scarce than a Ruth, Gehrig, or Ty Cobb.

Perhaps the best way to sum up the modern-day baseball autograph craze is to recall an incident at the 1980 New York Yankees annual Old Timer's Day game. As usual, all the Yankee living legends, from Joe DiMaggio to Mickey Mantle, Yogi Berra, and Whitey Ford, were on hand for the occasion and, accordingly, were besieged throughout the day for autographs. Reggie Jackson, the Yankees' star right fielder at the time, was attempting—

at least for public consumption—to express dismay at all the autograph badgering around him. "I don't understand all this idolatry," Reggie told the assembled writers. The next day, however, in the New York *Daily News* coverage of the Old Timer's Day festivities, there was a picture of Reggie Jackson—getting an autograph on a baseball from Joe DiMaggio.

Press Pins

Press pins from the World Series, the All Star Game, and Hall of Fame induction ceremonies are about the only baseball collectibles that are totally separated from the players themselves. They have nothing to do with the actual games themselves, other than being displayed on the sports coats of attending sportswriters, and they can't be autographed. Nevertheless, in conjunction with the baseball collecting boom of the 1970s and '80s, press pins have become among the most sought after (and subsequently highly valued) memorabilia items.

The origin of the baseball press pin dates back to 1911. According to legend John McGraw, manager of the New York Giants, had invited many of his cronies to attend the hotly contested games of September 1908. However, because of the scarcity of tickets, McGraw assigned his friends seats in the press box, where they became rowdy, distracting the members of the working press.

It was because of this unwelcome intrusion into their working domain that the Baseball Writers Association of America was formed. And as a part of this new union, press pins were used to establish proper identity for the World Series, when every seat was spoken for. No one was permitted into the press boxes without a press pin.

As years went on, press accreditation for the World Series became far more sophisticated, but the press pins continued to be a tradition. Each World Series team designed its own press pin for the games in its ballpark and though most sportswriters kept their pins through the years, they didn't look at them as valuable collectibles. Again, it was not until the early 1970s, when collectors began to realize how genuinely scarce all those old press pins were (because of limited distribution and the fact that so many of them were thrown away through the years) that they suddenly became a valued baseball collectible.

The earliest press pins are now valued at upwards of $10,000 apiece. But even the press pins from the 1940s, '50s, and '60s have considerable value. Of these, the most valued of all the World Series pins is that of the 1956 Brooklyn Dodgers—primarily because it isn't a pin at all; it's a tie clasp. For some reason, that year the Dodgers chose to break tradition and issue to the working press tie clasps with a blue Brooklyn cap affixed to it. Probably because the tie clasps were actually worn by the writers long after the Series was over (instead of being stuffed away in a drawer with all the old press pins), a good many of the tie clasps vanished from the scene. As a result, today the Brooklyn Dodgers 1956 World Series tie clasp has commanded as much as $3,000 in collectors' markets as opposed to the $300 that the 1956 New York Yankees World Series press pin generally sells for.

In 1937 baseball extended its press pin tradition to the All Star Game and those pins, too, have risen greatly in value. (The reason no press pins were issued prior to 1937 is that the All Star Game's creator and founder, sportswriter Arch Ward, had envisioned his "gala" as being a one-time event. (Actually, even the 1937 pin, from Griffith Stadium in Washington, may, in fact, be a one-of-a-kind item since only the one in the Halper collection is known to exist.)

The prices of All Star press pins vary greatly, based primarily on the issuing city. One of the hardest-to-find All Star press pins—and consequently one of the most sought-after and most prized—is the 1948 pin issued by the host St. Louis Browns. It is a beautiful pin depicting the white Brownies cap with the brown bill and gold piping; it is dated 1948, and it lists for upwards of $2,500.

Finally, in 1982, the Hall of Fame got into the press pin field. Beginning that year the Hall of Fame issued commemorative press pins, listing the names of each year's inductees. Because there is a far more limited number of media personnel covering the Hall of Fame ceremonies, the distribution of the pins is believed to be about one-tenth that of the World Series pins. As a result, the Hall of Fame pins have quickly shot past their contemporary World Series and All Star pins in value. That first Hall of Fame pin in 1982, engraved with the names of inductees Hank Aaron, Happy Chandler, Frank Robinson, and Travis Jackson, was going for $650 in the collectors' market.

In the early years of press pins, the Dieges & Clust Company of John Street in New York was the primary manufacturer. In 1946 the Balfour Company of Attleboro, Massachusetts, assumed the contract from Major League Baseball to produce the pins. They remain the prime producers of pins and rings for the World Series and All Star Game, although some teams have, in the interest of cost-cutting, sought local companies to produce their pins (the workmanship of those pins, particularly the colors and the enamel, has suffered noticeably).

The advent of the playoff system also caused economic problems for the contending clubs that were compelled to commission press pins. It had long been the custom of clubs to date the pins for each year's World Series. In many cases, though, the club would not make it to the Series and those press pins produced for the event were rendered unusable for any future Series. As such, these so-called "phantom" pins, such as the 1951 Brooklyn Dodgers (who lost out in a playoff to the Giants on Bobby Thomson's historic home run), the 1938 Pittsburgh Pirates (victims of the Cubs' Gabby Hartnett's memorable "homer in the gloamin'"), or the 1949 Cardinals are harder to come by and just as valuable as the "official" Series press pins of those years.

As John Scarpellini, Balfour's longtime representative to baseball recalled: "The elimination of the dating of the pins came about when Dick O'Connell, general manager of the Red Sox, was asked by us about the kind of press pin he wanted designed for the 1975 World Series. Instead of committing himself, O'Connell opened up a closet door in his office and produced what had to be nearly 50,000 press pins. 'Look at these,' he said. 'They're all dated and therefore no good to us. I've got all these pins, which we've paid for, and we can't do anything with them.'

"After that, we came up with the idea of labeling the pins with the phrase 'Our Second World Series' or whatever number that particular World Series was for that particular team. That way, if the club was beaten out in the playoffs, but had already had to produce their pins, they could just put them away in a vault and use them whenever they made it."

Uniforms

In the entire spectrum of baseball collecting there is probably no item more personal or intimate than a uniform. Unfortunately, the collecting of uniforms from modern-day players has oftentimes become a risky venture because of the increase in counterfeits on the market. Because the modern-day doubleknits are so easy to manufacture, it is very difficult to tell a counterfeit from the real thing. That's why the source of such uniforms is so important.

More often than not, the source for legitimate modern-day uniforms is the clubhouse man for the major league ballclubs. This, of course, has created a serious problem for Major League Baseball. They are aware of how little clubhouse men are paid and, as such, how they can become easy prey for dealers in baseball memorabilia.

In some cases, the players themselves can be sources for uniforms. Pete Rose, for example, reportedly had a deal with the Cincinnati Reds that he be given twenty-five or more uniforms during the course of the season to do with as he wished. And in the game in which Rose tied Ty Cobb's all-time hits record, he wore a different uniform top for each at bat. Presumably, Rose sold all those uniform tops to different collectors.

Similarly, Gaylord Perry, in winning his 300th game against the New York Yankees, wore two different Seattle Mariner uniforms. The reason I know that is that Perry had promised his uniform from that game to me. But a couple of days before he pitched, I got a call from the visiting clubhouse man in Baltimore, who was also a dealer in memorabilia. The clubhouse man offered me Perry's Seattle uniform from his 300th-win game. It seems that Gaylord had decided that two uniforms were better than one when it came to maximizing his profit on 300 wins, and he decided to make a change after four innings. I wound up having to make separate deals with both Perry and the clubhouse man from Baltimore in order to have what was surely the uniform in which Perry won his 300th game.

The values of modern-day players' uniforms vary greatly. Naturally, the uniforms players wore performing historic feats such as Perry's 300th win or Rose's 4,192nd hit (both of which are in the Halper collection) are of considerably more value than just an everyday game-worn uniform. In the uniform-collecting hobby of the '90s, common players' uniforms were selling in the $200 range, star-quality players' from $750 to $1,200, and superstar/Hall of Fame–caliber players' from $2,000 up.

Old-time uniforms are a far more challenging hobby, one that has been the most satisfying and exciting aspect of my collecting career. Why? Because I never believed so many of these old uniforms, particularly the ones from the pre-1900 Hall of Fame players, could still exist. And exist

in such remarkable condition! Through the years, I have managed to amass some 964 uniforms, which I have stored on a dry cleaner conveyer belt that is computerized to stop at whichever uniform number I punch in. Included among those 964 are uniforms of every Hall of Famer who played or managed, and even some minor league uniforms of Hall of Fame executives (such as longtime Yankee business manager Ed Barrow) who never wore a major league uniform.

As one might expect, values for the oldest, turn-of-the-century uniforms far exceed those for any of the more recent Hall of Famers of the '30s on up. I have had values in excess of $100,000 each placed on uniforms of Babe Ruth, Lou Gehrig, and Ty Cobb—all autographed—in my collection. But I could not even begin to put a value on the uniforms of turn-of-the-century Hall of Famers such as Pud Galvin (Buffalo, 1879), John Clarkson (Saginaw, 1883), King Kelly (NY Giants, 1893), Charles Comiskey (Cincinnati, 1893), Hoss Radbourn (Boston, 1886), Roger Connor (NY Giants, 1893), Joe McGinnity (NY Giants, 1904), and Cy Young (Boston, 1903)—most of which are almost certain to be the only ones worn by those players that still survive.

The existence of these uniforms only adds to and rounds out the lore and history of baseball. How they were uncovered after all these years—the treasure hunt—is the most fulfilling aspect of collecting baseballiana.

It was during a conversation I once had with Pete Sheehy, the venerable New York Yankee clubhouse man from the days of Ruth in the '20s right up until the Don Mattingly–Dave Winfield Yankees of the '80s, that I got my most valuable tip in regard to uniform collecting. I asked Sheehy: "Pete, where are all the Pete Sheehys of yesterday? The clubhouse men who kept a vigil over all the old uniforms?"

Not surprisingly, in his days as Yankee clubhouse man, Sheehy did become friends with the clubhouse men from other clubs and they would correspond frequently. Most of his contemporaries had died when I talked to him about this, but he kept track of many of their relatives.

One person Sheehy put me in contact with was a man from Coxsackie, New York, who, Sheehy thought, was in possession of most of the old Yankee uniforms from 1927, the year of Murderers' Row. Sure enough, upon getting in touch with the man, I was able to acquire the 1927 Yankee uniforms of Ruth, Gehrig, Earle Combs, Waite Hoyt, Bob Meusel, Mark Koenig, Bob Shawkey, and about a half dozen others. Sheehy also put me in contact with the relatives of the equipment manager at Columbia University during the early '20s when Gehrig played there. It was through that contact that I was able to uncover Gehrig's Columbia uniform and the first uniform he ever wore as a professional, with Hartford. He had played there under the assumed name of Lewis in 1921 to protect his amateur standing at Columbia; that name is sewn into the bottom flap of the shirt.

All the uniforms from that pre-1920s period are identified by the players' names sewn somewhere on them since numbers did not come into existence until 1929. The Yankees that year introduced numbers on the backs of their uniforms in the order in which the players appeared in the batting order.

Another valuable source of old uniforms was Dick Bartell, the pepperpot New York Giants and Detroit Tigers shortstop of the 1930s and '40s. Bartell put me in touch with Ollie O'Mara, an old ballplayer, then in his 80s, who lived in Reno, Nevada. O'Mara had had a brief major league career with the Brooklyn Dodgers from 1914 to 1919, a team that was managed by Hall of Famer Wilbert Robinson. Apparently O'Mara had maintained a close friendship with Robinson. That is the only explanation I can offer for the fact that he had in his possession the 1894 Baltimore Orioles uniforms of Robinson, Joe Kelley, Wee Willie Keeler, Dan Brouthers, and Hughie Jennings—Hall of Famers all. O'Mara never did tell me how he got the uniforms or why he had kept them all those years in near-perfect condition. In 1989 he went to his grave with that secret, but baseball historians can be forever grateful that he preserved so much of the game's valuable past.

Bats, Balls, Books

Until recent years vintage bats, balls, gloves, and other gear were a neglected area for collectors. One could find an antique glove or ball in a thrift store or flea market for just a few dollars; without an autograph or major-league player "association," the items were simply not viewed as desirable. The same could be said of baseball books and photos, though scorecards, guides (Spalding, Reach, Beadle, etc.), yearbooks, and programs—especially World Series programs— did attract collectors before the 1980s baseball-card boom.

A handful of early-baseball enthusiasts, myself included, picked up as many of these early items as we could, from club constitutions of the amateur era to thick-handled bats with "mushroom" knobs, from gold-painted trophy balls of the 1860s to sepia-toned photographs of unknown teams. These sorts of items increased in value over the years but not as spectacularly as, say, the cards of the 1950s. Where a 1952 Mickey Mantle card, of which may fine examples exist, might fetch $8,000, a genuinely rare 1868 book by Henry Chadwick might bring only $3,000. However, as card prices continued to soar sophisticated collectors and devoted fans who have been made nervous by the explosive speculation of the 1980s are beginning to see relative safety in the pursuit of older collectibles, where "the market" is driven by true scarcity more than widespread demand.

Despite dire predictions of a collapse in the market, I remain convinced that collecting baseball memorabilia is a hobby that is still in its infancy. Prices may go up or down with general economic conditions, but the lure of baseball and its collectibles is a constant.

PART TWO

Introduction

Part Two, the statistical section of *Total Baseball*, presents the record of major league contests played from 1871 through 1990—all 152,499 of them. It details the accomplishments of the game's 2,073 teams and 13,490 players more completely and more accurately than any other encyclopedic work; it applies to all of baseball's glorious past the "sabermetric" stats that fans first embraced in the 1980s; it introduces original measures of player performance. Yet for all its innovation, *Total Baseball* stands squarely in the tradition of baseball record keeping; it is—like each new spring of our national pastime—a link in a long, long chain. As the game of one hundred and fifty years ago lives on in the game of today, so is this volume enriched by the labors of statisticians from Henry Chadwick to Ernie Lanigan, from S. C. Thompson to David Neft to Bill James.

The Origins, 1845–1875

In fact, baseball and stats were a tandem from the outset of the game's history, as the editors of this volume first discussed in their earlier *Hidden Game of Baseball* (1984), from which portions of this introduction are adapted. The first box score appeared in the *New York Morning News* on October 22, 1845, just a month after Alexander Cartwright and his Knickerbocker teammates codified the first set of rules. Why did these early players and scribes measure individual performance rather than simply count the score? In part to imitate the custom of cricket; yet the larger explanation is that the numbers served to legitimize men's concern with a boys' pastime. The pioneers of baseball reporting—William Cauldwell of the *Sunday Mercury*, William Porter of *Spirit of the Times*, the unknown annalist at the *News*, and later Henry Chadwick—may indeed have reflected that if they did not cloak the game in the "importance" of statistics, it might not seem worthwhile for adults to read about, let alone play. Statistics elevated baseball from other boys' field games of the 1840s and '50s to make it somehow "serious," like business; its essential simplicity was adorned with intricate detail that suited it perfectly to quantification.

In the development of baseball statistics, no man is more important than Father Chadwick. Born in England in 1824, he came to these shores at age thirteen steeped in the tradition of cricket. In his teens he played the English game and in his twenties he reported on it for a variety of newspapers, including the *Long Island Star* and the *New York Times*. In the early 1840s, before the Knickerbocker rules eliminated the practice of retiring a base runner by throwing the ball at him rather than to the base, Chadwick occasionally played baseball too, but he was not favorably impressed, having received "some hard hits in the ribs." Not until 1856, by which time he had been a cricket reporter for a decade, were Chadwick's eyes opened to the possibilities in the American game, which had improved dramatically since his youth. In 1868 he recalled, "On returning from the early close of a cricket match on Fox Hill, I chanced to go through the Elysian Fields during the progress of a contest between the noted Eagle and Gotham clubs. The game was being sharply played on both sides, and I watched it with deeper interest than any previous ball game between clubs that I had seen. It was not long before I was struck with the idea that baseball was just the game for a national sport for Americans ... as much so as cricket in England. At the time I refer to I had been reporting cricket for years, and, in my method of taking notes of contests, I had a plan peculiarly my own. It was not long, therefore, after I had become interested in baseball, before I began to invent a method of giving detailed reports of leading contests at baseball ..."

Thus Chadwick's cricket background was largely the impetus to his method of scoring a baseball game, the format of his early box scores, and the copious if primitive statistics that appeared in his year-end summaries in the *New York Clipper*, Beadle's *Dime Base-Ball Player*, and other publications.

Actually, cricket had begun to shape baseball statistics even before Chadwick's conversion. The first box score reported on two categories, outs and runs: outs, or "hands out," counted both unsuccessful times at bat and outs run into on the basepaths; "runs" were runs scored, not those driven in. The reason for not recording hits in the early years, when coverage of baseball matches appeared alongside that of cricket matches, was that, unlike baseball, cricket had no such category as the successful hit which did not produce a run. To reach "base" in cricket is to run to the opposite wicket, which tallies a run; if you hit the ball and do not score a run, you have been put out.

Cricket box scores were virtual play-by-plays, a fact made possible by the lesser number of possible events. This play-by-play aspect was applied to a baseball box score as early as 1856; interestingly, despite the abundance of detail, hits were not accounted, nor did they appear in Chadwick's own box scores until 1867. The batting champion as declared by Chadwick, whose computations were immediately and universally accepted as "official," was the man with the highest average of runs per game. An inverse though imprecise measure of batting quality was outs per game. After 1863, when a fair ball caught on one bounce was no longer an out, fielding leaders were those with the greatest total of fly catches, assists, and "foul bounds" (fouls caught on one bounce). Pitching effectiveness was based purely on control, with the leader recognized as the one whose delivery offered the most opportunities for outs at first base and led to the fewest passed balls.

In a sense, Chadwick's measuring of baseball as if it were cricket can be viewed as correct in that when you strip the game to its basic elements, those that determine victory or defeat, outs and runs are all that count in the end. No individual statistic is meaningful to the team unless it relates directly to the scoring of runs. Chadwick's blind spot in his early years of baseball reporting lay in not recognizing the linear character of the game, the sequential nature whereby a string of base hits or men reaching base on error (there were no walks then) was necessary in most cases to produce a run. In cricket each successful hit must produce at least one run, while in baseball, more of a team game on offense, a successful hit may produce none.

Early player stats were of the most primitive kind, the counting kind. They'd tell you *how many* runs, or outs, or fly catches had occurred—later, how many hits or total bases. Counting is the most basic of all statistical processes; the next step up is averaging, and Chadwick was the first to put this into practice.

As professionalism infiltrated the game, teams began to bid for star-caliber players. Stars were known not by their stats but by their style until 1865, when Chadwick began to record in the *Clipper* a form of batting average taken from the cricket pages—runs per game. Two years later, in his newly founded baseball weekly, *The Ball Players' Chronicle,* he began to record not only average runs and outs per game, but also home runs, total bases, total bases per game—and hits per game. The averages were expressed not with decimal places but in the standard cricket format of the "average and over." Thus a batter with 23 hits in 6 games would have an average expressed not as 3.83 but as "3-5"—an average of 3 with an overage, or remainder, of 5. Another innovation was to remove from the individual accounting all bases gained through errors. Runs scored by a team, beginning in 1867, were divided between those scored after a man reached base on a clean hit and those arising from a runner's having reached base on an error. This was, of course, a precursor of today's earned run average.

In 1868, despite Chadwick's derision, the *Clipper* continued to award the prize for the batting championship to the player with the greatest average of runs per game. Actually, the old yardstick had been less preposterous a measure of batsmanship than one might imagine today, because team defense was so much poorer and the pitcher, with severe restrictions on his method of delivery, was so much less important. If you reached first base, whether by a hit or by an error, your chances of scoring were excellent; indeed, teams of the mid-1860s registered more runs than hits! By 1876, the caliber of both pitching and defense had improved to the extent that the ratio of runs to hits was about 6.5 to 10; today the ratio stands at roughly 5 to 10.

By the end of the decade Chadwick was recording total bases and home runs, but he placed little stock in either, as conscious attempts at slugging violated his cricket-bred

image of "form." Just as cricket aficionados watch the game for the many opportunities for fine fielding it affords, so was baseball from its inception perceived as a fielders' sport. The original Cartwright rules of 1845, in fact, specified that a ball hit out of the field—in fair territory or foul—was a foul ball! "Long hits are showy," Chadwick wrote in the *Clipper* in 1868, "but they do not pay in the long run. Sharp grounders insuring the first-base certain, and sometimes the second-base easily, are worth all the hits made for home-runs which players strive for."

Chadwick prevailed, and hits per game became the criterion for the *Clipper* batting championship and remained so until 1876, when the problem with using games as the denominator in the average at last became clear. If you were playing for a successful team, and thus were surrounded by good batters, or if your team played several weak rivals who committed many errors, the number of at-bats for each individual in that lineup would increase. The more at-bats one is granted in a game, the more hits one is likely to have. So, for example, if Player A had 10 at-bats in a game, which was not so unusual in the 1860s, he might have 4 base hits. In a more cleanly played game, Player B might bat only 6 times, and get 3 base hits. Yet Player A, with his 4-for-10, would achieve an average of 4.00; the average of Player B, who went 3-for-6, would be only 3.00. By modern standards, of course, Player A would be batting .400 while Player B would be batting .500.

In short, the batting average used in the 1860s is the same as that used today except in its denominator, with at-bats replacing games. Moreover, Chadwick created a measure in the 1860s that divided total bases by games played; change the denominator to at-bats and you have today's slugging average—which, incidentally, was not accepted by the National League as an official statistic until 1923 and by the American until 1946 (baseball was born and bred conservative).

Chadwick's "total bases average" represents the game's first attempt at a weighted average—an average in which the elements collected together in the numerator or the denominator are recognized numerically as being unequal. In this instance, a single is the unweighted unit, the double is weighted by a factor of two, the triple by three, and the home run by four. Statistically, this is a distinct leap forward from, first, counting, and next, averaging. The weighted average is in fact the cornerstone of today's statistical innovations, or "sabermetrics."

The 1870s gave rise to some new batting stats and to the first attempt to quantify thoroughly the other principal facets of the game, pitching and fielding. Although the *Clipper* recorded base hits and total bases as early as 1868, a significant wrinkle was added in 1870 when at-bats were listed as well. This was a critical introduction because it permitted the improvement of the batting average, first introduced in its current form by H. A. Dobson of Washington, D.C., in the *Dime Base-Ball Player* of 1872, and first computed officially—that is, for the National League—in 1876. Since then the batting average has not changed, except for 1876, when bases on balls were figured as outs, and 1887, when they were counted as hits. *Total Baseball* counts a walk as neither an at-bat nor an out for all years since 1871.

The objections to the batting average are well known, but to date have not dislodged it from its place as the most popular measure of hitting ability. First of all, the batting average makes no distinction between the single, the double, the triple, and the home run, treating all as the same unit. This objection had been addressed in 1868 by Chadwick's total bases average.

Second, it gives no indication of the effect of that base hit—that is, its value to the team. This was the reason Chadwick clung to runs per game as the best possible batting measure. Third, the batting average does not take into account those occasions when first base is reached via a walk, hit by pitch, or error. This last point was addressed at a surprisingly early date, too, as for 1879 the National League adopted as an official statistic a forerunner of the on-base percentage; it was called "reached first base," which included times reached by error as well as base on balls and base hits. (Being hit by a pitch did not give the batter first base until 1884 in the American Association, 1887 in the National League.)

The Flowering, 1876–1920

Ever since the Civil War, serial guides like Beadle and DeWitt and sporting columns like those in the *Clipper* had carried year-end tabulations of batting, fielding, and pitching exploits, varying from year to year with the brainstorms of Chadwick or other demon compilers like New York's M. J. Kelly or Philadelphia's Al Wright. But the year 1876 was special. It was significant not only for the founding of the National League and the official debut of the batting average in its current form, it was also the Centennial of the United States, which was marked by a giant exposition in Philadelphia celebrating the mechanical marvels of the day. American ingenuity reigned, and technology was seen as the new handmaiden of democracy. Baseball, that mirror of American life, reflected the fervor for things scientific with an explosion of statistics far more complex than those seen before, particularly in the previously neglected areas of pitching and fielding. The increasingly minute statistical examination of the game met a responsive audience, one primed to view complexity as a measure of worth.

The crossroads year of 1876 highlights how the game had changed to that point, as well as how it has changed since.

In that year, the number of offensive stats tabulated at season's end in any of the publications inspired by Chadwick or Spalding was six: games, at-bats, runs, hits, runs per game, and batting average. (And as with all the various guides until 1941, the stats of men who played in fewer than a specified minimum number of games were not noted.) Of these six, only runs and runs per game were common in the 1860s, while that decade's tabulation of total bases vanished. The number of offensive stats a hundred years later? Twenty. (Today the number is twenty-one, with the addition of on base percentage).

The number of pitching categories in 1876 was eleven, and there were some surprises, such as earned run average, hits allowed, hits per game, and opponents' batting average. Strikeouts were not recorded, for Chadwick saw them strictly as a sign of poor batting rather than good pitching (his view had such an impact that pitcher strike-

outs were not kept officially until 1889). The number of pitching stats today? Twenty-four.

The number of fielding categories in 1876 was six. One hundred years later it was still six (with the exception of the catcher, who gets a seventh: passed balls), dramatizing how the game, which originated as a showcase for fielders, had changed. The fielding stats of 1876 lumped "battery errors" with fielding errors, so that wild pitches and passed balls—in some years, even walks—diminished one's fielding percentage. This practice continued until 1887, but in *Total Baseball* battery errors are not included in fielding stats. Battery-mates' fielding stats were boosted by the awarding of an assist to the pitcher on strikeouts. This practice lasted until 1889, but is not reflected in *Total Baseball*.

The custom in 1876, as it is now, was to combine putouts, assists, and errors to form a "percentage of chances accepted," or what is today known as fielding average or fielding percentage. A "missing link" variant, devised by Al Wright in 1875, was to form averages by dividing the putouts by the number of games to yield a "putout average"; dividing the assists similarly to arrive at an "assist average"; and dividing putouts plus assists by games to get "fielding average." These averages took no account of errors. (Wright's "fielding average" was reborn a century later as Bill James's Range Factor.)

The public's appetite for new statistics was not sated by the outburst of 1876. New measures were introduced in dizzying profusion in the remaining years of the century. Some of these did not catch on and were soon dropped for all time, like the ridiculous "total bases run," while others fizzled only to reappear with new vigor in the twentieth century. These include (a) the above-mentioned "reached first base," which resurfaced in the early 1950s in an unofficial, improved form called on base percentage and became an official stat more than thirty years later, and (b) an 1860s stat, earned run average, which was periodically revived before dropping from sight in the 1880s, only to return triumphant to the NL in 1912 and the AL in 1913. In 1913 Ban Johnson not only proclaimed the ERA official but became so enamored with it that he also instructed American League scorers to compile *no* official won-lost records (this state of affairs lasted for seven years, 1913–1919).

Another stat that was "sent back to the minors" before its eventual adoption as an official stat in 1920 was the run batted in. Introduced by a Buffalo newspaper in 1879, the stat was picked up the following year by the *Chicago Tribune* and even became an official NL stat for the opening months of 1891. By season's end it had faded as most NL scorers declined to account for it in their summaries (The American Association, however, recorded it all year long.) Ernie Lanigan picked up the RBI baton with his reports to the *New York Press* in 1907, but only about a third of his data has been found, and he did not figure RBIs for men who played in fewer than ten games, or club totals for traded players. For *Total Baseball* we have placed much reliance upon the source material donated by Information Concepts, Inc. (ICI) to the National Baseball Library in Cooperstown following publication of its *Baseball Encyclopedia* for Macmillan in 1969. David Neft also kindly supplied us with his unpublished RBI data for the previously missing National League seasons of 1880–1885. The John Tattersall collection of nineteenth century game accounts and box scores was valuable as well.

Other statistics introduced officially before the turn of the century were stolen bases (though not caught stealing); doubles, triples, and homers; and sacrifice bunts (though an at-bat was charged from 1889 through 1894). Pitcher strikeouts, bases on balls, and the hit-by-pitch also appeared before 1900, but hit-by-pitch stats were not kept for batters on a systematic basis until 1917 in the NL and 1920 in the AL. Through newspaper research, we have filled in HBP data from 1884 through 1916 in the National League, Players League, and American Association, from 1909 through 1919 in the American League, and the 1914–1915 Federal League; research continues for the 1903–1908 period in both the American and National leagues. We are indebted in this area to Alex Haas, John Schwartz, John Tattersall, and Bob Davids.

Hit into double play—including line outs as well as groundouts—was recorded erratically in the nineteenth century, but separate stats for groundouts into double plays have been kept by the leagues only since 1933 in the NL and 1939 in the AL. Batters' strikeouts were reported unofficially in 1891, but not as a league stat until 1910 in the NL and 1913 in the AL. Innings pitched were not kept until 1908 in the AL and 1910 in the NL.

Stolen bases were awarded not only for clean steals but also for extra bases taken through daring, from the first year in which totals were kept, 1886, until 1898 (the Macmillan *Baseball Encyclopedia* begins its record of stolen bases with 1887). Because the figures reported in the guides were grossly inflated (such as Harry Stovey's ostensible 156 steals in 1888), the figures in *Total Baseball* reflect game-by-game research and refiguring. Caught-stealing (CS) figures are available on a very sketchy basis in some of the later years of the century, as some newspapers carried the data in the box scores of hometown games. From 1912 on, Lanigan recorded CS in box scores of the *New York Press,* but the leagues did not keep the figure officially until 1920. The AL has tabulated CS from that year to the present, excepting 1927, which members of the Society for American Baseball Research reconstructed from newspaper box scores. National League caught-stealing data exists for 1920–1925, and for 1951 to the present.

The new century added little in the way of *new* official statistics—ERA, RBI, and slugging average are better regarded as revivals despite their respective adoption dates of 1912, 1920, and 1923. But back in 1908 there was a classic case of a statistic rushing in to fill a void, as Phillies' manager Billy Murray observed that his outfielder Sherry Magee had the happy facility of providing a long fly ball whenever presented with a situation of a man on third and fewer than two outs. Taking up the cudgels on his player's behalf, Murray protested to the National League office that it was unfair to charge Magee with an unsuccessful time at bat when he was in fact succeeding, doing precisely what the situation demanded.

Murray won his point, but baseball flip-flopped a couple of times on this stat, in some years reverting to calling it a time at bat, in other years not even crediting an RBI. The sacrifice-fly rule was in effect from 1908 through 1930, with a sacrifice being given for advancing any runner, not just to home, for the final four years of this period. The rule was revived for one year in 1939. In none of these years was a distinction made between a sacrifice bunt or fly. When the rule came back into force in 1954, there was a breakdown of each.

More recent stats that have followed from this sort of perception—that something important was occurring on the field which had no verifiable reality because it was not yet being measured—are the save and the late, lamented game-winning RBI, which will be discussed later.

A signal event took place in 1912: the publication by *Baseball Magazine* editor John Lawres of *Who's Who in Baseball,* a small book that became the first to provide career statistics and personal facts for a group of players. Although thoroughly inadequate by today's standards—its only tabulations were games, batting average, and fielding average (even for pitchers, who were given no mound records!)—*Who's Who* was a groundbreaking work, giving rise to a much-expanded format in 1916 and inspiring two other significant encyclopedic works: in 1914, George Moreland's self-published opus called *Balldom* (grandiosely subtitled "The Britannica of Baseball," which it surely wasn't), and Ernest J. Lanigan's *Baseball Cyclopedia,* also sponsored by *Baseball Magazine,* which debuted in 1922 and was updated annually through 1933.

The Golden Age, 1920–1968

There have been other new statistical tabulations in this century, but generally of the counting sort: complete games (NL 1910, AL 1922), games started (AL 1926, NL 1938), games finished (NL 1920, AL 1926). And there were sacrifice bunts allowed (NL 1916, AL 1922), intentional bases on balls (only since 1955), and, in the next period, saves (1969) and game-winning RBIs (1980). The only new average since slugging average was adopted in 1923 has been the on base percentage, adopted in 1985. The ICI group computed saves for prior years. Another such stat that failed to survive, alas, was stolen bases off pitchers, which the American League recorded only in 1920–1924; it has been recorded on an unofficial basis in the 1980s by the Elias Sports Bureau and Project Scoresheet. The only new fielding measure was team double plays, added to the AL list in 1912 and the NL in 1919. Other new and more interesting stats appeared in the 1940s and '50s but have not yet gained the official stamp of approval, such as Ted Oliver's Weighted Rating System, Alfred P. Berry's Average Bases Allowed (opponents' slugging average), and Branch Rickey and Allan Roth's Isolated Power.

This period of baseball's history may have fielded its most dazzling array of stars, but strategically and statistically it was pretty dim. There was some excitement, however, in baseball record keeping. First came *Daguerreotypes,* issued by *The Sporting News* in 1934, featuring the playing records of many retired players both celebrated and obscure; most if not all of these statistical and biographical profiles originally appeared in the pages of *TSN.* Although its number of statistical categories was fewer than one might have wished, *Daguerreotypes* was very useful and, through its several editions ably edited by Paul MacFarlane, long-lived.

In 1940 came *The Sporting News's Baseball Register,* which supplied full records for active players, managers, coaches, and umpires, plus a grab bag of former stars. Since the expansion of the major leagues from sixteen teams to twenty-six, the *Register* has only accommodated contemporary players and managers, but it remains a valuable source. One year later, *TSN* issued a notable edition of its *Official Baseball Record Book,* giving for the first time full statistical lines for all men who played in a major league game the previous year.

In 1944 a little-known man named Ted Oliver published in obscurity a booklet called *Kings of the Mound.* It introduced a new stat called the Weighted Rating System for pitchers, a stat that we modified and continue to employ as Wins Above Team. Moved by the inadequacy of both the won-lost percentage and the ERA to reflect the value of a decent pitcher laboring for a lousy club, Oliver ingeniously subtracted the pitcher's decisions from his team's, then took the difference between the pitcher's won-lost percentage and his team's and multiplied that difference by the pitcher's number of decisions. Although his concept and his math were flawed, his principles—viewing a pitcher's record in relation to his team and weighting the result of his calculation by the number of decisions—were of unparalleled sophistication for the time. (Oliver's formula for his Weighted Rating System and its modification in *Total Baseball* are detailed in the Glossary, as are the calculations behind every statistic employed in this book.)

Then in 1951 came the first true encyclopedia of baseball, the claims of Moreland and Lanigan notwithstanding. Compiled by Hy Turkin and S. C. Thompson, *The Official Encyclopedia of Baseball* was published by the A. S. Barnes Company. Its 620 pages contained a wealth of features such as manager and umpire rosters, historical essays, playing tips, a bibliography, and much more. But the heart of the volume and the key to its subsequent success was a register of nearly nine thousand men who played one or more games at the major league level from 1871 through 1949 (the 1950 record of players appearing in ten games or more was tacked on to the end). In this register, Turkin/Thompson also offered birth and death data and what today seems fairly limited statistical information but by previous standards was a veritable cornucopia: year, club, league, position, games, and batting average or won-lost record. A landmark volume that did much to inspire this one, *The Official Encyclopedia of Baseball* lasted through ten revised editions, the last being published in 1979, ten years after the initial appearance of Macmillan's *Baseball Encyclopedia.*

The genesis of the Turkin/Thompson opus was one day in September 1944 when musician Thompson invited his neighbor, New York *Daily News* sportswriter Turkin, to "look over his baseball collection." What Turkin saw was a massive treasure chest of data, collected and collated over twenty years. "Tommy" Thompson was a baseball nut—a figure filbert, in the parlance of the time—who researched baseball just for the love of it. He was not alone in this pursuit, although very nearly so—other baseball archeologists of the time who contributed to this encyclopedia were Frank Marcellus, Tom Shea, Lee Allen, Ralph Lin Weber, Joe Overfield, Bob McConnell, and the aforementioned Ernie Lanigan.

The Official Encyclopedia of Baseball went a long way toward making the study of baseball history and records a respectable pursuit, just as a century earlier the statistical accounting of a boys' game had helped to make baseball a sport for grown men. The researchers' ranks expanded to include such men as Bob Davids, who in 1971, aided by other experts like Cliff Kachline, Bill Haber, Ray Nemec, John Pardon, and Joe Simenic, would create SABR, the Society for American Baseball Research (pronounced "saber"). Formerly the lonely pursuit of a handful of "nuts" like S. C. Thompson, baseball research and sabermetrics—a neologism coined in honor of SABR, signifying the statistical analysis of the game's records—would become the pastime of thousands.

An article in *Life* magazine by Branch Rickey on August 2, 1954, gave further impetus to the study of baseball statistics, but not just to set the historical record straight. Indeed, this article may be viewed as the opening shot of the sabermetric assault of the 1980s. In "Goodby to Some Old Baseball Ideas," Rickey, with the aid of some new mathematical tools supplied by Dodger statistician Allan Roth, sought to puncture some long-held conceptions about how the game was divided among its elements (batting, baserunning, pitching, fielding), who was best at playing it, and what caused one team to win and another to lose. This is a pretty fair statement of what sabermetrics is about.

Rickey attacked the batting average and proposed in its place the on base percentage; advocated the use of Isolated Power (extra bases beyond singles, divided by at-bats) as a better measure than slugging average; introduced a "clutch" measure of run-scoring efficiency for teams, and a similar concept for pitchers (earned runs divided by baserunners allowed); reaffirmed the basic validity of the ERA; saw the strikeout as the insubstantial thing it was—and more. But the most important thing Rickey did for baseball statistics was to pull it back from the wrong path it had taken with the introduction of the batting average in 1876: to strip the game and its stats to their essentials and start again, this time remembering that individual stats came into being as an attempt to apportion the players' contributions to achieving a team victory, for that is what the game is about.

Rickey and Roth devised a formula to measure a team's efficiency in turning its offensive and defensive statistics into runs, and thus wins. They realized, and had confirmed for them by mathematicians at the Massachusetts Institute of Technology, that just as the team which scores more runs in a game gets the win, so a team which over the course of a season scores more runs than it allows should win more games than it loses—and by an extent correlated to its run differential. From this startlingly simple (or rather, seemingly simple) observation in 1954 flowed: first, the trailblazing but little noted work of George Lindsey in the 1950s and early 1960s, when he developed a model for run-scoring probability from the twenty-four combinations of outs and bases occupied; the development of "percentage baseball" stats and strategies by Earnshaw Cook in the 1960s; the play-by-play analysis of complete seasons by the Mills brothers, Eldon and Harlan, in 1969–1970; and, over the next two decades, the statistical and historical works of several sabermetricians, most notably Bill James.

The Computer Age, 1969–

Despite the death of Turkin in 1957 and Thompson ten years later, their *Official Encyclopedia of Baseball* remained the dominant book of baseball statistics, although many fans were frustrated with the fragmentary records it presented. As Frank V. Phelps wrote in the 1987 edition of *The National Pastime,* "Gaps and obvious errors in official averages, the lack of many early records, difficulty in securing the records of players who appeared in only a few games, and frustrating discrepancies among existing guides and registers had long since created a desire for an ultimate, complete, correct set of major league records. But it wasn't until the mid-1960s that the development of sophisticated computers which could absorb, retain, order, and output huge amounts of data finally made a project feasible."

Beginning in 1967, a battalion of researchers commanded by David Neft foraged through the official records and newspaper box scores to provide freshly compiled figures for those who had no ERAs, RBIs, slugging averages, saves, and all manner of wonderful things. The material which finally appeared in the tome was entered into a data bank, and the book was the first typeset entirely by computer, now a common practice. Published in 1969, *The Baseball Encyclopedia* was a milestone in computer technology, but as indispensable as the computer were the old-fashioned scrapbooks and files of Lee Allen and John Tattersall. The result was a mammoth ledger book of the major leagues more thorough than any that had appeared before.

The Baseball Encyclopedia researchers not only found new data to correct old inaccuracies but also applied new yardsticks to men who had gone to their graves never having heard of an RBI or a save. They also raised the hackles of traditionalists with many of their findings, which prompted the formation of a Special Baseball Records Committee. Its members ruled upon such matters as whether, for the historical record, bases on balls should be counted as hits (as they were in 1887), outs (as they were in 1876), or neither (as has been the practice in all other years); or whether "sudden-death" home runs— thirty-seven game-winning blows with men on base that they identified as having occurred in the bottom half of the ninth or extra inning—would be credited as homers or, in the practice before 1920, would count for only as many bases as needed to push across the winning run. In the latter controversy, committee members first decided to count the disputed blows as homers, but then, when complaints arose that Babe Ruth's famous total of 714 would change to 715, they reversed themselves. They decided that the National Association of 1871–1875 was not a major league, while the Federal League, Union Association, and Players League were; and they ruled on several other issues, all of which were published in the Appendix to *The Baseball Encyclopedia.*

In *Total Baseball,* we have abided by most of the committee's decisions—not to preserve Ruth's total, but because there were many more such homers before 1920 than the thirty-seven the committee identified, and the disputes surrounding some of them are now beyond settling. We have, however, treated the National Association as a major league, as Turkin/Thompson and all previous record books did, and in accordance with the views of most historians. And we have differed from the committee's ruling on awarding pitchers wins and losses in the years before 1920. Not finding any official scoring rule or practice for that time, they chose to apply 1950 guidelines to decisions awarded in 1876–1920. This well-intentioned decision produced substantial alterations in the records of such hurlers as Cy Young, Christy Mathewson, Grover Alexander, and others. In the ensuing years, the notable research of Frank Williams (reported in "All the Record Books Are Wrong," *The National Pastime,* 1982) revealed that there was indeed a pattern and a rationale for the way decisions were awarded in those days; the data in *Total Baseball* conforms with his findings.

ICI research created new stars, launching several previously underappreciated heroes of old into the Hall of Fame. Sam Thompson, Addie Joss, Roger Connor, Amos Rusie—their phenomenal level of play was hidden simply because statisticians back then were not recording the particular numbers which would show them off to best advantage. If sabermetrics consists of finding things in the existing data that were not seen before, or collecting that data which makes possible the application of new statistics to old performances, the first edition of *The Baseball Encyclopedia* was a monument in the course of sabermetrics.

However, its subsequent editions declined from that standard, dropping valuable data, jimmying figures for star players in a misguided homage to tradition, and making a shambles of individual/team balance in the totals. As Phelps wrote of the second edition, edited by Joseph L. Reichler for the Macmillan Company after the ICI group broke up and relinquished supervision:

"Players' batting statistics were changed without compensating for changes in the records of other players on the same teams or in the corresponding team and league totals. Later editions included even more unbalanced adjustments . . .

"Quite apart from the problem of record-balancing, the numerous changes in players' totals and averages has caused serious misapprehensions and confusions for fans, writers, and researchers. The records of Fred Clarke and Cy Young differ in all six editions [to 1987] even without counting Clarke's astronomical 1899 BA [in the third edition, Clarke was credited with a batting average of .986 that boosted his lifetime mark by 15 points]. The figures for Burkett, Chesbro, Duffy, Hornsby, Walter Johnson, Radbourn, Speaker, and Waddell differ in five of the six books. The same is so in four of six for at least twenty-three other Hall of Famers, and many more less gifted players." The seventh edition was issued in 1988 and, like the five that preceded it, was less accurate than the classic first issue. The eighth edition, published in 1990, corrected many of the errors in the seventh but— perhaps because of its marketing link with Major League Baseball—retained many once-contested errors that historians had long since expunged from the record. (David Neft of ICI, along with *Baseball Encyclopedia* staff alumni Dick Cohen and Jordan Deutsch, went on to form Sport Products, Inc. Since 1974 they have issued the excellent *Sports Encyclopedia: Baseball,* which has endured as the baseball reference of choice for thousands of sophisticated fans.)

We will have more to add about accuracy and balance in the "Errors and Controversies" section of this Introduction.

There were two other interesting developments in 1969. The first and less celebrated was a research project launched by Eldon and Harlan Mills that, like the ICI encyclopedia, could not have been contemplated without the computer. The Mills brothers tracked the entire major league seasons of 1969 and 1970 on a play-by-play basis. Then they applied to that record the probabilities of winning which derived from each possible outcome of a plate appearance, as determined by a computer simulation incorporating nearly eight thousand possibilities. What, for example, was the visiting team's chance of winning the game before the first pitch was thrown? Fifty percent, if we are pitting two theoretical teams of equal or unknown ability on a neutral site. If the first man fails to get on base, the chances of the visiting team winning are reduced to 49.8 percent; should he hit a double, the visiting team's chance of victory is raised to 55.9 percent, as determined by the probabilistic simulation. Every possible situation—combining half inning, score, men on base, and men out—was tested by the simulator to arrive at "Win Points."

The Millses' purpose was to determine the clutch value of, say, hitting a homer with two men on and one man out in the bottom of the ninth, with the team trailing by two runs, the situation Bobby Thomson faced in the climactic National League game of 1951—oddly, the rookie year of the first modern computer. (It gained for him 1,472 Win Points; had it come with no one on in the eighth inning of a game in which his team led 4–0, the homer would have been worth only 12 Win Points.) What the Mills brothers were attempting to do was to evaluate not only the *what* of a performance, which traditional statistics indicate, but the *when,* or clutch factor, which no statistic to that time could provide.

This project, detailed in a small book issued in 1970 called *Player Win Averages,* proceeded from the same impulse that led to other measures of clutch performance: the game winning RBI, introduced as an official major league stat in 1980 and scrapped in 1989; the measure of batting performance in late-inning pressure situations first published by Seymour Siwoff, Steve Hirdt, and Peter Hirdt of the Elias Sports Bureau in 1985; and the historically complete indexes of clutch hitting and clutch pitching developed for this book.

The other noteworthy baseball event of 1969 (besides the centennial of professional baseball and the miracle of the Mets) was the adoption by the major leagues of the save, the stat associated with the most significant strategic development since the advent of the gopher ball. Now shown in the papers on a daily basis, saves were not officially recorded at all until 1960; it was at the instigation of Jerry Holtzman of the *Chicago Sun-Times,* with the cooperation of *The Sporting News,* that this statistic was finally accepted. (Although Pat McDonough, a founding member of SABR, had developed a similar stat in 1924 which he called "games finished by relief hurlers"; its first appearance in print came in the *New York Telegram* three years later.) The need for the save arose because relievers operated at a disadvantage when it came to picking up wins. The bullpen specialists were a new breed, and as their role increased, the need arose to identify excellence, as it had long ago for batters, starting pitchers, and fielders. The save's prime statistical drawback is that there is no negative to counteract the positive, no stat for saves blown (except, all too often, a victory for the "fireman"); unofficial attempts to develop such a stat have accelerated in recent years, and now are part of the formula for the Fireman of the Year award.

August 10, 1971, marked another milestone, the founding in Cooperstown of SABR, the group in whose annual publications most of today's sabermetricians cut their analytical teeth. Its statistical analysis research committee, headed for more than a decade by Pete Palmer, has served as a sounding board for the inventive approaches of such men as Dallas Adams, Dick Cramer, Steve Mann, Craig Wright, and Bill James.

James published *The Baseball Abstract* from his home in Lawrence, Kansas, for five years to a minute if appreciative audience (its 1977 publication budget: $112.73). In 1982 Ballantine Books, recognizing the increasing sophistication of baseball fans in the computer age, assumed publication of the *Abstract,* and the audience for sabermetrics became sizable indeed, with James's annuals reaching the bestseller lists and his *Historical Baseball Abstract* becoming an essential book for anyone who viewed himself as a serious fan. James has popularized a different approach to the whole question of what baseball statistics are for—that they are not brass knuckles to beat a barroom adversary with, but a means of achieving a better understanding of the game and heightening one's pleasure in it.

Among the many valuable analytical tools he has developed are the Brock-2 System of projecting career totals, the Victory Important RBI, Offensive and Defensive Winning Percentages, Secondary Average, Range Factor, and Runs Created. The last-mentioned, perhaps because James developed it earlier in his career, is the most widely known, and we apply it in this book to all batters, in all fourteen variations of the formula, bringing in data for stolen bases, caught stealing, hit-by-pitch, and grounded into double play for those years in which it is available. (See the Glossary for the formulas.)

The 1980s also brought attention to another attempt to redefine the measure of individual performance. In 1978 Barry Codell of Chicago distributed a paper describing his new statistic, the Base-Out Percentage, to fellow statisticians and figures in the sports media. At about the same time, Tom Boswell, not a statistician by trade or inclination but rather a sportswriter for the *Washington Post,* developed a stat called Total Average. Like the Base-Out Percentage, Total Average is a gauge of offensive proficiency which takes into account not only batting but also base-running skills. (See the Glossary.)

Dallas Adams and Dick Cramer devoted themselves in the late 1970s to a discussion of average batting, pitching, and fielding skill, which more than a decade later remains a subject of intense interest and passionate disagreement. The question, roughly put, is: *How would Cy Young do against the batters of today? Or Wade Boggs against the pitchers of the 1890s? How many homers would Babe Ruth hit if he were active today? Or how many strikeouts would Nolan Ryan have registered in 1880, pitching from a fifty-foot distance?* In other words, how can we adjust the statistics of players to reflect the certainty that the average batter, pitcher, and fielder have improved over time, thus narrowing the gap between each succeeding era's peak performance and its average one? (For more on this philosophically and mathematically complex subject, we refer you to *The Hidden Game of Baseball*.)

Adams and Cramer advanced a discussion that had begun in 1976 with the first article on cross-era comparison, in which David Shoebotham proposed a new statistic called the Relative Batting Average. Shoebotham recognized that a .320 batting average in 1893, when the National League batted .280, did not represent the same level of accomplishment as that average did in 1968 when, for a number of reasons, the National League batted a measly .243. His solution? To normalize the players' averages to their respective league averages simply by dividing the player's batting average by that of his league.

In this fashion he demonstrated, for example, that Pete Rose, who led the NL with a .335 BA in 1968, had a Relative BA of 1.38; while Ed Delahanty, who led the NL with a BA of .380 in 1893, had a Relative BA of only 1.36. Another way of stating this conclusion is that Rose's .335 was 38 percent above the average batting performance in the NL of 1968, while Delahanty exceeded his league's norm by 36 percent. The inferences that might be drawn from this approach are many: that batting skill has not declined since the days of Ruth, Gehrig, Foxx, et al., but that pitching skill might have increased; that no batting average of the years around 1930 ought to be taken without a carload of salt; that some of the most notable batting performances of all time, as measured by the batting average, have occurred right under our noses, unbeknownst to us.

Normalizing a statistic to its league average is a valuable analytical tool if employed logically. A Relative Batting Average, for example, tells a good deal more, and tells it more straightforwardly, than Relative Homers or Relative Strikeouts. The relativist approach works better with ratios such as batting average, on base percentage, or slugging average—or for that matter with Runs Created or Total Average—than it does for simple counter stats.

Another worthwhile adjustment to various averages is for home-park effects. The pioneering work in this area was done by Robert Kingsley, particularly in regard to why homers flew out of Atlanta's park despite its "normal" dimensions, but Pete Palmer was first to measure the effects of home parks on run totals and then to devise a park adjustment for the records of batters and pitchers. These were discussed in depth in *The Hidden Game of Baseball*, and the data base for park factor in this book has been upgraded to include runs scored *and* runs allowed at home parks instead of just the latter.

In 1984 the editors of this volume introduced, in *The Hidden Game*, the Linear Weights System of assessing players' contributions to their teams—at the bat, on the basepaths, in the field, or on the mound—in terms of runs, which are the currency of the game. Its back-to-basics foundation is the same as that underlying the Rickey formula of 1954 and most of the new statistics developed since then: that wins and losses are what the game is about; that wins and losses are proportional in some way to runs scored and runs allowed; and that runs in turn are proportional to the events which go into their making.

In the Linear Weights System, these events are expressed not in the familiar yet deceptive ratios—base hits to at-bats, wins to decisions, etc.—but in *runs themselves,* the runs contributed (by batting or base stealing) or saved (by pitching or fielding). Computer simulations of over 100,000 games produced the run values of, for example: a single (.47 runs), double (.78), triple (1.09), home run (1.40), walk (.33), steal (.30), caught stealing (−.60), out (−.25), and out made on base (−.50). Using a straightforward additive formula, one can calculate a batter or baserunner's contribution to his team in runs. These would be expressed in terms of runs contributed beyond what a league-average replacement player could contribute in his stead, and that average is defined as a baseline of zero. A team composed entirely of average performers would finish with a record of .500, as the league must—so each above-average player contributes positive runs toward a win, and each subpar player contributes negative runs.

Normalizing factors (to league average) are built into the formulas for all but base stealing, where league average is not a shaping force; these factors enable us to compute, for example, the number of runs (Batting Runs) that Cecil Fielder provided in 1990 beyond those an average hitter might have produced in an equivalent number of plate appearances. And by adjusting Fielder's Batting Runs for Detroit's homepark influences, the Linear Weights comparison may be extended to how many runs he accounted for beyond what an average player might have produced in the same number of at-bats *had he too played half his games in Tiger Stadium.*

Furthermore, having determined the number of runs above average required to transform a loss to a win in the final standings (generally around ten, historically in the range of nine to eleven; for more on the theory behind this, see the Glossary), we can convert a player's Linear Weights record—expressed as Batting Runs, Base Stealing Runs, Pitching Runs, or Fielding Runs—to the number of *wins above average* he alone contributed. What are individual statistics for if not to achieve some understanding of this? Last, by reviewing the win contributions of all a team's personnel, we may establish a solid assessment of that team's strength and weaknesses—either to predict a team's chances for success in the upcoming season or, in an encyclopedia like *Total Baseball*, to analyze how and even why it failed its reasonable statistical expectations or exceeded them.

Formulas for the Linear Weights measures for batting, baserunning, fielding, and pitching will be found in the Glossary.

Other developments of the decade include the previously mentioned adoption of the game-winning RBI (GWRBI) in 1980; it credited the batter who drove in a run to give his club a lead that it never relinquished. This stat was pilloried in the press from its introduction, with merit, until Major League Baseball finally gave up on it before the 1989 season. In 1984 on base percentage was made official, thirty years after its introduction to the general baseball public by Branch Rickey and Allan Roth. Subsequent years brought the Quality Start, which takes note of a pitcher who gives his club six innings or more while allowing three runs or less. Under this construction, an ERA of 4.50 in a mercifully shortened outing is held to be commendable. The editors of this book do not regard the Quality Start as a quality stat.

More interesting are the situational stats which are the specialty of the Elias Sports Bureau and Project Scoresheet—performance in day games vs. night, grass vs. artificial turf, lefty vs. righty, day game following night, bases-loaded situations, and so on. When the data is drawn from a large enough sample, these stats can be provocative and meaningful; too often, however, television announcers desperate to maintain conversation flow will burden their listeners with something like, "Over the last two seasons, he's batted .375 against this guy" (not bothering to add that the figure represents three hits in eight times at bat). Situational stats are the wave of the future in baseball, but are not yet of much use for reviewing the past—Elias has kept them systematically only since 1975.

Total Baseball

The next major event in the history of baseball record keeping may be the book you now hold. Founded upon a unique historical database that Pete Palmer has cultivated for over twenty years—in the tradition of baseball archivists like S. C. Thompson, Bradshaw Swales, Leonard Gettelson, and John Tattersall—*Total Baseball* is the third-generation encyclopedia of the game. Just as the advent of the Macmillan/ICI encyclopedia supplanted Turkin/Thompson, the standard for two decades, *Total Baseball* has taken advantage of new technology and new research, notably by members of the Society for American Baseball Research, to present more accurate data than ever before, and more of it. There are, of course, the traditional stats one would expect in a baseball reference work; there are many of the new, more revealing stats discussed above; there are stats never published before and developed now for this book. And as you have seen in Part One, there is a recognition that baseball history and knowledge resides not only in its numbers.

But returning to the statistics and records which make up this second part of *Total Baseball*, here is a brief rundown of what's coming (full descriptions will be found in the separate introduction to each section):

- *The Annual Record:* Season-by-season standings and records for all teams since 1871, plus the top five league leaders in generally forty-eight categories per season.
- *Home-Road Statistics:* Team stats for all years of major league play, including years before 1900.
- *The Rosters:* A completely revised manager roster, courtesy of some splendid research into the early years by SABR's Bob Tiemann and Richard Topp; and the application to all managers of the "actual vs. expected win" method introduced in the editors' *Baseball Annual 1990* (with Eliot Cohen); a definitive roster of the men in blue, compiled by expert Larry Gerlach; a roster of coaches, never before compiled; a roster of club owners and presidents; and a roster of all the teams of major league history, listing the starting lineups plus principal pitchers and substitutes.
- *The Player, Pitcher, and Fielding Registers:* The heart of this section of *Total Baseball,* presenting complete seasonal and lifetime records for every major leaguer, with twenty-three stats for players, twenty-five for pitchers, and seven for fielders.
- *All-Time Leaders:* The top one hundred lifetime and single-season performers in 219 categories, including important conventional stats not found in other encyclopedias and dozens of the sabermetric variety.

Now that the genealogy of the more significant records and record books has been described, it's time to say a few words about the measures you'll find in the main statistical sections of *Total Baseball:* the annual record and the player/pitcher registers. We will not attempt to define the basic counting stats such as games, at-bats, wins, losses, and so on; if these are puzzling to you, you have picked up the wrong book.

Batting

Let's start with the batting statistics, and the first of these to consider will be that venerable, uncannily durable fraud, the batting average. (It consists simply of hits divided by at-bats.) We know as well as anyone else that this monument just won't topple; the best that can be hoped is that in time fans and officials will recognize it as a bit of nostalgia, a throwback to the period of its invention when power counted for naught, bases on balls were scarce, and no one wanted to place a statistical accomplishment in historical context because there wasn't much history yet.

Time has given the batting average a powerful hold on the American baseball public; everyone knows that a man who hits .300 is a good hitter while one who hits .250 is not. Everyone knows that—no matter that it is not true. You want to trade Lenny Dykstra for Kevin Mitchell? Willie McGee for Will Clark? Batting average treats all hits in an egalitarian fashion. A two-out bunt single in the ninth with no one on base and your team trailing by six runs counts the same as Bobby Thomson's "shot heard 'round the world." And what about a walk? Say you foul off four 3–2 pitches, then watch a close one go by to take your base. Where's your credit for a neat bit of offensive work? Not in this stat. And a .250 batting average may have represented a distinct accomplishment in certain years, like 1968 when the American League mean was .230. That .250 hitter stood in the same relation to an average hitter of his season as a .282 hitter did in the American League in 1988—or a *.329* hitter in the National League of 1930! If .329 and .282 and .250 all mean roughly the same thing, it raises questions about the value of the measure.

And yet, the batting champion each year is declared to be the one with the highest batting average, and this will not soon change. And the Hall of Fame is filled with .300 hitters who couldn't carry the pine tar of many who will stay forever on the outside looking in. Knowledgeable fans have long realized that the ability to reach base and to produce runs are not adequately measured by batting average, and they have looked to other measures—for example, the other two components of the Triple Crown, home runs and RBIs. Still more sophisticated fans have looked to the slugging average or on base percentage, and in the 1980s to various sabermetric measures.

The slugging average does acknowledge the role of the

man whose talent is for the long ball and who may, with management's blessing, be sacrificing bat control and thus batting average in order to let'er rip. (Slugging average is the number of total bases divided by at-bats.) But the slugging average has its problems, too. It declares that a double is worth two singles, that a triple is worth one and a half doubles, and that a home run is worth four singles. All of these proportions are intuitively pleasing, for they relate to the number of bases touched on each hit, but in terms of the hits' value in generating runs, the proportions are wrong. One home run in four at-bats is not worth as much as four singles, for instance, in part because the total run potential for the team of four singles is greater, and in part because the man who hit the four singles did not also make three outs; yet the man who goes one for four at the plate, that one being a homer, has the same slugging percentage of 1.000 as a man who singles four times in four at-bats.

Moreover, it is possible to attain a high slugging average without being a slugger. In other words, if you have a high batting average, you must have a decent slugging average; it's difficult to hit .350 and have a slugging percentage of only .400. Even a bunt single boosts not only your batting average but also your slugging average. (The attempt to counteract this problem is a statistic called Isolated Power, which divides only extra bases by at-bats.) Other things the slugging average does not do are: indicate how many runs were produced by the hits; give any credit for other offensive categories, such as walks, hit-by-pitch, or steals; permit the comparison of sluggers from different eras (if Jimmie Foxx had a slugging percentage of .749 in 1932 and Mickey Mantle had one of .705 in 1957, was Fox 7 percent superior? The answer is no, and the reason is in the higher slugging average of the AL in 1932.

Well, how about on base percentage? (To calculate this stat, divide hits, walks, and hit-by-pitch by at-bats, walks, hit-by-pitch, and sacrifice flies.) On base percentage has the advantage of giving credit for walks and hit-by-pitch, but it is an unweighted average and thus makes no distinction between those two events and, say, a grand-slam homer. A fellow like Eddie Yost, who, in some years when he hit under .250, drew nearly a walk a game, gets his credit with this stat as does a Gene Tenace, one of those guys whose statistical line looks puny without his walks. Similarly, players like Mickey Rivers or Omar Moreno, leadoff hitters with a lot of speed, no power, and no patience, are exposed by the OBP as distinctly marginal major leaguers, even in years when their batting averages look respectable or excellent. In short, on base percentage does tell you more about a man's ability to get on than does the batting average, and thus is a better indicator of run generation, but it's not enough by itself to separate the "good" hitters from the "average" or "poor" ones.

Not by itself, no . . . but when you add it to slugging average, you come up with a very powerful indicator of batting ability. These two one-legged men, when joined together, make for a very sturdy tandem, the infirmity of the one being almost exactly compensated by the power of the other. The virtues of on base plus slugging, a combined stat called Production, are that it is easily computed from officially issued stats and that it is the most accurate of all the newer stats except those denominated directly in runs. Its weaknesses are that because it is stated as the sum of two averages, it is—like a batting average or earned run average or any other average—a measure of the *rate* of success rather than the *amount,* and the fan needs considerable context to know what it means. Is a Production mark of .750 poor, average, or outstanding? (Answer: pretty good, because the league average figure in recent years has been in the low .700s—although in the NL of 1930 it exceeded .800.)

This second drawback may be eliminated in the same manner for all averages: by normalizing, or adjusting, each individual performance to the league average in that category for the year in which it took place. If a batter's Production was .700 in a year when the league average was .700, he performed at a rate of 100 (his Production divided by the league's, discarding the decimal point for ease of expression). If his Production was .800, his league-adjusted mark would be 114. The meaningfulness of that performance might be further refined by adjusting it once more, to take into account the run-producing characteristics of the man's home park: a batter whose home park was a hitters' haven like Wrigley Field might have his Production adjusted downward, while another playing half his games in the Astrodome might have his adjusted upward. In *Total Baseball,* figures adjusted for league average and park factor are denoted by "/A" following the raw figure, and the Park Factor (PF) is expressed with a baseline of 100—a hitter's park might have a factor of 110, a pitcher's park 90. In this second edition of *Total Baseball,* we state Production in the Player Register only in its normalized, park-adjusted form, here termed "Production+."

RBIs? Don't they indicate run production and clutch ability? Yes and no. The RBI does tell you something about run-producing ability, but not enough: it's a situation-dependent statistic, inextricably tied to factors which vary wildly for individuals on the same team or on others (including, importantly, the position of each player in the batting order). And the RBI makes no distinction between being hit by a pitch to drive in the twelfth run of a game that concludes 14–3 and, again for comparison, the Thomson blast. RBIs tell how many runs a batter pushed across the plate, all right, but they don't tell how many fewer he might have driven in had he batted eighth rather than fourth, or how many more he might have driven in on a team that put more men on base. They don't even tell how many more runs a batter might have driven in if he had delivered a higher proportion of his hits with men on base.

The American League kept RBI Opportunities—men on base presented to each batter—as an official stat for the first three weeks of 1918, then saw how much work was involved and ditched it. The problem remains: how to assess run productivity for batters. Pitchers are easier. Their accomplishments are directly measured in runs allowed. But batters, baserunners, and fielders make their contributions in the constituent parts of runs—outs, hits, and a variety of more or less successful other events. (Even a batter who hits a solo homer contributes more than one run to his team, because he permits another player to bat who otherwise would not have, and each batter has a potential for producing further runs.)

You hear a lot in the media about the value of Runs

Produced, a stat we track in *Total Baseball* in the top five section of the Annual Record. Runs Produced is simply runs scored plus runs batted in, subtracting homers because a dinger gives a batter "double credit"—a run scored plus an RBI. The editors view Runs Produced as an odd linkage of one opportunity-dependent stat with another that depends upon largely the same factors, but we offer the stat for those who like that sort of thing.

And so we come to the recently formulated game-winning RBI (GWRBI)—a noble attempt at describing the value of a hit to the team, its "clutchness," but a measure which was misconceived in its presumption that a game could be won with a hit in the first inning. A man who drives in a run in the first inning is simply doing his job, not performing an extraordinary feat; if the pitcher makes that run hold up by throwing a shutout, bully for him, but why credit the hitter? Were he to drive in the lone run of the game in the seventh inning or later, that would be different. Nonetheless, the latest formulation of the stat gave the man who drove in that first-inning run a GWRBI even if his team eventually won 22–0, since it gave the team a lead that was never relinquished.

Worse, the GWRBI was situation-dependent to an even greater degree than the RBI. You can't play for a lousy team and lead the league in GWRBIs because there aren't enough games won to go around. And it's even harder to accumulate GWRBIs from the eighth place in the batting order than it is to accumulate RBIs. Last, if you put your team ahead with an RBI in the bottom of the eighth, why should you lose your GWRBI simply because the pitcher allows the lead to be lost? Wasn't your hit "clutch"? Say the pitcher allows the score to be tied, then a teammate might pick up the GWRBI that should have been safely tucked away for you. Nicely motivated, the GWRBI, but utterly without merit and thus we barred it from the first edition of *Total Baseball,* no matter that at the time we prepared that book the GWRBI was still an official Major League Baseball stat. It is no longer.

We do, however, present a measure called Clutch Hitting Index, which addresses the problem of run-producing opportunities on a historical basis. We offer this with several reservations, including the classic philosophical one about whether clutch ability exists at all. Is a man who hits .280 with men on base and .240 with the sacks clear a hero in the former situation or a bum in the latter? The Clutch Hitting Index measures actual RBIs over expected RBIs, which have been calculated on the basis of a man's extra-base hits and the opportunities he could have been expected to have, based on the average RBIs per league and where he batted in the lineup and who batted above him. This is, by admission, a rough measure indeed, but we think it's an interesting one. We included it in the Player Register in the first edition; this time we confine the stat to the Annual Record and Leaders Sections. For teams, the measure of clutch hitting is more elegant: the ratio of its actual runs to its runs as calculated by the Linear Weights method.

Previously discussed were Runs Created, Total Average, and Batting Runs. Total Average numbers will tend to look like those of Production, which measures largely the same things only in a different manner; for this reason we have removed it from the Player Register in this edition while retaining it in the Annual Record and Leaders.

The numerical expression of Runs Created exceeds that of Batting Runs, except that its baseline of zero defines the worst player in the league rather than the average one.

Base Stealing

Many fans understand, as a result of sabermetric findings of the 1980s, that a man with a lot of stolen bases is not necessarily the best baserunner, nor even an asset to his team; he might have been caught nearly as often as he stole and thus may have cost his team many runs on balance. The game's encyclopedic reference works have in years past contained stolen base totals, even if the tabulations for the early years were suspect because of unclear standards for what differentiated a steal from clever baserunning. What they have not offered is the flip side of the steal—the caught-stealing numbers that make sense of the steal itself.

As mentioned above, caught stealing was recorded officially in the AL beginning in 1920, then was dropped for 1927, was resumed in 1928, and has been continuously in use ever since. In the NL, it was computed for 1920–1925, then was dropped until 1951, when it resumed on a continuous basis. We have figures kept by Ernie Lanigan for the years 1914–1916 in the AL and for 1915–1916 in the NL, and for this second edition we have added caught-stealing data for 1927 from newspaper accounts (about 90 percent complete). In *Total Baseball* we present, for those years in which the data exists, the raw CS data, Stolen Base Averages, and Stolen Base Runs. This last is expressed in runs, based on the computer-derived value of .30 runs for a stolen base and −.60 runs for a thwarted steal. To make a positive contribution to his team, a base thief must be successful in more than two-thirds of his attempts.

Fielding

When, back in 1954, Rickey and Roth came up with their "efficiency formula" for run scoring and run prevention, the defensive half of the equation was divided into five segments. The first was opponents' batting average; the second was opponents' reaching base through bases on balls or hit batsmen; the third was a measure of a pitcher's clutch ability; the fourth was his strikeout capability; and the fifth was fielding, to which they assigned a mathematical value of zero. "There is nothing on earth," Rickey declared, "anyone can do with fielding." Besides, he added, good fielding might account for the critical run in a ballgame only four or five times a year.

Was Rickey right? The central weakness of the fielding average has long been known: you can't make an error on a ball you don't touch. To counter this weakness in fielding average and to credit the plays made as well as the plays not made, total chances per game is a more useful statistic—and when errors are deducted from chances, you have a fielder's Range Factor. James pointed out how absurd it had become, in a time when the best-fielding second baseman might commit ten errors a season and the worst twenty, to focus on this difference of ten rather than on the 250–300 in total chances which might separate the most agile keystoner from the exemplar of Lot's wife.

Another difficulty with the fielding average is that to

understand what figure represents mean performance (and thus be able to identify inferior and superior fielders), one must adjust for position: a shortstop who fields .980 has done quite well, but a first baseman, catcher, or outfielder with that figure would have been below average. Thus the fan must bring to the fielding average a great deal of background knowledge—the mean for each fielding average for each position in each season. This is a demand that, on first reflection, is not created by the batting average (all men stepping to the plate occupy the same position—batter). On second thought, however, the knowledgeable fan recognizes that a batting line of .267, 10 HRs, 80 RBIs will mean different things when applied to a shortstop or to a left fielder. In other words, just as any evaluation of fielding performance carries an inherent positional bias, so does batting performance.

High double-play totals are believed to indicate excellence among middle infielders, but the more double plays a club turns, as a rule, the worse the pitching. Which teams had the most double plays in major league history? In the 154-game season, the Philadelphia A's of 1949 and the Los Angeles Dodgers of 1958; in the 162-game season, Toronto and Boston of 1980 and Pittsburgh of 1966. Of these, only the last-mentioned had a team ERA better than the league average. If the pitchers are putting a lot of men on base, the team can get a lot of double plays even without a great-fielding shortstop and second baseman.

So what to do? How do we assess fielding excellence? The idea of crediting stellar fielding plays individually has been proposed occasionally ever since 1868, when Chadwick wrote: "The best player in a nine is he who makes the most good plays in a match, not the one who commits the fewest errors, and it is in the record of his good plays that we are to look for the most correct data for an estimate of his skill in the position he occupies." Father Chadwick was correct to see that fielding percentage emphasized failure rather than success, but in truth the fielding percentage was a far better measure of ability in the 1860s, when one play in four produced an error, than now, when only two plays in a hundred are flubbed.

The choice in *Total Baseball* has been to concentrate on Total Chances but not to disregard the error, as Range Factor does; nor to include it in Total Chances, as David Neft would favor; nor to subtract it from Total Chances, as Barry Codell once advocated. The error may be infrequent today but it is not insignificant; instead, it is a peculiarly damaging event, turning an out (with its computer-derived run value of −.25) to, in effect, a hit (with its run value of +.50). This is a turnaround of .75 runs, or *the equivalent of three outs;* an outfield error costs even more, because it so often produces more than one base for batter and runners both. Thus the defensive stats we favor in this book and include in the Player Register, Pitcher Register, and the new Fielding Register, are Linear Weights formulas, expressed in runs and computed differently for the different positions (see the Glossary for the formulas, which have significant refinements in this edition). However, in all cases the elements of the statistics are putouts, assists, double plays, and errors (and for catchers, passed balls).

Position players are gauged by Fielding Runs, a Linear Weights measure of the runs they saved (or allowed) through their play that an average man *at that position*

would not have (second baseman are compared with other second baseman rather than, say, with left fielders—even the worst-fielding second sacker would cost his team fewer runs at the position than the best defensive left fielder). Pitcher Defense (like Pitcher Batting) is to be found in the Pitcher Register. Raw fielding statistics, though of questionable value in and of themselves, have been included in the Fielding Register; the innovation for this second edition of *Total Baseball* is that each player's fielding totals are broken out by position.

Pitching

On to the pitching statistics you will see in the Annual Record and Pitcher Register. First to be reviewed are wins and losses, and won-lost percentage. Wins are a team statistic, obviously, as are losses, but we credit a win entirely to one pitcher in each game. Why not to the shortstop? Or the left fielder? Or some combination of the three? In a 13–11 game, several players may have had more to do with the win than any pitcher. No matter. We're not going to change this custom, though Ban Johnson gave it a good try when he banished it from the American League records for seven years beginning in 1913.

To win many games a pitcher generally must play for a team that wins many games. Look at Red Ruffing's won-lost record with the miserable Red Sox of the 1930s, then at his mark with the Yankees. Or at Danny Jackson, first with Kansas City, then with Cincinnati. There is an endless list of good pitchers traded to stronger offensive clubs who "emerge" as stars.

The recognition of the weakness of this statistic came early. Originally it was not computed by such men as Chadwick because most teams leaned heavily, if not exclusively, on one starter, and relievers as we know them today did not exist. As the season schedules lengthened, the need for a pitching staff became evident, and separating out the team's record on the basis of who was in the box seemed a good idea. However, it was not then nor is it now a good measure of performance, for the simple reason that one may pitch poorly and win, or pitch well and lose.

The natural corrective to this deficiency of the won-lost percentage is the earned run average—which, strangely, preceded it, gave way to it in the 1880s, and then returned in 1912. Originally, the ERA was computed as earned runs per game because pitchers almost invariably went nine innings. In this century it has been calculated as earned runs times nine, divided by innings pitched.

The purpose of the earned run average is noble: to give a pitcher credit for doing what *he* can to prevent runs from scoring, aside from his own fielding lapses and those of the men around him. It succeeds to a remarkable extent in isolating the performance of the pitcher from his situation, but objections to the statistic remain. Say a pitcher retires the first two men in an inning, then has the shortstop kick a ground ball to allow the batter to reach first base. Six runs follow before the third out is secured. How many of these runs are earned? None.

The prime difficulty with the ERA in the early days, say 1913, when one of every four runs scored was unearned, was that a pitcher got a lot of credit in his ERA for playing with a bad defensive club. The errors would serve to cover up in the ERA a good many runs which probably should not have scored. Those runs would hurt the team, but not the pitcher's record. This situation has been aggravated further by the use of newly computed ERAs for pitchers prior to 1913, the first year of its official status. Example: Bobby Mathews, sole pitcher for the New York Mutuals of 1876, allowed 7.19 runs per game, yet his ERA was only 2.86—almost a perfect illustration of the league's 40 percent proportion of earned runs.

It is not an accident that pitchers of the dead-ball era of this century (1900–1919) dominate the lifetime and seasonal leaders tables in ERA. Yes, there were circumstances away from the mound that depressed batting, but the pitchers of that period also benefited mightily in the ERA column from the high number of errors, as compared to today. How to compare the ERA of an Ed Walsh or Three Finger Brown with a Frank Viola or a Dwight Gooden? As with batting stats, normalize the ERA to league average and adjust for home park effects. A pitcher from 1908 whose Adjusted ERA was 150 can be compared to one from 1988 with the same Adjusted ERA—each stood in the same relation to his peers, that is, 50 percent better than average.

What gave rise to the ERA, and what we appreciate about it, is that like the batting average it is an attempt at an isolating stat, a measure of individual performance not dependent upon one's own team. Its principal shortcoming is that it indicates only a pitcher's *rate* of efficiency, not his actual benefit to the team. In a league with an ERA of 4.00, a starter who throws 300 innings with an ERA of 3.50 must be worth more to his team than a starter whose ERA is the same but who pitches in only half as many innings. Through the Linear Weights figures of Pitching Runs (broken out in the top-five section of the Annual Record as Starter Runs and Relief Runs), we can determine the number of runs a pitcher saved his team beyond what a pitcher performing at the league-average ERA would have allowed. A truly simple stat, it consists of nothing more than a pitcher's normalized, or league-adjusted, earned run average weighted by his innings pitched.

Because Pitching Runs has a built-in normalizing factor, when you see it in *Total Baseball* under a heading for "/A," that adjustment will be for park factor. Pitchers' park factor is calculated differently from batters' park factor, for a number of fairly complex reasons that technical-minded readers might best consult in the Glossary.

While the ERA is a far more accurate reflection of a pitcher's value than the BA is of a hitter's, it fails to a greater degree than the BA in offering an isolated measure. For a truly unalloyed individual pitching measure, we must look to the glamour statistic of strikeouts, the pitcher's mate to the home run (though home runs are highly dependent upon home park, strikeouts are to only a slight degree).

Is a strikeout artist a good pitcher? Maybe yes, maybe no; a good analogue would be to ask whether a home run slugger is a good hitter. The two stats run together: periods of high home run activity (as a percentage of all hits) invariably are accompanied by high strikeout totals. Strikeout totals, however, may soar even in the absence of overzealous swingers, say, as the result of a rules change

such as the legalization of overhand pitching in 1884, the introduction of the foul strike (NL, 1901; AL, 1903), or the expanded strike zone in 1963.

Just as home run totals are a function of the era in which one plays, so are strikeouts. The great nineteenth-century totals—Matches Kilroy's 513, Toad Ramsey's 499, One Arm Daily's 483—were achieved under different rules and fashions. No one in that era fanned batters at the rate of one per inning; indeed, among regular pitchers (those with 154 innings pitched or more), only Herb Score did until 1960. In the next five years the barrier was passed by Sandy Koufax, Jim Maloney, Bob Veale, Sam McDowell, and Sonny Siebert. Walter Johnson, Rube Waddell, and Bob Feller didn't run up numbers like that. Were they slower, or easier to hit, than Sonny Siebert?

Even in today's game, which lends itself to the accumulation of, by historic standards, high strikeout totals for a good many pitchers and batters, the strikeout is, as it always has been, just another way to make an out. Yes, it is a sure way to register an out without the risk of advancing baserunners and so is highly useful in a situation such as when there is a man on third with fewer than two outs; otherwise, it is a vastly overrated stat because it has nothing to do with victory or defeat—it is mere spectacle. A high strikeout total indicates raw talent and overpowering stuff, but the imperative of the pitcher is simply to retire the batter, not to crush him. What's not listed in your daily averages are strikeouts by batters—fans are not as interested in that because it's a negative measure—yet the strikeout may be a more significant stat for batters than it is for pitchers.

Bases on balls will drive a manager crazy and put lead in fielders' feet, but it is possible to survive, even to excel, without first-rate control—provided your stuff is good enough to hold down the number of hits. *Total Baseball* offers two stats that are, like strikeouts, highly interesting but ultimately of debatable value: Opponents' Batting Average and Opponents' On Base Percentage. (The same could be said of Fewest Hits Per Game and Fewest Walks Per Game, of course.) It is illuminating to compare one or the other with a pitcher's ERA or Pitching Runs, but both calculations are somewhat academic, for at the end of a game, season, or career, it doesn't matter how many men a pitcher puts on base. Theoretically he can put three men on every inning, leave the twenty-seven baserunners allowed, and pitch a shutout. A man who gives up one hit over nine innings can lose 1–0; it's even possible to allow no hits and lose. Who is the better pitcher? The man with the shutout and twenty-seven baserunners allowed, or the man who allows one hit? No matter how sophisticated your measurements for pitchers, the best ones are counted in runs.

The nature of baseball at all points is one man against nine. It's the pitcher against a series of batters. With that situation prevailing, we have tended to examine batting with intricate, ingenious stats, while viewing pitching through generally much weaker, though perhaps more copious, measurements. What if the game were to be turned around so that we had a "pitching order"— nine pitchers facing one batter? Think of that for a minute. The nature of the statistics would change, too, so that your batting stats would be vastly simplified. You wouldn't care about all the individual components of the batter's performance, all combining in some obscure fashion to reveal run production. You'd care only about *runs*. Yet what each of the nine pitchers did would bear intense scrutiny, and over the course of a year each pitcher's Opponents' Batting Average, Opponents' On Base Percentage, Opponents' Slugging Average, and so forth, would be recorded and spun to come up with a sense of how many runs each pitcher had saved.

A pitching stat with an interesting history is complete games. This is your basic counter stat, but it's taken to mean more than most of those measurements by baseball people and knowledgeable fans. When everyone was completing 90–100 percent of his starts, the stat was without meaning and thus was not kept. As relief pitchers crept into the game after 1905, the percentage of completed games declined rapidly. By the 1920s it became a point of honor to complete three quarters of one's starts; today the man who completes half is quite likely to lead his league. So with these shifting standards, what do CGs tell you? About pitchers, not a lot anymore: about managers and bullpens, a great deal.

Can we say that a pitcher with 18 complete games out of 37 starts is better than one with 12 complete games in 35 starts? Not without a lot of supporting help, we can't, not without a store of knowledge about the individuals, the teams, and especially the eras involved. The more uses to which we attempt to put the stat, the weaker it becomes, the more attenuated its force. If we declare the hurler with 18 CGs "better," how are we to compare him with another pitcher from, say, fifty years earlier who completed 27 out of 30 starts? Or another pitcher of eighty years ago who completed all the games he started? (Jack W. Taylor completed every one of the 187 games he started *over five years*.) Or what about Will White, who in 1880 started 75 games and completed every blessed one of them? But the rules were different, you say, or the ball was less resilient, or they pitched from a different distance, with a different motion, or this, or that. The point is, there are limits to what a traditional, unadjusted baseball statistic can tell you about a player's performance in any given year, let alone compare his efforts to those of a player from a different era.

Of shutouts there is little to say that is not perfectly obvious, except that historical totals have been revised because (a) in 1920–1939 the American League did not count games of less than nine innings as shutouts, and (b) in those years and before, in both leagues, a pitcher was credited with a shutout even if he was pulled midway, if he had pitched enough innings of a combined whitewash. *Total Baseball* counts only complete-game shutouts.

Wins Above Team is, as discussed, a variation of Ted Oliver's stat made public in 1944, which he called the Weighted Rating System. Apart from modifying his math, we have taken Oliver's "points"—the thousands of points his formula gave to hurlers who performed well for poor teams—and by retaining the decimal that he would have discarded, we have come up with a stat that is expressed quite properly in wins. In this second edition, Wins Above Team is recorded only for the top hundred lifetime and season marks.

Newly developed for the first edition of this book was a Clutch Pitching Index that, like the measure for clutch hitting, could be applied to historical data. The CPI is figured by taking how many earned runs the pitcher should have allowed, based on the performance of the batters who faced him, and how many he actually allowed (see the Glossary for the formula). The Clutch Pitching Index consists of expected runs over actual runs, so marks over 100 exceed league-average performance.

For relief pitchers, we have previously discussed saves, and Relief Runs (the Linear Weights category) are figured no differently than Starter Runs. Newly developed here is Relief Ranking, which adjusts Relief Runs for the greater situational importance of each run a bullpenner saves or yields. The other elements of the formula are wins, losses, and saves, in a proportion detailed in the Glossary.

Bringing It All Together

Pitcher Batting and Pitcher Defense are recorded in the Pitcher Register as Linear Weights figures, expressed in runs. (Pitcher batting has been removed from league stats for such computations, so that the batting records of everyday players are compared only with those of their peers and pitchers' batting records are compared only with those of *their* peers.) For this edition we have added to Pitcher Batting Runs the seasonal totals for hits and the pitchers' batting averages. The totals for Pitcher Batting Runs and Fielding Runs are seldom of a great magnitude—and for AL pitchers since 1973, the batting figure is, of course, zero—but in earlier years a pitcher's ability to help himself and his team off the mound has occasionally counted for a great deal in a given season; spitballer Ed Walsh in 1907, the year before he won 40 games for the White Sox, accounted for an astounding 2.3 Fielding Wins. The hitting ability of a Wes Ferrell or Don Drysdale certainly counted for something in their teams' prospects for victory. In *Total Baseball* a pitcher's overall contribution is reflected in the Total Pitcher Index, converted from Runs above average to Wins, based on the Runs required to create an extra Win in that year.

For everyday position players, add Fielding Runs to Stolen Base Runs to Batting Runs, then convert those combined Runs to Wins, and you have the best measure of the complete ballplayer: the Total Player Rating. We believe, however, that a positional adjustment must be made to the above combination to reflect the greater skill required to play, for example, second base than left field; this adjustment is based on the average batting skill required at that position to hold a major league job. Historically, left fielders have presented the best record in Batting Runs and middle infielders the worst. In other words, a left fielder who accounted for 10 Fielding Runs should not be regarded as having the same value to a team as a shortstop who also contributed 10 Fielding Runs: Have the two men switch positions and you would soon see who made more of a defensive contribution. And because some positions—shortstop, catcher, second base, and third base—are harder to play than others, we see a relative scarcity of good hitters at these positions and an abundance at the others. Again, see the Glossary for more detail.

The ultimate stat brings together batters, pitchers, fielders, and baserunners in the Total Baseball Ranking. The equivalent of a Most Valuable Player Award and Cy

Young Award wrapped into one, it reveals the best baseball player every season and the best ever. Relief pitchers and shortstops can compete on the same plane—wins contributed to their team through all their accomplishments. In 1978 the MVP question in the American League was whether to vote for Jim Rice, who had 46 homers, 139 RBIs, and 400 total bases (the first time for an American Leaguer in forty-one years), or for Ron Guidry, 25–3 with an .893 won-lost percentage that was the all-time high for a starter with 20 or more wins, and whose ERA of 1.74 was less than half the league average. Why don't you flip to the page in the Annual Record for 1978 and see for yourself who deserved the MVP Award that year.

Total Baseball also sums things up on the team level. Fielding Runs are expressed as Wins in the team stats section of the Annual Record, as are Batting Runs, Stolen Base Runs, and Pitching Runs. This enables one to see the component parts of a team's predicted success or failure—that is, the wins or losses beyond the average (a .500 season) that the players' performance could have been expected to produce. The Differential figure (DIF) in this section of the Annual Record states the spread between the team's actual won-lost record and that predicted by the Linear Weights measures of batting, base stealing, fielding, and pitching. The miracle Mets of 1969 exceeded expectations by 13 Wins—in other words, instead of finishing 87–75 as their players' performance would have warranted, they finished 100–62. Did the White Sox also do it with mirrors in 1990? Check for yourself.

Errors and Controversies

The data ICI reported in the first edition of *The Baseball Encyclopedia* upset many people in baseball, for their numbers were different from those traditionally accepted; however, their changes were responsible ones, the product of new research that corrected errors of long standing, or in response to the rulings of the Special Baseball Records Committee. For example, much of the statistical information on Hall of Fame plaques was rendered obsolete. The result has been that through the ensuing editions, the offending data has been fudged to bring it into line with tradition—more on this in a moment.

Despite the uproar that greeted ICI's revised numbers, 1969 was hardly the first time corrections had been made to official data. In 1929 Grover Cleveland Alexander won his 373rd game, breaking Christy Mathewson's National League record, then thought to be 372. He never won another game. A number of years later, Joe Reichler found a game in which, by today's rules, Matty should have gotten the win, this game taking place on May 21, 1902. The record was changed and they were given a tie. The problem was that no one checked all of Mathewson's other games to see how many times he received a win under the old rules that wouldn't have been credited that way today. When ICI did their research in 1968, they found Matty had only 367 wins total by today's rules, while Alexander had 374. (Further research, notably by Frank Williams, has restored Alexander and Mathewson to a tie at 373 wins.) The Records Committee decided that all wins and losses should be awarded according to the present rules, so Macmillan printed the totals as such

in the *Baseball Encyclopedia*. However, after the book came out, Commissioner Bowie Kuhn decided that it was better to show stats that agreed with previously published recognized sources, so all records—not only those of Mathewson and Alexander—were supposed to be changed back in accordance with the scoring practices at the time. What happened in the next edition was that some records, especially those of the stars, were changed, while others were not; team totals and the records of other players on the same team were not; and the data base was corrupted.

Here's another celebrated example of record-book flip-flops. When the American League was formed in 1901, Nap Lajoie was credited with a .422 average, with 220 hits in 543 at-bats. After a number of years, someone noticed that if you take these at-bats and hits, the average comes out only to .405, so his average was changed. (Turkin/Thompson gave Nap a mark of .409 in its first edition.) Later in the 1950s, John Tattersall had his doubts and decided to go through his newspaper collection of box scores. He found 229 hits for Lajoie, not 220—the error had been in the figure for hits, not in the figure for batting average. Thus his average was restored to .422, which happened to be the highest in American League history. Then ICI research in this area came up with a .426 mark (232 for 544, based on newspaper accounts), which was published in the first edition, then trimmed back to .422 in subsequent editions. The .426 figure is the one this book uses.

Nap seemed to be involved in a number of controversies. ICI research found four more hits for him in 1902, raising his average from .369 to .378. Later editions have changed Lajoie's stats back to the old values; we have not.

In 1910 there was a very close batting race between Cobb and Lajoie. At the end of the season, most people thought Nap had won, based on his getting seven hits in a doubleheader on the final day of the season. There was talk that the opposing Browns had let him get a number of bunts by playing back, so that the hated Cobb would lose. However, the AL office went over their figures and gave Cobb the title, .385 to .384. Nearly eighty years later, Pete Palmer discovered a critical error: a game in which Cobb had two hits in three at-bats had been entered twice. This was found because Sam Crawford had 157 games on his official sheet yet the Tigers only played 156. It turned out that Detroit played a doubleheader on September 24, but the second game inadvertently was inserted in the official sheets as being played on September 25. Later, this second game of the twenty-fourth, which appeared to have been missing, was put in the scoresheets again. The League Office discovered this mistake soon after its official announcement that Cobb had won the batting title, because the double entry was corrected for all the other Detroit players. However, Ban Johnson had made a big deal out of how carefully his people had checked the figures in order to settle the controversy, so they kept quiet about the gaffe, leaving Cobb the winner.

Appeals to Commissioner Kuhn in 1981 to set the matter straight officially were to no avail, because that would not only have changed the outcome of the 1910 batting race, it would also have altered Cobb's lifetime hit total, then being pursued to massive media attention by Pete Rose. Kuhn's statement read, in part, "The passage of 70 years, in our judgment . . . constitutes a certain statute of limitation as to recognizing any changes in the records with confidence of the accuracy of such changes. . . . Since a variety of questions have been raised through the years about the accuracy of the statistics of that period, the only way to make changes with confidence would be for a complete and thorough review of all team and individual statistics. That is not practical." It may not have not been practical, but we have done it, and are continuing to do it. A notable area of change reflected in this second edition of *Total Baseball* is the National Association period of 1871–1875, in which the research of Michael Stagno and a team of SABR researchers have not only supplied new, more accurate statistics but also a handful of new players, previously not included in any baseball encyclopedia.

In 1912, Heinie Zimmerman got credit for a Triple Crown victory, although it wasn't called that then. Ernie Lanigan's RBI figures gave him 98, compared to 94 for Honus Wagner. However, ICI research gave Wagner 102 and Zimmerman 99. Later editions of *The Baseball Encyclopedia* changed Zimmerman up to 103—giving him back his phony Triple Crown.

The National League batting data has been pretty accurate since 1910. That was the first year that the NL kept daily game records for teams as well as players and compared the team totals to the sum for the players for that team and tried to resolve any differences. Before then, the team totals simply *were* the sum for the players. The American League had team totals all the way back to 1905, but never compared them with the sum of the players and therefore had a great many errors. The AL, however, did introduce team pitching first in 1930, while the NL followed in 1941. The AL never published league totals, so the fact that the batter hits, strikeouts, walks, etc. did not agree with the corresponding pitcher totals was somewhat academic. However, the NL did publish league totals starting in 1926, and when they first presented team pitching, the totals did not agree. In order to make this look correct, they doctored the pitching totals to agree with the batting stats. After a few years, this was no longer necessary, as they took the time to resolve and correct differences. For the AL, most team totals did not agree with the sum of the players for that team until around 1935: the at-bats, runs, hits, and extra-base hits usually checked out, but walks and strikeouts did not add up until the 1960s. The AL converted to computer in 1973, while the NL did in 1981, improving accuracy.

On the whole there have been surprisingly few errors in the National League stats. Most of the bigger ones have involved innings pitched in the years before 1930. Because no one added up the innings and compared them to putouts to check for discrepancies, in 1926 Wayland Dean brought up the rear in ERA with a 6.10 mark. It turned out that his innings pitched had been added up incorrectly, and he should have had 204, not 164. This reduced his ERA to 4.90. For a game in 1920, Jimmy Ring had his faced batsman total of 35 put in the innings pitched column, giving him 26 extra innings pitched for the game. It would seem that someone adding up innings pitched would question a figure of 35 for one game, but it slipped through. Ring was also credited for nine extra innings in 1923. But the strangest mix-up in the NL was in

1909, the year before the team totals were kept. For some strange reason, 700 putouts were dropped from the team totals, all the result of adding mistakes for catchers. Pat Moran and Red Dooin each lost 200, while Peaches Graham, Bill Bergen, and Doc Marshall lost 100 each.

The American League has had many errors of 100 or more putouts or assists over the years due to addition mistakes, as well as quite a few blunders in innings pitched. Ed Willett in 1910 lost 77 innings, showing only 147 instead of 224. The correction lowered his ERA from 3.60 to 2.36. However, this was still more than a run behind the leader, Ed Walsh. Frank Williams discovered a dozen or more errors in entering wins and losses for pitchers in the AL *every year* from 1905 through 1919. And John Tattersall, in his home run research, found over 100 official errors, about 80 percent in the AL and most before 1920. George Sisler picked up 3 new homers, These were on April 12, 1916, September 22, 1921, and June 29, 1929.

From 1912 to 1914, the AL statistician decided not to enter anything for a player who had all zeroes for his line in any given game. Most of these were relief pitchers, but they had entries on their pitching sheets and these games were restored by the ICI researchers. There were about 600 other cases where nonpitchers had games omitted. These are included in *Total Baseball*. This kind of record keeping over the early years kept some men out of the encyclopedias altogether, like pinch runners or defensive replacements. SABR research has added several of these one-time ciphers to *The Baseball Encyclopedia* over the years, as well as to *Total Baseball*.

For the American League records of 1913, the official sheets disagree with the data published in the baseball guides for almost every player. The only logical explanation is that the official figures weren't ready when it came time to publish the guide, so they must have used data from another source. *Total Baseball* uses the official figures, as they have daily sheets to support the data.

An interesting quirk in the way records are kept—and another reminder, as if one needed it, that baseball record keeping remains subject to error and controversy—occurred as recently as 1981. The league rule was to round off the innings pitched at the end of the season, although the weekly reports showed thirds of innings. Baltimore's Sammy Stewart had 29 earned runs in 112⅓ innings, while Oakland's Steve McCatty had 48 in 185⅔ innings. This gave Stewart the ERA title, 2.323 to 2.327. But when the innings were rounded off, McCatty won, 2.32 to 2.33. McCatty got the title, but the next year both leagues decided to count thirds of innings.

Sources

The computer has made possible the rapid analysis of mountains of raw baseball data based upon observed games or mathematically accurate, probabilistic computer simulations. Questions once thought to be unanswerable are mysteries no longer. What is the worth, in terms of its run-producing capacity, of a single, or a walk, or a homer? How valuable is a stolen base? Who were the best clutch hitters? But as invaluable as the computer has been in producing the statistical data for *Total Baseball,* the editors owe more to the people who have contributed their time, their expertise, their love of the game, and their passion for getting things right. These individuals are listed here, in the Acknowledgments, or in the table at the end of the book of those readers of the first edition who helped us improve the accuracy of *Total Baseball* this time around. A collective debt is owed to the Society for American Baseball Research and the National Baseball Library.

The statistics were obtained primarily from the following sources:

- John Tattersall Collection of newspaper box scores and compilations for 1876–1890 NL.
- ICI computer printouts, National Baseball Library, 1891–1902 NL, 1882–1891 AA, 1884 UA, 1890 PL, 1901–1904 AL, 1914–1915 FL.
- Official league averages, 1903–date NL, 1905–date AL.
- Michael Stagno Collection of newspaper box scores and compilations for 1871–1875 NA, supplemented by research of SABR's nineteenth century research committee, headed by Bob Tiemann.

Supplemental sources were:

- For batters hit by pitch, 1884–1899 AA/NL/PL, 1909–1916 NL, 1909–1919 AL, research from newspapers by Alex Haas, Pete Palmer, John Schwartz, Bob Davids, John Tattersall, Lyle Spatz, and others. (Note: research continues for the 1903–1908 period.)
- For home runs allowed by pitchers, 1876–1950 AL/ NL, the Tattersall Collection, reviewed and corrected by Bob McConnell.
- For runs batted in, 1903–1919 NL, 1905–1919 AL, ICI research.
- For runs batted in, 1880–1885 NL, David Neft.
- For pitcher saves (except 1901–1919 AL) 1876–1968 NL/AA/UA/PL/AL.
- For stolen bases, 1886 NL, *Spalding Baseball Guide.*
- For wins and losses for pitchers, 1876–1900 NL/ AA/PL, and for wins, losses, games started, com-

plete games, shutouts, saves, 1900–1919 AL, and complete pitching data, 1892, research from newspapers and official sheets by Frank Williams.
- For shutouts, 1876–1939 AL, Joe Wayman.
- For biographical data, the biographical research committee of SABR, notably Richard Topp, Bill Carle.
- For caught-stealing data, 1914–1916 AL, 1915–1916 NL, Ernie Lanigan, courtesy of Bob Davids.
- For home/away data, 1876–1891 NL/AA/UA/PL, Bob McConnell.
- For game scores, 1876–1884 NL/AA/UA, Bob Tiemann.
- For game scores, 1885–1891 NL/AA/PL, Richard Topp.
- For runs and homers home/away, 1980s NL/AL, Bill Carr.

Missing data includes:

- Hit batters: 1903–1908 AL.
- Caught stealing: 1886–1914, 1916 (players with more than 20 steals), 1917–1919, 1926–1950 NL; 1886–1891 AA; 1890 PL; 1901–1913, 1916 (players with more than 20 steals), 1917–1919, 1914–15 FL.
- Sacrifice hits: 1927–1930 (fly balls advancing runners to any base counted as sacrifice hits).
- Sacrifice flies: 1908–1930, 1939, 1940–1953.
- Runs batted in, 1882–1887, 1890 AA; 1884 UA.
- Strikeouts for batters: 1882–1888, 1890 AA; 1884 UA; 1897–1909 NL; 1901–1912 AL.

Incomplete data for those years through 1902 NL and 1904 AL are available from the ICI computer printouts at the National Baseball Library. Additional research could turn up more data. If your research or sharp eye should detect errors or gaps in *Total Baseball,* please write us in care of the publisher and we'll be delighted to improve our data and credit your catch in the next edition.

Sabermetrics

Sabermetrics may be a new coinage for the statistical analysis of baseball but it is not a new phenomenon. Henry Chadwick, in the antebellum period, was as much a sabermetrician as Allan Roth or Bill James or Pete Palmer: he saw as clearly as they that because the object of the game is to win, runs are the best measure of player performance, just as they are of team performance at the end of a game.

After many decades in which this fundamental truth was lost (amid the general worship of false idols like batting average and pitcher won-lost percentage), today's sabermetricians have come around full circle to the game as it was originally understood. And what's remarkable about this is that in order to return to the primordial simplicity of the 1840s, '50s, and '60s, when runs and outs were all that went in to the box score, they have relied upon computer simulations and higher mathematics. In other words, with the new statistics, simplicity emerges from complexity; what baseball statistics have offered for the last hundred years or so has been, despite the appearance of simplicity, in fact extremely complex.

For the veteran fan as well as for Organized Baseball, new ideas, new statistics, and new discoveries that dispute long-held verities (Ty Cobb's hit total, Hoss Radbourn's number of victories in 1884, etc.) may represent a challenge to tradition and thus a threat to the very soul of baseball, its proud anachronism. Bernard Malamud wrote, "The whole history of baseball has the quality of mythology." The editors of *Total Baseball* relish the game's myths, from Abner Doubleday to the sacrifice bunt, and believe that in setting the record straight or turning conventional wisdom on its head, they are adding to the fan's enjoyment of the rich texture of the game. If you are one of the skeptics—like Earl Weaver, who once said, "There's no such thing as a new statistic"—please permit us to make the case for sabermetrics.

If you skipped over the preceding Introduction, which is largely taken up with an overview of baseball's traditional measures, we would encourage you to go back and read it before proceeding with this discussion of sabermetrics. As with the Introduction, much of the material in this section is adapted from the editors' earlier *The Hidden Game of Baseball*.

What's in a Number?

On April 27, 1983, the Montreal Expos came to bat in the bottom of the eighth inning trailing the Houston Astros 4–2. First up to face pitcher Nolan Ryan was Tim Blackwell, a lifetime .228 hitter who had struck out in his first time at bat. At this routine juncture of this commonplace game, Ryan stared down at Blackwell, but his invisible—yet, for all that, more substantial—opponent was a man who had died the month before Ryan was born, a man about whom Ryan knew nothing, he confessed, except his statistical line. For at this moment of his glorious big-league career, Ryan had accumulated a total of 3,507 strikeouts, only one short of the mark Walter Johnson set over twenty-one seasons, from 1907 to 1927. Long thought invulnerable, Johnson's record was in imminent danger of falling, in 1983, not only to Ryan but also to Steve Carlton and Gaylord Perry.

Ryan fanned Blackwell and then froze the next batter, pinch-hitter Brad Mills, with a 1-and-2 curveball. The pinnacle was his. Johnson had been baseball's all-time strikeout leader since 1921, when he surpassed Cy Young. Ryan would hold that title for just a few weeks, then would be overtaken by Carlton, only to display an incredible finishing kick and top the 5,000 mark in 1990. But at the time that Ryan topped Johnson, baseball savants scurried to assess the meaning of 3,509 for both the deposed King of K and the new.

In the aftermath of Ryan's feat, some writers pointed out that he only needed sixteen full seasons, plus fractions of two others, in which to record 3,509 strikeouts while Johnson needed twenty-one, or that Johnson pitched over 2,500 more innings than Ryan. Coming into the 1983 season, Ryan had fanned 9.44 men per nine innings, while Johnson was way down the list at 5.33. And Ryan allowed fewer hits per nine innings than Johnson, or, for that matter, anyone in the history of the game. So, it would seem 3,509 was not just one batter better than Johnson, but rather was mere confirmation for the masses of a superiority that was clear to the cognoscenti years before.

However, other writers introduced mitigating factors on Johnson's behalf, much as Ruth found supporters as the home run king even after Aaron hit number 715. These champions of the old order cited Johnson's won-lost record of 417–279 and earned run average of 2.17 while scoffing at Ryan's mark, entering 1983, of 205–186 with an ERA of 3.11. This tack led to further argument in print, bringing in the quality of the teams each man pitched for and against, the resiliency of the ball, the attitudes of the batters in each era toward the strikeout, the advent of night ball, integration, expansion, the designated hitter, the overall talent pool, competition from other professional sports . . . and on down into the black hole of subjectivism.

Why were so many things dragged into that discussion?

Because the underlying question about 3,509 was: Does this total make Ryan better than Johnson, or even a better *strikeout* pitcher than Johnson? At the least, does it make him a great pitcher? In our drive to identify excellence on the baseball field (or off it), we inevitably look to the numbers as a means of encapsulating and comprehending experience. This quantifying habit is at the heart of baseball's hidden game, the one ceaselessly played by Ryan and Johnson and Ruth and Aaron—and, thanks to baseball's voluminous records, more than 13,000 other players—in a stadium bounded only by the imagination.

What's in a number? The answer to "How Many?" and sometimes a great deal more. In this case, 3,509 men had come to the plate against Ryan and failed to put the ball in play, one more man than Johnson had returned to the dugout, cursing. So what's the big deal? That Ryan was .0002849 faster, scarier, tougher—better—than Johnson? An absolute number like 3,509, or 714 (the home-run record once thought invulnerable, too), or 4,191 (the erroneous hit total of Ty Cobb that Pete Rose finally surpassed) does not resound with meaning unless it is placed into some context that will give it life.

Baseball statistics are not the instruments of vivisection, taking the life out of the game in order to examine it; rather, statistics are themselves the vital part of baseball, the only tangible and imperishable remains of contests played yesterday or a hundred years ago. Baseball may be loved without statistics, but it cannot be understood without them. As the statistics reflect more accurately the reality of what happened on the field, greater understanding leads to a deeper love and appreciation of this great game—which is, essentially, the case for sabermetrics and the reason for *Total Baseball*.

The Linear Weights System

In 1982, Milwaukee's Robin Yount had the year of his life, batting .331 with 29 homers, 114 RBIs and 129 runs scored; he led the American League in hits, doubles, total bases, and slugging percentage, while finishing just one point behind the league leader in batting average. First of the two times in his career, he was voted the Most Valuable Player in the American League, being named first on all but one of the twenty-eight ballots cast by the baseball writers.

Over in the other league, Mike Schmidt of the Phillies was having an off year, batting only .280 with 35 homers and 87 RBIs; the previous year, when he was awarded the MVP, in only 102 games played he had totaled 31 homers and 91 RBIs. He did lead the league once again in 1982 in slugging percentage, and he did win the Gold Glove at third base for the seventh straight year, yet in the MVP balloting none of the ballots listed him higher than fourth; ten ballots were cast without listing him at all.

For Yount, 1982 was a crowning achievement; for Schmidt, a disappointment: That is the verdict reached by the baseball writers and conventional baseball statistics. Yet in terms of actual performance, as determined by the number of runs contributed, Schmidt's "off year" was scarcely different from Yount's. With the bat, Yount accounted for 50.3 runs beyond what an average batter might have contributed; Schmidt, 47.2. Through base

stealing, Yount added 2.4; Schmidt none. With the glove, Yount was 4 runs below league average at his position; Schmidt was 18.8 above average at *his* position. Total runs contributed: Yount 48.7, Schmidt 66.0. Total wins contributed beyond average by each: Yount 6.5, Schmidt 6.3. Both men had outstanding seasons, the best in their respective leagues, and both outstripped the second-best player by about the same margin.

Viewing player (and team) performance through this sort of prism frequently produces such illuminating results. Cecil Fielder had a wonderful year in 1990, with his 51 homers, 132 RBIs, and league-leading figures in slugging average and extra-base hits. But how did he convince any writer voting for MVP that he had a better year than Rickey Henderson? In *Total Baseball,* you could look it up: Fielder contributed 4.4 extra wins to his team (wins that an average player would not), which was the fourth-best figure in the American League that year; Henderson was responsible for a whopping 7.7, not only the top mark in 1990 but also the third-best mark in the AL since Ted Williams's epic season in 1941!

This is the kind of analysis of player performance possible with a variety of sabermetric measures, not just the Linear Weights System. The common ingredient of most of the new, as yet unofficial statistics is their creators' recognition of the relationship between runs and wins.

Runs and Wins

George Lindsey, in an article in *Operations Research* in 1963, was the first to assign run values to the various offensive events which lead to runs: Runs = (.41)1B + (.32)2B + (1.06)3B + (1.42)HR. He based these values on recorded play-by-play data and basic probability theory. Unlike Earnshaw Cook, who in the following year assigned run values on the basis of the sum of the individual scoring probabilities—that is, the *direct* run potential of the hit or walk plus those of the baserunners set in motion—Lindsey recognized that a substantial part of the run value of any non-out is that *it brings another man to the plate*. This additional batter has a one-in-three chance of reaching base and thus bringing another man to the plate with the same chance, as do the batters to follow. The *indirect* run potential of these batters cannot be ignored.

Steve Mann's Run Productivity Average (RPA) assigned these values based on observation of some 12,000 plate appearances: RPA = (.51)1B + (.82)2B + (1.38)3B + (2.63)HR + (.25)BB + (.15)SB − (.25)CS, all divided by plate appearances, then plus .016. His values were denominated in terms of the number of runs *and RBIs* each event produced. Bill James, at about the same time, came up with a similar formula, since shunned, with values based on runs plus RBIs *minus home runs*. The drawbacks to the approaches of Mann and James were the drawbacks of the RBI, which gives the entire credit for producing a run to the man who plates it, and of the run scored, which gives credit only to the man who touches home, no matter how he came to do so. For example, with no outs, a man reaches first on an error; the next batter hits a double, placing runners on second and third; the following batter taps a roller to short and is thrown out at first, with the run scoring from third. The man who produced the out is given the credit for producing a run, while the man who started the sequence by reaching first on an error is likewise credited with a run. The man who hit the double, which was surely the key event in the sequence which produced the run, and the only one reflecting batting skill, receives no credit whatsoever. In this regard, any formula based on "Runs Produced" (whether R + RBI or R + RBI − HR) is philosophically inferior to the formula Lindsey proposed, despite his failure to account for walks, steals, and other events.

The run values in the Linear Weights formula for identifying batters' real contribution are derived from Pete Palmer's 1978 computer simulation of all major-league games played since 1901. All the data available concerning the frequencies of the various events was collected; following a test run, these were tabulated. Unmeasured quantities, such as the probability of a man going from first to third on a single vs. that of his advancing only one base, were assigned values based on play-by-play analysis of over 100 World Series contests. The goal was to get all the measured quantities very nearly equal to the league statistics; then the simulation would provide run values of each event in terms of net runs produced above average. Expressing the values in those terms would give a meaningful base line to individual performances, because if you are told that a player contributed 87 runs you don't know what that signifies unless you know the average level of run contribution in that year: 87 may sound like a lot, but if the norm was 80, then you know the player contributed only 7 runs beyond average.

The values obtained from the simulation are remarkably similar from one era to the next, confounding expectations that the home run would prove more valuable today than in the dead-ball era, or that the steal was once a primary offensive weapon. These values are expressed in beyond average runs.

Run Values of Various Events, by Periods

Event	Period			
	1901–20	1921–40	1941–60	1961–77
home run	1.36	1.40	1.42	1.42
triple	1.02	1.05	1.03	1.00
double	.82	.83	.30	.77
single	.46	.50	.47	.45
walk/HBP	.32	.35	.35	.33
stolen base	.20	.22	.19	.19
caught stealing	−.33	−.39	−.36	−.32
out*	−.24	−.30	−.27	−.25

*An out is considered to be a hitless at bat and its value is set so that the sum of all events times their frequency is zero, thus establishing zero as the base line, or norm, for performance.

In the years since this simulation was conducted, statistician Dave Smith ("Maury Wills and the Value of the Stolen Base," *Baseball Research Journal*, 1980) convinced Pete to adjust the values of the stolen base and caught stealing because of their situation-dependent, elective nature: Attempts are apt to occur more frequently in close games, where they would be worth more than if they were distributed randomly the way an event like a single or a home run would be. Pete revised the value for the steal upward to .30 runs, while for the caught stealing it becomes −.60 runs.

Just as these run values change marginally with changing conditions of play, they differ slightly up and down the batting order (a homer is not worth as much to the leadoff hitter as it is to the fifth-place batter; a walk is worth more for the man batting second than for the man batting eighth); however, these differences have been averaged out in the figures above. For evaluating runs contributed by any batter at any time, there is no better method than Batting Runs, the Linear Weights formula derived from the computer simulation which is the basis of the table above.

The Formula

Runs = (.47)1B + (.78)2B + (1.09)3B + (1.40)HR + (.33)(BB + HB) + (.30)SB − (.60)CS − (.25)(AB − H) − .50(OOB).

The events not included in the formula that you might have thought to see are sacrifices, sacrifice hits, grounded into double plays, and reached on error. The last is not known for most years and in the official statistics is indistinguishable from outs on base (OOB). The sacrifice has essentially canceling values, trading an out for an advanced base which, often as not, leaves the team in a situation with poorer run potential than it had before the sacrifice. The sacrifice fly has dubious run value because it is entirely dependent upon a situation not under the batter's control: While a single or a walk always has a potential run value, a long fly does not unless a man happens to be poised at third base (whether it is achieved by accident or design is open to question, as well, but that is beside the question—getting hit by a pitch is not a product of intent, either). Last, the grounded into double play is to a far greater extent a function of one's place in the batting order than it is of poor speed or failure in the clutch, and thus it does not find a home in a formula applicable to all batters. It is no accident that Henry Aaron, who ran well for most of his long career and wasn't too bad in the clutch, hit into more DP's than anyone else, nor that Roberto Clemente, Al Kaline, and Frank Robinson, who fit the same description, are also among the ten "worst" in this department. If Boston's Luis Rivera doesn't hit into many twin killings, it's not because of adept bat handling or blazing speed but because he bats ninth.

The Linear Weights formula for batters may be long, but it calls for only addition, subtraction, and multiplication and thus is as simple as the slugging average, whose incorrect weights (1, 2, 3, and 4) it revises and expands upon. Each event has a value and a frequency, just as in slugging average, yet as in no batting statistic you have ever seen, outs are treated as offensive events with a run value of their own (albeit a negative one), a truth so obvious it somehow escaped notice. Just as the run potential for a team in a given half inning is boosted by a man reaching base, it is diminished by a man being retired; not only has he failed to change the situation on the bases but he has deprived his team of the services of a man further down the order who might have come up in this half inning, either with men on base and/or with scores already in.

What Batting Runs does is to take every offensive event

and treat it in terms of its impact upon the team—an average team, so that a man does not benefit in his individual record for having the good fortune to bat cleanup with the Giants or suffer for batting seventh with the Astros. The relationship of individual performance to team play is stated poorly or not at all in conventional baseball statistics. In Batting Runs it is crystal clear: The linear progression, the sum of the various offensive events, when weighted by their accurately predicted run values, will total the runs contributed by that batter or that team beyond the league average.

Recognizing some dedicated readers of *Total Baseball* will wish to keep track of batting performance by computing Batting Runs themselves over the course of a season, and that they may be frustrated by the difficulty of calculating the "At Bats–Hits" factor for the league, which is necessary to determine the negative value of an out, we advise that using a fixed value of −.25 for outs will tend to work quite well if you wish to include pitcher batting performance, and a fixed value of −.27 will serve if you wish to delete it. Actually, any fixed value will suffice in midseason; it's only when all the numbers are in and you care to compare this year's results with last year's (or with those of the 1927 Yankees) that more precision is desirable. At that point the value of the out may be calculated by the ambitious among you, but ideally, your newspaper or the sporting press will provide accurate Batting Runs figures. Who, after all, calculates ERA for himself?

Batting Runs and Production

For those to whom calculation is anathema, or at the least no pleasure, Batting Runs has a "shadow stat" that tracks its accuracy to a remarkable degree and is a breeze to calculate: Production, which consists simply of On Base Percentage Plus Slugging Average. While it is not expressed in runs and thus lacks the philosophical appeal of Batting Runs, the standard deviation of its most complete version is 20.4 runs compared to the 19.8 of Batting Runs. In other words, the correlation between Batting Runs and Production over the course of an average team season is 99.7 percent.

However, as an average or ratio, Production measures the *rate* of batting success (efficiency), while Batting Runs measures the *amount* of success. For example, a batter who goes 2-for-5 with a walk in one game, those 2 hits being doubles, will have an On Base Percentage of .500 and a Slugging Average of .800; his Production will be 1.3, or as stated for convenience in *Total Baseball,* 130. Another batter, who in 162 games gets 200 hits and 100 walks in 500 at bats, with 400 total bases, will have an identical OBP, SLG, and PRO. Which player has contributed more to his team? Clearly, longevity, or *amount* of production, is no less important than *rate* of production.

To cite a specific instance in which Production and Batting Runs differ, take George Brett's remarkable 1980 season in which he batted .390, had 298 total bases, 75 bases through walks or HBP, and 118 RBIs—all in only 117 games played. In the table of all-time single-season leaders in production, the Kansas City third baseman ranks 34th when his PRO of 1.124 is normalized to the league average and adjusted for home-park effects. Yet in

the table of park adjusted Batting Runs, Brett's season ranks only 106th because he missed 45 games, in which his team derived no benefit from his high rate of performance. (Had Brett played 162 games and continued to perform at the same level, his Batting Runs would have been not 64.8 but 89.7, the 21st best mark in history.)

Because PRO is not expressed in runs, it is less versatile than Batting Runs. For just as runs are proportional to the events that form them, so are they proportional to wins and losses. This statement, a truism today, was a novelty in 1954 when Rickey and Roth first stated the correlation between run differentials and team standings. But they did not take the next step, to recognize that not only a team's standing *but even its won-lost record* could be predicted from the run totals.

"The initial published attempt on this subject," Pete wrote in the 1982 issue of the SABR annual *The National Pastime,* "was Earnshaw Cook's *Percentage Baseball,* in 1964. Examining major-league results from 1950 through 1960 he found winning percentage equal to .484 times runs scored divided by runs allowed.... Arnold Soolman, in an unpublished paper which received some media attention, looked at results from 1901 through 1970 and came up with winning percentage equal to .102 times runs scored per game minus .103 times runs allowed per game plus .505.... Bill James, in the *Baseball Abstract,* developed winning percentage equal to runs scored raised to the power x, divided by the sum of runs scored and runs allowed each raised to the power x. Originally, x was equal to two but then better results were obtained when a value of 1.83 was used....

"My work showed that as a rough rule of thumb, each additional ten runs scored (or ten less runs allowed) produced one extra win, essentially the same as the Soolman study. However, breaking the teams into groups showed that high-scoring teams needed more runs to produce a win. This runs-per-win factor I determined to be ten times the square root of the average number of runs scored per inning by both teams. Thus in normal play, when 4.5 runs per game are scored by each club, each team scores .5 runs per inning—totaling one run, the square root of which is one, times ten."

Note that when Palmer refers to the need for approximately ten additional runs scored (or ten fewer allowed) to provide a team with an additional win, he does *not* mean that it takes ten runs to win any given game. Obviously, in a specific case, a one-run margin is all that is required; but statistics are designed for the long haul, not the short.

What does this have to do with Batting Runs? Remembering that Batting Runs are expressed not simply in runs but in beyond-average runs, the conversion from a batter's Linear Weights *runs* to his *wins* is a snap: simply divide Batting Runs by the number of runs it takes to gain an extra win in a given year. Taking the exploits of Babe Ruth in 1927, we see that through batting alone he contributed 100.7 runs, or 9.56 wins, since in the American League in 1927 it took 10.53 runs to produce an additional win. If every other player on the Yankees had performed at the league average, the New York record should have been 87–67; if each of the seven other batters had performed only half as well as Ruth and had added five extra wins (discounting reserves, pitchers, fielders, and stealers, whom we shall presume for this discussion to have been average), the Yankees would have gained another 35 wins (7×5) to finish with a won-lost mark of 122–32.

Stolen Base Runs

The Linear Weights formula for batters contains a factor for base stealers, expressed in runs. How do you judge the effectiveness of a base stealer? Conventional baseball statistics will lead you to the conclusion that whoever has the most steals is the best thief; that is the sole criterion for *The Sporting News* annual "Golden Shoe Award" in each league. How often the man with the most steals may have been thrown out is of no concern.

An article in the 1981 *Baseball Research Journal* by Bob Davids offered something more sophisticated yet utterly simple: a stolen base percentage, which is simply stolen bases divided by attempts. The best stolen base average of all time, insofar as we know and based on a minimum of 30 attempts, is Max Carey's in 1922 when he stole 51 bases in 53 attempts. The most times caught stealing in the course of a season was Ty Cobb's 38 in 1915, until 1982 when Rickey Henderson was nabbed 42 times. But the best method yet devised, and the one that is pleasingly simple, is to apply the Linear Weights method to get Stolen Base Runs. One multiplies the steals by their run value of .30 and the failed attempts by −.60, and adds the two products. The implication for such men as Ty Cobb, Rickey Henderson, and Vince Coleman is clear: It takes a fabulous stealing performance to produce as much as one extra win for the team.

In 1915 Ty Cobb, when he established the modern stolen base record of 96, can be seen to have contributed to his team 28.8 runs, while his 38 foiled larcenies cost 22.8. Thus Cobb, for all his whirling-dervish activity, accounted for only 6 non-par runs—not even a single win. Whoa! You mean that not a single one of Cobb's steals produced a victory? That is not what is being said: the fact is that while the gain from the stolen base is entirely visible—an extra base which may be followed by a hit that would otherwise not have produced a run—the cost of the caught stealing is entirely invisible, or conjectural, except with the aid of statistics. How many big innings did Cobb run his team out of? How many batters reached base in ensuing innings who might, in an earlier inning, have had their contributions count for runs? What Stolen Base Runs indicate are that, *on balance*, not on a specific-case basis, the stolen base is at best a dubious method of increasing a team's run production.

Now let's take a look at what Henderson did. His record 130 stolen bases in 1982 produced 39 runs for his team. His 42 failed attempts took away 25.2 possible runs. Net effect: approximately 14 runs, or one and a half wins, a performance nearly *three times* as good as Cobb's. In 1983, stealing 22 fewer bases, he was even better, accounting for 21.0 runs. However, the all-time best stealing record is that of Maury Wills in 1962, when he stole 104 bases and was caught only 13 times. Wills's 104 stolen bases produced 31.2 runs; his 13 failed attempts cost only 7.8. So, his baserunning contribution was 23.4, or a little over two wins.

Fielding Runs

As mentioned earlier, in 1954 when Branch Rickey and Allan Roth came up with their "efficiency formula" for run scoring and run prevention, the defensive half of the equation was divided into five segments, the last of which was fielding, to which they assigned a mathematical value of zero. "There is nothing on earth," Rickey declared, "anyone can do with fielding."

Since then many have tried, with mixed results, to improve upon the mere toting up of raw data—putouts, assists, errors, double plays. In this second edition of *Total Baseball*, we have improved upon the Fielding Runs formula by calculating innings played at each position, plate appearances for all players on the team, and then rating each fielder based on his chances per inning. (Formerly we had rated each position on each team based on totals for all players on that team at that position; then we split up the total based on putouts. For more on the formula, see the Introduction to the new Fielding Register, and the Glossary.)

In the current edition we have also rated left fielders against left fielders, center fielders against center fielders, and right fielders against right fielders; where previously all outfield positions had been grouped together. We revised thoroughly the formula for catchers, which retains the highest degree of subjectivism because their primary defensive contribution comes not with the glove but through calling the pitches.

More on this complex subject at the head of the Fielding Register.

Pitching Runs

Determining the run contributions of pitchers is much easier than determining those of fielders or batters, though not quite so simple as that of base stealers. Actual runs allowed are known, as are innings pitched. Let's assume that a pitcher is responsible only for earned runs. Then why, we hear some of you asking, is the ERA not measure enough of his ability? Because it tells only the pitcher's rate of efficiency, not his actual benefit to the team. In a league with an ERA of 3.50, a starter who throws 300 innings with an ERA of 2.50 must be worth twice as much to his team as a starter with the same ERA who appears in only 150 innings. Through Pitching Runs, we seek to determine the number of beyond-average runs a pitcher saved—the number he prevented from scoring that an average pitcher would have allowed.

The formula for Earned Run Average is:

$$\text{ERA} = \frac{\text{Earned Runs} \times 9}{\text{Innings Pitched}}$$

The number of average, or par, runs for a pitcher, which is represented by a Pitching Runs figure of zero, is equal to:

$$\frac{\text{League ERA} \times \text{IP}}{9}$$

If the league ERA is 3.79 (as the National League's was in 1990) and a pitcher's ERA is also 3.79, he will by definition have held batters in check at the league average no matter how many innings he pitched. If, however, his ERA was 2.67 and he hurled 249 innings (as Frank Viola did for the Mets in '90), he will have saved a certain number of runs that an average pitcher might have allowed in his place; to find that number we employ the Pitching Runs formula:

Pitcher's Runs =

$$\text{Innings Pitched} \times \left(\frac{\text{League ERA}}{9}\right) - \text{ER}$$

This represents the difference between the number of earned runs allowed at the league average for the innings pitched and the actual earned runs allowed. For the case of Viola, we get

$$\text{Runs} = 249 \times \frac{3.79}{9} - 74 = 31.2$$

Viola was 31.2 runs better than the average National League pitcher in 1990, and had he been transported to an average NL team—that mythical entity that scores as many runs as it allows while winning 81 and losing 81—he would have made that team's mark 84–78. An alternative way to calculate pitchers' Linear Weights, useful with oldtimers for whom you may have the ERA but not the number of earned runs allowed, is to use the pitcher's ERA, subtracted from the league's ERA, multiplying by the innings pitched, then dividing by nine. In Viola's case, this approach would look like:

$$(3.79 - 2.67) \times \frac{249}{9} = 31.0$$

The difference of two tenths of a point is accounted for because we are using the ERA of 2.69, which has been rounded off, rather than the absolute figure of the pitcher's earned runs allowed, 74.

The two parts of performance—efficiency and durability, or how well and how long—are incorporated into all Linear Weights measures. If you are performing at a better than average clip, the more regularly you do so, the more your team will benefit and thus the higher your Linear Weights measure. If you are stealing bases nine times out of ten, your team will benefit more from sixty attempts than from forty; if you are batting at an above average clip, it's better to play in 160 games than 110; if you're allowing one earned run per game less than the average pitcher, your LWTS will increase with innings pitched.

A problem emerges in this regard when trying to compare the Pitching Runs of a pitcher from 1978 like Ron Guidry, with that of Hoss Radbourn in 1884. In the "efficiency" component of the formula, which may be understood as the league ERA minus the individual's ERA, the two compare this way:

Guidry = 3.76 − 1.74 = 2.02
Radbourn = 2.98 − 1.38 = 1.60

Guidry's differential is "unfairly" boosted by the higher league ERA of 1978; in fact, if we had compared the two by their normalized ERAs, which is logically more sound, the results would have been:

Guidry = $\frac{3.76}{1.74}$ = 2.16   Radbourn = $\frac{2.98}{1.38}$ = 2.16

Yet because rules and playing conditions allowed Radbourn to extend his efficiency over 679 innings, while Guidry hurled "only" 274, their Pitching Runs look like this:

Guidry = 62.0   Radbourn = 120.6

There is a great deal more to say on the subject of pitching and sabermetric stats: see the Introduction to the Pitching Register and the Glossary.

Linear Weights in Practice

Having formulas for pitching, fielding, baserunning, and batting, we can assess the run-scoring contribution of every individual who has ever played the game, and thus the number of wins that he has contributed in a given season or over his career. The number of runs required to produce an additional win has varied over the years between 9 and 11 runs, with a very few league seasons outside those parameters.

Limited by conventional baseball statistics, one might, in 1990, have uttered something like, "Bobby Bonds hit .293 with 33 homers and 114 RBIs—the guy must have been worth 10 extra wins to Pittsburgh all by himself!" Or: "The White Sox are only one pitcher away from winning the division." Or: "The Yankees are only three players away from being a contender." Or, "Letting Darryl Strawberry get away was the worst thing the Mets ever did; they'll be a second-division club for a decade."

With Linear Weights, these statements, or rather the concerns they reflect, can be approached with some data and with some degree of objectivity. First: Bobby Bonds had a fine year in 1990, but to have contributed 10 wins by himself he would have had to account for nearly 100 Linear Weights runs, a mark that has been attained by only three men in major-league history. In fact, Bonds contributed 6.5 wins in '90.

As to the White Sox, they finished 94–68 in 1982, while their Linear Weights projected them to finish at 81–81. The Athletics, who won the AL West at 103–59, actually projected to finish 96–66. So, the Sox management might have asked, how to close ground on the Athletics? Could one pitcher—like Bob Welch, for whom they bid in the free-agent bazaar—make the difference? To do so, he would have to contribute about 150 Pitching Runs, a feat no pitcher has ever accomplished. In 1990, pitching for Oakland—and remember, the Linear Weights formula is divorced from considerations of batter support—Welch contributed 20.7 park-adjusted Pitching Runs. So presuming that he pitched as well for the White Sox as he did for the Athletics, or even slightly better, he would not be enough to "win" Chicago the flag on paper; Chicago would need help from other quarters.

Regarding the other statements, you get the picture: sabermetric analyses like the ones above that employed the Linear Weights System will tend to puncture fantasies.

Park Factor

A central issue for sabermetricians is the network of illusion created by home-park dimensions, atmospheric conditions, and visibility for batters. How many home runs would Mark McGwire hit if he played half his games in Fenway Park? Will the Atlanta Braves and Chicago Cubs keep "failing" to put together solid pitching staffs—or has their pitching been adequate all along? Why have the American League leaders in triples so often worn a Royals uniform? One's home park has a powerful effect on a player or pitcher's record, elevating some good players to greatness and denying the spotlight to some outstanding performers.

It should be understood that the average player does better at home *regardless* of the park—familarity breeds success, it seems. Individuals bat and pitch at a rate 10 percent higher at home, on average. But parks don't create performance; they only affect it. For example, a left-handed hitter at Fenway can do very well indeed, as Wade Boggs has, by learning to take the outside pitch to left field. Likewise, a righthanded batter can make the friendly Green Monster into his nemesis by trying to pull every pitch.

For hard luck in home parks, it is tough to top the record of Dave Winfield, who has had the misfortune to call both San Diego and Yankee stadiums home before landing in the more or less neutral Big A in Anaheim. Through 1990, his lifetime Production, normalized to league average but not adjusted for park effects, was 117th best on the all time list of those playing in 1,000 games. Had he played his home games instead in Fenway Park, his PRO would have projected to the 45th best of all time. Had he even played in an average hitters' park—which is what PRO⁺ measures—his record would show itself to be the 80th best ever.

If we desire to remove the silver spoon or the millstone that a home park can be, and measure individual ability alone, we must create a statistical balancer that diminishes the individual batting marks created in parks like Fenway and augments those created in San Diego. Pete Palmer developed an adjustment that enables us, for the first time, to measure a player's accomplishments apart from the influence of his home park.

Parks differ in so many ways that it may be hard to imagine how their differences can be quantified. The most obvious way in which they differ is in their dimensions, from home plate to the outfield walls, and from the base lines to the stands. The older arenas—Fenway Park, Wrigley Field, Tiger Stadium—tend to favor hitters in both regards, with reachable fences and little room to pursue a foul pop. The exception among the older parks was Chicago's Comiskey, which, in keeping with the theories of Charles Comiskey back in 1910 and the team's perceived strength, was built as a pitcher's park. Yet two parks can have nearly equal dimensions, like Pittsburgh's Three Rivers Stadium and Atlanta's Fulton County Stadium, yet have highly dissimilar impacts upon hitters because of climate (balls travel farther in hot weather), elevation (travel farther above sea level), and playing surface (travel faster and truer on artificial turf). Yet another factor is how well batters think they see the ball; Shea Stadium is notorious as a cause of complaints.

And perhaps more important than any of the objective park characteristics, suggested Robert Kingsley in a 1980 study of why so many homers were hit in Atlanta, is the attitude of the players, the way that the park changes their view of how the game must be played in order to win. Every team that comes into Atlanta in August knows that the ball is going to fly and, whether it is a team designed for power or not, it plays ball there as if it were the 1927 Yankees. In their own home park the Astros may peck and scratch for runs, but in Atlanta they will put the steal and

hit-and-run in mothballs. Conversely, a team which comes into the Astrodome and plays for the big inning will generally get what it deserves—a loss. The successful team is one that can play its game at home—the game for which the team was constructed—yet is flexible enough to adapt when on the road. How to quantify attitude?

Rather than try to assign a numerical value to each of the six or more variables that might go into establishing an estimator of homepark impact, Pete looked to the single measure in which all these variables are reflected—runs. After all, why would we assign one value to dimensions, another to climate, and so on, except to identify their impact on scoring? If a stadium is a "hitters' park," it stands to reason that more runs would be scored there than in a park perceived as neutral, just as a "pitchers' park" could be expected to depress scoring.

The full and lengthy explanation for the computation of the Park Factor is left to the Glossary, where hardy readers might consider taking a peek right now. For most of us, though, it will be enough to understand that the Park Factor consists mainly of the team's home-road ratio of runs allowed, computed as it was above for the league, compared to the league's home-road ratio.

Just as Dave Winfield's stats suffered for the home parks he played in until he joined the California Angels, Dean Chance, star pitcher of the Angels in the mid-1960s, benefited from playing in Chavez Ravine when it was notoriously rough on hitters. This is not to say Chance had anything but a marvelous year in 1964: 20 wins, a 1.65 ERA, and 11 shutouts are hard to argue with. Still, in 81 home games in 1964, the Angels allowed 226 runs; in 81 games on the road, they allowed 325—44 percent more, where a 10 to 11 percent increase would have been normal. If one is to compare Chance and, say, Bert Blyleven in his years with Minnesota fairly, you must deny one the benefit of his home park and remove from the other the onus of his. This is what Park Factor does.

For decades, the all-time scoring squelcher was Chicago's South Side Park, which saw service at the dawn of the American League. From 1901 through 1909, its last full year of service to the White Sox, this cavernous stadium produced home run totals like the 2 in 1904, 3 in 1906, and 4 in 1909; in two years the Sox failed to hit *any* homers at home, thus earning the nickname "Hitless Wonders." In 1906, Chicago pitchers held opponents to 180 runs at South Side Park, an average of 2.28 runs per game, earned *and* unearned, in a decade when 4 of every 10 runs were unearned. This mark held until 1981, when the Astrodome intimidated opposing hitters to such a point that in the 51 home dates of that strike-shortened season, Astro hurlers were touched for only 106 runs—2.08 per game. The Pitcher Park Factor of .817 for the Astrodome was the lowest ever. Those who suspected that men like Joe Niekro, Don Sutton, Vern Ruhle, et al., were perhaps not world beaters after all were right: Look at the ERAs the Astro starters registered that year, and what these ERAs might have been in an average park like Shea that year (BPF: 1.00) or a moderately difficult pitchers' park like San Francisco (BPF: 1.06).

Houston Pitchers, 1982

	ERA	BPF: 1.00	BPF: 1.06
Nolan Ryan	1.69	2.07	2.19
Joe Niekro	2.82	3.43	3.64
Vern Ruhle	2.91	3.56	3.77
Bob Knepper	2.18	2.66	2.82
Don Sutton	2.60	3.17	3.36
HOUSTON (all)	2.66	3.24	3.44
SAN FRANCISCO (all)	3.28	3.09	3.28

Some observations prompted by this table: San Francisco with its team ERA of 3.28 had a better pitching staff than Houston with its 2.66; and Houston batters, regarded as a Punch-and-Judy crew by all observers, must have been a lot more effective than heretofore suspected. In fact, when Houston batters' totals (eighth in runs scored, eighth in LWTS) are adjusted for park, the Astros emerge on ability as the *best* hitting team in the National League of 1981! Even without the application of Park Factor, one might have come to a similar conclusion by examining the runs scored totals for all NL clubs on the road in 1981. Houston's total was exceeded only by those of the Dodgers and Reds.

Proceeding from a similar hunch, we may look at the batting record of the "Hitless Wonders" of 1906, who won the pennant (and the World Series, in four straight over a Cubs team which went 116–36 during the season). Baseball lore has it that a magnificent pitching staff (Ed Walsh, Doc White, Nick Altrock, and others) overcame a puny batting attack (BA of .230, 6 homers, slugging percentage of .286). In fact, the Sox scored more runs on the road than all but one AL team, and their Batting Linear Weights, when adjusted for park, was third in the league—the same rank achieved by their pitching. (How they won the pennant remains a mystery, though, for both Cleveland and New York had vastly superior teams on paper.)

Relativity

Sabermetric statistics can be marvelous tools for cross-era comparisons, enabling us to determine if baseball's history is truly a seamless web or if its seams are real enough, but are camouflaged by traditional statistics.

If Batter A presented himself to you for approval with these statistics—.330 batting average, 16 home runs, 107 RBIs—what would your reaction be? You'd like to have him on your team, right? And what to make of Batter B, who presents these numbers—.257 batting average, 14 home runs, 53 RBIs? Not bad for a middle infielder with a good glove, you say, but otherwise undistinguished? In fact, the "impressive" figures of Batter A represent the *average* performance of a National League outfielder in 1930, while the "blah" figures of Batter B are those of the average American League outfielder of 1968: The former has more than twice the RBIs of the latter, along with a batting average 73 points higher, yet the two performed at identical levels, and an argument could be made that Batter B was superior.

In a similar comparison involving those two years of extremes, Bill Terry led the National League in 1930 with a BA of .401, a mark surpassed by Ted Williams in 1941 but not equaled since; Carl Yastrzemski led the American League of 1968 with a performance that oldtimers held to be a disgrace, a lowly BA of .301, the worst ever to win a batting championship. Terry's mark was achieved at a time when most pitchers had only two pitches, a fastball and a curve, and not enough confidence in the latter to throw it when behind in the count at 2–0 or 3–1. The parks were smaller; there was no night ball; the game was segregated racially; and you played 22 games with each team, none farther west of the Mississippi than St. Louis. Moreover, 1930 was the year in which National League officials, attempting to match the popularity of the slugging American League, juiced the ball to such an extent that the entire *league* batted .312 (if you remove pitcher batting). In other words, the average nonpitcher in the NL of 1930 batted higher than the AL leader in 1968! When Yaz hit .301, pitchers dominated the game and the average American League nonpitcher hit .238. How to compare Terry and Yaz, who played under such different conditions thirty-eight years apart?

You could view Terry's .401 in relation to his league's BA of .312, concluding that Memphis Bill was a better hitter (by BA alone, which despite its previously cited deficiencies remains the most comfortable stat by which to introduce this technique) by 28.5 percent. You could compare Yaz's .301 to *his* league's BA of .238 and conclude that he was a better than average hitter by 26.5 percent. A mere 2 percentage points separate the men— had they both played in the National League of 1983, when the league average was .255, the Terry of 1930 might have hit .328, the Yaz of 1968, .323. (A further refinement of this method would be to delete Terry's at bats and hits from his league's, and those of Yastrzemski from his league's, so that the batters are not in effect compared with themselves. This, however, necessitates the use of at bats and hits rather than simply the averages and does not significantly alter the results.)

Why do we need relative measures? Basically, for the same reason we need statistics altogether, to compare, to interpret, and to comprehend, but in a more reasonable and accurate manner when the disparity of the data sources makes the use of absolute, unadjusted numbers illogical. If the analysis involves data produced under widely varying conditions, such as a sample including performances 20, 50, or 100 years apart, any comparison will be meaningless without dragging in a series of rather complex historical understandings to modify the analysis—and in a highly subjective, unreliable manner. To compare Terry's .401 with Yastrzemski's .301 with no recognition of the *context* in which these marks were achieved, that is, to infer that Terry was 100 points *better* than Yaz, is equivalent to comparing Babe Ruth's salary of $80,000 in 1930 with Pete Rose's $806,250 of fifty years later and concluding that Rose was $726,250 richer. To understand those figures we must place them within a context which includes such factors as I.R.S. regulations and inflation: We might think to re-express the two salaries in terms of their purchasing power, multiplying each by the Consumer Price Index of its time as expressed in 1967 dollars; doing this would be to compute a "relative salary" for Ruth and Rose, just as we computed a Relative Batting Average for Terry and Yaz. (And just as we discovered there was little difference between the BAs of the latter couple, we would discover there is little difference between the salaries of the former pair.)

Few are the fans who could cite the context of Ross Barnes's .429 batting average of 1876, let alone evaluate its ingredients (these include considerations of equipment, schedule, travel, physiology, racial exclusion, daytime games, rules variations, attitudes, and customs). A statistic removed from its historical context can be as deceptive as a quotation pulled out of context. How, then, to compare Barnes's .429 with, say, Bill Madlock's league-leading figure of .339 a century later? Should we discount Barnes's average 10 percent because in his day batters could demand a pitch above the waist or below? Or should we augment it 17 percent because a pitcher could throw eight "balls" before allowing a walk?

We are confronted with a similar problem in trying to quantify the various differences between home parks; our solution there was to look at the single measure which reflected all the variables—runs—and from that measure we proceeded to devise a formula for Park Factor. Similarly, the many variables that supply the context for Barnes in 1876 supplied an identical context for every other batter in *that year*—and the context in which Bill Madlock hit .339 prevailed for every other National League batter in 1976 (except for home park, of course). Accordingly, if we form a ratio of Barnes's .429 to his league's average (.265) and another of Madlock's to his league's average (.263) we obtain figures (1.62 for Barnes, 1.28 for Madlock—stated for convenience in *Total Baseball* as 162 and 128), which may reasonably be compared with each other: Barnes was 62 percent better than his league in BA, while Madlock was 28 percent better than his; these become the comparables, not the .429 and .339. The method will not become a time machine—putting Barnes on a modern club and Madlock on an old-time one—any more than Park Factor is a place machine, switching Joe DiMaggio to Beantown and Ted Williams to the Bronx. However, the relativist approach offers suggestive truths and does measure precisely the extent to which Barnes's and Madlock's BAs dominated those of their contemporaries.

Until the 1970s, when David Shoebotham ("Relative Batting Averages," *Baseball Research Journal*, 1976) and Merritt Clifton ("Relative Baseball," *Samisdat*, 1979) introduced the relativist approach, all baseball stats were absolute. And for cross-era comparison, that favorite Hot Stove League activity, absolute stats were absolutely useless, generating plenty of heat and precious little light. What the theory of relativity, baseball-style, does beautifully is to eliminate the need for bringing historical baggage to statistical analysis. The normalized or relative versions of *any* statistic—batting average, Production, ERA, slugging average, you name it; even homers or strikeouts, though there are problems with these—will be greater than 1.00 for all above-average performers (1.41, for example, means 41 percent better than average in the given category) while relative statistics less than 1.00 will indicate a below average level of play (0.88 means 12 percent below the norm).

It is as simple as can be. So Early Wynn had a 3.20 ERA in 1950? What does that *mean*? Well, the league ERA was 4.58, so Wynn did very well indeed. His normalized ERA thus was 143, a mark better than that earned by Tom Seaver in 1968, when he had an absolute ERA a full run lower at 2.20.

We cannot employ a Relative Won-Lost record, for the league average is every year the same: .500. (A logical corollary is that one cannot fruitfully use relative measures of any sort for a single season's analysis, as all like figures will be compared to the same league average. The numbers may be changed into normalized form, but the players' rankings will be unchanged: The top ten in batting average in 1990, for example, will retain their ranks in Relative Batting Average.)

Relativism in baseball echoes not only Einstein but also Shakespeare, whose words in *Hamlet* might be modified to read "There is nothing either good or bad, but context makes it so." No longer must we accept arbitrary assessments of performance or regard with awe such old-time figures as Hugh Duffy's BA of .438 in 1894 (not the accomplishment that Rod Carew's .388 was in 1977) or George Sisler's .407 in 1920 (not as good as Roberto Clemente's .357 in 1967). Conversely, a "mediocre" performance of recent years, such as Bobby Murcer's .292 of 1972, for instance, stacks up as the equal of Eddie Collins' .360 in 1923, while Charlie Grimm's seemingly solid .298 in 1929 compares unfavorably to Mike Cubbage's .260 in 1976.

Relativism redefines our understanding not only of particular accomplishments but also of baseball history itself. We see that the men who batted .400 with numbing regularity in the 1890s and 1920s were not supermen (would you swap Wade Boggs for Tuck Turner? George Brett for Harry Heilmann?) anymore than the sub-2.00 ERA pitchers of the late 1960s (Gary Peters, Bob Bolin, Dave McNally, et al.). Absolute figures lie. Are hitters today worse because none has hit .400 since 1941? Or are they superior because a Dave Kingman can average nearly 30 homers a year while Cap Anson only averaged 4? Are infielders better today because they make fewer errors than their counterparts of 50, 75, or 100 years ago? Do modern outfielders have limp-noodle arms because their assist totals pale before those registered in the early decades of the 1900s? Is baseball improving or declining, and has its rise or fall been steady? One can spit absolute stats on the hot stove all winter long and get no closer to the answer, but with relative statistics, the issues are clarified.

In the May 1983 issue of *The Coffin Corner*, the newsletter of the Professional Football Researchers Association, Bob Carroll offered a witty and perceptive dissection of the relative approach to football statistics. It was based upon a comparison of two great running backs, Tuffy Leemans of the New York Giants of the late 1930s and early '40s and George Rogers, then with the New Orleans Saints. "I've always liked the story," Carroll wrote, "of the little old lady who scornfully toured a Picasso exhibit and then sniffed, 'If Rembrandt were alive today, *he* wouldn't paint this way!' To which a bystander replied, 'Ah, but if Rembrandt were alive today, he wouldn't be Rembrandt.'"

There are things that relative baseball stats won't do, questions they won't answer. What would Ty Cobb bat if he were playing today? Lefty O'Doul was asked this question by a fan at an offseason baseball banquet in 1960. "Maybe .340," O'Doul answered. "Then why do you say Cobb was so great," the fan remarked, "if he could only hit .340 with the lively ball today?" "Well," O'Doul said, "you have to take into consideration that the man is now 74 years old." Relative Batting Average cannot tell with certainty what Cobb would hit today, for as Carroll wrote of Tuffy Leemans, if Cobb were playing today he wouldn't be the same Cobb; he would be bigger, stronger, and faster, and he might choose to steal less and go for the long ball more.

Relief Pitching

Absent from the chapter to this point has been the relief pitcher, a modern specialist who because of his still-evolving role in baseball, presents a variety of sabermetric problems and opportunities. The nature of the job is such that his won-lost record is not meaningful (even less so today than ten or fifteen years ago, with the ace in most bullpens being called upon—in highly dubious wisdom—only when his team has a lead in the eighth or ninth inning). A reliever may pick up a win with as little as a third of an inning's work, if he is lucky, while a starter must go five innings; a reliever may also pick up a loss more easily, for if he allows a run there may be little or no opportunity for his teammates to get it back, as they can for a starter. Earned run average is meaningful for the reliever, but it must be .15 to .25 lower to equate with that of a starter of comparable ability: a reliever frequently begins his work with a man or two already out, and thus can put men on base and strand them without having to register three outs.

Ratios of hits to innings, strikeouts to innings, strikeouts to walks—all of these have their interest, but none is sufficient by itself to measure relief-pitcher effectiveness. Relievers may also have an edge in these ratios because they generally face each batter only once in a game, thus leading to fewer hits and more strikeouts per inning. Before discussing the modern alternatives of saves or Relief Points, and our own Relief Ranking, let's review briefly the rise of the relief pitcher from the role of a mere hanger-on to, some would say, the most indispensable part of a winning team.

Relief pitching before 1891 was limited, with rare exceptions, to the starting pitcher exchanging places with one of the fielders, who was known as the "change pitcher." Substitutions from the bench were not permitted except in case of injury until 1889, when a tenth man became entitled to designation as a substitute for all positions; free substitution came in two years later, but no relief specialists emerged until Claude Elliott, Cecil Ferguson, and Otis Crandall in the first decade of this century.

The next decade's best relievers were starters doing double duty—notably Ed Walsh, Chief Bender, and Three Finger Brown. The 1920s, and up to the end of World War II, brought the first firemen to be employed in the modern way, although they tended to work more innings and fewer games than today. These were men such as Firpo Marberry, Johnny Murphy, Ace Adams, and several other worthies.

When you think of a relief pitcher in the modern-day sense—that is, a man who can appear in 50 or more ballgames a year, all or nearly all in relief, and win/save 30 or more—you begin with Joe Page of the 1947–49 Yankees and Jim Konstanty of the 1950 Phils, though

Marberry had one such season in 1926. None of the three, however, ever heard of a "save" in his playing days—this term wasn't introduced until 1960, the year after Larry Sherry's heroic World Series in which he finished all four Dodger victories, garnering two for himself and saving the others; 1959 was also the year fireman Roy Face went 18–1, not losing until September 11.

Before Jerry Holtzman of the Chicago *Sun Times* devised the save, baseball people were looking at really only one figure to measure a reliever's work, and that was the number of games in which he appeared; any other appreciation of his efforts was expressed impressionistically. A reliever did not work enough innings to qualify for an ERA title (Hoyt Wilhelm in 1952 being the exception), nor could he expect to win 20 games. The introduction of a specialized statistic for the fireman was acknowledgment of his specialized employment and conferred upon it a status it had never enjoyed, not even after the exploits of Konstanty, Page, Wilhelm, and Face. Only when the save came into being did the majority of relievers take pride in their work and stop regarding their time in the bullpen as an extended audition for a starting role.

When *The Sporting News*, spurred by Holtzman, began recording saves in its weekly record of the 1960 season, the save was defined in a way different from today. Then, upon entering the game, a reliever had to confront the tying or winning run on base or at the plate, and of course finish the game with the lead. This definition later became eased, so that simply finishing a game would get the reliever a save; a memorably absurd result of the new ruling was that the Mets' Ron Taylor gained a save in 1969 by pitching the final inning of a 20–6 win over Atlanta. This outraged sportswriters and fans alike, so in 1973 the definition was changed yet again: a reliever had to work three innings *or* come in with the tying or winning run on base or at bat. This definition was relaxed yet again in 1975 so that the tying run could be *on deck*, thus giving the relief pitcher license to allow a baserunner. It was a good thing for statisticians when Dan Quisenberry surpassed John Hiller's 1973 record of 38 saves by a decisive margin of 7. Today, of course, Bobby Thigpen's 1990 mark of 57 saves seems beyond challenge . . . but back in 1920 so did Babe Ruth's 29 homers.

There was a blip in the relievers' trend of rising importance when the American League introduced the designated hitter in 1973. The predicted outcome, based on the first few years' experience of the DH, was: increased offensive production, no more need to pinch-hit for the pitcher, and thus a greater number of complete games and fewer saves. All those things did happen in 1973–76, although not quite to the degree expected—and soon the American League's use of relief pitchers became as extensive as it had been in the early 1970s. In 1982, despite the DH, American League starters completed only 19.6 percent of their games, an all-time league low (though still substantially higher than the National League, where CGs dropped below 15 percent the last few years). In 1990 the AL and NL each logged complete games at about a 16 percent rate.

Relief Points *is* an improvement over saves, in all of its various incarnations including the one that provides a penalty for a blown save as well as for a defeat.

Some folks still long for a measure of middle-relief

effectiveness, that statistical no-man's land. In April 1981 *Sports Illustrated* came up with an incredibly complicated series of tabulations to address these final injustices, and they were dazzling. However, the *SI* method dazzled in the same way that the Mills brothers' Player Win Average did—it was ingenious and well conceived, but involved too much work. Not only did it require play-by-play analysis, but it also reminded one (queasily) of the National Football League's quarterback-rating system. Quarterbacks are rated in four categories, variously weighted, to arrive at a number of "rating points." Not one fan in a thousand could tell you how the rating points are derived, and the same holds for the *SI* relievers' formulas.

The final relief statistic to be discussed is the one we think is the best—Relief Ranking, which is a weighted variant of park-adjusted Relief Runs (in the first edition of *Total Baseball*, we applied the measure to all pitchers who averaged less than three innings per appearance, and this resulted in some needless inclusions of pitchers who were primarily starters; this time around we have broken out all pitchers' relief innings). Relief Ranking tends to favor closers, while Relief Runs provides a good measure for middle-relief outings.

The Future

The most exciting frontier for sabermetrics is in situational stats, the type employed by Elias and Project Scoresheet; as the years go by and their data bases grow, the sampling sizes of the data will enlarge and their figures for day vs. night, turf vs. grass, and so on, will be statistically meaningful as well as statistically correct. Cross-era comparison remains a subject of intense interest, and the debate over average-player skill rages on. Fielding and relieving, as discussed, also provide fertile ground for invention.

Fantasy baseball aficionados seem caught up in the competition and deal-making (as well as player evaluation), but some of the newsletters, such as John Benson's, provide sound analysis and trend-spotting tips. It would not be surprising if Rotisserie-type Leagues, rather than SABR, furnish the best sabermetricians of the 1990s.

The Player Register

The Player Register

The Player Register consists of the central batting, baserunning, and fielding statistics of every man who has batted in major league play since 1871, excepting those men who were primarily pitchers. A pitcher's complete batting record, however, is included for those pitchers who also, over the course of their careers, played in 100 or more games at another position—including pinch hitter—or played in more than half of their total major league games at a position other than pitcher, or played more games at a position other than pitcher in at least one year. (Pitcher batting is also expressed in Batting Wins in the Pitcher Batting column of the Pitcher Register.)

The players are listed alphabetically by surname and, when more than one player bears the name, alphabetically by *given* name—not by "use name," by which we mean the name that may have been applied to him during his playing career. This is the standard method of alphabetizing used in other biographical reference works, and in the case of baseball it makes it easier to find a lesser-known player with a common surname like Smith or Johnson. This method also jibes with that employed in the Team Roster and Annual Record where, for example, Charles "Old Hoss" Radbourn is shown not as the puzzling O. Radbourn or H. Radbourn, as some reference books have it, but as C. Radbourn. On the whole, we have been conservative in ascribing nicknames, doing so only when the player was in fact known by that name during his playing days.

Each page of the Player Register is topped at the corner by a finding aid: in capital letters, the surname of, first, the player whose entry heads up the page and, second, the player whose entry concludes it. Another finding aid is the use of boldface numerals to indicate a league-leading total in those categories in which a player is truly attempting to excel (no boldface is given to the "leaders" in batter strikeouts, times caught stealing, at bats, or games played). An additional finding aid new to the second edition is an asterisk alongside the team for which a player appeared in postseason competition, thus making for easy cross-reference to the earlier section on postseason play. Condensed type appears occasionally throughout this section; it has no special significance but is designed simply to accommodate unusually wide figures, such as the 4.000 slugging average of a man who, in his only at bat of the year, hit a home run.

The record for each man who played in more than one season is given in a line for each season, plus a career total line. If he played for more than one team in a given year, his totals for each team are stated on separate lines. And if the teams for which he played in his "traded year" are in the same league, then his full record is stated in both separate and combined fashion. (In the odd case of a man playing for three or more clubs in one year, with some of these clubs being in the same league, the combined total line will reflect only his play in that one league.) A man who played in only one year will have no additional career total line, since it would be identical to his seasonal listing.

Batting records for the National Association are included in The Player Register because the editors, like most baseball historians, regard it as a major league, inasmuch as it was the only professional league of its day and supplied the National League of 1876 with most of its players. In this second edition of *Total Baseball*, we benefit from the SABR research project referred to in the Introduction to the Annual Record—which to date has produced extra-base hits, corrected averages, walks, some stolen bases, strikeouts, and other data heretofore unavailable; fielding data for the NA may be available for *Total Baseball 3*. Until Major League Baseball reverses the position it adopted in 1969 and restores the NA to offical major-league status, we will reluctantly continue the practice of carrying separate totals lines for the National Association years rather than integrating them into the career marks of those players whose major league tenures began before 1876 and concluded in that year or later.

Gaps remain elsewhere in the official record of baseball and in the ongoing process of sabermetric reconstruction. The reader will note occasional blank elements in biographical lines, or in single-season columns; these are not typographical lapses but signs that the information does not exist or has not yet been found. In the totals lines of many players, an underlined figure indicates that the total reflects partial data, such as caught stealing for a man whose career covers the National League of 1918–1930 (during which this data was available only for 1920–1925), or batter strikeouts for a man whose career spanned both sides of the year 1909.

For a discussion of which data is missing for particular years, see the general introduction to Part 2. Here is a quick summation of the missing data:

Hit batters, 1903–1908 NL/AL.
Caught stealing, 1886–1914, 1916 for players with fewer than 20 stolen bases, 1917–1919, 1926–1950 NL; 1886–1891 AA; 1890 PL; 1901–1913, 1916 for players with fewer than 20 stolen bases, 1917–1919 AL (1927 data, missing from the first edition, is now 90 percent complete); 1914–15 FL
Sacrifice hit, 1908–1930, 1939 (In these years fly balls scoring runners counted as sacrifice hits, and in

1927–1930 fly balls advancing runners to any base counted as sacrifices.)

Sacrifice fly, 1908–1930, 1939 (counted in these years but inseparable from sacrifice hits), 1940–1953 (not counted)

Runs batted in, 1882–1887, 1890 AA; 1884 UA

Strikeouts for batters, 1882–1888, 1890 AA; 1884 UA; 1897–1909 NL (although this second edition has filled most of the gaps for 1897–1899); 1901-1912 AL

For a key to the team and league abbreviations used in the Player Register, flip to the last page of this volume. For a guide to the other procedures and abbreviations employed in the Player Register, review the comments on the prodigiously extended playing record below.

Looking at the biographical line for any player, we see first his use name in full capitals, then his given name and nickname (and any other name he may have used or been born with, such as the matronymic of a Latin American

YEAR	TM/L	G	AB	R	H	2B	3B	HR	RBI	BB	SO	AVG	OBP	SLG	PRO+	BR	/A	RC	SB	CS	SBR	FR	POS	TPR
■ KID DE LEON	Ponce de Leon, Juan "Castilian Kid" (also played in 1874 as Kid Madrid)																						
	b: 3/13/1460, Madrid, Spain d: 2/25/1963, St. Augustine, Fl. BR/TR, 5'11", 173 lbs. Deb: 5/21/1874 MUCH																						
1874	Bos-n	52	277	73	94	7	4	1	14	2		.339	.342	.400	111	7	4	33					*2	0.2
1875	Wes-n	2	3	1	1	0	0	0		0		.333	.333	.333	95	0	0	0					/S	0.00
1883	Bal-a	28	121	12	33	2	1	1		8		.273	.318	.331	101	1	1	13				0	CO/S	0.0
1884	Was-U	86	371	75	107	12	5	1		11		.288	.309	.356	127	4	5	42	0			0	1OC	0.9
	KC-U	1	4	1	0	0	0	0		0		.000	.000	.000	-97	-0	0	0	0			0	/1	0.0
	Yr	87	375	76	107	12	5	1		11		.287	.308	.355	126	-0	-0	42	0			0		0.0
1890	Cin-P	1	1	1	1	0	0	1	1		0	1.000	1.000	4.000	700	1	1	2	0			0	/2	0.0
1908	Pit-N	1	0	0	0	0	0	0	0	0		—			—	-0	0	0	0			0	/3	0.0
	Phi-A	9	31	5	9	3	0	0	2	0		.290	.290	.387	113	1	0	3	0			-1	/3	0.0
1909	Phi-A	148	541	73	165	27	19	4	85	26		.305	.343	.447	146	27	26	88	20			-5	*3	3.0
1910	Phi-A	146	561	83	159	25	15	2	74	34		.283	.329	.392	123	14	13	77	21			3	*3	2.4
1911	Phi-A	148	592	96	198	40	4	11	115	50		.334	.379	.505	157	33	38	121	38			-8	*3	3.3
1912	Phi-A	149	577	116	200	40	21	10	130	50		.347	.404	.541	171	49	50	138	40			9	*3	5.4
1913	Phi-A	149	564	116	190	34	9	12	117	63	31	.337	.413	.493	171	46	48	130	34			7	*3	6.1
1914	Phi-A	150	570	84	182	23	10	9	89	53	37	.319	.380	.442	151	31	33	105	19	20	-6	8	*3	4.1
1915	Nwk-F	2	8	5	4	2	1	1	4	0	2	.500	.500	1.38	304	3	3	3	0			1	/3	0.1
1916	NY-A	100	360	46	97	23	2	10	52	36	30	.269	.344	.428	130	13	12	59	15			3	3	2.1
1917	NY-A	146	553	57	156	24	2	6	71	48	27	.282	.345	.365	109	10	6	76	18			11	*3	2.7
1918	NY-A	126	504	65	154	24	5	6	62	38	13	.306	.357	.409	138	17	20	79	8			11	*3	3.4
1919	NY-A	141	567	70	166	22	1	10	83	44	18	.293	.346	.388	100	4	-0	82	13			-2	*3	0.9
1921	NY-A	94	330	46	97	16	2	9	71	26	12	.294	.353	.436	98	-0	-2	55	8	5	-1	13	3	1.6
1922	NY-A	69	234	30	65	12	3	7	36	15	14	.278	.327	.444	98	-1	-2	36	1	3	-2	-8	3	-0.4
Total	2 n	54	280	74	95	7	4	1	14	2		.339	.348	.404	110	7	4	33					*2/S	0.2
Total	17	1694	6489	981	1983	329	100	100	$\overline{992}$	502	184	.306	.354	.446	130	247	246	1109	235	28		41	*3C/SO12	35.6

player). His date and place of birth follow "b" and his date and place of death follow "d." Years through 1900 are expressed fully, in four digits, and years after 1900 are expressed in their last two digits.

Then comes the player's manner of batting and throwing, abbreviated for a lefthanded batter who throws right as BL/TR (a switch-hitter would be shown as BB for "bats both" and a switch thrower as TB for "throws both").

Next, and for most players last, is the player's debut date in the major leagues, if known at this point. While we are able to report most of these thanks to SABR research, for some players we have had to list only the two digits representing their rookie years.

Some players continue in major league baseball after their playing days are through, as managers, coaches, or even umpires. A player whose biographical line concludes with an M can be located in the Manager Roster; one whose line bears a C will be listed in the Coach Roster; and one with a U occupies a place in the Umpire Roster. (In the last case we have placed a U on the biographical line only for those players who were employed as umpires by a league, for in the nineteenth century—and especially in the years of the National Association—literally hundreds of players were pressed into service as umpires for a game or two. It would be misleading to accord such players the same code we give to Bob Emslie or Babe Pinelli.) The select few who have been enshrined in the Baseball Hall of Fame at Cooperstown, NY, are noted with an H. They are also listed in the Hall of Fame Roster found toward the end of Bill Deane's "Awards and Honors" essay in Part One.

The explanations for the statistical column heads fol-

low; for more technical information about formulas and calculations, see the Glossary. The vertical rules in the column-header line separate the stats into seven logical groupings: year, team, league; fundamental counting stats for batters; hits and plate appearances broken out into their component counting stats; basic calculated averages; sabermetric figures of more complex calculation; baserunning stats; fielding stats and Total Player Rating.

Absent from the Player Register in this edition are some statistics present in the original: production as a raw, unadjusted figure (still available by simply adding OBP plus SLG, as well as in the Annual Record and Leaders sections); Park Factor for batters (still available from the Annual Record); Clutch Hitting Index, newly developed for *Total Baseball* but which we have judged to be of lesser interest and value than the more established sabermetric measures (like PRO, however, it is still present in the Annual Record and Leaders sections); and Total Average, a popular stat but one that is mirrored by Runs Created and Batting Runs, both of which are more accurate (TA is present in the Annual Record and Leaders sections). By deleting these statistics from the Register we have improved legibility, particularly by adding to the margin in the gutter of the book, and reduced some redundancy.

YEAR Year of play (when a space in the column is blank, this indicates that the man has played for two or more clubs in the last year stated in the column; if those clubs were in the same league, then the man will also have a combined total line, beginning with the abbreviation "Yr" placed in the TEAM/L column)

Yr   Year's totals for play with two or more clubs in same league (see comments for YEAR)

TM/L   Team and League (see comments for YEAR)

G   Games

AB   At-bats

R   Runs

H   Hits (Bases on balls were counted as hits by scorers in 1887, but in *Total Baseball* they are not figured as times at bat, nor as hits.)

2B   Doubles

3B   Triples

HR   Home Runs

RBI   Runs Batted In

BB   Bases on Balls (Bases on balls were counted as outs by scorers in 1876, but in *Total Baseball* they are not figured as times at bat nor as outs.)

SO   Strikeouts

AVG   Batting Average (Figured as hits over at-bats; mathematically meaningless averages created through a division by zero are rendered as dashes; see Kid De Leon's entry for 1908 with Pit-N.)

OBP   On Base Percentage (See comments for AVG)

SLG   Slugging Average (See comments for AVG, and note the use of condensed type to express Kid De Leon's maximum SLG in 1890.)

PRO+   Production Plus, or Adjusted Production (On Base Percentage plus Slugging Average, normalized to league average and adjusted for home-park factor.) See comments for /A.

BR   Batting Runs (Linear Weights measure of runs contributed *beyond* what a league-average batter or team might have contributed, defined as zero. Occasionally the curious figure of −0 will appear in this column, or in the columns of other Linear Weights measures of batting, baseruning, fielding, and the TPR. This "negative zero" figure signifies a run contribution that falls below the league average, but to so small a degree that it cannot be said to have cost the team a run.)

/A   Adjusted (This signifies that the stat to the immediate left, in this instance Batting Runs, is here normalized to league average and adjusted for home-park factor. A mark of 100 is a league-average performance. Pitcher batting is removed from all league batting statistics before normalization, for a variety of reasons expanded upon in the Glossary. An innovation for this edition is to use three-year averages for batting park factors. If a team moved or the park changed dramatically, then two-year averages are employed; if the park was used for only one year, then of course only that run-scoring data is used.)

RC   Runs Created (Bill James's formulation for run contribution from a variety of batting and base-

running events; calculated variably to make maximum use of the data available in a given year; see Glossary.)

SB   Stolen Bases (for 1886 to the present)

CS   Caught Stealing (Available 1915, 1916 for players with 20 or more stolen bases, 1920–1925, 1951–date NL; 1914–1915, 1916 for players with 20 or more stolen bases, 1920 to date AL with scattered data still missing from 1927.)

SBA   Stolen Base Average (Stolen bases divided by attempts; availability dependent upon CS as shown above.)

SBR   Stolen Base Runs (This is a Linear Weights measure of runs contributed *beyond* what a league-average base stealer might have gained, defined as zero and calculated on the basis of a 66.7 percent success rate, which computer simulations have shown to be the break-even point beyond which stolen bases have positive run value to the team; see the general introduction to Part Two and the Glossary. The presence of a figure in the SBR column in the Player Register is dependent upon the availability of CS as shown above. Lifetime Stolen Base Runs are not totaled where data is incomplete, but seasonal SBRs are reflected in the seasonal Total Player Ratings, which in turn are added to form the lifetime Total Player Rating.)

FR   Fielding Runs (The Linear Weights measure of runs saved *beyond* what a league-average player at that position might have saved, defined as zero; this stat is calculated to take account of the particular demands of the different positions; see Glossary for formulas, which have been refined for this edition to reflect innings played at each position and to more accurately portray the defensive contributions of catchers.)

POS   Positions played (This is a ranking from left to right by frequency of the positions played in the field or at designated hitter. An asterisk to the left of the position indicates, generally, that in a given year the man played about two-thirds of his team's scheduled games at that position; more precisely, it is figured at 20 games in 1871, 30 in 1872, 35 in 1873, 40 in 1874, and 50 in 1875; two-thirds of the scheduled games in 1876–1900, and 100 or more games since. When a slash separates positions, the man played those positions listed to the left of the slash in 10 or more games and the positions to the right of the slash in fewer than 10 games. If there is no slash, he played all positions listed in 10 or more games. For the POS [positions played] in the lifetime line, the asterisk signifies 1,000 games and the slash marks a dividing point of 100 games. The precise number of games played at each position, plus an array of fielding data, are available in the new Fielding Register. A player's POS column will list him as a pinch runner or pinch hitter in only those years in which he appeared at no other position. The positions and their abbreviations are)

1: First base	P: Pitcher
2: Second base	D: Designated hitter
S: Shortstop	R: Runner (pinch)
3: Third base	H: Hitter (pinch)
O: Outfield	M: Manager (playing)
C: Catcher	

TPR Total Player Rating (This is the sum of a player's Adjusted Batting Runs, Fielding Runs, and Base Stealing Runs, minus his positional adjustment, all divided by the Runs Per Win factor for that year—generally around 10, historically in the 9–11 range. For more information on the formula and the Runs Per Win concept, see the general introduction to Part 2 and the Glossary. In the lifetime line, the TPR is the sum of the seasonal TPRs. For men who were primarily pitchers but whose extent of play at other positions warrants a listing in the Player Register as well as the Pitcher Register, the TPR may be listed as 0.0; this signifies that their batting records are summed up in the Total Pitcher Index [TPI] column of the Pitcher Register.)

Total For players whose careers include play in the National Association a well as other major leagues, two totals are given, as described above and as illustrated in Kid De Leon's record, where the record of his years in the National Association is shown alongside the notation "Total 2 n," where *2* stands for the number of years totaled and *n* stands for National Association. For players whose careers began in 1876 or later, the lifetime record is shown alongside the notation "Total x," where *x* stands for the number of post-1875 years totaled. Note the underlined entries in the record for Kid De Leon, reflecting the partial data for RBI, batter strikeouts, stolen bases, and times caught stealing.

YEAR	TM/L	G	AB	R	H	2B	3B	HR	RBI	BB	SO	AVG	OBP	SLG	PRO+	BR	/A	RC	SB	CS	SBR	FR	POS	TPR

■ HANK AARON
Aaron, Henry Louis "Hammerin' Hank" b: 2/5/34, Mobile, Ala. BR/TR, 6', 180 lbs. Deb: 4/13/54 H

YEAR	TM/L	G	AB	R	H	2B	3B	HR	RBI	BB	SO	AVG	OBP	SLG	PRO+	BR	/A	RC	SB	CS	SBR	FR	POS	TPR
1954	Mil-N	122	468	58	131	27	6	13	69	28	39	.280	.325	.447	105	-2	1	64	2	2	-1	-3	*O	-0.6
1955	Mil-N	153	602	105	189	37	9	27	106	49	61	.314	.369	.540	144	31	35	114	3	1	0	6	*O2	4.0
1956	Mil-N	153	609	106	200	34	14	26	92	37	54	.328	.369	.558	154	36	41	115	2	4	-2	8	*O	4.2
1957	*Mil-N	151	615	118	198	27	6	44	132	57	58	.322	.379	.600	170	48	54	136	1	1	-0	9	*O	5.8
1958	*Mil-N	153	601	109	196	34	4	30	95	59	49	.326	.387	.546	157	37	43	121	4	1	1	4	*O	4.3
1959	Mil-N	154	629	116	223	46	7	39	123	51	54	.355	.406	.636	188	63	70	156	8	0	2	-2	*O/3	6.6
1960	Mil-N	153	590	102	172	20	11	40	126	60	63	.292	.359	.566	160	37	43	119	16	7	1	8	*O/3	4.8
1961	Mil-N	155	603	115	197	39	10	34	120	56	64	.327	.386	.594	165	46	51	132	21	9	1	-0	*O/3	4.2
1962	Mil-N	156	592	127	191	28	6	45	128	66	73	.323	.393	.618	171	54	56	140	15	7	0	-5	*O/1	4.2
1963	Mil-N	161	631	121	201	29	4	44	130	78	94	.319	.394	.586	180	63	64	149	31	5	6	-4	*O	6.1
1964	Mil-N	145	570	103	187	30	2	24	95	62	46	.328	.394	.514	158	42	41	112	22	4	4	9	*O2	5.2
1965	Mil-N	150	570	109	181	40	1	32	89	60	81	.318	.384	.560	161	46	46	122	24	4	5	9	*O	5.7
1966	Atl-N	158	603	117	168	23	1	44	127	76	96	.279	.360	.539	144	37	36	118	21	3	5	11	*O/2	4.8
1967	Atl-N	155	600	113	184	37	3	39	109	63	97	.307	.373	.573	169	50	51	126	17	6	2	12	*O/2	6.1
1968	Atl-N	160	606	84	174	33	4	29	86	64	62	.287	.356	.498	154	39	39	104	28	5	5	13	*O1	5.5
1969	*Atl-N	147	547	100	164	30	3	44	97	87	47	.300	.398	.607	177	56	56	128	9	10	-3	5	*O/1	5.1
1970	Atl-N	150	516	103	154	26	1	38	118	74	63	.298	.389	.574	146	39	35	116	9	0	3	5	*O1	3.3
1971	Atl-N	139	495	95	162	22	3	47	118	71	58	.327	.414	.669	190	65	62	137	1	1	-0	-9	1O	4.7
1972	Atl-N	129	449	75	119	10	0	34	77	92	55	.265	.391	.514	142	35	30	91	4	0	1	-0	*1O	2.4
1973	Atl-N	120	392	84	118	12	1	40	96	68	51	.301	.406	.643	173	45	42	104	1	1	-0	-2	*O	3.5
1974	Atl-N	112	340	47	91	16	0	20	69	39	29	.268	.343	.491	126	13	11	58	1	0	-0	-10	O	-0.1
1975	Mil-A	137	465	45	109	16	2	12	60	70	51	.234	.336	.355	95	-2	-2	56	0	1	-1	0	*D/O	-0.2
1976	Mil-A	85	271	22	62	8	0	10	35	35	38	.229	.317	.369	102	0	1	31	0	1	-1	0	D/O	0.0
Total	23	3298	12364	2174	3771	624	98	755	2297	1402	1383	.305	.377	.555	156	878	903	2550	240	73	28	60	*O1D/23	89.6

■ TOMMIE AARON
Aaron, Tommie Lee b: 8/5/39, Mobile, Ala. d: 8/16/84, Atlanta, Ga. BR/TR, 6'3", 190 lbs. Deb: 4/10/62 C

YEAR	TM/L	G	AB	R	H	2B	3B	HR	RBI	BB	SO	AVG	OBP	SLG	PRO+	BR	/A	RC	SB	CS	SBR	FR	POS	TPR
1962	Mil-N	141	334	54	77	20	2	8	38	41	58	.231	.315	.374	86	-8	-6	40	6	0	2	1	*1O/23	-0.8
1963	Mil-N	72	135	6	27	6	1	1	15	11	27	.200	.260	.281	57	-8	-7	8	0	3	-2	-9	1O/23	-2.0
1965	Mil-N	8	16	1	3	0	0	0	1	1	2	.188	.235	.188	21	-2	-2	1	0	0	0	0	/1	-0.1
1968	Atl-N	98	283	21	69	10	3	1	25	21	37	.244	.296	.311	82	-6	-6	24	3	4	-2	-4	O1/3	-1.7
1969	*Atl-N	49	60	13	15	2	0	1	5	6	6	.250	.318	.333	82	-1	-1	6	0	1	-1	1	1/O	-0.2
1970	Atl-N	44	63	3	13	2	0	2	7	3	10	.206	.242	.333	50	-4	-5	4	0	0	0	-1	1O	-0.7
1971	Atl-N	25	53	4	12	2	0	0	3	3	5	.226	.268	.264	48	-3	-4	3	0	0	0	2	1/3	-0.2
Total	7	437	944	102	216	42	6	13	94	86	145	.229	.293	.327	75	-32	-32	86	9	8	-2	-10	1O/32	-5.7

■ JOHN ABADIE
Abadie, John b: 11/4/1854, Philadelphia, Pa. d: 5/17/05, Pemberton, N.J. 6', 192 lbs. Deb: 6/10/1875

YEAR	TM/L	G	AB	R	H	2B	3B	HR	RBI	BB	SO	AVG	OBP	SLG	PRO+	BR	/A	RC	SB	CS	SBR	FR	POS	TPR
1875	Cen-n	11	45	3	10	0	0	0		0		.222	.222	.222	59	-2	-1	2				1		-0.1
	Atl-n	1	4	1	1	0	0	0		0		.250	.250	.250	84	-0	-0	0				/1		0.0
	Yr	12	49	4	11	0	0	0		0		.224	.224	.224	61	-2	-1	3						-0.1

■ ED ABBATICCHIO
Abbaticchio, Edward James "Batty" b: 4/15/1877, Latrobe, Pa. d: 1/6/57, Ft.Lauderdale, Fla. BR/TR, 5'11", 170 lbs. Deb: 9/04/1897

YEAR	TM/L	G	AB	R	H	2B	3B	HR	RBI	BB	SO	AVG	OBP	SLG	PRO+	BR	/A	RC	SB	CS	SBR	FR	POS	TPR
1897	Phi-N	3	10	0	3	0	0	0	0	1		.300	.364	.300	81	-0	-0	1	0			-2	/2	-0.1
1898	Phi-N	25	92	9	21	4	0	0	14	7		.228	.290	.272	66	-4	-4	9	4			-13	3/2O	-1.5
1903	Bos-N	136	489	61	111	18	5	1	46	52		.227	.301	.290	74	-18	-15	53	23			3	*2S	-0.3
1904	Bos-N	154	579	76	148	18	10	3	54	40		.256	.304	.337	103	-1	2	70	24			2	*S	0.5
1905	Bos-N	153	610	70	170	25	12	3	41	35		.279	.318	.374	110	4	6	85	30			-12	*S/O	-0.2
1907	Pit-N	147	496	63	130	14	7	2	82	65		.262	.348	.331	113	10	10	74	35			-23	*2	-1.2
1908	Pit-N	146	500	43	125	16	7	1	61	58		.250	.328	.316	108	6	6	60	22			-12	*2	-0.8
1909	*Pit-N	36	87	13	20	0	0	1	16	19		.230	.368	.264	89	1	-0	9	2			2	S/2O	0.2
1910	Pit-N	3	3	0	0	0	0	0	0	0	0	.000	.000	.000	-95	-1	-1	0	0			-0	/S	0.0
	Bos-N	52	178	20	44	4	2	0	10	12	16	.247	.295	.292	68	-7	-8	16	2			-3	S/2	-0.9
	Yr	55	181	20	44	4	2	0	10	12	16	.243	.290	.287	66	-7	-8	16	2			-3		-0.9
Total	9	855	3044	355	772	99	43	11	324	289	16	.254	.319	.325	98	-9	-4	377	142			-58	2S/3O	-4.3

■ CHARLIE ABBEY
Abbey, Charles S. b: 10/1868, Falls City, Neb. BL, 5'8.5", 169 lbs. Deb: 8/16/1893

YEAR	TM/L	G	AB	R	H	2B	3B	HR	RBI	BB	SO	AVG	OBP	SLG	PRO+	BR	/A	RC	SB	CS	SBR	FR	POS	TPR
1893	Was-N	31	116	11	30	1	4	0	12	12	6	.259	.333	.336	82	-3	-3	16	9			3	O	0.0
1894	Was-N	129	523	95	164	26	18	7	101	58	38	.314	.389	.472	112	7	11	111	31			14	*O	1.2
1895	Was-N	132	511	102	141	14	10	8	84	43	41	.276	.340	.389	91	-8	-7	79	28			10	*O	-0.6
1896	Was-N	79	301	47	79	12	6	1	49	27	20	.262	.331	.352	82	-8	-8	41	16			-6	O/P	-1.5
1897	Was-N	80	300	52	78	14	8	3	34	27		.260	.329	.390	92	-4	-4	43	9			2	O	-0.6
Total	5	451	1751	307	492	67	46	19	280	167	105	.281	.351	.404	96	-16	-10	291	93			21	O/P	-1.5

■ FRED ABBOTT
Abbott, Harry Frederick (b: Harry Frederick Winbigler)
b: 10/22/1874, Versailles, Ohio d: 6/11/35, Los Angeles, Cal. BR/TR, 5'10", 180 lbs. Deb: 4/25/03

YEAR	TM/L	G	AB	R	H	2B	3B	HR	RBI	BB	SO	AVG	OBP	SLG	PRO+	BR	/A	RC	SB	CS	SBR	FR	POS	TPR
1903	Cle-A	77	255	25	60	11	3	1	25	7		.235	.256	.314	73	-9	-8	24	8			10	C/1	1.1
1904	Cle-A	41	130	14	22	4	2	0	12	6		.169	.206	.231	40	-9	-9	7	2			-3	C/1	-0.8
1905	Phi-N	42	128	9	25	6	1	0	12	6		.195	.231	.258	49	-8	-8	9	4			-1	C/1	-0.5
Total	3	160	513	48	107	21	6	1	49	19		.209	.237	.279	59	-26	-25	41	14			6	C/1	-0.2

■ ODY ABBOTT
Abbott, Ody Cleon b: 9/5/1888, New Eagle, Pa. d: 4/13/33, Washington, D.C. BR/TR, 6'2", 180 lbs. Deb: 9/10/10

YEAR	TM/L	G	AB	R	H	2B	3B	HR	RBI	BB	SO	AVG	OBP	SLG	PRO+	BR	/A	RC	SB	CS	SBR	FR	POS	TPR
1910	StL-N	22	70	2	13	2	1	0	6	6	20	.186	.250	.243	46	-5	-5	5	3			3	O	-0.2

■ DAVE ABERCROMBIE
Abercrombie, David b: 5/1840, Falkirk, Scotland d: 9/2/16, Baltimore, Md. Deb: 10/21/1871

YEAR	TM/L	G	AB	R	H	2B	3B	HR	RBI	BB	SO	AVG	OBP	SLG	PRO+	BR	/A	RC	SB	CS	SBR	FR	POS	TPR
1871	Tro-n	1	4	0	0	0	0	0	0	0	0	.000	.000	.000	-99	-1	-1	0	0				/S	0.0

■ CLIFF ABERSON
Aberson, Clifford Alexander "Kif" b: 8/28/21, Chicago, Ill. d: 6/23/73, Vallejo, Cal. BR/TR, 6', 200 lbs. Deb: 7/18/47

YEAR	TM/L	G	AB	R	H	2B	3B	HR	RBI	BB	SO	AVG	OBP	SLG	PRO+	BR	/A	RC	SB	CS	SBR	FR	POS	TPR
1947	Chi-N	47	140	24	39	6	3	4	20	20	32	.279	.369	.450	121	3	4	23	0			-2	O	0.1
1948	Chi-N	12	32	1	6	1	0	1	6	5	10	.188	.297	.313	68	-2	-1	3	0			-1	/O	-0.2
1949	Chi-N	4	7	0	0	0	0	0	0	0	2	.000	.000	.000	-99	-2	-2	0	0			0	/O	-0.1
Total	3	63	179	25	45	7	3	5	26	25	44	.251	.343	.408	103	-0	1	26	0			-3	/O	-0.2

■ SHAWN ABNER
Abner, Shawn Wesley b: 6/17/66, Hamilton, Ohio BR/TR, 6'1", 190 lbs. Deb: 9/08/87

YEAR	TM/L	G	AB	R	H	2B	3B	HR	RBI	BB	SO	AVG	OBP	SLG	PRO+	BR	/A	RC	SB	CS	SBR	FR	POS	TPR
1987	SD-N	16	47	5	13	3	1	2	7	2	8	.277	.306	.511	116	1	1	8	1	0	0	1	O	0.1
1988	SD-N	37	83	16	15	3	0	2	5	4	19	.181	.227	.289	48	-6	-6	5	0	1	-1	2	O	-0.5
1989	SD-N	57	102	13	18	4	0	2	14	5	20	.176	.215	.275	39	-8	-8	6	1	0	0	2	O	-0.7
1990	SD-N	91	184	17	45	9	0	1	15	9	28	.245	.287	.310	63	-9	-9	16	2	3	-1	2	O	-1.0
Total	4	201	416	41	91	19	1	7	41	20	75	.219	.260	.320	61	-23	-23	35	4	4	-1	6	O	-2.1

■ CAL ABRAMS
Abrams, Calvin Ross b: 3/2/24, Philadelphia, Pa. BL/TL, 6', 185 lbs. Deb: 4/20/49

YEAR	TM/L	G	AB	R	H	2B	3B	HR	RBI	BB	SO	AVG	OBP	SLG	PRO+	BR	/A	RC	SB	CS	SBR	FR	POS	TPR
1949	Bro-N	8	24	6	2	1	0	0	0	7	6	.083	.290	.125	15	-3	-3	1	1			-1	/O	-0.4
1950	Bro-N	38	44	5	9	1	0	0	4	9	13	.205	.340	.227	51	-3	-3	4	0			0	O	-0.2
1951	Bro-N	67	150	27	42	8	0	3	19	36	26	.280	.419	.393	118	6	6	27	3	2	-0	-3	O	0.1
1952	Bro-N	10	10	1	2	0	0	0	0	2	4	.200	.333	.200	51	-1	-1	1	0	0	0	0	/O	0.0
	Cin-N	71	158	23	44	9	2	2	13	19	25	.278	.356	.399	109	2	2	25	1	0	0	0	O	0.2

YEAR	TM/L	G	AB	R	H	2B	3B	HR	RBI	BB	SO	AVG	OBP	SLG	PRO+	BR	/A	RC	SB	CS	SBR	FR	POS	TPR
	Yr	81	168	24	46	9	2	2	13	21	29	.274	.354	.387	106	2	2	25	1	0	0	0		0.2
1953	Pit-N	119	448	66	128	10	6	15	43	58	70	.286	.368	.435	109	6	7	77	4	4	-1	1	*O	0.2
1954	Pit-N	17	42	6	6	1	1	0	2	10	9	.143	.308	.214	39	-4	-4	3	0	0	0	0	O	-0.3
	Bal-A	115	423	67	124	22	7	6	25	72	67	.293	.401	.421	135	17	21	76	1	4	-2	1	*O	1.8
1955	Bal-A	118	309	56	75	12	3	6	32	89	69	.243	.416	.359	118	10	13	52	2	8	-4	0	O/1	0.4
1956	Chi-A	4	3	0	1	0	0	0	0	2	1	.333	.600	.333	150	1	1	1	0	0	0	0	/O	0.0
Total	8	567	1611	257	433	64	19	32	138	304	290	.269	.387	.392	113	33	40	268	12	18		-2	O/1	1.8

■ JOE ABREU
Abreu, Joseph Lawrence b: 5/24/16, Oakland, Cal. BR/TR, 5'8", 160 lbs. Deb: 4/23/42

YEAR	TM/L	G	AB	R	H	2B	3B	HR	RBI	BB	SO	AVG	OBP	SLG	PRO+	BR	/A	RC	SB	CS	SBR	FR	POS	TPR
1942	Cin-N	9	28	4	6	1	0	1	3	4	4	.214	.313	.357	96	-0	-0	3	0			-1	/32	0.0

■ BILL ABSTEIN
Abstein, William Henry "Big Bill" b: 2/2/1883, St.Louis, Mo. d: 4/8/40, St.Louis, Mo. BR/TR, 6', 185 lbs. Deb: 9/25/06

YEAR	TM/L	G	AB	R	H	2B	3B	HR	RBI	BB	SO	AVG	OBP	SLG	PRO+	BR	/A	RC	SB	CS	SBR	FR	POS	TPR
1906	Pit-N	8	20	2	4	0	0	0	3	0		.200	.200	.200	25	-2	-2	1	2			-1	/2O	-0.3
1909	*Pit-N	137	512	51	133	20	10	1	70	27		.260	.302	.344	93	-2	-6	59	16			-5	*1	-1.5
1910	StL-A	25	87	1	13	2	0	0	3	2		.149	.169	.172	7	-9	-9	3	3			2	1	-0.6
Total	3	170	619	54	150	22	10	1	76	29		.242	.281	.315	80	-13	-17	63	21			-5	1/2O	-2.4

■ MERITO ACOSTA
Acosta, Balmodero Pedro (Fernandez) b: 5/19/1896, Bauta, Cuba d: 11/17/63, Miami, Fla. BL/TL, 5'7", 140 lbs. Deb: 6/15/13

YEAR	TM/L	G	AB	R	H	2B	3B	HR	RBI	BB	SO	AVG	OBP	SLG	PRO+	BR	/A	RC	SB	CS	SBR	FR	POS	TPR
1913	Was-A	12	20	3	6	0	1	0	1	4	2	.300	.417	.400	136	1	1	4	2			-2	/O	-0.1
1914	Was-A	39	74	10	19	2	2	0	4	11	18	.257	.353	.338	105	1	1	8	3	4	-2	-2	O	-0.4
1915	Was-A	72	163	20	34	4	1	0	18	28	15	.209	.338	.245	74	-4	-4	17	8	4	0	-4	O	-1.0
1916	Was-A	5	8	0	1	0	0	0	0	2	0	.125	.300	.125	29	-1	-1	0	0			1	/O	0.0
1918	Was-A	3	2	0	0	0	0	0	0	0	1	.000	.000	.000	-99	-0	-0	0	0			0	H	0.0
	Phi-A	49	169	23	51	3	3	0	14	18	10	.302	.369	.355	117	4	4	24	4			-3	O	-0.1
	Yr	52	171	23	51	3	3	0	14	18	11	.298	.365	.351	115	4	3	24	4			-3		-0.1
Total	5	180	436	56	111	9	7	0	37	63	46	.255	.354	.307	97	2	1	53	17	8		-10	O	-1.6

■ JIMMY ADAIR
Adair, James Aubrey "Choppy" b: 1/25/07, Waxahachaie, Tex. d: 12/9/82, Dallas, Tex. BR/TR, 5'10.5", 154 lbs. Deb: 8/24/31 C

YEAR	TM/L	G	AB	R	H	2B	3B	HR	RBI	BB	SO	AVG	OBP	SLG	PRO+	BR	/A	RC	SB	CS	SBR	FR	POS	TPR
1931	Chi-N	18	76	9	21	3	1	0	3	1	8	.276	.286	.342	67	-4	-4	7	1			-1	S	-0.2

■ JERRY ADAIR
Adair, Kenneth Jerry b: 12/17/36, Sand Springs, Okla. d: 5/31/87, Tulsa, Okla. BR/TR, 6', 175 lbs. Deb: 9/02/58 C

YEAR	TM/L	G	AB	R	H	2B	3B	HR	RBI	BB	SO	AVG	OBP	SLG	PRO+	BR	/A	RC	SB	CS	SBR	FR	POS	TPR
1958	Bal-A	11	19	1	2	0	0	0	0	1	7	.105	.150	.105	-30	-3	-3	0	0	0	0	2	S/2	0.0
1959	Bal-A	12	35	3	11	0	1	0	2	1	5	.314	.333	.371	95	-0	-0	4	0	0	0	-4	2/S	-0.3
1960	Bal-A	3	5	1	1	0	0	1	1	0	0	.200	.200	.800	159	0	0	1	0	0	0	0	/2	0.1
1961	Bal-A	133	386	41	102	21	1	9	37	35	51	.264	.329	.394	94	-5	-4	51	5	2	0	-1	*2S/3	1.0
1962	Bal-A	139	538	67	153	29	4	11	48	27	77	.284	.321	.414	101	-4	-1	66	7	7	-2	-10	*S/23	-0.3
1963	Bal-A	109	382	34	87	21	3	6	30	9	51	.228	.249	.346	66	-19	-18	27	3	3	-1	-0	*2	-1.1
1964	Bal-A	155	569	56	141	20	3	9	47	28	72	.248	.284	.341	73	-21	-21	50	3	2	-0	9	*2	0.3
1965	Bal-A	157	582	51	151	26	3	7	66	35	65	.259	.304	.351	84	-12	-13	55	6	4	-1	12	*2	0.7
1966	Bal-A	17	52	3	15	1	0	0	3	4	8	.288	.339	.308	89	-1	-1	6	0	0	0	-1	2	0.0
	Chi-A	105	370	27	90	18	2	4	36	17	44	.243	.278	.335	81	-12	-9	31	3	2	-0	-2	S2	-0.3
	Yr	122	422	30	105	19	2	4	39	21	52	.249	.286	.332	82	-13	-10	37	3	2	-0	-3		-0.3
1967	Chi-A	28	98	6	20	4	0	0	9	4	17	.204	.243	.245	46	-7	-6	5	0	1	-1	-0	2	-0.6
	*Bos-A	89	316	41	92	13	1	3	26	13	35	.291	.323	.367	96	1	-2	34	1	4	-2	-8	3S2	-0.9
	Yr	117	414	47	112	17	1	3	35	17	52	.271	.304	.338	85	-6	-8	38	1	5	-3	-8		-1.5
1968	Bos-A	74	208	18	45	1	0	2	12	9	38	.216	.252	.250	49	-12	-13	11	0	0	0	-5	S2/31	-1.6
1969	KC-A	126	432	29	108	9	1	5	48	20	36	.250	.288	.310	67	-19	-20	32	1	3	-2	-22	*2/S3	-4.0
1970	KC-A	7	27	0	4	0	0	0	1	5	3	.148	.281	.148	22	-3	-3	1	0	1	-1	2	/2	0.0
Total	13	1165	4019	378	1022	163	19	57	366	208	499	.254	.294	.347	80	-117	-113	376	29	29	-9	-30	2S/31	-7.0

■ SPARKY ADAMS
Adams, Earl John b: 8/26/1894, Zerbe, Pa. d: 2/24/89, Pottsville, Pa. BR/TR, 5'5.5", 151 lbs. Deb: 9/18/22

YEAR	TM/L	G	AB	R	H	2B	3B	HR	RBI	BB	SO	AVG	OBP	SLG	PRO+	BR	/A	RC	SB	CS	SBR	FR	POS	TPR
1922	Chi-N	11	44	5	11	0	1	0	3	4	3	.250	.313	.295	56	-3	-3	4	1	2	-1	-4	2	-0.7
1923	Chi-N	95	311	40	90	12	0	4	35	26	10	.289	.346	.367	88	-5	-5	37	20	19	-5	-6	S/O	-0.8
1924	Chi-N	117	418	66	117	11	5	1	27	40	20	.280	.344	.337	83	-9	-9	48	15	17	-6	-8	S2	-1.6
1925	Chi-N	149	627	95	180	29	8	2	48	44	15	.287	.341	.368	80	-17	-19	80	26	12	1	**28**	*2/S	0.8
1926	Chi-N	154	624	95	193	35	3	0	39	52	27	.309	.367	.375	99	2	1	86	27			17	*23/S	2.3
1927	Chi-N	146	647	100	189	17	7	0	49	42	26	.292	.335	.340	81	-16	-17	73	26			-1	23S	-1.0
1928	Pit-N	135	539	91	149	14	6	0	38	64	18	.276	.357	.325	76	-14	-17	65	8			-10	*2S/O	-2.1
1929	Pit-N	74	196	37	51	8	1	0	11	15	5	.260	.316	.311	55	-13	-14	19	3			-15	S23/O	-2.0
1930	*StL-N	137	570	98	179	36	9	0	55	45	27	.314	.365	.409	84	-11	-14	84	7			-13	*32/S	-1.9
1931	*StL-N	143	608	97	178	**46**	5	1	40	42	24	.293	.340	.390	92	-4	-7	83	16			-12	*3/S	-0.9
1932	StL-N	31	127	22	35	3	1	0	13	14	5	.276	.352	.315	79	-3	-3	15	0			-4	3	-0.4
1933	StL-N	8	30	1	5	1	0	0	0	1	3	.167	.219	.200	19	-3	-3	1	0			-2	/S3	-0.4
	Cin-N	137	538	59	141	21	1	1	22	44	30	.262	.320	.310	82	-12	-11	56	3			-3	*3/S	-1.0
	Yr	145	568	60	146	22	1	1	22	45	33	.257	.315	.305	78	-15	-15	57	3			-5		-1.4
1934	Cin-N	87	278	38	70	16	1	0	14	20	10	.252	.307	.317	69	-13	-12	29	2			-3	32	-0.7
Total	13	1424	5557	844	1588	249	48	9	394	453	223	.286	.343	.353	82	-121	-133	679	154	50		-35	23S/O	-10.4

■ BUSTER ADAMS
Adams, Elvin Clark b: 6/24/15, Trinidad, Col. BR/TR, 6', 180 lbs. Deb: 4/27/39

YEAR	TM/L	G	AB	R	H	2B	3B	HR	RBI	BB	SO	AVG	OBP	SLG	PRO+	BR	/A	RC	SB	CS	SBR	FR	POS	TPR
1939	StL-N	2	1	1	0	0	0	0	0	0	0	.000	.000	.000	-94	-0	-0	0	0			0	H	0.0
1943	StL-N	8	11	1	1	1	0	0	1	4	4	.091	.333	.182	48	-1	-1	1	0			0	/O	0.0
	Phi-N	111	418	48	107	14	7	4	38	39	67	.256	.319	.352	98	-4	-2	48	2			-0	*O	-0.6
	Yr	119	429	49	108	15	7	4	39	43	71	.252	.320	.347	96	-4	-3	49	2			-0		-0.6
1944	Phi-N	151	584	86	165	35	3	17	64	74	74	.283	.370	.440	132	22	24	99	2			8	*O	2.1
1945	Phi-N	14	56	6	13	3	1	2	8	5	5	.232	.295	.429	103	-0	-0	7	0			-2	O	-0.2
	StL-N	140	578	98	169	26	0	20	101	57	75	.292	.359	.441	119	16	14	94	3			-5	*O	0.3
	Yr	154	634	104	182	29	1	22	109	62	80	.287	.353	.440	117	15	14	101	3			-7		0.1
1946	StL-N	81	173	21	32	6	0	5	22	29	27	.185	.312	.306	73	-5	-6	19	3			-2	O	-0.9
1947	Phi-N	69	182	21	45	11	1	2	15	26	29	.247	.341	.352	88	-4	-3	23	2			-4	O	-0.7
Total	6	576	2003	282	532	96	12	50	249	234	281	.266	.346	.400	110	24	27	290	12			-6	O	-0.0

■ GEORGE ADAMS
Adams, George b: Grafton, Mass. Deb: 6/14/1879

YEAR	TM/L	G	AB	R	H	2B	3B	HR	RBI	BB	SO	AVG	OBP	SLG	PRO+	BR	/A	RC	SB	CS	SBR	FR	POS	TPR
1879	Syr-N	4	13	0	3	0	0	0	0	1	1	.231	.286	.231	82	-0	-0	1				-0	/O1	0.0

■ GLENN ADAMS
Adams, Glenn Charles b: 10/4/47, Northbridge, Mass. BL/TR, 6'1", 180 lbs. Deb: 5/04/75

YEAR	TM/L	G	AB	R	H	2B	3B	HR	RBI	BB	SO	AVG	OBP	SLG	PRO+	BR	/A	RC	SB	CS	SBR	FR	POS	TPR
1975	SF-N	61	90	10	27	2	1	4	15	11	25	.300	.382	.478	132	5	4	17	1	0	0	-1	O	0.3
1976	SF-N	69	74	2	18	4	0	0	3	1	12	.243	.253	.297	54	-4	-5	5	1	0	0	-1	/O	-0.5
1977	Min-A	95	269	32	91	17	0	6	49	18	30	.338	.380	.468	132	11	11	46	0	2	-1	0	DO	0.7
1978	Min-A	116	310	27	80	18	1	7	35	17	32	.258	.297	.390	90	-4	-5	30	0	1	-1	0	*D/O	-0.5
1979	Min-A	119	326	34	98	13	1	8	50	25	27	.301	.356	.420	104	4	2	50	2	4	-1	-5	DO	-0.5
1980	Min-A	99	262	32	75	11	2	6	38	15	26	.286	.325	.412	94	-0	-3	31	2	4	-2	-1	DO	-0.5
1981	Min-A	72	220	13	46	10	0	2	24	20	26	.209	.275	.282	57	-11	-13	15	0	1	-1	0	D	-1.3
1982	Tor-A	30	66	2	17	4	0	1	11	4	5	.258	.300	.364	74	-2	-3	7	0	0	0	0	D	-0.2
Total	8	661	1617	152	452	79	5	34	225	111	183	.280	.327	.398	96	-2	-10	204	6	10	-4	-9	DO	-2.5

YEAR	TM/L	G	AB	R	H	2B	3B	HR	RBI	BB	SO	AVG	OBP	SLG	PRO+	BR	/A	RC	SB	CS	SBR	FR	POS	TPR

■ DOUG ADAMS
Adams, Harold Douglas b: 1/27/43, Blue River, Wis. BL/TR, 6'3", 185 lbs. Deb: 9/08/69

YEAR	TM/L	G	AB	R	H	2B	3B	HR	RBI	BB	SO	AVG	OBP	SLG	PRO+	BR	/A	RC	SB	CS	SBR	FR	POS	TPR
1969	Chi-A	8	14	1	3	0	0	0	1	1	3	.214	.267	.214	34	-1	-1	1	0	0	0	-1	/C	-0.1

■ HERB ADAMS
Adams, Herbert Loren b: 4/14/28, Hollywood, Cal. BL/TL, 5'9", 160 lbs. Deb: 9/17/48

YEAR	TM/L	G	AB	R	H	2B	3B	HR	RBI	BB	SO	AVG	OBP	SLG	PRO+	BR	/A	RC	SB	CS	SBR	FR	POS	TPR
1948	Chi-A	5	11	1	3	1	0	0	0	1	1	.273	.333	.364	88	-0	-0	2	0	0	0	2	/O	0.2
1949	Chi-A	56	208	26	61	5	3	0	16	9	16	.293	.323	.346	79	-7	-7	23	1	2	-1	1	O	-0.6
1950	Chi-A	34	118	12	24	2	3	0	2	12	7	.203	.288	.271	45	-10	-10	10	3	0	1	2	O	-0.6
Total	3	95	337	39	88	8	6	0	18	22	24	.261	.310	.320	67	-18	-16	35	4	2	0	5	/O	-1.0

■ BERT ADAMS
Adams, John Bertram b: 6/21/1891, Wharton, Tex. d: 6/24/40, Los Angeles, Cal. BB/TR, 6'1", 185 lbs. Deb: 8/30/10

YEAR	TM/L	G	AB	R	H	2B	3B	HR	RBI	BB	SO	AVG	OBP	SLG	PRO+	BR	/A	RC	SB	CS	SBR	FR	POS	TPR
1910	Cle-A	5	13	1	3	0	0	0	0	0		.231	.231	.231	44	-1	-1	1	0			3	/C	0.3
1911	Cle-A	2	5	0	1	0	0	0	0	1		.200	.333	.200	49	-0	-1	0	0			-1	/C	0.0
1912	Cle-A	20	54	5	11	2	1	0	6	4		.204	.259	.278	52	-3	-4	4	0			2	C	0.0
1915	Phi-N	24	27	1	3	0	0	0	2	2	3	.111	.172	.111	-13	-4	-4	1	0			-4	C/1	-0.6
1916	Phi-N	11	13	2	3	0	0	0	1	0	3	.231	.231	.231	40	-1	-1	1	0			1	C	0.1
1917	Phi-N	43	107	4	22	4	1	1	7	0	20	.206	.206	.290	49	-7	-7	6	0			1	C/1	-0.3
1918	Phi-N	84	227	10	40	4	0	0	12	10	26	.176	.214	.194	23	-20	-22	11	5			-1	C	-1.8
1919	Phi-N	78	232	14	54	7	2	1	17	6	27	.233	.252	.293	59	-11	-12	17	4			-2	C/1	-1.0
Total	8	267	678	37	137	17	4	2	45	23	79	.202	.229	.248	42	-46	-51	40	9			-0	C/1	-3.3

■ JOHN ADAMS
Adams, John J. b: 1868, E.St.Louis, Ill. TR , Deb: 4/21/1890

YEAR	TM/L	G	AB	R	H	2B	3B	HR	RBI	BB	SO	AVG	OBP	SLG	PRO+	BR	/A	RC	SB	CS	SBR	FR	POS	TPR
1890	StL-a	1	4	0	1	0	0	0		0		.250	.250	.250	43	-0	-0	0	0			-0	/C	0.0

■ DICK ADAMS
Adams, Richard Leroy b: 4/8/20, Tuolomne, Cal. BR/TL, 6', 185 lbs. Deb: 5/20/47

YEAR	TM/L	G	AB	R	H	2B	3B	HR	RBI	BB	SO	AVG	OBP	SLG	PRO+	BR	/A	RC	SB	CS	SBR	FR	POS	TPR
1947	Phi-A	37	89	9	18	2	3	2	11	2	18	.202	.220	.360	58	-6	-6	7	0	0	0	1	1/O	-0.4

■ RICKY ADAMS
Adams, Ricky Lee b: 1/21/59, Upland, Cal. BR/TR, 6'2", 180 lbs. Deb: 9/15/82

YEAR	TM/L	G	AB	R	H	2B	3B	HR	RBI	BB	SO	AVG	OBP	SLG	PRO+	BR	/A	RC	SB	CS	SBR	FR	POS	TPR
1982	Cal-A	8	14	1	2	0	0	0	0	0	2	.143	.200	.143	-4	-2	-2	0	1	0	0	-1	/S	-0.1
1983	Cal-A	58	112	22	28	2	0	2	6	5	12	.250	.300	.321	72	-4	-4	11	1	1	-0	21	S3/2	1.9
1985	SF-N	54	121	12	23	3	1	2	10	5	23	.190	.228	.281	44	-10	-9	7	1	1	-0	3	S3/2	-0.3
Total	3	120	247	35	53	5	1	4	16	10	37	.215	.260	.291	54	-16	-15	19	3	2	-0	24	/S32	1.5

■ BOBBY ADAMS
Adams, Robert Henry b: 12/14/21, Tuolomne, Cal. BR/TR, 5'10.5", 160 lbs. Deb: 4/16/46 C

YEAR	TM/L	G	AB	R	H	2B	3B	HR	RBI	BB	SO	AVG	OBP	SLG	PRO+	BR	/A	RC	SB	CS	SBR	FR	POS	TPR
1946	Cin-N	94	311	35	76	13	3	4	24	18	32	.244	.292	.344	83	-9	-8	31	16			25	2/O3	2.0
1947	Cin-N	81	217	39	59	11	2	4	20	25	23	.272	.358	.396	101	0	1	33	9			14	2	2.2
1948	Cin-N	87	262	33	78	20	3	1	21	25	23	.298	.361	.408	112	3	4	39	6			-12	2/3	-0.2
1949	Cin-N	107	277	32	70	16	2	0	25	26	36	.253	.317	.325	72	-11	-11	29	4			-9	23	-1.6
1950	Cin-N	115	348	57	98	21	8	3	25	43	29	.282	.361	.414	103	2	2	55	7			-9	23	-0.5
1951	Cin-N	125	403	57	107	12	5	5	24	43	40	.266	.338	.357	86	-7	-7	49	4	10	-5	-9	32/O	-2.0
1952	Cin-N	154	637	85	180	25	4	6	48	49	67	.283	.334	.363	93	-6	-6	77	11	9	-2	9	*3	0.5
1953	Cin-N	150	607	99	167	14	6	8	49	58	67	.275	.338	.357	81	-15	-16	78	3	2	-0	8	*3	-1.1
1954	Cin-N	110	390	69	105	25	6	3	23	55	46	.269	.364	.387	93	-1	-3	58	2	5	-2	1	3/2	-0.2
1955	Cin-N	64	150	23	41	11	2	2	20	20	21	.273	.370	.413	102	2	1	24	2	0	1	3	3/2	0.5
	Chi-A	28	21	8	2	0	1	0	3	4	4	.095	.240	.190	16	-3	-3	1	0	0	0	5	/32	0.3
1956	Bal-A	41	111	19	25	6	1	0	7	25	15	.225	.368	.297	84	-3	-1	15	1	1	-0	-6	32	-0.4
1957	Chi-N	60	187	21	47	10	2	1	10	17	28	.251	.320	.342	79	-6	-5	21	0	3	-2	-8	3/2	-1.3
1958	Chi-N	62	96	14	27	4	4	0	4	6	15	.281	.324	.406	93	-1	-1	13	2	0	1	-2	1/32	-0.2
1959	Chi-N	3	2	0	0	0	0	0	0	0	1	.000	.000	.000	-99	-1	-1	0	0	0	0	-0	/1	0.0
Total	14	1281	4019	591	1082	188	49	37	303	414	447	.269	.340	.368	90	-54	-54	523	67	30		12	32/1O	-2.0

■ BOB ADAMS
Adams, Robert Melvin b: 1/6/52, Pittsburgh, Pa. BR/TR, 6'2", 200 lbs. Deb: 7/10/77

YEAR	TM/L	G	AB	R	H	2B	3B	HR	RBI	BB	SO	AVG	OBP	SLG	PRO+	BR	/A	RC	SB	CS	SBR	FR	POS	TPR
1977	Det-A	15	24	2	6	1	0	2	2	0	5	.250	.250	.542	103	0	-0	3	0	0	0	-1	/1C	0.0

■ MIKE ADAMS
Adams, Robert Michael b: 7/24/48, Cincinnati, Ohio BR/TR, 5'9", 180 lbs. Deb: 9/10/72

YEAR	TM/L	G	AB	R	H	2B	3B	HR	RBI	BB	SO	AVG	OBP	SLG	PRO+	BR	/A	RC	SB	CS	SBR	FR	POS	TPR
1972	Min-A	3	6	0	2	0	0	0	0	0	1	.333	.333	.333	94	-0	-0	1	0	0	0	-0	/O	0.0
1973	Min-A	55	66	21	14	2	0	3	6	17	18	.212	.381	.379	110	2	2	11	2	1	0	4	O/D	0.5
1976	Chi-N	25	29	1	4	2	0	0	2	8	7	.138	.342	.207	54	-1	-2	3	0	0	0	-3	/O32	-0.4
1977	Chi-N	2	2	0	0	0	0	0	0	0	1	.000	.000	.000	-90	-1	-1	0	0	0	0	0	/O	0.0
1978	Oak-A	15	15	5	3	1	0	0	1	7	2	.200	.455	.267	113	1	1	3	0	0	0	0	/23D	0.2
Total	5	100	118	27	23	5	0	3	9	32	29	.195	.375	.314	93	1	0	17	2	1	0	2	/O23D	0.3

■ SPENCER ADAMS
Adams, Spencer Dewey b: 6/21/1898, Layton, Utah d: 11/24/70, Salt Lake City, Ut BL/TR, 5'9", 158 lbs. Deb: 5/08/23

YEAR	TM/L	G	AB	R	H	2B	3B	HR	RBI	BB	SO	AVG	OBP	SLG	PRO+	BR	/A	RC	SB	CS	SBR	FR	POS	TPR
1923	Pit-N	25	56	11	14	0	1	0	4	6	6	.250	.323	.286	60	-3	-3	5	2	1	0	-6	2/S	-0.7
1925	*Was-A	39	55	11	15	4	1	0	4	5	4	.273	.333	.382	83	-2	-2	7	1	1	-0	-2	2/S3	0.0
1926	*NY-A	28	25	7	3	1	0	0	1	3	7	.120	.214	.160	-1	-4	-4	1	1	0	0	4	/23	0.1
1927	StL-A	88	259	32	69	11	3	0	29	24	33	.266	.333	.332	71	-10	-11	27	1	8	-5	1	23	-0.9
Total	4	180	395	61	101	16	5	0	38	38	50	.256	.324	.322	66	-18	-20	40	5	10	-5	-3	/23S	-1.5

■ JOE ADCOCK
Adcock, Joseph Wilbur b: 10/30/27, Coushatta, La. BR/TR, 6'4", 210 lbs. Deb: 4/23/50 M

YEAR	TM/L	G	AB	R	H	2B	3B	HR	RBI	BB	SO	AVG	OBP	SLG	PRO+	BR	/A	RC	SB	CS	SBR	FR	POS	TPR
1950	Cin-N	102	372	46	109	16	1	8	55	24	24	.293	.336	.406	94	-4	-4	48	2			3	O1	-0.3
1951	Cin-N	113	395	40	96	16	4	10	47	24	29	.243	.288	.380	77	-13	-14	36	1	2	-1	-0	*O	-1.8
1952	Cin-N	117	378	43	105	22	4	13	52	23	38	.278	.321	.460	115	6	6	53	1	4	-2	2	O1	0.2
1953	Mil-N	157	590	71	168	33	6	18	80	42	82	.285	.334	.453	110	1	6	85	3	2	-0	-4	*1	-0.1
1954	Mil-N	133	500	73	154	27	5	23	87	44	58	.308	.367	.520	137	19	24	95	1	4	-2	-11	*1	0.5
1955	Mil-N	84	288	40	76	14	0	15	45	31	44	.264	.340	.469	118	6	8	42	0	2	-1	-5	1	-0.4
1956	Mil-N	137	454	76	132	23	1	38	103	32	86	.291	.339	.597	154	26	30	88	1	0	0	-6	*1	1.9
1957	*Mil-N	65	209	31	60	13	2	12	38	20	51	.287	.352	.541	146	10	12	38	0	0	0	-3	1	0.4
1958	*Mil-N	105	320	40	88	15	1	19	54	21	63	.275	.322	.506	125	5	9	47	0	0	0	-4	1O	0.0
1959	Mil-N	115	404	53	118	19	2	25	76	32	77	.292	.344	.535	141	16	20	73	0	0	0	8	1O	2.1
1960	Mil-N	138	514	55	153	21	4	25	91	46	86	.298	.357	.500	142	21	26	89	2	2	-1	3	*1	2.2
1961	Mil-N	152	562	77	160	20	0	35	108	59	94	.285	.357	.507	133	19	24	96	2	1	0	-4	*1	1.0
1962	Mil-N	121	391	48	97	12	1	29	78	50	91	.248	.335	.506	125	11	12	62	2	0	1	-4	*1	0.6
1963	Cle-A	97	283	28	71	7	1	13	49	30	53	.251	.323	.420	107	2	3	37	1	2	-1	-4	1	-0.4
1964	LA-A	118	366	39	98	13	0	21	64	48	61	.268	.353	.475	142	14	18	59	2	2	-1	-4	*1	1.0
1965	Cal-A	122	349	30	84	14	0	14	47	37	74	.241	.315	.401	104	1	2	43	2	2	-1	-3	1	-0.6
1966	Cal-A	83	231	33	63	10	3	18	48	31	48	.273	.359	.576	168	19	19	43	2	2	-1	0	1	1.8
Total	17	1959	6606	823	1832	295	35	336	1122	594	1059	.277	.339	.485	125	158	198	1033	20	25		-34	*1O	8.1

■ BOB ADDIS
Addis, Robert Gordon b: 11/6/25, Mineral, Ohio BL/TR, 6', 175 lbs. Deb: 9/01/50

YEAR	TM/L	G	AB	R	H	2B	3B	HR	RBI	BB	SO	AVG	OBP	SLG	PRO+	BR	/A	RC	SB	CS	SBR	FR	POS	TPR
1950	Bos-N	16	28	7	7	1	0	0	2	3	5	.250	.323	.286	66	-1	-1	3	1			-1	/O	-0.2
1951	Bos-N	85	199	23	55	7	0	1	24	9	10	.276	.308	.327	76	-8	-6	20	3	2	-0	0	O	-0.7
1952	Chi-N	93	292	38	86	13	2	1	20	23	30	.295	.346	.363	96	-1	-1	37	4	4	-1	0	O	-0.1
1953	Chi-N	10	12	2	2	0	0	0	1	2	0	.167	.286	.250	40	-1	-1	1	0	0	0	2	/O	0.0
	Pit-N	4	3	0	0	0	0	0	0	0	2	.000	.000	.000	-99	-1	-1	0	0	0	0	0	H	0.0
	Yr	14	15	2	2	1	0	0	1	2	2	.133	.235	.200	15	-2	-2	1	0	0	0	2		0.0

YEAR	TM/L	G	AB	R	H	2B	3B	HR	RBI	BB	SO	AVG	OBP	SLG	PRO+	BR	/A	RC	SB	CS	SBR	FR	POS	TPR
Total	4	208	534	70	150	22	2	2	47	37	47	.281	.327	.341	84	-13	-11	61	8	6		3	O	-1.0

■ JIM ADDUCI   Adduci, James David   b: 8/9/59, Chicago, Ill.   BL/TR, 6'5", 200 lbs.   Deb: 9/12/83

YEAR	TM/L	G	AB	R	H	2B	3B	HR	RBI	BB	SO	AVG	OBP	SLG	PRO+	BR	/A	RC	SB	CS	SBR	FR	POS	TPR
1983	StL-N	10	20	0	1	0	0	0	0	1	6	.050	.095	.050	-59	-4	-4	0	0	0	0	0	/1O	-0.4
1986	Mil-A	3	11	2	1	1	0	0	0	1	2	.091	.167	.182	-5	-2	-2	0	0	0	0	0	/1	-0.1
1988	Mil-A	44	94	8	25	6	1	1	15	0	15	.266	.266	.383	79	-3	-3	9	0	1	-1	1	OD/1	-0.2
1989	Phi-N	13	19	1	7	1	0	0	0	0	4	.368	.368	.421	125	1	1	3	0	0	0	0	/1O	0.1
Total	4	70	144	11	34	8	1	1	15	2	27	.236	.247	.326	58	-8	-8	12	0	1	-1	2	/O1D	-0.6

■ BOB ADDY   Addy, Robert Edward "Magnet"   b: 2/1845, Rochester, N.Y.   d: 4/9/10, Pocatello, Idaho   BL/TL, 5'8", 160 lbs.   Deb: 5/06/1871   M

YEAR	TM/L	G	AB	R	H	2B	3B	HR	RBI	BB	SO	AVG	OBP	SLG	PRO+	BR	/A	RC	SB	CS	SBR	FR	POS	TPR
1871	Rok-n	25	118	30	32	6	0	0	13	4	0	.271	.295	.322	81	-3	-2	14	8				*2/S	0.0
1873	Phi-n	10	51	12	16	1	0	0		2		.314	.340	.333	95	0	-0	6					2/M	0.0
	Bos-n	31	152	37	56	6	2	1		0		.368	.368	.454	130	7	5	26					*O	0.4
	Yr	41	203	49	72	7	2	1		2		.355	.361	.424	121	7	4	32						0.4
1874	Har-n	50	211	25	50	9	2	0		2		.237	.244	.299	68	-6	-8	16					*2/3S	-0.6
1875	Phi-n	69	311	60	79	11	4	0				.254	.254	.315	92	-1	-3	26					*O/2	-0.1
1876	Chi-N	32	142	36	40	4	1	0	16	5	0	.282	.306	.324	98	2	-1	14				-0	O	0.0
1877	Cin-N	57	245	27	68	2	3	0	31	6	5	.278	.295	.310	102	-2	2	23				4	*O/M	0.3
Total	4 n	185	843	164	233	33	8	1	13	8		.276	.283	.338	92	-4	-9	87					/O23S	-0.3
Total	2	89	387	63	108	6	4	0	47	11	5	.279	.299	.315	100	-1	1	37				4	/O	0.3

■ MORRIE ADERHOLT   Aderholt, Morris Woodrow   b: 9/13/15, Mt.Olive, N.C.   d: 3/18/55, Sarasota, Fla.   BL/TR, 6'1", 188 lbs.   Deb: 9/13/39

YEAR	TM/L	G	AB	R	H	2B	3B	HR	RBI	BB	SO	AVG	OBP	SLG	PRO+	BR	/A	RC	SB	CS	SBR	FR	POS	TPR
1939	Was-A	7	25	5	5	0	0	1	4	2	6	.200	.259	.320	51	-2	-2	2	0	1	-1	0	/2	-0.1
1940	Was-A	1	2	0	0	0	0	0	0	0	0	.000	.000	.000	-99	-1	-1	0	0	0	0	0	/2	0.0
1941	Was-A	11	14	3	2	0	0	0	1	1	3	.143	.200	.143	-8	-2	-2	0	0	0	0	0	/23	-0.1
1944	Bro-N	17	59	9	16	2	3	0	10	4	4	.271	.317	.407	105	0	0	8	0			-2	O	-0.2
1945	Bro-N	39	60	4	13	1	0	0	6	3	10	.217	.254	.233	36	-5	-5	4	0			-2	/O	-0.7
	Bos-N	31	102	15	34	4	0	2	11	9	6	.333	.387	.431	127	4	4	18	3			-1	O/2	0.1
	Yr	70	162	19	47	5	0	2	17	12	16	.290	.339	.358	94	-1	-1	20	3			-4		-0.6
Total	5	106	262	36	70	7	3	3	32	19	29	.267	.317	.351	85	-6	-6	32	3	1		-5	/O23	-1.0

■ DICK ADKINS   Adkins, Richard Earl   b: 3/3/20, Electra, Tex.   d: 9/12/55, Electra, Tex.   BR/TR, 5'10", 165 lbs.   Deb: 9/19/42

YEAR	TM/L	G	AB	R	H	2B	3B	HR	RBI	BB	SO	AVG	OBP	SLG	PRO+	BR	/A	RC	SB	CS	SBR	FR	POS	TPR
1942	Phi-A	3	7	2	1	0	0	0	0	2	2	.143	.333	.143	37	-0	-0	1	0	0	0	-1	/S	-0.1

■ HENRY ADKINSON   Adkinson, Henry Magee   b: 9/1/1874, Chicago, Ill.   d: 5/1/23, Salt Lake City, Ut.   Deb: 9/25/1895

YEAR	TM/L	G	AB	R	H	2B	3B	HR	RBI	BB	SO	AVG	OBP	SLG	PRO+	BR	/A	RC	SB	CS	SBR	FR	POS	TPR
1895	StL-N	1	5	1	2	0	0	0	0	0	2	.400	.400	.400	110	0	0	1	0			-0	/O	0.0

■ DAVE ADLESH   Adlesh, David George   b: 7/15/43, Long Beach, Cal.   BR/TR, 6', 187 lbs.   Deb: 5/12/63

YEAR	TM/L	G	AB	R	H	2B	3B	HR	RBI	BB	SO	AVG	OBP	SLG	PRO+	BR	/A	RC	SB	CS	SBR	FR	POS	TPR
1963	Hou-N	6	8	0	0	0	0	0	0	0	4	.000	.000	.000	-99	-2	-2	0	0	0	0	-2	/C	-0.3
1964	Hou-N	3	10	0	2	0	0	0	0	0	5	.200	.200	.200	14	-1	-1	0	0	0	0	-1	/C	-0.1
1965	Hou-N	15	34	2	5	1	0	0	3	2	12	.147	.216	.176	13	-4	-4	1	0	0	0	-1	C	-0.3
1966	Hou-N	3	6	0	0	0	0	0	0	0	4	.000	.000	.000	-99	-2	-2	0	0	0	0	1	/C	0.0
1967	Hou-N	39	94	4	17	1	0	1	4	11	28	.181	.267	.223	43	-7	-7	5	0	0	0	-2	C	-0.7
1968	Hou-N	40	104	3	19	1	1	0	4	5	27	.183	.227	.212	33	-8	-8	5	0	0	0	-2	C	-1.0
Total	6	106	256	9	43	3	1	1	11	18	80	.168	.228	.199	26	-24	-23	12	0	0	0	-7	/C	-2.4

■ TROY AFENIR   Afenir, Michael Troy   b: 9/21/63, Escondido, Cal.   BR/TR, 6'4", 185 lbs.   Deb: 9/14/87

YEAR	TM/L	G	AB	R	H	2B	3B	HR	RBI	BB	SO	AVG	OBP	SLG	PRO+	BR	/A	RC	SB	CS	SBR	FR	POS	TPR
1987	Hou-N	10	20	1	6	1	0	0	1	0	12	.300	.300	.350	74	-1	-1	2	0	0	0	-0	C	0.0
1990	Oak-A	14	14	0	2	0	0	0	2	0	6	.143	.143	.143	-20	-2	-2	0	0	0	0	-0	C/D	-0.1
Total	2	24	34	1	8	1	0	0	3	0	18	.235	.235	.265	36	-3	-3	2	0	0	0	-0	/CD	-0.1

■ TOMMIE AGEE   Agee, Tommie Lee   b: 8/9/42, Magnolia, Ala.   BR/TR, 5'11", 195 lbs.   Deb: 9/14/62

YEAR	TM/L	G	AB	R	H	2B	3B	HR	RBI	BB	SO	AVG	OBP	SLG	PRO+	BR	/A	RC	SB	CS	SBR	FR	POS	TPR
1962	Cle-A	5	14	0	3	0	0	0	2	0	4	.214	.214	.214	16	-2	-2	1	0	0	0	-0	/O	-0.1
1963	Cle-A	13	27	3	4	1	0	1	3	2	9	.148	.207	.296	39	-2	-2	1	0	0	0	1	O	-0.1
1964	Cle-A	13	12	0	2	0	0	0	0	0	3	.167	.167	.167	-7	-2	-2	0	0	0	0	0	O	-0.1
1965	Chi-A	10	19	2	3	1	0	0	3	2	6	.158	.238	.211	30	-2	-2	1	0	1	-1	1	/O	-0.1
1966	Chi-A	160	629	98	172	27	8	22	86	41	127	.273	.328	.447	129	15	20	88	44	18	2	9	*O	2.6
1967	Chi-A	158	529	73	124	26	2	14	52	44	129	.234	.303	.371	102	-2	0	58	28	10	2	-4	*O	-0.5
1968	NY-N	132	368	30	80	12	3	5	17	15	103	.217	.256	.307	68	-15	-15	27	13	8	-1	-12	*O	-3.9
1969	*NY-N	149	565	97	153	23	4	26	76	59	137	.271	.343	.464	121	17	15	91	12	9	-2	2	*O	0.8
1970	NY-N	153	636	107	182	30	7	24	75	55	156	.286	.345	.469	115	12	12	101	31	15	0	9	*O	1.4
1971	NY-N	113	425	58	121	19	0	14	50	50	84	.285	.363	.428	125	13	14	68	28	6	5	7	*O	2.4
1972	NY-N	114	422	52	96	23	0	13	47	53	92	.227	.319	.374	99	-2	-0	46	8	9	-3	3	*O	-0.5
1973	Hou-N	83	204	30	48	5	2	8	15	16	55	.235	.294	.397	90	-3	-3	22	2	5	-2	2	O	-0.6
	StL-N	26	62	8	11	3	1	3	7	5	13	.177	.239	.403	75	-3	-2	3	1	0	0	4	O	0.1
	Yr	109	266	38	59	8	3	11	22	21	68	.222	.281	.398	87	-6	-6	25	3	5	-2	6		-0.5
Total	12	1129	3912	558	999	170	27	130	433	342	918	.255	.321	.412	108	26	34	507	167	81	2	19	*O	1.4

■ HARRY AGGANIS   Agganis, Harry "The Golden Greek"   b: 4/30/30, Lynn, Mass.   d: 6/27/55, Cambridge, Mass.   BL/TL, 6'2", 200 lbs.   Deb: 4/13/54

YEAR	TM/L	G	AB	R	H	2B	3B	HR	RBI	BB	SO	AVG	OBP	SLG	PRO+	BR	/A	RC	SB	CS	SBR	FR	POS	TPR
1954	Bos-A	132	434	54	109	13	8	11	57	47	57	.251	.324	.394	86	-3	-9	57	6	3	0	7	*1	-0.5
1955	Bos-A	25	83	11	26	10	1	0	10	10	10	.313	.387	.458	116	3	2	15	2	0	1	0	1	0.2
Total	2	157	517	65	135	23	9	11	67	57	67	.261	.334	.404	91	-0	-7	72	8	3	1	7	1	-0.3

■ JOE AGLER   Agler, Joseph Abram   b: 6/12/1887, Coshocton, Ohio   d: 4/26/71, Massillon, Ohio   BL/TL, 5'11", 165 lbs.   Deb: 10/01/12

YEAR	TM/L	G	AB	R	H	2B	3B	HR	RBI	BB	SO	AVG	OBP	SLG	PRO+	BR	/A	RC	SB	CS	SBR	FR	POS	TPR
1912	Was-A	2	1	0	0	0	0	0	0	0		.000	.000	.000	-99	-0	-0	0	0			0	/1	0.0
1914	Buf-F	135	463	82	126	17	6	0	20	77	78	.272	.376	.335	102	6	5	70	21			5	1O	0.9
1915	Buf-F	25	73	11	13	1	2	0	2	20	14	.178	.355	.247	78	-1	-1	7	2			-2	O/1	-0.3
	Bal-F	72	214	28	46	4	2	0	14	34	38	.215	.325	.252	70	-6	-7	24	15			5	1/O2	-0.1
	Yr	97	287	39	59	5	4	0	16	54	52	.206	.333	.251	72	-7	-8	32	17			3		-0.4
Total	3	234	751	121	185	22	10	0	36	131	130	.246	.359	.302	91	-1	-3	101	38			7	1/O2	0.5

■ SAM AGNEW   Agnew, Samuel Lester "Slam"   b: 4/12/1887, Farmington, Mo.   d: 7/19/51, Sonoma, Cal.   BR/TR, 5'11", 185 lbs.   Deb: 4/10/13

YEAR	TM/L	G	AB	R	H	2B	3B	HR	RBI	BB	SO	AVG	OBP	SLG	PRO+	BR	/A	RC	SB	CS	SBR	FR	POS	TPR
1913	StL-A	105	307	27	64	9	5	2	24	20	49	.208	.272	.290	66	-14	-13	26	11			2	*C	-0.3
1914	StL-A	115	311	22	66	5	4	0	16	24	63	.212	.279	.254	63	-15	-14	23	10	8	-2	3	*C	-0.4
1915	StL-A	104	295	18	60	4	2	0	19	12	36	.203	.247	.231	45	-21	-20	18	5	2	0	6	*C	-0.5
1916	Bos-A	40	67	4	14	2	1	0	7	6	4	.209	.293	.269	69	-2	-3	6	0			8	C	0.8
1917	Bos-A	85	260	17	54	6	2	0	16	19	30	.208	.267	.246	57	-14	-13	17	2			-10	C	-1.9
1918	*Bos-A	72	199	11	33	8	0	0	6	11	26	.166	.221	.206	29	-17	-17	9	0			11	C	0.7
1919	Was-A	42	98	6	23	7	0	0	10	10	8	.235	.312	.306	74	-3	-3	10	1			8	C	0.7
Total	7	563	1537	105	314	41	14	2	98	102	216	.204	.265	.253	56	-87	-83	111	29	10		27	C	-1.6

■ LUIS AGUAYO   Aguayo, Luis (Muriel)   b: 3/13/59, Vega Baja, P.R.   BR/TR, 5'9", 173 lbs.   Deb: 4/19/80

YEAR	TM/L	G	AB	R	H	2B	3B	HR	RBI	BB	SO	AVG	OBP	SLG	PRO+	BR	/A	RC	SB	CS	SBR	FR	POS	TPR
1980	Phi-N	20	47	7	13	1	2	1	8	2	9	.277	.306	.447	102	0	-0	6	1	1	-0	1	2/S	0.2
1981	*Phi-N	45	84	11	18	4	0	1	7	6	15	.214	.268	.298	62	-4	-4	8	1	0	-0	-4	2S/3	-0.4
1982	Phi-N	50	56	11	15	1	2	3	7	5	7	.268	.339	.518	133	2	2	9	1	1	-0	3	2S/3	0.7
1983	Phi-N	2	4	1	1	0	0	0	0	1	2	.250	.400	.250	85	-0	-0	1	0	0	0	-1	/S	0.0

YEAR	TM/L	G	AB	R	H	2B	3B	HR	RBI	BB	SO	AVG	OBP	SLG	PRO+	BR	/A	RC	SB	CS	SBR	FR	POS	TPR
1984	Phi-N	58	72	15	20	4	0	3	11	8	16	.278	.350	.458	123	2	2	12	0	0	0	8	32S	1.2
1985	Phi-N	91	165	27	46	7	3	6	21	22	26	.279	.383	.467	133	9	8	29	1	0	0	3	S2/3	1.7
1986	Phi-N	62	133	17	28	6	1	4	13	8	26	.211	.271	.361	70	-5	-6	13	1	1	-0	-7	2S/3	-1.0
1987	Phi-N	94	209	25	43	9	1	12	21	15	56	.206	.275	.361	81	-6	-7	24	0	0	0	-9	S/23	-0.6
1988	Phi-N	49	97	9	24	3	0	3	5	13	17	.247	.336	.371	101	1	0	13	2	0	1	2	S3/2	0.5
	NY-A	50	140	12	35	4	0	3	8	7	33	.250	.291	.343	77	-5	-4	13	0	2	-1	-2	32/S	-0.5
1989	Cle-A	47	97	7	17	4	1	1	8	7	19	.175	.245	.268	44	-7	-7	6	0	0	0	5	3S2/D	0.0
Total	10	568	1104	142	260	43	10	37	109	94	220	.236	.307	.393	91	-13	-16	133	7	5	-1	-2	S2/3D	1.8

■ CHARLIE AHEARN
Ahearn, Charles　b: Troy, N.Y.　Deb: 6/19/1880

YEAR	TM/L	G	AB	R	H	2B	3B	HR	RBI	BB	SO	AVG	OBP	SLG	PRO+	BR	/A	RC	SB	CS	SBR	FR	POS	TPR
1880	Tro-N	1	4	1	1	0	0	0	0	0	0	.250	.250	.250	67	-0	-0	0				1	/C	0.1

■ WILLIE AIKENS
Aikens, Willie Mays　b: 10/14/54, Seneca, S.C.　BL/TR, 6'3", 220 lbs.　Deb: 5/17/77

YEAR	TM/L	G	AB	R	H	2B	3B	HR	RBI	BB	SO	AVG	OBP	SLG	PRO+	BR	/A	RC	SB	CS	SBR	FR	POS	TPR
1977	Cal-A	42	91	5	18	4	0	0	6	10	23	.198	.277	.242	45	-7	-7	6	1	2	-1	0	1D	-0.7
1979	Cal-A	116	379	59	106	18	0	21	81	61	79	.280	.381	.493	138	19	21	71	1	3	-2	-2	1D	1.4
1980	*KC-A	151	543	70	151	24	0	20	98	64	88	.278	.362	.433	116	13	13	82	1	0	0	-9	*1D	-0.4
1981	*KC-A	101	349	45	93	16	0	17	53	62	47	.266	.382	.458	142	20	21	62	0	0	0	-5	1	1.3
1982	KC-A	134	466	50	131	29	1	17	74	45	70	.281	.348	.457	119	12	12	69	0	1	-1	-3	*1	0.5
1983	KC-A	125	410	49	124	26	1	23	72	45	75	.302	.374	.539	148	26	26	78	0	0	0	-1	*1/D	2.0
1984	Tor-A	93	234	21	48	7	0	11	26	29	56	.205	.298	.372	82	-5	-6	26	0	0	0	0	D/1	-0.5
1985	Tor-A	12	20	2	4	1	0	1	5	3	6	.200	.304	.400	89	-0	-0	2	0	0	0	0	D	0.0
Total	8	774	2492	301	675	125	2	110	415	319	444	.271	.358	.455	123	78	79	398	3	6	-3	-19	1D	3.6

■ DANNY AINGE
Ainge, Daniel Ray　b: 3/17/59, Eugene, Ore.　BR/TR, 6'4", 175 lbs.　Deb: 5/21/79

YEAR	TM/L	G	AB	R	H	2B	3B	HR	RBI	BB	SO	AVG	OBP	SLG	PRO+	BR	/A	RC	SB	CS	SBR	FR	POS	TPR
1979	Tor-A	87	308	26	73	7	1	2	19	12	58	.237	.270	.286	50	-22	-22	23	1	0	0	-3	2	-2.0
1980	Tor-A	38	111	11	27	6	1	0	4	2	29	.243	.263	.315	55	-7	-7	9	3	0	1	4	O/32D	-0.2
1981	Tor-A	86	246	20	46	6	2	0	14	23	41	.187	.259	.228	39	-18	-20	15	8	5	-1	2	3/SO2D	-1.9
Total	3	211	665	57	146	19	4	2	37	37	128	.220	.265	.269	47	-46	-49	47	12	5	1	2	/23OSD	-4.1

■ EDDIE AINSMITH
Ainsmith, Edward Wilbur "Dorf"　b: 2/4/1892, Cambridge, Mass.　d: 9/6/81, Ft.Lauderdale, Fla　BR/TR, 5'11", 180 lbs.　Deb: 8/09/10

YEAR	TM/L	G	AB	R	H	2B	3B	HR	RBI	BB	SO	AVG	OBP	SLG	PRO+	BR	/A	RC	SB	CS	SBR	FR	POS	TPR
1910	Was-A	33	104	4	20	1	2	0	9	6		.192	.236	.240	52	-6	-6	6	0			-3	C	-0.6
1911	Was-A	61	149	12	33	2	3	0	14	10		.221	.275	.275	55	-9	-9	12	5			1	C	-0.2
1912	Was-A	61	186	22	42	7	2	0	22	14		.226	.280	.285	61	-10	-10	17	4			16	C	1.2
1913	Was-A	84	229	26	49	4	4	2	20	12	41	.214	.262	.293	61	-12	-12	20	17			6	C/P	0.0
1914	Was-A	62	151	11	34	7	0	0	13	9	28	.225	.273	.272	62	-7	-7	12	8	5	-1	8	C	0.3
1915	Was-A	47	120	13	24	4	2	0	6	10	18	.200	.267	.267	59	-6	-6	9	7	4	-0	5	C	0.2
1916	Was-A	51	100	11	17	4	0	0	8	8	14	.170	.231	.210	33	-8	-8	7	3			13	C	0.8
1917	Was-A	125	350	38	67	17	4	0	42	40	48	.191	.280	.263	66	-14	-14	30	16			15	*C	1.1
1918	Was-A	96	292	22	62	10	9	0	20	29	44	.212	.283	.308	80	-8	-8	27	6			8	C	1.0
1919	Det-A	114	364	42	99	17	12	3	32	45	30	.272	.354	.409	117	7	8	54	9			-11	*C	0.3
1920	Det-A	69	186	19	43	5	3	1	19	14	19	.231	.285	.306	58	-12	-11	17	4	3	-1	-3	C/1	-0.8
1921	Det-A	35	98	6	27	5	2	0	12	13	7	.276	.360	.367	87	-2	-2	14	1	0	0	-4	C	-0.3
	StL-N	27	62	5	18	0	1	0	5	3	4	.290	.323	.323	73	-2	-2	7	0	0	0	2	C/1	0.1
1922	StL-N	119	379	46	111	14	4	13	59	28	43	.293	.343	.454	109	1	4	58	2	3	-1	-2	*C	0.1
1923	StL-N	82	263	22	56	11	6	3	34	22	19	.213	.276	.335	62	-16	-15	26	4	0	1	-7	C	-1.6
	Bro-N	2	10	0	2	0	0	0	2	0	0	.200	.200	.200	6	-1	-1	0	0	1	-1	1	/C	0.0
	Yr	84	273	22	58	11	6	3	36	22	19	.212	.274	.330	60	-17	-16	26	4	1	1	-7		-1.6
1924	NY-N	10	5	0	3	0	0	0	0	0	0	.600	.600	.600	229	1	1	2	0	0	0	-0	/C	0.1
Total	15	1078	3048	299	707	108	54	22	317	263	315	.232	.296	.324	76	-105	-99	317	86	16		44	C/1P	1.7

■ GEORGE AITON
Aiton, George Wilson　b: 12/29/1890, Kingman, Kan.　d: 8/16/76, Van Nuys, Cal.　BB/TR, 5'11.5", 175 lbs.　Deb: 6/29/12

YEAR	TM/L	G	AB	R	H	2B	3B	HR	RBI	BB	SO	AVG	OBP	SLG	PRO+	BR	/A	RC	SB	CS	SBR	FR	POS	TPR
1912	StL-A	10	17	1	4	0	0	0	1	4		.235	.381	.235	80	-0	-0	1	0			-0	/O	0.0

■ JOHN AKE
Ake, John Leckie　b: 8/29/1861, Altoona, Pa.　d: 5/11/1887, LaCrosse, Wis.　6'1", 180 lbs.　Deb: 5/12/1884

YEAR	TM/L	G	AB	R	H	2B	3B	HR	RBI	BB	SO	AVG	OBP	SLG	PRO+	BR	/A	RC	SB	CS	SBR	FR	POS	TPR
1884	Bal-a	13	52	1	10	0	1	0		0		.192	.208	.231	43	-3	-3	3				-3	/3OS	-0.5

■ BILL AKERS
Akers, William G. "Bump"　b: 12/25/04, Chattanooga, Tenn.　d: 4/13/62, Chattanooga, Tenn.　BR/TR, 5'11", 178 lbs.　Deb: 9/08/29

YEAR	TM/L	G	AB	R	H	2B	3B	HR	RBI	BB	SO	AVG	OBP	SLG	PRO+	BR	/A	RC	SB	CS	SBR	FR	POS	TPR
1929	Det-A	24	83	15	22	4	1	1	9	10	9	.265	.351	.373	86	-2	-2	12	2	0	1	-9	S	-0.6
1930	Det-A	85	233	36	65	8	5	9	40	36	34	.279	.375	.472	111	5	4	42	5	5	-2	9	S3	1.6
1931	Det-A	29	66	5	13	2	2	0	3	7	6	.197	.274	.288	46	-5	-5	5	0	1	-1	-2	S/2	-0.4
1932	Bos-N	36	93	8	24	3	1	1	17	10	15	.258	.330	.344	85	-2	-2	11	0			-5	3/2S	-0.3
Total	4	174	475	64	124	17	9	11	69	63	64	.261	.349	.404	93	-4	-4	70	7	6		-6	/S32	0.3

■ GUS ALBERTS
Alberts, Augustus Peter　b: 1861, Reading, Pa.　d: 5/7/12, Idaho Springs, Colo　BR/TR, 5'6.5", 180 lbs.　Deb: 5/01/1884

YEAR	TM/L	G	AB	R	H	2B	3B	HR	RBI	BB	SO	AVG	OBP	SLG	PRO+	BR	/A	RC	SB	CS	SBR	FR	POS	TPR
1884	Pit-a	2	5	1	1	0	0	0		0		.200	.200	.200	32	-0	-0	0				-1	/S	-0.1
	Was-U	4	16	4	4	0	0	0		0	4	.250	.400	.250	128	1	1	2	0			2	/S	0.2
1888	Cle-a	102	364	51	75	10	6	1	48	41		.206	.299	.275	89	-3	-2	39	26			4	S3	0.4
1891	Mil-a	12	41	6	4	0	0	0	2	7	5	.098	.260	.098	4	-5	-6	1	1			-3	3	-0.7
Total	3	120	426	62	84	10	6	1	50	52	5	.197	.298	.256	79	-8	-8	42	27			2	/3S	-0.2

■ BUTCH ALBERTS
Alberts, Francis Burt　b: 5/4/50, Williamsport, Pa.　BR/TR, 6'2", 205 lbs.　Deb: 9/07/78

YEAR	TM/L	G	AB	R	H	2B	3B	HR	RBI	BB	SO	AVG	OBP	SLG	PRO+	BR	/A	RC	SB	CS	SBR	FR	POS	TPR
1978	Tor-A	6	18	1	5	1	0	0	0	0	2	.278	.278	.333	70	-1	-1	2	0	0	0	0	/D	0.0

■ JACK ALBRIGHT
Albright, Harold John　b: 6/30/21, St.Petersburg, Fl　BR/TR, 5'9", 175 lbs.　Deb: 5/19/47

YEAR	TM/L	G	AB	R	H	2B	3B	HR	RBI	BB	SO	AVG	OBP	SLG	PRO+	BR	/A	RC	SB	CS	SBR	FR	POS	TPR
1947	Phi-N	41	99	9	23	4	0	2	5	10	11	.232	.303	.333	71	-5	-4	10	1			3	S	0.1

■ LUIS ALCARAZ
Alcaraz, Angel Luis (Acosta)　b: 6/20/41, Humacao, P.R.　BR/TR, 5'9", 165 lbs.　Deb: 9/13/67

YEAR	TM/L	G	AB	R	H	2B	3B	HR	RBI	BB	SO	AVG	OBP	SLG	PRO+	BR	/A	RC	SB	CS	SBR	FR	POS	TPR
1967	LA-N	17	60	1	14	1	0	0	3	1	13	.233	.246	.250	46	-4	-4	3	1	1	-0	9	2	0.6
1968	LA-N	41	106	4	16	1	0	2	5	9	23	.151	.217	.217	33	-9	-8	5	1	1	-0	3	23/S	-0.3
1969	KC-A	22	79	15	20	2	1	1	7	7	9	.253	.314	.342	83	-2	-2	8	0	0	0	-5	2/3S	-0.5
1970	KC-A	35	120	10	20	5	1	1	14	4	13	.167	.194	.250	21	-13	-13	6	0	0	0	-8	2	-1.8
Total	4	115	365	30	70	9	2	4	29	21	58	.192	.236	.260	43	-28	-27	22	2	2	-1	-1	/23S	-2.0

■ SCOTTY ALCOCK
Alcock, John Forbes　b: 11/29/1885, Wooster, Ohio　d: 1/30/73, Wooster, Ohio　BR/TR, 5'9.5", 160 lbs.　Deb: 4/19/14

YEAR	TM/L	G	AB	R	H	2B	3B	HR	RBI	BB	SO	AVG	OBP	SLG	PRO+	BR	/A	RC	SB	CS	SBR	FR	POS	TPR
1914	Chi-A	54	156	12	27	4	2	0	7	7	14	.173	.213	.224	32	-13	-13	8	4	2	0	4	3/2	-0.8

■ MIKE ALDRETE
Aldrete, Michael Peter　b: 1/29/61, Carmel, Cal.　BL/TL, 5'11", 180 lbs.　Deb: 5/28/86

YEAR	TM/L	G	AB	R	H	2B	3B	HR	RBI	BB	SO	AVG	OBP	SLG	PRO+	BR	/A	RC	SB	CS	SBR	FR	POS	TPR
1986	SF-N	84	216	27	54	18	3	2	25	33	34	.250	.355	.389	110	2	4	31	1	3	-2	4	1O	0.4
1987	*SF-N	126	357	50	116	18	2	9	51	43	50	.325	.398	.462	133	15	17	68	6	0	2	-1	O1	1.3
1988	SF-N	139	389	44	104	15	0	3	50	56	65	.267	.360	.329	103	2	4	47	6	5	-1	-5	*O1	-0.5
1989	Mon-N	76	136	12	30	8	1	1	12	19	30	.221	.321	.316	81	-3	-3	14	1	3	-2	1	O1	-0.4
1990	Mon-N	96	161	22	39	7	1	1	18	37	31	.242	.387	.317	96	1	1	22	1	2	-1	1	O1	0.0
Total	5	521	1259	155	343	66	7	16	156	188	210	.272	.369	.374	110	17	23	182	15	13	-3	-0	O1	0.8

■ CHUCK ALENO
Aleno, Charles　b: 2/19/17, St.Louis, Mo.　BR/TR, 6'1.5", 215 lbs.　Deb: 5/15/41

YEAR	TM/L	G	AB	R	H	2B	3B	HR	RBI	BB	SO	AVG	OBP	SLG	PRO+	BR	/A	RC	SB	CS	SBR	FR	POS	TPR
1941	Cin-N	54	169	23	41	7	3	1	18	11	16	.243	.289	.337	76	-6	-6	16	3			-4	3/1	-0.9

YEAR	TM/L	G	AB	R	H	2B	3B	HR	RBI	BB	SO	AVG	OBP	SLG	PRO+	BR	/A	RC	SB	CS	SBR	FR	POS	TPR
1942	Cin-N	7	14	1	2	1	0	0	0	3	3	.143	.294	.214	50	-1	-1	1	0			1	/32	0.1
1943	Cin-N	7	10	0	3	0	0	0	1	2	1	.300	.417	.300	110	0	0	1	0			-0	/O	0.0
1944	Cin-N	50	127	10	21	3	0	1	15	15	15	.165	.259	.213	35	-11	-10	8	0			-4	3/1S	-1.2
Total	4	118	320	34	67	11	3	2	34	31	35	.209	.281	.281	60	-17	-17	26	3			-7	/31SO2	-2.0

■ DALE ALEXANDER

Alexander, David Dale "Moose" b: 4/26/03, Greenville, Tenn. d: 3/2/79, Greeneville, Tenn. BR/TR, 6'3", 210 lbs. Deb: 4/16/29

YEAR	TM/L	G	AB	R	H	2B	3B	HR	RBI	BB	SO	AVG	OBP	SLG	PRO+	BR	/A	RC	SB	CS	SBR	FR	POS	TPR
1929	Det-A	155	626	110	215	43	15	25	137	56	63	.343	.397	.580	148	43	42	140	5	9	-4	-4	*1	1.1
1930	Det-A	154	602	86	196	33	8	20	135	42	56	.326	.372	.507	118	17	15	112	6	5	-1	-7	*1	-0.9
1931	Det-A	135	517	75	168	47	3	3	87	64	35	.325	.401	.445	118	18	16	93	5	8	-3	-8	*1/O	-0.6
1932	Det-A	23	16	0	4	0	0	0	4	6	2	.250	.455	.250	84	0	0	2	0	0	0	0	/1	0.0
	Bos-A	101	376	58	140	27	3	8	56	55	19	.372	.454	.524	157	32	33	91	4	5	-2	2	*1	2.0
	Yr	124	392	58	144	27	3	8	60	61	21	.367	.454	.513	152	32	33	93	4	5	-2	2		2.0
1933	Bos-A	94	313	40	88	14	1	5	40	25	22	.281	.336	.380	90	-5	-5	40	0	1	-1	3	1	-0.7
Total	5	662	2450	369	811	164	30	61	459	248	197	.331	.394	.497	128	105	102	478	20	28	-11	-14	1/O	0.9

■ GARY ALEXANDER

Alexander, Gary Wayne b: 3/27/53, Los Angeles, Cal. BR/TR, 6'2", 195 lbs. Deb: 9/12/75

YEAR	TM/L	G	AB	R	H	2B	3B	HR	RBI	BB	SO	AVG	OBP	SLG	PRO+	BR	/A	RC	SB	CS	SBR	FR	POS	TPR
1975	SF-N	3	3	1	0	0	0	0	0	1	2	.000	.250	.000	-25	-0	-1	0	0	0	0	-1	/C	0.0
1976	SF-N	23	73	12	13	1	1	2	7	10	16	.178	.277	.301	62	-3	-4	7	1	0	0	-3	C	-0.5
1977	SF-N	51	119	17	36	4	2	5	20	20	33	.303	.411	.496	143	8	8	24	3	1	0	-8	C/O	0.0
1978	Oak-A	58	174	18	36	6	1	10	22	22	66	.207	.299	.425	107	-0	1	19	0	3	-2	-0	D/OC1	0.0
	Cle-A	90	324	39	76	14	3	17	62	35	100	.235	.311	.454	114	4	5	47	0	2	-1	-9	CD	-0.3
	Yr	148	498	57	112	20	4	27	84	57	166	.225	.307	.444	112	4	6	66	0	5	-3	-9		-0.3
1979	Cle-A	110	358	54	82	9	2	15	54	46	100	.229	.319	.391	90	-5	-5	46	4	2	0	-18	CD/O	-1.8
1980	Cle-A	76	178	22	40	7	1	5	31	17	52	.225	.292	.360	77	-6	-6	15	0	4	-2	0	DC/O	-0.7
1981	Pit-N	21	47	6	10	4	1	1	6	3	12	.213	.260	.404	84	-1	-1	5	0	0	0	1	/1O	-0.7
Total	7	432	1276	169	293	45	11	55	202	154	381	.230	.315	.411	99	-4	-3	163	8	12	-5	-37	CD/O1	-3.3

■ HUGH ALEXANDER

Alexander, Hugh b: 7/10/17, Buffalo, Mo. BR/TR, 6', 190 lbs. Deb: 8/15/37

YEAR	TM/L	G	AB	R	H	2B	3B	HR	RBI	BB	SO	AVG	OBP	SLG	PRO+	BR	/A	RC	SB	CS	SBR	FR	POS	TPR
1937	Cle-A	7	11	0	1	0	0	0	0	0	5	.091	.091	.091	-54	-3	-3	0	1	0	0	-1	/O	-0.2

■ MATT ALEXANDER

Alexander, Matthew b: 1/30/47, Shreveport, La. BB/TR, 5'11", 168 lbs. Deb: 8/23/73

YEAR	TM/L	G	AB	R	H	2B	3B	HR	RBI	BB	SO	AVG	OBP	SLG	PRO+	BR	/A	RC	SB	CS	SBR	FR	POS	TPR
1973	Chi-N	12	5	4	1	0	0	0	1	1	1	.200	.333	.200	48	-0	-1	1	2	0	1	1	/O	0.1
1974	Chi-N	45	54	15	11	2	1	0	0	12	12	.204	.358	.278	76	-1	-1	6	8	4	0	-1	3/O2	-0.1
1975	Oak-A	63	10	16	1	0	0	0	0	1	1	.100	.182	.100	-19	-2	-2	-7	17	10	-1	3	DO/23	0.0
1976	Oak-A	61	30	16	1	0	0	0	0	0	5	.033	.033	.033	-84	-7	-7	-2	20	7	2	4	OD	0.0
1977	Oak-A	90	42	24	10	1	0	0	2	4	6	.238	.304	.262	57	-2	-2	0	26	14	-1	3	OS/23D	0.1
1978	Pit-N	7	0	2	0	0	0	0	0	0	0	—	—	—	—		0	0	4	1	1	0	R	0.1
1979	*Pit-N	44	13	16	7	0	1	0	1	0	0	.538	.538	.692	223	2	2	7	13	1	3	4	O/S	1.0
1980	Pit-N	37	3	13	1	1	0	0	0	0	0	.333	.333	.667	170	0	0	-5	10	3	1	4	/O2	0.6
1981	Pit-N	15	11	5	4	0	0	0	0	0	1	.364	.364	.364	104	0	0	-1	3	2	-0	1	/O	0.1
Total	9	374	168	111	36	4	2	0	4	18	26	.214	.294	.262	56	-9	-9	1	103	42	6	21	/OD3S2	1.9

■ WALT ALEXANDER

Alexander, Walter Ernest b: 3/5/1891, Atlanta, Ga. d: 12/29/78, Fort Worth, Tex. BR/TR, 5'10.5", 165 lbs. Deb: 6/21/12

YEAR	TM/L	G	AB	R	H	2B	3B	HR	RBI	BB	SO	AVG	OBP	SLG	PRO+	BR	/A	RC	SB	CS	SBR	FR	POS	TPR
1912	StL-A	37	97	5	17	4	0	0	5	8		.175	.245	.216	34	-9	-8	6	1			-3	C	-0.6
1913	StL-A	43	110	5	15	2	1	0	7	4	36	.136	.174	.173	2	-14	-13	3	1			4	C	-0.6
1915	StL-A	1	1	0	0	0	0	0	0	0		.000	.000	.000	-99	-0	-0	0				0	/C	0.0
	NY-A	25	68	7	17	4	0	1	5	13	16	.250	.370	.353	117	2	2	10	2	1	0	9	C	1.3
	Yr	26	69	7	17	4	0	1	5	13	16	.246	.366	.348	114	2	2	10	2	1	0	9		1.3
1916	NY-A	36	78	8	20	6	1	0	3	13	20	.256	.376	.359	118	3	2	11	0			1	C	0.5
1917	NY-A	20	51	1	7	2	1	0	4	4	11	.137	.200	.216	27	-5	-5	3	1			-0	C	-0.3
Total	5	162	405	26	76	18	3	1	24	42	83	.188	.271	.254	56	-23	-22	32	5	1		12	C	0.3

■ NIN ALEXANDER

Alexander, William Henry b: 11/24/1858, Pana, Ill. d: 12/22/33, Pana, Ill. 5'4.5", 163 lbs. Deb: 6/07/1884

YEAR	TM/L	G	AB	R	H	2B	3B	HR	RBI	BB	SO	AVG	OBP	SLG	PRO+	BR	/A	RC	SB	CS	SBR	FR	POS	TPR
1884	KC-U	19	65	2	9	0	0	0		1		.138	.152	.138	-2	-7	-5	1	0			0	C/SO	-0.3
	StL-a	1	4	0	0	0	0	0				.000	.000	.000	-96	-1	-1	0				-0	/CO	0.0

■ LUIS ALICEA

Alicea, Luis Rene (De Jesus) b: 7/29/65, Santurce, P.R. BB/TR, 5'9", 165 lbs. Deb: 4/23/88

YEAR	TM/L	G	AB	R	H	2B	3B	HR	RBI	BB	SO	AVG	OBP	SLG	PRO+	BR	/A	RC	SB	CS	SBR	FR	POS	TPR
1988	StL-N	93	297	20	63	10	4	1	24	25	32	.212	.278	.283	61	-15	-15	22	1	1	-0	4	2	-0.8

■ ANDY ALLANSON

Allanson, Andrew Neal b: 12/22/61, Richmond, Va. BR/TR, 6'5", 220 lbs. Deb: 4/07/86

YEAR	TM/L	G	AB	R	H	2B	3B	HR	RBI	BB	SO	AVG	OBP	SLG	PRO+	BR	/A	RC	SB	CS	SBR	FR	POS	TPR
1986	Cle-A	101	293	30	66	7	3	1	29	14	36	.225	.263	.280	49	-21	-20	22	10	1	2	-6	C	-1.7
1987	Cle-A	50	154	17	41	6	0	3	16	9	30	.266	.307	.364	76	-5	-5	17	1	1	-0	-7	C	-0.7
1988	Cle-A	133	434	44	114	11	0	5	50	25	63	.263	.307	.323	75	-13	-15	42	5	9	-4	0	*C	-1.2
1989	Cle-A	111	323	30	75	9	1	3	17	23	47	.232	.291	.294	64	-15	-15	27	4	4	-1	4	*C	-0.7
Total	4	395	1204	121	296	33	4	12	112	71	176	.246	.292	.310	66	-54	-56	109	20	15	-3	-10	C	-4.3

■ NICK ALLEN

Allen, Artemus Ward b: 9/14/1888, Norton, Kan. d: 10/16/39, Hines, Ill. BR/TR, 6', 180 lbs. Deb: 5/01/14

YEAR	TM/L	G	AB	R	H	2B	3B	HR	RBI	BB	SO	AVG	OBP	SLG	PRO+	BR	/A	RC	SB	CS	SBR	FR	POS	TPR
1914	Buf-F	32	63	3	15	1	0	0	4	3	12	.238	.273	.254	50	-4	-4	6	4			2	C	0.0
1915	Buf-F	84	215	14	44	7	1	0	17	18	34	.205	.269	.247	52	-12	-13	16	4			8	C	-0.2
1916	Chi-N	5	16	1	1	0	0	0	1	0	3	.063	.063	.063	-56	-3	-3	0	0			-0	/C	-0.3
1918	Cin-N	37	96	6	25	2	2	0	5	4	7	.260	.297	.323	91	-1	-1	9	0			8	C	1.0
1919	Cin-N	15	25	7	8	0	1	0	5	2	0	.320	.393	.400	142	1	1	4	0			3	C	0.5
1920	Cin-N	43	85	10	23	3	1	0	4	6	11	.271	.340	.329	94	-1	-0	10	0	0	0	6	C	0.9
Total	6	216	500	41	116	13	5	0	36	33	73	.232	.288	.278	67	-20	-20	45	8	0		28	C	1.9

■ BERNIE ALLEN

Allen, Bernard Keith b: 4/16/39, E.Liverpool, O. BL/TR, 6', 175 lbs. Deb: 4/10/62

YEAR	TM/L	G	AB	R	H	2B	3B	HR	RBI	BB	SO	AVG	OBP	SLG	PRO+	BR	/A	RC	SB	CS	SBR	FR	POS	TPR
1962	Min-A	159	573	79	154	27	7	12	64	62	82	.269	.340	.403	96	-1	-3	80	0	1	-1	-17	*2	-0.9
1963	Min-A	139	421	52	101	20	1	9	43	38	52	.240	.304	.356	83	-9	-10	46	0	0	0	-24	*2	-2.5
1964	Min-A	74	243	28	52	8	1	6	20	33	30	.214	.310	.329	78	-7	-7	25	1	2	-1	-11	2	-1.1
1965	Min-A	19	39	2	9	2	0	0	6	6	8	.231	.333	.282	73	-1	-1	4	0	0	0	-2	2/3	-0.2
1966	Min-A	101	319	34	76	18	1	5	30	26	40	.238	.300	.348	80	-6	-8	31	2	3	-1	-7	2/3	-0.8
1967	Was-A	87	254	13	49	5	1	3	18	18	42	.193	.246	.256	51	-16	-15	17	1	2	-1	19	2	0.5
1968	Was-A	120	373	31	90	12	4	6	40	28	35	.241	.301	.343	98	-3	-1	38	2	0	1	5	*2/3	0.9
1969	Was-A	122	365	33	90	17	4	9	45	50	35	.247	.340	.389	108	2	4	48	5	4	-1	7	*2/3	1.5
1970	Was-A	104	261	31	61	7	1	8	29	43	21	.234	.342	.360	99	-1	0	34	0	2	-1	0	23	0.7
1971	Was-A	97	229	18	61	11	1	4	22	33	27	.266	.359	.376	115	3	5	33	2	1	0	-11	23	-0.5
1972	NY-A	84	220	26	50	9	0	4	21	23	42	.227	.300	.391	108	1	2	26	0	1	-1	-0	32	0.4
1973	NY-A	17	57	5	13	3	0	0	4	5	5	.228	.290	.281	64	-3	-3	5	0	0		3	2/D	0.1
	Mon-N	16	50	5	9	1	0	2	9	5	4	.180	.255	.320	56	-3	-3	4	0	0	0	-1	/23	-0.4
Total	12	1139	3404	357	815	140	21	73	351	370	424	.239	.315	.357	91	-44	-42	391	13	16	-6	-40	23/D	-2.3

■ JACK ALLEN

Allen, Cyrus Alban b: 10/2/1855, Woodstock, Ill. d: 4/21/15, Girard, Pa. Deb: 5/01/1879

YEAR	TM/L	G	AB	R	H	2B	3B	HR	RBI	BB	SO	AVG	OBP	SLG	PRO+	BR	/A	RC	SB	CS	SBR	FR	POS	TPR
1879	Syr-N	11	48	7	9	2	1	0	3	1	5	.188	.204	.271	62	-2	-1	3				-5	/3O	-0.5
	Cle-N	16	60	7	7	1	1	0	4	1	9	.117	.131	.167	-3	-6	-6	1				3	3/O	-0.1
	Yr	27	108	14	16	3	2	0	7	2	14	.148	.164	.213	24	-9	-8	4				-2		-0.6

YEAR	TM/L	G	AB	R	H	2B	3B	HR	RBI	BB	SO	AVG	OBP	SLG	PRO+	BR	/A	RC	SB	CS	SBR	FR	POS	TPR

■ ETHAN ALLEN
Allen, Ethan Nathan   b: 1/1/04, Cincinnati, Ohio   BR/TR, 6'1", 180 lbs.   Deb: 6/21/26

YEAR	TM/L	G	AB	R	H	2B	3B	HR	RBI	BB	SO	AVG	OBP	SLG	PRO+	BR	/A	RC	SB	CS	SBR	FR	POS	TPR
1926	Cin-N	18	13	3	4	1	0	0	0	0	3	.308	.308	.385	88	-0	-0	1	0			1	/O	0.1
1927	Cin-N	111	359	54	106	26	4	2	20	14	23	.295	.325	.407	98	-3	-2	46	12			-8	O	-1.3
1928	Cin-N	129	485	55	148	30	7	1	62	27	29	.305	.343	.402	96	-5	-4	65	6			-0	*O	-0.8
1929	Cin-N	143	538	69	157	27	11	6	64	20	21	.292	.317	.416	84	-18	-15	68	21			-1	*O	-2.4
1930	Cin-N	21	46	10	10	1	0	3	7	5	2	.217	.294	.435	77	-2	-2	6	1			0	O	-0.1
	NY-N	76	238	48	73	9	2	7	31	12	23	.307	.340	.450	91	-5	-4	35	5			0	O	-0.7
	Yr	97	284	58	83	10	2	10	38	17	25	.292	.332	.447	89	-7	-6	41	6			0		-0.8
1931	NY-N	94	298	58	98	18	2	5	43	15	15	.329	.363	.453	121	7	8	49	6			-5	O	0.0
1932	NY-N	54	103	13	18	6	2	1	7	1	12	.175	.198	.301	33	-10	-10	6	0			-0	O	-1.1
1933	StL-N	91	261	25	63	7	3	0	36	13	22	.241	.280	.291	60	-12	-14	22	3			12	O	-0.6
1934	Phi-N	145	581	87	192	42	4	10	85	34	47	.330	.370	.468	108	18	8	99	6			11	*O	1.1
1935	Phi-N	156	645	90	198	46	1	8	63	43	54	.307	.351	.419	96	5	-3	100	5			12	*O	0.2
1936	Phi-N	30	125	21	37	3	1	1	9	4	8	.296	.318	.360	75	-3	-5	14	4			2	O	-0.4
	Chi-N	91	373	47	110	18	6	3	39	13	30	.295	.322	.399	91	-4	-5	47	12			-2	O	-1.0
	Yr	121	498	68	147	21	7	4	48	17	38	.295	.321	.390	87	-8	-10	61	16			-0		-1.4
1937	StL-A	103	320	39	101	18	1	0	31	21	17	.316	.360	.378	86	-6	-7	43	3	4	-2	5	O	-0.5
1938	StL-A	19	33	4	10	3	1	0	4	2	4	.303	.343	.455	98	-0	-0	5	0	0	0	-0	/O	0.0
Total	13	1281	4418	623	1325	255	45	47	501	223	310	.300	.336	.410	92	-40	-55	606	84	4		27	*O	-7.5

■ SLED ALLEN
Allen, Fletcher Manson   b: 8/23/1886, West Plains, Mo.   d: 10/16/59, Lubbock, Tex.   TR, 6'1", 180 lbs.   Deb: 5/04/10

YEAR	TM/L	G	AB	R	H	2B	3B	HR	RBI	BB	SO	AVG	OBP	SLG	PRO+	BR	/A	RC	SB	CS	SBR	FR	POS	TPR
1910	StL-A	14	23	3	3	1	0	0	1	1		.130	.231	.174	29	-2	-2	1	0			-5	C/1	-0.6

■ HANK ALLEN
Allen, Harold Andrew   b: 7/23/40, Wampum, Pa.   BR/TR, 6', 190 lbs.   Deb: 9/09/66

YEAR	TM/L	G	AB	R	H	2B	3B	HR	RBI	BB	SO	AVG	OBP	SLG	PRO+	BR	/A	RC	SB	CS	SBR	FR	POS	TPR
1966	Was-A	9	31	2	12	0	0	1	6	3	6	.387	.441	.484	167	3	3	7	0	0	0	0	/O	0.3
1967	Was-A	116	292	34	68	8	4	3	17	13	53	.233	.266	.318	75	-11	-10	22	3	4	-2	-1	O	-1.5
1968	Was-A	68	128	16	28	2	2	1	9	7	16	.219	.265	.289	70	-5	-5	9	0	0	0	-3	O32	-0.8
1969	Was-A	109	271	42	75	9	3	1	17	13	28	.277	.312	.343	88	-6	-5	26	12	3	2	-10	O/32	-1.5
1970	Was-A	22	38	3	8	2	0	0	4	5	9	.211	.302	.263	60	-2	-2	3	0	0	0	0	O	-0.2
	Mil-A	28	61	4	14	4	0	0	4	7	5	.230	.309	.295	67	-3	-3	5	0	1	-1	1	O/21	-0.2
	Yr	50	99	7	22	6	0	0	8	12	14	.222	.306	.283	65	-5	-5	9	0	1	-1	1		-0.4
1972	Chi-A	9	21	1	3	0	0	0	0	0	2	.143	.143	.143	-15	-3	-3	0	0	0	0	3	/3	0.0
1973	Chi-A	28	39	2	4	2	0	0	0	1	9	.103	.125	.154	-21	-6	-6	0	0	1	-1	1	/310C2	-0.6
Total	7	389	881	104	212	27	9	6	57	49	128	.241	.282	.312	74	-34	-30	74	15	9	-1	-10	O/321C	-4.5

■ HEZEKIAH ALLEN
Allen, Hezekiah "Ki"   b: 2/25/1863, Westport, Conn.   d: 9/21/16, Saugatuck, Conn.   5'11", 160 lbs.   Deb: 5/16/1884

YEAR	TM/L	G	AB	R	H	2B	3B	HR	RBI	BB	SO	AVG	OBP	SLG	PRO+	BR	/A	RC	SB	CS	SBR	FR	POS	TPR
1884	Phi-N	1	3	0	2	0	0	0	0	0	0	.667	.667	.667	337	1	1	1				-0	/C	0.0

■ HAM ALLEN
Allen, Homer S.   b: 8/1854, Hamden, Conn.   d: 1/7/1892, Hamden, Conn.   Deb: 4/27/1872

YEAR	TM/L	G	AB	R	H	2B	3B	HR	RBI	BB	SO	AVG	OBP	SLG	PRO+	BR	/A	RC	SB	CS	SBR	FR	POS	TPR
1872	Man-n	15	59	8	15	2	0	0		0		.254	.254	.288	71	-2	-2	4					O/S	0.0

■ HORACE ALLEN
Allen, Horace Tanner "Pug"   b: 6/11/1899, Deland, Fla.   d: 7/5/81, Canton, N.C.   BL/TR, 6', 187 lbs.   Deb: 6/15/19

YEAR	TM/L	G	AB	R	H	2B	3B	HR	RBI	BB	SO	AVG	OBP	SLG	PRO+	BR	/A	RC	SB	CS	SBR	FR	POS	TPR
1919	Bro-N	4	7	0	0	0	0	0	0	0	2	.000	.000	.000	-98	-2	-2	0	0			1	/O	0.0

■ JAMIE ALLEN
Allen, James Bradley   b: 5/29/58, Yakima, Wash.   BR/TR, 6', 205 lbs.   Deb: 5/01/83

YEAR	TM/L	G	AB	R	H	2B	3B	HR	RBI	BB	SO	AVG	OBP	SLG	PRO+	BR	/A	RC	SB	CS	SBR	FR	POS	TPR
1983	Sea-A	86	273	23	61	10	0	4	21	33	52	.223	.309	.304	67	-11	-12	26	6	5	-1	-7	3/D	-1.9

■ PETE ALLEN
Allen, Jesse Hall   b: 5/1/1868, Columbiana, Ohio   d: 4/16/46, Philadelphia, Pa.   BR/TR, 5'8.5", 185 lbs.   Deb: 8/04/1893

YEAR	TM/L	G	AB	R	H	2B	3B	HR	RBI	BB	SO	AVG	OBP	SLG	PRO+	BR	/A	RC	SB	CS	SBR	FR	POS	TPR
1893	Cle-N	1	4	0	0	0	0	0	0	0	0	.000	.000	.000	-94	-1	-1	0	0			-1	/C	0.0

■ KIM ALLEN
Allen, Kim Bryant   b: 4/5/53, Fontana, Cal.   BR/TR, 5'11", 175 lbs.   Deb: 9/02/80

YEAR	TM/L	G	AB	R	H	2B	3B	HR	RBI	BB	SO	AVG	OBP	SLG	PRO+	BR	/A	RC	SB	CS	SBR	FR	POS	TPR
1980	Sea-A	23	51	9	12	3	0	0	3	8	3	.235	.350	.294	78	-1	-1	6	10	3	1	-2	2/OS	0.0
1981	Sea-A	19	3	1	0	0	0	0	0	0	2	.000	.000	.000	-96	-1	-1	-0	2	1	0	-0	/2OD	0.0
Total	2	42	54	10	12	3	0	0	3	8	5	.222	.333	.278	69	-2	-2	6	12	4	1	-2	/2ODS	0.0

■ MYRON ALLEN
Allen, Myron Smith "Zeke"   b: 3/22/1854, Kingston, N.Y.   d: 3/8/24, Kingston, N.Y.   5'8", 150 lbs.   Deb: 7/19/1883

YEAR	TM/L	G	AB	R	H	2B	3B	HR	RBI	BB	SO	AVG	OBP	SLG	PRO+	BR	/A	RC	SB	CS	SBR	FR	POS	TPR
1883	NY-N	1	4	0	0	0	0	0	1	0	2	.000	.000	.000	-99	-1	-1	0				0	/P	0.0
1886	Bos-N	1	3	0	0	0	0	0	0	0	1	.000	.000	.000	-99	-1	-1	0	0			0	/2	0.0
1887	Cle-a	117	463	66	128	22	10	4		36		.276	.335	.393	107	3	5	71	26			8	*O/3SP	0.7
1888	KC-a	37	136	23	29	6	4	0	10	9		.213	.267	.316	84	-2	-3	13	4			7	O/P	0.3
Total	4	156	606	89	157	28	14	4	11	45	3	.259	.317	.371	100	-1	0	84	30			15	O/P3S2	1.0

■ DICK ALLEN
Allen, Richard Anthony   b: 3/8/42, Wampum, Pa.   BR/TR, 5'11", 187 lbs.   Deb: 9/03/63

YEAR	TM/L	G	AB	R	H	2B	3B	HR	RBI	BB	SO	AVG	OBP	SLG	PRO+	BR	/A	RC	SB	CS	SBR	FR	POS	TPR
1963	Phi-N	10	24	6	7	2	1	0	2	0	5	.292	.292	.458	114	0	0	2	0	0	0	-1	/O3	0.0
1964	Phi-N	162	632	**125**	201	38	**13**	29	91	67	138	.318	.383	.557	163	50	51	135	3	4	-2	7	*3	5.0
1965	Phi-N	161	619	93	187	31	14	20	85	74	150	.302	.378	.494	146	36	38	119	15	2	3	-2	*3/S	3.4
1966	Phi-N	141	524	112	166	25	10	40	110	68	136	.317	.398	**.632**	181	57	57	131	10	6	-1	-10	3O	4.4
1967	Phi-N	122	463	89	142	31	10	23	77	75	117	.307	**.404**	.566	**173**	46	46	109	20	5	3	-6	*3/2S	3.9
1968	Phi-N	152	521	87	137	17	9	33	90	74	161	.263	.356	.520	160	38	38	97	7	7	-2	-14	*O3	1.6
1969	Phi-N	118	438	79	126	23	3	32	89	64	144	.288	.378	.573	168	36	37	95	9	3	1	-9	*1	2.0
1970	StL-N	122	459	88	128	17	5	34	101	71	118	.279	.378	.560	145	30	29	97	5	4	-1	-12	13/O	0.8
1971	LA-N	155	549	82	162	24	1	23	90	93	113	.295	.398	.468	154	35	39	102	8	1	2	-11	3O1	2.7
1972	Chi-A	148	506	90	156	28	5	**37**	**113**	99	126	.308	**.422**	.603	**199**	66	65	131	19	8	1	-4	*1/3	**5.3**
1973	Chi-A	72	250	39	79	20	3	16	41	33	51	.316	.398	.612	175	26	25	59	7	2	1	0	1/2D	2.2
1974	Chi-A	128	462	84	139	23	1	**32**	88	57	89	.301	.379	**.563**	164	39	38	96	7	1	2	-11	*1/2D	2.4
1975	Phi-N	119	416	54	97	21	3	12	62	58	109	.233	.330	.385	94	-1	-3	52	11	2	2	-1	*1	-0.8
1976	★Phi-N	85	298	52	80	16	1	15	49	37	63	.268	.349	.480	130	12	11	47	11	4	1	-3	1	0.5
1977	Oak-A	54	171	19	41	4	0	5	31	24	36	.240	.337	.351	89	-2	-2	20	1	3	-2	2	1/D	-0.4
Total	15	1749	6332	1099	1848	320	79	351	1119	894	1556	.292	.381	.534	156	470	469	1290	133	52	9	-76	130/2DS	33.0

■ BOB ALLEN
Allen, Robert   b: 1896,   BR/TR, 5'10", 180 lbs.   Deb: 8/20/19

YEAR	TM/L	G	AB	R	H	2B	3B	HR	RBI	BB	SO	AVG	OBP	SLG	PRO+	BR	/A	RC	SB	CS	SBR	FR	POS	TPR
1919	Phi-A	9	22	3	3	1	0	0	0	3	7	.136	.269	.182	27	-2	-2	1	0			-2	/O	-0.4

■ BOB ALLEN
Allen, Robert Gilman   b: 7/10/1867, Marion, Ohio   d: 5/14/43, Little Rock, Ark.   BR/TR, 5'11", 175 lbs.   Deb: 4/19/1890   M

YEAR	TM/L	G	AB	R	H	2B	3B	HR	RBI	BB	SO	AVG	OBP	SLG	PRO+	BR	/A	RC	SB	CS	SBR	FR	POS	TPR
1890	Phi-N	133	456	69	103	15	11	2	57	67	54	.226	.356	.320	97	-3	-3	58	13			**39**	*S/M	3.4
1891	Phi-N	118	438	46	97	7	4	1	51	43	44	.221	.291	.263	62	-19	-21	38	12			13	*S	-0.2
1892	Phi-N	152	563	77	128	20	14	2	64	61	60	.227	.304	.323	92	-6	-5	61	15			18	*S	1.8
1893	Phi-N	124	471	86	126	19	12	8	90	71	40	.268	.369	.410	109	7	7	76	8			18	*S	2.4
1894	Phi-N	40	149	26	38	10	3	0	19	17	11	.255	.335	.362	72	-7	-7	20	4			-2	S	-0.4
1897	Bos-N	34	119	33	38	5	0	1	24	18		.319	.409	.387	106	3	2	20	1			8	S/O2	0.9
1900	Cin-N	5	15	0	2	1	0	0	1	0		.133	.133	.200	-8	-2	-2	0	0			-0	/SM	-0.1
Total	7	606	2211	337	532	77	44	14	306	297	209	.241	.334	.334	90	-21	-25	273	53			94	S/2O	7.8

■ ROD ALLEN
Allen, Roderick Bernet   b: 10/5/59, Los Angeles, Cal.   BR/TR, 6'1", 185 lbs.   Deb: 4/07/83

YEAR	TM/L	G	AB	R	H	2B	3B	HR	RBI	BB	SO	AVG	OBP	SLG	PRO+	BR	/A	RC	SB	CS	SBR	FR	POS	TPR
1983	Sea-A	11	12	1	2	0	0	0	0	0	1	.167	.167	.167	-8	-2	-2	0	0	0	0	1	/OD	0.0

YEAR	TM/L	G	AB	R	H	2B	3B	HR	RBI	BB	SO	AVG	OBP	SLG	PRO+	BR	/A	RC	SB	CS	SBR	FR	POS	TPR
1984	Det-A	15	27	6	8	1	0	0	3	2	8	.296	.367	.333	96	-0	-0	4	1	0	0	0	D/O	0.0
1988	Cle-A	5	11	1	1	1	0	0	0	0	2	.091	.091	.182	-25	-2	-2	0	0	0	0	0	/D	-0.1
Total	3	31	50	8	11	2	0	0	3	2	11	.220	.264	.260	45	-4	-4	4	1	0	0	1	/DO	-0.1

■ RON ALLEN
Allen, Ronald Fredrick b: 12/23/43, Wampum, Pa. BB/TR, 6′3″, 205 lbs. Deb: 8/11/72

YEAR	TM/L	G	AB	R	H	2B	3B	HR	RBI	BB	SO	AVG	OBP	SLG	PRO+	BR	/A	RC	SB	CS	SBR	FR	POS	TPR
1972	StL-N	7	11	2	1	0	0	1	1	3	5	.091	.286	.364	84	-0	-0	1	0	0	0	-0	/1	0.0

■ GARY ALLENSON
Allenson, Gary Martin b: 2/4/55, Culver City, Cal. BR/TR, 5′11″, 185 lbs. Deb: 4/08/79

YEAR	TM/L	G	AB	R	H	2B	3B	HR	RBI	BB	SO	AVG	OBP	SLG	PRO+	BR	/A	RC	SB	CS	SBR	FR	POS	TPR
1979	Bos-A	108	241	27	49	10	2	3	22	20	42	.203	.267	.299	50	-16	-18	19	1	1	-0	10	*C/3	-0.3
1980	Bos-A	36	70	9	25	6	0	0	10	13	11	.357	.458	.443	141	6	5	15	2	2	-1	4	C/3D	0.9
1981	Bos-A	47	139	23	31	8	0	5	25	23	33	.223	.337	.388	102	2	1	18	0	0	0	1	C	0.4
1982	Bos-A	92	264	25	54	11	0	6	33	38	39	.205	.307	.314	67	-10	-12	26	0	3	-2	8	C	0.0
1983	Bos-A	84	230	19	53	11	0	3	30	27	43	.230	.317	.317	70	-7	-10	23	0	1	-1	4	C	-0.2
1984	Bos-A	35	83	9	19	2	0	2	8	9	14	.229	.304	.325	71	-3	-3	7	0	0	0	0	C	0.0
1985	Tor-A	14	34	2	4	1	0	0	3	0	10	.118	.118	.147	-27	-6	-6	0	0	0	0	-2	C	-0.6
Total	7	416	1061	114	235	49	2	19	131	130	192	.221	.309	.325	71	-35	-43	109	3	7	-3	26	C/3D	0.2

■ GENE ALLEY
Alley, Leonard Eugene b: 7/10/40, Richmond, Va. BR/TR, 5′10″, 160 lbs. Deb: 9/04/63

YEAR	TM/L	G	AB	R	H	2B	3B	HR	RBI	BB	SO	AVG	OBP	SLG	PRO+	BR	/A	RC	SB	CS	SBR	FR	POS	TPR
1963	Pit-N	17	51	3	11	1	0	0	0	2	12	.216	.245	.235	39	-4	-4	3	0	1	-1	1	/32S	-0.2
1964	Pit-N	81	209	30	44	3	1	6	13	21	56	.211	.289	.321	72	-8	-8	20	0	1	-1	24	S/32	2.1
1965	Pit-N	153	500	47	126	21	6	5	47	32	82	.252	.302	.348	82	-12	-12	52	7	2	1	30	*S2/3	3.4
1966	Pit-N	147	579	88	173	28	10	7	43	27	83	.299	.336	.418	108	6	6	79	8	8	-2	13	*S	2.9
1967	Pit-N	152	550	59	158	25	7	6	55	36	70	.287	.339	.391	108	6	6	70	10	5	0	8	*S	3.2
1968	Pit-N	133	474	48	116	20	2	4	39	39	78	.245	.309	.321	91	-6	-5	45	13	5	1	26	*S2	4.1
1969	Pit-N	82	285	28	70	3	2	8	32	19	48	.246	.295	.354	83	-8	-7	29	4	0	1	7	2S/3	0.8
1970	*Pit-N	121	426	46	104	16	5	8	41	31	70	.244	.300	.362	78	-15	-14	46	7	3	0	34	*S/23	3.4
1971	*Pit-N	114	348	38	79	8	7	6	28	35	43	.227	.298	.342	81	-9	-9	36	9	2	2	-16	*S/3	-0.9
1972	*Pit-N	119	347	30	86	12	2	3	36	38	52	.248	.322	.320	85	-7	-6	36	4	3	-1	-5	S/3	0.1
1973	Pit-N	76	158	25	32	3	2	2	8	20	28	.203	.292	.285	62	-8	-8	12	1	0	0	5	S/3	0.4
Total	11	1195	3927	442	999	140	44	55	342	300	622	.254	.312	.354	88	-65	-61	428	63	30	1	125	S2/3	19.3

■ GAIR ALLIE
Allie, Gair Roosevelt b: 10/28/31, Statesville, N.C. BR/TR, 6′1″, 190 lbs. Deb: 4/13/54

YEAR	TM/L	G	AB	R	H	2B	3B	HR	RBI	BB	SO	AVG	OBP	SLG	PRO+	BR	/A	RC	SB	CS	SBR	FR	POS	TPR
1954	Pit-N	121	418	38	83	8	6	3	30	56	84	.199	.296	.268	49	-31	-30	37	1	1	-0	-16	S3	-4.0

■ BOB ALLIETTA
Allietta, Robert George b: 5/1/52, New Bedford, Mass. BR/TR, 6′, 190 lbs. Deb: 5/06/75

YEAR	TM/L	G	AB	R	H	2B	3B	HR	RBI	BB	SO	AVG	OBP	SLG	PRO+	BR	/A	RC	SB	CS	SBR	FR	POS	TPR
1975	Cal-A	21	45	4	8	1	0	1	2	1	6	.178	.196	.267	32	-4	-4	2	0	0	0	2	C	-0.1

■ ANDY ALLISON
Allison, Andrew K. b: 1848, New York, N.Y. 5′10″, 150 lbs. Deb: 5/07/1872

YEAR	TM/L	G	AB	R	H	2B	3B	HR	RBI	BB	SO	AVG	OBP	SLG	PRO+	BR	/A	RC	SB	CS	SBR	FR	POS	TPR
1872	Eck-n	24	99	11	15	2	0	0		0		.152	.152	.172	-1	-11	-8	3					1/O	-0.3

■ ART ALLISON
Allison, Arthur Algernon b: 1/29/1849, Philadelphia, Pa. d: 2/25/16, Washington, D.C. 5′8″, 150 lbs. Deb: 5/04/1871

YEAR	TM/L	G	AB	R	H	2B	3B	HR	RBI	BB	SO	AVG	OBP	SLG	PRO+	BR	/A	RC	SB	CS	SBR	FR	POS	TPR
1871	Cle-n	29	137	28	40	4	5	0	19	2	5	.292	.302	.394	104	-0	1	18	3				*O	0.2
1872	Cle-n	19	85	13	23	6	0	0		0		.271	.271	.341	92	-1	-0	8					O	0.0
1873	Res-n	23	97	12	32	5	0	0		0		.330	.330	.381	118	1	3	13					O/1C	0.2
1875	Was-n	26	110	18	24	3	1	0		1		.218	.225	.264	71	-3	-3	7					1/OC	-0.2
	Har-n	40	173	26	41	6	0	1		0		.237	.237	.289	77	-3	-5	12					O/2	-0.3
	Yr	66	283	44	65	9	1	1		1		.230	.232	.279	75	-7	-7	19						-0.5
1876	Lou-N	31	130	9	27	2	1	0	10	2	6	.208	.220	.238	45	-6	-10	7				5	O/1	-0.3
Total	4 n	137	602	97	160	24	6	1	19	3	5	.266	.269	.331	91	-7	-4	57					O/1C2	-0.1

■ DOUG ALLISON
Allison, Douglas b: 1846, Philadelphia, Pa. d: 12/19/16, Washington, D.C. BR/TR, 5′10.5″, 160 lbs. Deb: 5/05/1871

YEAR	TM/L	G	AB	R	H	2B	3B	HR	RBI	BB	SO	AVG	OBP	SLG	PRO+	BR	/A	RC	SB	CS	SBR	FR	POS	TPR
1871	Oly-n	27	133	28	44	10	2	2	27	0	2	.331	.331	.481	137	5	6	22	1				*C	0.3
1872	Tro-n	23	118	23	34	5	2	0		0		.288	.288	.364	98	-0	-1	13					C/S	0.0
	Eck-n	18	79	18	27	2	1	0		2		.342	.358	.392	154	3	5	11					C	0.3
	Yr	41	197	41	61	7	3	0		2		.310	.317	.376	119	3	5	24						0.3
1873	Res-n	18	83	12	23	5	0	0		0		.277	.277	.337	86	-2	-1	8					C/O	0.0
	Mut-n	11	51	6	11	1	0	0		1		.216	.231	.235	38	-4	-4	3					C	-0.2
	Yr	29	134	18	34	6	0	0		1		.254	.259	.299	67	-6	-4	11						-0.2
1874	Mut-n	65	316	69	88	8	5	0		6		.278	.292	.335	96	-0	-2	32					*OC	0.0
1875	Har-n	61	267	38	67	7	0	0		7		.251	.270	.277	85	-2	-5	20					*C/1	-0.2
1876	Har-N	44	163	19	43	4	0	0	15	3	9	.264	.277	.288	82	-2	-4	13				9	C/O	0.6
1877	Har-N	29	115	14	17	2	0	0	6	3	7	.148	.169	.165	7	-12	-10	3				-1	C	-0.8
1878	Pro-n	19	76	9	22	2	0	0	7	1	8	.289	.299	.316	102	0	0	7				-0	C/P	0.0
1879	Pro-N	1	5	0	0	0	0	0	0	0	1	.000	.000	.000	-99	-1	-1	0				0	/C	0.0
1883	Bal-a	1	3	2	2	0	0	0	0	0	0	.667	.667	.667	321	1	1	1				-0	/OC	0.0
Total	5 n	223	1047	194	294	38	10	2	27	16	2	.281	.292	.342	99	-0	-0	109					C/O1S	0.2
Total	5	94	362	44	84	8	0	0	28	7	25	.232	.247	.254	63	-14	-14	25				7	/COP	-0.2

■ MILO ALLISON
Allison, Milo Henry b: 10/16/1890, Elk Rapids, Mich. d: 6/18/57, Kenosha, Wis. BL/TR, 6′, 163 lbs. Deb: 9/26/13

YEAR	TM/L	G	AB	R	H	2B	3B	HR	RBI	BB	SO	AVG	OBP	SLG	PRO+	BR	/A	RC	SB	CS	SBR	FR	POS	TPR
1913	Chi-N	2	6	1	2	0	0	0	0	0	1	.333	.333	.333	90	-0	-0	1	1			0	/O	0.0
1914	Chi-N	1	1	0	1	0	0	0	0	0	0	1.000	1.000	1.000	497	0	0	1	0			0	H	0.0
1916	Cle-A	14	18	10	5	0	0	0	0	6	1	.278	.458	.278	115	1	1	3	0			-1	/O	0.0
1917	Cle-A	32	35	4	5	0	0	0	0	9	7	.143	.318	.143	38	-2	-2	3	3			-3	O	-0.5
Total	4	49	60	15	13	0	0	0	0	15	9	.217	.373	.217	74	-0	-1	7	4			-4	/O	-0.5

■ BILL ALLISON
Allison, William Andrew b: 9/18/1848, Philadelphia, Pa. d: 6/12/23, Deb: 5/21/1872

YEAR	TM/L	G	AB	R	H	2B	3B	HR	RBI	BB	SO	AVG	OBP	SLG	PRO+	BR	/A	RC	SB	CS	SBR	FR	POS	TPR
1872	Eck-n	3	10	3	2	0	0	0		0		.200	.200	.200	28	-1	-1	0					/O2	0.0

■ BOB ALLISON
Allison, William Robert b: 7/11/34, Raytown, Mo. BR/TR, 6′3″, 205 lbs. Deb: 9/16/58

YEAR	TM/L	G	AB	R	H	2B	3B	HR	RBI	BB	SO	AVG	OBP	SLG	PRO+	BR	/A	RC	SB	CS	SBR	FR	POS	TPR
1958	Was-A	11	35	1	7	1	0	0	2	2	5	.200	.243	.229	31	-3	-3	1	0	2	-1	1	O	-0.4
1959	Was-A	150	570	83	149	18	9	30	85	60	92	.261	.334	.482	122	15	15	85	13	8	-1	-10	*O	-0.2
1960	Was-A	144	501	79	126	30	3	15	69	92	94	.251	.370	.413	113	10	11	79	11	9	-2	7	*O/1	1.0
1961	Min-A	159	556	83	136	21	3	29	105	103	100	.245	.367	.450	111	15	11	93	2	7	-4	4	*O1	0.4
1962	Min-A	149	519	102	138	24	8	29	102	84	115	.266	.372	.511	130	26	23	102	8	5	-1	6	*O	2.3
1963	Min-A	148	527	99	143	25	4	35	91	90	109	.271	.381	.533	150	39	37	113	6	1	1	11	*O	4.6
1964	Min-A	149	492	90	141	27	4	32	86	92	99	.287	.406	.553	163	45	44	119	10	1	1	1	1O	4.4
1965	*Min-A	135	438	71	102	14	5	23	78	73	114	.233	.345	.445	118	14	11	73	10	2	2	8	*O/1	1.7
1966	Min-A	70	168	34	37	6	1	8	19	30	34	.220	.348	.411	110	5	3	20	6	0	2	-1	O	0.2
1967	Min-A	153	496	73	128	21	6	24	75	74	114	.258	.357	.470	132	27	22	87	6	4	-1	-6	*O	1.3
1968	Min-A	145	469	63	116	16	8	22	52	52	98	.247	.325	.456	128	19	16	65	9	7	-2	-7	*O1	0.2
1969	*Min-A	81	189	18	43	8	2	8	27	29	39	.228	.333	.418	107	2	2	24	2	4	0	-0	O/1	-0.1
1970	*Min-A	47	72	15	15	5	0	1	7	14	20	.208	.345	.319	83	-1	-1	9	1	0	0	1	/O1	0.0
Total	13	1541	5032	811	1281	216	53	256	796	795	1033	.255	.360	.471	126	211	192	877	84	50	-5	13	*O1	15.2

■ BEAU ALLRED
Allred, Dale Le Beau b: 6/4/65, Mesa, Ariz. BL/TL, 6′, 190 lbs. Deb: 9/07/89

YEAR	TM/L	G	AB	R	H	2B	3B	HR	RBI	BB	SO	AVG	OBP	SLG	PRO+	BR	/A	RC	SB	CS	SBR	FR	POS	TPR
1989	Cle-A	13	24	0	6	3	0	0	1	2	10	.250	.308	.375	90	-0	-0	3	0	0	0	1	/OD	0.1

YEAR	TM/L	G	AB	R	H	2B	3B	HR	RBI	BB	SO	AVG	OBP	SLG	PRO+	BR	/A	RC	SB	CS	SBR	FR	POS	TPR
1990	Cle-A	4	16	2	3	1	0	1	2	2	3	.188	.278	.438	95	-0	-0	2	0	0	0	-1	/O	-0.1
Total	2	17	40	2	9	4	0	1	3	4	13	.225	.295	.400	92	-0	-1	5	0	0	0	0	/OD	0.0

■ MEL ALMADA
Almada, Baldomero Melo b: 2/7/13, Hwatabampo, Sonora, Mexico d: 8/13/88, Hermosillo, Mexico BL/TL, 6', 170 lbs. Deb: 9/08/33

YEAR	TM/L	G	AB	R	H	2B	3B	HR	RBI	BB	SO	AVG	OBP	SLG	PRO+	BR	/A	RC	SB	CS	SBR	FR	POS	TPR
1933	Bos-A	14	44	11	15	0	0	1	3	11	3	.341	.473	.409	137	3	3	10	3	1	0	-0	O	0.3
1934	Bos-A	23	90	7	21	2	1	0	10	6	8	.233	.281	.278	42	-7	-8	7	3	2	-0	4	O	-0.4
1935	Bos-A	151	607	85	176	27	9	3	59	55	34	.290	.350	.379	83	-10	-16	83	20	9	1	-7	*O/1	-2.2
1936	Bos-A	96	320	40	81	16	4	1	21	24	15	.253	.305	.338	55	-22	-24	33	2	4	-2	-2	O	-2.6
1937	Bos-A	32	110	17	26	6	2	1	9	15	6	.236	.328	.355	69	-5	-5	13	0	1	-1	-5	O/1	-1.1
	Was-A	100	433	74	134	21	4	4	33	38	21	.309	.365	.404	98	-4	-1	66	12	4	1	10	*O	0.6
	Yr	132	543	91	160	27	6	5	42	53	27	.295	.357	.394	91	-9	-7	79	12	5	1	5		-0.5
1938	Was-A	47	197	24	48	7	4	1	15	8	16	.244	.277	.335	56	-15	-13	19	4	1	1	9	O	-0.3
	StL-A	102	436	77	149	22	2	3	37	38	22	.342	.398	.422	106	5	5	74	9	5	-0	-3	*O	0.2
	Yr	149	633	101	197	29	6	4	52	46	38	.311	.362	.395	92	-10	-8	92	13	6	0	6		-0.1
1939	StL-A	42	134	17	32	2	1	1	7	10	8	.239	.292	.291	48	-10	-11	12	1	0	0	0	O	-0.9
	Bro-N	39	112	11	24	4	0	0	3	9	17	.214	.273	.250	40	-9	-10	8	2			5	O	-0.4
Total	7	646	2483	363	706	107	27	15	197	214	150	.284	.342	.367	79	-74	-80	324	56	27		11	O/1	-6.8

■ RAFAEL ALMEIDA
Almeida, Rafael D. "Mike" b: 7/30/1887, Havana, Cuba d: 3/68, Havana, Cuba BR/TR, 5'9", 164 lbs. Deb: 7/04/11

YEAR	TM/L	G	AB	R	H	2B	3B	HR	RBI	BB	SO	AVG	OBP	SLG	PRO+	BR	/A	RC	SB	CS	SBR	FR	POS	TPR
1911	Cin-N	36	96	9	30	5	1	0	15	9	16	.313	.383	.385	120	2	3	16	3			-2	3/2S	0.2
1912	Cin-N	16	59	9	13	4	3	0	10	5	8	.220	.281	.390	85	-2	-2	6	0			-2	3	-0.2
1913	Cin-N	50	130	14	34	4	2	3	21	11	16	.262	.324	.392	104	0	0	17	4			5	3/OS2	0.5
Total	3	102	285	32	77	13	6	3	46	25	40	.270	.335	.389	106	1	2	39	7			1	/3OS2	0.5

■ BILL ALMON
Almon, William Francis b: 11/21/52, Providence, R.I. BR/TR, 6'3", 180 lbs. Deb: 9/02/74

YEAR	TM/L	G	AB	R	H	2B	3B	HR	RBI	BB	SO	AVG	OBP	SLG	PRO+	BR	/A	RC	SB	CS	SBR	FR	POS	TPR
1974	SD-N	16	38	4	12	1	0	0	3	2	9	.316	.350	.342	98	-0	-0	5	1	0	0	-2	S	0.0
1975	SD-N	6	10	0	4	0	0	0	0	0	1	.400	.400	.400	131	0	0	2	0	0	0	1	/S	0.1
1976	SD-N	14	57	6	14	3	0	1	6	2	9	.246	.271	.351	82	-2	-2	6	3	1	0	1	S	0.1
1977	SD-N	155	613	75	160	18	11	2	43	37	114	.261	.303	.336	79	-25	-17	61	20	9	1	18	*S	2.3
1978	SD-N	138	405	39	102	19	2	0	21	33	74	.252	.308	.309	79	-14	-11	40	17	5	2	0	*3S/2	-0.7
1979	SD-N	100	198	20	45	3	0	1	8	21	48	.227	.301	.258	57	-12	-11	16	6	5	-1	16	2S/O	1.1
1980	Mon-N	18	38	2	10	1	1	0	3	1	5	.263	.282	.342	73	-1	-1	3	0	0	0	-2	S/2	-0.2
	NY-N	48	112	13	19	3	2	0	4	8	27	.170	.225	.232	29	-11	-11	6	2	0	1	9	S2/3	0.3
	Yr	66	150	15	29	4	3	0	7	9	32	.193	.239	.260	40	-12	-12	10	2	0	1	.7		0.1
1981	Chi-A	103	349	46	105	10	2	4	41	21	60	.301	.344	.375	109	3	4	46	16	6	1	14	*S	2.8
1982	Chi-A	111	308	40	79	10	4	4	26	25	49	.256	.314	.354	83	-7	-7	34	10	8	-2	26	*S/D	2.6
1983	Oak-A	143	451	45	120	29	1	4	63	26	67	.266	.309	.361	89	-10	-7	51	26	8	3	-26	S310/2D	-2.8
1984	Oak-A	106	211	24	47	11	0	7	16	10	42	.223	.258	.374	78	-8	-7	18	5	7	-3	0	O1D/3CS	-1.3
1985	Pit-N	88	244	33	66	17	0	6	29	22	61	.270	.333	.414	109	2	3	32	10	7	-1	-19	SO/13	-1.5
1986	Pit-N	102	196	29	43	7	2	7	27	30	38	.219	.323	.383	92	-2	-2	25	11	4	1	-7	O3S/1	-0.7
1987	Pit-N	19	20	5	4	1	0	0	1	1	5	.200	.238	.250	29	-2	-2	1	0	0	0	1	/SO3	0.0
	NY-N	49	54	8	13	3	0	0	4	8	16	.241	.339	.296	74	-2	-2	6	1	0	0	-3	S2/1O	-0.1
	Yr	68	74	13	17	4	0	0	5	9	21	.230	.313	.284	62	-4	-4	7	1	0	0	-1		-0.1
1988	Phi-N	20	26	1	3	2	0	0	1	3	11	.115	.207	.192	15	-3	-3	1	0	0	0	1	/3S1	-0.1
Total	15	1236	3330	390	846	138	25	36	296	250	636	.254	.307	.343	83	-95	-74	354	128	60	2	30	S302/1DC	1.9

■ ROBERTO ALOMAR
Alomar, Roberto (Velazquez) b: 2/5/68, Ponce, P.R. BB/TR, 6', 184 lbs. Deb: 4/22/88

YEAR	TM/L	G	AB	R	H	2B	3B	HR	RBI	BB	SO	AVG	OBP	SLG	PRO+	BR	/A	RC	SB	CS	SBR	FR	POS	TPR
1988	SD-N	143	545	84	145	24	6	9	41	47	83	.266	.328	.382	105	2	3	68	24	6	4	17	*2	2.9
1989	SD-N	158	623	82	184	27	1	7	56	53	76	.295	.352	.376	108	7	7	85	42	17	2	6	*2	1.7
1990	SD-N	147	586	80	168	27	5	6	60	48	72	.287	.343	.381	97	-1	-2	76	24	7	3	-1	*2/S	0.1
Total	3	448	1754	246	497	78	12	22	157	148	231	.283	.341	.379	103	8	8	230	90	30	9	21	2/S	4.7

■ SANDY ALOMAR
Alomar, Santos (Velazquez) Jr. b: 6/18/66, Salinas, P.R. BR/TR, 6'5", 200 lbs. Deb: 9/30/88

YEAR	TM/L	G	AB	R	H	2B	3B	HR	RBI	BB	SO	AVG	OBP	SLG	PRO+	BR	/A	RC	SB	CS	SBR	FR	POS	TPR
1988	SD-N	1	1	0	0	0	0	0	0	0	1	.000	.000	.000	-99	-0	-0	0	0	0	0	0	H	0.0
1989	SD-N	7	19	1	4	1	0	1	6	3	3	.211	.318	.421	110	0	0	2	0	0	0	-0	/C	0.0
1990	Cle-A	132	445	60	129	26	2	9	66	25	46	.290	.331	.418	106	4	3	60	4	1	1	-12	*C	-0.5
Total	3	140	465	61	133	27	2	10	72	28	50	.286	.329	.417	106	4	3	62	4	1	1	-13	C	-0.5

■ SANDY ALOMAR
Alomar, Santos Sr. (Conde) b: 10/19/43, Salinas, P.R. BB/TR, 5'9", 140 lbs. Deb: 9/15/64 C

YEAR	TM/L	G	AB	R	H	2B	3B	HR	RBI	BB	SO	AVG	OBP	SLG	PRO+	BR	/A	RC	SB	CS	SBR	FR	POS	TPR
1964	Mil-N	19	53	3	13	1	0	0	6	0	11	.245	.245	.264	43	-4	-4	3	1	0	0	8	S	0.6
1965	Mil-N	67	108	16	26	1	1	0	8	4	12	.241	.268	.269	51	-7	-7	7	12	5	1	14	S2	1.3
1966	Atl-N	31	44	4	4	1	0	0	2	1	10	.091	.111	.114	-37	-8	-8	1	0	0	0	3	2/S	-0.2
1967	NY-N	15	22	1	0	0	0	0	0	0	6	.000	.000	.000	-99	-6	-6	0	0	0	0	2	S/32	-0.1
	Chi-A	12	15	4	3	0	0	0	0	2	0	.200	.294	.200	50	-1	-1	1	2	0	1	2	/S2	0.3
1968	Chi-A	133	363	41	92	8	2	0	12	20	42	.253	.294	.287	76	-10	-11	32	21	8	2	-15	23/SO	-2.1
1969	Chi-A	22	58	8	13	2	0	0	4	4	6	.224	.274	.259	47	-4	-4	5	2	0	1	3	2	0.0
	Cal-A	134	559	60	140	10	2	1	30	36	48	.250	.296	.281	65	-28	-25	50	18	3	4	-10	*2	-2.6
	Yr	156	617	68	153	12	2	1	34	40	54	.248	.294	.279	63	-32	-29	54	20	3	4	-7		-2.6
1970	Cal-A	162	672	82	169	18	2	2	36	49	45	.251	.303	.293	68	-31	-28	64	35	6	3	9	*2S/3	0.0
1971	Cal-A	162	689	77	179	24	3	4	42	41	60	.260	.301	.321	82	-22	-16	70	39	10	6	21	*2S	2.1
1972	Cal-A	155	610	65	146	20	3	1	25	47	55	.239	.294	.287	78	-20	-16	52	20	12	-1	3	*2/S	-0.4
1973	Cal-A	136	470	45	112	7	1	0	28	34	44	.238	.290	.257	60	-27	-23	39	25	10	2	-8	*2S	-2.0
1974	Cal-A	46	54	12	12	0	1	0	1	2	8	.222	.250	.259	49	-4	-3	4	2	0	1	9	S2/3OD	0.9
	NY-A	76	279	35	75	8	0	1	27	14	25	.269	.304	.308	79	-9	-8	25	6	4	-1	-12	2	-1.7
	Yr	122	333	47	87	8	1	1	28	16	33	.261	.295	.300	74	-12	-11	29	8	4	0	-3		-0.8
1975	NY-A	151	489	61	117	18	4	2	39	26	58	.239	.278	.305	66	-23	-22	44	28	6	5	-12	*2/S	-2.4
1976	NY-A	67	163	20	39	4	0	1	10	13	12	.239	.295	.282	70	-6	-6	14	12	7	-1	-5	2/S310	-0.8
1977	Tex-A	69	83	21	22	3	0	1	11	8	13	.265	.337	.337	84	-2	-2	10	4	3	-1	15	D2/SO13	1.4
1978	Tex-A	24	29	3	6	1	0	0	1	1	7	.207	.233	.241	34	-3	-3	2	0	0	0	5	/123SD	0.3
Total	15	1481	4760	558	1168	126	19	13	282	302	482	.245	.291	.288	68	-213	-192	421	227	80	20	34	*2S/3D10	-5.4

■ FELIPE ALOU
Alou, Felipe Rojas (b: Felipe Rojas (Alou)) b: 5/12/35, Haina, D.R. BR/TR, 6', 195 lbs. Deb: 6/08/58 C

YEAR	TM/L	G	AB	R	H	2B	3B	HR	RBI	BB	SO	AVG	OBP	SLG	PRO+	BR	/A	RC	SB	CS	SBR	FR	POS	TPR
1958	SF-N	75	182	21	46	9	2	4	16	19	34	.253	.327	.390	91	-3	-2	24	4	2	0	-4	O	-0.7
1959	SF-N	95	247	38	68	13	2	10	33	17	38	.275	.322	.466	109	2	2	36	5	3	-0	-3	O	-0.1
1960	SF-N	106	322	48	85	17	3	8	44	16	42	.264	.303	.410	99	-4	-2	39	10	2	2	-5	O	-0.7
1961	SF-N	132	415	59	120	19	0	18	52	26	41	.289	.334	.465	113	5	6	62	11	4	1	-1	*O	0.0
1962	*SF-N	154	561	96	177	30	3	25	98	33	66	.316	.359	.513	133	23	24	103	10	7	-1	-1	*O	1.3
1963	SF-N	157	565	75	159	31	9	20	82	27	87	.281	.321	.474	127	17	17	83	11	2	2	-1	*O	1.4
1964	Mil-N	121	415	60	105	26	3	9	51	30	41	.253	.310	.395	96	-2	-2	51	5	2	0	-5	O1	-0.9
1965	Mil-N	143	555	80	165	29	2	23	78	31	63	.297	.340	.481	128	19	19	90	8	4	1	-4	O1/3S	0.9
1966	Atl-N	154	666	**122**	**218**	32	6	31	74	24	51	.327	.362	.533	143	38	37	123	5	7	-3	4	1O/3S	3.2
1967	Atl-N	140	574	76	157	26	3	15	43	32	50	.274	.320	.408	108	4	5	73	6	5	-1	-12	1O	-1.5
1968	Atl-N	160	662	72	**210**	37	5	11	57	48	56	.317	.367	.438	140	32	32	103	12	11	-3	4	*O	2.9
1969	*Atl-N	123	476	54	134	13	1	5	32	23	23	.282	.320	.345	86	-9	-9	51	4	6	-2	-1	*O	-2.0

YEAR	TM/L	G	AB	R	H	2B	3B	HR	RBI	BB	SO	AVG	OBP	SLG	PRO+	BR	/A	RC	SB	CS	SBR	FR	POS	TPR
1970	Oak-A	154	575	70	156	25	3	8	55	32	31	.271	.311	.367	89	-12	-9	63	10	5	0	6	*O/1	-0.9
1971	Oak-A	2	8	0	2	1	0	0	0	0	1	.250	.250	.375	77	-0	-0	1	0	0	0	1	/O	0.0
	NY-A	131	461	52	133	20	6	8	69	32	24	.289	.337	.410	118	6	9	59	5	5	-2	-12	O1	-0.9
	Yr	133	469	52	135	21	6	8	69	32	25	.288	.336	.409	117	5	9	60	5	5	-2	-11		-0.9
1972	NY-A	120	324	33	90	18	1	6	37	22	27	.278	.328	.395	118	5	6	41	1	0	0	3	1O	0.0
1973	NY-A	93	280	25	66	12	0	4	27	9	25	.236	.260	.321	65	-14	-13	22	0	1	-1	-4	1O	-2.3
	Mon-N	19	48	4	10	1	0	1	4	2	4	.208	.240	.292	45	-4	-4	2	0	1	-1	3	O/1	-0.2
1974	Mil-A	3	3	0	0	0	0	0	0	0	0	.000	.000	.000	-99	-1	-1	0	0	0	0	-0	/O	0.0
Total	17	2082	7339	985	2101	359	49	206	852	423	706	.286	.330	.433	114	101	115	1028	107	67	-8	-29	*O1/3S	-0.5

■ JESUS ALOU
Alou, Jesus Maria Rojas (b: Jesus Maria Rojas (Alou))   b: 3/24/42, Haina, D.R.   BR/TR, 6'2", 190 lbs.   Deb: 9/10/63   C

YEAR	TM/L	G	AB	R	H	2B	3B	HR	RBI	BB	SO	AVG	OBP	SLG	PRO+	BR	/A	RC	SB	CS	SBR	FR	POS	TPR
1963	SF-N	16	24	3	6	1	0	0	5	0	3	.250	.280	.292	66	-1	-1	1	0	1	-1	-1	O	-0.3
1964	SF-N	115	376	42	103	11	0	3	28	13	35	.274	.305	.327	77	-11	-12	35	6	6	-2	-1	*O	-1.8
1965	SF-N	143	543	76	162	19	4	9	52	13	40	.298	.318	.398	98	-1	-3	61	8	5	-1	-1	*O	-0.6
1966	SF-N	110	370	41	96	13	1	1	20	9	22	.259	.281	.308	62	-18	-19	28	5	5	-2	-8	*O	-3.3
1967	SF-N	129	510	55	149	15	4	5	30	14	39	.292	.316	.367	96	-4	-3	55	1	7	-4	-7	*O	-2.1
1968	SF-N	120	419	26	110	15	4	0	39	9	23	.263	.280	.317	79	-11	-11	31	1	4	-2	1	*O	-2.0
1969	Hou-N	115	452	49	112	19	4	5	34	15	30	.248	.278	.341	74	-18	-17	38	4	6	-2	-1	*O	-2.7
1970	Hou-N	117	458	59	140	27	3	1	44	21	15	.306	.338	.384	97	-5	-3	55	3	2	-0	-6	*O	-1.3
1971	Hou-N	122	433	41	121	21	4	2	40	13	17	.279	.307	.360	91	-8	-6	43	3	7	-3	4	*O	-0.9
1972	Hou-N	52	93	8	29	4	1	0	11	7	5	.312	.366	.376	114	2	2	11	0	2	-1	-0	O	-0.1
1973	Hou-N	28	55	7	13	2	0	1	8	1	6	.236	.276	.327	67	-3	-3	4	0	0	0	-2	O	-0.4
	*Oak-A	36	108	10	33	3	0	1	11	2	6	.306	.318	.361	96	-2	-1	12	0	0	0	0	O/D	0.0
1974	*Oak-A	96	220	13	59	8	0	2	15	5	9	.268	.291	.332	84	-6	-5	19	0	0	0	2	DO	-0.2
1975	NY-N	62	102	8	27	3	0	0	11	4	5	.265	.290	.294	68	-5	-4	8	0	1	-1	-0	O	-0.5
1978	Hou-N	77	139	7	45	5	1	2	19	6	5	.324	.352	.417	123	2	4	19	0	0	0	-4	O	0.0
1979	Hou-N	42	43	3	11	4	0	0	10	6	7	.256	.347	.349	96	-0	-0	4	0	0	0	-0	/O1	0.0
Total	15	1380	4345	448	1216	170	26	32	377	138	267	.280	.307	.353	87	-89	-82	426	31	46	-18	-23	*O/D1	-16.2

■ MATTY ALOU
Alou, Mateo Rojas (b: Mateo Rojas (Alou))   b: 12/22/38, Haina, D.R.   BL/TL, 5'9", 160 lbs.   Deb: 9/26/60

YEAR	TM/L	G	AB	R	H	2B	3B	HR	RBI	BB	SO	AVG	OBP	SLG	PRO+	BR	/A	RC	SB	CS	SBR	FR	POS	TPR
1960	SF-N	4	3	1	1	0	0	0	0	0	0	.333	.333	.333	88	-0	-0	0	0	0	0	0	/O	0.0
1961	SF-N	81	200	38	62	7	2	6	24	15	18	.310	.358	.455	118	4	5	32	3	2	-0	-3	O	0.0
1962	*SF-N	78	195	28	57	8	1	3	14	14	17	.292	.349	.390	100	-0	0	27	3	1	0	-1	O	-0.3
1963	SF-N	63	76	4	11	1	0	0	2	2	13	.145	.177	.158	-3	-10	-10	2	0	1	-1	1	O	-1.1
1964	SF-N	110	250	28	66	4	2	1	14	11	25	.264	.303	.308	71	-9	-9	23	5	3	-0	-5	O	-1.7
1965	SF-N	117	324	37	75	12	2	2	18	17	28	.231	.274	.299	60	-17	-18	24	10	2	2	-7	*O/P	-2.6
1966	Pit-N	141	535	86	183	18	9	2	27	24	44	.342	.375	.421	121	15	15	84	23	15	-2	-7	*O	0.2
1967	Pit-N	139	550	87	186	21	7	2	28	24	42	.338	.372	.413	124	17	17	85	16	10	-1	-6	*O/1	0.4
1968	Pit-N	146	558	59	185	28	4	0	52	27	26	.332	.365	.396	130	19	19	79	18	10	-1	-5	*O	0.7
1969	Pit-N	162	698	105	231	41	6	1	48	42	35	.331	.371	.411	121	17	19	109	22	8	2	-1	*O	1.2
1970	*Pit-N	155	677	97	201	21	8	1	47	30	18	.297	.331	.356	86	-15	-14	79	19	11	-1	0	*O	-2.1
1971	StL-N	149	609	85	192	28	6	7	74	34	27	.315	.355	.415	113	13	11	89	19	10	-0	2	O1	0.5
1972	StL-N	108	404	46	127	17	2	3	31	24	23	.314	.354	.389	112	6	6	54	11	4	1	-1	1O	0.5
	*Oak-A	32	121	11	34	5	0	1	16	11	12	.281	.346	.347	112	1	2	15	2	1	0	-4	O/1	-0.2
1973	NY-A	123	497	59	147	22	1	2	28	30	43	.296	.340	.356	100	-2	-0	57	5	2	0	-7	O1/D	-1.1
	StL-N	11	11	1	3	0	0	0	1	1	0	.273	.333	.273	70	-0	-0	1	0	0	0	1	/1O	0.0
1974	SD-N	48	81	8	16	3	0	0	3	5	6	.198	.244	.235	36	-7	-7	4	0	0	0	-2	O/1	-0.9
Total	15	1667	5789	780	1777	236	50	31	427	311	377	.307	.346	.381	105	30	35	764	156	80	-1	-45	*O1/DP	-7.0

■ MOISES ALOU
Alou, Moises Rojas   b: 7/3/66, Atlanta, Ga.   BR/TR, 6'3", 185 lbs.   Deb: 7/26/90

YEAR	TM/L	G	AB	R	H	2B	3B	HR	RBI	BB	SO	AVG	OBP	SLG	PRO+	BR	/A	RC	SB	CS	SBR	FR	POS	TPR
1990	Pit-N	2	5	0	1	0	0	0	0	0	0	.200	.200	.200	11	-1	-1	0	0	0	0	0	/O	0.0
	Mon-N	14	15	4	3	0	1	0	0	0	3	.200	.200	.333	44	-1	-1	1	0	0	0	1	/O	0.0
	Yr	16	20	4	4	0	1	0	0	0	3	.200	.200	.300	36	-2	-2	1	0	0	0	1		0.0

■ WHITEY ALPERMAN
Alperman, Charles Augustus   b: 11/11/1879, Etna, Pa.   d: 12/25/42, Pittsburgh, Pa.   BR/TR, 5'10", 180 lbs.   Deb: 4/13/06

YEAR	TM/L	G	AB	R	H	2B	3B	HR	RBI	BB	SO	AVG	OBP	SLG	PRO+	BR	/A	RC	SB	CS	SBR	FR	POS	TPR
1906	Bro-N	128	441	38	111	15	7	3	46	6		.252	.262	.338	96	-8	-4	46	13			2	*2S/3	-0.1
1907	Bro-N	141	558	44	130	23	16	2	39	13		.233	.250	.342	95	-11	-7	51	5			14	*23S	1.1
1908	Bro-N	70	213	17	42	3	1	1	15	9		.197	.230	.235	52	-12	-11	12	2			-5	2/3OS	-1.8
1909	Bro-N	111	420	35	104	19	12	1	41	2		.248	.262	.357	95	-7	-5	40	7			9	*2	0.4
Total	4	450	1632	134	387	60	36	7	141	30		.237	.254	.331	90	-38	-28	149	27			21	2/S3O	-0.4

■ TOM ALSTON
Alston, Thomas Edison   b: 1/31/31, Greensboro, N.C.   BL/TR, 6'5", 210 lbs.   Deb: 4/13/54

YEAR	TM/L	G	AB	R	H	2B	3B	HR	RBI	BB	SO	AVG	OBP	SLG	PRO+	BR	/A	RC	SB	CS	SBR	FR	POS	TPR
1954	StL-N	66	244	28	60	14	2	4	34	24	41	.246	.319	.369	78	-8	-8	27	3	5	-2	10	1	-0.2
1955	StL-N	13	8	0	1	0	0	0	0	0	0	.125	.125	.125	-33	-2	-2	0	0	0	0	0	/1	-0.1
1956	StL-N	3	2	0	0	0	0	0	0	0	0	.000	.000	.000	-99	-1	-1	0	0	0	0	0	/1	0.0
1957	StL-N	9	17	2	5	1	0	0	2	1	5	.294	.333	.353	83	-0	-0	2	0	0	0	-1	/1	-0.1
Total	4	91	271	30	66	15	2	4	36	25	46	.244	.312	.358	74	-10	-11	30	3	5	-2	10	1	-0.4

■ WALTER ALSTON
Alston, Walter Emmons "Smokey"   b: 12/1/11, Venice, Ohio   d: 10/1/84, Oxford, Ohio   BR/TR, 6'2", 195 lbs.   Deb: 9/27/36   MH

YEAR	TM/L	G	AB	R	H	2B	3B	HR	RBI	BB	SO	AVG	OBP	SLG	PRO+	BR	/A	RC	SB	CS	SBR	FR	POS	TPR
1936	StL-N	1	1	0	0	0	0	0	0	0	1	.000	.000	.000	-99	-0	-0	0	0			-0	/1	0.0

■ DELL ALSTON
Alston, Wendell   b: 9/22/52, Valhalla, N.Y.   BL/TR, 6', 180 lbs.   Deb: 5/17/77

YEAR	TM/L	G	AB	R	H	2B	3B	HR	RBI	BB	SO	AVG	OBP	SLG	PRO+	BR	/A	RC	SB	CS	SBR	FR	POS	TPR
1977	NY-A	22	40	10	13	4	0	1	4	3	4	.325	.372	.500	137	2	2	6	3	3	-1	1	D/O	0.2
1978	NY-A	3	3	0	0	0	0	0	0	0	2	.000	.000	.000	-99	-1	-1	0	0	0	0	0	H	0.0
	Oak-A	58	173	17	36	2	0	1	10	10	21	.208	.251	.237	40	-14	-13	10	11	10	-3	-6	O/1D	-2.4
	Yr	61	176	17	36	2	0	1	10	10	23	.205	.247	.233	38	-15	-14	10	11	10	-3	-6		-2.4
1979	Cle-A	54	62	10	18	0	2	1	12	10	10	.290	.389	.403	114	2	2	10	4	4	-1	1	O	0.0
1980	Cle-A	52	54	11	12	1	2	0	9	5	7	.222	.311	.315	72	-2	-2	5	2	4	-2	4	O/D	0.0
Total	4	189	332	48	79	7	4	3	35	28	44	.238	.301	.310	71	-13	-12	30	20	21	-7	-1	O/D1	-2.2

■ JESSE ALTENBURG
Altenburg, Jesse Howard   b: 1/2/1893, Ashley, Mich.   d: 3/12/73, Lansing, Mich.   BL/TR, 5'9", 158 lbs.   Deb: 9/19/16

YEAR	TM/L	G	AB	R	H	2B	3B	HR	RBI	BB	SO	AVG	OBP	SLG	PRO+	BR	/A	RC	SB	CS	SBR	FR	POS	TPR
1916	Pit-N	8	14	2	6	1	1	0	0	1	1	.429	.467	.643	237	2	2	4	0			-1	/O	0.1
1917	Pit-N	11	17	1	3	0	0	0	3	0	4	.176	.176	.176	8	-2	-2	1	0			-1	/O	-0.2
Total	2	19	31	3	9	1	1	0	3	1	5	.290	.313	.387	112	0	0	5	0			-1	/O	-0.1

■ DAVE ALTIZER
Altizer, David Tilden "Filipino"   b: 11/6/1876, Pearl, Ill.   d: 5/14/64, Pleasant Hill, Ill   BL/TR, 5'10.5", 160 lbs.   Deb: 5/29/06

YEAR	TM/L	G	AB	R	H	2B	3B	HR	RBI	BB	SO	AVG	OBP	SLG	PRO+	BR	/A	RC	SB	CS	SBR	FR	POS	TPR
1906	Was-A	115	433	56	111	9	5	1	27	35		.256	.312	.307	101	-1	1	56	37			-21	*S/O	-1.9
1907	Was-A	147	540	60	145	15	5	2	42	34		.269	.312	.326	114	3	8	71	38			-10	S1O	-0.1
1908	Was-A	67	205	19	46	1	1	0	18	13		.224	.271	.239	74	-7	-5	16	8			-2	23/1S	-0.7
	Cle-A	29	89	11	19	1	2	0	5	7		.213	.271	.270	77	-2	-2	9	7			4	O/S	0.0
	Yr	96	294	30	65	2	3	0	23	20		.221	.271	.248	75	-9	-7	25	15			1		-0.7
1909	Chi-A	116	382	47	89	6	7	1	20	39		.233	.330	.293	101	1	2	47	27			8	O1	0.9
1910	Cin-N	3	10	3	6	0	0	0	0	3		.600	.692	.600	290	3	3	4	0			-2	/S	0.1
1911	Cin-N	37	75	8	17	4	1	0	4	9	5	.227	.318	.307	78	-2	-2	8	2			1	S/12O	0.0
Total	6	514	1734	204	433	36	21	4	116	140	5	.250	.312	.302	101	-6	5	211	119			-22	SO1/23	-1.7

YEAR	TM/L	G	AB	R	H	2B	3B	HR	RBI	BB	SO	AVG	OBP	SLG	PRO+	BR	/A	RC	SB	CS	SBR	FR	POS	TPR
■ **GEORGE ALTMAN**				Altman, George Lee b: 3/20/33, Goldsboro, N.C. BL/TR, 6'4", 200 lbs. Deb: 4/11/59																					
1959	Chi-N	135	420	54	103	14	4	12	47	34	80	.245	.312	.383	85	-10	-9	51	1	0	0	-3	*O	-1.2
1960	Chi-N	119	334	50	89	16	4	13	51	32	67	.266	.332	.455	114	5	6	51	4	3	-1	-3	O1	-0.1
1961	Chi-N	138	518	77	157	28	12	27	96	40	92	.303	.358	.560	137	27	26	105	6	2	1	6	*O/1	2.4
1962	Chi-N	147	534	74	170	27	5	22	74	62	89	.318	.394	.511	136	31	29	110	19	7	2	1	*O1	2.3
1963	StL-N	135	464	62	127	18	7	9	47	47	93	.274	.343	.401	104	8	4	66	13	4	2	1	*O	0.0
1964	NY-N	124	422	48	97	14	1	9	47	18	70	.230	.263	.332	68	-19	-18	35	4	2	0	6	*O	-1.6
1965	Chi-N	90	196	24	46	7	1	4	23	19	36	.235	.302	.342	79	-5	-5	21	3	2	-0	-5	O/1	-1.2
1966	Chi-N	88	185	19	41	6	0	5	17	14	37	.222	.276	.335	68	-8	-8	17	2	2	-1	-3	O/1	-1.3
1967	Chi-N	15	18	1	2	2	0	0	1	2	8	.111	.200	.222	20	-2	-2	1	0	0	0	-1	/O1	-0.2
Total	9	991	3091	409	832	132	34	101	403	268	572	.269	.331	.432	105	29	22	456	52	22	2	-2	O/1	-0.9
■ **JOE ALTOBELLI**				Altobelli, Joseph Salvatore b: 5/26/32, Detroit, Mich. BL/TL, 6', 185 lbs. Deb: 4/14/55 MC																					
1955	Cle-A	42	75	8	15	3	0	2	5	5	14	.200	.259	.320	53	-5	-5	6	0	1	-1	-0	1	-0.8
1957	Cle-A	83	87	9	18	3	2	0	9	5	14	.207	.258	.287	49	-6	-6	7	3	2	-0	1	1/O	-0.6
1961	Min-A	41	95	10	21	2	1	3	14	13	14	.221	.315	.358	75	-3	-3	11	0	0	0	-2	O/1	-0.5
Total	3	166	257	27	54	8	3	5	28	23	42	.210	.280	.323	60	-14	-15	24	3	3	-1	-1	/1O	-1.9
■ **NICK ALTROCK**				Altrock, Nicholas b: 9/15/1876, Cincinnati, Ohio d: 1/20/65, Washington, D.C. BB/TL, 5'10", 197 lbs. Deb: 7/14/1898 C																					
1898	Lou-N	11	29	4	7	0	0	0	2	2		.241	.313	.241	63	-1	-1	3	1			2	P	0.0
1902	Bos-A	3	8	0	0	0	0	0	0	0		.000	.000	.000	-97	-2	-2	0	0			1	/P	0.0
1903	Bos-A	1	3	0	2	0	0	0	0	1		.667	.750	.667	315	1	1	2	0			1	/P	0.0
	Chi-A	13	30	6	9	0	0	0	3	3		.300	.364	.300	108	0	0	4	1			3	P	0.0
	Yr	14	33	6	11	0	0	0	3	4		.333	.405	.333	131	1	1	5	1			4		0.0
1904	Chi-A	41	111	13	22	1	0	1	8	4		.198	.226	.234	49	-6	-6	7	0			5	P/1	0.0
1905	Chi-A	40	112	8	14	1	0	0	5	6		.125	.169	.134	-2	-13	-12	3	0			9	P/1	0.0
1906	*Chi-A	38	100	4	16	2	0	0	3	8		.160	.222	.180	28	-8	-8	5	2			4	P/1	0.0
1907	Chi-A	30	72	7	13	3	0	0	2	3		.181	.213	.222	42	-5	-5	3	0			6	P	0.0
1908	Chi-A	23	49	6	10	2	0	0	3	0		.204	.204	.245	48	-3	-3	3	1			6	P	0.0
1909	Chi-A	1	3	0	0	0	0	0	0	0		.000	.000	.000	-99	-1	-1	0	0			0	/P	0.0
	Was-A	12	19	2	1	0	0	0	0	1		.053	.143	.053	-40	-3	-3	0	0			0	/PO	0.0
	Yr	13	22	2	1	0	0	0	0	1		.045	.125	.045	-48	-4	-3	0	0			0		0.0
1912	Was-A	1	1	0	0	0	0	0	0	0		.000	.000	.000	-99	-0	-0	0	0			-0	/P1	0.0
1913	Was-A	4	1	0	0	0	0	0	0	0		.000	.000	.000	-98	-0	-0	0	0			0	/P	0.0
1914	Was-A	1	0	0	0	0	0	0	0	0	0	—	—	—	—	0	0	0	0			0	/P	0.0
1915	Was-A	1	1	0	0	0	0	0	0	0	0	.000	.000	.000	-99	-0	-0	0	0			-0	/P	0.0
1918	Was-A	5	8	1	1	0	0	1	1	0	0	.125	.125	.500	90	-0	-0	0	0			0	/P1	0.0
1919	Was-A	1	0	0	0	0	0	0	0	0	0	—	—	—	—	0	0	0	0			0	/P	0.0
1924	Was-A	1	1	1	1	0	1	0	0	0	0	1.000	1.000	3.000	935	1	1	3	0	0	0	0	/P	0.0
1929	Was-A	1	1	0	1	0	0	0	0	0	0	1.000	1.000	1.000	413	0	0	1	0	0	0	-0	/O	0.0
1931	Was-A	1	0	0	0	0	0	0	0	1	0	—	1.000	—	182	0	0	0	0	1	-1	0	H	0.0
1933	Was-A	1	1	0	0	0	0	0	0	0	0	.000	.000	.000	-99	-0	-0	0	0	0	0	0	H	0.0
Total	19	230	550	52	97	9	1	2	27	29	0	.176	.220	.207	36	-40	-38	33	5	1		38	P/1O	0.0
■ **GEORGE ALUSIK**				Alusik, George Joseph b: 2/11/35, Ashley, Pa. BR/TR, 6'3.5", 175 lbs. Deb: 9/11/58																					
1958	Det-A	2	2	0	0	0	0	0	0	0	1	.000	.000	.000	-93	-1	-1	0	0	0	0	0	/O	0.0
1961	Det-A	15	14	0	2	0	0	0	2	1	4	.143	.200	.143	-6	-2	-2	1	0	0	0	0	/O	-0.1
1962	Det-A	2	2	0	0	0	0	0	0	0	0	.000	.000	.000	-97	-1	-1	0	0	0	0	0	H	0.0
	KC-A	90	209	29	57	10	1	11	35	16	29	.273	.327	.488	113	4	3	33	1	1	-0	-1	O/1	0.0
	Yr	92	211	29	57	10	1	11	35	16	29	.270	.325	.483	111	3	3	32	1	1	-0	-1		0.0
1963	KC-A	87	221	28	59	11	0	9	37	26	33	.267	.347	.439	114	6	5	33	0	1	-1	-2	O	0.0
1964	KC-A	102	204	18	49	10	1	3	19	30	36	.240	.343	.343	89	-1	-2	25	0	0	0	-5	O1	-0.9
Total	5	298	652	75	167	31	2	23	93	73	103	.256	.335	.416	102	5	2	91	1	2	-1	-7	O/1	-1.0
■ **LUIS ALVARADO**				Alvarado, Luis Cesar (Martinez) b: 1/15/49, LaJas, P.R. BR/TR, 5'9", 162 lbs. Deb: 9/13/68																					
1968	Bos-A	11	46	3	6	2	0	0	1	1	11	.130	.167	.174	3	-5	-6	1	0	0	0	-3	S	-0.9
1969	Bos-A	6	5	0	0	0	0	0	0	0	2	.000	.000	.000	-95	-1	-1	0	0	1	-1	2	/S	0.0
1970	Bos-A	59	183	19	41	11	0	1	10	9	30	.224	.260	.301	51	-12	-13	13	1	2	-1	5	3S	-0.6
1971	Chi-A	99	264	22	57	14	1	0	8	11	34	.216	.247	.277	47	-18	-19	18	1	2	-1	15	S2	0.4
1972	Chi-A	103	254	30	54	4	1	4	29	13	36	.213	.254	.283	58	-13	-13	15	2	2	-1	2	S2/3	-0.2
1973	Chi-A	80	203	21	47	7	2	0	20	4	20	.232	.250	.286	49	-14	-14	14	6	2	1	5	2S3/D	-0.4
1974	Chi-A	8	10	1	1	0	0	0	0	0	1	.100	.100	.100	-41	-2	-2	0	0	0	0	-1	/S23	0.0
	StL-N	17	36	3	5	2	0	0	1	2	6	.139	.184	.194	6	-5	-5	1	0	0	0	-2	S	-0.4
	Cle-A	61	114	12	25	2	0	0	12	6	14	.219	.258	.237	44	-8	-8	7	1	1	-0	11	2/SD	0.5
1976	StL-N	16	42	5	12	1	0	0	3	3	6	.286	.333	.310	82	-1	-1	5	0	0	0	-9	2	-0.9
1977	NY-N	1	2	0	0	0	0	0	0	0	0	.000	.000	.000	-99	-1	-1	0	0	0	0	0	/2	0.0
	Det-A	2	1	0	0	0	0	0	0	0	0	.000	.000	.000	-95	-0	-0	0	0	0	0	0	/3	0.0
Total	9	463	1160	116	248	43	4	5	84	49	160	.214	.248	.271	47	-79	-83	74	11	10	-3	26	S2/3D	-2.7
■ **ORLANDO ALVAREZ**				Alvarez, Jesus Manuel Orlando (Monge) b: 2/28/52, Rio Grande, P.R. BR/TR, 6', 165 lbs. Deb: 9/01/73																					
1973	LA-N	4	4	0	1	1	0	0	0	0	1	.250	.250	.500	108	-0	-0	1	0	0	0	0	H	0.0
1974	LA-N	2	1	0	0	0	0	0	0	0	0	.000	.000	.000	-99	-0	-0	0	0	0	0	0	/O	0.0
1975	LA-N	4	4	0	0	0	0	0	0	0	1	.000	.000	.000	-99	-1	-1	0	0	0	0	0	H	0.0
1976	Cal-A	15	42	4	7	1	0	2	8	0	3	.167	.167	.333	47	-3	-3	2	0	0	0	-0	O/D	-0.3
Total	4	25	51	4	8	2	0	2	8	0	5	.157	.157	.314	36	-5	-4	3	0	0	0	-0	/OD	-0.3
■ **OSSIE ALVAREZ**				Alvarez, Oswaldo (Gonzalez) b: 10/19/33, Matanzas, Cuba BR/TR, 5'10", 165 lbs. Deb: 4/19/58																					
1958	Was-A	87	196	20	41	3	0	0	5	16	26	.209	.269	.224	38	-16	-16	13	1	1	-0	12	S2/3	0.6
1959	Det-A	8	2	0	1	0	0	0	0	0	1	.500	.500	.500	166	0	0	1	0	0	0	0	H	0.0
Total	2	95	198	20	42	3	0	0	5	16	27	.212	.271	.227	39	-16	-16	13	1	1	-0	12	/S23	0.6
■ **ROGELIO ALVAREZ**				Alvarez, Rogelio (Hernandez) b: 4/18/38, Pinar Del Rio, Cuba BR/TR, 5'11", 183 lbs. Deb: 9/18/60																					
1960	Cin-N	3	9	1	1	0	0	0	0	0	3	.111	.111	.111	-38	-2	-2	0	0	0	0	-0	/1	-0.2
1962	Cin-N	14	28	1	6	0	0	0	2	1	10	.214	.241	.214	23	-3	-3	2	0	0	0	-1	1	-0.4
Total	2	17	37	2	7	0	0	0	2	1	13	.189	.211	.189	8	-5	-5	2	0	0	0	-1	/1	-0.6
■ **MAX ALVIS**				Alvis, Roy Maxwell b: 2/2/38, Jasper, Tex. BR/TR, 5'11", 185 lbs. Deb: 9/11/62																					
1962	Cle-A	12	51	1	11	0	0	3	2	13	.216	.245	.255	36	-5	-4	3	3	1	0	-4	3	-0.7	
1963	Cle-A	158	602	81	165	32	7	22	67	36	109	.274	.326	.460	118	12	13	90	9	7	-2	-5	*3	0.8
1964	Cle-A	107	381	51	96	14	3	18	53	29	77	.252	.315	.446	110	4	4	53	5	5	-2	-7	*3	-0.2
1965	Cle-A	159	604	88	149	24	2	21	61	47	121	.247	.311	.397	99	-1	-2	74	12	8	-1	-19	*3	-2.1
1966	Cle-A	157	596	67	146	22	3	17	55	50	98	.245	.306	.378	95	-4	-4	66	4	7	-3	-6	*3	-1.7
1967	Cle-A	161	637	66	163	23	4	21	70	38	107	.256	.302	.403	106	3	3	73	3	10	-5	-8	*3	-0.7
1968	Cle-A	131	452	38	101	17	3	8	37	41	91	.223	.294	.327	89	-7	-6	42	5	5	-2	-17	*3	-2.3

YEAR	TM/L	G	AB	R	H	2B	3B	HR	RBI	BB	SO	AVG	OBP	SLG	PRO+	BR	/A	RC	SB	CS	SBR	FR	POS	TPR
1969	Cle-A	66	191	13	43	6	0	1	15	14	26	.225	.278	.272	53	-12	-12	13	1	1	-0	-2	3/S	-1.3
1970	Mil-A	62	115	16	21	2	0	3	12	5	20	.183	.217	.278	35	-10	-10	5	1	2	-1	2	3	-0.9
Total	9	1013	3629	421	895	142	22	111	373	262	662	.247	.304	.390	97	-19	-19	420	43	46	-15	-63	3/S	-9.1

■ BILLY ALVORD   Alvord, William Charles "Uncle Bill"   b: 8/1863, St.Louis, Mo.   5'10", 187 lbs.   Deb: 4/30/1885

YEAR	TM/L	G	AB	R	H	2B	3B	HR	RBI	BB	SO	AVG	OBP	SLG	PRO+	BR	/A	RC	SB	CS	SBR	FR	POS	TPR
1885	StL-N	2	5	0	0	0	0	0	0	1	2	.000	.167	.000	-45	-1	-1	0				-1	/3	0.0
1889	KC-a	50	186	23	43	8	9	0	18	10	35	.231	.270	.371	79	-5	-7	20	3			5	3/S2	0.0
1890	Tol-a	116	495	69	135	13	16	2		22		.273	.304	.376	100	-1	-3	64	21			4	*3	0.0
1891	Cle-N	13	59	7	17	2	2	1	7	0	7	.288	.300	.441	112	1	0	8	0			-2	3	0.0
	Was-a	81	312	28	73	8	3	0	30	11	38	.234	.260	.279	59	-18	-16	24	3			17	3	0.3
1893	Cle-N	3	12	2	2	0	0	0	2	0	1	.167	.167	.167	-10	-2	-2	0	0			-1	/3	-0.2
Total	5	265	1069	129	270	31	30	3	57	44	83	.253	.283	.346	83	-26	-28	117	27			22	3/2S	0.1

■ BRANT ALYEA   Alyea, Garrabrant Ryerson   b: 12/8/40, Passaic, N.J.   BR/TR, 6'3", 215 lbs.   Deb: 9/11/65

YEAR	TM/L	G	AB	R	H	2B	3B	HR	RBI	BB	SO	AVG	OBP	SLG	PRO+	BR	/A	RC	SB	CS	SBR	FR	POS	TPR
1965	Was-A	8	13	3	3	0	0	2	6	1	4	.231	.286	.692	171	1	1	2	0	0	0	-1	/1O	0.0
1968	Was-A	53	150	18	40	11	1	6	23	10	39	.267	.317	.473	141	6	6	21	0	0	0	-1	O	0.5
1969	Was-A	104	237	29	59	4	0	11	40	34	67	.249	.346	.405	115	3	5	32	1	3	-2	-6	O/1	-0.4
1970	*Min-A	94	258	34	75	12	1	16	61	28	51	.291	.367	.531	143	15	15	46	3	3	-1	-7	O	0.3
1971	Min-A	79	158	13	28	4	0	2	15	24	38	.177	.290	.241	50	-10	-10	11	1	1	-0	-6	O	-1.9
1972	Oak-A	20	31	3	6	1	0	1	2	3	5	.194	.265	.323	78	-1	-1	3	0	0	0	4	/O	0.3
	StL-N	13	19	0	3	1	0	0	1	0	6	.158	.158	.211	4	-2	-2	1	0	0	0	1	/O	-0.1
Total	6	371	866	100	214	33	2	38	148	100	210	.247	.329	.421	113	12	13	115	5	7	-3	-15	O/1	-1.3

■ JOEY AMALFITANO   Amalfitano, John Joseph   b: 1/23/34, San Pedro, Cal.   BR/TR, 5'11", 175 lbs.   Deb: 5/03/54   MC

YEAR	TM/L	G	AB	R	H	2B	3B	HR	RBI	BB	SO	AVG	OBP	SLG	PRO+	BR	/A	RC	SB	CS	SBR	FR	POS	TPR
1954	NY-N	9	5	2	0	0	0	0	0	0	4	.000	.000	.000	-99	-1	-1	0	0	0	0	2	/32	0.1
1955	NY-N	36	22	8	5	1	1	0	1	2	2	.227	.292	.364	72	-1	-1	2	0	0	0	12	/S3	1.1
1960	SF-N	106	328	47	91	15	3	1	27	26	31	.277	.336	.351	94	-5	-2	39	2	3	-1	3	32/SO	0.1
1961	SF-N	109	384	64	98	11	4	2	23	44	59	.255	.332	.320	77	-13	-11	44	7	4	-0	-22	2/3	-2.1
1962	Hou-N	117	380	44	90	12	5	1	27	45	43	.237	.319	.303	73	-16	-12	36	4	4	-1	2	*2/3	-0.1
1963	SF-N	54	137	11	24	3	0	1	7	12	18	.175	.247	.219	36	-11	-11	6	2	6	-3	-3	2/3	-1.5
1964	Chi-N	100	324	51	78	19	6	4	27	40	42	.241	.333	.373	95	0	-1	38	2	7	-4	2	2/1S	0.5
1965	Chi-N	67	96	13	26	4	0	0	8	12	14	.271	.364	.313	90	-0	-1	12	2	2	-1	5	2/S	0.5
1966	Chi-N	41	38	8	6	2	0	0	3	4	10	.158	.238	.211	26	-4	-4	2	0	0	0	1	2/3S	-0.1
1967	Chi-N	4	1	0	0	0	0	0	0	0	1	.000	.000	.000	-96	-0	-0	0	0	0	0	0	H	0.0
Total	10	643	1715	248	418	67	19	9	123	185	224	.244	.322	.321	78	-52	-46	180	19	26	-10	2	2/3S10	-1.5

■ RUBEN AMARO   Amaro, Ruben (Mora)   b: 1/6/36, Vera Cruz, Mexico   BR/TR, 5'11", 170 lbs.   Deb: 6/29/58   C

YEAR	TM/L	G	AB	R	H	2B	3B	HR	RBI	BB	SO	AVG	OBP	SLG	PRO+	BR	/A	RC	SB	CS	SBR	FR	POS	TPR
1958	StL-N	40	76	8	17	2	1	0		5	8	.224	.272	.276	44	-6	-6	5	0	1	-1	3	S/2	-0.1
1960	Phi-N	92	264	25	61	9	1	0	16	21	32	.231	.293	.273	56	-16	-16	21	0	1	-1	-8	S	-2.1
1961	Phi-N	135	381	34	98	14	9	1	32	53	59	.257	.351	.349	88	-6	-5	49	1	0	0	14	*S/12	2.2
1962	Phi-N	79	226	24	55	10	0	0	19	30	28	.243	.335	.288	71	-9	-8	23	5	2	0	6	S/1	0.6
1963	Phi-N	115	217	25	47	9	2	2	19	19	31	.217	.280	.304	69	-9	-9	18	0	1	-1	2	S3/1	0.0
1964	Phi-N	129	299	31	79	11	0	4	34	16	37	.264	.308	.341	84	-7	-6	30	1	6	-3	-10	S1/230	-1.6
1965	Phi-N	118	184	26	39	7	0	0	15	27	22	.212	.316	.250	63	-8	-8	15	1	1	-0	-2	1S/2	-0.6
1966	NY-A	14	23	0	5	0	0	0	3	0	2	.217	.217	.217	26	-2	-2	1	0	0	0	5	S	0.4
1967	NY-A	130	417	31	93	12	0	1	17	43	49	.223	.297	.259	68	-17	-15	32	3	2	-0	8	*S/31	0.1
1968	NY-A	47	41	3	5	1	0	0	0	9	6	.122	.280	.146	33	-3	-3	2	0	0	0	-0	S1	-0.2
1969	Cal-A	41	27	4	6	0	0	0	1	4	6	.222	.323	.222	58	-1	-1	3	0	0	0	-0	1/2S3	-0.1
Total	11	940	2155	211	505	75	13	8	156	227	280	.234	.310	.292	70	-84	-79	200	11	14	-5	18	S1/320	-1.4

■ WAYNE AMBLER   Ambler, Wayne Harper   b: 11/8/15, Abington, Pa.   BR/TR, 5'8.5", 165 lbs.   Deb: 6/04/37

YEAR	TM/L	G	AB	R	H	2B	3B	HR	RBI	BB	SO	AVG	OBP	SLG	PRO+	BR	/A	RC	SB	CS	SBR	FR	POS	TPR
1937	Phi-A	56	162	3	35	5	0	0	11	13	8	.216	.274	.247	33	-17	-16	12	1	0	0	-4	2	-1.3
1938	Phi-A	120	393	42	92	21	2	0	38	48	31	.234	.317	.298	56	-27	-25	40	2	1	0	-19	*S/2	-3.4
1939	Phi-A	95	227	15	48	13	0	0	24	22	25	.211	.281	.269	42	-20	-19	17	1	0	0	-3	S2	-1.2
Total	3	271	782	60	175	39	2	0	73	83	64	.224	.298	.279	47	-64	-61	69	4	1	1	-26	S/2	-5.9

■ ED AMELUNG   Amelung, Edward Allen   b: 4/13/59, Fullerton, Cal.   BL/TL, 5'11", 180 lbs.   Deb: 7/28/84

YEAR	TM/L	G	AB	R	H	2B	3B	HR	RBI	BB	SO	AVG	OBP	SLG	PRO+	BR	/A	RC	SB	CS	SBR	FR	POS	TPR
1984	LA-N	34	46	7	10	0	0	0	4	2	4	.217	.250	.217	33	-4	-4	2	3	2	-0	2	O	-0.2
1986	LA-N	8	11	0	1	0	0	0	0	0	4	.091	.091	.091	-53	-2	-2	0	0	0	0	0	/O	-0.1
Total	2	42	57	7	11	0	0	0	4	2	8	.193	.220	.193	17	-6	-6	2	3	2	-0	2	/O	-0.3

■ SANDY AMOROS   Amoros, Edmundo (Isasi)   b: 1/30/30, Havana, Cuba   BL/TL, 5'7.5", 170 lbs.   Deb: 8/22/52

YEAR	TM/L	G	AB	R	H	2B	3B	HR	RBI	BB	SO	AVG	OBP	SLG	PRO+	BR	/A	RC	SB	CS	SBR	FR	POS	TPR
1952	*Bro-N	20	44	10	11	3	1	0	3	5	14	.250	.327	.364	90	-1	-1	6	1	0	0	-1	O	-0.1
1954	Bro-N	79	263	44	72	18	6	9	34	31	24	.274	.353	.490	113	6	5	45	1	4	-2	4	O	0.5
1955	*Bro-N	119	388	59	96	16	7	10	51	55	45	.247	.350	.402	96	0	-1	57	10	5	0	0	*O	-0.2
1956	*Bro-N	114	292	53	76	11	8	16	58	59	51	.260	.386	.517	130	18	15	61	3	4	-2	-10	O	0.0
1957	Bro-N	106	238	40	66	7	1	7	26	46	42	.277	.401	.403	107	8	5	41	3	2	-0	-2	O	0.0
1959	LA-N	5	5	1	1	0	0	0	1	0	1	.200	.200	.200	6	-1	-1	0	0	0	0	0	H	0.0
1960	LA-N	9	14	1	2	0	0	0	0	3	2	.143	.294	.143	23	-1	-1	1	0	0	0	1	/O	0.0
	Det-A	65	67	7	10	0	0	1	7	12	10	.149	.278	.194	29	-6	-7	4	0	0	0	1	O	-0.5
Total	7	517	1311	215	334	55	23	43	180	211	189	.255	.363	.430	105	23	14	215	18	15	-4	-7	O	-0.3

■ ALF ANDERSON   Anderson, Alfred Walton   b: 1/28/14, Gainesville, Ga.   d: 6/23/85, Albany, Ga.   BR/TR, 5'11", 165 lbs.   Deb: 4/20/41

YEAR	TM/L	G	AB	R	H	2B	3B	HR	RBI	BB	SO	AVG	OBP	SLG	PRO+	BR	/A	RC	SB	CS	SBR	FR	POS	TPR
1941	Pit-N	70	223	32	48	7	2	1	10	14	30	.215	.265	.278	53	-14	-14	17	2			-6	S	-1.5
1942	Pit-N	54	166	24	45	4	1	0	7	18	19	.271	.342	.307	89	-1	-2	18	4			-15	S	-1.4
1946	Pit-N	2	1	0	0	0	0	0	0	1	0	.000	.500	.000	47	0	0	0	0			0	H	0.0
Total	3	126	390	56	93	11	3	1	17	33	49	.238	.300	.290	68	-15	-16	35	6			-21	S	-2.9

■ ANDY ANDERSON   Anderson, Andy Holm   b: 11/13/22, Bremerton, Wash.   d: 7/18/82, Seattle, Wash.   BR/TR, 5'11", 172 lbs.   Deb: 5/10/48

YEAR	TM/L	G	AB	R	H	2B	3B	HR	RBI	BB	SO	AVG	OBP	SLG	PRO+	BR	/A	RC	SB	CS	SBR	FR	POS	TPR
1948	StL-A	51	87	13	24	5	1	1	12	8	15	.276	.337	.391	91	-1	-1	10	0	0	0	-2	2S/1	-0.1
1949	StL-A	71	136	10	17	3	0	1	5	14	21	.125	.207	.169	-0	-20	-21	5	0	1	-1	-7	S/23	-2.7
Total	2	122	223	23	41	8	1	2	17	22	36	.184	.267	.256	35	-21	-22	15	0	1	-1	-9	/S231	-2.8

■ BRADY ANDERSON   Anderson, Brady Kevin   b: 1/18/64, Silver Spring, Md.   BL/TL, 6'1", 170 lbs.   Deb: 4/04/88

YEAR	TM/L	G	AB	R	H	2B	3B	HR	RBI	BB	SO	AVG	OBP	SLG	PRO+	BR	/A	RC	SB	CS	SBR	FR	POS	TPR
1988	Bos-A	41	148	14	34	5	3	0	12	15	35	.230	.317	.304	72	-5	-5	16	4	2	0	-0	O	-0.6
	Bal-A	53	177	17	35	8	1	1	9	8	40	.198	.232	.271	42	-14	-14	11	6	4	-1	7	O	-0.7
	Yr	94	325	31	69	13	4	1	21	23	75	.212	.273	.286	57	-19	-19	27	10	6	-1	7		-1.3
1989	Bal-A	94	266	44	55	12	2	4	16	43	45	.207	.324	.312	82	-6	-5	31	16	4	2	5	O/D	0.1
1990	Bal-A	89	234	24	54	5	2	3	24	31	46	.231	.333	.308	82	-5	-4	28	15	5	3	4	OD	0.2
Total	3	277	825	99	178	30	8	8	61	97	166	.216	.307	.301	72	-30	-28	86	41	12	5	16	O/D	-1.0

■ DAVE ANDERSON   Anderson, David Carter   b: 8/1/60, Louisville, Ky.   BR/TR, 6'2", 185 lbs.   Deb: 5/08/83

YEAR	TM/L	G	AB	R	H	2B	3B	HR	RBI	BB	SO	AVG	OBP	SLG	PRO+	BR	/A	RC	SB	CS	SBR	FR	POS	TPR
1983	LA-N	61	115	12	19	4	2	1	2	12	15	.165	.244	.261	40	-9	-9	8	6	3	0	3	S/3	0.0
1984	LA-N	121	374	51	94	16	2	3	34	45	55	.251	.335	.329	88	-5	-5	44	15	5	2	19	*S3	2.9
1985	*LA-N	77	221	24	44	6	0	4	18	35	42	.199	.311	.281	69	-9	-8	21	5	4	-1	17	3S/2	1.1

YEAR	TM/L	G	AB	R	H	2B	3B	HR	RBI	BB	SO	AVG	OBP	SLG	PRO+	BR	/A	RC	SB	CS	SBR	FR	POS	TPR
1986	LA-N	92	216	31	53	9	0	1	15	22	39	.245	.315	.301	76	-8	-6	20	5	1	1	9	3S/2	0.6
1987	LA-N	108	265	32	62	12	3	1	13	24	43	.234	.300	.313	64	-14	-13	26	9	5	-0	6	S3/2	0.0
1988	*LA-N	116	285	31	71	10	2	2	20	32	45	.249	.327	.319	89	-4	-3	30	4	2	0	14	S32	1.8
1989	LA-N	87	140	15	32	2	0	1	14	17	26	.229	.312	.264	67	-6	-5	13	2	0	1	0	S3/2	-0.2
1990	SF-N	60	100	14	35	5	1	1	6	3	20	.350	.369	.450	126	3	3	15	1	2	-1	-6	S2/13	0.0
Total	8	722	1716	210	410	64	10	14	122	190	285	.239	.317	.312	78	-53	-47	177	47	22	1	63	S3/21	6.2

■ DWAIN ANDERSON

Anderson, Dwain Cleaven b: 11/23/47, Oakland, Cal. BR/TR, 5'11", 165 lbs. Deb: 9/03/71

YEAR	TM/L	G	AB	R	H	2B	3B	HR	RBI	BB	SO	AVG	OBP	SLG	PRO+	BR	/A	RC	SB	CS	SBR	FR	POS	TPR
1971	Oak-A	16	37	3	10	2	1	0	3	5	9	.270	.372	.378	115	1	1	5	0	1	-1	-0	S/23	0.1
1972	Oak-A	3	7	2	0	0	0	0	0	1	4	.000	.125	.000	-64	-1	-1	0	0	0	0	-0	/S3	-0.1
	StL-N	57	135	12	36	4	1	1	8	8	23	.267	.313	.333	85	-3	-3	13	0	1	-1	-3	S3/2	-0.1
1973	StL-N	18	17	5	2	0	0	0	0	4	4	.118	.286	.118	16	-2	-2	1	0	0	0	-2	/SO	-0.3
	SD-N	53	107	11	13	0	0	0	3	14	29	.121	.223	.121	-2	-15	-13	4	2	0	1	3	S/3	-0.3
	Yr	71	124	16	15	0	0	0	3	18	33	.121	.232	.121	1	-16	-15	5	2	0	1	2		-0.6
1974	Cle-A	2	3	0	1	0	0	0	0	0	1	.333	.333	.333	93	-0	-0	0	0	0	0	-1	/2	0.0
Total	4	149	306	33	62	6	2	1	14	32	70	.203	.282	.245	52	-20	-18	23	2	2	-1	-3	/S32O	-0.7

■ GOAT ANDERSON

Anderson, Edward John b: 1/13/1880, Cleveland, Ohio d: 3/15/23, South Bend, Ind. BL/TR, Deb: 4/11/07

YEAR	TM/L	G	AB	R	H	2B	3B	HR	RBI	BB	SO	AVG	OBP	SLG	PRO+	BR	/A	RC	SB	CS	SBR	FR	POS	TPR
1907	Pit-N	127	413	73	85	3	1	1	12	80		.206	.335	.225	77	-6	-6	43	27			-1	*O/2	-1.2

■ FERRELL ANDERSON

Anderson, Ferrell Jack "Andy" b: 1/9/18, Maple City, Kan. d: 3/12/78, Joplin, Mo. BR/TR, 6'1", 200 lbs. Deb: 4/16/46

YEAR	TM/L	G	AB	R	H	2B	3B	HR	RBI	BB	SO	AVG	OBP	SLG	PRO+	BR	/A	RC	SB	CS	SBR	FR	POS	TPR
1946	Bro-N	79	199	19	51	10	0	2	14	18	21	.256	.330	.337	89	-3	-3	22	1			-1	C	-0.1
1953	StL-N	18	35	1	10	2	0	0	1	0	4	.286	.286	.343	63	-2	-2	4	0	0	0	-1	C	-0.1
Total	2	97	234	20	61	12	0	2	15	18	25	.261	.324	.338	85	-5	-5	26	1	0		-2	/C	-0.2

■ GEORGE ANDERSON

Anderson, George Jendrus "Andy" (Born George Andrew Jendrus)
b: 9/26/1889, Cleveland, Ohio d: 5/28/62, Cleveland, Ohio BL/TR, 5'8.5", 160 lbs. Deb: 5/26/14

YEAR	TM/L	G	AB	R	H	2B	3B	HR	RBI	BB	SO	AVG	OBP	SLG	PRO+	BR	/A	RC	SB	CS	SBR	FR	POS	TPR
1914	Bro-F	98	364	58	115	13	3	3	24	31	50	.316	.376	.393	121	10	11	62	16			4	O	1.0
1915	Bro-F	136	511	70	135	23	9	2	39	52	54	.264	.342	.356	107	5	6	72	20			-8	*O	-0.8
1918	StL-N	35	132	20	39	4	5	0	6	15	7	.295	.380	.402	143	7	7	20	0			-5	O	0.1
Total	3	269	1007	148	289	40	17	5	69	98	111	.287	.359	.375	117	22	23	154	36			-8	O	0.3

■ SPARKY ANDERSON

Anderson, George Lee b: 2/22/34, Bridgewater, S.Dak BR/TR, 5'9", 170 lbs. Deb: 4/10/59 MC

YEAR	TM/L	G	AB	R	H	2B	3B	HR	RBI	BB	SO	AVG	OBP	SLG	PRO+	BR	/A	RC	SB	CS	SBR	FR	POS	TPR
1959	Phi-N	152	477	42	104	9	3	0	34	42	53	.218	.283	.249	43	-38	-39	32	6	9	-4	3	*2	-2.7

■ HAL ANDERSON

Anderson, Harold b: 2/10/04, St.Louis, Mo. d: 5/1/74, St.Louis, Mo. BR/TR, 5'11", 160 lbs. Deb: 4/12/32

YEAR	TM/L	G	AB	R	H	2B	3B	HR	RBI	BB	SO	AVG	OBP	SLG	PRO+	BR	/A	RC	SB	CS	SBR	FR	POS	TPR
1932	Chi-A	9	32	4	8	0	0	0	2	0	1	.250	.250	.250	32	-3	-3	2	0	1	-1	1	/O	-0.2

■ HARRY ANDERSON

Anderson, Harry Walter b: 9/10/31, North East, Md. BL/TR, 6'3", 205 lbs. Deb: 4/18/57

YEAR	TM/L	G	AB	R	H	2B	3B	HR	RBI	BB	SO	AVG	OBP	SLG	PRO+	BR	/A	RC	SB	CS	SBR	FR	POS	TPR
1957	Phi-N	118	400	53	107	15	4	17	61	36	61	.268	.337	.452	113	5	7	61	2	3	-1	1	*O	0.3
1958	Phi-N	140	515	80	155	34	6	23	97	59	95	.301	.376	.524	137	26	27	100	0	2	-1	-7	O1	1.2
1959	Phi-N	142	508	50	122	28	6	14	63	43	95	.240	.306	.402	85	-11	-12	62	1	1	-0	14	*O	0.0
1960	Phi-N	38	93	10	23	2	0	5	12	10	19	.247	.333	.430	107	1	1	13	0	0	0	-1	O1	0.0
	Cin-N	42	66	6	11	3	0	1	9	11	20	.167	.286	.258	49	-4	-5	6	0	0	0	-1	1/O	-0.5
	Yr	80	159	16	34	5	0	6	21	21	39	.214	.313	.358	82	-4	-4	19	0	0	0	-1		-0.5
1961	Cin-N	4	4	0	1	0	0	0	0	0	1	.250	.250	.250	33	-0	-0	1	0	0	0	0	H	0.0
Total	5	484	1586	199	419	82	16	60	242	159	291	.264	.337	.450	109	16	18	242	3	6	-3	7	O/1	1.0

■ JIM ANDERSON

Anderson, James Lea b: 2/23/57, Los Angeles, Cal. BR/TR, 6', 170 lbs. Deb: 7/02/78

YEAR	TM/L	G	AB	R	H	2B	3B	HR	RBI	BB	SO	AVG	OBP	SLG	PRO+	BR	/A	RC	SB	CS	SBR	FR	POS	TPR
1978	Cal-A	48	108	6	21	7	0	2	7	11	16	.194	.269	.259	51	-7	-7	7	0	0	0	3	S/2	0.0
1979	*Cal-A	96	234	33	58	13	1	3	23	17	31	.248	.302	.350	78	-8	-7	24	3	2	-0	-0	S3/2C	0.2
1980	Sea-A	116	317	46	72	7	0	8	30	27	39	.227	.294	.325	69	-13	-14	30	2	4	-2	6	S3/2CD	-0.4
1981	Sea-A	70	162	12	33	7	0	2	19	17	29	.204	.283	.284	61	-7	-8	12	3	5	-2	1	S/3	-0.3
1983	Tex-A	50	102	8	22	1	1	0	6	5	8	.216	.252	.245	38	-9	-8	6	1	2	-1	6	S2/3OCD	0.0
1984	Tex-A	39	47	2	5	0	0	0	1	4	7	.106	.176	.106	-8	-5	-4	1	0	0	0	10	S/32	0.5
Total	6	419	970	107	211	35	2	13	86	81	130	.218	.281	.298	60	-52	-52	81	9	13	-5	26	S/32DCO	0.0

■ JOHN ANDERSON

Anderson, John Joseph "Honest John" b: 12/14/1873, Sasbourg, Norway d: 7/23/49, Worcester, Mass. BB/TR, 6'2", 180 lbs. Deb: 9/08/1894

YEAR	TM/L	G	AB	R	H	2B	3B	HR	RBI	BB	SO	AVG	OBP	SLG	PRO+	BR	/A	RC	SB	CS	SBR	FR	POS	TPR
1894	Bro-N	17	63	14	19	1	3	1	19	3	3	.302	.333	.460	98	-1	-0	12	7			-5	O/3	-0.4
1895	Bro-N	102	419	76	120	11	14	9	87	12	29	.286	.314	.444	104	-5	1	68	24			-6	*O	-1.0
1896	Bro-N	108	430	70	135	23	17	1	55	18	23	.314	.344	.453	118	5	9	82	37			-3	O1	0.2
1897	Bro-N	117	492	93	160	28	12	4	85	17		.325	.355	.455	122	9	13	92	29			0	*O/1	0.4
1898	Bro-N	6	21	1	3	2	0	0	2	1		.143	.217	.238	32	-2	-2	1	0			0	/O	-0.1
	Was-N	110	430	70	131	28	18	9	71	23		.305	.357	.516	153	26	26	88	18			9	O1	2.7
	Bro-N	19	69	11	19	3	4	0	8	5		.275	.333	.435	123	2	2	11	2			-1	O/1	0.0
	Yr	135	520	82	153	33	22	9	81	29		.294	.348	.494	144	26	26	99	20			8		2.6
1899	Bro-N	117	439	65	118	18	7	4	92	27		.269	.317	.369	88	-7	-8	61	25			-4	O1	-1.4
1901	Mil-A	138	576	90	190	46	7	8	99	24		.330	.360	.476	139	23	27	114	35			5	*10	2.3
1902	StL-A	126	524	60	149	29	6	4	85	21		.284	.316	.385	97	-4	-3	71	15			-9	*1/O	-0.9
1903	StL-A	138	550	65	156	34	8	2	78	23		.284	.312	.385	113	6	6	73	16			4	*1/O	1.2
1904	NY-A	143	558	62	155	27	12	3	82	23		.278	.306	.385	115	11	8	75	20			-0	*O1	0.2
1905	NY-A	32	99	12	23	3	1	0	14	8		.232	.290	.283	75	-2	-3	11	9			-2	O/1	-0.6
	Was-A	101	400	50	116	21	6	1	38	22		.290	.327	.380	132	11	13	59	22			-0	O/1	0.8
	Yr	133	499	62	139	24	7	1	52	30		.279	.319	.361	118	9	9	70	31			-2		0.2
1906	Was-A	151	583	62	158	25	4	3	70	19		.271	.294	.343	106	-1	2	72	39			5	*O	0.1
1907	Was-A	87	333	33	96	12	4	0	44	34		.288	.354	.348	137	11	14	49	19			-0	1O	1.2
1908	Chi-A	123	355	36	93	17	1	0	47	30		.262	.319	.315	111	4	4	43	21			-6	O/1	-0.6
Total	14	1635	6341	870	1841	328	124	49	976	310	55	.290	.327	.404	116	85	110	982	338			-13	*O1/3	4.1

■ KENT ANDERSON

Anderson, Kent McKay b: 8/12/63, Florence, S.C. BR/TR, 6'1", 180 lbs. Deb: 4/15/89

YEAR	TM/L	G	AB	R	H	2B	3B	HR	RBI	BB	SO	AVG	OBP	SLG	PRO+	BR	/A	RC	SB	CS	SBR	FR	POS	TPR
1989	Cal-A	86	223	27	51	6	1	0	17	17	42	.229	.286	.265	57	-13	-12	17	1	2	-1	13	S/230D	0.6
1990	Cal-A	49	143	16	44	6	1	1	5	13	19	.308	.369	.385	111	2	2	20	0	2	-1	13	S3/2	1.6
Total	2	135	366	43	95	12	2	1	22	30	61	.260	.319	.311	79	-10	-10	37	1	4	-2	25	/S320D	2.2

■ MIKE ANDERSON

Anderson, Michael Allen b: 6/22/51, Florence, S.C. BR/TR, 6'2", 200 lbs. Deb: 9/02/71

YEAR	TM/L	G	AB	R	H	2B	3B	HR	RBI	BB	SO	AVG	OBP	SLG	PRO+	BR	/A	RC	SB	CS	SBR	FR	POS	TPR
1971	Phi-N	26	89	11	22	5	1	2	5	13	28	.247	.343	.393	108	1	1	13	0	0	0	2	O	0.3
1972	Phi-N	36	103	8	20	5	1	2	5	19	36	.194	.320	.320	80	-2	-2	12	1	0	0	5	O	0.1
1973	Phi-N	87	193	32	49	9	1	9	28	19	53	.254	.324	.451	110	3	2	27	0	3	-2	2	O	0.0
1974	Phi-N	145	395	35	99	22	2	5	34	37	75	.251	.315	.354	83	-7	-9	41	2	1	0	1	*O/1	-1.3
1975	Phi-N	115	247	24	64	10	3	4	28	17	66	.259	.312	.372	86	-4	-5	27	1	1	-1	-8	*O/1	-1.8
1976	StL-N	86	199	17	58	8	1	1	12	26	30	.291	.376	.357	108	3	3	27	1	1	-0	2	O/1	0.3
1977	StL-N	94	154	18	34	4	1	4	17	14	31	.221	.286	.338	68	-7	-7	14	2	3	-1	5	O	-0.5
1978	Bal-A	53	32	2	3	0	1	0	3	3	10	.094	.171	.156	-8	-5	-4	1	0	0	0	1	O	-0.4
1979	Phi-N	79	78	12	18	4	0	1	2	13	14	.231	.341	.321	79	-2	-2	9	1	2	-1	6	O/P	0.1
Total	9	721	1490	159	367	67	11	28	134	161	343	.246	.321	.362	88	-20	-24	173	8	12	-5	17	O/1P	-3.2

YEAR	TM/L	G	AB	R	H	2B	3B	HR	RBI	BB	SO	AVG	OBP	SLG	PRO+	BR	/A	RC	SB	CS	SBR	FR	POS	TPR

■ ERNIE ANDRES   Andres, Ernest Henry "Junie" b: 1/11/18, Jeffersonville, Ind. BR/TR, 6'1", 200 lbs. Deb: 4/16/46

| 1946 | Bos-A | 15 | 41 | 0 | 4 | 2 | 0 | 0 | 1 | 3 | 5 | .098 | .159 | .146 | -14 | -6 | -7 | 1 | 0 | 0 | 0 | 1 | 3 | -0.4 |

■ KIM ANDREW   Andrew, Kim Darrell b: 11/14/53, Glendale, Cal. BR/TR, 5'10", 160 lbs. Deb: 4/16/75

| 1975 | Bos-A | 2 | 2 | 0 | 1 | 0 | 0 | 0 | 0 | 0 | 0 | .500 | .500 | .500 | 169 | 0 | 0 | 1 | 0 | 0 | 0 | -0 | /2 | 0.0 |

■ FRED ANDREWS   Andrews, Fred b: 5/4/52, Lafayette, La. BR/TR, 5'8", 163 lbs. Deb: 9/26/76

1976	Phi-N	4	6	1	4	0	0	0	0	2	0	.667	.778	.667	304	2	2	4	1	1	-0	-0	/2	0.2
1977	Phi-N	12	23	3	4	0	1	0	2	1	5	.174	.208	.261	24	-2	-3	1	1	0	0	3	/2	0.1
Total	2	16	29	4	8	0	1	0	2	3	5	.276	.364	.345	90	-0	-0	5	2	1	0	3	/2	0.3

■ ED ANDREWS   Andrews, George Edward b: 4/5/1859, Painesville, Ohio d: 8/12/34, W.Palm Beach, Fla. BR/TR, 5'8", 160 lbs. Deb: 5/01/1884 U

1884	Phi-N	109	420	74	93	21	2	0	23	9	42	.221	.238	.281	66	-18	-15	29				-23	*2	-3.2
1885	Phi-N	103	421	77	112	15	3	0	23	32	25	.266	.318	.316	108	3	4	43				-1	*O/2	0.1
1886	Phi-N	107	437	93	109	15	4	2	28	31	35	.249	.299	.316	86	-6	-7	59	56			2	*O/2	-0.2
1887	Phi-N	104	464	110	151	19	7	4	67	21	21	.325	.359	.422	112	11	6	93	57			-7	*O/21	0.0
1888	Phi-N	124	528	75	126	14	4	3	44	21	41	.239	.272	.297	79	-10	-13	53	35			-6	*O	-1.9
1889	Phi-N	10	39	10	11	1	0	0	7	2	4	.282	.317	.308	70	-1	-2	6	7			-2	/O2	-0.3
	Ind-P	40	173	32	53	11	0	0	22	5	10	.306	.330	.370	95	-1	-2	24	7			-3	O/2	-0.5
	Yr	50	212	42	64	12	0	0	29	7	14	.302	.327	.358	90	-2	-3	30	14			-5		-0.8
1890	Bro-P	94	395	84	100	14	2	3	38	40	32	.253	.323	.322	70	-14	-19	49	21			1	*O	-1.7
1891	Cin-a	83	356	47	75	7	4	0	26	33	35	.211	.279	.253	50	-20	-25	32	22			17	O	-1.0
Total	8	774	3233	602	830	117	26	12	278	194	245	.257	.301	.320	83	-57	-72	389	205			-22	O2/1	-8.7

■ JIM ANDREWS   Andrews, James Pratt b: 6/5/1865, Shelburne Falls, Mass. d: 12/27/07, Chicago, Ill. Deb: 4/19/1890

| 1890 | Chi-N | 53 | 202 | 32 | 38 | 4 | 2 | 3 | 17 | 23 | 41 | .188 | .278 | .272 | 60 | -9 | -11 | 19 | 11 | | | 1 | O | -0.9 |

■ MIKE ANDREWS   Andrews, Michael Jay b: 7/9/43, Los Angeles, Cal. BR/TR, 6'3", 195 lbs. Deb: 9/18/66

1966	Bos-A	5	18	1	3	0	0	0	0	0	2	.167	.167	.167	-4	-2	-3	1	0	0	0	2	/2	0.0
1967	*Bos-A	142	494	79	130	20	4	8	40	62	72	.263	.348	.352	99	6	1	63	7	7	-2	-6	*2/S	-0.1
1968	Bos-A	147	536	77	145	22	1	7	45	81	57	.271	.369	.354	113	16	12	75	3	8	-4	1	*2/S3	1.7
1969	Bos-A	121	464	79	136	26	2	15	59	71	53	.293	.393	.455	129	24	21	88	1	1	-0	5	*2	3.2
1970	Bos-A	151	589	91	149	28	1	17	65	81	63	.253	.346	.390	96	-3	-2	84	2	1	0	-30	*2	-1.7
1971	Chi-A	109	330	45	93	16	0	12	47	67	36	.282	.405	.439	135	20	18	62	3	5	-2	-3	21	1.6
1972	Chi-A	148	505	58	111	18	0	7	50	70	78	.220	.317	.297	82	-8	-10	54	2	2	-1	-14	*2/1	-1.8
1973	Chi-A	52	159	10	32	9	0	0	10	23	28	.201	.302	.258	57	-8	-9	12	0	1	-1	-3	D/123	-1.2
	*Oak-A	18	21	1	4	1	0	0	0	3	1	.190	.292	.238	53	-1	-1	1	0	0	0	-1	/2D	-0.1
	Yr	70	180	11	36	10	0	0	10	26	29	.200	.301	.256	57	-9	-10	14	0	1	-1	-4		-1.3
Total	8	893	3116	441	803	140	4	66	316	458	390	.258	.356	.369	104	49	29	439	18	25	-10	-48	2/1DS3	1.6

■ ROB ANDREWS   Andrews, Robert Patrick b: 12/11/52, Santa Monica, Cal. BR/TR, 6', 185 lbs. Deb: 4/07/75

1975	Hou-N	103	277	29	66	5	4	0	19	31	34	.238	.315	.285	73	-12	-9	27	12	5	1	7	2/S	0.3
1976	Hou-N	109	410	42	105	8	5	0	23	33	27	.256	.312	.300	81	-13	-9	37	7	3	0	8	*2/S	0.5
1977	SF-N	127	436	60	115	11	3	0	25	56	33	.264	.348	.303	76	-13	-12	49	5	6	-2	-12	*2	-1.9
1978	SF-N	79	177	21	.39	3	3	1	11	20	18	.220	.299	.288	67	-8	-7	17	5	1	1	9	2/S	0.7
1979	SF-N	75	154	22	40	3	0	2	13	8	9	.260	.296	.318	73	-7	-6	14	4	1	1	4	2/3	0.2
Total	5	493	1454	174	365	30	15	3	91	148	121	.251	.320	.298	76	-52	-43	143	33	16	0	15	2/S3	-0.2

■ STAN ANDREWS   Andrews, Stanley Joseph "Polo" (b: Stanley Joseph Andruskewicz) b: 4/17/17, Lynn, Mass. BR/TR, 5'11", 178 lbs. Deb: 6/11/39

1939	Bos-N	13	26	1	6	0	0	0	1	1	2	.231	.259	.231	35	-2	-2	1	0			-1	C	-0.2
1940	Bos-N	19	33	1	6	0	0	0	2	0	3	.182	.182	.182	1	-4	-4	1	1			-0	C	-0.3
1944	Bro-N	4	8	1	1	0	0	0	1	1	2	.125	.222	.125	-1	-1	-1	0	0			0	/C	0.0
1945	Bro-N	21	49	5	8	0	1	0	2	5	4	.163	.255	.204	29	-5	-5	3	0			2	C	-0.1
	Phi-N	13	33	3	11	2	0	1	6	1	5	.333	.353	.485	135	1	1	6	1			-1	C	0.1
	Yr	34	82	8	19	2	1	1	8	6	9	.232	.292	.317	70	-4	-3	8	1			2		0.0
Total	4	70	149	11	32	2	1	1	12	8	16	.215	.259	.262	46	-11	-11	11	2			0	/C	-0.5

■ WALLY ANDREWS   Andrews, William Walter b: 9/18/1859, Philadelphia, Pa. d: 1/20/40, Indianapolis, Ind. 6'3", 170 lbs. Deb: 5/22/1884

1884	Lou-a	14	49	10	10	5	1	0	4			.204	.264	.347	105	0	0	5				-1	/13OS	0.0
1888	Lou-a	26	93	12	18	6	3	0	6	13		.194	.292	.323	102	0	1	10	5			2	1	0.0
Total	2	40	142	22	28	11	4	0	6	17		.197	.283	.331	103	0	1	15	5			1	/13SO	0.0

■ FRED ANDRUS   Andrus, Frederick Hotham b: 8/23/1850, Washington, Mich. d: 11/10/37, Detroit, Mich. BR/TR, 6'2", 185 lbs. Deb: 7/25/1876

1876	Chi-N	8	36	6	11	3	0	0	2	0	5	.306	.306	.389	116	1	1	4				-3	/O	-0.1
1884	Chi-N	1	5	3	1	0	0	0	0	1	0	.200	.333	.200	66	-0	-0	0				0	/P	0.0
Total	2	9	41	9	12	3	0	0	2	1	5	.293	.310	.366	110	1	0	5				-3	/OP	-0.1

■ BILL ANDRUS   Andrus, William Morgan "Andy" b: 7/25/07, Beaumont, Tex. d: 3/12/82, Washington, D.C. BR/TR, 6', 185 lbs. Deb: 9/19/31

1931	Was-A	3	7	0	0	0	0	0	1	0	1	.000	.000	.000	-99	-2	-2	0	0	0	0	-0	/3	-0.1
1937	Phi-N	3	2	0	0	0	0	0	0	0	2	.000	.000	.000	-93	-1	-1	0	0			0	/3	0.0
Total	2	6	9	0	0	0	0	0	1	0	3	.000	.000	.000	-98	-3	-3	0	0	0		-0	/3	-0.1

■ WYMAN ANDRUS   Andrus, Wyman W. b: 10/14/1858, Orono, Ontario, Can d: 6/17/35, Miles City, Mon. Deb: 9/15/1885

| 1885 | Pro-N | 1 | 4 | 0 | 0 | 0 | 0 | 0 | 0 | 0 | 1 | .000 | .000 | .000 | -99 | -1 | -1 | 0 | | | | 1 | /3 | 0.0 |

■ TOM ANGLEY   Angley, Thomas Samuel b: 10/2/04, Baltimore, Md. d: 10/26/52, Wichita, Kan. BL/TR, 5'8", 190 lbs. Deb: 4/23/29

| 1929 | Chi-N | 5 | 16 | 1 | 4 | 1 | 0 | 0 | 6 | 2 | 2 | .250 | .333 | .313 | 61 | -1 | -1 | 2 | 0 | | | 2 | /C | 0.1 |

■ PAT ANKENMAN   Ankenman, Frederick Norman b: 12/23/12, Houston, Tex. d: 1/13/89, Houston, Tex. BR/TR, 5'4", 125 lbs. Deb: 4/16/36

1936	StL-N	1	3	0	0	0	0	0	0	0	0	.000	.000	.000	-99	-1	-1	0	0			-1	/S	-0.1
1943	Bro-N	1	2	1	1	0	0	0	0	0	0	.500	.500	.500	189	0	0	1	0			1	/S	0.1
1944	Bro-N	13	24	1	6	1	0	0	3	0	2	.250	.250	.292	53	-2	-2	2	0			0	2/S	0.0
Total	3	15	29	2	7	1	0	0	3	0	5	.241	.241	.276	46	-2	-2	2	0			-0	/2S	0.0

■ BILL ANNIS   Annis, William Perley b: 3/8/1857, Stoneham, Mass. d: 6/10/23, Kennebunkport, Me BR, 5'7", 150 lbs. Deb: 5/01/1884

| 1884 | Bos-N | 27 | 96 | 17 | 17 | 2 | 0 | 0 | 3 | 0 | 8 | .177 | .177 | .198 | 18 | -9 | -9 | 3 | | | | -2 | O | -0.9 |

■ CAP ANSON   Anson, Adrian Constantine b: 4/11/1852, Marshalltown, Iowa d: 4/14/22, Chicago, Ill. BR/TR, 6', 227 lbs. Deb: 5/06/1871 MH

1871	Rok-n	25	120	29	39	11	3	0	16	2	1	.325	.336	.467	134	4	5	21	6			*3/C2O	0.2
1872	Ath-n	46	215	60	89	9	7	0		16		.414	.455	.521	199	26	25	52				*3	1.5
1873	Ath-n	52	252	53	99	9	2	0		5		.393	.405	.444	139	15	11	46				*13/2CO	0.3
1874	Ath-n	55	260	51	86	8	3	0		3		.331	.338	.385	119	8	4	35				13/OS	0.3
1875	Ath-n	69	324	84	105	17	4	1		6		.324	.336	.410	141	18	12	46				10C/3M	0.4
1876	Chi-N	66	309	63	110	9	7	2	59	12	8	.356	.380	.450	157	24	19	54			13	*3/C	2.6
1877	Chi-N	59	255	52	86	19	1	0	32	9	3	.337	.360	.420	129	13	8	39			9	*3C	1.8
1878	Chi-N	60	261	55	89	12	2	0	40	13	1	.341	.372	.402	145	15	13	40			-6	*O/23C	0.3

YEAR	TM/L	G	AB	R	H	2B	3B	HR	RBI	BB	SO	AVG	OBP	SLG	PRO+	BR	/A	RC	SB	CS	SBR	FR	POS	TPR
1879	Chi-N	51	227	40	72	20	1	0	34	2	2	.317	.323	.414	133	9	8	31				0	1/M	0.4
1880	Chi-N	86	356	54	120	24	1	1	74	14	12	.337	.362	.419	154	23	20	55				0	*1/3S2M	1.6
1881	Chi-N	84	343	67	**137**	21	7	1	82	26	4	**.399**	**.442**	.510	189	**39**	37	79				7	*1/CSM	3.0
1882	Chi-N	82	348	69	126	29	8	1	83	20	7	.362	.397	.500	177	33	30	71				-1	*1/CM	1.4
1883	Chi-N	98	413	70	127	36	5	0	68	18	9	.308	.336	.419	121	14	10	60				3	*1/POCM	0.0
1884	Chi-N	112	475	108	159	30	3	21	102	29	13	.335	.373	.543	170	45	38	99				-0	*1/CSPM	2.4
1885	*Chi-N	112	464	100	144	**35**	7	7	108	34	13	.310	.357	.461	142	32	22	78				-3	*1/CM	0.0
1886	*Chi-N	125	504	117	187	35	11	10	**147**	55	19	.371	.433	.544	170	58	46	134	29			9	*1CM	2.9
1887	Chi-N	122	472	107	164	33	13	7	102	60	18	.347	.422	.517	143	41	30	117	27			10	*1/CM	1.7
1888	Chi-N	134	515	101	177	20	12	12	84	47	24	**.344**	**.400**	.499	175	51	46	117	28			9	*1M	4.1
1889	Chi-N	134	518	100	161	32	7	7	117	86	19	.311	.414	.440	134	31	27	108	27			9	*1M	2.2
1890	Chi-N	139	504	95	157	14	5	7	107	**113**	23	.312	**.443**	.401	143	39	36	105	29			1	*1/C2M	2.4
1891	Chi-N	136	540	81	157	24	8	8	**120**	75	29	.291	.378	.409	132	23	23	92	17			8	*1/CM	2.4
1892	Chi-N	146	559	62	152	25	9	1	74	67	30	.272	.354	.354	115	12	12	77	13			-5	*1/M	-0.3
1893	Chi-N	103	398	70	125	24	2	0	91	68	12	.314	.415	.384	118	12	14	71	13			-4	*1/M	0.8
1894	Chi-N	83	340	82	132	28	4	5	99	40	15	.388	.457	.538	134	24	20	94	17			3	1/2M	1.8
1895	Chi-N	122	474	87	159	23	6	2	91	55	23	.335	.408	.422	109	14	8	89	12			-1	*1/M	0.8
1896	Chi-N	108	402	72	133	18	2	2	90	49	10	.331	.407	.400	111	11	9	77	24			0	*1C/M	1.1
1897	Chi-N	114	424	67	121	17	3	3	75	60		.285	.379	.361	95	1	-1	64	11			2	*1C/M	0.9
Total	5 n	247	1171	277	418	54	19	1	16	32	1	.357	.374	.438	145	71	58	201	6				/310C2S	3.8
Total	22	2276	9101	1719	2995	528	124	97	1879	952	<u>294</u>	.329	.395	.446	139	564	472	1751	247			63	*13/CO2PS	33.4

■ ERIC ANTHONY
Anthony, Eric Todd b: 11/8/67, San Diego, Cal. BL/TL, 6'2", 195 lbs. Deb: 7/29/89

YEAR	TM/L	G	AB	R	H	2B	3B	HR	RBI	BB	SO	AVG	OBP	SLG	PRO+	BR	/A	RC	SB	CS	SBR	FR	POS	TPR
1989	Hou-N	25	61	7	11	2	0	4	7	9	16	.180	.286	.410	100	-0	-0	7	0	0	0	0	O	0.0
1990	Hou-N	84	239	26	46	8	0	10	29	29	78	.192	.285	.351	76	-9	-8	26	5	0	2	-4	O	-1.2
Total	2	109	300	33	57	10	0	14	36	38	94	.190	.285	.363	80	-9	-8	33	5	0	2	-4	/O	-1.2

■ JOE ANTOLICK
Antolick, Joseph b: 4/11/16, Hokendauqua, Pa. BR/TR, 6', 185 lbs. Deb: 9/20/44

YEAR	TM/L	G	AB	R	H	2B	3B	HR	RBI	BB	SO	AVG	OBP	SLG	PRO+	BR	/A	RC	SB	CS	SBR	FR	POS	TPR
1944	Phi-N	4	6	1	2	0	0	0	0	1	0	.333	.429	.333	120	0	0	1	0			1	/C	0.1

■ JOHN ANTONELLI
Antonelli, John Lawrence b: 7/15/15, Memphis, Tenn. d: 4/18/90, Memphis, Tenn. BR/TR, 5'10.5", 165 lbs. Deb: 9/16/44

YEAR	TM/L	G	AB	R	H	2B	3B	HR	RBI	BB	SO	AVG	OBP	SLG	PRO+	BR	/A	RC	SB	CS	SBR	FR	POS	TPR
1944	StL-N	8	21	0	4	1	0	0	1	0	4	.190	.190	.238	20	-2	-2	1	0			1	/132	0.0
1945	StL-N	2	3	0	0	0	0	0	0	0	1	.000	.000	.000	-98	-1	-1	0	0			-0	/3	0.0
	Phi-N	125	504	50	129	27	2	1	28	24	24	.256	.292	.323	73	-21	-19	45	1			-9	*32/1S	-2.7
	Yr	127	507	50	129	27	2	1	28	24	25	.254	.291	.321	72	-21	-20	45	1			-9		-2.7
Total	2	135	528	50	133	28	2	1	29	24	29	.252	.287	.318	70	-24	-22	46	1			-8	3/21S	-2.7

■ BILL ANTONELLO
Antonello, William James b: 5/19/27, Brooklyn, N.Y. BR/TR, 5'11", 185 lbs. Deb: 4/30/53

YEAR	TM/L	G	AB	R	H	2B	3B	HR	RBI	BB	SO	AVG	OBP	SLG	PRO+	BR	/A	RC	SB	CS	SBR	FR	POS	TPR
1953	Bro-N	40	43	9	7	1	1	1	4	2	11	.163	.200	.302	28	-5	-5	2	0	0	0	2	O	-0.3

■ LUIS APARICIO
Aparicio, Luis Ernesto (Montiel) b: 4/29/34, Maracaibo, Venez. BR/TR, 5'9", 160 lbs. Deb: 4/17/56 H

YEAR	TM/L	G	AB	R	H	2B	3B	HR	RBI	BB	SO	AVG	OBP	SLG	PRO+	BR	/A	RC	SB	CS	SBR	FR	POS	TPR
1956	Chi-A	152	533	69	142	19	6	3	56	34	63	.266	.312	.341	71	-22	-23	59	**21**	4	**4**	0	*S	-0.4
1957	Chi-A	143	575	82	148	22	6	3	41	52	55	.257	.319	.332	78	-17	-17	65	**28**	8	4	-13	*S	-1.5
1958	Chi-A	145	557	76	148	20	9	2	40	35	38	.266	.310	.345	82	-15	-14	62	**29**	6	**5**	9	*S	2.1
1959	*Chi-A	152	612	98	157	18	5	6	51	53	40	.257	.319	.332	80	-17	-16	70	**56**	13	9	-4	*S	0.1
1960	Chi-A	153	600	86	166	20	7	2	61	43	39	.277	.326	.343	82	-15	-15	73	**51**	8	**11**	30	*S	**3.8**
1961	Chi-A	156	625	90	170	24	4	6	45	38	33	.272	.315	.352	79	-20	-19	72	**53**	13	8	6	*S	0.6
1962	Chi-A	153	581	72	140	23	5	7	40	32	36	.241	.282	.334	65	-29	-29	54	**31**	12	2	10	*S	-0.7
1963	Bal-A	146	601	73	150	18	8	5	45	36	35	.250	.294	.331	77	-20	-19	62	**40**	6	**8**	-5	*S	-0.8
1964	Bal-A	146	578	93	154	20	3	10	37	49	51	.266	.327	.362	92	-6	-6	71	**57**	17	**7**	3	*S	0.5
1965	Bal-A	144	564	67	127	20	10	8	40	46	56	.225	.287	.339	76	-17	-19	57	26	7	4	3	*S	-0.5
1966	*Bal-A	151	659	97	182	25	8	6	41	33	42	.276	.312	.366	95	-6	-5	74	25	11	1	10	*S	1.5
1967	Bal-A	134	546	55	127	22	5	4	31	29	44	.233	.273	.313	73	-19	-19	47	18	5	2	-19	*S	-2.9
1968	Chi-A	155	622	55	164	24	4	4	36	33	43	.264	.303	.342	92	-6	-7	61	17	11	-2	25	*S	3.1
1969	Chi-A	156	599	77	168	24	5	5	51	66	29	.280	.354	.362	96	2	-2	81	24	4	5	29	*S	4.0
1970	Chi-A	146	552	86	173	29	3	5	43	53	34	.313	.375	.404	110	12	9	85	8	3	1	18	*S	4.1
1971	Bos-A	125	491	56	114	23	0	4	45	35	43	.232	.286	.303	63	-22	-25	44	6	4	-1	-18	*S	-3.3
1972	Bos-A	110	436	47	112	26	3	3	39	26	28	.257	.302	.351	89	-4	-7	45	3	3	-1	-17	*S	-1.4
1973	Bos-A	132	499	56	135	17	1	0	49	43	33	.271	.328	.309	76	-12	-16	53	13	1	3	-16	*S	-1.1
Total	18	2599	10230	1335	2677	394	92	83	791	736	742	.262	.313	.343	82	-235	-246	1137	506	136	70	51	*S	7.2

■ LUKE APPLING
Appling, Lucius Benjamin b: 4/2/09, High Point, N.C. BR/TR, 5'10", 183 lbs. Deb: 9/10/30 MCH

YEAR	TM/L	G	AB	R	H	2B	3B	HR	RBI	BB	SO	AVG	OBP	SLG	PRO+	BR	/A	RC	SB	CS	SBR	FR	POS	TPR
1930	Chi-A	6	26	2	8	2	0	0	2	0	0	.308	.308	.385	77	-1	-1	3	2	0	1	-1	/S	0.0
1931	Chi-A	96	297	36	69	13	4	1	28	29	27	.232	.303	.313	66	-16	-14	30	9	2	2	-6	S/2	-0.9
1932	Chi-A	139	489	66	134	20	10	3	63	40	36	.274	.329	.374	87	-14	-9	60	9	8	-2	18	S23	1.4
1933	Chi-A	151	612	90	197	36	10	6	85	56	29	.322	.379	.443	122	15	18	100	6	11	-5	11	*S	3.4
1934	Chi-A	118	452	75	137	28	6	2	61	59	27	.303	.384	.405	100	4	2	73	3	1	0	-9	*S/2	0.1
1935	Chi-A	153	525	94	161	28	6	1	71	122	40	.307	.437	.389	112	20	17	100	12	6	0	21	*S	4.3
1936	Chi-A	138	526	111	204	31	7	6	128	85	25	**.388**	.474	.508	137	40	37	131	10	6	-1	15	*S	5.3
1937	Chi-A	154	574	98	182	42	8	4	77	86	28	.317	.407	.489	113	14	15	107	18	10	-1	14	*S	3.3
1938	Chi-A	81	294	41	89	14	0	0	44	42	17	.303	.392	.350	85	-4	-5	42	1	3	-2	1	S	0.0
1939	Chi-A	148	516	82	162	16	6	0	56	105	37	.314	.430	.368	103	11	9	90	16	9	-1	-2	*S	1.9
1940	Chi-A	150	566	96	197	27	13	0	79	69	35	.348	.420	.442	122	23	22	109	3	5	-2	-2	*S	2.9
1941	Chi-A	154	592	93	186	26	8	1	57	82	32	.314	.399	.390	111	11	12	98	12	8	-1	0	*S	1.5
1942	Chi-A	142	543	78	142	26	4	3	53	63	23	.262	.342	.341	94	-5	-3	70	17	5	2	-7	*S	0.0
1943	Chi-A	155	585	63	192	33	2	3	80	90	29	**.328**	**.419**	.407	142	35	35	109	27	8	3	7	*S	5.0
1945	Chi-A	18	57	12	21	2	2	1	10	12	7	.368	.478	.526	197	7	8	16	1	0	0	-0	S	0.8
1946	Chi-A	149	582	59	180	27	5	1	55	71	41	.309	.384	.378	118	13	15	88	6	4	-1	7	*S	2.5
1947	Chi-A	139	503	67	154	29	0	8	49	64	28	.306	.386	.412	126	16	18	81	8	6	-1	-7	*S/3	1.0
1948	Chi-A	139	497	63	156	16	2	0	47	94	35	.314	.423	.354	112	12	14	82	10	4	1	12	3S	2.3
1949	Chi-A	142	492	82	148	21	5	5	58	121	24	.301	.439	.394	125	22	25	90	7	12	-5	-1	*S	1.9
1950	Chi-A	50	128	11	30	3	4	0	13	12	8	.234	.300	.320	61	-8	-8	12	2	0	1	0	S1/2	-0.5
Total	20	2422	8856	1319	2749	440	102	45	1116	1302	528	.310	.399	.398	113	196	209	1493	179	108	-11	73	*S/321	36.2

■ JACK ARAGON
Aragon, Angel Valdes (Reyes) b: 11/20/15, Havana, Cuba d: 4/4/88, Clearwater, Fla. BR/TR, 5'10", 176 lbs. Deb: 8/13/41

YEAR	TM/L	G	AB	R	H	2B	3B	HR	RBI	BB	SO	AVG	OBP	SLG	PRO+	BR	/A	RC	SB	CS	SBR	FR	POS	TPR
1941	NY-N	1	0	0	0	0	0	0	0	0	0	—	—	—		0	0	0	0			0	R	0.0

■ ANGEL ARAGON
Aragon, Angel (Valdes) "Pete" b: 8/2/1890, Havana, Cuba d: 1/24/52, New York, N.Y. BR/TR, 5'5", 150 lbs. Deb: 8/20/14

YEAR	TM/L	G	AB	R	H	2B	3B	HR	RBI	BB	SO	AVG	OBP	SLG	PRO+	BR	/A	RC	SB	CS	SBR	FR	POS	TPR
1914	NY-A	6	7	1	1	0	0	0	0	1	2	.143	.333	.143	44	-0	-0	1	0			-0	/O	0.0
1916	NY-A	12	24	1	5	0	0	0	3	2	2	.208	.269	.208	43	-2	-2	2	2			1	/3O	0.0
1917	NY-A	14	45	2	3	1	0	0	2	2	2	.067	.106	.089	-40	-8	-8	1	0			1	/O3S	-0.7
Total	3	32	76	4	9	1	0	0	5	5	6	.118	.183	.132	-4	-10	-10	3	2			2	/3OS	-0.7

■ MAURICE ARCHDEACON
Archdeacon, Maurice John "Flash" b: 12/14/1898, St.Louis, Mo. d: 9/5/54, St.Louis, Mo. BL/TL, 5'8", 153 lbs. Deb: 9/17/23

YEAR	TM/L	G	AB	R	H	2B	3B	HR	RBI	BB	SO	AVG	OBP	SLG	PRO+	BR	/A	RC	SB	CS	SBR	FR	POS	TPR
1923	Chi-A	22	87	23	35	5	1	0	4	6	8	.402	.441	.483	145	5	6	17	2	3	-1	-2	O	0.1

YEAR	TM/L	G	AB	R	H	2B	3B	HR	RBI	BB	SO	AVG	OBP	SLG	PRO+	BR	/A	RC	SB	CS	SBR	FR	POS	TPR
1924	Chi-A	95	288	59	92	9	3	0	25	40	30	.319	.410	.372	106	3	5	47	11	7	-1	-5	O	-0.5
1925	Chi-A	10	9	2	1	0	0	0	0	2	1	.111	.273	.111	0	-1	-1	0	0	0	0	0	/O	0.0
Total	3	127	384	84	128	14	4	0	29	48	39	.333	.413	.391	112	7	9	65	13	10	-2	-7	/O	-0.4

■ JIMMY ARCHER
Archer, James Patrick   b: 5/13/1883, Dublin, Ireland   d: 3/29/58, Milwaukee, Wis.   BR/TR, 5'10", 168 lbs.   Deb: 9/06/04

YEAR	TM/L	G	AB	R	H	2B	3B	HR	RBI	BB	SO	AVG	OBP	SLG	PRO+	BR	/A	RC	SB	CS	SBR	FR	POS	TPR
1904	Pit-N	7	20	1	3	0	0	0	1	0		.150	.150	.150	-6	-2	-2	0	0			0	/CO	-0.1
1907	*Det-A	18	42	6	5	0	0	0	0	4		.119	.196	.119	2	-4	-5	1	0			2	C/2	0.0
1909	Chi-N	80	261	31	60	9	2	1	30	12		.230	.266	.291	71	-9	-10	22	5			-5	C	-0.9
1910	*Chi-N	98	313	36	81	17	6	2	41	14	49	.259	.293	.371	94	-5	-4	36	6			3	C1	0.0
1911	Chi-N	116	387	41	98	18	5	4	41	18	43	.253	.288	.357	80	-12	-12	41	5			-1	*C1/2	-0.6
1912	Chi-N	120	385	35	109	20	1	6	58	22	36	.283	.330	.387	96	-3	-3	51	7			-5	*C	-0.1
1913	Chi-N	111	368	38	98	14	7	2	44	19	27	.266	.311	.359	91	-5	-5	41	4			1	*C/1	0.2
1914	Chi-N	79	248	17	64	9	2	0	19	9	9	.258	.284	.310	77	-8	-8	21	1			6	C	0.1
1915	Chi-N	97	309	21	75	11	5	1	27	11	38	.243	.273	.320	79	-9	-9	27	5	6	-2	-1	C/1	-0.6
1916	Chi-N	77	205	11	45	6	2	1	30	12	24	.220	.269	.283	63	-7	-10	18	3			-4	C/3	-1.1
1917	Chi-N	2	2	0	0	0	0	0	0	0	1	.000	.000	.000	-93	-0	-0	0	0			0	H	0.0
1918	Pit-N	24	58	4	9	1	2	0	3	1	6	.155	.197	.241	32	-5	-5	3	0			4	C/1	0.1
	Bro-N	9	22	3	6	0	1	0	0	1	5	.273	.304	.364	104	-0	0	2	0			1	/C	0.2
	Cin-N	9	26	2	7	1	0	0	2	1	3	.269	.296	.308	86	-1	-0	2	0			2	/C1	0.2
	Yr	42	106	9	22	2	3	0	5	3	14	.208	.243	.283	59	-5	-5	7	0			7		0.5
Total	12	847	2646	246	660	106	33	17	296	124	241	.249	.288	.334	80	-70	-74	266	36	6		4	C/1230	-2.6

■ GEORGE ARCHIE
Archie, George Albert   b: 4/27/14, Nashville, Tenn.   BR/TR, 6', 170 lbs.   Deb: 9/14/38

YEAR	TM/L	G	AB	R	H	2B	3B	HR	RBI	BB	SO	AVG	OBP	SLG	PRO+	BR	/A	RC	SB	CS	SBR	FR	POS	TPR
1938	Det-A	3	2	1	0	0	0	0	0	0	1	.000	.000	.000	-95	-1	-1	0	0	0	0	0	H	0.0
1941	Was-A	105	379	45	102	20	4	3	48	30	42	.269	.324	.367	87	-10	-8	45	8	4	0	-4	31	-0.8
	StL-A	9	29	3	11	3	0	0	5	7	3	.379	.500	.483	156	3	3	8	2	0	1	0	/1	0.3
	Yr	114	408	48	113	23	4	3	53	37	45	.277	.339	.375	92	-7	-5	52	10	4	1	-4		-0.5
1946	StL-A	4	11	1	2	1	0	0	0	0	1	.182	.182	.273	25	-1	-1	1	0	0	0	2	/1	0.0
Total	3	121	421	50	115	24	4	3	53	37	47	.273	.333	.371	90	-9	-6	53	10	4	1	-2	/31	-0.5

■ JOSE ARCIA
Arcia, Jose Raimundo (Orta)   b: 8/22/43, Havana, Cuba   BR/TR, 6'3", 170 lbs.   Deb: 4/10/68

YEAR	TM/L	G	AB	R	H	2B	3B	HR	RBI	BB	SO	AVG	OBP	SLG	PRO+	BR	/A	RC	SB	CS	SBR	FR	POS	TPR
1968	Chi-N	59	84	15	16	4	0	0	8	3	24	.190	.218	.274	44	-6	-6	5	0	0	0	2	O2/S3	-0.3
1969	SD-N	120	302	35	65	11	3	0	10	14	47	.215	.255	.272	49	-21	-20	20	14	7	0	6	2S/3O1	-0.4
1970	SD-N	114	229	28	51	9	3	0	17	12	36	.223	.282	.288	55	-15	-14	18	3	6	-3	12	S2/3O	0.5
Total	3	293	615	78	132	24	6	1	35	29	107	.215	.260	.278	51	-42	-40	43	17	13	-3	20	S/2031	-0.2

■ DAN ARDELL
Ardell, Daniel Miers   b: 5/27/41, Seattle, Wash.   BL/TL, 6'2", 190 lbs.   Deb: 9/14/61

YEAR	TM/L	G	AB	R	H	2B	3B	HR	RBI	BB	SO	AVG	OBP	SLG	PRO+	BR	/A	RC	SB	CS	SBR	FR	POS	TPR
1961	LA-A	7	4	1	1	0	0	0	0	1	2	.250	.400	.250	70	-0	-0	1	0	0	0	0	/1	0.0

■ JOE ARDNER
Ardner, Joseph A. "Old Hoss"   b: 2/27/1858, Mt.Vernon, Ohio   d: 9/15/35, Cleveland, Ohio   BR/TR, 160 lbs.   Deb: 5/01/1884

YEAR	TM/L	G	AB	R	H	2B	3B	HR	RBI	BB	SO	AVG	OBP	SLG	PRO+	BR	/A	RC	SB	CS	SBR	FR	POS	TPR
1884	Cle-N	26	92	6	16	1	1	0	4	1	24	.174	.183	.207	21	-8	-8	4				-5	2/3	-1.1
1890	Cle-N	84	323	28	72	13	1	0	35	17	40	.223	.266	.269	59	-17	-16	26	9			-5	2	-1.5
Total	2	110	415	34	88	14	2	0	39	18	64	.212	.248	.255	51	-25	-25	30	9			-9	2/3	-2.6

■ HANK ARFT
Arft, Henry Irven "Bow Wow"   b: 1/28/22, Manchester, Mo.   BL/TL, 5'10.5", 190 lbs.   Deb: 7/27/48

YEAR	TM/L	G	AB	R	H	2B	3B	HR	RBI	BB	SO	AVG	OBP	SLG	PRO+	BR	/A	RC	SB	CS	SBR	FR	POS	TPR
1948	StL-A	69	248	25	59	10	3	5	38	45	43	.238	.355	.363	89	-3	-3	34	1	2	-1	-0	1	0.0
1949	StL-A	6	5	1	1	1	0	0	2	0	1	.200	.200	.400	55	-0	-0	0	0	0	0	0	H	0.0
1950	StL-A	98	280	45	75	16	4	1	32	46	48	.268	.375	.364	87	-3	-5	43	3	2	-0	2	1	-0.6
1951	StL-A	112	345	44	90	16	5	7	42	41	34	.261	.339	.397	96	-1	-2	48	4	6	-2	8	1	0.1
1952	StL-A	15	28	1	4	3	1	0	4	5	7	.143	.273	.321	63	-1	-2	3	0	0	0	-0	1	-0.2
Total	5	300	906	116	229	46	13	13	118	137	133	.253	.352	.375	90	-8	-12	128	8	10	-4	9	1	-0.7

■ BUZZ ARLETT
Arlett, Russell Loris   b: 1/3/1899, Elmhurst, Cal.   d: 5/16/64, Minneapolis, Minn.   BB/TR, 6'3.5", 225 lbs.   Deb: 4/14/31

YEAR	TM/L	G	AB	R	H	2B	3B	HR	RBI	BB	SO	AVG	OBP	SLG	PRO+	BR	/A	RC	SB	CS	SBR	FR	POS	TPR
1931	Phi-N	121	418	65	131	26	7	18	72	45	39	.313	.387	.538	135	27	22	90	3			4	O1	2.0

■ TONY ARMAS
Armas, Antonio Rafael (Machado)   b: 7/2/53, Anzoategui, Venez.   BR/TR, 5'11", 182 lbs.   Deb: 9/06/76

YEAR	TM/L	G	AB	R	H	2B	3B	HR	RBI	BB	SO	AVG	OBP	SLG	PRO+	BR	/A	RC	SB	CS	SBR	FR	POS	TPR
1976	Pit-N	4	6	0	2	0	0	0	1	0	2	.333	.333	.333	89	-0	-0	1	0	0	0	0	/O	0.0
1977	Oak-A	118	363	26	87	8	2	13	53	20	99	.240	.279	.380	79	-12	-11	37	1	2	-1	2	*O/S	-1.3
1978	Oak-A	91	239	17	51	6	1	2	13	10	62	.213	.251	.272	50	-17	-15	16	1	2	-1	8	O/D	-0.9
1979	Oak-A	80	278	29	69	9	3	11	34	16	67	.248	.292	.421	95	-5	-3	33	1	0	0	8	O/D	0.2
1980	Oak-A	158	628	87	175	18	8	35	109	29	128	.279	.313	.500	128	13	18	89	5	3	-0	12	*O	2.6
1981	*Oak-A	109	440	51	115	24	3	22	76	19	115	.261	.295	.480	126	9	11	61	5	1	1	6	*O	1.6
1982	Oak-A	138	536	58	125	19	2	28	89	33	128	.233	.279	.433	96	-8	-5	61	2	2	-1	8	*O/D	-0.1
1983	Bos-A	145	574	77	125	23	2	36	107	29	131	.218	.258	.453	85	-10	-15	55	0	1	-1	2	*OD	-1.4
1984	Bos-A	157	639	107	171	29	5	43	123	32	156	.268	.304	.531	120	18	18	97	1	3	-2	-5	*OD	0.4
1985	Bos-A	103	385	50	102	17	5	23	64	18	90	.265	.301	.514	114	8	6	54	0	0	0	-3	OD	0.3
1986	*Bos-A	121	425	40	112	21	4	11	58	24	77	.264	.306	.409	92	-5	-5	49	0	3	-2	-12	*O/D	-2.1
1987	Cal-A	28	81	8	16	3	1	3	9	1	11	.198	.207	.370	51	-6	-6	5	1	0	0	-3	O	-0.8
1988	Cal-A	120	368	42	100	20	2	13	49	22	87	.272	.313	.443	112	3	4	46	1	3	-2	-4	*O/D	-0.4
1989	Cal-A	60	202	22	52	7	1	11	30	7	48	.257	.282	.465	109	1	1	26	0	0	0	5	O/1D	0.5
Total	14	1432	5164	614	1302	204	39	251	815	260	1201	.252	.290	.453	103	-12	-6	629	18	20	-7	22	*O/D1S	-1.6

■ ED ARMBRISTER
Armbrister, Edison Rosanda   b: 7/4/48, Nassau, Bahamas   BR/TR, 5'11", 160 lbs.   Deb: 8/31/73

YEAR	TM/L	G	AB	R	H	2B	3B	HR	RBI	BB	SO	AVG	OBP	SLG	PRO+	BR	/A	RC	SB	CS	SBR	FR	POS	TPR
1973	*Cin-N	18	37	5	8	3	1	1	5	2	8	.216	.256	.432	92	-1	-1	4	0	0	0	0	O	0.0
1974	Cin-N	9	7	0	2	0	0	0	0	1	1	.286	.375	.286	88	-0	-0	1	0	0	0	0	/O	0.0
1975	*Cin-N	59	65	9	12	1	0	0	2	5	19	.185	.254	.200	27	-6	-6	4	3	1	0	-2	O	-0.8
1976	*Cin-N	73	78	20	23	3	2	2	7	6	22	.295	.345	.462	124	3	2	13	7	3	0	4	O	0.5
1977	Cin-N	65	78	12	20	4	3	1	5	10	21	.256	.341	.423	102	0	0	9	5	6	-2	1	O	-0.1
Total	5	224	265	46	65	11	6	4	19	24	71	.245	.310	.377	88	-4	-5	31	15	10	-2	3	/O	-0.4

■ CHARLIE ARMBRUSTER
Armbruster, Charles A.   b: 8/30/1880, Cincinnati, Ohio   d: 10/7/64, Grants Pass, Ore.   TR, 5'9", 180 lbs.   Deb: 7/17/05

YEAR	TM/L	G	AB	R	H	2B	3B	HR	RBI	BB	SO	AVG	OBP	SLG	PRO+	BR	/A	RC	SB	CS	SBR	FR	POS	TPR
1905	Bos-A	35	91	13	18	4	0	0	6	18		.198	.330	.242	84	-1	-1	9	3			-6	C	-0.2
1906	Bos-A	72	201	9	29	6	1	0	6	25		.144	.239	.184	34	-14	-14	10	2			1	C/1	-0.8
1907	Bos-A	23	60	2	6	1	0	0	0	8		.100	.206	.117	5	-6	-6	2	1			2	C	-0.1
	Chi-A	1	3	0	0	0	0	0	0	1		.000	.250	.000	-18	-0	-0	0	0			1	/C	0.0
	Yr	24	63	2	6	1	0	0	0	9		.095	.208	.111	4	-6	-6	2	1			3		-0.1
Total	3	131	355	24	53	11	1	0	12	52		.149	.258	.186	42	-21	-21	21	6			-2	C/1	-1.1

■ HARRY ARMBRUSTER
Armbruster, Henry "Army"   b: 3/20/1882, Cincinnati, Ohio   d: 12/10/53, Cincinnati, Ohio   BL/TL, 5'10", 190 lbs.   Deb: 4/30/06

YEAR	TM/L	G	AB	R	H	2B	3B	HR	RBI	BB	SO	AVG	OBP	SLG	PRO+	BR	/A	RC	SB	CS	SBR	FR	POS	TPR
1906	Phi-A	91	265	40	63	6	3	2	24	43		.238	.344	.306	103	4	3	36	13			0	O	0.0

■ GEORGE ARMSTRONG
Armstrong, George Noble "Dodo"   b: 6/3/24, Orange, N.J.   BR/TR. 5'10", 190 lbs.   Deb: 4/26/46

YEAR	TM/L	G	AB	R	H	2B	3B	HR	RBI	BB	SO	AVG	OBP	SLG	PRO+	BR	/A	RC	SB	CS	SBR	FR	POS	TPR
1946	Phi-A	8	6	0	1	1	0	0	0	1		.167	.286	.333	73	-0	-0	1	0	0	0	1	/C	0.0

■ SAM ARMSTRONG
Armstrong, Samuel   b: 1850, Baltimore, Md.   6'2", 160 lbs.   Deb: 6/26/1871

YEAR	TM/L	G	AB	R	H	2B	3B	HR	RBI	BB	SO	AVG	OBP	SLG	PRO+	BR	/A	RC	SB	CS	SBR	FR	POS	TPR
1871	Kek-n	12	49	9	11	2	1	0	5	0	1	.224	.224	.306	50	-3	-3	3	0				O	-0.1

YEAR	TM/L	G	AB	R	H	2B	3B	HR	RBI	BB	SO	AVG	OBP	SLG	PRO+	BR	/A	RC	SB	CS	SBR	FR	POS	TPR

■ HARRY ARNDT   Arndt, Harry J.   b: 2/12/1879, South Bend, Ind.   d: 3/24/21, South Bend, Ind.   TR,   Deb: 7/02/02

1902	Det-A	10	34	4	5	0	1	0	7	6		.147	.275	.206	35	-3	-3	2	0			0	O/1	-0.2
	Bal-A	68	248	41	63	7	4	2	28	35		.254	.353	.339	90	-1	-2	34	9			1	O/23S	-0.4
	Yr	78	282	45	68	7	5	2	35	41		.241	.344	.323	84	-3	-5	36	9			1		-0.6
1905	StL-N	113	415	40	101	11	6	2	36	24		.243	.285	.313	82	-11	-9	43	13			-14	2/O3S	-1.8
1906	StL-N	69	256	30	69	7	9	2	26	19		.270	.320	.391	129	6	7	35	5			12	3/1O	1.8
1907	StL-N	11	32	3	6	1	0	0	2	1		.188	.212	.219	38	-2	-2	2	0			0	/13	-0.1
Total	4	271	985	118	244	26	20	6	99	85		.248	.309	.333	93	-10	-9	116	27			-1	/2O3S1	-0.7

■ LARRY ARNDT   Arndt, Larry Wayne   b: 2/25/63, Fremont, Ohio   BR/TR, 6'1", 195 lbs.   Deb: 6/06/89

| 1989 | Oak-A | 2 | 6 | 1 | 1 | 0 | 0 | 0 | 0 | 0 | 1 | .167 | .167 | .167 | -6 | -1 | -1 | 0 | 0 | 0 | 0 | 0 | /13 | 0.0 |

■ CHRIS ARNOLD   Arnold, Christopher Paul   b: 11/6/47, Long Beach, Cal.   BR/TR, 5'10", 160 lbs.   Deb: 9/07/71

1971	SF-N	6	13	2	3	0	0	1	3	1	2	.231	.286	.462	110	0	0	2	0	0	0	-1	/2	0.0
1972	SF-N	51	84	8	19	3	1	1	4	8	12	.226	.293	.321	74	-3	-3	7	0	1	-1	3	3/2S	0.0
1973	SF-N	49	54	7	16	2	0	1	13	8	11	.296	.387	.389	111	1	1	8	0	0	0	-4	/C23	-0.2
1974	SF-N	78	174	22	42	7	3	1	26	15	27	.241	.305	.333	75	-5	-6	19	1	1	-0	-6	2/3S	-1.0
1975	SF-N	29	41	4	8	0	0	0	4	4	8	.195	.267	.195	28	-4	-4	2	0	0	0	1	/2O	-0.3
1976	SF-N	60	69	4	15	0	1	0	5	6	16	.217	.280	.246	49	-4	-5	4	0	0	0	3	/231S	0.0
Total	6	273	435	47	103	12	5	4	51	42	76	.237	.305	.315	72	-15	-16	42	1	2	-1	-4	/23CS01	-1.5

■ BILLY ARNOLD   Arnold, Willis S.   b: 3/2/1851, Middletown, Conn.   d: 1/17/1899, Albany, N.Y.   Deb: 4/26/1872

| 1872 | Man-n | 2 | 8 | 2 | 1 | 0 | 0 | 0 | | 0 | | .125 | .125 | .125 | -24 | -1 | -1 | 0 | | | | | /O | 0.0 |

■ MORRIE ARNOVICH   Arnovich, Morris "Snooker"   b: 11/16/10, Superior, Wis.   d: 7/20/59, Superior, Wis.   BR/TR, 5'10", 168 lbs.   Deb: 9/14/36

1936	Phi-N	13	48	4	15	3	0	1	7	1	3	.313	.353	.438	102	1	0	7	0			2	O	0.2
1937	Phi-N	117	410	60	119	27	4	10	60	34	32	.290	.349	.449	107	8	4	63	5			6	*O	0.4
1938	Phi-N	139	502	47	138	29	0	4	72	42	37	.275	.333	.357	92	-7	-5	60	2			18	*O	1.0
1939	Phi-N	134	491	68	159	25	2	5	67	58	28	.324	.397	.413	122	15	17	83	7			12	*O	2.6
1940	Phi-N	39	141	13	28	2	1	0	12	14	15	.199	.276	.227	42	-11	-10	9	0			1	O	-1.0
	*Cin-N	62	211	17	60	10	2	0	21	13	10	.284	.326	.351	86	-4	-4	23	1			3	O	-0.3
	Yr	101	352	30	88	12	3	0	33	27	25	.250	.305	.301	68	-15	-15	31	1			4		-1.3
1941	NY-N	85	207	25	58	8	3	2	22	23	14	.280	.352	.377	103	2	1	27	2			1	O	0.0
1946	NY-N	1	3	0	0	0	0	0	0	0	0	.000	.000	.000	-99	-1	-1	0	0			-0	/O	-0.1
Total	7	590	2013	234	577	104	12	22	261	185	139	.287	.350	.383	100	3	1	272	17			43	O	2.9

■ TUG ARUNDEL   Arundel, John Thomas   b: 6/30/1862, Romulus, N.Y.   d: 9/5/12, Auburn, N.Y.   Deb: 5/23/1882

1882	Phi-a	1	5	0	0	0	0	0		0		.000	.000	.000	-90	-1	-1	0				0	/C	0.0
1884	Tol-a	15	47	6	4	0	0	0		3		.085	.140	.085	-23	-6	-6	1				8	C	0.3
1887	Ind-N	43	157	13	31	4	0	0	13	8	12	.197	.241	.223	32	-14	-13	11	8			-3	C/O1	-0.9
1888	Was-N	17	51	2	10	0	1	0	3	5	10	.196	.268	.235	67	-2	-2	4	1			-5	C	-0.5
Total	4	76	260	21	45	4	1	0	16	16	22	.173	.224	.196	27	-23	-22	15	9			1	/CO1	-1.1

■ RANDY ASADOOR   Asadoor, Randall Carl   b: 10/20/62, Fresno, Cal.   BR/TR, 6'1", 185 lbs.   Deb: 9/14/86

| 1986 | SD-N | 15 | 55 | 9 | 20 | 5 | 0 | 0 | 7 | 3 | 13 | .364 | .397 | .455 | 137 | 3 | 3 | 9 | 1 | 2 | -1 | 0 | 3/2 | 0.2 |

■ JIM ASBELL   Asbell, James Marion "Big Train"   b: 6/22/14, Dallas Tex.   d: 7/6/67, San Mateo, Cal.   BR/TR, 6', 195 lbs.   Deb: 5/08/38

| 1938 | Chi-N | 17 | 33 | 6 | 6 | 2 | 0 | 0 | 3 | 3 | 9 | .182 | .250 | .242 | 35 | -3 | -3 | 2 | 0 | | | 0 | O | -0.2 |

■ CASPER ASBJORNSON   Asbjornson, Robert Anthony (Name Changed To Asby)   b: 6/19/09, Concord, Mass.   d: 1/21/70, Williamsport, Pa.   BR/TR, 6'1", 196 lbs.   Deb: 9/17/28

1928	Bos-A	6	16	0	3	1	0	0	1	1	1	.188	.235	.250	28	-2	-2	1	0	0	0	-2	/C	-0.2
1929	Bos-A	17	29	1	3	0	0	0	0	1	6	.103	.133	.103	-39	-6	-6	0	0	0	0	-2	C	-0.6
1931	Cin-N	45	118	13	36	7	1	0	22	7	23	.305	.349	.381	102	-1	0	16	0			0	C	0.2
1932	Cin-N	29	58	5	10	2	0	1	4	0	15	.172	.186	.259	19	-7	-6	3	0			0	C	-0.5
Total	4	97	221	19	52	10	1	1	27	9	45	.235	.272	.303	56	-15	-14	20	0		0	-4	/C	-1.1

■ RICHIE ASHBURN   Ashburn, Rich "Whitey"   b: 3/19/27, Tilden, Neb.   BL/TR, 5'10", 170 lbs.   Deb: 4/20/48

1948	Phi-N	117	463	78	154	17	4	2	40	60	22	.333	.410	.400	122	16	17	82	**32**			13	*O	2.1
1949	Phi-N	154	662	84	188	18	11	1	37	58	38	.284	.343	.349	88	-12	-10	82	9			19	*O	0.0
1950	*Phi-N	151	594	84	180	25	**14**	2	41	63	32	.303	.372	.402	105	4	6	91	14			3	*O	0.4
1951	Phi-N	154	643	92	**221**	31	5	4	63	50	37	.344	.393	.426	122	19	21	118	29	6	5	**25**	*O	4.5
1952	Phi-N	154	613	93	173	31	6	1	42	75	30	.282	.362	.357	101	2	3	86	16	11	-2	13	*O	1.1
1953	Phi-N	156	622	110	**205**	25	9	2	57	61	35	.330	.394	.408	110	11	12	109	14	6	1	22	*O	2.7
1954	Phi-N	153	559	111	175	16	8	1	41	**125**	46	.313	**.442**	.376	116	22	22	107	11	8	-2	13	*O	2.7
1955	Phi-N	140	533	91	180	32	9	3	42	105	36	**.338**	**.449**	.448	142	37	38	117	12	10	-2	6	*O	3.9
1956	Phi-N	154	628	94	190	26	8	3	50	79	45	.303	.385	.384	110	10	11	101	10	1	2	21	*O	2.9
1957	Phi-N	156	626	93	186	26	8	0	33	**94**	44	.297	.392	.364	108	9	12	95	13	10	-2	**27**	*O	3.2
1958	Phi-N	152	615	98	**215**	24	**13**	2	33	**97**	48	**.350**	**.441**	.441	136	36	38	129	30	12	2	15	*O	4.9
1959	Phi-N	153	564	86	150	16	2	1	20	79	42	.266	.362	.307	79	-12	-13	66	9	11	-4	-3	*O	-2.1
1960	Chi-N	151	547	99	159	16	5	0	40	**116**	50	.291	**.416**	.338	110	14	15	91	16	4	2	-7	*O	0.6
1961	Chi-N	109	307	49	79	7	4	0	19	55	27	.257	.375	.306	83	-5	-5	39	7	6	-2	-8	O	-1.8
1962	NY-N	135	389	60	119	7	3	7	28	81	39	.306	.426	.393	119	17	16	72	12	7	-1	4	O/2	1.4
Total	15	2189	8365	1322	2574	317	109	29	586	1198	571	.308	.397	.382	111	169	182	1386	234	92		163	*O/2	26.5

■ ALAN ASHBY   Ashby, Alan Dean   b: 7/8/51, Long Beach, Cal.   BB/TR, 6'2", 185 lbs.   Deb: 7/03/73

1973	Cle-A	11	29	4	5	1	0	1	3	2	11	.172	.226	.310	49	-2	-2	2	0	0	0	-2	C	-0.3
1974	Cle-A	10	7	1	1	0	0	0	0	1	2	.143	.250	.143	15	-1	-1	0	0	0	0	1	/C	0.0
1975	Cle-A	90	254	32	57	10	1	5	32	30	42	.224	.309	.331	81	-6	-6	26	3	2	-0	3	C/13D	0.0
1976	Cle-A	89	247	26	59	5	1	4	32	27	49	.239	.314	.316	86	-4	-4	24	0	2	-1	5	C/13	0.3
1977	Tor-A	124	396	25	83	16	3	2	29	50	51	.210	.301	.280	59	-21	-22	34	0	2	-1	-7	*C	-2.6
1978	Tor-A	81	264	27	69	15	0	9	29	28	32	.261	.334	.420	109	4	3	35	1	1	-0	-9	C	-0.4
1979	Hou-N	108	336	25	68	15	2	2	35	26	70	.202	.264	.277	51	-24	-22	24	0	0	0	-1	*C	-2.1
1980	*Hou-N	116	352	30	90	19	2	3	48	35	40	.256	.323	.347	94	-6	-3	38	0	0	0	4	*C	0.4
1981	*Hou-N	83	255	20	69	13	0	4	33	35	33	.271	.359	.369	112	3	5	34	0	2	-1	7	C	1.2
1982	Hou-N	100	339	40	87	14	2	12	49	27	53	.257	.313	.416	111	0	3	44	2	0	1	-4	C	0.0
1983	Hou-N	87	275	31	63	18	1	8	34	31	38	.229	.307	.389	98	-4	-1	31	0	0	0	-12	C	-1.1
1984	Hou-N	66	191	16	50	7	0	4	27	20	22	.262	.335	.361	103	-1	1	24	0	0	0	-1	C	0.2
1985	Hou-N	65	189	20	53	8	0	8	25	24	27	.280	.364	.450	130	7	8	29	0	0	0	1	C	1.2
1986	*Hou-N	120	315	24	81	15	0	7	38	39	56	.257	.339	.371	98	-1	-0	40	1	0	0	-4	*C	-0.1
1987	Hou-N	125	386	53	111	16	0	14	63	50	52	.288	.371	.438	118	8	10	61	0	1	-1	-4	*C	1.4
1988	Hou-N	73	227	19	54	7	0	7	33	29	36	.238	.324	.388	104	0	1	28	0	0	0	-11	C	-0.6
1989	Hou-N	22	61	4	10	1	0	0	3	7	8	.164	.261	.213	38	-5	-5	4	0	0	0	-3	C	-0.6
Total	17	1370	4123	397	1010	183	13	90	513	461	622	.245	.323	.361	93	-53	-35	478	7	10	-4	-37	*C/13D	-3.1

YEAR	TM/L	G	AB	R	H	2B	3B	HR	RBI	BB	SO	AVG	OBP	SLG	PRO+	BR	/A	RC	SB	CS	SBR	FR	POS	TPR

■ TUCKER ASHFORD
Ashford, Thomas Steven b: 12/4/54, Memphis, Tenn.   BR/TR, 6'1", 195 lbs.   Deb: 9/21/76

YEAR	TM/L	G	AB	R	H	2B	3B	HR	RBI	BB	SO	AVG	OBP	SLG	PRO+	BR	/A	RC	SB	CS	SBR	FR	POS	TPR
1976	SD-N	4	5	0	3	1	0	0	0	1	0	.600	.667	.800	343	2	2	4	2	0	1	0	/3	0.2
1977	SD-N	81	249	25	54	18	0	3	24	21	35	.217	.280	.325	69	-14	-10	22	2	3	-1	2	3S/2	-0.7
1978	SD-N	75	155	11	38	11	0	3	26	14	31	.245	.308	.374	97	-2	-1	18	1	0	0	-16	321	-1.7
1980	Tex-A	15	32	2	4	0	0	0	3	3	3	.125	.200	.125	-9	-5	-5	1	0	0	0	3	3/S	-0.1
1981	NY-A	3	0	0	0	0	0	0	0	0	0	—	—	—	—	0	0	0	0	0	0	0	/2	0.0
1983	NY-N	35	56	3	10	0	1	0	2	7	4	.179	.270	.214	36	-5	-5	3	0	0	0	-1	32/C	-0.5
1984	KC-A	9	13	1	2	1	0	0	0	1	2	.154	.214	.231	23	-1	-1	0	0	0	0	0	/3	0.0
Total	7	222	510	42	111	31	1	6	55	47	75	.218	.285	.318	70	-25	-20	48	5	3	-0	-12	3/21SC	-2.8

■ TOM ASMUSSEN
Asmussen, Thomas William b: 9/26/1876, Chicago, Ill. d: 8/21/63, Arlington Heights Ill.   TR ,   Deb: 8/10/07

YEAR	TM/L	G	AB	R	H	2B	3B	HR	RBI	BB	SO	AVG	OBP	SLG	PRO+	BR	/A	RC	SB	CS	SBR	FR	POS	TPR
1907	Bos-N	2	5	0	0	0	0	0	0	0	0	.000	.000	.000	-99	-1	-1	0	0			-1	/C	-0.1

■ KEN ASPROMONTE
Aspromonte, Kenneth Joseph b: 9/22/31, Brooklyn, N.Y.   BR/TR, 6', 180 lbs.   Deb: 9/02/57   M

YEAR	TM/L	G	AB	R	H	2B	3B	HR	RBI	BB	SO	AVG	OBP	SLG	PRO+	BR	/A	RC	SB	CS	SBR	FR	POS	TPR
1957	Bos-A	24	78	9	21	5	0	0	4	17	10	.269	.400	.333	97	1	1	11	0	1	-1	-3	2	-0.1
1958	Bos-A	6	16	0	2	0	0	0	0	3	1	.125	.263	.125	10	-2	-2	1	0	0	0	-3	/2	-0.4
	Was-A	92	253	15	57	9	1	5	27	25	28	.225	.297	.328	73	-10	-9	23	1	1	-0	3	23/S	0.0
	Yr	98	269	15	59	9	1	5	27	28	29	.219	.295	.316	69	-12	-11	24	1	1	-0	-0		-0.4
1959	Was-A	70	225	31	55	12	0	2	14	26	39	.244	.323	.324	79	-6	-6	23	2	1	0	-9	2S/1O	-1.2
1960	Was-A	4	3	0	0	0	0	0	0	0	1	.000	.000	.000	-99	-1	-1	0	0	0	0	0	H	0.0
	Cle-A	117	459	65	133	20	1	10	48	53	32	.290	.366	.403	111	6	8	69	4	1	1	-12	23	0.2
	Yr	121	462	65	133	20	1	10	48	53	33	.288	.364	.400	110	5	7	69	4	1	1	-12		0.2
1961	LA-A	66	238	29	53	10	0	2	14	33	21	.223	.322	.290	58	-11	-15	24	0	0	0	18	2	1.0
	Cle-A	22	70	5	16	6	1	0	5	6	3	.229	.289	.343	70	-3	-3	6	0	0	0	-1	2	-0.1
	Yr	88	308	34	69	16	1	2	19	39	24	.224	.315	.302	61	-14	-18	31	0	0	0	17		0.9
1962	Cle-A	20	28	4	4	2	0	0	1	6	5	.143	.294	.214	41	-2	-2	2	0	0	0	-1	/23	-0.2
	Mil-N	34	79	11	23	2	0	0	7	6	5	.291	.349	.316	82	-2	-2	7	0	1	-1	-0	2/3	0.0
1963	Chi-N	20	34	2	5	3	0	0	4	4	4	.147	.237	.235	35	-3	-3	2	0	0	0	3	/21	0.0
Total	7	475	1483	171	369	69	3	19	124	179	149	.249	.332	.338	82	-33	-34	169	7	5	-1	-6	2/3S10	-0.8

■ BOB ASPROMONTE
Aspromonte, Robert Thomas b: 6/19/38, Brooklyn, N.Y.   BR/TR, 6'2", 170 lbs.   Deb: 9/19/56

YEAR	TM/L	G	AB	R	H	2B	3B	HR	RBI	BB	SO	AVG	OBP	SLG	PRO+	BR	/A	RC	SB	CS	SBR	FR	POS	TPR
1956	Bro-N	1	1	0	0	0	0	0	0	0	1	.000	.000	.000	-93	-0	-0	0	0	0	0	0	H	0.0
1960	LA-N	21	55	1	10	1	0	1	6	0	6	.182	.196	.255	21	-6	-6	3	1	0	0	-2	S/3	-0.7
1961	LA-N	47	58	7	14	3	0	0	2	4	12	.241	.290	.293	51	-4	-4	5	0	0	0	-0	/3S2	-0.3
1962	Hou-N	149	534	59	142	18	4	11	59	46	54	.266	.333	.376	97	-7	-2	67	4	5	-2	1	*3S/2	0.2
1963	Hou-N	136	468	42	100	9	5	8	49	40	57	.214	.277	.306	72	-19	-16	38	3	1	0	-16	*3/1	-3.3
1964	Hou-N	157	553	51	155	20	3	12	69	35	54	.280	.332	.392	109	2	6	69	6	7	-2	-15	*3	-2.1
1965	Hou-N	152	578	53	152	15	2	5	52	38	54	.263	.312	.322	85	-16	-11	57	2	2	-1	1	*3/1S	-1.7
1966	Hou-N	152	560	55	141	16	3	8	52	35	63	.252	.298	.334	81	-18	-14	50	4	4	-2	-11	*3/1S	-3.0
1967	Hou-N	137	486	51	143	24	5	6	58	45	44	.294	.356	.401	121	11	13	67	2	2	-1	-4	*3	0.1
1968	Hou-N	124	409	25	92	9	2	1	46	35	57	.225	.286	.264	68	-16	-15	30	1	0	0	-7	3O/1S	-1.8
1969	*Atl-N	82	198	16	50	8	1	3	24	13	19	.253	.305	.348	82	-5	-5	21	0	1	-1	-0	O3S/2	-1.1
1970	Atl-N	62	127	5	27	3	0	0	7	13	13	.213	.286	.236	39	-10	-11	9	0	0	0	-0	3/S1O	-1.1
1971	NY-N	104	342	21	77	9	1	5	33	29	25	.225	.286	.301	67	-15	-15	27	0	2	-1	-5	3	-2.1
Total	13	1324	4369	386	1103	135	26	60	457	333	459	.252	.310	.336	86	-103	-81	441	19	24	-9	-57	*3/OS12	-16.9

■ BRIAN ASSELSTINE
Asselstine, Brian Hanly b: 9/23/53, Santa Barbara, Cal   BL/TR, 6'1", 175 lbs.   Deb: 9/14/76

YEAR	TM/L	G	AB	R	H	2B	3B	HR	RBI	BB	SO	AVG	OBP	SLG	PRO+	BR	/A	RC	SB	CS	SBR	FR	POS	TPR
1976	Atl-N	11	33	2	7	0	0	1	3	1	7	.212	.235	.303	49	-2	-2	3	0	0	0	0	/O	-0.2
1977	Atl-N	83	124	12	26	6	0	4	17	9	10	.210	.263	.355	57	-7	-8	12	1	0	0	3	O	-0.6
1978	Atl-N	39	103	11	28	3	3	2	13	11	16	.272	.353	.417	103	2	1	16	2	1	0	-1	O	-0.1
1979	Atl-N	8	10	1	1	0	0	0	0	1	2	.100	.182	.100	-20	-2	-2	0	0	0	0	-0	/O	-0.1
1980	Atl-N	87	218	18	62	13	1	3	25	11	37	.284	.322	.394	96	-1	-2	24	1	3	-2	-6	/O	-1.2
1981	Atl-N	56	86	8	22	5	0	2	10	5	7	.256	.297	.384	90	-1	-1	9	1	0	0	-1	O	-0.2
Total	6	284	574	52	146	27	4	12	68	38	74	.254	.304	.378	83	-10	-15	63	5	4	-1	-5	O	-2.4

■ JOE ASTROTH
Astroth, Joseph Henry b: 9/1/22, East Alton, Ill.   BR/TR, 5'9", 187 lbs.   Deb: 8/13/45

YEAR	TM/L	G	AB	R	H	2B	3B	HR	RBI	BB	SO	AVG	OBP	SLG	PRO+	BR	/A	RC	SB	CS	SBR	FR	POS	TPR
1945	Phi-A	10	17	1	1	0	0	0	1	0	1	.059	.111	.059	-50	-3	-3	0	0	0	0	-0	/C	-0.1
1946	Phi-A	4	7	0	1	0	0	0	0	0	1	.143	.143	.143	-20	-1	-1	0	0	0	0	-0	/C	0.0
1949	Phi-A	55	148	18	36	4	1	0	12	21	13	.243	.337	.284	67	-7	-6	15	1	0	0	2	C	-0.1
1950	Phi-A	39	110	11	36	3	1	1	18	18	3	.327	.422	.400	113	3	3	18	0	0	0	-5	C	0.0
1951	Phi-A	64	187	30	46	10	2	2	19	18	13	.246	.312	.353	78	-6	-6	21	0	1	-1	4	C	0.1
1952	Phi-A	104	337	24	84	7	2	1	36	25	27	.249	.305	.291	62	-15	-18	27	2	2	-1	-4	*C	-1.7
1953	Phi-A	82	260	28	77	15	2	3	24	27	12	.296	.367	.404	104	3	2	38	1	0	0	7	C	1.2
1954	Phi-A	77	226	22	50	8	1	1	23	21	19	.221	.286	.279	58	-13	-13	20	0	0	0	-2	C	-1.1
1955	KC-A	101	274	29	69	4	1	5	23	47	33	.252	.373	.328	89	-2	-2	35	2	3	-1	-3	*C	-0.2
1956	KC-A	8	13	0	1	0	0	0	0	0	1	.077	.077	.077	-59	-3	-3	0	0	0	0	2	/C	0.0
Total	10	544	1579	163	401	51	10	13	156	177	124	.254	.334	.324	77	-44	-48	175	6	6	-2	1	C	-1.9

■ CHARLIE ATHERTON
Atherton, Charles Morgan Herbert "Prexy" b: 10/19/1873, New Brunswick, N.J d: 12/19/34, Vienna, Austria 5'10", 160 lbs.   Deb: 5/30/1899

YEAR	TM/L	G	AB	R	H	2B	3B	HR	RBI	BB	SO	AVG	OBP	SLG	PRO+	BR	/A	RC	SB	CS	SBR	FR	POS	TPR
1899	Was-N	65	242	28	60	5	6	0	23	21		.248	.313	.318	76	-8	-7	25	2			-6	3/O	-1.2

■ ED ATKINSON
Atkinson, Edward b: 1851, Baltimore, Md.   Deb: 10/22/1873

YEAR	TM/L	G	AB	R	H	2B	3B	HR	RBI	BB	SO	AVG	OBP	SLG	PRO+	BR	/A	RC	SB	CS	SBR	FR	POS	TPR
1873	Was-n	2	8	2	0	0	0	0		0		.000	.000	.000	-99	-2	-2	0					/O	0.0

■ LEFTY ATKINSON
Atkinson, Hubert Berley b: 6/4/04, Chicago, Ill. d: 2/12/61, Chicago, Ill. BL/TL, 5'6.5", 149 lbs.   Deb: 8/05/27

YEAR	TM/L	G	AB	R	H	2B	3B	HR	RBI	BB	SO	AVG	OBP	SLG	PRO+	BR	/A	RC	SB	CS	SBR	FR	POS	TPR
1927	Was-A	1	1	1	0	0	0	0	0	0	0	.000	.000	.000	-99	-0	-0	0	0	0	0	0	H	0.0

■ DICK ATTREAU
Attreau, Richard Gilbert b: 4/8/1897, Chicago, Ill. d: 7/5/64, Chicago, Ill. BL/TL, 6', 160 lbs.   Deb: 9/14/26

YEAR	TM/L	G	AB	R	H	2B	3B	HR	RBI	BB	SO	AVG	OBP	SLG	PRO+	BR	/A	RC	SB	CS	SBR	FR	POS	TPR
1926	Phi-N	17	61	9	14	1	1	0	5	6	5	.230	.299	.279	53	-4	-4	5	0			-1	1	-0.5
1927	Phi-N	44	83	17	17	1	1	1	11	14	18	.205	.320	.277	60	-4	-4	8	1			-1	1	-0.7
Total	2	61	144	26	31	2	2	1	16	20	23	.215	.311	.278	57	-8	-8	13	1			-3	/1	-1.2

■ TOBY ATWELL
Atwell, Maurice Dailey b: 3/8/24, Leesburg, Va.   BL/TR, 5'9.5", 185 lbs.   Deb: 4/15/52

YEAR	TM/L	G	AB	R	H	2B	3B	HR	RBI	BB	SO	AVG	OBP	SLG	PRO+	BR	/A	RC	SB	CS	SBR	FR	POS	TPR
1952	Chi-N	107	362	36	105	16	3	2	31	46	22	.290	.362	.367	102	2	2	49	2	1	0	-6	*C	-0.2
1953	Chi-N	24	74	10	17	2	0	1	8	13	7	.230	.345	.297	68	-3	-3	9	0	0	0	1	C	0.0
	Pit-N	53	139	11	34	6	0	0	17	20	12	.245	.352	.288	70	-5	-5	14	0	0	0	-2	C	-0.4
	Yr	77	213	21	51	8	0	1	25	33	19	.239	.349	.291	69	-8	-8	23	0	0	0	-1		-0.4
1954	Pit-N	96	287	36	83	8	4	3	26	43	21	.289	.387	.376	101	2	2	42	2	3	-1	-2	C	0.1
1955	Pit-N	71	207	21	44	8	1	0	18	40	16	.213	.343	.266	65	-9	-9	21	0	1	-1	5	C	-0.1
1956	Pit-N	12	18	0	2	0	0	0	3	1	5	.111	.158	.111	-27	-3	-3	0	0	0	0	1	/C	-0.1
	Mil-N	15	30	2	5	1	0	0	7	4	1	.167	.265	.400	80	-1	-1	3	0	0	0	-0	C	0.0
	Yr	27	48	2	7	1	0	0	10	5	6	.146	.226	.292	40	-4	-4	3	0	0	0	1		-0.1
Total	5	378	1117	116	290	41	7	9	110	161	84	.260	.357	.333	86	-18	-17	139	4	5	-2	-4	C	-0.7

YEAR	TM/L	G	AB	R	H	2B	3B	HR	RBI	BB	SO	AVG	OBP	SLG	PRO+	BR	/A	RC	SB	CS	SBR	FR	POS	TPR

■ BILL ATWOOD
Atwood, William Franklin b: 9/25/11, Rome, Ga. BR/TR, 5'11.5", 190 lbs. Deb: 4/15/36

YEAR	TM/L	G	AB	R	H	2B	3B	HR	RBI	BB	SO	AVG	OBP	SLG	PRO+	BR	/A	RC	SB	CS	SBR	FR	POS	TPR
1936	Phi-N	71	192	21	58	9	2	2	29	11	15	.302	.346	.401	92	0	-2	27	0			-1	C	-0.1
1937	Phi-N	87	279	27	68	15	1	2	32	30	27	.244	.317	.326	69	-9	-12	32	3			-14	C	-2.2
1938	Phi-N	102	281	27	55	8	1	3	28	25	26	.196	.261	.263	46	-21	-20	19	0			1	C	-1.5
1939	Phi-N	4	6	0	0	0	0	0	1	2	3	.000	.250	.000	-29	-1	-1	0	1			-0	/C	0.0
1940	Phi-N	78	203	7	39	9	0	0	22	25	18	.192	.284	.236	47	-15	-14	14	0			1	C	-0.9
Total	5	342	961	82	220	41	4	7	112	93	89	.229	.299	.302	63	-46	-50	92	4			-12	C	-4.7

■ JAKE ATZ
Atz, John Jacob (b: John Jacob Zimmerman) b: 7/1/1879, Washington, D.C. d: 5/22/45, New Orleans, La. BR/TR, 5'9.5", 160 lbs. Deb: 9/24/02

YEAR	TM/L	G	AB	R	H	2B	3B	HR	RBI	BB	SO	AVG	OBP	SLG	PRO+	BR	/A	RC	SB	CS	SBR	FR	POS	TPR
1902	Was-A	3	10	1	1	0	0	0	0	0		.100	.100	.100	-44	-2	-2	0	0			0	/2	0.0
1907	Chi-A	4	8	0	1	0	0	0	0	0		.125	.125	.125	-20	-1	-1	0	0			1	/3O	0.0
1908	Chi-A	83	206	24	40	3	0	0	27	31		.194	.300	.209	69	-6	-5	17	9			-3	2S/3	-0.9
1909	Chi-A	119	381	39	90	18	3	0	22	38		.236	.309	.299	96	-3	-1	40	14			-7	*2/OS	-1.2
Total	4	209	605	64	132	21	3	0	49	69		.218	.300	.263	83	-11	-9	58	23			-8	2/SO3	-2.1

■ CHUB AUBREY
Aubrey, Harry Herbert "Harry" or "Chub" b: 7/5/1880, St.Joseph, Mo. d: 9/18/53, Baltimore, Md. TR , Deb: 4/22/03

YEAR	TM/L	G	AB	R	H	2B	3B	HR	RBI	BB	SO	AVG	OBP	SLG	PRO+	BR	/A	RC	SB	CS	SBR	FR	POS	TPR
1903	Bos-N	96	325	26	69	8	2	0	27	18		.212	.254	.249	47	-23	-21	24	7			-10	S/2O	-2.4

■ RICK AUERBACH
Auerbach, Frederick Steven b: 2/15/50, Woodland Hills, Cal BR/TR, 6', 165 lbs. Deb: 4/13/71

YEAR	TM/L	G	AB	R	H	2B	3B	HR	RBI	BB	SO	AVG	OBP	SLG	PRO+	BR	/A	RC	SB	CS	SBR	FR	POS	TPR
1971	Mil-A	79	236	22	48	10	0	1	9	20	40	.203	.271	.258	51	-15	-15	17	3	2	-0	-10	S	-1.7
1972	Mil-A	153	554	50	121	16	3	2	30	43	62	.218	.277	.269	64	-25	-24	42	24	8	2	-21	*S	-2.9
1973	Mil-A	6	10	2	1	1	0	0	0	0	1	.100	.100	.200	-18	-2	-2	0	0	1	-1	0	/S	-0.1
1974	*LA-N	45	73	12	25	0	0	1	4	8	9	.342	.407	.384	127	3	3	11	4	2	0	2	S2/3	0.8
1975	LA-N	85	170	18	38	9	0	0	12	18	22	.224	.298	.276	63	-9	-8	13	3	2	-0	-16	S/23	-1.5
1976	LA-N	36	47	7	6	0	0	0	1	6	6	.128	.226	.128	2	-6	-6	1	0	1	-1	11	S/32	0.6
1977	Cin-N	33	45	5	7	2	0	0	3	4	7	.156	.224	.200	15	-5	-6	2	0	0	0	6	2S	0.3
1978	Cin-N	63	55	17	18	6	0	2	5	7	12	.327	.413	.545	166	5	5	13	1	0	0	10	S2/3	1.9
1979	*Cin-N	62	100	17	21	8	1	1	12	14	19	.210	.307	.340	76	-3	-3	11	0	1	-1	7	3S/2	0.4
1980	Cin-N	24	33	5	11	1	1	0	4	3	5	.333	.389	.515	150	2	2	5	0	3	-2	-1	/S32	0.0
1981	Sea-A	38	84	12	13	3	0	1	6	4	15	.155	.202	.226	22	-8	-9	4	1	1	-0	2	S	-0.4
Total	11	624	1407	167	309	56	5	9	86	127	198	.220	.287	.286	65	-64	-62	119	36	21	-2	-10	S/23	-2.6

■ DAVE AUGUSTINE
Augustine, David Ralph b: 11/28/49, Follansbee, W.Va. BR/TR, 6'2", 174 lbs. Deb: 9/03/73

YEAR	TM/L	G	AB	R	H	2B	3B	HR	RBI	BB	SO	AVG	OBP	SLG	PRO+	BR	/A	RC	SB	CS	SBR	FR	POS	TPR
1973	Pit-N	11	7	1	2	1	0	0	0	0	1	.286	.286	.429	98	-0	-0	0	0	0	0	1	/O	0.1
1974	Pit-N	18	22	3	4	0	0	0	0	0	5	.182	.182	.182	2	-3	-3	0	0	1	-1	4	O	0.0
Total	2	29	29	4	6	1	0	0	0	0	6	.207	.207	.241	26	-3	-3	1	0	1	-1	5	/O	0.1

■ TEX AULDS
Aulds, Leycester Doyle b: 12/28/20, Farmerville, La. BR/TR, 6'2", 185 lbs. Deb: 5/25/47

YEAR	TM/L	G	AB	R	H	2B	3B	HR	RBI	BB	SO	AVG	OBP	SLG	PRO+	BR	/A	RC	SB	CS	SBR	FR	POS	TPR
1947	Bos-A	3	4	0	1	0	0	0	0	0	1	.250	.250	.250	37	-0	-0	0	0	0	0	0	/C	0.0

■ DOUG AULT
Ault, Douglas Reagan b: 3/9/50, Beaumont, Tex. BR/TL, 6'3", 200 lbs. Deb: 9/09/76

YEAR	TM/L	G	AB	R	H	2B	3B	HR	RBI	BB	SO	AVG	OBP	SLG	PRO+	BR	/A	RC	SB	CS	SBR	FR	POS	TPR
1976	Tex-A	9	20	0	6	1	0	0	0	1	3	.300	.333	.350	98	-0	-0	2	0	0	0	-1	/1D	0.0
1977	Tor-A	129	445	44	109	22	3	11	64	39	68	.245	.311	.382	87	-8	-9	48	4	4	-1	7	*1/D	-0.9
1978	Tor-A	54	104	10	25	1	1	3	7	17	14	.240	.352	.356	98	-0	-0	13	0	0	0	1	1/OD	-0.1
1980	Tor-A	64	144	12	28	5	1	3	15	14	23	.194	.275	.306	56	-8	-9	12	0	1	-1	3	1D/O	-0.8
Total	4	256	713	66	168	29	5	17	86	71	108	.236	.311	.362	82	-15	-18	75	4	5	-2	9	1/DO	-1.8

■ HENRY AUSTIN
Austin, Henry C. b: 1844, Brooklyn, N.Y. d: 9/3/1895, Amityville, N.Y. Deb: 4/28/1873

YEAR	TM/L	G	AB	R	H	2B	3B	HR	RBI	BB	SO	AVG	OBP	SLG	PRO+	BR	/A	RC	SB	CS	SBR	FR	POS	TPR
1873	Res-n	23	100	10	25	2	4	0		0		.250	.250	.350	81	-3	-2	9					O	0.0

■ JIMMY AUSTIN
Austin, James Philip "Pepper" b: 12/8/1879, Swansea, Wales d: 3/6/65, Laguna Beach, Cal. BB/TR, 5'7.5", 155 lbs. Deb: 4/19/09 MC

YEAR	TM/L	G	AB	R	H	2B	3B	HR	RBI	BB	SO	AVG	OBP	SLG	PRO+	BR	/A	RC	SB	CS	SBR	FR	POS	TPR
1909	NY-A	136	437	37	101	11	5	1	39	32		.231	.285	.286	80	-10	-10	45	30			13	*3S/2	0.9
1910	NY-A	133	432	46	94	11	4	2	36	47		.218	.305	.275	77	-8	-11	45	22			4	*3	-0.1
1911	StL-A	148	541	84	141	25	11	2	45	69		.261	.351	.359	102	-0	3	79	26			16	*3	1.9
1912	StL-A	149	536	57	135	14	8	2	44	38		.252	.306	.319	82	-15	-13	62	28			-1	*3	-1.6
1913	StL-A	142	489	56	130	18	6	2	42	45	51	.266	.338	.339	101	-1	1	66	37			7	*3M	1.2
1914	StL-A	130	466	55	111	16	4	0	30	40	59	.238	.300	.290	80	-13	-11	41	20	23	-8	1	*3	-1.6
1915	StL-A	141	477	61	127	6	6	1	30	64	60	.266	.355	.310	103	2	4	59	18	15	-4	10	*3	1.7
1916	StL-A	129	411	55	85	15	6	1	28	74	59	.207	.333	.280	89	-5	-3	47	19			-7	*3	-0.4
1917	StL-A	127	455	61	109	18	8	0	19	50	46	.240	.319	.314	97	-3	-1	50	13			3	*3/S	0.8
1918	StL-A	110	367	42	97	14	4	0	20	53	32	.264	.359	.324	109	4	6	49	18			-16	S3M	-0.7
1919	StL-A	106	396	54	94	9	9	1	21	42	31	.237	.314	.313	74	-12	-13	40	8			7	3	0.1
1920	StL-A	83	280	38	76	11	3	1	32	31	15	.271	.352	.343	82	-5	-7	35	2	4	-2	2	3	0.0
1921	StL-A	27	66	8	18	2	1	0	2	4	7	.273	.324	.333	64	-3	-4	7	2	1	0	-3	S/23	-0.3
1922	StL-A	15	31	6	9	3	1	0	1	3	2	.290	.353	.452	105	0	0	5	0	0	0	-3	/32	-0.1
1923	StL-A	1	0	0	0	0	0	0	0	0	0	—	—	—	—	0	0	0	0	0	0	0	/M	0.0
1925	StL-A	1	1	0	0	0	0	0	0	0	0	.000	.000	.000	-95	-0	-0	0	0	0	0	0	/3	0.0
1926	StL-A	1	2	1	1	1	0	0	1	0	0	.500	.500	1.000	272	0	0	1	1	0	0	0	/3	0.1
1929	StL-A	1	1	0	0	0	0	0	0	0	1	.000	.000	.000	-96	-0	-0	0	0	0	0	1	/3	0.0
Total	18	1580	5388	661	1328	174	76	13	390	592	363	.246	.326	.314	90	-70	-59	633	244	43		33	*3S/2	1.8

■ CHICK AUTRY
Autry, Martin Gordon b: 3/5/03, Martindale, Tex. d: 1/26/50, Savannah, Ga. BR/TR, 6', 180 lbs. Deb: 4/20/24

YEAR	TM/L	G	AB	R	H	2B	3B	HR	RBI	BB	SO	AVG	OBP	SLG	PRO+	BR	/A	RC	SB	CS	SBR	FR	POS	TPR
1924	NY-A	2	0	1	0	0	0	0	0	0	0	—	1.000	—	172	0	0	0	0	0	0	0	/C	0.0
1926	Cle-A	3	7	1	1	0	0	0	0	1	0	.143	.250	.143	4	-1	-1	0	0	0	0	-0	/C	0.0
1927	Cle-A	16	43	5	11	4	1	0	7	0	6	.256	.256	.395	66	-2	-2	4	0	0	0	2	C	0.0
1928	Cle-A	22	60	6	18	6	1	1	9	1	7	.300	.311	.483	105	-0	0	9	0	0	0	0	C	0.1
1929	Chi-A	43	96	7	20	6	0	1	12	1	8	.208	.224	.302	35	-10	-10	6	0	2	-1	-4	C	-1.1
1930	Chi-A	34	71	1	18	1	1	0	5	4	8	.254	.293	.296	52	-5	-5	6	0	0	0	8	C	0.5
Total	6	120	277	21	68	17	3	2	33	7	29	.245	.269	.350	59	-18	-18	26	0	2	-1	6	/C	-0.5

■ CHICK AUTRY
Autry, William Askew b: 1/2/1885, Humboldt, Tenn. d: 1/16/76, Santa Rosa, Cal. BL/TL, 5'11", 168 lbs. Deb: 9/18/07

YEAR	TM/L	G	AB	R	H	2B	3B	HR	RBI	BB	SO	AVG	OBP	SLG	PRO+	BR	/A	RC	SB	CS	SBR	FR	POS	TPR
1907	Cin-N	7	25	3	5	0	0	0	0	1		.200	.231	.200	35	-2	-2	1	0			-1	/O	-0.3
1909	Cin-N	9	33	3	6	2	0	0	4	2		.182	.229	.242	46	-2	-2	2	1			0	/1	-0.1
	Bos-N	65	199	16	39	4	0	0	13	21		.196	.279	.216	51	-10	-11	15	5			5	1/O	-0.8
	Yr	74	232	19	45	6	0	0	17	23		.194	.272	.220	51	-12	-13	17	6			5		-0.9
Total	2	81	257	22	50	6	0	0	17	24		.195	.269	.218	49	-14	-15	18	6			4	/1O	-1.2

■ EARL AVERILL
Averill, Earl Douglas b: 9/9/31, Cleveland, O. BR/TR, 5'10", 185 lbs. Deb: 4/19/56

YEAR	TM/L	G	AB	R	H	2B	3B	HR	RBI	BB	SO	AVG	OBP	SLG	PRO+	BR	/A	RC	SB	CS	SBR	FR	POS	TPR
1956	Cle-A	42	93	12	22	6	0	3	14	14	25	.237	.343	.398	93	-1	-1	13	0	1	-1	3	C	0.2
1958	Cle-A	17	55	2	10	1	0	2	7	4	7	.182	.250	.309	54	-4	-3	4	1	0	0	0	3	-0.1
1959	Chi-N	74	186	22	44	10	0	10	34	15	39	.237	.300	.452	98	-1	-1	25	0	1	-1	4	C3/O2	0.4
1960	Chi-N	52	102	14	24	4	0	1	13	11	16	.235	.316	.304	71	-4	-4	9	0	0	0	-9	C/3O	-1.1
	Chi-A	10	14	2	3	1	0	0	2	4	2	.214	.389	.214	68	-0	-0	2	0	0	0	2	/C	0.2
1961	LA-A	115	323	56	86	9	0	21	59	62	70	.266	.388	.489	119	16	11	64	1	0	0	-3	C/O2	0.7
1962	LA-A	92	187	21	41	9	0	4	22	43	47	.219	.368	.332	93	-1	-0	26	0	0	0	-3	O/C	-0.4

YEAR	TM/L	G	AB	R	H	2B	3B	HR	RBI	BB	SO	AVG	OBP	SLG	PRO+	BR	/A	RC	SB	CS	SBR	FR	POS	TPR
1963	Phi-N	47	71	8	19	2	0	3	8	9	14	.268	.350	.423	123	2	2	11	0	0	0	2	C/O13	0.4
Total	7	449	1031	137	249	41	0	44	159	162	220	.242	.349	.409	101	7	3	154	3	3	-1	-4	C/O321	0.3

■ EARL AVERILL

Averill, Howard Earl "Rock" b: 5/21/02, Snohomish, Wash. d: 8/16/83, Everett, Wash. BL/TR, 5'9.5", 172 lbs. Deb: 4/16/29 H

YEAR	TM/L	G	AB	R	H	2B	3B	HR	RBI	BB	SO	AVG	OBP	SLG	PRO+	BR	/A	RC	SB	CS	SBR	FR	POS	TPR
1929	Cle-A	151	597	110	198	43	13	18	96	63	53	.332	.398	.538	134	34	30	125	13	13	-4	-4	*O	1.5
1930	Cle-A	139	534	102	181	33	8	19	119	56	48	.339	.404	.537	131	29	26	116	10	7	-1	2	*O	1.9
1931	Cle-A	155	627	140	209	36	10	32	143	68	38	.333	.404	.576	147	48	43	144	9	9	-3	0	*O	2.8
1932	Cle-A	153	631	116	198	37	14	32	124	75	40	.314	.392	.569	137	41	35	140	5	8	-3	-4	*O	1.9
1933	Cle-A	151	599	83	180	39	16	11	92	54	29	.301	.363	.474	115	16	12	104	3	1	0	0	*O	0.7
1934	Cle-A	154	598	128	187	48	6	31	113	99	44	.313	.414	.569	149	46	44	145	5	3	-0	5	*O	4.3
1935	Cle-A	140	563	109	162	34	13	19	79	70	58	.288	.368	.496	119	16	15	105	8	4	0	-6	*O	0.7
1936	Cle-A	152	614	136	**232**	39	**15**	28	126	65	35	.378	.438	.627	159	56	56	168	3	3	-1	-8	*O	3.7
1937	Cle-A	156	609	121	182	33	11	21	92	88	65	.299	.387	.493	119	19	18	119	5	4	-1	-13	*O	-0.1
1938	Cle-A	134	482	101	159	27	15	14	93	81	48	.330	.429	.535	143	32	33	115	5	2	0	1	*O	3.1
1939	Cle-A	24	55	8	15	8	0	1	7	6	12	.273	.344	.473	111	0	1	9	0	1	-1	-3	O	-0.2
	Det-A	87	309	58	81	20	6	10	58	43	30	.262	.354	.463	100	3	-1	53	4	2	0	-4	O	-0.6
	Yr	111	364	66	96	28	6	11	65	49	42	.264	.353	.464	102	3	0	62	4	3	-1	-7		-0.8
1940	*Det-A	64	118	10	33	4	1	2	20	5	14	.280	.309	.381	71	-4	-6	14	0	0	0	-3	O	-0.9
1941	Bos-N	8	17	2	2	0	0	0	2	1	4	.118	.211	.118	-6	-2	-2	1	0			1	/O	-0.1
Total	13	1668	6353	1224	2019	401	128	238	1164	774	518	.318	.395	.534	132	334	305	1358	70	57		-36	*O	18.7

■ BOBBY AVILA

Avila, Roberto Francisco (Gonzalez) b: 4/2/24, Vera Cruz, Mexico BR/TR, 5'10", 175 lbs. Deb: 4/30/49

YEAR	TM/L	G	AB	R	H	2B	3B	HR	RBI	BB	SO	AVG	OBP	SLG	PRO+	BR	/A	RC	SB	CS	SBR	FR	POS	TPR
1949	Cle-A	31	14	3	3	0	0	0	3	1	3	.214	.267	.214	29	-1	-1	1	0	0	0	11	/2	0.9
1950	Cle-A	80	201	39	60	10	2	1	21	29	17	.299	.390	.383	102	0	1	32	5	0	2	-5	2/S	0.2
1951	Cle-A	141	542	76	165	21	3	10	58	60	31	.304	.374	.410	118	9	13	84	14	8	-1	-1	*2	1.7
1952	Cle-A	150	597	102	179	26	**11**	7	45	67	36	.300	.371	.415	127	15	20	93	12	10	-2	-18	*2	0.7
1953	Cle-A	141	559	85	160	22	3	8	55	58	27	.286	.355	.379	101	-1	1	75	10	8	-2	13	*2	2.1
1954	*Cle-A	143	555	112	189	27	2	15	67	59	31	.341	.405	.477	139	32	30	109	9	7	-2	8	*2/S	4.4
1955	Cle-A	141	537	83	146	22	4	13	61	82	47	.272	.370	.400	103	7	4	81	1	4	-2	-3	*2	0.8
1956	Cle-A	138	513	74	115	14	2	10	54	70	68	.224	.323	.318	68	-22	-23	57	17	4	3	-9	*2	-1.9
1957	Cle-A	129	463	60	124	19	3	5	48	46	47	.268	.335	.354	89	-7	-6	55	2	4	-2	-15	*23	-1.7
1958	Cle-A	113	375	54	95	21	3	5	30	55	45	.253	.350	.365	100	-0	1	50	5	7	-3	-21	23	-1.5
1959	Bal-A	20	47	1	8	0	0	0	0	4	5	.170	.235	.170	14	-6	-5	1	0	0	0	-4	O/23	-0.9
	Bos-A	22	45	7	11	0	0	3	6	6	11	.244	.333	.444	107	1	0	6	0	0	0	-2	2	0.0
	Yr	42	92	8	19	0	0	3	6	10	16	.207	.284	.304	61	-5	-5	6	0	0	0	-6		-0.9
	Mil-N	51	172	29	41	3	2	3	19	24	31	.238	.332	.331	84	-5	-3	22	3	0	1	-12	2	-0.9
Total	11	1300	4620	725	1296	185	35	80	467	561	399	.281	.360	.388	104	23	33	666	78	52	-8	-56	*2/3OS	3.9

■ RAMON AVILES

Aviles, Ramon Antonio (Miranda) b: 1/22/52, Manati, P.R. BR/TR, 5'9", 155 lbs. Deb: 7/10/77

YEAR	TM/L	G	AB	R	H	2B	3B	HR	RBI	BB	SO	AVG	OBP	SLG	PRO+	BR	/A	RC	SB	CS	SBR	FR	POS	TPR
1977	Bos-A	1	0	0	0	0	0	0	0	0	0	—	—	—	—	0	-0	0	0	0	0	0	/2	0.0
1979	Phi-N	27	61	7	17	2	0	0	12	8	8	.279	.371	.311	86	-1	-1	8	0	0	0	-7	2	-0.5
1980	*Phi-N	51	101	12	28	6	0	2	9	10	9	.277	.342	.396	100	1	0	13	0	0	0	-7	S2	-0.2
1981	*Phi-N	38	28	2	6	1	0	0	3	3	5	.214	.290	.250	52	-2	-2	2	0	0	0	4	23/S	0.4
Total	4	117	190	21	51	9	0	2	24	21	22	.268	.344	.347	88	-1	-2	24	0	0	0	-10	/2S3	-0.3

■ BENNY AYALA

Ayala, Benigno (Felix) b: 2/7/51, Yauco, P.R. BR/TR, 6'1", 185 lbs. Deb: 8/27/74

YEAR	TM/L	G	AB	R	H	2B	3B	HR	RBI	BB	SO	AVG	OBP	SLG	PRO+	BR	/A	RC	SB	CS	SBR	FR	POS	TPR
1974	NY-N	23	68	9	16	1	0	2	8	7	17	.235	.316	.338	84	-2	-1	7	0	0	0	-1	O	-0.2
1976	NY-N	22	26	2	3	0	0	1	2	5	8	.115	.179	.231	16	-3	-3	1	0	1	-1	1	/O	-0.2
1977	StL-N	1	3	0	1	0	0	0	0	0	1	.333	.333	.333	81	-0	-0	0	0	0	0	2	/O	0.2
1979	*Bal-A	42	86	15	22	5	0	6	13	6	9	.256	.304	.523	123	2	2	13	0	0	0	1	OD	0.2
1980	Bal-A	76	170	28	45	8	1	10	33	19	21	.265	.339	.500	128	6	6	28	0	0	0	1	DO	0.6
1981	Bal-A	44	86	12	24	2	0	3	13	11	9	.279	.367	.407	123	3	3	13	0	1	-1	1	D/O	0.3
1982	Bal-A	64	128	17	39	6	0	6	24	5	14	.305	.331	.492	123	3	3	19	1	1	-0	0	OD/1	0.3
1983	*Bal-A	47	104	12	23	7	0	4	13	9	18	.221	.283	.404	88	-2	-2	12	0	0	0	4	OD	0.1
1984	Bal-A	60	118	9	25	6	0	4	24	8	24	.212	.262	.364	73	-5	-5	10	1	1	-0	1	DO	-0.3
1985	Cle-A	46	76	10	19	7	0	2	15	6	17	.250	.287	.421	92	-1	-1	9	0	0	0	-0	O/D	-0.1
Total	10	425	865	114	217	42	1	38	145	71	136	.251	.309	.434	104	1	2	113	2	4	-2	9	OD/1	0.9

■ DICK AYLWARD

Aylward, Richard John "Dandy" b: 6/4/25, Baltimore, Md. d: 6/11/83, Spring Valley, Cal. BR/TR, 6', 190 lbs. Deb: 5/01/53

YEAR	TM/L	G	AB	R	H	2B	3B	HR	RBI	BB	SO	AVG	OBP	SLG	PRO+	BR	/A	RC	SB	CS	SBR	FR	POS	TPR
1953	Cle-A	4	3	0	0	0	0	0	0	0	1	.000	.000	.000	-99	-1	-1	0	0	0	0	0	/C	0.0

■ JOE AZCUE

Azcue, Jose Joaquin (Lopez) b: 8/18/39, Cienfuegos, Cuba BR/TR, 6', 190 lbs. Deb: 8/03/60

YEAR	TM/L	G	AB	R	H	2B	3B	HR	RBI	BB	SO	AVG	OBP	SLG	PRO+	BR	/A	RC	SB	CS	SBR	FR	POS	TPR
1960	Cin-N	14	31	1	3	0	0	0	3	2	6	.097	.152	.097	-30	-6	-6	0	0	1	-1	5	C	0.0
1962	KC-A	72	223	18	51	9	1	2	25	17	27	.229	.292	.305	59	-12	-13	20	1	0	0	4	C	-0.5
1963	KC-A	2	4	0	0	0	0	0	0	0	1	.000	.000	.000	-96	-1	-1	0	0	0	0	0	/C	0.0
	Cle-A	94	320	26	91	16	0	14	46	15	46	.284	.316	.466	117	6	6	42	1	1	-0	4	C	1.2
	Yr	96	324	26	91	16	0	14	46	15	47	.281	.313	.460	114	5	5	42	1	1	-0	4		1.2
1964	Cle-A	83	271	20	74	9	1	4	34	16	38	.273	.318	.358	88	-4	-4	30	0	2	-1	2	C	0.0
1965	Cle-A	111	335	16	77	7	0	2	35	27	54	.230	.293	.269	60	-17	-17	24	2	1	-0	-0	*C	-1.0
1966	Cle-A	98	302	22	83	10	1	9	37	20	22	.275	.324	.404	108	3	3	38	0	2	-1	-7	C	0.0
1967	Cle-A	86	295	33	74	12	5	11	34	22	35	.251	.309	.437	117	6	6	37	0	3	-2	7	C	1.7
1968	Cle-A	115	357	23	100	10	0	4	42	28	33	.280	.332	.342	106	2	3	40	1	1	-0	11	C	2.0
1969	Cle-A	7	24	1	7	0	0	1	1	4	3	.292	.393	.417	122	1	1	4	0	0	0	1	/C	0.3
	Bos-A	19	51	7	11	2	0	0	3	4	5	.216	.273	.255	46	-4	-4	3	0	0	0	3	C	0.1
	Cal-A	80	248	15	54	6	0	1	19	27	28	.218	.300	.254	59	-14	-12	17	0	1	-1	5	C	-0.2
	Yr	106	323	23	72	8	0	2	23	35	36	.223	.303	.266	62	-16	-15	24	0	1	-1	9		0.2
1970	Cal-A	114	351	19	85	13	1	2	25	24	40	.242	.294	.302	67	-17	-15	30	0	0	0	-4	*C	-1.7
1972	Cal-A	3	2	0	0	0	0	0	0	0	1	.000	.000	.000	-99	-0	-0	0	0	0	0	1	/C	0.0
	Mil-A	11	14	0	2	0	0	0	0	1	5	.143	.200	.143	3	-2	-2	0	0	0	0	2	/C	0.1
	Yr	14	16	0	2	0	0	0	0	1	6	.125	.176	.125	-10	-2	-2	0	0	0	0	3		0.1
Total	11	909	2828	201	712	94	9	50	304	207	344	.252	.307	.344	85	-59	-57	287	5	12	-6	33	C	2.0

■ OSCAR AZOCAR

Azocar, Oscar Gregorio (Azocar) b: 2/21/65, Soro, Venez. BL/TL, 6'1", 170 lbs. Deb: 7/17/90

YEAR	TM/L	G	AB	R	H	2B	3B	HR	RBI	BB	SO	AVG	OBP	SLG	PRO+	BR	/A	RC	SB	CS	SBR	FR	POS	TPR
1990	NY-A	65	214	18	53	8	0	5	19	2	15	.248	.258	.355	70	-9	-9	20	7	0	2	-1	O/D	-0.8

■ CHARLIE BABB

Babb, Charles Amos b: 2/20/1873, Milwaukie, Ore. d: 3/20/54, Portland, Ore. BB/TR, 5'10", 165 lbs. Deb: 4/17/03

YEAR	TM/L	G	AB	R	H	2B	3B	HR	RBI	BB	SO	AVG	OBP	SLG	PRO+	BR	/A	RC	SB	CS	SBR	FR	POS	TPR
1903	NY-N	121	424	68	105	15	8	0	46	45		.248	.320	.321	81	-8	-10	53	22			-1	*S/3	-0.4
1904	Bro-N	151	521	49	138	18	3	0	53	53		.265	.333	.311	104	2	4	68	34			-3	*S	0.1
1905	Bro-N	75	235	27	44	8	2	0	17	27		.187	.271	.238	58	-12	-10	19	10			5	S1/32	-0.5
Total	3	347	1180	144	287	41	13	0	116	125		.243	.316	.300	87	-18	-16	140	66			0	S/132	-0.8

■ LOREN BABE

Babe, Loren Rolland "Bee Bee" b: 1/11/28, Pisgah, Iowa d: 2/14/84, Omaha, Neb. BL/TR, 5'10", 180 lbs. Deb: 8/19/52 C

YEAR	TM/L	G	AB	R	H	2B	3B	HR	RBI	BB	SO	AVG	OBP	SLG	PRO+	BR	/A	RC	SB	CS	SBR	FR	POS	TPR
1952	NY-A	12	21	1	2	1	0	0	4	4	4	.095	.240	.143	9	-3	-2	1	0	0	0	2	/3	0.0
1953	NY-A	5	18	2	6	1	0	2	6	0	2	.333	.333	.722	185	2	2	4	0	0	0	3	/3	0.4
	Phi-A	103	343	34	77	16	2	0	20	35	20	.224	.300	.283	56	-20	-21	30	0	1	-1	1	3/S	-2.4

YEAR	TM/L	G	AB	R	H	2B	3B	HR	RBI	BB	SO	AVG	OBP	SLG	PRO+	BR	/A	RC	SB	CS	SBR	FR	POS	TPR
	Yr	108	361	36	83	17	2	2	26	35	22	.230	.302	.305	62	-18	-20	34	0	1	-1	5		-2.0
Total	2	120	382	37	85	18	2	2	26	39	26	.223	.298	.296	59	-21	-22	36	1	1	-0	6	3/S	-2.0

■ CHARLIE BABINGTON   Babington, Charles Percy   b: 5/4/1895, Cranston, R.I.   d: 3/22/57, Providence, R.I.   BR/TR, 6', 170 lbs.   Deb: 7/20/15

YEAR	TM/L	G	AB	R	H	2B	3B	HR	RBI	BB	SO	AVG	OBP	SLG	PRO+	BR	/A	RC	SB	CS	SBR	FR	POS	TPR
1915	NY-N	28	33	5	8	3	1	0	2	0	4	.242	.265	.394	104	-0	-0	4	1			-0	O/1	0.0

■ SHOOTY BABITT   Babitt, Mack Neal   b: 3/9/59, Oakland, Cal.   BR/TR, 5'8", 174 lbs.   Deb: 4/09/81

YEAR	TM/L	G	AB	R	H	2B	3B	HR	RBI	BB	SO	AVG	OBP	SLG	PRO+	BR	/A	RC	SB	CS	SBR	FR	POS	TPR
1981	Oak-A	54	156	10	40	1	3	0	14	13	13	.256	.314	.301	82	-4	-3	14	5	4	-1	-19	2	-2.2

■ WALLY BACKMAN   Backman, Walter Wayne   b: 9/22/59, Hillsboro, Ore.   BB/TR, 5'9", 160 lbs.   Deb: 9/02/80

YEAR	TM/L	G	AB	R	H	2B	3B	HR	RBI	BB	SO	AVG	OBP	SLG	PRO+	BR	/A	RC	SB	CS	SBR	FR	POS	TPR
1980	NY-N	27	93	12	30	1	1	0	9	11	14	.323	.400	.355	115	2	3	13	2	3	-1	-10	2/S	-0.6
1981	NY-N	26	36	5	10	2	0	0	0	4	7	.278	.350	.333	96	-0	-0	5	1	0	0	-3	2/3	-0.1
1982	NY-N	96	261	37	71	13	2	3	22	49	47	.272	.387	.372	114	7	7	39	8	7	-2	-11	2/3OS	-0.1
1983	NY-N	26	42	6	7	0	1	0	3	2	8	.167	.205	.214	16	-5	-5	2	0	0	0	-2	2/3	-0.6
1984	NY-N	128	436	68	122	19	2	1	26	56	63	.280	.362	.339	99	1	2	57	32	9	4	-12	*2/S	-0.1
1985	NY-N	145	520	77	142	24	5	1	38	36	72	.273	.321	.344	88	-10	-8	61	30	12	2	-9	*2/S	-1.5
1986	*NY-N	124	387	67	124	18	2	1	27	36	32	.320	.378	.385	114	7	7	59	13	7	-0	-3	*2	0.6
1987	NY-N	94	300	43	75	6	1	1	23	25	43	.250	.308	.287	62	-17	-15	28	11	3	2	-7	2	-1.8
1988	*NY-N	99	294	44	89	12	0	0	17	41	49	.303	.390	.344	118	7	8	42	9	5	-0	-9	2	0.3
1989	Min-A	87	299	33	69	9	2	1	26	32	45	.231	.307	.284	63	-12	-15	28	1	1	-0	-22	2/D	-3.6
1990	*Pit-N	104	315	62	92	21	3	2	28	42	53	.292	.377	.397	118	7	9	49	6	3	0	-19	32	-0.7
Total	11	956	2983	454	831	125	19	10	219	334	433	.279	.352	.343	96	-13	-6	384	113	50	4	-105	2/3SOD	-8.2

■ EDDIE BACON   Bacon, Edgar Suter   b: 4/8/1895, Franklin Co., Ky.   d: 10/2/63, Frankfurt, Ky.   Deb: 8/13/17

YEAR	TM/L	G	AB	R	H	2B	3B	HR	RBI	BB	SO	AVG	OBP	SLG	PRO+	BR	/A	RC	SB	CS	SBR	FR	POS	TPR
1917	Phi-A	4	6	1	3	1	0	0	2	0	0	.500	.500	.667	259	1	1	2	0			1	/P	0.2

■ ART BADER   Bader, Arthur Herman   b: 9/21/1886, St.Louis, Mo.   d: 4/5/57, St.Louis, Mo.   BR/TR, 5'10", 170 lbs.   Deb: 8/02/04

YEAR	TM/L	G	AB	R	H	2B	3B	HR	RBI	BB	SO	AVG	OBP	SLG	PRO+	BR	/A	RC	SB	CS	SBR	FR	POS	TPR
1904	StL-A	2	3	0	0	0	0	0	0		1	.000	.250	.000	-17	-0	-0	0	0			1	/O	0.0

■ RED BADGRO   Badgro, Morris Hiram   b: 12/1/02, Orilla, Wash.   BL/TR, 6', 190 lbs.   Deb: 6/20/29

YEAR	TM/L	G	AB	R	H	2B	3B	HR	RBI	BB	SO	AVG	OBP	SLG	PRO+	BR	/A	RC	SB	CS	SBR	FR	POS	TPR
1929	StL-A	54	148	27	42	12	0	1	18	11	15	.284	.342	.385	84	-3	-4	20	1	0	0	-4	O	-0.7
1930	StL-A	89	234	30	56	18	3	1	27	13	27	.239	.285	.355	59	-14	-16	23	3	5	-2	0	O	-1.7
Total	2	143	382	57	98	30	3	2	45	24	42	.257	.307	.366	69	-17	-19	43	4	5	-2	-4	/O	-2.4

■ CARLOS BAERGA   Baerga, Carlos Obed (Ortiz)   b: 11/4/68, San Juan, P.R.   BB/TR, 5'11", 165 lbs.   Deb: 4/14/90

YEAR	TM/L	G	AB	R	H	2B	3B	HR	RBI	BB	SO	AVG	OBP	SLG	PRO+	BR	/A	RC	SB	CS	SBR	FR	POS	TPR
1990	Cle-A	108	312	46	81	17	2	7	47	16	57	.260	.304	.394	92	-3	-4	37	0	2	-1	-9	3S/2	-0.9

■ JOSE BAEZ   Baez, Jose Antonio (b: Jose Antonio Mota (Baez))   b: 12/31/53, San Cristobal, D.R.   BR/TR, 5'8", 160 lbs.   Deb: 4/06/77

YEAR	TM/L	G	AB	R	H	2B	3B	HR	RBI	BB	SO	AVG	OBP	SLG	PRO+	BR	/A	RC	SB	CS	SBR	FR	POS	TPR
1977	Sea-A	91	305	39	79	14	1	1	17	19	20	.259	.305	.321	71	-12	-12	30	6	1	1	9	2/3D	0.4
1978	Sea-A	23	50	8	8	0	1	0	2	6	7	.160	.250	.200	28	-5	-5	3	1	0	0	12	2/3D	0.9
Total	2	114	355	47	87	14	2	1	19	25	27	.245	.297	.304	65	-17	-16	34	7	1	2	21	/2D3	1.3

■ KEVIN BAEZ   Baez, Kevin Richard   b: 1/10/67, Brooklyn, N.Y.   BR/TR, 6', 160 lbs.   Deb: 9/03/90

YEAR	TM/L	G	AB	R	H	2B	3B	HR	RBI	BB	SO	AVG	OBP	SLG	PRO+	BR	/A	RC	SB	CS	SBR	FR	POS	TPR
1990	NY-N	5	12	0	2	1	0	0	0	0	0	.167	.167	.250	13	-1	-1	0	0	0	0	0	/S	0.0

■ BILL BAGWELL   Bagwell, William Mallory "Big Bill"   b: 2/24/1896, Choudrant, La.   d: 10/5/76, Choudrant, La.   BL/TL, 6'1", 175 lbs.   Deb: 4/17/23

YEAR	TM/L	G	AB	R	H	2B	3B	HR	RBI	BB	SO	AVG	OBP	SLG	PRO+	BR	/A	RC	SB	CS	SBR	FR	POS	TPR
1923	Bos-N	56	93	8	27	4	2	2	10	6	12	.290	.333	.441	107	0	1	14	0	0	0	-1	O	0.0
1925	Phi-A	36	50	4	15	2	1	0	10	2	2	.300	.327	.380	74	-2	-2	6	0	0	0	-2	/O	-0.3
Total	2	92	143	12	42	6	3	2	20	8	14	.294	.331	.420	95	-2	-2	20	0	0	0	-2	/O	-0.3

■ FRANK BAHRET   Bahret, Frank J.   b: Baltimore, Md.   Deb: 4/17/1884

YEAR	TM/L	G	AB	R	H	2B	3B	HR	RBI	BB	SO	AVG	OBP	SLG	PRO+	BR	/A	RC	SB	CS	SBR	FR	POS	TPR
1884	Bal-U	2	8	0	0	0	0	0		0		.000	.000	.000	-91	-2	-2	0	0			0	/O	-0.1

■ GENE BAILEY   Bailey, Arthur Eugene   b: 11/25/1893, Pearsall, Tex.   d: 11/14/73, Houston, Tex.   BR/TR, 5'8", 160 lbs.   Deb: 9/10/17

YEAR	TM/L	G	AB	R	H	2B	3B	HR	RBI	BB	SO	AVG	OBP	SLG	PRO+	BR	/A	RC	SB	CS	SBR	FR	POS	TPR
1917	Phi-A	5	12	1	1	0	0	0	0	1	1	.083	.154	.083	-28	-2	-2	0				-1	/O	-0.3
1919	Bos-N	4	6	0	2	0	0	0	1	0	2	.333	.333	.333	105	-0	-0	1	1			0	/O	0.0
1920	Bos-N	13	24	2	2	0	0	0	0	3	3	.083	.185	.083	-22	-4	-4	1	0	1	-1	0	/O	-0.4
	Bos-A	46	135	14	31	2	0	0	5	9	15	.230	.283	.244	42	-11	-10	9	2	7	-4	-4	O	-2.1
1923	Bro-N	127	411	71	109	11	7	1	42	43	34	.265	.343	.344	81	-11	-9	49	9	7	-2	8	*O/1	-0.6
1924	Bro-N	18	46	7	11	3	0	1	4	7	6	.239	.340	.370	93	-1	-0	6	1	0	0	3	O	0.3
Total	5	213	634	95	156	16	7	2	52	63	61	.246	.321	.303	69	-28	-26	66	13	<u>15</u>		6	O/1	-3.1

■ FRED BAILEY   Bailey, Frederick Middleton "Penny"   b: 8/16/1895, Mt.Hope, W.Va.   d: 8/16/72, Huntington, W.Va.   BL/TL, 5'11", 150 lbs.   Deb: 8/19/16

YEAR	TM/L	G	AB	R	H	2B	3B	HR	RBI	BB	SO	AVG	OBP	SLG	PRO+	BR	/A	RC	SB	CS	SBR	FR	POS	TPR
1916	Bos-N	6	10	1	1	0	0	0	1	0	3	.100	.100	.100	-40	-2	-2					-0	/O	-0.2
1917	Bos-N	50	110	9	21	2	1	1	5	9	25	.191	.270	.255	65	-5	-4	8	3			1	O	-0.4
1918	Bos-N	4	4	1	1	0	0	0	0	0	1	.250	.250	.250	55	-0	-0	0	0			0	H	0.0
Total	3	60	124	10	23	2	1	1	6	9	29	.185	.257	.242	57	-7	-6	8	3			1	/O	-0.6

■ BILL BAILEY   Bailey, Harry Lewis   b: 11/19/1881, Shawnee, Ohio   d: 10/27/67, Seattle, Wash.   BL/TR, 5'10.5", 170 lbs.   Deb: 4/21/11

YEAR	TM/L	G	AB	R	H	2B	3B	HR	RBI	BB	SO	AVG	OBP	SLG	PRO+	BR	/A	RC	SB	CS	SBR	FR	POS	TPR
1911	NY-A	5	9	1	1	0	0	0	0	0		.111	.111	.111	-36	-2	-2	0	0			0	/O3	-0.1

■ MARK BAILEY   Bailey, John Mark   b: 11/4/61, Springfield, Mo.   BB/TR, 6'5", 195 lbs.   Deb: 4/27/84

YEAR	TM/L	G	AB	R	H	2B	3B	HR	RBI	BB	SO	AVG	OBP	SLG	PRO+	BR	/A	RC	SB	CS	SBR	FR	POS	TPR
1984	Hou-N	108	344	38	73	16	1	9	34	53	71	.212	.321	.343	93	-5	-2	40	0	1	-1	0	*C	0.0
1985	Hou-N	114	332	47	88	14	0	10	45	67	70	.265	.390	.398	124	12	13	51	0	2	-1	-8	*C/1	0.8
1986	Hou-N	57	153	9	27	5	0	4	15	28	45	.176	.304	.288	66	-7	-7	13	1	1	-0	1	C/1	-0.4
1987	Hou-N	35	64	5	13	1	0	0	3	10	21	.203	.311	.219	45	-5	-5	5	1	0	0	-1	C	-0.2
1988	Hou-N	8	23	1	3	0	0	0	0	5	6	.130	.286	.130	24	-2	-2	1	0	1	-1	-1	/C	-0.2
1990	SF-N	5	7	1	1	0	0	1	3	0	2	.143	.143	.571	88	-0	-0	1	0	0	0	-0	/C	0.0
Total	6	327	923	101	205	36	1	24	100	163	215	.222	.341	.341	95	-8	-2	110	2	5	-2	-9	C/1	0.0

■ ED BAILEY   Bailey, Lonas Edgar   b: 4/15/31, Strawberry Plains, Tenn.   BL/TR, 6'2", 205 lbs.   Deb: 9/26/53

YEAR	TM/L	G	AB	R	H	2B	3B	HR	RBI	BB	SO	AVG	OBP	SLG	PRO+	BR	/A	RC	SB	CS	SBR	FR	POS	TPR
1953	Cin-N	2	8	1	3	1	0	0	1	1	3	.375	.444	.500	145	1	1	2	0	0	0	-1	/C	0.0
1954	Cin-N	73	183	21	36	2	3	9	20	35	34	.197	.326	.388	83	-4	-5	26	1	0	0	-12	C	-1.4
1955	Cin-N	21	39	3	8	1	1	1	4	4	10	.205	.326	.359	77	-1	-1	4	0	0	0	3	C	0.2
1956	Cin-N	118	383	59	115	8	2	28	75	52	50	.300	.388	.551	140	27	24	83	2	0	1	3	*C	3.0
1957	Cin-N	122	391	54	102	15	2	20	48	73	69	.261	.380	.463	117	16	12	72	5	3	-0	-13	*C	0.5
1958	Cin-N	112	360	39	90	23	1	11	59	47	61	.250	.338	.411	92	-1	-4	51	2	2	-1	-4	*C	-0.3
1959	Cin-N	121	379	43	100	13	0	12	40	62	53	.264	.370	.393	101	4	2	58	2	0	1	1	*C	1.1
1960	Cin-N	133	441	52	115	19	3	13	67	59	70	.261	.351	.406	105	5	4	65	1	0	0	-13	*C	-0.2
1961	Cin-N	12	43	4	13	4	0	0	2	3	5	.302	.348	.395	95	-0	-0	6	0	0	0	-4	C	-0.3
	SF-N	107	340	39	81	9	1	13	51	42	41	.238	.329	.385	92	-5	-3	42	1	5	-2		*C/O	0.0
	Yr	119	383	43	94	13	1	13	53	45	46	.245	.331	.386	93	-5	-3	48	1	5	-3	-6	C	-0.3
1962	*SF-N	96	254	32	59	9	1	17	45	42	42	.232	.354	.476	123	8	8	44	1	1	-0	-6	C	0.3
1963	SF-N	105	308	41	81	8	0	21	68	50	42	.263	.368	.494	147	19	19	54	0	0	-4	-2	C	1.8
1964	Mil-N	95	271	30	71	10	1	5	34	34	39	.262	.346	.362	99	1	1	35	2	0	1	-10	C	-0.6
1965	SF-N	24	28	1	3	0	0	0	0	3	6	.107	.265	.107	9	-3	-3	3				3	C/1	0.0

YEAR	TM/L	G	AB	R	H	2B	3B	HR	RBI	BB	SO	AVG	OBP	SLG	PRO+	BR	/A	RC	SB	CS	SBR	FR	POS	TPR
	Chi-N	66	150	13	38	6	0	5	23	34	28	.253	.391	.393	119	6	5	23	0	1	-1	-6	C/1	0.1
	Yr	90	178	14	41	6	0	5	26	40	35	.230	.372	.348	102	3	2	23	0	1	-1	-3		0.1
1966	Cal-A	5	3	0	0	0	0	0	0	1	1	.000	.250	.000	-22	-0	-0	0	0	0	0	0	H	0.0
Total	14	1212	3581	432	915	128	15	155	540	545	577	.256	.358	.429	110	69	58	566	17	18	-6	-61	*C/1O	4.2

■ BOB BAILEY
Bailey, Robert Sherwood b: 10/13/42, Long Beach, Cal. BR/TR, 6'1", 180 lbs. Deb: 9/14/62

YEAR	TM/L	G	AB	R	H	2B	3B	HR	RBI	BB	SO	AVG	OBP	SLG	PRO+	BR	/A	RC	SB	CS	SBR	FR	POS	TPR
1962	Pit-N	14	42	6	7	2	1	0	6	6	10	.167	.271	.262	44	-3	-3	3	1	1	-0	0	3	-0.2
1963	Pit-N	154	570	60	130	15	3	12	45	58	98	.228	.305	.328	82	-12	-13	58	10	9	-2	6	*3/S	-0.9
1964	Pit-N	143	530	73	149	26	3	11	51	44	78	.281	.337	.404	108	5	6	68	10	8	-2	8	*3O/S	0.5
1965	Pit-N	159	626	87	160	28	3	11	49	70	93	.256	.330	.363	95	-3	-3	72	10	14	-5	-15	*3O	-3.2
1966	Pit-N	126	380	51	106	19	3	13	46	47	65	.279	.361	.447	123	13	13	60	5	3	-0	1	3O	1.2
1967	LA-N	116	322	21	73	8	2	4	28	40	50	.227	.314	.301	84	-9	-6	29	5	5	-2	2	3O/1S	-1.0
1968	LA-N	105	322	24	73	9	3	8	39	38	69	.227	.310	.348	105	-1	2	35	1	2	-1	-2	3/SO	-0.1
1969	Mon-N	111	358	46	95	16	6	9	53	40	76	.265	.341	.419	111	5	5	49	3	3	-1	5	1O/3	0.2
1970	Mon-N	131	352	77	101	19	3	28	84	72	70	.287	.409	.597	166	34	34	86	5	3	-0	-13	3O1	1.6
1971	Mon-N	157	545	65	137	21	4	14	83	97	105	.251	.364	.382	111	11	11	78	13	7	-0	-11	*3O/1	-0.2
1972	Mon-N	143	489	55	114	10	4	16	57	59	112	.233	.317	.368	92	-4	-5	56	6	7	-2	-8	*3/O1	-1.6
1973	Mon-N	151	513	77	140	25	4	26	86	88	99	.273	.380	.489	134	29	26	90	5	8	-3	-4	*3/O	1.6
1974	Mon-N	152	507	69	142	20	2	20	73	100	107	.280	.400	.446	129	28	24	89	4	7	-3	-20	O3	-0.2
1975	Mon-N	106	227	23	62	5	0	5	30	46	38	.273	.398	.361	107	6	5	34	4	4	-1	-6	O/3	-0.3
1976	Cin-N	69	124	17	37	6	1	6	23	16	26	.298	.379	.508	146	8	8	22	0	0	0	-2	O3	0.5
1977	Cin-N	49	79	9	20	2	1	2	11	12	10	.253	.352	.380	94	-0	-0	11	1	1	-0	0	1/O	-0.1
	Bos-A	2	2	0	0	0	0	0	0	0	1	.000	.000	.000	-90	-1	-1	0	0	0	0	0	H	0.0
1978	Bos-A	43	94	12	18	3	0	4	9	11	19	.191	.333	.351	84	-0	-2	12	2	1	0	0	D/3O	-0.1
Total	17	1931	6082	772	1564	234	43	189	773	852	1126	.257	.350	.403	111	106	101	852	85	83	-24	-58	*3O1/DS	-2.3

■ BOB BAILOR
Bailor, Robert Michael b: 7/10/51, Connellsville, Pa. BR/TR, 5'11", 170 lbs. Deb: 9/06/75

YEAR	TM/L	G	AB	R	H	2B	3B	HR	RBI	BB	SO	AVG	OBP	SLG	PRO+	BR	/A	RC	SB	CS	SBR	FR	POS	TPR
1975	Bal-A	5	7	0	1	0	0	0	0	1	0	.143	.250	.143	14	-1	-1	0	0	0	0	2	/S2	0.2
1976	Bal-A	9	6	2	2	0	1	0	0	0	0	.333	.333	.667	200	1	1	1	0	1	-1	-0	/SD	0.0
1977	Tor-A	122	496	62	154	21	5	5	32	17	26	.310	.336	.403	99	-0	-1	66	15	6	1	4	OS/D	0.8
1978	Tor-A	154	621	74	164	29	7	1	52	38	21	.264	.312	.338	81	-14	-16	66	5	6	-2	17	*O3/S	-0.3
1979	Tor-A	130	414	50	95	11	5	1	38	36	27	.229	.300	.287	59	-23	-23	37	14	8	-1	-1	*O/3	-2.8
1980	Tor-A	117	347	44	82	14	2	1	16	36	33	.236	.312	.297	65	-15	-17	33	12	8	-1	15	OS3/P2D	-0.3
1981	NY-N	51	81	11	23	3	1	0	8	8	11	.284	.356	.346	101	0	0	10	2	0	1	-2	S2O/3	0.2
1982	NY-N	110	376	44	104	14	1	0	31	20	17	.277	.317	.319	79	-11	-10	41	20	3	4	-22	S23	-2.2
1983	NY-N	118	340	33	85	8	0	1	30	20	23	.250	.294	.282	61	-18	-18	28	18	3	4	-5	S23/O	-1.1
1984	LA-N	65	131	11	36	4	0	0	8	8	1	.275	.317	.305	76	-4	-4	13	3	1	0	10	23S	0.9
1985	*LA-N	74	118	8	29	3	1	0	7	3	5	.246	.270	.288	58	-7	-7	9	1	0	0	15	32/SO	1.0
Total	11	955	2937	339	775	107	23	9	222	187	164	.264	.312	.325	76	-92	-95	305	90	36	5	33	OS23/DP	-3.6

■ HAROLD BAINES
Baines, Harold Douglass b: 3/15/59, Easton, Md. BL/TL, 6'2", 175 lbs. Deb: 4/10/80

YEAR	TM/L	G	AB	R	H	2B	3B	HR	RBI	BB	SO	AVG	OBP	SLG	PRO+	BR	/A	RC	SB	CS	SBR	FR	POS	TPR
1980	Chi-A	141	491	55	125	23	6	13	49	19	65	.255	.284	.405	87	-11	-11	50	2	4	-2	-15	*O/D	-2.9
1981	Chi-A	82	280	42	80	11	7	10	41	12	41	.286	.320	.482	131	9	9	41	6	2	1	-5	O/D	0.3
1982	Chi-A	161	608	89	165	29	8	25	105	49	95	.271	.326	.469	115	11	11	91	10	3	1	-2	*O	0.5
1983	*Chi-A	156	596	76	167	33	2	20	99	49	85	.280	.336	.443	108	9	6	85	7	5	-1	-2	*O	0.1
1984	Chi-A	147	569	72	173	28	10	29	94	54	75	.304	.364	.541	141	35	31	109	1	2	-1	-1	*O	2.5
1985	Chi-A	160	640	86	198	29	3	22	113	42	89	.309	.353	.467	118	19	15	98	1	1	-0	2	*O/D	1.4
1986	Chi-A	145	570	72	169	29	2	21	88	38	89	.296	.343	.465	114	12	10	87	2	1	0	7	*O/D	1.4
1987	Chi-A	132	505	59	148	26	4	20	93	46	82	.293	.353	.479	115	13	11	84	0	0	0	-1	*D/O	0.9
1988	Chi-A	158	599	55	166	39	1	13	81	67	109	.277	.351	.411	113	11	11	83	0	0	0	-1	*D/O	1.0
1989	Chi-A	96	333	55	107	20	1	13	56	60	52	.321	.426	.505	165	29	31	72	0	1	-1	-2	DO	2.7
	Tex-A	50	172	18	49	9	0	3	16	13	27	.285	.335	.390	102	1	0	21	0	2	-1	-0	D	0.0
	Yr	146	505	73	156	29	1	16	72	73	79	.309	.397	.465	144	30	31	93	0	3	-2	-2		2.7
1990	Tex-A	103	321	41	93	10	1	13	44	47	63	.290	.384	.449	129	14	13	53	0	1	-1	-0	D/O	1.3
	*Oak-A	32	94	11	25	5	0	3	21	20	17	.266	.395	.415	130	4	5	15	0	2	-1	-0	D	0.3
	Yr	135	415	52	118	15	1	16	65	67	80	.284	.384	.441	129	18	18	69	0	3	-2	-0		1.6
Total	11	1563	5778	731	1665	291	45	205	900	516	889	.288	.348	.461	119	155	144	891	29	24	-6	-20	*OD	9.5

■ AL BAIRD
Baird, Albert Wells b: 6/2/1895, Cleburne, Tex. d: 11/27/76, Shreveport, La. BR/TR, 5'9", 160 lbs. Deb: 9/10/17

YEAR	TM/L	G	AB	R	H	2B	3B	HR	RBI	BB	SO	AVG	OBP	SLG	PRO+	BR	/A	RC	SB	CS	SBR	FR	POS	TPR
1917	NY-N	10	24	1	7	0	0	0	4	2	2	.292	.346	.292	100	-0	-0	3	2			2	/2S	0.3
1919	NY-N	38	83	8	20	1	0	0	5	5	9	.241	.284	.253	63	-4	-4	6	3			8	2/S3	0.6
Total	2	48	107	9	27	1	0	0	9	7	11	.252	.298	.262	71	-4	-4	9	5			10	/2S3	0.9

■ DOUG BAIRD
Baird, Howard Douglas b: 9/27/1891, St.Charles, Mo. d: 6/13/67, Thomasville, Ga. BR/TR, 5'9.5", 148 lbs. Deb: 4/18/15

YEAR	TM/L	G	AB	R	H	2B	3B	HR	RBI	BB	SO	AVG	OBP	SLG	PRO+	BR	/A	RC	SB	CS	SBR	FR	POS	TPR
1915	Pit-N	145	512	49	112	26	12	1	53	37	88	.219	.277	.322	82	-13	-12	51	29	12	2	-1	*3O/2	-0.6
1916	Pit-N	128	430	41	93	10	7	1	28	24	49	.216	.263	.279	66	-17	-18	32	20	16	-4	-3	32O	-2.7
1917	Pit-N	43	135	17	35	6	1	0	18	20	19	.259	.355	.319	104	2	1	18	8			-4	3/2	-0.3
	StL-N	104	364	38	92	19	12	0	24	23	52	.253	.301	.371	108	1	3	45	18			14	*3/O	1.7
	Yr	147	499	55	127	25	13	0	42	43	71	.255	.316	.357	107	3	4	63	26			10		1.4
1918	StL-N	82	316	41	78	12	8	2	25	24	42	.247	.304	.354	104	-0	1	40	25			15	3/SO	1.9
1919	Phi-N	66	242	33	61	13	3	2	30	22	28	.252	.317	.355	95	1	-1	30	13			11	3	1.1
	StL-N	16	33	4	7	0	1	0	4	2	3	.212	.257	.273	63	-2	-1	3	2			-3	/32O	-0.4
	Bro-N	20	60	6	11	0	1	0	8	1	10	.183	.197	.217	24	-6	-6	3	3			1	3	-0.4
	Yr	102	335	43	79	13	5	2	42	25	41	.236	.291	.322	81	-7	-8	36	18			9		0.3
1920	Bro-N	6	6	1	2	0	0	0	1	2	1	.333	.556	.333	154	1	1	2	0	0	0	-0	/3	0.1
	NY-N	7	8	0	1	0	0	0	0	1	3	.125	.222	.125	1	-1	-1	0	0	0	0	2	/3	0.1
	Yr	13	14	1	3	0	0	0	1	3	4	.214	.389	.214	76	-0	-0	2	0	0	0	1		0.2
Total	6	617	2106	230	492	86	45	6	191	157	295	.234	.291	.326	88	-33	-33	223	118	28		32	3/O2S	0.5

■ CHARLIE BAKER
Baker, Charles A. b: 1856, Westboro, Mass. Deb: 8/01/1884

YEAR	TM/L	G	AB	R	H	2B	3B	HR	RBI	BB	SO	AVG	OBP	SLG	PRO+	BR	/A	RC	SB	CS	SBR	FR	POS	TPR
1884	CP-U	15	57	5	8	2	0	1	0	0		.140	.140	.228	23	-4	-4	2	0			-1	O/S2	-0.4

■ CHUCK BAKER
Baker, Charles Joseph b: 12/6/52, Seattle, Wash. BR/TR, 5'11", 180 lbs. Deb: 4/07/78

YEAR	TM/L	G	AB	R	H	2B	3B	HR	RBI	BB	SO	AVG	OBP	SLG	PRO+	BR	/A	RC	SB	CS	SBR	FR	POS	TPR
1978	SD-N	44	58	8	12	1	0	0	3	2	15	.207	.233	.224	31	-6	-5	3	0	0	0	14	2S	1.1
1980	SD-N	9	22	0	3	1	0	0	0	0	4	.136	.136	.182	-13	-3	-3	1	0	0	0	2	/S	0.0
1981	Min-A	40	66	6	12	0	3	0	6	1	8	.182	.194	.273	31	-6	-6	3	0	0	0	5	S/23D	0.1
Total	3	93	146	14	27	2	3	0	9	3	27	.185	.201	.240	25	-15	-14	7	0	0	0	20	/S2D3	1.2

■ DAVE BAKER
Baker, David Glenn b: 11/25/57, Lacona, Iowa BL/TR, 6', 185 lbs. Deb: 9/12/82

YEAR	TM/L	G	AB	R	H	2B	3B	HR	RBI	BB	SO	AVG	OBP	SLG	PRO+	BR	/A	RC	SB	CS	SBR	FR	POS	TPR
1982	Tor-A	9	20	3	5	1	0	0	2	3	3	.250	.400	.300	88	0	-0	3	0	0	0	1	/3	0.0

■ DEL BAKER
Baker, Delmer David b: 5/3/1892, Sherwood, Ore. d: 9/11/73, San Antonio, Tex. BR/TR, 5'11.5", 176 lbs. Deb: 4/16/14 MC

YEAR	TM/L	G	AB	R	H	2B	3B	HR	RBI	BB	SO	AVG	OBP	SLG	PRO+	BR	/A	RC	SB	CS	SBR	FR	POS	TPR
1914	Det-A	44	70	4	15	2	1	0	1	6	9	.214	.276	.271	63	-3	-3	5	0	2	-1	-5	C	-0.7
1915	Det-A	68	134	16	33	3	3	0	15	15	15	.246	.327	.313	87	-1	-2	16	3	1	0	-4	C	0.0
1916	Det-A	61	98	7	15	4	0	0	6	11	8	.153	.245	.194	31	-8	-8	6	2			-2	C	-0.8

YEAR	TM/L	G	AB	R	H	2B	3B	HR	RBI	BB	SO	AVG	OBP	SLG	PRO+	BR	/A	RC	SB	CS	SBR	FR	POS	TPR
Total	3	173	302	27	63	9	4	0	22	32	32	.209	.289	.265	63	-12	-14	27	5	3		-11	C	-1.5

■ DOUG BAKER
Baker, Douglas Lee b: 4/3/61, Fullerton, Cal. BB/TR, 5'9", 165 lbs. Deb: 7/02/84

YEAR	TM/L	G	AB	R	H	2B	3B	HR	RBI	BB	SO	AVG	OBP	SLG	PRO+	BR	/A	RC	SB	CS	SBR	FR	POS	TPR
1984	*Det-A	43	108	15	20	4	1	0	12	7	22	.185	.241	.241	34	-10	-10	7	3	0	1	2	S/2D	-0.2
1985	Det-A	15	27	4	5	1	0	0	1	0	9	.185	.185	.222	11	-3	-3	1	0	0	0	-2	S/2	-0.4
1986	Det-A	13	24	1	3	1	0	0	0	2	7	.125	.192	.167	-1	-3	-3	1	0	0	0	2	S/2D	0.0
1987	Det-A	8	1	0	0	0	0	0	0	0	1	.000	.000	.000	-99	-0	-0	0	0	0	0	3	/S23	0.3
1988	Min-A	11	7	1	0	0	0	0	0	0	5	.000	.000	.000	-97	-2	-2	0	0	0	0	1	/S23	0.0
1989	Min-A	43	78	17	23	5	1	0	9	9	18	.295	.382	.385	109	2	1	13	0	0	0	-3	2S	0.0
1990	Min-A	3	1	0	0	0	0	0	0	0	0	.000	.000	.000	-93	-0	-0	0	0	0	0	1	/2	0.0
Total	7	136	246	38	51	11	2	0	22	18	62	.207	.270	.268	49	-17	-17	22	3	0	1	4	/S23D	-0.3

■ GENE BAKER
Baker, Eugene Walter b: 6/15/25, Davenport, Iowa BR/TR, 6'1", 170 lbs. Deb: 9/20/53 C

YEAR	TM/L	G	AB	R	H	2B	3B	HR	RBI	BB	SO	AVG	OBP	SLG	PRO+	BR	/A	RC	SB	CS	SBR	FR	POS	TPR
1953	Chi-N	7	22	1	5	1	0	0	0	1	4	.227	.261	.273	39	-2	-2	2	1	0	0	-3	/2	-0.3
1954	Chi-N	135	541	68	149	32	5	13	61	47	55	.275	.336	.425	96	-3	-4	76	4	5	-2	-3	*2	0.0
1955	Chi-N	154	609	82	163	29	7	11	52	49	57	.268	.324	.392	89	-10	-10	76	9	7	-2	7	*2	0.8
1956	Chi-N	140	546	65	141	23	3	12	57	39	54	.258	.311	.377	85	-13	-11	62	4	3	-1	17	*2	1.7
1957	Chi-N	12	44	4	11	3	1	1	10	6	3	.250	.353	.432	111	1	1	7	0	0	0	-3	3	-0.2
	Pit-N	111	365	36	97	19	4	2	36	29	29	.266	.322	.356	84	-9	-8	41	3	2	-0	-4	3S2	-0.8
	Yr	123	409	40	108	22	5	3	46	35	32	.264	.325	.364	87	-8	-7	48	3	2	-0	-7		-1.0
1958	Pit-N	29	56	3	14	2	1	0	7	8	6	.250	.344	.321	80	-2	-1	6	0	0	0	-1	3/2	-0.1
1960	*Pit-N	33	37	5	9	0	0	0	4	2	9	.243	.282	.243	45	-3	-3	3	0	0	0	2	/32	0.0
1961	Pit-N	9	10	1	1	0	0	0	0	3	2	.100	.308	.100	15	-1	-1	0	0	0	0	1	/3	0.0
Total	8	630	2230	265	590	109	21	39	227	184	219	.265	.323	.385	88	-42	-39	272	21	17	-4	13	2/3S	1.1

■ FLOYD BAKER
Baker, Floyd Wilson b: 10/10/16, Luray, Va. BL/TR, 5'9", 160 lbs. Deb: 5/04/43 C

YEAR	TM/L	G	AB	R	H	2B	3B	HR	RBI	BB	SO	AVG	OBP	SLG	PRO+	BR	/A	RC	SB	CS	SBR	FR	POS	TPR
1943	StL-A	22	46	5	8	2	0	0	4	6	4	.174	.269	.217	42	-3	-3	3	0	1	-1	0	S/3	-0.3
1944	*StL-A	44	97	10	17	3	0	0	5	11	5	.175	.259	.206	32	-8	-9	6	2	0	1	-3	2S	-0.9
1945	Chi-A	82	208	22	52	8	0	0	19	23	12	.250	.325	.288	81	-5	-5	22	3	2	-0	2	32	-0.1
1946	Chi-A	9	24	2	6	1	0	0	3	2	3	.250	.308	.292	71	-1	-1	2	0	0	0	1	/3	0.1
1947	Chi-A	105	371	61	98	12	3	0	22	66	28	.264	.375	.313	96	-1	1	49	9	7	-2	18	*3/2S	2.1
1948	Chi-A	104	335	47	72	8	3	0	18	73	26	.215	.359	.257	68	-13	-12	35	4	10	-5	13	32/S	-0.5
1949	Chi-A	125	388	38	101	15	4	1	40	84	32	.260	.392	.327	94	-1	1	59	3	1	0	12	*3/S2	1.2
1950	Chi-A	83	186	26	59	7	0	0	11	32	10	.317	.417	.355	102	2	3	30	1	1	-0	3	3/2O	0.3
1951	Chi-A	82	133	24	35	6	1	0	14	25	12	.263	.380	.323	93	-0	-0	18	0	1	-1	-1	3/2S	-0.2
1952	Was-A	79	263	27	69	8	0	0	33	30	17	.262	.342	.293	81	-7	-6	30	1	0	0	-16	2/3S	-1.8
1953	Was-A	9	7	0	0	0	0	0	0	1	0	.000	.222	.000	-37	-1	-1	0	0	0	0	-0	/3	-0.1
	Bos-A	81	172	22	47	4	2	0	24	24	10	.273	.365	.320	82	-2	-3	21	0	2	-1	1	32	-0.4
	Yr	90	179	22	47	4	2	0	24	25	10	.263	.359	.307	78	-4	-5	21	0	2	-1	1		-0.5
1954	Bos-A	21	20	1	4	2	0	0	3	0	1	.200	.200	.300	32	-2	-2	1	0	0	0	1	/32	-0.1
	Phi-N	23	22	0	5	0	0	0	0	5	4	.227	.370	.227	60	-1	-1	2	0	0	0	4	/32	0.3
1955	Phi-N	5	8	0	0	0	0	0	0	0	1	.000	.000	.000	-99	-2	-2	0	0	0	0	1	/3	0.0
Total	13	874	2280	285	573	76	13	1	196	382	165	.251	.360	.297	82	-47	-41	279	23	25	-8	35	32/SO	-0.4

■ FRANK BAKER
Baker, Frank b: 1/11/44, Bartow, Fla. BL/TR, 5'10", 180 lbs. Deb: 7/27/69

YEAR	TM/L	G	AB	R	H	2B	3B	HR	RBI	BB	SO	AVG	OBP	SLG	PRO+	BR	/A	RC	SB	CS	SBR	FR	POS	TPR
1969	Cle-A	52	172	21	44	5	3	3	15	14	34	.256	.316	.372	89	-2	-3	20	2	1	0	-1	O	-0.5
1971	Cle-A	73	181	18	38	12	1	1	23	12	34	.210	.263	.304	55	-10	-12	13	1	3	-2	-4	/O	-2.0
Total	2	125	353	39	82	17	4	4	38	26	68	.232	.289	.337	71	-12	-14	33	3	4	-2	-6	/O	-2.5

■ FRANK BAKER
Baker, Frank Watts b: 10/29/46, Meridian, Miss. BL/TR, 6'2", 178 lbs. Deb: 8/09/70

YEAR	TM/L	G	AB	R	H	2B	3B	HR	RBI	BB	SO	AVG	OBP	SLG	PRO+	BR	/A	RC	SB	CS	SBR	FR	POS	TPR
1970	NY-A	35	117	6	27	4	1	0	11	14	26	.231	.323	.282	72	-5	-4	11	1	2	-1	4	S	0.3
1971	NY-A	43	79	9	11	2	0	0	2	16	22	.139	.284	.165	32	-7	-6	5	3	0	1	11	S	1.0
1973	*Bal-A	44	63	10	12	1	2	1	11	7	7	.190	.271	.317	66	-3	-3	6	0	0	0	4	S/213	0.5
1974	*Bal-A	24	29	3	5	1	0	0	0	3	5	.172	.250	.207	34	-2	-2	1	0	0	0	2	S/23	0.1
Total	4	146	288	28	55	8	3	1	24	40	60	.191	.294	.250	56	-17	-15	24	4	2	0	20	S/231	1.9

■ GEORGE BAKER
Baker, George F. b: 1859, St.Louis, Mo. Deb: 5/24/1883

YEAR	TM/L	G	AB	R	H	2B	3B	HR	RBI	BB	SO	AVG	OBP	SLG	PRO+	BR	/A	RC	SB	CS	SBR	FR	POS	TPR
1883	Bal-a	7	22	0	5	0	0	0		0		.227	.227	.227	45	-1	-1	1				-2	/SCO	-0.2
1884	StL-U	80	317	39	52	6	0	0		5		.164	.177	.183	21	-25	-27	11	0			6	C/203S	-1.4
1885	StL-N	38	131	5	16	0	0	0	5	9	28	.122	.179	.122	-1	-14	-13	3				-10	C/3O2	-1.8
1886	KC-N	1	4	1	1	0	0	0	0	0	1	.250	.250	.250	49	-0	-0	0	0			1	/C	0.1
Total	4	126	474	45	74	6	0	0	5	14	29	.156	.180	.169	17	-41	-41	15	0			-5	C/O3S2	-3.3

■ HOWARD BAKER
Baker, Howard Francis b: 3/1/1888, Bridgeport, Conn. d: 1/16/64, Bridgeport, Conn. BR/TR, 5'11", 175 lbs. Deb: 8/11/12

YEAR	TM/L	G	AB	R	H	2B	3B	HR	RBI	BB	SO	AVG	OBP	SLG	PRO+	BR	/A	RC	SB	CS	SBR	FR	POS	TPR
1912	Cle-A	11	30	1	5	0	0	0	2	5		.167	.286	.167	29	-3	-3	1	0			-1	3	-0.3
1914	Chi-A	15	47	4	13	1	1	0	5	3	8	.277	.320	.340	100	-0	-0	5	2	1	0	-4	3	-0.4
1915	Chi-A	2	2	0	0	0	0	0	0	0	2	.000	.000	.000	-97	-0	-0	0	0	0	0	0	H	0.0
	NY-N	1	3	0	0	0	0	0	0	0	0	.000	.000	.000	-99	-1	-1	0	0	0	0	0	/3	0.0
Total	3	29	82	5	18	1	1	0	7	8	10	.220	.289	.256	61	-4	-4	7	2	1		-5	/3	-0.7

■ JACK BAKER
Baker, Jack Edward b: 5/4/50, Birmingham, Ala. BR/TR, 6'5", 225 lbs. Deb: 9/11/76

YEAR	TM/L	G	AB	R	H	2B	3B	HR	RBI	BB	SO	AVG	OBP	SLG	PRO+	BR	/A	RC	SB	CS	SBR	FR	POS	TPR
1976	Bos-A	12	23	1	3	0	0	1	2	1	5	.130	.167	.261	21	-2	-3	1	0	0	0	-0	/1D	-0.2
1977	Bos-A	2	3	0	0	0	0	0	0	0	1	.000	.000	.000	-90	-1	-1	0	0	0	0	0	/1	0.0
Total	2	14	26	1	3	0	0	1	2	1	6	.115	.148	.231	8	-3	-3	1	0	0	0	0	/1D	-0.2

■ JESSE BAKER
Baker, Jesse (b: Michael Myron Silverman) b: 3/4/1895, Cleveland, Ohio d: 7/29/76, W.Los Angeles, Cal. 5'4", 140 lbs. Deb: 9/14/19

YEAR	TM/L	G	AB	R	H	2B	3B	HR	RBI	BB	SO	AVG	OBP	SLG	PRO+	BR	/A	RC	SB	CS	SBR	FR	POS	TPR
1919	Was-A	1	0	0	0	0	0	0	1	0	0	—	—	—	—	0	0	0	0	0	0	0	/S	0.0

■ FRANK BAKER
Baker, John Franklin "Home Run" b: 3/13/1886, Trappe, Md. d: 6/28/63, Trappe, Md. BL/TR, 5'11", 173 lbs. Deb: 9/21/08 H

YEAR	TM/L	G	AB	R	H	2B	3B	HR	RBI	BB	SO	AVG	OBP	SLG	PRO+	BR	/A	RC	SB	CS	SBR	FR	POS	TPR
1908	Phi-A	9	31	5	9	3	2	0				.290	.290	.387	114	1	0	4	0			2	/3	0.4
1909	Phi-A	148	541	73	165	27	19	4	85	26		.305	.343	.447	146	27	26	90	20			-8	*3	2.7
1910	*Phi-A	146	561	83	159	25	15	2	74	34		.283	.329	.392	127	14	15	79	21			6	*3	2.9
1911	Phi-A	148	592	96	198	42	14	11	115	40		.334	.379	.508	149	33	35	127	38			-0	*3	3.4
1912	Phi-A	149	577	116	200	40	21	10	130	50		.347	.404	.541	176	49	52	140	40			10	*3	5.8
1913	*Phi-A	149	564	116	190	34	9	12	117	63	31	.337	.413	.493	169	46	48	122	34			8	*3	6.1
1914	*Phi-A	150	570	84	182	23	10	9	89	53	37	.319	.380	.442	152	31	33	95	19	20	-6	10	*3	4.3
1916	NY-A	100	360	46	97	23	2	10	52	36	30	.269	.344	.428	129	13	12	58	15			2	3	1.9
1917	NY-A	146	553	57	156	24	2	6	71	48	27	.282	.345	.365	116	10	10	72	18			11	*3	3.0
1918	NY-A	126	504	65	154	24	5	6	62	38	13	.306	.357	.409	128	17	16	74	8			11	*3	3.0
1919	NY-A	141	567	70	166	22	1	10	83	44	18	.293	.346	.388	105	4	3	77	13			-2	*3	1.2
1921	*NY-A	94	330	46	97	16	2	9	71	26	12	.294	.353	.436	98	-1	-2	51	8	5	-1	-2	3	0.2
1922	*NY-A	69	234	30	65	12	3	7	36	15	14	.278	.327	.444	97	-1	-2	33	1	3	-2	-10	3	-0.6
Total	13	1575	5984	887	1838	315	103	96	987	473	182	.307	.363	.442	135	243	246	1020	235	28		37	*3	34.3

YEAR	TM/L	G	AB	R	H	2B	3B	HR	RBI	BB	SO	AVG	OBP	SLG	PRO+	BR	/A	RC	SB	CS	SBR	FR	POS	TPR

■ DUSTY BAKER   Baker, Johnnie B   b: 6/15/49, Riverside, Cal.   BR/TR, 6'2", 183 lbs.   Deb: 9/07/68   C

YEAR	TM/L	G	AB	R	H	2B	3B	HR	RBI	BB	SO	AVG	OBP	SLG	PRO+	BR	/A	RC	SB	CS	SBR	FR	POS	TPR
1968	Atl-N	6	5	0	2	0	0	0	0	0	1	.400	.400	.400	140	0	0	1	0	0	0	0	/O	0.0
1969	Atl-N	3	7	0	0	0	0	0	0	0	3	.000	.000	.000	-99	-2	-2	0	0	0	0	-0	/O	-0.2
1970	Atl-N	13	24	3	7	0	0	0	4	2	4	.292	.346	.292	69	-1	-1	2	0	0	0	0	O	-0.1
1971	Atl-N	29	62	2	14	2	0	0	4	1	14	.226	.238	.258	38	-5	-5	3	0	1	-1	1	O	-0.5
1972	Atl-N	127	446	62	143	27	2	17	76	45	68	.321	.388	.504	139	30	25	85	4	7	-3	9	*O	2.7
1973	Atl-N	159	604	101	174	29	4	21	99	67	72	.288	.364	.454	116	21	15	103	24	3	5	4	*O	1.8
1974	Atl-N	149	574	80	147	35	0	20	69	71	87	.256	.339	.422	107	8	5	83	18	7	1	14	*O	1.5
1975	Atl-N	142	494	63	129	18	2	19	72	67	57	.261	.349	.421	109	9	6	74	12	7	-1	5	*O	0.6
1976	LA-N	112	384	36	93	13	0	4	39	31	54	.242	.300	.307	74	-14	-13	33	2	4	-2	-7	*O	-2.7
1977	*LA-N	153	533	86	155	26	1	30	86	58	89	.291	.367	.512	134	24	25	99	2	6	-3	-14	*O	0.3
1978	*LA-N	149	522	62	137	24	1	11	66	47	66	.262	.327	.375	96	-3	-3	66	12	3	2	-4	*O	-1.0
1979	LA-N	151	554	86	152	29	1	23	88	56	70	.274	.342	.455	117	11	12	84	11	4	1	5	*O	1.4
1980	LA-N	153	579	80	170	26	4	29	97	43	66	.294	.346	.503	137	24	25	96	12	10	-2	-2	*O	1.6
1981	*LA-N	103	400	48	128	17	3	9	49	29	43	.320	.362	.445	134	15	16	63	10	7	-1	-2	*O	1.1
1982	LA-N	147	570	80	171	19	1	23	88	56	62	.300	.366	.458	132	22	24	96	17	10	-1	-11	*O	1.0
1983	*LA-N	149	531	71	138	25	1	15	73	72	59	.260	.350	.395	107	6	6	78	7	1	2	-6	*O	0.0
1984	SF-N	100	243	31	71	7	2	3	32	40	27	.292	.392	.374	120	7	8	39	4	1	1	-5	O	0.1
1985	Oak-A	111	343	48	92	15	1	14	52	50	47	.268	.361	.440	128	9	13	54	2	1	0	-4	1OD	0.4
1986	Oak-A	83	242	25	58	8	0	4	19	27	37	.240	.316	.322	80	-8	-6	24	0	1	-1	-3	OD/1	-1.0
Total	19	2039	7117	964	1981	320	23	242	1013	762	926	.278	.351	.432	116	153	152	1084	137	73	-3	-21	*O/1D	7.0

■ KIRTLEY BAKER   Baker, Kirtley "Whitey"   b: 6/24/1869, Aurora, Ind.   d: 4/15/27, Covington, Ky.   BR/TR, 5'9", 160 lbs.   Deb: 5/07/1890

YEAR	TM/L	G	AB	R	H	2B	3B	HR	RBI	BB	SO	AVG	OBP	SLG	PRO+	BR	/A	RC	SB	CS	SBR	FR	POS	TPR
1890	Pit-N	26	68	6	10	0	0	0	0	10	6	.147	.275	.147	29	-6	-5	3	1			-0	P	0.0
1893	Bal-N	19	57	9	17	1	1	0	6	8	6	.298	.385	.351	96	0	0	8	1			5	P/O	0.0
1894	Bal-N	2	4	0	0	0	0	0	0	0	1	.000	.000	.000	-96	-1	-1	0	0			1	/OP	0.0
1898	Was-N	6	18	3	5	0	1	0	3	3		.278	.381	.389	124	1	1	3	0			-0	/P	0.0
1899	Was-N	12	19	1	3	0	0	0	1	1		.158	.200	.158	0	-3	-2	1	0			2	P	0.0
Total	5	65	166	19	35	1	2	0	10	22	13	.211	.311	.241	59	-9	-8	15	2			7	/PO	0.0

■ PHIL BAKER   Baker, Philip   b: 9/19/1856, Philadelphia, Pa.   d: 6/4/40, Washington, D.C.   5'8", 152 lbs.   Deb: 5/01/1883

YEAR	TM/L	G	AB	R	H	2B	3B	HR	RBI	BB	SO	AVG	OBP	SLG	PRO+	BR	/A	RC	SB	CS	SBR	FR	POS	TPR
1883	Bal-a	28	121	22	33	2	1	1		8		.273	.318	.331	106	1	1	13				-6	CO/S	-0.2
1884	Was-U	86	371	75	107	12	5	1		11		.288	.309	.356	128	9	11	42	0			-14	1OC	-0.1
1886	Was-N	81	325	37	72	6	5	1	34	20	32	.222	.267	.280	70	-13	-10	29	16			-7	1O/C	-2.3
Total	3	195	817	134	212	20	11	3	34	39	32	.259	.293	.322	101	-3	2	84	16			-27	/1OCS	-2.6

■ TRACY BAKER   Baker, Tracy Lee   b: 11/7/1891, Pendleton, Ore.   d: 3/14/75, Placerville, Cal.   BR/TR, 6'1", 180 lbs.   Deb: 6/19/11

YEAR	TM/L	G	AB	R	H	2B	3B	HR	RBI	BB	SO	AVG	OBP	SLG	PRO+	BR	/A	RC	SB	CS	SBR	FR	POS	TPR
1911	Bos-A	1	0	0	0	0	0	0	0	0		—	—	—	—	0	0	0	0			0	/1	0.0

■ BILL BAKER   Baker, William Presley   b: 2/22/11, Paw Creek, N.C.   BR/TR, 6', 200 lbs.   Deb: 5/04/40   C

YEAR	TM/L	G	AB	R	H	2B	3B	HR	RBI	BB	SO	AVG	OBP	SLG	PRO+	BR	/A	RC	SB	CS	SBR	FR	POS	TPR
1940	*Cin-N	27	69	5	15	1	1	0	7	4	8	.217	.260	.261	44	-5	-5	4	2			4	C	0.0
1941	Cin-N	2	1	0	0	0	0	0	0	1	1	.000	.500	.000	49	0	0	0	0			0	/C	0.0
	Pit-N	35	67	5	15	3	0	0	6	11	0	.224	.333	.269	71	-2	-2	7	0			-0	C	0.1
	Yr	37	68	5	15	3	0	0	6	12	1	.221	.338	.265	71	-2	-2	7	0			0		0.1
1942	Pit-N	18	17	1	2	0	0	0	2	1	0	.118	.167	.118	-16	-2	-3	0	0			1	C	0.0
1943	Pit-N	63	172	12	47	6	3	1	26	22	6	.273	.365	.360	106	3	2	23	3			0	C	0.5
1946	Pit-N	53	113	7	27	4	0	1	8	12	6	.239	.312	.301	72	-4	-4	11	0			-5	C/1	-0.8
1948	StL-N	45	119	13	35	10	1	0	15	15	7	.294	.373	.395	102	2	1	17	1			-1	C	0.0
1949	StL-N	20	30	2	4	1	0	0	4	2	2	.133	.188	.167	-4	-4	-5	1	0			-2	C	-0.5
Total	7	263	588	45	145	25	5	2	68	68	30	.247	.328	.316	79	-13	-16	63	6			-3	C/1	-0.4

■ JOHN BALAZ   Balaz, John Lawrence   b: 11/24/50, Toronto, Ont., Can.   BR/TR, 6'3", 180 lbs.   Deb: 9/10/74

YEAR	TM/L	G	AB	R	H	2B	3B	HR	RBI	BB	SO	AVG	OBP	SLG	PRO+	BR	/A	RC	SB	CS	SBR	FR	POS	TPR
1974	Cal-A	14	42	4	10	0	0	1	5	2	10	.238	.289	.310	76	-2	-1	4	0	0	0	-2	O	-0.2
1975	Cal-A	45	120	10	29	8	1	1	10	5	25	.242	.272	.350	80	-4	-3	12	0	0	0	1	OD	-0.2
Total	2	59	162	14	39	8	1	2	15	7	35	.241	.276	.340	79	-6	-5	16	0	0	0	-0	/OD	-0.4

■ STEVE BALBONI   Balboni, Stephen Charles   b: 1/16/57, Brockton, Mass.   BR/TR, 6'3", 225 lbs.   Deb: 4/22/81

YEAR	TM/L	G	AB	R	H	2B	3B	HR	RBI	BB	SO	AVG	OBP	SLG	PRO+	BR	/A	RC	SB	CS	SBR	FR	POS	TPR
1981	NY-A	4	7	2	2	1	1	0	2	1	4	.286	.375	.714	211	1	1	2	0	0	0	0	/1D	0.1
1982	NY-A	33	107	8	20	2	1	2	4	6	34	.187	.230	.280	40	-9	-9	7	0	0	0	-0	1/D	-0.9
1983	NY-A	32	86	8	20	2	0	5	17	8	23	.233	.298	.430	101	-1	-0	11	0	0	0	-1	1/D	-0.1
1984	*KC-A	126	438	58	107	23	2	28	77	45	139	.244	.320	.498	122	12	11	69	0	0	0	-6	*1/D	-0.1
1985	*KC-A	160	600	74	146	28	2	36	88	52	166	.243	.309	.477	111	7	7	86	1	1	-0	-8	*1	-1.1
1986	KC-A	138	512	54	117	25	1	29	88	43	146	.229	.290	.451	96	-4	-5	67	0	0	0	-6	*1	-1.8
1987	KC-A	121	386	44	80	11	1	24	60	34	97	.207	.275	.427	80	-11	-13	43	0	0	0	2	1D	-1.4
1988	KC-A	21	63	2	9	2	0	2	5	1	20	.143	.156	.270	17	-7	-7	3	0	0	0	-1	1/D	-0.8
	Sea-A	97	350	44	88	15	1	21	61	23	67	.251	.299	.480	110	5	3	48	0	1	-1	-1	D1	0.0
	Yr	118	413	46	97	17	1	23	66	24	87	.235	.279	.448	96	-2	-4	49	0	1	-1	-2		-0.8
1989	NY-A	110	300	33	71	12	2	17	59	25	67	.237	.302	.460	113	3	4	39	0	0	0	-2	D1	0.1
1990	NY-A	116	266	24	51	6	0	17	34	35	91	.192	.293	.406	93	-3	-3	33	0	0	0	-3	D1	-0.7
Total	10	958	3115	351	711	127	11	181	495	273	854	.228	.294	.450	100	-6	-10	408	1	2	-1	-25	1D	-6.7

■ BOBBY BALCENA   Balcena, Robert Rudolph   b: 8/1/25, San Pedro, Cal.   d: 1/4/90, San Pedro, Cal.   BR/TL, 5'7", 160 lbs.   Deb: 9/16/56

YEAR	TM/L	G	AB	R	H	2B	3B	HR	RBI	BB	SO	AVG	OBP	SLG	PRO+	BR	/A	RC	SB	CS	SBR	FR	POS	TPR
1956	Cin-N	7	2	2	0	0	0	0	0	0	1	.000	.000	.000	-94	-1	-1	0	0	0	0	1	/O	0.0

■ LADY BALDWIN   Baldwin, Charles Busted   b: 4/8/1859, Ormel, N.Y.   d: 3/7/37, Hastings, Mich.   BL/TL, 5'11", 160 lbs.   Deb: 9/30/1884

YEAR	TM/L	G	AB	R	H	2B	3B	HR	RBI	BB	SO	AVG	OBP	SLG	PRO+	BR	/A	RC	SB	CS	SBR	FR	POS	TPR
1884	Mil-U	7	27	6	6	3	0	0		0		.222	.222	.333	158	-0	1	2	0			0	/OP	0.2
1885	Det-N	31	124	12	30	6	3	0	18	6	22	.242	.277	.339	98	-0	-0	12				0	PO	0.0
1886	Det-N	57	204	25	41	6	3	0	25	18	44	.201	.266	.260	59	-9	-10	15	3			2	P/O	0.0
1887	*Det-N	24	85	15	23	0	1	0	7	10	6	.271	.354	.294	81	-1	-2	11	4			1	P	0.0
1888	Det-N	6	23	5	6	0	0	0	3	3	3	.261	.346	.261	98	0	0	2	0			0	/PO	0.0
1890	Bro-N	2	3	1	0	0	0	0	0	1	1	.000	.250	.000	-24	-0	-0	0	0			0	/P	0.0
	Buf-P	7	28	4	8	1	0	0	2	2	1	.286	.333	.321	84	-1	-0	3	0			0	/P	0.0
Total	6	134	494	68	114	16	7	0	55	40	77	.231	.290	.291	78	-13	-12	45	7			4	P/O	0.2

■ KID BALDWIN   Baldwin, Clarence Geoghan   b: 11/1/1864, Newport, Ky.   d: 7/12/1897, Cincinnati, Ohio   BR/TR, 5'6", 147 lbs.   Deb: 7/27/1884

YEAR	TM/L	G	AB	R	H	2B	3B	HR	RBI	BB	SO	AVG	OBP	SLG	PRO+	BR	/A	RC	SB	CS	SBR	FR	POS	TPR
1884	KC-U	50	191	19	37	6	3	0		4		.194	.210	.257	66	-8	-4	11	0			-3	CO/23	-0.4
	CP-U	1	1	0	1	0	0	0		0		1.000	1.000	1.000	582	0	0	1	0			-0	/C	0.0
	Yr	51	192	19	38	6	3	0		4		.198	.214	.260	68	-8	-4	11	0			-4		-0.4
1885	Cin-a	34	126	9	17	1	0	1		3		.135	.155	.167	3	-13	-14	3				-3	C/O2P3	-1.1
1886	Cin-a	87	315	41	72	8	7	3		8		.229	.252	.327	80	-7	-9	30	12			-9	C3/O	-1.1
1887	Cin-a	96	388	46	98	15	10	1		6		.253	.271	.351	73	-14	-16	41	13			-4	*C/O	-0.2
1888	Cin-a	67	271	27	59	11	3	1	25	3		.218	.235	.292	67	-9	-11	20	4			-3	C/O1	-0.6
1889	Cin-a	60	223	34	55	14	2	1	34	15	32	.247	.273	.341	74	-8	-9	23	7			3	C/O31	0.0
1890	Cin-N	22	72	5	11	2	0	0	10	3	6	.153	.187	.153	0	-9	-9	2	2			4	C/O	-0.2
	Phi-a	24	90	5	21	1	2	0		4		.233	.274	.289	70	-4	-3	8	2			0	C/3	0.0

YEAR	TM/L	G	AB	R	H	2B	3B	HR	RBI	BB	SO	AVG	OBP	SLG	PRO+	BR	/A	RC	SB	CS	SBR	FR	POS	TPR
Total	7	441	1677	186	371	56	27	7	69	36	38	.221	.243	.299	65	-72	-74	140	40			-16	C/O321P	-3.6

■ FRANK BALDWIN
Baldwin, Frank De Witt b: 12/25/28, High Bridge, N.J. BR/TR, 5'11", 195 lbs. Deb: 4/22/53

YEAR	TM/L	G	AB	R	H	2B	3B	HR	RBI	BB	SO	AVG	OBP	SLG	PRO+	BR	/A	RC	SB	CS	SBR	FR	POS	TPR
1953	Cin-N	16	20	0	2	0	0	0	0	1	9	.100	.143	.100	-35	-4	-4	0	0	0	0	-1	/C	-0.3

■ HENRY BALDWIN
Baldwin, Henry Clay "Ted" b: 6/13/1894, Chadds Ford, Pa. d: 2/24/64, West Chester, Pa. BR/TR, 5'11", 180 lbs. Deb: 5/22/27

YEAR	TM/L	G	AB	R	H	2B	3B	HR	RBI	BB	SO	AVG	OBP	SLG	PRO+	BR	/A	RC	SB	CS	SBR	FR	POS	TPR
1927	Phi-N	6	16	1	5	0	0	0	1	1	2	.313	.353	.313	78	-0	-0	2	0			-2	/S3	-0.1

■ JEFF BALDWIN
Baldwin, Jeffrey Allen b: 9/5/65, Milford, Del. BL/TL, 6'1", 180 lbs. Deb: 5/22/90

YEAR	TM/L	G	AB	R	H	2B	3B	HR	RBI	BB	SO	AVG	OBP	SLG	PRO+	BR	/A	RC	SB	CS	SBR	FR	POS	TPR
1990	Hou-N	7	8	1	0	0	0	0	0	1	2	.000	.111	.000	-68	-2	-2	0	0	0	0	-0	/O	-0.1

■ REGGIE BALDWIN
Baldwin, Reginald Conrad b: 8/19/54, River Rouge, Mich. BR/TR, 6'1", 195 lbs. Deb: 5/25/78

YEAR	TM/L	G	AB	R	H	2B	3B	HR	RBI	BB	SO	AVG	OBP	SLG	PRO+	BR	/A	RC	SB	CS	SBR	FR	POS	TPR
1978	Hou-N	38	67	5	17	5	0	1	11	3	3	.254	.286	.373	89	-2	-1	6	0	0	0	-1	C	-0.1
1979	Hou-N	14	20	0	4	1	0	0	1	0	1	.200	.200	.250	23	-2	-2	1	0	0	0	-1	/C1	-0.2
Total	2	52	87	5	21	6	0	1	12	3	4	.241	.267	.345	74	-4	-3	7	0	0	0	-2	/C1	-0.3

■ BILLY BALDWIN
Baldwin, Robert Harvey b: 6/9/51, Tazewell, Va. BL/TL, 6', 175 lbs. Deb: 7/29/75

YEAR	TM/L	G	AB	R	H	2B	3B	HR	RBI	BB	SO	AVG	OBP	SLG	PRO+	BR	/A	RC	SB	CS	SBR	FR	POS	TPR
1975	Det-A	30	95	8	21	3	0	4	8	5	14	.221	.260	.379	75	-3	-4	10	2	1	0	5	O/D	0.1
1976	NY-N	9	22	4	6	1	1	1	5	1	2	.273	.304	.545	146	1	1	4	0	0	0	1	/O	0.2
Total	2	39	117	12	27	4	1	5	13	6	16	.231	.268	.410	87	-2	-3	13	2	1	0	7	/OD	0.3

■ MIKE BALENTI
Balenti, Michael Richard b: 7/3/1886, Calumet, Okla. d: 8/4/55, Altus, Okla. BR/TR, 5'11", 175 lbs. Deb: 7/19/11

YEAR	TM/L	G	AB	R	H	2B	3B	HR	RBI	BB	SO	AVG	OBP	SLG	PRO+	BR	/A	RC	SB	CS	SBR	FR	POS	TPR
1911	Cin-N	8	8	2	2	0	0	0	0	0	1	.250	.250	.250	42	-1	-1	1	3			1	/SO	0.0
1913	StL-A	70	211	17	38	2	4	0	11	6	32	.180	.206	.227	28	-20	-19	10	3			1	S/O	-1.4
Total	2	78	219	19	40	2	4	0	11	6	33	.183	.208	.228	28	-21	-20	12	6			1	/SO	-1.4

■ LEE BALES
Bales, Wesley Owen b: 12/4/44, Los Angeles, Cal. BB/TR, 5'10.5", 165 lbs. Deb: 8/07/66

YEAR	TM/L	G	AB	R	H	2B	3B	HR	RBI	BB	SO	AVG	OBP	SLG	PRO+	BR	/A	RC	SB	CS	SBR	FR	POS	TPR
1966	Atl-N	12	16	4	1	0	0	0	0	0	5	.063	.063	.063	-64	-3	-4	0	0	0	0	3	/23	0.0
1967	Hou-N	19	27	4	3	0	0	0	2	8	7	.111	.314	.111	28	-2	-2	2	1	1	-0	-2	/2S	-0.3
Total	2	31	43	8	4	0	0	0	2	8	12	.093	.235	.093	-3	-6	-6	2	1	1	-0	2	/23S	-0.3

■ ART BALL
Ball, Arthur Clark b: 1873, Indiana d: 12/26/15, Chicago, Ill. TR, Deb: 8/01/1894

YEAR	TM/L	G	AB	R	H	2B	3B	HR	RBI	BB	SO	AVG	OBP	SLG	PRO+	BR	/A	RC	SB	CS	SBR	FR	POS	TPR
1894	StL-N	1	3	0	1	0	0	0	0	0	1	.333	.333	.333	63	-0	-0	0	0			-1	/2	0.0
1898	Bal-N	32	81	7	15	2	0	0	8	7		.185	.258	.210	36	-6	-7	5	2			9	3S/2O	0.4
Total	2	33	84	7	16	2	0	0	8	7	1	.190	.261	.214	37	-7	-7	5	2			8	/3S2O	0.4

■ NEAL BALL
Ball, Cornelius b: 4/22/1881, Grand Haven, Mich. d: 10/15/57, Bridgeport, Conn. BR/TR, 5'7", 145 lbs. Deb: 9/12/07

YEAR	TM/L	G	AB	R	H	2B	3B	HR	RBI	BB	SO	AVG	OBP	SLG	PRO+	BR	/A	RC	SB	CS	SBR	FR	POS	TPR
1907	NY-A	15	44	5	9	1	1	0	4	1		.205	.222	.273	55	-2	-2	3	1			-3	S/2	-0.5
1908	NY-A	132	446	34	110	16	2	0	38	21		.247	.281	.291	87	-6	-7	45	32			-6	*S/2	-1.0
1909	NY-A	8	29	5	6	1	1	0	3	3		.207	.281	.310	86	-0	-0	3	2			-3	/2	-0.4
	Cle-A	96	324	29	83	13	2	1	25	17		.256	.295	.318	90	-3	-4	36	17			-11	S	-1.4
	Yr	104	353	34	89	14	3	1	28	20		.252	.294	.317	90	-4	-5	39	19			-14		-1.8
1910	Cle-A	53	119	13	25	3	1	0	12	9		.210	.266	.252	61	-5	-5	9	4			-2	S/2O3	-0.7
1911	Cle-A	116	412	45	122	14	9	3	45	27		.296	.339	.396	104	1	1	62	21			6	23/S	0.6
1912	Cle-A	40	132	12	30	4	1	0	14	9		.227	.277	.273	55	-7	-8	12	7			0	2	-0.7
	*Bos-A	18	45	10	9	2	0	0	6	3		.200	.250	.244	40	-3	-4	4	5			-3	2	-0.7
	Yr	58	177	22	39	6	1	0	20	12		.220	.270	.266	51	-11	-12	16	12			-3		-1.4
1913	Bos-A	23	58	9	10	2	0	0	4	9	13	.172	.294	.207	46	-4	-4	3	3			-2	2/S3	-0.5
Total	7	501	1609	162	404	56	17	4	151	99	13	.251	.295	.314	84	-30	-34	178	92			-24	S2/3O	-5.3

■ JIM BALL
Ball, James Chandler b: 2/22/1884, Hartford, Md. d: 4/7/63, Glendale, Cal. BR/TR, 5'11", 175 lbs. Deb: 9/21/07

YEAR	TM/L	G	AB	R	H	2B	3B	HR	RBI	BB	SO	AVG	OBP	SLG	PRO+	BR	/A	RC	SB	CS	SBR	FR	POS	TPR
1907	Bos-N	10	36	3	6	2	0	0	3	2		.167	.211	.222	37	-3	-3	2	0			-1	C	-0.2
1908	Bos-N	6	15	1	1	0	0	0	0	1		.067	.125	.067	-38	-2	-2	0	0			-0	/C	-0.2
Total	2	16	51	4	7	2	0	0	3	3		.137	.185	.176	15	-5	-5	2	0			-1	/C	-0.4

■ PELHAM BALLENGER
Ballenger, Pelham Ashby b: 2/6/1894, Gilreath Mill, S.C. d: 12/8/48, Greenville, County S.C. BR/TR, 5'11", 160 lbs. Deb: 5/07/28

YEAR	TM/L	G	AB	R	H	2B	3B	HR	RBI	BB	SO	AVG	OBP	SLG	PRO+	BR	/A	RC	SB	CS	SBR	FR	POS	TPR
1928	Was-A	3	9	0	1	0	0	0	0	0	1	.111	.111	.111	-42	-2	-2	0	0	0	0	1	/3	0.0

■ HAL BAMBERGER
Bamberger, Harold Earl "Dutch" b: 10/29/24, Lebanon, Pa. BL/TR, 6', 173 lbs. Deb: 9/15/48

YEAR	TM/L	G	AB	R	H	2B	3B	HR	RBI	BB	SO	AVG	OBP	SLG	PRO+	BR	/A	RC	SB	CS	SBR	FR	POS	TPR
1948	NY-N	7	12	0	1	0	0	0	0	1	2	.083	.154	.083	-34	-2	-2	0	0			0	/O	-0.1

■ STUD BANCKER
Bancker, John b: Philadelphia, Pa. Deb: 4/21/1875

YEAR	TM/L	G	AB	R	H	2B	3B	HR	RBI	BB	SO	AVG	OBP	SLG	PRO+	BR	/A	RC	SB	CS	SBR	FR	POS	TPR
1875	NH-n	19	72	3	11	0	0	0		0		.153	.153	.153	7	-7	-5	2					C/2S3	-0.3

■ DAVE BANCROFT
Bancroft, David James "Beauty" b: 4/20/1891, Sioux City, Iowa d: 10/9/72, Superior, Wis. BB/TR, 5'9.5", 160 lbs. Deb: 4/14/15 MCH

YEAR	TM/L	G	AB	R	H	2B	3B	HR	RBI	BB	SO	AVG	OBP	SLG	PRO+	BR	/A	RC	SB	CS	SBR	FR	POS	TPR
1915	*Phi-N	153	563	85	143	18	2	7	30	77	62	.254	.346	.330	104	6	5	64	15	27	-12	5	*S	0.2
1916	Phi-N	142	477	53	101	10	0	3	33	74	57	.212	.323	.252	75	-9	-11	46	15			25	*S	2.3
1917	Phi-N	127	478	56	116	22	5	4	43	44	42	.243	.307	.335	93	-2	-4	52	14			28	*S/2O	2.8
1918	Phi-N	125	499	69	132	19	4	0	26	54	36	.265	.338	.319	94	2	-2	55	11			18	*S	2.1
1919	Phi-N	92	335	45	91	13	7	0	25	31	30	.272	.333	.352	99	3	0	41	8			10	S	1.5
1920	Phi-N	42	171	23	51	7	2	0	5	9	12	.298	.337	.363	96	0	-1	19	1	7	-4	9	S	0.7
	NY-N	108	442	79	132	29	7	0	31	33	32	.299	.349	.361	115	8	8	61	7	5	-1	30	*S	4.4
	Yr	150	613	102	183	36	9	0	36	42	44	.299	.346	.387	109	8	7	80	8	12	-5	39		5.1
1921	*NY-N	153	606	121	193	26	15	6	67	66	23	.318	.389	.441	119	18	18	106	17	10	-1	17	*S	4.8
1922	*NY-N	156	651	117	209	41	5	4	60	79	27	.321	.397	.418	109	13	12	111	16	11	-2	22	*S	3.9
1923	*NY-N	107	444	80	135	33	3	1	31	62	23	.304	.391	.399	110	8	9	72	8	7	-2	21	S2	3.5
1924	Bos-N	79	319	49	89	11	1	2	21	37	24	.279	.356	.339	91	-5	-3	40	4	4	-1	-5	SM	-0.2
1925	Bos-N	128	479	75	153	29	8	2	49	64	22	.319	.400	.426	122	10	17	85	7	4	-0	10	*SM	3.4
1926	Bos-N	127	453	70	141	18	6	1	44	64	29	.311	.399	.384	122	10	16	72	3			-3	*S/3M	2.1
1927	Bos-N	111	375	44	91	13	4	1	31	43	36	.243	.322	.307	75	-15	-12	38	5			6	*S/3M	0.4
1928	Bro-N	149	515	47	127	19	5	0	51	59	20	.247	.326	.303	66	-25	-24	53	7			4	*S	0.0
1929	Bro-N	104	358	35	99	11	3	1	44	29	11	.277	.331	.332	66	-19	-18	40	7			-0	*S	-0.3
1930	NY-N	10	17	0	1	0	0	0	1	0	2	.059	.158	.118	-33	-4	-4	0	0			1	/S	-0.1
Total	16	1913	7182	1048	2004	320	77	32	591	827	487	.279	.355	.358	98	-1	8	954	145	75		198	*S/23O	31.5

■ CHRIS BANDO
Bando, Christopher Michael b: 2/4/56, Cleveland, Ohio BB/TR, 6', 195 lbs. Deb: 8/13/81

YEAR	TM/L	G	AB	R	H	2B	3B	HR	RBI	BB	SO	AVG	OBP	SLG	PRO+	BR	/A	RC	SB	CS	SBR	FR	POS	TPR
1981	Cle-A	21	47	3	10	3	0	0	6	2	2	.213	.245	.277	51	-3	-3	3	0	0	0	-2	C/D	-0.3
1982	Cle-A	66	184	13	39	6	1	3	16	24	30	.212	.303	.304	68	-8	-8	17	0	0	0	-6	C/3	-1.0
1983	Cle-A	48	121	15	31	3	0	4	15	15	19	.256	.338	.380	94	-0	-1	15	0	1	-1	-1	C	0.0
1984	Cle-A	75	220	38	64	11	0	12	41	33	35	.291	.383	.505	141	13	13	41	1	2	-1	-4	C/13D	1.2
1985	Cle-A	73	173	11	24	4	1	0	13	22	21	.139	.236	.173	14	-20	-20	7	0	1	-1	-4	C	-2.0
1986	Cle-A	92	254	28	68	9	0	2	26	22	49	.268	.329	.327	81	-7	-6	27	0	1	-1	-10	C	-1.0
1987	Cle-A	89	211	20	46	9	0	5	16	12	28	.218	.260	.332	55	-14	-14	17	0	0	0	-2	C	-0.7
1988	Cle-A	32	72	6	9	1	0	1	8	8	20	.125	.222	.181	14	-8	-8	3	0	0	0	1	C	-0.6
	Det-A	1	0	0	0	0	0	0	0	0	0	—	—	—		0	0	0	0	0	0	0	/C	0.0
	Yr	33	72	6	9	1	0	1	8	8	12	.125	.222	.181	14	-8	-8	3	0	0	0	1		-0.6

YEAR	TM/L	G	AB	R	H	2B	3B	HR	RBI	BB	SO	AVG	OBP	SLG	PRO+	BR	/A	RC	SB	CS	SBR	FR	POS	TPR
1989	Oak-A	1	2	0	1	0	0	0	1	0	1	.500	.500	.500	189	0	0	1	0	0	0	1	/C	0.1
Total	9	498	1284	134	292	46	2	27	142	138	197	.227	.303	.329	73	-47	-47	131	1	5	-3	-26	C/3D1	-4.3

■ SAL BANDO
Bando, Salvatore Leonard b: 2/13/44, Cleveland, O. BR/TR, 6', 195 lbs. Deb: 9/03/66 C

YEAR	TM/L	G	AB	R	H	2B	3B	HR	RBI	BB	SO	AVG	OBP	SLG	PRO+	BR	/A	RC	SB	CS	SBR	FR	POS	TPR
1966	KC-A	11	24	1	7	1	1	0	1	1	3	.292	.320	.417	113	0	0	3	0	0	0	4	/3	0.5
1967	KC-A	47	130	11	25	3	2	0	6	16	24	.192	.295	.246	64	-6	-5	11	1	0	0	8	3	0.4
1968	Oak-A	162	605	67	152	25	5	9	67	51	78	.251	.317	.354	108	2	5	69	13	4	2	-11	*3/O	0.0
1969	Oak-A	162	609	106	171	25	3	31	113	111	82	.281	.401	.484	153	41	45	124	1	4	-2	-13	*3	3.3
1970	Oak-A	155	502	93	132	20	2	20	75	118	88	.263	.409	.430	137	27	30	94	6	10	-4	-22	*3	0.4
1971	*Oak-A	153	538	75	146	23	1	24	94	86	55	.271	.380	.452	137	27	28	93	3	7	-3	-17	*3	0.2
1972	*Oak-A	152	535	64	126	20	3	15	77	78	55	.236	.342	.368	118	10	13	70	3	1	0	6	*3/2	2.7
1973	*Oak-A	162	592	97	170	32	3	29	98	82	84	.287	.378	.498	153	36	40	113	4	2	0	-23	*3/D	1.4
1974	*Oak-A	146	498	84	121	21	2	22	103	86	79	.243	.360	.426	134	18	22	80	2	3	-1	-13	*3/D	1.0
1975	*Oak-A	160	562	64	129	24	1	15	78	87	80	.230	.338	.356	98	-1	1	73	7	1	2	-16	*3	1.0
1976	Oak-A	158	550	75	132	18	2	27	84	76	74	.240	.337	.427	128	16	19	84	20	6	2	-5	*3/SD	1.7
1977	Mil-A	159	580	65	145	27	3	17	82	75	89	.250	.339	.395	99	0	0	81	4	2	0	-2	*3D/2S	-0.3
1978	Mil-A	152	540	85	154	20	6	17	78	72	52	.285	.375	.439	128	22	22	92	3	2	-0	12	*3D/1	3.2
1979	Mil-A	130	476	57	117	14	3	9	43	57	42	.246	.330	.345	82	-11	-11	54	2	0	1	-9	*3D/1P2	-1.6
1980	Mil-A	78	254	28	50	12	1	5	31	29	35	.197	.282	.311	64	-13	-12	22	5	3	-0	-3	3D/1	-1.6
1981	*Mil-A	32	65	10	13	4	0	2	9	6	3	.200	.268	.354	82	-2	-2	6	1	1	-0	1	3/1D	-0.1
Total	16	2019	7060	982	1790	289	38	242	1039	1031	923	.254	.355	.408	120	165	194	1069	75	46	-5	-102	*3/D1S2PO	10.2

■ ERNIE BANKS
Banks, Ernest b: 1/31/31, Dallas, Tex. BR/TR, 6'1", 180 lbs. Deb: 9/17/53 CH

YEAR	TM/L	G	AB	R	H	2B	3B	HR	RBI	BB	SO	AVG	OBP	SLG	PRO+	BR	/A	RC	SB	CS	SBR	FR	POS	TPR
1953	Chi-N	10	35	3	11	1	1	2	6	4	5	.314	.385	.571	142	2	2	8	0	0	0	3	S	0.5
1954	Chi-N	154	593	70	163	19	7	19	79	40	50	.275	.328	.427	94	-6	-7	80	6	10	-4	-1	*S	-0.1
1955	Chi-N	154	596	98	176	29	9	44	117	45	72	.295	.347	.596	145	34	35	117	9	3	1	5	*S	4.4
1956	Chi-N	139	538	82	160	25	8	28	85	52	62	.297	.359	.530	137	25	27	99	6	9	-4	-16	*S	1.7
1957	Chi-N	156	594	113	169	34	6	43	102	70	85	.285	.363	.579	150	39	40	123	8	4	0	-17	*S3	2.8
1958	Chi-N	154	617	119	193	23	11	47	129	52	87	.313	.370	.614	157	46	47	135	4	4	-1	-2	*S	5.3
1959	Chi-N	155	589	97	179	25	6	45	143	64	72	.304	.379	.596	156	44	45	126	2	4	-2	6	*S	5.4
1960	Chi-N	156	597	94	162	32	7	41	117	71	69	.271	.353	.554	145	34	35	113	1	3	-2	11	*S	5.0
1961	Chi-N	138	511	75	142	22	4	29	80	54	75	.278	.349	.507	122	16	15	88	1	2	-1	12	*SO/1	3.4
1962	Chi-N	154	610	87	164	20	6	37	104	30	71	.269	.311	.503	110	9	6	89	5	1	1	1	*1/3	0.3
1963	Chi-N	130	432	41	98	20	1	18	64	39	73	.227	.297	.403	94	-1	-4	50	0	3	-2	-1	*1	-0.9
1964	Chi-N	157	591	67	156	29	6	23	95	36	84	.264	.310	.450	107	7	4	77	1	2	-1	12	*1	1.0
1965	Chi-N	163	612	79	162	25	3	28	106	55	64	.265	.331	.453	116	14	12	87	3	5	-2	-3	*1	-0.1
1966	Chi-N	141	511	52	139	23	7	15	75	29	59	.272	.317	.432	105	3	5	66	0	1	-1	-0	*1/3	-0.5
1967	Chi-N	151	573	68	158	26	4	23	95	27	93	.276	.312	.455	112	10	7	74	2	2	-1	1	*1	0.1
1968	Chi-N	150	552	71	136	27	0	32	83	27	67	.246	.288	.469	116	13	9	72	2	0	1	-1	*1	0.4
1969	Chi-N	155	565	60	143	19	2	23	106	42	101	.253	.313	.416	91	0	-8	71	0	0	0	1	*1	-2.0
1970	Chi-N	72	222	25	56	6	2	12	44	20	33	.252	.317	.459	94	1	-3	32	0	0	0	-2	1	-0.9
1971	Chi-N	39	83	4	16	2	0	3	6	6	14	.193	.247	.325	53	-4	-6	7	0	0	0	1	1	-0.6
Total	19	2528	9421	1305	2583	407	90	512	1636	763	1236	.274	.333	.500	122	288	261	1513	50	53	-17	8	*1S/3O	25.3

■ GEORGE BANKS
Banks, George Edward b: 9/24/38, Pacolet Mills, S.C. d: 3/1/85, Spartanburg, S.C. BR/TR, 5'11", 185 lbs. Deb: 4/15/62

YEAR	TM/L	G	AB	R	H	2B	3B	HR	RBI	BB	SO	AVG	OBP	SLG	PRO+	BR	/A	RC	SB	CS	SBR	FR	POS	TPR
1962	Min-A	63	103	22	26	0	2	4	15	21	27	.252	.384	.408	109	3	2	16	0	0	0	-2	O/3	0.0
1963	Min-A	25	71	5	11	4	0	3	8	9	21	.155	.259	.338	65	-3	-4	6	0	0	0	2	3	-0.1
1964	Min-A	1	1	0	0	0	0	0	0	0	1	.000	.000	.000	-99	-0	-0	0	0	0	0	0	H	0.0
	Cle-A	9	17	6	5	1	0	2	3	6	6	.294	.478	.706	226	3	3	6	0	0	0	-0	/O23	0.3
	Yr	10	18	6	5	1	0	2	3	6	7	.278	.458	.667	210	3	3	6	0	0	0	-0		0.3
1965	Cle-A	4	5	0	1	1	0	0	1	3	4	.200	.333	.400	107	0	0	0	0	1	-1	0	/3	0.0
1966	Cle-A	4	4	0	1	0	0	0	1	0	1	.250	.250	.250	44	-0	-0	0	0	0	0	0	H	0.0
Total	5	106	201	33	44	6	2	9	27	37	59	.219	.346	.403	102	2	1	30	0	1	-1	-1	/3O2	0.2

■ BILL BANKSTON
Bankston, Wilborn Everett b: 5/25/1893, Barnesville, Ga. d: 2/26/70, Griffin, Ga. BL/TR, 5'11", 180 lbs. Deb: 8/15/15

YEAR	TM/L	G	AB	R	H	2B	3B	HR	RBI	BB	SO	AVG	OBP	SLG	PRO+	BR	/A	RC	SB	CS	SBR	FR	POS	TPR
1915	Phi-A	11	36	6	5	1	1	1	2	2	5	.139	.205	.306	54	-2	-2	2	1			-1	/O	-0.2

■ JIM BANNING
Banning, James M. b: 1866, New York, N.Y. BL/TR, 5'6", 150 lbs. Deb: 9/27/1888

YEAR	TM/L	G	AB	R	H	2B	3B	HR	RBI	BB	SO	AVG	OBP	SLG	PRO+	BR	/A	RC	SB	CS	SBR	FR	POS	TPR
1888	Was-N	1	0	0	0	0	0	0	0	0	0	—	—	—	—	0	0	0	0			-0	/C	0.0
1889	Was-N	2	1	0	0	0	0	0	0	0	0	.000	.000	.000	-99	-0	-0	0	0			1	/C	0.0
Total	2	3	1	0	0	0	0	0	0	0	0	.000	.000	.000	-99	-0	-0	0	0			1	/C	0.0

■ ALAN BANNISTER
Bannister, Alan b: 9/3/51, Montebello, Cal. BR/TR, 5'11", 170 lbs. Deb: 7/13/74

YEAR	TM/L	G	AB	R	H	2B	3B	HR	RBI	BB	SO	AVG	OBP	SLG	PRO+	BR	/A	RC	SB	CS	SBR	FR	POS	TPR
1974	Phi-N	26	25	4	3	0	0	0	1	3	7	.120	.241	.120	3	-3	-3	1	0	0	0	0	/OS	-0.2
1975	Phi-N	24	61	10	16	3	1	0	0	1	9	.262	.274	.344	68	-3	-3	5	2	2	-1	4	O/2S	0.0
1976	Chi-A	73	145	19	36	6	2	0	8	14	21	.248	.319	.317	86	-2	-2	17	12	4	1	5	OS/23D	0.4
1977	Chi-A	139	560	87	154	20	3	3	57	54	49	.275	.341	.338	86	-10	-9	66	4	3	-1	-33	*S/2O	-2.6
1978	Chi-A	49	107	16	24	3	2	0	8	11	12	.224	.303	.290	67	-4	-5	9	3	3	-1	-1	DO/S2	-0.5
1979	Chi-A	136	506	71	144	28	8	1	55	43	40	.285	.344	.383	96	-2	-2	69	22	6	3	-26	2O3/1D	-2.3
1980	Chi-A	45	130	16	25	6	0	0	9	12	16	.192	.261	.238	38	-11	-11	8	5	2	0	-1	O3	-1.1
	Cle-A	81	262	41	86	17	4	1	32	28	25	.328	.393	.435	126	10	10	46	9	2	2	-14	2O/3S	-1.1
	Yr	126	392	57	111	23	4	1	41	40	41	.283	.350	.370	97	-1	-1	52	14	4	2	-14		-1.1
1981	Cle-A	68	232	36	61	11	1	1	17	16	19	.263	.310	.332	86	-4	-4	27	16	2	4	-12	O2/1S	-1.2
1982	Cle-A	101	348	40	93	16	1	4	41	42	41	.267	.348	.353	94	-2	-2	48	18	5	2	-11	O2/S3D	-0.9
1983	Cle-A	117	377	51	100	25	4	5	45	31	43	.265	.326	.393	93	-2	-4	48	6	6	-2	-11	O2/1D	-1.6
1984	Hou-N	9	20	2	4	2	0	0	0	2	2	.200	.273	.300	65	-1	-1	2	0	0	0	-1	/SO	-0.1
	Tex-A	47	112	20	33	2	1	2	9	21	17	.295	.410	.384	118	4	4	20	3	0	1	-13	2/O13D	-0.6
1985	Tex-A	57	122	17	32	4	1	1	6	14	17	.262	.338	.336	84	-2	-2	15	8	2	1	3	DO2/31	0.0
Total	12	972	3007	430	811	143	28	19	288	292	318	.270	.337	.355	90	-32	-35	381	108	37	10	-109	O2S/D31	-10.6

■ JIMMY BANNON
Bannon, James Henry "Foxy Grandpa" b: 5/5/1871, Amesbury, Mass. d: 3/24/48, Glen Rock, N.J. BR, 5'5", 160 lbs. Deb: 6/15/1893

YEAR	TM/L	G	AB	R	H	2B	3B	HR	RBI	BB	SO	AVG	OBP	SLG	PRO+	BR	/A	RC	SB	CS	SBR	FR	POS	TPR
1893	StL-N	26	107	9	36	3	4	0	15	4	5	.336	.366	.439	115	2	2	21	8			-6	O/SP	-0.3
1894	Bos-N	128	494	130	166	29	10	13	114	62	42	.336	.414	.514	115	20	12	128	47			18	*O/P	1.6
1895	Bos-N	123	489	101	171	35	5	6	74	54	31	.350	.420	.479	124	25	18	113	28			10	*O/P	1.5
1896	Bos-N	89	343	52	86	9	5	0	50	32	23	.251	.316	.306	63	-16	-20	39	16			1	O/2S3	-2.0
Total	4	366	1433	292	459	76	24	19	253	152	101	.320	.390	.447	106	31	12	300	99			24	O/S23P	0.8

■ TOM BANNON
Bannon, Thomas Edward "Ward Six" b: 5/8/1869, Amesbury, Mass. d: 1/26/50, Lynn, Mass. 5'8", 175 lbs. Deb: 5/10/1895

YEAR	TM/L	G	AB	R	H	2B	3B	HR	RBI	BB	SO	AVG	OBP	SLG	PRO+	BR	/A	RC	SB	CS	SBR	FR	POS	TPR
1895	NY-N	37	159	33	43	6	2	0	8	7	8	.270	.301	.333	67	-8	-8	23	20			2	O1	-0.5
1896	NY-N	2	7	1	1	1	0	0	0	1	1	.143	.250	.286	44	-1	-1	1	0			-1	/O	0.0
Total	2	39	166	34	44	7	2	0	8	8	9	.265	.299	.331	66	-9	-8	23	20			1	/O1	-0.5

■ WALTER BARBARE
Barbare, Walter Lawrence "Dinty" b: 8/11/1891, Greenville, S.C. d: 10/28/65, Greenville, S.C. BR/TR, 6', 162 lbs. Deb: 9/17/14

YEAR	TM/L	G	AB	R	H	2B	3B	HR	RBI	BB	SO	AVG	OBP	SLG	PRO+	BR	/A	RC	SB	CS	SBR	FR	POS	TPR
1914	Cle-A	15	52	6	16	2	2	0	5	2	5	.308	.345	.423	126	2	1	7	1	4	-2	0	3/S	0.0
1915	Cle-A	77	246	15	47	3	1	0	11	10	27	.191	.235	.211	33	-20	-21	14	6	5	-1	7	3/1	-1.2

YEAR	TM/L	G	AB	R	H	2B	3B	HR	RBI	BB	SO	AVG	OBP	SLG	PRO+	BR	/A	RC	SB	CS	SBR	FR	POS	TPR
1916	Cle-A	13	48	3	11	1	0	0	3	4	9	.229	.288	.250	58	-2	-3	4	0			1	3	0.0
1918	Bos-A	13	29	2	5	3	0	0	2	0	1	.172	.172	.276	36	-2	-2	2	1			-3	3/S	-0.6
1919	Pit-N	85	293	34	80	11	5	1	34	18	18	.273	.317	.355	98	0	-1	36	11			-6	3/2	-0.7
1920	Pit-N	57	186	9	51	5	2	0	12	9	11	.274	.308	.323	79	-5	-5	18	5	3	-0	-5	S2/3	-0.8
1921	Bos-N	134	550	66	166	22	7	0	49	24	28	.302	.331	.367	89	-12	-8	68	11	4	1	-16	*S/23	-1.1
1922	Bos-N	106	373	38	86	5	4	0	40	21	22	.231	.272	.265	41	-34	-31	28	2	0	1	2	231	-2.4
Total	8	500	1777	173	462	52	21	1	156	88	121	.260	.297	.315	71	-73	-70	177	37	16		-21	3S/21	-6.8

■ RED BARBARY　Barbary, Donald Odell　b: 6/20/20, Simpsonville, S.C　BR/TR, 6'3", 190 lbs.　Deb: 5/22/43

YEAR	TM/L	G	AB	R	H	2B	3B	HR	RBI	BB	SO	AVG	OBP	SLG	PRO+	BR	/A	RC	SB	CS	SBR	FR	POS	TPR
1943	Was-A	1	1	0	0	0	0	0	0	0	0	.000	.000	.000	-99	-0	-0	0	0	0	0	0	H	0.0

■ JAP BARBEAU　Barbeau, William Joseph　b: 6/10/1882, New York, N.Y.　d: 9/10/69, Milwaukee, Wis.　BR/TR, 5'5", 140 lbs.　Deb: 9/27/05

YEAR	TM/L	G	AB	R	H	2B	3B	HR	RBI	BB	SO	AVG	OBP	SLG	PRO+	BR	/A	RC	SB	CS	SBR	FR	POS	TPR
1905	Cle-A	11	37	1	10	1	1	0	2	1		.270	.289	.351	103	0	0	4	1			1	2	0.1
1906	Cle-A	42	129	8	25	5	3	0	12	9		.194	.246	.279	67	-5	-5	11	5			-7	3/S	-1.0
1909	Pit-N	91	350	60	77	16	3	0	25	37		.220	.302	.283	75	-7	-10	35	19			-20	3	-3.2
	StL-N	48	175	23	44	3	0	0	5	28		.251	.370	.269	105	2	3	23	14			-11	3	-0.6
	Yr	139	525	83	121	19	3	0	30	65		.230	.326	.278	85	-5	-7	58	33			-31		-3.8
1910	StL-N	7	21	4	4	0	1	0	2	3	3	.190	.292	.286	71	-1	-1	2	0			2	/32	0.2
Total	4	199	712	96	160	25	8	0	46	78	3	.225	.309	.282	82	-11	-13	75	39			-34	3/2S	-4.5

■ DAVE BARBEE　Barbee, David Monroe　b: 5/7/05, Greensboro, N.C.　d: 7/1/68, Albermarle, N.C.　BR/TR, 5'11.5", 178 lbs.　Deb: 7/29/26

YEAR	TM/L	G	AB	R	H	2B	3B	HR	RBI	BB	SO	AVG	OBP	SLG	PRO+	BR	/A	RC	SB	CS	SBR	FR	POS	TPR
1926	Phi-A	19	47	7	8	1	1	1	5	2	4	.170	.204	.298	32	-5	-5	3	0	0	0	0	O	-0.5
1932	Pit-N	97	327	37	84	22	6	5	55	18	38	.257	.300	.407	89	-6	-5	40	1			0	O	-1.0
Total	2	116	374	44	92	23	7	6	60	20	42	.246	.290	.393	82	-11	-11	44	1	0		0	/O	-1.5

■ CHARLIE BARBER　Barber, Charles D.　b: 1854, Philadelphia, Pa.　d: 11/23/10, Philadelphia, Pa.　BR/TR,　Deb: 4/17/1884

YEAR	TM/L	G	AB	R	H	2B	3B	HR	RBI	BB	SO	AVG	OBP	SLG	PRO+	BR	/A	RC	SB	CS	SBR	FR	POS	TPR
1884	Cin-U	55	204	38	41	1	4	0	11			.201	.242	.245	60	-7	-10	12	0			4	3	-0.4

■ TURNER BARBER　Barber, Tyrus Turner　b: 7/9/1893, Lavinia, Tenn.　d: 10/20/68, Milan, Tenn.　BL/TR, 5'11", 170 lbs.　Deb: 8/19/15

YEAR	TM/L	G	AB	R	H	2B	3B	HR	RBI	BB	SO	AVG	OBP	SLG	PRO+	BR	/A	RC	SB	CS	SBR	FR	POS	TPR
1915	Was-A	20	53	9	16	1	1	0	6	6	7	.302	.383	.358	121	2	2	7	0	3	-2	-2	O	-0.2
1916	Was-A	15	33	3	7	0	1	1	5	2	3	.212	.257	.364	88	-1	-1	3	0			-3	O	-0.4
1917	Chi-N	7	28	2	6	1	0	0	2	2	8	.214	.267	.250	55	-1	-2	2	1			1	/O	0.0
1918	*Chi-N	55	123	11	29	3	2	0	10	9	16	.236	.293	.293	77	-3	-3	11	3			-1	O/1	-0.6
1919	Chi-N	76	230	26	72	9	4	0	21	14	17	.313	.355	.387	122	6	6	33	7			-2	O	0.1
1920	Chi-N	94	340	27	90	10	5	0	50	9	26	.265	.290	.324	74	-11	-12	31	5	6	-2	-6	1O/2	-2.2
1921	Chi-N	127	452	73	142	14	4	1	54	41	24	.314	.379	.369	99	1	1	64	5	9	-4	3	*O	-0.5
1922	Chi-N	84	226	35	70	7	4	0	29	30	9	.310	.391	.376	97	1	0	35	7	4	-0	-5	O1	-0.5
1923	Bro-N	13	46	3	10	2	0	0	8	2	2	.217	.250	.261	36	-4	-4	3	0	1	-1	-1	O	-0.5
Total	9	491	1531	189	442	47	21	2	185	115	112	.289	.343	.351	93	-10	-12	189	28	23		-14	O/12	-4.8

■ JIM BARBIERI　Barbieri, James Patrick　b: 9/15/41, Schenectady, N.Y.　BL/TR, 5'7", 155 lbs.　Deb: 7/05/66

YEAR	TM/L	G	AB	R	H	2B	3B	HR	RBI	BB	SO	AVG	OBP	SLG	PRO+	BR	/A	RC	SB	CS	SBR	FR	POS	TPR
1966	*LA-N	39	82	9	23	5	0	0	3	9	7	.280	.352	.341	102	-0	0	11	2	0	1	0	O	0.0

■ GEORGE BARCLAY　Barclay, George Oliver "Deerfoot"　b: 5/16/1876, Millville, Pa.　d: 4/3/09, Philadelphia, Pa.　TR, 5'10", 162 lbs.　Deb: 4/17/02

YEAR	TM/L	G	AB	R	H	2B	3B	HR	RBI	BB	SO	AVG	OBP	SLG	PRO+	BR	/A	RC	SB	CS	SBR	FR	POS	TPR
1902	StL-N	137	543	79	163	14	2	3	53	31		.300	.346	.350	122	11	13	79	30			-7	*O	-0.3
1903	StL-N	108	419	37	104	10	8	0	42	15		.248	.274	.310	70	-18	-16	40	12			-8	*O	-2.8
1904	StL-N	103	375	41	75	7	4	1	28	12		.200	.225	.248	50	-23	-21	26	14			-6	*O	-3.3
	Bos-N	24	93	5	21	3	1	0	10	2		.226	.242	.280	65	-4	-4	7	3			-3	O	-0.7
	Yr	127	468	46	96	10	5	1	38	14		.205	.228	.254	53	-27	-25	33	17			-9		-4.0
1905	Bos-N	29	108	5	19	1	0	0	7	2		.176	.191	.185	14	-11	-11	4	2			-4	O	-1.8
Total	4	401	1538	167	382	35	15	4	140	62		.248	.281	.298	79	-46	-39	157	61			-28	O	-8.9

■ JESSE BARFIELD　Barfield, Jesse Lee　b: 10/29/59, Joliet, Ill.　BR/TR, 6'4", 215 lbs.　Deb: 9/03/81

YEAR	TM/L	G	AB	R	H	2B	3B	HR	RBI	BB	SO	AVG	OBP	SLG	PRO+	BR	/A	RC	SB	CS	SBR	FR	POS	TPR
1981	Tor-A	25	95	7	22	3	2	2	9	4	19	.232	.270	.368	77	-2	-3	8	4	3	-1	2	O	-0.1
1982	Tor-A	139	394	54	97	13	2	18	58	42	79	.246	.323	.426	95	2	3	54	1	4	-2	-9	*O/D	-1.8
1983	Tor-A	128	388	58	98	13	3	27	68	22	110	.253	.300	.510	111	7	4	55	2	5	-2	-1	*O/D	0.0
1984	Tor-A	110	320	51	91	14	1	14	49	35	81	.284	.359	.466	122	11	10	55	8	2	1	4	O/D	1.2
1985	*Tor-A	155	539	94	156	34	9	27	84	66	143	.289	.371	.536	141	33	31	106	22	8	-2	17	*O	4.7
1986	Tor-A	158	589	107	170	35	2	**40**	108	69	146	.289	.371	.559	145	39	37	122	8	8	-2	20	*O	**5.0**
1987	Tor-A	159	590	89	155	25	3	28	84	58	141	.263	.332	.458	104	5	3	87	3	5	-2	14	*O	1.1
1988	Tor-A	137	468	62	114	21	5	18	56	41	108	.244	.306	.425	102	0	0	60	7	3	0	14	*O/D	1.2
1989	Tor-A	21	80	8	16	4	0	5	11	5	28	.200	.256	.438	94	-1	-1	9	0	2	-1	1	O	0.0
	NY-A	129	441	71	106	19	1	18	56	82	122	.240	.362	.410	119	12	13	70	5	3	-0	12	*O	2.3
	Yr	150	521	79	122	23	1	23	67	87	150	.234	.347	.415	115	11	12	78	5	5	-2	13		2.3
1990	NY-A	153	476	69	117	21	2	25	78	82	150	.246	.362	.456	127	19	18	84	4	3	-1	5	*O	2.2
Total	10	1314	4380	670	1142	202	30	222	661	506	1127	.261	.342	.473	119	125	110	708	64	46	-8	80	*O/D	15.8

■ AL BARKER　Barker, Alfred L　b: 1/18/1839, Rockford, Ill.　d: 9/15/12, Rockford, Ill.　Deb: 6/01/1871

YEAR	TM/L	G	AB	R	H	2B	3B	HR	RBI	BB	SO	AVG	OBP	SLG	PRO+	BR	/A	RC	SB	CS	SBR	FR	POS	TPR
1871	Rok-n	1	4	0	1	0	0	0	2	1	0	.250	.400	.250	97	0	0	0					/O	0.0

■ RAY BARKER　Barker, Raymond Herrell "Buddy"　b: 3/12/36, Martinsburg.W.Va.　BL/TR, 6', 192 lbs.　Deb: 9/13/60

YEAR	TM/L	G	AB	R	H	2B	3B	HR	RBI	BB	SO	AVG	OBP	SLG	PRO+	BR	/A	RC	SB	CS	SBR	FR	POS	TPR
1960	Bal-A	5	6	0	0	0	0	0	0	0	3	.000	.000	.000	-99	-2	-2	0	0	0	0	0	/O	-0.1
1965	Cle-A	11	6	0	0	0	0	0	0	2	2	.000	.250	.000	-22	-1	-1	0	0	0	0	0	/1	0.0
	NY-A	98	205	21	52	11	0	7	31	20	46	.254	.329	.410	109	2	2	28	1	0	0	-16	1/3	-1.6
	Yr	109	211	21	52	11	0	7	31	22	48	.246	.326	.398	105	1	1	28	1	0	0	-16		-1.6
1966	NY-A	61	75	11	14	5	0	3	13	4	20	.187	.228	.373	72	-3	-3	7	0	0	0	5	1	0.1
1967	NY-A	17	26	2	2	0	0	0	0	3	5	.077	.172	.077	-25	-4	-4	0	0	0	0	-1	1	-0.6
Total	4	192	318	34	68	16	0	10	44	29	76	.214	.286	.358	84	-8	-7	35	1	0	0	-12	1/3O	-2.2

■ RED BARKLEY　Barkley, John Duncan　b: 9/19/13, Childress, Tex.　BR/TR, 5'11", 160 lbs.　Deb: 9/02/37

YEAR	TM/L	G	AB	R	H	2B	3B	HR	RBI	BB	SO	AVG	OBP	SLG	PRO+	BR	/A	RC	SB	CS	SBR	FR	POS	TPR
1937	StL-A	31	101	9	27	6	0	0	14	14	17	.267	.357	.327	73	-4	-4	13	1	0	0	-4	2	-0.4
1939	Bos-N	12	11	1	0	0	0	0	0	1	2	.000	.083	.000	-82	-3	-3	0	0			4	/S3	0.1
1943	Bro-N	20	51	6	16	3	0	0	7	4	7	.314	.364	.373	113	1	1	7	1			-2	S	0.0
Total	3	63	163	16	43	9	0	0	21	19	26	.264	.341	.319	75	-6	-6	20	2	0		-3	/2S3	-0.3

■ SAM BARKLEY　Barkley, Samuel E　b: 5/24/1858, Wheeling, W.Va.　d: 4/20/12, Wheeling, W.Va.　BR/TR, 5'11.5",　Deb: 5/01/1884　M

YEAR	TM/L	G	AB	R	H	2B	3B	HR	RBI	BB	SO	AVG	OBP	SLG	PRO+	BR	/A	RC	SB	CS	SBR	FR	POS	TPR
1884	Tol-a	104	435	71	133	**39**	1	1	22			.306	.342	.444	152	26	24	68				25	*2/C	**4.6**
1885	*StL-a	106	418	67	112	18	10	3	25			.268	.312	.380	115	10	6	51				15	*21	2.2
1886	Pit-a	122	478	77	127	31	8	1	58			.266	.345	.370	127	15	16	70	22			-4	*2/O1	1.0
1887	Pit-N	89	340	44	76	10	4	1	35	30	24	.224	.294	.285	67	-16	-12	31	6			-4	12	-1.9
1888	KC-a	116	482	67	104	21	6	4	51	26		.216	.262	.309	80	-8	-13	44	15			-7	*2/M	-1.0
1889	KC-a	45	176	36	50	6	2	0	23	15	20	.284	.340	.341	91	-1	-2	24	8			-12	2/1	-1.1
Total	6	582	2329	362	602	125	39	10	109	176	44	.258	.314	.359	107	27	19	288	51			13	2/1OC	3.4

■ TOM BARLOW　Barlow, Thomas H.　Deb: 5/02/1872

YEAR	TM/L	G	AB	R	H	2B	3B	HR	RBI	BB	SO	AVG	OBP	SLG	PRO+	BR	/A	RC	SB	CS	SBR	FR	POS	TPR
1872	Atl-n	37	170	34	56	2	0	0	3			.329	.341	.341	94	2	-4	20					*C/S	-0.3

YEAR	TM/L	G	AB	R	H	2B	3B	HR	RBI	BB	SO	AVG	OBP	SLG	PRO+	BR	/A	RC	SB	CS	SBR	FR	POS	TPR
1873	Atl-n	55	272	48	71	2	2	1		3		.261	.269	.294	73	-11	-5	22					*C	-0.2
1874	Har-n	32	156	37	44	4	1	0		1		.282	.287	.321	89	-1	-3	15					S	-0.3
1875	NH-n	1	5	1	1	0	0	0		0		.200	.200	.200	45	-0	-0	0					/S	0.0
	Atl-n	1	4	0	0	0	0	0		0		.000	.000	.000	-99	-1	-1	0					/2	0.0
	Yr	2	9	1	1	0	0	0		0		.111	.111	.111	-27	-1	-1	0						0.0
Total	4 n	126	607	120	172	8	3	1		7		.283	.292	.311	83	-11	-13	57					/CS2	-0.8

■ BRUCE BARMES Barmes, Bruce Raymond "Squeaky" b: 10/23/29, Vincennes, Ind. BL/TR, 5'8", 165 lbs. Deb: 9/13/53

YEAR	TM/L	G	AB	R	H	2B	3B	HR	RBI	BB	SO	AVG	OBP	SLG	PRO+	BR	/A	RC	SB	CS	SBR	FR	POS	TPR
1953	Was-A	5	5	1	1	0	0	0	0	0	0	.200	.200	.200	8	-1	-1	0	0	0	0	0	/O	0.0

■ BABE BARNA Barna, Herbert Paul b: 3/2/15, Clarksburg, W.Va. d: 5/18/72, Charleston, W.Va. BL/TR, 6'2", 210 lbs. Deb: 9/16/37

YEAR	TM/L	G	AB	R	H	2B	3B	HR	RBI	BB	SO	AVG	OBP	SLG	PRO+	BR	/A	RC	SB	CS	SBR	FR	POS	TPR
1937	Phi-A	14	36	10	14	2	0	2	9	2	6	.389	.421	.611	159	3	3	9	1	0	0	-1	/O1	0.1
1938	Phi-A	9	30	4	4	0	0	0	2	3	5	.133	.212	.133	-12	-5	-5	1	0	0	0	-1	/O	-0.5
1941	NY-N	10	42	5	9	3	0	1	5	2	6	.214	.250	.357	68	-2	-2	4	0			-0	O	-0.2
1942	NY-N	104	331	39	85	8	7	6	58	38	48	.257	.333	.378	107	3	3	44	3			-4	O	-0.2
1943	NY-N	40	113	11	23	5	1	1	12	16	9	.204	.302	.292	72	-4	-4	11	3			-2	O	-0.7
	Bos-A	30	112	19	19	4	1	2	10	15	24	.170	.268	.277	58	-6	-6	9	2	1	0	-5	O	-1.2
Total	5	207	664	88	154	22	9	12	96	76	98	.232	.311	.346	88	-11	-11	78	9	1		-13	O/1	-2.7

■ RED BARNES Barnes, Emile Deering b: 12/25/03, Suggsville, Ala. d: 7/3/59, Mobile, Ala. BL/TR, 5'10.5", 158 lbs. Deb: 9/29/27

YEAR	TM/L	G	AB	R	H	2B	3B	HR	RBI	BB	SO	AVG	OBP	SLG	PRO+	BR	/A	RC	SB	CS	SBR	FR	POS	TPR
1927	Was-A	3	11	5	4	1	0	0		1	3	.364	.417	.455	127	0	0	2	0	0	0	0	/O	0.0
1928	Was-A	114	417	82	127	22	15	6	51	55	38	.305	.391	.472	127	16	17	80	7	3	0	4	*O	1.4
1929	Was-A	72	130	16	26	5	2	1	15	13	12	.200	.273	.292	45	-11	-11	11	1	0	0	-6	O	-1.6
1930	Was-A	12	12	1	2	1	0	0	0	0	3	.167	.167	.250	4	-2	-2	0	0	0	0	0	H	-0.1
	Chi-A	85	266	48	66	12	7	1	31	26	20	.248	.317	.357	73	-12	-11	31	4	2	0	-0	O	-1.1
	Yr	97	278	49	68	13	7	1	31	26	23	.245	.311	.353	70	-14	-12	32	4	2	0	-0		-1.2
Total	4	286	836	152	225	41	24	8	97	95	76	.269	.347	.404	95	-8	-6	125	12	5	1	-2	O	-1.4

■ EPPIE BARNES Barnes, Everett Duane b: 12/1/1900, Ossining, N.Y. d: 11/17/80, Mineola, N.Y. BL/TL, 5'9", 175 lbs. Deb: 9/25/23

YEAR	TM/L	G	AB	R	H	2B	3B	HR	RBI	BB	SO	AVG	OBP	SLG	PRO+	BR	/A	RC	SB	CS	SBR	FR	POS	TPR
1923	Pit-N	2	2	0	1	0	0	0	0	0	1	.500	.500	.500	161	0	0	0	0	0	0	0	/1	0.0
1924	Pit-N	2	5	0	0	0	0	0	0	0	1	.000	.000	.000	-98	-1	-1	0	0	0	0	0	/1	0.0
Total	2	4	7	0	1	0	0	0	0	0	2	.143	.143	.143	-23	-1	-1	0	0	0	0	1	/1	0.0

■ HONEY BARNES Barnes, John Francis b: 1/29/1900, Fulton, N.Y. d: 6/18/81, Lockport, N.Y. BL/TR, 5'10", 175 lbs. Deb: 4/20/26

YEAR	TM/L	G	AB	R	H	2B	3B	HR	RBI	BB	SO	AVG	OBP	SLG	PRO+	BR	/A	RC	SB	CS	SBR	FR	POS	TPR
1926	NY-A	1	0	0	0	0	0	0	0	1	0	—	1.000	—	179	0	0	0	0	0	0	0	/C	0.0

■ LUTE BARNES Barnes, Luther Owens b: 4/28/47, Forest City, Iowa BR/TR, 5'10", 160 lbs. Deb: 8/06/72

YEAR	TM/L	G	AB	R	H	2B	3B	HR	RBI	BB	SO	AVG	OBP	SLG	PRO+	BR	/A	RC	SB	CS	SBR	FR	POS	TPR
1972	NY-N	24	72	5	17	2	2	0	6	6	4	.236	.295	.319	76	-2	-2	6	0	1	-1	1	2/S	0.0
1973	NY-N	3	2	2	1	0	0	0	1	0	1	.500	.500	.500	181	0	0	1	0	0	0	0	H	0.0
Total	2	27	74	7	18	2	2	0	7	6	5	.243	.300	.324	79	-2	-2	7	0	1	-1	1	/2S	0.0

■ ROSS BARNES Barnes, Roscoe Charles b: 5/8/1850, Lima, N.Y. d: 2/5/15, Chicago, Ill. BR/TR, 5'8.5", 145 lbs. Deb: 5/05/1871 U

YEAR	TM/L	G	AB	R	H	2B	3B	HR	RBI	BB	SO	AVG	OBP	SLG	PRO+	BR	/A	RC	SB	CS	SBR	FR	POS	TPR
1871	Bos-n	31	157	**66**	63	10	9	0	34	13	1	.401	.447	.580	186	19	18	47	11				2S/3	1.1
1872	Bos-n	45	230	81	**97**	**28**	2	1		9		**.422**	.444	**.574**	**200**	29	27	60					*2	1.4
1873	Bos-n	60	320	125	137	28	10	3		18		.428	.459	.606	194	44	38	91					*23	2.3
1874	Bos-n	51	259	72	89	12	4	0		8		.344	.363	.421	141	14	11	41					*2	0.8
1875	Bos-n	78	393	114	**142**	22	6	1		7		.361	**.373**	.455	178	32	30	68					*2	2.3
1876	Chi-N	66	322	**126**	**138**	21	14	1	59	20	8	**.429**	.462	.590	222	50	44	90				5	*2/P	**4.2**
1877	Chi-N	22	92	16	25	1	0	0	5	7	4	.272	.323	.283	83	-0	-2	9				-8	2	-0.8
1879	Cin-N	77	323	55	86	9	2	1	30	16	25	.266	.301	.316	109	2	4	31				-1	*S2	0.8
1881	Bos-N	69	295	42	80	14	1	0	17	16	16	.271	.309	.325	104	0	2	30				-0	*S/2	0.6
Total	5 n	265	1359	458	528	100	31	5	34	55	1	.389	.412	.519	180	138	123	307					2S/3	7.9
Total	4	234	1032	239	329	45	17	2	111	59	53	.319	.356	.401	143	51	48	160				-5	S2/P	4.8

■ SAM BARNES Barnes, Samuel Thomas b: 12/18/1899, Suggsville, Ala. "Ed" d: 2/19/81, Montgomery, Ala. BL/TR, 5'8", 150 lbs. Deb: 9/14/21

YEAR	TM/L	G	AB	R	H	2B	3B	HR	RBI	BB	SO	AVG	OBP	SLG	PRO+	BR	/A	RC	SB	CS	SBR	FR	POS	TPR
1921	Det-A	7	11	2	2	1	0	0	0	2	1	.182	.357	.273	63	-1	-1	1	0	0	0	2	/2	0.1

■ BILL BARNES Barnes, William H. b: Indianapolis, Ind. Deb: 9/27/1884

YEAR	TM/L	G	AB	R	H	2B	3B	HR	RBI	BB	SO	AVG	OBP	SLG	PRO+	BR	/A	RC	SB	CS	SBR	FR	POS	TPR
1884	StP-U	8	30	2	6	1	0	0				.200	.200	.233	85	-2	0	1	0			-2	/O	0.0

■ SKEETER BARNES Barnes, William Henry b: 3/3/57, Cincinnati, Ohio BR/TR, 5'11", 175 lbs. Deb: 9/06/83

YEAR	TM/L	G	AB	R	H	2B	3B	HR	RBI	BB	SO	AVG	OBP	SLG	PRO+	BR	/A	RC	SB	CS	SBR	FR	POS	TPR
1983	Cin-N	15	34	5	7	0	0	1	4	7	3	.206	.372	.294	84	-0	-0	4	2	2	-1	-0	/13	-0.1
1984	Cin-N	32	42	5	5	0	0	1	3	4	6	.119	.196	.190	8	-5	-5	2	0	0	0	1	3/O	-0.4
1985	Mon-N	19	26	0	4	1	0	0	0	0	2	.154	.154	.192	-4	-4	-3	0	0	1	-1	2	/3O1	-0.2
1987	StL-N	4	4	1	1	0	0	1	3	0	0	.250	.250	1.000	208	1	1	1	0	0	0	0	3	0.1
1989	Cin-N	5	3	1	0	0	0	0	0	0	0	.000	.000	.000	-97	-1	-1	0	0	1	-1	0	H	0.0
Total	5	75	109	12	17	1	0	3	10	11	11	.156	.246	.248	37	-9	-9	7	2	4	-2	3	/31O	-0.6

■ ED BARNEY Barney, Edmund J. b: 1/23/1890, Amery, Wis. d: 10/4/67, Rice Lake, Wis. BL/TR, 5'10.5", 178 lbs. Deb: 7/22/15

YEAR	TM/L	G	AB	R	H	2B	3B	HR	RBI	BB	SO	AVG	OBP	SLG	PRO+	BR	/A	RC	SB	CS	SBR	FR	POS	TPR
1915	NY-A	11	36	1	7	0	0	0		3	6	.194	.256	.194	35	-3	-3	2	2	1	0	0	O	-0.3
	Pit-N	32	99	16	27	1	2	0	5	11	12	.273	.363	.323	110	2	2	13	7	3	0	2	O	0.4
1916	Pit-N	45	137	16	27	4	0	0	9	23	15	.197	.313	.226	66	-4	-4	13	8			6	O	0.0
Total	2	88	272	33	61	5	2	0	22	37	33	.224	.324	.257	78	-6	-6	29	17	4		9	/O	0.1

■ CLYDE BARNHART Barnhart, Clyde Lee "Pooch" b: 12/29/1895, Buck Valley, Pa. d: 1/21/80, Hagerstown, Md. BR/TR, 5'10", 155 lbs. Deb: 9/22/20

YEAR	TM/L	G	AB	R	H	2B	3B	HR	RBI	BB	SO	AVG	OBP	SLG	PRO+	BR	/A	RC	SB	CS	SBR	FR	POS	TPR
1920	Pit-N	12	46	5	15	4	2	0	5	1	2	.326	.340	.500	135	2	2	8	1	0	0	3		0.3
1921	Pit-N	124	449	66	116	15	13	3	62	32	36	.258	.312	.370	78	-13	-15	53	3	3	-1	-18	*3	-3.3
1922	Pit-N	75	209	30	69	7	5	1	38	25	7	.330	.402	.426	112	5	5	37	3	2	-0	-11	3O	-0.4
1923	Pit-N	114	327	60	106	25	13	9	72	47	21	.324	.409	.563	151	26	24	74	5	7	-3	2	O	1.9
1924	Pit-N	102	344	49	95	6	11	3	50	30	17	.276	.338	.384	91	-3	-4	46	8	4	0	0	O	-0.5
1925	*Pit-N	142	539	85	175	32	11	4	114	59	25	.325	.391	.447	106	12	7	96	9	5		-8	*O	-0.4
1926	Pit-N	76	203	26	39	3	0	0	10	23	13	.192	.278	.207	30	-19	-20	13	1			-3	O	-2.5
1927	*Pit-N	108	360	65	115	23	4	3	54	37	19	.319	.384	.431	110	10	6	59	2			1	O	0.3
1928	Pit-N	61	196	18	58	6	2	4	30	11	9	.296	.333	.408	89	-2	-3	26	3			-4	O/3	-0.8
Total	9	814	2673	404	788	121	61	27	436	265	149	.295	.360	.416	100	17	2	412	35	21		-41	O3	-5.4

■ VIC BARNHART Barnhart, Victor Dee b: 9/1/22, Hagerstown, Md. BR/TR, 6', 188 lbs. Deb: 10/01/44

YEAR	TM/L	G	AB	R	H	2B	3B	HR	RBI	BB	SO	AVG	OBP	SLG	PRO+	BR	/A	RC	SB	CS	SBR	FR	POS	TPR
1944	Pit-N	1	2	0	1	0	0	0		1		.500	.667	.500	222	1	1	1	0			1	/S	0.2
1945	Pit-N	71	201	21	54	7	0	0	19	9	11	.269	.300	.303	65	-9	-10	17	2			8	S/3	0.4
1946	Pit-N	2	1	0	0	0	0	0	0	0	0	.000	.000	.000	-98	-0	-0	0	0			0	H	0.0
Total	3	74	204	21	55	7	0	0	19	10	12	.270	.304	.304	67	-9	-10	17	2			9	S3	0.6

■ BILLY BARNIE Barnie, William Harrison "Bald Billy" b: 1/26/1853, New York, N.Y. d: 7/15/1900, Hartford, Conn. 5'7", 157 lbs. Deb: 5/07/1874 MU

YEAR	TM/L	G	AB	R	H	2B	3B	HR	RBI	BB	SO	AVG	OBP	SLG	PRO+	BR	/A	RC	SB	CS	SBR	FR	POS	TPR
1874	Har-n	45	188	21	34	3	2	0		0		.181	.181	.218	25	-15	-17	8					CO/S	-1.1
1875	Wes-n	10	36	3	4	1	0	0		0		.111	.111	.139	-13	-4	-4	1					/CO	-0.3
	Mut-n	9	35	1	5	1	0	0		0		.143	.143	.171	8	-3	-3	1					/CO	-0.2

YEAR	TM/L	G	AB	R	H	2B	3B	HR	RBI	BB	SO	AVG	OBP	SLG	PRO+	BR	/A	RC	SB	CS	SBR	FR	POS	TPR
	Yr	19	71	4	9	2	0	0		0		.127	.127	.155	-3	-7	-8	1						-0.5
1883	Bal-a	17	55	7	11	0	0	0		2		.200	.228	.200	38	-4	-4	3				2	C/OSM	0.0
1886	Bal-a	2	6	0	0	0	0	0		1		.000	.143	.000	-54	-1	-1	0	0			-1	/OC	0.0
Total	2 n	64	259	25	43	5	2	0		0		.166	.166	.201	18	-22	-24	9	0				/COS	-1.6
Total	2	19	61	7	11	0	0	0		3		.180	.219	.180	29	-5	-5	3	0			2	/COS	0.0

■ DICK BARONE
Barone, Richard Anthony   b: 10/13/32, San Jose, Cal.   BR/TR, 5'9", 165 lbs.   Deb: 9/22/60

YEAR	TM/L	G	AB	R	H	2B	3B	HR	RBI	BB	SO	AVG	OBP	SLG	PRO+	BR	/A	RC	SB	CS	SBR	FR	POS	TPR
1960	Pit-N	3	6	0	0	0	0	0	0	0	1	.000	.000	.000	-99	-2	-2	0	0	0	0	-0	/S	-0.1

■ SCOTTY BARR
Barr, Hyder Edward   b: 10/6/1886, Bristol, Tenn.   d: 12/2/34, Ft.Worth, Tex.   BR/TR, 6', 175 lbs.   Deb: 8/22/08

YEAR	TM/L	G	AB	R	H	2B	3B	HR	RBI	BB	SO	AVG	OBP	SLG	PRO+	BR	/A	RC	SB	CS	SBR	FR	POS	TPR
1908	Phi-A	19	56	4	8	2	0	0	1	3		.143	.186	.179	19	-5	-5	2	0			-7	2/31O	-1.4
1909	Phi-A	22	51	5	4	1	0	0	1	11		.078	.254	.098	12	-5	-5	2	2			-1	O/1	-0.7
Total	2	41	107	9	12	3	0	0	2	14		.112	.221	.140	16	-9	-10	4	2			-8	/O213	-2.1

■ CUNO BARRAGAN
Barragan, Facundo   b: 6/20/32, Sacramento, Cal.   BR/TR, 5'11", 180 lbs.   Deb: 9/01/61

YEAR	TM/L	G	AB	R	H	2B	3B	HR	RBI	BB	SO	AVG	OBP	SLG	PRO+	BR	/A	RC	SB	CS	SBR	FR	POS	TPR
1961	Chi-N	10	28	3	6	0	0	1	2	2	7	.214	.267	.321	54	-2	-2	2	0	0	0	-1	C	-0.1
1962	Chi-N	58	134	11	27	6	1	0	12	21	28	.201	.310	.261	53	-8	-9	11	0	2	-1	-6	C	-1.4
1963	Chi-N	1	1	0	0	0	0	0	0	0	1	.000	.000	.000	-95	-0	-0	0	0	0	0	0	/C	0.0
Total	3	69	163	14	33	6	1	1	14	23	36	.202	.301	.270	53	-10	-11	13	0	2	-1	-7	/C	-1.5

■ GERMAN BARRANCA
Barranca, German (Costales)   b: 10/19/56, Verzcruz, Mex.   BL/TR, 6', 160 lbs.   Deb: 9/02/79

YEAR	TM/L	G	AB	R	H	2B	3B	HR	RBI	BB	SO	AVG	OBP	SLG	PRO+	BR	/A	RC	SB	CS	SBR	FR	POS	TPR
1979	KC-A	5	5	3	3	1	0	0	0	0	0	.600	.600	.800	269	1	1	2	3	1	0	3	/23	0.4
1980	KC-A	7	0	3	0	0	0	0	0	0	0	—	—	—	—	0	0	0	0	0	0	0	/R	0.0
1981	Cin-N	9	6	2	2	0	0	0	1	0	0	.333	.333	.333	88	-0	-0	1	0	0	0	0	/H	0.0
1982	Cin-N	46	51	11	13	1	3	0	2	2	9	.255	.283	.392	85	-1	-1	6	2	0	1	-1	/2	-0.1
Total	4	67	62	19	18	2	3	0	3	2	9	.290	.313	.419	101	0	-0	9	5	1	1	2	/23	0.3

■ JIMMY BARRETT
Barrett, James Erigena   b: 3/28/1875, Athol, Mass.   d: 10/24/21, Detroit, Mich.   BL/TR, 5'9", 170 lbs.   Deb: 9/13/1899

YEAR	TM/L	G	AB	R	H	2B	3B	HR	RBI	BB	SO	AVG	OBP	SLG	PRO+	BR	/A	RC	SB	CS	SBR	FR	POS	TPR
1899	Cin-N	26	92	30	34	2	4	0	10	18		.370	.477	.478	163	10	9	23	4			-2	O	0.5
1900	Cin-N	137	545	114	172	11	7	5	42	72		.316	.399	.389	124	19	21	105	44			4	*O	1.2
1901	Det-A	135	542	110	159	16	9	4	65	76		.293	.386	.378	110	14	10	92	26			15	*O	2.1
1902	Det-A	136	509	93	154	19	6	4	44	74		.303	.397	.387	118	18	16	91	24			8	*O	1.4
1903	Det-A	136	517	95	163	13	10	2	31	**74**		.315	**.401**	.391	145	29	31	97	27			7	*O	3.0
1904	Det-A	162	624	83	167	10	5	0	31	**79**		.268	.350	.300	112	10	12	74	15			12	*O	1.6
1905	Det-A	20	67	2	17	1	0	0	3	6		.254	.315	.269	87	-1	-1	6	0			-3	O	-0.4
1906	Cin-N	5	12	1	0	0	0	0	0	2		.000	.143	.000	-52	-2	-2	0	0			0	/O	-0.2
1907	Bos-A	106	390	52	95	11	6	1	28	38		.244	.311	.310	101	1	1	41	3			4	O	0.0
1908	Bos-A	3	8	0	1	0	0	0	1	1		.125	.222	.125	15	-1	-1	0	0			-0	/O	-0.1
Total	10	866	3306	580	962	83	47	16	255	440		.291	.377	.359	119	97	97	529	143			44	O	9.1

■ JOHNNY BARRETT
Barrett, John Joseph "Jack"   b: 12/18/15, Lowell, Mass.   d: 8/17/74, Seabrook Beach, N.H.   BL/TL, 5'10.5", 170 lbs.   Deb: 4/14/42

YEAR	TM/L	G	AB	R	H	2B	3B	HR	RBI	BB	SO	AVG	OBP	SLG	PRO+	BR	/A	RC	SB	CS	SBR	FR	POS	TPR
1942	Pit-N	111	332	56	82	11	6	0	26	48	42	.247	.347	.316	92	-0	-1	40	10			5	O	0.2
1943	Pit-N	130	290	41	67	12	3	1	32	32	23	.231	.316	.303	77	-7	-8	30	5			-12	O	-2.5
1944	Pit-N	149	568	99	153	24	**19**	7	83	86	56	.269	.366	.415	115	16	13	93	**28**			9	*O	1.1
1945	Pit-N	142	507	97	130	29	4	15	67	79	68	.256	.357	.418	111	11	8	81	25			4	*O	0.6
1946	Pit-N	32	71	7	12	3	0	0	6	8	11	.169	.253	.211	32	-6	-6	4	1			-2	O	-0.8
	Bos-N	24	43	3	10	3	0	0	6	12	1	.233	.400	.302	100	1	1	6	0			-0	O	0.0
	Yr	56	114	10	22	6	0	0	12	20	12	.193	.313	.246	59	-5	-6	10	1			-2		-0.8
Total	5	588	1811	303	454	82	32	23	220	265	201	.251	.349	.369	100	14	6	255	69			5	O	-1.4

■ MARTY BARRETT
Barrett, Martin F.   b: 11/1860, Port Huron, N.Y.   d: 1/29/10, Holyoke, Mass.   BR/TR, 5'9", 170 lbs.   Deb: 6/24/1884

YEAR	TM/L	G	AB	R	H	2B	3B	HR	RBI	BB	SO	AVG	OBP	SLG	PRO+	BR	/A	RC	SB	CS	SBR	FR	POS	TPR
1884	Bos-N	3	6	0	0	0	0	0	0	0	4	.000	.000	.000	-99	-1	-1	0				-1	/C	-0.1
	Ind-a	5	13	1	1	1	0	0		0	1	.077	.143	.154	-2	-1	-1	0				-2	/CO	-0.2

■ MARTY BARRETT
Barrett, Martin Glenn   b: 6/23/58, Arcadia, Cal.   BR/TR, 5'10", 175 lbs.   Deb: 9/06/82

YEAR	TM/L	G	AB	R	H	2B	3B	HR	RBI	BB	SO	AVG	OBP	SLG	PRO+	BR	/A	RC	SB	CS	SBR	FR	POS	TPR
1982	Bos-A	8	18	0	1	0	0	0	0	0	1	.056	.056	.056	-66	-4	-4	0	0	0	0	5	/2	0.1
1983	Bos-A	33	44	7	10	1	1	0	2	3	1	.227	.277	.295	54	-3	-3	4	0	0	0	4	2/D	0.2
1984	Bos-A	139	475	56	144	23	3	3	45	42	25	.303	.361	.383	101	5	2	66	5	3	-0	0	*2	0.8
1985	Bos-A	156	534	59	142	26	0	5	56	56	50	.266	.338	.343	84	-8	-11	62	7	5	-1	15	*2	0.8
1986	*Bos-A	158	625	94	179	39	4	4	60	65	31	.286	.355	.381	100	1	1	87	15	7	0	-3	*2	0.7
1987	Bos-A	137	559	72	164	23	0	3	43	51	38	.293	.354	.351	85	-8	-10	74	15	2	3	**32**	*2	3.4
1988	*Bos-A	150	612	83	173	28	1	1	65	40	35	.283	.334	.337	85	-9	-12	69	7	3	0	2	*2	0.0
1989	Bos-A	86	336	31	86	18	0	1	27	32	12	.256	.324	.318	77	-7	-10	35	4	1	1	2	2/D	-0.7
1990	*Bos-A	62	159	15	36	4	0	0	13	15	13	.226	.297	.252	52	-9	-10	13	4	0	1	10	2/3D	0.4
Total	9	929	3362	417	935	162	9	17	311	304	206	.278	.341	.347	86	-42	-58	410	57	21	5	66	2/D3	5.7

■ BOB BARRETT
Barrett, Robert Schley "Jumbo"   b: 1/27/1899, Atlanta, Ga.   d: 1/18/82, Atlanta, Ga.   BR/TR, 5'11", 175 lbs.   Deb: 4/30/23

YEAR	TM/L	G	AB	R	H	2B	3B	HR	RBI	BB	SO	AVG	OBP	SLG	PRO+	BR	/A	RC	SB	CS	SBR	FR	POS	TPR
1923	Chi-N	3	3	0	1	0	0	0	0	0	0	.333	.333	.333	76	-0	-0	0	0	0	0	0	H	0.0
1924	Chi-N	54	133	12	32	2	3	5	21	7	29	.241	.279	.414	82	-4	-4	15	1	0	0	-1	21/3	-0.5
1925	Chi-N	14	32	1	10	1	0	0	7	1	4	.313	.333	.344	72	-1	-1	3	1	2	-1	-3	/32	-0.4
	Bro-N	1	1	0	0	0	0	0	1	0	0	.000	.000	.000	-99	-0	-0	0	0	0	0	0	H	0.0
	Yr	15	33	1	10	1	0	0	8	1	4	.303	.324	.333	67	-2	-2	3	1	2	-1	-3		-0.4
1927	Bro-N	99	355	29	92	10	2	5	38	14	22	.259	.289	.341	68	-17	-17	34	1			-8	3	-1.8
1929	Bos-A	68	126	15	34	10	0	0	19	10	6	.270	.324	.349	75	-5	-5	15	3	1	0	6	3/12O	0.3
Total	5	239	650	57	169	23	5	10	86	32	61	.260	.296	.357	72	-27	-27	68	6	<u>3</u>		-6	3/21O	-2.4

■ TOM BARRETT
Barrett, Thomas Loren   b: 4/2/60, San Fernando, Cal.   BB/TR, 5'9", 157 lbs.   Deb: 7/02/88

YEAR	TM/L	G	AB	R	H	2B	3B	HR	RBI	BB	SO	AVG	OBP	SLG	PRO+	BR	/A	RC	SB	CS	SBR	FR	POS	TPR
1988	Phi-N	36	54	5	11	1	0	0	3	7	8	.204	.306	.222	53	-3	-3	4	0	0	0	2	2	0.0
1989	Phi-N	14	27	3	6	0	0	0	1	1	7	.222	.250	.222	36	-2	-2	2	0	0	0	4	/2	0.2
Total	2	50	81	8	17	1	0	0	4	8	15	.210	.289	.222	48	-5	-5	6	0	0	0	6	/2	0.2

■ BILL BARRETT
Barrett, William   b: Washington, D.C.   Deb: 7/08/1871

YEAR	TM/L	G	AB	R	H	2B	3B	HR	RBI	BB	SO	AVG	OBP	SLG	PRO+	BR	/A	RC	SB	CS	SBR	FR	POS	TPR
1871	Kek-n	1	5	1	1	1	0	0	1	0	0	.200	.200	.400	66	-0	-0	0	0				/C3	0.0
1872	Oly-n	1	4	0	0	0	0	0		0	0	.000	.000	.000	-99	-1	-1	0					/C	0.0
	Atl-n	8	35	6	7	2	0	0		0		.200	.200	.257	34	-2	-4	2					/O	-0.1
	Yr	9	39	6	7	2	0	0		0		.179	.179	.231	22	-3	-5	2					/SO	-0.1
1873	Bal-n	1	4	0	1	0	0	0		0		.250	.250	.250	48	-0	-0	0					/SO	0.0
Total	3 n	11	48	7	9	3	0	0		0		.188	.188	.250	28	-4	-5	3					/OCS3	-0.1

■ BILL BARRETT
Barrett, William Joseph "Whispering Bill"   b: 5/28/1900, Cambridge, Mass.   d: 1/26/51, Cambridge, Mass.   BR/TR, 6', 175 lbs.   Deb: 5/13/21

YEAR	TM/L	G	AB	R	H	2B	3B	HR	RBI	BB	SO	AVG	OBP	SLG	PRO+	BR	/A	RC	SB	CS	SBR	FR	POS	TPR
1921	Phi-A	14	30	3	7	1	0	0		0	5	.233	.233	.367	51	-2	-2	2	0	0	0	2	/SP31	0.2
1923	Chi-A	44	162	17	44	7	2	2	23	9	24	.272	.310	.377	81	-5	-5	20	12	3	2	0	O/3	-0.5
1924	Chi-A	119	406	52	110	18	5	2	56	30	38	.271	.326	.355	78	-15	-14	47	15	10	-2	-15	SO/3	-2.1
1925	Chi-A	81	245	44	89	23	4	3	40	24	27	.363	.420	.518	145	14	16	52	5	6	-2	-7	2O/S3	0.6
1926	Chi-A	111	368	46	113	31	4	6	61	25	26	.307	.353	.462	115	4	6	59	9	7	-2	-6	*O/1	-0.7
1927	Chi-A	147	556	62	159	35	9	4	83	52	46	.286	.347	.403	96	-5	-3	72	20	13	-2	7	*O	-0.7

YEAR	TM/L	G	AB	R	H	2B	3B	HR	RBI	BB	SO	AVG	OBP	SLG	PRO+	BR	/A	RC	SB	CS	SBR	FR	POS	TPR
1928	Chi-A	76	235	34	65	11	2	3	26	14	30	.277	.320	.379	84	-6	-6	29	8	3	1	-5	O2	-0.9
1929	Chi-A	3	1	0	0	0	0	0	0	2	0	.000	.667	.000	87	0	0	0	0	0	0	0	H	0.0
	Bos-A	111	370	57	100	23	4	3	35	51	38	.270	.363	.378	93	-4	-2	53	11	8	-2	4	*O/3	-0.3
	Yr	114	371	57	100	23	4	3	35	53	38	.270	.365	.377	94	-4	-2	54	11	8	-2	4		-0.3
1930	Bos-A	6	18	3	3	1	0	0	1	1	3	.167	.211	.222	10	-2	-2	1	0	0	0	-1	/O	-0.3
	Was-A	6	4	0	0	0	0	0	0	1	2	.000	.200	.000	-44	-1	-1	0	0	0	0	-0	/O	0.0
	Yr	12	22	3	3	1	0	0	1	2	5	.136	.208	.182	-0	-3	-3	1	0	0	0	-1		-0.3
Total	9	718	2395	318	690	151	30	23	328	209	239	.288	.347	.405	97	-23	-14	335	80	50	-6	-20	O/S23P1	-4.7

■ **JOSE BARRIOS** Barrios, Jose Manuel b: 6/26/57, New York, N.Y. BR/TR, 6'4", 195 lbs. Deb: 4/23/82

YEAR	TM/L	G	AB	R	H	2B	3B	HR	RBI	BB	SO	AVG	OBP	SLG	PRO+	BR	/A	RC	SB	CS	SBR	FR	POS	TPR
1982	SF-N	10	19	2	3	0	0	0	0	1	4	.158	.200	.158	1	-2	-2	0	0	0	0	-1	/1	-0.3

■ **RED BARRON** Barron, David Irenus b: 6/21/1900, Clarksville, Ga. d: 10/4/82, Atlanta, Ga. BR/TR, 5'11.5", 185 lbs. Deb: 6/10/29

YEAR	TM/L	G	AB	R	H	2B	3B	HR	RBI	BB	SO	AVG	OBP	SLG	PRO+	BR	/A	RC	SB	CS	SBR	FR	POS	TPR
1929	Bos-N	10	21	3	4	1	0	0	1	1	4	.190	.227	.238	16	-3	-3	1	2			1	/O	-0.1

■ **JIM BARRON** Barron, James b: St.Louis.Mo. Deb: 6/19/1874

YEAR	TM/L	G	AB	R	H	2B	3B	HR	RBI	BB	SO	AVG	OBP	SLG	PRO+	BR	/A	RC	SB	CS	SBR	FR	POS	TPR
1874	Bal-n	17	78	6	20	0	0	0	0	1	0	.256	.256	.256	64	-3	-3	5					O	-0.1

■ **FRANK BARROWS** Barrows, Franklin L. b: 10/22/1846, Hudson, Ohio d: 2/6/22, Fitchburg, Mass. Deb: 5/20/1871

YEAR	TM/L	G	AB	R	H	2B	3B	HR	RBI	BB	SO	AVG	OBP	SLG	PRO+	BR	/A	RC	SB	CS	SBR	FR	POS	TPR
1871	Bos-n	18	86	13	13	2	1	0	11	0	0	.151	.151	.198	-1	-11	-12	3	1				O/2	-0.6

■ **CUKE BARROWS** Barrows, Roland b: 10/20/1883, Gray, Maine d: 2/10/55, Gorham, Maine BL/TR, 5'8", 158 lbs. Deb: 9/18/09

YEAR	TM/L	G	AB	R	H	2B	3B	HR	RBI	BB	SO	AVG	OBP	SLG	PRO+	BR	/A	RC	SB	CS	SBR	FR	POS	TPR
1909	Chi-A	5	20	1	3	0	0	0	2	0		.150	.190	.150	8	-2	-2	1	0			2	/O	0.0
1910	Chi-A	6	20	0	4	0	0	0	1	3		.200	.304	.200	61	-1	-1	1	0			-1	/O	-0.2
1911	Chi-A	13	46	5	9	2	0	0	4	7		.196	.315	.239	57	-3	-2	4	2			-2	O	-0.4
1912	Chi-A	8	13	0	3	0	0	0	2	2		.231	.333	.231	64	-1	-0	2	1			-0	/O	0.0
Total	4	32	99	6	19	2	0	0	9	12		.192	.292	.212	50	-6	-5	8	3			-1	/O	-0.6

■ **SHAD BARRY** Barry, John C. b: 10/27/1878, Newburgh, N.Y. d: 11/27/36, Los Angeles, Cal. BR/TR, Deb: 5/30/1899

YEAR	TM/L	G	AB	R	H	2B	3B	HR	RBI	BB	SO	AVG	OBP	SLG	PRO+	BR	/A	RC	SB	CS	SBR	FR	POS	TPR
1899	Was-N	78	247	31	71	7	5	1	33	12		.287	.328	.368	94	-3	-2	34	11			-16	O1S3/2	-1.5
1900	Bos-N	81	254	40	66	10	7	1	37	13		.260	.301	.366	76	-5	-10	31	9			-16	OS21/3	-2.2
1901	Bos-N	11	40	3	7	2	0	0	6	2		.175	.233	.225	32	-3	-4	3	1			-0	O	-0.4
	Phi-N	67	252	35	62	10	0	1	22	15		.246	.291	.298	71	-8	-9	27	13			-12	23O/S	-1.8
	Yr	78	292	38	69	12	0	1	28	17		.236	.283	.288	65	-12	-13	30	14			-12		-2.2
1902	Phi-N	138	543	65	156	20	6	3	58	44		.287	.344	.363	120	13	13	77	14			-5	*O/1	-1.3
1903	Phi-N	138	550	75	152	24	5	1	60	30		.276	.314	.344	92	-8	-6	71	26			-2	*O1/3	-1.3
1904	Phi-N	35	122	15	25	2	0	0	3	11		.205	.271	.221	56	-6	-6	8	2			13	O/3	0.7
	Chi-N	73	263	29	69	7	2	1	26	17		.262	.307	.316	94	-2	-2	31	12			-1	O13/S2	-0.3
	Yr	108	385	44	94	9	2	1	29	28		.244	.295	.286	82	-8	-7	39	14			12		0.4
1905	Chi-N	27	104	10	22	2	0	0	10	5		.212	.248	.231	43	-7	-7	7	5			0	1	-0.8
	Cin-N	125	494	90	160	11	12	1	56	33		.324	.366	.401	118	18	11	83	16			-8	*1/O	-0.1
	Yr	152	598	100	182	13	12	1	66	38		.304	.346	.371	106	11	4	89	21			-7		-0.9
1906	Cin-N	73	279	38	80	10	5	1	33	26		.287	.348	.369	120	8	7	42	11			1	1O	0.6
	StL-N	62	237	26	59	9	1	0	12	15		.249	.294	.295	89	-4	-3	24	6			-7	O1/3	-1.2
	Yr	135	516	64	139	19	6	1	45	41		.269	.323	.335	107	4	4	65	17			-6		-0.6
1907	StL-N	81	294	30	73	5	2	0	19	28		.248	.314	.279	91	-3	-2	30	4			-6	O	-1.3
1908	StL-N	74	268	24	61	8	1	0	11	19		.228	.279	.265	79	-7	-6	22	9			-1	O/S	-0.7
	NY-N	37	67	5	10	1	1	0	5	9		.149	.250	.194	42	-4	-4	4	1			-6	O	-1.2
	Yr	111	335	29	71	9	2	0	16	28		.212	.273	.251	70	-11	-10	26	10			-7		-1.9
Total	10	1100	4014	516	1073	128	47	10	391	279		.267	.317	.330	94	-22	-30	495	140			-64	O1/23S	-11.6

■ **JACK BARRY** Barry, John Joseph b: 4/26/1887, Meriden, Conn. d: 4/23/61, Shrewsbury, Mass. BR/TR, 5'9", 158 lbs. Deb: 7/13/08 M

YEAR	TM/L	G	AB	R	H	2B	3B	HR	RBI	BB	SO	AVG	OBP	SLG	PRO+	BR	/A	RC	SB	CS	SBR	FR	POS	TPR
1908	Phi-A	40	135	13	30	4	3	0	8	10		.222	.276	.296	82	-2	-3	12	1			-11	2S/3	-1.5
1909	Phi-A	124	409	56	88	11	2	1	23	44		.215	.307	.259	77	-8	-9	40	17			-31	*S	-4.2
1910	*Phi-A	145	487	64	126	19	5	3	60	52		.259	.336	.337	112	7	7	61	14			-22	*S	-1.3
1911	Phi-A	127	442	73	117	18	7	1	63	38		.265	.333	.344	91	-7	-5	62	30			-6	*S	0.0
1912	Phi-A	140	483	76	126	19	9	0	55	47		.261	.335	.337	96	-4	-2	63	22			-6	*S	0.4
1913	Phi-A	134	455	62	125	20	6	3	85	44	32	.275	.349	.365	112	5	7	64	15			-8	*S	1.1
1914	*Phi-A	140	467	57	113	12	0	0	42	53	34	.242	.324	.268	81	-11	-9	48	22	13	-1	-8	*S	0.8
1915	Phi-A	54	194	16	43	6	2	0	15	15	9	.222	.284	.273	69	-8	-7	16	6	5	-1	-4	S	-0.8
	*Bos-A	78	248	30	65	13	2	0	26	24	11	.262	.342	.331	104	1	2	32	0			-4	2	-0.2
	Yr	132	442	46	108	19	4	0	41	39	20	.244	.317	.305	89	-7	-6	48	6	5	-1	-8		-1.0
1916	Bos-A	94	330	28	67	6	1	0	20	17	24	.203	.277	.227	52	-19	-19	27	8			2	2	-1.6
1917	Bos-A	116	388	45	83	9	0	2	30	47	27	.214	.305	.253	71	-12	-12	39	12			-11	*2M	-1.6
1919	Bos-A	31	108	13	26	5	1	0	2	5	5	.241	.293	.306	72	-5	-4	11	2			-7	2	-0.8
Total	11	1223	4146	533	1009	142	38	10	429	396	142	.243	.320	.303	88	-63	-54	475	153	18		-104	S2/3	-9.7

■ **RICH BARRY** Barry, Richard Donovan b: 9/12/40, Berkeley, Cal. BR/TR, 6'4", 205 lbs. Deb: 7/04/69

YEAR	TM/L	G	AB	R	H	2B	3B	HR	RBI	BB	SO	AVG	OBP	SLG	PRO+	BR	/A	RC	SB	CS	SBR	FR	POS	TPR
1969	Phi-N	20	32	4	6	1	0	0	0	5	6	.188	.316	.219	54	-2	-2	2	0	0	0	0	/O	-0.1

■ **DICK BARTELL** Bartell, Richard William "Rowdy Richard" b: 11/22/07, Chicago, Ill. BR/TR, 5'9", 160 lbs. Deb: 10/02/27 C

YEAR	TM/L	G	AB	R	H	2B	3B	HR	RBI	BB	SO	AVG	OBP	SLG	PRO+	BR	/A	RC	SB	CS	SBR	FR	POS	TPR
1927	Pit-N	1	2	0	0	0	0	0	0	2	0	.000	.500	.000	41	0	0	0	0			0	/S	0.0
1928	Pit-N	72	233	27	71	8	4	1	36	21	18	.305	.377	.386	96	1	-1	34	4			2	2S3/3	0.5
1929	Pit-N	143	610	101	184	40	13	2	57	40	29	.302	.347	.420	87	-11	-14	86	11			4	S2	0.2
1930	Pit-N	129	475	69	152	32	13	4	75	39	34	.320	.378	.467	102	2	2	82	8			6	*S	1.7
1931	Phi-N	135	554	88	160	43	7	0	34	27	38	.289	.325	.392	85	-7	-13	72	6			3	*S/2	0.1
1932	Phi-N	154	614	118	189	48	7	1	53	64	47	.308	.379	.414	101	13	3	102	8			10	*S	2.5
1933	Phi-N	152	587	78	159	25	5	1	37	56	46	.271	.340	.336	83	-3	-13	73	6			9	*S	0.6
1934	Phi-N	146	604	102	187	30	4	0	37	64	59	.310	.384	.373	91	6	-5	92	13			14	*S	1.1
1935	NY-N	137	539	60	141	28	4	14	53	37	52	.262	.316	.406	94	-6	-5	72	5			10	*S	1.1
1936	*NY-N	145	510	71	152	31	3	8	42	40	38	.298	.355	.418	109	5	6	79	6			45	*S	5.6
1937	*NY-N	128	516	91	158	38	2	14	62	40	38	.306	.367	.469	124	18	17	92	5			38	*S	6.2
1938	NY-N	127	481	67	126	26	1	9	49	55	60	.262	.347	.376	98	0	-0	67	4			22	*S	3.1
1939	Chi-N	105	336	37	80	24	2	3	34	42	25	.238	.335	.348	82	-7	-8	41	6			-5	*S/3	-0.5
1940	*Det-A	139	528	70	123	24	3	7	53	76	53	.233	.335	.330	67	-20	-27	66	12	2	2	12	*S	0.0
1941	Det-A	5	12	0	2	1	0	0	1	2	2	.167	.333	.250	51	-1	-1	1	0	1	-1	1	/S	0.0
	NY-N	104	373	44	113	20	0	5	35	52	29	.303	.394	.397	121	13	13	60	6			-10	3S	0.5
1942	NY-N	90	316	53	77	10	3	5	24	44	34	.244	.351	.342	102	3	2	41	4			1	3S	0.6
1943	NY-N	99	337	48	91	14	0	5	28	47	27	.270	.371	.356	110	6	6	47	5			18	3S	2.9
1946	NY-N	5	2	0	0	0	0	0	0	0	0	.000	.000	.000	-99	-1	-1	0	0			1	/32	0.0
Total	18	2016	7629	1130	2165	442	71	79	710	748	627	.284	.355	.391	96	13	-36	1107	109	3		178	*S32	26.2

■ **TONY BARTIROME** Bartirome, Anthony Joseph b: 5/9/32, Pittsburgh, Pa. BL/TL, 5'10", 155 lbs. Deb: 4/19/52 C

YEAR	TM/L	G	AB	R	H	2B	3B	HR	RBI	BB	SO	AVG	OBP	SLG	PRO+	BR	/A	RC	SB	CS	SBR	FR	POS	TPR
1952	Pit-N	124	355	32	78	10	3	0	16	26	37	.220	.273	.265	48	-24	-25	28	3	3	-1	2	*1	-2.9

YEAR	TM/L	G	AB	R	H	2B	3B	HR	RBI	BB	SO	AVG	OBP	SLG	PRO+	BR	/A	RC	SB	CS	SBR	FR	POS	TPR

■ BOYD BARTLEY Bartley, Boyd Owen b: 2/11/20, Chicago, Ill. BR/TR, 5'8.5", 165 lbs. Deb: 5/30/43

| 1943 | Bro-N | 9 | 21 | 0 | 1 | 0 | 0 | 0 | 1 | 1 | 3 | .048 | .091 | .048 | -59 | -4 | -4 | 0 | 0 | | | 2 | /S | -0.1 |

■ IRV BARTLING Bartling, Irving Henry b: 6/27/14, Bay City, Mich. d: 6/12/73, Westland, Mich. BR/TR, 6', 175 lbs. Deb: 9/08/38

| 1938 | Phi-A | 14 | 46 | 5 | 8 | 1 | 1 | 0 | 5 | 3 | 7 | .174 | .224 | .239 | 17 | -6 | -6 | 3 | 0 | 0 | 0 | -3 | S/3 | -0.6 |

■ HARRY BARTON Barton, Harry Lamb b: 1/20/1875, Chester, Pa. d: 1/25/55, Upland, Pa. BB/TR, 5'6.5", 155 lbs. Deb: 4/15/05

| 1905 | Phi-A | 29 | 60 | 5 | 10 | 2 | 1 | 0 | 3 | 3 | | .167 | .206 | .233 | 40 | -4 | -4 | 4 | 2 | | | -5 | C/13O | -0.8 |

■ BOB BARTON Barton, Robert Wilbur b: 7/30/41, Norwood, O. BR/TR, 6', 175 lbs. Deb: 9/17/65

1965	SF-N	4	7	1	4	0	0	0	1	0	0	.571	.571	.571	217	1	1	2	0	0	0	0	/C	0.2
1966	SF-N	43	91	1	16	2	1	0	3	5	5	.176	.219	.220	22	-9	-10	4	0	0	0	7	C	-0.1
1967	SF-N	7	19	0	4	0	0	0	1	0	2	.211	.250	.211	34	-2	-2	1	0	0	0	1	/C	0.0
1968	SF-N	46	92	4	24	2	0	0	5	7	18	.261	.313	.283	80	-2	-2	9	0	0	0	12	C	1.3
1969	SF-N	49	106	5	18	2	0	0	1	9	19	.170	.241	.189	22	-11	-11	5	0	0	0	0	C	-0.7
1970	SD-N	61	188	15	41	6	0	4	16	15	37	.218	.279	.314	61	-11	-10	16	1	1	-0	6	C	-0.1
1971	SD-N	121	376	23	94	17	2	5	23	35	49	.250	.317	.346	94	-6	-3	36	0	5	-3	12	*C	0.9
1972	SD-N	29	88	1	17	1	0	0	9	2	19	.193	.211	.205	20	-9	-9	4	2	0	1	1	C	-0.5
1973	Cin-N	3	1	0	0	0	0	0	0	1	0	.000	.500	.000	52	0	0	0	0	0	0	1	/C	0.1
1974	SD-N	30	81	4	19	1	0	0	7	13	19	.235	.340	.247	69	-3	-3	8	0	0	0	9	C	0.8
Total	10	393	1049	54	237	31	3	9	66	87	168	.226	.288	.287	65	-52	-48	85	3	6	-3	49	C	1.9

■ VINCE BARTON Barton, Vincent David b: 2/1/08, Edmonton, Alberta, Canada d: 9/13/73, Toronto, Ont., Can BL/TR, 6', 180 lbs. Deb: 7/17/31

1931	Chi-N	66	239	45	57	10	1	13	50	21	40	.238	.323	.452	104	1	1	36	1			-5	O	-0.6
1932	Chi-N	36	134	19	30	2	3	3	15	8	22	.224	.273	.351	67	-7	-6	13	0			-2	O	-1.0
Total	2	102	373	64	87	12	4	16	65	29	62	.233	.306	.416	91	-5	-5	50	1			-7	/O	-1.6

■ DAVE BARTOSCH Bartosch, David Robert b: 3/24/17, St.Louis, Mo. BR/TR, 6'1", 190 lbs. Deb: 4/28/45

| 1945 | StL-N | 24 | 47 | 9 | 12 | 1 | 0 | 0 | 1 | 6 | 3 | .255 | .340 | .277 | 71 | -2 | -2 | 5 | 0 | | | 1 | /O | 0.0 |

■ MONTY BASGALL Basgall, Romanus b: 2/8/22, Pfeifer, Kan. BR/TR, 5'10.5", 175 lbs. Deb: 4/19/48 C

1948	Pit-N	38	51	12	11	1	0	2	6	3	5	.216	.259	.353	63	-3	-3	5	0			6	2	0.4
1949	Pit-N	107	308	25	67	9	1	2	26	31	32	.218	.291	.273	51	-21	-22	25	1			-7	2/3	-2.4
1951	Pit-N	55	153	15	32	5	2	0	9	12	14	.209	.271	.268	44	-12	-12	10	0	0	0	11	2	0.0
Total	3	200	512	52	110	15	3	4	41	46	51	.215	.282	.279	50	-35	-37	40	1	0		9	2/3	-2.0

■ AL BASHANG Bashang, Albert C. b: 8/22/1888, Cincinnati, Ohio d: 6/23/67, Cincinnati, Ohio BB/TR, 5'8", 150 lbs. Deb: 7/30/12

1912	Det-A	6	12	3	1	0	0	0	0	3		.083	.267	.083	1	-1	-1	0	0			-1	/O	-0.2
1918	Bro-N	2	5	0	1	0	0	0	0	0	0	.200	.200	.200	22	-0	-0	0	0			0	/O	0.0
Total	2	8	17	3	2	0	0	0	0	3	0	.118	.250	.118	8	-2	-2	0	0			-1	/O	-0.2

■ WALT BASHORE Bashore, Walter Franklin (b: Walter Franklin Beshore) b: 10/6/09, Harrisburg, Pa. d: 9/26/84, Sebring, Fla. BR/TR, 6', 170 lbs. Deb: 7/14/36

| 1936 | Phi-N | 10 | 10 | 1 | 2 | 0 | 0 | 0 | 0 | 1 | 3 | .200 | .273 | .200 | 26 | -1 | -1 | 1 | 0 | | | -1 | /O3 | -0.1 |

■ EDDIE BASINSKI Basinski, Edwin Frank "Bazooka" or "Fiddler" b: 11/4/22, Buffalo, N.Y. BR/TR, 6'1", 172 lbs. Deb: 5/20/44

1944	Bro-N	39	105	13	27	4	1	0	9	6	10	.257	.310	.314	77	-3	-3	11	1			-2	2/S	0.0
1945	Bro-N	108	336	30	88	9	4	0	33	11	33	.262	.293	.313	69	-15	-14	29	0			-10	*S/2	-1.2
1947	Pit-N	56	161	15	32	6	2	4	17	18	27	.199	.279	.335	61	-9	-10	15	0			-1	2	-0.4
Total	3	203	602	58	147	19	7	4	59	35	70	.244	.292	.319	68	-27	-27	55	1			-13	S/2	-1.6

■ JOHN BASS Bass, John E. b: 1850, Baltimore, Md. 5'6", 150 lbs. Deb: 5/04/1871

1871	Cle-n	22	89	18	27	1	10	3	18	3	4	.303	.326	.640	179	7	9	19	0				*3	0.4
1872	Atl-n	2	7	0	1	1	0	0		0		.143	.143	.286	24	-1	-1	0					/O	0.0
1877	Har-N	1	4	1	1	0	0	0	0	0	0	.250	.250	.250	65	-0	-0	0				0	/O	0.0
Total	2 n	24	96	18	28	2	10	3	18	3	4	.292	.313	.615	166	7	8	19					/3O	0.4

■ KEVIN BASS Bass, Kevin Charles b: 5/12/59, Menlo Park, Cal. BB/TR, 6', 183 lbs. Deb: 4/09/82

1982	Mil-A	18	9	4	0	0	0	0	0	1	1	.000	.100	.000	-74	-2	-2	0	0	0	0	1	O/D	-0.1
	Hou-N	12	24	2	1	0	0	0	1	0	8	.042	.042	.042	-83	-6	-5	0	0	0	0	-0	O	-0.5
1983	Hou-N	88	195	25	46	7	3	2	18	6	27	.236	.259	.333	67	-10	-9	16	2	2	-1	-5	O	-1.5
1984	Hou-N	121	331	33	86	17	5	2	29	6	57	.260	.279	.360	84	-10	-8	32	5	5	-2	-1	O	-1.3
1985	Hou-N	150	539	72	145	27	5	16	68	31	63	.269	.316	.427	109	3	4	71	19	8	1	2	*O	0.4
1986	*Hou-N	157	591	83	184	33	5	20	79	38	72	.311	.359	.486	134	23	25	97	22	13	-1	9	*O	3.1
1987	Hou-N	157	592	83	168	31	5	19	85	53	77	.284	.347	.449	113	7	10	90	21	8	2	6	*O	1.0
1988	Hou-N	157	541	57	138	27	2	14	72	42	65	.255	.316	.390	106	0	3	66	31	6	6	-3	*O	0.2
1989	Hou-N	87	313	42	94	19	4	5	44	29	44	.300	.362	.435	131	11	12	51	11	4	1	2	O	1.4
1990	SF-N	61	214	25	54	9	1	7	32	14	26	.252	.304	.402	94	-3	-2	25	2	2	-1	-8	O	-1.3
Total	9	1008	3349	426	916	170	30	85	428	220	440	.274	.324	.418	108	13	28	449	113	48	5	1	O/D	1.4

■ RANDY BASS Bass, Randy William b: 3/13/54, Lawton, Okla. BL/TR, 6'1", 210 lbs. Deb: 9/03/77

1977	Min-A	9	19	0	2	0	0	0	0	0	5	.105	.105	.105	-43	-4	-4	0	0	0	0	0	/D	-0.3
1978	KC-A	2	2	0	0	0	0	0	0	0	0	.000	.000	.000	-97	-1	-1	0	0	0	0	0	H	0.0
1979	Mon-N	2	1	0	0	0	0	0	0	0	0	.000	.000	-0	-99	-0	-0	0	0	0	0	0	/1	0.0
1980	SD-N	19	49	5	14	0	1	3	8	7	7	.286	.386	.510	157	3	4	10	0	0	0	-1	1	0.2
1981	SD-N	69	176	13	37	4	1	4	20	20	28	.210	.294	.313	78	-6	-5	15	0	1	-1	2	1	-0.5
1982	SD-N	13	30	1	6	0	0	1	8	2	4	.200	.273	.300	63	-2	-1	3	0	0	0	-0	/1	-0.2
	Tex-A	16	48	5	10	2	0	1	6	1	7	.208	.240	.313	53	-3	-3	4	0	0	0	0	/1D	-0.2
Total	6	130	325	24	69	6	2	9	42	30	51	.212	.287	.326	76	-12	-10	32	0	1	-1	0	/1D	-1.0

■ DOC BASS Bass, Williams Capers (Also Played One Game In 1918 Under Name Of Johnson) b: 12/4/1899, Macon, Ga. d: 1/12/70, Macon, Ga. BL/TL, 5'10", 165 lbs. Deb: 7/29/18

| 1918 | Bos-N | 2 | 1 | 1 | 1 | 0 | 0 | 0 | 0 | 0 | 0 | 1.000 | 1.000 | 1.000 | 533 | 0 | 0 | 2 | 1 | | | 0 | /H | 0.1 |

■ CHARLEY BASSETT Bassett, Charles Edwin b: 2/9/1863, Central Falls, R.I. d: 5/28/42, Pawtucket, R.I. BR/TR, 5'10", 150 lbs. Deb: 7/22/1884

1884	Pro-N	27	79	10	11	2	1	0	6	4	15	.139	.181	.190	17	-7	-7	3				1	3/SO2	-0.5
1885	Pro-N	82	285	21	41	8	2	0	16	19	60	.144	.197	.186	25	-23	-22	11				5	2S3/C	-0.9
1886	KC-N	90	342	41	89	19	8	2	32	36	43	.260	.331	.380	109	7	3	46	6			7	S/3	0.9
1887	Ind-N	119	452	41	104	14	6	1	47	25	31	.230	.278	.294	63	-23	-21	45	25			16	*2	0.2
1888	Ind-N	128	481	58	116	20	3	2	60	32	41	.241	.297	.308	93	-2	-3	52	24			-16	*2	-1.3
1889	Ind-N	127	477	64	117	12	5	4	68	37	38	.245	.304	.317	73	-16	-17	52	15			10	*2	0.2
1890	NY-N	100	410	52	98	13	8	0	54	29	25	.239	.300	.310	80	-10	-11	43	14			10	*2	0.3
1891	NY-N	130	524	60	136	19	8	4	68	36	29	.260	.312	.349	98	-5	-1	64	16			8	*3/2	1.0
1892	NY-N	35	130	9	27	2	3	0	16	6	10	.208	.254	.269	61	-6	-6	9	2			9	2/3	0.3
	Lou-N	79	313	36	67	5	5	2	35	15	19	.214	.250	.281	67	-15	-11	27	16			-0	3/2	-0.6
	Yr	114	443	45	94	7	8	2	51	21	29	.212	.251	.278	65	-21	-18	36	16			9		-0.3
Total	9	917	3493	392	806	114	49	15	402	239	311	.231	.285	.304	77	-101	-96	351	116			51	23S/OC	-0.4

YEAR	TM/L	G	AB	R	H	2B	3B	HR	RBI	BB	SO	AVG	OBP	SLG	PRO+	BR	/A	RC	SB	CS	SBR	FR	POS	TPR

■ JOHNNY BASSLER
Bassler, John Landis   b: 6/3/1895, Mechanics Grove, Pa.   d: 6/29/79, Santa Monica, Cal   BL/TR, 5'9", 170 lbs.   Deb: 7/11/13   C

1913	Cle-A	1	2	0	0	0	0	0	0	0	0	.000	.000	.000	-97	-0	-1	0	0			-1	/C	0.0
1914	Cle-A	43	77	5	14	1	1	0	6	15	8	.182	.323	.221	61	-3	-3	6	3	2	-0	-1	C/3O	-0.2
1921	Det-A	119	388	37	119	18	5	0	56	58	16	.307	.401	.379	101	3	3	63	2	1	0	3	*C	0.9
1922	Det-A	121	372	41	120	14	0	0	41	62	12	.323	.422	.360	109	7	9	62	2	1	0	-3	*C	0.9
1923	Det-A	135	383	45	114	12	3	0	49	76	13	.298	.414	.345	103	5	6	61	2	2	-1	12	*C	2.6
1924	Det-A	124	379	43	131	20	3	1	68	62	11	.346	.441	.422	125	17	18	76	2	1	0	-5	*C	1.9
1925	Det-A	121	344	40	96	19	3	0	52	74	6	.279	.408	.352	96	1	2	56	1	1	-0	-9	*C	0.0
1926	Det-A	66	174	20	53	8	1	0	22	45	6	.305	.447	.362	111	7	6	33	0	0	0	1	C	1.1
1927	Det-A	81	200	19	57	7	0	0	24	45	9	.285	.416	.320	92	1	1	30	1	0	0	-2	C	0.1
Total	9	811	2319	250	704	99	16	1	318	437	81	.304	.416	.361	104	37	42	387	13	8		-3	C/O3	7.3

■ CHARLIE BASTIAN
Bastian, Charles J.   b: 7/4/1860, Philadelphia, Pa.   d: 1/18/32, Pennsauken, N.J.   BR/TR, 5'6.5", 145 lbs.   Deb: 8/18/1884

1884	Wil-U	17	60	6	12	1	3	2		3		.200	.238	.417	114	1	1	6	0			10	2/PS	0.9
	KC-U	11	46	6	9	3	0	1		4		.196	.260	.326	112	-0	1	4	0			-0	2	0.0
	Yr	28	106	12	21	4	3	3		7		.198	.248	.377	112	1	2	10	0			10		0.9
1885	Phi-N	103	389	63	65	11	5	4	29	35	82	.167	.236	.252	59	-17	-16	24				5	*S	-0.5
1886	Phi-N	105	373	46	81	9	11	3	38	33	73	.217	.281	.316	81	-8	-9	42	29			-5	*2S/3	-0.8
1887	Phi-N	60	221	33	47	11	1	1	21	19	29	.213	.284	.285	57	-11	-14	22	11			-12	2S/3	-2.0
1888	Phi-N	80	275	30	53	4	1	1	17	27	41	.193	.282	.225	62	-9	-11	21	12			12	23/S	0.3
1889	Chi-N	46	155	19	21	0	0	0	10	25	46	.135	.256	.135	11	-17	-19	6	1			6	S/2	-0.9
1890	Chi-P	80	283	38	54	10	5	0	29	33	37	.191	.287	.261	46	-20	-23	23	4			-10	S2/3	-2.1
1891	Cin-a	1	4	0	0	0	0	0	0	0	0	.000	.000	.000	-92	-1	-1	0	0			1	/2	0.0
	Phi-N	1	0	0	0	0	0	0	0	0	0	—	—	—	0	0	0	0	0			0	/S	0.0
Total	8	504	1806	241	342	49	26	11	144	179	308	.189	.268	.264	59	-84	-90	148	57			6	S2/3P	-5.1

■ EMIL BATCH
Batch, Emil "Heinie" or "Ace"   b: 1/21/1880, Brooklyn, N.Y.   d: 8/23/26, Brooklyn, N.Y.   BR/TR, 5'7", 170 lbs.   Deb: 9/13/04

1904	Bro-N	28	94	9	24	1	2	2	7	1		.255	.263	.372	100	-1	-1	11	6			-2	3	0.0
1905	Bro-N	145	568	64	143	20	11	5	49	26		.252	.285	.352	98	-8	-3	65	21			-8	*3	0.0
1906	Bro-N	59	203	23	52	7	6	0	11	15		.256	.307	.350	116	1	3	24	3			1	O/3	0.3
1907	Bro-N	116	388	38	96	10	3	0	31	23		.247	.290	.289	90	-8	-4	38	7			-2	*O/32S	-1.1
Total	4	348	1253	134	315	38	22	7	98	65		.251	.288	.334	99	-15	-5	139	37			-11	3O/S2	-0.8

■ JOHN BATEMAN
Bateman, John Alvin   b: 7/21/42, Killeen, Tex.   BR/TR, 6'3", 210 lbs.   Deb: 4/19/63

1963	Hou-N	128	404	23	85	8	6	10	59	13	103	.210	.251	.334	71	-18	-15	33	0	0	0	3	*C	-0.9
1964	Hou-N	74	221	18	42	8	0	5	19	17	48	.190	.251	.294	56	-14	-12	14	0	1	-1	7	C	-0.4
1965	Hou-N	45	142	15	28	3	1	7	14	12	37	.197	.260	.380	83	-5	-3	11	0	1	-1	0	C	-0.2
1966	Hou-N	131	433	39	121	24	3	17	70	20	74	.279	.319	.467	123	8	11	58	0	0	0	3	*C	1.8
1967	Hou-N	76	252	16	48	9	0	2	17	17	53	.190	.247	.250	44	-19	-18	14	0	0	0	2	C	-1.2
1968	Hou-N	111	350	28	87	19	0	4	33	23	46	.249	.301	.337	93	-4	-3	31	1	1	-0	-2	*C	-0.1
1969	Mon-N	74	235	16	49	4	0	8	19	12	44	.209	.250	.328	60	-13	-13	17	0	2	-1	1	C	-0.9
1970	Mon-N	139	520	51	123	21	5	15	68	28	75	.237	.277	.383	75	-20	-20	51	8	4	0	-2	*C	-1.6
1971	Mon-N	139	492	34	119	17	3	10	56	19	87	.242	.276	.350	76	-17	-17	40	1	0	0	-10	*C	-2.5
1972	Mon-N	18	29	0	7	1	0	0	3	3	4	.241	.313	.276	67	-1	-1	2	0	0	0	-2	/C	-0.2
	Phi-N	82	252	10	56	9	0	3	17	8	39	.222	.249	.294	52	-16	-16	17	0	1	-1	1	C	-1.2
	Yr	100	281	10	63	10	0	3	20	11	43	.224	.256	.292	54	-17	-18	20	0	1	-1	-1		-1.4
Total	10	1017	3330	250	765	123	18	81	375	172	610	.230	.273	.350	77	-118	-109	289	10	10	-3	0	C	-7.4

■ CHARLIE BATES
Bates, Charles William   b: 9/17/07, Philadelphia, Pa.   d: 1/29/80, Topeka, Kan.   BR/TR, 5'10", 165 lbs.   Deb: 9/22/27

1927	Phi-A	9	38	5	9	2	2	0	2	3	5	.237	.293	.395	73	-1	-2	4	3	1	0	-0	/O	-0.1

■ DEL BATES
Bates, Delbert Oakley   b: 6/12/40, Seattle, Wash.   BL/TR, 6'2", 195 lbs.   Deb: 5/06/70

1970	Phi-N	22	60	1	8	2	0	0	1	6	15	.133	.257	.167	16	-7	-7	3	0	1	-1	-3	C	-0.9

■ BUD BATES
Bates, Hubert Edgar   b: 3/16/12, Los Angeles, Cal.   d: 4/29/87, Long Beach, Cal.   BR/TR, 6', 165 lbs.   Deb: 9/16/39

1939	Phi-N	15	58	8	15	2	0	1	2	2	8	.259	.283	.345	70	-3	-3	5	1			2	O	0.0

■ JOHNNY BATES
Bates, John William   b: 8/21/1882, Steubenville, Ohio   d: 2/10/49, Steubenville, Ohio   BL/TL, 5'7", 168 lbs.   Deb: 4/12/06

1906	Bos-N	140	504	52	127	21	5	6	54	36		.252	.302	.349	108	2	3	58	9			-10	*O	-1.0
1907	Bos-N	126	447	52	116	18	12	2	49	39		.260	.319	.367	117	8	8	59	11			-2	*O	0.1
1908	Bos-N	127	445	48	115	14	6	1	29	35		.258	.313	.324	107	3	3	52	25			-3	*O	0.0
1909	Bos-N	63	236	27	68	15	3	1	23	20		.288	.354	.390	125	8	7	37	15			5	O	1.1
	Phi-N	77	266	43	78	11	1	1	15	28		.293	.365	.353	122	8	7	43	22			-2	O	0.4
	Yr	140	502	70	146	26	4	2	38	48		.291	.360	.371	123	16	14	81	37			3		1.5
1910	Phi-N	135	498	91	152	26	11	3	61	61	49	.305	.385	.420	130	23	20	93	31			7	*O	2.4
1911	Cin-N	148	518	89	151	24	13	1	61	103	59	.292	.415	.394	131	24	27	99	33			0	*O	2.2
1912	Cin-N	81	239	45	69	12	7	1	29	47	16	.289	.406	.410	127	10	11	45	10			9	O	1.7
1913	Cin-N	131	407	63	113	13	7	6	51	67	30	.278	.387	.388	122	14	15	67	21			0	*O	1.3
1914	Cin-N	58	155	29	39	7	5	2	15	28	17	.252	.380	.400	128	7	7	25	4			-3	O	0.2
	Chi-N	9	8	2	1	0	0	0	1	1	1	.125	.300	.125	28	-1	-1	0	0			1	/O	0.0
	Yr	67	163	31	40	7	5	2	16	29	18	.245	.376	.387	124	7	6	25	4			-3		0.2
	Bal-F	59	190	24	58	6	3	1	29	38	18	.305	.429	.384	130	11	10	36	6			-1	O	0.6
Total	9	1154	3913	565	1087	167	73	25	417	503	190	.278	.364	.377	122	116	117	615	187			0	*O	9.0

■ RAY BATES
Bates, Raymond   b: 2/8/1890, Paterson, N.J.   d: 8/15/70, Tucson, Ariz.   BR/TR, 6', 165 lbs.   Deb: 5/31/13

1913	Cle-A	27	30	4	5	0	2	0	4	3	9	.167	.265	.300	63	-1	-2	3	3			0	3/O	-0.1
1917	Phi-A	127	485	47	115	20	7	2	66	21	39	.237	.277	.320	83	-12	-12	45	12			6	*3	0.0
Total	2	154	515	51	120	20	9	2	70	24	48	.233	.277	.318	82	-14	-13	48	15			6	3/O	-0.1

■ BILLY BATES
Bates, William Derrick   b: 12/7/63, Houston, Tex.   BL/TR, 5'7", 155 lbs.   Deb: 8/17/89

1989	Mil-A	7	14	3	3	0	0	0	0	1		.214	.214	.214	21	-1	-1	0	2	0	1	4	/2	0.3
1990	Mil-A	14	29	6	3	1	0	0	2	4	7	.103	.212	.138	-0	-4	-4	2	4	0	1	3	2	0.1
	*Cin-N	8	5	2	0	0	0	0	0	0	2	.000	.000	.000	-98	-1	-1	-0	2	1	0	1	/2	0.0
Total	2	29	48	11	6	1	0	0	2	4	10	.125	.192	.146	-4	-7	-7	2	8	1	2	8	/2	0.4

■ BILL BATHE
Bathe, William David   b: 10/14/60, Downey, Cal.   BR/TR, 6'2", 200 lbs.   Deb: 4/12/86

1986	Oak-A	39	103	9	19	3	0	5	11	2	20	.184	.208	.359	55	-7	-6	7	0	0	0	0	C	-0.3
1989	*SF-N	30	32	3	9	1	0	0	6	0	7	.281	.281	.313	72	-1	-1	3	0	0	0	-1	/C	-0.1
1990	SF-N	52	48	3	11	0	1	3	12	7	12	.229	.327	.458	115	1	1	7	0	0	0	-1	/C	0.0
Total	3	121	183	15	39	4	1	8	29	9	39	.213	.254	.377	75	-8	-7	17	0	0	0	-1	/C	-0.4

■ RAFAEL BATISTA
Batista, Rafael (Sanchez)   b: 10/20/47, San Pedro De Macoris, D.R.   BL/TL, 6'1", 195 lbs.   Deb: 6/17/73

1973	Hou-N	12	15	2	4	0	0	0	2	1	6	.267	.313	.267	62	-1	-1	1	0	0	0	-0	/1	0.0
1975	Hou-N	10	10	0	3	1	0	0	0	0	4	.300	.300	.400	100	-0	-0	1	0	0	0	0	H	0.0
Total	2	22	25	2	7	1	0	0	2	1	10	.280	.308	.320	76	-1	-1	2	0	0	0	-0	/1	0.0

YEAR	TM/L	G	AB	R	H	2B	3B	HR	RBI	BB	SO	AVG	OBP	SLG	PRO+	BR	/A	RC	SB	CS	SBR	FR	POS	TPR

■ KEVIN BATISTE · Batiste, Kevin Wade · b: 10/21/66, Galveston, Tex. · BR/TR, 6'2", 175 lbs. · Deb: 6/13/89

| 1989 | Tor-A | 6 | 8 | 1 | 2 | 0 | 0 | 0 | 0 | 0 | 5 | .250 | .250 | .250 | 42 | -1 | -1 | 1 | 0 | 0 | 0 | 1 | /O | 0.0 |

■ BILL BATSCH · Batsch, William McKinley · b: 5/18/1892, Mingo Junction, O. · d: 12/31/63, Canton, Ohio · BR/TR, 5'10.5", 168 lbs. · Deb: 9/09/16

| 1916 | Pit-N | 1 | 0 | 0 | 0 | 0 | 0 | 0 | 0 | 1 | 0 | — | 1.000 | — | 218 | 0 | 0 | 0 | 0 | | | 0 | H | 0.0 |

■ LARRY BATTAM · Battam, Lawrence J. · b: 5/1/1878, Brooklyn, N.Y. · d: 1/27/38, Brooklyn, N.Y. · 5'11" · Deb: 9/28/1895

| 1895 | NY-N | 2 | 4 | 0 | 1 | 0 | 0 | 0 | 0 | 2 | 1 | .250 | .500 | .250 | 102 | 0 | 0 | 1 | 0 | | | -1 | /3 | 0.0 |

■ GEORGE BATTEN · Batten, George Burnett · b: 10/7/1891, Haddonfield, N.J. · d: 8/4/72, New Port Richey, Fla. · BR/TR, 5'11", 165 lbs. · Deb: 9/28/12

| 1912 | NY-A | 1 | 3 | 0 | 0 | 0 | 0 | 0 | 0 | 0 | | .000 | .000 | .000 | -94 | -1 | -1 | 0 | 0 | | | -1 | /2 | -0.1 |

■ EARL BATTEY · Battey, Earl Jesse · b: 1/5/35, Los Angeles, Cal. · BR/TR, 6'1", 205 lbs. · Deb: 9/10/55

1955	Chi-A	5	7	1	2	0	0	0	0	1	1	.286	.444	.286	97	0	0	1	0	0	0	2	/C	0.2
1956	Chi-A	4	4	1	1	0	0	0	0	1	1	.250	.400	.250	74	-0	-0	0	0	0	0	-0	/C	0.0
1957	Chi-A	48	115	12	20	2	3	3	6	11	38	.174	.246	.322	54	-8	-8	8	0	2	-1	6	C	0.0
1958	Chi-A	68	168	24	38	8	0	8	26	24	34	.226	.330	.417	106	1	1	24	1	0	0	2	C	0.4
1959	Chi-A	26	64	9	14	1	2	2	7	8	13	.219	.306	.391	91	-1	-1	8	0	0	0	3	C	0.4
1960	Was-A	137	466	49	126	24	2	15	60	48	68	.270	.349	.427	110	6	6	67	4	5	-2	7	*C	1.9
1961	Min-A	133	460	70	139	24	1	17	55	53	66	.302	.378	.470	118	17	13	78	3	3	-1	7	*C	1.7
1962	Min-A	148	522	58	146	20	3	11	57	57	48	.280	.351	.393	96	0	-2	70	0	0		6	*C	1.2
1963	Min-A	147	508	64	145	17	1	26	84	61	75	.285	.371	.476	133	25	24	89	0	0	0	1	*C	2.8
1964	Min-A	131	405	33	110	17	1	12	52	51	49	.272	.354	.407	111	7	7	54	1	1	-0	-5	*C	0.6
1965	*Min-A	131	394	36	117	22	2	6	60	50	23	.297	.379	.409	119	14	12	63	0	0	0	-8	*C	1.3
1966	Min-A	115	364	30	93	12	1	4	34	43	30	.255	.339	.327	87	-2	-5	39	4	1	1	4	*C	0.6
1967	Min-A	48	109	6	18	3	1	0	8	13	24	.165	.254	.211	36	-8	-9	6	0	0	0	-2	C	-0.9
Total	13	1141	3586	393	969	150	17	104	449	421	470	.270	.351	.409	106	50	38	508	13	12	-3	22	*C	10.2

■ JOE BATTIN · Battin, Joseph V. · b: 11/11/1851, Philadelphia, Pa. · d: 12/10/37, Akron, Ohio · BR/TR, · Deb: 8/11/1871 · MU

1871	Cle-n	1	3	0	0	0	0	0	0	1	0	.000	.250	.000	-21	-0	-0	0	0				/O	0.0
1873	Ath-n	1	5	4	3	0	0	0		1		.600	.667	.600	257	1	1	2					/O	0.1
1874	Ath-n	51	226	40	52	11	1	0		1		.230	.233	.288	60	-9	-12	16					*2/OS	-0.9
1875	StL-n	67	284	31	71	7	3	0		0		.250	.250	.296	97	-3	1	22					*2/3	0.0
1876	StL-N	64	283	34	85	11	4	0	46	6	6	.300	.315	.367	134	8	10	34				14	*3/2	1.9
1877	StL-N	57	226	28	45	3	7	1	22	6	17	.199	.220	.288	62	-10	-9	15				-2	32/OP	-0.6
1882	Pit-a	34	133	13	28	5	1	1		3		.211	.228	.286	76	-4	-3	9				21	3	1.5
1883	Pit-a	98	388	42	83	9	6	1		11		.214	.236	.276	67	-15	-12	26				29	*3/PM	1.6
1884	Pit-a	43	158	10	28	1	2	0		3		.177	.198	.209	34	-11	-11	7				8	3M	-0.2
	CP-U	18	69	8	13	2	0	0		0		.188	.188	.217	37	-4	-4	3	0			11	3M	0.1
	Bal-U	17	59	3	6	1	0	0		0		.102	.102	.119	-23	-7	-8	1	0			2	3	-0.4
	Yr	35	128	11	19	3	0	0		0		.148	.148	.172	8	-12	-13	3	0			13		0.2
1890	Syr-a	29	119	15	25	2	1	0		8		.210	.260	.244	56	-7	-6	10	8			-4	3	-0.8
Total	4 n	120	518	75	126	18	4	0		3		.243	.248	.293	80	-11	-11	39	0				2/O3S	-0.8
Total	6	360	1435	153	313	34	21	3	68	37	23	.218	.238	.277	69	-52	-43	103	8			78	3/2OP	3.6

■ JIM BATTLE · Battle, James Milton · b: 3/26/01, Bailey, Tex. · d: 9/30/65, Chico, Cal. · BR/TR, 6'1", 170 lbs. · Deb: 9/09/27

| 1927 | Chi-A | 6 | 8 | 1 | 3 | 0 | 1 | 0 | 0 | 0 | 1 | .375 | .375 | .625 | 160 | 1 | 1 | 2 | 0 | 0 | 0 | -1 | /3S | 0.0 |

■ MATT BATTS · Batts, Matthew Daniel · b: 10/16/21, San Antonio, Tex. · BR/TR, 5'11", 200 lbs. · Deb: 9/10/47

1947	Bos-A	7	16	3	8	1	0	1	5	1	1	.500	.529	.750	236	3	3	7	0	0	0	-0	/C	0.3
1948	Bos-A	46	118	13	37	12	0	1	24	15	9	.314	.391	.441	115	4	3	21	0	0	0	-1	C	0.4
1949	Bos-A	60	157	23	38	9	1	3	31	25	22	.242	.350	.369	84	-2	-4	22	1	0	0	2	C	0.1
1950	Bos-A	75	238	27	65	15	3	4	34	18	19	.273	.327	.412	80	-5	-8	31	0	0	0	3	C	-0.2
1951	Bos-A	11	29	1	4	1	0	0	2	1	2	.138	.167	.172	-8	-4	-5	1	0	0	0	0	C	-0.3
	StL-A	79	248	26	75	17	1	5	31	21	21	.302	.357	.440	111	4	3	38	2	0	1	-7	C	0.1
	Yr	90	277	27	79	18	1	5	33	22	23	.285	.338	.412	98	-0	-1	38	2	0	1	-7		-0.2
1952	Det-A	56	173	11	41	4	1	3	13	14	22	.237	.298	.324	72	-7	-7	17	1	0	0	3	C	-0.2
1953	Det-A	116	374	38	104	24	3	6	43	24	36	.278	.322	.406	97	-4	-3	48	2	3	-1	-13	*C	-1.2
1954	Det-A	12	21	1	6	1	0	0	5	2	4	.286	.348	.333	89	-0	-0	3	0	0	0	1	/C	0.1
	Chi-A	55	158	16	36	7	1	3	19	17	15	.228	.303	.342	74	-5	-6	15	0	1	-1	6	C	0.2
	Yr	67	179	17	42	8	1	3	24	19	19	.235	.308	.341	76	-6	-6	17	0	1	-1	8		0.3
1955	Cin-N	26	71	4	18	4	1	0	13	4	11	.254	.293	.338	63	-3	-4	6	0	0	0	-1	C	-0.4
1956	Cin-N	3	2	0	0	0	0	0	0	1	1	.000	.333	.000	0	-0	-0	0	0	0	0	0	H	0.0
Total	10	546	1605	163	432	95	11	26	220	143	163	.269	.330	.391	89	-20	-28	208	6	4	-1	-7	C	-0.9

■ HANK BAUER · Bauer, Henry Albert · b: 7/31/22, E.St.Louis, Ill. · BR/TR, 6', 192 lbs. · Deb: 9/06/48 · MC

1948	NY-A	19	50	6	9	1	1	1	9	6	13	.180	.268	.300	51	-4	-4	5	1	0	0	-0	O	-0.3
1949	*NY-A	103	301	56	82	6	6	10	45	37	42	.272	.354	.432	107	2	2	47	2	2	-1	-0	O	0.0
1950	*NY-A	113	415	72	133	16	2	13	70	35	41	.320	.380	.463	118	9	10	75	2	3	-1	1	*O	0.7
1951	*NY-A	118	348	53	103	19	3	10	54	42	39	.296	.373	.454	128	11	13	60	5	2	0	-4	*O	0.4
1952	*NY-A	141	553	86	162	31	6	17	74	50	61	.293	.355	.463	134	18	22	91	6	7	-2	-2	*O	1.4
1953	*NY-A	133	437	77	133	20	6	10	57	59	45	.304	.394	.446	131	18	20	81	2	3	-1	-0	*O	1.4
1954	NY-A	114	377	73	111	16	5	12	54	40	42	.294	.362	.459	128	11	13	63	4	4	-1	-9	*O	0.0
1955	*NY-A	139	492	97	137	20	5	20	53	56	65	.278	.362	.461	122	13	14	86	8	4	0	2	*O/C	0.9
1956	*NY-A	147	539	96	130	18	7	26	84	59	72	.241	.318	.445	103	3	-0	77	4	2	0	-10	*O	-1.6
1957	*NY-A	137	479	70	124	22	9	18	65	42	64	.259	.324	.455	112	5	6	71	7	2	1	-11	*O	-1.1
1958	*NY-A	128	452	62	121	22	6	12	50	32	56	.268	.318	.423	106	-0	2	60	3	2	-0	-9	*O	-1.6
1959	NY-A	114	341	44	81	20	0	9	39	33	54	.238	.309	.375	90	-7	-5	41	4	2	0	-17	*O	-2.7
1960	KC-A	95	255	30	70	15	0	3	31	21	36	.275	.332	.369	89	-4	-4	30	1	0	0	-9	O	-1.4
1961	KC-A	43	106	11	28	3	1	3	18	9	8	.264	.322	.396	91	-2	-2	14	1	0	0	-3	OM	-0.5
Total	14	1544	5145	833	1424	229	57	164	703	521	638	.277	.347	.439	114	68	87	801	50	33	-5	-73	*O/C	-4.4

■ PADDY BAUMANN · Baumann, Charles John · b: 12/20/1885, Indianapolis, Ind. · d: 11/20/69, Indianapolis, Ind. · BR/TR, 5'9", 160 lbs. · Deb: 8/10/11

1911	Det-A	26	94	8	24	2	4	0	11	6		.255	.307	.362	82	-2	-3	11	1			6	2/O	0.2
1912	Det-A	16	42	3	11	1	0	0	7	6		.262	.354	.286	86	-1	-0	6	4			-2	/32O	-0.2
1913	Det-A	50	191	31	57	7	4	1	22	16	18	.298	.353	.393	120	4	4	28	4			-7	2	-0.3
1914	Det-A	3	11	1	0	0	0	0	0	2	1	.000	.154	.000	-52	-2	-2	0	0			-1	/2	-0.3
1915	NY-A	76	219	30	64	13	1	2	28	28	32	.292	.380	.388	130	9	9	33	9	10	-3	-2	23/O	0.4
1916	NY-A	79	237	35	68	5	3	1	25	19	16	.287	.352	.346	108	3	2	33	10			-7	O3/2	-0.5
1917	NY-A	49	110	10	24	2	1	0	8	4	9	.218	.246	.255	52	-7	-7	7	2			-12	2/O3	-2.0
Total	7	299	904	118	248	30	13	4	101	81	76	.274	.340	.350	103	4	3	117	30	10		-25	2/3O	-2.7

■ JIM BAUMER · Baumer, James Sloan · b: 1/29/31, Tulsa, Okla. · BR/TR, 6'2", 185 lbs. · Deb: 9/14/49

| 1949 | Chi-A | 8 | 10 | 2 | 4 | 1 | 1 | 0 | 2 | 2 | 1 | .400 | .571 | .700 | 243 | 2 | 2 | 5 | 0 | 0 | 0 | 1 | /S | 0.3 |
| 1961 | Cin-N | 10 | 24 | 0 | 3 | 0 | 0 | 0 | 0 | 0 | 9 | .125 | .125 | .125 | -33 | -5 | -5 | 0 | 0 | 0 | 0 | -0 | /2 | -0.3 |

YEAR	TM/L	G	AB	R	H	2B	3B	HR	RBI	BB	SO	AVG	OBP	SLG	PRO+	BR	/A	RC	SB	CS	SBR	FR	POS	TPR
Total	2	18	34	2	7	1	1	0	2	2	10	.206	.289	.294	55	-2	-2	5	0	0	0	1	/2S	0.0

■ JOHN BAUMGARTNER
Baumgartner, John Edward b: 5/29/31, Birmingham, Ala. BR/TR, 6'1", 190 lbs. Deb: 4/14/53

YEAR	TM/L	G	AB	R	H	2B	3B	HR	RBI	BB	SO	AVG	OBP	SLG	PRO+	BR	/A	RC	SB	CS	SBR	FR	POS	TPR
1953	Det-A	7	27	3	5	0	0	0	2	0	5	.185	.185	.185	0	-4	-4	1	0	0	0	-0	/3	-0.4

■ FRANK BAUMHOLTZ
Baumholtz, Frank Conrad b: 10/7/18, Midvale, Ohio BL/TL, 5'10.5", 175 lbs. Deb: 4/15/47

YEAR	TM/L	G	AB	R	H	2B	3B	HR	RBI	BB	SO	AVG	OBP	SLG	PRO+	BR	/A	RC	SB	CS	SBR	FR	POS	TPR
1947	Cin-N	151	643	96	182	32	9	5	45	56	53	.283	.341	.384	93	-7	-7	88	6			-2	*O	-1.3
1948	Cin-N	128	415	57	123	19	5	4	30	27	32	.296	.344	.395	103	-1	1	57	8			1	*O	-0.5
1949	Cin-N	27	81	12	19	5	3	1	8	6	8	.235	.295	.407	86	-2	-2	10	0			1	O	-0.2
	Chi-N	58	164	15	37	4	2	1	15	9	21	.226	.270	.293	52	-12	-11	14	2			-5	O	-1.7
	Yr	85	245	27	56	9	5	2	23	15	29	.229	.279	.331	64	-13	-13	24	2			-4		-1.9
1951	Chi-N	146	560	62	159	28	10	2	50	49	36	.284	.346	.380	94	-3	-5	74	5	4	-1	-21	*O	-3.0
1952	Chi-N	103	409	59	133	17	4	4	35	27	27	.325	.371	.416	116	10	9	64	5	7	-3	12	*O	1.7
1953	Chi-N	133	520	75	159	36	7	3	25	42	36	.306	.359	.419	100	2	0	82	3	3	-1	-15	*O	-1.9
1954	Chi-N	90	303	38	90	12	6	4	28	20	15	.297	.343	.416	95	-2	-2	42	1	3	-2	-1	O	-0.6
1955	Chi-N	105	280	23	81	12	5	1	27	16	24	.289	.330	.379	88	-5	-5	33	0	1	-1	1	O	-0.5
1956	Phi-N	76	100	13	27	0	0	0	9	6	6	.270	.318	.270	61	-5	-5	8	0	2	-1	0	O	-0.6
1957	Phi-N	2	2	0	0	0	0	0	0	0	0	.000	.000	.000	-99	-1	-1	0	0	0	0	0	H	0.0
Total	10	1019	3477	450	1010	165	51	25	272	258	258	.290	.342	.389	95	-26	-26	470	30	20		-28	O	-8.6

■ JIM BAXES
Baxes, Dimitrios Speros b: 7/5/28, San Francisco, Cal BR/TR, 6'1", 190 lbs. Deb: 4/11/59

YEAR	TM/L	G	AB	R	H	2B	3B	HR	RBI	BB	SO	AVG	OBP	SLG	PRO+	BR	/A	RC	SB	CS	SBR	FR	POS	TPR
1959	LA-N	11	33	4	10	1	0	2	5	4	7	.303	.395	.515	130	2	2	6	1	0	0	7	3	0.8
	Cle-A	77	247	35	59	11	0	15	34	21	47	.239	.299	.466	111	1	2	30	0	1	-1	-13	23	-0.9

■ MIKE BAXES
Baxes, Michael b: 12/18/30, San Francisco, Cal BR/TR, 5'10", 175 lbs. Deb: 4/17/56

YEAR	TM/L	G	AB	R	H	2B	3B	HR	RBI	BB	SO	AVG	OBP	SLG	PRO+	BR	/A	RC	SB	CS	SBR	FR	POS	TPR
1956	KC-A	73	106	9	24	3	1	1	5	18	15	.226	.339	.302	70	-4	-4	12	0	1	-1	4	S/2	0.5
1958	KC-A	73	231	31	49	10	1	0	8	21	24	.212	.286	.264	52	-15	-15	17	1	6	-3	-4	2/S	-1.8
Total	2	146	337	40	73	13	2	1	13	39	39	.217	.303	.276	58	-19	-19	29	1	7	-4	0	/S2	-1.3

■ JOHN BAXTER
Baxter, John b: Spokane, Wash. 6'3", Deb: 4/19/07

YEAR	TM/L	G	AB	R	H	2B	3B	HR	RBI	BB	SO	AVG	OBP	SLG	PRO+	BR	/A	RC	SB	CS	SBR	FR	POS	TPR
1907	StL-N	6	21	1	4	0	0	0	0	0		.190	.190	.190	21	-2	-2	1	0			-0	/1	-0.2

■ HARRY BAY
Bay, Harry Elbert "Deerfoot" b: 1/17/1878, Pontiac, Ill. d: 3/20/52, Peoria, Ill. BL/TL, 5'8", 138 lbs. Deb: 7/23/01

YEAR	TM/L	G	AB	R	H	2B	3B	HR	RBI	BB	SO	AVG	OBP	SLG	PRO+	BR	/A	RC	SB	CS	SBR	FR	POS	TPR
1901	Cin-N	41	157	25	33	1	2	1	3	13		.210	.271	.261	60	-8	-7	13	4			-1	O	-1.1
1902	Cin-N	6	16	3	6	0	0	0	1	2		.375	.474	.375	151	1	1	3	0			0	/O	0.1
	Cle-A	108	455	71	132	10	5	0	23	36		.290	.343	.334	94	-5	-2	64	22			4	*O	-0.4
1903	Cle-A	140	579	94	169	15	12	1	35	29		.292	.326	.364	111	6	7	88	45			-3	*O	-0.4
1904	Cle-A	132	506	69	122	12	9	3	36	43		.241	.301	.318	99	-1	-0	62	38			7	*O	0.0
1905	Cle-A	144	552	90	166	18	10	0	22	36		.301	.344	.370	127	17	16	88	36			1	*O	1.1
1906	Cle-A	68	280	47	77	8	3	0	14	26		.275	.337	.325	111	4	4	39	17			-2	O	0.0
1907	Cle-A	34	95	14	17	1	1	0	7	10		.179	.257	.211	51	-5	-5	8	7			0	O	-0.6
1908	Cle-A	2	0	0	0	0	0	0	0	0		—	—	—	—	0	0	0	0			0	R	0.0
Total	8	675	2640	413	722	65	42	5	141	195		.273	.324	.336	104	9	14	365	169			6	O	-1.3

■ DICK BAYLESS
Bayless, Harry Owen b: 9/6/1883, Joplin, Mo. d: 12/16/20, Santa Rita, N.M. 5'9", 178 lbs. Deb: 9/09/08

YEAR	TM/L	G	AB	R	H	2B	3B	HR	RBI	BB	SO	AVG	OBP	SLG	PRO+	BR	/A	RC	SB	CS	SBR	FR	POS	TPR
1908	Cin-N	19	71	7	16	1	0	1	3	6		.225	.286	.282	86	-1	-1	6	0			3	O	0.1

■ DON BAYLOR
Baylor, Don Edward b: 6/28/49, Austin, Tex. BR/TR, 6'1", 190 lbs. Deb: 9/18/70 C

YEAR	TM/L	G	AB	R	H	2B	3B	HR	RBI	BB	SO	AVG	OBP	SLG	PRO+	BR	/A	RC	SB	CS	SBR	FR	POS	TPR
1970	Bal-A	8	17	4	4	0	0	0	4	2	3	.235	.316	.235	54	-1	-1	1	1	1	-0	1	/O	0.0
1971	Bal-A	1	2	0	0	0	0	0	0	1	2	.000	.600	.000	83	0	0	0	0	0	0	0	O	0.1
1972	Bal-A	102	320	33	81	13	3	11	38	29	50	.253	.332	.416	118	8	7	47	24	2	6	-7	O/1	0.4
1973	*Bal-A	118	405	64	116	20	4	11	51	35	48	.286	.362	.437	125	13	14	65	32	9	4	-5	*O/1D	1.0
1974	*Bal-A	137	489	66	133	22	1	10	59	43	56	.272	.343	.382	112	6	8	65	29	12	2	-20	*O/1D	-1.4
1975	Bal-A	145	524	79	148	21	6	25	68	53	64	.282	.363	.489	148	26	30	90	32	17	-1	-6	*O/1D	2.0
1976	Oak-A	157	595	85	147	25	1	15	68	58	72	.247	.334	.368	110	5	8	80	52	12	8	-11	O1D	0.1
1977	Cal-A	154	561	87	141	27	0	25	75	62	76	.251	.339	.433	113	7	10	81	26	12	1	-3	OD1	0.4
1978	Cal-A	158	591	103	151	26	0	34	99	56	71	.255	.338	.472	131	19	22	93	22	9	1	-3	*DO1	1.8
1979	*Cal-A	162	628	120	186	33	3	36	139	71	51	.296	.377	.530	147	37	40	126	22	12	-1	-2	OD/1	3.2
1980	Cal-A	90	340	39	85	12	2	5	51	24	32	.250	.320	.341	83	-8	-7	36	6	6	-2	-1	OD	-1.0
1981	Cal-A	103	377	52	90	18	1	17	66	42	51	.239	.326	.427	116	7	7	51	3	3	-1	1	D/1O	0.8
1982	*Cal-A	157	608	80	160	24	1	24	93	57	69	.263	.333	.424	106	5	5	84	10	4	1	0	*D	0.5
1983	NY-A	144	534	82	162	33	3	21	85	40	53	.303	.366	.494	139	25	27	96	17	7	1	0	*D/O1	2.8
1984	NY-A	134	493	84	129	29	1	27	89	38	68	.262	.343	.489	132	18	20	83	1	1	-0	-1	*D/O	1.9
1985	NY-A	142	477	70	110	24	1	23	91	52	90	.231	.336	.430	111	6	7	70	0	4	-2	0	*D	0.5
1986	*Bos-A	160	585	93	139	23	1	31	94	62	111	.238	.346	.439	112	11	10	91	3	5	-2	-1	*D1/O	0.6
1987	Bos-A	108	339	64	81	8	0	16	57	40	47	.239	.360	.404	100	2	1	52	5	2	0	0	D	0.1
	*Min-A	20	49	3	14	1	0	0	6	5	12	.286	.397	.306	87	-0	-0	6	0	1	-1	0	D	0.0
	Yr	128	388	67	95	9	0	16	63	45	59	.245	.364	.392	98	2	1	58	5	3	-0	0		0.1
1988	*Oak-A	92	264	28	58	7	0	7	34	34	44	.220	.335	.326	89	-4	-2	30	0	1	-1	0	D	-0.2
Total	19	2292	8198	1236	2135	366	28	338	1276	805	1069	.260	.346	.436	119	181	206	1247	285	120	14	-55	*DO1	13.7

■ JACK BEACH
Beach, Stonewall Jackson b: 1862, Alexandria, Va. d: 7/23/1896, Alexandria, Va. Deb: 5/01/1884

YEAR	TM/L	G	AB	R	H	2B	3B	HR	RBI	BB	SO	AVG	OBP	SLG	PRO+	BR	/A	RC	SB	CS	SBR	FR	POS	TPR
1884	Was-a	8	31	3	3	2	0	0		0		.097	.097	.161	-18	-4	-3	0				-1	/O	-0.3

■ JOHNNY BEALL
Beall, John Woolf b: 3/12/1882, Beltsville, Md. d: 6/14/26, Beltsville, Md. BL/TR, 6', 180 lbs. Deb: 4/17/13

YEAR	TM/L	G	AB	R	H	2B	3B	HR	RBI	BB	SO	AVG	OBP	SLG	PRO+	BR	/A	RC	SB	CS	SBR	FR	POS	TPR
1913	Cle-A	6	6	0	1	0	0	0	1	0	2	.167	.167	.167	-2	-1	-1	0	0			0	H	0.0
	Chi-A	17	60	10	16	0	1	2	3	0		.267	.279	.400	99	-1	-1	6	1			1	O	0.0
	Yr	23	66	10	17	0	1	2	4	0	2	.258	.269	.379	89	-1	-1	6	1			1		0.0
1915	Cin-N	10	34	3	8	1	0	0	3	5	10	.235	.350	.265	86	-0	-0	3	0	1	-1	1	O	0.0
1916	Cin-N	6	21	3	7	2	0	1	4	3	7	.333	.417	.571	207	3	3	5	1			1	/O	0.3
1918	StL-N	19	49	2	11	1	0	0	6	3	6	.224	.269	.245	59	-2	-2	4	0			-0	O	-0.3
Total	4	58	170	18	43	4	1	3	17	11	25	.253	.306	.341	95	-2	-1	19	2	1		2	/O	0.0

■ BOB BEALL
Beall, Robert Brooks b: 4/24/48, Portland, Ore. BB/TL, 5'11", 180 lbs. Deb: 5/12/75

YEAR	TM/L	G	AB	R	H	2B	3B	HR	RBI	BB	SO	AVG	OBP	SLG	PRO+	BR	/A	RC	SB	CS	SBR	FR	POS	TPR
1975	Atl-N	20	31	2	7	1	0	0	1	6	9	.226	.351	.290	77	-1	-1	4	0	0	0	-0	/1	0.0
1978	Atl-N	108	185	29	45	8	0	1	16	36	27	.243	.369	.303	81	-1	-3	22	4	5	-2	0	1/O	-0.6
1979	Atl-N	17	15	1	2	2	0	0	1	3	4	.133	.278	.267	46	-1	-1	1	0	0	0	0	/1	0.0
1980	Pit-N	3	3	0	0	0	0	0	0	0	1	.000	.000	.000	-99	-1	-1	0	0	0	0	0	/H	0.0
Total	4	148	234	32	54	12	0	1	18	45	41	.231	.357	.295	76	-3	-6	28	4	5	-2	0	/1O	-0.6

■ TOMMY BEALS
Beals, Thomas L. (a.k.a. W.Thomas In 1871-1873) b: Hartford, Conn. d: 10/2/15, San Francisco, Cal. BR , 5'5", 144 lbs. Deb: 7/27/1871

YEAR	TM/L	G	AB	R	H	2B	3B	HR	RBI	BB	SO	AVG	OBP	SLG	PRO+	BR	/A	RC	SB	CS	SBR	FR	POS	TPR
1871	Oly-n	10	36	6	7	0	0	0	1	2	0	.194	.237	.194	27	-3	-3	2	2				/O2	-0.1
1872	Oly-n	9	36	7	12	0	2	0		1		.333	.351	.444	151	2	2	6					/2SO	0.1
1873	Was-n	37	170	33	46	4	8	0		1		.271	.275	.388	96	-2	-1	19					2C/O	-0.1
1874	Bos-n	19	97	20	19	3	4	0		0		.196	.196	.309	55	-4	-5	6					2/O	-0.3
1875	Bos-n	36	164	41	42	1	5	0		2		.256	.265	.323	99	0	-1	14					2O	0.0

YEAR	TM/L	G	AB	R	H	2B	3B	HR	RBI	BB	SO	AVG	OBP	SLG	PRO+	BR	/A	RC	SB	CS	SBR	FR	POS	TPR
1880	Chi-N	13	46	4	7	0	0	0	3	1	6	.152	.170	.152	10	-4	-4	1				-5	O/2	-0.9
Total	5 n	111	503	107	126	8	19	0		1	6	.250	.259	.342	87	-7	-7	47					/2OCS	-0.4

■ CHARLIE BEAMON
Beamon, Charles Alfonzo Jr. b: 12/4/53, Oakland, Cal. BL/TL, 6'1", 183 lbs. Deb: 9/11/78

YEAR	TM/L	G	AB	R	H	2B	3B	HR	RBI	BB	SO	AVG	OBP	SLG	PRO+	BR	/A	RC	SB	CS	SBR	FR	POS	TPR
1978	Sea-A	10	11	2	2	0	0	0	0	1	1	.182	.250	.182	23	-1	-1	1	0	0	0	1	/1D	0.0
1979	Sea-A	27	25	5	5	1	0	0	0	0	5	.200	.200	.240	18	-3	-3	1	1	0	0	1	/1O	-0.1
1981	Tor-A	8	15	1	3	1	0	0	0	2	2	.200	.294	.267	59	-1	-1	1	0	0	0	0	/D1	0.0
Total	3	45	51	8	10	2	0	0	0	3	8	.196	.241	.235	32	-5	-5	3	1	0	0	2	/D1O	-0.1

■ JOE BEAN
Bean, Joseph William b: 3/18/1874, Boston, Mass. d: 2/15/61, Atlanta, Ga. TR, 5'8", 138 lbs. Deb: 4/28/02

YEAR	TM/L	G	AB	R	H	2B	3B	HR	RBI	BB	SO	AVG	OBP	SLG	PRO+	BR	/A	RC	SB	CS	SBR	FR	POS	TPR
1902	NY-N	48	176	13	39	2	1	0	5	5		.222	.247	.244	54	-10	-9	14	9			-9	S	-1.7

■ BILL BEAN
Bean, William Daro b: 5/11/64, Santa Ana, Cal. BL/TL, 6'", 185 lbs. Deb: 4/25/87

YEAR	TM/L	G	AB	R	H	2B	3B	HR	RBI	BB	SO	AVG	OBP	SLG	PRO+	BR	/A	RC	SB	CS	SBR	FR	POS	TPR
1987	Det-A	26	66	6	17	2	0	0	4	5	11	.258	.310	.288	63	-4	-3	6	1	1	-0	3	O	0.0
1988	Det-A	10	11	2	2	0	1	0	0	0	2	.182	.182	.364	51	-1	-1	1	0	0	0	0	/O1D	0.0
1989	Det-A	9	11	0	0	0	0	0	0	2	3	.000	.214	.000	-36	-2	-2	0	0	0	0	-1	/O1	-0.2
	LA-N	51	71	7	14	4	0	0	3	4	10	.197	.250	.254	45	-5	-5	4	0	2	-1	2	O	-0.4
Total	3	96	159	15	33	6	1	0	7	11	26	.208	.267	.258	47	-12	-11	11	1	3	-2	5	/O1D	-0.6

■ BILLY BEANE
Beane, William Lamar b: 3/29/62, Orlando, Fla. BR/TR, 6'4", 195 lbs. Deb: 9/13/84

YEAR	TM/L	G	AB	R	H	2B	3B	HR	RBI	BB	SO	AVG	OBP	SLG	PRO+	BR	/A	RC	SB	CS	SBR	FR	POS	TPR
1984	NY-N	5	10	0	1	0	0	0	0	0	2	.100	.100	.100	-44	-2	-2	0	0	1	-1	-1	/O	-0.3
1985	NY-N	8	8	0	2	1	0	0	1	0	3	.250	.250	.375	74	-0	-0	1	0	0	0	0	/O	0.0
1986	Min-A	80	183	20	39	6	0	3	15	11	54	.213	.258	.295	49	-13	-13	12	2	3	-1	3	O/D	-1.2
1987	Min-A	12	15	1	4	2	0	0	1	0	6	.267	.267	.400	71	-1	-1	2	0	0	0	0	/O	0.0
1988	Det-A	6	6	1	1	0	0	0	1	0	2	.167	.167	.167	-7	-1	-1	0	0	0	0	0	/O	0.0
1989	Oak-A	37	79	8	19	5	0	0	11	0	13	.241	.241	.304	54	-5	-5	5	3	1	0	2	O/1C3D	-0.2
Total	6	148	301	30	66	14	0	3	29	11	80	.219	.247	.296	48	-22	-22	20	5	5	-2	5	O/D13C	-1.7

■ TED BEARD
Beard, Cramer Theodore b: 1/7/21, Woodsboro, Md. BL/TL, 5'8", 165 lbs. Deb: 9/05/48

YEAR	TM/L	G	AB	R	H	2B	3B	HR	RBI	BB	SO	AVG	OBP	SLG	PRO+	BR	/A	RC	SB	CS	SBR	FR	POS	TPR
1948	Pit-N	25	81	15	16	1	3	0	7	12	18	.198	.316	.284	62	-4	-4	8	5			2	O	-0.3
1949	Pit-N	14	24	1	2	0	0	0	1	2	2	.083	.154	.083	-34	-5	-5	0	0			-1	O	-0.5
1950	Pit-N	61	177	32	41	6	2	4	12	27	45	.232	.333	.356	79	-4	-5	22	3			2	O	-0.4
1951	Pit-N	22	48	7	9	1	0	1	3	6	14	.188	.291	.271	51	-3	-3	4	0	0	0	1	O	-0.2
1952	Pit-N	15	44	5	8	2	1	0	3	7	9	.182	.294	.273	57	-2	-3	4	2	0	1	0	O	-0.1
1957	Chi-A	38	78	15	16	1	0	0	7	18	14	.205	.354	.218	59	-3	-3	7	3	2	-0	1	O	-0.4
1958	Chi-A	19	22	5	2	0	0	1	2	6	5	.091	.286	.227	44	-2	-2	2	3	0	1	0	O	0.0
Total	7	194	474	80	94	11	6	6	35	78	107	.198	.315	.285	61	-24	-25	49	16	2		5	O	-1.9

■ OLLIE BEARD
Beard, Oliver Perry b: 5/2/1862, Lexington, Ky. d: 5/28/29, Cincinnati, Ohio BR/TR, 5'11", 180 lbs. Deb: 4/17/1889

YEAR	TM/L	G	AB	R	H	2B	3B	HR	RBI	BB	SO	AVG	OBP	SLG	PRO+	BR	/A	RC	SB	CS	SBR	FR	POS	TPR
1889	Cin-a	141	558	96	159	13	14	1	77	35	39	.285	.328	.364	96	-1	-4	80	36			20	*S	2.2
1890	Cin-N	122	492	64	132	17	15	3	72	44	13	.268	.331	.382	110	5	6	74	30			1	*S/3	0.5
1891	Lou-a	68	257	35	62	4	5	0	24	33	9	.241	.330	.296	83	-5	-5	28	7			7	3/S	0.4
Total	3	331	1307	195	353	34	34	4	173	112	61	.270	.330	.357	99	-1	-3	182	73			28	S/3	3.1

■ LEW BEASLEY
Beasley, Lewis Paige b: 8/27/48, Sparta, Va. BL/TR, 5'10", 172 lbs. Deb: 5/21/77

YEAR	TM/L	G	AB	R	H	2B	3B	HR	RBI	BB	SO	AVG	OBP	SLG	PRO+	BR	/A	RC	SB	CS	SBR	FR	POS	TPR
1977	Tex-A	25	32	5	7	1	0	0	3	2	2	.219	.265	.250	41	-3	-3	2	1	1	-0	-2	O/SD	-0.5

■ DAVE BEATLE
Beatle, David b: 1861, New York, N.Y. 6'2", 200 lbs. Deb: 6/17/1884

YEAR	TM/L	G	AB	R	H	2B	3B	HR	RBI	BB	SO	AVG	OBP	SLG	PRO+	BR	/A	RC	SB	CS	SBR	FR	POS	TPR
1884	Det-N	1	3	0	0	0	0	0	0	0	2	.000	.000	.000	-99	-1	-1	0				-1	/OC	-0.1

■ DESMOND BEATTY
Beatty, Aloysius Desmond "Desperate" b: 4/7/1893, Baltimore, Md. d: 10/6/69, Norway, Maine BR/TR, 5'8.5", 158 lbs. Deb: 9/28/14

YEAR	TM/L	G	AB	R	H	2B	3B	HR	RBI	BB	SO	AVG	OBP	SLG	PRO+	BR	/A	RC	SB	CS	SBR	FR	POS	TPR
1914	NY-N	2	3	0	0	0	0	0	1	0	0	.000	.000	.000	-99	-1	-1	-0	0			-0	/S3	0.0

■ JIM BEAUCHAMP
Beauchamp, James Edward b: 8/21/39, Vinita, Okla. BR/TR, 6'2", 190 lbs. Deb: 9/22/63

YEAR	TM/L	G	AB	R	H	2B	3B	HR	RBI	BB	SO	AVG	OBP	SLG	PRO+	BR	/A	RC	SB	CS	SBR	FR	POS	TPR
1963	StL-N	4	3	0	0	0	0	0	0	0	2	.000	.000	.000	-91	-1	-1	0	0	0	0	0	H	0.0
1964	Hou-N	23	55	6	9	2	0	2	4	5	16	.164	.246	.309	58	-3	-3	4	0	0	0	-1	O/1	-0.4
1965	Hou-N	24	53	5	10	1	0	0	4	5	11	.189	.259	.208	36	-5	-4	3	0	2	-1	2	/O1	-0.4
	Mil-N	4	3	0	0	0	0	0	0	1	0	.000	.250	.000	-23	-0	-0	0	0	1	-1	0	/1	0.0
	Yr	28	56	5	10	1	0	0	4	6	12	.179	.258	.196	32	-5	-5	2	0	3	-2	2		-0.4
1967	Atl-N	4	3	0	0	0	0	0	1	0	0	.000	.000	.000	-99	-1	-1	0				0	H	0.0
1968	Cin-N	31	57	10	15	2	0	2	14	4	19	.263	.311	.404	107	1	0	7	0	0	0	2	O/1	0.1
1969	Cin-N	43	60	8	15	1	0	1	8	5	13	.250	.308	.317	71	-2	-2	6	0	0	0	-0	/O1CS	-0.2
1970	Hou-N	31	26	3	5	0	0	1	4	3	7	.192	.276	.308	59	-2	-2	2	0	1	-1	0	O	-0.2
	StL-N	44	58	8	15	2	0	1	6	8	11	.259	.348	.345	85	-1	-1	8	2	0	1	2	O/1	0.0
	Yr	75	84	11	20	2	0	2	10	11	18	.238	.326	.333	78	-3	-3	10	2	1	0	2		-0.2
1971	StL-N	77	162	24	38	8	3	2	16	9	26	.235	.279	.358	76	-5	-6	16	3	1	0	-2	1/O	-1.1
1972	NY-N	58	120	10	29	1	0	5	19	7	33	.242	.289	.375	90	-2	-2	13	0	0	0	-3	1/O	-0.7
1973	*NY-N	50	61	5	17	1	1	0	14	7	11	.279	.353	.328	91	-1	-0	8	1	0	0	-1	1	-0.1
Total	10	393	661	79	153	18	4	14	90	54	150	.231	.292	.334	76	-21	-22	66	6	5	-1	-2	1/O	-3.0

■ GINGER BEAUMONT
Beaumont, Clarence Howeth b: 7/23/1876, Rochester, Wis. d: 4/10/56, Burlington, Wis. BL/TR, 5'8", 190 lbs. Deb: 4/21/1899

YEAR	TM/L	G	AB	R	H	2B	3B	HR	RBI	BB	SO	AVG	OBP	SLG	PRO+	BR	/A	RC	SB	CS	SBR	FR	POS	TPR
1899	Pit-N	111	437	90	154	15	8	3	38	41		.352	.416	.444	139	24	25	96	31			6	*O/1	2.2
1900	*Pit-N	138	567	105	158	14	9	5	50	40		.279	.331	.362	93	-5	-6	79	27			-12	*O	-2.7
1901	Pit-N	133	558	120	185	14	5	8	72	44		.332	.381	.418	130	24	22	106	36			-5	*O	0.3
1902	Pit-N	130	541	100	**193**	21	6	0	67	39		**.357**	.403	.418	151	55	33	109	33			0	*O	2.4
1903	*Pit-N	141	613	**137**	**209**	30	6	7	68	44		.341	.385	.444	134	29	27	118	23			-7	*O	1.1
1904	Pit-N	153	615	97	185	12	12	3	54	34		.301	.337	.374	118	14	13	92	28			-4	*O	0.3
1905	Pit-N	103	384	60	126	12	8	3	40	22		.328	.365	.424	134	16	15	70	21			-0	O	0.8
1906	Pit-N	80	310	48	82	9	3	2	32	19		.265	.307	.332	97	-0	-2	35	1			-5	O	-0.8
1907	Bos-N	150	580	67	**187**	19	14	4	62	37		.322	.363	.424	149	30	30	102	25			5	*O	3.3
1908	Bos-N	125	476	66	127	20	6	2	52	42		.267	.326	.347	119	9	10	58	13			-1	*O	0.9
1909	Bos-N	123	407	35	107	11	4	0	60	35		.263	.321	.310	92	-2	-4	45	12			1	O	-0.7
1910	*Chi-N	76	172	30	46	5	1	2	22	28	14	.267	.373	.343	110	3	3	24	4			2	O	0.3
Total	12	1463	5660	955	1759	182	82	39	617	425	14	.311	.361	.393	124	179	166	933	254			-19	*O/1	7.4

■ E. P. BEAVENS
Beavens, E. P. (a.k.a. E. P. Bevens) b: 1848, Troy, N.Y. TR, 5'8", 138 lbs. Deb: 5/09/1871

YEAR	TM/L	G	AB	R	H	2B	3B	HR	RBI	BB	SO	AVG	OBP	SLG	PRO+	BR	/A	RC	SB	CS	SBR	FR	POS	TPR
1871	Tro-n	3	15	7	6				5	0	0	.400	.400	.400	129	1	1	3	2				/2	0.0
1872	Atl-n	10	45	6	10	2	0	0		1		.222	.239	.267	47	-2	-4	3					/2SO	-0.3
Total	2 n	13	60	13	16	2	0	0		1		.267	.279	.300	66	-2	-3	6					/2OS	-0.3

■ BUCK BECANNON
Becannon, James Melvin b: 8/22/1859, New York, N.Y. d: 11/5/23, New York, N.Y. 5'10", 165 lbs. Deb: 10/15/1884

YEAR	TM/L	G	AB	R	H	2B	3B	HR	RBI	BB	SO	AVG	OBP	SLG	PRO+	BR	/A	RC	SB	CS	SBR	FR	POS	TPR
1884	*NY-a	1	3	0	0	0	0	0		0		.000	.000	.000	-99	-1	-1	0				0	/P	0.0
1885	NY-a	10	33	3	10	0	0	0		1		.303	.343	.303	118	0	1	4				1	P	0.0
1887	NY-N	1	5	0	0	0	0	0	0	0	2	.000	.000	.000	-99	-1	-1	0	0			-0	/3	-0.1
Total	3	12	41	3	10	0	0	0		1	2	.244	.279	.244	71	-2	-1	4	0			0	/P3	-0.1

YEAR	TM/L	G	AB	R	H	2B	3B	HR	RBI	BB	SO	AVG	OBP	SLG	PRO+	BR	/A	RC	SB	CS	SBR	FR	POS	TPR

■ GEORGE BECHTEL
Bechtel, George A. b: 1848, Philadelphia, Pa. 5'11", 165 lbs. Deb: 5/20/1871

YEAR	TM/L	G	AB	R	H	2B	3B	HR	RBI	BB	SO	AVG	OBP	SLG	PRO+	BR	/A	RC	SB	CS	SBR	FR	POS	TPR
1871	Ath-n	20	94	24	33	9	1	1	21	2	2	.351	.365	.500	147	5	6	19	4				O/P3	0.4
1872	Mut-n	51	246	60	74	11	2	0		6		.301	.317	.362	116	3	6	29					*O/1	0.6
1873	Phi-n	53	257	53	61	9	2	1		10		.237	.266	.300	64	-10	-12	21					*O/P	-0.6
1874	Phi-n	32	151	29	44	5	4	1		2		.291	.301	.397	116	3	2	18					O/P	0.3
1875	Cen-n	14	62	12	17	5	0	0		0		.274	.274	.355	126	1	2	6					P	0.0
	Ath-n	35	164	33	46	5	2	0		1		.280	.285	.335	102	2	-1	16					O/P	0.0
	Yr	49	226	45	63	10	2	0		1		.279	.282	.341	108	3	1	22						0.0
1876	Lou-N	14	55	2	10	1	0	0	2	0	1	.182	.182	.200	23	-4	-6	2				-3	O	-0.7
	NY-N	2	10	2	3	0	0	0	0	0	0	.300	.300	.300	115	-0	0	1				-1	/O	0.0
	Yr	16	65	4	13	1	0	0	2	0	1	.200	.200	.215	34	-4	-5	3				-4		-0.7
Total	5 n	205	974	211	275	44	11	3	21	21	2	.282	.297	.359	102	4	2	110					O/P31	0.7

■ CLYDE BECK
Beck, Clyde Eugene "Jersey" b: 1/6/1900, Bassett, Cal. d: 7/15/88, Temple City, Cal. BR/TR, 5'10", 176 lbs. Deb: 5/19/26

YEAR	TM/L	G	AB	R	H	2B	3B	HR	RBI	BB	SO	AVG	OBP	SLG	PRO+	BR	/A	RC	SB	CS	SBR	FR	POS	TPR
1926	Chi-N	30	81	10	16	0	0	1	4	7	15	.198	.261	.235	34	-7	-8	5				12	2	0.5
1927	Chi-N	117	391	44	101	20	5	2	44	43	37	.258	.332	.350	83	-9	-9	46	0			22	23/S	1.2
1928	Chi-N	131	483	72	124	18	4	3	52	58	58	.257	.341	.329	77	-16	-15	56	3			-1	3S/2	-0.7
1929	Chi-N	54	190	28	40	7	0	0	9	19	24	.211	.282	.247	32	-20	-20	14	3			5	3S	-0.8
1930	Chi-N	83	244	32	52	7	0	6	34	36	32	.213	.314	.316	53	-19	-19	26	2			0	S2/3	-0.9
1931	Cin-N	53	136	17	21	4	2	0	19	21	14	.154	.272	.213	34	-13	-12	10	1			-2	3/S	-1.0
Total	6	468	1525	203	354	56	11	12	162	184	180	.232	.317	.307	63	-83	-82	156	9			36	32S	-1.7

■ ERVE BECK
Beck, Ervin Thomas "Dutch" b: 7/19/1878, Toledo, Ohio d: 12/23/16, Toledo, Ohio BR/TR, 5'10", 168 lbs. Deb: 9/19/1899

YEAR	TM/L	G	AB	R	H	2B	3B	HR	RBI	BB	SO	AVG	OBP	SLG	PRO+	BR	/A	RC	SB	CS	SBR	FR	POS	TPR
1899	Bro-N	8	24	2	4	2	0	0	2	0		.167	.167	.250	14	-3	-3	1	0			-2	/2S	-0.3
1901	Cle-A	135	539	78	156	26	8	6	79	23		.289	.320	.401	105	-1	3	74	7			-11	*2	-1.2
1902	Cin-N	48	187	19	57	10	3	1	20	3		.305	.323	.406	116	5	3	26	2			-5	2/1O	0.0
	Det-A	41	162	23	48	4	0	2	22	4		.296	.313	.358	86	-3	-3	20	3			1	1/O	-0.1
Total	3	232	912	122	265	42	11	9	123	30		.291	.315	.390	101	-2	-1	121	12			-17	2/1OS	-1.6

■ FRANK BECK
Beck, Frank J. b: 1862, Poughkeepsie, N.Y. TR, Deb: 5/02/1884

YEAR	TM/L	G	AB	R	H	2B	3B	HR	RBI	BB	SO	AVG	OBP	SLG	PRO+	BR	/A	RC	SB	CS	SBR	FR	POS	TPR
1884	Pit-a	3	12	1	4	1	0	0		0		.333	.333	.417	144	1	1	2				0	/P	0.0
	Bal-U	5	20	1	2	1	0	0		0		.100	.100	.150	-15	-2	-3	0	0			-1	/OP	-0.3

■ FRED BECK
Beck, Frederick Thomas b: 11/17/1886, Havana, Ill. d: 3/12/62, Havana, Ill. BL/TL, 6'1", 180 lbs. Deb: 4/14/09

YEAR	TM/L	G	AB	R	H	2B	3B	HR	RBI	BB	SO	AVG	OBP	SLG	PRO+	BR	/A	RC	SB	CS	SBR	FR	POS	TPR
1909	Bos-N	96	334	20	66	4	6	3	27	17		.198	.245	.272	58	-16	-18	23	5			4	O1	-1.7
1910	Bos-N	154	571	52	157	32	9	10	64	19	55	.275	.307	.415	105	3	-0	75	8			-3	*O1	-0.7
1911	Cin-N	41	87	7	16	1	2	2	20	1	13	.184	.193	.310	41	-8	-7	5	2			-0	O/1	-0.8
	Phi-N	66	210	26	59	8	3	3	25	17	21	.281	.346	.390	105	1	1	29	3			-6	O	-0.6
	Yr	107	297	33	75	9	5	5	45	18	34	.253	.304	.367	88	-6	-6	34	5			-6		-1.4
1914	Chi-F	157	555	51	155	23	4	11	77	44	66	.279	.341	.395	117	7	11	81	9			-13	*1	0.1
1915	Chi-F	121	373	35	83	9	3	5	38	24	38	.223	.277	.303	76	-14	-11	34	4			-6	*1	-1.6
Total	5	635	2130	191	536	77	27	34	251	122	193	.252	.301	.361	93	-26	-24	247	31			-24	1O	-5.3

■ ZINN BECK
Beck, Zinn Bertram b: 9/30/1885, Steubenville, O. d: 3/19/81, W.Palm Beach, Fla. BR/TR, 5'10.5", 160 lbs. Deb: 9/14/13

YEAR	TM/L	G	AB	R	H	2B	3B	HR	RBI	BB	SO	AVG	OBP	SLG	PRO+	BR	/A	RC	SB	CS	SBR	FR	POS	TPR
1913	StL-N	10	30	4	5	1	0	0	2	4	10	.167	.265	.200	34	-2	-2	2	1			0	/S3	-0.1
1914	StL-N	137	457	42	106	15	11	3	45	28	32	.232	.282	.333	84	-11	-11	45	14			10	*3S	0.5
1915	StL-N	70	223	21	52	9	4	0	15	12	31	.233	.282	.309	79	-6	-6	18	3	10	-5	0	3/S2	-0.8
1916	StL-N	62	184	8	41	7	1	0	10	14	21	.223	.281	.272	71	-6	-6	15	3			-6	3/12	-1.3
1918	NY-A	11	8	0	0	0	0	0	1	0	1	.000	.000	.000	-98	-2	-2	-0	0			0	/13	-0.1
Total	5	290	902	75	204	32	16	3	73	58	95	.226	.279	.307	76	-28	-27	80	21	10		5	3/S12	-1.8

■ HEINE BECKENDORF
Beckendorf, Henry Ward b: 6/15/1884, New York, N.Y. d: 9/15/49, Jackson Heights, N.Y. BR/TR, 5'9", 174 lbs. Deb: 4/16/09

YEAR	TM/L	G	AB	R	H	2B	3B	HR	RBI	BB	SO	AVG	OBP	SLG	PRO+	BR	/A	RC	SB	CS	SBR	FR	POS	TPR
1909	Det-A	15	27	1	7	1	0	0	1	2		.259	.310	.296	88	-0	-0	3	0			-1	C	0.0
1910	Det-A	3	7	0	3	0	0	0	2	1		.429	.500	.429	179	1	1	1	0			-0	/C	0.1
	Was-A	37	103	8	15	1	0	0	10	5		.146	.207	.155	14	-10	-10	4	0			1	C	-0.5
	Yr	40	110	8	18	1	0	0	12	6		.164	.227	.173	26	-9	-9	5	0			1		-0.4
Total	2	55	137	9	25	2	0	0	13	8		.182	.243	.197	39	-10	-9	8	0			0	/C	-0.4

■ BEALS BECKER
Becker, David Beals b: 7/5/1886, ElDorado, Kan. d: 8/16/43, Huntington Park, Cal. BL/TL, 5'9", 170 lbs. Deb: 4/19/08

YEAR	TM/L	G	AB	R	H	2B	3B	HR	RBI	BB	SO	AVG	OBP	SLG	PRO+	BR	/A	RC	SB	CS	SBR	FR	POS	TPR
1908	Pit-N	20	65	4	10	0	1	0	0	2		.154	.179	.185	17	-6	-6	2	2			-1	O	-0.7
	Bos-N	43	171	13	47	3	1	0	7	7		.275	.303	.304	98	-1	-1	17	7			-4	O	-0.5
	Yr	63	236	17	57	3	2	0	7	9		.242	.269	.271	75	-7	-7	19	9			-5		-1.2
1909	Bos-N	152	562	60	138	15	6	6	24	47		.246	.305	.326	91	-4	-7	64	21			-1	*O	-1.3
1910	NY-N	80	126	18	36	2	4	3	24	14	25	.286	.357	.437	131	5	5	23	11			6	O/1	0.9
1911	*NY-N	88	172	28	45	11	1	1	20	26	22	.262	.359	.355	97	1	-0	28	19			1	O	0.0
1912	*NY-N	125	402	66	106	18	8	6	58	54	35	.264	.354	.393	101	3	1	66	30			4	*O	0.1
1913	Cin-N	30	108	11	32	5	3	0	14	6	12	.296	.333	.398	109	1	1	14	0			2	O	0.2
	Phi-N	88	306	53	99	19	10	9	44	22	30	.324	.369	.539	151	21	19	62	11			1	O/1	2.0
	Yr	118	414	64	131	24	13	9	58	28	42	.316	.360	.502	140	22	20	75	11			3		2.2
1914	Phi-N	138	514	76	167	25	5	9	66	37	59	.325	.370	.446	133	25	21	87	16			6	*O	2.5
1915	*Phi-N	112	338	38	83	16	4	11	35	26	48	.246	.301	.414	114	5	4	40	12	15	-5	-5	O	-0.9
Total	8	876	2764	367	763	114	43	45	292	241	231	.276	.335	.397	112	48	38	403	129	15		9	O/1	2.3

■ HEINZ BECKER
Becker, Heinz Reinhard "Dutch" b: 8/26/15, Berlin, Germany BB/TR, 6'2", 200 lbs. Deb: 4/21/43

YEAR	TM/L	G	AB	R	H	2B	3B	HR	RBI	BB	SO	AVG	OBP	SLG	PRO+	BR	/A	RC	SB	CS	SBR	FR	POS	TPR
1943	Chi-N	24	69	5	10	0	0	0	2	9	6	.145	.244	.145	14	-7	-7	3	0			1	1	-0.7
1945	*Chi-N	67	133	25	38	8	2	2	27	17	16	.286	.375	.421	124	4	4	22	0			-2	1	0.2
1946	Chi-N	9	7	0	2	0	0	0	1	1	1	.286	.375	.286	91	-0	-0	1	0			0	H	0.0
	Cle-A	50	147	15	44	10	1	0	17	23	18	.299	.401	.381	127	5	6	25	1	0	0	0	1	0.5
1947	Cle-A	2	2	0	0	0	0	0	0	0	1	.000	.000	.000	-99	-1	-1	0	0	0	0	0	H	0.0
Total	4	152	358	45	94	18	3	2	47	50	42	.263	.359	.346	102	1	3	50	1	0		0	/1	0.0

■ JOE BECKER
Becker, Joseph Edward b: 6/25/08, St.Louis, Mo. BR/TR, 6'1", 180 lbs. Deb: 5/10/36 C

YEAR	TM/L	G	AB	R	H	2B	3B	HR	RBI	BB	SO	AVG	OBP	SLG	PRO+	BR	/A	RC	SB	CS	SBR	FR	POS	TPR
1936	Cle-A	22	50	5	9	3	1	1	11	5	4	.180	.255	.340	45	-5	-5	4	0	0	0	-4	C	-0.6
1937	Cle-A	18	33	3	11	2	1	0	2	3	4	.333	.405	.455	116	1	1	6	0	0	0	-0	C	0.1
Total	2	40	83	8	20	5	2	1	13	8	8	.241	.315	.386	73	-4	-4	11	0	0	0	-5	/C	-0.5

■ MARTY BECKER
Becker, Martin Henry b: 12/25/1893, Tiffin, Ohio d: 9/25/57, Cincinnati, Ohio BB/TL, 5'8.5", 155 lbs. Deb: 9/08/15

YEAR	TM/L	G	AB	R	H	2B	3B	HR	RBI	BB	SO	AVG	OBP	SLG	PRO+	BR	/A	RC	SB	CS	SBR	FR	POS	TPR
1915	NY-N	17	52	5	13	2	0	0	3	2	9	.250	.278	.288	76	-2	-2	6	3			2	O	0.1

■ GLENN BECKERT
Beckert, Glenn Alfred b: 10/12/40, Pittsburgh, Pa. BR/TR, 6'1", 190 lbs. Deb: 4/12/65

YEAR	TM/L	G	AB	R	H	2B	3B	HR	RBI	BB	SO	AVG	OBP	SLG	PRO+	BR	/A	RC	SB	CS	SBR	FR	POS	TPR
1965	Chi-N	154	614	73	147	21	3	3	30	28	52	.239	.276	.298	60	-31	-33	47	6	8	-3	9	*2	-1.9
1966	Chi-N	153	656	73	188	23	7	1	59	26	36	.287	.318	.348	84	-13	-14	73	10	4	1	-20	*2/S	-2.5
1967	Chi-N	146	597	91	167	32	3	5	40	30	25	.280	.314	.369	91	-5	-8	68	10	3	1	4	*2	0.7
1968	Chi-N	155	643	98	189	28	4	4	37	31	20	.294	.328	.369	102	6	2	79	8	4	0	6	*2	1.9
1969	Chi-N	131	543	69	158	22	1	1	37	24	24	.291	.328	.341	78	-9	-17	60	6	0	2	6	*2	0.1

YEAR	TM/L	G	AB	R	H	2B	3B	HR	RBI	BB	SO	AVG	OBP	SLG	PRO+	BR	/A	RC	SB	CS	SBR	FR	POS	TPR
1970	Chi-N	143	591	99	170	15	6	3	36	32	22	.288	.324	.349	72	-17	-25	66	4	1	1	10	*2/O	0.1
1971	Chi-N	131	530	80	181	18	5	2	42	24	24	.342	.370	.406	104	13	4	76	3	2	-0	-3	*2	0.8
1972	Chi-N	120	474	51	128	22	2	3	43	23	17	.270	.307	.344	76	-10	-16	47	2	1	0	11	*2	0.3
1973	Chi-N	114	372	38	95	13	0	0	29	30	15	.255	.314	.290	64	-15	-18	32	0	2	-1	-12	2	-2.9
1974	SD-N	64	172	11	44	1	0	0	7	11	8	.256	.301	.262	61	-9	-8	14	0	0	0	-17	2/3	-2.4
1975	SD-N	9	16	2	6	1	0	0	0	1	0	.375	.412	.438	145	1	1	3	0	0	0	-1	/3	0.0
Total	11	1320	5208	685	1473	196	31	22	360	260	243	.283	.319	.345	81	-89	-133	565	49	25	-0	-6	*2/3OS	-5.8

■ JAKE BECKLEY

Beckley, Jacob Peter "Eagle Eye" b: 8/4/1867, Hannibal, Mo. d: 6/25/18, Kansas City, Mo. BL/TL, 5'10", 200 lbs. Deb: 6/20/1888 H

YEAR	TM/L	G	AB	R	H	2B	3B	HR	RBI	BB	SO	AVG	OBP	SLG	PRO+	BR	/A	RC	SB	CS	SBR	FR	POS	TPR
1888	Pit-N	71	283	35	97	15	3	0	27	7	22	.343	.363	.417	163	15	18	51	20			-3	1	0.8
1889	Pit-N	123	522	91	157	24	10	9	97	29	29	.301	.345	.437	132	11	19	84	11			3	*1/O	1.1
1890	Pit-P	121	516	109	167	38	22	9	120	42	32	.324	.381	.535	158	30	38	115	18			-0	*1	2.0
1891	Pit-N	133	554	94	162	20	19	4	73	44	46	.292	.353	.419	130	18	20	89	13			13	*1	2.5
1892	Pit-N	151	614	102	145	21	19	10	96	31	44	.236	.288	.381	103	-0	-0	78	30			21	*1	0.8
1893	Pit-N	131	542	108	164	32	19	5	106	54	26	.303	.386	.459	129	20	22	105	15			11	*1	2.6
1894	Pit-N	131	533	121	183	36	18	7	120	43	16	.343	.412	.518	146	21	22	125	21			5	*1	2.2
1895	Pit-N	129	530	104	174	31	19	5	110	24	20	.328	.381	.487	132	18	23	109	20			-7	*1	1.6
1896	Pit-N	59	217	44	55	7	5	3	32	22	28	.253	.349	.373	96	-2	-0	32	8			-1	1/O2	0.0
	NY-N	46	182	37	55	8	4	5	38	9	7	.302	.352	.473	122	4	5	35	11			-1	1/O	0.4
	Yr	105	399	81	110	15	9	8	70	31	35	.276	.351	.419	108	2	4	67	19			-2		0.4
1897	NY-N	17	68	8	17	2	3	1	11	2		.250	.301	.412	92	-1	-1	9	2			2	1	0.1
	Cin-N	97	365	76	126	17	9	7	76	18		.345	.395	.499	129	19	15	83	23			-3	*1	0.9
	Yr	114	433	84	143	19	12	8	87	20		.330	.380	.485	123	17	14	92	25			-1		1.0
1898	Cin-N	118	459	86	135	20	12	4	72	28		.294	.343	.416	112	10	6	69	6			-1	*1	0.5
1899	Cin-N	134	513	87	171	27	16	3	99	40		.333	.393	.466	135	26	25	104	20			5	*1	2.9
1900	Cin-N	141	558	98	190	26	10	2	94	40		.341	.386	.434	132	21	23	105	23			6	*1	2.7
1901	Cin-N	140	580	78	178	36	13	3	79	28		.307	.343	.429	134	17	22	91	4			-4	*1	1.9
1902	Cin-N	129	531	82	175	23	7	5	69	34		.330	.375	.427	137	30	24	94	15			-2	*1/P	1.7
1903	Cin-N	120	459	85	150	29	10	2	81	42		.327	.383	.447	125	22	15	91	23			4	*1	1.4
1904	StL-N	142	551	72	179	22	9	1	67	35		.325	.365	.403	146	24	27	91	17			-11	*1	1.0
1905	StL-N	134	514	48	147	20	10	1	57	30		.286	.325	.370	112	5	7	68	12			-9	*1	-0.7
1906	StL-N	87	320	29	79	16	6	0	44	13		.247	.276	.334	96	-4	-3	33	3			-4	1	-1.1
1907	StL-N	32	115	6	24	3	0	0	11	7		.209	.216	.235	44	-8	-7	6	0			-2	1	-1.1
Total	20	2386	9526	1600	2930	473	243	86	1575	616	270	.308	.359	.435	127	297	319	1668	315			20	*1/OP2	24.2

■ JULIO BECQUER

Becquer, Julio (Villegas) b: 12/20/31, Havana, Cuba BL/TL, 5'11.5", 178 lbs. Deb: 9/13/55

YEAR	TM/L	G	AB	R	H	2B	3B	HR	RBI	BB	SO	AVG	OBP	SLG	PRO+	BR	/A	RC	SB	CS	SBR	FR	POS	TPR
1955	Was-A	10	14	1	3	0	0	0	1	0	1	.214	.214	.214	16	-2	-2	1	0	0	0	1	/1	0.0
1957	Was-A	105	186	14	42	6	2	2	22	10	29	.226	.269	.312	59	-11	-11	13	3	3	-1	0	1	-1.2
1958	Was-A	86	164	10	39	3	0	0	12	8	21	.238	.273	.256	47	-12	-11	10	1	2	-1	6	1/O	-0.7
1959	Was-A	108	220	20	59	12	5	1	26	8	17	.268	.297	.382	85	-5	-5	22	3	2	-0	2	1	-0.1
1960	Was-A	110	298	41	75	15	7	4	35	12	35	.252	.283	.389	81	-9	-9	27	1	3	-2	-3	1/P	-1.8
1961	LA-A	11	8	0	0	0	0	0	0	1	5	.000	.111	.000	-61	-2	-2	0	0	0	0	0	/1	-0.1
	Min-A	57	84	13	20	1	2	5	18	2	12	.238	.256	.476	86	-2	-2	9	0	1	-1	-1	1/OP	-0.4
	Yr	68	92	13	20	1	2	5	18	3	17	.217	.242	.435	72	-4	-4	9	0	1	-1	-0		-0.5
1963	Min-A	1	0	1	0	0	0	0	0	0	0	—	—	—	—	0	0	0	0	0	0	0	H	0.0
Total	7	488	974	100	238	37	16	12	114	41	120	.244	.277	.352	70	-43	-42	82	8	11	-4	5	1/OP	-4.4

■ HOWIE BEDELL

Bedell, Howard William b: 9/29/35, Clearfield, Pa. BL/TR, 6'1", 185 lbs. Deb: 4/10/62 C

YEAR	TM/L	G	AB	R	H	2B	3B	HR	RBI	BB	SO	AVG	OBP	SLG	PRO+	BR	/A	RC	SB	CS	SBR	FR	POS	TPR
1962	Mil-N	58	138	15	27	1	2	0	2	11	22	.196	.255	.232	33	-13	-13	9	1	0	0	-3	O	-1.7
1968	Phi-N	9	7	0	1	0	0	0	1	1	0	.143	.250	.143	20	-1	-1	0	0	0	0	0	H	-0.0
Total	2	67	145	15	28	1	2	0	3	12	22	.193	.255	.228	32	-14	-13	9	1	0	0	-3	/O	-1.7

■ GENE BEDFORD

Bedford, William Eugene b: 12/2/1896, Dallas, Tex. d: 10/6/77, San Antonio, Tex. BB/TR, 5'8", 170 lbs. Deb: 6/25/25

YEAR	TM/L	G	AB	R	H	2B	3B	HR	RBI	BB	SO	AVG	OBP	SLG	PRO+	BR	/A	RC	SB	CS	SBR	FR	POS	TPR
1925	Cle-A	2	3	1	0	0	0	0	0	0	1	.000	.000	.000	-99	-1	-1	0	0	0	0	-1	/2	-0.1

■ ED BEECHER

Beecher, Edward "Scrap Iron" b: 5/1876, Indiana Deb: 9/26/1897

YEAR	TM/L	G	AB	R	H	2B	3B	HR	RBI	BB	SO	AVG	OBP	SLG	PRO+	BR	/A	RC	SB	CS	SBR	FR	POS	TPR
1897	StL-N	3	12	1	4	0	0	0	1	0		.333	.333	.333	80	-0	-0	2	1			-0	/O	0.0
1898	Cle-N	8	25	1	5	2	0	0	0	0		.200	.200	.280	39	-2	-2	1	0			-2	/O	-0.3
Total	2	11	37	2	9	2	0	0	1	0		.243	.243	.297	53	-2	-2	3	1			-2	/O	-0.3

■ ED BEECHER

Beecher, Edward H. b: 7/2/1860, Guilford, Conn. d: 9/12/35, Hartford, Conn. BL/TL, 5'10", 185 lbs. Deb: 6/28/1887

YEAR	TM/L	G	AB	R	H	2B	3B	HR	RBI	BB	SO	AVG	OBP	SLG	PRO+	BR	/A	RC	SB	CS	SBR	FR	POS	TPR
1887	Pit-N	41	169	15	41	8	0	2	22	7	8	.243	.281	.325	74	-7	-5	18	8			7	O	0.2
1889	Was-N	42	179	20	53	9	0	0	30	5	4	.296	.319	.346	93	-3	-2	21	3			-2	O/1	-0.3
1890	Buf-P	126	536	69	159	22	10	3	90	29	23	.297	.341	.392	106	-3	5	78	14			-5	*O/P	-0.3
1891	Was-a	58	235	35	57	11	3	2	28	27	9	.243	.333	.340	100	-1	1	33	17			3	O	0.1
	Phi-a	16	71	9	15	2	4	0	7	3	4	.211	.243	.352	70	-3	-3	8	7			-1	O	-0.3
	Yr	74	306	44	72	13	7	2	35	30	13	.235	.314	.343	93	-4	-3	41	24			2		-0.2
Total	4	283	1190	148	325	52	17	7	177	71	48	.273	.322	.363	96	-18	-5	159	49			3	O/1P	-0.6

■ JODIE BEELER

Beeler, Joseph Sam b: 11/26/21, Dallas, Tex. BR/TR, 6', 170 lbs. Deb: 9/21/44

YEAR	TM/L	G	AB	R	H	2B	3B	HR	RBI	BB	SO	AVG	OBP	SLG	PRO+	BR	/A	RC	SB	CS	SBR	FR	POS	TPR
1944	Cin-N	3	3	0	0	0	0	0	0	0	2	.000	.000	.000	-99	-1	-1	0	0			-1	/23	-0.1

■ GENE BEGLEY

Begley, Eugene T. b: 6/7/1861, Brooklyn, N.Y. Deb: 9/11/1886

YEAR	TM/L	G	AB	R	H	2B	3B	HR	RBI	BB	SO	AVG	OBP	SLG	PRO+	BR	/A	RC	SB	CS	SBR	FR	POS	TPR
1886	NY-N	5	16	1	2	0	0	0	1	1	3	.125	.176	.125	-7	-2	-2	1	1			0	/CO	0.0

■ JIM BEGLEY

Begley, James Lawrence "Imp" b: 9/19/02, San Francisco, Cal. d: 2/20/57, San Francisco, Cal BR/TR, 5'6", 145 lbs. Deb: 5/28/24

YEAR	TM/L	G	AB	R	H	2B	3B	HR	RBI	BB	SO	AVG	OBP	SLG	PRO+	BR	/A	RC	SB	CS	SBR	FR	POS	TPR
1924	Cin-N	2	5	1	1	0	0	0	0	2	0	.200	.429	.200	75	-0	-0	1	0	0	0	1	/2	0.1

■ STEVE BEHEL

Behel, Stephen Arnold Douglas b: 11/6/1860, Earlville, Ill. d: 2/15/45, Los Angeles, Cal. Deb: 9/27/1884

YEAR	TM/L	G	AB	R	H	2B	3B	HR	RBI	BB	SO	AVG	OBP	SLG	PRO+	BR	/A	RC	SB	CS	SBR	FR	POS	TPR
1884	Mil-U	9	33	5	8	1	0	0			3	.242	.306	.273	179	0	3	3	0			-1	/O	0.1
1886	NY-a	59	224	32	46	5	2	0			22	.205	.279	.246	70	-8	-6	20	16			-4	O	-1.0
Total	2	68	257	37	54	6	2	0			25	.210	.283	.249	78	-8	-4	23	16			-5	/O	-0.9

■ OLLIE BEJMA

Bejma, Alojzy Frank b: 9/12/07, South Bend, Ind. BR/TR, 5'10", 165 lbs. Deb: 4/24/34

YEAR	TM/L	G	AB	R	H	2B	3B	HR	RBI	BB	SO	AVG	OBP	SLG	PRO+	BR	/A	RC	SB	CS	SBR	FR	POS	TPR
1934	StL-A	95	262	39	71	16	3	2	29	40	36	.271	.376	.378	87	-1	-4	40	3	2	-0	-12	S23/O	-1.2
1935	StL-A	64	198	18	38	8	2	2	26	27	21	.192	.289	.283	46	-15	-17	18	1	0	0	-4	2/S3	-1.6
1936	StL-A	67	139	19	36	2	3	2	18	27	21	.259	.380	.360	81	-3	-4	21	0	0	0	-12	2/3S	-1.1
1939	Chi-A	90	307	52	77	9	3	8	44	36	27	.251	.331	.378	79	-9	-10	39	1	3	-2	-14	2/S3	-2.0
Total	4	316	906	128	222	35	11	14	117	130	105	.245	.343	.354	75	-28	-35	118	5	5	-2	-42	2/S3O	-5.9

■ MARK BELANGER

Belanger, Mark Henry b: 6/8/44, Pittsfield, Mass. BR/TR, 6'1", 170 lbs. Deb: 8/07/65

YEAR	TM/L	G	AB	R	H	2B	3B	HR	RBI	BB	SO	AVG	OBP	SLG	PRO+	BR	/A	RC	SB	CS	SBR	FR	POS	TPR
1965	Bal-A	11	3	1	1	0	0	0	0	0	0	.333	.333	.333	88	-0	-0	0	0	1	-1	3	/S	0.2
1966	Bal-A	8	19	2	3	1	0	0	0	0	3	.158	.158	.211	5	-2	-2	1	0	0	0	4	/S	0.2
1967	Bal-A	69	184	19	32	5	0	1	10	12	46	.174	.224	.217	31	-16	-16	10	6	1	1	7	S2/3	-0.4
1968	Bal-A	145	472	40	98	13	0	2	21	40	114	.208	.275	.248	59	-22	-22	35	10	1	2	12	*S	0.2
1969	*Bal-A	150	530	76	152	17	4	2	50	53	54	.287	.354	.345	95	-1	-2	66	14	6	1	-10	*S	-0.4

YEAR	TM/L	G	AB	R	H	2B	3B	HR	RBI	BB	SO	AVG	OBP	SLG	PRO+	BR	/A	RC	SB	CS	SBR	FR	POS	TPR
1970	*Bal-A	145	459	53	100	6	5	1	36	52	65	.218	.304	.259	56	-26	-26	42	13	2	3	8	*S	-0.3
1971	*Bal-A	150	500	67	133	19	4	0	35	73	48	.266	.367	.320	97	1	1	63	10	8	-2	0	*S	1.6
1972	Bal-A	113	285	36	53	9	1	2	16	18	53	.186	.239	.246	43	-20	-20	18	6	3	0	21	*S	1.3
1973	*Bal-A	154	470	60	106	15	1	0	27	49	54	.226	.305	.262	61	-23	-22	41	13	6	0	3	*S	0.1
1974	*Bal-A	155	493	54	111	14	4	5	36	51	69	.225	.300	.300	75	-16	-14	49	17	7	1	9	*S	0.8
1975	Bal-A	152	442	44	100	11	1	3	27	36	53	.226	.286	.276	63	-23	-20	40	16	4	2	28	*S	2.6
1976	Bal-A	153	522	66	141	22	2	1	40	51	64	.270	.337	.326	101	-2	2	60	27	17	-2	16	*S	2.6
1977	Bal-A	144	402	39	83	13	4	2	30	43	68	.206	.288	.274	58	-25	-22	34	15	8	-0	21	*S	1.5
1978	Bal-A	135	348	39	74	13	0	0	16	40	55	.213	.305	.250	61	-18	-15	29	6	6	-2	34	*S	2.8
1979	*Bal-A	101	198	28	33	6	2	0	9	29	33	.167	.276	.217	36	-18	-17	15	5	1	1	3	S	0.0
1980	Bal-A	113	268	37	61	7	3	0	22	12	25	.228	.261	.276	48	-19	-19	20	6	3	0	-1	*S	-1.0
1981	Bal-A	64	139	9	23	3	2	1	10	12	25	.165	.242	.237	39	-11	-11	8	2	1	0	5	S	-0.1
1982	LA-N	54	50	6	12	1	0	0	4	5	10	.240	.309	.260	62	-2	-2	4	1	0	0	8	S/2	1.0
Total	18	2016	5784	676	1316	175	33	20	389	576	839	.228	.302	.280	68	-245	-228	533	167	75	5	169	*S/23	12.7

■ WAYNE BELARDI
Belardi, Carroll Wayne b: 9/5/30, St.Helena, Cal. BL/TL, 6'1", 185 lbs. Deb: 4/18/50

YEAR	TM/L	G	AB	R	H	2B	3B	HR	RBI	BB	SO	AVG	OBP	SLG	PRO+	BR	/A	RC	SB	CS	SBR	FR	POS	TPR
1950	Bro-N	10	10	0	0	0	0	0	0	0	4	.000	.000	.000	-98	-3	-3	0	0			0	/1	-0.2
1951	Bro-N	3	3	1	1	0	1	0	0	0	2	.333	.333	1.000	240	1	1	1	0	0	0	0	H	0.1
1953	*Bro-N	69	163	19	39	3	2	11	34	16	40	.239	.311	.485	101	0	-0	26	0	0	0	-0	1	0.0
1954	Bro-N	11	9	0	2	0	0	0	1	2	3	.222	.364	.222	55	-0	-1	1	0	0	0	0	H	0.0
	Det-A	88	250	27	58	7	1	11	24	33	34	.232	.333	.400	102	-0	-0	35	1	0	0	2	1	0.0
1955	Det-A	3	3	0	0	0	0	0	0	0	1	.000	.000	.000	-99	-1	-1	0	0	0	0	0	H	0.0
1956	Det-A	79	154	24	43	3	1	6	15	15	13	.279	.373	.429	111	3	3	25	0	0	0	-1	1/O	0.1
Total	6	263	592	71	143	13	5	28	74	66	97	.242	.332	.422	100	-1	-1	88	1	0		1	1/O	0.0

■ KEVIN BELCHER
Belcher, Kevin Donnell b: 8/8/67, Waco, Tex. BR/TR, 6', 170 lbs. Deb: 9/03/90

YEAR	TM/L	G	AB	R	H	2B	3B	HR	RBI	BB	SO	AVG	OBP	SLG	PRO+	BR	/A	RC	SB	CS	SBR	FR	POS	TPR
1990	Tex-A	16	15	4	2	1	0	0	0	2	6	.133	.235	.200	22	-2	-2	1	0	0	0	1	/O	0.0

■ IRA BELDEN
Belden, Ira Allison b: 4/16/1874, Cleveland, Ohio d: 7/15/16, Lakewood, Ohio 5'11", 175 lbs. Deb: 9/17/1897

YEAR	TM/L	G	AB	R	H	2B	3B	HR	RBI	BB	SO	AVG	OBP	SLG	PRO+	BR	/A	RC	SB	CS	SBR	FR	POS	TPR
1897	Cle-N	8	30	5	8	0	2	0	4		2	.267	.333	.400	90	-0	-1	4	0			2	/O	0.0

■ CHARLIE BELL
Bell, Charles C. b: 8/12/1868, Cincinnati, Ohio d: 2/7/37, Cincinnati, Ohio TR, Deb: 10/13/1889

YEAR	TM/L	G	AB	R	H	2B	3B	HR	RBI	BB	SO	AVG	OBP	SLG	PRO+	BR	/A	RC	SB	CS	SBR	FR	POS	TPR
1889	KC-a	2	6	1	1	1	0	0	3	2	2	.167	.375	.333	99	0	0	1	0			0	/OP	0.0
1891	Lou-a	10	28	3	1	0	0	0	0	6	8	.036	.206	.036	-29	-4	-4	0	0			-1	P	0.0
	Cin-a	1	4	1	2	0	0	0	1	0	0	.500	.500	.500	175	0	0	1	0			0	/P	0.0
	Yr	11	32	4	3	0	0	0	1	6	8	.094	.237	.094	-3	-4	-4	1	0			-1		0.0
Total	2	13	38	5	4	1	0	0	4	8	10	.105	.261	.132	15	-4	-4	2	0			-1	/PO	0.0

■ BUDDY BELL
Bell, David Gus b: 8/27/51, Pittsburgh, Pa. BR/TR, 6'1", 180 lbs. Deb: 4/15/72

YEAR	TM/L	G	AB	R	H	2B	3B	HR	RBI	BB	SO	AVG	OBP	SLG	PRO+	BR	/A	RC	SB	CS	SBR	FR	POS	TPR
1972	Cle-A	132	466	49	119	21	1	9	36	34	29	.255	.310	.363	96	-1	-2	52	5	6	-2	12	*O/3	0.5
1973	Cle-A	156	631	86	169	23	7	14	59	49	47	.268	.327	.393	100	1	-1	76	7	15	-7	25	*3/O	1.5
1974	Cle-A	116	423	51	111	15	1	7	46	35	29	.262	.323	.352	95	-3	-3	46	1	3	-2	4	*3/D	0.1
1975	Cle-A	153	553	66	150	20	4	10	59	51	72	.271	.334	.376	100	0	0	69	6	5	-1	-3	*3	-0.1
1976	Cle-A	159	604	75	170	26	2	7	60	44	49	.281	.332	.366	105	3	4	71	3	8	-4	5	*3/1	0.5
1977	Cle-A	129	479	64	140	23	4	11	64	45	63	.292	.354	.426	115	8	10	68	1	8	-5	12	*3O	1.4
1978	Cle-A	142	556	71	157	27	8	6	62	39	43	.282	.329	.392	103	1	2	65	1	3	-2	28	*3/D	2.8
1979	Tex-A	162	670	89	200	42	3	18	101	30	45	.299	.331	.451	110	6	7	95	5	4	-1	12	*3S	2.3
1980	Tex-A	129	490	76	161	24	4	17	83	40	39	.329	.379	.498	143	25	27	88	3	1	0	22	*3/S	4.8
1981	Tex-A	97	360	44	106	16	1	10	64	42	30	.294	.373	.428	137	15	17	58	3	3	-1	30	3/S	4.7
1982	Tex-A	148	537	62	159	27	2	13	67	70	50	.296	.379	.426	127	17	21	87	5	4	-1	34	*3/S	5.1
1983	Tex-A	156	618	75	171	35	3	14	66	50	48	.277	.335	.411	106	3	5	78	3	5	-2	16	*3	1.9
1984	Tex-A	148	553	88	174	36	5	11	83	63	54	.315	.388	.458	129	26	24	95	2	1	0	20	*3	4.5
1985	Tex-A	84	313	33	74	13	3	4	32	33	21	.236	.311	.335	76	-10	-10	31	3	2	-1	13	3	0.0
	Cin-N	67	247	28	54	15	2	6	36	34	27	.219	.313	.368	86	-3	-5	27	0	1	-1	-9	3	-1.4
1986	Cin-N	155	568	89	158	29	3	20	75	73	49	.278	.365	.445	117	18	15	91	2	8	-4	1	*3/2	0.9
1987	Cin-N	143	522	74	148	19	2	17	70	71	39	.284	.370	.425	105	9	6	84	4	1	1	-17	3	-1.0
1988	Cin-N	21	54	3	10	0	0	0	3	7	3	.185	.279	.185	34	-4	-5	3	0	0	0	0	3/1	-0.4
	Hou-N	74	269	24	68	10	1	7	37	19	29	.253	.302	.375	97	-3	-2	29	1	1	-0	-11	3/1	-1.4
	Yr	95	323	27	78	10	1	7	40	26	32	.241	.298	.344	86	-7	-6	32	1	1	-0	-11		-1.8
1989	Tex-A	34	82	4	15	4	0	0	3	7	10	.183	.247	.232	35	-7	-7	4	0	0	0	1	D/31	-0.5
Total	18	2405	8995	1151	2514	425	56	201	1106	836	776	.279	.343	.406	108	102	104	1218	55	79	-31	195	*30/SD12	26.2

■ GUS BELL
Bell, David Russell b: 11/15/28, Louisville, Ky. BL/TR, 6'1.5", 190 lbs. Deb: 5/30/50

YEAR	TM/L	G	AB	R	H	2B	3B	HR	RBI	BB	SO	AVG	OBP	SLG	PRO+	BR	/A	RC	SB	CS	SBR	FR	POS	TPR
1950	Pit-N	111	422	62	119	22	11	8	53	28	46	.282	.333	.443	99	0	-2	63	4			2	*O	-0.3
1951	Pit-N	149	600	80	167	27	12	16	89	42	41	.278	.330	.443	103	3	1	88	1	4	-2	1	*O	-0.5
1952	Pit-N	131	468	53	117	21	5	16	59	36	72	.250	.306	.419	97	-2	-4	61	1	4	-2	-9	*O	-1.7
1953	Cin-N	151	610	102	183	37	5	30	105	48	72	.300	.354	.525	124	21	20	113	0	2	-1	9	*O	2.0
1954	Cin-N	153	619	104	185	38	7	17	101	48	58	.299	.353	.465	108	9	7	100	5	3	-0	-3	*O	0.0
1955	Cin-N	154	610	88	188	30	6	12	104	54	57	.308	.364	.510	122	24	20	114	4	4	-1	-13	*O	0.2
1956	Cin-N	150	603	82	176	31	4	29	84	50	66	.292	.349	.501	117	20	15	105	6	2	1	-12	*O	-0.1
1957	Cin-N	121	510	65	149	20	3	13	61	30	54	.292	.335	.420	95	0	-4	70	0	1	-1	-5	*O	-1.2
1958	Cin-N	112	385	42	97	16	2	10	46	36	40	.252	.318	.382	80	-9	-12	46	2	3	-1	-11	*O	-2.6
1959	Cin-N	148	580	59	170	27	2	19	115	29	44	.293	.329	.445	101	2	-0	81	2	3	-1	5	*O	0.2
1960	Cin-N	143	515	65	135	19	5	12	62	29	40	.262	.303	.388	86	-10	-11	60	4	3	-1	0	*O	-1.5
1961	*Cin-N	103	235	27	60	10	1	3	33	18	21	.255	.308	.345	72	-9	-9	25	1	1	-0	-3	O	-1.6
1962	NY-N	30	101	8	15	2	0	1	6	10	7	.149	.225	.198	14	-12	-12	5	0	1	-1	2	O	-1.1
	Mil-N	79	214	28	61	11	3	5	24	12	17	.285	.323	.435	104	-0	1	30	0	0	-1	-5	O	-0.6
	Yr	109	315	36	76	13	3	6	30	22	24	.241	.291	.359	74	-12	-12	33	0	1	-1	-2		-1.7
1963	Mil-N	3	3	0	1	0	0	0	0	0	0	.333	.333	.333	94	-0	-0	0	0	0	0	0	H	0.0
1964	Mil-N	3	3	0	0	0	0	0	0	0	1	.000	.000	.000	-99	-1	-1	0	0	0	0	0	H	0.0
Total	15	1741	6478	865	1823	311	66	206	942	470	636	.281	.333	.445	102	37	9	962	30	31		-42	*O	-8.8

■ FERN BELL
Bell, Fern Lee "Danny" b: 1/21/13, Ada, Okla. BR/TR, 6', 180 lbs. Deb: 4/17/39

YEAR	TM/L	G	AB	R	H	2B	3B	HR	RBI	BB	SO	AVG	OBP	SLG	PRO+	BR	/A	RC	SB	CS	SBR	FR	POS	TPR
1939	Pit-N	83	262	44	75	5	8	2	34	42	18	.286	.385	.389	110	5	5	42	2			1	O/3	0.5
1940	Pit-N	6	3	0	0	0	0	0	1	1	1	.000	.250	.000	-26	-0	-0	0	0			0	H	0.0
Total	2	89	265	44	75	5	8	2	35	43	19	.283	.383	.389	109	4	5	42	2			1	/O3	0.5

■ FRANK BELL
Bell, Frank Gustav b: 1863, Cincinnati, Ohio d: 4/14/1891, Cincinnati, Ohio Deb: 7/07/1885

YEAR	TM/L	G	AB	R	H	2B	3B	HR	RBI	BB	SO	AVG	OBP	SLG	PRO+	BR	/A	RC	SB	CS	SBR	FR	POS	TPR
1885	Bro-a	10	29	5	5	0	1	0			0	.172	.200	.241	40	-2	-2	1				1	/CO3	0.0

■ JAY BELL
Bell, Jay Stuart b: 12/11/65, Eglin A.F.B., Fla. BR/TR, 6'1", 180 lbs. Deb: 9/29/86

YEAR	TM/L	G	AB	R	H	2B	3B	HR	RBI	BB	SO	AVG	OBP	SLG	PRO+	BR	/A	RC	SB	CS	SBR	FR	POS	TPR
1986	Cle-A	5	14	3	5	2	0	1	4	2	3	.357	.438	.714	211	2	2	5	0	0	0	1	/2D	0.3
1987	Cle-A	38	125	14	27	9	1	2	13	8	31	.216	.269	.352	62	-7	-7	13	2	0	1	3	S	-0.1
1988	Cle-A	73	211	23	46	5	1	2	21	21	53	.218	.292	.280	59	-11	-11	18	4	2	0	-12	S/D	-2.0
1989	Pit-N	78	271	33	70	13	3	2	27	19	47	.258	.309	.351	91	-4	-3	28	5	3	-0	-14	S	-1.3

YEAR	TM/L	G	AB	R	H	2B	3B	HR	RBI	BB	SO	AVG	OBP	SLG	PRO+	BR	/A	RC	SB	CS	SBR	FR	POS	TPR
1990	*Pit-N	159	583	93	148	28	7	7	52	65	109	.254	.332	.362	95	-7	-3	72	10	6	-1	-3	*S	0.7
Total	5	353	1204	166	296	57	12	14	117	115	243	.246	.315	.348	85	-26	-23	136	21	11	-0	-26	S/D2	-2.4

■ RUDY BELL Bell, John (b: Rudolph Fred Baerwald) b: 1/1/1881, Wausau, Wis. d: 7/28/55, Albuquerque, N.M. BR/TR, 5'8.5", 158 lbs. Deb: 9/16/07

YEAR	TM/L	G	AB	R	H	2B	3B	HR	RBI	BB	SO	AVG	OBP	SLG	PRO+	BR	/A	RC	SB	CS	SBR	FR	POS	TPR
1907	NY-A	17	52	4	11	2	1	0	3	3		.212	.255	.288	69	-2	-2	5	4			-1	O	-0.3

■ GEORGE BELL Bell, Jorge (Mathey) b: 10/21/59, San Pedro De Macoris, D.R. BR/TR, 6'1", 190 lbs. Deb: 4/09/81

YEAR	TM/L	G	AB	R	H	2B	3B	HR	RBI	BB	SO	AVG	OBP	SLG	PRO+	BR	/A	RC	SB	CS	SBR	FR	POS	TPR
1981	Tor-A	60	163	19	38	2	1	5	12	5	27	.233	.256	.350	69	-6	-7	14	3	2	-0	2	O/D	-0.6
1983	Tor-A	39	112	5	30	5	4	2	17	4	17	.268	.305	.438	96	-0	-1	13	1	1	-0	-1	O/D	-0.2
1984	Tor-A	159	606	85	177	39	4	26	87	24	86	.292	.328	.498	121	18	15	95	11	2	2	-2	*O/3D	1.1
1985	*Tor-A	157	607	87	167	28	6	28	95	43	90	.275	.331	.479	116	14	12	97	21	6	3	0	*O/3	1.3
1986	Tor-A	159	641	101	198	38	6	31	108	41	62	.309	.352	.532	133	30	28	113	7	8	-3	-0	*OD/3	2.1
1987	Tor-A	156	610	111	188	32	4	47	134	39	75	.308	.357	.605	146	40	38	125	5	1	1	-5	*O/23D	2.9
1988	Tor-A	156	614	78	165	27	5	24	97	34	66	.269	.308	.446	108	5	4	78	4	2	0	-12	*O/D	-1.0
1989	*Tor-A	153	613	88	182	41	2	18	104	33	60	.297	.337	.458	124	16	17	89	4	3	-1	-10	*OD	0.5
1990	Tor-A	142	562	67	149	25	0	21	86	32	80	.265	.308	.422	104	-0	1	70	3	2	-0	-0	*OD	0.5
Total	9	1181	4528	641	1294	237	32	202	740	255	563	.286	.329	.486	120	116	108	695	59	27	2	-28	*O/D32	6.1

■ JUAN BELL Bell, Juan (Mathey) b: 3/29/68, San Pedro De Macoris, D.R. BR/TR, 5'11", 172 lbs. Deb: 9/06/89

YEAR	TM/L	G	AB	R	H	2B	3B	HR	RBI	BB	SO	AVG	OBP	SLG	PRO+	BR	/A	RC	SB	CS	SBR	FR	POS	TPR
1989	Bal-A	8	4	2	0	0	0	0	0	0	1	.000	.000	.000	-99	-1	-1	0	1	0	0	2	/2SD	0.2
1990	Bal-A	5	2	1	0	0	0	0	0	0	1	.000	.000	.000	-99	-1	-1	0	0	0	0	1	/S	0.1
Total	2	13	6	3	0	0	0	0	0	0	2	.000	.000	.000	-99	-2	-2	0	1	0	0	4	/DS2	0.3

■ KEVIN BELL Bell, Kevin Robert b: 7/13/55, Los Angeles, Cal. BR/TR, 6', 195 lbs. Deb: 6/16/76

YEAR	TM/L	G	AB	R	H	2B	3B	HR	RBI	BB	SO	AVG	OBP	SLG	PRO+	BR	/A	RC	SB	CS	SBR	FR	POS	TPR
1976	Chi-A	68	230	24	57	7	6	5	20	18	56	.248	.305	.396	104	1	0	28	2	1	0	3	3/D	0.3
1977	Chi-A	9	28	4	5	1	0	1	6	3	8	.179	.258	.321	57	-2	-2	3	0	0	0	0	/S3O	0.0
1978	Chi-A	54	68	9	13	0	0	2	5	5	19	.191	.257	.279	50	-4	-5	5	1	0	0	11	3/D	0.7
1979	Chi-A	70	200	20	49	8	1	4	22	15	43	.245	.298	.355	75	-7	-7	20	2	4	-2	12	3/S	0.4
1980	Chi-A	92	191	16	34	5	2	1	11	29	37	.178	.286	.241	46	-14	-14	15	0	0	0	7	3/SD	-0.6
1982	Oak-A	4	9	1	3	1	0	0	0	0	2	.333	.333	.444	117	0	0	1	0	0	0	0	/3D	0.0
Total	6	297	726	74	161	22	9	13	64	70	165	.222	.292	.331	73	-26	-26	72	5	5	-2	33	3/SDO	0.8

■ LES BELL Bell, Lester Rowland b: 12/14/01, Harrisburg, Pa. d: 12/26/85, Hershey, Pa. BR/TR, 5'11", 165 lbs. Deb: 9/18/23

YEAR	TM/L	G	AB	R	H	2B	3B	HR	RBI	BB	SO	AVG	OBP	SLG	PRO+	BR	/A	RC	SB	CS	SBR	FR	POS	TPR
1923	StL-N	15	51	5	19	2	1	0	9	9	7	.373	.467	.451	146	4	4	12	1	0	0	-1	S	0.4
1924	StL-N	17	57	5	14	3	2	1	5	3	7	.246	.295	.421	91	-1	-1	7	0	0	0	-4	S	-0.2
1925	StL-N	153	586	80	167	29	9	11	88	43	47	.285	.334	.422	89	-8	-10	82	4	5	-2	-1	*3/S	-0.2
1926	*StL-N	155	581	85	189	33	14	17	100	54	62	.325	.383	.518	135	32	29	112	9			-22	*3	0.8
1927	StL-N	115	390	48	101	26	6	9	65	34	63	.259	.320	.426	95	-2	-4	52	5			-14	*3S	-1.1
1928	Bos-N	153	591	58	164	36	7	10	91	40	45	.277	.323	.413	96	-9	-5	77	1			5	*3	0.2
1929	Bos-N	139	483	58	144	23	5	9	72	50	42	.298	.364	.422	98	-4	-1	74	4			-20	*3/2S	-0.9
1930	Chi-N	74	248	35	69	15	4	5	47	24	27	.278	.342	.431	85	-6	-6	36	1			0	3/1	-0.4
1931	Chi-N	75	252	30	71	17	1	4	32	19	22	.282	.332	.405	95	-1	-2	35	0			4	3	0.6
Total	9	896	3239	404	938	184	49	66	509	276	322	.290	.346	.438	102	3	3	486	25	5		-53	3/S12	-0.8

■ MIKE BELL Bell, Michael Allen b: 4/22/68, Lewiston, N.J. BL/TL, 6'1", 175 lbs. Deb: 5/02/90

YEAR	TM/L	G	AB	R	H	2B	3B	HR	RBI	BB	SO	AVG	OBP	SLG	PRO+	BR	/A	RC	SB	CS	SBR	FR	POS	TPR
1990	Atl-N	36	45	8	11	5	1	1	5	2	9	.244	.292	.467	103	0	-0	4	0	1	-1	1	1	0.0

■ BEAU BELL Bell, Roy Chester b: 8/20/07, Bellville, Tex. d: 9/14/77, College Station, Tex. BR/TR, 6'2", 185 lbs. Deb: 4/16/35

YEAR	TM/L	G	AB	R	H	2B	3B	HR	RBI	BB	SO	AVG	OBP	SLG	PRO+	BR	/A	RC	SB	CS	SBR	FR	POS	TPR
1935	StL-A	76	220	20	55	8	2	3	17	16	16	.250	.304	.345	65	-11	-12	23	1	1	-0	-5	O1/3	-1.8
1936	StL-A	155	616	100	212	40	12	11	123	60	55	.344	.403	.502	119	21	18	126	4	1	1	-3	*O1	0.8
1937	StL-A	156	642	82	218	51	8	14	117	53	54	.340	.391	.509	124	23	23	127	2	2	-0	-0	*O1/3	1.3
1938	StL-A	147	526	91	138	35	3	13	84	71	46	.262	.350	.414	91	-8	-8	79	1	3	-2	4	*O/1	-0.5
1939	StL-A	11	32	4	7	1	0	1	5	4	3	.219	.324	.344	69	-1	-2	4	0	0	0	-0	/O	-0.1
	Det-A	54	134	14	32	4	2	0	24	24	16	.239	.358	.299	65	-5	-7	15	0	1	-1	1	O	-0.6
	Yr	65	166	18	39	5	2	1	29	28	19	.235	.352	.307	66	-7	-8	19	0	1	-1	1		-0.7
1940	Cle-A	120	444	55	124	22	2	4	58	34	41	.279	.332	.365	83	-13	-11	55	2	2	-1	-5	O1	-2.2
1941	Cle-A	48	104	12	20	4	3	0	9	10	8	.192	.270	.288	50	-8	-7	8	1	2	-1	-2	O1	-1.1
Total	7	767	2718	378	806	165	32	46	437	272	239	.297	.362	.432	99	-2	-6	437	11	12	-4	-11	O/13	-4.2

■ TERRY BELL Bell, Terence William b: 10/27/62, Dayton, Ohio BR/TR, 6', 195 lbs. Deb: 9/03/86

YEAR	TM/L	G	AB	R	H	2B	3B	HR	RBI	BB	SO	AVG	OBP	SLG	PRO+	BR	/A	RC	SB	CS	SBR	FR	POS	TPR
1986	KC-A	8	3	0	0	0	0	0	0	2	1	.000	.400	.000	20	-0	-0	0	0	0	0	-0	/C	0.0
1987	Atl-N	1	1	0	0	0	0	0	0	0	1	.000	.000	.000	-95	-0	-0	0	0	0	0	0	/H	0.0
Total	2	9	4	0	0	0	0	0	0	2	2	.000	.333	.000	-0	-0	-0	0	0	0	0	-0	/C	0.0

■ ZEKE BELLA Bella, John b: 8/23/30, Greenwich, Conn. BR/TL, 5'11", 185 lbs. Deb: 9/11/57

YEAR	TM/L	G	AB	R	H	2B	3B	HR	RBI	BB	SO	AVG	OBP	SLG	PRO+	BR	/A	RC	SB	CS	SBR	FR	POS	TPR
1957	NY-A	5	10	0	1	0	0	0	0	1	2	.100	.182	.100	-21	-2	-2	0	0	0	0	1	/O	0.0
1959	KC-A	47	82	10	17	2	1	1	9	9	14	.207	.293	.293	60	-4	-4	6	0	0	0	-1	O/1	-0.6
Total	2	52	92	10	18	2	1	1	9	10	16	.196	.282	.272	52	-6	-6	7	0	0	0	-0	O/1	-0.6

■ STEVE BELLAN Bellan, Esteban Enrique b: 1850, Cuba d: 8/8/32, Havana, Cuba 5'6", 154 lbs. Deb: 5/09/1871

YEAR	TM/L	G	AB	R	H	2B	3B	HR	RBI	BB	SO	AVG	OBP	SLG	PRO+	BR	/A	RC	SB	CS	SBR	FR	POS	TPR
1871	Tro-n	29	128	26	32	3	3	0	23	9	2	.250	.299	.320	77	-3	-4	14	4				*3/S	-0.3
1872	Tro-n	23	118	22	30	4	1	0		0		.254	.254	.305	70	-4	-4	9					/S3O	-0.2
1873	Mut-n	7	34	4	7	2	0	0		0		.206	.206	.265	38	-3	-3	2					/3	-0.1
Total	3 n	59	280	52	69	9	4	0		9		.246	.270	.307	70	-10	-11	25					/3SO	-0.6

■ JOEY BELLE Belle, Albert Jojuan b: 8/25/66, Shreveport, La. BR/TR, 6'1", 190 lbs. Deb: 7/15/89

YEAR	TM/L	G	AB	R	H	2B	3B	HR	RBI	BB	SO	AVG	OBP	SLG	PRO+	BR	/A	RC	SB	CS	SBR	FR	POS	TPR
1989	Cle-A	62	218	22	49	8	4	7	37	12	55	.225	.272	.394	84	-5	-5	22	2	2	-1	-1	OD	-0.7
1990	Cle-A	9	23	1	4	0	0	1	3	1	6	.174	.208	.304	41	-2	-2	1	0	0	0	0	/OD	-0.1
Total	2	71	241	23	53	8	4	8	40	13	61	.220	.266	.386	80	-7	-7	24	2	2	-1	-1	/OD	-0.8

■ RAFAEL BELLIARD Belliard, Rafael Leonidas (Matias) b: 10/24/61, Pueblo Nuevo, D.R. BR/TR, 5'9", 139 lbs. Deb: 9/06/82

YEAR	TM/L	G	AB	R	H	2B	3B	HR	RBI	BB	SO	AVG	OBP	SLG	PRO+	BR	/A	RC	SB	CS	SBR	FR	POS	TPR
1982	Pit-N	9	2	3	1	0	0	0	0	0	0	.500	.500	.500	175	0	0	1	1	0	0	3	/S	0.3
1983	Pit-N	4	1	1	0	0	0	0	0	0	1	.000	.000	.000	-98	-0	-0	0	0	0	0	1	/S	0.1
1984	Pit-N	20	22	3	5	0	0	0	0	0	1	.227	.227	.227	28	-2	-2	1	4	1	1	1	S/2	0.1
1985	Pit-N	17	20	1	4	0	0	0	1	0	5	.200	.200	.200	12	-2	-2	1	0	0	0	6	S	0.5
1986	Pit-N	117	309	33	72	5	2	0	31	26	54	.233	.299	.262	55	-18	-19	26	12	6	2	13	S2	0.6
1987	Pit-N	81	203	26	42	4	3	1	15	20	25	.207	.288	.271	49	-15	-15	17	5	1	1	6	S/2	0.1
1988	Pit-N	122	286	28	61	0	4	0	11	26	47	.213	.288	.241	54	-16	-16	21	7	1	2	-11	*S/2	-1.8
1989	Pit-N	67	154	10	33	4	0	0	8	8	22	.214	.253	.240	43	-12	-11	10	5	2	0	7	S2/3	0.0
1990	Pit-N	47	54	10	11	3	0	0	6	5	13	.204	.283	.259	52	-4	-3	2	1	2	1	5	2S/3	0.2
Total	9	484	1051	115	229	16	9	1	72	85	168	.218	.283	.253	51	-69	-68	79	35	9	5	30	S/23	0.1

■ JACK BELLMAN Bellman, John Hutchins "Happy Jack" b: 3/4/1864, Taylorsville, Ky. d: 12/8/31, Louisville, Ky. Deb: 4/23/1889

YEAR	TM/L	G	AB	R	H	2B	3B	HR	RBI	BB	SO	AVG	OBP	SLG	PRO+	BR	/A	RC	SB	CS	SBR	FR	POS	TPR
1889	StL-a	1	2	1	1	0	0	0	0	1	0	.500	.667	.500	211	1	0	1				-0	/C	0.0

YEAR	TM/L	G	AB	R	H	2B	3B	HR	RBI	BB	SO	AVG	OBP	SLG	PRO+	BR	/A	RC	SB	CS	SBR	FR	POS	TPR

■ ROB BELLOIR
Belloir, Robert Edward   b: 7/13/48, Heidelberg, Ger.   BR/TR, 5'10", 155 lbs.   Deb: 8/02/75

YEAR	TM/L	G	AB	R	H	2B	3B	HR	RBI	BB	SO	AVG	OBP	SLG	PRO+	BR	/A	RC	SB	CS	SBR	FR	POS	TPR
1975	Atl-N	43	105	11	23	2	1	0	9	7	8	.219	.268	.257	45	-8	-8	7	0	0	0	-2	S/2	-0.5
1976	Atl-N	30	60	5	12	2	0	0	4	5	7	.200	.262	.233	39	-5	-5	4	0	0	0	-1	S3/2	-0.4
1977	Atl-N	6	1	2	0	0	0	0	0	0	0	.000	.000	.000	-89	-0	-0	0	0	0	0	2	/S	0.2
1978	Atl-N	2	1	0	1	1	0	0	0	0	0	1.000	1.000	2.000	647	1	1	2	0	0	0	-0	/S3	0.1
Total	4	81	167	18	36	5	1	0	13	12	15	.216	.268	.257	45	-12	-13	13	0	0	0	-1	/S32	-0.6

■ HARRY BEMIS
Bemis, Harry Parker   b: 2/1/1874, Farmington, N.H.   d: 5/23/47, Cleveland, Ohio   BR/TR, 5'6.5", 155 lbs.   Deb: 4/23/02

YEAR	TM/L	G	AB	R	H	2B	3B	HR	RBI	BB	SO	AVG	OBP	SLG	PRO+	BR	/A	RC	SB	CS	SBR	FR	POS	TPR
1902	Cle-A	93	317	42	99	12	7	1	29	19		.312	.366	.404	120	7	9	50	3			8	C/O2	2.2
1903	Cle-A	92	314	31	82	20	3	1	41	8		.261	.280	.354	92	-4	-3	34	5			-8	C1/2	-0.1
1904	Cle-A	97	336	35	76	11	6	0	25	8		.226	.244	.295	72	-11	-11	27	6			-4	C1/2	-0.6
1905	Cle-A	70	226	27	66	13	3	0	28	13		.292	.331	.376	124	6	6	30	3			-5	C/231	0.7
1906	Cle-A	93	297	28	82	13	5	2	30	12		.276	.304	.374	115	4	4	38	8			-9	C	0.1
1907	Cle-A	65	172	12	43	7	0	0	19	7		.250	.279	.291	83	-3	-3	17	5			-8	C/1	-0.6
1908	Cle-A	91	277	23	62	9	1	0	33	7		.224	.243	.264	66	-10	-11	21	14			-6	C/1	-0.9
1909	Cle-A	42	123	4	23	2	3	0	13	0		.187	.194	.252	39	-9	-9	6	2			-1	C	-0.7
1910	Cle-A	61	167	12	36	5	1	1	16	5		.216	.238	.275	60	-8	-8	12	3			-3	C	-0.6
Total	9	704	2229	214	569	92	29	5	234	79		.255	.284	.329	91	-29	-27	235	49			-35	C/1230	-0.6

■ JOHNNY BENCH
Bench, Johnny Lee   b: 12/7/47, Oklahoma City, Okla.   BR/TR, 6'1", 197 lbs.   Deb: 8/28/67   H

YEAR	TM/L	G	AB	R	H	2B	3B	HR	RBI	BB	SO	AVG	OBP	SLG	PRO+	BR	/A	RC	SB	CS	SBR	FR	POS	TPR
1967	Cin-N	26	86	7	14	3	1	1	6	5	19	.163	.209	.256	29	-8	-9	4	0	1	-1	5	C	-0.2
1968	Cin-N	154	564	67	155	40	2	15	82	31	96	.275	.315	.433	115	14	10	71	1	5	-3	7	*C	2.3
1969	Cin-N	148	532	83	156	23	1	26	90	49	86	.293	.357	.487	128	23	20	92	6	6	-2	-3	*C	2.5
1970	*Cin-N	158	605	97	177	35	4	**45**	**148**	54	102	.293	.351	.587	146	36	35	121	5	2	0	6	*CO1/3	4.5
1971	Cin-N	149	562	80	134	19	2	27	61	49	83	.238	.300	.423	105	-0	1	66	2	1	0	-3	*C1O/3	0.0
1972	*Cin-N	147	538	87	145	22	2	**40**	**125**	100	84	.270	.386	.541	171	44	48	110	6	6	-2	-6	*CO/13	4.9
1973	*Cin-N	152	557	83	141	17	3	25	104	83	83	.253	.350	.429	121	12	15	82	4	1	1	-2	*CO/13	2.1
1974	Cin-N	160	621	108	174	38	2	33	**129**	80	90	.280	.365	.507	144	33	35	114	5	4	-1	-7	*C3/1	3.2
1975	*Cin-N	142	530	83	150	39	1	28	110	65	108	.283	.363	.519	140	29	28	101	11	0	3	2	*CO/1	3.6
1976	*Cin-N	135	465	62	109	24	1	16	74	81	95	.234	.350	.394	108	8	7	69	13	2	3	-4	*CO/O1	1.2
1977	Cin-N	142	494	67	136	34	2	31	109	58	95	.275	.353	.540	133	23	22	92	2	4	-2	-13	*C/O13	0.4
1978	Cin-N	120	393	52	102	17	1	23	73	50	83	.260	.345	.483	129	14	14	65	4	2	0	-8	*C1/O	1.0
1979	*Cin-N	130	464	73	128	19	0	22	80	67	73	.276	.367	.459	123	16	16	79	4	2	0	-8	*C/1	1.1
1980	Cin-N	114	360	52	90	12	0	24	68	41	64	.250	.330	.483	124	11	11	57	4	2	0	-17	*C	-0.4
1981	Cin-N	52	178	14	55	8	0	8	25	17	21	.309	.369	.489	139	9	9	31	0	2	-1	-2	1/C	0.5
1982	Cin-N	119	399	44	103	16	0	13	38	37	58	.258	.321	.396	98	-1	-2	48	1	2	-1	-17	*3/1C	-2.3
1983	Cin-N	110	310	32	79	15	2	12	54	24	38	.255	.308	.432	100	0	-1	37	0	1	-1	-12	31/CO	-1.6
Total	17	2158	7658	1091	2048	381	24	389	1376	891	1278	.267	.345	.476	127	264	259	1240	68	43	-5	-81	*C31O	22.8

■ ART BENEDICT
Benedict, Arthur Melville   b: 3/31/1862, Cornwall, Ill.   d: 1/20/48, Denver, Colo.   BR/TR,   Deb: 5/14/1883

YEAR	TM/L	G	AB	R	H	2B	3B	HR	RBI	BB	SO	AVG	OBP	SLG	PRO+	BR	/A	RC	SB	CS	SBR	FR	POS	TPR
1883	Phi-N	3	15	3	4	1	0	0	4	0	4	.267	.267	.333	89	-0	-0	1				-4	/2	-0.3

■ BRUCE BENEDICT
Benedict, Bruce Edwin   b: 8/18/55, Birmingham, Ala.   BR/TR, 6'1", 175 lbs.   Deb: 8/18/78

YEAR	TM/L	G	AB	R	H	2B	3B	HR	RBI	BB	SO	AVG	OBP	SLG	PRO+	BR	/A	RC	SB	CS	SBR	FR	POS	TPR
1978	Atl-N	22	52	3	13	2	0	0	1	6	6	.250	.328	.288	66	-2	-2	5	0	0	0	2	C	0.0
1979	Atl-N	76	204	14	46	11	0	0	15	33	18	.225	.333	.279	64	-8	-10	20	1	3	-2	1	C	-0.7
1980	Atl-N	120	359	18	91	14	1	2	34	28	36	.253	.309	.315	72	-12	-13	34	3	3	-1	4	*C	-0.7
1981	Atl-N	90	295	26	78	12	1	5	35	33	21	.264	.344	.363	98	1	-0	37	1	1	-0	7	C	0.9
1982	*Atl-N	118	386	34	95	11	1	3	44	37	40	.246	.317	.303	71	-12	-14	37	4	4	-1	2	*C	-1.2
1983	Atl-N	134	423	43	126	13	1	2	43	61	24	.298	.388	.348	98	6	2	57	1	3	-2	7	*C	1.2
1984	Atl-N	95	300	26	67	8	1	0	25	34	25	.223	.304	.297	65	-12	-14	27	1	2	-1	-0	C	-1.2
1985	Atl-N	70	208	12	42	6	0	0	20	22	12	.202	.281	.231	42	-15	-16	13	0	1	-1	-3	C	-1.7
1986	Atl-N	64	160	11	36	10	1	0	13	15	10	.225	.299	.300	62	-7	-8	13	1	0	0	-4	C	-1.0
1987	Atl-N	37	95	4	14	1	0	1	5	17	15	.147	.277	.189	25	-10	-10	6	0	1	-1	4	C	-0.4
1988	Atl-N	90	236	11	57	7	0	0	19	19	26	.242	.298	.271	61	-10	-12	20	0	2	-1	7	C	0.0
1989	Atl-N	66	160	12	31	3	0	1	6	23	18	.194	.299	.231	52	-9	-9	13	0	0	0	16	C	1.2
Total	12	982	2878	214	696	98	6	18	260	328	251	.242	.322	.299	71	-90	-108	282	12	20	-8	44	C	-3.6

■ JOE BENES
Benes, Joseph Anthony "Bananas"   b: 1/8/01, Long Island City, N.Y.   d: 3/7/75, Elmhurst, N.J.   BR/TR, 5'8.5", 158 lbs.   Deb: 5/09/31

YEAR	TM/L	G	AB	R	H	2B	3B	HR	RBI	BB	SO	AVG	OBP	SLG	PRO+	BR	/A	RC	SB	CS	SBR	FR	POS	TPR
1931	StL-N	10	12	1	2	0	0	0	0	2	1	.167	.333	.167	37	-1	-1	1	0			1	/S23	0.0

■ BENNY BENGOUGH
Bengough, Bernard Oliver   b: 7/27/1898, Niagara Falls, N.Y.   d: 12/22/68, Philadelphia, Pa.   BR/TR, 5'7.5", 168 lbs.   Deb: 5/18/23   C

YEAR	TM/L	G	AB	R	H	2B	3B	HR	RBI	BB	SO	AVG	OBP	SLG	PRO+	BR	/A	RC	SB	CS	SBR	FR	POS	TPR
1923	NY-A	19	53	1	7	2	0	0	3	4	2	.132	.193	.170	-4	-8	-8	2	0	0	0	0	C	-0.5
1924	NY-A	11	16	4	5	1	1	0	3	2	0	.313	.389	.500	128	1	1	3	0	0	0	3	C	0.4
1925	NY-A	95	283	17	73	14	2	0	23	19	9	.258	.305	.322	60	-18	-17	28	0	2	-1	5	C	-0.6
1926	NY-A	36	84	9	32	6	0	0	14	7	4	.381	.435	.452	134	4	4	17	1	0	0	8	C	1.4
1927	*NY-A	31	85	6	21	3	3	0	10	4	4	.247	.281	.353	66	-5	-5	7	0	3	-2	11	C	0.6
1928	*NY-A	58	161	12	43	3	1	0	9	7	8	.267	.302	.298	60	-10	-9	15	0	0	0	6	C	0.1
1929	NY-A	23	62	5	12	2	1	0	7	0	2	.194	.194	.258	16	-8	-7	3	0	0	0	-5	C	-0.9
1930	NY-A	44	102	10	24	4	2	0	12	3	8	.235	.257	.314	46	-9	-8	8	1	0	0	9	C	0.5
1931	StL-A	40	140	6	35	4	1	0	12	4	4	.250	.271	.293	46	-11	-11	10	0	3	-1	-1	C	-1.0
1932	StL-A	54	139	13	35	7	1	0	15	12	4	.252	.311	.317	60	-8	-9	14	0	1	-1	7	C	0.0
Total	10	411	1125	83	287	46	12	0	108	62	45	.255	.295	.317	59	-71	-70	107	2	9	-5	44	C	0.0

■ JUAN BENIQUEZ
Beniquez, Juan Jose (Torres)   b: 5/13/50, San Sebastian, P.R.   BR/TR, 5'11", 150 lbs.   Deb: 9/04/71

YEAR	TM/L	G	AB	R	H	2B	3B	HR	RBI	BB	SO	AVG	OBP	SLG	PRO+	BR	/A	RC	SB	CS	SBR	FR	POS	TPR
1971	Bos-A	16	57	8	17	2	0	0	4	3	4	.298	.333	.333	83	-1	-1	6	3	1	0	-8	S	-0.7
1972	Bos-A	33	99	10	24	4	1	1	8	7	11	.242	.292	.333	81	-2	-2	10	2	0	1	5	S	0.6
1974	Bos-A	106	389	60	104	14	3	5	33	25	61	.267	.313	.357	86	-4	-7	41	19	11	-1	10	O/D	0.0
1975	*Bos-A	78	254	43	74	14	4	2	17	25	26	.291	.359	.402	106	5	2	34	7	10	-4	1	OD3	-0.1
1976	Tex-A	145	478	49	122	14	4	0	33	39	56	.255	.315	.301	79	-11	-12	47	17	6	2	14	*O/2	0.0
1977	Tex-A	123	424	56	114	19	6	10	50	43	43	.269	.338	.413	102	2	1	55	26	18	2	-0	*O	-0.5
1978	Tex-A	127	473	61	123	17	3	11	50	20	59	.260	.294	.378	88	-9	-9	48	10	12	-4	-5	*O	-2.1
1979	NY-A	62	142	19	36	6	1	4	17	9	17	.254	.307	.394	90	-3	-2	16	3	3	-1	6	O/3	0.0
1980	Sea-A	70	237	26	54	10	0	6	21	17	25	.228	.280	.346	70	-10	-10	20	2	3	-1	2	O/D	-1.0
1981	Cal-A	58	166	18	30	5	0	3	13	15	16	.181	.253	.265	49	-11	-11	11	2	1	0	-4	O/D	-1.6
1982	*Cal-A	112	196	25	52	11	2	3	24	15	21	.265	.321	.388	93	-2	-2	25	3	0	1	-10	*O	-1.3
1983	Cal-A	92	315	44	96	15	0	3	34	15	29	.305	.344	.381	110	-0	-0	39	4	2	0	-2	O/D	-0.2
1984	Cal-A	110	354	60	119	17	0	8	39	18	43	.336	.373	.452	128	13	13	55	0	3	-2	-4	O	0.4
1985	Cal-A	132	411	54	125	13	5	8	42	34	46	.304	.364	.418	114	8	9	59	4	3	-1	-7	O1D/3S	-0.2
1986	Bal-A	113	343	48	103	15	6	6	36	40	49	.300	.378	.397	114	7	7	51	2	3	-1	-5	O3D1	0.0
1987	KC-A	57	174	14	41	7	0	3	26	11	26	.236	.285	.328	60	-10	-10	14	0	0	0	-3	OD/13	-1.3
	Tor-A	39	81	6	23	5	1	5	21	5	13	.284	.333	.556	127	3	3	14	0	0	0	-1	D/O1	0.1
	Yr	96	255	20	64	12	1	8	47	16	39	.251	.300	.400	82	-6	-7	28	0	0	0	-4		-1.2
1988	Tor-A	27	58	9	17	2	0	1	8	8	6	.293	.379	.379	112	1	1	8	0	0	0	0	D/O	0.1
Total	17	1500	4651	610	1274	190	30	79	476	349	551	.274	.329	.379	95	-22	-30	553	104	76	-14	-10	*OD/13S2	-7.8

YEAR	TM/L	G	AB	R	H	2B	3B	HR	RBI	BB	SO	AVG	OBP	SLG	PRO+	BR	/A	RC	SB	CS	SBR	FR	POS	TPR

■ STAN BENJAMIN
Benjamin, Alfred Stanley   b: 5/20/14, Framingham, Mass.   BR/TR, 6'2", 194 lbs.   Deb: 9/16/39

YEAR	TM/L	G	AB	R	H	2B	3B	HR	RBI	BB	SO	AVG	OBP	SLG	PRO+	BR	/A	RC	SB	CS	SBR	FR	POS	TPR
1939	Phi-N	12	50	4	7	2	1	0	2	1	6	.140	.157	.220	0	-7	-7	1	1			0	/O3	-0.6
1940	Phi-N	8	9	1	2	0	0	0	1	1	1	.222	.300	.222	48	-1	-1	1	0			1	/O	0.0
1941	Phi-N	129	480	47	113	20	7	3	27	20	81	.235	.266	.325	68	-23	-21	39	17			-6	*O/123	-3.3
1942	Phi-N	78	210	24	47	8	3	2	8	10	27	.224	.262	.319	73	-9	-8	18	5			0	O1	-0.9
1945	Cle-A	14	21	1	7	2	0	0	3	0	0	.333	.333	.429	126	0	0	3	0	1	-1	2	/O	0.2
Total	5	241	770	77	176	32	11	5	41	32	115	.229	.260	.318	66	-39	-36	61	23	1		-3	O/132	-4.6

■ MIKE BENJAMIN
Benjamin, Michael Paul   b: 11/22/65, Euclid, Ohio   BR/TR, 6'3", 195 lbs.   Deb: 7/07/89

YEAR	TM/L	G	AB	R	H	2B	3B	HR	RBI	BB	SO	AVG	OBP	SLG	PRO+	BR	/A	RC	SB	CS	SBR	FR	POS	TPR
1989	SF-N	14	6	6	1	0	0	0	0	0	1	.167	.167	.167	-5	-1	-1	0	0	0	0	2	/S	0.2
1990	SF-N	22	56	7	12	3	1	2	3	3	10	.214	.254	.411	81	-2	-2	5	1	0	0	5	S	0.6
Total	2	36	62	13	13	3	1	2	3	3	11	.210	.246	.387	73	-3	-3	5	1	0	0	7	/S	0.8

■ IKE BENNERS
Benners, Isaac B.   b: Philadelphia, Pa.   BL, 175 lbs.   Deb: 5/01/1884

YEAR	TM/L	G	AB	R	H	2B	3B	HR	RBI	BB	SO	AVG	OBP	SLG	PRO+	BR	/A	RC	SB	CS	SBR	FR	POS	TPR
1884	Bro-a	49	189	25	38	11	5	1		7		.201	.237	.328	84	-3	-3	15				-5	O	-0.7
	Wil-U	6	22	0	1	0	0	0		1		.045	.087	.045	-53	-3	-4	0	0			0	/O	-0.2

■ CHARLIE BENNETT
Bennett, Charles Wesley   b: 11/21/1854, New Castle, Pa.   d: 2/24/27, Detroit, Mich.   BR/TR, 5'11", 180 lbs.   Deb: 5/01/1878

YEAR	TM/L	G	AB	R	H	2B	3B	HR	RBI	BB	SO	AVG	OBP	SLG	PRO+	BR	/A	RC	SB	CS	SBR	FR	POS	TPR
1878	Mil-N	49	184	16	45	9	0	1	12	10	26	.245	.284	.310	89	-1	-2	17				-16	CO	-1.7
1880	Wor-N	51	193	20	44	9	3	0	18	10	30	.228	.266	.306	86	-1	-3	16				-4	C/O	-0.3
1881	Det-N	76	299	44	90	18	7	7	64	18	37	.301	.341	.478	149	18	17	50				13	*C/3O	2.7
1882	Det-N	84	342	43	103	16	10	5	51	20	33	.301	.340	.450	151	19	19	54				2	*C3/2S1	2.3
1883	Det-N	92	371	56	113	34	7	5	55	26	59	.305	.350	.474	155	21	24	63				-8	*C2O	1.7
1884	Det-N	90	341	37	90	18	6	3	40	36	40	.264	.334	.378	132	10	13	44				-11	*C/OS321	0.8
1885	Det-N	91	349	49	94	24	13	5	60	47	37	.269	.356	.456	161	25	24	58				-4	CO3	2.3
1886	Det-N	72	235	37	57	13	5	4	34	48	29	.243	.371	.391	128	11	10	37	4			5	C/OS	1.7
1887	*Det-N	46	160	26	39	6	5	3	20	30	22	.244	.363	.400	110	4	3	26	7			-4	C/O1	0.3
1888	Det-N	74	258	32	68	12	4	5	29	31	40	.264	.347	.399	140	12	12	38	4			0	C/1	1.4
1889	Bos-N	82	247	42	57	8	2	4	28	21	43	.231	.296	.328	71	-8	-11	27	7			8	C	0.0
1890	Bos-N	85	281	59	60	17	2	3	40	72	56	.214	.377	.320	98	6	2	37	6			3	C	1.0
1891	Bos-N	75	256	35	55	9	3	5	39	42	61	.215	.332	.332	85	-0	-5	30	3			11	C	1.0
1892	*Bos-N	35	114	19	23	4	0	1	16	27	23	.202	.355	.263	82	0	-2	13	6			-0	C	0.0
1893	Bos-N	60	191	34	40	6	0	4	27	40	36	.209	.352	.304	71	-5	-8	23	5			-5	C	-0.5
Total	15	1062	3821	549	978	203	67	55	533	478	572	.256	.340	.387	119	111	93	532	42			-10	C/O32S1	12.7

■ HERSCHEL BENNETT
Bennett, Herschel Emmett   b: 9/21/1896, Elwood, Mo.   d: 9/9/64, Springfield, Mo.   BL/TR, 5'9.5", 160 lbs.   Deb: 4/19/23

YEAR	TM/L	G	AB	R	H	2B	3B	HR	RBI	BB	SO	AVG	OBP	SLG	PRO+	BR	/A	RC	SB	CS	SBR	FR	POS	TPR
1923	StL-A	5	4	0	0	0	0	0	0	1	1	.000	.200	.000	-42	-1	-1	0	0	0	0	-0	/O	0.0
1924	StL-A	41	94	16	31	4	3	1	11	3	6	.330	.364	.468	107	1	1	16	1	0	0	-4	O	-0.3
1925	StL-A	93	298	46	83	11	6	2	37	18	16	.279	.324	.376	73	-11	-13	34	4	8	-4	-2	O	-2.2
1926	StL-A	80	225	33	60	14	2	1	26	22	21	.267	.337	.360	78	-6	-7	28	2	1	0	3	O	-0.7
1927	StL-A	93	256	40	68	12	2	3	30	14	21	.266	.311	.363	72	-10	-11	28	6	2	1	1	O	-1.2
Total	5	312	877	135	242	41	13	7	104	58	65	.276	.327	.376	77	-27	-32	107	13	11	-3	-1	O	-4.4

■ FRED BENNETT
Bennett, James Fred "Red"   b: 3/15/02, Atkins, Ark.   d: 5/12/57, Atkins, Ark.   BR/TR, 5'9", 185 lbs.   Deb: 4/13/28

YEAR	TM/L	G	AB	R	H	2B	3B	HR	RBI	BB	SO	AVG	OBP	SLG	PRO+	BR	/A	RC	SB	CS	SBR	FR	POS	TPR
1928	StL-A	7	8	0	2	1	0	0	0	0	2	.250	.250	.375	60	-0	-1	1	0	0	0	0	/O	0.0
1931	Pit-N	32	89	6	25	5	0	1	7	7	4	.281	.333	.371	90	-1	-1	11	0			-2	O	-0.3
Total	2	39	97	6	27	6	0	1	7	7	6	.278	.327	.371	87	-2	-2	12	0	0		-2	/O	-0.3

■ JOE BENNETT
Bennett, Joseph Rosenblum   b: 7/2/1900, New York, N.Y.   d: 7/11/87, Morro Bay, Cal.   BR/TR, 5'9", 168 lbs.   Deb: 7/05/23

YEAR	TM/L	G	AB	R	H	2B	3B	HR	RBI	BB	SO	AVG	OBP	SLG	PRO+	BR	/A	RC	SB	CS	SBR	FR	POS	TPR
1923	Phi-N	1	0	0	0	0	0	0	0	0	0	—	—	—	—	0	0	0	0	0	0	0	/3	0.0

■ PUG BENNETT
Bennett, Justin Titus   b: 2/20/1874, Ponca, Neb.   d: 9/12/35, Kirkland, Wash.   TR, 5'11", 165 lbs.   Deb: 4/12/06

YEAR	TM/L	G	AB	R	H	2B	3B	HR	RBI	BB	SO	AVG	OBP	SLG	PRO+	BR	/A	RC	SB	CS	SBR	FR	POS	TPR
1906	StL-N	153	595	66	156	16	7	1	34	56		.262	.326	.318	107	2	5	73	20			-7	*2	-0.1
1907	StL-N	87	324	20	72	8	2	0	21	21		.222	.270	.259	70	-12	-11	26	7			-16	2/3	-2.9
Total	2	240	919	86	228	24	9	1	55	77		.248	.306	.297	94	-10	-6	99	27			-23	2/3	-3.0

■ VERN BENSON
Benson, Vernon Adair   b: 9/19/24, Granite Quarry, N.C.   BL/TR, 5'10", 160 lbs.   Deb: 7/31/43   MC

YEAR	TM/L	G	AB	R	H	2B	3B	HR	RBI	BB	SO	AVG	OBP	SLG	PRO+	BR	/A	RC	SB	CS	SBR	FR	POS	TPR
1943	Phi-A	2	2	0	0	0	0	0	0	0	0	.000	.000	.000	-99	-0	-0	0	0	0	0	0	H	0.0
1946	Phi-A	7	5	1	0	0	0	0	0	0	3	.000	.167	.000	-51	-1	-1	0	0	0	0	1	/O	0.0
1951	StL-N	13	46	8	12	3	1	1	7	6	8	.261	.346	.435	108	1	1	8	0	0	0	0	/3O	0.0
1952	StL-N	20	47	6	9	2	0	2	5	5	9	.191	.269	.362	73	-2	-2	5	0	0	0	-1	3	-0.1
1953	StL-N	13	4	2	0	0	0	0	0	1	2	.000	.200	.000	-42	-1	-1	0	0	0	0	0	H	0.0
Total	5	55	104	17	21	5	1	3	12	13	22	.202	.291	.356	75	-4	-4	13	0	0	0	0	/3O	-0.1

■ JACK BENTLEY
Bentley, John Needles   b: 3/8/1895, Sandy Spring, Md.   d: 10/24/69, Olney, Md.   BL/TL, 5'11.5", 200 lbs.   Deb: 9/06/13

YEAR	TM/L	G	AB	R	H	2B	3B	HR	RBI	BB	SO	AVG	OBP	SLG	PRO+	BR	/A	RC	SB	CS	SBR	FR	POS	TPR
1913	Was-A	3	3	0	0	0	0	0	0	0	0	.000	.000	.000	-98	-1	-1	0	0			0	/P	0.0
1914	Was-A	30	40	7	11	2	0	0	4	0	5	.275	.275	.325	78	-1	-1	4	0			-0	P	0.0
1915	Was-A	4	2	0	0	0	0	0	0	0	1	.000	.000	.000	-99	-0	-0	0	0			-0	/P	0.0
1916	Was-A	2	0	0	0	0	0	0	0	0	0	—	—	—	—	0	0	0	0			0	/P	0.0
1923	*NY-N	52	89	9	38	6	2	1	14	3	4	.427	.446	.573	169	8	8	22	0	0	0	-1	P	0.0
1924	*NY-N	46	98	12	26	5	1	0	6	3	13	.265	.287	.337	69	-5	-4	9	0	0	0	-1	P	0.0
1925	NY-N	64	99	10	30	5	2	3	18	9	11	.303	.361	.485	119	2	2	17	0	0	0	-1	P/O1	0.6
1926	Phi-N	75	240	19	62	12	3	2	27	5	4	.258	.273	.358	66	-11	-13	22	0			-2	1/P	-1.5
	NY-N	3	4	0	1	0	0	0	0	0	0	.250	.250	.250	35	-0	-0	0	0			0	/P	0.0
	Yr	78	244	19	63	12	3	2	27	5	4	.258	.273	.357	65	-12	-13	23	0			-2		-1.5
1927	NY-N	8	9	1	2	0	0	1	2	1	1	.222	.300	.556	125	0	0	1	0			-0	/P1	0.0
Total	9	287	584	58	170	30	8	7	71	21	39	.291	.316	.406	91	-8	-9	77	0	0		-5	P/1O	-0.9

■ BUTCH BENTON
Benton, Alfred Lee   b: 8/24/57, Tampa, Fla.   BR/TR, 6'1", 190 lbs.   Deb: 9/14/78

YEAR	TM/L	G	AB	R	H	2B	3B	HR	RBI	BB	SO	AVG	OBP	SLG	PRO+	BR	/A	RC	SB	CS	SBR	FR	POS	TPR
1978	NY-N	4	4	1	2	0	0	0	2	0	0	.500	.600	.500	218	1	1	1	0	0	0	0	/C	0.1
1980	NY-N	12	21	0	1	0	0	0	0	2	4	.048	.167	.048	-39	-4	-4	0	0	0	0	-1	/C	-0.4
1982	Chi-N	4	7	0	1	0	0	0	1	0	1	.143	.143	.143	-19	-1	-1	0	0	0	0	2	/C	0.1
1985	Cle-A	31	67	5	12	4	0	0	7	3	9	.179	.214	.239	24	-7	-7	3	0	0	0	-3	C	-0.8
Total	4	51	99	6	16	4	0	0	10	5	14	.162	.217	.202	16	-11	-11	5	0	0	0	-1	/C	-1.0

■ RABBIT BENTON
Benton, Stanley W. "Stan"   b: 9/29/01, Canal City, Ky.   d: 6/7/84, Mesquite, Tex.   BR/TR, 5'7", 150 lbs.   Deb: 9/13/22

YEAR	TM/L	G	AB	R	H	2B	3B	HR	RBI	BB	SO	AVG	OBP	SLG	PRO+	BR	/A	RC	SB	CS	SBR	FR	POS	TPR
1922	Phi-N	6	19	1	4	1	0	0	3	2	1	.211	.286	.263	39	-2	-2	2	0	0	0	0	/2	0.0

■ TODD BENZINGER
Benzinger, Todd Eric   b: 2/11/63, Dayton, Ky.   BB/TR, 6'1", 185 lbs.   Deb: 6/21/87

YEAR	TM/L	G	AB	R	H	2B	3B	HR	RBI	BB	SO	AVG	OBP	SLG	PRO+	BR	/A	RC	SB	CS	SBR	FR	POS	TPR
1987	Bos-A	73	223	36	62	11	1	8	43	22	41	.278	.348	.444	105	3	2	34	5	4	-1	3	O/1	0.2
1988	*Bos-A	120	405	47	103	28	1	13	70	22	80	.254	.294	.425	95	-2	-4	48	2	3	-1	-4	1O/D	-1.4
1989	Cin-N	161	628	79	154	28	3	17	76	44	120	.245	.297	.381	89	-8	-10	70	3	7	-3	-13	*1	-4.1
1990	*Cin-N	118	376	35	95	14	2	5	46	19	69	.253	.296	.340	73	-13	-14	38	3	4	-2	-3	1O	-2.5
Total	4	472	1632	197	414	81	7	43	235	107	310	.254	.303	.391	89	-21	-27	189	13	18	-7	-17	1O/D	-7.8

YEAR	TM/L	G	AB	R	H	2B	3B	HR	RBI	BB	SO	AVG	OBP	SLG	PRO+	BR	/A	RC	SB	CS	SBR	FR	POS	TPR

■ JOHNNY BERARDINO
Berardino, John "Bernie" b: 5/1/17, Los Angeles, Cal. BR/TR, 5'11.5", 175 lbs. Deb: 4/22/39

YEAR	TM/L	G	AB	R	H	2B	3B	HR	RBI	BB	SO	AVG	OBP	SLG	PRO+	BR	/A	RC	SB	CS	SBR	FR	POS	TPR
1939	StL-A	126	468	42	120	24	5	5	58	37	36	.256	.314	.361	71	-20	-22	53	6	2	1	4	*2/3S	-1.1
1940	StL-A	142	523	71	135	31	4	16	85	32	46	.258	.301	.424	84	-13	-15	64	6	8	-3	13	*S2/3	0.6
1941	StL-A	128	469	48	127	30	4	5	89	41	27	.271	.332	.384	86	-8	-10	57	3	5	-2	-14	*S/3	-2.1
1942	StL-A	29	74	11	21	6	0	1	10	4	2	.284	.329	.405	104	0	0	11	3	1	0	0	/S312	0.1
1946	StL-A	144	582	70	154	29	5	5	68	34	58	.265	.306	.357	81	-13	-16	61	2	4	-2	-2	*2	-0.8
1947	StL-A	90	306	29	80	22	1	1	20	44	26	.261	.358	.350	95	-0	-1	40	6	5	-1	-8	2	-0.6
1948	Cle-A	66	147	19	28	5	1	2	10	27	16	.190	.328	.279	64	-7	-7	14	0	1	-1	4	21S/3	-0.8
1949	Cle-A	50	116	11	23	6	1	0	13	14	14	.198	.295	.267	50	-9	-8	10	0	1	-1	-1	3/2S	-0.8
1950	Cle-A	4	5	1	2	0	0	0	3	1	0	.400	.500	.400	137	0	0	1	0	0	0	1	/23	0.1
	Pit-N	40	131	12	27	3	1	1	12	19	11	.206	.307	.267	51	-9	-9	11	0			3	2/3	-0.5
1951	StL-A	39	119	13	27	7	1	0	13	17	18	.227	.324	.303	68	-5	-5	12	1	1	-0	-6	3/210	-1.2
1952	Cle-A	35	32	5	3	0	0	0	2	10	8	.094	.310	.094	17	-3	-3	2	0	1	-1	2	/2S31	0.0
	Pit-N	19	56	2	8	4	0	0	4	4	6	.143	.200	.214	14	-7	-7	2	0	0	0	6	2	0.0
Total	11	912	3028	334	755	167	23	36	387	284	268	.249	.316	.355	77	-93	-102	339	27	29		2	2S/310	-6.4

■ LOU BERBERET
Berberet, Louis Joseph b: 11/20/29, Long Beach, Cal. BL/TR, 5'11", 200 lbs. Deb: 9/17/54

YEAR	TM/L	G	AB	R	H	2B	3B	HR	RBI	BB	SO	AVG	OBP	SLG	PRO+	BR	/A	RC	SB	CS	SBR	FR	POS	TPR
1954	NY-A	5	5	1	2	0	0	0	3	1	1	.400	.500	.400	154	0	0	1	0	0	0	1	/C	0.2
1955	NY-A	2	5	1	2	0	0	0	2	1	0	.400	.500	.400	147	0	0	1	0	0	0	1	/C	0.1
1956	Was-A	95	207	25	54	6	3	4	27	46	33	.261	.402	.377	107	4	4	33	0	0	0	-0	C	0.5
1957	Was-A	99	264	24	69	11	2	7	36	41	38	.261	.365	.398	110	4	4	37	0	1	-1	-3	C	0.5
1958	Was-A	5	6	0	1	0	0	0	0	4	1	.167	.500	.167	94	0	0	1	0	0	0	1	/C	0.1
	Bos-A	57	167	11	35	5	3	2	18	31	32	.210	.337	.311	74	-4	-5	18	0	2	-1	-6	C	-1.2
	Yr	62	173	11	36	5	3	2	18	35	33	.208	.344	.306	76	-3	-5	19	0	2	-1	-5		-1.1
1959	Det-A	100	338	38	73	8	2	13	44	35	59	.216	.290	.367	75	-10	-13	36	0	0	0	-11	C	-1.8
1960	Det-A	85	232	18	45	4	0	5	23	41	31	.194	.318	.276	60	-11	-12	22	2	0	1	-1	C	-0.7
Total	7	448	1224	118	281	34	10	31	153	200	195	.230	.341	.350	86	-16	-20	150	2	3	-1	-18	C	-2.3

■ MOE BERG
Berg, Morris b: 3/2/02, New York, N.Y. d: 5/29/72, Belleville, N.J. BR/TR, 6'1", 185 lbs. Deb: 7/04/23 C

YEAR	TM/L	G	AB	R	H	2B	3B	HR	RBI	BB	SO	AVG	OBP	SLG	PRO+	BR	/A	RC	SB	CS	SBR	FR	POS	TPR
1923	Bro-N	49	129	9	24	3	2	0	6	2	5	.186	.198	.240	16	-16	-15	6	1	0	0	-6	S/2	-1.6
1926	Chi-A	41	113	4	25	6	0	0	7	6	9	.221	.261	.274	41	-10	-10	8	0	2	-1	6	S/23	-0.2
1927	Chi-A	35	69	4	17	4	0	0	4	4	10	.246	.288	.304	55	-5	-5	6	0	0	0	-4	2C/S3	-0.5
1928	Chi-A	76	224	25	55	16	0	0	29	14	25	.246	.302	.317	64	-12	-12	23	2	1	0	5	C	0.0
1929	Chi-A	107	352	32	101	7	0	0	47	17	16	.287	.323	.307	64	-19	-18	36	5	1	1	-3	*C	-0.9
1930	Chi-A	20	61	4	7	3	0	0	7	1	5	.115	.129	.164	-27	-12	-11	0	0	0	0	-0	C	-0.8
1931	Cle-A	10	13	1	1	1	0	0	0	1	1	.077	.143	.154	-21	-2	-2	0	0	0	0	1	/C	0.0
1932	Was-A	75	195	16	46	8	1	1	26	8	13	.236	.266	.303	48	-16	-15	16	1	1	-0	7	C	-0.3
1933	Was-A	40	65	8	12	3	0	2	9	4	5	.185	.232	.323	46	-5	-5	5	0	0	0	3	C	0.0
1934	Was-A	33	86	5	21	4	0	0	6	6	4	.244	.301	.291	55	-6	-5	8	2	0	1	-4	C	-0.5
	Cle-A	29	97	4	25	3	1	0	9	1	7	.258	.265	.309	47	-8	-8	8	0	0	0	5	C	0.0
	Yr	62	183	9	46	7	1	0	15	7	11	.251	.283	.301	51	-14	-13	16	2	0	1	1		-0.5
1935	Bos-A	38	98	13	28	5	0	2	12	5	3	.286	.320	.398	79	-3	-3	12	0	0	0	2	C	0.0
1936	Bos-A	39	125	9	30	4	1	0	19	2	6	.240	.264	.288	34	-13	-14	10	0	0	0	12	C	0.1
1937	Bos-A	47	141	13	36	3	1	0	20	5	4	.255	.281	.291	43	-12	-13	12	0	0	0	3	C	-0.5
1938	Bos-A	10	12	0	4	0	0	0	0	0	1	.333	.333	.333	64	-1	-1	1	0	0	0	1	/C1	0.0
1939	Bos-A	14	33	3	9	1	0	1	5	2	3	.273	.314	.394	77	-1	-1	4	0	0	0	4	C	0.3
Total	15	663	1813	150	441	71	6	6	206	78	117	.243	.278	.299	49	-140	-139	156	11	5	0	31	C/S231	-4.9

■ AUGIE BERGAMO
Bergamo, August Samuel b: 2/14/17, Detroit, Mich. d: 8/19/74, Grosse Pointe City, Mich. BL/TL, 5'9", 165 lbs. Deb: 4/25/44

YEAR	TM/L	G	AB	R	H	2B	3B	HR	RBI	BB	SO	AVG	OBP	SLG	PRO+	BR	/A	RC	SB	CS	SBR	FR	POS	TPR
1944	*StL-N	80	192	35	55	6	3	2	19	35	23	.286	.399	.380	118	7	6	32	0			-7	O/1	-0.4
1945	StL-N	94	304	51	96	17	2	3	44	43	21	.316	.401	.414	124	12	11	55	0			-3	O/1	0.4
Total	2	174	496	86	151	23	5	5	63	78	44	.304	.400	.401	122	19	18	88	0			-10	O/1	0.0

■ MARTY BERGEN
Bergen, Martin b: 10/25/1871, N.Brookfield, Mass d: 1/19/1900, N.Brookfield, Mass TR, 5'10", 170 lbs. Deb: 4/17/1896

YEAR	TM/L	G	AB	R	H	2B	3B	HR	RBI	BB	SO	AVG	OBP	SLG	PRO+	BR	/A	RC	SB	CS	SBR	FR	POS	TPR
1896	Bos-N	65	245	39	66	6	4	4	37	11	22	.269	.309	.376	77	-7	-10	31	6			8	C/1	0.4
1897	*Bos-N	87	327	47	81	11	3	2	45	18		.248	.295	.318	60	-17	-20	33	5			4	C/O	-0.3
1898	Bos-N	120	446	62	125	16	5	3	60	13		.280	.302	.359	87	-6	-10	52	9			5	*C/1	0.4
1899	Bos-N	72	260	32	67	11	3	1	34	10		.258	.290	.335	67	-10	-14	27	4			2	C	-0.5
Total	4	344	1278	180	339	44	15	10	176	52	22	.265	.299	.347	74	-40	-53	143	24			20	C/1O	0.0

■ BILL BERGEN
Bergen, William Aloysius b: 6/13/1878, N.Brookfield, Mass. d: 12/19/43, Worcester, Mass. BR/TR, 6', 184 lbs. Deb: 5/06/01

YEAR	TM/L	G	AB	R	H	2B	3B	HR	RBI	BB	SO	AVG	OBP	SLG	PRO+	BR	/A	RC	SB	CS	SBR	FR	POS	TPR
1901	Cin-N	87	308	15	55	6	4	1	17	8		.179	.199	.234	28	-28	-26	16	2			-7	C	-2.1
1902	Cin-N	89	322	19	58	8	3	0	36	14		.180	.214	.224	33	-24	-27	17	2			15	C	-0.2
1903	Cin-N	58	207	21	47	4	2	0	19	7		.227	.252	.266	44	-14	-17	15	2			2	C	-0.8
1904	Bro-N	96	329	17	60	4	2	0	12	9		.182	.204	.207	29	-27	-26	16	3			13	C/1	-0.4
1905	Bro-N	79	247	12	47	3	2	0	22	7		.190	.213	.219	32	-21	-19	14	4			12	C	0.1
1906	Bro-N	103	353	9	56	3	3	0	19	7		.159	.175	.184	14	-35	-32	13	2			4	*C	-2.2
1907	Bro-N	51	138	2	22	3	0	0	14	1		.159	.165	.181	11	-14	-13	5	1			2	C	-0.7
1908	Bro-N	99	302	8	53	8	2	0	15	5		.175	.189	.215	31	-24	-22	13	1			15	C	-0.1
1909	Bro-N	112	346	16	48	1	1	1	15	10		.139	.163	.156	-1	-41	-40	14	4			21	*C	-1.1
1910	Bro-N	89	249	11	40	2	1	0	14	6	39	.161	.180	.177	4	-30	-30	9	0			18	C	-0.7
1911	Bro-N	84	227	8	30	3	1	0	10	14	42	.132	.183	.154	-6	-32	-31	7	2			15	C	-0.9
Total	11	947	3028	138	516	45	21	2	193	88	81	.170	.194	.201	21	-291	-283	134	23			110	C/1	-9.1

■ CLARENCE BERGER
Berger, Clarence Edward b: 11/1/1894, E.Cleveland, Ohio d: 6/30/59, Washington, D.C. BL/TR, 6', 185 lbs. Deb: 9/23/14

YEAR	TM/L	G	AB	R	H	2B	3B	HR	RBI	BB	SO	AVG	OBP	SLG	PRO+	BR	/A	RC	SB	CS	SBR	FR	POS	TPR
1914	Pit-N	6	13	2	1	0	0	0	0	1	4	.077	.143	.077	-36	-2	-2	0	0			-1	/O	-0.3

■ JOHNNY BERGER
Berger, John Henne b: 8/27/01, Philadelphia, Pa. d: 5/7/79, Lake Charles, La. BR/TR, 5'9", 165 lbs. Deb: 4/20/22

YEAR	TM/L	G	AB	R	H	2B	3B	HR	RBI	BB	SO	AVG	OBP	SLG	PRO+	BR	/A	RC	SB	CS	SBR	FR	POS	TPR
1922	Phi-A	2	1	0	1	0	0	0	0	0	0	1.000	1.000	1.000	412	0	0	1	1	0	0	1	/C	0.1
1927	Was-A	9	15	1	4	0	0	0	1	2	3	.267	.353	.267	63	-1	-1	2	0	0	0	0	/C	0.0
Total	2	11	16	1	5	0	0	0	1	2	3	.313	.389	.313	85	-0	-0	3	1	0	0	1	/C	0.1

■ TUN BERGER
Berger, John Henry b: 12/6/1867, Pittsburgh, Pa. d: 6/10/07, Pittsburgh, Pa. TR, 204 lbs. Deb: 5/09/1890

YEAR	TM/L	G	AB	R	H	2B	3B	HR	RBI	BB	SO	AVG	OBP	SLG	PRO+	BR	/A	RC	SB	CS	SBR	FR	POS	TPR
1890	Pit-N	104	391	64	104	18	4	0	40	35	23	.266	.337	.332	110	-1	7	49	11			-5	OSC/23	0.1
1891	Pit-N	43	134	15	32	2	1	1	14	12	10	.239	.315	.291	81	-3	-3	14	4			-13	C2/SO	-1.1
1892	Was-N	26	97	9	14	2	1	0	3	7	9	.144	.210	.186	21	-9	-9	5	3			-11	S/C	-1.6
Total	3	173	622	88	150	22	6	1	57	54	42	.241	.313	.301	89	-13	-5	67	18			-29	/SCO23	-2.6

■ JOE BERGER
Berger, Joseph August "Fats" b: 12/20/1886, St.Louis, Mo. d: 3/6/56, Rock Island, Ill. BR/TR, 5'10.5", 170 lbs. Deb: 4/11/13

YEAR	TM/L	G	AB	R	H	2B	3B	HR	RBI	BB	SO	AVG	OBP	SLG	PRO+	BR	/A	RC	SB	CS	SBR	FR	POS	TPR
1913	Chi-A	79	223	27	48	6	2	2	20	36	28	.215	.330	.287	82	-4	-4	23	5			3	2/S3	-0.1
1914	Chi-A	48	148	11	23	3	1	0	3	13	9	.155	.224	.189	25	-14	-13	6	2	8	-4	-2	S2/3	-1.8
Total	2	127	371	38	71	9	3	2	23	49	37	.191	.289	.248	60	-18	-17	29	7	8		1	/2S3	-1.9

■ BOZE BERGER
Berger, Louis William b: 5/13/10, Baltimore, Md. BR/TR, 6'2", 180 lbs. Deb: 8/17/32

YEAR	TM/L	G	AB	R	H	2B	3B	HR	RBI	BB	SO	AVG	OBP	SLG	PRO+	BR	/A	RC	SB	CS	SBR	FR	POS	TPR
1932	Cle-A	1	0	1	0	0	0	0	0	0	1	.000	.000	.000	-94	-0	-0	0	0	0	0	1	/S	0.1

YEAR	TM/L	G	AB	R	H	2B	3B	HR	RBI	BB	SO	AVG	OBP	SLG	PRO+	BR	/A	RC	SB	CS	SBR	FR	POS	TPR
1935	Cle-A	124	461	62	119	27	5	5	43	34	97	.258	.310	.371	74	-18	-19	53	7	5	-1	13	*2/S13	-0.1
1936	Cle-A	28	52	1	9	2	0	0	3	1	14	.173	.189	.212	-1	-8	-8	2	0	0	0	4	/123S	-0.3
1937	Chi-A	52	130	19	31	5	0	5	13	15	24	.238	.322	.392	79	-5	-5	17	1	1	-0	-1	3/2S	-0.3
1938	Chi-A	118	470	60	102	15	3	3	36	43	80	.217	.284	.281	41	-43	-44	40	4	1	1	-10	S2/3	-4.3
1939	Bos-A	20	30	4	9	2	0	0	2	1	10	.300	.323	.367	73	-1	-1	4	0	0	0	1	S/32	0.1
Total	6	343	1144	146	270	51	8	13	97	94	226	.236	.296	.329	57	-75	-78	116	12	7	-1	9	2/S31	-4.8

■ WALLY BERGER
Berger, Walter Antone b: 10/10/05, Chicago, Ill. d: 11/30/88, Redondo Beach, Cal BR/TR, 6'2", 198 lbs. Deb: 4/15/30

YEAR	TM/L	G	AB	R	H	2B	3B	HR	RBI	BB	SO	AVG	OBP	SLG	PRO+	BR	/A	RC	SB	CS	SBR	FR	POS	TPR
1930	Bos-N	151	555	98	172	27	14	38	119	54	69	.310	.375	.614	139	27	30	124	3			-4	*O	1.4
1931	Bos-N	156	617	94	199	44	8	19	84	55	70	.323	.380	.512	143	32	34	122	13			4	*O/1	3.0
1932	Bos-N	145	602	90	185	34	6	17	73	33	66	.307	.346	.468	121	13	16	98	5			-2	*O1	0.4
1933	Bos-N	137	528	84	165	37	8	27	106	41	77	.313	.365	.566	177	40	45	113	2			1	*O	3.9
1934	Bos-N	150	615	92	183	35	8	34	121	49	65	.298	.352	.546	148	29	35	119	2			-3	*O	2.4
1935	Bos-N	150	589	91	174	39	4	34	130	50	80	.295	.355	.548	151	30	36	115	3			7	*O	3.5
1936	Bos-N	138	534	88	154	23	3	25	91	53	84	.288	.361	.483	134	18	23	95	1			2	*O	1.8
1937	Bos-N	30	113	14	31	9	1	5	22	11	33	.274	.344	.504	140	4	5	21	0			-4	O	0.0
	*NY-N	59	199	40	58	11	2	12	43	18	30	.291	.359	.548	141	11	11	39	3			0	O	0.8
	Yr	89	312	54	89	20	3	17	65	29	63	.285	.354	.532	141	15	16	60	3			-3		0.8
1938	NY-N	16	32	5	6	0	0	0	4	2	4	.188	.235	.188	17	-4	-4	2	0			3	/O	0.0
	Cin-N	99	407	74	125	23	4	16	56	29	44	.307	.356	.501	137	17	18	73	2			-2	O	1.4
	Yr	115	439	79	131	23	4	16	60	31	48	.298	.347	.478	128	13	15	74	2			0		1.4
1939	*Cin-N	97	329	36	85	15	1	14	44	36	63	.258	.341	.438	107	3	3	50	1			-8	O	-0.6
1940	Cin-N	2	2	0	0	0	0	0	0	0	1	.000	.000	.000	-99	-1	-1	0	0			0	H	0.0
	Phi-N	20	41	3	13	2	0	1	5	4	8	.317	.378	.439	130	1	2	7	1			-1	O/1	0.0
	Yr	22	43	3	13	2	0	1	5	4	9	.302	.362	.419	119	1	1	6	1			-1		0.0
Total	11	1350	5163	809	1550	299	59	242	898	435	694	.300	.359	.522	140	222	255	977	36			-8	*O/1	18.0

■ JOHN BERGH
Bergh, John Baptist b: 10/8/1857, Boston, Mass. d: 4/16/1883, Boston, Mass. Deb: 8/05/1876

YEAR	TM/L	G	AB	R	H	2B	3B	HR	RBI	BB	SO	AVG	OBP	SLG	PRO+	BR	/A	RC	SB	CS	SBR	FR	POS	TPR
1876	Phi-N	1	4	0	0	0	0	0	0	0	2	.000	.000	.000	-99	-1	-1	0				1	/OC	0.0
1880	Bos-N	11	40	2	8	3	0	0	0	2	5	.200	.238	.275	76	-1	-1	3				-3	C	-0.3
Total	2	12	44	2	8	3	0	0	0	2	7	.182	.217	.250	59	-2	-2	3				-3	/CO	-0.3

■ MARTY BERGHAMMER
Berghammer, Martin Andrew "Pepper" b: 6/18/1888, Elliott, Pa. d: 12/21/57, Pittsburgh, Pa. BL/TR, 5'9", 172 lbs. Deb: 9/08/11

YEAR	TM/L	G	AB	R	H	2B	3B	HR	RBI	BB	SO	AVG	OBP	SLG	PRO+	BR	/A	RC	SB	CS	SBR	FR	POS	TPR
1911	Chi-A	2	5	0	0	0	0	0	0	0	0	.000	.167	.000	-54	-1	-1	0	0			-0	/2	0.0
1913	Cin-N	74	188	25	41	4	1	1	13	10	29	.218	.269	.266	53	-12	-11	17	16			5	S2	-0.3
1914	Cin-N	77	112	15	25	2	0	0	6	10	18	.223	.287	.241	56	-6	-6	8	4			7	S2	0.2
1915	Pit-F	132	469	96	114	10	6	0	33	83	44	.243	.371	.290	98	3	4	64	26			-16	*S	-0.1
Total	4	285	774	136	180	16	7	1	52	103	91	.233	.335	.275	80	-15	-14	90	46			-4	S/2	-0.2

■ AL BERGMAN
Bergman, Alfred Henry "Dutch" b: 9/27/1890, Peru, Ind. d: 6/20/61, Fort Wayne, Ind. BR/TR, 5'7", 155 lbs. Deb: 8/29/16

YEAR	TM/L	G	AB	R	H	2B	3B	HR	RBI	BB	SO	AVG	OBP	SLG	PRO+	BR	/A	RC	SB	CS	SBR	FR	POS	TPR
1916	Cle-A	8	14	2	3	0	1	0	0	2	4	.214	.313	.357	95	-0	-0	2	0			-2	/2	-0.1

■ DAVE BERGMAN
Bergman, David Bruce b: 6/6/53, Evanston, Ill. BL/TL, 6'1.5", 185 lbs. Deb: 8/26/75

YEAR	TM/L	G	AB	R	H	2B	3B	HR	RBI	BB	SO	AVG	OBP	SLG	PRO+	BR	/A	RC	SB	CS	SBR	FR	POS	TPR
1975	NY-A	7	17	0	0	0	0	0	0	2	4	.000	.105	.000	-70	-4	-4	0	0	0	0	1	/O	-0.2
1977	NY-A	5	4	1	1	0	0	0	1	0	0	.250	.250	.250	37	-0	-0	0	0	0	0	0	/O1	0.0
1978	Hou-N	104	186	15	43	5	1	0	12	39	32	.231	.364	.269	86	-3	-1	20	2	0	1	-2	1O	-0.5
1979	Hou-N	13	15	4	6	0	0	1	2	0	3	.400	.400	.600	179	1	1	4	0	0	0	-0	/1	0.1
1980	*Hou-N	90	78	12	20	6	1	0	3	10	10	.256	.341	.359	104	-0	0	10	1	0	0	3	1/O	0.1
1981	Hou-N	6	6	1	1	0	0	1	1	0	0	.167	.167	.667	134	0	0	1	0	0	0	0	/1	0.0
	SF-N	63	145	16	37	9	0	3	13	19	18	.255	.341	.379	106	1	1	19	2	0	1	2	1O	0.2
	Yr	69	151	17	38	9	0	4	14	19	18	.252	.335	.391	108	1	2	20	2	0	1	2		0.2
1982	SF-N	100	121	22	33	3	1	4	14	18	11	.273	.367	.413	118	3	3	20	3	0	1	1	1/O	0.2
1983	SF-N	90	140	16	40	4	1	6	24	24	21	.286	.394	.457	140	7	8	25	2	1	0	3	1/O	0.8
1984	*Det-A	120	271	42	74	8	5	7	44	33	40	.273	.358	.417	115	6	6	41	3	4	-2	9	*1/O	0.6
1985	Det-A	69	140	8	25	2	0	3	7	14	15	.179	.253	.257	41	-12	-11	9	0	0	0	1	1/OD	-1.2
1986	Det-A	65	130	14	30	6	1	1	9	21	16	.231	.338	.315	79	-3	-3	15	0	0	0	1	1/OD	-0.2
1987	*Det-A	91	172	25	47	7	3	6	22	30	23	.273	.384	.453	127	6	7	32	0	1	-1	1	1/OD	0.1
1988	Det-A	116	289	37	85	14	0	5	35	38	34	.294	.376	.394	121	7	9	43	0	2	-1	1	1DO	0.5
1989	Det-A	137	385	38	103	13	1	7	37	44	44	.268	.346	.361	102	1	2	50	1	3	-2	5	*1/OD	-0.2
1990	Det-A	100	205	21	57	10	1	2	26	33	17	.278	.378	.366	109	4	4	29	3	2	-0	-1	D1/O	0.1
Total	15	1176	2304	272	602	87	15	46	250	325	288	.261	.354	.372	105	14	22	318	17	13	-3	26	1DO	0.4

■ FRANK BERKELBACH
Berkelbach, Francis P. b: Philadelphia, Pa. 6', 182 lbs. Deb: 7/04/1884

YEAR	TM/L	G	AB	R	H	2B	3B	HR	RBI	BB	SO	AVG	OBP	SLG	PRO+	BR	/A	RC	SB	CS	SBR	FR	POS	TPR
1884	Cin-a	6	25	3	6	0	1	0		0		.240	.296	.320	99	0	-0	2				-1	/O	0.0

■ NATE BERKENSTOCK
Berkenstock, Nathan b: 1831, Pennsylvania d: 2/23/1900, Philadelphia, Pa. Deb: 10/30/1871

YEAR	TM/L	G	AB	R	H	2B	3B	HR	RBI	BB	SO	AVG	OBP	SLG	PRO+	BR	/A	RC	SB	CS	SBR	FR	POS	TPR
1871	Ath-n	1	4	0	0	0	0	0	0	0	3	.000	.000	.000	-99	-1	-1	0	0				/O	0.0

■ BOB BERMAN
Berman, Robert Leon b: 1/24/1899, New York, N.Y. d: 8/2/88, Bridgeport, Conn. BR/TR, 5'8", 147 lbs. Deb: 6/04/18

YEAR	TM/L	G	AB	R	H	2B	3B	HR	RBI	BB	SO	AVG	OBP	SLG	PRO+	BR	/A	RC	SB	CS	SBR	FR	POS	TPR
1918	Was-A	2	0	0	0	0	0	0	0	0	0	—	—	—	—	0	0	0				1	/C	0.1

■ CURT BERNARD
Bernard, Curtis Henry b: 2/18/1878, Parkersburg, W.Va. d: 4/10/55, Culver City, Cal. BL/TR, 5'10", 150 lbs. Deb: 9/17/00

YEAR	TM/L	G	AB	R	H	2B	3B	HR	RBI	BB	SO	AVG	OBP	SLG	PRO+	BR	/A	RC	SB	CS	SBR	FR	POS	TPR
1900	NY-N	20	71	9	18	2	0	0	8	6		.254	.329	.282	75	-2	-2	7	1			-2	O/S	-0.4
1901	NY-N	23	76	11	17	0	2	0	6	7		.224	.289	.276	69	-3	-3	7	2			-1	O/2S3	-0.4
Total	2	43	147	20	35	2	2	0	14	13		.238	.309	.279	72	-5	-5	14	3			-3	/O2S3	-0.8

■ TONY BERNAZARD
Bernazard, Antonio (Garcia) b: 8/24/56, Caguas, P.R. BB/TR, 5'9", 150 lbs. Deb: 7/13/79

YEAR	TM/L	G	AB	R	H	2B	3B	HR	RBI	BB	SO	AVG	OBP	SLG	PRO+	BR	/A	RC	SB	CS	SBR	FR	POS	TPR
1979	Mon-N	22	40	11	12	2	0	1	8	15	12	.300	.500	.425	156	5	5	9	1	2	-1	-1	2	0.3
1980	Mon-N	82	183	26	41	7	1	5	18	17	41	.224	.290	.355	79	-5	-5	19	9	2	2	2	2S	0.3
1981	Chi-A	106	384	53	106	14	4	6	34	54	66	.276	.368	.380	118	10	11	56	4	4	-1	-2	*2/S	1.1
1982	Chi-A	137	540	90	138	25	9	11	56	67	88	.256	.340	.396	101	2	2	78	11	0	3	25	*2	3.7
1983	Chi-A	59	233	30	61	16	2	2	26	17	45	.262	.312	.373	85	-4	-5	27	2	1	0	-2	2	-0.4
	Sea-A	80	300	35	80	18	1	6	30	38	52	.267	.353	.393	101	3	1	44	21	8	2	1	2	0.6
	Yr	139	533	65	141	34	3	8	56	55	97	.265	.336	.385	94	-1	-4	71	23	9	2	1		0.2
1984	Cle-A	140	439	44	97	15	4	2	38	43	70	.221	.293	.287	60	-22	-23	37	20	13	-2	-11	*2/D	-2.9
1985	Cle-A	153	500	73	137	26	3	11	59	69	72	.274	.363	.404	111	8	9	75	17	9	-0	-32	*2/S	-1.6
1986	Cle-A	146	562	88	169	28	4	17	73	53	77	.301	.367	.456	125	18	19	96	17	8	0	-1	*2	2.6
1987	Cle-A	79	293	39	70	12	1	11	30	25	49	.239	.301	.399	83	-7	-8	35	7	4	-0	-16	2	-1.6
	Oak-A	61	214	34	57	14	1	3	19	30	30	.266	.357	.383	103	-0	2	29	4	4	-1	-18	2/D	-1.2
	Yr	140	507	73	127	26	2	14	49	55	79	.250	.325	.393	91	-8	-6	65	11	8	-2	-34		-2.8
Total	9	1065	3688	523	968	177	30	75	391	428	602	.262	.342	.388	100	5	5	507	113	55	1	-55	2/SD	0.9

■ JUAN BERNHARDT
Bernhardt, Juan Ramon (Coradin) b: 8/31/53, San Pedro De Macoris, D.R. BR/TR, 5'11", 160 lbs. Deb: 7/10/76

YEAR	TM/L	G	AB	R	H	2B	3B	HR	RBI	BB	SO	AVG	OBP	SLG	PRO+	BR	/A	RC	SB	CS	SBR	FR	POS	TPR
1976	NY-A	10	21	1	4	1	0	0	1	0	4	.190	.190	.238	25	-2	-2	1	0	0	0	-0	/O3D	-0.2
1977	Sea-A	89	305	32	74	9	2	7	30	5	26	.243	.260	.354	66	-15	-15	25	2	3	-1	-1	D3/1	-1.7

YEAR	TM/L	G	AB	R	H	2B	3B	HR	RBI	BB	SO	AVG	OBP	SLG	PRO+	BR	/A	RC	SB	CS	SBR	FR	POS	TPR
1978	Sea-A	54	165	13	38	9	0	2	12	9	10	.230	.274	.321	67	-7	-7	14	1	1	-0	0	13/D	-0.8
1979	Sea-A	1	1	0	1	0	0	0	0	0	0	1.000	1.000	1.000	434	0	0	1	0	0	0	0	/H	0.0
Total	4	154	492	46	117	19	2	9	43	14	40	.238	.263	.339	66	-24	-24	41	3	4	-2	-1	/D31O	-2.7

■ CARLOS BERNIER   Bernier, Carlos (Rodriguez) b: 1/28/29, Juana Diaz, P.R. d: 4/6/89, Juana Diaz, P.R. BR/TR, 5'9", 180 lbs. Deb: 4/22/53

YEAR	TM/L	G	AB	R	H	2B	3B	HR	RBI	BB	SO	AVG	OBP	SLG	PRO+	BR	/A	RC	SB	CS	SBR	FR	POS	TPR
1953	Pit-N	105	310	48	66	7	8	3	31	51	53	.213	.332	.316	70	-13	-12	32	15	14	-4	-2	O	-2.0

■ JOHNNY BERO   Bero, John George b: 12/22/22, Gary, W.Va. d: 5/11/85, Gardena, Cal. BL/TR, 6', 170 lbs. Deb: 9/26/48

YEAR	TM/L	G	AB	R	H	2B	3B	HR	RBI	BB	SO	AVG	OBP	SLG	PRO+	BR	/A	RC	SB	CS	SBR	FR	POS	TPR
1948	Det-A	4	9	2	0	0	0	0	0	0	1	.000	.100	.000	-70	-2	-2	0	0	0	0	-1	/2	-0.2
1951	StL-A	61	160	24	34	5	0	5	17	26	30	.213	.323	.338	76	-5	-5	19	1	1	-0	-9	S/2	-1.0
Total	2	65	169	26	34	5	0	5	17	27	31	.201	.311	.320	69	-7	-8	19	1	1	-0	-10	/S2	-1.2

■ DALE BERRA   Berra, Dale Anthony b: 12/13/56, Ridgewood, N.J. BR/TR, 6', 180 lbs. Deb: 8/22/77

YEAR	TM/L	G	AB	R	H	2B	3B	HR	RBI	BB	SO	AVG	OBP	SLG	PRO+	BR	/A	RC	SB	CS	SBR	FR	POS	TPR
1977	Pit-N	17	40	0	7	1	0	0	3	1	8	.175	.195	.200	6	-5	-5	2	0	0	0	3	3	-0.2
1978	Pit-N	56	135	16	28	2	0	6	14	13	20	.207	.287	.356	75	-4	-5	14	3	1	0	1	3/S	-0.3
1979	Pit-N	44	123	11	26	5	0	3	15	11	17	.211	.276	.325	61	-6	-7	10	0	0	0	1	S3	-0.4
1980	Pit-N	93	245	21	54	8	2	6	31	16	52	.220	.271	.343	69	-10	-11	22	2	0	1	2	3S/2	-0.2
1981	Pit-N	81	232	21	56	12	0	2	27	17	34	.241	.302	.319	74	-7	-8	24	11	1	3	2	3S2	0.0
1982	Pit-N	156	529	64	139	25	5	10	61	33	83	.263	.311	.386	91	-5	-7	59	6	6	-2	-2	*S/3	0.0
1983	Pit-N	161	537	51	135	25	1	10	52	61	84	.251	.328	.358	88	-7	-9	63	8	5	-1	16	*S	2.1
1984	Pit-N	136	450	31	100	16	0	9	52	34	78	.222	.278	.318	67	-20	-20	38	1	3	-2	-2	*S/3	-0.9
1985	NY-A	48	109	8	25	5	1	1	8	7	20	.229	.276	.321	64	-6	-6	9	1	1	-0	4	3/S	-0.1
1986	NY-A	42	108	10	25	7	0	2	13	9	14	.231	.297	.352	77	-4	-4	12	0	0	0	-1	S3/D	-0.3
1987	Hou-N	19	45	3	8	3	0	0	2	8	12	.178	.302	.244	49	-3	-3	4	0	0	0	-3	S/2	-0.3
Total	11	853	2553	236	603	109	9	49	278	210	422	.236	.297	.344	76	-78	-84	258	32	17	-1	21	S3/2D	-0.6

■ YOGI BERRA   Berra, Lawrence Peter b: 5/12/25, St.Louis, Mo. BL/TR, 5'7.5", 185 lbs. Deb: 9/22/46 MCH

YEAR	TM/L	G	AB	R	H	2B	3B	HR	RBI	BB	SO	AVG	OBP	SLG	PRO+	BR	/A	RC	SB	CS	SBR	FR	POS	TPR
1946	NY-A	7	22	3	8	1	0	2	4	1	1	.364	.391	.682	193	3	3	6	0	0	0	2	/C	0.4
1947	*NY-A	83	293	41	82	15	3	11	54	13	12	.280	.310	.464	115	3	3	41	0	1	-1	-6	CO	0.0
1948	NY-A	125	469	70	143	24	10	14	98	25	24	.305	.341	.488	120	9	10	77	3	3	-1	-10	CO	0.2
1949	*NY-A	116	415	59	115	20	2	20	91	22	25	.277	.323	.480	111	2	2	65	2	1	0	11	*C	1.8
1950	*NY-A	151	597	116	192	30	6	28	124	55	12	.322	.383	.533	136	26	28	125	4	2	0	1	*C	3.2
1951	*NY-A	141	547	92	161	19	4	27	88	44	20	.294	.350	.492	131	17	19	92	5	4	-1	8	*C	3.5
1952	*NY-A	142	534	97	146	17	1	30	98	66	24	.273	.358	.478	139	21	25	95	2	3	-1	2	*C	3.3
1953	*NY-A	137	503	80	149	23	5	27	108	50	32	.296	.363	.523	142	24	28	98	0	3	-2	3	*C	3.1
1954	*NY-A	151	584	88	179	28	6	22	125	56	29	.307	.371	.488	139	26	28	107	0	1	-1	-1	*C/3	3.4
1955	*NY-A	147	541	84	147	20	3	27	108	60	20	.272	.352	.470	121	13	14	90	1	0	0	-2	*C	1.8
1956	*NY-A	140	521	93	155	29	2	30	105	65	29	.298	.381	.534	144	28	30	108	3	2	-0	7	*C/O	3.7
1957	*NY-A	134	482	74	121	14	2	24	82	57	24	.251	.331	.438	110	5	6	69	1	2	-1	17	*C/O	2.7
1958	*NY-A	122	433	60	115	17	3	22	90	35	35	.266	.323	.471	120	8	10	67	3	0	1	4	CO/1	1.4
1959	NY-A	131	472	64	134	25	1	19	69	43	38	.284	.349	.462	125	13	15	77	1	2	-1	5	*C/O	2.5
1960	*NY-A	120	359	46	99	14	1	15	62	38	23	.276	.350	.446	120	7	9	55	2	1	0	-11	CO	0.0
1961	*NY-A	119	395	62	107	11	0	22	61	35	28	.271	.333	.466	117	5	8	62	2	0	1	0	OC	0.5
1962	*NY-A	86	232	25	52	8	0	10	35	24	18	.224	.302	.388	87	-6	-5	26	0	1	-1	6	CO	0.1
1963	*NY-A	64	147	20	43	6	0	8	28	15	17	.293	.362	.497	139	7	7	26	1	0	0	8	C	1.7
1965	NY-N	4	9	1	2	0	0	0	0	0	0	.222	.222	.222	27	-1	-1	0	0	0	0	1	/C	0.0
Total	19	2120	7555	1175	2150	321	49	358	1430	704	414	.285	.350	.482	126	209	238	1284	30	26	-7	44	*CO/13	33.3

■ DENNIS BERRAN   Berran, Dennis Martin b: 10/8/1887, Merrimac, Mass. d: 4/28/43, Boston, Mass. BL/TL, Deb: 8/11/12

YEAR	TM/L	G	AB	R	H	2B	3B	HR	RBI	BB	SO	AVG	OBP	SLG	PRO+	BR	/A	RC	SB	CS	SBR	FR	POS	TPR
1912	Chi-A	2	4	1	1	0	0	0	0	0	0	.250	.250	.250	44	-0	-0	0	0			-1	/O	0.0

■ RAY BERRES   Berres, Raymond Frederick b: 8/31/07, Kenosha, Wis. BR/TR, 5'9", 170 lbs. Deb: 4/24/34 C

YEAR	TM/L	G	AB	R	H	2B	3B	HR	RBI	BB	SO	AVG	OBP	SLG	PRO+	BR	/A	RC	SB	CS	SBR	FR	POS	TPR
1934	Bro-N	39	79	7	17	4	0	0	3	1	16	.215	.225	.266	32	-8	-7	5	0			-1	C	-0.6
1936	Bro-N	105	267	16	64	10	1	1	13	14	35	.240	.280	.296	55	-17	-17	21	1			24	*C	0.9
1937	Pit-N	2	6	0	1	0	0	0	0	0	0	.167	.167	.167	-9	-1	-1	0	0			1	/C	0.0
1938	Pit-N	40	100	7	23	2	0	0	6	8	10	.230	.287	.250	48	-7	-7	7	0			4	C	0.0
1939	Pit-N	81	231	22	53	6	1	0	16	11	25	.229	.267	.264	44	-18	-18	15	1			-3	C	-1.7
1940	Pit-N	21	32	2	6	1	0	0	2	1	1	.188	.212	.188	11	-4	-4	1	0			3	C	0.0
	Bos-N	85	229	12	44	4	1	0	14	18	19	.192	.251	.218	32	-21	-20	13	0			0	C	-1.5
	Yr	106	261	14	50	4	1	0	16	19	20	.192	.246	.215	29	-25	-24	14	0			3		-1.5
1941	Bos-N	120	279	21	56	10	0	1	19	17	20	.201	.247	.247	41	-23	-21	15	2			9	*C	0.0
1942	NY-N	12	32	0	6	0	0	0	1	2	3	.188	.235	.188	24	-3	-3	1	0			-2	C	-0.4
1943	NY-N	20	28	1	4	1	0	0	0	1	2	.143	.172	.179	1	-4	-4	1	0			4	C	0.1
1944	NY-N	16	17	4	8	0	0	1	2	1	0	.471	.526	.647	230	3	3	5	0			0	C	0.4
1945	NY-N	20	30	4	5	0	0	0	2	2	3	.167	.219	.167	8	-4	-4	1	0			1	C	-0.1
Total	11	561	1330	96	287	37	3	3	78	76	134	.216	.260	.255	43	-106	-102	87	4			40	C	-2.9

■ GERONIMO BERROA   Berroa, Geronimo Emiliano b: 3/18/65, Santo Domingo, D.R. BR/TR, 6', 165 lbs. Deb: 4/05/89

YEAR	TM/L	G	AB	R	H	2B	3B	HR	RBI	BB	SO	AVG	OBP	SLG	PRO+	BR	/A	RC	SB	CS	SBR	FR	POS	TPR
1989	Atl-N	81	136	7	36	4	0	2	9	7	32	.265	.301	.338	80	-3	-4	13	0	1	-1	3	O	-0.1
1990	Atl-N	7	4	0	0	0	0	0	0	1	1	.000	.200	.000	-39	-1	-1	0	0	0	0	0	/O	0.0
Total	2	88	140	7	36	4	0	2	9	8	33	.257	.297	.329	77	-4	-4	13	0	1	-1	3	/O	-0.1

■ KEN BERRY   Berry, Allen Kent b: 5/10/41, Kansas City, Mo. BR/TR, 6', 175 lbs. Deb: 9/09/62

YEAR	TM/L	G	AB	R	H	2B	3B	HR	RBI	BB	SO	AVG	OBP	SLG	PRO+	BR	/A	RC	SB	CS	SBR	FR	POS	TPR
1962	Chi-A	3	6	2	2	0	0	0	0	0	0	.333	.333	.333	80	-0	-0	1	0	0	0	1	/O	0.1
1963	Chi-A	4	5	2	1	0	0	0	0	1	1	.200	.333	.200	55	-0	-0	0	0	0	0	0	/O2	0.0
1964	Chi-A	12	32	4	12	1	0	1	4	5	3	.375	.459	.500	171	3	3	7	0	1	-1	-1	O	0.1
1965	Chi-A	157	472	51	103	17	4	12	42	28	96	.218	.269	.347	79	-17	-14	45	4	2	0	-2	*O	-2.3
1966	Chi-A	147	443	50	120	20	2	8	34	28	63	.271	.317	.379	106	-1	3	51	7	10	-4	-8	*O	-1.5
1967	Chi-A	147	485	49	117	14	4	7	41	46	68	.241	.311	.330	93	-6	-4	49	9	8	-2	-4	*O	-1.5
1968	Chi-A	153	504	49	127	21	2	7	32	25	64	.252	.289	.343	90	-7	-7	46	6	6	-2	-3	*O	-2.0
1969	Chi-A	130	297	25	69	12	2	4	18	24	50	.232	.296	.327	71	-11	-12	27	1	2	-1	-11	*O	-2.8
1970	Chi-A	141	463	50	128	12	2	7	50	43	61	.276	.346	.356	90	-3	-5	54	6	4	-1	3	*O	-0.8
1971	Cal-A	111	298	29	66	17	0	3	22	18	33	.221	.273	.309	69	-14	-12	23	3	2	-0	1	*O	-1.5
1972	Cal-A	119	409	41	118	15	3	5	39	35	47	.289	.348	.377	122	8	10	56	5	3	-0	10	*O	1.9
1973	Cal-A	136	418	48	118	11	2	3	36	26	50	.284	.328	.342	96	-6	-2	41	1	6	-3	-0	*O	-0.9
1974	Mil-A	98	267	21	64	9	2	1	24	18	26	.240	.295	.300	72	-10	-10	24	3	1	0	10	OD	-0.4
1975	Cle-A	25	40	6	8	1	0	0	1	1	7	.200	.238	.225	31	-4	-4	2	0	1	-1	2	O/D	-0.2
Total	14	1383	4136	422	1053	150	23	58	343	298	569	.255	.309	.344	90	-67	-54	425	45	46	-14	-3	*O/D2	-11.4

■ CHARLIE BERRY   Berry, Charles Francis b: 10/18/02, Philipsburg, N.J. d: 9/6/72, Evanston, Ill. BR/TR, 6', 185 lbs. Deb: 6/15/25 UC

YEAR	TM/L	G	AB	R	H	2B	3B	HR	RBI	BB	SO	AVG	OBP	SLG	PRO+	BR	/A	RC	SB	CS	SBR	FR	POS	TPR
1925	Phi-A	10	14	1	3	1	0	0	3	0	2	.214	.214	.286	24	-2	-2	1	0	0	0	-0	/C	-0.1
1928	Bos-A	80	177	18	46	7	3	1	19	21	19	.260	.342	.350	84	-4	-4	22	1	1	-0	-10	C	-0.9
1929	Bos-A	77	207	19	50	11	4	1	21	15	29	.242	.302	.348	69	-11	-10	21	2	4	-2	3	C	-0.1
1930	Bos-A	88	256	31	74	9	6	6	35	16	22	.289	.331	.441	98	-3	-2	38	5	0	-0	7	C	1.2
1931	Bos-A	111	357	41	101	16	2	6	49	29	38	.283	.337	.389	96	-5	-3	48	4	0	1	-3	*C	0.3

YEAR	TM/L	G	AB	R	H	2B	3B	HR	RBI	BB	SO	AVG	OBP	SLG	PRO+	BR	/A	RC	SB	CS	SBR	FR	POS	TPR
1932	Bos-A	10	32	0	6	3	0	0	6	3	2	.188	.257	.281	40	-3	-3	2	0	0	0	-1	C	-0.2
	Chi-A	72	226	33	69	15	6	4	31	21	23	.305	.364	.478	124	5	7	40	3	0	1	-1	C	1.0
	Yr	82	258	33	75	18	6	4	37	24	25	.291	.351	.453	114	2	4	42	3	0	1	-2		0.8
1933	Chi-A	86	271	25	69	8	3	2	28	17	16	.255	.301	.328	70	-13	-12	27	0	0	0	-8	C	-1.4
1934	Phi-A	99	269	14	72	10	2	0	34	22	23	.268	.323	.320	69	-13	-12	29	1	0	0	0	C	-0.1
1935	Phi-A	62	190	14	48	7	3	3	29	10	20	.253	.290	.368	70	-9	-9	20	0	0	0	-1	C	-0.7
1936	Phi-A	13	17	0	1	1	0	0	1	6	2	.059	.304	.118	8	-2	-2	1	0	0	0	2	C	0.0
1938	Phi-A	1	2	0	0	0	0	0	0	0	0	.000	.000	.000	-99	-1	-1	0	0	0	0	0	/C	0.0
Total	11	709	2018	196	539	88	29	23	256	160	196	.267	.322	.374	83	-62	-51	251	13	5	1	-11	C	-1.0

■ CHARLIE BERRY
Berry, Charles Joseph   b: 9/6/1860, Elizabeth, N.J.   d: 1/22/40, Phillipsburg, N.J.   BR/TR, 5'11", 175 lbs.   Deb: 4/30/1884

YEAR	TM/L	G	AB	R	H	2B	3B	HR	RBI	BB	SO	AVG	OBP	SLG	PRO+	BR	/A	RC	SB	CS	SBR	FR	POS	TPR
1884	Alt-U	7	25	2	6	0	0	0		0		.240	.240	.240	62	-1	-1	1	0			-6	/2	-0.6
	KC-U	29	118	15	29	6	1	1		1		.246	.252	.339	113	-0	2	10	0			3	2/O3	0.3
	CP-U	7	27	4	3	2	0	0		0		.111	.111	.185	-1	-3	-3	1	0			1	/2	-0.1
	Yr	43	170	21	38	8	1	1		1		.224	.228	.300	84	-4	-2	12	0			-2		-0.4

■ CLAUDE BERRY
Berry, Claude Elzy "Admiral"   b: 2/14/1880, Losantville, Ind.   d: 2/1/74, Richmond, Ind.   BR/TR, 5'7", 165 lbs.   Deb: 4/22/04

YEAR	TM/L	G	AB	R	H	2B	3B	HR	RBI	BB	SO	AVG	OBP	SLG	PRO+	BR	/A	RC	SB	CS	SBR	FR	POS	TPR
1904	Chi-A	3	1	1	0	0	0	0	0	1		.000	.500	.000	71	0	0	0				1	/C	0.1
1906	Phi-A	10	30	2	7	0	0	0	2	2		.233	.281	.233	61	-1	-1	2	1			5	C	0.5
1907	Phi-A	8	19	2	4	2	0	0	1	2		.211	.286	.316	91	-0	-0	2	0			-2	C	-0.1
1914	Pit-F	124	411	35	98	18	9	2	36	26	50	.238	.284	.341	79	-12	-12	44	6			-37	*C	-4.5
1915	Pit-F	100	292	32	56	11	1	1	26	29	42	.192	.269	.247	54	-17	-16	23	7			-28	C	-4.6
Total	5	245	753	72	165	31	10	3	65	60	92	.219	.279	.299	69	-30	-30	72	14			-61	C	-8.6

■ NEIL BERRY
Berry, Cornelius John   b: 1/11/22, Kalamazoo, Mich.   BR/TR, 5'10", 168 lbs.   Deb: 4/20/48

YEAR	TM/L	G	AB	R	H	2B	3B	HR	RBI	BB	SO	AVG	OBP	SLG	PRO+	BR	/A	RC	SB	CS	SBR	FR	POS	TPR
1948	Det-A	87	256	46	68	8	1	0	16	37	23	.266	.358	.305	75	-7	-8	31	1	3	-2	4	S2	-0.4
1949	Det-A	109	329	38	78	9	1	0	18	27	24	.237	.299	.271	61	-23	-23	27	4	2	0	-0	2/S	-2.1
1950	Det-A	39	40	9	10	1	0	0	7	6	11	.250	.348	.275	59	-2	-2	5	0	0	0	2	S/23	0.1
1951	Det-A	67	157	17	36	5	2	0	9	10	15	.229	.275	.287	52	-11	-11	13	4	2	0	8	S2/3	0.0
1952	Det-A	73	189	22	43	4	3	0	13	22	19	.228	.311	.280	65	-8	-9	17	1	3	-2	4	S/3	-0.2
1953	StL-A	57	99	14	28	1	2	0	11	9	10	.283	.343	.333	82	-2	-2	11	1	2	-1	-1	32/S	-0.3
	Chi-A	5	8	1	1	0	0	0	0	1	1	.125	.222	.125	-4	-1	-1	0	0	0	0	2	/2	0.1
	Yr	62	107	15	29	1	2	0	11	10	11	.271	.333	.318	75	-3	-4	11	1	2	-1	2		-0.2
1954	Bal-A	5	9	1	1	0	0	0	0	1	2	.111	.200	.111	-14	-1	-1	0	0	0	0	0	/S	0.0
Total	7	442	1087	148	265	28	9	0	74	113	105	.244	.317	.286	62	-56	-58	104	11	12	-4	19	S2/3	-2.8

■ JOE BERRY
Berry, Joseph Howard Jr. "Nig"   b: 12/31/1894, Philadelphia, Pa.   d: 4/29/76, Philadelphia, Pa.   BB/TR, 5'10.5", 159 lbs.   Deb: 7/18/21

YEAR	TM/L	G	AB	R	H	2B	3B	HR	RBI	BB	SO	AVG	OBP	SLG	PRO+	BR	/A	RC	SB	CS	SBR	FR	POS	TPR
1921	NY-N	9	6	0	2	0	1	0	2	1	1	.333	.429	.667	185	1	1	2	0	0	0	0	/2	0.1
1922	NY-N	6	0	0	0	0	0	0	0	0	0	—	—	—	—	0	0	0	0	0	0	0	R	0.0
Total	2	15	6	0	2	0	1	0	2	1	1	.333	.429	.667	185	1	1	2	0	0	0	0	/2	0.1

■ JOE BERRY
Berry, Joseph Howard Sr. "Hodge"   b: 9/10/1872, Wheeling, W.Va.   d: 3/13/61, Allenwood, N.J.   BB/TR, 5'9", 172 lbs.   Deb: 9/04/02

YEAR	TM/L	G	AB	R	H	2B	3B	HR	RBI	BB	SO	AVG	OBP	SLG	PRO+	BR	/A	RC	SB	CS	SBR	FR	POS	TPR
1902	Phi-N	1	4	0	1	0	0	0	1	1		.250	.400	.250	103	0	0	1	1			-1	/C	0.0

■ SEAN BERRY
Berry, Sean Robert   b: 3/22/66, Santa Monica, Cal.   BR/TR, 5'11", 200 lbs.   Deb: 9/17/90

YEAR	TM/L	G	AB	R	H	2B	3B	HR	RBI	BB	SO	AVG	OBP	SLG	PRO+	BR	/A	RC	SB	CS	SBR	FR	POS	TPR
1990	KC-A	8	23	2	5	1	1	0	4	2	5	.217	.280	.348	76	-1	-1	2	0	0	0	1	/3	0.0

■ TOM BERRY
Berry, Thomas Haney   b: 12/31/1842, Chester, Pa.   d: 6/6/15, Chester, Pa.   5'6", 140 lbs.   Deb: 9/02/1871

YEAR	TM/L	G	AB	R	H	2B	3B	HR	RBI	BB	SO	AVG	OBP	SLG	PRO+	BR	/A	RC	SB	CS	SBR	FR	POS	TPR
1871	Ath-n	1	4	0	1	0	0	0	0			.250	.250	.250	45	-0	0	0	0				/O	0.0

■ DAMON BERRYHILL
Berryhill, Damon Scott   b: 12/3/63, South Laguna, Cal.   BB/TR, 6' ", 210 lbs.   Deb: 9/05/87

YEAR	TM/L	G	AB	R	H	2B	3B	HR	RBI	BB	SO	AVG	OBP	SLG	PRO+	BR	/A	RC	SB	CS	SBR	FR	POS	TPR
1987	Chi-N	12	28	2	5	1	0	0	1	3	5	.179	.258	.214	26	-3	-3	1	0	1	-1	-4	C	-0.6
1988	Chi-N	95	309	19	80	19	1	7	38	17	56	.259	.298	.395	93	-2	-4	33	1	0	0	-3	C	-0.1
1989	Chi-N	91	334	37	86	13	0	5	41	16	54	.257	.295	.341	76	-8	-11	31	1	0	0	-12	C	-1.7
1990	Chi-N	17	53	6	10	4	0	1	9	5	14	.189	.259	.321	54	-3	-4	4	0	0	0	-2	C	-0.5
Total	4	215	724	64	181	37	1	13	89	41	129	.250	.292	.358	79	-16	-22	69	2	1	0	-21	C	-2.9

■ HARRY BERTE
Berte, Harry Thomas   b: 5/10/1872, Covington, Ky.   d: 5/6/52, Los Angeles, Cal.   TR ,   Deb: 9/17/03

YEAR	TM/L	G	AB	R	H	2B	3B	HR	RBI	BB	SO	AVG	OBP	SLG	PRO+	BR	/A	RC	SB	CS	SBR	FR	POS	TPR
1903	StL-N	4	15	1	5	0	0	0	1	1		.333	.375	.333	108	0	0	2	0			-4	/2S	-0.3

■ DICK BERTELL
Bertell, Richard George   b: 11/21/35, Oak Park, Ill.   BR/TR, 6'0.5", 200 lbs.   Deb: 9/22/60

YEAR	TM/L	G	AB	R	H	2B	3B	HR	RBI	BB	SO	AVG	OBP	SLG	PRO+	BR	/A	RC	SB	CS	SBR	FR	POS	TPR
1960	Chi-N	5	15	0	2	0	0	0	2	3	1	.133	.278	.133	17	-2	-2	1	0	0	0	-1	/C	-0.2
1961	Chi-N	92	267	20	73	7	1	2	33	15	33	.273	.312	.330	70	-11	-12	26	0	0	0	7	C	0.2
1962	Chi-N	77	215	19	65	6	2	2	18	13	30	.302	.345	.377	90	-2	-3	27	0	1	-1	-11	C	-1.3
1963	Chi-N	100	322	15	75	7	2	2	14	24	41	.233	.286	.286	62	-14	-16	25	0	2	-1	16	C	0.2
1964	Chi-N	112	353	29	84	11	3	4	35	33	67	.238	.307	.320	74	-10	-12	34	2	1	0	-5	*C	-1.4
1965	Chi-N	34	84	6	18	2	0	0	7	11	10	.214	.305	.238	54	-5	-5	7	0	0	0	3	C	0.0
	SF-N	22	48	1	9	1	0	0	3	7	5	.188	.291	.208	42	-3	-4	3	0	0	0	3	C	0.0
	Yr	56	132	7	27	3	0	0	10	18	15	.205	.300	.227	50	-8	-8	10	0	0	0	5		0.0
1967	Chi-N	2	6	1	1	0	1	0	0	0	1	.167	.167	.500	80	-0	-0	1	0	0	0	0	/C	0.0
Total	7	444	1310	91	327	34	9	10	112	106	188	.250	.307	.312	70	-47	-53	124	2	4	-2	11	C	-2.5

■ HARRY BERTHRONG
Berthrong, Henry W.   b: 1/1/1844, Mumford, N.Y.   d: 4/28/28, Chelsea, Mass.   TR , 5'6.5", 140 lbs.   Deb: 5/05/1871

YEAR	TM/L	G	AB	R	H	2B	3B	HR	RBI	BB	SO	AVG	OBP	SLG	PRO+	BR	/A	RC	SB	CS	SBR	FR	POS	TPR
1871	Oly-n	17	73	17	17	1	1	0	8	4	2	.233	.273	.274	61	-4	-3	6	3				O/23	-0.1

■ RENO BERTOIA
Bertoia, Reno Peter   b: 1/8/35, St.Vito Udine, Italy   BR/TR, 5'11.5", 185 lbs.   Deb: 9/22/53

YEAR	TM/L	G	AB	R	H	2B	3B	HR	RBI	BB	SO	AVG	OBP	SLG	PRO+	BR	/A	RC	SB	CS	SBR	FR	POS	TPR
1953	Det-A	1	1	0	0	0	0	0	0	0	1	.000	.000	.000	-99	-0	-0	0	0	0	0	-0	/2	0.0
1954	Det-A	54	37	13	6	2	0	1	2	5	9	.162	.262	.297	54	-3	-2	3	1	0	0	17	2/3S	1.5
1955	Det-A	38	68	13	14	2	1	1	10	5	11	.206	.260	.309	54	-5	-5	6	0	0	0	7	3/2S	0.3
1956	Det-A	22	66	7	12	2	0	1	5	6	12	.182	.260	.258	37	-6	-6	4	0	0	0	10	2/3	0.5
1957	Det-A	97	295	28	81	16	2	4	28	19	43	.275	.327	.383	91	-3	-4	36	2	3	-1	-19	3/S2	-2.2
1958	Det-A	86	240	28	56	6	0	6	27	20	35	.233	.298	.333	68	-9	-11	25	5	2	0	4	3/SO	-0.2
1959	Was-A	90	308	33	73	10	0	8	29	29	46	.237	.305	.347	79	-9	-9	30	2	5	-2	-11	2/3S	-1.9
1960	Was-A	121	460	44	122	17	7	4	45	26	58	.265	.316	.359	83	-12	-11	50	3	5	-2	0	*32	-0.9
1961	Min-A	35	104	17	22	2	0	1	8	20	12	.212	.339	.260	59	-5	-6	10	0	0	0	0	3	-0.8
	KC-A	39	120	12	29	2	0	0	13	9	15	.242	.295	.258	49	-8	-8	9	1	0	0	5	3/2	0.0
	Det-A	24	46	6	10	1	0	1	4	3	8	.217	.265	.304	55	-3	-3	4	2	0	1	0	3/2S	-0.0
	Yr	98	270	35	61	5	0	2	25	32	35	.226	.308	.267	54	-17	-18	24	3	0	1	-0		-0.8
1962	Det-A	5	0	3	0	0	0	0	0	0	0	—	—	—	—	0	0	0	0	0	0	1	/2S3	0.1
Total	10	612	1745	204	425	60	10	27	171	142	252	.244	.306	.336	73	-63	-66	177	16	15	-4	8	32/SO	-3.6

■ BOB BESCHER
Bescher, Robert Henry   b: 2/25/1884, London, Ohio   d: 11/29/42, London, Ohio   BB/TL, 6'1", 200 lbs.   Deb: 9/05/08

YEAR	TM/L	G	AB	R	H	2B	3B	HR	RBI	BB	SO	AVG	OBP	SLG	PRO+	BR	/A	RC	SB	CS	SBR	FR	POS	TPR
1908	Cin-N	32	114	16	31	5	5	0	17	9		.272	.325	.404	138	4	9	18	10			4	O	0.9
1909	Cin-N	124	446	73	107	17	6	1	34	56		.240	.335	.312	102	2	3	63	54			-0	*O	0.0
1910	Cin-N	150	589	95	147	20	6	4	48	81	75	.250	.344	.338	104	1	4	91	70			7	*O	0.5
1911	Cin-N	153	599	106	165	32	10	1	45	102	78	.275	.385	.367	115	13	16	114	80			-6	*O	0.5

YEAR	TM/L	G	AB	R	H	2B	3B	HR	RBI	BB	SO	AVG	OBP	SLG	PRO+	BR	/A	RC	SB	CS	SBR	FR	POS	TPR
1912	Cin-N	145	548	**120**	154	29	11	4	38	83	61	.281	.381	.396	116	12	14	107	**67**			8	*O	1.7
1913	Cin-N	141	511	86	132	22	11	1	37	**94**	68	.258	.377	.350	109	10	10	77	38			7	*O	1.6
1914	NY-N	135	512	82	138	23	4	6	35	45	48	.270	.336	.365	112	5	7	70	36			2	*O	0.6
1915	StL-N	130	486	71	128	15	7	4	34	52	53	.263	.342	.348	109	6	6	61	27	19	-3	3	*O	0.2
1916	StL-N	151	561	78	132	24	8	6	43	60	50	.235	.316	.339	102	1	2	67	39	12	5	1	*O	0.2
1917	StL-N	42	110	10	17	1	1	1	8	20	13	.155	.290	.209	56	-5	-5	8	3			-3	O	-0.9
1918	Cle-A	25	60	12	20	2	1	0	6	17	5	.333	.487	.400	153	7	6	13	3			-0	O	0.5
Total	11	1228	4536	749	1171	190	74	28	345	619	451	.258	.353	.351	109	56	68	690	427	31		22	*O	5.8

■ BESTICK Bestick b: New York, N.Y. Deb: 6/10/1872

YEAR	TM/L	G	AB	R	H	2B	3B	HR	RBI	BB	SO	AVG	OBP	SLG	PRO+	BR	/A	RC	SB	CS	SBR	FR	POS	TPR
1872	Eck-n	4	14	0	3	0	0	0		0		.214	.214	.214	38	-1	-1	1					/C	0.0

■ JIM BESWICK Beswick, James William b: 2/12/58, Wilkinsburg, Pa. BB/TR, 6'1", 180 lbs. Deb: 8/09/78

YEAR	TM/L	G	AB	R	H	2B	3B	HR	RBI	BB	SO	AVG	OBP	SLG	PRO+	BR	/A	RC	SB	CS	SBR	FR	POS	TPR
1978	SD-N	17	20	2	1	0	0	0	1	1	7	.050	.095	.050	-63	-4	-4	0	0	0	0	1	/O	-0.3

■ FRANK BETCHER Betcher, Franklin Lyle (b: Franklin Lyle Bettger) b: 2/15/1888, Philadelphia, Pa. d: 11/27/81, Wynnewood, Pa. BB/TR, 5'11", 173 lbs. Deb: 5/21/10

YEAR	TM/L	G	AB	R	H	2B	3B	HR	RBI	BB	SO	AVG	OBP	SLG	PRO+	BR	/A	RC	SB	CS	SBR	FR	POS	TPR
1910	StL-N	35	89	7	18	2	0	0	6	7	14	.202	.276	.225	48	-6	-6	6	1			1	S/32O	-0.3

■ BILL BETHEA Bethea, William Lamar "Spot" b: 1/1/42, Houston, Tex. BR/TR, 6', 175 lbs. Deb: 9/13/64

YEAR	TM/L	G	AB	R	H	2B	3B	HR	RBI	BB	SO	AVG	OBP	SLG	PRO+	BR	/A	RC	SB	CS	SBR	FR	POS	TPR
1964	Min-A	10	30	4	5	1	0	0	2	4	4	.167	.265	.200	31	-3	-3	2	0	0	0	-1	/2S	-0.2

■ LARRY BETTENCOURT Bettencourt, Lawrence Joseph b: 9/22/05, Newark, Cal. d: 9/15/78, New Orleans, La. BR/TR, 5'11", 195 lbs. Deb: 6/02/28

YEAR	TM/L	G	AB	R	H	2B	3B	HR	RBI	BB	SO	AVG	OBP	SLG	PRO+	BR	/A	RC	SB	CS	SBR	FR	POS	TPR
1928	StL-A	67	159	30	45	9	4	4	24	22	19	.283	.377	.465	117	5	4	29	2	1	0	-10	3/OC	-0.5
1931	StL-A	74	206	27	53	9	2	3	26	31	35	.257	.357	.364	87	-2	-3	28	4	3	-1	-2	O	-0.8
1932	StL-A	27	30	4	4	1	0	1	3	7	6	.133	.297	.267	45	-2	-3	3	1	0	0	-1	/O3	-0.1
Total	3	168	395	61	102	19	6	8	53	60	60	.258	.360	.397	95	0	-2	60	7	4	-0	-12	/O3C	-1.4

■ BRUNO BETZEL Betzel, Christian Frederick Albert John Henry David b: 12/6/1894, Chattanooga, Ohio d: 2/7/65, W.Hollywood, Fla. BR/TR, 5'9", 158 lbs. Deb: 9/03/14

YEAR	TM/L	G	AB	R	H	2B	3B	HR	RBI	BB	SO	AVG	OBP	SLG	PRO+	BR	/A	RC	SB	CS	SBR	FR	POS	TPR
1914	StL-N	7	9	2	0	0	0	0	0	1	1	.000	.100	.000	-70	-2	-2	0	0			2	/23	0.0
1915	StL-N	117	367	42	92	12	4	0	27	18	48	.251	.291	.305	80	-9	-9	33	10	13	-5	5	*3/2S	-0.4
1916	StL-N	142	510	49	119	15	11	1	37	39	77	.233	.288	.312	85	-10	-10	47	22	16	-3	**29**	*23/O	2.2
1917	StL-N	106	328	24	71	4	3	1	17	20	47	.216	.266	.256	62	-15	-14	24	9			13	2O/3	0.2
1918	StL-N	76	230	18	51	6	7	0	13	12	16	.222	.260	.309	76	-8	-7	20	8			-1	3O2	-0.8
Total	5	448	1444	135	333	37	25	2	94	90	189	.231	.278	.295	76	-44	-42	124	49	29		48	23/OS	1.2

■ KURT BEVACQUA Bevacqua, Kurt Anthony b: 1/23/47, Miami Beach, Fla. BR/TR, 6', 180 lbs. Deb: 6/22/71

YEAR	TM/L	G	AB	R	H	2B	3B	HR	RBI	BB	SO	AVG	OBP	SLG	PRO+	BR	/A	RC	SB	CS	SBR	FR	POS	TPR
1971	Cle-A	55	137	9	28	3	1	3	13	4	28	.204	.227	.307	46	-9	-11	9	0	0	0	-8	2/O3S	-1.8
1972	Cle-A	19	35	2	4	0	0	1	1	3	10	.114	.184	.200	14	-4	-4	1	0	0	0	1	O/3	-0.3
1973	KC-A	99	276	39	71	8	3	2	40	25	42	.257	.321	.330	78	-6	-8	29	2	3	-1	-9	32DO/1	-1.9
1974	Pit-N	18	35	1	4	1	0	0	0	2	10	.114	.162	.143	-15	-5	-5	0	0	0	0	-0	/3O	-0.5
	KC-A	39	90	10	19	0	0	0	3	9	20	.211	.290	.211	43	-6	-7	6	1	1	-0	-3	13/2SD	-1.0
1975	Mil-A	104	258	30	59	14	0	2	24	26	45	.229	.302	.306	72	-9	-9	24	3	4	-2	1	32/S1D	-0.7
1976	Mil-A	12	7	3	1	0	0	0	0	0	0	.143	.143	.143	-17	-1	-1	0	0	0	0	2	/2D	0.1
1977	Tex-A	39	96	13	32	7	2	5	28	6	13	.333	.373	.604	159	8	7	18	0	1	-1	-4	O3/12D	0.2
1978	Tex-A	90	248	21	55	12	0	6	30	18	31	.222	.274	.343	72	-10	-10	22	1	2	-1	-4	3D2/1	-1.4
1979	SD-N	114	297	23	75	12	4	1	34	38	25	.253	.337	.330	88	-6	-4	31	2	5	-2	-3	32/1O	-1.1
1980	SD-N	62	71	4	19	6	1	0	12	6	1	.268	.325	.380	102	-0	0	9	1	1	-0	-3	3/O21	-0.2
	Pit-N	22	43	1	7	1	0	0	4	6	7	.163	.280	.186	32	-4	-4	2	0	0	0	0	/31	-0.3
	Yr	84	114	5	26	7	1	0	16	12	8	.228	.307	.307	75	-4	-4	11	1	1	-0	-3		-0.5
1981	Pit-N	29	27	2	7	1	0	1	4	4	6	.259	.355	.407	112	1	1	4	0	0	0	1	/23	0.2
1982	SD-N	64	123	15	31	9	0	0	24	17	22	.252	.343	.325	93	-2	-1	14	2	0	1	-2	1/O3	-0.3
1983	SD-N	74	156	17	38	7	0	2	24	18	33	.244	.322	.327	83	-4	-3	16	0	3	-2	0	13O	-0.6
1984	*SD-N	59	80	7	16	3	0	1	9	14	19	.200	.326	.275	71	-3	-3	7	0	0	0	-1	13/O	-0.4
1985	SD-N	71	138	17	33	6	0	3	25	25	17	.239	.356	.348	99	0	1	18	0	0	0	-2	3/1O	-0.6
Total	15	970	2117	214	499	90	11	27	275	221	329	.236	.309	.327	78	-60	-60	210	12	20	-8	-33	321/ODS	-10.0

■ HAL BEVAN Bevan, Joseph Harold b: 11/15/30, New Orleans, La. d: 10/5/68, New Orleans, La. BR/TR, 6'2", 198 lbs. Deb: 4/24/52

YEAR	TM/L	G	AB	R	H	2B	3B	HR	RBI	BB	SO	AVG	OBP	SLG	PRO+	BR	/A	RC	SB	CS	SBR	FR	POS	TPR
1952	Bos-A	1	1	0	0	0	0	0	0	0	0	.000	.000	.000	-93	-0	-0	0	0	0	0	0	/3	0.0
	Phi-A	8	17	1	6	0	0	0	4	0	1	.353	.353	.353	91	-0	-0	2	2	0	1	1	/3	0.1
	Yr	9	18	1	6	0	0	0	4	0	1	.333	.333	.333	81	-0	-0	2	2	0	1	1		0.1
1955	KC-A	3	3	0	0	0	0	0	0	0	0	.000	.000	.000	-99	-1	-1	0	0	0	0	0	/3	0.0
1961	Cin-N	3	3	1	1	0	0	1	1	0	2	.333	.333	1.333	311	1	1	1	0	0	0	0	H	0.1
Total	3	15	24	2	7	0	0	1	5	0	3	.292	.292	.417	89	-0	-1	3	2	0	1	1	/3	0.2

■ MONTE BEVILLE Beville, Henry Monte b: 2/24/1875, Dublin, Ind. d: 1/24/55, Grand Rapids, Mich BL/TR, 5'11", 180 lbs. Deb: 4/24/03

YEAR	TM/L	G	AB	R	H	2B	3B	HR	RBI	BB	SO	AVG	OBP	SLG	PRO+	BR	/A	RC	SB	CS	SBR	FR	POS	TPR
1903	NY-A	82	258	23	50	14	1	0	29	16		.194	.241	.256	48	-15	-17	18	4			-11	C/1	-1.9
1904	NY-A	9	22	2	6	2	0	0	2	2		.273	.333	.364	117	1	0	3	0			-2	/1C	0.0
	Det-A	54	174	14	36	5	1	0	13	8		.207	.242	.247	58	-8	-8	12	2			-2	C1	-0.6
	Yr	63	196	16	42	7	1	0	15	10		.214	.252	.260	65	-8	-7	15	2			-4		-0.6
Total	2	145	454	39	92	21	2	0	44	26		.203	.246	.258	55	-23	-24	33	6			-15	C/1	-2.5

■ BUDDY BIANCALANA Biancalana, Roland Americo b: 2/2/60, Larkspur, Cal. BB/TR, 5'11", 160 lbs. Deb: 9/12/82

YEAR	TM/L	G	AB	R	H	2B	3B	HR	RBI	BB	SO	AVG	OBP	SLG	PRO+	BR	/A	RC	SB	CS	SBR	FR	POS	TPR
1982	KC-A	3	2	0	1	0	0	0	0	0	0	.500	.667	1.500	474	1	1	1	0	0	0	3	/S	0.4
1983	KC-A	6	15	2	3	0	0	0	0	0	7	.200	.200	.200	10	-2	-2	1	1	0	0	3	/S	0.2
1984	*KC-A	66	134	18	26	6	1	2	9	6	44	.194	.229	.299	44	-10	-10	9	1	2	-1	7	S2/D	0.2
1985	*KC-A	81	138	21	26	5	1	1	6	17	34	.188	.277	.261	40	-10	-10	10	1	4	-2	23	S/2D	1.7
1986	KC-A	100	190	24	46	4	4	2	8	15	50	.242	.298	.337	71	-7	-8	20	5	1	1	2	S2	0.1
1987	KC-A	37	47	4	10	1	0	1	7	1	16	.213	.229	.298	37	-4	-4	3	0	0	0	4	S2/D	0.2
	Hou-N	18	24	1	1	0	0	0	0	1	12	.042	.080	.042	-69	-6	-6	0	0	0	0	-1	S/2	-0.4
Total	6	311	550	70	113	16	7	6	30	41	157	.205	.261	.293	50	-38	-39	44	8	7	-2	41	S/2D	2.2

■ TOMMY BIANCO Bianco, Thomas Anthony b: 12/16/52, Rockville Cntr, N.Y BB/TR, 5'11", 190 lbs. Deb: 5/28/75

YEAR	TM/L	G	AB	R	H	2B	3B	HR	RBI	BB	SO	AVG	OBP	SLG	PRO+	BR	/A	RC	SB	CS	SBR	FR	POS	TPR
1975	Mil-A	18	34	6	6	1	0	0		3	7	.176	.263	.206	34	-3	-3	2	0	0	0	-1	/31D	-0.3

■ HANK BIASATTI Biasatti, Henry Arcado b: 1/14/22, Beano, Italy BL/TL, 5'11", 175 lbs. Deb: 4/23/49

YEAR	TM/L	G	AB	R	H	2B	3B	HR	RBI	BB	SO	AVG	OBP	SLG	PRO+	BR	/A	RC	SB	CS	SBR	FR	POS	TPR
1949	Phi-A	21	24	6	2	0	0	0	2	8	5	.083	.313	.167	30	-2	-2	2	0	0	0	-1	/1	-0.2

■ DANTE BICHETTE Bichette, Alphonse Dante b: 11/18/63, W.Palm Beach, Fla. BR/TR, 6'3", 215 lbs. Deb: 9/05/88

YEAR	TM/L	G	AB	R	H	2B	3B	HR	RBI	BB	SO	AVG	OBP	SLG	PRO+	BR	/A	RC	SB	CS	SBR	FR	POS	TPR
1988	Cal-A	21	46	1	12	2	0	0	8	0	7	.261	.261	.304	59	-3	-2	4	0	0	0	3	O	0.0
1989	Cal-A	48	138	13	29	7	0	3	15	6	24	.210	.243	.326	60	-8	-8	11	3	0	1	4	O/D	-0.2
1990	Cal-A	109	349	40	89	15	1	5	53	16	79	.255	.293	.433	100	-1	-1	42	5	2	0	-1	*O	-0.2
Total	3	178	533	54	130	24	1	18	76	22	110	.244	.278	.394	87	-12	-11	56	8	2	1	6	O/D	-0.4

YEAR	TM/L	G	AB	R	H	2B	3B	HR	RBI	BB	SO	AVG	OBP	SLG	PRO+	BR	/A	RC	SB	CS	SBR	FR	POS	TPR

■ OSCAR BIELASKI Bielaski, Oscar b: 3/21/1847, Washington, D.C. d: 11/8/11, Washington, D.C. BR/TR, 5'7", Deb: 4/24/1872

1872	Nat-n	10	46	13	9	0	0	0			0	.196	.196	.196	18	-4	-6	2					O	-0.3
1873	Was-n	38	173	35	51	2	3	0			4	.295	.311	.341	95	-2	-0	19					*O	0.1
1874	Bal-n	27	113	18	27	1	0	0			2	.239	.252	.248	60	-5	-5	7					O/12	-0.2
1875	Chi-n	51	196	21	49	2	0	0			2	.250	.258	.260	79	-4	-4	13					*O	-0.2
1876	Chi-N	32	139	24	29	3	0	0	10	2	3	.209	.220	.230	45	-7	-10	7				-3	O	-1.0
Total	4 n	126	528	87	136	5	3	0			8	.258	.269	.278	74	-15	-15	41					O/21	-0.6

■ LOU BIERBAUER Bierbauer, Louis W. b: 9/28/1865, Erie, Pa. d: 1/31/26, Erie, Pa. BL/TR, 5'8", 140 lbs. Deb: 4/17/1886

1886	Phi-a	137	522	56	118	17	5	2			21	.226	.256	.289	71	-17	-18	45	19			-3	*2/CSP	-1.8
1887	Phi-a	126	530	74	144	19	7	1			13	.272	.289	.340	77	-17	-17	65	40			-8	*2/P	-1.9
1888	Phi-a	134	535	83	143	20	9	0	80	25		.267	.301	.338	109	4	4	66	34			22	*23/P	2.7
1889	Phi-a	130	549	80	167	27	7	7	105	29	30	.304	.344	.417	120	11	13	87	17			37	*2/C	4.3
1890	Bro-P	133	589	128	180	31	11	7	99	40	15	.306	.350	.431	103	6	-0	97	16			25	*2	2.5
1891	Pit-N	121	500	60	103	13	6	1	47	28	19	.206	.252	.262	53	-31	-29	37	12			-2	*2	-2.4
1892	Pit-N	152	649	81	153	20	9	8	65	25	29	.236	.264	.331	81	-17	-18	61	11			32	*2	1.4
1893	Pit-N	128	528	84	150	19	11	4	94	36	12	.284	.335	.384	94	-7	-5	73	11			16	*2	0.8
1894	Pit-N	130	525	86	159	19	13	3	107	26	9	.303	.337	.406	81	-18	-17	80	19			9	*2	0.0
1895	Pit-N	117	466	53	120	13	11	0	69	19	8	.258	.290	.333	65	-27	-23	51	18			14	*2	0.0
1896	Pit-N	59	258	33	74	10	6	0	39	5	7	.287	.300	.372	82	-9	-7	32	7			12	2	0.6
1897	StL-N	12	46	1	10	0	0	0	1	0		.217	.217	.217	17	-5	-5	3	2			-2	2	-0.4
1898	StL-N	4	9	0	0	0	0	0	0	1		.000	.100	.000	-68	-2	-2	0				-0	/2S3	-0.1
Total	13	1383	5706	819	1521	208	95	33	706	268	129	.267	.301	.354	85	-130	-125	697	206			151	*2/3CPS	5.7

■ CHARLIE BIERMAN Bierman, Charles S. b: 1845, Hoboken, N.J. d: 2/14/1879, Hoboken, N.J. 6', 180 lbs. Deb: 6/21/1871

| 1871 | Kek-n | 1 | 2 | 0 | 0 | 0 | 0 | 0 | | 1 | 0 | .000 | .333 | .000 | 6 | -0 | -0 | 0 | 0 | | | | /1 | 0.0 |

■ CARSON BIGBEE Bigbee, Carson Lee "Skeeter" b: 3/31/1895, Waterloo, Ore. d: 10/17/64, Portland, Ore. BL/TR, 5'9", 157 lbs. Deb: 8/25/16

1916	Pit-N	43	164	17	41	3	6	0	3	7	14	.250	.285	.341	91	-2	-2	19	8			-6	2O/3	-0.8
1917	Pit-N	133	469	46	112	11	6	0	21	37	16	.239	.301	.288	78	-10	-11	46	19			-3	*O2/S	-1.8
1918	Pit-N	92	310	47	79	11	3	1	19	42	10	.255	.344	.319	99	2	1	40	19			-1	O	-0.5
1919	Pit-N	125	478	61	132	11	4	2	27	37	26	.276	.332	.328	95	0	-2	59	31			11	*O	0.4
1920	Pit-N	137	550	78	154	19	15	4	32	45	28	.280	.341	.391	106	7	5	74	31	15	0	5	*O	0.3
1921	Pit-N	147	632	100	204	23	17	3	42	41	19	.323	.364	.427	106	8	6	94	21	20	-6	17	*O	0.9
1922	Pit-N	150	614	113	215	29	15	5	99	56	13	.350	.405	.471	124	24	23	116	24	15	-2	15	*O	2.8
1923	Pit-N	123	499	79	149	18	7	0	54	43	15	.299	.355	.363	88	-6	-8	65	10	9	-2	7	*O	-0.6
1924	Pit-N	89	282	42	74	4	1	0	15	26	12	.262	.331	.284	65	-12	-13	29	15	7	0	-1	O	-1.4
1925	*Pit-N	66	126	31	30	7	0	0	8	7	8	.238	.278	.294	43	-10	-11	10	2	2	-1	0	O	-1.1
1926	Pit-N	42	68	15	15	3	1	2	4	3	0	.221	.264	.382	69	-3	-3	7	2			0	O	-0.3
Total	11	1147	4192	629	1205	139	75	17	324	344	161	.287	.345	.369	96	-2	-16	558	182	68		44	*O/2S3	-2.1

■ LYLE BIGBEE Bigbee, Lyle Randolph "Al" b: 8/22/1893, Sweet Home, Ore. d: 8/5/42, Portland, Ore. BL/TR, 6', 180 lbs. Deb: 4/15/20

1920	Phi-A	38	75	5	14	2	0	1	8	9	12	.187	.282	.253	42	-6	-6	6	1	0	0	-2	OP	-0.6
1921	Pit-N	5	2	0	0	0	0	0	0	0	1	.000	.000	.000	-97	-1	-1	0	0	0	0	0	/P	0.0
Total	2	43	77	5	14	2	0	1	8	9	13	.182	.276	.247	39	-7	-7	6	1	0	0	-2	/PO	-0.6

■ ELLIOT BIGELOW Bigelow, Elliot Allardice "Babe" or "Gilly" b: 10/13/1897, Tarpon Springs, Fla. d: 8/10/33, Tampa, Fla. BL/TL, 5'11", 185 lbs. Deb: 4/18/29

| 1929 | Bos-A | 100 | 211 | 23 | 60 | 16 | 0 | 1 | 26 | 23 | 18 | .284 | .357 | .374 | 91 | -3 | -2 | 28 | 1 | 4 | -2 | -10 | O | -1.5 |

■ CRAIG BIGGIO Biggio, Craig Alan b: 12/14/65, Smithtown, N.Y. BR/TR, 5'11", 185 lbs. Deb: 6/26/88

1988	Hou-N	50	123	14	26	6	1	3	5	7	29	.211	.254	.350	74	-5	-4	11	6	1	1	16	C	1.6
1989	Hou-N	134	443	64	114	21	2	13	60	49	64	.257	.339	.402	115	7	9	65	21	3	5	-6	*C/O	1.7
1990	Hou-N	150	555	53	153	24	2	4	42	53	79	.276	.342	.348	92	-6	-5	68	25	11	5	-8	*CO	-0.7
Total	3	334	1121	131	293	51	5	20	107	109	172	.261	.332	.369	99	-4	-1	144	52	15	7	2	C/O	2.6

■ GEORGE BIGNELL Bignell, George William b: 7/18/1858, Taunton, Mass. d: 1/16/25, Providence, R.I. Deb: 9/27/1884

| 1884 | Mil-U | 4 | 9 | 4 | 2 | 0 | 0 | 0 | | 1 | | .222 | .300 | .222 | 146 | -0 | 1 | 1 | 0 | | | 4 | /C | 0.4 |

■ LARRY BIITTNER Biittner, Lawrence David b: 7/27/45, Pocahontas, Ia. BL/TL, 6'2", 205 lbs. Deb: 7/17/70

1970	Was-A	2	2	0	0	0	0	0	0	0	0	.000	.000	.000	-99	-1	-1	0	0	0	0	0	H	0.0
1971	Was-A	66	171	12	44	4	1	0	16	16	20	.257	.324	.292	80	-5	-4	16	1	0	0	-1	O/1	-0.6
1972	Tex-A	137	382	34	99	18	1	3	31	29	37	.259	.315	.335	98	-3	-1	40	1	3	-2	2	1O	-1.0
1973	Tex-A	83	258	19	65	8	2	1	12	20	21	.252	.308	.310	78	-9	-7	24	1	0	0	1	O1/D	-0.8
1974	Mon-N	18	26	2	7	1	0	0	3	0	2	.269	.269	.308	58	-1	-2	2	0	0	0	1	/O	0.0
1975	Mon-N	121	346	34	109	13	5	3	28	34	33	.315	.376	.408	113	9	7	51	2	1	0	-2	O	0.2
1976	Mon-N	11	32	2	6	1	0	0	1	0	3	.188	.188	.219	14	-4	-4	1	0	0	0	1	/O	-0.3
	Chi-N	78	192	21	47	13	1	0	17	10	6	.245	.286	.323	66	-7	-9	17	0	2	-1	6	1O	-0.7
	Yr	89	224	23	53	14	1	0	18	10	9	.237	.272	.308	59	-11	-13	17	0	2	-1	6		-1.0
1977	Chi-N	138	493	74	147	28	1	12	62	35	36	.298	.346	.432	97	5	-2	70	2	1	0	2	1O/P	-0.5
1978	Chi-N	120	343	32	88	15	1	4	50	23	37	.257	.305	.341	72	-9	-14	35	0	1	-1	5	1O	-1.3
1979	Chi-N	111	272	35	79	13	3	3	50	21	23	.290	.341	.393	91	-0	-3	34	1	1	-0	-3	O1	-0.8
1980	Chi-N	127	273	21	68	12	2	1	34	18	33	.249	.300	.319	68	-10	-12	25	1	3	-2	0	1O	-1.7
1981	Cin-N	42	61	1	13	4	0	0	8	4	4	.213	.262	.279	52	-4	-4	4	0	0	0	1	/1O	-0.2
1982	Cin-N	97	184	18	57	9	2	2	24	17	16	.310	.374	.413	118	5	5	27	1	0	0	0	O1	0.4
1983	Tex-A	66	116	5	32	5	1	0	18	9	16	.276	.328	.336	85	-2	-2	13	0	0	0	2	1/OD	-0.2
Total	14	1217	3151	310	861	144	20	29	354	236	287	.273	.326	.359	87	-37	-54	358	10	12	-4	15	O1/DP	-7.3

■ DANN BILARDELLO Bilardello, Dann James b: 5/26/59, Santa Cruz, Cal. BR/TR, 6', 185 lbs. Deb: 4/11/83

1983	Cin-N	109	298	27	71	18	0	9	38	15	49	.238	.277	.389	80	-8	-9	30	2	1	0	-1	*C	-0.7
1984	Cin-N	68	182	16	38	7	0	2	10	19	34	.209	.287	.280	57	-9	-10	14	0	1	-1	2	C	-0.7
1985	Cin-N	42	102	6	17	0	0	1	9	4	15	.167	.206	.196	12	-12	-12	3	0	0	0	8	C	-0.2
1986	Mon-N	79	191	12	37	5	0	4	17	14	32	.194	.249	.283	47	-14	-14	13	1	0	0	2	C	-1.0
1989	Pit-N	33	80	11	18	6	0	2	8	2	18	.225	.244	.375	77	-3	-3	6	1	2	-1	6	C	0.5
1990	Pit-N	19	37	1	2	0	0	0	3	4	10	.054	.146	.054	-44	-7	-7	1	0	0	0	3	C	-0.2
Total	6	350	890	73	183	36	0	18	85	58	158	.206	.257	.307	55	-54	-56	68	4	4	-1	19	C	-2.3

■ STEVE BILKO Bilko, Stephen Thomas b: 11/13/28, Nanticoke, Pa. d: 3/7/78, Wilkes-Barre, Pa. BR/TR, 6'1", 230 lbs. Deb: 9/22/49

1949	StL-N	6	17	3	5	1	0	2	5	6	6	.294	.455	.412	128	1	1	4	0			0	/1	0.1
1950	StL-N	10	33	1	6	1	0	0	2	5	10	.182	.270	.212	27	-3	-4	2	0			0	/1	-0.3
1951	StL-N	21	72	5	16	4	0	2	12	9	10	.222	.309	.361	79	-2	-2	9	0	0	0	-0	1	-0.2
1952	StL-N	20	72	7	19	6	1	1	6	4	15	.264	.303	.417	97	-1	-1	9	0	0	0	4	1	0.3
1953	StL-N	154	570	72	143	23	3	21	84	70	125	.251	.334	.412	93	-6	-6	79	0	1	-1	7	*1	-0.1
1954	StL-N	8	14	1	2	0	0	0	1	3	1	.143	.294	.143	18	-2	-2	0	0	0	0	2	/1	0.0
	Chi-N	47	92	11	22	8	1	4	12	11	24	.239	.320	.478	104	0	0	12	0	0	0	6	1	0.5

YEAR	TM/L	G	AB	R	H	2B	3B	HR	RBI	BB	SO	AVG	OBP	SLG	PRO+	BR	/A	RC	SB	CS	SBR	FR	POS	TPR
	Yr	55	106	12	24	8	1	4	13	14	25	.226	.317	.434	92	-1	-2	12	0	0	0	8		0.5
1958	Cin-N	31	87	12	23	4	2	4	17	10	20	.264	.340	.494	111	2	1	13	0	0	0	-1	1	0.0
	LA-N	47	101	13	21	1	2	7	18	8	37	.208	.266	.465	86	-2	-3	11	0	0	0	2	1	-0.2
	Yr	78	188	25	44	5	4	11	35	18	57	.234	.301	.479	98	-0	-1	24	0	0	0	1		-0.2
1960	Det-A	78	222	20	46	11	2	9	25	27	31	.207	.293	.396	82	-5	-6	25	0	1	-1	0	1	-1.0
1961	LA-A	114	294	49	82	16	1	20	59	58	81	.279	.398	.544	134	21	17	65	1	1	-0	4	1/O	1.2
1962	LA-A	64	164	26	47	9	1	8	38	25	35	.287	.387	.500	141	9	10	32	1	1	-0	-1	1	0.5
Total	10	600	1738	220	432	85	13	76	276	234	395	.249	.339	.444	103	13	6	262	2	4		24	1/O	0.8

■ JOSH BILLINGS
Billings, John Augustus b: 11/30/1891, Grantville, Kan. d: 12/30/81, Santa Monica, Cal. BR/TR, 5'11", 165 lbs. Deb: 9/09/13

YEAR	TM/L	G	AB	R	H	2B	3B	HR	RBI	BB	SO	AVG	OBP	SLG	PRO+	BR	/A	RC	SB	CS	SBR	FR	POS	TPR
1913	Cle-A	1	3	0	0	0	0	0	0	0	3	.000	.000	.000	-97	-1	-1	0	0			0	/C	0.0
1914	Cle-A	11	8	2	2	1	0	0	0	1	1	.250	.333	.375	109	0	0	1	1			2	/C	0.3
1915	Cle-A	8	21	2	4	1	0	0	0	0	6	.190	.190	.238	28	-2	-2	1	1			-1	/CO	-0.2
1916	Cle-A	22	31	2	5	0	0	0	1	2	11	.161	.212	.161	12	-3	-4	1	0			3	C	0.0
1917	Cle-A	66	129	8	23	3	2	0	9	8	21	.178	.243	.233	42	-9	-10	8	2			2	C	-0.3
1918	Cle-A	2	3	0	1	0	0	0	0	0	0	.333	.333	.333	92	-0	-0	0	0			-0	/C	0.0
1919	StL-A	38	76	9	15	1	1	0	3	1	12	.197	.218	.237	27	-7	-8	4	0			5	C/1	-0.1
1920	StL-A	66	155	19	43	5	2	0	11	11	10	.277	.353	.335	81	-3	-4	20	1	0	0	-5	C	-0.4
1921	StL-A	20	46	2	10	0	0	0	4	0	7	.217	.217	.217	11	-6	-6	2	0			2	C	-0.3
1922	StL-A	5	7	0	3	1	0	0	1	0	0	.429	.429	.571	153	1	1	2	0			0	/C	0.1
1923	StL-A	4	9	0	0	0	0	0	0	0	0	.000	.000	.000	-95	-3	-3	0	0			0	/C	-0.1
Total	11	243	488	44	106	12	5	0	29	23	73	.217	.268	.262	47	-33	-36	40	5	0		8	C/1O	-1.0

■ DICK BILLINGS
Billings, Richard Arlin b: 12/4/42, Detroit, Mich. BR/TR, 6'1", 195 lbs. Deb: 9/11/68

YEAR	TM/L	G	AB	R	H	2B	3B	HR	RBI	BB	SO	AVG	OBP	SLG	PRO+	BR	/A	RC	SB	CS	SBR	FR	POS	TPR
1968	Was-A	12	33	3	6	1	0	1	3	5	13	.182	.289	.303	82	-1	-1	3	0	0	0	-0	/O3	0.0
1969	Was-A	27	37	3	5	0	0	0	0	6	8	.135	.256	.135	13	-4	-4	1	0	1	-1	0	/O3	-0.4
1970	Was-A	11	24	3	6	2	0	1	1	2	3	.250	.308	.458	114	0	0	3	0	0	0	-1	/C	0.0
1971	Was-A	116	349	32	86	14	0	6	48	21	54	.246	.299	.338	85	-10	-7	34	2	5	-2	3	CO/3	-0.5
1972	Tex-A	133	469	41	119	15	1	5	58	29	77	.254	.300	.322	89	-9	-7	42	1	5	-3	-5	CO/31	-1.6
1973	Tex-A	81	280	17	50	11	0	3	32	20	43	.179	.238	.250	39	-23	-22	15	1	1	-0	-19	C/O1D	-4.1
1974	Tex-A	16	31	2	7	1	0	0	0	4	6	.226	.314	.258	68	-1	-1	3	2	0	1	1	C/OD	0.1
	StL-N	1	5	0	1	0	0	0	0	0	1	.200	.200	.200	12	-1	-1	0	0	0	0	0	/O	0.0
1975	StL-N	3	3	0	0	0	0	0	0	0	2	.000	.000	.000	-97	-1	-1	0	0	0	0	0	H	0.0
Total	8	400	1231	101	280	44	1	16	142	87	207	.227	.283	.304	73	-49	-43	102	6	12	-5	-21	C/O31D	-6.5

■ GEORGE BINKS
Binks, George Alvin "Bingo" (b: George Alvin Binkowski) b: 7/11/16, Chicago, Ill. BL/TL, 6', 175 lbs. Deb: 9/23/44

YEAR	TM/L	G	AB	R	H	2B	3B	HR	RBI	BB	SO	AVG	OBP	SLG	PRO+	BR	/A	RC	SB	CS	SBR	FR	POS	TPR
1944	Was-A	5	12	0	3	0	0	0	0	0	1	.250	.250	.250	45	-1	-1	1	0	0	0	-0	/O	0.0
1945	Was-A	145	550	62	153	32	6	6	81	34	52	.278	.324	.391	117	3	8	69	11	7	-1	-0	*O1	0.1
1946	Was-A	65	134	13	26	3	0	0	12	6	16	.194	.229	.216	26	-14	-13	7	1	0	0	2	O	-1.2
1947	Phi-A	104	333	33	86	19	4	2	34	23	36	.258	.308	.357	83	-8	-9	38	8	2	1	-1	O1	-1.2
1948	Phi-A	17	41	2	4	1	0	0	2	2	2	.098	.140	.122	-30	-8	-8	1	1	0	0	-1	O	-0.8
	StL-A	15	23	2	5	0	0	0	1	2	1	.217	.280	.217	32	-2	-2	2	0	0	0	-1	/O1	-0.2
	Yr	32	64	4	9	1	0	0	3	4	3	.141	.191	.156	-7	-10	-10	2	1	0	0	-1		-1.0
Total	5	351	1093	112	277	55	10	8	130	67	108	.253	.299	.344	86	-29	-24	117	21	9	1	-1	O/1	-3.3

■ STEVE BIRAS
Biras, Stephen Alexander b: 2/26/22, E.St.Louis, Ill. d: 4/21/65, St.Louis, Mo. BR/TR, 5'11", 185 lbs. Deb: 9/15/44

YEAR	TM/L	G	AB	R	H	2B	3B	HR	RBI	BB	SO	AVG	OBP	SLG	PRO+	BR	/A	RC	SB	CS	SBR	FR	POS	TPR
1944	Cle-A	2	2	0	2	0	0	0	2	0	0	1.000	1.000	1.000	491	1	1	2	0	0	0	0	/2	0.1

■ JUD BIRCHALL
Birchall, Adoniram Judson b: 1858, Germantown, Pa. d: 12/22/1887, Philadelphia, Pa. Deb: 5/02/1882

YEAR	TM/L	G	AB	R	H	2B	3B	HR	RBI	BB	SO	AVG	OBP	SLG	PRO+	BR	/A	RC	SB	CS	SBR	FR	POS	TPR
1882	Phi-a	75	338	65	89	12	1	0			8	.263	.280	.305	87	-1	-7	30				0	*O/2	-0.6
1883	Phi-a	96	449	95	108	10	1	1			19	.241	.271	.274	70	-11	-17	34				6	*O	-0.9
1884	Phi-a	54	221	36	57	2	2	0			4	.258	.287	.285	84	-2	-5	19				3	O/3	-0.1
Total	3	225	1008	196	254	24	4	1			31	.252	.278	.287	79	-15	-29	82				9	O/32	-1.6

■ FRANK BIRD
Bird, Frank Zepherin "Dodo" b: 3/10/1869, Spencer, Mass. d: 5/20/58, Worcester, Mass. BR/TR, 5'10", 195 lbs. Deb: 4/16/1892

YEAR	TM/L	G	AB	R	H	2B	3B	HR	RBI	BB	SO	AVG	OBP	SLG	PRO+	BR	/A	RC	SB	CS	SBR	FR	POS	TPR
1892	StL-N	17	50	9	10	3	1	1	1	6	11	.200	.286	.360	102	-0	0	6	2			-4	C	-0.1

■ GEORGE BIRD
Bird, George Raymond b: 6/23/1850, Stillman Valley, Ill. d: 11/9/40, Rockford, Ill. 5'9", 150 lbs. Deb: 5/06/1871

YEAR	TM/L	G	AB	R	H	2B	3B	HR	RBI	BB	SO	AVG	OBP	SLG	PRO+	BR	/A	RC	SB	CS	SBR	FR	POS	TPR
1871	Rok-n	25	106	19	28	2	5	0	13	3	2	.264	.284	.377	92	-2	-0	12	1				*O	0.0

■ DAVE BIRDSALL
Birdsall, David Solomon b: 7/16/1838, New York, N.Y. d: 12/30/1896, Boston, Mass. BR/TR, 5'9", 126 lbs. Deb: 5/05/1871

YEAR	TM/L	G	AB	R	H	2B	3B	HR	RBI	BB	SO	AVG	OBP	SLG	PRO+	BR	/A	RC	SB	CS	SBR	FR	POS	TPR
1871	Bos-n	29	152	51	46	3	3	0	24	4	4	.303	.321	.362	93	-1	-2	20	6				*O/C	0.0
1872	Bos-n	16	76	11	14	3	0	0			0	.184	.184	.224	24	-6	-7	3					C/O	-0.4
1873	Bos-n	3	11	4	1	0	0	0			2	.091	.231	.091	-1	-1	-2	0					/O	0.0
Total	3 n	48	239	66	61	6	3	0			6	.255	.273	.305	67	-9	-11	23					/OC	-0.4

■ JOE BIRMINGHAM
Birmingham, Joseph Leo "Dode" b: 8/6/1884, Elmira, N.Y. d: 4/24/46, Tampico, Mexico BR/TR, 5'10", 185 lbs. Deb: 9/12/06 M

YEAR	TM/L	G	AB	R	H	2B	3B	HR	RBI	BB	SO	AVG	OBP	SLG	PRO+	BR	/A	RC	SB	CS	SBR	FR	POS	TPR
1906	Cle-A	10	41	5	13	2	1	0	6	1		.317	.333	.415	138	1	2	6	2			1	/O3	0.3
1907	Cle-A	136	476	55	112	10	9	1	33	16		.235	.260	.300	80	-11	-12	45	23			12	*O/S	-0.6
1908	Cle-A	122	413	32	88	10	1	2	38	19		.213	.248	.257	65	-15	-16	29	15			6	*O/S	-1.7
1909	Cle-A	100	343	29	99	10	5	1	38	19		.289	.333	.356	113	6	5	44	12			4	O	0.6
1910	Cle-A	104	367	41	84	11	2	0	35	23		.229	.284	.270	72	-11	-12	33	18			14	*O/3	-0.2
1911	Cle-A	125	447	55	136	18	5	2	51	15		.304	.334	.380	98	-2	-3	61	16			8	*O3	-0.2
1912	Cle-A	107	369	49	94	19	3	1	45	26		.255	.311	.331	81	-9	-10	43	15			5	O/1M	-1.0
1913	Cle-A	47	131	16	37	9	1	0	15	8	22	.282	.324	.366	99	-0	-1	18	7			5	OM	-0.5
1914	Cle-A	19	47	2	6	0	0	0	4	2	5	.128	.163	.128	-12	-6	-7	1	0	1	-1	-2	OM	-1.1
Total	9	770	2634	284	669	89	27	7	265	129	27	.254	.293	.316	85	-48	-53	281	108	1		45	O/31S	-4.4

■ JOHN BISCHOFF
Bischoff, John George "Smiley" b: 10/28/1894, Granite City, Ill. d: 12/28/81, Granite City, Ill. BR/TR, 5'7", 165 lbs. Deb: 4/18/25

YEAR	TM/L	G	AB	R	H	2B	3B	HR	RBI	BB	SO	AVG	OBP	SLG	PRO+	BR	/A	RC	SB	CS	SBR	FR	POS	TPR
1925	Chi-A	7	11	1	1	0	0	0	0	1	5	.091	.167	.091	-35	-2	-2	0	0	0	0	0	/C	-0.1
	Bos-A	41	133	13	37	9	1	1	16	6	11	.278	.309	.383	75	-6	-6	15	1	2	-1	-3	C	-0.5
	Yr	48	144	14	38	9	1	1	16	7	16	.264	.298	.361	67	-8	-8	15	1	2	-1	-3		-0.6
1926	Bos-A	59	127	6	33	11	2	0	19	15	16	.260	.343	.378	91	-2	-2	16	1	3	-2	-1	C	-0.0
Total	2	107	271	20	71	20	3	1	35	22	32	.262	.320	.369	78	-10	-9	32	2	5	-2	-3	/C	-0.6

■ FRANK BISHOP
Bishop, Frank H. b: 9/21/1860, Belvidere, Ill. d: 6/18/29, Chicago, Ill. Deb: 5/27/1884

YEAR	TM/L	G	AB	R	H	2B	3B	HR	RBI	BB	SO	AVG	OBP	SLG	PRO+	BR	/A	RC	SB	CS	SBR	FR	POS	TPR
1884	CP-U	4	16	1	3	1	0	0		0		.188	.188	.250	47	-1	-1	1	0			-2	/3S	-0.1

■ MAX BISHOP
Bishop, Max Frederick "Tilly" or "Camera Eye" b: 9/5/1899, Waynesboro, Pa. d: 2/24/62, Waynesboro, Pa. BL/TR, 5'8.5", 165 lbs. Deb: 4/15/24

YEAR	TM/L	G	AB	R	H	2B	3B	HR	RBI	BB	SO	AVG	OBP	SLG	PRO+	BR	/A	RC	SB	CS	SBR	FR	POS	TPR
1924	Phi-A	91	294	52	75	13	2	2	21	54	30	.255	.380	.333	84	-4	-5	41	4	3	-1	6	2	0.3
1925	Phi-A	105	368	66	103	18	4	4	27	87	37	.280	.420	.383	98	7	3	65	5	9	-4	5	*2	0.8
1926	Phi-A	122	400	77	106	20	2	0	33	116	41	.265	.431	.325	94	8	4	67	4	5	-2	0	*2	0.7
1927	Phi-A	117	372	80	103	15	1	0	22	105	28	.277	.442	.323	95	9	5	60	8	6	-1	3	*2	1.1
1928	Phi-A	126	472	104	149	27	5	6	50	97	36	.316	.435	.432	125	25	23	95	9	9	-3	-11	*2	1.6
1929	*Phi-A	129	475	102	110	19	6	3	36	**128**	44	.232	.398	.316	83	-3	-6	70	1	4	-2	-26	*2	-2.9
1930	*Phi-A	130	441	117	111	27	6	10	38	128	60	.252	.426	.408	108	16	12	88	3	2	-0	-6	*2	0.6

YEAR	TM/L	G	AB	R	H	2B	3B	HR	RBI	BB	SO	AVG	OBP	SLG	PRO+	BR	/A	RC	SB	CS	SBR	FR	POS	TPR
1931	*Phi-A	130	497	115	146	30	4	5	37	112	51	.294	.426	.400	111	20	15	94	3	1	0	0	*2	2.1
1932	Phi-A	114	409	89	104	24	2	5	37	110	43	.254	.412	.359	98	7	4	69	2	2	-1	-10	*2	0.0
1933	Phi-A	117	391	80	115	27	1	4	42	106	46	.294	.446	.399	124	21	21	78	1	5	-3	-13	*2	0.3
1934	Bos-A	97	253	65	66	13	1	1	22	82	22	.261	.445	.332	96	7	4	46	3	2	-0	0	21	0.4
1935	Bos-A	60	122	19	28	3	1	1	14	28	14	.230	.377	.295	71	-3	-4	16	0	2	-1	-5	21/S	-0.9
Total	12	1338	4494	966	1216	236	35	41	379	1153	452	.271	.423	.366	102	109	77	789	43	50	-17	-56	*2/1S	4.1

■ MIKE BISHOP
Bishop, Michael   b: 11/5/58, Santa Maria, Cal.   BR/TR, 6'2", 188 lbs.   Deb: 4/16/83

YEAR	TM/L	G	AB	R	H	2B	3B	HR	RBI	BB	SO	AVG	OBP	SLG	PRO+	BR	/A	RC	SB	CS	SBR	FR	POS	TPR
1983	NY-N	3	8	2	1	1	0	0	0	3	4	.125	.364	.250	74	-0	-0	1	0	0	0	-0	/C	0.0

■ RIVINGTON BISLAND
Bisland, Rivington Martin   b: 2/17/1890, New York, N.Y.   d: 1/11/73, Salzburg, Austria   BR/TR, 5'9", 155 lbs.   Deb: 9/13/12

YEAR	TM/L	G	AB	R	H	2B	3B	HR	RBI	BB	SO	AVG	OBP	SLG	PRO+	BR	/A	RC	SB	CS	SBR	FR	POS	TPR
1912	Pit-N	1	1	0	0	0	0	0	0	0	0	.000	.000	.000	-99	-0	-0	0				0	H	0.0
1913	StL-A	12	44	3	6	0	0	0	3	2	5	.136	.191	.136	-4	-6	-6	1	0			-5	S	-1.0
1914	Cle-A	18	57	9	6	1	0	0	2	6	2	.105	.190	.123	-5	-7	-8	1	2	5	-2	0	S/3	-0.9
Total	3	31	102	12	12	1	0	0	5	8	7	.118	.189	.127	-6	-13	-13	2	2	5		-5	/S3	-1.9

■ DEL BISSONETTE
Bissonette, Adelphia Louis   b: 9/6/1899, Winthrop, Me.   d: 6/9/72, Augusta, Maine   BL/TL, 5'11", 180 lbs.   Deb: 4/11/28   MC

YEAR	TM/L	G	AB	R	H	2B	3B	HR	RBI	BB	SO	AVG	OBP	SLG	PRO+	BR	/A	RC	SB	CS	SBR	FR	POS	TPR
1928	Bro-N	155	587	90	188	30	13	25	106	70	75	.320	.396	.543	145	36	38	125	5			-3	*1	1.7
1929	Bro-N	116	431	68	121	28	10	12	75	46	58	.281	.351	.476	105	1	2	71	2			-9	*1	-1.1
1930	Bro-N	146	572	102	192	33	13	16	113	56	66	.336	.396	.523	121	18	19	115	4			-9	*1	0.4
1931	Bro-N	152	587	90	170	19	14	12	87	59	53	.290	.354	.431	111	8	9	93	4			-7	*1	-0.9
1933	Bro-N	35	114	9	28	7	0	1	10	2	17	.246	.259	.333	71	-5	-4	9	2			0	1	-0.4
Total	5	604	2291	359	699	117	50	66	391	233	269	.305	.371	.486	120	59	63	412	17			-28	1	-0.3

■ RED BITTMAN
Bittman, Henry Peter   b: 7/22/1862, Cincinnati, Ohio   d: 11/8/29, Cincinnati, Ohio   Deb: 10/10/1889

YEAR	TM/L	G	AB	R	H	2B	3B	HR	RBI	BB	SO	AVG	OBP	SLG	PRO+	BR	/A	RC	SB	CS	SBR	FR	POS	TPR
1889	KC-a	4	14	2	4	0	0	0	2	1	1	.286	.333	.286	75	-0	-0	2	1			1	/2	0.0

■ GEORGE BJORKMAN
Bjorkman, George Anton   b: 8/26/56, Ontario, Cal.   BR/TR, 6'2", 190 lbs.   Deb: 7/10/83

YEAR	TM/L	G	AB	R	H	2B	3B	HR	RBI	BB	SO	AVG	OBP	SLG	PRO+	BR	/A	RC	SB	CS	SBR	FR	POS	TPR
1983	Hou-N	29	75	8	17	4	0	2	14	16	29	.227	.370	.360	110	1	2	11	0	0	0	-2	C	0.0

■ JOHN BLACK
Black, John Falcnor "Jack (b: John Falcnor Haddow)   b: 2/23/1890, Covington, Ky.   d: 3/20/62, Rutherford, N.J.   BR/TR, 6'1", 185 lbs.   Deb: 6/20/11

YEAR	TM/L	G	AB	R	H	2B	3B	HR	RBI	BB	SO	AVG	OBP	SLG	PRO+	BR	/A	RC	SB	CS	SBR	FR	POS	TPR
1911	StL-A	54	186	13	28	4	0	0	7	10		.151	.202	.172	5	-24	-23	7	4			0	1	-2.1

■ BILL BLACK
Black, John William "Jigger"   b: 8/12/1899, Philadelphia, Pa.   d: 1/14/68, Philadelphia, Pa.   BL/TR, 5'11", 168 lbs.   Deb: 5/04/24

YEAR	TM/L	G	AB	R	H	2B	3B	HR	RBI	BB	SO	AVG	OBP	SLG	PRO+	BR	/A	RC	SB	CS	SBR	FR	POS	TPR
1924	Chi-N	6	5	0	1	0	0	0	0	0	0	.200	.200	.200	3	-1	-1	0	0			0	/2	0.0

■ BOB BLACK
Black, Robert Benjamin   b: 12/10/1862, Cincinnati, Ohio   d: 3/21/33, Sioux City, Iowa   Deb: 8/17/1884

YEAR	TM/L	G	AB	R	H	2B	3B	HR	RBI	BB	SO	AVG	OBP	SLG	PRO+	BR	/A	RC	SB	CS	SBR	FR	POS	TPR
1884	KC-U	38	146	25	36	14	2	1				.247	.295	.390	149	5	8	17	0			-1	OP/2S	0.6

■ ETHAN BLACKABY
Blackaby, Ethan Allen   b: 7/24/40, Cincinnati, O.   BL/TL, 5'11", 190 lbs.   Deb: 9/06/62

YEAR	TM/L	G	AB	R	H	2B	3B	HR	RBI	BB	SO	AVG	OBP	SLG	PRO+	BR	/A	RC	SB	CS	SBR	FR	POS	TPR
1962	Mil-N	6	13	0	2	1	0	0	0	1	8	.154	.214	.231	20	-1	-1	1	0	0	0	-1	/O	-0.1
1964	Mil-N	9	12	0	1	0	0	0	1	1	2	.083	.154	.083	-31	-2	-2	0	0	0	0	-1	/O	-0.2
Total	2	15	25	0	3	1	0	0	1	2	10	.120	.185	.160	-4	-4	-4	1	0	0	0	-1	/O	-0.3

■ EARL BLACKBURN
Blackburn, Earl Stuart   b: 11/1/1892, Leesville, Ohio   d: 8/3/66, Mansfield, Ohio   BR/TR, 5'11", 180 lbs.   Deb: 9/17/12

YEAR	TM/L	G	AB	R	H	2B	3B	HR	RBI	BB	SO	AVG	OBP	SLG	PRO+	BR	/A	RC	SB	CS	SBR	FR	POS	TPR
1912	Pit-N	1	0	0	0	0	0	0	0	0	0	—	—	—	—	0	0	0	0			0	/C	0.0
	Cin-N	1	0	0	0	0	0	0	0	1	0	—	1.000	—	191	0	0	0	0			0	/C	0.1
	Yr	2	0	0	0	0	0	0	0	1	0	—	1.000	—	190	0	0	0	0			0		0.1
1913	Cin-N	17	27	1	7	0	0	0	3	2	5	.259	.310	.259	64	-1	-1	3	2			-1	C	0.0
1915	Bos-N	3	6	0	1	0	0	0	0	2	1	.167	.375	.167	70	-0	-0	0	0			-0	/C	0.0
1916	Bos-N	47	110	12	30	4	4	0	7	9	21	.273	.328	.382	123	2	3	15	2			-1	C	0.4
1917	Chi-N	2	2	0	0	0	0	0	0	0	0	.000	.000	.000	-93	-0	-0	0	0			0	H	0.0
Total	5	71	145	13	38	4	4	0	10	14	27	.262	.327	.345	107	1	1	18	4			-2	/C	0.5

■ LENA BLACKBURNE
Blackburne, Russell Aubrey "Slats"   b: 10/23/1886, Clifton Heights, Pa.   d: 2/29/68, Riverside, N.J.   BR/TR, 5'11", 160 lbs.   Deb: 4/14/10   MC

YEAR	TM/L	G	AB	R	H	2B	3B	HR	RBI	BB	SO	AVG	OBP	SLG	PRO+	BR	/A	RC	SB	CS	SBR	FR	POS	TPR
1910	Chi-A	75	242	16	42	3	1	0	10	19		.174	.245	.194	39	-17	-16	13	4			19	S	0.5
1912	Chi-A	5	1	0	0	0	0	0	0	1		.000	.500	.000	48	0	0	1	1			1	/S3	0.1
1914	Chi-A	144	474	52	105	10	5	1	35	66	58	.222	.324	.270	80	-10	-9	49	25	15	-1	1	*2	-1.0
1915	Chi-A	96	283	33	61	5	1	0	25	35	34	.216	.304	.240	51	-12	-13	25	13	11	-3	-10	3/S	-2.2
1918	Cin-N	125	435	34	99	8	10	1	45	25	30	.228	.271	.299	75	-14	-13	36	6			10	*S	0.0
1919	Bos-N	31	80	5	21	3	1	0	4	6	7	.262	.322	.325	99	-0	-0	9	3			3	3/12S	0.4
	Phi-N	72	291	32	58	10	5	2	19	10	22	.199	.228	.289	51	-17	-19	20	2			6	3/1	-1.3
	Yr	103	371	37	79	13	6	2	23	16	29	.213	.249	.296	61	-17	-18	30	5			10		-0.9
1927	Chi-A	1	1	1	1	0	0	0	1	0	0	1.000	1.000	1.000	431	0	0	1	0	0	0	0	H	0.0
1929	Chi-A	1	0	0	0	0	0	0	0	0	0	—	—	—	—	0	0	0	0	0	0	0	/PM	0.0
Total	8	550	1807	173	387	39	23	4	139	162	151	.214	.284	.268	67	-69	-70	154	54	26		30	S32/1P	-3.5

■ GEORGE BLACKERBY
Blackerby, George Franklin   b: 11/10/03, Gluther, Okla.   BR/TR, 6'1", 176 lbs.   Deb: 8/10/28

YEAR	TM/L	G	AB	R	H	2B	3B	HR	RBI	BB	SO	AVG	OBP	SLG	PRO+	BR	/A	RC	SB	CS	SBR	FR	POS	TPR
1928	Chi-A	30	83	8	21	0	0	0	12	4	10	.253	.287	.253	44	-7	-7	6	2	1	0	-1	O	-0.8

■ FRED BLACKWELL
Blackwell, Fredrick William "   b: 9/7/1891, Bowling Green, Ky.   d: 12/8/75, Morgantown, Ky.   BL/TR, 5'1.5", 160 lbs.   Deb: 9/25/17

YEAR	TM/L	G	AB	R	H	2B	3B	HR	RBI	BB	SO	AVG	OBP	SLG	PRO+	BR	/A	RC	SB	CS	SBR	FR	POS	TPR
1917	Pit-N	3	10	1	2	0	0	0	2	0	3	.200	.200	.200	22	-1	-1	0	0			0	/C	0.0
1918	Pit-N	8	13	1	2	0	0	0	4	3	4	.154	.313	.154	42	-1	-1	1	0			0	/C	0.0
1919	Pit-N	24	65	3	14	3	0	0	4	3	9	.215	.261	.262	55	-3	-4	5	0			-1	C	-0.2
Total	3	35	88	5	18	3	0	0	10	6	16	.205	.263	.239	50	-5	-5	6	0			-1	/C	-0.2

■ TIM BLACKWELL
Blackwell, Timothy P   b: 8/19/52, San Diego, Cal.   BB/TR, 5'11", 170 lbs.   Deb: 7/03/74

YEAR	TM/L	G	AB	R	H	2B	3B	HR	RBI	BB	SO	AVG	OBP	SLG	PRO+	BR	/A	RC	SB	CS	SBR	FR	POS	TPR
1974	Bos-A	44	122	9	30	1	1	0	8	10	21	.246	.308	.270	63	-5	-6	10	1	1	-0	2	C	-0.2
1975	Bos-A	59	132	15	26	3	2	0	6	19	13	.197	.303	.250	53	-7	-8	11	0	0	0	7	C/D	0.1
1976	Phi-N	4	8	0	2	0	0	0	1	0	1	.250	.250	.250	41	-1	-1	1	0	0	0	1	/C	0.0
1977	Phi-N	1	0	1	0	0	0	0	0	0	0	—	—	—	—	0	0	0	0	0	0	0	/C	0.0
	Mon-N	16	22	3	2	1	0	0	0	2	7	.091	.167	.136	-18	-4	-4	0	0	0	0	-0	C	-0.3
	Yr	17	22	4	2	1	0	0	0	2	7	.091	.167	.136	-18	-4	-4	0	0	0	0	-0		-0.3
1978	Chi-N	49	103	8	23	3	0	0	7	23	17	.223	.370	.252	68	-2	-4	11	0	0	0	7	C	0.5
1979	Chi-N	63	122	8	20	3	1	0	12	32	25	.164	.342	.205	48	-7	-8	11	0	0	0	1	C	-0.5
1980	Chi-N	103	320	24	87	16	4	5	30	41	62	.272	.355	.394	101	4	2	46	0	1	-1	17	*C	2.1
1981	Chi-N	58	158	21	37	10	2	1	11	23	23	.234	.331	.342	87	-1	-2	19	2	1	0	2	C	0.0
1982	Mon-N	23	42	2	8	2	1	0	3	3	11	.190	.244	.286	47	-3	-3	3	0	0	0	2	C	0.0
1983	Mon-N	6	15	0	3	1	0	0	2	1	3	.200	.250	.267	43	-1	-1	1	0	0	0	0	/C	0.0
Total	10	426	1044	91	238	40	11	6	80	154	183	.228	.329	.305	73	-26	-35	113	3	3	-1	39	C/D	1.7

■ RAY BLADES
Blades, Francis Raymond   b: 8/6/1896, Mt. Vernon, Ill.   d: 5/18/79, Lincoln, Ill.   BR/TR, 5'7.5", 163 lbs.   Deb: 8/19/22   MC

YEAR	TM/L	G	AB	R	H	2B	3B	HR	RBI	BB	SO	AVG	OBP	SLG	PRO+	BR	/A	RC	SB	CS	SBR	FR	POS	TPR
1922	StL-N	37	130	27	39	2	4	3	21	25	21	.300	.428	.446	132	6	7	26	3	3	-1	-3	O/S3	0.3
1923	StL-N	98	317	48	78	21	5	5	44	37	46	.246	.342	.391	95	-3	-2	45	4	2	0	4	O/3	0.0
1924	StL-N	131	456	86	142	21	13	11	68	35	38	.311	.373	.487	131	18	19	81	7	9	-3	-3	*O/23	1.1

YEAR	TM/L	G	AB	R	H	2B	3B	HR	RBI	BB	SO	AVG	OBP	SLG	PRO+	BR	/A	RC	SB	CS	SBR	FR	POS	TPR
1925	StL-N	122	462	112	158	37	8	12	57	59	47	.342	.423	.535	140	31	30	105	6	8	-3	4	*O/3	2.6
1926	StL-N	107	416	81	127	17	12	8	43	62	57	.305	.409	.462	129	22	20	80	6			-2	*O	1.4
1927	StL-N	61	180	33	57	8	5	2	29	28	22	.317	.414	.450	127	9	8	34	3			-15	O	-0.7
1928	*StL-N	51	85	9	20	7	1	1	19	20	26	.235	.393	.376	100	1	1	14	0			-3	O	-0.1
1930	*StL-N	45	101	26	40	6	2	4	25	21	15	.396	.504	.614	163	13	12	32	1			0	O	0.9
1931	*StL-N	35	67	10	19	4	0	1	5	10	7	.284	.392	.388	106	2	1	11	1			-3	O	-0.2
1932	StL-N	80	201	35	46	10	1	3	29	34	31	.229	.340	.333	80	-4	-5	25	2			-3	O/3	-1.1
Total	10	767	2415	467	726	133	51	50	340	331	310	.301	.395	.460	123	95	92	453	33	22		-22	O/32S	4.2

■ RICK BLADT   Bladt, Richard Alan b: 12/9/46, Santa Cruz, Cal. BR/TR, 6'1", 160 lbs. Deb: 6/15/69

YEAR	TM/L	G	AB	R	H	2B	3B	HR	RBI	BB	SO	AVG	OBP	SLG	PRO+	BR	/A	RC	SB	CS	SBR	FR	POS	TPR
1969	Chi-N	10	13	1	2	0	0	0	1	0	5	.154	.154	.154	-12	-2	-2	0	0	0	0	2	/O	0.0
1975	NY-A	52	117	13	26	3	1	1	11	11	8	.222	.295	.291	68	-5	-5	11	6	2	1	7	O	0.2
Total	2	62	130	14	28	3	1	1	12	11	13	.215	.282	.277	59	-7	-7	11	6	2	1	9	/O	0.2

■ RAE BLAEMIRE   Blaemire, Rae Bertrum b: 2/8/11, Gary, Ind. d: 12/23/75, Champaign, Ill. BR/TR, 6', 178 lbs. Deb: 9/13/41

YEAR	TM/L	G	AB	R	H	2B	3B	HR	RBI	BB	SO	AVG	OBP	SLG	PRO+	BR	/A	RC	SB	CS	SBR	FR	POS	TPR
1941	NY-N	2	5	0	2	0	0	0	0	0	0	.400	.400	.400	123	0	0	1	0			-0	/C	0.0

■ FOOTSIE BLAIR   Blair, Clarence Vick b: 7/13/1900, Interprise, Okla. d: 7/1/82, Texarkana, Tex. BL/TR, 6'1", 180 lbs. Deb: 4/28/29

YEAR	TM/L	G	AB	R	H	2B	3B	HR	RBI	BB	SO	AVG	OBP	SLG	PRO+	BR	/A	RC	SB	CS	SBR	FR	POS	TPR
1929	*Chi-N	26	72	10	23	5	0	1	8	3	4	.319	.347	.431	91	-1	-1	10	1			1	/312	0.0
1930	Chi-N	134	578	97	158	24	12	6	59	20	58	.273	.308	.388	66	-33	-33	66	9			8	*23	-0.9
1931	Chi-N	86	240	31	62	19	4	3	29	14	26	.258	.302	.408	88	-4	-5	30	1			-6	21/3	-0.9
Total	3	246	890	138	243	48	16	10	96	37	88	.273	.308	.397	73	-38	-39	106	11			4	2/13	-1.8

■ BUDDY BLAIR   Blair, Louis Nathan b: 9/10/10, Columbia, Miss. BL/TR, 6', 186 lbs. Deb: 4/14/42

YEAR	TM/L	G	AB	R	H	2B	3B	HR	RBI	BB	SO	AVG	OBP	SLG	PRO+	BR	/A	RC	SB	CS	SBR	FR	POS	TPR
1942	Phi-A	137	484	48	135	26	8	5	66	30	30	.279	.325	.397	103	-0	0	59	1	6	-3	-7	*3	-0.8

■ PAUL BLAIR   Blair, Paul L b: 2/1/44, Cushing, Okla. BR/TR, 6', 168 lbs. Deb: 9/09/64

YEAR	TM/L	G	AB	R	H	2B	3B	HR	RBI	BB	SO	AVG	OBP	SLG	PRO+	BR	/A	RC	SB	CS	SBR	FR	POS	TPR
1964	Bal-A	8	1	0	0	0	0	0	0	0	1	.000	.000	.000	-99	-0	-0	0	0	1	-1	1	/O	0.0
1965	Bal-A	119	364	49	85	19	2	5	25	32	52	.234	.303	.338	80	-9	-10	38	8	5	-1	-2	*O	-1.7
1966	*Bal-A	133	303	35	84	20	2	6	33	15	36	.277	.311	.416	109	2	2	37	5	6	-2	-14	*O	-2.0
1967	Bal-A	151	552	72	162	27	12	11	64	50	68	.293	.357	.446	137	24	25	87	8	6	-1	16	*O	3.8
1968	Bal-A	141	421	48	89	22	1	7	38	37	60	.211	.278	.318	80	-10	-10	39	4	2	-0	4	*O/3	-2.1
1969	*Bal-A	150	625	102	178	32	5	26	76	40	72	.285	.330	.477	122	16	16	97	20	6	2	17	*O	3.2
1970	*Bal-A	133	480	79	128	24	2	18	65	56	93	.267	.347	.438	114	10	9	74	24	11	1	16	*O/3	2.1
1971	*Bal-A	141	516	75	135	24	8	10	44	32	94	.262	.306	.397	99	-3	-3	60	14	11	-2	0	*O	-0.9
1972	Bal-A	142	477	47	111	20	8	8	49	25	78	.233	.271	.358	84	-10	-11	41	7	8	-3	4	*O	-1.4
1973	*Bal-A	146	500	73	140	25	3	10	64	43	72	.280	.337	.402	108	4	5	67	18	8	1	5	*O/D	0.6
1974	*Bal-A	151	552	77	144	27	4	17	62	43	59	.261	.317	.417	113	5	7	73	27	9	3	5	*O	1.1
1975	Bal-A	140	440	51	96	13	4	5	31	25	82	.218	.260	.300	62	-25	-22	34	17	11	-2	-6	*O/1D	-3.3
1976	Bal-A	145	375	29	74	16	0	3	16	22	49	.197	.246	.264	52	-24	-21	23	15	6	1	-13	*O/D	-3.9
1977	*NY-A	83	164	20	43	4	3	4	25	9	16	.262	.309	.396	91	-2	-2	18	3	2	-0	4	O/D	-0.9
1978	*NY-A	75	125	10	22	5	0	2	13	9	17	.176	.231	.264	40	-10	-10	7	1	1	-0	2	O/2S3	-0.9
1979	NY-A	2	5	0	1	0	0	0	0	0	1	.200	.200	.200	8	-1	-1	0	0	0	0	1	/O	0.0
	Cin-N	75	140	7	21	4	1	2	15	11	27	.150	.212	.236	22	-15	-15	7	0	0	0	8	O	-0.9
1980	NY-A	12	2	2	0	0	0	0	0	0	0	.000	.000	.000	-99	-1	-1	0	0	0	0	1	O	0.1
Total	17	1947	6042	776	1513	282	55	134	620	449	877	.250	.305	.382	96	-49	-41	702	171	93	-5	40	*O/23SD1	-6.2

■ WALTER BLAIR   Blair, Walter Allen "Heavy" b: 10/13/1883, Landrus, Pa. d: 8/20/48, Lewisburg, Pa. BR/TR, 6', 185 lbs. Deb: 9/17/07 M

YEAR	TM/L	G	AB	R	H	2B	3B	HR	RBI	BB	SO	AVG	OBP	SLG	PRO+	BR	/A	RC	SB	CS	SBR	FR	POS	TPR
1907	NY-A	7	22	1	4	0	0	0	1	2		.182	.250	.182	37	-1	-2	1	0			2	/C	0.1
1908	NY-A	76	211	9	40	5	1	1	13	11		.190	.230	.237	53	-11	-11	12	4			-13	C/O1	-2.1
1909	NY-A	42	110	5	23	2	2	0	11	7		.209	.269	.264	68	-4	-4	8	2			-8	C	-0.9
1910	NY-A	6	22	2	5	0	1	0	2	0		.227	.227	.318	67	-1	-1	2	0			-2	/C	-0.2
1911	NY-A	85	222	18	43	9	2	0	26	16		.194	.257	.252	40	-17	-19	16	2			4	C/1	-0.5
1914	Buf-F	128	378	22	92	11	2	0	33	32	64	.243	.304	.283	67	-15	-16	36	6			4	*C	-0.5
1915	Buf-F	98	290	23	65	15	3	2	20	18	32	.224	.274	.317	73	-10	-10	27	4			4	CM	-0.3
Total	7	442	1255	80	272	42	11	3	106	86	96	.217	.271	.275	61	-59	-63	102	18			-10	C/O1	-4.4

■ HARRY BLAKE   Blake, Harry Cooper b: 6/16/1874, Portsmouth, Ohio d: 10/14/19, Chicago, Ill. 5'7", 165 lbs. Deb: 7/07/1894

YEAR	TM/L	G	AB	R	H	2B	3B	HR	RBI	BB	SO	AVG	OBP	SLG	PRO+	BR	/A	RC	SB	CS	SBR	FR	POS	TPR
1894	Cle-N	73	296	51	78	15	4	1	51	30	22	.264	.335	.351	65	-16	-18	36	1			2	O	-1.5
1895	*Cle-N	84	315	50	87	10	1	3	45	30	33	.276	.341	.343	74	-9	-13	42	11			-2	O	-1.7
1896	*Cle-N	104	383	66	92	12	5	1	43	46	30	.240	.322	.305	64	-17	-21	42	10			2	*O/S	-2.1
1897	Cle-N	32	117	17	30	3	1	1	15	12		.256	.331	.325	72	-4	-5	15	5			4	O	-0.2
1898	Cle-N	136	474	65	116	18	7	0	58	69		.245	.341	.312	91	-4	-3	56	12			8	*O/1	-0.4
1899	StL-N	97	292	50	70	9	4	2	41	43		.240	.341	.318	82	-5	-6	38	16			-2	O/2S1C	-1.1
Total	6	526	1877	299	473	67	22	8	253	230	85	.252	.336	.324	75	-55	-65	228	55			13	O/21SC	-6.8

■ LINC BLAKELY   Blakely, Lincoln Howard b: 2/12/12, Oakland, Cal. d: 9/28/76, Oakland, Cal. BR/TR, 6', 180 lbs. Deb: 4/29/34

YEAR	TM/L	G	AB	R	H	2B	3B	HR	RBI	BB	SO	AVG	OBP	SLG	PRO+	BR	/A	RC	SB	CS	SBR	FR	POS	TPR
1934	Cin-N	34	102	11	23	1	1	0	10	5	14	.225	.269	.255	42	-8	-8	6	1			5	O	-0.4

■ BOB BLAKISTON   Blakiston, Robert J. (b: Robert J. Blackstone) b: 10/2/1855, San Francisco, Cal. d: 12/25/18, San Francisco, Cal. 5'8.5", 180 lbs. Deb: 5/02/1882

YEAR	TM/L	G	AB	R	H	2B	3B	HR	RBI	BB	SO	AVG	OBP	SLG	PRO+	BR	/A	RC	SB	CS	SBR	FR	POS	TPR
1882	Phi-a	72	281	40	64	4	1	0			9	.228	.252	.249	62	-9	-13	18				0	O3/2	-1.3
1883	Phi-a	44	167	26	41	3	3	0			9	.246	.284	.299	81	-2	-4	15				-4	O/13	-0.6
1884	Phi-a	32	128	21	33	6	0	0			11	.258	.336	.305	106	2	1	13				2	O/312S	0.2
	Ind-a	6	18	0	4	1	0	0			1	.222	.263	.278	82	-0	-1	1				-1	/1O	0.0
	Yr	38	146	21	37	7	0	0			12	.253	.327	.301	104	2	1	15				1		0.2
Total	3	154	594	87	142	14	4	0			30	.239	.280	.276	78	-9	-17	47				-2	O/312S	-1.7

■ JOHNNY BLANCHARD   Blanchard, John Edwin b: 2/26/33, Minneapolis, Minn. BL/TR, 6'1", 193 lbs. Deb: 9/25/55

YEAR	TM/L	G	AB	R	H	2B	3B	HR	RBI	BB	SO	AVG	OBP	SLG	PRO+	BR	/A	RC	SB	CS	SBR	FR	POS	TPR
1955	NY-A	1	3	0	0	0	0	0	0	0	0	.000	.250	.000	-29	-1	-1	0	0	0	0	0	/C	0.0
1959	NY-A	49	59	6	10	1	0	2	4	7	12	.169	.258	.288	51	-4	-4	4	0	0	0	-1	C/O1	-0.3
1960	*NY-A	53	99	8	24	3	1	4	14	6	17	.242	.292	.414	94	-2	-1	12	0	0	0	10	C	1.0
1961	*NY-A	93	243	38	74	10	1	21	54	27	28	.305	.383	.613	170	20	22	56	1	0	0	-2	CO	1.9
1962	*NY-A	93	246	33	57	7	0	13	39	28	32	.232	.314	.419	98	-2	-1	33	0	0	0	-8	OC/1	-1.0
1963	*NY-A	76	218	22	49	4	0	16	45	26	30	.225	.307	.463	114	3	3	31	0	0	0	-9	CO	-0.8
1964	*NY-A	77	161	18	41	8	0	7	28	24	24	.255	.351	.435	115	4	4	24	1	0	0	-3	CO/1	0.1
1965	NY-A	12	34	1	5	1	0	1	3	7	3	.147	.293	.265	60	-2	-2	3	0	0	0	-1	C	-0.1
	KC-A	52	120	10	24	2	0	2	11	8	16	.200	.256	.267	49	-8	-8	8	0	0	0	-9	OC	-1.8
	Yr	64	154	11	29	3	0	3	14	15	19	.188	.265	.266	52	-10	-10	11	0	0	0	-10		-1.9
	Mil-N	10	10	1	1	0	0	1	2	2	1	.100	.250	.400	79	-0	-0	1	0	0	0	0	/O	0.0
Total	8	516	1193	137	285	36	2	67	200	136	163	.239	.320	.441	109	8	12	173	2	0	1	-23	OC/1	-1.0

■ DAMASO BLANCO   Blanco, Damaso (Caripe) b: 12/11/41, Curiepe, Venez. BR/TR, 5'10", 165 lbs. Deb: 5/26/72

YEAR	TM/L	G	AB	R	H	2B	3B	HR	RBI	BB	SO	AVG	OBP	SLG	PRO+	BR	/A	RC	SB	CS	SBR	FR	POS	TPR
1972	SF-N	39	20	5	7	1	0	0	2	4	3	.350	.458	.400	144	2	1	4	2	1	0	6	3/S2	0.9
1973	SF-N	28	12	4	0	0	0	0	0	1	2	.000	.077	.000	-74	-3	-3	0	0	0	0	2	/3S2	0.0

YEAR	TM/L	G	AB	R	H	2B	3B	HR	RBI	BB	SO	AVG	OBP	SLG	PRO+	BR	/A	RC	SB	CS	SBR	FR	POS	TPR
1974	SF-N	5	1	0	0	0	0	0	0	0	1	.000	.000	.000	-96	-0	-0	0	1	0	0	0	H	0.0
Total	3	72	33	9	7	1	0	0	2	5	6	.212	.316	.242	58	-2	-2	4	3	1	0	8	/3S2	0.9

■ OSSIE BLANCO
Blanco, Oswaldo Carlos (Diaz) b: 9/8/45, Caracas, Venez. BR/TR, 6', 185 lbs. Deb: 5/26/70

YEAR	TM/L	G	AB	R	H	2B	3B	HR	RBI	BB	SO	AVG	OBP	SLG	PRO+	BR	/A	RC	SB	CS	SBR	FR	POS	TPR
1970	Chi-A	34	66	4	13	0	0	0	8	3	14	.197	.232	.197	19	-7	-7	3	0	1	-1	-1	1/O	-0.9
1974	Cle-A	18	36	1	7	0	0	0	2	7	4	.194	.326	.194	53	-2	-2	2	0	3	-2	-1	1/D	-0.5
Total	2	52	102	5	20	0	0	0	10	10	18	.196	.268	.196	31	-9	-9	5	0	4	-2	-1	/1DO	-1.4

■ COONIE BLANK
Blank, Frank Ignatz b: 10/18/1892, St.Louis, Mo. d: 12/8/61, St.Louis, Mo. BR/TR, 5'11", 165 lbs. Deb: 8/15/09

YEAR	TM/L	G	AB	R	H	2B	3B	HR	RBI	BB	SO	AVG	OBP	SLG	PRO+	BR	/A	RC	SB	CS	SBR	FR	POS	TPR
1909	StL-N	1	2	0	0	0	0	0	0	0	0	.000	.000	.000	-99	-0	-0	0	0			-0	/C	0.0

■ CLIFF BLANKENSHIP
Blankenship, Clifford Douglas b: 4/10/1880, Columbus, Ga. d: 4/26/56, Oakland, Cal. BR/TR, 5'10.5", 165 lbs. Deb: 4/17/05

YEAR	TM/L	G	AB	R	H	2B	3B	HR	RBI	BB	SO	AVG	OBP	SLG	PRO+	BR	/A	RC	SB	CS	SBR	FR	POS	TPR
1905	Cin-N	19	56	8	11	1	1	0	7	4		.196	.250	.250	46	-3	-4	4	1			-2	1	-0.7
1907	Was-A	37	102	4	23	2	0	0	6	3		.225	.248	.245	64	-5	-4	7	3			0	C/1	-0.1
1909	Was-A	39	60	4	15	1	0	0	9	0		.250	.250	.267	66	-3	-2	4	2			-9	C/O	-1.0
Total	3	95	218	16	49	4	1	0	22	7		.225	.249	.252	59	-11	-10	16	6			-11	/C1O	-1.8

■ LANCE BLANKENSHIP
Blankenship, Lance Robert b: 12/6/63, Portland, Ore. BR/TR, 6', 190 lbs. Deb: 9/04/88

YEAR	TM/L	G	AB	R	H	2B	3B	HR	RBI	BB	SO	AVG	OBP	SLG	PRO+	BR	/A	RC	SB	CS	SBR	FR	POS	TPR
1988	Oak-A	10	3	1	0	0	0	0	0	0	1	.000	.000	.000	-99	-1	-1	0	0	1	-1	0	/2D	0.0
1989	*Oak-A	58	125	22	29	5	1	1	4	8	31	.232	.278	.312	68	-6	-5	12	5	1	1	7	O2D	0.3
1990	*Oak-A	86	136	18	26	3	0	0	10	20	23	.191	.295	.213	46	-10	-9	9	3	1	0	5	302/1D	-0.2
Total	3	154	264	41	55	8	1	1	14	28	55	.208	.284	.258	55	-16	-15	21	8	3	1	12	/O23D1	0.1

■ LARVELL BLANKS
Blanks, Larvell b: 1/28/50, Del Rio, Tex. BR/TR, 5'8", 167 lbs. Deb: 7/19/72

YEAR	TM/L	G	AB	R	H	2B	3B	HR	RBI	BB	SO	AVG	OBP	SLG	PRO+	BR	/A	RC	SB	CS	SBR	FR	POS	TPR
1972	Atl-N	33	85	10	28	5	0	1	7	7	12	.329	.380	.424	117	3	2	13	0	0	0	6	2/S3	1.1
1973	Atl-N	17	18	1	4	0	0	0	0	1	3	.222	.263	.222	33	-2	-2	1	0	0	0	-2	/32S	-0.3
1974	Atl-N	3	8	0	2	0	0	0	1	0	0	.250	.250	.250	38	-1	-1	1	0	0	0	-0	/S	0.0
1975	Atl-N	141	471	49	110	13	3	3	38	38	43	.234	.294	.293	61	-23	-25	40	4	3	-1	-12	*S2	-2.3
1976	Cle-A	104	328	45	92	8	7	5	41	30	31	.280	.341	.393	116	6	4	41	1	2	-1	-20	S2/3D	-0.8
1977	Cle-A	105	322	43	92	10	4	6	38	19	37	.286	.327	.398	100	-2	-1	42	3	0	1	-25	S32/D	-1.6
1978	Cle-A	70	193	19	49	10	0	2	20	10	16	.254	.291	.337	77	-6	-6	18	0	0	0	-9	S2/3D	-1.1
1979	Tex-A	68	120	13	24	5	0	1	15	11	9	.200	.267	.267	45	-9	-9	9	0	0	0	-9	S2	-1.1
1980	Atl-N	88	221	23	45	6	0	2	12	16	27	.204	.257	.258	43	-16	-17	14	1	2	-1	7	S3/2	-0.5
Total	9	629	1766	203	446	57	14	20	172	132	178	.253	.306	.335	78	-51	-52	179	9	7	-2	-65	S2/3D	-6.6

■ DON BLASINGAME
Blasingame, Don Lee b: 3/16/32, Corinth, Miss. BL/TR, 5'10", 160 lbs. Deb: 9/20/55

YEAR	TM/L	G	AB	R	H	2B	3B	HR	RBI	BB	SO	AVG	OBP	SLG	PRO+	BR	/A	RC	SB	CS	SBR	FR	POS	TPR
1955	StL-N	5	16	4	6	1	0	0	0	6	0	.375	.545	.438	165	2	2	4	1	1	-0	2	/2S	0.4
1956	StL-N	150	587	94	153	22	7	0	27	72	52	.261	.344	.322	81	-14	-14	70	8	8	-2	22	2S/3	1.7
1957	StL-N	154	650	108	176	25	7	8	58	71	49	.271	.343	.368	89	-7	-8	87	21	9	1	26	*2	3.1
1958	StL-N	143	547	71	150	19	10	2	36	57	47	.274	.344	.356	83	-10	-13	69	20	5	3	-1	*2	-0.2
1959	StL-N	150	615	90	178	26	7	1	24	67	42	.289	.361	.359	87	-4	-9	83	15	15	-5	**21**	*2	1.8
1960	SF-N	136	523	72	123	12	8	2	31	49	53	.235	.303	.300	70	-24	-20	52	14	2	3	-13	*2	-1.9
1961	SF-N	3	1	1	0	0	0	0	0	2	1	.000	.667	.000	100	0	0	0	0	0	0	0	H	0.0
	*Cin-N	123	450	59	100	18	4	1	21	39	38	.222	.287	.287	52	-30	-31	38	4	3	-1	-19	*2	-3.6
	Yr	126	451	60	100	18	4	1	21	41	39	.222	.289	.286	53	-30	-30	39	4	3	-1	-19		-3.6
1962	Cin-N	141	494	77	139	9	7	2	35	63	44	.281	.365	.340	88	-4	-6	66	4	3	-1	-9	*2	-0.3
1963	Cin-N	18	31	4	5	2	0	0	0	7	5	.161	.316	.226	57	-1	-2	3	0	1	-1	0	2/3	0.0
	Was-A	69	254	29	65	10	2	2	12	24	18	.256	.320	.335	84	-5	-5	29	3	2	-0	1	2	0.0
1964	Was-A	143	506	56	135	17	2	1	34	40	44	.267	.321	.314	84	-15	-14	54	8	5	-1	-30	*2	-3.2
1965	Was-A	129	403	47	90	8	8	1	18	35	45	.223	.289	.290	66	-18	-17	36	5	4	-1	1	*2	-1.2
1966	Was-A	68	200	18	43	9	0	1	11	18	21	.215	.280	.275	61	-10	-10	17	2	1	0	-1	2/S	-0.6
	KC-A	12	19	1	3	0	0	0	1	2	3	.158	.238	.158	11	-2	-2	1	0	1	-1	-0	/2	-0.2
	Yr	80	219	19	46	9	0	1	12	20	24	.210	.276	.265	57	-12	-12	17	2	2	-1	-2		-0.8
Total	12	1444	5296	731	1366	178	62	21	308	552	462	.258	.330	.327	78	-142	-149	610	105	60	-4	-2	*2/S3	-4.2

■ JOHNNY BLATNIK
Blatnik, John Louis b: 3/10/21, Bridgeport, Ohio BR/TR, 6', 195 lbs. Deb: 4/21/48

YEAR	TM/L	G	AB	R	H	2B	3B	HR	RBI	BB	SO	AVG	OBP	SLG	PRO+	BR	/A	RC	SB	CS	SBR	FR	POS	TPR
1948	Phi-N	121	415	56	108	27	8	6	45	31	77	.260	.315	.407	96	-5	-4	51	3			-1	*O	-1.1
1949	Phi-N	6	8	3	1	0	0	0	0	4	1	.125	.417	.125	53	-0	-0	1	0			-0	/O	0.0
1950	Phi-N	4	4	0	1	0	0	0	0	2	3	.250	.500	.250	106	0	0	1	0			0	/O	0.0
	StL-N	7	20	0	3	0	0	0	1	3	2	.150	.261	.150	11	-3	-3	1	0			-1	/O	-0.3
	Yr	11	24	0	4	0	0	0	1	5	5	.167	.310	.167	29	-2	-2	1	0			-1		-0.3
Total	3	138	447	59	113	27	8	6	46	40	83	.253	.317	.389	91	-7	-6	54	3			-2	O	-1.4

■ BUDDY BLATTNER
Blattner, Robert Garnett b: 2/8/20, St.Louis, Mo. BR/TR, 6'0.5", 180 lbs. Deb: 4/18/42

YEAR	TM/L	G	AB	R	H	2B	3B	HR	RBI	BB	SO	AVG	OBP	SLG	PRO+	BR	/A	RC	SB	CS	SBR	FR	POS	TPR
1942	StL-N	19	23	3	1	0	0	0	1	3	6	.043	.185	.043	-29	-4	-4	0	0			-0	S/2	-0.2
1946	NY-N	126	420	63	107	18	6	11	49	56	52	.255	.351	.405	113	8	8	63	12			1	*2/1	1.2
1947	NY-N	55	153	28	40	9	2	0	13	21	19	.261	.351	.346	85	-3	-3	20	4			-3	23	-0.2
1948	NY-N	8	20	3	4	1	0	0	0	3	2	.200	.304	.250	51	-1	-1	2	2			2	/2	0.2
1949	Phi-N	64	97	15	24	6	0	5	21	19	17	.247	.371	.464	126	3	4	18	0			-10	23/S	-0.5
Total	5	272	713	112	176	34	8	16	84	102	96	.247	.347	.384	102	4	3	103	18			-10	2/3S1	0.5

■ JEFF BLAUSER
Blauser, Jeffrey Michael b: 11/8/65, Los Gatos, Cal. BR/TR, 6'", 170 lbs. Deb: 7/05/87

YEAR	TM/L	G	AB	R	H	2B	3B	HR	RBI	BB	SO	AVG	OBP	SLG	PRO+	BR	/A	RC	SB	CS	SBR	FR	POS	TPR
1987	Atl-N	51	165	11	40	6	3	2	15	18	34	.242	.328	.352	76	-4	-6	19	7	3	0	10	S	1.1
1988	Atl-N	18	67	7	16	3	1	2	7	2	11	.239	.271	.403	87	-1	-1	7	0	1	-1	3	/2S	0.1
1989	Atl-N	142	456	63	123	24	2	12	46	38	101	.270	.327	.410	107	5	4	62	5	2	0	-16	32S/O	-1.0
1990	Atl-N	115	386	46	104	24	3	8	39	35	70	.269	.338	.409	103	2	2	54	3	5	-2	-2	S2/3O	0.6
Total	4	326	1074	127	283	57	9	24	107	93	216	.264	.328	.400	99	2	-2	142	15	11	-2	-5	S/32O	0.8

■ MARV BLAYLOCK
Blaylock, Marvin Edward b: 9/30/29, Ft.Smith, Ark. BL/TL, 6'1.5", 175 lbs. Deb: 9/26/50

YEAR	TM/L	G	AB	R	H	2B	3B	HR	RBI	BB	SO	AVG	OBP	SLG	PRO+	BR	/A	RC	SB	CS	SBR	FR	POS	TPR
1950	NY-N	1	1	0	0	0	0	0	0	0	0	.000	.000	.000	-99	-0	-0	0	0			0	H	0.0
1955	Phi-N	113	259	30	54	7	7	3	24	31	43	.208	.296	.324	66	-13	-13	27	6	1	1	3	1/O	-1.3
1956	Phi-N	136	460	61	117	14	8	10	50	50	86	.254	.330	.385	93	-5	-4	60	5	1	1	-5	*1/O	-1.3
1957	Phi-N	37	26	5	4	0	0	2	4	3	8	.154	.313	.385	89	-0	-0	4	0	0	0	0	1/O	0.0
Total	4	287	746	96	175	21	15	15	78	84	137	.235	.317	.363	83	-19	-17	90	11	2		-1	1/O	-2.6

■ CURT BLEFARY
Blefary, Curtis Le Roy b: 7/5/43, Brooklyn, N.Y. BL/TR, 6'2", 195 lbs. Deb: 4/14/65

YEAR	TM/L	G	AB	R	H	2B	3B	HR	RBI	BB	SO	AVG	OBP	SLG	PRO+	BR	/A	RC	SB	CS	SBR	FR	POS	TPR
1965	Bal-A	144	462	72	120	23	4	22	70	88	73	.260	.382	.470	138	27	26	87	4	2	0	0	*O	2.2
1966	*Bal-A	131	419	73	107	14	3	23	64	71	56	.255	.373	.468	142	24	25	77	1	4	-2	-9	*O1	0.9
1967	Bal-A	155	554	69	134	19	5	22	81	73	94	.242	.339	.413	122	15	16	81	4	4	-1	11	*O1	2.0
1968	Bal-A	137	451	50	90	8	1	15	39	65	66	.200	.306	.322	90	-4	-4	49	6	3	0	-8	OC1	-1.6
1969	Hou-N	155	542	66	137	26	7	12	67	77	79	.253	.350	.393	111	7	8	77	8	7	-2	6	*1/O	2.0
1970	NY-A	99	269	34	57	6	0	9	37	43	37	.212	.327	.335	87	-6	-4	31	1	3	-2	-12	O/1	-2.1
1971	NY-A	21	36	4	7	1	0	1	2	3	5	.194	.256	.306	62	-2	-2	2	0	0	0	0	/O1	-0.1
	*Oak-A	50	101	15	22	2	0	5	12	15	15	.218	.325	.386	103	0	0	13	0	1	-1	-2	CO/32	-0.1
	Yr	71	137	19	29	3	0	6	14	18	20	.212	.308	.365	93	-2	-1	16	0	1	-1	-2		-0.2

YEAR	TM/L	G	AB	R	H	2B	3B	HR	RBI	BB	SO	AVG	OBP	SLG	PRO+	BR	/A	RC	SB	CS	SBR	FR	POS	TPR
1972	Oak-A	8	11	1	5	2	0	0	1	0	1	.455	.455	.636	234	2	2	3	0	0	0	-0	/12O	0.1
	SD-N	74	102	10	20	3	0	3	9	19	18	.196	.322	.314	88	-2	-1	11	0	0	0	-7	C/13O	-0.7
Total	8	974	2947	394	699	104	20	112	382	456	444	.237	.345	.400	115	61	65	432	24	24	-7	-21	O1/C32	0.6

■ IKE BLESSITT
Blessitt, Isaiah b: 9/30/49, Detroit, Mich. BR/TR, 5'11", 185 lbs. Deb: 9/07/72

YEAR	TM/L	G	AB	R	H	2B	3B	HR	RBI	BB	SO	AVG	OBP	SLG	PRO+	BR	/A	RC	SB	CS	SBR	FR	POS	TPR
1972	Det-A	4	5	0	0	0	0	0	0	0	2	.000	.000	.000	-97	-1	-1	0	0	0	0	0	/O	0.0

■ NED BLIGH
Bligh, Edwin Forrest b: 6/30/1864, Brooklyn, N.Y. d: 4/18/1892, Brooklyn, N.Y. BR/TR, 5'11", 172 lbs. Deb: 6/26/1886

YEAR	TM/L	G	AB	R	H	2B	3B	HR	RBI	BB	SO	AVG	OBP	SLG	PRO+	BR	/A	RC	SB	CS	SBR	FR	POS	TPR
1886	Bal-a	3	9	0	0	0	0	0		1		.000	.100	.000	-69	-2	-2	0	0			-1	/C	-0.2
1888	Cin-a	3	5	0	0	0	0	0		0		.000	.000	.000	-96	-1	-1	0	0			-1	/CO	-0.1
1889	Col-a	28	93	6	13	1	1	0	5	4	14	.140	.200	.172	8	-11	-10	4	2			1	C	-0.5
1890	Col-a	8	29	2	6	2	0	0		2		.207	.258	.276	64	-2	-1	2	0			4	/C	0.3
	*Lou-a	24	73	9	15	0	0	1		9		.205	.293	.247	63	-3	-3	6	1			0	C	0.0
	Yr	32	102	11	21	2	0	1		11		.206	.283	.255	63	-5	-4	8	1			4		0.3
Total	4	66	209	17	34	3	1	1	5	16	14	.163	.232	.201	29	-19	-17	12	3			3	/CO	-0.5

■ ELMER BLISS
Bliss, Elmer Ward b: 3/9/1875, Penfield, Pa. d: 3/18/62, Bradford, Pa. BL/TR, 6', 180 lbs. Deb: 9/28/03

YEAR	TM/L	G	AB	R	H	2B	3B	HR	RBI	BB	SO	AVG	OBP	SLG	PRO+	BR	/A	RC	SB	CS	SBR	FR	POS	TPR
1903	NY-A	1	3	0	0	0	0	0	0	0		.000	.000	.000	-94	-1	-1	0	0			-0	/P	0.0
1904	NY-A	1	1	0	0	0	0	0	0	0		.000	.000	.000	-96	-0	-0	0	0			-0	/O	0.0
Total	2	2	4	0	0	0	0	0	0	0		.000	.000	.000	-94	-1	-1	0	0			-1	/OP	0.0

■ FRANK BLISS
Bliss, Frank Eugene b: 12/ 10, 52Chicago, Ill. d: 1/8/29, Nashville, Tenn. Deb: 6/20/1878

YEAR	TM/L	G	AB	R	H	2B	3B	HR	RBI	BB	SO	AVG	OBP	SLG	PRO+	BR	/A	RC	SB	CS	SBR	FR	POS	TPR
1878	Mil-N	2	8	1	1	0	0	0	0	0	0	.125	.125	.125	-17	-1	-1	0				1	/3C	0.0

■ JACK BLISS
Bliss, John Joseph Albert b: 1/9/1882, Vancouver, Wash. d: 10/23/68, Temple City, Cal. BR/TR, 5'9", 185 lbs. Deb: 5/10/08

YEAR	TM/L	G	AB	R	H	2B	3B	HR	RBI	BB	SO	AVG	OBP	SLG	PRO+	BR	/A	RC	SB	CS	SBR	FR	POS	TPR
1908	StL-N	44	136	9	29	4	0	1	5	8		.213	.257	.265	72	-5	-4	10	3			5	C	0.3
1909	StL-N	35	113	12	25	2	1	1	8	12		.221	.307	.283	89	-2	-1	11	2			1	C	0.3
1910	StL-N	16	33	2	2	0	0	0	3	4	8	.061	.162	.061	-36	-6	-5	0	0			-1	C	-0.6
1911	StL-N	97	258	36	59	6	4	1	27	42	25	.229	.341	.295	81	-6	-5	28	5			-10	C/S	-0.8
1912	StL-N	49	114	11	28	3	1	0	18	19	14	.246	.372	.289	84	-2	-1	14	3			-6	C	-0.4
Total	5	241	654	70	143	15	6	3	61	85	47	.219	.316	.274	75	-20	-17	63	13			-11	C/S	-1.2

■ BRUNO BLOCK
Block, James John (b: James John Blochowicz)
b: 3/13/1885, Wisconsin Rapids, Wis. d: 8/6/37, S.Milwaukee, Wis. BR/TR, 5'9", 185 lbs. Deb: 8/05/07

YEAR	TM/L	G	AB	R	H	2B	3B	HR	RBI	BB	SO	AVG	OBP	SLG	PRO+	BR	/A	RC	SB	CS	SBR	FR	POS	TPR
1907	Was-A	24	57	3	8	2	1	0	2	2		.140	.169	.211	24	-5	-5	2	0			-5	C	-0.8
1910	Chi-A	55	152	12	32	1	1	0	9	13		.211	.273	.230	60	-7	-6	11	3			1	C	0.0
1911	Chi-A	39	115	11	35	6	1	1	18	6		.304	.339	.400	109	0	1	15	0			-3	C	0.2
1912	Chi-A	46	136	8	35	5	6	0	26	7		.257	.294	.382	96	-2	-2	16	1			2	C	0.5
1914	Chi-F	44	105	8	21	4	1	0	14	11	17	.200	.276	.257	57	-6	-5	8	1			1	C	-0.2
Total	5	208	565	42	131	18	10	1	69	39	17	.232	.281	.304	76	-20	-17	52	5			-5	C	-0.3

■ CY BLOCK
Block, Seymour b: 5/4/19, Brooklyn, N.Y. BR/TR, 6', 180 lbs. Deb: 9/07/42

YEAR	TM/L	G	AB	R	H	2B	3B	HR	RBI	BB	SO	AVG	OBP	SLG	PRO+	BR	/A	RC	SB	CS	SBR	FR	POS	TPR
1942	Chi-N	9	33	6	12	1	1	0	4	3	3	.364	.417	.455	161	2	2	6	2			-2	/32	0.0
1945	*Chi-N	2	7	1	1	0	0	0	1	0	0	.143	.143	.143	-21	-1	-1	0	0			1	/23	0.0
1946	Chi-N	6	13	2	3	0	0	0	0	4	0	.231	.412	.231	86	0	0	2	0			1	/3	0.1
Total	3	17	53	9	16	1	1	0	5	7	3	.302	.383	.358	118	1	1	8	2			-0	/32	0.1

■ TERRY BLOCKER
Blocker, Terry Fennell b: 8/18/59, Columbia, S.C. BL/TL, 6'2", 195 lbs. Deb: 4/11/85

YEAR	TM/L	G	AB	R	H	2B	3B	HR	RBI	BB	SO	AVG	OBP	SLG	PRO+	BR	/A	RC	SB	CS	SBR	FR	POS	TPR
1985	NY-N	18	15	1	1	0	0	0	0	1	2	.067	.125	.067	-46	-3	-3	0	0	0	0	1	/O	-0.2
1988	Atl-N	66	198	13	42	4	2	2	10	10	20	.212	.250	.283	50	-12	-13	13	1	1	-0	1	O	-1.5
1989	Atl-N	26	31	1	7	1	0	0	1	1	5	.226	.250	.258	44	-2	-2	2	1	0	0	-0	/OP	-0.1
Total	3	110	244	15	50	5	2	2	11	12	27	.205	.242	.266	44	-17	-18	15	2	1	0	1	/OP	-1.8

■ WES BLOGG
Blogg, Wesley C. b: 1855, Norfolk, Va. d: 3/10/1897, Deb: 6/20/1883

YEAR	TM/L	G	AB	R	H	2B	3B	HR	RBI	BB	SO	AVG	OBP	SLG	PRO+	BR	/A	RC	SB	CS	SBR	FR	POS	TPR
1883	Pit-a	9	34	0	5	0	0	0		0		.147	.147	.147	-5	-4	-4	1				-1	/CO	-0.3

■ RON BLOMBERG
Blomberg, Ronald Mark "Boomer" b: 8/23/48, Atlanta, Ga. BL/TR, 6'1.5", 195 lbs. Deb: 9/10/69

YEAR	TM/L	G	AB	R	H	2B	3B	HR	RBI	BB	SO	AVG	OBP	SLG	PRO+	BR	/A	RC	SB	CS	SBR	FR	POS	TPR
1969	NY-A	4	6	0	3	0	0	0	0	1	0	.500	.571	.500	210	1	1	2	0	0	0	-0	/O	0.1
1971	NY-A	64	199	30	64	6	2	7	31	14	23	.322	.366	.477	146	9	10	33	2	4	-2	-5	O	0.2
1972	NY-A	107	299	36	80	22	1	14	49	38	26	.268	.356	.488	155	18	19	53	0	2	-1	-8	1	0.0
1973	NY-A	100	301	45	99	13	1	12	57	34	25	.329	.397	.498	156	20	22	60	2	0	1	3	D1	2.3
1974	NY-A	90	264	39	82	11	2	10	48	29	33	.311	.383	.481	151	16	17	49	2	1	0	1	DO	1.8
1975	NY-A	34	106	18	27	8	2	4	17	13	10	.255	.336	.481	132	4	4	17	0	0	0	0	D/O	0.4
1976	NY-A	1	2	0	0	0	0	0	0	0	0	.000	.000	.000	-99	-0	-0	0	0	0	0	0	/D	0.0
1978	Chi-A	61	156	16	36	7	0	5	22	11	17	.231	.281	.372	81	-4	-4	17	0	0	0	-1	D/1	-0.5
Total	8	461	1333	184	391	67	8	52	224	140	134	.293	.363	.473	142	64	68	231	6	7	-2	-10	D1/O	4.3

■ JOE BLONG
Blong, Joseph Myles b: 9/17/1853, St.Louis, Mo. d: 9/22/1892, St.Louis, Mo. BR/TR, Deb: 5/04/1875

YEAR	TM/L	G	AB	R	H	2B	3B	HR	RBI	BB	SO	AVG	OBP	SLG	PRO+	BR	/A	RC	SB	CS	SBR	FR	POS	TPR
1875	RS-n	16	68	3	10	2	0	0		0		.147	.147	.176	13	-6	-5	2					P/O	0.0
1876	StL-N	62	264	30	62	7	4	0	30	2	9	.235	.241	.292	81	-6	-4	19				0	*O/P	-0.3
1877	StL-N	58	218	17	47	8	3	0	13	4	22	.216	.230	.280	63	-10	-8	14				-2	*OP	-0.6
Total	2	120	482	47	109	15	7	0	43	6	31	.226	.236	.286	72	-16	-12	33				-2	O/P	-0.9

■ JIMMY BLOODWORTH
Bloodworth, James Henry b: 7/26/17, Tallahassee, Fla. BR/TR, 5'11", 180 lbs. Deb: 9/14/37

YEAR	TM/L	G	AB	R	H	2B	3B	HR	RBI	BB	SO	AVG	OBP	SLG	PRO+	BR	/A	RC	SB	CS	SBR	FR	POS	TPR
1937	Was-A	15	50	3	11	2	1	0	8	5	8	.220	.291	.300	51	-4	-4	4	0	1	-1	-1	2	-0.3
1939	Was-A	83	318	34	92	24	1	4	40	10	26	.289	.313	.409	90	-9	-8	37	3	1	0	14	2/O	1.0
1940	Was-A	119	469	47	115	17	8	11	70	16	71	.245	.272	.386	73	-24	-20	46	3	1	0	13	21/3	-0.1
1941	Was-A	142	506	59	124	24	3	7	66	41	58	.245	.303	.346	75	-22	-19	54	1	1	-0	35	*2/3S	2.7
1942	Det-A	137	533	62	129	23	1	13	57	35	63	.242	.295	.362	78	-13	-18	54	2	8	-4	10	*2/S	-0.7
1943	Det-A	129	474	41	114	23	4	6	52	29	59	.241	.289	.344	79	-11	-15	39	4	7	-3	17	*2	0.5
1946	Det-A	76	249	26	61	8	1	5	36	12	26	.245	.285	.345	71	-9	-11	22	3	3	-1	-2	*2	-0.6
1947	Pit-N	88	316	27	79	9	0	7	48	16	39	.250	.290	.345	66	-15	-16	30	1			-14	2	-2.0
1949	Cin-N	134	452	40	118	27	1	9	59	27	36	.261	.304	.385	83	-12	-12	51	2			-3	21/3	-1.1
1950	Cin-N	4	14	1	3	1	0	0	1	2	0	.214	.313	.286	58	-1	-1	1	0			-3	/2	-0.3
	*Phi-N	54	96	6	22	2	0	0	13	6	12	.229	.275	.250	40	-8	-8	7	0			-2	2/13	-0.9
	Yr	58	110	7	25	3	0	0	14	8	12	.227	.280	.255	42	-9	-9	8	0			-5		-1.2
1951	Phi-N	21	42	2	6	0	0	0	3	9		.143	.300	.143	-6	-6	-6	1	1	0	0	-1	/21	-0.6
Total	11	1002	3519	348	874	160	20	62	451	202	407	.248	.292	.358	74	-134	-135	346	19	22		65	2/130S	-2.4

■ BUD BLOOMFIELD
Bloomfield, Clyde Stalcup b: 1/5/36, Oklahoma City, Okla. BR/TR, 5'11.5", 175 lbs. Deb: 9/25/63

YEAR	TM/L	G	AB	R	H	2B	3B	HR	RBI	BB	SO	AVG	OBP	SLG	PRO+	BR	/A	RC	SB	CS	SBR	FR	POS	TPR
1963	StL-N	1	0	0	0	0	0	0	0	0	0	—	—	—	—	0	0	0	0	0	0	0	/3	0.0
1964	Min-A	7	7	1	1	0	0	0	0	0	0	.143	.143	.143	-20	-1	-1	0	0	0	0	1	/2S	0.1
Total	2	8	7	1	1	0	0	0	0	0	0	.143	.143	.143	-20	-1	-1	0	0	0	0	1	/2S3	0.1

■ JACK BLOTT
Blott, John Leonard b: 8/24/02, Girard, Ohio d: 6/11/64, Ann Arbor, Mich. BR/TR, 6', 210 lbs. Deb: 7/30/24

YEAR	TM/L	G	AB	R	H	2B	3B	HR	RBI	BB	SO	AVG	OBP	SLG	PRO+	BR	/A	RC	SB	CS	SBR	FR	POS	TPR
1924	Cin-N	2	1	0	0	0	0	0	0	0	0	.000	.000	.000	-99	-0	-0	0	0	0	0	0	/C	0.0

YEAR	TM/L	G	AB	R	H	2B	3B	HR	RBI	BB	SO	AVG	OBP	SLG	PRO+	BR	/A	RC	SB	CS	SBR	FR	POS	TPR

■ MIKE BLOWERS — Blowers, Michael Roy b: 4/24/65, Wurzburg, Germany BR/TR, 6'2", 190 lbs. Deb: 9/01/89

1989	NY-A	13	38	2	10	0	0	0	3	3	13	.263	.317	.263	66	-2	-2	3	0	0	0	-3	3	-0.3
1990	NY-A	48	144	16	27	4	0	5	21	12	50	.188	.255	.319	59	-8	-8	12	1	0	0	-8	3/D	-1.5
Total	2	61	182	18	37	4	0	5	24	15	63	.203	.268	.308	61	-10	-10	15	1	0	0	-11	/3D	-1.8

■ BERT BLUE — Blue, Bird Wayne b: 12/14/1876, Bettsville, Ohio d: 12/14/28, Detroit, Mich. TR, 6'3", 200 lbs. Deb: 6/15/08

1908	StL-A	11	24	2	9	1	2	0	1	3		.375	.444	.583	235	4	4	6	0			1	/C	0.6
	Phi-A	6	18	2	3	0	0	0	1	0		.167	.167	.167	9	-2	-2	0	0			2	/C	0.0
	Yr	17	42	4	12	1	2	0	2	3		.286	.333	.405	138	2	2	6	0			2		0.6

■ LU BLUE — Blue, Luzerne Atwell b: 3/5/1897, Washington, D.C. d: 7/28/58, Alexandria, Va. BB/TL, 5'10", 165 lbs. Deb: 4/14/21

1921	Det-A	153	585	103	180	33	11	5	75	103	47	.308	.416	.427	117	18	19	107	13	17	-6	-6	*1	0.5
1922	Det-A	145	584	131	175	31	9	6	45	82	48	.300	.392	.414	114	12	14	100	8	5	-1	0	*1	0.2
1923	Det-A	129	504	100	143	27	7	1	46	96	40	.284	.402	.371	106	8	9	81	9	11	-4	5	*1	0.4
1924	Det-A	108	395	81	123	26	7	2	53	64	26	.311	.413	.428	119	12	13	75	9	4	0	3	*1	1.1
1925	Det-A	150	532	91	163	18	9	3	94	83	29	.306	.403	.391	104	5	6	92	19	5	3	0	*1	0.5
1926	Det-A	128	429	92	123	24	14	1	52	90	18	.287	.413	.415	115	14	13	81	13	7	-0	-5	*1/O	0.3
1927	Det-A	112	365	71	95	17	9	1	42	71	28	.260	.384	.364	94	-0	-1	53	13	7	-0	-1	*1	-0.6
1928	StL-A	154	549	116	154	32	11	14	80	105	43	.281	.400	.455	120	22	20	107	12	7	-1	2	*1	1.2
1929	StL-A	151	573	111	168	40	10	6	61	126	32	.293	.422	.429	115	23	20	114	12	6	-1	-3	*1	-0.4
1930	StL-A	117	425	85	100	27	5	4	42	81	44	.235	.363	.351	79	-10	-12	60	12	7	-1	0	*1	-2.2
1931	Chi-A	155	589	119	179	23	15	1	62	127	60	.304	.430	.399	126	24	30	113	13	3	2	-3	*1	1.3
1932	Chi-A	112	373	51	93	21	2	0	43	64	21	.249	.364	.316	83	-10	-6	49	17	6	2	9	*1	-0.5
1933	Bro-N	1	1	0	0	0	0	0	0	0	0	.000	.000	.000	-99	-0	-0	0	0			0	/1	0.0
Total	13	1615	5904	1151	1696	319	109	44	695	1092	436	.287	.402	.401	109	119	125	1031	150	85		2	*1/O	1.8

■ OSSIE BLUEGE — Bluege, Oswald Louis b: 10/24/1900, Chicago, Ill. d: 10/14/85, Edina, Minn. BR/TR, 5'11", 162 lbs. Deb: 4/24/22 MC

1922	Was-A	19	61	5	12	1	0	0	2	7	7	.197	.300	.213	37	-6	-5	5	1	0	0	-3	3/S	-0.5
1923	Was-A	109	379	48	93	15	7	2	42	48	53	.245	.343	.338	84	-10	-8	48	5	3	-0	4	*3/2	0.8
1924	•Was-A	117	402	59	113	15	4	2	49	39	36	.281	.358	.353	86	-9	-7	53	7	5	-1	-12	*32/S	-0.9
1925	•Was-A	145	522	77	150	27	4	4	79	59	56	.287	.362	.377	89	-9	-7	73	16	13	-3	1	*3/S	0.0
1926	Was-A	139	487	69	132	19	8	3	65	70	46	.271	.368	.361	93	-5	-3	69	12	9	-2	-19	*3/S	-1.0
1927	Was-A	146	503	71	138	21	10	1	66	57	37	.274	.354	.362	87	-9	-8	71	15	5	2	15	*3	1.7
1928	Was-A	146	518	78	154	33	7	2	75	46	27	.297	.364	.400	101	1	1	79	18	6	2	12	*3/2	1.6
1929	Was-A	64	220	35	65	6	0	5	31	19	15	.295	.354	.391	91	-3	-3	31	6	4	-1	2	32S	0.2
1930	Was-A	134	476	64	138	27	7	3	69	51	40	.290	.368	.395	93	-3	-4	73	15	8	-0	-1	*3	0.0
1931	Was-A	152	570	82	155	25	7	8	98	50	39	.272	.336	.382	88	-10	-10	74	16	10	-1	-5	*3/S	-0.6
1932	Was-A	149	507	64	131	22	4	5	64	84	41	.258	.367	.347	87	-8	-7	71	9	7	-2	6	*3	0.7
1933	•Was-A	140	501	63	131	14	0	6	71	55	34	.261	.338	.325	77	-16	-15	58	6	7	-2	-8	*3	-1.3
1934	Was-A	99	285	39	70	9	2	0	11	23	15	.246	.306	.291	57	-19	-17	27	2	1	0	9	3S/2O	-0.5
1935	Was-A	100	320	44	84	14	3	0	34	37	21	.262	.341	.325	75	-12	-11	37	2	2	-1	1	3S/2	-0.6
1936	Was-A	90	319	43	92	12	1	1	55	38	16	.288	.375	.342	83	-9	-7	44	5	3	-0	0	2S3	0.0
1937	Was-A	42	127	12	36	4	2	1	13	13	9	.283	.355	.370	87	-3	-2	17	1	1	-0	2	S/13	0.1
1938	Was-A	58	184	25	48	12	1	0	21	21	11	.261	.340	.337	75	-8	-6	22	3	1	0	1	2S/13	-0.2
1939	Was-A	18	59	5	9	0	0	0	3	7	2	.153	.242	.153	3	-9	-8	2	1	0	0	1/2S3	-0.6
Total	18	1867	6440	883	1751	276	67	43	848	724	515	.272	.352	.356	85	-147	-126	847	140	85	-9	5	*3S2/10	-1.1

■ OTTO BLUEGE — Bluege, Otto Adam "Squeaky" b: 7/20/09, Chicago, Ill. d: 6/28/77, Chicago, Ill. BR/TR, 5'10", 154 lbs. Deb: 4/12/32

1932	Cin-N	1	0	1	0	0	0	0	0	0	0	—	—	—	—	0	0	0	0			0	R	0.0
1933	Cin-N	108	291	17	62	6	2	0	18	26	29	.213	.278	.247	52	-18	-17	19	0			-8	S2/3	-1.9
Total	2	109	291	18	62	6	2	0	18	26	29	.213	.278	.247	52	-18	-17	19	0			-8	/S23	-1.9

■ RED BLUHM — Bluhm, Harvey Fred b: 6/27/1894, Cleveland, Ohio d: 5/7/52, Flint, Mich. BR/TR, 5'11", 165 lbs. Deb: 7/03/18

| 1918 | Bos-A | 1 | 1 | 0 | 0 | 0 | 0 | 0 | 0 | 0 | 0 | .000 | .000 | .000 | -99 | -0 | -0 | 0 | 0 | | | 0 | H | 0.0 |

■ CHET BOAK — Boak, Chester Robert b: 6/19/35, New Castle, Pa. d: 11/28/83, Emporium, Pa. BR/TR, 6', 180 lbs. Deb: 9/18/60

1960	KC-A	5	13	1	2	0	0	0	1	0	2	.154	.214	.154	1	-2	-2	1	0	0	0	1	/2	0.0
1961	Was-A	5	7	0	0	0	0	0	0	1	1	.000	.125	.000	-64	-2	-2	0	1	0	0	-1	/2	-0.1
Total	2	10	20	1	2	0	0	0	1	1	3	.100	.182	.100	-22	-3	-3	1	1	0	0	0	/2	-0.1

■ FREDERICK BOARDMAN — Boardman, Frederick Deb: 8/29/1874

| 1874 | Bal-n | 1 | 3 | 0 | 1 | 0 | 0 | 0 | | 0 | | .333 | .333 | .333 | 114 | 0 | 0 | 0 | | | | | /O | 0.0 |

■ RANDY BOBB — Bobb, Mark Randall b: 1/1/48, Los Angeles, Cal. d: 6/13/82, Carnelian Bay, Cal BR/TR, 6'1", 185 lbs. Deb: 8/15/68

1968	Chi-N	7	8	0	1	0	0	0	0	1	2	.125	.222	.125	6	-1	-1	0	0	0	0	0	/C	0.0
1969	Chi-N	3	2	0	0	0	0	0	0	0	1	.000	.000	.000	-89	-1	-1	0	0	0	0	1	/C	0.0
Total	2	10	10	0	1	0	0	0	0	1	3	.100	.182	.100	-14	-1	-1	0	0	0	0	1	/C	0.0

■ JOHN BOCCABELLA — Boccabella, John Dominic b: 6/29/41, San Francisco, Cal BR/TR, 6'1", 195 lbs. Deb: 9/02/63

1963	Chi-N	24	74	7	14	4	1	0	5	6	21	.189	.250	.311	57	-4	-4	5	0	1	-1	-1	1	-0.6
1964	Chi-N	9	23	4	9	2	1	0	6	0	3	.391	.391	.565	159	2	2	5	0	0	0	-0	/1O	0.1
1965	Chi-N	6	12	2	4	0	0	2	4	1	2	.333	.385	.833	227	2	2	4	0	0	0	-0	/1O	0.0
1966	Chi-N	75	206	22	47	9	0	6	25	14	39	.228	.277	.359	74	-7	-7	19	0	1	-1	0	O1/C	-1.0
1967	Chi-N	25	35	0	6	1	1	0	8	3	7	.171	.256	.257	45	-2	-3	2	0	0	0	0	/O1C	-0.2
1968	Chi-N	7	14	0	1	0	0	0	1	2	2	.071	.188	.071	-19	-2	-2	0	0	0	0	-0	/CO	-0.2
1969	Mon-N	40	86	4	9	2	0	1	6	6	30	.105	.172	.163	-6	-12	-12	2	1	0	0	1	C	-0.8
1970	Mon-N	61	145	18	39	3	1	5	17	11	24	.269	.321	.407	94	-2	-2	18	0	1	-1	9	1C/3	0.5
1971	Mon-N	74	177	15	39	11	0	3	15	14	24	.220	.281	.333	73	-6	-7	15	0	1	-1	-0	C1/3	-1.0
1972	Mon-N	83	207	14	47	8	1	1	10	9	29	.227	.263	.290	56	-12	-12	15	1	2	-1	7	C/13	-0.2
1973	Mon-N	118	403	25	94	13	0	7	46	26	57	.233	.281	.318	63	-19	-21	33	1	1	-0	1	*C/1	-1.3
1974	SF-N	29	80	6	11	3	0	0	5	4	6	.138	.179	.175	-1	-11	-11	2	0	0	0	-2	C	-1.2
Total	12	551	1462	117	320	56	5	26	148	96	246	.219	.269	.317	62	-74	-77	122	3	7	-3	15	C1/O3	-5.8

■ MILT BOCEK — Bocek, Milton Frank b: 7/16/12, Chicago, Ill. BR/TR, 6'1", 185 lbs. Deb: 9/03/33

1933	Chi-A	11	22	3	8	1	0	1	3	4	6	.364	.462	.545	173	2	2	6	0	0	0	-1	/O	0.1
1934	Chi-A	19	38	3	8	1	0	0	3	5	5	.211	.302	.237	39	-3	-3	3	0	0	0	3	O	0.0
Total	2	30	60	6	16	2	0	1	6	9	11	.267	.362	.350	86	-1	-1	9	0	0	0	2	/O	0.1

■ BRUCE BOCHTE — Bochte, Bruce Anton b: 11/12/50, Pasadena, Cal. BL/TL, 6'3", 195 lbs. Deb: 7/19/74

1974	Cal-A	57	196	24	53	4	1	5	26	18	23	.270	.335	.378	111	1	3	24	6	3	0	-3	O1	-0.2
1975	Cal-A	107	375	41	107	19	3	3	48	45	43	.285	.365	.354	118	6	9	53	3	4	-2	-7	*1/D	-0.4
1976	Cal-A	146	466	53	120	17	1	2	49	64	53	.258	.350	.311	101	-1	-3	52	4	5	-2	-4	O1/D	-0.7
1977	Cal-A	25	100	12	29	4	0	2	8	7	4	.290	.336	.390	101	-0	0	11	3	2	-0	2	O/D	0.1
	Cle-A	112	392	52	119	19	1	5	43	40	38	.304	.368	.395	112	5	7	54	3	2	-0	0	O1/D	0.2
	Yr	137	492	64	148	23	1	7	51	47	42	.301	.362	.394	110	5	7	67	6	4	-1	2		0.3

YEAR	TM/L	G	AB	R	H	2B	3B	HR	RBI	BB	SO	AVG	OBP	SLG	PRO+	BR	/A	RC	SB	CS	SBR	FR	POS	TPR
1978	Sea-A	140	486	58	128	25	3	11	51	60	47	.263	.346	.395	108	6	6	67	3	4	-2	-3	OD/1	0.0
1979	Sea-A	150	554	81	175	38	6	16	100	67	64	.316	.392	.493	134	29	28	100	2	2	-1	5	*1	2.3
1980	Sea-A	148	520	62	156	34	4	13	78	72	81	.300	.385	.456	128	23	22	90	2	3	-1	5	*1D	1.7
1981	Sea-A	99	335	39	87	16	0	6	30	47	53	.260	.354	.361	102	4	3	44	1	3	-2	-4	1O/D	-0.5
1982	Sea-A	144	509	58	151	21	0	12	70	67	71	.297	.382	.409	114	14	12	79	8	5	-1	-6	O1D	0.2
1984	Oak-A	148	469	58	124	23	0	5	52	52	59	.264	.338	.345	96	-6	-1	54	2	5	-2	-13	*1/D	-2.5
1985	Oak-A	137	424	48	125	17	1	14	60	49	58	.295	.368	.439	129	12	16	67	3	1	0	-9	*1	0.0
1986	Oak-A	125	407	57	104	13	1	6	43	65	68	.256	.358	.337	98	-3	1	52	3	2	-0	2	*1/D	-0.4
Total	12	1538	5233	643	1478	250	21	100	658	653	662	.282	.363	.396	114	91	109	749	43	41	-12	-35	*1O/D	-0.2

■ BRUCE BOCHY   Bochy, Bruce Douglas   b: 4/16/55, Landes De Bussac, France   BR/TR, 6'3", 205 lbs.   Deb: 7/19/78

YEAR	TM/L	G	AB	R	H	2B	3B	HR	RBI	BB	SO	AVG	OBP	SLG	PRO+	BR	/A	RC	SB	CS	SBR	FR	POS	TPR
1978	Hou-N	54	154	8	41	8	0	3	15	11	35	.266	.315	.377	100	-2	-0	16	0	0	0	3	C	0.4
1979	Hou-N	56	129	11	28	4	0	1	6	13	25	.217	.294	.271	59	-8	-7	10	0	0	0	-1	C	-0.5
1980	*Hou-N	22	22	0	4	1	0	0	0	5	7	.182	.357	.227	72	-1	-0	2	0	0	0	-2	C/1	-0.2
1982	NY-N	17	49	4	15	4	0	2	8	4	6	.306	.358	.510	141	2	3	9	0	0	0	4	C/1	0.7
1983	SD-N	23	42	2	9	1	1	0	3	0	9	.214	.214	.286	39	-4	-3	2	0	0	0	2	C	0.0
1984	*SD-N	37	92	10	21	5	1	4	15	3	21	.228	.253	.435	90	-2	-2	9	0	1	-1	4	C	0.3
1985	SD-N	48	112	16	30	2	0	6	13	6	30	.268	.305	.446	109	1	1	15	0	0	0	1	C	0.3
1986	SD-N	63	127	16	32	9	0	8	22	14	23	.252	.326	.512	130	4	4	21	1	0	0	3	C	0.9
1987	SD-N	38	75	8	12	3	0	2	11	11	21	.160	.267	.280	47	-6	-6	5	0	1	-1	-4	C	-0.8
Total	9	358	802	75	192	37	2	26	93	67	177	.239	.300	.388	92	-14	-11	89	1	2	-1	9	C/1	1.1

■ EDDIE BOCKMAN   Bockman, Joseph Edward   b: 7/26/20, Santa Ana, Cal.   BR/TR, 5'9", 175 lbs.   Deb: 9/11/46

YEAR	TM/L	G	AB	R	H	2B	3B	HR	RBI	BB	SO	AVG	OBP	SLG	PRO+	BR	/A	RC	SB	CS	SBR	FR	POS	TPR
1946	NY-A	4	12	2	1	1	0	0	0	1	4	.083	.154	.167	-10	-2	-2	0	0	0	0	1	/3	0.0
1947	Cle-A	46	66	8	17	2	2	1	14	5	17	.258	.310	.394	97	-1	-1	9	0	0	0	9	3/2SO	0.9
1948	Pit-N	70	176	23	42	7	1	4	23	17	35	.239	.309	.358	79	-5	-6	19	2			8	3/2	0.1
1949	Pit-N	79	220	21	49	6	1	6	19	23	31	.223	.296	.341	69	-9	-10	23	3			6	3/2	-0.2
Total	4	199	474	54	109	16	4	11	56	46	87	.230	.299	.350	74	-17	-18	51	5	0		24	3/2OS	0.8

■ PING BODIE   Bodie, Frank Stephan (b: Francesco Stephano Pezzolo)   b: 10/8/1887, San Francisco, Cal.   d: 12/17/61, San Francisco, Cal   BR/TR, 5'8", 195 lbs.   Deb: 4/22/11

YEAR	TM/L	G	AB	R	H	2B	3B	HR	RBI	BB	SO	AVG	OBP	SLG	PRO+	BR	/A	RC	SB	CS	SBR	FR	POS	TPR
1911	Chi-A	145	551	75	159	27	13	4	97	49		.289	.348	.407	114	6	9	82	14			7	*O2	0.5
1912	Chi-A	138	472	58	139	24	7	5	72	43		.294	.358	.407	122	11	13	73	12			-13	*O	-0.7
1913	Chi-A	127	406	39	107	14	8	8	48	35	57	.264	.325	.397	112	4	4	54	5			-4	*O	-0.6
1914	Chi-A	107	327	21	75	9	5	3	29	21	35	.229	.278	.315	79	-10	-9	32	12	11	-3	-2	O	-2.1
1917	Phi-A	148	557	51	162	28	11	7	74	54	40	.291	.356	.418	138	22	23	86	13			5	*O/1	2.1
1918	NY-A	91	324	36	83	12	6	3	46	27	24	.256	.319	.358	102	1	-0	39	6			4	O	0.0
1919	NY-A	134	475	45	132	27	8	6	59	36	46	.278	.334	.406	107	3	3	67	15			-8	*O	-1.5
1920	NY-A	129	471	63	139	26	12	7	79	40	30	.295	.350	.446	106	5	3	70	6	14	-7	-10	*O	-2.3
1921	NY-A	31	87	5	15	2	2	0	12	8		.172	.242	.241	23	-10	-11	5	0	1	-1	-6	O	-1.7
Total	9	1050	3670	393	1011	169	72	43	516	312	240	.275	.335	.396	110	32	35	508	83	26		-27	O/21	-6.3

■ TONY BOECKEL   Boeckel, Norman Doxie   b: 8/25/1892, Los Angeles, Cal.   d: 2/16/24, Torrey Pines, Cal.   BR/TR, 5'10.5", 175 lbs.   Deb: 7/23/17

YEAR	TM/L	G	AB	R	H	2B	3B	HR	RBI	BB	SO	AVG	OBP	SLG	PRO+	BR	/A	RC	SB	CS	SBR	FR	POS	TPR
1917	Pit-N	64	219	16	58	11	1	1	23	8	31	.265	.297	.324	87	-3	-4	22	6			-4	3	-0.9
1919	Pit-N	45	152	18	38	9	2	0	16	18	20	.250	.333	.336	97	1	0	20	11			-8	3	-0.8
	Bos-N	95	365	42	91	11	5	1	26	35	13	.249	.317	.315	94	-4	-2	38	10			-4	3	-0.5
	Yr	140	517	60	129	20	7	1	42	53	33	.250	.322	.321	95	-3	-2	58	21			-11		-1.3
1920	Bos-N	153	582	70	156	28	5	3	62	38	50	.268	.314	.349	94	-8	-5	62	18	15	-4	-6	*3/S2	-0.7
1921	Bos-N	153	592	93	185	20	13	10	84	52	41	.313	.370	.441	120	12	16	95	20	15	-3	-12	*3	0.2
1922	Bos-N	119	402	61	116	19	6	6	47	35	32	.289	.349	.410	99	-3	-1	58	14	8	-1	-11	*3	-0.2
1923	Bos-N	148	568	72	169	32	4	7	79	51	31	.298	.357	.405	105	1	4	83	11	8	-2	-10	*3/S	-0.3
Total	6	777	2880	372	813	130	36	27	337	237	218	.282	.339	.381	102	-4	10	378	90	46		-54	3/S2	-3.2

■ LEN BOEHMER   Boehmer, Leonard Joseph Stephen   b: 6/28/41, Flint Hill, Mo.   BR/TR, 6'1", 192 lbs.   Deb: 6/18/67

YEAR	TM/L	G	AB	R	H	2B	3B	HR	RBI	BB	SO	AVG	OBP	SLG	PRO+	BR	/A	RC	SB	CS	SBR	FR	POS	TPR
1967	Cin-N	2	3	0	0	0	0	0	0	0	0	.000	.000	.000	-90	-1	-1	0	0	0	0	-0	/2	0.0
1969	NY-A	45	108	5	19	4	0	0	7	8	10	.176	.233	.213	26	-11	-10	5	0	1	-1	1	1/32S	-1.1
1971	NY-A	3	5	0	0	0	0	0	0	0	0	.000	.000	.000	-99	-1	-1	0	0	0	0	0	/3	-0.1
Total	3	50	116	5	19	4	0	0	7	8	10	.164	.218	.198	18	-13	-12	5	0	1	-1	1	/132S	-1.2

■ TERRY BOGENER   Bogener, Terry Wayne   b: 9/28/55, Hannibal, Mo.   BL/TL, 6', 193 lbs.   Deb: 6/14/82

YEAR	TM/L	G	AB	R	H	2B	3B	HR	RBI	BB	SO	AVG	OBP	SLG	PRO+	BR	/A	RC	SB	CS	SBR	FR	POS	TPR
1982	Tex-A	24	60	6	13	2	1	1	4	4	8	.217	.288	.333	74	-2	-2	6	2	0	1	-1	O/D	-0.2

■ WADE BOGGS   Boggs, Wade Anthony   b: 6/15/58, Omaha, Neb.   BL/TR, 6'2", 190 lbs.   Deb: 4/10/82

YEAR	TM/L	G	AB	R	H	2B	3B	HR	RBI	BB	SO	AVG	OBP	SLG	PRO+	BR	/A	RC	SB	CS	SBR	FR	POS	TPR
1982	Bos-A	104	338	51	118	14	1	5	44	35	21	.349	.410	.441	126	17	14	61	1	0	0	18	13/OD	3.0
1983	Bos-A	153	582	100	210	44	7	5	74	92	36	.361	.449	.486	147	51	45	130	3	3	-1	8	*3	5.1
1984	Bos-A	158	625	109	203	31	4	6	55	89	44	.325	.409	.416	123	29	25	110	3	2	-0	21	*3/D	4.7
1985	Bos-A	161	653	107	240	42	3	8	78	96	61	.368	.452	.478	149	55	51	143	2	1	0	8	*3	5.2
1986	*Bos-A	149	580	107	207	47	2	8	71	105	44	.357	.455	.486	156	52	51	133	0	4	-2	-1	*3	4.3
1987	Bos-A	147	551	108	200	40	6	24	89	105	48	.363	.467	.588	173	67	64	154	1	3	-2	3	*3/1D	6.0
1988	*Bos-A	155	584	128	214	45	6	5	58	125	34	.366	.480	.490	165	66	62	140	2	3	-1	-5	*3/D	5.6
1989	Bos-A	156	621	113	205	51	7	3	54	107	51	.330	.434	.449	141	47	41	122	2	6	-3	-4	*3/D	3.5
1990	*Bos-A	155	619	89	187	44	5	6	63	87	68	.302	.389	.418	120	24	20	103	0	0	0	-22	*3/D	0.0
Total	9	1338	5153	912	1784	358	41	70	586	841	407	.346	.440	.472	145	405	374	1097	14	22	-9	26	*3/1DO	37.4

■ CHARLIE BOHN   Bohn, Charles   b: 1857, Cleveland, Ohio   d: 8/1/03, Cleveland, Ohio   Deb: 6/20/1882

YEAR	TM/L	G	AB	R	H	2B	3B	HR	RBI	BB	SO	AVG	OBP	SLG	PRO+	BR	/A	RC	SB	CS	SBR	FR	POS	TPR
1882	Lou-a	4	13	0	2	0	0	0		0		.154	.154	.154	4	-1	-1	0				1	/OP	0.0

■ SAM BOHNE   Bohne, Samuel Arthur (b: Samuel Arthur Cohen)   b: 10/22/1896, San Francisco, Cal   d: 5/23/77, Palo Alto, Cal.   BR/TR, 5'8.5", 175 lbs.   Deb: 9/09/16

YEAR	TM/L	G	AB	R	H	2B	3B	HR	RBI	BB	SO	AVG	OBP	SLG	PRO+	BR	/A	RC	SB	CS	SBR	FR	POS	TPR
1916	StL-N	14	38	3	9	0	0	0	0	4	6	.237	.310	.237	69	-1	-1	4	3			-4	S	-0.4
1921	Cin-N	153	613	98	175	28	16	3	44	54	38	.285	.347	.398	101	-2	1	83	26	22	-5	8	*23	0.5
1922	Cin-N	112	383	53	105	14	5	3	51	39	18	.274	.344	.360	83	-10	-9	49	13	8	-1	11	2S	-0.1
1923	Cin-N	139	539	77	136	18	10	3	47	48	37	.252	.316	.340	74	-21	-19	56	16	19	-7	5	23/S1	-1.7
1924	Cin-N	100	349	42	89	15	9	4	46	18	24	.255	.293	.384	81	-11	-10	39	9	6	-1	-9	2S3	-1.8
1925	Cin-N	73	214	24	55	9	1	2	24	14	14	.257	.303	.336	65	-12	-11	22	6	4	-1	-7	S2/013	-1.3
1926	Cin-N	25	54	8	11	0	2	0	5	4	8	.204	.259	.278	46	-4	-4	4	1			-3	S	-0.5
	Bro-N	47	125	4	25	3	2	1	11	12	9	.200	.270	.280	49	-9	-9	10	1			11	23	0.3
	Yr	72	179	12	36	3	4	1	16	16	17	.201	.267	.279	48	-13	-13	14	2			8		-0.2
Total	7	663	2315	309	605	87	45	16	228	193	154	.261	.321	.359	81	-70	-62	266	75	59		13	2S3/01	-4.8

■ BRUCE BOISCLAIR   Boisclair, Bruce Armand   b: 12/9/52, Putnam, Conn.   BL/TL, 6'2", 185 lbs.   Deb: 9/11/74

YEAR	TM/L	G	AB	R	H	2B	3B	HR	RBI	BB	SO	AVG	OBP	SLG	PRO+	BR	/A	RC	SB	CS	SBR	FR	POS	TPR
1974	NY-N	7	12	0	3	1	0	0	1	4		.250	.308	.333	81	-0	-0	1	0	0	0	2	/O	0.2
1976	NY-N	110	286	42	82	13	3	2	13	28	55	.287	.350	.374	112	2	4	38	9	5	-0	0	O	0.1
1977	NY-N	127	307	41	90	21	1	4	44	31	57	.293	.360	.407	110	3	5	46	6	4	-1	-7	O/1	-0.6
1978	NY-N	107	214	24	48	7	1	4	15	23	43	.224	.300	.322	77	-7	-7	21	3	3	-1	1	O/1	-0.9
1979	NY-N	59	98	7	18	5	1	0	4	3	24	.184	.216	.255	29	-10	-9	5	0	2	-1	0	O/1	-1.1

YEAR	TM/L	G	AB	R	H	2B	3B	HR	RBI	BB	SO	AVG	OBP	SLG	PRO+	BR	/A	RC	SB	CS	SBR	FR	POS	TPR
Total	5	410	917	114	241	47	6	10	77	86	183	.263	.327	.360	94	-13	-7	111	18	14	-3	-4	O/1	-2.3

■ BOB BOKEN
Boken, Robert Anthony b: 2/23/08, Maryville, Ill. d: 10/6/88, Las Vegas, Nev. BR/TR, 6'2", 165 lbs. Deb: 4/25/33

YEAR	TM/L	G	AB	R	H	2B	3B	HR	RBI	BB	SO	AVG	OBP	SLG	PRO+	BR	/A	RC	SB	CS	SBR	FR	POS	TPR
1933	Was-A	55	133	19	37	5	2	3	26	9	16	.278	.324	.414	95	-2	-1	18	0	0	0	-2	23S	0.0
1934	Was-A	11	27	5	6	1	1	0	6	3	1	.222	.300	.333	66	-2	-1	3	2	0	1	1	/32	0.0
	Chi-A	81	297	30	70	9	1	3	40	15	32	.236	.275	.303	47	-23	-24	25	2	1	0	-10	2S	-2.7
	Yr	92	324	35	76	10	2	3	46	18	33	.235	.277	.306	49	-25	-26	28	4	1	1	-9		-2.7
Total	2	147	457	54	113	15	4	6	72	27	49	.247	.291	.337	62	-26	-27	46	4	1	1	-10	/2S3	-2.7

■ BOLAND
Boland Deb: 9/04/1875

YEAR	TM/L	G	AB	R	H	2B	3B	HR	RBI	BB	SO	AVG	OBP	SLG	PRO+	BR	/A	RC	SB	CS	SBR	FR	POS	TPR
1875	Atl-n	1	4	0	0	0	0	0	0			.000	.000	.000	-99	-1	-1	0					/O	0.0

■ ED BOLAND
Boland, Edward John b: 4/18/08, Long Island City, N.Y. BL/TL, 5'10", 165 lbs. Deb: 9/18/34

YEAR	TM/L	G	AB	R	H	2B	3B	HR	RBI	BB	SO	AVG	OBP	SLG	PRO+	BR	/A	RC	SB	CS	SBR	FR	POS	TPR
1934	Phi-N	8	30	2	9	1	1	0	5	0	2	.300	.300	.400	76	-1	-1	4	1			-2	/O	-0.2
1935	Phi-N	30	47	5	10	0	0	0	4	4	6	.213	.275	.213	30	-4	-5	3	1			-1	O	-0.6
1944	Was-A	19	59	4	16	4	0	0	14	0	6	.271	.271	.339	77	-2	-2	5	0	0	0	-1	O	-0.3
Total	3	57	136	11	35	5	1	0	23	4	14	.257	.279	.309	59	-7	-8	12	2	0		-4	/O	-1.1

■ CHARLIE BOLD
Bold, Charles Dickens "Dutch" b: 10/27/1894, Karlskrona, Sweden d: 7/29/78, Chelsea, Mass. BR/TR, 6'2", 185 lbs. Deb: 8/24/14

YEAR	TM/L	G	AB	R	H	2B	3B	HR	RBI	BB	SO	AVG	OBP	SLG	PRO+	BR	/A	RC	SB	CS	SBR	FR	POS	TPR
1914	StL-A	2	1	0	0	0	0	0	0		1	.000	.000	.000	-99	-0	-0	0	0			-0	/1	0.0

■ CARL BOLES
Boles, Carl Theodore b: 10/31/34, Center Point, Ark. BR/TR, 5'11", 185 lbs. Deb: 8/02/62

YEAR	TM/L	G	AB	R	H	2B	3B	HR	RBI	BB	SO	AVG	OBP	SLG	PRO+	BR	/A	RC	SB	CS	SBR	FR	POS	TPR
1962	SF-N	19	24	4	9	0	0	0	1	0	6	.375	.375	.375	104	0	0	3	0	0	0	-0	/O	0.0

■ JOE BOLEY
Boley, John Peter (b: John Peter Bolinsky) b: 7/19/1896, Mahanoy City, Pa. d: 12/30/62, Mahanoy City, Pa. BR/TR, 5'11", 170 lbs. Deb: 4/12/27

YEAR	TM/L	G	AB	R	H	2B	3B	HR	RBI	BB	SO	AVG	OBP	SLG	PRO+	BR	/A	RC	SB	CS	SBR	FR	POS	TPR
1927	Phi-A	118	370	49	115	18	8	1	52	26	14	.311	.361	.411	95	-0	-3	52	8	5	-1	-11	*S	-0.4
1928	Phi-A	132	425	49	112	20	3	0	49	32	11	.264	.317	.325	67	-19	-21	46	5	1	1	-17	*S	-2.3
1929	*Phi-A	91	303	36	76	17	6	2	47	24	16	.251	.310	.366	71	-13	-14	36	1	0	0	-10	S/3	-1.4
1930	*Phi-A	121	420	41	116	22	2	4	55	32	26	.276	.335	.367	74	-14	-17	53	0	0	0	-7	*S	-0.9
1931	*Phi-A	67	224	26	51	9	3	0	20	15	13	.228	.282	.295	49	-16	-18	19	1	1	-0	-13	S/2	-2.3
1932	Phi-A	10	34	2	7	2	0	0	4	1	4	.206	.229	.265	26	-4	-4	2	0	1	-1	-6	S	-0.9
	Cle-A	1	4	0	1	0	0	0	0	0	0	.250	.250	.250	28	-0	-0	0	0	0	0	0	/S	0.0
	Yr	11	38	2	8	2	0	0	4	1	4	.211	.231	.263	27	-4	-4	2	0	1	-1	-6		-0.9
Total	6	540	1780	203	478	88	22	7	227	130	84	.269	.323	.354	72	-66	-77	208	15	8	-0	-64	S/23	-8.2

■ JIM BOLGER
Bolger, James Cyril "Dutch" b: 2/23/32, Cincinnati, Ohio BR/TR, 6'2", 180 lbs. Deb: 6/24/50

YEAR	TM/L	G	AB	R	H	2B	3B	HR	RBI	BB	SO	AVG	OBP	SLG	PRO+	BR	/A	RC	SB	CS	SBR	FR	POS	TPR
1950	Cin-N	2	1	0	0	0	0	0	0	0	0	.000	.000	.000	-99	-0	-0	0	0			0	/O	0.0
1951	Cin-N	2	0	1	0	0	0	0	0	0	0	—	—	—		0	-0	-0	0	1	0	0	0	R	0.0
1954	Cin-N	5	3	1	1	0	0	0	0	0	1	.333	.333	.333	72	-0	-0	0	0	0	0	0	/O	0.0
1955	Chi-N	64	160	19	33	5	4	0	7	9	17	.206	.257	.287	45	-13	-13	11	2	2	-1	5	O	-0.8
1957	Chi-N	112	273	28	75	4	1	5	29	10	36	.275	.308	.352	78	-9	-9	27	0	1	-1	6	O/3	-0.4
1958	Chi-N	84	120	15	27	4	1	1	11	9	20	.225	.285	.300	56	-8	-8	10	0	1	-0	-0	O	-0.9
1959	Cle-N	8	7	0	0	0	0	0	0	1	1	.000	.125	.000	-65	-2	-2	0	0	0	0	0	H	-0.1
	Phi-N	35	48	1	4	1	0	0	1	3	8	.083	.137	.104	-34	-9	-9	0	0	0	0	0	/O	-0.9
Total	7	312	612	65	140	14	6	6	48	32	83	.229	.274	.301	54	-41	-40	49	3	4		12	O/3	-3.1

■ FRANK BOLLING
Bolling, Frank Elmore b: 11/16/31, Mobile, Ala. BR/TR, 6'1", 175 lbs. Deb: 4/13/54

YEAR	TM/L	G	AB	R	H	2B	3B	HR	RBI	BB	SO	AVG	OBP	SLG	PRO+	BR	/A	RC	SB	CS	SBR	FR	POS	TPR
1954	Det-A	117	368	46	87	15	2	6	38	36	51	.236	.304	.337	77	-13	-12	38	3	5	-2	-29	*2	-3.9
1956	Det-A	102	366	53	103	21	7	7	45	42	51	.281	.359	.434	108	4	4	60	6	2	1	-15	*2	-0.2
1957	Det-A	146	576	72	149	27	6	15	40	57	64	.259	.328	.405	96	-2	-3	73	4	9	-4	-3	*2	-0.2
1958	Det-A	154	610	91	164	25	4	14	75	54	54	.269	.332	.392	92	-1	-7	81	6	4	-1	8	*2	1.1
1959	Det-A	127	459	56	122	18	3	13	55	45	37	.266	.341	.403	98	2	-1	65	2	2	-1	-0	*2	0.2
1960	Det-A	139	536	64	136	20	4	9	59	40	48	.254	.308	.356	77	-16	-18	58	7	4	-0	-5	*2	-1.3
1961	Mil-N	148	585	86	153	16	4	15	56	57	62	.262	.330	.379	93	-10	-5	70	7	3	0	1	*2	1.4
1962	Mil-N	122	406	45	110	17	4	9	43	35	45	.271	.335	.399	99	-2	-1	55	2	2	-1	-9	*2	0.0
1963	Mil-N	142	542	73	132	18	2	5	43	41	47	.244	.300	.312	77	-16	-15	52	2	1	0	-2	*2	-0.8
1964	Mil-N	120	352	35	70	11	1	5	34	21	44	.199	.248	.278	48	-24	-25	24	0	1	-1	-9	*2	-2.5
1965	Mil-N	148	535	55	141	26	3	7	50	24	41	.264	.295	.363	84	-12	-12	54	0	4	-2	-16	*2	-2.4
1966	Atl-N	75	227	16	48	7	0	1	18	10	14	.211	.248	.256	40	-18	-18	14	1	1	-0	-15	2	-3.1
Total	12	1540	5562	692	1415	221	40	106	556	462	558	.254	.315	.366	85	-108	-114	643	40	38	-11	-94	*2	-11.7

■ JACK BOLLING
Bolling, John Edward b: 2/20/17, Mobile, Ala. BL/TL, 5'11", 168 lbs. Deb: 6/10/39

YEAR	TM/L	G	AB	R	H	2B	3B	HR	RBI	BB	SO	AVG	OBP	SLG	PRO+	BR	/A	RC	SB	CS	SBR	FR	POS	TPR
1939	Phi-N	69	211	27	61	11	0	3	13	11	10	.289	.324	.384	92	-3	-3	25	6			2	1	-0.5
1944	Bro-N	56	131	21	46	14	1	1	25	14	4	.351	.418	.496	159	10	10	27	0			1	1	0.9
Total	2	125	342	48	107	25	1	4	38	25	14	.313	.361	.427	118	7	8	52	6			3	/1	0.4

■ MILT BOLLING
Bolling, Milton Joseph b: 8/9/30, Mississippi City, Miss. BR/TR, 6'1", 177 lbs. Deb: 9/10/52

YEAR	TM/L	G	AB	R	H	2B	3B	HR	RBI	BB	SO	AVG	OBP	SLG	PRO+	BR	/A	RC	SB	CS	SBR	FR	POS	TPR
1952	Bos-A	11	36	4	8	1	0	1	3	3	5	.222	.282	.333	66	-2	-2	3	0	1	-1	6	S	0.4
1953	Bos-A	109	323	30	85	12	1	5	28	23	41	.263	.318	.353	77	-9	-11	37	1	4	-2	5	*S	0.0
1954	Bos-A	113	370	42	92	20	3	6	36	47	55	.249	.340	.368	84	-3	-8	49	2	4	-2	15	*S/3	1.4
1955	Bos-A	6	5	0	1	0	0	0	0	0	1	.200	.200	.200	7	-1	-1	0	0	0	0	0	/S	0.0
1956	Bos-A	45	118	19	25	3	2	3	8	18	20	.212	.321	.347	68	-4	-6	14	0	1	-1	-8	S3/2	-1.1
1957	Bos-A	1	1	0	0	0	0	0	0	0	0	.000	.000	.000	-95	-0	-0	0	0	0	0	0	H	0.0
	Was-A	91	277	29	63	12	1	4	19	18	59	.227	.279	.321	64	-14	-14	22	2	2	-1	8	2S/3	0.0
	Yr	92	278	29	63	12	1	4	19	18	59	.227	.279	.320	64	-15	-14	22	2	2	-1	8		0.0
1958	Det-A	24	31	3	6	2	0	0	0	5	7	.194	.306	.258	53	-2	-2	3	0	0	0	2	S/23	0.2
Total	7	400	1161	127	280	50	7	19	94	114	188	.241	.314	.345	74	-34	-44	129	5	12	-6	28	S/23	0.9

■ DON BOLLWEG
Bollweg, Donald Raymond b: 2/12/21, Wheaton, Ill. BL/TL, 6'1", 190 lbs. Deb: 9/28/50

YEAR	TM/L	G	AB	R	H	2B	3B	HR	RBI	BB	SO	AVG	OBP	SLG	PRO+	BR	/A	RC	SB	CS	SBR	FR	POS	TPR
1950	StL-N	4	11	1	2	0	0	0	1	1	1	.182	.250	.182	15	-1	-1	0				-1	/1	-0.1
1951	StL-N	6	9	1	1	1	0	0	2	0	1	.111	.111	.222	-13	-1	-1	0	0	0	0	-0	/1	-0.1
1953	*NY-A	70	155	24	46	6	4	6	24	21	31	.297	.384	.503	143	8	9	33	1	0	0	-4	1	0.4
1954	Phi-A	103	268	35	60	15	3	5	24	35	33	.224	.320	.358	85	-5	-5	33	1	0	0	2	1	-0.5
1955	KC-A	12	9	1	1	0	0	0	2	3	2	.111	.333	.111	23	-1	-0	0	0	0	0	-0	/1	0.0
Total	5	195	452	62	110	22	7	11	53	60	68	.243	.337	.396	100	-1	-0	67	2	0		-3	1	-0.3

■ CECIL BOLTON
Bolton, Cecil Glenford "Glenn" b: 2/13/04, Booneville, Miss. BL/TR, 6'4", 195 lbs. Deb: 9/21/28

YEAR	TM/L	G	AB	R	H	2B	3B	HR	RBI	BB	SO	AVG	OBP	SLG	PRO+	BR	/A	RC	SB	CS	SBR	FR	POS	TPR
1928	Cle-A	4	13	1	2	0	0	0	2	0	2	.154	.267	.462	87	-0	-0	2	0	0	0	-1	/1	0.0

■ CLIFF BOLTON
Bolton, William Clifton b: 4/10/07, High Point, N.C. d: 4/21/79, Lexington, N.C. BL/TR, 5'9", 160 lbs. Deb: 4/20/31

YEAR	TM/L	G	AB	R	H	2B	3B	HR	RBI	BB	SO	AVG	OBP	SLG	PRO+	BR	/A	RC	SB	CS	SBR	FR	POS	TPR
1931	Was-A	23	43	3	11	1	1	0	6	1	5	.256	.273	.326	56	-3	-3	4	0	0	0	-5	C	-0.6
1933	*Was-A	33	39	4	16	1	1	0	6	6	3	.410	.500	.487	164	4	4	10	0	0	0	-1	/CO	0.3
1934	Was-A	42	148	12	40	9	1	1	17	11	9	.270	.321	.365	80	-5	-5	18	2	0	1	-3	C	-0.3
1935	Was-A	110	375	47	114	18	11	2	55	57	13	.304	.397	.427	117	9	11	66	0	1	-1	-22	*C	-0.7
1936	Was-A	86	289	41	84	18	4	2	51	25	12	.291	.349	.401	90	-7	-5	41	1	2	-1	-3	C	0.0
1937	Det-A	27	57	6	15	2	0	1	7	8	6	.263	.354	.351	76	-2	-2	8	0	0	0	0	C	0.0

YEAR	TM/L	G	AB	R	H	2B	3B	HR	RBI	BB	SO	AVG	OBP	SLG	PRO+	BR	/A	RC	SB	CS	SBR	FR	POS	TPR
1941	Was-A	14	11	0	0	0	0	0	1	1	2	.000	.083	.000	-80	-3	-3	0	0	0	0	0	/C	-0.1
Total	7	335	962	113	280	49	18	6	143	109	50	.291	.365	.398	98	-7	-2	146	3	3	-1	-35	C/O	-1.4

■ TOMMY BOND
Bond, Thomas Henry b: 4/2/1856, Granard, Ireland d: 1/24/41, Boston, Mass. BR/TR, 5'7.5", 160 lbs. Deb: 5/05/1874 MU

YEAR	TM/L	G	AB	R	H	2B	3B	HR	RBI	BB	SO	AVG	OBP	SLG	PRO+	BR	/A	RC	SB	CS	SBR	FR	POS	TPR
1874	Atl-n	55	247	25	54	11	0	0		1		.219	.222	.263	61	-12	-7	15					*P	0.0
1875	Har-n	71	289	32	78	12	3	0		0		.270	.270	.332	102	2	-0	27					PO/12	0.0
1876	Har-N	45	182	18	50	8	0	0	21	0	4	.275	.275	.319	90	-1	-3	16				5	P	0.0
1877	Bos-N	61	259	32	59	4	3	0	30	1	15	.228	.231	.266	54	-13	-14	16				3	*P/O	0.0
1878	Bos-N	59	236	22	50	4	1	0	23	0	9	.212	.212	.237	44	-13	-16	12				2	*P/O	0.0
1879	Bos-N	65	257	35	62	3	1	0	21	6	8	.241	.259	.261	70	-8	-8	18				7	*P/O1	0.0
1880	Bos-N	76	282	27	62	4	1	0	24	8	14	.220	.241	.241	66	-10	-9	17				12	*PO/31	0.0
1881	Bos-N	3	10	0	2	0	0	0	0	0	0	.200	.200	.200	27	-1	-1	0				1	/P	0.0
1882	Wor-N	8	30	1	4	0	0	0	2	2	3	.133	.188	.133	5	-3	-3	1				-2	/OPM	-0.4
1884	Bos-U	37	162	21	48	8	0	0		4		.296	.313	.346	125	4	4	18	0			1	PO/3	0.0
	Ind-a	7	23	0	3	1	1	0		0		.130	.130	.261	27	-2	-2	1				-2	/PO	0.0
Total	2 n	126	536	57	132	23	3	0		1		.246	.248	.300	84	-11	-8	41					/PO21	0.0
Total	8	361	1441	156	340	32	7	0	121	21	53	.236	.247	.268	68	-46	-51	99				28	P/O31	-0.4

■ WALT BOND
Bond, Walter Franklin b: 10/19/37, Denmark, Tenn. d: 9/14/67, Houston, Tex. BL/TR, 6'7", 228 lbs. Deb: 4/19/60

YEAR	TM/L	G	AB	R	H	2B	3B	HR	RBI	BB	SO	AVG	OBP	SLG	PRO+	BR	/A	RC	SB	CS	SBR	FR	POS	TPR
1960	Cle-A	40	131	19	29	2	1	5	18	13	14	.221	.306	.366	84	-4	-3	15	4	1	1	1	O	-0.2
1961	Cle-A	38	52	7	9	1	1	2	7	6	10	.173	.271	.346	65	-3	-3	5	1	0	0	1	O	-0.1
1962	Cle-A	12	50	10	19	3	0	6	17	4	9	.380	.426	.800	228	8	8	17	1	0	0	-1	O	0.7
1964	Hou-N	148	543	63	138	16	7	20	85	38	90	.254	.312	.420	110	2	6	70	2	2	-1	-10	1O	-0.9
1965	Hou-N	117	407	46	107	17	2	7	47	42	51	.263	.339	.366	106	0	3	52	2	1	0	-2	1O	-0.2
1967	Min-A	10	16	4	5	1	0	1	5	3	1	.313	.421	.563	174	2	2	4	0	0	0	0	/O	0.2
Total	6	365	1199	149	307	40	11	41	179	106	175	.256	.325	.410	110	6	14	163	10	4	1	-11	O1	-0.5

■ BARRY BONDS
Bonds, Barry Lamar b: 7/24/64, Riverside, Cal. BL/TL, 6'1", 185 lbs. Deb: 5/30/86

YEAR	TM/L	G	AB	R	H	2B	3B	HR	RBI	BB	SO	AVG	OBP	SLG	PRO+	BR	/A	RC	SB	CS	SBR	FR	POS	TPR
1986	Pit-N	113	413	72	92	26	3	16	48	65	102	.223	.331	.416	102	3	2	64	36	7	7	10	*O	1.7
1987	Pit-N	150	551	99	144	34	9	25	59	54	88	.261	.331	.492	114	10	9	93	32	10	4	17	*O	2.3
1988	Pit-N	144	538	97	152	30	5	24	58	72	82	.283	.369	.491	147	32	32	100	17	11	-2	1	*O	3.0
1989	Pit-N	159	580	96	144	34	6	19	58	93	93	.248	.353	.426	126	18	20	92	32	10	4	14	*O	3.7
1990	*Pit-N	151	519	104	156	32	3	33	114	93	83	.301	.410	.565	172	48	51	128	52	13	8	11	*O	6.5
Total	5	717	2601	468	688	156	26	117	337	377	448	.265	.360	.479	133	110	114	477	169	51	20	53	O	17.2

■ BOBBY BONDS
Bonds, Bobby Lee b: 3/15/46, Riverside, Cal. BR/TR, 6'1", 190 lbs. Deb: 6/25/68 C

YEAR	TM/L	G	AB	R	H	2B	3B	HR	RBI	BB	SO	AVG	OBP	SLG	PRO+	BR	/A	RC	SB	CS	SBR	FR	POS	TPR
1968	SF-N	81	307	55	78	10	5	9	35	38	84	.254	.338	.407	123	9	9	46	16	7	1	6	O	1.3
1969	SF-N	158	622	120	161	25	6	32	90	81	187	.259	.353	.473	132	24	26	114	45	4	11	11	*O	4.1
1970	SF-N	157	663	134	200	36	10	26	78	77	189	.302	.376	.504	135	31	32	134	48	10	8	11	*O	4.3
1971	*SF-N	155	619	110	178	32	4	33	102	62	137	.288	.357	.512	146	34	35	115	26	8	3	7	*O	4.1
1972	SF-N	153	626	118	162	29	5	26	80	60	137	.259	.329	.446	116	13	12	96	44	6	10	10	*O	2.6
1973	SF-N	160	643	131	182	34	4	39	96	87	148	.283	.372	.530	141	40	37	130	43	17	3	8	*O	4.2
1974	SF-N	150	567	97	145	22	8	21	71	95	134	.256	.366	.434	118	19	16	100	41	11	6	4	*O	2.0
1975	NY-A	145	529	93	143	26	3	32	85	89	137	.270	.378	.512	154	35	37	103	30	17	-1	9	*OD	4.2
1976	Cal-A	99	378	48	100	10	3	10	54	41	90	.265	.341	.386	120	6	9	50	30	15	0	-7	O/D	0.0
1977	Cal-A	158	592	103	156	23	9	37	115	74	141	.264	.347	.520	138	26	29	107	41	18	2	-1	*OD	2.4
1978	Chi-A	26	90	8	25	4	0	2	8	10	10	.278	.350	.389	107	1	1	13	6	2	1	-1	O/D	0.0
	Tex-A	130	475	85	126	15	4	29	82	69	110	.265	.361	.497	139	24	24	82	37	20	-1	2	*OD	2.3
	Yr	156	565	93	151	19	4	31	90	79	120	.267	.359	.480	133	25	25	95	43	22	-0	1		2.3
1979	Cle-A	146	538	93	148	24	1	25	85	74	135	.275	.371	.463	123	19	18	92	34	23	-4	8	*OD	1.8
1980	StL-N	86	231	37	47	5	3	5	24	33	74	.203	.308	.316	72	-7	-8	25	15	5	2	-5	O	-1.5
1981	Chi-N	45	163	26	35	7	1	6	19	24	44	.215	.323	.380	95	-0	-1	19	5	6	-2	0	O	-0.3
Total	14	1849	7043	1258	1886	302	66	332	1024	914	1757	.268	.356	.471	129	274	276	1224	461	169	37	63	*O/D	31.5

■ GEORGE BONE
Bone, George Drummond b: 8/28/1876, New Haven, Conn. d: 5/26/18, West Haven, Conn. BB/TR, 5'7", 152 lbs. Deb: 9/18/01

YEAR	TM/L	G	AB	R	H	2B	3B	HR	RBI	BB	SO	AVG	OBP	SLG	PRO+	BR	/A	RC	SB	CS	SBR	FR	POS	TPR
1901	Mil-A	12	43	6	13	2	0	0	6	4		.302	.362	.349	105	0	0	6	0			-2	S	0.0

■ NINO BONGIOVANNI
Bongiovanni, Anthony Thomas b: 12/21/11, Pike's Peak, La. BL/TL, 5'10", 175 lbs. Deb: 4/23/38

YEAR	TM/L	G	AB	R	H	2B	3B	HR	RBI	BB	SO	AVG	OBP	SLG	PRO+	BR	/A	RC	SB	CS	SBR	FR	POS	TPR
1938	Cin-N	2	7	0	2	1	0	0	0	0	0	.286	.286	.429	97	-0	-0	1	0			0	/O	0.0
1939	*Cin-N	66	159	17	41	6	0	0	16	9	8	.258	.298	.296	60	-9	-9	15	0			2	O	-0.7
Total	2	68	166	17	43	7	0	0	16	9	8	.259	.297	.301	61	-9	-9	15	0			2	/O	-0.7

■ JUAN BONILLA
Bonilla, Juan Guillermo b: 2/12/55, Santurce, P.R. BR/TR, 5'9", 170 lbs. Deb: 4/09/81

YEAR	TM/L	G	AB	R	H	2B	3B	HR	RBI	BB	SO	AVG	OBP	SLG	PRO+	BR	/A	RC	SB	CS	SBR	FR	POS	TPR
1981	SD-N	99	369	30	107	13	2	1	25	25	23	.290	.338	.344	101	-3	0	41	4	9	-4	-11	2	-0.8
1982	SD-N	45	182	21	51	6	2	0	8	11	15	.280	.325	.335	90	-4	-2	20	0	1	-1	-8	2	-0.8
1983	SD-N	152	556	55	132	17	4	4	45	50	40	.237	.304	.304	71	-23	-21	50	3	0	1	-15	*2	-3.0
1985	NY-A	8	16	0	2	1	0	0	2	0	3	.125	.125	.188	-16	-3	-2	0	0	0	0	1	/2	0.0
1986	Bal-A	102	284	33	69	10	1	1	18	25	21	.243	.311	.296	67	-13	-12	25	0	0	0	-9	23/D	-1.7
1987	NY-A	23	55	6	14	3	0	1	3	5	6	.255	.317	.364	81	-2	-1	6	0	0	0	1	2/3D	0.1
Total	6	429	1462	145	375	50	9	7	101	116	108	.256	.315	.317	79	-46	-39	142	7	10	-4	-41	2/3D	-6.2

■ BOBBY BONILLA
Bonilla, Roberto Martin Antonio b: 2/23/63, New York, N.Y. BB/TR, 6'3", 210 lbs. Deb: 4/09/86

YEAR	TM/L	G	AB	R	H	2B	3B	HR	RBI	BB	SO	AVG	OBP	SLG	PRO+	BR	/A	RC	SB	CS	SBR	FR	POS	TPR
1986	Chi-A	75	234	27	63	10	2	2	26	33	49	.269	.362	.355	93	-0	-1	32	4	1	1	1	O1	-0.2
	Pit-N	63	192	28	46	6	2	1	17	29	39	.240	.342	.307	79	-4	-5	21	4	4	-1	-2	O/13	-0.9
1987	Pit-N	141	466	58	140	33	3	15	77	39	64	.300	.357	.481	119	12	12	78	3	5	-2	-16	3O/1	-0.8
1988	Pit-N	159	584	87	160	32	7	24	100	85	82	.274	.370	.476	143	32	33	106	3	5	-2	-1	*3	3.1
1989	Pit-N	163	616	96	173	37	10	24	86	76	93	.281	.361	.490	146	32	35	108	8	8	-1	6	*3/1O	3.9
1990	*Pit-N	160	625	112	175	39	7	32	120	45	103	.280	.329	.518	135	22	25	104	4	3	-1	-6	*O3/1	1.5
Total	5	761	2717	408	757	157	31	98	426	307	430	.279	.354	.467	128	95	99	449	26	26	-8	-19	3O/1	6.6

■ LUTHER BONIN
Bonin, Ernest Luther "Bonnie" b: 1/13/1888, Green Hill, Ind. d: 1/3/65, Sycamore, Ohio BL/TR, 5'9.5", 178 lbs. Deb: 4/13/13

YEAR	TM/L	G	AB	R	H	2B	3B	HR	RBI	BB	SO	AVG	OBP	SLG	PRO+	BR	/A	RC	SB	CS	SBR	FR	POS	TPR
1913	StL-A	1	1	0	0	0	0	0	0	0	0	.000	.000	.000	-99	-0	-0	0	0			1	H	0.0
1914	Buf-F	20	76	6	14	4	1	0	4	7	11	.184	.253	.263	47	-5	-5	6	3			1	O	-0.5
Total	2	21	77	6	14	4	1	0	4	7	11	.182	.250	.260	45	-5	-6	6	3			1	/O	-0.5

■ BARRY BONNELL
Bonnell, Robert Barry b: 10/27/53, Clermont County, O. BR/TR, 6'3", 190 lbs. Deb: 5/04/77

YEAR	TM/L	G	AB	R	H	2B	3B	HR	RBI	BB	SO	AVG	OBP	SLG	PRO+	BR	/A	RC	SB	CS	SBR	FR	POS	TPR
1977	Atl-N	100	360	41	108	11	0	1	45	37	32	.300	.368	.339	81	-3	-8	45	7	5	-1	10	O3	-0.1
1978	Atl-N	117	304	36	73	11	3	1	16	20	30	.240	.287	.306	59	-14	-18	32	13	6	0	9	*O3	-1.2
1979	Atl-N	127	375	47	97	20	3	12	45	26	55	.259	.312	.424	92	-2	-5	46	8	7	-2	-17	*O/3	-2.8
1980	Tor-A	130	463	55	124	22	4	13	56	37	59	.268	.325	.417	97	0	-2	59	3	4	-2	-7	*O/D	-1.2
1981	Tor-A	66	227	21	50	7	4	4	28	12	25	.220	.262	.339	68	-9	-10	18	4	3	-1	1	O	-1.1
1982	Tor-A	140	437	59	128	26	3	6	49	32	51	.293	.345	.407	97	4	-2	63	14	2	3	-10	*O/3D	-1.2
1983	Tor-A	121	377	49	120	21	3	10	54	33	52	.318	.373	.469	123	16	13	64	10	7	-1	-3	*O/3D	0.7
1984	Sea-A	110	363	42	96	15	4	8	48	25	51	.264	.315	.394	96	-3	-2	43	5	2	0	-6	O3/1D	-1.0
1985	Sea-A	48	111	9	27	8	0	1	10	6	19	.243	.282	.342	70	-5	-5	10	1	2	-1	0	O/1D	-0.5

YEAR	TM/L	G	AB	R	H	2B	3B	HR	RBI	BB	SO	AVG	OBP	SLG	PRO+	BR	/A	RC	SB	CS	SBR	FR	POS	TPR
1986	Sea-A	17	51	4	10	2	0	0	4	1	13	.196	.212	.235	21	-6	-6	2	0	1	-1	1	/O1D	-0.5
Total	10	976	3068	363	833	143	24	56	355	229	387	.272	.325	.389	89	-21	-46	374	64	39	-4	-21	O/3D1	-8.9

■ FRANK BONNER
Bonner, Frank J   b: 8/20/1869, Lowell, Mass.   d: 12/31/05, Kansas City, Mo.   BR/TR, 5'7.5", 169 lbs.   Deb: 4/26/1894

YEAR	TM/L	G	AB	R	H	2B	3B	HR	RBI	BB	SO	AVG	OBP	SLG	PRO+	BR	/A	RC	SB	CS	SBR	FR	POS	TPR
1894	*Bal-N	33	118	27	38	10	2	0	24	17	5	.322	.412	.441	103	2	1	27	12			-15	2/O3S	-0.9
1895	Bal-N	11	42	9	14	1	1	0	7	5	1	.333	.404	.405	108	1	1	9	4			-5	3	-0.3
	StL-N	15	59	3	8	0	1	1	8	1	8	.136	.164	.220	-1	-9	-9	3	2			-5	3/OC	-1.1
	Yr	26	101	12	22	1	2	1	15	6	9	.218	.269	.297	47	-8	-8	10	6			-10		-1.4
1896	Bro-N	9	34	8	6	2	0	0	5	2	8	.176	.263	.235	35	-3	-3	2	1			-1	/2	-0.2
1899	Was-N	85	347	41	95	20	4	2	44	18		.274	.313	.372	91	-6	-5	43	6			2	2	0.2
1902	Cle-A	34	132	14	37	6	0	0	14	5		.280	.312	.326	82	-4	-3	14	1			-10	2	-1.0
	Phi-A	11	44	2	8	0	0	0	3	0		.182	.200	.182	7	-5	-6	2	0			3	2	-0.1
	Yr	45	176	16	45	6	0	0	17	5		.256	.284	.290	62	-9	-9	15	1			-7		-1.1
1903	Bos-N	48	173	11	38	5	0	1	10	7		.220	.250	.266	50	-12	-11	13	2			-4	2S	-1.0
Total	6	246	949	115	244	44	8	4	115	55	22	.257	.303	.333	74	-36	-34	113	28			-34	2/S3OC	-4.4

■ BOBBY BONNER
Bonner, Robert Averill   b: 8/12/56, Uvalde, Tex.   BR/TR, 6', 185 lbs.   Deb: 9/12/80

YEAR	TM/L	G	AB	R	H	2B	3B	HR	RBI	BB	SO	AVG	OBP	SLG	PRO+	BR	/A	RC	SB	CS	SBR	FR	POS	TPR
1980	Bal-A	4	4	1	0	0	0	0	1	0	0	.000	.000	.000	-99	-1	-1	0	0	0	0	1	/S	0.0
1981	Bal-A	10	27	6	8	2	0	0	2	1	4	.296	.321	.370	99	-0	-0	4	1	0	0	1	/S	0.1
1982	Bal-A	41	77	8	13	3	1	0	5	3	12	.169	.200	.234	19	-9	-9	3	0	0	0	-5	S/2	-1.0
1983	Bal-A	6	0	0	0	0	0	0	0	0	0	—	—	—	—	0	0	0	0	0	0	-0	/2D	0.0
Total	4	61	108	15	21	5	1	0	8	4	16	.194	.223	.259	34	-10	-10	7	1	0	0	-3	/S2D	-0.9

■ ZEKE BONURA
Bonura, Henry John   b: 9/20/08, New Orleans, La.   d: 3/9/87, New Orleans, La.   BR/TR, 6', 210 lbs.   Deb: 4/17/34

YEAR	TM/L	G	AB	R	H	2B	3B	HR	RBI	BB	SO	AVG	OBP	SLG	PRO+	BR	/A	RC	SB	CS	SBR	FR	POS	TPR
1934	Chi-A	127	510	86	154	35	4	27	110	64	31	.302	.380	.545	132	25	23	106	0	2	-1	5	*1	0.4
1935	Chi-A	138	550	107	162	34	4	21	92	57	28	.295	.364	.485	115	13	11	99	4	0	1	2	*1	0.0
1936	Chi-A	148	587	120	194	39	7	12	138	94	29	.330	.426	.482	119	25	22	126	4	2	0	12	*1	1.2
1937	Chi-A	116	447	79	154	41	2	19	100	49	24	.345	.412	.573	146	30	30	107	5	1	1	-1	*1	1.4
1938	Was-A	137	540	72	156	27	3	22	114	44	29	.289	.346	.472	111	0	6	88	2	2	-1	3	*1	-0.8
1939	NY-N	123	455	75	146	26	6	11	85	46	22	.321	.388	.527	130	20	20	80	1			5	*1	1.1
1940	Was-A	79	311	41	85	16	3	3	45	40	13	.273	.358	.373	96	-4	-1	45	2	0	1	-4	1	-0.7
	Chi-N	49	182	20	48	14	0	4	20	10	4	.264	.302	.407	96	-2	-2	18	1			5	1	0.0
Total	7	917	3582	600	1099	232	29	119	704	404	180	.307	.380	.487	121	108	109	670	19	7		27	1	2.6

■ EVERETT BOOE
Booe, Everett Little   b: 9/28/1891, Mocksville, N.C.   d: 5/21/69, Kenedy, Tex.   BL/TR, 5'8.5", 165 lbs.   Deb: 4/13/13

YEAR	TM/L	G	AB	R	H	2B	3B	HR	RBI	BB	SO	AVG	OBP	SLG	PRO+	BR	/A	RC	SB	CS	SBR	FR	POS	TPR
1913	Pit-N	29	80	9	16	0	2	0	2	6	9	.200	.256	.250	47	-6	-5	5	2			1	O	-0.4
1914	Ind-F	20	31	5	7	1	0	0	6	7	6	.226	.368	.452	73	-0	-1	5	4			-1	/OS	-0.1
	Buf-F	76	241	29	54	9	2	0	14	21	50	.224	.289	.278	62	-11	-12	23	8			-4	O/S32	-1.8
	Yr	96	272	34	61	10	2	0	20	28	56	.224	.299	.276	63	-12	-13	28	12			-5		-1.9
Total	2	125	352	43	77	10	4	0	22	34	65	.219	.289	.270	60	-17	-18	33	14			-4	/OS32	-2.3

■ BUDDY BOOKER
Booker, Richard Lee   b: 5/28/42, Lynchburg, Va.   BL/TR, 5'10", 170 lbs.   Deb: 6/04/66

YEAR	TM/L	G	AB	R	H	2B	3B	HR	RBI	BB	SO	AVG	OBP	SLG	PRO+	BR	/A	RC	SB	CS	SBR	FR	POS	TPR
1966	Cle-A	18	28	6	6	1	0	2	5	2	6	.214	.267	.464	105	0	0	3	0	0	0	-5	C	-0.3
1968	Chi-A	5	5	0	0	0	0	0	0	1	2	.000	.167	.000	-46	-1	-1	0	0	0	0	-1	/C	-0.1
Total	2	23	33	6	6	1	0	2	5	3	8	.182	.250	.394	83	-1	-1	3	0	0	0	-5	/C	-0.4

■ ROD BOOKER
Booker, Roderick Stewart   b: 9/4/58, Los Angeles, Cal.   BL/TR, 6'", 175 lbs.   Deb: 4/29/87

YEAR	TM/L	G	AB	R	H	2B	3B	HR	RBI	BB	SO	AVG	OBP	SLG	PRO+	BR	/A	RC	SB	CS	SBR	FR	POS	TPR
1987	StL-N	44	47	9	13	1	1	0	8	7	7	.277	.370	.340	88	-0	-1	7	2	0	1	3	2/3S	0.4
1988	StL-N	18	35	6	12	3	0	0	3	4	3	.343	.410	.429	140	2	2	6	2	2	-1	-3	3/2	0.0
1989	StL-N	10	8	1	2	0	0	0	0	0	1	.250	.250	.250	42	-1	-1	1	0	0	0	2	/23	0.2
1990	Phi-N	73	131	19	29	5	2	0	10	15	26	.221	.301	.290	64	-6	-6	10	3	1	0	-6	S23	-0.8
Total	4	145	221	35	56	9	3	0	21	26	37	.253	.332	.321	80	-5	-5	24	7	3	0	-3	/2S3	-0.2

■ AL BOOL
Bool, Albert J.   b: 8/24/1897, Lincoln, Neb.   d: 9/27/81, Lincoln, Neb.   BR/TR, 5'11", 180 lbs.   Deb: 9/29/28

YEAR	TM/L	G	AB	R	H	2B	3B	HR	RBI	BB	SO	AVG	OBP	SLG	PRO+	BR	/A	RC	SB	CS	SBR	FR	POS	TPR
1928	Was-A	2	7	0	1	0	0	0	1	0	0	.143	.143	.143	-25	-1	-1	0	0	0	0	0	/C	0.0
1930	Pit-N	78	216	30	56	12	4	7	46	25	29	.259	.336	.449	87	-5	-5	32	0			-1	C	-0.1
1931	Bos-N	49	85	5	16	1	0	0	6	9	13	.188	.266	.200	28	-9	-8	5	0			-2	C	-0.7
Total	3	129	308	35	73	13	4	7	53	34	42	.237	.313	.373	71	-15	-14	38	0	0		-2	C	-0.8

■ IKE BOONE
Boone, Isaac Morgan   b: 2/17/1897, Samantha, Ala.   d: 8/1/58, Northport, Ala.   BL/TR, 6', 195 lbs.   Deb: 4/22/22

YEAR	TM/L	G	AB	R	H	2B	3B	HR	RBI	BB	SO	AVG	OBP	SLG	PRO+	BR	/A	RC	SB	CS	SBR	FR	POS	TPR
1922	NY-N	2	2	0	1	0	0	0	0	0	1	.500	.500	.500	157	0	0	0	0	0	0	0	H	0.0
1923	Bos-A	5	15	1	4	0	1	0	2	1	0	.267	.313	.400	86	-0	0	2	0	1	-1	0	/O	0.0
1924	Bos-A	128	487	72	164	31	4	13	98	54	32	.337	.404	.497	131	22	22	99	2	2	-1	-7	*O	0.6
1925	Bos-A	133	476	79	157	34	5	9	68	60	19	.330	.406	.479	124	18	18	94	1	4	-2	-7	*O	-0.1
1927	Chi-A	29	53	10	12	4	0	1	11	3	4	.226	.268	.358	63	-3	-3	5	0	0	0	-2	O	-0.5
1930	Bro-N	40	101	13	30	9	1	3	13	14	8	.297	.383	.495	112	2	2	19	0			-2	O	-0.1
1931	Bro-N	6	5	0	1	0	0	0	0	1	1	.200	.333	.200	47	-0	-0	0	0			0	H	-0.1
1932	Bro-N	13	21	2	3	1	0	0	2	5	2	.143	.308	.190	38	-2	-2	2	0			0	/O	-0.1
Total	8	356	1160	177	372	79	11	26	194	138	67	.321	.394	.475	121	36	37	221	3	7		-17	O	-0.2

■ LUKE BOONE
Boone, Lute Joseph "Danny"   b: 5/6/1890, Pittsburgh, Pa.   d: 7/29/82, Pittsburgh, Pa.   BR/TR, 5'9", 160 lbs.   Deb: 9/09/13

YEAR	TM/L	G	AB	R	H	2B	3B	HR	RBI	BB	SO	AVG	OBP	SLG	PRO+	BR	/A	RC	SB	CS	SBR	FR	POS	TPR
1913	NY-A	6	12	3	4	0	0	0	1	3	1	.333	.467	.333	134	1	1	2	0			-1	/S	0.0
1914	NY-A	106	370	34	82	8	2	0	21	31	41	.222	.285	.254	63	-17	-17	26	10	18	-8	23	2/3O	-0.1
1915	NY-A	130	431	44	88	12	2	5	43	41	53	.204	.285	.276	68	-17	-17	35	14	17	-6	**21**	*2S/3	-0.1
1916	NY-A	46	124	14	23	4	0	1	8	8	10	.185	.252	.242	47	-8	-8	10	7			7	3S/2	0.1
1918	Pit-N	27	91	7	18	3	0	0	3	8	6	.198	.263	.231	49	-5	-6	6	1			-0	S/2	-0.5
Total	5	315	1028	102	215	27	4	6	76	91	111	.209	.282	.261	63	-46	-47	79	32	35		50	2/S3O	-0.6

■ RAY BOONE
Boone, Raymond Otis "Ike"   b: 7/27/23, San Diego, Cal.   BR/TR, 6', 172 lbs.   Deb: 9/03/48

YEAR	TM/L	G	AB	R	H	2B	3B	HR	RBI	BB	SO	AVG	OBP	SLG	PRO+	BR	/A	RC	SB	CS	SBR	FR	POS	TPR
1948	*Cle-A	6	5	0	2	1	0	0	1	0	1	.400	.400	.600	168	0	0	1	0	0	0	1	/S	0.2
1949	Cle-A	86	258	39	65	4	4	4	26	38	17	.252	.352	.345	87	-5	-4	32	0	2	-1	2	S	-0.2
1950	Cle-A	109	365	53	110	14	6	7	58	56	27	.301	.397	.430	116	8	10	65	4	3	-1	-9	*S	0.4
1951	Cle-A	151	544	65	127	14	1	12	51	48	36	.233	.302	.329	75	-23	-19	55	5	3	-0	-7	*S	-1.6
1952	Cle-A	103	316	57	83	8	2	7	45	53	33	.263	.372	.367	113	4	7	45	0	1	-1	-10	S/32	0.1
1953	Cle-A	34	112	21	27	1	2	4	21	24	21	.241	.375	.393	110	2	2	18	1	2	-1	-1	S	0.3
	Det-A	101	385	73	120	16	6	22	93	48	47	.312	.395	.556	156	29	29	89	2	1	0	1	3/S	2.6
	Yr	135	497	94	147	17	8	26	114	72	68	.296	.390	.519	146	30	32	106	3	3	-1	0		2.9
1954	Det-A	148	543	76	160	19	7	20	85	71	53	.295	.378	.464	133	23	24	95	4	2	0	-1	*3/S	1.8
1955	Det-A	135	500	61	142	22	7	20	**116**	50	49	.284	.350	.476	123	12	14	80	1	1	-0	-5	*3	1.1
1956	Det-A	131	481	77	148	14	6	25	81	77	46	.308	.406	.518	142	30	30	103	0	0	0	-6	*3	2.6
1957	Det-A	129	462	48	126	25	3	12	65	57	47	.273	.356	.418	108	7	6	68	1	1	-0	-10	*1/3	-0.5
1958	Det-A	39	114	16	27	4	1	6	20	14	33	.237	.326	.447	103	1	0	16	0	2	-1	-1	*3	-0.2
	Chi-A	77	246	25	60	12	1	7	41	18	33	.244	.298	.386	89	-5	-4	27	1	1	-0	-2	1	-0.8
	Yr	116	360	41	87	16	2	13	61	32	46	.242	.307	.406	93	-4	-4	43	1	3	-2	-3		-1.0
1959	Chi-A	9	21	3	5	0	0	1	5	7	5	.238	.429	.381	126	1	1	5	1	0	0	0	/1	0.2

YEAR	TM/L	G	AB	R	H	2B	3B	HR	RBI	BB	SO	AVG	OBP	SLG	PRO+	BR	/A	RC	SB	CS	SBR	FR	POS	TPR
	KC-A	61	132	19	36	6	0	2	12	27	17	.273	.396	.364	108	3	3	21	1	0	0	1	1/3	0.4
	Yr	70	153	22	41	6	0	3	17	34	22	.268	.401	.366	111	4	4	25	2	0	1	1		0.6
	Mil-N	13	15	3	3	0	0	1	2	4	2	.200	.368	.400	114	0	0	2	0	0	0	-0	/1	0.0
1960	Mil-N	7	12	3	3	1	0	0	4	5	1	.250	.471	.333	135	1	1	2	0	0	0	0	/1	0.1
	Bos-N	34	78	6	16	1	0	1	11	11	15	.205	.303	.256	51	-5	-5	6	0	0	0	0	1	-0.6
Total	13	1373	4589	645	1260	162	46	151	737	608	463	.275	.363	.429	115	84	95	731	21	19	-5	-45	3S1/2	5.9

■ BOB BOONE   Boone, Robert Raymond b: 11/19/47, San Diego, Cal. BR/TR, 6'2.5", 195 lbs. Deb: 9/10/72

YEAR	TM/L	G	AB	R	H	2B	3B	HR	RBI	BB	SO	AVG	OBP	SLG	PRO+	BR	/A	RC	SB	CS	SBR	FR	POS	TPR
1972	Phi-N	16	51	4	14	1	0	1	4	5	7	.275	.339	.353	95	-0	-0	6	1	0	0	-6	C	-0.5
1973	Phi-N	145	521	42	136	20	2	10	61	41	36	.261	.315	.365	86	-9	-11	60	3	4	-2	7	*C	0.3
1974	Phi-N	146	488	41	118	24	3	3	52	35	29	.242	.298	.322	70	-18	-20	45	3	1	0	-7	*C	-2.1
1975	Phi-N	97	289	28	71	14	2	2	20	32	14	.246	.323	.329	78	-7	-8	30	1	3	-2	0	C/3	-0.6
1976	*Phi-N	121	361	40	98	18	2	4	54	45	44	.271	.354	.366	101	3	2	45	2	5	-2	-10	*C/1	-0.5
1977	*Phi-N	132	440	55	125	26	4	11	66	42	54	.284	.349	.436	105	6	3	66	5	5	-2	2	*C/3	0.1
1978	*Phi-N	132	435	48	123	18	4	12	62	46	37	.283	.353	.425	115	10	9	62	2	5	-2	-10	*C/1O	0.0
1979	Phi-N	119	398	38	114	21	3	9	58	49	33	.286	.367	.422	111	9	7	61	1	4	-2	-13	*C/3	-0.4
1980	*Phi-N	141	480	34	110	23	1	9	55	48	41	.229	.301	.338	74	-14	-17	48	3	4	-2	4	*C	-1.2
1981	*Phi-N	76	227	19	48	7	0	4	24	22	16	.211	.281	.295	61	-11	-12	18	2	2	-1	-3	C	-1.4
1982	*Cal-A	143	472	42	121	17	0	7	58	39	34	.256	.313	.337	79	-14	-14	51	2	2	-1	6	*C	0.0
1983	Cal-A	142	468	46	120	18	0	6	52	24	42	.256	.293	.353	77	-15	-15	44	4	3	-1	4	*C	-0.4
1984	Cal-A	139	450	33	91	16	1	3	32	25	45	.202	.244	.262	40	-37	-36	28	3	3	-1	7	*C	-2.2
1985	Cal-A	150	460	37	114	17	0	5	55	37	35	.248	.308	.317	72	-17	-17	45	1	2	-1	4	*C	-0.6
1986	*Cal-A	144	442	48	98	12	2	7	49	43	30	.222	.291	.305	63	-23	-22	39	1	0	0	11	*C	-0.1
1987	Cal-A	128	389	42	94	18	0	3	33	35	36	.242	.306	.311	66	-20	-18	37	0	2	-1	-1	*C/D	-0.8
1988	Cal-A	122	352	38	104	17	0	5	39	29	26	.295	.352	.386	110	4	5	47	2	2	-1	-10	*C	0.0
1989	KC-A	131	405	33	111	13	2	1	43	49	37	.274	.355	.323	93	-2	-2	47	3	2	-0	3	*C	0.6
1990	KC-A	40	117	11	28	3	0	0	9	17	12	.239	.336	.265	72	-4	-4	11	1	1	-0	2	C	0.0
Total	19	2264	7245	679	1838	303	26	105	826	663	608	.254	.318	.346	82	-160	-170	790	38	50	-19	-9	*C/13DO	-9.8

■ BOOTH   Booth *'", Deb: 5/01/1875

YEAR	TM/L	G	AB	R	H	2B	3B	HR	RBI	BB	SO	AVG	OBP	SLG	PRO+	BR	/A	RC	SB	CS	SBR	FR	POS	TPR
1875	NH-n	1	2	0	0	0	0	0		0		.000	.000	.000	-99	-0	-0	0					/S	0.0

■ AMOS BOOTH   Booth, Amos Smith "Darling" b: 9/14/1853, Cincinnati, O. d: 7/1/21, Miamisburg, Ohio BR/TR, Deb: 4/25/1876

YEAR	TM/L	G	AB	R	H	2B	3B	HR	RBI	BB	SO	AVG	OBP	SLG	PRO+	BR	/A	RC	SB	CS	SBR	FR	POS	TPR
1876	Cin-N	63	272	31	71	3	0	0	14	9	11	.261	.285	.272	101	-4	3	22				-16	3CS/OP	-1.1
1877	Cin-N	44	157	16	27	2	1	0	13	12	10	.172	.231	.197	41	-11	-8	7				-4	SCP2/3O	-0.7
1880	Cin-N	1	2	0	0	0	0	0	0	0	0	.000	.000	.000	-99	-0	-0	0				0	/3	0.0
1882	Bal-a	1	3	0	0	0	0	0		0		.000	.000	.000	-99	-1	-1	0				0	/3	0.0
	Lou-a	1	4	0	0	0	0	0		0		.000	.000	.000	-99	-1	-1	0				-1	/2	0.0
	Yr	2	7	0	0	0	0	0		0		.000	.000	.000	-99	-1	-1	0				-1		0.0
Total	4	110	438	47	98	5	1	0	27	21	21	.224	.259	.240	73	-16	-7	29				-20	/CS3P2O	-1.8

■ EDDIE BOOTH   Booth, Edward H. b: Brooklyn, N.Y. Deb: 4/26/1872

YEAR	TM/L	G	AB	R	H	2B	3B	HR	RBI	BB	SO	AVG	OBP	SLG	PRO+	BR	/A	RC	SB	CS	SBR	FR	POS	TPR
1872	Man-n	24	118	24	40	3	2	0		0		.339	.339	.398	134	3	5	16					2/O	0.2
	Atl-n	15	62	11	18	5	0	0		0		.290	.290	.371	87	0	-2	7					O/2	0.0
	Yr	39	180	35	58	8	2	0		0		.322	.322	.389	114	3	2	23						0.2
1873	Res-n	18	74	11	21	2	2	0		0		.284	.284	.365	97	-1	0	8					O/2	0.0
	Atl-n	16	69	8	14	3	1	0		3		.203	.236	.275	56	-4	-3	5					O	0.0
	Yr	34	143	19	35	5	3	0		3		.245	.260	.322	77	-5	-2	12						0.0
1874	Atl-n	44	187	24	47	2	4	1		3		.251	.263	.321	96	-3	1	16					*O	0.1
1875	Mut-n	68	278	33	55	3	4	0		1		.198	.201	.237	48	-13	16	14					*O/2P	-1.2
1876	NY-N	57	228	17	49	2	1	0	7	2	4	.215	.222	.232	59	-11	-7	12				-5	*O/2P	-1.0
Total	4 n	185	788	111	195	18	13	1		7		.247	.254	.307	80	-18	-15	65					O/2D	-0.9

■ FRENCHY BORDAGARAY   Bordagaray, Stanley George b: 1/3/10, Coalinga, Cal. BR/TR, 5'7.5", 175 lbs. Deb: 4/17/34

YEAR	TM/L	G	AB	R	H	2B	3B	HR	RBI	BB	SO	AVG	OBP	SLG	PRO+	BR	/A	RC	SB	CS	SBR	FR	POS	TPR
1934	Chi-A	29	87	12	28	3	1	0	2	3	8	.322	.344	.379	84	-2	-2	11	1	2	-1	-2	O	-0.4
1935	Bro-N	120	422	69	119	19	6	1	39	17	29	.282	.319	.363	85	-10	-9	51	18			5	*O	-0.8
1936	Bro-N	125	372	63	117	21	3	4	31	17	42	.315	.346	.419	104	2	2	54	12			3	O2/3	0.2
1937	StL-N	96	300	43	88	11	4	1	37	15	25	.293	.331	.367	88	-5	-5	37	11			-8	3O	-1.1
1938	StL-N	81	156	19	44	5	1	0	21	8	9	.282	.325	.327	76	-4	-5	17	2			2	O/3	-0.3
1939	*Cin-N	63	122	19	24	5	1	0	12	9	10	.197	.252	.254	36	-11	-11	8	3			0	O/2	-1.0
1941	*NY-A	36	73	10	19	1	0	0	4	6	8	.260	.325	.274	61	-4	-4	7	1	0	0	-1	O	-0.5
1942	Bro-N	48	58	11	14	2	0	0	5	3	3	.241	.279	.276	62	-3	-3	4	2			1	O	-0.2
1943	Bro-N	89	268	47	81	18	2	0	19	30	15	.302	.379	.384	120	8	8	42	6			-11	O3	-0.4
1944	Bro-N	130	501	85	141	26	4	6	51	36	22	.281	.331	.385	103	-0	1	64	2			-19	3O	-1.4
1945	Bro-N	113	273	32	70	9	6	2	49	29	15	.256	.328	.355	91	-4	-3	33	7			-6	3O	-1.1
Total	11	930	2632	410	745	120	28	14	270	173	186	.283	.331	.366	91	-32	-33	329	65	2		-34	O3/2	-7.0

■ PAT BORDERS   Borders, Patrick Lance b: 5/14/63, Columbus, Ohio BR/TR, 6'2", 190 lbs. Deb: 4/06/88

YEAR	TM/L	G	AB	R	H	2B	3B	HR	RBI	BB	SO	AVG	OBP	SLG	PRO+	BR	/A	RC	SB	CS	SBR	FR	POS	TPR
1988	Tor-A	56	154	15	42	6	3	5	21	3	24	.273	.287	.448	102	-0	-0	18	0	0	0	2	C/23D	0.3
1989	*Tor-A	94	241	22	62	11	1	3	29	11	45	.257	.292	.349	81	-7	-6	23	2	1	0	0	CD	-0.2
1990	Tor-A	125	346	36	99	24	2	15	49	18	57	.286	.321	.497	128	10	11	48	0	1	-1	-1	*C/D	1.2
Total	3	275	741	73	203	41	6	23	99	32	126	.274	.305	.439	108	3	4	89	2	2	-1	0	C/D32	1.3

■ MIKE BORDICK   Bordick, Michael Todd b: 7/21/65, Marquette, Mich. BR/TR, 5'11", 170 lbs. Deb: 4/11/90

YEAR	TM/L	G	AB	R	H	2B	3B	HR	RBI	BB	SO	AVG	OBP	SLG	PRO+	BR	/A	RC	SB	CS	SBR	FR	POS	TPR
1990	*Oak-A	25	14	0	1	0	0	0	0	1	4	.071	.133	.071	-42	-3	-3	0	0	0	0	-0	3/S2	-0.1

■ GLENN BORGMANN   Borgmann, Glenn Dennis b: 5/25/50, Paterson, N.J. BR/TR, 6'4", 210 lbs. Deb: 7/01/72

YEAR	TM/L	G	AB	R	H	2B	3B	HR	RBI	BB	SO	AVG	OBP	SLG	PRO+	BR	/A	RC	SB	CS	SBR	FR	POS	TPR
1972	Min-A	56	175	11	41	4	0	3	14	25	25	.234	.330	.309	86	-1	-2	18	0	0	0	-2	C	-0.3
1973	Min-A	12	34	7	9	2	0	0	9	6	10	.265	.375	.324	95	0	0	5	0	0	0	-3	C	-0.2
1974	Min-A	128	345	33	87	8	1	3	45	39	44	.252	.330	.307	81	-6	-8	36	2	1	0	-2	*C	-0.5
1975	Min-A	125	352	34	73	15	2	2	33	47	59	.207	.304	.278	64	-15	-16	31	0	1	-1	-5	*C	-1.7
1976	Min-A	24	65	10	16	3	0	1	6	19	7	.246	.417	.338	119	3	3	11	1	1	-0	1	C	0.5
1977	Min-A	17	43	12	11	1	0	2	7	11	9	.256	.407	.419	128	2	2	8	0	0	0	1	C	0.4
1978	Min-A	49	123	16	26	4	1	3	15	18	17	.211	.312	.333	80	-3	-3	15	0	0	0	5	C/D	0.3
1979	Min-A	31	70	4	14	3	0	0	8	12	11	.200	.317	.243	52	-4	-5	6	1	0	0	7	C	0.4
1980	Chi-A	32	87	10	19	2	0	2	14	14	9	.218	.327	.310	76	-3	-3	10	0	0	0	1	C	0.0
Total	9	474	1294	137	296	42	4	16	151	191	191	.229	.329	.304	79	-26	-31	140	4	3	-1	4	C/D	-1.1

■ BOB BORKOWSKI   Borkowski, Robert Vilarian b: 1/27/26, Dayton, Ohio BR/TR, 6', 182 lbs. Deb: 4/22/50

YEAR	TM/L	G	AB	R	H	2B	3B	HR	RBI	BB	SO	AVG	OBP	SLG	PRO+	BR	/A	RC	SB	CS	SBR	FR	POS	TPR
1950	Chi-N	85	256	27	70	7	4	4	29	16	30	.273	.319	.379	84	-7	-6	29	1			3	O/1	-0.5
1951	Chi-N	58	89	9	14	1	0	0	10	3	16	.157	.185	.169	-4	-13	-13	2	0	0	0	1	O	-1.2
1952	Cin-N	126	377	42	95	11	4	4	24	26	53	.252	.300	.334	76	-13	-13	39	1	3	-2	-12	*O/1	-2.9
1953	Cin-N	94	249	32	67	11	1	7	29	21	41	.269	.328	.406	89	-4	-4	34	0	1	-1	-8	O/1	-1.4
1954	Cin-N	73	162	13	43	12	1	1	19	8	18	.265	.304	.370	73	-6	-7	15	0	2	-1	-1	O/1	-0.9
1955	Cin-N	25	18	1	3	1	0	0	1	1	2	.167	.211	.222	14	-2	-2	1	0	0	0	1	O/1	-0.1

YEAR	TM/L	G	AB	R	H	2B	3B	HR	RBI	BB	SO	AVG	OBP	SLG	PRO+	BR	/A	RC	SB	CS	SBR	FR	POS	TPR
	Bro-N	9	19	2	2	0	0	0	0	1	6	.105	.150	.105	-30	-4	-4	0	0	0	0	-1	/O	-0.4
	Yr	34	37	3	5	1	0	0	1	2	8	.135	.179	.162	-8	-6	-6	1	0	0	0	-0		-0.5
Total	6	470	1170	126	294	43	10	16	112	76	166	.251	.299	.346	71	-48	-49	120	2	6		-17	O/1	-7.4

■ RED BOROM
Borom, Edward Jones b: 10/30/15, Spartanburg, S.C. BL/TR, 5'11", 180 lbs. Deb: 4/23/44

YEAR	TM/L	G	AB	R	H	2B	3B	HR	RBI	BB	SO	AVG	OBP	SLG	PRO+	BR	/A	RC	SB	CS	SBR	FR	POS	TPR
1944	Det-A	7	14	1	1	0	0	0	1	2	2	.071	.188	.071	-23	-2	-2	0	0	0	0	1	/2S	0.0
1945	*Det-A	55	130	19	35	4	0	0	9	7	8	.269	.307	.300	72	-4	-5	13	4	2	0	5	2/3S	0.1
Total	2	62	144	20	36	4	0	0	10	9	10	.250	.294	.278	62	-6	-7	13	4	2	0	6	/23S	0.1

■ STEVE BOROS
Boros, Stephen b: 9/3/36, Flint, Mich. BR/TR, 6', 185 lbs. Deb: 6/19/57 MC

YEAR	TM/L	G	AB	R	H	2B	3B	HR	RBI	BB	SO	AVG	OBP	SLG	PRO+	BR	/A	RC	SB	CS	SBR	FR	POS	TPR
1957	Det-A	24	41	4	6	1	0	0	2	1	8	.146	.167	.171	-7	-6	-6	1	0	0	0	3	/3S	-0.2
1958	Det-A	6	2	0	0	0	0	0	0	0	0	.000	.000	.000	-93	-1	-1	0	0	0	0	2	/2	0.1
1961	Det-A	116	396	51	107	18	2	5	62	68	42	.270	.388	.364	99	4	3	61	4	2	0	-21	*3	-1.0
1962	Det-A	116	356	46	81	14	1	16	47	53	62	.228	.333	.407	95	-1	-3	50	3	1	0	-15	*3/2	-1.5
1963	Chi-N	41	90	9	19	5	1	3	7	12	19	.211	.304	.389	93	-0	-1	11	0	2	-1	-2	1O	-0.4
1964	Cin-N	117	370	31	95	12	3	2	31	47	43	.257	.344	.322	86	-4	-6	41	4	1	1	4	*3	-0.7
1965	Cin-N	2	0	0	0	0	0	0	0	0	0	—	—	—	—	0	0	0	0	0	0	0	/3	0.0
Total	7	422	1255	141	308	50	7	26	149	181	174	.245	.346	.359	90	-7	-13	164	11	6	-0	-29	3/102S	-3.7

■ BABE BORTON
Borton, William Baker b: 8/14/1888, Marion, Ill. d: 7/29/54, Berkeley, Cal. BL/TL, 6', 178 lbs. Deb: 9/02/12

YEAR	TM/L	G	AB	R	H	2B	3B	HR	RBI	BB	SO	AVG	OBP	SLG	PRO+	BR	/A	RC	SB	CS	SBR	FR	POS	TPR
1912	Chi-A	31	105	15	39	3	1	0	17	8		.371	.416	.419	143	5	6	19	1			0	1	0.7
1913	Chi-A	28	80	9	22	5	0	0	13	23	5	.275	.442	.338	130	5	5	12	1			-1	1	0.4
	NY-A	33	108	8	14	2	0	0	11	18	19	.130	.260	.148	20	-10	-10	5	1			4	1	-0.6
	Yr	61	188	17	36	7	0	0	24	41	24	.191	.342	.229	68	-5	-5	16	2			3		-0.2
1915	StL-F	159	549	**97**	157	20	14	3	83	**92**	64	.286	.395	.390	126	27	23	96	17			-10	*1	1.7
1916	StL-A	66	98	10	22	1	2	1	12	19	13	.224	.350	.306	102	0	1	11	1			-1	1	0.0
Total	4	317	940	139	254	31	17	4	136	160	101	.270	.381	.352	114	27	24	144	21			-8	1	2.2

■ DON BOSCH
Bosch, Donald John b: 7/15/42, San Francisco, Cal BB/TR, 5'10", 160 lbs. Deb: 9/19/66

YEAR	TM/L	G	AB	R	H	2B	3B	HR	RBI	BB	SO	AVG	OBP	SLG	PRO+	BR	/A	RC	SB	CS	SBR	FR	POS	TPR
1966	Pit-N	3	2	0	0	0	0	0	0	0	0	.000	.000	.000	-99	-1	-1	0	0	0	0	0	/O	0.0
1967	NY-N	44	93	7	13	0	1	0	2	5	24	.140	.184	.161	-0	-12	-12	3	3	1	0	3	O	-1.1
1968	NY-N	50	111	14	19	1	0	3	7	9	33	.171	.233	.261	48	-7	-7	6	0	2	-1	6	O	-0.4
1969	Mon-N	49	112	13	20	5	0	1	4	8	20	.179	.233	.250	35	-10	-10	7	1	0	0	1	O	-1.0
Total	4	146	318	34	52	6	1	4	13	22	77	.164	.218	.226	28	-29	-29	16	4	3	-1	9	O	-2.5

■ RICK BOSETTI
Bosetti, Richard Alan b: 8/5/53, Redding, Cal. BR/TR, 5'11", 185 lbs. Deb: 9/09/76

YEAR	TM/L	G	AB	R	H	2B	3B	HR	RBI	BB	SO	AVG	OBP	SLG	PRO+	BR	/A	RC	SB	CS	SBR	FR	POS	TPR
1976	Phi-N	13	18	6	5	1	0	0	0	1	3	.278	.316	.333	82	-0	-0	2	3	0	1	1	/O	0.1
1977	StL-N	41	69	12	16	0	0	0	3	6	11	.232	.303	.232	47	-5	-5	5	4	4	-1	3	O	-0.3
1978	Tor-A	136	568	61	147	25	5	5	42	30	65	.259	.300	.347	80	-15	-16	58	6	10	-4	20	*O	-0.2
1979	Tor-A	162	619	59	161	35	2	8	65	22	70	.260	.289	.362	73	-23	-24	58	13	12	-3	11	*O	-2.2
1980	Tor-A	53	188	24	40	7	1	4	18	15	29	.213	.278	.324	62	-9	-10	16	4	6	-2	-1	O	-1.3
1981	Tor-A	25	47	5	11	2	0	0	4	2	6	.234	.265	.277	53	-3	-3	3	0	2	-1	2	O/D	-0.2
	*Oak-A	9	19	4	2	0	0	0	1	3	3	.105	.227	.105	-2	-2	-2	1	0	0	0	1	/OD	-0.1
	Yr	34	66	9	13	2	0	0	5	5	9	.197	.254	.227	38	-5	-5	3	0	2	-1	3		-0.3
1982	Oak-A	6	15	1	3	0	0	0	0	0	1	.200	.200	.200	11	-2	-2	0	0	0	0	2	/O	0.0
Total	7	445	1543	172	385	70	8	17	133	79	188	.250	.290	.338	71	-60	-63	143	30	34	-11	40	O/D	-4.2

■ THAD BOSLEY
Bosley, Thaddis b: 9/17/56, Oceanside, Cal. BL/TL, 6'3", 175 lbs. Deb: 6/29/77

YEAR	TM/L	G	AB	R	H	2B	3B	HR	RBI	BB	SO	AVG	OBP	SLG	PRO+	BR	/A	RC	SB	CS	SBR	FR	POS	TPR
1977	Cal-A	58	212	19	63	10	2	0	19	16	32	.297	.349	.363	98	-1	-0	27	5	4	-1	-0	O	-0.2
1978	Chi-A	66	219	25	59	5	1	2	13	13	32	.269	.310	.329	79	-6	-6	20	12	11	-3	3	O	-0.7
1979	Chi-A	36	77	13	24	1	1	1	8	9	14	.312	.384	.390	109	1	1	12	4	1	1	3	O	0.4
1980	Chi-A	70	147	12	33	2	0	2	14	10	27	.224	.274	.279	52	-10	-10	10	3	2	-0	0	O	-1.0
1981	*Mil-A	42	105	11	24	2	0	0	3	6	13	.229	.270	.248	53	-7	-6	7	2	1	0	-2	O/D	-0.9
1982	Sea-A	22	46	3	8	1	0	0	2	4	8	.174	.240	.196	21	-5	-5	2	3	1	0	-3	O	-0.7
1983	Chi-N	43	72	12	21	4	1	2	12	10	12	.292	.378	.458	125	3	3	13	1	1	-0	-0	O	0.2
1984	*Chi-N	55	98	17	29	2	2	2	14	13	22	.296	.378	.418	113	3	2	17	5	1	1	-1	O	0.1
1985	Chi-N	108	180	25	59	6	3	7	27	20	29	.328	.395	.511	137	12	10	37	5	1	1	1	O	1.1
1986	Chi-N	87	120	15	33	4	1	1	9	18	24	.275	.370	.350	92	1	-1	17	3	0	1	-4	O	-0.4
1987	KC-A	80	140	13	39	6	1	1	16	9	26	.279	.322	.357	78	-4	-4	16	0	0	0	-1	OD	-0.5
1988	KC-A	15	21	1	4	0	0	0	2	2	6	.190	.261	.190	28	-2	-2	1	0	0	0	0	/OD	-0.1
	Cal-A	35	75	9	21	5	0	0	7	6	12	.280	.333	.347	93	-1	-1	9	1	1	0	2	O/D	0.1
	Yr	50	96	10	25	5	0	0	9	8	18	.260	.317	.313	78	-3	-3	10	1	1	-0	2		0.0
1989	Tex-A	37	40	5	9	2	0	1	9	3	11	.225	.279	.350	75	-1	-1	4	2	0	1	2	/OD	0.1
1990	Tex-A	30	29	3	4	0	0	1	3	4	7	.138	.242	.241	35	-3	-3	2	1	0	0	0	/OD	-0.1
Total	14	784	1581	183	430	50	12	20	158	143	275	.272	.333	.357	89	-18	-22	194	47	24	-0	0	O/D	-2.6

■ HARLEY BOSS
Boss, Elmer Harley "Lefty" b: 11/19/08, Hodge, La. d: 5/15/64, Nashville, Tenn. BL/TL, 5'11.5", 185 lbs. Deb: 7/19/28

YEAR	TM/L	G	AB	R	H	2B	3B	HR	RBI	BB	SO	AVG	OBP	SLG	PRO+	BR	/A	RC	SB	CS	SBR	FR	POS	TPR
1928	Was-A	12	12	1	3	0	0	0	2	3	1	.250	.400	.250	75	-0	-0	1	0	0	0	-1	/1	0.0
1929	Was-A	28	66	9	18	2	1	0	6	2	6	.273	.294	.333	61	-4	-4	6	0	0	0	0	1	-0.5
1930	Was-A	3	3	0	0	0	0	0	0	0	0	.000	.000	.000	-99	-1	-1	0	0	0	0	0	/1	0.0
1933	Cle-A	112	438	54	118	17	7	1	53	25	27	.269	.310	.347	71	-17	-20	46	2	5	-2	6	*1	-2.2
Total	4	155	519	64	139	19	8	1	61	30	34	.268	.309	.341	69	-22	-25	54	2	5	-2	6	1	-2.7

■ HENRY BOSTICK
Bostick, Henry Landers (b: Henry Lipschitz) b: 1/12/1895, Boston, Mass. d: 9/16/68, Denver, Colo. BR/TR, Deb: 5/18/15

YEAR	TM/L	G	AB	R	H	2B	3B	HR	RBI	BB	SO	AVG	OBP	SLG	PRO+	BR	/A	RC	SB	CS	SBR	FR	POS	TPR
1915	Phi-A	2	7	0	0	0	0	0	2	1	1	.000	.125	.000	-64	-1	-1	0	0			-1	/3	-0.2

■ LYMAN BOSTOCK
Bostock, Lyman Wesley b: 11/22/50, Birmingham, Ala. d: 9/23/78, Gary, Ind. BL/TR, 6'1", 180 lbs. Deb: 4/08/75

YEAR	TM/L	G	AB	R	H	2B	3B	HR	RBI	BB	SO	AVG	OBP	SLG	PRO+	BR	/A	RC	SB	CS	SBR	FR	POS	TPR
1975	Min-A	98	369	52	104	21	5	0	29	28	42	.282	.332	.366	95	-1	-2	44	2	3	-1	-2	O/D	-0.7
1976	Min-A	128	474	75	153	21	9	4	60	33	37	.323	.368	.430	130	19	17	71	12	6	0	0	*O	1.6
1977	Min-A	153	593	104	199	36	12	14	90	51	59	.336	.394	.508	146	36	37	116	16	7	1	10	*O	4.2
1978	Cal-A	147	568	74	168	24	4	5	71	59	36	.296	.364	.379	113	8	11	72	15	12	-3	-2	*O/D	0.3
Total	4	526	2004	305	624	102	30	23	250	171	174	.311	.368	.427	124	62	63	303	45	28	-3	7	O/D	5.4

■ DARYL BOSTON
Boston, Daryl Lamont b: 1/4/63, Cincinnati, Ohio BL/TL, 6'3", 185 lbs. Deb: 5/13/84

YEAR	TM/L	G	AB	R	H	2B	3B	HR	RBI	BB	SO	AVG	OBP	SLG	PRO+	BR	/A	RC	SB	CS	SBR	FR	POS	TPR
1984	Chi-A	35	83	8	14	3	1	0	3	4	20	.169	.207	.229	20	-9	-9	5	6	0	2	2	O/D	-0.6
1985	Chi-A	95	232	20	53	13	1	3	15	14	44	.228	.272	.332	62	-12	-13	20	8	6	-1	-10	O/D	-2.5
1986	Chi-A	56	199	29	53	11	3	5	22	21	33	.266	.336	.427	103	2	1	28	9	5	-0	2	O/D	0.1
1987	Chi-A	103	337	51	87	21	2	10	29	25	68	.258	.309	.421	89	-5	-6	43	12	6	0	1	O/D	-0.5
1988	Chi-A	105	281	37	61	12	2	15	31	21	44	.217	.272	.434	95	-3	-3	32	9	3	1	0	O/D	-0.3
1989	Chi-A	101	218	34	55	3	4	5	23	24	31	.252	.326	.372	99	-1	-0	29	7	2	1	3	O/D	0.2
1990	Chi-A	5	1	0	0	0	0	0	0	0	0	.000	.000	.000	-99	-0	-0	0	1	0	0	0	/OD	0.0
	NY-N	115	366	65	100	21	2	12	45	28	50	.273	.328	.440	112	4	5	52	18	7	1	-10	*O	-0.7
Total	7	615	1717	244	423	84	15	50	168	137	290	.246	.303	.400	90	-25	-26	209	70	29	4	-13	O/D	-4.3

YEAR	TM/L	G	AB	R	H	2B	3B	HR	RBI	BB	SO	AVG	OBP	SLG	PRO+	BR	/A	RC	SB	CS	SBR	FR	POS	TPR

■ KEN BOSWELL Boswell, Kenneth George b: 2/23/46, Austin, Tex. BL/TR, 6', 170 lbs. Deb: 9/18/67

YEAR	TM/L	G	AB	R	H	2B	3B	HR	RBI	BB	SO	AVG	OBP	SLG	PRO+	BR	/A	RC	SB	CS	SBR	FR	POS	TPR
1967	NY-N	11	40	2	9	3	0	1	4	1	5	.225	.244	.375	76	-1	-1	3	0	0	0	2	/23	0.1
1968	NY-N	75	284	37	74	7	2	4	11	16	27	.261	.302	.342	93	-3	-3	29	7	2	1	-1	2	0.1
1969	*NY-N	102	362	48	101	14	7	3	32	36	47	.279	.348	.381	102	2	1	47	7	3	0	-15	2	-0.6
1970	NY-N	105	351	32	89	13	2	5	44	41	32	.254	.335	.345	82	-8	-8	39	5	4	-1	-15	*2	-1.2
1971	NY-N	116	392	46	107	20	1	5	40	36	31	.273	.337	.367	101	0	1	48	5	2	0	-29	*2	-2.4
1972	NY-N	100	355	35	75	9	1	9	33	32	35	.211	.276	.318	70	-15	-14	29	2	2	-1	-31	2	-4.3
1973	*NY-N	76	110	12	25	2	1	2	14	12	11	.227	.303	.318	74	-4	-4	11	0	0	0	0	3/2	-0.3
1974	NY-N	96	222	19	48	6	1	2	15	18	19	.216	.278	.279	57	-13	-13	16	0	1	-1	7	23/O	-0.5
1975	Hou-N	86	178	16	43	8	2	0	21	30	12	.242	.354	.309	92	-2	-1	19	0	3	-2	-9	23	-1.0
1976	Hou-N	91	126	12	33	8	1	0	18	8	8	.262	.306	.341	92	-3	-2	11	1	0	0	-5	3/2O	-0.6
1977	Hou-N	72	97	7	21	1	1	0	12	10	12	.216	.290	.247	50	-7	-6	6	0	0	0	-3	2/3	-0.7
Total	11	930	2517	266	625	91	19	31	244	240	239	.248	.316	.337	85	-55	-49	259	27	17	-2	-100	2/3O	-11.4

■ JOHN BOTTARINI Bottarini, John Charles b: 9/14/08, Crockett, Cal. d: 10/8/76, Jemez Springs, N.M. BR/TR, 6', 190 lbs. Deb: 4/22/37

YEAR	TM/L	G	AB	R	H	2B	3B	HR	RBI	BB	SO	AVG	OBP	SLG	PRO+	BR	/A	RC	SB	CS	SBR	FR	POS	TPR
1937	Chi-N	26	40	3	11	3	0	1	7	5	10	.275	.370	.425	111	1	1	7				0	1	C/O	0.3

■ JIM BOTTOMLEY Bottomley, James Leroy "Sunny Jim" b: 4/23/1900, Oglesby, Ill. d: 12/11/59, St.Louis, Mo. BL/TL, 6', 180 lbs. Deb: 8/18/22 MCH

YEAR	TM/L	G	AB	R	H	2B	3B	HR	RBI	BB	SO	AVG	OBP	SLG	PRO+	BR	/A	RC	SB	CS	SBR	FR	POS	TPR
1922	StL-N	37	151	29	49	8	5	5	35	6	13	.325	.358	.543	136	6	7	29	3	1	0	-2	1	0.4
1923	StL-N	134	523	79	194	34	14	8	94	45	44	.371	.425	.535	155	39	41	117	4	6	-2	-12	*1	1.6
1924	StL-N	137	528	87	167	31	12	14	111	35	35	.316	.362	.500	131	20	21	94	5	4	-1	-12	*1	0.2
1925	StL-N	153	619	92	227	44	12	21	128	47	36	.367	.413	.578	147	46	43	145	3	4	-2	-4	*1	2.1
1926	*StL-N	154	603	98	180	40	14	19	120	58	52	.299	.364	.506	127	25	22	109	4			-15	*1	0.1
1927	StL-N	152	574	95	174	31	15	19	124	74	49	.303	.387	.509	134	31	29	112	8			-11	*1	0.7
1928	*StL-N	149	576	123	187	42	20	31	136	71	54	.325	.402	.628	163	53	51	142	10			-14	*1	2.1
1929	StL-N	146	560	108	176	31	12	29	137	70	54	.314	.391	.568	133	29	28	122	3			-6	*1	1.3
1930	*StL-N	131	487	92	148	33	7	15	97	44	36	.304	.368	.493	102	4	1	86	5			-13	*1	-1.5
1931	*StL-N	108	382	73	133	34	5	9	75	34	24	.348	.403	.534	144	26	24	84	3			-3	1	1.4
1932	StL-N	91	311	45	92	16	3	11	48	25	32	.296	.350	.473	115	8	7	52	2			-3	1	0.0
1933	Cin-N	145	549	57	137	23	9	13	83	42	28	.250	.311	.395	102	-0	1	68	3			-9	*1	-1.1
1934	Cin-N	142	556	72	158	31	11	11	78	33	40	.284	.324	.439	105	0	2	80	1			-3	*1	-1.2
1935	Cin-N	107	399	44	103	21	1	1	49	18	24	.258	.294	.323	68	-19	-18	37	1			-2	1	-2.1
1936	StL-A	140	544	72	162	39	11	12	95	44	55	.298	.354	.476	100	0	-2	92	0	0	0	-10	*1	-2.7
1937	StL-A	65	109	11	26	7	0	1	12	18	15	.239	.346	.330	71	-4	-5	14	1	0	0	1	1M	-0.5
Total	16	1991	7471	1177	2313	465	151	219	1422	664	591	.310	.369	.500	124	262	252	1384	58	15		-119	*1/2	0.8

■ ED BOUCHEE Bouchee, Edward Francis b: 3/7/33, Livingston, Mont. BL/TL, 6', 200 lbs. Deb: 9/19/56

YEAR	TM/L	G	AB	R	H	2B	3B	HR	RBI	BB	SO	AVG	OBP	SLG	PRO+	BR	/A	RC	SB	CS	SBR	FR	POS	TPR
1956	Phi-N	9	22	0	6	2	0	0	1	5	6	.273	.407	.364	112	1	1	4	0	0	0	-0	/1	0.0
1957	Phi-N	154	574	78	168	35	8	17	76	84	91	.293	.396	.470	136	29	31	110	1	0	0	4	*1	2.2
1958	Phi-N	89	334	55	86	19	5	9	39	51	74	.257	.356	.425	107	3	4	51	1	0	0	0	1	0.0
1959	Phi-N	136	499	75	142	29	4	15	74	70	74	.285	.378	.449	117	15	14	85	0	4	-2	-0	*1	0.1
1960	Phi-N	22	65	1	17	4	0	0	8	9	11	.262	.360	.323	89	-1	-1	8	0	0	0	1	1	0.0
	Chi-N	98	299	33	71	11	1	5	44	45	51	.237	.341	.331	86	-5	-4	37	2	0	1	-0	1	-0.7
	Yr	120	364	34	88	15	1	5	52	54	62	.242	.344	.330	86	-6	-5	46	2	0	1	1		-0.7
1961	Chi-N	112	319	49	79	12	3	12	38	58	77	.248	.372	.417	108	6	5	53	1	4	-2	1	*1	-0.1
1962	NY-N	50	87	7	14	2	0	3	10	18	17	.161	.305	.287	59	-5	-5	8	0	0	0	4	1	-0.1
Total	7	670	2199	298	583	114	21	61	290	340	401	.265	.370	.419	112	43	45	357	5	8	-3	10	1	1.4

■ AL BOUCHER Boucher, Alexander Francis "Bo" b: 11/13/1881, Franklin, Mass. d: 6/23/74, Torrance, Cal. BR/TR, 5'8.5", 156 lbs. Deb: 4/16/14

YEAR	TM/L	G	AB	R	H	2B	3B	HR	RBI	BB	SO	AVG	OBP	SLG	PRO+	BR	/A	RC	SB	CS	SBR	FR	POS	TPR
1914	StL-F	147	516	62	119	26	4	2	49	52	88	.231	.304	.308	72	-16	-20	56	13			-4	*3	-2.1

■ MEDRIC BOUCHER Boucher, Medric Charles Francis b: 3/12/1886, St.Louis, Mo. d: 3/12/74, Martinez, Cal. BR/TR, 5'10", 165 lbs. Deb: 6/03/14

YEAR	TM/L	G	AB	R	H	2B	3B	HR	RBI	BB	SO	AVG	OBP	SLG	PRO+	BR	/A	RC	SB	CS	SBR	FR	POS	TPR
1914	Bal-F	16	16	2	5	1	1	0	2	1	1	.313	.353	.500	138	1	1	3	0			-0	/C1O	0.1
	Pit-F	1	1	0	0	0	0	0	0	0	0	.000	.000	.000	-99	-0	-0	0	0			0	H	0.0
	Yr	17	17	2	5	1	1	0	2	1	1	.294	.333	.471	125	1	1	3	0			-0		0.1

■ LOU BOUDREAU Boudreau, Louis b: 7/17/17, Harvey, Ill. BR/TR, 5'11", 185 lbs. Deb: 9/09/38 MH

YEAR	TM/L	G	AB	R	H	2B	3B	HR	RBI	BB	SO	AVG	OBP	SLG	PRO+	BR	/A	RC	SB	CS	SBR	FR	POS	TPR
1938	Cle-A	1	1	0	0	0	0	0	0	0	1	.000	.500	.000	36	0	0	0	0	0	0	0	/3	0.0
1939	Cle-A	53	225	42	58	15	4	0	19	28	24	.258	.340	.360	82	-7	-6	28	2	1	0	8	S	0.7
1940	Cle-A	155	627	97	185	46	10	9	101	73	39	.295	.370	.443	113	10	12	103	6	3	0	12	*S	3.5
1941	Cle-A	148	579	95	149	45	8	10	56	85	57	.257	.355	.415	108	3	7	92	9	4	0	13	*S	2.3
1942	Cle-A	147	506	57	143	18	10	2	58	75	39	.283	.379	.370	118	10	14	73	7	16	-8	-0	*SM	1.4
1943	Cle-A	152	539	69	154	32	7	3	67	90	31	.286	.388	.388	135	22	26	87	4	7	-3	28	*S/CM	5.5
1944	Cle-A	150	584	91	191	45	5	3	67	73	39	.327	.406	.437	146	33	36	112	11	3	2	26	*S/CM	7.3
1945	Cle-A	97	345	50	106	24	5	3	48	35	20	.307	.374	.409	133	12	14	53	0	4	-2	1	SM	1.7
1946	Cle-A	140	515	51	151	30	6	6	62	40	14	.293	.345	.410	118	6	10	72	6	7	-2	16	*SM	2.7
1947	Cle-A	150	538	79	165	45	3	4	67	67	10	.307	.388	.424	129	20	21	95	1	0	0	17	*SM	3.9
1948	*Cle-A	152	560	116	199	34	6	18	106	98	9	.355	.453	.534	166	53	55	143	3	2	-0	9	*S/CM	6.1
1949	Cle-A	134	475	53	135	20	3	4	60	70	19	.284	.381	.364	100	0	2	68	0	1	-1	5	S3/12M	0.7
1950	Cle-A	81	260	23	70	13	2	1	29	31	5	.269	.349	.346	81	-8	-7	32	1	2	-1	0	S/123M	-0.4
1951	Bos-A	82	273	37	73	18	1	5	47	30	12	.267	.353	.396	93	1	-3	39	1	0	0	-3	S3/1	0.0
1952	Bos-A	4	2	1	0	0	0	0	2	0	0	.000	.000	.000	-93	-1	-1	0	0	0	0	-0	/S3M	0.0
Total	15	1646	6029	861	1779	385	66	68	789	796	309	.295	.380	.415	121	154	181	996	51	50	-15	134	*S/312C	35.4

■ CHRIS BOURJOS Bourjos, Christopher b: 10/16/55, Chicago, Ill. BR/TR, 6', 185 lbs. Deb: 8/31/80

YEAR	TM/L	G	AB	R	H	2B	3B	HR	RBI	BB	SO	AVG	OBP	SLG	PRO+	BR	/A	RC	SB	CS	SBR	FR	POS	TPR
1980	SF-N	13	22	4	5	1	0	1	2	2	7	.227	.292	.409	96	-0	-0	2	0	0	0	-1	/O	0.0

■ PAT BOURQUE Bourque, Patrick Daniel b: 3/23/47, Worcester, Mass. BL/TL, 6', 210 lbs. Deb: 9/06/71

YEAR	TM/L	G	AB	R	H	2B	3B	HR	RBI	BB	SO	AVG	OBP	SLG	PRO+	BR	/A	RC	SB	CS	SBR	FR	POS	TPR
1971	Chi-N	14	37	3	7	0	1	1	3	3	9	.189	.250	.324	54	-2	-3	3	0	0	0	2	1	0.0
1972	Chi-N	11	27	3	7	1	0	0	5	2	2	.259	.310	.296	66	-1	-1	3	0	0	0	1	/1	0.0
1973	Chi-N	57	139	11	29	6	0	7	20	16	21	.209	.299	.403	86	-2	-3	18	1	1	-0	5	1	0.0
	*Oak-A	23	42	8	8	4	1	2	9	15	10	.190	.404	.476	155	3	4	9	0	0	0	-0	D/1	0.3
1974	Oak-A	73	96	6	22	4	0	1	16	15	20	.229	.330	.302	90	-2	-1	10	0	2	-1	-1	1/D	-0.4
	Min-A	23	64	5	14	2	0	1	8	7	11	.219	.296	.297	68	-2	-3	6	0	0	0	3	1	0.0
	Yr	96	160	11	36	6	0	2	24	22	31	.225	.319	.300	82	-4	-3	16	0	2	-1	2		-0.4
Total	4	201	405	36	87	17	2	12	61	58	73	.215	.316	.356	87	-5	-7	48	1	3	-2	10	1/D	-0.1

■ LARRY BOWA Bowa, Lawrence Robert b: 12/6/45, Sacramento, Cal. BB/TR, 5'10", 155 lbs. Deb: 4/07/70 MC

YEAR	TM/L	G	AB	R	H	2B	3B	HR	RBI	BB	SO	AVG	OBP	SLG	PRO+	BR	/A	RC	SB	CS	SBR	FR	POS	TPR
1970	Phi-N	145	547	50	137	11	6	0	34	24	48	.250	.284	.303	57	-35	-33	45	24	13	-1	-21	*S/2	-3.6
1971	Phi-N	159	650	74	162	18	5	0	25	36	61	.249	.294	.292	66	-28	-28	59	28	11	2	10	*S	0.5
1972	Phi-N	152	579	67	145	11	13	1	31	32	51	.250	.292	.320	72	-20	-22	54	17	9	-0	5	*S	0.0
1973	Phi-N	122	446	42	94	11	3	0	23	24	51	.211	.253	.249	38	-36	-38	28	10	6	-1	-0	*S	-2.2
1974	Phi-N	162	669	97	184	19	10	1	36	23	52	.275	.300	.338	75	-21	-24	69	39	11	5	-16	*S	-1.7
1975	Phi-N	136	583	79	178	18	9	2	38	24	32	.305	.335	.377	94	-3	-6	75	24	6	4	-12	*S	0.1
1976	*Phi-N	156	624	71	155	15	9	0	49	32	31	.248	.285	.301	65	-28	-30	55	30	8	4	-14	*S	-2.7

YEAR	TM/L	G	AB	R	H	2B	3B	HR	RBI	BB	SO	AVG	OBP	SLG	PRO+	BR	/A	RC	SB	CS	SBR	FR	POS	TPR
1977	*Phi-N	154	624	93	175	19	3	4	41	32	32	.280	.316	.340	73	-21	-25	70	32	3	8	1	*S	0.6
1978	*Phi-N	156	654	78	192	31	5	3	43	24	40	.294	.320	.370	91	-8	-9	80	27	5	5	2	*S	1.2
1979	Phi-N	147	539	74	130	17	11	0	31	61	32	.241	.319	.314	71	-19	-21	57	20	9	1	-13	*S	-1.8
1980	*Phi-N	147	540	57	144	16	4	2	39	24	28	.267	.302	.322	70	-19	-22	53	21	6	3	-13	*S	-1.6
1981	*Phi-N	103	360	34	102	14	3	0	31	26	17	.283	.332	.339	87	-4	-6	40	16	7	1	-10	*S	-0.4
1982	Chi-N	142	499	50	123	15	7	0	29	39	38	.246	.302	.305	68	-19	-21	47	8	3	1	-30	*S	-4.1
1983	Chi-N	147	499	73	133	20	5	2	43	35	30	.267	.315	.339	77	-13	-16	56	7	3	0	15	*S	1.3
1984	*Chi-N	133	391	33	87	14	2	0	17	28	24	.223	.274	.269	49	-24	-28	30	10	4	1	7	*S	-0.6
1985	Chi-N	72	195	13	48	6	4	0	13	11	20	.246	.286	.318	62	-8	-11	18	5	1	1	12	S	0.7
	NY-N	14	19	2	2	1	0	0	2	2	2	.105	.190	.158	-2	-3	-3	1	0	0	0	1	/S2	0.0
	Yr	86	214	15	50	7	4	0	15	13	22	.234	.278	.304	57	-11	-13	19	5	1	1	12		0.7
Total	16	2247	8418	987	2191	262	99	15	525	474	569	.260	.301	.320	71	-310	-341	836	318	105	32	-75	*S/2	-14.3

■ BENNY BOWCOCK

Bowcock, Benjamin James b: 10/28/1879, Fall River, Mass. d: 6/16/61, New Bedford, Mass BR/TR, 5'7", 150 lbs. Deb: 9/18/03

YEAR	TM/L	G	AB	R	H	2B	3B	HR	RBI	BB	SO	AVG	OBP	SLG	PRO+	BR	/A	RC	SB	CS	SBR	FR	POS	TPR
1903	StL-A	14	50	7	16	3	1	1	10	3		.320	.358	.480	156	3	3	9	1			-7	2	-0.3

■ TIM BOWDEN

Bowden, David Timon b: 8/15/1891, Mcdonough, Ga. d: 10/25/49, Emory, Ga. BL/TR, 5'10", 175 lbs. Deb: 9/17/14

YEAR	TM/L	G	AB	R	H	2B	3B	HR	RBI	BB	SO	AVG	OBP	SLG	PRO+	BR	/A	RC	SB	CS	SBR	FR	POS	TPR
1914	StL-A	7	9	0	2	0	0	0	0	1	6	.222	.300	.222	59	-0	-0	1	0			-1	/O	-0.1

■ CHICK BOWEN

Bowen, Emmons Joseph b: 7/26/1897, New Haven, Conn. d: 8/9/48, New Haven, Conn. BR/TR, 5'7", 165 lbs. Deb: 9/15/19

YEAR	TM/L	G	AB	R	H	2B	3B	HR	RBI	BB	SO	AVG	OBP	SLG	PRO+	BR	/A	RC	SB	CS	SBR	FR	POS	TPR
1919	NY-N	3	5	0	1	0	0	0	1	1	2	.200	.333	.200	63	-0	-0	0				0	/O	0.0

■ SAM BOWEN

Bowen, Samuel Thomas b: 9/18/52, Brunswick, Ga. BR/TR, 5'9", 170 lbs. Deb: 8/25/77

YEAR	TM/L	G	AB	R	H	2B	3B	HR	RBI	BB	SO	AVG	OBP	SLG	PRO+	BR	/A	RC	SB	CS	SBR	FR	POS	TPR
1977	Bos-A	3	2	0	0	0	0	0	0	0	2	.000	.000	.000	-90	-1	-1	0	0	0	0	0	/O	0.0
1978	Bos-A	6	7	3	1	0	0	1	1	1	2	.143	.250	.571	112	0	0	1	0	0	0	-0	/O	0.0
1980	Bos-A	7	13	0	2	0	0	0	0	2	3	.154	.267	.154	17	-1	-1	1	1	0	0	2	/O	0.1
Total	3	16	22	3	3	0	0	1	1	3	7	.136	.240	.273	38	-2	-2	2	1	0	0	2	/O	0.1

■ SAM BOWENS

Bowens, Samuel Edward b: 3/23/39, Wilmington, N.C. BR/TR, 6'1.5", 188 lbs. Deb: 9/07/63

YEAR	TM/L	G	AB	R	H	2B	3B	HR	RBI	BB	SO	AVG	OBP	SLG	PRO+	BR	/A	RC	SB	CS	SBR	FR	POS	TPR
1963	Bal-A	15	48	8	16	3	1	1	9	4	5	.333	.385	.500	149	3	3	9	1	1	-0	-2	O	0.1
1964	Bal-A	139	501	58	132	25	2	22	71	42	99	.263	.325	.453	114	8	9	71	4	3	-1	3	*O	0.6
1965	Bal-A	84	203	16	33	4	1	7	20	10	41	.163	.202	.296	39	-17	-17	10	7	1	2	2	O	-1.7
1966	Bal-A	89	243	26	51	9	1	6	20	17	52	.210	.275	.329	74	-9	-8	21	9	3	1	2	O	-0.7
1967	Bal-A	62	120	13	22	2	1	5	12	11	43	.183	.258	.342	76	-4	-4	10	3	4	-2	-1	O	-0.7
1968	Was-A	57	115	14	22	4	0	4	7	11	39	.191	.262	.330	81	-3	-3	11	0	0	-0	-1	O	-0.5
1969	Was-A	33	57	6	11	1	0	0	4	5	14	.193	.258	.211	34	-5	-5	3	1	1	-0	1	O	-0.5
Total	7	479	1287	141	287	48	6	45	143	100	293	.223	.284	.375	87	-26	-25	136	25	13	-0	5	O	-3.4

■ FRANK BOWERMAN

Bowerman, Frank Eugene "Mike" b: 12/5/1868, Romeo, Mich. d: 11/30/48, Romeo, Mich. BR/TR, 6'2", 190 lbs. Deb: 8/24/1895 M

YEAR	TM/L	G	AB	R	H	2B	3B	HR	RBI	BB	SO	AVG	OBP	SLG	PRO+	BR	/A	RC	SB	CS	SBR	FR	POS	TPR
1895	Bal-N	1	1	0	0	0	0	0	0	0	0	.000	.000	.000	-97	-0	-0	0	0			0	/C	0.0
1896	Bal-N	4	16	0	2	0	0	0	4	1	0	.125	.176	.125	-19	-3	-3	0	0			1	/C1	0.0
1897	*Bal-N	38	130	16	41	5	0	1	21	1		.315	.331	.377	89	-2	-2	18	3			6	C	0.7
1898	Bal-N	5	16	5	7	1	0	0	1	2		.438	.526	.500	195	2	2	5	1			1	/C	0.3
	Pit-N	69	241	17	66	6	3	0	29	7		.274	.297	.324	82	-7	-6	25	4			4	C/1	0.2
	Yr	74	257	22	73	7	3	0	30	9		.284	.313	.335	90	-4	-4	29	5			5		0.5
1899	Pit-N	109	424	49	110	16	10	3	53	11		.259	.286	.366	81	-13	-13	48	10			13	C1	0.5
1900	NY-N	80	270	25	65	5	3	1	42	6		.241	.263	.293	58	-17	-15	24	10			15	C/S	0.6
1901	NY-N	59	191	20	38	5	3	0	14	7		.199	.231	.257	44	-14	-13	13	3			15	C/2S31	0.8
1902	NY-N	107	367	38	93	14	6	0	26	13		.253	.279	.324	88	-6	-6	38	12			2	C/1	0.7
1903	NY-N	64	210	22	58	6	2	1	31	6		.276	.296	.338	79	-5	-6	24	5			1	C/1O	0.0
1904	NY-N	93	289	38	67	11	4	2	27	16		.232	.272	.318	80	-6	-7	28	7			-3	C/12P	-0.3
1905	NY-N	98	297	37	80	8	1	3	41	12		.269	.298	.333	88	-4	-5	33	6			-4	C1/2	-0.2
1906	NY-N	103	285	23	65	7	3	0	42	15		.228	.267	.284	72	-9	-10	24	5			3	C1	-0.1
1907	NY-N	96	311	31	81	8	2	0	32	17		.260	.299	.299	86	-4	-5	34	11			-4	C1	-0.5
1908	Bos-N	86	254	16	58	8	1	1	25	13		.228	.266	.280	77	-7	-7	19	4			-4	C1	-0.8
1909	Bos-N	33	99	6	21	2	0	0	4	2		.212	.228	.232	41	-7	-7	5	0			1	CM	-0.4
Total	15	1045	3401	343	852	102	38	13	392	129	0	.251	.280	.314	77	-101	-103	338	81			47	C1/2S3PO	1.5

■ BILLY BOWERS

Bowers, Grover Bill b: 3/25/23, Parkin, Ark. BL/TR, 5'9.5", 176 lbs. Deb: 4/24/49

YEAR	TM/L	G	AB	R	H	2B	3B	HR	RBI	BB	SO	AVG	OBP	SLG	PRO+	BR	/A	RC	SB	CS	SBR	FR	POS	TPR
1949	Chi-A	26	78	5	15	2	1	0	6	4	5	.192	.232	.244	27	-9	-8	4	1	1	-0	2	O	-0.7

■ STEW BOWERS

Bowers, Stewart Cole "Doc" b: 2/26/15, New Freedom, Pa. BB/TR, 6', 170 lbs. Deb: 8/05/35

YEAR	TM/L	G	AB	R	H	2B	3B	HR	RBI	BB	SO	AVG	OBP	SLG	PRO+	BR	/A	RC	SB	CS	SBR	FR	POS	TPR
1935	Bos-A	11	5	1	1	0	0	0	0	1	2	.200	.333	.200	38	-0	-0	0	0	0	0	0	P	0.0
1936	Bos-A	6	0	1	0	0	0	0	0	0	0	—	—	—	—	0	0	0	0	0	0	-0	/P	0.0
1937	Bos-A	1	0	1	0	0	0	0	0	0	0	—	—	—	—	0	0	0	0	0	0	0	R	0.0
Total	3	18	5	3	1	0	0	0	0	1	2	.200	.333	.200	38	-0	-0	0	0	0	0	0	/P	0.0

■ FRANK BOWES

Bowes, Frank M. b: 1865, Bath, N.Y. d: 1/21/1895, New York, N.Y. TR , 5'9", 160 lbs. Deb: 4/17/1890

YEAR	TM/L	G	AB	R	H	2B	3B	HR	RBI	BB	SO	AVG	OBP	SLG	PRO+	BR	/A	RC	SB	CS	SBR	FR	POS	TPR
1890	Bro-a	61	232	28	51	5	2	0		7		.220	.246	.259	52	-15	-13	18	11			-8	CO3/1S	-1.7

■ WELDON BOWLIN

Bowlin, Lois Weldon "Hoss" b: 12/10/40, Paragould, Ark. BR/TR, 5'9", 155 lbs. Deb: 9/27/67

YEAR	TM/L	G	AB	R	H	2B	3B	HR	RBI	BB	SO	AVG	OBP	SLG	PRO+	BR	/A	RC	SB	CS	SBR	FR	POS	TPR
1967	KC-A	2	5	0	1	0	0	0	0	0	0	.200	.200	.200	19	-1	-0	0	0	0	0	0	/3	0.0

■ STEVE BOWLING

Bowling, Stephen Shaddon b: 6/26/52, Tulsa, Okla. BR/TR, 6', 185 lbs. Deb: 9/07/76

YEAR	TM/L	G	AB	R	H	2B	3B	HR	RBI	BB	SO	AVG	OBP	SLG	PRO+	BR	/A	RC	SB	CS	SBR	FR	POS	TPR
1976	Mil-A	14	42	4	7	2	0	0	2	2	5	.167	.205	.214	23	-4	-4	2	0	0	0	3	O/D	-0.1
1977	Tor-A	89	194	19	40	8	1	1	13	37	42	.206	.333	.273	67	-8	-8	18	2	3	-1	10	O	-0.1
Total	2	103	236	23	47	10	1	1	15	39	47	.199	.313	.263	60	-12	-12	20	2	3	-1	13	O/D	-0.2

■ ELMER BOWMAN

Bowman, Elmari Wilhelm "Big Bow" b: 3/19/1897, Proctor, Vt. d: 12/17/85, Los Angeles, Cal. BR/TR, 6'0.5", 193 lbs. Deb: 8/03/20

YEAR	TM/L	G	AB	R	H	2B	3B	HR	RBI	BB	SO	AVG	OBP	SLG	PRO+	BR	/A	RC	SB	CS	SBR	FR	POS	TPR
1920	Was-A	2	1	0	0	0	0	0	0	1	0	.000	.500	.000	42	0	0	0	0	0	0	0	H	0.0

■ ERNIE BOWMAN

Bowman, Ernest Ferrell b: 7/28/35, Johnson City, Tenn. BR/TR, 5'10", 160 lbs. Deb: 4/12/61

YEAR	TM/L	G	AB	R	H	2B	3B	HR	RBI	BB	SO	AVG	OBP	SLG	PRO+	BR	/A	RC	SB	CS	SBR	FR	POS	TPR
1961	SF-N	38	38	10	8	0	2	0	2	1	8	.211	.231	.316	45	-3	-3	3	2	0	1	3	2S/3	0.3
1962	*SF-N	46	42	9	8	1	0	1	4	1	10	.190	.227	.286	37	-4	-4	2	0	1	-1	3	23S	0.1
1963	SF-N	81	125	10	23	3	0	0	4	0	15	.184	.184	.208	13	-14	-14	4	1	2	-1	4	S23	-0.5
Total	3	165	205	29	39	4	2	1	10	2	33	.190	.202	.244	24	-21	-20	9	3	3	-1	9	/S23	-0.1

■ JOE BOWMAN

Bowman, Joseph Emil b: 6/17/10, Argentine, Kan. BL/TR, 6'2", 190 lbs. Deb: 4/18/32

YEAR	TM/L	G	AB	R	H	2B	3B	HR	RBI	BB	SO	AVG	OBP	SLG	PRO+	BR	/A	RC	SB	CS	SBR	FR	POS	TPR
1932	Phi-A	7	1	0	1	0	0	0	0	0	0	1.000	1.000	1.000	405	0	0	1	0	0	0	1	/P	0.0
1934	NY-N	31	29	4	5	0	1	0	4	2	3	.172	.226	.241	26	-3	-3	2	0			-0	P	0.0
1935	Phi-N	49	67	6	13	1	1	1	7	4	7	.194	.239	.284	36	-6	-7	5	1			-0	P/O	0.0
1936	Phi-N	44	77	9	15	1	0	0	6	6	14	.195	.253	.208	23	-8	-9	4	0			-3	P	0.0
1937	Pit-N	35	47	3	10	1	0	0	4	5	9	.213	.288	.234	43	-4	-4	3	0			1	P	0.0
1938	Pit-N	18	21	5	7	0	1	0	1	1	3	.333	.364	.429	116	0	0	2	0			-1	P	0.0
1939	Pit-N	70	96	9	33	8	1	0	18	5	9	.344	.382	.448	124	3	3	17	0			0	P	0.0
1940	Pit-N	57	90	11	22	5	1	1	14	14	14	.244	.352	.356	96	-0	-0	12	0			0	P	0.0

YEAR	TM/L	G	AB	R	H	2B	3B	HR	RBI	BB	SO	AVG	OBP	SLG	PRO+	BR	/A	RC	SB	CS	SBR	FR	POS	TPR
1941	Pit-N	22	31	4	8	1	0	0	1	1	2	.258	.281	.290	61	-2	-2	2	0			0	P	0.0
1944	Bos-A	59	100	7	20	5	2	0	16	5	19	.200	.238	.290	51	-7	-7	7	1	0	0	-2	P	-0.4
1945	Bos-A	9	9	0	2	0	0	0	1	1	1	.222	.300	.222	51	-1	-1	1	0	0	0	0	/P	0.0
	Cin-N	29	71	4	5	2	1	0	3	2	9	.070	.096	.127	-39	-13	-13	1	1			-2	P	0.0
Total	11	430	639	62	141	24	8	2	75	46	90	.221	.275	.293	55	-39	-40	58	3	0		-6	P/O	-0.4

■ BOB BOWMAN
Bowman, Robert Leroy b: 5/10/31, Laytonville, Cal. BR/TR, 6'1", 195 lbs. Deb: 4/16/55

YEAR	TM/L	G	AB	R	H	2B	3B	HR	RBI	BB	SO	AVG	OBP	SLG	PRO+	BR	/A	RC	SB	CS	SBR	FR	POS	TPR
1955	Phi-N	3	3	0	0	0	0	0	0	0	0	.000	.000	.000	-99	-1	-1	0	0	0	0	0	/O	0.0
1956	Phi-N	6	16	2	3	0	1	1	2	0	6	.188	.188	.500	78	-1	-1	2	0	0	0	-1	/O	-0.1
1957	Phi-N	99	237	31	63	8	2	6	23	27	50	.266	.356	.392	104	1	2	35	0	0	0	-1	O	0.0
1958	Phi-N	91	184	31	53	11	2	8	24	16	30	.288	.345	.500	122	5	5	31	0	1	-1	-3	O	0.0
1959	Phi-N	57	79	7	10	0	0	2	5	5	23	.127	.179	.203	1	-11	-11	3	0	0	0	1	O/P	-0.9
Total	5	256	519	71	129	19	5	17	54	48	109	.249	.319	.403	93	-7	-6	70	0	1	-1	-2	O/P	-1.0

■ BILL BOWMAN
Bowman, William G. b: 1869, Chicago, Ill. d: 4/6/18, Arlington Heights, Ill. 5'11", 180 lbs. Deb: 6/18/1891

YEAR	TM/L	G	AB	R	H	2B	3B	HR	RBI	BB	SO	AVG	OBP	SLG	PRO+	BR	/A	RC	SB	CS	SBR	FR	POS	TPR
1891	Chi-N	15	45	2	4	1	0	0	5	5	9	.089	.196	.111	-9	-6	-6	1	0			-5	C	-0.8

■ RED BOWSER
Bowser, James H. b: Greensburg, Pa. Deb: 9/13/10

YEAR	TM/L	G	AB	R	H	2B	3B	HR	RBI	BB	SO	AVG	OBP	SLG	PRO+	BR	/A	RC	SB	CS	SBR	FR	POS	TPR
1910	Chi-A	1	2	0	0	0	0	0		0	0	.000	.000	.000	-99	-0	-0	0	0			0	/O	0.0

■ FRANK BOYD
Boyd, Frank Jay b: 4/2/1868, West Middletown, Pa d: 12/16/37, Oil City, Pa. BR/TR, Deb: 5/18/1893

YEAR	TM/L	G	AB	R	H	2B	3B	HR	RBI	BB	SO	AVG	OBP	SLG	PRO+	BR	/A	RC	SB	CS	SBR	FR	POS	TPR
1893	Cle-N	2	5	3	1	1	0	0	3	1	0	.200	.333	.400	91	-0	-0	1	0			-0	/C	0.0

■ JAKE BOYD
Boyd, Jacob Henry b: 1/19/1874, Martinsburg, W.Va. d: 8/12/32, Gettysburg, Pa. TL, 160 lbs. Deb: 9/20/1894

YEAR	TM/L	G	AB	R	H	2B	3B	HR	RBI	BB	SO	AVG	OBP	SLG	PRO+	BR	/A	RC	SB	CS	SBR	FR	POS	TPR
1894	Was-N	6	21	1	3	0	0	0	1	1	4	.143	.182	.143	-21	-4	-4	1	2			1	/OP	-0.1
1895	Was-N	51	157	29	42	5	1	1	16	20	28	.268	.375	.331	86	-2	-2	21	2			-14	OP2S3	-1.1
1896	Was-N	4	13	1	1	0	0	0	1	1	1	.077	.200	.077	-24	-2	-2	0	0			0	/P	0.0
Total	3	61	191	31	46	5	1	1	18	22	33	.241	.344	.293	67	-9	-8	22	4			-13	/OP2S3	-1.2

■ BOB BOYD
Boyd, Robert Richard "The Rope" b: 10/1/26, Potts Camp, Miss. BL/TL, 5'10", 170 lbs. Deb: 9/08/51

YEAR	TM/L	G	AB	R	H	2B	3B	HR	RBI	BB	SO	AVG	OBP	SLG	PRO+	BR	/A	RC	SB	CS	SBR	FR	POS	TPR
1951	Chi-A	12	18	3	3	0	1	0	4	3	3	.167	.286	.278	54	-1	-1	2	0	0	0	-0	/1	-0.1
1953	Chi-A	55	165	20	49	6	2	3	23	13	11	.297	.352	.412	103	1	1	23	1	4	-2	-1	1O	-0.3
1954	Chi-A	29	56	10	10	3	0	0	5	4	3	.179	.233	.232	27	-6	-6	3	2	0	1	-0	O1	-0.6
1956	Bal-A	70	225	28	70	8	3	2	11	30	14	.311	.395	.400	119	4	7	35	0	5	-3	-5	1/O	-0.3
1957	Bal-A	141	485	73	154	16	8	4	34	55	31	.318	.389	.408	126	14	18	80	2	4	-2	-3	*1/O	1.2
1958	Bal-A	125	401	58	124	21	5	7	36	25	24	.309	.353	.439	123	8	11	62	1	1	-0	-2	1	0.6
1959	Bal-A	128	415	42	110	20	2	3	41	29	14	.265	.315	.345	83	-11	-10	44	3	1	0	-9	*1	-1.8
1960	Bal-A	71	82	9	26	5	2	0	9	6	5	.317	.364	.427	114	1	2	12	0	0	0	-0	1	0.0
1961	KC-A	26	48	7	11	2	0	0	9	1	2	.229	.245	.271	38	-4	-4	2	0	2	-1	-1	/1	-0.6
	Mil-N	36	41	3	10	0	0	0	3	1	7	.244	.262	.244	38	-4	-3	3	0	0	0	1	/1	-0.1
Total	9	693	1936	253	567	81	23	19	175	167	114	.293	.351	.388	105	3	13	266	9	17	-8	-20	1/O	-2.0

■ BILL BOYD
Boyd, William J. b: 12/22/1852, New York, N.Y. d: 9/30/12, Jamaica, N.Y. Deb: 4/22/1872 M

YEAR	TM/L	G	AB	R	H	2B	3B	HR	RBI	BB	SO	AVG	OBP	SLG	PRO+	BR	/A	RC	SB	CS	SBR	FR	POS	TPR
1872	Mut-n	35	164	26	44	6	1	1			6	.268	.294	.335	100	-1	1	17					*3/SO	0.0
1873	Atl-n	48	228	31	63	10	5	1			1	.276	.279	.377	102	-3	2	25					*O/3	0.3
1874	Har-n	26	116	22	41	9	4	0			2	.353	.364	.500	164	9	8	22					3O	0.6
1875	Atl-n	36	148	14	44	8	2	1			1	.297	.302	.399	161	6	9	18					2O/3P1M	0.7
Total	4 n	145	656	93	192	33	12	3			10	.293	.303	.393	125	11	20	81					/O321PS	1.6

■ CLETE BOYER
Boyer, Cletis Leroy b: 2/9/37, Cassville, Mo. BR/TR, 6', 165 lbs. Deb: 6/05/55 C

YEAR	TM/L	G	AB	R	H	2B	3B	HR	RBI	BB	SO	AVG	OBP	SLG	PRO+	BR	/A	RC	SB	CS	SBR	FR	POS	TPR
1955	KC-A	47	79	3	19	1	0	0	6	3	17	.241	.268	.253	40	-7	-7	5	0	0	0	6	S32	0.1
1956	KC-A	67	129	15	28	3	1	1	4	11	24	.217	.284	.279	49	-10	-10	10	1	1	-0	18	2/3	1.2
1957	KC-A	10	0	0	0	0	0	0	0	0	0	—	—	—	—	0	0	0	0	0	0	0	/23	0.0
1959	NY-A	47	114	4	20	2	0	0	3	6	23	.175	.217	.193	14	-13	-13	5	1	0	0	6	S3	-0.4
1960	*NY-A	124	393	54	95	20	1	14	46	23	85	.242	.289	.405	90	-10	-7	44	2	3	-1	28	3S	2.4
1961	*NY-A	148	504	61	113	19	5	11	55	63	83	.224	.313	.347	80	-17	-13	55	1	3	-2	31	*3S/O	2.5
1962	*NY-A	158	566	85	154	24	1	18	68	51	106	.272	.335	.413	104	-0	2	76	3	2	-0	36	*3	4.0
1963	*NY-A	152	557	59	140	20	3	12	54	33	91	.251	.296	.363	84	-13	-12	60	4	2	0	22	*3/S2	1.2
1964	*NY-A	147	510	43	111	10	5	8	52	36	93	.218	.271	.304	59	-28	-29	41	6	1	1	19	*3S	-0.6
1965	NY-A	148	514	69	129	23	6	18	58	39	79	.251	.306	.424	106	2	3	63	4	1	1	25	*3/S	3.1
1966	NY-A	144	500	59	120	22	4	14	57	46	48	.240	.307	.384	101	-2	-0	66	6	0	2	20	3S	2.4
1967	Atl-N	154	572	63	140	18	3	26	96	39	81	.245	.295	.423	105	1	1	68	6	3	0	5	*3/S	0.0
1968	Atl-N	71	273	19	62	7	2	4	17	16	32	.227	.275	.311	75	-8	-8	22	2	0	1	0	3	-0.8
1969	*Atl-N	144	496	57	124	16	1	14	57	55	87	.250	.330	.371	96	-2	-3	58	3	7	-3	-1	*3	-0.1
1970	Atl-N	134	475	44	117	14	1	16	62	41	72	.246	.308	.381	79	-12	-16	53	2	5	-2	12	*3/S	-0.8
1971	Atl-N	30	98	10	24	1	0	6	19	8	11	.245	.302	.439	101	1	-0	13	0	0	0	3	3/S	0.3
Total	16	1725	5780	645	1396	200	33	162	654	470	931	.242	.301	.372	87	-119	-111	635	41	28	-5	233	*3S/2O	14.5

■ KEN BOYER
Boyer, Kenton Lloyd b: 5/20/31, Liberty, Mo. d: 9/7/82, St.Louis, Mo. BR/TR, 6'1.5", 190 lbs. Deb: 4/12/55 MC

YEAR	TM/L	G	AB	R	H	2B	3B	HR	RBI	BB	SO	AVG	OBP	SLG	PRO+	BR	/A	RC	SB	CS	SBR	FR	POS	TPR
1955	StL-N	147	530	78	140	27	2	18	62	37	67	.264	.313	.425	94	-6	-6	67	22	17	-4	4	*3S	-0.5
1956	StL-N	150	595	91	182	30	2	26	98	38	65	.306	.349	.494	123	18	18	97	8	3	1	9	*3	2.7
1957	StL-N	142	544	79	144	18	3	19	62	44	77	.265	.321	.414	94	-4	-5	70	12	8	-1	0	*O3	-0.8
1958	StL-N	150	570	101	175	21	9	23	90	49	53	.307	.365	.496	121	20	17	100	11	6	-0	24	*3/OS	4.1
1959	StL-N	149	563	86	174	18	5	28	94	67	77	.309	.384	.508	127	29	24	112	12	6	0	14	*3S	3.3
1960	StL-N	151	552	95	168	26	10	32	97	56	77	.304	.373	.562	139	38	32	111	8	7	-2	13	*3	4.2
1961	StL-N	153	589	109	194	26	11	24	95	68	91	.329	.400	.533	132	38	31	126	6	3	0	13	*3	3.6
1962	StL-N	160	611	92	178	27	5	24	98	75	104	.291	.370	.470	113	21	13	105	12	7	-1	4	*3	2.0
1963	StL-N	159	617	86	176	28	2	24	111	70	90	.285	.360	.454	121	26	20	98	1	0	0	-13	*3	0.8
1964	*StL-N	162	628	100	185	30	10	24	119	70	85	.295	.367	.489	128	32	26	107	3	5	-2	3	*3	1.9
1965	StL-N	144	535	71	139	18	2	13	75	57	73	.260	.332	.374	90	-0	-6	64	2	7	-4	-11	*3	-2.8
1966	NY-N	136	496	62	132	28	2	14	61	30	64	.266	.308	.415	101	-2	-0	59	4	3	-1	11	*3/1	0.8
1967	NY-N	56	166	17	39	7	2	3	13	26	22	.235	.339	.355	100	0	1	20	2	1	0	-2	3/1	-0.4
	Chi-A	57	180	17	47	5	1	4	21	7	25	.261	.289	.367	96	-2	-2	18	0	2	-1	1	31	-0.1
1968	Chi-A	10	24	0	3	0	0	0	0	1	6	.125	.160	.125	-13	-3	-3	0	0	0	0	-0	/31	-0.3
	LA-N	83	221	20	60	7	2	6	41	16	34	.271	.324	.403	127	4	6	29	2	2	-1	-4	31	0.0
1969	LA-N	25	34	2	7	2	0	0	4	2	7	.206	.250	.265	48	-3	-2	2	0	0	0	-0	/1	-0.2
Total	15	2034	7455	1104	2143	318	68	282	1141	713	1017	.287	.351	.462	115	207	162	1184	105	77	-15	66	*3O/1S	18.3

■ DOE BOYLAND
Boyland, Dorian Scott b: 1/6/55, Chicago, Ill. BL/TL, 6'4", 200 lbs. Deb: 9/04/78

YEAR	TM/L	G	AB	R	H	2B	3B	HR	RBI	BB	SO	AVG	OBP	SLG	PRO+	BR	/A	RC	SB	CS	SBR	FR	POS	TPR
1978	Pit-N	6	8	1	2	0	0	0	1	0	1	.250	.250	.250	38	-1	-1	1	0	0	0	-0	/1	0.0
1979	Pit-N	4	3	0	0	0	0	0	0	0	0	.000	.000	.000	-96	-1	-1	0	0	0	0	0	/H	0.0
1981	Pit-N	11	8	0	0	0	0	0	0	1	3	.000	.111	.000	-64	-2	-2	0	0	0	0	0	/H	-0.1
Total	3	21	19	1	2	0	0	0	1	1	6	.105	.150	.105	-26	-3	-3	1	0	0	0	-0	/1	-0.1

YEAR	TM/L	G	AB	R	H	2B	3B	HR	RBI	BB	SO	AVG	OBP	SLG	PRO+	BR	/A	RC	SB	CS	SBR	FR	POS	TPR

■ EDDIE BOYLE   Boyle, Edward J.   b: 5/8/1874, Cincinnati, Ohio   d: 2/9/41, Cincinnati, Ohio   6'3", 200 lbs.   Deb: 4/17/1896

YEAR	TM/L	G	AB	R	H	2B	3B	HR	RBI	BB	SO	AVG	OBP	SLG	PRO+	BR	/A	RC	SB	CS	SBR	FR	POS	TPR
1896	Lou-N	3	9	0	0	0	0	0	0	2	2	.000	.182	.000	-51	-2	-2	0	0			1	/C	0.0
	Pit-N	2	5	0	0	0	0	0	0	0	1	.000	.000	.000	-99	-1	-1	0	0			-0	/C	0.0
	Yr	5	14	0	0	0	0	0	0	2	3	.000	.125	.000	-67	-3	-3	0	0			0		0.0

■ HENRY BOYLE   Boyle, Henry J. "Handsome Henry"   b: 9/20/1860, Philadelphia, Pa.   d: 5/25/32, Philadelphia, Pa.   TR ,   Deb: 7/09/1884

YEAR	TM/L	G	AB	R	H	2B	3B	HR	RBI	BB	SO	AVG	OBP	SLG	PRO+	BR	/A	RC	SB	CS	SBR	FR	POS	TPR
1884	StL-U	65	262	41	68	10	3	4		9		.260	.284	.366	114	5	3	28	0			5	OP/3S21	0.8
1885	StL-N	72	258	24	52	9	1	1	21	13	38	.202	.240	.256	64	-11	-9	16				-2	PO/2	0.0
1886	StL-N	30	108	8	27	2	2	1	13	5	19	.250	.283	.333	93	-2	-1	10	0			1	P/O	0.0
1887	Ind-N	41	141	17	27	9	1	2	13	9	18	.191	.250	.312	59	-8	-7	12	2			-5	P/O	0.0
1888	Ind-N	37	125	13	18	2	0	1	6	6	31	.144	.189	.184	20	-11	-11	5	1			3	P/1	0.0
1889	Ind-N	46	155	17	38	10	0	1	17	9	23	.245	.291	.329	73	-6	-6	16	4			-4	P/3	0.0
Total	6	291	1049	120	230	42	7	10	70	51	129	.219	.258	.301	75	-33	-31	87	7			-3	P/O321S	0.8

■ JIM BOYLE   Boyle, James John   b: 1/19/04, Cincinnati, Ohio   d: 12/24/58, Cincinnati, Ohio   BR/TR, 6', 180 lbs.   Deb: 6/20/26

YEAR	TM/L	G	AB	R	H	2B	3B	HR	RBI	BB	SO	AVG	OBP	SLG	PRO+	BR	/A	RC	SB	CS	SBR	FR	POS	TPR
1926	NY-N	1	0	0	0	0	0	0	0	0	0	—	—	—	—	0	0	0	0			0	/C	0.0

■ JACK BOYLE   Boyle, John Anthony "Honest Jack"   b: 3/22/1866, Cincinnati, Ohio   d: 1/7/13, Cincinnati, Ohio   BL/TR, 6'4", 190 lbs.   Deb: 10/08/1886

YEAR	TM/L	G	AB	R	H	2B	3B	HR	RBI	BB	SO	AVG	OBP	SLG	PRO+	BR	/A	RC	SB	CS	SBR	FR	POS	TPR
1886	Cin-a	1	5	0	1	0	0	0		0		.200	.200	.200	26	-0	-0	0	0			0	/C	0.0
1887	*StL-a	88	350	48	66	3	1	2		20		.189	.237	.220	26	-33	-39	20	7			-15	C/O13	-3.2
1888	*StL-a	71	257	33	62	8	1	1	23	13		.241	.286	.292	79	-3	-7	25	11			12	C/O	1.1
1889	StL-a	99	347	54	85	11	4	4	42	21	42	.245	.301	.334	73	-8	-16	37	5			4	C3/012	-0.3
1890	Chi-P	100	369	56	96	9	5	1	49	44	29	.260	.347	.320	77	-9	-12	46	11			-6	C3S/10	-0.9
1891	StL-a	123	439	78	123	18	8	5	79	47	36	.280	.365	.392	104	12	0	72	19			-16	CS/3021	-0.8
1892	NY-N	120	436	52	80	8	8	0	32	36	40	.183	.252	.239	51	-26	-25	29	10			23	C1/OS	0.0
1893	Phi-N	116	504	105	144	29	9	4	81	41	30	.286	.351	.403	102	1	1	81	22			7	*1/C2	0.6
1894	Phi-N	114	495	98	149	21	10	4	88	45	26	.301	.363	.408	89	-10	-8	83	21			1	*1/32	0.0
1895	Phi-N	133	565	90	143	17	4	0	67	35	23	.253	.302	.297	56	-36	-36	56	13			-6	*1	-3.1
1896	Phi-N	40	145	17	43	4	1	1	28	6	7	.297	.346	.359	89	-2	-2	20	3			-6	C1	-0.3
1897	Phi-N	75	288	37	73	9	1	2	36	19		.253	.306	.313	67	-14	-13	29	3			-10	C1	-1.3
1898	Phi-N	6	22	0	2	0	1	0	3	1		.091	.130	.182	-10	-3	-3	1	0			0	/1C	-0.2
Total	13	1086	4222	668	1067	137	53	24	528	328	233	.253	.315	.327	74	-132	-160	499	125			-11	C1/3SO2	-8.7

■ JACK BOYLE   Boyle, John Bellew   b: 7/9/1889, Morris, Ill.   d: 4/3/71, Ft.Lauderdale, Fla.   BL/TR, 5'11.5", 165 lbs.   Deb: 6/28/12

YEAR	TM/L	G	AB	R	H	2B	3B	HR	RBI	BB	SO	AVG	OBP	SLG	PRO+	BR	/A	RC	SB	CS	SBR	FR	POS	TPR
1912	Phi-N	15	25	4	7	1	0	0	2	1	5	.280	.308	.320	67	-1	-1	2	0			5	/3S	0.4

■ BUZZ BOYLE   Boyle, Ralph Francis   b: 2/9/08, Cincinnati, Ohio   d: 11/12/78, Cincinnati, Ohio   BL/TL, 5'11.5", 170 lbs.   Deb: 9/11/29

YEAR	TM/L	G	AB	R	H	2B	3B	HR	RBI	BB	SO	AVG	OBP	SLG	PRO+	BR	/A	RC	SB	CS	SBR	FR	POS	TPR
1929	Bos-N	17	57	8	15	2	1	1	2	6	11	.263	.333	.386	81	-2	-2	7	2			-1	O	-0.3
1930	Bos-N	1	1	0	0	0	0	0	0	0	1	.000	.000	.000	-99	-0	-0	0	0			0	/O	0.0
1933	Bro-N	93	338	38	101	13	4	0	31	16	24	.299	.331	.361	102	-1	0	42	7			-5	O	-1.0
1934	Bro-N	128	472	88	144	26	10	7	48	51	44	.305	.376	.447	126	14	17	84	8			11	*O	2.1
1935	Bro-N	127	475	51	129	17	9	4	44	43	45	.272	.332	.371	90	-7	-6	62	7			2	*O	-0.8
Total	5	366	1343	185	389	58	24	12	125	116	125	.290	.347	.395	105	3	10	196	24			6	O	-0.0

■ GIBBY BRACK   Brack, Gilbert Herman   b: 3/29/08, Chicago, Ill.   d: 1/20/60, Greenville, Tex.   BR/TR, 5'9", 170 lbs.   Deb: 4/23/37

YEAR	TM/L	G	AB	R	H	2B	3B	HR	RBI	BB	SO	AVG	OBP	SLG	PRO+	BR	/A	RC	SB	CS	SBR	FR	POS	TPR
1937	Bro-N	112	372	60	102	27	9	5	38	44	93	.274	.351	.435	111	6	6	60	9			3	*O	0.3
1938	Bro-N	40	56	10	12	2	1	1	6	4	14	.214	.267	.339	64	-3	-3	5	1			4	O	0.1
	Phi-N	72	282	40	81	20	4	4	28	18	30	.287	.332	.429	111	2	3	41	2			0	O	0.2
	Yr	112	338	50	93	22	5	5	34	22	44	.275	.321	.414	102	-0	-0	46	3			4		0.3
1939	Phi-N	91	270	40	78	21	4	6	41	26	49	.289	.351	.463	121	6	7	45	1			-5	O1	0.0
Total	3	315	980	150	273	70	18	16	113	92	186	.279	.341	.436	111	12	13	151	13			2	O/1	0.6

■ BUDDY BRADFORD   Bradford, Charles William   b: 7/25/44, Mobile, Ala.   BR/TR, 5'11", 170 lbs.   Deb: 9/09/66

YEAR	TM/L	G	AB	R	H	2B	3B	HR	RBI	BB	SO	AVG	OBP	SLG	PRO+	BR	/A	RC	SB	CS	SBR	FR	POS	TPR
1966	Chi-A	14	28	3	4	0	0	0	0	2	6	.143	.200	.143	0	-4	-3	1	0	0	0	-2	/O	-0.5
1967	Chi-A	24	20	6	2	1	0	0	1	1	7	.100	.143	.150	-14	-3	-3	1	1	0	0	0	O	-0.2
1968	Chi-A	103	281	32	61	11	0	5	24	23	67	.217	.281	.310	78	-7	-8	24	8	4	0	-5	O	-1.8
1969	Chi-A	93	273	36	70	8	2	11	27	34	75	.256	.347	.421	109	5	4	42	5	2	0	-5	O	-0.3
1970	Chi-A	32	91	8	17	3	0	2	8	10	30	.187	.267	.286	51	-6	-6	6	1	2	-1	-1	O	-0.9
	Cle-A	75	163	25	32	6	1	7	23	21	43	.196	.292	.374	79	-4	-5	16	0	1	-1	6	O/3	-0.1
	Yr	107	254	33	49	9	1	9	31	31	73	.193	.283	.343	69	-10	-12	22	1	3	-2	5		-1.0
1971	Cle-A	20	38	4	6	2	1	0	3	6	10	.158	.273	.263	48	-2	-3	3	0	0	0	3	O	-0.2
	Cin-N	79	100	17	20	3	0	2	12	14	23	.200	.316	.290	74	-3	-3	10	4	2	0	3	O	-0.2
1972	Chi-A	35	48	13	13	2	0	2	8	4	13	.271	.340	.438	127	2	2	6	3	2	-0	2	O	0.3
1973	Chi-A	53	168	24	40	3	1	8	15	17	43	.238	.316	.411	100	0	-0	20	4	5	-2	9	O	0.5
1974	Chi-A	39	96	16	32	2	0	5	10	13	11	.333	.418	.510	162	8	8	20	1	2	-1	-2	O/D	0.5
1975	Chi-A	25	58	8	9	3	1	2	15	8	22	.155	.290	.345	78	-2	-2	6	3	2	-0	-1	O/D	-0.2
	StL-N	50	81	12	22	1	0	4	15	12	24	.272	.366	.432	117	2	2	12	0	2	-1	1	O	0.1
1976	Chi-A	55	160	20	35	5	2	4	14	19	37	.219	.309	.350	92	-1	-1	20	6	0	2	-3	O/D	-0.3
Total	11	697	1605	224	363	50	8	52	175	184	411	.226	.313	.364	91	-14	-19	185	36	24	-4	6	O/D3	-3.1

■ VIC BRADFORD   Bradford, Henry Victor   b: 3/5/15, Brownsville, Tenn.   BR/TR, 6'2", 190 lbs.   Deb: 5/01/43

YEAR	TM/L	G	AB	R	H	2B	3B	HR	RBI	BB	SO	AVG	OBP	SLG	PRO+	BR	/A	RC	SB	CS	SBR	FR	POS	TPR
1943	NY-N	6	5	1	1	0	0	0	1	1	1	.200	.333	.200	55	-0	-0	0	0			1	/O	0.0

■ AL BRADLEY   Bradley, Al   5'10", 185 lbs.   Deb: 5/21/1884

YEAR	TM/L	G	AB	R	H	2B	3B	HR	RBI	BB	SO	AVG	OBP	SLG	PRO+	BR	/A	RC	SB	CS	SBR	FR	POS	TPR
1884	Was-U	1	3	0	0	0	0	0		2		.000	.400	.000	47	0	0	0	0			0	/O	0.0

■ GEORGE BRADLEY   Bradley, George Washington "Grin"   b: 7/13/1852, Reading, Pa.   d: 10/2/31, Philadelphia, Pa.   BR/TR, 5'10.5", 175 lbs.   Deb: 5/04/1875

YEAR	TM/L	G	AB	R	H	2B	3B	HR	RBI	BB	SO	AVG	OBP	SLG	PRO+	BR	/A	RC	SB	CS	SBR	FR	POS	TPR
1875	StL-n	60	254	28	62	8	3	0		1		.244	.247	.299	97	-3	-1	19					*P/3O	0.0
1876	StL-N	64	265	29	66	7	6	0	28	3	12	.249	.257	.321	97	-2	-0	22				1	*P	0.0
1877	Chi-N	55	214	31	52	7	3	0	12	6	19	.243	.264	.304	70	-5	-9	18				-2	*P3/1O	0.0
1879	Tro-N	63	251	36	62	9	5	0	23	1	20	.247	.250	.323	93	-3	-1	21				7	P/310S	0.0
1880	Pro-N	82	309	32	70	7	6	0	23	5	38	.227	.239	.288	80	-7	-6	22				19	*3P/O1	1.4
1881	Det-N	1	4	0	0	0	0	0	0	0	0	.000	.000	.000	-96	-1	-1	0				-1	/S	-0.1
	Cle-N	60	241	21	60	10	1	2	18	4	25	.249	.261	.324	88	-5	-3	21				-9	3/PSO	-0.5
	Yr	61	245	21	60	10	1	2	18	4	25	.245	.257	.318	84	-6	-4	21				-9		-0.6
1882	Cle-N	30	115	16	21	5	0	0	6	4	16	.183	.210	.226	41	-7	-7	6				3	P/O1	0.0
1883	Cle-N	4	16	0	5	0	1	0	1	0	1	.313	.313	.438	126	0	0	2				0	/S	0.0
	Phi-a	76	312	47	73	8	5	1		8		.234	.253	.301	72	-8	-12	24				4	3PO/1	-0.2
1884	Cin-U	58	226	31	43	4	7	0		7		.190	.215	.270	58	-9	-11	13	0			-9	PO/S1	0.0
1886	Phi-a	13	48	1	4	0	1	0		1		.083	.102	.125	-28	-7	-7	1	2			1	S	-0.3
1888	Bal-a	1	3	0	0	0	0	0	0	0		.000	.000	.000	-99	-1	-1	0	0			-1	/S	0.0
Total	10	507	2004	244	456	57	35	3	111	39	131	.228	.242	.295	74	-55	-57	150	2			24	P3/OS1	0.3

■ GEORGE BRADLEY   Bradley, George Washington   b: 4/1/14, Greenwood, Ark.   d: 10/19/82, Lawrenceburg, Tenn.   BR/TR, 6'1.5", 185 lbs.   Deb: 4/28/46

YEAR	TM/L	G	AB	R	H	2B	3B	HR	RBI	BB	SO	AVG	OBP	SLG	PRO+	BR	/A	RC	SB	CS	SBR	FR	POS	TPR
1946	StL-A	4	12	2	2	1	0	0	3	0	1	.167	.167	.250	15	-1	-1	0	0	0	0	-0	/O	-0.1

YEAR	TM/L	G	AB	R	H	2B	3B	HR	RBI	BB	SO	AVG	OBP	SLG	PRO+	BR	/A	RC	SB	CS	SBR	FR	POS	TPR

■ HUGH BRADLEY
Bradley, Hugh Frederick "Corns"   b: 5/23/1885, Grafton, Mass.   d: 1/26/49, Worcester, Mass.   BR/TR, 5'10", 175 lbs.   Deb: 4/25/10

YEAR	TM/L	G	AB	R	H	2B	3B	HR	RBI	BB	SO	AVG	OBP	SLG	PRO+	BR	/A	RC	SB	CS	SBR	FR	POS	TPR
1910	Bos-A	32	83	8	14	6	2	0	7	5		.169	.216	.289	57	-4	-5	6	2			-2	1/CO	-0.6
1911	Bos-A	12	41	9	13	2	0	1	4	2		.317	.364	.439	125	1	1	7	1			1	1	0.2
1912	Bos-A	40	137	16	26	11	1	1	19	15		.190	.275	.307	63	-6	-7	13	3			0	1	-0.6
1914	Pit-F	118	427	41	131	20	6	0	61	27	27	.307	.359	.382	113	7	8	65	7			-0	*1	1.0
1915	Pit-F	26	66	3	18	4	1	0	6	4	5	.273	.314	.364	101	-0	-0	9	2			-2	O	-0.3
	Bro-F	37	126	7	31	3	2	0	18	4	9	.246	.269	.302	69	-5	-5	13	6			2	1/OC	-0.2
	New-F	12	33	0	5	0	0	0	2	2	3	.152	.243	.152	19	-3	-3	2	2			-1	/1	-0.4
	Yr	75	225	10	54	7	3	0	26	10	17	.240	.278	.298	72	-9	-8	23	10			-2		-0.9
Total	5	277	913	84	238	46	12	2	117	59	44	.261	.314	.344	91	-11	-11	113	23			-3	1/OC	-0.9

■ JACK BRADLEY
Bradley, John Thomas   b: 9/20/1893, Denver, Colo.   d: 3/18/69, Tulsa, Okla.   BR/TR, 5'11", 175 lbs.   Deb: 6/18/16

YEAR	TM/L	G	AB	R	H	2B	3B	HR	RBI	BB	SO	AVG	OBP	SLG	PRO+	BR	/A	RC	SB	CS	SBR	FR	POS	TPR
1916	Cle-A	2	3	0	0	0	0	0	0	0	1	.000	.000	.000	-94	-1	-1	0	0			-0	/C	0.0

■ MARK BRADLEY
Bradley, Mark Allen   b: 12/3/56, Elizabethtown, Ky.   BR/TR, 6'1", 180 lbs.   Deb: 9/03/81

YEAR	TM/L	G	AB	R	H	2B	3B	HR	RBI	BB	SO	AVG	OBP	SLG	PRO+	BR	/A	RC	SB	CS	SBR	FR	POS	TPR
1981	LA-N	9	6	2	1	1	0	0	0	0	1	.167	.167	.333	41	-1	-0	0	0	0	0	1	/O	0.0
1982	LA-N	8	3	1	1	0	0	0	0	0	0	.333	.333	.333	89	-0	-0	0	0	0	0	0	/O	0.0
1983	NY-N	73	104	10	21	4	0	3	5	11	35	.202	.278	.327	68	-5	-5	9	4	2	0	1	O	-0.4
Total	3	90	113	13	23	5	0	3	5	11	36	.204	.274	.327	67	-5	-5	10	4	2	0	2	/O	-0.4

■ PHIL BRADLEY
Bradley, Philip Poole   b: 3/11/59, Bloomington, Ind.   BR/TR, 6', 185 lbs.   Deb: 9/02/83

YEAR	TM/L	G	AB	R	H	2B	3B	HR	RBI	BB	SO	AVG	OBP	SLG	PRO+	BR	/A	RC	SB	CS	SBR	FR	POS	TPR
1983	Sea-A	23	67	8	18	2	0	0	5	8	5	.269	.347	.299	77	-2	-2	8	3	1	0	-2	O/D	-0.3
1984	Sea-A	124	322	49	97	12	4	0	24	34	61	.301	.373	.363	106	3	4	46	21	8	2	-2	*O/D	0.0
1985	Sea-A	159	641	100	192	33	8	26	88	55	129	.300	.366	.498	133	29	29	116	22	9	1	4	*O	3.1
1986	Sea-A	143	526	88	163	27	4	12	50	77	134	.310	.406	.445	130	26	26	99	21	12	-1	-3	*O	1.8
1987	Sea-A	158	603	101	179	38	10	14	67	84	119	.297	.390	.463	119	24	19	113	40	10	6	-5	*O	1.6
1988	Phi-N	154	569	77	150	30	5	11	56	54	106	.264	.344	.392	109	9	8	78	11	9	-2	6	*O	0.7
1989	Bal-A	144	545	83	151	23	10	11	55	70	103	.277	.367	.417	124	16	18	87	20	6	2	-8	*O/D	1.0
1990	Bal-A	72	289	39	78	9	1	4	26	30	35	.270	.353	.349	99	-0	1	36	10	4	1	-5	O/D	-0.3
	Chi-A	45	133	20	30	5	1	0	5	20	26	.226	.344	.278	78	-3	-3	15	7	3	0	-2	O/D	-0.4
	Yr	117	422	59	108	14	2	4	31	50	61	.256	.350	.327	92	-3	-2	51	17	7	1	-6		-0.7
Total	8	1022	3695	565	1058	179	43	78	376	432	718	.286	.371	.421	117	103	100	598	155	62	9	-17	O/D	7.2

■ SCOTT BRADLEY
Bradley, Scott William   b: 3/22/60, Glen Ridge, N.J.   BL/TR, 5'11", 185 lbs.   Deb: 9/09/84

YEAR	TM/L	G	AB	R	H	2B	3B	HR	RBI	BB	SO	AVG	OBP	SLG	PRO+	BR	/A	RC	SB	CS	SBR	FR	POS	TPR
1984	NY-A	9	21	3	6	1	0	0	2	1	1	.286	.318	.333	84	-1	-0	2	0	0	0	-1	/OC	-0.1
1985	NY-A	19	49	4	8	2	1	0	1	1	5	.163	.196	.245	20	-5	-5	2	0	0	0	2	/CD	-0.3
1986	Chi-A	9	21	3	6	0	0	0	0	1	0	.286	.375	.286	81	-0	-0	2	0	2	-1	0	/OD	-0.1
	Sea-A	68	199	17	60	8	3	5	28	12	7	.302	.347	.447	113	4	4	27	1	0	0	-12	C/D	-0.4
	Yr	77	220	20	66	8	3	5	28	13	7	.300	.350	.432	110	3	3	28	1	2	-1	-12		-0.5
1987	Sea-A	102	342	34	95	15	1	5	43	15	18	.278	.314	.371	77	-10	-12	36	1	0	-1	-8	C/3OD	-1.2
1988	Sea-A	103	335	45	86	17	1	4	33	17	16	.257	.297	.349	77	-9	-11	32	1	1	-0	4	C/O31	-0.3
1989	Sea-A	103	270	21	74	16	0	3	37	21	23	.274	.329	.367	93	-2	-3	32	1	1	-0	2	C/1OD	0.2
1990	Sea-A	101	233	11	52	9	0	1	28	15	20	.223	.270	.275	52	-15	-15	17	0	1	-1	1	C/31D	-1.2
Total	7	514	1470	138	387	68	6	18	172	83	90	.263	.308	.354	79	-38	-43	151	3	6	-3	-11	C/D301	-3.4

■ BILL BRADLEY
Bradley, William Joseph   b: 2/13/1878, Cleveland, Ohio   d: 3/11/54, Cleveland, Ohio   BR/TR, 6', 185 lbs.   Deb: 8/26/1899   M

YEAR	TM/L	G	AB	R	H	2B	3B	HR	RBI	BB	SO	AVG	OBP	SLG	PRO+	BR	/A	RC	SB	CS	SBR	FR	POS	TPR
1899	Chi-N	35	129	26	40	6	1	2	18	12		.310	.373	.419	123	4	4	22	4			-3	3/S	0.1
1900	Chi-N	122	444	63	125	21	8	5	49	27		.282	.330	.399	107	1	3	65	14			17	*31	1.9
1901	Cle-A	133	516	95	151	28	13	1	55	26		.293	.336	.403	111	4	7	77	15			10	*3/P	1.2
1902	Cle-A	137	550	104	187	39	12	11	77	27		.340	.375	.515	153	32	35	114	11			12	*3	4.0
1903	Cle-A	136	536	101	168	36	22	6	68	25		.313	.344	.496	155	31	32	103	21			12	*3	4.3
1904	Cle-A	154	609	94	183	32	8	5	83	26		.300	.329	.404	134	21	22	93	23			9	*3	4.0
1905	Cle-A	146	541	63	145	34	6	0	51	27		.268	.303	.353	108	5	4	68	22			13	*3	2.5
1906	Cle-A	82	302	32	83	15	2	2	25	18		.275	.316	.358	114	4	4	41	13			5	3	1.6
1907	Cle-A	139	498	48	111	20	1	0	34	35		.223	.274	.267	74	-14	-14	48	20			5	*3	-0.1
1908	Cle-A	148	548	70	133	24	7	1	46	29		.243	.281	.318	96	-3	-3	57	18			-31	*3S	-2.9
1909	Cle-A	95	334	30	62	6	3	0	22	19		.186	.236	.222	43	-21	-23	20	8			-10	3/12	-3.3
1910	Cle-A	61	214	12	42	3	0	0	12	10		.196	.236	.210	39	-15	-15	12	6			-0	3	-1.4
1914	Bro-F	7	6	1	3	1	0	0	3	0	0	.500	.500	.667	234	1	1	2	0			0	HM	0.1
1915	KC-F	66	203	15	38	9	1	0	9	18		.187	.225	.241	40	-16	-15	13	6			-6	3	-2.1
Total	14	1461	5430	754	1471	274	84	33	552	290	18	.271	.311	.371	108	34	43	737	181			29	*3/S12P	9.9

■ DALLAS BRADSHAW
Bradshaw, Dallas Carl "Windy"   b: 11/23/1895, Wolf Creek, Ill.   d: 12/11/39, Herrin, Ill.   BL/TR, 5'7", 145 lbs.   Deb: 6/05/17

YEAR	TM/L	G	AB	R	H	2B	3B	HR	RBI	BB	SO	AVG	OBP	SLG	PRO+	BR	/A	RC	SB	CS	SBR	FR	POS	TPR
1917	Phi-A	2	4	0	0	0	0	0	0	0	1	.000	.000	.000	-99	-1	-1	0	0			1	/2	0.0

■ GEORGE BRADSHAW
Bradshaw, George Thomas   b: 9/12/24, Salisbury, N.C.   BR/TR, 6'2", 185 lbs.   Deb: 8/10/52

YEAR	TM/L	G	AB	R	H	2B	3B	HR	RBI	BB	SO	AVG	OBP	SLG	PRO+	BR	/A	RC	SB	CS	SBR	FR	POS	TPR
1952	Was-A	10	23	3	5	2	0	0	6	1	2	.217	.280	.304	65	-1	-1	2	0	0	0	-3	/C	-0.3

■ BRADY
Brady   Deb: 9/25/1875

YEAR	TM/L	G	AB	R	H	2B	3B	HR	RBI	BB	SO	AVG	OBP	SLG	PRO+	BR	/A	RC	SB	CS	SBR	FR	POS	TPR
1875	Chi-n	1	4	1	1	0	1	0		0		.250	.250	.750	230	1	1	1					/O	0.0

■ BRIAN BRADY
Brady, Brian Phelan   b: 7/11/62, Elmhurst, N.Y.   BL/TL, 5'11", 185 lbs.   Deb: 4/16/89

YEAR	TM/L	G	AB	R	H	2B	3B	HR	RBI	BB	SO	AVG	OBP	SLG	PRO+	BR	/A	RC	SB	CS	SBR	FR	POS	TPR
1989	Cal-A	2	2	0	1	1	0	0	1	0	0	.500	.500	1.000	319	1	1	1	0	0	0	0	/O	0.1

■ CLIFF BRADY
Brady, Clifford Francis   b: 3/6/1897, St.Louis, Mo.   d: 9/25/74, Belleville, Ill.   BR/TR, 5'5.5", 140 lbs.   Deb: 8/08/20

YEAR	TM/L	G	AB	R	H	2B	3B	HR	RBI	BB	SO	AVG	OBP	SLG	PRO+	BR	/A	RC	SB	CS	SBR	FR	POS	TPR
1920	Bos-A	53	180	16	41	5	1	0	12	13	12	.228	.284	.267	48	-14	-13	14	0	1	-1	17	2	0.5

■ BOB BRADY
Brady, Robert Jay   b: 11/8/22, Lewistown, Pa.   BL/TR, 6'1", 175 lbs.   Deb: 8/24/46

YEAR	TM/L	G	AB	R	H	2B	3B	HR	RBI	BB	SO	AVG	OBP	SLG	PRO+	BR	/A	RC	SB	CS	SBR	FR	POS	TPR
1946	Bos-N	3	5	0	1	0	0	0	0	1	1	.200	.333	.200	52	-0	-0	0	0			0	/C	0.0
1947	Bos-N	1	1	0	0	0	0	0	0	0	0	.000	.000	.000	-99	-0	-0	0	0			0	H	0.0
Total	2	4	6	0	1	0	0	0	0	1	1	.167	.286	.167	29	-1	-1	0	0			0	/C	0.0

■ STEVE BRADY
Brady, Stephen A.   b: 7/14/1851, Worcester, Mass.   d: 11/1/17, Hartford, Conn.   5'9.5", 165 lbs.   Deb: 7/23/1874

YEAR	TM/L	G	AB	R	H	2B	3B	HR	RBI	BB	SO	AVG	OBP	SLG	PRO+	BR	/A	RC	SB	CS	SBR	FR	POS	TPR
1874	Har-n	27	115	19	38	5	2	0		3		.330	.347	.409	133	5	4	17					3/O	0.3
1875	Was-n	21	90	6	13	1	1	0		0		.144	.144	.178	11	-8	-7	2					2/O1	-0.6
1883	NY-a	97	432	69	117	12	6	0		11		.271	.289	.326	94	-1	-4	42				3	*1O	-0.6
1884	*NY-a	112	485	102	122	11	3	1		21		.252	.283	.293	93	-5	-3	41				1	*O/12	-0.2
1885	NY-a	108	434	60	128	14	5	3		25		.295	.342	.371	139	14	19	56				-5	*O/123	0.7
1886	NY-a	124	466	56	112	8	5	0		35		.240	.298	.279	86	-8	-5	45	16			-5	*O/1	-1.2
Total	2 n	48	205	25	51	6	3	0		3		.249	.260	.307	85	-3	-3	19	0				/3201	-0.3
Total	4	441	1817	287	479	45	19	4		92		.264	.302	.316	102	-0	8	184	16			-6	O/123	-1.3

■ TOM BRADY
Brady, Thomas A.   b: Hartford, Conn.   d: 8/27/22, Hartford, Conn.   Deb: 9/25/1875

YEAR	TM/L	G	AB	R	H	2B	3B	HR	RBI	BB	SO	AVG	OBP	SLG	PRO+	BR	/A	RC	SB	CS	SBR	FR	POS	TPR
1875	Har-n	1	4	0	0		0	0	0		0		.000	.000	.000	-95	-1	-1	0					/O	0.0

BOBBY BRAGAN

Bragan, Robert Randall "Nig" b: 10/30/17, Birmingham, Ala. BR/TR, 5'10.5", 175 lbs. Deb: 4/16/40 MC

YEAR	TM/L	G	AB	R	H	2B	3B	HR	RBI	BB	SO	AVG	OBP	SLG	PRO+	BR	/A	RC	SB	CS	SBR	FR	POS	TPR
1940	Phi-N	132	474	36	105	14	1	7	44	28	34	.222	.265	.300	58	-29	-27	37	2			1	*S/3	-1.3
1941	Phi-N	154	557	37	140	19	3	4	69	26	29	.251	.285	.318	72	-23	-21	48	7			-7	*S/23	-1.4
1942	Phi-N	109	335	17	73	12	2	2	15	20	21	.218	.264	.284	63	-17	-15	24	0			10	SC/23	0.0
1943	Bro-N	74	220	17	58	7	2	2	24	15	16	.264	.311	.341	88	-4	-4	23	0			4	C3	0.3
1944	Bro-N	94	266	26	71	8	4	0	17	13	14	.267	.304	.327	79	-8	-8	25	2			-1	SC/32	0.0
1947	*Bro-N	25	36	3	7	2	0	0	3	7	3	.194	.326	.250	53	-2	-2	4	1			3	C	0.1
1948	Bro-N	9	12	0	2	0	0	0	0	1	0	.167	.231	.167	9	-2	-2	1	0			-0	/C	-0.1
Total	7	597	1900	136	456	62	12	15	172	110	117	.240	.282	.309	69	-86	-79	160	12			10	SC/32	-2.4

GLENN BRAGGS

Braggs, Glenn Erick b: 10/17/62, San Bernardino, Cal BR/TR, 6'3", 210 lbs. Deb: 7/18/86

YEAR	TM/L	G	AB	R	H	2B	3B	HR	RBI	BB	SO	AVG	OBP	SLG	PRO+	BR	/A	RC	SB	CS	SBR	FR	POS	TPR
1986	Mil-A	58	215	19	51	8	2	4	18	11	47	.237	.278	.349	67	-10	-10	20	1	1	-0	-2	O/D	-1.3
1987	Mil-A	132	505	67	136	28	7	13	77	47	96	.269	.336	.430	98	1	-1	69	12	5	1	10	*O/D	0.6
1988	Mil-A	72	272	30	71	14	0	10	42	14	60	.261	.309	.423	102	0	0	34	6	4	-1	-2	OD	-0.2
1989	Mil-A	144	514	77	127	12	3	15	66	42	111	.247	.309	.370	91	-7	-6	58	17	5	2	-4	*OD	-0.9
1990	Mil-A	37	113	17	28	5	0	3	13	12	21	.248	.336	.372	101	-0	0	15	5	3	-0	1	O/D	0.1
	*Cin-N	72	201	22	60	9	1	6	28	26	43	.299	.387	.443	125	8	8	35	3	4	-2	5	O	0.9
Total	5	515	1820	232	473	76	13	51	244	152	378	.260	.324	.400	97	-7	-7	230	44	22	0	8	O/D	-0.8

DAVE BRAIN

Brain, David Leonard b: 1/24/1879, Hereford, England d: 5/25/59, Los Angeles, Cal. BR/TR, 5'10", 170 lbs. Deb: 4/24/01

YEAR	TM/L	G	AB	R	H	2B	3B	HR	RBI	BB	SO	AVG	OBP	SLG	PRO+	BR	/A	RC	SB	CS	SBR	FR	POS	TPR
1901	Chi-A	5	20	2	7	1	0	0	5	1		.350	.381	.400	122	1	1	3	0			1	/2	0.1
1903	StL-N	119	464	44	107	8	15	1	60	25		.231	.270	.319	71	-19	-17	47	21			10	S3	-0.2
1904	StL-N	127	488	57	130	24	12	7	72	17		.266	.291	.408	122	7	10	66	18			3	S302/1	1.4
1905	StL-N	44	158	11	36	4	5	1	17	8		.228	.265	.335	83	-4	-4	16	4			-9	S/3O	-1.2
	Pit-N	85	307	31	79	17	6	3	46	15		.257	.292	.381	99	-0	-1	38	8			6	3/S	1.0
	Yr	129	465	42	115	21	11	4	63	23		.247	.283	.366	94	-5	-5	54	12			-3		-0.2
1906	Bos-N	139	525	43	131	19	5	5	45	29		.250	.289	.333	98	-4	-3	57	11			26	*3	2.0
1907	Bos-N	133	509	60	142	24	9	**10**	56	29		.279	.318	.420	134	16	17	74	10			25	*3/O	4.6
1908	Cin-N	16	55	4	6	0	0	0	1	8		.109	.222	.109	8	-5	-5	1	0			-0	O	-0.6
	NY-N	11	17	2	3	0	0	0	1	2		.176	.263	.176	41	-1	-1	1	1			-3	/2O3S	-0.3
	Yr	27	72	6	9	0	0	0	2	10		.125	.232	.125	16	-6	-6	2	1			-3		-0.9
Total	7	679	2543	254	641	97	52	27	303	134		.252	.290	.363	102	-11	-5	304	73			59	3S/O21	6.8

ASA BRAINARD

Brainard, Asa "Count" b: 1841, Albany, N.Y. d: 12/29/1888, Denver, Colo. TR, 5'8.5", 150 lbs. Deb: 5/05/1871

YEAR	TM/L	G	AB	R	H	2B	3B	HR	RBI	BB	SO	AVG	OBP	SLG	PRO+	BR	/A	RC	SB	CS	SBR	FR	POS	TPR
1871	Oly-n	30	134	24	30	4	0	0	21	7	2	.224	.262	.254	52	-8	-7	10	4				*P	0.0
1872	Oly-n	9	41	8	16	3	0	0		1		.390	.405	.463	175	3	4	8					/P	0.0
	Man-n	6	25	2	5	0	0	0		1		.200	.231	.200	36	-2	-2	1					/2P	0.0
	Yr	15	66	10	21	3	0	0		2		.318	.338	.364	123	1	2	8						0.0
1873	Bal-n	16	69	18	18	2	0	0		0		.261	.261	.290	62	-3	-3	5					P/O	0.0
1874	Bal-n	46	198	19	50	5	0	0		2		.253	.260	.278	72	-6	-6	15					P2/O	0.0
Total	4 n	107	467	71	119	14	0	0		11		.255	.272	.285	71	-16	-14	39					/P2O	0.0

FRED BRAINERD

Brainerd, Frederick F. b: 2/17/1892, Champaign, Ill. d: 4/17/59, Galveston, Tex. BR/TR, 6', 176 lbs. Deb: 10/06/14

YEAR	TM/L	G	AB	R	H	2B	3B	HR	RBI	BB	SO	AVG	OBP	SLG	PRO+	BR	/A	RC	SB	CS	SBR	FR	POS	TPR
1914	NY-N	2	5	1	1	0	0	0	0	1	0	.200	.333	.200	62	-0	-0	1	0			1	/2	0.1
1915	NY-N	91	249	31	50	7	2	1	21	21	44	.201	.266	.257	62	-12	-11	17	6	7	-2	7	13/S2O	-0.7
1916	NY-N	2	7	0	0	0	0	0	0	0	0	.000	.000	.000	-99	-2	-2	0	0			-1	/3	-0.2
Total	3	95	261	32	51	7	2	1	21	22	44	.195	.261	.249	58	-14	-12	17	6	7		7	/13S2O	-0.8

ART BRAMHALL

Bramhall, Arthur Washington b: 2/22/09, Oak Park, Ill. d: 9/4/85, Madison, Wis. BR/TR, 5'11", 170 lbs. Deb: 4/18/35

YEAR	TM/L	G	AB	R	H	2B	3B	HR	RBI	BB	SO	AVG	OBP	SLG	PRO+	BR	/A	RC	SB	CS	SBR	FR	POS	TPR
1935	Phi-N	2	1	0	0	0	0	0	0	0	0	.000	.000	.000	-91	-0	-0	0	0			1	/S3	0.0

AL BRANCATO

Brancato, Albert "Bronk" b: 5/29/19, Philadelphia, Pa. BR/TR, 5'9.5", 188 lbs. Deb: 9/07/39

YEAR	TM/L	G	AB	R	H	2B	3B	HR	RBI	BB	SO	AVG	OBP	SLG	PRO+	BR	/A	RC	SB	CS	SBR	FR	POS	TPR
1939	Phi-A	21	68	12	14	5	0	1	8	8	4	.206	.299	.324	60	-4	-4	7	1	0	0	-1	3/S	-0.4
1940	Phi-A	107	298	42	57	11	2	1	23	28	36	.191	.265	.252	36	-29	-28	20	3	1	0	0	S3	-1.7
1941	Phi-A	144	530	60	124	20	9	2	49	59	49	.234	.311	.317	68	-26	-24	54	1	5	-3	-19	*S/3	-4.0
1945	Phi-A	10	34	3	4	1	0	0	0	1	3	.118	.143	.147	-16	-5	-5	1	0	0	0	-1	S	-0.5
Total	4	282	930	117	199	37	11	4	80	96	92	.214	.290	.290	54	-64	-61	81	5	6	-2	-21	S/3	-6.6

RON BRAND

Brand, Ronald George b: 1/13/40, Los Angeles, Cal. BR/TR, 5'7.5", 167 lbs. Deb: 5/26/63

YEAR	TM/L	G	AB	R	H	2B	3B	HR	RBI	BB	SO	AVG	OBP	SLG	PRO+	BR	/A	RC	SB	CS	SBR	FR	POS	TPR
1963	Pit-N	46	66	8	19	2	0	1	7	10	11	.288	.390	.364	118	2	2	10	0	0	0	8	C/23	1.2
1965	Hou-N	117	391	27	92	6	3	2	37	19	34	.235	.281	.281	63	-21	-18	28	10	5	0	-5	*C/3O	-2.0
1966	Hou-N	56	123	12	30	2	0	0	10	9	13	.244	.306	.260	64	-6	-5	9	0	2	-1	-5	C/2O3	-1.0
1967	Hou-N	84	215	22	52	8	1	0	18	23	17	.242	.321	.288	78	-6	-5	21	4	0	1	-2	C/2O	-0.1
1968	Hou-N	43	81	7	13	2	0	0	4	9	11	.160	.261	.185	36	-6	-6	5	1	1	-0	3	C/3O	-0.2
1969	Mon-N	103	287	19	74	12	0	0	20	30	19	.258	.330	.300	77	-8	-8	27	2	3	-1	-8	C/O	-1.1
1970	Mon-N	72	126	10	30	2	3	0	9	9	16	.238	.289	.302	59	-7	-7	12	2	1	0	4	S3/CO2	-0.9
1971	Mon-N	47	56	3	12	0	0	0	1	3	5	.214	.254	.214	34	-5	-5	3	1	1	-0	4	S/3OC2	0.2
Total	8	568	1345	108	322	34	7	3	106	112	126	.239	.305	.282	68	-57	-52	114	20	13	-2	-10	C/S3O2	-3.9

JACKIE BRANDT

Brandt, John George b: 4/28/34, Omaha, Neb. BR/TR, 5'11", 165 lbs. Deb: 4/21/56

YEAR	TM/L	G	AB	R	H	2B	3B	HR	RBI	BB	SO	AVG	OBP	SLG	PRO+	BR	/A	RC	SB	CS	SBR	FR	POS	TPR
1956	StL-N	27	42	9	12	3	0	1	3	4	5	.286	.362	.429	111	1	1	6	0	1	-1	2	O	0.1
	NY-N	98	351	45	105	16	8	11	47	17	31	.299	.332	.484	116	7	7	55	3	4	-2	-1	O	0.0
	Yr	125	393	54	117	19	8	12	50	21	36	.298	.335	.478	116	7	7	61	3	5	-2	0		0.1
1958	SF-N	18	52	7	13	1	0	0	3	6	5	.250	.328	.269	62	-3	-3	5	1	0	0	-1	O	-0.2
1959	SF-N	137	429	63	116	16	5	12	57	35	69	.270	.325	.415	98	-3	-2	58	11	4	1	-8	*O3/12	-1.0
1960	Bal-A	145	511	73	130	24	6	15	65	47	69	.254	.321	.413	98	-3	-2	69	5	3	-0	-9	*O/31	-1.7
1961	Bal-A	139	516	93	153	18	5	16	72	62	51	.297	.373	.444	120	13	15	85	10	2	2	-7	*O/3	0.4
1962	Bal-A	143	505	76	129	29	5	19	75	55	64	.255	.333	.446	113	5	8	76	9	3	1	1	*O/3	0.5
1963	Bal-A	142	451	49	112	15	5	15	61	34	85	.248	.301	.404	98	-4	-2	51	4	5	-2	-6	*O/3	-1.5
1964	Bal-A	137	523	66	127	25	1	13	47	45	104	.243	.306	.369	87	-9	-9	59	1	4	-2	11	*O	-0.5
1965	Bal-A	96	243	35	59	17	0	8	24	21	40	.243	.303	.412	99	-0	-1	30	1	2	-1	5	O	0.0
1966	Phi-N	82	164	16	41	6	1	1	15	17	36	.250	.320	.317	78	-4	-4	16	0	2	-1	0	O	-0.7
1967	Phi-N	16	19	1	2	1	0	0	1	0	6	.105	.105	.158	-25	-3	-3	0	0	0	-0	0	/O	-0.3
	Hou-N	41	89	7	21	4	1	1	15	8	9	.236	.299	.337	85	-2	-2	9	0	0	0	-1	1/O3	-0.3
	Yr	57	108	8	23	5	1	1	16	8	15	.213	.267	.306	65	-5	-5	9	0	0	0	-1		-0.6
Total	11	1221	3895	540	1020	175	37	112	485	351	574	.262	.325	.412	101	-7	1	520	45	30	-4	-15	*O/312	-5.2

OTIS BRANNAN

Brannan, Otis Owen b: 3/13/1899, Greenbrier, Ark. d: 6/6/67, Little Rock, Ark. BR/TR, 5'9", 160 lbs. Deb: 4/11/28

YEAR	TM/L	G	AB	R	H	2B	3B	HR	RBI	BB	SO	AVG	OBP	SLG	PRO+	BR	/A	RC	SB	CS	SBR	FR	POS	TPR
1928	StL-A	135	483	68	118	18	3	10	66	60	19	.244	.333	.356	79	-13	-15	59	3	9	-5	-8	*2	-1.9
1929	StL-A	23	51	4	15	1	0	1	8	4	4	.294	.345	.373	82	-1	-1	7	0	0	0	-1	2	-0.1
Total	2	158	534	72	133	19	3	11	74	64	23	.249	.334	.358	79	-14	-16	66	3	9	-5	-9	2	-2.0

MIKE BRANNOCK

Brannock, Michael J. b: 1853, Guelph, Ont., Canada 5'8", 162 lbs. Deb: 10/21/1871

YEAR	TM/L	G	AB	R	H	2B	3B	HR	RBI	BB	SO	AVG	OBP	SLG	PRO+	BR	/A	RC	SB	CS	SBR	FR	POS	TPR
1871	Chi-n	3	14	2	1	0	0	0	0	0	0	.071	.071	.071	-53	-3	-3	0	0				/3	-0.1
1875	Chi-n	2	9	2	1	0	0	0		0	0	.111	.111	.111	-23	-1	-1	0					/3	0.0

YEAR	TM/L	G	AB	R	H	2B	3B	HR	RBI	BB	SO	AVG	OBP	SLG	PRO+	BR	/A	RC	SB	CS	SBR	FR	POS	TPR
Total	2 n	5	23	4	2	0	0	0		0		.087	.087	.087	-43	-4	-4	0					/3	-0.1

■ DUD BRANOM
Branom, Edgar Dudley b: 11/30/1897, Sulphur Springs, Tex. d: 2/4/80, Sun City, Ariz. BL/TL, 6'1", 190 lbs. Deb: 4/12/27

YEAR	TM/L	G	AB	R	H	2B	3B	HR	RBI	BB	SO	AVG	OBP	SLG	PRO+	BR	/A	RC	SB	CS	SBR	FR	POS	TPR
1927	Phi-A	30	94	8	22	1	0	0	13	2	5	.234	.250	.245	27	-10	-11	6	2	1	0	-0	1	-1.0

■ KITTY BRANSFIELD
Bransfield, William Edward b: 1/7/1875, Worcester, Mass. d: 5/1/47, Worcester, Mass. BR/TR, 5'11", 207 lbs. Deb: 8/22/1898 U

YEAR	TM/L	G	AB	R	H	2B	3B	HR	RBI	BB	SO	AVG	OBP	SLG	PRO+	BR	/A	RC	SB	CS	SBR	FR	POS	TPR
1898	Bos-N	5	9	2	2	0	1	0	1	0		.222	.222	.444	87	-0	-0	1	0			-1	/C1	0.0
1901	Pit-N	139	566	92	167	26	16	0	91	29		.295	.335	.398	111	9	7	86	23			-10	*1	-0.2
1902	Pit-N	102	413	49	126	21	8	0	69	17		.305	.334	.395	123	11	10	65	23			-6	*1	0.0
1903	*Pit-N	127	505	69	134	23	7	2	57	33		.265	.310	.350	87	-7	-9	62	13			6	*1	-0.6
1904	Pit-N	139	520	47	116	17	9	0	60	22		.223	.255	.290	68	-19	-21	44	11			-3	*1	-3.1
1905	Phi-N	151	580	55	150	23	9	3	76	27		.259	.292	.345	95	-8	-5	70	27			-2	*1	-1.3
1906	Phi-N	140	524	47	144	28	5	1	60	16		.275	.296	.353	104	-0	0	61	12			-2	*1	-0.7
1907	Phi-N	94	348	25	81	15	2	0	38	14		.233	.262	.287	75	-11	-11	30	8			-2	1	-1.7
1908	Phi-N	144	527	53	160	25	7	3	71	23		.304	.333	.395	130	18	16	78	30			-1	*1	1.4
1909	Phi-N	140	527	47	154	27	6	1	59	18		.292	.319	.372	113	6	6	68	17			7	*1	1.2
1910	Phi-N	123	427	39	102	17	4	3	52	20	34	.239	.275	.319	71	-16	-18	40	10			-4	*1	-2.4
1911	Phi-N	23	43	4	11	1	1	0	3	0	5	.256	.256	.326	61	-2	-2	4	1			0	/1	-0.2
	Chi-N	3	10	0	4	2	0	0	0	2	2	.400	.500	.600	207	2	2	3	0			-0	/1	0.1
	Yr	26	53	4	15	3	1	0	3	2	7	.283	.309	.377	91	-1	-1	6	1			-0		-0.1
Total	12	1330	4999	529	1351	225	75	13	637	221	41	.270	.302	.353	98	-17	-26	611	175			-18	*1/C	-7.5

■ MARSHALL BRANT
Brant, Marshall Lee b: 9/17/55, Garberville, Cal. BR/TR, 6'5", 185 lbs. Deb: 10/01/80

YEAR	TM/L	G	AB	R	H	2B	3B	HR	RBI	BB	SO	AVG	OBP	SLG	PRO+	BR	/A	RC	SB	CS	SBR	FR	POS	TPR
1980	NY-A	3	6	0	0	0	0	0	0	0	3	.000	.000	.000	-99	-2	-2	0	0	0	0	0	/1D	-0.1
1983	Oak-A	5	14	2	2	0	0	0	2	0	3	.143	.143	.143	-22	-2	-2	0	0	0	0	-1	/1D	-0.2
Total	2	8	20	2	2	0	0	0	2	0	6	.100	.100	.100	-47	-4	-4	0	0	0	0	-1	/1D	-0.3

■ MICKEY BRANTLEY
Brantley, Michael Charles b: 6/17/61, Catskill, N.Y. BR/TR, 5'10", 180 lbs. Deb: 8/09/86

YEAR	TM/L	G	AB	R	H	2B	3B	HR	RBI	BB	SO	AVG	OBP	SLG	PRO+	BR	/A	RC	SB	CS	SBR	FR	POS	TPR
1986	Sea-A	27	102	12	20	3	2	3	7	10	21	.196	.268	.353	67	-5	-5	9	1	1	-0	1	O	-0.4
1987	Sea-A	92	351	52	106	23	2	14	54	24	44	.302	.347	.499	115	10	7	62	13	4	2	-6	O/D	0.1
1988	Sea-A	149	577	76	152	25	4	15	56	26	64	.263	.298	.399	89	-7	-10	66	18	7	1	5	*O/D	-0.5
1989	Sea-A	34	108	14	17	5	0	0	8	7	7	.157	.209	.204	16	-12	-12	5	2	2	-1	0	O/D	-1.2
Total	4	302	1138	154	295	56	8	32	125	67	136	.259	.302	.407	89	-14	-20	142	34	14	2	1	O/D	-2.0

■ KITTY BRASHEAR
Brashear, Norman C. b: 8/27/1877, Mansfield, Ohio d: 12/22/34, Los Angeles, Cal. 5'11", 205 lbs. Deb: 4/25/02

YEAR	TM/L	G	AB	R	H	2B	3B	HR	RBI	BB	SO	AVG	OBP	SLG	PRO+	BR	/A	RC	SB	CS	SBR	FR	POS	TPR
1902	StL-N	110	388	36	107	8	2	1	40	32		.276	.333	.314	106	2	3	46	9			-9	12O/S	-0.8

■ ROY BRASHEAR
Brashear, Roy Parks b: 1/3/1874, Ashtabula, Ohio d: 4/20/51, Los Angeles, Cal. TR, Deb: 6/25/1899

YEAR	TM/L	G	AB	R	H	2B	3B	HR	RBI	BB	SO	AVG	OBP	SLG	PRO+	BR	/A	RC	SB	CS	SBR	FR	POS	TPR
1899	Lou-N	3	2	0	1	0	0	0	0	0		.500	.500	.500	178	0	0	1	0			0	/P	0.0
1903	Phi-N	20	75	9	17	3	0	0	4	6		.227	.284	.267	61	-4	-4	7	2			-4	2/1	-0.5
Total	2	23	77	9	18	3	0	0	4	6		.234	.289	.273	64	-4	-3	7	2			-4	/2P1	-0.5

■ JOE BRATCHER
Bratcher, Joseph Warlick "Goobers" b: 7/22/1898, Grand Saline, Tex d: 10/13/77, Fort Worth, Tex. BL/TR, 5'8.5", 140 lbs. Deb: 8/26/24

YEAR	TM/L	G	AB	R	H	2B	3B	HR	RBI	BB	SO	AVG	OBP	SLG	PRO+	BR	/A	RC	SB	CS	SBR	FR	POS	TPR
1924	StL-N	4	1	1	0	0	0	0	0	0	0	.000	.000	.000	-99	-0	-0	0	0	0	0	0	/O	0.0

■ FRED BRATSCHI
Bratschi, Frederick Oscar "Fritz" b: 1/16/1892, Alliance, Ohio d: 1/10/62, Massillon, Ohio BR/TR, 5'10", 170 lbs. Deb: 7/24/21

YEAR	TM/L	G	AB	R	H	2B	3B	HR	RBI	BB	SO	AVG	OBP	SLG	PRO+	BR	/A	RC	SB	CS	SBR	FR	POS	TPR
1921	Chi-A	16	28	0	8	1	0	0	3	0	2	.286	.286	.321	55	-2	-2	2	0	0	0	1	/O	-0.1
1926	Bos-A	72	167	12	46	10	1	0	19	14	15	.275	.335	.347	81	-5	-5	20	0	1	-1	-7	O	-1.3
1927	Bos-A	1	1	0	0	0	0	0	0	0	0	.000	.000	.000	-99	-0	-0	0	0	0	0	0	H	0.0
Total	3	89	196	12	54	11	1	0	22	14	17	.276	.327	.342	76	-8	-7	22	0	1	-1	-6	/O	-1.4

■ STEVE BRAUN
Braun, Stephen Russell b: 5/8/48, Trenton, N.J. BL/TR, 5'10", 180 lbs. Deb: 4/06/71 C

YEAR	TM/L	G	AB	R	H	2B	3B	HR	RBI	BB	SO	AVG	OBP	SLG	PRO+	BR	/A	RC	SB	CS	SBR	FR	POS	TPR
1971	Min-A	128	343	51	87	12	2	5	35	48	50	.254	.354	.344	95	1	-0	44	8	3	1	-12	32S/O	-1.2
1972	Min-A	121	402	40	116	21	0	2	50	45	38	.289	.363	.356	109	8	6	51	4	5	-2	-13	32S/O	-0.4
1973	Min-A	115	361	46	102	28	5	6	42	74	48	.283	.409	.438	133	22	20	68	4	3	-1	-11	*3/O	0.6
1974	Min-A	129	453	53	127	12	1	8	40	56	51	.280	.362	.364	105	7	5	62	4	4	-1	-5	*O3	-0.3
1975	Min-A	136	453	70	137	18	3	11	45	66	55	.302	.392	.428	129	21	20	79	0	2		-6	*O/132D	0.9
1976	Min-A	122	417	38	120	13	3	3	61	67	43	.288	.388	.353	114	13	11	63	12	4	1	-3	DO3	0.9
1977	Sea-A	139	451	51	106	19	1	5	31	80	59	.235	.353	.315	84	-7	-7	54	8	3	1	2	*OD/3	-0.7
1978	Sea-A	32	74	11	17	4	0	3	15	9	5	.230	.313	.405	101	-0	0	9	1	0	-0	D/O		0.0
	*KC-A	64	137	16	36	10	1	0	14	28	16	.263	.388	.350	106	3	3	21	3	2	-0	-7	O3	-0.5
	Yr	96	211	27	53	14	1	3	29	37	21	.251	.363	.370	105	3	3	30	4	2	0	-7		-0.5
1979	KC-A	58	116	15	31	2	0	4	10	22	11	.267	.384	.388	107	2	2	19	0	0	0	4	OD/3	0.5
1980	KC-A	14	23	0	1	0	0	0	1	2	2	.043	.120	.043	-53	-5	-5	0	0	0	0	-1	/OD	0.0
	Tor-A	37	55	4	15	2	0	1	9	8	5	.273	.365	.364	96	-0	-0	7	0	0	0	0	D/3	0.0
	Yr	51	78	4	16	2	0	1	10	10	7	.205	.295	.269	54	-5	-5	6	0	0	0	-0		-0.5
1981	StL-N	44	46	9	9	2	1	0	2	15	7	.196	.393	.283	92	1	0	7	1	0	0	1	O/3	0.1
1982	*StL-N	58	62	6	17	4	0	0	4	11	10	.274	.384	.339	103	1	1	8	0	0	0	-3	O/3	-0.1
1983	StL-N	78	92	8	25	2	1	3	7	21	7	.272	.407	.413	128	4	4	17	0	1	-1	-2	O/3	0.2
1984	StL-N	86	98	6	27	3	1	0	16	17	17	.276	.383	.327	104	1	1	14	0	0	0	-3	O/3	-0.2
1985	*StL-N	64	67	7	16	4	0	0	9	9	9	.239	.346	.343	94	-0	0	9	0	0	0	0	O	0.0
Total	15	1425	3650	466	989	155	19	52	388	579	433	.271	.373	.367	108	72	61	532	45	27	-3	-58	O3D/2S1	-0.7

■ ANGEL BRAVO
Bravo, Angel Alfonso (Urdaneta) b: 8/4/42, Maracaibo, Venez. BL/TL, 5'8", 150 lbs. Deb: 6/06/69

YEAR	TM/L	G	AB	R	H	2B	3B	HR	RBI	BB	SO	AVG	OBP	SLG	PRO+	BR	/A	RC	SB	CS	SBR	FR	POS	TPR
1969	Chi-A	27	90	10	26	4	2	1	3	3	5	.289	.319	.411	98	-0	-0	12	2	0	1	-2	O	-0.2
1970	*Cin-N	65	65	10	18	1	1	0	3	9	13	.277	.365	.323	86	-1	-1	8	0	1	-1	0	O	-0.1
1971	Cin-N	5	5	0	1	0	0	0	0	0	0	.200	.200	.200	14	-1	-1	0	0	0	0	0	H	0.0
	SD-N	52	58	6	9	2	0	0	6	8	12	.155	.269	.190	34	-5	-5	3	0	1	-1	-2	/O	-0.7
	Yr	57	63	6	10	2	0	0	6	8	13	.159	.264	.190	33	-6	-5	4	0	1	-1	-2		-0.7
Total	3	149	218	26	54	7	3	1	12	20	31	.248	.317	.321	77	-6	-7	24	2	2	-1	-4	/O	-1.0

■ BUSTER BRAY
Bray, Clarence Wilbur b: 4/1/13, Birmingham, Ala. d: 9/4/82, Evansville, Ind. BL/TL, 6', 170 lbs. Deb: 4/18/41

YEAR	TM/L	G	AB	R	H	2B	3B	HR	RBI	BB	SO	AVG	OBP	SLG	PRO+	BR	/A	RC	SB	CS	SBR	FR	POS	TPR
1941	Bos-N	4	11	2	1	1	0	0	1	1	2	.091	.167	.182	-2	-2	-1	0	0			0	/O	-0.1

■ FRANK BRAZILL
Brazill, Frank Leo b: 8/11/1899, Spangler, Pa. d: 11/3/76, Oakland, Cal. BL/TR, 5'11.5", 175 lbs. Deb: 4/13/21

YEAR	TM/L	G	AB	R	H	2B	3B	HR	RBI	BB	SO	AVG	OBP	SLG	PRO+	BR	/A	RC	SB	CS	SBR	FR	POS	TPR
1921	Phi-A	66	177	17	48	3	1	0	19	23	21	.271	.361	.299	70	-7	-7	20	2	4	-2	-1	1/3	-0.8
1922	Phi-A	6	13	0	1	0	0	0	1	0	1	.077	.077	.077	-58	-3	-3	0	0	0	0	-2	/3	-0.4
Total	2	72	190	17	49	3	1	0	20	23	22	.258	.344	.284	62	-10	-10	20	2	4	-2	-3	/13	-1.2

■ SID BREAM
Bream, Sidney Eugene b: 8/3/60, Carlisle, Pa. BL/TL, 6'4", 215 lbs. Deb: 9/01/83

YEAR	TM/L	G	AB	R	H	2B	3B	HR	RBI	BB	SO	AVG	OBP	SLG	PRO+	BR	/A	RC	SB	CS	SBR	FR	POS	TPR
1983	LA-N	15	11	0	2	0	0	0	2	2	1	.182	.308	.182	39	-1	-1	1	0	0	0	0	/1	0.0
1984	LA-N	27	49	2	9	3	0	0	6	6	9	.184	.273	.245	47	-3	-3	4	1	0	0	2	1	-0.1
1985	LA-N	24	53	4	7	0	0	3	6	7	10	.132	.233	.302	50	-4	-4	4	0	0	0	2	1	-0.1
	Pit-N	26	95	14	27	7	0	3	15	11	14	.284	.358	.453	127	3	3	14	0	2	-1	2	1	0.3
	Yr	50	148	18	34	7	0	6	21	18	24	.230	.313	.399	100	-1	-0	18	0	2	-1	4		0.2
1986	Pit-N	154	522	73	140	37	5	16	77	60	73	.268	.345	.450	115	12	10	79	13	7	-0	23	*1/O	2.9

YEAR	TM/L	G	AB	R	H	2B	3B	HR	RBI	BB	SO	AVG	OBP	SLG	PRO+	BR	/A	RC	SB	CS	SBR	FR	POS	TPR
1987	Pit-N	149	516	64	142	25	3	13	65	49	69	.275	.338	.411	97	-2	-3	66	9	8	-2	11	*1	-0.1
1988	Pit-N	148	462	50	122	37	0	10	65	47	64	.264	.333	.409	114	7	8	61	9	9	-3	21	*1	2.0
1989	Pit-N	19	36	3	8	3	0	0	4	12	10	.222	.417	.306	113	1	1	5	0	4	-2	-0	1	-0.1
1990	*Pit-N	147	389	39	105	23	2	15	67	48	65	.270	.353	.455	126	11	13	64	8	4	0	10	*1	1.5
Total	8	709	2133	249	562	135	10	60	307	242	316	.263	.340	.421	109	24	26	297	40	34	-8	70	1/O	6.3

■ JIM BREAZEALE
Breazeale, James Leo   b: 10/3/49, Houston, Tex.   BL/TR, 6'2", 210 lbs.   Deb: 9/13/69

YEAR	TM/L	G	AB	R	H	2B	3B	HR	RBI	BB	SO	AVG	OBP	SLG	PRO+	BR	/A	RC	SB	CS	SBR	FR	POS	TPR
1969	Atl-N	2	1	1	0	0	0	0	0	2	0	.000	.667	.000	101	0	0	0	0	0	0	-0	/1	0.0
1971	Atl-N	10	21	1	4	0	0	1	3	0	3	.190	.190	.333	43	-2	-2	1	0	0	0	-0	/1	-0.1
1972	Atl-N	52	85	10	21	2	0	5	17	6	12	.247	.297	.447	100	1	-0	10	0	1	-1	-2	1/3	-0.3
1978	Chi-A	25	72	8	15	3	0	3	13	8	10	.208	.287	.375	84	-2	-2	8	0	0	0	-3	1/D	-0.4
Total	4	89	179	20	40	5	0	9	33	16	25	.223	.287	.402	88	-2	-3	20	0	1	-1	-5	/1D3	-0.8

■ DANNY BREEDEN
Breeden, Danny Richard   b: 6/27/42, Albany, Ga.   BR/TR, 5'11.5", 185 lbs.   Deb: 7/24/69

YEAR	TM/L	G	AB	R	H	2B	3B	HR	RBI	BB	SO	AVG	OBP	SLG	PRO+	BR	/A	RC	SB	CS	SBR	FR	POS	TPR
1969	Cin-N	3	8	0	1	0	0	0	0	0	3	.125	.125	.125	-28	-1	-1	0	0	0	0	0	/C	0.0
1971	Chi-N	25	65	3	10	1	0	0	4	9	18	.154	.267	.169	23	-6	-7	4	0	0	0	4	C	-0.2
Total	2	28	73	3	11	1	0	0	5	9	21	.151	.253	.164	18	-7	-9	4	0	0	0	5	/C	-0.2

■ HAL BREEDEN
Breeden, Harold Noel   b: 6/28/44, Albany, Ga.   BR/TL, 6'2", 200 lbs.   Deb: 4/07/71

YEAR	TM/L	G	AB	R	H	2B	3B	HR	RBI	BB	SO	AVG	OBP	SLG	PRO+	BR	/A	RC	SB	CS	SBR	FR	POS	TPR
1971	Chi-N	23	36	1	5	1	0	1	2	2	7	.139	.184	.250	19	-4	-4	2	0	0	0	1	/1	-0.3
1972	Mon-N	42	87	6	20	2	0	3	10	7	15	.230	.287	.356	80	-2	-2	9	0	0	0	-1	1/O	-0.4
1973	Mon-N	105	258	36	71	10	6	15	43	29	45	.275	.353	.535	138	14	13	47	0	1	-1	3	1	1.3
1974	Mon-N	79	190	14	47	13	0	2	20	24	35	.247	.332	.347	85	-2	-4	21	0	1	-1	1	1	-0.5
1975	Mon-N	24	37	4	5	2	0	0	1	7	5	.135	.273	.189	29	-3	-4	2	0	0	0	-0	1	-0.4
Total	5	273	608	61	148	28	6	21	76	69	107	.243	.323	.413	99	2	-1	81	0	2	-1	4	1/O	-0.3

■ MARV BREEDING
Breeding, Marvin Eugene   b: 3/8/34, Decatur, Ala.   BR/TR, 6', 175 lbs.   Deb: 4/19/60

YEAR	TM/L	G	AB	R	H	2B	3B	HR	RBI	BB	SO	AVG	OBP	SLG	PRO+	BR	/A	RC	SB	CS	SBR	FR	POS	TPR
1960	Bal-A	152	551	69	147	25	2	3	43	35	80	.267	.314	.336	77	-19	-18	59	10	4	1	5	*2	-0.1
1961	Bal-A	90	244	32	51	8	0	1	16	14	33	.209	.252	.254	36	-22	-22	16	5	2	0	7	2	-0.4
1962	Bal-A	95	240	27	59	10	1	2	18	8	41	.246	.273	.321	62	-14	-13	21	2	2	-1	21	2/S3	1.3
1963	Was-A	58	197	20	54	7	2	1	14	7	21	.274	.299	.345	80	-5	-5	20	1	1	-0	-9	32/S	-1.2
	LA-N	20	36	6	6	0	0	0	1	2	5	.167	.211	.167	11	-4	-4	2	1	0	0	-4	2/S3	-0.6
Total	4	415	1268	154	317	50	5	7	92	66	180	.250	.289	.314	65	-64	-61	118	19	9	0	20	2/3S	-1.0

■ HERB BREMER
Bremer, Herbert Frederick   b: 10/26/13, Chicago, Ill.   d: 11/28/79, Columbus, Ga.   BR/TR, 6', 195 lbs.   Deb: 9/16/37

YEAR	TM/L	G	AB	R	H	2B	3B	HR	RBI	BB	SO	AVG	OBP	SLG	PRO+	BR	/A	RC	SB	CS	SBR	FR	POS	TPR
1937	StL-N	11	33	2	7	1	0	0	3	2	4	.212	.257	.242	36	-3	-3	2	0			-0	C	-0.2
1938	StL-N	50	151	14	33	5	1	2	14	9	36	.219	.262	.305	53	-9	-10	13	1			4	C	-0.4
1939	StL-N	9	9	0	1	0	0	0	1	0	2	.111	.111	.111	-38	-2	-2	0	0			1	/C	0.0
Total	3	70	193	16	41	6	1	2	18	11	42	.212	.255	.285	45	-14	-15	15	1			4	/C	-0.6

■ SAM BRENEGAN
Brenegan, Olaf Selmar   b: 9/1/1890, Galesville, Wis.   d: 4/20/56, Galesville, Wis.   BL/TR, 6'2", 185 lbs.   Deb: 4/24/14

YEAR	TM/L	G	AB	R	H	2B	3B	HR	RBI	BB	SO	AVG	OBP	SLG	PRO+	BR	/A	RC	SB	CS	SBR	FR	POS	TPR
1914	Pit-N	1	0	0	0	0	0	0	0	0	0	—	—	—	—	0	0	0	0			0	/C	0.0

■ BOB BRENLY
Brenly, Robert Earl   b: 2/25/54, Coshocton, Ohio   BR/TR, 6'2", 210 lbs.   Deb: 8/14/81

YEAR	TM/L	G	AB	R	H	2B	3B	HR	RBI	BB	SO	AVG	OBP	SLG	PRO+	BR	/A	RC	SB	CS	SBR	FR	POS	TPR
1981	SF-N	19	45	5	15	2	1	4	6	4	4	.333	.423	.489	161	4	4	9	0	1	-1	-3	C/3O	0.0
1982	SF-N	65	180	26	51	4	1	4	15	18	26	.283	.352	.383	106	2	2	25	6	2	1	0	C/3	0.3
1983	SF-N	104	281	36	63	12	2	7	34	37	48	.224	.319	.356	89	-5	-4	30	10	7	-1	2	C1/O	0.0
1984	SF-N	145	506	74	147	28	0	20	80	48	52	.291	.355	.464	133	19	21	79	6	9	-4	-17	*C1/O	0.4
1985	SF-N	133	440	41	97	16	1	19	56	57	62	.220	.313	.391	100	-3	-0	55	1	4	-2	-5	*C31	-0.3
1986	SF-N	149	472	60	116	26	0	16	62	74	97	.246	.352	.403	113	6	9	71	10	6	-1	-6	*C31	0.3
1987	*SF-N	123	375	55	100	19	1	18	51	47	85	.267	.353	.467	121	8	10	63	10	7	-1	10	*C/13	2.7
1988	SF-N	73	206	13	39	7	0	5	22	20	40	.189	.268	.296	64	-10	-9	17	1	2	-1	-3	C	-0.9
1989	Tor-A	48	88	9	15	3	1	1	6	10	17	.170	.255	.261	47	-6	-6	6	1	0	0	2	DC/1	-0.3
	SF-N	12	22	2	4	2	0	0	3	1	7	.182	.217	.273	40	-2	-2	1	0	0	0	1	C	0.0
Total	9	871	2615	321	647	119	7	91	333	318	438	.247	.333	.403	107	12	24	356	45	38	-9	-19	C/13DO	2.2

■ JACK BRENNAN
Brennan, John Gottlieb (b: John Gottlieb Dorn)   b: 1862, St.Louis, Mo.   d: 10/18/04, Philadelphia, Pa.   Deb: 7/14/1884

YEAR	TM/L	G	AB	R	H	2B	3B	HR	RBI	BB	SO	AVG	OBP	SLG	PRO+	BR	/A	RC	SB	CS	SBR	FR	POS	TPR
1884	StL-U	56	231	38	50	6	1	0		12		.216	.255	.251	69	-6	-8	15	0			-5	CO/3S	-0.9
1885	StL-N	3	10	0	1	0	0	0	1	1	1	.100	.182	.100	-7	-1	-1	0				-2	/O3	-0.2
1888	KC-a	34	118	5	20	2	0	0	6	3		.169	.203	.186	26	-9	-10	5	3			-3	C/O3	-0.9
1889	Phi-a	31	113	12	25	4	0	0	15	10	15	.221	.285	.257	57	-6	-6	9	1			-3	C/O23	-0.6
1890	Cle-P	59	233	32	59	3	7	0	26	13	29	.253	.304	.326	76	-10	-7	26	8			-19	C3/O	-1.8
Total	5	183	705	87	155	15	8	0	48	39	45	.220	.267	.264	61	-33	-32	55	12			-33	C/O32S	-4.4

■ BILL BRENZEL
Brenzel, William Richard   b: 3/3/10, Oakland, Cal.   d: 6/12/79, Oakland, Cal.   BR/TR, 5'10", 173 lbs.   Deb: 4/13/32

YEAR	TM/L	G	AB	R	H	2B	3B	HR	RBI	BB	SO	AVG	OBP	SLG	PRO+	BR	/A	RC	SB	CS	SBR	FR	POS	TPR
1932	Pit-N	9	24	0	1	1	0	0	2	0	4	.042	.042	.083	-69	-6	-6	0	0			2	/C	-0.2
1934	Cle-A	15	51	4	11	3	0	0	3	2	1	.216	.245	.275	33	-5	-5	4	0	0	0	3	C	0.0
1935	Cle-A	52	142	12	31	5	1	0	14	6	10	.218	.250	.268	33	-14	-14	10	2	2	-1	-6	C	-1.8
Total	3	76	217	16	43	9	1	0	19	8	15	.198	.227	.249	23	-25	-25	13	2	2		-2	/C	-2.0

■ ROGER BRESNAHAN
Bresnahan, Roger Philip "The Duke Of Tralee"   b: 6/11/1879, Toledo, Ohio   d: 12/4/44, Toledo, Ohio   BR/TR, 5'9", 200 lbs.   Deb: 8/27/1897   MCH

YEAR	TM/L	G	AB	R	H	2B	3B	HR	RBI	BB	SO	AVG	OBP	SLG	PRO+	BR	/A	RC	SB	CS	SBR	FR	POS	TPR
1897	Was-N	6	16	1	6	0	0	0	3	1		.375	.412	.375	112	0	0	3	0			-1	/PO	0.0
1900	Chi-N	2	2	0	0	0	0	0	0	0		.000	.000	.000	-99	-1	-1	0	0			0	/C	0.0
1901	Bal-A	86	295	40	79	9	9	1	32	23		.268	.321	.369	89	-3	-5	40	10			-19	C/O3P2	-1.5
1902	Bal-A	65	235	30	64	8	6	4	34	21		.272	.335	.409	102	2	1	37	12			-9	3CO	-0.7
	NY-N	51	178	16	51	9	3	1	22	16		.287	.352	.388	131	6	7	28	6			-0	OC/1S3	0.6
1903	NY-N	113	406	87	142	30	8	4	55	61		.350	.435	.493	160	37	35	105	34			0	O1C/3	2.9
1904	NY-N	109	402	81	114	22	7	5	33	58		.284	.374	.410	139	22	20	69	13			0	O1/S23	1.8
1905	*NY-N	104	331	58	100	18	3	0	46	50		.302	.394	.375	129	15	14	56	11			-0	C/O	2.3
1906	NY-N	124	405	69	114	22	4	0	43	81		.281	.401	.356	136	23	22	70	25			6	CO	3.6
1907	NY-N	110	328	57	83	9	7	4	38	61		.253	.370	.360	127	14	13	51	15			-7	C/1O3	1.5
1908	NY-N	140	449	70	127	25	3	1	54	83		.283	.395	.359	137	26	24	71	14			-17	*C	1.6
1909	StL-N	72	234	27	57	4	1	0	23	46		.244	.370	.269	105	3	4	28	11			-7	C/23M	0.2
1910	StL-N	88	234	35	65	15	3	0	27	55	17	.278	.419	.368	135	12	14	42	13			-8	C/OPM	1.0
1911	StL-N	81	227	22	63	17	8	3	41	45	19	.278	.404	.463	146	14	15	44	4			-1	C/2M	1.9
1912	StL-N	48	108	8	36	7	2	1	15	14	9	.333	.419	.463	145	7	7	22	4			7	CM	1.5
1913	Chi-N	69	162	20	37	5	2	1	21	21	11	.228	.324	.302	79	-4	-4	18	7			-3	C	-0.2
1914	Chi-N	101	248	42	69	10	4	0	24	49	20	.278	.401	.351	125	10	10	40	14			-3	C2/O	1.1
1915	Chi-N	77	221	19	45	8	1	1	19	29	23	.204	.296	.262	70	-7	-7	22	19	3	4	2	CM	0.3
Total	17	1446	4481	682	1252	218	71	26	530	714	99	.279	.380	.377	125	178	169	746	212	3		-57	CO/312PS	17.9

■ RUBE BRESSLER
Bressler, Raymond Bloom   b: 10/23/1894, Coder, Pa.   d: 11/7/66, Cincinnati, Ohio   BR/TL, 6', 187 lbs.   Deb: 4/24/14

YEAR	TM/L	G	AB	R	H	2B	3B	HR	RBI	BB	SO	AVG	OBP	SLG	PRO+	BR	/A	RC	SB	CS	SBR	FR	POS	TPR
1914	Phi-A	29	51	6	11	1	1	0	4	6	7	.216	.310	.275	79	-1	-1	5	0			-3	P	0.0
1915	Phi-A	33	55	9	8	0	1	0	4	9	13	.145	.277	.236	55	-3	-3	4	0			1	P	0.0

YEAR	TM/L	G	AB	R	H	2B	3B	HR	RBI	BB	SO	AVG	OBP	SLG	PRO+	BR	/A	RC	SB	CS	SBR	FR	POS	TPR
1916	Phi-A	4	5	1	1	0	1	0	1	0	0	.200	.200	.600	146	0	0	1	0			-0	/P	0.0
1917	Cin-N	3	5	0	1	0	0	0	0	0	2	.200	.200	.200	24	-0	-0	0	0			-0	/P	0.0
1918	Cin-N	23	62	10	17	5	0	0	6	5	4	.274	.328	.355	110	1	1	7	0			3	P/O	0.0
1919	Cin-N	61	165	22	34	3	4	2	17	23	15	.206	.311	.309	89	-2	-2	17	2			1	OP	0.0
1920	Cin-N	21	30	4	8	1	0	0	3	1	4	.267	.290	.300	71	-1	-1	3	1	0	0	-0	P/O1	0.0
1921	Cin-N	109	323	41	99	18	6	1	54	39	20	.307	.385	.409	115	6	8	52	5	5	-2	-9	O/1	-0.6
1922	Cin-N	52	53	7	14	0	2	0	8	4	4	.264	.316	.340	70	-2	-2	6	1	0	0	-1	/1O	-0.2
1923	Cin-N	54	119	25	33	3	1	0	18	20	4	.277	.399	.319	93	-0	-0	17	3	1	0	-2	1/O	-0.2
1924	Cin-N	115	383	41	133	14	13	4	49	22	20	.347	.389	.483	134	17	18	69	9	10	-3	1	1O	1.2
1925	Cin-N	97	319	43	111	17	6	4	61	40	16	.348	.424	.476	133	16	17	66	9	5	-0	-4	1O	0.5
1926	Cin-N	86	297	58	106	15	9	1	51	37	20	.357	.433	.478	149	20	21	61	3			-8	O/1	1.0
1927	Cin-N	124	467	43	136	14	8	3	77	32	22	.291	.338	.375	94	-6	-4	58	4			3	*O	-0.6
1928	Bro-N	145	501	78	148	29	13	4	70	80	33	.295	.398	.429	118	15	16	88	2			-8	*O	0.2
1929	Bro-N	136	456	72	145	22	8	9	77	67	27	.318	.406	.461	117	12	14	86	4			-2	*O	0.1
1930	Bro-N	109	335	53	100	12	8	3	52	51	19	.299	.394	.409	96	-1	-0	56	4			1	O/1	-0.4
1931	Bro-N	67	153	22	43	4	5	0	26	11	10	.281	.329	.373	89	-3	-2	19	0			-4	O/1	-0.7
1932	Phi-N	27	83	9	19	6	1	0	6	2	5	.229	.247	.325	47	-6	-7	7	0			2	O	-0.5
	StL-N	10	19	0	3	0	0	0	2	0	1	.158	.158	.158	-14	-3	-3	1	0			-0	/O	-0.3
	Yr	37	102	9	22	6	1	0	8	2	6	.216	.231	.294	37	-9	-10	7	0			2		-0.8
Total	19	1305	3881	544	1170	164	87	32	586	449	246	.301	.378	.413	110	58	69	623	47	21		-30	O1P	-0.5

■ EDDIE BRESSOUD   Bressoud, Edward Francis b: 5/2/32, Los Angeles, Cal. BR/TR, 6'1", 175 lbs. Deb: 6/14/56

YEAR	TM/L	G	AB	R	H	2B	3B	HR	RBI	BB	SO	AVG	OBP	SLG	PRO+	BR	/A	RC	SB	CS	SBR	FR	POS	TPR
1956	NY-N	49	163	15	37	4	2	0	9	12	20	.227	.284	.276	52	-11	-11	13	1	0	0	-9	S	-1.6
1957	NY-N	49	127	11	34	2	2	5	10	4	19	.268	.301	.433	94	-1	-1	16	0	1	-1	1	S3	0.1
1958	SF-N	66	137	19	36	5	3	0	8	14	22	.263	.331	.343	81	-4	-4	16	0	1	-1	-2	2/3S	-0.1
1959	SF-N	104	315	36	79	17	2	9	26	28	55	.251	.312	.403	91	-6	-5	40	0	0	0	-6	S/123	-0.7
1960	SF-N	116	386	37	87	19	6	9	43	35	72	.225	.293	.376	87	-10	-8	41	1	2	-1	6	*S	0.2
1961	SF-N	59	114	14	24	6	0	3	11	11	23	.211	.280	.342	66	-6	-5	9	1	1	-0	-9	S/32	-1.1
1962	Bos-A	153	599	79	166	40	9	14	68	46	118	.277	.331	.444	103	4	2	85	2	3	-1	25	*S	3.4
1963	Bos-A	140	497	61	129	23	6	20	60	52	93	.260	.332	.451	113	11	9	75	1	1	-0	-9	*S	0.7
1964	Bos-A	158	566	86	166	41	3	15	55	72	99	.293	.374	.456	123	24	20	99	1	1	-0	-14	*S	0.7
1965	Bos-A	107	296	29	67	11	1	8	25	29	77	.226	.298	.351	79	-6	-9	32	0	1	-1	-5	S/3O	-1.0
1966	NY-N	133	405	48	91	15	5	10	49	47	107	.225	.307	.360	87	-8	-7	45	2	2	-1	8	S3/12	0.8
1967	*StL-N	52	67	8	9	1	1	1	1	9	18	.134	.237	.224	33	-6	-6	4	0	0	0	-4	S/3	-0.4
Total	12	1186	3672	443	925	184	40	94	365	359	723	.252	.321	.401	96	-20	-24	474	9	13	-5	-18	*S/2310	1.0

■ JIM BRETON   Breton, John Frederick b: 7/15/1891, Chicago, Ill. d: 5/30/73, Beloit, Wis. BR/TR, 5'10.5", 178 lbs. Deb: 8/25/13

YEAR	TM/L	G	AB	R	H	2B	3B	HR	RBI	BB	SO	AVG	OBP	SLG	PRO+	BR	/A	RC	SB	CS	SBR	FR	POS	TPR
1913	Chi-A	12	30	1	5	1	1	0	2	1	5	.167	.194	.267	35	-3	-3	1	0			3	/S3	0.1
1914	Chi-A	81	231	21	49	7	2	0	24	24	42	.212	.292	.260	67	-9	-9	20	9	6	-1	3	3	-0.5
1915	Chi-A	16	36	3	5	1	0	0	1	5	9	.139	.262	.167	27	-3	-3	3	2	1	0	-2	3/2S	-0.4
Total	3	109	297	25	59	9	3	0	27	30	56	.199	.279	.249	59	-15	-15	24	11	7		4	/3S2	-0.8

■ GEORGE BRETT   Brett, George Howard b: 5/15/53, Glen Dale, W.Va. BL/TR, 6', 185 lbs. Deb: 8/02/73

YEAR	TM/L	G	AB	R	H	2B	3B	HR	RBI	BB	SO	AVG	OBP	SLG	PRO+	BR	/A	RC	SB	CS	SBR	FR	POS	TPR
1973	KC-A	13	40	2	5	2	0	0	0	0	5	.125	.125	.175	-15	-6	-6	1	0	0	0	3	3	-0.3
1974	KC-A	133	457	49	129	21	5	2	47	21	38	.282	.314	.363	89	-4	-7	50	8	5	-1	-10	*3/S	-1.5
1975	KC-A	159	634	84	195	35	13	11	89	46	49	.308	.356	.456	125	22	20	102	13	10	-2	-6	*3/S	1.4
1976	*KC-A	159	645	94	215	34	14	7	67	49	36	.333	.381	.462	145	36	36	114	21	11	-0	3	*3/S	4.1
1977	*KC-A	139	564	105	176	32	13	22	88	55	24	.312	.375	.532	143	33	33	108	14	12	-3	17	*3/SD	4.3
1978	*KC-A	128	510	79	150	45	8	9	62	39	35	.294	.345	.467	123	16	15	83	23	7	3	5	*3/S	2.2
1979	KC-A	154	645	119	212	42	20	23	107	51	36	.329	.378	.563	147	43	41	134	17	10	-1	13	*3/1	5.3
1980	*KC-A	117	449	87	175	33	9	24	118	58	22	.390	.461	.664	203	65	64	135	15	6	1	4	*3/1	6.6
1981	*KC-A	89	347	42	109	27	7	6	43	27	23	.314	.365	.484	144	18	19	60	14	6	1	-9	3	1.1
1982	KC-A	144	552	101	166	32	9	21	82	71	51	.301	.381	.505	141	32	32	107	6	1	1	-6	*3O	2.4
1983	KC-A	123	464	90	144	38	2	25	93	57	39	.310	.387	.563	157	36	36	100	0	1	-1	-25	*31O/D	1.0
1984	*KC-A	104	377	42	107	21	3	13	69	38	37	.284	.349	.459	121	11	10	58	0	2	-1	-5	*3	0.6
1985	*KC-A	155	550	108	184	38	5	30	112	103	49	.335	.442	.585	178	63	63	146	9	1	2	10	*3/D	6.8
1986	KC-A	124	441	70	128	28	4	16	73	80	45	.290	.404	.481	137	27	26	89	1	2	-1	-2	*3/SD	2.0
1987	KC-A	115	427	71	124	18	2	22	78	72	47	.290	.394	.496	131	23	21	85	6	3	0	-5	1D3	0.8
1988	KC-A	157	589	90	180	42	3	24	103	82	51	.306	.393	.509	149	41	40	119	14	3	2	-9	*1D/S	2.7
1989	KC-A	124	457	67	129	26	3	12	80	59	47	.282	.368	.431	125	16	16	71	14	4	2	4	*1D/O	1.5
1990	KC-A	142	544	82	179	45	7	14	87	56	63	.329	.392	.515	155	37	39	106	9	2	2	-1	*1D/O3	3.2
Total	18	2279	8692	1382	2707	559	127	281	1398	964	697	.311	.382	.502	142	509	497	1669	184	86	4	-17	*31D/OS	44.2

■ TONY BREWER   Brewer, Anthony Bruce b: 11/25/57, Shreveport, La. BR/TR, 5'11", 190 lbs. Deb: 8/01/84

YEAR	TM/L	G	AB	R	H	2B	3B	HR	RBI	BB	SO	AVG	OBP	SLG	PRO+	BR	/A	RC	SB	CS	SBR	FR	POS	TPR
1984	LA-N	24	37	3	4	1	0	1	4	4	9	.108	.195	.216	16	-4	-4	2	1	0	0	-1	O	-0.5

■ MIKE BREWER   Brewer, Michael Quinn b: 10/24/59, Shreveport, La. BR/TR, 6'5", 190 lbs. Deb: 6/11/86

YEAR	TM/L	G	AB	R	H	2B	3B	HR	RBI	BB	SO	AVG	OBP	SLG	PRO+	BR	/A	RC	SB	CS	SBR	FR	POS	TPR
1986	KC-A	12	18	0	3	1	0	0	2		6	.167	.250	.222	29	-2	-2	1	0	1	-1	1	/OD	-0.1

■ ROD BREWER   Brewer, Rodney Lee b: 2/24/66, Eustis, Fla. BL/TL, 6'3", 210 lbs. Deb: 9/05/90

YEAR	TM/L	G	AB	R	H	2B	3B	HR	RBI	BB	SO	AVG	OBP	SLG	PRO+	BR	/A	RC	SB	CS	SBR	FR	POS	TPR
1990	StL-N	14	25	4	6	1	0	0	2	0	4	.240	.240	.280	41	-2	-2	1	0	0	0	1	/1	-0.1

■ CHARLIE BREWSTER   Brewster, Charles Lawrence b: 12/27/16, Marthaville, La. BR/TR, 5'8.5", 175 lbs. Deb: 5/02/43

YEAR	TM/L	G	AB	R	H	2B	3B	HR	RBI	BB	SO	AVG	OBP	SLG	PRO+	BR	/A	RC	SB	CS	SBR	FR	POS	TPR
1943	Cin-N	7	8	0	1	0	0	0	0	0	1	.125	.125	.125	-28	-1	-1	0	0			0	/2	0.0
	Phi-N	49	159	13	35	2	0	0	12	10	19	.220	.275	.233	49	-11	-10	11	1			-20	S	-2.7
	Yr	56	167	13	36	2	0	0	12	10	20	.216	.268	.228	45	-12	-11	11	1			-20		-2.7
1944	Chi-N	10	44	4	11	2	0	0	2	5	7	.250	.327	.295	76	-1	-1	4	0			0	S	0.0
1946	Cle-A	3	2	0	0	0	0	0	0	1	1	.000	.333	.000	-1	-0	-0	0	0	0	0	0	/S	0.0
Total	3	69	213	17	47	4	0	0	14	16	28	.221	.281	.239	52	-13	-13	15	1	0		-20	/S2	-2.7

■ FRITZ BRICKELL   Brickell, Fritz Darrell b: 3/19/35, Wichita, Kan. d: 10/15/65, Wichita, Kan. BR/TR, 5'5", 157 lbs. Deb: 4/30/58

YEAR	TM/L	G	AB	R	H	2B	3B	HR	RBI	BB	SO	AVG	OBP	SLG	PRO+	BR	/A	RC	SB	CS	SBR	FR	POS	TPR
1958	NY-A	2	0	0	0	0	0	0	0	0	0	—	—	—	—	0	0	0	0			0	/2	0.0
1959	NY-A	18	39	4	10	1	0	0	4	1	10	.256	.275	.359	75	-2	-1	4	0	0	0	0	S/2	0.0
1961	LA-A	21	49	3	6	0	0	1	3	6	9	.122	.218	.122	-6	-7	-8	1	0	0	0	0	S	-0.6
Total	3	41	88	7	16	1	0	1	7	7	19	.182	.242	.227	26	-9	-9	5	0	0	0	0	/S2	-0.6

■ FRED BRICKELL   Brickell, George Frederick b: 11/9/06, Saffordville, Kan. d: 4/8/61, Wichita, Kan. BL/TR, 5'7", 160 lbs. Deb: 8/19/26

YEAR	TM/L	G	AB	R	H	2B	3B	HR	RBI	BB	SO	AVG	OBP	SLG	PRO+	BR	/A	RC	SB	CS	SBR	FR	POS	TPR
1926	Pit-N	24	55	11	19	3	1	0	4	3	6	.345	.379	.436	113	1	1	9	0			0	O	0.1
1927	*Pit-N	32	21	6	6	1	0	1	4	1	0	.286	.318	.476	103	0	-0	3	0			2	/O	0.2
1928	Pit-N	81	202	34	65	4	4	3	41	20	18	.322	.383	.426	107	4	3	33	5			1	O	0.2
1929	Pit-N	60	118	13	37	4	2	0	17	7	12	.314	.352	.381	80	-3	-4	15	3			2	O	-0.3
1930	Pit-N	68	219	36	65	9	3	1	14	15	20	.297	.342	.379	74	-9	-9	28	3			1	O	-1.0
	Phi-N	53	240	33	59	12	6	0	17	13	21	.246	.290	.346	49	-19	-21	24	1			5	O	-1.7
	Yr	121	459	69	124	21	9	1	31	28	41	.270	.315	.362	61	-28	-30	51	4			7		-2.7
1931	Phi-N	130	514	77	130	14	5	1	31	42	39	.253	.316	.305	63	-22	-28	52	5			-2	*O	-3.5

YEAR	TM/L	G	AB	R	H	2B	3B	HR	RBI	BB	SO	AVG	OBP	SLG	PRO+	BR	/A	RC	SB	CS	SBR	FR	POS	TPR
1932	Phi-N	45	66	9	22	6	1	0	2	4	5	.333	.389	.455	112	3	2	12	2			2	O	0.3
1933	Phi-N	8	13	2	4	1	1	0	1	1	1	.308	.357	.538	136	1	1	3	0			2	/O	0.2
Total	8	501	1448	221	407	54	23	6	131	106	121	.281	.334	.363	75	-45	-56	178	19			13	O	-5.5

■ GEORGE BRICKLEY
Brickley, George Vincent b: 7/19/1894, Everett, Mass. d: 2/23/47, Everett, Mass. BR/TR, 5'9", 180 lbs. Deb: 9/26/13

YEAR	TM/L	G	AB	R	H	2B	3B	HR	RBI	BB	SO	AVG	OBP	SLG	PRO+	BR	/A	RC	SB	CS	SBR	FR	POS	TPR
1913	Phi-A	5	12	0	2	0	1	0	0	0	4	.167	.231	.333	66	-1	-1	1	0			-1	/O	-0.1

■ JIM BRIDEWESER
Brideweser, James Ehrenfeld b: 2/13/27, Lancaster, Ohio d: 8/25/89, ElToro, Cal. BR/TR, 6', 165 lbs. Deb: 9/29/51

YEAR	TM/L	G	AB	R	H	2B	3B	HR	RBI	BB	SO	AVG	OBP	SLG	PRO+	BR	/A	RC	SB	CS	SBR	FR	POS	TPR
1951	NY-A	2	8	1	3	0	0	0	0	0	1	.375	.375	.375	107	0	0	1	0	0	0	0	/S	0.0
1952	NY-A	42	38	12	10	0	0	0	2	3	5	.263	.317	.263	67	-2	-2	3	0	0	0	2	S/23	0.2
1953	NY-A	7	3	3	3	0	1	0	3	1	0	1.000	1.000	1.667	631	2	2	5	0	0	0	0	/S	0.3
1954	Bal-A	73	204	18	54	7	2	0	12	15	27	.265	.318	.319	81	-7	-5	20	1	1	-0	-12	S2	-1.2
1955	Chi-A	34	58	6	12	3	2	0	4	3	7	.207	.246	.328	52	-4	-4	4	0	0	0	6	S/32	0.4
1956	Chi-A	10	11	0	2	1	0	0	1	0	3	.182	.250	.273	37	-1	-1	1	0	0	0	0	S	0.0
	Det-A	70	156	23	34	4	0	0	10	20	19	.218	.307	.244	47	-11	-12	13	3	1	0	14	S2/3	0.7
	Yr	80	167	23	36	5	0	0	11	20	22	.216	.303	.246	46	-12	-13	13	3	1	0	14		0.7
1957	Bal-A	91	142	16	38	7	1	1	18	21	15	.268	.362	.352	102	-0	-1	19	2	0	1	5	S/32	1.3
Total	7	329	620	79	156	22	6	1	50	63	77	.252	.323	.311	75	-23	-20	66	6	2	1	15	S/23	1.7

■ ROCKY BRIDGES
Bridges, Everett Lamar b: 8/7/27, Refugio, Tex. BR/TR, 5'8", 170 lbs. Deb: 4/17/51 C

YEAR	TM/L	G	AB	R	H	2B	3B	HR	RBI	BB	SO	AVG	OBP	SLG	PRO+	BR	/A	RC	SB	CS	SBR	FR	POS	TPR
1951	Bro-N	63	134	13	34	7	0	1	15	10	10	.254	.306	.328	69	-6	-6	12	0	0	0	3	32/S	-0.1
1952	Bro-N	51	56	9	11	3	0	0	2	7	9	.196	.286	.250	49	-4	-4	4	0	1	-1	12	2S/3	0.9
1953	Cin-N	122	432	52	98	13	2	1	21	37	42	.227	.288	.273	47	-33	-33	35	6	3	0	11	*2/S3	-1.6
1954	Cin-N	53	52	4	12	1	0	0	2	7	7	.231	.322	.250	50	-3	-4	4	0	1	-1	11	S23	0.9
1955	Cin-N	95	168	20	48	4	0	1	18	15	19	.286	.344	.327	75	-4	-6	19	1	1	-0	7	3S/2	0.2
1956	Cin-N	71	19	9	4	0	0	0	1	4	3	.211	.348	.211	52	-1	-1	1	1	2	-1	9	3/2SO	0.7
1957	Cin-N	5	1	1	0	0	0	0	0	1	1	.000	.500	.000	46	0	0	0	0	0	0	-1	/2S3	0.0
	Was-A	120	391	40	89	17	2	3	47	40	32	.228	.303	.304	67	-18	-17	34	0	2	-1	29	*S2/3	2.1
1958	Was-A	116	377	38	99	14	3	5	28	27	32	.263	.317	.355	86	-8	-7	38	0	3	-2	3	*S/23	1.1
1959	Det-A	116	381	38	102	16	3	3	35	30	35	.268	.323	.349	80	-8	-11	40	1	2	-1	-5	*S/2	-0.7
1960	Det-A	10	5	0	1	0	0	0	0	0	0	.200	.200	.200	8	-1	-1	0	0	0	0	3	/3S	0.3
	Cle-A	10	27	1	9	0	0	0	3	1	2	.333	.357	.333	91	-0	-0	3	0	0	0	3	/S3	0.3
	Yr	20	32	1	10	0	0	0	3	1	2	.313	.333	.313	76	-1	-1	3	0	0	0	6		0.6
	StL-N	3	0	0	0	0	0	0	0	0	0	—	—	—	—	0	0	0	0	0	0	0	/2	0.1
1961	LA-A	84	229	20	55	5	1	2	15	26	37	.240	.320	.297	59	-10	-14	23	1	0	0	10	2S/3	0.5
Total	11	919	2272	245	562	80	11	16	187	205	229	.247	.312	.313	67	-96	-103	215	10	15	-6	95	S23/O	4.7

■ AL BRIDWELL
Bridwell, Albert Henry b: 1/4/1884, Friendship, Ohio d: 1/23/69, Portsmouth, Ohio BL/TR, 5'9", 170 lbs. Deb: 4/16/05

YEAR	TM/L	G	AB	R	H	2B	3B	HR	RBI	BB	SO	AVG	OBP	SLG	PRO+	BR	/A	RC	SB	CS	SBR	FR	POS	TPR
1905	Cin-N	82	254	17	64	3	1	0	17	19		.252	.304	.272	67	-8	-11	26	8			0	30/2S1	-0.8
1906	Bos-N	120	459	41	104	9	1	0	22	44		.227	.294	.251	74	-14	-12	38	6			17	*S/O	1.2
1907	Bos-N	140	509	49	111	8	2	0	26	61		.218	.302	.242	73	-14	-14	45	17			7	*S	0.0
1908	NY-N	147	467	53	133	14	1	0	46	52		.285	.356	.319	113	12	9	61	20			11	*S	2.0
1909	NY-N	145	476	59	140	11	5	0	55	67		.294	.386	.338	123	17	16	75	32			-0	*S	1.9
1910	NY-N	142	492	74	136	15	7	0	48	73	23	.276	.374	.335	107	8	7	68	14			6	*S	1.9
1911	NY-N	76	263	28	71	10	1	0	31	33	10	.270	.358	.316	86	-3	-4	33	8			6	S	0.5
	Bos-N	51	182	29	53	5	0	0	10	33	8	.291	.403	.319	95	3	1	25	2			-11	S	-0.7
	Yr	127	445	57	124	15	1	0	41	66	18	.279	.377	.317	90	0	-3	59	10			-5		-0.2
1912	Bos-N	31	106	6	25	5	1	0	14	5	5	.236	.270	.302	55	-7	-7	9	2			-6	S	-0.9
1913	Chi-N	136	405	35	97	6	6	1	37	74	28	.240	.358	.291	86	-3	-4	47	12			2	*S	0.7
1914	StL-F	117	381	46	90	6	5	1	33	71	18	.236	.359	.286	82	-3	-6	47	9			-11	*S2	-1.0
1915	StL-F	65	175	20	40	3	2	0	9	25	6	.229	.328	.269	74	-4	-5	19	6			1	23/1	-0.2
Total	11	1252	4169	457	1064	95	32	2	348	557	98	.255	.345	.295	90	-16	-29	496	136			21	*S/2301	4.6

■ BUNNY BRIEF
Brief, Anthony Vincent (b: Antonio Bordetzki) b: 7/3/1892, Remus, Mich. d: 2/10/63, Milwaukee, Wis. BR/TR, 6', 185 lbs. Deb: 9/22/12

YEAR	TM/L	G	AB	R	H	2B	3B	HR	RBI	BB	SO	AVG	OBP	SLG	PRO+	BR	/A	RC	SB	CS	SBR	FR	POS	TPR
1912	StL-A	15	42	9	13	3	0	0	5	6		.310	.408	.381	131	2	2	8	2			-1	/O1	0.0
1913	StL-A	85	258	24	56	11	6	1	26	21	46	.217	.284	.318	78	-9	-8	24	3			-1	1/O	-0.9
1915	Chi-A	48	154	13	33	6	2	2	17	16	28	.214	.305	.318	84	-3	-3	16	8	6	-1	-2	1	-0.8
1917	Pit-N	36	115	15	25	5	1	2	11	15	21	.217	.318	.330	96	0	-0	14	4			2	1	0.1
Total	4	184	569	61	127	25	9	5	59	58	95	.223	.306	.325	87	-9	-9	62	17	6		-2	1/O	-1.6

■ CHARLIE BRIGGS
Briggs, Charles R. b: 1861, Batavia, Ill. 5'7", 170 lbs. Deb: 5/02/1884

YEAR	TM/L	G	AB	R	H	2B	3B	HR	RBI	BB	SO	AVG	OBP	SLG	PRO+	BR	/A	RC	SB	CS	SBR	FR	POS	TPR
1884	CP-U	49	182	29	31	8	2	1		11		.170	.218	.253	59	-7	-7	10	0			-5	O2/S	-1.1

■ DAN BRIGGS
Briggs, Dan Lee b: 11/18/52, Scotia, Cal. BL/TL, 6', 180 lbs. Deb: 9/10/75

YEAR	TM/L	G	AB	R	H	2B	3B	HR	RBI	BB	SO	AVG	OBP	SLG	PRO+	BR	/A	RC	SB	CS	SBR	FR	POS	TPR
1975	Cal-A	13	31	3	7	1	0	1	3	2	6	.226	.273	.355	82	-1	-1	2	0	2	-1	-1	/1OD	-0.2
1976	Cal-A	77	248	19	53	13	2	1	14	13	47	.214	.256	.294	65	-13	-11	17	0	3	-2	2	1O/D	-1.4
1977	Cal-A	59	74	6	12	2	0	1	4	8	14	.162	.244	.230	31	-7	-7	4	0	0	0	3	1O	-0.6
1978	Cle-A	15	49	4	8	0	1	1	1	4	9	.163	.226	.265	38	-4	-4	3	0	0	0	2	O	-0.2
1979	SD-N	104	227	34	47	4	3	8	30	18	45	.207	.280	.357	77	-9	-7	23	2	1	0	5	1O	-0.5
1981	Mon-N	9	11	0	1	0	0	0	0	0	3	.091	.091	.091	-48	-2	-2	0	0	1	-1	1	/1O	-0.1
1982	Chi-N	48	48	1	6	0	0	0	1	0	9	.125	.143	.125	-24	-8	-8	1	0	0	0	1	O/1	-0.7
Total	7	325	688	67	134	20	6	12	53	45	133	.195	.251	.294	56	-44	-40	50	2	7	-4	13	1O/D	-3.7

■ GRANT BRIGGS
Briggs, Grant b: 3/16/1865, Pittsburgh, Pa. d: 5/31/28, Pittsburgh, Pa. Deb: 4/17/1890

YEAR	TM/L	G	AB	R	H	2B	3B	HR	RBI	BB	SO	AVG	OBP	SLG	PRO+	BR	/A	RC	SB	CS	SBR	FR	POS	TPR
1890	Syr-a	86	316	44	57	6	5	0		16		.180	.222	.231	39	-26	-21	18	7			-2	CO/3S	-1.6
1891	Lou-a	1	4	0	1	0	0	0	0	0	0	.250	.250	.250	46	-0	-0	0	0			-0	/C	0.0
1892	StL-N	23	57	2	4	1	0	0	1	6	16	.070	.172	.088	-21	-8	-8	1	3			-8	C/O	-1.4
1895	Lou-N	1	3	0	0	0	0	0	0	0	1	.000	.000	.000	-99	-1	-1	0	0			-1	/C	0.0
Total	4	111	380	46	62	7	5	0	1	22	17	.163	.213	.208	28	-35	-30	20	10			-11	/CO3S	-3.0

■ JOHN BRIGGS
Briggs, John Edward b: 3/10/44, Paterson, N.J. BL/TL, 6'1", 190 lbs. Deb: 4/17/64

YEAR	TM/L	G	AB	R	H	2B	3B	HR	RBI	BB	SO	AVG	OBP	SLG	PRO+	BR	/A	RC	SB	CS	SBR	FR	POS	TPR
1964	Phi-N	61	66	16	17	2	0	1	6	9	12	.258	.347	.333	94	-0	-0	8	1	1	-0	1	O/1	0.0
1965	Phi-N	93	229	47	54	9	4	4	23	42	44	.236	.354	.362	104	2	3	33	3	2	-0	-2	O	-0.1
1966	Phi-N	81	255	43	72	13	5	10	23	41	44	.282	.382	.490	140	15	15	50	3	2	-0	-7	O	0.6
1967	Phi-N	106	332	47	77	12	4	9	30	41	72	.232	.316	.373	96	-1	-1	40	3	5	-2	-5	O	-1.3
1968	Phi-N	110	338	36	86	13	1	7	31	58	72	.254	.365	.361	119	10	10	49	6	5	-1	-2	O1	0.3
1969	Phi-N	124	361	51	86	20	3	12	46	64	78	.238	.353	.410	116	7	9	56	9	6	-1	1	*O/1	0.3
1970	Phi-N	110	341	43	92	15	7	9	47	39	65	.270	.345	.434	110	3	4	48	5	4	-1	5	O	0.4
1971	Phi-N	10	22	3	4	1	0	0	3	6	2	.182	.357	.227	69	-1	-1	2	0	0	0	-1	/O	-0.1
	Mil-A	125	375	51	99	11	1	21	59	71	79	.264	.383	.467	141	21	22	71	1	2	-1	1	O1	1.8
1972	Mil-A	135	418	58	111	14	1	21	65	54	67	.266	.351	.455	141	20	20	67	1	2	-1	-4	*O1	1.2
1973	Mil-A	142	488	78	120	20	7	18	57	87	83	.246	.362	.428	124	16	17	80	15	9	-1	2	*O/D	1.5
1974	Mil-A	154	554	72	140	30	8	17	73	71	102	.253	.338	.428	120	13	14	82	9	7	-2	-4	*O/D	0.5
1975	Mil-A	28	74	12	22	1	0	3	5	20	13	.297	.447	.432	149	6	6	15	0	2	-1	0	O/D	0.5
	Min-A	87	264	44	61	9	2	7	39	60	41	.231	.373	.360	106	5	4	41	6	2	1	7	1O/D	0.8

YEAR	TM/L	G	AB	R	H	2B	3B	HR	RBI	BB	SO	AVG	OBP	SLG	PRO+	BR	/A	RC	SB	CS	SBR	FR	POS	TPR
	Yr	115	338	56	83	10	2	10	44	80	54	.246	.390	.376	115	11	11	56	6	4	-1	7		1.3
Total	12	1366	4117	601	1041	170	43	139	507	663	785	.253	.357	.416	121	116	121	643	64	49	-10	-7	*O1/D	6.4

■ HARRY BRIGHT
Bright, Harry James b: 9/22/29, Kansas City, Mo. BR/TR, 6', 190 lbs. Deb: 8/07/58

YEAR	TM/L	G	AB	R	H	2B	3B	HR	RBI	BB	SO	AVG	OBP	SLG	PRO+	BR	/A	RC	SB	CS	SBR	FR	POS	TPR
1958	Pit-N	15	24	4	6	1	0	1	3	1	6	.250	.280	.417	84	-1	-1	3	0	0	0	0	/3	0.0
1959	Pit-N	40	48	4	12	1	0	3	8	5	10	.250	.321	.458	105	0	0	7	0	0	0	-1	/O32	0.0
1960	Pit-N	4	4	0	0	0	0	0	0	0	2	.000	.000	.000	-99	-1	-1	0	0	0	0	0	H	0.0
1961	Was-A	72	183	20	44	6	0	4	21	19	23	.240	.312	.339	75	-7	-6	18	0	2	-1	7	3/C2	0.2
1962	Was-A	113	392	55	107	15	4	17	67	26	51	.273	.321	.462	109	3	3	54	2	1	0	-1	1/C3	-0.3
1963	Cin-N	1	1	0	0	0	0	0	0	0	1	.000	.000	.000	-97	-0	-0	0	0	0	0	0	/1	0.0
	*NY-A	60	157	15	37	7	0	7	23	13	31	.236	.298	.414	98	-1	-1	19	0	0	0	-4	13	-0.6
1964	NY-A	4	5	0	1	0	0	0	0	1	1	.200	.333	.200	52	-0	-0	0	0	0	0	-0	/1	0.0
1965	Chi-N	27	25	1	7	1	0	0	4	0	8	.280	.280	.320	67	-1	-1	2	0	0	0	0	H	0.0
Total	8	336	839	99	214	31	4	32	126	65	133	.255	.311	.416	96	-8	-7	104	2	3	-1	1	1/3CO2	-0.7

■ GREG BRILEY
Briley, Gregory "Peewee" b: 5/24/65, Greenville, N.C. BL/TR, 5'9", 175 lbs. Deb: 6/27/88

YEAR	TM/L	G	AB	R	H	2B	3B	HR	RBI	BB	SO	AVG	OBP	SLG	PRO+	BR	/A	RC	SB	CS	SBR	FR	POS	TPR
1988	Sea-A	13	36	6	9	2	0	1	4	5	6	.250	.341	.389	100	0	0	5	0	1	-1	-2	O	-0.2
1989	Sea-A	115	394	52	105	22	4	13	52	39	82	.266	.340	.442	115	9	8	59	11	5	0	-8	*O2/D	-0.1
1990	Sea-A	125	337	40	83	18	2	5	29	37	48	.246	.323	.356	89	-4	-5	41	16	4	2	-7	*O/D	-1.0
Total	3	253	767	98	197	42	6	19	85	81	136	.257	.333	.402	103	5	3	105	27	10	2	-18	O/2D	-1.3

■ BILL BRINKER
Brinker, William Hutchinson "Dode" b: 8/30/1883, Warrensburg, Mo. d: 2/5/65, Arcadia, Cal. BB/TR, 6'1", 190 lbs. Deb: 4/24/12

YEAR	TM/L	G	AB	R	H	2B	3B	HR	RBI	BB	SO	AVG	OBP	SLG	PRO+	BR	/A	RC	SB	CS	SBR	FR	POS	TPR
1912	Phi-N	9	18	1	4	1	0	0	2	2	3	.222	.300	.278	55	-1	-1	1	0			-0	/3O	0.0

■ CHUCK BRINKMAN
Brinkman, Charles Ernest b: 9/16/44, Cincinnati, O. BR/TR, 6'1", 185 lbs. Deb: 7/10/69

YEAR	TM/L	G	AB	R	H	2B	3B	HR	RBI	BB	SO	AVG	OBP	SLG	PRO+	BR	/A	RC	SB	CS	SBR	FR	POS	TPR
1969	Chi-A	14	15	2	1	0	0	0	0	1	5	.067	.125	.067	-43	-3	-3	0	0	0	0	1	C	0.0
1970	Chi-A	9	20	4	5	1	0	0	3	3	3	.250	.348	.300	77	-0	0	2	0	0	0	1	/C	0.1
1971	Chi-A	15	20	0	4	0	0	0	1	3	5	.200	.304	.200	44	-1	-1	1	0	0	0	3	C	0.2
1972	Chi-A	35	52	1	7	0	0	0	4	7	7	.135	.196	.135	-0	-6	-6	1	0	0	0	8	C	0.1
1973	Chi-A	63	139	13	26	6	0	1	10	11	37	.187	.252	.252	41	-11	-11	9	0	0	0	11	C	0.1
1974	Chi-A	8	14	1	2	0	0	0	0	1	3	.143	.200	.143	-0	-2	-2	0	0	0	0	-1	/C	-0.1
	Pit-N	4	7	1	1	0	0	0	1	0	0	.143	.143	.143	-21	-1	-1	0	0	0	0	-0	/C	0.0
Total	6	148	267	22	46	7	0	1	12	23	60	.172	.241	.210	28	-25	-26	15	0	0	0	22	C	0.4

■ ED BRINKMAN
Brinkman, Edwin Albert b: 12/8/41, Cincinnati, O. BR/TR, 6', 170 lbs. Deb: 9/06/61 C

YEAR	TM/L	G	AB	R	H	2B	3B	HR	RBI	BB	SO	AVG	OBP	SLG	PRO+	BR	/A	RC	SB	CS	SBR	FR	POS	TPR
1961	Was-A	4	11	0	1	0	0	0	0	1	1	.091	.167	.091	-30	-2	-2	0	0	0	0	0	/3	-0.1
1962	Was-A	54	133	8	22	7	1	0	4	11	28	.165	.229	.233	25	-14	-14	6	1	0	0	2	S3	-0.9
1963	Was-A	145	514	44	117	20	3	7	45	31	86	.228	.277	.319	67	-23	-23	46	5	3	-0	7	*S	-0.9
1964	Was-A	132	447	54	100	20	3	8	34	26	99	.224	.273	.336	68	-20	-20	41	2	2	-1	-3	*S	-2.3
1965	Was-A	154	444	35	82	13	2	5	35	38	82	.185	.252	.257	46	-32	-31	28	1	2	-1	4	*S	-2.2
1966	Was-A	158	582	42	133	18	9	7	48	29	105	.229	.265	.326	70	-24	-23	45	7	9	-3	12	*S	-0.6
1967	Was-A	109	320	21	60	9	2	1	18	24	58	.188	.253	.237	47	-21	-20	20	1	3	-2	14	*S	0.0
1968	Was-A	77	193	12	36	3	0	0	6	19	31	.187	.259	.202	43	-13	-13	10	0	0	0	3	S/2O	-0.4
1969	Was-A	151	576	71	153	18	5	2	43	50	42	.266	.330	.325	88	-12	-8	59	2	2	-1	15	*S	1.3
1970	Was-A	158	625	63	164	17	2	1	40	60	41	.262	.332	.301	79	-19	-15	62	8	9	-3	31	*S	2.7
1971	Det-A	159	527	40	120	18	2	1	37	44	54	.228	.296	.275	60	-25	-28	42	1	4	-2	12	*S	0.0
1972	*Det-A	156	516	42	105	19	1	6	49	38	51	.203	.262	.279	59	-25	-27	37	0	0	0	2	*S	-0.9
1973	Det-A	162	515	55	122	16	4	7	40	34	79	.237	.285	.324	67	-20	-24	44	0	1	-1	-13	*S	-1.6
1974	Det-A	153	502	55	111	15	3	14	54	29	72	.221	.268	.347	73	-17	-19	45	2	0	1	13	*S/3	0.7
1975	StL-N	28	75	6	18	4	0	1	6	7	10	.240	.313	.333	77	-2	-2	7	0	0	0	3	S	0.1
	Tex-A	1	2	0	0	0	0	0	0	0	1	.000	.000	.000	-99	-1	-1	0	0	0	0	0	/3	0.0
	NY-A	44	63	2	11	4	1	0	2	3	6	.175	.224	.270	40	-5	-5	3	0	0	0	-3	S/23	-0.3
	Yr	45	65	2	11	4	1	0	2	3	7	.169	.217	.262	36	-6	-6	3	0	0	0	-3		-0.3
Total	15	1845	6045	550	1355	201	38	60	461	444	845	.224	.282	.300	65	-276	-275	497	30	35	-12	95	*S/32O	-5.4

■ LEON BRINKOPF
Brinkopf, Leon Clarence b: 10/20/26, Cape Girardeau, Mo BR/TR, 5'11.5", 185 lbs. Deb: 4/18/52

YEAR	TM/L	G	AB	R	H	2B	3B	HR	RBI	BB	SO	AVG	OBP	SLG	PRO+	BR	/A	RC	SB	CS	SBR	FR	POS	TPR
1952	Chi-N	9	22	1	4	0	0	0	2	4	5	.182	.308	.182	38	-2	-2	2	0	0	0	-2	/S	-0.3

■ FATTY BRIODY
Briody, Charles F. "Alderman" b: 8/13/1858, Lansingburg, N.Y. d: 6/22/03, Chicago, Ill. TR, 5'8.5", 190 lbs. Deb: 6/16/1880

YEAR	TM/L	G	AB	R	H	2B	3B	HR	RBI	BB	SO	AVG	OBP	SLG	PRO+	BR	/A	RC	SB	CS	SBR	FR	POS	TPR
1880	Tro-N	1	4	0	0	0	0	0	0	0	0	.000	.000	.000	-95	-1	-1	0				1	/C	0.0
1882	Cle-N	53	194	30	50	13	0	0	13	9	13	.258	.291	.325	100	-1	-1	19				5	C	0.8
1883	Cle-N	40	145	23	34	5	1	0	10	3	13	.234	.250	.283	62	-7	-6	11				3	C/213	-0.1
1884	Cle-N	43	148	17	25	6	0	1	12	6	19	.169	.201	.230	34	-11	-12	7				6	C/O	-0.1
	Cin-U	22	89	11	30	2	2	0		1		.337	.344	.404	141	5	3	13	0			11	C	1.3
1885	StL-N	62	215	14	42	9	0	1	17	12	23	.195	.238	.251	62	-10	-8	13				-11	C/O32	-1.2
1886	KC-N	56	215	14	51	10	3	0	29	3	35	.237	.248	.312	65	-8	-10	17	0			-3	C/O1	-0.8
1887	Det-N	33	128	24	29	6	1	1	26	9	10	.227	.283	.313	64	-6	-6	13	6			3	C	-0.3
1888	KC-a	13	48	1	10	1	0	0	8	1		.208	.224	.229	45	-3	-3	3	0			-2	C	-0.3
Total	8	323	1186	134	271	52	7	3	115	44	113	.228	.257	.292	70	-40	-42	95	6			11	C/2013	-0.4

■ GEORGE BRISTOW
Bristow, George T. b: 5/1870, Paw Paw, Ill. TR, Deb: 4/15/1899

YEAR	TM/L	G	AB	R	H	2B	3B	HR	RBI	BB	SO	AVG	OBP	SLG	PRO+	BR	/A	RC	SB	CS	SBR	FR	POS	TPR
1899	Cle-N	3	8	0	1	1	0	0	0	0		.125	.222	.250	34	-1	-1	0	0			0	/O	0.0

■ GUS BRITTAIN
Brittain, August Schuster b: 11/29/09, Wilmington, N.C. d: 2/16/74, Wilmington, N.C. BR/TR, 5'10", 192 lbs. Deb: 7/22/37

YEAR	TM/L	G	AB	R	H	2B	3B	HR	RBI	BB	SO	AVG	OBP	SLG	PRO+	BR	/A	RC	SB	CS	SBR	FR	POS	TPR
1937	Cin-N	3	6	0	1	0	0	0	0	0	3	.167	.167	.167	-10	-1	-1	0	0			-0	/C	0.0

■ GIL BRITTON
Britton, Stephen Gilbert b: 9/21/1891, Parsons, Kan. d: 6/20/83, Parsons, Kan. BR/TR, 5'10", 160 lbs. Deb: 9/20/13

YEAR	TM/L	G	AB	R	H	2B	3B	HR	RBI	BB	SO	AVG	OBP	SLG	PRO+	BR	/A	RC	SB	CS	SBR	FR	POS	TPR
1913	Pit-N	3	12	0	0	0	0	0	0	0	2	.000	.000	.000	-99	-3	-3	0	0			-1	/S	-0.3

■ GREG BROCK
Brock, Gregory Allen b: 6/14/57, McMinnville, Ore. BL/TR, 6'3", 200 lbs. Deb: 9/01/82

YEAR	TM/L	G	AB	R	H	2B	3B	HR	RBI	BB	SO	AVG	OBP	SLG	PRO+	BR	/A	RC	SB	CS	SBR	FR	POS	TPR
1982	LA-N	18	17	1	2	1	0	1	1	1	5	.118	.167	.176	-4	-2	-2	1	0	0	0	-0	/1	-0.2
1983	*LA-N	146	455	64	102	14	2	20	66	83	81	.224	.345	.396	105	4	5	64	5	1	1	5	*1	0.4
1984	LA-N	88	271	33	61	6	0	14	34	39	37	.225	.323	.402	104	1	1	37	8	0	2	7	1	0.9
1985	*LA-N	129	438	64	110	19	0	21	66	54	72	.251	.333	.438	118	8	9	65	4	2	0	2	*1	0.8
1986	LA-N	115	325	33	76	13	0	16	52	37	60	.234	.312	.422	108	-1	2	42	2	5	-2	12	1	0.8
1987	Mil-A	141	532	81	159	29	3	13	85	57	63	.299	.373	.438	111	12	10	88	5	4	-1	3	*1	0.0
1988	Mil-A	115	364	53	77	16	1	6	50	63	48	.212	.333	.310	81	-7	-8	39	6	2	1	9	*1/D	-0.4
1989	Mil-A	107	373	40	99	16	0	12	52	43	49	.265	.346	.405	112	6	6	53	6	1	1	-5	*1/D	-0.3
1990	Mil-A	123	367	42	91	23	0	7	50	43	45	.248	.330	.368	98	-2	-1	46	4	2	0	-4	*1	-1.3
Total	9	982	3142	411	777	137	6	109	456	420	460	.247	.339	.399	105	18	23	435	40	17	2	29	1/D	0.7

■ JOHN BROCK
Brock, John Roy b: 10/16/1896, Hamilton, Ill. d: 10/27/51, Clayton, Mo. BR/TR, 5'6.5", 165 lbs. Deb: 8/10/17

YEAR	TM/L	G	AB	R	H	2B	3B	HR	RBI	BB	SO	AVG	OBP	SLG	PRO+	BR	/A	RC	SB	CS	SBR	FR	POS	TPR
1917	StL-N	7	15	4	6	1	0	0	2	0	2	.400	.400	.467	170	1	1	3	2			-0	/C	0.1
1918	StL-N	27	52	9	11	2	0	0	4	3	10	.212	.255	.250	56	-3	-3	4	5			-1	C/O	-0.1
Total	2	34	67	13	17	3	0	0	6	3	12	.254	.286	.299	81	-2	-2	8	7			-1	/CO	0.0

YEAR	TM/L	G	AB	R	H	2B	3B	HR	RBI	BB	SO	AVG	OBP	SLG	PRO+	BR	/A	RC	SB	CS	SBR	FR	POS	TPR

■ LOU BROCK   Brock, Louis Clark   b: 6/18/39, ElDorado, Ark.   BL/TL, 5'11.5", 170 lbs.   Deb: 9/10/61

YEAR	TM/L	G	AB	R	H	2B	3B	HR	RBI	BB	SO	AVG	OBP	SLG	PRO+	BR	/A	RC	SB	CS	SBR	FR	POS	TPR
1961	Chi-N	4	11	1	1	0	0	0	0	1	3	.091	.167	.091	-29	-2	-2	0	0	0	0	-0	/O	-0.2
1962	Chi-N	123	434	73	114	24	7	9	35	35	96	.263	.322	.412	92	-3	-5	58	16	7	1	-4	*O	-1.3
1963	Chi-N	148	547	79	141	19	11	9	37	31	122	.258	.302	.382	91	-4	-7	64	24	12	0	11	*O	-0.3
1964	Chi-N	52	215	30	54	9	2	2	14	13	40	.251	.300	.340	77	-6	-7	23	10	3	1	-0	O	-0.7
	*StL-N	103	419	81	146	21	9	12	44	27	87	.348	.391	.527	143	30	26	86	33	15	1	0	*O	2.5
	Yr	155	634	111	200	30	11	14	58	40	127	.315	.360	.464	121	24	19	107	43	18	2	-0		1.8
1965	StL-N	155	631	107	182	35	8	16	69	45	116	.288	.345	.445	110	17	10	99	63	27	3	1	*O	0.9
1966	StL-N	156	643	94	183	24	12	15	46	31	134	.285	.321	.429	106	4	4	91	74	18	11	-2	*O	0.9
1967	*StL-N	159	689	113	206	32	12	21	76	24	109	.299	.328	.472	128	21	21	106	52	18	5	-0	*O	2.0
1968	*StL-N	159	660	92	184	46	14	6	51	46	124	.279	.329	.418	125	17	18	98	62	12	11	-5	*O	1.9
1969	StL-N	157	655	97	195	33	10	12	47	50	115	.298	.349	.434	118	15	15	105	53	14	8	-7	*O	0.7
1970	StL-N	155	664	114	202	29	5	13	57	60	99	.304	.363	.422	107	9	7	105	51	15	6	-8	*O	0.0
1971	StL-N	157	640	126	200	37	7	7	61	76	107	.313	.386	.425	125	27	24	114	64	19	8	-11	*O	1.6
1972	StL-N	153	621	81	193	26	8	3	42	47	93	.311	.360	.393	114	11	12	93	63	18	8	-7	*O	0.7
1973	StL-N	160	650	110	193	29	8	7	63	71	112	.297	.366	.398	112	12	12	101	70	20	9	-6	*O	0.7
1974	StL-N	153	635	105	194	25	7	3	48	61	88	.306	.368	.381	111	9	10	98	118	33	16	-6	*O	1.4
1975	StL-N	136	528	78	163	27	6	3	47	38	64	.309	.359	.400	106	7	5	79	56	16	7	-3	*O	0.5
1976	StL-N	133	498	73	150	24	5	4	67	35	75	.301	.348	.394	109	6	6	65	56	19	5	-7	*O	0.0
1977	StL-N	141	489	69	133	22	6	2	46	30	74	.272	.317	.354	81	-14	-13	52	35	24	-4	-20	*O	-4.2
1978	StL-N	92	298	31	66	9	0	0	12	17	29	.221	.263	.252	45	-22	-21	21	17	5	2	-11	O	-3.5
1979	StL-N	120	405	56	123	15	4	5	38	23	43	.304	.346	.398	101	1	1	54	21	12	-1	-14	O	-1.6
Total	19	2616	10332	1610	3023	486	141	149	900	761	1730	.293	.344	.410	109	135	114	1512	938	307	97	-100	*O	2.0

■ MATT BRODERICK   Broderick, Matthew Thomas   b: 12/1/1877, Lattimer Mines, Pa.   d: 2/26/40, Freeland, Pa.   TR, 5'6.5", 135 lbs.   Deb: 5/01/03

YEAR	TM/L	G	AB	R	H	2B	3B	HR	RBI	BB	SO	AVG	OBP	SLG	PRO+	BR	/A	RC	SB	CS	SBR	FR	POS	TPR
1903	Bro-N	2	2	0	0	0	0	0	0	0		.000	.000	.000	-99	-1	-0	0	0			0	/2	0.0

■ STEVE BRODIE   Brodie, Walter Scott   b: 9/11/1868, Warronton, Va.   d: 10/30/35, Baltimore, Md.   BL, 5'11", 180 lbs.   Deb: 4/21/1890

YEAR	TM/L	G	AB	R	H	2B	3B	HR	RBI	BB	SO	AVG	OBP	SLG	PRO+	BR	/A	RC	SB	CS	SBR	FR	POS	TPR
1890	Bos-N	132	514	77	152	19	9	0	67	66	20	.296	.387	.368	114	18	11	87	29			6	*O	1.2
1891	Bos-N	133	523	84	136	13	6	2	78	63	39	.260	.351	.319	87	1	-9	69	25			10	*O	-0.4
1892	StL-N	154	602	85	152	10	9	4	60	52	31	.252	.316	.319	99	-4	0	71	28			8	*O2/3	0.4
1893	StL-N	107	469	71	149	16	8	2	79	33	16	.318	.376	.399	108	6	5	88	41			9	*O	0.9
	Bal-N	25	97	18	35	7	2	0	19	12	2	.361	.446	.474	144	7	7	25	8			-3	O	0.2
	Yr	132	566	89	184	23	10	2	98	45	18	.325	.389	.412	114	13	12	112	49			6		1.1
1894	*Bal-N	129	573	134	210	25	11	3	113	18	8	.366	.399	.464	105	9	4	126	42			-5	*O	-0.7
1895	*Bal-N	131	528	85	184	27	10	2	134	26	15	.348	.394	.449	116	15	12	110	35			5	*O	0.5
1896	*Bal-N	132	516	98	153	19	11	3	87	36	17	.297	.363	.388	98	1	-1	84	25			11	*O	0.1
1897	Pit-N	100	370	47	108	7	12	2	53	25		.292	.348	.392	101	-1	1	56	11			-0	O	-0.5
1898	Pit-N	42	156	15	41	5	0	0	21	6		.263	.303	.295	75	-5	-5	15	3			3	O	-0.3
	Bal-N	23	98	12	30	3	2	0	19	5		.306	.346	.378	108	1	1	14	3			3	O	0.2
	Yr	65	254	27	71	8	2	0	40	11		.280	.320	.327	88	-4	-4	29	6			6		-0.1
1899	Bal-N	137	531	82	164	26	1	3	87	31		.309	.373	.379	103	8	3	84	19			1	*O	-0.3
1901	Bal-A	83	306	41	95	6	6	2	41	25		.310	.376	.389	110	7	5	51	9			-3	O	0.0
1902	NY-N	109	416	37	117	8	2	3	42	22		.281	.328	.332	107	3	3	51	11			7	*O	0.2
Total	12	1437	5699	886	1726	191	89	25	900	420	148	.303	.364	.381	104	64	38	930	289			51	*O/23	1.5

■ JACK BROHAMER   Brohamer, John Anthony   b: 2/26/50, Maywood, Cal.   BL/TR, 5'10", 165 lbs.   Deb: 4/18/72

YEAR	TM/L	G	AB	R	H	2B	3B	HR	RBI	BB	SO	AVG	OBP	SLG	PRO+	BR	/A	RC	SB	CS	SBR	FR	POS	TPR
1972	Cle-A	136	527	49	123	13	2	5	35	27	46	.233	.272	.294	66	-21	-23	42	3	2	-0	6	*2/3	-1.0
1973	Cle-A	102	300	29	66	12	1	4	29	32	23	.220	.295	.307	69	-12	-13	28	0	2	-1	17	2	0.7
1974	Cle-A	101	315	33	85	11	1	2	30	26	22	.270	.331	.330	92	-3	-3	36	2	1	0	-4	2	-0.2
1975	Cle-A	69	217	15	53	5	0	6	16	14	14	.244	.290	.350	80	-6	-6	21	2	2	-1	4	2	0.0
1976	Chi-A	119	354	33	89	12	2	2	40	44	28	.251	.339	.356	103	2	2	43	1	3	-2	18	*2/3	2.7
1977	Chi-A	59	152	26	39	10	3	2	20	21	8	.257	.351	.401	105	1	1	23	0	0	0	2	32/D	0.4
1978	Bos-A	81	244	34	57	14	1	1	25	25	13	.234	.305	.311	67	-8	-12	23	1	3	-2	-3	3D2	-1.5
1979	Bos-A	64	192	25	51	7	1	1	11	15	15	.266	.319	.328	71	-7	-8	18	0	3	-2	0	23	-0.7
1980	Bos-A	21	57	5	18	2	0	1	6	4	3	.316	.361	.404	104	1	0	8	0	0	0	-1	3/2D	0.0
	Cle-A	53	142	13	32	5	1	1	15	14	6	.225	.295	.296	62	-7	-7	12	0	1	-1	-3	2/D	-0.8
	Yr	74	199	18	50	7	1	2	21	18	9	.251	.313	.327	74	-6	-7	19	0	1	-1	-5		-0.8
Total	9	805	2500	262	613	91	12	30	227	222	178	.245	.309	.327	79	-60	-67	253	9	17	-8	34	23/D	-0.4

■ HERMAN BRONKIE   Bronkie, Herman Charles "Dutch"   b: 3/31/1885, S.Manchester, Conn   d: 5/27/68, Somers, Conn.   BR/TR, 5'9", 165 lbs.   Deb: 9/20/10

YEAR	TM/L	G	AB	R	H	2B	3B	HR	RBI	BB	SO	AVG	OBP	SLG	PRO+	BR	/A	RC	SB	CS	SBR	FR	POS	TPR
1910	Cle-A	5	9	1	2	0	0	0	0	1		.222	.300	.222	63	-0	-0	1	1			-1	/3S	-0.1
1911	Cle-A	2	6	0	1	0	0	0	0	0		.167	.167	.167	-7	-1	-1	0	0			-1	/3	-0.1
1912	Cle-A	6	16	1	0	0	0	0	0	1		.000	.059	.000	-80	-4	-4	0	0			2	/3	-0.1
1914	Chi-N	1	1	1	1	1	0	0	1	0	0	1.000	1.000	2.000	786	1	1	2	0			-0	/3	0.0
1918	StL-N	18	68	7	15	3	0	1	7	2	4	.221	.243	.309	70	-3	-3	5	0			-1	3	-0.3
1919	StL-A	67	196	23	50	6	4	0	14	23	23	.255	.336	.327	84	-3	-4	22	2			4	32/1	0.4
1922	StL-A	23	64	7	18	4	1	0	2	6	7	.281	.343	.375	84	-1	-2	8	0	2	-1	-0	3	0.0
Total	7	122	360	40	87	14	5	1	24	33	34	.242	.307	.317	75	-11	-12	38	3	2		3	/321S	-0.2

■ TOM BROOKENS   Brookens, Thomas Dale   b: 8/10/53, Chambersburg, Pa.   BR/TR, 5'10", 165 lbs.   Deb: 7/10/79

YEAR	TM/L	G	AB	R	H	2B	3B	HR	RBI	BB	SO	AVG	OBP	SLG	PRO+	BR	/A	RC	SB	CS	SBR	FR	POS	TPR
1979	Det-A	60	190	23	50	5	2	4	21	11	40	.263	.310	.374	81	-5	-5	23	10	3	1	11	32	0.8
1980	Det-A	151	509	64	140	25	9	10	66	32	71	.275	.319	.418	98	-1	-2	64	13	11	-3	4	*3/2SD	0.0
1981	Det-A	71	239	19	58	10	1	4	25	14	43	.243	.290	.343	79	-6	-7	23	5	3	-0	-4	3	-1.1
1982	Det-A	140	398	40	92	15	3	9	58	27	63	.231	.280	.352	72	-16	-16	36	5	9	-4	8	*32/SO	-1.1
1983	Det-A	138	332	50	71	13	3	6	32	29	46	.214	.281	.325	68	-15	-14	32	10	4	1	5	*3S2/D	-0.6
1984	*Det-A	113	224	32	55	11	4	5	26	19	33	.246	.307	.397	94	-2	-2	27	6	6	-2	20	3S2/D	2.0
1985	Det-A	156	485	54	115	34	6	7	47	27	78	.237	.277	.375	77	-17	-16	50	14	5	1	3	*3/3S2CD	-1.6
1986	Det-A	98	281	42	76	11	2	3	25	20	42	.270	.321	.356	84	-6	-6	32	11	8	-2	-0	32SD/O	-0.1
1987	*Det-A	143	444	59	107	15	3	13	59	33	63	.241	.296	.376	80	-15	-13	49	7	4	-0	2	*3S2	-0.9
1988	Det-A	136	441	62	107	23	5	5	38	44	74	.243	.316	.351	90	-8	-5	49	4	4	-1	-3	*3/S2	-0.9
1989	NY-A	66	168	14	38	6	0	4	14	11	27	.226	.274	.333	71	-7	-7	14	1	3	-2	-4	3/S2OD	-1.1
1990	Cle-A	64	154	18	41	7	2	1	20	14	25	.266	.327	.357	90	-2	-2	18	0	0	0	4	32/S1D	0.4
Total	12	1336	3865	477	950	175	40	71	431	281	605	.246	.299	.367	83	-99	-96	417	86	60	-10	49	*32S/DO1C	-4.2

■ HARRY BROOKS   Brooks, Harry Frank   b: 11/30/1865, Philadelphia   d: 12/5/45, Philadelphia, Pa.   Deb: 7/24/1886

YEAR	TM/L	G	AB	R	H	2B	3B	HR	RBI	BB	SO	AVG	OBP	SLG	PRO+	BR	/A	RC	SB	CS	SBR	FR	POS	TPR
1886	NY-a	1	1	0	0	0	0	0		0		.000	.000	.000	-99	-0	-0	0	0			-0	/OP	0.0

■ HUBIE BROOKS   Brooks, Hubert   b: 9/24/56, Los Angeles, Cal.   BR/TR, 6', 178 lbs.   Deb: 9/04/80

YEAR	TM/L	G	AB	R	H	2B	3B	HR	RBI	BB	SO	AVG	OBP	SLG	PRO+	BR	/A	RC	SB	CS	SBR	FR	POS	TPR
1980	NY-N	24	81	8	25	1	1	1	10	5	9	.309	.364	.395	115	1	2	12	1	1	-0	-1	3	0.0
1981	NY-N	98	358	34	110	21	2	4	38	23	65	.307	.351	.411	117	7	7	50	9	5	-0	-2	3/OS	0.1
1982	NY-N	126	457	40	114	21	2	2	40	28	76	.249	.300	.317	73	-17	-16	43	6	3	0	-8	*3	-2.7
1983	NY-N	150	586	53	147	18	4	5	58	24	96	.251	.285	.321	68	-26	-26	51	6	4	-1	3	*3/2	-2.9
1984	NY-N	153	561	61	159	23	2	16	73	48	79	.283	.342	.417	114	9	10	75	6	5	-1	-18	*3S	0.7

YEAR	TM/L	G	AB	R	H	2B	3B	HR	RBI	BB	SO	AVG	OBP	SLG	PRO+	BR	/A	RC	SB	CS	SBR	FR	POS	TPR
1985	Mon-N	156	605	67	163	34	7	13	100	34	79	.269	.314	.413	108	-0	4	71	6	9	-4	-34	*S	-2.2
1986	Mon-N	80	306	50	104	18	5	14	58	25	60	.340	.393	.569	164	25	25	65	4	2	0	-14	S	1.9
1987	Mon-N	112	430	57	113	22	3	14	72	24	72	.263	.303	.426	88	-7	-9	54	4	3	-1	-26	*S	-2.2
1988	Mon-N	151	588	61	164	35	2	20	90	35	108	.279	.321	.447	113	12	9	78	7	3	0	-7	*O	-0.2
1989	Mon-N	148	542	56	145	30	1	14	70	39	108	.268	.321	.404	105	3	3	65	6	11	-5	-8	*O	-1.2
1990	LA-N	153	568	74	151	28	1	20	91	33	108	.266	.313	.424	107	-1	3	71	2	5	-2	-7	*O	-1.0
Total	11	1351	5082	561	1395	252	30	123	700	318	860	.274	.321	.409	103	5	11	633	57	51	-14	-121	3OS/2	-11.1

■ MANDY BROOKS

Brooks, Jonathan Joseph (b: Jonathan Joseph Brozek)
b: 8/18/1897, Milwaukee, Wis.   d: 6/17/62, Kirkwood, Mo.   BR/TR, 5'9", 165 lbs.   Deb: 5/30/25

YEAR	TM/L	G	AB	R	H	2B	3B	HR	RBI	BB	SO	AVG	OBP	SLG	PRO+	BR	/A	RC	SB	CS	SBR	FR	POS	TPR
1925	Chi-N	90	349	55	98	25	7	14	72	19	28	.281	.322	.513	108	3	2	57	10	3	1	3	O	0.3
1926	Chi-N	26	48	7	9	1	0	1	6	5	5	.188	.278	.271	48	-3	-4	4	0			1	O	-0.3
Total	2	116	397	62	107	26	7	15	78	24	33	.270	.316	.484	101	-1	-2	61	10	3		4	O	0.0

■ BOBBY BROOKS

Brooks, Robert   b: 11/1/45, Los Angeles, Cal.   BR/TR, 5'8.5", 165 lbs.   Deb: 9/01/69

YEAR	TM/L	G	AB	R	H	2B	3B	HR	RBI	BB	SO	AVG	OBP	SLG	PRO+	BR	/A	RC	SB	CS	SBR	FR	POS	TPR
1969	Oak-A	29	79	13	19	5	0	3	10	20	24	.241	.400	.418	135	4	4	15	0	2	-1	-1	O	0.1
1970	Oak-A	7	18	2	6	1	0	2	5	1	7	.333	.368	.722	201	2	2	4	0	1	-1	-1	/O	0.0
1972	Oak-A	15	39	4	7	0	0	0	5	8	8	.179	.319	.179	54	-2	-2	2	0	1	-1	2	/O	0.0
1973	Cal-A	4	7	0	1	0	0	0	0	0	3	.143	.143	.143	-21	-1	-1	0	0	0	0	0	/O	0.0
Total	4	55	143	19	33	6	0	5	20	29	42	.231	.364	.378	116	3	4	21	0	4	-2	0	/O	0.1

■ SIG BROSKIE

Broskie, Sigmund Theodore "Chops"   b: 3/23/11, Iselin, Pa.   d: 5/17/75, Canton, Ohio   BR/TR, 5'11.5", 200 lbs.   Deb: 9/11/40

YEAR	TM/L	G	AB	R	H	2B	3B	HR	RBI	BB	SO	AVG	OBP	SLG	PRO+	BR	/A	RC	SB	CS	SBR	FR	POS	TPR
1940	Bos-N	11	22	1	6	1	0	0	4	1	2	.273	.304	.318	76	-1	-1	2	0			0	C	0.0

■ TONY BROTTEM

Brottem, Anton Christian   b: 4/30/1892, Halstead, Minn.   d: 8/5/29, Chicago, Ill.   BR/TR, 6'0.5", 176 lbs.   Deb: 4/17/16

YEAR	TM/L	G	AB	R	H	2B	3B	HR	RBI	BB	SO	AVG	OBP	SLG	PRO+	BR	/A	RC	SB	CS	SBR	FR	POS	TPR
1916	StL-N	26	33	3	6	1	0	0	4	3	10	.182	.250	.212	43	-2	-2	2	1			0	C/O	-0.1
1918	StL-N	2	4	0	0	0	0	0	0	1	0	.000	.200	.000	-39	-1	-1	0	0			1	/1	0.0
1921	Was-A	4	7	1	1	0	0	0	0	2	1	.143	.333	.143	26	-1	-1	0	0	0	0	1	/C	0.1
	Pit-N	30	91	6	22	2	0	0	9	3	11	.242	.266	.264	40	-8	-8	6	0	1	-1	-2	C	-0.8
Total	3	62	135	10	29	3	0	0	13	9	22	.215	.264	.237	38	-11	-11	9	1	1		0	/C1O	-0.8

■ CAL BROUGHTON

Broughton, Cecil Calvert   b: 12/28/1860, Magnolia, Wis.   d: 3/15/39, Evansville, Wis.   BR/TR,   Deb: 5/02/1883

YEAR	TM/L	G	AB	R	H	2B	3B	HR	RBI	BB	SO	AVG	OBP	SLG	PRO+	BR	/A	RC	SB	CS	SBR	FR	POS	TPR
1883	Cle-N	4	10	2	2	0	0	0	1	2	2	.200	.333	.200	68	-0	-0	1				0	/C	0.0
	Bal-a	9	32	1	6	0	0	0		0	1	.188	.212	.188	29	-2	-3	1				0	/CO	0.0
1884	Mil-U	11	39	5	12	5	0	0		0		.308	.308	.436	275	2	5	5	0			0	/CO	0.4
1885	StL-a	4	17	1	1	0	0	0		0		.059	.059	.059	-59	-3	-3	0				-1	/C	-0.2
	NY-a	11	41	1	6	1	0	0		0	1	.146	.167	.171	9	-4	-4	1				-1	C	-0.2
	Yr	15	58	2	7	1	0	0		0	1	.121	.136	.138	-13	-7	-7	1				-2		-0.4
1888	Det-N	1	4	0	0	0	0	0	0	0	0	.000	.000	.000	-99	-1	-1	0	0			1	/C	0.0
Total	4	40	143	10	27	6	0	0	1	4	2	.189	.211	.231	50	-9	-6	9	0			-1	/CO	0.0

■ MARK BROUHARD

Brouhard, Mark Steven   b: 5/22/56, Burbank.Cal.   BR/TR, 6'1", 210 lbs.   Deb: 4/12/80

YEAR	TM/L	G	AB	R	H	2B	3B	HR	RBI	BB	SO	AVG	OBP	SLG	PRO+	BR	/A	RC	SB	CS	SBR	FR	POS	TPR
1980	Mil-A	45	125	17	29	6	0	5	16	7	24	.232	.278	.400	86	-3	-3	13	1	0	0	1	DO1	-0.2
1981	Mil-A	60	186	19	51	6	3	2	20	7	41	.274	.308	.371	100	-2	-1	19	1	1	-0	2	O/D	0.0
1982	*Mil-A	40	108	16	29	4	1	4	10	9	17	.269	.336	.435	117	1	2	14	0	3	-2	2	O/D	0.2
1983	Mil-A	56	185	25	51	10	1	7	23	9	39	.276	.316	.454	118	2	4	23	0	4	-2	0	OD	0.1
1984	Mil-A	66	197	20	47	7	0	6	22	16	36	.239	.302	.365	87	-4	-3	21	0	3	-2	2	O/D	-0.4
1985	Mil-A	37	108	11	28	7	2	1	13	5	26	.259	.298	.389	87	-2	-2	12	0	0	0	-3	O/D	-0.5
Total	6	304	909	108	235	40	7	25	104	53	183	.259	.307	.400	99	-8	-3	103	2	11	-6	4	O/D1	-0.8

■ ART BROUTHERS

Brouthers, Arthur H.   b: 11/25/1882, Montgomery, Ala.   d: 9/28/59, Charleston, S.C.   TR , 6'1",   Deb: 4/14/06

YEAR	TM/L	G	AB	R	H	2B	3B	HR	RBI	BB	SO	AVG	OBP	SLG	PRO+	BR	/A	RC	SB	CS	SBR	FR	POS	TPR
1906	Phi-A	37	144	18	30	5	1	0	14	5		.208	.235	.257	54	-7	-8	11	4			-4	3/2	-1.0

■ DAN BROUTHERS

Brouthers, Dennis Joseph "Big Dan"   b: 5/8/1858, Sylvan Lake, N.Y.   d: 8/2/32, E.Orange, N.J.   BL/TL, 6'2", 207 lbs.   Deb: 6/23/1879   H

YEAR	TM/L	G	AB	R	H	2B	3B	HR	RBI	BB	SO	AVG	OBP	SLG	PRO+	BR	/A	RC	SB	CS	SBR	FR	POS	TPR
1879	Tro-N	39	168	17	46	12	1	4	17	1	18	.274	.278	.429	138	5	6	21				-5	1/P	0.0
1880	Tro-N	3	12	0	2	0	0	0	1	1	0	.167	.231	.167	35	-1	-1	0				-1	/1	-0.1
1881	Buf-N	65	270	60	86	18	9	8	45	18	22	.319	.361	.541	182	24	25	54				-4	O1	1.5
1882	Buf-N	84	351	71	129	23	11	6	63	21	7	.368	.403	.547	198	39	38	79				1	*1	2.3
1883	Buf-N	98	425	85	159	41	17	3	97	16	17	.374	.397	.572	186	44	43	99				2	*1/3P	2.8
1884	Buf-N	94	398	82	130	22	15	14	79	33	20	.327	.378	.563	186	41	39	87				0	*1/3	2.6
1885	Buf-N	98	407	87	146	32	11	7	59	34	10	.359	.408	.543	200	47	45	92				-2	*1	2.4
1886	Det-N	121	489	139	181	40	15	11	72	66	16	.370	.445	.581	204	66	64	139	21			-8	*1	3.0
1887	*Det-N	123	500	153	169	36	20	12	101	71	9	.338	.426	.562	169	52	49	138	34			-5	*1	2.0
1888	Det-N	129	522	118	160	33	11	9	66	68	13	.307	.399	.464	177	48	48	113	34			-2	*1	3.3
1889	Bos-N	126	485	105	181	26	9	7	118	66	6	.373	.462	.507	163	51	46	127	22			1	*1	3.2
1890	Bos-P	123	460	117	152	36	9	1	97	99	17	.330	.466	.454	139	40	33	113	28			2	*1	1.8
1891	Bos-a	130	486	117	170	26	19	5	109	87	20	.350	.471	.512	188	59	60	135	31			-7	*1	4.0
1892	Bro-N	152	588	121	197	30	20	5	124	84	30	.335	.432	.480	185	58	62	138	31			12	*1	5.7
1893	Bro-N	77	282	57	95	21	11	2	59	52	10	.337	.450	.511	165	25	28	71	9			3	1	2.5
1894	*Bal-N	123	525	137	182	39	23	9	128	67	9	.347	.425	.560	132	32	27	145	38			-1	*1	2.1
1895	Bal-N	5	23	2	6	2	0	0	5	1	1	.261	.292	.348	64	-1	-1	2	0			0	/1	0.0
	Lou-N	24	97	13	30	10	1	2	15	11	2	.309	.380	.495	135	4	5	19	1			-2	1	0.2
	Yr	29	120	15	36	12	1	2	20	12	3	.300	.364	.467	121	2	3	21	1			-2		0.2
1896	Phi-N	57	218	42	75	13	3	1	41	44	11	.344	.462	.445	144	17	17	49	7			-3	1	1.3
1904	NY-N	2	5	0	0	0	0	0	0	0		.000	.000	.000	-96	-1	-1	0	0			0	/1	0.0
Total	19	1673	6711	1523	2296	460	205	106	1296	840	238	.342	.423	.519	171	648	632	1622	256			-15	*1/OP3	40.5

■ JOE BROVIA

Brovia, Joseph John "Ox"   b: 2/18/22, Davenport, Cal.   BL/TR, 6'3", 195 lbs.   Deb: 7/03/55

YEAR	TM/L	G	AB	R	H	2B	3B	HR	RBI	BB	SO	AVG	OBP	SLG	PRO+	BR	/A	RC	SB	CS	SBR	FR	POS	TPR
1955	Cin-N	21	18	0	2	0	0	0	4	1	6	.111	.158	.111	-25	-3	-3	0	0	0	0	0	H	-0.2

■ FRANK BROWER

Brower, Frank Willard "Turkeyfoot"   b: 3/26/1893, Gainesville, Va.   d: 11/20/60, Baltimore, Md.   BL/TR, 6'2", 180 lbs.   Deb: 8/14/20

YEAR	TM/L	G	AB	R	H	2B	3B	HR	RBI	BB	SO	AVG	OBP	SLG	PRO+	BR	/A	RC	SB	CS	SBR	FR	POS	TPR
1920	Was-A	36	119	21	37	7	2	1	13	9	11	.311	.374	.429	115	2	3	19	1	1	-0	-0	O/13	0.0
1921	Was-A	83	203	31	53	12	3	1	35	18	7	.261	.330	.365	81	-7	-6	25	1	1	-0	3	O/1	-0.5
1922	Was-A	139	471	61	138	20	6	9	71	52	25	.293	.375	.418	112	5	9	76	8	6	-1	-3	*O/1	-0.4
1923	Cle-A	126	397	77	113	25	8	16	66	62	32	.285	.392	.509	136	21	21	82	6	5	-1	-3	*1/O	1.1
1924	Cle-A	66	107	16	30	10	1	3	20	27	9	.280	.434	.477	133	7	7	24	1	1	-0	-1	1/PO	0.4
Total	5	450	1297	206	371	74	20	30	205	168	84	.286	.379	.443	117	28	33	227	17	14	-3	-4	O1/P3	0.6

■ LOUIS BROWER

Brower, Louis Lester   b: 7/1/1900, Cleveland, Ohio   BR/TR, 5'10", 155 lbs.   Deb: 6/13/31

YEAR	TM/L	G	AB	R	H	2B	3B	HR	RBI	BB	SO	AVG	OBP	SLG	PRO+	BR	/A	RC	SB	CS	SBR	FR	POS	TPR
1931	Det-A	21	62	3	10	1	0	0	6	8	5	.161	.278	.177	21	-7	-7	4	1	0	0	-7	S/2	-1.0

■ BOB BROWER

Brower, Robert Richard   b: 1/10/60, Jamaica, N.Y.   BR/TR, 5'11", 185 lbs.   Deb: 9/03/86

YEAR	TM/L	G	AB	R	H	2B	3B	HR	RBI	BB	SO	AVG	OBP	SLG	PRO+	BR	/A	RC	SB	CS	SBR	FR	POS	TPR
1986	Tex-A	21	9	3	1	1	0	0	0	2	1	.111	.111	.222	-12	-1	-1	-0	1	2	-1	1	O/D	0.0
1987	Tex-A	127	303	63	79	10	3	14	46	36	66	.261	.339	.452	107	3	3	47	15	9	-1	2	*O/D	0.1
1988	Tex-A	82	201	29	45	7	0	1	11	27	38	.224	.316	.274	65	-8	-9	18	10	5	0	1	OD	-0.8
1989	NY-A	26	69	9	16	3	0	2	3	6	11	.232	.293	.362	85	-2	-1	7	3	1	0	4	O	0.3

YEAR	TM/L	G	AB	R	H	2B	3B	HR	RBI	BB	SO	AVG	OBP	SLG	PRO+	BR	/A	RC	SB	CS	SBR	FR	POS	TPR
Total	4	256	582	104	141	21	3	17	60	69	118	.242	.323	.376	89	-8	-9	73	29	17	-2	8	O/D	-0.4

■ BROWN Brown Deb: 7/29/1874

YEAR	TM/L	G	AB	R	H	2B	3B	HR	RBI	BB	SO	AVG	OBP	SLG	PRO+	BR	/A	RC	SB	CS	SBR	FR	POS	TPR
1874	Bal-n	2	9	0	0	0	0	0		0		.000	.000	.000	-99	-2	-2	0					/S	-0.1

■ CURTIS BROWN Brown, Curtis b: 9/14/45, Sacramento, Cal. BR/TR, 5'11", 180 lbs. Deb: 5/27/73

YEAR	TM/L	G	AB	R	H	2B	3B	HR	RBI	BB	SO	AVG	OBP	SLG	PRO+	BR	/A	RC	SB	CS	SBR	FR	POS	TPR
1973	Mon-N	1	4	0	0	0	0	0	0	0	0	.000	.000	.000	-97	-1	-1	0	0	0	0	0	/O	0.0

■ DARRELL BROWN Brown, Darrell Wayne b: 10/29/55, Oklahoma City, Okla BB/TR, 6', 184 lbs. Deb: 4/11/81

YEAR	TM/L	G	AB	R	H	2B	3B	HR	RBI	BB	SO	AVG	OBP	SLG	PRO+	BR	/A	RC	SB	CS	SBR	FR	POS	TPR
1981	Det-A	16	4	4	1	0	0	0	0	0	1	.250	.250	.250	43	-0	-0	0	1	0	0	0	/OD	0.0
1982	Oak-A	8	18	2	6	0	1	0	3	1	2	.333	.368	.444	128	1	1	3	1	0	0	0	/OD	0.1
1983	Min-A	91	309	40	84	6	2	0	22	10	28	.272	.297	.304	64	-14	-16	26	3	3	-1	-7	O/D	-2.4
1984	Min-A	95	260	36	71	9	3	1	19	14	16	.273	.310	.342	77	-7	-8	27	4	1	1	5	OD	-0.4
Total	4	210	591	82	162	15	6	1	44	25	47	.274	.305	.325	71	-21	-24	57	9	4	0	-2	O/D	-2.7

■ DELOS BROWN Brown, Delos Hight b: 10/4/1892, Anna, Ill. d: 12/21/64, Carbondale, Ill. BR/TR, 5'9", 160 lbs. Deb: 6/12/14

YEAR	TM/L	G	AB	R	H	2B	3B	HR	RBI	BB	SO	AVG	OBP	SLG	PRO+	BR	/A	RC	SB	CS	SBR	FR	POS	TPR
1914	Chi-A	1	1	0	0	0	0	0	0	0	1	.000	.000	.000	-99	-0	-0	0	0			0	H	0.0

■ DRUMMOND BROWN Brown, Drummond Nicol b: 1/31/1885, Los Angeles, Cal. d: 1/27/27, Parkville, Mo. BR/TR, 6', 180 lbs. Deb: 4/25/13

YEAR	TM/L	G	AB	R	H	2B	3B	HR	RBI	BB	SO	AVG	OBP	SLG	PRO+	BR	/A	RC	SB	CS	SBR	FR	POS	TPR
1913	Bos-N	15	34	3	11	1	0	1	2	2	9	.324	.361	.441	126	1	1	5	0			-4	C	-0.1
1914	KC-F	31	58	4	11	3	0	0	5	7	6	.190	.277	.241	51	-4	-3	5	1			0	C/1	-0.1
1915	KC-F	77	227	13	55	10	1	1	26	12	23	.242	.289	.308	80	-7	-6	23	3			-20	C/1	-2.6
Total	3	123	319	20	77	14	1	2	33	21	38	.241	.294	.310	80	-9	-8	33	4			-24	C/1	-2.8

■ EARL BROWN Brown, Earl James "Snitz" b: 3/5/11, Louisville, Ky. BL/TL, 6', 175 lbs. Deb: 9/12/35

YEAR	TM/L	G	AB	R	H	2B	3B	HR	RBI	BB	SO	AVG	OBP	SLG	PRO+	BR	/A	RC	SB	CS	SBR	FR	POS	TPR
1935	Pit-N	9	32	6	8	2	0	0	6	2	8	.250	.294	.313	61	-2	-2	3	0			0	/1	-0.1
1936	Pit-N	8	23	7	7	1	2	0	3	1	4	.304	.333	.522	124	1	1	3	0			0	/O1	0.1
1937	Phi-N	105	332	42	97	19	3	6	52	21	41	.292	.342	.422	98	2	-1	48	4			2	O1	-0.2
1938	Phi-N	21	74	4	19	4	0	0	8	5	11	.257	.304	.311	71	-3	-3	7	0			-0	1/O	-0.4
Total	4	143	461	59	131	26	5	6	69	29	64	.284	.332	.401	93	-2	-5	60	4			2	/O1	-0.6

■ ED BROWN Brown, Edward P. b: Chicago, Ill. TR, Deb: 8/19/1882

YEAR	TM/L	G	AB	R	H	2B	3B	HR	RBI	BB	SO	AVG	OBP	SLG	PRO+	BR	/A	RC	SB	CS	SBR	FR	POS	TPR
1882	StL-a	17	60	4	11	0	0	0			4	.183	.234	.183	41	-3	-4	3				-2	O/2P	-0.5
1884	Tol-a	42	153	13	27	3	0	0			2	.176	.187	.196	26	-12	-12	6				-8	3/OCP	-1.8
Total	2	59	213	17	38	3	0	0			6	.178	.201	.192	30	-15	-16	8				-10	/3OP2C	-2.3

■ EDDIE BROWN Brown, Edward William "Glass Arm Eddie" b: 7/17/1891, Milligan, Neb. d: 9/10/56, Vallejo, Cal. BR/TR, 6'3", 190 lbs. Deb: 9/26/20

YEAR	TM/L	G	AB	R	H	2B	3B	HR	RBI	BB	SO	AVG	OBP	SLG	PRO+	BR	/A	RC	SB	CS	SBR	FR	POS	TPR
1920	NY-N	3	8	1	1	0	0	0	0	0	3	.125	.125	.125	6	-1	-1	0	0	0	0	0	/O	0.0
1921	NY-N	70	128	16	36	6	2	0	12	4	11	.281	.324	.359	80	-4	-4	15	1	0	0	1	O	-0.3
1924	Bro-N	114	455	56	140	30	4	5	78	26	15	.308	.345	.424	109	3	4	65	3	5	-2	0	*O	0.0
1925	Bro-N	153	618	88	189	39	11	5	99	22	18	.306	.332	.429	95	-8	-6	86	3	4	-2	5	*O	-0.5
1926	Bos-N	153	612	71	**201**	31	8	2	84	23	20	.328	.355	.415	117	5	12	86	5			7	*O	1.2
1927	Bos-N	155	558	64	171	35	6	2	75	28	20	.306	.340	.401	106	-3	3	73	11			-3	*O/1	-0.5
1928	Bos-N	142	523	45	140	28	2	2	59	24	22	.268	.305	.340	72	-25	-21	53	6			1	*O/1	-2.4
Total	7	790	2902	341	878	170	33	16	407	127	109	.303	.334	.400	99	-33	-12	379	29	9		11	O/1	-2.5

■ RANDY BROWN Brown, Edwin Randolph b: 8/29/44, Leesburg, Fla. BL/TR, 5'7", 170 lbs. Deb: 9/11/69

YEAR	TM/L	G	AB	R	H	2B	3B	HR	RBI	BB	SO	AVG	OBP	SLG	PRO+	BR	/A	RC	SB	CS	SBR	FR	POS	TPR
1969	Cal-A	13	25	3	4	1	0	0	0	6	1	.160	.323	.200	52	-1	-1	2	0	0	0	-1	C/O	-0.1
1970	Cal-A	5	4	0	0	0	0	0	0	0	0	.000	.000	.000	-99	-1	-1	0	0	0	0	0	/C	0.0
Total	2	18	29	3	4	1	0	0	0	6	1	.138	.286	.172	32	-3	-2	2	0	0	0	-1	/CO	-0.1

■ FRED BROWN Brown, Fred Herbert b: 4/12/1879, Ossipee, N.H. d: 2/3/55, Somersworth, N.H. BR/TR, 5'10.5", 190 lbs. Deb: 5/04/01

YEAR	TM/L	G	AB	R	H	2B	3B	HR	RBI	BB	SO	AVG	OBP	SLG	PRO+	BR	/A	RC	SB	CS	SBR	FR	POS	TPR
1901	Bos-N	7	14	1	2	0	0	0	2	0		.143	.143	.143	-15	-2	-2	0	0			0	/O	-0.2
1902	Bos-N	2	6	1	2	1	0	0	0	0		.333	.333	.500	157	0	0	1	0			0	/O	0.0
Total	2	9	20	2	4	1	0	0	2	0		.200	.200	.250	32	-2	-2	1	0			0	/O	-0.2

■ IKE BROWN Brown, Isaac b: 4/13/42, Memphis, Tenn. BR/TR, 6', 190 lbs. Deb: 6/17/69

YEAR	TM/L	G	AB	R	H	2B	3B	HR	RBI	BB	SO	AVG	OBP	SLG	PRO+	BR	/A	RC	SB	CS	SBR	FR	POS	TPR
1969	Det-A	70	170	24	39	4	3	5	12	26	43	.229	.338	.376	96	0	-1	21	2	3	-1	-5	23/OS	-0.4
1970	Det-A	56	94	17	27	5	0	4	15	13	26	.287	.380	.468	132	4	4	17	0	0	0	-3	2/O3	0.4
1971	Det-A	59	110	20	28	1	0	8	19	19	25	.255	.364	.482	133	6	5	19	0	1	-1	-0	1/O23S	0.3
1972	*Det-A	51	84	12	21	3	0	2	10	17	23	.250	.376	.357	115	3	2	11	1	2	-1	0	O1/2S3	0.5
1973	Det-A	42	76	12	22	2	1	1	9	15	13	.289	.407	.382	115	3	2	12	0	1	-1	0	1O/3D	0.1
1974	Det-A	2	2	0	0	0	0	0	0	0	0	.000	.000	.000	-97	-1	-1	0	0	0	0	0	/3	0.0
Total	6	280	536	85	137	15	4	20	65	90	130	.256	.366	.410	115	16	13	80	3	7	-3	-3	/2103SD	0.9

■ JIM BROWN Brown, James Donaldson "Don" or "Moose" b: 3/31/1897, Laurel, Md. BR/TR, 6', 178 lbs. Deb: 9/13/15

YEAR	TM/L	G	AB	R	H	2B	3B	HR	RBI	BB	SO	AVG	OBP	SLG	PRO+	BR	/A	RC	SB	CS	SBR	FR	POS	TPR
1915	StL-N	1	2	0	1	0	0	0	0	2	1	.500	.750	.500	281	1	1	1	0			-0	/O	0.1
1916	Phi-A	14	42	6	10	2	1	1	5	4	9	.238	.304	.405	118	0	1	6	0			-1	O	0.0
Total	2	15	44	6	11	2	1	1	5	6	10	.250	.340	.409	130	1	1	6	0			-1	/O	0.1

■ JIMMY BROWN Brown, James Roberson b: 4/25/10, Jamesville, N.C. d: 12/29/77, Bath, N.C. BB/TR, 5'8.5", 165 lbs. Deb: 4/23/37 C

YEAR	TM/L	G	AB	R	H	2B	3B	HR	RBI	BB	SO	AVG	OBP	SLG	PRO+	BR	/A	RC	SB	CS	SBR	FR	POS	TPR
1937	StL-N	138	525	86	145	20	9	2	53	27	29	.276	.313	.360	81	-13	-15	50	10			-14	*2S3	-2.1
1938	StL-N	108	382	50	115	12	6	0	38	27	9	.301	.350	.364	91	-1	-4	50	7			1	2S3	0.2
1939	StL-N	147	645	88	192	31	8	3	51	32	18	.298	.335	.384	87	-7	-12	83	4			-5	*S2	-0.8
1940	StL-N	107	454	56	127	17	4	0	30	24	15	.280	.317	.335	76	-12	-15	48	9			-22	23S	-3.2
1941	StL-N	132	549	81	168	28	9	3	56	45	22	.306	.363	.406	109	12	7	83	2			3	*32	1.2
1942	*StL-N	145	606	75	155	28	4	1	71	52	11	.256	.315	.320	80	-11	-16	63	4			-12	23S	-2.2
1943	StL-N	34	110	6	20	4	2	0	8	6	1	.182	.224	.255	37	-9	-10	7	0			2	2/3S	-0.6
1946	Pit-N	79	241	23	58	6	0	0	12	18	5	.241	.293	.266	58	-13	-13	18	3			-2	S2/3	-1.3
Total	8	890	3512	465	980	146	42	9	319	231	110	.279	.326	.352	84	-55	-78	411	39			-49	23S	-8.8

■ JIM BROWN Brown, James W. H. b: 12/12/1860, Clinton Co., Pa. d: 4/6/08, Williamsport, Pa. Deb: 4/17/1884

YEAR	TM/L	G	AB	R	H	2B	3B	HR	RBI	BB	SO	AVG	OBP	SLG	PRO+	BR	/A	RC	SB	CS	SBR	FR	POS	TPR
1884	Alt-U	21	88	12	22	2	2	1			1	.250	.258	.352	103	0	0	8	0			-3	OP	0.0
	NY-N	1	3	0	0	0	0	0	0	0	1	.000	.000	.000	-98	-1	-1	0	0			-0	/P	0.0
	StP-U	6	16	5	5	4	0	0			1	.313	.353	.563	378	2	3	3	0			0	/P1O	0.0
1886	Phi-a	1	3	0	0	0	0	0			0	.000	.000	.000	-99	-1	-1	0	0			0	/P	0.0
Total	2	29	110	17	27	6	2	1	0	2	1	.245	.259	.364	114	1	2	11	0			-3	/PO1	0.0

■ JAKE BROWN Brown, Jerald Ray b: 3/22/48, Sumrall, Miss. d: 12/18/81, Houston, Tex. BR/TR, 6'2", 200 lbs. Deb: 5/17/75

YEAR	TM/L	G	AB	R	H	2B	3B	HR	RBI	BB	SO	AVG	OBP	SLG	PRO+	BR	/A	RC	SB	CS	SBR	FR	POS	TPR
1975	SF-N	41	43	6	9	3	0	0	4	5	13	.209	.292	.279	57	-2	-3	4	0	0	0	0	O	-0.2

■ CHRIS BROWN Brown, John Christopher b: 8/15/61, Jackson, Miss. BR/TR, 6', 185 lbs. Deb: 9/03/84

YEAR	TM/L	G	AB	R	H	2B	3B	HR	RBI	BB	SO	AVG	OBP	SLG	PRO+	BR	/A	RC	SB	CS	SBR	FR	POS	TPR
1984	SF-N	23	84	6	24	7	0	1	11	9	19	.286	.362	.405	119	2	2	12	2	1	0	-2	3	0.0
1985	SF-N	131	432	50	117	20	3	16	61	38	78	.271	.345	.442	125	10	13	61	2	3	-1	5	*3	1.8
1986	SF-N	116	416	57	132	16	3	7	49	33	43	.317	.380	.421	127	12	15	65	13	9	-2	-14	*3/S	-0.2
1987	SF-N	38	132	17	32	6	0	6	17	9	16	.242	.306	.424	95	-2	-1	14	1	3	-2	-2	3/S	-0.4

YEAR	TM/L	G	AB	R	H	2B	3B	HR	RBI	BB	SO	AVG	OBP	SLG	PRO+	BR	/A	RC	SB	CS	SBR	FR	POS	TPR
	SD-N	44	155	17	36	3	0	6	23	11	30	.232	.296	.368	77	-6	-5	16	3	1	0	-4	3	-0.8
	Yr	82	287	34	68	9	0	12	40	20	46	.237	.300	.394	86	-8	-6	30	4	4	-1	-5		-1.2
1988	SD-N	80	247	14	58	6	0	2	19	19	49	.235	.297	.283	69	-10	-9	20	0	0	0	5	3	-0.4
1989	Det-A	17	57	3	11	3	0	0	4	1	17	.193	.207	.246	28	-6	-5	2	0	0	0	-1	3	-0.6
Total	6	449	1523	164	410	61	6	38	184	120	252	.269	.335	.392	105	1	9	190	21	17	-4	-12	3/S	-0.6

■ LINDSAY BROWN   Brown, John Lindsay "Red" b: 7/22/11, Mason, Tex. d: 1/1/67, San Antonio, Tex. BR/TR, 5'10", 160 lbs. Deb: 7/13/37

YEAR	TM/L	G	AB	R	H	2B	3B	HR	RBI	BB	SO	AVG	OBP	SLG	PRO+	BR	/A	RC	SB	CS	SBR	FR	POS	TPR
1937	Bro-N	48	115	16	31	3	1	0	6	3	17	.270	.288	.313	62	-6	-6	10	1			6	S	0.4

■ JOE BROWN   Brown, Joseph E. b: 4/4/1859, Warren, Pa. d: 6/28/1888, Warren, Pa. Deb: 8/16/1884

YEAR	TM/L	G	AB	R	H	2B	3B	HR	RBI	BB	SO	AVG	OBP	SLG	PRO+	BR	/A	RC	SB	CS	SBR	FR	POS	TPR
1884	Chi-N	15	61	6	13	1	0	0	3	0	15	.213	.213	.230	36	-4	-5	3				-1	/OP1C	-0.4
1885	Bal-a	5	19	2	3	0	0	0		0		.158	.158	.158	1	-2	-2	0				0	/P2	0.0
Total	2	20	80	8	16	1	0	0	3	0	15	.200	.200	.213	29	-6	-7	4				-1	/PO2C1	-0.4

■ LARRY BROWN   Brown, Larry Leslie b: 3/1/40, Shinnston, W.Va. BR/TR, 5'10", 160 lbs. Deb: 7/06/63

YEAR	TM/L	G	AB	R	H	2B	3B	HR	RBI	BB	SO	AVG	OBP	SLG	PRO+	BR	/A	RC	SB	CS	SBR	FR	POS	TPR
1963	Cle-A	74	247	28	63	6	0	5	18	22	27	.255	.319	.340	85	-5	-5	27	4	3	-1	-8	S2	-0.9
1964	Cle-A	115	335	33	77	12	1	12	40	24	55	.230	.285	.379	84	-8	-8	34	1	2	-1	11	*2/S	1.3
1965	Cle-A	124	438	52	111	22	2	8	40	38	62	.253	.316	.368	93	-4	-4	51	5	7	-3	3	S2	0.2
1966	Cle-A	105	340	29	78	12	0	3	17	36	58	.229	.309	.291	73	-11	-11	30	0	1	-1	-4	S2	-0.9
1967	Cle-A	152	485	38	110	16	2	7	37	53	62	.227	.311	.311	84	-9	-9	48	4	4	-1	1	*S	0.2
1968	Cle-A	154	495	43	116	18	3	6	35	43	46	.234	.302	.319	90	-7	-6	47	1	1	-0	-14	*S	-1.0
1969	Cle-A	132	469	48	112	10	2	4	24	44	43	.239	.305	.294	66	-19	-21	43	5	3	-0	-17	*S3/2	-3.5
1970	Cle-A	72	155	17	40	5	2	0	15	20	14	.258	.343	.316	79	-3	-4	17	1	0	0	-2	S32	-0.1
1971	Cle-A	13	50	4	11	1	0	0	5	3	3	.220	.278	.240	44	-3	-4	3	0	0	0	-6	S	-0.8
	Oak-A	70	189	14	37	2	1	1	9	7	19	.196	.228	.233	31	-17	-17	9	1	2	-1	4	S23	-1.0
	Yr	83	239	18	48	3	1	1	14	10	22	.201	.239	.234	35	-21	-21	12	1	2	-1	-2		-1.8
1972	Oak-A	47	142	11	26	2	0	0	4	13	8	.183	.252	.197	37	-11	-10	6	0	0	0	-8	2/3	-1.7
1973	*Bal-A	17	28	4	7	0	0	1	5	5	4	.250	.364	.357	104	0	0	4	0	0	0	-2	3/2	-0.1
1974	Tex-A	54	76	10	15	2	0	0	5	9	13	.197	.282	.224	48	-5	-5	4	0	0	0	8	3/2S	0.4
Total	12	1129	3449	331	803	108	13	47	254	317	414	.233	.301	.313	76	-102	-103	324	22	23	-7	-33	S23	-7.9

■ LEON BROWN   Brown, Leon b: 11/16/49, Sacramento, Cal. BR/TR, 6', 185 lbs. Deb: 5/19/76

YEAR	TM/L	G	AB	R	H	2B	3B	HR	RBI	BB	SO	AVG	OBP	SLG	PRO+	BR	/A	RC	SB	CS	SBR	FR	POS	TPR
1976	NY-N	64	70	11	15	3	0	0	2	4	4	.214	.257	.257	49	-5	-5	3	2	4	-2	6	O	-0.1

■ LEW BROWN   Brown, Lewis J. "Blower" b: 2/1/1858, Leominster, Mass. d: 1/16/1889, Boston, Mass. BR/TR, 5'10.5", 185 lbs. Deb: 6/17/1876

YEAR	TM/L	G	AB	R	H	2B	3B	HR	RBI	BB	SO	AVG	OBP	SLG	PRO+	BR	/A	RC	SB	CS	SBR	FR	POS	TPR
1876	Bos-N	45	195	23	41	6	6	2	21	3	22	.210	.222	.333	82	-3	-4	15				-2	C/O	-0.3
1877	Bos-N	58	221	27	56	12	8	1	31	6	33	.253	.273	.394	104	2	2	24				13	*C/1	1.3
1878	Pro-N	58	243	44	74	21	6	1	43	7	37	.305	.324	.453	153	13	13	37				3	*C1/OP	1.7
1879	Pro-N	53	229	23	59	13	4	2	38	4	24	.258	.270	.376	112	2	3	24				-6	C/O	-0.2
	Chi-N	6	21	2	6	1	0	0	3	1	4	.286	.318	.333	109	0	0	2				0	/1M	0.0
	Yr	59	250	25	65	14	4	2	41	5	28	.260	.275	.372	112	3	3	26				-6		-0.2
1881	Det-N	27	108	16	26	3	1	3	14	3	16	.241	.261	.370	93	-1	-1	11				-0	1	-0.4
	Pro-N	18	75	9	18	3	1	0	10	4	13	.240	.278	.307	85	-1	-1	7				-4	O/1	-0.5
	Yr	45	183	25	44	6	2	3	24	7	29	.240	.268	.344	90	-2	-2	17				-4		-0.9
1883	Bos-N	14	54	5	13	4	1	0	9	3	6	.241	.281	.352	89	-1	-1	5				-2	1	-0.3
	Lou-a	14	60	6	11	2	1	0		1		.183	.197	.250	46	-4	-3	3				-1	1/C	-0.3
1884	Bos-U	85	325	50	75	18	3	1		13		.231	.260	.314	95	-2	-1	27	0			12	C1/OP	1.1
Total	7	378	1531	205	379	83	31	10	169	45	155	.248	.269	.362	104	6	6	155	0			13	C1/OP	2.0

■ MARTY BROWN   Brown, Marty Leo b: 1/23/63, Lawton, Okla. BR/TR, 6'1", 190 lbs. Deb: 9/04/88

YEAR	TM/L	G	AB	R	H	2B	3B	HR	RBI	BB	SO	AVG	OBP	SLG	PRO+	BR	/A	RC	SB	CS	SBR	FR	POS	TPR
1988	Cin-N	10	16	0	3	1	0	0	2	1	2	.188	.235	.250	38	-1	-1	1	0	1	-1	1	/3	0.0
1989	Cin-N	16	30	2	5	1	0	0	4	4	9	.167	.265	.200	34	-2	-3	2	0	0	0	2	3	0.0
1990	Bal-A	9	15	1	3	0	0	0	0	1	7	.200	.250	.200	28	-1	-1	1	0	0	0	0	/23D	0.0
Total	3	35	61	3	11	2	0	0	6	6	18	.180	.254	.213	33	-5	-5	3	0	1	-1	3	/3D2	0.0

■ MIKE BROWN   Brown, Michael Charles b: 12/29/59, San Francisco, Cal. BR/TR, 6'2", 195 lbs. Deb: 7/21/83

YEAR	TM/L	G	AB	R	H	2B	3B	HR	RBI	BB	SO	AVG	OBP	SLG	PRO+	BR	/A	RC	SB	CS	SBR	FR	POS	TPR
1983	Cal-A	31	104	12	24	5	1	3	9	7	20	.231	.279	.385	81	-3	-3	11	1	0	0	-1	O	-0.3
1984	Cal-A	62	148	19	42	8	3	7	22	13	23	.284	.342	.520	136	6	7	22	0	2	-1	-2	O/D	0.2
1985	Cal-A	60	153	23	41	9	1	4	20	7	21	.268	.304	.418	96	-1	-1	16	0	1	-1	1	O/D	0.0
	Pit-N	57	205	29	68	18	2	5	33	22	27	.332	.396	.512	154	14	15	40	2	2	-1	-6	O	0.6
1986	Pit-N	87	243	18	53	7	0	4	26	27	32	.218	.296	.296	62	-12	-12	20	2	3	-1	-4	O	-1.9
1988	Cal-A	18	50	4	11	2	0	0	3	1	12	.220	.235	.260	40	-4	-4	3	0	0	0	0	O	-0.3
Total	5	315	903	105	239	49	7	23	113	77	135	.265	.323	.411	102	1	1	112	5	8	-3	-13	O/D	-1.7

■ OLIVER BROWN   Brown, Oliver S. b: 1849, Brooklyn, N.Y. d: 9/23/32, Brooklyn, N.Y. Deb: 8/01/1872

YEAR	TM/L	G	AB	R	H	2B	3B	HR	RBI	BB	SO	AVG	OBP	SLG	PRO+	BR	/A	RC	SB	CS	SBR	FR	POS	TPR
1872	Atl-n	4	16	0	1	0	0	0		0		.063	.063	.063	-52	-3	-3	0					/O	-0.1
1875	Atl-n	3	10	0	0	0	0	0		0		.000	.000	.000	-99	-2	-2	0					/1	-0.1
Total	2 n	7	26	0	1	0	0	0		0		.038	.038	.038	-71	-5	-5	0					/O1	-0.2

■ OLLIE BROWN   Brown, Ollie Lee "Downtown" b: 2/11/44, Tuscaloosa, Ala. BR/TR, 6'2", 178 lbs. Deb: 9/10/65

YEAR	TM/L	G	AB	R	H	2B	3B	HR	RBI	BB	SO	AVG	OBP	SLG	PRO+	BR	/A	RC	SB	CS	SBR	FR	POS	TPR
1965	SF-N	6	10	0	2	1	0	0	0	0	2	.200	.200	.300	38	-1	-1	1	0	0	0	0	/O	0.0
1966	SF-N	115	348	32	81	7	1	7	33	33	66	.233	.303	.319	71	-12	-13	30	2	5	-2	-2	*O	-2.2
1967	SF-N	120	412	44	110	12	1	13	53	25	65	.267	.315	.396	104	1	1	47	0	2	-1	-4	*O	-0.9
1968	SF-N	40	95	7	22	4	0	0	11	3	23	.232	.270	.274	64	-4	-4	7	1	0	0	-3	O	-0.9
1969	SD-N	151	568	76	150	18	3	20	61	44	97	.264	.320	.412	108	2	4	73	10	6	-1	5	*O	0.0
1970	SD-N	139	534	79	156	34	1	23	89	34	78	.292	.335	.489	123	11	14	82	5	3	-0	4	*O	1.1
1971	SD-N	145	484	36	132	16	0	9	55	52	74	.273	.347	.362	108	2	5	61	3	3	-1	3	*O	0.3
1972	SD-N	23	70	3	12	2	0	0	3	5	9	.171	.227	.200	24	-7	-7	3	0	0	0	0	O	-0.7
	Oak-A	20	54	5	13	1	0	1	4	6	14	.241	.317	.315	93	-1	-0	6	1	1	-0	-0	O	-0.1
	Mil-A	66	179	21	50	8	0	3	25	17	24	.279	.345	.374	116	3	4	20	0	2	-1	7	O/3	0.9
	Yr	86	233	26	63	9	0	4	29	23	38	.270	.339	.361	111	3	3	26	1	3	-2	6		0.8
1973	Mil-A	97	296	28	83	10	1	7	32	33	53	.280	.356	.392	113	5	5	42	4	1	1	0	D/O	0.6
1974	Hou-N	27	69	8	15	1	0	3	6	4	15	.217	.260	.362	76	-3	-3	6	0	0	0	0	O	-0.2
	Phi-N	43	99	11	24	5	2	4	13	6	20	.242	.286	.455	101	-0	-1	11	0	1	-1	-4	O	-0.6
	Yr	70	168	19	39	6	2	7	19	10	35	.232	.275	.417	91	-3	-4	17	0	1	-1	-4		-0.8
1975	Phi-N	84	145	19	44	12	1	6	26	15	33	.303	.369	.510	137	8	7	28	1	1	-0	-2	O	0.2
1976	*Phi-N	92	209	30	53	10	1	5	30	33	33	.254	.355	.383	106	3	3	31	2	1	0	-0	O	0.0
1977	*Phi-N	53	70	5	17	3	1	1	13	4	14	.243	.284	.357	68	-3	-3	6	1	1	-0	-1	O	-0.4
Total	13	1221	3642	404	964	144	11	102	454	314	616	.265	.326	.394	103	3	11	455	30	27	-7	2	O/D3	-2.9

■ OSCAR BROWN   Brown, Oscar Lee b: 2/8/46, Long Beach, Cal. BR/TR, 6', 175 lbs. Deb: 9/03/69

YEAR	TM/L	G	AB	R	H	2B	3B	HR	RBI	BB	SO	AVG	OBP	SLG	PRO+	BR	/A	RC	SB	CS	SBR	FR	POS	TPR
1969	Atl-N	7	4	2	1	0	0	0	0	0	0	.250	.250	.250	40	-0	-0	0	0	0	0	0	/O	0.0
1970	Atl-N	28	47	6	18	2	1	1	7	7	7	.383	.473	.532	159	5	5	11	0	2	-1	-1	O	0.1
1971	Atl-N	27	43	4	9	4	0	0	5	3	8	.209	.261	.302	56	-2	-3	4	0	0	0	1	O	-0.1
1972	Atl-N	76	164	19	37	5	1	3	16	4	29	.226	.244	.323	55	-9	-11	11	0	2	-1	4	O	-1.1

YEAR	TM/L	G	AB	R	H	2B	3B	HR	RBI	BB	SO	AVG	OBP	SLG	PRO+	BR	/A	RC	SB	CS	SBR	FR	POS	TPR
1973	Atl-N	22	58	3	12	3	0	0	0	3	10	.207	.246	.259	37	-5	-5	4	0	0	0	1	O	-0.4
Total	5	160	316	34	77	14	2	4	28	17	55	.244	.284	.339	68	-11	-14	30	0	4	-2	5	O	-1.5

■ DICK BROWN
Brown, Richard Ernest   b: 1/17/35, Shinnston, W.Va.   d: 4/17/70, Baltimore, Md.   BR/TR, 6'2", 176 lbs.   Deb: 6/20/57

YEAR	TM/L	G	AB	R	H	2B	3B	HR	RBI	BB	SO	AVG	OBP	SLG	PRO+	BR	/A	RC	SB	CS	SBR	FR	POS	TPR
1957	Cle-A	34	114	10	30	4	0	4	22	4	23	.263	.288	.404	88	-3	-2	13	1	1	-0	1	C	0.0
1958	Cle-A	68	173	20	41	5	0	7	20	14	27	.237	.305	.387	91	-3	-2	21	1	0	0	8	C	0.6
1959	Cle-A	48	141	15	31	7	0	5	16	11	39	.220	.290	.376	85	-4	-3	16	0	0	0	3	C	0.2
1960	Chi-A	16	43	4	7	0	0	3	5	3	11	.163	.217	.372	57	-3	-3	3	0	0	0	3	C	0.1
1961	Det-A	93	308	32	82	12	2	16	45	22	57	.266	.315	.474	105	2	1	42	0	2	-1	-1	C	-0.1
1962	Det-A	134	431	40	104	12	0	12	40	21	66	.241	.280	.353	67	-20	-22	40	0	1	-1	2	*C	-1.3
1963	Bal-A	59	171	13	42	7	0	2	13	15	35	.246	.310	.322	79	-5	-4	18	1	0	0	6	C	0.3
1964	Bal-A	88	230	24	59	6	0	8	32	12	45	.257	.296	.387	89	-4	-4	24	2	0	1	4	C	0.4
1965	Bal-A	96	255	17	59	9	1	5	30	17	53	.231	.282	.333	73	-9	-9	22	2	2	-1	9	C	0.6
Total	9	636	1866	175	455	62	3	62	223	119	356	.244	.293	.380	82	-48	-49	199	7	6	-2	34	C	0.8

■ BOBBY BROWN
Brown, Robert William "Doc"   b: 10/25/24, Seattle, Wash.   BL/TR, 6'1", 180 lbs.   Deb: 9/22/46

YEAR	TM/L	G	AB	R	H	2B	3B	HR	RBI	BB	SO	AVG	OBP	SLG	PRO+	BR	/A	RC	SB	CS	SBR	FR	POS	TPR
1946	NY-A	7	24	1	8	1	0	0	1	4	0	.333	.429	.375	124	1	1	4	0	0	0	-3	/S3	-0.1
1947	*NY-A	69	150	21	45	6	1	1	18	21	9	.300	.390	.373	114	3	4	23	0	2	-1	-10	3S/O	-0.7
1948	NY-A	113	363	62	109	19	5	3	48	48	16	.300	.383	.405	111	6	6	60	0	1	-1	-18	3S2/O	-1.2
1949	*NY-A	104	343	61	97	14	4	6	61	38	18	.283	.359	.399	101	-0	-0	50	4	3	-1	-4	3/O	-0.4
1950	*NY-A	95	277	33	74	4	2	4	37	39	18	.267	.360	.339	82	-8	-6	35	3	1	0	-4	3	-1.1
1951	*NY-A	103	313	44	84	15	2	6	51	47	18	.268	.369	.387	108	3	5	49	1	1	-0	-5	3	-0.3
1952	NY-A	29	89	6	22	2	0	1	14	9	6	.247	.323	.303	80	-3	-2	9	1	1	-0	3	3	0.0
1954	NY-A	28	60	5	13	1	0	1	7	8	3	.217	.309	.283	65	-3	-3	5	0	1	-1	-0	3	-0.4
Total	8	548	1619	233	452	62	14	22	237	214	88	.279	.367	.376	100	-0	4	234	9	10	-3	-40	3/S2O	-4.2

■ BOBBY BROWN
Brown, Rogers Lee   b: 5/24/54, Norfolk, Va.   BB/TR, 6'2", 190 lbs.   Deb: 4/05/79

YEAR	TM/L	G	AB	R	H	2B	3B	HR	RBI	BB	SO	AVG	OBP	SLG	PRO+	BR	/A	RC	SB	CS	SBR	FR	POS	TPR
1979	Tor-A	4	10	1	0	0	0	0	0	2	1	.000	.167	.000	-50	-2	-2	0	0	0	0	0	/O	-0.1
	NY-A	30	68	7	17	3	1	0	3	2	17	.250	.271	.324	61	-4	-4	6	2	1	0	2	O	-0.2
	Yr	34	78	8	17	3	1	0	3	4	18	.218	.256	.282	46	-6	-6	6	2	1	0	2		-0.3
1980	*NY-A	137	412	65	107	12	5	14	47	29	82	.260	.308	.415	98	-3	-2	52	27	8	3	4	*O/D	0.2
1981	*NY-A	31	62	5	14	1	0	0	6	5	15	.226	.284	.242	53	-4	-4	5	4	2	0	4	O/D	0.0
1982	Sea-A	79	245	29	59	7	1	4	17	17	32	.241	.290	.327	67	-10	-11	25	28	6	5	3	O/D	-0.5
1983	SD-N	57	225	40	60	5	3	5	22	23	38	.267	.335	.342	102	-1	0	31	27	9	3	-6	O	-0.3
1984	*SD-N	85	171	28	43	7	2	3	29	11	33	.251	.297	.368	86	-4	-4	18	16	4	2	2	O	0.0
1985	SD-N	79	84	8	13	3	0	0	6	5	20	.155	.202	.190	11	-10	-10	3	6	4	-1	1	O	-1.0
Total	7	502	1277	183	313	38	12	26	130	94	238	.245	.297	.355	80	-37	-36	140	110	34	13	10	O/D	-1.9

■ SAM BROWN
Brown, Samuel Wakefield   b: 5/21/1878, Webster, Pa.   d: 11/8/31, Mount Pleasant, Pa.   BR/TR,   Deb: 4/21/06

YEAR	TM/L	G	AB	R	H	2B	3B	HR	RBI	BB	SO	AVG	OBP	SLG	PRO+	BR	/A	RC	SB	CS	SBR	FR	POS	TPR
1906	Bos-N	71	231	12	48	6	1	0	20	13		.208	.250	.242	57	-12	-11	16	4			-0	C03/12	-1.0
1907	Bos-N	70	208	17	40	6	0	0	14	12		.192	.236	.221	45	-13	-13	12	0			7	C/1	0.0
Total	2	141	439	29	88	12	1	0	34	25		.200	.244	.232	51	-25	-24	28	4			7	/CO312	-1.0

■ TOMMY BROWN
Brown, Thomas Michael "Buckshot"   b: 12/6/27, Brooklyn, N.Y.   BR/TR, 6'1", 170 lbs.   Deb: 8/03/44

YEAR	TM/L	G	AB	R	H	2B	3B	HR	RBI	BB	SO	AVG	OBP	SLG	PRO+	BR	/A	RC	SB	CS	SBR	FR	POS	TPR
1944	Bro-N	46	146	17	24	4	0	0	8	8	17	.164	.208	.192	13	-17	-16	6	0			-9	S	-2.0
1945	Bro-N	57	196	13	48	3	4	2	19	6	16	.245	.267	.332	66	-10	-10	17	3			-4	S/O	-0.7
1947	Bro-N	15	34	3	8	1	0	0	2	1	6	.235	.257	.265	37	-3	-3	2	0			2	/3OS	0.0
1948	Bro-N	54	145	18	35	4	0	2	20	7	17	.241	.281	.310	58	-8	-9	12	1			-1	3/1	-1.0
1949	*Bro-N	41	89	14	27	2	0	3	18	6	8	.303	.347	.427	102	1	0	13	0			1	O	0.0
1950	Bro-N	48	86	15	25	2	1	8	20	1	9	.291	.378	.616	153	7	6	19	0			0	O	0.6
1951	Bro-N	11	25	2	4	2	0	0	1	2	4	.160	.222	.240	24	-3	-3	1	0	0	0	0	/O	-0.2
	Phi-N	78	196	24	43	2	1	10	32	15	21	.219	.278	.393	80	-7	-6	19	1	2	-1	-8	O21/3	-1.5
	Yr	89	221	26	47	4	1	10	33	17	25	.213	.272	.376	73	-9	-9	21	1	2	-1	-8		-1.7
1952	Phi-N	18	25	2	4	1	0	1	2	4	3	.160	.276	.320	65	-1	-1	3	0	0	0	0	/1O	-1.0
	Chi-N	61	200	24	64	11	0	3	24	12	24	.320	.358	.420	114	4	4	29	1	2	-1	-19	S2/1	-1.5
	Yr	79	225	26	68	12	0	4	26	16	27	.302	.349	.409	109	3	2	32	1	2	-1	-19		-1.5
1953	Chi-N	65	138	19	27	7	1	2	13	13	17	.196	.279	.304	51	-10	-10	11	1	0	0	-5	S/O	-1.2
Total	9	494	1280	151	309	39	7	31	159	85	142	.241	.292	.355	74	-47	-48	132	7	4		-43	S/O321	-7.5

■ TOM BROWN
Brown, Thomas T.   b: 9/21/1860, Liverpool, England   d: 10/25/27, Washington, D.C.   BL/TR, 5'10", 168 lbs.   Deb: 7/06/1882   MU

YEAR	TM/L	G	AB	R	H	2B	3B	HR	RBI	BB	SO	AVG	OBP	SLG	PRO+	BR	/A	RC	SB	CS	SBR	FR	POS	TPR
1882	Bal-a	45	181	30	55	5	2	1		6		.304	.326	.370	146	6	8	22				0	O/P	0.7
1883	Col-a	97	420	69	115	12	7	5		20		.274	.307	.371	128	8	13	49				-2	*O/P	1.1
1884	Col-a	107	451	93	123	9	11	5		24		.273	.315	.375	138	13	19	55				-6	*O/P	1.1
1885	Pit-a	108	437	81	134	16	12	4		34		.307	.366	.426	155	26	27	70				-3	*O/P	1.7
1886	Pit-a	115	460	106	131	11	11	1		56		.285	.365	.363	131	18	18	74	30			6	*O/P	1.8
1887	Pit-N	47	192	30	47	3	4	0	6	11	40	.245	.289	.302	70	-9	-7	21	12			3	O	-0.1
	Ind-N	36	140	20	25	3	0	2	9	8	25	.179	.228	.243	33	-13	-12	11	13			-1	O	-1.0
	Yr	83	332	50	72	6	4	2	15	19	65	.217	.263	.277	54	-21	-18	32	25			2		-1.1
1888	Bos-N	107	420	62	104	10	7	9	49	30	68	.248	.299	.369	112	7	6	62	46			-4	*O	0.1
1889	Bos-N	90	362	93	84	10	5	2	24	59	56	.232	.341	.304	78	-6	-10	61	63			2	*O	-0.9
1890	Bos-P	128	543	146	150	23	14	4	61	86	84	.276	.378	.392	101	8	1	113	79			4	*O	0.0
1891	Bos-a	137	589	177	189	30	21	5	71	70	96	.321	.397	.469	153	38	39	155	106			-10	*O	2.0
1892	Lou-N	153	660	105	150	16	8	2	45	47	94	.227	.284	.285	80	-21	-13	77	78			19	*O	0.0
1893	Lou-N	122	529	104	127	15	7	5	54	56	63	.240	.319	.323	78	-21	-13	77	66			27	*O	0.7
1894	Lou-N	129	536	122	136	22	14	9	57	60	73	.254	.332	.397	82	-22	-14	95	66			3	*O	-1.5
1895	StL-N	83	350	72	76	11	4	1	31	48	44	.217	.315	.280	57	-22	-21	43	34			8	O	-1.5
	Was-N	34	134	25	32	8	3	2	16	18	16	.239	.329	.388	87	-3	-3	20	8			-7	O	-0.9
	Yr	117	484	97	108	19	7	3	47	66	60	.223	.319	.310	65	-25	-23	63	42			2		-2.4
1896	Was-N	116	435	87	128	17	6	2	59	58	49	.294	.385	.375	103	4	4	75	28			-5	*O	-0.7
1897	Was-N	116	469	91	137	17	2	5	45	52		.292	.364	.369	96	-1	-1	74	25			1	*O	-0.7
1898	Was-N	16	55	8	9	1	0	0	2	5		.164	.233	.182	21	-5	-5	3	3			0	O/M	-0.5
Total	17	1786	7363	1521	1952	239	138	64	529	748	708	.265	.337	.361	103	6	37	1157	657			37	*O/P	1.4

■ TOM BROWN
Brown, Thomas William   b: 12/12/40, Laureldale, Pa.   BB/TL, 6'1", 190 lbs.   Deb: 4/08/63

YEAR	TM/L	G	AB	R	H	2B	3B	HR	RBI	BB	SO	AVG	OBP	SLG	PRO+	BR	/A	RC	SB	CS	SBR	FR	POS	TPR
1963	Was-A	61	116	8	17	4	0	1	4	11	45	.147	.227	.207	23	-12	-12	6	2	1	0	-1	O1	-1.4

■ WILLARD BROWN
Brown, Willard "Big Bill" or "California"   b: 1866, San Francisco, Cal.   d: 12/20/1897, San Francisco, Cal   BR/TR, 6'2", 190 lbs.   Deb: 5/10/1887

YEAR	TM/L	G	AB	R	H	2B	3B	HR	RBI	BB	SO	AVG	OBP	SLG	PRO+	BR	/A	RC	SB	CS	SBR	FR	POS	TPR
1887	NY-N	49	170	17	37	3	2	0	25	10	15	.218	.273	.259	52	-11	-10	15	10			4	C/3O	0.0
1888	*NY-N	20	59	4	16	1	0	0	6	1	8	.271	.283	.288	86	-1	-1	5	1			7	C	0.6
1889	*NY-N	40	139	16	36	10	0	1	29	9	9	.259	.318	.353	88	-2	-2	18	6			-4	C/O	-0.5
1890	NY-P	60	230	47	64	8	4	4	43	13	13	.278	.320	.400	86	-3	-7	32	5			-17	CO/132	-1.8
1891	Phi-N	115	440	62	107	20	4	0	50	34	35	.243	.303	.306	86	-11	-13	44	7			6	*1C/O	-0.7
1893	Bal-N	7	32	5	4	3	0	0	5	1	3	.125	.152	.219	-1	-5	-5	1	0			-0	/1	-0.3
	Lou-N	111	461	80	140	23	7	1	85	50	32	.304	.373	.390	114	4	10	72	9			-2	*1/C	0.7

YEAR	TM/L	G	AB	R	H	2B	3B	HR	RBI	BB	SO	AVG	OBP	SLG	PRO+	BR	/A	RC	SB	CS	SBR	FR	POS	TPR
	Yr	118	493	85	144	26	7	1	90	51	35	.292	.360	.379	106	-1	5	72	9			-2		0.4
1894	Lou-N	13	48	5	10	2	0	0	9	5	7	.208	.283	.250	33	-5	-5	4	1			4	1	0.0
	StL-N	3	9	0	1	0	0	0	0	0	2	.111	.111	.111	-46	-2	-2	0	0			0	/1	0.0
	Yr	16	57	5	11	2	0	0	9	5	9	.193	.258	.228	20	-7	-7	4	1			4		0.0
Total	7	418	1589	236	415	70	17	6	252	123	124	.261	.319	.338	84	-37	-34	191	39			-3	1C/O32	-2.0

■ WILLARD BROWN
Brown, Willard Jessie b: 6/26/15, Shreveport, La. BR/TR, 5'11.5", 200 lbs. Deb: 7/19/47

YEAR	TM/L	G	AB	R	H	2B	3B	HR	RBI	BB	SO	AVG	OBP	SLG	PRO+	BR	/A	RC	SB	CS	SBR	FR	POS	TPR
1947	StL-A	21	67	4	12	3	0	1	6	0	7	.179	.179	.269	23	-7	-7	2	2	2	-1	2	O	-0.6

■ GATES BROWN
Brown, William James b: 5/2/39, Crestline, O. BL/TR, 5'11", 220 lbs. Deb: 6/19/63 C

YEAR	TM/L	G	AB	R	H	2B	3B	HR	RBI	BB	SO	AVG	OBP	SLG	PRO+	BR	/A	RC	SB	CS	SBR	FR	POS	TPR
1963	Det-A	55	82	16	22	3	1	2	14	8	13	.268	.341	.402	104	1	1	11	2	1	0	4	O	0.4
1964	Det-A	123	426	65	116	22	6	15	54	31	53	.272	.328	.458	114	8	7	64	11	4	1	3	*O	0.8
1965	Det-A	96	227	33	58	14	2	10	43	17	33	.256	.307	.467	115	4	4	34	6	0	2	1	O	0.5
1966	Det-A	88	169	27	45	5	1	7	27	18	19	.266	.344	.432	119	5	4	26	3	0	1	-3	O	0.1
1967	Det-A	51	91	17	17	1	1	2	9	13	15	.187	.288	.286	68	-3	-3	8	0	0	0	-2	O	-0.6
1968	*Det-A	67	92	15	34	7	2	6	15	12	4	.370	.442	.685	231	15	15	28	0	0	0	-1	O/1	1.5
1969	Det-A	60	93	13	19	1	2	1	6	5	17	.204	.253	.290	49	-6	-7	7	0	0	0	0	O	-0.6
1970	Det-A	81	124	18	28	3	0	3	24	20	14	.226	.338	.323	82	-2	-2	15	0	0	0	-2	O	-0.4
1971	Det-A	82	195	37	66	2	3	11	29	21	17	.338	.408	.549	163	18	17	44	4	2	0	-6	O	1.0
1972	*Det-A	103	252	33	58	5	0	10	31	26	28	.230	.307	.369	97	-0	-1	29	3	0	1	-0	O	-0.2
1973	Det-A	125	377	48	89	11	1	12	50	52	41	.236	.330	.366	90	-1	-5	44	1	1	-0	0	*D/O	-0.4
1974	Det-A	73	99	7	24	2	0	4	17	10	15	.242	.312	.384	96	-0	-1	12	0	0	0	0	D	0.0
1975	Det-A	47	35	1	6	2	0	1	3	9	6	.171	.356	.314	87	-0	-0	4	0	0	0	0	H	0.0
Total	13	1051	2262	330	582	78	19	84	322	242	275	.257	.333	.420	109	37	28	324	30	8	4	-5	OD/1	2.1

■ BILL BROWN
Brown, William Verna "Verna" b: 7/8/1893, Coleman, Tex. d: 5/13/65, Lubbock, Tex. BL/TL, 5'8", 185 lbs. Deb: 8/15/12

YEAR	TM/L	G	AB	R	H	2B	3B	HR	RBI	BB	SO	AVG	OBP	SLG	PRO+	BR	/A	RC	SB	CS	SBR	FR	POS	TPR
1912	StL-A	9	20	0	4	0	0	0	1	0		.200	.200	.200	15	-2	-2	1	0			-1	/O	-0.3

■ BYRON BROWNE
Browne, Byron Ellis b: 12/27/42, St.Joseph, Mo. BR/TR, 6'2", 190 lbs. Deb: 9/09/65

YEAR	TM/L	G	AB	R	H	2B	3B	HR	RBI	BB	SO	AVG	OBP	SLG	PRO+	BR	/A	RC	SB	CS	SBR	FR	POS	TPR
1965	Chi-N	4	6	0	0	0	0	0	0	0	2	.000	.000	.000	-98	-2	-2	0	0	0	0	-0	/O	-0.1
1966	Chi-N	120	419	46	102	15	7	16	51	40	143	.243	.317	.427	103	2	2	57	3	3	-1	-3	*O	-0.5
1967	Chi-N	10	19	3	3	2	0	0	2	4	5	.158	.304	.263	61	-1	-1	2	1	1	-0	0	/O	-0.1
1968	Hou-N	10	13	0	3	0	0	0	1	4	6	.231	.412	.231	99	0	0	1	0	0	0	2	/O	0.2
1969	StL-N	22	53	9	12	0	1	1	7	11	14	.226	.359	.321	92	0	-0	6	0	0	0	4	O	0.3
1970	Phi-N	104	270	29	67	17	2	10	36	33	72	.248	.330	.437	107	1	2	36	1	2	-1	-3	O	-0.5
1971	Phi-N	58	68	5	14	3	0	3	5	8	23	.206	.289	.382	89	-1	-1	8	0	0	0	-1	O	-0.3
1972	Phi-N	21	21	2	4	0	0	0	0	1	8	.190	.227	.190	19	-2	-2	1	0	0	0	-1	O	-0.3
Total	8	349	869	94	205	37	10	30	102	101	273	.236	.319	.405	98	-2	-2	111	5	6	-2	-2	O	-1.3

■ GEORGE BROWNE
Browne, George Edward b: 1/12/1876, Richmond, Va. d: 12/9/20, Hyde Park, N.Y. BL/TR, 5'10.5", 160 lbs. Deb: 9/27/01

YEAR	TM/L	G	AB	R	H	2B	3B	HR	RBI	BB	SO	AVG	OBP	SLG	PRO+	BR	/A	RC	SB	CS	SBR	FR	POS	TPR
1901	Phi-N	8	26	2	5	1	0	0	4	1		.192	.222	.231	32	-2	-2	2				-1	/O	-0.3
1902	Phi-N	70	281	41	73	7	1	0	26	16		.260	.304	.292	86	-4	-4	30	11			8	O	-0.1
	NY-N	53	216	30	69	9	5	0	14	9		.319	.352	.407	138	8	9	37	13			-0	O	0.5
	Yr	123	497	71	142	16	6	0	40	25		.286	.325	.342	108	4	4	66	24			7		0.4
1903	NY-N	141	591	105	185	20	3	3	45	43		.313	.360	.372	107	8	5	93	27			-4	*O	-0.6
1904	NY-N	150	596	99	169	16	5	4	39	39		.284	.328	.347	106	7	4	80	24			-5	*O	-0.6
1905	*NY-N	127	536	95	157	16	14	4	43	20		.293	.318	.397	112	8	6	79	26			-9	*O	-1.1
1906	NY-N	122	477	61	126	10	4	0	38	27		.264	.304	.302	89	-6	-7	58	32			-5	*O	-1.5
1907	NY-N	127	458	54	119	11	10	5	37	31		.260	.307	.360	107	4	3	59	15			-9	*O	-1.1
1908	Bos-N	138	536	61	122	10	6	1	34	36		.228	.276	.274	79	-13	-12	45	17			4	*O	-1.0
1909	Chi-N	12	39	7	8	0	1	0	1	5		.205	.295	.256	70	-1	-1	4	3			-2	O	-0.3
	Was-A	103	393	40	107	15	5	1	16	17		.272	.308	.344	111	1	3	45	13			-2	*O	-0.2
1910	Was-A	7	22	1	4	0	0	0	0	1		.182	.217	.182	26	-2	-2	1	0			-2	/O	-0.3
	Chi-A	30	112	17	27	4	1	0	4	12		.241	.315	.295	95	-1	-0	12	5			-3	O	-0.5
	Yr	37	134	18	31	4	1	0	4	13		.231	.299	.276	84	-3	-2	12	5			-5		-0.8
1911	Bro-N	8	12	1	4	0	0	0	2	1	1	.333	.385	.333	106	0	0	2	2			0	/O	0.0
1912	Phi-N	5	5	0	1	0	0	0	0	1	0	.200	.333	.200	45	-0	-0	0	0			0	H	0.0
Total	12	1102	4300	614	1176	119	55	18	303	259	1	.273	.316	.339	101	8	1	547	190			-30	*O	-7.1

■ JERRY BROWNE
Browne, Jerome Austin b: 2/13/66, Christiansted, V.I. BB/TR, 5'10", 140 lbs. Deb: 9/06/86

YEAR	TM/L	G	AB	R	H	2B	3B	HR	RBI	BB	SO	AVG	OBP	SLG	PRO+	BR	/A	RC	SB	CS	SBR	FR	POS	TPR
1986	Tex-A	12	24	6	10	2	0	0	3	1	4	.417	.440	.500	151	2	2	4	0	2	-1	-1	/2	0.0
1987	Tex-A	132	454	63	123	16	6	1	38	61	50	.271	.360	.339	87	-6	-7	59	27	17	-2	-17	*2/D	-1.4
1988	Tex-A	73	214	26	49	9	2	1	17	25	32	.229	.310	.304	71	-7	-8	20	7	5	-1	-25	2/D	-2.9
1989	Cle-A	153	598	83	179	31	4	5	45	68	64	.299	.372	.390	113	13	12	90	14	6	1	-48	*2/D	-3.3
1990	Cle-A	140	513	92	137	26	5	6	50	72	46	.267	.359	.372	103	5	4	72	12	7	-1	-21	*2	-0.9
Total	5	510	1803	270	498	84	17	13	153	227	196	.276	.359	.363	99	7	4	245	60	37	-4	-111	2/D	-8.5

■ PIDGE BROWNE
Browne, Prentice Almont b: 3/21/29, Peekskill, N.Y. BL/TL, 6'1", 190 lbs. Deb: 4/13/62

YEAR	TM/L	G	AB	R	H	2B	3B	HR	RBI	BB	SO	AVG	OBP	SLG	PRO+	BR	/A	RC	SB	CS	SBR	FR	POS	TPR
1962	Hou-N	65	100	8	21	4	2	1	10	13	9	.210	.301	.320	72	-5	-4	8	0	0	0	1	1	-0.2

■ PETE BROWNING
Browning, Louis Rogers "The Gladiator" b: 6/17/1861, Louisville, Ky. d: 9/10/05, Louisville, Ky. BR/TR, 6', 180 lbs. Deb: 5/02/1882

YEAR	TM/L	G	AB	R	H	2B	3B	HR	RBI	BB	SO	AVG	OBP	SLG	PRO+	BR	/A	RC	SB	CS	SBR	FR	POS	TPR
1882	Lou-a	69	288	67	109	17	3	5		26		.378	.430	.510	230	35	38	65				12	2S3	4.7
1883	Lou-a	84	358	95	121	15	9	4		23		.338	.378	.464	184	27	32	64				-7	OS3/21	2.1
1884	Lou-a	103	447	101	150	33	8	4		13		.336	.357	.472	180	33	36	77				-9	3O1/2P	2.3
1885	Lou-a	112	481	98	174	34	10	9		25		.362	.393	.530	193	48	49	103				5	*O	4.2
1886	Lou-a	112	467	86	159	29	6	2		30		.340	.389	.441	153	32	28	92	26			-10	*O	1.2
1887	Lou-a	134	547	137	220	35	16	4		55		.402	.464	.547	181	62	61	191	103			-2	*O	4.3
1888	Lou-a	99	383	58	120	22	8	3	72	37		.313	.380	.436	169	28	29	79	36			-1	*O	2.2
1889	Lou-a	83	324	39	83	19	5	2	32	34	30	.256	.327	.364	101	-1	1	47	21			-3	O	-0.4
1890	Cle-P	118	493	112	184	40	8	5	93	75	36	.373	.459	.517	177	47	55	136	35			4	*O	4.2
1891	Pit-N	50	203	35	59	14	1	4	28	27	31	.291	.377	.429	140	10	10	35	4			5	O	1.2
	Cin-N	55	216	29	74	10	3	0	33	24	23	.343	.413	.417	143	13	13	43	12			-1	O	0.8
	Yr	105	419	64	133	24	4	4	61	51	54	.317	.395	.422	142	23	23	78	16			5		2.0
1892	Lou-N	21	77	10	19	4	0	0	4	12	7	.247	.348	.299	107	0	1	10	5			-1	O	0.0
	Cin-N	83	307	47	93	12	5	3	52	40	25	.303	.383	.404	142	16	16	52	8			-2	O/1	1.0
	Yr	104	384	57	112	16	5	3	56	52	32	.292	.376	.383	135	16	18	62	13			-3		1.0
1893	Lou-N	57	220	38	78	11	3	1	37	44	15	.355	.466	.445	157	17	21	51	8			-3	O	1.2
1894	StL-N	2	7	1	1	0	0	0	0	0	0	.143	.143	.143	-30	-1	-1	0	0			-1	/O	-0.1
	Bro-N	1	2	1	2	0	0	0	2	1	0	1.000	1.000	1.000	417	1	1	2	0			-0	/O	0.1
	Yr	3	9	2	3	0	0	0	2	1	0	.333	.400	.333	82	-0	-0	1	0			-1		0.0
Total	13	1183	4820	954	1646	295	85	46	353	466	167	.341	.403	.467	166	368	388	1048	258			-15	O/32S1P	29.0

■ BILL BRUBAKER
Brubaker, Wilbur Lee b: 11/7/10, Cleveland, Ohio d: 4/2/78, Laguna Hills, Cal. BR/TR, 6'2", 185 lbs. Deb: 9/08/32

YEAR	TM/L	G	AB	R	H	2B	3B	HR	RBI	BB	SO	AVG	OBP	SLG	PRO+	BR	/A	RC	SB	CS	SBR	FR	POS	TPR
1932	Pit-N	7	24	3	10	3	0	0	4	3	4	.417	.481	.542	178	3	3	6	1			0	/3	0.3
1933	Pit-N	2	2	0	0	0	0	0	0	0	0	.000	.000	.000	-99	-1	-1	0	0			0	/3	0.0

YEAR	TM/L	G	AB	R	H	2B	3B	HR	RBI	BB	SO	AVG	OBP	SLG	PRO+	BR	/A	RC	SB	CS	SBR	FR	POS	TPR
1934	Pit-N	3	6	0	2	1	0	0	1	1	0	.333	.429	.500	144	0	0	1	0			1	/3	0.1
1935	Pit-N	6	11	1	0	0	0	0	0	2	5	.000	.154	.000	-53	-2	-2	0	0			-0	/3	-0.2
1936	Pit-N	145	554	77	160	27	4	6	102	50	96	.289	.352	.384	96	-1	-2	76	5			-15	*3	-0.5
1937	Pit-N	120	413	57	105	20	4	6	48	47	51	.254	.335	.366	90	-5	-5	52	2			2	*3/S1	0.2
1938	Pit-N	45	112	18	33	5	0	3	19	9	14	.295	.347	.420	109	1	1	16	2			-1	3/1SO	0.2
1939	Pit-N	100	345	41	80	23	1	7	43	29	51	.232	.297	.365	78	-12	-11	36	3			10	23/S	0.2
1940	Pit-N	38	78	8	15	3	1	0	7	8	16	.192	.267	.256	45	-6	-6	6	0			6	3/S1	0.0
1943	Bos-N	13	19	3	8	3	0	0	1	2	2	.421	.476	.579	207	3	3	5	0			-1	/31	0.2
Total	10	479	1564	208	413	85	10	22	225	151	239	.264	.333	.373	90	-19	-20	200	13			2	3/21SO	0.3

■ LOU BRUCE
Bruce, Louis R. b: 1/16/1877, St.Regis, N.Y. d: 2/9/68, Ilion, N.Y. BL/TR, 5'5", 145 lbs. Deb: 6/22/04

YEAR	TM/L	G	AB	R	H	2B	3B	HR	RBI	BB	SO	AVG	OBP	SLG	PRO+	BR	/A	RC	SB	CS	SBR	FR	POS	TPR
1904	Phi-A	30	101	9	27	3	0	0	8	5		.267	.302	.297	87	-1	-1	11	2			-2	O/P23	-0.4

■ EARLE BRUCKER
Brucker, Earle Francis Jr. b: 8/29/25, Los Angeles, Cal. BL/TR, 6'2", 210 lbs. Deb: 10/02/48

YEAR	TM/L	G	AB	R	H	2B	3B	HR	RBI	BB	SO	AVG	OBP	SLG	PRO+	BR	/A	RC	SB	CS	SBR	FR	POS	TPR
1948	Phi-A	2	6	0	1	1	0	0	0	1	1	.167	.286	.333	64	-0	-0	1	0	0	0	-0	/C	0.0

■ EARLE BRUCKER
Brucker, Earle Francis Sr. b: 5/6/01, Albany, N.Y. d: 5/8/81, San Diego, Cal. BR/TR, 5'11", 175 lbs. Deb: 4/19/37 MC

YEAR	TM/L	G	AB	R	H	2B	3B	HR	RBI	BB	SO	AVG	OBP	SLG	PRO+	BR	/A	RC	SB	CS	SBR	FR	POS	TPR
1937	Phi-A	102	317	40	82	16	5	6	37	48	30	.259	.356	.397	91	-5	-4	47	1	2	-1	-7	C	-0.4
1938	Phi-A	53	171	26	64	21	1	3	35	19	16	.374	.437	.561	152	13	14	42	1	1	-0	-2	C/1	1.1
1939	Phi-A	62	172	18	50	15	1	3	31	24	16	.291	.381	.442	112	3	3	28	0	1	-1	-5	C	0.1
1940	Phi-A	23	46	3	9	1	1	0	2	6	3	.196	.288	.261	44	-4	-4	3	0	0	0	2	C	0.0
1943	Phi-A	1	1	0	0	0	0	0	0	0	0	.000	.000	.000	-99	-0	-0	0	0	0	0	0	H	0.0
Total	5	241	707	87	205	53	8	12	105	97	65	.290	.376	.438	108	7	9	120	2	4	-2	-12	C/1	0.8

■ FRANK BRUGGY
Bruggy, Frank Leo b: 5/4/1891, Elizabeth, N.J. d: 4/5/59, Elizabeth, N.J. BR/TR, 5'11", 195 lbs. Deb: 4/13/21

YEAR	TM/L	G	AB	R	H	2B	3B	HR	RBI	BB	SO	AVG	OBP	SLG	PRO+	BR	/A	RC	SB	CS	SBR	FR	POS	TPR
1921	Phi-N	96	277	28	86	11	2	5	28	23	37	.310	.370	.419	100	4	1	44	6	2	1	-8	C/1	-0.1
1922	Phi-N	53	111	10	31	7	0	0	9	6	11	.279	.322	.342	71	-4	-5	12	1	2	-1	-1	C	-0.5
1923	Phi-A	54	105	4	22	3	0	1	6	4	9	.210	.245	.267	34	-10	-10	7	1	1	-0	1	C/1	-0.6
1924	Phi-A	50	113	9	30	6	0	0	8	8	15	.265	.314	.319	63	-6	-6	12	4	0	1	-7	C	-0.8
1925	Cin-N	6	14	2	3	0	0	0	1	2	0	.214	.313	.214	38	-1	-1	1	0	0	0	-0	/C	0.0
Total	5	259	620	53	172	27	2	6	52	43	72	.277	.329	.356	76	-18	-22	76	12	5	1	-16	C/1	-2.0

■ MIKE BRUMLEY
Brumley, Anthony Michael b: 4/9/63, Oklahoma City, Okla. BB/TR, 5'10", 165 lbs. Deb: 6/16/87

YEAR	TM/L	G	AB	R	H	2B	3B	HR	RBI	BB	SO	AVG	OBP	SLG	PRO+	BR	/A	RC	SB	CS	SBR	FR	POS	TPR
1987	Chi-N	39	104	8	21	2	2	1	9	10	30	.202	.278	.288	49	-7	-8	9	7	1	2	4	S/2	0.1
1989	Det-A	92	212	33	42	5	2	1	11	14	45	.198	.251	.255	44	-16	-15	14	8	4	0	-6	S23/OD	-1.7
1990	Sea-A	62	147	19	33	5	4	0	7	10	22	.224	.274	.313	63	-7	-7	12	2	0	1	-1	S/23O	-0.4
Total	3	193	463	60	96	12	8	2	27	34	97	.207	.265	.281	51	-31	-31	35	17	5	2	-3	S/23DO	-2.0

■ MIKE BRUMLEY
Brumley, Tony Mike b: 7/10/38, Granite, Okla. BL/TR, 5'10", 195 lbs. Deb: 4/18/64

YEAR	TM/L	G	AB	R	H	2B	3B	HR	RBI	BB	SO	AVG	OBP	SLG	PRO+	BR	/A	RC	SB	CS	SBR	FR	POS	TPR
1964	Was-A	136	426	36	104	19	2	2	35	40	54	.244	.310	.312	74	-14	-14	40	1	1	-0	-13	*C	-2.3
1965	Was-A	79	216	15	45	4	0	3	15	20	33	.208	.282	.269	58	-12	-11	16	1	1	-0	1	C	-0.5
1966	Was-A	9	18	1	2	1	0	0	0	0	2	.111	.111	.167	-22	-3	-3	0	0	0	0	-0	/C	-0.2
Total	3	224	660	52	151	24	2	5	50	60	89	.229	.296	.294	67	-29	-28	57	2	2	-1	-12	C	-3.0

■ GLENN BRUMMER
Brummer, Glenn Edward b: 11/23/54, Olney, Ill. BR/TR, 6', 200 lbs. Deb: 5/25/81

YEAR	TM/L	G	AB	R	H	2B	3B	HR	RBI	BB	SO	AVG	OBP	SLG	PRO+	BR	/A	RC	SB	CS	SBR	FR	POS	TPR
1981	StL-N	21	30	2	6	1	0	0	1	2	1	.200	.226	.233	30	-3	-3	2	0	0	0	2	C	0.0
1982	*StL-N	35	64	4	15	4	0	0	8	0	12	.234	.234	.297	47	-5	-5	5	2	0	1	3	C	0.0
1983	StL-N	45	87	7	24	7	0	0	9	10	11	.276	.351	.356	96	-0	-0	10	1	3	-2	0	C	0.0
1984	StL-N	28	58	3	12	0	0	1	3	3	7	.207	.246	.259	43	-4	-4	3	0	0	0	4	C	0.0
1985	Tex-A	49	108	7	30	4	0	0	5	11	22	.278	.355	.315	84	-2	-2	11	1	5	-3	-2	C/OD	-0.4
Total	5	178	347	23	87	16	0	1	27	25	54	.251	.305	.305	70	-14	-14	30	4	8	-4	7	C/DO	-0.4

■ TOM BRUNANSKY
Brunansky, Thomas Andrew b: 8/20/60, Covina, Cal. BR/TR, 6'4", 205 lbs. Deb: 4/09/81

YEAR	TM/L	G	AB	R	H	2B	3B	HR	RBI	BB	SO	AVG	OBP	SLG	PRO+	BR	/A	RC	SB	CS	SBR	FR	POS	TPR
1981	Cal-A	11	33	7	5	0	0	3	6	8	10	.152	.317	.424	112	1	1	5	1	0	0	2	O	0.3
1982	Min-A	127	463	77	126	30	1	20	46	71	101	.272	.378	.471	128	22	20	84	1	2	-1	16	*O	3.1
1983	Min-A	151	542	70	123	24	5	28	82	61	95	.227	.310	.445	101	2	-0	72	2	5	-2	19	*O/D	1.4
1984	Min-A	155	567	75	144	21	0	32	85	57	94	.254	.322	.460	109	9	6	81	4	5	-2	-0	*O/D	1.1
1985	Min-A	157	567	71	137	28	4	27	90	71	86	.242	.326	.448	103	7	2	83	5	3	-0	-0	*O	0.0
1986	Min-A	157	593	69	152	28	1	23	75	53	98	.256	.318	.423	97	-1	-3	78	12	4	1	3	*O/D	-0.1
1987	*Min-A	155	532	83	138	22	2	32	85	74	104	.259	.354	.489	116	16	13	90	11	11	-3	3	*OD	0.9
1988	Min-A	14	49	5	9	1	0	1	6	7	11	.184	.286	.265	54	-3	-3	4	1	2	-1	-3	O/D	-0.6
	StL-N	143	523	69	128	22	4	22	79	79	82	.245	.348	.428	121	16	15	79	16	6	1	-1	*O	1.2
1989	StL-N	158	556	67	133	29	3	20	85	59	107	.239	.314	.410	102	3	1	70	5	9	-4	-3	*O/1	-0.8
1990	StL-N	19	57	5	9	3	0	1	2	12	10	.158	.314	.263	59	-3	-3	6	0	0	0	-0	O	-0.3
	*Bos-A	129	461	61	123	24	5	15	71	54	105	.267	.347	.438	113	11	8	67	5	10	-5	6	*O/D	0.8
Total	10	1376	4943	659	1227	232	25	224	712	606	903	.248	.334	.441	108	80	57	718	63	57	-15	41	*O/D1	5.9

■ ARLO BRUNSBERG
Brunsberg, Arlo Adolph b: 8/15/40, Fertile, Minn. BL/TR, 6', 195 lbs. Deb: 9/23/66

YEAR	TM/L	G	AB	R	H	2B	3B	HR	RBI	BB	SO	AVG	OBP	SLG	PRO+	BR	/A	RC	SB	CS	SBR	FR	POS	TPR
1966	Det-A	2	3	1	1	1	0	0	0	0	0	.333	.500	.667	227	1	1	1	0	0	0	-1	/C	0.0

■ BOB BRUSH
Brush, Robert b: 3/8/1875, Osage, Iowa d: 4/2/44, San Bernadino, Cal. Deb: 4/20/07

YEAR	TM/L	G	AB	R	H	2B	3B	HR	RBI	BB	SO	AVG	OBP	SLG	PRO+	BR	/A	RC	SB	CS	SBR	FR	POS	TPR
1907	Bos-N	2	2	0	0	0	0	0	0	0		.000	.000	.000	-99	-0	-0	0	0			0	/1	0.0

■ BILL BRUTON
Bruton, William Haron b: 12/22/25, Panola, Ala. BL/TR, 6'0.5", 169 lbs. Deb: 4/13/53

YEAR	TM/L	G	AB	R	H	2B	3B	HR	RBI	BB	SO	AVG	OBP	SLG	PRO+	BR	/A	RC	SB	CS	SBR	FR	POS	TPR
1953	Mil-N	151	613	82	153	18	14	1	41	44	100	.250	.306	.330	70	-31	-25	65	**26**	11	1	4	*O	-2.4
1954	Mil-N	142	567	89	161	20	7	4	30	40	78	.284	.336	.365	88	-14	-10	73	**34**	13	2	-3	*O	-1.4
1955	Mil-N	149	636	106	175	30	12	9	47	43	72	.275	.325	.403	97	-8	-4	86	**25**	11	1	9	*O	0.3
1956	Mil-N	147	525	73	143	23	**15**	8	56	26	63	.272	.308	.419	99	-6	-2	66	8	6	-1	-2	*O	-1.0
1957	Mil-N	79	306	41	85	16	9	5	30	19	35	.278	.322	.438	110	0	3	44	11	4	1	-3	O	0.0
1958	*Mil-N	100	325	47	91	11	3	3	28	27	37	.280	.339	.360	93	-6	-3	41	4	1	1	-11	O	-1.6
1959	Mil-N	133	478	72	138	22	6	6	41	35	54	.289	.339	.397	104	-3	2	64	13	5	1	-3	*O	-0.1
1960	Mil-N	151	629	**112**	180	27	**13**	12	54	41	97	.286	.332	.428	115	4	10	89	22	13	-1	-2	*O	0.2
1961	Det-A	160	596	99	153	15	5	17	63	61	66	.257	.329	.384	87	-9	-11	79	22	6	3	4	*O	-0.8
1962	Det-A	147	561	90	156	27	5	16	74	55	67	.278	.348	.430	104	6	4	84	14	7	0	12	*O	1.0
1963	Det-A	145	524	84	134	21	8	8	48	59	70	.256	.331	.372	93	-2	-4	67	14	7	0	3	*O	-0.5
1964	Det-A	106	296	42	82	11	5	5	33	32	54	.277	.348	.399	105	3	3	42	14	5	1	4	O	0.5
Total	12	1610	6056	937	1651	241	102	94	545	482	793	.273	.329	.393	96	-65	-38	801	207	89	9	13	*O	-5.8

■ ED BRUYETTE
Bruyette, Edward T. b: 8/31/1874, Wanawa, Wis. d: 8/5/40, Peshastin, Wash. BL, 5'10", 170 lbs. Deb: 8/06/01

YEAR	TM/L	G	AB	R	H	2B	3B	HR	RBI	BB	SO	AVG	OBP	SLG	PRO+	BR	/A	RC	SB	CS	SBR	FR	POS	TPR
1901	Mil-A	26	82	7	15	3	0	0	4	12		.183	.295	.220	48	-5	-5	6	1			-6	O/2S3	-0.9

■ BILLY BRYAN
Bryan, William Ronald b: 12/4/38, Morgan, Ga. BL/TR, 6'4", 200 lbs. Deb: 9/12/61

YEAR	TM/L	G	AB	R	H	2B	3B	HR	RBI	BB	SO	AVG	OBP	SLG	PRO+	BR	/A	RC	SB	CS	SBR	FR	POS	TPR
1961	KC-A	9	19	2	3	0	0	1	2	2	7	.158	.238	.316	47	-2	-2	1	0	0	0	-1	/C	-0.2
1962	KC-A	25	74	5	11	2	1	2	7	5	32	.149	.203	.284	28	-8	-8	5	0	0	0	-2	C	-0.8
1963	KC-A	24	65	11	11	1	1	3	7	9	22	.169	.270	.354	70	-2	-3	6	0	0	0	5	C	0.2
1964	KC-A	93	220	19	53	9	2	13	36	16	69	.241	.292	.477	107	2	1	29	0	0	0	-9	C	-0.4

YEAR	TM/L	G	AB	R	H	2B	3B	HR	RBI	BB	SO	AVG	OBP	SLG	PRO+	BR	/A	RC	SB	CS	SBR	FR	POS	TPR
1965	KC-A	108	325	36	82	11	5	14	51	29	87	.252	.317	.446	116	5	6	47	0	0	0	-5	C	0.8
1966	KC-A	32	76	0	10	4	0	0	7	6	17	.132	.195	.184	10	-9	-9	3	0	0	0	-1	C/1	-0.8
	NY-A	27	69	5	15	2	0	4	5	5	19	.217	.270	.420	99	-1	-0	8	0	0	0	-0	C/1	0.0
	Yr	59	145	5	25	6	0	4	12	11	36	.172	.231	.297	52	-10	-9	10	0	0	0	-1		-0.8
1967	NY-A	16	12	1	2	0	0	1	2	5	3	.167	.412	.417	151	1	1	3	0	0	0	1	/C	0.2
1968	Was-A	40	108	7	22	3	0	3	8	14	27	.204	.301	.315	90	-2	-1	11	0	1	-1	-3	C	-0.3
Total	8	374	968	86	209	32	9	41	125	91	283	.216	.285	.395	91	-14	-14	112	0	1	-1	-15	C/1	-1.3

■ DEREK BRYANT
Bryant, Derek Roszell b: 10/9/51, Lexington, Ky. BR/TR, 5'11", 185 lbs. Deb: 4/24/79

YEAR	TM/L	G	AB	R	H	2B	3B	HR	RBI	BB	SO	AVG	OBP	SLG	PRO+	BR	/A	RC	SB	CS	SBR	FR	POS	TPR
1979	Oak-A	39	106	8	19	2	1	0	13	10	10	.179	.250	.217	29	-11	-10	6	0	0	0	-1	O/D	-1.1

■ DON BRYANT
Bryant, Donald Ray b: 7/13/41, Jasper, Fla. BR/TR, 6'5", 200 lbs. Deb: 7/17/66 C

YEAR	TM/L	G	AB	R	H	2B	3B	HR	RBI	BB	SO	AVG	OBP	SLG	PRO+	BR	/A	RC	SB	CS	SBR	FR	POS	TPR
1966	Chi-N	13	26	2	8	2	0	0	4	1	4	.308	.357	.385	105	0	0	4	1	0	0	0	C	0.1
1969	Hou-N	31	59	2	11	1	0	1	6	4	13	.186	.250	.254	42	-5	-4	4	0	0	0	3	C	0.1
1970	Hou-N	15	24	2	5	0	0	0	3	1	8	.208	.240	.208	22	-3	-3	1	0	0	0	0	C	-0.1
Total	3	59	109	6	24	3	0	1	13	6	25	.220	.274	.275	53	-7	-7	9	1	0	0	4	/C	0.1

■ G. BRYANT
Bryant, G. Deb: 8/06/1885

YEAR	TM/L	G	AB	R	H	2B	3B	HR	RBI	BB	SO	AVG	OBP	SLG	PRO+	BR	/A	RC	SB	CS	SBR	FR	POS	TPR
1885	Det-N	1	4	0	0	0	0	0	1	0	2	.000	.000	.000	-99	-1	-1	0				-1	/2	-0.1

■ RALPH BRYANT
Bryant, Ralph Wendell b: 5/20/61, Fort Gaines, Ga. BL/TR, 6'2", 200 lbs. Deb: 9/08/85

YEAR	TM/L	G	AB	R	H	2B	3B	HR	RBI	BB	SO	AVG	OBP	SLG	PRO+	BR	/A	RC	SB	CS	SBR	FR	POS	TPR
1985	LA-N	6	6	0	2	0	0	0	1	0	2	.333	.333	.333	90	-0	-0	1	0	0	0	0	/O	0.0
1986	LA-N	27	75	15	19	4	2	6	13	5	25	.253	.309	.600	156	4	4	13	0	1	-1	-0	O	0.3
1987	LA-N	46	69	7	17	2	1	2	10	10	24	.246	.350	.391	99	-0	0	10	2	1	0	-2	O	-0.2
Total	3	79	150	22	38	6	3	8	24	15	51	.253	.329	.493	125	4	4	24	2	2	-1	-2	/O	0.1

■ STEVE BRYE
Brye, Stephen Robert b: 2/4/49, Alameda, Cal. BR/TR, 6', 190 lbs. Deb: 9/03/70

YEAR	TM/L	G	AB	R	H	2B	3B	HR	RBI	BB	SO	AVG	OBP	SLG	PRO+	BR	/A	RC	SB	CS	SBR	FR	POS	TPR
1970	Min-A	9	11	1	2	1	0	0	2	4	2	.182	.308	.273	60	-1	-1	1	0	0	0	-0	/O	0.0
1971	Min-A	28	107	10	24	1	0	3	11	7	15	.224	.272	.318	65	-5	-5	9	3	1	0	1	O	-0.5
1972	Min-A	100	253	18	61	9	3	0	12	17	38	.241	.292	.300	73	-7	-9	22	3	1	0	2	O	-0.9
1973	Min-A	92	278	39	73	9	5	6	33	35	43	.263	.345	.396	104	3	2	38	3	5	-2	8	O/D	0.5
1974	Min-A	135	488	52	138	32	1	2	41	22	59	.283	.320	.365	93	-3	-5	54	1	3	-2	12	*O	0.2
1975	Min-A	86	246	41	62	13	1	9	34	21	37	.252	.316	.423	105	2	1	32	2	1	0	-0	O/D	0.0
1976	Min-A	87	258	33	68	11	0	2	23	13	31	.264	.299	.329	82	-6	-7	24	1	2	-1	-2	O/D	-1.1
1977	Mil-A	94	241	27	60	14	3	7	28	16	39	.249	.298	.419	93	-3	-3	30	1	1	0	10	O/D	0.4
1978	Pit-N	66	115	16	27	7	0	1	9	11	10	.235	.307	.322	73	-4	-4	12	2	1	0	0	O	-0.5
Total	9	697	1997	237	515	97	13	30	193	144	276	.258	.311	.365	89	-23	-30	222	16	14	-4	29	O/D	-1.9

■ HAL BUBSER
Bubser, Harold Fred b: 9/28/1895, Chicago, Ill. d: 6/22/59, Melrose Park, Ill BR/TR, 5'11", 170 lbs. Deb: 4/15/22

YEAR	TM/L	G	AB	R	H	2B	3B	HR	RBI	BB	SO	AVG	OBP	SLG	PRO+	BR	/A	RC	SB	CS	SBR	FR	POS	TPR
1922	Chi-A	3	3	0	0	0	0	0	0	0	2	.000	.000	.000	-99	-1	-1	0	0	0	0	0	H	0.0

■ JOHNNY BUCHA
Bucha, John George b: 1/22/25, Allentown, Pa. BR/TR, 5'11", 190 lbs. Deb: 5/02/48

YEAR	TM/L	G	AB	R	H	2B	3B	HR	RBI	BB	SO	AVG	OBP	SLG	PRO+	BR	/A	RC	SB	CS	SBR	FR	POS	TPR
1948	StL-N	2	1	0	0	0	0	0	0	1	0	.000	.500	.000	43	0	0	0	0			0	/C	0.0
1950	StL-N	22	36	1	5	1	0	0	1	4	7	.139	.225	.167	5	-5	-5	1	0			0	C	-0.3
1953	Det-A	60	158	17	35	9	0	1	14	20	14	.222	.309	.297	65	-8	-7	16	1	1	-0	-4	C	-0.9
Total	3	84	195	18	40	10	0	1	15	25	21	.205	.295	.272	53	-13	-13	17	1	1		-3	/C	-1.2

■ JERRY BUCHEK
Buchek, Gerald Peter b: 5/9/42, St.Louis, Mo. BR/TR, 5'11", 185 lbs. Deb: 6/30/61

YEAR	TM/L	G	AB	R	H	2B	3B	HR	RBI	BB	SO	AVG	OBP	SLG	PRO+	BR	/A	RC	SB	CS	SBR	FR	POS	TPR
1961	StL-N	31	90	6	12	2	0	0	9	0	28	.133	.152	.156	-16	-15	-16	1	0	0	0	-6	S	-1.9
1963	StL-N	3	4	0	1	0	0	0	0	0	2	.250	.250	.250	41	-0	-0	0	0	0	0	0	/S	0.0
1964	*StL-N	35	30	7	6	0	2	0	1	3	11	.200	.273	.333	64	-1	-2	3	0	0	0	7	S/23	0.8
1965	StL-N	55	166	17	41	8	3	3	21	13	46	.247	.302	.386	84	-2	-4	19	1	0	0	10	2S/3	1.1
1966	StL-N	100	284	23	67	10	4	4	25	23	71	.236	.293	.342	75	-9	-9	26	0	5	-3	-12	2S/3	-1.8
1967	NY-N	124	411	35	97	11	2	14	41	26	101	.236	.285	.375	89	-8	-7	41	3	5	-2	4	23/S	0.1
1968	NY-N	73	192	8	35	4	0	1	11	10	53	.182	.234	.219	36	-15	-15	9	1	1	-0	1	32/O	-1.6
Total	7	421	1177	96	259	35	11	22	108	75	312	.220	.271	.325	67	-50	-53	98	5	11	-5	3	2S/3O	-3.3

■ JIM BUCHER
Bucher, James Quinter b: 3/11/11, Manassas, Va. BL/TR, 5'11", 170 lbs. Deb: 4/18/34

YEAR	TM/L	G	AB	R	H	2B	3B	HR	RBI	BB	SO	AVG	OBP	SLG	PRO+	BR	/A	RC	SB	CS	SBR	FR	POS	TPR
1934	Bro-N	47	84	12	19	5	2	0	8	4	7	.226	.261	.333	61	-5	-5	7	1			-1	2/3	-0.2
1935	Bro-N	123	473	72	143	22	1	7	58	10	33	.302	.317	.397	93	-7	-6	58	4			-10	23O	-1.2
1936	Bro-N	110	370	49	93	12	8	2	41	29	27	.251	.306	.343	74	-13	-14	40	5			-9	32O	-1.8
1937	Bro-N	125	380	44	96	11	2	4	37	20	18	.253	.295	.324	67	-17	-18	37	5			-13	23/O	-2.6
1938	StL-N	17	57	7	13	3	1	0	7	2	2	.228	.254	.316	53	-4	-4	4	0			-4	2/3	-0.6
1944	Bos-A	80	277	39	76	9	2	4	31	19	13	.274	.326	.365	98	-1	-3	39	3	3	-1	-9	32	-1.0
1945	Bos-A	52	151	19	34	4	3	0	11	7	13	.225	.264	.291	60	-8	-8	11	1	3	-2	-2	3/2	-1.1
Total	7	554	1792	242	474	66	19	17	193	91	113	.265	.302	.351	78	-56	-55	192	19	6		-46	32/O	-8.5

■ KEVIN BUCKLEY
Buckley, Kevin John b: 1/16/59, Quincy, Mass. BR/TR, 6'1", 200 lbs. Deb: 9/04/84

YEAR	TM/L	G	AB	R	H	2B	3B	HR	RBI	BB	SO	AVG	OBP	SLG	PRO+	BR	/A	RC	SB	CS	SBR	FR	POS	TPR
1984	Tex-A	5	7	1	2	1	0	0	0	2	4	.286	.444	.429	138	1	1	2	0	0	0	0	/D	0.1

■ DICK BUCKLEY
Buckley, Richard D. b: 9/21/1858, Troy, N.Y. d: 12/12/29, Pittsburgh, Pa. TR, 5'10", Deb: 4/20/1888

YEAR	TM/L	G	AB	R	H	2B	3B	HR	RBI	BB	SO	AVG	OBP	SLG	PRO+	BR	/A	RC	SB	CS	SBR	FR	POS	TPR
1888	Ind-N	71	260	28	71	9	3	5	22	6	24	.273	.289	.388	114	4	3	31	4			-21	C3/O1	-1.5
1889	Ind-N	68	260	35	67	11	0	8	41	15	32	.258	.301	.392	92	-3	-4	33	5			-23	C3/O1	-2.2
1890	NY-N	70	266	39	68	11	0	2	26	23	35	.256	.324	.320	90	-3	-3	29	3			11	C/3	1.1
1891	NY-N	75	253	23	55	9	1	4	31	11	30	.217	.258	.308	69	-11	-10	21	3			17	C/3	1.1
1892	StL-N	121	410	43	93	17	4	5	52	22	34	.227	.275	.324	87	-10	-7	39	7			-11	*C/1	-1.0
1893	StL-N	9	23	2	4	1	0	0	1	0	0	.174	.174	.217	5	-3	-3	1	0			2	/C	0.0
1894	StL-N	29	89	5	16	1	2	1	3	6	3	.180	.240	.270	24	-11	-11	6	1			2	C/1	-0.4
	Phi-N	43	160	18	47	7	3	1	26	6	13	.294	.327	.394	77	-7	-6	21	0			4	C/1	0.1
	Yr	72	249	23	63	8	5	2	29	12	16	.253	.295	.349	57	-18	-18	27	1			6		-0.3
1895	Phi-N	38	112	20	28	6	1	0	14	9	17	.250	.333	.321	71	-5	-5	13	2			6	C	0.4
Total	8	524	1833	213	449	72	14	26	216	98	188	.245	.291	.342	82	-49	-46	195	25			-14	C/31O	-2.4

■ BILL BUCKNER
Buckner, William Joseph b: 12/14/49, Vallejo, Cal. BL/TL, 6', 185 lbs. Deb: 9/21/69

YEAR	TM/L	G	AB	R	H	2B	3B	HR	RBI	BB	SO	AVG	OBP	SLG	PRO+	BR	/A	RC	SB	CS	SBR	FR	POS	TPR
1969	LA-N	1	1	0	0	0	0	0	0	0	0	.000	.000	.000	-99	-0	-0	0	0	0	0	0	H	0.0
1970	LA-N	28	68	6	13	3	1	0	4	3	7	.191	.225	.265	32	-7	-6	4	0	1	-1	1	O/1	-0.6
1971	LA-N	108	358	37	99	15	1	5	41	11	18	.277	.307	.366	96	-5	-3	40	4	1	1	0	O1	-0.5
1972	LA-N	105	383	47	122	14	3	5	37	17	13	.319	.349	.410	118	7	8	52	10	3	1	-2	O1	0.2
1973	LA-N	140	575	68	158	20	0	8	46	17	34	.275	.299	.351	83	-17	-14	58	12	2	2	-7	1O	-2.5
1974	*LA-N	145	580	83	182	30	3	7	58	30	24	.314	.352	.412	118	9	12	81	31	13	2	-10	*O/1	-0.1
1975	LA-N	92	288	30	70	11	2	6	31	17	15	.243	.290	.358	82	-9	-8	27	8	3	1	0	O	-0.9
1976	LA-N	154	642	76	193	28	4	7	60	26	26	.301	.329	.389	105	1	2	82	28	9	3	-1	*O/1	-0.1
1977	Chi-N	122	426	40	121	27	0	11	60	21	17	.284	.319	.425	88	-3	-8	52	7	5	-1	-1	1	-1.4
1978	Chi-N	117	446	47	144	26	1	5	74	18	17	.323	.349	.419	102	7	1	59	7	5	-1	8	*1	0.5
1979	Chi-N	149	591	72	168	34	7	14	66	30	28	.284	.321	.437	96	2	-5	78	9	4	0	18	*1	0.7
1980	Chi-N	145	578	69	187	41	3	10	68	30	18	.324	.357	.457	117	18	13	90	1	2	-1	4	1O	1.1

YEAR	TM/L	G	AB	R	H	2B	3B	HR	RBI	BB	SO	AVG	OBP	SLG	PRO+	BR	/A	RC	SB	CS	SBR	FR	POS	TPR
1981	Chi-N	106	421	45	131	**35**	3	10	75	26	16	.311	.353	.480	129	17	15	65	5	2	0	1	*1	1.3
1982	Chi-N	161	657	93	201	34	5	15	105	36	26	.306	.347	.441	116	15	13	98	15	5	2	16	*1	2.3
1983	Chi-N	153	626	79	175	**38**	6	16	66	25	30	.280	.313	.436	101	2	-2	83	12	4	1	21	*1O	1.4
1984	Chi-N	21	43	3	9	0	0	0	2	1	1	.209	.244	.209	26	-4	-4	2	0	0	0	1	/1O	-0.3
	Bos-A	114	439	51	122	21	2	11	67	24	38	.278	.323	.410	97	0	-2	55	2	2	-1	5	*1	-0.5
1985	Bos-A	162	673	89	201	46	3	16	110	30	36	.299	.330	.447	106	8	5	96	18	4	3	25	*1	2.2
1986	*Bos-A	153	629	73	168	39	2	18	102	40	25	.267	.315	.421	98	-3	-3	76	6	4	-1	20	*1D	0.7
1987	Bos-A	75	286	23	78	6	1	2	42	13	19	.273	.304	.322	65	-14	-15	25	1	3	-2	2	1	-1.9
	Cal-A	57	183	16	56	12	1	3	32	9	7	.306	.339	.432	106	0	1	26	1	0	0	-0	D/1	0.1
	Yr	132	469	39	134	18	2	5	74	22	26	.286	.318	.365	80	-13	-13	51	2	3	-1	2		-1.8
1988	Cal-A	19	43	1	9	0	0	0	9	4	0	.209	.277	.209	39	-3	-3	3	2	0	1	0	D/1	-0.1
	KC-A	89	242	18	62	14	0	3	34	13	19	.256	.294	.351	79	-7	-7	24	3	1	0	-0	D1	-0.7
	Yr	108	285	19	71	14	0	3	43	17	19	.249	.291	.330	73	-10	-10	27	5	1	1	0		-0.8
1989	KC-A	79	176	7	38	4	1	1	16	6	11	.216	.242	.267	43	-13	-13	11	1	0	0	-0	1D	-1.4
1990	Bos-A	22	43	4	8	0	0	1	3	3	2	.186	.239	.256	37	-4	-4	3	0	0	0	-0	1	-0.4
Total	22	2517	9397	1077	2715	498	49	174	1208	450	453	.289	.324	.408	99	-2	-27	1190	183	73	11	103	*1OD	-0.9

■ MARK BUDASKA
Budaska, Mark David   b: 12/27/52, Sharon, Pa.   BB/TL, 6', 180 lbs.   Deb: 6/06/78

YEAR	TM/L	G	AB	R	H	2B	3B	HR	RBI	BB	SO	AVG	OBP	SLG	PRO+	BR	/A	RC	SB	CS	SBR	FR	POS	TPR
1978	Oak-A	4	4	0	1	1	0	0	0	1	2	.250	.400	.500	160	0	0	1	0	0	0	-0	/O	0.0
1981	Oak-A	9	32	3	5	1	0	0	2	4	10	.156	.250	.188	29	-3	-3	2	0	1	-1	0	/D	-0.3
Total	2	13	36	3	6	2	0	0	2	5	12	.167	.268	.222	44	-3	-2	2	0	1	-1	-0	/DO	-0.3

■ BUDD
Budd   Deb: 9/10/1890

YEAR	TM/L	G	AB	R	H	2B	3B	HR	RBI	BB	SO	AVG	OBP	SLG	PRO+	BR	/A	RC	SB	CS	SBR	FR	POS	TPR
1890	Cle-P	1	4	0	0	0	0	0	0	0	3	.000	.000	.000	-99	-1	-1	0	0			0	/O	0.0

■ DON BUDDIN
Buddin, Donald Thomas   b: 5/5/34, Turbeville, S.C.   BR/TR, 5'11", 178 lbs.   Deb: 4/17/56

YEAR	TM/L	G	AB	R	H	2B	3B	HR	RBI	BB	SO	AVG	OBP	SLG	PRO+	BR	/A	RC	SB	CS	SBR	FR	POS	TPR
1956	Bos-A	114	377	49	90	24	0	5	37	65	62	.239	.357	.342	76	-6	-13	49	2	0	1	14	*S	1.1
1958	Bos-A	136	497	74	118	25	2	12	43	82	106	.237	.350	.368	92	1	-4	66	0	4	-2	15	*S	2.8
1959	Bos-A	151	485	75	117	24	1	10	53	92	99	.241	.368	.357	95	3	0	72	6	1	1	-17	*S	-0.3
1960	Bos-A	124	428	62	105	21	5	6	36	62	59	.245	.342	.360	87	-5	-7	53	4	2	0	-5	*S	-0.1
1961	Bos-A	115	339	58	89	22	3	6	42	72	45	.263	.395	.398	110	9	8	58	2	1	0	-1	*S	1.4
1962	Hou-N	40	80	10	13	4	1	2	10	17	17	.162	.316	.313	75	-3	-2	8	0	0	0	3	S/3	0.3
	Det-A	31	83	14	19	3	0	0	4	20	16	.229	.385	.265	76	-1	-2	11	1	0	0	-2	S/23	-0.1
Total	6	711	2289	342	551	123	12	41	225	410	404	.241	.360	.359	90	-3	-20	317	15	8	-0	7	S/32	5.1

■ STEVE BUECHELE
Buechele, Steven Bernard   b: 9/26/61, Lancaster, Cal.   BR/TR, 6'2", 190 lbs.   Deb: 7/19/85

YEAR	TM/L	G	AB	R	H	2B	3B	HR	RBI	BB	SO	AVG	OBP	SLG	PRO+	BR	/A	RC	SB	CS	SBR	FR	POS	TPR
1985	Tex-A	69	219	22	48	6	3	6	21	14	38	.219	.272	.356	70	-9	-10	18	3	2	-0	5	3/2	-0.6
1986	Tex-A	153	461	54	112	19	4	18	54	35	98	.243	.303	.410	90	-6	-8	54	5	8	-3	18	*32/O	0.6
1987	Tex-A	136	363	45	86	20	0	13	50	28	66	.237	.293	.399	81	-10	-11	42	2	2	-1	3	*32/O	-0.7
1988	Tex-A	155	503	68	126	21	4	16	58	65	79	.250	.342	.404	105	6	5	71	2	4	-2	8	*3/2	1.1
1989	Tex-A	155	486	60	114	22	2	16	59	36	107	.235	.294	.387	89	-7	-7	50	1	3	-2	15	*32/SD	0.6
1990	Tex-A	91	251	30	54	10	0	7	30	27	63	.215	.296	.339	76	-8	-8	26	1	0	0	6	3/2	0.0
Total	6	759	2283	279	540	98	11	76	272	205	451	.237	.305	.389	88	-35	-40	261	14	19	-7	56	3/2ODS	1.0

■ CHARLIE BUELOW
Buelow, Charles John   b: 1/12/1877, Dubuque, Iowa   d: 5/4/51, Dubuque, Iowa   BR/TR,   Deb: 6/01/01

YEAR	TM/L	G	AB	R	H	2B	3B	HR	RBI	BB	SO	AVG	OBP	SLG	PRO+	BR	/A	RC	SB	CS	SBR	FR	POS	TPR
1901	NY-N	22	72	3	8	4	0	0	4	2		.111	.147	.167	-9	-10	-9	2	0			3	3/2	-0.4

■ FRITZ BUELOW
Buelow, Frederick William   b: 2/13/1876, Berlin, Germany   d: 12/27/33, Detroit, Mich.   BR/TR, 5'10.5", 170 lbs.   Deb: 9/28/1899

YEAR	TM/L	G	AB	R	H	2B	3B	HR	RBI	BB	SO	AVG	OBP	SLG	PRO+	BR	/A	RC	SB	CS	SBR	FR	POS	TPR
1899	StL-N	7	15	4	7	0	2	0	2	2		.467	.556	.733	250	3	3	6	0			-2	/CO	0.1
1900	StL-N	6	17	2	4	0	0	0	3	0		.235	.235	.235	32	-2	-2	1	0			-1	/CO	-0.1
1901	Det-A	70	231	28	52	5	5	2	29	11		.225	.269	.316	61	-11	-13	22	2			5	C	-0.1
1902	Det-A	66	224	23	50	5	2	2	29	9		.223	.253	.290	51	-15	-15	18	3			-1	C/1	-1.0
1903	Det-A	63	192	24	41	3	6	1	13	6		.214	.237	.307	66	-8	-8	16	4			1	C/1	0.0
1904	Det-A	42	136	6	15	1	1	0	5	8		.110	.160	.132	-6	-16	-15	4	2			2	C	-0.9
	Cle-A	42	119	11	21	4	1	0	5	11		.176	.246	.227	52	-6	-6	8	2			2	C	0.0
	Yr	84	255	17	36	5	2	0	10	19		.141	.201	.176	22	-22	-21	11	4			4		-0.9
1905	Cle-A	75	239	11	41	4	1	1	18	6		.172	.192	.209	28	-19	-19	12	7			-7	C/O13	-2.2
1906	Cle-A	34	86	7	14	2	0	0	7	9		.163	.242	.186	37	-6	-6	5	0			4	C/1	0.1
1907	StL-A	26	75	9	11	1	0	0	1	7		.147	.220	.160	23	-6	-6	3	0			0	C	-0.3
Total	9	431	1334	125	256	25	18	6	112	69		.192	.234	.251	46	-86	-87	95	20			3	C/O13	-4.4

■ ART BUES
Bues, Arthur Frederick   b: 3/3/1888, Milwaukee, Wis.   d: 11/7/54, Whitefish Bay, Wis.   BR/TR, 5'11", 184 lbs.   Deb: 4/17/13

YEAR	TM/L	G	AB	R	H	2B	3B	HR	RBI	BB	SO	AVG	OBP	SLG	PRO+	BR	/A	RC	SB	CS	SBR	FR	POS	TPR
1913	Bos-N	2	1	0	0	0	0	0	0	0	1	.000	.000	.000	-98	-0	-0	0	0			0	/23	0.0
1914	Chi-N	14	45	3	10	1	1	0	4	5	6	.222	.300	.289	76	-1	-1	4	1			-2	3	-0.3
Total	2	16	46	3	10	1	1	0	4	5	7	.217	.294	.283	72	-2	-2	4	1			-2	/32	-0.3

■ CHARLIE BUFFINTON
Buffinton, Charles G.   b: 6/14/1861, Fall River, Mass.   d: 9/23/07, Fall River, Mass.   BR/TR, 6'1", 180 lbs.   Deb: 5/17/1882   M

YEAR	TM/L	G	AB	R	H	2B	3B	HR	RBI	BB	SO	AVG	OBP	SLG	PRO+	BR	/A	RC	SB	CS	SBR	FR	POS	TPR
1882	Bos-N	15	50	5	13	1	0	0	4	2	3	.260	.288	.280	83	-1	-1	4				-1	/OP1	-0.1
1883	Bos-N	86	341	28	81	8	3	1	26	6	24	.238	.251	.287	62	-15	-16	25				-6	OP/1	-1.1
1884	Bos-N	87	352	48	94	18	3	1	39	16	12	.267	.299	.344	102	0	1	37				-0	PO1	0.0
1885	Bos-N	82	338	26	81	12	3	1	33	3	26	.240	.246	.302	80	-9	-8	26				0	PO1	0.0
1886	Bos-N	44	176	27	51	4	1	1	30	6	12	.290	.313	.341	103	-0	1	20	3			-1	1P	0.0
1887	Phi-N	66	269	34	72	12	1	1	46	11	3	.268	.299	.331	72	-8	-11	30	8			3	PO1	0.0
1888	Phi-N	46	160	14	29	4	1	0	12	7	5	.181	.216	.219	38	-10	-11	8	1			9	P/O	0.0
1889	Phi-N	47	154	16	32	2	0	0	21	9	5	.208	.256	.221	32	-13	-15	9	0			1	P/O	0.0
1890	Phi-P	42	150	24	41	3	2	1	24	9	3	.273	.319	.340	76	-5	-5	17	1			0	P/O1M	0.0
1891	Bos-a	58	181	16	34	2	1	1	16	19	15	.188	.269	.227	45	-13	-12	11	0			3	PO/1	0.0
1892	Bal-N	13	43	7	15	1	1	0	4	3	6	.349	.391	.419	142	2	2	8	1			2	P	0.0
Total	11	586	2214	245	543	67	16	7	255	91	114	.245	.276	.299	72	-72	-76	195	14			10	PO/1	-1.2

■ DON BUFORD
Buford, Donald Alvin   b: 2/2/37, Linden, Tex.   BB/TR, 5'7", 160 lbs.   Deb: 9/14/63   C

YEAR	TM/L	G	AB	R	H	2B	3B	HR	RBI	BB	SO	AVG	OBP	SLG	PRO+	BR	/A	RC	SB	CS	SBR	FR	POS	TPR
1963	Chi-A	12	42	9	12	1	2	0	5	5	7	.286	.362	.405	116	1	1	6	1	0	0	-5	/32	-0.2
1964	Chi-A	135	442	62	116	14	6	4	30	46	62	.262	.339	.348	94	-4	-2	54	12	7	-1	-16	23	-0.9
1965	Chi-A	155	586	93	166	22	5	10	47	67	76	.283	.361	.389	120	12	16	87	17	7	1	3	*23	2.8
1966	Chi-A	163	607	85	148	26	7	8	52	69	71	.244	.324	.349	100	-4	1	74	51	22	2	1	*32O	0.4
1967	Chi-A	156	535	61	129	10	9	4	32	65	55	.241	.324	.316	93	-5	-3	58	34	21	-2	4	*32/O	0.3
1968	Bal-A	130	426	65	120	13	4	15	46	57	46	.282	.372	.437	144	24	24	74	27	12	1	-6	O2/3	2.1
1969	*Bal-A	144	554	99	161	31	3	11	64	96	62	.291	.400	.417	128	25	25	97	19	18	-5	-7	*O2/3	1.0
1970	*Bal-A	144	504	99	137	15	2	17	66	109	55	.272	.409	.411	125	24	23	97	16	8	0	-1	*O/23	1.8
1971	*Bal-A	122	449	**99**	130	19	4	19	54	89	62	.290	.415	.477	153	34	35	97	15	7	0	-3	*O	3.0
1972	Bal-A	125	408	46	84	6	2	5	22	69	83	.206	.326	.267	76	-8	-9	40	8	3	1	-5	*O	-1.8
Total	10	1286	4553	718	1203	157	44	93	418	672	575	.264	.364	.379	115	98	109	686	200	105	-3	-35	O23	8.5

■ JAY BUHNER
Buhner, Jay Campbell   b: 8/13/64, Louisville, Ky.   BR/TR, 6'3", 205 lbs.   Deb: 9/11/87

YEAR	TM/L	G	AB	R	H	2B	3B	HR	RBI	BB	SO	AVG	OBP	SLG	PRO+	BR	/A	RC	SB	CS	SBR	FR	POS	TPR
1987	NY-A	7	22	0	5	2	0	0	1	1	6	.227	.261	.318	53	-2	-1	2	0	0	0	1	/O	0.0

YEAR	TM/L	G	AB	R	H	2B	3B	HR	RBI	BB	SO	AVG	OBP	SLG	PRO+	BR	/A	RC	SB	CS	SBR	FR	POS	TPR
1988	NY-A	25	69	8	13	0	0	3	13	3	25	.188	.253	.319	60	-4	-4	6	0	0	0	3	O	-0.1
	Sea-A	60	192	28	43	13	1	10	25	25	68	.224	.323	.458	111	4	3	29	1	1	-0	6	O	0.7
	Yr	85	261	36	56	13	1	13	38	28	93	.215	.305	.421	98	-0	-1	34	1	1	-0	9		0.6
1989	Sea-A	58	204	27	56	15	1	9	33	19	55	.275	.342	.490	128	8	7	34	1	4	-2	-1	O	0.3
1990	Sea-A	51	163	16	45	12	0	7	33	17	50	.276	.359	.479	131	7	7	27	2	2	-1	-5	OD	0.1
Total	4	201	650	79	162	42	2	29	105	65	204	.249	.329	.454	114	13	11	97	4	7	-3	3	O/D	1.0

■ HARRY BUKER
Buker, Henry L. "Happy" b: 1859, Chicago, Ill. d: 8/10/1899, Chicago, Ill. Deb: 6/11/1884

YEAR	TM/L	G	AB	R	H	2B	3B	HR	RBI	BB	SO	AVG	OBP	SLG	PRO+	BR	/A	RC	SB	CS	SBR	FR	POS	TPR
1884	Det-N	30	111	5	15	1	0	0	3	4	15	.135	.165	.144	-2	-13	-12	3				1	SO	-0.7

■ GEORGE BULLARD
Bullard, George Donald "Curly" b: 10/24/28, Lynn, Mass. BR/TR, 5'9.5", 165 lbs. Deb: 9/17/54

YEAR	TM/L	G	AB	R	H	2B	3B	HR	RBI	BB	SO	AVG	OBP	SLG	PRO+	BR	/A	RC	SB	CS	SBR	FR	POS	TPR
1954	Det-A	4	1	0	0	0	0	0	0	0	0	.000	.000	.000	-99	-0	-0	0	0	0	0	2	/S	0.2

■ SIM BULLAS
Bullas, Simeon Edward b: 4/10/1861, Cleveland, Ohio d: 1/14/08, Cleveland, Ohio 5'7.5", 150 lbs. Deb: 5/02/1884

YEAR	TM/L	G	AB	R	H	2B	3B	HR	RBI	BB	SO	AVG	OBP	SLG	PRO+	BR	/A	RC	SB	CS	SBR	FR	POS	TPR
1884	Tol-a	13	45	4	4	0	1	0		1		.089	.109	.133	-20	-6	-6	1				-2	C/O	-0.6

■ BUD BULLING
Bulling, Terry Charles "Terry" b: 12/15/52, Lynwood, Cal. BR/TR, 6'1", 200 lbs. Deb: 7/03/77

YEAR	TM/L	G	AB	R	H	2B	3B	HR	RBI	BB	SO	AVG	OBP	SLG	PRO+	BR	/A	RC	SB	CS	SBR	FR	POS	TPR
1977	Min-A	15	32	2	5	1	0	0	5	5	5	.156	.270	.188	28	-3	-3	2	0	0	0	-0	C/D	-0.2
1981	Sea-A	62	154	15	38	3	0	2	15	21	20	.247	.341	.305	84	-2	-3	18	0	0	0	-2	C	-0.1
1982	Sea-A	56	154	17	34	7	0	1	8	19	16	.221	.306	.286	62	-7	-8	13	2	1	0	7	C	0.2
1983	Sea-A	5	5	0	0	0	0	0	0	0	0	.000	.000	.000	-96	-1	-1	0	0	0	0	2	/C	0.0
Total	4	138	345	34	77	11	0	3	28	45	41	.223	.315	.281	66	-13	-15	33	2	1	0	6	C/D	-0.1

■ ERIC BULLOCK
Bullock, Eric Gerald b: 2/16/60, Los Angeles, Cal. BL/TL, 5'11", 185 lbs. Deb: 8/26/85

YEAR	TM/L	G	AB	R	H	2B	3B	HR	RBI	BB	SO	AVG	OBP	SLG	PRO+	BR	/A	RC	SB	CS	SBR	FR	POS	TPR
1985	Hou-N	18	25	3	7	2	0	0	2	1	3	.280	.308	.360	89	-1	-0	2	0	1	-1	-1	/O	-0.1
1986	Hou-N	6	21	0	1	0	0	0	1	0	3	.048	.048	.048	-76	-5	-5	0	2	0	1	-1	/O	-0.5
1988	Min-A	16	17	3	5	0	0	0	3	3	1	.294	.400	.294	95	0	0	3	1	0	0	1	/OD	0.1
1989	Phi-N	6	4	1	0	0	0	0	0	0	2	.000	.000	.000	-99	-1	-1	0	0	0	0	0	/O	0.0
1990	Mon-N	4	2	0	1	0	0	0	0	0	0	.500	.500	.500	177	0	0	1	0	0	0	0	/H	0.0
Total	5	50	69	7	14	2	0	0	6	4	9	.203	.247	.232	35	-6	-6	6	3	1	0	-1	/OD	-0.5

■ AL BUMBRY
Bumbry, Alonza Benjamin (b: Alonza Benjamin Bumbrey) b: 4/21/47, Fredericksburg, Va. BL/TR, 5'8", 170 lbs. Deb: 9/05/72 C

YEAR	TM/L	G	AB	R	H	2B	3B	HR	RBI	BB	SO	AVG	OBP	SLG	PRO+	BR	/A	RC	SB	CS	SBR	FR	POS	TPR
1972	Bal-A	9	11	5	4	0	1	0	0	0	0	.364	.364	.545	164	1	1	2	1	1	-0	0	/O	0.1
1973	*Bal-A	110	356	73	120	15	11	7	34	34	49	.337	.399	.500	153	24	25	72	23	10	1	-11	O/D	1.3
1974	*Bal-A	94	270	35	63	10	3	1	19	21	46	.233	.291	.304	74	-10	-9	25	12	4	1	8	O/D	-0.1
1975	Bal-A	114	349	47	94	19	4	2	32	32	81	.269	.338	.364	105	-1	2	47	16	3	3	5	DO/3	1.0
1976	Bal-A	133	450	71	113	15	7	9	36	43	76	.251	.318	.376	109	1	5	57	42	10	7	-2	*OD	0.7
1977	Bal-A	133	518	74	164	31	3	4	41	45	88	.317	.373	.411	121	11	15	83	19	8	1	-5	*O	0.6
1978	Bal-A	33	114	21	27	5	2	2	6	17	15	.237	.346	.368	108	1	1	15	5	3	-0	-1	O	0.0
1979	*Bal-A	148	569	80	162	29	1	7	49	43	74	.285	.338	.376	96	-6	-3	76	37	12	4	-6	*O	-1.0
1980	Bal-A	160	645	118	205	29	9	9	53	78	75	.318	.394	.433	128	26	27	118	44	11	7	11	*O	4.0
1981	Bal-A	101	392	61	107	18	2	1	27	51	51	.273	.360	.337	102	3	3	49	22	15	-2	0	*O	-0.1
1982	Bal-A	150	562	77	147	20	4	5	40	44	77	.262	.315	.338	80	-15	-15	60	10	5	0	2	*O/D	-1.7
1983	*Bal-A	124	378	63	104	14	4	3	31	31	33	.275	.330	.357	91	-5	-4	47	12	5	1	-10	*OD	-1.4
1984	Bal-A	119	344	47	93	12	1	3	24	25	35	.270	.320	.337	84	-8	-7	35	9	5	-0	-9	*O	-1.9
1985	SD-N	68	95	6	19	3	0	1	10	7	9	.200	.255	.263	46	-7	-7	6	2	0	1	-0	O	-0.6
Total	14	1496	5053	778	1422	220	52	54	402	471	709	.281	.345	.378	104	14	33	692	254	92	21	-18	*O/D3	0.9

■ JOSH BUNCE
Bunce, Joshua b: 5/10/1847, Brooklyn, N.Y. d: 4/28/12, Brooklyn, N.Y. Deb: 8/27/1877

YEAR	TM/L	G	AB	R	H	2B	3B	HR	RBI	BB	SO	AVG	OBP	SLG	PRO+	BR	/A	RC	SB	CS	SBR	FR	POS	TPR
1877	Har-N	1	4	0	0	0	0	0	0	0	0	.000	.000	.000	-99	-1	-1	0				-0	/O	0.0

■ NELSON BURBRINK
Burbrink, Nelson Edward b: 12/28/21, Cincinnati, Ohio BR/TR, 5'10", 195 lbs. Deb: 6/05/55

YEAR	TM/L	G	AB	R	H	2B	3B	HR	RBI	BB	SO	AVG	OBP	SLG	PRO+	BR	/A	RC	SB	CS	SBR	FR	POS	TPR
1955	StL-N	58	170	11	47	8	1	0	15	14	13	.276	.335	.335	79	-5	-5	19	1	1	-0	0	C	-0.3

■ AL BURCH
Burch, Albert William b: 10/7/1883, Albany, N.Y. d: 10/5/26, Brooklyn, N.Y. BL/TR, 5'8.5", 160 lbs. Deb: 6/19/06

YEAR	TM/L	G	AB	R	H	2B	3B	HR	RBI	BB	SO	AVG	OBP	SLG	PRO+	BR	/A	RC	SB	CS	SBR	FR	POS	TPR
1906	StL-N	91	335	40	89	5	1	0	11	37		.266	.339	.287	101	0	2	40	15			1	O	0.1
1907	StL-N	48	154	18	35	3	1	0	5	17		.227	.304	.260	81	-3	-3	15	7			0	O	-0.4
	Bro-N	40	120	12	35	2	2	0	12	11		.292	.351	.342	130	3	4	17	5			2	O/2	0.5
	Yr	88	274	30	70	5	3	0	17	28		.255	.325	.296	102	-0	1	31	12			2		0.1
1908	Bro-N	123	456	45	111	8	4	2	18	33		.243	.294	.292	93	-5	-3	43	15			13	*O	0.9
1909	Bro-N	152	601	80	163	20	6	1	30	51		.271	.329	.329	108	3	5	76	38			6	*O/1	0.7
1910	Bro-N	103	352	41	83	8	3	1	20	22	30	.236	.281	.284	67	-16	-15	31	13			-3	O1	-2.1
1911	Bro-N	54	167	18	38	2	3	0	7	15	22	.228	.291	.275	61	-9	-8	14	3			4	O/2	-0.4
Total	6	611	2185	254	554	48	20	4	103	186	52	.254	.312	.299	92	-28	-18	236	96			23	O/12	-0.7

■ ERNIE BURCH
Burch, Earnest W. b: 1856, Dekalb Co., Ill. BL, Deb: 8/15/1884

YEAR	TM/L	G	AB	R	H	2B	3B	HR	RBI	BB	SO	AVG	OBP	SLG	PRO+	BR	/A	RC	SB	CS	SBR	FR	POS	TPR
1884	Cle-N	32	124	9	26	4	0	0	7	5	24	.210	.240	.242	50	-7	-7	7				5	O	-0.2
1886	Bro-a	113	456	78	119	22	6	2		39		.261	.321	.349	110	6	5	58	16			-12	*O	-0.9
1887	Bro-a	49	188	47	55	4	4	2		29		.293	.395	.388	120	7	6	36	15			1	O	0.4
Total	3	194	768	134	200	30	10	4	7	73	24	.260	.328	.341	104	6	4	101	31			-7	O	-0.7

■ BOB BURDA
Burda, Edward Robert b: 7/16/38, St.Louis, Mo. BL/TL, 5'11", 174 lbs. Deb: 8/25/62

YEAR	TM/L	G	AB	R	H	2B	3B	HR	RBI	BB	SO	AVG	OBP	SLG	PRO+	BR	/A	RC	SB	CS	SBR	FR	POS	TPR
1962	StL-N	7	14	0	1	0	0	0	0	3	1	.071	.235	.071	-12	-2	-2	1	0	0	0	0	/O	-0.1
1965	SF-N	31	27	0	3	0	0	0	5	5	6	.111	.250	.111	6	-3	-3	1	0	0	0	-1	1/O	-0.4
1966	SF-N	37	43	3	7	3	0	0	2	2	5	.163	.200	.233	19	-5	-5	2	0	0	0	0	/1O	-0.5
1969	SF-N	97	161	20	37	8	0	6	27	21	12	.230	.319	.391	100	-1	-0	21	0	1	-1	0	1O	-0.5
1970	SF-N	28	23	1	6	0	0	0	3	5	2	.261	.414	.261	86	-0	-0	3	0	0	0	-1	/1O	0.0
	Mil-A	78	222	19	55	9	0	4	20	16	17	.248	.307	.342	78	-7	-7	24	1	0	0	-7	O/1	-1.7
1971	StL-N	65	71	6	21	0	0	1	12	10	11	.296	.390	.338	104	1	1	10	0	0	0	0	1/O	0.0
1972	Bos-A	45	73	4	12	1	0	2	9	8	11	.164	.247	.260	48	-4	-5	4	0	0	0	0	1/O	-0.6
Total	7	388	634	53	142	21	0	13	78	70	65	.224	.306	.319	74	-20	-21	64	2	1	0	-7	1/O	-3.8

■ JACK BURDOCK
Burdock, John Joseph "Black Jack" b: 1851, Brooklyn, N.Y. d: 11/28/31, Brooklyn, N.Y. BR/TR, 5'9.5", 158 lbs. Deb: 5/02/1872 M

YEAR	TM/L	G	AB	R	H	2B	3B	HR	RBI	BB	SO	AVG	OBP	SLG	PRO+	BR	/A	RC	SB	CS	SBR	FR	POS	TPR
1872	Atl-n	37	174	26	45	2	1	0		1		.259	.263	.282	58	-6	-13	13					*S/C2	-0.8
1873	Atl-n	55	244	56	62	9	2	2		7		.254	.275	.332	87	-7	-1	23					*2	-0.3
1874	Mut-n	61	272	45	76	16	3	2		1		.279	.282	.382	106	3	1	30					*3	0.0
1875	Har-n	74	347	72	102	14	5	0		5		.294	.304	.363	123	10	7	39					*2/3	0.4
1876	Har-N	69	309	66	80	9	1	0	23	13	16	.259	.289	.294	87	-1	-5	27				1	*2/3	-0.3
1877	Har-N	58	277	35	72	6	0	0	9	2	16	.260	.265	.282	81	-9	-4	21				7	*2/3	0.4
1878	Bos-N	60	246	37	64	12	6	0	25	3	17	.260	.269	.358	97	1	-2	24				21	*2	2.2
1879	Bos-N	84	359	64	86	10	3	0	36	9	28	.240	.258	.284	77	-8	-9	27				10	*2	0.8
1880	Bos-N	86	356	58	90	17	4	2	35	8	26	.253	.269	.340	108	2	3	33				12	*2	1.7
1881	Bos-N	73	282	36	67	12	4	1	24	7	18	.238	.259	.319	84	-7	-5	24				-11	*2/S	-1.1
1882	Bos-N	83	319	36	76	6	7	0	27	9	24	.238	.259	.301	79	-7	-7	25				4	*2	-0.1
1883	Bos-N	96	400	80	132	27	8	5	88	14	35	.330	.353	.475	145	23	21	69				-1	*2/M	1.4
1884	Bos-N	87	361	65	97	14	4	6	49	15	52	.269	.298	.380	112	4	5	42				2	*2/3	0.7

YEAR	TM/L	G	AB	R	H	2B	3B	HR	RBI	BB	SO	AVG	OBP	SLG	PRO+	BR	/A	RC	SB	CS	SBR	FR	POS	TPR
1885	Bos-N	45	169	18	24	5	0	0	7	8	18	.142	.181	.172	15	-16	-15	5				-4	2	-1.3
1886	Bos-N	59	221	26	48	6	1	0	25	11	27	.217	.254	.253	57	-12	-10	15	3			-8	2	-1.3
1887	Bos-N	65	237	36	61	6	0	0	29	18	22	.257	.320	.283	70	-8	-9	28	19			-18	2	-1.9
1888	Bos-N	22	79	5	16	0	0	0	4	2	5	.203	.232	.203	40	-5	-5	4	1			0	2	-0.3
	Bro-a	70	246	15	30	1	2	0	8	8		.122	.166	.154	5	-25	-25	8	9			2	2	-1.9
1891	Bro-N	3	12	1	1	0	0	0	1	1	1	.083	.154	.083	-30	-2	-2	0	0			-1	/2	-0.1
Total	4 n	227	1037	199	285	41	11	4		14		.275	.284	.347	97	-0	-6	105	0				2/3SC	-0.7
Total	14	960	3873	578	944	131	40	15	390	128	305	.244	.270	.310	84	-70	-69	354	32			17	2/3S	-1.1

■ PETE BURG   Burg, Joseph Peter b: 6/4/1882, Chicago, Ill. d: 4/28/69, Joliet, Ill. TR , 5'1", 150 lbs. Deb: 9/26/10

YEAR	TM/L	G	AB	R	H	2B	3B	HR	RBI	BB	SO	AVG	OBP	SLG	PRO+	BR	/A	RC	SB	CS	SBR	FR	POS	TPR
1910	Bos-N	13	46	7	15	0	0	0	10	7	12	.326	.415	.370	124	2	2	9	5			3	3/S	0.5

■ SMOKY BURGESS   Burgess, Forrest Harrill b: 2/6/27, Caroleen, N.C. BL/TR, 5'8.5", 185 lbs. Deb: 4/19/49

YEAR	TM/L	G	AB	R	H	2B	3B	HR	RBI	BB	SO	AVG	OBP	SLG	PRO+	BR	/A	RC	SB	CS	SBR	FR	POS	TPR
1949	Chi-N	46	56	4	15	0	0	1	12	4	4	.268	.317	.321	73	-2	-2	6	0			1	/C	0.0
1951	Chi-N	94	219	21	55	4	2	2	20	21	12	.251	.317	.315	69	-9	-9	21	2	0	1	-2	C	-1.0
1952	Phi-N	110	371	49	110	27	2	6	56	49	21	.296	.380	.429	125	13	13	65	3	1	0	-7	*C	0.9
1953	Phi-N	102	312	31	91	17	5	4	36	37	17	.292	.370	.417	105	3	3	48	3	2	-0	-8	C	0.1
1954	Phi-N	108	345	41	127	27	5	4	46	42	11	.368	.437	.510	146	25	25	75	1	5	-3	-8	C	1.6
1955	Phi-N	7	21	4	4	2	0	1	1	3	1	.190	.292	.429	90	-0	-0	2	0	0	0	1	/C	0.1
	Cin-N	116	421	67	129	15	3	20	77	47	35	.306	.377	.499	123	18	15	78	1	1	-0	-10	*C	0.8
	Yr	123	442	71	133	17	3	21	78	50	36	.301	.373	.495	122	18	18	80	1	1	-0	-9		0.9
1956	Cin-N	90	229	28	63	10	0	12	39	26	18	.275	.349	.476	112	6	4	37	0	1	-1	-2	C	0.3
1957	Cin-N	90	205	29	58	14	1	14	39	24	16	.283	.358	.566	134	12	10	41	0	0	0	-5	C	0.7
1958	Cin-N	99	251	28	71	12	1	6	31	22	20	.283	.343	.410	93	-1	-2	34	0	0	0	4	C	0.5
1959	Pit-N	114	377	41	112	28	5	11	59	31	16	.297	.354	.485	122	11	11	62	0	0	0	-17	*C	0.0
1960	*Pit-N	110	337	33	99	15	2	7	39	35	13	.294	.360	.412	110	6	5	50	0	1	-1	0	C	0.9
1961	Pit-N	100	323	37	98	17	3	12	52	30	16	.303	.366	.486	123	11	11	57	1	0	0	-14	C	0.4
1962	Pit-N	103	360	38	118	19	2	13	61	31	19	.328	.381	.500	134	17	17	68	0	1	-1	-12	*C	0.6
1963	Pit-N	91	264	20	74	10	1	6	37	24	14	.280	.343	.394	111	4	4	32	0	1	-1	-11	C	-0.6
1964	Pit-N	68	171	9	42	3	1	2	17	13	14	.246	.303	.310	73	-6	-6	14	2	1	0	-9	C	-1.3
	Chi-A	7	5	1	1	0	0	1	1	2	0	.200	.429	.800	239	1	1	2	0	0	0	0	H	0.1
1965	Chi-A	80	77	2	22	4	0	2	24	11	7	.286	.375	.416	132	3	3	12	0	0	0	-0	/C	0.4
1966	Chi-A	79	67	0	21	5	0	0	15	11	8	.313	.418	.388	143	4	4	12	0	0	0	-0	/C	0.4
1967	Chi-A	77	60	2	8	1	0	0	2	11	14	.133	.307	.250	69	-2	-2	5	0	0	0	0	H	-0.1
Total	18	1691	4471	485	1318	230	33	126	673	477	270	.295	.364	.446	116	112	105	722	13	14		-99	*C	4.8

■ TOM BURGESS   Burgess, Thomas Roland "Tim" b: 9/1/27, London, Ont., Can. BL/TL, 6', 180 lbs. Deb: 4/17/54 C

YEAR	TM/L	G	AB	R	H	2B	3B	HR	RBI	BB	SO	AVG	OBP	SLG	PRO+	BR	/A	RC	SB	CS	SBR	FR	POS	TPR
1954	StL-N	17	21	2	1	1	0	0	1	3	9	.048	.167	.095	-29	-4	-4	0	0	0	0	-1	/O	-0.4
1962	LA-A	87	143	17	28	7	1	2	13	36	20	.196	.358	.301	82	-3	-2	18	2	0	1	-2	1/O	-0.5
Total	2	104	164	19	29	8	1	2	14	39	29	.177	.335	.274	67	-7	-6	19	2	0	1	-3	/1O	-0.9

■ BILL BURGO   Burgo, William Ross b: 11/5/19, Johnstown, Pa. d: 10/19/88, Morgan City, La. BR/TR, 5'8", 185 lbs. Deb: 9/22/43

YEAR	TM/L	G	AB	R	H	2B	3B	HR	RBI	BB	SO	AVG	OBP	SLG	PRO+	BR	/A	RC	SB	CS	SBR	FR	POS	TPR
1943	Phi-A	17	70	12	26	4	2	1	9	4	1	.371	.421	.529	178	7	7	16	0	2	-1	1	O	0.7
1944	Phi-A	27	88	6	21	2	0	1	3	7	3	.239	.316	.295	76	-3	-2	8	1	3	-2	1	O	-0.3
Total	2	44	158	18	47	6	2	2	12	11	4	.297	.362	.399	121	4	4	23	1	5	-3	2	/O	0.4

■ BILL BURICH   Burich, William Max b: 5/29/18, Calumet, Mich. BR/TR, 6', 180 lbs. Deb: 4/15/42

YEAR	TM/L	G	AB	R	H	2B	3B	HR	RBI	BB	SO	AVG	OBP	SLG	PRO+	BR	/A	RC	SB	CS	SBR	FR	POS	TPR
1942	Phi-N	25	80	3	23	1	0	0	7	6	13	.287	.337	.300	92	-1	-1	8	2			-5	S/3	-0.4
1946	Phi-N	2	1	1	0	0	0	0	0	0	0	.000	.000	.000	-99	-0	-0	0	0			0	/3	0.0
Total	2	27	81	4	23	1	0	0	7	6	13	.284	.333	.296	89	-1	-1	8	2			-5	/S3	-0.4

■ MACK BURK   Burk, Mack Edwin b: 4/21/35, Nacogdoches, Tex. BR/TR, 6'4", 180 lbs. Deb: 5/25/56

YEAR	TM/L	G	AB	R	H	2B	3B	HR	RBI	BB	SO	AVG	OBP	SLG	PRO+	BR	/A	RC	SB	CS	SBR	FR	POS	TPR
1956	Phi-N	15	1	3	1	0	0	0	0	0	0	1.000	1.000	1.000	449	0	0	1	0	0	0	5	/C	0.5
1958	Phi-N	1	1	0	0	0	0	0	0	0	1	.000	.000	.000	-99	-0	-0	0	0	0	0	0	H	0.0
Total	2	16	2	3	1	0	0	0	0	0	1	.500	.500	.500	171	0	0	1	0	0	0	5	/C	0.5

■ CHRIS BURKAM   Burkam, Chauncey De Pew b: 10/13/1892, Benton Harbor, Mich. d: 5/9/64, Kalamazoo, Mich. BL/TR, 5'11", 175 lbs. Deb: 6/24/15

YEAR	TM/L	G	AB	R	H	2B	3B	HR	RBI	BB	SO	AVG	OBP	SLG	PRO+	BR	/A	RC	SB	CS	SBR	FR	POS	TPR
1915	StL-A	1	1	0	0	0	0	0	0	0	1	.000	.000	.000	-99	-0	-0	0	0			0	H	0.0

■ DAN BURKE   Burke, Daniel L. b: 10/25/1868, Abington, Mass. d: 3/20/33, Taunton, Mass. BR/TR, 5'10", 190 lbs. Deb: 4/18/1890

YEAR	TM/L	G	AB	R	H	2B	3B	HR	RBI	BB	SO	AVG	OBP	SLG	PRO+	BR	/A	RC	SB	CS	SBR	FR	POS	TPR
1890	Roc-a	32	102	14	22	1	0	0		17		.216	.333	.225	73	-3	-2	9	2			-6	O/C1	-0.7
	Syr-a	9	20	1	0	0	0	0		5		.000	.231	.000	-33	-3	-3	0	0			3	/C	0.1
	Yr	41	122	15	22	1	0	0		22		.180	.315	.189	55	-6	-4	8	2			-3		-0.6
1892	Bos-N	1	4	0	0	0	0	0	0	0	2	.000	.000	.000	-92	-1	-1	0	0			1	/C	0.0
Total	2	42	126	15	22	1	0	0	0	22	2	.175	.307	.183	50	-7	-5	9	2			-2	/OC1	-0.6

■ EDDIE BURKE   Burke, Edward D. b: 10/6/1866, Northumberland, Pa. d: 11/26/07, Utica, N.Y. BR/TR, 5'6", 161 lbs. Deb: 4/19/1890

YEAR	TM/L	G	AB	R	H	2B	3B	HR	RBI	BB	SO	AVG	OBP	SLG	PRO+	BR	/A	RC	SB	CS	SBR	FR	POS	TPR
1890	Phi-N	100	430	85	113	16	11	4	50	49	40	.263	.349	.379	112	8	7	72	38			4	*O/2	0.7
	Pit-N	31	124	17	26	5	2	1	7	14	9	.210	.295	.306	87	-3	-1	13	6			0	O	0.0
	Yr	131	554	102	139	21	13	5	57	63	49	.251	.337	.363	107	5	6	85	44			4		0.7
1891	Mil-a	35	144	31	34	9	0	2	21	12	19	.236	.337	.340	80	-0	-5	19	7			3	O	-0.3
1892	Cin-N	15	41	6	6	1	0	0	4	9	4	.146	.300	.171	45	-2	-2	3	2			-3	O/3	-0.4
	NY-N	89	363	81	94	10	5	6	41	46	37	.259	.350	.364	120	9	10	62	42			-3	2O	0.6
	Yr	104	404	87	100	11	5	6	45	55	41	.248	.345	.344	112	7	7	65	44			-6		0.2
1893	NY-N	135	537	122	150	23	10	9	80	51	32	.279	.369	.410	108	7	7	104	54			2	*O	0.3
1894	*NY-N	136	566	121	172	23	11	4	77	37	35	.304	.357	.405	86	-14	-13	96	34			-4	*O	-2.0
1895	NY-N	39	167	38	43	6	2	1	12	7	9	.257	.299	.335	67	-9	-8	21	14			2	O	-0.7
	Cin-N	56	228	52	61	8	6	1	25	22	14	.268	.343	.368	82	-5	-7	36	19			2	O	0.0
	Yr	95	395	90	104	14	8	2	37	29	23	.263	.325	.354	76	-14	-15	58	33			4		-1.4
1896	Cin-N	122	521	120	177	24	9	1	52	41	29	.340	.392	.426	110	14	8	111	53			3	*O	0.2
1897	Cin-N	95	387	71	103	17	1	1	41	29		.266	.327	.323	69	-14	-18	49	22			7	*O	-1.5
Total	8	853	3508	744	979	142	57	30	410	317	228	.279	.352	.378	95	-9	-24	587	291			14	O/23	-3.8

■ FRANK BURKE   Burke, Frank Aloysius b: 2/16/1880, Carbon, Co., Pa. d: 9/17/46, Los Angeles, Cal. TR , Deb: 9/14/06

YEAR	TM/L	G	AB	R	H	2B	3B	HR	RBI	BB	SO	AVG	OBP	SLG	PRO+	BR	/A	RC	SB	CS	SBR	FR	POS	TPR
1906	NY-N	8	9	2	3	1	1	0	1	1		.333	.400	.667	230	1	1	3	1			-2	/O	0.0
1907	Bos-N	43	129	6	23	0	1	0	8	11		.178	.243	.194	39	-9	-9	8	3			-4	O	-1.5
Total	2	51	138	8	26	1	2	0	9	12		.188	.253	.225	51	-7	-7	10	4			-5	/O	-1.5

■ GLENN BURKE   Burke, Glenn Lawrence b: 11/16/52, Oakland, Cal. BR/TR, 6', 195 lbs. Deb: 4/09/76

YEAR	TM/L	G	AB	R	H	2B	3B	HR	RBI	BB	SO	AVG	OBP	SLG	PRO+	BR	/A	RC	SB	CS	SBR	FR	POS	TPR
1976	LA-N	25	46	9	11	2	0	0	5	3	8	.239	.300	.283	67	-2	-2	4	3	2	-0	1	O	-0.1
1977	*LA-N	83	169	16	43	8	0	1	13	5	22	.254	.280	.320	61	-10	-9	15	13	5	1	1	O	-1.0
1978	LA-N	16	19	3	4	0	0	0	2	0	4	.211	.211	.211	18	-2	-2	1	1	0	0	0	O	-0.2
	Oak-A	78	200	19	47	6	1	1	14	10	26	.235	.271	.290	61	-11	-10	14	15	8	-0	3	O/1D	-0.8
1979	Oak-A	23	89	4	19	2	1	0	4	4	10	.213	.247	.258	39	-8	-7	5	3	1	0	-1	O	-0.8
Total	4	225	523	50	124	18	2	2	38	22	70	.237	.271	.291	56	-33	-31	38	35	16	1	3	O/D1	-2.9

YEAR	TM/L	G	AB	R	H	2B	3B	HR	RBI	BB	SO	AVG	OBP	SLG	PRO+	BR	/A	RC	SB	CS	SBR	FR	POS	TPR

■ JIMMY BURKE
Burke, James Timothy "Sunset Jimmy"   b: 10/12/1874, St.Louis, Mo.   d: 3/26/42, St.Louis, Mo.   BR/TR, 5'7", 160 lbs.   Deb: 10/06/1898   MC

YEAR	TM/L	G	AB	R	H	2B	3B	HR	RBI	BB	SO	AVG	OBP	SLG	PRO+	BR	/A	RC	SB	CS	SBR	FR	POS	TPR
1898	Cle-N	13	38	1	4	1	0	0	1	2		.105	.150	.132	-18	-6	-6	1	1			-4	3	-0.8
1899	StL-N	2	6	1	2	0	0	0	0	1		.333	.429	.333	111	0	0	1	0			1	/2	0.1
1901	Mil-A	64	233	24	48	8	0	0	26	17		.206	.266	.240	45	-17	-16	18	6			-7	3	-2.1
	Chi-A	42	148	20	39	5	0	0	21	12		.264	.327	.297	78	-4	-4	19	11			-2	S3	-0.2
	Yr	106	381	44	87	13	0	0	47	29		.228	.290	.262	58	-22	-19	37	17			-9		-2.3
	Pit-N	14	51	4	10	0	0	0	4	4		.196	.268	.196	36	-4	-4	3	0			3	3	0.0
1902	Pit-N	60	203	24	60	12	2	0	26	17		.296	.356	.374	123	7	6	32	9			-5	2O/3S	0.2
1903	StL-N	115	431	55	123	13	3	0	42	23		.285	.322	.329	90	-7	-5	57	28			6	32/O	0.2
1904	StL-N	118	406	37	92	10	3	0	37	15		.227	.254	.266	65	-18	-16	34	17			-7	*3	-1.8
1905	StL-N	122	431	34	97	9	5	1	30	21		.225	.261	.276	64	-20	-19	37	15			3	*3M	-0.7
Total	7	550	1947	200	475	58	13	1	187	112		.244	.288	.289	73	-69	-62	201	87			-12	3/2SO	-5.1

■ JOHN BURKE
Burke, John Patrick   b: 1/27/1877, Hazelton, Pa.   d: 8/4/50, Jersey City, N.J.   BR/TR,   Deb: 6/27/02

YEAR	TM/L	G	AB	R	H	2B	3B	HR	RBI	BB	SO	AVG	OBP	SLG	PRO+	BR	/A	RC	SB	CS	SBR	FR	POS	TPR
1902	NY-N	4	13	0	2	0	0	0	0	0		.154	.154	.154	-4	-2	-2	0	0			-1	/PO	-0.2

■ JOE BURKE
Burke, Joseph A.   b: Cincinnati, Ohio   5'7", 160 lbs.   Deb: 9/26/1890

YEAR	TM/L	G	AB	R	H	2B	3B	HR	RBI	BB	SO	AVG	OBP	SLG	PRO+	BR	/A	RC	SB	CS	SBR	FR	POS	TPR
1890	StL-a	2	6	3	4	0	0	0		1		.667	.750	.667	283	2	2	3	0			-0	/3	0.1
1891	Cin-a	1	4	0	1	0	0	0	1	0	2	.250	.250	.250	42	-0	-0	0	0			1	/2	0.1
Total	2	3	10	3	5	0	0	0	1	1	2	.500	.583	.500	196	2	2	3	0			1	/32	0.2

■ LEO BURKE
Burke, Leo Patrick   b: 5/6/34, Hagerstown, Md.   BR/TR, 5'11", 185 lbs.   Deb: 9/07/58

YEAR	TM/L	G	AB	R	H	2B	3B	HR	RBI	BB	SO	AVG	OBP	SLG	PRO+	BR	/A	RC	SB	CS	SBR	FR	POS	TPR
1958	Bal-A	7	11	4	5	1	0	1	4	1	2	.455	.500	.818	271	2	2	5	0	0	0	-1	/O3	0.1
1959	Bal-A	5	10	0	2	0	0	0	1	0	5	.200	.273	.200	33	-1	-1	0	0	0	0	-2	/23	-0.2
1961	LA-A	6	5	0	0	0	0	0	0	0	1	.000	.000	.000	-90	-1	-1	0	0	0	0	0	H	0.0
1962	LA-A	19	64	8	17	1	0	4	14	5	11	.266	.329	.469	115	1	1	10	0	0	0	-1	O/3S	0.0
1963	StL-N	30	49	6	10	2	1	1	5	4	12	.204	.264	.347	68	-2	-2	4	0	0	0	-0	O/3	-0.2
	Chi-N	27	49	4	9	0	0	2	7	4	13	.184	.245	.306	55	-3	-3	3	0	1	-1	3	2/1	0.0
	Yr	57	98	10	19	2	1	3	12	8	25	.194	.255	.327	61	-4	-5	8	0	1	-1	3		-0.2
1964	Chi-N	59	103	11	27	3	1	1	14	7	31	.262	.315	.340	81	-2	-3	11	0	0	0	-1	0/231C	-0.3
1965	Chi-N	12	10	0	2	0	0	0	0	0	4	.200	.200	.200	13	-1	-1	0	0	0	0	0	/CO	0.0
Total	7	165	301	33	72	7	2	9	45	21	79	.239	.295	.365	81	-7	-8	34	0	1	-1	-3	/0231CS	-0.6

■ LES BURKE
Burke, Leslie Kingston "Buck"   b: 12/18/02, Lynn, Mass.   d: 5/6/75, Danvers, Mass.   BL/TR, 5'9", 168 lbs.   Deb: 5/02/23

YEAR	TM/L	G	AB	R	H	2B	3B	HR	RBI	BB	SO	AVG	OBP	SLG	PRO+	BR	/A	RC	SB	CS	SBR	FR	POS	TPR
1923	Det-A	7	10	2	1	0	0	0	2	0	1	.100	.100	.100	-48	-2	-2	0	0	0	0	-1	/32	-0.2
1924	Det-A	72	241	30	61	10	4	0	17	22	20	.253	.321	.328	69	-12	-11	26	2	4	-2	-6	2/S	-1.5
1925	Det-A	77	180	32	52	6	3	0	24	17	8	.289	.357	.356	82	-5	-4	25	4	1	1	2	2	0.0
1926	Det-A	38	75	9	17	1	0	0	4	7	3	.227	.301	.240	42	-6	-6	6	1	2	1	4	2/3S	-0.1
Total	4	194	506	73	131	17	7	0	47	46	32	.259	.327	.320	67	-25	-24	56	7	7	-2	-1	2/3S	-1.8

■ MIKE BURKE
Burke, Michael E.   b: Cincinnati, Ohio   d: 6/9/1889, Albany, N.Y.   BR/TR, 6', 190 lbs.   Deb: 5/01/1879

YEAR	TM/L	G	AB	R	H	2B	3B	HR	RBI	BB	SO	AVG	OBP	SLG	PRO+	BR	/A	RC	SB	CS	SBR	FR	POS	TPR
1879	Cin-N	28	117	13	26	3	0	0	8	2	5	.222	.235	.248	63	-5	-4	7				-7	S/O3	-0.8

■ PAT BURKE
Burke, Patrick Edward   b: 5/13/01, St.Louis, Mo.   d: 7/7/65, St.Louis, Mo.   BR/TR, 5'10.5", 170 lbs.   Deb: 9/23/24

YEAR	TM/L	G	AB	R	H	2B	3B	HR	RBI	BB	SO	AVG	OBP	SLG	PRO+	BR	/A	RC	SB	CS	SBR	FR	POS	TPR
1924	StL-A	1	3	0	0	0	0	0	1	0	0	.000	.000	.000	-94	-1	-1	0	0	0	0	0	/3	0.0

■ WALTER BURKE
Burke, Walter R.   b: California   d: 3/3/11, Memphis, Tenn.   6', 200 lbs.   Deb: 6/10/1882

YEAR	TM/L	G	AB	R	H	2B	3B	HR	RBI	BB	SO	AVG	OBP	SLG	PRO+	BR	/A	RC	SB	CS	SBR	FR	POS	TPR
1882	Buf-N	1	4	0	0	0	0	0	0	0	1	.000	.000	.000	-98	-1	-1	0				1	/OP	0.0
1883	Buf-N	1	5	0	1	0	0	0	1	0	3	.200	.200	.200	22	-0	-0	0				-1	/OP	0.0
1884	Bos-U	47	184	21	41	8	3	0		6		.223	.247	.299	85	-3	-3	14	0			-4	PO	0.0
1887	Det-N	2	8	1	2	0	0	0	1	0	1	.250	.250	.250	39	-1	-1	1	0			-0	/PO	0.0
Total	4	51	201	22	44	8	3	0	2	6	5	.219	.242	.289	77	-5	-5	15	0			-4	/PO	0.0

■ JESSE BURKETT
Burkett, Jesse Cail "Crab"   b: 12/4/1868, Wheeling, W.Va.   d: 5/27/53, Worcester, Mass.   BL/TL, 5'8", 155 lbs.   Deb: 4/22/1890   CH

YEAR	TM/L	G	AB	R	H	2B	3B	HR	RBI	BB	SO	AVG	OBP	SLG	PRO+	BR	/A	RC	SB	CS	SBR	FR	POS	TPR
1890	NY-N	101	401	67	124	23	3	4	60	33	52	.309	.366	.461	143	20	20	75	14			3	OP	2.2
1891	Cle-N	40	167	29	45	7	4	0	13	23	19	.269	.358	.359	107	3	2	22	1			-3	O	-0.2
1892	*Cle-N	145	608	119	167	15	14	6	66	67	59	.275	.348	.375	116	15	12	94	36			3	*O	0.9
1893	Cle-N	125	511	145	178	25	15	6	82	98	23	.348	.459	.491	146	45	39	137	39			-8	*O	2.1
1894	Cle-N	125	523	138	187	27	14	8	94	84	27	.358	.447	.509	127	30	26	135	28			-4	*O/P	1.1
1895	*Cle-N	131	550	153	**225**	22	13	5	83	74	31	**.409**	.486	.524	154	56	50	164	41			-3	*O	2.8
1896	*Cle-N	133	586	160	**240**	27	16	6	72	49	19	**.410**	.461	.541	157	56	51	166	34			-2	*O	3.3
1897	Cle-N	127	517	129	198	28	7	2	60	76		.383	.468	.476	145	44	39	132	28			-2	*O	2.3
1898	Cle-N	150	624	114	213	18	9	0	42	69		.341	.415	.399	139	33	34	114	19			-8	*O	1.5
1899	StL-N	141	558	116	221	21	8	7	71	67		.396	.463	.500	163	54	52	144	25			-3	*O/2	3.5
1900	StL-N	141	559	88	203	11	15	7	68	62		.363	.429	.474	153	41	42	131	32			4	*O	3.0
1901	StL-N	142	601	**142**	**226**	20	15	10	75	59		**.376**	.434	.509	**185**	**58**	**62**	**149**	27			-1	*O	4.5
1902	StL-A	138	553	97	169	29	9	5	52	71		.306	.389	.418	127	21	22	102	23			6	*O/PS3	1.9
1903	StL-A	132	513	75	151	20	7	3	40	52		.293	.358	.377	126	16	17	78	17			-4	*O	0.5
1904	StL-A	147	575	72	156	15	10	2	27	78		.271	.358	.343	133	19	23	77	12			5	*O	2.2
1905	Bos-A	148	573	78	147	12	13	4	47	67		.257	.334	.344	116	13	12	73	13			-1	*O	0.4
Total	16	2066	8421	1720	2850	320	182	75	952	1029	230	.338	.414	.446	142	525	504	1792	389			-18	*O/P3S2	32.0

■ ELLIS BURKS
Burks, Ellis Rena   b: 9/11/64, Vicksburg, Miss.   BR/TR, 6'2", 175 lbs.   Deb: 4/30/87

YEAR	TM/L	G	AB	R	H	2B	3B	HR	RBI	BB	SO	AVG	OBP	SLG	PRO+	BR	/A	RC	SB	CS	SBR	FR	POS	TPR
1987	Bos-A	133	558	94	152	30	2	20	59	41	98	.272	.324	.441	98	-1	-3	85	27	6	5	11	*O/D	0.9
1988	*Bos-A	144	540	93	159	37	5	18	92	62	89	.294	.370	.481	131	27	24	99	25	9	2	6	*O/D	2.9
1989	Bos-A	97	399	73	121	19	6	12	61	36	52	.303	.368	.471	127	18	15	71	21	5	3	5	O/D	2.2
1990	*Bos-A	152	588	89	174	33	8	21	89	48	82	.296	.350	.486	126	23	20	92	9	11	-4	-4	*O/D	1.0
Total	4	526	2085	349	606	119	21	71	301	187	321	.291	.352	.470	120	67	56	347	82	31	6	17	O/D	7.0

■ RICK BURLESON
Burleson, Richard Paul "Rooster"   b: 4/29/51, Lynwood, Cal.   BR/TR, 5'10", 165 lbs.   Deb: 5/04/74

YEAR	TM/L	G	AB	R	H	2B	3B	HR	RBI	BB	SO	AVG	OBP	SLG	PRO+	BR	/A	RC	SB	CS	SBR	FR	POS	TPR
1974	Bos-A	114	384	36	109	22	0	4	44	21	34	.284	.324	.372	93	-1	-4	43	3	5	-1	-5	S2/3	-0.1
1975	*Bos-A	158	580	66	146	25	1	6	62	45	44	.252	.309	.329	74	-15	-21	58	8	5	-1	-1	*S	-0.6
1976	Bos-A	152	540	75	157	27	1	7	42	60	37	.291	.367	.383	107	15	6	76	14	9	-1	-7	*S	0.8
1977	Bos-A	154	663	80	194	36	7	3	52	47	69	.293	.341	.382	87	-3	-13	83	13	12	-3	12	*S	1.4
1978	Bos-A	145	626	75	155	32	5	5	49	40	71	.248	.297	.339	71	-18	-27	60	8	8	-2	19	*S	0.2
1979	Bos-A	153	627	93	174	32	5	5	60	35	54	.278	.319	.368	80	-14	-18	72	9	5	-0	22	*S	2.1
1980	Bos-A	155	644	89	179	29	2	8	51	62	51	.278	.343	.366	90	-4	-8	76	12	13	-4	26	*S	2.5
1981	Cal-A	109	430	53	126	17	1	5	33	42	38	.293	.360	.372	111	7	7	58	6	6	-2	21	*S	3.5
1982	Cal-A	11	45	4	7	1	0	0	2	6	3	.156	.255	.178	21	-5	-5	2	0	0	0	7	S	0.0
1983	Cal-A	33	119	22	34	7	0	0	11	12	12	.286	.351	.345	93	-1	-1	13	0	2	-1	-0	S	0.0
1984	Cal-A	7	4	2	0	0	0	0	0	0	0	.000	.000	.000	-99	-1	-1	0	0	0	0	0	/H	0.0
1986	*Cal-A	93	271	35	77	14	0	5	29	33	32	.284	.364	.391	107	3	3	40	1	5	-2	-7	DS/23	-0.2
1987	Bal-A	62	206	26	43	14	1	2	14	17	30	.209	.279	.316	59	-13	-12	17	0	2	-1	-1	2/D	-0.8
Total	13	1346	5139	656	1401	256	23	50	449	420	477	.273	.331	.361	87	-49	-92	599	72	68	-19	87	*S/2D3	9.1

YEAR	TM/L	G	AB	R	H	2B	3B	HR	RBI	BB	SO	AVG	OBP	SLG	PRO+	BR	/A	RC	SB	CS	SBR	FR	POS	TPR

■ HERCULES BURNETT
Burnett, Hercules H.   b: 8/13/1865, Louisville, Ky.   d: 10/4/36, Louisville, Ky.   BR ,   Deb: 6/26/1888

YEAR	TM/L	G	AB	R	H	2B	3B	HR	RBI	BB	SO	AVG	OBP	SLG	PRO+	BR	/A	RC	SB	CS	SBR	FR	POS	TPR
1888	Lou-a	1	4	1	0	0	0	0	0	0	1	.000	.200	.000	-32	-1	-1	0	1			-0	/O	0.0
1895	Lou-N	5	17	6	7	0	1	2	3	2	2	.412	.474	.882	264	3	4	8	2			-0	/O1	0.2
Total	2	6	21	7	7	0	1	2	3	3	2	.333	.417	.714	214	3	3	8	3			-0	/O1	0.2

■ JOHNNY BURNETT
Burnett, John Henderson   b: 11/1/04, Bartow, Fla.   d: 8/13/59, Tampa, Fla.   BL/TR, 5'11", 175 lbs.   Deb: 5/07/27

YEAR	TM/L	G	AB	R	H	2B	3B	HR	RBI	BB	SO	AVG	OBP	SLG	PRO+	BR	/A	RC	SB	CS	SBR	FR	POS	TPR
1927	Cle-A	17	8	5	0	0	0	0	0	0	3	.000	.000	.000	-99	-2	-2	0	1	0	0	5	/2	0.3
1928	Cle-A	3	10	3	5	0	0	0	1	0	1	.500	.500	.500	162	1	1	2	0	0	0	0	/S	0.1
1929	Cle-A	19	33	2	5	1	0	0	2	1	2	.152	.200	.182	-1	-5	-5	1	0	0	0	6	S/2	0.1
1930	Cle-A	54	170	28	53	13	0	0	20	17	8	.312	.378	.388	91	-1	-2	26	2	2	-1	-5	3S	-0.3
1931	Cle-A	111	427	85	128	25	5	1	52	39	25	.300	.360	.389	92	-2	-5	61	5	2	0	-15	S23/O	-0.9
1932	Cle-A	129	512	81	152	23	5	4	53	46	27	.297	.359	.385	87	-5	-10	72	2	5	-2	-22	*S2	-2.3
1933	Cle-A	83	261	39	71	11	2	1	29	23	14	.272	.333	.341	76	-8	-9	31	3	2	-0	-5	S23	-0.9
1934	Cle-A	72	208	28	61	11	2	3	30	18	11	.293	.352	.409	94	-1	-2	30	1	1	-0	-7	3/S2O	-0.7
1935	StL-A	70	206	17	46	10	1	0	26	19	16	.223	.289	.282	46	-16	-17	18	1	0	0	-5	3S2	-1.9
Total	9	558	1835	288	521	94	15	9	213	163	107	.284	.345	.366	81	-38	-52	241	15	12	-3	-49	S32/O	-6.5

■ JACK BURNETT
Burnett, John P.   b: 12/2/1889, Missouri   d: 9/8/29, Taft, Cal.   Deb: 7/02/07

YEAR	TM/L	G	AB	R	H	2B	3B	HR	RBI	BB	SO	AVG	OBP	SLG	PRO+	BR	/A	RC	SB	CS	SBR	FR	POS	TPR
1907	StL-N	59	206	18	49	8	4	0	12	15		.238	.290	.316	95	-2	-2	22	5			-4	O	-0.9

■ C.B. BURNS
Burns, Charles Birmingham   b: 5/15/1879, Bay View, Md.   d: 6/6/68, Havre De Grace, Md   BR/TR, 6', 175 lbs.   Deb: 8/19/02

YEAR	TM/L	G	AB	R	H	2B	3B	HR	RBI	BB	SO	AVG	OBP	SLG	PRO+	BR	/A	RC	SB	CS	SBR	FR	POS	TPR
1902	Bal-A	1	1	0	1	0	0	0	0	0		1.000	1.000	1.000	441	0	0	1	0			0	H	0.0

■ ED BURNS
Burns, Edward James   b: 10/31/1888, San Francisco, Cal   d: 6/1/42, Monterey, Cal.   BR/TR, 5'6", 165 lbs.   Deb: 6/25/12

YEAR	TM/L	G	AB	R	H	2B	3B	HR	RBI	BB	SO	AVG	OBP	SLG	PRO+	BR	/A	RC	SB	CS	SBR	FR	POS	TPR
1912	StL-N	1	1	0	0	0	0	0	1	0	0	.000	.000	.000	-99	-0	-0	0	0			0	/C	0.0
1913	Phi-N	17	30	3	6	3	0	0	3	6	3	.200	.351	.300	83	-0	-0	4	2			-4	C	-0.2
1914	Phi-N	70	139	8	36	3	4	0	16	20	12	.259	.352	.338	99	2	0	18	5			-2	C	0.0
1915	*Phi-N	67	174	11	42	5	0	0	16	20	12	.241	.327	.270	81	-3	-3	16	1			-6	C	-0.5
1916	Phi-N	78	219	14	51	8	1	0	14	16	18	.233	.294	.279	74	-6	-7	20	3			-10	C/SO	-1.4
1917	Phi-N	20	49	2	10	1	0	0	6	1	5	.204	.220	.224	35	-4	-4	3	2			-1	C	-0.4
1918	Phi-N	68	184	10	38	1	1	0	9	20	9	.207	.288	.223	53	-9	-10	12	1			-4	C	-0.8
Total	7	321	796	48	183	21	6	0	65	83	59	.230	.308	.271	73	-20	-24	72	14			-26	C/OS	-3.3

■ GEORGE BURNS
Burns, George Henry "Tioga George"   b: 1/31/1893, Niles, Ohio   d: 1/7/78, Kirkland, Wash.   BR/TR, 6'1.5", 180 lbs.   Deb: 4/14/14

YEAR	TM/L	G	AB	R	H	2B	3B	HR	RBI	BB	SO	AVG	OBP	SLG	PRO+	BR	/A	RC	SB	CS	SBR	FR	POS	TPR
1914	Det-A	137	478	55	139	22	5	5	57	32	56	.291	.351	.389	119	12	10	70	23	13	-1	-5	*1	0.5
1915	Det-A	105	392	49	99	18	3	5	50	22	51	.253	.301	.352	91	-4	-7	45	9	3	1	-3	*1	-1.4
1916	Det-A	135	479	60	137	22	6	4	73	22	30	.286	.327	.382	109	5	3	66	12			-10	*1	-0.9
1917	Det-A	119	407	42	92	14	10	1	40	15	33	.226	.264	.317	77	-13	-13	34	3			-4	*1	-2.2
1918	Phi-A	130	505	61	**178**	22	9	6	70	23	25	.352	.390	.467	157	33	32	91	8			6	*1/O	3.3
1919	Phi-A	126	470	63	139	29	9	8	57	19	18	.296	.339	.447	118	10	9	72	15			2	1O	0.2
1920	Phi-A	22	60	1	14	3	0	1	7	6	7	.233	.313	.333	71	-2	-3	7	4	0	1	1	O	-0.1
	*Cle-A	44	56	7	15	4	1	0	13	4	3	.268	.339	.375	86	-1	-1	8	1	0	0	1	1/O	0.0
	Yr	66	116	8	29	7	1	1	20	10	10	.250	.326	.353	78	-3	-4	15	5	0	2	1		-0.1
1921	Cle-A	84	244	52	88	21	4	0	49	13	19	.361	.398	.480	121	8	8	46	2	1	0	2	1	0.8
1922	Bos-A	147	558	71	171	32	5	12	73	20	28	.306	.341	.446	104	1	1	85	8	2	1	-1	*1	-0.8
1923	Bos-A	146	551	91	181	47	5	7	82	45	33	.328	.386	.470	124	19	18	100	9	7	-2	-1	*1	1.0
1924	Cle-A	129	462	64	143	37	5	4	68	29	27	.310	.370	.437	106	4	4	77	14	5	1	8	*1	0.7
1925	Cle-A	127	488	69	164	41	4	6	79	24	24	.336	.371	.473	112	8	7	83	16	11	-2	-1	*1	0.1
1926	Cle-A	151	603	97	**216**	**64**	3	4	114	28	33	.358	.394	.494	129	25	24	116	13	7	-0	1	*1	1.8
1927	Cle-A	140	549	84	175	51	2	3	78	42	27	.319	.375	.435	109	8	7	84	13	11	-3	3	*1	0.2
1928	Cle-A	82	209	29	52	12	1	5	30	17	11	.249	.323	.388	85	-5	-5	26	2	3	-1	2	1	-0.6
	NY-A	4	4	1	2	0	0	0	0	0	1	.500	.500	.500	169	0	0	1	0	0	0	0	/1	0.0
	Yr	86	213	30	54	12	1	5	30	17	12	.254	.326	.390	87	-4	-4	27	2	3	-1	2		-0.6
1929	NY-A	9	9	0	0	0	0	0	0	0	4	.000	.000	.000	-99	-3	-3	0	0	0	0	0	H	-0.1
	*Phi-A	29	49	5	13	5	0	1	11	2	3	.265	.294	.429	81	-1	-2	6	1	0	0	-0	1	-0.3
	Yr	38	58	5	13	5	0	1	11	2	7	.224	.250	.362	55	-4	-4	5	1	0	0	-0		-0.4
Total	16	1866	6573	901	2018	444	72	72	951	363	433	.307	.354	.429	112	104	93	1017	153	63		1	*1/O	2.2

■ GEORGE BURNS
Burns, George Joseph   b: 11/24/1889, Utica, N.Y.   d: 8/15/66, Gloversville, N.Y.   BR/TR, 5'7", 160 lbs.   Deb: 10/03/11   C

YEAR	TM/L	G	AB	R	H	2B	3B	HR	RBI	BB	SO	AVG	OBP	SLG	PRO+	BR	/A	RC	SB	CS	SBR	FR	POS	TPR
1911	NY-N	6	17	2	1	0	0	0	0	1		.059	.111	.059	-50	-3	-4	0	0			-1	/O	-0.4
1912	NY-N	29	51	11	15	4	0	0	3	8	8	.294	.400	.373	109	1	1	10	7			1	O	0.1
1913	*NY-N	150	605	81	173	37	4	2	54	58	74	.286	.352	.370	106	6	5	88	40			7	*O	1.0
1914	NY-N	154	561	**100**	170	35	10	3	60	89	53	.303	.403	.417	149	34	36	**113**	62			4	*O	3.8
1915	NY-N	155	622	83	169	27	14	3	51	56	57	.272	.333	.375	121	10	14	79	27	20	-4	-2	*O	0.3
1916	NY-N	155	623	**105**	174	24	8	5	41	63	47	.279	.346	.368	126	15	19	82	37	26	-5	2	*O	1.2
1917	*NY-N	152	597	103	180	25	13	5	45	**75**	55	.302	.380	.412	148	32	34	**102**	40			6	*O	3.9
1918	NY-N	119	465	80	135	22	6	4	51	43	37	.290	.354	.389	129	15	16	74	40			7	*O	1.8
1919	NY-N	139	534	**86**	162	30	9	2	46	**82**	37	.303	**.396**	.404	142	30	31	**96**	**40**			1	*O	2.9
1920	NY-N	154	631	**115**	181	35	9	6	46	**76**	48	.287	.365	.399	121	18	18	91	22	22	-7	-0	*O	0.3
1921	*NY-N	149	605	111	181	28	9	4	60	**80**	24	.299	.386	.395	107	10	9	93	19	20	-6	-9	*O/3	-1.2
1922	Cin-N	156	631	104	180	20	10	1	53	78	38	.285	.366	.353	88	-10	-9	83	30	23	-5	-3	*O	-2.0
1923	Cin-N	154	614	99	168	27	13	3	45	**101**	46	.274	.376	.375	101	2	4	90	12	14	-5	-3	*O	-0.8
1924	Cin-N	93	336	43	86	19	2	2	33	29	21	.256	.315	.342	77	-11	-11	36	5	6	-3	1	O	-1.4
1925	Phi-N	88	349	65	102	29	1	1	22	33	20	.292	.353	.390	82	-5	-9	47	4	8	-4	-2	O	-1.5
Total	15	1853	7241	1188	2077	362	108	41	611	872	565	.287	.366	.384	115	143	156	1085	383	139		10	*O/3	8.0

■ JIM BURNS
Burns, James M.   b: Quincy, Ill.   5'7", 168 lbs.   Deb: 9/25/1888

YEAR	TM/L	G	AB	R	H	2B	3B	HR	RBI	BB	SO	AVG	OBP	SLG	PRO+	BR	/A	RC	SB	CS	SBR	FR	POS	TPR
1888	KC-a	15	66	13	20	0	0	0	4	1		.303	.343	.303	104	1	0	9	6			2	O	0.1
1889	KC-a	134	579	103	176	23	11	5	97	20	68	.304	.334	.408	107	8	2	100	56			-7	*O/3	-0.8
1891	Was-a	20	82	15	26	6	0	0	10	6	10	.317	.378	.390	129	2	3	13	2			-4	O/S	0.0
Total	3	169	727	131	222	29	11	5	111	27	78	.305	.341	.396	109	11	5	123	64			-9	O/S3	-0.7

■ JACK BURNS
Burns, John Irving "Slug"   b: 8/31/07, Cambridge, Mass.   d: 4/18/75, Brighton, Mass.   BL/TL, 5'10.5", 175 lbs.   Deb: 9/17/30   C

YEAR	TM/L	G	AB	R	H	2B	3B	HR	RBI	BB	SO	AVG	OBP	SLG	PRO+	BR	/A	RC	SB	CS	SBR	FR	POS	TPR
1930	StL-A	8	30	5	9	3	0	0	2	5	5	.300	.400	.400	100	0	0	5	0	0	0	1	/1	0.0
1931	StL-A	144	570	75	148	27	7	4	70	42	58	.260	.312	.353	72	-22	-25	63	19	12	-2	18	*1	-1.9
1932	StL-A	150	617	111	188	33	8	11	70	61	43	.305	.368	.438	102	7	2	100	17	11	-2	4	*1	-0.9
1933	StL-A	144	556	89	160	43	4	7	71	56	51	.288	.353	.417	97	2	-3	81	11	11	-3	3	*1	-1.3
1934	StL-A	154	612	86	157	28	8	13	73	62	47	.257	.327	.392	78	-15	-23	81	9	3	1	0	*1	-4.5
1935	StL-A	143	549	77	157	48	1	5	67	68	49	.286	.366	.368	86	-6	-10	78	3	2	-0	0	*1	-3.0
1936	StL-A	9	14	2	3	1	0	0	1	3	1	.214	.353	.286	58	-1	-1	2	0	0	0	0	/1	0.0
	Det-A	138	558	96	158	36	3	4	63	79	45	.283	.375	.380	87	-10	-10	82	4	8	-4	1	*1	-2.8
	Yr	147	572	98	161	37	3	4	64	82	46	.281	.374	.378	86	-11	-11	84	4	8	-4	1		-2.8
Total	7	890	3506	541	980	199	31	44	417	376	299	.280	.351	.392	87	-44	-69	493	63	47	-9	19	1	-14.4

YEAR	TM/L	G	AB	R	H	2B	3B	HR	RBI	BB	SO	AVG	OBP	SLG	PRO+	BR	/A	RC	SB	CS	SBR	FR	POS	TPR

■ JACK BURNS   Burns, John Joseph   b: 5/13/1880, Avoca, Pa.   d: 6/24/57, Waterford, Conn.   BR/TR, 5'10", 160 lbs.   Deb: 9/11/03

YEAR	TM/L	G	AB	R	H	2B	3B	HR	RBI	BB	SO	AVG	OBP	SLG	PRO+	BR	/A	RC	SB	CS	SBR	FR	POS	TPR
1903	Det-A	11	37	2	10	0	0	0	3	1		.270	.289	.270	73	-1	-1	3	0			1	2	0.0
1904	Det-A	4	16	3	2	0	0	0	1	1		.125	.176	.125	-3	-2	-2	1	1			-1	/2	-0.3
Total	2	15	53	5	12	0	0	0	4	2		.226	.255	.226	50	-3	-3	4	1			-1	/2	-0.3

■ JOE BURNS   Burns, Joseph Francis   b: 3/26/1889, Ipswich, Mass.   d: 7/12/87, Beverly, Ma.   BL/TL, 5'11", 170 lbs.   Deb: 6/19/10

YEAR	TM/L	G	AB	R	H	2B	3B	HR	RBI	BB	SO	AVG	OBP	SLG	PRO+	BR	/A	RC	SB	CS	SBR	FR	POS	TPR
1910	Cin-N	1	1	0	1	0	0	0	0	0	0	1.000	1.000	1.000	506	0	0	2				0	H	0.0
1913	Det-A	4	13	0	5	0	0	0	1	2	4	.385	.500	.385	162	1	1	2	0			-0	/O	0.1
Total	2	5	14	0	6	0	0	0	1	2	4	.429	.529	.429	184	2	2	4	1			-0	/O	0.1

■ JOE BURNS   Burns, Joseph Francis   b: 2/25/1900, Trenton, N.J.   d: 1/7/86, Trenton, N.J.   BR/TR, 6', 175 lbs.   Deb: 4/18/24

YEAR	TM/L	G	AB	R	H	2B	3B	HR	RBI	BB	SO	AVG	OBP	SLG	PRO+	BR	/A	RC	SB	CS	SBR	FR	POS	TPR
1924	Chi-A	8	19	1	2	0	0	0	0	0	2	.105	.105	.105	-47	-4	-4	0	0	0	0	-2	/C	-0.5

■ JOE BURNS   Burns, Joseph James   b: 6/17/16, Bryn Mawr, Pa.   d: 6/24/74, Bryn Mawr, Pa.   BR/TR, 5'10.5", 175 lbs.   Deb: 4/24/43

YEAR	TM/L	G	AB	R	H	2B	3B	HR	RBI	BB	SO	AVG	OBP	SLG	PRO+	BR	/A	RC	SB	CS	SBR	FR	POS	TPR
1943	Bos-N	52	135	12	28	3	0	1	5	8	25	.207	.262	.252	49	-9	-9	8	2			0	3/O	-0.8
1944	Phi-A	28	75	5	18	2	0	1	8	4	8	.240	.278	.307	68	-3	-3	7	0	1	-1	-8	3/2	-1.1
1945	Phi-A	31	90	7	23	1	1	0	3	4	17	.256	.287	.289	68	-4	-4	7	0	1	-1	-4	O/31	-0.9
Total	3	111	300	24	69	6	1	2	16	16	50	.230	.274	.277	60	-16	-16	22	2	2		-11	/3O21	-2.8

■ PAT BURNS   Burns, Patrick   Deb: 8/11/1884

YEAR	TM/L	G	AB	R	H	2B	3B	HR	RBI	BB	SO	AVG	OBP	SLG	PRO+	BR	/A	RC	SB	CS	SBR	FR	POS	TPR
1884	Bal-a	6	25	3	5	2	1	0	3			.200	.286	.360	108	0	0	3				-0	/1	0.0
	Bal-U	1	4	0	2	0	0	0	0			.500	.500	.500	217	1	0	1	0			-0	/1	0.0

■ DICK BURNS   Burns, Richard Simon   b: 12/26/1863, Holyoke, Mass.   d: 11/11/37, Holyoke, Mass.   BL , 140 lbs.   Deb: 5/03/1883

YEAR	TM/L	G	AB	R	H	2B	3B	HR	RBI	BB	SO	AVG	OBP	SLG	PRO+	BR	/A	RC	SB	CS	SBR	FR	POS	TPR
1883	Det-N	37	140	11	26	7	1	0	5	2	22	.186	.197	.250	36	-11	-10	7				-5	OP	-0.9
1884	Cin-U	79	350	84	107	17	12	4		5		.306	.315	.457	147	20	16	52	0			-3	OP/S	-0.3
1885	StL-N	14	54	2	12	2	1	0	4	3	8	.222	.263	.296	86	-1	-1	4				-4	O/P	-0.3
Total	3	130	544	97	145	26	14	4	9	10	30	.267	.280	.388	112	8	5	63				-12	/OPS	-1.2

■ TOM BURNS   Burns, Thomas Everett   b: 3/30/1857, Honesdale, Pa.   d: 3/19/02, Jersey City, N.J.   BR/TR, 5'7", 152 lbs.   Deb: 5/01/1880   MU

YEAR	TM/L	G	AB	R	H	2B	3B	HR	RBI	BB	SO	AVG	OBP	SLG	PRO+	BR	/A	RC	SB	CS	SBR	FR	POS	TPR
1880	Chi-N	85	333	47	103	17	3	0	43	12	23	.309	.333	.378	133	14	11	43				-24	*S/3CP	-0.8
1881	Chi-N	84	342	41	95	20	3	4	42	14	22	.278	.306	.389	112	6	4	42				-5	*S/32	0.5
1882	Chi-N	84	355	55	88	23	6	0	48	15	28	.248	.278	.346	95	-0	-3	35				-1	2S	0.1
1883	Chi-N	97	405	69	119	37	7	2	67	13	31	.294	.316	.435	118	12	8	57				-2	*S2/O	0.7
1884	Chi-N	83	343	54	84	14	2	7	44	13	50	.245	.272	.359	89	-2	-6	34				-1	*S/3	0.3
1885	*Chi-N	111	445	82	121	23	9	7	71	16	48	.272	.297	.411	111	12	3	56				-3	*S/2	0.5
1886	*Chi-N	112	445	64	123	18	10	3	65	14	40	.276	.298	.382	92	2	-8	57	15			14	*3	0.9
1887	Chi-N	115	424	57	112	20	10	3	60	34	32	.264	.320	.380	84	-3	-12	63	32			21	*3/O	0.8
1888	Chi-N	134	483	60	115	12	6	3	70	26	49	.238	.281	.306	83	-5	-10	52	34			18	*3	1.3
1889	Chi-N	136	525	64	127	27	6	4	66	32	57	.242	.288	.339	73	-18	-22	58	18			4	*3	-0.7
1890	Chi-N	139	538	86	149	17	6	5	86	57	45	.277	.348	.359	104	6	3	85	44			0	*3	0.8
1891	Chi-N	59	243	36	55	8	1	1	17	21	21	.226	.288	.280	68	-10	-10	25	18			-2	3/SO	-0.6
1892	Pit-N	12	39	7	8	0	0	0	4	3	8	.205	.262	.205	43	-3	-3	2	1			-5	/3OM	-0.6
Total	13	1251	4920	722	1299	236	69	39	683	270	454	.264	.303	.364	96	12	-45	610	162			13	3S/20CP	2.8

■ OYSTER BURNS   Burns, Thomas P.   b: 9/6/1864, Philadelphia, Pa.   d: 11/11/28, Brooklyn, N.Y.   BR/TR, 5'8", 183 lbs.   Deb: 8/18/1884

YEAR	TM/L	G	AB	R	H	2B	3B	HR	RBI	BB	SO	AVG	OBP	SLG	PRO+	BR	/A	RC	SB	CS	SBR	FR	POS	TPR
1884	Wil-U	2	7	0	1	0	1	0			1	.143	.250	.429	122	0	0	1	0			-0	/S	0.0
	Bal-a	35	131	34	39	2	6	6			7	.298	.348	.542	182	12	12	25				-5	O2/P3	0.6
1885	Bal-a	78	321	47	74	11	6	5			16	.231	.280	.349	102	0	1	32	0			0	OPS/321	0.1
1887	Bal-a	140	551	122	188	33	19	9			63	.341	.414	.519	172	46	52	146	58			-19	*S3/P2	2.4
1888	Bal-a	79	325	54	97	18	9	4	42		24	.298	.349	.446	162	20	21	60	23			-5	OS/P32	1.5
	Bro-a	52	204	40	58	9	6	2	25		14	.284	.339	.417	146	10	10	37	21			-13	SO/2	0.0
	Yr	131	529	94	155	27	15	6	67		38	.293	.345	.435	155	30	31	97	44			-17		1.5
1889	*Bro-N	131	504	105	153	19	13	5	100	68	26	.304	.391	.423	134	24	24	98	32			-8	*OS	1.0
1890	*Bro-N	119	472	102	134	22	12	13	128	51	42	.284	.359	.464	141	23	23	88	21			-4	*O/3	1.5
1891	Bro-N	123	470	75	134	24	13	4	83	53	30	.285	.358	.417	128	16	16	80	21			2	*O/S3	1.1
1892	Bro-N	141	542	88	171	27	18	4	96	65	42	.315	.395	.454	165	39	42	113	33			-13	*O/3S	2.3
1893	Bro-N	109	415	68	112	22	8	7	60	36	16	.270	.334	.412	104	-2	2	63	14			-1	*O/S	-0.2
1894	Bro-N	125	505	106	179	32	14	5	107	44	18	.354	.409	.503	130	17	24	119	30			-4	*O	0.9
1895	Bro-N	20	76	7	14	0	1	0	7	8	2	.184	.271	.211	29	-8	-7	4	0			1	O	-0.5
	NY-N	33	114	21	35	5	3	1	25	14	6	.307	.388	.430	115	2	3	23	10			-4	O/1	-0.3
	Yr	53	190	28	49	5	4	1	32	22	8	.258	.341	.342	82	-6	-4	26	10			-3		-0.8
Total	11	1187	4637	869	1389	224	129	65	673	464	182	.300	.368	.446	137	199	222	890	263			-73	OS/3P21	10.4

■ ALEX BURR   Burr, Alexander Thomson   b: 11/1/1893, Chicago, Ill.   d: 11/1/18, France   BR/TR, 6'3.5", 190 lbs.   Deb: 4/21/14

YEAR	TM/L	G	AB	R	H	2B	3B	HR	RBI	BB	SO	AVG	OBP	SLG	PRO+	BR	/A	RC	SB	CS	SBR	FR	POS	TPR
1914	NY-A	1	0	0	0	0	0	0	0	0	0	—	—	—		0	0	0	0			-0	/O	0.0

■ BUSTER BURRELL   Burrell, Frank Andrew   b: 12/22/1866, E.Weymouth, Mass.   d: 5/8/62, S.Weymouth, Mass.   BR/TR, 5'10", 165 lbs.   Deb: 8/01/1891

YEAR	TM/L	G	AB	R	H	2B	3B	HR	RBI	BB	SO	AVG	OBP	SLG	PRO+	BR	/A	RC	SB	CS	SBR	FR	POS	TPR
1891	NY-N	15	53	1	5	0	0	0	1	3	12	.094	.158	.094	-26	-8	-8	1	2			-4	C/O	-0.9
1895	Bro-N	12	28	7	4	0	0	1	5	4	3	.143	.250	.250	33	-3	-3	2	0			-2	C	-0.2
1896	Bro-N	62	206	61	62	11	3	0	23	15	13	.301	.348	.383	100	-2	0	29	1			-11	C	-0.4
1897	Bro-N	33	103	15	25	2	0	2	18	10		.243	.310	.320	72	-5	-4	11	1			-4	C/1	-0.3
Total	4	122	390	42	96	13	3	3	47	32	28	.246	.305	.318	72	-17	-14	42	4			-21	C/1O	-1.8

■ LARRY BURRIGHT   Burright, Larry Allen "Possum"   b: 7/10/37, Roseville, Ill.   BR/TR, 5'11", 170 lbs.   Deb: 4/12/62

YEAR	TM/L	G	AB	R	H	2B	3B	HR	RBI	BB	SO	AVG	OBP	SLG	PRO+	BR	/A	RC	SB	CS	SBR	FR	POS	TPR
1962	LA-N	115	249	35	51	6	5	4	30	21	67	.205	.267	.317	60	-16	-14	20	4	3	-1	14	*2/S	0.9
1963	NY-N	41	100	9	22	2	1	0	3	8	25	.220	.291	.260	59	-5	-5	8	1	0	0	12	S2/3	1.1
1964	NY-N	3	7	0	0	0	0	0	0	0	0	.000	.000	.000	-99	-2	-2	0	0	0	0	4	/2	0.3
Total	3	159	356	44	73	8	6	4	33	29	92	.205	.269	.295	56	-23	-21	29	5	3	-0	30	2/S3	2.3

■ PAUL BURRIS   Burris, Paul Robert   b: 7/21/23, Hickory, N.C.   BR/TR, 6', 190 lbs.   Deb: 10/02/48

YEAR	TM/L	G	AB	R	H	2B	3B	HR	RBI	BB	SO	AVG	OBP	SLG	PRO+	BR	/A	RC	SB	CS	SBR	FR	POS	TPR
1948	Bos-N	2	4	0	2	0	0	0				.500	.500	.500	174	0	0	1	0			1	/C	0.1
1950	Bos-N	10	23	1	4	1	0	0	3	1	2	.174	.208	.217	13	-3	-3	1	0			2	/C	0.0
1952	Bos-N	55	168	14	37	4	0	2	21	7	19	.220	.256	.280	50	-12	-11	10	0	0	0	-3	C	-1.3
1953	Mil-N	2	1	0	0	0	0	0	0	0	0	.000	.000	.000	-99	-0	-0	0	0	0	0		C	0.0
Total	4	69	196	15	43	5	0	2	24	8	21	.219	.254	.276	47	-15	-14	12	0	0		-1	/C	-1.2

■ HENRY BURROUGHS   Burroughs, Henry F.   b: 1845, Detroit, Mich.   5'8", 147 lbs.   Deb: 5/05/1871

YEAR	TM/L	G	AB	R	H	2B	3B	HR	RBI	BB	SO	AVG	OBP	SLG	PRO+	BR	/A	RC	SB	CS	SBR	FR	POS	TPR
1871	Oly-n	12	63	11	15	2	3	1	14	1	1	.238	.250	.413	91	-1	-0	7	0				/O3	0.0
1872	Oly-n	2	7	1	1	1	0	0		1		.143	.250	.286	68	-0	-0	1					/O	0.0
Total	2 n	14	70	12	16	3	3	1		2		.229	.250	.400	89	-1	-1	7					/O3	0.0

■ JEFF BURROUGHS   Burroughs, Jeffrey Alan   b: 3/7/51, Long Beach, Cal.   BR/TR, 6'1", 200 lbs.   Deb: 7/20/70

YEAR	TM/L	G	AB	R	H	2B	3B	HR	RBI	BB	SO	AVG	OBP	SLG	PRO+	BR	/A	RC	SB	CS	SBR	FR	POS	TPR
1970	Was-A	6	12	1	2	0	0	0	0	2	5	.167	.286	.167	29	-1	-1	1	0	0	0	-0	/O	0.0
1971	Was-A	59	181	20	42	9	0	5	25	22	55	.232	.319	.365	99	-2	-0	22	1	0	0	-5	O	-0.6

YEAR	TM/L	G	AB	R	H	2B	3B	HR	RBI	BB	SO	AVG	OBP	SLG	PRO+	BR	/A	RC	SB	CS	SBR	FR	POS	TPR
1972	Tex-A	22	65	4	12	1	0	1	3	5	22	.185	.243	.246	48	-4	-4	3	0	2	-1	-1	O/1	-0.7
1973	Tex-A	151	526	71	147	17	1	30	85	67	88	.279	.362	.487	143	25	28	95	0	0	0	7	*O/1D	3.1
1974	Tex-A	152	554	84	167	33	2	25	**118**	91	104	.301	.405	.504	164	**45**	**47**	113	2	3	-1	-13	*O/1D	2.9
1975	Tex-A	152	585	81	132	20	0	29	94	79	155	.226	.319	.409	105	3	3	76	4	4	-1	-12	*O/D	-1.4
1976	Tex-A	158	604	71	143	22	2	18	86	69	93	.237	.317	.369	98	0	-1	69	0	0	0	-7	*O/D	-1.1
1977	Atl-N	154	579	91	157	19	1	41	114	86	126	.271	.365	.520	120	28	19	114	4	1	1	-8	*O	0.6
1978	Atl-N	153	488	72	147	30	6	23	77	**117**	92	.301	**.436**	.529	151	50	41	116	1	2	-1	-9	*O	2.9
1979	Atl-N	116	397	49	89	14	1	11	47	73	75	.224	.349	.348	84	-3	-7	50	2	2	-1	-6	*O	-1.7
1980	Atl-N	99	278	35	73	14	0	13	51	35	57	.263	.349	.453	118	8	7	45	1	1	-0	-8	O	-0.3
1981	Sea-A	89	319	32	81	13	1	10	41	41	64	.254	.339	.395	107	5	3	43	0	1	-1	-14	O/D	-1.3
1982	Oak-A	113	285	42	79	13	2	16	48	45	61	.277	.376	.505	146	16	18	54	1	3	-2	0	DO	1.5
1983	Oak-A	121	401	43	108	15	1	10	56	47	79	.269	.346	.387	108	1	5	51	0	2	-1	0	*D	0.3
1984	Oak-A	58	71	5	15	1	0	2	8	18	23	.211	.371	.310	97	-0	1	9	0	0	0	0	D/O	0.1
1985	*Tor-A	86	191	19	49	9	3	6	28	34	36	.257	.369	.429	115	6	5	30	0	1	-1	0	D	0.4
Total	16	1689	5536	720	1443	230	20	240	882	831	1135	.261	.359	.439	120	177	164	892	16	22	-8	-76	*OD/1	4.7

■ DICK BURRUS
Burrus, Maurice Lennon b: 1/29/1898, Hatteras, N.C. d: 2/2/72, Elizabeth City, N.C BL/TL, 5'11", 175 lbs. Deb: 6/23/19

YEAR	TM/L	G	AB	R	H	2B	3B	HR	RBI	BB	SO	AVG	OBP	SLG	PRO+	BR	/A	RC	SB	CS	SBR	FR	POS	TPR
1919	Phi-A	70	194	17	50	3	4	0	8	9	25	.258	.294	.314	70	-8	-8	18	2			-4	1O	-1.6
1920	Phi-A	71	135	11	25	8	0	0	10	5	7	.185	.225	.244	24	-15	-15	7	0	3	-2	-1	1/O	-1.7
1925	Bos-N	152	588	82	200	41	4	5	87	51	29	.340	.396	.449	126	15	22	104	8	9	-3	1	*1	0.4
1926	Bos-N	131	486	59	131	21	1	3	61	37	16	.270	.324	.335	85	-15	-9	53	4			12	*1	-0.1
1927	Bos-N	72	220	22	70	8	3	0	32	17	10	.318	.370	.382	110	1	3	31	3			1	1	0.0
1928	Bos-N	64	137	15	37	6	0	3	13	19	8	.270	.367	.380	101	-0	1	20	1			-2	1	-0.4
Total	6	560	1760	206	513	87	12	11	211	138	95	.291	.347	.373	97	-22	-6	231	18	<u>12</u>		7	1/O	-3.4

■ FRANK BURT
Burt, Frank J. b: Camden, N.J. Deb: 5/02/1882

YEAR	TM/L	G	AB	R	H	2B	3B	HR	RBI	BB	SO	AVG	OBP	SLG	PRO+	BR	/A	RC	SB	CS	SBR	FR	POS	TPR
1882	Bal-a	10	36	2	4	2	1	0			1	.111	.135	.222	20	-3	-3	1				-0	O	-0.2

■ ELLIS BURTON
Burton, Ellis Narrington b: 8/12/36, Los Angeles, Cal. BB/TR, 5'11", 160 lbs. Deb: 9/18/58

YEAR	TM/L	G	AB	R	H	2B	3B	HR	RBI	BB	SO	AVG	OBP	SLG	PRO+	BR	/A	RC	SB	CS	SBR	FR	POS	TPR
1958	StL-N	8	30	5	7	0	1	2	4	3	8	.233	.324	.500	110	0	0	4	0	1	-1	-1	/O	0.0
1960	StL-N	29	28	5	6	1	0	0	2	4	14	.214	.313	.250	52	-2	-2	2	0	2	-1	-1	O	-0.5
1963	Cle-A	26	31	6	6	3	0	1	1	4	4	.194	.286	.387	87	-1	-1	3	0	0	0	0	O	0.0
	Chi-N	93	322	45	74	16	1	12	41	36	59	.230	.315	.398	98	2	-0	41	6	3	-0	-10	/O	-1.5
1964	Chi-N	42	105	12	20	3	2	2	7	17	22	.190	.303	.314	71	-3	-4	11	4	0	1	-2	O	-0.5
1965	Chi-N	17	40	6	7	1	0	0	4	1	10	.175	.195	.200	11	-5	-5	2	1	0	0	1	O	-0.3
Total	5	215	556	79	120	24	4	17	59	65	117	.216	.304	.365	85	-8	-11	64	11	6	-0	-13	O	-2.8

■ JIM BUSBY
Busby, James Franklin b: 1/8/27, Kenedy, Tex. BR/TR, 6'1", 175 lbs. Deb: 4/23/50 C

YEAR	TM/L	G	AB	R	H	2B	3B	HR	RBI	BB	SO	AVG	OBP	SLG	PRO+	BR	/A	RC	SB	CS	SBR	FR	POS	TPR
1950	Chi-A	18	48	5	10	0	0	0	4	1	5	.208	.224	.208	12	-6	-6	2	0	2	-1	1	O	-0.5
1951	Chi-A	143	477	59	135	15	2	5	68	40	46	.283	.344	.354	91	-7	-6	58	26	11	1	-3	*O	-1.2
1952	Chi-A	16	39	5	5	0	0	0	0	2	7	.128	.171	.128	-16	-6	-6	1	0	2	-1	3	O	-0.4
	Was-A	129	512	58	125	24	4	2	47	22	48	.244	.281	.318	69	-24	-22	44	5	6	-2	7	*O	-2.1
	Yr	145	551	63	130	24	4	2	47	24	55	.236	.273	.305	62	-30	-29	44	5	8	-3	10		-2.5
1953	Was-A	150	586	68	183	28	7	6	82	38	45	.312	.358	.415	111	6	6	90	13	6	0	14	*O	1.7
1954	Was-A	155	628	83	187	22	7	7	80	43	56	.298	.346	.389	107	-0	4	88	17	2	**4**	8	*O	1.2
1955	Was-A	47	191	23	44	6	2	6	14	13	22	.230	.279	.377	79	-8	-6	20	5	0	2	2	O	-0.4
	Chi-A	99	337	38	82	13	4	1	27	25	37	.243	.296	.315	62	-17	-19	32	7	3	0	-1	O	-2.4
	Yr	146	528	61	126	19	6	7	41	38	59	.239	.290	.337	68	-25	-25	52	12	3	2	1		-2.8
1956	Cle-A	135	494	72	116	17	3	12	50	43	47	.235	.301	.354	71	-21	-22	52	8	3	1	-0	*O	-2.7
1957	Cle-A	30	74	9	14	2	1	2	4	1	8	.189	.200	.324	79	-6	-6	4	0	1	-1	2	O	-0.6
	Bal-A	86	288	31	72	10	1	3	19	23	36	.250	.305	.323	77	-11	-9	30	6	3	0	5	O	-0.8
	Yr	116	362	40	86	12	2	5	23	24	44	.238	.285	.323	69	-17	-15	33	6	4	-1	7		-1.4
1958	Bal-A	113	215	32	51	7	2	3	19	24	37	.237	.322	.330	84	-5	-4	24	6	4	-1	-11	*O/3	-2.3
1959	Bos-A	61	102	16	23	8	0	1	5	5	18	.225	.269	.333	61	-5	-6	8	0	1	-1	1	O	-0.6
1960	Bos-A	1	0	0	0	0	0	0	0	0	0	—	—	—	—	0	0	0	0	0	0	0	/O	0.0
	Bal-A	79	159	25	41	7	1	0	12	20	14	.258	.341	.314	79	-4	-4	17	2	3	-1	-1	O	-0.8
	Yr	80	159	25	41	7	1	0	12	20	14	.258	.341	.314	79	-4	-4	17	2	3	-1	-1		-0.8
1961	Bal-A	75	89	15	23	3	1	0	6	8	10	.258	.320	.315	72	-4	-3	10	2	1	-1	6	O	0.1
1962	Hou-N	15	11	2	2	0	0	0	1	2	3	.182	.308	.182	38	-1	-1	1	0	1	-1	-0	O/C	-0.1
Total	13	1352	4250	541	1113	162	35	48	438	310	439	.262	.316	.350	82	-121	-109	481	97	48	0	32	*O/C3	-11.9

■ PAUL BUSBY
Busby, Paul Miller "Red" b: 8/25/18, Waynesboro, Miss. BL/TR, 6'1", 175 lbs. Deb: 9/14/41

YEAR	TM/L	G	AB	R	H	2B	3B	HR	RBI	BB	SO	AVG	OBP	SLG	PRO+	BR	/A	RC	SB	CS	SBR	FR	POS	TPR
1941	Phi-N	10	16	3	5	0	0	0	2	0	1	.313	.313	.313	79	-1	-0	2	0			-0	/O	0.0
1943	Phi-N	26	40	13	10	1	0	0	5	2	1	.250	.286	.275	65	-2	-2	3	2			1	O	0.0
Total	2	36	56	16	15	1	0	0	7	2	2	.268	.293	.286	69	-2	-2	5	2			1	/O	0.0

■ ED BUSCH
Busch, Edgar John b: 11/16/17, Lebanon, Ill. d: 1/17/87, St.Clair Co., Ill. BR/TR, 5'10", 175 lbs. Deb: 9/30/43

YEAR	TM/L	G	AB	R	H	2B	3B	HR	RBI	BB	SO	AVG	OBP	SLG	PRO+	BR	/A	RC	SB	CS	SBR	FR	POS	TPR
1943	Phi-A	4	17	2	5	0	0	0	0	1	2	.294	.368	.294	95	-0	-0	2	0	1	-1	-3	/S	-0.3
1944	Phi-A	140	484	41	131	11	3	0	40	29	17	.271	.313	.306	78	-14	-13	44	5	3	-0	-30	*S2/3	-3.8
1945	Phi-A	126	416	37	104	10	3	0	35	32	9	.250	.305	.288	73	-14	-14	37	2	3	-1	1	*S/231	-1.0
Total	3	270	917	80	240	21	6	0	75	62	28	.262	.311	.298	76	-29	-28	82	7	7	-2	-32	S/231	-5.1

■ DONIE BUSH
Bush, Owen Joseph b: 10/8/1887, Indianapolis, Ind. d: 3/28/72, Indianapolis, Ind. BB/TR, 5'6", 140 lbs. Deb: 9/18/08 M

YEAR	TM/L	G	AB	R	H	2B	3B	HR	RBI	BB	SO	AVG	OBP	SLG	PRO+	BR	/A	RC	SB	CS	SBR	FR	POS	TPR
1908	Det-A	20	68	13	20	1	1	0	4	7		.294	.360	.338	125	2	2	9	2			-3	S	0.0
1909	*Det-A	157	532	114	145	18	2	0	33	**88**		.273	.380	.314	114	17	14	89	53			4	*S	2.5
1910	Det-A	142	496	90	130	13	4	3	34	**78**		.262	.365	.323	108	12	8	78	49			9	*S/3	2.2
1911	Det-A	150	561	126	130	18	5	1	36	**98**		.232	.349	.287	74	-12	-17	73	40			17	*S	1.4
1912	Det-A	144	511	107	118	14	8	2	38	**117**		.231	.377	.301	98	3	5	72	35			29	*S	4.6
1913	Det-A	153	597	98	150	19	10	1	40	80	32	.251	.344	.322	96	-2	-1	77	44			2	*S	1.5
1914	Det-A	157	596	97	150	18	4	0	32	**112**	54	.252	.373	.295	98	7	7	71	35	26	-5	**34**	*S	5.1
1915	Det-A	155	561	99	128	12	8	1	44	**118**	44	.228	.364	.283	89	2	-2	65	35	27	-6	9	*S	1.6
1916	Det-A	145	550	73	124	5	9	0	34	75	42	.225	.319	.267	74	-14	-16	57	19			-15	*S	-0.1
1917	Det-A	147	581	**112**	163	18	3	0	24	80	40	.281	.370	.322	111	11	11	78	34			-18	*S	-1.8
1918	Det-A	128	500	74	117	10	3	0	22	79	31	.234	.340	.266	86	-7	-5	48	9			-20	*S	-1.1
1919	Det-A	129	509	82	124	11	6	0	26	75	36	.244	.343	.289	80	-12	-10	57	22			-12	*S	-1.1
1920	Det-A	141	590	85	133	18	5	1	33	73	32	.263	.357	.324	83	-11	-9	66	15	7	0	-17	*S	-1.2
1921	Det-A	104	402	72	113	6	5	0	27	45	23	.281	.355	.321	74	-15	-14	48	8	11	-4	-5	S2	-1.1
	Was-A	23	84	15	18	1	0	0	2	12	4	.214	.313	.226	41	-7	-7	7	2	2	-1	-4	S	-0.8
	Yr	127	486	87	131	7	5	0	29	57	27	.270	.347	.305	69	-22	-21	55	10	13	-5	-10		-1.9
1922	Was-A	41	134	17	32	4	1	0	7	21	7	.239	.342	.284	68	-6	-5	14	1	1	-0	-2	3/2	-0.3
1923	Was-A	10	22	6	9	0	0	0	0	0	1	.409	.409	.409	122	0	1	3	0	1	-1	-2	/32M	0.0
Total	16	1946	7210	1280	1804	186	74	9	436	1158	<u>346</u>	.250	.356	.300	91	-32	-40	911	403	<u>75</u>		5	*S/32	10.4

■ RANDY BUSH
Bush, Robert Randall b: 10/5/58, Dover, Del. BL/TR, 6'1", 186 lbs. Deb: 5/01/82

YEAR	TM/L	G	AB	R	H	2B	3B	HR	RBI	BB	SO	AVG	OBP	SLG	PRO+	BR	/A	RC	SB	CS	SBR	FR	POS	TPR
1982	Min-A	55	119	13	29	6	1	4	13	8	28	.244	.308	.412	93	-1	-1	16	0	0	0	0	D/O	0.0

YEAR	TM/L	G	AB	R	H	2B	3B	HR	RBI	BB	SO	AVG	OBP	SLG	PRO+	BR	/A	RC	SB	CS	SBR	FR	POS	TPR
1983	Min-A	124	373	43	93	24	3	11	56	34	51	.249	.324	.418	99	1	-1	50	0	1	-1	1	*D/1	0.0
1984	Min-A	113	311	46	69	17	1	11	43	31	60	.222	.301	.389	85	-5	-7	38	1	2	-1	0	D/1	-0.7
1985	Min-A	97	234	26	56	13	3	10	35	24	30	.239	.323	.449	103	3	1	36	3	0	1	-3	OD/1	-0.1
1986	Min-A	130	357	50	96	19	7	7	45	39	63	.269	.348	.420	105	4	3	53	5	3	-0	-11	*O/1D	-1.0
1987	*Min-A	122	293	46	74	10	2	11	46	43	49	.253	.354	.413	99	2	0	45	10	3	1	-7	O/1D	-0.7
1988	Min-A	136	394	51	103	20	3	14	51	58	49	.261	.369	.434	120	14	13	64	8	6	-1	-9	*O/1D	0.0
1989	Min-A	141	391	60	103	17	4	14	54	48	73	.263	.348	.435	112	10	7	54	5	8	-3	-6	*O1/D	-0.5
1990	Min-A	73	181	17	44	8	0	6	18	21	27	.243	.341	.387	96	1	-1	24	0	3	-2	-0	OD/1	-0.2
Total	9	991	2653	352	667	134	24	88	361	306	430	.251	.339	.420	103	29	14	380	32	26	-6	-35	OD/1	-3.2

■ DOC BUSHONG
Bushong, Albert John b: 9/15/1856, Philadelphia, Pa. d: 8/19/08, Brooklyn, N.Y. BR/TR, 5'11", 165 lbs. Deb: 7/19/1875

YEAR	TM/L	G	AB	R	H	2B	3B	HR	RBI	BB	SO	AVG	OBP	SLG	PRO+	BR	/A	RC	SB	CS	SBR	FR	POS	TPR
1875	Atl-n	1	5	0	3	0	1	0			0	.600	.600	1.000	509	2	2	3					/C	0.1
1876	Phi-N	5	21	4	1	0	0	0	0	1	0	.048	.048	.048	-69	-4	-4	0				1	/C	-0.1
1880	Wor-N	41	146	13	25	3	0	0	19	1	16	.171	.177	.192	23	-11	-13	5				14	C/O3	0.4
1881	Wor-N	76	275	35	64	7	4	0	21	21	23	.233	.287	.287	77	-5	-7	23				6	*C	-0.1
1882	Wor-N	69	253	20	40	4	1	1	15	5	17	.158	.174	.194	18	-22	-23	9				-5	*C	-2.1
1883	Cle-N	63	215	15	37	5	0	0	9	7	19	.172	.198	.195	21	-20	-20	9				10	C	-0.5
1884	Cle-N	62	203	24	48	6	1	0	10	17	11	.236	.295	.276	78	-4	-5	17				6	C/O	0.5
1885	*StL-a	85	300	42	80	13	5	0			11	.267	.297	.343	100	1	-1	31				8	*C/3	1.7
1886	*StL-a	107	386	56	86	8	0	1			31	.223	.281	.251	66	-13	-16	31	12			5	*C/1	-0.3
1887	*StL-a	53	201	35	51	4	0	0			11	.254	.299	.274	56	-10	-14	21	14			5	C/O3	0.0
1888	Bro-a	69	253	23	53	5	1	0	16	5		.209	.231	.237	53	-13	-13	16	9			-9	C	-1.3
1889	*Bro-a	25	84	15	13	1	0	0	8	9	7	.155	.237	.167	17	-9	-9	4	2			-1	C	-0.5
1890	*Bro-N	16	55	5	13	2	0	0	7	6	4	.236	.311	.273	72	-2	-2	5	2			0	C/O	0.0
Total	12	671	2392	287	511	58	12	2	106	124	97	.214	.254	.250	56	-111	-126	172	39			40	C/O31	-2.3

■ JOE BUSKEY
Buskey, Joseph Henry "Jazzbow" b: 12/18/02, Cumberland, Md. d: 4/11/49, Cumberland, Md. BR/TR, 5'10", 175 lbs. Deb: 4/19/26

YEAR	TM/L	G	AB	R	H	2B	3B	HR	RBI	BB	SO	AVG	OBP	SLG	PRO+	BR	/A	RC	SB	CS	SBR	FR	POS	TPR
1926	Phi-N	5	8	1	0	0	0	0	0	1	1	.000	.111	.000	-65	-2	-2	0	0			0	/S	-0.1

■ MIKE BUSKEY
Buskey, Michael Thomas b: 1/13/49, San Francisco, Cal. BR/TR, 5'11", 160 lbs. Deb: 9/02/77

YEAR	TM/L	G	AB	R	H	2B	3B	HR	RBI	BB	SO	AVG	OBP	SLG	PRO+	BR	/A	RC	SB	CS	SBR	FR	POS	TPR
1977	Phi-N	6	7	1	2	0	1	0	1	0	1	.286	.375	.571	143	0	0	2	0	0	0	2	/S	0.3

■ RAY BUSSE
Busse, Raymond Edward b: 9/25/48, Daytona Beach, Fla. BR/TR, 6'4", 175 lbs. Deb: 7/24/71

YEAR	TM/L	G	AB	R	H	2B	3B	HR	RBI	BB	SO	AVG	OBP	SLG	PRO+	BR	/A	RC	SB	CS	SBR	FR	POS	TPR
1971	Hou-N	10	34	2	5	3	0	0	4	2	9	.147	.194	.235	22	-4	-3	2	0	0	0	-2	/S3	-0.4
1973	StL-N	24	70	6	10	4	2	2	5	5	21	.143	.200	.343	48	-5	-5	3	0	1	-1	-2	S	-0.4
	Hou-N	15	17	1	1	0	0	0	0	1	12	.059	.111	.059	-52	-3	-3	0	0	0	0	1	/S3	-0.1
	Yr	39	87	7	11	4	2	2	5	6	33	.126	.183	.287	28	-9	-9	3	0	1	-1	-1		-0.5
1974	Hou-N	19	34	3	7	1	0	0	0	3	12	.206	.270	.235	44	-3	-2	2	0	0	0	-0	/3	-0.2
Total	3	68	155	12	23	8	2	2	9	11	54	.148	.205	.265	31	-15	-15	7	0	1	-1	-3	/S3	-1.1

■ HANK BUTCHER
Butcher, Henry Joseph b: 7/12/1886, Chicago, Ill. d: 12/28/79, Hazel Crest, Ill. BR/TR, 5'10", 180 lbs. Deb: 7/08/11

YEAR	TM/L	G	AB	R	H	2B	3B	HR	RBI	BB	SO	AVG	OBP	SLG	PRO+	BR	/A	RC	SB	CS	SBR	FR	POS	TPR
1911	Cle-A	38	133	21	32	7	3	1	11	11		.241	.303	.361	84	-3	-3	17	9			0	O	-0.5
1912	Cle-A	26	82	9	16	4	1	1	10	6		.195	.250	.305	57	-5	-5	6	1			1	O	-0.4
Total	2	64	215	30	48	11	4	2	21	17		.223	.283	.340	74	-8	-8	23	10			2	/O	-0.9

■ SAL BUTERA
Butera, Salvatore Philip b: 9/25/52, Richmond Hill, N.Y BR/TR, 6', 190 lbs. Deb: 4/10/80

YEAR	TM/L	G	AB	R	H	2B	3B	HR	RBI	BB	SO	AVG	OBP	SLG	PRO+	BR	/A	RC	SB	CS	SBR	FR	POS	TPR
1980	Min-A	34	85	4	23	1	0	0	2	3	6	.271	.303	.282	57	-4	-5	7	0	0	0	-1	C/D	-0.4
1981	Min-A	62	167	13	40	7	1	0	18	22	14	.240	.328	.293	75	-4	-5	16	0	0	0	1	C/1D	0.0
1982	Min-A	54	126	9	32	2	0	0	8	17	12	.254	.347	.270	70	-4	-4	12	0	0	0	6	C	0.4
1983	Det-A	4	5	1	1	0	0	0	0	0	0	.200	.200	.200	11	-1	-1	0	0	0	0	1	/C	0.1
1984	Mon-N	3	3	0	0	0	0	0	0	1	0	.000	.250	.000	-26	-0	-0	0	0	0	0	1	/C	0.0
1985	Mon-N	67	120	11	24	1	0	3	12	13	12	.200	.284	.283	63	-6	-6	11	0	0	0	0	C/P	-0.2
1986	Cin-N	56	113	14	27	6	1	2	16	21	10	.239	.358	.363	95	1	-0	15	0	0	0	1	C/P	0.2
1987	Cin-N	5	11	1	2	0	0	1	2	1	6	.182	.250	.455	78	-0	-0	1	0	0	0	1	/C	0.1
	*Min-A	51	111	7	19	5	0	1	12	7	16	.171	.220	.243	22	-12	-13	5	0	0	0	1	C	-0.6
1988	Tor-A	23	60	3	14	2	1	1	6	1	9	.233	.246	.350	65	-3	-3	5	0	0	0	3	C	0.1
Total	9	359	801	63	182	24	3	8	76	86	85	.227	.304	.295	65	-35	-38	71	0	0	0	14	C/DP1	-0.3

■ ED BUTKA
Butka, Edward Luke "Babe" b: 1/7/16, Canonsburg, Pa. BR/TR, 6'3", 193 lbs. Deb: 9/26/43

YEAR	TM/L	G	AB	R	H	2B	3B	HR	RBI	BB	SO	AVG	OBP	SLG	PRO+	BR	/A	RC	SB	CS	SBR	FR	POS	TPR
1943	Was-A	3	9	0	3	1	0	0	1	0	3	.333	.333	.444	132	0	0	1	0	0	0	1	/1	0.1
1944	Was-A	15	41	1	8	1	0	0	1	2	11	.195	.233	.220	31	-4	-4	2	0	0	0	0	1	-0.4
Total	2	18	50	1	11	2	0	0	2	2	14	.220	.250	.260	48	-4	-3	4	0	0	0	1	/1	-0.3

■ ART BUTLER
Butler, Arthur Edward (b: Arthur Edward Bouthillier) b: 12/19/1887, Fall River, Mass. d: 10/7/84, Fall River, Mass. BR/TR, 5'9", 160 lbs. Deb: 4/14/11

YEAR	TM/L	G	AB	R	H	2B	3B	HR	RBI	BB	SO	AVG	OBP	SLG	PRO+	BR	/A	RC	SB	CS	SBR	FR	POS	TPR
1911	Bos-N	27	68	11	12	2	0	0	2	6	6	.176	.263	.206	30	-6	-7	4	0			-3	3/2S	-0.9
1912	Pit-N	43	154	19	42	4	2	1	17	15	13	.273	.337	.344	88	-3	-2	19	2			-22	2	-2.6
1913	Pit-N	82	214	40	60	9	3	0	20	32	14	.280	.379	.350	114	4	5	31	9			-11	2S/3O	-0.4
1914	StL-N	86	274	29	55	12	3	1	24	39	23	.201	.311	.277	76	-7	-7	28	14			-18	S/O	-2.4
1915	StL-N	130	469	73	119	12	5	1	31	47	34	.254	.323	.307	91	-4	-4	52	26	14	-1	-34	*S/2	-3.9
1916	StL-N	86	110	9	23	5	0	0	7	7	12	.209	.256	.255	57	-6	-5	8	3			-4	O/2S3	-1.0
Total	6	454	1289	181	311	44	13	3	101	146	102	.241	.323	.303	85	-22	-20	141	54	14		-93	S/2O3	-11.2

■ BRETT BUTLER
Butler, Brett Morgan b: 6/15/57, Los Angeles, Cal. BL/TL, 5'10", 160 lbs. Deb: 8/20/81

YEAR	TM/L	G	AB	R	H	2B	3B	HR	RBI	BB	SO	AVG	OBP	SLG	PRO+	BR	/A	RC	SB	CS	SBR	FR	POS	TPR
1981	Atl-N	40	126	17	32	2	3	0	4	19	17	.254	.352	.317	89	-1	-1	17	9	1	2	-0	O	0.0
1982	*Atl-N	89	240	35	52	2	0	0	7	25	35	.217	.291	.225	44	-17	-18	19	21	8	2	-5	O	-2.3
1983	Atl-N	151	549	84	154	21	13	5	37	54	56	.281	.347	.393	98	4	-1	75	39	23	-2	8	*O	0.2
1984	Cle-A	159	602	108	162	25	9	3	49	86	62	.269	.364	.355	98	3	2	86	52	22	2	5	*O	0.4
1985	Cle-A	152	591	106	184	28	14	5	50	63	42	.311	.379	.431	122	19	19	100	47	20	2	14	*O/D	3.2
1986	Cle-A	161	587	92	163	17	14	4	51	70	65	.278	.359	.375	102	2	3	84	32	15	1	1	*O	0.1
1987	Cle-A	137	522	91	154	25	8	9	41	91	55	.295	.401	.425	119	18	18	97	33	16	0	11	*O	2.5
1988	SF-N	157	568	109	163	27	9	6	43	97	64	.287	.395	.398	134	25	28	99	43	20	1	-0	*O	2.6
1989	*SF-N	154	594	100	168	22	4	4	36	59	69	.283	.351	.354	105	3	3	78	31	16	-0	6	*O	0.9
1990	SF-N	160	622	108	192	20	9	3	44	90	62	.309	.401	.384	119	19	20	108	51	19	4	-3	*O	1.7
Total	10	1360	5001	850	1424	189	83	39	362	654	527	.285	.370	.379	108	75	75	764	358	160	11	36	*O/D	9.3

■ FRANK BUTLER
Butler, Frank Dean "Stuffy" or "Goldbrick" b: 7/18/1860, Savannah, Ga. d: 7/10/45, Jacksonville, Fla BL/TL, Deb: 7/30/1895

YEAR	TM/L	G	AB	R	H	2B	3B	HR	RBI	BB	SO	AVG	OBP	SLG	PRO+	BR	/A	RC	SB	CS	SBR	FR	POS	TPR
1895	NY-N	5	22	5	6	1	0	0	2	1	1	.273	.304	.318	64	-1	-1	2	0			-0	/O	-0.1

■ KID BUTLER
Butler, Frank Edward b: 1862, Boston, Mass. d: 4/9/21, S.Boston, Mass. Deb: 5/20/1884

YEAR	TM/L	G	AB	R	H	2B	3B	HR	RBI	BB	SO	AVG	OBP	SLG	PRO+	BR	/A	RC	SB	CS	SBR	FR	POS	TPR
1884	Bos-U	71	255	36	43	15	0	0			12	.169	.206	.227	47	-14	-13	12	0			-6	O2/S3	-1.7

■ JOHN BUTLER
Butler, John Albert (a.k.a. Frederick King In 1901) b: 7/26/1879, Boston, Mass. d: 2/2/50, Boston, Mass. BR/TR, 5'7", 170 lbs. Deb: 9/28/01

YEAR	TM/L	G	AB	R	H	2B	3B	HR	RBI	BB	SO	AVG	OBP	SLG	PRO+	BR	/A	RC	SB	CS	SBR	FR	POS	TPR
1901	Mil-A	1	3	0	0	0	0	0	0	0	1	.000	.250	.000	-26	-0	-0	0	0			-1	/C	0.0
1904	StL-N	12	37	0	6	1	0	0	1	4		.162	.244	.189	37	-3	-2	2	0			-2	C	-0.3
1906	Bro-N	1	0	0	0	0	0	0	0	0		—	—	—	—	0	0	0	0			0	/C	0.0

YEAR	TM/L	G	AB	R	H	2B	3B	HR	RBI	BB	SO	AVG	OBP	SLG	PRO+	BR	/A	RC	SB	CS	SBR	FR	POS	TPR
1907	Bro-N	30	79	6	10	1	0	0	2	9		.127	.216	.139	14	-8	-7	3	0			-4	C/O	-0.9
Total	4	44	119	6	16	2	0	0	3	14		.134	.226	.151	20	-11	-10	5	0			-7	/CO	-1.2

■ JOHNNY BUTLER   Butler, John Stephen "Trolley Line"   b: 3/20/1893, Fall River, Kan.   d: 4/29/67, Seal Beach, Cal.   BR/TR, 6', 175 lbs.   Deb: 4/18/26   C

YEAR	TM/L	G	AB	R	H	2B	3B	HR	RBI	BB	SO	AVG	OBP	SLG	PRO+	BR	/A	RC	SB	CS	SBR	FR	POS	TPR
1926	Bro-N	147	501	54	135	27	5	1	68	54	44	.269	.346	.349	89	-7	-6	62	6			-7	*S3/2	-0.5
1927	Bro-N	149	521	39	124	13	6	2	57	34	33	.238	.292	.298	58	-31	-31	46	9			-1	S3	-2.0
1928	Chi-N	62	174	17	47	7	0	0	16	19	7	.270	.352	.310	75	-6	-5	20	2			10	3/S	0.6
1929	StL-N	17	55	5	9	1	1	0	5	4	5	.164	.220	.218	9	-8	-8	3	0			1	/3S	-0.4
Total	4	375	1251	115	315	48	12	3	146	111	89	.252	.320	.317	70	-52	-51	130	17			3	S3/2	-2.3

■ DICK BUTLER   Butler, Richard H.   b: Brooklyn, N.Y.   Deb: 6/16/1897

YEAR	TM/L	G	AB	R	H	2B	3B	HR	RBI	BB	SO	AVG	OBP	SLG	PRO+	BR	/A	RC	SB	CS	SBR	FR	POS	TPR
1897	Lou-N	10	38	3	7	0	0	0	2	0		.184	.184	.184	-2	-5	-5	2	1			-2	C	-0.5
1899	Was-N	12	36	4	10	0	1	0	1	2		.278	.316	.333	81	-1	-1	4	1			-3	C	-0.2
Total	2	22	74	7	17	0	1	0	3	2		.230	.250	.257	39	-6	-6	6	2			-5	/C	-0.7

■ BILL BUTLER   Butler, William J.   b: 1861, New Orleans, La.   Deb: 6/29/1884

YEAR	TM/L	G	AB	R	H	2B	3B	HR	RBI	BB	SO	AVG	OBP	SLG	PRO+	BR	/A	RC	SB	CS	SBR	FR	POS	TPR
1884	Ind-a	9	31	7	7	3	2	0		1		.226	.250	.452	131	1	1	4				-2	/O	0.0

■ KID BUTLER   Butler, Willis Everett   b: 8/9/1887, Franklin, Pa.   d: 2/22/64, Richmond, Cal.   BR/TR, 5'11", 155 lbs.   Deb: 4/30/07

YEAR	TM/L	G	AB	R	H	2B	3B	HR	RBI	BB	SO	AVG	OBP	SLG	PRO+	BR	/A	RC	SB	CS	SBR	FR	POS	TPR
1907	StL-A	20	59	4	13	2	0	0	6	2		.220	.246	.254	61	-3	-3	4	1			-1	2/3S	-0.3

■ FRANK BUTTERY   Buttery, Frank   b: 5/13/1851, Silver Mine, Conn.   d: 12/16/02, Silver Mine, Conn.   Deb: 4/26/1872

YEAR	TM/L	G	AB	R	H	2B	3B	HR	RBI	BB	SO	AVG	OBP	SLG	PRO+	BR	/A	RC	SB	CS	SBR	FR	POS	TPR
1872	Man-n	18	93	18	25	0	0	0		0		.269	.269	.269	70	-4	-2	7					/P3O	0.0

■ JOE BUZAS   Buzas, Joseph John   b: 10/2/19, Alpha, N.J.   BR/TR, 6'1", 180 lbs.   Deb: 4/17/45

YEAR	TM/L	G	AB	R	H	2B	3B	HR	RBI	BB	SO	AVG	OBP	SLG	PRO+	BR	/A	RC	SB	CS	SBR	FR	POS	TPR
1945	NY-A	30	65	8	17	2	1	0	6	2	5	.262	.284	.323	73	-2	-3	6	2	0	1	-3	S	-0.4

■ BURLEY BYERS   Byers, Burley (b: Christopher A. Bayer)   b: 12/19/1875, Louisville, Ky.   d: 5/30/33, Louisville, Ky.   175 lbs.   Deb: 6/17/1899

YEAR	TM/L	G	AB	R	H	2B	3B	HR	RBI	BB	SO	AVG	OBP	SLG	PRO+	BR	/A	RC	SB	CS	SBR	FR	POS	TPR
1899	Lou-N	1	3	0	0	0	0	0	0	0		.000	.000	.000	-99	-1	-1	0	0			-1	/S	-0.1

■ BILL BYERS   Byers, James William   b: 10/3/1877, Bridgeton, Ind.   d: 9/8/48, Baltimore, Md.   TR, 5'7",   Deb: 4/15/04

YEAR	TM/L	G	AB	R	H	2B	3B	HR	RBI	BB	SO	AVG	OBP	SLG	PRO+	BR	/A	RC	SB	CS	SBR	FR	POS	TPR
1904	StL-N	19	60	3	13	0	0	0	4	1		.217	.230	.217	41	-4	-4	3	0			-1	C/1	-0.3

■ RANDY BYERS   Byers, Randell Parker   b: 10/2/64, Bridgeton, N.J.   BL/TR, 6'2", 180 lbs.   Deb: 9/07/87

YEAR	TM/L	G	AB	R	H	2B	3B	HR	RBI	BB	SO	AVG	OBP	SLG	PRO+	BR	/A	RC	SB	CS	SBR	FR	POS	TPR
1987	SD-N	10	16	1	5	1	0	0	1	1	5	.313	.353	.375	96	-0	-0	2	1	0	0	1	/O	0.1
1988	SD-N	11	10	0	2	1	0	0	0	0	5	.200	.200	.300	42	-1	-1	1	0	0	0	0	/O	0.0
Total	2	21	26	1	7	2	0	0	1	1	10	.269	.296	.346	77	-1	-1	3	1	0	0	1	/O	0.1

■ SAMMY BYRD   Byrd, Samuel Dewey "Babe Ruth's Legs"   b: 10/15/07, Bremen, Ga.   d: 5/11/81, Mesa, Ariz.   BR/TR, 5'10.5", 175 lbs.   Deb: 5/11/29

YEAR	TM/L	G	AB	R	H	2B	3B	HR	RBI	BB	SO	AVG	OBP	SLG	PRO+	BR	/A	RC	SB	CS	SBR	FR	POS	TPR
1929	NY-A	62	170	32	53	12	0	5	28	28	18	.312	.409	.471	135	7	9	33	1	4	-2	-0	O	0.4
1930	NY-A	92	218	46	62	12	2	6	31	30	18	.284	.371	.440	110	2	3	38	5	1	1	-12	O	-0.9
1931	NY-A	115	248	51	67	18	2	3	32	29	26	.270	.349	.395	101	-2	0	36	5	0	2	-13	O	-1.5
1932	*NY-A	105	209	49	62	12	1	8	30	30	20	.297	.385	.478	129	7	9	39	1	2	-1	4	O	0.8
1933	NY-A	85	107	26	30	6	1	2	11	15	12	.280	.369	.411	113	1	2	17	0	1	-1	4	O	0.3
1934	NY-A	106	191	32	47	8	0	3	23	18	22	.246	.318	.335	73	-9	-7	21	1	2	-1	-13	*O	-2.0
1935	Cin-N	121	416	51	109	25	4	9	52	37	51	.262	.322	.406	97	-4	-2	56	4			-3	*O	-0.9
1936	Cin-N	59	141	17	35	8	2	2	13	11	11	.248	.303	.348	80	-5	-4	15	0			3	O	-0.2
Total	8	745	1700	304	465	101	10	38	220	198	178	.274	.350	.412	104	-2	11	255	17	10		-30	O	-4.0

■ BOBBY BYRNE   Byrne, Robert Matthew   b: 12/31/1884, St.Louis, Mo.   d: 12/31/64, Wayne, Pa.   BR/TR, 5'7.5", 145 lbs.   Deb: 4/11/07

YEAR	TM/L	G	AB	R	H	2B	3B	HR	RBI	BB	SO	AVG	OBP	SLG	PRO+	BR	/A	RC	SB	CS	SBR	FR	POS	TPR
1907	StL-N	149	559	55	143	11	5	0	29	35		.256	.300	.293	91	-8	-6	60	21			21	*3/S	1.7
1908	StL-N	127	439	27	84	7	1	0	14	23		.191	.232	.212	46	-27	-25	26	16			9	*3/S	-1.5
1909	StL-N	105	421	61	90	13	6	1	33	46		.214	.302	.280	86	-9	-6	42	21			16	*3	1.4
	*Pit-N	46	168	31	43	6	2	0	7	32		.256	.387	.315	109	6	4	24	8			5	3	1.1
	Yr	151	589	92	133	19	8	1	40	78		.226	.327	.290	93	-3	-2	65	29			21		2.5
1910	Pit-N	148	602	101	**178**	43	12	2	52	66	27	.296	.366	.417	121	21	16	104	36			-7	*3	1.1
1911	Pit-N	153	598	96	155	24	17	2	52	67	41	.259	.342	.366	95	-1	0	82	23			-3	*3	0.0
1912	Pit-N	130	528	99	152	31	11	3	35	54	40	.288	.358	.405	110	6	7	83	10			-23	*3	-1.4
1913	Pit-N	113	448	54	121	22	0	1	47	29	28	.270	.322	.326	89	-9	-6	49	10			-11	*3	-1.8
	Phi-N	19	58	9	13	1	0	1	4	5	3	.224	.308	.293	69	-2	-2	6	2			3	3	0.0
	Yr	132	506	63	134	23	0	2	51	34	31	.265	.320	.322	86	-11	-9	54	12			-8		-1.8
1914	Phi-N	126	467	61	127	12	1	0	26	45	44	.272	.339	.302	85	-4	-7	49	9			-3	*23	-1.0
1915	*Phi-N	105	387	50	81	6	4	0	21	39	28	.209	.290	.245	62	-16	-17	28	4	12	-6	-6	*3	-2.7
1916	Phi-N	48	141	22	33	10	1	0	9	14	7	.234	.308	.319	89	-1	-2	17	6			3	3	0.2
1917	Phi-N	13	14	1	5	0	0	0	0	1	2	.357	.400	.357	128	1	1	2	0			-1	/3	0.0
	Chi-A	1	1	0	0	0	0	0	0	0	0	.000	.000	.000	-98	-0	-0	0	0			0	/2	0.0
Total	11	1283	4831	667	1225	186	60	10	329	456	220	.254	.323	.323	91	-44	-48	571	176	12		2	*32/S	-2.9

■ JIM BYRNES   Byrnes, James Joseph   b: 1/5/1880, San Francisco, Cal.   d: 7/31/41, San Francisco, Cal   BR/TR, 5'9", 150 lbs.   Deb: 4/19/06

YEAR	TM/L	G	AB	R	H	2B	3B	HR	RBI	BB	SO	AVG	OBP	SLG	PRO+	BR	/A	RC	SB	CS	SBR	FR	POS	TPR
1906	Phi-A	10	23	2	4	0	1	0	0	0		.174	.174	.261	36	-2	-2	1	0			0	/C	0.0

■ MILT BYRNES   Byrnes, Milton John "Skippy"   b: 11/15/16, St.Louis, Mo.   d: 2/1/79, St.Louis, Mo.   BL/TL, 5'10.5", 170 lbs.   Deb: 4/21/43

YEAR	TM/L	G	AB	R	H	2B	3B	HR	RBI	BB	SO	AVG	OBP	SLG	PRO+	BR	/A	RC	SB	CS	SBR	FR	POS	TPR
1943	StL-A	129	429	58	120	28	7	4	50	54	49	.280	.362	.406	122	13	12	65	1	4	-2	3	*O	1.1
1944	*StL-A	128	407	63	120	20	4	4	45	68	50	.295	.396	.393	119	16	13	67	1	7	-4	-15	*O	-0.9
1945	StL-A	133	442	53	110	29	4	8	59	78	84	.249	.363	.387	112	12	9	69	1	3	-2	11	*O/1	1.4
Total	3	390	1278	174	350	77	15	16	154	200	183	.274	.373	.395	117	41	35	201	3	14	-8	-0	O/1	1.6

■ PUTSY CABALLERO   Caballero, Ralph Joseph   b: 11/5/27, New Orleans, La.   BR/TR, 5'10", 170 lbs.   Deb: 9/14/44

YEAR	TM/L	G	AB	R	H	2B	3B	HR	RBI	BB	SO	AVG	OBP	SLG	PRO+	BR	/A	RC	SB	CS	SBR	FR	POS	TPR
1944	Phi-N	4	4	0	0	0	0	0	0	0	1	.000	.000	.000	-99	-1	-1	0	0			2	/3	0.1
1945	Phi-N	9	1	1	0	0	0	0	1	0	0	.000	.000	.000	-99	-0	-0	0	0			2	/3	0.2
1947	Phi-N	2	7	2	1	0	0	0	0	1	0	.143	.250	.143	7	-1	-1	0	0			0	/23	0.0
1948	Phi-N	113	351	33	86	12	1	0	19	24	18	.245	.293	.285	58	-21	-20	29	7			6	32	-1.3
1949	Phi-N	29	68	8	19	3	0	0	3	0	3	.279	.279	.324	63	-4	-4	6	0			4	2/S	0.1
1950	*Phi-N	46	24	12	4	0	0	0	0	2	2	.167	.231	.167	7	-3	-3	1	1			9	/23S	0.6
1951	Phi-N	84	161	15	30	3	2	1	11	12	7	.186	.243	.248	33	-15	-15	9	1	2	-1	9	/23S	-0.4
1952	Phi-N	35	42	10	10	3	0	0	6	2	3	.238	.273	.310	62	-2	-2	2	1	0	0	2	/S23	0.1
Total	8	322	658	81	150	21	3	1	40	41	34	.228	.273	.274	49	-48	-46	47	10	2		35	23/S	-0.6

■ ENOS CABELL   Cabell, Enos Milton   b: 10/8/49, Fort Riley, Kan.   BR/TR, 6'4", 170 lbs.   Deb: 9/17/72

YEAR	TM/L	G	AB	R	H	2B	3B	HR	RBI	BB	SO	AVG	OBP	SLG	PRO+	BR	/A	RC	SB	CS	SBR	FR	POS	TPR
1972	Bal-A	3	5	0	0	0	0	0	0	1	0	.000	.000	.000	-97	-1	-1	0	0	0	0	-0	/1	-0.1
1973	Bal-A	32	47	12	10	2	0	1	3	3	7	.213	.260	.319	63	-2	-2	3	1	3	-2	-1	1/3	-0.1
1974	*Bal-A	80	174	24	42	4	2	3	17	7	20	.241	.271	.339	77	-6	-6	14	5	3	-0	5	103/2D	-0.1
1975	Hou-N	117	348	43	92	17	6	2	43	18	53	.264	.306	.365	92	-8	-5	38	12	3	2	1	O13	-0.5
1976	Hou-N	144	586	85	160	13	7	2	43	29	79	.273	.310	.329	89	-15	-9	61	35	8	6	-9	*3/1	-1.4
1977	Hou-N	150	625	101	176	36	7	16	68	27	55	.282	.315	.438	109	-2	4	82	42	22	-1	-6	*3/1S	-0.3
1978	Hou-N	162	660	92	195	31	8	7	71	22	80	.295	.323	.398	109	-1	4	81	33	15	1	-16	*31/S	-1.2

YEAR	TM/L	G	AB	R	H	2B	3B	HR	RBI	BB	SO	AVG	OBP	SLG	PRO+	BR	/A	RC	SB	CS	SBR	FR	POS	TPR
1979	Hou-N	155	603	60	164	30	5	6	67	21	68	.272	.300	.368	86	-17	-13	60	37	18	0	-23	*31	-4.4
1980	*Hou-N	152	604	69	167	23	8	2	55	26	84	.276	.307	.351	90	-14	-9	61	21	13	-2	-19	*3/1	-3.1
1981	SF-N	96	396	41	101	20	1	2	36	10	47	.255	.275	.326	71	-16	-16	33	6	7	-2	-1	13	-2.3
1982	Det-A	125	464	45	121	17	3	2	37	15	48	.261	.285	.323	67	-21	-21	41	15	6	1	-9	13/O	-3.2
1983	Det-A	121	392	62	122	23	5	5	46	16	41	.311	.340	.434	114	5	6	51	4	8	-4	7	*1/3SD	0.5
1984	Hou-N	127	436	52	135	17	3	8	44	21	47	.310	.343	.417	121	6	10	56	8	11	-4	-0	*1	0.2
1985	Hou-N	60	143	20	35	8	1	2	14	16	15	.245	.321	.357	92	-2	-1	16	3	1	0	-1	1	-0.3
	*LA-N	57	192	20	56	11	0	0	22	14	21	.292	.340	.349	96	-2	-1	24	6	2	1	-1	31/O	-0.1
	Yr	117	335	40	91	19	1	2	36	30	36	.272	.332	.352	94	-4	-2	40	9	3	1	-2		-0.4
1986	LA-N	107	277	27	71	11	0	2	29	14	26	.256	.297	.318	75	-12	-9	26	10	4	1	0	1O/3	-1.1
Total	15	1688	5952	753	1647	263	56	60	596	259	691	.277	.309	.370	93	-108	-68	646	238	124	-3	-72	310/DS2	-18.0

■ AL CABRERA   Cabrera, Alfredo A. b: 1883, Canary Islands d: Havana, Cuba TR, Deb: 5/16/13

YEAR	TM/L	G	AB	R	H	2B	3B	HR	RBI	BB	SO	AVG	OBP	SLG	PRO+	BR	/A	RC	SB	CS	SBR	FR	POS	TPR
1913	StL-N	1	2	0	0	0	0	0	0	0	0	.000	.000	.000	-99	-1	-1	0	0			0	/S	0.0

■ FRANCISCO CABRERA   Cabrera, Francisco (Paulino) b: 10/10/66, Santo Domingo, D.R. BR/TR, 6'4", 195 lbs. Deb: 7/24/89

YEAR	TM/L	G	AB	R	H	2B	3B	HR	RBI	BB	SO	AVG	OBP	SLG	PRO+	BR	/A	RC	SB	CS	SBR	FR	POS	TPR
1989	Tor-A	3	12	1	2	1	0	0	0	1	3	.167	.231	.250	36	-1	-1	1	0	0	0	0	/D	0.0
	Atl-N	4	14	0	3	2	0	0	0	0	3	.214	.214	.357	59	-1	-1	1	0	0	0	-1	/1C	-0.1
1990	Atl-N	63	137	14	38	5	1	7	25	5	21	.277	.303	.482	110	2	1	19	1	0	0	-2	1/C	-0.2
Total	2	70	163	15	43	8	1	7	25	6	27	.264	.290	.454	101	-0	-0	20	1	0	0	-2	/1CD	-0.3

■ CRAIG CACEK   Cacek, Craig Thomas b: 9/10/54, Hollywood, Cal. BR/TR, 6'1", 200 lbs. Deb: 6/18/77

YEAR	TM/L	G	AB	R	H	2B	3B	HR	RBI	BB	SO	AVG	OBP	SLG	PRO+	BR	/A	RC	SB	CS	SBR	FR	POS	TPR
1977	Hou-N	7	20	0	1	0	0	0	1	1	3	.050	.095	.050	-66	-5	-4	0	0	0	0	-1	/1	-0.5

■ CHARLIE CADY   Cady, Charles B. b: 12/1865, Chicago, Ill. d: 6/7/09, Kankakee, Ill. 5'11", 180 lbs. Deb: 9/05/1883

YEAR	TM/L	G	AB	R	H	2B	3B	HR	RBI	BB	SO	AVG	OBP	SLG	PRO+	BR	/A	RC	SB	CS	SBR	FR	POS	TPR
1883	Cle-N	3	11	0	0	0	0	0	0	1	5	.000	.083	.000	-73	-2	-2	0				-1	/OP	-0.2
1884	CP-U	6	20	4	2	1	1	0			1	.100	.143	.250	31	-1	-1	1	0			0	/PO	0.0
	KC-U	2	3	0	0	0	0	0			0	.000	.000	.000	-99	-1	-1	0	0			-1	/C2	0.0
	Yr	8	23	4	2	1	1	0			1	.087	.125	.217	14	-2	-2	1	0			-1		0.0
Total	2	11	34	4	2	1	1	0	0	2	5	.059	.111	.147	-17	-4	-4	1	0			-2	/PO2C	-0.2

■ HICK CADY   Cady, Forrest Leroy b: 1/26/1886, Bishop Hill, Ill. d: 3/3/46, Cedar Rapids, Iowa BR/TR, 6'2", 179 lbs. Deb: 4/26/12

YEAR	TM/L	G	AB	R	H	2B	3B	HR	RBI	BB	SO	AVG	OBP	SLG	PRO+	BR	/A	RC	SB	CS	SBR	FR	POS	TPR
1912	*Bos-A	47	135	19	35	13	2	0	9	10		.259	.324	.385	98	0	-1	17	0			11	C/1	1.4
1913	Bos-A	40	96	10	24	5	2	0	6	5	14	.250	.294	.344	84	-2	-2	10	1			9	C	1.0
1914	Bos-A	61	159	14	41	6	1	0	8	12	22	.258	.310	.308	86	-3	-3	16	2	1	0	-3	C	-0.1
1915	*Bos-A	78	205	25	57	10	2	0	17	19	25	.278	.342	.346	109	1	2	25	0	2	-1	-1	C	0.6
1916	*Bos-A	78	162	5	31	6	3	0	13	15	16	.191	.264	.265	59	-8	-8	12	0			-13	C/1	-2.0
1917	Bos-A	17	46	4	7	1	1	0	2	1	6	.152	.170	.217	18	-5	-5	2	0			1	C	-0.2
1919	Phi-N	34	98	6	21	6	0	1	19	4	8	.214	.252	.306	63	-4	-5	8	1			-6	C	-1.0
Total	7	355	901	83	216	47	11	1	74	66	91	.240	.297	.320	82	-21	-22	89	4	3		-3	C/1	-0.3

■ TOM CAFEGO   Cafego, Thomas b: 8/21/11, Whipple, W.Va. d: 10/29/61, Detroit, Mich. BL/TR, 5'10", 160 lbs. Deb: 9/03/37

YEAR	TM/L	G	AB	R	H	2B	3B	HR	RBI	BB	SO	AVG	OBP	SLG	PRO+	BR	/A	RC	SB	CS	SBR	FR	POS	TPR
1937	StL-A	4	4	1	0	0	0	0	0	0	1	.000	.000	.000	-99	-1	-1	0	0	0	0	0	/O	0.0

■ JOE CAFFIE   Caffie, Joseph Clifford "Rabbit" b: 2/14/31, Ramer, Ala. BL/TR, 5'10.5", 180 lbs. Deb: 9/13/56

YEAR	TM/L	G	AB	R	H	2B	3B	HR	RBI	BB	SO	AVG	OBP	SLG	PRO+	BR	/A	RC	SB	CS	SBR	FR	POS	TPR
1956	Cle-A	12	38	7	13	0	0	0	1	4	8	.342	.432	.342	104	1	1	6	3	2	-0	0	O	0.0
1957	Cle-A	32	89	14	24	2	1	3	10	4	11	.270	.301	.416	95	-1	-1	11	0	1	-1	-1	O	-0.3
Total	2	44	127	21	37	2	1	3	11	8	19	.291	.343	.394	99	-0	-0	17	3	3	-1	-1	/O	-0.3

■ BEN CAFFYN   Caffyn, Benjamin Thomas b: 2/10/1880, Peoria, Ill. d: 11/22/42, Peoria, Ill. BL/TL, Deb: 8/21/06

YEAR	TM/L	G	AB	R	H	2B	3B	HR	RBI	BB	SO	AVG	OBP	SLG	PRO+	BR	/A	RC	SB	CS	SBR	FR	POS	TPR
1906	Cle-A	30	103	16	20	4	0	0	3		12	.194	.278	.233	63	-4	-4	8	2			-4	O	-0.9

■ WAYNE CAGE   Cage, Wayne Levell b: 11/23/51, Monroe, La. BL/TL, 6'4", 205 lbs. Deb: 4/22/78

YEAR	TM/L	G	AB	R	H	2B	3B	HR	RBI	BB	SO	AVG	OBP	SLG	PRO+	BR	/A	RC	SB	CS	SBR	FR	POS	TPR
1978	Cle-A	36	98	11	24	6	1	4	13	9	28	.245	.308	.449	112	1	1	13	1	2	-1	1	D1	0.1
1979	Cle-A	29	56	6	13	2	0	1	6	5	16	.232	.295	.321	66	-3	-3	5	0	2	-1	1	/1D	-0.3
Total	2	65	154	17	37	8	1	5	19	14	44	.240	.304	.403	94	-2	-2	17	1	4	-2	2	/D1	-0.2

■ JOHN CAHILL   Cahill, John Patrick Francis "Patsy" b: 1864, San Francisco, Cal. d: 11/1/01, Pleasanton, Cal. BR/TR, 5'7.5", 168 lbs. Deb: 5/31/1884

YEAR	TM/L	G	AB	R	H	2B	3B	HR	RBI	BB	SO	AVG	OBP	SLG	PRO+	BR	/A	RC	SB	CS	SBR	FR	POS	TPR
1884	Col-a	59	210	28	46	3	3	0		6		.219	.248	.262	75	-7	-4	14				-0	O/SP	-0.4
1886	StL-N	125	463	43	92	17	6	1	32	9	79	.199	.214	.268	49	-30	-26	31	16			3	*O/PS3	-1.8
1887	Ind-N	68	263	22	54	4	3	0	26	9	5	.205	.234	.243	35	-23	-21	24	34			-7	O/3PS	-2.2
Total	3	252	936	93	192	24	12	1	58	24	84	.205	.227	.260	50	-60	-52	68	50			-4	O/3PS	-4.4

■ TOM CAHILL   Cahill, Thomas H. b: 10/1868, Fall River, Mass. d: 12/25/1894, Scranton, Pa. Deb: 4/09/1891

YEAR	TM/L	G	AB	R	H	2B	3B	HR	RBI	BB	SO	AVG	OBP	SLG	PRO+	BR	/A	RC	SB	CS	SBR	FR	POS	TPR
1891	Lou-a	120	433	70	111	18	7	3	47	41	51	.256	.329	.351	98	-2	-1	64	39			-2	CSO/23	0.1

■ BOB CAIN   Cain, Robert Max "Sugar" b: 10/16/24, Longford, Kan. BL/TL, 6', 165 lbs. Deb: 9/18/49

YEAR	TM/L	G	AB	R	H	2B	3B	HR	RBI	BB	SO	AVG	OBP	SLG	PRO+	BR	/A	RC	SB	CS	SBR	FR	POS	TPR
1949	Chi-A	6	3	0	0	0	0	0	0	0	1	.000	.000	.000	-99	-1	-1	0	0	0	0	-0	/P	0.0
1950	Chi-A	35	61	7	12	2	0	0	2	3	15	.197	.234	.230	20	-8	-7	4	0	0	0	-0	P	0.0
1951	Chi-A	4	9	1	3	1	0	0	0	0	3	.333	.333	.444	111	0	0	1	0	0	0	-0	/P	0.0
	Det-A	35	53	9	13	3	0	0	9	6	9	.245	.322	.302	69	-2	-2	5	0	0	0	0	P	0.0
	Yr	39	62	10	16	4	0	0	9	6	12	.258	.324	.323	75	-2	-2	7	0	0	0	0		0.0
1952	StL-A	35	58	7	8	0	1	0	1	4	14	.138	.194	.172	2	-8	-8	2	0	0	0	-2	P	0.0
1953	StL-A	34	30	3	6	2	0	0	2	1	3	.200	.226	.267	32	-3	-3	2	0	0	0	-1	P	0.0
1954	Chi-A	1	0	1	0	0	0	0	0	0	0	—	—	—	—	0	0	0	0	0	0	0	R	0.0
Total	6	150	214	28	42	8	1	0	14	14	45	.196	.246	.243	31	-21	-21	14	0	0	0	-4	P	0.0

■ GEORGE CAITHAMER   Caithamer, George Theodore "Sidel" b: 7/22/10, Chicago, Ill. d: 6/1/54, Chicago, Ill. BR/TR, 5'7.5", 160 lbs. Deb: 9/17/34

YEAR	TM/L	G	AB	R	H	2B	3B	HR	RBI	BB	SO	AVG	OBP	SLG	PRO+	BR	/A	RC	SB	CS	SBR	FR	POS	TPR
1934	Chi-A	5	19	1	6	1	0	0	3	1	5	.316	.350	.368	83	-0	-0	2	0	0	0	-1	/C	0.0

■ IVAN CALDERON   Calderon, Ivan (Perez) b: 3/19/62, Fajardo, P.R. BR/TR, 5'11", 160 lbs. Deb: 8/10/84

YEAR	TM/L	G	AB	R	H	2B	3B	HR	RBI	BB	SO	AVG	OBP	SLG	PRO+	BR	/A	RC	SB	CS	SBR	FR	POS	TPR
1984	Sea-A	11	24	2	5	1	0	1		2	5	.208	.269	.375	77	-1	-1	2	1	0	0	1	O	0.0
1985	Sea-A	67	210	37	60	16	4	8	28	19	45	.286	.351	.514	132	9	9	34	4	2	0	1	O/1D	0.9
1986	Sea-A	37	131	13	31	5	0	2	13	6	33	.237	.275	.321	61	-7	-7	12	3	1	0	-2	O	-0.9
	Chi-A	13	33	3	10	2	1	0	2	3	6	.303	.361	.424	109	1	0	5	0	0	0	-0	/OD	0.0
	Yr	50	164	16	41	7	1	2	15	9	39	.250	.293	.341	71	-6	-7	17	3	1	0	-3		-0.9
1987	Chi-A	144	542	93	159	38	2	28	83	60	109	.293	.365	.526	129	25	23	102	10	5	0	1	*O/D	1.9
1988	Chi-A	73	264	40	56	14	0	14	35	34	66	.212	.302	.424	101	-0	-0	33	4	4	-1	-5	O/D	-0.7
1989	Chi-A	157	622	83	178	34	9	14	87	43	94	.286	.335	.437	119	12	14	87	7	1	2	-1	*OD1	1.1
1990	Chi-A	158	607	85	166	44	2	14	74	51	79	.273	.331	.422	111	6	8	76	32	16	0	-0	*OD/1	0.6
Total	7	660	2433	356	665	154	18	81	323	218	437	.273	.335	.451	115	44	46	351	61	29	1	-6	O/D1	2.9

■ SAM CALDERONE   Calderone, Samuel Francis b: 2/6/26, Beverly, N.J. BR/TR, 5'10.5", 185 lbs. Deb: 4/19/50

YEAR	TM/L	G	AB	R	H	2B	3B	HR	RBI	BB	SO	AVG	OBP	SLG	PRO+	BR	/A	RC	SB	CS	SBR	FR	POS	TPR
1950	NY-N	34	67	9	20	1	0	1	12	2	5	.299	.319	.358	77	-2	-2	7	0			-4	C	-0.4
1953	NY-N	35	45	4	10	2	0	0	8	1	4	.222	.239	.267	31	-4	-5	3	0	0	0	-1	C	-0.2
1954	Mil-N	22	29	3	11	2	0	0	5	4	4	.379	.455	.448	146	2	2	6	0	0	0	3	C	0.5

YEAR	TM/L	G	AB	R	H	2B	3B	HR	RBI	BB	SO	AVG	OBP	SLG	PRO+	BR	/A	RC	SB	CS	SBR	FR	POS	TPR
Total	3	91	141	16	41	5	0	1	25	7	13	.291	.324	.348	76	-5	-5	16	0	0		-1	/C	-0.1

■ BRUCE CALDWELL
Caldwell, Bruce b: 2/8/06, Ashton, R.I. d: 2/15/59, West Haven, Conn. BR/TR, 6′, 195 lbs. Deb: 6/30/28

YEAR	TM/L	G	AB	R	H	2B	3B	HR	RBI	BB	SO	AVG	OBP	SLG	PRO+	BR	/A	RC	SB	CS	SBR	FR	POS	TPR
1928	Cle-A	18	27	2	6	1	1	0	3	2	2	.222	.300	.333	66	-1	-1	3	1	0	0	-1	O/1	-0.2
1932	Bro-N	7	11	2	1	0	0	0	2	2	2	.091	.231	.091	-10	-2	-2	0	0			-1	/1	-0.2
Total	2	25	38	4	7	1	1	0	5	4	4	.184	.279	.263	44	-3	-3	3	1	0		-3	/O1	-0.4

■ RAY CALDWELL
Caldwell, Raymond Benjamin "Rube" or "Slim" b: 4/26/1888, Corydon, Pa. d: 8/17/67, Salamanca, N.Y. BL/TR, 6′2″, 190 lbs. Deb: 9/09/10

YEAR	TM/L	G	AB	R	H	2B	3B	HR	RBI	BB	SO	AVG	OBP	SLG	PRO+	BR	/A	RC	SB	CS	SBR	FR	POS	TPR
1910	NY-A	6	6	0	0	0	0	0	0	0		.000	.000	.000	-95	-1	-1	0	0			-0	/P	0.0
1911	NY-A	59	147	14	40	4	1	0	17	11		.272	.323	.313	73	-4	-6	16	5			-2	PO	0.0
1912	NY-A	44	76	18	18	1	2	0	6	5		.237	.284	.303	64	-3	-4	7	4			2	P/O	0.0
1913	NY-A	59	97	10	28	3	2	0	11	3	15	.289	.310	.361	96	-1	-1	11	3			-2	P/O	0.2
1914	NY-A	59	113	9	22	4	0	0	10	7	24	.195	.248	.230	44	-8	-8	7	2	1	0	-4	P/1	0.0
1915	NY-A	72	144	27	35	4	1	4	20	9	32	.243	.288	.368	96	-2	-2	15	4	3	-1	-3	P	0.0
1916	NY-A	45	93	6	19	2	0	0	4	2	17	.204	.221	.226	34	-8	-8	5	1			-1	P/O	-0.6
1917	NY-A	63	124	12	32	6	1	2	12	16	16	.258	.343	.371	117	3	3	16	2			-3	P/O	0.0
1918	NY-A	65	151	14	44	10	0	1	18	13	23	.291	.352	.377	117	3	3	20	2			-2	PO	0.4
1919	Bos-A	33	48	5	13	1	1	0	4	0	9	.271	.271	.333	73	-2	-2	4	0			-1	P/O	0.0
	Cle-A	6	23	4	8	4	0	0	2	0	4	.348	.348	.522	134	1	1	4	0			-1	/P	0.0
	Yr	39	71	9	21	5	1	0	6	0	13	.296	.296	.394	97	-1	-1	8	0			-3		0.0
1920	*Cle-A	41	89	17	19	3	0	0	7	10	13	.213	.300	.247	45	-7	-7	7	0	2	-1	-3	P	0.0
1921	Cle-A	38	53	2	11	4	0	1	3	2	5	.208	.236	.340	45	-5	-5	4	0	0	0	-1	P	0.0
Total	12	590	1164	138	289	46	8	8	114	78	158	.248	.297	.322	78	-34	-36	117	23	6		-21	P/O1	-0.0

■ JACK CALHOUN
Calhoun, John Charles "Red" b: 12/14/1879, Pittsburgh, Pa. d: 2/27/47, Cincinnati, Ohio BR/TR, 6′, 185 lbs. Deb: 6/27/02

YEAR	TM/L	G	AB	R	H	2B	3B	HR	RBI	BB	SO	AVG	OBP	SLG	PRO+	BR	/A	RC	SB	CS	SBR	FR	POS	TPR
1902	StL-N	20	64	3	10	2	1	0	8	8		.156	.260	.219	52	-3	-3	4	1			-2	3/1O	-0.5

■ BILL CALHOUN
Calhoun, William Davitte "Mary" b: 6/23/1890, Rockmart, Ga. d: 2/11/55, Sandersville, Ga. BL/TL, 6′, 180 lbs. Deb: 4/24/13

YEAR	TM/L	G	AB	R	H	2B	3B	HR	RBI	BB	SO	AVG	OBP	SLG	PRO+	BR	/A	RC	SB	CS	SBR	FR	POS	TPR
1913	Bos-N	6	13	0	1	0	0	0	0	0	3	.077	.077	.077	-55	-3	-3	0	0			-0	/1	-0.2

■ MARTY CALLAGHAN
Callaghan, Martin Francis b: 6/9/1900, Norwood, Mass. d: 6/23/75, Norfolk, Mass. BL/TL, 5′10″, 157 lbs. Deb: 4/13/22

YEAR	TM/L	G	AB	R	H	2B	3B	HR	RBI	BB	SO	AVG	OBP	SLG	PRO+	BR	/A	RC	SB	CS	SBR	FR	POS	TPR
1922	Chi-N	74	175	31	45	7	4	0	20	17	17	.257	.326	.343	71	-7	-7	20	2	3	-1	-4	O	-1.3
1923	Chi-N	61	129	18	29	1	3	0	14	8	18	.225	.275	.279	47	-10	-10	9	2	5	-2	-1	O	-1.4
1928	Cin-N	81	238	29	69	11	4	0	24	27	10	.290	.362	.370	93	-2	-2	33	5			-3	O	-0.7
1930	Cin-N	79	225	28	62	9	2	0	16	19	25	.276	.335	.333	66	-13	-11	25	1			3	O	-1.0
Total	4	295	767	106	205	28	13	0	74	71	70	.267	.332	.338	72	-32	-31	87	10	8		-6	O	-4.4

■ DAVE CALLAHAN
Callahan, David Joseph b: 7/20/1888, Ottawa, Ill. d: 10/28/69, Ottawa, Ill. BL/TR, 5′10″, 165 lbs. Deb: 9/14/10

YEAR	TM/L	G	AB	R	H	2B	3B	HR	RBI	BB	SO	AVG	OBP	SLG	PRO+	BR	/A	RC	SB	CS	SBR	FR	POS	TPR
1910	Cle-A	13	44	6	8	1	0	0	2	4		.182	.265	.205	47	-3	-3	4	5			0	O	-0.2
1911	Cle-A	6	16	1	4	0	1	0	0	1		.250	.294	.375	85	-0	-0	2	0			0	/O	0.0
Total	2	19	60	7	12	1	1	0	2	5		.200	.273	.250	58	-3	-3	5	5			1	/O	-0.2

■ ED CALLAHAN
Callahan, Edward Joseph b: 12/11/1857, Boston, Mass. d: 2/5/47, New York, N.Y. Deb: 7/19/1884

YEAR	TM/L	G	AB	R	H	2B	3B	HR	RBI	BB	SO	AVG	OBP	SLG	PRO+	BR	/A	RC	SB	CS	SBR	FR	POS	TPR
1884	StL-U	1	3	0	0	0	0	0		0		.000	.000	.000	-97	-1	-1	0	0			0	/O	0.0
	KC-U	3	11	0	4	0	0	0		0		.364	.364	.364	168	0	1	1	0			1	/S	0.1
	Bos-U	4	13	2	5	0	0	0		1		.385	.429	.385	180	1	1	2	0			-1	/O	0.0
	Yr	8	27	2	9	0	0	0		1		.333	.357	.333	142	1	1	3	0			0		0.1

■ NIXEY CALLAHAN
Callahan, James Joseph b: 3/18/1874, Fitchburg, Mass. d: 10/4/34, Boston, Mass. BR/TR, 5′10.5″, 180 lbs. Deb: 5/12/1894 M

YEAR	TM/L	G	AB	R	H	2B	3B	HR	RBI	BB	SO	AVG	OBP	SLG	PRO+	BR	/A	RC	SB	CS	SBR	FR	POS	TPR
1894	Phi-N	9	21	4	5	0	0	0	0	0	7	.238	.238	.238	17	-3	-3	1	0			1	/P	0.0
1897	Chi-N	94	360	60	105	18	6	3	47	10		.292	.320	.400	88	-6	-8	51	12			5	2POS/3	0.2
1898	Chi-N	43	164	27	43	7	5	0	22	4		.262	.280	.366	87	-4	-3	18	3			-1	P/OS21	0.0
1899	Chi-N	47	150	21	39	4	3	0	18	8		.260	.306	.327	78	-5	-4	18	9			3	P/OS2	0.0
1900	Chi-N	32	115	10	27	3	2	0	9	6		.235	.273	.296	61	-6	-6	11	5			6	P	0.0
1901	Chi-A	45	118	15	39	7	3	1	19	10		.331	.383	.466	141	6	6	26	10			4	P/32	0.0
1902	Chi-A	70	218	27	51	7	2	0	13	6		.234	.261	.284	55	-14	-13	19	4			2	PO/S	-0.1
1903	Chi-A	118	439	47	128	26	5	2	56	20		.292	.322	.387	119	7	9	65	24			-6	*3/OPM	0.3
1904	Chi-A	132	482	66	126	23	2	0	54	39		.261	.317	.317	107	2	5	63	29			-16	*O2M	-1.9
1905	Chi-A	96	345	50	94	18	6	1	43	29		.272	.329	.368	128	9	11	53	26			-8	O	-0.1
1911	Chi-A	120	466	64	131	13	5	3	60	15		.281	.306	.350	86	-12	-10	63	45			-9	*O	-2.8
1912	Chi-A	111	408	45	111	9	7	1	52	12		.272	.298	.336	84	-11	-10	47	19			-16	*OM	-3.2
1913	Chi-A	6	9	0	2	0	0	0	1	0	2	.222	.222	.222	30	-1	-1	0	0			0	/OM	0.0
Total	13	923	3295	442	901	135	46	11	394	159	9	.273	.310	.352	95	-38	-27	435	186			-35	OP3/2S1	-7.6

■ JIM CALLAHAN
Callahan, James Timothy "Red" (b: James Timothy Callaghan)
b: 1/12/1879, Allegheny Co., Pa. d: 3/9/68, Carnegie, Pa. 5′9″, 145 lbs. Deb: 5/25/02

YEAR	TM/L	G	AB	R	H	2B	3B	HR	RBI	BB	SO	AVG	OBP	SLG	PRO+	BR	/A	RC	SB	CS	SBR	FR	POS	TPR
1902	NY-N	1	4	0	0	0	0	0	0	0	1	.000	.200	.000	-37	-1	-1	0	0			-0	/O	0.0

■ LEO CALLAHAN
Callahan, Leo David b: 8/9/1890, Jamaica Plain, Mass d: 5/2/82, Erie, Pa. BL/TL, 5′8″, 142 lbs. Deb: 4/09/13

YEAR	TM/L	G	AB	R	H	2B	3B	HR	RBI	BB	SO	AVG	OBP	SLG	PRO+	BR	/A	RC	SB	CS	SBR	FR	POS	TPR
1913	Bro-N	33	41	6	7	3	1	0	3	4	5	.171	.244	.293	52	-3	-3	3	0			-0	/O	-0.2
1919	Phi-N	81	235	26	54	14	4	1	9	29	19	.230	.317	.336	90	-1	-2	26	5			1	O	-0.3
Total	2	114	276	32	61	17	5	1	12	33	24	.221	.306	.330	84	-3	-5	29	5			1	/O	-0.5

■ PAT CALLAHAN
Callahan, Patrick Henry b: 10/15/1866, Cleveland, Ohio d: 2/4/40, Louisville, Ky. Deb: 5/01/1884

YEAR	TM/L	G	AB	R	H	2B	3B	HR	RBI	BB	SO	AVG	OBP	SLG	PRO+	BR	/A	RC	SB	CS	SBR	FR	POS	TPR
1884	Ind-a	61	258	38	67	8	5	2		8		.260	.282	.353	112	2	3	26				-7	3	-0.2

■ WESLEY CALLAHAN
Callahan, Wesley Leroy b: 7/3/1888, Lyons, Ind. d: 9/13/53, Dayton, Ohio TR , 5′7.5″, 155 lbs. Deb: 9/07/13

YEAR	TM/L	G	AB	R	H	2B	3B	HR	RBI	BB	SO	AVG	OBP	SLG	PRO+	BR	/A	RC	SB	CS	SBR	FR	POS	TPR
1913	StL-N	7	14	0	4	0	0	0	1	2	2	.286	.375	.286	91	-0	-0	2	1			1	/S	0.1

■ FRANK CALLAWAY
Callaway, Frank Burnett b: 2/26/1898, Knoxville, Tenn. d: 8/21/87, Knoxville, Tenn. BR/TR, 6′, 170 lbs. Deb: 9/17/21

YEAR	TM/L	G	AB	R	H	2B	3B	HR	RBI	BB	SO	AVG	OBP	SLG	PRO+	BR	/A	RC	SB	CS	SBR	FR	POS	TPR
1921	Phi-A	14	50	7	12	1	1	0	4	2	11	.240	.283	.300	49	-4	-4	5	1	0	0	-5	S	-0.5
1922	Phi-A	29	48	5	13	0	2	0	4	0	13	.271	.271	.354	60	-3	-3	4	0	0	0	1	2/3S	0.0
Total	2	43	98	12	25	1	3	0	8	2	24	.255	.277	.327	54	-7	-7	9	1	0	0	-3	/S23	-0.5

■ JOHNNY CALLISON
Callison, John Wesley b: 3/12/39, Qualls, Okla. BL/TR, 5′10″, 175 lbs. Deb: 9/09/58

YEAR	TM/L	G	AB	R	H	2B	3B	HR	RBI	BB	SO	AVG	OBP	SLG	PRO+	BR	/A	RC	SB	CS	SBR	FR	POS	TPR
1958	Chi-A	18	64	10	19	4	2	1	12	6	14	.297	.357	.469	128	2	2	11	1	0	0	1	O	0.3
1959	Chi-A	49	104	12	18	3	0	3	12	13	20	.173	.271	.288	54	-7	-6	7	0	1	-1	0	O	-0.8
1960	Phi-N	99	288	36	75	11	5	9	30	45	70	.260	.360	.427	114	7	7	46	0	4	-2	4	O	0.5
1961	Phi-N	138	455	74	121	20	11	9	47	69	76	.266	.366	.418	109	6	9	74	10	4	1	1	*O	0.2
1962	Phi-N	157	603	107	181	26	10	23	83	54	96	.300	.363	.491	131	22	24	110	10	3	1	25	*O	4.2
1963	Phi-N	157	626	96	178	36	11	26	78	50	111	.284	.339	.502	140	29	30	107	8	3	1	21	*O	4.6
1964	Phi-N	162	654	101	179	30	10	31	104	36	95	.274	.318	.492	126	19	19	103	6	3	0	18	*O	3.4
1965	Phi-N	160	619	93	162	25	16	32	101	57	117	.262	.330	.509	135	25	26	105	6	5	-1	18	*O	4.0
1966	Phi-N	155	612	93	169	40	7	11	55	56	83	.276	.340	.418	109	8	9	86	8	8	-2	5	*O	0.7
1967	Phi-N	149	556	62	145	30	5	14	64	55	63	.261	.331	.408	109	7	7	72	6	12	-5	8	*O	0.3
1968	Phi-N	121	398	46	97	18	4	14	40	42	70	.244	.321	.415	119	9	9	54	4	3	-1	2	*O	0.6

YEAR	TM/L	G	AB	R	H	2B	3B	HR	RBI	BB	SO	AVG	OBP	SLG	PRO+	BR	/A	RC	SB	CS	SBR	FR	POS	TPR
1969	Phi-N	134	495	66	131	29	5	16	64	49	73	.265	.335	.440	119	9	11	74	2	1	0	14	*O	1.9
1970	Chi-N	147	477	65	126	23	2	19	68	60	63	.264	.350	.440	98	7	-1	75	7	2	1	-2	*O	-0.8
1971	Chi-N	103	290	27	61	12	1	8	38	36	55	.210	.302	.341	71	-7	-12	31	2	1	0	-4	O	-2.0
1972	NY-A	92	275	28	71	10	0	9	34	18	34	.258	.304	.393	110	1	2	33	2	3	0	-1	O	-0.2
1973	NY-A	45	136	10	24	4	0	1	10	4	24	.176	.200	.228	21	-14	-14	5	1	1	-0	1	OD	-1.4
Total	16	1886	6652	926	1757	321	89	226	840	650	1064	.264	.333	.441	114	123	120	992	74	51	-8	108	*O/D	15.5

■ JACK CALVO
Calvo, Jacinto (Gonzalez) (Born Jacinto Del Calvo) b: 6/11/1894, Havana, Cuba d: 6/15/65, Miami, Fla. BL/TL, 5'10", 156 lbs. Deb: 5/09/13

YEAR	TM/L	G	AB	R	H	2B	3B	HR	RBI	BB	SO	AVG	OBP	SLG	PRO+	BR	/A	RC	SB	CS	SBR	FR	POS	TPR
1913	Was-A	17	33	5	8	0	0	1	2	1	4	.242	.265	.333	73	-1	-1	3	0			-2	O	-0.4
1920	Was-A	17	23	5	1	0	1	0	2	2	2	.043	.120	.130	-35	-5	-4	0	0	0	0	-4	O	-0.8
Total	2	34	56	10	9	0	1	1	4	3	6	.161	.203	.250	27	-6	-6	4	0	0		-6	/O	-1.2

■ HANK CAMELLI
Camelli, Henry Richard b: 12/12/14, Gloucester, Mass. BR/TR, 5'11", 190 lbs. Deb: 10/03/43

YEAR	TM/L	G	AB	R	H	2B	3B	HR	RBI	BB	SO	AVG	OBP	SLG	PRO+	BR	/A	RC	SB	CS	SBR	FR	POS	TPR
1943	Pit-N	1	3	1	0	0	0	0	0	1	0	.000	.250	.000	-24	-0	-0	0	0			0	/C	0.0
1944	Pit-N	63	125	14	37	5	1	1	10	18	12	.296	.385	.376	110	3	2	18	0			3	C	0.9
1945	Pit-N	1	2	0	0	0	0	0	0	1	0	.000	.333	.000	-3	-0	-0	0	0			0	/C	0.0
1946	Pit-N	42	96	8	20	2	2	0	5	8	9	.208	.269	.271	52	-6	-6	7	0			4	C	-0.1
1947	Bos-N	52	150	10	29	8	1	1	11	18	18	.193	.280	.280	50	-11	-11	11	0			7	C	-0.2
Total	5	159	376	33	86	15	4	2	26	46	39	.229	.313	.306	70	-15	-15	36	0			14	C	0.6

■ JACK CAMERON
Cameron, John William "Happy Jack" b: 1885, Canada d: 8/17/51, Boston, Mass. Deb: 9/13/06

YEAR	TM/L	G	AB	R	H	2B	3B	HR	RBI	BB	SO	AVG	OBP	SLG	PRO+	BR	/A	RC	SB	CS	SBR	FR	POS	TPR
1906	Bos-N	18	61	3	11	0	0	0	4	2		.180	.206	.180	22	-5	-5	2	0			-1	O/P	-0.6

■ DOLPH CAMILLI
Camilli, Adolph Louis b: 4/23/07, San Francisco, Cal BL/TL, 5'10", 185 lbs. Deb: 9/09/33

YEAR	TM/L	G	AB	R	H	2B	3B	HR	RBI	BB	SO	AVG	OBP	SLG	PRO+	BR	/A	RC	SB	CS	SBR	FR	POS	TPR
1933	Chi-N	16	58	8	13	2	1	2	7	4	11	.224	.274	.397	90	-1	-1	6	3			2	1	0.1
1934	Chi-N	32	120	17	33	8	0	4	19	5	25	.275	.315	.442	102	-0	-0	18	1			2	1	0.0
	Phi-N	102	378	52	100	20	3	12	68	48	69	.265	.350	.429	95	4	-3	59	3			-3	*1	-1.3
	Yr	134	498	69	133	28	3	16	87	53	94	.267	.342	.432	96	4	-3	77	4			-2		-1.3
1935	Phi-N	156	602	88	157	23	5	25	83	65	113	.261	.336	.440	97	5	-3	93	9			-1	*1	-0.6
1936	Phi-N	151	530	106	167	29	13	28	102	116	84	.315	.441	.577	156	58	50	148	5			-10	*1	2.7
1937	Phi-N	131	475	101	161	23	7	27	80	90	82	.339	.446	.587	165	55	49	137	6			4	*1	4.5
1938	Bro-N	146	509	106	128	25	11	24	100	119	101	.251	.393	.485	137	31	30	110	6			-1	*1	1.6
1939	Bro-N	157	565	105	164	30	12	26	104	110	107	.290	.409	.524	144	42	39	128	1			10	*1	3.0
1940	Bro-N	142	512	92	147	29	13	23	96	89	83	.287	.397	.529	145	39	34	114	9			-4	*1	1.8
1941	*Bro-N	149	529	92	151	29	6	34	120	104	115	.285	.407	.556	162	50	47	128	3			3	*1	2.9
1942	Bro-N	150	524	89	132	23	7	26	109	97	85	.252	.372	.471	144	32	30	97	10			-1	*1	1.9
1943	Bro-N	95	353	56	87	15	6	6	43	65	48	.246	.365	.374	113	8	8	52	2			-0	1	0.4
1945	Bos-A	63	198	24	42	5	2	2	19	35	38	.212	.330	.288	78	-4	-5	21	2	0	1	2	1	-0.3
Total	12	1490	5353	936	1482	261	86	239	950	947	961	.277	.388	.492	134	319	277	1111	60	0		2	*1	16.7

■ DOUG CAMILLI
Camilli, Douglas Joseph b: 9/22/36, Philadelphia, Pa. BR/TR, 5'11", 195 lbs. Deb: 9/25/60 C

YEAR	TM/L	G	AB	R	H	2B	3B	HR	RBI	BB	SO	AVG	OBP	SLG	PRO+	BR	/A	RC	SB	CS	SBR	FR	POS	TPR
1960	LA-N	6	24	4	8	2	0	1	3	1	4	.333	.385	.542	141	2	1	5	0	0	0	0	/C	0.2
1961	LA-N	13	30	3	4	0	0	3	4	1	9	.133	.161	.433	47	-2	-3	2	0	0	0	2	C	0.1
1962	LA-N	45	88	16	25	5	2	4	22	12	21	.284	.370	.523	145	4	5	16	0	0	0	-5	C	0.0
1963	LA-N	49	117	9	19	1	1	3	10	11	22	.162	.234	.265	47	-9	-8	7	0	0	0	8	C	0.2
1964	LA-N	50	123	1	22	3	0	0	10	8	19	.179	.229	.203	25	-12	-11	6	0	0	0	8	C	-0.1
1965	Was-A	75	193	13	37	6	1	3	18	16	34	.192	.257	.280	53	-12	-12	14	0	0	0	1	C	-0.6
1966	Was-A	44	107	5	22	4	0	2	8	3	19	.206	.234	.299	53	-7	-7	7	0	0	0	4	C	0.0
1967	Was-A	30	82	5	15	1	0	2	5	4	16	.183	.221	.268	46	-6	-5	5	0	0	0	0	C	-0.3
1969	Was-A	1	3	0	1	0	0	0	0	0	2	.333	.333	.333	92	-0	-0	0	0	0	0	-0	/C	0.0
Total	9	313	767	56	153	22	4	18	80	56	146	.199	.257	.309	61	-42	-39	61	0	0	0	19	C	-0.5

■ LOU CAMILLI
Camilli, Louis Steven b: 9/24/46, ElPaso, Tex. BB/TR, 5'10", 170 lbs. Deb: 8/09/69

YEAR	TM/L	G	AB	R	H	2B	3B	HR	RBI	BB	SO	AVG	OBP	SLG	PRO+	BR	/A	RC	SB	CS	SBR	FR	POS	TPR
1969	Cle-A	13	14	0	0	0	0	0	0	0	3	.000	.000	.000	-97	-4	-4	-0	0	0	0	3	3	0.0
1970	Cle-A	16	15	0	0	0	0	0	0	2	2	.000	.118	.000	-62	-3	-3	0	0	0	0	-1	/S23	-0.3
1971	Cle-A	39	81	5	16	2	0	0	8	10	10	.198	.270	.222	37	-6	-7	5	0	0	0	1	S2	-0.2
1972	Cle-A	39	41	2	6	2	0	0	3	3	8	.146	.205	.195	19	-4	-4	2	0	0	0	-2	S2	-0.5
Total	4	107	151	7	22	4	0	0	13	13	23	.146	.213	.172	11	-17	-18	7	0	0	0	2	/S23	-1.0

■ KEN CAMINITI
Caminiti, Kenneth Gene b: 4/21/63, Hanford, Cal. BB/TR, 6'3", 200 lbs. Deb: 7/16/87

YEAR	TM/L	G	AB	R	H	2B	3B	HR	RBI	BB	SO	AVG	OBP	SLG	PRO+	BR	/A	RC	SB	CS	SBR	FR	POS	TPR
1987	Hou-N	63	203	10	50	7	1	3	23	12	44	.246	.288	.335	67	-10	-10	19	0	0	0	3	3	-0.6
1988	Hou-N	30	83	5	15	2	0	1	7	5	18	.181	.227	.241	36	-7	-7	4	0	0	0	-0	3	-0.7
1989	Hou-N	161	585	71	149	31	3	10	72	51	93	.255	.318	.369	99	-3	-1	70	4	1	1	13	*3	1.2
1990	Hou-N	153	541	52	131	20	2	4	51	48	97	.242	.304	.309	70	-22	-21	50	9	4	0	-11	*3	-2.7
Total	4	407	1412	138	345	60	6	18	153	116	252	.244	.303	.334	80	-43	-38	143	13	5	1	6	3	-2.8

■ HOWIE CAMP
Camp, Howard Lee "Red" b: 7/1/1893, Mumford, Ala. d: 5/8/60, Eastaboga, Ala. BL/TR, 5'9", 169 lbs. Deb: 9/19/17

YEAR	TM/L	G	AB	R	H	2B	3B	HR	RBI	BB	SO	AVG	OBP	SLG	PRO+	BR	/A	RC	SB	CS	SBR	FR	POS	TPR
1917	NY-A	5	21	3	6	1	0	0	0	0		.286	.318	.333	98	-0	-0	2	0			1	/O	0.0

■ LEW CAMP
Camp, Llewellyn Robert b: 2/22/1868, Columbus, Ohio d: 10/1/48, Omaha, Neb. BL/TR, 6', 175 lbs. Deb: 8/26/1892

YEAR	TM/L	G	AB	R	H	2B	3B	HR	RBI	BB	SO	AVG	OBP	SLG	PRO+	BR	/A	RC	SB	CS	SBR	FR	POS	TPR
1892	StL-N	42	145	19	30	3	1	2	13	17	27	.207	.294	.283	80	-4	-3	16	12			-16	3/O	-1.4
1893	Chi-N	38	156	37	41	7	7	2	17	19	19	.263	.347	.436	111	2	2	35	30			-10	3O/2S	-0.6
1894	Chi-N	8	33	1	6	2	0	0	1	1	6	.182	.206	.242	8	-5	-5	2	0			-2	/2	-0.5
Total	3	88	334	57	77	12	8	4	31	37	52	.231	.311	.350	87	-7	-6	53	42			-28	/32OS	-2.5

■ ROY CAMPANELLA
Campanella, Roy b: 11/19/21, Philadelphia, Pa. BR/TR, 5'9.5", 190 lbs. Deb: 4/20/48 H

YEAR	TM/L	G	AB	R	H	2B	3B	HR	RBI	BB	SO	AVG	OBP	SLG	PRO+	BR	/A	RC	SB	CS	SBR	FR	POS	TPR
1948	Bro-N	83	279	32	72	11	3	9	45	36	45	.258	.345	.416	102	2	1	42	3			9	C	1.5
1949	*Bro-N	130	436	65	125	22	2	22	82	67	36	.287	.385	.498	130	22	20	86	3			4	*C	2.7
1950	Bro-N	126	437	70	123	19	3	31	89	55	51	.281	.364	.551	134	22	21	84	1			-5	*C	1.9
1951	Bro-N	143	505	90	164	33	1	33	108	53	51	.325	.393	.590	158	42	40	114	1	2	-1	7	*C	4.7
1952	*Bro-N	128	468	73	126	18	1	22	97	57	59	.269	.352	.453	120	14	13	72	8	4	0	-7	*C	0.9
1953	*Bro-N	144	519	103	162	26	3	41	142	67	58	.312	.395	.611	154	43	41	128	4	2	0	1	*C	4.8
1954	Bro-N	111	397	43	82	14	3	19	51	42	49	.207	.286	.401	74	-15	-17	42	1	4	-2	-3	*C	-1.9
1955	*Bro-N	123	446	81	142	20	1	32	107	56	41	.318	.402	.583	153	37	35	101	2	3	-1	0	*C	3.6
1956	*Bro-N	124	388	39	85	6	1	20	73	66	61	.219	.334	.394	88	-2	-6	49	1	0	0	3	*C	0.0
1957	Bro-N	103	330	31	80	9	0	13	62	34	50	.242	.321	.388	81	-5	-9	40	1	0	0	16	*C	1.2
Total	10	1215	4205	627	1161	178	18	242	856	533	501	.276	.362	.500	123	159	139	759	25	15		27	*C	19.4

■ BERT CAMPANERIS
Campaneris, Dagoberto (Blanco) "Campy" (b: Dagoberto Campaneria (Blanco))
b: 3/9/42, Pueblo Nuevo, Cuba BR/TR, 5'10", 160 lbs. Deb: 7/23/64

YEAR	TM/L	G	AB	R	H	2B	3B	HR	RBI	BB	SO	AVG	OBP	SLG	PRO+	BR	/A	RC	SB	CS	SBR	FR	POS	TPR
1964	KC-A	67	269	27	69	14	3	4	22	15	41	.257	.306	.375	86	-5	-5	32	10	2	2	-7	SO/3	-1.2
1965	KC-A	144	578	67	156	23	12	6	42	41	71	.270	.328	.382	103	1	2	76	51	19	4	-16	*SO/PC123	-0.6
1966	KC-A	142	573	82	153	29	10	5	42	25	72	.267	.303	.379	98	-5	-3	70	52	10	10	-16	*S	-0.2
1967	KC-A	147	601	85	149	29	6	3	32	32	82	.248	.298	.331	89	-11	-9	64	55	16	7	-19	*S	-1.1
1968	Oak-A	159	642	87	177	25	9	4	38	50	69	.276	.332	.361	116	8	11	82	62	22	5	1	*S/O	3.2

YEAR	TM/L	G	AB	R	H	2B	3B	HR	RBI	BB	SO	AVG	OBP	SLG	PRO+	BR	/A	RC	SB	CS	SBR	FR	POS	TPR
1969	Oak-A	135	547	71	142	15	2	2	25	30	62	.260	.303	.305	74	-22	-19	59	62	8	14	-5	*S	-0.4
1970	Oak-A	147	603	97	168	28	4	22	64	36	73	.279	.323	.448	115	6	9	91	42	10	7	-9	*S	1.9
1971	*Oak-A	134	569	80	143	18	4	5	47	29	64	.251	.290	.323	75	-21	-19	56	34	7	6	-5	*S	-0.3
1972	*Oak-A	149	625	85	150	25	2	8	32	32	88	.240	.279	.325	84	-17	-14	59	52	14	7	7	*S	1.7
1973	*Oak-A	151	601	89	150	17	6	4	46	50	79	.250	.311	.318	82	-17	-14	63	34	10	4	-7	*S	0.3
1974	*Oak-A	134	527	77	153	18	8	2	41	47	81	.290	.348	.366	113	4	9	70	34	15	1	-9	*S/D	1.1
1975	*Oak-A	137	509	69	135	15	3	4	46	50	71	.265	.339	.330	92	-6	-4	60	24	12	0	-31	*S	-2.1
1976	Oak-A	149	536	67	137	14	1	1	52	63	80	.256	.337	.291	89	-8	-5	64	54	12	9	-6	*S	0.7
1977	Tex-A	150	552	77	140	19	7	5	46	47	86	.254	.317	.341	78	-15	-16	60	27	20	-4	18	*S	1.5
1978	Tex-A	98	269	30	50	5	3	1	17	20	36	.186	.247	.238	37	-22	-22	19	22	4	4	4	S/D	-0.7
1979	Tex-A	8	9	2	1	0	0	0	0	1	3	.111	.200	.111	-14	-1	-1	0	1	0	0	4	/S	0.3
	*Cal-A	85	239	27	56	4	4	0	15	19	32	.234	.296	.285	59	-14	-13	21	12	4	1	4	S	0.2
	Yr	93	248	29	57	4	4	0	15	20	35	.230	.293	.278	57	-15	-14	21	13	4	2	7		0.5
1980	Cal-A	77	210	32	53	8	1	2	18	14	33	.252	.302	.329	75	-8	-7	21	10	5	0	-5	S/2D	-0.6
1981	Cal-A	55	82	11	21	2	1	1	10	5	10	.256	.299	.341	84	-2	-2	9	5	2	0	-2	3/S2	-0.2
1983	NY-A	60	143	19	46	5	0	0	11	8	9	.322	.358	.357	101	-0	0	16	6	7	-2	-2	23	-0.3
Total	19	2328	8684	1181	2249	313	86	79	646	618	1142	.259	.313	.342	89	-154	-123	992	649	199	75	-104	*S/3O2D1C	3.2

■ AL CAMPANIS
Campanis, Alexander Sebastian (b: Alessandro Campani) b: 11/2/16, Cos, Greece BB/TR, 6', 185 lbs. Deb: 9/23/43

YEAR	TM/L	G	AB	R	H	2B	3B	HR	RBI	BB	SO	AVG	OBP	SLG	PRO+	BR	/A	RC	SB	CS	SBR	FR	POS	TPR
1943	Bro-N	7	20	3	2	0	0	0	0	4	5	.100	.250	.100	3	-2	-2	1	0			4	/2	0.1

■ JIM CAMPANIS
Campanis, James Alexander b: 2/9/44, New York, N.Y. BR/TR, 6', 195 lbs. Deb: 9/20/66

YEAR	TM/L	G	AB	R	H	2B	3B	HR	RBI	BB	SO	AVG	OBP	SLG	PRO+	BR	/A	RC	SB	CS	SBR	FR	POS	TPR
1966	LA-N	1	1	0	0	0	0	0	0	0	0	.000	.000	.000	-99	-0	-0	0	0	0	0	0	/C	0.0
1967	LA-N	41	62	3	10	1	0	2	2	9	14	.161	.268	.274	60	-4	-3	5	0	0	0	0	C	-0.1
1968	LA-N	4	11	0	1	0	0	0	0	1	2	.091	.167	.091	-23	-2	-2	0	0	0	0	1	/C	0.0
1969	KC-A	30	83	4	13	5	0	0	5	5	19	.157	.205	.217	18	-9	-9	3	0	0	0	2	C	-0.4
1970	KC-A	31	54	6	7	0	0	2	2	4	14	.130	.203	.241	22	-6	-6	2	0	0	0	2	C/O	-0.3
1973	Pit-N	6	6	0	1	0	0	0	0	0	0	.167	.167	.167	-8	-1	-1	0	0	0	0	0	H	0.0
Total	6	113	217	13	32	6	0	4	9	19	49	.147	.219	.230	27	-21	-21	10	0	0	0	5	/CO	-0.8

■ COUNT CAMPAU
Campau, Charles Columbus b: 10/17/1863, Detroit, Mich. d: 4/3/38, New Orleans, La. BL/TR, 5'11", 160 lbs. Deb: 7/07/1888 M

YEAR	TM/L	G	AB	R	H	2B	3B	HR	RBI	BB	SO	AVG	OBP	SLG	PRO+	BR	/A	RC	SB	CS	SBR	FR	POS	TPR
1888	Det-N	70	251	28	51	5	3	1	18	19	36	.203	.259	.259	68	-9	-9	24	27			-4	O	-1.3
1890	StL-a	75	314	68	101	9	12	9		26		.322	.374	.513	144	22	15	75	36			3	O/31M	1.3
1894	Was-N	2	7	1	1	0	0	0	0	1	4	.143	.250	.143	-2	-1	-1	0	0			-0	/O	0.0
Total	3	147	572	97	153	14	15	10	18	46	40	.267	.322	.397	112	13	6	100	63			-1	O/13	0.0

■ VIN CAMPBELL
Campbell, Arthur Vincent b: 1/30/1888, St.Louis, Mo. d: 11/16/69, Towson, Md. BL/TR, 6', 185 lbs. Deb: 6/06/08

YEAR	TM/L	G	AB	R	H	2B	3B	HR	RBI	BB	SO	AVG	OBP	SLG	PRO+	BR	/A	RC	SB	CS	SBR	FR	POS	TPR
1908	Chi-N	1	1	0	0	0	0	0	0	0		.000	.000	.000	-96	-0	-0	0	0			0	H	0.0
1910	Pit-N	97	282	42	92	9	5	4	21	26	23	.326	.391	.436	133	15	12	55	17			-5	O	0.6
1911	Pit-N	42	93	12	29	3	1	0	10	8	7	.312	.366	.366	101	1	0	14	6			-2	O	-0.2
1912	Bos-N	145	624	102	185	32	9	3	48	32	44	.296	.334	.391	96	-4	-5	87	19			-1	*O	-1.0
1914	Ind-F	134	544	92	173	23	11	7	44	37	47	.318	.368	.439	118	21	13	101	26			-5	*O	0.1
1915	New-F	127	525	78	163	18	10	1	44	29	35	.310	.352	.389	126	12	15	83	24			-5	*O	0.5
Total	6	546	2069	326	642	85	36	15	167	132	156	.310	.357	.408	114	44	36	341	92			-18	O	0.0

■ BRUCE CAMPBELL
Campbell, Bruce Douglas b: 10/20/09, Chicago, Ill. BL/TR, 6'1", 185 lbs. Deb: 9/12/30

YEAR	TM/L	G	AB	R	H	2B	3B	HR	RBI	BB	SO	AVG	OBP	SLG	PRO+	BR	/A	RC	SB	CS	SBR	FR	POS	TPR
1930	Chi-A	5	10	4	5	1	1	0	5	1	2	.500	.545	.800	245	2	2	4	0	0	0	0	/O	0.2
1931	Chi-A	4	17	4	7	2	0	2	5	0	4	.412	.444	.882	256	3	3	7	0	0	0	-0	/O	0.3
1932	Chi-A	7	18	3	4	1	0	0	2	0	2	.222	.222	.278	31	-2	-2	1	0	1	-1	-1	/O	-0.2
	StL-A	139	593	83	169	35	11	14	85	40	102	.285	.336	.452	97	0	-5	90	7	5	-1	1	*O	-0.9
	Yr	146	611	86	173	36	11	14	87	40	104	.283	.333	.447	95	-2	-6	90	7	6	-2	0		-1.1
1933	StL-A	148	567	87	157	38	8	16	106	69	77	.277	.357	.457	108	11	6	95	10	4	1	-7	*O	-0.4
1934	StL-A	138	481	62	134	25	6	9	74	51	64	.279	.350	.412	88	-3	-9	71	5	4	-1	-1	*O	-1.1
1935	Cle-A	80	308	56	100	26	3	7	54	31	33	.325	.390	.497	126	12	12	60	2	1	0	-11	O	0.0
1936	Cle-A	76	172	35	64	15	2	6	30	19	17	.372	.440	.587	150	14	14	45	2	1	0	-2	O	0.9
1937	Cle-A	134	448	82	135	42	11	4	61	67	49	.301	.392	.471	116	12	12	85	4	5	-2	-4	*O	0.1
1938	Cle-A	133	511	90	148	27	12	12	72	53	57	.290	.360	.460	106	2	3	85	11	7	-1	-0	*O	0.2
1939	Cle-A	130	450	84	129	23	13	8	72	67	48	.287	.383	.449	116	9	11	81	7	6	-2	-6	*O	0.0
1940	*Det-A	103	297	56	84	15	5	8	44	45	28	.283	.381	.448	104	7	3	51	2	7	-4	-4	*O	-0.9
1941	Det-A	141	512	72	141	28	10	15	93	68	67	.275	.364	.457	105	11	4	90	3	3	-1	-11	*O	-1.5
1942	Was-A	122	378	41	105	17	5	5	63	37	34	.278	.344	.389	107	3	3	51	0	6	-4	-1	O	-0.7
Total	13	1360	4762	759	1382	295	87	106	766	548	584	.290	.367	.455	108	81	57	815	53	50	-14	-48	*O	-4.0

■ SOUP CAMPBELL
Campbell, Clarence b: 3/7/15, Sparta, Va. BL/TR, 6'1", 188 lbs. Deb: 4/21/40

YEAR	TM/L	G	AB	R	H	2B	3B	HR	RBI	BB	SO	AVG	OBP	SLG	PRO+	BR	/A	RC	SB	CS	SBR	FR	POS	TPR
1940	Cle-A	35	62	8	14	1	0	0	2	7	12	.226	.304	.242	45	-5	-5	5	0	0	0	1	O	-0.4
1941	Cle-A	104	328	36	82	10	4	3	35	31	21	.250	.317	.332	75	-13	-11	32	1	9	-5	4	O	-1.6
Total	2	139	390	44	96	11	4	3	37	38	33	.246	.315	.318	70	-18	-16	37	1	9	-5	5	/O	-2.0

■ DAVE CAMPBELL
Campbell, David Wilson b: 1/14/42, Manistee, Mich. BR/TR, 6'1", 180 lbs. Deb: 9/17/67

YEAR	TM/L	G	AB	R	H	2B	3B	HR	RBI	BB	SO	AVG	OBP	SLG	PRO+	BR	/A	RC	SB	CS	SBR	FR	POS	TPR
1967	Det-A	2	2	0	0	0	0	0	0	0	1	.000	.000	.000	-97	-0	-0	0	0	0	0	-0	/1	0.0
1968	Det-A	9	8	1	1	0	0	1	2	1	3	.125	.222	.500	111	0	0	1	0	0	0	0	/2	0.1
1969	Det-A	32	39	4	4	1	0	0	2	4	15	.103	.205	.128	-5	-5	-6	1	0	1	-1	-1	1/23	-0.8
1970	SD-N	154	581	71	127	28	2	12	40	40	115	.219	.270	.336	64	-33	-30	54	18	6	2	12	*2	0.1
1971	SD-N	108	365	38	83	14	2	7	29	37	75	.227	.299	.334	85	-10	-7	38	9	6	-1	-1	23/S10	-0.6
1972	SD-N	33	100	6	24	5	0	0	3	11	12	.240	.315	.290	79	-3	-2	8	0	4	-2	4	3/2	0.0
1973	SD-N	33	98	2	22	3	0	0	8	7	15	.224	.276	.255	52	-7	-6	6	1	1	-0	-1	2/13	-0.6
	StL-N	13	21	1	0	0	0	0	1	1	6	.000	.045	.000	-87	-5	-5	0	0	0	0	-2	/2	-0.7
	Hou-N	9	15	1	4	2	0	0	2	0	4	.267	.267	.400	83	-0	-0	2	0	0	0	2	/31O	-0.1
	Yr	55	134	4	26	5	0	0	11	8	25	.194	.239	.231	33	-12	-12	7	1	1	-0	-2		-1.2
1974	Hou-N	35	23	4	2	1	0	0	2	1	8	.087	.125	.130	-30	-4	-4	1	1	0	0	6	/213O	0.2
Total	8	428	1252	128	267	54	4	20	89	102	254	.213	.274	.311	64	-69	-62	110	29	18	-2	17	2/310S	-2.2

■ JIM CAMPBELL
Campbell, James Robert b: 6/24/37, Palo Alto, Cal. BR/TR, 6', 190 lbs. Deb: 7/17/62

YEAR	TM/L	G	AB	R	H	2B	3B	HR	RBI	BB	SO	AVG	OBP	SLG	PRO+	BR	/A	RC	SB	CS	SBR	FR	POS	TPR
1962	Hou-N	27	86	6	19	4	0	3	6	6	23	.221	.272	.372	77	-4	-3	7	0	0	0	7	C	0.4
1963	Hou-N	55	158	9	35	3	0	4	19	10	40	.222	.268	.316	72	-7	-6	12	0	0	0	-2	C	-0.6
Total	2	82	244	15	54	7	0	7	25	16	63	.221	.269	.336	74	-11	-9	20	0	0	0	4	/C	-0.2

■ JIM CAMPBELL
Campbell, James Robert b: 1/10/43, Hartsville, S.C. BL/TR, 6', 205 lbs. Deb: 4/11/70

YEAR	TM/L	G	AB	R	H	2B	3B	HR	RBI	BB	SO	AVG	OBP	SLG	PRO+	BR	/A	RC	SB	CS	SBR	FR	POS	TPR
1970	StL-N	13	13	0	3	0	0	0	1	0	3	.231	.231	.231	24	-1	-1	1	0	0	0	0	H	0.0

■ JOE CAMPBELL
Campbell, Joseph Earl b: 3/10/44, Louisville, Ky. BR/TR, 6'1", 175 lbs. Deb: 5/03/67

YEAR	TM/L	G	AB	R	H	2B	3B	HR	RBI	BB	SO	AVG	OBP	SLG	PRO+	BR	/A	RC	SB	CS	SBR	FR	POS	TPR
1967	Chi-N	1	3	0	0	0	0	0	0	0	3	.000	.000	.000	-96	-1	-1	0	0	0	0	0	/O	0.0

■ MARC CAMPBELL
Campbell, Marc Thaddeus b: 11/29/1884, Punxsutawney, Pa. d: 2/13/46, New Bethlehem, Pa. BL/TR, 5'10", 155 lbs. Deb: 9/30/07

YEAR	TM/L	G	AB	R	H	2B	3B	HR	RBI	BB	SO	AVG	OBP	SLG	PRO+	BR	/A	RC	SB	CS	SBR	FR	POS	TPR
1907	Pit-N	2	4	0	1	0	0	0	1	1		.250	.400	.250	105	0	-0	0	0			0	/S	0.0

YEAR	TM/L	G	AB	R	H	2B	3B	HR	RBI	BB	SO	AVG	OBP	SLG	PRO+	BR	/A	RC	SB	CS	SBR	FR	POS	TPR

■ MAT CAMPBELL Campbell, Mathew b: New Jersey Deb: 4/28/1873

1873	Res-n	21	82	9	12	0	0	0		2		.146	.167	.146	-8	-11	-9	2					1/SO	-0.5

■ PAUL CAMPBELL Campbell, Paul McLaughlin b: 9/1/17, Paw Creek, N.C. BL/TL, 5'10", 185 lbs. Deb: 4/15/41

1941	Bos-A	1	0	0	0	0	0	0	0	0	0	—	—	—	—	0	0	0	0	0	0	0	R	0.0
1942	Bos-A	26	15	4	1	0	0	0	0	1	5	.067	.125	.067	-44	-3	-3	0	1	0	0	1	/O	-0.1
1946	*Bos-A	28	26	3	3	1	0	0	0	2	7	.115	.179	.154	-6	-4	-4	1	0	0	0	0	/1	-0.4
1948	Det-A	59	83	15	22	1	1	1	11	0	10	.265	.274	.337	60	-5	-5	8	0	0	0	3	1	0.0
1949	Det-A	87	255	38	71	15	4	3	30	24	32	.278	.343	.404	97	-2	-2	38	3	3	-1	-3	1	-0.4
1950	Det-A	3	1	1	0	0	0	0	0	0	0	.000	.000	.000	-97	-0	-0	0	0	0	0	0	H	0.0
Total	6	204	380	61	97	17	5	4	41	28	54	.255	.308	.358	76	-14	-14	47	4	3	-1	1	1/O	-0.9

■ RON CAMPBELL Campbell, Ronald Thomas b: 4/5/40, Chattanooga, Tenn. BR/TR, 6'1", 180 lbs. Deb: 9/01/64

1964	Chi-N	26	92	7	25	6	1	1	10	1	21	.272	.280	.391	83	-2	-2	10	0	1	-1	14	2	1.3
1965	Chi-N	2	2	0	0	0	0	0	0	0	0	.000	.000	.000	-98	-1	-1	0	0	0	0	0	H	0.0
1966	Chi-N	24	60	4	13	1	0	0	4	6	5	.217	.288	.233	46	-4	-4	4	1	1	-0	4	S/3	0.0
Total	3	52	154	11	38	7	1	1	14	7	26	.247	.280	.325	67	-6	-7	13	1	2	-1	18	/2S3	1.3

■ SAM CAMPBELL Campbell, Samuel b: Philadelphia, Pa. Deb: 10/11/1890

1890	Phi-a	2	5	0	0	0	0	0		1		.000	.167	.000	-51	-1	-1	0	0			-2	/2	-0.2

■ GILLY CAMPBELL Campbell, William Gilthorpe b: 2/13/08, Kansas City, Kan. d: 2/21/73, Los Angeles, Cal. BL/TR, 5'7.5", 182 lbs. Deb: 4/25/33

1933	Chi-N	46	89	11	25	3	1	1	10	7	4	.281	.347	.371	105	1	1	12	0			-2	C	0.0
1935	Cin-N	88	218	26	56	7	0	3	30	42	7	.257	.379	.330	95	-0	1	30	3			1	C/1O	0.1
1936	Cin-N	89	235	28	63	13	1	1	40	43	14	.268	.384	.345	104	1	3	35	2			6	C/1	1.1
1937	Cin-N	18	40	3	11	2	0	0	2	5	1	.275	.356	.325	90	-1	-0	5	0			-0	C	0.0
1938	Bro-N	54	126	10	31	5	0	0	11	19	9	.246	.354	.286	76	-3	-3	13	0			0	C	0.0
Total	5	295	708	78	186	30	2	5	93	116	35	.263	.371	.332	96	-2	1	95	5			5	C/1O	1.2

■ FRANK CAMPOS Campos, Francisco Jose (Lopez) b: 5/11/24, Havana, Cuba BL/TL, 5'11", 180 lbs. Deb: 9/11/51

1951	Was-A	8	26	4	11	3	1	0	3	0	1	.423	.423	.615	182	3	3	7	0	0	0	-2	/O	0.0
1952	Was-A	53	112	9	29	6	1	0	8	1	13	.259	.278	.330	71	-5	-5	11	0	0	0	-2	O	-0.6
1953	Was-A	10	9	0	1	0	0	0	2	1	0	.111	.200	.111	-14	-1	-1	0	0	0	0	0	H	0.0
Total	3	71	147	13	41	9	2	0	13	2	14	.279	.298	.367	86	-4	-3	18	0	0	0	-4	/O	-0.6

■ SIL CAMPUSANO Campusano, Silvestre (Diaz) b: 12/31/65, Santo Domingo, D.R. BR/TR, 6', 160 lbs. Deb: 4/04/88

1988	Tor-A	73	142	14	31	10	2	2	12	9	33	.218	.284	.359	78	-4	-4	16	0	0	0	3	O/D	-0.1
1990	Phi-N	66	85	10	18	1	1	2	9	6	16	.212	.272	.318	62	-5	-5	8	1	0	0	-1	O	-0.6
Total	2	139	227	24	49	11	3	4	21	15	49	.216	.279	.344	72	-9	-9	23	1	0	0	3	O/D	-0.7

■ GEORGE CANALE Canale, George Anthony b: 8/11/65, Memphis, Tenn. BL/TR, 6'1", 190 lbs. Deb: 9/03/89

1989	Mil-A	13	26	5	5	1	0	1	3	2	3	.192	.250	.346	67	-1	-1	2	0	1	-1	-0	1	-0.2
1990	Mil-A	10	13	4	1	1	0	0	0	2	5	.077	.200	.154	0	-2	-2	0	0	1	-1	1	/1D	-0.1
Total	2	23	39	9	6	2	0	1	3	4	8	.154	.233	.282	45	-3	-3	2	0	2	-1	1	/1D	-0.3

■ JIM CANAVAN Canavan, James Edward b: 11/26/1866, New Bedford, Mass. d: 5/27/49, New Bedford, Mass. BR/TR, 5'8", 160 lbs. Deb: 4/08/1891

1891	Cin-a	101	426	74	97	13	14	7	66	27	44	.228	.282	.373	82	-8	-14	52	21			-11	*S	-1.7
	Mil-a	35	142	33	38	2	4	3	21	16	10	.268	.342	.401	96	2	-2	22	7			-2	2S	-0.1
	Yr	136	568	107	135	15	18	10	87	43	54	.238	.297	.380	86	-6	-17	74	28			-13		-1.8
1892	Chi-N	118	439	48	73	10	11	0	32	48	48	.166	.248	.239	49	-27	-27	35	33			-2	*2/OS	-2.6
1893	Cin-N	121	461	65	104	13	7	5	64	51	20	.226	.305	.317	65	-22	-24	55	31			-1	*O/23	-2.4
1894	Cin-N	101	356	77	97	16	9	13	70	62	25	.272	.380	.478	103	4	1	71	13			-2	*O/S321	-0.5
1897	Bro-N	63	240	25	52	9	3	2	34	26		.217	.296	.304	64	-14	-11	25	9			-21	2	-2.3
Total	5	539	2064	322	461	63	48	30	287	230	147	.223	.304	.344	75	-64	-78	261	114			-39	O2S/31	-9.6

■ CASEY CANDAELE Candaele, Casey Todd b: 1/12/61, Lompoc, Cal. BB/TR, 5'9", 160 lbs. Deb: 6/05/86

1986	Mon-N	30	104	9	24	4	1	0	6	5	15	.231	.266	.288	53	-7	-7	6	3	5	-2	-1	2/3	-1.0
1987	Mon-N	138	449	62	122	23	4	1	23	38	28	.272	.331	.347	78	-12	-14	51	7	10	-4	1	2OS/1	-1.5
1988	Mon-N	36	116	9	20	5	1	0	4	10	11	.172	.238	.233	34	-10	-10	6	1	0	0	1	2	-0.7
	Hou-N	21	31	2	5	3	0	0	1	1	6	.161	.188	.258	28	-3	-3	1	0	1	-1	3	2/O3	0.0
	Yr	57	147	11	25	8	1	0	5	11	17	.170	.228	.238	33	-13	-13	7	1	1	-0	4		-0.7
1990	Hou-N	130	262	30	75	8	6	3	22	31	42	.286	.364	.397	111	4	5	38	7	5	-1	-1	O2S/3	0.2
Total	4	355	962	112	246	43	12	4	56	85	102	.256	.318	.338	78	-28	-29	103	18	21	-7	2	2O/S31	-3.0

■ JOHN CANGELOSI Cangelosi, John Anthony b: 3/10/63, Brooklyn, N.Y. BB/TL, 5'8", 150 lbs. Deb: 6/03/85

1985	Chi-A	5	2	2	0	0	0	0	0	0	1	.000	.333	.000	1	-0	-0	0	0	0	0	0	/OD	0.0
1986	Chi-A	137	438	65	103	16	3	2	32	71	61	.235	.351	.299	77	-10	-12	55	50	17	5	1	*O/D	-0.8
1987	Pit-N	104	182	44	50	8	3	4	18	46	33	.275	.429	.418	125	9	9	39	21	6	3	-2	O	0.8
1988	Pit-N	75	118	18	30	4	1	0	8	17	16	.254	.353	.305	92	-1	-1	15	9	4	0	-1	O/P	-0.3
1989	Pit-N	112	160	18	35	4	2	0	9	35	20	.219	.369	.269	88	-1	-0	19	11	8	-2	-1	O	-0.3
1990	Pit-N	58	76	13	15	2	0	0	1	11	12	.197	.307	.224	50	-5	-5	6	7	2	1	-0	O	-0.4
Total	6	491	976	160	233	34	9	6	68	180	143	.239	.366	.310	88	-8	-8	134	98	37	7	-2	O/DP	-0.7

■ RIP CANNELL Cannell, Virgin Wirt b: 1/23/1880, S.Bridgton, Maine d: 8/26/48, Bridgton, Maine BL/TR, 5'10.5", 180 lbs. Deb: 4/14/04

1904	Bos-N	100	346	32	81	5	1	0	18	23		.234	.282	.254	70	-12	-11	29	10			-11	O	-2.6
1905	Bos-N	154	567	52	140	14	4	0	36	51		.247	.309	.286	81	-13	-11	58	17			-8	*O	-3.1
Total	2	254	913	84	221	19	5	0	54	74		.242	.299	.274	77	-25	-22	87	27			-19	O	-5.7

■ CHRIS CANNIZZARO Cannizzaro, Christopher John b: 5/3/38, Oakland, Cal. BR/TR, 6', 190 lbs. Deb: 4/17/60 C

1960	StL-N	7	9	0	2	0	0	0	1	1	3	.222	.300	.222	42	-1	-1	1	0	0	0	1	/C	0.1
1961	StL-N	6	2	0	1	0	0	0	0	0	0	.500	.500	.500	151	0	0	1	0	0	0	1	/C	0.1
1962	NY-N	59	133	9	32	2	1	0	9	19	26	.241	.340	.271	65	-6	-6	13	1	1	-0	3	C/O	-0.1
1963	NY-N	16	33	4	8	1	0	0	4	1	8	.242	.265	.273	54	-2	-2	3	0	0	0	-1	C	-0.1
1964	NY-N	60	164	11	51	10	0	0	10	14	28	.311	.369	.372	112	2	3	21	0	5	-3	2	C	0.3
1965	NY-N	114	251	17	46	8	2	0	7	28	60	.183	.270	.231	44	-18	-17	16	0	2	-1	11	*C	-0.2
1968	Pit-N	25	58	5	14	2	2	1	7	9	13	.241	.343	.397	123	2	2	8	0	0	0	-1	C	0.2
1969	SD-N	134	418	23	92	14	3	4	33	42	81	.220	.291	.297	68	-19	-17	34	0	1	-1	-14	*C	-2.4
1970	SD-N	111	341	27	95	13	3	5	42	48	49	.279	.369	.378	105	2	4	47	2	7	-4	-18	*C	-1.2
1971	SD-N	21	63	2	12	1	0	1	8	11	10	.190	.320	.254	69	-3	-2	4	0	0	0	-1	C	-0.2
	Chi-N	71	197	18	42	8	1	5	23	28	24	.213	.314	.340	74	-4	-7	19	0	0	0	-11	C	-1.7
	Yr	92	260	20	54	9	1	6	31	39	34	.208	.316	.319	73	-6	-9	24	0	0	0	-12		-1.9
1972	LA-N	73	200	14	48	6	0	2	18	31	38	.240	.342	.300	86	-3	-3	22	0	1	-1	-8	C	-0.6
1973	LA-N	17	21	0	4	0	0	0	3	3	3	.190	.292	.190	38	-2	-2	1	0	0	0	-0	C	0.0
1974	SD-N	26	60	2	11	1	0	0	4	6	11	.183	.258	.200	31	-6	-5	3	0	0	0	5	C	0.1
Total	13	740	1950	132	458	66	12	18	169	241	354	.235	.321	.309	77	-56	-53	192	3	17	-9	-29	C/O	-5.7

YEAR	TM/L	G	AB	R	H	2B	3B	HR	RBI	BB	SO	AVG	OBP	SLG	PRO+	BR	/A	RC	SB	CS	SBR	FR	POS	TPR

■ JOE CANNON
Cannon, Joseph Jerome   b: 7/13/53, Camp Lejune, N.C.   BL/TR, 6'3", 193 lbs.   Deb: 9/22/77

YEAR	TM/L	G	AB	R	H	2B	3B	HR	RBI	BB	SO	AVG	OBP	SLG	PRO+	BR	/A	RC	SB	CS	SBR	FR	POS	TPR
1977	Hou-N	9	17	3	2	2	0	0	1	0	5	.118	.118	.235	-9	-3	-2	0	1	1	-0	0	/O	-0.2
1978	Hou-N	8	18	1	4	0	0	0	1	0	1	.222	.222	.222	26	-2	-2	1	0	1	-1	-1	/O	-0.2
1979	Tor-A	61	142	14	30	1	1	1	5	1	34	.211	.217	.254	26	-15	-15	8	12	2	2	2	O	-1.2
1980	Tor-A	70	50	16	4	0	0	0	4	0	14	.080	.098	.080	-48	-10	-10	0	2	2	-1	5	O/D	-0.6
Total	4	148	227	34	40	3	1	1	11	1	54	.176	.183	.211	7	-29	-29	9	15	6	1	6	/OD	-2.2

■ JOSE CANSECO
Canseco, Jose (Capas)   b: 7/2/64, Havana, Cuba   BR/TR, 6'3", 195 lbs.   Deb: 9/02/85

YEAR	TM/L	G	AB	R	H	2B	3B	HR	RBI	BB	SO	AVG	OBP	SLG	PRO+	BR	/A	RC	SB	CS	SBR	FR	POS	TPR
1985	Oak-A	29	96	16	29	3	0	5	13	4	31	.302	.330	.490	130	2	3	15	1	1	-0	0	O	0.3
1986	Oak-A	157	600	85	144	29	1	33	117	65	175	.240	.322	.457	118	6	13	89	15	7	0	-4	*O/D	0.5
1987	Oak-A	159	630	81	162	35	3	31	113	50	157	.257	.314	.470	111	2	8	91	15	3	3	6	*OD	1.2
1988	*Oak-A	158	610	120	187	34	0	42	124	78	128	.307	.394	**.569**	172	54	57	136	40	16	2	4	*OD	**6.0**
1989	*Oak-A	65	227	40	61	9	1	17	57	23	69	.269	.341	.542	151	13	14	41	6	3	0	-1	O/D	1.2
1990	*Oak-A	131	481	83	132	14	2	37	101	72	158	.274	.375	.543	158	34	36	98	19	10	-0	-2	OD	3.3
Total	6	699	2644	425	715	124	7	165	525	292	718	.270	.349	.510	139	112	130	470	96	40	5	3	O/D	12.5

■ OZZIE CANSECO
Canseco, Osvaldo Capas   b: 7/2/64, Havana, Cuba   BR/TR, 6'2", 220 lbs.   Deb: 7/18/90

YEAR	TM/L	G	AB	R	H	2B	3B	HR	RBI	BB	SO	AVG	OBP	SLG	PRO+	BR	/A	RC	SB	CS	SBR	FR	POS	TPR
1990	Oak-A	9	19	1	2	1	0	0	1	1	10	.105	.150	.158	-14	-3	-3	0	0	0	0	0	/OD	-0.2

■ BART CANTZ
Cantz, Bartholomew L.   b: 1/29/1860, Philadelphia, Pa.   d: 2/12/43, Philadelphia, Pa.   Deb: 7/25/1888

YEAR	TM/L	G	AB	R	H	2B	3B	HR	RBI	BB	SO	AVG	OBP	SLG	PRO+	BR	/A	RC	SB	CS	SBR	FR	POS	TPR
1888	Bal-a	37	126	7	21	2	1	0	9	2		.167	.180	.198	24	-11	-10	5	0			-8	C/O	-1.3
1889	Bal-a	20	69	6	12	2	0	0	8	4	14	.174	.219	.203	21	-7	-7	4	2			-7	C/O	-1.0
1890	Phi-a	5	22	1	1	0	0	0		0		.045	.045	.045	-75	-5	-5	0	0			-2	/C	-0.5
Total	3	62	217	14	34	4	1	0	17	6	14	.157	.179	.184	13	-22	-22	8	2			-17	/CO	-2.8

■ NICK CAPRA
Capra, Nick Lee   b: 3/8/58, Denver, Colo.   BR/TR, 5'8", 165 lbs.   Deb: 9/06/82

YEAR	TM/L	G	AB	R	H	2B	3B	HR	RBI	BB	SO	AVG	OBP	SLG	PRO+	BR	/A	RC	SB	CS	SBR	FR	POS	TPR
1982	Tex-A	13	15	2	4	0	0	1	1	3	4	.267	.421	.467	151	1	1	3	2	1	0	3	/O	0.4
1983	Tex-A	8	2	2	0	0	0	0	0	0	0	.000	.000	.000	-99	-1	-1	0	0	0	0	0	/O	0.0
1985	Tex-A	8	8	1	1	0	0	0	0	0	0	.125	.125	.125	-31	-1	-1	0	0	0	0	1	/O	0.0
1988	KC-A	14	29	3	4	1	0	0	0	2	3	.138	.194	.172	3	-4	-4	1	1	0	0	0	O/D	-0.3
Total	4	43	54	8	9	1	0	1	1	5	7	.167	.250	.241	37	-5	-5	4	3	1	0	4	/OD	0.1

■ PAT CAPRI
Capri, Patrick Nicholas   b: 11/27/18, New York, N.Y.   d: 6/14/89, New York.N.Y.   BR/TR, 6'0.5", 170 lbs.   Deb: 7/16/44

YEAR	TM/L	G	AB	R	H	2B	3B	HR	RBI	BB	SO	AVG	OBP	SLG	PRO+	BR	/A	RC	SB	CS	SBR	FR	POS	TPR
1944	Bos-N	7	1	1	0	0	0	0	0	1	.000	.000	.000	-96	-0	-0	0	0			3	/2	0.3

■ RALPH CAPRON
Capron, Ralph Earl   b: 6/16/1889, Minneapolis, Minn   d: 9/19/80, Los Angeles, Cal.   BL/TR, 5'11.5", 165 lbs.   Deb: 4/25/12

YEAR	TM/L	G	AB	R	H	2B	3B	HR	RBI	BB	SO	AVG	OBP	SLG	PRO+	BR	/A	RC	SB	CS	SBR	FR	POS	TPR
1912	Pit-N	1	0	0	0	0	0	0	0	0	0	—	—	—	—	0	0	0	0			0	R	0.0
1913	Phi-N	2	1	1	0	0	0	0	0	0	0	.000	.000	.000	-96	-0	-0	0	0			0	/O	0.0
Total	2	3	1	1	0	0	0	0	0	0	0	.000	.000	.000	-96	-0	-0	0	0			0	/O	0.0

■ JOHN CARBINE
Carbine, John C.   b: 10/12/1855, Syracuse, N.Y.   d: 9/11/15, Chicago, Ill.   6', 187 lbs.   Deb: 5/08/1875

YEAR	TM/L	G	AB	R	H	2B	3B	HR	RBI	BB	SO	AVG	OBP	SLG	PRO+	BR	/A	RC	SB	CS	SBR	FR	POS	TPR
1875	Wes-n	10	36	0	3	0	0	0		0		.083	.083	.083	-40	-5	-5	0				1		-0.4
1876	Lou-N	7	25	3	4	0	0	0	1	0	0	.160	.160	.160	6	-2	-3	1				-0	/1O	-0.2

■ BERNIE CARBO
Carbo, Bernardo   b: 8/5/47, Detroit, Mich.   BL/TR, 5'11", 173 lbs.   Deb: 9/02/69

YEAR	TM/L	G	AB	R	H	2B	3B	HR	RBI	BB	SO	AVG	OBP	SLG	PRO+	BR	/A	RC	SB	CS	SBR	FR	POS	TPR
1969	Cin-N	4	3	0	0	0	0	0	0	0	2	.000	.000	.000	-95	-1	-1	0	0	0	0	0	H	0.0
1970	*Cin-N	125	365	54	113	19	3	21	63	94	77	.310	.456	.551	168	40	40	100	10	4	1	-8	*O	2.7
1971	Cin-N	106	310	33	68	20	1	5	20	54	56	.219	.339	.339	94	-2	-1	38	2	1	0	-6	O	-0.9
1972	Cin-N	19	21	2	3	0	0	0	0	6	3	.143	.357	.143	50	-1	-1	2	0	0	0	0	/O	0.0
	StL-N	99	302	42	78	13	1	7	34	57	56	.258	.385	.377	119	9	10	47	0	1	-1	3	O/3	0.8
	Yr	118	323	44	81	13	1	7	34	63	59	.251	.383	.362	115	8	9	48	0	1	-1	3		0.8
1973	StL-N	111	308	42	88	18	0	8	40	58	52	.286	.401	.422	128	14	14	56	2	0	1	2	O	1.3
1974	Bos-A	117	338	40	84	20	0	12	61	58	90	.249	.365	.414	116	12	9	52	4	3	-1	-4	OD	0.2
1975	Bos-A	107	319	64	82	21	3	15	50	83	69	.257	.412	.483	140	25	22	68	2	4	-2	-5	OD	1.3
1976	Bos-A	17	55	5	13	4	0	2	6	8	17	.236	.333	.418	106	1	0	8	1	0	0	0	OD	0.1
	Mil-A	69	183	20	43	7	0	3	15	33	55	.235	.352	.322	100	1	1	22	1	2	-1	2	OD	0.2
	Yr	86	238	25	56	11	0	5	21	41	72	.235	.348	.345	102	2	2	30	2	2	-1	2		0.3
1977	Bos-A	86	228	36	66	6	1	15	34	47	72	.289	.411	.522	136	18	14	51	1	2	-1	-1	O/D	1.0
1978	Bos-A	17	46	7	12	3	0	1	6	8	8	.261	.370	.391	103	1	0	6	1	1	-0	1	/OD	0.1
	Cle-A	60	174	21	50	8	0	4	16	20	31	.287	.364	.402	117	4	4	25	1	0	0	0	D/O	0.5
	Yr	77	220	28	62	11	0	5	22	28	39	.282	.365	.400	113	5	5	31	2	1	0	1		0.6
1979	StL-N	52	64	6	18	1	0	3	12	10	22	.281	.378	.438	121	2	2	12	1	0	0	-3	O	0.0
1980	StL-N	14	11	0	2	0	0	0	0	1	0	.182	.250	.182	22	-1	-1	0	0	0	0	0	H	0.0
	Pit-N	7	6	0	2	0	0	0	1	1	1	.333	.429	.333	114	0	0	1	0	0	0	0	/H	0.0
	Yr	21	17	0	4	0	0	0	1	2	1	.235	.316	.235	55	-1	-1	2	0	0	0	0		0.0
Total	12	1010	2733	372	722	140	9	96	358	538	611	.264	.389	.427	125	125	114	489	26	18	-3	-17	OD/3	7.3

■ JOSE CARDENAL
Cardenal, Jose Rosario Domec (b: Jose Rosario Domec (Cardenal))   b: 10/7/43, Matanzas, Cuba   BR/TR, 5'10", 150 lbs.   Deb: 4/14/63

YEAR	TM/L	G	AB	R	H	2B	3B	HR	RBI	BB	SO	AVG	OBP	SLG	PRO+	BR	/A	RC	SB	CS	SBR	FR	POS	TPR
1963	SF-N	9	5	1	1	0	0	0	2	1	1	.200	.333	.200	58	-0	-0	0	0	1	-1	0	/O	0.0
1964	SF-N	20	15	3	0	0	0	0	0	2	3	.000	.118	.000	-62	-3	-3	0	2	0	-1	2	O	-0.1
1965	Cal-A	134	512	58	128	23	2	11	57	27	72	.250	.290	.367	87	-11	-9	54	37	17	1	5	*O/32	-0.8
1966	Cal-A	154	561	67	155	15	3	16	48	34	69	.276	.322	.399	109	4	5	72	24	11	1	8	*O	0.8
1967	Cal-A	108	381	40	90	13	5	6	27	15	63	.236	.269	.344	83	-10	-9	35	10	5	0	-1	*O	-1.4
1968	Cle-A	157	583	78	150	21	7	7	44	39	74	.257	.306	.353	101	-1	-0	65	40	18	1	8	*O	0.3
1969	Cle-A	146	557	75	143	26	3	11	45	49	58	.257	.317	.373	89	-6	-9	67	36	6	7	4	*O/3	0.0
1970	StL-N	148	552	73	162	32	6	10	74	49	70	.293	.348	.428	104	4	3	81	26	9	2	-5	*O	-0.4
1971	StL-N	89	301	37	73	12	4	7	48	29	35	.243	.309	.379	90	-3	-4	35	12	3	2	7	O	0.2
	Mil-A	53	198	20	51	10	0	3	32	13	20	.258	.307	.354	88	-4	-4	21	9	5	-0	6	O	0.0
1972	Chi-N	143	533	96	155	24	6	17	70	55	58	.291	.358	.454	117	20	14	83	25	14	-1	-5	*O	0.2
1973	Chi-N	145	522	80	158	33	2	11	68	58	62	.303	.378	.437	116	19	14	86	19	7	2	-4	*O	0.5
1974	Chi-N	143	542	75	159	35	3	13	72	56	67	.293	.361	.441	118	16	14	84	23	9	2	5	*O	1.5
1975	Chi-N	154	574	85	182	30	2	9	68	77	50	.317	.402	.423	124	25	22	103	34	12	3	10	*O	3.0
1976	Chi-N	136	521	64	156	25	2	8	47	32	39	.299	.341	.401	101	6	7	71	23	14	2	0	*O	-0.5
1977	Chi-N	100	226	33	54	12	1	3	18	28	30	.239	.325	.341	71	-6	-10	24	5	4	-1	-7	O/2S	-1.9
1978	*Phi-N	87	201	27	50	12	0	4	33	23	16	.249	.326	.368	93	-2	-2	23	2	3	-1	-5	1O	-1.0
1979	Phi-N	29	48	4	10	3	0	0	9	8	8	.208	.321	.271	61	-2	-2	4	1	0	0	-2	O/1	-0.3
	NY-N	11	37	8	11	4	0	2	4	6	3	.297	.409	.568	170	3	4	10	1	0	1	-1	/O1	0.2
	Yr	40	85	12	21	7	0	2	13	14	11	.247	.360	.400	106	1	1	13	2	0	1	-3		-0.1
1980	NY-N	26	42	4	7	1	0	0	4	6	4	.167	.271	.190	32	-2	-2	2	0	1	-1	0	O/1	-0.4
	*KC-A	25	53	8	18	2	0	0	5	5	5	.340	.397	.377	112	1	1	9	0	0	0	-1	O	0.0
Total	18	2017	6964	936	1913	333	46	138	775	608	807	.275	.335	.395	102	46	21	928	329	139	15	24	*O/132S	-0.1

■ LEO CARDENAS
Cardenas, Leonardo Lazaro (Alfonso) "Chico"   b: 12/17/38, Matanzas, Cuba   BR/TR, 5'11", 150 lbs.   Deb: 7/25/60

YEAR	TM/L	G	AB	R	H	2B	3B	HR	RBI	BB	SO	AVG	OBP	SLG	PRO+	BR	/A	RC	SB	CS	SBR	FR	POS	TPR
1960	Cin-N	48	142	13	33	2	4	1	12	6	32	.232	.264	.324	59	-8	-8	12	0	0	0	7	S	0.0
1961	*Cin-N	74	198	23	61	18	1	5	24	15	39	.308	.357	.485	119	6	5	33	1	0	0	-5	S	0.7

YEAR	TM/L	G	AB	R	H	2B	3B	HR	RBI	BB	SO	AVG	OBP	SLG	PRO+	BR	/A	RC	SB	CS	SBR	FR	POS	TPR
1962	Cin-N	153	589	77	173	31	4	10	60	39	99	.294	.343	.411	98	1	-2	79	2	5	-2	-7	*S	0.3
1963	Cin-N	158	565	42	133	22	4	7	48	23	101	.235	.270	.326	69	-22	-24	46	3	5	-2	-3	*S	-1.5
1964	Cin-N	163	597	61	150	32	2	9	69	41	110	.251	.302	.357	82	-12	-15	63	4	4	-1	-10	*S	-1.5
1965	Cin-N	156	557	65	160	25	11	11	57	60	100	.287	.311	.431	113	16	11	81	1	4	-2	-1	*S	2.7
1966	Cin-N	160	568	59	145	25	4	20	81	45	87	.255	.311	.419	93	-0	-6	69	9	4	0	-14	*S	-0.7
1967	Cin-N	108	379	30	97	14	3	2	21	34	77	.256	.320	.325	76	-7	-12	38	4	5	-2	-10	*S	-1.1
1968	Cin-N	137	452	45	106	13	2	7	41	36	83	.235	.294	.319	79	-9	-12	39	2	1	0	-23	*S	-2.0
1969	*Min-A	160	578	67	162	24	4	10	70	66	96	.280	.358	.388	106	8	6	78	5	6	-2	34	*S	4.6
1970	*Min-A	160	588	67	145	34	4	11	65	42	101	.247	.301	.374	84	-13	-14	65	2	5	-2	3	*S	0.0
1971	Min-A	153	554	59	146	25	4	18	75	51	69	.264	.327	.421	107	6	4	73	3	3	-1	-0	*S	2.1
1972	Cal-A	150	551	25	123	11	2	6	42	35	73	.223	.272	.283	69	-24	-21	41	1	2	-1	3	*S	-0.2
1973	Cle-A	72	195	9	42	4	0	0	12	13	42	.215	.264	.236	41	-15	-15	11	1	4	-2	-8	S/3	-1.7
1974	Tex-A	34	92	5	25	3	0	0	7	2	14	.272	.287	.304	72	-4	-3	8	1	0	0	2	3S/D	0.0
1975	Tex-A	55	102	15	24	2	0	1	5	14	12	.235	.328	.284	75	-3	-3	11	0	0	0	11	3/S2	0.9
Total	16	1941	6707	662	1725	285	49	118	689	522	1135	.257	.313	.367	88	-80	-107	748	39	48	-17	-21	*S/3D2	2.6

■ ROD CAREW

Carew, Rodney Cline b: 10/1/45, Gatun, C.Z. BL/TR, 6', 170 lbs. Deb: 4/11/67

YEAR	TM/L	G	AB	R	H	2B	3B	HR	RBI	BB	SO	AVG	OBP	SLG	PRO+	BR	/A	RC	SB	CS	SBR	FR	POS	TPR
1967	Min-A	137	514	66	150	22	7	8	51	37	91	.292	.342	.409	112	13	8	68	5	9	-4	-10	*2	-0.1
1968	Min-A	127	461	46	126	27	2	1	42	26	71	.273	.314	.347	95	-1	-3	49	12	4	1	-14	*2/S	-1.2
1969	*Min-A	123	458	79	152	30	4	8	56	37	72	.332	.386	.467	135	22	21	83	19	8	1	-17	*2	1.0
1970	*Min-A	51	191	27	70	12	3	4	28	11	28	.366	.407	.524	153	14	13	39	4	6	-2	-11	2/1	0.4
1971	Min-A	147	577	88	177	16	10	2	48	45	81	.307	.358	.380	106	7	5	73	6	7	-2	-25	*2/3	-1.7
1972	Min-A	142	535	61	170	21	6	0	51	43	60	.318	.371	.379	118	16	13	75	12	6	0	0	*2	2.4
1973	Min-A	149	580	98	203	30	11	6	62	62	55	.350	.415	.471	143	39	36	113	41	16	3	7	*2	5.1
1974	Min-A	153	599	86	218	30	5	3	55	74	49	.364	.435	.446	148	45	42	118	38	16	2	9	*2	6.0
1975	Min-A	143	535	89	192	24	4	14	80	64	40	.359	.428	.497	158	44	43	118	35	9	5	2	*21/D	5.3
1976	Min-A	156	605	97	200	29	12	9	90	67	52	.331	.398	.463	147	40	38	111	49	22	2	-2	*1/2	3.2
1977	Min-A	155	616	128	239	38	16	14	100	69	55	.388	.452	.570	179	67	68	160	23	13	-1	6	*1/2D	6.3
1978	Min-A	152	564	85	188	26	10	5	70	78	62	.333	.415	.441	138	34	32	105	27	7	4	1	*1/2O	3.2
1979	*Cal-A	110	409	78	130	15	3	3	44	73	46	.318	.421	.391	125	16	18	73	18	8	1	-7	*1/D	0.6
1980	Cal-A	144	540	74	179	34	7	3	59	59	38	.331	.398	.437	132	23	25	92	23	15	-2	-4	*1D	1.1
1981	Cal-A	93	364	57	111	17	1	2	21	45	45	.305	.381	.374	118	10	10	53	16	9	-1	-1	*1/D	0.6
1982	*Cal-A	138	523	88	167	25	5	3	44	67	49	.319	.399	.403	121	18	18	83	10	17	-7	1	*1	0.8
1983	Cal-A	129	472	66	160	24	2	2	44	57	48	.339	.411	.411	128	20	21	78	6	7	-2	-9	1D/2	0.5
1984	Cal-A	93	329	42	97	8	1	3	31	40	39	.295	.371	.353	102	2	3	44	4	3	-1	-4	1/D	-0.6
1985	Cal-A	127	443	69	124	17	3	2	39	64	47	.280	.372	.345	99	1	2	60	5	5	-2	-8	*1	-1.4
Total	19	2469	9315	1424	3053	445	112	92	1015	1018	1028	.328	.395	.429	131	431	414	1595	353	187	-6	-87	*12/DS3O	31.5

■ ANDY CAREY

Carey, Andrew Arthur (b: Andrew Arthur Nordstrom) b: 10/18/31, Oakland, Cal. BR/TR, 6'1.5", 190 lbs. Deb: 5/02/52

YEAR	TM/L	G	AB	R	H	2B	3B	HR	RBI	BB	SO	AVG	OBP	SLG	PRO+	BR	/A	RC	SB	CS	SBR	FR	POS	TPR
1952	NY-A	16	40	6	6	0	0	0	1	3	10	.150	.209	.150	1	-5	-5	1	0	0	0	-1	3/S	-0.5
1953	NY-A	51	81	14	26	5	0	4	8	9	12	.321	.389	.531	152	5	5	17	2	1	0	8	3/S2	1.2
1954	NY-A	122	411	60	124	14	6	8	65	43	38	.302	.377	.423	123	11	13	64	5	5	-2	17	*3	2.2
1955	*NY-A	135	510	73	131	19	11	7	47	44	51	.257	.317	.378	88	-11	-10	60	3	3	-1	14	*3	0.6
1956	*NY-A	132	422	54	100	18	2	7	50	45	53	.237	.313	.339	75	-17	-15	45	9	6	-1	-3	*3	-1.5
1957	*NY-A	85	247	30	63	6	5	6	33	15	42	.255	.311	.393	92	-4	-3	29	2	2	-1	3	3	0.1
1958	*NY-A	102	315	39	90	19	4	12	45	34	43	.286	.366	.486	137	14	15	57	1	2	-1	10	3	2.9
1959	NY-A	41	101	11	26	1	0	3	9	7	17	.257	.306	.356	84	-3	-2	10	1	1	-0	2	3	0.0
1960	NY-A	4	3	1	1	0	0	0	0	1	0	.333	.333	.333	86	-0	-0	0	0	0	0	-0	/3O	0.0
	KC-A	102	343	30	80	14	4	12	53	26	52	.233	.289	.402	84	-8	-9	36	0	0	0	-0	3	-0.7
	Yr	106	346	31	81	14	4	12	54	26	53	.234	.290	.402	85	-9	-9	36	0	0	0	-0		-0.7
1961	KC-A	39	123	20	30	6	2	3	11	15	23	.244	.336	.398	95	-1	-1	17	0	0	0	-1	3	0.0
	Chi-A	56	143	21	38	12	3	0	14	11	24	.266	.327	.392	93	-2	-2	19	0	1	-1	-5	3	-0.3
	Yr	95	266	41	68	18	5	3	25	26	47	.256	.331	.395	94	-3	-2	36	0	1	-1	-6		-0.3
1962	LA-N	53	111	12	26	5	1	2	13	16	23	.234	.336	.351	90	-2	-1	14	0	0	0	1	3	0.1
Total	11	938	2850	371	741	119	38	64	350	268	389	.260	.329	.396	97	-23	-14	369	23	21	-6	46	3/SO2	4.1

■ SCOOPS CAREY

Carey, George C. b: 12/4/1870, E.Liverpool, Ohio d: 12/17/16, E.Liverpool, Ohio BR/TR, 175 lbs. Deb: 4/26/1895

YEAR	TM/L	G	AB	R	H	2B	3B	HR	RBI	BB	SO	AVG	OBP	SLG	PRO+	BR	/A	RC	SB	CS	SBR	FR	POS	TPR
1895	*Bal-N	123	490	59	128	21	6	1	75	27	32	.261	.305	.335	65	-25	-27	52	2			-6	*1/OS3	-2.4
1898	Lou-N	8	32	1	6	1	1	0		1	1	.188	.212	.281	43	-2	-2	2	0			0	/1	-0.1
1902	Was-A	120	452	46	142	35	11	0	60	20		.314	.350	.440	119	11	11	73	3			4	*1	1.5
1903	Was-A	48	183	8	37	3	2	0	23	4		.202	.219	.240	38	-13	-14	10	0			-3	1	-1.6
Total	4	299	1157	114	313	60	20	1	159	52	32	.271	.307	.360	81	-29	-33	137	5			-5	1/3SO	-2.6

■ MAX CAREY

Carey, Max George "Scoops" (b: Maximilian Carnarius)
b: 1/11/1890, Terre Haute, Ind. d: 5/30/76, Miami, Fla. BB/TR, 5'11.5", 170 lbs. Deb: 10/03/10 MCH

YEAR	TM/L	G	AB	R	H	2B	3B	HR	RBI	BB	SO	AVG	OBP	SLG	PRO+	BR	/A	RC	SB	CS	SBR	FR	POS	TPR
1910	Pit-N	2	6	2	3	0	1	0	2	2	1	.500	.625	.833	307	2	2	3	0			2	/O	0.3
1911	Pit-N	129	427	77	110	15	10	5	43	44	75	.258	.337	.375	95	-1	-3	64	27			0	*O	-0.6
1912	Pit-N	150	587	114	177	23	8	5	66	61	79	.302	.372	.394	111	9	10	104	45			14	*O	1.8
1913	Pit-N	154	620	99	172	23	10	5	49	55	67	.277	.339	.371	107	2	6	92	61			20	*O	2.3
1914	Pit-N	156	593	76	144	25	17	1	31	59	56	.243	.313	.347	101	-3	-0	72	38			5	O	0.1
1915	Pit-N	140	564	76	143	26	5	3	27	57	58	.254	.326	.333	101	1	2	66	36	17	1	18	*O	1.7
1916	Pit-N	154	599	90	158	23	11	7	42	59	58	.264	.337	.374	117	13	13	87	63	19	8	23	*O	4.3
1917	Pit-N	155	588	82	174	21	12	1	51	58	38	.296	.369	.378	125	22	20	94	46			20	*O	3.9
1918	Pit-N	126	468	70	128	14	6	3	48	62	25	.274	.363	.348	113	12	10	76	58			13	*O	1.9
1919	Pit-N	66	244	41	75	10	2	0	9	25	24	.307	.376	.365	119	8	7	38	18			4	O	0.9
1920	Pit-N	130	485	74	140	18	4	1	35	59	31	.289	.369	.348	104	7	5	72	52	10	10	-3	*O	0.4
1921	Pit-N	140	521	85	161	34	4	7	56	70	30	.309	.395	.430	115	16	14	95	37	12	4	11	*O	2.2
1922	Pit-N	155	629	140	207	28	12	10	70	80	26	.329	.408	.459	122	24	23	131	51	2	14	15	*O	4.3
1923	Pit-N	153	610	120	188	32	19	6	63	73	28	.308	.388	.452	119	20	18	117	51	8	11	15	*O	3.6
1924	Pit-N	149	599	113	178	30	9	7	55	58	17	.297	.366	.412	106	8	7	97	49	13	7	6	*O	1.6
1925	*Pit-N	133	542	109	186	39	13	5	44	66	19	.343	.418	.491	123	28	22	118	46	11	7	7	O	3.0
1926	Pit-N	86	324	46	72	14	5	0	28	30	14	.222	.288	.296	55	-19	-22	28	10			3	O	-2.1
	Bro-N	27	100	18	26	3	1	0	7	8	5	.260	.315	.310	70	-4	-4	10	0			-1	O	-0.5
	Yr	113	424	64	98	17	6	0	35	38	19	.231	.294	.300	58	-24	-26	38	10			2		-2.6
1927	Bro-N	144	538	70	143	30	10	3	54	64	18	.266	.345	.364	90	-7	-7	69	32			12	*O	0.0
1928	Bro-N	108	296	41	73	11	0	2	19	47	24	.247	.354	.304	74	-10	-9	34	18			-9	O	-2.1
1929	Bro-N	19	23	2	7	0	0	0	1	3	2	.304	.407	.304	81	-0	-0	3	0			0	/O	0.0
Total	20	2476	9363	1545	2665	419	159	69	800	1040	695	.285	.361	.385	107	127	112	1471	738	92		172	*O	27.0

■ ROGER CAREY

Carey, Roger J. Deb: 7/09/1887

YEAR	TM/L	G	AB	R	H	2B	3B	HR	RBI	BB	SO	AVG	OBP	SLG	PRO+	BR	/A	RC	SB	CS	SBR	FR	POS	TPR
1887	NY-N	1	4	0	0	0	0	0	2	0	1	.000	.000	.000	-99	-1	-1	0	0			1	/2	0.0

■ TOM CAREY

Carey, Thomas Francis Aloysius "Scoops" b: 10/11/06, Hoboken, N.J. d: 2/21/70, Rochester, N.Y. BR/TR, 5'8.5", 170 lbs. Deb: 7/19/35 C

YEAR	TM/L	G	AB	R	H	2B	3B	HR	RBI	BB	SO	AVG	OBP	SLG	PRO+	BR	/A	RC	SB	CS	SBR	FR	POS	TPR
1935	StL-A	76	296	29	86	18	4	0	42	13	11	.291	.320	.378	77	-9	-11	35	0	2	-1	-1	2	-0.8

YEAR	TM/L	G	AB	R	H	2B	3B	HR	RBI	BB	SO	AVG	OBP	SLG	PRO+	BR	/A	RC	SB	CS	SBR	FR	POS	TPR
1936	StL-A	134	488	58	133	27	6	1	57	27	25	.273	.315	.359	64	-27	-29	55	2	1	0	-1	*2/S	-1.8
1937	StL-A	130	487	54	134	24	1	1	40	21	26	.275	.306	.335	61	-29	-29	49	1	2	-1	2	2S/3	-1.5
1939	Bos-A	54	161	17	39	6	2	0	20	3	9	.242	.265	.304	44	-14	-14	12	0	0	0	6	2S	-0.5
1940	Bos-A	43	62	4	20	4	0	0	7	2	1	.323	.344	.387	86	-1	-1	8	0	0	0	5	S/23	0.5
1941	Bos-A	25	21	7	4	0	0	0	0	0	0	.190	.190	.190	1	-3	-3	1	0	0	0	4	/2S3	0.2
1942	Bos-A	1	1	0	1	0	0	0	1	0	0	1.000	1.000	1.000	448	0	0	1	0	0	0	-0	/2	0.0
1946	Bos-A	3	5	0	1	0	0	0	1	0	1	.200	.200	.200	11	-1	-1	0	0	0	0	1	/2	0.1
Total	8	466	1521	169	418	79	13	2	167	66	73	.275	.308	.348	63	-83	-89	162	3	5	-2	17	2/S3	-3.8

■ TOM CAREY — Carey, Thomas John (b: J. J. Norton) b: 1849, Brooklyn, N.J. d: 2/13/1899, Los Angeles, Cal. TR, 5'8", 145 lbs. Deb: 5/04/1871 M

YEAR	TM/L	G	AB	R	H	2B	3B	HR	RBI	BB	SO	AVG	OBP	SLG	PRO+	BR	/A	RC	SB	CS	SBR	FR	POS	TPR
1871	Kek-n	19	87	16	20	2	0	0	10	2	1	.230	.247	.253	43	-6	-7	7	5				2/S	-0.3
1872	Bal-n	42	197	43	58	7	1	2			1	.294	.298	.371	100	1	-1	22					2/S301	-0.2
1873	Bal-n	56	291	76	98	18	3	2			1	.337	.339	.440	128	9	10	44					*2/S3M	0.3
1874	Mut-n	64	286	54	82	10	3	1			2	.287	.292	.353	101	1	-1	30					*S2M	-0.2
1875	Har-n	86	382	63	101	6	2	0			2	.264	.268	.291	89	-3	-6	31					*S	-0.6
1876	Har-N	68	289	51	78	7	0	0	26	3	4	.270	.277	.294	84	-3	-6	24				-1	*S	-0.6
1877	Har-N	60	274	38	70	3	2	1	20	0	9	.255	.255	.292	81	-9	-4	21				-6	*S	-0.7
1878	Pro-N	61	253	33	60	10	3	0	24	0	14	.237	.237	.300	76	-7	-7	18				1	*S	0.0
1879	Cle-N	80	335	30	80	14	1	0	32	5	20	.239	.250	.287	77	-8	-8	25				-3	*S	-0.4
Total	5 n	267	1243	252	359	43	9	5	10	8	1	.289	.293	.350	99	3	-4	134					S2/301	-1.0
Total	4	269	1151	152	288	34	6	1	102	8	47	.250	.255	.293	70	-26	-25	88				-9	S	-1.7

■ BOBBY CARGO — Cargo, Robert J. b: 1871, Pittsburgh, Pa. d: 4/27/04, Atlanta, Ga. BR/TR. Deb: 10/06/1892

YEAR	TM/L	G	AB	R	H	2B	3B	HR	RBI	BB	SO	AVG	OBP	SLG	PRO+	BR	/A	RC	SB	CS	SBR	FR	POS	TPR
1892	Pit-N	2	4	0	1	0	0	0	0	0	0	.250	.250	.250	52	-0	-0	0	0			1	/S	0.0

■ FRED CARISCH — Carisch, Frederick Behlmer b: 11/14/1881, Fountain City, Wis d: 4/19/77, San Gabriel, Cal. BR/TR, 5'10.5", 174 lbs. Deb: 8/31/03 C

YEAR	TM/L	G	AB	R	H	2B	3B	HR	RBI	BB	SO	AVG	OBP	SLG	PRO+	BR	/A	RC	SB	CS	SBR	FR	POS	TPR
1903	Pit-N	5	18	4	6	4	0	1	5		0	.333	.333	.722	194	2	2	4	0			1	/C	0.3
1904	Pit-N	37	125	9	31	3	1	0	8		9	.248	.299	.288	81	-2	-3	12	3			2	C1	0.1
1905	Pit-N	32	107	7	22	0	3	0	8		2	.206	.220	.262	44	-7	-8	7	1			1	C	-0.2
1906	Pit-N	4	12	0	1	0	0	0	0		1	.083	.154	.083	-24	-2	-2	0	1			-0	/C	-0.1
1912	Cle-A	25	70	4	19	3	1	0	5		1	.271	.282	.343	76	-2	-3	7	3			6	C	0.6
1913	Cle-A	82	222	11	48	4	2	0	26	21	19	.216	.287	.252	56	-12	-12	17	6			13	C	0.7
1914	Cle-A	40	102	8	22	3	2	0	5	12	18	.216	.298	.284	72	-3	-3	9	2	2	-1	-0	C	-0.1
1923	Det-A	2	0	0	0	0	0	0	0	0	0	—	—	—	—	0	0	0	0	0	0	0	/C	0.0
Total	8	227	656	43	149	17	9	1	57	46	37	.227	.279	.285	66	-26	-29	57	16	2		23	C/1	1.3

■ FRED CARL — Carl, Frederick E. b: 1856, Washington, D.C. d: 5/4/19, Washington, D.C. TL, 5'6", 158 lbs. Deb: 7/25/1889

YEAR	TM/L	G	AB	R	H	2B	3B	HR	RBI	BB	SO	AVG	OBP	SLG	PRO+	BR	/A	RC	SB	CS	SBR	FR	POS	TPR
1889	Lou-a	25	99	13	20	2	2	0	13	16	22	.202	.313	.263	68	-4	-3	8	0			0	O/23	-0.2

■ LEW CARL — Carl, Lewis b: Baltimore, Md. Deb: 9/09/1874

YEAR	TM/L	G	AB	R	H	2B	3B	HR	RBI	BB	SO	AVG	OBP	SLG	PRO+	BR	/A	RC	SB	CS	SBR	FR	POS	TPR
1874	Bal-n	1	3	0	0	0	0	0			0	.000	.000	.000	-99	-1	-1	0					/C	0.0

■ JIM CARLETON — Carleton, James b: 1849, New York 5'8", 155 lbs. Deb: 5/04/1871

YEAR	TM/L	G	AB	R	H	2B	3B	HR	RBI	BB	SO	AVG	OBP	SLG	PRO+	BR	/A	RC	SB	CS	SBR	FR	POS	TPR
1871	Cle-n	29	127	31	32	8	1	0	18	8	3	.252	.296	.331	85	-3	-1	13	2				*1	0.0
1872	Cle-n	7	38	8	12	3	0	0			1	.316	.333	.395	130	1	1	5					1	0.2
Total	2 n	36	165	39	44	11	1	0			9	.267	.305	.345	94	-2	0	18					/1	0.2

■ JIM CARLIN — Carlin, James Arthur b: 2/23/18, Wylam, Ala. BR/TR, 5'11", 165 lbs. Deb: 7/26/41

YEAR	TM/L	G	AB	R	H	2B	3B	HR	RBI	BB	SO	AVG	OBP	SLG	PRO+	BR	/A	RC	SB	CS	SBR	FR	POS	TPR
1941	Phi-N	16	21	2	3	1	0	0	2	3	4	.143	.250	.333	66	-1	-1	2	0			-2	/O3	-0.3

■ WALTER CARLISLE — Carlisle, Walter G. "Rosy" b: 7/6/1883, Yorkshire, England d: 5/27/45, Los Angeles, Cal. BB/TR, 5'9", 154 lbs. Deb: 5/08/08

YEAR	TM/L	G	AB	R	H	2B	3B	HR	RBI	BB	SO	AVG	OBP	SLG	PRO+	BR	/A	RC	SB	CS	SBR	FR	POS	TPR
1908	Bos-A	3	10	0	1	0	0	0			0	.100	.182	.100	-6	-1	-1	0	1			1	/O	0.0

■ SWEDE CARLSTROM — Carlstrom, Albin Oscar b: 10/26/1886, Elizabeth, N.J. d: 4/28/35, Elizabeth, N.J. BR/TR, 6', 167 lbs. Deb: 9/13/11

YEAR	TM/L	G	AB	R	H	2B	3B	HR	RBI	BB	SO	AVG	OBP	SLG	PRO+	BR	/A	RC	SB	CS	SBR	FR	POS	TPR
1911	Bos-A	2	6	0	1	0	0	0	0	0		.167	.167	.167	-7	-1	-1	0	0			0	/S	0.0

■ CLEO CARLYLE — Carlyle, Hiram Cleo b: 9/7/02, Fairburn, Ga. d: 11/12/67, Los Angeles, Cal. BL/TR, 6', 170 lbs. Deb: 5/16/27

YEAR	TM/L	G	AB	R	H	2B	3B	HR	RBI	BB	SO	AVG	OBP	SLG	PRO+	BR	/A	RC	SB	CS	SBR	FR	POS	TPR
1927	Bos-A	95	278	31	65	12	8	1	28	36	40	.234	.324	.345	75	-11	-10	31	4	4	-1	-6	O	-2.1

■ ROY CARLYLE — Carlyle, Roy Edward "Dizzy" b: 12/10/1900, Buford, Ga. d: 11/22/56, Norcross, Ga. BL/TR, 6'2.5", 195 lbs. Deb: 4/16/25

YEAR	TM/L	G	AB	R	H	2B	3B	HR	RBI	BB	SO	AVG	OBP	SLG	PRO+	BR	/A	RC	SB	CS	SBR	FR	POS	TPR
1925	Was-A	1	1	0	0	0	0	0	0	0	1	.000	.000	.000	-99	-0	-0	0	0			0	H	0.0
	Bos-A	93	276	36	90	20	3	7	49	16	28	.326	.365	.496	117	6	6	49	1	1	-0	-6	O	-0.5
	Yr	94	277	36	90	20	3	7	49	16	29	.325	.364	.495	116	5	5	49	1	1	-0	-6		-0.5
1926	Bos-A	45	165	22	47	6	2	2	16	4	18	.285	.310	.382	82	-6	-5	19	0	0	0	-3	O	-1.0
	NY-A	35	52	3	20	5	1	0	11	4	9	.385	.439	.519	151	4	4	12	0	0	0	-3	O	0.0
	Yr	80	217	25	67	11	3	2	27	8	27	.309	.342	.415	99	-2	-1	30	0	0	0	-6		-1.0
Total	2	174	494	61	157	31	6	9	76	24	56	.318	.354	.460	109	4	4	80	1	1	-0	-12	O	-1.5

■ GEORGE CARMAN — Carman, George Wartman b: 3/29/1866, Philadelphia, Pa. d: 6/16/29, Lancaster, Pa. Deb: 9/04/1890

YEAR	TM/L	G	AB	R	H	2B	3B	HR	RBI	BB	SO	AVG	OBP	SLG	PRO+	BR	/A	RC	SB	CS	SBR	FR	POS	TPR
1890	Phi-a	28	97	9	17	2	0	0		8		.175	.245	.196	33	-8	-8	6	5			-9	SO/23	-1.3

■ DUKE CARMEL — Carmel, Leon James b: 4/23/37, New York, N.Y. BL/TL, 6'3", 202 lbs. Deb: 9/10/59

YEAR	TM/L	G	AB	R	H	2B	3B	HR	RBI	BB	SO	AVG	OBP	SLG	PRO+	BR	/A	RC	SB	CS	SBR	FR	POS	TPR
1959	StL-N	10	23	2	3	1	0	0	3	1	6	.130	.167	.174	-9	-4	-4	1	0	1	-1	0	O	-0.3
1960	StL-N	4	3	0	0	0	0	0	0	1	1	.000	.250	.000	-23	-1	-1	0	1	1	-0	1	/1O	0.0
1963	StL-N	57	44	9	10	1	0	1	2	9	11	.227	.358	.318	88	0	-0	6	0	0	0	4	O/1	0.2
	NY-N	47	149	11	35	5	3	3	18	16	37	.235	.309	.369	93	-1	-1	18	2	2	-1	-0	O1	-0.3
	Yr	104	193	20	45	6	3	4	20	25	48	.233	.321	.358	90	-1	-2	24	2	2	-1	3		-0.1
1965	NY-A	6	8	0	0	0	0	0	0	0	5	.000	.000	.000	-99	-2	-2	0	0	0	0	-0	/1	-0.2
Total	4	124	227	22	48	7	3	4	23	27	60	.211	.295	.322	73	-7	-8	24	3	4	-2	4	/O1	-0.6

■ EDDIE CARNETT — Carnett, Edwin Elliott "Lefty" b: 10/21/16, Springfield, Mo. BL/TL, 6', 185 lbs. Deb: 4/19/41

YEAR	TM/L	G	AB	R	H	2B	3B	HR	RBI	BB	SO	AVG	OBP	SLG	PRO+	BR	/A	RC	SB	CS	SBR	FR	POS	TPR
1941	Bos-N	2	0	0	0	0	0	0	0	0	0	—	—	—	—	0	0	0	0			0	/P	0.0
1944	Chi-A	126	457	51	126	18	8	1	60	26	35	.276	.322	.357	95	-4	-4	55	5	2	0	-2	O1/P	-0.9
1945	Cle-A	30	73	5	16	7	0	0	7	2	9	.219	.250	.315	66	-4	-3	5	0	1	-1	-0	O/P	-0.4
Total	3	158	530	56	142	25	8	1	67	28	44	.268	.312	.351	91	-8	-7	60	5	3		-2	O/1P	-1.3

■ JOHN CARNEY — Carney, John Joseph "Handsome Jack" b: 11/10/1866, Salem, Mass. d: 10/19/25, Litchfield, N.H. BR/TR, 5'10.5", 175 lbs. Deb: 4/24/1889

YEAR	TM/L	G	AB	R	H	2B	3B	HR	RBI	BB	SO	AVG	OBP	SLG	PRO+	BR	/A	RC	SB	CS	SBR	FR	POS	TPR
1889	Was-N	69	273	25	63	7	0	1	29	14	14	.231	.271	.267	55	-17	-15	24	12			-7	1O	-2.2
1890	Buf-P	28	107	11	29	3	0	0	13	7	14	.271	.333	.299	78	-4	-2	12	2			-2	1/O	-0.5
	Cle-P	25	89	15	31	5	3	0	21	14	5	.348	.442	.472	160	6	8	22	6			-3	O/1	0.3
	Yr	53	196	26	60	8	3	0	34	21	19	.306	.385	.378	115	2	6	32	8			-5		-0.2
1891	Cin-a	99	367	47	102	10	8	3	43	35	18	.278	.346	.373	100	4	-2	54	15			1	1	-0.4
	Mil-a	31	110	22	33	5	2	3	23	13	8	.300	.389	.464	122	7	3	22	5			4	1	0.4
	Yr	130	477	69	135	15	10	6	66	48	26	.283	.356	.394	105	10	1	76	20			5		0.0
Total	3	252	946	120	258	30	13	7	129	83	59	.273	.338	.354	94	-5	-8	133	40			-8	1/O	-2.4

YEAR	TM/L	G	AB	R	H	2B	3B	HR	RBI	BB	SO	AVG	OBP	SLG	PRO+	BR	/A	RC	SB	CS	SBR	FR	POS	TPR

■ PAT CARNEY
Carney, Patrick Joseph "Doc" b: 8/7/1876, Holyoke, Mass. d: 1/9/53, Worcester, Mass. BL/TL, 6', 200 lbs. Deb: 9/20/01

YEAR	TM/L	G	AB	R	H	2B	3B	HR	RBI	BB	SO	AVG	OBP	SLG	PRO+	BR	/A	RC	SB	CS	SBR	FR	POS	TPR
1901	Bos-N	13	55	6	16	2	1	0	6	3		.291	.339	.364	97	0	-0	7	0			-3	O	-0.3
1902	Bos-N	137	522	75	141	17	4	2	65	42		.270	.337	.330	107	6	6	69	27			-9	*O/P	-1.3
1903	Bos-N	110	392	37	94	12	4	1	49	28		.240	.290	.298	73	-15	-13	38	10			-6	OP/1	-2.1
1904	Bos-N	78	279	24	57	5	2	0	11	12		.204	.237	.237	50	-17	-16	18	6			-2	O/P1	-2.0
Total	4	338	1248	142	308	36	11	3	131	85		.247	.301	.300	83	-25	-23	133	43			-19	O/P1	-5.7

■ BILL CARNEY
Carney, William John b: 3/25/1874, St.Paul, Minn. d: 7/31/38, Hopkins, Minn. BB/TR, 5'10", Deb: 8/22/04

YEAR	TM/L	G	AB	R	H	2B	3B	HR	RBI	BB	SO	AVG	OBP	SLG	PRO+	BR	/A	RC	SB	CS	SBR	FR	POS	TPR
1904	Chi-N	2	7	0	0	0	0	0	0	1		.000	.125	.000	-60	-1	-1	0	0			0	/O	0.0

■ HICK CARPENTER
Carpenter, Warren William b: 8/16/1855, Grafton, Mass. d: 4/18/37, San Diego, Cal. BR/TL, 5'11", 186 lbs. Deb: 5/01/1879

YEAR	TM/L	G	AB	R	H	2B	3B	HR	RBI	BB	SO	AVG	OBP	SLG	PRO+	BR	/A	RC	SB	CS	SBR	FR	POS	TPR
1879	Syr-N	65	261	30	53	6	0	0	20	2	15	.203	.209	.226	49	-15	-11	13				-4	13O/2	-1.5
1880	Cin-N	77	300	32	72	6	4	0	23	2	15	.240	.245	.287	80	-6	-6	22				-0	*3/1S	-0.6
1881	Wor-N	83	347	40	75	12	2	2	31	3	19	.216	.223	.280	54	-17	-20	22				3	*3	-0.9
1882	Cin-a	80	351	78	120	15	5	1			10	.342	.360	.422	153	22	19	55				-1	*3	1.3
1883	Cin-a	95	436	99	129	18	4	3		18		.296	.324	.376	118	12	7	54				-5	*3	0.3
1884	Cin-a	108	474	80	121	16	2	4		6		.255	.271	.323	91	-3	-6	42				-9	*3/O	-1.2
1885	Cin-a	112	473	89	131	12	8	2		9		.277	.295	.349	103	2	1	50				-6	*3	0.0
1886	Cin-a	111	458	67	101	8	5	2		18		.221	.262	.273	67	-16	-18	36	8			-6	*3	-1.6
1887	Cin-a	127	498	70	124	12	6	1		19		.249	.282	.303	64	-23	-25	56	44			-13	*3	-3.3
1888	Cin-a	136	551	68	147	14	5	3	67	5		.267	.280	.327	93	-3	-7	69	59			-12	*3	-1.6
1889	Cin-a	123	486	67	127	23	6	0	63	18	41	.261	.293	.333	78	-14	-16	63	47			-25	*3/1	-3.4
1892	StL-N	1	3	0	1	0	0	0	0	1	1	.333	.500	.333	164	0	0	1	0			0	/3	0.0
Total	12	1118	4638	720	1201	142	47	18	204	111	91	.259	.281	.321	87	-62	-81	482	158			-78	*3/102S	-12.5

■ CHARLIE CARR
Carr, Charles Carbitt b: 12/27/1876, Coatesville, Pa. d: 11/25/32, Memphis, Tenn. BR/TR, 6'2", 195 lbs. Deb: 9/15/1898

YEAR	TM/L	G	AB	R	H	2B	3B	HR	RBI	BB	SO	AVG	OBP	SLG	PRO+	BR	/A	RC	SB	CS	SBR	FR	POS	TPR
1898	Was-N	20	73	6	14	2	0	0	4	2		.192	.213	.219	26	-7	-7	4	2			-2	1	-0.7
1901	Phi-A	2	8	0	1	0	0	0	0	0		.125	.125	.125	-29	-1	-1	0	0			0	/1	0.0
1903	Det-A	135	548	59	154	23	11	2	79	10		.281	.294	.374	104	-1	1	66	10			12	*1	1.5
1904	Det-A	92	360	29	77	13	3	0	40	14		.214	.243	.267	65	-15	-14	27	6			16	1	0.5
	Cle-A	32	120	9	27	5	1	0	7	4		.225	.250	.283	71	-4	-4	9	0			0	1	-0.3
	Yr	124	480	38	104	18	4	0	47	18		.217	.245	.271	66	-19	-18	37	6			16		0.2
1905	Cle-A	89	306	29	72	12	4	1	31	13		.235	.266	.310	83	-6	-6	31	12			-2	1	-1.0
1906	Cin-N	22	94	9	18	2	3	0	10	2		.191	.208	.277	50	-5	-6	6	0			1	1	-0.6
1914	Ind-F	115	441	44	129	11	10	3	69	26	47	.293	.333	.383	95	2	-4	66	19			1	*1	0.2
Total	7	507	1950	185	492	68	32	6	240	71	47	.252	.279	.329	84	-37	-41	209	49			27	1	-0.6

■ CHUCK CARR
Carr, Charles Lee Glenn b: 8/10/67, San Bernardino, Cal. BB/TR, 5'10", 155 lbs. Deb: 4/28/90

YEAR	TM/L	G	AB	R	H	2B	3B	HR	RBI	BB	SO	AVG	OBP	SLG	PRO+	BR	/A	RC	SB	CS	SBR	FR	POS	TPR
1990	NY-N	4	2	0	0	0	0	0	0	0	2	.000	.000	.000	-99	-1	-1	0	1	0	0	0	/O	0.0

■ LEW CARR
Carr, Lewis Smith b: 8/15/1872, Union Springs, N.Y d: 6/15/54, Moravia, N.Y. TR, 6'2", 200 lbs. Deb: 7/04/01

YEAR	TM/L	G	AB	R	H	2B	3B	HR	RBI	BB	SO	AVG	OBP	SLG	PRO+	BR	/A	RC	SB	CS	SBR	FR	POS	TPR
1901	Pit-N	9	28	2	7	1	1	0	4	2		.250	.344	.357	102	0	0	4	0			-4	/S3	-0.2

■ CHICO CARRASQUEL
Carrasquel, Alfonso (Colon) b: 1/23/28, Caracas, Venez. BR/TR, 6', 170 lbs. Deb: 4/18/50

YEAR	TM/L	G	AB	R	H	2B	3B	HR	RBI	BB	SO	AVG	OBP	SLG	PRO+	BR	/A	RC	SB	CS	SBR	FR	POS	TPR
1950	Chi-A	141	524	72	148	21	5	4	46	66	46	.282	.368	.365	91	-8	-6	73	0	2	-1	11	*S	1.0
1951	Chi-A	147	538	41	142	22	4	2	58	46	39	.264	.325	.331	79	-17	-15	60	14	4	2	13	*S	0.8
1952	Chi-A	100	359	36	89	7	4	1	42	33	27	.248	.315	.298	71	-14	-14	36	2	2	-1	-15	*S	-2.5
1953	Chi-A	149	552	72	154	30	4	2	47	38	47	.279	.330	.359	83	-11	-13	65	5	3	-0	3	*S	0.1
1954	Chi-A	155	620	106	158	28	3	12	62	85	67	.255	.349	.368	93	-2	-4	84	7	6	-2	11	*S	1.9
1955	Chi-A	145	523	83	134	11	2	11	52	61	59	.256	.338	.348	83	-11	-12	64	1	1	-0	0	*S	0.3
1956	Cle-A	141	474	60	115	15	1	7	48	52	61	.243	.325	.323	70	-19	-20	51	0	4	-2	-25	*S/3	-3.4
1957	Cle-A	125	392	37	108	14	1	8	57	41	53	.276	.356	.378	102	1	2	51	0	2	-1	-5	*S	0.5
1958	Cle-A	49	156	14	40	6	0	2	21	14	12	.256	.318	.333	81	-4	-4	16	0	0	0	-19	S3	-1.8
	KC-A	59	160	19	34	5	1	2	13	21	15	.213	.304	.294	64	-7	-8	15	0	1	-1	-6	3S	-0.9
	Yr	108	316	33	74	11	1	4	34	35	27	.234	.311	.313	72	-12	-11	31	0	1	-1	-25		-2.7
1959	Bal-A	114	346	28	77	13	0	4	34	41	42	.223	.294	.295	64	-14	-17	30	2	3	-1	-14	S2/31	-2.3
Total	10	1325	4644	568	1199	172	25	55	474	491	467	.258	.334	.342	82	-108	-112	546	31	28	-8	-46	*S/321	-6.3

■ CAM CARREON
Carreon, Camilo b: 8/6/37, Colton, Cal. d: 9/2/87, Tucson, Ariz. BR/TR, 6'1.5", 190 lbs. Deb: 9/27/59

YEAR	TM/L	G	AB	R	H	2B	3B	HR	RBI	BB	SO	AVG	OBP	SLG	PRO+	BR	/A	RC	SB	CS	SBR	FR	POS	TPR
1959	Chi-A	1	1	0	0	0	0	0	0	0	0	.000	.000	.000	-99	-0	-0	0	0	0	0	0	/C	0.0
1960	Chi-A	8	17	2	4	0	0	0	2	1	3	.235	.278	.235	41	-1	-1	1	0	0	0	0	/C	0.0
1961	Chi-A	78	229	32	62	5	1	4	27	21	24	.271	.332	.354	85	-5	-5	26	0	1	-1	8	C	0.2
1962	Chi-A	106	313	31	80	19	1	4	37	33	37	.256	.329	.361	86	-6	-6	36	1	1	-0	8	C	0.6
1963	Chi-A	101	270	28	74	10	1	2	35	23	32	.274	.333	.341	91	-3	-3	30	1	1	-0	8	C	-0.1
1964	Chi-A	37	95	12	26	5	0	0	4	7	13	.274	.330	.326	86	-2	-2	9	0	0	0	-4	C	-0.4
1965	Cle-A	19	52	6	12	2	1	1	7	9	6	.231	.344	.365	101	0	0	6	1	1	-0	1	C	0.2
1966	Bal-A	4	9	2	2	2	0	0	2	3	2	.222	.417	.444	150	1	1	2	0	0	0	0	/C	0.1
Total	8	354	986	113	260	43	4	11	114	97	117	.264	.331	.349	87	-17	-16	111	3	4	-2	14	C	0.6

■ MARK CARREON
Carreon, Mark Steven b: 7/19/63, Chicago, Ill. BR/TL, 6'", 170 lbs. Deb: 9/08/87

YEAR	TM/L	G	AB	R	H	2B	3B	HR	RBI	BB	SO	AVG	OBP	SLG	PRO+	BR	/A	RC	SB	CS	SBR	FR	POS	TPR
1987	NY-N	9	12	0	3	0	0	0	1	1	1	.250	.308	.250	53	-1	-1	1	0	1	-1	-0	/O	-0.1
1988	NY-N	7	9	5	5	2	0	1	1	2	1	.556	.636	1.111	413	4	4	7	0	0	0	-1	/O	0.3
1989	NY-N	68	133	20	41	6	0	6	16	12	17	.308	.370	.489	151	7	8	24	2	3	-1	-1	O	0.5
1990	NY-N	82	188	30	47	12	0	10	26	15	29	.250	.312	.473	116	3	3	29	1	0	0	-1	O	0.0
Total	4	166	342	55	96	20	0	17	44	30	48	.281	.344	.488	134	13	14	60	3	4	-2	-3	O	0.7

■ BILL CARRIGAN
Carrigan, William Francis "Rough" b: 10/22/1883, Lewiston, Me. d: 7/8/69, Lewiston, Me. BR/TR, 5'9", 175 lbs. Deb: 7/07/06 M

YEAR	TM/L	G	AB	R	H	2B	3B	HR	RBI	BB	SO	AVG	OBP	SLG	PRO+	BR	/A	RC	SB	CS	SBR	FR	POS	TPR
1906	Bos-A	37	109	5	23	0	0	0	10	5		.211	.246	.211	45	-7	-7	7	3			-1	C	-0.4
1908	Bos-A	57	149	13	35	5	2	0	14	3		.235	.250	.295	77	-4	-4	11	1			6	C/1	0.8
1909	Bos-A	94	280	25	83	13	2	1	36	17		.296	.341	.368	121	7	6	36	2			1	C/1	1.5
1910	Bos-A	114	342	36	85	11	1	3	53	23		.249	.307	.313	92	-2	-3	37	10			-19	*C	-1.1
1911	Bos-A	72	232	19	67	6	1	1	30	26		.289	.373	.336	99	1	1	31	5			-2	C/1	0.6
1912	*Bos-A	87	266	34	70	7	1	0	24	38		.263	.359	.297	84	-2	-4	31	7			-12	C	-0.6
1913	Bos-A	87	256	17	62	15	5	0	28	27	26	.242	.319	.340	91	-2	-3	29	6			-8	CM	-0.4
1914	Bos-A	82	178	18	45	5	1	1	22	40	18	.253	.395	.309	112	5	5	24	1	2	-1	3	CM	1.3
1915	*Bos-A	46	95	10	19	3	0	0	7	16	12	.200	.321	.232	68	-3	-3	8	0			9	CM	0.9
1916	*Bos-A	33	63	7	17	2	1	0	11	11	3	.270	.378	.333	113	2	2	9	2			6	CM	1.0
Total	10	709	1970	194	506	67	14	6	235	206	59	.257	.333	.314	94	-6	-11	224	37	2		-16	C/1	3.6

■ DIXIE CARROLL
Carroll, Dorsey Lee b: 5/9/1891, Paducah, Ky. d: 10/13/84, Jacksonville, Fla BL/TR, 5'11", 165 lbs. Deb: 9/12/19

YEAR	TM/L	G	AB	R	H	2B	3B	HR	RBI	BB	SO	AVG	OBP	SLG	PRO+	BR	/A	RC	SB	CS	SBR	FR	POS	TPR
1919	Bos-N	15	49	10	13	3	1	0	7	7	1	.265	.379	.367	130	2	2	8	5			2	O	0.4

■ CHICK CARROLL
Carroll, Edward b: 1868, Arkansas d: 7/13/08, Chicago, Ill. Deb: 4/17/1884

YEAR	TM/L	G	AB	R	H	2B	3B	HR	RBI	BB	SO	AVG	OBP	SLG	PRO+	BR	/A	RC	SB	CS	SBR	FR	POS	TPR
1884	Was-U	4	16	1	4	0	0	0	0			.250	.250	.250	72	-1	-0	1	0			-1	/O	0.0

YEAR	TM/L	G	AB	R	H	2B	3B	HR	RBI	BB	SO	AVG	OBP	SLG	PRO+	BR	/A	RC	SB	CS	SBR	FR	POS	TPR

■ FRED CARROLL　　Carroll, Frederick Herbert　b: 7/2/1864, Sacramento, Cal.　d: 11/7/04, San Rafael, Cal.　BR/TR, 5'11", 185 lbs.　Deb: 5/01/1884

YEAR	TM/L	G	AB	R	H	2B	3B	HR	RBI	BB	SO	AVG	OBP	SLG	PRO+	BR	/A	RC	SB	CS	SBR	FR	POS	TPR
1884	Col-a	69	252	46	70	13	5	6		13		.278	.326	.440	164	14	17	37				15	CO	3.2
1885	Pit-a	71	280	45	75	13	8	0		7		.268	.298	.371	115	4	4	32				5	CO	1.5
1886	Pit-a	122	486	92	140	28	11	5		52		.288	.362	.422	148	27	27	83	20			13	CO1/S	3.6
1887	Pit-N	102	421	71	138	24	15	6	54	36	21	.328	.383	.499	155	25	30	92	23			-14	OC1/S	1.5
1888	Pit-N	97	366	62	91	14	5	2	48	32	31	.249	.326	.331	121	6	10	46	18			-9	CO/13	0.2
1889	Pit-N	91	318	80	105	21	11	2	51	85	26	.330	**.486**	.484	**192**	39	45	86	19			-8	CO/13	3.0
1890	Pit-P	111	416	95	124	20	7	2	71	75	22	.298	.418	.394	130	16	23	85	35			-39	CO/1	-1.2
1891	Pit-N	91	353	55	77	13	4	4	48	48	36	.218	.315	.312	87	-6	-5	43	22			6	O	-0.2
Total	8	754	2892	546	820	146	66	27	<u>272</u>	348	<u>136</u>	.284	.370	.408	139	124	151	504	137			-30	CO/13S	11.6

■ SCRAPPY CARROLL　　Carroll, John E.　b: 8/27/1860, Buffalo, N.Y.　d: 11/14/42, Buffalo, N.Y.　5'7.5",　Deb: 9/27/1884

YEAR	TM/L	G	AB	R	H	2B	3B	HR	RBI	BB	SO	AVG	OBP	SLG	PRO+	BR	/A	RC	SB	CS	SBR	FR	POS	TPR
1884	StP-U	9	31	3	3	1	0	0		2		.097	.152	.129	-8	-3	-1	1	0			3	/O3	0.2
1885	Buf-N	13	40	1	3	0	0	0	1	2	8	.075	.119	.075	-35	-6	-6	0				2	O	-0.4
1887	Cle-a	57	216	30	43	5	1	0		15		.199	.264	.231	41	-17	-16	19	19			-5	O/32	-1.8
Total	3	79	287	34	49	6	1	0	<u>1</u>	19	<u>8</u>	.171	.232	.199	29	-26	-23	20	19			-1	/O32	-2.0

■ PAT CARROLL　　Carroll, Patrick　b: Philadelphia, Pa.　d: 2/14/16, Philadelphia, Pa.　Deb: 5/10/1884

YEAR	TM/L	G	AB	R	H	2B	3B	HR	RBI	BB	SO	AVG	OBP	SLG	PRO+	BR	/A	RC	SB	CS	SBR	FR	POS	TPR
1884	Alt-U	11	49	4	13	1	0	0		1		.265	.280	.286	90	-0	-1	4	0			-8	/CO	-0.6
	Phi-U	5	19	1	3	1	0	0		0		.158	.158	.211	25	-1	-1	1	0			4	/C	0.3
	Yr	16	68	5	16	2	0	0		1		.235	.246	.265	74	-2	-2	5	0			-3		-0.3

■ DOC CARROLL　　Carroll, Ralph Arthur "Red"　b: 12/28/1891, Worcester, Mass.　d: 6/27/83, Worcester, Mass.　BR/TR, 6', 170 lbs.　Deb: 6/27/16

YEAR	TM/L	G	AB	R	H	2B	3B	HR	RBI	BB	SO	AVG	OBP	SLG	PRO+	BR	/A	RC	SB	CS	SBR	FR	POS	TPR
1916	Phi-A	10	22	1	2	0	0	0	0	1	8	.091	.167	.091	-23	-3	-3	1	0			1	C	-0.1

■ CLIFF CARROLL　　Carroll, Samuel Clifford　b: 10/18/1859, Clay Grove, Iowa　d: 6/12/23, Portland, Ore.　BB , 5'8", 163 lbs.　Deb: 8/03/1882

YEAR	TM/L	G	AB	R	H	2B	3B	HR	RBI	BB	SO	AVG	OBP	SLG	PRO+	BR	/A	RC	SB	CS	SBR	FR	POS	TPR
1882	Pro-N	10	41	4	5	0	0	0	2	0	4	.122	.122	.122	-21	-5	-5	1				1	O	-0.3
1883	Pro-N	58	238	37	63	12	3	1	20	4	28	.265	.277	.353	87	-3	-4	24				4	O	0.1
1884	*Pro-N	113	452	90	118	16	4	3	54	29	39	.261	.306	.334	103	1	2	47				2	*O	0.3
1885	Pro-N	104	426	62	99	12	3	1	40	29	29	.232	.281	.282	86	-8	-5	35				3	*O	-0.4
1886	Was-N	111	433	73	99	11	6	2	22	44	26	.229	.300	.296	87	-8	-5	49	31			-2	*O	-0.4
1887	Was-N	103	420	79	104	17	4	4	37	17	30	.248	.291	.336	79	-14	-10	54	40			0	*O	-0.7
1888	Pit-N	5	20	1	0	0	0	0	0	0	8	.000	.000	.000	-99	-4	-4	0	2			-1	/O	-0.5
1890	Chi-N	136	582	134	166	16	6	7	65	53	34	.285	.352	.369	108	10	6	90	34			11	*O	1.2
1891	Chi-N	130	515	87	132	20	8	7	80	50	42	.256	.340	.367	108	6	6	77	31			-5	*O	-0.4
1892	StL-N	101	407	82	111	14	8	4	49	47	22	.273	.363	.376	132	14	17	68	30			4	*O	1.6
1893	Bos-N	120	438	80	98	7	5	2	54	88	28	.224	.360	.276	86	-14	-20	55	29			2	*O	-1.9
Total	11	991	3972	729	995	125	47	31	423	361	290	.251	.320	.329	94	-26	-23	499	197			18	O	-1.4

■ TOM CARROLL　　Carroll, Thomas Edward　b: 9/17/36, Jamaica, N.Y.　BR/TR, 6'3", 186 lbs.　Deb: 5/07/55

YEAR	TM/L	G	AB	R	H	2B	3B	HR	RBI	BB	SO	AVG	OBP	SLG	PRO+	BR	/A	RC	SB	CS	SBR	FR	POS	TPR
1955	*NY-A	14	6	3	2	0	0	0	0	0	2	.333	.333	.333	81	-0	-0	1	0	0	0	4	/S	0.4
1956	NY-A	36	17	11	6	0	0	0	0	1	3	.353	.389	.353	100	-0	0	3	1	0	0	7	3/S	0.7
1959	KC-A	14	7	1	1	0	0	0	1	0	1	.143	.143	.143	-21	-1	-1	0	0	0	0	4	/S3	0.3
Total	3	64	30	15	9	0	0	0	1	1	6	.300	.323	.300	69	-1	-1	3	1	0	0	15	/3S	1.4

■ KID CARSEY　　Carsey, Wilfred　b: 10/22/1870, New York, N.Y.　d: 3/29/60, Miami, Fla.　BL/TR, 5'7", 168 lbs.　Deb: 4/08/1891

YEAR	TM/L	G	AB	R	H	2B	3B	HR	RBI	BB	SO	AVG	OBP	SLG	PRO+	BR	/A	RC	SB	CS	SBR	FR	POS	TPR
1891	Was-a	61	187	25	28	5	2	0	15	19	38	.150	.236	.198	27	-18	-16	9	2			5	P/OS	0.0
1892	Phi-N	44	131	8	20	2	1	1	10	9	24	.153	.207	.206	26	-12	-12	6	1			2	P/O	0.0
1893	Phi-N	39	145	12	27	1	1	0	10	5	14	.186	.229	.207	17	-17	-17	8	2			2	P	0.0
1894	Phi-N	35	125	30	34	2	2	0	18	16	11	.272	.359	.320	68	-6	-6	16	3			2	P	0.0
1895	Phi-N	44	141	24	41	2	0	0	20	15	12	.291	.363	.305	75	-4	-4	17	2			-1	P	0.0
1896	Phi-N	27	81	13	18	2	2	0	7	11	12	.222	.315	.296	64	-4	-4	8	1			1	P	0.0
1897	Phi-N	4	13	1	3	0	0	0	1	0		.231	.231	.231	24	-1	-1	1	0			0	/P	0.0
	StL-N	13	43	2	13	2	2	0	5	1		.302	.318	.442	103	-0	-1	7	1			1	P	0.0
	Yr	17	56	3	16	2	2	0	6	1		.286	.298	.393	85	-2	-1	7	1			1		0.0
1898	StL-N	38	105	8	21	0	1	1	10	10		.200	.270	.248	49	-6	-7	8	3			-5	P2/O	0.0
1899	Cle-N	11	36	5	10	0	0	0	4	3		.278	.333	.278	76	-1	-1	3	0			3	P/S	0.0
	Was-N	4	11	1	0	0	0	0	0	0		.000	.000	.000	-99	-3	-3	0	0			1	/P	0.0
	NY-N	5	18	2	6	1	0	0	1	2		.333	.400	.389	124	1	1	4	2			-1	/3S	0.0
	Yr	20	65	8	16	1	0	0	5	5		.246	.300	.262	60	-4	-3	6	2			3		0.0
1901	Bro-N	2	2	0	0	0	0	0	0	0		.000	.000	.000	-97	-0	-0	0	0			-0	/P	0.0
Total	10	327	1038	131	221	17	11	2	101	91	<u>111</u>	.213	.281	.256	48	-73	-70	86	17			10	P/O2S3	0.0

■ KIT CARSON　　Carson, Walter Lloyd　b: 11/15/12, Colton, Cal.　d: 6/21/83, Long Beach, Cal.　BL/TL, 6', 180 lbs.　Deb: 7/21/34

YEAR	TM/L	G	AB	R	H	2B	3B	HR	RBI	BB	SO	AVG	OBP	SLG	PRO+	BR	/A	RC	SB	CS	SBR	FR	POS	TPR
1934	Cle-A	5	18	4	5	2	1	0	1	2	3	.278	.350	.500	115	0	0	3	0	0	0	-2	/O	0.0
1935	Cle-A	16	22	1	5	2	0	0	1	2	6	.227	.292	.318	57	-1	-1	2	0	1	-1	0	/O	-0.1
Total	2	21	40	5	10	4	1	0	2	4	9	.250	.318	.400	83	-1	-1	5	0	1	-1	-2	/O	-0.1

■ FRANK CARSWELL　　Carswell, Frank Willis "Tex" or "Wheels"　b: 11/6/19, Palestine, Tex.　BR/TR, 6', 195 lbs.　Deb: 4/17/53

YEAR	TM/L	G	AB	R	H	2B	3B	HR	RBI	BB	SO	AVG	OBP	SLG	PRO+	BR	/A	RC	SB	CS	SBR	FR	POS	TPR
1953	Det-A	16	15	2	4	0	0	0	2	3	1	.267	.389	.267	81	-0	-0	2	0	0	0	-0	/O	0.0

■ GARY CARTER　　Carter, Gary Edmund　b: 4/8/54, Culver City, Cal.　BR/TR, 6'2", 205 lbs.　Deb: 9/16/74

YEAR	TM/L	G	AB	R	H	2B	3B	HR	RBI	BB	SO	AVG	OBP	SLG	PRO+	BR	/A	RC	SB	CS	SBR	FR	POS	TPR
1974	Mon-N	9	27	5	11	0	1	1	6	1	2	.407	.429	.593	174	3	3	7	2	0	1	-1	/CO	0.3
1975	Mon-N	144	503	58	136	20	1	17	68	72	83	.270	.363	.416	111	11	9	80	5	2	0	-19	OC/3	-1.0
1976	Mon-N	91	311	31	68	8	1	6	38	30	43	.219	.289	.309	67	-12	-14	28	0	2	-1	4	CO	-0.9
1977	Mon-N	154	522	86	148	29	2	31	84	58	103	.284	.361	.525	138	24	26	98	5	5	-2	2	*C/O	2.5
1978	Mon-N	157	533	76	136	27	1	20	72	62	70	.255	.338	.422	113	8	9	77	10	6	-1	8	*C/1	2.0
1979	Mon-N	141	505	74	143	26	5	22	75	40	62	.283	.342	.485	124	14	15	82	3	2	-0	11	*C	3.0
1980	Mon-N	154	549	76	145	25	5	29	101	58	78	.264	.336	.486	127	18	18	89	3	2	-0	13	*C	3.5
1981	*Mon-N	100	374	48	94	20	2	16	68	35	35	.251	.317	.444	113	6	5	51	1	5	-3	2	*C/1	0.6
1982	Mon-N	154	557	91	163	32	1	29	97	78	64	.293	.385	.510	146	37	35	107	2	5	-2	13	*C	4.9
1983	Mon-N	145	541	63	146	37	3	17	79	51	57	.270	.341	.444	116	11	11	80	1	1	-0	8	*C/1	2.4
1984	Mon-N	159	596	75	175	32	1	27	**106**	64	57	.294	.368	.487	145	30	33	108	2	2	-1	-6	*C1	3.1
1985	NY-N	149	555	83	156	17	1	32	100	69	46	.281	.367	.488	141	28	29	97	1	1	-0	4	*C/1O	3.9
1986	*NY-N	132	490	81	125	14	2	24	105	62	63	.255	.346	.439	118	10	12	72	1	0	0	6	*C/1O3	2.0
1987	NY-N	139	523	55	123	18	2	20	83	42	73	.235	.293	.392	84	-17	-13	58	0	0	0	-1	*C/1O	-0.3
1988	*NY-N	130	455	39	110	16	2	11	46	34	52	.242	.304	.358	94	-6	-4	50	0	2	-1	-3	*C1/3	-0.2
1989	NY-N	50	153	14	28	8	0	2	15	12	15	.183	.242	.275	50	-11	-10	10	0	0	0	-2	C/1	-0.8
1990	SF-N	92	244	24	62	10	0	9	27	25	31	.254	.326	.406	105	-0	0	33	1	1	-0	-3	C/1	0.0
Total	17	2100	7438	979	1969	339	30	313	1170	793	934	.265	.340	.445	118	153	164	1127	37	36	-11	36	*CO/13	25.0

■ HOWIE CARTER　　Carter, John Howard　b: 10/13/04, New York, N.Y.　BR/TR, 5'10", 154 lbs.　Deb: 6/21/26

YEAR	TM/L	G	AB	R	H	2B	3B	HR	RBI	BB	SO	AVG	OBP	SLG	PRO+	BR	/A	RC	SB	CS	SBR	FR	POS	TPR
1926	Cin-N	5	1	0	0	0	0	0	0	0	0	.000	.000	.000	-99	-0	-0	0	0			0	/2S	0.0

YEAR	TM/L	G	AB	R	H	2B	3B	HR	RBI	BB	SO	AVG	OBP	SLG	PRO+	BR	/A	RC	SB	CS	SBR	FR	POS	TPR

■ JOE CARTER   Carter, Joseph b: 3/7/60, Oklahoma City, Okla.   BR/TR, 6'3", 215 lbs.   Deb: 7/30/83

YEAR	TM/L	G	AB	R	H	2B	3B	HR	RBI	BB	SO	AVG	OBP	SLG	PRO+	BR	/A	RC	SB	CS	SBR	FR	POS	TPR
1983	Chi-N	23	51	6	9	1	1	0	1	0	21	.176	.176	.235	13	-6	-6	2	1	0	0	0	O	-0.5
1984	Cle-A	66	244	32	67	6	1	13	41	11	48	.275	.309	.467	109	3	2	34	2	4	-2	-0	O/1	-0.1
1985	Cle-A	143	489	64	128	27	0	15	59	25	74	.262	.300	.409	93	-6	-6	60	24	6	4	2	*O1/23D	-0.2
1986	Cle-A	162	663	108	200	36	9	29	121	32	95	.302	.339	.514	130	23	25	116	29	7	5	1	*O1	2.3
1987	Cle-A	149	588	83	155	27	2	32	106	27	105	.264	.306	.480	103	1	1	87	31	6	6	-11	1O/D	-1.3
1988	Cle-A	157	621	85	168	36	6	27	98	35	82	.271	.317	.478	116	.13	11	96	27	5	5	6	*O	2.0
1989	Cle-A	162	651	84	158	32	4	35	105	39	112	.243	.294	.465	109	6	5	89	13	5	1	-4	*O1/D	-0.1
1990	SD-N	162	634	79	147	27	1	24	115	48	93	.232	.293	.391	85	-13	-14	72	22	6	3	2	*O1	-1.4
Total	8	1024	3941	541	1032	192	24	175	646	217	630	.262	.307	.456	106	21	17	555	149	39	21	-4	O1/D32	0.7

■ BLACKIE CARTER   Carter, Otis Leonard b: 9/30/02, Langley, S.C.   d: 9/10/76, Greenville, S.C.   BR/TR, 5'10", 175 lbs.   Deb: 10/03/25

YEAR	TM/L	G	AB	R	H	2B	3B	HR	RBI	BB	SO	AVG	OBP	SLG	PRO+	BR	/A	RC	SB	CS	SBR	FR	POS	TPR
1925	NY-N	1	4	0	0	0	0	0	0	0	1	.000	.000	.000	-99	-1	-1	0	0	0	0	1	/O	0.0
1926	NY-N	5	17	4	4	1	0	1	1	1	0	.235	.278	.471	100	-0	-0	2	0			-0	/O	0.0
Total	2	6	21	4	4	1	0	1	1	1	1	.190	.227	.381	61	-1	-1	2	0	0		0	/O	0.0

■ STEVE CARTER   Carter, Steven Jerome b: 12/3/64, Charlottesville, Va.   BL/TR, 6'4", 201 lbs.   Deb: 4/16/89

YEAR	TM/L	G	AB	R	H	2B	3B	HR	RBI	BB	SO	AVG	OBP	SLG	PRO+	BR	/A	RC	SB	CS	SBR	FR	POS	TPR
1989	Pit-N	9	16	2	2	1	0	1	3	2	5	.125	.222	.375	70	-1	-1	1	0	0	0	-1	/O	-0.1
1990	Pit-N	5	5	0	1	0	0	0	0	0	1	.200	.200	.200	11	-1	-1	0	0	0	0	0	/O	0.0
Total	2	14	21	2	3	1	0	1	3	2	6	.143	.217	.333	56	-1	-1	2	0	0	0	-0	/O	-0.1

■ ED CARTWRIGHT   Cartwright, Edward Charles "Jumbo" b: 10/6/1859, Johnstown, Pa.   d: 9/3/33, St.Petersburg, Fla   BR/TR, 5'10", 220 lbs.   Deb: 7/10/1890

YEAR	TM/L	G	AB	R	H	2B	3B	HR	RBI	BB	SO	AVG	OBP	SLG	PRO+	BR	/A	RC	SB	CS	SBR	FR	POS	TPR
1890	StL-a	75	300	70	90	12	4	8		29		.300	.367	.447	125	15	8	60	26			-1	1	0.4
1894	Was-N	132	507	88	149	35	13	12	106	57	43	.294	.374	.485	111	5	8	106	31			-1	*1	0.6
1895	Was-N	122	472	95	156	34	17	3	90	54	41	.331	.400	.494	134	22	23	116	50			14	*1	3.2
1896	Was-N	133	499	76	138	15	10	1	62	54	44	.277	.350	.353	87	-8	-8	73	28			-0	*1	-0.2
1897	Was-N	33	124	19	29	4	0	0	15	8		.234	.286	.266	48	-9	-9	12	9			2	1	-0.5
Total	5	495	1902	348	562	100	44	24	273	202	128	.295	.368	.432	108	25	23	368	144			14	1	3.5

■ RICO CARTY   Carty, Ricardo Adolfo Jacobo (b: Ricardo Adolfo Jacobo (Carty)) b: 9/1/39, San Pedro De Macoris, D.R.   BR/TR, 6'3", 200 lbs.   Deb: 9/15/63

YEAR	TM/L	G	AB	R	H	2B	3B	HR	RBI	BB	SO	AVG	OBP	SLG	PRO+	BR	/A	RC	SB	CS	SBR	FR	POS	TPR
1963	Mil-N	2	2	0	0	0	0	0	0	0	2	.000	.000	.000	-99	-1	-1	0	0	0	0	0	H	0.0
1964	Mil-N	133	455	72	150	28	4	22	88	43	78	.330	.391	.554	162	37	37	94	1	2	-1	-8	*O	2.6
1965	Mil-N	83	271	37	84	18	1	10	35	17	44	.310	.357	.494	136	13	13	44	1	4	-2	-4	O	0.5
1966	Atl-N	151	521	73	170	25	2	15	76	60	74	.326	.396	.468	137	29	28	94	4	6	-2	-1	*OC/13	2.3
1967	Atl-N	134	444	41	113	16	2	15	64	49	70	.255	.330	.401	110	5	5	55	4	3	-1	-1	*O/1	-0.1
1969	*Atl-N	104	304	47	104	15	0	16	58	32	28	.342	.405	.549	164	26	26	61	0	2	-1	-9	O	1.2
1970	Atl-N	136	478	84	175	23	3	25	101	77	46	.366	.456	.584	167	54	51	125	1	2	-1	-6	*O	3.7
1972	Atl-N	86	271	31	75	12	2	6	29	44	33	.277	.378	.402	111	9	6	42	0	1	-1	-5	O	-0.1
1973	Tex-A	86	306	24	71	12	0	3	33	36	39	.232	.315	.301	77	-10	-8	30	2	0	1	-4	OD	-1.3
	Chi-N	22	70	4	15	0	0	1	8	6	10	.214	.276	.257	45	-5	-5	4	0	0	0	-1	O	-0.7
	Oak-A	7	8	1	2	0	0	1	1	2	1	.250	.400	.750	230	1	1	3	0	0	0	0	/D	0.1
1974	Cle-A	33	91	6	33	5	0	1	16	5	9	.363	.396	.451	144	5	5	15	0	0	-1	0	D/1	0.3
1975	Cle-A	118	383	57	118	19	1	18	64	45	31	.308	.384	.504	149	25	25	70	2	2	-1	-1	D1O	2.2
1976	Cle-A	152	552	67	171	34	0	13	83	67	45	.310	.384	.442	143	30	31	92	1	1	-0	-2	*D1/O	2.9
1977	Cle-A	127	461	50	129	23	1	15	80	56	51	.280	.358	.432	118	10	12	68	1	2	-1	1	*D/1	1.1
1978	Tor-A	104	387	51	110	16	0	20	68	36	41	.284	.345	.481	127	14	13	64	1	1	-0	0	*D	1.3
	Oak-A	41	141	19	39	5	1	11	31	21	16	.277	.370	.560	167	11	12	27	0	0	0	0	D	1.2
	Yr	145	528	70	149	21	1	31	99	57	57	.282	.352	.502	138	25	25	91	1	1	-0	0		2.5
1979	Tor-A	132	461	48	118	26	0	12	55	46	45	.256	.325	.390	91	-5	-6	54	3	1	0	0	*D	-0.5
Total	15	1651	5606	712	1677	278	17	204	890	642	663	.299	.372	.464	132	248	244	941	21	26	-9	-41	OD/1C3	16.7

■ BOB CARUTHERS   Caruthers, Robert Lee "Parisian Bob" b: 1/5/1864, Memphis, Tenn.   d: 8/5/11, Peoria, Ill.   BL/TR, 5'7", 138 lbs.   Deb: 9/07/1884   MU

YEAR	TM/L	G	AB	R	H	2B	3B	HR	RBI	BB	SO	AVG	OBP	SLG	PRO+	BR	/A	RC	SB	CS	SBR	FR	POS	TPR
1884	StL-a	23	82	15	21	2	0	2		4		.256	.291	.354	108	1	1	9				-6	OP	0.0
1885	*StL-a	60	222	37	50	10	2	1		20		.225	.289	.302	85	-2	-4	20				-0	P/O	0.0
1886	*StL-a	87	317	91	106	21	14	4		64		.334	.448	.527	198	42	39	89	26			-5	PO/2	0.0
1887	*StL-a	98	364	102	130	23	11	8		66		.357	.463	.547	166	44	36	118	49			9	OP/1	4.0
1888	Bro-a	94	335	58	77	10	5	5	53	45		.230	.328	.334	116	7	8	45	23			1	OP	1.2
1889	*Bro-a	59	172	45	43	8	3	2	31	44	17	.250	.408	.366	123	8	8	30	9			1	P/O1	0.0
1890	*Bro-N	71	238	46	63	7	4	1	29	47	18	.265	.397	.340	117	8	8	38	13			-4	OP	0.0
1891	Bro-N	56	171	24	48	5	3	2	23	25	13	.281	.372	.380	122	5	6	26	4			-2	PO/2	0.0
1892	StL-N	143	513	76	142	16	8	3	69	86	29	.277	.386	.357	134	21	25	82	24			-10	*OP/21M	1.2
1893	Chi-N	1	3	0	0	0	0	0	0	0	0	.000	.000	.000	-99	-1	-1	0	0			-0	/O	0.0
	Cin-N	13	48	14	14	2	0	0	8	16	1	.292	.477	.396	132	4	4	11	4			-1	O	0.2
	Yr	14	51	14	14	2	0	1	8	16	2	.275	.456	.373	121	3	3	11	4			-1		0.2
Total	10	705	2465	508	694	104	50	29	213	417	79	.282	.391	.400	137	138	129	468	152			-18	OP/12	6.6

■ PAUL CASANOVA   Casanova, Paulino (Ortiz) b: 12/21/41, Colon, Matanzas, Cuba   BR/TR, 6'4", 180 lbs.   Deb: 9/18/65

YEAR	TM/L	G	AB	R	H	2B	3B	HR	RBI	BB	SO	AVG	OBP	SLG	PRO+	BR	/A	RC	SB	CS	SBR	FR	POS	TPR
1965	Was-A	5	13	2	4	1	0	1	1	1	3	.308	.357	.385	112	0	0	2	0	0	0	-2	/C	-0.1
1966	Was-A	122	429	45	109	16	5	13	44	14	78	.254	.279	.406	95	-5	-4	46	1	2	-1	-11	*C	-1.1
1967	Was-A	141	528	47	131	19	1	9	53	17	65	.248	.274	.339	84	-14	-12	44	1	1	-0	-5	*C	-0.8
1968	Was-A	96	322	19	63	6	0	4	25	7	52	.196	.213	.252	42	-24	-23	16	0	1	-1	-9	C	-3.2
1969	Was-A	124	379	26	82	9	2	4	37	18	52	.216	.257	.282	54	-25	-23	26	0	0	0	-6	*C	-2.2
1970	Was-A	104	328	25	75	17	3	6	30	10	47	.229	.254	.354	69	-16	-15	28	0	0	0	-2	*C	-1.5
1971	Was-A	94	311	19	63	9	1	5	26	14	52	.203	.239	.286	51	-22	-20	19	0	3	-2	-5	C	-2.4
1972	Atl-N	49	136	8	28	3	0	2	10	4	28	.206	.229	.272	38	-11	-12	6	0	1	-1	-6	C	-1.6
1973	Atl-N	82	236	18	51	7	0	7	18	11	36	.216	.254	.335	58	-13	-15	18	0	2	-1	7	C	-0.4
1974	Atl-N	42	104	5	21	0	0	0	8	5	17	.202	.239	.202	23	-10	-11	5	0	0	0	-1	C	-1.0
Total	10	859	2786	214	627	87	12	50	252	101	430	.225	.254	.319	64	-140	-134	210	2	10	-5	-40	C	-14.3

■ GEORGE CASE   Case, George Washington b: 11/11/15, Trenton, N.J.   d: 1/23/89, Trenton, N.J.   BR/TR, 6', 183 lbs.   Deb: 9/08/37   C

YEAR	TM/L	G	AB	R	H	2B	3B	HR	RBI	BB	SO	AVG	OBP	SLG	PRO+	BR	/A	RC	SB	CS	SBR	FR	POS	TPR
1937	Was-A	22	90	14	26	6	2	0	11	3	5	.289	.312	.400	82	-3	-3	11	2	1	0	-0	O	-0.3
1938	Was-A	107	433	69	132	27	3	2	40	39	28	.305	.362	.395	96	-7	-2	63	11	6	-0	-2	*O	-0.3
1939	Was-A	128	530	103	160	20	7	2	35	56	36	.302	.369	.377	98	-6	0	80	51	17	5	10	*O	1.0
1940	Was-A	154	656	109	192	29	5	5	56	52	39	.293	.349	.375	94	-11	-5	94	35	10	5	-3	*O	-1.3
1941	Was-A	153	649	95	176	32	8	2	53	51	37	.271	.325	.354	84	-19	-15	82	33	9	5	14	*O	-0.6
1942	Was-A	125	513	101	164	26	2	5	43	44	30	.320	.377	.407	122	14	15	88	44	6	10	-1	*O	1.5
1943	Was-A	141	613	102	180	36	5	1	52	41	27	.294	.341	.374	113	6	8	88	61	14	10	-2	*O	1.2
1944	Was-A	119	464	63	116	14	2	2	32	49	22	.250	.326	.302	83	-11	-9	50	49	18	4	8	*O	0.0
1945	Was-A	123	504	72	148	19	5	1	31	49	27	.294	.360	.357	118	6	11	68	30	16	-1	15	*O	2.1
1946	Cle-A	118	484	46	109	23	4	1	22	34	38	.225	.280	.295	65	-26	-22	43	28	11	2	-5	*O	-3.2
1947	Was-A	36	80	11	12	1	0	0	4	9	7	.150	.227	.162	10	-10	-9	4	5	1	0	1	O	-0.8
Total	11	1226	5016	785	1415	233	43	21	377	426	297	.282	.341	.358	95	-67	-32	670	349	109	39	33	*O	-0.7

DENNIS CASEY
Casey, Dennis Patrick b: 3/30/1858, Binghamton, N.Y. d: 1/19/09, Binghamton, N.Y. BL/TR, 5'9", 164 lbs. Deb: 8/18/1884

YEAR	TM/L	G	AB	R	H	2B	3B	HR	RBI	BB	SO	AVG	OBP	SLG	PRO+	BR	/A	RC	SB	CS	SBR	FR	POS	TPR
1884	Wil-U	2	8	1	2	1	0	0	0			.250	.250	.375	106	0	0	1	0			0	/O	0.0
	Bal-a	37	149	20	37	7	4	3	5			.248	.273	.409	118	3	2	17				-0	O	0.1
1885	Bal-a	63	264	50	76	10	5	3	21			.288	.347	.398	140	12	12	37				-5	O	0.3
Total	2	102	421	71	115	18	9	6	26			.273	.320	.401	132	15	15	55				-5	O	0.4

DOC CASEY
Casey, James Patrick b: 3/15/1870, Lawrence, Mass. d: 12/31/36, Detroit, Mich. BB/TR, 5'6", Deb: 9/14/1898

YEAR	TM/L	G	AB	R	H	2B	3B	HR	RBI	BB	SO	AVG	OBP	SLG	PRO+	BR	/A	RC	SB	CS	SBR	FR	POS	TPR
1898	Was-N	28	112	13	31	2	0	0	15	3		.277	.302	.295	74	-4	-4	15	15			-3	3/SC	-0.4
1899	Was-N	9	34	3	4	2	0	0	2	2		.118	.167	.176	-5	-5	-5	1	1			-0	/3	-0.4
	Bro-N	134	525	75	141	14	8	1	43	25		.269	.313	.331	77	-15	-17	64	27			-19	*3	-3.2
	Yr	143	559	78	145	16	8	1	45	27		.259	.304	.322	73	-20	-21	65	28			-19		-3.6
1900	Bro-N	1	3	0	1	0	0	0	1	0		.333	.500	.333	128	0	0	1				0	/3	0.0
1901	Det-A	128	540	105	153	16	9	2	46	32		.283	.335	.357	90	-4	-7	79	34			5	*3	-0.4
1902	Det-A	132	520	69	142	18	7	3	55	44		.273	.338	.352	91	-4	-5	72	22			1	*3	-0.7
1903	Chi-N	112	435	56	126	8	3	1	40	19		.290	.319	.329	89	-8	-6	53	11			-19	*3	-2.3
1904	Chi-N	136	548	71	147	20	4	1	43	18		.268	.292	.325	92	-6	-6	62	21			-10	*3/C	-1.0
1905	Chi-N	144	526	66	122	21	10	1	56	41		.232	.287	.316	78	-12	-15	58	22			-9	*3/S	-1.3
1906	Bro-N	149	571	71	133	17	8	0	34	52		.233	.297	.291	92	-9	-4	59	22			-16	*3	-2.8
1907	Bro-N	141	527	55	122	19	3	0	19	34		.231	.278	.279	83	-14	-10	50	16			-6	*3	-1.8
Total	10	1114	4341	584	1122	137	52	9	354	270		.258	.306	.320	86	-81	-79	515	191			-75	*3/CS	-14.3

JOE CASEY
Casey, Joseph Felix b: 8/15/1887, Boston, Mass. d: 6/2/66, Melrose, Mass. BR/TR, 5'9", 180 lbs. Deb: 10/01/09

YEAR	TM/L	G	AB	R	H	2B	3B	HR	RBI	BB	SO	AVG	OBP	SLG	PRO+	BR	/A	RC	SB	CS	SBR	FR	POS	TPR
1909	Det-A	3	5	1	0	0	0	0	0	1		.000	.167	.000	-45	-1	-1	0	0			2	/C	0.1
1910	Det-A	23	62	3	12	3	0	0	2	2		.194	.231	.242	45	-4	-4	4	1			6	C	0.4
1911	Det-A	15	33	2	5	0	0	0	3	3		.152	.222	.152	5	-4	-4	1	0			-3	C/O	-0.5
1918	Was-A	9	17	3	4	0	0	0	2	2	2	.235	.316	.235	68	-1	-1	1	0			2	/C	0.2
Total	4	50	117	9	21	3	0	0	7	8	2	.179	.238	.205	32	-9	-10	6	1			6	/CO	0.2

BOB CASEY
Casey, Orrin Robinson b: 1/26/1859, Adolphustown, Ontario, Canada 5'11", 190 lbs. Deb: 7/17/1882

YEAR	TM/L	G	AB	R	H	2B	3B	HR	RBI	BB	SO	AVG	OBP	SLG	PRO+	BR	/A	RC	SB	CS	SBR	FR	POS	TPR
1882	Det-N	9	39	5	9	2	1	1	7	0	15	.231	.231	.410	101	-0	-0	4				-5	/32	-0.4

DAVE CASH
Cash, David b: 6/11/48, Utica, N.Y. BR/TR, 5'11", 170 lbs. Deb: 9/13/69

YEAR	TM/L	G	AB	R	H	2B	3B	HR	RBI	BB	SO	AVG	OBP	SLG	PRO+	BR	/A	RC	SB	CS	SBR	FR	POS	TPR
1969	Pit-N	18	61	8	17	3	1	0	4	9	9	.279	.371	.361	108	1	1	9	2	0	1	5	2	0.8
1970	*Pit-N	64	210	30	66	7	6	1	28	17	25	.314	.368	.419	113	3	4	30	5	2	0	6	2	1.6
1971	*Pit-N	123	478	79	138	17	4	2	34	46	33	.289	.351	.354	101	1	1	61	13	5	1	6	*23/S	1.5
1972	*Pit-N	99	425	58	120	22	4	3	30	22	31	.282	.318	.374	98	-3	-2	48	9	9	-3	28	2	3.1
1973	Pit-N	116	436	59	118	21	2	2	31	38	36	.271	.329	.342	88	-8	-6	49	2	5	-2	6	23	0.0
1974	Phi-N	162	687	89	206	26	11	2	58	46	33	.300	.352	.378	100	4	4	93	20	8	1	29	*2	4.0
1975	Phi-N	162	699	111	213	40	3	4	57	56	34	.305	.360	.388	103	7	4	100	13	6	0	9	*2	2.1
1976	*Phi-N	160	666	92	189	14	12	1	56	54	13	.284	.339	.345	92	-4	-6	75	10	12	-4	-2	*2	-0.4
1977	Mon-N	153	650	91	188	42	7	0	43	52	33	.289	.344	.375	96	-6	-4	82	21	12	-1	-11	*2	-0.6
1978	Mon-N	159	658	66	166	26	3	3	43	37	29	.252	.292	.315	70	-27	-26	58	12	6	0	-30	*2	-4.9
1979	Mon-N	76	187	24	60	11	1	2	19	12	12	.321	.362	.422	114	3	4	27	7	4	-0	-5	2	0.1
1980	SD-N	130	397	25	90	14	2	1	23	35	21	.227	.289	.280	63	-21	-18	30	6	5	-1	4	*2	-0.7
Total	12	1422	5554	732	1571	243	56	21	426	424	309	.283	.336	.358	93	-50	-49	661	120	74	-8	43	*2/3S	6.6

NORM CASH
Cash, Norman Dalton b: 11/10/34, Justiceburg, Tex. d: 10/12/86, Beaver Island, Mich. BL/TL, 6', 185 lbs. Deb: 6/18/58

YEAR	TM/L	G	AB	R	H	2B	3B	HR	RBI	BB	SO	AVG	OBP	SLG	PRO+	BR	/A	RC	SB	CS	SBR	FR	POS	TPR
1958	Chi-A	13	8	2	2	0	0	0	0	0	1	.250	.250	.250	39	-1	-1	1	0	0	0	1	/O	0.0
1959	*Chi-A	58	104	16	25	0	1	4	16	18	9	.240	.378	.375	109	2	2	17	1	1	-0	-1	1	0.1
1960	Det-A	121	353	64	101	16	3	18	63	65	58	.286	.406	.501	140	24	22	79	4	2	0	-1	1/O	1.5
1961	Det-A	159	535	119	193	22	8	41	132	124	85	.361	.488	.662	198	86	84	178	11	5	0	6	*1	7.3
1962	Det-A	148	507	94	123	16	2	39	89	104	82	.243	.385	.513	134	30	28	104	6	3	0	7	*1/O	2.4
1963	Det-A	147	493	67	133	19	1	26	79	89	76	.270	.388	.471	135	29	27	94	2	3	-1	2	*1	2.4
1964	Det-A	144	479	63	123	15	5	23	83	70	66	.257	.355	.453	121	16	15	78	2	1	0	4	*1	1.6
1965	Det-A	142	467	79	124	23	1	30	82	77	62	.266	.374	.512	147	31	30	91	6	6	-2	7	*1	3.1
1966	Det-A	160	603	98	168	18	3	32	93	66	79	.279	.354	.478	133	28	27	101	2	1	0	6	*1	2.9
1967	Det-A	152	488	64	118	16	5	22	72	81	100	.242	.354	.430	127	20	19	78	3	2	-0	10	*1	1.9
1968	*Det-A	127	411	50	108	15	1	25	63	39	70	.263	.331	.487	141	21	20	63	1	1	-0	10	*1	2.7
1969	Det-A	142	483	81	135	15	4	22	74	63	80	.280	.370	.464	126	21	18	85	2	1	0	6	*1	1.5
1970	Det-A	130	370	58	96	18	2	15	53	72	58	.259	.387	.441	127	16	16	64	0	1	-1	2	*1	1.2
1971	Det-A	135	452	72	128	10	3	32	91	59	86	.283	.375	.531	148	32	30	93	1	0	0	-0	*1	2.5
1972	*Det-A	137	440	51	114	16	0	22	61	50	64	.259	.340	.445	128	17	16	66	0	2	-1	-0	*1	0.1
1973	Det-A	121	363	51	95	19	0	19	40	47	73	.262	.359	.471	124	16	12	63	1	0	0	2	*1/D	0.8
1974	Det-A	53	149	17	34	3	2	7	12	19	30	.228	.327	.416	109	2	2	21	1	1	-0	-2	1	-0.1
Total	17	2089	6705	1046	1820	241	41	377	1103	1043	1091	.271	.377	.488	138	390	366	1278	43	30	-5	59	*1/OD	31.9

RON CASH
Cash, Ronald Forrest b: 11/20/49, Atlanta, Ga. BR/TR, 6', 180 lbs. Deb: 9/04/73

YEAR	TM/L	G	AB	R	H	2B	3B	HR	RBI	BB	SO	AVG	OBP	SLG	PRO+	BR	/A	RC	SB	CS	SBR	FR	POS	TPR
1973	Det-A	14	39	8	16	1	0	0	6	5	5	.410	.477	.487	161	4	4	9	0	0	0	-2	/O3	0.2
1974	Det-A	20	62	6	14	2	0	0	5	0	11	.226	.226	.258	38	-5	-5	3	0	1	-1	-2	1/3	-0.8
Total	2	34	101	14	30	3	1	0	11	5	16	.297	.330	.347	89	-1	-1	12	0	1	-1	-3	/13O	-0.6

ED CASKIN
Caskin, Edward James b: 12/30/1851, Danvers, Mass. d: 10/9/24, Danvers, Mass. BR/TR, 5'9.5", 165 lbs. Deb: 5/01/1879

YEAR	TM/L	G	AB	R	H	2B	3B	HR	RBI	BB	SO	AVG	OBP	SLG	PRO+	BR	/A	RC	SB	CS	SBR	FR	POS	TPR
1879	Tro-N	70	304	32	78	13	2	0	21	2	14	.257	.261	.313	95	-4	-4	25				10	SC/2	1.1
1880	Tro-N	82	333	36	75	5	4	0	28	7	24	.225	.241	.264	68	-10	-12	22				7	*S/C	0.0
1881	Tro-N	63	234	33	53	7	1	0	21	13	29	.226	.267	.265	65	-8	-10	17				1	*S	-0.3
1883	NY-N	95	383	47	91	11	2	1	40	14	25	.238	.264	.285	68	-15	-14	30				-7	*S2/C	-1.5
1884	NY-N	100	351	49	81	11	1	1	40	34	55	.231	.299	.276	80	-6	-7	30				5	*S/C	0.6
1885	StL-N	71	262	31	47	3	0	0	12	12	22	.179	.215	.191	34	-19	-17	11				-4	3/CS	-1.8
1886	NY-N	1	4	1	2	0	0	0	1	0	1	.500	.500	.500	203	0	0	1	0			-1	/S	0.0
Total	7	482	1871	229	427	50	10	2	163	82	170	.228	.261	.269	70	-61	-61	136	0			11	S/3C2	-1.9

HARRY CASSADY
Cassady, Harry Delbert (b: Harry Delbert Cassaday) b: 7/20/1880, Belleflower, Ill. d: 4/19/69, Fresno, Cal. BL, 5'8", 145 lbs. Deb: 8/08/04

YEAR	TM/L	G	AB	R	H	2B	3B	HR	RBI	BB	SO	AVG	OBP	SLG	PRO+	BR	/A	RC	SB	CS	SBR	FR	POS	TPR
1904	Pit-N	12	44	8	9	0	0	0	3	2		.205	.239	.205	38	-3	-3	3	2			-1	O	-0.4
1905	Was-A	10	30	1	4	0	0	0	1	0		.133	.133	.133	-15	-4	-4	1	0			0	/O	-0.3
Total	2	22	74	9	13	0	0	0	4	2		.176	.197	.176	18	-7	-7	3	2			-1	/O	-0.7

JOHN CASSIDY
Cassidy, John P. b: 1857, Brooklyn, N.Y. d: 7/2/1891, Brooklyn, N.Y. TL, 5'8", 168 lbs. Deb: 4/24/1875

YEAR	TM/L	G	AB	R	H	2B	3B	HR	RBI	BB	SO	AVG	OBP	SLG	PRO+	BR	/A	RC	SB	CS	SBR	FR	POS	TPR
1875	Atl-n	41	165	14	29	3	2	1		1		.176	.181	.236	49	-9	-6	7					PO/1	0.0
	NH-n	6	22	3	3	1	0	0		0		.136	.136	.182	11	-2	-1	1					/1	0.0
	Yr	47	187	17	32	4	2	1		1		.171	.176	.230	45	-11	-7	8						0.0
1876	Har-N	12	47	6	13	2	0	0	8	1	0	.277	.292	.319	95	-0	-0	4				1	/O1	0.0
1877	Har-N	60	251	43	95	10	5	0	27	3	3	.378	.386	.458	184	18	22	45				-5	*O/P	1.3
1878	Chi-N	60	256	33	68	7	1	0	29	9	11	.266	.291	.301	89	-1	-4	23				7	*O/C	0.0
1879	Tro-N	9	37	4	7	1	0	0	1	2	4	.189	.231	.216	52	-2	-2	2				-1	/O1	-0.2

YEAR	TM/L	G	AB	R	H	2B	3B	HR	RBI	BB	SO	AVG	OBP	SLG	PRO+	BR	/A	RC	SB	CS	SBR	FR	POS	TPR
1880	Tro-N	83	352	40	89	14	8	0	29	12	34	.253	.277	.338	102	3	0	34				-5	*O/2	-0.7
1881	Tro-N	85	370	57	82	13	3	1	11	18	21	.222	.258	.281	66	-12	-15	27				-9	*O/S	-2.3
1882	Tro-N	29	121	14	21	3	1	0	9	3	16	.174	.194	.215	32	-9	-8	5				-9	O3	-1.6
1883	Pro-N	89	366	46	87	16	5	0	42	9	38	.238	.256	.309	69	-13	-14	30				0	*O/21	-0.9
1884	Bro-a	106	433	57	109	11	6	2		19		.252	.286	.319	99	0	-0	41				-8	*O/3S	-0.8
1885	Bro-a	54	221	36	47	6	2	1		8		.213	.250	.271	66	-8	-8	15				-7	O	-1.6
Total	10	587	2454	336	618	83	31	4	<u>156</u>	84	<u>127</u>	.252	.278	.316	89	-25	-30	227				-37	O/31S2PC	-6.8

■ JOE CASSIDY
Cassidy, Joseph Phillip b: 2/8/1883, Chester, Pa. d: 3/25/06, Chester, Pa. BR/TR. Deb: 4/18/04

YEAR	TM/L	G	AB	R	H	2B	3B	HR	RBI	BB	SO	AVG	OBP	SLG	PRO+	BR	/A	RC	SB	CS	SBR	FR	POS	TPR
1904	Was-A	152	581	63	140	12	19	1	33	15		.241	.260	.332	90	-9	-8	58	17			12	SO3	0.4
1905	Was-A	151	576	67	124	16	4	1	43	25		.215	.248	.262	66	-24	-21	47	23			33	*S	1.8
Total	2	303	1157	130	264	28	23	2	76	40		.228	.254	.297	78	-33	-29	104	40			45	S/O3	2.2

■ PETE CASSIDY
Cassidy, Peter Francis b: 4/8/1873, Wilmington, Del. d: 7/9/29, Wilmington, Del. BR/TR, 5'10", 165 lbs. Deb: 4/18/1896

YEAR	TM/L	G	AB	R	H	2B	3B	HR	RBI	BB	SO	AVG	OBP	SLG	PRO+	BR	/A	RC	SB	CS	SBR	FR	POS	TPR
1896	Lou-N	49	184	16	39	1	1	0	12	7	7	.212	.256	.228	31	-18	-17	12	5			-7	1S	-1.9
1899	Bro-N	6	20	2	3	1	0	0	4	1		.150	.261	.200	28	-2	-2	1	1			-4	/3S	-0.5
	Was-N	46	178	21	56	13	0	3	32	9		.315	.361	.438	123	5	5	31	5			-1	1/3S	0.4
	Yr	52	198	23	59	14	0	3	36	10		.298	.350	.414	113	3	3	32	6			-5		-0.1
Total	2	101	382	39	98	15	1	3	48	17	<u>7</u>	.257	.306	.325	73	-15	-14	44	11			-12	/1S3	-2.0

■ JACK CASSINI
Cassini, Jack Dempsey "Gabby" or "Scat" b: 10/26/19, Dearborn, Mich. BR/TR, 5'10", 175 lbs. Deb: 4/19/49

YEAR	TM/L	G	AB	R	H	2B	3B	HR	RBI	BB	SO	AVG	OBP	SLG	PRO+	BR	/A	RC	SB	CS	SBR	FR	POS	TPR
1949	Pit-N	8	0	3	0	0	0	0	0	0	0	—	—	—	—	0	0	0	0			0	R	0.0

■ JIM CASTIGLIA
Castiglia, James Vincent b: 9/30/18, Passaic, N.J. BL/TR, 5'11", 200 lbs. Deb: 4/14/42

YEAR	TM/L	G	AB	R	H	2B	3B	HR	RBI	BB	SO	AVG	OBP	SLG	PRO+	BR	/A	RC	SB	CS	SBR	FR	POS	TPR
1942	Phi-A	16	18	2	7	0	0	0	2	1	3	.389	.421	.389	129	1	1	3	0	0	0	-0	/C	0.1

■ PETE CASTIGLIONE
Castiglione, Peter Paul b: 2/13/21, Greenwich, Conn. BR/TR, 5'11", 175 lbs. Deb: 9/10/47

YEAR	TM/L	G	AB	R	H	2B	3B	HR	RBI	BB	SO	AVG	OBP	SLG	PRO+	BR	/A	RC	SB	CS	SBR	FR	POS	TPR
1947	Pit-N	13	50	6	14	0	0	0	1	2	5	.280	.308	.280	55	-3	-3	4	0			1	S	0.0
1948	Pit-N	4	2	0	0	0	0	0	0	0	0	.000	.000	.000	-98	-1	-1	0	1			1	/S	0.0
1949	Pit-N	118	448	57	120	20	2	6	43	20	43	.268	.299	.362	74	-16	-17	49	2			-1	3S/O	-1.4
1950	Pit-N	94	263	29	67	10	3	3	22	23	23	.255	.317	.350	73	-9	-11	29	1			-17	3S/21	-2.4
1951	Pit-N	132	482	62	126	19	4	7	42	34	28	.261	.311	.361	78	-14	-16	55	2			4	3S	-1.0
1952	Pit-N	67	214	27	57	9	1	4	18	17	8	.266	.323	.374	90	-2	-3	27	3	3	-1	6	3/1O	0.4
1953	Pit-N	45	159	14	33	2	1	4	21	5	14	.208	.236	.308	41	-14	-14	11	1	1	-0	4	3	-1.1
	StL-N	67	52	9	9	2	0	0	3	2	5	.173	.204	.212	9	-7	-7	2	0	0	0	8	3/2S	0.0
	Yr	112	211	23	42	4	1	4	24	7	19	.199	.228	.284	33	-21	-21	13	1	1	-0	12		-1.1
1954	StL-N	5	0	1	0	0	0	0	0	0	0	—	—	—	—	0	0	0	0	0	0	0	/3	0.0
Total	8	545	1670	205	426	62	11	24	150	103	126	.255	.300	.349	71	-66	-71	178	10	<u>6</u>		5	3/S21O	-5.5

■ TONY CASTILLO
Castillo, Anthony b: 6/14/57, San Jose, Cal. BR/TR, 6'4", 190 lbs. Deb: 9/22/78

YEAR	TM/L	G	AB	R	H	2B	3B	HR	RBI	BB	SO	AVG	OBP	SLG	PRO+	BR	/A	RC	SB	CS	SBR	FR	POS	TPR
1978	SD-N	5	8	0	1	0	0	0	1	0	2	.125	.125	.125	-33	-1	-1	0	0	0	0	1	/C	0.0

■ MANNY CASTILLO
Castillo, Esteban Manuel Antonio (Cabrera) b: 4/1/57, Santo Domingo, D.R. BB/TR, 5'9", 160 lbs. Deb: 9/01/80

YEAR	TM/L	G	AB	R	H	2B	3B	HR	RBI	BB	SO	AVG	OBP	SLG	PRO+	BR	/A	RC	SB	CS	SBR	FR	POS	TPR
1980	KC-A	7	10	1	2	0	0	0	0	0	0	.200	.200	.200	10	-1	-1	0	0	0	0	2	/32D	0.0
1982	Sea-A	138	506	49	130	29	1	3	49	22	35	.257	.291	.336	70	-20	-22	46	2	8	-4	-28	*3/2	-5.6
1983	Sea-A	91	203	13	42	6	3	0	24	7	20	.207	.237	.266	37	-17	-18	12	1	1	-0	8	31/2PD	-1.0
Total	3	236	719	63	174	35	4	3	73	29	55	.242	.274	.314	59	-38	-41	58	3	9	-5	-18	3/21DP	-6.6

■ JUAN CASTILLO
Castillo, Juan (Bryas) b: 1/25/62, San Pedro De Macoris, D.R. BB/TR, 5'11", 162 lbs. Deb: 4/12/86

YEAR	TM/L	G	AB	R	H	2B	3B	HR	RBI	BB	SO	AVG	OBP	SLG	PRO+	BR	/A	RC	SB	CS	SBR	FR	POS	TPR
1986	Mil-A	26	54	6	9	0	1	0	5	5	12	.167	.250	.204	24	-6	-6	3	1	1	-0	5	2/S3OD	0.0
1987	Mil-A	116	321	44	72	11	4	3	28	33	76	.224	.303	.312	62	-17	-18	33	15	7	0	-9	2S/3	-1.6
1988	Mil-A	54	90	10	20	0	0	0	2	3	14	.222	.247	.222	32	-8	-8	5	2	0	1	7	23S/OD	0.1
1989	Mil-A	3	4	0	0	0	0	0	3	0	2	.000	.000	.000	-99	-1	-1	0	0	0	0	1	/2	0.0
Total	4	199	469	60	101	11	5	3	38	41	104	.215	.284	.279	51	-31	-33	41	18	8	1	4	2/S3DO	-1.5

■ MARTY CASTILLO
Castillo, Martin Horace b: 1/16/57, Long Beach, Cal. BR/TR, 6'1", 190 lbs. Deb: 8/19/81

YEAR	TM/L	G	AB	R	H	2B	3B	HR	RBI	BB	SO	AVG	OBP	SLG	PRO+	BR	/A	RC	SB	CS	SBR	FR	POS	TPR
1981	Det-A	6	8	1	1	0	0	0	0	0	2	.125	.125	.125	-27	-1	-1	0	0	0	0	3	/3CO	0.1
1982	Det-A	1	0	0	0	0	0	0	0	0	0	—	—	—	—	0	0	0	0	0	0	0	/C	0.0
1983	Det-A	67	119	10	23	4	0	2	10	7	22	.193	.238	.277	42	-10	-9	8	2	0	1	4	3C	-0.3
1984	*Det-A	70	141	16	33	5	2	4	17	10	33	.234	.285	.383	83	-4	-3	15	1	0	0	3	C3/D	0.2
1985	Det-A	57	84	4	10	2	0	2	5	2	19	.119	.140	.214	-5	-12	-12	2	0	2	-1	7	C3	-0.5
Total	5	201	352	31	67	11	2	8	32	19	76	.190	.232	.301	46	-27	-26	25	3	2	-0	17	3/CDO	-0.5

■ CARMELO CASTILLO
Castillo, Monte Carmelo b: 6/8/58, San Pedro De Macoris, D.R. BR/TR, 6'1", 185 lbs. Deb: 7/17/82

YEAR	TM/L	G	AB	R	H	2B	3B	HR	RBI	BB	SO	AVG	OBP	SLG	PRO+	BR	/A	RC	SB	CS	SBR	FR	POS	TPR
1982	Cle-A	47	120	11	25	4	0	2	11	6	17	.208	.258	.292	51	-8	-8	9	0	0	0	3	O/D	-0.5
1983	Cle-A	23	36	9	10	2	1	1	3	4	6	.278	.366	.472	124	1	1	6	1	1	-0	2	O/D	0.3
1984	Cle-A	87	211	36	55	9	2	10	36	21	32	.261	.333	.464	116	5	4	30	1	3	-2	3	O/D	-0.2
1985	Cle-A	67	184	27	45	5	1	11	25	11	40	.245	.298	.462	105	0	1	24	3	0	1	1	O/D	0.2
1986	Cle-A	85	205	34	57	9	0	8	32	9	48	.278	.312	.439	103	-0	0	25	2	1	0	7	OD	0.6
1987	Cle-A	89	220	27	55	17	0	11	31	16	52	.250	.301	.477	101	-0	-0	33	1	1	-0	2	DO	0.1
1988	Cle-A	66	176	12	48	8	0	4	14	5	31	.273	.297	.386	87	-3	-3	19	6	2	1	-2	O/D	-0.5
1989	Min-A	94	218	23	56	13	3	8	33	15	40	.257	.308	.454	105	3	1	29	1	2	-1	4	OD	0.3
1990	Min-A	64	137	11	30	4	0	0	12	3	23	.219	.241	.248	35	-12	-13	8	0	1	-1	-0	DO	-1.3
Total	9	622	1507	190	381	71	7	55	197	90	289	.253	.300	.419	94	-14	-17	183	15	11	-2	14	OD	-1.0

■ JOHN CASTINO
Castino, John Anthony b: 10/23/54, Evanston, Ill. BR/TR, 5'11", 175 lbs. Deb: 4/06/79

YEAR	TM/L	G	AB	R	H	2B	3B	HR	RBI	BB	SO	AVG	OBP	SLG	PRO+	BR	/A	RC	SB	CS	SBR	FR	POS	TPR
1979	Min-A	148	393	49	112	13	8	5	52	27	72	.285	.333	.397	92	-3	-5	52	5	2	0	18	*3/S	1.6
1980	Min-A	150	546	67	165	17	7	13	64	29	67	.302	.337	.430	101	5	0	75	7	5	-1	28	*3S	2.8
1981	Min-A	101	381	41	102	13	9	6	36	18	52	.268	.303	.396	94	-1	-4	45	4	5	-2	11	3/2	0.6
1982	Min-A	117	410	48	99	12	6	6	37	36	51	.241	.306	.344	76	-12	-14	41	2	5	-2	5	23/OD	-0.6
1983	Min-A	142	563	83	156	30	4	11	57	62	54	.277	.350	.403	103	6	3	81	4	2	0	7	*2/3D	1.4
1984	Min-A	8	27	5	12	1	0	0	3	5	2	.444	.531	.481	174	4	3	6	0	0	0	-1	/3	0.2
Total	6	666	2320	293	646	86	34	41	249	177	298	.278	.331	.398	95	-1	-15	300	22	19	-5	67	32/SOD	6.0

■ VINCE CASTINO
Castino, Vincent Charles b: 10/11/17, Willisville, Ill. d: 3/6/67, Sacramento, Cal. BR/TR, 5'9", 175 lbs. Deb: 6/24/43

YEAR	TM/L	G	AB	R	H	2B	3B	HR	RBI	BB	SO	AVG	OBP	SLG	PRO+	BR	/A	RC	SB	CS	SBR	FR	POS	TPR
1943	Chi-A	33	101	14	23	1	0	2	16	12	11	.228	.310	.297	78	-3	-3	10	0	0	0	-9	C	-1.0
1944	Chi-A	29	78	8	18	5	0	0	3	10	13	.231	.326	.295	79	-2	-2	8	0	1	-1	1	C	0.0
1945	Chi-A	26	36	2	8	1	0	0	4	3	7	.222	.282	.250	56	-2	-2	2	0	0	0	-2	C	-0.1
Total	3	88	215	24	49	7	0	2	23	25	31	.228	.311	.288	75	-7	-6	20	0	1	-1	-10	/C	-1.1

■ DON CASTLE
Castle, Donald Hardy b: 2/1/50, Kokomo, Ind. BL/TL, 6'1", 205 lbs. Deb: 9/11/73

YEAR	TM/L	G	AB	R	H	2B	3B	HR	RBI	BB	SO	AVG	OBP	SLG	PRO+	BR	/A	RC	SB	CS	SBR	FR	POS	TPR
1973	Tex-A	4	13	0	4	1	0	0	2	1	3	.308	.357	.385	114	0	0	1	0	0	0	0	/D	0.0

■ JOHN CASTLE
Castle, John Francis b: 6/1/1883, Honey Brook, Pa. d: 4/13/29, Philadelphia, Pa. 5'10.5". Deb: 4/30/10

YEAR	TM/L	G	AB	R	H	2B	3B	HR	RBI	BB	SO	AVG	OBP	SLG	PRO+	BR	/A	RC	SB	CS	SBR	FR	POS	TPR
1910	Phi-N	3	4	1	1	0	0	0	0	0	0	.250	.250	.250	44	-0	-0	0	1			0	/O	0.0

YEAR	TM/L	G	AB	R	H	2B	3B	HR	RBI	BB	SO	AVG	OBP	SLG	PRO+	BR	/A	RC	SB	CS	SBR	FR	POS	TPR

■ FOSTER CASTLEMAN
Castleman, Foster Ephraim b: 1/1/31, Nashville, Tenn. BR/TR, 6', 175 lbs. Deb: 8/04/54

YEAR	TM/L	G	AB	R	H	2B	3B	HR	RBI	BB	SO	AVG	OBP	SLG	PRO+	BR	/A	RC	SB	CS	SBR	FR	POS	TPR
1954	NY-N	13	12	0	3	0	0	0	1	0	3	.250	.308	.250	47	-1	-1	1	0	0	0	0	/3	0.0
1955	NY-N	15	28	3	6	1	0	2	4	2	4	.214	.267	.464	89	-1	-1	4	0	0	0	-2	/23	-0.2
1956	NY-N	124	385	33	87	16	3	14	45	15	50	.226	.259	.392	72	-16	-16	37	2	1	0	7	*3/S2	-0.9
1957	NY-N	18	37	7	6	2	0	1	1	2	8	.162	.205	.297	33	-4	-4	2	0	0	0	-2	/32S	-0.4
1958	Bal-A	98	200	15	34	5	0	3	14	16	34	.170	.242	.240	35	-18	-17	12	2	0	1	-19	S/23O	-2.3
Total	5	268	662	58	136	24	3	20	65	35	99	.205	.252	.341	60	-40	-38	55	4	1	1	-17	3/S2O	-3.8

■ LOUIS CASTRO
Castro, Louis Manuel "Jud" b: 1877, Columbia, South America d: Venezuela TR, 5'7", Deb: 4/23/02

YEAR	TM/L	G	AB	R	H	2B	3B	HR	RBI	BB	SO	AVG	OBP	SLG	PRO+	BR	/A	RC	SB	CS	SBR	FR	POS	TPR
1902	Phi-A	42	143	18	35	8	1	1	15	4		.245	.270	.336	66	-6	-7	14	2			-16	2/OS	-2.1

■ DANNY CATER
Cater, Danny Anderson b: 2/25/40, Austin, Tex. BR/TR, 6', 170 lbs. Deb: 4/14/64

YEAR	TM/L	G	AB	R	H	2B	3B	HR	RBI	BB	SO	AVG	OBP	SLG	PRO+	BR	/A	RC	SB	CS	SBR	FR	POS	TPR
1964	Phi-N	60	152	13	45	9	1	1	13	7	15	.296	.327	.388	102	-0	0	18	1	0	0	1	O/13	0.0
1965	Chi-A	142	514	74	139	18	4	14	55	33	65	.270	.318	.403	110	1	5	61	3	3	-1	-12	*O3/1	-1.2
1966	Chi-A	21	60	3	11	1	1	0	4	0	10	.183	.197	.233	25	-6	-5	3	3	1	0	-4	O	-1.0
	KC-A	116	425	47	124	16	3	7	52	28	37	.292	.337	.393	113	5	6	53	1	4	-2	-5	13O	-0.4
	Yr	137	485	50	135	17	4	7	56	28	47	.278	.320	.373	102	-1	1	55	4	5	-2	-8		-1.4
1967	KC-A	142	529	55	143	17	4	4	46	34	56	.270	.319	.340	98	-3	-2	54	4	5	-2	-16	3O1	-2.5
1968	Oak-A	147	504	53	146	28	3	6	62	35	43	.290	.338	.393	127	12	14	61	8	7	-2	-1	*1O/2	0.6
1969	Oak-A	152	584	64	153	24	2	10	76	28	40	.262	.298	.361	87	-14	-11	55	1	4	-2	7	*1O/2	-1.7
1970	NY-A	155	582	64	175	26	5	6	76	34	44	.301	.341	.393	108	1	5	74	4	2	0	-4	*13/O	-0.6
1971	NY-A	121	428	39	118	16	5	4	50	19	25	.276	.310	.364	96	-6	-4	42	0	3	-2	8	13	-0.2
1972	Bos-A	92	317	32	75	17	1	8	39	15	33	.237	.275	.372	87	-5	-6	28	0	1	-1	6	1	-1.1
1973	Bos-A	63	195	30	61	12	0	1	24	10	22	.313	.350	.390	102	2	0	25	0	0	0	2	13/D	0.0
1974	Bos-A	56	126	14	31	5	0	5	20	10	13	.246	.312	.405	98	1	-1	15	1	0	0	1	1D	0.0
1975	StL-N	22	35	3	8	2	0	0	2	1	3	.229	.250	.286	47	-3	-3	3	0	0	0	0	1	-0.3
Total	12	1289	4451	491	1229	191	29	66	519	254	406	.276	.318	.377	102	-16	-1	492	26	30	-10	-17	103/D2	-8.4

■ ELI CATES
Cates, Eli Eldo b: 1/26/1877, Greensfork, Ind. d: 5/29/64, Richmond, Ind. BR/TR, 5'9.5", 175 lbs. Deb: 4/20/08

YEAR	TM/L	G	AB	R	H	2B	3B	HR	RBI	BB	SO	AVG	OBP	SLG	PRO+	BR	/A	RC	SB	CS	SBR	FR	POS	TPR
1908	Was-A	40	59	5	11	1	1	0	3	6		.186	.262	.237	70	-2	-2	4	0			0	P/2	0.1

■ TED CATHER
Cather, Theodore P b: 5/20/1889, Chester, Pa. d: 4/9/45, Elkton, Md. BR/TR, 5'10.5", 178 lbs. Deb: 9/23/12

YEAR	TM/L	G	AB	R	H	2B	3B	HR	RBI	BB	SO	AVG	OBP	SLG	PRO+	BR	/A	RC	SB	CS	SBR	FR	POS	TPR
1912	StL-N	5	19	4	8	1	1	0	2	0	4	.421	.421	.579	176	2	2	5	1			2	/O	0.3
1913	StL-N	67	183	16	39	8	4	0	12	9	24	.213	.250	.301	58	-11	-10	15	7			-5	O/P1	-1.6
1914	StL-N	39	99	11	27	7	0	0	13	3	15	.273	.294	.343	90	-2	-2	11	4			1	O	0.0
	*Bos-N	50	145	19	43	11	2	0	27	7	28	.297	.338	.400	120	3	3	21	7			-4	O	-0.2
	Yr	89	244	30	70	18	2	0	40	10	43	.287	.320	.377	108	1	1	32	11			-3		-0.2
1915	Bos-N	40	102	10	21	3	1	2	18	15	19	.206	.319	.314	96	-1	-0	11	2	4	-2	-5	O	-0.8
Total	4	201	548	60	138	30	8	2	72	34	90	.252	.300	.347	91	-8	-7	62	21	4		-11	O/1P	-2.3

■ HOWDY CATON
Caton, James Howard "Buster" b: 7/16/1896, Zanesville, Ohio d: 1/8/48, Zanesville, Ohio BR/TR, 5'6", 165 lbs. Deb: 9/17/17

YEAR	TM/L	G	AB	R	H	2B	3B	HR	RBI	BB	SO	AVG	OBP	SLG	PRO+	BR	/A	RC	SB	CS	SBR	FR	POS	TPR
1917	Pit-N	14	57	6	12	1	2	0	4	6	7	.211	.286	.298	77	-1	-2	5	0			-2	S	-0.3
1918	Pit-N	80	303	37	71	5	7	0	17	32	16	.234	.312	.297	83	-4	-6	31	12			-7	S	-1.1
1919	Pit-N	39	102	13	18	1	2	0	5	12	10	.176	.263	.225	46	-6	-7	7	2			-11	S3/O	-1.8
1920	Pit-N	98	352	29	83	11	5	0	27	33	19	.236	.305	.295	71	-12	-13	32	4	9	-4	-22	S	-3.7
Total	4	231	814	85	184	18	16	0	53	83	52	.226	.301	.287	72	-24	-27	74	18	9		-42	S/3O	-6.9

■ TOM CATTERSON
Catterson, Thomas Henry b: 8/25/1884, Warwick, R.I. d: 2/5/20, Portland, Maine BL, 5'10", 170 lbs. Deb: 9/19/08

YEAR	TM/L	G	AB	R	H	2B	3B	HR	RBI	BB	SO	AVG	OBP	SLG	PRO+	BR	/A	RC	SB	CS	SBR	FR	POS	TPR
1908	Bro-N	19	68	5	13	1	1	1	2	5		.191	.247	.279	72	-2	-2	5	0			0	O	-0.1
1909	Bro-N	9	18	0	4	0	0	0	1	3		.222	.333	.222	75	-0	-0	1	0			-2	/O	-0.2
Total	2	28	86	5	17	1	1	1	3	8		.198	.266	.267	73	-3	-2	6	0			-2	/O	-0.3

■ JAKE CAULFIELD
Caulfield, John Joseph b: 11/23/17, Los Angles, Cal. d: 12/16/86, San Francisco, Cal BR/TR, 5'11", 170 lbs. Deb: 4/24/46

YEAR	TM/L	G	AB	R	H	2B	3B	HR	RBI	BB	SO	AVG	OBP	SLG	PRO+	BR	/A	RC	SB	CS	SBR	FR	POS	TPR
1946	Phi-A	44	94	13	26	8	0	0	10	4	11	.277	.306	.362	87	-2	-2	10	0	0	0	-6	S/3	-0.7

■ WAYNE CAUSEY
Causey, James Wayne b: 12/26/36, Ruston, La. BL/TR, 5'10.5", 175 lbs. Deb: 6/05/55

YEAR	TM/L	G	AB	R	H	2B	3B	HR	RBI	BB	SO	AVG	OBP	SLG	PRO+	BR	/A	RC	SB	CS	SBR	FR	POS	TPR
1955	Bal-A	68	175	14	34	2	1	1	9	17	25	.194	.269	.234	39	-16	-14	12	0	1	-1	-8	3/2S	-2.1
1956	Bal-A	53	88	7	15	0	1	1	4	8	23	.170	.240	.227	26	-10	-9	5	0	0	0	2	3/2	-0.4
1957	Bal-A	14	10	2	2	0	0	0	1	5	2	.200	.500	.200	105	1	1	2	0	0	0	3	/23	0.4
1961	KC-A	104	312	37	86	14	1	8	49	37	28	.276	.352	.404	101	1	1	46	0	0	0	20	3S/2	2.7
1962	KC-A	117	305	40	77	14	1	4	38	41	30	.252	.345	.344	84	-5	-6	38	2	0	1	2	S3/2	0.0
1963	KC-A	139	554	72	155	32	4	8	44	56	54	.280	.346	.393	103	6	3	77	4	2	0	5	*S/3	1.5
1964	KC-A	157	604	82	170	31	4	8	49	88	65	.281	.379	.386	110	14	12	90	0	1	-1	-1	*S2/3	1.3
1965	KC-A	144	513	48	134	17	8	3	34	61	48	.261	.342	.343	97	-2	-1	63	1	3	-2	-19	S23	-1.6
1966	KC-A	28	79	1	18	0	0	0	5	7	6	.228	.291	.228	53	-5	-4	5	1	0	0	-6	3S	-1.0
	Chi-A	78	164	23	40	8	2	0	13	24	13	.244	.340	.317	97	-1	0	20	2	0	1	-16	2/S3	-1.0
	Yr	106	243	24	58	8	2	0	18	31	19	.239	.325	.288	83	-6	-4	25	3	0	1	-21		-2.0
1967	Chi-A	124	292	21	66	10	3	1	28	32	35	.226	.305	.291	80	-8	-7	27	2	5	-2	-8	2/S	-1.5
1968	Chi-A	59	100	8	18	2	0	0	7	14	7	.180	.287	.200	49	-6	-6	7	0	0	0	-13	2	-1.9
	Cal-A	4	11	0	0	0	0	0	0	0	1	.000	.000	.000	-99	-3	-3	0	0	0	0	1	/2	-0.1
	Yr	63	111	8	18	2	0	0	7	14	8	.162	.262	.180	36	-8	-8	6	0	0	0	-13		-2.0
	Atl-N	16	37	2	4	0	1	1	4	4	4	.108	.108	.243	3	-4	-4	1	0	0	0	-4	/2S3	-0.9
Total	11	1105	3244	357	819	130	26	35	285	390	341	.252	.335	.341	90	-37	-37	394	12	12	-4	-41	S23	-4.6

■ JOHN CAVANAUGH
Cavanaugh, John J. b: 6/5/1900, Scranton, Pa. d: 1/14/61, New Brunswick, N.J 5'9", 158 lbs. Deb: 7/07/19

YEAR	TM/L	G	AB	R	H	2B	3B	HR	RBI	BB	SO	AVG	OBP	SLG	PRO+	BR	/A	RC	SB	CS	SBR	FR	POS	TPR
1919	Phi-N	1	1	0	0	0	0	0	0	0	1	.000	.000	.000	-93	-0	-0	0	0			0	/3	0.0

■ PHIL CAVARRETTA
Cavarretta, Philip Joseph b: 7/19/16, Chicago, Ill. BL/TL, 5'11.5", 175 lbs. Deb: 9/16/34 MC

YEAR	TM/L	G	AB	R	H	2B	3B	HR	RBI	BB	SO	AVG	OBP	SLG	PRO+	BR	/A	RC	SB	CS	SBR	FR	POS	TPR
1934	Chi-N	7	21	5	8	0	1	1	6	2	3	.381	.435	.619	182	2	2	6	1			1	/1	0.3
1935	*Chi-N	146	589	85	162	28	12	8	82	39	61	.275	.322	.404	93	-6	-6	79	4			2	*1	-0.6
1936	Chi-N	124	458	55	125	18	1	9	56	17	36	.273	.306	.376	81	-12	-13	53	8			-2	*1	-2.4
1937	Chi-N	106	329	43	94	18	7	5	56	32	35	.286	.349	.429	106	4	3	50	7			3	O1	0.1
1938	*Chi-N	92	268	29	64	11	4	1	28	14	27	.239	.287	.321	65	-12	-13	25	4			-3	O1	-1.9
1939	Chi-N	22	55	4	15	3	1	0	0	4	3	.273	.322	.364	82	-1	-1	6	2			-1	1/O	-0.3
1940	Chi-N	65	193	34	54	11	4	2	22	31	18	.280	.388	.409	122	6	7	33	3			-1	1	0.1
1941	Chi-N	107	346	46	99	18	4	6	40	53	28	.286	.384	.413	129	13	14	58	7			-10	O1	-0.2
1942	Chi-N	136	482	59	130	28	4	3	54	71	42	.270	.365	.363	118	10	12	71	7			4	O1	1.0
1943	Chi-N	143	530	93	154	27	9	8	73	75	42	.291	.382	.421	134	23	24	89	3			-10	*1/O	0.8
1944	Chi-N	152	614	106	**197**	35	15	5	82	67	42	.321	.390	.451	137	30	31	111	4			-7	*1O	1.2
1945	*Chi-N	132	498	94	177	34	10	6	97	81	34	**.355**	**.449**	.500	167	46	48	119	5			-1	*1O	4.0
1946	Chi-N	139	510	89	150	28	10	8	78	88	54	.294	.401	.435	140	28	29	92	2			5	O1	2.9
1947	Chi-N	127	459	56	144	22	5	2	63	58	35	.314	.391	.397	114	8	11	76	2			-1	*O1	0.5
1948	Chi-N	111	334	41	93	16	5	3	40	35	29	.278	.349	.383	102	1	1	48	4			-0	1O	-0.1
1949	Chi-N	105	360	46	106	22	4	8	49	45	31	.294	.374	.444	122	10	11	62	2			9	1O	1.8
1950	Chi-N	82	256	49	70	11	1	10	31	40	31	.273	.376	.441	115	6	6	45	1			0	1/O	0.3

YEAR	TM/L	G	AB	R	H	2B	3B	HR	RBI	BB	SO	AVG	OBP	SLG	PRO+	BR	/A	RC	SB	CS	SBR	FR	POS	TPR
1951	Chi-N	89	206	24	64	7	1	6	28	27	28	.311	.393	.442	122	8	7	39	0	0	0	4	1M	1.0
1952	Chi-N	41	63	7	15	1	1	1	8	9	3	.238	.333	.333	84	-1	-1	8	0	0	0	1	1M	0.0
1953	Chi-N	27	21	3	6	3	0	0	3	6	3	.286	.444	.429	126	1	1	5	0	0	0	0	HM	0.1
1954	Chi-A	71	158	21	50	6	0	3	24	26	12	.316	.419	.411	124	7	7	31	4	0	1	-3	1/O	0.4
1955	Chi-A	6	4	1	0	0	0	0	0	0	1	.000	.000	.000	-97	-1	-1	0	0	0	0	0	/1	0.0
Total	22	2030	6754	990	1977	347	99	95	920	820	598	.293	.372	.416	118	170	178	1106	65	0		-11	*1O	9.0

■ IKE CAVENEY
Caveney, James Christopher b: 12/10/1894, San Francisco, Cal d: 7/6/49, San Francisco, Cal BR/TR, 5'9", 168 lbs. Deb: 4/12/22

YEAR	TM/L	G	AB	R	H	2B	3B	HR	RBI	BB	SO	AVG	OBP	SLG	PRO+	BR	/A	RC	SB	CS	SBR	FR	POS	TPR
1922	Cin-N	118	394	41	94	12	9	3	54	29	33	.239	.301	.338	66	-21	-20	41	6	6	-2	-6	*S	-1.9
1923	Cin-N	138	488	58	135	21	9	4	63	26	41	.277	.315	.381	84	-13	-12	58	5	4	-1	-0	*S	0.0
1924	Cin-N	95	337	36	92	19	1	4	32	14	21	.273	.310	.371	83	-9	-9	38	2	3	-1	3	S/2	0.0
1925	Cin-N	115	358	38	89	9	5	2	47	28	31	.249	.303	.318	60	-22	-21	36	2	0	1	9	*S	-1.9
Total	4	466	1577	173	410	61	24	13	196	97	126	.260	.307	.354	74	-66	-61	174	15	13	-3	6	S/2	-1.9

■ ANDUJAR CEDENO
Cedeno, Andujar b: 8/21/69, LaRomana, D.R. BR/TR, 6'1", 170 lbs. Deb: 9/02/90

YEAR	TM/L	G	AB	R	H	2B	3B	HR	RBI	BB	SO	AVG	OBP	SLG	PRO+	BR	/A	RC	SB	CS	SBR	FR	POS	TPR
1990	Hou-N	7	8	0	0	0	0	0	0	0	5	.000	.000	.000	-99	-2	-2	0	0	0	0	-0	/S	-0.1

■ CESAR CEDENO
Cedeno, Cesar (Encarnacion) b: 2/25/51, Santo Domingo, D.R. BR/TR, 6'2", 175 lbs. Deb: 6/20/70

YEAR	TM/L	G	AB	R	H	2B	3B	HR	RBI	BB	SO	AVG	OBP	SLG	PRO+	BR	/A	RC	SB	CS	SBR	FR	POS	TPR
1970	Hou-N	90	355	46	110	21	4	7	42	15	57	.310	.341	.451	115	4	6	53	17	4	3	0	0	0.4
1971	Hou-N	161	611	85	161	40	6	10	81	25	102	.264	.296	.398	97	-6	-5	70	20	9	1	-7	*O/1	-1.6
1972	Hou-N	139	559	103	179	39	8	22	82	56	62	.320	.387	.537	163	43	44	115	55	21	4	5	*O	4.9
1973	Hou-N	139	525	86	168	35	2	25	70	41	79	.320	.377	.537	151	34	34	102	56	15	8	10	*O	4.7
1974	Hou-N	160	610	95	164	29	5	26	102	64	103	.269	.342	.461	129	17	20	99	57	17	7	16	*O	3.8
1975	Hou-N	131	500	93	144	31	3	13	63	62	52	.288	.374	.440	135	18	22	85	50	17	5	1	*O	2.4
1976	Hou-N	150	575	89	171	26	5	18	83	55	51	.297	.360	.454	143	22	28	94	58	15	8	3	*O	3.5
1977	Hou-N	141	530	92	148	36	8	14	71	47	50	.279	.350	.457	126	10	17	89	61	14	10	5	*O	2.7
1978	Hou-N	50	192	31	54	8	2	7	23	15	24	.281	.333	.453	127	4	6	31	23	2	6	6	O	1.6
1979	Hou-N	132	470	57	123	27	4	6	54	64	52	.262	.354	.374	105	1	4	63	30	13	1	-5	1O	-0.4
1980	*Hou-N	137	499	71	154	32	8	10	73	66	72	.309	.390	.465	150	27	31	93	48	15	5	-0	*O	3.2
1981	*Hou-N	82	306	42	83	19	0	5	34	24	31	.271	.326	.382	106	-0	2	37	12	7	-1	-1	1O	-0.2
1982	Cin-N	138	492	52	142	35	1	8	57	41	41	.289	.348	.413	110	8	7	67	16	11	-2	-2	*O/1	0.1
1983	Cin-N	98	332	40	77	16	0	9	39	33	53	.232	.307	.361	82	-7	-9	38	13	9	-2	-3	O1	-1.5
1984	Cin-N	110	380	59	105	24	2	10	47	25	54	.276	.323	.429	105	4	2	52	19	3	4	-0	O1	0.1
1985	Cin-N	83	220	24	53	12	0	3	30	19	35	.241	.310	.336	77	-6	-7	23	9	5	-0	-0	O1	-1.0
	*StL-N	28	76	14	33	4	1	6	19	5	7	.434	.469	.750	238	13	13	26	5	1	1	-3	1/O	1.1
	Yr	111	296	38	86	16	1	9	49	24	42	.291	.350	.443	116	8	6	45	14	6	1	-4		0.1
1986	LA-N	37	78	5	18	2	1	0	6	7	13	.231	.294	.282	64	-4	-4	7	1	1	-0	-0	O	-0.6
Total	17	2006	7310	1084	2087	436	60	199	976	664	938	.285	.350	.443	124	180	212	1144	550	179	58	22	*O1	23.2

■ ORLANDO CEPEDA
Cepeda, Orlando Manuel (Penne) "Baby Bull" or "Cha Cha" b: 9/17/37, Ponce, P.R. BR/TR, 6'2", 210 lbs. Deb: 4/15/58 C

YEAR	TM/L	G	AB	R	H	2B	3B	HR	RBI	BB	SO	AVG	OBP	SLG	PRO+	BR	/A	RC	SB	CS	SBR	FR	POS	TPR
1958	SF-N	148	603	88	188	38	4	25	96	29	84	.312	.346	.512	126	18	20	97	15	11	-2	-3	*1	0.6
1959	SF-N	151	605	92	192	35	4	27	105	33	100	.317	.358	.522	134	25	26	110	23	9	2	-7	*1O/3	1.1
1960	SF-N	151	569	81	169	36	3	24	96	34	91	.297	.345	.497	135	20	24	95	15	6	1	-5	O1	1.4
1961	SF-N	152	585	105	182	28	4	46	142	39	91	.311	.363	.609	158	41	44	118	12	8	-1	-5	1O	2.7
1962	*SF-N	162	625	105	191	26	1	35	114	37	97	.306	.350	.518	132	24	25	108	10	4	1	-7	*1/O	1.3
1963	SF-N	156	579	100	183	33	4	34	97	37	70	.316	.350	.563	166	45	45	113	8	3	1	-7	*1/O	3.9
1964	SF-N	142	529	75	161	27	2	31	97	43	83	.304	.366	.539	148	35	33	101	9	4	0	-3	*1/O	2.7
1965	SF-N	33	34	1	6	1	0	1	5	3	9	.176	.243	.294	49	-2	-2	2	0	0	0	-0	/1O	-0.2
1966	SF-N	19	49	5	14	2	0	3	15	4	11	.286	.352	.510	132	2	2	9	0	1	-1	-2	/O1	0.0
	StL-N	123	452	65	137	24	0	17	58	34	69	.303	.369	.469	130	19	19	75	9	8	-2	-6	*1	0.4
	Yr	142	501	70	151	26	0	20	73	38	80	.301	.367	.473	130	22	21	83	9	9	-3	-8		0.4
1967	*StL-N	151	563	91	183	37	0	25	111	62	75	.325	.403	.524	166	47	48	118	11	2	2	-0	*1	4.6
1968	*StL-N	157	600	71	149	26	2	16	73	43	96	.248	.306	.378	107	3	4	68	8	6	-1	-5	*1	-0.9
1969	*Atl-N	154	573	74	147	28	2	22	88	55	76	.257	.327	.428	109	6	6	79	12	5	1	3	*1	-0.2
1970	Atl-N	148	567	87	173	33	0	34	111	47	75	.305	.368	.543	133	31	26	108	6	5	-1	3	*1	1.6
1971	Atl-N	71	250	31	69	10	1	14	44	22	29	.276	.335	.492	124	9	8	35	3	6	-3	2	1	0.2
1972	Atl-N	28	84	6	25	3	0	4	9	7	17	.298	.352	.476	122	3	3	14	0	0	0	1	1	0.2
	Oak-A	3	3	0	0	0	0	0	0	0	0	.000	.000	.000	-99	-1	-1	0	0	0	0	0	H	0.0
1973	Bos-A	142	550	51	159	25	0	20	86	50	81	.289	.352	.444	116	16	12	79	0	2	-1	0	*D	1.1
1974	KC-A	33	107	3	23	5	0	1	18	9	16	.215	.282	.290	61	-5	-6	8	1	0	0	0	D	-0.5
Total	17	2124	7927	1131	2351	417	27	379	1365	588	1170	.297	.353	.499	133	337	337	1338	142	80	-5	-41	*1OD/3	20.0

■ ED CERMAK
Cermak, Edward Hugo b: 3/10/1882, Cleveland, Ohio d: 11/22/11, Cleveland, Ohio BR/TR, 5'11", 170 lbs. Deb: 9/09/01

YEAR	TM/L	G	AB	R	H	2B	3B	HR	RBI	BB	SO	AVG	OBP	SLG	PRO+	BR	/A	RC	SB	CS	SBR	FR	POS	TPR
1901	Cle-A	1	4	0	0	0	0	0	0	0	0	.000	.000	.000	-99	-1	-1	0	0			1	/O	0.0

■ RICK CERONE
Cerone, Richard Aldo b: 5/19/54, Newark, N.J. BR/TR, 5'11", 192 lbs. Deb: 8/17/75

YEAR	TM/L	G	AB	R	H	2B	3B	HR	RBI	BB	SO	AVG	OBP	SLG	PRO+	BR	/A	RC	SB	CS	SBR	FR	POS	TPR
1975	Cle-A	7	12	1	3	1	0	0	0	1	0	.250	.308	.333	81	-0	-0	1	0	0	0	-0	/C	0.0
1976	Cle-A	7	16	1	2	0	0	0	1	0	2	.125	.125	.125	-27	-3	-2	0	0	0	0	1	/CD	-0.1
1977	Tor-A	31	100	7	20	4	0	1	10	6	12	.200	.245	.270	40	-8	-8	6	0	0	0	-2	C	-0.9
1978	Tor-A	88	282	25	63	8	2	3	20	23	32	.223	.284	.298	63	-13	-14	23	0	3	-2	3	C/D	-1.0
1979	Tor-A	136	469	47	112	27	4	7	61	37	40	.239	.296	.358	75	-17	-17	50	1	4	-2	-9	*C	-2.2
1980	*NY-A	147	519	70	144	30	4	14	85	32	56	.277	.327	.432	108	3	4	70	1	3	-2	6	*C	1.6
1981	*NY-A	71	234	23	57	13	2	2	21	12	24	.244	.280	.342	80	-7	-7	20	0	2	-1	-6	C	-1.1
1982	NY-A	89	300	29	68	10	0	5	28	19	27	.227	.275	.310	61	-16	-16	23	2	2	-1	-7	C	-1.8
1983	NY-A	80	246	18	54	7	0	2	22	15	29	.220	.267	.272	51	-17	-16	18	0	0	0	-1	C/3	-1.2
1984	NY-A	38	120	8	25	3	0	2	13	9	15	.208	.269	.283	55	-8	-7	9	1	0	0	3	C	0.0
1985	Atl-N	96	282	15	61	9	0	3	25	29	25	.216	.292	.280	57	-14	-16	20	0	3	-2	-8	C	-2.3
1986	Mil-A	68	216	22	56	14	0	4	18	15	28	.259	.310	.380	84	-4	-5	25	1	1	-0	7	C	0.6
1987	NY-A	113	284	28	69	12	1	4	23	30	46	.243	.324	.335	76	-10	-9	31	0	1	-1	5	*C/P1	0.4
1988	Bos-A	84	264	31	71	13	1	3	27	20	32	.269	.328	.360	89	-3	-4	31	0	0	0	-4	C/D	-0.4
1989	Bos-A	102	296	28	72	16	1	4	48	34	40	.243	.325	.345	84	-4	-6	33	0	0	0	2	C/OD	0.0
1990	NY-A	49	139	12	42	6	0	2	11	5	13	.302	.326	.388	99	-0	-1	17	0	0	0	-3	C/2D	-0.1
Total	16	1206	3779	365	919	173	15	56	413	287	421	.243	.300	.341	76	-121	-125	377	4	19	-10	-12	*C/D1P203	-8.5

■ BOB CERV
Cerv, Robert Henry b: 5/5/26, Weston, Neb. BR/TR, 6', 200 lbs. Deb: 8/01/51

YEAR	TM/L	G	AB	R	H	2B	3B	HR	RBI	BB	SO	AVG	OBP	SLG	PRO+	BR	/A	RC	SB	CS	SBR	FR	POS	TPR
1951	NY-A	12	28	4	6	1	0	0	2	4	6	.214	.313	.250	55	-2	-2	2	0	0	0	-1	O	-0.2
1952	NY-A	36	87	11	21	3	2	1	8	9	22	.241	.313	.356	91	-2	-1	10	0	1	-1	1	O	-0.1
1953	NY-A	8	6	0	0	0	0	0	0	1	1	.000	.143	.000	-61	-1	-1	0	0	0	0	0	H	0.0
1954	NY-A	56	100	14	26	6	0	5	13	11	17	.260	.333	.470	122	5	4	14	0	2	-1	-4	O	-0.2
1955	*NY-A	55	85	17	29	4	2	5	25	7	16	.341	.411	.541	157	6	7	20	0	0	-1	-1	O	0.6
1956	*NY-A	54	115	16	35	5	6	3	25	18	13	.304	.398	.530	148	7	8	24	0	1	-1	1	O	0.6
1957	KC-A	124	345	35	94	14	2	11	44	20	64	.272	.314	.420	97	-2	-2	42	1	1	-0	-3	O	-1.0
1958	KC-A	141	515	93	157	20	7	38	104	50	82	.305	.372	.592	158	41	40	106	3	3	-1	13	*O	4.4
1959	KC-A	125	463	61	132	22	4	20	87	35	87	.285	.339	.479	120	13	11	72	3	2	-1	2	*O	0.8

YEAR	TM/L	G	AB	R	H	2B	3B	HR	RBI	BB	SO	AVG	OBP	SLG	PRO+	BR	/A	RC	SB	CS	SBR	FR	POS	TPR
1960	KC-A	23	78	14	20	1	1	6	12	10	17	.256	.341	.526	130	3	3	14	0	0	0	1	O	0.3
	*NY-A	87	216	32	54	11	1	8	28	30	36	.250	.349	.421	114	2	4	32	0	0	0	2	O/1	0.4
	Yr	110	294	46	74	12	2	14	40	40	53	.252	.347	.449	119	6	7	46	0	0	0	3		0.7
1961	LA-A	18	57	3	9	3	0	2	6	1	8	.158	.172	.316	25	-6	-7	2	0	0	0	-3	O	-0.9
	NY-A	57	118	17	32	5	1	6	20	12	17	.271	.344	.483	125	3	4	18	1	0	0	2	O/1	0.5
	Yr	75	175	20	41	8	1	8	26	13	25	.234	.291	.429	91	-3	-3	19	1	0	0	-1		-0.4
1962	NY-A	14	17	1	2	1	0	0	0	2	3	.118	.250	.176	18	-2	-2	1	0	0	0	0	/O	-0.1
	Hou-N	19	31	2	7	0	0	2	3	2	10	.226	.273	.419	89	-1	-1	3	0	0	0	-1	/O	-0.1
Total	12	829	2261	320	624	96	26	105	374	212	392	.276	.343	.481	122	62	63	361	12	10	-2	11	O/1	5.0

■ RON CEY
Cey, Ronald Charles b: 2/15/48, Tacoma, Wash.   BR/TR, 5'10", 185 lbs.   Deb: 9/03/71

YEAR	TM/L	G	AB	R	H	2B	3B	HR	RBI	BB	SO	AVG	OBP	SLG	PRO+	BR	/A	RC	SB	CS	SBR	FR	POS	TPR
1971	LA-N	2	2	0	0	0	0	0	0	0	2	.000	.000	.000	-99	-1	-1	0	0	0	0	0	H	0.0
1972	LA-N	11	37	3	10	1	0	1	3	7	10	.270	.400	.378	125	1	2	6	0	0	0	-2	3	0.0
1973	LA-N	152	507	60	124	18	4	15	80	74	77	.245	.343	.385	106	2	5	66	1	1	-0	16	*3	1.8
1974	*LA-N	159	577	88	151	20	2	18	97	76	68	.262	.355	.397	115	9	12	82	1	1	-0	17	*3	2.6
1975	LA-N	158	566	72	160	29	2	25	101	78	74	.283	.376	.473	141	27	30	101	5	2	0	-4	*3	2.6
1976	LA-N	145	502	69	139	18	3	23	80	89	74	.277	.389	.462	144	29	30	92	0	4	-2	11	*3	3.9
1977	*LA-N	153	564	77	136	22	3	30	110	93	106	.241	.351	.450	114	11	11	92	3	4	-2	17	*3	2.5
1978	*LA-N	159	555	84	150	32	0	23	84	96	96	.270	.384	.452	134	27	27	99	2	5	-2	5	*3	3.0
1979	LA-N	150	487	77	137	20	1	28	81	86	85	.281	.391	.499	143	29	30	97	3	3	-1	-1	*3	2.3
1980	LA-N	157	551	81	140	25	0	28	77	69	92	.254	.342	.452	122	14	16	84	2	2	-1	7	*3	2.2
1981	*LA-N	85	312	42	90	15	2	13	50	40	55	.288	.375	.474	145	16	18	55	0	2	-1	7	3	2.1
1982	LA-N	150	556	62	141	23	1	24	79	57	99	.254	.327	.428	113	6	8	76	3	2	-0	11	*3	1.7
1983	Chi-N	159	581	73	160	33	1	24	90	62	85	.275	.350	.460	117	17	14	90	0	0	-0	-20	*3	-1.2
1984	*Chi-N	146	505	71	121	27	0	25	97	61	108	.240	.329	.442	105	9	3	74	3	2	-0	-20	*3	-1.7
1985	Chi-N	145	500	64	116	18	2	22	63	58	106	.232	.317	.408	91	0	-6	65	1	1	-0	-7	*3	-1.3
1986	Chi-N	97	256	42	70	21	0	13	36	44	66	.273	.386	.508	134	16	14	53	0	0	0	-6	3	0.6
1987	Oak-A	45	104	12	23	6	0	4	11	22	32	.221	.362	.394	108	1	2	16	0	0	0	-1	D/13	0.0
Total	17	2073	7162	977	1868	328	21	316	1139	1012	1235	.261	.357	.445	121	216	215	1149	24	29	-10	31	*3/D1	21.1

■ ELIO CHACON
Chacon, Elio (Rodirguez) b: 10/26/36, Caracas, Venez.   BR/TR, 5'9", 160 lbs.   Deb: 4/20/60

YEAR	TM/L	G	AB	R	H	2B	3B	HR	RBI	BB	SO	AVG	OBP	SLG	PRO+	BR	/A	RC	SB	CS	SBR	FR	POS	TPR
1960	Cin-N	49	116	14	21	1	0	0	7	14	23	.181	.275	.190	29	-11	-11	8	7	1	2	6	2/O	0.0
1961	*Cin-N	61	132	26	35	4	2	2	5	21	22	.265	.374	.371	97	1	0	20	1	4	-2	3	2/O	0.6
1962	NY-N	118	368	49	87	10	3	2	27	76	64	.236	.369	.296	80	-6	-7	44	12	7	-1	-3	*S/23	0.0
Total	3	228	616	89	143	15	5	4	39	111	109	.232	.353	.292	74	-17	-18	71	20	12	-1	6	S/2O3	0.6

■ CHET CHADBOURNE
Chadbourne, Chester James "Pop" b: 10/28/1884, Parkman, Me.   d: 6/21/43, Los Angeles, Cal.   BL/TR, 5'9", 170 lbs.   Deb: 9/17/06

YEAR	TM/L	G	AB	R	H	2B	3B	HR	RBI	BB	SO	AVG	OBP	SLG	PRO+	BR	/A	RC	SB	CS	SBR	FR	POS	TPR
1906	Bos-A	11	43	7	13	1	0	0	3		3	.302	.348	.326	113	1	1	5	1			3	2/S	0.4
1907	Bos-A	10	38	0	11	0	0	0	1		7	.289	.400	.289	124	2	2	5	1			-0	O	0.1
1914	KC-F	147	581	92	161	22	8	1	37	69	49	.277	.359	.344	107	5	8	91	42			9	*O	0.9
1915	KC-F	152	587	75	133	16	9	1	35	62	29	.227	.307	.290	80	-15	-12	65	29			1	*O	-2.0
1918	Bos-N	27	104	9	27	2	1	0	6	5	5	.260	.300	.298	86	-2	-2	11	5			-1	O	-0.4
Total	5	347	1353	183	345	41	18	2	82	146	83	.255	.333	.316	95	-11	-4	178	78			11	O/2S	-1.0

■ DAVE CHALK
Chalk, David Lee b: 8/30/50, Del Rio, Tex.   BR/TR, 5'10", 175 lbs.   Deb: 9/04/73

YEAR	TM/L	G	AB	R	H	2B	3B	HR	RBI	BB	SO	AVG	OBP	SLG	PRO+	BR	/A	RC	SB	CS	SBR	FR	POS	TPR
1973	Cal-A	24	69	14	16	2	0	0	6	9	13	.232	.329	.261	74	-3	-2	6	0	0	0	2	S	0.3
1974	Cal-A	133	465	44	117	9	3	5	31	30	57	.252	.307	.316	84	-12	-9	41	10	10	-3	-2	S3	-0.5
1975	Cal-A	149	513	59	140	24	2	3	56	66	49	.273	.358	.345	107	2	6	64	6	9	-4	6	*3	1.1
1976	Cal-A	142	438	39	95	14	1	0	33	49	62	.217	.310	.253	71	-17	-13	36	0	0	0	4	*S3	-0.2
1977	Cal-A	149	519	58	144	27	2	3	45	52	69	.277	.349	.355	96	-4	-1	65	12	8	-1	3	*3/2S	-0.7
1978	Cal-A	135	470	42	119	12	0	1	34	38	34	.253	.318	.285	74	-17	-15	43	5	8	-3	-20	S23/D	-2.9
1979	Tex-A	9	8	0	2	0	0	0	0	0	0	.250	.250	.250	36	-1	-1	0	0	0	0	-0	/S2	0.0
	Oak-A	66	212	15	47	6	0	2	13	29	14	.222	.318	.278	66	-10	-9	20	2	1	0	-17	2S3	-2.1
	Yr	75	220	15	49	6	0	2	13	29	14	.223	.316	.277	65	-11	-10	20	2	1	0	-17		-2.1
1980	*KC-A	69	167	19	42	10	1	1	20	18	27	.251	.332	.341	84	-3	-3	19	1	1	-0	-3	32/SD	-0.5
1981	KC-A	27	49	2	11	3	0	0	5	4	2	.224	.283	.286	62	-2	-2	4	0	1	-1	-2	32/S	-0.3
Total	9	903	2910	292	733	107	9	15	243	295	327	.252	.328	.310	85	-67	-48	299	36	38	-12	-35	3S2/D	-5.8

■ JOE CHAMBERLAIN
Chamberlain, Joseph Jeremiah b: 5/10/10, San Francisco, Cal d: 1/28/83, San Francisco, Cal.   BR/TR, 6'1", 175 lbs.   Deb: 4/17/34

YEAR	TM/L	G	AB	R	H	2B	3B	HR	RBI	BB	SO	AVG	OBP	SLG	PRO+	BR	/A	RC	SB	CS	SBR	FR	POS	TPR
1934	Chi-A	43	141	13	34	5	1	2	17	6	38	.241	.272	.333	54	-10	-10	13	1	1	-0	-6	S3/2	-1.3

■ WES CHAMBERLAIN
Chamberlain, Wesley Polk b: 4/13/66, Chicago, Ill.   BR/TR, 6'2", 210 lbs.   Deb: 8/31/90

YEAR	TM/L	G	AB	R	H	2B	3B	HR	RBI	BB	SO	AVG	OBP	SLG	PRO+	BR	/A	RC	SB	CS	SBR	FR	POS	TPR
1990	Phi-N	18	46	9	13	3	0	2	4	1	9	.283	.298	.478	110	0	0	7	4	0	1	-0	O	0.1

■ AL CHAMBERS
Chambers, Albert Eugene b: 3/24/61, Harrisburg, Pa.   BL/TL, 6'4", 217 lbs.   Deb: 7/23/83

YEAR	TM/L	G	AB	R	H	2B	3B	HR	RBI	BB	SO	AVG	OBP	SLG	PRO+	BR	/A	RC	SB	CS	SBR	FR	POS	TPR
1983	Sea-A	31	67	11	14	3	0	1	7	18	20	.209	.376	.299	85	-0	-1	9	0	1	-1	0	D/O	0.0
1984	Sea-A	22	49	4	11	1	0	1	4	3	12	.224	.269	.306	60	-3	-3	4	2	1	0	-1	O/D	-0.4
1985	Sea-A	4	4	0	0	0	0	0	0	0	2	.000	.000	.000	-99	-1	-1	0	0	0	0	0	/H	0.0
Total	3	57	120	15	25	4	0	2	11	21	34	.208	.326	.292	71	-4	-4	13	2	2	-1	-1	/DO	-0.4

■ CHRIS CHAMBLISS
Chambliss, Carroll Christopher b: 12/26/48, Dayton, O.   BL/TR, 6'1", 195 lbs.   Deb: 5/28/71   C

YEAR	TM/L	G	AB	R	H	2B	3B	HR	RBI	BB	SO	AVG	OBP	SLG	PRO+	BR	/A	RC	SB	CS	SBR	FR	POS	TPR
1971	Cle-A	111	415	49	114	20	4	9	48	40	83	.275	.341	.407	102	6	2	58	2	0	1	-5	*1	-0.7
1972	Cle-A	121	466	51	136	27	2	6	44	26	63	.292	.329	.397	112	8	6	59	3	4	-2	-6	*1	-1.4
1973	Cle-A	155	572	70	156	30	2	11	53	58	76	.273	.343	.390	104	5	4	74	4	8	-4	7	*1	-0.1
1974	Cle-A	17	67	8	22	4	0	0	7	5	5	.328	.375	.388	121	2	2	9	0	1	-1	-2	1	-0.1
	NY-A	110	400	38	97	16	3	6	43	23	43	.243	.284	.343	82	-11	-10	38	0	0	0	7	*1	-0.7
	Yr	127	467	46	119	20	3	6	50	28	48	.255	.297	.349	87	-10	-8	47	0	1	-1	5		-0.8
1975	NY-A	150	562	66	171	38	4	9	72	29	50	.304	.340	.434	102	11	13	77	0	1	-1	3	*1	0.7
1976	*NY-A	156	641	79	188	32	6	17	96	27	80	.293	.325	.441	124	15	16	90	2	1	0	-2	*1/D	0.7
1977	*NY-A	157	600	90	172	32	6	17	90	45	73	.287	.338	.445	113	9	10	85	4	0	1	-5	*1	-0.2
1978	*NY-A	162	625	81	171	26	3	12	90	41	73	.274	.323	.382	100	-3	-1	79	2	1	0	4	*1/D	-0.2
1979	NY-A	149	554	61	155	27	3	18	63	34	53	.280	.327	.437	106	2	3	78	3	2	-0	0	*1D	-0.3
1980	Atl-N	158	602	83	170	37	2	18	72	49	73	.282	.340	.440	113	12	10	90	7	3	0	-2	*1	0.1
1981	Atl-N	107	404	44	110	25	2	8	51	44	41	.272	.345	.403	109	6	5	56	4	1	1	7	*1	1.0
1982	*Atl-N	157	534	57	144	25	2	20	86	57	57	.270	.340	.436	111	11	8	79	7	3	0	14	*1	1.5
1983	Atl-N	131	447	59	125	24	2	20	78	63	68	.280	.369	.481	124	20	16	78	2	7	-4	0	*1	0.7
1984	Atl-N	135	389	47	100	14	0	9	44	58	54	.257	.355	.362	95	3	-1	51	1	2	-1	2	*1	-0.3
1985	Atl-N	101	170	16	40	7	0	3	21	18	22	.235	.309	.329	74	-5	-6	17	0	0	0	2	1	-0.5
1986	Atl-N	97	122	13	38	8	0	2	14	15	24	.311	.387	.426	117	4	4	20	0	2	-1	2	1	0.0
1988	NY-A	1	1	0	0	0	0	0	0	0	1	.000	.000	.000	-99	-0	-0	0	0	0	0	0	/H	0.0
Total	17	2175	7571	912	2109	392	42	185	972	632	926	.279	.336	.415	108	94	80	1036	40	35	-9	25	*1/D	0.2

■ MIKE CHAMPION
Champion, Robert Michael b: 2/10/55, Montgomery, Ala.   BR/TR, 6', 185 lbs.   Deb: 9/14/76

YEAR	TM/L	G	AB	R	H	2B	3B	HR	RBI	BB	SO	AVG	OBP	SLG	PRO+	BR	/A	RC	SB	CS	SBR	FR	POS	TPR
1976	SD-N	11	38	4	9	2	0	1	2	1	3	.237	.256	.368	82	-1	-1	3	0	0	0	-4	2	-0.4
1977	SD-N	150	507	35	116	14	6	1	43	27	85	.229	.271	.286	55	-36	-30	39	3	3	-1	-26	*2	-4.9

YEAR	TM/L	G	AB	R	H	2B	3B	HR	RBI	BB	SO	AVG	OBP	SLG	PRO+	BR	/A	RC	SB	CS	SBR	FR	POS	TPR
1978	SD-N	32	53	3	12	0	2	0	4	5	13	.226	.293	.302	72	-2	-2	5	0	0	0	2	2/3	0.1
Total	3	193	598	42	137	16	8	2	49	33	101	.229	.272	.293	58	-40	-33	47	3	3	-1	-28	2/3	-5.2

■ FRANK CHANCE

Chance, Frank Leroy "Husk" or "The Peerless Leader"
b: 9/9/1877, Fresno, Cal. d: 9/15/24, Los Angeles, Cal. BR/TR, 6', 190 lbs. Deb: 4/29/1898 MH

YEAR	TM/L	G	AB	R	H	2B	3B	HR	RBI	BB	SO	AVG	OBP	SLG	PRO+	BR	/A	RC	SB	CS	SBR	FR	POS	TPR
1898	Chi-N	53	147	32	41	4	3	1	14	7		.279	.338	.367	105	1	1	21	7			-4	CO/1	-0.1
1899	Chi-N	64	192	37	55	6	2	1	22	15		.286	.344	.354	97	-1	-0	28	10			-4	C/O1	0.0
1900	Chi-N	56	149	26	44	9	3	0	13	15		.295	.403	.396	129	6	7	28	8			2	C/1	1.3
1901	Chi-N	69	241	38	67	12	4	0	36	29		.278	.367	.361	118	6	7	43	27			-6	OC/1	-0.2
1902	Chi-N	75	240	39	69	9	4	1	31	35		.287	.396	.371	143	13	14	47	27			-4	1C/O	1.2
1903	Chi-N	125	441	83	144	24	10	2	81	78		.327	.428	.440	154	32	34	115	67			-3	*1/C	2.6
1904	Chi-N	124	451	89	140	16	10	6	49	36		.310	.361	.430	146	24	24	88	42			12	*1/C	3.1
1905	Chi-N	118	392	92	124	16	12	2	70	78		.316	.430	.434	154	33	31	93	38			2	*1M	2.8
1906	*Chi-N	136	474	103	151	24	10	3	71	70		.319	.406	.430	154	37	33	111	57			-0	*1M	3.0
1907	*Chi-N	111	382	58	112	19	2	1	49	51		.293	.376	.361	126	16	14	67	35			7	*1M	2.1
1908	*Chi-N	129	452	65	123	27	4	2	55	37		.272	.327	.363	117	11	9	62	27			4	*1M	1.2
1909	Chi-N	93	324	53	88	16	4	0	46	30		.272	.341	.346	110	5	4	48	29			-1	1M	0.1
1910	*Chi-N	88	295	54	88	12	8	0	36	37	15	.298	.395	.393	131	13	13	52	16			-2	1M	1.1
1911	Chi-N	31	88	23	21	6	3	1	17	25	13	.239	.432	.409	136	6	6	20	9			-2	1M	0.3
1912	Chi-N	2	5	2	1	0	0	0	0	3		.200	.500	.200	96	0	0	1	1			-0	/1M	0.0
1913	NY-A	12	24	3	5	0	0	0	6	8	1	.208	.406	.208	81	0	0	3	1			1	/1M	0.1
1914	NY-A	1	0	0	0	0	0	0	0	0	0	—	—	—	—	0	0	0	0			0	/1M	0.0
Total	17	1287	4297	797	1273	200	79	20	596	554	29	.296	.383	.394	134	202	197	827	401			1	1C/O	18.6

■ BOB CHANCE

Chance, Robert b: 9/10/40, Statesboro, Ga. BL/TR, 6'2", 196 lbs. Deb: 9/04/63

YEAR	TM/L	G	AB	R	H	2B	3B	HR	RBI	BB	SO	AVG	OBP	SLG	PRO+	BR	/A	RC	SB	CS	SBR	FR	POS	TPR
1963	Cle-A	16	52	5	15	4	0	2	7	1	10	.288	.302	.481	116	1	1	7	0	1	-1	-2	O	-0.1
1964	Cle-A	120	390	45	109	16	1	14	75	40	101	.279	.351	.433	118	9	9	58	3	3	-1	-11	1O	-0.6
1965	Was-A	72	199	20	51	9	0	4	14	18	44	.256	.318	.362	94	-2	-2	23	0	1	-1	-1	1/O	-0.5
1966	Was-A	37	57	1	10	3	0	1	8	2	23	.175	.203	.281	38	-5	-5	3	0	0	0	-1	1	-0.6
1967	Was-A	27	42	5	9	2	0	3	7	7	13	.214	.340	.476	144	2	2	8	0	0	0	-0	1	0.1
1969	Cal-A	5	7	0	1	0	0	0	1	0	4	.143	.143	.143	-21	-1	-1	0	0	0	0	-0	/1	-0.1
Total	6	277	747	76	195	34	1	24	112	68	195	.261	.326	.406	106	4	5	98	3	5	-2	-16	1/O	-1.8

■ DARREL CHANEY

Chaney, Darrel Lee b: 3/9/48, Hammond, Ind. BB/TR, 6'2", 188 lbs. Deb: 4/11/69

YEAR	TM/L	G	AB	R	H	2B	3B	HR	RBI	BB	SO	AVG	OBP	SLG	PRO+	BR	/A	RC	SB	CS	SBR	FR	POS	TPR
1969	Cin-N	93	209	21	40	5	2	0	15	24	75	.191	.278	.234	43	-15	-16	15	1	0	0	-12	S	-1.8
1970	*Cin-N	57	95	7	22	3	0	1	4	3	26	.232	.263	.295	49	-7	-7	8	1	1	-0	5	S2/3	0.3
1971	Cin-N	10	24	2	3	0	0	0	1	1	3	.125	.160	.125	-19	-4	-4	0	0	1	-1	-0	/S23	-0.3
1972	*Cin-N	83	196	29	49	7	2	2	19	29	28	.250	.347	.337	101	-0	1	24	1	3	-2	-7	S23	0.0
1973	*Cin-N	105	227	27	41	7	1	0	14	26	50	.181	.268	.220	39	-19	-18	15	4	3	-1	12	S23	0.5
1974	Cin-N	117	135	27	27	6	1	2	16	26	33	.200	.329	.304	79	-3	-3	14	1	2	-1	17	32S	1.5
1975	*Cin-N	71	160	18	35	6	0	2	26	14	38	.219	.282	.294	59	-9	-9	14	3	0	1	17	S23	1.4
1976	Atl-N	153	496	42	125	20	8	1	50	54	92	.252	.327	.331	82	-8	-11	54	5	7	-3	0	*S/23	0.0
1977	Atl-N	74	209	22	42	7	2	3	15	17	44	.201	.261	.297	44	-15	-18	15	0	0	0	4	S2	-0.6
1978	Atl-N	89	245	27	55	9	1	3	20	25	48	.224	.296	.306	62	-10	-13	24	1	0	0	-6	S/32	-1.2
1979	Atl-N	63	117	15	19	5	0	0	10	19	34	.162	.279	.205	32	-10	-11	8	2	1	0	-3	S/23C	-1.0
Total	11	915	2113	237	458	75	17	14	190	238	471	.217	.297	.288	61	-101	-110	191	19	18	-5	26	S23/C	-1.2

■ LES CHANNELL

Channell, Lester Clark "Goat" or "Gint" b: 3/3/1886, Crestline, Ohio d: 5/8/54, Denver, Colo. BL/TL, 6', 180 lbs. Deb: 5/11/10

YEAR	TM/L	G	AB	R	H	2B	3B	HR	RBI	BB	SO	AVG	OBP	SLG	PRO+	BR	/A	RC	SB	CS	SBR	FR	POS	TPR
1910	NY-A	6	19	3	6	0	0	0	3	2		.316	.381	.316	112	0	0	3	2			-1	/O	0.0
1914	NY-A	1	1	0	1	0	0	0	0	0		1.000	1.000	2.000	803	1	1	2	0			0	H	0.1
Total	2	7	20	3	7	1	0	0	3	2	0	.350	.409	.400	145	1	1	5	2			-1	/O	0.1

■ CHARLIE CHANT

Chant, Charles Joseph b: 8/7/51, Bell, Cal. BR/TR, 6', 190 lbs. Deb: 9/12/75

YEAR	TM/L	G	AB	R	H	2B	3B	HR	RBI	BB	SO	AVG	OBP	SLG	PRO+	BR	/A	RC	SB	CS	SBR	FR	POS	TPR
1975	Oak-A	5	5	1	0	0	0	0	0	0	0	.000	.000	.000	-99	-1	-1	0	0	0	0	0	/OD	0.0
1976	StL-N	15	14	0	2	0	0	0	0	0	4	.143	.143	.143	-19	-2	-2	0	0	0	0	2	O	0.0
Total	2	20	19	1	2	0	0	0	0	0	4	.105	.105	.105	-40	-3	-3	0	0	0	0	2	/OD	0.0

■ ED CHAPLIN

Chaplin, Bert Edgar (b: Bert Edgar Chapman) b: 9/25/1893, Pelzer, S.C. d: 8/15/78, Sanford, Fla. BL/TR, 5'7", 158 lbs. Deb: 9/04/20

YEAR	TM/L	G	AB	R	H	2B	3B	HR	RBI	BB	SO	AVG	OBP	SLG	PRO+	BR	/A	RC	SB	CS	SBR	FR	POS	TPR
1920	Bos-A	4	5	2	1	1	0	0	1	4	1	.200	.556	.400	163	1	1	2	0	0	0	-0	/C	0.1
1921	Bos-A	3	2	0	0	0	0	0	0	0	0	.000	.000	.000	-99	-1	-1	0	0	0	0	-0	/C	0.0
1922	Bos-A	28	69	8	13	1	1	0	6	9	9	.188	.282	.232	35	-6	-6	5	2	1	0	-3	C	-0.7
Total	3	35	76	10	14	2	1	0	7	13	11	.184	.303	.237	43	-6	-6	5	2	1	0	-3	/C	-0.6

■ CALVIN CHAPMAN

Chapman, Calvin Louis b: 12/20/10, Courtland, Miss. BL/TR, 5'9", 160 lbs. Deb: 9/10/35

YEAR	TM/L	G	AB	R	H	2B	3B	HR	RBI	BB	SO	AVG	OBP	SLG	PRO+	BR	/A	RC	SB	CS	SBR	FR	POS	TPR
1935	Cin-N	15	53	6	18	1	0	0	3	4	5	.340	.386	.358	105	1	0	8	2			-2	S/2	0.0
1936	Cin-N	96	219	35	54	7	3	1	22	16	19	.247	.301	.320	72	-10	-8	22	5			-13	O2/3	-2.0
Total	2	111	272	41	72	8	3	1	25	20	24	.265	.317	.327	78	-10	-8	30	7			-16	/O2S3	-2.0

■ GLENN CHAPMAN

Chapman, Glenn Justice "Pete" b: 1/21/06, Cambridge City, Ind. d: 11/5/88, Richmond, Ind. BR/TR, 5'11.5", 170 lbs. Deb: 4/18/34

YEAR	TM/L	G	AB	R	H	2B	3B	HR	RBI	BB	SO	AVG	OBP	SLG	PRO+	BR	/A	RC	SB	CS	SBR	FR	POS	TPR
1934	Bro-N	67	93	19	26	5	1	1	10	7	19	.280	.330	.387	96	-1	-1	12	1			5	O2	0.4

■ HARRY CHAPMAN

Chapman, Harry E. b: 10/26/1887, Severance, Kan. d: 10/21/18, Nevada, Mo. BR/TR, 5'11", 160 lbs. Deb: 10/06/12

YEAR	TM/L	G	AB	R	H	2B	3B	HR	RBI	BB	SO	AVG	OBP	SLG	PRO+	BR	/A	RC	SB	CS	SBR	FR	POS	TPR
1912	Chi-N	1	4	1	1	0	1	0	1	0	0	.250	.250	.750	169	0	0	1	1			1	/C	0.1
1913	Cin-N	2	2	0	1	0	0	0	0	0	1	.500	.500	.500	187	0	0	0	0			0	H	0.0
1914	StL-F	64	181	16	38	2	1	0	14	13	27	.210	.270	.232	42	-13	-14	13	2			-4	C/12O	-1.6
1915	StL-F	62	186	19	37	6	3	1	29	22	24	.199	.284	.280	64	-7	-9	17	4			7	C	0.0
1916	StL-A	18	31	2	3	0	0	0	0	2	5	.097	.152	.097	-27	-5	-5	1	0			2	C	-0.1
Total	5	147	404	38	80	8	5	1	44	37	57	.198	.269	.250	50	-24	-27	32	7			6	C/O21	-1.6

■ JACK CHAPMAN

Chapman, John Curtis "Death To Flying Things" b: 5/8/1843, Brooklyn, N.Y. d: 6/10/16, Brooklyn, N.Y. TR, 5'11", 170 lbs. Deb: 5/05/1874 M

YEAR	TM/L	G	AB	R	H	2B	3B	HR	RBI	BB	SO	AVG	OBP	SLG	PRO+	BR	/A	RC	SB	CS	SBR	FR	POS	TPR
1874	Atl-n	53	238	32	64	7	3	0		5		.269	.284	.324	105	-2	3	22					*O/1	0.3
1875	StL-n	43	195	28	44	6	3	0		1		.226	.230	.287	85	-4	-1	13					O	0.0
1876	Lou-N	17	67	4	16	1	0	0	5	1	3	.239	.250	.254	58	-2	-4	4				-3	O/3	-0.5
Total	2 n	96	433	60	108	13	6	0		6		.249	.260	.307	96	-6	2	36					/O1	0.3

■ JOHN CHAPMAN

Chapman, John Joseph b: 10/15/1899, Centralia, Pa. d: 11/3/53, Philadelphia, Pa. BR/TR, 5'10.5", 175 lbs. Deb: 6/28/24

YEAR	TM/L	G	AB	R	H	2B	3B	HR	RBI	BB	SO	AVG	OBP	SLG	PRO+	BR	/A	RC	SB	CS	SBR	FR	POS	TPR
1924	Phi-A	19	71	7	20	4	1	0	7	4	8	.282	.329	.366	78	-2	-2	9	0	0	0	-10	S	-0.9

■ KELVIN CHAPMAN

Chapman, Kelvin Keith b: 6/2/56, Willits, Cal. BR/TR, 5'11", 173 lbs. Deb: 4/05/79

YEAR	TM/L	G	AB	R	H	2B	3B	HR	RBI	BB	SO	AVG	OBP	SLG	PRO+	BR	/A	RC	SB	CS	SBR	FR	POS	TPR
1979	NY-N	35	80	7	12	1	2	0	4	5	15	.150	.200	.213	13	-10	-9	4	0	0	0	-4	2/3	-1.1
1984	NY-N	75	197	27	57	13	0	3	23	19	30	.289	.358	.401	115	4	4	26	8	7	-2	1	2/3	0.5
1985	NY-N	62	144	16	25	3	0	0	7	9	15	.174	.232	.194	21	-15	-15	7	5	4	-1	-6	2/3	-2.2
Total	3	172	421	50	94	17	2	3	34	33	60	.223	.286	.295	64	-21	-20	36	13	11	-3	-8	2/3	-2.8

■ RAY CHAPMAN

Chapman, Raymond Johnson b: 1/15/1891, Beaver Dam, Ky. d: 8/17/20, New York, N.Y. BR/TR, 5'10", 170 lbs. Deb: 8/30/12

YEAR	TM/L	G	AB	R	H	2B	3B	HR	RBI	BB	SO	AVG	OBP	SLG	PRO+	BR	/A	RC	SB	CS	SBR	FR	POS	TPR
1912	Cle-A	31	109	29	34	6	3	0	19	10		.312	.375	.422	124	4	3	22	10			-10	S	-0.3

YEAR	TM/L	G	AB	R	H	2B	3B	HR	RBI	BB	SO	AVG	OBP	SLG	PRO+	BR	/A	RC	SB	CS	SBR	FR	POS	TPR
1913	Cle-A	141	508	78	131	19	7	3	39	46	51	.258	.322	.341	91	-5	-6	66	29			-9	*S/O	-0.3
1914	Cle-A	106	375	59	103	16	10	2	42	48	48	.275	.358	.387	119	11	9	58	24	9	2	-15	S2	0.3
1915	Cle-A	154	570	101	154	14	17	3	67	70	82	.270	.353	.370	114	12	10	84	36	15	2	9	*S	3.6
1916	Cle-A	109	346	50	80	10	5	0	27	50	46	.231	.330	.289	81	-5	-7	41	21	14	-2	13	S32	1.0
1917	Cle-A	156	563	98	170	28	13	2	36	61	65	.302	.370	.409	128	25	20	105	52			24	*S	5.4
1918	Cle-A	128	446	84	119	19	8	1	32	84	46	.267	.390	.352	113	17	12	74	30			6	*S/O	2.8
1919	Cle-A	115	433	75	130	23	10	3	53	31	38	.300	.351	.420	109	8	5	72	18			0	*S	1.5
1920	Cle-A	111	435	97	132	27	8	3	49	52	38	.303	.380	.423	109	9	7	72	13	9	-2	12	*S	2.6
Total	9	1051	3785	671	1053	162	81	17	364	452	414	.278	.358	.377	110	76	52	595	233	47			30	S/23O	16.6

■ SAM CHAPMAN

Chapman, Samuel Blake   b: 4/11/16, Tiburon, Cal.   BR/TR, 6', 180 lbs.   Deb: 5/16/38

YEAR	TM/L	G	AB	R	H	2B	3B	HR	RBI	BB	SO	AVG	OBP	SLG	PRO+	BR	/A	RC	SB	CS	SBR	FR	POS	TPR
1938	Phi-A	114	406	60	105	17	7	17	63	55	94	.259	.353	.461	105	0	2	67	3	4	-2	-1	*O	0.0
1939	Phi-A	140	498	74	134	24	6	15	64	51	62	.269	.338	.432	98	-5	-3	73	11	4	1	0	*O1	-0.6
1940	Phi-A	134	508	88	140	26	3	23	75	46	96	.276	.337	.474	110	4	6	78	2	6	-3	3	*O	-0.2
1941	Phi-A	143	552	97	178	29	9	25	106	47	49	.322	.378	.543	145	30	32	110	6	9	-4	11	*O	2.9
1945	Phi-A	9	30	3	6	2	0	0	1	2	4	.200	.250	.267	50	-2	-2	2	0	0	0	-0	/O	-0.2
1946	Phi-A	146	545	77	142	22	5	20	67	54	66	.261	.327	.429	111	6	6	73	1	3	-2	15	*O	1.3
1947	Phi-A	149	551	84	139	18	5	14	83	65	70	.252	.331	.379	95	-3	-4	71	3	4	-2	5	*O	-0.6
1948	Phi-A	123	445	58	115	18	6	13	70	55	50	.258	.341	.413	100	-1	-1	63	6	1	1	3	*O	-0.1
1949	Phi-A	154	589	89	164	24	4	24	108	80	68	.278	.367	.455	121	12	15	97	3	4	-2	8	*O	1.7
1950	Phi-A	144	553	93	139	20	6	23	95	68	79	.251	.338	.434	98	-5	-4	83	3	3	-1	7	*O	0.0
1951	Phi-A	18	65	7	11	1	0	0	5	12	12	.169	.299	.185	32	-6	-6	4	0	0	0	-0	*O	-0.6
	Cle-A	94	246	24	56	9	1	6	36	27	32	.228	.304	.346	80	-9	-7	27	3	0	1	-4	O/1	-1.3
	Yr	112	311	31	67	10	1	6	41	39	44	.215	.303	.312	69	-15	-13	31	3	0	1	-4		-1.9
Total	11	1368	4988	754	1329	210	52	180	773	562	682	.266	.342	.438	107	22	33	749	41	38	-11	48	*O/1	2.3

■ BEN CHAPMAN

Chapman, William Benjamin   b: 12/25/08, Nashville, Tenn.   BR/TR, 6', 190 lbs.   Deb: 4/15/30   MC

YEAR	TM/L	G	AB	R	H	2B	3B	HR	RBI	BB	SO	AVG	OBP	SLG	PRO+	BR	/A	RC	SB	CS	SBR	FR	POS	TPR
1930	NY-A	138	513	74	162	31	10	10	81	43	58	.316	.371	.474	118	9	13	91	14	6	1	-6	32	1.0
1931	NY-A	149	600	120	189	28	11	17	122	75	77	.315	.396	.483	138	27	32	119	61	23	5	8	*O2	3.4
1932	*NY-A	151	581	101	174	41	15	10	107	71	55	.299	.381	.473	126	17	22	107	38	18	1	1	*O	1.6
1933	NY-A	147	565	112	176	36	4	9	98	72	45	.312	.393	.437	127	18	23	99	27	18	-3	11	*O	2.4
1934	NY-A	149	588	82	181	21	13	5	86	67	68	.308	.381	.413	113	6	11	94	26	16	-2	1	*O	0.7
1935	NY-A	140	553	118	160	38	8	8	74	61	39	.289	.361	.430	110	3	7	87	17	10	-1	13	*O	1.6
1936	NY-A	36	139	19	37	14	3	1	21	15	20	.266	.338	.432	92	-3	-2	20	1	2	-1	5	O	0.1
	Was-A	97	401	91	133	36	7	4	60	69	18	.332	.431	.486	133	19	23	89	19	7	2	1	O	2.0
	Yr	133	540	110	170	50	10	5	81	84	38	.315	.408	.472	123	16	20	109	20	9	1	6		2.1
1937	Was-A	35	130	23	34	7	1	0	12	26	7	.262	.385	.381	86	-3	-2	20	8	0	2	1	O	0.0
	Bos-A	113	423	76	130	23	11	7	57	57	35	.307	.391	.463	110	10	8	79	27	12	1	7	*O/S	1.0
	Yr	148	553	99	164	30	12	7	69	83	42	.297	.389	.432	105	7	6	99	35	12	3	8		1.0
1938	Bos-A	127	480	92	163	40	8	6	80	65	33	.340	.418	.494	122	22	18	102	13	6	0	6	*O/3	2.2
1939	Cle-A	149	545	101	158	31	9	6	82	87	30	.290	.384	.413	109	7	10	91	18	6	2	-9	*O	-0.1
1940	Cle-A	143	548	82	157	40	6	4	50	78	45	.286	.377	.403	105	4	6	85	13	7	-0	2	*O	0.0
1941	Was-A	28	110	9	28	6	0	1	10	10	6	.255	.317	.336	76	-4	-4	10	2	2	-1	-1	O	-0.5
	Chi-A	57	190	26	43	9	1	2	19	19	14	.226	.297	.311	63	-11	-10	19	2	2	-1	2	O	-1.1
	Yr	85	300	35	71	15	1	3	29	29	20	.237	.304	.323	68	-15	-14	29	4	4	-1	2		-1.6
1944	Bro-N	20	38	11	14	4	0	0	11	5	4	.368	.442	.474	161	3	3	9	1			-2	P	0.0
1945	Bro-N	13	22	2	3	0	0	0	3	2	1	.136	.208	.136	-3	-3	-3	1	0			1	P	0.0
	Phi-N	24	51	4	16	2	0	0	4	2	1	.314	.340	.353	95	-1	-0	5	0			-2	O/3PM	-0.1
	Yr	37	73	6	19	2	0	0	7	4	2	.260	.299	.288	65	-4	-3	5	0			-1		-0.1
1946	Phi-N	1	1	1	0	0	0	0	0	0	0	.000	.000	.000	-99	-0	-0	0	0			0	/PM	0.0
Total	15	1717	6478	1144	1958	407	107	90	977	824	556	.302	.383	.440	115	120	155	1127	287	135		38	*O/32PS	14.2

■ FRED CHAPMAN

Chapman, William Fred "Chappie"   b: 7/17/16, Liberty, S.C.   BR/TR, 6'1", 185 lbs.   Deb: 9/15/39

YEAR	TM/L	G	AB	R	H	2B	3B	HR	RBI	BB	SO	AVG	OBP	SLG	PRO+	BR	/A	RC	SB	CS	SBR	FR	POS	TPR
1939	Phi-A	15	49	5	14	1	1	0	1	1	3	.286	.300	.347	66	-3	-3	5	1	0	0	-4	S	-0.3
1940	Phi-A	26	69	6	11	1	0	0	4	6	10	.159	.227	.174	6	-10	-9	3	1	1	-0	-5	S	-1.2
1941	Phi-A	35	69	1	11	1	0	0	4	4	15	.159	.205	.174	1	-10	-10	2	1	2	-1	-2	S/32	-1.0
Total	3	76	187	12	36	3	1	0	9	11	28	.193	.237	.219	20	-22	-22	11	3	3	-1	-10	/S32	-2.5

■ HARRY CHAPPAS

Chappas, Harry Perry   b: 10/26/57, Mt.Ranier, Md.   BB/TR, 5'3", 150 lbs.   Deb: 9/07/78

YEAR	TM/L	G	AB	R	H	2B	3B	HR	RBI	BB	SO	AVG	OBP	SLG	PRO+	BR	/A	RC	SB	CS	SBR	FR	POS	TPR
1978	Chi-A	20	75	11	20	1	0	0	6	6	11	.267	.329	.280	72	-2	-3	8	1	2	-1	0	S	-0.1
1979	Chi-A	26	59	9	17	1	0	1	4	5	5	.288	.354	.356	92	-0	-0	7	1	1	-0	3	S	0.4
1980	Chi-A	26	50	6	8	2	0	0	2	4	10	.160	.236	.200	21	-5	-5	2	0	2	-1	-1	S/2D	-0.5
Total	3	72	184	26	45	4	0	1	12	15	26	.245	.312	.283	65	-8	-8	17	2	5	-2	2	/SD2	-0.2

■ LARRY CHAPPELL

Chappell, La Verne Ashford   b: 2/19/1890, McClusky, Ill.   d: 11/8/18, San Francisco, Cal.   BL/TR, 6', 186 lbs.   Deb: 7/18/13

YEAR	TM/L	G	AB	R	H	2B	3B	HR	RBI	BB	SO	AVG	OBP	SLG	PRO+	BR	/A	RC	SB	CS	SBR	FR	POS	TPR
1913	Chi-A	60	208	20	48	8	1	0	15	18	22	.231	.295	.279	69	-8	-8	18	7			-1	O	-1.3
1914	Chi-A	21	39	3	9	0	0	0	1	4	11	.231	.302	.231	61	-2	-2	3	0			-2	/O	-0.3
1915	Chi-A	1	1	0	0	0	0	0	0	0	0	.000	.000	.000	-97	-0	-0	0	0			0	H	0.0
1916	Cle-A	3	2	0	0	0	0	0	0	1	0	.000	.333	.000	1	-0	-0	0	1			0	H	0.0
	Bos-N	20	53	4	12	1	1	0	9	2	8	.226	.268	.283	72	-2	-2	4	1			-2	O	-0.4
1917	Bos-N	4	2	0	0	0	0	0	1	0	1	.000	.000	.000	-99	-0	-0	0	0			0	/O	0.0
Total	5	109	305	27	69	9	2	0	26	25	42	.226	.289	.269	66	-13	-12	26	9			-4	/O	-2.0

■ JOE CHARBONEAU

Charboneau, Joseph   b: 6/17/55, Belvidere, Ill.   BR/TR, 6'2", 205 lbs.   Deb: 4/11/80

YEAR	TM/L	G	AB	R	H	2B	3B	HR	RBI	BB	SO	AVG	OBP	SLG	PRO+	BR	/A	RC	SB	CS	SBR	FR	POS	TPR
1980	Cle-A	131	453	76	131	17	2	23	87	49	70	.289	.362	.488	130	19	19	72	2	4	-2	-0	OD	1.5
1981	Cle-A	48	138	14	29	7	1	4	18	7	22	.210	.248	.362	75	-5	-5	11	1	0	0	-2	OD	-0.5
1982	Cle-A	22	56	7	12	2	1	2	9	5	7	.214	.290	.393	86	-1	-1	6	0	0	0	-2	O/D	-0.3
Total	3	201	647	97	172	26	4	29	114	61	99	.266	.333	.453	115	12	12	90	3	4	-2	-3	O/D	0.7

■ ED CHARLES

Charles, Edwin Douglas   b: 4/29/33, Daytona Beach, Fla.   BR/TR, 5'10", 170 lbs.   Deb: 4/11/62

YEAR	TM/L	G	AB	R	H	2B	3B	HR	RBI	BB	SO	AVG	OBP	SLG	PRO+	BR	/A	RC	SB	CS	SBR	FR	POS	TPR
1962	KC-A	147	535	81	154	24	7	17	74	54	70	.288	.358	.454	113	12	10	89	20	4	4	4	*3/2	2.0
1963	KC-A	158	603	82	161	28	2	15	79	58	79	.267	.336	.395	100	4	1	77	15	8	-0	-8	*3	-0.6
1964	KC-A	150	557	69	134	25	2	16	63	64	92	.241	.323	.379	92	-4	-6	66	12	7	-1	-15	*3	-1.9
1965	KC-A	134	480	55	129	19	7	8	56	44	72	.269	.335	.387	106	3	4	64	13	4	2	-1	*3/2S	0.6
1966	KC-A	118	385	52	110	18	8	9	42	30	53	.286	.337	.444	127	11	10	56	12	5	1	-5	*3/1O	0.5
1967	KC-A	19	61	5	15	1	0	0	5	12	13	.246	.378	.262	95	0	0	7	1	0	0	0	3	0.1
	NY-N	101	323	32	77	13	2	3	31	24	58	.238	.305	.319	80	-9	-8	33	4	1	1	9	3	-0.3
1968	NY-N	117	369	41	102	11	1	15	53	28	57	.276	.331	.434	127	12	12	52	5	4	-1	1	*3/1	1.3
1969	*NY-N	61	169	21	35	8	1	3	18	18	31	.207	.287	.320	68	-7	-7	15	4	2	0	-0	3	-0.7
Total	8	1005	3482	438	917	147	30	86	421	332	525	.263	.332	.397	104	23	18	458	86	35	5	-15	3/12OS	1.0

■ CHAPPY CHARLES

Charles, Raymond (b: Charles Shuh Achenbach)
b: 3/25/1881, Phillipsburg, N.J.   d: 8/4/59, Bethlehem, Pa.   BR/TR, 5'11", 175 lbs.   Deb: 4/15/08

YEAR	TM/L	G	AB	R	H	2B	3B	HR	RBI	BB	SO	AVG	OBP	SLG	PRO+	BR	/A	RC	SB	CS	SBR	FR	POS	TPR
1908	StL-N	121	454	39	93	14	3	1	17	19		.205	.237	.256	62	-21	-19	31	15			-12	2S3	-3.7
1909	StL-N	99	339	33	80	7	3	0	29	31		.236	.309	.274	87	-7	-4	31	7			-1	2S/3	-0.6

YEAR	TM/L	G	AB	R	H	2B	3B	HR	RBI	BB	SO	AVG	OBP	SLG	PRO+	BR	/A	RC	SB	CS	SBR	FR	POS	TPR
	Cin-N	13	43	3	11	2	0	0	5	4		.256	.319	.302	94	-0	-0	5	2			-3	2/S	-0.2
	Yr	112	382	36	91	9	3	0	34	35		.238	.310	.277	87	-7	-5	36	9			-4		-0.8
1910	Cin-N	4	15	1	2	0	1	0	0	0	1	.133	.133	.267	17	-2	-2	0	0			-1	/S	-0.2
Total	3	237	851	96	186	23	7	1	51	54	1	.219	.269	.266	73	-30	-25	67	24			-18	2/S3	-4.7

■ MIKE CHARTAK

Chartak, Michael George "Shotgun" b: 4/28/16, Brooklyn, N.Y. d: 7/25/67, Cedar Rapids, Ia. BL/TL, 6'2", 180 lbs. Deb: 9/13/40

YEAR	TM/L	G	AB	R	H	2B	3B	HR	RBI	BB	SO	AVG	OBP	SLG	PRO+	BR	/A	RC	SB	CS	SBR	FR	POS	TPR
1940	NY-A	11	15	2	2	1	0	0	3	5	5	.133	.350	.200	49	-1	-1	2	0	0	0	-1	/O	-0.1
1942	NY-A	5	5	0	0	0	0	0	0	0	0	.000	.000	.000	-99	-1	-1	0	0	0	0	0	H	0.0
	Was-A	24	92	11	20	4	2	1	8	14	16	.217	.321	.337	86	-2	-2	10	0	1	-1	-1	O	-0.5
	StL-A	73	237	37	59	11	2	9	43	40	27	.249	.362	.426	119	7	7	39	3	3	-1	4	O	0.5
	Yr	102	334	48	79	15	4	10	51	54	43	.237	.346	.395	107	4	4	48	3	4	-2	3		0.0
1943	StL-A	108	344	38	88	16	2	10	37	39	55	.256	.333	.401	112	6	5	47	1	3	-2	-6	O1	-0.5
1944	*StL-A	35	72	8	17	2	1	1	7	6	9	.236	.304	.333	77	-2	-2	8	0	0	0	0	1/O	-0.2
Total	4	256	765	96	186	34	7	21	98	104	112	.243	.337	.388	105	7	5	105	4	7	-3	-4	O/1	-0.8

■ HAL CHASE

Chase, Harold Homer "Prince Hal" b: 2/13/1883, Los Gatos, Cal. d: 5/18/47, Colusa, Cal. BR/TL, 6', 175 lbs. Deb: 4/14/05 M

YEAR	TM/L	G	AB	R	H	2B	3B	HR	RBI	BB	SO	AVG	OBP	SLG	PRO+	BR	/A	RC	SB	CS	SBR	FR	POS	TPR
1905	NY-A	128	465	60	116	16	6	3	49	15		.249	.273	.329	83	-5	-11	51	22			-9	*1/S2	-2.4
1906	NY-A	151	597	84	193	23	10	0	76	13		.323	.338	.395	119	19	12	94	28			-2	*1/2	0.6
1907	NY-A	125	498	72	143	23	3	2	68	19		.287	.313	.357	107	7	3	68	32			1	*1/O	0.2
1908	NY-A	106	405	50	104	11	3	1	36	15		.257	.283	.306	93	-4	-4	42	27			-4	1/2O3	-1.1
1909	NY-A	118	474	60	134	17	3	4	63	20		.283	.317	.357	112	5	5	61	25			-2	*1/S	0.3
1910	NY-A	130	524	67	152	20	5	3	73	16		.290	.312	.365	106	5	1	71	40			-4	*1M	0.2
1911	NY-A	133	527	82	166	32	7	3	62	21		.315	.342	.419	105	6	1	87	36			-2	*1/O2M	0.2
1912	NY-A	131	522	61	143	21	9	4	58	17		.274	.299	.372	86	-8	-13	67	33			-2	*1/2	-1.2
1913	NY-A	39	146	15	31	2	4	0	9	11	13	.212	.268	.281	60	-8	-8	12	5			-5	1/2O	-1.3
	Chi-A	102	384	49	110	11	10	2	39	16	41	.286	.320	.383	107	1	1	48	9			1	*1	0.2
	Yr	141	530	64	141	13	14	2	48	27	54	.266	.305	.355	94	-7	-6	59	14			-4		-1.1
1914	Chi-A	58	206	27	55	10	5	0	20	23	19	.267	.343	.364	114	3	3	28	9	4	0	2	1	0.6
	Buf-F	75	291	43	101	19	9	3	48	6	31	.347	.365	.505	144	16	15	59	10			-1	1	1.6
1915	Buf-F	145	567	85	165	31	10	17	89	20	50	.291	.316	.471	129	18	16	95	23			0	*1/O	2.0
1916	Cin-N	142	542	66	184	29	12	4	82	19	48	.339	.363	.459	155	30	31	93	22	11	0	-5	1O2	2.5
1917	Cin-N	152	602	71	167	28	15	4	86	15	49	.277	.296	.394	115	5	7	72	21			-3	*1	0.3
1918	Cin-N	74	259	30	78	12	6	2	38	13	15	.301	.339	.417	133	8	9	37	5			-2	1/O	0.6
1919	NY-N	110	408	58	116	17	7	5	45	17	40	.284	.318	.397	115	6	6	54	16			-1	*1	0.4
Total	15	1919	7417	980	2158	322	124	57	941	276	306	.291	.318	.391	112	103	77	1038	363	15		-38	*1/O2S3	3.7

■ BUSTER CHATHAM

Chatham, Charles L b: 12/25/01, West, Tex. d: 12/15/75, Waco, Tex. BR/TR, 5'5", 150 lbs. Deb: 6/01/30

YEAR	TM/L	G	AB	R	H	2B	3B	HR	RBI	BB	SO	AVG	OBP	SLG	PRO+	BR	/A	RC	SB	CS	SBR	FR	POS	TPR
1930	Bos-N	112	404	48	108	20	11	5	56	37	41	.267	.332	.408	80	-15	-13	54	8			-14	3S	-2.1
1931	Bos-N	17	44	4	10	1	0	1	3	6	6	.227	.320	.318	75	-2	-1	5	0			-5	/S3	-0.5
Total	2	129	448	52	118	21	11	6	59	43	47	.263	.331	.400	80	-17	-14	59	8			-20	/3S	-2.6

■ JIM CHATTERTON

Chatterton, James M. b: 10/14/1864, Brooklyn, N.Y. d: 12/15/44, Tewksbury, Mass. Deb: 6/07/1884

YEAR	TM/L	G	AB	R	H	2B	3B	HR	RBI	BB	SO	AVG	OBP	SLG	PRO+	BR	/A	RC	SB	CS	SBR	FR	POS	TPR
1884	KC-U	4	15	4	2	1	0	0			2	.133	.235	.200	56	-1	-1	1	0			0	/O1P	0.0

■ OSSIE CHAVARRIA

Chavarria, Osvaldo (Quijano) b: 8/5/40, Colon, Panama BR/TR, 5'11", 155 lbs. Deb: 4/14/66

YEAR	TM/L	G	AB	R	H	2B	3B	HR	RBI	BB	SO	AVG	OBP	SLG	PRO+	BR	/A	RC	SB	CS	SBR	FR	POS	TPR
1966	KC-A	86	191	26	46	10	0	2	10	18	43	.241	.306	.325	84	-4	-4	19	3	2	-0	-2	OS2/13	-0.4
1967	KC-A	38	59	2	6	2	0	0	4	7	16	.102	.209	.136	4	-7	-7	2	1	0	0	3	2/3OS	-0.2
Total	2	124	250	28	52	12	0	2	14	25	59	.208	.283	.280	65	-11	-10	21	4	2	0	1	/2OS31	-0.6

■ HARRY CHEEK

Cheek, Harry G. b: 1879, Sedalia, Mo. d: 6/25/56, Paramas, N.J. TR , Deb: 5/12/10

YEAR	TM/L	G	AB	R	H	2B	3B	HR	RBI	BB	SO	AVG	OBP	SLG	PRO+	BR	/A	RC	SB	CS	SBR	FR	POS	TPR
1910	Phi-N	2	4	1	2	1	0	0	0	0	0	.500	.500	.750	255	1	1	1	0			-1	/C	0.0

■ PAUL CHERVINKO

Chervinko, Paul b: 7/28/10, Trauger, Pa. d: 6/3/76, Danville, Ill. BR/TR, 5'8", 185 lbs. Deb: 5/30/37

YEAR	TM/L	G	AB	R	H	2B	3B	HR	RBI	BB	SO	AVG	OBP	SLG	PRO+	BR	/A	RC	SB	CS	SBR	FR	POS	TPR
1937	Bro-N	30	48	1	7	0	1	0	2	3	16	.146	.196	.188	5	-6	-6	2	0			1	C	-0.4
1938	Bro-N	12	27	0	4	0	0	0	3	2	0	.148	.207	.148	-1	-4	-4	1	0			0	C	-0.2
Total	2	42	75	1	11	0	1	0	5	5	16	.147	.200	.173	3	-10	-10	2	0			1	/C	-0.6

■ CUPID CHILDS

Childs, Clarence Algernon b: 8/14/1867, Calvert Co., Md. d: 11/8/12, Baltimore, Md. BL/TR, 5'8", 185 lbs. Deb: 4/23/1888

YEAR	TM/L	G	AB	R	H	2B	3B	HR	RBI	BB	SO	AVG	OBP	SLG	PRO+	BR	/A	RC	SB	CS	SBR	FR	POS	TPR
1888	Phi-N	2	4	0	0	0	0	0	0	0	0	.000	.000	.000	-95	-1	-1	0	0			0	/2	0.0
1890	Syr-a	126	493	109	170	33	14	2		72		.345	.434	.481	191	47	55	130	56			12	*2/S	6.1
1891	Cle-N	141	551	120	155	21	12	2	83	97	32	.281	.395	.374	122	23	20	99	39			-12	*2	1.0
1892	*Cle-N	145	558	136	177	14	11	3	53	117	20	.317	.443	.398	151	47	43	113	26			-6	*2	3.5
1893	Cle-N	124	485	145	158	19	10	3	65	120	12	.326	.463	.425	131	36	30	109	23			10	*2	3.1
1894	Cle-N	118	479	143	169	21	12	2	52	107	11	.353	.475	.459	124	30	26	116	17			-3	*2	2.3
1895	*Cle-N	119	462	96	133	15	3	4	90	74	24	.288	.393	.359	92	-2	-4	75	20			10	*2	1.0
1896	*Cle-N	132	498	106	177	24	9	1	106	100	18	.355	.467	.446	136	39	33	118	25			42	*2	6.6
1897	Cle-N	114	444	105	150	15	9	1	61	74		.338	.435	.419	122	23	18	94	25			17	*2	3.8
1898	Cle-N	110	413	90	119	9	4	1	31	69		.288	.395	.337	115	11	12	60	9			9	*2	2.3
1899	StL-N	125	464	73	123	11	11	1	48	74		.265	.369	.343	96	2	0	64	11			-11	*2	-0.3
1900	Chi-N	137	531	67	128	14	5	0	44	57		.241	.318	.286	72	-20	-17	54	15			16	*2	0.5
1901	Chi-N	63	236	24	61	9	0	0	31	30		.258	.342	.297	95	-1	0	26	3			9	2	1.4
Total	13	1456	5618	1214	1720	205	100	20	654	991	117	.306	.415	.389	121	237	216	1059	269			92	*2/S	31.3

■ PETE CHILDS

Childs, Peter Pierre b: 11/15/1871, Philadelphia, Pa. d: 2/15/22, Philadelphia, Pa. TR , Deb: 4/24/01

YEAR	TM/L	G	AB	R	H	2B	3B	HR	RBI	BB	SO	AVG	OBP	SLG	PRO+	BR	/A	RC	SB	CS	SBR	FR	POS	TPR
1901	StL-N	29	79	12	21	1	0	0	8	14		.266	.376	.278	99	0	1	9	0			-6	2/OS	-0.3
	Chi-N	60	210	23	48	5	1	0	14	26		.229	.314	.262	72	-7	-6	19	4			13	2	1.1
	Yr	89	289	35	69	6	1	0	22	40		.239	.331	.266	80	-7	-5	28	4			7		0.8
1902	Phi-N	123	403	25	78	5	0	0	25	34		.194	.260	.206	45	-24	-24	25	6			-9	*2	-2.5
Total	2	212	692	60	147	11	1	0	47	74		.212	.290	.231	60	-31	-29	53	10			-2	2/OS	-1.7

■ PEARCE CHILES

Chiles, Pearce Nuget "What's the Use" b: 5/28/1867, Deepwater, Mo. 5'11", 185 lbs. Deb: 4/18/1899

YEAR	TM/L	G	AB	R	H	2B	3B	HR	RBI	BB	SO	AVG	OBP	SLG	PRO+	BR	/A	RC	SB	CS	SBR	FR	POS	TPR
1899	Phi-N	97	338	57	108	28	7	2	76	16		.320	.352	.462	129	10	12	58	6			-16	O12	-0.4
1900	Phi-N	33	111	13	24	6	2	1	23	6		.216	.256	.333	64	-6	-6	11	4			-3	12/O	-0.6
Total	2	130	449	70	132	34	9	3	99	22		.294	.328	.430	113	4	6	69	10			-19	/O12	-1.0

■ RICH CHILES

Chiles, Richard Francis b: 11/22/49, Sacramento, Cal. BL/TL, 5'11", 170 lbs. Deb: 9/20/71

YEAR	TM/L	G	AB	R	H	2B	3B	HR	RBI	BB	SO	AVG	OBP	SLG	PRO+	BR	/A	RC	SB	CS	SBR	FR	POS	TPR
1971	Hou-N	67	119	12	27	5	1	2	15	6	20	.227	.270	.336	73	-5	-5	10	0	1	-1	-3	O	-0.9
1972	Hou-N	9	11	0	3	1	0	0	2	1	1	.273	.333	.364	100	-0	0	1	0	0	0	0	/O	0.0
1973	NY-N	8	25	2	3	2	0	0	1	0	2	.120	.120	.200	-13	-4	-4	0	0	0	0	3	/O	-0.1
1976	Hou-N	5	4	1	2	1	0	0	0	0	0	.500	.500	.750	276	1	1	2	0	0	0	0	/O	0.1
1977	Min-A	108	261	31	69	16	1	3	36	23	17	.264	.329	.368	91	-4	-3	32	0	1	-1	-2	DO	-0.6
1978	Min-A	87	198	22	53	12	0	1	22	20	25	.268	.341	.343	91	-1	-2	22	1	2	-1	0	O/D	-0.3
Total	6	284	618	68	157	37	2	6	76	50	65	.254	.315	.350	85	-13	-12	67	1	4	-2	-2	O/D	-1.8

■ DINO CHIOZZA

Chiozza, Dino Joseph "Dynamo" b: 6/30/12, Memphis, Tenn. d: 4/23/72, Memphis, Tenn. BL/TR, 6', 170 lbs. Deb: 7/14/35

YEAR	TM/L	G	AB	R	H	2B	3B	HR	RBI	BB	SO	AVG	OBP	SLG	PRO+	BR	/A	RC	SB	CS	SBR	FR	POS	TPR
1935	Phi-N	2	0	1	0	0	0	0	0	0	0	—	—	—	—	0	0	0	0			-0	/S	0.0

YEAR	TM/L	G	AB	R	H	2B	3B	HR	RBI	BB	SO	AVG	OBP	SLG	PRO+	BR	/A	RC	SB	CS	SBR	FR	POS	TPR

■ LOU CHIOZZA
Chiozza, Louis Peo b: 5/17/10, Tallulah, La. d: 2/28/71, Memphis, Tenn. BL/TR, 6', 172 lbs. Deb: 4/17/34

YEAR	TM/L	G	AB	R	H	2B	3B	HR	RBI	BB	SO	AVG	OBP	SLG	PRO+	BR	/A	RC	SB	CS	SBR	FR	POS	TPR
1934	Phi-N	134	484	66	147	28	5	0	44	34	35	.304	.357	.382	86	-1	-9	68	9			-24	23O	-2.2
1935	Phi-N	124	472	71	134	26	6	3	47	33	44	.284	.333	.383	84	-5	-12	64	5			3	*2/3	0.1
1936	Phi-N	144	572	83	170	32	6	1	48	37	39	.297	.346	.379	87	-3	-11	80	17			-3	O23	-1.3
1937	*NY-N	117	439	49	102	11	2	4	29	20	30	.232	.266	.294	51	-30	-30	36	6			2	3O/2	-2.4
1938	NY-N	57	179	15	42	7	2	3	17	12	7	.235	.283	.346	72	-7	-7	18	5			-7	2O/3	-1.1
1939	NY-N	40	142	19	38	3	1	3	12	9	10	.268	.311	.366	81	-4	-4	17	3			-3	3/S	-0.5
Total	6	616	2288	303	633	107	22	14	197	145	165	.277	.324	.361	78	-50	-73	283	45			-32	23O/S	-7.4

■ WALT CHIPPLE
Chipple, Walter John (b: Walter John Chlipala) b: 9/26/18, Utica, N.Y. d: 6/8/88, Tonawanda, N.Y. BR/TR, 6'0.5", 168 lbs. Deb: 4/17/45

YEAR	TM/L	G	AB	R	H	2B	3B	HR	RBI	BB	SO	AVG	OBP	SLG	PRO+	BR	/A	RC	SB	CS	SBR	FR	POS	TPR
1945	Was-A	18	44	4	6	0	0	0	5	5	6	.136	.224	.136	6	-5	-5	1	0	1	-1	4	O	-0.1

■ TOM CHISM
Chism, Thomas Raymond b: 5/9/55, Chester, Pa. BL/TL, 6'1", 195 lbs. Deb: 9/13/79

YEAR	TM/L	G	AB	R	H	2B	3B	HR	RBI	BB	SO	AVG	OBP	SLG	PRO+	BR	/A	RC	SB	CS	SBR	FR	POS	TPR
1979	Bal-A	6	3	0	0	0	0	0	0	0	0	.000	.000	.000	-99	-1	-1	0	0	0	0	0	/1	0.0

■ HARRY CHITI
Chiti, Harry b: 11/16/32, Kincaid, Ill. BR/TR, 6'2.5", 221 lbs. Deb: 9/27/50

YEAR	TM/L	G	AB	R	H	2B	3B	HR	RBI	BB	SO	AVG	OBP	SLG	PRO+	BR	/A	RC	SB	CS	SBR	FR	POS	TPR
1950	Chi-N	3	6	0	2	0	0	0	0	0	0	.333	.333	.333	77	-0	-0	1	0			-1	/C	0.0
1951	Chi-N	9	31	1	11	2	0	0	5	2	2	.355	.394	.419	117	1	1	4	0	0	0	0	/C	0.1
1952	Chi-N	32	113	14	31	5	0	5	13	5	8	.274	.305	.451	106	1	0	15	0	1	-1	6	C	0.7
1955	Chi-N	113	338	24	78	6	1	11	41	25	68	.231	.286	.352	68	-16	-16	33	0	0	0	2	*C	-1.0
1956	Chi-N	72	203	17	43	6	4	4	18	19	35	.212	.283	.340	68	-10	-9	18	0	0	0	3	C	-0.4
1958	KC-A	103	295	32	79	11	3	9	44	18	48	.268	.316	.417	98	-1	-1	37	3	2	-0	5	C	0.4
1959	KC-A	55	162	20	44	11	1	5	25	17	26	.272	.344	.444	113	3	3	22	0	1	-1	2	C	0.7
1960	KC-A	58	190	16	42	7	0	5	28	17	33	.221	.288	.337	68	-9	-9	18	1	0	0	-0	C	-0.5
	Det-A	37	104	9	17	0	0	2	5	10	12	.163	.237	.221	24	-11	-11	4	0	3	-2	1	C	-0.9
	Yr	95	294	25	59	7	0	7	33	27	45	.201	.270	.296	52	-20	-20	21	1	3	-2	1		-1.4
1961	Det-A	5	12	0	1	0	0	0	0	1	2	.083	.154	.083	-34	-2	-2	0	0	0	0	1	/C	-0.1
1962	NY-N	15	41	2	8	1	0	0	0	1	8	.195	.233	.220	22	-4	-5	2	0	0	0	-1	C	-0.5
Total	10	502	1495	135	356	49	9	41	179	115	242	.238	.296	.365	77	-48	-50	153	4	7		18	C	-1.5

■ FELIX CHOUINARD
Chouinard, Felix George b: 10/5/1887, Hines, Ill. d: 4/28/55, Hines, Ill. BR/TR, 5'7", 150 lbs. Deb: 9/11/10

YEAR	TM/L	G	AB	R	H	2B	3B	HR	RBI	BB	SO	AVG	OBP	SLG	PRO+	BR	/A	RC	SB	CS	SBR	FR	POS	TPR
1910	Chi-A	24	82	6	16	3	2	0	9	8		.195	.275	.280	77	-2	-2	7	4			4	O/2	0.1
1911	Chi-A	14	17	3	3	0	0	0	0	0		.176	.176	.176	-2	-2	-2	1	0			1	/2O	-0.1
1914	Pit-F	9	30	2	9	1	0	1	3	0	4	.300	.300	.433	109	0	0	4	1			-0	/2OS	0.0
	Bro-F	32	79	7	20	1	2	0	8	4	13	.253	.289	.316	74	-3	-3	8	3			-0	/O	-0.4
	Bal-F	5	9	3	4	0	0	0	1	0	1	.444	.444	.444	150	1	1	2	0			-0	/O	0.0
	Yr	46	118	12	33	2	2	1	12	4	18	.280	.303	.356	89	-2	-2	15	4			-1		-0.4
1915	Bro-F	4	4	1	2	0	0	0	2	0	0	.500	.500	.500	198	0	0	1	0			-1	/O	0.0
Total	4	88	221	22	54	5	4	1	23	12	18	.244	.286	.317	80	-6	-6	24	8			4	/O2S	-0.4

■ HARRY CHOZEN
Chozen, Harry b: 9/27/15, Winnebago, Minn. BR/TR, 5'9.5", 190 lbs. Deb: 9/21/37

YEAR	TM/L	G	AB	R	H	2B	3B	HR	RBI	BB	SO	AVG	OBP	SLG	PRO+	BR	/A	RC	SB	CS	SBR	FR	POS	TPR
1937	Cin-N	1	4	0	1	0	0	0	0	0	0	.250	.250	.250	38	-0	-0	0	0			-0	/C	0.0

■ NEIL CHRISLEY
Chrisley, Barbra O'Neil b: 12/16/31, Calhoun Falls, S.C BL/TR, 6'3", 187 lbs. Deb: 4/15/57

YEAR	TM/L	G	AB	R	H	2B	3B	HR	RBI	BB	SO	AVG	OBP	SLG	PRO+	BR	/A	RC	SB	CS	SBR	FR	POS	TPR
1957	Was-A	26	51	6	8	2	1	0	3	7	7	.157	.259	.235	36	-5	-4	4	0	0	0	-2	O	-0.6
1958	Was-A	105	233	19	50	7	4	5	26	16	18	.215	.265	.343	67	-11	-11	19	1	3	-2	3	O/3	-1.3
1959	Det-A	65	106	7	14	3	0	6	11	12	10	.132	.227	.330	48	-8	-8	8	0	0	0	-2	O	-1.1
1960	Det-A	96	220	27	56	10	3	5	24	19	26	.255	.317	.395	89	-3	-4	28	2	0	1	-1	O/1	-0.5
1961	Mil-N	10	9	1	2	0	0	0	0	1	1	.222	.300	.222	44	-1	-1	1	0	0	0	0	H	0.0
Total	5	302	619	60	130	22	8	16	64	55	62	.210	.277	.349	69	-27	-28	60	3	3	-1	-1	O/13	-3.5

■ LLOYD CHRISTENBURY
Christenbury, Lloyd Reid "Low"
b: 10/19/1893, Mecklenburg Co., N.C. d: 12/13/44, Birmingham, Ala. BL/TR, 5'7", 165 lbs. Deb: 9/20/19

YEAR	TM/L	G	AB	R	H	2B	3B	HR	RBI	BB	SO	AVG	OBP	SLG	PRO+	BR	/A	RC	SB	CS	SBR	FR	POS	TPR
1919	Bos-N	7	31	5	9	1	0	0	4	2	2	.290	.333	.323	102	-0	-0	3	0			1	/O	0.1
1920	Bos-N	65	106	17	22	2	2	0	14	13	12	.208	.300	.264	66	-5	-4	9	0	1	-1	-4	O/S23	-0.8
1921	Bos-N	62	125	34	44	6	2	3	16	21	7	.352	.449	.504	161	10	11	28	3	4	-2	-12	2/S	-0.1
1922	Bos-N	71	152	22	38	5	2	1	13	18	11	.250	.337	.329	76	-6	-5	17	2	4	-2	0	O/23	-0.6
Total	4	205	414	78	113	14	6	4	47	54	32	.273	.362	.365	101	-0	3	58	5	9		-15	/O2S3	-1.4

■ BRUCE CHRISTENSEN
Christensen, Bruce Ray b: 2/22/48, Madison, Wis. BL/TR, 5'11", 160 lbs. Deb: 7/17/71

YEAR	TM/L	G	AB	R	H	2B	3B	HR	RBI	BB	SO	AVG	OBP	SLG	PRO+	BR	/A	RC	SB	CS	SBR	FR	POS	TPR
1971	Cal-A	29	63	4	17	1	0	0	3	6	5	.270	.333	.286	83	-2	-1	6	0	1	-1	2	S	0.3

■ JOHN CHRISTENSEN
Christensen, John Lawrence b: 9/5/60, Downey, Cal. BR/TR, 6'3", 205 lbs. Deb: 9/13/84

YEAR	TM/L	G	AB	R	H	2B	3B	HR	RBI	BB	SO	AVG	OBP	SLG	PRO+	BR	/A	RC	SB	CS	SBR	FR	POS	TPR
1984	NY-N	5	11	2	3	2	0	0	3	1	2	.273	.333	.455	121	0	0	1	0	1	-1	-1	/O	-0.1
1985	NY-N	51	113	10	21	4	1	3	13	19	23	.186	.303	.319	76	-4	-3	11	1	2	-1	-3	O	-0.8
1987	Sea-A	53	132	19	32	6	1	2	12	12	28	.242	.306	.348	69	-5	-6	14	2	0	1	1	O/D	-0.4
1988	Min-A	23	38	5	10	4	0	0	5	3	5	.263	.349	.368	98	0	0	5	0	0	0	0	O/D	0.0
Total	4	132	294	36	66	16	2	5	33	35	58	.224	.311	.344	77	-8	-9	32	3	3	-1	-3	O/D	-1.3

■ CUCKOO CHRISTENSEN
Christensen, Walter Niels "Seacap"
b: 10/24/1899, San Francisco, Cal d: 12/20/84, Menlo Park, Cal. BL/TL, 5'6.5", 156 lbs. Deb: 4/13/26

YEAR	TM/L	G	AB	R	H	2B	3B	HR	RBI	BB	SO	AVG	OBP	SLG	PRO+	BR	/A	RC	SB	CS	SBR	FR	POS	TPR
1926	Cin-N	114	329	41	115	15	7	0	41	40	18	.350	.426	.438	136	17	19	62	8			-10	O	0.5
1927	Cin-N	57	185	25	47	6	0	0	16	20	16	.254	.330	.286	68	-8	-7	18	4			-1	O	-0.9
Total	2	171	514	66	162	21	7	0	57	60	34	.315	.392	.383	112	9	11	80	12			-10	O	-0.4

■ BOB CHRISTIAN
Christian, Robert Charles b: 10/17/45, Chicago, Ill. d: 2/20/74, San Diego, Cal. BR/TR, 5'10", 180 lbs. Deb: 9/02/68

YEAR	TM/L	G	AB	R	H	2B	3B	HR	RBI	BB	SO	AVG	OBP	SLG	PRO+	BR	/A	RC	SB	CS	SBR	FR	POS	TPR
1968	Det-A	3	3	0	1	1	0	0	0	0	0	.333	.333	.667	191	0	0	1	0	0	0	-0	/1O	0.0
1969	Chi-A	39	129	11	28	4	0	3	16	10	19	.217	.279	.318	63	-6	-7	12	3	0	1	-2	O	-0.8
1970	Chi-A	12	15	3	4	0	0	1	3	1	4	.267	.313	.467	108	0	0	2	0	0	0	-0	/O	0.0
Total	3	54	147	14	33	5	0	4	19	11	23	.224	.283	.340	70	-6	-6	15	3	0	1	-2	/O1	-0.8

■ MARK CHRISTMAN
Christman, Marquette Joseph b: 10/21/13, Maplewood, Mo. d: 10/9/76, St.Louis, Mo. BR/TR, 5'11", 175 lbs. Deb: 4/20/38

YEAR	TM/L	G	AB	R	H	2B	3B	HR	RBI	BB	SO	AVG	OBP	SLG	PRO+	BR	/A	RC	SB	CS	SBR	FR	POS	TPR
1938	Det-A	95	318	35	79	6	4	1	44	27	21	.248	.307	.302	50	-23	-26	31	5	2	0	9	3S	-1.1
1939	Det-A	6	16	0	4	2	0	0	2	0	2	.250	.250	.375	54	-1	-1	1	0	0	0	-1	/3	-0.1
	StL-A	79	222	27	48	6	3	0	20	20	10	.216	.281	.270	41	-20	-20	16	2	1	0	21	S/2	0.7
	Yr	85	238	27	52	8	3	0	20	20	12	.218	.279	.277	42	-21	-22	17	2	1	0	20		0.6
1943	StL-A	98	336	31	91	11	5	2	35	19	19	.271	.318	.351	94	-3	-3	38	0	3	-2	-0	3S12	-0.4
1944	*StL-A	148	547	56	148	25	1	6	83	47	37	.271	.332	.353	90	-3	-7	64	5	2	0	4	*3/1	-0.3
1945	StL-A	78	289	32	80	7	4	0	34	19	19	.277	.328	.370	98	0	-1	36	1	0	0	-3	3	-0.1
1946	StL-A	128	458	40	118	22	2	1	41	22	29	.258	.295	.321	68	-18	-20	41	0	2	-1	-5	3S	-0.5
1947	Was-A	110	374	27	83	15	2	1	33	33	16	.222	.287	.281	60	-21	-20	30	4	4	-1	-10	*S/2	-3.2
1948	Was-A	120	409	38	106	17	2	1	40	25	19	.259	.303	.318	67	-21	-19	37	0	3	-2	-32	*S/32	-5.1
1949	Was-A	49	112	8	24	2	0	3	18	8	7	.214	.273	.313	56	-8	-8	9	0	0	0	3	3/1S2	-0.4
Total	9	911	3081	294	781	113	23	19	348	220	179	.253	.306	.324	71	-117	-126	302	17	17	-5	0	3S/12	-10.5

YEAR	TM/L	G	AB	R	H	2B	3B	HR	RBI	BB	SO	AVG	OBP	SLG	PRO+	BR	/A	RC	SB	CS	SBR	FR	POS	TPR

■ STEVE CHRISTMAS　Christmas, Stephen Randall　b: 12/9/57, Orlando, Fla.　BL/TR, 6′, 190 lbs.　Deb: 9/01/83

1983	Cin-N	9	17	0	1	0	0	0	1	1	3	.059	.111	.059	-50	-3	-4	0	0	0	0	0	/C	-0.3
1984	Chi-A	12	11	1	4	1	0	1	4	0	2	.364	.364	.727	185	1	1	3	0	0	0	0	/C	0.1
1986	Chi-N	3	9	0	1	1	0	0	2	0	1	.111	.111	.222	-10	-1	-1	0	0	0	0	-0	/C1	-0.1
Total	3	24	37	1	6	2	0	1	7	1	6	.162	.184	.297	30	-4	-4	3	0	0	0	0	/C1	-0.3

■ JOE CHRISTOPHER　Christopher, Joseph O'Neal　b: 12/13/35, Frederiksted, V.I.　BR/TR, 5′10″, 175 lbs.　Deb: 5/26/59

1959	Pit-N	15	12	6	0	0	0	0	0	1	4	.000	.077	.000	-78	-3	-3	0	0	0	0	0	/O	-0.2
1960	*Pit-N	50	56	21	13	2	0	1	3	5	8	.232	.295	.321	68	-2	-2	6	1	0	0	2	O	0.0
1961	Pit-N	76	186	25	49	7	3	0	14	18	24	.263	.328	.333	76	-6	-6	19	6	4	-1	-2	O	-1.1
1962	NY-N	119	271	36	66	10	2	6	32	35	42	.244	.339	.362	87	-4	-5	36	11	3	2	-0	O	-0.7
1963	NY-N	64	149	19	33	5	1	1	8	13	21	.221	.297	.289	68	-6	-6	13	1	3	-2	-3	O	-1.3
1964	NY-N	154	543	78	163	26	8	16	76	48	92	.300	.363	.466	135	23	24	88	6	5	-1	-1	*O	1.9
1965	NY-N	148	437	38	109	18	3	5	40	35	82	.249	.314	.339	87	-9	-7	46	4	4	-1	-7	*O	-1.9
1966	Bos-A	12	13	1	1	0	0	0	0	2	4	.077	.200	.077	-15	-2	-2	0	0	0	0	-0	O	-0.2
Total	8	638	1667	224	434	68	17	29	173	157	277	.260	.331	.374	96	-9	-7	208	29	19	-3	-11	O	-3.5

■ LOYD CHRISTOPHER　Christopher, Loyd Eugene　b: 12/31/19, Richmond, Cal.　BR/TR, 6′2″, 190 lbs.　Deb: 4/20/45

1945	Bos-A	8	14	4	4	0	0	0	4	3	2	.286	.412	.286	101	0	0	2	0	0	0	-0	/O	0.0
	Chi-N	1	0	0	0	0	0	0	0	0	0	—	—	—	—	0	0	0	0			0	/O	0.0
1947	Chi-A	7	23	1	5	0	1	0	0	2	4	.217	.280	.304	65	-1	-1	1	0	1	-1	2	/O	0.0
Total	2	16	37	5	9	0	1	0	4	5	6	.243	.333	.297	80	-1	-1	3	0	1		1	/O	0.0

■ HI CHURCH　Church, Hiram Lincoln　b: Central Square, N.Y.　Deb: 8/28/1890

1890	Bro-a	3	9	1	1	0	0	0		0		.111	.111	.111	-35	-1	-1	0	0			-1	/O	-0.2

■ JOHN CHURRY　Churry, John　b: 11/26/1900, Johnstown, Pa.　d: 2/8/70, Zanesville, Ohio　BR/TR, 5′9″, 172 lbs.　Deb: 5/24/24

1924	Chi-N	6	7	0	1	1	0	0	2	0		.143	.333	.286	67	-0	-0	1	0	0	0	0	/C	0.0
1925	Chi-N	3	6	1	3	0	0	0	1	0	0	.500	.500	.500	154	1	1	1	0	0	0	0	/C	0.0
1926	Chi-N	2	4	0	0	0	0	0	0	1	2	.000	.000	.000	-42	-1	-1	0	0			0	/C	0.0
1927	Chi-N	1	1	0	1	0	0	0	0	0	0	1.000	1.000	1.000	436	0	0	1	0			0	/C	0.1
Total	4	12	18	1	5	1	0	0	1	3	2	.278	.381	.333	89	-0	-0	3	0	0		0	/C	0.1

■ LARRY CIAFFONE　Ciaffone, Lawrence Thomas "Symphony Larry"　b: 8/17/24, Brooklyn, N.Y.　BR/TR, 5′9.5″, 185 lbs.　Deb: 4/17/51

1951	StL-N	5	5	0	0	0	0	0	0	1	2	.000	.167	.000	-51	-1	-1	0	0	0	0	0	/O	0.0

■ DARRYL CIAS　Cias, Darryl Richard　b: 4/23/57, New York, N.Y.　BR/TR, 5′11″, 190 lbs.　Deb: 4/27/83

1983	Oak-A	19	18	1	6	1	0	0	1	2	4	.333	.400	.389	126	1	1	3	1	0	0	0	C	0.2

■ JOE CICERO　Cicero, Joseph Francis "Dode"　b: 11/18/10, Atlantic City, N.J　d: 3/30/83, Clearwater, Fla.　BR/TR, 5′8″, 167 lbs.　Deb: 9/20/29

1929	Bos-A	10	32	6	10	2	2	0	4	0	2	.313	.313	.500	108	0	0	5	0	0	0	-1	/O	0.0
1930	Bos-A	18	30	5	5	1	2	0	4	1	5	.167	.194	.333	32	-3	-3	2	0	0	0	-2	/O3	-0.4
1945	Phi-A	12	19	3	3	0	0	0	0	1	6	.158	.238	.158	16	-2	-2	1	0	0	0	-1	/O	-0.2
Total	3	40	81	14	18	3	4	0	8	2	13	.222	.250	.358	60	-5	-5	8	0	0	0	-3	/O3	-0.6

■ TED CIESLAK　Cieslak, Thaddeus Walter　b: 11/22/16, Milwaukee, Wis.　BR/TR, 5′10″, 175 lbs.　Deb: 4/18/44

1944	Phi-N	85	220	18	54	10	0	2	11	21	17	.245	.314	.318	81	-6	-5	22	1			-16	3/O	-1.9

■ AL CIHOCKI　Cihocki, Albert Joseph　b: 5/7/24, Nanticoke, Pa.　BR/TR, 5′11″, 185 lbs.　Deb: 4/17/45

1945	Cle-A	92	283	21	60	9	3	0	24	11	48	.212	.241	.265	49	-20	-18	19	2	1	0	1	S32	-1.5

■ ED CIHOCKI　Cihocki, Edward Joseph "Cy"　b: 5/9/07, Wilmington, Del.　d: 11/9/87, Newark, Del.　BR/TR, 5′8″, 163 lbs.　Deb: 5/29/32

1932	Phi-A	1	1	0	0	0	0	0	0	0	0	.000	.000	.000	-97	-0	-0	0	0	0	0	0	H	0.0
1933	Phi-A	33	97	6	14	2	3	0	9	7	16	.144	.200	.227	13	-12	-13	5	0	0	0	-2	S/23	-1.1
Total	2	34	98	6	14	2	3	0	9	7	16	.143	.200	.224	12	-13	-13	5	0	0	0	-2	/S32	-1.1

■ GINO CIMOLI　Cimoli, Gino Nicholas　b: 12/18/29, San Francisco, Cal.　BR/TR, 6′1″, 180 lbs.　Deb: 4/19/56

1956	*Bro-N	73	36	3	4	1	0	0	4	1	8	.111	.135	.139	-24	-6	-7	1	1	0	0	4	O	-0.4
1957	Bro-N	142	532	88	156	22	5	10	57	39	86	.293	.346	.410	93	2	-5	76	3	1	0	4	*O	-0.4
1958	LA-N	109	325	35	80	6	3	9	27	18	49	.246	.292	.366	71	-13	-14	30	3	3	-1	0	*O	-1.7
1959	StL-N	143	519	61	145	40	7	8	72	37	83	.279	.330	.430	94	-1	-5	70	7	0	2	-9	*O	-1.2
1960	*Pit-N	101	307	36	82	14	4	0	28	32	43	.267	.338	.339	85	-5	-5	35	1	0	0	1	O	-0.6
1961	Pit-N	21	67	4	20	3	1	0	6	2	13	.299	.319	.373	83	-2	-2	7	0	0	0	-0	O	-0.2
	Mil-N	37	117	12	23	5	0	3	4	11	15	.197	.266	.316	57	-8	-7	10	1	0	0	-1	O	-0.9
	Yr	58	184	16	43	8	1	3	10	13	28	.234	.284	.337	67	-10	-9	17	1	0	0	-2		-1.1
1962	KC-A	152	550	67	151	20	15	10	71	40	89	.275	.326	.420	96	-2	-4	74	2	1	0	-8	*O	-1.7
1963	KC-A	145	529	56	139	19	11	4	48	39	72	.263	.316	.363	86	-7	-10	60	3	1	0	4	*O	-0.9
1964	KC-A	4	9	1	0	0	0	0	0	0	1	.000	.000	.000	-97	-2	-2	0	0	0	0	-0	/O	-0.2
	Bal-A	38	58	6	8	3	2	0	3	2	13	.138	.167	.259	16	-7	-7	2	0	0	0	-2	O	-0.9
	Yr	42	67	6	8	3	2	0	3	2	14	.119	.145	.224	1	-9	-9	2	0	0	0	-1		-1.1
1965	Cal-A	4	5	1	0	0	0	0	1	0	2	.000	.000	.000	-99	-1	-1	0	0	0	0	0	/O	0.0
Total	10	969	3054	370	808	133	48	44	321	221	474	.265	.317	.383	85	-52	-69	365	21	6	3	-6	O	-9.1

■ FRANK CIPRIANI　Cipriani, Frank Dominick　b: 4/14/41, Buffalo, N.Y.　BR/TR, 6′, 180 lbs.　Deb: 9/08/61

1961	KC-A	13	36	2	9	0	0	0	2	2	4	.250	.289	.250	46	-3	-3	3	0	0	0	-0	O	-0.2

■ GEORGE CISAR　Cisar, George Joseph　b: 8/25/12, Chicago, Ill.　BR/TR, 6′, 175 lbs.　Deb: 9/09/37

1937	Bro-N	20	29	8	6	0	0	0	4	2	6	.207	.258	.207	27	-3	-3	1	3			0	O	-0.2

■ BILL CISSELL　Cissell, Chalmer William　b: 1/3/04, Perryville, Mo.　d: 3/15/49, Chicago, Ill.　BR/TR, 5′11″, 170 lbs.　Deb: 4/11/28

1928	Chi-A	125	443	66	115	22	3	1	60	29	41	.260	.307	.330	68	-21	-20	46	18	6	2	-2	*S	-0.7
1929	Chi-A	152	618	83	173	27	12	5	62	28	53	.280	.312	.381	80	-21	-20	72	26	17	-3	-3	*S	-1.0
1930	Chi-A	141	562	82	152	28	9	2	48	28	32	.270	.307	.363	72	-27	-24	62	16	9	-1	-11	*23S	-2.9
1931	Chi-A	109	409	42	90	13	5	1	46	16	26	.220	.256	.284	44	-35	-32	31	18	6	2	-10	S2/3	-2.8
1932	Chi-A	12	43	7	11	1	1	1	5	1	0	.256	.273	.395	76	-2	-2	5	0	0	0	0	S	0.0
	Cle-A	131	541	78	173	35	6	6	93	28	25	.320	.354	.440	98	3	-2	80	18	15	-4	11	*2/S	1.0
	Yr	143	584	85	184	36	7	7	98	29	25	.315	.349	.437	97	1	-4	85	18	15	-4	11		1.0
1933	Cle-A	112	409	53	94	21	3	6	33	31	29	.230	.284	.340	62	-22	-24	39	6	6	-2	-7	2S/3	-2.9
1934	Bos-A	102	416	71	111	13	4	4	44	28	23	.267	.315	.346	66	-19	-23	46	11	4	1	-4	2/S3	-1.9
1937	Phi-A	34	117	15	31	7	0	1	14	17	10	.265	.358	.350	81	-3	-3	16	0	0	0	3	2	0.3
1938	NY-N	38	149	19	40	6	0	2	18	6	11	.268	.297	.349	76	-5	-5	14	1			9	2/3	0.6
Total	9	956	3707	516	990	173	43	29	423	212	250	.267	.308	.360	73	-153	-156	412	114	63		-14	2S/3	-10.3

■ MOOSE CLABAUGH　Clabaugh, John William　b: 11/13/01, Albany, Mo.　d: 7/11/84, Tucson, Arizona　BL/TR, 6′, 185 lbs.　Deb: 8/30/26

1926	Bro-N	11	14	2	1	1	0	0	1	0	1	.071	.133	.143	-26	-3	-2	0	0			-1	/O	-0.2

YEAR	TM/L	G	AB	R	H	2B	3B	HR	RBI	BB	SO	AVG	OBP	SLG	PRO+	BR	/A	RC	SB	CS	SBR	FR	POS	TPR

■ BOBBY CLACK
Clack, Robert S. "Gentlemanly Bob" (b: Robert S. Clark)
b: 1851, Brooklyn, N.Y.   d: 10/22/33, Danvers, Mass.   BR/TR, 5'9", 153 lbs.   Deb: 5/15/1874

1874	Atl-n	33	134	22	23	2	0	0		2		.172	.184	.187	21	-12	-9	5					O/1	-0.6
1875	Atl-n	17	59	1	6	0	0	0		0		.102	.102	.102	-34	-7	-6	1					O	-0.4
1876	Cin-N	32	118	10	19	0	1	0	5	5	12	.161	.195	.178	29	-9	-6	4				1	O/213P	-0.4
Total	2 n	50	193	23	29	2	0	0		2		.150	.159	.161	5	-19	-15	5					/O1D	-1.0

■ DANNY CLAIRE
Claire, David Matthew   b: 11/17/1897, Ludington, Mich.   d: 1/7/56, Las Vegas, Nev.   BR/TR, 5'8", 164 lbs.   Deb: 9/17/20

1920	Det-A	3	7	1	1	0	0	0	0	0	0	.143	.143	.143	-25	-1	-1	0	0	0	0	-0	/S	0.0

■ AL CLANCY
Clancy, Albert Harrison   b: 8/14/1888, Santa Fe, N.Mex.   d: 10/17/51, Las Cruces, N.Mex.   BR/TR, 5'10.5", 175 lbs.   Deb: 6/20/11

1911	StL-A	3	5	0	0	0	0	0	0	0		.000	.167	.000	-54	-1	-1	0	0			0	/3	0.0

■ BUD CLANCY
Clancy, John William   b: 9/15/1900, Odell, Ill.   d: 9/26/68, Ottumwa, Iowa   BL/TL, 6', 170 lbs.   Deb: 8/29/24

1924	Chi-A	13	35	5	9	1	0	0	6	3	2	.257	.316	.286	58	-2	-2	3	3	2	-0	-2	/1	-0.3
1925	Chi-A	4	3	0	0	0	0	0	0	1	0	.000	.250	.000	-34	-1	-1	0	0	0	0	0	H	0.0
1926	Chi-A	12	38	3	13	2	2	0	7	1	1	.342	.375	.500	131	1	1	7	0	0	0	0	1	0.1
1927	Chi-A	130	464	46	139	21	2	3	53	24	24	.300	.337	.373	86	-11	-10	56	4	3	-1	0	*1	-1.3
1928	Chi-A	130	487	64	132	19	11	2	37	42	25	.271	.331	.368	85	-12	-11	60	6	9	-4	5	*1	-1.6
1929	Chi-A	92	290	36	82	14	6	3	45	16	19	.283	.320	.403	86	-7	-7	38	3	1	0	2	1	-1.3
1930	Chi-A	68	234	28	57	8	3	3	27	12	18	.244	.286	.342	61	-15	-14	23	3	1	0	-3	1	-2.1
1932	Bro-N	53	196	14	60	4	2	0	16	6	13	.306	.327	.347	83	-5	-5	22	0			3	1	-0.4
1934	Phi-N	20	49	8	12	0	0	1	7	6	4	.245	.339	.306	65	-2	-2	6	0			-1	1	-0.3
Total	9	522	1796	204	504	69	26	12	198	111	106	.281	.325	.368	81	-54	-49	215	19	16		4	1	-7.2

■ BILL CLANCY
Clancy, William Edward   b: 4/12/1879, Redfield, N.Y.   d: 2/10/48, Oriskany, N.Y.   BR/TR, 6'2", 180 lbs.   Deb: 4/14/05

1905	Pit-N	56	227	23	52	11	3	2	34	4		.229	.242	.330	70	-9	-9	20	3			-4	1/O	-1.6

■ UKE CLANTON
Clanton, Eucal "Cat"   b: 2/19/1898, Powell, Mo.   d: 2/24/60, Antlers, Okla.   BL/TL, 5'8", 165 lbs.   Deb: 9/21/22

1922	Cle-A	1	1	0	0	0	0	0	0	0	1	.000	.000	.000	-99	-0	-0	0	0	0	0	-0	/1	0.0

■ AARON CLAPP
Clapp, Aaron Bronson   b: 7/1856, Ithaca, N.Y.   d: 1/13/14, Sayre, Pa.   TR, 5'8", 175 lbs.   Deb: 5/01/1879

1879	Tro-N	36	146	24	39	9	3	0	18	6	10	.267	.296	.370	126	3	4	16				-3	1O	0.0

■ JOHN CLAPP
Clapp, John Edgar   b: 7/17/1851, Ithaca, N.Y.   d: 12/18/04, Ithaca, N.Y.   BR/TR, 5'7", 194 lbs.   Deb: 4/26/1872   M

1872	Man-n	19	97	30	32	8	0	1		1		.330	.337	.443	147	4	5	15					CM	0.3
1873	Ath-n	44	204	36	62	11	2	1		2		.304	.311	.392	98	1	-2	25					*C/S2	0.0
1874	Ath-n	39	165	46	48	8	4	3		1		.291	.295	.442	121	5	3	22					CO/S	0.3
1875	Ath-n	60	291	65	77	7	8	0		8		.265	.284	.344	104	5	-0	29					C	0.1
1876	StL-N	64	298	60	91	4	2	0	29	8	2	.305	.324	.332	125	6	8	33				9	*C/O2	1.8
1877	StL-N	60	255	47	81	6	6	0	34	8	6	.318	.338	.388	135	8	10	34				-5	*CO/1	0.5
1878	Ind-N	63	263	42	80	10	2	0	29	13	8	.304	.337	.357	148	8	13	32				-8	*O1/CS2M	0.3
1879	Buf-N	70	292	47	77	12	5	1	36	11	11	.264	.290	.349	107	3	2	30				-13	*C/OM	-1.0
1880	Cin-N	80	323	33	91	16	4	1	20	21	10	.282	.326	.365	135	12	12	39				14	*COM	2.9
1881	Cle-N	68	261	47	66	12	2	0	25	35	6	.253	.341	.314	113	4	6	29				-3	CO	0.2
1883	NY-N	20	73	6	13	0	0	0	5	5	4	.178	.231	.178	27	-6	-6	3				7	C/OM	0.2
Total	4 n	162	757	177	219	34	14	5		12		.289	.300	.391	111	16	6	92					C/OS2	0.7
Total	7	425	1765	282	499	60	21	2	178	101	47	.283	.322	.344	122	35	46	201				1	CO/1S2	4.9

■ DENNY CLARE
Clare, Dennis J.   b: 1852, Brooklyn, N.Y.   d: 11/26/28, Brooklyn, N.Y.   Deb: 9/14/1872

1872	Atl-n	2	7	1	1	0	0	0		0		.143	.143	.143	-10	-1	-1	0					/2	0.0

■ DOUG CLAREY
Clarey, Douglas William   b: 4/20/54, Los Angeles, Cal.   BR/TR, 6', 180 lbs.   Deb: 4/20/76

1976	StL-N	9	4	2	1	0	0	1	2	0	1	.250	.250	1.000	240	1	1	1	0	0	0	0	/2	0.1

■ ALLIE CLARK
Clark, Alfred Aloysius   b: 6/16/23, S.Amboy, N.J.   BR/TR, 6', 185 lbs.   Deb: 8/05/47

1947	*NY-A	24	67	9	25	5	0	1	14	5	2	.373	.417	.493	154	5	5	12	0	0	0	-0	O	0.4
1948	*Cle-A	81	271	43	84	5	2	9	38	23	13	.310	.364	.443	117	5	5	41	0	2	-1	-9	O/31	-0.6
1949	Cle-A	35	74	8	13	4	0	1	9	4	7	.176	.218	.270	29	-8	-8	4	0	0	0	-4	O/1	-1.1
1950	Cle-A	59	163	19	35	6	1	6	21	11	10	.215	.264	.374	64	-10	-10	12	0	1	-1	-2	O	-1.1
1951	Cle-A	3	10	3	3	2	0	1	3	1	2	.300	.364	.800	221	1	1	3	0	0	0	-1	/O	0.1
	Phi-A	56	161	20	40	10	1	4	22	15	7	.248	.320	.398	91	-2	-2	20	2	0	1	-2	O3	-0.4
	Yr	59	171	23	43	12	1	5	25	16	9	.251	.323	.421	98	-1	-1	23	2	0	1	-3		-0.3
1952	Phi-A	71	186	23	51	12	0	7	29	10	19	.274	.315	.452	105	2	0	24	0	2	-1	-4	O/1	-0.6
1953	Phi-A	20	74	6	15	4	0	3	13	3	5	.203	.234	.378	61	-4	-5	6	0	0	0	-1	O	-0.6
	Chi-A	9	15	0	1	0	0	0	0	0	5	.067	.067	.067	-62	-3	-3	-0	0	0	0	-0	/1O	-0.3
	Yr	29	89	6	16	4	0	3	13	3	10	.180	.207	.326	40	-8	-8	5	0	0	0	-2		-0.9
Total	7	358	1021	131	267	48	4	32	149	72	70	.262	.312	.410	92	-16	-16	123	2	5	-2	-22	O/31	-4.2

■ DAD CLARK
Clark, Alfred Robert "Fred"   b: 7/16/1873, San Francisco, Cal   d: 7/26/56, Ogden, Utah   BL/TL, 5'11", 170 lbs.   Deb: 7/03/02

1902	Chi-N	12	43	1	8	1	0	0	2	4		.186	.255	.209	46	-3	-2	3	1			-1	1	-0.4

■ EARL CLARK
Clark, Bailey Earl   b: 11/6/07, Washington, D.C.   d: 1/16/38, Washington, D.C.   BR/TR, 5'10", 160 lbs.   Deb: 8/17/27

1927	Bos-N	13	44	6	12	1	0	0	3	2	4	.273	.304	.295	66	-2	-2	4	0			-0	O	-0.2
1928	Bos-N	28	112	18	34	9	1	0	10	4	8	.304	.339	.402	98	-1	-1	15	0			0	O	0.0
1929	Bos-N	84	279	43	88	13	3	1	30	12	30	.315	.346	.394	86	-7	-6	37	6			1	O	-0.9
1930	Bos-N	82	233	29	69	11	3	3	28	7	22	.296	.320	.408	77	-10	-9	29	3			7	O	-0.5
1931	Bos-N	16	50	8	11	2	0	0	4	7	4	.220	.316	.260	58	-3	-3	5	1			0	O	-0.2
1932	Bos-N	50	44	11	11	2	0	0	4	2	7	.250	.283	.295	58	-3	-2	4	1			4	O	0.0
1933	Bos-N	7	23	3	8	1	0	0	1	2	1	.348	.400	.391	138	1	1	4	0			-1	/O	0.0
1934	StL-A	13	41	4	7	2	0	0	1	1	3	.171	.190	.220	5	-6	-6	2	0	0	0	-0	/O	-0.5
Total	8	293	826	122	240	41	7	4	81	37	79	.291	.324	.372	78	-32	-27	98	11	0		11	O	-2.3

■ DANNY CLARK
Clark, Daniel Curran   b: 1/18/1894, Meridian, Miss.   d: 5/23/37, Meridian, Miss.   BL/TL, 5'9", 167 lbs.   Deb: 4/12/22

1922	Det-A	83	185	31	54	11	3	3	26	15	11	.292	.345	.432	105	-0	1	28	1	0	0	-6	2/O3	-0.1
1924	Bos-N	104	325	36	90	23	3	2	54	51	19	.277	.378	.385	97	-0	-0	49	4	7	-3	-6	3	-0.1
1927	StL-N	58	72	8	17	2	2	0	13	8	7	.236	.313	.319	67	-3	-3	7	0			2	/O	-0.1
Total	3	245	582	75	161	36	8	5	93	74	37	.277	.360	.392	96	-3	-3	85	5	7		-10	/32O	-0.3

■ DAVE CLARK
Clark, David Earl   b: 9/3/62, Tupelo, Miss.   BL/TL, 6'2", 200 lbs.   Deb: 9/03/86

1986	Cle-A	18	58	10	16	1	0	3	9	7	11	.276	.354	.448	119	1	2	10	1	0	0	1	O/D	0.3
1987	Cle-A	29	87	11	18	5	0	3	12	2	24	.207	.225	.368	53	-6	-6	6	1	0	0	1	OD	-0.2
1988	Cle-A	63	156	11	41	4	1	3	18	17	28	.263	.335	.359	92	-1	-1	17	0	2	-1	1	DO	-0.1
1989	Cle-A	102	253	21	60	12	0	8	29	30	63	.237	.318	.379	94	-1	-2	29	0	2	-1	-1	DO	-0.4
1990	Chi-N	84	171	22	47	4	3	5	20	8	40	.275	.307	.409	88	-2	-3	21	7	1	2	-3	O	-0.5
Total	5	296	725	75	182	26	3	22	88	64	166	.251	.312	.386	89	-9	-11	83	9	5	-0	-1	OD	-1.1

YEAR	TM/L	G	AB	R	H	2B	3B	HR	RBI	BB	SO	AVG	OBP	SLG	PRO+	BR	/A	RC	SB	CS	SBR	FR	POS	TPR

■ GLEN CLARK
Clark, Glen Ester b: 3/7/41, Austin, Tex. BB/TR, 6'1", 190 lbs. Deb: 6/03/67

| 1967 | Atl-N | 4 | 4 | 0 | 0 | 0 | 0 | 0 | 0 | 0 | 1 | .000 | .000 | .000 | -99 | -1 | -1 | 0 | 0 | 0 | 0 | 0 | H | 0.0 |

■ PEP CLARK
Clark, Harry b: 3/20/1883, Union City, Ohio d: 6/8/65, Milwaukee, Wis. BR/TR, 5'7.5", 175 lbs. Deb: 9/11/03

| 1903 | Chi-A | 15 | 65 | 7 | 20 | 4 | 2 | 0 | 9 | 2 | | .308 | .328 | .431 | 134 | 2 | 2 | 11 | 5 | | | -0 | 3 | 0.2 |

■ JACK CLARK
Clark, Jack Anthony b: 11/10/55, New Brighton, Pa. BR/TR, 6'2", 175 lbs. Deb: 9/12/75

1975	SF-N	8	17	3	4	0	0	0	2	1	2	.235	.278	.235	42	-1	-1	1	1	0	0	0	/O3	0.0
1976	SF-N	26	102	14	23	6	2	2	10	8	18	.225	.282	.382	85	-2	-2	12	6	2	1	3	O	0.1
1977	SF-N	136	413	64	104	17	4	13	51	49	73	.252	.334	.407	98	-1	-1	58	12	4	1	4	*O	0.0
1978	SF-N	156	592	90	181	46	8	25	98	50	72	.306	.363	.537	155	36	39	109	15	11	-2	10	*O	4.2
1979	SF-N	143	527	84	144	25	2	26	86	63	95	.273	.352	.476	133	17	21	88	11	8	-2	5	*O/3	2.1
1980	SF-N	127	437	77	124	20	8	22	82	74	52	.284	.390	.517	155	31	32	87	2	5	-2	-3	*O	2.3
1981	SF-N	99	385	60	103	19	2	17	53	45	45	.268	.346	.460	129	13	14	59	1	1	-0	5	O	1.7
1982	SF-N	157	563	90	154	30	3	27	103	90	91	.274	.375	.481	138	30	30	98	6	9	-4	-3	*O	2.2
1983	SF-N	135	492	82	132	25	0	20	66	74	79	.268	.365	.441	126	16	18	80	5	3	-0	7	*O/1	2.3
1984	SF-N	57	203	33	65	9	1	11	44	43	29	.320	.439	.537	179	22	22	47	1	1	-0	-4	O1	1.7
1985	*StL-N	126	442	71	124	26	3	22	87	83	88	.281	.397	.502	151	32	32	89	1	4	-2	-8	*1O	1.9
1986	StL-N	65	232	34	55	12	2	9	23	45	61	.237	.363	.422	117	6	6	38	1	1	-0	-6	1	-0.2
1987	*StL-N	131	419	93	120	23	1	35	106	**136**	139	.286	**.461**	**.597**	174	54	53	127	1	2	-1	-8	*1/O	3.6
1988	NY-A	150	496	81	120	14	0	27	93	113	141	.242	.385	.433	130	23	24	88	3	2	-0	-1	*DO1	2.1
1989	SD-N	142	455	76	110	19	1	26	94	**132**	145	.242	.413	.459	149	36	36	95	6	2	1	0	*1O	2.7
1990	SD-N	115	334	59	89	12	1	25	62	**104**	91	.266	.443	.533	165	37	36	84	4	3	-1	-3	*1	2.7
Total	16	1773	6109	1011	1652	303	38	307	1060	1110	1221	.270	.384	.483	141	346	358	1161	76	58	-12	-2	*O1D/3	29.4

■ JIM CLARK
Clark, James (b: James Petrosky) b: 9/21/27, Bagley, Pa. BR/TR, 5'9", 150 lbs. Deb: 8/17/48

| 1948 | Was-A | 9 | 12 | 1 | 3 | 0 | 0 | 0 | 0 | 0 | 2 | .250 | .250 | .250 | 34 | -1 | -1 | 1 | 0 | 0 | 0 | -0 | /S3 | 0.0 |

■ JIM CLARK
Clark, James Edward b: 4/30/47, Kansas City, Kan. BR/TR, 6'1", 190 lbs. Deb: 7/16/71

| 1971 | Cle-A | 13 | 18 | 2 | 3 | 0 | 1 | 0 | 2 | 0 | 7 | .167 | .250 | .278 | 45 | -1 | -1 | 1 | 0 | 0 | 0 | 0 | /O1 | 0.0 |

■ JIM CLARK
Clark, James Francis b: 12/26/1887, Brooklyn, N.Y. d: 3/20/69, Beaumont, Tex. BR/TR, 5'11", 175 lbs. Deb: 9/02/11

1911	StL-N	14	18	2	3	0	1	0	3	3	4	.167	.286	.278	60	-1	-1	2	2			-1	/O	-0.1
1912	StL-N	2	1	0	0	0	0	0	0	0	1	.000	.000	.000	-99	-0	-0	0	0			0	H	0.0
Total	2	16	19	2	3	0	1	0	3	3	5	.158	.273	.263	51	-1	-1	2	2			-1	/O	-0.1

■ JERALD CLARK
Clark, Jerald Dwayne b: 8/10/63, Crockett, Tex. BR/TR, 6'4", 189 lbs. Deb: 9/19/88

1988	SD-N	6	15	0	3	1	0	0	3	0	4	.200	.200	.267	33	-1	-1	1	0	0	0	1	/O	0.0
1989	SD-N	17	41	5	8	2	0	1	7	3	9	.195	.250	.317	61	-2	-2	3	0	1	-1	0	O	-0.2
1990	SD-N	53	101	12	27	4	1	5	11	5	24	.267	.302	.475	109	1	1	14	0	0	-0	-0	1O	0.0
Total	3	76	157	17	38	7	1	6	21	8	37	.242	.279	.414	90	-3	-3	17	0	1	-1	1	/O1	-0.2

■ CAP CLARK
Clark, John Carrol b: 9/19/06, Snow Camp, N.C. d: 2/16/57, Fayetteville, N.C. BL/TR, 5'11", 180 lbs. Deb: 4/23/38

| 1938 | Phi-N | 52 | 74 | 11 | 19 | 1 | 1 | 0 | 4 | 9 | 10 | .257 | .337 | .297 | 78 | -2 | -2 | 8 | 0 | | | -2 | C | -0.2 |

■ MEL CLARK
Clark, Melvin Earl b: 7/7/26, Letart, W.Va. BR/TR, 6', 180 lbs. Deb: 9/11/51

1951	Phi-N	10	31	2	10	1	0	0	3	0	3	.323	.323	.452	108	0	0	4	0	1	-1	-1	/O	-0.1
1952	Phi-N	47	155	20	52	6	4	1	15	6	13	.335	.364	.445	125	4	5	25	2	1	0	1	O/3	0.5
1953	Phi-N	60	198	31	59	10	4	0	19	11	17	.298	.338	.389	89	-3	-3	24	1	0	0	-2	O	-0.6
1954	Phi-N	83	233	26	56	9	7	1	24	17	21	.240	.292	.352	67	-12	-12	21	0	1	-1	1	O	-1.3
1955	Phi-N	10	32	3	5	3	0	1	3	4	4	.156	.229	.250	27	-3	-3	2	0	0	0	3	/O	0.0
1957	Det-A	5	7	0	0	0	0	0	1	0	3	.000	.000	.000	-97	-2	-2	0	0	0	0	0	/O	-0.1
Total	6	215	656	82	182	29	15	3	63	37	61	.277	.318	.381	85	-16	-15	75	3	3	-1	3	O/3	-1.6

■ SPIDER CLARK
Clark, Owen F. b: 9/16/1867, Brooklyn, N.Y. d: 2/8/1892, Brooklyn, N.Y. TR, 5'10", 150 lbs. Deb: 5/02/1889

1889	Was-N	38	145	19	37	7	2	3	22	6	18	.255	.285	.393	96	-3	-1	19	8			4	CS/O32	0.3
1890	Buf-P	69	260	45	69	11	1	1	25	20	16	.265	.325	.327	83	-9	-5	31	8			-5	OC2/13SP	-0.7
Total	2	107	405	64	106	18	3	4	47	26	34	.262	.311	.351	87	-11	-6	50	16			-0	/OC2S13P	-0.4

■ BOB CLARK
Clark, Robert Cale b: 6/13/55, Sacramento, Cal. BR/TR, 6', 190 lbs. Deb: 8/21/79

1979	*Cal-A	19	54	8	16	2	2	1	5	5	11	.296	.356	.463	123	1	2	8	1	1	-0	4	O	0.4
1980	Cal-A	78	261	26	60	10	1	5	23	11	42	.230	.266	.333	65	-14	-13	21	0	1	-1	13	O	-0.1
1981	Cal-A	34	88	12	22	2	1	4	19	7	18	.250	.305	.432	110	1	1	11	0	0	0	4	O	0.5
1982	*Cal-A	102	90	11	19	1	0	2	8	0	29	.211	.211	.289	36	-8	-8	5	1	0	0	5	*O	-0.5
1983	Cal-A	76	212	17	49	9	1	5	21	9	45	.231	.262	.354	68	-10	-10	18	0	0	0	4	O/3D	-1.4
1984	Mil-A	58	169	17	44	7	2	2	16	16	35	.260	.328	.361	94	-2	-1	17	1	5	-3	-4	O	-0.9
1985	Mil-A	29	93	6	21	3	0	0	8	7	19	.226	.280	.258	49	-6	-6	6	1	1	-0	2	O	-0.4
Total	7	396	967	97	231	34	7	19	100	55	199	.239	.282	.347	74	-38	-35	87	4	8	-4	20	O/D3	-2.4

■ BOB CLARK
Clark, Robert H. b: 3/18/1863, Covington, Ky. d: 8/21/19, Covington, Ky. BR/TR, 5'10", 175 lbs. Deb: 4/17/1886

1886	Bro-a	71	269	37	58	8	2	0		17		.216	.241	.260	65	-11	-11	23	14			-13	COS	-1.8
1887	Bro-a	48	177	24	47	3	1	0		7		.266	.297	.294	66	-8	-8	20	15			-2	C/O	-0.1
1888	Bro-a	45	150	23	36	5	3	1	20	9		.240	.292	.333	103	0	1	18	11			-2	C/O1	0.2
1889	*Bro-a	53	182	32	50	5	2	0	22	15	7	.275	.368	.324	100	1	1	29	18			5	C	0.9
1890	*Bro-N	43	151	24	33	3	3	0	15	15	8	.219	.306	.278	72	-5	-5	16	10			-12	C/O	-1.2
1891	Cin-N	16	54	2	6	0	0	0	3	6	9	.111	.213	.111	-3	-7	-7	2	3			-5	C	-0.9
1893	Lou-N	12	28	3	3	1	0	0	3	5	5	.107	.242	.143	5	-4	-3	1	0			-2	C/OS	-0.3
Total	7	288	1011	145	233	25	11	1	63	85	29	.230	.296	.280	73	-32	-32	110	71			-31	C/OS1	-3.2

■ RON CLARK
Clark, Ronald Bruce b: 1/14/43, Ft.Worth, Tex. BR/TR, 5'10", 175 lbs. Deb: 9/11/66 C

1966	Min-A	5	1	1	1	0	0	0	0	0	0	1.000	1.000	1.000	448	0	0	1	0	0	0	0	/3	0.0
1967	Min-A	20	60	7	10	3	1	2	11	4	9	.167	.219	.350	61	-3	-3	4	0	0	0	-1	3	-0.3
1968	Min-A	104	227	14	42	5	1	1	13	16	44	.185	.245	.229	42	-15	-16	14	3	2	-0	-8	3S2	-2.2
1969	Min-A	8	8	0	1	0	0	0	0	0	0	.125	.125	.125	-29	-1	-1	0	0	0	0	-1	/3	-0.1
	Sea-A	57	163	9	32	5	0	0	12	13	29	.196	.260	.227	38	-14	-13	11	1	0	0	-9	S3/21	-2.0
	Yr	62	171	9	33	5	0	0	12	13	29	.193	.254	.222	35	-15	-15	10	1	0	0	-10		-2.1
1971	Oak-A	2	1	0	0	0	0	0	0	0	0	.000	.000	.000	53	0	0	0	0	0	0	0	H	0.0
1972	Oak-A	14	15	1	4	2	0	0	1	2	4	.267	.353	.400	130	0	1	2	0	0	0	0	2/3	0.2
	Mil-A	22	54	8	10	1	1	2	5	5	11	.185	.254	.352	81	-2	-1	5	0	0	0	5	23	0.5
	Yr	36	69	9	14	3	1	2	6	7	15	.203	.276	.362	92	-1	-1	6	0	0	0	6		0.7
1975	Phi-N	1	0	0	0	0	0	0	0	0	0	.000	.000	.000	-96	-0	-0	0	0	0	0	0	H	0.0
Total	7	230	530	40	100	16	3	5	43	41	98	.189	.251	.258	49	-34	-35	35	4	2	0	-12	/3S21	-3.9

■ ROY CLARK
Clark, Roy Elliott "Pepper" b: 5/11/1874, New Haven, Conn. d: 11/1/25, Bridgeport, Conn. BL/TR, 5'8", 170 lbs. Deb: 4/19/02

| 1902 | NY-N | 21 | 76 | 4 | 11 | 1 | 0 | 0 | 3 | 1 | | .145 | .156 | .158 | -2 | -9 | -9 | 3 | 5 | | | -3 | O | -1.3 |

YEAR	TM/L	G	AB	R	H	2B	3B	HR	RBI	BB	SO	AVG	OBP	SLG	PRO+	BR	/A	RC	SB	CS	SBR	FR	POS	TPR

■ WILL CLARK   Clark, William Nuschler b: 3/13/64, New Orleans, La. BL/TL, 6'2", 190 lbs. Deb: 4/08/86

YEAR	TM/L	G	AB	R	H	2B	3B	HR	RBI	BB	SO	AVG	OBP	SLG	PRO+	BR	/A	RC	SB	CS	SBR	FR	POS	TPR
1986	SF-N	111	408	66	117	27	2	11	41	34	76	.287	.346	.444	122	8	11	62	4	7	-3	-1	*1	0.3
1987	*SF-N	150	529	89	163	29	5	35	91	49	98	.308	.372	.580	155	34	38	109	5	17	-9	2	*1	2.3
1988	SF-N	162	575	102	162	31	6	29	109	100	129	.282	.392	.508	163	44	47	120	9	1	2	-3	*1	4.1
1989	*SF-N	159	588	104	196	38	9	23	111	74	103	.333	.412	.546	177	56	58	136	8	3	1	0	*1	4.8
1990	SF-N	154	600	91	177	25	5	19	95	62	97	.295	.364	.448	124	18	19	101	8	2	1	1	*1	1.3
Total	5	736	2700	452	815	150	27	117	447	319	503	.302	.380	.507	149	161	173	528	34	30	-8	-1	1	12.8

■ WILLIE CLARK   Clark, William Otis "Wee Willie" b: 8/16/1872, Pittsburgh, Pa. d: 11/13/32, Pittsburgh, Pa. Deb: 6/20/1895

YEAR	TM/L	G	AB	R	H	2B	3B	HR	RBI	BB	SO	AVG	OBP	SLG	PRO+	BR	/A	RC	SB	CS	SBR	FR	POS	TPR
1895	NY-N	23	88	9	23	3	2	0	16	5	6	.261	.301	.341	69	-4	-4	10	1			1	1	-0.1
1896	NY-N	72	247	38	72	12	4	0	33	15	12	.291	.352	.372	96	-2	-1	36	8			-4	1	-0.2
1897	NY-N	116	431	63	122	17	12	1	75	37		.283	.352	.385	100	-2	0	66	18			2	*1/O3	0.1
1898	Pit-N	57	209	29	64	9	7	1	31	22		.306	.378	.431	137	9	10	35	0			0	1	1.0
1899	Pit-N	80	298	49	85	13	10	0	44	35		.285	.379	.396	116	8	8	50	11			1	1	0.9
Total	5	348	1273	188	366	54	35	2	199	114	18	.288	.359	.390	106	9	13	197	38			0	1/O3	1.7

■ BILL CLARK   Clark, William Winfield b: 4/11/1875, Circleville, Ohio d: 4/15/59, Los Angeles, Cal. BR/TR, 5'10", 175 lbs. Deb: 7/12/1897

YEAR	TM/L	G	AB	R	H	2B	3B	HR	RBI	BB	SO	AVG	OBP	SLG	PRO+	BR	/A	RC	SB	CS	SBR	FR	POS	TPR
1897	Lou-N	4	16	2	3	0	0	0	2	1		.188	.235	.188	14	-2	-2	1	1			-1	/23	-0.2

■ ARTIE CLARKE   Clarke, Arthur Franklin b: 5/6/1865, Providence, R.I. d: 11/14/49, Brookline, Mass. BR/TR, 5'8", 155 lbs. Deb: 4/19/1890

YEAR	TM/L	G	AB	R	H	2B	3B	HR	RBI	BB	SO	AVG	OBP	SLG	PRO+	BR	/A	RC	SB	CS	SBR	FR	POS	TPR
1890	NY-N	101	395	55	89	12	8	0	49	32	38	.225	.290	.296	73	-14	-14	48	44			-2	CO32/S	-1.1
1891	NY-N	48	174	17	33	2	2	0	21	15	16	.190	.254	.224	43	-13	-12	11	5			-9	C/3O	-1.4
Total	2	149	569	72	122	14	10	0	70	47	54	.214	.279	.274	64	-26	-25	59	49			-11	/CO32S	-2.5

■ FRED CLARKE   Clarke, Fred Clifford "Cap" b: 10/3/1872, Winterset, Iowa d: 8/14/60, Winfield, Kan. BL/TR, 5'10.5", 165 lbs. Deb: 6/30/1894   MH

YEAR	TM/L	G	AB	R	H	2B	3B	HR	RBI	BB	SO	AVG	OBP	SLG	PRO+	BR	/A	RC	SB	CS	SBR	FR	POS	TPR
1894	Lou-N	75	310	54	83	11	7	7	48	25	27	.268	.330	.416	86	-11	-7	52	25			4	O	-0.5
1895	Lou-N	132	550	96	191	21	5	4	82	34	24	.347	.396	.425	121	12	18	111	40			11	*O	1.5
1896	Lou-N	131	517	96	168	15	18	9	79	43	34	.325	.392	.476	135	22	26	113	34			0	*O	1.4
1897	Lou-N	128	518	120	202	30	13	6	67	45		.390	.461	.533	170	50	53	157	57			6	*OM	4.2
1898	Lou-N	149	599	116	184	23	12	3	47	48		.307	.373	.401	127	20	21	107	40			6	*OM	1.6
1899	Lou-N	148	602	122	206	23	9	5	70	49		.342	.405	.435	134	29	29	129	49			1	*O/SM	1.8
1900	Pit-N	106	399	84	110	15	12	3	32	51		.276	.366	.396	112	8	8	67	21			3	*OM	0.1
1901	Pit-N	129	527	118	171	24	15	6	60	51		.324	.391	.461	145	33	31	108	23			2	*O/S3M	1.9
1902	Pit-N	113	459	103	145	27	14	2	53	51		.316	.408	.449	161	38	36	99	29			-1	*OM	2.8
1903	*Pit-N	104	427	88	150	32	15	5	70	41		.351	.408	.532	164	37	35	105	21			-8	*O/SM	2.0
1904	Pit-N	72	278	51	85	7	11	0	25	22		.306	.357	.410	135	12	11	47	11			0	OM	0.9
1905	Pit-N	141	525	95	157	18	15	2	51	55		.299	.366	.402	128	20	19	91	24			4	*OM	1.4
1906	Pit-N	118	417	69	129	14	13	1	39	40		.309	.370	.412	140	22	20	74	18			6	*OM	2.5
1907	Pit-N	148	501	97	145	18	13	2	59	68		.289	.374	.389	140	26	25	91	37			6	*OM	2.8
1908	Pit-N	151	551	83	146	18	15	2	53	65		.265	.343	.363	128	18	18	77	24			10	*OM	3.0
1909	*Pit-N	152	550	97	158	16	11	3	68	80		.287	.384	.373	124	25	20	92	31			7	*OM	2.5
1910	Pit-N	123	429	57	113	23	9	2	63	53	23	.263	.350	.373	105	6	3	62	12			7	*OM	0.6
1911	Pit-N	110	392	73	127	25	13	5	49	53	27	.324	.407	.492	146	27	25	82	10			2	*OM	2.3
1913	Pit-N	9	13	0	1	1	0	0	0	0	0	.077	.077	.154	-37	-2	-2	0	0			-0	/OM	-0.2
1914	Pit-N	2	2	0	0	0	0	0	0	0	0	.000	.000	.000	-99	-0	-0	0	0			0	/HM	0.0
1915	Pit-N	1	2	0	1	0	0	0	0	0	0	.500	.500	.500	206	0	0	1	0			0	/OM	0.0
Total	21	2242	8568	1619	2672	361	220	67	1015	874	135	.312	.384	.429	133	393	388	1665	506			65	*O/S3	32.6

■ HARRY CLARKE   Clarke, Harry Corson b: 1861, d: 3/3/23, Long Beach, Cal. Deb: 8/28/1889

YEAR	TM/L	G	AB	R	H	2B	3B	HR	RBI	BB	SO	AVG	OBP	SLG	PRO+	BR	/A	RC	SB	CS	SBR	FR	POS	TPR
1889	Was-N	1	3	0	0	0	0	0	0	0	1	.000	.000	.000	-99	-1	-1	0	0			1	/O	0.1

■ HENRY CLARKE   Clarke, Henry Tefft b: 8/28/1875, Bellevue, Neb. d: 3/28/50, Colorado Springs, Colo. BR/TR, Deb: 6/26/1897

YEAR	TM/L	G	AB	R	H	2B	3B	HR	RBI	BB	SO	AVG	OBP	SLG	PRO+	BR	/A	RC	SB	CS	SBR	FR	POS	TPR
1897	Cle-N	7	25	3	7	0	0	0	3	2		.280	.333	.280	62	-1	-1	2	0			-1	/PO	0.0
1898	Chi-N	2	4	0	1	0	0	0	0	1		.250	.400	.250	90	0	0	0	0			-1	/OP	0.0
Total	2	9	29	3	8	0	0	0	3	3		.276	.344	.276	66	-1	-1	3	0			-2	/PO	0.0

■ HORACE CLARKE   Clarke, Horace Meredith b: 6/2/40, Frederiksted, St.Croix, V.I. BB/TR, 5'9", 170 lbs. Deb: 5/13/65

YEAR	TM/L	G	AB	R	H	2B	3B	HR	RBI	BB	SO	AVG	OBP	SLG	PRO+	BR	/A	RC	SB	CS	SBR	FR	POS	TPR
1965	NY-A	51	108	13	28	1	0	1	9	6	6	.259	.298	.296	70	-4	-4	10	2	1	0	3	3/2S	0.0
1966	NY-A	96	312	37	83	10	4	6	28	27	24	.266	.326	.381	107	1	2	40	5	3	-0	-19	S2/3	-1.3
1967	NY-A	143	588	74	160	17	0	3	29	42	64	.272	.321	.316	92	-8	-5	64	21	4	4	15	*2	1.9
1968	NY-A	148	579	52	133	6	1	2	26	23	46	.230	.259	.254	58	-31	-29	39	20	7	2	30	*2	0.8
1969	NY-A	156	641	82	183	26	7	4	48	53	41	.285	.340	.367	101	-2	1	83	33	13	2	-4	*2	0.5
1970	NY-A	158	686	81	172	24	2	4	46	35	35	.251	.289	.309	68	-33	-29	62	23	7	3	-7	*2	-1.7
1971	NY-A	159	625	76	156	23	7	2	41	64	43	.250	.321	.318	87	-14	-10	66	17	7	1	-3	*2	-0.5
1972	NY-A	147	547	65	132	20	2	3	37	56	44	.241	.316	.302	87	-9	-7	56	18	6	2	6	*2	1.1
1973	NY-A	148	590	60	155	21	0	2	35	47	48	.263	.319	.308	80	-17	-14	56	11	10	-3	6	*2	-0.5
1974	NY-A	24	47	3	11	1	0	0	1	4	5	.234	.294	.255	61	-2	-2	4	1	0	0	-5	2/D	-0.6
	SD-N	42	90	5	17	1	0	0	4	8	6	.189	.255	.200	30	-8	-8	5	0	0	0	-4	2	-1.1
Total	10	1272	4813	548	1230	150	23	27	304	365	362	.256	.310	.313	82	-128	-106	482	151	58	11	17	*2/S3D	-1.4

■ NIG CLARKE   Clarke, Jay Justin b: 12/15/1882, Amherstburg, Ont., Canada d: 6/15/49, River Rouge, Mich BL/TR, 5'8", 165 lbs. Deb: 4/26/05

YEAR	TM/L	G	AB	R	H	2B	3B	HR	RBI	BB	SO	AVG	OBP	SLG	PRO+	BR	/A	RC	SB	CS	SBR	FR	POS	TPR
1905	Cle-A	5	9	2	1	1	0	0	1	1		.111	.200	.222	35	-1	-1	0	0			-1	/C	-0.1
	Det-A	3	7	1	3	0	0	1	1	0		.429	.429	.857	305	1	1	3	0			1	/C	0.3
	Cle-A	37	114	9	23	5	1	0	8	10		.202	.266	.263	69	-4	-4	8	0			-0	C	0.0
	Yr	45	130	12	27	6	1	1	10	11		.208	.270	.292	79	-3	-3	11	0			-1		0.2
1906	Cle-A	57	179	22	64	12	4	1	21	13		.358	.401	.486	182	16	16	37	3			-1	C	2.0
1907	Cle-A	120	390	44	105	19	6	3	33	35		.269	.329	.372	125	11	11	50	3			-10	*C	1.2
1908	Cle-A	97	290	34	70	8	6	1	27	30		.241	.313	.321	108	3	3	31	6			-7	C	0.6
1909	Cle-A	55	164	15	45	4	2	0	14	9		.274	.316	.323	98	0	-1	17	1			-1	C	0.1
1910	Cle-A	21	58	4	9	2	0	0	2	8		.155	.258	.190	40	-4	-4	3	0			3	C	0.1
1911	StL-A	82	256	22	55	10	1	0	18	26		.215	.287	.262	56	-16	-14	20	2			-5	C/1	-1.0
1919	Phi-N	26	62	4	15	3	0	0	2	4	5	.242	.299	.290	72	-2	-2	5	1			1	C	0.0
1920	Pit-N	3	7	0	0	0	0	0	0	2	4	.000	.222	.000	-32	-1	-1	0	0			1	/C	0.0
Total	9	506	1536	157	390	64	20	6	127	138	9	.254	.316	.333	102	5	5	175	16	0		-21	C/1	3.2

■ JOSH CLARKE   Clarke, Joshua Baldwin "Pepper" b: 3/8/1879, Winfield, Kan. d: 7/2/62, Ventura, Cal. BL/TR, 5'10", 180 lbs. Deb: 6/15/1898

YEAR	TM/L	G	AB	R	H	2B	3B	HR	RBI	BB	SO	AVG	OBP	SLG	PRO+	BR	/A	RC	SB	CS	SBR	FR	POS	TPR
1898	Lou-N	6	18	0	3	0	0	0	0	0	1	.167	.211	.167	10	-2	-2	1	0			-1	/O	-0.2
1905	StL-N	50	167	31	43	3	2	3	18	27		.257	.361	.353	119	4	5	25	8			-8	O2/S	-0.3
1908	Cle-A	131	492	70	119	8	4	1	21	76		.242	.343	.280	105	7	7	60	37			-3	*O	-0.2
1909	Cle-A	4	12	1	0	0	0	0	0	2		.000	.143	.000	-52	-2	-2	0	0			-1	/O	-0.4
1911	Bos-N	32	120	16	28	7	3	1	4	29	22	.233	.387	.367	103	3	2	19	6			3	O	0.4
Total	5	223	809	118	193	18	9	5	43	135	22	.239	.348	.302	103	10	9	105	51			-10	O/2S	-0.7

■ GREY CLARKE   Clarke, Richard Grey "Noisy" b: 9/26/12, Fulton, Ala. BR/TR, 5'9", 183 lbs. Deb: 4/19/44

YEAR	TM/L	G	AB	R	H	2B	3B	HR	RBI	BB	SO	AVG	OBP	SLG	PRO+	BR	/A	RC	SB	CS	SBR	FR	POS	TPR
1944	Chi-A	63	169	14	44	10	1	0	27	22	6	.260	.352	.331	97	-0	0	19	0	4	-2	1	3	-0.1

YEAR	TM/L	G	AB	R	H	2B	3B	HR	RBI	BB	SO	AVG	OBP	SLG	PRO+	BR	/A	RC	SB	CS	SBR	FR	POS	TPR

■ SUMPTER CLARKE Clarke, Sumpter Mills b: 10/18/1897, Savannah, Ga. d: 3/16/62, Knoxville, Tenn. BR/TR, 5'11", 170 lbs. Deb: 9/27/20

1920	Chi-N	1	3	0	1	0	0	0	0	0	1	.333	.333	.333	90	-0	-0	0	0	0	0	-0	/3	0.0
1923	Cle-A	1	3	0	0	0	0	0	0	0	0	.000	.000	.000	-99	-1	-1	0	0	0	0	-0	/O	0.0
1924	Cle-A	35	104	17	24	6	1	0	11	6	12	.231	.273	.308	49	-8	-8	9	0	0	0	-5	O	-1.4
Total	3	37	110	17	25	6	1	0	11	6	13	.227	.267	.300	46	-9	-9	9	0	0	0	-6	/O3	-1.4

■ TOMMY CLARKE Clarke, Thomas Aloysius b: 5/9/1888, New York, N.Y. d: 8/14/45, Corona, N.Y. BR/TR, 5'11", 175 lbs. Deb: 8/26/09

1909	Cin-N	18	52	8	13	3	2	0	10	6		.250	.328	.385	122	1	1	8	3			4	C	0.7
1910	Cin-N	64	151	19	42	6	5	1	20	19	17	.278	.370	.404	131	5	6	23	1			-0	C	0.9
1911	Cin-N	86	203	20	49	6	7	1	25	25	22	.241	.328	.355	94	-3	-2	26	4			2	C/1	0.6
1912	Cin-N	72	146	19	41	7	2	0	22	28	14	.281	.400	.356	111	3	4	25	9			5	C	1.2
1913	Cin-N	114	330	29	87	11	8	1	38	39	40	.264	.345	.355	100	1	1	39	2			-9	*C	-0.1
1914	Cin-N	113	313	30	82	13	7	2	25	31	30	.262	.332	.367	105	3	2	39	6			-3	*C	0.3
1915	Cin-N	96	226	23	65	7	2	0	21	33	22	.288	.381	.336	116	7	6	32	7	3	0	-5	C	0.6
1916	Cin-N	78	177	10	42	10	1	0	17	24	20	.237	.328	.305	97	-0	0	20	8			-11	C	-0.8
1917	Cin-N	58	110	11	32	3	3	1	13	11	12	.291	.361	.400	139	4	5	16	2			-5	C	0.1
1918	Chi-N	1	0	0	0	0	0	0	0	0	0	—	—	—	—	0	0	0	0			0	/C	0.0
Total	10	700	1708	169	453	66	37	6	191	216	177	.265	.351	.358	109	21	23	227	42	3		-23	C/1	3.5

■ BOILERYARD CLARKE Clarke, William Jones b: 10/18/1868, New York, N.Y. d: 7/29/59, Princeton, N.J. BR/TR, 5'11.5", 170 lbs. Deb: 5/01/1893

1893	Bal-N	49	183	23	32	1	3	1	24	19	14	.175	.274	.230	35	-17	-17	12	2			-2	C1	-1.2
1894	Bal-N	28	100	18	24	8	0	1	19	16	14	.240	.361	.350	71	-4	-5	14	2			-3	C/1	-0.3
1895	*Bal-N	67	241	38	70	15	3	0	35	13	18	.290	.350	.378	87	-4	-5	35	8			5	C/1	0.4
1896	Bal-N	80	300	48	89	14	7	2	71	14	12	.297	.345	.410	99	-0	-1	46	7			-11	C1	-0.4
1897	*Bal-N	64	241	32	65	7	1	1	38	9		.270	.320	.320	71	-10	-10	27	5			-16	C/1	-1.4
1898	Bal-N	82	285	26	69	5	2	0	27	4		.242	.289	.274	63	-13	-14	24	2			4	C/1	-0.3
1899	Bos-N	60	223	25	50	3	2	2	32	10		.224	.270	.283	49	-14	-17	18	2			-2	C	-1.3
1900	Bos-N	81	270	35	85	5	2	1	30	9		.315	.344	.359	86	-1	-6	34	0			9	C/1	0.8
1901	Was-A	110	422	58	118	15	5	3	54	23		.280	.335	.360	96	-3	-2	56	7			-10	*C/1	-0.1
1902	Was-A	87	291	31	78	16	0	6	40	23		.268	.334	.385	100	0	0	39	1			-4	C	0.3
1903	Was-A	126	465	35	111	14	6	2	38	15		.239	.262	.308	71	-16	-17	42	12			-12	1C	-2.4
1904	Was-A	85	275	23	58	8	1	0	17	17		.211	.257	.247	63	-11	-11	20	5			0	C1	-0.4
1905	NY-N	31	50	2	9	0	0	1	4	4		.180	.241	.240	44	-3	-3	3	1			-1	1C	-0.3
Total	13	950	3346	394	858	111	32	20	429	176	58	.256	.308	.327	76	-95	-108	371	54			-41	C1	-6.6

■ STU CLARKE Clarke, William Stuart b: 1/24/06, San Francisco, Cal d: 8/26/85, Hayward, Cal. BR/TR, 5'8.5", 160 lbs. Deb: 7/17/29

1929	Pit-N	57	178	20	47	5	7	2	21	19	21	.264	.338	.404	81	-5	-6	24	3			-8	S3/2	-0.5
1930	Pit-N	4	9	2	4	0	1	0	2	1	0	.444	.500	.667	178	1	1	3	0			-1	/2	0.1
Total	2	61	187	22	51	5	8	2	23	20	21	.273	.346	.417	86	-4	-4	27	3			-9	/S32	-0.4

■ BUZZ CLARKSON Clarkson, James Buster b: 3/13/18, Hopkins, S.C. d: 1/18/89, Jeannette, Pa. BR/TR, 5'11", 210 lbs. Deb: 4/30/52

| 1952 | Bos-N | 14 | 25 | 3 | 5 | 0 | 0 | 0 | 1 | 3 | 3 | .200 | .286 | .200 | 38 | -2 | -2 | 2 | 0 | 0 | 0 | -2 | /S3 | -0.3 |

■ ELLIS CLARY Clary, Ellis "Cat" b: 9/11/16, Valdosta, Ga. BR/TR, 5'8", 160 lbs. Deb: 6/07/42 C

1942	Was-A	76	240	34	66	9	0	0	16	45	25	.275	.394	.313	101	3	3	35	2	0	1	-17	2/3	-1.0
1943	Was-A	73	254	36	65	19	1	0	19	44	31	.256	.370	.339	112	4	5	35	8	4	0	-8	3/S	0.0
	StL-A	23	69	15	19	2	0	0	5	11	6	.275	.375	.304	98	1	0	9	1	2	-1	-1	3/2	0.0
	Yr	96	323	51	84	21	1	0	24	55	37	.260	.371	.331	109	5	6	43	9	6	-1	-9		0.0
1944	*StL-A	25	49	6	13	1	1	0	4	12	9	.265	.410	.327	106	2	1	8	1	0	0	-1	3/2	0.0
1945	StL-A	26	38	6	8	1	0	1	2	3		.211	.250	.316	61	-2	-2	3	0	2	-1	3	3/2	0.0
Total	4	223	650	97	171	32	2	1	46	114	74	.263	.376	.323	103	7	8	89	12	8	-1	-24	3/2S	-1.0

■ DAIN CLAY Clay, Dain Elmer "Sniffy" or "Ding-A-Ling" b: 7/10/19, Hicksville, Ohio BR/TR, 5'1.5", 160 lbs. Deb: 6/12/43

1943	Cin-N	49	93	19	25	2	4	0	9	8	14	.269	.333	.376	106	0	1	12	1			-2	O	-0.1
1944	Cin-N	110	356	51	89	15	0	0	17	17	18	.250	.290	.292	67	-17	-15	31	8			-4	O	-2.7
1945	Cin-N	153	656	81	184	29	2	1	50	37	58	.280	.321	.335	84	-16	-14	71	19			1	*O	-1.9
1946	Cin-N	121	435	52	99	17	0	2	22	53	40	.228	.318	.280	73	-15	-14	43	11			2	*O	-1.4
Total	4	433	1540	203	397	63	6	3	98	115	130	.258	.314	.312	79	-48	-42	157	39			-4	O	-6.1

■ BILL CLAY Clay, Frederick C. b: 11/23/1874, Baltimore, Md. d: 10/12/17, York, Pa. TR , Deb: 8/08/02

| 1902 | Phi-N | 3 | 8 | 1 | 2 | 0 | 0 | 0 | 1 | 0 | | .250 | .250 | .250 | 56 | -0 | -0 | 1 | 0 | | | -1 | /O | -0.1 |

■ CHET CLEMENS Clemens, Chester Spurgeon b: 5/10/17, San Fernando, Cal. BR/TR, 6', 175 lbs. Deb: 9/13/39

1939	Bos-N	9	23	2	5	0	0	0	1	1	3	.217	.250	.217	29	-2	-2	1	1			-0	/O	-0.2
1944	Bos-N	19	17	7	3	1	1	0	2	2	2	.176	.263	.353	69	-1	-1	2	0			0	/O	0.0
Total	2	28	40	9	8	1	1	0	3	3	5	.200	.256	.275	46	-3	-3	3	1			0	/O	-0.2

■ CLEM CLEMENS Clemens, Clement Lambert "Count" (b: Clement Lambert Ulatowski)
b: 11/21/1886, Chicago, Ill. d: 11/2/67, St.Petersburg, Fla. BR/TR, 5'11", 176 lbs. Deb: 5/15/14

1914	Chi-F	13	27	4	4	0	0	0	2	3	0	.148	.233	.148	11	-3	-3	1	0			-1	/C	-0.2
1915	Chi-F	11	22	3	3	1	0	0	3	1	0	.136	.174	.182	6	-3	-2	1	0			-0	/C2	-0.2
1916	Chi-N	10	15	0	0	0	0	0	0	1	6	.000	.063	.000	-72	-3	-3	0	0			1	/C	-0.1
Total	3	34	64	7	7	1	0	0	5	5	6	.109	.174	.125	-12	-9	-9	2	0			1	/C2	-0.5

■ DOUG CLEMENS Clemens, Douglas Horace b: 6/9/39, Leesport, Pa. BL/TR, 6', 180 lbs. Deb: 10/02/60

1960	StL-N	1	0	0	0	0	0	0	0	0	0	—	—	—		0	0	0	0	0	0	0	/O	0.0
1961	StL-N	6	12	1	2	1	0	0	0	3	1	.167	.333	.250	53	-1	-1	1	0	0	0	-1	/O	-0.1
1962	StL-N	48	93	12	22	1	1	1	12	17	19	.237	.355	.301	71	-2	-4	11	0	0	0	-3	O	-0.7
1963	StL-N	5	6	1	1	0	0	1	2	1	2	.167	.286	.667	151	0	0	1	0	0	0	1	/O	0.1
1964	StL-N	33	78	8	16	4	3	1	9	6	16	.205	.271	.372	73	-2	-3	8	0	0	0	-0	O	-0.4
	Chi-N	54	140	23	39	10	2	2	12	18	22	.279	.365	.421	116	4	4	22	0	0	0	1	O	0.3
	Yr	87	218	31	55	14	5	3	21	24	38	.252	.332	.404	100	2	0	30	0	0	0			-0.1
1965	Chi-N	128	340	36	75	11	0	4	26	38	53	.221	.303	.288	66	-14	-15	29	5	8	-3	-8	*O	-3.1
1966	Phi-N	79	121	10	31	1	0	1	15	16	25	.256	.353	.289	81	-2	-2	14	1	0	0	1	O/1	-0.1
1967	Phi-N	69	73	2	13	5	0	0	4	8	15	.178	.268	.247	48	-5	-5	5	0	0	0	1	O	-0.6
1968	Phi-N	29	57	6	12	1	1	2	8	7	13	.211	.297	.368	99	-0	-0	6	0	0	0	0	O	0.0
Total	9	452	920	99	211	34	7	12	88	114	166	.229	.319	.321	78	-22	-26	98	6	8	-3	-11	O/1	-4.6

■ BOB CLEMENS Clemens, Robert Baxter b: 8/9/1886, Mt.Hebron, Mo. d: 4/5/64, Marshall, Mo. BR/TR, 5'9", 163 lbs. Deb: 9/17/14

| 1914 | StL-A | 7 | 13 | 1 | 3 | 0 | 1 | 0 | 3 | 2 | 1 | .231 | .375 | .385 | 133 | 1 | 1 | 1 | 0 | 2 | -1 | -1 | /O | -0.1 |

■ WALLY CLEMENT Clement, Wallace Oakes b: 7/21/1881, Auburn, Me. d: 11/1/53, Coral Gables, Fla. BL/TR, 5'11", 175 lbs. Deb: 8/17/08

1908	Phi-N	16	36	0	8	3	0	0	1	0		.222	.222	.306	67	-1	-1	3	2			4	/O	0.2
1909	Phi-N	3	3	0	0	0	0	0	0	0		.000	.000	.000	-99	-0	-0	0	0			0	H	0.0
	Bro-N	92	340	35	88	8	4	0	17	18		.259	.296	.306	90	-6	-5	35	11			4	O	-0.3

YEAR	TM/L	G	AB	R	H	2B	3B	HR	RBI	BB	SO	AVG	OBP	SLG	PRO+	BR	/A	RC	SB	CS	SBR	FR	POS	TPR
	Yr	95	343	35	88	8	4	0	17	18		.257	.294	.303	88	-7	-5	34	11			4		-0.3
Total	2	111	379	35	96	11	4	0	18	18		.253	.287	.303	86	-8	-7	38	13			8	/O	-0.1

■ ROBERTO CLEMENTE
Clemente, Roberto (Walker) "Bob" b: 8/18/34, Carolina, P.R. d: 12/31/72, San Juan, P.R. BR/TR, 5'11", 175 lbs. Deb: 4/17/55 H

YEAR	TM/L	G	AB	R	H	2B	3B	HR	RBI	BB	SO	AVG	OBP	SLG	PRO+	BR	/A	RC	SB	CS	SBR	FR	POS	TPR
1955	Pit-N	124	474	48	121	23	11	5	47	18	60	.255	.285	.382	76	-18	-17	46	2	5	-2	12	*O	-0.8
1956	Pit-N	147	543	66	169	30	7	7	60	13	58	.311	.332	.431	105	1	3	72	6	6	-2	6	*O/23	0.2
1957	Pit-N	111	451	42	114	17	7	4	30	23	45	.253	.289	.348	72	-19	-18	41	0	4	-2	13	*O	-1.0
1958	Pit-N	140	519	69	150	24	10	6	50	31	41	.289	.329	.408	96	-5	-3	67	8	2	1	21	*O	1.4
1959	Pit-N	105	432	60	128	17	7	4	50	15	51	.296	.324	.396	91	-6	-6	52	2	3	-1	7	*O	0.0
1960	*Pit-N	144	570	89	179	22	6	16	94	39	72	.314	.360	.458	121	17	16	87	4	5	-2	2	*O	1.2
1961	Pit-N	146	572	100	201	30	10	23	89	35	59	.351	.392	.559	148	39	38	119	4	1	1	13	*O	4.3
1962	Pit-N	144	538	95	168	28	9	10	74	35	73	.312	.355	.454	115	11	11	81	6	4	-1	13	*O	1.5
1963	Pit-N	152	600	77	192	23	8	17	76	31	64	.320	.357	.470	135	26	26	94	12	2	2	-5	*O	1.7
1964	Pit-N	155	622	95	211	40	7	12	87	51	87	.339	.391	.484	145	37	37	118	5	2	0	8	*O	4.3
1965	Pit-N	152	589	91	194	21	14	10	65	43	78	.329	.380	.463	136	28	28	101	8	0	2	10	*O	3.7
1966	Pit-N	154	638	105	202	31	11	29	119	46	109	.317	.363	.536	146	38	38	119	7	5	-1	16	*O	4.9
1967	Pit-N	147	585	103	209	26	10	23	110	41	103	.357	.402	.554	170	52	52	126	9	1	2	9	*O	5.9
1968	Pit-N	132	502	74	146	18	12	18	57	51	77	.291	.357	.482	152	30	31	82	2	3	-1	11	*O	3.8
1969	Pit-N	138	507	87	175	20	12	19	91	56	73	.345	.413	.544	170	45	46	109	4	1	1	6	*O	4.7
1970	*Pit-N	108	412	65	145	22	10	14	60	38	66	.352	.409	.556	159	32	33	93	3	0	1	5	*O	3.3
1971	*Pit-N	132	522	82	178	29	8	13	86	26	65	.341	.372	.502	146	29	29	90	1	2	-1	8	*O	3.4
1972	*Pit-N	102	378	68	118	19	7	10	60	29	49	.312	.361	.479	140	17	18	61	0	0	0	5	O	1.9
Total	18	2433	9454	1416	3000	440	166	240	1305	621	1230	.317	.362	.475	130	354	362	1557	83	46	-3	159	*O/23	44.4

■ ED CLEMENTS
Clements, Edward b: Philadelphia, Pa. Deb: 6/24/1890

YEAR	TM/L	G	AB	R	H	2B	3B	HR	RBI	BB	SO	AVG	OBP	SLG	PRO+	BR	/A	RC	SB	CS	SBR	FR	POS	TPR
1890	Pit-N	1	1	0	0	0	0	0	0	0	0	.000	.000	.000	-99	-0	-0	0	0			-0	/S	0.0

■ JACK CLEMENTS
Clements, John J. b: 7/24/1864, Philadelphia, Pa. d: 5/23/41, Norristown, Pa. BL/TL, 5'8.5", 204 lbs. Deb: 4/22/1884 M

YEAR	TM/L	G	AB	R	H	2B	3B	HR	RBI	BB	SO	AVG	OBP	SLG	PRO+	BR	/A	RC	SB	CS	SBR	FR	POS	TPR
1884	Phi-U	41	177	37	50	13	2	3		9		.282	.317	.429	162	9	11	25	0			4	OC/S	1.4
	Phi-N	9	30	3	7	0	0	0	0	4	8	.233	.324	.233	82	-1	-0	2				1	/C	0.1
1885	Phi-N	52	188	14	36	11	3	1	14	2	30	.191	.200	.298	61	-9	-8	11				-5	CO	-0.9
1886	Phi-N	54	185	15	38	5	1	0	11	7	34	.205	.234	.243	45	-12	-12	12	4			9	C/O	0.0
1887	Phi-N	66	246	48	69	13	7	1	47	9	24	.280	.317	.402	95	-0	-3	34	7			7	C/3S	0.9
1888	Phi-N	86	326	26	80	8	4	1	32	10	36	.245	.276	.304	82	-5	-7	29	3			-3	C/O	-0.6
1889	Phi-N	78	310	51	88	17	1	4	35	29	21	.284	.347	.384	97	2	-2	43	3			-8	C	-0.7
1890	Phi-N	97	381	64	120	23	8	7	74	45	30	.315	.392	.472	150	26	24	76	10			1	C/1M	2.7
1891	Phi-N	107	423	58	131	29	4	4	75	43	19	.310	.380	.426	133	20	18	71	3			-7	*C/1	1.8
1892	Phi-N	109	402	50	106	25	6	8	76	43	40	.264	.339	.415	130	14	14	61	7			3	*C	2.1
1893	Phi-N	94	376	64	107	20	3	17	80	39	29	.285	.360	.489	127	12	12	69	3			-15	*C/1	0.5
1894	Phi-N	45	159	26	55	6	5	3	36	24	7	.346	.455	.503	136	10	11	40	6			-3	C	0.9
1895	Phi-N	88	322	64	127	27	2	13	75	22	7	.394	.446	.612	173	34	34	91	3			-12	*C	2.4
1896	Phi-N	57	184	35	66	5	7	5	45	17	14	.359	.427	.543	159	15	15	45	2			-3	C	1.4
1897	Phi-N	55	185	18	44	4	2	6	36	12		.238	.305	.378	84	-5	-5	23	3			-3	C	0.0
1898	StL-N	99	335	39	86	19	5	3	41	21		.257	.314	.370	96	-1	-2	40	1			-6	C	-0.1
1899	Cle-N	4	12	1	3	0	0	0	0	0		.250	.308	.250	60	-1	-1	1	0			0	/C	0.0
1900	Bos-N	16	42	6	13	1	0	1	10	3		.310	.370	.405	103	1	0	6	0			0	C	0.1
Total	17	1157	4283	619	1226	226	60	77	687	339	299	.286	.347	.421	119	109	100	681	55			-39	*C/O13S	12.0

■ VERNE CLEMONS
Clemons, Verne James "Stinger" or "Tubby" b: 9/8/1891, Clemons, Iowa d: 5/5/59, Bay Pines, Fla. BR/TR, 5'9.5", 190 lbs. Deb: 4/22/16

YEAR	TM/L	G	AB	R	H	2B	3B	HR	RBI	BB	SO	AVG	OBP	SLG	PRO+	BR	/A	RC	SB	CS	SBR	FR	POS	TPR
1916	StL-A	4	7	0	1	0	0	0	0	0	1	.143	.143	.286	30	-1	-1	0	0			0	/C	0.0
1919	StL-N	88	239	14	63	13	2	2	22	26	13	.264	.336	.360	116	3	5	29	4			2	C	1.2
1920	StL-N	112	338	17	95	10	6	1	36	30	12	.281	.340	.355	103	0	2	42	1	1	-0	-6	*C	0.3
1921	StL-N	117	341	29	109	16	2	2	48	33	17	.320	.380	.396	108	4	5	53	0	0	0	-4	*C	0.7
1922	StL-N	71	160	9	41	4	0	0	15	18	5	.256	.331	.281	62	-9	-8	16	1	0	0	2	C	-0.3
1923	StL-N	57	130	6	37	9	1	0	13	10	11	.285	.345	.369	90	-2	-2	17	0	0	0	5	C	0.5
1924	StL-N	25	56	3	18	3	0	0	6	2	3	.321	.345	.375	94	-1	-0	7	0	0	0	-1	C	0.0
Total	7	474	1271	78	364	56	11	5	140	119	62	.286	.348	.360	99	-5	1	164	6	1		-1	C	2.4

■ DONN CLENDENON
Clendenon, Donn Alvin b: 7/15/35, Neosho, Mo. BR/TR, 6'4", 209 lbs. Deb: 9/22/61

YEAR	TM/L	G	AB	R	H	2B	3B	HR	RBI	BB	SO	AVG	OBP	SLG	PRO+	BR	/A	RC	SB	CS	SBR	FR	POS	TPR
1961	Pit-N	9	35	7	11	1	1	0	2	5	10	.314	.400	.400	113	1	1	6	0	0	0	0	/O	0.0
1962	Pit-N	80	222	39	67	8	5	7	28	26	58	.302	.378	.477	128	9	9	42	16	4	2	-2	1O	0.6
1963	Pit-N	154	563	65	155	28	7	15	57	39	136	.275	.328	.430	116	11	11	75	22	13	-1	7	*1	1.5
1964	Pit-N	133	457	53	129	23	8	12	64	26	96	.282	.324	.446	115	8	8	62	12	8	-1	-0	*1	0.9
1965	Pit-N	162	612	89	184	32	14	14	96	48	128	.301	.356	.467	129	24	23	99	9	9	-3	6	*1/3	1.9
1966	Pit-N	155	571	80	171	22	10	28	98	52	142	.299	.360	.520	141	31	31	102	8	7	-2	-1	*1	2.1
1967	Pit-N	131	478	46	119	15	2	13	56	34	107	.249	.300	.399	90	-6	-7	49	4	4	-1	5	*1	-0.9
1968	Pit-N	158	584	63	150	20	6	17	87	47	163	.257	.313	.399	114	8	9	72	10	3	1	10	*1	1.6
1969	Mon-N	38	129	14	31	6	1	4	14	6	32	.240	.274	.395	85	-3	-3	11	0	2	-1	3	1O	-0.3
	*NY-N	72	202	31	51	5	0	12	37	19	62	.252	.323	.455	113	4	3	30	3	2	-0	-3	1/O	-0.5
	Yr	110	331	45	82	11	1	16	51	25	94	.248	.304	.432	103	1	-0	40	3	4	-2	0		-0.8
1970	NY-N	121	396	65	114	18	3	22	97	39	91	.288	.353	.515	129	15	15	68	4	1	-1	-2	*1	0.5
1971	NY-N	88	263	29	65	10	0	11	37	21	78	.247	.305	.411	103	-0	0	29	1	2	-1	-2	1	-0.8
1972	StL-N	61	136	13	26	4	0	4	9	17	37	.191	.281	.309	68	-6	-6	10	1	2	-1	3	1	-0.5
Total	12	1362	4648	594	1273	192	57	159	682	379	1140	.274	.331	.442	117	94	94	657	90	57	-7	24	*1/O3	5.5

■ ELMER CLEVELAND
Cleveland, Elmer Ellsworth b: 9/15/1862, Washington, D.C. d: 10/8/13, Zimmerman, Pa. BR/TR, Deb: 8/29/1884

YEAR	TM/L	G	AB	R	H	2B	3B	HR	RBI	BB	SO	AVG	OBP	SLG	PRO+	BR	/A	RC	SB	CS	SBR	FR	POS	TPR
1884	Cin-U	29	115	24	37	9	2	0		4		.322	.345	.435	150	7	6	18	0			2	3	0.7
1888	NY-N	9	34	6	8	0	2	2	5	3	1	.235	.297	.529	163	2	2	6	1			-6	/3	-0.3
	Pit-N	30	108	10	24	2	1	2	11	5	23	.222	.270	.315	95	-1	-0	10	3			-9	3	-0.7
	Yr	39	142	16	32	2	3	4	16	8	24	.225	.276	.366	112	1	2	16	4			-15		-1.0
1891	Col-a	12	41	12	7	0	0	0	4	12	9	.171	.370	.171	62	-1	-1	4	4			3	3	0.2
Total	3	80	298	52	76	11	5	4	20	24	33	.255	.317	.366	120	7	7	38	8			-10	/3	-0.1

■ STAN CLIBURN
Cliburn, Stanley Gene b: 12/19/56, Jackson, Miss. BR/TR, 6', 195 lbs. Deb: 5/06/80

YEAR	TM/L	G	AB	R	H	2B	3B	HR	RBI	BB	SO	AVG	OBP	SLG	PRO+	BR	/A	RC	SB	CS	SBR	FR	POS	TPR
1980	Cal-A	54	56	7	10	2	0	2	6	3	9	.179	.220	.321	48	-4	-4	4	0	0	0	5	C	0.3

■ HARLOND CLIFT
Clift, Harlond Benton "Darkie" b: 8/12/12, ElReno, Okla. BR/TR, 5'11", 180 lbs. Deb: 4/17/34

YEAR	TM/L	G	AB	R	H	2B	3B	HR	RBI	BB	SO	AVG	OBP	SLG	PRO+	BR	/A	RC	SB	CS	SBR	FR	POS	TPR
1934	StL-A	147	572	104	149	30	10	14	56	84	100	.260	.357	.421	92	0	-7	91	7	2	1	-16	*3	-2.0
1935	StL-A	137	475	101	140	26	4	11	69	83	39	.295	.406	.436	113	15	12	89	0	3	-2	-6	*3/2	0.5
1936	StL-A	152	576	145	174	40	11	20	73	115	68	.302	.424	.514	127	31	28	134	12	4	1	3	*3	2.9
1937	StL-A	155	571	103	175	36	7	29	118	98	80	.306	.413	.546	139	36	35	134	8	5	-1	41	*3	7.0
1938	StL-A	149	534	119	155	25	7	34	118	118	67	.290	.423	.546	143	38	38	133	10	5	1	14	*3	5.0
1939	StL-A	151	526	90	142	25	2	15	84	111	55	.270	.402	.411	106	11	9	97	4	3	-1	12	*3	1.6
1940	StL-A	150	523	92	143	29	5	20	87	104	62	.273	.396	.463	119	20	18	103	9	8	-2	4	*3	2.6
1941	StL-A	154	584	108	149	33	9	17	84	113	93	.255	.376	.430	109	13	10	102	6	4	-1	1	*3	1.7

YEAR	TM/L	G	AB	R	H	2B	3B	HR	RBI	BB	SO	AVG	OBP	SLG	PRO+	BR	/A	RC	SB	CS	SBR	FR	POS	TPR
1942	StL-A	143	541	108	148	39	4	7	55	106	48	.274	.394	.399	122	21	20	95	6	4	-1	-1	*3/S	2.0
1943	StL-A	105	379	43	88	11	3	3	25	54	37	.232	.329	.301	83	-6	-7	40	5	4	-1	19	*3	1.4
	Was-A	8	30	4	9	0	0	0	4	5	3	.300	.417	.300	115	1	1	4	0	0	0	-0	/3	0.1
	Yr	113	409	47	97	11	3	3	29	59	40	.237	.336	.301	85	-5	-6	44	5	4	-1	18		1.5
1944	Was-A	12	44	4	7	3	0	0	3	3	3	.159	.213	.227	27	-4	-4	2	0	0	0	-2	3	-0.6
1945	Was-A	119	375	49	79	12	0	8	53	76	58	.211	.349	.307	99	-1	3	48	2	1	0	-3	*3	0.2
Total	12	1582	5730	1070	1558	309	62	178	829	1070	713	.272	.390	.441	115	173	155	1072	69	43	-5	64	*3/2S	22.4

■ FLEA CLIFTON
Clifton, Herman Earl   b: 12/12/09, Cincinnati, Ohio   BR/TR, 5'10", 160 lbs.   Deb: 4/29/34

YEAR	TM/L	G	AB	R	H	2B	3B	HR	RBI	BB	SO	AVG	OBP	SLG	PRO+	BR	/A	RC	SB	CS	SBR	FR	POS	TPR
1934	Det-A	16	16	3	1	0	0	0	1	1	2	.063	.118	.063	-52	-4	-4	0	0	0	0	2	/32	-0.1
1935	*Det-A	43	110	15	28	5	0	0	9	5	13	.255	.293	.300	56	-8	-7	10	2	1	0	-1	3/2S	-0.6
1936	Det-A	13	26	5	5	1	0	0	1	4	3	.192	.300	.231	33	-3	-3	2	0	1	-1	-0	/S32	-0.2
1937	Det-A	15	43	4	5	1	0	0	2	7	10	.116	.240	.140	-2	-7	-7	2	3	0	1	-0	/3S2	-0.4
Total	4	87	195	27	39	7	0	0	13	17	28	.200	.268	.236	30	-21	-20	14	5	2	0	0	/3S2	-1.3

■ MONK CLINE
Cline, John P.   b: 3/3/1858, Ohio   d: 9/23/16, Louisville, Ky.   BL/TL, 5'4", 150 lbs.   Deb: 7/04/1882

YEAR	TM/L	G	AB	R	H	2B	3B	HR	RBI	BB	SO	AVG	OBP	SLG	PRO+	BR	/A	RC	SB	CS	SBR	FR	POS	TPR
1882	Bal-a	44	172	18	38	6	2	0			3	.221	.234	.279	79	-5	-3	12				6	O/S23	0.3
1884	Lou-a	94	396	91	115	16	7	2		27		.290	.342	.381	146	17	20	53				6	*O/S	2.2
1885	Lou-a	2	9	0	2	1	0	0		0		.222	.222	.333	76	-0	-0	1				-1	/O3	0.0
1888	KC-a	73	293	45	69	13	2	0	19	20		.235	.289	.294	84	-3	-6	34	29			5	O/23	-0.2
1891	Lou-a	21	76	13	23	3	1	0	12	19	3	.303	.442	.368	137	5	5	14	2			-3	O	0.1
Total	5	234	946	167	247	39	12	2	31	69	3	.261	.315	.334	113	14	16	113	31			14	O/S23	2.4

■ TY CLINE
Cline, Tyrone Alexander   b: 6/15/39, Hampton, S.C.   BL/TL, 6'0.5", 170 lbs.   Deb: 9/14/60

YEAR	TM/L	G	AB	R	H	2B	3B	HR	RBI	BB	SO	AVG	OBP	SLG	PRO+	BR	/A	RC	SB	CS	SBR	FR	POS	TPR
1960	Cle-A	7	26	2	8	1	1	0	2	0	4	.308	.308	.423	99	-0	-0	3	0	0	0	2	/O	0.1
1961	Cle-A	12	43	9	9	2	1	0	1	6	1	.209	.333	.302	73	-2	-1	5	1	0	0	-2	O	-0.2
1962	Cle-A	118	375	53	93	15	5	2	28	28	50	.248	.309	.331	74	-15	-13	39	5	4	-1	-3	*O	-2.0
1963	Mil-N	72	174	17	41	2	1	0	10	10	31	.236	.285	.259	58	-9	-9	14	2	1	0	9	O	-0.3
1964	Mil-N	101	116	22	35	4	2	1	13	8	22	.302	.362	.397	113	2	2	18	0	1	-1	5	O/1	0.5
1965	Mil-N	123	220	27	42	5	3	0	10	16	50	.191	.246	.241	37	-18	-18	14	2	2	-1	8	O/1	-1.4
1966	Chi-N	7	17	3	6	0	0	0	2	0	2	.353	.353	.353	96	-0	-0	2	1	0	0	-0	/O	0.0
	Atl-N	42	71	12	18	0	0	0	6	3	11	.254	.303	.254	56	-4	-4	5	2	1	0	0	O/1	-0.4
	Yr	49	88	15	24	0	0	0	8	3	13	.273	.312	.273	63	-4	-4	7	3	1	0	0		-0.4
1967	Atl-N	10	8	0	0	0	0	0	0	0	3	.000	.111	.000	-66	-2	-2	0	0	0	0	0	/O	-0.1
	SF-N	64	122	18	33	5	5	0	4	9	13	.270	.326	.393	106	1	1	16	2	1	0	-1	O	-0.1
	Yr	74	130	18	33	5	5	0	4	9	16	.254	.312	.369	96	-1	-1	16	2	1	0	-1		-0.2
1968	SF-N	116	291	37	65	6	3	1	28	11	26	.223	.254	.275	59	-15	-15	20	0	2	-1	-0	O1	-2.3
1969	Mon-N	101	209	26	50	5	3	2	12	32	22	.239	.346	.321	87	-2	-2	25	4	3	-1	1	O1	-0.5
1970	Mon-N	2	2	0	1	0	0	0	0	0	0	.500	.500	.500	169	0	0	1	0	0	0	0	H	0.0
	*Cin-N	48	63	13	17	7	1	0	8	12	11	.270	.387	.413	114	2	2	11	1	2	-1	1	O/1	0.1
	Yr	50	65	13	18	7	1	0	8	12	11	.277	.390	.415	115	2	2	11	1	2	-1	1		0.1
1971	Cin-N	69	97	12	19	1	0	0	1	18	16	.196	.333	.206	57	-5	-4	8	2	2	-1	-2	O/1	-0.7
Total	12	892	1834	251	437	53	25	6	125	153	262	.238	.304	.304	72	-66	-64	180	22	19	-5	19	O/1	-7.3

■ GENE CLINES
Clines, Eugene Anthony   b: 10/6/46, San Pablo, Cal.   BR/TR, 5'9", 170 lbs.   Deb: 6/28/70   C

YEAR	TM/L	G	AB	R	H	2B	3B	HR	RBI	BB	SO	AVG	OBP	SLG	PRO+	BR	/A	RC	SB	CS	SBR	FR	POS	TPR
1970	Pit-N	31	37	4	15	2	0	0	3	2	5	.405	.436	.459	143	2	2	7	2	1	0	-1	/O	0.1
1971	*Pit-N	97	273	52	84	12	4	1	24	22	36	.308	.366	.392	115	6	6	42	15	6	1	6	O	1.0
1972	*Pit-N	107	311	52	104	15	6	0	17	16	47	.334	.371	.421	127	10	10	47	12	6	0	-3	O	0.4
1973	Pit-N	110	304	42	80	11	3	1	23	26	36	.263	.327	.329	84	-7	-6	30	8	7	-2	-0	O	-1.1
1974	*Pit-N	107	276	29	62	5	1	0	14	30	40	.225	.310	.250	60	-15	-13	23	14	2	3	7	O	-0.5
1975	NY-N	82	203	25	46	6	3	0	10	11	21	.227	.270	.286	57	-13	-12	15	4	4	-1	6	O	-0.9
1976	Tex-A	116	446	52	123	12	3	0	38	16	52	.276	.307	.316	81	-10	-11	39	11	9	-2	0	*OD	-1.5
1977	Chi-N	101	239	27	70	12	2	3	41	25	25	.293	.362	.397	93	2	-2	34	1	2	-1	-9	O	-1.3
1978	Chi-N	109	229	31	59	10	2	0	17	21	28	.258	.323	.319	71	-6	-9	24	4	3	-1	-3	O	-1.5
1979	Chi-N	10	10	0	2	0	0	0	0	0	1	.200	.200	.200	9	-1	-1	0	0	0	0	0	/H	0.0
Total	10	870	2328	314	645	85	24	5	187	169	291	.277	.331	.341	88	-32	-36	260	71	40	-3	3	O/D	-5.3

■ BILLY CLINGMAN
Clingman, William Frederick   b: 11/21/1869, Cincinnati, Ohio   d: 5/14/58, Cincinnati, Ohio   BB/TR, 5'11", 150 lbs.   Deb: 9/09/1890

YEAR	TM/L	G	AB	R	H	2B	3B	HR	RBI	BB	SO	AVG	OBP	SLG	PRO+	BR	/A	RC	SB	CS	SBR	FR	POS	TPR
1890	Cin-N	7	27	2	7	1	0	0	5	1	0	.259	.286	.296	72	-1	-1	2	0			-1	/S2	-0.1
1891	Cin-a	1	5	0	1	1	0	0	0	0	0	.200	.200	.400	67	-0	-0	0	0			-1	/2	0.0
1895	Pit-N	106	382	69	99	16	4	0	45	41	43	.259	.334	.322	76	-15	-11	49	19			14	*3	0.3
1896	Lou-N	121	423	57	99	10	2	0	37	57	51	.234	.329	.281	66	-20	-17	47	19			24	*3	1.0
1897	Lou-N	113	395	59	90	14	7	2	47	37		.228	.302	.314	67	-20	-18	43	14			29	*3	1.0
1898	Lou-N	154	538	65	138	12	6	0	50	51		.257	.327	.301	84	-10	-9	59	15			15	3S/O2	1.1
1899	Lou-N	109	366	67	96	15	4	2	44	46		.262	.349	.342	92	-2	-2	49	13			-4	*S	0.0
1900	Chi-N	47	159	15	33	6	0	0	11	17		.208	.292	.245	53	-10	-9	13	6			-14	S	-1.6
1901	Was-A	137	480	66	116	10	7	2	55	42		.242	.308	.304	73	-17	-16	51	10			18	*S	0.9
1903	Cle-A	21	64	10	18	1	1	0	7	11		.281	.387	.328	121	2	2	9	2			0	2/S3	0.3
Total	10	816	2839	410	697	86	31	8	301	303	94	.246	.323	.306	76	-94	-81	323	98			79	3S/2O	2.9

■ JIM CLINTON
Clinton, James Lawrence "Big Jim"   b: 8/10/1850, New York, N.Y.   d: 9/3/21, Brooklyn, N.Y.   BR/TR, 5'8.5", 174 lbs.   Deb: 5/18/1872   MU

YEAR	TM/L	G	AB	R	H	2B	3B	HR	RBI	BB	SO	AVG	OBP	SLG	PRO+	BR	/A	RC	SB	CS	SBR	FR	POS	TPR
1872	Eck-n	25	97	13	23	2	1	0		0		.234	.234	.277	67	-5	-2	6					/3/OS2M	-0.1
1873	Res-n	9	37	5	9	1	0	0		1		.243	.263	.270	62	-2	-1	3					/3O	0.0
1874	Atl-n	2	11	3	2	1	0	0				.182	.182	.273	48	-1	-0	1					/2O	0.0
1875	Atl-n	22	81	3	10	0	0	0				.123	.123	.123	-16	-9	-7	1					P/O12	0.0
1876	Lou-N	16	65	8	22	2	0	0	0	0	0	.338	.338	.369	115	2	1	8				-1	O/1P	0.0
1882	Wor-N	26	98	9	16	2	0	0	3	7	13	.163	.219	.184	30	-7	-8	4				-4	O	-1.0
1883	Bal-a	94	399	69	125	16	8	0		27		.313	.357	.393	137	19	17	57				5	*O/2	2.0
1884	Bal-a	104	437	82	118	12	6	4		29		.270	.334	.352	122	14	11	53				-1	*O/2	0.8
1885	Cin-a	105	408	48	97	5	5	0		15		.238	.277	.275	76	-10	-11	32				-0	*O	-1.5
1886	Bal-a	23	83	8	15	1	0	0		4		.181	.227	.193	34	-6	-6	4	3			-0	O	-0.5
Total	4 n	57	223	23	43	4	1	0		1		.193	.196	.220	37	-16	-11	11	0				/P3O21S	-0.1
Total	6	368	1490	224	393	38	19	4	3	82	13	.264	.311	.323	102	12	4	159	3			-1	O/2P1	-0.2

■ LOU CLINTON
Clinton, Lucien Louis   b: 10/13/37, Ponca City, Okla.   BR/TR, 6'1", 185 lbs.   Deb: 4/22/60

YEAR	TM/L	G	AB	R	H	2B	3B	HR	RBI	BB	SO	AVG	OBP	SLG	PRO+	BR	/A	RC	SB	CS	SBR	FR	POS	TPR
1960	Bos-A	96	298	37	68	17	5	6	37	20	66	.228	.283	.379	75	-10	-12	29	4	3	-1	-0	O	-1.5
1961	Bos-A	17	51	4	13	2	1	0	3	2	10	.255	.283	.333	63	-3	-3	5	0	0	0	3	O	0.0
1962	Bos-A	114	398	63	117	24	10	18	75	34	79	.294	.351	.540	132	18	17	75	2	1	0	-3	*O	1.0
1963	Bos-A	148	560	71	130	23	7	22	77	49	118	.232	.295	.416	94	-4	-6	65	0	0	0	8	*O	-1.2
1964	Bos-A	37	120	15	31	4	3	3	6	9	33	.258	.310	.417	95	-0	-1	15	1	0	0	4	O	0.2
	LA-A	91	306	30	76	18	0	9	38	31	40	.248	.320	.395	108	-1	3	40	3	0	1	2	O	0.2
	Yr	128	426	45	107	22	3	12	44	40	73	.251	.317	.401	104	-1	2	55	4	0	1	6		0.4
1965	Cal-A	89	222	29	54	12	3	1	8	23	37	.243	.317	.338	88	-4	-3	23	2	3	-1	2	O	-0.5
	KC-A	1	1	0	0	0	0	0	0	0	0	.000	.000	.000	-99	-0	-0	0	0	0	0	0	/O	0.0

YEAR	TM/L	G	AB	R	H	2B	3B	HR	RBI	BB	SO	AVG	OBP	SLG	PRO+	BR	/A	RC	SB	CS	SBR	FR	POS	TPR
	Cle-A	12	34	2	6	1	0	1	2	3	7	.176	.243	.294	51	-2	-2	3	0	0	0	0	/O	-0.1
	Yr	102	257	31	60	13	3	2	10	26	44	.233	.306	.331	83	-6	-6	26	2	3	-1	2		-0.6
1966	NY-A	80	159	18	35	10	2	5	21	16	27	.220	.291	.403	101	-1	-0	19	0	0	0	0	O	-0.2
1967	NY-A	6	4	1	2	1	0	0	2	1	1	.500	.600	.750	308	1	1	2	0	0	0	0	/O	0.1
Total	8	691	2153	270	532	112	31	65	269	188	418	.247	.310	.418	99	-6	-7	275	12	7	-1	16	O	-1.0

■ ED CLOUGH
Clough, Edgar George "Big Ed" or "Spec" b: 10/28/06, Wiconisco, Pa. d: 1/30/44, Harrisburg, Pa. BL/TL, 6′, 188 lbs. Deb: 8/28/24

YEAR	TM/L	G	AB	R	H	2B	3B	HR	RBI	BB	SO	AVG	OBP	SLG	PRO+	BR	/A	RC	SB	CS	SBR	FR	POS	TPR
1924	StL-N	7	14	0	1	0	0	0	1	0	3	.071	.071	.071	-63	-3	-3	0	0	0	0	2	/O	-0.1
1925	StL-N	3	4	0	1	0	0	0	0	0	0	.250	.250	.250	28	-0	-0	0	0	0	0	-0	/P	0.0
1926	StL-N	1	1	0	0	0	0	0	0	0	0	.000	.000	.000	-96	-0	-0	0	0			0	/P	0.0
Total	3	11	19	0	2	0	0	0	1	0	3	.105	.105	.105	-44	-4	-4	0	0	0	0	1	/OP	-0.1

■ OTIS CLYMER
Clymer, Otis Edgar b: 1/27/1876, Pine Grove, Pa. d: 2/27/26, St.Paul, Minn. BB/TR, 5′11″, 180 lbs. Deb: 4/14/05

YEAR	TM/L	G	AB	R	H	2B	3B	HR	RBI	BB	SO	AVG	OBP	SLG	PRO+	BR	/A	RC	SB	CS	SBR	FR	POS	TPR
1905	Pit-N	96	365	74	108	11	5	0	23	19		.296	.331	.353	103	2	1	52	23			-2	O/1	-0.7
1906	Pit-N	11	45	7	11	0	1	0	1	3		.244	.292	.289	79	-1	-1	4	1			-1	O	-0.1
1907	Pit-N	22	66	8	15	2	0	0	4	5		.227	.282	.258	70	-2	-2	6	4			-3	O/1	-0.5
	Was-A	57	206	30	65	5	5	1	16	18		.316	.371	.403	161	11	13	39	18			-4	O/1	0.7
1908	Was-A	110	368	32	93	11	4	1	35	20		.253	.291	.313	107	-1	-2	38	19			-7	O2/3	-1.0
1909	Was-A	45	138	11	27	5	2	0	6	17		.196	.284	.261	76	-4	-3	12	7			-4	O	-0.9
1913	Chi-N	30	105	16	24	5	1	0	7	14	18	.229	.319	.295	76	-3	-3	12	9			-2	O	-0.4
	Bos-N	14	37	4	12	3	1	0	6	3	3	.324	.375	.459	135	2	2	7	2			-1	O	0.1
	Yr	44	142	20	36	8	2	0	13	17	21	.254	.333	.338	91	-1	-1	18	11			-2		-0.3
Total	6	385	1330	182	355	42	19	2	98	99	21	.267	.318	.332	106	4	8	171	83			-22	O/213	-2.8

■ BILL CLYMER
Clymer, William Johnston "Derby Day Bill" b: 12/18/1873, Philadelphia, Pa. d: 12/26/36, Philadelphia, Pa. Deb: 6/26/1891 C

YEAR	TM/L	G	AB	R	H	2B	3B	HR	RBI	BB	SO	AVG	OBP	SLG	PRO+	BR	/A	RC	SB	CS	SBR	FR	POS	TPR
1891	Phi-a	3	11	0	0	0	0	0	0	1	2	.000	.154	.000	-53	-2	-2	0	1			-2	/S	-0.2

■ PETE COACHMAN
Coachman, Bobby Dean b: 11/11/61, Cottonwood, Ala. BR/TR, 5′9″, 175 lbs. Deb: 8/18/90

YEAR	TM/L	G	AB	R	H	2B	3B	HR	RBI	BB	SO	AVG	OBP	SLG	PRO+	BR	/A	RC	SB	CS	SBR	FR	POS	TPR
1990	Cal-A	16	45	3	14	3	0	0	5	1	7	.311	.354	.378	104	0	0	6	0	1	-1	3	/32D	0.3

■ GIL COAN
Coan, Gilbert Fitzgerald b: 5/18/22, Monroe, N.C. BL/TR, 6′, 180 lbs. Deb: 4/27/46

YEAR	TM/L	G	AB	R	H	2B	3B	HR	RBI	BB	SO	AVG	OBP	SLG	PRO+	BR	/A	RC	SB	CS	SBR	FR	POS	TPR
1946	Was-A	59	134	17	28	3	2	3	9	7	37	.209	.269	.328	70	-6	-6	12	2	2	-1	-2	O	-0.9
1947	Was-A	11	42	5	21	3	2	0	3	5	6	.500	.553	.667	245	8	8	17	2	1	0	-0	O	0.7
1948	Was-A	138	513	56	119	13	9	7	60	41	78	.232	.298	.333	70	-25	-23	55	23	9	2	11	*O	-1.4
1949	Was-A	111	358	36	78	7	8	3	25	29	58	.218	.278	.307	56	-25	-24	32	9	6	-1	2	O	-2.4
1950	Was-A	104	366	58	111	17	4	7	50	28	46	.303	.359	.429	106	-0	-2	60	10	5	0	-3	O	-0.1
1951	Was-A	135	538	85	163	25	7	9	62	39	62	.303	.357	.426	113	7	8	85	8	5	-1	24	*O	2.6
1952	Was-A	107	332	50	68	11	6	5	20	32	35	.205	.277	.319	68	-16	-15	32	9	4	0	0	O	-1.7
1953	Was-A	68	168	28	33	1	4	2	17	22	23	.196	.301	.286	60	-9	-9	17	7	0	2	1	O	-0.6
1954	Bal-A	94	265	29	74	11	1	2	20	16	17	.279	.323	.351	91	-6	-4	31	9	4	0	-1	O	-0.5
1955	Bal-A	61	130	18	31	7	1	1	11	13	15	.238	.313	.331	79	-5	-4	14	4	2	0	-1	O	-0.6
	Chi-A	17	17	0	3	0	0	0	1	0	5	.176	.176	.176	-5	-2	-3	1	0	0	0	0	/O	-0.2
	Yr	78	147	18	34	7	1	1	12	13	20	.231	.298	.313	68	-7	-7	14	4	2	0	-1		-0.8
	NY-N	9	13	0	2	0	0	0	0	0	1	.154	.154	.154	-18	-2	-2	0	0	0	0	-0	/O	-0.2
1956	NY-N	4	1	2	0	0	0	0	0	0	1	.000	.000	.000	-99	-0	-0	0	0	0	0	0	H	0.0
Total	11	918	2877	384	731	98	44	39	278	232	384	.254	.316	.359	84	-83	-70	355	83	38	2	31	O	-5.3

■ JOE COBB
Cobb, Joseph Stanley (b: Joseph Stanley Serafin) b: 1/24/1895, Hudson, Pa. d: 12/24/47, Allentown, Pa. BR/TR, 5′9″, 170 lbs. Deb: 4/25/18

YEAR	TM/L	G	AB	R	H	2B	3B	HR	RBI	BB	SO	AVG	OBP	SLG	PRO+	BR	/A	RC	SB	CS	SBR	FR	POS	TPR
1918	Det-A	1	0	0	0	0	0	0	0	1	0	—	1.000	—	210	0	0	0	0			0	H	0.0

■ TY COBB
Cobb, Tyrus Raymond "The Georgia Peach" b: 12/18/1886, Narrows, Ga. d: 7/17/61, Atlanta, Ga. BL/TR, 6′1″, 175 lbs. Deb: 8/30/05 MH

YEAR	TM/L	G	AB	R	H	2B	3B	HR	RBI	BB	SO	AVG	OBP	SLG	PRO+	BR	/A	RC	SB	CS	SBR	FR	POS	TPR
1905	Det-A	41	150	19	36	6	0	1	15	10		.240	.287	.300	88	-2	-2	14	2			2	O	-0.2
1906	Det-A	98	358	45	113	15	5	1	34	19		.316	.350	.394	131	13	12	60	23			6	O	1.6
1907	*Det-A	150	605	97	212	28	14	5	119	24		.350	.375	.468	165	44	42	129	49			11	*O	4.9
1908	*Det-A	150	581	88	188	36	20	4	108	34		.324	.361	.475	167	44	41	112	39			4	*O	4.2
1909	*Det-A	156	573	116	216	33	10	9	107	48		.377	.431	.517	191	63	61	159	76			3	*O	6.4
1910	Det-A	140	506	106	194	35	13	8	91	64		.383	.456	.551	202	68	64	156	65			9	*O	7.2
1911	Det-A	146	591	147	248	47	24	8	127	44		.420	.467	.621	193	78	74	207	83			11	*O	7.0
1912	Det-A	140	553	119	227	30	23	7	83	43		.410	.458	.586	204	68	70	174	61			0	*O	6.0
1913	Det-A	122	428	70	167	18	16	4	67	58	31	.390	.467	.535	196	52	53	124	51			3	*O	5.2
1914	Det-A	98	345	69	127	22	11	2	57	57	22	.368	.466	.513	188	42	41	89	35	17	0	-10	O	2.8
1915	Det-A	156	563	144	208	31	13	3	99	118	43	.369	.486	.487	182	72	68	155	96	38	6	-3	*O	6.5
1916	Det-A	145	542	113	201	31	10	5	68	78	39	.371	.452	.493	177	58	55	136	68	24	6	-1	*O/1	5.6
1917	Det-A	152	588	107	225	44	24	6	102	61	34	.383	.444	.570	210	74	75	164	55			13	*O	8.4
1918	Det-A	111	421	83	161	19	14	3	64	41	21	.382	.440	.515	196	44	46	105	34			2	O1/P23	4.7
1919	Det-A	124	497	92	191	36	13	1	70	38	22	.384	.429	.515	168	42	43	116	28			-2	*O	3.3
1920	Det-A	112	428	86	143	28	8	2	63	58	28	.334	.416	.451	133	20	22	82	14	10	-2	-7	*O	0.3
1921	Det-A	128	507	124	197	37	16	12	101	56	19	.389	.452	.596	167	50	51	134	22	15	-2	13	*OM	4.8
1922	Det-A	137	526	99	211	42	16	4	99	55	24	.401	.462	.565	172	52	55	133	9	13	-5	4	*OM	4.1
1923	Det-A	145	556	103	189	40	7	6	88	66	14	.340	.413	.469	135	27	28	108	9	10	-3	5	*OM	1.6
1924	Det-A	155	625	115	211	38	10	4	78	85	18	.338	.418	.450	126	25	26	118	23	14	-2	5	*OM	1.7
1925	Det-A	121	415	97	157	31	12	12	102	65	12	.378	.468	.598	171	45	46	118	13	9	-2	-2	*O/PM	3.1
1926	Det-A	79	233	48	79	18	5	4	62	26	2	.339	.408	.511	137	13	13	49	9	4	0	-5	OM	0.4
1927	Phi-A	134	490	104	175	32	7	5	93	67	12	.357	.440	.482	131	31	27	97	22	16	-3	-5	*O	1.0
1928	Phi-A	95	353	54	114	27	4	1	40	34	16	.323	.389	.431	112	8	7	58	5	8	-3	-1	O	0.0
Total	24	3035	11434	2245	4190	724	295	117	1937	1249	357	.366	.432	.512	167	1032	1018	2799	891	178		56	*O/1P32	90.6

■ DAVE COBLE
Coble, David Lamar b: 12/24/12, Monroe, N.C. d: 10/15/71, Orlando, Fla. BR/TR, 6′1″, 183 lbs. Deb: 5/01/39

YEAR	TM/L	G	AB	R	H	2B	3B	HR	RBI	BB	SO	AVG	OBP	SLG	PRO+	BR	/A	RC	SB	CS	SBR	FR	POS	TPR
1939	Phi-N	15	25	2	7	1	0	0	0	0	3	.280	.280	.320	63	-1	-1	2	0			-1	C	-0.1

■ GEORGE COCHRAN
Cochran, George Leslie b: 2/12/1889, Rusk, Tex. d: 5/21/60, Harbor City, Cal. TR , Deb: 7/29/18

YEAR	TM/L	G	AB	R	H	2B	3B	HR	RBI	BB	SO	AVG	OBP	SLG	PRO+	BR	/A	RC	SB	CS	SBR	FR	POS	TPR
1918	Bos-A	24	60	7	7	0	0	0	3	10	6	.117	.264	.117	15	-6	-6	2	3			-4	3/S	-0.9

■ DAVE COCHRANE
Cochrane, David Carter b: 1/31/63, Riverside, Cal. BB/TR, 6′2″, 180 lbs. Deb: 9/02/86

YEAR	TM/L	G	AB	R	H	2B	3B	HR	RBI	BB	SO	AVG	OBP	SLG	PRO+	BR	/A	RC	SB	CS	SBR	FR	POS	TPR
1986	Chi-A	19	62	4	12	2	0	1	2	5	22	.194	.254	.274	42	-5	-5	4	0	0	0	-3	3/S	-0.7
1989	Sea-A	54	102	13	24	4	1	3	7	14	27	.235	.333	.382	98	-0	-0	13	0	2	-1	-13	S/1320C	-1.2
1990	Sea-A	15	20	0	3	0	0	0	0	0	8	.150	.150	.150	-16	-3	-3	0	0	0	0	0	/S13C	-0.2
Total	3	88	184	17	39	6	1	4	9	19	57	.212	.289	.321	67	-8	-8	17	0	2	-1	-15	/S312CO	-2.1

■ MICKEY COCHRANE
Cochrane, Gordon Stanley b: 4/6/03, Bridgewater, Mass. d: 6/28/62, Lake Forest, Ill. BL/TR, 5′10.5″, 180 lbs. Deb: 4/14/25 MCH

YEAR	TM/L	G	AB	R	H	2B	3B	HR	RBI	BB	SO	AVG	OBP	SLG	PRO+	BR	/A	RC	SB	CS	SBR	FR	POS	TPR
1925	Phi-A	134	420	69	139	21	5	6	55	44	19	.331	.397	.448	107	9	5	76	7	4	-0	-9	*C	0.4
1926	Phi-A	120	370	50	101	8	9	8	47	56	15	.273	.369	.408	97	2	-1	60	7	5	2	12	*C	1.8
1927	Phi-A	126	432	80	146	20	6	12	80	50	7	.338	.409	.495	127	22	18	84	9	6	-1	3	*C	2.4
1928	Phi-A	131	468	92	137	26	12	10	57	76	25	.293	.395	.464	122	19	17	89	7	7	-2	2	*C	2.4
1929	*Phi-A	135	514	113	170	37	8	7	95	69	8	.331	.412	.475	123	23	20	103	7	6	-2	8	*C	3.6

YEAR	TM/L	G	AB	R	H	2B	3B	HR	RBI	BB	SO	AVG	OBP	SLG	PRO+	BR	/A	RC	SB	CS	SBR	FR	POS	TPR
1930	*Phi-A	130	487	110	174	42	5	10	85	55	18	.357	.424	.526	133	30	27	111	5	0	2	6	*C	4.1
1931	*Phi-A	122	459	87	160	31	6	17	89	56	21	.349	.423	.553	146	37	33	108	2	3	-1	10	*C	4.5
1932	Phi-A	139	518	118	152	35	4	23	112	100	22	.293	.412	.510	132	31	28	115	0	1	-1	12	*C/O	4.2
1933	Phi-A	130	429	104	138	30	4	15	60	106	22	.322	.459	.515	156	42	41	109	8	6	-1	-7	*C	3.6
1934	*Det-A	129	437	74	140	32	1	2	76	78	26	.320	.428	.412	117	16	16	83	8	4	0	-5	*CM	2.0
1935	*Det-A	115	411	93	131	33	3	5	47	96	15	.319	.452	.450	139	27	29	91	5	5	-2	-5	*CM	2.4
1936	Det-A	44	126	24	34	8	0	2	17	46	15	.270	.465	.381	111	6	5	27	1	1	-0	-8	CM	0.0
1937	Det-A	27	98	27	30	10	1	2	12	25	4	.306	.452	.490	134	7	7	23	0	1	-1	-2	CM	0.5
Total	13	1482	5169	1041	1652	333	64	119	832	857	217	.320	.419	.478	127	269	244	1079	64	46	-8	17	*C/O	31.9

■ JIM COCKMAN
Cockman, James b: 4/26/1873, Guelph, Ont., Can. d: 9/28/47, Guelph, Ont., Can. BR/TR, 5'6", 145 lbs. Deb: 9/28/05

YEAR	TM/L	G	AB	R	H	2B	3B	HR	RBI	BB	SO	AVG	OBP	SLG	PRO+	BR	/A	RC	SB	CS	SBR	FR	POS	TPR
1905	NY-A	13	38	5	4	0	0	0	2	4		.105	.190	.105	-4	-4	-5	1	2			-2	3	-0.6

■ JACK COFFEY
Coffey, John Francis b: 1/28/1887, New York, N.Y. d: 2/14/66, Bronx, N.Y. BR/TR, 5'11", 178 lbs. Deb: 6/23/09

YEAR	TM/L	G	AB	R	H	2B	3B	HR	RBI	BB	SO	AVG	OBP	SLG	PRO+	BR	/A	RC	SB	CS	SBR	FR	POS	TPR
1909	Bos-N	73	257	21	48	4	4	0	20	11		.187	.229	.233	41	-17	-19	14	2			-11	S	-3.3
1918	Det-A	22	67	7	14	0	2	0	4	8	6	.209	.303	.269	75	-2	-2	6	2			0	2	0.0
	Bos-N	15	44	5	7	1	0	1	2	3	2	.159	.213	.250	40	-3	-3	3	2			2	3/2	0.0
	Yr	37	111	12	21	1	2	1	6	11	8	.189	.268	.261	62	-6	-5	9	4			2		0.0
Total	2	110	368	33	69	5	6	1	26	22	8	.188	.241	.242	47	-23	-24	22	6			-9	/S23	-3.3

■ FRANK COGGINS
Coggins, Franklin b: 5/22/44, Griffin, Ga. BB/TR, 6'2", 187 lbs. Deb: 9/10/67

YEAR	TM/L	G	AB	R	H	2B	3B	HR	RBI	BB	SO	AVG	OBP	SLG	PRO+	BR	/A	RC	SB	CS	SBR	FR	POS	TPR
1967	Was-A	19	75	9	23	3	0	1	8	2	17	.307	.325	.387	114	1	1	9	1	0	0	3	2	0.6
1968	Was-A	62	171	15	30	6	1	0	7	9	33	.175	.217	.222	34	-14	-13	8	1	1	-0	4	2	-0.8
1972	Chi-N	6	1	1	0	0	0	0	0	1	0	.000	.500	.000	48	0	0	0	0	0	0	0	H	0.0
Total	3	87	247	25	53	9	1	1	15	12	50	.215	.251	.271	59	-13	-12	17	2	1	0	7	/2	-0.2

■ RICH COGGINS
Coggins, Richard Allen b: 12/7/50, Indianapolis, Ind. BL/TL, 5'8", 170 lbs. Deb: 8/29/72

YEAR	TM/L	G	AB	R	H	2B	3B	HR	RBI	BB	SO	AVG	OBP	SLG	PRO+	BR	/A	RC	SB	CS	SBR	FR	POS	TPR
1972	Bal-A	16	39	5	13	4	0	0	1	1	6	.333	.350	.436	129	1	1	5	0	2	-1	4	O	0.4
1973	*Bal-A	110	389	54	124	19	9	7	41	28	24	.319	.365	.468	134	16	16	65	17	9	-0	3	*O/D	1.7
1974	*Bal-A	113	411	53	100	13	3	4	32	29	31	.243	.301	.319	81	-11	-10	42	26	6	4	-1	*O	-0.9
1975	Mon-N	13	37	1	10	3	1	0	4	1	7	.270	.289	.405	87	-1	-1	4	0	0	0	-1	O	-0.1
	NY-A	51	107	7	24	1	0	1	6	7	16	.224	.272	.262	53	-7	-6	8	3	3	-1	3	O/D	-0.4
1976	NY-A	7	4	1	1	0	0	0	1	0	1	.250	.250	.250	47	-0	-0	0	1	0	0	1	/O	0.1
	Chi-A	32	96	4	15	2	0	0	5	6	15	.156	.206	.177	13	-10	-11	4	3	1	0	-2	O/D	-1.3
	Yr	39	100	5	16	2	0	0	6	6	16	.160	.208	.180	14	-11	-11	4	4	1	1	-1		-1.2
Total	5	342	1083	125	287	42	13	12	90	72	100	.265	.314	.361	94	-12	-10	129	50	21	2	8	O/D	-0.5

■ ED COGSWELL
Cogswell, Edward b: 2/25/1854, England d: 7/27/1888, Fitchburg, Mass. BR/TR, 5'8", 150 lbs. Deb: 7/11/1879

YEAR	TM/L	G	AB	R	H	2B	3B	HR	RBI	BB	SO	AVG	OBP	SLG	PRO+	BR	/A	RC	SB	CS	SBR	FR	POS	TPR
1879	Bos-N	49	236	51	76	8	1	1	18	8	5	.322	.344	.377	135	9	9	31				1	1	0.5
1880	Tro-N	47	209	41	63	7	3	0	13	11	10	.301	.336	.364	130	8	7	26				1	1	0.5
1882	Wor-N	13	51	10	7	1	0	0	1	6	6	.137	.228	.157	26	-4	-4	2				-1	1	-0.6
Total	3	109	496	102	146	16	4	1	32	25	21	.294	.328	.349	121	13	11	59				1	1	0.4

■ ALTA COHEN
Cohen, Alta Albert "Schoolboy" b: 12/25/08, New York, N.Y. BL/TL, 5'10.5", 170 lbs. Deb: 4/15/31

YEAR	TM/L	G	AB	R	H	2B	3B	HR	RBI	BB	SO	AVG	OBP	SLG	PRO+	BR	/A	RC	SB	CS	SBR	FR	POS	TPR
1931	Bro-N	1	3	1	2	0	0	0	0	0	0	.667	.667	.667	261	1	1	1	0			2	/O	0.2
1932	Bro-N	9	32	1	5	1	0	0	3	3	7	.156	.229	.188	14	-4	-4	2	0			1	/O	-0.3
1933	Phi-N	19	32	6	6	1	0	0	1	6	4	.188	.316	.219	49	-2	-2	2	0			0	/O	-0.2
Total	3	29	67	8	13	2	0	0	2	9	11	.194	.289	.224	42	-5	-5	5	0			2	/O	-0.3

■ ANDY COHEN
Cohen, Andrew Howard b: 10/25/04, Baltimore, Md. d: 10/29/88, ElPaso, Tex. BR/TR, 5'8", 155 lbs. Deb: 6/06/26 MC

YEAR	TM/L	G	AB	R	H	2B	3B	HR	RBI	BB	SO	AVG	OBP	SLG	PRO+	BR	/A	RC	SB	CS	SBR	FR	POS	TPR
1926	NY-N	32	35	4	9	0	1	0	8	1	2	.257	.278	.314	60	-2	-2	3	0			2	2S/3	0.1
1928	NY-N	129	504	64	138	24	7	9	59	31	17	.274	.318	.403	87	-11	-11	63	3			3	*2/S3	-0.5
1929	NY-N	101	347	40	102	12	2	5	47	11	15	.294	.319	.383	73	-15	-15	41	3			12	2/S3	-0.4
Total	3	262	886	108	249	36	10	14	114	43	34	.281	.317	.392	81	-28	-28	106	6			16	2/S3	-0.4

■ JIMMIE COKER
Coker, James Goodwin b: 3/28/36, Holly Hill, S.C. BR/TR, 5'11", 195 lbs. Deb: 9/11/58

YEAR	TM/L	G	AB	R	H	2B	3B	HR	RBI	BB	SO	AVG	OBP	SLG	PRO+	BR	/A	RC	SB	CS	SBR	FR	POS	TPR
1958	Phi-N	2	6	0	1	0	0	0	0	0	0	.167	.167	.167	-12	-1	-1	0	0	0	0	1	/C	0.0
1960	Phi-N	81	252	18	54	5	3	6	34	23	45	.214	.290	.329	69	-11	-11	24	0	3	-2	2	C	-0.6
1961	Phi-N	11	25	3	10	1	0	1	4	7	4	.400	.531	.560	193	4	4	9	1	0	0	1	C	0.6
1962	Phi-N	5	3	0	0	0	0	0	1	1	2	.000	.250	.000	-27	-1	-1	0	0	0	0	0	H	0.0
1963	SF-N	4	5	0	1	0	0	0	0	1	2	.200	.333	.200	58	-0	-0	0	0	0	0	-1	/C	0.0
1964	Cin-N	11	32	3	10	2	0	1	4	3	5	.313	.371	.469	130	1	1	5	0	0	0	3	C	0.4
1965	Cin-N	24	61	3	15	2	0	2	9	8	16	.246	.333	.377	93	0	-0	8	0	0	0	6	C	0.6
1966	Cin-N	50	111	9	28	3	0	4	14	8	5	.252	.303	.387	83	-2	-3	13	0	1	-1	4	C/O	0.2
1967	Cin-N	45	97	8	18	2	1	2	4	4	20	.186	.218	.289	39	-7	-8	5	0	1	-1	-1	C	-0.7
Total	9	233	592	44	137	15	4	16	70	55	99	.231	.301	.351	77	-16	-19	64	1	5	-3	15	C/O	0.5

■ ROCKY COLAVITO
Colavito, Rocco Domenico b: 8/10/33, New York, N.Y. BR/TR, 6'3", 190 lbs. Deb: 9/10/55 C

YEAR	TM/L	G	AB	R	H	2B	3B	HR	RBI	BB	SO	AVG	OBP	SLG	PRO+	BR	/A	RC	SB	CS	SBR	FR	POS	TPR
1955	Cle-A	5	9	3	4	2	0	0	0	0	2	.444	.444	.667	189	1	1	3	0	0	0	2	/O	0.3
1956	Cle-A	101	322	55	89	11	4	21	65	49	46	.276	.375	.531	134	16	15	67	0	1	-1	-3	O	0.7
1957	Cle-A	134	461	66	116	26	0	25	84	71	80	.252	.353	.471	124	14	15	76	1	6	-3	7	*O	0.9
1958	Cle-A	143	489	80	148	26	3	41	113	84	89	.303	.407	.620	183	53	54	122	0	2	-1	2	*O1/P	4.7
1959	Cle-A	154	588	90	151	24	0	42	111	71	86	.257	.339	.512	135	22	25	101	3	3	-1	5	*O	2.2
1960	Det-A	145	555	67	138	18	1	35	87	53	80	.249	.319	.474	108	6	5	78	3	6	-3	4	*O	0.0
1961	Det-A	163	583	129	169	30	2	45	140	113	75	.290	.407	.580	156	52	49	141	1	2	-1	7	*O	4.8
1962	Det-A	161	601	90	164	30	2	37	112	96	68	.273	.375	.514	132	31	29	117	2	0	1	14	*O	3.7
1963	Det-A	160	597	91	162	29	2	22	91	84	78	.271	.362	.437	119	20	17	95	0	0	0	4	*O	1.7
1964	KC-A	160	588	89	161	31	2	34	102	83	56	.274	.366	.507	136	33	31	110	3	1	0	1	*O	2.7
1965	Cle-A	162	592	92	170	25	2	26	108	93	63	.287	.387	.468	140	35	34	110	1	1	-0	3	*O	3.1
1966	Cle-A	151	533	68	127	13	0	30	72	76	81	.238	.337	.432	119	14	14	74	2	1	0	3	*O	1.2
1967	Cle-A	63	191	10	46	9	0	5	21	24	31	.241	.329	.366	104	2	1	23	2	2	-1	-3	O	-0.3
	Chi-A	60	190	20	42	4	1	3	29	25	10	.221	.312	.300	85	-4	-3	19	1	1	-0	-6	O	-1.2
	Yr	123	381	30	88	13	1	8	50	49	41	.231	.320	.333	95	-2	-2	42	3	3	-1	-9		-1.5
1968	LA-N	40	113	6	23	3	0	3	11	15	18	.204	.297	.310	89	-2	-2	13	0	1	-0	-2	O	-0.5
	NY-A	39	91	13	20	2	2	5	13	14	17	.220	.330	.451	139	4	4	14	0	0	0	-5	O/P	-0.5
Total	14	1841	6503	971	1730	283	21	374	1159	951	880	.266	.362	.489	132	297	290	1157	19	27	-11	32	*O/1P	24.1

■ MIKE COLBERN
Colbern, Michael Malloy b: 4/19/55, Santa Monica, Cal. BR/TR, 6'3", 205 lbs. Deb: 7/18/78

YEAR	TM/L	G	AB	R	H	2B	3B	HR	RBI	BB	SO	AVG	OBP	SLG	PRO+	BR	/A	RC	SB	CS	SBR	FR	POS	TPR
1978	Chi-A	48	141	11	38	5	1	2	20	1	36	.270	.285	.362	80	-4	-4	14	0	1	-1	-0	C/D	-0.3
1979	Chi-A	32	83	5	20	5	1	0	8	4	25	.241	.276	.325	61	-5	-5	8	0	0	0	3	C	0.0
Total	2	80	224	16	58	10	2	2	28	5	61	.259	.281	.348	73	-9	-9	22	0	1	-1	3	/CD	-0.3

■ NATE COLBERT
Colbert, Nathan b: 4/9/46, St.Louis, Mo. BR/TR, 6'2", 190 lbs. Deb: 4/14/66

YEAR	TM/L	G	AB	R	H	2B	3B	HR	RBI	BB	SO	AVG	OBP	SLG	PRO+	BR	/A	RC	SB	CS	SBR	FR	POS	TPR
1966	Hou-N	19	7	3	0	0	0	0	0	0	4	.000	.000	.000	-99	-2	-2	0	0	0	0	0	H	-0.1
1968	Hou-N	20	53	5	8	1	0	0	4	1	23	.151	.167	.170	1	-6	-6	1	1	1	-0	-0	O/1	-0.8

YEAR	TM/L	G	AB	R	H	2B	3B	HR	RBI	BB	SO	AVG	OBP	SLG	PRO+	BR	/A	RC	SB	CS	SBR	FR	POS	TPR
1969	SD-N	139	483	64	123	20	9	24	66	45	123	.255	.322	.482	128	12	15	72	6	4	-1	1	*1	0.4
1970	SD-N	156	572	84	148	17	6	38	86	56	150	.259	.329	.509	126	14	17	93	3	5	-2	-8	*1/3	-0.5
1971	SD-N	156	565	81	149	25	3	27	84	63	119	.264	.342	.462	135	18	23	87	5	2	0	1	*1	1.3
1972	SD-N	151	563	87	141	27	2	38	111	70	127	.250	.335	.508	147	25	30	95	15	6	1	7	*1	2.9
1973	SD-N	145	529	73	143	25	2	22	80	54	146	.270	.347	.450	130	13	18	80	9	8	-2	3	*1	1.2
1974	SD-N	119	368	53	76	16	0	14	54	62	108	.207	.323	.364	96	-4	-2	46	10	2	2	6	1O	0.0
1975	Det-A	45	156	16	23	4	2	4	18	17	52	.147	.231	.276	41	-12	-13	9	0	2	-1	-3	1/D	-1.9
	Mon-N	38	81	10	14	4	1	4	11	5	31	.173	.230	.395	68	-4	-4	7	0	0	0	-1	1	-0.6
1976	Mon-N	14	40	5	8	2	0	2	6	9	16	.200	.347	.400	107	1	1	6	3	1	0	1	/O1	0.1
	Oak-A	2	5	0	0	0	0	0	0	1	3	.000	.167	.000	-50	-1	-1	0	0	0	0	0	/D	0.0
Total	10	1004	3422	481	833	141	25	173	520	383	902	.243	.324	.451	120	55	75	497	52	31	-3	5	1/OD3	2.0

■ ALEX COLE   Cole, Alexander   b: 8/17/65, Fayetteville, N.C.   BL/TL, 6'2", 170 lbs.   Deb: 7/27/90

YEAR	TM/L	G	AB	R	H	2B	3B	HR	RBI	BB	SO	AVG	OBP	SLG	PRO+	BR	/A	RC	SB	CS	SBR	FR	POS	TPR
1990	Cle-A	63	227	43	68	5	4	0	13	28	38	.300	.379	.357	105	3	3	37	40	9	7	1	O	0.9

■ DICK COLE   Cole, Richard Roy   b: 5/6/26, Long Beach, Cal.   BR/TR, 6'2", 175 lbs.   Deb: 4/27/51   C

YEAR	TM/L	G	AB	R	H	2B	3B	HR	RBI	BB	SO	AVG	OBP	SLG	PRO+	BR	/A	RC	SB	CS	SBR	FR	POS	TPR
1951	StL-N	15	36	4	7	1	0	0	3	6	5	.194	.310	.222	45	-3	-3	3	0	0	0	5	2	0.2
	Pit-N	42	106	9	25	4	0	1	11	15	9	.236	.331	.302	69	-4	-4	11	0	1	-1	-2	2/S	-0.4
	Yr	57	142	13	32	5	0	1	14	21	14	.225	.325	.282	63	-6	-7	14	0	1	-1	2		-0.2
1953	Pit-N	97	235	29	64	13	1	0	23	38	26	.272	.374	.336	87	-3	-3	32	2	2	-1	-3	S/21	0.0
1954	Pit-N	138	486	40	131	22	5	1	40	41	48	.270	.326	.342	75	-18	-17	52	0	0	0	-11	S32	-2.2
1955	Pit-N	77	239	16	54	8	3	0	21	18	22	.226	.286	.285	53	-16	-16	19	0	0	0	1	32S	-1.2
1956	Pit-N	72	99	7	21	2	1	0	9	11	9	.212	.291	.253	49	-7	-7	7	0	0	0	-8	32/S	-1.3
1957	Mil-N	15	14	1	1	0	0	0	0	3	5	.071	.235	.071	-13	-2	-2	0	0	0	0	0	2/13	0.0
Total	6	456	1215	106	303	50	10	2	107	132	124	.249	.324	.312	69	-53	-51	125	2	3	-1	-18	S23/1	-4.9

■ WILLIS COLE   Cole, Willis Russell   b: 1/6/1882, Milton Junction, Wis.   d: 10/11/65, Madison, Wis.   BR/TR, 5'8", 170 lbs.   Deb: 8/22/09

YEAR	TM/L	G	AB	R	H	2B	3B	HR	RBI	BB	SO	AVG	OBP	SLG	PRO+	BR	/A	RC	SB	CS	SBR	FR	POS	TPR
1909	Chi-A	46	165	17	39	7	3	0	16	16		.236	.308	.315	101	-1	0	17	3			-4	O	-0.5
1910	Chi-A	22	80	6	14	2	1	0	2	4		.175	.224	.225	42	-6	-5	4	0			1	O	-0.5
Total	2	68	245	23	53	9	4	0	18	20		.216	.281	.286	82	-6	-5	21	3			-3	/O	-1.0

■ CHOO CHOO COLEMAN   Coleman, Clarence   b: 8/25/37, Orlando, Fla.   BL/TR, 5'9", 165 lbs.   Deb: 4/16/61

YEAR	TM/L	G	AB	R	H	2B	3B	HR	RBI	BB	SO	AVG	OBP	SLG	PRO+	BR	/A	RC	SB	CS	SBR	FR	POS	TPR
1961	Phi-N	34	47	3	6	1	0	0	4	2	8	.128	.180	.149	-12	-8	-7	1	0	0	0	-1	C	-0.6
1962	NY-N	55	152	24	38	7	2	6	17	11	24	.250	.305	.441	96	-1	-1	19	2	4	-2	-9	C	-1.0
1963	NY-N	106	247	22	44	0	0	3	9	24	49	.178	.264	.215	39	-19	-19	15	5	5	-2	4	C/O	-1.4
1966	NY-N	6	16	2	3	0	0	0	0	0	4	.188	.188	.188	5	-2	-2	1	0	0	0	0	/C	-0.1
Total	4	201	462	51	91	8	2	9	30	37	85	.197	.267	.281	52	-29	-30	36	7	9	-3	-5	C/O	-3.1

■ CURT COLEMAN   Coleman, Curtis Hancock   b: 2/18/1887, Salem, Ore.   d: 7/1/80, Newport, Ore.   BR/TR, 5'11", 180 lbs.   Deb: 4/13/12

YEAR	TM/L	G	AB	R	H	2B	3B	HR	RBI	BB	SO	AVG	OBP	SLG	PRO+	BR	/A	RC	SB	CS	SBR	FR	POS	TPR
1912	NY-A	12	37	8	9	4	0	0	4	7		.243	.364	.351	99	0	0	5	0			0	3	0.0

■ DAVE COLEMAN   Coleman, David Lee   b: 10/26/50, Dayton, Ohio   BR/TR, 6'3", 195 lbs.   Deb: 4/13/77

YEAR	TM/L	G	AB	R	H	2B	3B	HR	RBI	BB	SO	AVG	OBP	SLG	PRO+	BR	/A	RC	SB	CS	SBR	FR	POS	TPR
1977	Bos-A	11	12	1	0	0	0	0	0	1	3	.000	.077	.000	-69	-3	-3	0	0	0	0	-0	/O	-0.3

■ JERRY COLEMAN   Coleman, Gerald Francis   b: 9/14/24, San Jose, Cal.   BR/TR, 6', 165 lbs.   Deb: 4/20/49   M

YEAR	TM/L	G	AB	R	H	2B	3B	HR	RBI	BB	SO	AVG	OBP	SLG	PRO+	BR	/A	RC	SB	CS	SBR	FR	POS	TPR
1949	*NY-A	128	447	54	123	21	5	2	42	63	44	.275	.367	.358	92	-4	-4	62	8	6	-1	1	*2/S	-0.1
1950	*NY-A	153	522	69	150	19	6	6	69	67	38	.287	.372	.381	96	-4	-2	79	3	2	-0	-15	*2/S	-0.6
1951	*NY-A	121	362	48	90	11	2	3	43	31	36	.249	.315	.315	73	-15	-13	37	6	1	1	3	*2S	-0.2
1952	NY-A	11	42	6	17	2	1	0	4	5	4	.405	.468	.500	180	4	4	10	0	1	-1	3	2	0.7
1953	NY-A	8	10	1	2	0	0	0	0	0	2	.200	.200	.200	9	-1	-1	0	0	0	0	2	/2S	0.1
1954	NY-A	107	300	39	65	7	1	3	21	26	29	.217	.279	.277	54	-20	-18	24	3	0	1	18	2S/3	0.6
1955	*NY-A	43	96	12	22	5	0	0	8	11	11	.229	.321	.281	64	-5	-5	9	0	2	-1	-2	S2/3	-0.3
1956	*NY-A	80	183	15	47	5	1	0	18	12	33	.257	.306	.295	61	-11	-10	16	1	2	-1	17	2S3	1.1
1957	*NY-A	72	157	23	42	7	2	2	12	20	21	.268	.354	.376	101	0	1	20	1	1	-0	5	23/S	0.8
Total	9	723	2119	267	558	77	18	16	217	235	218	.263	.341	.339	83	-55	-48	257	22	15	-2	31	2S/3	2.1

■ GORDY COLEMAN   Coleman, Gordon Calvin   b: 7/5/34, Rockville, Md.   BL/TR, 6'3", 208 lbs.   Deb: 9/19/59

YEAR	TM/L	G	AB	R	H	2B	3B	HR	RBI	BB	SO	AVG	OBP	SLG	PRO+	BR	/A	RC	SB	CS	SBR	FR	POS	TPR
1959	Cle-A	6	15	5	8	0	1	0	2	1	2	.533	.563	.667	245	3	3	6	0	0	0	0	/1	0.3
1960	Cin-N	66	251	26	68	10	1	6	32	12	32	.271	.309	.390	89	-4	-4	31	1	1	-0	7	1	0.0
1961	*Cin-N	150	520	63	149	27	4	26	87	45	67	.287	.346	.504	120	15	14	88	1	3	-2	7	*1	1.0
1962	Cin-N	136	476	73	132	13	1	28	86	36	68	.277	.332	.485	113	9	7	73	2	3	-1	-2	*1	0.0
1963	Cin-N	123	365	38	90	20	2	14	59	29	51	.247	.306	.427	105	3	2	47	1	0	0	1	*1	0.2
1964	Cin-N	89	198	18	48	6	2	5	27	13	30	.242	.292	.369	82	-4	-5	20	2	0	1	4	1	-0.2
1965	Cin-N	108	325	39	98	19	0	14	57	24	38	.302	.351	.489	125	14	11	55	0	0	0	1	1	0.8
1966	Cin-N	91	227	20	57	7	0	5	37	16	45	.251	.300	.348	73	-6	-9	24	2	1	0	-1	1	-1.3
1967	Cin-N	4	7	0	0	0	0	0	0	1	0	.000	.125	.000	-55	-1	-2	0	0	0	0	0	/1	-0.1
Total	9	773	2384	282	650	102	11	98	387	177	333	.273	.326	.448	106	29	18	344	9	8	-2	17	1	0.7

■ JOHN COLEMAN   Coleman, John Francis   b: 3/6/1863, Saratoga Spgs., N.Y   d: 5/31/22, Detroit, Mich.   BL/TR, 5'9.5", 170 lbs.   Deb: 5/01/1883

YEAR	TM/L	G	AB	R	H	2B	3B	HR	RBI	BB	SO	AVG	OBP	SLG	PRO+	BR	/A	RC	SB	CS	SBR	FR	POS	TPR
1883	Phi-N	90	354	33	83	12	8	0	32	15	39	.234	.266	.314	83	-10	-5	30				10	PO/2	0.0
1884	Phi-N	43	171	16	42	7	2	0	22	8	20	.246	.279	.310	89	-3	-2	15				4	OP/1	0.4
	Phi-a	28	107	16	22	2	3	2		5		.206	.241	.336	83	-1	-2	9				-1	O/P1	-0.2
1885	Phi-a	96	398	71	119	15	11	3		25		.299	.345	.415	134	19	15	58				-1	*O/P	0.9
1886	Phi-a	121	492	67	121	18	16	0		33		.246	.296	.348	102	1	0	60	28			2	*O/1P2	0.0
	Pit-a	11	43	3	15	2	1	0		2		.349	.378	.442	159	3	3	8	1			-2	O	0.0
	Yr	132	535	70	136	20	17	0		35		.254	.302	.355	107	4	3	68	29			-0		0.0
1887	Pit-N	115	475	75	139	21	11	2	54	31	40	.293	.337	.396	111	3	8	74	25			-2	*O/1	0.6
1888	Pit-N	116	438	49	101	11	4	0	26	29	52	.231	.285	.274	87	-9	-4	39	15			2	O1	-0.5
1889	Phi-a	6	19	1	1	0	0	0	1	1	3	.053	.100	.053	-56	-4	-4	0	1			0	/PO	0.0
1890	Pit-N	3	11	1	2	0	0	0	0	3	0	.182	.357	.182	69	-0	-0	1	1			-0	/OP	0.0
Total	8	629	2508	332	645	88	56	7	135	152	154	.257	.302	.345	102	-2	9	295	71			12	OP/12	1.2

■ ED COLEMAN   Coleman, Parke Edward   b: 12/1/01, Canby, Ore.   d: 8/5/64, Oregon City, Ore.   BL/TR, 6'2", 200 lbs.   Deb: 4/15/32

YEAR	TM/L	G	AB	R	H	2B	3B	HR	RBI	BB	SO	AVG	OBP	SLG	PRO+	BR	/A	RC	SB	CS	SBR	FR	POS	TPR
1932	Phi-A	26	73	13	25	7	1	1	13	1	6	.342	.351	.507	115	2	1	13	1	0	0	0	O	0.1
1933	Phi-A	102	388	48	109	26	3	6	68	19	51	.281	.318	.410	91	-6	-7	50	0	0	0	-5	O	-1.3
1934	Phi-A	101	329	53	92	14	6	14	60	29	34	.280	.342	.486	116	4	6	55	0	1	-1	-4	O	0.0
1935	Phi-A	10	13	0	1	0	0	0	0	0	3	.077	.077	.077	-61	-3	-3	0	0	0	0	0	/O	-0.2
	StL-A	108	397	66	114	15	9	17	71	53	41	.287	.373	.499	118	13	10	75	0	2	-1	-6	*O	0.2
	Yr	118	410	66	115	15	9	17	71	53	44	.280	.364	.485	113	10	7	74	0	2	-1	-6		0.0
1936	StL-A	92	137	13	40	5	4	2	34	15	17	.292	.366	.431	93	-1	-2	22	0	0	0	-4	O	-0.4
Total	5	439	1337	193	381	67	23	40	246	117	152	.285	.345	.459	105	8	6	215	1	3	-2	-18	O	-1.6

■ RAY COLEMAN   Coleman, Raymond Leroy   b: 6/4/22, Dunsmuir, Cal.   BL/TR, 5'11", 170 lbs.   Deb: 4/22/47

YEAR	TM/L	G	AB	R	H	2B	3B	HR	RBI	BB	SO	AVG	OBP	SLG	PRO+	BR	/A	RC	SB	CS	SBR	FR	POS	TPR
1947	StL-A	110	343	34	89	9	7	2	30	26	32	.259	.314	.344	81	-9	-9	33	2	5	-2	-3	O	-1.9
1948	StL-A	17	29	2	5	0	1	0	2	2	5	.172	.226	.241	24	-3	-3	1	1	0	0	-1	/O	-0.3

YEAR	TM/L	G	AB	R	H	2B	3B	HR	RBI	BB	SO	AVG	OBP	SLG	PRO+	BR	/A	RC	SB	CS	SBR	FR	POS	TPR
	Phi-A	68	210	32	51	6	6	0	21	31	17	.243	.340	.329	78	-6	-6	23	4	3	-1	2	O	-0.6
	Yr	85	239	34	56	6	7	0	23	33	22	.234	.327	.318	72	-9	-10	24	5	3	-0	1		-0.9
1950	StL-A	117	384	54	104	25	6	8	55	32	37	.271	.330	.430	90	-6	-8	52	7	5	-1	6	O	-0.3
1951	StL-A	91	341	41	96	16	5	5	55	24	32	.282	.329	.402	94	-3	-4	43	3	4	-2	4	O	-0.4
	Chi-A	51	181	21	50	8	7	3	21	15	14	.276	.332	.448	112	1	2	26	2	3	-1	6	O	0.4
	Yr	142	522	62	146	24	12	8	76	39	46	.280	.330	.418	100	-1	-2	69	5	7	-3	9		0.0
1952	Chi-A	85	195	19	42	7	1	2	14	13	17	.215	.264	.292	54	-12	-12	15	0	0	0	6	O	-0.8
	StL-A	20	46	5	9	3	0	0	1	5	4	.196	.288	.261	52	-3	-3	4	0	0	0	-0	O	-0.3
	Yr	105	241	24	51	10	1	2	15	18	21	.212	.269	.286	54	-15	-15	19	0	0	0	6		-1.1
Total	5	559	1729	208	446	74	33	20	199	148	158	.258	.318	.374	84	-40	-44	198	19	20	-6	19	O	-4.2

■ BOB COLEMAN
Coleman, Robert Hunter b: 9/26/1890, Huntingburg, Ind. d: 7/16/59, Boston, Mass. BR/TR, 6'2", 190 lbs. Deb: 6/13/13 MC

YEAR	TM/L	G	AB	R	H	2B	3B	HR	RBI	BB	SO	AVG	OBP	SLG	PRO+	BR	/A	RC	SB	CS	SBR	FR	POS	TPR
1913	Pit-N	24	50	5	9	2	0	0	9	7	8	.180	.281	.220	46	-3	-3	3	0			-3	C	-0.4
1914	Pit-N	73	150	11	40	4	1	1	14	15	32	.267	.333	.327	101	-0	0	17	3			2	C	0.5
1916	Cle-A	19	28	3	6	2	0	0	4	7	6	.214	.371	.286	92	0	0	3	0			-2	C	-0.1
Total	3	116	228	19	55	8	1	1	27	29	46	.241	.327	.298	87	-4	-3	23	3			-4	C	-0.0

■ VINCE COLEMAN
Coleman, Vincent Maurice b: 9/22/60, Jacksonville, Fla. BB/TR, 6', 170 lbs. Deb: 4/18/85

YEAR	TM/L	G	AB	R	H	2B	3B	HR	RBI	BB	SO	AVG	OBP	SLG	PRO+	BR	/A	RC	SB	CS	SBR	FR	POS	TPR
1985	*StL-N	151	636	107	170	20	10	1	40	50	115	.267	.321	.335	84	-14	-13	79	110	25	18	7	*O	0.9
1986	StL-N	154	600	94	139	13	8	0	29	60	98	.232	.304	.280	63	-30	-29	67	107	14	24	1	*O	-0.6
1987	*StL-N	151	623	121	180	14	10	3	43	70	126	.289	.364	.358	90	-5	-6	96	109	22	20	2	*O	0.9
1988	StL-N	153	616	77	160	20	10	3	38	49	111	.260	.315	.339	87	-9	-10	71	81	27	8	2	*O	-0.3
1989	StL-N	145	563	94	143	21	9	2	28	50	90	.254	.317	.334	84	-10	-12	70	65	10	14	-10	*O	-1.0
1990	StL-N	124	497	73	145	18	9	6	39	35	88	.292	.341	.400	100	2	0	74	77	17	13	4	*O	1.4
Total	6	878	3535	566	937	106	56	15	217	314	628	.265	.327	.339	84	-65	-70	457	549	115	96	6	O	1.3

■ CAD COLES
Coles, Cadwallader R. b: 1/17/1889, Rockhill, S.C. d: 6/30/42, Miami, Fla. BL/TR, 6'0.5", 174 lbs. Deb: 4/16/14

YEAR	TM/L	G	AB	R	H	2B	3B	HR	RBI	BB	SO	AVG	OBP	SLG	PRO+	BR	/A	RC	SB	CS	SBR	FR	POS	TPR
1914	KC-F	78	194	17	49	7	3	1	25	5	30	.253	.271	.335	76	-7	-6	20	6			-7	O/1	-1.5

■ CHUCK COLES
Coles, Charles Edward b: 6/27/31, Fredericktown, Pa BL/TL, 5'9", 180 lbs. Deb: 9/19/58

YEAR	TM/L	G	AB	R	H	2B	3B	HR	RBI	BB	SO	AVG	OBP	SLG	PRO+	BR	/A	RC	SB	CS	SBR	FR	POS	TPR
1958	Cin-N	5	11	0	2	1	0	0	2	2	6	.182	.308	.273	52	-1	-1	1	0	0	0	1	/O	0.0

■ DARNELL COLES
Coles, Darnell b: 6/2/62, San Bernardino, Cal BR/TR, 6'1", 170 lbs. Deb: 9/04/83

YEAR	TM/L	G	AB	R	H	2B	3B	HR	RBI	BB	SO	AVG	OBP	SLG	PRO+	BR	/A	RC	SB	CS	SBR	FR	POS	TPR
1983	Sea-A	27	92	9	26	7	0	1	6	7	12	.283	.333	.391	95	-0	-1	8	0	3	-2	-4	3	-0.5
1984	Sea-A	48	143	15	23	3	1	0	6	17	26	.161	.259	.196	28	-14	-13	8	2	1	0	-3	3/OD	-1.5
1985	Sea-A	27	59	8	14	4	0	1	5	9	17	.237	.348	.356	93	-0	-0	8	0	1	-1	7	S/3OD	0.7
1986	Det-A	142	521	67	142	30	2	20	86	45	84	.273	.337	.453	113	9	9	81	6	2	1	-5	*3/SOD	0.2
1987	Det-A	53	149	14	27	5	1	4	15	15	23	.181	.265	.309	54	-11	-10	13	0	1	-1	-3	3/10SD	-1.3
	Pit-N	40	119	20	27	8	0	6	24	19	20	.227	.338	.445	105	1	1	17	1	3	-2	-3	O3/1	-0.4
1988	Pit-N	68	211	20	49	13	1	5	36	20	41	.232	.308	.374	96	-1	-1	25	1	1	-0	-6	O/13	-0.9
	Sea-A	55	195	32	57	10	1	10	34	17	26	.292	.361	.508	134	10	9	35	3	2	-0	-7	O/1D	0.1
1989	Sea-A	146	535	54	135	21	3	10	59	27	61	.252	.296	.359	81	-12	-15	54	5	4	-1	6	O31D	-1.2
1990	Sea-A	37	107	9	23	5	1	2	16	4	17	.215	.250	.336	62	-6	-6	9	0	0	0	2	O/31D	-0.4
	Det-A	52	108	13	22	2	0	1	4	12	21	.204	.283	.250	51	-7	-7	7	0	4	-2	2	DO/3	-0.6
	Yr	89	215	22	45	7	1	3	20	16	38	.209	.267	.293	56	-13	-13	16	0	4	-2	4		-1.0
Total	8	695	2239	261	545	108	10	60	291	192	348	.243	.311	.381	90	-32	-34	265	18	22	-8	-14	30/D1S	-5.8

■ CHRIS COLETTA
Coletta, Christopher Michael b: 8/2/44, Brooklyn, N.Y. BL/TL, 5'11", 190 lbs. Deb: 8/15/72

YEAR	TM/L	G	AB	R	H	2B	3B	HR	RBI	BB	SO	AVG	OBP	SLG	PRO+	BR	/A	RC	SB	CS	SBR	FR	POS	TPR
1972	Cal-A	14	30	5	9	1	0	1	7	1	4	.300	.323	.433	131	1	1	4	0	0	0	-2	/O	-0.1

■ ED COLGAN
Colgan, William H. b: E.St.Louis, Ill. d: 8/13/1895, Great Falls, Mont. 180 lbs. Deb: 5/03/1884

YEAR	TM/L	G	AB	R	H	2B	3B	HR	RBI	BB	SO	AVG	OBP	SLG	PRO+	BR	/A	RC	SB	CS	SBR	FR	POS	TPR
1884	Pit-a	48	161	10	25	4	1	0	3			.155	.171	.193	20	-13	-14	5				3	C/O	-0.6

■ BILL COLIVER
Coliver, William J. b: 1867, Detroit, Mich. d: 3/24/1888, Detroit, Mich. Deb: 7/04/1885

YEAR	TM/L	G	AB	R	H	2B	3B	HR	RBI	BB	SO	AVG	OBP	SLG	PRO+	BR	/A	RC	SB	CS	SBR	FR	POS	TPR
1885	Bos-N	1	4	0	0	0	0	0	0	0	1	.000	.000	.000	-99	-1	-1	0				-0	/O	0.0

■ CHUB COLLINS
Collins, Charles b: 1862, Dundas, Ont., Canada d: 5/20/14, Dundas, Ont., Can. Deb: 5/01/1884

YEAR	TM/L	G	AB	R	H	2B	3B	HR	RBI	BB	SO	AVG	OBP	SLG	PRO+	BR	/A	RC	SB	CS	SBR	FR	POS	TPR
1884	Buf-N	45	169	24	30	6	0	0	20	14	36	.178	.240	.213	43	-10	-11	9				0	2/S	-0.8
	Ind-a	38	138	18	31	3	1	0		9		.225	.272	.261	80	-3	-2	10				-8	2	-0.8
1885	Det-N	14	55	8	10	0	2	0	6	0	11	.182	.182	.255	40	-4	-4	3				-8	S	-0.9
Total	2	97	362	50	71	9	3	0	26	23	47	.196	.244	.238	56	-17	-17	22				-16	/2S	-2.5

■ WILSON COLLINS
Collins, Cyril Wilson b: 5/7/1889, Pulaski, Tenn. d: 2/28/41, Knoxville, Tenn. BR/TR, 5'9.5", 165 lbs. Deb: 5/12/13

YEAR	TM/L	G	AB	R	H	2B	3B	HR	RBI	BB	SO	AVG	OBP	SLG	PRO+	BR	/A	RC	SB	CS	SBR	FR	POS	TPR
1913	Bos-N	16	3	3	1	0	0	0	0	0	1	.333	.333	.333	89	-0	-0	0	0			1	/O	0.1
1914	Bos-N	27	35	5	9	0	0	0	1	2	8	.257	.297	.257	66	-1	-1	3	0			1	O	0.0
Total	2	43	38	8	10	0	0	0	1	2	9	.263	.300	.263	68	-2	-1	3	0			2	/O	0.1

■ DAN COLLINS
Collins, Daniel Thomas b: 7/12/1854, St.Louis, Mo. d: 9/21/1883, New Orleans, La. Deb: 6/08/1874

YEAR	TM/L	G	AB	R	H	2B	3B	HR	RBI	BB	SO	AVG	OBP	SLG	PRO+	BR	/A	RC	SB	CS	SBR	FR	POS	TPR
1874	Chi-n	3	12	1	1	0	0	0		0		.083	.083	.083	-46	-2	-2	0					/POS	0.0
1876	Lou-N	7	28	3	4	1	0	0	9	0	2	.143	.143	.179	5	-3	-3	1				0	/O	-0.2

■ DAVE COLLINS
Collins, David S b: 10/20/52, Rapid City, S.D. BB/TL, 5'11", 175 lbs. Deb: 6/07/75

YEAR	TM/L	G	AB	R	H	2B	3B	HR	RBI	BB	SO	AVG	OBP	SLG	PRO+	BR	/A	RC	SB	CS	SBR	FR	POS	TPR
1975	Cal-A	93	319	41	85	13	4	3	29	36	55	.266	.343	.361	106	0	3	42	24	10	1	-2	OD	0.0
1976	Cal-A	99	365	45	96	12	1	4	28	40	55	.263	.336	.334	103	-1	2	43	32	19	-2	-2	OD	-0.3
1977	Sea-A	120	402	46	96	9	3	5	28	33	66	.239	.301	.313	69	-17	-17	41	25	10	2	-2	OD	-1.9
1978	Cin-N	102	102	13	22	1	0	0	7	15	18	.216	.316	.225	54	-6	-6	7	7	7	-2	2	O	-0.6
1979	*Cin-N	122	396	59	126	16	4	3	35	27	48	.318	.365	.402	108	5	5	58	16	9	-1	-13	O1	-1.1
1980	Cin-N	144	551	94	167	20	4	3	35	53	68	.303	.367	.370	106	6	6	84	79	21	11	-7	*O	0.5
1981	Cin-N	95	360	63	98	18	6	3	23	41	41	.272	.356	.381	107	5	5	52	26	10	2	-5	O	0.0
1982	NY-A	111	348	41	88	12	3	3	25	28	49	.253	.318	.330	80	-10	-9	37	13	8	-1	-0	O1/D	-1.3
1983	Tor-A	118	402	55	109	12	4	1	34	43	67	.271	.345	.328	81	-6	-9	51	31	7	5	4	*O/1D	-0.1
1984	Tor-A	128	441	59	136	24	15	2	44	33	41	.308	.369	.444	119	14	12	81	60	14	10	-2	*O/1D	1.6
1985	Oak-A	112	379	52	95	16	4	4	29	29	37	.251	.306	.346	84	-11	-8	42	29	8	4	2	O	-0.2
1986	Det-A	124	419	44	113	18	2	1	27	44	49	.270	.342	.329	84	-8	-8	49	27	12	1	1	OD	-0.7
1987	Cin-N	57	85	19	25	5	0	0	5	11	14	.294	.388	.353	94	0	0	14	9	0	3	0	O	0.2
1988	Cin-N	99	174	12	41	6	2	0	14	11	27	.236	.289	.293	65	-7	-8	16	7	2	1	-3	O/1	-1.1
1989	Cin-N	78	106	12	25	4	0	0	7	10	17	.236	.302	.274	63	-5	-5	9	3	1	0	2	O	-0.2
1990	StL-N	99	58	12	13	1	0	0	3	13	10	.224	.366	.241	69	-2	-2	7	7	1	2	-1	1O	-0.4
Total	16	1701	4907	667	1335	187	52	32	373	467	660	.272	.340	.351	93	-42	-39	633	395	139	35	-26	*O1D	-5.6

■ EDDIE COLLINS
Collins, Edward Trowbridge Jr. b: 11/23/16, Lansdowne, Pa. BL/TR, 5'10", 175 lbs. Deb: 7/04/39

YEAR	TM/L	G	AB	R	H	2B	3B	HR	RBI	BB	SO	AVG	OBP	SLG	PRO+	BR	/A	RC	SB	CS	SBR	FR	POS	TPR
1939	Phi-A	32	21	6	5	1	0	0	3			.238	.238	.286	34	-2	-2	2	1	0	0	3	/O2	0.1
1941	Phi-A	80	219	29	53	6	3	0	12	20	24	.242	.305	.297	61	-13	-12	21	2	1	0	-1	O	-1.4
1942	Phi-A	20	34	6	8	2	0	0	4	4	2	.235	.316	.294	72	-1	-1	4	1	0	0	-2	/O	-0.3
Total	3	132	274	41	66	9	3	0	16	24	29	.241	.302	.296	61	-16	-15	26	4	1	1	1	/O2	-1.6

YEAR	TM/L	G	AB	R	H	2B	3B	HR	RBI	BB	SO	AVG	OBP	SLG	PRO+	BR	/A	RC	SB	CS	SBR	FR	POS	TPR

■ EDDIE COLLINS

Collins, Edward Trowbridge Sr. "Cocky" (a.k.a. Edward T. Sullivan In 1906)
b: 5/2/1887, Millerton, N.Y. d: 3/25/51, Boston, Mass. BL/TR, 5'9", 175 lbs. Deb: 9/17/06 MCH

YEAR	TM/L	G	AB	R	H	2B	3B	HR	RBI	BB	SO	AVG	OBP	SLG	PRO+	BR	/A	RC	SB	CS	SBR	FR	POS	TPR
1906	Phi-A	6	15	2	3	0	0	0	0	0		.200	.200	.200	26	-1	-1	1	0			-0	/S23	-0.1
1907	Phi-A	14	20	0	5	0	0	0	2	0		.250	.250	.250	60	-1	-1	1	0			1	/S	0.0
1908	Phi-A	102	330	39	90	18	7	1	40	16		.273	.306	.379	117	8	5	41	8			-12	2SO	-0.7
1909	Phi-A	153	572	104	198	30	10	3	56	62		.346	.416	.449	170	49	48	134	67			8	*2/S	5.7
1910	Phi-A	153	583	81	188	16	15	3	81	49		.322	.381	.417	151	33	34	122	81			35	*2	6.4
1911	Phi-A	132	493	92	180	22	13	3	73	62		.365	.451	.481	163	43	44	124	38			3	*2	4.5
1912	Phi-A	153	543	137	189	25	11	0	64	101		.348	.450	.435	159	44	47	136	63			15	*2	5.8
1913	Phi-A	148	534	125	184	23	13	3	73	85	37	.345	.441	.453	166	46	47	126	55			16	*2	6.1
1914	Phi-A	152	526	122	181	23	14	2	85	97	31	.344	.452	.452	178	52	54	120	58	30	-1	0	*2	5.7
1915	Chi-A	155	521	118	173	22	10	4	77	119	27	.332	.460	.436	163	52	50	116	46	30	-4	13	*2	5.9
1916	Chi-A	155	545	87	168	14	17	0	52	86	36	.308	.405	.396	139	31	30	99	40	21	-1	-6	*2	3.0
1917	Chi-A	156	564	91	163	18	12	0	67	89	16	.289	.389	.363	127	24	22	98	53			-25	*2	0.7
1918	Chi-A	97	330	51	91	8	2	2	30	73	13	.276	.407	.330	121	14	13	54	22			-0	2	1.9
1919	Chi-A	140	518	87	165	19	7	4	80	68	27	.319	.400	.405	126	21	20	97	33			3	*2	3.7
1920	Chi-A	153	601	115	222	37	13	3	75	69	19	.369	.436	.489	145	41	41	132	19	8	1	10	*2	5.3
1921	Chi-A	139	526	79	177	20	10	2	58	66	11	.337	.412	.424	115	14	15	94	12	10	-2	27	*2	4.0
1922	Chi-A	154	598	92	194	20	12	1	69	73	16	.324	.401	.403	110	12	12	101	20	12	-1	-9	*2	1.2
1923	Chi-A	145	505	89	182	22	5	5	67	84	8	.360	.455	.453	141	34	35	109	49	29	-3	-4	*2	3.2
1924	Chi-A	152	556	108	194	27	7	6	86	89	16	.349	.441	.455	136	30	33	119	42	17	2	-7	*2	3.0
1925	Chi-A	118	425	80	147	26	3	3	80	87	8	.346	.461	.442	137	26	29	96	19	6	2	-9	*2M	2.5
1926	Chi-A	106	375	66	129	32	4	1	62	62	8	.344	.441	.459	140	22	24	80	13	8	-1	-6	*2M	2.0
1927	Phi-A	95	226	50	76	12	1	1	15	56	9	.336	.468	.412	123	14	12	46	6	2	1	-7	2/S	0.8
1928	Phi-A	36	33	3	10	3	0	0	7	4	4	.303	.378	.394	100	0	0	5	0	0	0	-2	/2S	0.0
1929	Phi-A	9	7	0	0	0	0	0	0	2	0	.000	.222	.000	-37	-1	-1	0	0	0	0	0	H	0.0
1930	Phi-A	3	2	1	1	0	0	0	0	0	0	.500	.500	.500	148	0	0	0	0	0	0	0	H	0.0
Total	25	2826	9948	1819	3310	437	186	47	1299	1499	286	.333	.424	.428	141	604	613	2054	744	173		44	*2/SO3	70.6

■ HUB COLLINS

Collins, Hubert B. b: 4/15/1864, Louisville, Ky. d: 5/21/1892, Brooklyn, N.Y. BR/TR, 5'8", 160 lbs. Deb: 9/04/1886

YEAR	TM/L	G	AB	R	H	2B	3B	HR	RBI	BB	SO	AVG	OBP	SLG	PRO+	BR	/A	RC	SB	CS	SBR	FR	POS	TPR
1886	Lou-a	27	101	12	29	3	2	0		5		.287	.321	.356	108	1	0	14	7			-2	0/3S21	-0.1
1887	Lou-a	130	559	122	162	22	8	1		39		.290	.338	.363	96	-2	-3	95	71			-8	*02/1S3	-1.1
1888	Lou-a	116	485	117	149	26	11	2	50	41		.307	.366	.419	158	29	31	99	62			13	O2S	3.8
	Bro-a	12	42	16	13	5	1	0	3	9		.310	.442	.476	199	5	5	13	9			-3	2	0.3
	Yr	128	527	133	162	31	12	2	53	50		.307	.373	.423	162	35	36	112	71			10		4.1
1889	*Bro-a	138	560	139	149	18	3	2	73	80	41	.266	.365	.320	97	2	2	91	65			-2	*2	0.2
1890	*Bro-N	129	510	148	142	32	7	3	69	85	47	.278	.385	.386	127	21	20	111	85			6	*2	2.7
1891	Bro-N	107	435	82	120	16	5	3	31	59	63	.276	.365	.356	113	9	9	70	32			-22	2O	-1.1
1892	Bro-N	21	87	17	26	5	1	0	17	14	13	.299	.396	.356	142	4	5	15	4			-2	O	0.2
Total	7	680	2779	653	790	127	38	11	243	332	164	.284	.365	.369	118	70	70	509	335			-20	20/S13	4.9

■ HUGH COLLINS

Collins, Hugh 150 lbs. Deb: 8/01/1887

YEAR	TM/L	G	AB	R	H	2B	3B	HR	RBI	BB	SO	AVG	OBP	SLG	PRO+	BR	/A	RC	SB	CS	SBR	FR	POS	TPR
1887	NY-a	1	4	0	1	0	0	0		0		.250	.250	.250	43	-0	-0	0	0			0	/C	0.0

■ RIPPER COLLINS

Collins, James Anthony b: 3/30/04, Altoona, Pa. d: 4/15/70, New Haven, Conn. BB/TL, 5'9", 165 lbs. Deb: 4/18/31 C

YEAR	TM/L	G	AB	R	H	2B	3B	HR	RBI	BB	SO	AVG	OBP	SLG	PRO+	BR	/A	RC	SB	CS	SBR	FR	POS	TPR
1931	*StL-N	89	279	34	84	20	10	4	59	18	24	.301	.350	.487	118	8	7	48	1			4	1/O	0.5
1932	StL-N	149	549	82	153	28	8	21	91	38	67	.279	.329	.474	110	8	6	87	4			-4	1O	-0.5
1933	StL-N	132	493	66	153	26	7	10	68	38	49	.310	.363	.452	125	20	17	81	7			3	*1	1.8
1934	*StL-N	154	600	116	200	40	12	35	128	57	50	.333	.393	.615	155	53	48	148	2			8	*1	4.1
1935	StL-N	150	578	109	181	36	10	23	122	65	45	.313	.385	.529	138	35	32	125	0			1	*1	2.8
1936	StL-N	103	277	48	81	15	3	13	48	48	30	.292	.399	.509	143	18	18	61	1			-1	1/O	1.0
1937	Chi-N	115	456	77	125	16	5	16	71	32	46	.274	.329	.436	102	3	0	64	2			1	*1	-0.4
1938	*Chi-N	143	490	78	131	22	8	13	61	54	48	.267	.344	.424	107	7	5	73	1			10	*1	0.3
1941	Pit-N	49	62	5	13	2	2	0	11	6	14	.210	.279	.306	65	-3	-3	6	0			1	1/O	-0.3
Total	9	1084	3784	615	1121	205	65	135	659	356	373	.296	.360	.492	125	149	130	694	18			22	1/O	9.3

■ JIMMY COLLINS

Collins, James Joseph b: 1/16/1870, Buffalo, N.Y. d: 3/6/43, Buffalo, N.Y. BR/TR, 5'9", 178 lbs. Deb: 4/19/1895 MH

YEAR	TM/L	G	AB	R	H	2B	3B	HR	RBI	BB	SO	AVG	OBP	SLG	PRO+	BR	/A	RC	SB	CS	SBR	FR	POS	TPR
1895	Bos-N	11	38	10	8	3	0	1	8	4	4	.211	.302	.368	69	-2	-2	4	0			-2	O	-0.3
	Lou-N	96	373	65	104	17	5	6	49	33	16	.279	.352	.399	102	-3	2	58	12			21	3O/2S	1.8
	Yr	107	411	75	112	20	5	7	57	37	20	.273	.347	.397	98	-4	-0	62	12			19		1.5
1896	Bos-N	84	304	48	90	10	9	1	46	30	12	.296	.374	.398	100	3	0	50	10			21	3	2.1
1897	*Bos-N	134	529	103	183	28	13	6	132	41		.346	.400	.482	127	26	20	110	14			21	*3	3.5
1898	Bos-N	152	597	107	196	35	5	15	111	40		.328	.377	.479	140	34	30	115	12			15	*3	4.4
1899	Bos-N	151	599	98	166	28	11	5	92	40		.277	.335	.386	91	-1	-10	83	12			21	*3	1.0
1900	Bos-N	142	586	104	178	25	5	6	95	34		.304	.351	.394	96	6	-5	91	23			10	*3/S	0.6
1901	Bos-A	138	564	108	187	42	16	6	94	34		.332	.375	.495	144	30	32	116	19			14	*3M	3.8
1902	Bos-A	108	429	71	138	21	10	6	61	24		.322	.362	.459	125	15	14	82	18			9	*3M	1.8
1903	*Bos-A	130	540	88	160	33	17	5	72	24		.296	.326	.448	126	19	16	90	23			12	*3M	2.7
1904	Bos-A	156	631	85	171	33	13	3	67	27		.271	.301	.379	110	10	6	81	19			7	*3M	2.1
1905	Bos-A	131	508	66	140	26	5	4	65	37		.276	.325	.370	121	12	12	70	18			6	*3M	2.5
1906	Bos-A	37	142	17	39	8	4	1	16	4		.275	.295	.408	121	3	3	18	1			3	3M	0.8
1907	Bos-A	41	158	13	46	8	0	0	10	10		.291	.333	.342	118	3	3	21	4			-7	3	-0.1
	Phi-A	100	365	38	100	22	0	0	35	24		.274	.319	.334	108	4	3	42	4			-2	3	0.7
	Yr	141	523	51	146	30	0	0	45	34		.279	.323	.337	111	7	6	63	8			-9		0.6
1908	Phi-A	115	433	34	94	14	3	0	30	20		.217	.252	.263	65	-15	-18	30	5			-6	*3	-1.6
Total	14	1726	6796	1055	2000	353	116	65	983	426	32	.294	.341	.409	113	147	106	1061	194			140	*3/OS2	25.6

■ ZIP COLLINS

Collins, John Edgar b: 5/2/1892, Brooklyn, N.Y. d: 12/19/83, Manassas, Va. BL/TL, 5'11", 152 lbs. Deb: 7/31/14

YEAR	TM/L	G	AB	R	H	2B	3B	HR	RBI	BB	SO	AVG	OBP	SLG	PRO+	BR	/A	RC	SB	CS	SBR	FR	POS	TPR
1914	Pit-N	49	182	14	44	2	0	5	15	8	10	.242	.277	.253	61	-9	-9	13	3			0	O	-1.0
1915	Pit-N	101	354	51	104	8	5	1	23	24	38	.294	.340	.353	112	4	5	44	6	7	-2	1	O	0.1
	Bos-N	5	14	3	4	1	1	0	0	2	1	.286	.375	.500	171	1	1	3	1			0	/O	0.2
	Yr	106	368	54	108	9	6	1	23	26	39	.293	.342	.359	114	5	6	47	7	7	-2	2		0.3
1916	Bos-N	93	268	39	56	1	6	1	18	18	42	.209	.261	.269	66	-12	-11	21	4			-3	O	-1.8
1917	Bos-N	9	27	3	4	0	1	0	2	0	4	.148	.148	.222	14	-3	-3	1	0			0	O	-0.2
1921	Phi-A	24	71	14	20	5	1	0	5	6	5	.282	.354	.380	87	-1	-1	9	1	2	-1	0	O	-0.2
Total	5	281	916	124	232	17	14	2	63	58	100	.253	.301	.309	85	-20	-17	92	15	9		-1	O	-2.9

■ SHANO COLLINS

Collins, John Francis b: 12/4/1885, Charlestown, Mass. d: 9/10/55, Newton, Mass. BR/TR, 6', 185 lbs. Deb: 4/21/10 M

YEAR	TM/L	G	AB	R	H	2B	3B	HR	RBI	BB	SO	AVG	OBP	SLG	PRO+	BR	/A	RC	SB	CS	SBR	FR	POS	TPR
1910	Chi-A	97	315	29	62	10	8	0	24	25		.197	.258	.289	74	-11	-10	26	10			4	O1	-0.8
1911	Chi-A	106	370	48	97	16	12	4	48	20		.262	.309	.403	101	-3	-1	50	14			4	1/2O	0.4
1912	Chi-A	153	579	75	168	34	10	2	81	29		.290	.323	.403	110	2	5	83	26			2	*O1	0.2
1913	Chi-A	148	535	53	128	26	9	1	47	32	60	.239	.286	.327	80	-16	-15	55	22			1	*O	-2.2
1914	Chi-A	154	598	61	164	34	9	3	65	27	49	.274	.312	.376	108	2	3	71	30	24	-5	9	*O	-0.3
1915	Chi-A	153	576	73	148	24	17	2	85	28	50	.257	.298	.368	96	-4	-6	70	38	19	0	2	*O1	-1.2

YEAR	TM/L	G	AB	R	H	2B	3B	HR	RBI	BB	SO	AVG	OBP	SLG	PRO+	BR	/A	RC	SB	CS	SBR	FR	POS	TPR
1916	Chi-A	143	527	74	128	28	12	0	42	59	51	.243	.323	.342	98	-1	-1	65	16			8	*O/1	-0.1
1917	*Chi-A	82	252	38	59	13	3	1	14	10	27	.234	.269	.321	78	-7	-8	24	14			-2	O	-1.5
1918	Chi-A	103	365	30	100	18	11	1	56	17	19	.274	.310	.392	111	3	2	45	7			14	O/1	1.3
1919	*Chi-A	63	179	21	50	6	3	1	16	7	11	.279	.317	.363	90	-3	-3	21	3			1	O/1	-0.5
1920	Chi-A	133	495	70	150	21	10	1	63	23	24	.303	.339	.392	93	-6	-6	65	12	9	-2	-9	*1O	-1.6
1921	Bos-A	141	542	63	155	29	12	4	69	18	38	.286	.314	.406	85	-16	-14	68	15	8	-0	4	*O/1	-2.0
1922	Bos-A	135	472	33	128	24	7	1	52	7	30	.271	.289	.358	68	-24	-23	46	7	9	-3	-7	*O/1	-4.1
1923	Bos-A	97	342	41	79	10	5	0	18	11	29	.231	.265	.289	46	-27	-28	25	7	8	-3	-2	O	-3.9
1924	Bos-A	89	240	37	70	17	5	0	28	18	17	.292	.349	.404	94	-3	-3	33	4	6	-2	-10	O1	-1.8
1925	Bos-A	2	3	1	1	0	0	0	1	0	0	.333	.333	.333	70	-0	-0	0	0	0	0	-1	/O	0.0
Total	16	1799	6390	747	1687	310	133	22	709	331	405	.264	.306	.364	90	-114	-108	748	225	83		19	*O1/2	-18.1

■ JOE COLLINS

Collins, Joseph Edward (b: Joseph Edward Kollonige) b: 12/3/22, Scranton, Pa. d: 8/30/89, Union, N.J. BL/TL, 6', 185 lbs. Deb: 9/25/48

YEAR	TM/L	G	AB	R	H	2B	3B	HR	RBI	BB	SO	AVG	OBP	SLG	PRO+	BR	/A	RC	SB	CS	SBR	FR	POS	TPR
1948	NY-A	5	5	0	1	1	0	0	2	0	1	.200	.200	.400	58	-0	-0	0	0	0	0	0	H	0.0
1949	NY-A	7	10	2	1	0	0	0	4	6	2	.100	.438	.100	46	-0	-0	1	0	0	0	-1	/1	-0.1
1950	*NY-A	108	205	47	48	8	3	8	28	31	34	.234	.335	.420	95	-3	-2	31	5	0	2	1	1/O	-0.4
1951	*NY-A	125	262	52	75	8	5	9	48	34	23	.286	.368	.458	127	8	9	44	9	7	-2	5	*1O	1.1
1952	*NY-A	122	428	69	120	16	8	18	59	55	47	.280	.364	.481	142	18	22	77	4	2	0	-3	*1	1.2
1953	*NY-A	127	387	72	104	11	2	17	44	59	36	.269	.365	.439	121	9	11	65	2	6	-3	0	*1/O	0.6
1954	NY-A	130	343	67	93	20	2	12	46	51	37	.271	.365	.446	126	10	12	58	2	2	-1	1	*1	0.9
1955	*NY-A	105	278	40	65	9	1	13	45	44	32	.234	.343	.414	104	1	1	40	0	2	-1	5	1O	0.0
1956	*NY-A	100	262	38	59	5	3	7	43	34	33	.225	.316	.347	78	-10	-8	30	3	1	0	6	O1	-0.5
1957	*NY-A	79	149	17	30	1	0	2	10	24	18	.201	.312	.248	56	-9	-8	12	2	1	0	-1	1O	-1.0
Total	10	908	2329	404	596	79	24	86	329	338	263	.256	.351	.421	112	25	36	360	27	21	-5	14	1O	1.8

■ KEVIN COLLINS

Collins, Kevin Michael "Casey" b: 8/4/46, Springfield, Mass. BL/TR, 6'1", 180 lbs. Deb: 9/01/65

YEAR	TM/L	G	AB	R	H	2B	3B	HR	RBI	BB	SO	AVG	OBP	SLG	PRO+	BR	/A	RC	SB	CS	SBR	FR	POS	TPR
1965	NY-N	11	23	3	4	1	0	0	0	1	9	.174	.208	.217	21	-2	-2	1	0	1	-1	-1	/3S	-0.4
1967	NY-N	4	10	1	1	0	0	0	0	0	3	.100	.100	.100	-43	-2	-2	0	1	0	0	0	/2	-0.1
1968	NY-N	58	154	12	31	5	2	1	13	7	37	.201	.236	.279	54	-9	-9	10	0	1	-1	-6	3/2S	-1.7
1969	NY-N	16	40	1	6	3	0	1	2	3	10	.150	.209	.300	40	-3	-3	3	0	0	0	3	3	0.0
	Mon-N	52	96	5	23	5	1	2	12	8	16	.240	.298	.375	87	-2	-2	11	0	0	0	-7	23	-0.7
	Yr	68	136	6	29	8	1	3	14	11	26	.213	.272	.353	73	-5	-5	13	0	0	0	-4		-0.7
1970	Det-A	25	24	2	5	1	0	1	3	1	10	.208	.240	.375	67	-1	-1	2	0	0	0	0	/1	0.0
1971	Det-A	35	41	6	11	2	1	1	4	0	12	.268	.268	.439	94	-0	-1	4	0	0	0	1	/3O2	0.0
Total	6	201	388	30	81	17	4	6	34	20	97	.209	.248	.320	62	-20	-20	31	1	2	-1	-11	/32SO1	-2.9

■ ORTH COLLINS

Collins, Orth Stein "Buck" b: 4/27/1880, Lafayette, Ind. d: 12/13/49, Ft.Lauderdale, Fla BL/TR, 6', 150 lbs. Deb: 6/01/04

YEAR	TM/L	G	AB	R	H	2B	3B	HR	RBI	BB	SO	AVG	OBP	SLG	PRO+	BR	/A	RC	SB	CS	SBR	FR	POS	TPR
1904	NY-A	5	17	3	6	1	1	0	1	1	1	.353	.389	.529	183	2	2	4	0			2	/O	0.4
1909	Was-A	8	7	0	0	0	0	0	0	0		.000	.000	.000	-99	-2	-2	0	0			-1	/OP	-0.1
Total	2	13	24	3	6	1	1	0	1	1	1	.250	.280	.375	105	0	0	4	0			1	/OP	0.3

■ RIP COLLINS

Collins, Robert Joseph b: 9/18/09, Pittsburgh, Pa. d: 4/19/69, Pittsburgh, Pa. BR/TR, 5'11", 176 lbs. Deb: 4/28/40

YEAR	TM/L	G	AB	R	H	2B	3B	HR	RBI	BB	SO	AVG	OBP	SLG	PRO+	BR	/A	RC	SB	CS	SBR	FR	POS	TPR
1940	Chi-N	47	120	11	25	3	0	1	14	14	18	.208	.296	.258	55	-7	-7	9	4			-2	C	-0.6
1944	NY-A	3	3	0	1	0	0	0	0	1	0	.333	.500	.333	136	0	0	1	0	0	0	0	/C	0.1
Total	2	50	123	11	26	3	0	1	14	15	18	.211	.302	.260	58	-7	-7	10	4	0		-2	/C	-0.5

■ PAT COLLINS

Collins, Tharon Leslie b: 9/13/1896, Sweet Sprgs., Mo. d: 5/20/60, Kansas City, Kan. BR/TR, 5'9", 178 lbs. Deb: 9/05/19

YEAR	TM/L	G	AB	R	H	2B	3B	HR	RBI	BB	SO	AVG	OBP	SLG	PRO+	BR	/A	RC	SB	CS	SBR	FR	POS	TPR
1919	StL-A	11	21	2	3	1	0	0	1	4	2	.143	.280	.190	32	-2	-2	1	0			-0	/C	-0.1
1920	StL-A	23	28	5	6	1	0	0	6	3	5	.214	.290	.250	43	-2	-2	2	0	0	0	-2	/C	-0.3
1921	StL-A	58	111	9	27	3	0	1	10	16	17	.243	.339	.297	60	-6	-7	12	1	0	0	-1	C	-0.5
1922	StL-A	63	127	14	39	6	0	8	23	21	21	.307	.405	.543	140	9	8	28	0	1	-1	6	C/1	1.3
1923	StL-A	85	181	9	32	8	0	3	30	15	45	.177	.240	.271	32	-18	-19	13	0	0	0	-1	C	-1.6
1924	StL-A	32	54	9	17	2	0	1	11	11	14	.315	.431	.407	110	2	1	10	0	1	-1	-1	C	0.1
1926	*NY-A	102	290	41	83	11	3	7	35	73	55	.286	.433	.417	124	14	14	59	3	2	-0	2	*C	2.2
1927	*NY-A	92	251	38	69	9	3	7	36	54	24	.275	.407	.418	118	8	9	45	0	1	-1	-7	C	0.5
1928	*NY-A	70	136	18	30	5	0	6	14	35	16	.221	.380	.390	106	2	2	23	0	0	0	-5	C	0.2
1929	Bos-N	7	5	1	0	0	0	0	2	3	1	.000	.375	.000	2	-1	-1	1	0			1	/C	0.1
Total	10	543	1204	146	306	46	6	33	168	235	200	.254	.378	.385	98	5	4	194	4	5		-7	C/1	1.9

■ BILL COLLINS

Collins, William J. b: 1863, Dublin, Ireland d: 6/8/1893, New York, N.Y. BR Deb: 10/05/1889

YEAR	TM/L	G	AB	R	H	2B	3B	HR	RBI	BB	SO	AVG	OBP	SLG	PRO+	BR	/A	RC	SB	CS	SBR	FR	POS	TPR
1889	Phi-a	1	4	0	1	0	0	0	1	1	0	.250	.400	.250	91	0	0	1	1			-1	/C	0.0
1890	Phi-a	1	1	0	0	0	0	0	0			.000	.000	.000	-99	-0	-0	0	0			-0	/S	0.0
1891	Cle-N	2	3	0	0	0	0	0	0	0	0	.000	.000	.000	-96	-1	-1	0	0			1	/OC	0.1
Total	3	4	8	0	1	0	0	0	1	1	0	.125	.222	.125	2	-1	-1	1	1			1	/COS	0.1

■ BILL COLLINS

Collins, William Shirley b: 3/27/1882, Chesterton, Ind. d: 6/26/61, San Bernadino, Cal. BB/TR, 6', 170 lbs. Deb: 4/14/10

YEAR	TM/L	G	AB	R	H	2B	3B	HR	RBI	BB	SO	AVG	OBP	SLG	PRO+	BR	/A	RC	SB	CS	SBR	FR	POS	TPR
1910	Bos-N	151	584	67	141	6	7	3	40	43	48	.241	.308	.291	72	-18	-22	63	36			18	*O	-0.9
1911	Bos-N	17	44	8	6	1	1	0	8	1	8	.136	.156	.205	0	-6	-6	2	4			2	O/3	-0.4
	Chi-N	7	3	2	1	1	0	0	0	1	0	.333	.500	.667	225	1	1	1	0			0	/O	0.1
	Yr	24	47	10	7	2	1	0	8	2	8	.149	.184	.234	16	-5	-6	3	4			2		-0.3
1913	Bro-N	32	95	8	18	1	0	0	4	8	11	.189	.267	.200	33	-8	-8	5	2			-1	O	-0.9
1914	Buf-F	21	47	6	7	2	2	0	2	1	8	.149	.167	.277	25	-5	-5	2	0			-1	O	-0.6
Total	4	228	773	91	173	11	10	3	54	54	75	.224	.287	.276	61	-36	-41	74	42			18	O/3	-2.7

■ FRANK COLMAN

Colman, Frank Lloyd b: 3/2/18, London, Ont., Canada d: 2/19/83, London, Ont., Can. BL/TL, 5'11", 186 lbs. Deb: 9/12/42

YEAR	TM/L	G	AB	R	H	2B	3B	HR	RBI	BB	SO	AVG	OBP	SLG	PRO+	BR	/A	RC	SB	CS	SBR	FR	POS	TPR
1942	Pit-N	10	37	2	5	0	1	2	2	2		.135	.179	.216	15	-4	-4	2	0			0	/O	-0.4
1943	Pit-N	32	59	9	16	2	2	0	4	8	7	.271	.358	.373	108	1	1	9	0			-0	O	0.0
1944	Pit-N	99	226	30	61	9	5	6	53	25	27	.270	.345	.434	113	5	4	34	0			-3	O/1	-0.3
1945	Pit-N	77	153	18	32	11	1	4	30	9	16	.209	.253	.373	70	-7	-7	14	0			-1	1O	-0.9
1946	Pit-N	26	53	3	9	3	0	1	6	2	7	.170	.214	.283	39	-4	-5	3	0			0	/O1	-0.4
	NY-A	5	15	2	4	0	0	1	5	1	1	.267	.313	.467	114	0	0	2	0	0	0	0	/O	0.0
1947	NY-A	22	28	2	3	0	0	2	6	2	6	.107	.167	.321	34	-3	-3	2	0	0	0	1	/O	-0.2
Total	6	271	571	66	130	25	8	15	106	49	66	.228	.291	.378	85	-11	-14	65	0	0		-3	O/1	-2.2

■ BOB COLUCCIO

Coluccio, Robert Pasquali b: 10/2/51, Centralia, Wash. BR/TR, 5'11", 183 lbs. Deb: 4/15/73

YEAR	TM/L	G	AB	R	H	2B	3B	HR	RBI	BB	SO	AVG	OBP	SLG	PRO+	BR	/A	RC	SB	CS	SBR	FR	POS	TPR
1973	Mil-A	124	438	65	98	21	8	15	58	54	92	.224	.313	.411	105	1	2	58	13	6	0	8	*OD	0.7
1974	Mil-A	138	394	42	88	13	4	6	31	43	61	.223	.305	.322	81	-10	-9	40	15	9	-1	13	*O/D	0.0
1975	Mil-A	22	62	8	12	0	1	1	5	11	11	.194	.324	.274	70	-2	-2	5	1	4	-2	1	O	-0.3
	Chi-A	61	161	22	33	4	2	4	13	13	34	.205	.269	.329	67	-7	-7	15	4	0	1	1	O/D	-0.7
	Yr	83	223	30	45	4	3	5	18	24	45	.202	.285	.314	68	-9	-9	20	5	4	-1	2		-1.0
1977	Chi-A	20	37	4	10	0	0	0	7	6	2	.270	.372	.270	79	-1	-1	4	0	2	-1	2	O	0.0
1978	StL-N	5	3	0	0	0	0	0	0	1	2	.000	.250	.000	-25	-0	-0	0	0	0	0	0	/O	0.0
Total	5	370	1095	141	241	38	15	26	114	128	202	.220	.306	.353	87	-19	-18	122	33	21	-3	25	O/D	-0.3

YEAR	TM/L	G	AB	R	H	2B	3B	HR	RBI	BB	SO	AVG	OBP	SLG	PRO+	BR	/A	RC	SB	CS	SBR	FR	POS	TPR

■ EARLE COMBS
Combs, Earle Bryan "The Kentucky Colonel" b: 5/14/1899, Pebworth, Ky. d: 7/21/76, Richmond, Ky. BL/TR, 6', 185 lbs. Deb: 4/16/24 CH

YEAR	TM/L	G	AB	R	H	2B	3B	HR	RBI	BB	SO	AVG	OBP	SLG	PRO+	BR	/A	RC	SB	CS	SBR	FR	POS	TPR
1924	NY-A	24	35	10	14	5	0	0	2	4	2	.400	.462	.543	159	3	3	8	0	1	-1	-3	O	0.0
1925	NY-A	150	593	117	203	36	13	3	61	65	43	.342	.411	.462	123	20	22	112	12	13	-4	4	*O	0.8
1926	*NY-A	145	606	113	181	31	12	8	56	47	23	.299	.352	.429	105	1	2	92	8	6	-1	1	*O	-0.8
1927	*NY-A	152	648	137	231	36	23	6	64	62	31	.356	.414	.511	143	37	40	131	15	6	1	2	*O	3.1
1928	*NY-A	149	626	118	194	33	21	7	56	77	33	.310	.387	.463	127	21	24	114	10	8	-2	8	*O	2.1
1929	NY-A	142	586	119	202	33	15	3	65	69	32	.345	.414	.468	135	25	31	115	11	7	-1	-3	*O	1.9
1930	NY-A	137	532	129	183	30	22	7	82	74	26	.344	.424	.523	145	33	37	120	16	10	-1	-4	*O	2.3
1931	NY-A	138	563	120	179	31	13	5	58	68	34	.318	.394	.446	128	18	23	103	11	3	2	-0	*O	1.5
1932	*NY-A	144	591	143	190	32	10	9	65	81	16	.321	.405	.455	129	22	27	110	3	9	-5	-6	*O	0.9
1933	NY-A	122	417	86	125	22	16	5	64	47	19	.300	.372	.465	128	12	16	73	6	4	-1	-6	*O	0.5
1934	NY-A	63	251	47	80	13	5	2	25	40	9	.319	.412	.434	127	8	11	48	3	1	0	-1	O	0.9
1935	NY-A	89	298	47	84	7	4	3	35	36	10	.282	.359	.362	92	-5	-3	40	1	3	-2	-5	O	-0.8
Total	12	1455	5746	1186	1866	309	154	58	633	670	278	.325	.397	.462	127	196	232	1066	96	71	-14	-13	*O	12.4

■ MERL COMBS
Combs, Merrill Russell b: 12/11/19, Los Angeles, Cal. d: 7/8/81, Riverside, Cal. BL/TR, 6', 172 lbs. Deb: 9/12/47 C

YEAR	TM/L	G	AB	R	H	2B	3B	HR	RBI	BB	SO	AVG	OBP	SLG	PRO+	BR	/A	RC	SB	CS	SBR	FR	POS	TPR
1947	Bos-A	17	68	8	15	1	0	1	6	9	9	.221	.329	.279	65	-2	-3	7	0	0	0	4	3	0.2
1949	Bos-A	14	24	5	5	1	0	0	1	9	0	.208	.424	.250	75	-0	-0	4	0	0	0	-0	/3S	0.0
1950	Bos-A	1	0	0	0	0	0	0	0	1	0	—	1.000	—	158	0	0	0	0	0	0	0	H	0.0
	Was-A	37	102	19	25	1	0	0	6	22	16	.245	.379	.255	68	-4	-3	12	0	0	0	-0	S	-0.1
	Yr	38	102	19	25	1	0	0	6	23	16	.245	.384	.255	69	-4	-3	12	0	0	0	-0		-0.1
1951	Cle-A	19	28	2	5	2	0	0	2	2	3	.179	.233	.250	32	-3	-3	2	0	0	0	5	S	0.3
1952	Cle-A	52	139	11	23	1	1	1	10	14	15	.165	.242	.209	28	-14	-13	8	0	1	-1	9	S/2	-0.1
Total	5	140	361	45	73	6	1	2	25	57	43	.202	.314	.241	52	-23	-22	32	0	1	-1	17	/S32	0.3

■ WAYNE COMER
Comer, Harry Wayne b: 2/3/44, Shenandoah, Va. BR/TR, 5'1", 175 lbs. Deb: 9/17/67

YEAR	TM/L	G	AB	R	H	2B	3B	HR	RBI	BB	SO	AVG	OBP	SLG	PRO+	BR	/A	RC	SB	CS	SBR	FR	POS	TPR
1967	Det-A	4	3	0	1	0	0	0	0	0	0	.333	.333	.333	95	-0	-0	0	0	0	0	0	/O	0.0
1968	*Det-A	48	48	8	6	0	1	1	3	2	7	.125	.160	.229	16	-5	-5	1	0	0	0	1	O/C	-0.5
1969	Sea-A	147	481	88	118	18	1	15	54	82	79	.245	.356	.380	108	6	7	70	18	7	1	1	*O/C3	0.5
1970	Mil-A	13	17	1	1	0	0	0	1	0	3	.059	.059	.059	-67	-4	-4	0	0	0	0	0	/O	-0.3
	Was-A	77	129	21	30	4	0	0	8	22	16	.233	.349	.264	75	-4	-3	14	4	1	1	0	O/3	-0.4
	Yr	90	146	22	31	4	0	0	9	22	19	.212	.320	.240	59	-8	-7	13	4	1	1	0		-0.7
1972	Det-A	27	9	1	1	0	0	0	1	0	1	.111	.111	.111	-33	-1	-1	0	0	1	-1	1	O	-0.1
Total	5	316	687	119	157	22	2	16	67	106	106	.229	.333	.336	90	-8	-7	85	22	9	1	3	O/3C	-0.8

■ CHARLIE COMISKEY
Comiskey, Charles Albert "Commy" or "The Old Roman" b: 8/15/1859, Chicago, Ill. d: 10/26/31, Eagle River, Wis. BR/TR, 6', 180 lbs. Deb: 5/02/1882 MH

YEAR	TM/L	G	AB	R	H	2B	3B	HR	RBI	BB	SO	AVG	OBP	SLG	PRO+	BR	/A	RC	SB	CS	SBR	FR	POS	TPR
1882	StL-a	78	329	58	80	9	5	1		4		.243	.252	.310	85	-4	-6	26				-1	*1/P	-0.6
1883	StL-a	96	401	87	118	17	9	2		11		.294	.313	.397	120	11	8	51				-2	*1/OM	-0.2
1884	StL-a	108	460	76	110	17	6	2		5		.239	.255	.315	84	-6	-9	38				2	*1/2PM	-1.1
1885	*StL-a	83	340	68	87	15	7	2		14		.256	.293	.359	103	3	0	37				1	*1M	-0.4
1886	*StL-a	131	578	95	147	15	9	3		10		.254	.267	.327	83	-10	-14	63	41			4	*1/2OM	-1.4
1887	*StL-a	125	538	139	180	22	5	4		27		.335	.374	.416	111	16	6	131	117			3	*1/2OM	0.5
1888	*StL-a	137	576	102	157	22	5	6	83	12		.273	.292	.359	100	5	-4	84	72			-6	*1/O2M	-1.6
1889	StL-a	137	587	105	168	28	10	3	102	19	19	.286	.312	.383	88	-3	-15	93	65			-1	*1/02PM	-2.3
1890	Chi-P	88	377	53	92	11	3	0	59	14	17	.244	.277	.289	51	-26	-28	41	34			-2	1M	-3.1
1891	StL-a	141	580	86	152	16	2	3	93	33	25	.262	.310	.312	70	-15	-29	70	41			3	*1/OM	-2.8
1892	Cin-N	141	551	61	125	14	6	3	71	32	16	.227	.274	.290	73	-19	-18	53	30			1	*1M	-2.5
1893	Cin-N	64	259	38	57	12	1	0	26	11	2	.220	.257	.274	42	-22	-23	21	9			-6	1M	-2.3
1894	Cin-N	61	220	26	58	8	0	0	33	5	5	.264	.289	.300	42	-20	-22	23	10			-4	1/OM	-1.8
Total	13	1390	5796	994	1531	206	68	29	467	197	84	.264	.293	.338	83	-90	-154	730	419			-7	*1/2OP	-19.6

■ JIM COMMAND
Command, James Dalton "Igor" b: 10/15/28, Grand Rapids, Mich BL/TR, 6'2", 200 lbs. Deb: 6/20/54

YEAR	TM/L	G	AB	R	H	2B	3B	HR	RBI	BB	SO	AVG	OBP	SLG	PRO+	BR	/A	RC	SB	CS	SBR	FR	POS	TPR
1954	Phi-N	9	18	1	4	1	0	1	6	2	4	.222	.300	.444	91	-0	-0	3	0	0	0	-0	/3	0.0
1955	Phi-N	5	5	0	0	0	0	0	0	0	0	.000	.000	.000	-99	-1	-1	0	0	0	0	0	H	0.0
Total	2	14	23	1	4	1	0	1	6	2	4	.174	.240	.348	52	-2	-2	3	0	0	0	-0	/3	0.0

■ ADAM COMOROSKY
Comorosky, Adam b: 12/9/05, Swoyersville, Pa. d: 3/2/51, Swoyersville, Pa. BR/TR, 5'10", 167 lbs. Deb: 9/13/26

YEAR	TM/L	G	AB	R	H	2B	3B	HR	RBI	BB	SO	AVG	OBP	SLG	PRO+	BR	/A	RC	SB	CS	SBR	FR	POS	TPR
1926	Pit-N	8	15	2	4	1	0	0	0	1	2	.267	.313	.467	102	0	-0	2	1			-0	/O	0.0
1927	Pit-N	18	61	5	14	1	0	0	4	3	1	.230	.266	.246	35	-5	-6	4	0			1	O	-0.4
1928	Pit-N	51	176	22	52	6	3	2	34	15	6	.295	.354	.398	92	-1	-2	25	1			1	O	-0.2
1929	Pit-N	127	473	86	152	26	11	6	97	40	22	.321	.377	.461	104	5	3	80	19			-6	*O	-1.1
1930	Pit-N	152	597	112	187	47	23	12	119	51	33	.313	.371	.529	114	12	12	114	14			-1	*O	0.0
1931	Pit-N	99	350	37	85	12	1	1	48	34	28	.243	.310	.291	63	-18	-17	34	11			-1	O	-2.2
1932	Pit-N	108	370	54	106	18	4	4	46	25	20	.286	.337	.389	96	-3	-2	50	7			6	O	-0.1
1933	Pit-N	64	162	18	46	8	1	1	15	4	9	.284	.301	.364	89	-3	-3	16	2			-2	O	-0.6
1934	Cin-N	127	446	46	115	12	6	0	40	34	23	.258	.315	.312	70	-19	-18	44	1			-1	*O	-2.3
1935	Cin-N	59	137	22	34	3	1	2	14	7	14	.248	.290	.328	68	-7	-6	13	1			1	O	-0.5
Total	10	813	2787	404	795	134	51	28	417	214	158	.285	.339	.400	91	-38	-38	382	57			-1	O	-7.4

■ PETE COMPTON
Compton, Anna Sebastian "Bash" b: 9/28/1889, San Marcos, Tex. d: 2/3/78, Kansas City, Mo. BL/TL, 5'11", 170 lbs. Deb: 9/06/11

YEAR	TM/L	G	AB	R	H	2B	3B	HR	RBI	BB	SO	AVG	OBP	SLG	PRO+	BR	/A	RC	SB	CS	SBR	FR	POS	TPR
1911	StL-A	28	107	9	29	4	0	0	5	8		.271	.322	.308	79	-3	-3	11	2			1	O	-0.3
1912	StL-A	103	268	26	75	6	4	2	30	22		.280	.339	.354	102	-1	1	36	11			0	O	-0.2
1913	StL-A	63	100	14	18	5	2	2	17	13	13	.180	.274	.330	79	-3	-3	9	2			-4	O	-0.8
1915	StL-F	2	8	0	2	0	0	0	3	0	0	.250	.250	.250	46	-1	-1	1	0			-1	/O	0.0
	Bos-N	35	116	10	28	7	1	1	12	8	11	.241	.290	.345	96	-1	-1	13	4	1	1	1	O	0.0
1916	Bos-N	34	98	13	20	2	0	0	8	7	7	.204	.264	.224	53	-6	-5	7	5			1	O	-0.5
	Pit-N	5	16	1	1	0	0	0	0	2	5	.063	.211	.063	-14	-2	-2	0	0			-0	/O	-0.2
	Yr	39	114	14	21	2	0	0	8	9	12	.184	.256	.202	43	-8	-7	8	5			0		-0.7
1918	NY-N	21	60	5	13	0	1	0	5	5	4	.217	.277	.250	62	-3	-3	4	2			1	O	-0.2
Total	6	291	773	78	186	24	8	5	80	65	40	.241	.303	.312	83	-20	-16	81	26	1		-1	O	-2.2

■ MIKE COMPTON
Compton, Michael Lynn b: 8/15/44, Stamford, Tex. BR/TR, 5'10", 180 lbs. Deb: 4/17/70

YEAR	TM/L	G	AB	R	H	2B	3B	HR	RBI	BB	SO	AVG	OBP	SLG	PRO+	BR	/A	RC	SB	CS	SBR	FR	POS	TPR
1970	Phi-N	47	110	8	18	0	1	1	7	9	22	.164	.240	.209	22	-12	-12	6	0	0	0	8	C	-0.1

■ CLINT CONATSER
Conatser, Clinton Astor "Connie" b: 7/24/21, Los Angeles, Cal. BR/TR, 5'11", 182 lbs. Deb: 4/21/48

YEAR	TM/L	G	AB	R	H	2B	3B	HR	RBI	BB	SO	AVG	OBP	SLG	PRO+	BR	/A	RC	SB	CS	SBR	FR	POS	TPR
1948	*Bos-N	90	224	30	62	9	3	3	23	32	27	.277	.370	.384	106	2	3	34	0			2	O	0.0
1949	Bos-N	53	152	10	40	6	0	3	16	14	19	.263	.325	.362	89	-3	-2	17	0			2	O	-0.2
Total	2	143	376	40	102	15	3	6	39	46	46	.271	.352	.375	99	-1	0	51	0			4	O	-0.2

■ DAVE CONCEPCION
Concepcion, David Ismael (Benitez) b: 6/17/48, Aragua, Venez. BR/TR, 6'2", 155 lbs. Deb: 4/06/70

YEAR	TM/L	G	AB	R	H	2B	3B	HR	RBI	BB	SO	AVG	OBP	SLG	PRO+	BR	/A	RC	SB	CS	SBR	FR	POS	TPR
1970	*Cin-N	101	265	38	69	6	3	1	19	23	45	.260	.326	.317	73	-10	-10	27	10	2	2	-7	S/2	-0.2
1971	Cin-N	130	327	24	67	4	4	1	20	18	51	.205	.246	.251	42	-25	-25	19	9	3	1	-4	*S2/3O	-1.2
1972	*Cin-N	119	378	40	79	13	2	2	29	32	65	.209	.274	.270	58	-22	-20	27	13	6	0	3	*S/32	-0.2
1973	Cin-N	89	328	39	94	18	3	8	46	21	55	.287	.331	.433	116	4	6	47	22	5	4	2	S/O	2.4

YEAR	TM/L	G	AB	R	H	2B	3B	HR	RBI	BB	SO	AVG	OBP	SLG	PRO+	BR	/A	RC	SB	CS	SBR	FR	POS	TPR
1974	Cin-N	160	594	70	167	25	1	14	82	44	79	.281	.337	.397	106	3	4	80	41	6	9	9	*S/O	4.0
1975	*Cin-N	140	507	62	139	23	1	5	49	39	51	.274	.328	.353	88	-8	-9	59	33	6	6	8	*S/3	2.1
1976	*Cin-N	152	576	74	162	28	7	9	69	49	68	.281	.339	.401	107	6	5	77	21	10	0	17	*S	3.7
1977	Cin-N	156	572	59	155	26	3	8	64	46	77	.271	.325	.369	84	-11	-13	69	8	7	5	8	*S	2.1
1978	Cin-N	153	565	75	170	33	4	6	67	51	83	.301	.360	.405	113	10	10	82	23	10	1	-5	*S	2.0
1979	*Cin-N	149	590	91	166	25	3	16	84	64	73	.281	.352	.415	108	7	7	85	19	7	2	14	*S	3.8
1980	Cin-N	156	622	72	162	31	8	5	77	37	107	.260	.303	.360	84	-14	-14	65	12	2	2	-13	*S/2	-0.7
1981	Cin-N	106	421	57	129	28	0	5	67	37	61	.306	.364	.409	117	10	10	60	4	5	-2	4	*S	2.4
1982	Cin-N	147	572	48	164	25	4	5	53	45	61	.287	.339	.371	96	-1	-2	68	13	6	0	13	*S/13	2.2
1983	Cin-N	143	528	54	123	22	0	1	47	56	81	.233	.307	.280	61	-25	-27	43	14	9	-1	-22	*S/31	-3.9
1984	Cin-N	154	531	46	130	26	1	4	58	52	72	.245	.312	.320	75	-15	-18	56	22	6	3	-34	*S3/1	-4.0
1985	Cin-N	155	560	59	141	19	2	7	48	50	67	.252	.316	.330	77	-14	-17	54	16	12	-2	-32	*S/3	-4.1
1986	Cin-N	90	311	42	81	13	2	3	30	26	43	.260	.318	.344	79	-7	-9	33	13	2	3	-2	S123	-0.2
1987	Cin-N	104	279	32	89	15	0	1	33	28	24	.319	.381	.384	99	2	1	39	4	3	-1	0	213/S	0.0
1988	Cin-N	84	197	11	39	9	0	0	8	18	23	.198	.265	.244	45	-13	-14	13	3	2	-0	1	21S/3P	-1.2
Total	19	2488	8723	993	2326	389	48	101	950	736	1186	.267	.325	.357	88	-122	-135	1005	321	109	31	-41	*S23/10P	9.0

■ ONIX CONCEPCION

Concepcion, Onix Cardona (Cardona) b: 10/5/57, Dorado, P.R. BR/TR, 5'6", 160 lbs. Deb: 8/30/80

YEAR	TM/L	G	AB	R	H	2B	3B	HR	RBI	BB	SO	AVG	OBP	SLG	PRO+	BR	/A	RC	SB	CS	SBR	FR	POS	TPR
1980	*KC-A	12	15	1	2	0	0	0	2	0	1	.133	.133	.133	-26	-3	-3	0	0	0	0	1	/S	-0.1
1981	KC-A	2	0	0	0	0	0	0	0	0	0	—	—	—	—	0	0	0	0	0	0	0	/S	0.0
1982	KC-A	74	205	17	48	9	1	0	15	5	18	.234	.256	.288	49	-14	-14	14	2	1	0	-1	S2/D	-1.0
1983	KC-A	80	219	22	53	11	3	0	20	12	12	.242	.284	.320	66	-10	-10	20	10	3	1	6	32S/D	0.0
1984	*KC-A	90	287	36	81	9	2	1	23	14	33	.282	.322	.338	82	-6	-7	31	9	6	-1	2	S/23	0.2
1985	*KC-A	131	314	32	64	5	1	2	20	16	29	.204	.256	.245	38	-26	-27	19	4	4	-1	-9	*S/2	-2.6
1987	Pit-N	1	1	0	1	0	0	0	0	0	0	1.000	1.000	1.000	429	0	0	1	0	0	0	0	/H	0.0
Total	7	390	1041	108	249	34	7	3	80	47	93	.239	.279	.294	58	-60	-60	86	25	14	-1	-1	S/23D	-3.5

■ RAMON CONDE

Conde, Ramon Luis (Roman) "Wito" b: 12/29/34, Juana Diaz, P.R. BR/TR, 5'8", 172 lbs. Deb: 7/17/62

YEAR	TM/L	G	AB	R	H	2B	3B	HR	RBI	BB	SO	AVG	OBP	SLG	PRO+	BR	/A	RC	SB	CS	SBR	FR	POS	TPR
1962	Chi-A	14	16	0	0	0	0	0	1	3	3	.000	.158	.000	-54	-4	-3	0	0	0	0	-1	/3	-0.3

■ FRED CONE

Cone, Joseph Frederick b: 5/1848, Rockford, Ill. d: 4/13/09, Chicago, Ill. 5'9.5", 171 lbs. Deb: 5/05/1871

YEAR	TM/L	G	AB	R	H	2B	3B	HR	RBI	BB	SO	AVG	OBP	SLG	PRO+	BR	/A	RC	SB	CS	SBR	FR	POS	TPR
1871	Bos-n	19	77	17	20	3	1	0	16	8	2	.260	.329	.325	86	-1	-1	12	12				O	0.0

■ BUNK CONGALTON

Congalton, William Millar b: 1/24/1875, Guelph, Ont., Can. d: 8/16/37, Cleveland, Ohio BL/TL, 5'11", 190 lbs. Deb: 4/18/02

YEAR	TM/L	G	AB	R	H	2B	3B	HR	RBI	BB	SO	AVG	OBP	SLG	PRO+	BR	/A	RC	SB	CS	SBR	FR	POS	TPR
1902	Chi-N	45	179	14	40	3	0	1	24	7		.223	.253	.257	61	-9	-8	13	3			0	O	-1.1
1905	Cle-A	12	47	4	17	0	0	0	5	2		.362	.388	.362	139	2	2	8	3			-1	O	0.1
1906	Cle-A	117	419	51	134	13	5	3	50	24		.320	.357	.396	140	17	18	68	12			-9	*O	0.5
1907	Cle-A	9	22	2	4	0	0	0	2	4		.182	.308	.182	58	-1	-1	1	0			0	/O	0.0
	Bos-A	124	496	44	142	11	8	2	47	20		.286	.314	.353	116	7	7	62	13			-2	*O	-0.1
	Yr	133	518	46	146	11	8	2	49	24		.282	.314	.346	113	6	6	63	13			-2		-0.1
Total	4	307	1163	115	337	27	13	6	128	57		.290	.323	.351	116	17	18	152	31			-12	O	-0.6

■ TONY CONIGLIARO

Conigliaro, Anthony Richard b: 1/7/45, Revere, Mass. d: 2/24/90, Salem, Mass. BR/TR, 6'3", 185 lbs. Deb: 4/16/64

YEAR	TM/L	G	AB	R	H	2B	3B	HR	RBI	BB	SO	AVG	OBP	SLG	PRO+	BR	/A	RC	SB	CS	SBR	FR	POS	TPR
1964	Bos-A	111	404	69	117	21	2	24	52	35	78	.290	.354	.530	135	22	19	72	2	4	-2	2	*O	1.6
1965	Bos-A	138	521	82	140	21	5	**32**	82	51	116	.269	.340	.512	131	25	21	91	4	2	0	12	*O	3.0
1966	Bos-A	150	558	77	148	26	7	28	93	52	112	.265	.333	.487	120	22	16	91	0	2	-1	-4	*O	0.5
1967	Bos-A	95	349	59	100	11	5	20	67	27	58	.287	.346	.519	141	21	18	62	4	6	-2	2	*O	1.6
1969	Bos-A	141	506	57	129	21	3	20	82	48	111	.255	.324	.427	103	4	1	68	2	4	-2	-12	*O	-1.6
1970	Bos-A	146	560	89	149	20	1	36	116	43	93	.266	.327	.498	116	16	11	90	4	2	0	-2	*O	0.3
1971	Cal-A	74	266	23	59	18	0	4	15	23	52	.222	.286	.335	81	-9	-7	23	3	3	-1	2	O	-0.7
1975	Bos-A	21	57	8	7	1	0	2	9	8	9	.123	.231	.246	32	-5	-6	4	1	0	0	0	D	-0.5
Total	8	876	3221	464	849	139	23	166	516	287	629	.264	.330	.476	118	97	74	501	20	23	-8	0	O/D	4.2

■ BILLY CONIGLIARO

Conigliaro, William Michael b: 8/15/47, Revere, Mass. BR/TR, 6', 180 lbs. Deb: 4/11/69

YEAR	TM/L	G	AB	R	H	2B	3B	HR	RBI	BB	SO	AVG	OBP	SLG	PRO+	BR	/A	RC	SB	CS	SBR	FR	POS	TPR
1969	Bos-A	32	80	14	23	6	2	4	7	9	23	.287	.367	.563	149	6	5	17	1	1	-0	-4	O	0.0
1970	Bos-A	114	398	59	108	16	3	18	58	35	73	.271	.341	.462	112	10	6	59	3	7	-3	9	*O	0.1
1971	Bos-A	101	351	42	92	26	1	11	33	25	68	.262	.311	.436	102	3	0	45	3	2	-0	1	*O	-0.1
1972	Mil-A	52	191	22	44	8	2	7	16	8	54	.230	.261	.393	95	-3	-2	18	1	0	0	4	O	0.1
1973	*Oak-A	48	110	5	22	2	2	0	14	9	26	.200	.261	.255	48	-8	-7	8	1	0	0	4	O/2	-0.3
Total	5	347	1130	142	289	56	10	40	128	86	244	.256	.313	.429	103	8	2	147	9	10	-3	8	O/2	-0.2

■ JEFF CONINE

Conine, Jeffrey Guy b: 6/27/66, Tacoma, Wash. BR/TR, 6'1", 205 lbs. Deb: 9/16/90

YEAR	TM/L	G	AB	R	H	2B	3B	HR	RBI	BB	SO	AVG	OBP	SLG	PRO+	BR	/A	RC	SB	CS	SBR	FR	POS	TPR
1990	KC-A	9	20	3	5	2	0	0	2	2	5	.250	.318	.350	89	-0	-0	2	0	0	0	0	/1	0.0

■ JOCKO CONLAN

Conlan, John Bertrand b: 12/6/1899, Chicago, Ill. d: 4/16/89, Scottsdale, Ariz. BL/TL, 5'7.5", 165 lbs. Deb: 7/06/34   UH

YEAR	TM/L	G	AB	R	H	2B	3B	HR	RBI	BB	SO	AVG	OBP	SLG	PRO+	BR	/A	RC	SB	CS	SBR	FR	POS	TPR
1934	Chi-A	63	225	35	56	11	3	0	16	19	7	.249	.310	.324	62	-12	-13	24	2	2	-1	1	O	-1.2
1935	Chi-A	65	140	20	40	7	1	0	15	14	6	.286	.355	.350	81	-3	-4	18	3	3	-1	1	O	-0.3
Total	2	128	365	55	96	18	4	0	31	33	13	.263	.327	.334	69	-15	-17	41	5	5	-2	1	/O	-1.5

■ JOCKO CONLON

Conlon, Arthur Joseph b: 12/10/1897, Woburn, Mass. d: 8/5/87, Falmouth, Mass. BR/TR, 5'7", 145 lbs. Deb: 4/17/23

YEAR	TM/L	G	AB	R	H	2B	3B	HR	RBI	BB	SO	AVG	OBP	SLG	PRO+	BR	/A	RC	SB	CS	SBR	FR	POS	TPR
1923	Bos-N	59	147	23	32	3	0	0	17	11	11	.218	.299	.238	45	-12	-11	11	0	3	-2	1	2/S3	-0.9

■ BERT CONN

Conn, Albert Thomas b: 9/22/1879, Philadelphia, Pa. d: 11/2/44, Philadelphia, Pa. TR, Deb: 9/16/1898

YEAR	TM/L	G	AB	R	H	2B	3B	HR	RBI	BB	SO	AVG	OBP	SLG	PRO+	BR	/A	RC	SB	CS	SBR	FR	POS	TPR
1898	Phi-N	1	3	1	1	0	1	0	1	0		.333	.333	1.000	293	1	1	1	0			-0	/P	0.0
1900	Phi-N	6	9	4	3	1	0	0	1	0		.333	.333	.444	117	0	0	1	0			-1	/P	0.0
1901	Phi-N	5	18	2	4	1	0	0	0	0		.222	.263	.278	57	-1	-1	1	0			-1	/2	0.0
Total	3	12	30	7	8	2	1	0	2	0		.267	.290	.400	97	-0	-0	4	0			-1	/2P	0.0

■ FRITZIE CONNALLY

Connally, Fritzie Lee b: 5/19/58, Bryan, Tex. BR/TR, 6'3", 210 lbs. Deb: 9/09/83

YEAR	TM/L	G	AB	R	H	2B	3B	HR	RBI	BB	SO	AVG	OBP	SLG	PRO+	BR	/A	RC	SB	CS	SBR	FR	POS	TPR
1983	Chi-N	8	10	0	1	0	0	0	0	0	5	.100	.100	.100	-42	-2	-2	0	0	0	0	0	/3	-0.1
1985	Bal-A	50	112	16	26	4	0	3	15	19	21	.232	.348	.348	94	-1	-0	15	0	0	0	-3	3/1D	-0.4
Total	2	58	122	16	27	4	0	3	15	19	26	.221	.331	.328	83	-3	-2	15	0	0	0	-3	/31D	-0.5

■ BRUCE CONNATSER

Connatser, Broadus Milburn b: 9/19/02, Sevierville, Tenn. d: 1/27/71, Terre Haute, Ind. BR/TR, 5'11.5", 170 lbs. Deb: 9/15/31

YEAR	TM/L	G	AB	R	H	2B	3B	HR	RBI	BB	SO	AVG	OBP	SLG	PRO+	BR	/A	RC	SB	CS	SBR	FR	POS	TPR
1931	Cle-A	12	49	5	14	3	0	0	4	2	3	.286	.327	.347	73	-2	-2	6	0	0	0	1	1	-0.1
1932	Cle-A	23	60	8	14	3	1	0	4	4	8	.233	.281	.317	51	-4	-5	6	1	0	0	0	1	-0.4
Total	2	35	109	13	28	6	1	0	8	6	11	.257	.302	.330	61	-6	-7	11	1	0	0	2	/1	-0.5

■ FRANK CONNAUGHTON

Connaughton, Frank H. b: 1/1/1869, Clinton, Mass. d: 12/1/42, Boston, Mass. BR/TR, 5'9", 165 lbs. Deb: 5/29/1894

YEAR	TM/L	G	AB	R	H	2B	3B	HR	RBI	BB	SO	AVG	OBP	SLG	PRO+	BR	/A	RC	SB	CS	SBR	FR	POS	TPR
1894	Bos-N	46	171	42	59	9	2	2	33	16	8	.345	.407	.456	102	3	0	34	3			-2	S/CO	0.0
1896	NY-N	88	315	53	82	3	2	2	43	25	7	.260	.319	.302	68	-15	-13	38	22			3	SO	-1.0
1906	Bos-N	12	44	3	9	0	0	0	1	3		.205	.255	.205	46	-3	-3	3	1			-3	S/2	-0.4
Total	3	146	530	98	150	12	4	4	77	44	15	.283	.343	.343	79	-15	-16	75	26			-2	/SOC2	-1.4

■ GENE CONNELL

Connell, Eugene Joseph b: 5/10/06, Hazelton, Pa. d: 8/31/37, Waverly, N.Y. BR/TR, 6'0.5", 180 lbs. Deb: 7/04/31

YEAR	TM/L	G	AB	R	H	2B	3B	HR	RBI	BB	SO	AVG	OBP	SLG	PRO+	BR	/A	RC	SB	CS	SBR	FR	POS	TPR
1931	Phi-N	6	12	1	3	0	0	0	0	0	3	.250	.250	.250	32	-1	-1	1	0			-0	/C	0.0

YEAR	TM/L	G	AB	R	H	2B	3B	HR	RBI	BB	SO	AVG	OBP	SLG	PRO+	BR	/A	RC	SB	CS	SBR	FR	POS	TPR

■ JOE CONNELL
Connell, Joseph Bernard b: 1/16/02, Bethlehem, Pa. d: 9/21/77, Trexlertown, Pa. BL/TL, 5'8", 165 lbs. Deb: 6/15/26

YEAR	TM/L	G	AB	R	H	2B	3B	HR	RBI	BB	SO	AVG	OBP	SLG	PRO+	BR	/A	RC	SB	CS	SBR	FR	POS	TPR
1926	NY-N	2	1	1	0	0	0	0	0	0	0	.000	.000	.000	-99	-0	-0	0	0			0	H	0.0

■ PETE CONNELL
Connell, Peter J. b: Brooklyn, N.Y. Deb: 9/03/1886

YEAR	TM/L	G	AB	R	H	2B	3B	HR	RBI	BB	SO	AVG	OBP	SLG	PRO+	BR	/A	RC	SB	CS	SBR	FR	POS	TPR
1886	NY-a	1	5	0	0	0	0	0	0		0	.000	.000	.000	-99	-1	-1	0	0			-1	/3	-0.1

■ TERRY CONNELL
Connell, Terence G. b: 6/17/1855, Philadelphia, Pa. d: 3/25/24, Philadelphia, Pa. Deb: 6/20/1874

YEAR	TM/L	G	AB	R	H	2B	3B	HR	RBI	BB	SO	AVG	OBP	SLG	PRO+	BR	/A	RC	SB	CS	SBR	FR	POS	TPR
1874	Chi-n	1	4	0	0	0	0	0	0			.000	.000	.000	-99	-1	-1	0					/C	0.0

■ TOM CONNELLY
Connelly, Thomas Martin b: 10/20/1897, Chicago, Ill. d: 2/18/41, Hines, Ill. BL/TR, 5'11.5", 165 lbs. Deb: 9/24/20

YEAR	TM/L	G	AB	R	H	2B	3B	HR	RBI	BB	SO	AVG	OBP	SLG	PRO+	BR	/A	RC	SB	CS	SBR	FR	POS	TPR
1920	NY-A	1	1	0	0	0	0	0	0	0	0	.000	.000	.000	-97	-0	-0	0	0	0	0	0	H	0.0
1921	NY-A	4	5	0	1	0	0	0	0	1	0	.200	.333	.200	38	-0	-0	0	0	0	0	0	/O	0.0
Total	2	5	6	0	1	0	0	0	0	1	0	.167	.286	.167	18	-1	-1	0	0	0	0	0	/O	0.0

■ ED CONNOLLY
Connolly, Edward Joseph Sr b: 7/17/08, Brooklyn, N.Y. d: 11/12/63, Pittsfield, Mass. BR/TR, 5'8.5", 180 lbs. Deb: 9/20/29

YEAR	TM/L	G	AB	R	H	2B	3B	HR	RBI	BB	SO	AVG	OBP	SLG	PRO+	BR	/A	RC	SB	CS	SBR	FR	POS	TPR
1929	Bos-A	5	8	0	0	0	0	0	0	0	2	.000	.000	.000	-99	-2	-2	0	0	0	0	-1	/C	-0.2
1930	Bos-A	27	48	1	9	2	0	0	7	4	3	.188	.250	.229	23	-6	-5	3	0	0	0	-1	C	-0.3
1931	Bos-A	42	93	3	7	1	0	0	3	5	18	.075	.131	.086	-44	-19	-19	1	0	0	0	-1	C	-1.4
1932	Bos-A	75	222	9	50	8	4	0	21	20	27	.225	.289	.297	54	-16	-15	20	0	1	-1	3	C	-0.7
Total	4	149	371	13	66	11	4	0	31	29	50	.178	.239	.229	23	-43	-41	24	0	1	-1	1	C	-2.6

■ RED CONNOLLY
Connolly, John M. b: 1863, New York, N.Y. d: 3/2/1896, New York, N.Y. Deb: 7/01/1886

YEAR	TM/L	G	AB	R	H	2B	3B	HR	RBI	BB	SO	AVG	OBP	SLG	PRO+	BR	/A	RC	SB	CS	SBR	FR	POS	TPR
1886	StL-N	2	7	0	0	0	0	0	0	0	3	.000	.000	.000	-99	-2	-2	0	0			-1	/O	-0.1

■ JOE CONNOLLY
Connolly, Joseph Aloysius b: 2/12/1888, N.Smithfield, R.I. d: 9/1/43, Springfield, R.I. BL/TR, 5'7.5", 165 lbs. Deb: 4/10/13

YEAR	TM/L	G	AB	R	H	2B	3B	HR	RBI	BB	SO	AVG	OBP	SLG	PRO+	BR	/A	RC	SB	CS	SBR	FR	POS	TPR
1913	Bos-N	126	427	79	120	18	11	5	57	60	47	.281	.379	.410	123	16	15	72	18			-4	*O	0.8
1914	*Bos-N	120	399	64	122	28	10	9	65	49	36	.306	.393	.494	164	31	31	80	12			-9	*O	2.1
1915	Bos-N	104	305	48	91	14	8	0	23	39	35	.298	.387	.397	144	15	17	48	13	12	-3	-1	O	1.0
1916	Bos-N	62	110	11	25	5	2	0	12	14	13	.227	.320	.309	98	-0	0	13	5			1	O	0.0
Total	4	412	1241	202	358	65	31	14	157	168	131	.288	.380	.425	139	61	63	212	48	12		-13	O	3.9

■ JOE CONNOLLY
Connolly, Joseph George "Coaster Joe" b: 6/4/1896, San Francisco, Cal d: 3/30/60, San Francisco, Cal BR/TR, 6', 170 lbs. Deb: 10/01/21

YEAR	TM/L	G	AB	R	H	2B	3B	HR	RBI	BB	SO	AVG	OBP	SLG	PRO+	BR	/A	RC	SB	CS	SBR	FR	POS	TPR
1921	NY-N	2	4	0	0	0	0	0	0	1	1	.000	.200	.000	-42	-1	-1	0	0	0	0	0	/O	0.0
1922	Cle-A	12	45	6	11	2	1	0	6	5	8	.244	.320	.333	70	-2	-2	5	1	0	0	2	O	0.0
1923	Cle-A	52	109	25	33	10	1	3	25	13	7	.303	.377	.495	129	4	4	20	1	2	-1	-10	O	-0.9
1924	Bos-A	14	10	1	1	0	0	0	1	2	2	.100	.250	.100	-8	-2	-2	0	0	0	0	-1	/O	-0.1
Total	4	80	168	32	45	12	2	3	32	21	18	.268	.349	.417	100	-0	-0	26	2	2	-1	-9	/O	-1.0

■ BUD CONNOLLY
Connolly, Mervin Thomas "Mike" b: 5/25/01, San Francisco, Cal d: 6/12/64, Berkeley, Cal. BR/TR, 5'8", 154 lbs. Deb: 5/03/25

YEAR	TM/L	G	AB	R	H	2B	3B	HR	RBI	BB	SO	AVG	OBP	SLG	PRO+	BR	/A	RC	SB	CS	SBR	FR	POS	TPR
1925	Bos-A	43	107	12	28	7	1	0	21	23	9	.262	.392	.346	88	-1	-1	15	0	3	-2	-11	S/3	-0.7

■ TOM CONNOLLY
Connolly, Thomas Francis "Blackie" or "Ham" b: 12/30/1892, Boston, Mass. d: 5/14/66, Boston, Mass. BL/TR, 5'11", 175 lbs. Deb: 5/12/15

YEAR	TM/L	G	AB	R	H	2B	3B	HR	RBI	BB	SO	AVG	OBP	SLG	PRO+	BR	/A	RC	SB	CS	SBR	FR	POS	TPR
1915	Was-A	50	141	14	26	3	2	0	7	14	19	.184	.268	.234	50	-9	-9	9	5	4	-1	-6	3O/S	-1.6

■ NED CONNOR
Connor, Edward b: 1850, New York 5'9", 156 lbs. Deb: 5/18/1871

YEAR	TM/L	G	AB	R	H	2B	3B	HR	RBI	BB	SO	AVG	OBP	SLG	PRO+	BR	/A	RC	SB	CS	SBR	FR	POS	TPR
1871	Tro-n	7	33	6	7	0	0	0	2	0	0	.212	.212	.212	22	-3	-3	2	0				/1O2	-0.1

■ JIM CONNOR
Connor, James Matthew (b: James Matthew O'Connor) b: 5/11/1863, Port Jervis, N.Y. d: 9/3/50, Providence, R.I. BR/TR, Deb: 7/11/1892

YEAR	TM/L	G	AB	R	H	2B	3B	HR	RBI	BB	SO	AVG	OBP	SLG	PRO+	BR	/A	RC	SB	CS	SBR	FR	POS	TPR
1892	Chi-N	9	34	0	2	0	0	0	0	1	7	.059	.111	.059	-47	-6	-6	0	0			-6	/2	-1.1
1897	Chi-N	77	285	40	83	10	5	3	38	24		.291	.355	.393	96	-0	-2	44	10			22	2	2.2
1898	Chi-N	138	505	51	114	9	9	0	67	42		.226	.289	.279	65	-22	-22	45	11			-4	*2	-1.8
1899	Chi-N	69	234	26	48	7	1	0	24	18		.205	.265	.244	43	-18	-17	17	6			6	23	-0.7
Total	4	293	1058	117	247	26	15	3	129	85	7	.233	.296	.295	66	-46	-47	107	27			19	2/3	-1.4

■ JOE CONNOR
Connor, Joseph Francis b: 12/8/1874, Waterbury, Conn. d: 11/8/57, Waterbury, Conn. BR/TR, 6'2", 185 lbs. Deb: 9/09/1895

YEAR	TM/L	G	AB	R	H	2B	3B	HR	RBI	BB	SO	AVG	OBP	SLG	PRO+	BR	/A	RC	SB	CS	SBR	FR	POS	TPR
1895	StL-N	2	7	0	0	0	0	0	1	0	2	.000	.000	.000	-99	-2	-2	0	0			1	/3	0.0
1900	Bos-N	7	19	2	4	0	0	0	4	2		.211	.286	.211	36	-1	-2	1	1			3	/C	0.2
1901	Mil-A	38	102	10	28	3	1	1	9	6		.275	.321	.353	93	-2	-1	14	4			0	C/23O	0.2
	Cle-A	37	121	13	17	3	1	0	6	7		.140	.206	.182	10	-15	-14	5	2			2	C/OS	-0.8
	Yr	75	223	23	45	6	2	1	15	13		.202	.258	.260	48	-16	-14	18	6			2		-0.6
1905	NY-A	8	22	4	5	1	0	0	2	3		.227	.320	.273	81	-0	-0	3	1			3	/C1	0.3
Total	4	92	271	29	54	7	2	1	22	18	2	.199	.259	.251	45	-20	-19	23	8			8	/CO31S2	-0.1

■ ROGER CONNOR
Connor, Roger b: 7/1/1857, Waterbury, Conn. d: 1/4/31, Waterbury, Conn. BL/TR, 6'3", 220 lbs. Deb: 5/01/1880 MH

YEAR	TM/L	G	AB	R	H	2B	3B	HR	RBI	BB	SO	AVG	OBP	SLG	PRO+	BR	/A	RC	SB	CS	SBR	FR	POS	TPR
1880	Tro-N	83	340	53	113	18	8	3	47	13	21	.332	.357	.459	166	25	23	57				-10	*3	1.2
1881	Tro-N	85	367	55	107	17	6	2	31	15	20	.292	.319	.387	115	9	6	46				2	*1	-0.3
1882	Tro-N	81	349	65	115	22	18	1	42	13	20	.330	.354	.530	188	30	32	67				3	1O3	2.5
1883	NY-N	98	409	80	146	28	15	1	50	25	16	.357	.394	.506	173	35	35	84				3	*1	2.2
1884	NY-N	116	477	98	151	28	4	4	82	38	32	.317	.367	.417	143	26	24	75				1	2O3	2.2
1885	NY-N	110	455	102	169	23	15	1	65	51	8	.371	.435	.495	203	52	53	100				3	*1	3.4
1886	NY-N	118	485	105	172	29	20	7	71	41	15	.355	.405	.540	183	49	48	116	17			10	*1	3.2
1887	NY-N	127	471	113	134	26	22	17	104	75	50	.285	.392	.541	166	38	43	120	43			5	*1	2.2
1888	*NY-N	134	481	98	140	15	17	14	71	73	44	.291	.389	.480	181	45	46	103	27			2	*1/2	3.3
1889	*NY-N	131	496	117	157	32	17	13	130	93	46	.317	.426	.528	168	47	47	124	21			-8	*1/3	2.5
1890	NY-P	123	484	133	169	24	15	14	103	88	32	.349	.450	.548	155	49	41	132	22			11	*1	3.1
1891	NY-N	129	479	112	139	29	13	7	94	83	39	.290	.399	.449	155	32	36	99	27			1	*1	2.9
1892	Phi-N	155	564	123	166	37	11	12	73	116	39	.294	.420	.463	170	52	52	122	22			-6	*1	3.1
1893	NY-N	135	511	111	156	25	8	11	105	91	26	.305	.413	.450	131	26	25	108	24			2	*1/3	2.1
1894	NY-N	22	82	10	24	7	0	1	14	8	0	.293	.356	.415	87	-2	-2	13	2			2	1/O	0.1
	StL-N	99	380	83	122	28	25	7	79	51	17	.321	.410	.582	138	22	22	100	17			5	*1	2.2
	Yr	121	462	93	146	35	25	8	93	59	17	.316	.400	.552	130	21	21	112	19			7		2.3
1895	StL-N	103	398	78	131	29	9	8	77	63	10	.329	.423	.508	144	26	27	92	9			4	*1	2.7
1896	StL-N	126	483	71	137	21	9	11	72	52	14	.284	.356	.433	114	6	9	80	10			13	*1M	2.1
1897	StL-N	22	83	13	19	3	1	1	12	9	3	.229	.333	.325	78	-3	-2	10	3			0	1	0.1
Total	18	1997	7794	1620	2467	441	233	138	1322	1002	449	.317	.397	.486	155	564	564	1647	244			40	*13/2O	40.6

■ JERRY CONNORS
Connors, Jeremiah b: Philadelphia, Pa. Deb: 7/11/1882

YEAR	TM/L	G	AB	R	H	2B	3B	HR	RBI	BB	SO	AVG	OBP	SLG	PRO+	BR	/A	RC	SB	CS	SBR	FR	POS	TPR
1892	Phi-N	1	3	0	0	0	0	0	0	0	1	.000	.000	.000	-99	-1	-1	0	0			-0	/O	0.0

■ JOE CONNORS
Connors, Joseph P. b: Paterson, N.J. Deb: 5/03/1884

YEAR	TM/L	G	AB	R	H	2B	3B	HR	RBI	BB	SO	AVG	OBP	SLG	PRO+	BR	/A	RC	SB	CS	SBR	FR	POS	TPR
1884	Alt-U	3	11	0	1	0	0	0		0		.091	.091	.091	-38	-2	-2	0	0			0	/P3O	0.0
	KC-U	3	11	2	1	0	0	0		1		.091	.167	.091	-12	-1	-1	0	0			1	/OP	0.0
	Yr	6	22	2	2	0	0	0		1		.091	.130	.091	-25	-3	-3	0	0			1		0.0

■ CHUCK CONNORS
Connors, Kevin Joseph Aloysius b: 4/10/21, Brooklyn, N.Y. BL/TL, 6'5", 190 lbs. Deb: 5/01/49

YEAR	TM/L	G	AB	R	H	2B	3B	HR	RBI	BB	SO	AVG	OBP	SLG	PRO+	BR	/A	RC	SB	CS	SBR	FR	POS	TPR
1949	Bro-N	1	1	0	0	0	0	0	0	0	0	.000	.000	.000	-96	-0	-0	0	0			0	H	0.0

YEAR	TM/L	G	AB	R	H	2B	3B	HR	RBI	BB	SO	AVG	OBP	SLG	PRO+	BR	/A	RC	SB	CS	SBR	FR	POS	TPR
1951	Chi-N	66	201	16	48	5	1	2	18	12	25	.239	.282	.303	56	-12	-13	19	4	0	1	-1	1	-1.3
Total	2	67	202	16	48	5	1	2	18	12	25	.238	.280	.302	56	-12	-13	19	4	0		-1	/1	-1.3

■ MERV CONNORS
Connors, Mervyn James   b: 1/23/14, Berkeley, Cal.   BR/TR, 6'2", 192 lbs.   Deb: 9/04/37

YEAR	TM/L	G	AB	R	H	2B	3B	HR	RBI	BB	SO	AVG	OBP	SLG	PRO+	BR	/A	RC	SB	CS	SBR	FR	POS	TPR
1937	Chi-A	28	103	12	24	4	1	2	12	14	19	.233	.325	.350	70	-5	-5	12	2	1	0	-3	3	-0.6
1938	Chi-A	24	62	14	22	4	0	6	13	9	17	.355	.437	.710	178	8	7	19	0	0	0	0	1	0.5
Total	2	52	165	26	46	8	1	8	25	23	36	.279	.367	.485	111	3	3	32	2	1	0	-3	/31	-0.1

■ BEN CONROY
Conroy, Bernard Patrick   b: 3/14/1871, Philadelphia, Pa.   d: 11/25/37, Philadelphia, Pa.   160 lbs.   Deb: 4/21/1890

YEAR	TM/L	G	AB	R	H	2B	3B	HR	RBI	BB	SO	AVG	OBP	SLG	PRO+	BR	/A	RC	SB	CS	SBR	FR	POS	TPR
1890	Phi-a	117	404	45	69	13	1	0		45		.171	.262	.208	42	-29	-27	27	17			-6	S2/O	-2.3

■ WID CONROY
Conroy, William Edward   b: 4/5/1877, Camden, N.J.   d: 12/6/59, Mt.Holly, N.J.   BR/TR, 5'9", 158 lbs.   Deb: 4/25/01   C

YEAR	TM/L	G	AB	R	H	2B	3B	HR	RBI	BB	SO	AVG	OBP	SLG	PRO+	BR	/A	RC	SB	CS	SBR	FR	POS	TPR
1901	Mil-A	131	503	74	129	20	6	5	64	36		.256	.316	.350	91	-9	-5	65	21			20	*S3	1.9
1902	Pit-N	99	365	55	89	10	6	1	47	24		.244	.299	.312	88	-4	-5	39	10			8	S/O	0.7
1903	NY-A	126	503	74	137	23	12	1	45	32		.272	.316	.372	101	4	1	72	33			3	*3/S	0.3
1904	NY-A	140	489	58	119	18	12	1	52	43		.243	.305	.335	100	3	0	62	30			4	*3S/O	0.9
1905	NY-A	101	385	55	105	19	11	2	45	32		.273	.329	.395	118	13	8	60	25			7	30S1/2	1.7
1906	NY-A	148	567	67	139	17	10	4	54	47		.245	.303	.332	91	0	-6	70	32			-1	OS/3	-1.1
1907	NY-A	140	530	58	124	12	11	3	51	30		.234	.275	.315	83	-7	-11	60	41			12	*OS	-0.4
1908	NY-A	141	531	44	126	22	3	1	39	14		.237	.257	.296	80	-12	-13	46	23			13	*32O	0.8
1909	Was-A	139	488	44	119	13	4	1	20	37		.244	.298	.293	91	-7	-5	51	24			0	*32/OS	0.2
1910	Was-A	103	351	36	89	11	3	1	27	30		.254	.314	.311	100	-2	0	38	11			2	30/2	0.2
1911	Was-A	106	349	40	81	11	4	2	28	20		.232	.282	.304	64	-18	-17	33	12			6	30/2	-1.1
Total	11	1374	5061	605	1257	176	82	22	452	345		.248	.299	.329	92	-38	-53	597	262			72	3SO/21	3.9

■ BILL CONROY
Conroy, William Frederick "Pep"   b: 1/9/1899, Chicago, Ill.   d: 1/23/70, Chicago, Ill.   BR/TR, 5'8.5", 160 lbs.   Deb: 4/18/23

YEAR	TM/L	G	AB	R	H	2B	3B	HR	RBI	BB	SO	AVG	OBP	SLG	PRO+	BR	/A	RC	SB	CS	SBR	FR	POS	TPR
1923	Was-A	18	60	6	8	2	2	0	2	4	9	.133	.188	.233	11	-8	-8	3	0	0	0	-2	3/1O	-0.8

■ BILL CONROY
Conroy, William Gordon   b: 2/26/15, Bloomington, Ill.   BR/TR, 6', 185 lbs.   Deb: 9/21/35

YEAR	TM/L	G	AB	R	H	2B	3B	HR	RBI	BB	SO	AVG	OBP	SLG	PRO+	BR	/A	RC	SB	CS	SBR	FR	POS	TPR
1935	Phi-A	1	4	0	1	1	0	0	0	1	0	.250	.400	.500	133	0	0	1	0	0	0	1	/C	0.1
1936	Phi-A	1	2	0	1	0	0	0	0	0	1	.500	.500	.500	151	0	0	0	0	0	0	0	/C	0.1
1937	Phi-A	26	60	4	12	1	1	0	3	7	9	.200	.284	.250	36	-6	-6	5	1	0	0	-1	C/1	-0.4
1942	Bos-A	83	250	22	50	4	2	4	20	40	47	.200	.315	.280	66	-10	-11	26	2	0	1	0	C	0.0
1943	Bos-A	39	89	13	16	5	0	1	6	18	19	.180	.336	.270	77	-2	-2	9	0	0	0	2	C	0.2
1944	Bos-A	19	47	6	10	2	0	0	4	11	9	.213	.362	.255	79	-1	-1	5	0	0	0	-0	C	0.0
Total	6	169	452	45	90	13	3	5	33	77	85	.199	.322	.274	66	-18	-19	46	3	0	1	2	C/1	0.0

■ BILLY CONSOLO
Consolo, William Angelo   b: 8/18/34, Cleveland, Ohio   BR/TR, 5'11", 180 lbs.   Deb: 4/20/53   C

YEAR	TM/L	G	AB	R	H	2B	3B	HR	RBI	BB	SO	AVG	OBP	SLG	PRO+	BR	/A	RC	SB	CS	SBR	FR	POS	TPR
1953	Bos-A	47	65	9	14	2	1	1	6	2	23	.215	.239	.323	48	-5	-5	5	1	2	-1	10	32	0.4
1954	Bos-A	91	242	23	55	7	1	1	11	33	69	.227	.325	.277	59	-10	-14	24	2	1	0	-2	S32	-1.2
1955	Bos-A	8	18	4	4	0	0	0	0	5	4	.222	.391	.222	63	-0	-1	2	0	0	0	-3	/2	-0.2
1956	Bos-A	48	11	13	2	0	0	0	1	3	5	.182	.357	.182	41	-1	-1	1	0	0	0	12	2	1.2
1957	Bos-A	68	196	26	53	6	1	4	19	23	48	.270	.347	.372	91	-1	-2	25	1	3	-2	12	S2/3	1.3
1958	Bos-A	46	72	13	9	2	1	0	5	6	14	.125	.192	.181	3	-10	-10	2	0	0	0	7	2S/3	0.0
1959	Bos-A	10	14	3	3	1	0	0	0	2	5	.214	.313	.286	63	-1	-1	1	0	0	0	-1	/S	-0.1
	Was-A	79	202	25	43	5	3	0	10	36	54	.213	.332	.267	67	-8	-8	21	1	0	0	10	S/2	0.9
	Yr	89	216	28	46	6	3	0	10	38	59	.213	.331	.269	66	-9	-9	22	1	0	0	9		0.8
1960	Was-A	100	174	23	36	4	2	3	15	25	29	.207	.310	.305	68	-8	-8	17	1	1	-0	-1	S2/3	-0.1
1961	Min-A	11	5	1	0	0	0	0	0	0	1	.000	.000	.000	-95	-1	-1	0	0	0	0	0	/2S3	0.0
1962	Phi-N	13	5	3	2	0	0	0	0	0	1	.400	.400	.400	119	0	0	1	0	0	0	0	/3	0.0
	LA-A	28	20	4	2	0	0	0	0	3	11	.100	.217	.100	-12	-3	-3	1	2	0	1	3	3/S2	0.1
	KC-A	54	154	11	37	4	2	0	16	23	33	.240	.339	.292	70	-5	-6	16	1	3	-2	-1	S	-0.5
	Yr	82	174	15	39	4	2	0	16	26	44	.224	.325	.270	62	-9	-9	17	3	3	-1	2		-0.4
Total	10	603	1178	158	260	31	11	9	83	161	297	.221	.316	.289	63	-53	-59	116	9	10	-3	45	S2/3	1.8

■ CHARLIE CONWAY
Conway, Charles Connell   b: 4/28/1886, Youngstown, Ohio   d: 9/12/68, Youngstown, Ohio   BR/TR,   Deb: 4/15/11

YEAR	TM/L	G	AB	R	H	2B	3B	HR	RBI	BB	SO	AVG	OBP	SLG	PRO+	BR	/A	RC	SB	CS	SBR	FR	POS	TPR
1911	Was-A	2	3	0	1	0	1	0	0	0		.333	.333	1.000	272	1	1	1				-1	/O	0.0

■ JACK CONWAY
Conway, Jack Clements   b: 7/30/19, Bryan, Tex.   BR/TR, 5'11.5", 175 lbs.   Deb: 9/09/41

YEAR	TM/L	G	AB	R	H	2B	3B	HR	RBI	BB	SO	AVG	OBP	SLG	PRO+	BR	/A	RC	SB	CS	SBR	FR	POS	TPR
1941	Cle-A	2	2	0	1	0	0	0	1	0	0	.500	.500	.500	174	0	0	1	0	0	0	1	/S	0.1
1946	Cle-A	68	258	24	58	6	2	0	18	20	36	.225	.281	.264	56	-16	-14	20	2	2	-1	-7	2S/3	-1.7
1947	Cle-A	34	50	3	9	2	0	0	5	3	8	.180	.226	.220	25	-5	-5	2	0	0	0	0	S/23	-0.4
1948	NY-N	24	49	8	12	2	1	1	3	5	10	.245	.315	.388	89	-1	-1	6	0			6	2/S3	0.6
Total	4	128	359	35	80	10	3	1	27	28	54	.223	.279	.276	57	-22	-20	28	2	2		0	/2S3	-1.4

■ OWEN CONWAY
Conway, Owen Sylvester   b: 10/23/1890, New York, N.Y.   d: 3/12/42, Philadelphia, Pa.   TR,   Deb: 6/21/15

YEAR	TM/L	G	AB	R	H	2B	3B	HR	RBI	BB	SO	AVG	OBP	SLG	PRO+	BR	/A	RC	SB	CS	SBR	FR	POS	TPR
1915	Phi-A	4	15	2	1	0	0	0	0	0	3	.067	.067	.067	-62	-3	-3	0	0			1	/3	-0.1

■ PETE CONWAY
Conway, Peter J.   b: 10/30/1866, Burmont, Pa.   d: 1/13/03, Clifton Heights, Pa.   BR/TR, 5'10.5",   Deb: 8/10/1885

YEAR	TM/L	G	AB	R	H	2B	3B	HR	RBI	BB	SO	AVG	OBP	SLG	PRO+	BR	/A	RC	SB	CS	SBR	FR	POS	TPR
1885	Buf-N	29	90	7	10	5	0	1	7	5	28	.111	.158	.200	15	-8	-9	3				-1	P/OS1	0.0
1886	KC-N	51	194	22	47	8	2	1	18	5	34	.242	.261	.320	71	-6	-8	17	3			-2	OP	-0.3
	Det-N	12	43	10	8	1	0	2	3	1	8	.186	.205	.349	64	-2	-2	3	0			-0	P/O	0.0
	Yr	63	237	32	55	9	2	3	21	6	42	.232	.251	.325	70	-8	-10	21	3			-2		-0.3
1887	*Det-N	24	95	16	22	5	1	1	7	2	9	.232	.247	.337	60	-5	-5	8	0			2	P/O	0.0
1888	Det-N	45	167	28	46	4	2	3	23	8	25	.275	.320	.377	124	4	4	21	1			2	P/O	0.0
1889	Pit-N	3	10	2	1	0	0	1	2	1	3	.100	.182	.400	68	-1	-0	1	1			0	/PO	0.0
Total	5	164	599	85	134	23	5	9	60	22	107	.224	.255	.324	74	-17	-20	54	5			2	P/O1S	-0.3

■ RIP CONWAY
Conway, Richard Daniel   b: 4/18/1896, White Bear, Minn.   d: 12/3/71, St.Paul, Minn.   5'6", 160 lbs.   Deb: 4/16/18

YEAR	TM/L	G	AB	R	H	2B	3B	HR	RBI	BB	SO	AVG	OBP	SLG	PRO+	BR	/A	RC	SB	CS	SBR	FR	POS	TPR
1918	Bos-N	14	24	4	4	0	0	0	2	2	4	.167	.231	.167	23	-2	-2	1	1			-4	/23	-0.5

■ BILL CONWAY
Conway, William F.   b: 11/28/1861, Lowell, Mass.   d: 12/28/43, Somerville, Mass.   5'8", 170 lbs.   Deb: 7/28/1884

YEAR	TM/L	G	AB	R	H	2B	3B	HR	RBI	BB	SO	AVG	OBP	SLG	PRO+	BR	/A	RC	SB	CS	SBR	FR	POS	TPR
1884	Phi-N	1	4	0	0	0	0	0	0	0	1	.000	.000	.000	-99	-1	-1	0				1	/C	0.0
1886	Bal-a	7	14	4	2	0	0	0		7		.143	.429	.143	87	0	1	1	0			-2	/C	0.0
Total	2	8	18	4	2	0	0	0	0	7	1	.111	.360	.111	54	-0	-0	1	0			-1	/C	0.0

■ ED CONWELL
Conwell, Edward James "Irish"   b: 1/29/1890, Chicago, Ill.   d: 5/1/26, Norwood Park, Ill.   BR/TR, 5'11", 155 lbs.   Deb: 9/22/11

YEAR	TM/L	G	AB	R	H	2B	3B	HR	RBI	BB	SO	AVG	OBP	SLG	PRO+	BR	/A	RC	SB	CS	SBR	FR	POS	TPR
1911	StL-N	1	1	0	0	0	0	0	0	0	1	.000	.000	.000	-99	-0	-0	0	0			-0	/3	0.0

■ HERB CONYERS
Conyers, Herbert Leroy   b: 1/8/21, Cowgill, Mo.   d: 9/16/64, Cleveland, Ohio   BL/TR, 6'5", 210 lbs.   Deb: 4/18/50

YEAR	TM/L	G	AB	R	H	2B	3B	HR	RBI	BB	SO	AVG	OBP	SLG	PRO+	BR	/A	RC	SB	CS	SBR	FR	POS	TPR
1950	Cle-A	7	9	2	3	0	0	1	1	1	2	.333	.400	.667	175	1	1	3	1	0	0	-0	/1	0.1

■ DALE COOGAN
Coogan, Dale Roger   b: 8/14/30, Los Angeles, Cal.   d: 3/8/89, Mission Viejo, Cal.   BL/TL, 6'1", 190 lbs.   Deb: 4/22/50

YEAR	TM/L	G	AB	R	H	2B	3B	HR	RBI	BB	SO	AVG	OBP	SLG	PRO+	BR	/A	RC	SB	CS	SBR	FR	POS	TPR
1950	Pit-N	53	129	19	31	6	1	1	13	17	24	.240	.338	.326	73	-4	-5	15	0			2	1	-0.3

YEAR	TM/L	G	AB	R	H	2B	3B	HR	RBI	BB	SO	AVG	OBP	SLG	PRO+	BR	/A	RC	SB	CS	SBR	FR	POS	TPR

■ DAN COOGAN   Coogan, Daniel George b: 2/16/1875, Philadelphia, Pa. d: 10/28/42, Philadelphia, Pa. 128 lbs. Deb: 4/25/1895

YEAR	TM/L	G	AB	R	H	2B	3B	HR	RBI	BB	SO	AVG	OBP	SLG	PRO+	BR	/A	RC	SB	CS	SBR	FR	POS	TPR
1895	Was-N	26	77	9	17	2	1	0	7	13	6	.221	.333	.273	60	-4	-4	8	1			-11	S/CO3	-1.0

■ JIM COOK   Cook, James Fitchie b: 11/10/1879, Dundee, Ill. d: 6/17/49, St.Louis, Mo. BR/TR, 5'9", 163 lbs. Deb: 7/02/03

YEAR	TM/L	G	AB	R	H	2B	3B	HR	RBI	BB	SO	AVG	OBP	SLG	PRO+	BR	/A	RC	SB	CS	SBR	FR	POS	TPR
1903	Chi-N	8	26	3	4	1	0	0	2	2		.154	.214	.192	18	-3	-3	1	1			-1	/O21	-0.3

■ DOC COOK   Cook, Luther Almus b: 6/24/1886, Witt, Tex. d: 6/30/73, Lawrenceburg, Tenn. BL/TR, 6', 170 lbs. Deb: 8/07/13

YEAR	TM/L	G	AB	R	H	2B	3B	HR	RBI	BB	SO	AVG	OBP	SLG	PRO+	BR	/A	RC	SB	CS	SBR	FR	POS	TPR
1913	NY-A	20	72	9	19	2	1	0		10	4	.264	.369	.319	102	1	1	9	1			1	O	0.0
1914	NY-A	132	470	59	133	11	3	1	40	44	60	.283	.356	.326	105	4	4	53	26	32	-11	-5	*O	-2.1
1915	NY-A	132	476	70	129	16	5	2	33	62	43	.271	.364	.338	111	8	8	63	29	18	-2	1	*O	0.0
1916	NY-A	4	10	0	1	0	0	0	1	0	2	.100	.100	.100	-39	-2	-2	0	0			-1	/O	-0.2
Total	4	288	1028	138	282	29	9	3	75	116	109	.274	.359	.329	106	11	11	125	56	50		-4	O	-2.3

■ PAUL COOK   Cook, Paul b: 5/5/1863, Caledonia, N.Y. d: 5/25/05, Rochester, N.Y. BR/TR, Deb: 9/13/1884

YEAR	TM/L	G	AB	R	H	2B	3B	HR	RBI	BB	SO	AVG	OBP	SLG	PRO+	BR	/A	RC	SB	CS	SBR	FR	POS	TPR
1884	Phi-N	3	12	0	1	0	0	0	0	0	2	.083	.083	.083	-50	-2	-2	0				-1	/C	-0.1
1886	Lou-a	66	262	28	54	5	2	0		10		.206	.235	.240	48	-15	-17	17	6			-7	1C/O	-2.1
1887	Lou-a	61	223	34	55	4	2	0		11		.247	.294	.283	62	-11	-11	24	15			-10	C/1	-0.9
1888	Lou-a	57	185	20	34	2	0	0	13	5		.184	.222	.195	37	-13	-12	10	9			-11	C/OS	-1.5
1889	Lou-a	81	286	34	65	10	1	0	15	15	48	.227	.287	.269	62	-14	-13	26	11			9	C/OS1	0.3
1890	Bro-P	58	218	32	55	3	3	0	31	14	18	.252	.303	.294	58	-12	-14	22	7			-0	C1/O	-1.1
1891	Lou-a	45	153	21	35	3	1	0	23	11	17	.229	.285	.261	59	-8	-8	13	4			-8	C1	-1.2
	StL-a	7	25	3	5	0	0	0	1	1	2	.200	.259	.200	29	-2	-3	1	0			3	/C	0.0
	Yr	52	178	24	40	3	1	0	24	12	19	.225	.281	.253	55	-10	-10	14	4			-5		-1.2
Total	7	378	1364	172	304	27	9	0	83	67	87	.223	.270	.256	54	-76	-80	113	52			-24	C/1OS	-6.6

■ CLIFF COOK   Cook, Raymond Clifford b: 8/20/36, Dallas, Tex. BR/TR, 6', 185 lbs. Deb: 9/09/59

YEAR	TM/L	G	AB	R	H	2B	3B	HR	RBI	BB	SO	AVG	OBP	SLG	PRO+	BR	/A	RC	SB	CS	SBR	FR	POS	TPR
1959	Cin-N	9	21	3	8	2	1	0	5	2	8	.381	.435	.571	161	2	2	6	1	0	0	1	/3	0.3
1960	Cin-N	54	149	9	31	7	0	3	13	8	51	.208	.248	.315	52	-10	-10	12	0	0	0	5	3/O	-0.5
1961	Cin-N	4	5	0	0	0	0	0	0	0	4	.000	.000	.000	-99	-1	-1	0	0	0	0	0	/3	0.0
1962	Cin-N	6	5	0	0	0	0	0	0	0	2	.000	.000	.000	-97	-1	-1	0	0	0	0	-0	/3	-0.1
	NY-N	40	112	12	26	6	1	2	9	4	34	.232	.277	.357	68	-5	-5	12	1	0	0	-8	3O	-1.2
	Yr	46	117	12	26	6	1	2	9	4	36	.222	.266	.342	61	-7	-7	11	1	0	0	-8		-1.3
1963	NY-N	50	106	9	15	2	1	2	8	12	37	.142	.229	.236	34	-9	-9	6	0	1	-1	1	O/31	-1.0
Total	5	163	398	33	80	17	3	7	35	26	136	.201	.255	.312	54	-25	-26	35	2	1	0	-0	/3O1	-2.5

■ DUSTY COOKE   Cooke, Allen Lindsey b: 6/23/07, Swepsonville, N.C. d: 11/21, 87 Raleigh, N.C. BL/TR, 6'1", 205 lbs. Deb: 4/15/30 MC

YEAR	TM/L	G	AB	R	H	2B	3B	HR	RBI	BB	SO	AVG	OBP	SLG	PRO+	BR	/A	RC	SB	CS	SBR	FR	POS	TPR
1930	NY-A	92	216	43	55	12	3	6	29	32	61	.255	.353	.421	100	-1	0	32	4	6	-2	-6	O	-0.9
1931	NY-A	27	39	10	13	1	0	1	6	8	11	.333	.447	.436	141	2	3	9	4	1	1	-1	O	0.1
1932	NY-A	3	0	1	0	0	0	0	0	1	0	—	1.000	—	191	0	0	0	0	0	0	0	H	0.0
1933	Bos-A	119	454	86	133	35	10	5	54	67	71	.293	.386	.447	121	14	15	81	7	5	-1	-10	*O	-0.9
1934	Bos-A	74	168	34	41	8	5	1	26	36	25	.244	.377	.369	87	-1	-3	26	7	2	1	-4	O	-0.4
1935	Bos-A	100	294	51	90	18	6	3	34	46	24	.306	.400	.439	109	9	6	52	6	8	-3	-2	O	0.0
1936	Bos-A	111	341	58	93	20	3	6	47	72	48	.273	.401	.402	93	2	-2	60	4	3	-1	0	O	-0.3
1938	Cin-N	82	233	41	64	15	1	2	33	28	36	.275	.355	.373	103	1	2	33	0			1	O	0.2
Total	8	608	1745	324	489	109	28	24	229	290	276	.280	.384	.416	106	26	21	294	32	25		-20	O	-1.3

■ FRED COOKE   Cooke, Frederick B. b: Paulding, Ohio Deb: 7/30/1897

YEAR	TM/L	G	AB	R	H	2B	3B	HR	RBI	BB	SO	AVG	OBP	SLG	PRO+	BR	/A	RC	SB	CS	SBR	FR	POS	TPR
1897	Cle-N	5	17	2	5	2	0	0	3	3		.294	.400	.412	111	1	0	3	0			1	/O	0.1

■ SCOTT COOLBAUGH   Coolbaugh, Scott Robert b: 6/13/66, Binghamton, N.Y. BR/TR, 5'11", 185 lbs. Deb: 9/02/89

YEAR	TM/L	G	AB	R	H	2B	3B	HR	RBI	BB	SO	AVG	OBP	SLG	PRO+	BR	/A	RC	SB	CS	SBR	FR	POS	TPR
1989	Tex-A	25	51	7	14	1	0	2	7	4	12	.275	.327	.412	105	0	0	6	0	0	0	5	3/D	0.5
1990	Tex-A	67	180	21	36	6	0	2	13	15	47	.200	.265	.267	48	-12	-13	14	1	0	0	7	3	-0.4
Total	2	92	231	28	50	7	0	4	20	19	59	.216	.279	.299	61	-12	-12	20	1	0	0	12	/3D	0.1

■ DUFF COOLEY   Cooley, Duff Gordan "Dick" b: 3/14/1873, Dallas, Tex. d: 8/9/37, Dallas, Tex. BL/TR, Deb: 7/27/1893

YEAR	TM/L	G	AB	R	H	2B	3B	HR	RBI	BB	SO	AVG	OBP	SLG	PRO+	BR	/A	RC	SB	CS	SBR	FR	POS	TPR
1893	StL-N	29	107	20	37	2	3	0	21	8	9	.346	.391	.421	117	3	3	21	8			-8	OC/S	-0.3
1894	StL-N	54	206	35	61	3	1	1	21	12	16	.296	.335	.335	63	-12	-12	26	7			-11	O3/S1	-1.9
1895	StL-N	132	563	106	191	9	20	7	75	36	29	.339	.382	.464	121	15	17	113	27			11	*O/3SC	1.4
1896	StL-N	40	166	29	51	5	3	0	13	7	3	.307	.335	.373	92	-3	-2	25	12			-1	O	-0.4
	Phi-N	64	287	63	88	6	4	2	22	18	16	.307	.348	.376	94	-3	-3	45	18			-4	O	-0.9
	Yr	104	453	92	139	11	7	2	35	25	19	.307	.343	.375	93	-6	-4	70	30			-5		-1.3
1897	Phi-N	133	566	124	186	14	13	4	40	51		.329	.386	.420	118	13	16	106	31			7	*O/1	1.1
1898	Phi-N	149	629	123	196	24	12	4	55	48		.312	.364	.407	129	19	22	102	17			4	*O	1.6
1899	Phi-N	94	406	75	112	15	8	1	31	29		.276	.330	.360	95	-5	-3	55	15			-5	1O/2	-0.6
1900	Pit-N	66	249	30	50	8	1	0	22	14		.201	.243	.241	35	-21	-22	17	9			-5	1	-2.4
1901	Bos-N	63	240	27	62	13	3	0	27	14		.258	.302	.338	80	-4	-7	28	5			2	O1	-0.9
1902	Bos-N	135	548	73	162	26	8	0	58	34		.296	.339	.372	120	13	12	82	27			-6	*O/1	-0.2
1903	Bos-N	138	553	76	160	26	10	1	70	44		.289	.342	.378	111	5	8	83	27			-5	*O1	-0.4
1904	Bos-N	122	467	41	127	18	7	5	70	24		.272	.308	.373	116	5	7	59	14			-7	*O/1	-0.4
1905	Det-A	97	377	25	93	11	9	1	32	26		.247	.295	.332	100	0	-0	42	7			7	O	0.2
Total	13	1316	5364	847	1576	180	102	26	557	365	73	.294	.341	.380	106	24	37	804	224			-20	*O1/3CS2	-4.1

■ CECIL COOMBS   Coombs, Cecil Lysander b: 3/18/1888, Moweaqua, Ill. d: 11/25/75, Fort Worth, Tex. BR/TR, 5'9", 160 lbs. Deb: 8/07/14

YEAR	TM/L	G	AB	R	H	2B	3B	HR	RBI	BB	SO	AVG	OBP	SLG	PRO+	BR	/A	RC	SB	CS	SBR	FR	POS	TPR
1914	Chi-A	7	23	1	4	1	0	0	1	1	7	.174	.208	.217	28	-2	-2	1	0	1	-1	1	/O	-0.2

■ JACK COOMBS   Coombs, John Wesley "Colby Jack" b: 11/18/1882, LeGrand, Iowa d: 4/15/57, Palestine, Tex. BB/TR, 6', 185 lbs. Deb: 7/05/06 MC

YEAR	TM/L	G	AB	R	H	2B	3B	HR	RBI	BB	SO	AVG	OBP	SLG	PRO+	BR	/A	RC	SB	CS	SBR	FR	POS	TPR
1906	Phi-A	24	67	9	16	2	0	0	3	1		.239	.250	.269	62	-3	-3	5	2			0	P	0.0
1907	Phi-A	24	48	4	8	0	0	1	4	0		.167	.167	.229	26	-4	-4	2	1			0	P	0.0
1908	Phi-A	78	220	24	56	9	5	1	23	9		.255	.284	.355	102	1	-0	24	6			6	OP/1	0.8
1909	Phi-A	37	83	4	14	4	0	0	10	4		.169	.216	.217	36	-6	-6	4	1			-6	P	0.0
1910	*Phi-A	46	132	20	29	3	0	0	9	7		.220	.270	.242	61	-6	-6	9	3			-6	P	0.0
1911	*Phi-A	52	141	31	45	6	1	2	23	8		.319	.356	.418	118	2	3	22	5			-3	P	0.0
1912	Phi-A	56	110	10	28	2	0	0	13	14		.255	.344	.273	80	-3	-2	11	1			-1	P	0.0
1913	Phi-A	2	3	1	1	1	0	0	0	0	2	.333	.333	.667	196	0	0	1				-0	/P	0.0
1914	Phi-A	5	11	0	3	1	0	0	2	1	1	.273	.333	.364	113	0	0	1	0	1	-1	-0	/PO	0.0
1915	Bro-N	29	75	8	21	1	1	0	5	2	17	.280	.299	.320	86	-1	-1	7	0	1	-1	-3	P	-0.3
1916	*Bro-N	27	61	2	11	2	0	0	3	2	10	.180	.206	.213	28	-5	-5	3	1			-5	P	0.0
1917	Bro-N	32	44	4	10	0	1	0	2	4	9	.227	.292	.273	72	-1	-1	4	1			-2	P	0.0
1918	Bro-N	46	113	6	19	3	2	0	3	7	5	.168	.223	.230	38	-8	-8	6	1			-4	PO	0.0
1920	Det-A	2	2	0	0	0	0	0	0	0	0	.000	.000	.000	-99	-1	-1	0	0	0	0	0	/P	0.0
Total	14	460	1110	123	261	34	10	4	100	59	44	.235	.277	.295	74	-34	-35	98	21	2		-18	P/O1	0.8

■ WILLIAM COON   Coon, William K. b: 3/21/1855, Pennsylvania d: 8/30/15, Burlington, N.J. Deb: 9/04/1875

YEAR	TM/L	G	AB	R	H	2B	3B	HR	RBI	BB	SO	AVG	OBP	SLG	PRO+	BR	/A	RC	SB	CS	SBR	FR	POS	TPR
1875	Ath-n	3	12	1	2	0	0	0		0		.167	.167	.167	14	-1	-1	0					/C	0.0
1876	Phi-N	54	220	30	50	5	1	0	22	2	4	.227	.234	.259	65	-8	-8	14				-13	OC/32P	-1.7

YEAR	TM/L	G	AB	R	H	2B	3B	HR	RBI	BB	SO	AVG	OBP	SLG	PRO+	BR	/A	RC	SB	CS	SBR	FR	POS	TPR

■ JIMMY COONEY   Cooney, James Edward "Scoops"   b: 8/24/1894, Cranston, R.I.   BR/TR, 5'11", 160 lbs.   Deb: 9/22/17

YEAR	TM/L	G	AB	R	H	2B	3B	HR	RBI	BB	SO	AVG	OBP	SLG	PRO+	BR	/A	RC	SB	CS	SBR	FR	POS	TPR
1917	Bos-A	11	36	4	8	1	0	0	3	6	2	.222	.333	.250	79	-1	-1	4	0			5	2/S	0.5
1919	NY-N	5	14	3	3	0	0	0	1	0	0	.214	.214	.214	29	-1	-1	1	0			-1	/S2	-0.1
1924	StL-N	110	383	44	113	20	8	1	57	20	20	.295	.330	.397	96	-4	-3	48	12	10	-2	1	S/32	0.4
1925	StL-N	54	187	27	51	11	2	0	18	4	5	.273	.292	.353	62	-10	-11	18	1	3	-2	-10	S2/O	-1.8
1926	Chi-N	141	513	52	129	18	5	1	47	23	10	.251	.288	.312	61	-28	-29	45	11			19	*S	0.0
1927	Chi-N	33	132	16	32	2	0	0	6	8	7	.242	.286	.258	46	-10	-10	10	1			-2	S	-0.8
	Phi-N	76	259	33	70	12	1	0	15	13	9	.270	.305	.324	68	-12	-12	25	4			17	S	1.1
	Yr	109	391	49	102	14	1	0	21	21	16	.261	.299	.302	61	-21	-22	35	5			15		0.3
1928	Bos-N	18	51	2	7	0	0	0	3	2	5	.137	.170	.137	-20	-9	-8	1	1			2	S/2	-0.4
Total	7	448	1575	181	413	64	16	2	150	76	58	.262	.298	.327	67	-74	-75	153	30	13		30	S/23O	-1.1

■ JIMMY COONEY   Cooney, James Joseph   b: 7/9/1865, Cranston, R.I.   d: 7/1/03, Cranston, R.I.   BB/TR, 5'9", 155 lbs.   Deb: 4/19/1890

YEAR	TM/L	G	AB	R	H	2B	3B	HR	RBI	BB	SO	AVG	OBP	SLG	PRO+	BR	/A	RC	SB	CS	SBR	FR	POS	TPR
1890	Chi-N	135	574	114	156	19	10	4	52	73	23	.272	.360	.361	108	11	7	93	45			-2	*S/C	0.3
1891	Chi-N	118	465	84	114	15	3	0	42	48	17	.245	.318	.290	80	-11	-10	51	21			8	*S	0.3
1892	Chi-N	65	238	18	41	1	0	0	20	23	5	.172	.248	.176	30	-19	-19	13	10			-8	S	-2.1
	Was-N	6	25	5	4	0	1	0	4	4	3	.160	.276	.240	60	-1	-1	2	1			-3	/S	-0.3
	Yr	71	263	23	45	1	1	0	24	27	8	.171	.251	.183	33	-20	-20	15	11			-11		-2.4
Total	3	324	1302	221	315	35	14	4	118	148	48	.242	.324	.300	84	-20	-24	159	77			-4	S/C	-1.8

■ JOHNNY COONEY   Cooney, John Walter   b: 3/18/01, Cranston, R.I.   d: 7/8/86, Sarasota, Fla.   BR/TL, 5'10", 165 lbs.   Deb: 4/19/21   MC

YEAR	TM/L	G	AB	R	H	2B	3B	HR	RBI	BB	SO	AVG	OBP	SLG	PRO+	BR	/A	RC	SB	CS	SBR	FR	POS	TPR
1921	Bos-N	8	5	0	1	0	0	0	0	0	1	.200	.200	.200	7	-1	-1	0	0	0	0	0	/P	0.0
1922	Bos-N	4	8	0	0	0	0	0	0	0	1	.000	.000	.000	-99	-2	-2	0	0	0	0	0	/P	0.0
1923	Bos-N	42	66	7	25	1	0	0	3	4	2	.379	.414	.394	119	2	2	11	0	1	-1	2	PO/1	0.0
1924	Bos-N	55	130	10	33	2	1	0	4	9	5	.254	.302	.285	61	-7	-7	11	0	4	-2	0	PO/1	0.0
1925	Bos-N	54	103	17	33	7	0	0	13	3	6	.320	.346	.388	96	-2	-1	14	1	0	0	1	P/1O	0.0
1926	Bos-N	64	126	17	38	3	2	0	18	13	7	.302	.367	.357	105	-0	1	17	6			5	1P/O	0.7
1927	Bos-N	10	1	3	0	0	0	0	0	0	0	.000	.000	.000	-99	-0	-0	0	0			0	H	0.0
1928	Bos-N	33	41	2	7	0	0	0	2	4	3	.171	.244	.171	11	-5	-5	2	0			3	P/1O	0.0
1929	Bos-N	41	72	10	23	4	1	0	6	3	3	.319	.355	.403	91	-1	-1	10	1			3	OP	0.3
1930	Bos-N	4	3	0	0	0	0	0	0	0	0	.000	.000	.000	-99	-1	-1	0	0			1	/P	0.0
1935	Bro-N	10	29	3	9	0	1	0	1	3	1	.310	.375	.379	106	0	0	5	0			1	O	0.1
1936	Bro-N	130	507	71	143	17	5	0	30	24	15	.282	.315	.335	74	-18	-18	54	3			3	*O	-2.1
1937	Bro-N	120	430	61	126	18	5	0	37	22	10	.293	.327	.358	85	-8	-9	49	5			2	*O/1	-1.2
1938	Bro-N	120	432	45	117	25	5	0	17	22	12	.271	.308	.352	90	-12	-6	47	2			-7	*O1	-1.6
1939	Bos-N	118	368	39	101	8	1	2	27	21	8	.274	.317	.318	77	-15	-11	37	2			-9	*O/1	-2.2
1940	Bos-N	108	365	40	116	14	3	0	21	25	9	.318	.363	.373	109	2	5	50	4			-3	O/1	-0.1
1941	Bos-N	123	442	52	141	25	2	0	29	27	15	.319	.358	.385	114	5	7	59	3			1	*O/1	0.3
1942	Bos-N	74	198	23	41	6	0	0	7	23	5	.207	.290	.237	56	-11	-10	15	2			-4	O1	-1.8
1943	Bro-N	37	34	7	7	0	0	0	2	4	3	.206	.289	.206	44	-2	-2	2	1			0	/1O	-0.1
1944	Bro-N	7	4	0	3	0	0	0	1	0	0	.750	.750	.750	329	1	1	2	0			1	/O	0.2
	NY-A	10	8	1	1	0	0	0	1	1	0	.125	.222	.125	1	-1	-1	0	0	0	0	1	/O	0.0
Total	20	1172	3372	408	965	130	26	2	219	208	107	.286	.329	.342	87	-77	-60	383	30	5		-3	OP/1	-7.5

■ PHIL COONEY   Cooney, Philip Clarence (b: Philip Clarence Cohen)   b: 9/14/1882, New York, N.Y.   d: 10/6/57, New York, N.Y.   BL/TR, 5'8", 155 lbs.   Deb: 9/27/05

YEAR	TM/L	G	AB	R	H	2B	3B	HR	RBI	BB	SO	AVG	OBP	SLG	PRO+	BR	/A	RC	SB	CS	SBR	FR	POS	TPR
1905	NY-A	1	3	0	0	0	0	0	0	0	0	.000	.000	.000	-90	-1	-1	0	0			-0	/3	0.0

■ BILL COONEY   Cooney, William A. "Cush"   b: 4/4/1887, Boston, Mass.   d: 11/6/28, Roxbury, Mass.   TR ,   Deb: 9/22/09

YEAR	TM/L	G	AB	R	H	2B	3B	HR	RBI	BB	SO	AVG	OBP	SLG	PRO+	BR	/A	RC	SB	CS	SBR	FR	POS	TPR
1909	Bos-N	5	10	0	3	0	0	0	0	0	0	.300	.300	.300	82	-0	-0	1	0			-0	/P2S	0.0
1910	Bos-N	8	12	2	3	0	0	0	1	2	0	.250	.357	.250	74	-0	-0	1	0			0	/O	0.0
Total	2	13	22	2	6	0	0	0	1	2	0	.273	.333	.273	78	-0	-1	2	0			-0	/POS2	0.0

■ CECIL COOPER   Cooper, Cecil Celester   b: 12/20/49, Brenham, Tex.   BL/TL, 6'2", 165 lbs.   Deb: 9/08/71

YEAR	TM/L	G	AB	R	H	2B	3B	HR	RBI	BB	SO	AVG	OBP	SLG	PRO+	BR	/A	RC	SB	CS	SBR	FR	POS	TPR
1971	Bos-A	14	42	9	13	4	1	0	3	5	4	.310	.396	.452	130	2	2	8	1	0	0	-2	1	0.0
1972	Bos-A	12	17	0	4	1	0	0	2	2	5	.235	.316	.294	78	-0	-0	2	0	0	0	-0	/1	0.0
1973	Bos-A	30	101	12	24	2	0	3	11	7	12	.238	.287	.347	73	-3	-4	10	1	2	-1	-1	1	-0.6
1974	Bos-A	121	414	55	114	24	1	8	43	32	74	.275	.329	.396	101	4	0	54	2	5	-2	-1	1D	-0.6
1975	*Bos-A	106	305	49	95	17	6	14	44	19	33	.311	.358	.544	140	19	16	57	1	4	-2	2	D1	1.4
1976	Bos-A	123	451	66	127	22	6	15	78	16	62	.282	.308	.457	109	10	3	64	7	1	2	-1	1D	0.6
1977	Mil-A	160	643	86	193	31	7	20	78	28	110	.300	.329	.463	113	10	10	93	13	8	-1	5	*1D	0.6
1978	Mil-A	107	407	60	127	23	2	13	54	32	72	.312	.362	.474	133	17	17	69	3	4	-2	0	1D	1.4
1979	Mil-A	150	590	83	182	44	1	24	106	56	77	.308	.368	.508	134	27	27	110	15	3	3	-8	*1D	1.4
1980	Mil-A	153	622	96	219	33	4	25	122	39	42	.352	.392	.539	157	43	45	126	17	6	2	4	*1D	4.1
1981	*Mil-A	106	416	70	133	35	1	12	60	28	30	.320	.367	.495	154	24	26	70	5	4	-1	0	*1/D	2.3
1982	*Mil-A	155	654	104	205	38	3	32	121	32	53	.313	.345	.528	145	29	34	118	2	3	-1	-1	*1/D	2.8
1983	Mil-A	160	661	106	203	37	3	30	126	37	63	.307	.345	.508	142	26	32	110	2	1	0	-10	*1D	1.5
1984	Mil-A	148	603	63	166	28	3	11	67	27	59	.275	.309	.386	95	-8	-5	70	8	2	1	3	*1D	-0.8
1985	Mil-A	154	631	82	185	39	8	16	99	30	77	.293	.327	.456	112	9	9	86	10	3	1	-1	*1D	0.1
1986	Mil-A	134	542	46	140	24	1	12	75	41	87	.258	.312	.373	83	-11	-14	60	1	2	-1	-4	1D	-2.3
1987	Mil-A	63	250	25	62	13	0	6	36	17	51	.248	.296	.372	74	-9	-10	27	1	1	-0	0	D	-0.9
Total	17	1896	7349	1012	2192	415	47	241	1125	448	911	.298	.340	.466	121	186	188	1134	89	49	-3	-12	*1D	10.4

■ CLAUDE COOPER   Cooper, Claude William   b: 4/1/1892, Troupe, Tex.   d: 1/21/74, Plainview, Tex.   BL/TL, 5'9", 158 lbs.   Deb: 4/14/13

YEAR	TM/L	G	AB	R	H	2B	3B	HR	RBI	BB	SO	AVG	OBP	SLG	PRO+	BR	/A	RC	SB	CS	SBR	FR	POS	TPR
1913	*NY-N	27	30	11	9	4	0	0	4	4	6	.300	.382	.433	132	1	1	6	3			1	O	0.2
1914	Bro-F	113	399	56	96	14	11	0	25	26	60	.241	.294	.346	83	-10	-9	50	25			-1	*O	-1.5
1915	Bro-F	153	527	75	155	26	12	2	63	77	78	.294	.388	.400	135	25	25	98	31			18	*O1	4.0
1916	Phi-N	56	104	9	20	2	0	0	11	7	15	.192	.250	.212	41	-7	-7	6	1			0	O/1	-0.8
1917	Phi-N	24	29	5	3	1	0	0	1	5	4	.103	.235	.138	15	-3	-3	1	0			-0	O/1	-0.3
Total	5	373	1089	156	283	47	23	4	104	119	163	.260	.338	.356	104	7	7	161	60			18	O/1	1.6

■ GARY COOPER   Cooper, Gary Nathaniel   b: 12/22/56, Savannah, Ga.   BB/TR, 6'3", 175 lbs.   Deb: 8/25/80

YEAR	TM/L	G	AB	R	H	2B	3B	HR	RBI	BB	SO	AVG	OBP	SLG	PRO+	BR	/A	RC	SB	CS	SBR	FR	POS	TPR
1980	Atl-N	21	2	3	0	0	0	0	0	0	1	.000	.000	.000	-97	-1	-1	-1	2	1	0	3	O	0.2

■ PAT COOPER   Cooper, Orge Patterson   b: 11/26/17, Albemarle, N.C.   BR/TR, 6'3", 180 lbs.   Deb: 5/11/46

YEAR	TM/L	G	AB	R	H	2B	3B	HR	RBI	BB	SO	AVG	OBP	SLG	PRO+	BR	/A	RC	SB	CS	SBR	FR	POS	TPR
1946	Phi-A	1	0	0	0	0	0	0	0	0	0	—	—	—		0	0	0	0	0	0	0	/P	0.0
1947	Phi-A	13	16	0	4	2	0	0	3	0	5	.250	.250	.375	71	-1	-1	2	0	0	0	-0	/1	0.0
Total	2	14	16	0	4	2	0	0	3	0	5	.250	.250	.375	71	-1	-1	2	0	0	0	-0	/1P	0.0

■ SCOTT COOPER   Cooper, Scott Kendrick   b: 10/13/67, St.Louis, Mo.   BL/TR, 6'3", 200 lbs.   Deb: 9/05/90

YEAR	TM/L	G	AB	R	H	2B	3B	HR	RBI	BB	SO	AVG	OBP	SLG	PRO+	BR	/A	RC	SB	CS	SBR	FR	POS	TPR
1990	Bos-A	2	1	0	0	0	0	0	0	0	1	.000	.000	.000	-96	-0	-0	0	0	0	0	0	/H	0.0

■ WALKER COOPER   Cooper, William Walker "Walk"   b: 1/8/15, Atherton, Mo.   BR/TR, 6'3", 210 lbs.   Deb: 9/25/40   C

YEAR	TM/L	G	AB	R	H	2B	3B	HR	RBI	BB	SO	AVG	OBP	SLG	PRO+	BR	/A	RC	SB	CS	SBR	FR	POS	TPR
1940	StL-N	6	19	3	6	1	0	0	2	2	2	.316	.381	.368	102	0	0	3	1			-0	/C	0.0
1941	StL-N	68	200	19	49	9	1	1	20	13	14	.245	.291	.315	66	-8	-10	17	1			4	C	0.0
1942	*StL-N	125	438	58	123	32	7	7	65	29	29	.281	.327	.434	113	10	6	57	4			3	*C	1.2

YEAR	TM/L	G	AB	R	H	2B	3B	HR	RBI	BB	SO	AVG	OBP	SLG	PRO+	BR	/A	RC	SB	CS	SBR	FR	POS	TPR
1943	*StL-N	122	449	52	143	30	4	9	81	19	19	.318	.349	.463	128	17	14	69	1			-2	*C	1.8
1944	*StL-N	112	397	56	126	25	5	13	72	20	19	.317	.352	.504	136	18	17	65	4			3	C	2.6
1945	StL-N	4	18	3	7	0	0	0	1	0	1	.389	.389	.389	114	0	0	3	0			1	/C	0.2
1946	NY-N	87	280	29	75	10	1	8	46	17	12	.268	.310	.396	99	-1	-2	32	0			-12	C	-1.2
1947	NY-N	140	515	79	157	24	8	35	122	24	43	.305	.339	.586	141	26	25	97	2			-10	*C	1.8
1948	NY-N	91	290	40	77	12	0	16	54	28	29	.266	.332	.472	115	5	5	42	1			-13	C	-0.2
1949	NY-N	42	147	14	31	4	2	4	21	7	8	.211	.261	.347	62	-8	-8	11	0			-2	C	-0.9
	Cin-N	82	307	34	86	9	2	16	62	21	24	.280	.330	.479	113	5	4	46	0			-2	C	0.5
	Yr	124	454	48	117	13	4	20	83	28	32	.258	.308	.436	97	-4	-4	56	0			-4		-0.4
1950	Cin-N	15	47	3	9	3	0	0	4	0	5	.191	.191	.255	16	-6	-6	2	0			1	C	-0.4
	Bos-N	102	337	52	111	19	3	14	60	30	26	.329	.389	.528	148	18	21	69	1			-5	C	1.8
	Yr	117	384	55	120	22	3	14	64	30	31	.313	.367	.495	132	13	16	69	1			-4		1.4
1951	Bos-N	109	342	42	107	14	1	18	59	28	18	.313	.367	.518	145	16	19	64	1	1	-0	-1	C	1.8
1952	Bos-N	102	349	33	82	12	1	10	55	22	32	.235	.282	.361	80	-12	-10	36	1	0	0	-4	C	-1.2
1953	Mil-N	53	137	12	30	6	0	3	16	12	15	.219	.287	.328	64	-8	-7	12	1	0	0	-5	C	-0.9
1954	Pit-N	14	15	0	3	2	0	0	1	2	1	.200	.294	.333	64	-1	-1	1	0	0	0	0	/C	0.0
	Chi-N	57	158	21	49	10	2	7	32	21	23	.310	.398	.532	138	9	9	32	0	0	0	-2	C	0.8
	Yr	71	173	21	52	12	2	7	33	23	24	.301	.389	.514	132	9	8	33	0	0	0	-2		0.8
1955	Chi-N	54	111	11	31	8	1	7	15	6	19	.279	.322	.559	128	4	4	19	0	0	0	-11	C	-0.5
1956	StL-N	40	68	5	18	5	1	2	14	3	8	.265	.296	.456	98	-0	-0	8	0	0	0	-3	C	-0.2
1957	StL-N	48	78	7	21	5	1	3	10	5	10	.269	.313	.474	106	1	0	9	0	0	0	-2	C	0.0
Total	18	1473	4702	573	1341	240	40	173	812	309	357	.285	.332	.464	116	84	82	695	18	1		-62	*C	7.0

■ JOEY CORA
Cora, Jose Manuel (Amaro) b: 5/14/65, Caguas, P.R. BB/TR, 5'8", 150 lbs. Deb: 4/06/87

YEAR	TM/L	G	AB	R	H	2B	3B	HR	RBI	BB	SO	AVG	OBP	SLG	PRO+	BR	/A	RC	SB	CS	SBR	FR	POS	TPR
1987	SD-N	77	241	23	57	7	2	0	13	28	26	.237	.319	.282	63	-13	-12	22	15	11	-2	-2	2/S	-1.3
1989	SD-N	12	19	5	6	1	0	0	1	1	0	.316	.350	.368	105	0	0	3	1	0	0	2	/S32	0.3
1990	SD-N	51	100	12	27	3	0	0	2	6	9	.270	.311	.300	68	-4	-4	10	8	3	1	-3	S2/C	-0.4
Total	3	140	360	40	90	11	2	0	16	35	35	.250	.318	.292	66	-17	-16	35	24	14	-1	-3	/2S3C	-1.4

■ GENE CORBETT
Corbett, Eugene Louis b: 10/25/13, Winona, Minn. BL/TR, 6'1.5", 190 lbs. Deb: 9/19/36

YEAR	TM/L	G	AB	R	H	2B	3B	HR	RBI	BB	SO	AVG	OBP	SLG	PRO+	BR	/A	RC	SB	CS	SBR	FR	POS	TPR
1936	Phi-N	6	21	1	3	0	0	0	2	2	3	.143	.217	.143	-1	-3	-3	1	0			-0	/1	-0.3
1937	Phi-N	7	12	4	4	2	0	0	1	0	0	.333	.333	.500	114	0	0	2	0			-1	/32	0.0
1938	Phi-N	24	75	7	6	1	0	2	7	6	11	.080	.148	.173	-12	-12	-11	2	0			-1	1	-1.3
Total	3	37	108	12	13	3	0	2	10	8	14	.120	.181	.204	5	-14	-14	5	0			-2	/132	-1.6

■ CLAUDE CORBITT
Corbitt, Claude Elliott b: 7/21/15, Sunbury, N.C. d: 5/1/78, Cincinnati, Ohio BR/TR, 5'10", 170 lbs. Deb: 9/23/45

YEAR	TM/L	G	AB	R	H	2B	3B	HR	RBI	BB	SO	AVG	OBP	SLG	PRO+	BR	/A	RC	SB	CS	SBR	FR	POS	TPR
1945	Bro-N	2	4	1	2	0	0	0	0	1	0	.500	.600	.500	209	1	1	1	0			0	/3	0.1
1946	Cin-N	82	274	25	68	10	1	1	16	23	13	.248	.309	.303	77	-9	-8	27	3			-13	S	-1.6
1948	Cin-N	87	258	24	66	11	0	0	18	14	16	.256	.297	.298	64	-14	-13	24	4			-8	23S	-1.5
1949	Cin-N	44	94	10	17	1	0	0	3	9	1	.181	.252	.191	20	-10	-11	5	1			-5	S2/3	-1.3
Total	4	215	630	60	153	22	1	1	37	47	30	.243	.297	.286	63	-33	-31	57	8			-26	S/23	-4.3

■ ART CORCORAN
Corcoran, Arthur Andrew "Bunny" b: 11/23/1894, Roxbury, Mass. d: 7/27/58, Chelsea, Mass. TR, Deb: 9/09/15

YEAR	TM/L	G	AB	R	H	2B	3B	HR	RBI	BB	SO	AVG	OBP	SLG	PRO+	BR	/A	RC	SB	CS	SBR	FR	POS	TPR
1915	Phi-A	1	4	0	0	0	0	0	0	0	2	.000	.000	.000	-99	-1	-1	0	0			-0	/3	0.0

■ JOHN CORCORAN
Corcoran, John A. b: 1873, Cincinnati, Ohio d: 11/1/01, Cincinnati, Ohio TL, Deb: 9/17/1895

YEAR	TM/L	G	AB	R	H	2B	3B	HR	RBI	BB	SO	AVG	OBP	SLG	PRO+	BR	/A	RC	SB	CS	SBR	FR	POS	TPR
1895	Pit-N	6	20	0	3	0	0	0	1	0	2	.150	.150	.150	-23	-4	-3	0	0			-1	/S3	-0.3

■ JACK CORCORAN
Corcoran, John H. b: 1860, Lowell, Mass. Deb: 5/01/1884

YEAR	TM/L	G	AB	R	H	2B	3B	HR	RBI	BB	SO	AVG	OBP	SLG	PRO+	BR	/A	RC	SB	CS	SBR	FR	POS	TPR
1884	Bro-a	52	185	17	39	4	3	0		8		.211	.251	.265	70	-6	-6	13				-6	C/O2SP	-0.7

■ LARRY CORCORAN
Corcoran, Lawrence J. b: 8/10/1859, Brooklyn, N.Y. d: 10/14/1891, Newark, N.J. BL/TB, 120 lbs. Deb: 5/01/1880

YEAR	TM/L	G	AB	R	H	2B	3B	HR	RBI	BB	SO	AVG	OBP	SLG	PRO+	BR	/A	RC	SB	CS	SBR	FR	POS	TPR
1880	Chi-N	72	286	41	66	11	1	0	25	10	33	.231	.257	.276	76	-5	-8	21				5	*P/OS	0.0
1881	Chi-N	47	189	25	42	8	0	0	9	5	22	.222	.242	.265	57	-9	-10	12				-1	P/SO	0.0
1882	Chi-N	40	169	23	35	10	2	1	24	6	18	.207	.234	.308	69	-5	-6	12				-0	P/3	0.0
1883	Chi-N	68	263	40	55	12	7	0	25	6	62	.209	.227	.308	57	-12	-15	19				-2	PO/S2	0.0
1884	Chi-N	64	251	43	61	3	4	1	19	10	33	.243	.272	.299	73	-6	-9	21				8	P/OS	0.0
1885	Chi-N	7	22	6	6	1	0	0	4	6	1	.273	.429	.318	126	2	1	3	0			0	/PS	0.0
	NY-N	3	14	3	5	0	0	0	2	0	1	.357	.357	.357	133	0	0	2				1	/P	0.0
	Yr	10	36	9	11	1	0	0	6	6	2	.306	.405	.333	128	2	1	5				1		0.0
1886	NY-N	1	4	0	0	0	0	0	0	0	2	.000	.000	.000	-99	-1	-1	0	0			-1	/O	-0.1
	Was-N	21	81	9	15	2	1	0	3	7	14	.185	.250	.235	51	-5	-4	6	3			-3	O/SP	-0.5
	Yr	22	85	9	15	2	1	0	3	7	16	.176	.239	.224	44	-6	-5	5	3			-3		-0.6
1887	Ind-N	3	10	2	2	0	0	0	0	2	1	.200	.333	.200	55	-1	-0	1	2			0	/OP	0.0
Total	8	326	1289	192	287	47	15	2	111	52	187	.223	.253	.287	67	-42	-52	97	5			7	P/OS23	-0.6

■ MICKEY CORCORAN
Corcoran, Michael Joseph b: 8/26/1882, Buffalo, N.Y. d: 12/9/50, Buffalo, N.Y. BR/TR, 5'8", 165 lbs. Deb: 9/15/10

YEAR	TM/L	G	AB	R	H	2B	3B	HR	RBI	BB	SO	AVG	OBP	SLG	PRO+	BR	/A	RC	SB	CS	SBR	FR	POS	TPR
1910	Cin-N	14	46	3	10	3	0	0	7	5	9	.217	.308	.283	76	-2	-1	4	0			-0	2	-0.1

■ TOMMY CORCORAN
Corcoran, Thomas William "Corky" b: 1/4/1869, New Haven, Conn. d: 6/25/60, Plainfield, Conn. BR/TR, 5'9", 164 lbs. Deb: 4/19/1890 U

YEAR	TM/L	G	AB	R	H	2B	3B	HR	RBI	BB	SO	AVG	OBP	SLG	PRO+	BR	/A	RC	SB	CS	SBR	FR	POS	TPR
1890	Pit-P	123	503	80	117	14	13	1	61	38	45	.233	.289	.318	69	-27	-19	60	43			4	*S	-0.5
1891	Phi-a	133	511	84	130	11	15	7	71	29	56	.254	.307	.376	95	-4	-6	70	30			12	*S	1.0
1892	Bro-N	151	613	77	145	11	6	1	74	34	51	.237	.281	.279	74	-22	-18	61	39			-2	*S	-1.1
1893	Bro-N	115	459	61	126	11	10	2	58	27	12	.275	.318	.355	84	-14	-10	58	14			14	*S	0.6
1894	Bro-N	129	576	123	173	21	20	5	92	25	17	.300	.329	.432	90	-11	-10	95	33			-4	*S	-0.4
1895	Bro-N	127	535	81	142	17	10	2	69	23	11	.265	.299	.346	74	-26	-19	62	17			18	*S	0.8
1896	Bro-N	132	532	63	154	15	7	3	73	15	13	.289	.310	.361	83	-18	-13	66	16			24	*S	0.9
1897	Cin-N	109	445	76	128	30	5	3	57	13		.288	.311	.398	83	-9	-14	61	15			5	S2	-0.2
1898	Cin-N	153	619	80	155	28	15	2	87	26		.250	.281	.354	78	-15	-21	68	19			14	*S	0.0
1899	Cin-N	137	537	91	149	11	8	0	81	28		.277	.316	.328	77	-15	-17	67	32			4	*S	-0.3
1900	Cin-N	127	523	64	128	21	9	1	54	22		.245	.277	.325	69	-24	-22	56	27			-4	*S/2	-1.1
1901	Cin-N	31	115	14	24	3	3	0	15	11		.209	.278	.287	70	-5	-4	11	6			4	S	0.2
1902	Cin-N	138	538	54	136	18	4	0	54	11		.253	.269	.301	71	-15	-21	51	20			-13	*S/2	-2.8
1903	Cin-N	115	459	61	113	18	7	2	73	12		.246	.265	.329	63	-19	-26	44	12			6	*S	-1.2
1904	Cin-N	150	578	55	133	17	9	2	74	19		.230	.255	.301	67	-19	-25	62	19			2	*S	-2.3
1905	Cin-N	151	605	70	150	21	11	2	85	23		.248	.275	.329	74	-15	-23	66	28			20	*S	0.0
1906	Cin-N	117	430	29	89	13	1	1	33	19		.207	.241	.249	52	-23	-25	29	8			8	*S	-1.2
1907	NY-N	62	226	21	60	9	2	0	24	7		.265	.288	.323	90	-3	-3	25	9			-5	2	-0.8
Total	18	2200	8804	1184	2252	289	155	34	1135	382	205	.256	.289	.335	76	-289	-295	1003	387			107	*S2	-8.4

■ TIM CORCORAN
Corcoran, Timothy Michael b: 3/19/53, Glendale, Cal. BL/TL, 5'11", 175 lbs. Deb: 5/18/77

YEAR	TM/L	G	AB	R	H	2B	3B	HR	RBI	BB	SO	AVG	OBP	SLG	PRO+	BR	/A	RC	SB	CS	SBR	FR	POS	TPR
1977	Det-A	55	103	13	29	3	0	3	15	6	9	.282	.321	.398	90	-1	-2	12	0	1	-1	4	O/D	0.1
1978	Det-A	116	324	37	86	13	1	1	27	24	27	.265	.326	.321	80	-7	-8	33	3	2	-0	-13	*O/D	-2.4
1979	Det-A	18	22	4	5	1	0	0	6	4	2	.227	.346	.273	67	-1	-1	2	1	1	-0	1	/O1	0.0
1980	Det-A	84	153	20	44	7	1	3	18	22	10	.288	.381	.405	113	4	4	23	0	2	-1	0	1O/D	0.0

YEAR	TM/L	G	AB	R	H	2B	3B	HR	RBI	BB	SO	AVG	OBP	SLG	PRO+	BR	/A	RC	SB	CS	SBR	FR	POS	TPR
1981	Min-A	22	51	4	9	3	0	0	4	6	7	.176	.263	.235	42	-4	-4	3	0	0	0	1	1/D	-0.3
1983	Phi-N	3	0	0	0	0	0	0	0	0	0	—	—	—	—	0	0	0	0	0	0	0	/1	0.0
1984	Phi-N	102	208	30	71	13	1	5	36	37	27	.341	.443	.486	158	19	18	45	0	1	-1	-2	1O	1.4
1985	Phi-N	103	182	11	39	6	1	0	22	29	20	.214	.322	.258	63	-8	-8	16	0	0	0	-1	1/O	-1.1
1986	NY-N	6	7	1	0	0	0	0	0	2	0	.000	.222	.000	-34	-1	-1	0	0	0	0	0	/1	0.0
Total	9	509	1050	120	283	46	4	12	128	130	102	.270	.354	.355	96	2	-2	136	4	7	-3	-10	1O/D	-2.3

■ FRED COREY
Corey, Frederick Harrison b: 1857, S.Kingston, R.I. d: 11/27/12, Providence, R.I. BR/TR, Deb: 5/01/1878

YEAR	TM/L	G	AB	R	H	2B	3B	HR	RBI	BB	SO	AVG	OBP	SLG	PRO+	BR	/A	RC	SB	CS	SBR	FR	POS	TPR
1878	Pro-N	7	21	3	3	0	0	0	1	0	2	.143	.143	.143	-6	-2	-2	0				0	/P21	0.0
1880	Wor-N	41	138	11	24	8	1	0	6	4	27	.174	.197	.246	45	-7	-9	7				-11	OP/S31	0.0
1881	Wor-N	51	203	22	45	8	4	0	10	5	10	.222	.240	.300	65	-7	-9	15				1	OP/S	-0.3
1882	Wor-N	64	255	33	63	7	12	0	29	5	31	.247	.262	.369	97	-0	-1	25				-8	SPO/31	-0.5
1883	Phi-a	71	298	45	77	16	2	1		12		.258	.287	.336	92	-0	-4	29				-2	3PO/2SC	-0.1
1884	Phi-a	104	439	64	121	17	16	5		17		.276	.306	.421	129	17	13	58				13	*3	2.4
1885	Phi-a	94	384	61	94	14	8	1		17		.245	.282	.331	90	-2	-5	37				8	*3/SP	0.7
Total	7	432	1738	239	427	70	43	7	46	60	70	.246	.273	.348	94	-2	-18	172				0	3/POS21C	2.2

■ MARK COREY
Corey, Mark Mundell b: 11/3/55, Tucumcari, N.Mex. BR/TR, 6'2", 200 lbs. Deb: 9/01/79

YEAR	TM/L	G	AB	R	H	2B	3B	HR	RBI	BB	SO	AVG	OBP	SLG	PRO+	BR	/A	RC	SB	CS	SBR	FR	POS	TPR
1979	Bal-A	13	13	1	2	0	0	0	0	0	4	.154	.154	.154	-17	-2	-2	0	1	0	0	1	O	0.0
1980	Bal-A	36	36	7	10	2	0	1	2	5	7	.278	.366	.417	115	1	1	6	0	1	-1	-1	O	0.0
1981	Bal-A	10	8	2	0	0	0	0	0	2	2	.000	.200	.000	-38	-1	-1	0	0	0	0	1	/O	0.0
Total	3	59	57	10	12	2	0	1	3	7	13	.211	.297	.298	65	-3	-3	6	1	1	-0	1	/O	0.0

■ CHUCK CORGAN
Corgan, Charles Howard b: 12/4/02, Wagoner, Okla. d: 6/13/28, Wagoner, Okla. BB/TR, 5'11", 180 lbs. Deb: 9/19/25

YEAR	TM/L	G	AB	R	H	2B	3B	HR	RBI	BB	SO	AVG	OBP	SLG	PRO+	BR	/A	RC	SB	CS	SBR	FR	POS	TPR
1925	Bro-N	14	47	4	8	1	1	0	0	3	9	.170	.220	.234	16	-6	-6	3	0	0	0	4	S	0.0
1927	Bro-N	19	57	3	15	1	0	0	1	4	4	.263	.311	.281	59	-3	-3	5	0			-1	2/S	-0.3
Total	2	33	104	7	23	2	1	0	1	7	13	.221	.270	.260	40	-9	-9	8	0	0		3	/S2	-0.3

■ ROY CORHAN
Corhan, Roy George "Irish" b: 10/21/1887, Indianapolis, Ind. d: 11/24/58, San Francisco, Cal BR/TR, 5'9.5", 165 lbs. Deb: 4/20/11

YEAR	TM/L	G	AB	R	H	2B	3B	HR	RBI	BB	SO	AVG	OBP	SLG	PRO+	BR	/A	RC	SB	CS	SBR	FR	POS	TPR
1911	Chi-A	43	131	14	28	6	2	0	8	15		.214	.304	.290	68	-6	-5	12	2			11	S	0.9
1916	StL-N	92	295	30	62	6	3	0	18	20	31	.210	.265	.251	59	-14	-14	24	15			1	S	-0.8
Total	2	135	426	44	90	12	5	0	26	35	31	.211	.277	.263	62	-20	-19	36	17			12	S	0.1

■ POP CORKHILL
Corkhill, John Stewart b: 4/11/1858, Parkesburg, Pa. d: 4/4/21, Pennsauken, N.J. BL/TR, 5'10", 180 lbs. Deb: 5/01/1883

YEAR	TM/L	G	AB	R	H	2B	3B	HR	RBI	BB	SO	AVG	OBP	SLG	PRO+	BR	/A	RC	SB	CS	SBR	FR	POS	TPR
1883	Cin-a	88	375	53	81	10	8	2		3		.216	.222	.301	63	-14	-17	26				1	*O/S21	-1.3
1884	Cin-a	110	452	85	124	13	11	4		6		.274	.290	.378	114	8	5	51				10	*OS/13P	1.2
1885	Cin-a	112	440	64	111	10	8	1		7		.252	.275	.318	88	-5	-7	40				17	*O/P1	0.5
1886	Cin-a	129	540	81	143	9	7	5		23		.265	.302	.335	99	-0	-2	64	24			-0	*O3/1SP	-0.4
1887	Cin-a	128	541	79	168	19	11	5		14		.311	.333	.414	108	5	3	87	30			15	*O/P	1.2
1888	Cin-a	118	490	68	133	11	9	1	74	15		.271	.299	.337	102	3	-1	59	27			7	*O/P12	0.1
	Bro-a	19	71	17	27	4	3	1	19	4		.380	.429	.563	222	9	9	19	3			2	O	0.9
	Yr	137	561	85	160	15	12	2	93	19		.285	.316	.365	116	12	9	76	30			8		1.0
1889	*Bro-a	138	537	91	134	21	9	8	78	42	24	.250	.308	.367	93	-6	-6	69	22			12	*O/S1	0.1
1890	Bro-N	51	204	23	46	4	2	1	21	15	11	.225	.279	.279	64	-9	-9	18	6			6	O/1	-0.3
1891	Phi-a	83	349	50	73	7	7	0	31	26	15	.209	.268	.269	54	-20	-22	29	12			7	O	-1.5
	Cin-N	1	4	0	0	0	0	0	0	0	1	.000	.000	.000	-99	-1	-1	0	1				/O	0.0
	Pit-N	41	145	16	33	1	1	3	20	7	10	.228	.268	.310	72	-6	-5	14	7			2	O	-0.4
	Yr	42	149	16	33	1	1	3	20	7	11	.221	.261	.302	67	-7	-6	14	7			3		-0.4
1892	Pit-N	68	256	23	47	1	4	1	25	12	19	.184	.229	.219	37	-19	-20	15	6			7	O	-1.3
Total	10	1086	4404	650	1120	110	80	31	268	174	80	.254	.288	.337	89	-55	-72	489	137			86	*O/1PS32	-1.2

■ PAT CORRALES
Corrales, Patrick b: 3/20/41, Los Angeles, Cal. BR/TR, 6', 180 lbs. Deb: 8/02/64 MC

YEAR	TM/L	G	AB	R	H	2B	3B	HR	RBI	BB	SO	AVG	OBP	SLG	PRO+	BR	/A	RC	SB	CS	SBR	FR	POS	TPR
1964	Phi-N	2	1	1	0	0	0	0	0	1	0	.000	.500	.000	55	0	0	0	0	0	0	0	H	0.0
1965	Phi-N	63	174	16	39	8	1	2	15	25	42	.224	.325	.316	83	-4	-3	19	0	0	0	-4	C	-0.4
1966	StL-N	28	72	5	13	2	0	0	3	2	17	.181	.224	.208	21	-8	-8	3	1	0	0	9	C	0.3
1968	Cin-N	20	56	3	15	4	0	0	6	6	16	.268	.349	.339	101	1	0	7	0	0	0	-0	C	0.1
1969	Cin-N	29	72	10	19	5	0	1	5	8	17	.264	.346	.375	97	-0	0	9	0	1	-1	3	C	0.5
1970	*Cin-N	43	106	9	25	5	1	1	10	8	22	.236	.289	.330	65	-5	-5	9	0	0	0	4	C	0.1
1971	Cin-N	40	94	6	17	2	0	0	6	6	17	.181	.230	.202	24	-9	-9	5	0	0	0	2	C	-0.7
1972	Cin-N	2	1	0	0	0	0	0	0	2	0	.000	.667	.000	110	0	0	0	0	0	0	1	/C	0.2
	SD-N	44	119	6	23	0	0	0	6	11	26	.193	.267	.193	35	-10	-9	7	0	0	0	3	C	-0.3
	Yr	46	120	6	23	0	0	0	6	13	26	.192	.276	.192	38	-10	-9	7	0			5		-0.1
1973	SD-N	29	72	7	15	2	1	0	3	6	10	.208	.278	.264	55	-5	-4	6	0	0	0	-0	C	-0.2
Total	9	300	767	63	166	28	3	4	54	75	167	.216	.292	.276	61	-39	-38	64	1	1	-0	19	C	-0.4

■ VIC CORRELL
Correll, Victor Crosby b: 2/5/46, Washington, D.C. BR/TR, 5'10", 185 lbs. Deb: 10/04/72

YEAR	TM/L	G	AB	R	H	2B	3B	HR	RBI	BB	SO	AVG	OBP	SLG	PRO+	BR	/A	RC	SB	CS	SBR	FR	POS	TPR
1972	Bos-A	1	4	1	2	0	0	0	1	0	1	.500	.500	.500	188	0	0	1	0	0	0	1	/C	0.1
1974	Atl-N	73	202	20	48	15	1	4	29	21	38	.238	.322	.381	92	-1	-2	25	0	0	0	7	C	0.8
1975	Atl-N	103	325	37	70	12	1	11	39	42	66	.215	.307	.360	82	-7	-9	34	0	2	-1	-1	C	-0.7
1976	Atl-N	69	200	26	45	6	2	5	16	21	37	.225	.302	.350	80	-4	-6	20	0	1	-1	4	C	0.1
1977	Atl-N	54	144	16	30	7	0	7	16	22	33	.208	.317	.403	82	-2	-4	18	2	3	-1	4	C	-0.1
1978	Cin-N	52	105	9	25	7	0	1	6	8	17	.238	.292	.333	74	-4	-4	8	0	2	-1	2	C	-0.1
1979	Cin-N	48	133	14	31	12	0	1	15	14	26	.233	.311	.346	78	-4	-4	14	0	0	0	7	C	0.4
1980	Cin-N	10	19	1	8	1	0	0	3	0	2	.421	.421	.474	149	1	1	4	0	0	0	0	C	0.1
Total	8	410	1132	124	259	60	4	29	125	128	220	.229	.312	.366	83	-20	-27	125	2	8	-4	24	C	0.6

■ PHIL CORRIDAN
Corridan, Philip Deb: 7/16/1884

YEAR	TM/L	G	AB	R	H	2B	3B	HR	RBI	BB	SO	AVG	OBP	SLG	PRO+	BR	/A	RC	SB	CS	SBR	FR	POS	TPR
1884	CP-U	2	7	1	1	0	0	0		0		.143	.143	.143	-3	-1	-1	0	0			-1	/2O	-0.1

■ JOHN CORRIDEN
Corriden, John Michael Jr. b: 10/6/18, Logansport, Ind. BB/TR, 5'6", 160 lbs. Deb: 4/20/46

YEAR	TM/L	G	AB	R	H	2B	3B	HR	RBI	BB	SO	AVG	OBP	SLG	PRO+	BR	/A	RC	SB	CS	SBR	FR	POS	TPR
1946	Bro-N	1	0	1	0	0	0	0	0	0	0	—	—	—	—	0	0	0	0			0	R	0.0

■ RED CORRIDEN
Corriden, John Michael Sr. b: 9/4/1887, Logansport, Ind. d: 9/28/59, Indianapolis, Ind BR/TR, 5'9", 165 lbs. Deb: 9/08/10 MC

YEAR	TM/L	G	AB	R	H	2B	3B	HR	RBI	BB	SO	AVG	OBP	SLG	PRO+	BR	/A	RC	SB	CS	SBR	FR	POS	TPR
1910	StL-A	26	84	19	13	3	0	1	4	13		.155	.297	.226	68	-3	-2	8	5			4	S3	0.3
1912	Det-A	38	138	22	28	6	0	0	5	15		.203	.286	.246	54	-8	-8	11	4			-4	3/2S	-1.1
1913	Chi-N	46	97	13	17	3	0	2	9	10	14	.175	.252	.268	48	-7	-7	7	4			-1	S/23	-0.5
1914	Chi-N	107	318	42	73	9	5	3	29	35	33	.230	.323	.318	91	-3	-3	37	13			-33	S/32	-3.4
1915	Chi-N	6	3	1	0	0	0	0	0	2	1	.000	.571	.000	79	1	1	0	0			-0	/3O	0.0
Total	5	223	640	97	131	21	5	6	47	75	48	.205	.304	.281	74	-20	-19	63	26			-34	S/32O	-4.7

■ JESS CORTAZZO
Cortazzo, John Francis b: 9/26/04, Wilmerding, Pa. d: 3/4/63, Pittsburgh, Pa. BR/TR, 5'3.5", 142 lbs. Deb: 9/01/23

YEAR	TM/L	G	AB	R	H	2B	3B	HR	RBI	BB	SO	AVG	OBP	SLG	PRO+	BR	/A	RC	SB	CS	SBR	FR	POS	TPR
1923	Chi-A	1	1	0	0	0	0	0	0	0	0	.000	.000	.000	-99	-0	-0	0	0	0	0	0	H	0.0

■ JOE COSCARART
Coscarart, Joseph Marvin b: 11/18/09, Escondido, Cal. BR/TR, 6', 185 lbs. Deb: 4/26/35

YEAR	TM/L	G	AB	R	H	2B	3B	HR	RBI	BB	SO	AVG	OBP	SLG	PRO+	BR	/A	RC	SB	CS	SBR	FR	POS	TPR
1935	Bos-N	86	284	30	67	11	2	1	29	16	28	.236	.277	.299	59	-18	-15	23	2			-4	3S2	-1.4
1936	Bos-N	104	367	28	90	11	2	2	44	19	37	.245	.292	.302	64	-20	-17	31	0			2	3/S2	-0.7

YEAR	TM/L	G	AB	R	H	2B	3B	HR	RBI	BB	SO	AVG	OBP	SLG	PRO+	BR	/A	RC	SB	CS	SBR	FR	POS	TPR
Total	2	190	651	58	157	22	4	3	73	35	65	.241	.285	.301	62	-38	-32	55	2			-3	3/S2	-2.1

■ PETE COSCARART
Coscarart, Peter Joseph b: 6/16/13, Escondido, Cal. BR/TR, 5'11.5", 175 lbs. Deb: 4/26/38

YEAR	TM/L	G	AB	R	H	2B	3B	HR	RBI	BB	SO	AVG	OBP	SLG	PRO+	BR	/A	RC	SB	CS	SBR	FR	POS	TPR
1938	Bro-N	32	79	10	12	3	0	0	6	9	18	.152	.256	.190	24	-8	-8	5	0			1	2	-0.4
1939	Bro-N	115	419	59	116	22	2	4	43	46	56	.277	.354	.368	91	-2	-4	58	10			-8	*2/3S	-0.7
1940	Bro-N	143	506	55	120	24	4	9	58	53	59	.237	.311	.354	78	-12	-16	56	5			-31	*2	-3.8
1941	*Bro-N	43	62	13	8	1	0	0	5	7	12	.129	.217	.145	3	-8	-8	2	1			5	2/S	-0.1
1942	Pit-N	133	487	57	111	12	4	3	29	38	56	.228	.288	.287	67	-19	-21	42	2			-18	*S2	-3.1
1943	Pit-N	133	491	57	119	19	6	0	48	46	48	.242	.307	.305	75	-14	-16	47	4			-4	2S/3	-1.3
1944	Pit-N	139	554	89	146	30	4	4	42	41	57	.264	.315	.354	85	-9	-12	62	10			-7	*2/SO	-0.4
1945	Pit-N	123	392	59	95	17	2	8	38	55	55	.242	.341	.357	91	-2	-8	50	2			21	*2/S	2.7
1946	Pit-N	3	2	0	1	1	0	0	0	0	0	.500	.500	1.000	312	1	1	1	0			0	/S	0.1
Total	9	864	2992	399	728	129	22	28	269	295	361	.243	.314	.329	78	-75	-89	322	34			-40	2S/3O	-7.0

■ RAY COSEY
Cosey, Donald Ray b: 2/15/56, San Raphael, Cal. BL/TL, 5'10", 185 lbs. Deb: 4/14/80

YEAR	TM/L	G	AB	R	H	2B	3B	HR	RBI	BB	SO	AVG	OBP	SLG	PRO+	BR	/A	RC	SB	CS	SBR	FR	POS	TPR
1980	Oak-A	9	9	0	1	0	0	0	0	0	0	.111	.111	.111	-42	-2	-2	0	0	0	0	0	/H	-0.1

■ DAN COSTELLO
Costello, Daniel Francis "Dashing Dan" b: 9/9/1891, Jessup, Pa. d: 3/26/36, Pittsburgh, Pa. BL/TR, 6'0.5", 185 lbs. Deb: 7/02/13

YEAR	TM/L	G	AB	R	H	2B	3B	HR	RBI	BB	SO	AVG	OBP	SLG	PRO+	BR	/A	RC	SB	CS	SBR	FR	POS	TPR
1913	NY-A	2	2	1	1	0	0	0	0	0	0	.500	.500	.500	192	0	0	0	0			0	H	0.0
1914	Pit-N	21	64	7	19	1	0	0	5	8	16	.297	.375	.313	110	1	1	8	2			-1	O	0.0
1915	Pit-N	71	125	16	27	4	1	0	11	7	23	.216	.258	.264	59	-6	-6	10	7	1	2	-5	O/1	-1.0
1916	Pit-N	60	159	11	38	1	3	0	8	6	23	.239	.267	.283	68	-6	-6	13	3			-2	O	-1.0
Total	4	154	350	35	85	6	4	0	24	21	62	.243	.286	.283	73	-11	-11	32	12	1		-7	/O1	-2.0

■ HENRY COTE
Cote, Henry Joseph b: 2/19/1864, Troy, N.Y. d: 4/28/40, Troy, N.Y. Deb: 9/16/1894

YEAR	TM/L	G	AB	R	H	2B	3B	HR	RBI	BB	SO	AVG	OBP	SLG	PRO+	BR	/A	RC	SB	CS	SBR	FR	POS	TPR
1894	Lou-N	10	31	7	9	2	2	0	3	5	6	.290	.389	.484	119	1	1	7	2			5	C	0.5
1895	Lou-N	10	33	10	10	0	0	0	5	3	3	.303	.361	.303	79	-1	-1	4	2			-3	C	-0.1
Total	2	20	64	17	19	2	2	0	8	8	9	.297	.375	.391	99	-1	0	11	4			2	/C	0.4

■ PETE COTE
Cote, Warren Peter b: 8/30/02, Cambridge, Mass. d: 10/17/87, Middleton, Mass. BR/TR, 5'6", 148 lbs. Deb: 6/18/26

YEAR	TM/L	G	AB	R	H	2B	3B	HR	RBI	BB	SO	AVG	OBP	SLG	PRO+	BR	/A	RC	SB	CS	SBR	FR	POS	TPR
1926	NY-N	2	1	0	0	0	0	0	0	0	0	.000	.000	.000	-99	-0	-0	0	0			0	H	0.0

■ ED COTTER
Cotter, Edward Chrsitopher b: 7/4/04, Hartford, Conn. d: 6/14/59, Hartford, Conn. BR/TR, 6', 185 lbs. Deb: 6/12/26

YEAR	TM/L	G	AB	R	H	2B	3B	HR	RBI	BB	SO	AVG	OBP	SLG	PRO+	BR	/A	RC	SB	CS	SBR	FR	POS	TPR
1926	Phi-N	17	26	3	8	0	1	0	1	1	4	.308	.333	.385	88	-0	-0	3	1			0	/3S	0.0

■ HOOKS COTTER
Cotter, Harvey Louis b: 5/22/1900, Holden, Mo. d: 8/6/55, Los Angeles, Cal. BL/TL, 5'10", 160 lbs. Deb: 4/15/22

YEAR	TM/L	G	AB	R	H	2B	3B	HR	RBI	BB	SO	AVG	OBP	SLG	PRO+	BR	/A	RC	SB	CS	SBR	FR	POS	TPR
1922	Chi-N	1	1	0	1	1	0	0	0	0	0	1.000	1.000	2.000	644	1	1	2	0	0	0	0	H	0.1
1924	Chi-N	98	310	39	81	16	4	4	33	36	31	.261	.338	.377	91	-3	-4	40	3	5	-2	4	1	-0.5
Total	2	99	311	39	82	17	4	4	33	36	31	.264	.340	.383	92	-3	-3	42	3	5	-2	4	/1	-0.4

■ DICK COTTER
Cotter, Richard Raphael b: 10/12/1889, Manchester, N.H. d: 4/4/45, Brooklyn, N.Y. TR, 5'11", 172 lbs. Deb: 8/17/11

YEAR	TM/L	G	AB	R	H	2B	3B	HR	RBI	BB	SO	AVG	OBP	SLG	PRO+	BR	/A	RC	SB	CS	SBR	FR	POS	TPR
1911	Phi-N	20	46	2	13	0	0	0	5	5	7	.283	.353	.283	78	-1	-1	5	1			-1	C	0.0
1912	Chi-N	26	54	6	15	0	2	0	10	6	13	.278	.361	.352	96	-0	-0	7	1			-3	C	-0.1
Total	2	46	100	8	28	0	2	0	15	11	20	.280	.357	.320	87	-1	-1	12	2			-4	/C	-0.1

■ TOM COTTER
Cotter, Thomas B. b: 9/30/1866, Waltham, Mass. d: 11/22/06, Brookline, Mass. BR/TR, 5'10.5", 149 lbs. Deb: 9/03/1891

YEAR	TM/L	G	AB	R	H	2B	3B	HR	RBI	BB	SO	AVG	OBP	SLG	PRO+	BR	/A	RC	SB	CS	SBR	FR	POS	TPR
1891	Bos-a	6	12	1	3	0	0	0	4	1	2	.250	.308	.250	63	-1	-1	1	0			-1	/CO	0.0

■ CHUCK COTTIER
Cottier, Charles Keith b: 1/8/36, Delta, Colo. BR/TR, 5'10.5", 175 lbs. Deb: 4/17/59 MC

YEAR	TM/L	G	AB	R	H	2B	3B	HR	RBI	BB	SO	AVG	OBP	SLG	PRO+	BR	/A	RC	SB	CS	SBR	FR	POS	TPR
1959	Mil-N	10	24	1	3	1	0	0	1	3	7	.125	.222	.167	6	-3	-3	1	0	0	0	1	2	-0.1
1960	Mil-N	95	229	29	52	8	0	3	19	14	21	.227	.278	.301	63	-13	-11	20	1	0	0	17	2	1.4
1961	Det-A	10	7	2	2	0	0	0	1	1	1	.286	.375	.286	77	-0	-0	1	0	0	0	2	/S2	0.2
	Was-A	101	337	37	79	14	4	2	34	30	51	.234	.299	.318	66	-17	-16	34	9	1	2	15	*2	1.3
	Yr	111	344	39	81	14	4	2	35	31	52	.235	.301	.317	66	-17	-16	35	9	1	2	17		1.5
1962	Was-A	136	443	50	107	14	6	6	40	44	57	.242	.313	.341	76	-15	-14	49	14	8	-1	21	*2	1.5
1963	Was-A	113	337	30	69	16	4	5	21	24	63	.205	.258	.320	61	-18	-18	28	2	1	0	11	2S/3	0.0
1964	Was-A	73	137	16	23	6	2	3	10	19	33	.168	.269	.307	60	-7	-7	12	2	0	1	14	2/3S	1.3
1965	Was-A	7	1	1	0	0	0	0	0	0	0	.000	.000	.000	-99	-0	-0	0	0	0	0	0	H	0.0
1968	Cal-A	33	67	2	13	4	1	0	1	2	15	.194	.217	.284	53	-4	-4	4	0	0	0	2	3/2	-0.1
1969	Cal-A	2	2	0	0	0	0	0	0	0	0	.000	.000	.000	-99	-1	-1	0	0	0	0	-0	/2	0.0
Total	9	580	1584	168	348	63	17	19	127	137	248	.220	.284	.317	65	-79	-75	150	28	10	2	81	2/S3	5.5

■ HENRY COTTO
Cotto, Henry b: 1/5/61, New York, N.Y. BR/TR, 6'2", 178 lbs. Deb: 4/05/84

YEAR	TM/L	G	AB	R	H	2B	3B	HR	RBI	BB	SO	AVG	OBP	SLG	PRO+	BR	/A	RC	SB	CS	SBR	FR	POS	TPR
1984	*Chi-N	105	146	24	40	5	0	0	8	10	23	.274	.325	.308	72	-4	-5	16	9	3	1	10	O	0.2
1985	NY-A	34	56	4	17	1	0	1	6	3	12	.304	.339	.375	98	-0	-0	7	1	1	-0	2	O	0.1
1986	NY-A	35	80	11	17	3	0	1	6	2	17	.213	.232	.287	41	-7	-7	5	3	0	1	4	O/D	-0.2
1987	NY-A	68	149	21	35	10	0	5	20	6	35	.235	.269	.403	76	-6	-6	14	4	2	0	2	O	-0.3
1988	Sea-A	133	386	50	100	18	1	8	33	23	53	.259	.304	.373	85	-6	-9	46	27	3	6	-10	*O/D	-1.3
1989	Sea-A	100	295	44	78	11	2	9	33	12	44	.264	.300	.407	94	-2	-3	35	10	4	1	2	O/D	-0.1
1990	Sea-A	127	355	40	92	14	3	4	33	22	52	.259	.310	.349	83	-8	-8	38	21	3	5	-8	*O/D	-1.3
Total	7	602	1467	194	379	62	6	28	139	78	236	.258	.301	.366	82	-33	-38	160	75	16	13	2	O/D	-2.9

■ DENNIS COUGHLIN
Coughlin, Dennis F. Deb: 4/27/1872

YEAR	TM/L	G	AB	R	H	2B	3B	HR	RBI	BB	SO	AVG	OBP	SLG	PRO+	BR	/A	RC	SB	CS	SBR	FR	POS	TPR
1872	Nat-n	8	38	5	12	0	0	0		0	0	.316	.316	.316	81	-0	-2	4					/OS2	0.0

■ ED COUGHLIN
Coughlin, Edward E. b: 8/5/1861, Hartford, Conn. d: 12/25/52, Hartford, Conn. Deb: 5/15/1884

YEAR	TM/L	G	AB	R	H	2B	3B	HR	RBI	BB	SO	AVG	OBP	SLG	PRO+	BR	/A	RC	SB	CS	SBR	FR	POS	TPR
1884	Buf-N	1	4	0	1	0	0	0	1	0	2	.250	.250	.250	56	-0	-0	0				0	/OP	0.0

■ BILL COUGHLIN
Coughlin, William Paul "Scranton Bill" b: 7/12/1878, Scranton, Pa. d: 5/7/43, Scranton, Pa. BR/TR, 5'9", 140 lbs. Deb: 8/09/1899

YEAR	TM/L	G	AB	R	H	2B	3B	HR	RBI	BB	SO	AVG	OBP	SLG	PRO+	BR	/A	RC	SB	CS	SBR	FR	POS	TPR
1899	Was-N	6	24	2	3	0	1	0	3	1		.125	.160	.208	2	-3	-3	1	1			-1	/3	-0.3
1901	Was-A	137	506	75	139	17	13	6	68	25		.275	.315	.395	100	-2	-1	71	16			0	*3	-0.3
1902	Was-A	123	469	84	141	27	4	6	71	26		.301	.348	.414	111	7	7	80	29			12	3S2	1.9
1903	Was-A	125	473	56	116	18	3	1	31	9		.245	.259	.302	68	-18	-19	46	30			4	*3/S2	-1.6
1904	Was-A	65	265	28	73	15	4	0	17	9		.275	.299	.362	112	3	3	33	10			2	3	0.9
	Det-A	56	206	22	47	6	0	0	17	5		.228	.246	.257	63	-9	-8	14	1			-3	3	-1.0
	Yr	121	471	50	120	21	4	0	34	14		.255	.276	.316	91	-6	-5	47	11			-1		-0.1
1905	Det-A	137	489	48	123	20	6	0	44	34		.252	.300	.317	97	-1	-2	55	16			-9	*3	-0.6
1906	Det-A	147	498	54	117	15	5	2	60	36		.235	.287	.297	82	-9	-10	56	31			-10	*3	-1.0
1907	*Det-A	134	519	80	126	10	2	0	46	35		.243	.291	.270	78	-11	-13	49	15			-10	*3	-1.5
1908	*Det-A	119	405	32	87	5	1	0	23	23		.215	.257	.232	59	-17	-18	27	10			-15	*3	-2.9
Total	9	1049	3854	481	972	133	39	15	380	203		.252	.292	.319	86	-59	-64	433	159			-31	3/S2	-6.4

■ MARLAN COUGHTRY
Coughtry, James Marlan b: 9/11/34, Hollywood, Cal. BL/TR, 6'1", 170 lbs. Deb: 9/02/60

YEAR	TM/L	G	AB	R	H	2B	3B	HR	RBI	BB	SO	AVG	OBP	SLG	PRO+	BR	/A	RC	SB	CS	SBR	FR	POS	TPR
1960	Bos-A	15	19	3	3	0	0	0	0	6	8	.158	.333	.158	36	-1	-2	1	0	0	0	1	2/3	0.1
1962	LA-A	11	22	0	4	0	0	0	2	0	6	.182	.182	.182	-2	-3	-3	1	0	0	0	3	/32	0.0
	KC-A	6	11	1	2	0	0	0	1	4	3	.182	.400	.182	61	-0	-0	1	0	0	0	1	/3	0.1

YEAR	TM/L	G	AB	R	H	2B	3B	HR	RBI	BB	SO	AVG	OBP	SLG	PRO+	BR	/A	RC	SB	CS	SBR	FR	POS	TPR
	Cle-A	3	2	1	1	0	0	0	1	1	1	.500	.667	.500	226	1	1	1	0	0	0	0	H	0.1
	Yr	20	35	2	7	0	0	0	4	5	10	.200	.300	.200	38	-3	-3	3	0	0	0	4		0.2
Total 2		35	54	5	10	0	0	0	4	10	18	.185	.313	.185	37	-4	-4	4	0	0	0	6	/23	0.3

■ BOB COULSON
Coulson, Robert Jackson b: 6/17/1887, Courtney, Pa. d: 9/11/53, Washington, Pa. BR/TR, 5'10.5", 175 lbs. Deb: 8/04/08

YEAR	TM/L	G	AB	R	H	2B	3B	HR	RBI	BB	SO	AVG	OBP	SLG	PRO+	BR	/A	RC	SB	CS	SBR	FR	POS	TPR
1908	Cin-N	8	18	3	6	1	1	0	1	1	3	.333	.429	.500	205	2	2	4	0			1	/O	0.4
1910	Bro-N	25	89	14	22	3	4	1	13	6	14	.247	.302	.404	109	0	0	13	9			-0	O	0.0
1911	Bro-N	146	521	52	122	23	7	0	50	42	78	.234	.301	.305	73	-21	-18	57	32			-3	*O	-2.5
1914	Pit-F	18	64	7	13	1	0	0	3	7	10	.203	.282	.219	45	-4	-4	5	2			-2	O	-0.7
Total 4		197	692	76	163	28	12	1	67	58	102	.236	.303	.315	78	-24	-20	79	43			-4	O	-2.8

■ CHIP COULTER
Coulter, Thomas Lee b: 6/5/45, Steubenville, O. BB/TR, 5'10", 172 lbs. Deb: 9/18/69

YEAR	TM/L	G	AB	R	H	2B	3B	HR	RBI	BB	SO	AVG	OBP	SLG	PRO+	BR	/A	RC	SB	CS	SBR	FR	POS	TPR
1969	StL-N	6	19	3	6	1	1	0	4	2	6	.316	.381	.474	138	1	1	3	0	1	-1	0	/2	0.1

■ CLINT COURTNEY
Courtney, Clinton Dawson "Scrap Iron" b: 3/16/27, Hall Summit, La. d: 6/16/75, Rochester, N.Y. BL/TR, 5'8", 180 lbs. Deb: 9/29/51 C

YEAR	TM/L	G	AB	R	H	2B	3B	HR	RBI	BB	SO	AVG	OBP	SLG	PRO+	BR	/A	RC	SB	CS	SBR	FR	POS	TPR
1951	NY-A	1	2	0	0	0	0	0	0	1	1	.000	.333	.000	-5	-0	-0	0	0	0	0	0	C	0.0
1952	StL-A	119	413	38	118	24	3	5	50	39	26	.286	.349	.395	104	3	2	58	0	2	-1	4	*C	1.1
1953	StL-A	106	355	28	89	12	2	4	19	25	20	.251	.302	.330	69	-15	-16	33	0	1	-1	-5	*C	-1.7
1954	Bal-A	122	397	25	107	18	3	4	37	30	7	.270	.326	.360	95	-7	-4	46	2	1	0	-2	*C	0.0
1955	Chi-A	19	37	7	14	3	0	1	10	7	0	.378	.477	.541	168	4	4	9	0	0	0	-1	C	0.4
	Was-A	75	238	26	71	8	4	2	30	19	9	.298	.353	.391	105	-0	1	33	0	0	0	-14	C	-0.9
	Yr	94	275	33	85	11	4	3	40	26	9	.309	.371	.411	114	4	5	42	0	0	0	-14		-0.5
1956	Was-A	101	283	31	85	20	3	5	44	20	10	.300	.365	.445	113	5	5	43	0	5	-3	-15	C	-1.1
1957	Was-A	91	232	23	62	14	1	6	27	16	11	.267	.346	.414	108	2	3	33	0	0	0	-0	C	0.5
1958	Was-A	134	450	46	113	18	0	8	62	48	23	.251	.335	.344	89	-7	-6	52	1	5	-3	-4	*C	-1.1
1959	Was-A	72	189	19	44	4	1	2	18	20	19	.233	.310	.296	68	-8	-8	18	0	1	-1	-13	C	-1.8
1960	Bal-A	83	154	14	35	3	0	1	12	30	14	.227	.380	.266	79	-3	-2	18	0	1	-1	4	C	0.4
1961	KC-A	1	1	0	0	0	0	0	0	0	0	.000	.000	.000	-99	-0	-0	0	0	0	0	0	H	0.0
	Bal-A	22	45	3	12	2	0	0	4	10	3	.267	.400	.311	95	0	0	6	0	0	0	2	C	0.2
	Yr	23	46	3	12	2	0	0	4	10	3	.261	.393	.304	91	-0	-0	6	0	0	0	2		0.2
Total 11		946	2796	260	750	126	17	38	313	265	143	.268	.341	.366	94	-26	-21	349	3	16	-9	-44	C	-4.0

■ ERNIE COURTNEY
Courtney, Edward Ernest b: 1/20/1875, Des Moines, Iowa d: 2/29/20, Buffalo, N.Y. BL/TR, 5'10", Deb: 4/17/02

YEAR	TM/L	G	AB	R	H	2B	3B	HR	RBI	BB	SO	AVG	OBP	SLG	PRO+	BR	/A	RC	SB	CS	SBR	FR	POS	TPR
1902	Bos-N	48	165	23	36	3	0	0	17	13		.218	.295	.236	65	-6	-6	13	3			-0	O/S	-0.9
	Bal-A	1	4	3	2	0	1	0	1	1		.500	.600	1.000	327	1	1	2	0			0	/3	0.1
1903	NY-A	25	79	7	21	3	3	1	8	7		.266	.326	.418	116	2	2	12	1			-2	S/21	0.1
	Det-A	23	74	7	17	0	0	0	6	5		.230	.278	.230	57	-4	-3	5	1			-4	3/S	-0.6
	Yr	48	153	14	38	3	3	1	14	12		.248	.303	.327	89	-2	-2	17	2			-5		-0.5
1905	Phi-N	155	601	77	165	14	7	2	77	47		.275	.327	.331	102	-1	2	76	17			-17	*3	-0.4
1906	Phi-N	116	398	53	94	12	2	0	42	45		.236	.314	.276	86	-5	-5	38	6			-11	31/OS	-2.2
1907	Phi-N	130	440	42	107	17	4	2	43	55		.243	.327	.314	105	3	4	49	6			-8	31/O2S	-0.5
1908	Phi-N	60	160	14	29	3	0	0	8	15		.181	.251	.200	45	-9	-10	9	1			-7	31/2S	-1.8
Total 6		558	1921	226	471	52	17	5	200	188		.245	.314	.298	91	-18	-15	204	35			-48	3/1OS2	-6.2

■ DEE COUSINEAU
Cousineau, Edward Thomas b: 12/16/1898, Watertown, Mass. d: 7/14/51, Watertown, Mass. BR/TR, 6', 170 lbs. Deb: 10/06/23

YEAR	TM/L	G	AB	R	H	2B	3B	HR	RBI	BB	SO	AVG	OBP	SLG	PRO+	BR	/A	RC	SB	CS	SBR	FR	POS	TPR
1923	Bos-N	1	2	1	2	0	0	0	2	0	0	1.000	1.000	1.000	447	1	1	2	0	0	0	0	/C	0.1
1924	Bos-N	3	2	0	0	0	0	0	0	0	0	.000	.000	.000	-99	-1	-1	0	0	0	0	-1	/C	0.0
1925	Bos-N	1	0	0	0	0	0	0	0	0	0	—	—	—		0	0	0	0	0	0	0	/C	0.0
Total 3		5	4	1	2	0	0	0	2	0	0	.500	.500	.500	174	0	0	2	0	0	0	-1	/C	0.1

■ JACK COVENEY
Coveney, John Patrick b: 6/10/1880, S.Natick, Mass. d: 3/28/61, Waverly, Mass. TR, 5'9", 175 lbs. Deb: 9/19/03

YEAR	TM/L	G	AB	R	H	2B	3B	HR	RBI	BB	SO	AVG	OBP	SLG	PRO+	BR	/A	RC	SB	CS	SBR	FR	POS	TPR
1903	StL-N	4	14	0	2	0	0	0	0	0	0	.143	.143	.143	-18	-2	-2	0	0			1	/C	0.0

■ SAM COVINGTON
Covington, Clarence Otto b: 12/17/1892, Henryville, Tenn. d: 1/4/63, Denison, Tex. BL/TR, 6'1", 190 lbs. Deb: 8/25/13

YEAR	TM/L	G	AB	R	H	2B	3B	HR	RBI	BB	SO	AVG	OBP	SLG	PRO+	BR	/A	RC	SB	CS	SBR	FR	POS	TPR
1913	StL-A	20	60	3	9	0	1	0	4	4	6	.150	.203	.183	14	-7	-6	3	3			3	1	-0.2
1917	Bos-N	17	66	8	13	2	0	1	10	5	5	.197	.264	.273	69	-3	-2	7	1			0	1	-0.2
1918	Bos-N	3	3	0	1	0	0	0	0	0	0	.333	.333	.333	108	0	0	0	0			0	H	0.0
Total 3		40	129	11	23	2	1	1	14	9	11	.178	.237	.233	43	-9	-9	8	4			3	/1	-0.4

■ WES COVINGTON
Covington, John Wesley b: 3/27/32, Laurinburg, N.C. BL/TR, 6'1", 205 lbs. Deb: 4/19/56

YEAR	TM/L	G	AB	R	H	2B	3B	HR	RBI	BB	SO	AVG	OBP	SLG	PRO+	BR	/A	RC	SB	CS	SBR	FR	POS	TPR
1956	Mil-N	75	138	17	39	4	0	2	16	16	20	.283	.361	.355	100	-1	0	19	1	0	0	-4	O	-0.4
1957	*Mil-N	96	328	51	93	4	8	21	65	29	44	.284	.345	.537	143	14	17	61	4	1	1	-2	O	1.3
1958	*Mil-N	90	294	43	97	12	1	24	74	20	35	.330	.382	.622	175	24	27	68	0	0	0	-10	O	1.5
1959	Mil-N	103	373	58	104	17	3	7	45	26	41	.279	.331	.397	101	-4	-0	46	0	1	-1	-5	O	-0.7
1960	Mil-N	95	281	25	70	16	1	10	35	15	37	.249	.290	.420	99	-4	-2	31	1	2	-1	-9	O	-1.3
1961	Mil-N	9	21	3	4	1	0	0	0	2	4	.190	.261	.238	36	-2	-2	1	0	0	0	-2	/O	-0.3
	Chi-A	22	59	5	17	1	0	4	15	4	5	.288	.333	.508	123	2	2	9	0	0	0	-2	O	0.0
	KC-A	17	44	3	7	0	0	1	6	4	7	.159	.260	.227	31	-4	-4	3	0	0	0	-2	O	-0.6
	Yr	39	103	8	24	1	0	5	21	8	12	.233	.301	.388	83	-3	-3	11	0	0	0	-4		-0.6
	Phi-N	57	165	23	50	9	0	7	26	15	17	.303	.361	.485	124	5	5	28	0	0	0	-5	O	-0.2
1962	Phi-N	116	304	36	86	12	1	9	44	19	44	.283	.329	.418	102	-1	-0	40	0	0	0	-10	O	-1.4
1963	Phi-N	119	353	46	107	24	1	17	64	26	56	.303	.354	.521	150	21	21	63	1	0	0	-11	*O	0.6
1964	Phi-N	129	339	37	95	18	0	13	58	38	50	.280	.358	.448	127	12	12	55	0	0	0	-12	*O	-0.2
1965	Phi-N	101	235	27	58	10	1	15	45	26	47	.247	.324	.489	128	7	8	37	0	0	0	-3	O	0.3
1966	Chi-N	9	11	0	1	0	0	0	0	1	2	.091	.167	.091	-26	-2	-2	0	0	0	0	0	O	-0.1
	*LA-N	37	33	1	4	0	1	1	6	6	5	.121	.293	.273	63	-2	-1	3	0	0	0	-0	/O	-0.1
	Yr	46	44	1	5	0	1	1	6	7	7	.114	.264	.227	41	-4	-3	3	0	0	0	-0		-0.2
Total 11		1075	2978	355	832	128	17	131	499	247	414	.279	.339	.466	123	65	83	463	7	4	-0	-77	O	-1.6

■ BILLY COWAN
Cowan, Billy Rolland b: 8/28/38, Calhoun City, Miss. BR/TR, 6', 170 lbs. Deb: 9/09/63

YEAR	TM/L	G	AB	R	H	2B	3B	HR	RBI	BB	SO	AVG	OBP	SLG	PRO+	BR	/A	RC	SB	CS	SBR	FR	POS	TPR
1963	Chi-N	14	36	1	9	1	1	1	2	0	11	.250	.250	.417	84	-1	-1	3	0	1	-1	-1	O	-0.2
1964	Chi-N	139	497	52	120	16	4	19	50	18	128	.241	.269	.404	83	-10	-12	53	12	3	2	-8	*O	-2.3
1965	NY-N	82	156	16	28	8	2	3	9	4	45	.179	.205	.314	45	-12	-11	9	3	2	-0	3	O/2S	-1.0
	Mil-N	19	27	4	5	1	0	0	0	0	9	.185	.185	.222	14	-3	-3	1	0	0	0	0	O	-0.3
	Yr	101	183	20	33	9	2	3	9	4	54	.180	.202	.301	41	-15	-14	11	3	2	-0	3		-1.3
1967	Phi-N	34	59	11	9	0	0	3	6	4	14	.153	.206	.305	44	-4	-4	4	1	0	0	-2	O/23	-0.7
1969	NY-A	32	48	5	8	0	0	1	3	3	9	.167	.216	.229	25	-5	-5	2	1	0	0	0	O	-0.4
	Cal-A	28	56	10	17	1	0	4	10	3	9	.304	.350	.536	152	3	3	10	0	0	0	1	O/1	0.4
	Yr	60	104	15	25	1	0	5	13	6	18	.240	.288	.394	93	-2	-1	11	0	0	0	1		0.0
1970	Cal-A	68	134	20	37	9	1	5	25	11	29	.276	.336	.470	124	3	4	21	0	1	-1	-4	O1/3	-0.2
1971	Cal-A	74	174	12	48	8	0	4	20	7	41	.276	.304	.391	103	-2	-0	20	1	1	-0	-2	O/1	-0.3
1972	Cal-A	3	3	0	0	0	0	0	0	0	2	.000	.000	.000	-99	-1	-0	0	0	0	0	0	H	0.0
Total 8		493	1190	131	281	44	8	40	125	50	297	.236	.269	.387	83	-31	-31	124	17	8	0	-12	O/132S	-5.0

AL COWENS

Cowens, Alfred Edward b: 10/25/51, Los Angeles, Cal. BR/TR, 6'1", 197 lbs. Deb: 4/06/74

YEAR	TM/L	G	AB	R	H	2B	3B	HR	RBI	BB	SO	AVG	OBP	SLG	PRO+	BR	/A	RC	SB	CS	SBR	FR	POS	TPR
1974	KC-A	110	269	28	65	7	1	1	25	23	38	.242	.304	.286	67	-10	-12	23	5	0	2	5	*O/3D	-0.7
1975	KC-A	120	328	44	91	13	8	4	42	28	36	.277	.342	.402	107	4	3	44	12	7	-1	-6	*O/D	-0.6
1976	*KC-A	152	581	71	154	23	6	3	59	26	50	.265	.300	.341	87	-10	-11	57	23	16	-3	4	*O/D	-1.2
1977	*KC-A	162	606	98	189	32	14	23	112	41	64	.312	.363	.525	138	31	30	109	16	12	-2	2	*O/D	2.4
1978	*KC-A	132	485	63	133	24	8	5	63	31	54	.274	.326	.388	97	-1	-2	62	14	6	1	4	*O/3D	0.0
1979	KC-A	136	516	69	152	18	7	9	73	40	44	.295	.349	.409	102	3	1	71	10	8	-2	-3	*O	-0.8
1980	Cal-A	34	119	11	27	5	0	1	17	12	21	.227	.303	.294	66	-6	-5	11	1	2	-1	-0	O/D	-0.6
	Det-A	108	403	58	113	15	3	5	42	37	40	.280	.342	.370	93	-2	-3	51	5	6	-2	-5	*O/D	-1.2
	Yr	142	522	69	140	20	3	6	59	49	61	.268	.333	.352	87	-8	-9	61	6	8	-3	-5		-1.8
1981	Det-A	85	253	27	66	11	4	1	18	22	36	.261	.322	.348	90	-2	-3	29	3	3	-1	-11	O	-1.7
1982	Sea-A	146	560	72	151	39	8	20	78	46	81	.270	.326	.475	114	11	9	84	11	7	-1	2	*O/D	0.5
1983	Sea-A	110	356	39	73	19	2	7	35	23	38	.205	.257	.329	58	-20	-22	28	10	2	2	1	OD	-1.9
1984	Sea-A	139	524	60	145	34	2	15	78	27	83	.277	.315	.435	106	2	3	66	9	5	-0	-5	*O/D	-0.6
1985	Sea-A	122	452	59	120	32	5	14	69	30	56	.265	.313	.451	105	3	2	56	0	0	0	-2	*O/D	-0.1
1986	Sea-A	28	82	5	15	4	0	0	6	3	18	.183	.212	.232	20	-9	-9	4	1	0	0	-1	O/D	-1.0
Total	13	1584	5534	704	1494	276	68	108	717	389	659	.270	.322	.403	98	-6	-18	694	120	74	-8	-17	*O/D3	-7.5

DICK COX

Cox, Elmer Joseph b: 9/30/1897, Pasadena, Cal. d: 6/1/66, Morro Bay, Cal. BR/TR, 5'7.5", 158 lbs. Deb: 4/16/25

YEAR	TM/L	G	AB	R	H	2B	3B	HR	RBI	BB	SO	AVG	OBP	SLG	PRO+	BR	/A	RC	SB	CS	SBR	FR	POS	TPR
1925	Bro-N	122	434	68	143	23	10	7	64	37	29	.329	.382	.477	121	12	13	79	4	3	-1	-7	*O	0.3
1926	Bro-N	124	398	53	118	17	4	1	45	46	20	.296	.375	.367	102	2	3	56	6			-9	*O	-1.0
Total	2	246	832	121	261	40	14	8	109	83	49	.314	.379	.424	112	14	16	135	10	3		-16	O	-0.7

FRANK COX

Cox, Francis Bernhard "Runt" b: 8/29/1857, Waltham, Mass. d: 6/24/28, Hartford, Conn. 5'6", Deb: 8/13/1884

YEAR	TM/L	G	AB	R	H	2B	3B	HR	RBI	BB	SO	AVG	OBP	SLG	PRO+	BR	/A	RC	SB	CS	SBR	FR	POS	TPR
1884	Det-N	27	102	6	13	3	1	0	4	2	36	.127	.144	.176	0	-11	-10	3				-4	S	-1.0

JIM COX

Cox, James Charles b: 5/28/50, Bloomington, Ill. BR/TR, 5'11", 175 lbs. Deb: 7/19/73

YEAR	TM/L	G	AB	R	H	2B	3B	HR	RBI	BB	SO	AVG	OBP	SLG	PRO+	BR	/A	RC	SB	CS	SBR	FR	POS	TPR
1973	Mon-N	9	15	1	2	1	0	0	0	1	4	.133	.188	.200	7	-2	-2	1	0	0	0	-0	/2	-0.1
1974	Mon-N	77	236	29	52	9	1	2	26	23	36	.220	.292	.292	61	-11	-13	20	2	3	-1	15	2	0.4
1975	Mon-N	11	27	1	7	1	0	1	5	1	2	.259	.286	.407	87	-0	-1	2	1	0	0	0	/2	0.0
1976	Mon-N	13	29	2	5	0	1	0	2	2	2	.172	.226	.241	31	-3	-3	1	0	0	0	1	2	0.0
Total	4	110	307	33	66	11	2	3	33	27	44	.215	.281	.293	58	-16	-18	24	3	3	-1	16	/2	0.3

JEFF COX

Cox, Jeffrey Lindon b: 11/9/55, Los Angeles, Cal. BR/TR, 5'11", 170 lbs. Deb: 7/01/80

YEAR	TM/L	G	AB	R	H	2B	3B	HR	RBI	BB	SO	AVG	OBP	SLG	PRO+	BR	/A	RC	SB	CS	SBR	FR	POS	TPR
1980	Oak-A	59	169	20	36	3	0	0	9	14	23	.213	.273	.231	43	-14	-12	12	8	5	-1	-18	2	-2.7
1981	Oak-A	2	0	0	0	0	0	0	0	0	0	—	—	—	—	0	0	0	0	0	0	1	/2	0.1
Total	2	61	169	20	36	3	0	0	9	14	23	.213	.273	.231	43	-14	-12	12	8	5	-1	-17	/2	-2.6

LARRY COX

Cox, Larry Eugene b: 9/11/47, Bluffton, Ohio d: 2/17/90, Bellefontaine, Ohio BR/TR, 5'10", 178 lbs. Deb: 4/18/73 C

YEAR	TM/L	G	AB	R	H	2B	3B	HR	RBI	BB	SO	AVG	OBP	SLG	PRO+	BR	/A	RC	SB	CS	SBR	FR	POS	TPR
1973	Phi-N	1	0	0	0	0	0	0	0	0	0	—	—	—	—	0	0	0	0	0	0	0	/C	0.0
1974	Phi-N	30	53	5	9	2	0	0	4	4	9	.170	.241	.208	25	-5	-5	3	0	0	0	0	C	-0.3
1975	Phi-N	11	5	0	1	0	0	0	1	1	0	.200	.333	.200	49	-0	-0	0	1	0	0	0	C	0.0
1977	Sea-A	35	93	6	23	6	0	2	6	10	12	.247	.320	.376	90	-1	-1	11	1	1	-0	0	C	0.0
1978	Chi-N	59	121	10	34	5	0	2	18	12	16	.281	.346	.372	90	0	-1	15	0	0	0	2	C	0.2
1979	Sea-A	100	293	32	63	11	3	4	36	22	39	.215	.270	.314	56	-18	-19	24	2	1	0	-3	C	-1.6
1980	Sea-A	105	243	18	49	6	2	4	20	19	36	.202	.260	.292	50	-17	-17	17	1	2	-1	11	*C	-0.1
1981	Tex-A	5	13	0	3	1	0	0	0	0	4	.231	.231	.308	57	-1	-1	1	0	0	0	4	/C	0.3
1982	Chi-N	2	4	1	0	0	0	0	0	2	1	.000	.333	.000	1	-0	-0	0	0	0	0	1	/C	0.0
Total	9	348	825	72	182	31	5	12	85	70	117	.221	.282	.314	61	-42	-45	71	5	4	-1	14	C	-1.5

BOBBY COX

Cox, Robert Joseph b: 5/21/41, Tulsa, Okla. BR/TR, 5'11", 180 lbs. Deb: 4/14/68 MC

YEAR	TM/L	G	AB	R	H	2B	3B	HR	RBI	BB	SO	AVG	OBP	SLG	PRO+	BR	/A	RC	SB	CS	SBR	FR	POS	TPR
1968	NY-A	135	437	33	100	15	1	7	41	41	85	.229	.302	.316	90	-6	-5	42	3	2	-0	-5	*3	-0.6
1969	NY-A	85	191	17	41	7	1	2	17	34	41	.215	.336	.293	80	-5	-4	19	0	1	-1	11	3/2	0.8
Total	2	220	628	50	141	22	2	9	58	75	126	.225	.313	.309	87	-11	-9	61	3	3	-1	6	3/2	0.2

BILLY COX

Cox, William Richard b: 8/29/19, Newport, Pa. d: 3/30/78, Harrisburg, Pa. BR/TR, 5'10", 150 lbs. Deb: 9/20/41

YEAR	TM/L	G	AB	R	H	2B	3B	HR	RBI	BB	SO	AVG	OBP	SLG	PRO+	BR	/A	RC	SB	CS	SBR	FR	POS	TPR
1941	Pit-N	10	37	4	10	3	1	0	2	3	2	.270	.325	.405	105	0	0	5	1			2	S	0.3
1946	Pit-N	121	411	32	119	22	6	2	36	26	15	.290	.333	.387	101	1	-0	54	4			-16	*S	-0.8
1947	Pit-N	132	529	75	145	30	7	15	54	29	28	.274	.313	.442	96	-4	-6	74	5			-12	*S	-0.7
1948	Bro-N	88	237	36	59	13	2	3	15	38	19	.249	.353	.359	90	-1	-3	31	3			-4	3/S2	-0.7
1949	*Bro-N	100	390	48	91	18	2	8	40	30	18	.233	.290	.351	68	-17	-19	39	5			9	*3	-0.8
1950	Bro-N	119	451	62	116	17	2	8	44	35	24	.257	.311	.357	74	-17	-18	48	6			12	*32/S	-0.4
1951	Bro-N	142	455	62	127	25	4	9	51	37	30	.279	.336	.411	98	-1	-2	64	5	5	-2	-8	*3/S	-1.1
1952	*Bro-N	116	455	56	118	12	3	6	34	25	32	.259	.301	.338	76	-15	-15	43	10	12	-4	-9	*3S2	-2.5
1953	*Bro-N	100	327	44	95	18	1	10	44	37	21	.291	.363	.443	106	4	3	54	2	2	-1	-2	3/S2	0.0
1954	Bro-N	77	226	26	53	9	2	2	17	21	13	.235	.300	.319	59	-13	-14	21	0	0		2	32/S	-0.9
1955	Bal-A	53	194	25	41	7	2	3	14	17	16	.211	.275	.314	63	-12	-10	16	1	2	-1	-9	32/S	-1.7
Total	11	1058	3712	470	974	174	32	66	351	298	218	.262	.318	.380	85	-73	-82	448	42	21		-35	3S/2	-9.3

TED COX

Cox, William Ted b: 1/24/55, Oklahoma City, Okla BR/TR, 6'3", 195 lbs. Deb: 9/18/77

YEAR	TM/L	G	AB	R	H	2B	3B	HR	RBI	BB	SO	AVG	OBP	SLG	PRO+	BR	/A	RC	SB	CS	SBR	FR	POS	TPR
1977	Bos-A	13	58	11	21	3	1	1	6	3	6	.362	.393	.500	127	3	2	12	0	0	0	0	D	0.2
1978	Cle-A	82	227	14	53	7	0	1	19	16	30	.233	.287	.278	60	-12	-12	18	0	1	-1	-1	O3D/1S	-1.5
1979	Cle-A	78	189	17	40	6	0	4	22	14	27	.212	.273	.307	56	-12	-12	14	3	4	-2	2	3O/2	-1.0
1980	Sea-A	83	247	17	60	9	0	2	23	19	25	.243	.297	.304	64	-12	-12	21	0	0	0	-4	3	-1.6
1981	Tor-A	16	50	6	15	4	0	2	9	5	10	.300	.364	.500	138	3	3	9	0	1	-1	-4	3/1D	-0.2
Total	5	272	771	65	189	29	1	10	79	57	98	.245	.300	.324	71	-29	-31	75	3	6	-3	-8	3/OD12S	-4.1

TOOTS COYNE

Coyne, TR , Deb: 9/28/14

YEAR	TM/L	G	AB	R	H	2B	3B	HR	RBI	BB	SO	AVG	OBP	SLG	PRO+	BR	/A	RC	SB	CS	SBR	FR	POS	TPR
1914	Phi-A	1	2	0	0	0	0	0	0	0	2	.000	.000	.000	-99	-0	-0	0	0			-0	/3	0.0

ESTEL CRABTREE

Crabtree, Estel Crayton "Crabby" b: 8/19/03, Crabtree, Ohio d: 1/4/67, Logan, Ohio BL/TR, 6', 168 lbs. Deb: 4/18/29 C

YEAR	TM/L	G	AB	R	H	2B	3B	HR	RBI	BB	SO	AVG	OBP	SLG	PRO+	BR	/A	RC	SB	CS	SBR	FR	POS	TPR
1929	Cin-N	1	1	0	0	0	0	0	0	0	0	.000	.000	.000	-99	-0	-0	0	0			0	H	0.0
1931	Cin-N	117	443	70	119	12	12	4	37	23	33	.269	.309	.377	89	-11	-8	53	3			13	*O/31	0.0
1932	Cin-N	108	402	38	110	14	9	2	35	23	26	.274	.316	.368	86	-9	-8	48	2			2	O	-1.1
1933	StL-N	23	34	6	9	3	0	0	3	2	3	.265	.306	.353	83	-1	-1	4	1			1	/O	0.0
1941	StL-N	77	167	27	57	6	3	5	28	26	24	.341	.439	.503	154	15	14	39	1			-2	O/3	1.0
1942	StL-N	10	9	1	3	2	0	0	2	1	3	.333	.400	.556	166	1	1	2	0			0	H	0.1
1943	Cin-N	95	254	25	70	12	0	2	29	25	17	.276	.345	.346	101	1	1	29	1			-3	O	-0.4
1944	Cin-N	58	98	7	28	4	1	0	11	13	3	.286	.369	.347	106	1	1	12	0			-4	O/1	-0.3
Total	8	489	1408	174	396	53	25	13	142	113	109	.281	.339	.382	100	-4	0	186	8			7	O/31	-0.7

HARRY CRAFT

Craft, Harry Francis "Wildfire" b: 4/19/15, Ellisville, Miss. BR/TR, 6'1", 185 lbs. Deb: 9/19/37 MC

YEAR	TM/L	G	AB	R	H	2B	3B	HR	RBI	BB	SO	AVG	OBP	SLG	PRO+	BR	/A	RC	SB	CS	SBR	FR	POS	TPR
1937	Cin-N	10	42	7	13	2	1	0	4	1	3	.310	.326	.405	102	-0	-0	5				0	O	0.0
1938	Cin-N	151	612	70	165	28	9	15	83	29	46	.270	.305	.418	100	-5	-3	77	3			11	*O	0.5
1939	*Cin-N	134	502	58	129	20	7	13	67	27	54	.257	.299	.402	86	-11	-11	61	5			-1	*O	-1.4

YEAR	TM/L	G	AB	R	H	2B	3B	HR	RBI	BB	SO	AVG	OBP	SLG	PRO+	BR	/A	RC	SB	CS	SBR	FR	POS	TPR
1940	*Cin-N	115	422	47	103	18	5	6	48	17	46	.244	.277	.353	72	-17	-17	41	2			4	*O/1	-1.7
1941	Cin-N	119	413	48	103	15	2	10	59	33	43	.249	.308	.368	90	-6	-7	46	4			-1	*O	-1.2
1942	Cin-N	37	113	7	20	2	1	0	6	3	11	.177	.205	.212	22	-11	-11	5	0			4	O	-0.8
Total	6	566	2104	237	533	85	25	44	267	110	203	.253	.294	.380	85	-51	-49	236	14			17	O/1	-4.6

■ ROD CRAIG
Craig, Rodney Paul   b: 1/12/58, Los Angeles, Cal.   BB/TR, 6'1", 195 lbs.   Deb: 9/11/79

YEAR	TM/L	G	AB	R	H	2B	3B	HR	RBI	BB	SO	AVG	OBP	SLG	PRO+	BR	/A	RC	SB	CS	SBR	FR	POS	TPR
1979	Sea-A	16	52	9	20	8	1	0	6	1	5	.385	.396	.577	156	4	4	12	1	1	-0	-2	O	0.1
1980	Sea-A	70	240	30	57	15	1	3	20	17	35	.237	.293	.346	74	-9	-9	22	3	6	-3	-1	O	-1.3
1982	Cle-A	49	65	7	15	2	0	0	1	4	6	.231	.275	.262	49	-5	-4	4	3	1	0	1	O/D	-0.3
1986	Chi-A	10	10	3	2	0	0	0	0	2	2	.200	.333	.200	48	-1	-1	1	0	0	0	0	/O	0.0
Total	4	145	367	49	94	25	2	3	27	24	48	.256	.305	.360	80	-10	-10	39	7	8	-3	-2	O/D	-1.5

■ DOC CRAMER
Cramer, Roger Maxwell "Flit"   b: 7/22/05, Beach Haven, N.J.   d: 9/9/90, Manahawkin, N.J.   BL/TR, 6'2", 185 lbs.   Deb: 9/18/29   C

YEAR	TM/L	G	AB	R	H	2B	3B	HR	RBI	BB	SO	AVG	OBP	SLG	PRO+	BR	/A	RC	SB	CS	SBR	FR	POS	TPR
1929	Phi-A	2	6	0	0	0	0	0	0	0	2	.000	.000	.000	-97	-2	-2	0	0	0	0	1	/O	0.0
1930	Phi-A	30	82	12	19	1	1	0	6	2	8	.232	.250	.268	30	-9	-9	5	0	0	0	-2	O/S	-1.0
1931	*Phi-A	65	223	37	58	8	2	2	20	11	15	.260	.301	.341	64	-11	-12	23	2	1	0	1	O	-1.3
1932	Phi-A	92	384	73	129	27	6	3	46	17	27	.336	.367	.461	109	7	5	64	3	1	0	11	O	1.2
1933	Phi-A	152	661	109	195	27	8	8	75	36	24	.295	.331	.396	91	-9	-10	86	5	4	-1	2	*O	-1.2
1934	Phi-A	153	649	93	202	29	9	6	46	40	35	.311	.353	.411	100	-4	-1	93	1	5	-3	2	*O	-0.2
1935	Phi-A	149	644	96	214	37	4	3	70	37	34	.332	.373	.416	105	4	4	99	6	7	-2	-1	*O	0.0
1936	Bos-A	154	643	99	188	31	7	0	41	49	20	.292	.347	.362	71	-25	-30	82	4	6	-2	11	*O	-2.2
1937	Bos-A	133	560	90	171	22	11	0	51	35	14	.305	.351	.384	82	-13	-16	76	8	6	-1	2	*O	-1.8
1938	Bos-A	148	658	116	198	36	8	0	71	51	19	.301	.354	.380	80	-16	-21	87	4	9	-4	5	*O/P	-1.7
1939	Bos-A	137	589	110	183	30	6	0	56	36	17	.311	.352	.382	85	-11	-14	77	3	3	-1	-3	*O	-2.0
1940	Bos-A	150	661	94	**200**	27	12	1	51	36	29	.303	.340	.384	84	-13	-16	86	3	5	-2	-12	*O	-3.8
1941	Was-A	154	660	93	180	25	6	2	66	37	15	.273	.317	.338	77	-26	-22	71	4	1	1	-10	*O	-3.9
1942	Det-A	151	630	71	166	26	4	0	43	43	18	.263	.314	.317	72	-19	-25	63	4	4	-1	-3	*O	-4.0
1943	Det-A	140	606	79	182	18	4	1	43	31	13	.300	.335	.348	93	-1	-6	73	4	3	-1	-0	*O	-1.1
1944	Det-A	143	578	69	169	20	9	2	42	37	21	.292	.337	.369	96	0	-3	74	6	5	-1	-10	*O	-1.9
1945	*Det-A	141	541	62	149	22	8	6	58	36	21	.275	.324	.379	97	1	-3	65	2	9	-5	-11	*O	-2.6
1946	Det-A	68	204	26	60	8	2	1	26	15	8	.294	.342	.368	93	-1	-2	26	3	0	1	-4	O	-0.7
1947	Det-A	73	157	21	42	2	2	2	30	20	5	.268	.350	.344	91	-1	-2	17	0	4	-2	1	O	-0.4
1948	Det-A	4	4	1	0	0	0	0	0	0	0	.000	.429	.000	19	-0	-0	0	0	0	0	0	/O	0.0
Total	20	2239	9140	1357	2705	396	109	37	842	572	345	.296	.340	.375	87	-146	-184	1168	62	73	-25	-20	*O/PS	-28.6

■ DICK CRAMER
Cramer, William B.   b: Brooklyn, N.Y.   d: 8/12/1885, Camden, N.J.   Deb: 5/12/1883

YEAR	TM/L	G	AB	R	H	2B	3B	HR	RBI	BB	SO	AVG	OBP	SLG	PRO+	BR	/A	RC	SB	CS	SBR	FR	POS	TPR
1883	NY-N	2	6	0	0	0	0	0	0	1	5	.000	.143	.000	-52	-1	-1	0				0	/O	0.0

■ DEL CRANDALL
Crandall, Delmar Wesley   b: 3/5/30, Ontario, Cal.   BR/TR, 6'1.5", 180 lbs.   Deb: 6/17/49   MC

YEAR	TM/L	G	AB	R	H	2B	3B	HR	RBI	BB	SO	AVG	OBP	SLG	PRO+	BR	/A	RC	SB	CS	SBR	FR	POS	TPR
1949	Bos-N	67	228	21	60	10	1	4	34	9	18	.263	.291	.368	80	-8	-7	22	2			6	C	0.1
1950	Bos-N	79	255	21	56	11	0	4	37	13	24	.220	.257	.310	52	-20	-17	20	0			2	C/1	-1.2
1953	Mil-N	116	382	55	104	13	1	15	51	33	47	.272	.330	.429	102	-3	0	53	2	1	0	14	*C	2.0
1954	Mil-N	138	463	60	112	18	2	21	64	40	56	.242	.306	.425	94	-10	-6	57	0	3	-2	13	*C	0.9
1955	Mil-N	133	440	61	104	15	2	26	62	40	56	.236	.303	.457	103	-3	0	58	2	1	0	-3	*C	0.1
1956	Mil-N	112	311	37	74	14	2	16	48	35	30	.238	.317	.450	110	1	3	44	1	2	-1	2	*C	0.7
1957	*Mil-N	118	383	45	97	11	2	15	46	30	38	.253	.309	.410	98	-5	-2	45	1	2	-1	-8	*C/O1	-0.5
1958	*Mil-N	131	427	50	116	23	1	18	63	48	38	.272	.351	.457	122	7	12	66	4	1	1	5	*C	2.3
1959	Mil-N	150	518	65	133	19	2	21	72	46	48	.257	.321	.423	105	-4	2	65	5	1	1	5	*C	1.6
1960	Mil-N	142	537	81	158	14	1	19	77	34	36	.294	.341	.430	118	6	11	74	4	6	-2	-15	*C	0.0
1961	Mil-N	15	30	3	6	3	0	0	1	1	0	.200	.226	.300	40	-3	-2	2	0	0	0	-2	/C	-0.3
1962	Mil-N	107	350	35	104	12	3	8	45	27	24	.297	.351	.417	108	3	4	46	3	4	-2	-5	C/1	-0.1
1963	Mil-N	86	259	18	52	4	0	3	28	18	22	.201	.253	.251	46	-18	-18	14	1	4	-2	2	C/1	-1.6
1964	SF-N	69	195	12	45	8	1	3	11	22	21	.231	.309	.328	78	-5	-5	18	0	3	-2	12	C	0.7
1965	Pit-N	60	140	11	30	2	0	2	10	14	10	.214	.290	.271	59	-7	-7	11	1	0	0	4	C	0.0
1966	Cle-A	50	108	10	25	2	0	4	8	14	9	.231	.320	.361	95	-1	-1	12	0	0	0	15	C	1.7
Total	16	1573	5026	585	1276	179	18	179	657	424	477	.254	.315	.404	97	-69	-33	607	26	<u>28</u>		48	*C/1O	6.4

■ DOC CRANDALL
Crandall, James Otis   b: 10/8/1887, Wadena, Ind.   d: 8/17/51, Bell, Cal.   BR/TR, 5'10.5", 180 lbs.   Deb: 4/27/08

YEAR	TM/L	G	AB	R	H	2B	3B	HR	RBI	BB	SO	AVG	OBP	SLG	PRO+	BR	/A	RC	SB	CS	SBR	FR	POS	TPR
1908	NY-N	34	72	8	16	4	0	2	6		4	.222	.263	.361	96	-0	-1	7	0			-1	P/2	0.0
1909	NY-N	30	41	4	10	0	1	1	1		1	.244	.262	.366	93	-1	-1	4	0			2	P	0.0
1910	NY-N	45	73	10	25	2	4	1	13	5	7	.342	.385	.521	163	5	5	15	0			-1	P/S	0.0
1911	*NY-N	61	113	12	27	1	4	2	21	8	16	.239	.295	.372	83	-3	-3	13	2			0	P/S2	0.0
1912	NY-N	50	80	9	25	6	2	0	19	6	7	.313	.360	.438	114	2	1	13	0			0	P/21	0.0
1913	*NY-N	31	25	4	7	2	1	0	2	1	5	.280	.308	.440	111	0	0	3	0			1	P/2	0.0
	StL-N	2	2	0	0	0	0	0	0	0	2	.000	.000	.000	-99	-1	-1	0	0			0	H	0.0
	*NY-N	15	22	3	8	2	0	0	2	2	3	.364	.417	.455	148	1	1	4	0			1	P	0.0
	Yr	48	49	7	15	4	1	0	4	3	10	.306	.346	.429	120	1	1	7	0			2		0.0
1914	StL-F	118	278	40	86	16	5	2	41	58	32	.309	.429	.424	138	19	17	54	3			-18	2P/SO	0.5
1915	StL-F	84	141	18	40	2	2	1	19	27	15	.284	.406	.348	118	6	5	22	4			2	P	0.0
1916	StL-A	16	12	0	1	0	0	0	0	2	4	.083	.214	.083	-11	-2	-1	0	0			-0	/P	-0.1
1918	Bos-N	14	28	1	8	0	0	0	2	4	3	.286	.375	.286	107	0	0	3	0			-0	/PO	0.1
Total	10	500	887	109	253	35	19	9	126	118	94	.285	.371	.398	119	29	25	137	9			-14	P/2SO1	0.5

■ ED CRANE
Crane, Edward Nicholas "Cannon-Ball"   b: 5/1862, Boston, Mass.   d: 9/19/1896, Rochester, N.Y.   BR/TR, 5'10.5", 204 lbs.   Deb: 4/17/1884

YEAR	TM/L	G	AB	R	H	2B	3B	HR	RBI	BB	SO	AVG	OBP	SLG	PRO+	BR	/A	RC	SB	CS	SBR	FR	POS	TPR
1884	Bos-U	101	428	83	122	23	6	12			14	.285	.308	.451	156	23	24	61	0			-2	OC/1P	2.0
1885	Pro-N	1	2	0	0	0	0	0	0	1	1	.000	.333	.000	16	-0	-0	0	0			0	/O	0.0
	Buf-N	13	51	5	14	0	1	2	9	3	8	.275	.315	.431	136	2	2	7				-3	O	0.0
	Yr	14	53	5	14	0	1	2	9	4	9	.264	.316	.415	132	2	2	7				-3		0.0
1886	Was-N	80	292	50	50	11	3	0	20	13	54	.171	.207	.229	34	-23	-21	16	8			3	OP/C	-1.3
1888	*NY-N	12	37	3	6	2	0	1	2	3	11	.162	.225	.297	68	-1	-1	3	1			1	P	0.0
1889	*NY-N	29	103	16	21	1	0	2	11	13	21	.204	.293	.272	60	-5	-5	10	6			-4	P/1	0.0
1890	NY-P	43	146	27	46	5	4	0	16	10	26	.315	.363	.404	98	1	-1	24	5			-3	P	0.0
1891	Cin-a	34	110	13	17	0	0	1	7	8	28	.155	.212	.182	13	-12	-14	5	4			-3	P/O	0.0
	Cin-N	15	46	3	5	0	0	0	2	3	12	.109	.163	.109	-19	-7	-7	1	3			0	P	0.0
1892	NY-N	48	163	20	40	1	1	0	14	11	30	.245	.297	.264	73	-5	-5	14	2			-1	P/O	0.0
1893	NY-N	12	26	8	12	1	0	0	3	7	0	.462	.576	.500	189	4	4	8	0			-1	P/1O	0.0
	Bro-N	3	5	1	2	1	0	0	0	0	0	.400	.400	.600	174	1	1	1	0			-1	/PO	0.0
	Yr	15	31	9	14	2	0	0	3	7	0	.452	.553	.516	189	5	5	9	0			-2		0.0
Total	9	391	1409	199	335	45	15	18	84	86	191	.238	.283	.329	87	-24	-24	150	29			-13	PO/C1	0.7

■ FRED CRANE
Crane, Frederic William Hotchkiss   b: 11/4/1840, Saybrook, Conn.   d: 4/27/25, Brooklyn, N.Y.   Deb: 5/26/1873

YEAR	TM/L	G	AB	R	H	2B	3B	HR	RBI	BB	SO	AVG	OBP	SLG	PRO+	BR	/A	RC	SB	CS	SBR	FR	POS	TPR
1873	Res-n	1	4	0	1	0	0	0		0		.250	.250	.250	52	-0	-0	0					/2	0.0
1875	Atl-n	21	80	7	17	1	0	0		0		.213	.213	.225	59	-4	-2	4					1/O	-0.2
Total	2 n	22	84	7	18	1	0	0		0		.214	.214	.226	59	-4	-2	4					/1O2	-0.2

YEAR	TM/L	G	AB	R	H	2B	3B	HR	RBI	BB	SO	AVG	OBP	SLG	PRO+	BR	/A	RC	SB	CS	SBR	FR	POS	TPR

■ SAM CRANE
Crane, Samuel Byren "Lucky" or "Red"　b: 9/13/1894, Harrisburg, Pa.　d: 11/12/55, Philadelphia, Pa.　BR/TR, 5'11.5", 154 lbs.　Deb: 10/02/14

YEAR	TM/L	G	AB	R	H	2B	3B	HR	RBI	BB	SO	AVG	OBP	SLG	PRO+	BR	/A	RC	SB	CS	SBR	FR	POS	TPR
1914	Phi-A	2	6	0	0	0	0	0	0	2	3	.000	.250	.000	-25	-1	-1	0	0			1	/S	0.0
1915	Phi-A	8	23	3	2	2	0	0	1	0	4	.087	.087	.174	-23	-4	-3	0	0			2	/S2	0.0
1916	Phi-A	2	4	1	1	0	0	0	0	2	1	.250	.500	.250	131	0	0	1	0			-0	/S	0.0
1917	Was-A	32	95	6	17	2	0	0	4	4	14	.179	.212	.200	26	-9	-8	4	0			-4	S	-1.2
1920	Cin-N	54	144	20	31	4	0	0	9	7	9	.215	.261	.243	46	-10	-10	9	5	4	-1	-8	S3/2O	-1.7
1921	Cin-N	73	215	20	50	10	2	0	16	14	14	.233	.292	.298	59	-13	-12	19	2	5	-2	-16	S/3O	-2.4
1922	Bro-N	3	8	1	2	1	0	0	0	0	1	.250	.333	.375	83	-0	-0	1	0	0	0	2	/S	0.2
Total	7	174	495	51	103	19	2	0	30	29	46	.208	.262	.255	46	-36	-34	34	7	9		-23	S/32O	-5.1

■ SAM CRANE
Crane, Samuel Newhall　b: 1/2/1854, Springfield, Mass.　d: 6/26/25, New York, N.Y.　BR/TR,　Deb: 5/01/1880　M

YEAR	TM/L	G	AB	R	H	2B	3B	HR	RBI	BB	SO	AVG	OBP	SLG	PRO+	BR	/A	RC	SB	CS	SBR	FR	POS	TPR
1880	Buf-N	10	31	4	4	0	0	0	2	1	8	.129	.156	.129	-2	-3	-3	1				-2	2/OM	-0.4
1883	NY-a	96	349	57	82	8	5	0		13		.235	.262	.287	74	-9	-11	27				-11	*2/O	-1.7
1884	Cin-U	80	309	56	72	9	3	1		11		.233	.259	.291	80	-4	-8	24	0			-9	*2M	-1.7
1885	Det-N	68	245	23	47	4	6	1	20	13	45	.192	.233	.269	62	-10	-10	16				-4	2	-0.6
1886	Det-N	47	185	24	26	2	2	1	12	8	34	.141	.176	.189	11	-19	-20	8	8			2	2/SO	-1.5
	StL-N	39	116	10	20	3	1	0	7	13	27	.172	.256	.216	48	-7	-6	8	6			-7	2	-1.0
	Yr	86	301	34	46	5	3	1	19	21	61	.153	.208	.199	25	-27	-26	16	14			-6		-2.5
1887	Was-N	7	30	6	9	1	1	0	1	1	6	.300	.323	.400	107	-0	0	6	5			-1	/S	0.0
1890	NY-N	2	6	0	0	0	0	0	0	0	0	.000	.000	.000	-99	-1	-1	0	1			-1	/1O	-0.1
	Pit-N	22	82	3	16	3	0	0	3	0	5	.195	.205	.232	32	-7	-6	5	5			4	2/SO	-0.1
	NY-N	2	6	0	0	0	0	0	0	0	0	.000	.000	.000	-99	-1	-1	0	1			-1	/2	-0.1
	Yr	26	94	3	16	3	0	0	3	0	5	.170	.179	.202	13	-10	-9	5	7			3		-0.3
Total	7	373	1359	183	276	30	18	3	45	60	125	.203	.237	.258	57	-64	-68	94	26			-28	2/SO1	-7.2

■ GAVVY CRAVATH
Cravath, Clifford Carlton "Cactus"　b: 3/23/1881, Escondido, Cal.　d: 5/23/63, Laguna Beach, Cal.　BR/TR, 5'10.5", 186 lbs.　Deb: 4/18/08　MC

YEAR	TM/L	G	AB	R	H	2B	3B	HR	RBI	BB	SO	AVG	OBP	SLG	PRO+	BR	/A	RC	SB	CS	SBR	FR	POS	TPR
1908	Bos-A	94	277	43	71	10	11	1	34	38		.256	.346	.383	135	13	12	39	6			-1	O/1	0.7
1909	Chi-A	19	50	7	9	0	0	1	8	19		.180	.406	.240	109	2	2	6	3			-2	O	0.0
	Was-A	4	6	0	0	0	0	0	1	1		.000	.143	.000	-57	-1	-1	0	0			1	/O	0.0
	Yr	23	56	7	9	0	0	1	9	20		.161	.382	.214	93	1	1	6	3			-2		0.0
1912	Phi-N	130	436	63	124	30	9	11	70	47	77	.284	.358	.470	118	14	10	78	15			5	*O	1.1
1913	Phi-N	147	525	78	179	34	14	19	128	55	63	.341	.407	.568	169	50	48	120	10			-11	*O	3.5
1914	Phi-N	149	499	76	149	27	8	19	100	83	72	.299	.402	.499	157	43	39	103	14			-1	*O	3.6
1915	*Phi-N	150	522	89	149	31	7	24	115	86	77	.285	.393	.510	170	47	46	105	11	9	-2	2	*O	4.5
1916	Phi-N	137	448	70	127	21	8	11	70	64	89	.283	.379	.440	146	29	27	80	9			-9	*O	1.5
1917	Phi-N	140	503	70	141	29	16	12	83	70	57	.280	.369	.473	151	35	32	88	6			-10	*O	2.0
1918	Phi-N	121	426	43	99	27	5	8	54	54	46	.232	.320	.376	105	6	3	51	7			-9	*O	-1.3
1919	Phi-N	83	214	34	73	18	5	12	45	35	21	.341	.438	.640	207	32	30	61	8			-6	OM	2.4
1920	Phi-N	46	45	2	13	5	0	1	11	9	12	.289	.407	.467	144	3	3	9	0	0	0	-1	/OM	0.1
Total	11	1220	3951	575	1134	232	83	119	719	561	514	.287	.379	.478	149	272	251	741	89	9		-44	*O/1	18.1

■ BILL CRAVER
Craver, William H.　b: 1844, Troy, N.Y.　d: 6/17/01, Troy, N.Y.　BR/TR, 5'9", 160 lbs.　Deb: 5/09/1871　M

YEAR	TM/L	G	AB	R	H	2B	3B	HR	RBI	BB	SO	AVG	OBP	SLG	PRO+	BR	/A	RC	SB	CS	SBR	FR	POS	TPR
1871	Tro-n	27	118	26	38	8	1	0	26	3	0	.322	.339	.407	112	2	2	19	6				2/SC1M	0.1
1872	Bal-n	35	180	55	50	5	3	0			4	.278	.293	.339	90	-1	-3	18					C/O32M	-0.2
1873	Bal-n	40	189	40	58	7	4	0			2	.307	.314	.386	105	1	1	24					CS/O1	0.1
1874	Phi-n	55	267	68	94	13	11	0			4	.352	.362	.483	161	19	17	48					*2/CM	1.3
1875	Cen-n	14	65	8	18	5	2	0			0	.277	.277	.415	148	2	3	8					/S31M	0.3
	Ath-n	54	260	71	83	11	11	2			4	.319	.330	.469	156	18	14	41					2/C	1.0
	Yr	68	325	79	101	16	13	2			4	.311	.319	.458	155	21	17	49						1.3
1876	NY-N	56	246	24	55	4	0	0	22	2	7	.224	.230	.240	65	-11	-6	14				-23	2C/S	-2.4
1877	Lou-N	57	238	33	63	5	2	0	29	5	11	.265	.280	.303	71	-4	-11	21				-1	*S	-0.8
Total	5 n	225	1079	268	341	49	32	2	26	17		.316	.327	.426	131	42	34	157					2/CSO31	2.6
Total	2	113	484	57	118	9	2	0	51	7	18	.244	.255	.271	69	-15	-17	35				-23	/S2C	-3.2

■ PAT CRAWFORD
Crawford, Clifford Rankin　b: 1/28/02, Society Hill, S.C.　BL/TR, 5'11", 170 lbs.　Deb: 4/18/29

YEAR	TM/L	G	AB	R	H	2B	3B	HR	RBI	BB	SO	AVG	OBP	SLG	PRO+	BR	/A	RC	SB	CS	SBR	FR	POS	TPR
1929	NY-N	65	57	13	17	3	0	3	24	11	5	.298	.412	.509	127	3	3	12	1			-0	/13	0.2
1930	NY-N	25	76	11	21	3	2	3	17	7	2	.276	.345	.487	100	-0	-0	13	0			-4	2/1	-0.1
	Cin-N	76	224	24	65	7	1	3	26	23	10	.290	.359	.371	81	-8	-6	30	2			-8	21	-0.7
	Yr	101	300	35	86	10	3	6	43	30	12	.287	.355	.400	86	-8	-6	43	2			-12		-0.8
1933	StL-N	91	224	24	60	8	2	0	21	14	9	.268	.317	.321	78	-5	-6	23	1			3	12/3	-0.2
1934	*StL-N	61	70	3	19	2	0	0	16	5	3	.271	.320	.300	63	-3	-4	7	0			2	/32	0.0
Total	4	318	651	75	182	23	5	9	104	60	29	.280	.344	.372	85	-14	-13	85	4			-8	/213	-0.8

■ FORREST CRAWFORD
Crawford, Forrest A.　b: 5/10/1881, Rockdale, Tex.　d: 3/29/08, Austin, Tex.　TR ,　Deb: 7/30/06

YEAR	TM/L	G	AB	R	H	2B	3B	HR	RBI	BB	SO	AVG	OBP	SLG	PRO+	BR	/A	RC	SB	CS	SBR	FR	POS	TPR
1906	StL-N	45	145	8	30	3	1	0	11	7		.207	.243	.241	55	-8	-7	9	1			-10	S/3	-1.6
1907	StL-N	7	22	0	5	0	0	0	3	2		.227	.292	.227	67	-1	-1	2	0			-1	/S	0.0
Total	2	52	167	8	35	3	1	0	14	9		.210	.250	.240	57	-9	-8	11	1			-10	/S3	-1.6

■ GEORGE CRAWFORD
Crawford, George　Deb: 10/09/1890

YEAR	TM/L	G	AB	R	H	2B	3B	HR	RBI	BB	SO	AVG	OBP	SLG	PRO+	BR	/A	RC	SB	CS	SBR	FR	POS	TPR
1890	Phi-a	5	17	1	2	0	0	0		0		.118	.118	.118	-31	-3	-3	0	1			1	/OS	-0.1

■ GLENN CRAWFORD
Crawford, Glenn Martin "Shorty"　b: 12/2/13, North Branch, Mich.　d: 1/2/72, Saginaw, Mich.　BL/TR, 5'9", 165 lbs.　Deb: 4/22/45

YEAR	TM/L	G	AB	R	H	2B	3B	HR	RBI	BB	SO	AVG	OBP	SLG	PRO+	BR	/A	RC	SB	CS	SBR	FR	POS	TPR
1945	StL-N	4	3	0	0	0	0	0	0	1	0	.000	.250	.000	-26	-0	-0	0	0			0	/O	0.0
	Phi-N	82	302	41	89	13	2	2	24	36	15	.295	.372	.371	110	4	5	45	5			-4	OS2	0.4
	Yr	86	305	41	89	13	2	2	24	37	15	.292	.370	.367	108	3	4	45	5			-4		0.4
1946	Phi-N	1	1	0	0	0	0	0	0	0	0	.000	.000	.000	-99	-0	-0	0	0			0	H	0.0
Total	2	87	306	41	89	13	2	2	24	37	15	.291	.369	.366	108	3	4	45	5			-4	/OS2	0.4

■ KEN CRAWFORD
Crawford, Kenneth Daniel　b: 10/31/1894, South Bend, Ind.　d: 11/11/76, Pittsburgh, Pa.　BL/TR, 5'9", 145 lbs.　Deb: 9/06/15

YEAR	TM/L	G	AB	R	H	2B	3B	HR	RBI	BB	SO	AVG	OBP	SLG	PRO+	BR	/A	RC	SB	CS	SBR	FR	POS	TPR
1915	Bal-F	23	82	4	20	2	1	0	7	1	18	.244	.253	.293	59	-4	-4	6	0			-2	1/O	-0.6

■ JAKE CRAWFORD
Crawford, Rufus　b: 3/20/28, Campbell, Mo.　BR/TR, 6'1.5", 185 lbs.　Deb: 9/07/52

YEAR	TM/L	G	AB	R	H	2B	3B	HR	RBI	BB	SO	AVG	OBP	SLG	PRO+	BR	/A	RC	SB	CS	SBR	FR	POS	TPR
1952	StL-A	7	11	1	2	1	0	0	0	1	5	.182	.250	.273	44	-1	-1	1	1	0	0	0	/O	0.0

■ SAM CRAWFORD
Crawford, Samuel Earl "Wahoo Sam"　b: 4/18/1880, Wahoo, Neb.　d: 6/15/68, Hollywood, Cal.　BL/TL, 6', 190 lbs.　Deb: 9/10/1899　H

YEAR	TM/L	G	AB	R	H	2B	3B	HR	RBI	BB	SO	AVG	OBP	SLG	PRO+	BR	/A	RC	SB	CS	SBR	FR	POS	TPR
1899	Cin-N	31	127	25	39	3	7	1	20	2		.307	.318	.465	114	2	1	21	6			2	O	0.1
1900	Cin-N	101	389	68	101	15	15	7	59	28		.260	.314	.429	109	2	3	58	14			12	*O	0.6
1901	Cin-N	131	515	91	170	20	16	16	104	37		.330	.377	.524	174	36	43	110	13			3	*O	3.1
1902	Cin-N	140	555	92	185	18	22	3	78	47		.333	.386	.461	150	40	34	108	16			4	*O	2.9
1903	Det-A	137	550	88	184	23	25	4	89	25		.335	.363	.489	161	35	37	109	18			4	*O	3.3
1904	Det-A	150	562	49	143	22	16	2	73	44		.254	.309	.361	117	9	10	72	20			4	*O	0.6
1905	Det-A	154	575	73	171	38	10	6	75	50		.297	.354	.430	149	32	31	98	22			11	*O1	3.9
1906	Det-A	145	563	65	166	25	16	2	72	38		.295	.339	.407	132	21	20	89	24			1	*O1	1.7
1907	*Det-A	144	582	102	188	34	17	4	81	37		.323	.363	.460	159	39	37	108	18			8	*O/1	4.0
1908	*Det-A	152	591	102	184	33	16	7	80	37		.311	.352	.457	158	39	36	99	15			-8	*O1	2.4

YEAR	TM/L	G	AB	R	H	2B	3B	HR	RBI	BB	SO	AVG	OBP	SLG	PRO+	BR	/A	RC	SB	CS	SBR	FR	POS	TPR
1909	*Det-A	156	589	83	185	35	14	6	97	47		.314	.366	.452	151	37	34	108	30			-7	*O1	2.4
1910	Det-A	154	588	83	170	26	19	5	120	37		.289	.332	.423	128	21	17	89	20			-10	*O/1	0.0
1911	Det-A	146	574	109	217	36	14	7	115	61		.378	.438	.526	160	52	48	147	37			-12	*O	2.4
1912	Det-A	149	581	81	189	30	21	4	109	42		.325	.373	.470	145	28	30	116	41			-17	*O	0.4
1913	Det-A	153	609	78	193	32	23	9	83	52	28	.317	.371	.489	154	36	37	110	13			-10	*O1	2.0
1914	Det-A	157	582	74	183	22	26	8	104	69	31	.314	.388	.483	157	42	40	113	25	16	-2	-8	*O	2.3
1915	Det-A	156	612	81	183	31	19	5	112	66	29	.299	.367	.436	134	28	24	102	24	14	-1	-13	*O	0.2
1916	Det-A	100	322	41	92	11	13	0	42	37	10	.286	.359	.401	124	11	9	51	10			-10	O/1	-0.5
1917	Det-A	61	104	6	18	4	0	2	12	4	6	.173	.204	.269	44	-7	-7	6	0			-3	1/O	-1.1
Total	19	2517	9570	1391	2961	458	309	98	1525	760	104	.309	.361	.453	144	505	487	1712	366	30		-50	*O1	30.7

■ WILLIE CRAWFORD
Crawford, Willie Murphy b: 9/7/46, Los Angeles, Cal. BL/TL, 6'1", 197 lbs. Deb: 9/16/64

YEAR	TM/L	G	AB	R	H	2B	3B	HR	RBI	BB	SO	AVG	OBP	SLG	PRO+	BR	/A	RC	SB	CS	SBR	FR	POS	TPR
1964	LA-N	10	16	3	5	1	0	0	0	1	7	.313	.353	.375	113	0	0	2	1	1	-0	0	/O	0.0
1965	*LA-N	52	27	10	4	0	0	0	0	2	8	.148	.207	.148	2	-3	-3	1	2	0	1	4	/O	0.1
1966	LA-N	6	0	1	0	0	0	0	0	0	0	—	—	—	—	0	0	0	0	0	0	0	R	0.0
1967	LA-N	4	4	0	1	0	0	0	0	1	3	.250	.400	.250	98	0	0	1	0	0	0	-0	/O	0.0
1968	LA-N	61	175	25	44	12	1	4	14	20	64	.251	.335	.400	130	4	6	24	1	3	-2	1	*O	0.3
1969	LA-N	129	389	64	96	17	5	11	41	49	85	.247	.331	.401	112	2	5	52	4	5	-2	-6	*O	-0.8
1970	LA-N	109	299	48	70	8	6	8	40	33	88	.234	.314	.381	89	-7	-5	36	4	4	-1	4	O	-0.5
1971	LA-N	114	342	64	96	16	6	9	40	28	49	.281	.337	.442	126	8	10	51	5	2	0	-9	O	-0.1
1972	LA-N	96	243	28	61	7	3	8	27	35	55	.251	.350	.403	116	5	6	34	4	2	0	-5	O	-0.2
1973	LA-N	145	457	75	135	26	2	14	66	78	91	.295	.399	.453	142	25	27	88	12	5	1	0	*O	2.3
1974	*LA-N	139	468	73	138	23	4	11	61	64	88	.295	.380	.432	132	18	20	77	7	8	-3	-10	*O	0.2
1975	LA-N	124	373	46	98	15	2	9	46	49	43	.263	.348	.386	108	2	4	52	5	5	-2	-6	*O	-0.7
1976	StL-N	120	392	49	119	17	5	9	50	37	53	.304	.365	.441	127	14	14	62	2	1	0	-2	*O	0.8
1977	Hou-N	42	114	14	29	3	0	2	18	16	10	.254	.346	.333	91	-2	-1	14	0	0	0	-4	O	-0.6
	Oak-A	59	136	7	25	7	1	1	16	18	20	.184	.279	.272	52	-9	-9	10	0	0	0	1	OD	-0.7
Total	14	1210	3435	507	921	152	35	86	419	431	664	.268	.351	.408	117	56	74	505	47	36	-8	-31	O/D	0.1

■ GEORGE CREAMER
Creamer, George W. (b: George W. Triebel) b: 1855, Philadelphia, Pa. d: 6/27/1886, Philadelphia, Pa. BR/TR, 6'2", Deb: 5/01/1878 M

YEAR	TM/L	G	AB	R	H	2B	3B	HR	RBI	BB	SO	AVG	OBP	SLG	PRO+	BR	/A	RC	SB	CS	SBR	FR	POS	TPR
1878	Mil-N	50	193	30	41	7	3	0	15	5	15	.212	.232	.280	63	-7	-8	13				-3	2O/3	-0.9
1879	Syr-N	15	60	3	13	2	0	0	3	1	2	.217	.230	.250	65	-3	-2	4				-10	2/SO	-0.9
1880	Wor-N	85	306	40	61	6	3	0	27	4	21	.199	.210	.239	47	-15	-18	16				-7	*2	-2.1
1881	Wor-N	80	309	42	64	9	2	0	25	11	27	.207	.234	.249	49	-16	-19	18				-9	*2	-2.3
1882	Wor-N	81	286	27	65	16	6	1	29	14	24	.227	.263	.336	88	-3	-4	26				12	*2	0.8
1883	Pit-a	91	369	54	94	7	9	0		20		.255	.293	.322	103	-0	2	36				9	*2	1.1
1884	Pit-a	98	339	38	62	8	5	0		16		.183	.224	.236	52	-17	-18	18				16	*2M	0.0
Total	7	500	1862	234	400	55	28	1	99	71	89	.215	.244	.276	68	-61	-66	131				8	2/O3S	-4.3

■ BIRDIE CREE
Cree, William Franklin b: 10/23/1882, Khedive, Pa. d: 11/8/42, Sunbury, Pa. BR/TR, 5'6", 150 lbs. Deb: 9/17/08

YEAR	TM/L	G	AB	R	H	2B	3B	HR	RBI	BB	SO	AVG	OBP	SLG	PRO+	BR	/A	RC	SB	CS	SBR	FR	POS	TPR
1908	NY-A	21	78	5	21	0	2	0	4	7		.269	.329	.321	113	1	1	8	1			1	O	0.1
1909	NY-A	104	343	48	90	6	3	2	27	30		.262	.338	.315	105	3	3	40	10			-6	O/S23	-0.6
1910	NY-A	134	467	58	134	19	16	4	73	40		.287	.353	.422	135	22	19	79	28			-12	*O	0.0
1911	NY-A	137	520	90	181	30	22	4	88	56		.348	.415	.513	149	40	35	129	48			0	*O/S2	2.5
1912	NY-A	50	190	25	63	11	6	0	22	20		.332	.409	.453	138	12	10	39	12			6	O	1.3
1913	NY-A	145	534	51	145	25	6	1	63	50	51	.272	.338	.346	100	0	0	68	22			-4	*O	-1.1
1914	NY-A	77	275	45	85	18	5	0	40	30	24	.309	.389	.411	141	14	14	43	4	9	-4	7	O	1.4
1915	NY-A	74	196	23	42	8	2	0	15	36	22	.214	.353	.276	88	-1	-1	20	7	8	-3	-3	O	-0.9
Total	8	742	2603	345	761	117	62	11	332	269	97	.292	.368	.398	124	92	82	427	132	17		-11	O/S23	2.7

■ CONNIE CREEDEN
Creeden, Cornelius Stephen b: 7/21/15, Danvers, Mass. d: 11/30/69, Santa Ana, Cal. BL/TL, 6'1", 200 lbs. Deb: 4/28/43

YEAR	TM/L	G	AB	R	H	2B	3B	HR	RBI	BB	SO	AVG	OBP	SLG	PRO+	BR	/A	RC	SB	CS	SBR	FR	POS	TPR
1943	Bos-N	5	4	0	1	0	0	0	1	1	0	.250	.400	.250	91	0	0	1	0			0	H	0.0

■ PAT CREEDEN
Creeden, Patrick Francis "Whoops" b: 5/23/06, Newburyport, Mass. BL/TR, 5'8", 175 lbs. Deb: 4/14/31

YEAR	TM/L	G	AB	R	H	2B	3B	HR	RBI	BB	SO	AVG	OBP	SLG	PRO+	BR	/A	RC	SB	CS	SBR	FR	POS	TPR
1931	Bos-A	5	8	0	0	0	0	0	0	1	3	.000	.111	.000	-73	-2	-2	0	0	0	0	0	/2	-0.1

■ MARTY CREEGAN
Creegan, Martin b: San Francisco, Cal. Deb: 4/17/1884

YEAR	TM/L	G	AB	R	H	2B	3B	HR	RBI	BB	SO	AVG	OBP	SLG	PRO+	BR	/A	RC	SB	CS	SBR	FR	POS	TPR
1884	Was-U	9	33	4	5	0	0	0		1		.152	.176	.152	12	-3	-3	1	0			1	/OC31	0.0

■ GUS CREELY
Creely, August L. b: 6/6/1870, Florissant, Mo. d: 4/22/34, St.Louis, Mo. 5'6", 150 lbs. Deb: 10/09/1890

YEAR	TM/L	G	AB	R	H	2B	3B	HR	RBI	BB	SO	AVG	OBP	SLG	PRO+	BR	/A	RC	SB	CS	SBR	FR	POS	TPR
1890	StL-a	4	15	0	0	0	0	0	0			.000	.000	.000	-88	-4	-4	0	1			-3	/S	-0.5

■ PETE CREGAN
Cregan, Peter James "Peekskill Pete" b: 4/13/1875, Kingston, N.Y. d: 5/18/45, New York, N.Y. BR/TR, 5'7.5", 150 lbs. Deb: 9/08/1899

YEAR	TM/L	G	AB	R	H	2B	3B	HR	RBI	BB	SO	AVG	OBP	SLG	PRO+	BR	/A	RC	SB	CS	SBR	FR	POS	TPR
1899	NY-N	1	2	0	0	0	0	0	0	0		.000	.000	.000	-99	-1	-1	0	0			-0	/O	0.0
1903	Cin-N	6	19	0	2	0	0	0	0	1		.105	.150	.105	-23	-3	-3	0	0			-1	/O	-0.4
Total	2	7	21	0	2	0	0	0	0	1		.095	.136	.095	-30	-4	-4	0	0			-1	/O	-0.4

■ BERNIE CREGER
Creger, Bernard Odell b: 3/21/27, Wytheville, Va. BR/TR, 6', 175 lbs. Deb: 4/29/47

YEAR	TM/L	G	AB	R	H	2B	3B	HR	RBI	BB	SO	AVG	OBP	SLG	PRO+	BR	/A	RC	SB	CS	SBR	FR	POS	TPR
1947	StL-N	15	16	3	3	1	0	0	0	1	3	.188	.235	.250	28	-2	-2	1	1			-3	S	-0.3

■ CREEPY CRESPI
Crespi, Frank Angelo Joseph b: 2/16/18, St.Louis, Mo. d: 3/1/90, Florissant, Mo. BR/TR, 5'8.5", 175 lbs. Deb: 9/14/38

YEAR	TM/L	G	AB	R	H	2B	3B	HR	RBI	BB	SO	AVG	OBP	SLG	PRO+	BR	/A	RC	SB	CS	SBR	FR	POS	TPR
1938	StL-N	7	19	2	5	2	0	0	1	2	7	.263	.333	.368	88	-0	-0	2	0			-2	/S	-0.1
1939	StL-N	15	29	3	5	1	0	0	6	3	6	.172	.250	.207	23	-3	-3	2	0			-0	/2S	-0.2
1940	StL-N	3	11	2	3	1	0	0	0	1	2	.273	.333	.364	87	-0	-0	1	1			-1	/3S	0.0
1941	StL-N	146	560	85	156	24	2	4	46	57	58	.279	.355	.350	93	1	-4	72	3			0	*2	0.6
1942	*StL-N	93	292	33	71	4	2	0	35	27	29	.243	.309	.271	65	-10	-13	26	4			-5	2/S	-1.1
Total	5	264	911	125	240	32	4	4	88	90	102	.263	.326	.321	82	-13	-21	104	8			-7	2/S3	-0.8

■ LOU CRIGER
Criger, Louis b: 2/3/1872, Elkhart, Ind. d: 5/14/34, Tucson, Ariz. BR/TR, 5'10", 165 lbs. Deb: 9/21/1896

YEAR	TM/L	G	AB	R	H	2B	3B	HR	RBI	BB	SO	AVG	OBP	SLG	PRO+	BR	/A	RC	SB	CS	SBR	FR	POS	TPR
1896	Cle-N	2	5	0	0	0	0	0	0	1	0	.000	.167	.000	-50	-1	-1	0	1			1	/C	0.0
1897	Cle-N	39	138	15	31	4	1	0	22	23		.225	.340	.268	60	-6	-8	15	5			-2	C/1	-0.3
1898	Cle-N	84	287	43	80	13	4	1	32	40		.279	.373	.362	115	7	7	40	2			15	C	2.6
1899	StL-N	77	258	39	66	4	5	2	44	28		.256	.333	.333	84	-4	-5	34	14			1	C	0.0
1900	StL-N	80	288	31	78	8	6	2	38	4		.271	.286	.361	84	-9	-8	32	5			4	C/3	0.2
1901	Bos-A	76	268	26	62	6	3	0	24	11		.231	.270	.276	54	-17	-16	23	7			21	C/1	1.0
1902	Bos-A	83	266	32	68	16	6	0	28	27		.256	.324	.361	89	-3	-4	35	7			14	C/O	1.5
1903	*Bos-A	96	317	41	61	7	10	0	31	26		.192	.254	.306	65	-12	-14	28	5			22	C	2.1
1904	Bos-A	98	299	34	63	10	5	2	34	27		.211	.276	.298	79	-5	-7	26	1			18	C	2.3
1905	Bos-A	109	313	33	62	6	7	1	36	54		.198	.316	.272	88	-1	-2	30	5			6	*C	1.6
1906	Bos-A	7	17	0	3	1	0	0	1	1		.176	.222	.235	45	-1	-1	1	1			4	/C	0.4
1907	Bos-A	75	226	12	41	4	0	0	14	19		.181	.245	.199	44	-14	-13	13	2			0	C	-0.6
1908	Bos-A	84	237	12	45	4	2	0	25	13		.190	.232	.224	49	-13	-13	13	1			15	C	1.1
1909	StL-A	74	212	15	36	1	1	0	9	25		.170	.261	.184	44	-13	-12	12	2			8	C	0.2
1910	NY-A	27	69	3	13	2	0	0	4	10		.188	.291	.217	56	-3	-3	4	0			-1	C	-0.1
1912	StL-A	1	2	1	0	0	0	0	0	0		.000	.000	.000	-99	-1	-1	0	0			1	/C	0.0

YEAR	TM/L	G	AB	R	H	2B	3B	HR	RBI	BB	SO	AVG	OBP	SLG	PRO+	BR	/A	RC	SB	CS	SBR	FR	POS	TPR
Total	16	1012	3202	337	709	86	50	11	342	309	0	.221	.292	.290	73	-96	-101	307	58			126	C/1O3	12.0

■ DAVE CRIPE
Cripe, David Gordon b: 4/7/51, Ramona, Cal. BR/TR, 6′, 180 lbs. Deb: 9/10/78

YEAR	TM/L	G	AB	R	H	2B	3B	HR	RBI	BB	SO	AVG	OBP	SLG	PRO+	BR	/A	RC	SB	CS	SBR	FR	POS	TPR
1978	KC-A	7	13	1	2	0	0	0	1	0	2	.154	.154	.154	-13	-2	-2	0	0	0	0	-2	/3	-0.3

■ DAVE CRISCIONE
Criscione, David Gerald b: 9/2/51, Dunkirk, N.Y. BR/TR, 5′8″, 185 lbs. Deb: 7/17/77

YEAR	TM/L	G	AB	R	H	2B	3B	HR	RBI	BB	SO	AVG	OBP	SLG	PRO+	BR	/A	RC	SB	CS	SBR	FR	POS	TPR
1977	Bal-A	7	9	1	3	0	0	1	1	0	1	.333	.333	.667	176	1	1	2	0	0	0	-1	/C	0.0

■ TONY CRISCOLA
Criscola, Anthony Paul b: 7/9/15, Walla Walla, Wash. BL/TR, 5′11.5″, 180 lbs. Deb: 4/15/42

YEAR	TM/L	G	AB	R	H	2B	3B	HR	RBI	BB	SO	AVG	OBP	SLG	PRO+	BR	/A	RC	SB	CS	SBR	FR	POS	TPR
1942	StL-A	91	158	17	47	9	2	1	13	8	13	.297	.331	.399	103	0	0	22	2	2	-1	-3	O	-0.6
1943	StL-A	29	52	4	8	0	0	0	1	8	7	.154	.267	.154	24	-5	-5	3	0	0	0	-1	O	-0.6
1944	Cin-N	64	157	14	36	3	2	0	14	14	12	.229	.297	.274	64	-8	-7	13	0			-1	O	-1.0
Total	3	184	367	35	91	12	4	1	28	30	32	.248	.307	.311	75	-12	-12	38	2	2		-4	O	-2.2

■ PAT CRISHAM
Crisham, Patrick J. b: 6/4/1877, Amesbury, Mass. d: 6/12/15, Syracuse, N.Y. 6′, 168 lbs. Deb: 5/05/1899

YEAR	TM/L	G	AB	R	H	2B	3B	HR	RBI	BB	SO	AVG	OBP	SLG	PRO+	BR	/A	RC	SB	CS	SBR	FR	POS	TPR
1899	Bal-N	53	172	23	50	5	3	0	20	4		.291	.311	.355	80	-4	-5	21	4			-5	1C	-0.7

■ JOE CRISP
Crisp, Joseph Shelby b: 7/8/1889, Higginsville, Mo. d: 2/5/39, Kansas City, Mo. BR/TR, 6′4″, 200 lbs. Deb: 9/02/10

YEAR	TM/L	G	AB	R	H	2B	3B	HR	RBI	BB	SO	AVG	OBP	SLG	PRO+	BR	/A	RC	SB	CS	SBR	FR	POS	TPR
1910	StL-A	1	1	0	0	0	0	0	0	0	0	.000	.000	.000	-99	-0	-0	0	0			0	/C	0.0
1911	StL-A	1	1	0	1	0	0	0	0	0	0	1.000	1.000	1.000	477	0	0	1	0			0	/H	0.0
Total	2	2	2	0	1	0	0	0	0	0	0	.500	.500	.500	206	0	0	1	0			0	/C	0.0

■ DODE CRISS
Criss, Dode b: 3/12/1885, Sherman, Miss. d: 9/8/55, Sherman, Miss. BL/TR, 6′2″, 200 lbs. Deb: 4/20/08

YEAR	TM/L	G	AB	R	H	2B	3B	HR	RBI	BB	SO	AVG	OBP	SLG	PRO+	BR	/A	RC	SB	CS	SBR	FR	POS	TPR
1908	StL-A	64	82	15	28	6	0	0	14	9		.341	.407	.415	169	6	6	14	1			-1	O/P1	0.7
1909	StL-A	35	48	2	14	6	1	0	7	0		.292	.306	.458	152	2	2	6	0			-1	P	0.3
1910	StL-A	70	91	11	21	4	2	1	11	11		.231	.320	.352	118	1	2	11	2			-1	1/P	0.2
1911	StL-A	58	83	10	21	3	1	2	15	11		.253	.347	.386	109	1	1	11	0			-2	1/P	0.0
Total	4	227	304	38	84	19	4	3	47	31		.276	.349	.395	133	10	11	42	3			-5	/P1O	1.2

■ CHES CRIST
Crist, Chester Arthur "Squak" b: 2/10/1882, Cozaddale, Ohio d: 1/7/57, Cincinnati, Ohio TR , 5′11″, 165 lbs. Deb: 5/18/06

YEAR	TM/L	G	AB	R	H	2B	3B	HR	RBI	BB	SO	AVG	OBP	SLG	PRO+	BR	/A	RC	SB	CS	SBR	FR	POS	TPR
1906	Phi-N	6	11	1	0	0	0	0	0	0		.000	.000	.000	-99	-2	-2	0	0			-3	/C	-0.5

■ HUGHIE CRITZ
Critz, Hugh Melville b: 9/17/1900, Starkville, Miss. d: 1/10/80, Greenwood, Miss. BR/TR, 5′8″, 147 lbs. Deb: 5/31/24

YEAR	TM/L	G	AB	R	H	2B	3B	HR	RBI	BB	SO	AVG	OBP	SLG	PRO+	BR	/A	RC	SB	CS	SBR	FR	POS	TPR
1924	Cin-N	102	413	67	133	15	14	3	35	19	18	.322	.352	.448	115	7	7	63	19	11	-1	2	2/S	0.3
1925	Cin-N	144	541	74	150	14	8	2	51	34	17	.277	.321	.344	72	-24	-22	59	13	13	-4	22	*2	-0.5
1926	Cin-N	155	607	96	164	24	14	3	79	39	25	.270	.316	.371	87	-14	-12	70	7			**24**	*2	1.9
1927	Cin-N	113	396	50	110	10	8	4	49	16	18	.278	.306	.374	84	-11	-10	44	7			-1	*2	-1.2
1928	Cin-N	153	641	95	190	21	11	5	52	37	24	.296	.335	.387	90	-12	-10	81	18			-16	*2	-2.4
1929	Cin-N	107	425	55	105	17	9	1	50	27	21	.247	.292	.336	58	-31	-27	41	9			4	*2/S	-1.8
1930	Cin-N	28	104	15	24	3	2	0	11	6	6	.231	.273	.298	40	-11	-10	8	1			-3	2	-0.8
	NY-N	124	558	93	148	17	11	4	50	24	26	.265	.296	.357	58	-40	-38	57	7			5	*2	-1.6
	Yr	152	662	108	172	20	13	4	61	30	32	.260	.292	.347	55	-50	-48	65	8			2		-2.4
1931	NY-N	66	238	33	69	7	2	4	17	8	17	.290	.313	.387	89	-5	-4	29	4			0	2	0.0
1932	NY-N	151	659	90	182	32	7	2	50	34	27	.276	.313	.355	81	-19	-17	74	3			1	*2	-0.4
1933	*NY-N	133	558	68	137	18	5	2	33	23	24	.246	.279	.306	68	-24	-23	48	4			**47**	*2	3.4
1934	NY-N	137	571	77	138	17	1	6	40	19	24	.242	.269	.306	55	-38	-36	47	3			**25**	*2	0.3
1935	NY-N	65	219	19	41	0	3	2	14	3	10	.187	.198	.242	18	-25	-25	10	2			3	2	-1.6
Total	12	1478	5930	832	1591	195	95	38	531	289	257	.268	.303	.352	74	-247	-228	631	97	24		111	*2/S	-4.4

■ DAVEY CROCKETT
Crockett, Daniel Solomon b: 10/5/1875, Roanoke, Va. d: 2/23/61, Charlottesville, Va. BL/TR, 6′1″, 175 lbs. Deb: 7/11/01

YEAR	TM/L	G	AB	R	H	2B	3B	HR	RBI	BB	SO	AVG	OBP	SLG	PRO+	BR	/A	RC	SB	CS	SBR	FR	POS	TPR
1901	Det-A	28	102	10	29	2	2	0	14	6		.284	.336	.343	87	-1	-2	13	1			-0	1	-0.2

■ ART CROFT
Croft, Arthur F. b: 1/23/1855, St.Louis, Mo. d: 3/16/1884, St.Louis, Mo. Deb: 5/04/1875

YEAR	TM/L	G	AB	R	H	2B	3B	HR	RBI	BB	SO	AVG	OBP	SLG	PRO+	BR	/A	RC	SB	CS	SBR	FR	POS	TPR
1875	RS-n	19	75	5	15	3	0	0		0		.200	.200	.240	57	-4	-2	4					O	-0.1
1877	StL-N	54	220	23	51	5	2	0	27	1	15	.232	.235	.273	63	-10	-8	14				-2	1O/2	-1.0
1878	Ind-N	60	222	22	35	6	0	0	16	5	23	.158	.176	.185	22	-19	-15	7				-2	*1/O	-1.4
Total	2	114	442	45	86	11	2	0	43	6	38	.195	.205	.229	43	-29	-23	22				-4	/1O2	-2.4

■ HARRY CROFT
Croft, Henry T. b: 8/1/1875, Chicago, Ill. d: 12/11/33, Oak Park, Ill. Deb: 5/19/1899

YEAR	TM/L	G	AB	R	H	2B	3B	HR	RBI	BB	SO	AVG	OBP	SLG	PRO+	BR	/A	RC	SB	CS	SBR	FR	POS	TPR
1899	Lou-N	2	2	0	0	0	0	0	0	0	0	.000	.000	.000	-99	-1	-1	0	0			0		0.0
	Phi-N	2	7	0	1	0	0	0	0	0	1	.143	.250	.143	11	-1	-1	0	0			-1	/2	0.0
	Yr	4	9	0	1	0	0	0	0	0	1	.111	.200	.111	-13	-1	-1	0	0			-1		0.0
1901	Chi-N	3	12	1	4	0	0	0	4	0		.333	.333	.333	99	-0	-0	1	0			2	/O	0.2
Total	2	7	21	1	5	0	0	0	4	1		.238	.273	.238	48	-1	-1	2	0			1	/O2	0.2

■ FRED CROLIUS
Crolius, Fred Joseph b: 12/16/1876, Jersey City, N.J. d: 8/25/60, Ormond Beach, Fla. Deb: 4/19/01

YEAR	TM/L	G	AB	R	H	2B	3B	HR	RBI	BB	SO	AVG	OBP	SLG	PRO+	BR	/A	RC	SB	CS	SBR	FR	POS	TPR
1901	Bos-N	49	200	22	48	4	1	1	13	9		.240	.303	.285	67	-6	-9	20	6			-7	O	-2.1
1902	Pit-N	9	38	4	10	2	1	0	7	0		.263	.263	.368	93	-0	-1	4	0			-1	/O	-0.1
Total	2	58	238	26	58	6	2	1	20	9		.244	.297	.298	70	-7	-9	24	6			-8	/O	-2.2

■ WARREN CROMARTIE
Cromartie, Warren Livingston b: 9/29/53, Miami Beach, Fla. BL/TL, 6′, 180 lbs. Deb: 9/06/74

YEAR	TM/L	G	AB	R	H	2B	3B	HR	RBI	BB	SO	AVG	OBP	SLG	PRO+	BR	/A	RC	SB	CS	SBR	FR	POS	TPR
1974	Mon-N	8	17	2	3	0	0	0	0	3	3	.176	.300	.176	34	-1	-1	1	1	0	0	-0	/O	-0.1
1976	Mon-N	33	81	8	17	1	0	0	2	1	5	.210	.220	.222	25	-8	-8	3	1	2	-1	-2	O	-1.1
1977	Mon-N	155	620	64	175	41	7	5	50	33	40	.282	.323	.395	94	-8	-6	77	10	3	1	2	*O	-0.7
1978	Mon-N	159	607	77	180	32	6	10	56	33	60	.297	.340	.418	112	8	8	82	8	8	-2	15	*O/1	1.6
1979	Mon-N	158	659	84	181	46	5	8	46	38	78	.275	.315	.396	94	-8	-7	79	8	7	-2	12	*O	-0.1
1980	Mon-N	162	597	74	172	33	5	14	70	51	64	.288	.346	.430	115	12	12	80	8	8	-2	-4	*1/O	-0.1
1981	*Mon-N	99	358	41	109	19	2	6	42	39	27	.304	.373	.419	123	12	11	55	2	3	-1	-4	1O	0.3
1982	Mon-N	144	497	59	126	24	3	14	62	69	60	.254	.348	.398	106	7	5	71	3	0	1	6	*O/1	1.1
1983	Mon-N	120	360	37	100	26	2	3	43	43	48	.278	.356	.386	106	4	4	49	8	3	1	8	*O/1	1.1
Total	9	1038	3796	446	1063	222	30	60	371	310	385	.280	.337	.402	104	16	18	497	49	34	-6	34	O1	2.0

■ NED CROMPTON
Crompton, Edward b: 2/12/1889, Liverpool, England d: 9/28/50, Aspinwall, Pa. BL/TL, 5′10.5″, 175 lbs. Deb: 9/13/09

YEAR	TM/L	G	AB	R	H	2B	3B	HR	RBI	BB	SO	AVG	OBP	SLG	PRO+	BR	/A	RC	SB	CS	SBR	FR	POS	TPR
1909	StL-A	17	63	7	10	2	1	0	2	7		.159	.254	.222	54	-3	-3	4	1			1	O	-0.2
1910	Cin-N	1	2	0	0	0	0	0	0	0	2	.000	.000	.000	-99	-1	-0	0	0			0	/O	0.0
Total	2	18	65	7	10	2	1	0	2	7	2	.154	.247	.215	49	-4	-3	4	1			1	/O	-0.2

■ HERB CROMPTON
Crompton, Herbert Bryan "Workhorse" b: 11/7/11, Taylor Ridge, Ill. d: 8/5/63, Moline, Ill. BR/TR, 6′, 185 lbs. Deb: 4/26/37

YEAR	TM/L	G	AB	R	H	2B	3B	HR	RBI	BB	SO	AVG	OBP	SLG	PRO+	BR	/A	RC	SB	CS	SBR	FR	POS	TPR
1937	Was-A	2	3	0	1	0	0	0	0	0	0	.333	.333	.333	72	-0	-0	0	0	0	0	0	/C	0.0
1945	NY-A	36	99	6	19	3	0	0	12	2	7	.192	.208	.222	24	-10	-10	4	0	0	0	1	C	-0.6
Total	2	38	102	6	20	3	0	0	12	2	7	.196	.212	.225	25	-10	-10	5	0	0	0	1	/C	-0.6

■ DAN CRONIN
Cronin, Daniel T. b: 4/1857, S.Boston, Mass. d: 11/30/1885, Boston, Mass. 5′8″, 170 lbs. Deb: 7/08/1884

YEAR	TM/L	G	AB	R	H	2B	3B	HR	RBI	BB	SO	AVG	OBP	SLG	PRO+	BR	/A	RC	SB	CS	SBR	FR	POS	TPR
1884	CP-U	1	4	1	1	0	0	0		0	0	.250	.250	.250	70	-0	-0	0				-2	/2	-0.1
	StL-U	1	5	0	0	0	0	0		0	0	.000	.000	.000	-97	-1	-1	0	0			-1	/O	-0.1
	Yr	2	9	1	1	0	0	0		0	0	.111	.111	.111	-24	-1	-1	0	0			-2		-0.2

YEAR	TM/L	G	AB	R	H	2B	3B	HR	RBI	BB	SO	AVG	OBP	SLG	PRO+	BR	/A	RC	SB	CS	SBR	FR	POS	TPR

■ JIM CRONIN
Cronin, James John b: 8/7/05, Richmond, Cal. d: 6/10/83, Concord, Cal.   BB/TR, 5'10.5", 150 lbs. Deb: 7/04/29

| 1929 | Phi-A | 25 | 56 | 7 | 13 | 2 | 1 | 0 | 4 | 5 | 7 | .232 | .295 | .304 | 52 | -4 | -4 | 5 | 0 | 0 | 0 | 5 | 2/S3 | 0.2 |

■ JOE CRONIN
Cronin, Joseph Edward b: 10/12/06, San Francisco, Cal d: 9/7/84, Osterville, Mass.   BR/TR, 5'11.5", 180 lbs. Deb: 4/29/26 MH

1926	Pit-N	38	83	9	22	2	2	0	11	6	15	.265	.315	.337	72	-3	-3	9	0			6	2/S	0.4
1927	Pit-N	12	22	2	5	1	0	0	3	2	3	.227	.292	.273	48	-1	-2	2	0			-4	/2S1	-0.5
1928	Was-A	63	227	23	55	10	4	0	25	22	27	.242	.309	.322	66	-11	-11	25	4	0	1	8	S	0.4
1929	Was-A	145	494	72	139	29	8	8	61	85	85	.281	.388	.421	107	8	8	84	5	9	-4	6	*S/2	2.2
1930	Was-A	154	587	127	203	41	9	13	126	72	36	.346	.422	.513	135	34	33	129	17	10	-1	26	*S	6.6
1931	Was-A	156	611	103	187	44	13	12	126	81	52	.306	.391	.480	127	25	25	116	10	9	-2	13	*S	4.6
1932	Was-A	143	557	95	177	43	18	6	116	66	45	.318	.393	.492	129	23	24	109	7	5	-1	6	*S	3.7
1933	*Was-A	152	602	89	186	45	11	5	118	87	49	.309	.398	.445	124	22	23	111	5	4	-1	10	*SM	4.1
1934	Was-A	127	504	68	143	30	9	7	101	53	28	.284	.353	.421	103	-1	1	78	8	0	2	18	*SM	2.9
1935	Bos-A	144	556	70	164	37	14	9	95	63	40	.295	.370	.460	106	11	5	96	3	3	-1	-13	*S/1M	-0.1
1936	Bos-A	81	295	36	83	22	4	2	43	32	21	.281	.354	.403	82	-6	-9	43	1	3	-2	-2	S3M	-0.7
1937	Bos-A	148	570	102	175	40	4	18	110	84	73	.307	.402	.486	118	21	18	116	5	3	-0	-12	*SM	1.2
1938	Bos-A	143	530	98	172	51	5	17	94	91	60	.325	.428	.536	134	35	31	126	7	5	-1	7	*SM	4.0
1939	Bos-A	143	520	97	160	33	3	19	107	87	48	.308	.407	.492	124	24	21	104	6	6	-2	6	*SM	3.6
1940	Bos-A	149	548	104	156	35	6	24	111	83	65	.285	.380	.502	122	22	18	112	7	5	-1	2	*S/3M	3.0
1941	Bos-A	143	518	98	161	38	8	16	95	82	55	.311	.406	.508	137	31	29	107	1	4	-2	-8	*S3/OM	2.3
1942	Bos-A	45	79	7	24	3	0	4	24	15	21	.304	.415	.494	150	6	6	16	0	1	-1	-0	3/1SM	0.5
1943	Bos-A	59	77	8	24	4	0	5	29	11	4	.312	.398	.558	176	7	7	17	0	0	0	3	3M	0.8
1944	Bos-A	76	191	24	46	7	0	5	28	34	19	.241	.358	.356	106	2	2	25	1	4	-2	-2	1M	-0.4
1945	Bos-A	3	8	1	3	0	0	0	1	3	2	.375	.545	.375	165	1	1	2	0	0	0	1	/3M	0.2
Total	20	2124	7579	1233	2285	515	118	170	1424	1059	700	.301	.390	.468	119	250	229	1426	87	71		70	*S/3120	38.8

■ BILL CRONIN
Cronin, William Patrick "Crungy" b: 12/26/02, W.Newton, Mass. d: 10/26/66, Newton, Mass.   BR/TR, 5'9", 167 lbs. Deb: 7/04/28

1928	Bos-N	3	2	1	0	0	0	0	0	1	0	.000	.333	.000	-6	-0	-0	0	0			-0	/C	0.0
1929	Bos-N	6	9	0	1	0	0	0	0	0	0	.111	.111	.111	-47	-2	-2	0	0			1	/C	0.0
1930	Bos-N	66	178	19	45	9	1	0	17	4	8	.253	.277	.315	44	-17	-16	15	0			8	C	-0.3
1931	Bos-N	51	107	8	22	6	1	0	10	7	5	.206	.267	.280	49	-8	-7	8	0			1	C	-0.3
Total	4	126	296	28	68	15	2	0	27	12	13	.230	.269	.294	43	-27	-25	24	0			9	C	-0.6

■ TOM CROOKE
Crooke, Thomas Aloysius b: 7/26/1884, Washington, D.C. d: 4/5/29, Quantico, Va.   BR/TR, 6', 180 lbs. Deb: 9/29/09

1909	Was-A	3	7	2	2	1	0	0	2	2		.286	.444	.429	185	1	1	2	1			-1	/1	0.0
1910	Was-A	8	21	1	4	1	0	0	1	1		.190	.227	.238	48	-1	-1	1	0			0	/1	0.0
Total	2	11	28	3	6	2	0	0	3	3		.214	.290	.286	85	-1	-0	3	1			-1	/1	0.0

■ JACK CROOKS
Crooks, John Charles b: 11/9/1865, St.Paul, Minn. d: 2/2/18, St.Louis, Mo.   BR/TR, 170 lbs. Deb: 9/26/1889 M

1889	Col-a	12	43	13	14	2	3	0	7	10	4	.326	.463	.512	190	5	6	15	10			5	2	0.9
1890	Col-a	135	485	86	107	5	4	1		96		.221	.357	.254	89	-4	1	66	57			-3	*2/3O	0.3
1891	Col-a	138	519	110	127	19	13	0	46	103	47	.245	.379	.331	113	10	15	86	50			20	*2	3.7
1892	StL-N	128	445	82	95	7	4	7	38	136	52	.213	.400	.294	119	17	20	63	23			-7	*23/OM	1.4
1893	StL-N	128	448	93	106	10	9	1	48	121	37	.237	.400	.306	93	4	3	70	31			5	*3/SC	0.8
1895	Was-N	117	409	80	114	19	8	6	57	68	39	.279	.392	.408	110	8	9	82	36			12	*2	2.2
1896	Was-N	25	84	20	24	3	0	3	20	16	8	.286	.406	.429	122	3	3	16	2			-2	2/3	0.1
	Lou-N	39	122	19	29	5	1	2	15	20	8	.238	.354	.344	90	-2	-1	18	8			4	2	0.4
	Yr	64	206	39	53	8	1	5	35	36	16	.257	.376	.379	104	2	2	34	10			2		0.5
1898	StL-N	72	225	33	52	4	2	1	20	40		.231	.359	.280	85	-1	-2	24	3			8	2/3SO	0.8
Total	8	794	2780	536	668	74	44	21	251	610	195	.240	.385	.321	104	38	55	440	220			41	23/SOC	10.6

■ ED CROSBY
Crosby, Edward Carlton b: 5/26/49, Long Beach, Cal.   BL/TR, 6'2", 175 lbs. Deb: 7/12/70

1970	StL-N	38	95	9	24	4	1	0	7	5	5	.253	.311	.316	67	-4	-4	10	0	0	0	-1	S/32	0.0
1972	StL-N	101	276	27	60	9	1	0	19	18	27	.217	.270	.257	51	-18	-17	18	1	1	-0	-6	S23	-1.6
1973	StL-N	22	39	4	5	2	1	0	1	4	4	.128	.209	.231	22	-4	-4	2	0	0	0	-3	/S23	-0.6
	*Cin-N	36	51	4	11	1	1	0	5	7	12	.216	.333	.275	74	-2	-1	5	0	1	-1	5	S/2	0.7
	Yr	58	90	8	16	3	2	0	6	11	16	.178	.282	.256	52	-6	-6	7	0	1	-1	2		0.1
1974	Cle-A	37	86	11	18	3	0	0	6	6	12	.209	.261	.244	46	-6	-6	8	0	1	-1	-10	3S/2	-1.5
1975	Cle-A	61	128	12	30	3	0	0	7	13	14	.234	.305	.258	60	-6	-6	9	0	4	-2	4	S23	0.0
1976	Cle-A	2	2	0	1	0	0	0	0	0	0	.500	.500	.500	195	0	0	1	0	0	0	1	/3D	0.1
Total	6	297	677	67	149	22	4	0	44	55	74	.220	.284	.264	55	-40	-39	50	1	7	-4	-10	S/23D	-2.9

■ FRANKIE CROSETTI
Crosetti, Frank Peter Joseph "Crow" b: 10/4/10, San Francisco, Cal.   BR/TR, 5'10", 165 lbs. Deb: 4/12/32 C

1932	*NY-A	116	398	47	96	20	9	5	57	51	51	.241	.335	.374	88	-10	-6	53	3	2	-0	-5	S3/2	-0.2
1933	NY-A	136	451	71	114	20	5	9	60	55	40	.253	.337	.379	95	-7	-3	61	4	1	1	-8	*S	0.0
1934	NY-A	138	554	85	147	22	10	11	67	61	58	.265	.344	.401	98	-8	-2	78	5	6	-2	-10	*S3/2	-0.4
1935	NY-A	87	305	49	78	17	6	8	50	41	27	.256	.351	.430	107	0	3	48	3	1	0	-7	S	0.1
1936	*NY-A	151	632	137	182	35	7	15	78	90	83	.288	.387	.437	107	4	8	113	18	7	1	-8	*S	1.0
1937	*NY-A	149	611	127	143	29	5	11	49	86	105	.234	.340	.352	74	-23	-24	79	13	7	-0	2	*S	-1.2
1938	*NY-A	157	631	113	166	35	3	9	55	106	97	.263	.382	.371	90	-7	-6	98	27	12	1	18	*S	1.9
1939	*NY-A	152	656	109	153	25	5	10	56	65	81	.233	.315	.332	67	-34	-33	71	11	7	-1	8	*S	-0.9
1940	NY-A	145	546	84	106	23	4	4	31	72	77	.194	.299	.273	52	-40	-37	47	14	8	-1	-14	*S	-3.7
1941	NY-A	50	148	13	33	2	2	1	22	18	14	.223	.320	.284	62	-8	-8	13	0	2	-1	10	S3	0.2
1942	*NY-A	74	285	50	69	5	5	4	23	31	31	.242	.335	.337	91	-3	-3	35	1	1	-0	-2	3/S2	-0.3
1943	*NY-A	95	348	36	81	8	1	2	20	36	47	.233	.317	.279	74	-10	-10	33	4	4	-1	3	S	-0.7
1944	NY-A	55	197	20	47	4	2	5	30	11	21	.239	.299	.355	84	-4	-5	20	3	0	1	-9	S	-0.9
1945	NY-A	130	441	57	105	12	0	4	48	59	65	.238	.341	.293	81	-6	-9	52	7	1	2	8	*S	-1.0
1946	NY-A	28	59	4	17	3	0	0	3	8	2	.288	.382	.339	101	1	1	8	0	3	-2	7	S	0.6
1947	NY-A	3	1	0	0	0	0	0	0	0	0	.000	.000	.000	-99	-0	-0	0	0	0	0	0	/2S	0.0
1948	NY-A	17	14	4	4	0	1	0	0	2	0	.286	.375	.429	115	0	0	3	0	0	0	0	/2S	0.1
Total	17	1683	6277	1006	1541	260	65	98	649	792	799	.245	.341	.354	84	-155	-134	812	113	62	-3	-23	*S3/2	-5.4

■ AMOS CROSS
Cross, Amos C. b: 1861, Czechoslovakia d: 7/16/1888, Cleveland, Ohio   Deb: 4/22/1885

1885	Lou-a	35	130	11	37	2	1	0		0		.285	.290	.315	94	-1	-1	12				0	C	0.3
1886	Lou-a	74	283	51	78	14	6	1		44		.276	.375	.378	131	14	11	46	13			-15	C1/SO	0.0
1887	Lou-a	8	28	0	3	0	0	0		1		.107	.138	.107	-30	-5	-5	0	0			-5	/C1O	-0.6
Total	3	117	441	62	118	16	7	1		45		.268	.338	.342	110	8	5	59	13			-19	/C1OS	-0.3

■ CLARENCE CROSS
Cross, Clarence (b: Clarence Crause) b: 3/4/1856, St.Louis, Mo. d: 6/23/31, Seattle, Wash. Deb: 5/05/1884

1884	Alt-U	2	7	1	4	1	0	0		2		.571	.667	.714	362	2	2	3	0			-2	/3	0.0
	Phi-U	2	9	0	2	0	0	0		0		.222	.222	.222	55	-0	-0	0	0			-2	/S	-0.1
	KC-U	25	93	13	20	1	0	0		6		.215	.263	.226	76	-3	-1	6	0			3	S/3	0.2
	Yr	29	109	14	26	2	0	0		8		.239	.291	.257	98	-1	1	8	0			-1		0.1
1887	NY-a	16	55	9	11	2	1	0		2		.200	.267	.273	55	-3	-3	4	0			-3	S/3	-0.5

YEAR	TM/L	G	AB	R	H	2B	3B	HR	RBI	BB	SO	AVG	OBP	SLG	PRO+	BR	/A	RC	SB	CS	SBR	FR	POS	TPR
Total	2	45	164	23	37	4	1	0		10		.226	.282	.262	81	-5	-2	14	0			-4	/S3	-0.4

■ **FRANK CROSS**   Cross, Frank Atwell "Mickey" b: 1/20/1873, Cleveland, Ohio d: 11/2/32, Geauga Lake, Ohio TR , Deb: 5/20/01

YEAR	TM/L	G	AB	R	H	2B	3B	HR	RBI	BB	SO	AVG	OBP	SLG	PRO+	BR	/A	RC	SB	CS	SBR	FR	POS	TPR
1901	Cle-A	1	5	0	3	0	0	0	0	0	0	.600	.600	.600	247	1	1	2	0			-0	/O	0.0

■ **JEFF CROSS**   Cross, Joffre James b: 8/28/18, Tulsa, Okla. BR/TR, 5'11", 160 lbs. Deb: 9/27/42

YEAR	TM/L	G	AB	R	H	2B	3B	HR	RBI	BB	SO	AVG	OBP	SLG	PRO+	BR	/A	RC	SB	CS	SBR	FR	POS	TPR
1942	StL-N	1	4	0	1	0	0	0	1	0	0	.250	.250	.250	43	-0	-0	0	0			-0	/S	0.0
1946	StL-N	49	69	17	15	3	0	0	6	10	8	.217	.316	.261	62	-3	-3	6	4			6	S/23	0.4
1947	StL-N	51	49	4	5	1	0	0	3	10	6	.102	.254	.122	3	-7	-7	2	0			5	3S/2	0.0
1948	StL-N	2	0	0	0	0	0	0	0	0	0	—	—	—	—	0	0	0	0			0	R	0.0
	Chi-N	16	20	1	2	0	0	0	0	0	4	.100	.100	.100	-48	-4	-4	0	0			-4	/S2	-0.6
	Yr	18	20	1	2	0	0	0	0	0	4	.100	.100	.100	-47	-4	-4	0	0			-4		-0.6
Total	4	119	142	22	23	4	0	0	10	20	18	.162	.265	.190	26	-14	-15	9	4			7	/S32	-0.2

■ **LAVE CROSS**   Cross, Lafayette Napoleon b: 5/12/1866, Milwaukee, Wis. d: 9/6/27, Toledo, Ohio BR/TR, 5'8.5", 155 lbs. Deb: 4/23/1887 M

YEAR	TM/L	G	AB	R	H	2B	3B	HR	RBI	BB	SO	AVG	OBP	SLG	PRO+	BR	/A	RC	SB	CS	SBR	FR	POS	TPR
1887	Lou-a	54	203	32	54	8	3	0		15		.266	.320	.335	83	-4	-5	27	15			0	CO	0.2
1888	Lou-a	47	181	20	41	3	0	0	15	2		.227	.239	.243	58	-9	-8	13	10			-1	CO/S	-0.4
1889	Phi-a	55	199	22	44	8	2	0	23	14	9	.221	.272	.281	60	-11	-10	19	11			16	C	1.0
1890	Phi-P	63	245	42	73	7	8	3	47	12	6	.298	.331	.429	101	0	-1	37	5			-0	CO	0.0
1891	Phi-a	110	402	66	121	20	14	5	52	38	23	.301	.366	.458	134	18	16	74	14			-5	OC3/S2	1.0
1892	Phi-N	140	541	84	149	15	10	4	69	39	16	.275	.328	.362	111	6	6	72	18			-3	3CO2/S	0.9
1893	Phi-N	96	415	81	124	17	6	4	78	26	7	.299	.342	.398	98	-2	-2	64	18			14	C3OS/1	1.3
1894	Phi-N	119	529	123	204	34	9	7	125	29	7	.386	.421	.524	132	24	26	128	21			22	*3C/S2	3.7
1895	Phi-N	125	535	95	145	26	9	2	101	35	8	.271	.319	.364	77	-18	-19	71	21			33	*3	1.3
1896	Phi-N	106	406	63	104	23	5	1	73	32	14	.256	.312	.345	76	-15	-14	47	8			14	3S/2OC	0.3
1897	Phi-N	88	344	37	89	17	5	3	51	10		.259	.282	.363	73	-15	-14	39	10			3	32/OS	-0.6
1898	StL-N	151	602	71	191	28	8	3	79	28		.317	.348	.405	116	12	10	92	14			18	*3/S	3.0
1899	Cle-N	38	154	15	44	5	0	1	20	8		.286	.325	.338	91	-3	-2	18	2			4	3M	0.2
	StL-N	103	403	61	122	14	5	4	64	17		.303	.333	.392	99	-1	-2	58	11			29	*3	2.4
	Yr	141	557	76	166	19	5	5	84	25		.298	.330	.377	97	-4	-4	76	13			33		2.6
1900	StL-N	16	61	6	18	1	0	0	6	1		.295	.306	.311	73	-2	-2	6	1			1	3	0.0
	*Bro-N	117	461	73	135	14	6	4	67	25		.293	.331	.375	91	-2	-7	65	20			2	*3	-0.2
	Yr	133	522	79	153	15	6	4	73	26		.293	.328	.368	89	-5	-9	72	21			4		-0.2
1901	Phi-A	100	424	82	139	28	12	2	73	19		.328	.358	.465	124	15	12	81	23			5	*3	1.4
1902	Phi-A	137	559	90	191	39	8	0	108	27		.342	.374	.440	122	19	16	105	25			7	*3	1.8
1903	Phi-A	137	559	60	163	22	4	2	90	10		.292	.304	.356	95	-1	-4	67	14			-3	*3/1	-0.8
1904	Phi-A	155	607	73	176	31	10	1	71	13		.290	.305	.379	112	10	7	76	10			-10	*3	0.3
1905	*Phi-A	147	587	69	156	29	5	0	77	26		.266	.297	.332	100	-0	-1	64	8			-9	*3	-0.4
1906	Was-A	130	494	55	130	14	6	1	46	28		.263	.303	.322	102	-2	1	57	19			-4	*3	0.7
1907	Was-A	41	161	13	32	8	0	0	10	10		.199	.246	.248	64	-7	-6	11	3			7	3	0.4
Total	21	2275	9072	1333	2645	411	135	47	1345	464	90	.292	.328	.382	101	11	-1	1293	301			143	*3CO/S21	17.5

■ **MONTE CROSS**   Cross, Montford Montgomery b: 8/31/1869, Philadelphia, Pa. d: 6/21/34, Philadelphia, Pa. BR/TR, 6'2", 180 lbs. Deb: 9/27/1892 U

YEAR	TM/L	G	AB	R	H	2B	3B	HR	RBI	BB	SO	AVG	OBP	SLG	PRO+	BR	/A	RC	SB	CS	SBR	FR	POS	TPR
1892	Bal-N	15	50	5	8	0	0	0	2	4	10	.160	.222	.160	17	-5	-5	2	2			-3	S	-0.6
1894	Pit-N	13	43	14	19	1	5	2	13	5	4	.442	.520	.837	227	9	9	22	6			2	S	0.9
1895	Pit-N	108	393	67	101	14	13	3	54	38	38	.257	.327	.382	89	-10	-6	63	39			-13	*S/2	-0.7
1896	StL-N	125	427	66	104	10	6	6	52	58	48	.244	.342	.337	85	-10	-7	65	40			-11	*S	-1.5
1897	StL-N	131	462	59	132	17	11	4	55	62		.286	.379	.396	109	6	8	86	38			28	*S	3.3
1898	Phi-N	149	525	68	135	25	5	1	50	55		.257	.337	.330	98	-3	1	67	20			14	*S	2.0
1899	Phi-N	154	557	85	143	25	6	3	65	56		.257	.335	.339	91	-8	-5	74	26			2	*S	0.5
1900	Phi-N	131	466	59	94	11	3	0	62	51		.202	.289	.258	54	-28	-27	41	19			-2	*S	-1.4
1901	Phi-N	139	483	49	95	14	1	1	44	52		.197	.281	.236	52	-27	-28	41	24			-16	*S	-3.6
1902	Phi-A	137	497	72	115	22	2	3	59	32		.231	.289	.302	63	-23	-26	52	17			11	*S	-0.2
1903	Phi-A	137	470	44	116	21	2	3	45	49		.247	.318	.319	89	-2	-5	60	31			8	*S/2	1.0
1904	Phi-A	153	503	33	95	23	4	1	38	46		.189	.257	.256	61	-19	-22	41	19			-16	*S	-4.1
1905	*Phi-A	79	252	28	67	17	2	0	24	19		.266	.317	.349	112	4	3	34	8			-5	S/2	0.1
1906	Phi-A	134	445	32	89	23	3	1	40	50		.200	.281	.272	73	-12	-13	44	22			4	*S	-0.7
1907	Phi-A	77	248	37	51	9	5	0	18	39		.206	.314	.282	90	-1	-1	30	17			13	S	1.4
Total	15	1682	5821	718	1364	232	68	31	621	616	100	.234	.313	.314	81	-128	-125	722	328			16	*S/2	-3.6

■ **FRANK CROSSIN**   Crossin, Frank Patrick b: 6/15/1891, Avondale, Pa. d: 12/6/65, Kingston, Pa. BR/TR, 5'10", 160 lbs. Deb: 9/24/12

YEAR	TM/L	G	AB	R	H	2B	3B	HR	RBI	BB	SO	AVG	OBP	SLG	PRO+	BR	/A	RC	SB	CS	SBR	FR	POS	TPR
1912	StL-A	8	22	2	5	0	0	0	2	1		.227	.261	.227	41	-2	-2	1	1			-5	/C	-0.5
1913	StL-A	4	4	1	1	0	0	0	0	1	1	.250	.500	.250	124	0	0	1	0			-1	/C	0.0
1914	StL-A	43	90	5	11	1	1	0	5	10	10	.122	.225	.156	15	-9	-9	4	3			-1	C	-0.6
Total	3	55	116	8	17	1	1	0	7	12	11	.147	.244	.172	25	-11	-10	6	4			-6	/C	-1.1

■ **JOE CROTTY**   Crotty, Joseph P. b: 12/24/1860, Cincinnati, O. d: 6/22/26, Minneapolis, Minn BR , Deb: 5/04/1882

YEAR	TM/L	G	AB	R	H	2B	3B	HR	RBI	BB	SO	AVG	OBP	SLG	PRO+	BR	/A	RC	SB	CS	SBR	FR	POS	TPR
1882	Lou-a	5	20	1	2	0	0	0		0		.100	.100	.100	-34	-3	-2	0				-0	/C	-0.2
	StL-a	8	28	2	4	1	0	0		3		.143	.226	.179	37	-2	-2	1				-1	/CO	-0.2
	Yr	13	48	3	6	1	0	0		3		.125	.176	.146	10	-4	-4	1				-1		-0.4
1884	Cin-U	21	84	11	22	4	2	1		1		.262	.271	.393	113	2	1	9	0			-8	C	-0.5
1885	Lou-a	39	129	14	20	2	0	0		3		.155	.193	.171	17	-12	-12	4				5	C/1	0.0
1886	NY-a	14	47	6	8	0	1	0		4		.170	.250	.213	49	-3	-2	3	3			-2	C	-0.2
Total	4	87	308	34	56	7	3	1		11		.182	.220	.234	48	-17	-18	18	3			-7	/C1O	-1.1

■ **JACK CROUCH**   Crouch, Jack Albert "Roxy" b: 6/12/03, Salisbury, N.C. d: 8/25/72, Leesburg, Fla. BR/TR, 5'9", 165 lbs. Deb: 9/18/30

YEAR	TM/L	G	AB	R	H	2B	3B	HR	RBI	BB	SO	AVG	OBP	SLG	PRO+	BR	/A	RC	SB	CS	SBR	FR	POS	TPR
1930	StL-A	6	14	1	2	1	0	0	1	1	3	.143	.200	.214	5	-2	-2	1	0	0	0	1	/C	0.0
1931	StL-A	8	12	0	0	0	0	0	1	0	4	.000	.000	.000	-97	-3	-4	0	0	0	0	1	/C	-0.1
1933	StL-A	19	30	1	5	0	0	1	5	2	6	.167	.219	.267	26	-3	-3	2	0	0	0	-0	/C	-0.2
	Cin-N	10	16	5	2	0	0	0	1	0	0	.125	.222	.125	1	-2	-2	1	1			2	/C	0.0
Total	3	43	72	7	9	1	0	1	8	3	13	.125	.182	.181	-3	-11	-11	3	1	0		3	/C	-0.3

■ **FRANK CROUCHER**   Croucher, Frank Donald "Dingle" b: 7/23/14, San Antonio, Tex. d: 5/21/80, Houston, Tex. BR/TR, 5'11", 165 lbs. Deb: 4/18/39

YEAR	TM/L	G	AB	R	H	2B	3B	HR	RBI	BB	SO	AVG	OBP	SLG	PRO+	BR	/A	RC	SB	CS	SBR	FR	POS	TPR
1939	Det-A	97	324	38	87	15	0	5	40	16	42	.269	.303	.361	64	-16	-19	33	2	2	-1	-8	S/2	-1.6
1940	*Det-A	37	57	3	6	0	0	0	2	4	5	.105	.164	.105	-26	-11	-12	1	0	0	0	-2	S/23	-1.0
1941	Det-A	136	489	51	124	21	4	2	39	33	72	.254	.305	.325	61	-24	-30	50	2	0	1	-3	*S	-2.8
1942	Was-A	26	65	2	18	1	1	0	5	3	9	.277	.309	.323	79	-2	-2	6	0	0	0	5	2	0.4
Total	4	296	935	94	235	37	5	7	86	56	128	.251	.296	.324	58	-52	-63	90	4	2	0	-8	S/23	-5.0

■ **BUCK CROUSE**   Crouse, Clyde Elsworth b: 1/6/1897, Anderson, Ind. d: 10/23/83, Muncie, Ind. BL/TR, 5'8", 158 lbs. Deb: 8/01/23

YEAR	TM/L	G	AB	R	H	2B	3B	HR	RBI	BB	SO	AVG	OBP	SLG	PRO+	BR	/A	RC	SB	CS	SBR	FR	POS	TPR
1923	Chi-A	23	70	6	18	2	1	1	7	3	4	.257	.297	.357	73	-3	-3	7	0	0	0	-2	C	-0.3
1924	Chi-A	94	305	30	79	10	1	1	44	26	12	.259	.319	.308	64	-16	-16	32	3	2	-0	1	C	-0.8
1925	Chi-A	54	131	18	46	7	0	2	25	12	4	.351	.410	.450	125	4	5	24	1	2	-1	-3	C	0.4
1926	Chi-A	49	135	10	32	4	1	0	17	14	7	.237	.309	.281	57	-9	-8	13	0	0	0	3	C	-0.2
1927	Chi-A	85	222	22	53	11	0	0	20	21	10	.239	.307	.288	57	-14	-14	20	4	1	1	7	C	-0.2

YEAR	TM/L	G	AB	R	H	2B	3B	HR	RBI	BB	SO	AVG	OBP	SLG	PRO+	BR	/A	RC	SB	CS	SBR	FR	POS	TPR
1928	Chi-A	78	218	17	55	5	2	2	20	19	14	.252	.315	.321	68	-10	-10	22	3	4	-2	-2	C	-0.7
1929	Chi-A	45	107	11	29	7	0	2	12	5	7	.271	.316	.393	82	-3	-3	14	2	0	1	6	C	0.7
1930	Chi-A	42	118	14	30	8	1	0	15	17	10	.254	.348	.339	78	-4	-3	15	1	1	-0	7	C	0.6
Total	8	470	1306	128	342	54	6	8	160	114	68	.262	.326	.331	72	-57	-52	146	14	10	-2	17	C	-0.5

■ DON CROW
Crow, Donald Le Roy   b: 8/18/58, Yakima, Wash.   BR/TR, 6'4", 200 lbs.   Deb: 7/25/82

YEAR	TM/L	G	AB	R	H	2B	3B	HR	RBI	BB	SO	AVG	OBP	SLG	PRO+	BR	/A	RC	SB	CS	SBR	FR	POS	TPR
1982	LA-N	4	4	0	0	0	0	0	0	0	3	.000	.000	.000	-99	-1	-1	0	0	0	0	1	/C	0.0

■ GEORGE CROWE
Crowe, George Daniel "Big George"   b: 3/22/23, Whiteland, Ind.   BL/TL, 6'2", 210 lbs.   Deb: 4/16/52

YEAR	TM/L	G	AB	R	H	2B	3B	HR	RBI	BB	SO	AVG	OBP	SLG	PRO+	BR	/A	RC	SB	CS	SBR	FR	POS	TPR
1952	Bos-N	73	217	25	56	13	1	4	20	18	25	.258	.329	.382	100	-1	-0	28	0	1	-1	2	1	0.0
1953	Mil-N	47	42	6	12	2	0	2	6	2	7	.286	.333	.476	115	0	1	7	0	0	0	0	/1	0.1
1955	Mil-N	104	303	41	85	12	4	15	55	45	44	.281	.375	.495	135	13	15	59	1	0	0	2	1	1.1
1956	Cin-N	77	144	22	36	2	1	10	23	11	28	.250	.312	.486	104	2	0	22	0	0	0	2	1	0.1
1957	Cin-N	133	494	71	134	20	1	31	92	32	62	.271	.317	.504	108	9	5	77	1	1	-0	-1	*1	-0.7
1958	Cin-N	111	345	31	95	12	5	7	61	41	51	.275	.352	.400	94	-0	-2	50	1	0	0	-2	1/2	-1.0
1959	StL-N	77	103	14	31	6	0	8	29	5	12	.301	.333	.592	132	5	4	18	0	0	0	2	1	0.6
1960	StL-N	73	72	5	17	3	0	4	13	5	16	.236	.286	.444	89	-1	-1	8	0	0	0	0	/1	-0.1
1961	StL-N	7	7	0	1	0	0	0	0	0	1	.143	.143	.143	-22	-1	-1	0	0	0	0	0	H	0.0
Total	9	702	1727	215	467	70	12	81	299	159	246	.270	.335	.466	109	26	20	269	3	2	-0	4	1/2	0.1

■ ED CROWLEY
Crowley, Edgar Jewel   b: 8/20/06, Watkinsville, Ga.   d: 4/14/70, Birmingham, Ala.   BR/TR, 6'1", 180 lbs.   Deb: 6/21/28

YEAR	TM/L	G	AB	R	H	2B	3B	HR	RBI	BB	SO	AVG	OBP	SLG	PRO+	BR	/A	RC	SB	CS	SBR	FR	POS	TPR
1928	Was-A	2	1	0	0	0	0	0	0	0	0	.000	.000	.000	-99	-0	-0	0	0	0	0	-0	/3	0.0

■ JOHN CROWLEY
Crowley, John A.   b: 1/12/1862, Lawrence, Mass.   d: 9/23/1896, Lawrence, Mass.   5'10", 164 lbs.   Deb: 5/01/1884

YEAR	TM/L	G	AB	R	H	2B	3B	HR	RBI	BB	SO	AVG	OBP	SLG	PRO+	BR	/A	RC	SB	CS	SBR	FR	POS	TPR
1884	Phi-N	48	168	26	41	7	3	0	19	15	21	.244	.306	.321	102	-0	1	17				-20	C	-1.3

■ TERRY CROWLEY
Crowley, Terrence Michael   b: 2/16/47, Staten Island, N.Y.   BL/TL, 6', 180 lbs.   Deb: 9/04/69   C

YEAR	TM/L	G	AB	R	H	2B	3B	HR	RBI	BB	SO	AVG	OBP	SLG	PRO+	BR	/A	RC	SB	CS	SBR	FR	POS	TPR
1969	Bal-A	7	18	2	6	0	0	0	3	1	4	.333	.368	.333	97	-0	-0	2	0	0	0	0	/1O	0.0
1970	*Bal-A	83	152	25	39	5	0	5	20	35	26	.257	.396	.388	116	5	5	25	2	0	1	-4	O1	0.0
1971	Bal-A	18	23	2	4	0	0	0	1	3	4	.174	.269	.174	28	-2	-2	1	0	0	0	-1	/O1	-0.2
1972	Bal-A	97	247	30	57	10	0	11	29	32	26	.231	.321	.405	112	5	4	32	0	0	0	-5	O1	-0.4
1973	*Bal-A	54	131	16	27	4	0	3	15	16	14	.206	.297	.305	71	-5	-5	12	0	0	0	1	DO/1	-0.4
1974	Cin-N	84	125	11	30	12	0	1	20	10	16	.240	.301	.360	86	-3	-3	13	1	0	0	-1	O1	-0.3
1975	*Cin-N	66	71	8	19	6	0	1	11	7	6	.268	.333	.394	100	0	-0	8	0	0	0	2	/1O	0.1
1976	Atl-N	7	6	0	0	0	0	0	1	0	0	.000	.000	.000	-94	-2	-2	-0	0	0	0	0	H	-0.1
	Bal-A	33	61	5	15	1	0	0	5	7	11	.246	.333	.262	81	-2	-1	6	0	0	0	1	D1	0.0
1977	Bal-A	18	22	3	8	1	0	1	9	1	3	.364	.391	.545	162	2	2	5	0	0	0	0	/1D	0.2
1978	Bal-A	62	95	9	24	2	0	0	12	8	12	.253	.317	.274	72	-4	-3	8	0	0	0	1	D/O1	-0.2
1979	*Bal-A	61	63	8	20	5	1	1	8	14	13	.317	.449	.476	155	5	6	14	0	0	0	0	D/1	0.5
1980	Bal-A	92	233	33	67	8	0	12	50	29	21	.288	.366	.476	130	9	10	40	0	0	0	1	D/1	1.1
1981	Bal-A	68	134	12	33	6	0	4	25	29	12	.246	.380	.381	120	5	5	21	0	0	0	0	D/1	0.5
1982	Bal-A	65	93	8	22	2	0	3	17	21	9	.237	.377	.355	103	1	1	13	0	0	0	0	D1	0.1
1983	Mon-N	50	44	2	8	0	0	0	3	9	4	.182	.333	.182	47	-3	-3	3	0	0	0	-1	/1	-0.3
Total	15	865	1518	174	379	62	1	42	229	222	181	.250	.348	.375	104	12	13	202	3	0	1	-5	DO/1	0.6

■ BILL CROWLEY
Crowley, William Michael   b: 4/8/1857, Philadelphia, Pa.   d: 7/14/1891, Gloucester, N.J.   BR/TR, 5'7.5", 159 lbs.   Deb: 4/26/1875

YEAR	TM/L	G	AB	R	H	2B	3B	HR	RBI	BB	SO	AVG	OBP	SLG	PRO+	BR	/A	RC	SB	CS	SBR	FR	POS	TPR
1875	Phi-n	9	37	4	3	0	0	0			1	.081	.105	.081	-33	-5	-5	0					/O312	-0.3
1877	Lou-N	61	238	30	67	9	3	1	23	4	13	.282	.293	.357	88	1	-5	26				7	*O/SC32	0.0
1879	Buf-N	60	261	41	75	9	5	0	30	6	14	.287	.303	.360	115	5	4	29				-3	OC/12	0.0
1880	Buf-N	85	354	57	95	16	4	0	20	19	23	.268	.306	.336	115	7	6	37				1	*OC	0.6
1881	Bos-N	72	279	33	71	12	0	0	31	14	15	.254	.290	.297	89	-4	-3	25				-4	*O	-0.6
1883	Phi-a	23	96	16	24	4	3	0			3	.250	.273	.354	92	-0	-1	10				-2	O/1	-0.2
	Cle-N	11	41	3	12	5	0	0	5	1	7	.293	.310	.415	119	1	1	5				-3	O	0.0
1884	Bos-N	108	407	50	110	14	6	6	61	33	74	.270	.325	.378	121	10	10	51				-5	*O	0.4
1885	Buf-N	92	344	29	83	14	1	1	36	21	32	.241	.285	.297	86	-4	-6	30				-4	*O	-1.0
Total	7	512	2020	259	537	83	22	8	206	101	178	.266	.301	.341	103	14	6	213				-12	O/C12S3	-0.8

■ WALTON CRUISE
Cruise, Walton Edwin   b: 5/6/1890, Childersburg, Ala.   d: 1/9/75, Sylacauga, Ala.   BL/TR, 6', 175 lbs.   Deb: 4/14/14

YEAR	TM/L	G	AB	R	H	2B	3B	HR	RBI	BB	SO	AVG	OBP	SLG	PRO+	BR	/A	RC	SB	CS	SBR	FR	POS	TPR
1914	StL-N	95	256	20	58	9	3	4	28	25	42	.227	.303	.332	90	-4	-3	26	3			1	O	-0.4
1916	StL-N	3	3	0	2	0	0	0	0	1	0	.667	.750	.667	339	1	1	2	0			0	/O	0.1
1917	StL-N	153	529	70	156	20	10	5	59	38	73	.295	.343	.399	131	16	18	76	16			-4	*O	1.1
1918	StL-N	70	240	34	65	5	4	6	39	30	26	.271	.359	.400	136	10	11	35	2			-9	O	-0.1
1919	StL-N	9	21	0	2	1	0	0	0	1	6	.095	.136	.143	-17	-3	-3	0	0			-1	/O1	-0.4
	Bos-N	73	241	23	52	7	0	1	21	17	29	.216	.267	.257	61	-12	-11	18	8			-3	O	-1.8
	Yr	82	262	23	54	8	0	1	21	18	35	.206	.257	.248	55	-15	-14	18	8			-4		-2.2
1920	Bos-N	91	288	40	80	7	5	3	21	31	26	.278	.352	.347	106	1	3	37	5	3	-0	-9	O	-1.1
1921	Bos-N	108	344	47	119	16	7	8	55	48	24	.346	.429	.503	154	24	27	75	10	8	-2	-6	*O/1	1.4
1922	Bos-N	104	352	51	98	15	10	4	46	44	20	.278	.360	.412	103	-0	2	54	4	4	-1	-2	O/1	-0.4
1923	Bos-N	21	38	4	8	2	0	0	0	3	2	.211	.268	.263	42	-3	-3	3	1	0	0	0	/O	-0.2
1924	Bos-N	9	9	4	4	1	0	1	3	0	2	.444	.444	.889	260	2	2	3	0	0	0	0	H	0.2
Total	10	736	2321	293	644	83	39	30	272	238	250	.277	.348	.386	114	32	43	329	49	15		-31	O/1	-1.6

■ GENE CRUMLING
Crumling, Eugene Leon   b: 4/5/22, Wrightsville, Pa.   BR/TR, 6', 180 lbs.   Deb: 9/11/45

YEAR	TM/L	G	AB	R	H	2B	3B	HR	RBI	BB	SO	AVG	OBP	SLG	PRO+	BR	/A	RC	SB	CS	SBR	FR	POS	TPR
1945	StL-N	6	12	0	1	0	0	0	1	0	1	.083	.083	.083	-52	-2	-2	0	0			2	/C	0.0

■ BUDDY CRUMP
Crump, Arthur Elliott   b: 11/29/01, Norfolk, Va.   d: 9/7/76, Raleigh, N.C.   BL/TL, 5'10", 156 lbs.   Deb: 9/28/24

YEAR	TM/L	G	AB	R	H	2B	3B	HR	RBI	BB	SO	AVG	OBP	SLG	PRO+	BR	/A	RC	SB	CS	SBR	FR	POS	TPR
1924	NY-N	1	4	0	0	0	0	0	1	0	1	.000	.000	.000	-99	-1	-1	0	0	0	0	-1	/O	-0.1

■ PRESS CRUTHERS
Cruthers, Charles Preston   b: 9/8/1890, Marshallton, Del.   d: 12/27/76, Kenosha, Wis.   BR/TR, 5'9", 152 lbs.   Deb: 9/29/13

YEAR	TM/L	G	AB	R	H	2B	3B	HR	RBI	BB	SO	AVG	OBP	SLG	PRO+	BR	/A	RC	SB	CS	SBR	FR	POS	TPR
1913	Phi-A	3	12	0	3	1	0	0	0	0	0	.250	.250	.333	72	-1	-0	1	0			-2	/2	-0.3
1914	Phi-A	4	15	1	3	0	1	0	0	0	4	.200	.200	.333	62	-1	-1	1	0	1	-1	2	/2	0.0
Total	2	7	27	1	6	1	1	0	0	0	4	.222	.222	.333	67	-1	-1	2	0	1		-1	/2	-0.3

■ TOMMY CRUZ
Cruz, Cirilo (Dilan)   b: 2/15/51, Arroyo, P.R.   BL/TL, 5'9", 165 lbs.   Deb: 9/04/73

YEAR	TM/L	G	AB	R	H	2B	3B	HR	RBI	BB	SO	AVG	OBP	SLG	PRO+	BR	/A	RC	SB	CS	SBR	FR	POS	TPR
1973	StL-N	3	0	0	0	0	0	0	0	0	0	—	—	—	—	0	0	0	0	0	0	0	/O	0.0
1977	Chi-A	4	2	1	0	0	0	0	0	0	0	.000	.000	.000	-99	-1	-1	0	0	0	0	0	/O	0.0
Total	2	7	2	1	0	0	0	0	0	0	0	.000	.000	.000	-99	-1	-1	0	0	0	0	0	/O	0.0

■ HECTOR CRUZ
Cruz, Hector Louis (Dilan) "Heity"   b: 4/2/53, Arroyo, P.R.   BR/TR, 5'11", 170 lbs.   Deb: 8/11/73

YEAR	TM/L	G	AB	R	H	2B	3B	HR	RBI	BB	SO	AVG	OBP	SLG	PRO+	BR	/A	RC	SB	CS	SBR	FR	POS	TPR
1973	StL-N	11	11	1	0	0	0	0	0	1	3	.000	.083	.000	-75	-3	-3	0	0	0	0	1	/O	-0.1
1975	StL-N	23	48	7	7	2	2	0	6	6	4	.146	.180	.271	23	-5	-5	2	0	0	0	-2	3/O	-0.7
1976	StL-N	151	526	54	120	17	1	13	71	42	119	.228	.288	.338	77	-17	-17	50	1	0	0	-21	*3	-4.2
1977	StL-N	118	339	50	80	19	2	6	42	46	56	.236	.329	.357	85	-7	-6	41	4	3	-1	-6	*O/3	-1.6
1978	Chi-N	30	76	8	18	5	0	2	9	3	6	.237	.266	.382	70	-2	-3	6	0	0	0	1	O/3	-0.2
	SF-N	79	197	19	44	8	1	6	24	21	39	.223	.301	.365	89	-4	-3	20	0	2	-1	-1	O3	-0.6
	Yr	109	273	27	62	13	1	8	33	24	45	.227	.292	.370	83	-7	-7	27	0	2	-1	1		-0.8

YEAR	TM/L	G	AB	R	H	2B	3B	HR	RBI	BB	SO	AVG	OBP	SLG	PRO+	BR	/A	RC	SB	CS	SBR	FR	POS	TPR
1979	SF-N	16	25	2	3	0	0	0	1	3	7	.120	.214	.120	-7	-4	-3	1	0	0	0	-1	/O3	-0.4
	*Cin-N	74	182	24	44	10	2	4	27	31	39	.242	.352	.385	100	1	1	24	0	1	-1	6	O	0.4
	Yr	90	207	26	47	10	2	4	28	34	46	.227	.336	.353	89	-3	-3	24	0	1	-1	5		0.0
1980	Cin-N	52	75	5	16	4	1	1	5	8	16	.213	.289	.333	73	-3	-3	7	0	0	0	1	O	-0.2
1981	Chi-N	53	109	15	25	5	0	7	15	17	24	.229	.333	.468	120	3	3	17	2	2	-1	-4	3O	-0.2
1982	Chi-N	17	19	1	4	1	0	0	0	2	4	.211	.286	.263	53	-1	-1	1	0	0	0	-1	/O	-0.1
Total	9	624	1607	186	361	71	9	39	200	176	317	.225	.303	.353	81	-41	-42	170	7	8	-3	-26	O3	-7.9

■ HENRY CRUZ
Cruz, Henry (Acosta)   b: 2/27/52, Christiansted, V.I.   BL/TL, 6', 175 lbs.   Deb: 4/18/75

YEAR	TM/L	G	AB	R	H	2B	3B	HR	RBI	BB	SO	AVG	OBP	SLG	PRO+	BR	/A	RC	SB	CS	SBR	FR	POS	TPR
1975	LA-N	53	94	8	25	3	1	0	5	7	6	.266	.317	.319	80	-3	-2	10	1	1	-0	-1	O	-0.4
1976	LA-N	49	88	8	16	2	1	4	14	9	11	.182	.258	.364	76	-3	-3	8	0	2	-1	-0	O	-0.5
1977	Chi-A	16	21	3	6	0	0	2	5	1	3	.286	.318	.571	137	1	1	4	0	0	0	-1	/O	0.0
1978	Chi-A	53	77	13	17	2	1	2	10	8	11	.221	.302	.351	82	-2	-2	8	0	1	-1	5	O/D	0.2
Total	4	171	280	32	64	7	3	8	34	25	31	.229	.294	.361	84	-7	-6	29	1	4	-2	4	O/D	-0.7

■ JOSE CRUZ
Cruz, Jose (Dilan)   b: 8/8/47, Arroyo, P.R.   BL/TL, 6', 170 lbs.   Deb: 9/19/70

YEAR	TM/L	G	AB	R	H	2B	3B	HR	RBI	BB	SO	AVG	OBP	SLG	PRO+	BR	/A	RC	SB	CS	SBR	FR	POS	TPR
1970	StL-N	6	17	2	6	1	0	0	1	4	0	.353	.500	.412	144	2	2	4	0	0	0	1	/O	0.2
1971	StL-N	83	292	46	80	13	2	9	27	49	35	.274	.380	.425	123	12	11	49	6	3	0	-1	O	0.7
1972	StL-N	117	332	33	78	14	4	2	23	36	54	.235	.312	.319	81	-8	-8	35	9	3	1	-1	*O	-1.3
1973	StL-N	132	406	51	92	22	5	10	57	51	66	.227	.314	.379	92	-5	-5	50	10	4	1	-4	*O	-1.3
1974	StL-N	107	161	24	42	4	3	5	20	20	27	.261	.343	.416	112	2	3	23	4	2	0	2	O/1	0.3
1975	Hou-N	120	315	44	81	15	2	9	49	52	44	.257	.364	.403	121	6	9	49	6	3	0	2	O	0.9
1976	Hou-N	133	439	49	133	21	5	4	61	53	46	.303	.378	.431	133	13	18	70	28	11	2	6	*O	2.2
1977	Hou-N	157	579	87	173	31	10	17	87	69	67	.299	.373	.475	138	21	28	104	44	23	-1	2	*O	2.5
1978	Hou-N	153	565	79	178	34	9	10	83	57	57	.315	.378	.460	144	25	30	102	37	9	6	-1	*O/1	3.0
1979	Hou-N	157	558	73	161	33	7	9	72	72	66	.289	.370	.421	122	13	17	91	36	14	2	1	*O	1.6
1980	*Hou-N	160	612	79	185	29	7	11	91	60	66	.302	.365	.426	130	17	22	97	36	11	4	6	*O	2.8
1981	*Hou-N	107	409	53	109	16	5	13	55	35	49	.267	.324	.425	117	5	7	54	5	7	-3	5	*O	0.7
1982	Hou-N	155	570	62	157	27	2	9	68	60	67	.275	.345	.377	110	2	8	75	21	11	-0	9	*O	1.5
1983	Hou-N	160	594	85	**189**	28	8	14	92	65	86	.318	.386	.463	143	28	33	109	30	16	-1	3	*O	3.3
1984	Hou-N	160	600	96	187	28	13	12	95	73	68	.312	.386	.462	148	31	36	111	22	8	2	4	*O	3.7
1985	Hou-N	141	544	69	163	34	4	9	79	43	74	.300	.351	.426	120	11	13	81	16	5	2	2	*O	1.4
1986	*Hou-N	141	479	48	133	22	4	10	72	55	86	.278	.352	.403	111	6	7	68	3	4	-2	-2	*O	0.1
1987	Hou-N	126	365	47	88	17	4	11	38	36	65	.241	.309	.400	90	-8	-6	47	4	1	1	-0	*O	-0.7
1988	NY-A	38	80	9	16	2	0	1	7	8	8	.200	.273	.262	51	-5	-5	5	0	1	-1	-0	D/O	-0.6
Total	19	2353	7917	1036	2251	391	94	165	1077	898	1031	.284	.358	.420	122	169	220	1223	317	136	14	36	*O/D1	21.0

■ JULIO CRUZ
Cruz, Julio Luis   b: 12/2/54, Brooklyn, N.Y.   BB/TR, 5'9", 165 lbs.   Deb: 7/04/77

YEAR	TM/L	G	AB	R	H	2B	3B	HR	RBI	BB	SO	AVG	OBP	SLG	PRO+	BR	/A	RC	SB	CS	SBR	FR	POS	TPR
1977	Sea-A	60	199	25	51	3	1	1	7	24	29	.256	.336	.296	75	-6	-6	22	15	6	1	2	2/D	0.1
1978	Sea-A	147	550	77	129	14	1	1	25	69	66	.235	.321	.269	68	-21	-21	58	59	10	12	8	*2/SD	0.7
1979	Sea-A	107	414	70	112	16	2	1	29	62	61	.271	.366	.326	87	-4	-5	59	49	9	9	17	*2	2.4
1980	Sea-A	119	422	66	88	9	3	2	16	59	49	.209	.307	.258	56	-24	-24	42	45	7	9	-3	*2/D	-1.1
1981	Sea-A	94	352	57	90	12	3	2	24	39	40	.256	.335	.324	87	-3	-5	45	43	8	8	8	2/S	1.4
1982	Sea-A	154	549	83	133	22	5	8	49	57	71	.242	.317	.344	79	-13	-15	66	46	13	6	3	*2/S3D	0.2
1983	Sea-A	61	181	24	46	10	1	2	12	20	22	.254	.335	.354	86	-2	-3	25	33	6	6	7	*2/D	1.2
	*Chi-A	99	334	47	84	9	4	1	40	29	44	.251	.315	.311	71	-12	-13	35	24	6	4	10	2	0.3
	Yr	160	515	71	130	19	5	3	52	49	66	.252	.322	.326	76	-14	-16	60	57	12	10	17		1.5
1984	Chi-A	143	415	42	92	14	4	5	43	45	58	.222	.298	.311	66	-17	-20	40	14	6	1	22	*2	1.0
1985	Chi-A	91	234	28	46	2	3	0	15	32	40	.197	.299	.231	46	-16	-17	17	8	5	-1	13	2/D	0.0
1986	Chi-A	81	209	38	45	2	0	0	19	42	28	.215	.347	.225	58	-10	-11	20	7	2	1	2	2/D	-0.3
Total	10	1156	3859	557	916	113	27	23	279	478	508	.237	.324	.299	71	-129	-141	430	343	78	56	88	*2/DS3	5.9

■ TODD CRUZ
Cruz, Todd Ruben   b: 11/23/55, Highland Park, Mich   BR/TR, 6', 175 lbs.   Deb: 9/04/78

YEAR	TM/L	G	AB	R	H	2B	3B	HR	RBI	BB	SO	AVG	OBP	SLG	PRO+	BR	/A	RC	SB	CS	SBR	FR	POS	TPR
1978	Phi-N	3	4	0	2	0	0	0	2	0	0	.500	.500	.500	178	0	0	1	0	1	-1	2	/S	0.1
1979	KC-A	55	118	9	24	7	0	2	15	3	19	.203	.230	.314	44	-9	-10	8	0	1	-1	4	S/3	0.0
1980	Cal-A	18	40	5	11	3	0	1	5	5	8	.275	.356	.425	116	1	1	6	0	0	0	-6	S/32O	-0.3
	Chi-A	90	293	23	68	11	1	2	18	9	54	.232	.260	.297	52	-19	-19	22	2	1	0	5	S	-0.6
	Yr	108	333	28	79	14	1	3	23	14	62	.237	.272	.312	60	-19	-18	28	2	1	0	-1		-0.9
1982	Sea-A	136	492	44	113	20	2	16	57	12	95	.230	.248	.376	67	-23	-24	37	2	10	-5	17	*S	0.0
1983	Sea-A	65	216	21	41	4	2	7	21	7	56	.190	.222	.324	46	-16	-17	15	1	3	-2	20	S	0.5
	*Bal-A	81	221	16	46	9	1	3	27	15	52	.208	.262	.299	55	-14	-14	14	3	4	-2	5	3/2	-0.9
	Yr	146	437	37	87	13	3	10	48	22	108	.199	.242	.311	51	-30	-30	29	4	7	-3	25		-0.4
1984	Bal-A	96	142	15	31	4	0	3	9	8	33	.218	.265	.310	60	-8	-8	11	1	4	-2	12	3/PD	0.3
Total	6	544	1526	133	336	58	6	34	154	59	317	.220	.253	.333	59	-88	-90	113	9	24	-12	58	S3/2DPO	-0.9

■ MIKE CUBBAGE
Cubbage, Michael Lee   b: 7/21/50, Charlottesville, Va.   BL/TR, 6', 180 lbs.   Deb: 4/07/74   C

YEAR	TM/L	G	AB	R	H	2B	3B	HR	RBI	BB	SO	AVG	OBP	SLG	PRO+	BR	/A	RC	SB	CS	SBR	FR	POS	TPR
1974	Tex-A	9	15	0	0	0	0	0	0	0	4	.000	.000	.000	-99	-4	-4	0	0	0	0	2	/32	-0.1
1975	Tex-A	58	143	12	32	6	0	4	21	18	14	.224	.311	.350	87	-3	-2	17	0	0	0	2	2/3D	0.0
1976	Tex-A	14	32	2	7	0	0	0	0	7	7	.219	.359	.219	70	-1	-1	3	0	0	0	-0	/23D	0.0
	Min-A	104	342	40	89	19	5	3	49	42	37	.260	.346	.371	107	5	4	44	1	1	-0	1	3/2D	0.6
	Yr	118	374	42	96	19	5	3	49	49	44	.257	.347	.358	104	4	3	47	1	1	-0	1		0.6
1977	Min-A	129	417	60	110	16	5	9	55	37	49	.264	.324	.391	95	-4	-3	53	1	4	-2	9	*3/D	0.1
1978	Min-A	125	394	40	111	12	7	7	57	40	44	.282	.349	.401	108	6	5	56	3	1	0	2	*3/2	0.6
1979	Min-A	94	243	26	67	10	1	2	23	39	26	.276	.376	.350	94	1	-1	33	1	8	-5	-12	3D/12	-1.5
1980	Min-A	103	285	29	70	9	0	8	42	23	37	.246	.304	.361	76	-7	-10	32	0	1	-1	7	13/2D	-0.7
1981	NY-N	67	80	9	17	2	2	1	4	9	15	.213	.292	.325	76	-3	-3	8	0	0	0	1	3	-0.1
Total	8	703	1951	218	503	74	20	34	251	215	233	.258	.333	.369	94	-9	-15	245	6	15	-7	11	3/12D	-1.1

■ AL CUCCINELLO
Cuccinello, Alfred Edward   b: 11/26/14, Long Island City, N.Y.   BR/TR, 5'10", 165 lbs.   Deb: 5/17/35

YEAR	TM/L	G	AB	R	H	2B	3B	HR	RBI	BB	SO	AVG	OBP	SLG	PRO+	BR	/A	RC	SB	CS	SBR	FR	POS	TPR
1935	NY-N	54	165	27	41	7	1	4	20	1	20	.248	.262	.376	70	-8	-7	15	0			6	2/3	0.2

■ TONY CUCCINELLO
Cuccinello, Anthony Francis "Cooch" or "Chick"   b: 11/8/07, Long Island City, N.Y.   BR/TR, 5'7", 160 lbs.   Deb: 4/15/30   C

YEAR	TM/L	G	AB	R	H	2B	3B	HR	RBI	BB	SO	AVG	OBP	SLG	PRO+	BR	/A	RC	SB	CS	SBR	FR	POS	TPR
1930	Cin-N	125	443	64	138	22	5	10	78	47	44	.312	.380	.451	105	1	4	75	5			-19	*32/S	-0.8
1931	Cin-N	154	575	67	181	39	11	2	93	54	28	.315	.374	.431	123	13	18	96	5			5	*2	2.9
1932	Bro-N	154	597	76	168	32	6	12	77	46	47	.281	.337	.415	103	1	2	86	5			19	*2	3.2
1933	Bro-N	134	485	58	122	31	4	9	65	44	40	.252	.316	.388	105	-0	2	57	4			-19	*23	-0.7
1934	Bro-N	140	528	59	138	32	2	14	94	49	45	.261	.325	.409	100	-4	-0	73	0			12	*23	2.4
1935	Bro-N	102	360	49	105	20	3	8	53	40	35	.292	.366	.431	116	7	8	57	3			6	23	2.0
1936	Bos-N	150	565	68	174	26	3	7	86	58	49	.308	.374	.402	116	9	14	89	1			22	*2	4.3
1937	Bos-N	152	575	77	156	36	4	11	80	61	40	.271	.341	.405	112	2	8	83	2			-9	*2	0.5
1938	Bos-N	147	555	62	147	35	2	9	76	52	32	.265	.331	.366	102	-6	1	67	4			-25	*2	-1.4
1939	Bos-N	81	310	42	95	17	1	2	40	26	26	.306	.360	.387	109	1	4	43	1			-3	2	0.3
1940	Bos-N	34	126	14	34	9	0	0	19	8	9	.270	.319	.341	87	-3	-2	13	1			1	3	0.0
	NY-N	88	307	26	64	9	2	5	36	16	42	.208	.248	.300	50	-21	-22	21	1			5	23	-1.3

YEAR	TM/L	G	AB	R	H	2B	3B	HR	RBI	BB	SO	AVG	OBP	SLG	PRO+	BR	/A	RC	SB	CS	SBR	FR	POS	TPR
	Yr	122	433	40	98	18	2	5	55	24	51	.226	.269	.312	60	-24	-24	34	2			6		-1.3
1942	Bos-N	40	104	8	21	3	0	1	8	9	11	.202	.265	.260	55	-6	-6	7	1			-4	32	-0.8
1943	Bos-N	13	19	0	0	0	0	0	2	3	1	.000	.136	.000	-60	-4	-4	0	0			0	/32S	-0.3
	Chi-A	34	103	5	28	5	0	2	11	13	13	.272	.353	.379	114	2	2	15	3	1	0	-1	3	0.1
1944	Chi-A	38	130	5	34	3	0	0	17	8	16	.262	.304	.285	70	-5	-5	12	0	0	0	-2	3/2	-0.6
1945	Chi-A	118	402	50	124	25	3	2	49	45	19	.308	.379	.400	130	14	15	64	6	2	1	-5	*3	1.4
Total	15	1704	6184	730	1729	334	46	94	884	579	497	.280	.343	.394	105	-1	40	857	42	3		-17	*23/S	11.2

■ JIM CUDWORTH
Cudworth, James Alaric "Cuddy" b: 8/22/1858, Fairhaven, Mass. d: 12/21/43, Middleboro, Mass. BR/TR, 6', 165 lbs. Deb: 7/27/1884

YEAR	TM/L	G	AB	R	H	2B	3B	HR	RBI	BB	SO	AVG	OBP	SLG	PRO+	BR	/A	RC	SB	CS	SBR	FR	POS	TPR
1884	KC-U	32	116	7	17	3	1	0		2		.147	.161	.190	21	-10	-7	4	0			2	1O/P	-0.4

■ MANUEL CUETO
Cueto, Manuel "Potato" b: 2/8/1892, Guanajay, Cuba d: 6/29/42, Regla, Havana, Cuba BR/TR, 5'5", 157 lbs. Deb: 6/25/14

YEAR	TM/L	G	AB	R	H	2B	3B	HR	RBI	BB	SO	AVG	OBP	SLG	PRO+	BR	/A	RC	SB	CS	SBR	FR	POS	TPR
1914	StL-F	19	43	2	4	0	0	0	2	5	0	.093	.188	.093	-17	-6	-7	1	0			-1	3/S2	-0.7
1917	Cin-N	56	140	10	28	3	0	1	11	16	17	.200	.287	.243	66	-6	-5	11	4			1	O/2C	-0.4
1918	Cin-N	47	108	14	32	5	1	0	14	19	5	.296	.406	.361	137	6	6	18	4			-14	O2/SC	-0.8
1919	Cin-N	29	88	10	22	2	0	0	4	10	4	.250	.340	.273	88	-1	-1	10	5			2	O/3	0.1
Total	4	151	379	36	86	10	1	1	31	50	26	.227	.323	.266	81	-7	-7	39	13			-11	/O2SC3	-1.8

■ JOHN CUFF
Cuff, John J. b: 6/1864, Jersey City, N. J. Deb: 9/11/1884

YEAR	TM/L	G	AB	R	H	2B	3B	HR	RBI	BB	SO	AVG	OBP	SLG	PRO+	BR	/A	RC	SB	CS	SBR	FR	POS	TPR
1884	Bal-U	3	11	1	1	1	0	0		1		.091	.167	.182	16	-1	-1	0	0			2	/C	0.1

■ LEON CULBERSON
Culberson, Delbert Leon "Lee" b: 8/6/19, Hall's Station, Ga. d: 9/17/89, Rome, Ga. BR/TR, 5'11", 180 lbs. Deb: 5/16/43

YEAR	TM/L	G	AB	R	H	2B	3B	HR	RBI	BB	SO	AVG	OBP	SLG	PRO+	BR	/A	RC	SB	CS	SBR	FR	POS	TPR
1943	Bos-A	81	312	36	85	16	6	3	34	31	35	.272	.338	.391	111	5	4	46	14	0	4	9	O	1.5
1944	Bos-A	75	282	41	67	11	5	2	21	20	20	.238	.288	.333	78	-9	-9	27	6	4	-1	5	O	-0.5
1945	Bos-A	97	331	26	91	21	6	6	45	20	37	.275	.316	.429	113	4	4	41	4	3	-1	2	O	0.2
1946	*Bos-A	59	179	34	56	10	1	3	18	16	19	.313	.369	.430	116	5	4	29	3	2	-0	-3	O/3	0.0
1947	Bos-A	47	84	10	20	1	0	0	11	12	10	.238	.354	.250	65	-3	-4	9	1	1	-0	-1	O/3	-0.5
1948	Was-A	12	29	1	5	0	0	0	2	8	5	.172	.351	.172	43	-2	-2	2	0	0	0	-1	O	-0.2
Total	6	371	1217	148	324	59	18	14	131	107	126	.266	.327	.379	100	1	-2	153	28	10	2	12	O/3	0.5

■ JOHN CULLEN
Cullen, John J. b: 3/E, Cal. Deb: 8/18/1884

YEAR	TM/L	G	AB	R	H	2B	3B	HR	RBI	BB	SO	AVG	OBP	SLG	PRO+	BR	/A	RC	SB	CS	SBR	FR	POS	TPR
1884	Wil-U	9	31	2	6	0	0	0		1		.194	.219	.194	39	-2	-2	1	0			-1	/OS	-0.2

■ TIM CULLEN
Cullen, Timothy Leo b: 2/16/42, San Francisco, Cal. BR/TR, 6'1", 185 lbs. Deb: 8/08/66

YEAR	TM/L	G	AB	R	H	2B	3B	HR	RBI	BB	SO	AVG	OBP	SLG	PRO+	BR	/A	RC	SB	CS	SBR	FR	POS	TPR
1966	Was-A	18	34	8	8	1	0	0	2	2	8	.235	.278	.265	57	-2	-2	3	0	0	0	1	/32	0.0
1967	Was-A	124	402	35	95	7	0	2	31	40	47	.236	.307	.269	74	-13	-12	35	4	5	-2	15	S23/O	0.9
1968	Chi-A	72	155	16	31	7	0	2	13	15	23	.200	.275	.284	69	-6	-6	12	0	0	0	6	2	0.3
	Was-A	47	114	8	31	4	2	1	16	7	12	.272	.325	.368	113	1	2	14	0	0	0	-1	S2/3	0.4
	Yr	119	269	24	62	11	2	3	29	22	35	.230	.296	.320	87	-4	-4	26	0	0	0	5		0.7
1969	Was-A	119	249	22	52	7	0	1	15	14	27	.209	.257	.249	44	-19	-18	14	1	1	-0	12	*2/S3	-0.1
1970	Was-A	123	262	22	56	10	2	1	18	31	38	.214	.304	.279	65	-13	-11	22	3	2	-0	27	*2/S	2.7
1971	Was-A	125	403	34	77	13	4	2	26	33	47	.191	.252	.258	47	-29	-27	26	2	0	1	21	2S	0.5
1972	*Oak-A	72	142	10	37	8	1	0	15	5	17	.261	.286	.331	88	-3	-3	13	0	1	-1	-1	2/3S	-0.1
Total	7	700	1761	155	387	57	9	9	134	147	219	.220	.283	.278	65	-85	-76	138	10	9	-2	80	2S/3O	4.7

■ ROY CULLENBINE
Cullenbine, Roy Joseph b: 10/18/15, Nashville, Tenn. BB/TR, 6'1", 190 lbs. Deb: 4/19/38

YEAR	TM/L	G	AB	R	H	2B	3B	HR	RBI	BB	SO	AVG	OBP	SLG	PRO+	BR	/A	RC	SB	CS	SBR	FR	POS	TPR
1938	Det-A	25	67	12	19	1	3	0	9	12	9	.284	.392	.388	91	-0	-1	11	2	0	1	-1	O	0.0
1939	Det-A	75	179	31	43	9	2	6	23	34	29	.240	.362	.413	91	-0	-2	29	0	1	-1	-3	O/1	-0.6
1940	Bro-N	22	61	8	11	1	0	1	9	23	11	.180	.405	.246	78	-0	-0	8	2			-0	O	0.0
	StL-A	86	257	41	59	11	2	7	31	50	34	.230	.359	.370	87	-3	-4	38	0	1	-1	-4	O/1	-1.1
1941	StL-A	149	501	82	159	29	9	9	98	121	43	.317	.452	.465	138	38	36	120	6	4	-1	1	*O1	2.7
1942	StL-A	38	109	15	21	7	1	2	14	30	20	.193	.367	.330	95	1	1	16	0	1	-1	-0	O/1	-0.1
	Was-A	64	241	30	69	19	0	2	35	44	18	.286	.396	.390	123	9	9	41	1	2	-1	8	O3	1.4
	*NY-A	21	77	16	28	7	0	2	17	18	2	.364	.484	.532	190	10	10	22	0	1	-1	1	O/1	0.9
	Yr	123	427	61	118	33	1	6	66	92	40	.276	.405	.400	127	19	20	77	1	4	-2	9		2.2
1943	Cle-A	138	488	66	141	24	4	8	56	96	58	.289	.407	.404	146	27	31	89	3	4	-2	-1	*O1	2.6
1944	Cle-A	154	571	98	162	34	5	16	80	87	49	.284	.380	.445	141	28	30	102	4	4	-1	-6	*O	1.9
1945	Cle-A	8	13	3	1	1	0	0	0	11	0	.077	.500	.154	97	1	1	2	0	0	0	-2	/O3	0.0
	*Det-A	146	523	80	145	27	5	18	93	102	36	.277	.398	.451	137	34	30	103	2	0	1	10	*O	3.6
	Yr	154	536	83	146	28	5	18	93	**113**	36	.272	.402	.444	137	35	31	106	2	0	1	8		3.6
1946	Det-A	113	328	63	110	21	0	15	56	88	39	.335	.477	.537	172	42	39	95	3	0	1	-0	O1	3.6
1947	Det-A	142	464	82	104	18	1	24	78	137	51	.224	.401	.422	125	24	22	91	3	2	-0	16	*1	3.6
Total	10	1181	3879	627	1072	209	32	110	599	853	399	.276	.408	.432	132	211	202	769	26	20		18	O1/3	18.4

■ DICK CULLER
Culler, Richard Broadus b: 1/15/15, High Point, N.C. d: 6/16/64, Chapel Hill, N.C. BR/TR, 5'9.5", 155 lbs. Deb: 9/19/36

YEAR	TM/L	G	AB	R	H	2B	3B	HR	RBI	BB	SO	AVG	OBP	SLG	PRO+	BR	/A	RC	SB	CS	SBR	FR	POS	TPR
1936	Phi-A	9	38	3	9	0	0	0	1	1	3	.237	.256	.237	23	-5	-4	2	0	0	0	-3	/2S	-0.6
1943	Chi-A	53	148	9	32	5	1	0	11	16	11	.216	.297	.264	65	-6	-6	11	4	5	-2	11	32/S	0.4
1944	Bos-N	8	28	2	2	0	0	0	0	4	2	.071	.188	.071	-24	-5	-5	0	0			2	/S	-0.1
1945	Bos-N	136	527	87	138	12	1	2	30	50	35	.262	.328	.300	75	-16	-17	54	7			-8	*S/3	-1.1
1946	Bos-N	134	482	70	123	15	3	0	33	62	18	.255	.342	.299	82	-9	-10	51	7			-8	*S	-0.8
1947	Bos-N	77	214	20	53	5	1	0	19	19	15	.248	.309	.280	59	-13	-12	19	1			3	S	-0.2
1948	Chi-N	48	89	4	15	2	0	0	5	13	3	.169	.275	.191	29	-9	-8	5	0			**16**	S/2	1.2
1949	NY-N	7	1	0	0	0	0	0	0	1	0	.000	.500	.000	45	0	0	0	0			2	/S	0.3
Total	8	472	1527	195	372	39	6	2	99	166	87	.244	.320	.281	68	-62	-62	144	19	5		14	S/32	-0.9

■ NICK CULLOP
Cullop, Henry Nicholas "Tomato Face" b: 10/16/1900, St.Louis, Mo. d: 12/8/78, Westerville, Ohio BR/TR, 6', 200 lbs. Deb: 4/14/26

YEAR	TM/L	G	AB	R	H	2B	3B	HR	RBI	BB	SO	AVG	OBP	SLG	PRO+	BR	/A	RC	SB	CS	SBR	FR	POS	TPR
1926	NY-A	2	2	0	1	0	0	0	0	0	1	.500	.500	.500	164	0	0	0	0	0	0	0	H	0.0
1927	Was-A	15	23	2	5	2	0	0	1	1	6	.217	.250	.304	44	-2	-2	2	0	0	0	-1	/O1	-0.1
	Cle-A	32	68	9	16	2	3	1	8	9	19	.235	.333	.397	88	-1	-1	8	0	4	-2	3	O/P	-0.1
	Yr	47	91	11	21	4	3	1	9	10	25	.231	.314	.374	78	-3	-3	9	0	4	-2	2		-0.3
1929	Bro-N	13	41	7	8	2	2	1	5	8	7	.195	.327	.415	84	-1	-1	6	0			0	O/1	-0.1
1930	Cin-N	7	22	2	4	0	0	1	5	1	9	.182	.217	.318	29	-3	-3	1	0			1	/O	-0.1
1931	Cin-N	104	334	29	88	23	7	8	48	21	86	.263	.309	.446	107	-1	1	47	1			-4	O	-0.5
Total	5	173	490	49	122	29	12	11	67	40	128	.249	.308	.424	96	-8	-5	64	1	4		-1	O/1P	-1.0

■ WIL CULMER
Culmer, Wilfred Hillard b: 11/11/58, Nassau, Bahamas BR/TR, 6'4", 210 lbs. Deb: 4/12/83

YEAR	TM/L	G	AB	R	H	2B	3B	HR	RBI	BB	SO	AVG	OBP	SLG	PRO+	BR	/A	RC	SB	CS	SBR	FR	POS	TPR
1983	Cle-A	7	19	0	2	0	0	0	1	0	4	.105	.105	.105	-40	-4	-4	0	0	1	-1	-0	/OD	-0.4

■ BENNY CULP
Culp, Benjamin Baldy b: 1/19/14, Philadelphia, Pa. BR/TR, 5'9", 175 lbs. Deb: 9/17/42 C

YEAR	TM/L	G	AB	R	H	2B	3B	HR	RBI	BB	SO	AVG	OBP	SLG	PRO+	BR	/A	RC	SB	CS	SBR	FR	POS	TPR
1942	Phi-N	1	0	0	0	0	0	0	0	0		—	—	—	—	0	0	0	0			-0	/C	0.0
1943	Phi-N	10	24	4	5	1	0	0	2	3	3	.208	.296	.250	61	-1	-1	2	0			-2	C	-0.2
1944	Phi-N	4	2	1	0	0	0	0	0	0	0	.000	.000	.000	-99	-1	-1	0	0			1	/C	0.0
Total	3	15	26	5	5	1	0	0	2	3	3	.192	.276	.231	49	-2	-2	2	0			-2	/C	-0.2

■ JACK CUMMINGS
Cummings, John William b: 4/1/04, Pittsburgh, Pa. d: 10/5/62, W.Mifflin, Pa. BR/TR, 6', 195 lbs. Deb: 9/11/26

YEAR	TM/L	G	AB	R	H	2B	3B	HR	RBI	BB	SO	AVG	OBP	SLG	PRO+	BR	/A	RC	SB	CS	SBR	FR	POS	TPR
1926	NY-N	7	16	3	5	3	0	0	4	4	2	.313	.450	.500	157	1	1	4	0			0	/C	0.2

YEAR	TM/L	G	AB	R	H	2B	3B	HR	RBI	BB	SO	AVG	OBP	SLG	PRO+	BR	/A	RC	SB	CS	SBR	FR	POS	TPR
1927	NY-N	43	80	8	29	6	1	2	14	5	10	.363	.407	.538	151	6	6	17	0			-5	C	0.3
1928	NY-N	33	27	4	9	2	0	2	9	3	4	.333	.400	.630	165	2	2	7	0			0	/C	0.3
1929	NY-N	3	3	0	1	0	0	0	0	0	0	.333	.333	.333	66	-0	-0	0	0			0	/C	0.0
	Bos-N	3	6	0	1	0	0	0	1	0	2	.167	.167	.167	-18	-1	-1	0	0			-1	/C	-0.1
	Yr	6	9	0	2	0	0	0	1	0	2	.222	.222	.222	11	-1	-1	0	0			-1		-0.1
Total	4	89	132	15	45	11	1	4	28	12	18	.341	.400	.530	145	8	8	28	0			-6	/C	0.7

■ GEORGE CUNNINGHAM
Cunningham, George Harold   b: 7/13/1894, Sturgeon Lake, Minn.   d: 3/10/72, Chattanooga, Tenn.   BR/TR, 5'11", 185 lbs.   Deb: 4/14/16

YEAR	TM/L	G	AB	R	H	2B	3B	HR	RBI	BB	SO	AVG	OBP	SLG	PRO+	BR	/A	RC	SB	CS	SBR	FR	POS	TPR
1916	Det-A	35	41	7	11	2	2	0	3	8	12	.268	.388	.415	136	2	2	7	0			1	P	0.0
1917	Det-A	44	34	5	6	0	0	1	3	3	13	.176	.243	.265	55	-2	-2	2	0			0	P	0.0
1918	Det-A	56	112	11	25	4	1	0	2	16	34	.223	.320	.277	84	-2	-2	11	2			-5	PO	-0.4
1919	Det-A	26	23	4	5	0	0	0	5	9	8	.217	.438	.217	89	0	0	2	0			0	P	0.0
1921	Det-A	1	0	0	0	0	0	0	0	0	0	—	—	—	—	0	0	0	0	0	0	-0	/O	0.0
Total	5	162	210	27	47	6	3	1	13	36	67	.224	.337	.295	91	-2	-1	22	2	0		-4	P/O	-0.4

■ JOE CUNNINGHAM
Cunningham, Joseph Robert   b: 8/27/31, Paterson, N.J.   BL/TL, 6', 180 lbs.   Deb: 6/30/54   C

YEAR	TM/L	G	AB	R	H	2B	3B	HR	RBI	BB	SO	AVG	OBP	SLG	PRO+	BR	/A	RC	SB	CS	SBR	FR	POS	TPR
1954	StL-N	85	310	40	88	11	3	11	50	43	40	.284	.375	.445	112	6	6	55	1	1	-0	2	1	0.4
1956	StL-N	4	3	1	0	0	0	0	0	0	1	.000	.250	.000	-25	-1	-1	0	0	0	0	0	/1	0.0
1957	StL-N	122	261	50	83	15	0	9	52	56	29	.318	.447	.479	146	22	21	61	3	3	-1	-6	1O	0.8
1958	StL-N	131	337	61	105	20	3	12	57	82	23	.312	.450	.496	144	29	27	80	4	4	-1	-8	1O	1.2
1959	StL-N	144	458	65	158	28	6	7	60	88	47	.345	**.456**	.478	140	38	34	104	2	6	-3	-7	*O1	2.0
1960	StL-N	139	492	68	138	28	3	6	39	59	59	.280	.364	.386	97	6	0	70	1	7	-4	-8	*O1	-1.5
1961	StL-N	113	322	60	92	11	2	7	40	53	32	.286	.404	.398	104	9	5	58	1	0	0	-12	O1	-1.1
1962	Chi-A	149	526	91	155	32	7	8	70	101	59	.295	.415	.428	128	25	26	102	3	3	-1	-5	*1/O	1.0
1963	Chi-A	67	210	32	60	12	1	1	31	33	23	.286	.393	.367	116	6	6	33	1	0	0	-7	1	-0.1
1964	Chi-A	40	108	13	27	7	0	0	10	14	15	.250	.352	.315	90	-1	-1	13	0	1	-1	-0	1	-0.2
	Was-A	49	126	15	27	4	0	0	7	23	13	.214	.344	.246	68	-4	-4	12	0	1	-1	-4	1	-1.0
	Yr	89	234	28	54	11	0	0	17	37	28	.231	.348	.278	78	-6	-5	25	0	2	-1	-4		-1.2
1965	Was-A	95	201	29	46	9	1	3	20	46	27	.229	.375	.328	103	3	3	27	0	1	-1	-3	1	-0.3
1966	Was-A	3	8	0	1	0	0	0	0	0	1	.125	.125	.125	-28	-1	-1	0	0	0	0	1	/1	0.0
Total	12	1141	3362	525	980	177	26	64	436	599	369	.291	.406	.417	119	136	121	614	16	27	-11	-54	1O	1.2

■ RAY CUNNINGHAM
Cunningham, Raymond Lee   b: 1/17/08, Mesquite, Tex.   BR/TR, 5'7.5", 150 lbs.   Deb: 9/16/31

YEAR	TM/L	G	AB	R	H	2B	3B	HR	RBI	BB	SO	AVG	OBP	SLG	PRO+	BR	/A	RC	SB	CS	SBR	FR	POS	TPR
1931	StL-N	3	4	0	0	0	0	0	1	0	0	.000	.000	.000	-96	-1	-1	0	0			1	/3	0.0
1932	StL-N	11	22	4	4	1	0	0	0	3	4	.182	.280	.227	37	-2	-2	2	0			3	/32	0.2
Total	2	14	26	4	4	1	0	0	1	3	4	.154	.241	.192	18	-3	-3	2	0			4	/32	0.2

■ BILL CUNNINGHAM
Cunningham, William Aloysius   b: 7/30/1895, San Francisco, Cal   d: 9/26/53, Colusa, Cal.   BR/TR, 5'8", 155 lbs.   Deb: 7/14/21   C

YEAR	TM/L	G	AB	R	H	2B	3B	HR	RBI	BB	SO	AVG	OBP	SLG	PRO+	BR	/A	RC	SB	CS	SBR	FR	POS	TPR
1921	NY-N	40	76	10	21	2	1	1	12	3	3	.276	.313	.368	79	-2	-2	8	0	1	-1	-0	O	-0.3
1922	*NY-N	85	229	37	75	15	2	2	33	7	9	.328	.350	.437	101	-0	-0	33	4	5	-2	6	O/3	0.1
1923	*NY-N	79	203	22	55	7	1	5	27	10	9	.271	.305	.389	83	-6	-5	24	5	2	0	6	O/2	0.0
1924	Bos-N	114	437	44	119	15	8	1	40	32	27	.272	.326	.350	85	-11	-9	51	8	5	-1	8	*O	-0.3
Total	4	318	945	113	270	39	12	9	112	52	48	.286	.326	.381	88	-19	-17	116	17	13	-3	20	O/23	-0.5

■ BILL CUNNINGHAM
Cunningham, William James   b: 6/9/1888, Schenectady, N.Y.   d: 2/21/46, Schenectady, N.Y.   BR/TR, 5'9", 170 lbs.   Deb: 9/12/10

YEAR	TM/L	G	AB	R	H	2B	3B	HR	RBI	BB	SO	AVG	OBP	SLG	PRO+	BR	/A	RC	SB	CS	SBR	FR	POS	TPR
1910	Was-A	21	74	3	22	5	1	0	14	12		.297	.402	.392	156	5	5	14	4			-4	2	0.0
1911	Was-A	94	331	34	63	10	5	3	37	19		.190	.239	.278	45	-26	-25	25	10			-13	2	-3.8
1912	Was-A	8	27	5	5	1	0	1	8	3		.185	.267	.333	71	-1	-1	3	2			-3	/2S	-0.3
Total	3	123	432	42	90	16	6	4	59	34		.208	.271	.301	64	-22	-21	41	16			-20	2/S	-4.1

■ DOC CURLEY
Curley, Walter James   b: 3/12/1874, Upton, Mass.   d: 9/23/20, Framingham, Mass.   BR/TR,   Deb: 9/12/1899

YEAR	TM/L	G	AB	R	H	2B	3B	HR	RBI	BB	SO	AVG	OBP	SLG	PRO+	BR	/A	RC	SB	CS	SBR	FR	POS	TPR
1899	Chi-N	10	37	7	4	0	1	0	2	3		.108	.214	.162	6	-5	-5	1	0			-5	2	-0.8

■ PETE CURREN
Curren, Peter   b: Baltimore, Md.   Deb: 9/12/1876

YEAR	TM/L	G	AB	R	H	2B	3B	HR	RBI	BB	SO	AVG	OBP	SLG	PRO+	BR	/A	RC	SB	CS	SBR	FR	POS	TPR
1876	Phi-N	3	12	5	4	1	0	0	2	0	0	.333	.333	.417	150	1	1	2				-1	/CO	0.0

■ PERRY CURRIN
Currin, Perry Gilmore   b: 9/27/28, Washington, D.C.   BL/TL, 6', 175 lbs.   Deb: 6/29/47

YEAR	TM/L	G	AB	R	H	2B	3B	HR	RBI	BB	SO	AVG	OBP	SLG	PRO+	BR	/A	RC	SB	CS	SBR	FR	POS	TPR
1947	StL-A	3	2	0	0	0	0	0	0	1	0	.000	.333	.000	-3	-0	-0	0	0	0	0	1	/S	0.1

■ TONY CURRY
Curry, George Anthony   b: 12/22/38, Nassau, Bahamas   BL/TL, 5'11", 185 lbs.   Deb: 4/12/60

YEAR	TM/L	G	AB	R	H	2B	3B	HR	RBI	BB	SO	AVG	OBP	SLG	PRO+	BR	/A	RC	SB	CS	SBR	FR	POS	TPR
1960	Phi-N	95	245	26	64	14	2	6	34	16	53	.261	.309	.408	94	-2	-2	31	0	2	-1	-8	O	-1.3
1961	Phi-N	15	36	3	7	2	0	0	3	1	8	.194	.216	.250	24	-4	-4	2	0	0	0	-0	/O	-0.4
1966	Cle-A	19	16	4	2	0	0	0	3	3	8	.125	.263	.125	16	-2	-2	1	0	0	0	0	H	-0.1
Total	3	129	297	33	73	16	2	6	40	20	69	.246	.296	.374	82	-8	-8	34	0	2	-1	-8	/O	-1.8

■ JIM CURRY
Curry, James E.   b: 3/10/1893, Camden, N.J.   d: 8/2/38, Lakeland, N.J.   BR/TR, 5'11", 160 lbs.   Deb: 10/02/09

YEAR	TM/L	G	AB	R	H	2B	3B	HR	RBI	BB	SO	AVG	OBP	SLG	PRO+	BR	/A	RC	SB	CS	SBR	FR	POS	TPR
1909	Phi-A	1	4	1	1	0	0	0	0	0		.250	.250	.250	57	-0	-0	0	0			-1	/2	0.0
1911	NY-A	4	11	3	2	0	0	0	0	1		.182	.250	.182	20	-1	-1	1	0			-1	/2	-0.2
1918	Det-A	5	20	1	5	1	0	0	0	0	0	.250	.286	.300	80	-1	-1	2	0			-2	/2	-0.2
Total	3	10	35	5	8	1	0	0	0	1	0	.229	.270	.257	56	-2	-2	2	0			-4	/2	-0.4

■ GENE CURTIS
Curtis, Eugene Holmes "Eude"   b: 5/5/1883, Bethany, W.Va.   d: 1/1/19, Steubenville, Ohio   BR/TR, 6'3", 220 lbs.   Deb: 9/21/03

YEAR	TM/L	G	AB	R	H	2B	3B	HR	RBI	BB	SO	AVG	OBP	SLG	PRO+	BR	/A	RC	SB	CS	SBR	FR	POS	TPR
1903	Pit-N	5	19	2	8	1	0	0	3	1		.421	.450	.474	161	2	2	4	0			-0	/O	0.1

■ FRED CURTIS
Curtis, Frederick Marion   b: 10/30/1880, Beaver Lake, Mich.   d: 4/5/39, Minneapolis, Minn.   BR/TR, 6'1",   Deb: 7/24/05

YEAR	TM/L	G	AB	R	H	2B	3B	HR	RBI	BB	SO	AVG	OBP	SLG	PRO+	BR	/A	RC	SB	CS	SBR	FR	POS	TPR
1905	NY-A	2	9	0	2	1	0	0	2	1		.222	.300	.333	92	0	-0	1	1			0	/1	0.0

■ HARRY CURTIS
Curtis, Harry Albert   b: 2/19/1883, Portland, Maine   d: 8/1/51, Evanston, Ill.   TR, 5'10.5", 170 lbs.   Deb: 8/28/07

YEAR	TM/L	G	AB	R	H	2B	3B	HR	RBI	BB	SO	AVG	OBP	SLG	PRO+	BR	/A	RC	SB	CS	SBR	FR	POS	TPR
1907	NY-N	6	9	2	2	0	0	0	1	2		.222	.364	.222	83	0	-0	1	2			0	/C	0.1

■ JIM CURTIS
Curtis, James D.   b: 12/27/1861, Coldwater, Mich.   d: 2/14/45, N.Adams, Mass.   BL, 5'8.5", 157 lbs.   Deb: 7/15/1891

YEAR	TM/L	G	AB	R	H	2B	3B	HR	RBI	BB	SO	AVG	OBP	SLG	PRO+	BR	/A	RC	SB	CS	SBR	FR	POS	TPR
1891	Cin-N	27	108	11	29	3	3	1	13	9	19	.269	.331	.380	123	1	1	15	3			-0	O	0.0
	Was-a	29	103	17	26	3	2	0	12	13	16	.252	.347	.320	99	-0	0	12	2			-1	O	-0.1

■ GUY CURTRIGHT
Curtright, Guy Paxton   b: 10/18/12, Holliday, Mo.   BR/TR, 5'11", 200 lbs.   Deb: 4/21/43

YEAR	TM/L	G	AB	R	H	2B	3B	HR	RBI	BB	SO	AVG	OBP	SLG	PRO+	BR	/A	RC	SB	CS	SBR	FR	POS	TPR
1943	Chi-A	138	488	67	142	20	7	3	48	69	60	.291	.382	.379	123	16	16	74	13	12	-3	-2	*O	0.8
1944	Chi-A	72	198	22	50	8	2	2	23	23	21	.253	.330	.343	94	-2	-1	23	4	3	-1	1	O	-0.2
1945	Chi-A	98	324	51	91	15	7	4	32	39	29	.281	.358	.407	125	9	10	49	3	4	-2	2	O	0.7
1946	Chi-A	23	55	7	11	2	0	0	5	11	14	.200	.333	.236	63	-2	-2	4	0	1	-1	1	O	-0.2
Total	4	331	1065	147	294	45	16	9	108	142	124	.276	.363	.374	115	21	23	150	20	20	-6	2	O	1.1

■ TONY CUSICK
Cusick, Andrew Daniel   b: 1860, Fall River, Mass.   d: 8/6/29, Chicago, Ill.   BR/TR, 5'9.5", 190 lbs.   Deb: 8/21/1884

YEAR	TM/L	G	AB	R	H	2B	3B	HR	RBI	BB	SO	AVG	OBP	SLG	PRO+	BR	/A	RC	SB	CS	SBR	FR	POS	TPR
1884	Wil-U	11	34	0	5	0	0	0		1		.147	.171	.147	8	-3	-3	1	0			2	/CSO23	0.0
	Phi-N	9	29	2	4	0	0	0	1	0	3	.138	.138	.138	-14	-4	-3	1				6	/C	0.2
1885	Phi-N	39	141	12	25	1	0	0	5	1	24	.177	.183	.184	19	-12	-12	5				-3	C/O	-1.0
1886	Phi-N	29	104	10	23	5	1	0	4	3	14	.221	.243	.288	60	-5	-5	8	1			-6	C/O1	-0.8

YEAR	TM/L	G	AB	R	H	2B	3B	HR	RBI	BB	SO	AVG	OBP	SLG	PRO+	BR	/A	RC	SB	CS	SBR	FR	POS	TPR
1887	Phi-N	7	24	3	7	1	0	0	5	3	1	.292	.393	.333	100	0	0	3	0			-3	/C12	-0.1
Total	4	95	332	27	64	7	1	0	15	8	42	.193	.214	.220	37	-24	-24	17	1			-4	/C01S23	-1.7

■ JACK CUSICK
Cusick, John Peter   b: 6/12/28, Weehawken, N.J.   d: 11/17/89, Edgewood, N.J.   BR/TR, 6', 170 lbs.   Deb: 4/24/51

YEAR	TM/L	G	AB	R	H	2B	3B	HR	RBI	BB	SO	AVG	OBP	SLG	PRO+	BR	/A	RC	SB	CS	SBR	FR	POS	TPR
1951	Chi-N	65	164	16	29	3	2	2	16	17	29	.177	.254	.256	37	-15	-15	11	2	1	0	-2	S	-1.1
1952	Bos-N	49	78	5	13	1	0	0	6	6	9	.167	.226	.179	14	-9	-9	2	0	1	-1	-2	S/3	-1.0
Total	2	114	242	21	42	4	2	2	22	23	38	.174	.245	.231	30	-24	-24	13	2	2	-1	-4	/S3	-2.1

■ NED CUTHBERT
Cuthbert, Edgar Edward   b: 6/20/1845, Philadelphia, Pa.   d: 2/6/05, St.Louis, Mo.   BR/TR, 5'6", 140 lbs.   Deb: 5/20/1871   MU

YEAR	TM/L	G	AB	R	H	2B	3B	HR	RBI	BB	SO	AVG	OBP	SLG	PRO+	BR	/A	RC	SB	CS	SBR	FR	POS	TPR
1871	Ath-n	28	150	47	37	7	5	3	30	10	2	.247	.294	.420	103	0	1	24	16				*O/C	0.1
1872	Ath-n	47	258	82	90	9	0	1	6			.349	.364	.395	133	10	10	38					*O	0.8
1873	Phi-n	51	278	78	78	5	5	1	2			.281	.286	.345	82	-5	-7	28					*O	-0.3
1874	Chi-n	58	293	65	81	6	1	1	7			.276	.293	.314	93	-2	-2	28					*O/C	0.0
1875	StL-n	68	318	68	77	9	2	0	3			.242	.249	.283	92	-5	-0	23					*O/C	0.0
1876	StL-N	63	283	46	70	10	1	0	25	7	4	.247	.266	.290	90	-4	-2	22				-9	*O	-0.9
1877	Cin-N	12	56	6	10	5	0	0	2	1	2	.179	.193	.268	49	-4	-3	3				5	O	0.1
1882	StL-a	60	233	28	52	16	5	0	17			.223	.276	.335	101	2	0	22				-4	*OM	-0.3
1883	StL-a	21	71	3	12	1	0	0	4			.169	.213	.183	27	-5	-6	3				-1	O/1	-0.5
1884	Bal-U	44	168	29	34	5	0	0	10			.202	.247	.232	57	-6	-9	10	0			-5	O/1	-1.2
Total	5 n	252	1297	340	363	36	13	6	30	28	2	.280	.295	.342	100	-2	0	141	16				O/C	0.6
Total	5	200	811	112	178	37	6	0	27	39	6	.219	.255	.280	77	-18	-19	60	0			-14	O/1	-2.8

■ GEORGE CUTSHAW
Cutshaw, George William "Clancy"   b: 7/27/1887, Wilmington, Ill.   d: 8/22/73, San Diego, Cal.   BR/TR, 5'9", 160 lbs.   Deb: 4/25/12

YEAR	TM/L	G	AB	R	H	2B	3B	HR	RBI	BB	SO	AVG	OBP	SLG	PRO+	BR	/A	RC	SB	CS	SBR	FR	POS	TPR
1912	Bro-N	102	357	41	100	14	4	0	28	31	16	.280	.341	.342	91	-6	-4	47	16			8	2/3S	0.1
1913	Bro-N	147	592	72	158	23	13	3	80	39	22	.267	.315	.385	97	-2	-4	80	39			18	*2	1.0
1914	Bro-N	153	583	69	150	22	12	2	78	30	32	.257	.297	.346	89	-8	-10	67	34			28	*2	1.8
1915	Bro-N	154	566	68	139	18	9	0	62	34	35	.246	.293	.309	81	-13	-14	53	28	23	-5	17	*2	0.0
1916	*Bro-N	154	581	58	151	21	4	2	63	25	32	.260	.292	.320	85	-9	-11	58	27	20	-4	8	*2	-0.2
1917	Bro-N	135	487	42	126	17	7	4	49	21	26	.259	.292	.347	93	-4	-5	54	22			-9	*2	-0.6
1918	Pit-N	126	463	56	132	16	10	5	68	27	18	.285	.326	.395	115	9	7	66	25			-3	*2	1.3
1919	Pit-N	139	512	49	124	15	8	3	51	30	22	.242	.287	.320	79	-11	-14	54	36			-11	*2	-2.2
1920	Pit-N	131	488	56	123	16	8	0	47	23	10	.252	.287	.318	71	-17	-19	44	17	14	-3	1	*2	-1.9
1921	Pit-N	98	350	46	119	18	4	0	53	11	11	.340	.362	.414	102	2	1	52	14	5	1	-15	2	-1.1
1922	Det-A	132	499	57	133	14	8	2	61	20	13	.267	.300	.339	68	-25	-23	52	11	5	0	9	*2	-0.4
1923	Det-A	45	143	15	32	1	2	0	13	9	5	.224	.279	.259	43	-12	-12	12	2	1	0	12	2/3	0.2
Total	12	1516	5621	629	1487	195	89	25	653	300	242	.265	.305	.344	86	-96	-106	639	271	68		62	*2/3S	-2.0

■ KIKI CUYLER
Cuyler, Hazen Shirley   b: 8/30/1899, Harrisville, Mich.   d: 2/11/50, Ann Arbor, Mich.   BR/TR, 5'10.5", 180 lbs.   Deb: 9/29/21   CH

YEAR	TM/L	G	AB	R	H	2B	3B	HR	RBI	BB	SO	AVG	OBP	SLG	PRO+	BR	/A	RC	SB	CS	SBR	FR	POS	TPR
1921	Pit-N	1	3	0	0	0	0	0	0	0	1	.000	.000	.000	-97	-1	-1	0	0			-0	/O	0.0
1922	Pit-N	1	0	0	0	0	0	0	0	0	0	—	—	—	—	0	0	0	0			0	R	0.0
1923	Pit-N	11	40	4	10	1	1	0	2	5	3	.250	.348	.325	77	-1	-1	4	2	3	-1	0	O	-0.2
1924	Pit-N	117	466	94	165	27	16	9	85	30	62	.354	.402	.539	147	32	31	101	32	11	3	6	*O	3.7
1925	*Pit-N	153	617	**144**	220	43	**26**	18	102	58	56	.357	.423	.598	148	53	47	158	41	13	5	6	*O	4.9
1926	Pit-N	157	614	**113**	197	31	15	8	92	50	56	.321	.380	.459	119	22	17	105	**35**			14	*O	2.4
1927	Pit-N	85	285	60	88	13	7	3	31	37	36	.309	.394	.435	114	10	7	49	20			4	O	0.8
1928	Chi-N	133	499	92	142	25	9	17	79	51	61	.285	.359	.473	117	11	12	84	**37**			7	*O	1.3
1929	*Chi-N	139	509	111	183	29	7	15	102	66	56	.360	.438	.532	139	33	33	118	**43**			7	*O	2.6
1930	Chi-N	156	642	155	228	50	17	13	134	72	49	.355	.428	.547	133	37	36	148	**37**			16	*O	3.6
1931	Chi-N	154	613	100	202	37	12	9	88	72	54	.330	.404	.473	133	32	31	122	13			3	*O	2.5
1932	*Chi-N	110	446	58	130	19	9	10	77	29	43	.291	.340	.442	109	5	5	68	9			-3	*O	-0.5
1933	Chi-N	70	262	37	83	13	3	5	35	21	29	.317	.376	.447	135	12	12	43	4			-8	O	0.0
1934	Chi-N	142	559	80	189	**42**	8	6	69	31	62	.338	.377	.474	129	20	22	101	15			-3	*O	1.1
1935	Chi-N	45	157	22	42	5	1	4	18	10	16	.268	.331	.389	92	-2	-2	21	3			3	O	0.0
	Cin-N	62	223	36	56	8	3	2	22	27	18	.251	.337	.341	85	-5	-4	28	5			-2	O	-0.7
	Yr	107	380	58	98	13	4	6	40	37	34	.258	.335	.361	88	-6	-5	49	8			1		-0.7
1936	Cin-N	144	567	96	185	29	11	7	74	47	67	.326	.380	.453	132	19	23	102	16			-12	*O	0.5
1937	Cin-N	117	406	48	110	12	4	0	32	36	50	.271	.333	.320	82	-11	-9	43	10			-7	*O	-2.0
1938	Bro-N	82	253	45	69	10	8	2	23	34	23	.273	.363	.399	107	4	3	39	6			0	O	0.2
Total	18	1879	7161	1295	2299	394	157	128	1065	676	752	.321	.386	.474	125	270	263	1336	328	27		30	*O	20.2

■ MILT CUYLER
Cuyler, Milton   b: 10/7/68, Macon, Ga.   BB/TR, 5'10", 175 lbs.   Deb: 9/06/90

YEAR	TM/L	G	AB	R	H	2B	3B	HR	RBI	BB	SO	AVG	OBP	SLG	PRO+	BR	/A	RC	SB	CS	SBR	FR	POS	TPR
1990	Det-A	19	51	8	13	3	1	0	8	5	10	.255	.321	.353	89	-1	-1	5	1	2	-1	2	O	0.0

■ AL CYPERT
Cypert, Alfred Boyd "Cy"   b: 8/8/1889, Little Rock, Ark.   d: 1/9/73, Washington, D.C.   BR/TR, 5'10.5", 150 lbs.   Deb: 6/27/14

YEAR	TM/L	G	AB	R	H	2B	3B	HR	RBI	BB	SO	AVG	OBP	SLG	PRO+	BR	/A	RC	SB	CS	SBR	FR	POS	TPR
1914	Cle-A	1	1	0	0	0	0	0	0	0	1	.000	.000	.000	-96	-0	-0	0	0			0	/3	0.0

■ PAUL DADE
Dade, Lonnie Paul   b: 12/7/51, Seattle, Wash.   BR/TR, 6'1", 185 lbs.   Deb: 9/12/75

YEAR	TM/L	G	AB	R	H	2B	3B	HR	RBI	BB	SO	AVG	OBP	SLG	PRO+	BR	/A	RC	SB	CS	SBR	FR	POS	TPR
1975	Cal-A	11	30	5	6	4	0	0	1	6	7	.200	.333	.333	96	-0	-0	4	0	0	0	0	/O3D	0.0
1976	Cal-A	13	9	2	1	0	0	0	1	3	3	.111	.333	.111	36	-1	-0	0	0	0	0	1	/O23D	0.1
1977	Cle-A	134	461	65	134	15	3	3	45	32	58	.291	.339	.356	93	-6	-4	54	16	8	0	-6	O3/2D	-1.3
1978	Cle-A	93	307	37	78	12	1	3	20	34	45	.254	.332	.329	88	-5	-4	35	12	9	-2	1	O/D	-0.6
1979	Cle-A	44	170	22	48	4	1	3	18	12	22	.282	.330	.371	88	-3	-3	21	12	6	0	-2	O/3D	-0.5
	SD-N	76	283	38	78	19	2	1	19	14	48	.276	.314	.367	91	-6	-4	32	13	5	1	7	3/O	0.1
1980	SD-N	68	53	17	10	0	0	0	3	12	10	.189	.338	.189	54	-3	-2	4	4	5	2	4	3/O2	0.1
Total	6	439	1313	186	355	54	7	10	107	113	193	.270	.331	.345	89	-23	-18	151	57	33	-3	5	O3/D2	-2.2

■ ANGELO DAGRES
Dagres, Angelo George "Junior"   b: 8/22/34, Newburyport, Mass.   BL/TL, 5'11", 175 lbs.   Deb: 9/11/55

YEAR	TM/L	G	AB	R	H	2B	3B	HR	RBI	BB	SO	AVG	OBP	SLG	PRO+	BR	/A	RC	SB	CS	SBR	FR	POS	TPR
1955	Bal-A	8	15	5	4	0	0	0	3	1	2	.267	.313	.267	61	-1	-1	2	0	0	0	-0	/O	-0.1

■ BILL DAHLEN
Dahlen, William Frederick "Bad Bill"   b: 1/5/1870, Helliston, N.Y.   d: 12/5/50, Brooklyn, N.Y.   BR/TR, 5'9", 180 lbs.   Deb: 4/22/1891   M

YEAR	TM/L	G	AB	R	H	2B	3B	HR	RBI	BB	SO	AVG	OBP	SLG	PRO+	BR	/A	RC	SB	CS	SBR	FR	POS	TPR
1891	Chi-N	135	549	114	143	18	13	9	76	67	60	.260	.348	.390	118	12	13	84	21			9	3OS	2.0
1892	Chi-N	143	581	114	169	23	19	5	58	45	56	.291	.347	.422	133	22	21	109	60			25	S3/O2	5.0
1893	Chi-N	116	485	113	146	28	15	5	64	58	30	.301	.381	.452	125	16	17	98	31			3	*SO2/3	1.8
1894	Chi-N	121	502	149	179	32	14	15	107	76	33	.357	.444	.566	137	37	31	148	42			32	S3	**4.9**
1895	Chi-N	129	516	106	131	19	10	7	62	61	51	.254	.344	.370	81	-10	-16	81	38			35	*S/O	2.3
1896	Chi-N	125	474	137	167	30	19	9	74	64	36	.352	.438	.553	156	44	40	140	51			25	*S	5.4
1897	Chi-N	75	276	67	80	18	8	6	40	43		.290	.399	.478	129	14	12	60	15			28	S	3.5
1898	Chi-N	142	521	96	151	35	8	1	79	58		.290	.385	.393	126	20	20	92	27			25	*S	**4.8**
1899	Bro-N	121	484	87	121	22	7	4	76	67		.283	.398	.395	118	16	14	81	29			19	*S3	3.5
1900	*Bro-N	133	483	87	125	16	11	3	69	73		.259	.360	.344	91	1	-4	73	31			19	*S	2.6
1901	Bro-N	131	511	69	136	17	9	4	82	30		.266	.309	.358	93	-4	-5	66	23			14	*S/2	1.4
1902	Bro-N	138	527	67	139	25	8	2	74	43		.264	.329	.353	112	8	8	71	20			-6	*S	0.8
1903	Bro-N	138	474	71	124	17	9	1	64	82		.262	.371	.342	109	7	9	76	34			18	*S	3.2
1904	NY-N	145	523	70	140	26	2	2	**80**	44		.268	.325	.337	102	4	2	75	47			28	*S	3.1
1905	*NY-N	148	520	67	126	20	4	7	81	62		.242	.323	.337	97	0	-1	71	37			20	*S/O	2.2

YEAR	TM/L	G	AB	R	H	2B	3B	HR	RBI	BB	SO	AVG	OBP	SLG	PRO+	BR	/A	RC	SB	CS	SBR	FR	POS	TPR
1906	NY-N	143	471	63	113	18	3	1	49	76		.240	.346	.297	101	5	4	56	16			0	*S	1.2
1907	NY-N	143	464	40	96	20	1	0	34	51		.207	.285	.254	69	-14	-16	39	11			7	*S	-0.2
1908	Bos-N	144	524	50	125	23	2	3	48	35		.239	.286	.307	93	-5	-4	49	10			**38**	*S	3.5
1909	Bos-N	69	197	22	46	6	1	2	16	29		.234	.332	.305	93	0	-1	21	4			9	S/23	1.0
1910	Bro-N	3	2	0	0	0	0	0	0	0	0	.000	.000	.000	-99	-1	-0	-0	0			0	HM	0.0
1911	Bro-N	1	3	0	0	0	0	0	0	0	3	.000	.000	.000	-99	-1	-1	0	0			2	/SM	0.1
Total	21	2443	9031	1589	2457	413	163	84	1233	1064	269	.272	.355	.382	111	171	143	1490	547			349	*S3/O2	52.1

■ BABE DAHLGREN
Dahlgren, Ellsworth Tenney b: 6/15/12, San Francisco, Cal   BR/TR, 6', 190 lbs.   Deb: 4/16/35   C

YEAR	TM/L	G	AB	R	H	2B	3B	HR	RBI	BB	SO	AVG	OBP	SLG	PRO+	BR	/A	RC	SB	CS	SBR	FR	POS	TPR
1935	Bos-A	149	525	77	138	27	7	9	63	56	67	.263	.337	.392	83	-10	-15	71	6	5	-1	-7	*1	-3.6
1936	Bos-A	16	57	6	16	3	1	1	7	7	1	.281	.359	.421	87	-1	-1	9	2	1	0	-0	1	-0.3
1937	NY-A	1	1	0	0	0	0	0	0	0	0	.000	.000	.000	-99	-0	-0	0	0	0	0	0	H	0.0
1938	NY-A	27	43	8	8	1	0	0	1	1	7	.186	.205	.209	4	-6	-6	2	0	0	0	-1	/31	-0.7
1939	*NY-A	144	531	71	125	18	6	15	89	57	54	.235	.312	.377	76	-21	-20	61	2	3	-1	-7	*1	-3.8
1940	NY-A	155	568	51	150	24	4	12	73	46	54	.264	.325	.384	86	-15	-12	69	1	1	-0	-10	*1	-2.7
1941	Bos-N	44	166	20	39	8	1	7	30	16	13	.235	.306	.422	108	0	1	20	0			2	1/3	-0.1
	Chi-N	99	359	50	101	20	1	16	59	43	39	.281	.360	.476	139	15	17	62	2			-8	1	-0.4
	Yr	143	525	70	140	28	2	23	89	59	52	.267	.343	.459	129	16	18	82	2			-6		-0.5
1942	Chi-N	17	56	4	12	1	0	0	6	4	2	.214	.267	.232	48	-4	-3	3	0			1	1	-0.3
	StL-A	2	2	0	0	0	0	0	0	0	0	.000	.000	.000	-99	-1	-1	0	0	0	0	0	H	0.0
	Bro-N	17	19	2	1	0	0	0	0	4	5	.053	.217	.053	-19	-3	-3	0	0			1	1	-0.2
1943	Phi-N	136	508	55	146	19	2	5	56	50	39	.287	.354	.362	111	5	7	62	2			-22	13S/C	-1.6
1944	Pit-N	158	599	67	173	28	7	12	101	47	56	.289	.347	.419	110	11	8	84	2			8	*1	0.3
1945	Pit-N	144	531	57	133	24	8	5	75	51	51	.250	.318	.354	84	-10	-13	57	1			1	*1	-1.7
1946	StL-A	28	80	2	14	1	0	0	9	8	13	.175	.250	.188	22	-8	-9	4	0	1	-1	1	1	-0.9
Total	12	1137	4045	470	1056	174	37	82	569	390	401	.261	.329	.383	92	-47	-49	505	18	11		-43	*1/3SC	-16.0

■ JOHN DAILEY
Dailey, John G. b: Brooklyn, N.Y.   Deb: 7/12/1875

YEAR	TM/L	G	AB	R	H	2B	3B	HR	RBI	BB	SO	AVG	OBP	SLG	PRO+	BR	/A	RC	SB	CS	SBR	FR	POS	TPR
1875	Was-n	27	106	17	20	3	5	0			0	.189	.189	.311	72	-3	-2	6					S/32	-0.1
	Atl-n	2	8	3	1	0	0	0			0	.125	.125	.125	-15	-1	-1	0					/1O	0.0
	Yr	29	114	20	21	3	5	0			0	.184	.184	.298	67	-4	-3	6						-0.1

■ VINCE DAILEY
Dailey, Vincent Perry b: 12/25/1864, Osceola, Pa.   d: 11/14/19, Hornell, N.Y.   6', 200 lbs.   Deb: 4/21/1890

YEAR	TM/L	G	AB	R	H	2B	3B	HR	RBI	BB	SO	AVG	OBP	SLG	PRO+	BR	/A	RC	SB	CS	SBR	FR	POS	TPR
1890	Cle-N	64	246	41	71	5	7	0	32	33	23	.289	.373	.366	120	6	7	41	17			1	O/P	0.6

■ CON DAILY
Daily, Cornelius F. b: 9/11/1864, Blackstone, Mass.   d: 6/14/28, Brooklyn, N.Y.   BL, 6', 192 lbs.   Deb: 6/09/1884

YEAR	TM/L	G	AB	R	H	2B	3B	HR	RBI	BB	SO	AVG	OBP	SLG	PRO+	BR	/A	RC	SB	CS	SBR	FR	POS	TPR
1884	Phi-U	2	8	0	0	0	0	0		0		.000	.000	.000	-99	-2	-2	0	0			0	/C	0.0
1885	Pro-N	60	223	20	58	6	1	0	19	12	20	.260	.298	.296	96	-2	-1	20				-1	C/1O	0.1
1886	Bos-N	50	180	25	43	4	2	0	21	19	29	.239	.312	.283	85	-3	-2	17	2			-12	C	-0.9
1887	Bos-N	36	120	12	19	5	0	0	13	9	8	.158	.229	.200	21	-12	-12	7	7			-2	C	-1.1
1888	Ind-N	57	202	14	44	6	1	0	14	10	28	.218	.255	.257	64	-8	-8	17	15			2	C/O312	-0.4
1889	Ind-N	62	219	35	55	6	2	0	26	28	21	.251	.347	.297	81	-4	-5	28	14			-10	C/O13	-1.2
1890	Bro-P	46	168	20	42	6	3	0	35	15	14	.250	.315	.321	68	-7	-9	19	6			-8	C/10	-1.1
1891	Bro-N	60	206	25	66	10	1	0	30	15	13	.320	.378	.379	124	6	6	33	7			-2	C/OS1	0.7
1892	Bro-N	80	278	38	65	10	1	0	28	38	21	.234	.328	.277	88	-4	-2	32	18			-2	CO	0.0
1893	Bro-N	61	215	33	57	4	2	1	32	20	12	.265	.342	.316	81	-6	-5	28	13			-2	C/O	-0.1
1894	Bro-N	67	234	40	60	14	7	0	32	31	22	.256	.351	.376	83	-9	-5	35	8			-3	C/1	-0.1
1895	Bro-N	40	142	17	30	3	2	1	11	10	18	.211	.268	.282	47	-12	-10	12	3			-4	C/O	-0.7
1896	Chi-N	9	27	1	2	0	0	0	1	1	2	.074	.107	.074	-49	-6	-6	0	1			-1	/C	-0.4
Total	13	630	2222	280	541	74	22	2	262	208	208	.243	.314	.299	77	-67	-59	249	94			-43	C/O13S2	-4.9

■ ED DAILY
Daily, Edward M. b: 9/7/1862, Providence, R.I.   d: 10/21/1891, Washington, D.C.   BR/TR, 5'10.5", 174 lbs.   Deb: 5/04/1885

YEAR	TM/L	G	AB	R	H	2B	3B	HR	RBI	BB	SO	AVG	OBP	SLG	PRO+	BR	/A	RC	SB	CS	SBR	FR	POS	TPR
1885	Phi-N	50	184	22	38	8	2	1	13	0	25	.207	.207	.288	60	-9	-8	11				-3	P	0.0
1886	Phi-N	79	309	40	70	17	1	4	50	7	34	.227	.244	.327	72	-11	-11	31	23			5	OP	0.0
1887	Phi-N	26	106	18	30	11	1	1	17	3	9	.283	.303	.434	98	0	-1	17	8			-3	O/P	-0.1
	Was-N	78	311	39	78	6	10	2	36	14	27	.251	.285	.354	82	-9	-7	40	26			-7	O/P	-1.0
	Yr	104	417	57	108	17	11	3	53	17	36	.259	.290	.374	87	-9	-8	56	34			-10		-1.1
1888	Was-N	110	453	56	102	8	4	7	39	7	42	.225	.239	.307	79	-13	-10	45	44			3	*O/P1	-0.5
1889	Col-a	136	578	105	148	22	8	3	70	38	65	.256	.303	.337	89	-13	-8	79	60			-3	*O/P	-1.3
1890	Bro-a	91	394	68	94	15	7	1		24		.239	.284	.320	83	-11	-9	51	49			5	OP	0.0
	NY-N	4	15	1	2	1	0	0	1	0	4	.133	.133	.200	-2	-2	-2	0	0			1	/OP	0.0
	*Lou-a	23	80	24	20	0	2	0		13		.250	.355	.300	98	0	0	13	13			1	PO	0.0
1891	Lou-a	22	64	10	16	2	0	0	8	8	6	.250	.342	.281	82	-1	-1	8	4			1	P/O	0.0
	Was-a	21	79	13	18	2	0	0	6	11	10	.228	.322	.253	71	-3	-2	9	8			-4	O	-0.5
	Yr	43	143	23	34	4	0	0	14	19	16	.238	.331	.266	76	-4	-3	17	12			-3		-0.5
Total	7	640	2573	396	616	92	35	19	240	125	222	.239	.276	.325	81	-71	-58	304	235			-4	OP/1	-3.4

■ GEORGE DAISEY
Daisey, George K. b: Altoona, Pa.   5'11", 190 lbs.   Deb: 5/31/1884

YEAR	TM/L	G	AB	R	H	2B	3B	HR	RBI	BB	SO	AVG	OBP	SLG	PRO+	BR	/A	RC	SB	CS	SBR	FR	POS	TPR
1884	Alt-U	1	4	0	0	0	0	0		0		.000	.000	.000	-99	-1	-1	0				-1	/O	0.0

■ PETE DALENA
Dalena, Peter Martin b: 6/26/60, Fresno, Cal.   BL/TR, 5'11", 200 lbs.   Deb: 7/07/89

YEAR	TM/L	G	AB	R	H	2B	3B	HR	RBI	BB	SO	AVG	OBP	SLG	PRO+	BR	/A	RC	SB	CS	SBR	FR	POS	TPR
1989	Cle-A	5	7	0	1	1	0	0	0	0	3	.143	.143	.286	18	-1	-1	0	0	0	0	0	/D	0.0

■ JOHN DALEY
Daley, John Francis b: 5/25/1887, Pittsburgh, Pa.   d: 8/31/88, Mansfield, Ohio   BR/TR, 5'7.5", 155 lbs.   Deb: 7/19/12

YEAR	TM/L	G	AB	R	H	2B	3B	HR	RBI	BB	SO	AVG	OBP	SLG	PRO+	BR	/A	RC	SB	CS	SBR	FR	POS	TPR
1912	StL-A	18	52	7	9	0	0	1	3	9		.173	.317	.231	60	-2	-2	5	4			-4	S	-0.4

■ JUD DALEY
Daley, Judson Lawrence b: 3/14/1884, S.Coventry, Conn.   d: 1/26/67, Gasden, Ala.   BL/TR, 5'8", 172 lbs.   Deb: 9/19/11

YEAR	TM/L	G	AB	R	H	2B	3B	HR	RBI	BB	SO	AVG	OBP	SLG	PRO+	BR	/A	RC	SB	CS	SBR	FR	POS	TPR
1911	Bro-N	19	65	8	15	2	1	0	7	2	8	.231	.286	.292	65	-3	-3	6	2			1	O	-0.2
1912	Bro-N	61	199	22	51	9	1	1	13	24	17	.256	.342	.327	87	-4	-3	24	2			1	O	-0.2
Total	2	80	264	30	66	11	2	1	20	26	25	.250	.329	.318	82	-7	-6	30	4			2	/O	-0.4

■ PETE DALEY
Daley, Peter Harvey b: 1/14/30, Grass Valley, Cal.   BR/TR, 6', 195 lbs.   Deb: 5/03/55

YEAR	TM/L	G	AB	R	H	2B	3B	HR	RBI	BB	SO	AVG	OBP	SLG	PRO+	BR	/A	RC	SB	CS	SBR	FR	POS	TPR
1955	Bos-A	17	50	4	11	2	1	0	5	3	6	.220	.264	.300	47	-4	-4	4	0	0	0	3	C	0.0
1956	Bos-A	59	187	22	50	11	3	5	29	18	30	.267	.338	.439	92	0	-3	25	1	0	0	-9	C	-1.0
1957	Bos-A	78	191	17	43	10	0	3	25	16	31	.225	.288	.325	64	-9	-10	16	0	0	0	-3	C	-0.9
1958	Bos-A	27	56	10	18	2	1	2	8	7	11	.321	.397	.500	136	4	3	10	0	0	0	2	C	0.5
1959	Bos-A	65	169	9	38	7	0	1	11	13	31	.225	.280	.284	53	-10	-11	14	1	1	-0	3	C	-0.5
1960	KC-A	73	228	19	60	10	2	5	25	16	41	.263	.311	.390	88	-4	-4	26	0	0	0	-4	C/O	-0.6
1961	Was-A	72	203	12	39	7	1	2	17	14	37	.192	.244	.266	37	-19	-18	11	0	1	-1	7	C	-1.2
Total	7	391	1084	93	259	49	8	18	120	87	187	.239	.297	.349	71	-41	-48	106	2	2	-1	-2	C/O	-3.5

■ TOM DALEY
Daley, Thomas Francis "Pete" b: 11/13/1884, Dubois, Pa.   d: 12/2/34, Los Angeles, Cal.   BL/TR, 5'5", 168 lbs.   Deb: 8/29/08

YEAR	TM/L	G	AB	R	H	2B	3B	HR	RBI	BB	SO	AVG	OBP	SLG	PRO+	BR	/A	RC	SB	CS	SBR	FR	POS	TPR
1908	Cin-N	14	46	5	5	0	0	0	1	3		.109	.163	.109	-12	-6	-5	1	1			-0	O	-0.6
1913	Phi-A	62	141	13	36	2	1	0	11	13	28	.255	.327	.284	81	-3	-3	14	4			-1	O	-0.6
1914	Phi-A	28	86	17	22	1	3	0	7	12	14	.256	.347	.337	109	1	1	9	4	7	-3	2	O	-0.1

YEAR	TM/L	G	AB	R	H	2B	3B	HR	RBI	BB	SO	AVG	OBP	SLG	PRO+	BR	/A	RC	SB	CS	SBR	FR	POS	TPR
	NY-A	69	191	36	48	6	4	0	9	38	13	.251	.378	.325	112	5	5	25	8	8	-2	6	O	0.5
	Yr	97	277	53	70	7	7	0	16	50	27	.253	.369	.329	111	5	6	35	12	15	-5	7		0.4
1915	NY-A	10	8	2	2	0	0	0	1	2	2	.250	.400	.250	95	0	0	1	1			-0	/O	0.0
Total	4	183	472	73	113	9	8	0	29	68	57	.239	.339	.292	91	-3	-2	51	18	15		6	O	-0.8

■ DOM DALLESSANDRO

Dallessandro, Nicholas Dominic "Dim Dom" b: 10/3/13, Reading, Pa. d: 4/29/88, Indianapolis, Ind. BL/TL, 5'6", 168 lbs. Deb: 4/24/37

YEAR	TM/L	G	AB	R	H	2B	3B	HR	RBI	BB	SO	AVG	OBP	SLG	PRO+	BR	/A	RC	SB	CS	SBR	FR	POS	TPR
1937	Bos-A	68	147	18	34	7	1	0	11	27	16	.231	.351	.293	61	-7	-8	17	2	1	0	-5	O	-1.2
1940	Chi-N	107	287	33	77	19	6	1	36	34	13	.268	.348	.387	104	1	2	40	4			-2	O	-0.2
1941	Chi-N	140	486	73	132	36	2	6	85	68	37	.272	.362	.391	116	9	11	72	3			-0	*O	0.6
1942	Chi-N	96	264	30	69	12	4	4	43	36	18	.261	.350	.383	119	5	6	35	4			-1	O	0.4
1943	Chi-N	87	176	13	39	8	3	1	31	40	14	.222	.369	.318	101	2	2	24	1			-3	O	-0.2
1944	Chi-N	117	381	53	116	19	4	8	74	61	29	.304	.400	.438	137	20	20	70	1			-3	*O	1.0
1946	Chi-N	65	89	4	20	2	2	1	9	23	12	.225	.384	.326	104	1	2	12	1			-2	O	0.0
1947	Chi-N	66	115	18	33	7	1	1	14	21	11	.287	.397	.391	115	3	3	18	0			-1	O	0.1
Total	8	746	1945	242	520	110	23	22	303	310	150	.267	.369	.381	112	34	39	287	16	1		-16	O	0.5

■ ABNER DALRYMPLE

Dalrymple, Abner Frank b: 9/9/1857, Warren, Ill. d: 1/25/39, Warren, Ill. BL/TR, 5'10.5", 175 lbs. Deb: 5/01/1878

YEAR	TM/L	G	AB	R	H	2B	3B	HR	RBI	BB	SO	AVG	OBP	SLG	PRO+	BR	/A	RC	SB	CS	SBR	FR	POS	TPR
1878	Mil-N	61	271	52	96	10	4	0	15	6	29	.354	.368	.421	149	16	14	43				6	*O	1.4
1879	Chi-N	71	333	47	97	25	1	0	23	4	29	.291	.300	.372	113	7	4	38				-13	*O	-1.0
1880	Chi-N	86	382	91	126	25	12	0	36	3	18	.330	.335	.458	157	25	22	60				4	*O	2.1
1881	Chi-N	82	362	72	117	22	4	1	37	15	22	.323	.350	.414	133	16	14	54				-8	*O	0.4
1882	Chi-N	84	397	96	117	25	11	1	36	14	18	.295	.319	.421	129	15	12	55				-1	*O	0.9
1883	Chi-N	80	363	78	108	24	4	2	37	11	29	.298	.318	.402	110	7	4	48				-2	*O	0.3
1884	Chi-N	111	521	111	161	18	9	22	69	14	39	.309	.327	.505	145	32	25	88				1	*O	2.2
1885	*Chi-N	113	492	109	135	27	12	11	61	46	42	.274	.336	.445	131	28	17	76				-1	*O	1.2
1886	*Chi-N	82	331	62	77	7	12	3	26	33	44	.233	.302	.353	86	-0	-8	41	16			3	O	-0.3
1887	Pit-N	92	358	45	76	18	5	2	31	45	43	.212	.311	.307	79	-11	-7	44	29			4	O	-0.2
1888	Pit-N	57	227	19	50	9	2	0	14	6	28	.220	.247	.278	74	-8	-6	18	7			-2	O	-0.7
1891	Mil-a	32	135	31	42	7	5	1	22	7	18	.311	.345	.459	110	5	0	24	6			-1	O	0.0
Total	12	951	4172	813	1202	217	81	43	407	204	359	.288	.323	.410	121	131	90	588	58			-11	O	6.3

■ CLAY DALRYMPLE

Dalrymple, Clayton Errol b: 12/3/36, Chico, Cal. BL/TR, 6', 190 lbs. Deb: 4/24/60

YEAR	TM/L	G	AB	R	H	2B	3B	HR	RBI	BB	SO	AVG	OBP	SLG	PRO+	BR	/A	RC	SB	CS	SBR	FR	POS	TPR
1960	Phi-N	82	158	11	43	6	2	4	21	15	21	.272	.347	.411	106	2	2	22	0	0	0	-5	C	0.0
1961	Phi-N	129	378	23	83	11	1	5	42	30	30	.220	.284	.294	54	-25	-24	30	0	2	-1	0	*C	-1.5
1962	Phi-N	123	370	40	102	13	3	11	54	70	32	.276	.396	.416	122	13	14	65	1	3	-2	-12	*C	0.3
1963	Phi-N	142	452	40	114	15	3	10	40	45	55	.252	.327	.365	100	-0	1	54	0	2	-1	-0	*C	0.3
1964	Phi-N	127	382	36	91	16	3	6	46	39	40	.238	.309	.343	84	-8	-7	41	0	1	-1	3	*C	-0.1
1965	Phi-N	103	301	14	64	5	5	4	23	34	37	.213	.293	.302	69	-12	-12	27	0	1	-1	18	*C	1.0
1966	Phi-N	114	331	30	81	13	3	4	39	60	57	.245	.365	.338	97	1	1	46	0	0	0	-4	*C	0.0
1967	Phi-N	101	268	12	46	7	1	3	21	36	49	.172	.272	.239	47	-18	-18	18	1	2	-1	20	C	0.7
1968	Phi-N	85	241	19	50	9	1	3	26	22	57	.207	.277	.290	70	-9	-9	19	1	2	-1	-2	C	-0.9
1969	*Bal-A	37	80	8	19	1	1	3	6	13	8	.237	.344	.387	103	1	1	10	0	0	0	1	C	0.4
1970	Bal-A	13	32	4	7	1	0	1	3	7	4	.219	.359	.344	94	-0	-0	4	0	0	0	6	C	0.6
1971	Bal-A	23	49	6	10	1	0	1	6	16	13	.204	.409	.286	101	1	1	8	0	0	0	2	C	0.4
Total	12	1079	3042	243	710	98	23	55	327	387	403	.233	.324	.335	85	-54	-51	343	3	13	-7	26	*C	1.2

■ BILL DALRYMPLE

Dalrymple, William Dunn b: 2/7/1891, Baltimore, Md. d: 7/14/67, San Diego, Cal. TR, Deb: 7/06/15

YEAR	TM/L	G	AB	R	H	2B	3B	HR	RBI	BB	SO	AVG	OBP	SLG	PRO+	BR	/A	RC	SB	CS	SBR	FR	POS	TPR
1915	StL-A	3	2	0	0	0	0	0	0	0	0	.000	.000	.000	-99	-0	-0	0	0			0	/3	0.0

■ JACK DALTON

Dalton, Talbot Percy b: 7/3/1885, Henderson, Tenn. BR/TR, 5'10.5", 187 lbs. Deb: 6/20/10

YEAR	TM/L	G	AB	R	H	2B	3B	HR	RBI	BB	SO	AVG	OBP	SLG	PRO+	BR	/A	RC	SB	CS	SBR	FR	POS	TPR
1910	Bro-N	77	273	33	62	9	4	1	21	26	30	.227	.304	.300	79	-8	-7	27	5			1	O	-0.9
1914	Bro-N	128	442	65	141	13	8	1	45	53	39	.319	.396	.391	131	20	19	74	19			-9	*O	0.8
1915	Buf-F	132	437	68	128	17	3	2	46	50	38	.293	.368	.359	113	10	9	72	28			-5	*O	-0.1
1916	Det-A	8	11	1	2	0	0	0	0	0	5	.182	.182	.182	9	-1	-1	0	0			-1	/O	-0.2
Total	4	345	1163	167	333	39	15	4	112	129	112	.286	.362	.356	111	21	20	174	52			-15	O	-0.4

■ BERT DALY

Daly, Albert Joseph b: 4/8/1881, Bayonne, N.J. d: 9/3/52, Bayonne, N.J. BR/TR, 5'9", 170 lbs. Deb: 8/07/03

YEAR	TM/L	G	AB	R	H	2B	3B	HR	RBI	BB	SO	AVG	OBP	SLG	PRO+	BR	/A	RC	SB	CS	SBR	FR	POS	TPR
1903	Phi-A	10	21	2	4	0	2	0	4	1		.190	.227	.381	78	-1	-1	2	0			-4	/23S	-0.4

■ SUN DALY

Daly, James J. b: 1/6/1865, Rutland, Vt. d: 4/30/38, Albany, N.Y. Deb: 9/30/1892

YEAR	TM/L	G	AB	R	H	2B	3B	HR	RBI	BB	SO	AVG	OBP	SLG	PRO+	BR	/A	RC	SB	CS	SBR	FR	POS	TPR
1892	Bal-N	13	48	5	12	0	2	0	7	1	4	.250	.265	.333	80	-1	-1	4	0			0	O	-0.1

■ JOE DALY

Daly, Joseph John b: 9/21/1868, Conshohocken, Pa. d: 3/21/43, Philadelphia, Pa. TR, 5'8", 157 lbs. Deb: 9/19/1890

YEAR	TM/L	G	AB	R	H	2B	3B	HR	RBI	BB	SO	AVG	OBP	SLG	PRO+	BR	/A	RC	SB	CS	SBR	FR	POS	TPR
1890	Phi-a	21	75	8	21	4	1	0		3		.280	.308	.360	102	-0	-0	9	1			-6	O/C	-0.4
1891	Cle-N	1	3	0	0	0	0	0	0	0		.000	.000	.000	-96	-1	-1	0	0			0	/O	0.0
1892	Bos-N	1	0	0	0	0	0	0	0	0	0	—	—	—	—	0	0	0	0			0	/C	0.0
Total	3	23	78	8	21	4	1	0	0	3	2	.269	.296	.346	94	-1	-1	9	1			-6	/OC	-0.4

■ TOM DALY

Daly, Thomas Daniel b: 12/12/1891, St.John, N.B., Can. d: 11/7/46, Medford, Mass. BR/TR, 5'11.5", 171 lbs. Deb: 9/23/13 C

YEAR	TM/L	G	AB	R	H	2B	3B	HR	RBI	BB	SO	AVG	OBP	SLG	PRO+	BR	/A	RC	SB	CS	SBR	FR	POS	TPR
1913	Chi-A	1	3	0	0	0	0	0	0	0	0	.000	.000	.000	-99	-1	-1	0				1	/C	0.0
1914	Chi-A	62	133	13	31	2	0	0	8	7	13	.233	.271	.248	57	-7	-7	9	3	4	-2	-10	O/3C1	-2.1
1915	Chi-A	29	47	5	9	1	0	0	3	5	9	.191	.269	.213	43	-3	-3	3	0			-2	C/1	-0.4
1916	Cle-A	31	73	3	16	1	1	0	8	1	2	.219	.230	.260	45	-5	-5	4	0			-2	C/O	-0.6
1918	Chi-N	1	1	0	0	0	0	0	0	0	0	.000	.000	.000	-98	-0	-0	0				-0	/C	0.0
1919	Chi-N	25	50	4	11	0	1	0	1	2	5	.220	.250	.260	53	-3	-3	3	0			-2	C	-0.4
1920	Chi-N	44	90	12	28	6	0	0	13	2	6	.311	.333	.378	102	0	0	11	1	1	-0	-3	C	-0.1
1921	Chi-N	51	143	12	34	7	1	0	22	8	8	.238	.278	.301	53	-10	-10	12	1	2	-1	4	C	-0.3
Total	8	244	540	49	129	17	3	0	55	25	43	.239	.274	.281	59	-28	-29	42	5	7		-16	C/O31	-3.9

■ TOM DALY

Daly, Thomas Peter "Tido" b: 2/7/1866, Philadelphia, Pa. d: 10/29/39, Brooklyn, N.Y. BB/TR, 5'7", 170 lbs. Deb: 4/30/1887

YEAR	TM/L	G	AB	R	H	2B	3B	HR	RBI	BB	SO	AVG	OBP	SLG	PRO+	BR	/A	RC	SB	CS	SBR	FR	POS	TPR
1887	Chi-N	74	256	45	53	10	4	2	17	22	25	.207	.270	.301	53	-14	-19	29	29			35	C/OS21	1.9
1888	Chi-N	65	219	34	42	2	6	0	29	10	26	.192	.230	.256	53	-10	-12	16	10			20	C/O	0.9
1889	Was-N	71	250	39	75	13	5	1	40	38	28	.300	.394	.404	133	10	12	48	18			1	C/120S	1.2
1890	*Bro-N	82	292	55	71	9	4	5	43	32	43	.243	.326	.353	100	-0	-0	41	20			4	C1/O	0.7
1891	Bro-N	58	200	29	50	11	5	2	27	21	34	.250	.327	.385	110	2	2	28	7			-7	C1S/O	0.5
1892	Bro-N	124	446	76	114	15	6	4	51	64	61	.256	.355	.343	118	9	12	68	34			-9	3OC2	0.6
1893	Bro-N	126	470	94	136	21	14	8	70	76	65	.289	.388	.445	129	16	20	96	32			-18	23	0.2
1894	Bro-N	123	492	135	168	22	10	8	82	77	42	.341	.436	.476	131	20	28	127	51			-19	*2	1.3
1895	Bro-N	120	455	89	128	17	8	2	68	52	52	.281	.359	.367	97	-6	1	72	28			-19	*2	-0.8
1896	Bro-N	67	224	43	63	13	6	3	29	33	25	.281	.385	.433	125	6	9	46	19			-3	2/C	0.7
1898	Bro-N	23	73	11	24	3	1	0	11	14		.329	.443	.397	145	5	5	16	6			3	2	0.8
1899	Bro-N	141	498	95	156	24	9	5	88	69		.313	.409	.428	130	25	23	107	43			16	*2	4.2
1900	*Bro-N	97	343	72	107	17	3	4	55	46		.312	.395	.414	119	14	10	68	27			-9	2/1O	0.5
1901	Bro-N	133	520	88	164	38	10	3	90	42		.315	.370	.444	134	23	23	100	31			11	*2	4.2
1902	Chi-A	137	489	57	110	22	3	1	54	55		.225	.305	.288	70	-21	-17	52	19			-15	*2	-2.5

YEAR	TM/L	G	AB	R	H	2B	3B	HR	RBI	BB	SO	AVG	OBP	SLG	PRO+	BR	/A	RC	SB	CS	SBR	FR	POS	TPR
1903	Chi-A	43	150	20	31	11	0	0	19	20		.207	.300	.280	80	-4	-3	15	6			-13	2	-1.5
	Cin-N	80	307	42	90	14	9	1	38	16		.293	.328	.407	100	3	-1	44	5			-10	2	-0.6
Total	16	1564	5684	1024	1582	262	103	49	811	687	401	.278	.361	.387	109	82	93	975	385			-32	*2C3/O1S	11.6

■ BILL DAM
Dam, Elbridge Rust b: 4/4/1885, Cambridge, Mass. d: 6/22/30, Quincy, Mass. Deb: 8/23/09

YEAR	TM/L	G	AB	R	H	2B	3B	HR	RBI	BB	SO	AVG	OBP	SLG	PRO+	BR	/A	RC	SB	CS	SBR	FR	POS	TPR
1909	Bos-N	1	2	1	1	1	0	0	0	1		.500	.667	1.000	398	1	1	1	0			-0	/O	0.1

■ JACK DAMASKA
Damaska, Jack Lloyd b: 8/21/37, Beaver Falls, Pa. BR/TR, 5'11", 168 lbs. Deb: 7/03/63

YEAR	TM/L	G	AB	R	H	2B	3B	HR	RBI	BB	SO	AVG	OBP	SLG	PRO+	BR	/A	RC	SB	CS	SBR	FR	POS	TPR
1963	StL-N	5	5	1	1	0	0	0	1	0	4	.200	.200	.200	14	-1	-1	0	0	0	0	0	/2O	0.0

■ HARRY DAMRAU
Damrau, Harry Robert (Also Known As Arthur Lee Whitehorn) b: 9/11/1890, Newburgh, N.Y. d: 8/21/57, Staten Island, N.Y BR/TR, 5'10", 178 lbs. Deb: 9/17/15

YEAR	TM/L	G	AB	R	H	2B	3B	HR	RBI	BB	SO	AVG	OBP	SLG	PRO+	BR	/A	RC	SB	CS	SBR	FR	POS	TPR
1915	Phi-A	16	56	4	11	1	0	0	3	5	17	.196	.262	.214	44	-4	-4	3	1	1	-0	-4	3	-0.7

■ JAKE DANIEL
Daniel, Handley Jacob b: 4/22/11, Roanoke, Ala. BL/TL, 5'11", 175 lbs. Deb: 7/24/37

YEAR	TM/L	G	AB	R	H	2B	3B	HR	RBI	BB	SO	AVG	OBP	SLG	PRO+	BR	/A	RC	SB	CS	SBR	FR	POS	TPR
1937	Bro-N	12	27	3	5	1	0	0	3	4		.185	.267	.222	34	-2	-2	2	0			-0	/1	-0.2

■ BERT DANIELS
Daniels, Bernard Elmer b: 10/13/1882, Danville, Ill. d: 6/6/58, Cedar Grove, N.J. BR/TR, 5'9.5", 180 lbs. Deb: 6/25/10

YEAR	TM/L	G	AB	R	H	2B	3B	HR	RBI	BB	SO	AVG	OBP	SLG	PRO+	BR	/A	RC	SB	CS	SBR	FR	POS	TPR
1910	NY-A	95	356	68	90	13	8	1	17	41		.253	.356	.343	112	10	7	58	41			3	O/31	0.7
1911	NY-A	131	462	74	132	16	9	2	31	48		.286	.375	.372	102	7	3	80	40			1	*O	-0.5
1912	NY-A	135	496	72	136	25	11	2	41	51		.274	.363	.381	106	9	5	82	37			8	*O	0.5
1913	NY-A	94	320	52	69	13	5	0	22	44	36	.216	.343	.287	85	-4	-4	38	27			1	O	-0.7
1914	Cin-N	71	269	29	59	9	7	0	19	19	40	.219	.276	.305	70	-10	-11	25	14			-3	O	-1.6
Total	5	526	1903	295	486	76	40	5	130	203	76	.255	.349	.345	98	13	0	283	159			10	O/31	-1.6

■ TONY DANIELS
Daniels, Frederick Clinton b: 12/28/24, Gastonia, N.C. BR/TR, 5'9.5", 185 lbs. Deb: 6/12/45

YEAR	TM/L	G	AB	R	H	2B	3B	HR	RBI	BB	SO	AVG	OBP	SLG	PRO+	BR	/A	RC	SB	CS	SBR	FR	POS	TPR
1945	Phi-N	76	230	15	46	3	2	0	10	12	22	.200	.249	.230	35	-21	-20	13	1			7	2/3	-0.5

■ JACK DANIELS
Daniels, Harold Jack "Sour Mash Jack" b: 12/21/27, Chester, Pa. BL/TL, 5'10", 165 lbs. Deb: 4/18/52

YEAR	TM/L	G	AB	R	H	2B	3B	HR	RBI	BB	SO	AVG	OBP	SLG	PRO+	BR	/A	RC	SB	CS	SBR	FR	POS	TPR
1952	Bos-N	106	219	31	41	5	1	2	14	28	30	.187	.288	.247	51	-14	-13	18	3	3	-1	-0	O	-1.7

■ KAL DANIELS
Daniels, Kalvoski b: 8/20/63, Vienna, Ga. BL/TR, 5'11", 195 lbs. Deb: 4/09/86

YEAR	TM/L	G	AB	R	H	2B	3B	HR	RBI	BB	SO	AVG	OBP	SLG	PRO+	BR	/A	RC	SB	CS	SBR	FR	POS	TPR
1986	Cin-N	74	181	34	58	10	4	6	23	22	30	.320	.400	.519	145	13	12	40	15	2	3	-3	O	1.2
1987	Cin-N	108	368	73	123	24	1	26	64	60	62	.334	.429	.617	166	40	37	100	26	8	3	-6	O	3.0
1988	Cin-N	140	495	95	144	29	1	18	64	87	94	.291	.400	.463	141	33	31	98	27	6	5	0	*O	3.4
1989	Cin-N	44	133	26	29	11	0	2	9	36	28	.218	.392	.346	109	4	4	21	6	4	-1	-2	O	0.1
	LA-N	11	38	7	13	2	0	2	8	7	5	.342	.444	.553	187	4	4	10	3	0	1	-1	O	0.4
	Yr	55	171	33	42	13	0	4	17	43	33	.246	.403	.392	125	9	8	31	9	4	0	-3		0.5
1990	LA-N	130	450	81	133	23	1	27	94	68	104	.296	.392	.531	160	32	36	96	4	3	-1	-2	*O	2.9
Total	5	507	1665	316	500	99	7	81	262	280	323	.300	.404	.514	151	127	124	366	81	23	11	-13	O	11.0

■ LAW DANIELS
Daniels, Lawrence Long b: 7/14/1862, Newton, Mass. d: 1/7/29, Waltham, Mass. 5'10", 170 lbs. Deb: 4/25/1887

YEAR	TM/L	G	AB	R	H	2B	3B	HR	RBI	BB	SO	AVG	OBP	SLG	PRO+	BR	/A	RC	SB	CS	SBR	FR	POS	TPR
1887	Bal-a	48	165	23	41	5	1	0		8		.248	.287	.291	67	-8	-6	16	7			-4	CO/12S3	-0.5
1888	KC-a	61	218	32	45	2	0	2	28	14		.206	.264	.243	62	-8	-10	20	20			-0	OC/3S	-0.7
Total	2	109	383	55	86	7	1	2	28	22		.225	.274	.264	64	-16	-16	36	27			-5	/CO13S2	-1.2

■ BUCK DANNER
Danner, Henry Frederick b: 6/8/1891, Dedham, Mass. d: 9/21/49, Boston, Mass. BR/TR, 5'6", 135 lbs. Deb: 9/17/15

YEAR	TM/L	G	AB	R	H	2B	3B	HR	RBI	BB	SO	AVG	OBP	SLG	PRO+	BR	/A	RC	SB	CS	SBR	FR	POS	TPR
1915	Phi-A	3	12	1	3	0	0	0	0	0	1	.250	.250	.250	51	-1	-1	1	1			-3	/S	-0.2

■ HARRY DANNING
Danning, Harry "Harry The Horse" b: 9/6/11, Los Angeles, Cal. BR/TR, 6'1", 190 lbs. Deb: 7/30/33

YEAR	TM/L	G	AB	R	H	2B	3B	HR	RBI	BB	SO	AVG	OBP	SLG	PRO+	BR	/A	RC	SB	CS	SBR	FR	POS	TPR
1933	NY-N	3	2	0	0	0	0	0	0	1	0	.000	.333	.000	2	-0	-0	0	0			0	/C	0.0
1934	NY-N	53	97	8	32	7	0	1	7	1	9	.330	.337	.433	107	0	1	12	1			-1	C	0.1
1935	NY-N	65	152	16	37	11	1	2	20	9	16	.243	.286	.368	76	-6	-5	16	0			2	C	-0.2
1936	*NY-N	32	69	3	11	2	2	0	4	1	5	.159	.183	.246	15	-8	-8	2	0			2	C	-0.5
1937	*NY-N	93	292	30	84	12	4	8	51	18	20	.288	.331	.438	106	2	2	42	0			-5	C	0.0
1938	NY-N	120	448	59	137	26	3	9	60	23	40	.306	.345	.438	113	7	7	66	1			-8	*C	0.3
1939	NY-N	135	520	79	163	28	5	16	74	35	42	.313	.359	.479	122	15	15	87	4			7	*C	2.6
1940	NY-N	140	524	65	157	34	4	13	91	35	31	.300	.349	.454	119	13	13	79	3			7	*C	2.5
1941	NY-N	130	459	58	112	22	4	7	56	30	25	.244	.292	.355	80	-12	-14	46	1			7	*C/1	0.4
1942	NY-N	119	408	45	114	20	3	1	34	34	29	.279	.335	.350	79	0	0	46	3			-6	*C	-0.3
Total	10	890	2971	363	847	162	26	57	397	187	217	.285	.330	.415	104	12	9	395	13			5	C/1	4.9

■ IKE DANNING
Danning, Ike b: 1/20/05, Los Angeles, Cal. d: 3/30/83, Santa Monica, Cal BR/TR, 5'10", 160 lbs. Deb: 9/21/28

YEAR	TM/L	G	AB	R	H	2B	3B	HR	RBI	BB	SO	AVG	OBP	SLG	PRO+	BR	/A	RC	SB	CS	SBR	FR	POS	TPR
1928	StL-A	2	6	0	3	0	0	0	1	1	2	.500	.571	.500	178	1	1	2	0	0	0	1	/C	0.2

■ FATS DANTONIO
Dantonio, John James b: 12/31/19, New Orleans, La. BR/TR, 5'8", 165 lbs. Deb: 9/18/44

YEAR	TM/L	G	AB	R	H	2B	3B	HR	RBI	BB	SO	AVG	OBP	SLG	PRO+	BR	/A	RC	SB	CS	SBR	FR	POS	TPR
1944	Bro-N	3	7	0	1	0	0	0	0	0	1	.143	.143	.143	-20	-1	-1	0	0			0	/C	0.0
1945	Bro-N	47	128	12	32	6	1	0	12	11	6	.250	.309	.313	74	-5	-4	13	3			-6	C	-0.8
Total	2	50	135	12	33	6	1	0	12	11	7	.244	.301	.304	69	-6	-6	13	3			-6	/C	-0.8

■ BABE DANZIG
Danzig, Harold P. b: 4/30/1887, Binghamton, N.Y. d: 7/14/31, San Francisco, Cal BR/TR, 6'2", 205 lbs. Deb: 4/12/09

YEAR	TM/L	G	AB	R	H	2B	3B	HR	RBI	BB	SO	AVG	OBP	SLG	PRO+	BR	/A	RC	SB	CS	SBR	FR	POS	TPR
1909	Bos-A	6	13	0	2	0	0	0	0	2		.154	.313	.154	47	-1	-1	1	0			-1	/1	-0.1

■ CLIFF DAPPER
Dapper, Clifford Roland b: 1/2/20, Los Angeles, Cal. BR/TR, 6'2", 190 lbs. Deb: 4/19/42

YEAR	TM/L	G	AB	R	H	2B	3B	HR	RBI	BB	SO	AVG	OBP	SLG	PRO+	BR	/A	RC	SB	CS	SBR	FR	POS	TPR
1942	Bro-N	8	17	2	8	1	0	1	9	2	2	.471	.526	.706	255	3	3	7	0			-0	/C	0.3

■ CLIFF DARINGER
Daringer, Clifford Clarence "Shanty" b: 4/10/1885, Hayden, Ind. d: 12/26/71, Sacramento, Cal. BL/TR, 5'7.5", 155 lbs. Deb: 4/20/14

YEAR	TM/L	G	AB	R	H	2B	3B	HR	RBI	BB	SO	AVG	OBP	SLG	PRO+	BR	/A	RC	SB	CS	SBR	FR	POS	TPR
1914	KC-F	64	160	12	42	2	1	0	16	11		.262	.322	.287	79	-5	-4	19	9			6	S32	0.5

■ ROLLA DARINGER
Daringer, Rolla Harrison b: 11/15/1888, N.Vernon, Ind. d: 5/23/74, Seymour, Ind. BL/TR, 5'10", 155 lbs. Deb: 9/19/14

YEAR	TM/L	G	AB	R	H	2B	3B	HR	RBI	BB	SO	AVG	OBP	SLG	PRO+	BR	/A	RC	SB	CS	SBR	FR	POS	TPR
1914	StL-N	2	4	1	2	1	0	0	0	1	2	.500	.600	.750	304	1	1	2	0			-1	/S	0.0
1915	StL-N	10	23	3	2	0	0	0	0	9	5	.087	.344	.087	33	-1	-1	1	0	1	-1	-3	S	-0.4
Total	2	12	27	4	4	1	0	0	0	10	7	.148	.378	.185	72	-0	-0	3	0	1		-4	/S	-0.4

■ AL DARK
Dark, Alvin Ralph "Blackie" b: 1/7/22, Comanche, Okla. BR/TR, 5'11", 185 lbs. Deb: 7/14/46 MC

YEAR	TM/L	G	AB	R	H	2B	3B	HR	RBI	BB	SO	AVG	OBP	SLG	PRO+	BR	/A	RC	SB	CS	SBR	FR	POS	TPR
1946	Bos-N	15	13	0	3	3	0	0	1	0	3	.231	.231	.462	93	-0	-0	1	0			3	S/O	0.3
1948	*Bos-N	137	543	85	175	39	6	3	48	24	36	.322	.353	.433	114	8	9	84	4			-12	*S	1.1
1949	Bos-N	130	529	74	146	23	5	3	53	31	43	.276	.317	.355	85	-15	-12	59	5			-3	*S/3	-0.1
1950	NY-N	154	587	79	164	36	5	16	67	39	60	.279	.331	.440	100	-1	-1	85	9			-14	*S	0.0
1951	*NY-N	156	646	114	196	41	7	14	69	42	39	.303	.352	.454	104	14	12	104	12	7	-1	1	*S	2.5
1952	NY-N	151	589	92	177	29	3	14	73	47	39	.301	.357	.420	117	14	13	92	6	6	-2	3	*S	1.9
1953	NY-N	155	647	126	194	41	6	23	88	28	34	.300	.335	.488	109	8	7	102	7	2	1	9	*S2O/3P	2.5
1954	*NY-N	154	644	98	189	26	6	20	70	20	48	.293	.327	.446	98	-3	-3	89	5	3	-0	4	*S	0.9
1955	NY-N	115	475	77	134	20	3	9	45	22	32	.282	.321	.394	88	-8	-8	60	2	1	0	-14	*S	-1.8
1956	NY-N	48	206	19	52	12	0	2	17	8	13	.252	.284	.340	67	-10	-10	19	0	0	0	-5	S	-1.1
	StL-N	100	413	54	118	14	7	4	37	21	33	.286	.323	.383	89	-7	-7	50	3	1	0	-2	S	-0.1
	Yr	148	619	73	170	26	7	6	54	29	46	.275	.310	.368	82	-16	-16	69	3	1	0	-7		-1.2

YEAR	TM/L	G	AB	R	H	2B	3B	HR	RBI	BB	SO	AVG	OBP	SLG	PRO+	BR	/A	RC	SB	CS	SBR	FR	POS	TPR
1957	StL-N	140	583	80	169	25	8	4	64	29	56	.290	.328	.381	88	-9	-10	72	3	4	-2	6	*S/3	0.0
1958	StL-N	18	64	7	19	0	0	1	5	2	6	.297	.318	.344	72	-2	-3	6	0	0	0	-3	/S3	-0.4
	Chi-N	114	464	54	137	16	4	3	43	29	23	.295	.343	.366	89	-7	-6	57	1	1	-0	-3	*3	-0.9
	Yr	132	528	61	156	16	4	4	48	31	29	.295	.340	.364	87	-10	-9	63	1	1	-0	-6		-1.3
1959	Chi-N	136	477	60	126	22	9	6	45	55	50	.264	.344	.386	95	-3	-3	66	1	1	-0	-2	*3/1S	-0.8
1960	Phi-N	55	198	29	48	5	1	3	14	19	14	.242	.315	.323	75	-6	-6	20	1	1	-0	-8	3/1	-1.5
	Mil-N	50	141	16	42	6	2	1	18	7	13	.298	.336	.390	106	-0	1	18	0	0	0	-4	O1/32	-0.3
	Yr	105	339	45	90	11	3	4	32	26	27	.265	.323	.351	88	-7	-5	38	1	1	-0	-11		-1.8
Total	14	1828	7219	1064	2089	358	72	126	757	430	534	.289	.334	.411	98	-31	-29	987	59	27		-44	*S3/O21P	2.2

■ DELL DARLING

Darling, Conrad b: 12/21/1861, Erie, Pa. d: 11/20/04, Erie, Pa. BR/TR, 5'8", 170 lbs. Deb: 7/03/1883

YEAR	TM/L	G	AB	R	H	2B	3B	HR	RBI	BB	SO	AVG	OBP	SLG	PRO+	BR	/A	RC	SB	CS	SBR	FR	POS	TPR
1883	Buf-N	6	18	1	3	0	0	0	1	2	5	.167	.250	.167	29	-1	-1	1				0	/C	0.0
1887	Chi-N	38	141	28	45	7	4	3	20	22	18	.319	.411	.489	134	10	7	37	19			6	OC	1.3
1888	Chi-N	20	75	12	16	3	1	2	7	3	12	.213	.253	.360	89	-0	-1	7	0			4	C	0.4
1889	Chi-N	36	120	14	23	1	1	0	7	25	22	.192	.331	.217	53	-6	-7	11	5			5	C	-0.1
1890	Chi-P	58	221	45	57	12	4	2	39	29	28	.258	.352	.376	92	-1	-3	32	5			-9	1S/CO23	-1.0
1891	StL-a	17	53	9	7	1	3	0	9	10	11	.132	.270	.264	48	-3	-4	4	0			4	C/2S	0.0
Total	6	175	628	109	151	24	13	7	83	91	96	.240	.340	.354	89	-1	-10	91	29			10	C/1OS23	0.6

■ JACK DARRAGH

Darragh, James S. b: 7/17/1866, Ebensburg, Pa. d: 8/12/39, Rochester, Pa. Deb: 5/13/1891

YEAR	TM/L	G	AB	R	H	2B	3B	HR	RBI	BB	SO	AVG	OBP	SLG	PRO+	BR	/A	RC	SB	CS	SBR	FR	POS	TPR
1891	Lou-a	1	2	0	1	0	0	0	0	0	0	.500	.500	.500	193	0	0	1	0			0	/1	0.0

■ BOBBY DARWIN

Darwin, Arthur Bobby Lee b: 2/16/43, Los Angeles, Cal. BR/TR, 6'2", 190 lbs. Deb: 9/30/62

YEAR	TM/L	G	AB	R	H	2B	3B	HR	RBI	BB	SO	AVG	OBP	SLG	PRO+	BR	/A	RC	SB	CS	SBR	FR	POS	TPR
1962	LA-A	1	1	0	0	0	0	0	0	0	1	.000	.000	.000	-99	-0	-0	0	0	0	0	-0	/P	0.0
1969	LA-N	6	0	1	0	0	0	0	0	0	0	—	—	—	—	-0	-0	0	0	0	0	-0	/P	0.0
1971	LA-N	11	20	2	5	1	0	1	4	2	9	.250	.318	.450	123	0	0	3	0	0	0	0	/O	0.0
1972	Min-A	145	513	48	137	20	2	22	80	38	145	.267	.327	.442	122	16	13	67	2	3	-1	-10	*O	-0.1
1973	Min-A	145	560	69	141	20	2	18	90	46	137	.252	.312	.391	93	-3	-6	64	5	2	0	-18	*O/D	-2.7
1974	Min-A	152	575	67	152	13	7	25	94	37	127	.264	.324	.442	114	12	9	80	1	3	-2	-21	*O	-1.7
1975	Min-A	48	169	26	37	6	0	5	18	18	44	.219	.309	.343	82	-3	-4	17	2	0	1	1	OD	-0.2
	Mil-A	55	186	19	46	6	2	8	23	11	54	.247	.300	.430	104	0	0	24	4	1	1	-2	O/D	-0.2
	Yr	103	355	45	83	12	2	13	41	29	98	.234	.304	.389	94	-3	-4	41	6	1	1	-1		-0.4
1976	Mil-A	25	73	6	18	3	1	1	5	6	16	.247	.321	.356	100	-0	0	8	0	0	0	-1	O/D	-0.1
	Bos-A	43	106	9	19	5	2	3	13	2	35	.179	.216	.349	57	-5	-7	8	1	0	0	0	OD	-0.6
	Yr	68	179	15	37	8	3	4	18	8	51	.207	.260	.352	73	-6	-7	16	1	0	0	-1		-0.7
1977	Bos-A	4	9	1	2	1	0	0	1	0	4	.222	.222	.333	44	-1	-1	0	0	0	0	-0	/OD	0.0
	Chi-N	11	12	2	2	1	0	0	0	0	5	.167	.167	.250	9	-2	-2	1	0	0	0	-0	/O	-0.1
Total	9	646	2224	250	559	76	16	83	328	160	577	.251	.312	.412	103	14	4	272	15	9	-1	-51	O/DP	-5.7

■ DOUG DASCENZO

Dascenzo, Douglas Craig b: 6/30/64, Cleveland, Ohio BB/TL, 5'7", 150 lbs. Deb: 9/02/88

YEAR	TM/L	G	AB	R	H	2B	3B	HR	RBI	BB	SO	AVG	OBP	SLG	PRO+	BR	/A	RC	SB	CS	SBR	FR	POS	TPR
1988	Chi-N	26	75	9	16	3	0	0	4	9	4	.213	.298	.253	57	-4	-4	6	6	1	1	3	O	0.0
1989	Chi-N	47	139	20	23	1	0	1	12	13	13	.165	.237	.194	23	-13	-15	7	6	3	0	2	O	-1.4
1990	Chi-N	113	241	27	61	9	5	1	26	21	18	.253	.316	.344	75	-6	-9	27	15	6	1	-11	*O/P	-2.2
Total	3	186	455	56	100	13	5	2	42	43	35	.220	.289	.284	57	-23	-27	41	27	10	2	-6	O/P	-3.6

■ WALLY DASHIELL

Dashiell, John Wallace b: 5/9/02, Jewett, Tex. d: 5/20/72, Pensacola, Fla. BR/TR, 5'9.5", 170 lbs. Deb: 4/20/24

YEAR	TM/L	G	AB	R	H	2B	3B	HR	RBI	BB	SO	AVG	OBP	SLG	PRO+	BR	/A	RC	SB	CS	SBR	FR	POS	TPR
1924	Chi-A	1	2	0	0	0	0	0	0	0	0	.000	.000	.000	-99	-1	-1	0	0	0	0	-1	/S	0.0

■ JEFF DATZ

Datz, Jeffrey William b: 11/28/59, Camden, N.J. BR/TR, 6'4", 220 lbs. Deb: 9/05/89

YEAR	TM/L	G	AB	R	H	2B	3B	HR	RBI	BB	SO	AVG	OBP	SLG	PRO+	BR	/A	RC	SB	CS	SBR	FR	POS	TPR
1989	Det-A	7	10	0	2	0	0	0	0	1	1	.200	.333	.200	55	-1	-0	1	0	0	0	0	/CD	0.0

■ HARRY DAUBERT

Daubert, Harry "Jake" b: 6/19/1892, Columbus, Ohio d: 1/8/44, Detroit, Mich. BR/TR, 6', 160 lbs. Deb: 9/04/15

YEAR	TM/L	G	AB	R	H	2B	3B	HR	RBI	BB	SO	AVG	OBP	SLG	PRO+	BR	/A	RC	SB	CS	SBR	FR	POS	TPR
1915	Pit-N	1	1	0	0	0	0	0	0	0	1	.000	.000	.000	-99	-0	-0	0				0	H	0.0

■ JAKE DAUBERT

Daubert, Jacob Ellsworth b: 4/7/1884, Shamokin, Pa. d: 10/9/24, Cincinnati, Ohio BL/TL, 5'10.5", 160 lbs. Deb: 4/14/10

YEAR	TM/L	G	AB	R	H	2B	3B	HR	RBI	BB	SO	AVG	OBP	SLG	PRO+	BR	/A	RC	SB	CS	SBR	FR	POS	TPR
1910	Bro-N	144	552	67	146	15	15	8	50	47	53	.264	.328	.389	112	4	6	79	23			-3	*1	0.2
1911	Bro-N	149	573	89	176	17	8	5	45	51	56	.307	.366	.391	117	9	12	94	32			2	*1	0.8
1912	Bro-N	145	559	81	172	19	16	3	66	48	45	.308	.369	.415	119	11	14	95	29			0	*1	0.8
1913	Bro-N	139	508	76	178	17	7	2	52	44	40	.350	.405	.423	133	25	24	94	25			3	*1	2.0
1914	Bro-N	126	474	89	156	17	7	6	45	30	34	.329	.375	.432	137	22	21	85	25			-6	*1	1.3
1915	Bro-N	150	544	62	164	21	8	2	47	57	48	.301	.369	.381	125	19	18	81	11	13	-5	9	*1	1.6
1916	*Bro-N	127	478	75	151	16	7	3	33	38	39	.316	.371	.397	132	21	19	80	21	7	2	4	*1	2.2
1917	Bro-N	125	468	59	122	4	4	2	30	51	30	.261	.341	.299	94	1	1	53	11			6	*1	0.4
1918	Bro-N	108	396	50	122	12	15	2	47	27	18	.308	.360	.429	141	18	18	63	10			0	*1	1.8
1919	*Cin-N	140	537	79	148	10	12	2	44	35	23	.276	.322	.350	105	1	3	66	11			-1	*1	0.0
1920	Cin-N	142	553	97	168	28	13	4	48	47	29	.304	.362	.423	127	18	19	83	11	13	-5	-9	*1	0.4
1921	Cin-N	136	516	69	158	18	12	2	64	24	16	.306	.341	.399	100	-4	-1	70	12	6	0	2	*1	-0.1
1922	Cin-N	156	610	114	205	15	22	12	66	56	21	.336	.395	.492	130	25	26	115	14	17	-6	-0	*1	1.7
1923	Cin-N	125	500	63	146	27	10	2	54	40	20	.292	.349	.398	99	-2	-1	68	11	12	-4	6	*1	-0.6
1924	Cin-N	102	405	47	114	14	9	1	31	28	17	.281	.331	.368	88	-7	-6	48	5	10	-5	7	*1	-0.7
Total	15	2014	7673	1117	2326	250	165	56	722	623	489	.303	.360	.401	117	159	170	1174	251	78		19	*1	11.8

■ RICH DAUER

Dauer, Richard Fremont b: 7/27/52, San Bernardino, Cal. BR/TR, 6', 180 lbs. Deb: 9/11/76 C

YEAR	TM/L	G	AB	R	H	2B	3B	HR	RBI	BB	SO	AVG	OBP	SLG	PRO+	BR	/A	RC	SB	CS	SBR	FR	POS	TPR
1976	Bal-A	11	39	0	4	0	0	0	3	1	3	.103	.146	.103	-28	-6	-6	1	0	0	0	-3	2	-0.8
1977	Bal-A	96	304	38	74	15	1	5	25	20	28	.243	.294	.349	79	-11	-9	30	1	0	0	6	2/3D	0.4
1978	Bal-A	133	459	57	121	23	0	6	46	26	22	.264	.303	.353	89	-10	-7	44	0	4	-2	3	23/D	-0.1
1979	*Bal-A	142	479	63	123	20	0	9	61	36	36	.257	.310	.355	82	-14	-12	51	0	1	-1	-5	*23	-1.1
1980	Bal-A	152	557	71	158	32	0	2	63	46	19	.284	.342	.352	91	-6	-6	64	3	2	-0	-4	*23	-0.2
1981	Bal-A	96	369	41	97	27	0	4	38	27	18	.263	.318	.369	98	-1	-1	44	0	0	0	-15	2/3	-1.3
1982	Bal-A	158	558	75	156	24	2	8	57	50	34	.280	.340	.373	96	-3	-2	70	0	1	-1	-36	*23	-3.3
1983	*Bal-A	140	459	49	108	19	0	5	41	47	29	.235	.309	.309	72	-17	-16	42	1	1	-0	-32	*23	-4.5
1984	Bal-A	127	397	49	101	26	0	2	24	24	23	.254	.297	.335	76	-14	-13	36	1	3	-2	-19	*2/3	-2.7
1985	Bal-A	85	208	25	42	7	0	2	14	20	7	.202	.275	.264	50	-14	-14	14	0	1	-1	4	23/1	-0.7
Total	10	1140	3829	448	984	193	3	43	372	297	219	.257	.313	.343	83	-98	-86	396	6	13	-6	-101	23/D1	-14.3

■ DOC DAUGHERTY

Daugherty, Harold Ray b: 10/12/27, Paris, Pa. BR/TR, 6', 180 lbs. Deb: 4/22/51

YEAR	TM/L	G	AB	R	H	2B	3B	HR	RBI	BB	SO	AVG	OBP	SLG	PRO+	BR	/A	RC	SB	CS	SBR	FR	POS	TPR
1951	Det-A	1	1	0	0	0	0	0	0	0	1	.000	.000	.000	-99	-0	-0	0	0	0	0	0	H	0.0

■ JACK DAUGHERTY

Daugherty, John Michael b: 7/3/60, Hialeah, Fla. BB/TL, 6'", 188 lbs. Deb: 9/01/87

YEAR	TM/L	G	AB	R	H	2B	3B	HR	RBI	BB	SO	AVG	OBP	SLG	PRO+	BR	/A	RC	SB	CS	SBR	FR	POS	TPR
1987	Mon-N	11	10	1	1	1	0	0	0	0	3	.100	.100	.200	-22	-2	-2	0	0	0	0	0	/1	-0.1
1989	Tex-A	52	106	15	32	4	2	1	10	11	21	.302	.373	.406	117	3	3	17	2	1	0	2	1/OD	0.3
1990	Tex-A	125	310	36	93	20	2	6	47	22	49	.300	.350	.435	116	7	7	48	0	0	0	-1	O1D	0.3
Total	3	188	426	52	126	25	4	7	58	33	73	.296	.351	.423	113	8	7	65	2	1	0	2	/1OD	0.5

■ BOB DAUGHTERS

Daughters, Robert Francis "Red" b: 8/5/14, Cincinnati, Ohio d: 8/22/88, Southbury, Conn. BR/TR, 6'2", 185 lbs. Deb: 4/24/37

YEAR	TM/L	G	AB	R	H	2B	3B	HR	RBI	BB	SO	AVG	OBP	SLG	PRO+	BR	/A	RC	SB	CS	SBR	FR	POS	TPR
1937	Bos-A	1	0	1	0	0	0	0	0	0	0	—	—	—	—	0	0	0	0	0	0	0	R	0.0

■ DARREN DAULTON
Daulton, Darren Arthur b: 1/3/62, Arkansas City, Kan. BL/TR, 6', 185 lbs. Deb: 9/25/83

YEAR	TM/L	G	AB	R	H	2B	3B	HR	RBI	BB	SO	AVG	OBP	SLG	PRO+	BR	/A	RC	SB	CS	SBR	FR	POS	TPR
1983	Phi-N	2	3	1	1	0	0	0	0	1	1	.333	.500	.333	137	0	0	1	0	0	0	0	/C	0.0
1985	Phi-N	36	103	14	21	3	1	4	11	16	37	.204	.311	.369	87	-1	-2	13	3	0	1	1	C	0.1
1986	Phi-N	49	138	18	31	4	0	8	21	38	41	.225	.395	.428	123	7	6	26	2	3	-1	-4	C	0.2
1987	Phi-N	53	129	10	25	6	0	3	13	16	37	.194	.283	.310	55	-8	-9	13	0	0	0	1	C/1	-0.4
1988	Phi-N	58	144	13	30	6	0	1	12	17	26	.208	.292	.271	61	-7	-7	12	2	1	0	-6	C/1	-1.0
1989	Phi-N	131	368	29	74	12	2	8	44	52	58	.201	.303	.310	76	-11	-11	37	2	1	0	-12	*C	-1.4
1990	Phi-N	143	459	62	123	30	1	12	57	72	72	.268	.370	.416	116	12	12	76	7	1	2	-10	*C	1.0
Total	7	472	1344	147	305	61	4	36	158	212	272	.227	.334	.359	92	-8	-10	178	16	6	1	-30	C/1	-1.5

■ YO-YO DAVALILLO
Davalillo, Pompeyo Antonio (Romero) b: 6/30/31, Caracas, Venez. BR/TR, 5'3", 140 lbs. Deb: 8/01/53

YEAR	TM/L	G	AB	R	H	2B	3B	HR	RBI	BB	SO	AVG	OBP	SLG	PRO+	BR	/A	RC	SB	CS	SBR	FR	POS	TPR
1953	Was-A	19	58	10	17	1	0	0	2	1	7	.293	.305	.310	68	-3	-3	6	1	0	0	2	S	0.1

■ VIC DAVALILLO
Davalillo, Victor Jose (Romero) b: 7/31/36, Cabimas, Venez. BL/TR, 5'7", 150 lbs. Deb: 4/09/63

YEAR	TM/L	G	AB	R	H	2B	3B	HR	RBI	BB	SO	AVG	OBP	SLG	PRO+	BR	/A	RC	SB	CS	SBR	FR	POS	TPR
1963	Cle-A	90	370	44	108	18	5	7	36	16	41	.292	.323	.424	108	3	3	50	3	3	-1	12	O	1.2
1964	Cle-A	150	577	64	156	26	2	6	51	34	77	.270	.312	.354	85	-12	-12	65	21	11	-0	8	*O	-0.9
1965	Cle-A	142	505	67	152	19	1	5	40	35	50	.301	.346	.372	103	3	2	68	26	7	4	10	*O	1.2
1966	Cle-A	121	344	42	86	6	4	3	19	24	37	.250	.299	.317	77	-10	-10	32	8	6	-1	-3	*O	-1.9
1967	Cle-A	139	359	47	103	17	5	2	22	10	30	.287	.308	.379	101	-0	-1	39	6	7	-2	-12	*O	-2.0
1968	Cle-A	51	180	15	43	2	3	2	13	3	19	.239	.255	.317	74	-6	-6	13	8	6	-1	1	O	-0.9
	Cal-A	93	339	34	101	15	4	1	18	15	34	.298	.328	.375	117	4	5	41	17	10	-1	1	O	0.3
	Yr	144	519	49	144	17	7	3	31	18	53	.277	.303	.355	102	-2	-1	54	25	16	-2	2		-0.6
1969	Cal-A	33	71	10	11	1	1	0	1	6	5	.155	.231	.197	22	-8	-7	4	3	0	1	-1	O/1	-0.8
	StL-N	63	98	15	26	3	0	2	10	7	8	.265	.314	.357	87	-2	-2	10	1	1	-0	1	O/P	-0.1
1970	StL-N	111	183	29	57	14	3	1	33	13	19	.311	.357	.437	109	3	2	28	4	1	1	1	O	0.1
1971	*Pit-N	99	295	48	84	14	6	1	33	11	31	.285	.315	.383	97	-2	-2	36	10	2	2	1	O1	-0.1
1972	*Pit-N	117	368	59	117	19	2	4	28	26	44	.318	.368	.413	124	10	11	59	14	1	4	-2	O1	0.8
1973	Pit-N	59	83	9	15	1	0	1	3	2	7	.181	.200	.229	19	-9	-9	3	0	2	-1	2	1O	-0.9
	*Oak-A	38	64	5	12	1	0	0	4	3	4	.188	.224	.203	22	-7	-6	3	0	0	0	1	O/1D	-0.5
1974	Oak-A	17	23	0	4	0	0	0	1	2	2	.174	.240	.174	22	-2	-2	1	0	0	0	0	/OD	-0.1
1977	*LA-N	24	48	3	15	2	0	0	4	0	6	.313	.313	.354	79	-2	-1	5	0	0	0	-2	O	-0.3
1978	LA-N	75	77	15	24	1	1	1	11	3	7	.312	.338	.390	103	0	0	10	2	1	0	0	O/1	0.0
1979	LA-N	29	27	2	7	1	0	0	2	2	0	.259	.310	.296	67	-1	-1	3	0	0	1	0	/O	0.0
1980	LA-N	7	6	1	1	0	0	0	0	0	1	.167	.167	.167	-7	-1	-1	0	0	0	0	0	/1	0.0
Total	16	1458	4017	509	1122	160	37	36	329	212	422	.279	.317	.364	94	-38	-35	472	125	58	3	20	*O/1DP	-4.9

■ JERRY DaVANON
DaVanon, Frank Gerald b: 8/21/45, Oceanside, Cal. BR/TR, 5'11", 175 lbs. Deb: 4/11/69

YEAR	TM/L	G	AB	R	H	2B	3B	HR	RBI	BB	SO	AVG	OBP	SLG	PRO+	BR	/A	RC	SB	CS	SBR	FR	POS	TPR
1969	SD-N	24	59	4	8	1	0	0	3	3	12	.136	.177	.153	-7	-8	-8	1	0	3	-2	0	2/S	-0.7
	StL-N	16	40	7	12	3	0	1	7	6	8	.300	.391	.450	135	2	2	7	0	0	0	1	S	0.5
	Yr	40	99	11	20	4	0	1	10	9	20	.202	.269	.273	53	-6	-6	8	0	3	-2	1		-0.2
1970	StL-N	11	18	2	2	1	0	0	0	2	5	.111	.200	.167	-1	-3	-3	1	0	0	0	3	/32	0.0
1971	Bal-A	38	81	14	19	5	0	0	4	12	20	.235	.340	.296	82	-2	-1	8	0	0	0	-3	2S/31	-0.2
1973	Cal-A	41	49	6	12	3	0	0	2	3	9	.245	.288	.306	73	-2	-2	4	1	2	-1	5	S2/3	0.5
1974	StL-N	30	40	4	6	1	0	0	4	4	5	.150	.261	.175	24	-4	-4	2	0	1	-1	-2	S/32O	-0.4
1975	Hou-N	32	97	15	27	4	2	1	10	16	7	.278	.386	.392	125	3	4	16	2	0	1	2	S/23	1.0
1976	Hou-N	61	107	19	31	3	3	1	20	21	12	.290	.411	.402	144	6	7	18	0	2	-1	3	2S/3	1.2
1977	StL-N	9	8	2	0	0	0	0	0	1	2	.000	.111	.000	-68	-2	-2	0	0	0	0	1	/2	0.0
Total	8	262	499	73	117	21	5	3	50	68	80	.234	.332	.315	86	-10	-7	56	3	8	-4	12	S/2301	1.9

■ JIM DAVENPORT
Davenport, James Houston b: 8/17/33, Siluria, Ala. BR/TR, 5'11", 170 lbs. Deb: 4/15/58 MC

YEAR	TM/L	G	AB	R	H	2B	3B	HR	RBI	BB	SO	AVG	OBP	SLG	PRO+	BR	/A	RC	SB	CS	SBR	FR	POS	TPR
1958	SF-N	134	434	70	111	22	3	12	41	33	64	.256	.319	.403	92	-7	-6	57	1	3	-2	-4	*3/S	-1.0
1959	SF-N	123	469	65	121	16	3	6	38	28	65	.258	.303	.343	73	-19	-18	50	0	1	-1	-3	*3/S	-2.5
1960	SF-N	112	363	43	91	15	3	6	38	26	58	.251	.308	.358	87	-9	-7	39	0	2	-1	-0	*3/S	-0.9
1961	SF-N	137	436	64	121	28	4	12	65	46	65	.278	.348	.443	112	5	7	67	4	3	-1	8	*3	0.8
1962	*SF-N	144	485	83	144	25	5	14	58	45	76	.297	.359	.456	119	11	12	76	2	5	-2	4	*3	1.7
1963	SF-N	147	460	40	116	19	3	4	36	32	87	.252	.301	.333	83	-11	-10	46	5	2	0	1	*32/S	-0.6
1964	SF-N	116	297	24	70	10	6	2	26	29	46	.236	.304	.330	77	-8	-9	29	2	0	1	-3	S32	-0.6
1965	SF-N	106	271	29	68	14	3	4	31	21	47	.251	.307	.369	87	-4	-5	30	0	0	0	-21	3S2	-2.2
1966	SF-N	111	305	42	76	6	2	9	30	22	40	.249	.302	.370	83	-6	-7	33	1	1	-0	-17	S32/1	-2.0
1967	SF-N	124	295	42	81	10	3	5	30	39	50	.275	.367	.380	116	7	7	41	1	4	-2	1	3S2	0.7
1968	SF-N	113	272	27	61	1	1	1	17	26	32	.224	.292	.246	63	-12	-11	19	0	3	-2	-7	3S/2	-2.0
1969	SF-N	112	303	20	73	10	1	2	42	29	37	.241	.307	.300	72	-11	-11	27	0	1	-1	1	*3/1SO	-0.9
1970	SF-N	22	37	3	9	1	0	0	4	7	6	.243	.364	.270	73	-1	-1	4	0	0	0	-3	3	-0.4
Total	13	1501	4427	552	1142	177	37	77	456	382	673	.258	.320	.367	90	-65	-57	519	16	25	-10	-42	*3S2/10	-9.9

■ ANDRE DAVID
David, Andre Anter b: 5/18/58, Hollywood, Cal. BL/TL, 6', 170 lbs. Deb: 6/29/84

YEAR	TM/L	G	AB	R	H	2B	3B	HR	RBI	BB	SO	AVG	OBP	SLG	PRO+	BR	/A	RC	SB	CS	SBR	FR	POS	TPR
1984	Min-A	33	48	5	12	2	0	1	5	7	11	.250	.357	.354	93	0	-0	6	0	0	0	-1	O/D	-0.1
1986	Min-A	5	5	0	1	0	0	0	0	0	2	.200	.333	.200	48	-0	-0	0	0	0	0	0	/D	0.0
Total	2	38	53	5	13	2	0	1	5	7	13	.245	.355	.340	89	-0	-1	6	0	0	0	-1	/OD	-0.1

■ CLAUDE DAVIDSON
Davidson, Claude Boucher "Davey" b: 10/13/1896, Boston, Mass. d: 4/18/56, Weymouth, Mass. BL/TR, 5'11", 155 lbs. Deb: 4/25/18

YEAR	TM/L	G	AB	R	H	2B	3B	HR	RBI	BB	SO	AVG	OBP	SLG	PRO+	BR	/A	RC	SB	CS	SBR	FR	POS	TPR
1918	Phi-A	31	81	4	15	1	0	0	4	5	9	.185	.233	.198	29	-7	-7	4	0			-7	2/O3	-1.4
1919	Was-A	2	7	1	3	0	0	0	0	1	1	.429	.500	.429	163	1	1	2	0			-0	/3	0.1
Total	2	33	88	5	18	1	0	0	4	6	10	.205	.255	.216	41	-6	-6	6	0			-7	/2O3	-1.3

■ HOMER DAVIDSON
Davidson, Homer Hurd "Divvy" b: 10/14/1884, Cleveland, Ohio d: 7/26/48, Detroit, Mich. TR, 5'10.5", 155 lbs. Deb: 4/25/08

YEAR	TM/L	G	AB	R	H	2B	3B	HR	RBI	BB	SO	AVG	OBP	SLG	PRO+	BR	/A	RC	SB	CS	SBR	FR	POS	TPR
1908	Cle-A	9	4	2	0	0	0	0	0	0		.000	.000	.000	-99	-1	-1	0	1			2	/CO	0.1

■ MARK DAVIDSON
Davidson, John Mark b: 2/15/61, Knoxville, Tenn. BR/TR, 6'2", 180 lbs. Deb: 6/20/86

YEAR	TM/L	G	AB	R	H	2B	3B	HR	RBI	BB	SO	AVG	OBP	SLG	PRO+	BR	/A	RC	SB	CS	SBR	FR	POS	TPR
1986	Min-A	36	68	5	8	3	0	0	2	6	22	.118	.189	.162	-3	-10	-10	2	2	3	-1	2	O/D	-0.9
1987	*Min-A	102	150	32	40	4	1	1	14	13	26	.267	.325	.327	71	-5	-6	17	9	2	2	7	O/D	0.0
1988	Min-A	100	106	22	23	7	0	1	10	10	20	.217	.291	.311	67	-4	-5	9	3	3	-1	9	O/3D	0.2
1989	Hou-N	33	65	7	13	2	1	1	5	7	14	.200	.278	.308	70	-3	-3	6	1	0	0	0	O	-0.2
1990	Hou-N	57	130	12	38	5	1	1	11	10	18	.292	.343	.369	98	-1	-0	16	0	3	-2	4	O	0.1
Total	5	328	519	78	122	21	3	4	42	46	100	.235	.299	.310	66	-23	-24	50	15	11	-2	22	O/D3	-0.8

■ BILL DAVIDSON
Davidson, William Simpson b: 5/10/1884, Lafayette, Ind. d: 5/23/54, Lincoln, Neb. BR/TR, 5'10", 170 lbs. Deb: 9/29/09

YEAR	TM/L	G	AB	R	H	2B	3B	HR	RBI	BB	SO	AVG	OBP	SLG	PRO+	BR	/A	RC	SB	CS	SBR	FR	POS	TPR
1909	Chi-N	2	7	2	1	0	0	0	0	1		.143	.250	.143	22	-1	-1	0	1			-0	/O	0.0
1910	Bro-N	136	509	48	121	13	7	0	34	24	54	.238	.277	.291	68	-23	-22	48	27			-11	*O	-3.9
1911	Bro-N	87	292	33	68	3	4	1	26	16	21	.233	.275	.281	58	-18	-16	27	18			-7	O	-2.5
Total	3	225	808	83	190	16	11	1	60	41	75	.235	.276	.286	64	-42	-38	75	46			-18	O	-6.4

■ CHICK DAVIES
Davies, Lloyd Garrison b: 3/6/1892, Peabody, Mass. d: 9/5/73, Middletown, Conn. BL/TL, 5'8", 145 lbs. Deb: 7/11/14

YEAR	TM/L	G	AB	R	H	2B	3B	HR	RBI	BB	SO	AVG	OBP	SLG	PRO+	BR	/A	RC	SB	CS	SBR	FR	POS	TPR
1914	Phi-A	19	46	6	11	3	1	0	5	5	13	.239	.314	.348	102	-0	0	6	1			0	O/P	0.0
1915	Phi-A	56	132	13	24	5	3	0	11	14	31	.182	.270	.265	62	-7	-6	10	2	4	-2	4	O/P	-0.4

YEAR	TM/L	G	AB	R	H	2B	3B	HR	RBI	BB	SO	AVG	OBP	SLG	PRO+	BR	/A	RC	SB	CS	SBR	FR	POS	TPR
1925	NY-N	4	6	1	0	0	0	0	0	0	1	.000	.000	.000	-99	-2	-2	0	0	0	0	0	/PO	0.0
1926	NY-N	38	18	4	4	0	0	0	1	3	5	.222	.333	.222	53	-1	-1	1	0			1	P	0.0
Total	4	117	202	24	39	8	4	0	17	22	50	.193	.279	.272	64	-10	-9	17	3	4		6	/PO	-0.4

■ LEFTY DAVIS
Davis, Alphonzo De Ford b: 2/4/1875, Nashville, Tenn. d: 2/4/19, Collins, N.Y. BL/TL, 5'10", 170 lbs. Deb: 4/18/01

YEAR	TM/L	G	AB	R	H	2B	3B	HR	RBI	BB	SO	AVG	OBP	SLG	PRO+	BR	/A	RC	SB	FR	POS	TPR
1901	Bro-N	25	91	11	19	2	0	0	7	10		.209	.287	.231	52	-5	-5	8	4	-5	O/2	-1.2
	Pit-N	87	335	87	105	8	11	2	33	56		.313	.412	.421	140	21	20	70	22	7	O	1.8
	Yr	112	426	98	124	10	11	2	40	66		.291	.386	.380	122	16	15	76	26	2		0.6
1902	Pit-N	59	232	52	65	7	3	0	20	35		.280	.379	.336	119	8	7	39	19	-2	O	0.1
1903	NY-A	104	372	54	88	10	0	0	20	43		.237	.316	.263	72	-8	-11	38	11	-7	*O/S	-2.5
1907	Cin-N	73	266	28	61	5	5	1	25	23		.229	.291	.297	83	-4	-5	27	9	5	O	-0.3
Total	4	348	1296	232	338	32	19	3	110	167		.261	.346	.322	99	12	5	181	65	-2	O/S2	-2.1

■ ALVIN DAVIS
Davis, Alvin Glenn b: 9/9/60, Riverside, Cal. BL/TR, 6'1", 195 lbs. Deb: 4/11/84

YEAR	TM/L	G	AB	R	H	2B	3B	HR	RBI	BB	SO	AVG	OBP	SLG	PRO+	BR	/A	RC	SB	CS	SBR	FR	POS	TPR
1984	Sea-A	152	567	80	161	34	3	27	116	97	78	.284	.395	.497	147	38	39	117	5	4	-1	-4	*1/D	2.4
1985	Sea-A	155	578	78	166	33	1	18	78	90	71	.287	.385	.441	125	23	23	101	1	2	-1	-5	*1	0.7
1986	Sea-A	135	479	66	130	18	1	18	72	76	68	.271	.375	.426	116	14	13	78	0	3	-2	-0	*1D	0.4
1987	Sea-A	157	580	86	171	37	2	29	100	72	84	.295	.375	.516	126	28	23	111	0	0	0	-7	*1	0.2
1988	Sea-A	140	478	67	141	24	1	18	69	95	53	.295	.416	.462	139	34	31	95	1	1	-0	-6	*1D	1.8
1989	Sea-A	142	498	84	152	30	1	21	95	101	49	.305	.428	.496	155	44	42	109	0	1	-1	-3	*1D	3.0
1990	Sea-A	140	494	63	140	21	0	17	68	85	68	.283	.393	.429	128	23	22	87	0	2	-1	-1	D1	1.6
Total	7	1021	3674	524	1061	197	9	148	598	616	471	.289	.395	.468	134	202	192	697	7	13	-6	-25	1D	10.1

■ BILL DAVIS
Davis, Arthur Willard b: 6/6/42, Graceville, Minn. BL/TL, 6'7", 215 lbs. Deb: 9/16/65

YEAR	TM/L	G	AB	R	H	2B	3B	HR	RBI	BB	SO	AVG	OBP	SLG	PRO+	BR	/A	RC	SB	CS	SBR	FR	POS	TPR
1965	Cle-A	10	10	0	3	1	0	0	0	0	1	.300	.300	.400	96	-0	-0	1	0	0	0	0	H	0.0
1966	Cle-A	23	38	2	6	1	0	1	4	6	9	.158	.273	.263	55	-2	-2	3	0	0	0	0	/1	-0.2
1969	SD-N	31	57	1	10	1	0	0	1	8	18	.175	.288	.193	39	-5	-4	3	0	0	0	-1	1	-0.6
Total	3	64	105	3	19	3	0	1	5	14	28	.181	.283	.238	50	-7	-6	8	0	0	0	-1	/1	-0.8

■ BROCK DAVIS
Davis, Bryshear Barnett b: 10/19/43, Oakland, Cal. BL/TL, 5'10", 160 lbs. Deb: 4/09/63

YEAR	TM/L	G	AB	R	H	2B	3B	HR	RBI	BB	SO	AVG	OBP	SLG	PRO+	BR	/A	RC	SB	CS	SBR	FR	POS	TPR
1963	Hou-N	34	55	7	11	2	0	0	2	4	10	.200	.254	.291	60	-3	-3	4	0	0	0	-0	O	-0.3
1964	Hou-N	1	3	0	0	0	0	0	0	1	1	.000	.250	.000	-24	-0	-0	0	0	0	0	0	/O	0.0
1966	Hou-N	10	27	2	4	1	0	0	1	5	4	.148	.281	.185	35	-2	-2	2	1	0	0	0	/O	-0.1
1970	Chi-N	6	3	0	0	0	0	0	0	0	1	.000	.000	.000	-89	-1	-1	0	0	0	0	0	/O	0.0
1971	Chi-N	106	301	22	77	7	5	0	28	35	34	.256	.337	.312	74	-5	-10	33	0	6	-4	-0	O	-1.7
1972	Mil-A	85	154	17	49	2	0	0	12	12	23	.318	.367	.331	111	2	2	18	6	4	-1	-1	O	0.0
Total	6	242	543	48	141	12	5	0	43	57	73	.260	.332	.306	79	-10	-14	58	7	10	-4	-2	O	-2.1

■ CHILI DAVIS
Davis, Charles Theodore b: 1/17/60, Kingston, Jamaica BB/TR, 6'3", 195 lbs. Deb: 4/10/81

YEAR	TM/L	G	AB	R	H	2B	3B	HR	RBI	BB	SO	AVG	OBP	SLG	PRO+	BR	/A	RC	SB	CS	SBR	FR	POS	TPR
1981	SF-N	8	15	1	2	0	0	0	0	1	2	.133	.188	.133	-8	-2	-2	0	2	0	1	-0	/O	-0.1
1982	SF-N	154	641	86	167	27	6	19	76	45	115	.261	.311	.410	100	-2	-1	79	24	13	-1	10	*O	0.7
1983	SF-N	137	486	54	113	21	2	11	59	55	108	.233	.311	.352	86	-11	-9	52	10	12	-4	5	*O	-1.0
1984	SF-N	137	499	87	157	21	6	21	81	42	74	.315	.369	.507	149	28	30	89	12	8	-1	12	*O	3.7
1985	SF-N	136	481	53	130	25	2	13	56	62	74	.270	.354	.412	119	9	12	68	15	7	0	12	*O	2.2
1986	SF-N	153	526	71	146	28	3	13	70	84	96	.278	.378	.416	125	16	19	83	16	13	-3	5	*O	1.9
1987	*SF-N	149	500	80	125	22	1	24	76	72	109	.250	.347	.442	113	5	9	78	16	9	-1	-8	*O	-0.4
1988	Cal-A	158	600	81	161	29	3	21	93	56	118	.268	.331	.432	115	9	11	82	9	10	-3	-6	*O/D	0.3
1989	Cal-A	154	560	81	152	24	1	22	90	61	109	.271	.343	.436	120	13	14	80	3	0	1	-10	*O/D	0.3
1990	Cal-A	113	412	58	109	17	1	12	58	61	89	.265	.359	.398	111	8	7	59	1	2	-1	5	DO	1.1
Total	10	1299	4720	652	1262	214	25	156	659	539	894	.267	.343	.422	115	73	89	669	108	74	-12	24	*O/D	8.4

■ DOUG DAVIS
Davis, Douglas Raymond b: 9/24/62, Bloomsburg, Pa. BR/TR, 6', 180 lbs. Deb: 7/08/88

YEAR	TM/L	G	AB	R	H	2B	3B	HR	RBI	BB	SO	AVG	OBP	SLG	PRO+	BR	/A	RC	SB	CS	SBR	FR	POS	TPR
1988	Cal-A	6	12	1	0	0	0	0	0	0	3	.000	.077	.000	-79	-3	-3	0	0	0	0	-3	/C3	-0.5

■ ERIC DAVIS
Davis, Eric Keith b: 5/29/62, Los Angeles, Cal. BR/TR, 6'2", 165 lbs. Deb: 5/19/84

YEAR	TM/L	G	AB	R	H	2B	3B	HR	RBI	BB	SO	AVG	OBP	SLG	PRO+	BR	/A	RC	SB	CS	SBR	FR	POS	TPR
1984	Cin-N	57	174	33	39	10	1	10	30	24	48	.224	.322	.466	114	4	3	28	10	2	2	8	O	1.1
1985	Cin-N	56	122	26	30	3	3	8	18	7	39	.246	.287	.516	114	2	2	19	16	3	3	4	O	0.8
1986	Cin-N	132	415	97	115	15	3	27	71	68	100	.277	.380	.523	140	27	24	95	80	11	17	3	*O	4.4
1987	Cin-N	129	474	120	139	23	4	37	100	84	134	.293	.401	.593	152	41	38	124	50	6	11	22	*O	**6.4**
1988	Cin-N	135	472	81	129	18	3	26	93	65	124	.273	.365	.489	138	27	24	90	35	3	9	-6	*O	2.5
1989	Cin-N	131	462	74	130	14	2	34	101	68	116	.281	.375	.541	154	35	33	91	21	7	2	-5	*O	3.0
1990	*Cin-N	127	453	84	118	26	2	24	86	60	100	.260	.350	.486	124	16	15	81	21	3	5	8	*O	2.4
Total	7	767	2572	515	700	109	18	166	499	376	661	.272	.367	.522	139	152	140	528	233	35	49	33	O	20.6

■ GEORGE DAVIS
Davis, George Stacey b: 8/23/1870, Cohoes, N.Y. d: 10/17/40, Philadelphia, Pa. BB/TR, 5'9", 180 lbs. Deb: 4/19/1890 M

YEAR	TM/L	G	AB	R	H	2B	3B	HR	RBI	BB	SO	AVG	OBP	SLG	PRO+	BR	/A	RC	SB	FR	POS	TPR
1890	Cle-N	136	526	98	139	22	9	6	73	53	34	.264	.336	.375	111	6	7	75	22	12	*O/2S	1.4
1891	Cle-N	136	570	115	165	35	12	3	89	53	29	.289	.354	.409	119	17	13	100	42	14	*O3/P	1.9
1892	*Cle-N	144	597	95	144	27	12	5	82	58	51	.241	.312	.352	98	1	-2	79	36	-10	3OS/2	-0.6
1893	NY-N	133	549	112	195	22	27	11	119	42	20	.355	.410	.554	157	42	41	143	37	0	*3/S	3.5
1894	*NY-N	122	477	120	168	26	19	8	91	66	10	.352	.435	.537	136	28	29	132	40	-1	*3	2.0
1895	NY-N	110	430	108	146	36	9	5	101	55	12	.340	.417	.500	141	25	27	112	48	15	312/OM	3.4
1896	NY-N	124	494	98	158	25	12	6	99	50	24	.320	.387	.455	127	17	19	108	48	11	3S/O1	2.8
1897	NY-N	130	519	112	183	31	10	10	**136**	41		.353	.406	.509	147	31	34	137	65	22	*S	4.9
1898	NY-N	121	486	80	149	20	5	2	86	32		.307	.351	.381	116	7	9	76	26	**36**	*S	4.7
1899	NY-N	108	416	68	140	21	5	1	57	37		.337	.393	.418	130	15	17	84	34	**46**	*S	**6.2**
1900	NY-N	114	426	69	136	20	4	3	61	35		.319	.374	.406	123	11	14	77	29	29	*SM	4.9
1901	NY-N	130	491	69	148	26	7	7	65	40		.301	.355	.426	133	17	20	86	27	23	*S3M	4.8
1902	Chi-A	132	485	76	145	27	7	3	93	65		.299	.387	.402	127	16	19	91	31	-2	*S/1	2.7
1903	NY-N	4	15	2	4	0	0	0	1	1		.267	.313	.267	65	-1	-1	1	0	-1	/S	-0.1
1904	Chi-A	152	563	75	142	27	15	1	69	43		.252	.305	.359	116	7	10	75	32	17	*S	3.0
1905	Chi-A	151	550	74	153	28	3	1	55	60		.278	.349	.345	128	16	18	84	31	16	*S	**4.2**
1906	*Chi-A	133	484	63	134	26	6	0	80	41		.277	.333	.355	121	10	11	69	27	10	*S/2	2.5
1907	Chi-A	132	466	59	111	16	2	1	52	47		.238	.308	.288	95	-3	-1	49	15	9	*S	1.2
1908	Chi-A	128	419	41	91	14	1	0	26	46		.217	.287	.255	80	-8	-8	39	22	4	2S/1	-0.6
1909	Chi-A	28	68	5	9	1	0	0	2	10		.132	.253	.147	28	-5	-5	4	4	1	1/2	-0.4
Total	20	2368	9031	1539	2660	450	165	73	1437	870	180	.295	.360	.405	123	249	273	1624	616	250	*S3O2/1P	52.4

■ KIDDO DAVIS
Davis, George Willis b: 2/12/02, Bridgeport, Conn. d: 3/4/83, Bridgeporrrconn. BR/TR, 5'11", 178 lbs. Deb: 6/15/26

YEAR	TM/L	G	AB	R	H	2B	3B	HR	RBI	BB	SO	AVG	OBP	SLG	PRO+	BR	/A	RC	SB	CS	SBR	FR	POS	TPR
1926	NY-A	1	0	0	0	0	0	0	0	0	0	—	—	—		0	0	0	0	0	0	-0	/O	0.0
1932	Phi-N	137	576	100	178	39	6	5	57	44	56	.309	.359	.424	98	8	-1	90	16			8	*O	-0.2
1933	*NY-N	126	434	61	112	20	4	7	37	25	30	.258	.298	.371	92	-6	-5	47	10			-12	*O	-2.6
1934	StL-N	16	33	6	10	3	0	1	4	3	1	.303	.361	.485	117	1	1	6	1			2	/O	0.2
	Phi-N	100	393	50	115	25	5	3	48	27	28	.293	.338	.405	86	-1	-8	55	1			15	*O	0.2
	Yr	116	426	56	125	28	5	4	52	30	29	.293	.340	.411	89	-0	-7	60	2			17		0.4
1935	NY-N	47	91	16	24	7	1	2	6	10	4	.264	.343	.429	108	1	1	14	2			-1	O	0.0

YEAR	TM/L	G	AB	R	H	2B	3B	HR	RBI	BB	SO	AVG	OBP	SLG	PRO+	BR	/A	RC	SB	CS	SBR	FR	POS	TPR
1936	*NY-N	47	67	6	16	1	0	0	5	6	5	.239	.301	.254	51	-4	-4	6	0			5	O	0.0
1937	NY-N	56	76	20	20	10	0	0	9	10	7	.263	.356	.395	103	1	0	11	1			0	O	0.0
	Cin-N	40	136	19	35	6	0	1	5	16	6	.257	.340	.324	85	-3	-2	16	1			2	O	-0.1
	Yr	96	212	39	55	16	0	1	14	26	13	.259	.346	.349	90	-3	-2	27	2			2		-0.1
1938	Cin-N	5	18	3	5	1	0	0	0	1	4	.278	.316	.333	81	-1	-0	2	0			0	/O	0.0
Total	8	575	1824	281	515	112	16	19	171	142	141	.282	.336	.393	92	-5	-19	246	32	0		18	O	-2.5

■ GERRY DAVIS
Davis, Gerald Edward b: 12/25/58, Trenton, N.J. BR/TR, 6', 185 lbs. Deb: 9/20/83

YEAR	TM/L	G	AB	R	H	2B	3B	HR	RBI	BB	SO	AVG	OBP	SLG	PRO+	BR	/A	RC	SB	CS	SBR	FR	POS	TPR
1983	SD-N	5	15	3	5	2	0	0	1	3	4	.333	.444	.467	158	1	1	3	1	0	0	0	/O	0.2
1985	SD-N	44	58	10	17	3	1	0	2	5	7	.293	.349	.379	105	0	0	7	0	0	0	0	O	0.0
Total	2	49	73	13	22	5	1	0	3	8	11	.301	.370	.397	117	2	2	11	1	0	0	0	/O	0.2

■ GLENN DAVIS
Davis, Glenn Earle b: 3/28/61, Jacksonville, Fla. BR/TR, 6'3", 210 lbs. Deb: 9/02/84

YEAR	TM/L	G	AB	R	H	2B	3B	HR	RBI	BB	SO	AVG	OBP	SLG	PRO+	BR	/A	RC	SB	CS	SBR	FR	POS	TPR
1984	Hou-N	18	61	6	13	5	0	2	8	4	12	.213	.262	.393	88	-2	-1	7	0	0	0	2	1	0.0
1985	Hou-N	100	350	51	95	11	0	20	64	27	68	.271	.336	.474	128	10	11	53	0	0	0	-2	1/O	0.7
1986	*Hou-N	158	574	91	152	32	3	31	101	64	72	.265	.348	.493	133	22	24	100	3	1	0	2	*1	2.0
1987	Hou-N	151	578	70	145	35	2	27	93	47	84	.251	.313	.458	105	-1	2	80	4	1	1	3	*1	-0.2
1988	Hou-N	152	561	78	152	26	0	30	99	53	77	.271	.346	.478	140	24	26	91	4	3	-1	3	*1	2.0
1989	Hou-N	158	581	87	156	26	1	34	89	69	123	.269	.353	.492	144	29	31	102	4	2	0	3	*1	2.3
1990	Hou-N	93	327	44	82	15	4	22	64	46	54	.251	.357	.523	142	17	18	62	8	3	1	-3	1	1.1
Total	7	830	3032	427	795	150	10	166	518	310	490	.262	.340	.483	130	99	111	494	23	10	1	4	1/O	7.9

■ HARRY DAVIS
Davis, Harry Albert "Stinky" b: 5/7/08, Shreveport, La. BL/TL, 5'10.5", 160 lbs. Deb: 4/13/32

YEAR	TM/L	G	AB	R	H	2B	3B	HR	RBI	BB	SO	AVG	OBP	SLG	PRO+	BR	/A	RC	SB	CS	SBR	FR	POS	TPR
1932	Det-A	141	590	92	159	32	13	4	74	60	53	.269	.339	.388	84	-11	-14	80	12	7	-1	-5	*1	-3.1
1933	Det-A	66	173	24	37	8	2	0	14	22	8	.214	.303	.283	55	-11	-11	16	2	3	-1	-5	1	-1.9
1937	StL-A	120	450	89	124	25	3	3	35	71	26	.276	.374	.364	86	-7	-7	65	7	6	-2	-4	*1/O	-2.4
Total	3	327	1213	205	320	65	18	7	123	153	87	.264	.347	.364	81	-28	-33	161	21	16	-3	-13	1/O	-7.4

■ HARRY DAVIS
Davis, Harry H (b: Harry Davis) "Jasper" b: 7/19/1873, Philadelphia, Pa. d: 8/11/47, Philadelphia, Pa. BR/TR, 5'10", 180 lbs. Deb: 9/21/1895 M

YEAR	TM/L	G	AB	R	H	2B	3B	HR	RBI	BB	SO	AVG	OBP	SLG	PRO+	BR	/A	RC	SB	CS	SBR	FR	POS	TPR
1895	NY-N	7	24	1	7	0	1	0	6	2	0	.292	.346	.375	90	-0	-0	4	1			0	/1	0.0
1896	NY-N	64	233	43	64	11	10	2	50	31	20	.275	.372	.433	117	5	6	45	16			-4	O1	0.0
	Pit-N	44	168	24	32	5	6	0	23	13	21	.190	.257	.292	48	-13	-12	15	9			1	1O/S	-0.9
	Yr	108	401	67	96	16	16	2	73	44	41	.239	.325	.374	89	-8	-6	58	25			-3		-0.9
1897	Pit-N	111	429	70	131	10	28	2	63	26		.305	.356	.473	125	11	13	82	21			-12	13O/S	0.0
1898	Pit-N	58	222	31	65	9	13	1	24	12		.293	.332	.464	132	7	8	37	7			-2	1/O	0.5
	Lou-N	37	138	18	30	5	2	1	16	7		.217	.255	.304	63	-7	-7	13	6			0	1/2O	-0.5
	Was-N	1	3	0	0	0	0	0	0	0		.000	.000	.000	-99	-1	-1	0	0			-0	/1	0.0
	Yr	96	363	49	95	14	15	2	40	19		.262	.300	.399	104	-1	0	49	13			-2		0.0
1899	Was-N	18	64	3	12	2	3	0	8	8		.188	.288	.313	67	-3	-3	6	2			-1	1	-0.2
1901	Phi-A	117	496	92	152	28	10	8	76	23		.306	.338	.452	115	11	8	85	21			9	*1	1.0
1902	Phi-A	133	561	89	172	43	8	6	92	30		.307	.344	.444	114	13	9	98	28			7	*1/O	1.7
1903	Phi-A	106	420	77	125	28	7	6	55	24		.298	.336	.440	127	16	14	72	24			-1	*1/O	1.4
1904	Phi-A	102	404	54	125	21	11	10	62	23		.309	.347	.490	158	28	26	75	12			-1	*1	3.0
1905	*Phi-A	150	607	93	173	47	6	8	83	43		.285	.332	.422	139	26	25	100	36			1	*1	2.4
1906	Phi-A	145	551	94	161	40	8	12	96	49		.292	.350	.459	150	33	31	100	23			0	*1	2.9
1907	Phi-A	149	582	84	155	37	8	8	87	42		.266	.336	.399	126	17	16	83	20			4	*1	2.0
1908	Phi-A	147	513	65	127	23	9	5	62	61		.248	.328	.357	117	15	11	67	20			1	*1	0.9
1909	Phi-A	149	530	73	142	22	11	4	75	51		.268	.338	.374	122	15	14	73	20			-5	*1	0.9
1910	*Phi-A	139	492	61	122	19	4	1	41	53		.248	.332	.309	102	2	3	57	17			-4	*1	0.4
1911	*Phi-A	57	183	27	36	9	1	1	22	24		.197	.297	.273	60	-10	-9	16	2			2	1	-0.5
1912	Cle-A	2	5	0	0	0	0	0	0	0		.000	.000	.000	-97	-1	-1	0	0			0	/1M	0.0
1913	Phi-A	7	17	2	6	2	0	0	4	1	4	.353	.389	.471	155	1	1	3	0			1	/1	0.2
1914	Phi-A	5	7	0	3	0	0	0	2	1	0	.429	.556	.429	203	1	1	1	0	2	-1	-0	/1	0.0
1915	Phi-A	5	3	0	1	0	0	0	4	0	0	.333	.333	.333	102	-0	-0	0	0			0	/1	0.0
1916	Phi-A	1	0	0	0	0	0	0	0	1	0	—	1.000	—	211	0	0	0	0			0	H	0.0
1917	Phi-A	1	1	0	0	0	0	0	0	0	0	.000	.000	.000	-99	-0	-0	0	0			0	H	0.0
Total	22	1755	6653	1001	1841	361	146	75	951	525	45	.277	.333	.409	120	166	153	1033	285	2		-5	*1/O32S	15.2

■ TOMMY DAVIS
Davis, Herman Thomas b: 3/21/39, Brooklyn, N.Y. BR/TR, 6'2", 195 lbs. Deb: 9/22/59 C

YEAR	TM/L	G	AB	R	H	2B	3B	HR	RBI	BB	SO	AVG	OBP	SLG	PRO+	BR	/A	RC	SB	CS	SBR	FR	POS	TPR
1959	LA-N	1	1	0	0	0	0	0	0	0	1	1.000	1.000	1.000	-93	-0	-0	0	0	0	0	0	H	0.0
1960	LA-N	110	352	43	97	18	1	11	44	13	35	.276	.305	.426	92	-2	-5	45	6	2	1	-6	O/3	-1.3
1961	LA-N	132	460	60	128	13	2	15	58	32	53	.278	.328	.413	87	-4	-9	59	10	4	1	-2	O3	-1.7
1962	LA-N	163	665	120	230	27	9	27	153	33	65	.346	.379	.535	151	37	42	129	18	6	2	-5	*O3	3.1
1963	*LA-N	146	556	69	181	19	3	16	88	29	59	.326	.363	.457	144	24	28	86	15	10	-2	-11	*O3	0.9
1964	LA-N	152	592	70	163	20	5	14	86	29	68	.275	.314	.397	106	-2	3	69	11	8	-2	4	*O	0.1
1965	LA-N	17	60	3	15	1	1	0	9	2	4	.250	.274	.300	66	-3	-3	3	2	1	0	-3	O	-0.5
1966	*LA-N	100	313	27	98	11	1	3	27	16	36	.313	.347	.383	111	1	4	38	3	3	-1	-7	O/3	-0.5
1967	NY-N	154	577	72	174	32	0	16	73	31	71	.302	.345	.440	125	16	17	84	9	3	1	-9	*O/1	0.3
1968	Chi-A	132	456	30	122	5	3	8	50	16	48	.268	.292	.344	91	-5	-6	42	4	2	0	-9	*O/1	-2.2
1969	Sea-A	123	454	52	123	29	1	6	80	30	46	.271	.322	.379	97	-4	-3	53	19	4	3	-9	*O/1	-1.1
	Hou-N	24	79	2	19	3	0	1	9	8	9	.241	.318	.316	80	-2	-2	8	1	1	-0	-2	O	-0.5
1970	Hou-N	57	213	24	60	12	2	3	30	7	25	.282	.305	.399	91	-5	-4	25	8	3	1	-5	O	-0.9
	Chi-N	11	42	4	11	2	0	2	8	1	1	.262	.279	.452	83	-1	-1	5	0	0	0	-2	O	-0.2
	Yr	68	255	28	71	14	2	5	38	8	26	.278	.300	.408	89	-5	-5	31	8	3	1	-6		-1.1
	Oak-A	66	200	17	58	9	1	1	27	8	18	.290	.321	.360	91	-4	-3	21	2	4	-2	-8	O/1	-1.5
1971	*Oak-A	79	219	26	71	8	1	3	42	15	19	.324	.368	.411	123	6	6	31	7	1	2	2	1O/23	0.8
1972	Chi-N	15	26	3	7	1	0	0	6	2	3	.269	.321	.308	72	-1	-1	2	0	1	-1	-0	/1O	-0.2
	Bal-A	26	82	9	21	3	0	0	6	6	18	.256	.307	.293	77	-2	-2	7	2	0	1	-1	O/1	-0.3
1973	*Bal-A	137	552	53	169	20	3	7	89	30	56	.306	.343	.391	107	4	4	72	11	3	2	-0	*D/1	0.6
1974	*Bal-A	158	626	67	181	20	1	11	84	34	49	.289	.329	.377	106	1	3	73	6	2	1	0	*D	0.4
1975	Bal-A	116	460	43	130	14	1	6	57	23	52	.283	.317	.357	96	-7	-3	49	2	0	1	0	*D	-0.2
1976	Cal-A	72	219	16	58	5	0	3	26	15	18	.265	.315	.329	95	-3	-1	20	0	1	-1	0	D/1	-0.1
	KC-A	8	19	1	5	0	0	0	0	1	0	.263	.300	.263	65	-1	-1	1	0	0	0	0	/D	0.0
	Yr	80	238	17	63	5	0	3	26	16	18	.265	.314	.324	92	-4	-2	21	0	1	-1	0		-0.1
Total	18	1999	7223	811	2121	272	35	153	1052	381	754	.294	.332	.405	109	44	65	923	136	59	5	-72	*OD3/12	-5.0

■ IKE DAVIS
Davis, Isaac Marion b: 6/14/1895, Pueblo, Col. d: 4/2/84, Tucson, Ariz. BR/TR, 5'7", 140 lbs. Deb: 4/23/19

YEAR	TM/L	G	AB	R	H	2B	3B	HR	RBI	BB	SO	AVG	OBP	SLG	PRO+	BR	/A	RC	SB	CS	SBR	FR	POS	TPR
1919	Was-A	8	14	0	0	0	0	0	0	0	6	.000	.000	.000	-99	-4	-4	0	0			-2	/S	-0.5
1924	Chi-A	10	33	5	8	1	1	0	4	2	5	.242	.286	.333	61	-2	-2	3	0	0	0	1	S	0.0
1925	Chi-A	146	562	105	143	31	9	0	61	71	58	.240	.333	.327	72	-27	-22	66	19	14	-3	8	*S	0.5
Total	3	164	609	110	143	32	10	0	65	73	69	.235	.324	.320	68	-33	-28	69	19	14		8	S	0.0

■ IRA DAVIS
Davis, J. Ira "Slats" b: 7/8/1870, Philadelphia, Pa. d: 12/21/42, Brooklyn, N.Y. 162 lbs. Deb: 4/22/1899

YEAR	TM/L	G	AB	R	H	2B	3B	HR	RBI	BB	SO	AVG	OBP	SLG	PRO+	BR	/A	RC	SB	CS	SBR	FR	POS	TPR
1899	NY-N	6	17	3	4	1	1	0	2	0		.235	.235	.412	81	-1	-1	2	1			-0	/S1	0.0

YEAR	TM/L	G	AB	R	H	2B	3B	HR	RBI	BB	SO	AVG	OBP	SLG	PRO+	BR	/A	RC	SB	CS	SBR	FR	POS	TPR

■ JACKE DAVIS   Davis, Jacke Sylvesta b: 3/5/36, Carthage, Tex.   BR/TR, 5'11", 160 lbs.   Deb: 4/19/62

| 1962 | Phi-N | 48 | 75 | 9 | 16 | 0 | 1 | 1 | 6 | 4 | 20 | .213 | .253 | .280 | 44 | -6 | -6 | 5 | 1 | 0 | 0 | -1 | O | -0.7 |

■ JUMBO DAVIS   Davis, James J. b: 9/5/1861, New York, N.Y. d: 2/14/21, St.Louis, Mo.   BL/TR, 5'11", 195 lbs.   Deb: 7/27/1884 U

1884	KC-U	7	29	3	6	0	0	0			0	.207	.207	.207	46	-2	-1	1	0			-2	/3	-0.2
1886	Bal-a	60	216	23	42	5	2	1			11	.194	.240	.250	56	-11	-10	16	12			5	3	-0.2
1887	Bal-a	130	485	81	150	23	**19**	8			28	.309	.353	.485	143	20	25	103	49			4	3S	2.1
1888	KC-a	121	491	70	131	22	8	3	61	20		.267	.304	.363	109	8	3	68	42			30	*3/S	3.1
1889	KC-a	62	241	40	64	4	3	0	30	17	35	.266	.319	.307	76	-6	-8	32	25			-0	3	-0.6
	StL-a	2	4	1	0	0	0	0	0	1	1	.000	.200	.000	-35	-1	-1	0	0			-0	/SO	0.0
	Yr	64	245	41	64	4	3	0	30	18	36	.261	.317	.302	74	-6	-9	32	25			-1		-0.6
1890	StL-a	21	71	8	18	3	1	0			9	.254	.338	.324	85	-0	-2	10	5			-1	3	-0.2
	Bro-a	38	142	33	43	9	2	2			15	.303	.385	.437	150	8	9	28	10			-5	3	0.3
	Yr	59	213	41	61	12	3	2			24	.286	.369	.399	126	8	7	38	15			-6		0.1
1891	Was-a	12	44	7	14	3	2	0	9	7	5	.318	.422	.477	165	3	4	12	8			-2	3	0.2
Total	7	453	1723	266	468	69	37	14	100	108	41	.272	.322	.379	110	20	19	272	151			28	3/SO	4.5

■ JODY DAVIS   Davis, Jody Richard b: 11/12/56, Gainesville, Ga.   BR/TR, 6'4", 192 lbs.   Deb: 4/21/81

1981	Chi-N	56	180	14	46	5	1	4	21	21	28	.256	.337	.361	94	-0	-1	21	0	1	-1	-1	C	-0.1
1982	Chi-N	130	418	41	109	20	2	12	52	36	92	.261	.321	.404	99	0	-1	55	0	1	-1	8	*C	0.8
1983	Chi-N	151	510	56	138	31	2	24	84	33	93	.271	.317	.480	113	10	7	72	0	2	-1	-12	*C	-0.1
1984	*Chi-N	150	523	55	134	25	2	19	94	47	99	.256	.319	.421	97	3	-3	63	5	6	-2	4	*C	0.4
1985	Chi-N	142	482	47	112	30	0	17	58	48	83	.232	.302	.400	85	-4	-11	57	1	0	0	0	*C	-0.5
1986	Chi-N	148	528	61	132	27	2	21	74	41	110	.250	.304	.428	92	-2	-7	66	0	1	-1	4	*C/1	0.0
1987	Chi-N	125	428	57	106	12	2	19	51	52	91	.248	.332	.418	93	-2	-4	58	1	2	-1	-2	*C	0.3
1988	Chi-N	88	249	19	57	9	0	6	33	29	51	.229	.312	.337	83	-4	-5	25	0	3	-2	-4	C	-0.7
	Atl-N	2	8	2	2	0	0	1	3	0	1	.250	.250	.625	137	0	0	1	0	0	0	1	/C	0.1
	Yr	90	257	21	59	9	0	7	36	29	52	.230	.310	.346	84	-4	-5	27	0	3	-2	-3		-0.6
1989	Atl-N	78	231	12	39	5	0	4	19	23	61	.169	.247	.242	39	-18	-19	13	0	0	0	-9	C/1	-2.4
1990	Atl-N	12	28	0	2	0	0	0	1	3	3	.071	.161	.071	-33	-5	-5	0	0	0	0	1	/1C	-0.4
Total	10	1082	3585	364	877	164	11	127	490	333	712	.245	.310	.403	91	-22	-49	432	7	16	-8	-10	*C/1	-2.6

■ JOHN DAVIS   Davis, John Humphrey "Red" b: 7/15/15, Laurel Run, Pa.   BR/TR, 5'11", 172 lbs.   Deb: 9/09/41

| 1941 | NY-N | 21 | 70 | 8 | 15 | 3 | 0 | 0 | 5 | 8 | 12 | .214 | .295 | .257 | 55 | -4 | -4 | 6 | 0 | | | 1 | 3 | -0.2 |

■ CRASH DAVIS   Davis, Lawrence Columbus b: 7/14/19, Canon, Ga.   BR/TR, 6', 173 lbs.   Deb: 6/15/40

1940	Phi-A	23	67	4	18	1	1	0	9	3	10	.269	.310	.313	63	-4	-4	7	1	0	0	4	2/S	0.1
1941	Phi-A	39	105	8	23	3	0	0	8	11	16	.219	.293	.248	45	-8	-8	9	0	0	0	2	21	-0.3
1942	Phi-A	86	272	31	61	8	1	2	26	21	30	.224	.282	.283	60	-15	-15	22	1	0	0	-5	2S/1	-1.6
Total	3	148	444	43	102	12	2	2	43	35	56	.230	.289	.279	57	-27	-26	37	2	0	1	0	/2S1	-1.8

■ MIKE DAVIS   Davis, Michael Dwayne b: 6/11/59, San Diego, Cal.   BL/TL, 6'2", 175 lbs.   Deb: 4/10/80

1980	Oak-A	51	95	11	20	2	1	1	8	7	14	.211	.265	.284	54	-6	-6	7	2	1	0	4	O/1D	-0.1
1981	*Oak-A	17	20	0	1	1	0	0	0	2	4	.050	.136	.100	-33	-3	-3	0	0	0	0	0	/O1D	-0.2
1982	Oak-A	23	75	12	30	4	0	1	10	2	8	.400	.416	.493	155	5	5	15	3	2	-0	-1	O/1	0.4
1983	Oak-A	128	443	61	122	24	4	8	62	27	74	.275	.324	.402	105	-1	2	56	32	15	1	9	*O/D	1.0
1984	Oak-A	134	382	47	88	18	3	9	46	31	66	.230	.290	.364	85	-11	-8	40	14	9	-1	1	*O	-1.1
1985	Oak-A	154	547	92	157	34	1	24	82	50	99	.287	.349	.484	135	18	24	91	24	10	1	7	*O	2.9
1986	Oak-A	142	489	77	131	28	3	19	55	34	91	.268	.317	.454	115	3	8	72	27	4	6	6	*O	1.7
1987	Oak-A	139	494	69	131	32	1	22	72	42	94	.265	.324	.468	114	3	8	72	19	7	2	-11	*OD	-0.3
1988	*LA-N	108	281	29	55	11	2	2	17	25	59	.196	.261	.270	55	-17	-16	20	7	3	0	-6	O	-2.5
1989	LA-N	67	173	21	43	7	1	5	19	16	28	.249	.312	.387	101	-0	-0	20	6	5	-1	-4	O	-0.5
Total	10	963	2999	419	778	161	16	91	371	236	537	.259	.316	.415	105	-10	14	395	134	56	7	7	O/D1	1.3

■ ODIE DAVIS   Davis, Odie Ernest b: 8/13/55, San Antonio, Tex.   BR/TR, 6'1", 178 lbs.   Deb: 9/03/80

| 1980 | Tex-A | 17 | 8 | 0 | 1 | 0 | 0 | 0 | 0 | 0 | 2 | .125 | .125 | .125 | -32 | -1 | -1 | 0 | 0 | 0 | 0 | 5 | S/3 | 0.4 |

■ OTIS DAVIS   Davis, Otis Allen "Scat" b: 9/24/20, Charleston, Ark.   BL/TL, 6', 160 lbs.   Deb: 4/22/46

| 1946 | Bro-N | 1 | 0 | 1 | 0 | 0 | 0 | 0 | 0 | 0 | 0 | — | — | — | — | 0 | 0 | 0 | 0 | | | 0 | R | 0.0 |

■ DICK DAVIS   Davis, Richard Earl b: 9/25/53, Long Beach, Cal.   BR/TR, 6'3", 190 lbs.   Deb: 7/12/77

1977	Mil-A	22	51	7	14	2	0	0	6	1	8	.275	.288	.314	64	-3	-3	4	0	0	0	-1	O/D	-0.3
1978	Mil-A	69	218	28	54	10	1	5	26	7	23	.248	.278	.372	81	-6	-6	20	2	5	-2	-0	DO	-0.9
1979	Mil-A	91	335	51	89	13	1	12	41	16	46	.266	.299	.418	91	-5	-5	38	3	3	-1	-2	DO	-0.9
1980	Mil-A	106	365	50	99	26	2	4	30	11	43	.271	.298	.386	89	-8	-6	40	5	3	-0	1	DO	-0.6
1981	*Phi-N	45	96	12	32	6	1	2	19	8	13	.333	.392	.479	139	6	5	18	1	2	-1	-2	O	0.1
1982	Phi-N	28	68	5	19	3	1	2	7	2	9	.279	.300	.441	103	0	-0	8	1	0	0	-1	O	0.0
	Tor-A	3	7	0	2	0	0	0	2	0	1	.286	.286	.286	53	-0	-0	0	0	0	0	0	/OD	0.0
	Pit-N	39	77	7	14	2	1	2	10	5	9	.182	.230	.312	49	-5	-5	6	1	0	0	-2	O	-0.7
Total	6	403	1217	160	323	62	7	27	141	50	152	.265	.298	.394	89	-22	-21	134	13	13	-4	-7	OD	-3.3

■ BRANDY DAVIS   Davis, Robert Brandon b: 9/10/28, Newark, Del.   BR/TR, 6', 170 lbs.   Deb: 4/15/52 C

1952	Pit-N	55	95	14	17	1	1	0	1	11	28	.179	.264	.211	32	-8	-9	7	9	2	2	2	O	-0.6
1953	Pit-N	12	39	5	8	2	0	0	2	0	3	.205	.205	.256	20	-5	-5	2	0	2	-1	-0	/O	-0.5
Total	2	67	134	19	25	3	1	0	3	11	31	.187	.248	.224	29	-13	-13	9	9	4	0	1	/O	-1.1

■ BOB DAVIS   Davis, Robert John Eugene b: 3/1/52, Pryor, Okla.   BR/TR, 6', 180 lbs.   Deb: 4/06/73

1973	SD-N	5	11	1	1	0	0	0	0	0	5	.091	.091	.091	-54	-2	-2	0	0	0	0	2	/C	0.0
1975	SD-N	43	128	6	30	3	2	0	7	11	31	.234	.310	.289	71	-5	-5	12	0	0	0	3	C	0.0
1976	SD-N	51	83	7	17	0	1	0	5	5	13	.205	.250	.229	40	-7	-6	5	0	0	0	4	C	0.0
1977	SD-N	48	94	9	17	2	0	1	10	5	24	.181	.238	.234	30	-10	-8	5	0	0	0	-2	C	-1.0
1978	SD-N	19	40	3	8	1	0	0	2	1	5	.200	.220	.225	26	-4	-4	1	0	1	-1	-2	C	-0.6
1979	Tor-A	32	89	6	11	2	0	1	8	6	15	.124	.188	.180	-0	-13	-13	2	0	0	0	-2	C	-1.2
1980	Tor-A	91	218	18	47	11	0	4	19	12	25	.216	.260	.321	56	-13	-14	17	0	0	0	-3	C	-1.2
1981	Cal-A	1	2	0	0	0	0	0	0	0	0	.000	.000	.000	-99	-1	-1	0	0	0	0	0	/C	0.0
Total	8	290	665	50	131	19	3	6	51	40	118	.197	.250	.262	42	-54	-52	42	0	1	-1	0	C	-4.0

■ RON DAVIS   Davis, Ronald Everette b: 10/21/41, Roanoke Rapids, N.C.   BR/TR, 6', 175 lbs.   Deb: 8/01/62

1962	Hou-N	6	14	1	3	0	0	0	1	1	7	.214	.267	.214	33	-1	-1	1	1	0	0	0	/O	0.0
1966	Hou-N	48	194	21	48	10	1	2	19	13	26	.247	.308	.340	86	-5	-3	20	2	2	-1	6	O	0.0
1967	Hou-N	94	285	31	73	19	1	7	38	17	48	.256	.303	.404	104	-1	-1	34	5	3	-0	-2	O	-0.5
1968	Hou-N	52	217	22	46	10	1	1	12	13	48	.212	.269	.281	67	-9	-9	16	0	4	-2	5	O	-0.9
	*StL-N	33	79	11	14	4	2	0	5	5	17	.177	.226	.278	51	-5	-5	5	1	0	0	3	O	-0.2
	Yr	85	296	33	60	14	3	1	17	18	65	.203	.258	.280	63	-14	-13	21	1	4	-2	8		-1.1
1969	Pit-N	62	64	10	15	1	1	0	4	7	14	.234	.310	.281	68	-3	-3	6	0	0	0	0	O	-0.5

YEAR	TM/L	G	AB	R	H	2B	3B	HR	RBI	BB	SO	AVG	OBP	SLG	PRO+	BR	/A	RC	SB	CS	SBR	FR	POS	TPR
Total	5	295	853	96	199	44	6	10	79	56	160	.233	.288	.334	82	-24	-20	83	9	9	-3	12	O	-2.1

■ STEVE DAVIS
Davis, Steven Michael b: 12/30/53, Oakland, Cal. BR/TR, 6'1", 200 lbs. Deb: 9/23/79

YEAR	TM/L	G	AB	R	H	2B	3B	HR	RBI	BB	SO	AVG	OBP	SLG	PRO+	BR	/A	RC	SB	CS	SBR	FR	POS	TPR
1979	Chi-N	3	4	0	0	0	0	0	0	0	0	.000	.000	.000	-91	-1	-1	0	0	0	0	0	/23	0.0

■ TOD DAVIS
Davis, Thomas Oscar b: 7/24/24, Los Angeles, Cal. d: 12/31/78, W.Covina, Cal. BR/TR, 6'2", 190 lbs. Deb: 4/27/49

YEAR	TM/L	G	AB	R	H	2B	3B	HR	RBI	BB	SO	AVG	OBP	SLG	PRO+	BR	/A	RC	SB	CS	SBR	FR	POS	TPR
1949	Phi-A	31	75	7	20	0	1	1	6	9	16	.267	.345	.333	83	-2	-2	10	0	0	0	-0	S3/2	-0.1
1951	Phi-A	11	15	0	1	0	0	0	0	1	3	.067	.125	.067	-46	-3	-3	0	0	0	0	-0	/23	-0.2
Total	2	42	90	7	21	0	1	1	6	10	19	.233	.310	.289	61	-5	-5	10	0	0	0	-1	/S32	-0.3

■ TRENCH DAVIS
Davis, Trench Neal b: 9/12/60, Baltimore, Md. BL/TL, 6'3", 171 lbs. Deb: 6/04/85

YEAR	TM/L	G	AB	R	H	2B	3B	HR	RBI	BB	SO	AVG	OBP	SLG	PRO+	BR	/A	RC	SB	CS	SBR	FR	POS	TPR
1985	Pit-N	2	7	1	1	0	0	0	0	0	0	.143	.143	.143	-20	-1	-1	0	1	0	0	-1	/O	-0.1
1986	Pit-N	15	23	2	3	0	0	0	1	0	4	.130	.130	.130	-27	-4	-4	0	0	0	0	1	/O	-0.2
1987	Atl-N	6	3	0	0	0	0	0	0	0	1	.000	.000	.000	-95	-1	-1	0	0	0	0	0	/H	0.0
Total	3	23	33	3	4	0	0	0	1	0	5	.121	.121	.121	-32	-6	-6	0	1	0	0	0	/O	-0.3

■ SPUD DAVIS
Davis, Virgil Lawrence b: 12/20/04, Birmingham, Ala. d: 8/14/84, Birmingham, Ala. BR/TR, 6'1", 197 lbs. Deb: 4/30/28 MC

YEAR	TM/L	G	AB	R	H	2B	3B	HR	RBI	BB	SO	AVG	OBP	SLG	PRO+	BR	/A	RC	SB	CS	SBR	FR	POS	TPR
1928	StL-N	2	5	1	1	0	0	0	1	1	0	.200	.333	.200	42	-0	-0	0	0			-1	/C	0.0
	Phi-N	67	163	16	46	2	0	3	18	15	11	.282	.343	.350	79	-4	-5	19	0			4	C	0.2
	Yr	69	168	17	47	2	0	3	19	16	11	.280	.342	.345	78	-5	-5	20	0			3		0.2
1929	Phi-N	98	263	31	90	18	0	7	48	19	17	.342	.391	.490	110	7	4	49	1			-12	C	0.0
1930	Phi-N	106	329	41	103	16	1	14	65	17	20	.313	.349	.495	94	-0	-4	54	1			-3	C	-0.1
1931	Phi-N	120	393	30	128	32	1	4	51	36	28	.326	.382	.443	112	12	8	68	0			1	*C	1.4
1932	Phi-N	125	402	44	135	23	5	14	70	40	39	.336	.399	.522	130	26	20	86	1			-4	*C	1.9
1933	Phi-N	141	495	51	173	28	3	9	65	32	24	.349	.395	.473	130	30	23	89	2			-11	*C	1.7
1934	*StL-N	107	347	45	104	22	4	9	65	34	27	.300	.366	.464	113	10	7	58	0			1	C	1.0
1935	StL-N	102	315	28	100	24	2	1	60	33	30	.317	.386	.416	111	8	6	54	0			-5	C/1	0.1
1936	StL-N	112	363	24	99	26	2	4	59	35	34	.273	.342	.388	97	-2	-2	48	0			-14	*C/3	-1.1
1937	Cin-N	76	209	19	56	10	1	3	33	23	15	.268	.341	.368	97	-2	-1	26	0			11	C	1.2
1938	Cin-N	12	36	3	6	1	0	0	1	5	6	.167	.286	.194	35	-3	-3	2	0			1	C	-0.1
	Phi-N	70	215	11	53	7	0	2	23	14	14	.247	.293	.307	67	-10	-10	17	1			-12	C	-1.9
	Yr	82	251	14	59	8	0	2	24	19	20	.235	.292	.291	62	-13	-12	19	1			-12		-2.0
1939	Phi-N	87	202	10	62	8	1	0	23	24	20	.307	.383	.356	103	1	2	29	0			-2	C	0.2
1940	Pit-N	99	285	23	93	14	1	5	39	35	20	.326	.404	.435	132	13	14	48	0			-7	C	1.1
1941	Pit-N	57	107	3	27	4	1	0	6	11	11	.252	.322	.308	78	-3	-3	10	0			-2	C	0.0
1944	Pit-N	54	93	6	28	7	0	2	14	10	8	.301	.369	.441	122	3	3	15	0			-1	C	0.3
1945	Pit-N	23	33	2	8	2	0	0	6	2	2	.242	.306	.303	67	-1	-2	3	0			-0	C	-0.1
Total	16	1458	4255	388	1312	244	22	77	647	386	326	.308	.369	.430	108	84	58	676	6			-56	*C/13	5.8

■ WILLIE DAVIS
Davis, William Henry b: 4/15/40, Mineral Springs, Ark. BL/TL, 5'11", 180 lbs. Deb: 9/08/60

YEAR	TM/L	G	AB	R	H	2B	3B	HR	RBI	BB	SO	AVG	OBP	SLG	PRO+	BR	/A	RC	SB	CS	SBR	FR	POS	TPR
1960	LA-N	22	88	12	28	6	1	2	10	4	12	.318	.348	.477	116	3	2	12	3	5	-2	1	O	0.0
1961	LA-N	128	339	56	86	19	6	12	45	27	46	.254	.318	.451	93	-0	-4	49	12	5	1	-7	*O	-1.6
1962	LA-N	157	600	103	171	18	10	21	85	42	72	.285	.338	.453	117	7	12	92	32	7	5	6	*O	1.5
1963	*LA-N	156	515	60	126	19	8	9	60	25	61	.245	.284	.365	92	-11	-7	51	25	11	1	9	*O	-0.4
1964	LA-N	157	613	91	180	23	7	12	77	22	59	.294	.319	.413	112	2	7	82	42	13	5	19	*O	2.8
1965	*LA-N	142	558	52	133	24	3	10	57	14	81	.238	.266	.346	76	-23	-18	51	25	9	2	3	*O	-1.8
1966	*LA-N	153	624	74	177	31	6	11	61	15	68	.284	.305	.405	104	-5	0	76	21	10	0	3	*O	0.0
1967	LA-N	143	569	65	146	27	9	6	41	29	65	.257	.296	.367	97	-9	-4	62	20	6	2	0	*O	-0.7
1968	LA-N	160	643	86	161	24	10	7	31	31	88	.250	.286	.351	96	-9	-4	68	36	10	5	2	*O	-0.5
1969	LA-N	129	498	66	155	23	8	11	59	33	39	.311	.359	.456	136	17	21	79	24	10	1	-0	*O	1.6
1970	LA-N	146	593	92	181	23	16	8	93	29	54	.305	.339	.438	111	4	7	88	38	14	3	10	*O	1.4
1971	LA-N	158	641	84	198	33	10	10	74	23	47	.309	.333	.438	124	12	16	88	20	8	1	5	*O	1.8
1972	LA-N	149	615	81	178	22	7	19	79	27	61	.289	.320	.441	117	9	11	87	20	3	4	5	*O	1.3
1973	LA-N	152	599	82	171	29	9	16	77	29	62	.285	.324	.444	116	6	10	86	17	5	2	-2	*O	0.3
1974	Mon-N	153	611	86	180	27	9	12	89	27	69	.295	.328	.427	104	5	2	85	25	7	3	1	*O	0.0
1975	Tex-A	42	169	16	42	8	2	5	17	4	25	.249	.270	.408	90	-3	-3	18	13	5	1	1	O	-0.2
	StL-N	98	350	41	102	19	6	6	50	14	27	.291	.326	.431	105	3	1	50	10	1	2	-6	O	-0.5
1976	SD-N	141	493	61	132	18	10	5	46	19	34	.268	.298	.375	98	-8	-4	56	14	2	3	2	*O	-0.3
1979	*Cal-A	43	56	9	14	2	1	0	2	4	7	.250	.300	.321	70	-3	-2	5	1	0	0	0	/OD	-0.1
Total	18	2429	9174	1217	2561	395	138	182	1053	418	977	.279	.314	.412	106	-2	42	1186	398	131	41	52	*O/D	4.6

■ BUTCH DAVIS
Davis, Wallace McArthur b: 6/19/58, Martin Co., N.C. BR/TR, 6', 185 lbs. Deb: 8/23/83

YEAR	TM/L	G	AB	R	H	2B	3B	HR	RBI	BB	SO	AVG	OBP	SLG	PRO+	BR	/A	RC	SB	CS	SBR	FR	POS	TPR
1983	KC-A	33	122	13	42	2	6	2	18	4	19	.344	.365	.508	137	6	6	21	4	3	-1	-3	O	0.2
1984	KC-A	41	116	11	17	3	0	2	12	10	19	.147	.214	.224	21	-12	-13	5	4	3	-1	0	O/D	-1.4
1987	Pit-N	7	7	3	1	1	0	0	0	1	3	.143	.250	.286	41	-1	-1	1	0	0	0	0	/O	0.0
1988	Bal-A	13	25	2	6	1	0	0	0	0	8	.240	.240	.280	46	-2	-2	1	1	0	0	2	O/D	0.0
1989	Bal-A	5	6	1	1	1	0	0	0	0	3	.167	.167	.333	39	-1	-0	0	0	0	0	0	/O	0.0
Total	5	99	276	30	67	8	6	4	30	15	52	.243	.282	.359	75	-10	-10	28	9	6	-1	-0	/OD	-1.2

■ ANDRE DAWSON
Dawson, Andre Fernando b: 7/10/54, Miami, Fla. BR/TR, 6'3", 180 lbs. Deb: 9/11/76

YEAR	TM/L	G	AB	R	H	2B	3B	HR	RBI	BB	SO	AVG	OBP	SLG	PRO+	BR	/A	RC	SB	CS	SBR	FR	POS	TPR
1976	Mon-N	24	85	9	20	4	1	0	7	5	13	.235	.278	.306	63	-4	-4	7	1	2	-1	2	O	-0.4
1977	Mon-N	139	525	64	148	26	9	19	65	34	93	.282	.328	.474	114	7	9	82	21	7	2	3	*O	0.9
1978	Mon-N	157	609	84	154	24	8	25	72	30	128	.253	.301	.442	106	1	2	80	28	11	2	15	*O	1.4
1979	Mon-N	155	639	90	176	24	12	25	92	27	115	.275	.311	.468	111	5	6	91	35	10	5	-2	*O	0.4
1980	Mon-N	151	577	96	178	41	7	17	87	44	69	.308	.364	.492	137	27	27	105	34	9	5	11	*O	3.9
1981	*Mon-N	103	394	71	119	21	3	24	64	35	50	.302	.369	.553	157	29	28	83	26	4	5	13	*O	4.6
1982	Mon-N	148	608	107	183	37	7	23	83	34	96	.301	.346	.498	131	25	23	106	39	10	6	14	*O	4.2
1983	Mon-N	159	633	104	189	36	10	32	113	38	81	.299	.347	.539	143	32	33	113	25	11	1	6	*O	3.8
1984	Mon-N	138	533	73	132	23	6	17	86	41	80	.248	.304	.409	103	-3	-0	65	13	5	1	11	*O	0.8
1985	Mon-N	139	529	65	135	27	2	23	91	29	92	.255	.299	.444	112	1	5	67	13	4	2	-1	*O	0.2
1986	Mon-N	130	496	65	141	32	2	20	78	37	79	.284	.341	.478	125	14	15	75	18	12	-2	-4	*O	0.7
1987	Chi-N	153	621	90	178	24	2	49	137	32	103	.287	.329	.568	127	25	22	111	11	3	2	2	*O	1.8
1988	Chi-N	157	591	78	179	31	8	24	79	37	73	.303	.348	.504	136	30	27	100	12	4	1	-4	*O	2.1
1989	*Chi-N	118	416	62	105	18	6	21	77	35	62	.252	.312	.476	114	10	7	55	8	5	-1	-0	*O	0.5
1990	Chi-N	147	529	72	164	28	5	27	100	42	65	.310	.363	.535	132	30	24	101	16	2	4	-4	*O	2.0
Total	15	2018	7785	1130	2201	396	88	346	1231	500	1199	.283	.332	.490	124	230	223	1241	300	99	31	63	*O	26.9

■ BOOTS DAY
Day, Charles Frederick b: 8/31/47, Ilion, N.Y. BL/TL, 5'9", 160 lbs. Deb: 6/15/69

YEAR	TM/L	G	AB	R	H	2B	3B	HR	RBI	BB	SO	AVG	OBP	SLG	PRO+	BR	/A	RC	SB	CS	SBR	FR	POS	TPR
1969	StL-N	11	6	1	0	0	0	0	0	1	1	.000	.143	.000	-57	-1	-1	0	0	0	0	0	/O	0.0
1970	Chi-N	11	8	2	2	0	0	0	0	0	3	.250	.250	.250	31	-1	-1	0	0	0	0	1	/O	0.0
	Mon-N	41	108	14	29	4	0	0	5	6	18	.269	.307	.306	65	-5	-5	10	3	2	-0	4	O	-0.2
	Yr	52	116	16	31	4	0	0	5	6	21	.267	.303	.302	61	-6	-6	10	3	2	-0	6		-0.2
1971	Mon-N	127	371	53	105	10	2	4	33	33	39	.283	.343	.353	97	-1	-1	47	9	4	0	1	*O	-0.5
1972	Mon-N	128	386	32	90	7	3	0	30	29	44	.233	.288	.272	59	-20	-21	31	3	6	-3	-11	*O	-4.2
1973	Mon-N	101	207	36	57	7	0	4	28	21	28	.275	.342	.367	93	-1	-2	26	0	3	-2	-1	O	-0.7

YEAR	TM/L	G	AB	R	H	2B	3B	HR	RBI	BB	SO	AVG	OBP	SLG	PRO+	BR	/A	RC	SB	CS	SBR	FR	POS	TPR
1974	Mon-N	52	65	8	12	0	0	0	2	5	8	.185	.243	.185	20	-7	-7	3	0	0	0	-0	O	-0.8
Total	6	471	1151	146	295	28	6	8	98	95	141	.256	.314	.312	75	-35	-38	117	15	15	-5	-7	O	-6.4

■ BRIAN DAYETT
Dayett, Brian Kelly   b: 1/22/57, New London, Conn.   BR/TR, 5'10", 180 lbs.   Deb: 9/11/83

YEAR	TM/L	G	AB	R	H	2B	3B	HR	RBI	BB	SO	AVG	OBP	SLG	PRO+	BR	/A	RC	SB	CS	SBR	FR	POS	TPR
1983	NY-A	11	29	3	6	0	1	0	5	2	4	.207	.258	.276	49	-2	-2	2	0	0	0	1	/O	0.0
1984	NY-A	64	127	14	31	8	0	4	23	9	14	.244	.299	.402	96	-2	-1	15	0	0	0	1	O/D	-0.1
1985	Chi-N	22	26	1	6	0	0	1	4	0	6	.231	.259	.346	61	-1	-2	2	0	0	0	0	O	-0.1
1986	Chi-N	24	67	7	18	4	0	4	11	6	10	.269	.329	.507	118	2	2	10	0	1	-1	-1	O	0.0
1987	Chi-N	97	177	20	49	14	1	5	25	20	37	.277	.350	.452	106	3	2	29	0	0	0	-2	O	-0.3
Total	5	218	426	45	110	26	2	14	68	37	71	.258	.320	.427	99	-0	-1	58	0	1	-1	-1	O/D	-0.5

■ CHARLIE DEAL
Deal, Charles Albert   b: 10/30/1891, Wilkinsburg, Pa.   d: 9/16/79, Covina, Cal.   BR/TR, 6', 160 lbs.   Deb: 7/19/12

YEAR	TM/L	G	AB	R	H	2B	3B	HR	RBI	BB	SO	AVG	OBP	SLG	PRO+	BR	/A	RC	SB	CS	SBR	FR	POS	TPR
1912	Det-A	42	142	13	32	4	2	0	11	9		.225	.272	.282	60	-8	-7	12	4			10	3	0.2
1913	Det-A	16	50	3	11	0	2	0	3	1	7	.220	.235	.300	57	-3	-3	4	2			2	3	0.0
	Bos-N	10	36	6	11	1	0	0	3	2	1	.306	.359	.333	96	0	-0	5	1			-6	2	-0.6
1914	*Bos-N	79	257	17	54	13	2	0	23	20	23	.210	.270	.276	63	-12	-12	21	4			-5	3/S	-1.5
1915	StL-F	65	223	21	72	12	4	1	27	12	16	.323	.357	.426	125	8	6	40	10			5	3	1.4
1916	StL-A	23	74	7	10	1	0	0	10	6	8	.135	.200	.149	5	-9	-8	3	4			-2	3/2	-0.9
	Chi-N	2	8	2	2	1	0	0	3	0		.250	.250	.375	82	-0	-0	1	0			2	/3	0.2
1917	Chi-N	135	449	46	114	11	3	0	47	19	18	.254	.284	.292	71	-13	-16	41	10			7	*3	-1.2
1918	*Chi-N	119	414	43	99	9	3	2	34	21	13	.239	.279	.290	72	-13	-14	37	11			-2	*3	-1.6
1919	Chi-N	116	405	37	117	23	5	2	52	12	12	.289	.316	.385	110	4	4	52	11			7	*3	1.2
1920	Chi-N	129	450	48	108	10	5	3	39	20	14	.240	.285	.304	68	-18	-19	39	5	8	-3	10	*3	-0.6
1921	Chi-N	115	422	52	122	19	8	3	66	13	9	.289	.310	.393	85	-10	-10	50	3	5	-2	14	*3	0.2
Total	10	851	2930	295	752	104	34	11	318	135	121	.257	.293	.327	79	-74	-81	304	65	13		41	3/2S	-3.2

■ LINDSAY DEAL
Deal, Fred Lindsay   b: 9/3/11, Lenoir, N.C.   d: 4/18/79, Little Rock, Ark.   BL/TR, 6', 175 lbs.   Deb: 9/13/39

YEAR	TM/L	G	AB	R	H	2B	3B	HR	RBI	BB	SO	AVG	OBP	SLG	PRO+	BR	/A	RC	SB	CS	SBR	FR	POS	TPR
1939	Bro-N	4	7	0	0	0	0	0	0	0	2	.000	.000	.000	-97	-2	-2	0	0			0	/O	-0.1

■ SNAKE DEAL
Deal, John Wesley   b: 1/21/1879, Lancaster, Pa.   d: 5/9/44, Harrisburg, Pa.   BR/TR, 6', 164 lbs.   Deb: 7/09/06

YEAR	TM/L	G	AB	R	H	2B	3B	HR	RBI	BB	SO	AVG	OBP	SLG	PRO+	BR	/A	RC	SB	CS	SBR	FR	POS	TPR
1906	Cin-N	65	231	13	48	4	3	0	21	6		.208	.228	.251	49	-14	-15	18	15			2	1	-1.6

■ PAT DEALY
Dealy, Patrick E.   b: Burlington, Vt.   d: 12/16/24, Buffalo, N.Y.   BR/TR,   Deb: 9/30/1884

YEAR	TM/L	G	AB	R	H	2B	3B	HR	RBI	BB	SO	AVG	OBP	SLG	PRO+	BR	/A	RC	SB	CS	SBR	FR	POS	TPR
1884	StP-U	5	15	2	2	0	0	0		0		.133	.133	.133	-18	-2	-1	0	0			3	/CO	0.2
1885	Bos-N	35	130	18	29	4	1	1	9	2	14	.223	.235	.292	72	-4	-4	9				-0	C/3OS1	-0.1
1886	Bos-N	15	46	9	15	1	1	0	3	4	4	.326	.380	.391	140	2	2	9	5			0	C/O	0.3
1887	Was-N	58	212	33	55	8	2	1	18	8	8	.259	.293	.330	78	-7	-5	32	36			-7	CS/O3	-0.7
1890	Syr-a	18	66	9	12	1	0	0		5		.182	.250	.197	37	-5	-4	4	4			-6	C/3O	-0.8
Total	5	131	469	71	113	14	4	2	30	19	26	.241	.275	.301	76	-17	-12	55	45			-11	/CS301	-1.1

■ CHUBBY DEAN
Dean, Alfred Lovill   b: 8/24/16, Mt.Airy, N.C.   d: 12/21/70, Riverside, Cal.   BL/TR, 5'11", 181 lbs.   Deb: 4/14/36

YEAR	TM/L	G	AB	R	H	2B	3B	HR	RBI	BB	SO	AVG	OBP	SLG	PRO+	BR	/A	RC	SB	CS	SBR	FR	POS	TPR
1936	Phi-A	111	342	41	98	21	3	1	48	24	24	.287	.337	.374	77	-14	-12	44	3	2	-0	-1	1	-2.1
1937	Phi-A	104	309	36	81	14	4	2	31	42	10	.262	.350	.353	79	-10	-9	41	2	1	0	-2	1/P	-1.8
1938	Phi-A	16	20	3	6	2	0	0	1	1	4	.300	.333	.400	85	-1	-0	3	0	0	0	0	/P	0.1
1939	Phi-A	80	77	12	27	4	0	0	19	8	4	.351	.412	.403	111	1	2	12	0	0	0	1	P	0.0
1940	Phi-A	67	90	6	26	2	0	0	6	16	9	.289	.396	.311	88	-1	-1	13	0	0	0	1	P/1	0.5
1941	Phi-A	27	37	0	9	2	0	0	9	4	3	.243	.317	.297	65	-2	-2	4	0	0	0	0	P/1	0.0
	Cle-A	17	25	2	4	1	0	0	2	3	2	.160	.250	.200	21	-3	-3	1	0	0	0	1	/P	0.0
	Yr	44	62	2	13	3	0	0	11	7	5	.210	.290	.258	48	-5	-4	5	0	0	0	1		0.0
1942	Cle-A	70	101	4	27	1	0	0	7	11	7	.267	.339	.277	79	-3	-2	10	0	0	0	-3	P	0.0
1943	Cle-A	41	46	2	9	0	0	0	5	6	2	.196	.288	.196	45	-3	-3	3	0	0	0	-1	P	-0.1
Total	8	533	1047	106	287	47	7	3	128	115	65	.274	.347	.341	79	-34	-31	129	5	3	-0	-4	P1	-3.4

■ TOMMY DEAN
Dean, Tommy Douglas   b: 8/30/45, Iuka, Miss.   BR/TR, 6', 165 lbs.   Deb: 9/17/67

YEAR	TM/L	G	AB	R	H	2B	3B	HR	RBI	BB	SO	AVG	OBP	SLG	PRO+	BR	/A	RC	SB	CS	SBR	FR	POS	TPR
1967	LA-N	12	28	4	4	1	0	0	2	0	9	.143	.143	.179	-9	-4	-4	1	0	0	0	6	S	0.4
1969	SD-N	101	273	14	48	9	2	2	9	27	54	.176	.252	.245	42	-22	-21	17	0	3	-2	4	S/2	-0.6
1970	SD-N	61	158	18	35	5	1	2	13	11	29	.222	.272	.304	56	-10	-10	13	2	0	1	6	S	0.4
1971	SD-N	41	70	2	8	0	0	0	1	4	13	.114	.162	.114	-22	-11	-10	2	1	0	0	6	S3/2	0.0
Total	4	215	529	35	95	15	3	4	25	42	105	.180	.241	.242	36	-47	-44	33	3	3	-1	23	S/32	0.2

■ HARRY DEANE
Deane, John Henry   b: 5/6/1846, Trenton, N.J.   d: 5/31/25, Indianapolis, Ind.   5'7", 150 lbs.   Deb: 7/20/1871   M

YEAR	TM/L	G	AB	R	H	2B	3B	HR	RBI	BB	SO	AVG	OBP	SLG	PRO+	BR	/A	RC	SB	CS	SBR	FR	POS	TPR
1871	Kek-n	6	22	3	4	0	1	0	2	2	0	.182	.250	.273	49	-1	-1	2	0				/OM	0.0
1874	Bal-n	47	204	29	50	9	2	0		4		.245	.260	.309	81	-4	-4	17					*O/2	-0.1
Total	2 n	53	226	32	54	9	3	0		6		.239	.259	.305	77	-6	-6	18					/O2	-0.1

■ BUDDY DEAR
Dear, Paul Stanford   b: 12/1/05, Norfolk, Va.   BR/TR, 5'8", 143 lbs.   Deb: 9/09/27

YEAR	TM/L	G	AB	R	H	2B	3B	HR	RBI	BB	SO	AVG	OBP	SLG	PRO+	BR	/A	RC	SB	CS	SBR	FR	POS	TPR
1927	Was-A	2	1	1	0	0	0	0	0	0	0	.000	.000	.000	-99	-0	-0	0	0	0	0	0	/2	0.0

■ CHARLIE DeARMOND
DeArmond, Charles Hommer "Hummer"   b: 2/13/1877, Okeana, Ohio   d: 12/17/33, Morning Sun, Ohio   BR/TR, 5'10", 165 lbs.   Deb: 9/19/03

YEAR	TM/L	G	AB	R	H	2B	3B	HR	RBI	BB	SO	AVG	OBP	SLG	PRO+	BR	/A	RC	SB	CS	SBR	FR	POS	TPR
1903	Cin-N	11	39	10	11	2	1	0	7	3		.282	.333	.385	96	0	-0	6	1			-1	3	-0.1

■ JOHN DEASLEY
Deasley, John   b: 1/1861, Philadelphia, Pa.   d: 12/25/10, Philadelphia, Pa.   Deb: 6/17/1884

YEAR	TM/L	G	AB	R	H	2B	3B	HR	RBI	BB	SO	AVG	OBP	SLG	PRO+	BR	/A	RC	SB	CS	SBR	FR	POS	TPR
1884	Was-U	31	134	20	29	1	1	0		3		.216	.234	.239	62	-5	-5	8	0			0	S	-0.2
	KC-U	13	40	3	7	2	0	0		2		.175	.214	.225	56	-2	-1	2	0			0	S	0.0
	Yr	44	174	23	36	3	1	0		5		.207	.229	.236	61	-7	-6	10	0			0		-0.2

■ PAT DEASLEY
Deasley, Thomas H.   b: 11/17/1857, Ireland   d: 4/1/43, Philadelphia, Pa.   BR/TR, 5'8.5", 154 lbs.   Deb: 5/18/1881

YEAR	TM/L	G	AB	R	H	2B	3B	HR	RBI	BB	SO	AVG	OBP	SLG	PRO+	BR	/A	RC	SB	CS	SBR	FR	POS	TPR
1881	Bos-N	43	147	13	35	5	2	0	8	5	10	.238	.263	.299	80	-4	-3	12				-2	C/OS1	-0.4
1882	Bos-N	67	264	36	70	8	0	0	29	7	4	.265	.284	.295	86	-4	-4	23				1	*CO/S	0.1
1883	StL-a	58	206	27	53	2	1	0		6		.257	.278	.277	75	-5	-6	16				1	C/O	0.0
1884	StL-a	75	254	27	52	5	4	0		7		.205	.235	.256	60	-10	-11	16				7	*C/O1	0.1
1885	NY-N	54	207	22	53	5	1	0	24	9	20	.256	.287	.290	88	-3	-3	18				8	C/OS	0.9
1886	NY-N	41	143	18	38	6	1	0	17	4	12	.266	.286	.322	84	-3	-3	14	2			8	CO	0.6
1887	NY-N	30	118	12	37	5	0	0	23	9	7	.314	.367	.356	109	1	2	17	3			-14	C/3S	-0.7
1888	Was-N	34	127	6	20	1	0	0	4	2	18	.157	.171	.165	9	-13	-12	4	2			9	C/OS2	-0.1
Total	8	402	1466	161	358	37	9	0	105	49	89	.244	.271	.282	75	-40	-40	119	7			16	C/OS312	0.5

■ HANK DeBERRY
DeBerry, John Herman   b: 12/29/1894, Savannah, Tenn.   d: 9/10/51, Savannah, Tenn.   BR/TR, 5'11", 195 lbs.   Deb: 9/12/16

YEAR	TM/L	G	AB	R	H	2B	3B	HR	RBI	BB	SO	AVG	OBP	SLG	PRO+	BR	/A	RC	SB	CS	SBR	FR	POS	TPR
1916	Cle-A	15	33	7	9	4	0	0	4	6	9	.273	.385	.394	126	2	1	5	0			-3	C	0.0
1917	Cle-A	25	33	3	9	2	0	0	1	2	7	.273	.333	.333	96	0	-0	3	0			1	/C	0.1
1922	Bro-N	85	259	29	78	10	1	3	35	20	9	.301	.354	.382	91	-4	-3	36	4	1	1	-1	C	-0.2
1923	Bro-N	78	235	21	67	11	6	1	48	20	12	.285	.346	.396	98	-2	-1	33	2	1	0	8	C	1.0
1924	Bro-N	77	218	20	53	10	3	3	26	20	21	.243	.307	.358	80	-7	-6	24	0	1	-1	23	C	1.7
1925	Bro-N	67	193	26	50	8	1	2	24	16	8	.259	.322	.342	72	-9	-8	22	2	2	-1	20	C	1.3
1926	Bro-N	48	115	6	33	11	0	0	13	8	5	.287	.333	.383	94	-1	-1	14	0			8	C	0.8

YEAR	TM/L	G	AB	R	H	2B	3B	HR	RBI	BB	SO	AVG	OBP	SLG	PRO+	BR	/A	RC	SB	CS	SBR	FR	POS	TPR
1927	Bro-N	68	201	15	47	3	2	1	21	17	8	.234	.294	.284	55	-13	-13	17	1			23	C	1.4
1928	Bro-N	82	258	19	65	8	2	0	23	18	15	.252	.301	.298	58	-16	-16	23	3			18	C	0.7
1929	Bro-N	68	210	13	55	11	1	1	25	17	15	.262	.317	.338	64	-12	-12	23	1			6	C	0.0
1930	Bro-N	35	95	11	28	3	0	0	14	4	10	.295	.323	.326	58	-6	-6	10	0			13	C	0.8
Total	11	648	1850	170	494	81	16	11	234	148	119	.267	.323	.346	76	-68	-64	210	13	5		116	C	7.6

■ **ADAM DEBUS**   Debus, Adam Joseph   b: 10/7/1892, Chicago, Ill.   d: 5/13/77, Chicago, Ill.   BR/TR, 5'10.5", 150 lbs.   Deb: 7/14/17

YEAR	TM/L	G	AB	R	H	2B	3B	HR	RBI	BB	SO	AVG	OBP	SLG	PRO+	BR	/A	RC	SB	CS	SBR	FR	POS	TPR
1917	Pit-N	38	131	9	30	5	4	0	7	7	14	.229	.279	.328	83	-2	-3	12	2			-6	S3	-0.9

■ **DOUG DeCINCES**   DeCinces, Douglas Vernon   b: 8/29/50, Burbank, Cal.   BR/TR, 6'2", 190 lbs.   Deb: 9/09/73

YEAR	TM/L	G	AB	R	H	2B	3B	HR	RBI	BB	SO	AVG	OBP	SLG	PRO+	BR	/A	RC	SB	CS	SBR	FR	POS	TPR
1973	Bal-A	10	18	2	2	0	0	0	3	1	5	.111	.158	.111	-23	-3	-3	0	0	0	0	3	/32S	0.0
1974	Bal-A	1	1	0	0	0	0	0	0	1	0	.000	.500	.000	55	0	0	0	0	0	0	0	/3	0.0
1975	Bal-A	61	167	20	42	6	3	4	23	13	32	.251	.309	.395	105	-1	0	20	0	1	-1	3	3S2/1	0.5
1976	Bal-A	129	440	36	103	17	2	11	42	29	68	.234	.285	.357	93	-8	-5	43	8	4	0	-1	*321/SD	-0.5
1977	Bal-A	150	522	63	135	28	3	19	69	64	86	.259	.342	.433	117	7	11	75	8	8	-2	10	*3/12D	1.6
1978	Bal-A	142	511	72	146	37	1	28	80	46	81	.286	.347	.526	152	27	30	89	7	7	-2	10	*32	3.8
1979	•Bal-A	120	422	67	97	27	1	16	61	54	68	.230	.322	.412	100	-3	-0	56	5	3	-0	-3	*3	0.0
1980	Bal-A	145	489	64	122	23	2	16	64	49	83	.249	.322	.403	98	-2	-2	59	11	6	-0	25	*3/1	2.2
1981	Bal-A	100	346	49	91	23	2	13	55	41	32	.263	.343	.454	128	12	12	51	0	3	-2	-2	*3/1S	0.9
1982	•Cal-A	153	575	94	173	42	5	30	97	66	80	.301	.374	.548	149	38	38	113	7	5	-1	19	*3/S	5.2
1983	Cal-A	95	370	49	104	19	3	18	65	32	56	.281	.338	.495	127	12	13	59	2	0	1	9	3D	2.2
1984	Cal-A	146	547	77	147	23	3	20	82	53	79	.269	.333	.431	111	7	7	77	4	1	1	-6	*3/D	0.4
1985	Cal-A	120	427	50	104	22	1	20	78	47	71	.244	.321	.440	107	3	3	55	1	4	-2	-10	*3/D	-1.1
1986	•Cal-A	140	512	69	131	20	3	26	96	52	74	.256	.327	.459	112	7	8	72	2	2	-1	-8	*3/SD	-0.3
1987	Cal-A	133	453	65	106	23	0	16	63	70	87	.234	.339	.391	96	-4	-1	61	3	4	-2	-3	*3/1SD	-0.6
	StL-N	4	9	1	2	2	0	0	1	0	2	.222	.222	.444	70	-0	-0	1	0	0	0	1	/3	0.1
Total	15	1649	5809	778	1505	312	29	237	879	618	904	.259	.333	.445	116	91	112	832	58	48	-11	49	*3/2D1SO	14.4

■ **HARRY DECKER**   Decker, Earl Harry   b: 9/3/1854, Lockport, Ill.   BR/TR, 5'11", 180 lbs.   Deb: 8/23/1884

YEAR	TM/L	G	AB	R	H	2B	3B	HR	RBI	BB	SO	AVG	OBP	SLG	PRO+	BR	/A	RC	SB	CS	SBR	FR	POS	TPR
1884	Ind-a	4	15	1	4	1	0	0			1	.267	.313	.333	118	0	0	2				-3	/C	-0.1
	KC-U	23	75	8	10	2	0	0			5	.133	.188	.160	21	-6	-4	2	0			3	OC	0.0
1886	Det-N	14	54	2	12	1	0	0	5	2	9	.222	.250	.241	48	-3	-3	3	0			5	C/O	0.2
	Was-N	7	23	0	5	1	1	0	2	1	5	.217	.250	.348	85	-1	-0	2	0			2	/C3S	0.2
	Yr	21	77	2	17	2	1	0	7	3	14	.221	.250	.273	59	-4	-4	5	0			7		0.4
1889	Phi-N	11	30	4	3	0	0	0	2	2	5	.100	.156	.100	-25	-5	-5	1	1			-1	/2CO	-0.4
1890	Phi-N	5	19	5	7	1	0	0	2	4	1	.368	.478	.421	162	2	2	6	4			-1	/1OC	0.1
	Pit-N	92	354	52	97	14	3	5	38	26	36	.274	.324	.373	119	1	8	46	8			-26	C1/O2S	-1.2
	Yr	97	373	57	104	15	3	5	40	30	37	.279	.333	.375	122	3	10	52	12			-26		-1.1
Total	4	156	570	72	138	20	4	5	49	41	56	.242	.293	.318	91	-11	-4	62	13			-20	C/O12S3	-1.2

■ **FRANK DECKER**   Decker, Frank   b: 2/26/1856, St.Louis, Mo.   d: 2/5/40, St.Louis, Mo.   BR/TR,   Deb: 6/25/1879

YEAR	TM/L	G	AB	R	H	2B	3B	HR	RBI	BB	SO	AVG	OBP	SLG	PRO+	BR	/A	RC	SB	CS	SBR	FR	POS	TPR
1879	Syr-N	3	10	0	1	0	0	0	0	0	3	.100	.100	.100	-38	-1	-1	0				-1	/CO1	-0.2
1882	StL-a	2	8	0	2	0	0	0	0	0		.250	.250	.250	66	-0	-0	1				-0	/2	0.0
Total	2	5	18	0	3	0	0	0	0	0	3	.167	.167	.167	12	-2	-2	1				-1	/2C1O	-0.2

■ **GEORGE DECKER**   Decker, George A "Gentleman George"   b: 6/1/1869, York, Pa.   d: 6/9/09, Compton, Cal.   BL/TL, 6'1", 180 lbs.   Deb: 7/11/1892

YEAR	TM/L	G	AB	R	H	2B	3B	HR	RBI	BB	SO	AVG	OBP	SLG	PRO+	BR	/A	RC	SB	CS	SBR	FR	POS	TPR
1892	Chi-N	78	291	32	66	6	7	1	28	20	49	.227	.277	.306	77	-8	-9	28	9			-12	O2	-2.0
1893	Chi-N	81	328	57	89	9	8	2	48	24	22	.271	.325	.366	87	-8	-7	47	22			-9	O12/S	-1.3
1894	Chi-N	91	384	74	120	17	6	8	92	24	17	.313	.361	.451	91	-3	-7	72	23			-8	10/32S	-1.2
1895	Chi-N	73	297	51	82	9	7	2	41	17	22	.276	.324	.374	76	-9	-12	41	11			-7	O1/3S2	-1.8
1896	Chi-N	107	421	68	118	23	11	5	61	23	14	.280	.318	.423	92	-4	-7	64	20			-3	O1	-1.1
1897	Chi-N	111	428	72	124	12	7	5	63	24		.290	.333	.386	88	-6	-8	60	11			-3	O1/2	-1.4
1898	StL-N	76	286	26	74	10	0	1	45	20		.259	.314	.304	78	-7	-8	29	4			-7	1	-1.3
	Lou-N	42	148	27	44	4	3	0	19	9		.297	.342	.365	107	1	1	22	9			-1	1/O	0.0
	Yr	118	434	53	118	14	3	1	64	29		.272	.323	.325	88	-6	-7	51	13			-9		-1.3
1899	Lou-N	38	135	13	36	8	0	1	18	12		.267	.336	.348	90	-2	-2	17	3			-2	1	-0.2
	Was-N	4	9	0	0	0	0	0	0	0		.000	.000	.000	-99	-2	-2	0				-0	/10	-0.2
	Yr	42	144	13	36	8	0	1	18	12		.250	.316	.326	79	-4	-4	16	3			-3		-0.4
Total	8	701	2727	420	753	98	49	25	415	173	124	.276	.324	.376	86	-48	-61	381	112			-53	O1/23S	-10.5

■ **STEVE DECKER**   Decker, Steven Michael   b: 10/25/65, Rock Island, Ill.   BR/TR, 6'3", 205 lbs.   Deb: 9/18/90

YEAR	TM/L	G	AB	R	H	2B	3B	HR	RBI	BB	SO	AVG	OBP	SLG	PRO+	BR	/A	RC	SB	CS	SBR	FR	POS	TPR
1990	SF-N	15	54	5	16	2	0	3	8	1	10	.296	.309	.500	120	1	1	8	0	0	0	2	C	0.4

■ **ARTIE DEDE**   Dede, Arthur Richard   b: 7/12/1895, Brooklyn, N.Y.   d: 9/6/71, Keene, N.H.   BR/TR, 5'9", 155 lbs.   Deb: 10/04/16

YEAR	TM/L	G	AB	R	H	2B	3B	HR	RBI	BB	SO	AVG	OBP	SLG	PRO+	BR	/A	RC	SB	CS	SBR	FR	POS	TPR
1916	Bro-N	1	1	0	0	0	0	0	0	0	0	.000	.000	.000	-97	-0	-0	0				0	/C	0.0

■ **ROD DEDEAUX**   Dedeaux, Raoul Martial   b: 2/17/15, New Orleans, La.   BR/TR, 5'11", 160 lbs.   Deb: 9/28/35

YEAR	TM/L	G	AB	R	H	2B	3B	HR	RBI	BB	SO	AVG	OBP	SLG	PRO+	BR	/A	RC	SB	CS	SBR	FR	POS	TPR
1935	Bro-N	2	4	0	1	0	0	0	1	0	0	.250	.250	.250	36	-0	-0	0				0	/S	0.0

■ **JIM DEE**   Dee, James D.   b: Buffalo, N.Y.   Deb: 7/30/1884

YEAR	TM/L	G	AB	R	H	2B	3B	HR	RBI	BB	SO	AVG	OBP	SLG	PRO+	BR	/A	RC	SB	CS	SBR	FR	POS	TPR
1884	Pit-a	12	40	0	5	0	0	0			1	.125	.146	.125	-9	-5	-5	1				1	S	-0.3

■ **SHORTY DEE**   Dee, Maurice Leo   b: 10/4/1889, Halifax, N.S., Can.   d: 8/12/71, Jamaica Plain, Mass.   BR/TR, 5'6", 155 lbs.   Deb: 9/14/15

YEAR	TM/L	G	AB	R	H	2B	3B	HR	RBI	BB	SO	AVG	OBP	SLG	PRO+	BR	/A	RC	SB	CS	SBR	FR	POS	TPR
1915	StL-A	1	3	1	0	0	0	0	0	1	0	.000	.250	.000	-26	-0	-0	0	0	1	-1	-1	/S	-0.2

■ **ROB DEER**   Deer, Robert George   b: 9/29/60, Orange, Cal.   BR/TR, 6'3", 210 lbs.   Deb: 9/04/84

YEAR	TM/L	G	AB	R	H	2B	3B	HR	RBI	BB	SO	AVG	OBP	SLG	PRO+	BR	/A	RC	SB	CS	SBR	FR	POS	TPR
1984	SF-N	13	24	5	4	0	0	3	3	7	10	.167	.375	.542	160	2	2	5	1	1	-0	0	/O	0.2
1985	SF-N	78	162	22	30	5	1	8	20	23	71	.185	.286	.377	88	-4	-3	19	0	1	-1	-3	O1	-0.7
1986	Mil-A	134	466	75	108	17	3	33	86	72	179	.232	.338	.494	119	14	12	82	5	2	0	3	*O/1	1.2
1987	Mil-A	134	474	71	113	15	2	28	80	86	186	.238	.361	.456	117	11	9	85	12	4	1	5	*O1/D	1.1
1988	Mil-A	135	492	71	124	24	0	23	85	51	153	.252	.331	.441	113	9	8	74	9	5	-0	4	*O/D	1.0
1989	Mil-A	130	466	72	98	18	2	26	65	60	158	.210	.306	.425	105	1	2	59	4	8	-4	3	*O/D	0.0
1990	Mil-A	134	440	57	92	15	1	27	69	64	147	.209	.315	.432	110	3	5	64	2	3	-1	5	*O1	0.6
Total	7	758	2524	373	569	94	9	148	408	363	904	.225	.328	.446	111	37	36	389	33	24	-5	16	O/1D	3.4

■ **CHARLIE DEES**   Dees, Charles Henry   b: 6/24/35, Birmingham, Ala.   BL/TL, 6'1", 173 lbs.   Deb: 5/26/63

YEAR	TM/L	G	AB	R	H	2B	3B	HR	RBI	BB	SO	AVG	OBP	SLG	PRO+	BR	/A	RC	SB	CS	SBR	FR	POS	TPR
1963	LA-A	60	202	23	62	11	1	3	27	11	31	.307	.367	.416	126	5	7	30	3	3	-1	-2	1	0.2
1964	LA-A	26	26	3	2	1	0	0	1	1	4	.077	.143	.115	-30	-4	-4	0	1	2	-1	0	1	-0.5
1965	Cal-A	12	32	1	5	0	0	0	1	1	8	.156	.182	.156	-3	-4	-4	1	1	2	-1	-1	/1	-0.6
Total	3	98	260	27	69	12	1	3	29	13	43	.265	.323	.354	95	-3	-2	31	5	7	-3	-3	O/1	-0.9

■ **TONY DeFATE**   DeFate, Clyde Herbert   b: 2/22/1895, Kansas City, Mo.   d: 9/3/63, New Orleans, La.   BR/TR, 5'8.5", 158 lbs.   Deb: 4/18/17

YEAR	TM/L	G	AB	R	H	2B	3B	HR	RBI	BB	SO	AVG	OBP	SLG	PRO+	BR	/A	RC	SB	CS	SBR	FR	POS	TPR
1917	StL-N	14	14	0	2	0	0	0	1	4	5	.143	.333	.143	50	-1	-1	1	0			-0	/32	0.0
	Det-A	3	2	1	0	0	0	0	0	0	1	.000	.000	.000	-99	-0	-0	0				-0	/2	0.0

YEAR	TM/L	G	AB	R	H	2B	3B	HR	RBI	BB	SO	AVG	OBP	SLG	PRO+	BR	/A	RC	SB	CS	SBR	FR	POS	TPR

■ ARTURO DeFREITAS
DeFreitas, Arturo Marcelino (Simon) b: 4/26/53, San Pedro De Macoris, D.R. BR/TR, 6'2", 195 lbs. Deb: 9/07/78

YEAR	TM/L	G	AB	R	H	2B	3B	HR	RBI	BB	SO	AVG	OBP	SLG	PRO+	BR	/A	RC	SB	CS	SBR	FR	POS	TPR
1978	Cin-N	9	19	1	4	1	0	1	2	1	4	.211	.250	.421	84	-1	-1	2	0	0	0	0	/1	0.0
1979	Cin-N	23	34	2	7	2	0	0	4	0	16	.206	.206	.265	27	-3	-3	2	0	0	0	-1	/1O	-0.4
Total	2	32	53	3	11	3	0	1	6	1	20	.208	.222	.321	47	-4	-4	4	0	0	0	-1	/1O	-0.4

■ RUBE DeGROFF
DeGroff, Edward Arthur b: 9/2/1879, Hyde Park, N.Y. d: 12/17/55, Poughkeepsie, N.Y. BL, 5'11", Deb: 9/22/05

YEAR	TM/L	G	AB	R	H	2B	3B	HR	RBI	BB	SO	AVG	OBP	SLG	PRO+	BR	/A	RC	SB	CS	SBR	FR	POS	TPR
1905	StL-N	15	56	3	14	2	1	0	5	5		.250	.311	.321	94	-1	-1	6	1			0	O	0.0
1906	StL-N	1	4	1	0	0	0	0	0	0		.000	.000	.000	-99	-1	-1	0				-0	/O	-0.1
Total	2	16	60	4	14	2	1	0	5	5		.233	.292	.300	82	-1	-1	6	1			0	/O	-0.1

■ HERMAN DEHLMAN
Dehlman, Herman J. "Dutch" b: 1850, Catasaqua, Pa. d: 3/13/1885, Wilkes-Barre, Pa. Deb: 5/02/1872

YEAR	TM/L	G	AB	R	H	2B	3B	HR	RBI	BB	SO	AVG	OBP	SLG	PRO+	BR	/A	RC	SB	CS	SBR	FR	POS	TPR
1872	Atl-n	37	164	30	36	3	0	0			2	.220	.229	.238	37	-10	-16	9					*1	-0.8
1873	Atl-n	54	223	50	53	5	2	0			9	.238	.267	.278	68	-10	-5	17					*1	-0.2
1874	Atl-n	53	216	40	50	5	1	0			7	.231	.256	.264	74	-8	-3	15					*1	-0.1
1875	StL-n	67	254	42	57	12	2	0			11	.224	.257	.287	97	-3	1	19					*1	0.0
1876	StL-N	64	245	40	45	6	0	0	9	0	10	.184	.213	.208	43	-15	-13	11				0	*1	-0.9
1877	StL-N	32	119	24	22	4	0	0	11	7	21	.185	.230	.218	44	-7	-7	6				-3	1/O	-0.9
Total	4 n	211	857	162	196	25	5	0			29	.229	.254	.270	70	-31	-24	60					1/D	-1.1
Total	2	96	364	64	67	10	0	0	20	16	31	.184	.218	.212	43	-22	-19	17				-3	/1O	-1.8

■ JIM DEIDEL
Deidel, James Lawrence b: 6/6/49, Denver, Col. BR/TR, 6'2", 195 lbs. Deb: 5/31/74

YEAR	TM/L	G	AB	R	H	2B	3B	HR	RBI	BB	SO	AVG	OBP	SLG	PRO+	BR	/A	RC	SB	CS	SBR	FR	POS	TPR
1974	NY-A	2	2	0	0	0	0	0	0	0	0	.000	.000	.000	-99	-1	-0	0	0	0	0	1	/C	0.1

■ PEP DEININGER
Deininger, Otto Charles b: 10/10/1877, Wasseralfingen, Germany d: 9/25/50, Boston, Mass. BL/TL, 5'8.5", 180 lbs. Deb: 4/26/02

YEAR	TM/L	G	AB	R	H	2B	3B	HR	RBI	BB	SO	AVG	OBP	SLG	PRO+	BR	/A	RC	SB	CS	SBR	FR	POS	TPR
1902	Bos-A	2	6	0	2	1	1	0	0	0		.333	.333	.833	212	1	1	2	0			-0	/P	0.0
1908	Phi-N	1	0	0	0	0	0	0	0	0		—	—	—	—	0	0	0	0			-0	/O	0.0
1909	Phi-N	55	169	22	44	9	0	0	16	11		.260	.309	.314	93	-2	-2	18	5			-2	O/2	-0.5
Total	3	58	175	22	46	10	1	0	16	11		.263	.310	.331	97	-1	-1	19	5			-3	/OP2	-0.5

■ PAT DEISEL
Deisel, Edward b: 4/29/1876, Ripley, Ohio d: 4/17/48, Cincinnati, Ohio BR/TR, 5'5", 145 lbs. Deb: 8/21/02

YEAR	TM/L	G	AB	R	H	2B	3B	HR	RBI	BB	SO	AVG	OBP	SLG	PRO+	BR	/A	RC	SB	CS	SBR	FR	POS	TPR
1902	Bro-N	1	3	0	2	0	0	0	1	1		.667	.750	.667	340	1	1	2	0			0	/C	0.1
1903	Cin-N	2	0	0	0	0	0	0	0	1		—	1.000	—	180	0	0	0	0			0	/C	0.0
Total	2	3	3	0	2	0	0	0	1	2		.667	.800	.667	345	1	1	2	0			0	/C	0.1

■ BILL DEITRICK
Deitrick, William Alexander b: 4/20/02, Hanover Co., Va. d: 5/6/46, Bethesda, Md. BR/TR, 5'10", 160 lbs. Deb: 9/19/27

YEAR	TM/L	G	AB	R	H	2B	3B	HR	RBI	BB	SO	AVG	OBP	SLG	PRO+	BR	/A	RC	SB	CS	SBR	FR	POS	TPR
1927	Phi-N	5	6	1	1	0	0	0	0	0	0	.167	.167	.167	-10	-1	-1	0	0			-1	/S	0.0
1928	Phi-N	52	100	13	20	6	0	0	7	17	10	.200	.322	.260	52	-6	-7	9	1			-1	O/S	-0.6
Total	2	57	106	14	21	6	0	0	7	17	10	.198	.315	.255	49	-7	-8	9	1			-2	/OS	-0.6

■ MIKE DEJAN
Dejan, Michael Dan b: 1/13/15, Cleveland, Ohio d: 2/2/53, W.Los Angeles, Cal. BL/TL, 6'1", 185 lbs. Deb: 7/13/40

YEAR	TM/L	G	AB	R	H	2B	3B	HR	RBI	BB	SO	AVG	OBP	SLG	PRO+	BR	/A	RC	SB	CS	SBR	FR	POS	TPR
1940	Cin-N	12	16	1	3	0	1	0	2	3	3	.188	.316	.313	73	-1	-1	2	0			-0	/O	0.0

■ IVAN DeJESUS
DeJesus, Ivan (Alvarez) b: 1/9/53, Santurce, P.R. BR/TR, 5'11", 175 lbs. Deb: 9/13/74

YEAR	TM/L	G	AB	R	H	2B	3B	HR	RBI	BB	SO	AVG	OBP	SLG	PRO+	BR	/A	RC	SB	CS	SBR	FR	POS	TPR
1974	LA-N	3	3	1	1	0	0	0	0	0		.333	.333	.333	91	-0	-0	0	0	0	0	-1	/S	0.0
1975	LA-N	63	87	10	16	2	1	0	2	11	15	.184	.276	.230	43	-7	-6	6	1	2	-1	7	S	0.7
1976	LA-N	22	41	4	7	2	1	0	2	4	9	.171	.244	.268	46	-3	-3	2	0	1	-1	5	S/3	0.3
1977	Chi-N	155	624	91	166	31	7	3	40	56	90	.266	.330	.353	75	-14	-23	75	24	12	0	36	*S	3.4
1978	Chi-N	160	619	**104**	172	24	7	3	35	74	78	.278	.357	.354	88	-1	-8	84	41	12	5	13	*S	2.4
1979	Chi-N	160	636	92	180	26	10	5	52	59	82	.283	.346	.379	89	-1	-9	83	24	20	-5	0	*S	0.2
1980	Chi-N	157	618	78	160	26	3	3	33	60	81	.259	.328	.325	77	-13	-18	72	44	16	4	8	*S	1.1
1981	Chi-N	106	403	49	78	8	4	0	13	46	61	.194	.276	.233	44	-28	-30	30	21	9	1	10	*S	-0.8
1982	Phi-N	161	536	53	128	21	5	3	59	54	70	.239	.311	.313	73	-17	-19	55	14	4	2	-7	*S/3	-1.3
1983	*Phi-N	158	497	60	126	15	7	4	45	53	77	.254	.325	.336	85	-10	-10	56	11	4	1	-14	*S	-0.8
1984	Phi-N	144	435	40	112	15	3	0	35	43	76	.257	.327	.306	77	-11	-12	43	12	5	1	-21	*S	-1.8
1985	StL-N	59	72	11	16	5	0	0	7	4	16	.222	.263	.292	55	-4	-4	6	2	2	-1	2	3S	0.0
1986	NY-A	7	4	1	0	0	0	0	0	1	1	.000	.200	.000	-40	-1	-1	0	0	0	0	0	/S	0.0
1987	SF-N	9	10	0	2	0	0	0	1	0	2	.200	.200	.200	7	-1	-1	0	0	1	-1	2	/S	0.2
1988	Det-A	7	17	1	3	0	0	0	0	1	4	.176	.222	.176	14	-2	-2	1	0	0	0	1	/S	0.0
Total	15	1371	4602	595	1167	175	48	21	324	466	664	.254	.324	.326	76	-111	-145	514	194	88	5	41	*S/3	3.6

■ MARK DeJOHN
DeJohn, Mark Stephen b: 9/18/53, Middletown, Conn. BB/TR, 5'11", 170 lbs. Deb: 4/28/82

YEAR	TM/L	G	AB	R	H	2B	3B	HR	RBI	BB	SO	AVG	OBP	SLG	PRO+	BR	/A	RC	SB	CS	SBR	FR	POS	TPR
1982	Det-A	24	21	1	4	2	0	0	1	4	4	.190	.320	.286	68	-1	-1	3	1	0	0	6	S/32	0.7

■ BILL DeKONING
DeKoning, William Callahan b: 12/19/18, Brooklyn, N.Y. d: 7/26/79, Palm Harbor, Fla. BR/TR, 5'11", 185 lbs. Deb: 5/27/45

YEAR	TM/L	G	AB	R	H	2B	3B	HR	RBI	BB	SO	AVG	OBP	SLG	PRO+	BR	/A	RC	SB	CS	SBR	FR	POS	TPR
1945	NY-N	3	1	0	0	0	0	0	0	0	1	.000	.000	.000	-99	-0	-0	0	0			0	/C	0.0

■ ED DELAHANTY
Delahanty, Edward James "Big Ed" b: 10/30/1867, Cleveland, Ohio d: 7/2/03, Niagara Falls, N.Y. BR/TR, 6'1", 170 lbs. Deb: 5/22/1888

YEAR	TM/L	G	AB	R	H	2B	3B	HR	RBI	BB	SO	AVG	OBP	SLG	PRO+	BR	/A	RC	SB	CS	SBR	FR	POS	TPR
1888	Phi-N	74	290	40	66	12	2	1	31	12	26	.228	.261	.293	74	-7	-9	33	38			-10	2O	-1.7
1889	Phi-N	56	246	37	72	13	3	0	27	14	17	.293	.333	.370	90	-1	-4	38	19			-13	O2/S	-1.4
1890	Cle-P	115	517	107	154	26	13	3	64	24	30	.298	.339	.416	112	0	8	83	25			-7	S20/31	0.5
1891	Phi-N	128	543	92	132	19	9	5	86	33	50	.243	.296	.339	84	-10	-12	63	25			1	*O1/2	-1.4
1892	Phi-N	123	477	79	146	30	**21**	6	91	31	32	.306	.360	**.495**	160	31	32	98	29			10	*O/3	3.5
1893	Phi-N	132	595	145	219	35	18	**19**	**146**	47	20	.368	.423	**.583**	169	55	55	167	37			31	*O2/1	**6.5**
1894	Phi-N	114	489	147	199	39	18	4	131	60	16	.407	.478	.585	161	48	50	151	21			16	*O1/3S2	4.6
1895	Phi-N	116	480	149	194	**49**	10	11	106	86	31	.404	**.500**	.617	**189**	68	68	175	46			2	*O/S23	4.9
1896	Phi-N	123	499	131	198	**44**	17	**13**	126	62	22	.397	.472	**.631**	**194**	66	67	170	37			15	*O1/2	6.3
1897	Phi-N	129	530	109	200	40	15	5	96	60		.377	.444	.538	165	47	49	141	26			9	*O/1	4.1
1898	Phi-N	144	548	115	183	36	9	4	92	77		.334	.426	.454	163	43	**46**	**134**	58			5	*O	3.9
1899	Phi-N	146	581	135	**238**	**55**	9	9	**137**	55		**.410**	.464	**.582**	**196**	70	**73**	175	30			0	*O	5.7
1900	Phi-N	131	539	82	174	32	10	2	109	41		.323	.377	.430	126	18	19	96	16			-3	*1	1.5
1901	Phi-N	139	542	106	192	**38**	16	8	108	65		.354	.426	.528	175	55	53	139	29			-5	O1	3.8
1902	Was-A	123	473	103	178	**43**	14	10	93	62		**.376**	**.454**	**.590**	**189**	58	58	137	16			2	*O1	5.0
1903	Was-A	42	156	22	52	11	1	1	21	12		.333	.381	.436	144	9	9	28	3			2	O/1	0.8
Total	16	1835	7505	1599	2597	522	185	101	1464	741	<u>244</u>	.346	.411	.505	155	550	561	1828	455			55	*O12/S3	46.6

■ FRANK DELAHANTY
Delahanty, Frank George "Pudgie" b: 1/29/1883, Cleveland, Ohio d: 7/22/66, Cleveland, Ohio BR/TR, 5'9", 160 lbs. Deb: 8/23/05

YEAR	TM/L	G	AB	R	H	2B	3B	HR	RBI	BB	SO	AVG	OBP	SLG	PRO+	BR	/A	RC	SB	CS	SBR	FR	POS	TPR
1905	NY-A	9	27	0	6	1	0	0	2	1		.222	.250	.259	57	-1	-1	2	0			-1	/1O	-0.2
1906	NY-A	92	307	37	73	11	8	2	41	16		.238	.276	.345	87	-2	-6	35	11			3	O	-0.5
1907	Cle-A	15	52	3	9	0	1	0	4	4		.173	.232	.212	43	-3	-3	3	2			-0	O	-0.4
1908	NY-A	37	125	12	32	1	2	0	10	10		.256	.311	.296	99	0	0	14	9			-1	O	-0.2
1914	Buf-F	79	274	29	55	4	7	2	27	23	19	.201	.265	.288	57	-15	-16	28	21			-5	O	-2.6
	Pit-F	41	159	25	38	4	4	1	7	11	11	.239	.297	.333	81	-4	-4	19	7			-3	O/2	-0.8
	Yr	120	433	54	93	8	11	3	34	34	30	.215	.277	.305	66	-19	-20	47	28			-8		-3.4
1915	Pit-F	14	42	3	10	1	0	0	3	0		.238	.238	.262	54	-2	-2	2	3			1	O	-0.2
Total	6	287	986	109	223	22	22	5	94	66	<u>30</u>	.226	.277	.308	74	-28	-33	103	50			-6	O/12	-4.9

YEAR	TM/L	G	AB	R	H	2B	3B	HR	RBI	BB	SO	AVG	OBP	SLG	PRO+	BR	/A	RC	SB	CS	SBR	FR	POS	TPR

■ JIM DELAHANTY
Delahanty, James Christopher b: 6/20/1879, Cleveland, Ohio d: 10/17/53, Cleveland, Ohio BR/TR, 5'10.5", 170 lbs. Deb: 4/19/01

YEAR	TM/L	G	AB	R	H	2B	3B	HR	RBI	BB	SO	AVG	OBP	SLG	PRO+	BR	/A	RC	SB	CS	SBR	FR	POS	TPR
1901	Chi-N	17	63	4	12	2	0	0	4	3		.190	.239	.222	37	-5	-5	5	5			-1	3/2	-0.4
1902	NY-N	7	26	3	6	1	0	0	3	1		.231	.259	.269	65	-1	-1	2	0			-1	/O	-0.1
1904	Bos-N	142	499	56	142	27	8	3	60	27		.285	.321	.389	125	11	13	70	16			1	*32/OP	1.9
1905	Bos-N	125	461	50	119	11	8	5	55	28		.258	.301	.349	97	-3	-2	54	12			-7	*O/P	-1.8
1906	Cin-N	115	379	63	106	21	4	1	39	45		.280	.356	.364	121	12	11	60	21			-19	*3/SO	-1.2
1907	StL-A	33	95	8	21	3	0	0	6	5		.221	.260	.253	65	-4	-4	8	6			-1	3/O2	-0.3
	Was-A	108	404	44	118	18	7	2	54	36		.292	.350	.386	148	17	20	64	18			-13	23/O1	0.9
	Yr	141	499	52	139	21	7	2	60	41		.279	.333	.361	131	13	16	71	24			-14		0.6
1908	Was-A	83	287	33	91	11	4	1	30	24		.317	.370	.394	164	16	18	47	16			3	2	2.2
1909	Was-A	90	302	18	67	13	5	1	21	23		.222	.290	.308	93	-4	-2	28	4			-3	2	-0.8
	*Det-A	46	150	29	38	10	1	0	20	17		.253	.364	.333	115	5	4	22	9			-7	2	-0.4
	Yr	136	452	47	105	23	6	1	41	40		.232	.316	.316	101	1	1	50	13			-10		-1.2
1910	Det-A	106	378	67	111	16	2	3	45	43		.294	.379	.370	126	17	14	59	15			-14	*2	-0.7
1911	Det-A	144	542	83	184	30	14	3	94	56		.339	.411	.463	137	33	29	110	15			-10	123	2.0
1912	Det-A	79	266	34	76	14	1	0	41	42		.286	.397	.346	117	7	8	41	9			-5	2O	0.1
1914	Bro-F	74	214	28	62	13	5	0	15	25	21	.290	.372	.397	121	6	7	36	4			-18	2/1	-1.1
1915	Bro-F	17	25	0	6	1	0	0	2	3	3	.240	.345	.280	87	-0	-0	3	1			-1	/2	0.0
Total	13	1186	4091	520	1159	191	59	19	489	378	24	.283	.351	.373	122	106	109	608	151			-94	23O/1SP	0.3

■ JOE DELAHANTY
Delahanty, Joseph Nicholas b: 10/18/1875, Cleveland, Ohio d: 1/9/36, Cleveland, Ohio BR/TR, 5'9", 168 lbs. Deb: 9/30/07

YEAR	TM/L	G	AB	R	H	2B	3B	HR	RBI	BB	SO	AVG	OBP	SLG	PRO+	BR	/A	RC	SB	CS	SBR	FR	POS	TPR
1907	StL-N	7	22	3	7	0	0	1	2	0		.318	.318	.455	149	1	1	4	3			-0	/O	0.0
1908	StL-N	140	499	37	127	14	11	1	44	32		.255	.299	.333	109	1	4	53	11			-5	*O	-0.1
1909	StL-N	123	411	28	88	16	4	2	54	42		.214	.292	.287	85	-10	-7	37	10			-16	O2	-2.7
Total	3	270	932	68	222	30	15	4	100	74		.238	.296	.315	99	-7	-2	94	24			-20	O/2	-2.8

■ TOM DELAHANTY
Delahanty, Thomas James b: 3/9/1872, Cleveland, Ohio d: 1/10/51, Sanford, Fla. TR , 5'8", 175 lbs. Deb: 9/29/1894

YEAR	TM/L	G	AB	R	H	2B	3B	HR	RBI	BB	SO	AVG	OBP	SLG	PRO+	BR	/A	RC	SB	CS	SBR	FR	POS	TPR
1894	Phi-N	1	4	0	1	0	0	0	0	0	1	.250	.250	.250	23	-0	-0	0	0			0	/2	0.0
1896	Cle-N	16	56	11	13	4	0	0	4	8	4	.232	.338	.304	68	-2	-3	7	4			-1	3	-0.2
	Pit-N	1	3	1	1	0	0	0	0	0	0	.333	.333	.333	81	-0	-0	0	0			-1	/S	0.0
	Yr	17	59	12	14	4	0	0	4	8	4	.237	.338	.305	69	-2	-3	8	4			-2		-0.2
1897	Lou-N	1	4	1	1	1	0	0	2	0		.250	.250	.500	100	-0	-0	1	0			-2	/2	-0.1
Total	3	19	67	13	16	5	0	0	6	8	5	.239	.329	.313	68	-3	-3	8	4			-4	/32S	-0.3

■ MIKE de la HOZ
de la Hoz, Miguel Angel (Piloto) b: 10/2/38, Havana, Cuba BR/TR, 5'11", 175 lbs. Deb: 7/22/60

YEAR	TM/L	G	AB	R	H	2B	3B	HR	RBI	BB	SO	AVG	OBP	SLG	PRO+	BR	/A	RC	SB	CS	SBR	FR	POS	TPR
1960	Cle-A	49	160	20	41	6	2	6	23	9	12	.256	.300	.431	98	-2	-1	19	0	0	0	-15	S/3	-1.2
1961	Cle-A	61	173	20	45	10	0	3	23	7	10	.260	.297	.370	79	-6	-5	18	0	0	0	3	2S3	0.2
1962	Cle-A	12	12	0	1	0	0	0	0	0	3	.083	.083	.083	-57	-3	-3	0	0	0	0	-0	/2	-0.2
1963	Cle-A	67	150	15	40	10	0	5	25	9	29	.267	.313	.433	107	1	1	20	0	0	0	5	2/3SO	0.9
1964	Mil-N	78	189	25	55	7	1	4	12	14	22	.291	.346	.402	109	3	2	25	1	1	-0	-4	23/S	0.0
1965	Mil-N	81	176	15	45	3	2	2	11	8	21	.256	.296	.330	75	-6	-6	16	0	1	-1	-10	S32/1	-1.0
1966	Atl-N	71	110	11	24	3	0	2	7	5	18	.218	.252	.300	52	-7	-7	8	0	1	-1	-2	3/2S	-1.0
1967	Atl-N	74	143	10	29	3	0	3	14	4	14	.203	.224	.287	46	-10	-10	8	1	0	0	-4	23/S	-1.4
1969	Cin-N	1	1	0	0	0	0	0	0	0	1	.000	.000	.000	-95	-0	-0	0	0	0	0	0	H	0.0
Total	9	494	1114	116	280	42	5	25	115	56	130	.251	.292	.365	82	-30	-29	114	2	3	-1	-27	32S/O1	-3.9

■ BILL DeLANCEY
DeLancey, William Pinkney b: 11/28/11, Greensboro, N.C. d: 11/28/46, Phoenix, Ariz. BL/TR, 5'11.5", 185 lbs. Deb: 9/11/32

YEAR	TM/L	G	AB	R	H	2B	3B	HR	RBI	BB	SO	AVG	OBP	SLG	PRO+	BR	/A	RC	SB	CS	SBR	FR	POS	TPR
1932	StL-N	8	26	1	5	0	2	0	2	2	1	.192	.250	.346	57	-2	-2	2	0			1	/C	0.0
1934	*StL-N	93	253	41	80	18	3	13	40	41	37	.316	.414	.565	150	22	20	62	1			5	C	2.6
1935	StL-N	103	301	37	84	14	5	6	41	42	34	.279	.369	.419	107	6	4	50	0			-1	C	0.2
1940	StL-N	15	18	0	4	0	0	0	2	0	2	.222	.222	.222	22	-2	-2	1	0			1	C	0.0
Total	4	219	598	79	173	32	10	19	85	85	74	.289	.380	.472	121	24	20	115	1			5	C	2.8

■ BILL DELANEY
Delaney, William L. b: 3/4/1863, Cincinnati, O. d: 3/1/42, Canton, Ohio BR/TR, Deb: 8/21/1890

YEAR	TM/L	G	AB	R	H	2B	3B	HR	RBI	BB	SO	AVG	OBP	SLG	PRO+	BR	/A	RC	SB	CS	SBR	FR	POS	TPR
1890	Cle-N	36	116	16	22	1	1	1	7	21	19	.190	.314	.241	66	-4	-4	11	5			-9	2	-1.0

■ JESUS De La ROSA
De La Rosa, Jesus (b: Jesus De Los Santos (De La Rosa)) b: 8/5/53, Santo Domingo, D.R BR/TR, 6'1", 153 lbs. Deb: 8/02/75

YEAR	TM/L	G	AB	R	H	2B	3B	HR	RBI	BB	SO	AVG	OBP	SLG	PRO+	BR	/A	RC	SB	CS	SBR	FR	POS	TPR
1975	Hou-N	3	3	1	1	1	0	0	0	0	0	.333	.333	.667	186	0	0	1	0	0	0	0	H	0.0

■ PUCHY DELGADO
Delgado, Luis Felipe (Robles) b: 2/2/54, Hatillo, P.R. BB/TL, 5'11", 170 lbs. Deb: 9/06/77

YEAR	TM/L	G	AB	R	H	2B	3B	HR	RBI	BB	SO	AVG	OBP	SLG	PRO+	BR	/A	RC	SB	CS	SBR	FR	POS	TPR
1977	Sea-A	13	22	4	4	0	0	0	2	1	8	.182	.217	.182	10	-3	-3	1	0	0	0	1	O	-0.1

■ BOBBY Del GRECO
Del Greco, Robert George b: 4/7/33, Pittsburgh, Pa. BR/TR, 5'10.5", 185 lbs. Deb: 4/16/52

YEAR	TM/L	G	AB	R	H	2B	3B	HR	RBI	BB	SO	AVG	OBP	SLG	PRO+	BR	/A	RC	SB	CS	SBR	FR	POS	TPR
1952	Pit-N	99	341	34	74	14	2	1	20	38	70	.217	.301	.279	60	-17	-18	30	6	5	-1	4	O	-1.8
1956	Pit-N	14	20	4	4	0	0	2	3	3	3	.200	.304	.500	114	0	0	3	0	0	0	0	/O3	0.0
	StL-N	102	270	29	58	16	2	5	18	32	50	.215	.312	.344	76	-9	-9	31	1	1	-0	-11	O	-2.4
	Yr	116	290	33	62	16	2	7	21	35	53	.214	.311	.355	79	-9	-8	34	1	1	-0	-11		-2.4
1957	Chi-N	20	40	2	8	2	0	0	3	10	17	.200	.360	.250	69	-1	-1	5	1	0	0	2	O	0.0
	NY-A	8	7	3	3	0	0	0	0	2	2	.429	.556	.429	175	1	1	2	1	0	0	0	/O	0.1
1958	NY-A	12	5	1	1	0	0	0	0	1	1	.200	.333	.200	52	-0	-0	0	0	1	-1	0	/O	0.0
1960	Phi-N	100	300	48	71	16	4	10	26	54	64	.237	.355	.417	110	5	5	46	1	5	-3	8	O	0.8
1961	Phi-N	41	112	14	29	5	0	2	11	12	17	.259	.346	.357	88	-2	-2	14	0	0	0	3	O/23	-0.2
	KC-A	74	239	34	55	14	1	5	21	30	31	.230	.319	.360	81	-6	-7	29	1	0	0	2	O	-0.6
1962	KC-A	132	338	61	86	21	1	9	38	49	62	.254	.370	.402	105	5	4	55	4	1	1	-5	*O	-0.4
1963	KC-A	121	306	40	65	7	1	8	29	40	52	.212	.313	.320	75	-8	-10	32	1	2	-1	-12	*O/3	-2.7
1965	Phi-N	8	4	1	0	0	0	0	0	0	3	.000	.000	.000	-99	-1	-1	0	0	0	0	0	/O	0.0
Total	9	731	1982	271	454	95	11	42	169	271	372	.229	.331	.352	85	-33	-37	247	16	15	-4	-9	O/32	-7.0

■ JUAN DELIS
Delis, Juan Francisco b: 2/27/28, Santiago, Cuba BR/TR, 5'11", 170 lbs. Deb: 4/16/55

YEAR	TM/L	G	AB	R	H	2B	3B	HR	RBI	BB	SO	AVG	OBP	SLG	PRO+	BR	/A	RC	SB	CS	SBR	FR	POS	TPR
1955	Was-A	54	132	12	25	3	1	0	11	3	15	.189	.219	.227	21	-15	-14	6	1	2	-1	-2	3/O2	-1.6

■ EDDIE DELKER
Delker, Edward Alberts b: 4/17/07, DeAlto, Pa. BR/TR, 5'10.5", 170 lbs. Deb: 4/28/29

YEAR	TM/L	G	AB	R	H	2B	3B	HR	RBI	BB	SO	AVG	OBP	SLG	PRO+	BR	/A	RC	SB	CS	SBR	FR	POS	TPR
1929	StL-N	22	40	5	6	0	1	0	3	2	12	.150	.209	.200	2	-6	-6	2	0			-2	/S23	-0.6
1931	StL-N	1	2	0	1	1	0	0	2	0	0	.500	.500	1.000	283	1	0	1	0			-0	/3	0.0
1932	StL-N	20	42	1	5	4	0	0	2	8	7	.119	.260	.214	28	-4	-4	3	0			4	2/3S	0.1
	Phi-N	30	62	7	10	1	1	0	7	6	14	.161	.235	.258	29	-6	-7	4	0			-2	2	-0.6
	Yr	50	104	8	15	5	1	0	9	14	21	.144	.246	.240	29	-10	-11	7	0			3		-0.5
1933	Phi-N	25	41	6	7	3	1	0	1	0	12	.171	.171	.293	27	-4	-4	2	0			6	2/3	0.3
Total	4	98	187	19	29	9	3	1	15	16	45	.155	.225	.251	25	-20	-22	12	0			6	/23S	-0.8

■ BERT DELMAS
Delmas, Albert Charles b: 5/20/11, San Francisco, Cal d: 12/4/79, Huntington Beach, Cal. BL/TR, 5'11", 165 lbs. Deb: 9/10/33

YEAR	TM/L	G	AB	R	H	2B	3B	HR	RBI	BB	SO	AVG	OBP	SLG	PRO+	BR	/A	RC	SB	CS	SBR	FR	POS	TPR
1933	Bro-N	12	28	4	7	0	0	0	1	7		.250	.276	.250	53	-2	-2	2	0			-3	2	-0.3

■ LUIS De Los SANTOS
De Los Santos, Luis Manuel (Martinez) b: 12/29/66, San Cristobal, D.R. BR/TR, 6'5", 205 lbs. Deb: 9/07/88

YEAR	TM/L	G	AB	R	H	2B	3B	HR	RBI	BB	SO	AVG	OBP	SLG	PRO+	BR	/A	RC	SB	CS	SBR	FR	POS	TPR
1988	KC-A	11	22	1	2	1	1	0	1	4	4	.091	.231	.227	29	-2	-2	1	0	0	0	-0	/1D	-0.2

YEAR	TM/L	G	AB	R	H	2B	3B	HR	RBI	BB	SO	AVG	OBP	SLG	PRO+	BR	/A	RC	SB	CS	SBR	FR	POS	TPR
1989	KC-A	28	87	6	22	3	1	0	6	5	14	.253	.293	.310	71	-3	-3	8	0	0	0	0	1	-0.4
Total	2	39	109	7	24	4	2	0	7	9	18	.220	.280	.294	62	-6	-6	8	0	0	0	-0	/1D	-0.6

■ GARTON Del SAVIO
Del Savio, Garton Orville b: 11/26/13, New York, N.Y. BR/TR, 5'9.5", 165 lbs. Deb: 4/24/43

YEAR	TM/L	G	AB	R	H	2B	3B	HR	RBI	BB	SO	AVG	OBP	SLG	PRO+	BR	/A	RC	SB	CS	SBR	FR	POS	TPR
1943	Phi-N	4	11	0	1	0	0	0	0	1	0	.091	.167	.091	-26	-2	-2	0	0			0	/S	0.0

■ JIM DELSING
Delsing, James Henry b: 11/13/25, Rudolph, Wis. BL/TR, 5'10", 175 lbs. Deb: 4/21/48

YEAR	TM/L	G	AB	R	H	2B	3B	HR	RBI	BB	SO	AVG	OBP	SLG	PRO+	BR	/A	RC	SB	CS	SBR	FR	POS	TPR
1948	Chi-A	20	63	5	12	0	0	0	5	5	12	.190	.261	.190	22	-7	-7	3	0	0	0	-1	O	-0.7
1949	NY-A	9	20	5	7	1	0	1	3	1	2	.350	.381	.550	145	1	1	4	0	0	0	-1	/O	0.0
1950	NY-A	12	10	2	4	0	0	0	2	2	0	.400	.500	.400	137	1	1	2	0	0	0	0	H	0.1
	StL-A	69	209	25	55	5	2	0	15	20	23	.263	.328	.306	61	-11	-12	21	1	4	-2	6	O	-0.8
	Yr	81	219	27	59	5	2	0	17	22	23	.269	.336	.311	65	-11	-12	23	1	4	-2	6		-0.7
1951	StL-A	131	449	59	112	20	2	8	45	56	39	.249	.338	.356	85	-7	-9	52	2	9	-5	4	*O	-1.3
1952	StL-A	93	298	34	76	13	6	1	34	26	29	.255	.323	.349	85	-5	-6	33	3	3	-1	5	O	-0.3
	Det-A	33	113	14	31	2	1	3	15	11	8	.274	.344	.389	103	1	0	16	1	0	0	-1	O	-0.1
	Yr	126	411	48	107	15	7	4	49	37	37	.260	.329	.365	90	-5	-6	49	4	3	-1	4		-0.4
1953	Det-A	138	479	77	138	26	6	11	62	66	39	.288	.380	.436	121	14	15	84	1	3	-2	-6	*O	0.4
1954	Det-A	122	371	39	92	24	2	6	38	49	38	.248	.337	.372	96	-3	-2	48	4	4	-1	-2	*O	-0.7
1955	Det-A	114	356	49	85	15	2	10	60	48	40	.239	.331	.376	92	-5	-4	47	2	0	1	-7	*O	-1.5
1956	Det-A	10	12	0	0	0	0	0	0	3	3	.000	.250	.000	-29	-2	-2	0	0	0	0	-0	/O	-0.2
	Chi-A	55	41	11	5	3	0	0	2	10	13	.122	.294	.195	31	-4	-4	3	1	0	0	2	O	-0.2
	Yr	65	53	11	5	3	0	0	2	13	16	.094	.284	.151	17	-6	-6	4	1	0	0	2		-0.4
1960	KC-A	16	40	2	10	3	0	0	5	3	5	.250	.302	.325	69	-2	-2	4	0	0	0	1	O	0.0
Total	10	822	2461	322	627	112	21	40	286	300	251	.255	.340	.366	91	-30	-31	320	15	23	-9	0	O	-5.3

■ JOE DeMAESTRI
DeMaestri, Joseph Paul "Oats" b: 12/9/28, San Francisco, Cal. BR/TR, 6', 170 lbs. Deb: 4/19/51

YEAR	TM/L	G	AB	R	H	2B	3B	HR	RBI	BB	SO	AVG	OBP	SLG	PRO+	BR	/A	RC	SB	CS	SBR	FR	POS	TPR
1951	Chi-A	56	74	8	15	0	1	1	3	5	11	.203	.253	.297	49	-6	-5	5	0	4	-2	6	S2/3	0.0
1952	StL-A	81	186	13	42	9	1	1	18	8	25	.226	.258	.301	54	-12	-12	14	0	1	-1	2	S/23	-0.6
1953	Phi-A	111	420	53	107	17	3	6	35	24	39	.255	.297	.352	72	-16	-18	42	0	1	-1	-16	*S	-2.6
1954	Phi-A	146	539	49	124	16	3	8	40	20	63	.230	.262	.315	57	-33	-33	42	1	4	-2	-6	*S/23	-3.0
1955	KC-A	123	457	42	114	14	1	6	37	20	47	.249	.285	.324	63	-24	-25	39	3	5	-2	-12	*S	-2.5
1956	KC-A	133	434	41	101	16	1	6	39	25	73	.233	.279	.316	57	-28	-28	37	3	3	-1	6	*S/2	-1.0
1957	KC-A	135	461	44	113	14	6	9	33	22	82	.245	.282	.360	73	-18	-18	44	6	1	1	-7	*S	-1.3
1958	KC-A	139	442	32	97	11	1	6	38	16	84	.219	.248	.290	47	-32	-33	29	1	0	0	11	*S	-0.2
1959	KC-A	118	352	31	86	16	5	6	34	28	65	.244	.307	.369	83	-8	-8	38	1	0	0	5	*S	0.6
1960	*NY-A	49	35	8	8	1	0	0	2	0	9	.229	.229	.257	33	-3	-3	2	0	0	0	7	2S	0.7
1961	NY-A	30	41	1	6	0	0	0	2	0	13	.146	.146	.146	-23	-7	-7	1	0	0	0	7	S/23	0.2
Total	11	1121	3441	322	813	114	23	49	281	168	511	.236	.275	.325	62	-186	-192	293	15	19	-7	4	*S/23	-9.7

■ FRANK DEMAREE
Demaree, Joseph Franklin (b: Joseph Franklin Dimaria)
b: 6/10/10, Winters, Cal. d: 8/30/58, Los Angeles, Cal. BR/TR, 5'11.5", 185 lbs. Deb: 7/22/32

YEAR	TM/L	G	AB	R	H	2B	3B	HR	RBI	BB	SO	AVG	OBP	SLG	PRO+	BR	/A	RC	SB	CS	SBR	FR	POS	TPR
1932	*Chi-N	23	56	4	14	3	0	0	6	2	7	.250	.288	.304	60	-3	-3	5	0			1	O	-0.2
1933	Chi-N	134	515	68	140	24	6	6	51	22	42	.272	.304	.377	94	-5	-5	59	4			-3	*O	-1.6
1935	*Chi-N	107	385	60	125	19	4	2	66	26	23	.325	.369	.410	108	5	5	58	6			-6	O	-0.4
1936	Chi-N	154	605	93	212	34	3	16	96	49	30	.350	.400	.496	137	34	32	119	4			-4	*O	2.0
1937	Chi-N	154	615	104	199	36	6	17	115	57	31	.324	.382	.485	129	28	25	112	6			-1	*O	1.7
1938	*Chi-N	129	476	63	130	15	7	8	62	45	34	.273	.341	.384	96	-0	-2	62	1			-9	*O	-1.2
1939	NY-N	150	560	68	170	27	2	11	79	66	40	.304	.381	.418	114	13	12	89	2			-5	*O	0.5
1940	NY-N	121	460	68	139	18	6	7	61	45	39	.302	.364	.413	113	9	9	71	5			-11	*O	-0.6
1941	NY-N	16	35	3	6	0	0	0	1	4	1	.171	.256	.171	22	-4	-4	1	0			1	O	-0.2
	Bos-N	48	113	20	26	5	2	2	15	12	5	.230	.304	.363	91	-2	-2	12	2			-3	O	-0.5
	Yr	64	148	23	32	5	2	2	16	16	6	.216	.293	.318	74	-6	-5	13	2			-3		-0.7
1942	Bos-N	64	187	18	42	5	0	3	24	17	10	.225	.289	.299	74	-7	-6	15	2			2	O	-0.4
1943	*StL-N	39	86	5	25	2	0	0	9	8	4	.291	.351	.314	89	-1	-1	9	1			-2	O	-0.3
1944	StL-A	16	51	4	13	2	0	0	6	6	3	.255	.333	.294	76	-1	-1	6	0	0	0	-0	O	-0.2
Total	12	1155	4144	578	1241	190	36	72	591	359	269	.299	.357	.415	110	67	59	616	33	0		-40	*O	-1.4

■ BILLY DeMARS
DeMars, William Lester "Kid" b: 8/26/25, Brooklyn, N.Y. BR/TR, 5'10", 160 lbs. Deb: 5/18/48 C

YEAR	TM/L	G	AB	R	H	2B	3B	HR	RBI	BB	SO	AVG	OBP	SLG	PRO+	BR	/A	RC	SB	CS	SBR	FR	POS	TPR
1948	Phi-A	18	29	3	5	0	0	0	1	5	3	.172	.294	.172	26	-3	-3	2	0	0	0	4	/S23	0.1
1950	StL-A	61	178	25	44	5	1	0	13	22	13	.247	.330	.287	57	-11	-12	17	0	1	-1	-7	S/3	-1.5
1951	StL-A	1	4	1	1	0	0	0	0	1	0	.250	.400	.250	76	-0	-0	1	0	0	0	-0	/S	0.0
Total	3	80	211	29	50	5	1	0	14	28	16	.237	.326	.270	53	-14	-15	20	0	1	-1	-4	/S32	-1.4

■ JOHN DeMERIT
DeMerit, John Stephen "Thumper" b: 1/8/36, West Bend, Wis. BR/TR, 6'1.5", 195 lbs. Deb: 6/18/57

YEAR	TM/L	G	AB	R	H	2B	3B	HR	RBI	BB	SO	AVG	OBP	SLG	PRO+	BR	/A	RC	SB	CS	SBR	FR	POS	TPR
1957	*Mil-N	33	34	8	5	0	0	0	1	0	8	.147	.147	.147	-22	-6	-5	1	1	0	0	3	O	-0.2
1958	Mil-N	3	3	1	2	0	0	0	0	0	0	.667	.667	.667	278	1	1	1	0	0	0	0	/O	0.1
1959	Mil-N	11	5	4	1	0	0	0	0	1	2	.200	.333	.200	51	-0	-0	0	0	0	0	2	/O	0.1
1961	Mil-N	32	74	5	12	3	0	2	5	5	19	.162	.225	.284	36	-7	-7	5	0	0	0	2	O	-0.5
1962	NY-N	14	16	3	3	0	0	1	1	2	4	.188	.278	.375	72	-1	-1	2	0	0	0	-1	/O	-0.1
Total	5	93	132	21	23	3	0	3	7	8	33	.174	.227	.265	32	-13	-12	9	1	0	0	5	/O	-0.6

■ DON DEMETER
Demeter, Donald Lee b: 6/25/35, Oklahoma City, Okla BR/TR, 6'4", 190 lbs. Deb: 9/18/56

YEAR	TM/L	G	AB	R	H	2B	3B	HR	RBI	BB	SO	AVG	OBP	SLG	PRO+	BR	/A	RC	SB	CS	SBR	FR	POS	TPR
1956	Bro-N	3	3	1	1	0	0	0	1	0	1	.333	.333	1.333	297	1	1	1	0	0	0	0	/O	0.1
1958	LA-N	43	106	11	20	2	0	5	8	5	32	.189	.225	.349	48	-8	-9	8	2	3	-1	2	O	-0.8
1959	*LA-N	139	371	55	95	11	1	18	70	16	87	.256	.298	.437	86	-5	-9	45	5	6	-2	-12	*O	-2.4
1960	LA-N	64	168	23	46	7	1	9	29	8	34	.274	.311	.488	108	3	1	25	0	1	-1	1	O	0.0
1961	LA-N	15	29	3	5	0	0	1	2	3	6	.172	.250	.276	36	-3	-3	2	0	0	0	1	O	-0.1
	Phi-N	106	382	54	98	18	4	20	68	19	74	.257	.300	.482	105	0	1	54	2	1	0	11	O1	0.5
	Yr	121	411	57	103	18	4	21	70	22	80	.251	.297	.467	99	-2	-2	55	2	1	0	12		0.4
1962	Phi-N	153	550	85	169	24	3	29	107	41	93	.307	.366	.520	139	26	28	101	2	7	-4	-6	*3O/1	1.7
1963	Phi-N	154	515	63	133	20	2	22	83	31	93	.258	.308	.433	112	6	7	66	1	4	-2	-5	*O31	-0.7
1964	Det-A	134	441	57	113	22	1	22	80	17	85	.256	.292	.460	104	1	1	58	4	1	1	-10	O1	-1.3
1965	Det-A	122	389	50	108	16	4	16	58	23	65	.278	.328	.463	121	10	10	56	4	2	0	-5	O1	0.3
1966	Det-A	32	99	12	21	5	0	5	12	3	19	.212	.235	.414	81	-3	-3	8	1	0	0	6	O/1	0.3
	Bos-A	73	226	31	66	13	1	9	29	5	42	.292	.310	.478	111	6	3	33	1	0	0	-3	O/1	-0.1
	Yr	105	325	43	87	18	1	14	41	8	61	.268	.287	.458	102	3	0	40	2	0	1	3		0.2
1967	Bos-A	20	43	7	12	5	0	1	4	3	11	.279	.326	.465	122	2	1	7	0	0	0	0	O/3	0.1
	Cle-A	51	121	15	25	4	0	5	12	5	16	.207	.256	.364	80	-3	-3	10	0	0	0	4	O/3	0.0
	Yr	71	164	22	37	9	0	6	16	8	27	.226	.274	.390	92	-2	-2	17	0	0	0	4		0.1
Total	11	1109	3443	467	912	147	17	163	563	180	658	.265	.309	.459	108	32	25	474	22	25	-8	-15	O31	-2.7

■ STEVE DEMETER
Demeter, Stephen b: 1/27/35, Homer City, Pa. BR/TR, 5'9.5", 185 lbs. Deb: 7/29/59 C

YEAR	TM/L	G	AB	R	H	2B	3B	HR	RBI	BB	SO	AVG	OBP	SLG	PRO+	BR	/A	RC	SB	CS	SBR	FR	POS	TPR
1959	Det-A	11	18	1	2	1	0	0	1	0	1	.111	.111	.167	-24	-3	-3	0	0	0	0	1	/3	-0.1
1960	Cle-A	4	5	0	0	0	0	0	0	0	1	.000	.000	.000	-99	-1	-1	0	0	0	0	0	/3	0.0
Total	2	15	23	1	2	1	0	0	1	0	2	.087	.087	.130	-40	-4	-5	0	0	0	0	1	/3	-0.1

YEAR	TM/L	G	AB	R	H	2B	3B	HR	RBI	BB	SO	AVG	OBP	SLG	PRO+	BR	/A	RC	SB	CS	SBR	FR	POS	TPR

■ RAY DEMMITT   Demmitt, Charles Raymond   b: 2/2/1884, Illiopolis, Ill.   d: 2/19/56, Glen Ellyn, Ill.   BL/TR, 5'8", 170 lbs.   Deb: 4/12/09

1909	NY-A	123	427	68	105	12	12	4	30	55		.246	.340	.358	120	11	11	57	16			5	*O	1.3
1910	StL-A	10	23	4	4	1	0	0	2	3		.174	.296	.217	65	-1	-1	2	0			1	/O	0.0
1914	Det-A	1	0	0	0	0	0	0	0	0	0	—	—	—	—	0	0	0	0			0	R	0.0
	Chi-A	146	515	63	133	13	12	2	46	61	48	.258	.344	.342	108	5	6	60	12	20	-8	-5	*O	-1.7
	Yr	147	515	63	133	13	12	2	46	61	48	.258	.344	.342	108	5	6	60	12	20	-8	-5		-1.7
1915	Chi-A	9	6	0	0	0	0	0	0	1	2	.000	.143	.000	-55	-1	-1	0	0			-1	/O	-0.2
1917	StL-A	14	53	6	15	1	2	0	7	0	8	.283	.296	.377	109	-0	0	6	1			-3	O	-0.3
1918	StL-A	116	405	45	114	23	5	1	61	38	35	.281	.346	.370	120	7	9	55	10			7	*O	1.2
1919	StL-A	79	202	19	48	11	2	1	19	14	27	.238	.290	.327	71	-8	-8	19	3			-7	O	-1.9
Total	7	498	1631	205	419	61	33	8	165	172	120	.257	.334	.349	108	14	15	199	42	20		-3	O	-1.6

■ GENE DeMONTREVILLE   DeMontreville, Eugene Napoleon   b: 3/26/1874, St.Paul, Minn.   d: 2/18/35, Memphis, Tenn.   BR/TR, 5'8", 165 lbs.   Deb: 8/20/1894

1894	Pit-N	2	8	0	2	0	0	0	0	1	4	.250	.333	.250	44	-1	-1	1	0			-1	/S	0.0
1895	Was-N	12	46	7	10	1	3	0	9	3	4	.217	.265	.370	65	-3	-3	6	5			4	S	0.1
1896	Was-N	133	533	94	183	24	5	8	77	29	27	.343	.381	.452	121	15	15	105	28			16	*S	2.6
1897	Was-N	133	566	92	193	27	8	3	93	21		.341	.366	.433	113	9	9	103	30			10	*S2	2.0
1898	Bal-N	151	567	93	186	19	2	0	86	52		.328	.394	.369	120	19	17	104	49			0	*2S	2.2
1899	Chi-N	82	310	43	87	6	3	0	40	17		.281	.328	.319	82	-8	-7	42	26			9	S	0.7
	Bal-N	60	240	40	67	13	4	1	36	10		.279	.313	.379	87	-3	-5	36	21			9	2	0.6
	Yr	142	550	83	154	19	7	1	76	27		.280	.322	.345	85	-11	-12	78	47			18		1.3
1900	Bro-N	69	234	34	57	8	1	0	28	10		.244	.280	.286	55	-13	-15	25	21			2	2S/301	-0.8
1901	Bos-N	140	577	83	173	14	4	5	72	17		.300	.320	.364	92	-1	-8	80	25			6	*23	0.7
1902	Bos-N	124	481	51	125	16	5	0	53	12		.260	.279	.314	84	-10	-10	53	23			-17	*2S	-2.0
1903	Was-A	12	44	0	12	2	0	0	3	0		.273	.273	.318	77	-1	-1	4	0			-4	2/S	-0.5
1904	StL-A	4	9	0	1	0	0	0	0	2		.111	.273	.111	27	-1	-1	0	0			-0	/2	0.0
Total	11	922	3615	537	1096	130	35	17	497	174	35	.303	.339	.373	99	2	-9	559	228			32	2S/310	5.6

■ LEE DeMONTREVILLE   DeMontreville, Leon   b: 9/23/1879, St.Paul, Minn.   d: 3/22/62, Pelham Manor, N.Y.   TR, 5'7", 140 lbs.   Deb: 7/10/03

| 1903 | StL-N | 26 | 70 | 8 | 17 | 3 | 1 | 0 | 7 | 8 | | .243 | .321 | .314 | 86 | -1 | -1 | 8 | 3 | | | -3 | S/2O | -0.2 |

■ RICK DEMPSEY   Dempsey, John Rikard   b: 9/13/49, Fayetteville, Tenn.   BR/TR, 6', 190 lbs.   Deb: 9/23/69

1969	Min-A	5	6	1	3	1	0	0	0	1	0	.500	.571	.667	240	1	1	2	0	0	0	-1	/C	0.0
1970	Min-A	5	7	1	0	0	0	0	0	1	1	.000	.125	.000	-62	-2	-2	0	0	0	0	0	/C	-0.1
1971	Min-A	6	13	2	4	1	0	0	0	1	1	.308	.357	.385	107	0	0	2	0	0	0	2	/C	0.2
1972	Min-A	25	40	0	8	1	0	0	0	6	8	.200	.304	.225	56	-2	-2	3	0	0	0	-1	C	-0.2
1973	NY-A	6	11	0	2	0	0	0	0	1	3	.182	.250	.182	24	-1	-1	0	0	0	0	-2	/C	-0.3
1974	NY-A	43	109	12	26	3	0	2	12	8	7	.239	.291	.321	78	-3	-3	9	1	0	0	5	C/OD	0.3
1975	NY-A	71	145	18	38	8	0	1	11	21	15	.262	.355	.338	100	0	1	18	0	0	0	2	CD/O3	0.3
1976	NY-A	21	42	1	5	0	0	0	2	5	4	.119	.213	.119	-1	-5	-5	1	0	0	0	3	/CO	-0.2
	Bal-A	59	174	11	37	2	0	0	10	13	17	.213	.275	.224	50	-11	-10	11	1	1	-0	6	C/O	-0.2
	Yr	80	216	12	42	2	0	0	12	18	21	.194	.263	.204	40	-16	-15	13	1	1	-0	8		-0.4
1977	Bal-A	91	270	27	61	7	4	3	34	34	34	.226	.317	.315	78	-9	-7	27	2	3	-1	-3	C	-0.8
1978	Bal-A	136	441	44	114	25	0	6	32	48	54	.259	.331	.356	99	-3	0	53	7	3	0	-5	*C	0.0
1979	*Bal-A	124	368	48	88	23	0	6	41	38	37	.239	.310	.351	81	-11	-10	39	0	1	-1	18	*C	1.3
1980	Bal-A	119	362	51	95	26	3	9	40	36	45	.262	.334	.425	108	3	3	50	3	1	0	11	*C/O1D	1.9
1981	Bal-A	92	251	24	54	10	1	6	15	32	36	.215	.306	.335	85	-5	-5	24	0	1	-1	3	C/D	0.2
1982	Bal-A	125	344	35	88	15	1	5	36	46	37	.256	.344	.349	91	-3	-3	42	0	3	-2	0	*C/D	0.2
1983	*Bal-A	128	347	33	80	16	2	4	32	40	54	.231	.315	.323	78	-11	-10	36	1	1	-0	20	*C	1.5
1984	Bal-A	109	330	37	76	11	0	11	34	40	58	.230	.315	.364	89	-5	-4	37	1	2	-1	-6	*C	-0.4
1985	Bal-A	132	362	54	92	19	0	12	52	50	87	.254	.346	.406	108	3	5	55	0	1	-1	-12	*C	-0.2
1986	Bal-A	122	327	42	68	15	1	13	29	45	78	.208	.309	.379	87	-6	-6	41	1	0	0	3	*C	0.5
1987	Cle-A	60	141	16	25	10	0	1	9	23	29	.177	.297	.270	51	-10	-10	12	0	0	0	0	C	-0.3
1988	*LA-N	77	167	25	42	13	0	7	30	25	44	.251	.349	.455	133	6	7	27	1	0	0	5	C	1.7
1989	LA-N	79	151	16	27	7	0	4	16	30	37	.179	.319	.305	80	-3	-3	16	1	0	0	3	C	0.5
1990	LA-N	62	128	13	25	5	0	2	15	23	29	.195	.318	.281	70	-5	-4	11	1	0	0	0	C	-0.1
Total	22	1697	4536	508	1058	218	12	92	450	567	715	.233	.321	.347	88	-83	-67	520	20	17	-4	50	*C/OD13	5.8

■ TOD DENNEHEY   Dennehey, Thomas Francis   b: 5/12/1899, Philadelphia, Pa.   d: 8/8/77, Philadelphia, Pa.   BL/TL, 5'10", 180 lbs.   Deb: 4/21/23

| 1923 | Phi-N | 9 | 24 | 4 | 7 | 2 | 0 | 0 | 2 | 1 | 3 | .292 | .320 | .375 | 74 | -1 | -1 | 3 | 0 | 0 | 0 | 0 | /O | 0.0 |

■ OTTO DENNING   Denning, Otto George "Dutch"   b: 12/28/12, Hays, Kan.   BR/TR, 6', 180 lbs.   Deb: 4/15/42

1942	Cle-A	92	214	15	45	14	0	1	19	18	14	.210	.275	.290	62	-12	-10	18	0	0	0	-2	C/O	-0.3
1943	Cle-A	37	129	8	31	6	0	0	13	5	1	.240	.269	.287	67	-6	-6	9	3	1	0	-3	1	-1.0
Total	2	129	343	23	76	20	0	1	32	23	15	.222	.272	.289	64	-18	-16	27	3	1	0	-5	/C1O	-1.3

■ JERRY DENNY   Denny, Jeremiah Dennis (b: Jeremiah Dennis Eldridge)   b: 3/16/1859, New York, N.Y.   d: 8/16/27, Houston, Tex.   BR/TR, 5'11.5", 180 lbs.   Deb: 5/02/1881

1881	Pro-N	85	320	38	77	16	2	1	24	5	44	.241	.252	.313	78	-9	-8	26				6	*3	0.4
1882	Pro-N	84	329	54	81	10	9	2	42	4	46	.246	.255	.350	92	-3	-3	30				14	*3	1.1
1883	Pro-N	98	393	73	108	26	8	8	55	9	48	.275	.291	.443	116	8	7	52				10	*3	1.5
1884	*Pro-N	110	439	57	109	22	9	6	59	14	58	.248	.272	.380	105	1	2	46				-1	*3/12C	-0.4
1885	Pro-N	83	318	40	71	14	4	3	24	12	53	.223	.252	.321	87	-6	-4	26				-0	*3	-0.2
1886	StL-N	119	475	58	122	24	6	9	62	14	68	.257	.278	.389	108	-1	4	57	16			28	*3/S	3.3
1887	Ind-N	122	510	86	165	34	12	11	97	13	22	.324	.344	.502	139	21	24	101	29			23	*3/SO2	4.0
1888	Ind-N	126	524	52	137	27	7	12	63	9	79	.261	.277	.408	116	9	8	70	32			25	*3S/20P	3.6
1889	Ind-N	133	578	96	163	24	0	18	112	27	63	.282	.314	.417	103	1	-1	85	22			12	*3/2S	1.7
1890	NY-N	114	437	50	93	18	7	3	42	28	62	.213	.270	.307	69	-18	-18	40	11			4	*3/S2	-0.7
1891	NY-N	4	16	0	4	1	0	0	1	0	3	.250	.250	.313	68	-1	-1	2	2			-3	/3	-0.2
	Cle-N	36	138	17	31	5	0	0	21	12	23	.225	.291	.261	60	-6	-7	12	3			-3	3/O	-0.3
	Phi-N	19	73	5	21	1	1	0	11	4	6	.288	.325	.329	90	-1	-1	8	1			-1	1/3	-0.1
	Yr	59	227	22	56	7	1	0	33	16	32	.247	.299	.286	70	-8	-9	22	6			-7		-1.1
1893	Lou-N	44	175	22	43	5	4	1	22	9	15	.246	.283	.337	71	-9	-7	18	4			1	S/3	-0.3
1894	Lou-N	60	221	26	61	11	7	0	32	12	15	.276	.325	.389	78	-10	-7	32	10			3	3	-0.3
Total	13	1237	4946	714	1286	238	76	74	667	173	602	.260	.287	.384	100	-24	-13	605	130			117	*3/S120PC	12.6

■ DREW DENSON   Denson, Andrew   b: 11/16/65, Cincinnati, Ohio   BB/TR, 6'5", 210 lbs.   Deb: 9/13/89

| 1989 | Atl-N | 12 | 36 | 1 | 9 | 1 | 0 | 0 | 5 | 3 | 9 | .250 | .308 | .278 | 67 | -1 | -2 | 3 | 1 | 0 | 0 | 2 | 1 | 0.0 |

■ BUCKY DENT   Dent, Russell Earl (b: Russell Earl O'Dey)   b: 11/25/51, Savannah, Ga.   BR/TR, 5'9", 170 lbs.   Deb: 6/01/73   M

1973	Chi-A	40	117	17	29	2	0	0	10	10	18	.248	.313	.265	62	-5	-6	10	2	3	-1	5	S/23	0.3
1974	Chi-A	154	496	55	136	15	3	5	45	28	48	.274	.317	.347	89	-6	-8	54	3	4	-2	9	*S	1.2
1975	Chi-A	157	602	52	159	29	4	3	58	36	48	.264	.306	.341	81	-15	-16	60	2	4	-2	27	*S	2.5
1976	Chi-A	158	562	44	138	18	4	2	52	43	45	.246	.301	.302	77	-16	-16	52	3	5	-2	-5	*S	-1.5

YEAR	TM/L	G	AB	R	H	2B	3B	HR	RBI	BB	SO	AVG	OBP	SLG	PRO+	BR	/A	RC	SB	CS	SBR	FR	POS	TPR
1977	*NY-A	158	477	54	118	18	4	8	49	39	28	.247	.306	.352	80	-14	-13	52	1	1	-0	-11	*S	-0.5
1978	*NY-A	123	379	40	92	11	1	5	40	23	24	.243	.290	.317	72	-15	-14	34	3	1	0	-8	*S	-1.1
1979	NY-A	141	431	47	99	14	2	2	32	37	30	.230	.292	.285	58	-26	-25	39	0	0	0	32	*S	2.3
1980	*NY-A	141	489	57	128	26	2	5	52	48	37	.262	.330	.354	89	-8	-7	59	0	3	-2	13	*S	1.5
1981	NY-A	73	227	20	54	11	0	7	27	19	17	.238	.302	.379	97	-2	-1	27	0	1	-1	-2	S	0.1
1982	NY-A	59	160	11	27	1	1	0	9	8	11	.169	.208	.188	10	-20	-19	6	0	0	0	17	S	0.3
	Tex-A	46	146	16	32	9	0	1	14	13	10	.219	.283	.301	64	-8	-7	13	0	0	0	-2	S	-0.4
	Yr	105	306	27	59	10	1	1	23	21	21	.193	.245	.242	35	-27	-26	18	0	0	0	15		-0.1
1983	Tex-A	131	417	36	99	15	2	2	34	23	31	.237	.279	.297	60	-23	-22	34	3	7	-3	-8	*S/D	-2.5
1984	KC-A	11	9	2	3	0	0	0	1	1	2	.333	.400	.333	105	0	0	1	0	0	0	-1	/S3	0.0
Total	12	1392	4512	451	1114	169	23	40	423	328	349	.247	.300	.321	74	-157	-154	442	17	29	-12	66	*S/32D	2.2

■ SAM DENTE
Dente, Samuel Joseph "Blackie"   b: 4/26/22, Harrison, N.J.   BR/TR, 5'11", 175 lbs.   Deb: 7/10/47

YEAR	TM/L	G	AB	R	H	2B	3B	HR	RBI	BB	SO	AVG	OBP	SLG	PRO+	BR	/A	RC	SB	CS	SBR	FR	POS	TPR
1947	Bos-A	46	168	14	39	4	2	0	11	19	15	.232	.310	.280	60	-8	-9	15	0	1	-1	-3	3	-1.2
1948	StL-A	98	267	26	72	11	2	0	22	22	8	.270	.328	.326	72	-10	-11	29	1	3	-2	-2	S/3	-1.3
1949	Was-A	153	590	48	161	24	4	1	53	31	24	.273	.309	.332	71	-27	-26	58	4	4	-1	-9	*S	-3.3
1950	Was-A	155	603	56	144	20	5	2	59	39	19	.239	.286	.299	52	-47	-42	49	1	1	-0	1	*S2	-3.1
1951	Was-A	88	273	21	65	8	1	0	29	25	10	.238	.302	.275	58	-16	-16	22	3	0	1	3	S2/3	-0.6
1952	Chi-A	62	145	12	32	0	1	0	11	5	8	.221	.257	.234	37	-12	-12	8	0	0	0	3	S3/201	-0.7
1953	Chi-A	2	0	0	0	0	0	0	0	0	0	—	—	—	—	0	0	0	0	0	0	0	/S	0.0
1954	*Cle-A	68	169	18	45	7	1	1	19	14	4	.266	.322	.337	79	-4	-5	18	0	0	0	-3	S/2	-0.1
1955	Cle-A	73	105	10	27	4	0	0	10	12	8	.257	.333	.295	68	-4	-5	11	0	0	0	7	S3/2	0.9
Total	9	745	2320	205	585	78	16	4	214	167	96	.252	.303	.305	62	-129	-126	211	9	9	-3	-3	S/3201	-9.4

■ MIKE DePANGHER
DePangher, Michael Anthony b: 9/11/1858, Marysville, Cal. d: 7/7/15, San Francisco, Cal 5'8", 190 lbs. Deb: 8/01/1884

YEAR	TM/L	G	AB	R	H	2B	3B	HR	RBI	BB	SO	AVG	OBP	SLG	PRO+	BR	/A	RC	SB	CS	SBR	FR	POS	TPR
1884	Phi-N	4	10	0	2	0	0	0	0	1	3	.200	.273	.200	54	-1	-0	1				2	/C	0.1

■ TONY DePHILLIPS
DePhillips, Anthony Andrew b: 9/20/12, New York, N.Y. BR/TR, 6'2", 185 lbs. Deb: 4/25/43

YEAR	TM/L	G	AB	R	H	2B	3B	HR	RBI	BB	SO	AVG	OBP	SLG	PRO+	BR	/A	RC	SB	CS	SBR	FR	POS	TPR
1943	Cin-N	35	20	0	2	1	0	0	2	1	5	.100	.143	.150	-16	-3	-3	1	0			5	C	0.4

■ GENE DERBY
Derby, Eugene A. b: 2/1860, New Hampshire d: 10/12/28, Buffalo, N.Y. Deb: 9/03/1885

YEAR	TM/L	G	AB	R	H	2B	3B	HR	RBI	BB	SO	AVG	OBP	SLG	PRO+	BR	/A	RC	SB	CS	SBR	FR	POS	TPR
1885	Bal-a	10	31	4	4	0	0	0		1		.129	.182	.129	1	-3	-3	1				-0	/CO	-0.1

■ BOB DERNIER
Dernier, Robert Eugene b: 1/5/57, Kansas City, Mo. BR/TR, 6', 160 lbs. Deb: 9/07/80

YEAR	TM/L	G	AB	R	H	2B	3B	HR	RBI	BB	SO	AVG	OBP	SLG	PRO+	BR	/A	RC	SB	CS	SBR	FR	POS	TPR
1980	Phi-N	10	7	5	4	0	0	0	1	1	0	.571	.625	.571	224	1	1	4	3	0	1	2	/O	0.4
1981	Phi-N	10	4	0	3	0	0	0	0	0	0	.750	.750	.750	313	1	1	2	2	1	0	1	/O	0.2
1982	Phi-N	122	370	56	92	10	2	4	21	36	69	.249	.317	.319	77	-10	-11	41	42	12	5	6	*O	0.0
1983	*Phi-N	122	221	41	51	10	0	1	15	18	21	.231	.289	.290	61	-12	-11	22	35	7	6	11	*O	0.4
1984	*Chi-N	143	536	94	149	26	5	3	32	63	60	.278	.356	.362	94	-3	-3	75	45	17	3	-0	*O	-0.4
1985	Chi-N	121	469	63	119	20	3	1	21	40	44	.254	.316	.316	70	-14	-20	51	31	8	5	4	*O	-1.4
1986	Chi-N	108	324	32	73	14	1	4	18	22	41	.225	.275	.312	57	-17	-20	30	27	2	7	-3	*O	-1.8
1987	Chi-N	93	199	38	63	4	4	8	21	19	19	.317	.379	.497	125	8	7	37	16	7	1	-2	O	0.3
1988	Phi-N	68	166	19	48	3	1	1	10	9	19	.289	.330	.337	90	-2	-2	19	13	6	0	3	O	0.0
1989	Phi-N	107	187	26	32	5	0	1	13	14	28	.171	.229	.214	27	-18	-18	10	4	3	-1	0	O	-2.0
Total	10	904	2483	374	634	92	16	23	152	222	301	.255	.318	.333	77	-58	-75	290	218	63	28	20	O	-4.3

■ CLAUD DERRICK
Derrick, Claud Lester "Deek" b: 6/11/1886, Burton, Ga. d: 7/15/74, Clayton, Ga. BR/TR, 6', 175 lbs. Deb: 9/08/10

YEAR	TM/L	G	AB	R	H	2B	3B	HR	RBI	BB	SO	AVG	OBP	SLG	PRO+	BR	/A	RC	SB	CS	SBR	FR	POS	TPR
1910	Phi-A	2	1	0	0	0	0	0	0	0		.000	.000	.000	-99	-0	-0	0	0			-0	/S	0.0
1911	Phi-A	36	100	14	23	1	2	0	5	7		.230	.294	.280	61	-5	-5	11	7			1	2/S13	-0.3
1912	Phi-A	21	58	7	14	0	1	0	7	5		.241	.313	.276	71	-2	-2	6	1			1	S	0.2
1913	NY-A	23	65	7	19	1	0	1	7	5	8	.292	.352	.354	106	1	1	8	2			0	S/32	0.2
1914	Cin-N	3	6	2	2	1	0	0	1	0		.333	.333	.500	142	0	0	1	1			0	/S	0.1
	Chi-N	28	96	5	21	3	1	0	13	5	13	.219	.257	.271	57	-5	-5	7	2			3	/S	-0.1
	Yr	31	102	7	23	4	1	0	14	5	13	.225	.262	.284	62	-5	-5	8	3			3		0.0
Total	5	113	326	35	79	6	4	1	33	22	21	.242	.298	.294	72	-12	-12	33	13			4	/S231	-0.1

■ MIKE DERRICK
Derrick, James Michael b: 9/19/43, Columbia, S.C. BL/TR, 6', 190 lbs. Deb: 4/09/70

YEAR	TM/L	G	AB	R	H	2B	3B	HR	RBI	BB	SO	AVG	OBP	SLG	PRO+	BR	/A	RC	SB	CS	SBR	FR	POS	TPR
1970	Bos-A	24	33	3	7	1	0	0	5	0	11	.212	.212	.242	23	-3	-4	1	0	1	-1	-0	/O1	-0.4

■ RUSS DERRY
Derry, Alva Russell b: 10/7/16, Princeton, Mo. BL/TR, 6'1", 180 lbs. Deb: 7/04/44

YEAR	TM/L	G	AB	R	H	2B	3B	HR	RBI	BB	SO	AVG	OBP	SLG	PRO+	BR	/A	RC	SB	CS	SBR	FR	POS	TPR
1944	NY-A	38	114	14	29	3	0	4	14	20	19	.254	.366	.386	111	3	2	19	1	0	0	-3	O	-0.1
1945	NY-A	78	253	37	57	6	2	13	45	31	49	.225	.312	.419	107	3	1	34	1	0	0	3	O	0.2
1946	Phi-A	69	184	17	38	8	5	0	14	27	54	.207	.311	.304	73	-6	-6	20	0	0	0	5	O	-0.3
1949	StL-N	2	2	0	0	0	0	0	0	0	2	.000	.000	.000	-96	-1	-1	0	0			0	H	0.0
Total	4	187	553	68	124	17	7	17	73	78	124	.224	.322	.373	95	-2	-2	72	2	0		5	O	-0.2

■ JOE DeSA
DeSa, Joseph b: 7/27/59, Honolulu, Hawaii d: 12/20/86, San Juan, P.R. BL/TL, 5'11", 170 lbs. Deb: 9/06/80

YEAR	TM/L	G	AB	R	H	2B	3B	HR	RBI	BB	SO	AVG	OBP	SLG	PRO+	BR	/A	RC	SB	CS	SBR	FR	POS	TPR
1980	StL-N	7	11	0	3	0	0	0	0	0	2	.273	.273	.273	51	-1	-1	1	0	0	0	-0	/1O	0.0
1985	Chi-A	28	44	5	8	2	0	2	7	3	6	.182	.234	.364	58	-3	-3	4	0	0	0	1	/1OD	-0.1
Total	2	35	55	5	11	2	0	2	7	3	8	.200	.241	.345	57	-3	-3	4	0	0	0	1	/1DO	-0.1

■ GENE DESAUTELS
Desautels, Eugene Abraham "Red" b: 6/13/07, Worcester, Mass. BR/TR, 5'11", 170 lbs. Deb: 6/22/30

YEAR	TM/L	G	AB	R	H	2B	3B	HR	RBI	BB	SO	AVG	OBP	SLG	PRO+	BR	/A	RC	SB	CS	SBR	FR	POS	TPR
1930	Det-A	42	126	13	24	4	2	0	9	7	9	.190	.239	.254	25	-15	-15	8	2	0	1	9	C	-0.1
1931	Det-A	3	11	1	1	0	0	0	1	0	1	.091	.091	.091	-50	-2	-2	0	0	0	0	-1	/C	-0.2
1932	Det-A	28	72	8	17	2	0	0	2	13	11	.236	.360	.264	62	-3	-4	8	0	0	0	4	C	0.1
1933	Det-A	30	42	5	6	1	0	0	4	4	6	.143	.234	.167	8	-6	-6	2	0	0	0	2	C	-0.1
1937	Bos-A	96	305	33	74	10	3	0	27	36	26	.243	.325	.295	55	-19	-21	31	1	2	-1	3	C	-1.0
1938	Bos-A	108	333	47	97	16	2	0	48	57	31	.291	.396	.369	89	-1	-4	53	1	1	-0	5	*C	0.3
1939	Bos-A	76	226	26	55	14	0	0	21	33	13	.243	.340	.305	64	-11	-12	27	3	1	0	9	C	0.2
1940	Bos-A	71	222	19	50	7	1	0	17	32	13	.225	.328	.266	54	-13	-15	21	0	1	-1	-4	C	-1.2
1941	Cle-A	66	189	20	38	5	1	1	17	14	12	.201	.260	.254	38	-17	-16	14	1	0	0	5	C	-0.6
1942	Cle-A	62	162	14	40	5	0	0	9	12	13	.247	.303	.278	68	-8	-6	15	1	0	0	-9	C	-0.7
1943	Cle-A	68	185	14	38	6	1	0	19	11	16	.205	.250	.249	49	-13	-12	12	2	0	1	1	C	-0.6
1945	Cle-A	10	9	1	1	0	0	0	1	1	1	.111	.200	.111	-9	-1	-1	0	0	0	0	0	C	0.0
1946	Phi-A	52	130	10	28	3	1	0	13	12	16	.215	.282	.254	51	-9	-8	10	1	1	-0	1	C	-0.4
Total	13	712	2012	211	469	73	11	3	187	232	168	.233	.315	.285	58	-118	-122	201	12	6	0	26	C	-4.3

■ DELINO DeSHIELDS
DeShields, Delino Lamont b: 1/15/69, Seaford, Del. BL/TR, 6'1", 170 lbs. Deb: 4/09/90

YEAR	TM/L	G	AB	R	H	2B	3B	HR	RBI	BB	SO	AVG	OBP	SLG	PRO+	BR	/A	RC	SB	CS	SBR	FR	POS	TPR
1990	Mon-N	129	499	69	144	28	6	4	45	66	96	.289	.376	.393	112	10	11	75	42	22	-1	-8	*2	0.3

■ ORESTES DESTRADE
Destrade, Orestes (Cucuas) b: 5/8/62, Santiago, Cuba BB/TR, 6'4", 210 lbs. Deb: 9/11/87

YEAR	TM/L	G	AB	R	H	2B	3B	HR	RBI	BB	SO	AVG	OBP	SLG	PRO+	BR	/A	RC	SB	CS	SBR	FR	POS	TPR
1987	NY-A	9	19	5	5	0	0	0	1	5	5	.263	.417	.263	87	-0	-0	2	0	0	0	-0	/1D	0.0
1988	Pit-N	36	47	2	7	1	0	1	3	5	17	.149	.231	.234	34	-4	-4	3	0	0	0	-1	/1	-0.5
Total	2	45	66	7	12	1	0	1	4	10	22	.182	.289	.242	51	-4	-4	5	0	0	0	-1	/1D	-0.5

YEAR	TM/L	G	AB	R	H	2B	3B	HR	RBI	BB	SO	AVG	OBP	SLG	PRO+	BR	/A	RC	SB	CS	SBR	FR	POS	TPR

■ BOB DETHERAGE   Detherage, Robert Wayne   b: 9/20/54, Springfield, Mo.   BR/TR, 6', 180 lbs.   Deb: 4/11/80

| 1980 | KC-A | 20 | 26 | 2 | 8 | 2 | 0 | 1 | 7 | 1 | 4 | .308 | .333 | .500 | 124 | 1 | 1 | 4 | 1 | 1 | -0 | -1 | O | 0.0 |

■ GEORGE DETORE   Detore, George Francis   b: 11/11/06, Utica, N.Y.   BR/TR, 5'8", 170 lbs.   Deb: 9/14/30

1930	Cle-A	3	12	0	2	1	0	0	2	0	2	.167	.167	.250	4	-2	-2	1	0	0	0	-2	/3	-0.2
1931	Cle-A	30	56	3	15	6	0	0	7	8	2	.268	.359	.375	88	-0	-1	7	0	2	-1	4	3S/2	0.3
Total	2	33	68	3	17	7	0	0	9	8	4	.250	.329	.353	74	-2	-3	8	0	2	-1	2	/3S2	0.1

■ DUCKY DETWEILER   Detweiler, Robert Sterling   b: 2/15/19, Trumbauersville, Pa.   BR/TR, 5'11", 178 lbs.   Deb: 9/12/42

1942	Bos-N	12	44	3	14	2	1	0	5	2	7	.318	.348	.409	123	1	1	6	0			-4	3	-0.2
1946	Bos-N	1	1	0	0	0	0	0	0	0	0	.000	.000	.000	-99	-0	-0	0	0			0	H	0.0
Total	2	13	45	3	14	2	1	0	5	2	7	.311	.340	.400	118	1	1	6	0			-4	/3	-0.2

■ MIKE DEVEREAUX   Devereaux, Michael   b: 4/10/63, Casper, Wyo.   BR/TR, 6'", 195 lbs.   Deb: 9/02/87

1987	LA-N	19	54	7	12	3	0	0	4	3	10	.222	.263	.278	45	-4	-4	4	3	1	0	-1	O	-0.5
1988	LA-N	30	43	4	5	1	0	0	2	2	10	.116	.156	.140	-15	-6	-6	1	0	1	-1	1	O	-0.6
1989	Bal-A	122	391	55	104	14	3	8	46	36	60	.266	.331	.379	103	-0	1	49	22	11	0	-7	*O/D	-0.6
1990	Bal-A	108	367	48	88	18	1	12	49	28	48	.240	.294	.392	92	-6	-5	38	13	12	-3	1	*O/D	-0.8
Total	4	279	855	114	209	36	4	20	101	69	128	.244	.302	.366	89	-17	-14	92	38	25	-4	-6	O/D	-2.5

■ JIM DEVINE   Devine, Walter James   b: 10/5/1858, Brooklyn, N.Y.   d: 1/11/05, Syracuse, N.Y.   TL ,   Deb: 5/08/1883

1883	Bal-a	2	9	4	2	0	0	0		0		.222	.222	.222	42	-1	-1	0				-1	/PO	0.0
1886	NY-N	1	3	0	0	0	0	0	0	0	1	.000	.000	.000	-99	-1	-1	0	0			-0	/O	0.0
Total	2	3	12	4	2	0	0	0	0	0	1	.167	.167	.167	6	-1	-1	0	0			-1	/OP	0.0

■ MICKEY DEVINE   Devine, William Patrick   b: 5/9/1892, Albany, N.Y.   d: 10/1/37, Albany, N.Y.   BR/TR, 5'10", 165 lbs.   Deb: 8/02/18

1918	Phi-N	4	8	0	1	1	0	0	0	0	1	.125	.125	.250	13	-1	-1	0	0			0	/C	0.0
1920	Bos-A	8	12	1	2	0	0	0	0	1	2	.167	.231	.167	7	-2	-2	1	1	0	0	1	/C	0.0
1925	NY-N	21	33	6	9	3	0	0	4	2	3	.273	.314	.364	76	-1	-1	4	0	0	0	2	C/3	0.1
Total	3	33	53	7	12	4	0	0	4	3	6	.226	.268	.302	51	-4	-4	5	1	0		3	/C3	0.1

■ BERNIE DeVIVEIROS   DeViveiros, Bernard John   b: 4/19/01, Oakland, Cal.   BR/TR, 5'7", 160 lbs.   Deb: 9/13/24

1924	Chi-A	1	1	0	0	0	0	0	0	0	0	.000	.000	-0	-99	-0	-0	0	0	0	0	-1	/S	0.0
1927	Det-A	24	22	4	5	1	0	0	2	2	8	.227	.292	.273	46	-2	-2	2	1	0	0	0	S/3	0.0
Total	2	25	23	4	5	1	0	0	2	2	8	.217	.280	.261	40	-2	-2	2	1	0	0	-1	/S3	0.0

■ ART DEVLIN   Devlin, Arthur McArthur   b: 10/16/1879, Washington, D.C.   d: 9/18/48, Jersey City, N.J.   BR/TR, 6', 175 lbs.   Deb: 4/14/04   C

1904	NY-N	130	474	81	133	16	8	1	66	62		.281	.364	.354	119	16	13	78	33			7	*3	2.7
1905	*NY-N	153	525	74	129	14	7	2	61	66		.246	.330	.310	91	-2	-4	76	59			5	*3	1.3
1906	NY-N	148	498	76	149	23	8	2	65	74		.299	.390	.390	143	29	27	101	54			28	*3	5.5
1907	NY-N	143	491	61	136	16	2	1	54	63		.277	.359	.324	113	12	10	77	38			0	*3/S	1.1
1908	NY-N	157	534	59	135	18	4	2	45	62		.253	.331	.313	103	6	4	62	19			13	*3	2.4
1909	NY-N	143	491	61	130	19	8	0	56	65		.265	.362	.336	115	12	11	70	26			14	*3	3.2
1910	NY-N	147	493	71	128	17	5	2	67	62	32	.260	.353	.327	98	1	1	69	28			5	*3	0.7
1911	NY-N	95	260	42	71	16	2	0	25	42	19	.273	.386	.350	103	4	3	40	9			2	3/12S	0.8
1912	Bos-N	124	436	59	126	18	8	0	54	51	37	.289	.367	.362	99	2	1	62	11			-0	1S3/O	0.0
1913	Bos-N	73	210	19	48	7	5	0	12	29	17	.229	.328	.310	81	-4	-5	23	8			8	3	0.3
Total	10	1313	4412	603	1185	164	57	10	505	576	105	.269	.357	.338	108	76	62	657	285			82	*3/1S20	18.0

■ JIM DEVLIN   Devlin, James Alexander   b: 1849, Philadelphia, Pa.   d: 10/10/1883, Philadelphia, Pa.   BR/TR, 5'11", 175 lbs.   Deb: 4/21/1873

1873	Phi-n	23	99	18	25	4	4	0			2	.253	.267	.374	83	-2	-2	10					1/3SO	-0.1
1874	Chi-n	45	203	26	59	5	1	0			2	.291	.298	.325	97	-0	-1	20					1O/3	0.0
1875	Chi-n	69	315	60	92	18	5	0			5	.292	.303	.381	134	11	10	37					1P/O	1.0
1876	Lou-N	68	298	38	94	14	1	0	28	1	11	.315	.318	.369	109	8	8	36				2	*P/1	0.0
1877	Lou-N	61	268	38	72	6	3	1	27	7	27	.269	.287	.325	78	-2	-9	26				2	*P	0.0
Total	3 n	137	617	104	176	27	10	0			9	.285	.296	.361	112	9	7	68					/1PO3S	0.9
Total	2	129	566	76	166	20	4	1	55	8	38	.293	.303	.348	94	6	-9	61				4	P/1	0.0

■ JIM DEVLIN   Devlin, James Raymond   b: 8/25/22, Plains, Pa.   BL/TR, 5'11.5", 165 lbs.   Deb: 4/27/44

| 1944 | Cle-A | 1 | 1 | 0 | 0 | 0 | 0 | 0 | 0 | 0 | 0 | .000 | .000 | .000 | -99 | -0 | -0 | 0 | 0 | 0 | 0 | 0 | /C | 0.0 |

■ REX DeVOGT   DeVogt, Rex Eugene   b: 1/4/1888, Clare, Mich.   d: 11/9/35, Alma, Mich.   BR/TR, 5'9", 170 lbs.   Deb: 4/17/13

| 1913 | Bos-N | 3 | 6 | 0 | 0 | 0 | 0 | 0 | 0 | 0 | 3 | .000 | .000 | .000 | -98 | -2 | -2 | 0 | 0 | | | 2 | /C | 0.0 |

■ JOSH DEVORE   Devore, Joshua D.   b: 11/13/1887, Murray City, Ohio   d: 10/6/54, Chillicothe, Ohio   BL/TL, 5'6", 160 lbs.   Deb: 9/25/08

1908	NY-N	5	6	1	1	0	0	0	2	1		.167	.286	.167	45	-0	-0	1	1			-1	/O	0.0
1909	NY-N	22	28	6	4	1	0	0	1	2		.143	.250	.179	33	-2	-2	2	3			-4	O	-0.6
1910	NY-N	133	490	92	149	11	10	2	27	46	67	.304	.371	.380	119	12	12	84	43			-9	*O	0.0
1911	*NY-N	149	565	96	158	19	10	3	50	81	69	.280	.376	.365	104	8	6	99	61			2	*O	0.3
1912	*NY-N	106	327	66	90	14	6	2	37	51	43	.275	.381	.373	104	5	3	56	27			-5	O	-0.3
1913	NY-N	16	21	4	4	0	1	0	1	3	4	.190	.320	.286	73	-1	-1	3	6			-0	/O	0.0
	Cin-N	66	217	30	58	6	4	3	14	12	21	.267	.309	.373	95	-2	-2	29	17			-0	O	-0.3
	Phi-N	23	39	9	11	1	0	0	5	4	7	.282	.364	.308	89	-0	-0	4	0			-0	O	0.0
	Yr	105	277	43	73	7	5	3	20	19	32	.264	.318	.357	92	-3	-3	37	23			-0		-0.3
1914	Phi-N	30	53	5	16	2	0	0	7	4	5	.302	.351	.340	99	-0	-0	6	0			2	/O	0.2
	*Bos-N	51	128	22	29	4	0	1	5	18	14	.227	.327	.281	82	-2	-2	12	2			-5	O	-0.8
	Yr	81	181	27	45	6	0	1	12	22	19	.249	.333	.298	87	-2	-2	19	2			-3		-0.6
Total	7	601	1874	331	520	58	31	11	149	222	230	.277	.361	.359	103	18	13	297	160			-19	O	-1.5

■ AL DeVORMER   DeVormer, Albert E.   b: 8/19/1891, Grand Rapids, Mich   d: 8/29/66, Grand Rapids, Mich   BR/TR, 6'0.5", 175 lbs.   Deb: 8/04/18

1918	Chi-A	8	19	2	5	2	0	0	0	0	4	.263	.263	.368	90	-0	-0	2	1			-2	/CO	-0.1
1921	*NY-A	22	49	6	17	4	0	0	7	2	4	.347	.373	.429	102	0	0	8	2	0	1	-1	C	0.0
1922	NY-A	24	59	8	12	4	1	0	11	1	6	.203	.217	.305	34	-6	-6	4	0	0	0	-0	C/1	-0.5
1923	Bos-A	74	209	20	54	7	3	0	18	6	21	.258	.282	.321	58	-13	-13	19	3	0	1	1	C/1	-0.6
1927	NY-N	68	141	14	35	3	1	2	21	11	11	.248	.312	.326	71	-6	-6	14	1			-4	C/1	-0.5
Total	5	196	477	50	123	20	5	2	57	20	46	.258	.292	.333	65	-25	-25	48	7	0		-6	C/1O	-1.7

■ WALT DEVOY   Devoy, Walter Joseph   b: 3/14/1886, St.Louis, Mo.   d: 12/17/53, St.Louis, Mo.   5'11", 165 lbs.   Deb: 9/13/09

| 1909 | StL-A | 19 | 69 | 7 | 17 | 3 | 1 | 0 | 8 | 3 | | .246 | .278 | .319 | 95 | -1 | -1 | 7 | 4 | | | -1 | O/1 | -0.2 |

■ JEFF DeWILLIS   DeWillis, Jeffrey Allen   b: 4/13/65, Houston, Tex.   BR/TR, 6'2", 170 lbs.   Deb: 4/19/87

| 1987 | Tor-A | 13 | 25 | 2 | 3 | 1 | 0 | 1 | 2 | 2 | 12 | .120 | .185 | .280 | 21 | -3 | -3 | 1 | 0 | 0 | 0 | 1 | C | 0.0 |

■ CHARLIE DEXTER   Dexter, Charles Dana   b: 6/15/1876, Evansville, Ind.   d: 6/9/34, Cedar Rapids, Iowa   BR/TR, 5'7", 155 lbs.   Deb: 4/17/1896

| 1896 | Lou-N | 107 | 402 | 65 | 112 | 18 | 7 | 3 | 37 | 17 | 34 | .279 | .318 | .381 | 89 | -9 | -7 | 57 | 21 | | | -3 | CO | -0.6 |
| 1897 | Lou-N | 76 | 257 | 43 | 72 | 12 | 5 | 2 | 46 | 21 | | .280 | .342 | .389 | 98 | -2 | -1 | 39 | 12 | | | -5 | OC3/S | -0.3 |

YEAR	TM/L	G	AB	R	H	2B	3B	HR	RBI	BB	SO	AVG	OBP	SLG	PRO+	BR	/A	RC	SB	CS	SBR	FR	POS	TPR
1898	Lou-N	112	421	76	132	13	5	1	66	26		.314	.361	.375	116	7	8	75	44			-0	O/2C	0.3
1899	Lou-N	80	295	47	76	7	1	1	33	21		.258	.316	.298	71	-11	-11	35	21			3	O/S	-1.0
1900	Chi-N	40	125	7	25	5	0	2	20	1		.200	.213	.288	40	-11	-10	8	2			6	CO/2	-0.2
1901	Chi-N	116	460	46	123	9	5	1	66	16		.267	.296	.315	82	-12	-10	51	22			3	1302/C	-0.5
1902	Chi-N	69	266	30	60	12	0	2	26	19		.226	.290	.293	84	-5	-4	29	13			-13	31O	-1.8
	Bos-N	48	183	33	47	3	0	1	18	16		.257	.323	.290	90	-1	-1	24	16			-3	S2/O3	-0.2
	Yr	117	449	63	107	15	0	3	44	35		.238	.303	.292	87	-7	-6	52	29			-16		-2.0
1903	Bos-N	123	457	82	102	15	1	3	34	61		.223	.316	.280	75	-15	-12	53	32			-9	*O/SC	-2.5
Total	8	771	2866	429	749	94	24	16	346	198	34	.261	.316	.328	86	-59	-48	371	183			-21	OC/312S	-6.8

■ BO DIAZ
Diaz, Baudilio Jose (Seijas) b: 3/23/53, Cua, Venezuela BR/TR, 5'11", 185 lbs. Deb: 9/06/77

YEAR	TM/L	G	AB	R	H	2B	3B	HR	RBI	BB	SO	AVG	OBP	SLG	PRO+	BR	/A	RC	SB	CS	SBR	FR	POS	TPR
1977	Bos-A	2	1	0	0	0	0	0	0	0	1	.000	.000	.000	-90	-0	-0	0	0	0	0	1	/C	0.0
1978	Cle-A	44	127	12	30	4	0	2	11	4	17	.236	.260	.315	61	-7	-7	10	0	0	0	-0	C	-0.5
1979	Cle-A	15	32	0	5	2	0	0	1	2	6	.156	.206	.219	15	-4	-4	1	0	0	0	4	C	0.0
1980	Cle-A	76	207	15	47	11	2	3	32	7	27	.227	.252	.343	61	-11	-12	14	1	0	0	2	C	-0.5
1981	Cle-A	63	182	25	57	19	0	7	38	13	23	.313	.362	.533	157	12	12	32	2	2	-1	-3	C/D	1.1
1982	Phi-N	144	525	69	151	29	1	18	85	36	87	.288	.337	.450	116	11	10	72	3	6	-3	-9	*C	0.0
1983	*Phi-N	136	471	49	111	17	0	15	64	38	57	.236	.295	.367	84	-12	-11	49	1	4	-2	14	*C	0.5
1984	Phi-N	27	75	5	16	4	0	1	9	5	13	.213	.262	.307	58	-4	-4	5	0	0	0	-0	C	-0.3
1985	Phi-N	26	76	9	16	5	1	2	16	6	7	.211	.268	.382	78	-2	-3	6	0	0	0	2	C	0.0
	Cin-N	51	161	12	42	8	0	3	15	15	18	.261	.328	.366	89	-1	-2	19	0	0	0	8	C	0.8
	Yr	77	237	21	58	13	1	5	31	21	25	.245	.309	.371	86	-4	-5	25	0	0	0	10		0.8
1986	Cin-N	134	474	50	129	21	0	10	56	40	52	.272	.329	.380	91	-4	-6	59	1	1	-0	-6	*C	-0.9
1987	Cin-N	140	496	49	134	28	1	15	82	19	73	.270	.304	.421	86	-9	-11	59	1	0	0	-6	*C	-0.5
1988	Cin-N	92	315	26	69	9	0	10	35	7	41	.219	.238	.343	63	-15	-17	20	0	2	-1	-3	C	-1.7
1989	Cin-N	43	132	6	27	5	0	1	8	6	7	.205	.239	.265	43	-10	-10	7	0	2	-1	-0	C	-0.8
Total	13	993	3274	327	834	162	5	87	452	198	429	.255	.300	.387	87	-56	-65	354	9	17	-8	3	C/D	-2.8

■ CARLOS DIAZ
Diaz, Carlos Francisco b: 12/24/64, Elizabeth, N.J. BR/TR, 6'3", 195 lbs. Deb: 5/08/90

YEAR	TM/L	G	AB	R	H	2B	3B	HR	RBI	BB	SO	AVG	OBP	SLG	PRO+	BR	/A	RC	SB	CS	SBR	FR	POS	TPR
1990	Tor-A	9	3	1	1	0	0	0	0	0	2	.333	.333	.333	89	-0	-0	0	0	0	0	2	/C	0.3

■ EDGAR DIAZ
Diaz, Edgar (Serrano) b: 2/8/64, Santurce, P.R. BR/TR, 6', 155 lbs. Deb: 9/16/86

YEAR	TM/L	G	AB	R	H	2B	3B	HR	RBI	BB	SO	AVG	OBP	SLG	PRO+	BR	/A	RC	SB	CS	SBR	FR	POS	TPR
1986	Mil-A	5	13	0	3	0	0	0	0	1	3	.231	.286	.231	41	-1	-1	1	0	0	0	-1	/S	0.0
1990	Mil-A	86	218	27	59	2	2	0	14	21	32	.271	.338	.298	82	-5	-4	23	3	2	-0	-1	S2/3	0.0
Total	2	91	231	27	62	2	2	0	14	22	35	.268	.335	.294	79	-6	-5	24	3	2	-0	-2	/S23	0.0

■ MARIO DIAZ
Diaz, Mario Rafael (Torres) b: 1/10/62, Humacao, P.R. BR/TR, 5'10", 145 lbs. Deb: 9/12/87

YEAR	TM/L	G	AB	R	H	2B	3B	HR	RBI	BB	SO	AVG	OBP	SLG	PRO+	BR	/A	RC	SB	CS	SBR	FR	POS	TPR
1987	Sea-A	11	23	4	7	0	1	0	3	0	4	.304	.304	.391	79	-1	-1	3	0	0	0	4	S	0.3
1988	Sea-A	28	72	6	22	5	0	0	9	3	5	.306	.333	.375	94	-0	-1	8	0	0	0	-4	S/213	-0.3
1989	Sea-A	52	74	9	10	0	0	1	7	7	7	.135	.210	.176	9	-9	-9	3	0	0	0	-9	S2/3	-1.4
1990	NY-N	16	22	0	3	1	0	0	1	0	3	.136	.136	.182	-14	-3	-3	1	0	0	0	2	S/2	0.0
Total	4	107	191	19	42	6	1	1	20	10	19	.220	.259	.277	48	-13	-14	15	0	0	0	-7	/S231	-1.4

■ MIKE DIAZ
Diaz, Michael Anthony b: 4/15/60, San Francisco, Cal. BR/TR, 6'2", 195 lbs. Deb: 9/15/83

YEAR	TM/L	G	AB	R	H	2B	3B	HR	RBI	BB	SO	AVG	OBP	SLG	PRO+	BR	/A	RC	SB	CS	SBR	FR	POS	TPR
1983	Chi-N	6	7	2	2	0	0	0	1	0	0	.286	.286	.429	91	-0	-0	1	0	0	0	-0	/C	0.0
1986	Pit-N	97	209	22	56	9	0	12	36	19	43	.268	.335	.483	120	6	5	33	0	1	-1	-5	O1/3C	-0.1
1987	Pit-N	103	241	28	58	8	2	16	48	31	42	.241	.335	.490	114	5	4	40	1	0	0	-4	O1/C	-0.2
1988	Pit-N	47	74	6	17	3	0	0	5	16	13	.230	.367	.270	87	-1	-0	8	0	0	0	-2	1/D	-0.2
	Chi-A	40	152	12	36	6	0	3	12	5	30	.237	.266	.336	67	-7	-7	12	0	1	-1	-2	1/D	-1.1
Total	4	293	683	70	169	27	2	31	102	71	128	.247	.324	.429	103	3	2	94	1	2	-1	-12	/10C3D	-1.5

■ PAUL DICKEN
Dicken, Paul Franklin b: 10/2/43, Deland, Fla. BR/TR, 6'5", 195 lbs. Deb: 6/07/64

YEAR	TM/L	G	AB	R	H	2B	3B	HR	RBI	BB	SO	AVG	OBP	SLG	PRO+	BR	/A	RC	SB	CS	SBR	FR	POS	TPR
1964	Cle-A	11	11	0	0	0	0	0	0	0	5	.000	.000	.000	-99	-3	-3	0	0	0	0	0	H	-0.2
1966	Cle-A	2	2	0	0	0	0	0	0	0	1	.000	.000	.000	-99	-1	-1	0	0	0	0	0	H	0.0
Total	2	13	13	0	0	0	0	0	0	0	6	.000	.000	.000	-99	-3	-3	0	0	0	0	0		-0.2

■ BUTTERCUP DICKERSON
Dickerson, Lewis Pessano b: 10/11/1858, Tyaskin, Md. d: 7/23/20, Baltimore, Md. BL/TR, 5'6", 140 lbs. Deb: 7/15/1878

YEAR	TM/L	G	AB	R	H	2B	3B	HR	RBI	BB	SO	AVG	OBP	SLG	PRO+	BR	/A	RC	SB	CS	SBR	FR	POS	TPR
1878	Cin-N	29	123	17	38	5	1	0	9	0	7	.309	.309	.366	134	2	4	14				-2	O	0.0
1879	Cin-N	81	350	73	102	18	14	2	57	3	27	.291	.297	.440	147	14	16	47				-4	*O	0.9
1880	Tro-N	30	119	15	23	2	2	0	10	2	3	.193	.207	.244	49	-6	-7	6				5	O/S	-0.1
	Wor-N	31	133	22	39	8	6	0	20	1	2	.293	.299	.444	136	6	5	18				-3	O	0.0
	Yr	61	252	37	62	10	8	0	30	3	5	.246	.255	.349	96	0	-2	23				2		-0.1
1881	Wor-N	80	367	48	116	18	6	1	31	8	8	.316	.331	.406	123	12	9	51				9	*O	-0.1
1883	Pit-a	85	355	62	88	15	1	0		17		.248	.282	.296	91	-5	-2	30				0	*O/S2	-0.1
1884	StL-U	46	211	49	77	15	1	0		8		.365	.388	.445	175	17	16	37	0			5	O/3	1.8
	Bal-a	13	56	9	12	2	1	0		4		.214	.290	.286	88	-0	-1	5				-2	O/3	-0.2
	Lou-a	8	28	6	4	0	2	1		3		.143	.226	.393	105	0	0	3				-0	/O	0.0
	Yr	21	84	15	16	2	3	1		7		.190	.269	.321	94	-0	-0	7				-2		-0.2
1885	Buf-N	21	21	1	1	1	0	0		0	1	.048	.095	.095	-39	-3	-3	0				0	0	-0.2
Total	7	408	1763	302	500	84	34	4	127	47	51	.284	.303	.377	121	38	38	211				8	O/S32	3.6

■ GEORGE DICKEY
Dickey, George Willard "Skeets" b: 7/10/15, Kensett, Ark. d: 6/16/76, Dewitt, Ark. BB/TR, 6'2", 180 lbs. Deb: 9/21/35

YEAR	TM/L	G	AB	R	H	2B	3B	HR	RBI	BB	SO	AVG	OBP	SLG	PRO+	BR	/A	RC	SB	CS	SBR	FR	POS	TPR
1935	Bos-A	5	11	1	0	0	0	0	1	1	3	.000	.083	.000	-72	-3	-3	0	0	0	0	-1	/C	-0.3
1936	Bos-A	10	23	0	1	1	0	0	0	2	3	.043	.120	.087	-46	-6	-6	0	0	0	0	1	C	-0.3
1941	Chi-A	32	55	6	11	1	0	2	8	5	7	.200	.267	.327	57	-4	-4	5	0	0	0	1	C	-0.1
1942	Chi-A	59	116	6	27	3	0	1	17	9	11	.233	.288	.284	63	-6	-6	10	0	0	0	-4	C	-0.5
1946	Chi-A	37	78	8	15	1	0	0	1	12	13	.192	.300	.205	45	-6	-5	5	0	2	-1	2	C	-0.2
1947	Chi-A	83	211	15	47	6	0	1	27	34	25	.223	.331	.265	69	-8	-7	22	4	2	0	3	C	0.2
Total	6	226	494	36	101	12	0	4	54	63	62	.204	.294	.253	53	-32	-31	41	4	4	-1	1	C	-1.2

■ BILL DICKEY
Dickey, William Malcolm b: 6/6/07, Bastrop, La. BL/TR, 6'1.5", 185 lbs. Deb: 8/15/28 MCH

YEAR	TM/L	G	AB	R	H	2B	3B	HR	RBI	BB	SO	AVG	OBP	SLG	PRO+	BR	/A	RC	SB	CS	SBR	FR	POS	TPR
1928	NY-A	10	15	1	3	1	1	0	2	0	2	.200	.200	.400	56	-1	-1	1	0	0	0	-1	/C	-0.1
1929	NY-A	130	447	60	145	30	6	10	65	14	16	.324	.346	.485	120	6	10	73	4	3	-1	1	*C	2.0
1930	NY-A	109	366	55	124	25	7	5	65	21	14	.339	.375	.486	122	8	11	67	7	1	2	-12	*C	0.8
1931	NY-A	130	477	65	156	17	10	6	78	39	20	.327	.378	.442	122	10	14	80	2	1	0	3	*C	2.4
1932	*NY-A	108	423	66	131	20	4	15	84	34	13	.310	.361	.482	123	9	12	72	2	4	-2	-2	*C	1.3
1933	NY-A	130	478	58	152	24	8	14	97	47	14	.318	.381	.490	138	19	23	89	3	4	-2	1	*C	2.7
1934	NY-A	104	395	56	127	24	4	12	72	38	18	.322	.384	.494	134	14	18	74	0	3	-2	-1	*C	2.2
1935	NY-A	120	448	54	125	26	6	14	81	35	11	.279	.339	.458	111	1	5	70	1	1	-0	-1	*C	0.6
1936	*NY-A	112	423	99	153	26	8	22	107	46	16	.362	.428	.617	161	35	38	111	0	2	-1	-0	*C	3.9
1937	*NY-A	140	530	87	176	35	2	29	133	73	22	.332	.417	.570	145	37	37	128	3	2	-0	11	*C	5.2
1938	*NY-A	132	454	84	142	27	4	27	115	75	22	.313	.412	.568	144	30	31	111	3	0	1	3	*C	3.3
1939	*NY-A	128	480	98	145	23	3	24	105	77	37	.302	.403	.512	135	24	26	104	5	0	2	7	*C	3.8
1940	NY-A	106	372	45	92	11	1	9	54	48	32	.247	.336	.355	83	-11	-9	46	0	3	-2	-1	*C	-0.3
1941	*NY-A	109	348	35	99	15	5	7	71	45	17	.284	.371	.417	110	5	5	56	2	1	0	-0	*C	1.1

YEAR	TM/L	G	AB	R	H	2B	3B	HR	RBI	BB	SO	AVG	OBP	SLG	PRO+	BR	/A	RC	SB	CS	SBR	FR	POS	TPR
1942	*NY-A	82	268	28	79	13	1	2	38	26	11	.295	.359	.373	108	2	3	34	2	2	-1	2	C	1.5
1943	*NY-A	85	242	29	85	18	2	4	33	41	12	.351	.445	.492	173	24	24	57	2	1	0	-2	C	2.7
1946	NY-A	54	134	10	35	8	0	2	10	19	12	.261	.357	.366	101	1	1	17	0	1	-1	9	CM	1.1
Total	17	1789	6300	930	1969	343	72	202	1210	678	289	.313	.382	.486	128	216	247	1193	36	29	-7	18	*C	34.2

■ JOHNNY DICKSHOT
Dickshot, John Oscar "Ugly" (b: John Oscar Dicksus) b: 1/24/10, Waukegan, Ill. BR/TR, 6', 195 lbs. Deb: 4/16/36

YEAR	TM/L	G	AB	R	H	2B	3B	HR	RBI	BB	SO	AVG	OBP	SLG	PRO+	BR	/A	RC	SB	CS	SBR	FR	POS	TPR
1936	Pit-N	9	9	2	2	0	0	0	1	1	2	.222	.300	.222	42	-1	-1	1	0			0	/O	0.0
1937	Pit-N	82	264	42	67	8	4	3	33	26	36	.254	.323	.348	82	-6	-6	29	0			-4	O	-1.3
1938	Pit-N	29	35	3	8	0	0	0	4	8	5	.229	.372	.229	68	-1	-1	4	3			0	O	0.0
1939	NY-N	10	34	3	8	0	0	0	5	5	3	.235	.333	.235	55	-2	-2	3	0			-1	O	-0.2
1944	Chi-A	62	162	18	41	8	5	0	15	13	10	.253	.313	.364	94	-2	-2	20	2	0	1	-3	O	-0.5
1945	Chi-A	130	486	74	147	19	10	4	58	48	41	.302	.366	.407	128	15	16	75	18	3	**4**	-1	*O	1.4
Total	6	322	990	142	273	35	19	7	116	101	97	.276	.345	.371	104	3	5	131	23	3		-9	O	-0.6

■ BOB DIDIER
Didier, Robert Daniel b: 2/16/49, Hattiesburg, Miss. BB/TR, 6', 190 lbs. Deb: 4/07/69 C

YEAR	TM/L	G	AB	R	H	2B	3B	HR	RBI	BB	SO	AVG	OBP	SLG	PRO+	BR	/A	RC	SB	CS	SBR	FR	POS	TPR
1969	*Atl-N	114	352	30	90	16	1	0	32	34	39	.256	.321	.307	76	-10	-10	36	1	3	-2	1	*C	-0.3
1970	Atl-N	57	168	9	25	2	1	0	7	12	11	.149	.210	.173	3	-23	-24	6	1	0	0	2	C	-1.9
1971	Atl-N	51	155	9	34	4	1	0	5	6	17	.219	.248	.258	41	-12	-13	10	0	0	0	4	C	-0.8
1972	Atl-N	13	40	5	12	1	0	0	5	2	4	.300	.349	.400	103	1	0	6	0	0	0	2	C	0.3
1973	Det-A	7	22	3	10	1	0	0	1	3	0	.455	.520	.500	177	3	3	6	0	0	0	2	/C	0.5
1974	Bos-A	5	14	0	1	0	0	0	1	2	1	.071	.188	.071	-22	-2	-2	0	0	0	0	1	/C	-0.1
Total	6	247	751	56	172	25	4	0	51	59	72	.229	.287	.273	55	-43	-47	64	2	3	-1	12	C	-2.3

■ ERNIE DIEHL
Diehl, Ernest Guy b: 10/2/1877, Cincinnati, Ohio d: 11/6/58, Miami, Fla. BR/TR, 6'1", 190 lbs. Deb: 5/31/03

YEAR	TM/L	G	AB	R	H	2B	3B	HR	RBI	BB	SO	AVG	OBP	SLG	PRO+	BR	/A	RC	SB	CS	SBR	FR	POS	TPR
1903	Pit-N	1	3	0	1	0	0	0		0	0	.333	.333	.333	89	-0	-0	0				-0	/O	0.0
1904	Pit-N	12	37	6	6	0	0	0		4	6	.162	.279	.162	38	-2	-2	3	3			1	/OS	-0.1
1906	Bos-N	3	11	1	5	0	1	0		0	0	.455	.455	.636	249	2	2	3	0			0	/OS	0.2
1909	Bos-N	1	4	1	2	1	0	0		0	0	.500	.500	.750	274	1	1	1	0			1	/O	0.1
Total	4	17	55	8	14	1	1	0		4	6	.255	.328	.309	97	0	-0	8	3			2	/OS	0.2

■ CHUCK DIERING
Diering, Charles Edward Allen b: 2/5/23, St.Louis, Mo. BR/TR, 5'10", 165 lbs. Deb: 4/15/47

YEAR	TM/L	G	AB	R	H	2B	3B	HR	RBI	BB	SO	AVG	OBP	SLG	PRO+	BR	/A	RC	SB	CS	SBR	FR	POS	TPR
1947	StL-N	105	74	22	16	3	1	2	11	19	22	.216	.383	.365	95	1	0	12	3			6	O	0.3
1948	StL-N	7	7	2	0	0	0	0	0	2	2	.000	.222	.000	-33	-1	-1	0	1			1	/O	0.0
1949	StL-N	131	369	60	97	21	8	3	38	35	49	.263	.328	.388	87	-5	-7	49	1			-7	*O	-2.0
1950	StL-N	89	204	34	51	12	0	3	18	35	38	.250	.360	.353	84	-2	-4	28	1			-3	O	-0.9
1951	StL-N	64	85	9	22	5	1	0	8	6	15	.259	.308	.341	74	-3	-3	9	0	1	-1	7	O	0.2
1952	NY-N	41	23	2	4	1	1	0	2	4	3	.174	.296	.304	66	-1	-1	2	0	2	-1	3	O	0.0
1954	Bal-A	128	418	35	108	14	1	2	29	56	57	.258	.351	.311	89	-8	-4	46	3	7	-3	10	*O	0.0
1955	Bal-A	137	371	38	95	16	2	3	31	57	45	.256	.355	.334	93	-6	-2	45	5	8	-3	1	*O3S	-0.9
1956	Bal-A	50	97	15	18	4	0	1	4	23	19	.186	.342	.258	65	-5	-4	10	2	5	-2	4	O/3	-0.3
Total	9	752	1648	217	411	76	14	14	141	237	250	.249	.346	.338	86	-31	-26	201	16	23		19	O/3S	-3.6

■ DICK DIETZ
Dietz, Richard Allen b: 9/18/41, Crawfordsville, Ind. BR/TR, 6'1", 195 lbs. Deb: 6/18/66

YEAR	TM/L	G	AB	R	H	2B	3B	HR	RBI	BB	SO	AVG	OBP	SLG	PRO+	BR	/A	RC	SB	CS	SBR	FR	POS	TPR
1966	SF-N	13	23	1	1	0	0	0	0	0	9	.043	.083	.043	-62	-5	-5	0	0	0	0	-0	/C	-0.5
1967	SF-N	56	120	10	27	3	0	4	19	25	44	.225	.363	.350	106	2	2	16	0	1	-1	0	C	0.5
1968	SF-N	98	301	21	82	14	2	6	38	34	68	.272	.348	.392	122	9	9	42	1	1	-0	-6	C	0.6
1969	SF-N	79	244	28	56	8	1	11	35	53	53	.230	.373	.406	120	8	8	38	0	0	0	-4	C	0.9
1970	SF-N	148	493	82	148	36	2	22	107	109	106	.300	.430	.515	154	41	42	113	0	1	-1	-16	*C	3.0
1971	*SF-N	142	453	58	114	19	0	19	72	97	86	.252	.388	.419	131	21	22	79	1	3	-2	-11	*C	1.3
1972	LA-N	27	56	4	9	1	0	1	6	14	11	.161	.329	.232	63	-2	-2	5	2	0	1	4	C	0.3
1973	Atl-N	83	139	22	41	8	1	3	24	49	25	.295	.479	.432	143	14	13	32	0	0	0	2	1C	1.4
Total	8	646	1829	226	478	89	6	66	301	381	402	.261	.392	.425	130	87	88	326	4	6	-2	-32	C/1	7.5

■ ROY DIETZEL
Dietzel, Leroy Louis b: 1/9/31, Baltimore, Md. BR/TR, 6', 190 lbs. Deb: 9/02/54

YEAR	TM/L	G	AB	R	H	2B	3B	HR	RBI	BB	SO	AVG	OBP	SLG	PRO+	BR	/A	RC	SB	CS	SBR	FR	POS	TPR
1954	Was-A	9	21	1	5	0	0	0	1	5	4	.238	.385	.238	78	-0	-0	2	0	0	0	-2	/23	-0.1

■ JAY DIFANI
Difani, Clarence Joseph b: 12/21/23, Crystal City, Mo. BR/TR, 6', 170 lbs. Deb: 4/23/48

YEAR	TM/L	G	AB	R	H	2B	3B	HR	RBI	BB	SO	AVG	OBP	SLG	PRO+	BR	/A	RC	SB	CS	SBR	FR	POS	TPR
1948	Was-A	2	2	0	0	0	0	0	0	0	2	.000	.000	.000	-99	-1	-1	0	0	0	0	0	H	0.0
1949	Was-A	2	1	0	1	1	0	0	0	0	0	1.000	1.000	2.000	700	1	1	2	0	0	0	0	/2	0.1
Total	2	4	3	0	1	1	0	0	0	0	2	.333	.333	.667	166	0	0	2	0	0	0	0	/2	0.1

■ STEVE DIGNAN
Dignan, Stephen E. b: 5/16/1859, Boston, Mass. d: 7/11/1881, Boston, Mass. Deb: 6/01/1880

YEAR	TM/L	G	AB	R	H	2B	3B	HR	RBI	BB	SO	AVG	OBP	SLG	PRO+	BR	/A	RC	SB	CS	SBR	FR	POS	TPR
1880	Bos-N	8	34	4	11	1	0	0	4	0	3	.324	.324	.353	133	1	1	4				-0	/O	0.0
	Wor-N	3	10	1	3	0	1	0	2	0	1	.300	.300	.500	153	1	1	2				-1	/O	0.0
	Yr	11	44	5	14	1	1	0	6	0	4	.318	.318	.386	137	2	2	6				-1		0.0

■ DON DILLARD
Dillard, David Donald b: 1/8/37, Greenville, S.C. BL/TR, 6'1", 200 lbs. Deb: 4/24/59

YEAR	TM/L	G	AB	R	H	2B	3B	HR	RBI	BB	SO	AVG	OBP	SLG	PRO+	BR	/A	RC	SB	CS	SBR	FR	POS	TPR
1959	Cle-A	10	10	0	4	0	0	0	0	0	2	.400	.400	.400	125	0	0	2	0	0	0	0	H	0.0
1960	Cle-A	6	7	0	1	0	0	0	0	1	3	.143	.250	.143	9	-1	-1	0	0	0	0	0	/O	0.0
1961	Cle-A	74	147	27	40	5	0	7	17	15	28	.272	.340	.449	112	2	2	23	0	0	0	0	O	0.1
1962	Cle-A	95	174	22	40	5	1	5	14	11	25	.230	.276	.356	71	-8	-7	16	0	0	-1	-4	O	-1.3
1963	Mil-N	67	119	9	28	6	4	1	12	5	21	.235	.272	.378	86	-3	-2	11	0	2	-1	1	O	-0.4
1965	Mil-N	20	19	1	3	0	0	1	3	0	6	.158	.158	.316	30	-2	-2	0	0	0	0	0	/O	-0.1
Total	6	272	476	59	116	16	5	14	47	32	85	.244	.293	.387	86	-12	-10	53	0	3	-2	-3	O	-1.7

■ PAT DILLARD
Dillard, Robert Lee b: 6/12/1874, Chattanooga, Tenn d: 7/22/07, Denver, Colo. Deb: 4/21/00

YEAR	TM/L	G	AB	R	H	2B	3B	HR	RBI	BB	SO	AVG	OBP	SLG	PRO+	BR	/A	RC	SB	CS	SBR	FR	POS	TPR
1900	StL-N	57	183	24	42	5	2	0	12	13		.230	.284	.279	58	-10	-10	17	7			-5	O3/S	-1.4

■ STEVE DILLARD
Dillard, Stephen Bradley b: 2/8/51, Memphis, Tenn. BR/TR, 6'1", 180 lbs. Deb: 9/28/75

YEAR	TM/L	G	AB	R	H	2B	3B	HR	RBI	BB	SO	AVG	OBP	SLG	PRO+	BR	/A	RC	SB	CS	SBR	FR	POS	TPR
1975	Bos-A	1	5	2	2	0	0	0	0	0	0	.400	.400	.400	117	0	0	1	1	0	0	1	/2	0.1
1976	Bos-A	57	167	22	46	14	0	1	15	17	20	.275	.342	.377	99	2	-0	20	6	4	-1	-4	32S/D	-0.2
1977	Bos-A	66	141	22	34	7	0	1	13	7	13	.241	.277	.312	54	-8	-10	12	4	3	-1	8	2/SD	0.2
1978	Det-A	56	130	21	29	5	2	0	7	6	11	.223	.257	.292	53	-8	-8	9	1	2	-1	40	2/D	3.2
1979	Chi-N	89	166	31	47	6	1	5	24	17	24	.283	.353	.422	101	2	0	25	1	0	0	9	2/3	1.4
1980	Chi-N	100	244	31	55	8	1	4	27	20	54	.225	.287	.316	63	-11	-13	22	2	2	-1	2	32/S	-0.8
1981	Chi-N	53	119	18	26	7	1	2	11	8	20	.218	.268	.345	70	-5	-5	11	2	0	0	2	2/3S	0.0
1982	Chi-A	16	41	1	7	3	1	0	5	1	5	.171	.190	.293	30	-4	-4	2	0	1	-1	-1	2	-0.4
Total	8	438	1013	148	246	50	6	13	102	76	147	.243	.297	.343	73	-30	-40	102	15	12	-3	57	2/3SD	3.5

■ PICKLES DILLHOEFER
Dillhoefer, William Martin b: 10/13/1894, Cleveland, Ohio d: 2/23/22, St.Louis, Mo. BR/TR, 5'7", 154 lbs. Deb: 4/16/17

YEAR	TM/L	G	AB	R	H	2B	3B	HR	RBI	BB	SO	AVG	OBP	SLG	PRO+	BR	/A	RC	SB	CS	SBR	FR	POS	TPR
1917	Chi-N	42	95	3	12	1	1	0	8	2	9	.126	.144	.158	-7	-12	-13	3	1			9	C	-0.1
1918	Phi-N	8	11	0	1	0	0	0	0	1	1	.091	.167	.091	-19	-2	-2	0	2			-1	/C	-0.1
1919	StL-N	45	108	11	23	3	2	0	12	8	6	.213	.267	.278	68	-5	-4	9	5			-3	C	-0.4
1920	StL-N	76	224	26	59	8	3	0	13	13	7	.263	.304	.326	84	-6	-5	22	2	1	0	-0	C	0.2
1921	StL-N	76	162	19	39	4	4	0	15	11	7	.241	.289	.315	61	-9	-9	15	2	1	0	2	C	-0.1
Total	5	247	600	59	134	16	10	0	48	35	30	.223	.266	.283	58	-33	-32	49	12	2		7	C	-0.7

■ BOB DILLINGER

Dillinger, Robert Bernard "Duke" "Duke" b: 9/17/18, Glendale, Cal. BR/TR, 5'11.5", 170 lbs. Deb: 4/16/46

YEAR	TM/L	G	AB	R	H	2B	3B	HR	RBI	BB	SO	AVG	OBP	SLG	PRO+	BR	/A	RC	SB	CS	SBR	FR	POS	TPR
1946	StL-A	83	225	33	63	6	3	0	11	19	30	.280	.341	.333	85	-3	-4	27	8	1	2	-3	3/S	0.0
1947	StL-A	137	571	70	168	23	6	3	37	56	38	.294	.361	.371	102	4	2	80	34	13	2	2	*3	1.1
1948	StL-A	153	644	110	207	34	10	2	44	65	34	.321	.385	.415	110	12	10	105	28	11	2	-15	*3	-0.9
1949	StL-A	137	544	68	176	22	13	1	51	51	40	.324	.385	.417	108	9	6	87	20	14	-2	-25	*3	-2.0
1950	Phi-A	84	356	55	110	21	9	3	41	31	20	.309	.366	.444	109	3	4	57	5	3	-0	-2	3	-0.1
	Pit-N	58	222	23	64	8	2	1	9	13	22	.288	.328	.356	77	-6	-7	24	4			2	3	-0.5
1951	Pit-N	12	43	3	10	3	0	0	0	1	0	.233	.255	.302	47	-3	-3	2	2	0	1	-2	3	-0.4
	Chi-A	89	299	39	90	6	4	0	20	15	17	.301	.337	.348	87	-6	-6	34	5	5	-2	-6	3	-1.4
Total	6	753	2904	401	888	123	47	10	213	251	201	.306	.363	.391	100	9	1	417	106	47		-50	3/S	-4.2

■ POP DILLON

Dillon, Frank Edward b: 10/17/1873, Normal, Ill. d: 9/12/31, Pasadena, Cal. BL Deb: 9/08/1899

YEAR	TM/L	G	AB	R	H	2B	3B	HR	RBI	BB	SO	AVG	OBP	SLG	PRO+	BR	/A	RC	SB	CS	SBR	FR	POS	TPR
1899	Pit-N	30	121	21	31	5	0	0	20	5		.256	.286	.298	62	-6	-6	12	5			1	1	-0.3
1900	Pit-N	5	18	3	2	1	0	0	1	0		.111	.111	.167	-23	-3	-3	0	0			1	/1	-0.1
1901	Det-A	74	281	40	81	14	6	1	42	15		.288	.324	.391	95	-1	-2	42	14			3	1	-0.2
1902	Det-A	66	243	21	50	6	3	0	22	16		.206	.255	.255	42	-18	-19	17	2			5	1	-1.1
	Bal-A	2	7	1	2	0	1	0	0	2		.286	.444	.571	175	1	1	2	0			0	/1	0.1
	Yr	68	250	22	52	6	4	0	22	18		.208	.261	.264	46	-18	-18	19	2			6		-1.0
1904	Bro-N	135	511	60	132	18	6	0	31	40		.258	.312	.317	99	-2	-0	57	13			3	*1	-0.2
Total	5	312	1181	146	298	44	16	1	116	78		.252	.299	.319	80	-29	-30	130	34			14	1	-1.8

■ J. DILLON

Dillon, J. Deb: 5/98/1875

YEAR	TM/L	G	AB	R	H	2B	3B	HR	RBI	BB	SO	AVG	OBP	SLG	PRO+	BR	/A	RC	SB	CS	SBR	FR	POS	TPR
1875	RS-n	1	1	0	0	0	0	0		0		.000	.000	.000	-99	-0	-0	0					/S	0.0

■ PACKY DILLON

Dillon, Packard Andrew b: St.Louis, Mo. d: 1/8/1890, Guelph, Ont., Canada Deb: 5/04/1875

YEAR	TM/L	G	AB	R	H	2B	3B	HR	RBI	BB	SO	AVG	OBP	SLG	PRO+	BR	/A	RC	SB	CS	SBR	FR	POS	TPR
1875	RS-n	3	13	1	3	1	0	0	0			.231	.231	.308	93	-0	-0	1					/C	0.0

■ MIGUEL DILONE

Dilone, Miguel Angel (Reyes) b: 11/1/54, Santiago, D.R. BB/TR, 6', 160 lbs. Deb: 9/02/74

YEAR	TM/L	G	AB	R	H	2B	3B	HR	RBI	BB	SO	AVG	OBP	SLG	PRO+	BR	/A	RC	SB	CS	SBR	FR	POS	TPR
1974	Pit-N	12	2	3	0	0	0	0	0	1	0	.000	.333	.000	-1	-0	-0	0	2	0	1	1	/O	0.1
1975	Pit-N	18	6	8	0	0	0	0	0	0	1	.000	.000	.000	-99	-2	-2	-0	2	2	-1	2	/O	0.1
1976	Pit-N	16	17	7	4	0	0	0	0	0	0	.235	.235	.235	34	-1	-1	1	5	1	1	2	/O	0.1
1977	Pit-N	29	44	5	6	0	0	0	0	2	3	.136	.174	.136	-15	-7	-7	2	12	0	4	1	O	-0.3
1978	Oak-A	135	258	34	59	8	0	1	14	23	30	.229	.294	.271	63	-13	-13	21	50	23	1	-12	OD/3	-2.5
1979	Oak-A	30	91	15	17	1	2	1	6	6	7	.187	.237	.275	40	-8	-7	5	6	5	-1	-3	O	-1.2
	Chi-N	43	36	14	11	0	0	0	1	2	5	.306	.342	.306	71	-1	-1	4	15	5	2	4	O	0.3
1980	Cle-A	132	528	82	180	30	9	0	40	28	45	.341	.376	.432	120	15	15	89	61	18	8	1	*OD	2.0
1981	Cle-A	72	269	33	78	5	5	0	19	18	28	.290	.334	.346	98	-1	-1	31	29	10	3	5	OD	0.5
1982	Cle-A	104	379	50	89	12	3	3	25	25	36	.235	.286	.306	63	-19	-19	35	33	5	7	-6	O/D	-2.1
1983	Cle-A	32	68	15	13	3	1	0	7	10	5	.191	.295	.265	53	-4	-4	6	5	1	1	1	O	-0.2
	Chi-N	4	3	1	0	0	0	0	0	0	0	.000	.000	.000	-96	-1	-1	0	1	0	0	0	/OD	0.0
	Yr	36	71	16	13	3	1	0	7	10	5	.183	.284	.254	47	-5	-5	6	6	1	1	1		-0.2
	Pit-N	7	0	1	0	0	0	0	0	0	0	—	—	—	—	0	0	0	2	0	1	0	/R	0.1
1984	Mon-N	88	169	28	47	8	2	1	10	17	18	.278	.348	.367	106	1	1	26	27	2	7	-0	O	0.7
1985	Mon-N	51	84	10	16	0	2	0	6	6	11	.190	.244	.238	38	-7	-7	4	7	3	0	1	O	-0.6
	SD-N	27	46	8	10	0	1	0	1	4	8	.217	.280	.261	53	-3	-3	4	10	3	1	0	O	-0.1
	Yr	78	130	18	26	0	3	0	7	10	19	.200	.257	.246	43	-10	-9	8	17	6	2	1		-0.7
Total	12	800	2000	314	530	67	25	6	129	142	197	.265	.316	.333	81	-53	-49	229	267	78	33	-5	O/D3	-3.2

■ DOM DiMAGGIO

DiMaggio, Dominic Paul "The Little Professor" b: 2/12/17, San Francisco, Cal BR/TR, 5'9", 168 lbs. Deb: 4/16/40

YEAR	TM/L	G	AB	R	H	2B	3B	HR	RBI	BB	SO	AVG	OBP	SLG	PRO+	BR	/A	RC	SB	CS	SBR	FR	POS	TPR
1940	Bos-A	108	418	81	126	32	6	8	46	41	46	.301	.367	.464	109	8	6	73	7	6	-2	15	O	1.2
1941	Bos-A	144	584	117	165	37	6	8	58	90	57	.283	.385	.408	107	11	9	101	13	6	0	3	*O	0.3
1942	Bos-A	151	622	110	178	36	8	14	48	70	52	.286	.364	.437	121	20	17	103	16	10	-1	14	*O	2.0
1946	*Bos-A	142	534	85	169	24	7	7	73	66	58	.316	.393	.427	122	22	18	92	10	6	-1	4	*O	1.5
1947	Bos-A	136	513	75	145	21	5	8	71	74	62	.283	.376	.390	105	11	6	80	10	6	-1	14	*O	1.4
1948	Bos-A	155	648	127	185	40	4	9	87	101	58	.285	.383	.401	104	10	6	110	10	2	2	10	*O	1.1
1949	Bos-A	145	605	126	186	34	5	8	60	96	55	.307	.404	.420	110	18	12	110	9	7	-2	11	*O	1.8
1950	Bos-A	141	588	131	193	30	11	7	70	82	68	.328	.414	.452	111	21	13	117	15	4	2	6	*O	1.7
1951	Bos-A	146	639	113	189	34	4	12	72	73	53	.296	.370	.418	103	12	3	101	4	7	-3	-3	*O	-0.7
1952	Bos-A	128	486	81	143	20	1	6	33	57	61	.294	.371	.377	100	7	2	70	6	8	-3	-6	*O	-1.0
1953	Bos-A	3	3	1	1	0	0	0	0	0	1	.333	.333	.333	76	-0	-0	0	0	0	0	0	H	0.0
Total	11	1399	5640	1046	1680	308	57	87	618	750	571	.298	.383	.419	109	140	92	958	100	62	-7	69	*O	9.3

■ JOE DiMAGGIO

DiMaggio, Joseph Paul "Joltin' Joe" or "The Yankee Clipper" b: 11/25/14, Martinez, Cal. BR/TR, 6'2", 193 lbs. Deb: 5/03/36 CH

YEAR	TM/L	G	AB	R	H	2B	3B	HR	RBI	BB	SO	AVG	OBP	SLG	PRO+	BR	/A	RC	SB	CS	SBR	FR	POS	TPR
1936	*NY-A	138	637	132	206	44	15	29	125	24	39	.323	.352	.576	130	19	23	127	4	0	1	1	O	1.8
1937	*NY-A	151	621	151	215	35	15	46	167	64	37	.346	.412	.673	168	61	61	173	3	0	1	6	*O	5.6
1938	*NY-A	145	599	129	194	32	13	32	140	59	21	.324	.386	.581	140	33	33	136	6	1	1	0	*O	3.1
1939	*NY-A	120	462	108	176	32	6	30	126	52	20	.381	.448	.671	185	56	57	139	3	0	1	4	*O	5.3
1940	NY-A	132	508	93	179	28	9	31	133	61	30	.352	.425	.626	176	51	54	135	1	2	-1	0	*O	4.1
1941	NY-A	139	541	122	193	43	11	30	125	76	13	.357	.440	.643	186	64	65	162	4	2	0	7	*O	6.0
1942	*NY-A	154	610	123	186	29	13	21	114	68	36	.305	.376	.498	148	34	36	120	4	2	0	-0	*O	2.5
1946	NY-A	132	503	81	146	20	8	25	95	59	24	.290	.367	.511	142	28	27	96	1	0	0	1	*O	2.2
1947	NY-A	141	534	97	168	31	10	20	97	64	32	.315	.391	.522	154	37	37	112	3	0	1	2	*O	3.5
1948	NY-A	153	594	110	190	26	11	39	155	67	30	.320	.396	.598	164	49	49	140	1	1	-0	-1	*O	4.0
1949	NY-A	76	272	58	94	14	6	14	67	55	18	.346	.459	.596	178	32	32	76	0	1	-1	-3	O	2.5
1950	*NY-A	139	525	114	158	33	10	32	122	80	33	.301	.394	.585	152	35	38	125	0	0	0	-2	*O/1	3.1
1951	*NY-A	116	415	72	109	22	4	12	71	61	36	.263	.365	.422	117	8	10	65	0	0	0	0	*O	0.5
Total	13	1736	6821	1390	2214	389	131	361	1537	790	369	.325	.398	.579	156	507	522	1606	30	9	4	14	*O/1	44.2

■ VINCE DiMAGGIO

DiMaggio, Vincent Paul b: 9/6/12, Martinez, Cal. d: 10/3/86, N.Hollywood, Cal. BR/TR, 5'11", 183 lbs. Deb: 4/19/37

YEAR	TM/L	G	AB	R	H	2B	3B	HR	RBI	BB	SO	AVG	OBP	SLG	PRO+	BR	/A	RC	SB	CS	SBR	FR	POS	TPR
1937	Bos-N	132	493	56	126	18	4	13	69	39	111	.256	.311	.387	98	-9	-3	61	8			10	*O	0.1
1938	Bos-N	150	540	71	123	28	3	14	61	65	134	.228	.313	.369	96	-10	-3	68	11			8	*O/2	0.2
1939	Cin-N	8	14	1	1	1	0	0	2	2	10	.071	.188	.143	-10	-2	-2	0	0			1	/O	0.0
1940	Cin-N	2	4	2	1	0	0	0	0	1	0	.250	.400	.250	82	-0	-0	0	0			0	/O	0.0
	Pit-N	110	356	59	103	26	0	19	54	37	83	.289	.364	.522	143	19	20	68	11			-4	*O	1.2
	Yr	112	360	61	104	26	0	19	54	38	83	.289	.365	.519	142	19	20	68	11			-4		1.2
1941	Pit-N	151	528	73	141	27	5	21	100	66	100	.267	.354	.456	128	18	19	88	10			2	*O	1.5
1942	Pit-N	143	496	57	118	22	3	15	75	52	87	.238	.311	.385	101	1	-1	59	10			14	*O	1.1
1943	Pit-N	157	580	64	144	41	2	15	88	70	126	.248	.329	.403	107	7	5	80	11			9	*O/S	0.9
1944	Pit-N	109	342	41	82	20	4	9	50	33	83	.240	.307	.401	94	-2	-4	42	6			-8	*O/3	-1.9
1945	Phi-N	127	452	64	116	25	3	19	84	43	91	.257	.322	.451	117	6	7	67	12			7	*O	0.8
1946	Phi-N	6	19	1	4	1	0	0	1	0	7	.211	.211	.263	35	-2	-2	1	0			-0	/O	-0.1
	NY-N	15	25	3	0	0	0	0	0	2	5	.000	.074	.000	-78	-6	-6	0	0			2	O	-0.3
	Yr	21	44	3	4	1	0	0	1	2	12	.091	.130	.114	-31	-8	-8	0	0			2		-0.4
Total	10	1110	3849	491	959	209	24	125	584	412	837	.249	.324	.413	108	21	31	535	79			41	*O/3S2	3.5

YEAR	TM/L	G	AB	R	H	2B	3B	HR	RBI	BB	SO	AVG	OBP	SLG	PRO+	BR	/A	RC	SB	CS	SBR	FR	POS	TPR

■ MIKE DIMMEL   Dimmel, Michael Wayne   b: 10/16/54, Albert Lea, Minn.   BR/TR, 6', 180 lbs.   Deb: 9/02/77

1977	Bal-A	25	5	8	0	0	0	0	0	0	1	.000	.000	.000	-99	-1	-1	0	1	0	0	3	O	0.1
1978	Bal-A	8	0	2	0	0	0	0	0	0	0	—	—	—	—	0	0	0	0	1	-1	0	/O	0.0
1979	StL-N	6	3	1	1	0	0	0	0	0	0	.333	.333	.333	82	-0	-0	0	0	1	-1	0	/O	0.0
Total	3	39	8	11	1	0	0	0	0	0	1	.125	.125	.125	-33	-1	-1	0	1	2	-1	4	/O	0.1

■ KERRY DINEEN   Dineen, Kerry Michael   b: 7/1/52, Englewood, N.J.   BL/TL, 5'11", 165 lbs.   Deb: 6/14/75

1975	NY-A	7	22	3	8	1	0	0	1	2	1	.364	.417	.409	138	1	1	4	0	0	0	1	/O	0.2
1976	NY-A	4	7	0	2	0	0	0	1	1	2	.286	.375	.286	96	0	0	1	1	1	-0	1	/O	0.0
1978	Phi-N	5	8	0	2	1	0	0	0	1	0	.250	.333	.375	97	-0	-0	1	0	0	0	-0	/O	0.0
Total	3	16	37	3	12	2	0	0	2	4	3	.324	.390	.378	121	1	1	5	1	1	-0	1	/O	0.2

■ VANCE DINGES   Dinges, Vance George   b: 5/29/15, Elizabeth, N.J.   BL/TL, 6'2", 175 lbs.   Deb: 4/17/45

1945	Phi-N	109	397	46	114	15	4	1	36	35	17	.287	.346	.353	87	-3	-1	49	5			1	O1	-0.4
1946	Phi-N	50	104	7	32	5	1	1	10	9	12	.308	.363	.404	121	2	3	15	2			0	1/O	0.1
Total	2	159	501	53	146	20	5	2	46	44	29	.291	.350	.363	102	-0	1	64	7			1	/1O	-0.3

■ BOB DiPIETRO   DiPietro, Robert Louis Paul   b: 9/1/27, San Francisco, Cal   BR/TR, 5'11", 185 lbs.   Deb: 9/23/51

| 1951 | Bos-A | 4 | 11 | 0 | 1 | 0 | 0 | 0 | 0 | 1 | 1 | .091 | .167 | .091 | -26 | -2 | -2 | 0 | 0 | 0 | 0 | 0 | /O | -0.1 |

■ GARY DISARCINA   Disarcina, Gary Thomas   b: 11/19/67, Malden, Mass.   BR/TR, 6'1", 170 lbs.   Deb: 9/23/89

1989	Cal-A	2	0	0	0	0	0	0	0	0	0	—	—	—	—	0	0	0	0	0	0	0	/S	0.0
1990	Cal-A	18	57	8	8	1	1	0	0	3	10	.140	.183	.193	5	-7	-7	2	1	0	0	2	S/2	-0.3
Total	2	20	57	8	8	1	1	0	0	3	10	.140	.183	.193	5	-7	-7	2	1	0	0	2	/S2	-0.3

■ BENNY DISTEFANO   Distefano, Benito James   b: 1/23/62, Brooklyn, N.Y.   BL/TL, 6'1", 195 lbs.   Deb: 5/18/84

1984	Pit-N	45	78	10	13	1	2	3	9	5	13	.167	.226	.346	59	-5	-5	5	0	1	-1	3	O1	-0.3
1986	Pit-N	31	39	3	7	1	0	1	5	1	5	.179	.200	.282	31	-4	-4	2	0	0	0	0	/O1	-0.3
1988	Pit-N	16	29	6	10	3	1	1	6	3	4	.345	.406	.621	194	3	3	7	0	0	0	0	/1O	0.3
1989	Pit-N	96	154	12	38	8	0	2	15	17	30	.247	.333	.338	96	-1	-0	17	1	0	0	-3	1/CO	-0.6
Total	4	188	300	31	68	13	3	7	35	26	52	.227	.297	.360	87	-6	-6	32	1	1	-0	1	/1OC	-0.9

■ DUTCH DISTEL   Distel, George Adam   b: 4/15/1896, Madison, Ind.   d: 2/12/67, Madison, Ind.   BR/TR, 5'9", 165 lbs.   Deb: 6/21/18

| 1918 | StL-N | 8 | 17 | 3 | 3 | 1 | 1 | 0 | 1 | 2 | 3 | .176 | .263 | .353 | 90 | -0 | -0 | 2 | | | | -1 | /2SO | -0.1 |

■ JACK DITTMER   Dittmer, John Douglas   b: 1/10/28, Elkader, Iowa   BL/TR, 6'1", 175 lbs.   Deb: 6/17/52

1952	Bos-N	93	326	26	63	7	2	7	41	26	26	.193	.255	.291	53	-22	-21	24	1	0	0	6	2	-1.0
1953	Mil-N	138	504	54	134	22	1	9	63	18	35	.266	.293	.367	75	-22	-18	53	1	0	0	-29	*2	-3.9
1954	Mil-N	66	192	22	47	8	0	6	20	19	17	.245	.322	.380	88	-5	-3	24	0	1	-1	-3	2	-0.3
1955	Mil-N	38	72	4	9	1	1	1	4	4	15	.125	.171	.208	0	-10	-10	3	0	0	0	-1	2	-0.8
1956	Mil-N	44	102	8	25	4	0	1	6	8	8	.245	.300	.314	69	-5	-4	10	0	0	0	3	2	0.2
1957	Det-A	16	22	3	5	1	0	0	2	2	1	.227	.292	.273	54	-1	-1	2	0	0	0	-1	/32	-0.1
Total	6	395	1218	117	283	43	4	24	136	77	102	.232	.281	.333	66	-66	-58	116	2	1	0	-26	2/3	-5.9

■ MOXIE DIVIS   Divis, Edward G.   b: 1/16/1894, Cleveland, Ohio   d: 12/19/55, Lakewood, Ohio   Deb: 8/04/16

| 1916 | Phi-A | 3 | 6 | 0 | 1 | 0 | 0 | 0 | 1 | 0 | 2 | .167 | .167 | .167 | 0 | -1 | -1 | 0 | 0 | | | 1 | /O | 0.0 |

■ LEO DIXON   Dixon, Leo Moses   b: 9/4/1894, Chicago, Ill.   d: 4/11/84, Chicago, Ill.   BR/TR, 5'11", 170 lbs.   Deb: 4/14/25

1925	StL-A	76	205	27	46	11	1	1	19	24	42	.224	.318	.302	55	-13	-15	21	3	2	-0	9	C	0.0
1926	StL-A	33	89	7	17	3	1	0	8	11	14	.191	.294	.247	40	-7	-8	7	1	4	-2	4	C	-0.3
1927	StL-A	36	103	6	20	3	1	0	12	7	6	.194	.245	.243	26	-11	-12	6	0	1	-1	3	C	-0.7
1929	Cin-N	14	30	0	5	2	0	0	2	3	7	.167	.242	.233	19	-4	-4	2	0			4	C	0.1
Total	4	159	427	40	88	19	3	1	41	45	69	.206	.291	.272	43	-36	-38	36	4	7		20	C	-0.9

■ WALT DOANE   Doane, Walter Rudolph   b: 3/12/1887, Bellevue, Idaho   d: 10/19/35, W.Brandywine, Pa.   BL/TR, 6', 165 lbs.   Deb: 9/20/09

1909	Cle-A	4	9	1	1	0	0	0	0	1		.111	.200	.111	-1	-1	-1	0	0			1	/OP	0.0
1910	Cle-A	6	7	0	2	1	0	0	2	1		.286	.375	.429	150	0	0	1	0			-1	/P	0.0
Total	2	10	16	1	3	1	0	0	2	2		.188	.278	.250	64	-1	-1	1	0			-0	/PO	0.0

■ DAN DOBBEK   Dobbek, Daniel John   b: 12/6/34, Ontonagon, Mich.   BL/TR, 6', 195 lbs.   Deb: 9/09/59

1959	Was-A	16	60	8	15	1	2	1	5	5	13	.250	.308	.383	89	-1	-1	7	0	0	0	-1	O	-0.2
1960	Was-A	110	248	32	54	8	2	10	30	35	41	.218	.317	.387	90	-4	-4	31	4	3	-1	4	O	-0.2
1961	Min-A	72	125	12	21	3	1	4	14	13	18	.168	.257	.304	47	-9	-10	10	1	2	-1	1	O	-1.1
Total	3	198	433	52	90	12	5	15	49	53	72	.208	.299	.363	77	-14	-15	48	5	5	-2	4	O	-1.5

■ JOHN DOBBS   Dobbs, John Gordon   b: 6/3/1876, Chattanooga, Tenn.   d: 9/9/34, Charlotte, N.C.   BL/TR, 5'9.5", 170 lbs.   Deb: 4/20/01

1901	Cin-N	109	435	71	119	17	4	2	27	36		.274	.333	.345	106	0	4	59	19			-6	*O/3	-1.1
1902	Cin-N	63	256	39	76	7	3	1	16	19		.297	.345	.359	109	6	3	37	7			8	O	0.6
	Chi-N	59	235	31	71	8	2	0	35	18		.302	.357	.353	125	6	7	33	3			1	O	0.4
	Yr	122	491	70	147	15	5	1	51	37		.299	.351	.356	116	12	10	70	10			8		1.0
1903	Chi-N	16	61	8	14	1	1	0	4	7		.230	.309	.279	72	-2	-2	6	0			1	O	-0.1
	Bro-N	111	414	61	98	15	7	2	59	48		.237	.316	.321	86	-8	-6	52	23			4	*O	-0.8
	Yr	127	475	69	112	16	8	2	63	55		.236	.315	.316	84	-10	-8	58	23			4		-0.9
1904	Bro-N	101	363	36	90	16	2	0	30	28		.248	.302	.303	91	-4	-3	39	11			0	O/2S	-0.6
1905	Bro-N	123	460	59	117	21	4	2	36	31		.254	.301	.330	97	-6	-2	53	15			-6	*O	-1.6
Total	5	582	2224	305	585	85	23	7	207	187		.263	.322	.331	99	-8	1	279	78			0	O/3S2	-3.2

■ LARRY DOBY   Doby, Lawrence Eugene   b: 12/13/24, Camden, S.C.   BL/TR, 6'1", 180 lbs.   Deb: 7/05/47   MC

1947	Cle-A	29	32	3	5	1	0	0	2	1	11	.156	.182	.188	3	-4	-4	1	0	0	0	-1	/21S	-0.4
1948	*Cle-A	121	439	83	132	23	9	14	66	54	77	.301	.384	.490	135	19	20	84	9	9	-3	9	*O	2.2
1949	Cle-A	147	547	106	153	25	3	24	85	91	90	.280	.389	.468	129	21	22	104	10	9	-2	-9	*O	0.7
1950	Cle-A	142	503	110	164	25	5	25	102	98	71	.326	**.442**	.545	**156**	42	44	130	8	6	-1	-8	*O	2.9
1951	Cle-A	134	447	84	132	27	5	20	69	101	81	.295	.428	.512	**163**	37	41	108	4	1	1	-6	*O	2.9
1952	Cle-A	140	519	**104**	143	26	8	**32**	104	90	111	.276	.383	**.541**	**166**	38	42	116	5	2	0	3	*O	**4.3**
1953	Cle-A	149	513	92	135	18	5	29	102	96	121	.263	.385	.487	138	26	28	105	3	2	-0	-12	*O	1.1
1954	*Cle-A	153	577	94	157	18	4	**32**	**126**	85	94	.272	.368	.484	130	25	23	108	3	1	0	2	*O	2.2
1955	Cle-A	131	491	91	143	17	5	26	75	61	100	.291	.372	.505	129	22	20	95	2	0	1	-2	*O	1.2
1956	Chi-A	140	504	89	135	22	3	24	102	102	105	.268	.395	.466	125	22	21	100	0	1	-1	0	*O	1.3
1957	Chi-A	119	416	57	120	27	2	14	79	56	79	.288	.376	.464	127	17	16	71	2	3	-1	-9	*O	0.0
1958	Cle-A	89	247	41	70	10	1	13	45	26	49	.283	.352	.490	132	9	10	41	0	2	-1	-2	O	0.3
1959	Det-A	18	55	5	12	3	1	0	4	8	9	.218	.317	.309	69	-2	-2	6	0	0	0	0	O	-0.4
	Chi-A	21	58	1	14	1	1	0	9	2	13	.241	.267	.293	54	-4	-4	5	1	0	0	-1	O/1	-0.4
	Yr	39	113	6	26	4	2	0	13	10	22	.230	.293	.301	62	-6	-6	11	1	0	0	-2		-0.7
Total	13	1533	5348	960	1515	243	52	253	970	871	1011	.283	.387	.490	137	267	278	1074	47	36	-8	-36	*O/21S	18.0

YEAR	TM/L	G	AB	R	H	2B	3B	HR	RBI	BB	SO	AVG	OBP	SLG	PRO+	BR	/A	RC	SB	CS	SBR	FR	POS	TPR

■ ORAN DODD Dodd, Oran A. b: 9/14/1889, Bagwell, Tex. d: 3/31/29, Newport, Ark. BR/TR, 5'8", 150 lbs. Deb: 7/26/12

YEAR	TM/L	G	AB	R	H	2B	3B	HR	RBI	BB	SO	AVG	OBP	SLG	PRO+	BR	/A	RC	SB	CS	SBR	FR	POS	TPR
1912	Pit-N	5	9	0	0	0	0	0	1	1	3	.000	.100	.000	-73	-2	-2	0	0			0	/32	-0.1

■ TOM DODD Dodd, Thomas Marion b: 8/15/58, Portland, Ore. BR/TR, 6', 190 lbs. Deb: 7/25/86

YEAR	TM/L	G	AB	R	H	2B	3B	HR	RBI	BB	SO	AVG	OBP	SLG	PRO+	BR	/A	RC	SB	CS	SBR	FR	POS	TPR
1986	Bal-A	8	13	1	3	0	0	1	2	2	2	.231	.375	.462	128	1	1	2	0	0	0	-0	/3D	0.0

■ JOHN DODGE Dodge, John Lewis b: 4/27/1889, Bolivar, Tenn. d: 6/19/16, Mobile, Ala. BR/TR, 5'11.5", 165 lbs. Deb: 8/29/12

YEAR	TM/L	G	AB	R	H	2B	3B	HR	RBI	BB	SO	AVG	OBP	SLG	PRO+	BR	/A	RC	SB	CS	SBR	FR	POS	TPR
1912	Phi-N	30	92	3	11	1	0	0	3	4	11	.120	.156	.130	-20	-15	-16	2	2			8	3/2S	-0.8
1913	Phi-N	3	3	0	1	0	0	0	0	2	0	.333	.600	.333	164	1	1	-1	0			-1	/S	0.0
	Cin-N	94	323	35	78	8	8	4	45	10	34	.241	.269	.353	77	-11	-11	32	11			0	3	-1.1
	Yr	97	326	35	79	8	8	4	45	12	34	.242	.274	.353	78	-11	-10	31	11			-0		-1.1
Total	2	127	418	38	90	9	8	4	48	16	45	.215	.248	.304	55	-26	-27	35	13			7	3/2S	-1.9

■ PAT DODSON Dodson, Patrick Neal b: 10/11/59, Santa Monica, Cal. BL/TL, 6'4", 210 lbs. Deb: 9/05/86

YEAR	TM/L	G	AB	R	H	2B	3B	HR	RBI	BB	SO	AVG	OBP	SLG	PRO+	BR	/A	RC	SB	CS	SBR	FR	POS	TPR
1986	Bos-A	9	12	3	5	2	0	1	3	3	3	.417	.533	.833	264	3	3	6	0	0	0	-0	/1	0.2
1987	Bos-A	26	42	4	7	3	0	2	6	8	13	.167	.300	.381	77	-1	-1	5	0	0	0	-1	1/D	-0.3
1988	Bos-A	17	45	5	8	3	1	1	1	6	17	.178	.275	.356	72	-2	-2	5	0	0	0	2	1	0.0
Total	3	52	99	12	20	8	1	4	10	17	33	.202	.319	.424	97	0	-0	16	0	0	0	1	/1D	-0.1

■ BOBBY DOERR Doerr, Robert Pershing b: 4/7/18, Los Angeles, Cal. BR/TR, 5'11", 175 lbs. Deb: 4/20/37 CH

YEAR	TM/L	G	AB	R	H	2B	3B	HR	RBI	BB	SO	AVG	OBP	SLG	PRO+	BR	/A	RC	SB	CS	SBR	FR	POS	TPR
1937	Bos-A	55	147	22	33	5	1	2	14	18	25	.224	.313	.313	56	-9	-10	15	2	4	-2	4	2	-0.3
1938	Bos-A	145	509	70	147	26	7	5	80	59	39	.289	.363	.397	86	-7	-11	74	5	10	-5	6	*2	-0.3
1939	Bos-A	127	525	75	167	28	2	12	73	38	52	.318	.365	.448	103	5	2	78	1	10	-6	27	*2	2.6
1940	Bos-A	151	595	87	173	37	10	22	105	57	53	.291	.353	.497	113	14	10	104	10	5	0	18	*2	3.4
1941	Bos-A	132	500	74	141	28	4	16	93	43	43	.282	.339	.450	105	3	2	78	1	3	-2	-6	*2	0.6
1942	Bos-A	144	545	71	158	35	5	15	102	67	55	.290	.369	.455	127	22	19	95	4	4	-1	11	*2	3.4
1943	Bos-A	155	604	78	163	32	3	16	75	62	59	.270	.339	.412	117	13	12	86	8	8	-2	15	*2	3.3
1944	Bos-A	125	468	95	152	30	10	15	81	58	31	.325	.399	.528	166	38	39	103	5	2	0	4	*2	4.8
1946	*Bos-A	151	583	95	158	34	9	18	116	66	67	.271	.346	.453	115	16	12	90	5	6	-2	27	*2	5.0
1947	Bos-A	146	561	79	145	23	10	17	95	59	47	.258	.329	.426	101	5	-0	74	3	3	-1	24	*2	3.0
1948	Bos-A	140	527	94	150	23	6	27	111	83	49	.285	.386	.505	129	26	22	107	3	2	-0	8	*2	3.2
1949	Bos-A	139	541	91	167	30	9	18	109	75	33	.309	.393	.497	126	26	20	101	2	2	-1	28	*2	4.7
1950	Bos-A	149	586	103	172	29	11	27	120	67	42	.294	.367	.519	114	19	10	109	3	4	-2	9	*2	2.6
1951	Bos-A	106	402	60	116	21	2	13	73	57	33	.289	.378	.448	112	13	8	71	2	1	0	6	*2	1.8
Total	14	1865	7093	1094	2042	381	89	223	1247	809	608	.288	.362	.461	114	181	135	1185	54	64	-22	181	*2	37.8

■ JOHN DOHERTY Doherty, John Michael b: 8/22/51, Woburn, Mass. BL/TL, 5'11", 185 lbs. Deb: 6/01/74

YEAR	TM/L	G	AB	R	H	2B	3B	HR	RBI	BB	SO	AVG	OBP	SLG	PRO+	BR	/A	RC	SB	CS	SBR	FR	POS	TPR
1974	Cal-A	74	223	20	57	14	1	3	15	8	13	.256	.281	.368	91	-5	-3	23	2	1	0	-1	1/D	-0.7
1975	Cal-A	30	94	7	19	3	0	1	12	8	12	.202	.265	.266	54	-6	-5	7	1	1	-0	-1	1/D	-0.7
Total	2	104	317	27	76	17	1	4	27	16	25	.240	.276	.338	80	-11	-9	29	3	2	-0	-1	/1D	-1.4

■ COZY DOLAN Dolan, Albert J. (b: James Alberts) b: 12/23/1889, Chicago, Ill. d: 12/10/58, Chicago, Ill. BR/TR, 5'10", 160 lbs. Deb: 8/15/09 C

YEAR	TM/L	G	AB	R	H	2B	3B	HR	RBI	BB	SO	AVG	OBP	SLG	PRO+	BR	/A	RC	SB	CS	SBR	FR	POS	TPR
1909	Cin-N	3	6	2	1	0	0	0	0	2		.167	.375	.167	69	-0	-0	1	0			-1	/3	0.0
1911	NY-A	19	69	19	21	1	2	0	6	8		.304	.385	.377	106	1	1	14	12			-1	3	0.0
1912	NY-A	18	60	15	12	1	3	0	11	5		.200	.273	.317	64	-3	-3	7	5			-5	3	-0.8
	Phi-N	11	50	8	14	2	2	0	7	1	10	.280	.294	.400	83	-1	-1	6	3			-1	3	-0.1
1913	Phi-N	55	126	15	33	4	0	0	8	1	21	.262	.273	.294	59	-6	-7	12	9			-6	OS/231	-1.3
	Pit-N	35	133	22	27	5	2	0	9	15	14	.203	.289	.271	63	-7	-6	13	14			-2	3	-0.8
	Yr	90	259	37	60	9	2	0	17	16	35	.232	.282	.282	61	-13	-13	25	23			-8		-2.1
1914	StL-N	126	421	76	101	16	3	4	32	55	74	.240	.335	.321	96	-1	-0	57	42			-11	O3	-1.3
1915	StL-N	111	322	53	90	14	9	2	38	34	37	.280	.356	.398	127	11	11	49	17	11	-2	-7	O	0.0
1922	NY-N	1	0	0	0	0	0	0	0	0	0	—	—	—	—	0	0	0	0	0	0	0	R	0.0
Total	7	379	1187	210	299	43	21	6	111	121	156	.252	.328	.339	95	-5	-6	159	102	11		-34	O3/S21	-4.3

■ JOE DOLAN Dolan, Joseph b: 2/24/1873, Baltimore, Md. d: 3/24/38, Omaha, Neb. TR, 5'10", 155 lbs. Deb: 8/11/1896

YEAR	TM/L	G	AB	R	H	2B	3B	HR	RBI	BB	SO	AVG	OBP	SLG	PRO+	BR	/A	RC	SB	CS	SBR	FR	POS	TPR
1896	Lou-N	44	165	14	35	2	1	3	18	9	12	.212	.253	.291	46	-13	-12	14	6			9	S	-0.2
1897	Lou-N	36	133	10	28	2	2	0	7	8		.211	.271	.256	43	-11	-10	11	6			-3	S2	-0.9
1899	Phi-N	61	222	27	57	8	3	1	30	11		.257	.298	.324	75	-8	-7	23	3			-11	2	-1.2
1900	Phi-N	74	257	39	51	7	3	1	27	16		.198	.256	.261	45	-19	-19	20	10			3	32S	-1.1
1901	Phi-N	10	37	0	3	0	0	0	2	2		.081	.128	.081	-37	-6	-6	0	0			-3	2	-0.8
	Phi-A	98	338	50	73	21	2	1	38	26		.216	.280	.299	59	-17	-19	31	3			17	S3/2O	0.0
Total	5	323	1152	140	247	38	11	6	122	72	12	.214	.268	.282	52	-75	-74	99	28			11	S2/3O	-4.2

■ BIDDY DOLAN Dolan, Leon Mark b: 7/9/1881, Onalaska, Wis. d: 7/15/50, Indianapolis, Ind BR, 6', Deb: 4/16/14

YEAR	TM/L	G	AB	R	H	2B	3B	HR	RBI	BB	SO	AVG	OBP	SLG	PRO+	BR	/A	RC	SB	CS	SBR	FR	POS	TPR
1914	Ind-F	32	103	13	23	4	2	1	15	12	13	.223	.316	.330	77	-2	-3	14	5			1	1	-0.1

■ COZY DOLAN Dolan, Patrick Henry b: 12/3/1872, Cambridge, Mass. d: 3/29/07, Louisville, Ky. BL/TL, 5'10", 160 lbs. Deb: 8/09/1892

YEAR	TM/L	G	AB	R	H	2B	3B	HR	RBI	BB	SO	AVG	OBP	SLG	PRO+	BR	/A	RC	SB	CS	SBR	FR	POS	TPR
1892	Was-N	5	13	1	3	0	0	0	1	2	5	.231	.333	.231	75	-0	-0	1	0			-0	/P	0.0
1895	Bos-N	26	83	12	20	4	1	0	7	6	7	.241	.300	.313	55	-5	-6	9	3			4	P/O	0.0
1896	Bos-N	6	14	4	2	0	0	0	0	0	1	.143	.143	.143	-22	-2	-3	0	0			-0	/P	0.0
1900	Chi-N	13	48	5	13	1	0	0	2	2		.271	.300	.292	68	-2	-2	5	2			-2	O	-0.3
1901	Chi-N	43	171	29	45	1	2	0	16	7		.263	.296	.292	76	-6	-5	16	3			2	O	-0.6
	Bro-N	66	253	33	66	11	1	0	29	17		.261	.307	.312	80	-6	-6	27	7			-2	O	-1.4
	Yr	109	424	62	111	12	3	0	45	24		.262	.303	.304	78	-11	-11	44	10			0		-2.0
1902	Bro-N	141	592	72	166	16	7	1	54	33		.280	.324	.336	105	4	3	75	24			-9	*O	-1.6
1903	Chi-A	27	104	16	27	5	1	0	7	6		.260	.300	.327	94	-1	-1	12	5			2	1/O	0.1
	Cin-N	93	385	64	111	20	3	0	58	28		.288	.337	.356	89	-0	-6	52	11			-7	O	-1.7
1904	Cin-N	129	465	88	132	8	10	6	51	39		.284	.339	.383	115	13	8	70	19			-4	*O1	0.0
1905	Cin-N	22	77	7	18	2	1	0	4	7		.234	.298	.286	69	-2	-3	8	2			-4	1/O	-0.8
	Bos-N	112	433	44	119	11	7	3	48	27		.275	.317	.353	104	0	2	58	21			4	*O/P1	-0.1
	Yr	134	510	51	137	13	8	3	52	34		.269	.314	.343	98	-2	-2	65	23			-0		-0.9
1906	Bos-N	152	549	54	136	20	4	0	39	55		.248	.316	.299	96	-3	-1	60	17			-2	O/2P1	-0.5
Total	10	835	3187	429	858	99	37	10	316	229	13	.269	.320	.333	95	-10	-21	394	114			-18	O/1P2	-6.9

■ TOM DOLAN Dolan, Thomas J. b: 1/10/1859, New York, N.Y. d: 1/16/13, St.Louis, Mo. BR/TR, Deb: 9/30/1879

YEAR	TM/L	G	AB	R	H	2B	3B	HR	RBI	BB	SO	AVG	OBP	SLG	PRO+	BR	/A	RC	SB	CS	SBR	FR	POS	TPR
1879	Chi-N	1	4	0	0	0	0	0	0	0	2	.000	.000	.000	-94	-1	-1	0				1	/C	0.0
1882	Buf-N	22	89	12	14	0	1	0	8	2	11	.157	.176	.180	14	-8	-8	3				-5	C/O3	-1.0
1883	StL-a	81	295	32	63	9	2	1		9		.214	.237	.268	59	-12	-15	19				10	CO/P	0.0
1884	StL-a	35	137	19	36	6	2	0		6		.263	.299	.336	105	1	1	14				-9	C/O	-0.4
	StL-U	19	69	9	13	3	0	0		4		.188	.233	.232	56	-3	-3	4	0			10	C/3O	0.7
1885	StL-N	3	9	1	2	0	0	0	0	2	1	.222	.364	.222	99	0	0	1				0	/C	0.1
1886	StL-N	15	44	8	11	3	0	0	7	5		.250	.353	.318	112	1	1	6	2			8	C	0.9
	Bal-a	38	125	13	19	3	2	0		8		.152	.203	.208	31	-10	-9	7	8			-5	C/O	-1.0
1888	StL-a	11	36	1	7	1	0	0	1	1		.194	.216	.222	39	-2	-3	2	1			-0	C	-0.1
Total	7	225	808	95	165	25	7	1	10	39	23	.204	.242	.256	59	-34	-38	56	11			10	C/O3P	-0.8

YEAR	TM/L	G	AB	R	H	2B	3B	HR	RBI	BB	SO	AVG	OBP	SLG	PRO+	BR	/A	RC	SB	CS	SBR	FR	POS	TPR
■ **LESTER DOLE**			Dole, Lester Carrington		b: 7/8/1855, Meriden, Conn.			d: 12/10/18, Concord, N.H.		5'11",		Deb: 5/27/1875												
1875	NH-n	1	4	1	2	0	0	0		0		.500	.500	.500	289	1	1	1					/O	0.1
■ **FRANK DOLJACK**			Doljack, Frank Joseph "Dolie"		b: 10/5/07, Cleveland, Ohio			d: 1/23/48, Cleveland, Ohio		BR/TR, 5'11", 175 lbs.		Deb: 9/04/30												
1930	Det-A	20	74	10	19	5	1	3	17	2	11	.257	.286	.473	87	-2	-2	9	0	1	-1	0	O	-0.2
1931	Det-A	63	187	20	52	13	3	4	20	15	17	.278	.335	.444	100	0	-1	28	3	2	-0	3	O	-0.1
1932	Det-A	8	26	5	10	1	0	1	7	2	2	.385	.429	.538	143	2	2	6	1	0	0	-2	/O	0.0
1933	Det-A	42	147	18	42	5	2	0	22	14	13	.286	.348	.347	83	-3	-3	17	2	6	-3	1	O	-0.5
1934	*Det-A	56	120	15	28	7	1	1	19	13	15	.233	.313	.333	67	-6	-6	13	2	1	0	0	O/1	-0.5
1943	Cle-A	3	7	0	0	0	0	0	0	1	2	.000	.125	.000	-66	-1	-1	0	0	0	0	-0	/O	-0.1
Total	6	192	561	68	151	31	7	9	85	47	60	.269	.329	.398	87	-10	-12	73	8	10	-4	2	O/1	-1.4
■ **ART DOLL**			Doll, Arthur James "Moose"		b: 5/7/13, Chicago, Ill.			d: 4/28/78, Calumet City, Ill.		BR/TR, 6'1", 190 lbs.		Deb: 9/21/35												
1935	Bos-N	3	10	0	1	0	0	0	0	0	1	.100	.100	.100	-50	-2	-2	0	0			0	/C	-0.1
1936	Bos-N	1	2	0	0	0	0	0	0	0	2	.000	.000	.000	-99	-1	-1	0	0			0	/P	0.0
1938	Bos-N	3	1	0	1	0	0	0	0	0	0	1.000	1.000	1.000	501	0	0	1	0			0	/P	0.0
Total	3	7	13	0	2	0	0	0	0	0	3	.154	.154	.154	-18	-2	-2	1	0			0	/PC	-0.1
■ **SHE DONAHUE**			Donahue, Charles Michael		b: 6/29/1877, Oswego, N.Y.			d: 8/24/47, New York, N.Y.		BR/TR, 5'9",		Deb: 4/29/04												
1904	StL-N	4	15	1	4	0	0	0	2	0		.267	.267	.267	70	-1	-1	2	3			-3	/2S	-0.3
	Phi-N	58	200	21	43	4	0	0	14	3		.215	.227	.235	46	-13	-12	13	7			-17	S3/12	-3.0
	Yr	62	215	22	47	4	0	0	16	3		.219	.229	.237	47	-14	-13	15	10			-19		-3.3
■ **JIM DONAHUE**			Donahue, James Augustus		b: 1/8/1862, Lockport, Ill.			d: 4/19/35, Lockport, Ill.		TR, 6', 175 lbs.		Deb: 4/19/1886												
1886	NY-a	49	186	14	37	0	0	0		10		.199	.251	.199	45	-12	-10	10	1			-1	OC	-0.9
1887	NY-a	60	220	33	62	4	1	1		21		.282	.350	.323	94	-2	-0	28	6			-7	C/O132	0.1
1888	KC-a	88	337	29	79	11	3	1	28	21		.234	.281	.294	82	-5	-8	32	12			-12	CO/32	-1.2
1889	KC-a	67	252	30	59	5	4	0	32	21	20	.234	.293	.286	63	-11	-13	25	12			-9	CO3	-1.4
1891	Col-a	77	280	27	61	4	3	0	35	31	18	.218	.298	.254	64	-14	-11	22	2			1	C/O1	-0.5
Total	5	341	1275	133	298	24	11	2	95	104	38	.234	.295	.275	71	-42	-42	117	33			-28	C/O312	-3.9
■ **JIGGS DONAHUE**			Donahue, John Augustus		b: 7/13/1879, Springfield, Ohio			d: 7/19/13, Columbus, Ohio		BL/TL, 6'1", 178 lbs.		Deb: 9/10/00												
1900	Pit-N	3	10	1	2	0	1	0	3	0		.200	.200	.400	64	-1	-1	1	1			-1	/CO	-0.1
1901	Pit-N	2	0	0	0	0	0	0	0	0		—	—	—		0	0	0	0			-0	/CO	0.0
	Mil-A	37	107	10	34	5	4	0	16	10		.318	.387	.439	138	5	5	20	4			-2	C1	0.4
1902	StL-N	30	89	11	21	1	1	1	7	12		.236	.327	.303	78	-2	-2	10	2			0	C/1	0.0
1904	Chi-A	102	367	46	91	9	7	1	48	25		.248	.296	.319	100	-1	0	42	18			7	*1	1.1
1905	Chi-A	149	533	71	153	22	4	1	76	44		.287	.341	.349	127	13	16	79	32			8	*1	2.2
1906	*Chi-A	154	556	70	143	17	7	1	57	48		.257	.316	.318	103	1	3	73	36			9	*1	0.8
1907	Chi-A	157	609	75	158	16	4	0	68	28		.259	.292	.299	95	-7	-5	64	27			21	*1	1.5
1908	Chi-A	93	304	22	62	8	2	0	22	25		.204	.264	.243	68	-10	-10	23	14			5	1	-0.7
1909	Chi-A	2	4	0	0	0	0	0	2	1		.000	.200	.000	-38	-1	-1	0	0			-0	/1	0.0
	Was-A	84	283	13	67	12	1	0	28	22		.237	.294	.286	87	-5	-4	27	9			-4	1	-0.8
	Yr	86	287	13	67	12	1	0	30	23		.233	.293	.282	86	-6	-4	27	9			-4		-0.8
Total	9	813	2862	319	731	90	31	4	327	215		.255	.308	.313	100	-8	3	341	143			42	1/CO	4.4
■ **JOHN DONAHUE**			Donahue, John Frederick "Jiggs"		b: 4/19/1894, Roxbury, Mass.			d: 10/3/49, Boston, Mass.		BB/TR, 5'8", 170 lbs.		Deb: 9/25/23												
1923	Bos-A	10	36	5	10	4	0	0	1	4	5	.278	.350	.389	94	-0	-0	5	0	1	-1	3	/O	0.1
■ **PAT DONAHUE**			Donahue, Patrick William		b: 11/8/1884, Springfield, Ohio			d: 1/31/66, Springfield, Ohio		BR/TR, 6', 175 lbs.		Deb: 5/29/08												
1908	Bos-A	35	86	8	17	2	0	1	6	9		.198	.274	.256	72	-2	-2	6	0			0	C/1	0.1
1909	Bos-A	64	176	14	42	4	1	2	25	17		.239	.309	.307	93	-1	-1	18	2			-1	C	0.2
1910	Bos-A	2	4	0	0	0	0	0	0	0		.000	.000	.000	-98	-1	-1	0	0			0	/C	0.0
	Phi-A	14	34	2	5	0	0	0	4	3		.147	.237	.147	21	-3	-3	2	1			3	C	0.2
	Cle-A	2	6	0	1	0	0	0	0	0		.167	.167	.167	4	-1	-1	0	0			-1	/C1	0.0
	Phi-A	1	1	0	0	0	0	0	0	0		.000	.000	.000	-99	-0	-0	0	0			1	/C.	0.1
	Yr	19	45	2	6	0	0	0	4	3		.133	.204	.133	6	-5	-5	2	1			4		0.3
Total	3	118	307	24	65	6	1	3	35	29		.212	.284	.267	74	-8	-9	26	3			2	C/1	0.6
■ **TIM DONAHUE**			Donahue, Timothy Cornelius "Bridget"		b: 6/8/1870, Raynham, Mass.			d: 6/12/02, Taunton, Mass.		BL/TR, 5'11", 180 lbs.		Deb: 7/28/1891												
1891	Bos-a	4	7	0	0	0	0	0	0	0	5	.000	.000	.000	-99	-2	-2	0	0			-1	/C	-0.2
1895	Chi-N	63	219	29	59	9	1	2	36	20	25	.269	.339	.347	74	-7	-9	28	5			-2	C	-0.4
1896	Chi-N	57	188	27	41	10	1	0	20	11	15	.218	.276	.282	47	-14	-15	18	11			5	C	-0.3
1897	Chi-N	58	188	28	45	7	3	0	21	9		.239	.281	.309	55	-12	-13	18	3			7	C/S1	0.2
1898	Chi-N	122	396	52	87	12	3	0	39	49		.220	.318	.265	70	-13	-13	40	17			4	*C	0.0
1899	Chi-N	92	278	39	69	9	3	0	29	34		.248	.345	.302	83	-6	-5	33	10			3	C/1	0.4
1900	Chi-N	67	216	21	51	10	1	0	17	19		.236	.310	.292	71	-9	-7	23	8			-10	C/2	-1.0
1902	Was-A	3	8	0	2	0	0	0	1	0		.250	.250	.250	40	-1	-1	1	0			0	/C	0.0
Total	8	466	1500	196	354	57	12	2	163	142	45	.236	.314	.294	68	-62	-64	160	54			6	C/1S2	-1.3
■ **JOHN DONALDSON**			Donaldson, John David		b: 5/5/43, Charlotte, N.C.			BL/TR, 5'11", 160 lbs.		Deb: 8/26/66														
1966	KC-A	15	30	4	4	0	0	0	1	3	4	.133	.212	.133	2	-4	-4	1	1	0	0	-2	/2	-0.4
1967	KC-A	105	377	27	104	16	5	0	28	37	39	.276	.344	.345	107	3	4	47	6	3	0	-18	*2/S	-1.1
1968	Oak-A	127	363	37	80	9	2	2	27	45	44	.220	.310	.273	82	-9	-7	32	5	5	-2	-4	2/3S	-0.9
1969	Oak-A	12	13	1	1	0	0	0	0	2	4	.077	.200	.077	-21	-2	-2	0	0	0	0	0	/2	-0.1
	Sea-A	95	338	22	79	8	3	1	19	36	36	.234	.307	.284	67	-15	-14	32	6	1	1	-0	2/3S	-0.9
	Yr	107	351	23	80	8	3	1	19	38	40	.228	.303	.276	64	-17	-16	32	6	1	1	0		-1.0
1970	Oak-A	41	89	4	22	2	1	1	11	9	6	.247	.316	.326	80	-3	-2	9	1	0	0	-3	2/S3	-0.1
1974	Oak-A	10	15	1	2	0	0	0	0	0	0	.133	.133	.133	-25	-2	-2	0	0	0	0	1	/23	0.0
Total	6	405	1225	96	292	35	11	4	86	132	133	.238	.314	.295	81	-31	-27	121	19	9	0	-26	2/3S	-3.5
■ **LEN DONDERO**			Dondero, Leonard Peter "Mike"		b: 9/12/03, Newark, Cal.			BR/TR, 5'11", 178 lbs.		Deb: 4/21/29														
1929	StL-A	19	31	2	6	0	0	1	8	0	4	.194	.194	.290	22	-4	-4	2	0	0	0	-3	3/2	-0.5
■ **MIKE DONLIN**			Donlin, Michael Joseph "Turkey Mike"		b: 5/30/1878, Peoria, Ill.			d: 9/24/33, Hollywood, Cal.		BL/TL, 5'9", 170 lbs.		Deb: 7/19/1899												
1899	StL-N	66	266	49	86	9	6	6	27	17		.323	.366	.470	128	10	9	54	20			-7	O1/SP	0.0
1900	StL-N	78	276	40	90	8	6	10	48	14		.326	.361	.507	142	14	14	57	14			-4	O1	0.6
1901	Bal-A	121	476	107	162	23	13	5	67	53		.340	.409	.475	141	31	28	109	33			9	O1	3.0
1902	Cin-N	34	143	30	41	5	4	0	9	9		.287	.333	.378	111	3	2	22	9			-1	O/PS	0.0
1903	Cin-N	126	496	110	174	25	18	7	67	56		.351	.417	.516	151	**43**	35	121	26			-2	*O/1	2.5
1904	Cin-N	60	236	42	84	11	7	1	38	18		.356	.402	.475	159	19	17	55	21			-3	O1/1	1.3
	NY-N	42	132	17	37	7	3	2	14	10		.280	.331	.424	129	5	4	19	1			-7	O	-0.3
	Yr	102	368	59	121	18	10	3	52	28		.329	.376	.457	149	24	21	74	22			-9		1.0
1905	*NY-N	150	606	**124**	216	31	16	7	80	56		.356	.411	.495	169	52	51	141	33			-11	*O	3.0
1906	NY-N	37	121	15	38	5	1	1	14	11		.314	.371	.397	139	6	5	22	9			-6	O1/1	0.0

YEAR	TM/L	G	AB	R	H	2B	3B	HR	RBI	BB	SO	AVG	OBP	SLG	PRO+	BR	/A	RC	SB	CS	SBR	FR	POS	TPR
1908	NY-N	155	593	71	198	26	13	6	106	23		.334	.359	.452	154	37	34	106	30			0	*O	3.7
1911	NY-N	12	12	3	4	0	0	1	1	0	1	.333	.333	.583	150	1	1	3	2			0	/O	0.0
	Bos-N	56	222	33	70	16	1	2	34	22	17	.315	.377	.423	115	7	4	38	7			1	O	0.4
	Yr	68	234	36	74	16	1	3	35	22	18	.316	.375	.432	117	8	5	41	9			1		0.4
1912	Pit-N	77	244	27	77	9	8	2	35	20	16	.316	.370	.443	124	7	7	43	8			-4	O	0.1
1914	NY-N	35	31	1	5	1	1	1	3	3	5	.161	.235	.355	77	-1	-1	2	0			0	H	0.0
Total	12	1049	3854	669	1282	176	97	51	543	312	39	.333	.384	.468	144	234	211	794	213			-33	O/1PS	14.3

■ JIM DONNELLY
Donnelly, James B. b: 7/19/1865, New Haven, Conn. d: 3/5/15, Meriden, Conn. BR, Deb: 7/11/1884

YEAR	TM/L	G	AB	R	H	2B	3B	HR	RBI	BB	SO	AVG	OBP	SLG	PRO+	BR	/A	RC	SB	CS	SBR	FR	POS	TPR
1884	KC-U	6	23	2	3	1	0	0		1		.130	.167	.174	18	-2	-1	1	0			-3	/3C	-0.3
	Ind-a	40	134	22	34	2	2	0		5		.254	.301	.299	102	0	1	12				-5	3/SO2	-0.2
1885	Det-N	56	211	24	49	4	3	1	22	10	29	.232	.267	.294	81	-4	-4	17				-3	3/1	-0.5
1886	KC-N	113	438	51	88	11	3	0	38	36	57	.201	.262	.240	50	-24	-28	32	16			-0	*3	-2.0
1887	Was-N	117	425	51	85	9	6	1	46	16	26	.200	.234	.256	39	-35	-32	36	42			17	*3/S	-1.1
1888	Was-N	122	428	43	86	9	4	0	23	20	16	.201	.242	.241	59	-20	-17	36	44			-6	*3/S	-1.7
1889	Was-N	4	13	3	2	0	0	0	0	2	0	.154	.267	.154	21	-1	-1	1	1			-1	/3	-0.1
1890	StL-a	11	42	11	14	0	0	0		8		.333	.451	.333	118	3	2	9	5			-2	3	0.0
1891	Col-a	17	54	6	13	0	0	0	9	13	5	.241	.388	.241	89	-0	0	8	7			3	3	0.3
1896	Bal-N	106	396	70	130	14	10	0	71	34	11	.328	.387	.414	112	8	7	80	38			-2	*3	0.9
1897	Pit-N	44	161	22	31	4	0	0	14	16		.193	.270	.217	32	-15	-14	14	14			2	3	-1.0
	NY-N	23	85	19	16	3	0	0	11	9		.188	.266	.224	32	-8	-8	7	6			-6	3	-1.1
	Yr	67	246	41	47	7	0	0	25	25		.191	.268	.220	32	-24	-22	20	20			-4		-2.1
1898	StL-N	1	1	0	1	0	0	0	0	0		1.000	1.000	1.000	470	0	0	1	0			0	/3	0.0
Total	11	660	2411	324	552	57	28	2	234	170	144	.229	.284	.278	66	-99	-96	254	173			-7	3/SO21C	-6.8

■ JOHN DONNELLY
Donnelly, John b: Elizabeth, N.J. Deb: 4/14/1873

YEAR	TM/L	G	AB	R	H	2B	3B	HR	RBI	BB	SO	AVG	OBP	SLG	PRO+	BR	/A	RC	SB	CS	SBR	FR	POS	TPR
1873	Was-n	30	137	15	35	3	0	0		1		.255	.261	.277	60	-7	-6	10					S2/O	-0.4
1874	Phi-n	6	22	2	5	0	0	0		0		.227	.227	.227	44	-1	-1	1					/SO2	0.0
Total	2 n	36	159	17	40	3	0	0		1		.252	.256	.270	58	-8	-7	11					/S2O	-0.4

■ PETER DONNELLY
Donnelly, Peter J. b: Philadelphia, Pa. d: 10/2/1890, Jersey City,N.J. Deb: 5/13/1871

YEAR	TM/L	G	AB	R	H	2B	3B	HR	RBI	BB	SO	AVG	OBP	SLG	PRO+	BR	/A	RC	SB	CS	SBR	FR	POS	TPR
1871	Kek-n	9	34	7	7	1	1	0	3	1	2	.206	.229	.294	48	-2	-2	2	0				/O3	0.0

■ JOE DONOHUE
Donohue, Joseph F. b: 1869, Syracuse, N.Y. Deb: 8/24/1891

YEAR	TM/L	G	AB	R	H	2B	3B	HR	RBI	BB	SO	AVG	OBP	SLG	PRO+	BR	/A	RC	SB	CS	SBR	FR	POS	TPR
1891	Phi-N	6	22	2	7	1	0	0	2	1	3	.318	.375	.364	115	1	0	3	0			-0	/OS	0.0

■ TOM DONOHUE
Donohue, Thomas James b: 11/15/52, Mineola, N.Y. BR/TR, 6', 185 lbs. Deb: 4/06/79

YEAR	TM/L	G	AB	R	H	2B	3B	HR	RBI	BB	SO	AVG	OBP	SLG	PRO+	BR	/A	RC	SB	CS	SBR	FR	POS	TPR
1979	Cal-A	38	107	13	24	3	1	3	14	3	29	.224	.259	.355	66	-6	-5	10	2	0	1	-2	C	-0.4
1980	Cal-A	84	218	18	41	4	1	2	14	7	63	.188	.217	.243	26	-22	-22	12	5	1	1	-10	C	-2.6
Total	2	122	325	31	65	7	2	5	28	10	92	.200	.231	.280	40	-28	-27	23	7	1	2	-12	C	-3.0

■ FRED DONOVAN
Donovan, Frederick Maurice b: 7/4/1864, New Hampshire d: 3/7/16, Bloomington, Ill. BR/TR, Deb: 6/23/1895

YEAR	TM/L	G	AB	R	H	2B	3B	HR	RBI	BB	SO	AVG	OBP	SLG	PRO+	BR	/A	RC	SB	CS	SBR	FR	POS	TPR
1895	Cle-N	3	12	1	1	0	0	0	1	1	2	.083	.154	.083	-35	-2	-3	0				1	/C	0.0

■ JERRY DONOVAN
Donovan, Jeremiah Francis b: 9/3/1876, Lock Haven, Pa. d: 6/27/38, St.Petersburg, Fla. BR/TR, Deb: 4/12/06

YEAR	TM/L	G	AB	R	H	2B	3B	HR	RBI	BB	SO	AVG	OBP	SLG	PRO+	BR	/A	RC	SB	CS	SBR	FR	POS	TPR
1906	Phi-N	61	166	11	33	4	0	0	15	6		.199	.227	.223	42	-11	-11	9	2			-5	C/SO	-1.2

■ MIKE DONOVAN
Donovan, Michael Berchman b: 10/18/1881, Brooklyn, N.Y. d: 2/3/38, New York, N.Y. BR/TR, 5'8", 155 lbs. Deb: 5/29/04

YEAR	TM/L	G	AB	R	H	2B	3B	HR	RBI	BB	SO	AVG	OBP	SLG	PRO+	BR	/A	RC	SB	CS	SBR	FR	POS	TPR
1904	Cle-A	2	2	0	0	0	0	0	0	0		.000	.000	.000	-99	-0	-0	0	0			0	/S	0.0
1908	NY-A	5	19	2	5	1	0	0	2	0		.263	.263	.316	89	-0	-0	1	0			1	/3	0.1
Total	2	7	21	2	5	1	0	0	2	0		.238	.238	.286	71	-1	-1	1	0			1	/3S	0.1

■ PATSY DONOVAN
Donovan, Patrick Joseph b: 3/16/1865, County Cork, Ireland d: 12/25/53, Lawrence, Mass. BL/TL, 5'11.5", 175 lbs. Deb: 4/19/1890 M

YEAR	TM/L	G	AB	R	H	2B	3B	HR	RBI	BB	SO	AVG	OBP	SLG	PRO+	BR	/A	RC	SB	CS	SBR	FR	POS	TPR
1890	Bos-N	32	140	17	36	0	0	0	9	8	17	.257	.307	.257	62	-6	-7	14	10			-5	O	-1.1
	*Bro-N	28	105	17	23	5	1	0	8	5	5	.219	.268	.286	63	-5	-5	9	3			1	O	-0.3
	Yr	60	245	34	59	5	1	0	17	13	22	.241	.290	.269	62	-11	-12	23	13			-4		-1.4
1891	Lou-a	105	439	73	141	10	3	2	53	30	18	.321	.375	.371	118	10	11	73	27			5	*O	0.9
	Was-a	17	70	9	14	1	0	0	3	4	5	.200	.243	.214	35	-6	-5	4	1			-2	O	-0.7
	Yr	122	509	82	155	11	3	2	56	34	23	.305	.358	.350	107	4	5	75	28			2		0.2
1892	Was-N	40	163	29	39	3	3	0	12	11	13	.239	.295	.294	83	-4	-3	19	16			1	O	-0.3
	Pit-N	90	388	77	114	15	3	2	26	20	16	.294	.333	.363	112	5	5	62	40			-3	O	0.0
	Yr	130	551	106	153	18	6	2	38	31	29	.278	.322	.343	104	1	2	81	56			-2		-0.3
1893	Pit-N	113	499	114	158	5	8	2	56	42	8	.317	.373	.371	102	1	2	88	46			-1	*O	-0.1
1894	Pit-N	132	576	145	174	21	10	4	76	33	12	.302	.345	.394	80	-20	-19	95	41			8	*O	-1.4
1895	Pit-N	125	519	114	160	17	6	1	58	47	19	.308	.375	.370	100	-2	3	88	36			-5	*O	-1.0
1896	Pit-N	131	573	113	183	20	5	3	59	35	18	.319	.370	.387	106	2	6	102	48			7	*O	0.3
1897	Pit-N	120	479	82	154	16	7	0	57	25		.322	.360	.384	103	-1	2	80	34			1	*OM	-0.5
1898	Pit-N	147	610	112	184	16	8	1	37	34		.302	.346	.359	107	4	5	92	41			0	*O	-0.2
1899	Pit-N	121	531	82	156	11	7	1	55	17		.294	.322	.347	86	-11	-11	69	26			-12	*OM	-2.7
1900	StL-N	126	503	78	159	11	1	0	61	38		.316	.368	.342	100	1	2	82	45			-5	*O	-1.2
1901	StL-N	130	531	92	161	23	5	1	73	27		.303	.339	.371	114	5	9	80	28			4	*OM	0.0
1902	StL-N	126	502	70	158	12	4	0	35	28		.315	.363	.355	129	14	17	80	34			10	*OM	1.9
1903	StL-N	105	410	63	134	15	3	0	39	25		.327	.366	.378	118	7	9	69	25			-1	*OM	0.2
1904	Was-A	125	436	30	100	6	0	0	19	24		.229	.270	.243	66	-17	-16	36	17			9	*OM	-1.5
1906	Bro-N	7	21	1	5	0	0	0	0	0		.238	.238	.238	54	-1	-1	1	0			-1	/OM	-0.1
1907	Bro-N	1	1	0	0	0	0	0	0	0		.000	.000	.000	-99	-0	-0	0	0			0	/OM	0.0
Total	17	1821	7496	1318	2253	207	74	17	736	453	131	.301	.347	.355	100	-23	3	1145	518			13	*O	-7.8

■ TOM DONOVAN
Donovan, Thomas Joseph b: 1/1/1873, West Troy, N.Y. d: 3/25/33, Watervliet, N.Y. BR/TR, 6'2", 168 lbs. Deb: 9/10/01

YEAR	TM/L	G	AB	R	H	2B	3B	HR	RBI	BB	SO	AVG	OBP	SLG	PRO+	BR	/A	RC	SB	CS	SBR	FR	POS	TPR
1901	Cle-A	18	71	9	18	3	1	0	5	0		.254	.254	.324	63	-4	-3	6	1			-1	O/P	-0.3

■ BILL DONOVAN
Donovan, William Edward "Wild Bill" b: 10/13/1876, Lawrence, Mass. d: 12/9/23, Forsyth, N.Y. BR/TR, 5'11", 190 lbs. Deb: 4/22/1898 M

YEAR	TM/L	G	AB	R	H	2B	3B	HR	RBI	BB	SO	AVG	OBP	SLG	PRO+	BR	/A	RC	SB	CS	SBR	FR	POS	TPR
1898	Was-N	39	103	11	17	2	3	1	8	4		.165	.211	.272	40	-8	-8	6	2			1	OP/S2	-0.4
1899	Bro-N	5	13	2	3	1	0	0	0	0		.231	.231	.308	48	-1	-1	1	0			-0	/P	0.0
1900	Bro-N	5	10	0	0	0	0	0	2	0		.000	.000	.000	-94	-3	-4	0	0			1	/P	0.0
1901	Bro-N	46	135	16	23	3	0	2	13	8		.170	.217	.237	32	-11	-12	8	1			-2	P	0.0
1902	Bro-N	48	161	16	28	3	2	1	16	9		.174	.222	.236	42	-11	-11	10	7			1	P/1O2	0.0
1903	Det-A	40	124	11	30	3	2	0	12	4		.242	.266	.298	73	-4	-4	12	3			-3	P/S2O	0.0
1904	Det-A	46	140	12	38	2	1	1	6	3		.271	.287	.321	97	-1	-1	14	2			-4	P/1O	0.0
1905	Det-A	44	130	16	25	4	0	0	5	12		.192	.261	.223	55	-6	-6	11	8			-1	P/O2	0.0
1906	Det-A	28	91	5	11	0	1	0	2	6		.121	.143	.143	-13	-12	-12	3	6			-1	P/2O	0.0
1907	*Det-A	37	109	20	29	7	2	0	19	6		.266	.304	.367	112	2	1	14	4			-6	P	0.0
1908	*Det-A	30	82	5	13	1	0	0	2	10		.159	.250	.171	37	-5	-5	4	2			-7	P	0.0
1909	*Det-A	22	45	6	9	0	0	0	1	2		.200	.250	.200	41	-3	-3	3	0			-3	P	0.0
1910	Det-A	26	69	6	10	1	0	0	5	5		.145	.203	.159	13	-7	-7	2	0			-7	P	0.0

YEAR	TM/L	G	AB	R	H	2B	3B	HR	RBI	BB	SO	AVG	OBP	SLG	PRO+	BR	/A	RC	SB	CS	SBR	FR	POS	TPR
1911	Det-A	24	60	11	12	3	1	1	6	11		.200	.324	.333	79	-1	-2	7	1			-5	P	0.0
1912	Det-A	6	13	3	1	0	0	0	0	1		.077	.143	.077	-38	-2	-2	0	0			-2	/P1O	-0.3
1915	NY-A	10	12	1	1	0	0	0	0	1	6	.083	.154	.083	-29	-2	-2	0	0			-1	/PM	0.0
1916	NY-A	1	0	0	0	0	0	0	0	0	0	—	—	—		0	0	0	0			0	/PM	0.0
1918	Det-A	2	2	1	1	0	0	0	1	0	0	.500	.500	.500	210	0	0	0	0			-0	/P	0.0
Total	18	459	1302	142	251	30	12	6	93	77	6	.193	.240	.248	50	-76	-78	97	36			-37	P/O12S	-0.7

■ RED DOOIN   Dooin, Charles Sebastian   b: 6/12/1879, Cincinnati, Ohio   d: 5/14/52, Rochester, N.Y.   BR/TR, 5'9.5", 165 lbs.   Deb: 4/18/02   M

YEAR	TM/L	G	AB	R	H	2B	3B	HR	RBI	BB	SO	AVG	OBP	SLG	PRO+	BR	/A	RC	SB	CS	SBR	FR	POS	TPR
1902	Phi-N	94	333	20	77	7	3	0	35	10		.231	.260	.270	65	-14	-14	27	8			4	C/O	-0.1
1903	Phi-N	62	188	18	41	5	1	0	14	8		.218	.250	.255	47	-13	-12	15	9			-3	C/1O	-1.0
1904	Phi-N	108	355	41	86	11	4	6	36	8		.242	.259	.346	91	-6	-5	37	15			8	C/1O3	1.2
1905	Phi-N	113	380	45	95	13	5	0	36	10		.250	.269	.311	77	-13	-11	37	12			7	*C/3	0.7
1906	Phi-N	113	351	25	86	19	1	0	32	13		.245	.272	.305	82	-8	-8	35	15			-12	*C	-1.2
1907	Phi-N	101	313	18	66	8	4	0	14	15		.211	.247	.262	62	-14	-14	24	10			3	C/2O	-0.3
1908	Phi-N	133	435	28	108	17	4	0	41	17		.248	.277	.306	85	-7	-8	42	20			12	*C	1.2
1909	Phi-N	141	468	42	105	14	1	2	38	21		.224	.264	.271	65	-20	-20	37	14			4	*C	-0.5
1910	Phi-N	103	331	30	80	13	4	0	30	22	17	.242	.289	.305	71	-12	-13	31	10			-2	C/OM	-1.1
1911	Phi-N	74	247	18	81	15	1	1	16	14	12	.328	.366	.409	115	5	5	39	6			4	CM	1.4
1912	Phi-N	69	184	20	43	9	0	0	22	5	12	.234	.262	.283	46	-13	-15	15	8			1	CM	-0.9
1913	Phi-N	55	129	6	33	4	1	0	13	3	9	.256	.273	.302	62	-6	-7	10	1			5	CM	0.1
1914	Phi-N	53	118	10	21	2	0	1	8	4	14	.178	.205	.220	25	-11	-12	6	4			0	C/OM	-1.0
1915	Cin-N	10	31	2	10	0	0	0	0	2	5	.323	.364	.323	106	0	0	4	1			-3	C	-0.2
	NY-N	46	124	9	27	2	2	0	9	3	15	.218	.236	.266	55	-7	-7	8	0	2	-1	1	C	-0.4
	Yr	56	155	11	37	2	2	0	9	5	20	.239	.262	.277	66	-7	-6	11	1	2	-1	-3		-0.6
1916	NY-N	15	17	1	2	0	0	0	0	0	3	.118	.118	.118	-29	-3	-2	0	0			0	C	0.0
Total	15	1290	4004	333	961	139	31	10	344	155	87	.240	.270	.298	72	-142	-143	367	133	2		29	*C/O132	-2.1

■ MICKEY DOOLAN   Doolan, Michael Joseph "Doc" (b: Michael Joseph Doolittle)   b: 5/7/1880, Ashland, Pa.   d: 11/1/51, Orlando, Fla.   BR/TR, 5'10.5", 170 lbs.   Deb: 4/14/05   C

YEAR	TM/L	G	AB	R	H	2B	3B	HR	RBI	BB	SO	AVG	OBP	SLG	PRO+	BR	/A	RC	SB	CS	SBR	FR	POS	TPR
1905	Phi-N	136	492	53	125	27	11	1	48	24		.254	.289	.360	98	-5	-2	58	17			-9	*S	-0.9
1906	Phi-N	154	535	41	123	19	7	1	55	27		.230	.267	.297	78	-15	-15	50	16			6	*S	-0.1
1907	Phi-N	145	509	33	104	19	7	1	47	25		.204	.242	.275	64	-22	-22	40	18			14	*S	0.0
1908	Phi-N	129	445	29	104	25	4	2	49	17		.234	.262	.321	85	-7	-9	39	5			0	*S	-1.1
1909	Phi-N	147	493	39	108	12	10	1	35	37		.219	.276	.290	75	-15	-15	43	10			25	*S	1.2
1910	Phi-N	148	536	58	141	31	6	2	57	35	56	.263	.315	.354	92	-5	-7	64	16			21	*S	2.0
1911	Phi-N	146	512	51	122	23	6	1	49	44	65	.238	.301	.313	71	-20	-21	52	14			20	*S	0.5
1912	Phi-N	146	532	47	137	26	6	1	62	34	59	.258	.305	.335	70	-20	-24	56	6			8	*S	-0.1
1913	Phi-N	151	518	32	113	12	6	1	43	29	68	.218	.262	.270	50	-33	-35	40	17			17	*S/2	-0.8
1914	Bal-F	145	486	58	119	23	6	1	53	40	47	.245	.311	.323	79	-11	-13	63	30			29	*S	2.7
1915	Bal-F	119	404	41	75	13	7	2	21	24	39	.186	.238	.267	48	-26	-27	31	10			32	*S	1.4
	Chi-F	24	86	9	23	1	1	0	9	2	7	.267	.292	.302	81	-3	-2	10	5			0	S	0.0
	Yr	143	490	50	98	14	8	2	30	26	46	.200	.248	.273	53	-29	-30	40	15			32		1.4
1916	Chi-N	28	70	4	15	2	1	0	5	8	7	.214	.295	.271	67	-2	-3	6	0			3	S	0.1
	NY-N	18	51	4	12	3	1	1	3	2	4	.235	.264	.392	106	-0	0	6	1			2	S/2	0.3
	Yr	46	121	8	27	5	2	1	8	10	11	.223	.282	.322	82	-2	-3	12	1			4		0.4
1918	Bro-N	92	308	14	55	8	2	0	18	22	24	.179	.233	.218	38	-23	-23	18	8			10	2	-0.8
Total	13	1728	5977	513	1376	244	81	15	554	370	376	.230	.278	.306	72	-206	-218	576	173			177	*S/2	4.4

■ HARRY DOOMS   Dooms, Henry E. "Jack"   b: 1/30/1867, St.Louis, Mo.   d: 12/14/1899, St.Louis, Mo.   Deb: 8/07/1892

YEAR	TM/L	G	AB	R	H	2B	3B	HR	RBI	BB	SO	AVG	OBP	SLG	PRO+	BR	/A	RC	SB	CS	SBR	FR	POS	TPR
1892	Lou-N	1	4	0	0	0	0	0	0	1	3	.000	.200	.000	-41	-1	-1	0	0			-1	/O	0.0

■ TOM DORAN   Doran, Thomas J. "Long Tom"   b: 12/2/1880, Westchester Co., N.Y.   d: 6/22/10, New York, N.Y.   TR, 5'11", 152 lbs.   Deb: 4/19/04

YEAR	TM/L	G	AB	R	H	2B	3B	HR	RBI	BB	SO	AVG	OBP	SLG	PRO+	BR	/A	RC	SB	CS	SBR	FR	POS	TPR
1904	Bos-A	12	32	1	4	0	1	0	0	4		.125	.222	.188	30	-2	-3	2	1			-4	C	-0.6
1905	Bos-A	3	3	0	0	0	0	0	0	0		.000	.000	.000	-99	-1	-1	0	0			0	/C	0.0
	Det-A	34	94	8	15	3	0	0	4	8		.160	.225	.191	34	-7	-7	5	2			-6	C	-1.0
	Yr	37	97	8	15	3	0	0	4	8		.155	.219	.186	30	-7	-7	5	2			-6		-1.0
1906	Bos-A	2	3	1	0	0	0	0	0	0		.000	.000	.000	-99	-0	-1	0	0			-0	/C	0.0
Total	3	51	132	10	19	3	1	0	4	12		.144	.215	.182	27	-10	-11	7	3			-10	/C	-1.6

■ BILL DORAN   Doran, William Donald   b: 5/28/58, Cincinnati, Ohio   BB/TR, 5'11", 175 lbs.   Deb: 9/06/82

YEAR	TM/L	G	AB	R	H	2B	3B	HR	RBI	BB	SO	AVG	OBP	SLG	PRO+	BR	/A	RC	SB	CS	SBR	FR	POS	TPR
1982	Hou-N	26	97	11	27	3	0	0	6	4	11	.278	.307	.309	79	-4	-3	10	5	0	2	-3	2	-0.2
1983	Hou-N	154	535	70	145	12	7	8	39	86	67	.271	.372	.364	112	7	11	76	12	12	-4	5	*2	1.8
1984	Hou-N	147	548	92	143	18	11	4	41	66	69	.261	.343	.356	104	-1	4	70	21	12	-1	6	*2S	1.4
1985	Hou-N	148	578	84	166	31	6	14	59	71	69	.287	.365	.434	126	18	20	92	23	15	-2	7	*2	2.7
1986	*Hou-N	145	550	92	152	29	3	6	37	81	57	.276	.371	.373	109	7	9	81	42	19	1	-41	*2	-3.0
1987	Hou-N	162	625	82	177	23	3	16	79	82	64	.283	.369	.406	109	7	10	99	31	11	3	-16	*2/S	0.0
1988	Hou-N	132	480	66	119	18	1	7	53	65	60	.248	.339	.333	97	-2	0	59	17	4	3	-3	*2	0.4
1989	Hou-N	142	507	65	111	25	2	8	58	59	63	.219	.303	.323	82	-13	-11	54	22	3	5	-27	*2	-3.4
1990	Hou-N	109	344	49	99	21	2	6	32	71	53	.288	.410	.413	129	16	17	65	18	9	0	-11	2	0.7
	Cin-N	17	59	10	22	8	0	1	5	8	5	.373	.448	.559	171	6	6	16	5	0	2	1	2/3	0.9
	Yr	126	403	59	121	29	2	7	37	79	58	.300	.415	.434	136	22	23	81	23	9	2	-10		1.6
Total	9	1182	4323	621	1161	188	35	70	409	593	518	.269	.358	.377	109	41	63	623	196	85	8	-83	*2/S3	1.3

■ BILL DORAN   Doran, William James   b: 6/14/1898, San Francisco, Cal.   d: 3/9/78, Santa Monica, Cal.   BL/TR, 5'11.5", 175 lbs.   Deb: 6/23/22

YEAR	TM/L	G	AB	R	H	2B	3B	HR	RBI	BB	SO	AVG	OBP	SLG	PRO+	BR	/A	RC	SB	CS	SBR	FR	POS	TPR
1922	Cle-A	3	2	0	1	0	0	0	0	1	0	.500	.667	.500	206	0	0	1	0	0	0	0	/3	0.1

■ JERRY DORGAN   Dorgan, Jeremiah F.   b: 1856, Meriden, Conn.   d: 6/10/1891, New Haven, Conn.   BL/TR,   Deb: 7/08/1880

YEAR	TM/L	G	AB	R	H	2B	3B	HR	RBI	BB	SO	AVG	OBP	SLG	PRO+	BR	/A	RC	SB	CS	SBR	FR	POS	TPR
1880	Wor-N	10	35	2	7	1	0	0	1	0	1	.200	.200	.229	41	-2	-2	2				-3	/OC	-0.5
1882	Phi-a	44	181	25	51	9	1	0		4		.282	.297	.343	103	3	-0	19				-0	CO/3	0.4
1884	Ind-a	34	141	22	42	6	1	0		2		.298	.317	.355	126	3	4	16				0	O/C	0.4
	Bro-a	4	13	2	4	0	0	0		0		.308	.308	.308	104	0	0	1				3	/C	0.3
	Yr	38	154	24	46	6	1	0		2		.299	.316	.351	124	3	4	18				4		0.7
1885	Det-N	39	161	23	46	6	2	0	24	8	10	.286	.320	.348	115	3	3	18				-3	O	-0.1
Total	4	131	531	74	150	22	4	0	25	14	11	.282	.303	.339	108	6	4	56				-3	/OC3	0.1

■ MIKE DORGAN   Dorgan, Michael Cornelius   b: 10/2/1853, Middletown, Conn.   d: 4/26/09, Syracuse, N.Y.   BR/TR, 5'9", 180 lbs.   Deb: 5/08/1877   M

YEAR	TM/L	G	AB	R	H	2B	3B	HR	RBI	BB	SO	AVG	OBP	SLG	PRO+	BR	/A	RC	SB	CS	SBR	FR	POS	TPR
1877	StL-N	60	266	45	82	9	7	0	23	9	13	.308	.331	.395	135	8	10	36				-11	*OC/3S2	0.0
1879	Syr-N	59	270	38	72	11	5	1	17	4	13	.267	.277	.356	120	2	6	27				-6	1O3/SCP2	0.0
1880	Pro-N	79	321	45	79	10	1	0	31	10	18	.246	.269	.283	90	-0	-3	25				-0	*O/3PM	-0.5
1881	Wor-N	51	220	36	61	5	0	0	18	8	4	.277	.303	.300	85	-2	-4	20				0	1O/SM	-0.6
	Det-N	8	34	5	8	1	0	0	5	1	0	.235	.257	.265	62	-1	-2	2				0	/O31	-0.1
	Yr	59	254	41	69	6	0	0	23	9	4	.272	.297	.295	82	-4	-6	23				0		-0.6
1883	NY-N	64	261	32	61	11	3	0	27	2	23	.234	.240	.299	63	-12	-11	19				-4	O/CP	-1.1
1884	NY-N	83	341	61	94	13	6	1	48	13	27	.276	.302	.352	103	2	0	37				-1	OP/C2	0.1
1885	NY-N	89	347	60	113	17	8	0	46	11	24	.326	.346	.421	149	17	18	52				-3	*O/1	1.1

YEAR	TM/L	G	AB	R	H	2B	3B	HR	RBI	BB	SO	AVG	OBP	SLG	PRO+	BR	/A	RC	SB	CS	SBR	FR	POS	TPR
1886	NY-N	118	442	61	129	19	4	2	79	29	37	.292	.335	.367	112	7	6	59	9			-11	*O/1	-0.2
1887	NY-N	71	283	41	73	10	0	0	34	15	20	.258	.302	.293	71	-12	-9	33	22			-3	O/1	-1.0
1890	Syr-a	33	139	19	30	8	0	0		16		.216	.301	.273	79	-5	-2	14	8			-2	O	-0.5
Total	10	715	2924	443	802	112	34	4	328	118	179	.274	.303	.340	103	0	10	325	39			-41	O/1CP3S2	-2.8

■ CHARLIE DORMAN
Dorman, Charles William "Slats" b: 4/23/1898, San Francisco, Cal d: 11/15/28, San Francisco, Cal BR/TR, 6'2", 185 lbs. Deb: 5/14/23

YEAR	TM/L	G	AB	R	H	2B	3B	HR	RBI	BB	SO	AVG	OBP	SLG	PRO+	BR	/A	RC	SB	CS	SBR	FR	POS	TPR
1923	Chi-A	1	2	0	1	0	0	0	0	0	0	.500	.500	.500	166	0	0	0	0	0	0	0	/C	0.0

■ RED DORMAN
Dorman, Dwight Dexter "Curlie" b: 10/3/05, Jacksonville, Ill. d: 12/7/74, Anaheim, Cal. BR/TR, 5'10.5", 180 lbs. Deb: 8/21/28

YEAR	TM/L	G	AB	R	H	2B	3B	HR	RBI	BB	SO	AVG	OBP	SLG	PRO+	BR	/A	RC	SB	CS	SBR	FR	POS	TPR
1928	Cle-A	25	77	12	28	6	0	0	11	9	6	.364	.430	.442	128	4	4	15	1	0	0	-3	O	0.0

■ BRIAN DORSETT
Dorsett, Brian Richard b: 4/9/61, Terre Haute, Ind. BR/TR, 6'3", 215 lbs. Deb: 9/08/87

YEAR	TM/L	G	AB	R	H	2B	3B	HR	RBI	BB	SO	AVG	OBP	SLG	PRO+	BR	/A	RC	SB	CS	SBR	FR	POS	TPR
1987	Cle-A	5	11	2	3	0	0	1	3	0	3	.273	.333	.545	127	0	0	2	0	0	0	-2	/C	0.0
1988	Cal-A	7	11	0	1	0	0	0	2	1	5	.091	.167	.091	-26	-2	-2	0	0	0	0	1	/C	0.0
1989	NY-A	8	22	3	8	1	0	0	4	1	3	.364	.391	.409	127	1	1	4	0	0	0	-0	/C	0.1
1990	NY-A	14	35	2	5	2	0	0	0	2	4	.143	.189	.200	9	-4	-4	1	0	0	0	-1	/CD	-0.5
Total	4	34	79	7	17	3	0	1	9	4	15	.215	.262	.291	54	-5	-5	7	0	0	0	-2	/CD	-0.4

■ JERRY DORSEY
Dorsey, Jeremiah b: 1885, Oakland, Cal. BL/TL, 5'11", 175 lbs. Deb: 9/23/11

YEAR	TM/L	G	AB	R	H	2B	3B	HR	RBI	BB	SO	AVG	OBP	SLG	PRO+	BR	/A	RC	SB	CS	SBR	FR	POS	TPR
1911	Pit-N	2	6	0	0	0	0	0	0	0	1	.000	.000	.000	-96	-2	-2	0	0			0	/O	0.0

■ JERRY DORSEY
Dorsey, Michael Jeremiah b: 1854, Canada d: 11/3/38, Auburn, N.Y. Deb: 7/09/1884

YEAR	TM/L	G	AB	R	H	2B	3B	HR	RBI	BB	SO	AVG	OBP	SLG	PRO+	BR	/A	RC	SB	CS	SBR	FR	POS	TPR
1884	Bal-U	1	3	0	0	0	0	0		0		.000	.000	.000	-91	-1	-1	0	0			-0	/OP	0.0

■ HERM DOSCHER
Doscher, John Henry Sr. b: 12/20/1852, New York, N.Y. d: 3/20/34, Buffalo, N.Y. BR/TR, 5'10", 182 lbs. Deb: 9/04/1872 U

YEAR	TM/L	G	AB	R	H	2B	3B	HR	RBI	BB	SO	AVG	OBP	SLG	PRO+	BR	/A	RC	SB	CS	SBR	FR	POS	TPR
1872	Atl-n	6	25	4	9	1	0	0		0		.360	.360	.400	114	1	0	4					/O	0.0
1873	Atl-n	1	6	1	1	0	0	0		0		.167	.167	.167	-2	-1	-1	0					/O	0.0
1875	Was-n	22	81	5	15	2	0	0		0		.185	.185	.210	38	-5	-5	3					3/S	-0.2
1879	Tro-N	47	191	16	42	8	0	0	18	2	10	.220	.228	.262	65	-8	-6	12				-4	3	-0.7
	Chi-N	3	11	1	2	0	0	0	1	0	3	.182	.182	.182	19	-1	-1	0				-1	/3	-0.1
	Yr	50	202	17	44	8	0	0	19	2	13	.218	.225	.257	62	-9	-7	12				-5		-0.8
1881	Cle-N	5	19	2	4	0	0	0	0	0	2	.211	.211	.211	35	-1	-1	1				-0	/3	0.0
1882	Cle-N	25	104	7	25	2	0	0	10	0	11	.240	.240	.260	62	-5	-4	7				-1	3/OS	-0.4
Total	3 n	29	112	10	25	3	0	0		0		.223	.223	.250	57	-5	-5	7					/3OS	-0.2
Total	3	80	325	26	73	10	0	0	29	2	26	.225	.229	.255	61	-15	-12	20				-7	/3OS	-1.2

■ DUTCH DOTTERER
Dotterer, Henry John b: 11/11/31, Syracuse, N.Y. BR/TR, 6', 209 lbs. Deb: 9/25/57

YEAR	TM/L	G	AB	R	H	2B	3B	HR	RBI	BB	SO	AVG	OBP	SLG	PRO+	BR	/A	RC	SB	CS	SBR	FR	POS	TPR
1957	Cin-N	4	12	0	1	0	0	0	2	1	2	.083	.154	.083	-32	-2	-2	0	0	0	0	-0	/C	-0.2
1958	Cin-N	11	28	1	7	1	0	1	2	2	4	.250	.300	.393	77	-1	-1	3	0	0	0	4	/C	0.3
1959	Cin-N	52	161	21	43	7	0	2	17	16	23	.267	.333	.348	79	-4	-5	19	0	0	0	0	C	-0.1
1960	Cin-N	33	79	4	18	5	0	2	11	13	10	.228	.337	.367	91	-1	-1	10	0	1	-1	1	C	0.1
1961	Was-N	7	19	1	5	2	0	0	1	3	5	.263	.364	.368	98	-0	-1	3	0	0	0	2	/C	0.2
Total	5	107	299	27	74	15	0	5	33	35	44	.247	.326	.348	79	-8	-9	36	0	1	-1	7	C	0.3

■ CHARLIE DOUGHERTY
Dougherty, Charles William b: 2/7/1862, Darlington, Wis. d: 2/18/25, Milwaukee, Wis. Deb: 4/17/1884

YEAR	TM/L	G	AB	R	H	2B	3B	HR	RBI	BB	SO	AVG	OBP	SLG	PRO+	BR	/A	RC	SB	CS	SBR	FR	POS	TPR
1884	Alt-U	23	85	6	22	5	0	0		2		.259	.276	.318	99	-0	-0	8	0			0	2/OS	0.0

■ PATSY DOUGHERTY
Dougherty, Patrick Henry b: 10/27/1876, Andover, N.Y. d: 4/30/40, Bolivar, N.Y. BL/TR, 6'2", 190 lbs. Deb: 4/19/02

YEAR	TM/L	G	AB	R	H	2B	3B	HR	RBI	BB	SO	AVG	OBP	SLG	PRO+	BR	/A	RC	SB	CS	SBR	FR	POS	TPR
1902	Bos-A	108	438	77	150	12	6	0	34	42		.342	.411	.397	123	18	17	82	20			-9	*O/3	0.1
1903	*Bos-A	139	590	106	195	19	12	4	59	33		.331	.366	.424	132	27	23	109	35			4	*O	1.8
1904	Bos-A	49	195	33	53	5	4	0	4	25		.272	.355	.338	116	6	5	28	10			0	O	0.2
	NY-A	106	452	80	128	13	10	6	22	19		.283	.312	.396	120	12	9	61	11			-8	*O	-0.5
	Yr	155	647	113	181	18	14	6	26	44		.280	.326	.379	119	17	14	90	21			-8		-0.3
1905	NY-A	116	418	56	110	9	6	3	29	28		.263	.309	.335	96	3	-2	51	17			-6	*O/3	-1.4
1906	NY-A	12	52	3	10	2	0	0	4	0		.192	.192	.231	30	-4	-5	2	0			2	O	-0.2
	*Chi-A	75	253	30	59	9	4	1	27	19		.233	.287	.312	92	-3	-2	28	11			-1	O	-0.6
	Yr	87	305	33	69	11	4	1	31	19		.226	.272	.298	81	-7	-7	30	11			1		-0.8
1907	Chi-A	148	533	69	144	17	2	1	59	36		.270	.316	.315	107	2	4	67	33			-7	*O	-1.1
1908	Chi-A	138	482	68	134	11	6	0	45	58		.278	.356	.326	126	15	16	73	47			-15	*O	-0.5
1909	Chi-A	139	491	71	140	23	13	1	55	51		.285	.359	.391	143	21	24	82	36			-15	*O	0.3
1910	Chi-A	127	443	45	110	8	6	1	43	41		.248	.318	.300	98	-3	-1	48	22			-13	*O	-2.1
1911	Chi-A	76	211	39	61	10	9	0	32	26		.289	.380	.422	128	7	8	41	19			-5	O	-0.1
Total	10	1233	4558	677	1294	138	78	17	413	378		.284	.342	.360	117	101	95	672	261			-74	*O/3	-4.1

■ JOHN DOUGLAS
Douglas, John Franklin b: 9/14/17, Thayer, W.Va. d: 2/11/84, Miami, Fla. BL/TL, 6'2.5", 195 lbs. Deb: 4/21/45

YEAR	TM/L	G	AB	R	H	2B	3B	HR	RBI	BB	SO	AVG	OBP	SLG	PRO+	BR	/A	RC	SB	CS	SBR	FR	POS	TPR
1945	Bro-N	5	9	0	0	0	0	0	0	2	4	.000	.182	.000	-47	-2	-2	0	0			-1	/1	-0.2

■ ASTYANAX DOUGLASS
Douglass, Astyanax Saunders b: 9/19/1899, Covington, Tex. d: 1/26/75, El Paso, Tex. BL/TR, 6'1", 190 lbs. Deb: 7/30/21

YEAR	TM/L	G	AB	R	H	2B	3B	HR	RBI	BB	SO	AVG	OBP	SLG	PRO+	BR	/A	RC	SB	CS	SBR	FR	POS	TPR
1921	Cin-N	4	7	1	1	0	0	0	0	0		.143	.143	.143	-25	-1	-1	0	0	0	0	0	/C	0.0
1925	Cin-N	7	17	1	3	0	0	0	1	1	3	.176	.222	.176	3	-2	-2	1	0	0	0	-1	/C	-0.2
Total	2	11	24	2	4	0	0	0	1	1	4	.167	.200	.167	-4	-4	-4	1	0	0	0	-0	/C	-0.2

■ KLONDIKE DOUGLASS
Douglass, William Bingham b: 5/10/1872, Boston, Pa. d: 12/13/53, Bend, Ore. BL/TR, 6', 200 lbs. Deb: 4/23/1896

YEAR	TM/L	G	AB	R	H	2B	3B	HR	RBI	BB	SO	AVG	OBP	SLG	PRO+	BR	/A	RC	SB	CS	SBR	FR	POS	TPR
1896	StL-N	81	296	42	78	6	4	1	28	35	15	.264	.351	.321	83	-7	-5	41	18			-6	O/CS	-1.3
1897	StL-N	125	516	77	170	15	3	6	50	52		.329	.403	.405	119	15	16	91	12			-17	CO1/3S	0.3
1898	Phi-N	146	582	105	150	26	4	2	48	55		.258	.333	.326	96	-5	-1	71	18			2	*1	0.1
1899	Phi-N	77	275	26	70	6	6	0	27	10		.255	.296	.320	73	-11	-10	29	7			-5	C/31O	-0.8
1900	Phi-N	50	160	23	48	9	4	0	25	13		.300	.360	.406	115	3	3	27	7			-1	C/3	0.6
1901	Phi-N	51	173	14	56	6	1	0	23	11		.324	.368	.370	114	4	3	28	10			2	C/1O	1.0
1902	Phi-N	109	408	37	95	12	3	0	37	23		.233	.274	.277	72	-13	-13	35	6			-9	1CO	-2.3
1903	Phi-N	105	377	43	96	5	4	1	36	28		.255	.306	.297	76	-12	-11	39	6			-1	1	-1.3
1904	Phi-N	3	10	1	3	0	0	0	1	0		.300	.300	.300	91	-0	-0	1	0			-0	/1	0.0
Total	9	747	2797	368	766	85	29	10	275	227	15	.274	.336	.336	93	-27	-17	361	84			-34	1CO/3S	-3.7

■ TAYLOR DOUTHIT
Douthit, Taylor Lee b: 4/22/01, Little Rock, Ark. d: 5/28/86, Fremont, Cal. BR/TR, 5'11.5", 175 lbs. Deb: 9/14/23

YEAR	TM/L	G	AB	R	H	2B	3B	HR	RBI	BB	SO	AVG	OBP	SLG	PRO+	BR	/A	RC	SB	CS	SBR	FR	POS	TPR
1923	StL-N	9	27	3	5	0	2	0	0	0	4	.185	.185	.333	35	-3	-3	2	1	0	0	0	/O	-0.1
1924	StL-N	53	173	24	48	13	1	0	13	16	19	.277	.349	.364	93	-2	-1	23	4	3	-1	4	O	0.1
1925	StL-N	30	73	13	20	3	1	1	8	2	6	.274	.312	.384	75	-3	-3	9	0	0	0	2	O	-0.1
1926	*StL-N	139	530	96	163	20	4	3	52	55	44	.308	.375	.377	99	4	1	76	23			15	*O	1.1
1927	StL-N	130	488	81	128	29	6	5	50	52	45	.262	.336	.377	88	-6	-6	62	6			3	*O	-1.0
1928	*StL-N	154	648	111	191	35	3	3	43	84	36	.295	.384	.372	97	2	1	95	11			21	*O	1.5
1929	StL-N	150	613	128	206	42	7	9	62	79	49	.336	.416	.471	118	21	20	120	8			-1	*O	0.5
1930	*StL-N	154	664	109	201	41	10	7	93	60	38	.303	.364	.426	87	-10	-13	102	4			6	*O	-1.5
1931	StL-N	36	133	21	44	11	2	1	21	19	9	.331	.386	.466	123	5	5	25	1			2	O	0.5
	Cin-N	95	374	42	98	9	1	0	24	42	24	.262	.340	.291	76	-13	-10	40	4			1	O	-1.4
	Yr	131	507	63	142	20	3	1	45	53	33	.280	.352	.337	89	-8	-6	64	5			3		-0.9

YEAR	TM/L	G	AB	R	H	2B	3B	HR	RBI	BB	SO	AVG	OBP	SLG	PRO+	BR	/A	RC	SB	CS	SBR	FR	POS	TPR
1932	Cin-N	96	333	28	81	12	1	0	25	31	29	.243	.311	.285	64	-17	-15	32	3			8	O	-1.2
1933	Cin-N	1	0	1	0	0	0	0	0	0	0	—	—	—	—	0	0	0	0			0	R	0.0
	Chi-N	27	71	8	16	5	0	0	5	11	7	.225	.329	.296	80	-2	-1	6	2			0	O	-0.2
	Yr	28	71	9	16	5	0	0	5	11	7	.225	.329	.296	80	-2	-1	6	2			0		-0.2
Total	11	1074	4127	665	1201	220	38	29	396	443	312	.291	.336	.384	93	-22	-29	592	67	3		62	*O	-1.8

■ CLARENCE DOW
Dow, Clarence G.   b: 10/11/1854, Charlestown, Mass.   d: 3/11/1893, West Somerville, Mass.   Deb: 9/22/1884

YEAR	TM/L	G	AB	R	H	2B	3B	HR	RBI	BB	SO	AVG	OBP	SLG	PRO+	BR	/A	RC	SB	CS	SBR	FR	POS	TPR
1884	Bos-U	1	6	1	2	0	0	0		0		.333	.333	.333	128	0	0	1	0			2	/O	0.1

■ JOHN DOWD
Dowd, John Leo   b: 1/3/1891, S.Weymouth, Mass.   d: 1/31/81, Ft.Lauderdale, Fla   BR/TR, 5'8", 170 lbs.   Deb: 7/03/12

YEAR	TM/L	G	AB	R	H	2B	3B	HR	RBI	BB	SO	AVG	OBP	SLG	PRO+	BR	/A	RC	SB	CS	SBR	FR	POS	TPR
1912	NY-A	10	31	1	6	1	0	0	0	6		.194	.342	.226	60	-1	-1	2	0			-4	S	-0.4

■ SNOOKS DOWD
Dowd, Raymond Bernard   b: 12/20/1897, Springfield, Mass.   d: 4/4/62, Northampton, Mass.   BR/TR, 5'8", 163 lbs.   Deb: 4/27/19

YEAR	TM/L	G	AB	R	H	2B	3B	HR	RBI	BB	SO	AVG	OBP	SLG	PRO+	BR	/A	RC	SB	CS	SBR	FR	POS	TPR
1919	Det-A	1	0	0	0	0	0	0	0	0	0	—	—	—	—	0	0	0	0			0	R	0.0
	Phi-A	13	18	4	3	0	0	0	6	0	5	.167	.167	.167	-6	-3	-3	1	2			1	/2S3O	0.0
	Yr	14	18	4	3	0	0	0	6	0	5	.167	.167	.167	-6	-3	-3	1	2			1		0.0
1926	Bro-N	2	8	0	0	0	0	0	0	0	0	.000	.000	.000	-99	-2	-2	0	0			-2	/2	-0.4
Total	2	16	26	4	3	0	0	0	6	0	5	.115	.115	.115	-36	-5	-5	1	2			-1	/2SO3	-0.4

■ TOMMY DOWD
Dowd, Thomas Jefferson "Buttermilk Tommy"   b: 4/20/1869, Holyoke, Mass.   d: 7/2/33, Holyoke, Mass.   BR/TR, 5'8", 173 lbs.   Deb: 4/08/1891   M

YEAR	TM/L	G	AB	R	H	2B	3B	HR	RBI	BB	SO	AVG	OBP	SLG	PRO+	BR	/A	RC	SB	CS	SBR	FR	POS	TPR
1891	Bos-a	4	11	1	1	0	0	0	0	0	1	.091	.091	.091	-48	-2	-2	0	0			-1	/O	-0.2
	Was-a	112	464	66	120	9	10	1	44	19	44	.259	.291	.328	83	-14	-11	57	39			-17	*2/O	-1.7
	Yr	116	475	67	121	9	10	1	44	19	45	.255	.286	.322	80	-16	-13	56	39			-19		-1.9
1892	Was-N	144	584	94	142	9	10	1	50	34	49	.243	.286	.298	81	-16	-14	65	49			-32	2O3/S	-4.1
1893	StL-N	132	581	114	164	18	7	1	54	49	23	.282	.340	.343	83	-13	-14	90	59			3	*O/2	-1.2
1894	StL-N	123	524	92	142	16	8	4	62	54	33	.271	.341	.355	70	-25	-25	76	31			-7	*O/23	-3.0
1895	StL-N	129	505	95	163	19	17	5	74	30	31	.323	.364	.469	118	10	11	100	30			-7	*O3/2	-0.3
1896	StL-N	126	521	93	138	17	11	5	46	42	19	.265	.322	.369	87	-13	-9	77	40			-13	2OM	-1.9
1897	StL-N	35	145	25	38	9	1	0	9	6		.262	.291	.338	69	-7	-6	18	11			-6	O/2M	-1.2
	Phi-N	91	391	68	114	14	4	0	43	19		.292	.324	.348	82	-12	-10	55	30			-6	O2	-1.6
	Yr	126	536	93	152	23	5	0	52	25		.284	.316	.345	78	-19	-16	73	41			-12		-2.8
1898	StL-N	139	586	70	143	17	7	0	32	30		.244	.287	.297	68	-23	-25	56	16			-17	*O2	-4.6
1899	Cle-N	147	605	81	168	17	6	2	35	48		.278	.334	.336	93	-10	-4	79	28			-2	O	-1.3
1901	Bos-A	138	594	104	159	18	7	3	52	38		.268	.315	.337	84	-13	-12	76	33			1	*O/13	-1.0
Total	10	1320	5511	903	1492	163	88	24	501	369	200	.271	.319	.345	84	-139	-120	749	366			-105	O2/3S1	-22.1

■ KEN DOWELL
Dowell, Kenneth Allen   b: 1/19/61, Sacramento, Cal.   BR/TR, 5'9", 160 lbs.   Deb: 6/24/87

YEAR	TM/L	G	AB	R	H	2B	3B	HR	RBI	BB	SO	AVG	OBP	SLG	PRO+	BR	/A	RC	SB	CS	SBR	FR	POS	TPR
1987	Phi-N	15	39	4	5	0	0	0	1	2	5	.128	.171	.128	-19	-7	-7	1	0	0	0	0	S	-0.4

■ JOE DOWIE
Dowie, Joseph E.   b: 7/1865, New Orleans, La.   5'8", 150 lbs.   Deb: 7/10/1889

YEAR	TM/L	G	AB	R	H	2B	3B	HR	RBI	BB	SO	AVG	OBP	SLG	PRO+	BR	/A	RC	SB	CS	SBR	FR	POS	TPR
1889	Bal-a	20	75	12	17	5	0	0	8	2	10	.227	.266	.293	60	-4	-4	7	5			0	O	-0.3

■ RED DOWNEY
Downey, Alexander Cummings   b: 2/6/1889, Aurora, Ind.   d: 7/10/49, Detroit, Mich.   BL/TL, 5'11", 174 lbs.   Deb: 9/15/09

YEAR	TM/L	G	AB	R	H	2B	3B	HR	RBI	BB	SO	AVG	OBP	SLG	PRO+	BR	/A	RC	SB	CS	SBR	FR	POS	TPR
1909	Bro-N	19	78	7	20	1	0	0	8	2		.256	.275	.269	71	-3	-3	7	4			-1	O	-0.4

■ TOM DOWNEY
Downey, Thomas Edward   b: 1/1/1884, Lewiston, Me.   d: 8/3/61, Passaic, N.J.   BR/TR, 5'10", 178 lbs.   Deb: 5/07/09

YEAR	TM/L	G	AB	R	H	2B	3B	HR	RBI	BB	SO	AVG	OBP	SLG	PRO+	BR	/A	RC	SB	CS	SBR	FR	POS	TPR
1909	Cin-N	119	416	39	96	9	6	1	32	32		.231	.287	.288	79	-11	-10	40	16			-6	*S/C	-1.6
1910	Cin-N	111	378	43	102	9	3	2	32	34	28	.270	.335	.325	97	-3	-1	46	12			-7	S3	-0.5
1911	Cin-N	111	360	50	94	16	7	0	36	44	38	.261	.345	.344	97	-3	-1	46	10			-11	S/2310	-0.8
1912	Phi-N	54	171	27	50	6	3	1	23	21	20	.292	.370	.380	99	2	-0	26	3			-3	3/S	-0.1
	Chi-N	13	22	4	4	0	2	0	4	1	5	.182	.217	.364	58	-1	-1	2	0			1	/S32	0.0
	Yr	67	193	31	54	6	5	1	27	22	25	.280	.353	.378	95	0	-1	28	3			-2		-0.1
1914	Buf-F	151	541	69	118	20	3	2	42	40	55	.218	.273	.277	57	-29	-31	54	35			13	*2S/3	-1.6
1915	Buf-F	92	282	24	56	9	1	1	19	26	26	.199	.269	.248	52	-16	-17	23	11			2	23/S1	-1.3
Total	6	651	2170	256	520	69	25	7	188	198	172	.240	.306	.304	77	-62	-62	238	87			-12	S23/10C	-5.9

■ BRIAN DOWNING
Downing, Brian Jay   b: 10/9/50, Los Angeles, Cal.   BR/TR, 5'10", 170 lbs.   Deb: 5/31/73

YEAR	TM/L	G	AB	R	H	2B	3B	HR	RBI	BB	SO	AVG	OBP	SLG	PRO+	BR	/A	RC	SB	CS	SBR	FR	POS	TPR
1973	Chi-A	34	73	5	13	1	0	2	4	10	17	.178	.277	.274	54	-4	-5	6	0	0	0	2	OC/3D	-0.2
1974	Chi-A	108	293	41	66	12	1	10	39	51	72	.225	.344	.375	104	4	3	38	0	1	-1	-4	CO/D	0.0
1975	Chi-A	138	420	58	101	12	1	7	41	76	75	.240	.361	.324	93	0	-1	54	13	4	2	3	*C/D	0.8
1976	Chi-A	104	317	38	81	14	0	3	30	40	55	.256	.341	.328	96	-0	-1	39	7	3	0	-13	CD	-0.9
1977	Chi-A	69	169	28	48	4	2	4	25	34	21	.284	.410	.402	123	7	7	30	1	2	-1	3	C/OD	1.0
1978	Cal-A	133	412	42	105	15	0	7	46	52	47	.255	.347	.342	98	-1	1	49	3	2	-0	-8	*C/D	-0.3
1979	*Cal-A	148	509	87	166	27	3	12	75	77	57	.326	.420	.462	142	30	33	99	3	3	-1	-22	*CD	1.5
1980	Cal-A	30	93	5	27	6	0	2	25	12	12	.290	.371	.419	119	2	3	13	0	2	-1	-4	CD	-0.1
1981	Cal-A	93	317	47	79	14	0	9	41	46	35	.249	.351	.379	110	5	5	43	1	1	-0	-10	OC/D	-0.4
1982	*Cal-A	158	623	109	175	37	2	28	84	86	58	.281	.373	.482	132	29	29	114	2	1	0	-4	*O	1.9
1983	Cal-A	113	403	68	99	15	1	19	53	62	59	.246	.353	.429	115	9	9	63	1	2	-1	-3	OD	0.4
1984	Cal-A	156	539	65	148	28	2	23	91	70	66	.275	.365	.462	128	21	21	89	0	4	-2	-3	*OD	1.1
1985	Cal-A	150	520	80	137	23	1	20	85	78	61	.263	.373	.427	119	16	16	86	5	3	-0	-4	*OD	1.0
1986	*Cal-A	152	513	90	137	27	4	20	95	90	84	.267	.394	.452	131	25	26	96	4	4	-1	-5	*OD	1.6
1987	Cal-A	155	567	110	154	29	3	29	77	106	85	.272	.401	.487	139	32	35	117	5	5	-2	-2	*DO	2.9
1988	Cal-A	135	484	80	117	18	2	25	64	81	63	.242	.366	.442	129	19	20	81	3	4	-2	0	*D	1.9
1989	Cal-A	142	544	59	154	25	2	14	59	56	87	.283	.356	.414	118	12	14	83	0	2	-1	0	*D	1.3
1990	Cal-A	96	330	47	90	18	2	14	51	50	45	.273	.378	.467	133	15	17	59	0	0	0	0	D	1.6
Total	18	2114	7126	1059	1897	325	26	248	985	1077	999	.266	.371	.424	121	221	232	1160	48	43	-11	-73	OCD/3	15.1

■ RED DOWNS
Downs, Jerome Willis   b: 8/22/1883, Neola, Iowa   d: 10/19/39, Council Bluffs, Ia   BR/TR, 5'11", 155 lbs.   Deb: 5/02/07

YEAR	TM/L	G	AB	R	H	2B	3B	HR	RBI	BB	SO	AVG	OBP	SLG	PRO+	BR	/A	RC	SB	CS	SBR	FR	POS	TPR
1907	Det-A	105	374	28	82	13	5	1	42	13		.219	.245	.289	69	-12	-14	29	3			-25	2O/S3	-4.4
1908	*Det-A	84	289	29	64	10	3	1	35	5		.221	.235	.287	68	-10	-11	19	2			1	2/3	-1.3
1912	Bro-N	9	32	2	8	3	0	0	3	1	5	.250	.273	.344	71	-2	-1	4	3			-1	/2	-0.2
	Chi-N	43	95	9	25	4	3	1	14	9	17	.263	.327	.400	99	-1	-0	14	5			2	2/S3	0.2
	Yr	52	127	11	33	7	3	1	17	10	22	.260	.314	.386	92	-2	-2	18	8			1		0.0
Total	3	241	790	68	179	30	11	3	94	28	22	.227	.253	.304	73	-24	-27	66	13			-23	2/OS3	-5.7

■ TOM DOWSE
Dowse, Thomas Joseph   b: 8/12/1866, Ireland   d: 12/14/46, Riverside, Cal.   BR/TR, 5'11", 175 lbs.   Deb: 4/21/1890

YEAR	TM/L	G	AB	R	H	2B	3B	HR	RBI	BB	SO	AVG	OBP	SLG	PRO+	BR	/A	RC	SB	CS	SBR	FR	POS	TPR
1890	Cle-N	40	159	20	33	2	1	0	9	12	22	.208	.267	.233	49	-10	-10	11	3			-1	O1/CP	-1.0
1891	Col-a	55	201	24	45	7	0	0	22	13	22	.224	.278	.259	59	-11	-10	15	2			-6	C/O	-1.1
1892	Lou-N	41	145	10	21	2	0	0	7	2	15	.145	.173	.159	2	-17	-15	4	1			2	C1/O2	-1.1
	Cin-N	1	4	0	0	0	0	0	0	0	0	.000	.000	.000	-99	-1	-1	0	0			-1	/C	-0.1
	Phi-N	16	54	3	10	0	0	0	6	2	4	.185	.228	.185	27	-5	-5	3	1			-1	C	-0.4
	Was-N	7	27	5	7	1	0	0	2	0	3	.259	.259	.296	71	-1	-1	2	0			0	/OC	0.0
	Yr	65	230	18	38	3	0	0	15	4	22	.165	.193	.178	14	-24	-22	9	2			1		-1.6
Total	3	160	590	62	116	12	1	0	46	29	66	.197	.243	.220	40	-45	-41	35	7			-6	C/O12P	-3.7

YEAR	TM/L	G	AB	R	H	2B	3B	HR	RBI	BB	SO	AVG	OBP	SLG	PRO+	BR	/A	RC	SB	CS	SBR	FR	POS	TPR

■ BRIAN DOYLE Doyle, Brian Reed b: 1/26/55, Glasgow, Ky. BL/TR, 5'10", 160 lbs. Deb: 4/30/78

1978	*NY-A	39	52	6	10	0	0	0	0	0	3	.192	.192	.192	9	-6	-6	1	0	3	-2	13	2/S3	0.7
1979	NY-A	20	32	2	4	2	0	0	5	3	1	.125	.200	.188	5	-4	-4	1	0	0	0	1	2/3	-0.2
1980	NY-A	34	75	8	13	1	0	1	5	6	7	.173	.235	.227	27	-8	-7	4	1	1	-0	5	2S/3	0.0
1981	Oak-A	17	40	2	5	0	0	0	3	1	2	.125	.146	.125	-22	-6	-6	1	0	1	-1	1	2	-0.5
Total	4	110	199	18	32	3	0	1	13	10	13	.161	.201	.191	10	-24	-24	7	1	5	-3	19	/2S3	0.0

■ CONNY DOYLE Doyle, Cornelius J. b: 1858, Holyoke, Mass. d: 1/18/27, E.Orange, N.J. 5'10", 185 lbs. Deb: 6/23/1883

| 1883 | Phi-N | 16 | 68 | 3 | 15 | 3 | 2 | 0 | 3 | 0 | 15 | .221 | .221 | .324 | 69 | -3 | -2 | 5 | | | | -2 | O | -0.2 |

■ ED DOYLE Doyle, Edward H. b: 1853, LaSalle, Ill. d: 2/6/29, Havre, Mont. Deb: 8/22/1884

| 1884 | Pit-a | 15 | 58 | 8 | 17 | 3 | 2 | 0 | | 2 | | .293 | .317 | .414 | 137 | 2 | 2 | 8 | | | | -1 | O/S | 0.1 |

■ DANNY DOYLE Doyle, Howard James b: 1/24/17, Mcloud, Okla. BB/TR, 6'1", 195 lbs. Deb: 9/14/43

| 1943 | Bos-A | 13 | 43 | 2 | 9 | 1 | 0 | 0 | 6 | 7 | 9 | .209 | .320 | .233 | 62 | -2 | -2 | 3 | 0 | 1 | -1 | -3 | C | -0.4 |

■ JIM DOYLE Doyle, James Francis b: 12/25/1881, Detroit, Mich. d: 2/1/12, Syracuse, N.Y. BR/TR, 5'10", 168 lbs. Deb: 5/04/10

1910	Cin-N	7	13	1	2	2	0	0	1	0	2	.154	.154	.308	36	-1	-1	1	0			-1	/3O	-0.1
1911	Chi-N	130	472	69	133	23	12	5	62	40	54	.282	.340	.413	110	5	5	73	19			10	*3	1.9
Total	2	137	485	70	135	25	12	5	63	40	56	.278	.336	.410	108	4	4	73	19			9	3/O	1.8

■ JEFF DOYLE Doyle, Jeffrey Donald b: 10/2/56, Havre, Mont. BB/TR, 5'9", 160 lbs. Deb: 9/13/83

| 1983 | StL-N | 13 | 37 | 4 | 11 | 1 | 2 | 0 | 2 | 1 | 3 | .297 | .316 | .432 | 105 | 0 | 0 | 4 | 0 | 0 | 0 | 1 | 2 | 0.2 |

■ JACK DOYLE Doyle, John Joseph "Dirty Jack" b: 10/25/1869, Killorgin, Ireland d: 12/31/58, Holyoke, Mass. BR/TR, 5'9", 155 lbs. Deb: 8/27/1889 MU

1889	Col-a	11	36	6	10	1	1	0	3	6	6	.278	.381	.361	120	1	1	9	9			-3	/CO2	0.0
1890	Col-a	77	298	47	80	17	7	2		13		.268	.299	.393	114	0	3	44	27			-6	CS/023	0.2
1891	Cle-N	69	250	43	69	14	4	0	43	26	44	.276	.351	.364	106	4	2	41	24			-1	CO3/S	0.3
1892	Cle-N	24	88	17	26	4	1	1	14	6	10	.295	.340	.398	120	2	2	14	5			-1	O/C1S	0.1
	NY-N	90	366	61	109	22	1	5	55	18	30	.298	.336	.404	128	10	10	65	42			-14	2CO3/S	0.0
	Yr	114	454	78	135	26	2	6	69	24	40	.297	.337	.403	126	12	12	79	47			-15		0.1
1893	NY-N	82	318	56	102	17	5	1	51	27	12	.321	.383	.415	113	6	6	67	40			4	CO/S31	1.1
1894	*NY-N	105	422	90	155	30	8	3	100	35	3	.367	.420	.498	123	16	16	108	42			-1	*1/C	1.3
1895	NY-N	82	319	52	100	21	3	1	66	24	12	.313	.365	.408	104	1	2	62	35			-1	12/3CM	0.2
1896	*Bal-N	118	487	116	165	29	4	1	101	42	15	.339	.400	.421	117	14	13	114	73			-11	*1/2	0.5
1897	*Bal-N	114	460	91	163	29	4	2	87	29		.354	.394	.448	124	16	16	108	62			5	*1	1.6
1898	Was-N	43	177	26	54	2	2	2	26	7		.305	.335	.373	106	1	1	26	9			-2	1/2M	0.0
	NY-N	82	297	42	84	15	3	1	43	12		.283	.317	.364	101	-2	-0	40	14			0	O1S/3C	0.0
	Yr	125	474	68	138	17	5	3	69	19		.291	.324	.367	103	-1	1	65	23			-2		0.0
1899	NY-N	118	448	55	134	15	7	1	76	33		.299	.353	.384	108	3	5	75	35			6	*1/C	1.2
1900	NY-N	133	505	69	135	24	1	1	66	34		.267	.314	.325	82	-14	-11	64	34			6	*1	-0.2
1901	Chi-N	75	285	21	66	9	2	0	39	7		.232	.258	.277	59	-16	-14	23	8			7	1	-0.6
1902	NY-N	49	186	21	56	13	0	1	19	10		.301	.340	.387	127	5	5	29	12			3	1	0.2
	Was-A	78	312	52	77	15	2	1	20	29		.247	.315	.317	77	-9	-9	35	6			-11	2/1OC	-1.6
1903	Bro-N	139	524	84	164	27	6	0	91	54		.313	.377	.387	124	15	17	93	34			2	*1	1.4
1904	Bro-N	8	22	2	5	1	0	0	2	6		.227	.393	.273	112	1	1	3	1			1	/1	0.2
	Phi-N	66	236	20	52	10	3	1	22	19		.220	.278	.301	84	-5	-4	22	4			4	1/2	-0.3
	Yr	74	258	22	57	11	3	1	24	25		.221	.290	.298	87	-5	-4	25	5			5		-0.1
1905	NY-A	1	3	0	0	0	0	0	0	0		.000	.000	.000	-90	-1	-1	0	0			-1	/1	-0.1
Total	17	1564	6039	971	1806	315	64	26	924	437	132	.299	.350	.385	108	48	62	1042	516			-13	*1CO2/S3	6.0

■ JOE DOYLE Doyle, Joseph K. b: Cincinnati, Ohio Deb: 4/20/1872

| 1872 | Nat-n | 9 | 42 | 7 | 12 | 0 | 0 | 0 | | 0 | | .286 | .286 | .286 | 66 | -1 | -3 | 4 | | | | | /S23 | -0.1 |

■ LARRY DOYLE Doyle, Lawrence Joseph "Laughing Larry" b: 7/31/1886, Caseyville, Ill. d: 3/1/74, Saranac Lake, N.Y. BL/TR, 5'10", 165 lbs. Deb: 7/22/07

1907	NY-N	69	227	16	59	3	0	0	16	20		.260	.320	.273	85	-3	-3	22	3			-22	*2	-2.7
1908	NY-N	104	377	65	116	16	9	0	33	22		.308	.346	.398	133	16	14	58	17			-10	*2	0.3
1909	NY-N	147	570	86	172	27	11	6	49	45		.302	.360	.419	140	26	25	96	31			-20	*2	0.5
1910	NY-N	151	575	97	164	21	14	8	69	71	26	.285	.369	.412	128	20	20	101	39			-17	*2	0.7
1911	*NY-N	143	526	102	163	25	**25**	13	77	71	39	.310	.397	.527	153	39	37	124	38			-24	*2	0.9
1912	*NY-N	143	558	98	184	33	8	10	90	56	20	.330	.393	.471	132	27	25	116	36			-8	*2	1.2
1913	*NY-N	132	482	67	135	25	6	5	73	59	29	.280	.364	.388	114	11	10	78	38			-14	*2	-0.6
1914	NY-N	145	539	87	140	19	8	5	63	58	25	.260	.343	.353	111	6	8	69	17			-19	*2	-1.2
1915	NY-N	150	591	86	**189**	40	10	4	70	32	28	**.320**	.358	.442	150	27	31	94	22	18	-4	-7	*2	2.3
1916	NY-N	113	441	55	118	24	10	2	47	27	23	.268	.316	.381	120	6	8	60	17			16	*2	3.0
	Chi-N	9	38	6	15	5	1	1	7	1	1	.395	.410	.658	203	5	5	11	2			5	/2	1.0
	Yr	122	479	61	133	29	11	3	54	28	24	.278	.323	.403	127	11	13	70	19			20		4.0
1917	Chi-N	135	476	48	121	19	5	6	61	48	28	.254	.323	.353	99	4	0	56	5			-2	*2	0.6
1918	NY-N	75	257	48	67	7	4	3	36	37	10	.261	.354	.354	118	6	7	34	10			-12	2	0.0
1919	NY-N	113	381	61	110	14	10	7	52	31	17	.289	.350	.433	136	16	16	59	12			2	*2	2.3
1920	NY-N	137	471	48	134	21	2	4	50	47	28	.285	.352	.363	107	4	5	61	11	9	-2	-26	*2	-2.1
Total	14	1766	6509	960	1887	299	123	74	793	625	274	.290	.356	.408	126	211	207	1040	298	27		-157	*2	6.2

■ DENNY DOYLE Doyle, Robert Dennis b: 1/17/44, Glasgow, Ky. BL/TR, 5'9", 175 lbs. Deb: 4/07/70

1970	Phi-N	112	413	46	86	10	7	2	16	33	64	.208	.267	.281	48	-31	-30	31	6	5	-1	-16	*2	-3.5
1971	Phi-N	95	342	34	79	12	1	3	24	19	31	.231	.281	.298	64	-16	-16	29	4	2	0	4	2	-0.8
1972	Phi-N	123	442	33	110	14	2	1	26	31	33	.249	.298	.296	68	-17	-19	38	6	7	-2	-9	*2	-2.3
1973	Phi-N	116	370	45	101	9	3	3	26	31	32	.273	.329	.338	83	-7	-8	41	1	3	-2	9	*2	0.4
1974	Cal-A	147	511	47	133	19	2	1	34	25	49	.260	.296	.311	79	-17	-13	46	6	7	-2	16	2/S	0.7
1975	Cal-A	8	15	0	1	0	0	0	0	1	1	.067	.125	.067	-48	-3	-3	0	0	0	0	2	/23	0.0
	*Bos-A	89	310	50	96	21	2	4	36	14	11	.310	.342	.429	107	6	3	43	5	7	-3	-31	2/3S	-2.8
	Yr	97	325	50	97	21	2	4	36	15	12	.298	.331	.412	102	3	0	42	5	7	-3	-29		-2.8
1976	Bos-A	117	432	51	108	15	5	0	26	22	39	.250	.286	.308	66	-15	-21	37	8	5	-1	-25	*2	-4.2
1977	Bos-A	137	455	54	109	13	6	2	49	29	50	.240	.291	.308	57	-23	-30	40	2	4	-2	-10	*2	-3.0
Total	8	944	3290	357	823	113	28	16	237	205	310	.250	.296	.316	70	-123	-138	305	38	40	-13	-60	2/3S	-15.5

■ DRAKE Drake Deb: 6/29/1884

| 1884 | Was-a | 2 | 7 | 0 | 2 | 1 | 0 | 0 | | 0 | | .286 | .286 | .429 | 150 | 0 | 0 | 1 | | | | -1 | /O | 0.0 |

■ DELOS DRAKE Drake, Delos Daniel b: 12/3/1886, Girard, Ohio d: 10/3/65, Findlay, Ohio BR/TL, 5'11.5", 170 lbs. Deb: 4/30/11

1911	Det-A	95	315	37	88	9	9	1	36	17		.279	.324	.375	90	-3	-5	44	20			-10	O/1	-2.1
1914	StL-F	138	514	51	129	18	8	3	42	31	57	.251	.295	.335	76	-14	-17	59	17			-1	*O1	-2.4
1915	StL-F	102	343	32	91	23	4	1	41	23	27	.265	.313	.364	95	-1	-3	43	6			-5	O/1	-1.2
Total	3	335	1172	120	308	50	21	5	119	71	84	.263	.308	.354	85	-18	-25	146	43			-16	O/1	-5.7

YEAR	TM/L	G	AB	R	H	2B	3B	HR	RBI	BB	SO	AVG	OBP	SLG	PRO+	BR	/A	RC	SB	CS	SBR	FR	POS	TPR

■ LARRY DRAKE   Drake, Larry Francis   b: 5/4/21, McKinney, Tex.   d: 7/14/85, Houston, Tex.   BL/TR, 6'1.5", 195 lbs.   Deb: 7/20/45

1945	Phi-A	1	2	0	0	0	0	0	0	0	2	.000	.000	.000	-99	-1	-1	0	0	0	0	0	/O	0.0
1948	Was-A	4	7	0	2	0	0	0	1	1	3	.286	.375	.286	79	-0	-0	1	0	0	0	-0	/O	0.0
Total	2	5	9	0	2	0	0	0	1	1	5	.222	.300	.222	44	-1	-1	1	0	0	0	0	/O	0.0

■ SAMMY DRAKE   Drake, Samuel Harrison   b: 10/7/34, Little Rock, Ark.   BB/TR, 5'11", 175 lbs.   Deb: 4/17/60

1960	Chi-N	15	15	5	1	0	0	0	0	1	4	.067	.125	.067	-46	-3	-3	0	0	0	0	-1	/32	-0.3
1961	Chi-N	13	5	1	0	0	0	0	0	1	1	.000	.167	.000	-50	-1	-1	0	0	0	0	1	/O	0.0
1962	NY-N	25	52	2	10	0	0	0	7	6	12	.192	.276	.192	28	-5	-5	3	0	0	0	-2	2/3	-0.5
Total	3	53	72	8	11	0	0	0	7	8	17	.153	.237	.153	8	-9	-9	3	0	0	0	-2	/23O	-0.8

■ SOLLY DRAKE   Drake, Solomon Louis   b: 10/23/30, Little Rock, Ark.   BB/TR, 6', 170 lbs.   Deb: 4/17/56

1956	Chi-N	65	215	29	55	9	1	2	15	23	35	.256	.331	.335	81	-6	-5	26	9	5	-0	5	O	-0.1
1959	LA-N	9	8	2	2	0	0	0	0	1	3	.250	.333	.250	54	-0	-1	1	1	0	0	-0	O	0.0
	Phi-N	67	62	10	9	1	0	0	3	8	15	.145	.243	.161	10	-8	-8	3	5	5	-2	3	O	-0.7
	Yr	76	70	12	11	1	0	0	3	9	18	.157	.253	.171	15	-8	-8	3	6	5	-1	2		-0.7
Total	2	141	285	41	66	10	1	2	18	32	53	.232	.311	.295	64	-14	-14	29	15	10	-2	8	/O	-0.8

■ JAKE DRAUBY   Drauby, Jacob C.   b: 1865, Harrisburg, Pa.   5'10", 163 lbs.   Deb: 10/03/1892

| 1892 | Was-N | 10 | 34 | 3 | 7 | 0 | 1 | 0 | 3 | 2 | 12 | .206 | .250 | .265 | 59 | -2 | -2 | 2 | 0 | | | -2 | 3 | -0.2 |

■ BILL DREESEN   Dreesen, William Richard   b: 7/26/04, New York, N.Y.   d: 11/9/71, Mt.Vernon, N.Y.   BL/TR, 5'7.5", 160 lbs.   Deb: 5/01/31

| 1931 | Bos-N | 48 | 180 | 38 | 40 | 10 | 4 | 1 | 10 | 23 | 23 | .222 | .310 | .339 | 77 | -6 | -6 | 20 | 1 | | | -7 | 3 | -0.9 |

■ BILL DRESCHER   Drescher, William Clayton "Dutch"   b: 5/23/21, Congers, N.Y.   d: 5/15/68, Hammerstraw, N.Y.   BL/TR, 6'2", 190 lbs.   Deb: 4/19/44

1944	NY-A	4	7	0	1	0	0	0	0	0	0	.143	.143	.143	-18	-1	-1	0	0	0	0	0	/C	0.0
1945	NY-A	48	126	10	34	3	1	0	15	8	5	.270	.313	.310	77	-3	-4	12	0	2	-1	-8	C	-1.0
1946	NY-A	5	6	0	2	1	0	0	1	0	0	.333	.333	.500	129	0	0	1	0	0	0	1	/C	0.1
Total	3	57	139	10	37	4	1	0	16	8	5	.266	.306	.309	75	-4	-5	13	0	2	-1	-7	/C	-0.9

■ CHUCK DRESSEN   Dressen, Charles Walter   b: 9/20/1898, Decatur, Ill.   d: 8/10/66, Detroit, Mich.   BR/TR, 5'5.5", 146 lbs.   Deb: 4/17/25   MC

1925	Cin-N	76	215	35	59	8	2	3	19	12	4	.274	.319	.372	78	-8	-7	26	5	3	-0	2	3/2O	-0.1
1926	Cin-N	127	474	76	126	27	11	4	48	49	31	.266	.338	.395	99	-2	-1	63	0			17	*3/SO	1.7
1927	Cin-N	144	548	78	160	36	10	2	55	71	32	.292	.376	.405	113	9	11	85	7			12	*3/S	3.1
1928	Cin-N	135	498	72	145	26	3	1	59	43	22	.291	.355	.361	89	-8	-7	64	10			-2	*3	-0.6
1929	Cin-N	110	401	49	98	22	3	1	36	41	21	.244	.321	.322	63	-25	-22	42	8			-20	3/2	-3.1
1930	Cin-N	33	19	0	4	0	0	0	1	1	3	.211	.250	.211	14	-3	-3	1	0			3	3/2	0.1
1931	Cin-N	5	15	0	1	0	0	0	0	1	1	.067	.125	.067	-50	-3	-3	0	0			0	/3	-0.2
1933	NY-N	16	45	3	10	4	0	0	3	1	4	.222	.239	.311	57	-3	-3	3	0			0	3	-0.1
Total	8	646	2215	313	603	123	29	11	221	219	118	.272	.343	.369	89	-43	-34	285	30	3		13	3/2OS	0.8

■ LEE DRESSEN   Dressen, Lee August   b: 7/23/1889, Ellinwood, Kan.   d: 6/30/31, Diller, Neb.   BL/TL, 6', 165 lbs.   Deb: 4/21/14

1914	StL-N	46	103	16	24	2	1	0	7	11	20	.233	.307	.272	73	-3	-3	9	2			-1	1	-0.5
1918	Det-A	31	107	10	19	1	2	0	3	21	10	.178	.323	.224	68	-3	-3	9	2			-3	1	-0.8
Total	2	77	210	26	43	3	3	0	10	32	30	.205	.316	.248	71	-7	-6	18	4			-5	/1	-1.3

■ CAMERON DREW   Drew, Cameron Steward   b: 2/12/64, Boston, Mass.   BL/TR, 6'5", 230 lbs.   Deb: 9/09/88

| 1988 | Hou-N | 7 | 16 | 1 | 3 | 0 | 1 | 0 | 1 | 0 | 1 | .188 | .188 | .313 | 43 | -1 | -1 | 1 | 0 | 0 | 0 | 1 | /O | 0.0 |

■ DAVE DREW   Drew, David   Deb: 5/14/1884

1884	Phi-U	2	9	1	4	0	0	0		0		.444	.444	.444	217	1	1	2	0			0	/P2S	0.1
	Was-U	13	53	8	16	1	2	0		1		.302	.315	.396	144	2	2	7	0			1	/S1O	0.3
	Yr	15	62	9	20	1	2	0		1		.323	.333	.403	154	3	3	9	0			1		0.4

■ FRANK DREWS   Drews, Frank John   b: 5/25/16, Buffalo, N.Y.   d: 4/22/72, Buffalo, N.Y.   BR/TR, 5'10", 175 lbs.   Deb: 8/13/44

1944	Bos-N	46	141	14	29	9	1	0	10	25	14	.206	.329	.284	71	-4	-5	15	0			1	2	0.0
1945	Bos-N	49	147	13	30	4	1	0	19	16	18	.204	.282	.245	47	-10	-10	12	0			5	2	-0.1
Total	2	95	288	27	59	13	2	0	29	41	32	.205	.306	.264	59	-14	-15	27	0			5	/2	-0.1

■ DAN DRIESSEN   Driessen, Daniel   b: 7/29/51, Hilton Head, S.C.   BL/TR, 5'11", 187 lbs.   Deb: 6/09/73

1973	*Cin-N	102	366	49	110	15	2	4	47	24	37	.301	.347	.385	108	1	3	48	8	3	1	-10	31/O	-0.9
1974	Cin-N	150	470	63	132	23	6	7	56	48	62	.281	.349	.400	111	6	6	66	10	5	0	-20	*31/O	-1.8
1975	Cin-N	88	210	38	59	8	1	7	38	35	30	.281	.389	.429	124	9	8	36	10	3	1	-3	1O	0.3
1976	*Cin-N	98	219	32	54	11	0	7	44	43	32	.247	.370	.402	116	7	6	35	14	1	4	-2	1O	0.5
1977	Cin-N	151	536	75	161	31	4	17	91	64	85	.300	.378	.468	123	20	19	95	31	13	2	-3	*1	0.9
1978	Cin-N	153	524	68	131	23	3	16	70	75	79	.250	.348	.397	108	7	7	76	28	9	3	3	*1	0.8
1979	*Cin-N	150	515	72	129	24	3	18	75	62	77	.250	.334	.414	102	2	2	74	11	5	0	-3	*1	-0.7
1980	Cin-N	154	524	81	139	36	1	14	74	93	68	.265	.382	.418	123	20	20	88	19	6	2	-4	*1	1.1
1981	Cin-N	82	233	35	55	14	0	7	33	40	31	.236	.353	.386	108	4	3	33	2	4	-2	-5	1	-0.6
1982	Cin-N	149	516	64	139	25	1	17	57	82	62	.269	.372	.421	119	17	15	85	11	6	0	-7	*1	0.1
1983	Cin-N	122	386	57	107	17	1	12	57	75	51	.277	.395	.420	121	16	15	66	4	4	-1	-2	*1	0.7
1984	Cin-N	81	218	27	61	13	0	7	28	37	25	.280	.384	.436	124	10	8	38	2	1	0	-3	1	0.3
	Mon-N	51	169	20	43	11	0	9	32	17	15	.254	.323	.479	128	4	5	24	0	1	-1	-1	1	0.2
	Yr	132	387	47	104	24	0	16	60	54	40	.269	.358	.454	126	14	14	63	2	2	-1	-5		0.5
1985	Mon-N	91	312	31	78	18	0	6	25	33	29	.250	.326	.365	99	-3	-1	36	2	2	-1	3	1	0.0
	SF-N	54	181	22	42	8	0	3	22	17	22	.232	.302	.326	79	-6	-5	19	0	0	0	-1	1	-0.7
	Yr	145	493	53	120	26	0	9	47	50	51	.243	.317	.351	92	-9	-5	55	2	2	-1	1		-0.7
1986	SF-N	15	16	2	3	2	0	0	0	4	4	.188	.350	.313	89	-0	-0	2	0	0	0	1	/1	0.0
	Hou-N	17	24	5	7	1	0	1	3	5	2	.292	.414	.458	144	2	2	5	0	0	0	-0	1	0.1
	Yr	32	40	7	10	3	0	1	3	9	6	.250	.388	.400	122	1	2	7	0	0	0	0		0.1
1987	*StL-N	24	60	5	14	2	0	1	11	7	8	.233	.313	.317	66	-3	-3	6	0	0	0	-0	1	-0.4
Total	15	1732	5479	746	1464	282	23	153	763	761	719	.267	.359	.411	113	111	111	830	154	63	8	-58	*13/O	-0.1

■ LEW DRILL   Drill, Lewis L   b: 5/9/1877, Browerville, Minn.   d: 7/4/69, St.Paul, Minn.   BR/TR, 5'6", 186 lbs.   Deb: 4/23/02

1902	Was-A	38	123	21	34	7	2	1	16	16		.276	.369	.390	112	3	2	19	0			-10	C/2O3	-0.4
	Bal-A	2	8	2	2	0	0	0	0	0		.250	.250	.250	38	-1	-1	1	0			1	/C1	0.0
	Was-A	33	98	12	24	3	2	0	13	10		.245	.327	.316	80	-2	-2	12	5			-4	C/O2	-0.3
	Yr	73	229	35	60	10	4	1	29	26		.262	.347	.354	96	-0	-1	32	5			-13		-0.7
1903	Was-A	51	154	11	39	9	3	0	23	15		.253	.320	.351	101	1	0	19	4			-4	C/1	0.2
1904	Was-A	46	142	17	38	7	2	1	11	21		.268	.362	.366	135	6	6	21	3			-7	CO	0.1
	Det-A	51	160	7	39	6	1	0	13	20		.244	.328	.294	103	1	1	17	2			-8	C/1	-0.1
	Yr	97	302	24	77	13	3	1	24	41		.255	.344	.328	118	7	8	37	5			-15		0.0
1905	Det-A	72	211	17	55	9	0	0	24	32		.261	.358	.303	112	5	5	27	7			-3	C	1.0
Total	4	293	896	87	231	41	10	2	100	114		.258	.344	.333	108	12	12	116	21			-35	C/O123	0.5

YEAR	TM/L	G	AB	R	H	2B	3B	HR	RBI	BB	SO	AVG	OBP	SLG	PRO+	BR	/A	RC	SB	CS	SBR	FR	POS	TPR

■ JIM DRISCOLL Driscoll, James Bernard b: 5/14/44, Medford, Mass. BL/TR, 5'11", 175 lbs. Deb: 6/17/70

YEAR	TM/L	G	AB	R	H	2B	3B	HR	RBI	BB	SO	AVG	OBP	SLG	PRO+	BR	/A	RC	SB	CS	SBR	FR	POS	TPR
1970	Oak-A	21	52	2	10	0	0	1	2	2	15	.192	.236	.250	35	-5	-4	3	0	0	0	-2	/2S	-0.5
1972	Tex-A	15	18	0	0	0	0	0	0	2	3	.000	.100	.000	-72	-4	-4	0	0	0	0	1	/23	-0.2
Total	2	36	70	2	10	0	0	1	2	4	18	.143	.200	.186	9	-8	-8	3	0	0	0	-1	/2S3	-0.7

■ DENNY DRISCOLL Driscoll, John F. b: 11/19/1855, Lowell, Mass. d: 7/11/1886, Lowell, Mass. BL/TL, 5'10.5", 160 lbs. Deb: 7/01/1880

YEAR	TM/L	G	AB	R	H	2B	3B	HR	RBI	BB	SO	AVG	OBP	SLG	PRO+	BR	/A	RC	SB	CS	SBR	FR	POS	TPR
1880	Buf-N	18	65	1	10	1	0	0	4	1	7	.154	.167	.169	14	-6	-6	2				-0	O/P	-0.5
1882	Pit-a	23	80	12	11	2	0	1		3		.138	.169	.200	25	-6	-6	3				-3	P	0.0
1883	Pit-a	41	148	19	27	2	1	0		4		.182	.204	.209	35	-11	-10	6				4	P/O3	0.0
1884	Lou-a	13	48	5	9	1	0	0		2		.188	.220	.208	45	-3	-3	2				2	P/O	0.0
1885	Buf-N	7	19	2	3	0	0	0	0	2	5	.158	.238	.158	29	-1	-1	1				-5	/2	-0.4
Total	5	102	360	39	60	6	1	1	4	12	12	.167	.194	.197	30	-27	-25	14				-2	/PO23	-0.9

■ PADDY DRISCOLL Driscoll, John Leo b: 1/11/1895, Evanston, Ill. d: 6/29/68, Chicago, Ill. BR/TR, 5'8.5", 155 lbs. Deb: 6/12/17

YEAR	TM/L	G	AB	R	H	2B	3B	HR	RBI	BB	SO	AVG	OBP	SLG	PRO+	BR	/A	RC	SB	CS	SBR	FR	POS	TPR
1917	Chi-N	13	28	2	3	1	0	0	3	2	6	.107	.167	.143	-4	-3	-4	1	2			2	/23S	0.0

■ MIKE DRISSEL Drissel, Michael F. b: 12/19/1864, St.Louis, Mo. d: 2/26/13, St.Louis, Mo. BR/TR, 5'11", Deb: 9/05/1885

YEAR	TM/L	G	AB	R	H	2B	3B	HR	RBI	BB	SO	AVG	OBP	SLG	PRO+	BR	/A	RC	SB	CS	SBR	FR	POS	TPR
1885	StL-a	6	20	0	1	0	0	0	0			.050	.050	.050	-65	-4	-4	0				2	/C	0.0

■ WALT DROPO Dropo, Walter "Moose" b: 1/30/23, Moosup, Conn. BR/TR, 6'5", 220 lbs. Deb: 4/19/49

YEAR	TM/L	G	AB	R	H	2B	3B	HR	RBI	BB	SO	AVG	OBP	SLG	PRO+	BR	/A	RC	SB	CS	SBR	FR	POS	TPR
1949	Bos-A	11	41	3	6	2	0	0	1	3	7	.146	.205	.195	6	-6	-6	1	0	0	0	-1	1	-0.6
1950	Bos-A	136	559	101	180	28	8	34	144	45	75	.322	.378	.583	130	32	24	122	0	0	0	-4	*1	1.2
1951	Bos-A	99	360	37	86	14	0	11	57	38	52	.239	.312	.369	76	-9	-14	40	0	0	0	-1	1	-1.5
1952	Bos-A	37	132	13	35	7	1	6	27	11	22	.265	.331	.470	112	3	2	18	0	0	0	-1	1	-0.1
	Det-A	115	459	56	128	17	3	23	70	26	63	.279	.320	.479	120	9	9	66	2	2	-1	-1	*1	0.0
	Yr	152	591	69	163	24	4	29	97	37	85	.276	.323	.477	118	12	11	84	2	2	-1	-2		-0.1
1953	Det-A	152	606	61	150	30	3	13	96	29	69	.248	.289	.371	78	-22	-21	61	2	0	1	12	*1	-1.1
1954	Det-A	107	320	27	90	14	2	4	44	24	41	.281	.331	.375	95	-3	-3	37	0	1	-1	1	1	-0.5
1955	Chi-A	141	453	55	127	15	2	19	79	42	71	.280	.344	.448	109	6	4	66	0	1	-1	-5	*1	-0.8
1956	Chi-A	125	361	42	96	13	1	8	52	37	51	.266	.339	.374	87	-6	-7	44	1	0	0	-3	*1	-1.3
1957	Chi-A	93	223	24	57	2	0	13	49	16	40	.256	.305	.439	101	-1	-1	26	0	1	-1	2	1	0.0
1958	Chi-A	28	52	3	10	1	0	2	8	5	11	.192	.276	.327	67	-3	-2	4	0	0	0	1	1	-0.1
	Cin-N	63	162	18	47	7	2	7	31	12	31	.290	.343	.488	111	3	2	25	0	0	0	1	1	0.1
1959	Cin-N	26	39	4	4	1	0	1	2	4	7	.103	.205	.205	9	-5	-5	1	0	0	0	2	1	-0.4
	Bal-A	62	151	17	42	9	0	6	21	12	20	.278	.331	.457	117	2	3	21	0	0	0	-2	1/3	0.1
1960	Bal-A	79	179	16	48	8	0	4	21	20	19	.268	.345	.380	97	-1	-1	22	0	1	-1	1	1/3	-0.5
1961	Bal-A	14	27	1	7	0	0	1	2	4	3	.259	.355	.370	96	-0	-0	3	0	0	1	1	1	0.0
Total	13	1288	4124	478	1113	168	22	152	704	328	582	.270	.327	.432	100	0	-15	559	5	6	-2	-0	*1/3	-5.5

■ KEITH DRUMRIGHT Drumright, Keith Alan b: 10/21/54, Springfield, Mo. BL/TR, 5'10", 170 lbs. Deb: 9/01/78

YEAR	TM/L	G	AB	R	H	2B	3B	HR	RBI	BB	SO	AVG	OBP	SLG	PRO+	BR	/A	RC	SB	CS	SBR	FR	POS	TPR
1978	Hou-N	17	55	5	9	0	0	0	2	3	4	.164	.207	.164	5	-7	-6	2	0	1	-1	-1	2	-0.7
1981	*Oak-A	31	86	8	25	1	1	0	11	4	4	.291	.322	.326	91	-1	-1	9	0	0	0	-3	2/D	-0.3
Total	2	48	141	13	34	1	1	0	13	7	8	.241	.277	.262	58	-8	-7	10	0	1	-1	-4	/2D	-1.0

■ JEAN DUBUC Dubuc, Jean Joseph Octave Arthur "Chauncey" b: 9/15/1888, St.Johnsbury, Vt. d: 8/28/58, Fort Myers, Fla. BR/TR, 5'10.5", 185 lbs. Deb: 6/25/08 C

YEAR	TM/L	G	AB	R	H	2B	3B	HR	RBI	BB	SO	AVG	OBP	SLG	PRO+	BR	/A	RC	SB	CS	SBR	FR	POS	TPR
1908	Cin-N	15	29	2	4	1	0	0				.138	.138	.172	-0	-3	-3	1	0			1	P	0.0
1909	Cin-N	19	18	1	3	0	0	0	0		2	.167	.250	.167	30	-1	-1	1	0			0	P	0.0
1912	Det-A	40	108	16	29	6	2	1	9		3	.269	.295	.389	98	-1	-1	12	0			4	P/O	0.0
1913	Det-A	68	135	17	36	5	3	2	11	2	17	.267	.277	.393	97	-2	-2	14	1			6	P/O	0.0
1914	Det-A	71	124	9	28	8	1	1	11	7	11	.226	.273	.331	79	-3	-4	12	1			4	P	0.0
1915	Det-A	60	112	7	23	2	1	0	14	8	15	.205	.258	.241	47	-7	-8	7	0			2	P	0.0
1916	Det-A	52	78	3	20	0	2	0	7	7	12	.256	.318	.308	85	-1	-1	8	0			5	P	0.0
1918	*Bos-A	5	6	0	1	0	0	0	0	1	2	.167	.286	.167	37	-0	-0	0	0			0	/P	0.0
1919	NY-N	37	42	2	6	1	1	0	2	0	6	.143	.143	.214	7	-5	-5	1	0			2	P	0.0
Total	9	367	652	57	150	23	10	4	56	30	63	.230	.266	.314	72	-25	-25	57	2			24	P/O	0.0

■ ROB DUCEY Ducey, Robert Thomas b: 5/24/65, Toronto, Ont., Can. BL/TR, 6'2", 175 lbs. Deb: 5/01/87

YEAR	TM/L	G	AB	R	H	2B	3B	HR	RBI	BB	SO	AVG	OBP	SLG	PRO+	BR	/A	RC	SB	CS	SBR	FR	POS	TPR
1987	Tor-A	34	48	12	9	1	0	1	6	8	10	.188	.304	.271	53	-3	-3	5	2	0	1	1	O/D	-0.1
1988	Tor-A	27	54	15	17	4	1	0	6	5	7	.315	.373	.426	123	2	2	9	1	0	0	0	O/D	0.2
1989	Tor-A	41	76	5	16	4	0	0	7	9	25	.211	.294	.263	59	-4	-4	6	2	1	0	4	O/D	0.0
1990	Tor-A	19	53	7	16	5	0	0	7	7	15	.302	.393	.396	124	2	2	9	1	1	-0	-0	O	0.1
Total	4	121	231	39	58	14	1	1	26	29	57	.251	.337	.333	87	-4	-3	29	6	2	1	5	O/D	0.2

■ JOHN DUDRA Dudra, John Joseph b: 5/27/16, Assumption, Ill. d: 10/24/65, Pana, Ill. BR/TR, 5'11.5", 175 lbs. Deb: 9/07/41

YEAR	TM/L	G	AB	R	H	2B	3B	HR	RBI	BB	SO	AVG	OBP	SLG	PRO+	BR	/A	RC	SB	CS	SBR	FR	POS	TPR
1941	Bos-N	14	25	3	9	3	1	0	3	3	4	.360	.429	.560	185	3	3		0			0	/231S	0.3

■ PAT DUFF Duff, Patrick Henry b: 5/6/1875, Providence, R.I. d: 9/11/25, Providence, R.I. TR, Deb: 4/16/06

YEAR	TM/L	G	AB	R	H	2B	3B	HR	RBI	BB	SO	AVG	OBP	SLG	PRO+	BR	/A	RC	SB	CS	SBR	FR	POS	TPR
1906	Was-A	1	1	0	0	0	0	0	0			.000	.000	.000	-99	-0	-0	0	0			0	H	0.0

■ CHARLIE DUFFEE Duffee, Charles Edward "Home Run" b: 1/27/1866, Mobile, Ala. d: 12/24/1894, Mobile, Ala. BR, Deb: 4/17/1889

YEAR	TM/L	G	AB	R	H	2B	3B	HR	RBI	BB	SO	AVG	OBP	SLG	PRO+	BR	/A	RC	SB	CS	SBR	FR	POS	TPR
1889	StL-a	137	509	93	124	15	12	15	86	60	81	.244	.327	.409	98	6	-5	77	21			18	*O/32	0.6
1890	StL-a	98	378	68	104	11	7	3		37		.275	.343	.365	97	5	-4	56	20			10	O3/S	0.3
1891	Col-a	137	552	86	166	28	4	10	90	42	36	.301	.353	.420	132	15	20	99	41			11	*O/3S	2.2
1892	Was-N	132	492	64	122	12	11	6	51	36	33	.248	.302	.354	103	-1	1	63	28			19	*O/31	1.4
1893	Cin-N	4	12	3	2	1	0	0	0	5	0	.167	.412	.250	78	-0	-0	1	0			-2	/O	-0.1
Total	5	508	1943	314	518	67	34	34	227	180	150	.267	.332	.389	108	25	12	295	110			56	O/31S2	4.4

■ ED DUFFY Duffy, Edward Charles b: 1844, Ireland d: 6/21/1889, Brooklyn, N.Y. 5'7.5", 152 lbs. Deb: 5/08/1871

YEAR	TM/L	G	AB	R	H	2B	3B	HR	RBI	BB	SO	AVG	OBP	SLG	PRO+	BR	/A	RC	SB	CS	SBR	FR	POS	TPR
1871	Chi-n	26	121	30	28	5	0	0	15	3	2	.231	.250	.273	45	-8	-11	11	11				S/3	-0.6

■ FRANK DUFFY Duffy, Frank Thomas b: 10/14/46, Oakland, Cal. BR/TR, 6'1", 180 lbs. Deb: 9/04/70

YEAR	TM/L	G	AB	R	H	2B	3B	HR	RBI	BB	SO	AVG	OBP	SLG	PRO+	BR	/A	RC	SB	CS	SBR	FR	POS	TPR
1970	Cin-N	6	11	1	2	2	0	0	0	1	2	.182	.250	.364	62	-1	-1	1	-1	0	0	1	/S	0.1
1971	Cin-N	13	16	0	3	1	0	0	1	1	2	.188	.235	.250	38	-1	-1	1	0	0	0	5	S	0.5
	*SF-N	21	28	4	5	0	0	0	2	0	10	.179	.179	.179	1	-4	-4	1	0	0	0	5	/S23	0.2
	Yr	34	44	4	8	1	0	0	3	1	12	.182	.200	.205	15	-5	-5	2	0	0	0	10		0.7
1972	Cle-A	130	385	23	92	16	4	5	27	31	54	.239	.297	.325	82	-7	-9	36	6	2	1	3	*S	0.9
1973	Cle-A	116	361	34	95	16	4	8	50	25	41	.263	.314	.396	97	-1	-2	41	6	6	-2	12	*S	2.4
1974	Cle-A	158	549	62	128	18	0	8	48	30	64	.233	.273	.310	68	-24	-23	45	7	8	-3	-7	*S	-2.1
1975	Cle-A	146	482	44	117	22	2	1	47	27	60	.243	.286	.303	66	-22	-22	39	10	10	-3	14	*S	0.4
1976	Cle-A	133	392	38	83	11	2	2	30	29	50	.212	.270	.265	58	-21	-21	29	10	4	0	11	*S	0.1
1977	Cle-A	122	334	30	67	13	2	4	31	21	47	.201	.248	.287	47	-26	-24	24	8	3	1	3	*S	-0.5
1978	Bos-A	64	104	14	27	5	0	0	6	4	16	.260	.306	.308	66	-4	-5	10	1	1	-0	6	3S2/D	0.3
1979	Bos-A	6	3	0	0	0	0	0	0	0	1	.000	.000	.000	-95	-1	-1	0	0	0	0	1	/21	0.0
Total	10	915	2665	248	619	104	14	26	240	171	342	.232	.281	.311	69	-111	-111	227	49	30	-3	53	S/32D1	2.3

YEAR	TM/L	G	AB	R	H	2B	3B	HR	RBI	BB	SO	AVG	OBP	SLG	PRO+	BR	/A	RC	SB	CS	SBR	FR	POS	TPR

■ HUGH DUFFY   Duffy, Hugh b: 11/26/1866, Cranston, R.I. d: 10/19/54, Boston, Mass. BR/TR, 5'7", 168 lbs. Deb: 6/23/1888 MCH

YEAR	TM/L	G	AB	R	H	2B	3B	HR	RBI	BB	SO	AVG	OBP	SLG	PRO+	BR	/A	RC	SB	CS	SBR	FR	POS	TPR
1888	Chi-N	71	298	60	84	10	4	7	41	9	32	.282	.305	.413	121	9	6	43	13			4	O/S3	1.0
1889	Chi-N	136	584	144	172	21	7	12	89	46	30	.295	.348	.416	109	10	5	105	52			-15	*OS	-1.2
1890	Chi-P	138	596	**161**	**191**	36	16	7	82	59	20	.320	.384	.470	124	24	19	**141**	78			13	*O	2.1
1891	Bos-a	127	536	134	180	20	8	9	**110**	61	29	.336	.408	.453	152	35	36	137	85			0	*O/3S	2.6
1892	*Bos-N	147	612	125	184	28	12	5	81	60	37	.301	.364	.410	125	26	18	113	51			-9	*O/3	0.3
1893	Bos-N	131	560	147	203	23	7	6	118	50	13	.363	.416	.461	125	28	20	129	44			-2	*O	1.0
1894	Bos-N	125	539	160	**237**	51	16	18	145	66	15	**.440**	**.502**	**.694**	174	77	68	217	48			5	*O/S	4.9
1895	Bos-N	130	531	110	187	30	6	9	100	63	16	.352	.425	.482	126	30	22	130	42			6	*O	1.3
1896	Bos-N	131	527	97	158	16	8	5	113	52	19	.300	.365	.389	95	1	-4	91	39			1	*O/2S	-0.9
1897	*Bos-N	134	550	130	187	25	10	11	129	52		.340	.403	.482	128	28	22	126	41			-1	*O/2S	1.0
1898	Bos-N	152	568	97	169	13	3	8	108	59		.298	.365	.373	109	12	7	90	29			2	*O/31C	0.0
1899	Bos-N	147	588	103	164	29	7	5	102	39		.279	.327	.378	87	-5	-13	83	26			-4	*O	-2.3
1900	Bos-N	55	181	27	55	5	4	2	31	16		.304	.360	.409	102	4	0	31	11			-1	O/2	-0.4
1901	Mil-A	79	285	40	86	15	9	2	45	16		.302	.341	.439	123	6	8	49	12			-6	OM	0.1
1904	Phi-N	18	46	10	13	1	1	0	5	13		.283	.441	.348	153	4	4	9	3			-3	OM	0.1
1905	Phi-N	15	40	7	12	2	1	0	3	1		.300	.317	.400	120	1	1	5	0			1	/OM	0.1
1906	Phi-N	1	1	0	0	0	0	0	0	0		.000	.000	.000	-99	-0	-0	0	0			0	HM	0.0
Total	17	1737	7042	1552	2282	325	119	106	1302	662	211	.324	.384	.449	123	288	219	1499	574			-9	*O/S23C1	9.7

■ JOE DUGAN   Dugan, Joseph Anthony "Jumping Joe" b: 5/12/1897, Mahanoy City, Pa. d: 7/7/82, Norwood, Mass. BR/TR, 5'11", 160 lbs. Deb: 7/05/17

YEAR	TM/L	G	AB	R	H	2B	3B	HR	RBI	BB	SO	AVG	OBP	SLG	PRO+	BR	/A	RC	SB	CS	SBR	FR	POS	TPR
1917	Phi-A	43	134	9	26	8	0	0	16	3	16	.194	.229	.254	48	-9	-9	8	0			1	S/2	-0.6
1918	Phi-A	121	411	26	80	11	3	3	34	16	55	.195	.230	.258	47	-28	-28	25	4			17	S2	-0.3
1919	Phi-A	104	387	25	105	17	2	1	30	11	30	.271	.300	.333	77	-12	-13	40	9			1	S/23	-0.2
1920	Phi-A	123	491	65	158	40	5	3	60	19	51	.322	.351	.442	108	5	4	73	5	8	-3	-1	3S2	0.0
1921	Phi-A	119	461	54	136	22	6	10	58	28	45	.295	.342	.434	96	-4	-4	69	5	1	1	-25	*3	-1.7
1922	Bos-A	84	341	45	98	22	3	3	38	9	28	.287	.308	.396	83	-10	-10	40	2	3	-1	-9	3S	-1.0
	*NY-A	60	252	44	72	9	1	3	25	13	21	.286	.331	.365	79	-7	-8	31	1	0	0	-9	3	-1.0
	Yr	144	593	89	170	31	4	6	63	22	49	.287	.318	.383	81	-17	-18	72	3	3	-1	-18		-2.0
1923	*NY-A	146	644	111	182	30	7	7	67	25	41	.283	.311	.384	81	-19	-20	76	4	2	0	-12	*3	-1.3
1924	NY-A	148	610	105	184	31	7	3	56	31	32	.302	.341	.390	88	-12	-12	81	1	3	-2	-14	*3/2	-1.4
1925	NY-A	102	404	50	118	19	4	0	31	19	20	.292	.330	.359	76	-16	-15	47	2	4	-2	7	3	-0.3
1926	*NY-A	123	434	39	125	19	5	1	64	25	16	.288	.328	.362	81	-13	-12	52	2	4	-2	-16	*3	-1.8
1927	*NY-A	112	387	44	104	24	3	2	43	27	37	.269	.321	.362	79	-14	-12	43	1	4	-2	-19	*3	-2.4
1928	*NY-A	94	312	33	86	15	0	6	34	16	15	.276	.317	.381	85	-8	-7	38	1	0	0	-18	3/2	-2.2
1929	Bos-N	60	125	14	38	10	0	0	15	8	8	.304	.346	.384	84	-4	-3	16	0			-8	3/S2O	-0.7
1931	Det-A	8	17	1	4	0	0	0	0	0	3	.235	.235	.235	23	-2	-2	1	0	0	0	-1	/3	-0.1
Total	14	1447	5410	665	1516	277	46	42	571	250	418	.280	.317	.372	82	-154	-151	641	37	29		-105	*3S/2O	-14.3

■ BILL DUGAN   Dugan, William H. b: 1864, New York, N.Y. d: 7/24/21, New York, N.Y. Deb: 8/05/1884

YEAR	TM/L	G	AB	R	H	2B	3B	HR	RBI	BB	SO	AVG	OBP	SLG	PRO+	BR	/A	RC	SB	CS	SBR	FR	POS	TPR
1884	Ric-a	9	28	4	2	1	0	0		0		.071	.103	.107	-31	-4	-4	0				-1	/C	-0.3
	KC-U	3	6	0	0	0	0	0		0		.000	.000	.000	-99	-1	-1	0	0			-1	/O	-0.1

■ GUS DUGAS   Dugas, Augustin Joseph b: 3/24/07, St.Jean Dematha, Que., Canada BL/TL, 5'9", 165 lbs. Deb: 9/17/30

YEAR	TM/L	G	AB	R	H	2B	3B	HR	RBI	BB	SO	AVG	OBP	SLG	PRO+	BR	/A	RC	SB	CS	SBR	FR	POS	TPR
1930	Pit-N	9	31	8	9	2	0	1	7	4		.290	.421	.355	90	-0	-0	5	0			-1	/O	0.0
1932	Pit-N	55	97	13	23	3	3	3	12	7	11	.237	.288	.423	90	-2	-2	12	0			-1	O	-0.3
1933	Phi-N	37	71	4	12	3	0	0	9	1	9	.169	.181	.211	10	-8	-9	2	0			0	1/O	-0.9
1934	Was-A	24	19	2	1	1	0	0	1	3	3	.053	.182	.105	-25	-4	-4	0	0	0	0	1	/O	-0.2
Total	4	125	218	27	45	9	3	3	23	18	27	.206	.267	.317	54	-14	-14	20	0	0		-1	/O1	-1.4

■ DAN DUGDALE   Dugdale, Daniel Edward b: 10/28/1864, Peoria, Ill. d: 3/9/34, Seattle, Wash. Deb: 5/20/1886

YEAR	TM/L	G	AB	R	H	2B	3B	HR	RBI	BB	SO	AVG	OBP	SLG	PRO+	BR	/A	RC	SB	CS	SBR	FR	POS	TPR
1886	KC-N	12	40	4	7	0	0	0	2	2	13	.175	.214	.175	18	-4	-4	2	1			-0	/CO	-0.3
1894	Was-N	38	134	19	32	4	2	0	16	13	14	.239	.306	.299	49	-11	-10	15	7			-5	C/3O	-0.9
Total	2	50	174	23	39	4	2	0	18	15	27	.224	.286	.270	43	-15	-15	17	8			-5	/CO3	-1.2

■ OSCAR DUGEY   Dugey, Oscar Joseph "Jake" b: 10/25/1887, Palestine, Tex. d: 1/1/66, Dallas, Tex. BR/TR, 5'8", 160 lbs. Deb: 9/13/13 C

YEAR	TM/L	G	AB	R	H	2B	3B	HR	RBI	BB	SO	AVG	OBP	SLG	PRO+	BR	/A	RC	SB	CS	SBR	FR	POS	TPR
1913	Bos-N	5	8	1	2	0	0	0	0	1	1	.250	.333	.250	67	-0	-0	1	0			-1	/32S	0.0
1914	Bos-N	58	109	17	21	2	0	1	10	10	15	.193	.267	.239	51	-7	-6	9	10			-1	O2/3	-0.8
1915	*Phi-N	42	39	4	6	1	0	0	0	7	5	.154	.283	.179	41	-2	-3	2	2	1	0	3	2	0.0
1916	Phi-N	41	50	9	11	3	0	0	1	9	8	.220	.339	.280	88	-0	-0	6	3			3	2	0.3
1917	Phi-N	44	72	12	14	4	1	0	9	4	9	.194	.237	.278	55	-4	-4	5	2			0	2/O	-0.3
1920	Bos-N	5	0	2	0	0	0	0	0	0	0	—	—	—	—	0	0	0	0	0	0	0	R	0.0
Total	6	195	278	45	54	10	1	1	20	31	38	.194	.277	.248	58	-13	-14	23	17	1		4	/2O3S	-0.8

■ JIM DUGGAN   Duggan, James Elmer "Mer" b: 6/3/1884, Whiteland, Ind. d: 12/5/51, Indianapolis, Ind. BL/TL, 5'10", 165 lbs. Deb: 6/29/11

YEAR	TM/L	G	AB	R	H	2B	3B	HR	RBI	BB	SO	AVG	OBP	SLG	PRO+	BR	/A	RC	SB	CS	SBR	FR	POS	TPR
1911	StL-A	1	4	1	0	0	0	0	1	1		.000	.200	.000	-44	-1	-1	0	0			0	/1	0.0

■ TOM DUNBAR   Dunbar, Thomas Jerome b: 11/24/59, Graniteville, S.C. BL/TL, 6'2", 192 lbs. Deb: 9/07/83

YEAR	TM/L	G	AB	R	H	2B	3B	HR	RBI	BB	SO	AVG	OBP	SLG	PRO+	BR	/A	RC	SB	CS	SBR	FR	POS	TPR
1983	Tex-A	12	24	3	6	0	0	0	3	5	7	.250	.379	.250	79	-0	-0	3	3	1	0	-1	/OD	-0.1
1984	Tex-A	34	97	9	25	2	0	2	10	6	16	.258	.301	.340	75	-3	-3	10	1	0	0	-3	O/D	-0.5
1985	Tex-A	45	104	7	21	4	0	1	5	12	9	.202	.291	.269	54	-6	-6	7	0	3	-2	-0	DO	-0.8
Total	3	91	225	19	52	6	0	3	18	23	32	.231	.305	.298	66	-10	-10	20	4	4	-1	-4	/OD	-1.4

■ DAVE DUNCAN   Duncan, David Edwin b: 9/26/45, Dallas, Tex. BR/TR, 6'2", 190 lbs. Deb: 5/06/64 C

YEAR	TM/L	G	AB	R	H	2B	3B	HR	RBI	BB	SO	AVG	OBP	SLG	PRO+	BR	/A	RC	SB	CS	SBR	FR	POS	TPR
1964	KC-A	25	53	2	9	0	1	1	5	2	20	.170	.200	.264	27	-5	-5	3	0	0	0	4	C	0.0
1967	KC-A	34	101	9	19	4	0	5	11	4	50	.188	.219	.376	75	-4	-4	8	0	1	-1	-6	C	-0.8
1968	Oak-A	82	246	15	47	4	0	7	28	25	68	.191	.268	.293	73	-9	-8	19	1	2	-1	1	C	-0.4
1969	Oak-A	58	127	11	16	3	0	3	22	19	41	.126	.240	.220	31	-12	-11	7	0	0	0	-11	C	-2.0
1970	Oak-A	86	232	21	60	7	0	10	29	22	38	.259	.323	.418	107	0	1	31	0	0	0	3	C	0.6
1971	*Oak-A	103	363	39	92	13	1	15	40	28	77	.253	.309	.419	106	1	2	47	1	1	-0	3	*C	0.9
1972	*Oak-A	121	403	39	88	13	0	19	59	34	68	.218	.287	.392	106	-1	1	43	0	2	-1	2	*C	0.3
1973	Cle-A	95	344	43	80	11	1	17	43	35	86	.233	.309	.419	101	1	0	44	3	3	1	1	C/D	0.2
1974	Cle-A	136	425	45	85	10	1	16	46	42	91	.200	.275	.341	77	-14	-13	38	0	4	-2	-9	*C/1D	-2.0
1975	Bal-A	96	307	30	63	7	0	12	41	16	82	.205	.247	.345	70	-15	-13	25	0	0	0	-7	C	-1.7
1976	Bal-A	93	284	20	58	7	0	4	17	25	56	.204	.271	.271	63	-15	-12	21	0	0	0	-12	C	-2.1
Total	11	929	2885	274	617	79	4	109	341	252	677	.214	.280	.357	85	-72	-62	285	5	13	-6	-32	C/D1	-7.0

■ JIM DUNCAN   Duncan, James William b: 7/1/1871, Saltsburg, Pa. d: 10/16/01, Foxburg, Pa. BR/TR, 5'8", 140 lbs. Deb: 7/18/1899

YEAR	TM/L	G	AB	R	H	2B	3B	HR	RBI	BB	SO	AVG	OBP	SLG	PRO+	BR	/A	RC	SB	CS	SBR	FR	POS	TPR
1899	Was-N	15	47	5	11	2	0	0	5	4		.234	.294	.277	60	-3	-2	4	1			-0	C	-0.1
	Cle-N	31	105	9	24	2	3	2	9	4		.229	.257	.362	76	-5	-4	10	0			-4	1C	-0.5
	Yr	46	152	14	35	4	3	2	14	8		.230	.269	.336	71	-7	-6	14	1			-4		-0.6

■ PAT DUNCAN   Duncan, Louis Baird b: 10/6/1893, Coalton, Ohio d: 7/17/60, Columbus, Ohio BR/TR, 5'9", 170 lbs. Deb: 7/16/15

YEAR	TM/L	G	AB	R	H	2B	3B	HR	RBI	BB	SO	AVG	OBP	SLG	PRO+	BR	/A	RC	SB	CS	SBR	FR	POS	TPR
1915	Pit-N	3	5	0	1	0	0	0	0	0	1	.200	.200	.200	22	-0	-0	0	0			-0	/O	0.0
1919	*Cin-N	31	90	9	22	3	3	2	17	8	7	.244	.306	.411	118	1	2	12	2			-0	O	0.0

YEAR	TM/L	G	AB	R	H	2B	3B	HR	RBI	BB	SO	AVG	OBP	SLG	PRO+	BR	/A	RC	SB	CS	SBR	FR	POS	TPR
1920	Cin-N	154	576	75	170	16	11	2	83	42	42	.295	.350	.372	109	6	7	74	18	18	-5	3	*O	-0.4
1921	Cin-N	145	532	57	164	27	10	2	60	44	33	.308	.367	.408	110	4	8	76	7	18	-9	10	*O	0.2
1922	Cin-N	151	607	94	199	44	12	8	94	40	31	.328	.370	.479	120	14	16	97	12	28	-13	0	*O	-0.2
1923	Cin-N	147	566	92	185	26	8	7	83	30	27	.327	.363	.438	113	8	9	87	15	13	-3	-4	*O	-0.2
1924	Cin-N	96	319	34	86	21	6	2	37	20	23	.270	.313	.392	89	-6	-6	37	1	7	-4	-16	O	-2.6
Total	7	727	2695	361	827	137	50	23	374	184	164	.307	.355	.420	110	27	36	383	55	84		-7	O	-3.2

■ MARIANO DUNCAN
Duncan, Mariano (Nalasco) b: 3/13/63, San Pedro De Macoris, D.R. BB/TR, 6', 160 lbs. Deb: 4/09/85

YEAR	TM/L	G	AB	R	H	2B	3B	HR	RBI	BB	SO	AVG	OBP	SLG	PRO+	BR	/A	RC	SB	CS	SBR	FR	POS	TPR
1985	*LA-N	142	562	74	137	24	6	6	39	38	113	.244	.295	.340	79	-18	-16	60	38	8	7	-8	*S2	-0.7
1986	LA-N	109	407	47	93	7	0	8	30	30	78	.229	.285	.305	67	-21	-17	38	48	13	7	-2	*S	-0.2
1987	LA-N	76	261	31	56	8	1	6	18	17	62	.215	.268	.322	57	-17	-16	24	11	1	3	-0	S/2O	-0.5
1989	LA-N	49	84	9	21	5	1	0	8	0	15	.250	.267	.333	72	-3	-3	7	3	3	-1	2	S/2O	0.0
	Cin-N	45	174	23	43	10	1	3	13	8	36	.247	.292	.368	85	-3	-4	19	6	2	1	-7	S/2	-0.8
	Yr	94	258	32	64	15	2	3	21	8	51	.248	.284	.357	81	-7	-7	26	9	5	-0	-5		-0.8
1990	*Cin-N	125	435	67	133	22	11	10	55	24	67	.306	.348	.476	121	13	12	69	13	7	-0	1	*2S/O	1.4
Total	5	546	1923	251	483	76	20	33	163	117	371	.251	.300	.363	84	-49	-45	216	119	34	15	-15	S2/O	-0.8

■ TAYLOR DUNCAN
Duncan, Taylor McDowell b: 5/12/53, Memphis, Tenn. BR/TR, 6', 170 lbs. Deb: 9/15/77

YEAR	TM/L	G	AB	R	H	2B	3B	HR	RBI	BB	SO	AVG	OBP	SLG	PRO+	BR	/A	RC	SB	CS	SBR	FR	POS	TPR
1977	StL-N	8	12	2	4	0	0	1	2	2	1	.333	.429	.583	172	1	1	3	0	0	0	-2	/3	0.0
1978	Oak-A	104	319	25	82	15	2	2	37	19	38	.257	.299	.335	82	-10	-8	32	1	2	-1	-21	32/SD	-3.0
Total	2	112	331	27	86	15	2	3	39	21	39	.260	.304	.344	86	-8	-6	35	1	2	-1	-23	/32DS	-3.0

■ VERN DUNCAN
Duncan, Vernon Van Duke b: 1/6/1890, Clayton, N.C. d: 6/1/54, Daytona Beach, Fla BL/TR, 5'9", 155 lbs. Deb: 9/11/13

YEAR	TM/L	G	AB	R	H	2B	3B	HR	RBI	BB	SO	AVG	OBP	SLG	PRO+	BR	/A	RC	SB	CS	SBR	FR	POS	TPR
1913	Phi-N	8	12	3	5	1	0	0	1	0	3	.417	.417	.500	155	1	1	2	0			0	/O	0.1
1914	Bal-F	157	557	99	160	20	8	2	53	67	55	.287	.375	.363	108	11	9	87	13			-3	*O/32	-0.1
1915	Bal-F	146	531	68	142	18	4	2	43	54	40	.267	.337	.328	94	-1	-3	71	19			0	*O3/2	-0.8
Total	3	311	1100	170	307	39	12	4	97	121	98	.279	.357	.347	102	12	7	160	32			-3	O/32	-0.8

■ GUS DUNDON
Dundon, Augustus Joseph b: 7/10/1874, Columbus, Ohio d: 9/1/40, Pittsburgh, Pa. BR/TR, 5'10", 165 lbs. Deb: 4/14/04

YEAR	TM/L	G	AB	R	H	2B	3B	HR	RBI	BB	SO	AVG	OBP	SLG	PRO+	BR	/A	RC	SB	CS	SBR	FR	POS	TPR
1904	Chi-A	108	373	40	85	9	3	0	36	30		.228	.285	.268	81	-9	-7	36	19			-15	*2/3S	-2.3
1905	Chi-A	106	364	30	70	7	3	0	22	23		.192	.240	.228	53	-20	-18	26	14			13	*2/S	-0.5
1906	Chi-A	33	96	7	13	1	0	0	4	11		.135	.224	.146	18	-9	-8	4	4			7	2S	-0.1
Total	3	247	833	77	168	17	6	0	62	64		.202	.259	.236	61	-37	-33	66	37			5	2/S3	-2.9

■ ED DUNDON
Dundon, Edward Joseph "Dummy" b: 7/10/1859, Columbus, Ohio d: 8/18/1893, Columbus, Ohio TR Deb: 6/02/1883

YEAR	TM/L	G	AB	R	H	2B	3B	HR	RBI	BB	SO	AVG	OBP	SLG	PRO+	BR	/A	RC	SB	CS	SBR	FR	POS	TPR
1883	Col-a	26	93	8	15	1	0	0			3	.161	.188	.172	18	-8	-7	3				1	P/O2	0.0
1884	Col-a	26	86	6	12	2	2	0			5	.140	.196	.209	37	-6	-5	4				4	OP/1	0.0
Total	2	52	179	14	27	3	2	0			8	.151	.191	.190	27	-14	-12	7				4	/PO12	0.0

■ SAM DUNGAN
Dungan, Samuel Morrison b: 1/29/1866, Ferndale, Cal. d: 3/16/39, Santa Ana, Cal. BR , 5'11", 180 lbs. Deb: 4/12/1892

YEAR	TM/L	G	AB	R	H	2B	3B	HR	RBI	BB	SO	AVG	OBP	SLG	PRO+	BR	/A	RC	SB	CS	SBR	FR	POS	TPR
1892	Chi-N	113	433	46	123	19	7	0	53	35	19	.284	.346	.360	115	8	8	61	15			-6	*O	-0.1
1893	Chi-N	107	465	86	138	23	7	2	64	29	8	.297	.350	.389	100	-2	-0	69	11			4	*O	0.0
1894	Chi-N	10	39	5	9	2	0	0	3	7	1	.231	.348	.282	52	-3	-3	4	1			0	O	-0.2
	Lou-N	8	32	6	11	1	0	0	3	4	1	.344	.417	.375	101	-0	0	6	2			0	/O	0.0
	Yr	18	71	11	20	3	0	0	6	11	2	.282	.378	.324	72	-3	-3	10	3			1		-0.2
1900	Chi-N	6	15	1	4	0	0	0	1	1		.267	.313	.267	65	-1	-1	1	0			-1	/O	-0.1
1901	Was-A	138	559	70	179	26	12	1	73	40		.320	.368	.415	121	14	16	92	9			-5	*O1	0.7
Total	5	382	1543	214	464	71	26	3	197	116	29	.301	.356	.386	109	17	20	233	38			-8	O/1	0.3

■ LEE DUNHAM
Dunham, Leland Huffield b: 6/9/02, Atlanta, Ill. d: 5/11/61, Atlanta, Ill. BL/TL, 5'11", 185 lbs. Deb: 4/17/26

YEAR	TM/L	G	AB	R	H	2B	3B	HR	RBI	BB	SO	AVG	OBP	SLG	PRO+	BR	/A	RC	SB	CS	SBR	FR	POS	TPR
1926	Phi-N	5	4	0	1	0	0	0	1	0	1	.250	.250	.250	33	-0	-0	0	0			0	/1	0.0

■ FRED DUNLAP
Dunlap, Frederick C. "Sure Shot" b: 5/21/1859, Philadelphia, Pa. d: 12/1/02, Philadelphia, Pa. BR/TR, 5'8", 165 lbs. Deb: 5/01/1880 M

YEAR	TM/L	G	AB	R	H	2B	3B	HR	RBI	BB	SO	AVG	OBP	SLG	PRO+	BR	/A	RC	SB	CS	SBR	FR	POS	TPR
1880	Cle-N	85	373	61	103	27	9	4	30	7	32	.276	.289	.429	143	15	16	47				8	*2	2.5
1881	Cle-N	80	351	60	114	25	4	3	24	18	24	.325	.358	.444	159	20	23	57				6	*2/3	2.9
1882	Cle-N	84	364	68	102	19	4	0	28	23	26	.280	.323	.354	121	7	9	43				18	*2M	2.5
1883	Cle-N	93	396	81	129	34	2	4	37	22	21	.326	.361	.452	147	21	22	66				9	*2/O	2.3
1884	StL-U	101	449	160	185	39	8	13		29		.412	.448	.621	249	72	70	128	0			31	*2/OPM	8.1
1885	StL-N	106	423	70	114	11	5	2	25	41	24	.270	.334	.333	124	9	13	48				25	*2M	4.5
1886	StL-N	71	285	53	76	15	2	3	32	28	30	.267	.332	.365	119	5	7	38	7			22	2	2.9
	Det-N	51	196	32	56	8	3	4	37	16	21	.286	.340	.418	126	7	6	33	13			3	2/O	1.0
	Yr	122	481	85	132	23	5	7	69	44	51	.274	.335	.387	122	11	13	71	20			25		3.9
1887	*Det-N	65	272	60	72	13	10	5	45	25	12	.265	.327	.441	109	4	3	45	15			22	2/P	2.4
1888	Pit-N	82	321	41	84	12	4	1	36	16	30	.262	.303	.333	114	2	5	41	24			13	2	2.0
1889	Pit-N	121	451	59	106	19	0	2	65	46	33	.235	.309	.290	77	-18	-10	48	21			1	*2M	0.1
1890	Pit-N	17	64	9	11	1	1	0	3	7	6	.172	.264	.219	48	-4	-3	4	2			-3	2	-0.4
	NY-P	1	4	1	2	0	0	0	0	0	0	.500	.500	.500	156	0	0	1	0			-1	/2	0.0
1891	Was-a	8	25	4	5	1	1	0	4	5	4	.200	.355	.320	101	0	0	4	3			-3	/2	0.0
Total	12	965	3974	759	1159	224	53	41	366	283	263	.292	.340	.406	136	141	160	604	85			149	2/OP3	30.7

■ GRANT DUNLAP
Dunlap, Grant Lester "Snap" b: 12/20/23, Stockton, Cal. BR/TR, 6'2", 180 lbs. Deb: 4/21/53

YEAR	TM/L	G	AB	R	H	2B	3B	HR	RBI	BB	SO	AVG	OBP	SLG	PRO+	BR	/A	RC	SB	CS	SBR	FR	POS	TPR
1953	StL-N	16	17	2	6	0	1	1	3	0	2	.353	.353	.647	154	1	1	3	0	0	0	0	/O	0.1

■ BILL DUNLAP
Dunlap, William James b: 5/1/09, Three Rivers, Mass. d: 11/29/80, Reading, Pa. BR/TR, 5'11", 170 lbs. Deb: 9/02/29

YEAR	TM/L	G	AB	R	H	2B	3B	HR	RBI	BB	SO	AVG	OBP	SLG	PRO+	BR	/A	RC	SB	CS	SBR	FR	POS	TPR
1929	Bos-N	10	29	6	12	0	1	1	4	4	4	.414	.485	.586	171	3	3	8	0			-1	/O	0.1
1930	Bos-N	16	29	3	2	1	0	0	0	0	6	.069	.069	.103	-61	-7	-7	0	0			1	/O	-0.6
Total	2	26	58	9	14	1	1	1	4	4	10	.241	.290	.345	57	-4	-4	8	0			-1	/O	-0.5

■ JACK DUNLEAVY
Dunleavy, John Francis b: 9/14/1879, Harrison, N.J. d: 4/12/44, S.Norwalk, Conn. TL , 5'6", 167 lbs. Deb: 5/30/03

YEAR	TM/L	G	AB	R	H	2B	3B	HR	RBI	BB	SO	AVG	OBP	SLG	PRO+	BR	/A	RC	SB	CS	SBR	FR	POS	TPR
1903	StL-N	61	193	23	48	3	3	0	10	13		.249	.296	.295	73	-7	-6	21	10			6	OP	0.1
1904	StL-N	51	172	23	40	7	3	1	14	16		.233	.298	.326	99	-1	-0	20	8			1	O/P	0.0
1905	StL-N	119	435	52	105	8	8	1	25	55		.241	.327	.303	93	-3	-2	51	15			2	*O/2	-0.8
Total	3	231	800	98	193	18	14	2	49	84		.241	.313	.306	89	-12	-8	91	33			8	O/P2	-0.7

■ GEORGE DUNLOP
Dunlop, George Henry b: 7/19/1888, Meriden, Conn. d: 12/12/72, Meriden, Conn. BR/TR, 5'10", 170 lbs. Deb: 9/09/13

YEAR	TM/L	G	AB	R	H	2B	3B	HR	RBI	BB	SO	AVG	OBP	SLG	PRO+	BR	/A	RC	SB	CS	SBR	FR	POS	TPR
1913	Cle-A	7	17	3	4	1	0	0	0	0	5	.235	.235	.294	53	-1	-1	1	0			1	/S3	0.1
1914	Cle-A	1	3	0	0	0	0	0	0	1	1	.000	.250	.000	-23	-0	-0	0	0			-1	/S	-0.1
Total	2	8	20	3	4	1	0	0	0	1	6	.200	.238	.250	42	-1	-2	1	0			0	/S3	0.0

■ JACK DUNN
Dunn, John Joseph b: 10/6/1872, Meadville, Pa. d: 10/22/28, Towson, Md. BR/TR, 5'9", Deb: 5/06/1897

YEAR	TM/L	G	AB	R	H	2B	3B	HR	RBI	BB	SO	AVG	OBP	SLG	PRO+	BR	/A	RC	SB	CS	SBR	FR	POS	TPR
1897	Bro-N	36	131	20	29	4	0	0	17	4		.221	.244	.252	35	-13	-11	9	2			-1	P/203S	0.0
1898	Bro-N	51	167	21	41	0	1	0	19	7		.246	.280	.257	57	-9	-9	13	3			-0	P/OS3	0.0
1899	Bro-N	43	122	21	30	2	1	0	16	3		.246	.270	.279	51	-8	-8	10	3			3	P/S	0.0
1900	Bro-N	10	26	2	6	0	0	0	1	1		.231	.259	.231	35	-2	-2	2	0			1	P	0.0
	Phi-N	10	33	3	10	1	0	0	5	0		.303	.303	.333	78	-1	-1	4	1			-0	P	0.0
	Yr	20	59	5	16	1	0	0	6	1		.271	.283	.288	58	-3	-3	5	1			1		0.0

YEAR	TM/L	G	AB	R	H	2B	3B	HR	RBI	BB	SO	AVG	OBP	SLG	PRO+	BR	/A	RC	SB	CS	SBR	FR	POS	TPR
1901	Phi-N	2	1	1	1	0	0	0	0	1		1.000	1.000	1.000	478	1	1	1	0			0	/P	0.0
	Bal-A	96	362	41	90	9	4	0	36	21		.249	.301	.296	65	-15	-18	38	10			-8	3S/P2O	-2.1
1902	NY-N	100	342	26	72	11	1	0	14	20		.211	.254	.249	57	-17	-17	28	13			-10	OS3/P2	-2.7
1903	NY-N	78	257	35	62	15	1	0	37	15		.241	.283	.307	67	-10	-12	27	12			-7	S32/O	-1.4
1904	NY-N	64	181	27	56	12	2	1	19	11		.309	.349	.414	132	7	7	31	11			-8	3S/2OP	0.0
Total	8	490	1622	197	397	54	10	1	164	83		.245	.285	.292	67	-67	-71	163	55			-29	3P/SO2	-6.2

■ JOE DUNN
Dunn, Joseph Edward b: 3/11/1885, Springfield, Ohio d: 3/19/44, Springfield, Ohio BR/TR, 5'9", 160 lbs. Deb: 9/12/08

YEAR	TM/L	G	AB	R	H	2B	3B	HR	RBI	BB	SO	AVG	OBP	SLG	PRO+	BR	/A	RC	SB	CS	SBR	FR	POS	TPR
1908	Bro-N	20	64	3	11	3	0	0	5	0		.172	.172	.219	27	-5	-5	2	0			7	C	0.4
1909	Bro-N	10	25	1	4	1	0	0	2	0		.160	.192	.200	22	-2	-2	1	0			-1	/C	-0.3
Total	2	30	89	4	15	4	0	0	7	0		.169	.178	.213	26	-8	-7	3	0			6	/C	0.1

■ RON DUNN
Dunn, Ronald Ray b: 1/24/50, Oklahoma City, Okla BR/TR, 5'11", 180 lbs. Deb: 9/03/74

YEAR	TM/L	G	AB	R	H	2B	3B	HR	RBI	BB	SO	AVG	OBP	SLG	PRO+	BR	/A	RC	SB	CS	SBR	FR	POS	TPR
1974	Chi-N	23	68	6	20	7	0	2	15	12	8	.294	.400	.485	141	5	4	12	0	0	0	-6	2/3	-0.1
1975	Chi-N	32	44	2	7	3	0	1	6	6	17	.159	.260	.295	52	-3	-3	4	0	0	0	0	3/O2	-0.2
Total	2	55	112	8	27	10	0	3	21	18	25	.241	.346	.411	106	2	1	16	0	0	0	-6	/23O	-0.3

■ STEVE DUNN
Dunn, Stephen b: 12/21/1858, London, Ont., Can. d: 5/5/33, London, Ont., Can. Deb: 9/27/1884

YEAR	TM/L	G	AB	R	H	2B	3B	HR	RBI	BB	SO	AVG	OBP	SLG	PRO+	BR	/A	RC	SB	CS	SBR	FR	POS	TPR
1884	StP-U	9	32	2	8	2	0	0				.250	.250	.313	164	-0	2	3	0			1	/13	0.2

■ SHAWON DUNSTON
Dunston, Shawon Donnell b: 3/21/63, Brooklyn, N.Y. BR/TR, 6'1", 175 lbs. Deb: 4/09/85

YEAR	TM/L	G	AB	R	H	2B	3B	HR	RBI	BB	SO	AVG	OBP	SLG	PRO+	BR	/A	RC	SB	CS	SBR	FR	POS	TPR
1985	Chi-N	74	250	40	65	12	4	4	18	19	42	.260	.312	.388	85	-2	-5	31	11	3	2	13	S	1.6
1986	Chi-N	150	581	66	145	37	3	17	68	21	114	.250	.279	.411	82	-12	-17	64	13	11	-3	20	*S	1.5
1987	Chi-N	95	346	40	85	18	3	5	22	10	68	.246	.269	.358	62	-18	-20	32	12	3	2	5	S	-0.2
1988	Chi-N	155	575	69	143	23	6	9	56	16	108	.249	.272	.357	76	-17	-20	55	30	9	4	6	*S	0.0
1989	*Chi-N	138	471	52	131	20	6	9	60	30	86	.278	.323	.403	99	3	-1	59	19	11	-1	7	*S	1.4
1990	Chi-N	146	545	73	143	22	8	17	66	15	87	.262	.286	.426	85	-8	-13	65	25	5	5	6	*S	1.0
Total	6	758	2768	340	712	132	30	61	290	111	505	.257	.288	.393	82	-54	-77	306	110	42	8	57	S	5.3

■ DAN DURAN
Duran, Daniel James b: 3/16/54, Palo Alto, Cal. BL/TL, 5'11", 190 lbs. Deb: 4/17/81

YEAR	TM/L	G	AB	R	H	2B	3B	HR	RBI	BB	SO	AVG	OBP	SLG	PRO+	BR	/A	RC	SB	CS	SBR	FR	POS	TPR
1981	Tex-A	13	16	1	4	0	0	0	0	1	1	.250	.294	.250	61	-1	-1	1	0	0	0	0	/O1	0.0

■ KID DURBIN
Durbin, Blaine Alphonsus b: 9/10/1886, Kansas d: 9/11/43, Kirkwood, Mo. BL/TL, 5'8", 155 lbs. Deb: 4/24/07

YEAR	TM/L	G	AB	R	H	2B	3B	HR	RBI	BB	SO	AVG	OBP	SLG	PRO+	BR	/A	RC	SB	CS	SBR	FR	POS	TPR
1907	Chi-N	11	18	2	6	0	0	0	0	1		.333	.368	.333	115	0	0	2	0			0	/PO	0.2
1908	Chi-N	14	28	3	7	1	0	0	0	2		.250	.300	.286	86	-0	-0	2	0			-3	O	-0.3
1909	Cin-N	6	5	1	1	0	0	0	0	1		.200	.333	.200	66	-0	-0	0	0			0	H	0.0
	Pit-N	1	0	0	0	0	0	0	0	0		—	—	—	—	0	0	0	0			0	R	0.0
	Yr	7	5	1	1	0	0	0	0	1		.200	.333	.200	65	-0	-0	0	0			0		0.0
Total	3	32	51	6	14	1	0	0	0	4		.275	.327	.294	94	0	-0	5	0			-2	/OP	-0.1

■ JOE DURHAM
Durham, Joseph Vann "Pop" b: 7/31/31, Newport News, Va. BR/TR, 6'1", 186 lbs. Deb: 9/10/54

YEAR	TM/L	G	AB	R	H	2B	3B	HR	RBI	BB	SO	AVG	OBP	SLG	PRO+	BR	/A	RC	SB	CS	SBR	FR	POS	TPR
1954	Bal-A	10	40	4	9	0	0	1	3	4	7	.225	.295	.300	68	-2	-2	4	0	0	0	-1	O	-0.2
1957	Bal-A	77	157	19	29	2	0	4	17	16	42	.185	.260	.274	49	-12	-11	11	1	1	-0	-3	O	-1.7
1959	StL-N	6	5	2	0	0	0	0	0	0	1	.000	.000	.000	-94	-1	-1	0	0	0	0	0	/O	0.0
Total	3	93	202	25	38	2	0	5	20	20	50	.188	.261	.272	49	-15	-14	15	1	1	-0	-4	/O	-1.9

■ LEON DURHAM
Durham, Leon b: 7/31/57, Cincinnati, Ohio BL/TL, 6'1", 185 lbs. Deb: 5/27/80

YEAR	TM/L	G	AB	R	H	2B	3B	HR	RBI	BB	SO	AVG	OBP	SLG	PRO+	BR	/A	RC	SB	CS	SBR	FR	POS	TPR
1980	StL-N	96	303	42	82	15	4	8	42	18	55	.271	.314	.426	101	1	-0	40	8	5	-1	4	O/1	0.0
1981	Chi-N	87	328	42	95	14	6	10	35	27	53	.290	.344	.460	121	10	9	50	25	11	1	-4	O/1	0.4
1982	Chi-N	148	539	84	168	33	7	22	90	66	77	.312	.389	.521	148	38	36	108	28	14	0	-9	*O/1	2.6
1983	Chi-N	100	337	58	87	18	8	12	55	66	83	.258	.384	.466	120	17	15	64	12	6	0	0	O/1	0.7
1984	*Chi-N	137	473	86	132	30	4	23	96	69	86	.279	.372	.505	132	28	23	90	16	8	0	6	*1	2.6
1985	Chi-N	153	542	58	153	32	2	21	75	64	99	.282	.358	.465	116	20	13	90	7	6	-2	3	*1	1.0
1986	Chi-N	141	484	66	127	18	7	20	65	67	98	.262	.353	.452	112	14	9	78	8	7	-2	-7	*1	-0.4
1987	Chi-N	131	439	70	120	22	1	27	63	51	92	.273	.349	.513	120	15	12	79	2	2	-1	-9	*1	-0.4
1988	Chi-N	24	73	10	16	6	1	3	6	9	20	.219	.305	.452	110	1	1	10	0	1	-1	1	*1	0.0
	Cin-N	21	51	4	11	3	0	1	2	5	12	.216	.286	.333	74	-2	-2	5	0	0	0	-1	1	-0.3
	Yr	45	124	14	27	9	1	4	8	14	32	.218	.297	.403	95	-0	-1	15	0	1	-1	-0		-0.3
1989	StL-N	29	18	2	1	1	0	0	1	2	4	.056	.190	.111	-11	-3	-3	0	0	1	-1	1	1	-0.3
Total	10	1067	3587	522	992	192	40	147	530	444	679	.277	.358	.475	122	140	113	615	106	61	-5	-21	1O	5.9

■ BOBBY DURNBAUGH
Durnbaugh, Robert Eugene "Scroggy" b: 1/15/33, Dayton, Ohio BR/TR, 5'8", 170 lbs. Deb: 9/22/57

YEAR	TM/L	G	AB	R	H	2B	3B	HR	RBI	BB	SO	AVG	OBP	SLG	PRO+	BR	/A	RC	SB	CS	SBR	FR	POS	TPR
1957	Cin-N	2	1	0	0	0	0	0	0	0	0	.000	.000	.000	-93	-0	-0	0	0	0	0	-0	/S	0.0

■ GEORGE DURNING
Durning, George Dewey b: 5/9/1898, Philadelphia, Pa. d: 4/18/86, Tampa, Fla. BR/TR, 5'11", 175 lbs. Deb: 9/12/25

YEAR	TM/L	G	AB	R	H	2B	3B	HR	RBI	BB	SO	AVG	OBP	SLG	PRO+	BR	/A	RC	SB	CS	SBR	FR	POS	TPR
1925	Phi-N	5	14	3	5	0	0	0	1	2	1	.357	.438	.357	97	0	0	2	0	0	0	2	/O	0.2

■ LEO DUROCHER
Durocher, Leo Ernest "Lippy" b: 7/27/05, W.Springfield, Mass. BR/TR, 5'10", 160 lbs. Deb: 10/02/25 MC

YEAR	TM/L	G	AB	R	H	2B	3B	HR	RBI	BB	SO	AVG	OBP	SLG	PRO+	BR	/A	RC	SB	CS	SBR	FR	POS	TPR
1925	NY-A	2	1	1	0	0	0	0	0	0	0	.000	.000	.000	-99	-0	-0	0	0	0	0	0	H	0.0
1928	*NY-A	102	296	46	80	8	6	0	31	22	52	.270	.327	.338	77	-11	-9	33	1	4	-2	12	2S	0.6
1929	NY-A	106	341	53	84	4	5	0	32	34	33	.246	.320	.287	62	-21	-17	34	3	1	0	26	S2	1.7
1930	Cin-N	119	354	31	86	15	3	3	32	20	45	.243	.287	.328	51	-30	-27	33	0			10	*S2	-0.4
1931	Cin-N	121	361	26	82	11	5	1	29	18	32	.227	.264	.294	53	-26	-23	29	0			-4	*S	-1.7
1932	Cin-N	143	457	43	99	22	5	1	33	36	40	.217	.275	.293	55	-30	-28	39	3			-14	*S	-2.9
1933	Cin-N	16	51	6	11	1	0	1	3	4	5	.216	.273	.294	63	-3	-2	4	0			6	S	0.4
	StL-N	123	395	45	102	18	4	2	41	26	32	.258	.306	.339	80	-8	-11	44	3			-1	*S	-0.3
	Yr	139	446	51	113	19	4	3	44	30	37	.253	.302	.334	78	-11	-13	44	3			5		0.1
1934	*StL-N	146	500	62	130	26	5	3	70	33	40	.260	.308	.350	71	-17	-21	53	2			1	*S	-1.6
1935	StL-N	143	513	62	136	23	5	8	78	29	46	.265	.304	.376	79	-14	-16	57	4			9	*S	0.0
1936	StL-N	136	510	57	146	22	3	1	58	29	47	.286	.327	.347	79	-13	-13	56	3			-11	*S	-1.4
1937	StL-N	135	477	46	97	11	3	1	47	38	36	.203	.262	.245	38	-40	-42	30	6			-11	*S	-4.1
1938	Bro-N	141	479	41	105	18	5	1	56	47	30	.219	.293	.284	58	-26	-28	42	3			-5	*S	-2.2
1939	Bro-N	116	390	42	108	21	6	1	34	27	24	.277	.325	.369	83	-8	-10	46	2			-7	*S/3M	-0.9
1940	Bro-N	62	160	10	37	9	1	1	14	12	13	.231	.285	.319	62	-7	-9	14	1			1	S/2M	-0.2
1941	Bro-N	18	42	2	12	1	0	0	6	1	3	.286	.302	.310	70	-2	-2	4	0			-0	S/2M	0.0
1943	Bro-N	6	18	1	4	0	0	0	1	1	2	.222	.263	.222	41	-1	-1	1	0			2	/SM	0.2
1945	Bro-N	2	5	1	1	0	0	0	2	0	0	.200	.200	.200	11	-1	-1	0	0			1	/2M	0.0
Total	17	1637	5350	575	1320	210	56	24	567	377	480	.247	.299	.320	66	-257	-260	513	31	5		17	*S/23	-12.8

■ RED DURRETT
Durrett, Elmer Charles b: 2/3/21, Sherman, Tex. BL/TL, 5'10", 170 lbs. Deb: 9/14/44

YEAR	TM/L	G	AB	R	H	2B	3B	HR	RBI	BB	SO	AVG	OBP	SLG	PRO+	BR	/A	RC	SB	CS	SBR	FR	POS	TPR
1944	Bro-N	11	32	3	5	1	0	1	1	7	10	.156	.308	.281	68	-1	-1	3	0			2	/O	0.0
1945	Bro-N	8	16	2	2	0	0	0	0	3	3	.125	.263	.125	10	-2	-2	1	0			-0	/O	-0.1
Total	2	19	48	5	7	1	0	1	1	10	13	.146	.293	.229	48	-3	-3	4	0			2	/O	-0.1

■ CEDRIC DURST
Durst, Cedric Montgomery b: 8/23/1896, Austin, Tex. d: 2/16/71, San Diego, Cal. BL/TL, 5'11", 160 lbs. Deb: 5/30/22

YEAR	TM/L	G	AB	R	H	2B	3B	HR	RBI	BB	SO	AVG	OBP	SLG	PRO+	BR	/A	RC	SB	CS	SBR	FR	POS	TPR
1922	StL-A	15	12	5	4	1	1	0	0	0	1	.333	.333	.417	91	-0	-0	2	0	0	0	-2	/O	-0.2

YEAR	TM/L	G	AB	R	H	2B	3B	HR	RBI	BB	SO	AVG	OBP	SLG	PRO+	BR	/A	RC	SB	CS	SBR	FR	POS	TPR
1923	StL-A	45	85	12	18	2	0	5	11	8	14	.212	.280	.412	76	-3	-4	10	0	0	0	-2	O/1	-0.6
1926	StL-A	80	219	32	52	7	5	3	16	22	19	.237	.310	.356	70	-9	-11	24	0	5	-3	2	O/1	-1.5
1927	*NY-A	65	129	18	32	4	3	0	25	6	7	.248	.281	.326	59	-8	-8	11	0	3	-2	-7	O/1	-1.7
1928	*NY-A	74	135	18	34	2	1	2	10	7	9	.252	.289	.326	63	-8	-7	13	1	0	0	-3	O/1	-1.0
1929	NY-A	92	202	32	52	3	3	4	31	15	25	.257	.309	.361	77	-8	-7	23	3	2	-0	-0	O/1	-0.9
1930	NY-A	8	19	0	3	1	0	0	5	0	1	.158	.158	.211	-8	-3	-3	1	0	0	0	-0	/O	-0.2
	Bos-A	102	302	29	74	19	5	1	24	17	24	.245	.290	.351	64	-18	-16	31	3	1	0	-2	O	-1.8
	Yr	110	321	29	77	20	5	1	29	17	25	.240	.282	.343	60	-21	-19	32	3	1	0	-2		-2.0
Total	7	481	1103	146	269	39	17	15	122	75	100	.244	.294	.351	67	-59	-56	114	7	11	-5	-14	O/1	-7.9

■ ERV DUSAK
Dusak, Ervin Frank "Four Sack" b: 7/29/20, Chicago, Ill. BR/TR, 6'2", 185 lbs. Deb: 9/18/41

YEAR	TM/L	G	AB	R	H	2B	3B	HR	RBI	BB	SO	AVG	OBP	SLG	PRO+	BR	/A	RC	SB	CS	SBR	FR	POS	TPR
1941	StL-N	6	14	1	2	0	0	0	3	2	6	.143	.250	.143	12	-2	-2	1	1			2	/O	0.0
1942	StL-N	12	27	4	5	3	0	0	3	3	7	.185	.267	.296	60	-1	-1	2	0			2	/O3	0.0
1946	*StL-N	100	275	38	66	9	1	9	42	33	63	.240	.321	.378	94	-1	-3	34	7			7	O3/2	0.3
1947	StL-N	111	328	56	93	7	3	6	28	50	34	.284	.378	.378	97	2	0	50	1			3	O/3	0.0
1948	StL-N	114	311	60	65	9	2	6	19	49	55	.209	.317	.309	66	-12	-15	34	3			3	O2/3PS	-1.4
1949	StL-N	1	0	1	0	0	0	0	0	0	0	—	—	—	—	0	0	0	0			0	R	0.0
1950	StL-N	23	12	0	1	1	0	0	0	0	3	.083	.083	.167	-34	-2	-2	0	0			1	P/O	0.0
1951	StL-N	5	2	1	1	0	0	1	1	0	1	.500	.500	2.000	537	1	1	2	0	0	0	0	/P	0.0
	Pit-N	21	39	6	12	3	0	1	7	3	11	.308	.357	.462	115	1	1	7	0	0	0	-3	O/P23	-0.1
	Yr	26	41	7	13	3	0	2	8	3	12	.317	.364	.537	136	2	2	8	0	0	0	-3		-0.1
1952	Pit-N	20	27	1	6	0	0	1	3	2	8	.222	.276	.333	66	-1	-1	2	0	0	0	0	O	0.0
Total	9	413	1035	168	251	32	6	24	106	142	188	.243	.334	.355	84	-16	-22	132	12	0		14	O/23PS	-1.2

■ AL DWIGHT
Dwight, Albert Ward b: 1/4/1856, New York, N.Y. d: 2/20/03, San Francisco, Cal Deb: 6/19/1884

YEAR	TM/L	G	AB	R	H	2B	3B	HR	RBI	BB	SO	AVG	OBP	SLG	PRO+	BR	/A	RC	SB	CS	SBR	FR	POS	TPR
1884	KC-U	12	43	8	10	2	0	0		2		.233	.267	.279	97	-1	0	3	0			-1	C/O2	0.0

■ JIM DWYER
Dwyer, James Edward b: 1/3/50, Evergreen Park, Ill. BL/TL, 5'10", 165 lbs. Deb: 6/10/73

YEAR	TM/L	G	AB	R	H	2B	3B	HR	RBI	BB	SO	AVG	OBP	SLG	PRO+	BR	/A	RC	SB	CS	SBR	FR	POS	TPR
1973	StL-N	28	57	7	11	1	1	0	0	1	5	.193	.207	.246	25	-6	-6	2	0	0	0	1	O	-0.5
1974	StL-N	74	86	13	24	1	0	2	11	11	16	.279	.367	.360	105	1	1	12	0	0	0	1	O/1	0.1
1975	StL-N	21	31	4	6	1	0	0	1	4	6	.194	.286	.226	42	-2	-2	2	0	0	0	1	/O	-0.1
	Mon-N	60	175	22	50	7	1	3	20	23	30	.286	.369	.389	106	3	2	28	4	1	1	-0	O	0.0
	Yr	81	206	26	56	8	1	3	21	27	36	.272	.356	.364	96	1	-0	30	4	1	1	0		-0.1
1976	Mon-N	50	92	7	17	3	1	0	5	11	10	.185	.272	.239	44	-6	-7	6	0	0	0	-3	O	-1.0
	NY-N	11	13	2	2	0	0	0	0	2	1	.154	.267	.154	23	-1	-1	1	0	0	0	0	/O	0.0
	Yr	61	105	9	19	3	1	0	5	13	11	.181	.271	.229	42	-8	-8	7	0	0	0	-3		-1.0
1977	StL-N	13	31	3	7	1	0	0	2	4	5	.226	.351	.258	68	-1	-1	3	0	0	0	-1	O	-0.1
1978	StL-N	34	65	8	14	3	0	1	4	9	3	.215	.320	.308	77	-2	-2	7	1	0	0	-3	O	-0.5
	SF-N	73	173	22	39	9	2	5	22	28	29	.225	.333	.387	105	0	1	25	6	0	2	2	O1	0.3
	Yr	107	238	30	53	12	2	6	26	37	32	.223	.330	.366	97	-1	-1	33	7	0	2	-0		-0.2
1979	Bos-A	76	113	19	30	7	0	2	14	17	9	.265	.366	.381	96	1	-0	15	3	1	0	2	1O	0.2
1980	Bos-A	93	260	41	74	11	1	9	38	39	23	.285	.359	.438	111	6	5	41	3	2	-0	0	OD/1	0.2
1981	Bal-A	68	134	16	30	0	1	3	10	20	19	.224	.325	.306	83	-2	-2	14	0	2	-1	-0	O/1D	-0.5
1982	Bal-A	71	148	28	45	4	3	6	15	27	24	.304	.411	.493	148	11	11	33	2	0	1	-3	O/1D	0.6
1983	*Bal-A	100	196	37	56	17	1	8	38	31	29	.286	.383	.505	145	12	12	39	1	1	0	4	OD/1	1.5
1984	Bal-A	76	161	22	41	9	1	2	21	23	24	.255	.348	.360	98	-0	0	21	0	2	-1	-2	O/D	-0.4
1985	Bal-A	101	233	35	58	8	3	7	36	37	31	.249	.354	.399	109	3	4	33	0	3	-2	-1	O/D	0.6
1986	Bal-A	94	160	18	39	13	1	8	31	23	31	.244	.346	.488	126	5	6	27	0	2	-1	3	OD/1	0.6
1987	Bal-A	92	241	54	66	7	1	15	33	37	57	.274	.373	.498	132	10	11	46	4	1	1	-1	DO	0.9
1988	Bal-A	35	53	3	12	0	0	0	3	12	11	.226	.369	.226	73	-1	-1	5	0	0	0	0	D/O	0.0
	Min-A	20	41	6	12	1	0	2	15	13	8	.293	.473	.463	159	5	4	10	0	0	0	0	D	0.4
	Yr	55	94	9	24	1	0	2	18	25	19	.255	.417	.330	113	3	3	15	0	0	0	0		0.4
1989	Min-A	88	225	34	71	11	0	3	23	28	23	.316	.391	.404	117	8	6	36	2	0	1	0	D/O	0.7
	Mon-N	13	10	1	3	1	0	0	2	1	1	.300	.364	.400	116	0	0	2	0	0	0	0	H	0.0
1990	Min-A	37	63	7	12	0	0	1	5	12	7	.190	.320	.238	55	-3	-4	5	0	0	0	0	D/O	-0.3
Total	18	1328	2761	409	719	115	17	77	349	402	402	.260	.357	.398	107	39	37	417	26	15	-1	-1	OD/1	1.9

■ JOHN DWYER
Dwyer, John E. Deb: 5/16/1882

YEAR	TM/L	G	AB	R	H	2B	3B	HR	RBI	BB	SO	AVG	OBP	SLG	PRO+	BR	/A	RC	SB	CS	SBR	FR	POS	TPR
1882	Cle-N	1	3	0	0	0	0	0	1	0	0	.000	.000	.000	-99	-1	-1	0				-1	/OC	0.0

■ DOUBLE JOE DWYER
Dwyer, Joseph Michael b: 3/27/04, Orange, N.J. BL/TL, 5'9", 186 lbs. Deb: 4/20/37

YEAR	TM/L	G	AB	R	H	2B	3B	HR	RBI	BB	SO	AVG	OBP	SLG	PRO+	BR	/A	RC	SB	CS	SBR	FR	POS	TPR
1937	Cin-N	12	11	2	3	0	0	0	1	1	0	.273	.333	.273	70	-0	-0	1	0			0	H	0.0

■ JERRY DYBZINSKI
Dybzinski, Jerome Matthew b: 7/7/55, Cleveland, Ohio BR/TR, 6'2", 180 lbs. Deb: 4/11/80

YEAR	TM/L	G	AB	R	H	2B	3B	HR	RBI	BB	SO	AVG	OBP	SLG	PRO+	BR	/A	RC	SB	CS	SBR	FR	POS	TPR
1980	Cle-A	114	248	32	57	11	1	1	23	13	35	.230	.274	.294	55	-15	-15	21	4	1	1	21	S2/3D	1.4
1981	Cle-A	48	57	10	17	0	0	0	6	5	8	.298	.355	.298	91	-1	-0	8	7	1	2	8	S/23D	1.2
1982	Cle-A	80	212	19	49	6	2	0	22	21	25	.231	.309	.278	63	-10	-10	18	3	5	-2	17	S/3	1.1
1983	*Chi-A	127	256	30	59	10	1	1	32	18	29	.230	.286	.289	57	-14	-15	21	11	4	1	1	*S/3	-0.6
1984	Chi-A	94	132	17	31	5	1	1	10	13	12	.235	.313	.311	70	-5	-5	14	7	2	1	20	S3/2D	2.1
1985	Pit-N	5	4	0	0	0	0	0	0	0	0	.000	.000	.000	-99	-1	-1	0	0	0	0	1	/S	0.0
Total	6	468	909	108	213	32	5	3	93	70	109	.234	.296	.290	61	-46	-48	81	32	13	2	69	S/32D	5.2

■ JIM DYCK
Dyck, James Robert b: 2/3/22, Omaha, Neb. BR/TR, 6'2", 200 lbs. Deb: 9/27/51

YEAR	TM/L	G	AB	R	H	2B	3B	HR	RBI	BB	SO	AVG	OBP	SLG	PRO+	BR	/A	RC	SB	CS	SBR	FR	POS	TPR
1951	StL-A	4	15	1	1	0	0	0	0	1	1	.067	.125	.067	-46	-3	-3	0	0	0	0	0	/3	-0.2
1952	StL-A	122	402	60	108	22	3	15	64	50	68	.269	.354	.450	119	12	10	67	0	4	-2	9	3O	1.6
1953	StL-A	112	334	38	71	15	1	9	27	38	40	.213	.299	.344	72	-13	-14	33	3	2	-0	1	O3	-1.6
1954	Cle-A	2	1	0	1	0	0	0	1	1	0	1.000	1.000	1.000	441	1	1	1	0	0	0	1	H	0.1
1955	Bal-A	61	197	32	55	13	1	2	22	28	21	.279	.372	.386	112	2	4	29	1	0	0	1	O3	0.2
1956	Bal-A	11	23	3	5	2	0	0	4	10	5	.217	.455	.304	112	1	1	4	0	0	0	-0	/O	0.0
	Cin-N	18	11	5	1	0	0	0	0	3	5	.091	.286	.091	7	-1	-1	0	0	0	0	0	/13	0.0
Total	6	330	983	139	242	52	5	26	114	131	140	.246	.339	.389	98	-2	-3	135	4	6	-2	11	O3/1	0.1

■ BEN DYER
Dyer, Benjamin Franklin b: 2/13/1893, Chicago, Ill. d: 8/7/59, Kenosha, Wis. BR/TR, 5'10", 170 lbs. Deb: 5/23/14

YEAR	TM/L	G	AB	R	H	2B	3B	HR	RBI	BB	SO	AVG	OBP	SLG	PRO+	BR	/A	RC	SB	CS	SBR	FR	POS	TPR
1914	NY-N	7	4	1	1	0	0	0	0	0	1	.250	.250	.250	50	-0	-0	0	1			1	/S2	0.1
1915	NY-N	7	19	4	4	0	1	0	0	4	3	.211	.375	.316	117	1	1	2	0			-0	/3S	0.1
1916	Det-A	4	14	4	4	1	0	0	1	1	1	.286	.333	.357	104	0	0	2	0			-2	/S	-0.1
1917	Det-A	30	67	6	14	5	0	0	0	2	17	.209	.232	.284	57	-4	-4	5	3			2	S/3	0.0
1918	Det-A	13	18	1	5	0	0	0	2	0	6	.278	.278	.278	71	-1	-1	1	0			0	/P1O2	0.0
1919	Det-A	44	85	11	21	4	0	0	15	8	19	.247	.312	.294	72	-3	-3	8	0			6	3S/O	0.6
Total	6	105	207	27	49	10	1	0	18	15	47	.237	.291	.295	74	-7	-7	18	4			7	/3SO1P2	0.7

■ DUFFY DYER
Dyer, Don Robert b: 8/15/45, Dayton, Ohio BR/TR, 6', 187 lbs. Deb: 9/21/68 C

YEAR	TM/L	G	AB	R	H	2B	3B	HR	RBI	BB	SO	AVG	OBP	SLG	PRO+	BR	/A	RC	SB	CS	SBR	FR	POS	TPR
1968	NY-N	1	3	0	1	0	0	0	0	0	1	.333	.500	.333	153	0	0	1	0	0	0	0	/C	0.0
1969	*NY-N	29	74	5	19	3	1	3	12	4	22	.257	.295	.446	103	0	-0	9	0	0	0	-1	C	0.0
1970	NY-N	59	148	8	31	1	0	2	12	21	32	.209	.308	.257	53	-9	-9	12	1	1	-0	1	C	-0.5

YEAR	TM/L	G	AB	R	H	2B	3B	HR	RBI	BB	SO	AVG	OBP	SLG	PRO+	BR	/A	RC	SB	CS	SBR	FR	POS	TPR
1971	NY-N	59	169	13	39	7	1	2	18	14	45	.231	.293	.320	75	-6	-6	16	1	0	0	-0	C	-0.4
1972	NY-N	94	325	33	75	17	3	8	36	28	71	.231	.302	.375	94	-4	-3	36	0	1	-1	17	C/O	1.9
1973	NY-N	70	189	9	35	6	1	1	9	13	40	.185	.245	.243	36	-16	-16	11	0	1	-1	-1	C	-1.4
1974	NY-N	63	142	14	30	1	1	0	10	18	15	.211	.304	.232	53	-9	-8	10	0	0	0	-4	C	-1.0
1975	*Pit-N	48	132	8	30	5	2	3	16	6	22	.227	.266	.364	74	-5	-5	12	0	0	0	6	C	0.2
1976	Pit-N	69	184	12	41	8	0	3	9	29	35	.223	.338	.315	85	-2	-3	21	0	0	0	7	C	0.7
1977	Pit-N	94	270	27	65	11	1	3	19	54	49	.241	.373	.322	86	-2	-3	36	6	0	2	4	C	0.1
1978	Pit-N	58	175	7	37	8	1	0	13	18	32	.211	.296	.269	56	-9	-10	14	2	1	0	5	C	-0.3
1979	Mon-N	28	74	4	18	6	0	1	8	9	17	.243	.325	.365	89	-1	-1	9	0	0	0	6	C	0.6
1980	Det-A	48	108	11	20	1	0	4	11	13	34	.185	.273	.306	57	-6	-7	9	0	0	0	3	CD	-0.1
1981	Det-A	2	0	0	0	0	0	0	0	0	0	—	—	—	—	0	0	0	0	0	0	0	/C	0.0
Total	14	722	1993	151	441	74	11	30	173	228	415	.221	.307	.315	73	-71	-71	195	10	4	1	43	C/DO	-0.2

■ EDDIE DYER

Dyer, Edwin Hawley   b: 10/11/1900, Morgan City, La.   d: 4/20/64, Houston, Tex.   BL/TL, 5'11.5", 168 lbs.   Deb: 7/08/22   M

YEAR	TM/L	G	AB	R	H	2B	3B	HR	RBI	BB	SO	AVG	OBP	SLG	PRO+	BR	/A	RC	SB	CS	SBR	FR	POS	TPR
1922	StL-N	6	3	1	1	1	0	0	0	0	0	.333	.333	.667	159	-0	-0	1	0	0	0	0	/P	0.1
1923	StL-N	35	45	17	12	3	0	2	5	3	5	.267	.313	.467	105	-0	-0	7	1	0	0	-0	/OP	0.0
1924	StL-N	50	76	8	18	2	3	0	8	3	8	.237	.266	.342	63	-4	-4	7	1	0	0	1	P/O	0.0
1925	StL-N	31	31	4	3	1	0	0	0	3	1	.097	.176	.129	-20	-6	-6	1	1	1	-0	0	P	0.0
1926	StL-N	6	2	1	1	0	0	0	0	0	0	.500	.500	.500	164	0	0	0	0			0	/P	0.0
1927	StL-N	1	0	0	0	0	0	0	0	0	1	—	1.000	—	181	0	0	0	0			0	/P	0.0
Total	6	129	157	31	35	7	3	2	13	10	14	.223	.269	.344	61	-9	-9	16	3	1		1	/PO	0.1

■ JIMMY DYKES

Dykes, James Joseph   b: 11/10/1896, Philadelphia, Pa.   d: 6/15/76, Philadelphia, Pa.   BR/TR, 5'9", 185 lbs.   Deb: 5/06/18   MC

YEAR	TM/L	G	AB	R	H	2B	3B	HR	RBI	BB	SO	AVG	OBP	SLG	PRO+	BR	/A	RC	SB	CS	SBR	FR	POS	TPR
1918	Phi-A	59	186	13	35	3	3	0	13	19	32	.188	.267	.237	51	-11	-11	13	3			10	2/3	0.2
1919	Phi-A	17	49	4	9	1	0	0	1	7	11	.184	.286	.204	38	-4	-4	3	0			6	2	0.3
1920	Phi-A	142	546	81	140	25	4	8	35	55	73	.256	.334	.361	83	-12	-13	68	6	9	-4	17	*23	0.5
1921	Phi-A	155	613	88	168	32	13	16	77	60	75	.274	.353	.447	102	1	1	99	6	5	-1	25	*2	2.8
1922	Phi-A	145	501	66	138	23	7	12	68	55	98	.275	.359	.421	100	2	0	79	6	2	1	-7	*3/2	0.8
1923	Phi-A	124	416	50	105	28	1	4	43	35	40	.252	.318	.353	76	-15	-16	48	4		-1	4	*2S/3	-0.5
1924	Phi-A	110	410	68	128	26	6	3	50	38	59	.312	.372	.427	105	3	3	65	1	4	-2	16	23/S	2.0
1925	Phi-A	122	465	93	150	32	11	5	55	46	49	.323	.393	.471	111	13	8	88	3	1	0	10	32/S	2.3
1926	Phi-A	124	429	54	123	32	5	1	44	49	34	.287	.370	.392	93	0	-3	66	6	2	1	**26**	32/S	3.1
1927	Phi-A	121	417	61	135	33	6	3	60	44	23	.324	.394	.453	113	12	9	73	2	3	-1	-3	13/SO2P	0.4
1928	Phi-A	85	242	39	67	11	0	5	30	27	21	.277	.361	.384	93	-1	-2	36	2	1	0	-1	2S3/10	0.2
1929	*Phi-A	119	401	76	131	34	6	13	79	51	25	.327	.412	.539	138	26	24	91	8	3	1	-11	S32	2.1
1930	*Phi-A	125	435	69	131	28	4	6	73	74	53	.301	.414	.425	109	13	9	82	3	3	-1	-13	*3/O	0.0
1931	*Phi-A	101	355	48	97	28	2	3	46	49	47	.273	.371	.389	94	1	-2	54	1	2	-1	-2	3S	0.2
1932	Phi-A	153	558	71	148	29	5	7	90	77	65	.265	.358	.373	87	-7	-10	80	8	2	1	-5	*3S/2	-0.2
1933	Chi-A	151	554	49	144	22	6	1	68	69	37	.260	.354	.327	85	-12	-9	67	3	7	-3	-1	*3	-0.1
1934	Chi-A	127	456	52	122	17	4	7	82	64	28	.268	.363	.368	86	-6	-8	65	1	1	-0	-5	312M	-1.5
1935	Chi-A	117	403	45	116	24	2	4	61	59	28	.288	.381	.387	97	1	-0	63	4	3	-1	-5	31/2M	-0.6
1936	Chi-A	127	435	62	116	16	3	7	60	61	36	.267	.362	.366	77	-13	-15	61	1	3	-2	-6	*3M	-1.9
1937	Chi-A	30	85	10	26	5	0	1	23	9	7	.306	.372	.400	95	-1	-1	13	0	0	0	0	13M	-0.1
1938	Chi-A	26	89	9	27	4	2	2	13	10	8	.303	.374	.461	105	1	1	16	0	0	0	1	2/S3M	0.3
1939	Chi-A	2	1	0	0	0	0	0	0	0	0	.000	.000	.000	-97	-0	-0	0	0	0	0	0	/3M	0.0
Total	22	2282	8046	1108	2256	453	90	108	1071	958	849	.280	.365	.399	96	-7	-40	1230	70	55		58	*321S/OP	10.1

■ LENNY DYKSTRA

Dykstra, Leonard Kyle   b: 2/10/63, Santa Ana, Cal.   BL/TL, 5'10", 160 lbs.   Deb: 5/03/85

YEAR	TM/L	G	AB	R	H	2B	3B	HR	RBI	BB	SO	AVG	OBP	SLG	PRO+	BR	/A	RC	SB	CS	SBR	FR	POS	TPR
1985	NY-N	83	236	40	60	9	3	1	19	30	24	.254	.341	.331	91	-3	-2	30	15	2	3	10	O	0.9
1986	*NY-N	147	431	77	127	27	7	8	45	58	55	.295	.378	.445	130	16	18	80	31	7	5	-2	*O	1.9
1987	NY-N	132	431	86	123	37	3	10	43	40	67	.285	.352	.455	118	7	10	74	27	7	4	-5	*O	0.4
1988	*NY-N	126	429	57	116	19	3	8	33	30	43	.270	.323	.385	107	1	3	56	30	8	4	2	*O	0.7
1989	NY-N	56	159	27	43	12	1	3	13	23	15	.270	.370	.415	130	6	7	28	13	1	3	5	O	1.5
	Phi-N	90	352	39	78	20	3	4	19	37	38	.222	.297	.330	79	-10	-10	35	17	11	-2	3	O	-1.0
	Yr	146	511	66	121	32	4	7	32	60	53	.237	.321	.356	95	-4	-3	62	30	12		8		0.5
1990	Phi-N	149	590	106	**192**	35	3	9	60	89	48	.325	.420	.441	138	34	35	121	33	5	7	11	*O	4.9
Total	6	783	2628	432	739	159	23	43	232	307	290	.281	.360	.408	116	52	61	424	166	41	25	24	O	9.3

■ JOHN DYLER

Dyler, John F.   b: 6/1852, Louisville, Ky.   Deb: 7/22/1882   U

YEAR	TM/L	G	AB	R	H	2B	3B	HR	RBI	BB	SO	AVG	OBP	SLG	PRO+	BR	/A	RC	SB	CS	SBR	FR	POS	TPR
1882	Lou-a	1	4	0	0	0	0	0		0		.000	.000	.000	-99	-1	-1	0				-0	/O	0.0

■ DON EADDY

Eaddy, Donald Johnson   b: 2/16/34, Grand Rapids, Mich   BR/TR, 5'11", 165 lbs.   Deb: 4/24/59

YEAR	TM/L	G	AB	R	H	2B	3B	HR	RBI	BB	SO	AVG	OBP	SLG	PRO+	BR	/A	RC	SB	CS	SBR	FR	POS	TPR
1959	Chi-N	15	1	3	0	0	0	0	0	0	1	.000	.000	.000	-99	-0	-0	0	0	0	0	3	/3	0.3

■ TRUCK EAGAN

Eagan, Charles Eugene   b: 8/10/1877, San Francisco, Cal   d: 3/19/49, San Francisco, Cal   5'11", 190 lbs.   Deb: 5/01/01

YEAR	TM/L	G	AB	R	H	2B	3B	HR	RBI	BB	SO	AVG	OBP	SLG	PRO+	BR	/A	RC	SB	CS	SBR	FR	POS	TPR
1901	Pit-N	4	12	0	1	0	0	0	0	2	0	.083	.083	.083	-50	-2	-2	0				-1	/S	-0.2
	Cle-A	5	18	2	3	0	1	0	2	2	1	.167	.211	.278	37	-2	-1	1	0			0	/23	-0.1

■ BILL EAGAN

Eagan, William "Bad Bill"   b: 6/1/1869, Camden, N.J.   d: 2/14/05, Denver, Colo.   Deb: 4/08/1891

YEAR	TM/L	G	AB	R	H	2B	3B	HR	RBI	BB	SO	AVG	OBP	SLG	PRO+	BR	/A	RC	SB	CS	SBR	FR	POS	TPR
1891	StL-a	83	302	49	65	11	4	4	43	44	54	.215	.321	.318	74	-5	-13	38	21			20	2	1.1
1893	Chi-N	6	19	3	5	0	0	0	2	5	5	.263	.417	.263	86	-0	0	4	4			0	/2	0.0
1898	Pit-N	19	61	14	20	2	3	0	5	8		.328	.446	.459	166	6	6	13	1			3	2	0.9
Total	3	108	382	66	90	13	7	4	50	57	59	.236	.347	.338	88	1	-7	56	26			23	2	2.0

■ BILL EAGLE

Eagle, William Lycurgus   b: 7/25/1877, Rockville, Md.   d: 4/27/51, Churchton, Md.   Deb: 8/20/1898

YEAR	TM/L	G	AB	R	H	2B	3B	HR	RBI	BB	SO	AVG	OBP	SLG	PRO+	BR	/A	RC	SB	CS	SBR	FR	POS	TPR
1898	Was-N	4	13	0	4	1	0	0	2	0		.308	.308	.385	101	-0	-0	2	0			0	/O	0.0

■ CHARLIE EAKLE

Eakle, Charles Emory   b: 9/27/1887, Maryland   d: 6/15/59, Baltimore, Md.   Deb: 8/20/15

YEAR	TM/L	G	AB	R	H	2B	3B	HR	RBI	BB	SO	AVG	OBP	SLG	PRO+	BR	/A	RC	SB	CS	SBR	FR	POS	TPR
1915	Bal-F	2	7	0	2	1	0	0	0	0	0	.286	.286	.429	107	0	0	1	1			-2	/2	-0.2

■ HOWARD EARL

Earl, Howard J. "Slim Jim"   b: 2/27/1869, Massachusetts   d: 12/22/16, North Bay, N.Y.   6'2", 180 lbs.   Deb: 4/19/1890

YEAR	TM/L	G	AB	R	H	2B	3B	HR	RBI	BB	SO	AVG	OBP	SLG	PRO+	BR	/A	RC	SB	CS	SBR	FR	POS	TPR
1890	Chi-N	92	384	57	95	10	3	7	51	18	47	.247	.285	.344	81	-9	-11	43	17			-5	O2/S1	-1.3
1891	Mil-a	31	129	21	32	5	2	1	17	5	13	.248	.281	.341	67	-4	-8	14	3			-1	O/1	-0.8
Total	2	123	513	78	127	15	5	8	68	23	60	.248	.284	.343	77	-13	-19	57	20			-6	/O21S	-2.1

■ SCOTT EARL

Earl, William Scott   b: 9/18/60, Seymour, Ind.   BR/TR, 5'11", 165 lbs.   Deb: 9/10/84

YEAR	TM/L	G	AB	R	H	2B	3B	HR	RBI	BB	SO	AVG	OBP	SLG	PRO+	BR	/A	RC	SB	CS	SBR	FR	POS	TPR
1984	Det-A	14	35	3	4	1	0	1	0	9		.114	.114	.171	-22	-6	-6	1	1	0	0	1	2	-0.3

■ BILLY EARLE

Earle, William Moffat "The Little Globetrotter"
b: 11/10/1867, Philadelphia, Pa.   d: 5/30/46, Omaha, Neb.   BR/TR, 5'10.5", 170 lbs.   Deb: 4/27/1889

YEAR	TM/L	G	AB	R	H	2B	3B	HR	RBI	BB	SO	AVG	OBP	SLG	PRO+	BR	/A	RC	SB	CS	SBR	FR	POS	TPR
1889	Cin-a	53	169	37	45	4	7	4	31	30	24	.266	.386	.444	134	9	8	40	26			-1	OC/1	0.7
1890	StL-a	22	73	16	17	3	1	0		7		.233	.317	.301	74	-1	-3	9	6			5	C/OS32	0.3
1892	Pit-N	5	13	5	7	2	0	0	3	4	1	.538	.647	.692	307	4	4	7	2			-1	/C	0.3
1893	Pit-N	27	95	21	24	4	4	2	15	7	6	.253	.304	.442	101	-1	-1	13	1			1	C	0.2
1894	Lou-N	21	65	10	23	1	0	0	7	9	3	.354	.432	.369	104	0	1	12	2			3	C/1230	0.5
	Bro-N	14	50	13	17	6	0	0	6	6	2	.340	.421	.460	123	1	2	12	4			-2	C/2	0.1

YEAR	TM/L	G	AB	R	H	2B	3B	HR	RBI	BB	SO	AVG	OBP	SLG	PRO+	BR	/A	RC	SB	CS	SBR	FR	POS	TPR
	Yr	35	115	23	40	7	0	0	13	15	5	.348	.427	.409	112	2	3	23	6			2		0.6
Total	5	142	465	102	133	20	12	6	62	63	36	.286	.378	.419	116	13	12	93	41			5	C/0123S	2.1

■ **JAKE EARLY**   Early, Jacob Willard b: 5/19/15, King's Mountain, N.C. d: 5/31/85, Melbourne, Fla.   BL/TR, 5'11", 168 lbs. Deb: 5/04/39

YEAR	TM/L	G	AB	R	H	2B	3B	HR	RBI	BB	SO	AVG	OBP	SLG	PRO+	BR	/A	RC	SB	CS	SBR	FR	POS	TPR
1939	Was-A	32	84	8	22	7	2	0	14	5	14	.262	.303	.393	83	-3	-2	10	0	0	0	-1	C	-0.1
1940	Was-A	80	206	26	53	8	4	5	14	23	22	.257	.335	.408	98	-3	-1	29	0	1	-1	6	C	0.8
1941	Was-A	104	355	42	102	20	7	10	54	24	38	.287	.338	.468	117	4	6	57	0	1	-1	-9	*C	0.2
1942	Was-A	104	353	31	72	14	2	3	46	37	37	.204	.281	.280	59	-20	-19	30	0	0	0	-2	C	-0.9
1943	Was-A	126	423	37	109	23	3	5	60	53	43	.258	.346	.362	111	4	6	57	5	3	-0	-7	*C	0.5
1946	Was-A	64	189	13	38	6	0	4	18	23	27	.201	.288	.296	67	-9	-8	17	0	0	0	4	C	0.0
1947	StL-A	87	214	25	48	9	3	3	19	54	34	.224	.381	.336	98	2	2	32	0	1	-1	-3	C	0.6
1948	Was-A	97	246	22	54	7	2	1	28	36	33	.220	.322	.276	62	-13	-12	25	2	1	0	3	C	-0.2
1949	Was-A	53	138	12	34	4	0	1	11	26	11	.246	.370	.297	79	-3	-3	17	0	1	-1	-3	C	-0.3
Total	9	747	2208	216	532	98	23	32	264	281	259	.241	.330	.350	89	-41	-32	275	7	8	-3	-13	C	0.6

■ **MIKE EASLER**   Easler, Michael Anthony b: 11/29/50, Cleveland, Ohio BL/TR, 6', 190 lbs. Deb: 9/05/73

YEAR	TM/L	G	AB	R	H	2B	3B	HR	RBI	BB	SO	AVG	OBP	SLG	PRO+	BR	/A	RC	SB	CS	SBR	FR	POS	TPR
1973	Hou-N	6	7	1	0	0	0	0	0	2	4	.000	.222	.000	-34	-1	-1	0	0	0	0	-0	/O	-0.1
1974	Hou-N	15	15	0	1	0	0	0	0	0	5	.067	.067	.067	-65	-3	-3	0	0	0	0	0	H	-0.2
1975	Hou-N	5	5	0	0	0	0	0	0	0	1	.000	.000	.000	-99	-1	-1	0	0	0	0	0	H	0.0
1976	Cal-A	21	54	6	13	1	1	0	4	2	11	.241	.268	.296	69	-2	-2	4	1	1	-0	0	D	-0.2
1977	Pit-N	10	18	3	8	2	0	1	5	0	1	.444	.444	.722	202	3	2	6	0	0	0	0	/O	0.2
1979	*Pit-N	55	54	8	15	1	1	2	11	8	13	.278	.371	.444	116	2	1	9	0	1	-1	0	/O	0.1
1980	Pit-N	132	393	66	133	27	3	21	74	43	65	.338	.404	.583	170	37	36	88	5	9	-4	-8	*O	2.0
1981	Pit-N	95	339	43	97	18	5	7	42	24	45	.286	.333	.431	112	6	5	44	4	7	-3	6	O	0.5
1982	Pit-N	142	475	52	131	27	2	15	58	40	85	.276	.340	.436	112	9	7	69	1	1	-0	-3	*O	0.2
1983	Pit-N	115	381	44	117	17	2	10	54	22	64	.307	.350	.441	115	8	7	57	4	2	-0	-7	*O	-0.1
1984	Bos-A	156	601	87	188	31	5	27	91	58	134	.313	.377	.516	138	36	32	118	1	1	-0	2	*D1	3.2
1985	Bos-A	155	568	71	149	29	4	16	74	53	129	.262	.329	.412	97	1	-2	75	0	1	-1	-3	*DO	-0.5
1986	NY-A	146	490	64	148	26	2	14	78	49	87	.302	.365	.449	122	14	15	76	3	2	-0	-1	*DO	1.3
1987	Phi-N	33	110	7	31	4	0	1	10	6	20	.282	.319	.345	74	-4	-4	12	0	1	-1	1	O	-0.4
	NY-A	65	167	13	47	6	0	4	21	14	32	.281	.341	.389	94	-2	-1	22	1	0	-0	0	DO	
Total	14	1151	3677	465	1078	189	25	118	522	321	696	.293	.353	.454	118	102	91	581	20	26	-10	-13	OD/1	6.0

■ **CARL EAST**   East, Carlton William b: 8/27/1894, Marietta, Ga. d: 1/15/53, Whitesburg, Ga.   BL/TR, 6'2", 178 lbs. Deb: 8/24/15

YEAR	TM/L	G	AB	R	H	2B	3B	HR	RBI	BB	SO	AVG	OBP	SLG	PRO+	BR	/A	RC	SB	CS	SBR	FR	POS	TPR
1915	StL-A	1	1	0	0	0	0	0	0	0	0	.000	.000	.000	-99	-0	-0	0	0			-0	/P	0.0
1924	Was-A	2	6	1	2	1	0	0	2	2	1	.333	.500	.500	163	1	1	2	0	0	0	-0	/O	0.0
Total	2	3	7	1	2	1	0	0	2	2	1	.286	.444	.429	134	0	0	2	0	0		-0	/OP	0.0

■ **HARRY EAST**   East, Henry H. b: 4/1863, St.Louis, Mo. Deb: 6/17/1882

YEAR	TM/L	G	AB	R	H	2B	3B	HR	RBI	BB	SO	AVG	OBP	SLG	PRO+	BR	/A	RC	SB	CS	SBR	FR	POS	TPR
1882	Bal-a	1	4	0	0	0	0	0		0		.000	.000	.000	-99	-1	-1	0				-0	/3	0.0

■ **LUKE EASTER**   Easter, Luscious Luke b: 8/4/15, Jonestown, Miss. d: 3/29/79, Euclid, Ohio BL/TR, 6'4.5", 240 lbs. Deb: 8/11/49 C

YEAR	TM/L	G	AB	R	H	2B	3B	HR	RBI	BB	SO	AVG	OBP	SLG	PRO+	BR	/A	RC	SB	CS	SBR	FR	POS	TPR
1949	Cle-A	21	45	6	10	3	0	0	2	8	6	.222	.340	.289	68	-2	-2	4	0	1	-1	-4	O	-0.5
1950	Cle-A	141	540	65	151	20	4	28	107	70	95	.280	.373	.487	123	14	16	100	0	3	-2	-0	*1O	0.7
1951	Cle-A	128	486	65	131	12	5	27	103	37	71	.270	.333	.481	125	9	13	77	0	1	-1	-7	*1	0.3
1952	Cle-A	127	437	63	115	10	3	31	97	44	84	.263	.337	.513	144	17	21	79	1	1	-0	4	*1	1.7
1953	Cle-A	68	211	26	64	9	0	7	31	15	35	.303	.361	.445	120	5	5	30	0	2	-1	-2	1	0.1
1954	Cle-A	6	6	0	1	0	0	0	0	0	2	.167	.167	.167	-8	-1	-1	0	0	0	0	0	H	0.0
Total	6	491	1725	256	472	54	12	93	340	174	293	.274	.350	.481	126	42	53	290	1	8	-5	-9	1/O	2.3

■ **HENRY EASTERDAY**   Easterday, Henry P. b: 9/16/1864, Philadelphia, Pa. d: 3/30/1895, Philadelphia, Pa. BR/TR, 5'6", 145 lbs. Deb: 6/23/1884

YEAR	TM/L	G	AB	R	H	2B	3B	HR	RBI	BB	SO	AVG	OBP	SLG	PRO+	BR	/A	RC	SB	CS	SBR	FR	POS	TPR
1884	Phi-U	28	115	12	28	5	0	0		5		.243	.275	.287	97	-1	0	9	0			6	S	0.6
1888	KC-a	115	401	42	76	7	6	3	37	31		.190	.256	.259	64	-13	-17	33	23			26	*S	1.3
1889	Col-a	95	324	43	56	5	8	4	34	41	57	.173	.270	.275	60	-18	-15	27	10			12	S/23	0.3
1890	Col-a	58	197	25	31	5	1	1		23		.157	.249	.208	39	-15	-13	12	5			6	S	-0.2
	Phi-a	19	68	17	10	1	0	1		10		.147	.256	.206	39	-5	-5	5	4			-2	S	-0.4
	Lou-a	7	24	2	2	0	0	0		2		.083	.185	.083	-20	-3	-3	1	1			1	/S3	-0.1
	Yr	84	289	44	43	6	1	2		35		.149	.245	.197	34	-24	-21	17	10			5		-0.7
Total	4	322	1129	141	203	23	15	9	71	112	57	.180	.259	.251	58	-56	-53	87	43			50	S/23	1.5

■ **PAUL EASTERLING**   Easterling, Paul b: 9/28/05, Reidsville, Ga. BR/TR, 5'11", 180 lbs. Deb: 4/11/28

YEAR	TM/L	G	AB	R	H	2B	3B	HR	RBI	BB	SO	AVG	OBP	SLG	PRO+	BR	/A	RC	SB	CS	SBR	FR	POS	TPR
1928	Det-A	43	114	17	37	7	1	3	12	8	24	.325	.374	.482	122	4	3	21	2	1	0	-2	O	0.0
1930	Det-A	29	79	7	16	6	0	1	14	6	18	.203	.259	.316	44	-7	-7	6	0	1	-1	-2	O	-0.9
1938	Phi-A	4	7	1	2	0	0	0	0	1	2	.286	.375	.286	70	-0	-1	1	0	0	0	-0	/O	0.0
Total	3	76	200	25	55	13	1	4	26	15	44	.275	.329	.410	88	-4	-4	28	2	2	-1	-4	O	-0.9

■ **TED EASTERLY**   Easterly, Theodore Harrison b: 4/20/1885, Lincoln, Neb. d: 7/6/51, Clearlake Highlands, Cal. BL/TR, 5'8", 165 lbs. Deb: 4/17/09

YEAR	TM/L	G	AB	R	H	2B	3B	HR	RBI	BB	SO	AVG	OBP	SLG	PRO+	BR	/A	RC	SB	CS	SBR	FR	POS	TPR
1909	Cle-A	98	287	32	75	14	10	1	27	13		.261	.293	.390	111	3	2	34	8			0	C	0.9
1910	Cle-A	110	363	34	111	16	6	0	55	21		.306	.344	.383	126	10	10	51	10			-27	CO	-1.2
1911	Cle-A	99	287	34	93	19	5	1	37	8		.324	.345	.436	116	5	4	45	6			-12	OC	-0.9
1912	Cle-A	65	186	17	55	4	0	2	21	7		.296	.328	.349	91	-2	-3	22	3			-4	C	0.0
	Chi-A	30	55	5	20	2	0	0	14	2		.364	.386	.400	129	2	2	9	1			-4	C/O	0.0
	Yr	95	241	22	75	6	0	2	35	9		.311	.341	.361	100	-0	-1	31	4			-8		0.0
1913	Chi-A	60	97	3	23	1	0	0	8	4	9	.237	.267	.247	51	-6	-6	7	2			2	C	-0.1
1914	KC-F	134	436	58	146	20	12	1	67	31	25	.335	.384	.443	142	20	23	81	10			-54	*C	-2.6
1915	KC-F	110	309	32	84	12	5	3	32	21	15	.272	.320	.372	109	1	3	39	2			-21	C	-1.6
Total	7	706	2020	215	607	88	38	8	261	107	49	.300	.338	.394	116	34	35	288	42			-119	C/O	-5.5

■ **ROY EASTERWOOD**   Easterwood, Roy Charles "Shag" b: 1/12/15, Waxahachie, Tex. d: 8/24/84, Graham, Tex. BR/TR, 6'0.5", 196 lbs. Deb: 4/21/44

YEAR	TM/L	G	AB	R	H	2B	3B	HR	RBI	BB	SO	AVG	OBP	SLG	PRO+	BR	/A	RC	SB	CS	SBR	FR	POS	TPR
1944	Chi-N	17	33	1	7	2	0	1	2	1	11	.212	.235	.364	67	-2	-2	2	0			-0	C	0.0

■ **JOHN EASTON**   Easton, John David "Goose" b: 3/4/33, Trenton, N.J. BR/TR, 6'2", 185 lbs. Deb: 6/19/55

YEAR	TM/L	G	AB	R	H	2B	3B	HR	RBI	BB	SO	AVG	OBP	SLG	PRO+	BR	/A	RC	SB	CS	SBR	FR	POS	TPR
1955	Phi-N	1	0	0	0	0	0	0	0	0	0	—	—	—		0	0	0	0	0	0	0	R	0.0
1959	Phi-N	3	3	0	0	0	0	0	0	0	3	.000	.000	.000	-98	-1	-1	0	0	0	0	0	H	0.0
Total	2	4	3	0	0	0	0	0	0	0	3	.000	.000	.000	-98	-1	-1	0	0	0	0	0		0.0

■ **EDDIE EAYRS**   Eayrs, Edwin b: 11/10/1890, Blackstone, Mass. d: 11/30/69, Warwick, R.I. BL/TL, 5'7", 160 lbs. Deb: 6/30/13

YEAR	TM/L	G	AB	R	H	2B	3B	HR	RBI	BB	SO	AVG	OBP	SLG	PRO+	BR	/A	RC	SB	CS	SBR	FR	POS	TPR
1913	Pit-N	4	6	0	1	0	0	0	0	0	1	.167	.167	.167	-5	-1	-1	0	0			0	/P	0.0
1920	Bos-N	87	244	31	80	5	2	1	24	30	18	.328	.410	.377	133	10	12	40	4	3	-1	-6	O/P	0.2
1921	Bos-N	15	15	0	1	0	0	0	1	0	4	.067	.067	.067	-68	-3	-3	0	0	0	0	-0	/P	-0.2
	Bro-N	8	6	1	1	0	0	0	1	2	0	.167	.375	.167	47	-0	-0	1	0	0	0	0	/O	0.0
	Yr	23	21	1	2	0	0	0	2	2	4	.095	.174	.095	-27	-4	-4	0	0	0	0	-0		-0.2
Total	3	114	271	32	83	5	2	1	26	32	23	.306	.388	.351	116	6	7	41	4	3		-7	OP	0.0

■ **HI EBRIGHT**   Ebright, Hiram C. "Buck" b: 6/12/1859, Lancaster Co., Pa d: 10/24/16, Milwaukee, Wis. BR/TR, Deb: 4/24/1889

YEAR	TM/L	G	AB	R	H	2B	3B	HR	RBI	BB	SO	AVG	OBP	SLG	PRO+	BR	/A	RC	SB	CS	SBR	FR	POS	TPR
1889	Was-N	16	59	7	15	2	2	1	6	3	8	.254	.302	.407	105	-0	0	8	1			3	/COS	0.3

YEAR	TM/L	G	AB	R	H	2B	3B	HR	RBI	BB	SO	AVG	OBP	SLG	PRO+	BR	/A	RC	SB	CS	SBR	FR	POS	TPR

■ JOHNNY ECHOLS
Echols, John Gresham   b: 1/9/17, Atlanta, Ga.   d: 11/13/72, Atlanta, Ga.   BR/TR, 5'10.5", 175 lbs.   Deb: 5/24/39

YEAR	TM/L	G	AB	R	H	2B	3B	HR	RBI	BB	SO	AVG	OBP	SLG	PRO+	BR	/A	RC	SB	CS	SBR	FR	POS	TPR
1939	StL-N	2	0	0	0	0	0	0	0	0	0	—	—	—	—	0	0	0				0	R	0.0

■ OX ECKHARDT
Eckhardt, Oscar George   b: 12/23/01, Yorktown, Tex.   d: 4/22/51, Yorktown, Tex.   BL/TR, 6'1", 185 lbs.   Deb: 4/16/32

YEAR	TM/L	G	AB	R	H	2B	3B	HR	RBI	BB	SO	AVG	OBP	SLG	PRO+	BR	/A	RC	SB	CS	SBR	FR	POS	TPR
1932	Bos-N	8	8	1	2	0	0	0	1	0	1	.250	.250	.250	36	-1	-1	0				0	H	0.0
1936	Bro-N	16	44	5	8	1	0	1	6	5	2	.182	.265	.273	45	-3	-3	4	0			1	O	-0.2
Total	2	24	52	6	10	1	0	1	7	5	3	.192	.263	.269	43	-4	-4	4	0			1	/O	-0.2

■ CHARLIE EDEN
Eden, Charles M.   b: 1/18/1855, Lexington, Ky.   d: 9/17/20, Cincinnati, Ohio   BR/TR,   Deb: 8/17/1877

YEAR	TM/L	G	AB	R	H	2B	3B	HR	RBI	BB	SO	AVG	OBP	SLG	PRO+	BR	/A	RC	SB	CS	SBR	FR	POS	TPR
1877	Chi-N	15	55	9	12	0	1	0	5	3	6	.218	.259	.255	56	-2	-3	4				-2	O	-0.4
1879	Cle-N	81	353	40	96	31	7	3	34	6	20	.272	.284	.425	131	11	11	44				-5	*O/1C	0.3
1884	Pit-a	32	122	12	33	7	4	1		7		.270	.341	.418	147	7	6	18				-4	O/P	0.2
1885	Pit-a	98	405	57	103	18	6	0		17		.254	.298	.328	102	0	1	41				-15	*O/P3	-1.6
Total	4	226	935	118	244	56	18	4	39	33	26	.261	.296	.372	116	16	16	106				-27	O/P13C	-1.5

■ MIKE EDEN
Eden, Edward Michael   b: 5/22/49, Fort Clayton, Canal Zone   BB/TR, 5'10", 170 lbs.   Deb: 8/02/76

YEAR	TM/L	G	AB	R	H	2B	3B	HR	RBI	BB	SO	AVG	OBP	SLG	PRO+	BR	/A	RC	SB	CS	SBR	FR	POS	TPR
1976	Atl-N	5	8	0	0	0	0	0	1	0	0	.000	.000	.000	-94	-2	-2	0	0	0	0	1	/2	0.0
1978	Chi-A	10	17	1	2	0	0	0	0	4	0	.118	.286	.118	17	-2	-2	1	0	0	0	-0	/S2	0.0
Total	2	15	25	1	2	0	0	0	1	4	0	.080	.207	.080	-16	-4	-4	1	0	0	0	1	/2S	0.0

■ STUMP EDINGTON
Edington, Jacob Frank   b: 7/4/1891, Roleen, Ind.   d: 11/11/69, Bastrop, La.   BL/TL, 5'8", 170 lbs.   Deb: 6/20/12

YEAR	TM/L	G	AB	R	H	2B	3B	HR	RBI	BB	SO	AVG	OBP	SLG	PRO+	BR	/A	RC	SB	CS	SBR	FR	POS	TPR
1912	Pit-N	15	53	4	16	0	2	0	12	3	1	.302	.339	.377	97	-0	-0	7	0			-0	O	0.0

■ DAVE EDLER
Edler, David Delmar   b: 8/5/56, Sioux City, Iowa   BR/TR, 6', 185 lbs.   Deb: 9/04/80

YEAR	TM/L	G	AB	R	H	2B	3B	HR	RBI	BB	SO	AVG	OBP	SLG	PRO+	BR	/A	RC	SB	CS	SBR	FR	POS	TPR
1980	Sea-A	28	89	11	20	1	0	3	9	8	16	.225	.289	.337	70	-4	-4	8	2	3	-1	3	3	-0.1
1981	Sea-A	29	78	7	11	3	0	0	5	11	13	.141	.256	.179	26	-7	-7	4	3	3	-1	-4	3/S	-1.2
1982	Sea-A	40	104	14	29	2	2	2	18	11	13	.279	.348	.394	100	1	0	14	4	2	0	4	3/OD	0.3
1983	Sea-A	29	63	2	12	1	1	1	4	5	11	.190	.261	.286	49	-4	-5	4	3	3	-1	0	3/1OD	-0.5
Total	4	126	334	34	72	7	3	6	36	35	53	.216	.294	.308	66	-14	-16	30	12	11	-3	2	/3D1OS	-1.5

■ BOB EDMONDSON
Edmondson, Robert E.   b: 4/30/1879, Paris, Ky.   d: 8/14/31, Lawrence, Kan.   BR/TR, 5'11", 185 lbs.   Deb: 9/15/06

YEAR	TM/L	G	AB	R	H	2B	3B	HR	RBI	BB	SO	AVG	OBP	SLG	PRO+	BR	/A	RC	SB	CS	SBR	FR	POS	TPR
1906	Was-A	3	3	1	1	0	0	0	0	0	0	.333	.333	.333	116	0	0	0	0			0	/PO	0.0
1908	Was-A	26	80	5	15	4	1	0	2	7		.188	.253	.262	76	-3	-2	5	0			-2	O	-0.5
Total	2	29	83	6	16	4	1	0	2	7		.193	.256	.265	77	-3	-2	5	0			-2	/OP	-0.5

■ EDDIE EDMONSON
Edmonson, Earl Edward   b: 11/20/1889, Hopewell, Pa.   d: 5/10/71, Leesburg, Fla.   BL/TR, 6', 175 lbs.   Deb: 10/04/13

YEAR	TM/L	G	AB	R	H	2B	3B	HR	RBI	BB	SO	AVG	OBP	SLG	PRO+	BR	/A	RC	SB	CS	SBR	FR	POS	TPR
1913	Cle-A	2	5	0	0	0	0	0	0	0	0	.000	.000	.000	-97	-1	-1	0	0			-0	/1O	-0.1

■ EDWARDS
Edwards   Deb: 9/17/15

YEAR	TM/L	G	AB	R	H	2B	3B	HR	RBI	BB	SO	AVG	OBP	SLG	PRO+	BR	/A	RC	SB	CS	SBR	FR	POS	TPR
1915	Phi-A	2	5	0	0	0	0	0	0	0	3	.000	.000	.000	-99	-1	-1	0	0			-1	/2	-0.2

■ BRUCE EDWARDS
Edwards, Charles Bruce "Bull"   b: 7/15/23, Quincy, Ill.   d: 4/25/75, Sacramento, Cal.   BR/TR, 5'8", 180 lbs.   Deb: 6/23/46

YEAR	TM/L	G	AB	R	H	2B	3B	HR	RBI	BB	SO	AVG	OBP	SLG	PRO+	BR	/A	RC	SB	CS	SBR	FR	POS	TPR
1946	Bro-N	92	292	24	78	13	5	1	25	34	20	.267	.348	.356	99	0	0	37	1			6	C	0.9
1947	*Bro-N	130	471	53	139	15	8	9	80	49	55	.295	.364	.418	103	5	3	73	2			6	*C	1.1
1948	Bro-N	96	286	36	79	17	2	8	54	26	28	.276	.341	.434	105	3	1	41	4			-6	CO3/1	-0.2
1949	*Bro-N	64	148	24	31	3	0	8	25	25	15	.209	.324	.392	87	-2	-3	19	0			-2	C/O3	-0.3
1950	Bro-N	50	142	16	26	4	1	8	16	13	22	.183	.256	.394	67	-7	-8	13	1			-4	C/1	-0.9
1951	Bro-N	17	36	6	9	2	0	1	8	1	3	.250	.270	.389	74	-1	-1	4	0	0	0	0	/C	0.0
	Chi-N	51	141	19	33	9	2	3	17	16	14	.234	.316	.390	87	-2	-3	17	1	2	-1	-2	C/1	-0.5
	Yr	68	177	25	42	11	2	4	25	17	17	.237	.308	.390	85	-4	-4	21	1	2	-1	-2		-0.5
1952	Chi-N	50	94	7	23	2	2	1	12	8	12	.245	.304	.340	77	-3	-3	9	0	0	0	-3	C/2	-0.4
1954	Chi-N	4	3	1	0	0	0	0	1	2	2	.000	.400	.000	15	-0	-0	0	0	0	0	0	H	0.0
1955	Was-A	30	57	5	10	2	0	0	3	16	6	.175	.356	.211	58	-3	-2	5	0	1	-1	7	C/3	0.5
1956	Cin-N	7	5	0	1	0	0	0	0	1	0	.200	.200	.200	8	-1	-1	0	0	0	0	-1	/C23	0.0
Total	10	591	1675	191	429	67	20	39	241	190	179	.256	.335	.390	93	-11	-17	217	9	3		2	C/0312	0.2

■ DAVE EDWARDS
Edwards, David Leonard   b: 2/24/54, Los Angeles, Cal.   BR/TR, 6', 170 lbs.   Deb: 9/11/78

YEAR	TM/L	G	AB	R	H	2B	3B	HR	RBI	BB	SO	AVG	OBP	SLG	PRO+	BR	/A	RC	SB	CS	SBR	FR	POS	TPR
1978	Min-A	15	44	7	11	3	0	1	3	7	13	.250	.377	.386	113	1	1	7	1	1	-0	3	O	0.3
1979	Min-A	96	229	42	57	8	0	8	35	24	45	.249	.323	.389	88	-3	-4	29	6	3	0	-1	O	-0.7
1980	Min-A	81	200	26	50	9	1	2	20	12	51	.250	.296	.335	68	-8	-9	19	2	1	0	6	O/D	-0.4
1981	SD-N	58	112	13	24	4	1	2	13	11	24	.214	.285	.321	77	-4	-3	10	3	1	0	2	O	-0.1
1982	SD-N	71	55	7	10	2	0	1	2	1	14	.182	.196	.273	32	-5	-5	2	0	0	0	3	O/1	-0.2
Total	5	321	640	95	152	26	2	14	73	55	147	.237	.302	.350	77	-19	-21	67	12	6	0	13	O/D1	-1.1

■ HANK EDWARDS
Edwards, Henry Albert   b: 1/29/19, Elmwood Place, O.   d: 6/22/88, Santa Ana, Cal.   BL/TL, 6', 190 lbs.   Deb: 9/10/41

YEAR	TM/L	G	AB	R	H	2B	3B	HR	RBI	BB	SO	AVG	OBP	SLG	PRO+	BR	/A	RC	SB	CS	SBR	FR	POS	TPR
1941	Cle-A	16	68	10	15	1	1	1	6	2	4	.221	.243	.309	47	-6	-5	5	0	0	0	-2	O	-0.7
1942	Cle-A	13	48	6	12	2	1	0	7	5	8	.250	.321	.333	89	-1	-1	6	2	1	0	-0	O	-0.1
1943	Cle-A	92	297	38	82	18	6	3	28	30	34	.276	.343	.407	127	6	9	41	4	8	-4	-0	O	0.3
1946	Cle-A	124	458	62	138	33	16	10	54	43	48	.301	.361	.509	151	23	27	88	1	3	-2	-1	*O	1.8
1947	Cle-A	108	393	54	102	12	3	15	59	31	55	.260	.315	.420	106	-0	1	53	1	3	-2	-5	*O	-0.9
1948	Cle-A	55	160	27	43	9	2	3	18	14	18	.269	.346	.406	102	-0	-0	24	1	1	-0	-4	O	-0.4
1949	Cle-A	5	15	3	4	0	0	1	1	1	2	.267	.313	.467	107	-0	-0	2	0	0	0	-1	/O	0.0
	Chi-N	58	176	25	51	8	4	7	21	19	22	.290	.359	.500	131	6	7	31	0			-5	O	0.0
1950	Chi-N	41	110	13	40	11	1	2	21	10	13	.364	.417	.536	150	8	8	25	0			-4	O	0.3
1951	Bro-N	35	31	1	7	3	0	0	3	4	9	.226	.314	.323	70	-1	-1	3	0	0	0	0	H	0.0
	Cin-N	41	127	14	40	9	1	3	20	13	17	.315	.379	.472	126	5	5	22	0	2	-1	-4	O	-0.1
	Yr	76	158	15	47	12	1	3	23	17	26	.297	.366	.443	115	4	3	25	0	2	-1	-4		-0.1
1952	Cin-N	74	184	24	52	7	6	3	28	19	22	.283	.350	.484	129	7	7	31	0	3	-2	-4	O	0.0
	Chi-A	8	18	2	6	0	0	0	1	0	2	.333	.333	.333	85	-0	-0	2	0	0		0	/O	0.0
1953	StL-A	65	106	6	21	3	0	0	9	13	10	.198	.286	.226	39	-9	-9	8	0	1	-1	0	O	-0.9
Total	11	735	2191	285	613	116	41	51	276	208	264	.280	.343	.440	119	38	46	340	9	22		-30	O	-0.7

■ DOC EDWARDS
Edwards, Howard Rodney   b: 12/10/36, Red Jacket, W.Va.   BR/TR, 6'2", 215 lbs.   Deb: 4/21/62   MC

YEAR	TM/L	G	AB	R	H	2B	3B	HR	RBI	BB	SO	AVG	OBP	SLG	PRO+	BR	/A	RC	SB	CS	SBR	FR	POS	TPR
1962	Cle-A	53	143	13	39	6	0	3	9	9	14	.273	.325	.378	91	-2	-2	18	0	0	0	8	C	0.8
1963	Cle-A	10	31	6	8	2	0	0	0	2	6	.258	.303	.323	76	-1	-1	3	0	0	0	5	C	0.4
	KC-A	71	240	16	60	12	0	6	35	11	23	.250	.289	.375	81	-5	-7	24	0	1	-1	-6	C	-1.2
	Yr	81	271	22	68	14	0	6	35	13	29	.251	.290	.369	81	-6	-8	27	0	1	-1	-1		-0.8
1964	KC-A	97	294	25	66	10	0	5	28	13	40	.224	.265	.310	57	-16	-17	21	0	1	-1	1	C/1	-1.4
1965	KC-A	6	20	1	3	0	0	0	0	1	2	.150	.190	.150	-2	-3	-3	0	0	0	0	-0	/C	-0.2
	NY-A	45	100	3	19	3	0	1	9	13	14	.190	.289	.250	55	-6	-6	6	1	2	-1	3	C	0.0
	Yr	51	120	4	22	3	0	1	9	14	16	.183	.274	.233	46	-8	-8	6	1	2	-1	2		-0.1
1970	Phi-N	35	78	5	21	0	0	0	6	4	10	.269	.313	.269	59	-4	-4	6	0	0	0	6	C	0.3
Total	5	317	906	69	216	33	0	15	87	53	109	.238	.287	.325	68	-38	-39	79	1	4	-2	17	C/1	-1.3

YEAR	TM/L	G	AB	R	H	2B	3B	HR	RBI	BB	SO	AVG	OBP	SLG	PRO+	BR	/A	RC	SB	CS	SBR	FR	POS	TPR

■ JOHNNY EDWARDS   Edwards, John Alban   b: 6/10/38, Columbus, Ohio   BL/TR, 6'4", 220 lbs.   Deb: 6/27/61

YEAR	TM/L	G	AB	R	H	2B	3B	HR	RBI	BB	SO	AVG	OBP	SLG	PRO+	BR	/A	RC	SB	CS	SBR	FR	POS	TPR
1961	*Cin-N	52	145	14	27	5	0	2	14	18	28	.186	.280	.262	45	-11	-12	11	1	0	0	-2	C	-0.8
1962	Cin-N	133	452	47	115	28	5	8	50	45	70	.254	.323	.392	88	-6	-8	58	1	1	-0	14	*C	0.7
1963	Cin-N	148	495	46	128	19	4	11	67	45	93	.259	.325	.380	99	2	0	61	1	5	-3	12	*C	1.5
1964	Cin-N	126	423	47	119	23	1	7	55	34	65	.281	.336	.390	100	2	1	56	1	2	-1	22	*C	2.7
1965	Cin-N	114	371	47	99	22	2	17	51	50	45	.267	.355	.474	123	16	13	64	0	0	0	4	*C	2.1
1966	Cin-N	98	282	24	54	8	0	6	39	31	42	.191	.272	.284	50	-17	-20	21	1	3	-2	9	C	-1.0
1967	Cin-N	80	209	10	43	6	0	2	20	16	28	.206	.262	.263	46	-13	-16	14	1	4	-2	15	C	0.1
1968	*StL-N	85	230	14	55	9	1	3	29	16	20	.239	.291	.326	86	-4	-4	21	1	1	-0	1	C	-0.1
1969	Hou-N	151	496	52	115	20	6	6	50	53	69	.232	.309	.333	81	-13	-12	49	2	1	0	5	*C	0.2
1970	Hou-N	140	458	46	101	16	4	7	49	51	63	.221	.300	.319	69	-22	-20	44	1	0	0	11	*C	-0.1
1971	Hou-N	106	317	18	74	13	4	1	23	26	38	.233	.292	.309	72	-12	-11	30	1	1	0	8	*C	-0.1
1972	Hou-N	108	332	33	89	16	2	5	40	50	39	.268	.366	.373	113	6	7	47	2	4	-2	-8	*C	0.3
1973	Hou-N	79	250	24	61	10	2	5	27	19	23	.244	.303	.360	83	-6	-6	27	1	0	0	-2	C	-0.3
1974	Hou-N	50	117	8	26	7	1	1	10	11	12	.222	.295	.325	76	-4	-4	11	1	1	-0	5	C	0.2
Total	14	1470	4577	430	1106	202	32	81	524	465	635	.242	.314	.353	85	-84	-92	515	15	23	-9	92	*C	5.4

■ MARSHALL EDWARDS   Edwards, Marshall Lynn   b: 8/27/52, Fort Lewis, Wash.   BL/TL, 5'9", 157 lbs.   Deb: 4/11/81

YEAR	TM/L	G	AB	R	H	2B	3B	HR	RBI	BB	SO	AVG	OBP	SLG	PRO+	BR	/A	RC	SB	CS	SBR	FR	POS	TPR
1981	*Mil-A	40	58	10	14	1	1	0	4	0	2	.241	.241	.293	56	-4	-4	4	6	2	1	3	O/D	0.0
1982	*Mil-A	69	178	24	44	4	1	2	14	4	8	.247	.264	.315	62	-10	-9	14	10	4	1	3	O/D	-0.6
1983	Mil-A	51	74	14	22	1	1	0	5	1	9	.297	.307	.338	84	-2	-2	6	5	5	-2	7	O/D	0.3
Total	3	160	310	48	80	6	3	2	23	5	19	.258	.270	.316	66	-16	-14	24	21	11	-0	13	O/D	-0.3

■ MIKE EDWARDS   Edwards, Michael Lewis   b: 8/27/52, Fort Lewis, Wash.   BR/TR, 5'10", 154 lbs.   Deb: 9/10/77

YEAR	TM/L	G	AB	R	H	2B	3B	HR	RBI	BB	SO	AVG	OBP	SLG	PRO+	BR	/A	RC	SB	CS	SBR	FR	POS	TPR
1977	Pit-N	7	6	1	0	0	0	0	0	0	3	.000	.143	.000	-56	-1	-1	-0	0	2	-1	3	/2	0.1
1978	Oak-A	142	414	48	113	16	2	1	23	16	32	.273	.303	.329	82	-13	-10	37	27	21	-5	-30	*2/SD	-3.7
1979	Oak-A	122	400	35	93	12	2	1	23	15	37	.233	.264	.280	49	-30	-27	27	10	6	-1	-14	*2/S	-3.5
1980	Oak-A	46	59	10	14	0	0	0	3	1	5	.237	.250	.237	37	-5	-5	3	1	1	-0	9	2/OD	0.5
Total	4	317	879	94	220	28	4	2	49	32	77	.250	.281	.298	63	-49	-43	68	38	30	-7	-31	2/SDO	-6.6

■ BEN EGAN   Egan, Arthur Augustus   b: 11/20/1883, Augusta, N.Y.   d: 2/18/68, Sherrill, N.Y.   BR/TR, 6', 195 lbs.   Deb: 9/29/08   C

YEAR	TM/L	G	AB	R	H	2B	3B	HR	RBI	BB	SO	AVG	OBP	SLG	PRO+	BR	/A	RC	SB	CS	SBR	FR	POS	TPR
1908	Phi-A	2	6	1	1	1	0	0	0	1		.167	.286	.333	97	0	-0	1	0			0	/C	0.0
1912	Phi-A	49	138	9	24	3	4	0	13	6		.174	.208	.254	33	-13	-12	7	3			4	C	-0.3
1914	Cle-A	29	88	7	20	2	1	0	11	3	20	.227	.277	.273	63	-4	-4	7	0	1	-1	5	C	0.2
1915	Cle-A	42	120	4	13	3	0	0	6	8	14	.108	.164	.133	-11	-16	-17	3	0			9	C	-0.4
Total	4	122	352	21	58	9	5	0	30	18	34	.165	.212	.219	27	-33	-33	18	3	1		17	C	-0.5

■ JIM EGAN   Egan, James K. "Troy Terrier"   b: 1858, Derby, Conn.   d: 9/26/1884, New Haven, Conn.   TL   Deb: 5/15/1882

YEAR	TM/L	G	AB	R	H	2B	3B	HR	RBI	BB	SO	AVG	OBP	SLG	PRO+	BR	/A	RC	SB	CS	SBR	FR	POS	TPR
1882	Tro-N	30	115	15	23	3	2	0	10	1	21	.200	.207	.261	51	-6	-6	6				-6	OP/C	-0.9

■ DICK EGAN   Egan, Richard Joseph   b: 6/23/1884, Portland, Ore.   d: 7/7/47, Oakland, Cal.   BR/TR, 5'11", 162 lbs.   Deb: 9/15/08

YEAR	TM/L	G	AB	R	H	2B	3B	HR	RBI	BB	SO	AVG	OBP	SLG	PRO+	BR	/A	RC	SB	CS	SBR	FR	POS	TPR
1908	Cin-N	18	68	8	14	3	1	0	5	2		.206	.229	.279	65	-3	-3	6	7			-3	2	-0.6
1909	Cin-N	127	480	59	132	14	3	2	53	37		.275	.329	.329	105	2	3	66	39			24	*2S	2.9
1910	Cin-N	135	474	70	116	11	5	0	46	53	38	.245	.322	.289	82	-12	-9	59	41			-11	*2/S	-1.7
1911	Cin-N	153	558	80	139	11	5	1	56	59	50	.249	.322	.292	75	-20	-17	65	37			10	*2	-0.9
1912	Cin-N	149	507	69	125	14	5	0	52	56	26	.247	.324	.294	72	-20	-18	58	24			3	*2	-1.9
1913	Cin-N	60	195	15	55	7	3	0	22	15	13	.282	.333	.349	95	-1	-1	25	6			-5	2S/3	-0.5
1914	Bro-N	106	337	30	76	10	3	1	21	22	25	.226	.273	.282	64	-15	-16	28	8			-8	S3/O21	-2.2
1915	Bro-N	3	3	0	0	0	0	0	0	0	0	.000	.000	.000	-98	-1	-1	0	0			0	H	0.0
	Bos-N	83	220	20	57	9	1	0	21	28	18	.259	.343	.309	102	0	2	24	3	4	-2	-0	O2S/13	0.0
	Yr	86	223	20	57	9	1	0	21	28	18	.256	.339	.305	100	-0	1	24	3	4	-2	-0		0.0
1916	Bos-N	83	238	23	53	8	3	0	16	19	21	.223	.280	.282	76	-8	-6	21	2			-21	2S/3	-2.9
Total	9	917	3080	374	767	87	29	4	292	291	191	.249	.315	.300	82	-77	-67	353	167	4		-11	2S/O31	-7.8

■ TOM EGAN   Egan, Thomas Patrick   b: 6/9/46, Los Angeles, Cal.   BR/TR, 6'4", 218 lbs.   Deb: 5/27/65

YEAR	TM/L	G	AB	R	H	2B	3B	HR	RBI	BB	SO	AVG	OBP	SLG	PRO+	BR	/A	RC	SB	CS	SBR	FR	POS	TPR
1965	Cal-A	18	38	3	10	0	1	0	1	3	12	.263	.317	.316	82	-1	-1	4	0	0	0	1	C	0.1
1966	Cal-A	7	11	0	0	0	0	0	0	1	5	.000	.083	.000	-76	-2	-2	0	0	0	0	2	/C	0.0
1967	Cal-A	1	1	0	0	0	0	0	0	0	0	.000	.000	.000	-99	-0	-0	0	0	0	0	0	/C	0.0
1968	Cal-A	16	43	2	5	1	0	1	4	2	15	.116	.156	.209	10	-5	-5	1	0	0	0	2	C	-0.1
1969	Cal-A	46	120	7	17	1	0	5	16	17	41	.142	.254	.275	50	-9	-8	9	0	1	-1	7	C	0.2
1970	Cal-A	79	210	14	50	6	0	4	20	14	67	.238	.289	.324	71	-9	-8	20	0	0	0	0	C	-0.6
1971	Chi-A	85	251	29	60	11	1	10	34	26	94	.239	.320	.410	102	1	1	35	1	0	0	5	C/1	0.9
1972	Chi-A	50	141	8	27	3	0	2	9	4	48	.191	.224	.255	42	-10	-10	7	0	0	0	3	C	-0.7
1974	Cal-A	43	94	4	11	0	0	0	4	8	40	.117	.194	.117	-9	-13	-12	3	1	0	0	16	C	0.5
1975	Cal-A	28	70	7	16	3	1	0	3	5	14	.229	.280	.300	69	-3	-3	6	0	0	0	4	C	0.2
Total	10	373	979	74	196	25	3	22	91	80	336	.200	.267	.299	62	-51	-49	83	2	1	-0	40	C/1	0.5

■ ELMER EGGERT   Eggert, Elmer Albert "Mose"   b: 1/29/02, Rochester, N.Y.   d: 4/9/71, Rochester, N.Y.   BR/TR, 5'9", 160 lbs.   Deb: 4/27/27

YEAR	TM/L	G	AB	R	H	2B	3B	HR	RBI	BB	SO	AVG	OBP	SLG	PRO+	BR	/A	RC	SB	CS	SBR	FR	POS	TPR
1927	Bos-A	5	3	0	0	0	0	0	0	0	1	.000	.250	.000	-31	-1	-1	0	0	0	0	0	/2	0.0

■ DAVE EGGLER   Eggler, David Daniel   b: 4/30/1851, Brooklyn, N.Y.   d: 4/5/02, Buffalo, N.Y.   BR/TR, 5'9", 165 lbs.   Deb: 5/18/1871

YEAR	TM/L	G	AB	R	H	2B	3B	HR	RBI	BB	SO	AVG	OBP	SLG	PRO+	BR	/A	RC	SB	CS	SBR	FR	POS	TPR
1871	Mut-n	33	147	37	47	3	0	0	18	4	3	.320	.338	.408	124	2	6	26	14			*O		0.5
1872	Mut-n	56	287	95	97	20	0	0		4	9	.338	.358	.408	144	12	16	43				*O		1.3
1873	Mut-n	53	268	81	91	16	5	0		6		.340	.354	.437	132	10	11	42				*O		0.9
1874	Phi-n	58	296	71	96	14	7	0		6		.324	.338	.419	135	13	11	43				*O/2		0.9
1875	Ath-n	66	293	66	89	15	7	0		2		.304	.308	.403	130	12	7	37				*O		0.7
1876	Phi-N	39	174	28	52	4	0	0	19	2	4	.299	.307	.322	111	2	2	18				4	O	0.5
1877	Chi-N	33	136	20	36	3	0	0	20	1	5	.265	.270	.287	67	-4	-6	11				1	O	-0.4
1879	Buf-N	78	317	41	66	5	7	0	27	11	41	.208	.235	.268	64	-11	-12	20				-7	*O	-2.0
1883	Bal-a	53	202	15	38	2	0	0		1		.188	.192	.198	25	-16	-17	8				1	O	-1.3
	Buf-N	38	153	13	38	2	1	0	13	2	29	.248	.258	.275	61	-7	-7	11				-2	O	-0.7
1884	Buf-N	63	241	25	47	3	1	0	20	6	54	.195	.215	.216	35	-17	-18	11				-1	O	-1.7
1885	Buf-N	6	24	0	2	0	0	0	0	2	4	.083	.154	.083	-21	-3	-3	0				0	/O	-0.2
Total	5 n	266	1291	350	420	72	22	0	18	27	3	.325	.339	.415	133	49	50	191					O/2	4.3
Total	6	310	1247	142	279	19	9	0	99	25	137	.224	.239	.253	56	-57	-63	80				-4	O	-5.8

■ RED EHRET   Ehret, Philip Sydney   b: 8/31/1868, Louisville, Ky.   d: 7/28/40, Cincinnati, Ohio   BR/TR, 6', 175 lbs.   Deb: 7/07/1888

YEAR	TM/L	G	AB	R	H	2B	3B	HR	RBI	BB	SO	AVG	OBP	SLG	PRO+	BR	/A	RC	SB	CS	SBR	FR	POS	TPR
1888	KC-a	17	63	4	12	4	0	0	4	1		.190	.203	.254	45	-4	-4	1				-3	O/P21	-0.6
1889	Lou-a	67	258	27	65	6	6	1	31	4	23	.252	.263	.333	73	-11	-10	24	4			-1	PO/S32	0.0
1890	*Lou-a	43	146	11	31	2	1	0		1		.212	.218	.240	37	-12	-11	8	1			-2	P	0.0
1891	Lou-a	26	91	9	22	2	1	0	9	5	15	.242	.281	.286	65	-4	-4	8	3			0	P	0.0
1892	Pit-N	40	132	12	34	2	0	0	19	7	22	.258	.295	.273	73	-4	-4	11	1			-3	P	0.0
1893	Pit-N	40	136	16	24	3	0	1	17	10	18	.176	.233	.221	22	-15	-15	7	1			1	P	0.0
1894	Pit-N	46	135	6	23	4	1	0	11	8	22	.170	.217	.215	5	-21	-21	6	2			-1	P	0.0
1895	StL-N	37	96	13	21	2	1	1	9	6	12	.219	.265	.292	45	-8	-8	8	0			0	P	0.0

YEAR	TM/L	G	AB	R	H	2B	3B	HR	RBI	BB	SO	AVG	OBP	SLG	PRO+	BR	/A	RC	SB	CS	SBR	FR	POS	TPR
1896	Cin-N	34	102	10	20	2	0	1	20	10	12	.196	.268	.245	35	-9	-10	7	2			0	P/1	0.0
1897	Cin-N	34	66	6	13	2	0	0	6	4		.197	.254	.227	27	-7	-7	4	2			-1	P	0.0
1898	Lou-N	13	40	3	9	3	1	0	4	1		.225	.262	.350	78	-1	-1	4	0			-1	P	0.0
Total	11	397	1265	117	274	32	11	4	130	57	124	.217	.252	.269	45	-96	-96	92	15			-11	P/0123S	-0.6

■ HACK EIBEL

Eibel, Henry Hack b: 12/6/1893, Brooklyn, N.Y. d: 10/16/45, Macon, Ga. BL/TL, 5'11", 220 lbs. Deb: 6/13/12

YEAR	TM/L	G	AB	R	H	2B	3B	HR	RBI	BB	SO	AVG	OBP	SLG	PRO+	BR	/A	RC	SB	CS	SBR	FR	POS	TPR
1912	Cle-A	1	3	0	0	0	0	0	0			.000	.000	.000	-97	-1	-1	0	0			-0	/O	0.0
1920	Bos-A	29	43	4	8	2	0	0	6	3	6	.186	.239	.233	26	-5	-4	2	1	1	-0	-2	/OP1	-0.6
Total	2	30	46	4	8	2	0	0	6	3	6	.174	.224	.217	19	-5	-5	2	1	1		-2	/OP1	-0.6

■ IKE EICHRODT

Eichrodt, Frederick George b: 1/6/03, Chicago, Ill. d: 7/14/65, Indianapolis, Ind BR/TR, 5'11.5", 167 lbs. Deb: 9/07/25

YEAR	TM/L	G	AB	R	H	2B	3B	HR	RBI	BB	SO	AVG	OBP	SLG	PRO+	BR	/A	RC	SB	CS	SBR	FR	POS	TPR
1925	Cle-A	15	52	4	12	3	1	0	4	2	7	.231	.259	.327	48	-4	-4	4	0	0	0	-2	O	-0.6
1926	Cle-A	37	80	14	25	7	1	0	7	2	11	.313	.329	.425	95	-1	-1	11	1	0	-0	-3	O	-0.5
1927	Cle-A	85	267	24	59	19	2	0	25	16	25	.221	.265	.307	48	-21	-21	21	2	3	-1	1	O	-2.5
1931	Chi-A	34	117	9	25	5	1	0	15	1	8	.214	.220	.274	31	-12	-11	7	0	0	0	-4	O	-1.6
Total	4	171	516	51	121	34	5	0	51	21	51	.234	.264	.320	52	-39	-38	43	3	3	-1	-9	O	-5.2

■ JIM EISENREICH

Eisenreich, James Michael b: 4/18/59, St.Cloud, Minn. BL/TL, 5'11", 180 lbs. Deb: 4/06/82

YEAR	TM/L	G	AB	R	H	2B	3B	HR	RBI	BB	SO	AVG	OBP	SLG	PRO+	BR	/A	RC	SB	CS	SBR	FR	POS	TPR
1982	Min-A	34	99	10	30	6	0	2	9	11	13	.303	.378	.424	117	3	3	17	0	0	0	1	O	0.3
1983	Min-A	2	7	1	2	1	0	0	0	1	1	.286	.375	.429	116	0	0	1	0	0	0	1	/O	0.1
1984	Min-A	12	32	1	7	1	0	0	3	2	4	.219	.265	.250	41	-2	-3	2	2	0	1	0	/OD	-0.1
1987	KC-A	44	105	10	25	8	2	4	21	7	13	.238	.286	.467	93	-1	-2	13	1	1	-0	0	D	-0.1
1988	KC-A	82	202	26	44	8	1	1	19	6	31	.218	.240	.282	45	-15	-15	14	9	3	1	0	OD	-1.4
1989	KC-A	134	475	64	139	33	7	9	59	37	44	.293	.344	.448	122	13	13	73	27	8	3	3	*OD	1.7
1990	KC-A	142	496	61	139	29	7	5	51	42	51	.280	.338	.397	107	3	4	64	12	14	-5	-2	*O/D	-0.3
Total	7	450	1416	173	386	86	17	21	162	106	157	.273	.324	.402	102	0	1	185	51	26	-0	3	O/D	0.2

■ ELAND

Eland Deb: 4/14/1873

YEAR	TM/L	G	AB	R	H	2B	3B	HR	RBI	BB	SO	AVG	OBP	SLG	PRO+	BR	/A	RC	SB	CS	SBR	FR	POS	TPR
1873	Mar-n	1	3	0	0	0	0	0		0		.000	.000	.000	-99	-1	-1	0					/O	0.0

■ KID ELBERFELD

Elberfeld, Norman Arthur "The Tabasco Kid"
b: 4/13/1875, Pomeroy, Ohio d: 1/13/44, Chattanooga, Tenn. BR/TR, 5'7", 158 lbs. Deb: 5/30/1898 M

YEAR	TM/L	G	AB	R	H	2B	3B	HR	RBI	BB	SO	AVG	OBP	SLG	PRO+	BR	/A	RC	SB	CS	SBR	FR	POS	TPR
1898	Phi-N	14	38	1	9	4	0	0	7	5		.237	.420	.342	128	2	2	6	0			-5	3	-0.1
1899	Cin-N	41	138	23	36	4	2	0	22	15		.261	.378	.319	93	0	-0	19	5			-4	S3	-0.2
1901	Det-A	121	432	76	133	21	11	3	76	57		.308	.396	.428	125	20	17	86	23			23	*S	4.1
1902	Det-A	130	488	70	127	17	6	1	64	55		.260	.348	.326	88	-5	-6	65	19			9	*S	1.4
1903	Det-A	35	132	29	45	5	3	0	19	11		.341	.392	.424	151	8	8	25	6			6	S/3	1.6
	NY-A	90	349	49	100	18	5	0	45	22		.287	.329	.367	104	4	2	49	16			7	S	1.4
	Yr	125	481	78	145	23	8	0	64	33		.301	.346	.383	116	12	10	74	22			13		3.0
1904	NY-A	122	445	55	117	13	5	2	46	37		.263	.320	.328	102	4	2	56	18			15	*S	2.0
1905	NY-A	111	390	48	102	18	2	0	53	23		.262	.303	.318	89	-1	-6	46	18			-5	*S	-0.7
1906	NY-A	99	346	59	106	12	4	2	31	30		.306	.362	.382	122	14	10	57	19			-3	S	0.9
1907	NY-A	120	447	61	121	17	6	0	51	36		.271	.325	.336	104	7	3	58	22			11	*S	1.8
1908	NY-A	19	56	11	11	3	0	0	5	6		.196	.274	.250	72	-1	-2	4	1			-3	SM	-0.3
1909	NY-A	106	379	47	90	9	5	0	26	28		.237	.314	.288	89	-3	-4	41	23			-2	S3	-0.2
1910	Was-A	127	455	53	114	9	2	2	42	35		.251	.322	.292	97	-3	-0	49	19			-10	*32/S	-0.6
1911	Was-A	127	404	58	110	19	4	0	47	65		.272	.405	.339	110	10	11	66	24			10	23	2.0
1914	Bro-N	30	62	7	14	1	0	0	1	2	4	.226	.304	.242	62	-3	-3	4	0			-4	S/2	-0.5
Total	14	1292	4561	647	1235	170	55	10	535	427	4	.271	.345	.339	103	54	35	631	213			46	S3/2	12.6

■ GEORGE ELDER

Elder, George Rezin b: 3/10/21, Lebanon, Ky. BL/TR, 5'11", 180 lbs. Deb: 7/22/49

YEAR	TM/L	G	AB	R	H	2B	3B	HR	RBI	BB	SO	AVG	OBP	SLG	PRO+	BR	/A	RC	SB	CS	SBR	FR	POS	TPR
1949	StL-A	41	44	9	11	3	0	0	4	4	11	.250	.313	.318	64	-2	-2	5	0	0	0	1	O	-0.1

■ LEE ELIA

Elia, Lee Constantine b: 7/16/37, Philadelphia, Pa. BR/TR, 5'11", 175 lbs. Deb: 4/23/66 MC

YEAR	TM/L	G	AB	R	H	2B	3B	HR	RBI	BB	SO	AVG	OBP	SLG	PRO+	BR	/A	RC	SB	CS	SBR	FR	POS	TPR
1966	Chi-A	80	195	16	40	5	2	3	22	15	39	.205	.269	.297	67	-9	-8	14	0	1	-1	4	S	0.0
1968	Chi-N	15	17	1	3	0	0	0	3	0	6	.176	.222	.176	20	-2	-2	1	0	0	0	-1	/S23	-0.2
Total	2	95	212	17	43	5	2	3	25	15	45	.203	.265	.288	63	-11	-10	15	0	1	-1	3	/S32	-0.2

■ PETE ELKO

Elko, Peter "Piccolo Pete" b: 6/17/18, Wilkes-Barre, Pa. BR/TR, 5'11", 185 lbs. Deb: 9/17/43

YEAR	TM/L	G	AB	R	H	2B	3B	HR	RBI	BB	SO	AVG	OBP	SLG	PRO+	BR	/A	RC	SB	CS	SBR	FR	POS	TPR
1943	Chi-N	9	30	1	4	0	0	0	4	4	5	.133	.235	.133	8	-3	-3	1	0			-2	/3	-0.5
1944	Chi-N	7	22	2	5	1	0	0	0	0	0	.227	.227	.273	40	-2	-2	1	0			-0	/3	-0.1
Total	2	16	52	3	9	1	0	0	4	4	5	.173	.232	.192	22	-5	-5	2	0			-2	/3	-0.6

■ ROY ELLAM

Ellam, Roy "Whitey" or "Slippery" b: 2/8/1886, W.Conshohocken, Pa. d: 10/28/48, Conshohocken, Pa. BR/TR, 5'10.5", 203 lbs. Deb: 9/18/09

YEAR	TM/L	G	AB	R	H	2B	3B	HR	RBI	BB	SO	AVG	OBP	SLG	PRO+	BR	/A	RC	SB	CS	SBR	FR	POS	TPR
1909	Cin-N	10	21	4	4	0	1	1	4	7		.190	.393	.429	156	2	2	4	1			-1	/S	0.1
1918	Pit-N	26	77	9	10	1	1	0	2	17	17	.130	.302	.169	43	-4	-4	5	2			-8	S	-1.3
Total	2	36	98	13	14	1	2	1	6	24	17	.143	.323	.224	67	-2	-3	9	3			-9	/S	-1.2

■ FRANK ELLERBE

Ellerbe, Francis Rogers "Governor" b: 12/25/1895, Marion Co., S.C. d: 7/8/88, Latta, S.C. BR/TR, 5'10.5", 165 lbs. Deb: 8/28/19

YEAR	TM/L	G	AB	R	H	2B	3B	HR	RBI	BB	SO	AVG	OBP	SLG	PRO+	BR	/A	RC	SB	CS	SBR	FR	POS	TPR
1919	Was-A	28	105	13	29	4	1	0	16	2	15	.276	.290	.333	75	-4	-4	12	5			-4	S	-0.5
1920	Was-A	101	336	38	98	14	2	0	36	19	23	.292	.331	.345	82	-10	-9	39	5	4	-1	-5	3S/O	-0.7
1921	Was-A	10	10	1	2	0	1	0	1	0	2	.200	.200	.400	52	-1	-1	1	0	0	0	0	H	0.0
	StL-A	105	430	65	124	20	12	2	49	22	42	.288	.327	.405	81	-10	-14	56	1	6	-3	3	*3	-0.5
	Yr	115	440	66	126	20	13	2	50	22	44	.286	.325	.405	81	-11	-14	56	1	6	-3	3		-0.5
1922	StL-A	91	342	42	84	16	3	1	33	25	37	.246	.303	.319	60	-19	-21	35	1	0	0	16	3	0.4
1923	StL-A	18	49	6	9	0	0	0	1	1	5	.184	.200	.184	1	-7	-7	2	0	1	-1	-3	3	-0.8
1924	StL-A	21	61	7	12	3	0	0	2	2	3	.197	.222	.246	19	-7	-8	3	0	1	-1	3	3	-0.3
	Cle-A	46	120	7	31	1	3	1	14	1	9	.258	.270	.342	56	-8	-8	11	0	0	-1	5	3/2	0.0
	Yr	67	181	14	43	4	3	1	16	3	12	.238	.254	.309	44	-16	-16	14	0	1	-1	8		-0.3
Total	6	420	1453	179	389	58	22	4	152	72	136	.268	.306	.346	68	-67	-72	158	12	12		14	3/S2O	-2.4

■ JOE ELLICK

Ellick, Joseph J. b: 4/3/1854, Cincinnati, Ohio d: 4/21/23, Kansas City, Kan. 5'10", 162 lbs. Deb: 5/13/1875 MU

YEAR	TM/L	G	AB	R	H	2B	3B	HR	RBI	BB	SO	AVG	OBP	SLG	PRO+	BR	/A	RC	SB	CS	SBR	FR	POS	TPR
1875	RS-n	7	27	1	6	1	0	0		0		.222	.222	.259	73	-1	-0	2					/3OS	0.0
1878	Mil-N	3	13	2	2	0	0	0	1	0	1	.154	.154	.154	1	-1	-1	0				-1	/C3P	-0.1
1880	Wor-N	5	18	1	1	0	0	0	0	1	2	.056	.105	.056	-40	-3	-3	0				0	/3	-0.2
1884	CP-U	92	394	71	93	11	0	0		16		.236	.266	.264	80	-8	-8	28	0			-2	OS/2M	-0.8
	KC-U	2	8	0	0	0	0	0		0		.000	.000	.000	-99	-2	-1	0	0			-1	/2O	-0.1
	Bal-U	7	27	2	4	0	0	0		2		.148	.207	.148	20	-2	-3	1	0			-1	/SO	-0.2
	Yr	101	429	73	97	11	0	0	1	18		.226	.257	.252	73	-12	-12	28	0			-3		-1.1
Total	3	109	460	76	100	11	0	0	1	19	3	.217	.248	.241	66	-16	-16	30	0			-4	/OS32CP	-1.4

■ LARRY ELLIOT

Elliot, Lawrence Lee b: 3/5/38, San Diego, Cal. BL/TL, 6'2", 200 lbs. Deb: 4/19/62

YEAR	TM/L	G	AB	R	H	2B	3B	HR	RBI	BB	SO	AVG	OBP	SLG	PRO+	BR	/A	RC	SB	CS	SBR	FR	POS	TPR
1962	Pit-N	8	10	2	3	0	0	0	2	0	1	.300	.300	.300	135	0	0	2	0	0	0	0	/O	0.0
1963	Pit-N	4	4	0	0	0	0	0	0	0	3	.000	.000	.000	-99	-1	-1	0	0	0	0	0	H	0.0
1964	NY-N	80	224	27	51	8	0	9	22	28	55	.228	.322	.384	100	-0	0	27	1	2	-1	1	O	0.0
1966	NY-N	65	199	24	49	14	2	5	32	17	46	.246	.306	.412	100	-1	-0	25	0	1	-1	-1	O	-0.3

YEAR	TM/L	G	AB	R	H	2B	3B	HR	RBI	BB	SO	AVG	OBP	SLG	PRO+	BR	/A	RC	SB	CS	SBR	FR	POS	TPR
Total	4	157	437	53	103	22	2	15	56	45	105	.236	.311	.398	99	-2	-1	54	1	3	-2	0	O	-0.3

■ ALLEN ELLIOTT Elliott, Allen Clifford "Ace" b: 12/25/1897, St.Louis, Mo. d: 5/6/79, St.Louis, Mo. BL/TR, 6', 170 lbs. Deb: 6/14/23

YEAR	TM/L	G	AB	R	H	2B	3B	HR	RBI	BB	SO	AVG	OBP	SLG	PRO+	BR	/A	RC	SB	CS	SBR	FR	POS	TPR
1923	Chi-N	53	168	21	42	8	2	2	29	2	12	.250	.267	.357	63	-9	-9	15	3	3	-1	-2	1	-1.4
1924	Chi-N	10	14	0	2	0	0	0	0	0	1	.143	.143	.143	-23	-2	-2	0	0	0	0	-0	1	-0.2
Total	2	63	182	21	44	8	2	2	29	2	13	.242	.258	.341	57	-12	-12	16	3	3	-1	-2	/1	-1.6

■ CARTER ELLIOTT Elliott, Carter Ward b: 11/29/1893, Atchison, Kan. d: 5/21/59, Palm Springs, Cal. BL/TR, 5'11", 165 lbs. Deb: 9/10/21

YEAR	TM/L	G	AB	R	H	2B	3B	HR	RBI	BB	SO	AVG	OBP	SLG	PRO+	BR	/A	RC	SB	CS	SBR	FR	POS	TPR
1921	Chi-N	12	28	5	7	2	0	0	0	5	3	.250	.364	.321	83	-0	-0	4	0	0	0	4	S	0.4

■ GENE ELLIOTT Elliott, Eugene Birminghouse b: 2/8/1889, Fayette Co., Pa. d: 1/5/76, Huntingdon, Pa. BL/TR, 5'7", 150 lbs. Deb: 4/13/11

YEAR	TM/L	G	AB	R	H	2B	3B	HR	RBI	BB	SO	AVG	OBP	SLG	PRO+	BR	/A	RC	SB	CS	SBR	FR	POS	TPR
1911	NY-A	5	13	1	1	1	0	0		1	2	.077	.200	.154	-1	-2	-2	0	0			-1	/O3	-0.2

■ ROWDY ELLIOTT Elliott, Harold B. b: 7/8/1890, Kokomo, Ind. d: 2/12/34, San Francisco, Cal BR/TR, 5'9", 160 lbs. Deb: 9/24/10

YEAR	TM/L	G	AB	R	H	2B	3B	HR	RBI	BB	SO	AVG	OBP	SLG	PRO+	BR	/A	RC	SB	CS	SBR	FR	POS	TPR
1910	Bos-N	3	2	0	0	0	0	0	0	0	0	.000	.000	.000	-96	-1	-1	0	0			-0	/C	0.0
1916	Chi-N	23	55	5	14	3	0	0	3	3	5	.255	.293	.309	77	-1	-2	6	1			-1	C	-0.1
1917	Chi-N	85	223	18	56	8	5	0	28	11	11	.251	.292	.332	84	-3	-5	22	4			4	C	0.4
1918	Chi-N	5	10	0	0	0	0	0	0	2	1	.000	.167	.000	-47	-2	-2	0	0			0	/C	0.0
1920	Bro-N	41	112	13	27	4	0	1	13	3	6	.241	.267	.304	62	-5	-6	9	0	0	0	4	C	0.1
Total	5	157	402	36	97	15	5	1	44	19	23	.241	.281	.311	73	-11	-14	37	5	0		9	C	0.4

■ HARRY ELLIOTT Elliott, Harry Lewis b: 12/30/23, San Francisco, Cal BR/TR, 5'9", 175 lbs. Deb: 8/01/53

YEAR	TM/L	G	AB	R	H	2B	3B	HR	RBI	BB	SO	AVG	OBP	SLG	PRO+	BR	/A	RC	SB	CS	SBR	FR	POS	TPR
1953	StL-N	24	59	6	15	6	1	1	6	3	8	.254	.302	.441	91	-1	-1	7	0	0	0	1	O	0.0
1955	StL-N	68	117	9	30	4	0	1	12	11	9	.256	.326	.316	71	-5	-5	10	0	2	-1	-1	O	-0.6
Total	2	92	176	15	45	10	1	2	18	14	17	.256	.318	.358	78	-6	-6	17	0	2	-1	0	/O	-0.6

■ RANDY ELLIOTT Elliott, Randy Lee b: 6/5/51, Oxnard, Cal. BR/TR, 6'2", 190 lbs. Deb: 9/10/72

YEAR	TM/L	G	AB	R	H	2B	3B	HR	RBI	BB	SO	AVG	OBP	SLG	PRO+	BR	/A	RC	SB	CS	SBR	FR	POS	TPR
1972	SD-N	14	49	5	10	3	1	0	6	2	11	.204	.235	.306	57	-3	-3	3	0	0	0	0	O	-0.2
1974	SD-N	13	33	5	7	1	0	1	2	7	9	.212	.350	.333	96	-0	0	4	0	1	-1	-3	O/1	-0.3
1977	SF-N	73	167	17	40	5	1	7	26	8	24	.240	.278	.407	82	-5	-5	17	0	2	-1	1	O	-0.6
1980	Oak-A	14	39	4	5	3	0	0	1	1	13	.128	.150	.205	-4	-6	-5	1	0	0	0	D	-0.5
Total	4	114	288	31	62	12	2	8	35	18	57	.215	.264	.354	69	-14	-13	25	0	3	-2	-2	/OD1	-1.6

■ BOB ELLIOTT Elliott, Robert Irving "Mr. Team" b: 11/26/16, San Francisco, Cal d: 5/4/66, San Diego, Cal. BR/TR, 6', 185 lbs. Deb: 9/02/39 MC

YEAR	TM/L	G	AB	R	H	2B	3B	HR	RBI	BB	SO	AVG	OBP	SLG	PRO+	BR	/A	RC	SB	CS	SBR	FR	POS	TPR
1939	Pit-N	32	129	18	43	10	3	3	19	9	4	.333	.377	.527	143	7	7	24	0			3	O	0.9
1940	Pit-N	148	551	88	161	34	11	5	64	45	28	.292	.348	.421	112	8	8	81	13			1	*O	0.4
1941	Pit-N	141	527	74	144	24	10	3	76	64	52	.273	.353	.374	105	4	5	72	6			-6	*O	-0.6
1942	Pit-N	143	560	75	166	26	7	9	89	52	35	.296	.358	.416	123	18	16	84	2			-2	*3/O	1.5
1943	Pit-N	156	581	82	183	30	12	7	101	56	24	.315	.376	.444	132	26	24	96	4			-7	*3/2S	1.8
1944	Pit-N	143	538	85	160	28	16	10	108	75	42	.297	.383	.465	132	28	25	100	9			-1	*3/S	3.2
1945	Pit-N	144	541	80	157	36	6	8	108	64	38	.290	.366	.423	115	14	11	84	5			7	3O	1.4
1946	Pit-N	140	486	50	128	25	3	5	68	64	44	.263	.351	.358	99	2	1	62	6			0	O3	0.0
1947	Bos-N	150	555	93	176	35	5	22	113	87	60	.317	.410	.517	148	37	39	120	3			-2	*3	3.1
1948	*Bos-N	151	540	99	153	24	5	23	100	**131**	57	.283	.423	.474	145	38	39	117	6			-10	*3	2.6
1949	Bos-N	139	482	77	135	29	5	17	76	90	38	.280	.395	.467	138	23	27	92	0			11	*3	3.8
1950	Bos-N	142	531	94	162	28	5	24	107	68	67	.305	.386	.512	143	26	31	103	2			-17	*3	1.3
1951	Bos-N	136	480	73	137	29	2	15	70	65	56	.285	.371	.448	128	14	18	81	2	0	1	-7	*3	1.0
1952	NY-N	98	272	33	62	6	2	10	35	36	20	.228	.323	.375	92	-3	-3	35	1	0	0	-5	O3	-0.8
1953	StL-A	48	160	19	40	7	1	5	29	30	18	.250	.368	.400	105	2	2	25	0	1	-1	-2	3	-0.1
	Chi-A	67	208	24	54	11	1	4	32	31	21	.260	.358	.380	96	0	-0	31	1	1	-0	-10	3/O	-1.3
	Yr	115	368	43	94	18	2	9	61	61	39	.255	.363	.389	100	3	1	56	1	2	-1	-12		-1.4
Total	15	1978	7141	1064	2061	382	94	170	1195	967	604	.289	.375	.440	124	245	250	1206	60	2		-46	*3O/S2	18.2

■ BEN ELLIS Ellis, Benjamin Franklin b: 7/1870, New York, N.Y. Deb: 7/16/1896

YEAR	TM/L	G	AB	R	H	2B	3B	HR	RBI	BB	SO	AVG	OBP	SLG	PRO+	BR	/A	RC	SB	CS	SBR	FR	POS	TPR
1896	Phi-N	4	16	0	1	0	0	0	0	3	6	.063	.211	.063	-25	-3	-3	0	0			-1	/S3	-0.2

■ RUBE ELLIS Ellis, George William b: 11/17/1885, Downey, Cal. d: 3/13/38, Rivera, Cal. BL/TL, 6', 170 lbs. Deb: 4/15/09

YEAR	TM/L	G	AB	R	H	2B	3B	HR	RBI	BB	SO	AVG	OBP	SLG	PRO+	BR	/A	RC	SB	CS	SBR	FR	POS	TPR
1909	StL-N	149	575	76	154	10	9	3	46	54		.268	.334	.332	114	5	9	68	16			13	*O	1.9
1910	StL-N	142	550	87	142	18	8	4	54	62	70	.258	.339	.342	102	-1	2	72	25			5	*O	0.2
1911	StL-N	155	555	69	139	20	11	2	66	66	64	.250	.332	.337	90	-9	-7	66	9			3	O	-0.8
1912	StL-N	109	305	47	82	18	2	4	33	34	36	.269	.342	.380	100	-1	-0	42	6			0	O	-0.1
Total	4	555	1985	279	517	66	30	13	199	216	170	.260	.336	.344	101	-6	4	248	56			21	O	1.2

■ JOHN ELLIS Ellis, John Charles b: 8/21/48, New London, Conn. BR/TR, 6'2.5", 225 lbs. Deb: 5/17/69

YEAR	TM/L	G	AB	R	H	2B	3B	HR	RBI	BB	SO	AVG	OBP	SLG	PRO+	BR	/A	RC	SB	CS	SBR	FR	POS	TPR
1969	NY-A	22	62	2	18	4	0	1	8	1	11	.290	.313	.403	103	-0	-0	7	0	2	-1	0	C	0.0
1970	NY-A	78	226	24	56	12	1	7	29	18	47	.248	.309	.403	100	-2	-1	27	0	1	-1	1	1/3C	-0.2
1971	NY-A	83	238	16	58	12	1	3	34	23	42	.244	.326	.340	95	-3	-1	25	0	0	0	-3	1/C	-0.7
1972	NY-A	52	136	13	40	5	1	5	25	8	22	.294	.333	.456	138	5	5	17	0	0	0	1	C/1	0.6
1973	Cle-A	127	437	59	118	12	2	14	68	46	57	.270	.344	.403	108	6	5	60	0	0	0	-17	CD1	-1.0
1974	Cle-A	128	477	58	136	23	6	10	64	32	53	.285	.331	.421	116	8	9	62	1	2	-1	-8	1CD	-0.1
1975	Cle-A	92	296	22	68	11	1	7	32	14	33	.230	.269	.345	72	-12	-12	24	0	1	-1	-7	C/1D	-1.7
1976	Tex-A	11	31	4	13	2	0	1	8	0	4	.419	.419	.581	187	3	3	7	0	0	0	-1	/CD	0.3
1977	Tex-A	49	119	7	28	7	0	4	15	8	26	.235	.283	.395	82	-3	-3	13	0	0	0	-2	CD/1	-0.5
1978	Tex-A	34	94	7	23	4	0	3	17	6	20	.245	.290	.383	88	-2	-2	11	0	1	-1	-1	C/D	-0.2
1979	Tex-A	111	316	33	90	12	0	12	61	15	55	.285	.321	.437	103	0	1	44	2	2	-1	-3	D1/C	-0.3
1980	Tex-A	73	182	12	43	9	1	1	23	14	23	.236	.294	.313	69	-8	-8	17	3	0	1	-2	1D/C	-1.1
1981	Tex-A	23	58	2	8	3	0	1	7	5	10	.138	.219	.241	34	-5	-5	2	0	1	-1	-1	1/D	-0.6
Total	13	883	2672	259	699	116	13	69	391	190	403	.262	.315	.392	99	-14	-9	317	6	10	-4	-43	1CD/3	-5.5

■ ROB ELLIS Ellis, Robert Walter b: 7/3/50, Grand Rapids, Mich. BR/TR, 5'11", 180 lbs. Deb: 6/18/71

YEAR	TM/L	G	AB	R	H	2B	3B	HR	RBI	BB	SO	AVG	OBP	SLG	PRO+	BR	/A	RC	SB	CS	SBR	FR	POS	TPR
1971	Mil-A	36	111	9	22	2	0	0	6	12	24	.198	.282	.216	43	-8	-8	7	0	2	-1	-7	3O	-1.8
1974	Mil-A	22	48	4	14	2	0	0	4	4	11	.292	.346	.333	97	-0	-0	6	0	0	0	2	O/3D	0.1
1975	Mil-A	6	7	0	2	0	0	0	0	0	0	.286	.286	.286	62	-0	-0	0	0	0	0	-0	/OD	0.0
Total	3	64	166	16	38	4	0	0	10	16	35	.229	.301	.253	59	-9	-8	13	0	2	-1	-6	/O3D	-1.7

■ BABE ELLISON Ellison, Herbert Spencer "Bert" b: 11/15/1895, Rutland, Ark. d: 8/11/55, San Francisco, Cal BR/TR, 5'11", 170 lbs. Deb: 9/18/16

YEAR	TM/L	G	AB	R	H	2B	3B	HR	RBI	BB	SO	AVG	OBP	SLG	PRO+	BR	/A	RC	SB	CS	SBR	FR	POS	TPR
1916	Det-A	2	7	0	1	0	0	0	1	0	1	.143	.143	.143	-14	-1	-1	0	0			-1	/3	-0.2
1917	Det-A	9	29	2	5	1	2	1	4	6	3	.172	.333	.448	139	1	1	4	0			-2	/1	0.0
1918	Det-A	7	23	1	6	1	0	0	2	3	1	.261	.346	.304	100	-0	-0	3	1			-0	/O2	0.0
1919	Det-A	56	134	18	29	4	0	0	11	13	24	.216	.291	.246	53	-8	-8	11	4			-7	2O/S	-1.3
1920	Det-A	61	155	11	34	7	2	0	21	8	26	.219	.258	.290	46	-13	-12	12	4	1	1	2	1/O3	-0.9
Total	5	135	348	32	75	13	4	1	39	30	55	.216	.282	.284	58	-21	-20	30	9	1		-9	/1203S	-2.4

▼ VERDO ELMORE Elmore, Verdo Wilson "Ellie" b: 12/10/1899, Gordo, Ala. d: 8/5/69, Birmingham, Ala. BL/TR, 5'11", 185 lbs. Deb: 9/11/24

YEAR	TM/L	G	AB	R	H	2B	3B	HR	RBI	BB	SO	AVG	OBP	SLG	PRO+	BR	/A	RC	SB	CS	SBR	FR	POS	TPR
1924	StL-A	7	17	2	3	3	0	0	0	1	3	.176	.222	.353	44	-2	-2	1	0	0	0	-2	/O	-0.2

YEAR	TM/L	G	AB	R	H	2B	3B	HR	RBI	BB	SO	AVG	OBP	SLG	PRO+	BR	/A	RC	SB	CS	SBR	FR	POS	TPR

■ ROY ELSH Elsh, Eugene Reybold b: 3/1/1892, Penns Grove, N.J. d: 11/12/78, Philadelphia, Pa. BR/TR, 5'9", 165 lbs. Deb: 4/19/23

1923	Chi-A	81	209	28	52	7	2	0	24	16	23	.249	.305	.301	61	-12	-12	20	15	8	-0	1	O	-1.5
1924	Chi-A	60	147	21	45	9	1	0	11	10	14	.306	.350	.381	91	-3	-2	20	6	2	1	-6	O/1	-0.9
1925	Chi-A	32	48	6	9	1	0	0	4	5	7	.188	.264	.208	22	-6	-5	3	2	0	1	-1	O/1	-0.6
Total	3	173	404	55	106	17	3	0	39	31	44	.262	.317	.319	67	-21	-19	43	23	10	1	-6	O/1	-3.0

■ KEVIN ELSTER Elster, Kevin Daniel b: 8/3/64, San Pedro, Cal. BR/TR, 6'2", 180 lbs. Deb: 9/02/86

1986	*NY-N	19	30	3	5	1	0	0	0	3	8	.167	.242	.200	24	-3	-3	2	0	0	0	4	S	0.3
1987	NY-N	5	10	1	4	2	0	0	1	0	1	.400	.400	.600	169	1	1	2	0	0	0	-0	/S	0.1
1988	*NY-N	149	406	41	87	11	1	9	37	35	47	.214	.282	.313	74	-16	-13	37	2	0	1	7	*S	0.3
1989	NY-N	151	458	52	106	25	2	10	55	34	77	.231	.287	.360	88	-10	-8	45	4	3	-1	7	*S	0.8
1990	NY-N	92	314	36	65	20	1	9	45	30	54	.207	.278	.363	77	-11	-11	33	2	0	1	15	S	1.3
Total	5	416	1218	133	267	59	4	28	138	102	187	.219	.283	.343	80	-40	-34	118	8	3	1	32	S	2.8

■ BONES ELY Ely, William Frederick b: 6/7/1863, N.Girard, Pa. d: 1/10/52, Berkeley, Cal. BR/TR, 6'1", 155 lbs. Deb: 6/19/1884

1884	Buf-N	1	4	0	0	0	0	0	0	0	2	.000	.000	.000	-97	-1	-1	0				-1	/OP	0.0
1886	Lou-a	10	32	5	5	0	0	0			2	.156	.206	.156	14	-3	-3	1	1			-0	/PO	0.0
1890	Syr-a	119	496	72	130	16	6	0			31	.262	.307	.319	96	-9	-2	64	44			19	OS/123P	1.4
1891	Bro-N	31	111	9	17	0	1	0	11	7	9	.153	.203	.171	11	-12	-12	5	4			8	S/32	-0.1
1893	StL-N	44	178	25	45	1	6	0	16	17	13	.253	.318	.326	73	-7	-7	20	2			-3	S	-0.6
1894	StL-N	127	510	85	156	20	12	12	89	30	34	.306	.344	.463	95	-7	-7	91	23			1	*S/2P	0.1
1895	StL-N	117	467	68	121	16	2	1	46	19	17	.259	.288	.308	56	-31	-30	51	28			6	*S	-1.1
1896	Pit-N	128	537	85	153	15	9	3	77	33	33	.285	.326	.363	87	-13	-10	71	18			-2	*S	-0.9
1897	Pit-N	133	516	63	146	20	8	2	74	25		.283	.317	.364	85	-14	-11	64	10			3	*S	-0.3
1898	Pit-N	148	519	49	110	14	5	2	44	24		.212	.247	.270	51	-34	-32	37	6			8	*S	-1.5
1899	Pit-N	138	522	66	145	18	6	3	72	22		.278	.313	.352	85	-12	-11	62	8			5	*S/2	0.1
1900	*Pit-N	130	475	60	116	6	6	0	51	17		.244	.282	.282	54	-29	-29	39	6			13	*S	-0.2
1901	Pit-N	65	240	18	50	6	3	0	28	6		.208	.234	.258	43	-17	-18	17	5			-9	S/3	-2.2
	Phi-A	45	171	11	37	6	2	0	16	3		.216	.230	.275	39	-14	-15	13	6			1	S	-0.9
1902	Was-A	105	381	39	100	11	2	1	62	21		.262	.303	.310	71	-14	-15	39	9			-9	*S	-1.3
Total	14	1341	5159	655	1331	149	68	24	586	257	108	.258	.295	.327	71	-216	-203	574	164			41	*S/O2P31	-7.5

■ CHESTER EMERSON Emerson, Chester Arthur "Chuck" b: 10/27/1889, Stow, Me. d: 7/2/71, Augusta, Me. BL/TR, 5'8", 165 lbs. Deb: 9/27/11

1911	Phi-A	7	18	2	4	0	0	0	0	6		.222	.417	.222	82	0	0	2	1			1	/O	0.0
1912	Phi-A	1	1	0	0	0	0	0	0	0		.000	.000	.000	-99	-0	-0	0	0			0	H	0.0
Total	2	8	19	2	4	0	0	0	0	6		.211	.400	.211	74	-0	-0	2	1			1	/O	0.0

■ CAL EMERY Emery, Calvin Wayne b: 6/28/37, Centre Hall, Pa. BL/TL, 6'2", 205 lbs. Deb: 7/15/63 C

| 1963 | Phi-N | 16 | 19 | 0 | 3 | 1 | 0 | 0 | 0 | 0 | 2 | .158 | .158 | .211 | 5 | -2 | -2 | 1 | 0 | 0 | 0 | -0 | /1 | -0.2 |

■ SPOKE EMERY Emery, Herrick Smith b: 12/10/1898, Bay City, Mich. d: 6/2/75, Cape Canaveral, Fla. BR/TR, 5'9", 165 lbs. Deb: 7/18/24

| 1924 | Phi-N | 5 | 3 | 3 | 2 | 0 | 0 | 0 | 0 | 0 | 0 | .667 | .667 | .667 | 230 | 1 | 1 | 1 | 0 | 1 | -1 | 1 | /O | 0.1 |

■ FRANK EMMER Emmer, Frank William b: 2/17/1896, Crestline, Ohio d: 10/18/63, Homestead, Fla. BR/TR, 5'8", 150 lbs. Deb: 4/25/16

1916	Cin-N	42	89	8	13	3	1	0	2	7	27	.146	.208	.202	27	-8	-7	4	1			5	S/O23	0.0
1926	Cin-N	80	224	22	44	7	6	0	18	13	30	.196	.244	.281	42	-19	-18	16	1			-7	S	-1.9
Total	2	122	313	30	57	10	7	0	20	20	57	.182	.234	.259	38	-27	-26	20	2			-2	S/O32	-1.9

■ BOB EMMERICH Emmerich, Robert G. b: 8/1/1897, New York, N.Y. d: 11/22/48, Bridgeport, Conn. BR/TR, 5'3", 155 lbs. Deb: 9/22/23

| 1923 | Bos-N | 13 | 24 | 3 | 2 | 0 | 0 | 0 | 0 | 2 | 3 | .083 | .154 | .083 | -37 | -5 | -5 | 0 | 1 | 1 | -0 | 1 | /O | -0.3 |

■ BILL ENDICOTT Endicott, William Franklin b: 9/4/18, Acorn, Mo. BL/TL, 5'11.5", 175 lbs. Deb: 4/21/46

| 1946 | StL-N | 20 | 20 | 2 | 4 | 3 | 0 | 0 | 3 | 4 | 4 | .200 | .333 | .350 | 90 | -0 | -0 | 2 | 0 | | | 0 | /O | 0.0 |

■ CLYDE ENGLE Engle, Arthur Clyde "Hack" b: 3/19/1884, Dayton, Ohio d: 12/26/39, Boston, Mass. BR/TR, 5'10", 190 lbs. Deb: 4/12/09

1909	NY-A	135	492	66	137	20	5	3	71	47		.278	.347	.358	122	13	13	68	18			14	*O	2.5
1910	NY-A	5	13	0	3	0	0	0	0	2		.231	.333	.231	73	-0	-0	1	1			-0	/O	0.0
	Bos-A	106	363	59	96	18	7	2	38	31		.264	.326	.369	115	7	6	47	12			1	32O/S	0.7
	Yr	111	376	59	99	18	7	2	38	33		.263	.326	.364	113	6	5	49	13			0		0.7
1911	Bos-A	146	514	58	139	13	3	2	48	51		.270	.343	.319	86	-9	-8	65	24			-4	132O	-1.0
1912	*Bos-A	58	171	32	40	5	3	0	18	28		.234	.348	.298	81	-2	-3	22	12			-8	123/SO	-1.0
1913	Bos-A	143	498	75	144	17	12	2	50	53	41	.289	.363	.384	116	12	10	76	28			-7	*1/O	0.3
1914	Bos-A	59	134	14	26	2	0	0	9	14	11	.194	.275	.209	46	-8	-8	7	4	9	-4	-4	1/23O	-1.8
	Buf-F	32	110	12	28	4	1	0	12	11	18	.255	.328	.309	81	-2	-2	14	5			-7	3/O	-0.9
1915	Buf-F	141	501	56	131	22	8	3	71	34	43	.261	.312	.355	95	-2	-4	66	24			-3	*O23/1	-1.0
1916	Cle-A	11	26	1	4	0	0	0	1	0	6	.154	.154	.154	-7	-3	-4	1	0			-2	/31O	-0.6
Total	8	836	2822	373	748	101	39	12	318	271	119	.265	.335	.341	99	4	-1	367	128	9		-20	O13/2S	-2.8

■ CHARLIE ENGLE Engle, Charlie August "Cholly" b: 8/27/03, New York, N.Y. d: 10/12/83, San Antonio, Tex. BR/TR, 5'8", 145 lbs. Deb: 9/14/25

1925	Phi-A	1	0	0	0	0	0	0	0	0	0	—	—	—		0	0	0	0	0	0	0	/S	0.0
1926	Phi-A	19	19	7	2	0	0	0	0	10	6	.105	.433	.105	43	-1	-1	2	0	0	0	2	S	0.2
1930	Pit-N	67	216	34	57	10	1	0	15	22	20	.264	.335	.319	59	-14	-14	24	1			-0	3S2	-0.9
Total	3	87	235	41	59	10	1	0	15	32	26	.251	.346	.302	59	-14	-15	26	1	0		2	/S32	-0.7

■ DAVE ENGLE Engle, Ralph David b: 11/30/56, San Diego, Cal. BR/TR, 6'3", 210 lbs. Deb: 4/14/81

1981	Min-A	82	248	29	64	14	4	5	32	13	37	.258	.298	.407	95	-0	-2	27	0	1	-1	-5	O/3D	-0.9
1982	Min-A	58	186	20	42	7	2	4	16	10	22	.226	.269	.349	67	-8	-9	16	0	0	0	1	OD	-0.8
1983	Min-A	120	374	46	114	22	4	8	43	28	39	.305	.355	.449	115	10	8	57	2	1	0	-18	CD/O	-0.6
1984	Min-A	109	391	56	104	20	1	4	38	26	22	.266	.312	.353	80	-9	-11	39	0	1	-1	-8	CD	-1.4
1985	Min-A	70	172	28	44	8	2	7	25	21	28	.256	.337	.448	106	3	2	26	2	2	-1	-1	DC/O	0.1
1986	Det-A	35	86	6	22	7	0	4	7	7	13	.256	.312	.337	77	-3	-3	9	0	0	0	0	1/OCD	-0.3
1987	Mon-N	59	84	7	19	4	0	1	14	6	11	.226	.278	.310	54	-5	-6	6	1	0	0	-0	O/C13	-0.5
1988	Mon-N	34	37	4	8	3	0	0	1	5	5	.216	.310	.297	72	-1	-1	3	0	0	0	-0	/CO3	-0.1
1989	Mil-A	27	65	5	14	3	0	2	8	4	13	.215	.261	.354	72	-3	-3	6	0	0	0	-0	1/CD	-0.3
Total	9	594	1643	201	431	88	13	31	181	120	190	.262	.314	.388	90	-17	-25	189	5	5	-2	-31	COD/13	-4.8

■ CHARLIE ENGLISH English, Charles Dewie b: 4/8/10, Darlington, S.C. BR/TR, 5'9.5", 160 lbs. Deb: 7/23/32

1932	Chi-A	24	63	7	20	3	1	1	8	3	7	.317	.348	.444	111	0	1	10	0	0	0	-2	3/S	0.0
1933	Chi-A	3	9	2	4	2	0	0	1	1	1	.444	.500	.667	216	1	1	3	0	0	0	-1	/2	0.1
1936	NY-N	6	1	0	0	0	0	0	0	0	0	.000	.000	.000	-99	-0	-0	0	0			0	/2	0.0
1937	Cin-N	17	63	1	15	3	1	0	4	0	2	.238	.238	.317	52	-5	-4	4	0			2	3/2	-0.1
Total	4	50	136	10	39	8	2	1	13	4	10	.287	.307	.397	90	-3	-2	17	0	0		-1	/32S	0.0

■ WOODY ENGLISH English, Elwood George b: 3/2/07, Fredonia, Ohio BR/TR, 5'10", 155 lbs. Deb: 4/26/27

| 1927 | Chi-N | 87 | 334 | 46 | 97 | 14 | 4 | 1 | 28 | 16 | 26 | .290 | .325 | .365 | 84 | -8 | -8 | 39 | 1 | | | 7 | S/3 | 0.7 |

YEAR	TM/L	G	AB	R	H	2B	3B	HR	RBI	BB	SO	AVG	OBP	SLG	PRO+	BR	/A	RC	SB	CS	SBR	FR	POS	TPR
1928	Chi-N	116	475	68	142	22	4	2	34	30	28	.299	.343	.375	89	-9	-8	60	4			6	*S/3	1.3
1929	*Chi-N	144	608	131	168	29	3	1	52	68	50	.276	.352	.339	72	-25	-25	74	13	·		15	*S	0.9
1930	Chi-N	156	638	152	214	36	17	14	59	100	72	.335	.430	.511	125	31	30	141	3			-13	3S	2.3
1931	Chi-N	156	634	117	202	38	8	2	53	68	80	.319	.391	.413	114	17	16	108	12			1	*S3	2.8
1932	*Chi-N	127	522	70	142	23	7	3	47	55	73	.272	.344	.360	90	-6	-6	68	5			-2	3S	0.3
1933	Chi-N	105	398	54	104	19	2	3	41	53	44	.261	.348	.342	98	0	1	51	5			-15	*3/S	-1.1
1934	Chi-N	109	421	65	117	26	5	3	31	48	65	.278	.353	.385	99	-1	1	61	6			-10	S3/2	-0.3
1935	Chi-N	34	84	11	17	2	0	2	8	20	4	.202	.368	.298	81	-1	-1	12	1			-5	3S	-0.4
1936	Chi-N	64	182	33	45	9	0	0	20	40	28	.247	.394	.297	86	-0	-1	26	1			1	S3/2	0.4
1937	Bro-N	129	378	45	90	16	2	1	42	65	55	.238	.350	.299	77	-9	-10	42	4			-17	*S2	-1.7
1938	Bro-N	34	72	9	18	2	0	0	7	8	11	.250	.333	.278	68	-3	-3	7	2			1	3/2S	-0.1
Total	12	1261	4746	801	1356	236	52	32	422	571	536	.286	.366	.378	95	-12	-14	690	57			-30	S3/2	5.1

■ GIL ENGLISH
English, Gilbert Raymond b: 7/2/09, Glenola, N.C. BR/TR, 5'11", 180 lbs. Deb: 9/20/31

YEAR	TM/L	G	AB	R	H	2B	3B	HR	RBI	BB	SO	AVG	OBP	SLG	PRO+	BR	/A	RC	SB	CS	SBR	FR	POS	TPR
1931	NY-N	3	8	0	0	0	0	0	0	1	3	.000	.111	.000	-69	-2	-2	0	0			-1	/3	-0.1
1932	NY-N	59	204	22	46	7	5	2	19	5	20	.225	.244	.338	56	-13	-13	17	0			4	3S	-0.3
1936	Det-A	1	1	0	0	0	0	0	0	0	0	.000	.000	.000	-99	-0	-0	0	0	0	0	0	/3	0.0
1937	Det-A	18	65	6	17	1	0	1	6	6	4	.262	.333	.323	65	-3	-3	7	1	1	-0	-8	2/3	-0.9
	Bos-N	79	269	25	78	5	2	2	37	23	27	.290	.348	.346	98	-3	-0	32	3			-7	3	-0.3
1938	Bos-N	53	165	17	41	6	0	2	21	15	16	.248	.315	.321	84	-5	-3	16	1			-3	3/O2S	-0.6
1944	Bro-N	27	79	4	12	3	0	1	7	6	7	.152	.212	.228	24	-8	-8	4	0			-3	3/S2	-0.8
Total	6	240	791	74	194	22	7	8	90	56	78	.245	.298	.321	72	-36	-30	76	5	1		-17	3/S2O	-3.0

■ DEL ENNIS
Ennis, Delmer b: 6/8/25, Philadelphia, Pa. BR/TR, 6', 195 lbs. Deb: 4/28/46

YEAR	TM/L	G	AB	R	H	2B	3B	HR	RBI	BB	SO	AVG	OBP	SLG	PRO+	BR	/A	RC	SB	CS	SBR	FR	POS	TPR
1946	Phi-N	141	540	70	169	30	6	17	73	39	65	.313	.364	.485	144	25	27	96	5			12	*O	3.8
1947	Phi-N	139	541	71	149	25	6	12	81	37	51	.275	.325	.410	98	-6	-3	69	9			6	*O	-0.1
1948	Phi-N	152	589	86	171	40	4	30	95	47	58	.290	.345	.525	135	23	25	106	2			-2	*O	1.2
1949	Phi-N	154	610	92	184	39	11	25	110	59	61	.302	.367	.525	140	29	32	118	2			3	*O	2.5
1950	*Phi-N	153	595	92	185	34	8	31	126	56	59	.311	.372	.551	142	32	33	115	2			-4	*O	2.3
1951	Phi-N	144	532	76	142	20	5	15	73	68	42	.267	.352	.408	105	4	5	77	4	2	0	-1	*O	0.0
1952	Phi-N	151	592	90	171	30	10	20	107	47	65	.289	.341	.475	125	17	18	94	6	4	-1	-5	*O	0.9
1953	Phi-N	152	578	79	165	22	3	29	125	57	53	.285	.355	.484	117	13	13	100	1	3	-2	2	*O	0.7
1954	Phi-N	145	556	73	145	23	2	25	119	50	60	.261	.324	.444	98	-3	-3	75	2	1	0	2	*O/1	-0.6
1955	Phi-N	146	564	82	167	24	7	29	120	46	46	.296	.351	.518	129	20	21	99	4	2	0	3	*O	2.1
1956	Phi-N	153	630	80	164	23	3	26	95	33	62	.260	.300	.430	95	-8	-6	77	7	3		-7	*O	-1.8
1957	StL-N	136	490	61	140	24	3	24	105	37	50	.286	.337	.494	117	12	11	73	1	3	-2	-19	*O	-1.2
1958	StL-N	106	329	22	86	18	1	3	47	15	35	.261	.296	.350	67	-14	-16	29	0	1	-1	-2	*O	-2.1
1959	Cin-N	5	12	1	4	0	0	0	1	2	2	.333	.429	.333	103	0	0	2	0	0	0	-0	/O	0.0
	Chi-A	26	96	10	21	6	0	2	7	4	10	.219	.250	.344	62	-5	-5	8	0	0	0	-5	O	-1.1
Total	14	1903	7254	985	2063	358	69	288	1284	597	719	.284	.341	.472	117	139	151	1137	45	19		-17	*O/1	6.6

■ RUSS ENNIS
Ennis, Russell Elwood "Hack" b: 3/10/1897, Superior, Wis. d: 1/21/49, Superior, Wis. BR/TR, 5'11.5", 160 lbs. Deb: 9/19/26

YEAR	TM/L	G	AB	R	H	2B	3B	HR	RBI	BB	SO	AVG	OBP	SLG	PRO+	BR	/A	RC	SB	CS	SBR	FR	POS	TPR
1926	Was-A	1	0	0	0	0	0	0	0	0	0	—	—	—	—	0	0	0	0	0	0	0	/C	0.0

■ GEORGE ENRIGHT
Enright, George Albert b: 5/9/54, New Britain, Conn. BR/TR, 5'11", 175 lbs. Deb: 8/08/76

YEAR	TM/L	G	AB	R	H	2B	3B	HR	RBI	BB	SO	AVG	OBP	SLG	PRO+	BR	/A	RC	SB	CS	SBR	FR	POS	TPR
1976	Chi-A	2	1	0	0	0	0	0	0	0	0	.000	.000	.000	-99	-0	-0	0	0	0	0	1	/C	0.0

■ MUTZ ENS
Ens, Anton b: 11/8/1884, St.Louis, Mo. d: 6/28/50, St.Louis, Mo. BL/TL, 6'1", 180 lbs. Deb: 9/02/12

YEAR	TM/L	G	AB	R	H	2B	3B	HR	RBI	BB	SO	AVG	OBP	SLG	PRO+	BR	/A	RC	SB	CS	SBR	FR	POS	TPR
1912	Chi-A	3	6	0	0	0	0	0	0	0	0	.000	.000	.000	-99	-2	-2	0	0			-1	/1	-0.1

■ JEWEL ENS
Ens, Jewel Winklemeyer b: 8/24/1889, St.Louis, Mo. d: 1/17/50, Syracuse, N.Y. BR/TR, 5'10.5", 165 lbs. Deb: 4/29/22 MC

YEAR	TM/L	G	AB	R	H	2B	3B	HR	RBI	BB	SO	AVG	OBP	SLG	PRO+	BR	/A	RC	SB	CS	SBR	FR	POS	TPR
1922	Pit-N	47	142	18	42	7	3	0	17	7	9	.296	.338	.387	85	-3	-3	19	3	0	1	-16	2/31S	-1.6
1923	Pit-N	12	29	3	8	1	1	0	5	0	3	.276	.276	.379	70	-1	-1	3	2	0	1	-0	/13	0.0
1924	Pit-N	5	10	2	3	0	0	0	0	0	3	.300	.300	.300	60	-1	-1	1	0	0	0	-0	/1	0.0
1925	Pit-N	3	5	2	1	0	0	1	2	0	1	.200	.200	.800	133	0	0	2	0	0	0	-0	/1	0.0
Total	4	67	186	25	54	8	4	1	24	7	16	.290	.323	.392	83	-5	-5	24	5	0	2	-16	/213S	-1.6

■ CHARLIE ENWRIGHT
Enwright, Charles Massey b: 10/6/1887, Sacramento, Cal. d: 1/19/17, Sacramento, Cal. BL/TR, 5'10", Deb: 4/19/09

YEAR	TM/L	G	AB	R	H	2B	3B	HR	RBI	BB	SO	AVG	OBP	SLG	PRO+	BR	/A	RC	SB	CS	SBR	FR	POS	TPR
1909	StL-N	3	7	1	1	0	0	0		1	2	.143	.333	.143	51	-0	-0	0	0			-3	/S	-0.3

■ JACK ENZENROTH
Enzenroth, Clarence Herman b: 11/4/1885, Mineral Point, Wis. d: 2/21/44, Detroit, Mich. BR/TR, 5'10", 164 lbs. Deb: 5/01/14

YEAR	TM/L	G	AB	R	H	2B	3B	HR	RBI	BB	SO	AVG	OBP	SLG	PRO+	BR	/A	RC	SB	CS	SBR	FR	POS	TPR
1914	StL-A	3	6	0	1	0	0	0	0	2	3	.167	.444	.167	88	0	0	0	0	1	-1	-1	/C	-0.1
	KC-F	26	67	7	12	4	1	0	5	5	19	.179	.236	.269	46	-5	-5	4	0			-7	C	-1.0
1915	KC-F	14	19	3	3	0	0	0	3	6	0	.158	.360	.158	58	-1	-1	1	0			0	/C	0.0
Total	2	43	92	10	16	4	1	0	8	13	22	.174	.283	.239	54	-5	-5	6	0	1		-8	/C	-1.1

■ JIM EPPARD
Eppard, James Gerhard b: 4/27/60, South Bend, Ind. BL/TL, 6'2", 180 lbs. Deb: 9/08/87

YEAR	TM/L	G	AB	R	H	2B	3B	HR	RBI	BB	SO	AVG	OBP	SLG	PRO+	BR	/A	RC	SB	CS	SBR	FR	POS	TPR
1987	Cal-A	8	9	2	3	0	0	0	0	2	0	.333	.455	.333	118	0	0	1	0	0	0	-0	/O	0.0
1988	Cal-A	56	113	7	32	3	1	0	14	11	15	.283	.347	.327	92	-1	-1	13	0	0	0	4	OD/1	0.2
1989	Cal-A	12	12	0	3	0	0	0	2	1	4	.250	.308	.250	60	-1	-1	1	0	0	0	-0	/1	0.0
1990	Tor-A	6	5	0	1	0	0	0	0	0	2	.200	.333	.200	54	-0	-0	0	0	0	0	0	/H	0.0
Total	4	82	139	9	39	3	1	0	16	14	21	.281	.351	.317	90	-2	-1	15	0	0	0	4	/O1D	0.2

■ AUBREY EPPS
Epps, Aubrey Lee "Yo-Yo" b: 3/3/12, Memphis, Tenn. d: 11/13/84, Ackerman, Miss. BR/TR, 5'10", 170 lbs. Deb: 9/29/35

YEAR	TM/L	G	AB	R	H	2B	3B	HR	RBI	BB	SO	AVG	OBP	SLG	PRO+	BR	/A	RC	SB	CS	SBR	FR	POS	TPR
1935	Pit-N	1	4	1	3	0	0	0	3	0	0	.750	.750	1.250	414	2	2	4	0			-0	/C	0.1

■ HAL EPPS
Epps, Harold Franklin b: 3/26/14, Athens, Ga. BL/TL, 6', 175 lbs. Deb: 9/09/38

YEAR	TM/L	G	AB	R	H	2B	3B	HR	RBI	BB	SO	AVG	OBP	SLG	PRO+	BR	/A	RC	SB	CS	SBR	FR	POS	TPR
1938	StL-N	17	50	8	15	0	0	1	3	2	4	.300	.327	.360	84	-1	-1	6	2			-0	O	-0.1
1940	StL-N	11	15	6	3	0	0	0	1	0	3	.200	.200	.200	10	-2	-2	1	0			-0	/O	-0.1
1943	StL-A	8	35	2	10	4	0	0	3	1	3	.286	.342	.400	114	1	1	1	1	1	-0	-1	/O	0.0
1944	StL-A	22	62	15	11	1	1	0	3	14	14	.177	.338	.226	59	-2	-3	6	0	1	-1	3	O	0.0
	Phi-A	67	229	27	60	8	8	0	13	18	18	.262	.316	.367	96	-2	-2	28	2	1	0	1	O	-0.2
	Yr	89	291	42	71	9	9	0	16	32	32	.244	.321	.337	88	-4	-4	34	2	2	-1	4		-0.2
Total	4	125	391	58	99	13	9	1	21	37	43	.253	.319	.340	86	-6	-7	44	5	3		3	/O	-0.4

■ MIKE EPSTEIN
Epstein, Michael Peter "Superjew" b: 4/4/43, Bronx, N.Y. BL/TL, 6'3.5", 230 lbs. Deb: 9/16/66

YEAR	TM/L	G	AB	R	H	2B	3B	HR	RBI	BB	SO	AVG	OBP	SLG	PRO+	BR	/A	RC	SB	CS	SBR	FR	POS	TPR
1966	Bal-A	6	11	1	2	0	0	1	3	1	3	.182	.250	.364	75	-0	-0	1	0	0	0	0	/1	0.0
1967	Bal-A	9	13	0	2	0	0	0	0	3	5	.154	.313	.154	42	-1	-1	1	0	0	0	-0	/1	0.0
	Was-A	96	284	32	65	7	4	9	29	38	74	.229	.332	.377	114	4	5	37	1	4	-2	-1	1	-0.4
	Yr	105	297	32	67	7	4	9	29	41	79	.226	.331	.367	110	3	4	37	1	4	-2	-1		-0.4
1968	Was-A	123	385	40	90	8	2	13	33	48	91	.234	.339	.366	117	8	9	48	1	1	-0	2	*1	0.6
1969	Was-A	131	403	73	112	18	1	30	85	85	99	.278	.416	.551	178	40	42	96	2	5	-2	-1	*1	3.2
1970	Was-A	140	430	55	110	15	3	20	56	73	117	.256	.375	.444	131	16	19	76	2	3	-1	-3	*1	0.9
1971	Was-A	24	85	6	21	1	1	1	9	12	31	.247	.366	.318	101	0	1	12	1	0	0	-1	1	0.0
	*Oak-A	104	329	43	77	13	0	18	51	62	71	.234	.368	.438	130	14	14	57	0	0	-2	-2	1	0.7
	Yr	128	414	49	98	14	1	19	60	74	102	.237	.368	.413	124	14	15	69	1	3	-2	-2		0.7

YEAR	TM/L	G	AB	R	H	2B	3B	HR	RBI	BB	SO	AVG	OBP	SLG	PRO+	BR	/A	RC	SB	CS	SBR	FR	POS	TPR
1972	*Oak-A	138	455	63	123	18	2	26	70	68	68	.270	.378	.490	166	33	36	88	0	1	-1	-2	*1	2.1
1973	Tex-A	27	85	9	16	3	0	1	6	14	19	.188	.324	.259	69	-3	-3	8	0	0	0	-1	1	-0.5
	Cal-A	91	312	30	67	8	2	8	32	34	54	.215	.302	.330	84	-9	-6	31	0	0	0	0	1	-1.1
	Yr	118	397	39	83	11	2	9	38	48	73	.209	.307	.315	81	-12	-9	40	0	0	0	-1		-1.6
1974	Cal-A	18	62	10	10	2	0	4	6	10	13	.161	.288	.387	98	-1	-0	8	0	0	0	1	1	0.0
Total	9	907	2854	362	695	93	16	130	380	448	645	.244	.360	.424	130	100	116	461	7	17	-8	-8	1	5.5

■ JOE ERAUTT   Erautt, Joseph Michael "Stubby"   b: 9/1/21, Vibank, Sask., Can.   d: 10/6/76, Portland, Ore.   BR/TR, 5'9", 175 lbs.   Deb: 5/09/50

YEAR	TM/L	G	AB	R	H	2B	3B	HR	RBI	BB	SO	AVG	OBP	SLG	PRO+	BR	/A	RC	SB	CS	SBR	FR	POS	TPR
1950	Chi-A	16	18	0	4	0	0	0	1	1	3	.222	.263	.222	26	-2	-2	1	0	0	0	1	/C	0.0
1951	Chi-A	16	25	3	4	1	0	0	0	3	2	.160	.276	.200	31	-2	-2	1	0	0	0	3	C	0.1
Total	2	32	43	3	8	1	0	0	1	4	5	.186	.271	.209	29	-4	-4	2	0	0	0	4	/C	0.1

■ HANK ERICKSON   Erickson, Henry Nels "Popeye"   b: 11/11/07, Chicago, Ill.   d: 12/13/64, Louisville, Ky.   BR/TR, 6'1", 185 lbs.   Deb: 4/17/35

YEAR	TM/L	G	AB	R	H	2B	3B	HR	RBI	BB	SO	AVG	OBP	SLG	PRO+	BR	/A	RC	SB	CS	SBR	FR	POS	TPR
1935	Cin-N	37	88	9	23	3	2	1	4	6	4	.261	.323	.375	90	-2	-1	11	0			3	C	0.1

■ CAL ERMER   Ermer, Calvin Coolidge   b: 11/10/23, Baltimore, Md.   BR/TR, 6'0.5", 175 lbs.   Deb: 9/26/47   MC

YEAR	TM/L	G	AB	R	H	2B	3B	HR	RBI	BB	SO	AVG	OBP	SLG	PRO+	BR	/A	RC	SB	CS	SBR	FR	POS	TPR
1947	Was-A	1	3	0	0	0	0	0	0	0	0	.000	.000	.000	-99	-1	-1	0	0	0	0	1	/2	0.0

■ FRANK ERNAGA   Ernaga, Frank John   b: 8/22/30, Susanville, Cal.   BR/TR, 6'1", 195 lbs.   Deb: 5/24/57

YEAR	TM/L	G	AB	R	H	2B	3B	HR	RBI	BB	SO	AVG	OBP	SLG	PRO+	BR	/A	RC	SB	CS	SBR	FR	POS	TPR
1957	Chi-N	20	35	9	11	3	2	2	7	9	14	.314	.455	.686	204	5	5	12	0	0	0	-0	O	0.5
1958	Chi-N	9	8	0	1	0	0	0	0	0	2	.125	.125	.125	-34	-2	-1	0	0	0	0	0	H	-0.1
Total	2	29	43	9	12	3	2	2	7	9	16	.279	.404	.581	163	4	4	12	0	0	0	-0	/O	0.4

■ TEX ERWIN   Erwin, Ross Emil   b: 12/22/1885, Forney, Tex.   d: 4/5/53, Rochester, N.Y.   BL/TR, 6', 185 lbs.   Deb: 8/26/07

YEAR	TM/L	G	AB	R	H	2B	3B	HR	RBI	BB	SO	AVG	OBP	SLG	PRO+	BR	/A	RC	SB	CS	SBR	FR	POS	TPR
1907	Det-A	4	5	0	1	0	0	0	1	1		.200	.333	.200	70	-0	-0	0	0			0	/C	0.1
1910	Bro-N	81	202	15	38	3	1	1	10	24	12	.188	.278	.228	49	-13	-12	14	3			-1	C	-0.9
1911	Bro-N	91	218	30	59	13	2	7	34	31	23	.271	.367	.445	132	8	9	37	5			-6	C	0.8
1912	Bro-N	59	133	14	28	3	0	2	14	18	16	.211	.305	.278	62	-7	-6	12	1			-1	C	-0.5
1913	Bro-N	20	31	6	8	1	0	0	3	4	5	.258	.343	.290	80	-1	-1	3	0			-3	C	-0.2
1914	Bro-N	9	11	0	5	0	0	0	1	2	1	.455	.538	.455	192	2	1	3	1			-1	/C	0.1
	Cin-N	12	35	5	11	3	0	1	7	2	3	.314	.351	.486	144	2	2	6	0			2	C	0.4
	Yr	21	46	5	16	3	0	1	8	4	4	.348	.400	.478	157	3	3	9	1			1		0.5
Total	6	276	635	70	150	23	3	11	70	82	60	.236	.326	.334	90	-10	-7	75	10			-9	C	-0.2

■ NICK ESASKY   Esasky, Nicholas Andrew   b: 2/24/60, Hialeah, Fla.   BR/TR, 6'3", 200 lbs.   Deb: 6/19/83

YEAR	TM/L	G	AB	R	H	2B	3B	HR	RBI	BB	SO	AVG	OBP	SLG	PRO+	BR	/A	RC	SB	CS	SBR	FR	POS	TPR
1983	Cin-N	85	302	41	80	10	5	12	46	27	99	.265	.331	.450	111	5	4	46	6	2	1	-10	3	-0.8
1984	Cin-N	113	322	30	62	10	5	10	45	52	103	.193	.305	.348	79	-7	-9	36	1	2	-1	-8	31	-2.0
1985	Cin-N	125	413	61	108	21	0	21	66	41	102	.262	.334	.465	115	11	8	63	3	4	-2	-7	3O1	-0.1
1986	Cin-N	102	330	35	76	17	2	12	41	47	97	.230	.328	.403	96	0	-2	44	0	2	-1	-3	1O/3	-0.9
1987	Cin-N	100	346	48	94	19	2	22	59	29	76	.272	.328	.529	117	9	8	57	0	0	0	-11	1/3O	-0.8
1988	Cin-N	122	391	40	95	17	2	15	62	48	104	.243	.332	.412	108	6	5	56	7	2	1	-9	*1	-0.9
1989	Bos-A	154	564	79	156	26	5	30	108	66	117	.277	.355	.500	130	28	23	100	1	2	-1	4	*1/O	1.6
1990	Atl-N	9	35	2	6	0	0	0	0	4	14	.171	.256	.171	20	-4	-4	2	0	0	0	-1	/1	-0.5
Total	8	810	2703	336	677	120	21	122	427	314	712	.250	.332	.446	109	49	33	403	18	14	-3	-45	13/O	-4.4

■ NINO ESCALERA   Escalera, Saturnino Cuadrado   b: 12/1/29, Santurce, P.R.   BL/TR, 5'10", 165 lbs.   Deb: 4/17/54

YEAR	TM/L	G	AB	R	H	2B	3B	HR	RBI	BB	SO	AVG	OBP	SLG	PRO+	BR	/A	RC	SB	CS	SBR	FR	POS	TPR
1954	Cin-N	73	69	15	11	1	1	0	3	7	11	.159	.237	.203	15	-9	-9	4	1	0	0	4	O/1S	-0.4

■ JIM ESCHEN   Eschen, James Godrich   b: 8/21/1891, Brooklyn, N.Y.   d: 9/27/60, Sloatsburg, N.Y.   BR/TR, 5'10.5", 160 lbs.   Deb: 7/10/15

YEAR	TM/L	G	AB	R	H	2B	3B	HR	RBI	BB	SO	AVG	OBP	SLG	PRO+	BR	/A	RC	SB	CS	SBR	FR	POS	TPR
1915	Cle-A	15	42	11	10	1	0	0	2	5	9	.238	.319	.262	73	-1	-1	4	0	1	-1	1	O	0.0

■ LARRY ESCHEN   Eschen, Lawrence Edward   b: 9/22/20, Suffern, N.Y.   BR/TR, 6', 180 lbs.   Deb: 6/16/42

YEAR	TM/L	G	AB	R	H	2B	3B	HR	RBI	BB	SO	AVG	OBP	SLG	PRO+	BR	/A	RC	SB	CS	SBR	FR	POS	TPR
1942	Phi-A	12	11	0	0	0	0	0	0	4	6	.000	.267	.000	-22	-2	-2	0	0	0	0	-1	/S2	-0.2

■ ANGEL ESCOBAR   Escobar, Angel Rubenque (Rivas)   b: 5/12/65, LaSabana, Venez.   BB/TR, 6', 160 lbs.   Deb: 5/17/1988

YEAR	TM/L	G	AB	R	H	2B	3B	HR	RBI	BB	SO	AVG	OBP	SLG	PRO+	BR	/A	RC	SB	CS	SBR	FR	POS	TPR
1988	SF-N	3	3	1	1	0	0	0	0	0	0	.333	.333	.333	96	-0	-0	0	0	0	0	0	/S3	0.0

■ JIMMY ESMOND   Esmond, James J.   b: 10/8/1889, Albany, N.Y.   d: 6/26/48, Troy, N.Y.   BR/TR, 5'11", 167 lbs.   Deb: 4/20/11

YEAR	TM/L	G	AB	R	H	2B	3B	HR	RBI	BB	SO	AVG	OBP	SLG	PRO+	BR	/A	RC	SB	CS	SBR	FR	POS	TPR
1911	Cin-N	73	198	27	54	4	6	1	11	17	30	.273	.330	.369	99	-2	-1	26	7			1	S3/2	0.2
1912	Cin-N	82	231	24	45	5	3	1	40	20	31	.195	.259	.255	42	-19	-18	19	11			-7	S	-1.7
1914	Ind-F	151	542	74	160	23	15	2	49	40	48	.295	.344	.404	103	9	1	88	25			-7	*S	0.5
1915	New-F	155	569	79	147	20	10	5	62	59	54	.258	.329	.355	109	2	6	78	18			6	*S	2.5
Total	4	461	1540	204	406	52	34	9	162	136	163	.264	.324	.359	95	-10	-12	211	61			-8	S/32	1.5

■ JUAN ESPINO   Espino, Juan (Reyes)   b: 3/16/56, Bonao, D.R.   BR/TR, 6'1", 190 lbs.   Deb: 6/25/82

YEAR	TM/L	G	AB	R	H	2B	3B	HR	RBI	BB	SO	AVG	OBP	SLG	PRO+	BR	/A	RC	SB	CS	SBR	FR	POS	TPR
1982	NY-A	3	2	0	0	0	0	0	0	0	1	.000	.000	.000	-99	-1	-1	0	0	0	0	0	/C	0.0
1983	NY-A	10	23	1	6	0	0	1	3	1	5	.261	.292	.391	89	-0	-0	3	0	0	0	-0	C	0.0
1985	NY-A	9	11	0	4	0	0	0	0	0	0	.364	.364	.364	102	-0	0	1	0	0	0	1	/C	0.1
1986	NY-A	27	37	1	6	2	0	0	5	2	9	.162	.205	.216	15	-4	-4	2	0	0	0	3	C	0.0
Total	4	49	73	2	16	2	0	1	8	3	15	.219	.250	.288	48	-5	-5	6	0	0	0	4	/C	0.1

■ ALVARO ESPINOZA   Espinoza, Alvaro Alberto   b: 2/19/62, Valencia, Venez.   BR/TR, 6', 170 lbs.   Deb: 9/14/84

YEAR	TM/L	G	AB	R	H	2B	3B	HR	RBI	BB	SO	AVG	OBP	SLG	PRO+	BR	/A	RC	SB	CS	SBR	FR	POS	TPR
1984	Min-A	1	0	0	0	0	0	0	0	0	0	—	—	—	—	0	0	0	0	0	0	0	/S	0.0
1985	Min-A	32	57	5	15	2	0	0	9	1	9	.263	.288	.298	58	-3	-3	4	0	1	-1	7	S	0.5
1986	Min-A	37	42	4	9	1	0	0	1	1	10	.214	.233	.238	28	-4	-4	2	0	1	-1	6	2S	0.3
1988	NY-A	3	3	0	0	0	0	0	0	0	0	.000	.000	.000	-99	-1	-1	0	0	0	0	1	/2S	0.0
1989	NY-A	146	503	51	142	23	1	0	41	14	60	.282	.303	.332	80	-15	-14	48	3	3	-1	17	*S	1.4
1990	NY-A	150	438	31	98	12	2	2	20	16	54	.224	.259	.274	49	-30	-30	29	1	2	-1	21	*S	0.0
Total	6	369	1043	91	264	38	3	2	71	32	133	.253	.280	.301	63	-52	-52	84	4	7	-3	51	S/2	2.2

■ SAMMY ESPOSITO   Esposito, Samuel   b: 12/15/31, Chicago, Ill.   BR/TR, 5'9", 165 lbs.   Deb: 9/28/52

YEAR	TM/L	G	AB	R	H	2B	3B	HR	RBI	BB	SO	AVG	OBP	SLG	PRO+	BR	/A	RC	SB	CS	SBR	FR	POS	TPR
1952	Chi-A	1	4	0	1	0	0	0	0	0	2	.250	.250	.250	39	-0	-0	0	0	1	-1	-1	/S	-0.2
1955	Chi-A	3	4	3	0	0	0	0	0	1	0	.000	.200	.000	-41	-1	-1	0	0	0	0	-1	/3	-0.1
1956	Chi-A	81	184	30	42	8	2	3	25	41	19	.228	.374	.342	89	-1	-1	26	1	2	-1	4	3S/2	0.4
1957	Chi-A	94	176	26	36	3	0	2	15	38	27	.205	.346	.256	66	-7	-7	19	5	1	1	17	3S/2O	1.4
1958	Chi-A	98	81	16	20	3	0	0	3	12	6	.247	.358	.284	81	-2	-1	9	1	1	-0	11	3S/2O	1.5
1959	*Chi-A	69	66	12	11	1	0	0	5	11	16	.167	.286	.227	43	-5	-5	5	0	1	-1	9	3S/2	0.4
1960	Chi-A	57	77	14	14	5	0	1	11	10	20	.182	.276	.286	53	-5	-5	6	0	0	0	1	3S/2	-0.1
1961	Chi-A	63	94	12	16	5	0	1	8	12	21	.170	.264	.255	40	-8	-8	7	0	0	0	12	3S2	0.8
1962	Chi-A	75	81	14	19	1	0	0	4	17	13	.235	.367	.247	69	-3	-3	8	0	1	-1	3	3S/2	0.2
1963	Chi-A	1	0	0	0	0	0	0	0	0	0	—	—	—	—	0	0	0	0	0	0	0	R	0.0
	KC-A	18	25	3	5	1	0	0	2	3	3	.200	.286	.240	47	-2	-2	2	0	0	0	-2	/2S3	-0.2
	Yr	19	25	3	5	1	0	0	2	3	3	.200	.286	.240	47	-2	-2	2	0	0	0	-2		-0.2
Total	10	560	792	130	164	27	2	8	73	145	127	.207	.333	.277	66	-33	-33	81	7	7	-2	52	3S/2O	4.1

YEAR	TM/L	G	AB	R	H	2B	3B	HR	RBI	BB	SO	AVG	OBP	SLG	PRO+	BR	/A	RC	SB	CS	SBR	FR	POS	TPR

■ CECIL ESPY   Espy, Cecil Edward   b: 1/20/63, San Diego, Cal.   BB/TR, 6'3", 195 lbs.   Deb: 9/02/83

YEAR	TM/L	G	AB	R	H	2B	3B	HR	RBI	BB	SO	AVG	OBP	SLG	PRO+	BR	/A	RC	SB	CS	SBR	FR	POS	TPR
1983	LA-N	20	11	4	3	1	0	0	1	1	2	.273	.333	.364	94	-0	-0	1	0	0	0	1	O	0.1
1987	Tex-A	14	8	1	0	0	0	0	0	1	3	.000	.111	.000	-67	-2	-2	0	2	0	1	2	/O	0.1
1988	Tex-A	123	347	46	86	17	6	2	39	20	83	.248	.291	.349	76	-10	-12	37	33	10	4	1	OD/SC12	-0.7
1989	Tex-A	142	475	65	122	12	7	3	31	38	99	.257	.315	.331	81	-11	-12	52	45	20	2	-6	*O/D	-1.8
1990	Tex-A	52	71	10	9	0	0	0	1	10	20	.127	.235	.127	4	-9	-9	3	11	5	0	4	O/2D	-0.5
Total	5	351	912	126	220	30	13	5	72	70	207	.241	.297	.319	72	-33	-35	94	91	35	6	3	O/DS2C1	-2.8

■ CHUCK ESSEGIAN   Essegian, Charles Abraham   b: 8/9/31, Boston, Mass.   BR/TR, 5'11", 200 lbs.   Deb: 4/15/58

YEAR	TM/L	G	AB	R	H	2B	3B	HR	RBI	BB	SO	AVG	OBP	SLG	PRO+	BR	/A	RC	SB	CS	SBR	FR	POS	TPR
1958	Phi-N	39	114	15	28	5	2	5	16	12	34	.246	.317	.456	103	-0	0	17	0	0	0	-2	O	-0.2
1959	StL-N	17	39	2	7	2	1	0	5	1	13	.179	.200	.282	25	-4	-4	1	0	0	0	-1	/O	-0.5
	*LA-N	24	46	6	14	6	0	1	5	4	11	.304	.360	.500	118	2	1	8	0	0	0	-2	O	0.0
	Yr	41	85	8	21	8	1	1	10	5	24	.247	.289	.400	76	-3	-3	9	0	0	0	-3		-0.5
1960	LA-N	52	79	8	17	3	0	3	11	8	24	.215	.287	.367	73	-3	-3	9	0	0	0	1	O	-0.2
1961	Bal-A	1	1	0	0	0	0	0	0	0	0	.000	.000	.000	-99	-0	-0	0	0	0	0	0	H	0.0
	KC-A	4	6	1	2	1	0	0	1	1	2	.333	.429	.500	147	0	0	1	0	0	0	0	/O	0.1
	Cle-A	60	166	25	48	7	1	12	35	10	33	.289	.333	.560	138	7	7	29	0	0	0	2	O	0.8
	Yr	65	173	26	50	8	1	12	36	11	35	.289	.335	.555	137	7	8	30	0	0	0	3		0.9
1962	Cle-A	106	336	59	92	12	0	21	50	42	68	.274	.366	.497	134	14	16	62	0	0	0	-8	O	0.4
1963	KC-A	101	231	23	52	9	0	5	27	19	48	.225	.287	.329	69	-9	-10	21	0	0	0	-3	O	-1.4
Total	6	404	1018	139	260	45	4	47	150	97	233	.255	.326	.446	106	7	7	148	0	0	0	-12	O	-1.0

■ JIM ESSIAN   Essian, James Sarkis   b: 1/2/51, Detroit, Mich.   BR/TR, 6'2", 195 lbs.   Deb: 9/15/73

YEAR	TM/L	G	AB	R	H	2B	3B	HR	RBI	BB	SO	AVG	OBP	SLG	PRO+	BR	/A	RC	SB	CS	SBR	FR	POS	TPR
1973	Phi-N	2	3	0	0	0	0	0	0	0	1	.000	.000	.000	-97	-1	-1	0	0	0	0	0	/C	0.0
1974	Phi-N	17	20	1	2	0	0	0	0	2	1	.100	.182	.100	-19	-3	-3	0	0	0	0	1	C/13	-0.1
1975	Phi-N	2	1	1	1	0	0	0	1	1	0	1.000	1.000	1.000	439	1	1	1	0	0	0	0	/C	0.1
1976	Chi-A	78	199	20	49	7	0	0	21	23	28	.246	.327	.281	79	-4	-5	19	2	1	0	3	C/13	0.1
1977	Chi-A	114	322	50	88	18	2	10	44	52	35	.273	.376	.435	120	10	10	53	1	4	-2	5	*C/3	1.6
1978	Oak-A	126	278	21	62	9	1	3	26	44	22	.223	.329	.295	81	-7	-5	28	2	1	0	13	*C/12D	1.1
1979	Oak-A	98	313	34	76	16	0	8	40	25	29	.243	.303	.371	85	-9	-7	33	0	1	-1	11	C3/10D	0.7
1980	Oak-A	87	285	19	66	11	0	5	29	30	18	.232	.305	.323	78	-11	-8	25	1	3	-2	3	CD/1	-0.2
1981	Chi-A	27	52	6	16	3	0	1	5	4	5	.308	.357	.365	111	1	1	6	0	1	-1	5	C/3	0.6
1982	Sea-A	48	153	14	42	8	0	3	20	11	7	.275	.327	.386	92	-1	-2	20	2	0	1	6	C	0.7
1983	Cle-A	48	93	11	19	4	0	2	11	16	8	.204	.321	.312	72	-3	-3	10	0	1	-1	4	C/3	0.2
1984	Oak-A	63	136	17	32	9	0	2	10	23	17	.235	.350	.346	100	-1	1	18	1	1	-0	11	C/3D	1.4
Total	12	710	1855	194	453	85	3	33	207	231	171	.244	.330	.347	90	-28	-21	214	9	13	-5	61	C/3D102	6.2

■ BOBBY ESTALELLA   Estalella, Roberto (Ventoza)   b: 4/25/11, Cardenas, Cuba   BR/TR, 5'8", 180 lbs.   Deb: 9/07/35

YEAR	TM/L	G	AB	R	H	2B	3B	HR	RBI	BB	SO	AVG	OBP	SLG	PRO+	BR	/A	RC	SB	CS	SBR	FR	POS	TPR
1935	Was-A	15	51	7	16	0	0	2	10	17	7	.314	.485	.471	153	5	5	13	1	0	0	2	3	0.7
1936	Was-A	13	9	2	2	0	2	0	0	4	5	.222	.462	.667	186	1	1	3	0	0	0	0	H	0.1
1939	Was-A	82	280	51	77	18	6	8	41	40	27	.275	.368	.468	121	5	8	48	2	3	-1	-4	O	0.1
1941	StL-A	46	83	7	20	6	1	0	14	18	13	.241	.376	.337	87	-1	-1	12	0	0	0	-4	O	-0.5
1942	Was-A	133	429	68	119	24	5	8	65	85	42	.277	.400	.413	130	20	20	74	5	2	0	-14	3O	0.5
1943	Phi-A	117	367	43	95	14	4	11	63	52	44	.259	.352	.409	123	11	11	52	1	3	-2	-1	O	0.5
1944	Phi-A	140	506	54	151	17	9	7	60	59	60	.298	.374	.409	125	16	17	80	3	3	-1	-6	*O/1	0.6
1945	Phi-A	126	451	45	135	25	6	8	52	74	46	.299	.399	.435	142	26	26	79	1	6	-3	-1	*O	1.8
1949	Phi-A	8	20	2	5	0	0	0	3	1	2	.250	.286	.250	44	-2	-2	0	0	0	0	1	/O	0.0
Total	9	680	2196	279	620	106	33	44	308	350	246	.282	.383	.421	127	82	87	361	13	17	-6	-27	O/31	3.8

■ DUDE ESTERBROOK   Esterbrook, Thomas John   b: 6/20/1857, Staten Is., N.Y.   d: 4/30/01, Middletown, N.Y.   BR/TR, 5'11", 167 lbs.   Deb: 5/01/1880   M

YEAR	TM/L	G	AB	R	H	2B	3B	HR	RBI	BB	SO	AVG	OBP	SLG	PRO+	BR	/A	RC	SB	CS	SBR	FR	POS	TPR
1880	Buf-N	64	253	20	61	12	1	0	35	0	15	.241	.241	.296	80	-5	-6	19				-2	10/2SC	-0.9
1882	Cle-N	45	179	13	44	4	3	0	19	5	12	.246	.266	.302	85	-4	-3	15				9	O/1	0.5
1883	NY-a	97	407	55	103	9	7	0			15	.253	.280	.310	86	-5	-7	36				-5	*3	-0.8
1884	*NY-a	112	477	110	150	29	11	1			12	.314	.345	.428	158	27	29	72				9	*3	3.5
1885	NY-N	88	359	48	92	14	5	2	44	4	28	.256	.264	.340	96	-3	-2	33				2	*3/O	0.1
1886	NY-N	123	473	62	125	20	6	3	43	8	43	.264	.277	.351	89	-7	-8	51	13			-8	*3	-0.9
1887	NY-a	26	101	16	17	1	0	0			6	.168	.222	.178	14	-11	-11	6	8			-7	/1OS2	-1.4
1888	Ind-N	64	246	21	54	8	0	0	17	2	20	.220	.232	.252	55	-12	-13	17	11			-3	1/3	-2.0
	Lou-a	23	93	9	21	6	0	0	7	3		.226	.265	.290	82	-2	-2	9	5			0	1	-0.2
1889	Lou-a	11	44	8	14	3	0	0	9	5	2	.318	.400	.386	129	2	2	9	6			-1	/1OSM	0.1
1890	NY-N	45	197	29	57	14	1	0	29	10	8	.289	.333	.371	107	1	1	29	12			0	1	-0.1
1891	Bro-N	3	8	1	3	0	0	0	0	0	1	.375	.444	.375	143	0	0	1	0			-1	/O2	0.0
Total	11	701	2837	387	741	120	34	6	203	70	129	.261	.284	.334	95	-18	-18	297	55			-6	31/O2SC	-2.1

■ FRANK ESTRADA   Estrada, Francisco (Soto)   b: 2/12/48, Navojoa, Sonora, Mex   BR/TR, 5'8", 182 lbs.   Deb: 9/14/71

YEAR	TM/L	G	AB	R	H	2B	3B	HR	RBI	BB	SO	AVG	OBP	SLG	PRO+	BR	/A	RC	SB	CS	SBR	FR	POS	TPR
1971	NY-N	1	2	0	1	0	0	0	0	0	0	.500	.500	.500	187	0	0	1	0	0	0	-1	/C	0.0

■ ANDY ETCHEBARREN   Etchebarren, Andrew Auguste   b: 6/20/43, Whittier, Cal.   BR/TR, 6'1", 190 lbs.   Deb: 9/26/62   C

YEAR	TM/L	G	AB	R	H	2B	3B	HR	RBI	BB	SO	AVG	OBP	SLG	PRO+	BR	/A	RC	SB	CS	SBR	FR	POS	TPR
1962	Bal-A	2	6	0	2	0	0	0	1	0	2	.333	.333	.333	84	-0	-0	1	0	0	0	-1	/C	0.0
1965	Bal-A	5	6	1	1	0	0	1	4	0	2	.167	.167	.667	123	0	0	1	0	0	0	3	/C	0.3
1966	*Bal-A	121	412	49	91	14	6	11	50	38	106	.221	.295	.364	89	-7	-6	42	0	1	-1	-3	*C	-0.2
1967	Bal-A	112	330	29	71	13	0	7	35	38	80	.215	.300	.318	83	-7	-6	31	1	0	0	-0	*C	0.1
1968	Bal-A	74	189	20	44	11	2	5	20	19	46	.233	.313	.392	112	3	3	23	0	0	0	9	C	1.6
1969	*Bal-A	73	217	29	54	9	2	3	26	28	42	.249	.353	.350	96	0	-0	25	1	2	-1	1	C	0.5
1970	*Bal-A	78	230	19	56	10	1	4	28	21	41	.243	.315	.348	82	-5	-6	24	4	1	1	1	C	-0.2
1971	*Bal-A	70	222	21	60	8	0	9	29	16	40	.270	.322	.428	112	2	3	28	1	4	-2	1	C	0.5
1972	Bal-A	71	188	11	38	6	1	2	21	17	43	.202	.279	.277	64	-8	-8	14	0	2	-1	6	C	-0.2
1973	*Bal-A	54	152	16	39	9	1	2	23	12	21	.257	.319	.368	94	-1	-1	16	1	1	-0	1	C	0.1
1974	*Bal-A	62	180	13	40	8	0	2	15	6	26	.222	.251	.300	60	-10	-9	13	1	0	0	1	C	-0.5
1975	Bal-A	8	20	0	4	1	0	0	3	0	3	.200	.200	.250	28	-2	-2	1	0	0	0	0	/C	0.0
	Cal-A	31	100	10	28	0	1	3	17	14	19	.280	.368	.390	123	2	3	15	1	0	0	-3	C	0.1
	Yr	39	120	10	32	1	1	3	20	14	22	.267	.343	.367	108	0	1	15	1	0	0	-3		0.1
1976	Cal-A	103	247	15	56	9	1	0	21	24	37	.227	.305	.271	74	-9	-7	20	0	2	-1	5	*C	0.1
1977	Cal-A	80	114	11	29	2	0	2	14	12	19	.254	.325	.307	77	-4	-3	12	3	1	0	0	C	0.0
1978	Mil-A	4	5	1	2	1	0	0	2	1	2	.400	.500	.600	207	1	1	2	0	0	0	2	/C	0.3
Total	15	948	2618	245	615	101	17	49	309	246	529	.235	.308	.343	88	-44	-39	268	13	14	-5	23	C	2.5

■ BUCK ETCHISON   Etchison, Clarence Hampton   b: 1/27/15, Baltimore, Md.   d: 1/24/80, E.New Market, Md.   BL/TL, 6'1", 190 lbs.   Deb: 9/22/43

YEAR	TM/L	G	AB	R	H	2B	3B	HR	RBI	BB	SO	AVG	OBP	SLG	PRO+	BR	/A	RC	SB	CS	SBR	FR	POS	TPR
1943	Bos-N	10	19	2	6	3	0	0	2	2	2	.316	.381	.474	148	1	1	4	0			-1	/1	0.0
1944	Bos-N	109	308	30	66	16	0	8	33	33	50	.214	.292	.344	76	-9	-11	32	1			-1	1	-1.8
Total	2	119	327	32	72	19	0	8	35	35	52	.220	.298	.352	79	-8	-10	35	1			-2	/1	-1.8

■ BOBBY ETHERIDGE   Etheridge, Bobby Lamar "Luke"   b: 11/25/42, Greenville, Miss.   BR/TR, 5'9", 170 lbs.   Deb: 7/16/67

YEAR	TM/L	G	AB	R	H	2B	3B	HR	RBI	BB	SO	AVG	OBP	SLG	PRO+	BR	/A	RC	SB	CS	SBR	FR	POS	TPR
1967	SF-N	40	115	13	26	7	2	1	16	7	12	.226	.299	.348	86	-2	-2	12	0	0	0	-1	3	-0.5

YEAR	TM/L	G	AB	R	H	2B	3B	HR	RBI	BB	SO	AVG	OBP	SLG	PRO+	BR	/A	RC	SB	CS	SBR	FR	POS	TPR
1969	SF-N	56	131	13	34	9	0	1	10	19	26	.260	.358	.351	101	0	1	15	0	0	0	-2	3/S	0.0
Total	2	96	246	26	60	16	2	2	25	26	38	.244	.331	.350	94	-2	-1	27	0	0	0	-4	/3S	-0.5

■ NICK ETTEN
Etten, Nicholas Raymond Thomas b: 9/19/13, Spring Grove, Ill d: 10/18/90, Hinsdale, Ill. BL/TL, 6'2", 198 lbs. Deb: 9/08/38

YEAR	TM/L	G	AB	R	H	2B	3B	HR	RBI	BB	SO	AVG	OBP	SLG	PRO+	BR	/A	RC	SB	CS	SBR	FR	POS	TPR
1938	Phi-A	22	81	6	21	6	2	0	11	9	7	.259	.333	.383	81	-3	-2	11	1	0	0	-2	1	-0.5
1939	Phi-A	43	155	20	39	11	2	3	29	16	11	.252	.322	.406	87	-4	-3	20	0	0	0	-2	1	-0.8
1941	Phi-N	151	540	78	168	27	4	14	79	82	33	.311	.405	.454	147	32	35	104	9			-3	*1	1.1
1942	Phi-N	139	459	37	121	21	3	8	41	67	26	.264	.357	.375	120	10	12	65	3			1	*1	0.2
1943	*NY-A	154	583	78	158	35	5	14	107	76	31	.271	.355	.420	126	19	19	89	3	7	-3	-11	*1	0.0
1944	NY-A	154	573	88	168	25	4	**22**	91	**97**	29	.293	.399	.466	142	37	35	114	4	2	0	4	*1	3.0
1945	NY-A	152	565	77	161	24	4	18	**111**	90	23	.285	.387	.437	133	30	27	98	2	3	-1	-9	*1	1.2
1946	NY-A	108	323	37	75	14	1	9	49	38	35	.232	.315	.365	88	-5	-5	39	0	1	-1	-0	1	-1.1
1947	Phi-N	14	41	5	10	4	0	1	8	5	4	.244	.326	.415	99	-0	-0	5	0			1	1	0.0
Total	9	937	3320	426	921	167	25	89	526	480	199	.277	.371	.423	125	116	116	544	22	<u>13</u>		-22	1	3.1

■ FRED EUNICK
Eunick, Fernandas Bowen b: 4/22/1892, Baltimore, Md. d: 12/9/59, Baltimore, Md. BR/TR, 5'6", 148 lbs. Deb: 8/29/17

YEAR	TM/L	G	AB	R	H	2B	3B	HR	RBI	BB	SO	AVG	OBP	SLG	PRO+	BR	/A	RC	SB	CS	SBR	FR	POS	TPR
1917	Cle-A	1	2	0	0	0	0	0	0	0	0	.000	.000	.000	-93	-0	-0	0	0			-0	/3	0.0

■ FRANK EUSTACE
Eustace, Frank John b: 11/7/1873, New York, N.Y. d: 10/20/32, Pottsville, Pa. 5'9", 160 lbs. Deb: 4/17/1896

YEAR	TM/L	G	AB	R	H	2B	3B	HR	RBI	BB	SO	AVG	OBP	SLG	PRO+	BR	/A	RC	SB	CS	SBR	FR	POS	TPR
1896	Lou-N	25	100	18	17	2	2	1	11	6	14	.170	.217	.260	28	-11	-10	7	4			-5	S/2	-1.2

■ EVANS
Evans Deb: 6/01/1875

YEAR	TM/L	G	AB	R	H	2B	3B	HR	RBI	BB	SO	AVG	OBP	SLG	PRO+	BR	/A	RC	SB	CS	SBR	FR	POS	TPR
1875	NH-n	1	4	1	2	1	0	0		0		.500	.500	.750	381	1	1	2					/O	0.1

■ AL EVANS
Evans, Alfred Hubert b: 9/28/16, Kenly, N.C. d: 4/6/79, Wilson, N.C. BR/TR, 5'11", 190 lbs. Deb: 9/13/39

YEAR	TM/L	G	AB	R	H	2B	3B	HR	RBI	BB	SO	AVG	OBP	SLG	PRO+	BR	/A	RC	SB	CS	SBR	FR	POS	TPR
1939	Was-A	7	21	2	7	0	0	0	1	5	2	.333	.462	.333	115	1	1	4	0	0	0	-1	/C	0.1
1940	Was-A	14	25	1	8	2	0	0	7	6	7	.320	.452	.400	131	1	2	6	1	0	0	-0	/C	0.2
1941	Was-A	53	159	16	44	8	4	1	19	9	18	.277	.315	.396	91	-3	-2	19	0	3	-2	2	C	0.0
1942	Was-A	74	223	22	51	4	1	0	10	25	36	.229	.309	.256	60	-11	-11	19	3	0	1	-2	C	-0.3
1944	Was-A	14	22	5	2	0	0	0	0	2	6	.091	.167	.091	-27	-4	-3	0	0	0	0	-1	/C	-0.3
1945	Was-A	51	150	19	39	11	2	2	19	17	22	.260	.339	.400	125	3	4	21	2	1	0	-5	C	0.2
1946	Was-A	88	272	30	69	10	4	2	30	30	28	.254	.332	.342	94	-4	-2	32	1	2	-1	-10	C	-0.9
1947	Was-A	99	319	17	77	8	3	2	23	28	25	.241	.303	.304	71	-13	-12	29	2	1	0	-2	C	-0.6
1948	Was-A	93	228	19	59	6	3	2	28	38	20	.259	.367	.338	91	-3	-2	29	1	1	-0	-3	C	0.0
1949	Was-A	109	321	32	87	12	3	2	42	50	19	.271	.369	.346	92	-4	-3	45	4	1	1	-16	*C	-1.1
1950	Was-A	90	289	24	68	8	3	2	30	29	21	.235	.309	.301	61	-19	-17	28	0	0	0	-13	C	-2.4
1951	Bos-A	12	24	1	3	1	0	0	2	4	2	.125	.250	.167	13	-3	-3	1	0	0	0	-1	C	-0.1
Total	12	704	2053	188	514	70	23	13	211	243	206	.250	.332	.326	82	-59	-49	234	14	9	-1	-52	C	-5.2

■ BARRY EVANS
Evans, Barry Steven b: 11/30/56, Atlanta, Ga. BR/TR, 6'1", 180 lbs. Deb: 9/04/78

YEAR	TM/L	G	AB	R	H	2B	3B	HR	RBI	BB	SO	AVG	OBP	SLG	PRO+	BR	/A	RC	SB	CS	SBR	FR	POS	TPR
1978	SD-N	24	90	7	24	1	1	0	4	4	10	.267	.298	.300	73	-4	-3	8	0	0	0	1	3	-0.1
1979	SD-N	56	162	9	35	5	0	1	14	5	16	.216	.240	.265	40	-14	-13	10	0	2	-1	1	3/S2	-0.4
1980	SD-N	73	125	11	29	3	2	1	14	17	21	.232	.324	.312	83	-3	-2	14	1	1	-0	-3	32/S1	-0.3
1981	SD-N	54	93	11	30	5	0	0	7	9	9	.323	.382	.376	125	2	3	12	2	2	-1	-4	31/2S	-0.1
1982	NY-A	17	31	2	8	3	0	0	2	6	6	.258	.395	.355	109	1	1	5	0	0	0	1	/23S	0.3
Total	5	224	501	40	126	17	3	2	41	41	62	.251	.309	.309	77	-18	-15	49	3	5	-2	8	3/2S1	-0.6

■ DARRELL EVANS
Evans, Darrell Wayne b: 5/26/47, Pasadena, Cal. BL/TR, 6'2", 200 lbs. Deb: 4/20/69 C

YEAR	TM/L	G	AB	R	H	2B	3B	HR	RBI	BB	SO	AVG	OBP	SLG	PRO+	BR	/A	RC	SB	CS	SBR	FR	POS	TPR
1969	Atl-N	12	26	3	6	1	0	0	1	1	8	.231	.259	.231	38	-2	-2	2	0	0	0	-2	/3	-0.3
1970	Atl-N	12	44	4	14	1	1	0	9	7	5	.318	.423	.386	112	2	1	7	0	0	0	-1	3	0.0
1971	Atl-N	89	260	42	63	11	1	12	38	39	54	.242	.343	.431	111	6	4	39	2	3	-1	4	3/O	0.7
1972	Atl-N	125	418	67	106	12	0	19	71	90	58	.254	.391	.419	119	20	15	76	4	2	0	9	*3	2.5
1973	Atl-N	161	595	114	167	25	8	41	104	**124**	104	.281	.407	.556	153	55	49	**143**	6	3	0	8	*31	5.3
1974	Atl-N	160	571	99	137	21	3	25	79	**126**	88	.240	.383	.419	119	23	19	100	4	2	0	16	*3	3.3
1975	Atl-N	156	567	82	138	22	2	22	73	105	106	.243	.364	.406	109	12	10	91	12	3	2	23	*3/1	3.5
1976	Atl-N	44	139	11	24	0	0	1	10	30	33	.173	.320	.194	45	-8	-9	11	3	0	1	0	1/3	-0.9
	SF-N	92	257	42	57	9	1	10	36	42	38	.222	.331	.381	99	1	0	36	6	1	1	9	1/3	0.6
	Yr	136	396	53	81	9	1	11	46	72	71	.205	.327	.316	80	-7	-9	46	9	1	2	9		-0.3
1977	SF-N	144	461	64	117	18	3	17	72	69	50	.254	.355	.416	106	5	5	71	9	6	-1	-6	O13	-0.6
1978	SF-N	159	547	82	133	24	2	20	78	105	64	.243	.365	.404	119	13	16	87	4	5	-2	10	*3	2.4
1979	SF-N	160	562	68	142	23	2	17	70	91	80	.253	.359	.391	112	6	11	83	6	7	-2	**22**	*3	2.5
1980	SF-N	154	556	69	147	23	0	20	78	83	65	.264	.362	.414	119	14	15	87	17	5	2	17	*31	3.5
1981	SF-N	102	357	51	92	13	4	12	48	54	33	.258	.358	.417	122	10	11	56	2	3	-1	7	31	1.3
1982	SF-N	141	465	64	119	20	4	16	61	77	64	.256	.364	.419	119	13	13	74	5	4	-1	-2	31S	0.7
1983	SF-N	142	523	94	145	29	3	30	82	84	81	.277	.379	.516	151	33	35	104	6	6	-2	1	*13/S	2.9
1984	*Det-A	131	401	60	93	11	1	16	63	77	70	.232	.356	.384	105	5	5	58	0	2	-1		D13	0.4
1985	Det-A	151	505	81	125	17	0	**40**	94	85	85	.248	.357	.519	137	25	26	96	0	4	-2	11	*1D/3	2.6
1986	Det-A	151	507	78	122	15	0	29	85	91	105	.241	.357	.442	116	13	13	85	3	2	-0	11	*1D/3	1.6
1987	*Det-A	150	499	90	128	20	0	34	99	100	84	.257	.383	.501	138	25	28	103	6	5	-1	12	*1D/3	2.7
1988	Det-A	144	437	48	91	9	0	22	64	84	89	.208	.337	.380	104	2	4	57	1	4	-2	5	D1	0.3
1989	Atl-N	107	276	31	57	6	1	11	39	41	46	.207	.309	.355	87	-4	-4	33	0	1	-1	6	13	-0.3
Total	21	2687	8973	1344	2223	329	36	414	1354	1605	1410	.248	.364	.431	119	268	266	1499	98	68	-11	161	*31D/OS	34.7

■ DWIGHT EVANS
Evans, Dwight Michael "Dewey" b: 11/3/51, Santa Monica, Cal. BR/TR, 6'2", 180 lbs. Deb: 9/16/72

YEAR	TM/L	G	AB	R	H	2B	3B	HR	RBI	BB	SO	AVG	OBP	SLG	PRO+	BR	/A	RC	SB	CS	SBR	FR	POS	TPR
1972	Bos-A	18	57	2	15	3	1	1	6	7	13	.263	.344	.404	115	2	1	8	0	0	0	1	O	0.1
1973	Bos-A	119	282	46	63	13	1	10	32	40	52	.223	.322	.383	92	-1	-3	36	5	0	2	0	*O/D	-0.3
1974	Bos-A	133	463	60	130	19	8	10	70	38	77	.281	.338	.421	110	10	6	65	4	4	-1	8	*O/D	1.0
1975	*Bos-A	128	412	61	113	24	6	13	56	47	60	.274	.354	.456	118	15	10	66	3	4	-2	15	*O/D	2.1
1976	Bos-A	146	501	61	121	34	5	17	62	57	92	.242	.326	.431	107	12	4	69	6	7	-2	7	*O/D	0.6
1977	Bos-A	73	230	39	66	9	2	14	36	28	58	.287	.364	.526	125	12	9	45	4	2	0	-2	O/D	0.4
1978	Bos-A	147	497	75	123	24	2	24	63	65	119	.247	.337	.449	108	12	5	74	8	5	-1	4	*O/D	0.6
1979	Bos-A	152	489	69	134	24	1	21	58	69	76	.274	.365	.456	114	14	11	79	6	9	-4	6	*O/D	0.7
1980	Bos-A	148	463	72	123	37	5	18	60	64	98	.266	.361	.484	123	19	16	85	3	1	0	-6	*O/D	0.7
1981	Bos-A	108	412	84	122	19	4	**22**	71	**85**	85	.296	.418	.522	160	**40**	**37**	**95**	3	2	-0	7	*O	4.2
1982	Bos-A	162	609	122	178	37	7	32	98	112	125	.292	**.403**	.534	146	48	44	134	3	2	-0	0	*O	3.8
1983	Bos-A	126	470	74	112	19	4	22	58	70	97	.238	.339	.436	104	8	3	71	3	0	1	2	OD	0.3
1984	Bos-A	162	630	**121**	186	37	8	32	104	96	115	.295	.392	.532	146	47	43	**132**	3	1	0	-3	*O/D	3.4
1985	Bos-A	159	617	110	162	29	1	29	78	**114**	105	.263	.382	.454	123	27	23	112	7	2	1	-3	*O/D	1.9
1986	Bos-A	152	529	86	137	33	2	26	97	97	117	.259	.380	.476	131	25	25	100	3	3	-1	0	*O/D	2.0
1987	Bos-A	154	541	109	165	37	2	34	123	**106**	98	.305	.422	.569	155	50	47	134	4	6	-2	-14	1O/D	2.1
1988	*Bos-A	149	559	96	164	31	7	21	111	76	99	.293	.379	.487	135	28	28	104	5	5	-1	-8	O1/D	1.6
1989	*Bos-A	146	520	82	148	27	3	20	100	99	98	.285	.402	.463	135	33	29	100	3	4	-1	-1	OD	2.6
1990	*Bos-A	123	445	66	111	18	3	13	63	67	73	.249	.353	.391	103	6	3	60	3	4	-2	0	*D	0.2
Total	19	2505	8726	1435	2373	474	72	379	1346	1337	1643	.272	.372	.473	126	410	340	1568	76	56	-11	12	*OD1	28.2

YEAR	TM/L	G	AB	R	H	2B	3B	HR	RBI	BB	SO	AVG	OBP	SLG	PRO+	BR	/A	RC	SB	CS	SBR	FR	POS	TPR

■ JAKE EVANS
Evans, Jacob "Bloody Jake" b: Baltimore, Md. d: 2/3/07, Baltimore, Md. TR, 5'8", 154 lbs. Deb: 5/01/1879

YEAR	TM/L	G	AB	R	H	2B	3B	HR	RBI	BB	SO	AVG	OBP	SLG	PRO+	BR	/A	RC	SB	CS	SBR	FR	POS	TPR
1879	Tro-N	72	280	30	65	9	5	0	17	5	18	.232	.246	.300	84	-6	-4	21				17	*O	1.0
1880	Tro-N	47	180	31	46	8	1	0	22	7	15	.256	.283	.311	96	0	-1	16				-1	O/P	-0.3
1881	Tro-N	83	315	35	76	11	5	0	28	14	30	.241	.274	.308	78	-6	-8	27				12	*O	0.2
1882	Wor-N	80	334	33	71	10	4	0	25	7	22	.213	.229	.266	57	-15	-16	21				19	*OS/32P	0.2
1883	Cle-N	90	332	36	79	13	2	0	31	8	38	.238	.256	.289	66	-13	-13	25				6	*O/S32P	-0.3
1884	Cle-N	80	313	32	81	18	3	1	38	15	49	.259	.293	.345	97	-0	-2	32				6	*O/2S	0.3
1885	Bal-a	20	77	18	17	1	1	0		6	7	.221	.318	.260	88	-1	-0	7				2	O	0.0
Total	7	472	1831	215	435	70	21	1	161	63	172	.238	.264	.300	78	-41	-44	150				59	O/S23P	1.1

■ JOE EVANS
Evans, Joseph Patton "Doc" b: 5/15/1895, Meridian, Miss. d: 8/9/53, Gulfport, Miss. BR/TR, 5'9", 160 lbs. Deb: 7/03/15

YEAR	TM/L	G	AB	R	H	2B	3B	HR	RBI	BB	SO	AVG	OBP	SLG	PRO+	BR	/A	RC	SB	CS	SBR	FR	POS	TPR
1915	Cle-A	42	109	17	28	4	2	0	11	22	18	.257	.382	.330	111	3	2	17	6	1	1	-0	3/2	0.5
1916	Cle-A	33	82	4	12	1	0	0	1	7	12	.146	.213	.159	11	-9	-9	4	4			4	3	-0.4
1917	Cle-A	132	385	30	73	4	5	2	33	42	44	.190	.271	.242	53	-20	-23	19	12			3	*3	-1.5
1918	Cle-A	79	243	38	64	6	7	1	22	30	29	.263	.344	.358	102	4	1	32	7			4	3	0.6
1919	Cle-A	21	14	9	1	0	0	0	0	2	1	.071	.188	.071	-24	-2	-2	0	1			4	/S	0.2
1920	*Cle-A	56	172	32	60	9	9	0	23	15	3	.349	.404	.506	136	10	9	36	6	2	1	-3	O/S	0.3
1921	Cle-A	57	153	36	51	11	0	0	21	19	5	.333	.410	.405	107	3	3	27	4	1	1	-1	O	0.0
1922	Cle-A	75	145	35	39	6	2	0	22	8	4	.269	.307	.338	67	-7	-7	16	11	2	2	-7	O	-1.4
1923	Was-A	106	372	42	98	15	3	0	38	27	18	.263	.313	.320	70	-18	-15	38	6	5	-1	-4	O3/1	-2.3
1924	StL-A	77	209	30	53	3	3	0	19	24	12	.254	.330	.297	59	-11	-13	21	1	4	-2	-2	O	-1.5
1925	StL-A	55	159	27	50	12	0	0	20	16	6	.314	.377	.390	90	-1	-2	25	6	2	1	4	O	0.0
Total	11	733	2043	306	529	71	31	3	210	212	152	.259	.329	.328	79	-49	-58	247	64	17		6	O3/S12	-5.5

■ STEVE EVANS
Evans, Louis Richard b: 2/17/1885, Cleveland, Ohio d: 12/28/43, Cleveland, Ohio BL/TL, 5'10", 175 lbs. Deb: 4/16/08

YEAR	TM/L	G	AB	R	H	2B	3B	HR	RBI	BB	SO	AVG	OBP	SLG	PRO+	BR	/A	RC	SB	CS	SBR	FR	POS	TPR
1908	NY-N	2	2	0	1	0	0	0	0	0	0	.500	.500	.500	213	0	0	0	0			-0	/O	0.0
1909	StL-N	143	498	67	129	17	6	2	56	66		.259	.362	.329	122	11	15	65	14			-4	*O/1	0.7
1910	StL-N	151	506	73	122	21	8	2	73	78	63	.241	.376	.326	109	8	11	66	10			-11	*O 1	-0.4
1911	StL-N	154	547	74	161	24	13	5	71	46	52	.294	.369	.413	122	14	16	88	13			-6	*O	0.4
1912	StL-N	135	491	59	139	23	9	6	72	36	51	.283	.353	.403	109	4	6	73	11			-8	*O	-0.6
1913	StL-N	97	245	18	61	15	6	1	31	20	28	.249	.321	.371	99	-1	-1	29	5			-10	O/1	-1.2
1914	Bro-F	145	514	93	179	41	15	12	96	50	49	.348	.416	.556	178	51	51	130	18			-5	*O1	4.2
1915	Bro-F	63	216	44	64	14	4	3	30	35	22	.296	.411	.440	153	16	16	43	7			-2	O/1	1.2
	Bal-F	88	340	50	107	20	6	1	37	28	34	.315	.379	.418	131	15	14	59	8			-5	O/1	0.5
	Yr	151	556	94	171	34	10	4	67	63	56	.308	.392	.426	140	31	30	102	15			-7		1.7
Total	8	978	3359	478	963	175	67	32	466	359	299	.287	.374	.407	129	118	128	554	86			-51	O/1	4.8

■ BILL EVERETT
Everett, William L. "Wild Bill" b: 12/13/1868, Ft.Wayne, Ind. d: 1/19/38, Denver, Colo. BL/TR, 6'.5", 185 lbs. Deb: 4/18/1895

YEAR	TM/L	G	AB	R	H	2B	3B	HR	RBI	BB	SO	AVG	OBP	SLG	PRO+	BR	/A	RC	SB	CS	SBR	FR	POS	TPR
1895	Chi-N	133	550	129	197	16	10	3	88	33	42	.358	.399	.440	111	15	9	118	47			-8	*3/2	0.2
1896	Chi-N	132	575	130	184	16	13	2	46	41	43	.320	.367	.403	101	4	0	105	46			-10	*3O	-0.5
1897	Chi-N	92	379	63	119	14	7	5	39	36		.314	.373	.427	109	7	5	72	26			-5	3/O	0.0
1898	Chi-N	149	596	102	190	15	6	0	69	53		.319	.377	.364	116	14	14	95	28			-2	*1	1.1
1899	Chi-N	136	536	87	166	17	5	1	74	31		.310	.351	.366	102	-0	2	81	30			8	*1	1.1
1900	Chi-N	23	91	10	24	4	0	0	17	3		.264	.287	.308	69	-4	-4	9	2			-1	1	-0.4
1901	Was-A	33	115	14	22	3	2	0	8	15		.191	.301	.252	57	-6	-6	12	7			-4	1	-0.9
Total	7	698	2842	535	902	85	43	11	341	212	85	.317	.368	.389	105	29	20	491	186			-22	13/O2	0.6

■ JOHNNY EVERS
Evers, John Joseph "Crab" or "Trojan" b: 7/22/1883, Troy, N.Y. d: 3/28/47, Albany, N.Y. BL/TR, 5'9", 125 lbs. Deb: 9/01/02 MCH

YEAR	TM/L	G	AB	R	H	2B	3B	HR	RBI	BB	SO	AVG	OBP	SLG	PRO+	BR	/A	RC	SB	CS	SBR	FR	POS	TPR
1902	Chi-N	26	90	7	20	0	0	0	2	3		.222	.263	.222	53	-5	-5	6	1			-0	2/S	-0.3
1903	Chi-N	124	464	70	136	27	7	0	52	19		.293	.321	.381	105	-0	1	68	25			-14	*2S/3	-0.5
1904	Chi-N	152	532	49	141	14	7	0	47	28		.265	.302	.318	93	-5	-5	63	26			31	*2	3.2
1905	Chi-N	99	340	44	94	11	2	1	37	27		.276	.330	.329	95	-0	-2	47	19			3	2	0.7
1906	*Chi-N	154	533	65	136	17	6	1	51	36		.255	.302	.315	89	-4	-7	70	49			6	*2/3	-0.1
1907	*Chi-N	151	508	66	127	18	4	2	51	38		.250	.302	.313	89	-3	-7	65	46			28	*2	2.6
1908	*Chi-N	126	416	83	125	19	6	0	37	66		.300	.396	.375	143	26	24	77	36			-0	*2/O	2.6
1909	Chi-N	127	463	88	122	19	6	1	24	73		.263	.369	.337	116	13	12	68	28			2	*2	1.5
1910	Chi-N	125	433	87	114	11	7	0	28	108	18	.263	.413	.321	115	15	16	70	28			-4	*2	1.5
1911	Chi-N	46	155	29	35	4	3	0	7	34	10	.226	.372	.290	86	-1	-1	19	6			-6	23	-0.7
1912	Chi-N	143	478	73	163	23	11	1	63	74	18	.341	.431	.441	139	29	29	98	16			6	*2	3.0
1913	Chi-N	136	446	81	127	20	5	3	49	50	14	.285	.361	.372	109	7	6	64	11			30	*2M	3.4
1914	*Bos-N	139	491	81	137	20	3	1	40	87	26	.279	.390	.338	118	15	15	72	12			5	*2	2.0
1915	Bos-N	83	278	38	73	4	1	0	22	50	16	.263	.375	.295	109	4	6	35	7	8	-3	-1	2	0.3
1916	Bos-N	71	241	33	52	4	1	0	15	40	19	.216	.330	.241	80	-5	-3	23	5			-17	2	-2.1
1917	Bos-N	24	83	5	16	0	0	0	0	13	8	.193	.302	.193	56	-4	-3	5	1			-7	2	-1.0
	Phi-N	56	183	20	41	5	1	1	12	30	13	.224	.333	.279	85	-1	-2	19	8			-5	2/3	-0.4
	Yr	80	266	25	57	5	1	1	12	43	21	.214	.324	.252	77	-5	-5	24	9			-12		-1.4
1922	Chi-A	1	3	0	0	0	0	0	1	2	0	.000	.400	.000	12	-0	-0	0	0	0	0	-0	/2	0.0
1929	Bos-N	1	0	0	0	0	0	0	0	0	0	—	—	—	—	0	0	0	0			-1	/2	0.0
Total	18	1784	6137	919	1659	216	70	12	538	778	142	.270	.354	.334	106	81	75	869	324	8		55	*2/3SO	15.7

■ JOE EVERS
Evers, Joseph Francis b: 9/10/1891, Troy, N.Y. d: 1/4/49, Albany, N.Y. BR/TR, 5'9", 135 lbs. Deb: 4/24/13

YEAR	TM/L	G	AB	R	H	2B	3B	HR	RBI	BB	SO	AVG	OBP	SLG	PRO+	BR	/A	RC	SB	CS	SBR	FR	POS	TPR
1913	NY-N	1	0	0	0	0	0	0	0	0	0	—	—	—	—	0	0	0	0			0	R	0.0

■ TOM EVERS
Evers, Thomas Francis b: 3/31/1852, Troy, N.Y. d: 3/23/25, Washington, D.C. Deb: 5/25/1882

YEAR	TM/L	G	AB	R	H	2B	3B	HR	RBI	BB	SO	AVG	OBP	SLG	PRO+	BR	/A	RC	SB	CS	SBR	FR	POS	TPR
1882	Bal-a	1	4	0	0	0	0	0		0		.000	.000	.000	-99	-1	-1	0				-2	/2	-0.2
1884	Was-U	109	427	54	99	6	1	0		7		.232	.244	.251	70	-14	-12	27	0			11	*2	-0.3
Total	2	110	431	54	99	6	1	0		7		.230	.242	.248	68	-15	-13	27				10	2	-0.5

■ HOOT EVERS
Evers, Walter Arthur b: 2/8/21, St.Louis, Mo. BR/TR, 6'2", 180 lbs. Deb: 9/16/41 C

YEAR	TM/L	G	AB	R	H	2B	3B	HR	RBI	BB	SO	AVG	OBP	SLG	PRO+	BR	/A	RC	SB	CS	SBR	FR	POS	TPR
1941	Det-A	1	4	0	0	0	0	0	0	0	0	.000	.000	.000	-91	-1	-1	0	0	0	0	0	/O	0.0
1946	Det-A	81	304	42	81	8	4	4	33	34	43	.266	.344	.359	91	-1	-3	41	7	1	2	-1	O	-0.6
1947	Det-A	126	460	67	136	24	5	10	67	45	49	.296	.366	.435	119	13	12	73	8	7	-2	3	*O	0.8
1948	Det-A	139	538	86	169	33	6	10	103	51	31	.314	.378	.454	117	15	13	92	3	4	-2	-2	O	0.4
1949	Det-A	132	432	68	131	21	6	7	72	70	38	.303	.403	.428	120	14	14	76	6	7	-2	13	*O	2.0
1950	Det-A	143	526	100	170	35	11	21	103	71	40	.323	.408	.551	139	34	31	116	5	9	-4	9	*O	3.1
1951	Det-A	116	393	47	88	15	2	11	46	40	47	.224	.297	.356	76	-14	-15	40	5	3	-0	4	*O	-1.4
1952	Det-A	1	1	0	1	0	0	0	0	0	0	1.000	1.000	1.000	454	0	0	1	0	0	0	0	H	0.0
	Bos-A	106	401	53	105	17	4	14	59	29	55	.262	.318	.429	99	2	-2	54	5	2	0	3	*O	-0.1
	Yr	107	402	53	106	17	4	14	59	29	55	.264	.320	.430	100	2	-2	55	5	2	0	3		-0.1
1953	Bos-A	99	300	39	72	10	1	11	31	23	41	.240	.301	.390	81	-7	-9	35	2	1	0	-7	O	-1.9
1954	Bos-A	6	8	1	0	0	0	0	0	0	2	.000	.000	.000	-90	-2	-2	0	0	0	0	0	/O	-0.2
	NY-N	12	11	1	1	0	0	1	3	0	6	.091	.091	.364	12	-2	-2	0	0	0	0	1	/O	0.0
	Det-A	30	60	5	11	4	0	0	5	5	8	.183	.258	.250	40	-5	-5	4	0	0	0	0	O	-0.4
1955	Bal-A	60	185	21	44	10	1	6	30	19	28	.238	.309	.400	96	-3	-2	21	2	1	0	-3	O	-0.6

YEAR	TM/L	G	AB	R	H	2B	3B	HR	RBI	BB	SO	AVG	OBP	SLG	PRO+	BR	/A	RC	SB	CS	SBR	FR	POS	TPR
	Cle-A	39	66	10	19	7	1	2	9	3	12	.288	.319	.515	117	1	1	10	0	1	-1	2	O	0.1
	Yr	99	251	31	63	17	2	8	39	22	40	.251	.311	.430	101	-2	-1	30	2	2	-1	-1		-0.5
1956	Cle-A	3	0	1	0	0	0	0	0	1	0	—	1.000	—	180	0	0	0	0	0	0	0	H	0.0
	Bal-A	48	112	20	27	3	0	1	4	24	18	.241	.375	.295	85	-2	-1	15	1	0	0	-1	O	-0.3
	Yr	51	112	21	27	3	0	1	4	25	18	.241	.380	.295	86	-2	-1	15	1	0	0	-1		-0.3
Total	12	1142	3801	556	1055	187	41	98	565	415	420	.278	.353	.426	106	41	29	578	45	36	-8	19	*O	0.9

■ GEORGE EWELL　Ewell, George　b: Philadelphia, Pa.　Deb: 6/26/1871

YEAR	TM/L	G	AB	R	H	2B	3B	HR	RBI	BB	SO	AVG	OBP	SLG	PRO+	BR	/A	RC	SB	CS	SBR	FR	POS	TPR
1871	Cle-n	1	3	0	0	0	0	0	0	0	0	.000	.000	.000	-99	-1	-1	0	0				/O	0.0

■ JOHN EWING　Ewing, John "Long Jong"　b: 6/1/1863, Cincinnati, Ohio　d: 4/23/1895, Denver, Colo.　TR ,　Deb: 6/18/1883

YEAR	TM/L	G	AB	R	H	2B	3B	HR	RBI	BB	SO	AVG	OBP	SLG	PRO+	BR	/A	RC	SB	CS	SBR	FR	POS	TPR
1883	StL-a	1	5	0	0	0	0	0		0		.000	.000	.000	-94	-1	-1	0				-1	/O	-0.1
1884	Cin-U	1	4	0	0	0	0	0		0		.000	.000	.000	-93	-1	-1	0	0			-0	/O	0.0
	Was-U	1	5	1	1	0	1	0		0		.200	.200	.600	166	0	0	1	0			0	/O	0.0
	Yr	2	9	1	1	0	1	0		0		.111	.111	.333	44	-1	-1	0	0			0		0.0
1888	Lou-a	21	79	6	16	1	1	0	5	1		.203	.213	.241	48	-5	-4	6	7			0	P	0.0
1889	Lou-a	41	134	12	23	2	0	0	6	9	30	.172	.234	.187	22	-13	-13	7	5			2	P/1	0.0
1890	NY-P	35	114	18	24	2	1	2	17	5	35	.211	.244	.298	42	-9	-11	9	2			-1	P	0.0
1891	NY-N	33	113	10	23	1	0	0	8	3	14	.204	.224	.212	30	-10	-9	6	4			0	P	0.0
Total	6	133	454	47	87	6	3	2	36	18	79	.192	.226	.231	33	-39	-39	29	18			1	P/O1	-0.1

■ REUBEN EWING　Ewing, Reuben (b: Reuben Cohen)　b: 11/30/1899, Odessa, Russia　d: 10/5/70, W.Hartford, Conn.　5'4.5", 150 lbs.　Deb: 6/21/21

YEAR	TM/L	G	AB	R	H	2B	3B	HR	RBI	BB	SO	AVG	OBP	SLG	PRO+	BR	/A	RC	SB	CS	SBR	FR	POS	TPR
1921	StL-N	3	1	0	0	0	0	0	0	0	1	.000	.000	.000	-99	-0	-0	0	0	0	0	1	/S	0.1

■ SAM EWING　Ewing, Samuel James　b: 4/9/49, Lewisburg, Tenn.　BL/TL, 6'3", 200 lbs.　Deb: 9/11/73

YEAR	TM/L	G	AB	R	H	2B	3B	HR	RBI	BB	SO	AVG	OBP	SLG	PRO+	BR	/A	RC	SB	CS	SBR	FR	POS	TPR
1973	Chi-A	11	20	1	3	1	0	0	2	2	6	.150	.227	.200	20	-2	-2	1	0	0	0	1	/1	-0.1
1976	Chi-A	19	41	3	9	2	1	0	2	2	8	.220	.256	.317	67	-2	-2	3	0	0	0	0	D/1	-0.1
1977	Tor-A	97	244	24	70	8	2	4	34	19	42	.287	.338	.385	95	-1	-1	30	1	1	-0	-3	OD/1	-0.5
1978	Tor-A	40	56	3	10	0	0	2	9	5	9	.179	.246	.286	48	-4	-4	4	0	0	0	1	/OD	-0.3
Total	4	167	361	31	92	11	3	6	47	28	65	.255	.308	.352	81	-9	-9	39	1	1	-0	-2	/OD1	-1.0

■ BUCK EWING　Ewing, William　b: 10/17/1859, Hoaglands, Ohio　d: 10/20/06, Cincinnati, Ohio　BR/TR, 5'10", 188 lbs.　Deb: 9/09/1880　MH

YEAR	TM/L	G	AB	R	H	2B	3B	HR	RBI	BB	SO	AVG	OBP	SLG	PRO+	BR	/A	RC	SB	CS	SBR	FR	POS	TPR
1880	Tro-N	13	45	1	8	1	0	0	5	1	3	.178	.196	.200	33	-3	-3	2				-5	C/O	-0.6
1881	Tro-N	67	272	40	68	14	7	0	25	7	8	.250	.269	.353	89	-2	-4	26				23	CS/O3	1.9
1882	Tro-N	74	328	67	89	16	11	2	29	10	15	.271	.293	.405	127	7	10	40				11	3C/2O1P	2.1
1883	NY-N	88	376	90	114	11	13	10	41	20	14	.303	.338	.481	147	20	21	63				-6	CO2/S3	1.6
1884	NY-N	94	382	90	106	15	20	3	41	28	22	.277	.327	.445	137	17	16	57				-2	*CO/S3P	1.8
1885	NY-N	81	342	81	104	15	12	6	63	13	17	.304	.330	.471	159	20	21	54				7	CO/3S1P	3.1
1886	NY-N	73	275	59	85	11	7	4	31	16	17	.309	.347	.444	138	12	12	50	18			-2	CO1	1.1
1887	NY-N	77	318	83	97	17	13	6	44	30	33	.305	.370	.497	148	17	20	70	26			-2	32/C	1.7
1888	*NY-N	103	415	83	127	18	15	6	58	24	28	.306	.348	.465	162	27	28	88	53			9	C3/SP	3.9
1889	*NY-N	99	407	91	133	23	13	4	87	37	32	.327	.383	.477	141	21	21	89	34			15	*C/PO	3.2
1890	NY-P	83	352	98	119	19	15	8	72	39	12	.338	.406	.545	142	26	20	95	36			16	C/2PM	3.1
1891	NY-N	14	49	8	17	2	1	0	18	5	5	.347	.407	.429	152	3	3	11	5			-2	/2C	0.1
1892	NY-N	105	393	58	122	10	15	8	76	38	26	.310	.371	.473	160	26	26	87	42			11	1C/2	3.0
1893	Cle-N	116	407	117	172	28	15	6	122	41	18	.344	.394	.496	130	25	20	119	47			-1	*O/21C	1.2
1894	Cle-N	53	211	32	53	12	4	2	39	24	9	.251	.328	.374	68	-11	-12	33	18			-2	O/2	-1.3
1895	Cin-N	105	434	90	138	24	13	5	94	30	22	.318	.363	.468	111	8	5	88	34			8	*1M	1.2
1896	Cin-N	69	263	41	73	14	4	1	38	29	13	.278	.349	.373	86	-3	-6	50	41			4	1M	0.1
1897	Cin-N	1	1	0	0	0	0	0	0	0	0	.000	.500	.000	39	0	0	0	0			-0	/1M	0.0
Total	18	1315	5363	1129	1625	250	178	71	883	392	294	.303	.351	.456	131	212	197	1021	354			82	C103/2SP	27.2

■ ART EWOLDT　Ewoldt, Arthur Lee "Sheriff"　b: 1/8/1894, Paullina, Iowa　d: 12/8/77, Des Moines, Iowa　BR/TR, 5'10", 165 lbs.　Deb: 9/17/19

YEAR	TM/L	G	AB	R	H	2B	3B	HR	RBI	BB	SO	AVG	OBP	SLG	PRO+	BR	/A	RC	SB	CS	SBR	FR	POS	TPR
1919	Phi-A	9	32	2	7	1	0	0	2	1	5	.219	.242	.250	38	-3	-3	2	0			0	/3	-0.1

■ HOMER EZZELL　Ezzell, Homer Estell　b: 2/28/1896, Victoria, Tex.　d: 8/3/76, San Antonio, Tex.　BR/TR, 5'10", 158 lbs.　Deb: 4/22/23

YEAR	TM/L	G	AB	R	H	2B	3B	HR	RBI	BB	SO	AVG	OBP	SLG	PRO+	BR	/A	RC	SB	CS	SBR	FR	POS	TPR
1923	StL-A	88	279	31	68	6	0	0	14	15	20	.244	.287	.265	44	-22	-24	22	4	3	-1	8	3/2	-0.6
1924	Bos-A	90	277	35	75	8	4	0	32	14	21	.271	.311	.329	65	-15	-15	29	12	5	1	9	3S/C	0.2
1925	Bos-A	58	186	40	53	6	4	0	15	19	18	.285	.351	.360	81	-5	-5	24	9	7	-2	-7	3/2	-0.9
Total	3	236	742	106	196	20	8	0	61	48	59	.264	.312	.313	61	-42	-44	75	25	15	-1	10	3/S2C	-1.3

■ JAY FAATZ　Faatz, Jayson S.　b: 10/24/1860, Weedsport, N.Y.　d: 4/10/23, Syracuse, N.Y.　BR/TR, 6'4",　Deb: 8/22/1884　M

YEAR	TM/L	G	AB	R	H	2B	3B	HR	RBI	BB	SO	AVG	OBP	SLG	PRO+	BR	/A	RC	SB	CS	SBR	FR	POS	TPR
1884	Pit-a	29	112	18	27	2	3	0		1		.241	.274	.313	92	-1	-1	10				-1	1	-0.2
1888	Cle-a	120	470	73	124	10	2	0	51	12		.264	.312	.294	100	-1	1	65	64			2	*1	-0.3
1889	Cle-N	117	442	50	102	12	5	2	38	17	28	.231	.275	.294	61	-24	-22	44	27			6	*1	-2.2
1890	Buf-P	32	111	18	21	0	2	1	16	9	5	.189	.297	.252	53	-8	-6	9	2			-2	1	-0.8
Total	4	298	1135	159	274	24	12	3	105	39	33	.241	.293	.292	78	-33	-28	128	93			4	1	-3.5

■ BUNNY FABRIQUE　Fabrique, Albert La Verne　b: 12/23/1887, Clinton, Mich.　d: 1/10/60, Ann Arbor, Mich.　BB/TR, 5'8.5", 150 lbs.　Deb: 10/04/16

YEAR	TM/L	G	AB	R	H	2B	3B	HR	RBI	BB	SO	AVG	OBP	SLG	PRO+	BR	/A	RC	SB	CS	SBR	FR	POS	TPR
1916	Bro-N	2	2	0	0	0	0	0	0	0	1	.000	.000	.000	-97	-0	-0	0	0			0	/S	0.0
1917	Bro-N	25	88	8	18	3	0	1	3	8	9	.205	.271	.273	65	-3	-4	6	0			-2	S	-0.5
Total	2	27	90	8	18	3	0	1	3	8	10	.200	.265	.267	62	-4	-4	6	0			-2	/S	-0.5

■ LENNY FAEDO　Faedo, Leonardo Lago　b: 5/13/60, Tampa, Fla.　BR/TR, 6', 170 lbs.　Deb: 9/06/80

YEAR	TM/L	G	AB	R	H	2B	3B	HR	RBI	BB	SO	AVG	OBP	SLG	PRO+	BR	/A	RC	SB	CS	SBR	FR	POS	TPR
1980	Min-A	5	8	1	2	1	0	0	0	0	0	.250	.250	.375	64	-0	-0	1	0	0	0	-1	/S	0.0
1981	Min-A	12	41	3	8	0	1	0	6	1	5	.195	.214	.244	30	-4	-4	2	0	0	0	3	S	0.0
1982	Min-A	90	255	16	62	8	0	3	22	16	22	.243	.290	.310	63	-12	-13	22	1	0	0	3	S/D	-0.1
1983	Min-A	51	173	16	48	7	0	1	18	4	19	.277	.294	.335	70	-7	-7	16	0	0	0	-15	S	-1.9
1984	Min-A	16	52	6	13	1	0	1	6	4	3	.250	.304	.327	71	-2	-2	5	0	0	0	-5	S/D	-0.5
Total	5	174	529	42	133	17	1	5	52	25	49	.251	.286	.316	64	-24	-27	46	1	0	0	-15	S/D	-2.5

■ FRED FAGIN　Fagin, Frederick H.　b: Cincinnati, Ohio　Deb: 6/25/1895

YEAR	TM/L	G	AB	R	H	2B	3B	HR	RBI	BB	SO	AVG	OBP	SLG	PRO+	BR	/A	RC	SB	CS	SBR	FR	POS	TPR
1895	StL-N	1	3	0	1	0	0	0	2	0	0	.333	.333	.333	75	-0	-0	0	0			1	/C	0.1

■ FRANK FAHEY　Fahey, Francis Raymond　b: 1/22/1896, Milford, Mass.　d: 3/19/54, Boston, Mass.　BB/TR, 6'1", 190 lbs.　Deb: 4/25/18

YEAR	TM/L	G	AB	R	H	2B	3B	HR	RBI	BB	SO	AVG	OBP	SLG	PRO+	BR	/A	RC	SB	CS	SBR	FR	POS	TPR
1918	Phi-A	10	17	2	3	1	0	0	1	0	3	.176	.176	.235	24	-2	-2	1	0			-2	/OP	-0.3

■ HOWARD FAHEY　Fahey, Howard Simpson "Cap" or "Kid"　b: 6/24/1892, Medford, Mass.　d: 10/24/71, Clearwater, Fla.　BR/TR, 5'7.5", 145 lbs.　Deb: 7/23/12

YEAR	TM/L	G	AB	R	H	2B	3B	HR	RBI	BB	SO	AVG	OBP	SLG	PRO+	BR	/A	RC	SB	CS	SBR	FR	POS	TPR
1912	Phi-A	5	8	0	0	0	0	0		0	0	.000	.000	.000	-99	-2	-2	0	0			-1	/32S	-0.2

■ BILL FAHEY　Fahey, William Roger　b: 6/14/50, Detroit, Mich.　BL/TR, 6', 200 lbs.　Deb: 9/26/71　C

YEAR	TM/L	G	AB	R	H	2B	3B	HR	RBI	BB	SO	AVG	OBP	SLG	PRO+	BR	/A	RC	SB	CS	SBR	FR	POS	TPR
1971	Was-A	2	8	0	0	0	0	0	0	0	0	.000	.000	.000	-99	-0	-0	0	0	0	0	-0	/C	-0.2
1972	Tex-A	39	119	8	20	2	0	1	10	12	23	.168	.250	.210	40	-9	-8	7	4	0	1	10	C	0.4
1974	Tex-A	6	16	1	4	0	0	0	0	0	1	.250	.250	.250	45	-1	-1	1	0	0	0	-1	/C	-0.2
1975	Tex-A	21	37	3	11	1	1	0	3	1	10	.297	.316	.378	96	-0	-0	4	0	0	0	-1	C	0.0
1976	Tex-A	38	80	12	20	2	0	1	9	11	6	.250	.348	.313	92	-0	-0	9	1	0	0	2	C	0.3

YEAR	TM/L	G	AB	R	H	2B	3B	HR	RBI	BB	SO	AVG	OBP	SLG	PRO+	BR	/A	RC	SB	CS	SBR	FR	POS	TPR
1977	Tex-A	37	68	3	15	4	0	0	5	1	8	.221	.232	.279	38	-6	-6	4	0	0	0	-1	C	-0.5
1979	SD-N	73	209	14	60	8	1	3	19	21	17	.287	.352	.378	106	0	2	28	1	1	-0	-3	C	0.0
1980	SD-N	93	241	18	62	4	0	1	22	21	16	.257	.317	.286	74	-9	-8	23	2	0	1	-4	C	-0.9
1981	Det-A	27	67	5	17	2	0	1	9	2	4	.254	.275	.328	71	-2	-2	6	0	1	-1	3	C	0.1
1982	Det-A	28	67	7	10	2	0	0	4	0	5	.149	.149	.179	-10	-10	-10	2	1	0	0	5	C	-0.2
1983	Det-A	19	22	4	6	1	0	0	2	5	3	.273	.407	.318	106	0	0	3	0	0	0	1	C	0.2
Total	11	383	934	75	225	26	2	7	83	74	93	.241	.298	.296	69	-40	-36	87	9	2	2	10	C	-1.0

■ FERRIS FAIN
Fain, Ferris Roy "Burrhead"　b: 5/29/21, San Antonio, Tex.　BL/TL, 5'11", 180 lbs.　Deb: 4/15/47

YEAR	TM/L	G	AB	R	H	2B	3B	HR	RBI	BB	SO	AVG	OBP	SLG	PRO+	BR	/A	RC	SB	CS	SBR	FR	POS	TPR
1947	Phi-A	136	461	70	134	28	6	7	71	95	34	.291	.414	.423	130	25	24	86	4	5	-2	1	*1	2.0
1948	Phi-A	145	520	81	146	27	6	7	88	113	37	.281	.412	.396	115	17	17	93	10	5	0	9	*1	3.1
1949	Phi-A	150	525	81	138	21	5	3	78	136	51	.263	.415	.339	104	8	11	87	8	1	2	4	*1	1.7
1950	Phi-A	151	522	83	147	25	4	10	83	133	26	.282	.430	.402	116	18	20	101	8	5	-1	8	*1	1.9
1951	Phi-A	117	425	63	146	30	3	6	57	80	20	.344	.451	.471	146	34	33	96	0	3	-2	14	*1O	4.1
1952	Phi-A	145	538	82	176	43	3	2	59	105	26	.327	.438	.429	133	36	32	107	3	5	-2	16	*1	3.8
1953	Chi-A	128	446	73	114	18	2	6	52	108	28	.256	.405	.345	101	9	7	72	3	2	-0	10	*1	1.3
1954	Chi-A	65	235	30	71	10	1	5	51	40	14	.302	.406	.417	121	10	9	44	5	1	1	-4	1	0.4
1955	Det-A	58	140	23	37	8	0	2	23	52	12	.264	.464	.364	128	9	10	28	2	1	0	0	1	0.8
	Cle-A	56	118	9	30	3	0	0	8	42	13	.254	.453	.280	97	4	3	19	3	0	1	3	1	0.5
	Yr	114	258	32	67	11	0	2	31	94	25	.260	.459	.326	113	13	13	48	5	1	1	4		1.3
Total	9	1151	3930	595	1139	213	30	48	570	904	261	.290	.425	.396	120	169	163	735	46	28	-3	60	*1/O	19.6

■ GEORGE FAIR
Fair, George T.　b: 1/14/1856, Boston, Mass.　d: 2/12/39, Roslindale, Mass.　5'7.5", 140 lbs.　Deb: 7/29/1876

YEAR	TM/L	G	AB	R	H	2B	3B	HR	RBI	BB	SO	AVG	OBP	SLG	PRO+	BR	/A	RC	SB	CS	SBR	FR	POS	TPR
1876	NY-N	1	4	0	0	0	0	0	0	0	0	.000	.000	.000	-99	-1	-1	0				0	/2	0.0

■ JIM FAIREY
Fairey, James Burke　b: 9/22/44, Orangeburg, S.C.　BL/TL, 5'10", 190 lbs.　Deb: 4/14/68

YEAR	TM/L	G	AB	R	H	2B	3B	HR	RBI	BB	SO	AVG	OBP	SLG	PRO+	BR	/A	RC	SB	CS	SBR	FR	POS	TPR
1968	LA-N	99	156	17	31	3	3	1	10	9	32	.199	.242	.276	60	-9	-7	10	1	1	-0	1	O	-1.0
1969	Mon-N	20	49	6	14	1	0	1	6	1	7	.286	.300	.367	86	-1	-1	4	0	2	-1	0	O	-0.2
1970	Mon-N	92	211	35	51	9	3	3	25	14	38	.242	.295	.355	74	-8	-8	21	1	3	-2	-2	O	-1.4
1971	Mon-N	92	200	19	49	8	1	1	19	12	23	.245	.288	.310	69	-8	-8	18	3	3	-1	2	O	-0.9
1972	Mon-N	86	141	9	33	7	0	1	15	10	21	.234	.285	.305	66	-6	-6	12	1	3	-2	-3	O	-1.3
1973	LA-N	10	9	0	2	0	0	0	0	1	1	.222	.300	.222	49	-1	-1	1	0	0	0	0	H	0.0
Total	6	399	766	86	180	28	7	7	75	47	122	.235	.281	.317	69	-33	-32	65	6	12	-5	-2	O	-4.8

■ RON FAIRLY
Fairly, Ronald Ray　b: 7/12/38, Macon, Ga.　BL/TL, 5'10", 175 lbs.　Deb: 9/09/58

YEAR	TM/L	G	AB	R	H	2B	3B	HR	RBI	BB	SO	AVG	OBP	SLG	PRO+	BR	/A	RC	SB	CS	SBR	FR	POS	TPR
1958	LA-N	15	53	6	15	1	0	2	8	6	7	.283	.356	.415	100	0	0	8	0	0	0	-0	O	0.0
1959	*LA-N	118	244	27	58	12	1	4	23	31	29	.238	.326	.344	73	-7	-9	28	0	4	-2	-1	O	-1.3
1960	LA-N	14	37	6	4	0	3	1	3	7	12	.108	.250	.351	59	-2	-2	3	0	0	0	-1	O	-0.3
1961	LA-N	111	245	42	79	15	2	10	48	48	22	.322	.435	.522	140	21	18	60	0	0	0	2	O1	1.4
1962	LA-N	147	460	80	128	15	7	14	71	75	59	.278	.383	.433	126	14	18	80	1	1	-0	-12	*1O	0.0
1963	*LA-N	152	490	62	133	21	0	12	77	58	69	.271	.350	.388	120	9	13	68	5	2	0	-7	*1O	0.1
1964	LA-N	150	454	62	116	19	5	10	74	65	59	.256	.351	.385	116	6	10	66	4	0	1	-1	*1	0.6
1965	*LA-N	158	555	79	152	28	1	9	70	76	72	.274	.364	.377	117	9	14	82	2	0	1	3	O1	1.3
1966	*LA-N	117	351	53	101	20	0	14	61	52	38	.288	.383	.464	146	18	21	63	3	2	-0	-13	O1	0.4
1967	LA-N	153	486	45	107	19	0	10	55	54	51	.220	.299	.321	85	-14	-9	46	1	4	-2	5	O1	-1.4
1968	LA-N	141	441	32	103	15	1	4	43	41	61	.234	.305	.299	89	-9	-5	40	0	2	-1	0	*O1	-1.4
1969	LA-N	30	64	3	14	3	2	0	8	9	6	.219	.315	.328	86	-2	-1	7	0	0	0	1	1O	-0.1
	Mon-N	70	253	35	73	13	4	12	39	28	22	.289	.359	.514	142	13	13	46	1	0	0	2	1O	1.1
	Yr	100	317	38	87	16	6	12	47	37	28	.274	.350	.476	132	12	13	53	1	0	0	3		1.0
1970	Mon-N	119	385	54	111	19	0	15	61	72	64	.288	.406	.455	130	19	19	76	10	2	2	6	*1/O	1.6
1971	Mon-N	146	447	58	115	23	0	13	71	81	65	.257	.377	.396	119	14	14	71	1	3	-2	7	*1O	1.0
1972	Mon-N	140	446	51	124	15	1	17	68	46	45	.278	.349	.430	118	12	11	66	3	4	-2	5	O1	0.7
1973	Mon-N	142	413	70	123	13	1	17	49	86	33	.298	.422	.458	139	29	27	85	2	2	-1	-13	*O/1	0.7
1974	Mon-N	101	282	35	69	9	1	12	43	57	28	.245	.374	.411	113	9	7	46	2	1	0	10	10	0.4
1975	StL-N	107	229	32	69	13	2	7	37	45	22	.301	.422	.467	142	16	15	46	0	1	-1	1	1O	1.2
1976	StL-N	73	110	13	29	4	0	3	21	23	12	.264	.391	.300	97	1	1	14	0	0	0	3	1	0.3
	Oak-A	15	46	9	11	1	0	3	10	9	12	.239	.364	.457	145	2	3	8	0	0	0	1	1	0.3
1977	Tor-A	132	458	60	128	24	2	19	64	58	58	.279	.363	.465	122	16	15	75	0	4	-2	0	D1O	0.9
1978	Cal-A	91	235	23	51	5	0	10	40	25	31	.217	.295	.366	88	-5	-4	25	0	1	-1	-2	1/D	-0.9
Total	21	2442	7184	931	1913	307	33	215	1044	1052	877	.266	.363	.408	117	170	187	1107	35	33	-9	-15	*1O/D	6.6

■ ANTON FALCH
Falch, Anton C.　b: 12/4/1860, Milwaukee, Wis.　d: 3/31/36, Wauwatosa, Wis.　6'6", 220 lbs.　Deb: 9/30/1884

YEAR	TM/L	G	AB	R	H	2B	3B	HR	RBI	BB	SO	AVG	OBP	SLG	PRO+	BR	/A	RC	SB	CS	SBR	FR	POS	TPR
1884	Mil-U	5	18	0	2	0	0	0		0			.111	.111	.111	-45	-2	-1	0				0	/OC	0.0

■ BIBB FALK
Falk, Bibb August "Jockey"　b: 1/27/1899, Austin, Tex.　d: 6/8/89, Austin, Tex.　BL/TL, 6', 175 lbs.　Deb: 9/17/20 MC

YEAR	TM/L	G	AB	R	H	2B	3B	HR	RBI	BB	SO	AVG	OBP	SLG	PRO+	BR	/A	RC	SB	CS	SBR	FR	POS	TPR
1920	Chi-A	7	17	1	5	1	1	0	2	0	5	.294	.294	.471	100	-0	-0	2	0	0	0	-1	/O	0.0
1921	Chi-A	152	585	62	167	31	11	5	82	37	69	.285	.330	.402	87	-14	-13	78	4	4	-1	-14	*O	-3.7
1922	Chi-A	131	483	58	144	27	1	12	79	27	55	.298	.335	.433	99	-2	-2	68	2	6	-3	-9	*O	-2.3
1923	Chi-A	87	274	44	84	18	6	5	38	25	12	.307	.367	.471	121	7	7	47	4	5	-2	-7	O	-0.7
1924	Chi-A	138	526	77	185	37	8	6	99	47	21	.352	.406	.487	134	23	25	103	6	6	-2	10	*O	2.2
1925	Chi-A	154	602	80	181	35	9	4	99	51	25	.301	.357	.409	99	-6	-1	89	4	5	-2	-4	*O	-1.9
1926	Chi-A	155	566	86	195	43	4	8	108	66	22	.345	.415	.477	137	28	31	112	9	10	-3	8	*O	2.2
1927	Chi-A	145	535	76	175	35	6	9	83	52	19	.327	.391	.465	125	17	19	93	5	7	-3	18	*O	2.3
1928	Chi-A	98	286	42	83	18	4	1	37	25	16	.290	.347	.392	95	-3	-2	40	5	1	1	2	O	-0.3
1929	Cle-A	125	426	65	133	30	7	13	93	42	14	.312	.374	.507	120	15	12	80	4	4	-1	-4	*O	0.2
1930	Cle-A	82	191	34	62	12	1	4	36	23	8	.325	.397	.461	113	5	4	36	2	0	1	1	O	0.4
1931	Cle-A	79	161	30	49	13	1	2	28	17	13	.304	.371	.435	105	3	1	26	1	1	-0	-3	O	-0.3
Total	12	1353	4652	655	1463	300	59	69	784	412	279	.314	.372	.449	113	71	81	775	46	49	-16	-3	*O	-1.9

■ CHARLIE FALLON
Fallon, Charles Augustus　b: 3/7/1881, New York, N.Y.　d: 6/10/60, Kings Park, N.Y.　BR/TR, 5'6", Deb: 6/30/05

YEAR	TM/L	G	AB	R	H	2B	3B	HR	RBI	BB	SO	AVG	OBP	SLG	PRO+	BR	/A	RC	SB	CS	SBR	FR	POS	TPR
1905	NY-A	1	0	0	0	0	0	0	0	0	0	—	—	—	—	0	0	0				0	R	0.0

■ GEORGE FALLON
Fallon, George Decatur "Flash"　b: 7/8/16, Jersey City, N.J.　BR/TR, 5'9", 155 lbs.　Deb: 9/27/37

YEAR	TM/L	G	AB	R	H	2B	3B	HR	RBI	BB	SO	AVG	OBP	SLG	PRO+	BR	/A	RC	SB	CS	SBR	FR	POS	TPR
1937	Bro-N	4	8	0	2	1	0	0	0	1	0	.250	.333	.375	91	-0	-0	0	0			1	/2	0.1
1943	StL-N	36	78	6	18	1	0	0	5	2	9	.231	.259	.244	44	-5	-6	5	0			15	2	1.1
1944	*StL-N	69	141	16	28	6	0	1	9	16	11	.199	.285	.262	54	-8	-9	11	1			4	2S/3	0.3
1945	StL-N	24	55	4	13	2	1	0	7	6	6	.236	.311	.309	71	-2	-2	6	1			-2	S/2	-0.1
Total	4	133	282	26	61	10	1	1	21	25	26	.216	.285	.270	56	-16	-17	22	2			18	/2S3	1.4

■ PETE FALSEY
Falsey, Peter James　b: 4/24/1891, New Haven, Conn.　d: 5/23/76, Los Angeles, Cal.　BL/TL, 5'6.5", 132 lbs.　Deb: 7/16/14

YEAR	TM/L	G	AB	R	H	2B	3B	HR	RBI	BB	SO	AVG	OBP	SLG	PRO+	BR	/A	RC	SB	CS	SBR	FR	POS	TPR
1914	Pit-N	3	1	0	0	0	0	0	0	0	1	.000	.000	.000	-99	-0	-0	0	0			0	H	0.0

■ JIM FANNING
Fanning, William James　b: 9/14/27, Chicago, Ill.　BR/TR, 5'11", 180 lbs.　Deb: 9/11/54 MC

YEAR	TM/L	G	AB	R	H	2B	3B	HR	RBI	BB	SO	AVG	OBP	SLG	PRO+	BR	/A	RC	SB	CS	SBR	FR	POS	TPR
1954	Chi-N	11	38	2	7	0	0	0	1	1	7	.184	.205	.184	2	-5	-5	1	0	0	0	-1	C	-0.6
1955	Chi-N	5	10	0	0	0	0	0	0	1	2	.000	.091	.000	-73	-3	-3	0	0	0	0	3	/C	0.1

YEAR	TM/L	G	AB	R	H	2B	3B	HR	RBI	BB	SO	AVG	OBP	SLG	PRO+	BR	/A	RC	SB	CS	SBR	FR	POS	TPR
1956	Chi-N	1	4	0	1	0	0	0	0	0	0	.250	.250	.250	36	-0	-0	0	0	0	0	1	/C	0.0
1957	Chi-N	47	89	3	16	2	0	0	4	4	17	.180	.223	.202	16	-11	-10	4	0	0	0	3	C	-0.5
Total	4	64	141	5	24	2	0	0	5	6	26	.170	.209	.184	6	-19	-19	4	0	0	0	6	/C	-1.0

■ CARMEN FANZONE
Fanzone, Carmen Ronald   b: 8/30/43, Detroit, Mich.   BR/TR, 6', 200 lbs.   Deb: 7/21/70

YEAR	TM/L	G	AB	R	H	2B	3B	HR	RBI	BB	SO	AVG	OBP	SLG	PRO+	BR	/A	RC	SB	CS	SBR	FR	POS	TPR
1970	Bos-A	10	15	0	3	1	0	0	3	2	2	.200	.333	.267	63	-1	-1	1	0	0	0	0	/3	0.0
1971	Chi-N	12	43	5	8	2	0	2	5	2	7	.186	.222	.372	57	-2	-3	3	0	0	0	0	/O31	-0.3
1972	Chi-N	86	222	26	50	11	0	8	42	35	45	.225	.338	.383	95	2	-1	28	2	3	-1	3	312/SO	0.0
1973	Chi-N	64	150	22	41	7	0	6	22	20	38	.273	.359	.440	112	4	3	24	1	2	-1	-3	31/O	-0.2
1974	Chi-N	65	158	13	30	6	0	4	22	15	27	.190	.269	.304	57	-9	-10	13	0	1	-1	-1	32/1O	-1.1
Total	5	237	588	66	132	27	0	20	94	74	119	.224	.317	.372	86	-5	-11	70	3	6	-3	-0	3/120S	-1.6

■ PAUL FARIES
Faries, Paul Tyrell   b: 2/20/65, Berkeley, Cal.   BR/TR, 5'10", 165 lbs.   Deb: 9/06/90

YEAR	TM/L	G	AB	R	H	2B	3B	HR	RBI	BB	SO	AVG	OBP	SLG	PRO+	BR	/A	RC	SB	CS	SBR	FR	POS	TPR
1990	SD-N	14	37	4	7	1	0	0	2	4	7	.189	.286	.216	40	-3	-3	3	0	1	-1	6	/2S3	0.3

■ BOB FARLEY
Farley, Robert Jacob   b: 11/15/37, Watsontown, Pa.   BL/TL, 6'2", 200 lbs.   Deb: 4/15/61

YEAR	TM/L	G	AB	R	H	2B	3B	HR	RBI	BB	SO	AVG	OBP	SLG	PRO+	BR	/A	RC	SB	CS	SBR	FR	POS	TPR
1961	SF-N	13	20	3	2	0	0	0	1	3	5	.100	.217	.100	-13	-3	-3	1	0	0	0	-1	/O1	-0.3
1962	Chi-A	35	53	7	10	1	1	1	4	13	13	.189	.348	.302	77	-1	-1	6	0	1	-1	-1	1	-0.3
	Det-A	36	50	9	8	2	0	1	4	14	10	.160	.344	.260	63	-2	-2	6	0	0	0	-2	O/1	-0.5
	Yr	71	103	16	18	3	1	2	8	27	23	.175	.346	.282	70	-3	-4	12	0	1	-1	-3		-0.8
Total	2	84	123	19	20	3	1	2	9	30	28	.163	.327	.252	58	-7	-7	13	0	1	-1	-4	/1O	-1.1

■ TOM FARLEY
Farley, Thomas T.   b: Chicago, Ill.   Deb: 6/24/1884

YEAR	TM/L	G	AB	R	H	2B	3B	HR	RBI	BB	SO	AVG	OBP	SLG	PRO+	BR	/A	RC	SB	CS	SBR	FR	POS	TPR
1884	Was-a	14	52	5	11	4	0	0		1		.212	.241	.288	84	-1	-1	4				1	O	0.1

■ ALEX FARMER
Farmer, Alexander Johnson   b: 5/9/1880, New York, N.Y.   d: 3/5/20, New York, N.Y.   BR/TR, 6', 175 lbs.   Deb: 9/01/08

YEAR	TM/L	G	AB	R	H	2B	3B	HR	RBI	BB	SO	AVG	OBP	SLG	PRO+	BR	/A	RC	SB	CS	SBR	FR	POS	TPR
1908	Bro-N	12	30	1	5	1	0	0	2	1		.167	.194	.200	28	-2	-2	1	0			-0	C	-0.1

■ JACK FARMER
Farmer, Floyd Haskell   b: 7/14/1892, Granville, Tenn.   d: 5/21/70, Columbia, La.   BR/TR, 6', 180 lbs.   Deb: 7/08/16

YEAR	TM/L	G	AB	R	H	2B	3B	HR	RBI	BB	SO	AVG	OBP	SLG	PRO+	BR	/A	RC	SB	CS	SBR	FR	POS	TPR
1916	Pit-N	55	166	10	45	6	4	0	14	7	24	.271	.309	.355	103	0	0	19	1			-8	2O/S3	-0.8
1918	Cle-A	7	9	1	2	0	0	0	1	0	3	.222	.300	.222	53	-0	-1	1	2			-2	/O	-0.2
Total	2	62	175	11	47	6	4	0	15	7	27	.269	.308	.349	100	-0	-0	20	3			-10	/2OS3	-1.0

■ BILL FARMER
Farmer, William   b: 12/27/1870,   BR/TR, 5'11.5",   Deb: 5/01/1888

YEAR	TM/L	G	AB	R	H	2B	3B	HR	RBI	BB	SO	AVG	OBP	SLG	PRO+	BR	/A	RC	SB	CS	SBR	FR	POS	TPR
1888	Pit-N	2	4	0	0	0	0	0	0	0	1	.000	.000	.000	-99	-1	-1	0	0			0	/CO	0.0
	Phi-a	3	12	0	2	0	0	0	1	0		.167	.167	.167	9	-1	-1	0	0			0	/C	0.0

■ SID FARRAR
Farrar, Sidney Douglas   b: 8/10/1859, Paris Hill, Me.   d: 5/7/35, New York, N.Y.   TR , 5'10", 185 lbs.   Deb: 5/01/1883

YEAR	TM/L	G	AB	R	H	2B	3B	HR	RBI	BB	SO	AVG	OBP	SLG	PRO+	BR	/A	RC	SB	CS	SBR	FR	POS	TPR
1883	Phi-N	99	377	41	88	19	8	0	29	4	37	.233	.241	.326	77	-13	-8	30				0	*1	-1.8
1884	Phi-N	111	428	62	105	16	6	1	45	9	25	.245	.261	.318	85	-10	-7	36				4	*1	-1.2
1885	Phi-N	111	420	49	103	20	3	3	36	28	34	.245	.292	.329	103	0	2	41				2	*1	-1.4
1886	Phi-N	118	439	55	109	19	7	5	50	16	47	.248	.275	.358	90	-6	-6	47	10			3	*1	-2.2
1887	Phi-N	116	443	83	125	20	9	4	72	42	29	.282	.358	.395	105	8	3	73	24			3	*1	-1.0
1888	Phi-N	131	508	53	124	24	7	1	53	31	38	.244	.304	.325	98	2	-1	58	21			3	*1	-1.0
1889	Phi-N	130	477	70	128	22	2	3	58	52	36	.268	.348	.342	87	-2	-9	68	28			-5	*1	-2.0
1890	Phi-P	127	481	84	122	17	11	1	69	51	23	.254	.331	.341	80	-12	-14	59	9			-2	*1	-2.2
Total	8	943	3573	497	904	157	53	18	412	233	269	.253	.305	.342	91	-32	-41	413	92			8	1	-12.8

■ DUKE FARRELL
Farrell, Charles Andrew   b: 8/31/1866, Oakdale, Mass.   d: 2/15/25, Boston, Mass.   BB/TR, 6'1", 208 lbs.   Deb: 4/21/1888

YEAR	TM/L	G	AB	R	H	2B	3B	HR	RBI	BB	SO	AVG	OBP	SLG	PRO+	BR	/A	RC	SB	CS	SBR	FR	POS	TPR
1888	Chi-N	64	241	34	56	6	3	3	19	4	41	.232	.245	.320	75	-6	-8	21	8			-10	CO/1	-1.6
1889	Chi-N	101	407	66	101	19	7	11	75	41	21	.248	.318	.410	99	1	-2	59	13			6	CO	0.3
1890	Chi-P	117	451	79	131	21	12	2	84	42	28	.290	.352	.404	99	2	-2	69	8			20	C1O	1.5
1891	Bos-a	122	473	108	143	19	13	**12**	**110**	59	48	.302	.384	.474	151	29	30	97	21			21	3CO/1	**4.5**
1892	Pit-N	152	605	96	130	10	13	8	77	46	53	.215	.276	.314	80	-16	-16	59	20			-3	*3O	-0.9
1893	Was-N	124	511	84	143	13	13	4	75	47	12	.280	.346	.380	97	-4	-2	73	11			13	C3/1	1.5
1894	*NY-N	114	401	47	114	20	12	4	66	35	15	.284	.346	.424	87	-10	-9	64	9			31	*C/31	2.4
1895	NY-N	90	312	38	90	16	9	1	58	38	18	.288	.371	.407	105	2	3	52	11			5	C3/1	1.1
1896	NY-N	58	191	23	54	7	3	1	37	19	7	.283	.351	.366	94	-2	-1	26	2			-6	CS/3	-0.2
	Was-N	37	130	18	39	7	3	1	30	7	3	.300	.345	.423	104	0	0	20	2			0	C3	0.2
	Yr	95	321	41	93	14	6	2	67	26	10	.290	.349	.389	98	-2	-1	46	4			-6		0.0
1897	Was-N	78	261	41	84	9	6	0	53	17		.322	.366	.402	105	2	2	42	8			9	C/1	1.6
1898	Was-N	99	338	47	106	12	6	1	53	34		.314	.383	.393	126	12	12	57	12			-8	C1	0.8
1899	Was-N	5	12	2	4	1	0	0	1	2		.333	.429	.417	137	1	1	3	1			-0	/C	0.0
	Bro-N	80	254	40	76	10	7	2	55	35		.299	.399	.417	124	11	10	46	6			9	C	2.1
	Yr	85	266	42	80	11	7	2	56	37		.301	.400	.417	125	11	11	48	7			8		2.1
1900	*Bro-N	76	273	33	75	11	5	0	39	11		.275	.308	.352	79	-6	-9	31	3			-5	C	-0.6
1901	Bro-N	80	284	38	84	10	6	1	31	7		.296	.317	.384	102	1	0	38	7			7	C1	1.4
1902	Bro-N	74	264	14	64	5	2	0	24	12		.242	.286	.277	75	-7	-8	24	6			7	C1	0.4
1903	*Bos-A	17	52	5	21	5	1	0	8	5		.404	.456	.538	190	6	6	14	1			1	C	0.9
1904	Bos-A	68	198	11	42	9	2	0	15	15		.212	.268	.278	70	-5	-7	16	1			-6	C	-0.7
1905	Bos-A	7	21	2	6	1	0	0	2	1		.286	.318	.333	108	0	0	2	0			2	/C	0.3
Total	18	1563	5679	826	1563	211	123	51	912	477	246	.275	.336	.383	101	10	1	813	150			93	*C301/S	15.0

■ DOC FARRELL
Farrell, Edward Stephen   b: 12/26/01, Johnson City, N.Y.   d: 12/20/66, Livingston, N.J.   BR/TR, 5'8", 160 lbs.   Deb: 6/23/25

YEAR	TM/L	G	AB	R	H	2B	3B	HR	RBI	BB	SO	AVG	OBP	SLG	PRO+	BR	/A	RC	SB	CS	SBR	FR	POS	TPR
1925	NY-N	27	56	6	12	1	0	0	4	4	6	.214	.267	.232	30	-6	-6	3	0	1	-1	2	S/32	-0.2
1926	NY-N	67	171	19	49	10	1	2	23	12	17	.287	.341	.392	98	-1	-1	22	4			-11	S/2	-0.7
1927	NY-N	42	142	13	55	10	1	3	34	12	11	.387	.442	.535	161	12	12	33	0			-1	S/3	1.5
	Bos-N	110	424	44	124	13	2	1	58	14	21	.292	.315	.340	82	-15	-15	44	4			-4	S23	-0.8
	Yr	152	566	57	179	23	3	4	92	26	32	.316	.348	.389	103	-3	2	74	4			-4		0.7
1928	Bos-N	134	483	36	104	14	2	3	43	26	26	.215	.263	.271	42	-43	-39	35	3			-17	*S/2	-3.7
1929	Bos-N	5	8	0	1	0	0	0	2	0	1	.125	.125	.125	-39	-2	-2	0	0			-0	/2S	-0.1
	NY-N	63	178	18	38	6	0	0	16	9	17	.213	.251	.247	24	-21	-21	11	2			7	32/S	-0.9
	Yr	68	186	18	39	6	0	0	18	9	18	.210	.246	.242	22	-23	-23	11	2			7		-1.0
1930	StL-N	23	61	3	13	1	1	0	6	4	2	.213	.262	.262	26	-7	-8	4	1			2	S/21	-0.2
	Chi-N	46	113	21	33	6	0	1	16	9	5	.292	.344	.372	73	-5	-5	14	0			3	S/2	0.0
	Yr	69	174	24	46	7	1	1	22	13	7	.264	.316	.333	56	-12	-12	18	1			5		0.0
1932	NY-A	26	63	4	11	1	1	0	4	2	8	.175	.212	.222	13	-8	-8	3	0	0	0	-1	2/S13	-0.6
1933	NY-A	44	93	16	25	0	0	0	6	16	6	.269	.376	.269	78	-3	-2	11	0	0	0	-4	S2	-0.4
1935	Bos-A	4	7	1	2	1	0	0	1	1	0	.286	.375	.429	101	0	0	1	0	0	0	-0	/2	0.0
Total	9	591	1799	181	467	63	8	10	213	109	120	.260	.306	.320	66	-98	-89	182	14	1		-23	S2/31	-5.9

■ JACK FARRELL
Farrell, John "Hartford Jack"   b: 1/2/1856, Hartford, Conn.   d: 11/15/16, Hartford, Conn.   Deb: 10/27/1874

YEAR	TM/L	G	AB	R	H	2B	3B	HR	RBI	BB	SO	AVG	OBP	SLG	PRO+	BR	/A	RC	SB	CS	SBR	FR	POS	TPR
1874	Har-n	3	14	3	5	0	0	0		0		.357	.357	.357	122	0	0	2					/O	0.0

■ JACK FARRELL
Farrell, John A. "Moose"   b: 7/5/1857, Newark, N.J.   d: 2/10/14, Overbrook, N.J.   BR/TR, 5'9", 165 lbs.   Deb: 5/01/1879 M

YEAR	TM/L	G	AB	R	H	2B	3B	HR	RBI	BB	SO	AVG	OBP	SLG	PRO+	BR	/A	RC	SB	CS	SBR	FR	POS	TPR
1879	Syr-N	54	241	40	73	6	2	1	21	3	13	.303	.311	.357	135	5	9	27				-15	2	0.0

YEAR	TM/L	G	AB	R	H	2B	3B	HR	RBI	BB	SO	AVG	OBP	SLG	PRO+	BR	/A	RC	SB	CS	SBR	FR	POS	TPR
	Pro-N	12	51	5	13	2	0	0	5	0	0	.255	.255	.294	82	-1	-1	4				7	2	0.7
	Yr	66	292	45	86	8	2	1	26	3	13	.295	.302	.346	125	4	8	31				-7		0.7
1880	Pro-N	80	339	46	92	12	5	3	36	10	6	.271	.292	.363	125	7	8	37				-9	*2	0.2
1881	Pro-N	84	345	69	82	16	5	5	36	29	23	.238	.297	.357	106	2	3	37				-5	*2/OM	0.0
1882	Pro-N	84	366	67	93	21	6	2	31	16	23	.254	.285	.361	106	2	2	39				-2	*2	0.2
1883	Pro-N	95	420	92	128	24	11	3	61	15	21	.305	.329	.436	126	14	13	62				24	*2	2.8
1884	*Pro-N	111	469	70	102	13	6	1	37	35	44	.217	.272	.277	75	-14	-12	36				-2	*2/3	-1.1
1885	Pro-N	68	257	27	53	7	1	1	19	10	25	.206	.236	.253	60	-12	-10	16				-16	2	-1.7
1886	Phi-N	17	60	7	11	0	1	0	3	3	11	.183	.222	.217	34	-5	-5	3	1			-3	2	-0.5
	Was-N	47	171	24	41	11	4	2	18	15	12	.240	.301	.386	114	1	3	24	12			-13	2	-0.7
	Yr	64	231	31	52	11	5	2	21	18	23	.225	.281	.342	92	-3	-2	27	13			-16		-1.2
1887	Was-N	87	339	40	75	14	9	0	41	20	12	.221	.267	.316	66	-17	-14	38	31			-7	S2	-1.7
1888	Bal-a	103	398	72	81	19	5	4	36	26		.204	.256	.307	85	-8	-6	40	29			11	S2	0.8
1889	Bal-a	42	157	25	33	3	0	1	26	15	15	.210	.287	.248	54	-9	-9	16	14			-6	S	-0.9
Total	11	884	3613	584	877	148	55	23	370	197	205	.243	.283	.333	94	-33	-20	378	87			-35	2S/3O	-1.9

■ JACK FARRELL
Farrell, John J. b: 6/16/1892, Chicago, Ill. d: 3/24/18, Chicago, Ill. BB/TR, 5'8", 145 lbs. Deb: 4/16/14

YEAR	TM/L	G	AB	R	H	2B	3B	HR	RBI	BB	SO	AVG	OBP	SLG	PRO+	BR	/A	RC	SB	CS	SBR	FR	POS	TPR
1914	Chi-F	156	524	58	123	23	4	0	35	52	65	.235	.307	.294	77	-18	-13	54	12			0	*2/S	-1.1
1915	Chi-F	70	222	27	48	10	1	0	14	25	18	.216	.298	.270	73	-8	-6	22	8			-4	2/S	-1.0
Total	2	226	746	85	171	33	5	0	49	77	83	.229	.305	.287	76	-26	-20	77	20			-4	2/S	-2.1

■ JOHN FARRELL
Farrell, John Sebastian b: 12/4/1876, Covington, Ky. d: 5/13/21, Kansas City, Mo. BR/TR, 5'10", 160 lbs. Deb: 4/26/01

YEAR	TM/L	G	AB	R	H	2B	3B	HR	RBI	BB	SO	AVG	OBP	SLG	PRO+	BR	/A	RC	SB	CS	SBR	FR	POS	TPR
1901	Was-A	135	555	100	151	32	11	3	63	52		.272	.336	.386	103	1	3	83	25			17	2O/3	1.4
1902	StL-N	138	565	68	141	13	5	0	25	43		.250	.308	.290	90	-8	-5	56	9			**33**	*2S	3.9
1903	StL-N	130	519	83	141	25	8	1	32	48		.272	.333	.356	102	-1	2	70	17			**28**	*2O	3.4
1904	StL-N	131	509	72	130	23	3	0	20	46		.255	.317	.312	101	-1	2	58	16			16	*2	2.2
1905	StL-N	7	24	6	4	0	1	0	1	4		.167	.286	.250	64	-1	-1	2	1			-3	/2	-0.2
Total	5	541	2172	329	567	93	28	4	141	193		.261	.333	.335	99	-9	0	268	68			92	2/OS3	10.7

■ JOE FARRELL
Farrell, Joseph F. b: 1857, Brooklyn, N.Y. d: 4/18/1893, Brooklyn, N.Y. R , 5'6", 160 lbs. Deb: 5/01/1882

YEAR	TM/L	G	AB	R	H	2B	3B	HR	RBI	BB	SO	AVG	OBP	SLG	PRO+	BR	/A	RC	SB	CS	SBR	FR	POS	TPR
1882	Det-N	69	283	34	70	12	2	1	24	4	20	.247	.258	.314	83	-6	-6	24				-12	32/S	-1.3
1883	Det-N	101	444	58	108	13	5	0	36	5	29	.243	.252	.295	69	-18	-15	34				13	*3	0.0
1884	Det-N	110	461	59	104	10	5	3	41	14	66	.226	.248	.289	73	-17	-13	34				-7	*3/O	-2.2
1886	Bal-a	73	301	36	63	8	3	1			12	.209	.240	.266	61	-14	-13	21	5			-15	23/O	-2.4
Total	4	353	1489	187	345	43	15	5	101	35	115	.232	.249	.291	71	-55	-46	112	5			-22	3/2SO	-5.9

■ KERBY FARRELL
Farrell, Major Kerby b: 9/3/13, Leapwood, Tenn. d: 12/17/75, Nashville, Tenn. BL/TL, 5'11", 172 lbs. Deb: 4/24/43 MC

YEAR	TM/L	G	AB	R	H	2B	3B	HR	RBI	BB	SO	AVG	OBP	SLG	PRO+	BR	/A	RC	SB	CS	SBR	FR	POS	TPR
1943	Bos-N	85	280	11	75	14	1	0	21	16	15	.268	.307	.325	84	-7	-6	26	1			2	1/P	-0.6
1945	Chi-A	103	396	44	102	11	3	0	34	24	18	.258	.300	.301	76	-13	-12	35	4	9	-4	-0	1	-2.0
Total	2	188	676	55	177	25	4	0	55	40	33	.262	.303	.311	80	-20	-18	61	5	9		2	1/P	-2.6

■ BILL FARRELL
Farrell, William Deb: 5/03/1882

YEAR	TM/L	G	AB	R	H	2B	3B	HR	RBI	BB	SO	AVG	OBP	SLG	PRO+	BR	/A	RC	SB	CS	SBR	FR	POS	TPR
1882	Phi-a	2	7	2	2	1	0	0			1	.286	.375	.429	153	1	0	1				-1	/OC	0.0
1883	Bal-a	2	7	0	0	0	0	0			1	.000	.125	.000	-55	-1	-1	0				-1	/S	-0.1
Total	2	4	14	2	2	1	0	0			2	.143	.250	.214	51	-1	-1	1				-1	/SOC	-0.1

■ JOHN FARROW
Farrow, John Jacob b: 1852, Verplanck's Point, N.Y. d: 12/31/14, Perth Amboy, N.J. BL/TR, Deb: 4/28/1873

YEAR	TM/L	G	AB	R	H	2B	3B	HR	RBI	BB	SO	AVG	OBP	SLG	PRO+	BR	/A	RC	SB	CS	SBR	FR	POS	TPR
1873	Res-n	12	48	2	8	0	0	0			0	.167	.167	.167	-2	-6	-5	1					/CSO1	-0.3
1874	Atl-n	27	121	16	26	3	0	0				.215	.221	.240	53	-7	-4	7					C2	-0.2
1884	Bro-a	16	58	7	11	2	0	0			3	.190	.230	.224	50	-3	-3	3				-1	C	-0.1
Total	2 n	39	169	18	34	3	0	0			1	.201	.206	.219	36	-13	-10	8					/C2OS1	-0.5

■ BUCK FAUSETT
Fausett, Robert Shaw "Leaky" b: 4/8/08, Sheridan, Ark. BL/TR, 5'10", 170 lbs. Deb: 4/18/44

YEAR	TM/L	G	AB	R	H	2B	3B	HR	RBI	BB	SO	AVG	OBP	SLG	PRO+	BR	/A	RC	SB	CS	SBR	FR	POS	TPR
1944	Cin-N	13	31	2	3	0	1	0	1	1	2	.097	.125	.161	-21	-5	-5	0	0			3	/3P	0.0

■ JOE FAUTSCH
Fautsch, Joseph Roamon b: 2/28/1887, Minneapolis, Minn. d: 3/16/71, New Hope, Minn. BR/TR, 5'10", 162 lbs. Deb: 4/24/16

YEAR	TM/L	G	AB	R	H	2B	3B	HR	RBI	BB	SO	AVG	OBP	SLG	PRO+	BR	/A	RC	SB	CS	SBR	FR	POS	TPR
1916	Chi-A	1	1	0	0	0	0	0	0	0	0	.000	.000	.000	-99	-0	-0	0	0			0	H	0.0

■ ERNIE FAZIO
Fazio, Ernest Joseph b: 1/25/42, Oakland, Cal. BR/TR, 5'7", 165 lbs. Deb: 7/03/62

YEAR	TM/L	G	AB	R	H	2B	3B	HR	RBI	BB	SO	AVG	OBP	SLG	PRO+	BR	/A	RC	SB	CS	SBR	FR	POS	TPR
1962	Hou-N	12	12	3	1	0	0	0	1	2	5	.083	.214	.083	-18	-2	-2	0	0	0	0	0	S	0.0
1963	Hou-N	102	228	31	42	10	3	2	5	27	70	.184	.273	.281	64	-12	-10	18	4	4	-1	-10	2/S3	-1.7
1966	KC-A	27	34	3	7	0	1	0	2	4	10	.206	.289	.265	62	-2	-2	3	1	0	0	2	2/S	0.1
Total	3	141	274	37	50	10	4	2	8	33	85	.182	.273	.270	60	-15	-13	22	5	4		-9	/2S3	-1.6

■ AL FEDEROFF
Federoff, Alfred "Whitey" b: 7/11/24, Bairdford, Pa. BR/TR, 5'10.5", 165 lbs. Deb: 9/27/51

YEAR	TM/L	G	AB	R	H	2B	3B	HR	RBI	BB	SO	AVG	OBP	SLG	PRO+	BR	/A	RC	SB	CS	SBR	FR	POS	TPR
1951	Det-A	2	4	0	0	0	0	0	0	0		.000	.000	.000	-99	-1	-1	0	0	0	0	1	/2	0.0
1952	Det-A	74	231	14	56	4	2	0	14	16	13	.242	.294	.277	59	-12	-13	20	1	0	0	0	2/S	-0.8
Total	2	76	235	14	56	4	2	0	14	16	13	.238	.290	.272	56	-14	-14	20	1	0	0	1	/2S	-0.8

■ BILL FEHRING
Fehring, William Paul "Dutch" b: 5/31/12, Columbus, Ind. BB/TR, 6', 195 lbs. Deb: 6/25/34

YEAR	TM/L	G	AB	R	H	2B	3B	HR	RBI	BB	SO	AVG	OBP	SLG	PRO+	BR	/A	RC	SB	CS	SBR	FR	POS	TPR
1934	Chi-A	1	0	0	0	0	0	0	0		1	.000	.000	.000	-97	-0	-0	0	0	0	0	0	/C	0.0

■ EDDIE FEINBERG
Feinberg, Edward Isadore "Itzzy" b: 9/29/17, Philadelphia, Pa. d: 4/20/86, Hollywood, Fla. BB/TR, 5'9", 165 lbs. Deb: 9/11/38

YEAR	TM/L	G	AB	R	H	2B	3B	HR	RBI	BB	SO	AVG	OBP	SLG	PRO+	BR	/A	RC	SB	CS	SBR	FR	POS	TPR
1938	Phi-N	10	20	0	3	0	0	0	0		1	.150	.150	.150	-18	-3	-3	0	0			4	/SO	0.1
1939	Phi-N	6	18	2	4	1	0	0		2	0	.222	.300	.278	58	-1	-1	2	0			-4	/2S	-0.4
Total	2	16	38	2	7	1	0	0		2	1	.184	.225	.211	20	-4	-4	2	0			-1	/S2O	-0.3

■ MIKE FELDER
Felder, Michael Otis b: 11/18/61, Vallejo, Cal. BB/TR, 5'8", 160 lbs. Deb: 9/11/85

YEAR	TM/L	G	AB	R	H	2B	3B	HR	RBI	BB	SO	AVG	OBP	SLG	PRO+	BR	/A	RC	SB	CS	SBR	FR	POS	TPR
1985	Mil-A	15	56	8	11	1	0	0		5	6	.196	.262	.214	33	-5	-5	3	4	1	1	-0	O	-0.4
1986	Mil-A	44	155	24	37	2	4	1	13	13	16	.239	.298	.323	67	-7	-7	17	16	2	4	-1	O/D	-0.4
1987	Mil-A	108	289	48	77	5	7	2	31	28	23	.266	.331	.353	79	-7	-8	38	34	8	5	9	O/2D	0.3
1988	Mil-A	50	81	14	14	1	0	0	5	0	11	.173	.183	.185	3	-10	-10	3	8	2	1	2	OD/2	-0.6
1989	Mil-A	117	315	50	76	11	3	3	23	23	38	.241	.293	.324	74	-11	-11	33	26	5	5	10	OD2	0.3
1990	Mil-A	121	237	38	65	7	2	3	27	22	17	.274	.336	.359	97	-2	-1	31	20	9	1	7	*O/23D	0.6
Total	6	455	1133	182	280	27	16	9	99	91	111	.247	.304	.323	72	-42	-42	125	108	27	16	27	O/D23	-0.2

■ MARV FELDERMAN
Felderman, Marvin Wilfred "Coonie" b: 12/20/15, Bellevue, Iowa BR/TR, 6'1", 187 lbs. Deb: 4/19/42

YEAR	TM/L	G	AB	R	H	2B	3B	HR	RBI	BB	SO	AVG	OBP	SLG	PRO+	BR	/A	RC	SB	CS	SBR	FR	POS	TPR
1942	Chi-N	3	6	0	1	0	0	0		1	4	.167	.286	.167	35	-0	-0	0	0			1	/C	0.0

■ GUS FELIX
Felix, August Guenther b: 5/24/1895, Cincinnati, Ohio d: 5/12/60, Montgomery, Ala. BR/TR, 6', 180 lbs. Deb: 4/19/23

YEAR	TM/L	G	AB	R	H	2B	3B	HR	RBI	BB	SO	AVG	OBP	SLG	PRO+	BR	/A	RC	SB	CS	SBR	FR	POS	TPR
1923	Bos-N	139	506	64	138	17	2	6	44	51	65	.273	.348	.350	88	-10	-7	62	8	13	-5	-1	*O/23	-1.6
1924	Bos-N	59	204	25	43	7	1	1	10	18	16	.211	.275	.270	48	-15	-14	15	0	3	-2	2	O	-1.4
1925	Bos-N	121	459	60	141	25	7	2	66	30	34	.307	.356	.405	103	-4	2	66	5	5	-2	6	*O	0.3
1926	Bro-N	134	432	64	121	21	7	3	53	51	32	.280	.360	.382	101	1	2	60	9			-8	*O	-0.9
1927	Bro-N	130	445	43	118	21	8	0	57	39	47	.265	.327	.348	81	-12	-12	51	6			-5	*O	-2.1
Total	5	583	2046	256	561	91	25	12	230	189	194	.274	.341	.361	89	-40	-29	254	28	21		-5	O/23	-5.7

YEAR	TM/L	G	AB	R	H	2B	3B	HR	RBI	BB	SO	AVG	OBP	SLG	PRO+	BR	/A	RC	SB	CS	SBR	FR	POS	TPR

■ JUNIOR FELIX Felix, Junior Francisco (Sanchez) b: 10/3/67, Laguna Sabada, D.R. BB/TR, 6′, 170 lbs. Deb: 5/03/89

YEAR	TM/L	G	AB	R	H	2B	3B	HR	RBI	BB	SO	AVG	OBP	SLG	PRO+	BR	/A	RC	SB	CS	SBR	FR	POS	TPR
1989	*Tor-A	110	415	62	107	14	8	9	46	33	101	.258	.317	.395	101	-1	0	51	18	12	-2	4	*O/D	0.1
1990	Tor-A	127	463	73	122	23	7	15	65	45	99	.263	.331	.441	116	8	9	69	13	8	-1	-0	*O/D	0.7
Total	2	237	878	135	229	37	15	24	111	78	200	.261	.325	.419	109	7	9	120	31	20	-3	4	O/D	0.8

■ JACK FELLER Feller, Jack Leland b: 12/10/36, Adrian, Mich. BR/TR, 5′10.5″, 185 lbs. Deb: 9/13/58

YEAR	TM/L	G	AB	R	H	2B	3B	HR	RBI	BB	SO	AVG	OBP	SLG	PRO+	BR	/A	RC	SB	CS	SBR	FR	POS	TPR
1958	Det-A	1	0	0	0	0	0	0	0	0	0	—	—	—	—	0	0	0	0	0	0	0	/C	0.0

■ HAPPY FELSCH Felsch, Oscar Emil b: 8/22/1891, Milwaukee, Wis. d: 8/17/64, Milwaukee, Wis. BR/TR, 5′11″, 175 lbs. Deb: 4/14/15

YEAR	TM/L	G	AB	R	H	2B	3B	HR	RBI	BB	SO	AVG	OBP	SLG	PRO+	BR	/A	RC	SB	CS	SBR	FR	POS	TPR
1915	Chi-A	121	427	65	106	18	11	3	53	51	59	.248	.334	.363	105	4	2	52	16	18	-6	-3	*O	-1.3
1916	Chi-A	146	546	73	164	24	12	7	70	31	67	.300	.341	.427	129	17	16	85	13			7	*O	1.6
1917	*Chi-A	152	575	75	177	17	10	6	102	33	52	.308	.352	.403	128	19	17	87	26			19	*O	3.0
1918	Chi-A	53	206	16	52	2	5	1	20	15	13	.252	.306	.325	90	-3	-3	22	6			5	O	0.0
1919	*Chi-A	135	502	68	138	34	11	7	86	40	35	.275	.336	.428	113	7	7	76	19			21	*O	2.0
1920	Chi-A	142	556	88	188	40	15	14	115	37	25	.338	.384	.540	143	31	31	109	8	13	-5	18	*O	3.0
Total	6	749	2812	385	825	135	64	38	446	207	251	.293	.347	.427	123	75	71	431	88	31		67	O	8.3

■ JOHN FELSKE Felske, John Frederick b: 5/30/42, Chicago, Ill. BR/TR, 6′3″, 195 lbs. Deb: 7/26/68 MC

YEAR	TM/L	G	AB	R	H	2B	3B	HR	RBI	BB	SO	AVG	OBP	SLG	PRO+	BR	/A	RC	SB	CS	SBR	FR	POS	TPR
1968	Chi-N	4	2	0	0	0	0	0	0	0	1	.000	.000	.000	-94	-0	-0	0	0	0	0	1	/C	0.0
1972	Mil-A	37	80	6	11	3	0	1	5	8	23	.138	.216	.213	28	-7	-7	4	0	0	0	-2	C/1	-1.1
1973	Mil-A	13	22	1	3	0	1	0	4	1	11	.136	.174	.227	12	-3	-3	1	0	0	0	0	/C1	-0.2
Total	3	54	104	7	14	3	1	1	9	9	35	.135	.204	.212	23	-10	-10	5	0	0	0	-2	/C1	-1.3

■ FRANK FENNELLY Fennelly, Francis John b: 2/18/1860, Fall River, Mass. d: 8/4/20, Fall River, Mass. BR/TR, 5′8″, 168 lbs. Deb: 5/01/1884

YEAR	TM/L	G	AB	R	H	2B	3B	HR	RBI	BB	SO	AVG	OBP	SLG	PRO+	BR	/A	RC	SB	CS	SBR	FR	POS	TPR
1884	Was-a	62	257	52	75	17	7	2		20		.292	.343	.436	176	15	20	39				13	S/2	2.8
	Cin-a	28	122	42	43	5	8	2		11		.352	.415	.574	213	16	15	30				-6	S	0.8
	Yr	90	379	94	118	22	15	4		31		.311	.367	.480	190	32	36	68				7		3.6
1885	Cin-a	112	454	82	124	14	17	10		38		.273	.333	.445	144	24	23	69				-11	*S	1.1
1886	Cin-a	132	497	113	124	13	17	6		60		.249	.351	.380	128	20	18	80	32			14	*S	3.3
1887	Cin-a	134	526	133	140	15	16	8		82		.266	.369	.401	115	14	12	108	74			-9	*S	0.1
1888	Cin-a	120	448	64	88	8	7	2	56	63		.196	.297	.259	78	-7	-10	48	43			17	*S/2O	1.1
	Phi-a	15	47	13	11	2	2	1	12	9		.234	.357	.426	155	3	3	9	5			-1	S	0.3
	Yr	135	495	77	99	10	9	3	68	72		.200	.303	.275	85	-3	-7	57	48			16		1.4
1889	Phi-a	138	513	70	132	20	5	1	64	65	78	.257	.344	.322	94	-3	-2	64	15			-20	*S	-0.9
1890	Bro-a	45	178	40	44	8	3	2		30		.247	.356	.360	118	4	5	26	6			0	S/3	0.6
Total	7	786	3042	609	781	102	82	34	132	378	78	.257	.345	.378	121	87	84	472	175			-4	S/23O	9.2

■ BOBBY FENWICK Fenwick, Robert Richard b: 12/10/46, Naha, Okinawa BR/TR, 5′9″, 165 lbs. Deb: 4/26/72

YEAR	TM/L	G	AB	R	H	2B	3B	HR	RBI	BB	SO	AVG	OBP	SLG	PRO+	BR	/A	RC	SB	CS	SBR	FR	POS	TPR
1972	Hou-N	36	50	7	9	3	0	0	4	3	13	.180	.226	.240	33	-4	-4	2	0	1	-1	3	2/S3	0.0
1973	StL-N	5	6	0	1	0	0	0	1	0	2	.167	.167	.167	-7	-1	-1	0	0	0	0	-1	/2	0.0
Total	2	41	56	7	10	3	0	0	5	3	15	.179	.220	.232	29	-5	-5	3	0	1	-1	3	/2S3	0.0

■ JOE FERGUSON Ferguson, Joseph Vance b: 9/19/46, San Francisco, Cal. BR/TR, 6′2″, 200 lbs. Deb: 9/12/70 C

YEAR	TM/L	G	AB	R	H	2B	3B	HR	RBI	BB	SO	AVG	OBP	SLG	PRO+	BR	/A	RC	SB	CS	SBR	FR	POS	TPR
1970	LA-N	5	4	0	1	0	0	0	1	2	2	.250	.500	.250	112	0	0	1	0	0	0	0	/C	0.0
1971	LA-N	36	102	13	22	3	0	2	7	12	15	.216	.304	.304	77	-3	-3	10	1	0	0	-2	C	-0.3
1972	LA-N	8	24	2	7	3	0	1	5	2	4	.292	.346	.542	152	1	1	4	0	0	0	2	/CO	0.4
1973	LA-N	136	487	84	128	26	0	25	88	87	81	.263	.376	.470	139	23	26	92	1	1	-0	2	*CO	3.5
1974	*LA-N	111	349	54	88	14	1	16	57	75	73	.252	.384	.436	134	16	18	60	2	2	-1	-8	CO	1.1
1975	LA-N	66	202	15	42	2	1	5	23	35	47	.208	.328	.302	79	-6	-5	22	2	1	0	-1	CO	-0.5
1976	LA-N	54	185	24	41	7	0	6	18	25	41	.222	.318	.357	93	-2	-2	22	2	0	1	-2	OC	-0.3
	StL-N	71	189	22	38	8	4	4	21	32	40	.201	.320	.349	89	-2	-2	22	4	2	0	7	CO	0.7
	Yr	125	374	46	79	15	4	10	39	57	81	.211	.319	.353	91	-4	-4	44	6	2	1	5		0.4
1977	Hou-N	132	421	59	108	21	3	16	61	85	79	.257	.381	.435	130	13	19	74	6	2	1	-9	*C/1	0.9
1978	Hou-N	51	150	20	31	5	0	7	22	37	30	.207	.367	.380	118	3	5	22	0	0	0	-5	C	0.1
	*LA-N	67	198	20	47	11	0	7	28	34	41	.237	.352	.399	110	3	3	27	1	2	-1	-9	C/O	-0.5
	Yr	118	348	40	78	16	0	14	50	71	71	.224	.359	.391	113	6	8	49	1	2	-1	-15		-0.4
1979	LA-N	122	363	54	95	14	0	20	69	70	68	.262	.384	.466	133	17	18	68	2	2	-1	-10	CO	0.8
1980	LA-N	77	172	20	41	3	0	9	29	38	46	.238	.376	.436	128	7	8	27	2	2	-1	-3	C/O	0.5
1981	LA-N	17	14	2	2	1	0	0	1	2	5	.143	.250	.214	34	-1	-1	1	0	0	0	0	/O	0.0
	Cal-A	12	30	5	7	1	0	1	5	9	8	.233	.410	.367	125	2	2	5	0	0	0	1	/CO	0.3
1982	Cal-A	36	84	10	19	2	0	3	8	12	19	.226	.323	.357	87	-1	-1	9	0	0	0	6	C/O	0.6
1983	Cal-A	12	27	3	2	0	0	0	2	5	8	.074	.219	.074	-15	-4	-4	0	0	0	0	-1	/CO	-0.4
Total	14	1013	3001	407	719	121	11	122	445	562	607	.240	.361	.409	117	66	80	465	22	12	-1	-34	CO/1	6.9

■ BOB FERGUSON Ferguson, Robert V. b: 1/31/1845, Brooklyn, N.Y. d: 5/3/1894, Brooklyn, N.Y. BB/TR, 5′9.5″, 149 lbs. Deb: 5/18/1871 MU

YEAR	TM/L	G	AB	R	H	2B	3B	HR	RBI	BB	SO	AVG	OBP	SLG	PRO+	BR	/A	RC	SB	CS	SBR	FR	POS	TPR
1871	Mut-n	33	158	30	38	6	1	0	25	3	2	.241	.255	.291	62	-9	-5	13	4				32/CPM	-0.4
1872	Atl-n	37	166	33	45	6	0	0		2		.271	.280	.307	69	-4	-10	15					*3M	-0.8
1873	Atl-n	51	231	36	60	5	5	0		3		.260	.269	.325	83	-7	-2	21					*3/PM	-0.1
1874	Atl-n	56	246	34	63	5	1	0		1		.256	.259	.285	82	-7	-2	19					*3/CP	-0.1
1875	Har-n	85	366	66	88	12	4	0		2		.240	.245	.295	82	-5	-8	27					*3/PM	-0.3
1876	Har-N	69	310	48	82	8	5	0	32	2	11	.265	.269	.323	89	-1	-5	28				2	*3M	-0.4
1877	Har-N	58	254	40	65	7	2	0	35	3	10	.256	.265	.299	86	-6	-2	21				17	*3/PM	1.7
1878	Chi-N	61	259	44	91	10	2	0	39	10	12	.351	.375	.405	147	16	13	40				18	*S/2CM	3.1
1879	Tro-N	30	123	18	31	5	2	0	4	4	3	.252	.276	.325	104	-0	1	11				3	3/2M	0.4
1880	Tro-N	82	332	55	87	9	0	0	22	24	24	.262	.312	.289	100	3	0	31				-3	*2M	0.4
1881	Tro-N	85	339	56	96	13	5	1	35	29	12	.283	.340	.360	114	9	6	42				-10	*2M	0.0
1882	Tro-N	81	319	44	82	15	2	0	32	23	21	.257	.307	.317	106	1	3	32				-13	*2/SM	-0.6
1883	Phi-N	86	329	39	85	9	2	0	27	18	21	.258	.297	.298	89	-7	-2	30				-7	*2/PM	-1.1
1884	Pit-a	10	41	2	6	0	0	0		0		.146	.146	.146	-3	-4	-4	1				-3	/O13M	-0.7
Total	5 n	262	1167	199	294	34	11	0	25	11	2	.252	.259	.300	77	-32	-27	94					3/2PC	-1.7
Total	9	562	2306	346	625	76	20	1	226	113	114	.271	.305	.323	102	8	8	236				3	23/SOP1C	2.4

■ FELIX FERMIN Fermin, Felix Jose (Minaya) b: 10/9/63, Mao Valverde, D.R. BR/TR, 5′11″, 160 lbs. Deb: 7/08/87

YEAR	TM/L	G	AB	R	H	2B	3B	HR	RBI	BB	SO	AVG	OBP	SLG	PRO+	BR	/A	RC	SB	CS	SBR	FR	POS	TPR
1987	Pit-N	23	68	6	17	0	0	0	4	4	9	.250	.301	.250	48	-5	-5	5	0	0	0	1	S	0.0
1988	Pit-N	43	87	9	24	0	2	0	2	8	10	.276	.357	.322	98	0	0	10	3	1	0	-5	S	-0.1
1989	Cle-A	156	484	50	115	9	1	0	21	41	27	.238	.302	.260	69	-24	-25	40	6	4	-1	18	*S/2	0.4
1990	Cle-A	148	414	47	106	13	2	1	40	26	22	.256	.300	.304	68	-17	-18	36	3	3	-1	4	*S/2	-0.4
Total	4	370	1053	112	262	22	5	1	67	79	68	.249	.306	.282	65	-46	-48	91	12	8	-1	18	S/2	-0.1

■ ED FERNANDES Fernandes, Edward Paul b: 3/11/18, Oakland, Cal. d: 11/27/68, Hayward, Cal. BB/TR, 5′9″, 185 lbs. Deb: 6/09/40

YEAR	TM/L	G	AB	R	H	2B	3B	HR	RBI	BB	SO	AVG	OBP	SLG	PRO+	BR	/A	RC	SB	CS	SBR	FR	POS	TPR
1940	Pit-N	28	33	1	4	1	0	0	2	7	6	.121	.275	.152	21	-3	-3	2	0			0	C	-0.1
1946	Chi-A	14	32	4	8	2	0	0	4	8	7	.250	.400	.313	105	1	1	5	0	0	0	-1	C	0.0
Total	2	42	65	5	12	3	0	0	6	15	13	.185	.338	.231	61	-3	-3	6	0	0		-1	/C	-0.1

YEAR	TM/L	G	AB	R	H	2B	3B	HR	RBI	BB	SO	AVG	OBP	SLG	PRO+	BR	/A	RC	SB	CS	SBR	FR	POS	TPR

■ FRANK FERNANDEZ
Fernandez, Frank b: 4/16/43, Staten Island, N.Y.   BR/TR, 6', 185 lbs.   Deb: 9/12/67

YEAR	TM/L	G	AB	R	H	2B	3B	HR	RBI	BB	SO	AVG	OBP	SLG	PRO+	BR	/A	RC	SB	CS	SBR	FR	POS	TPR
1967	NY-A	9	28	1	6	2	0	1	4	2	7	.214	.290	.393	104	-0	0	3	1	1	-0	0	/CO	0.0
1968	NY-A	51	135	15	23	6	1	7	30	35	50	.170	.341	.385	124	4	5	20	1	0	0	5	C/O	1.4
1969	NY-A	89	229	34	51	6	1	12	29	65	68	.223	.401	.415	133	12	13	42	1	3	-2	-7	CO	0.9
1970	Oak-A	94	252	30	54	5	0	15	44	40	76	.214	.327	.413	106	-1	2	35	1	0	0	-1	C/O	0.3
1971	Oak-A	2	4	0	0	0	0	0	0	1	2	.000	.200	.000	-40	-1	-1	0	0	0	0	2	/C	0.1
	Was-A	18	30	0	3	0	0	0	4	4	10	.100	.206	.100	-12	-4	-4	1	0	0	0	-1	/OC	-0.5
	Oak-A	2	5	1	1	1	0	0	1	0	1	.200	.200	.400	68	-0	-0	0	0	0	0	-0	/C	0.0
	Yr	22	39	1	4	1	0	0	5	5	13	.103	.205	.128	-4	-5	-5	1	0	0	0	0		-0.4
	Chi-N	17	41	11	7	1	0	4	17	17	15	.171	.414	.488	135	4	3	10	0	0	0	0	C	0.4
1972	Chi-N	3	3	0	0	0	0	0	0	0	2	.000	.000	.000	-90	-1	-1	0	0	0	0	0	/C	0.0
Total	6	285	727	92	145	21	2	39	116	164	231	.199	.351	.395	114	15	17	111	4	4	-1	-1	C/O	2.6

■ NANNY FERNANDEZ
Fernandez, Froilan b: 10/25/18, Wilmington, Cal.   BR/TR, 5'9", 170 lbs.   Deb: 4/14/42

YEAR	TM/L	G	AB	R	H	2B	3B	HR	RBI	BB	SO	AVG	OBP	SLG	PRO+	BR	/A	RC	SB	CS	SBR	FR	POS	TPR
1942	Bos-N	145	577	63	147	29	3	6	55	38	61	.255	.303	.347	92	-9	-7	58	15			3	3O	-0.4
1946	Bos-N	115	372	37	95	15	2	2	42	30	44	.255	.313	.323	79	-10	-10	37	1			-1	3SO	-0.9
1947	Bos-N	83	209	16	43	4	0	2	21	22	20	.206	.281	.254	44	-17	-16	16	2			-11	S/O3	-2.2
1950	Pit-N	65	198	23	51	11	0	6	27	19	17	.258	.326	.404	88	-3	-4	24	2			-3	3	-0.6
Total	4	408	1356	139	336	59	5	16	145	109	142	.248	.306	.334	80	-38	-38	135	20			-11	3/SO	-4.1

■ CHICO FERNANDEZ
Fernandez, Humberto (Perez) b: 3/2/32, Havana, Cuba   BR/TR, 6', 165 lbs.   Deb: 7/14/56

YEAR	TM/L	G	AB	R	H	2B	3B	HR	RBI	BB	SO	AVG	OBP	SLG	PRO+	BR	/A	RC	SB	CS	SBR	FR	POS	TPR
1956	Bro-N	34	66	11	15	2	0	1	9	3	10	.227	.261	.303	47	-5	-5	4	2	3	-1	7	S	0.2
1957	Phi-N	149	500	42	131	14	4	5	51	31	64	.262	.306	.336	75	-19	-17	48	18	5	2	-25	*S	-3.4
1958	Phi-N	148	522	38	120	18	5	6	51	37	48	.230	.283	.318	60	-31	-30	45	12	6	0	-12	*S	-3.1
1959	Phi-N	45	123	15	26	5	1	0	3	10	11	.211	.271	.268	43	-10	-10	9	2	1	0	-3	S/2	-1.0
1960	Det-N	133	435	44	105	13	3	4	35	39	50	.241	.305	.313	66	-20	-21	41	13	4	2	-4	*S	-1.3
1961	Det-N	133	435	41	108	15	4	3	40	36	45	.248	.306	.322	66	-20	-21	41	8	5	-1	-7	*S/3	-2.0
1962	Det-N	141	503	64	125	17	2	20	59	42	69	.249	.306	.410	88	-8	-10	62	10	3	1	-27	*S/31	-2.7
1963	Det-N	15	49	3	7	1	0	0	2	6	11	.143	.236	.163	14	-6	-6	1	0	1	-1	2	S	-0.3
	NY-N	58	145	12	29	6	0	1	9	9	30	.200	.247	.262	46	-10	-10	10	3	0	1	-16	S/32	-2.2
Total	8	856	2778	270	666	91	19	40	259	213	338	.240	.295	.329	67	-127	-131	262	68	28	4	-85	S/321	-15.8

■ CHICO FERNANDEZ
Fernandez, Lorenzo Marto (Mosquera) b: 4/23/39, Havana, Cuba   BR/TR, 5'10", 160 lbs.   Deb: 4/20/68

YEAR	TM/L	G	AB	R	H	2B	3B	HR	RBI	BB	SO	AVG	OBP	SLG	PRO+	BR	/A	RC	SB	CS	SBR	FR	POS	TPR
1968	Bal-A	24	18	0	2	0	0	0	0	1	2	.111	.158	.111	-17	-3	-3	0	0	0	0	3	/S2	0.1

■ TONY FERNANDEZ
Fernandez, Octavio Antonio (Castro) (b: Octavio Antonio Fernando (Castro))
b: 8/6/62, San Pedro De Macoris, D.R.   BB/TR, 6'2", 165 lbs.   Deb: 9/02/83

YEAR	TM/L	G	AB	R	H	2B	3B	HR	RBI	BB	SO	AVG	OBP	SLG	PRO+	BR	/A	RC	SB	CS	SBR	FR	POS	TPR
1983	Tor-A	15	34	5	9	1	1	0	2	2	2	.265	.324	.353	81	-1	-1	4	0	1	-1	-3	S/D	-0.3
1984	Tor-A	88	233	29	63	5	3	3	19	17	15	.270	.320	.356	84	-4	-5	25	5	7	-3	3	S3/D	0.0
1985	*Tor-A	161	564	71	163	31	10	2	51	43	41	.289	.342	.390	97	0	-2	75	13	6	0	5	*S	1.5
1986	Tor-A	163	687	91	213	33	9	10	65	27	52	.310	.340	.428	105	6	4	99	25	12	0	3	*S	1.7
1987	Tor-A	146	578	90	186	29	8	5	67	51	48	.322	.382	.426	112	13	11	94	32	12	2	6	*S	2.5
1988	Tor-A	154	648	76	186	41	4	5	70	45	65	.287	.337	.386	101	2	1	86	15	5	2	10	*S	2.0
1989	*Tor-A	140	573	64	147	25	9	11	64	29	51	.257	.296	.389	93	-8	-7	66	22	6	3	18	*S	2.6
1990	Tor-A	161	635	84	175	27	17	4	66	71	70	.276	.355	.391	110	8	10	88	26	13	0	9	*S	2.9
Total	8	1028	3952	510	1142	192	61	40	404	285	344	.289	.341	.399	102	16	12	536	138	62	4	50	*S/3D	12.9

■ AL FERRARA
Ferrara, Alfred John "The Bull" b: 12/22/39, Brooklyn, N.Y.   BR/TR, 6'1", 200 lbs.   Deb: 7/30/63

YEAR	TM/L	G	AB	R	H	2B	3B	HR	RBI	BB	SO	AVG	OBP	SLG	PRO+	BR	/A	RC	SB	CS	SBR	FR	POS	TPR
1963	LA-N	21	44	2	7	0	0	1	1	6	9	.159	.275	.227	50	-3	-3	3	0	0	0	0	O	-0.2
1965	LA-N	41	81	5	17	2	1	1	10	9	20	.210	.297	.296	72	-3	-3	8	0	0	0	-4	O	-0.7
1966	*LA-N	63	115	15	31	4	0	5	23	9	35	.270	.339	.435	123	2	3	17	0	0	0	-1	O	0.1
1967	LA-N	122	347	41	96	16	1	16	50	33	73	.277	.345	.467	142	13	16	56	0	1	-1	-10	O	0.2
1968	LA-N	2	7	0	1	0	0	0	0	0	2	.143	.143	.143	-15	-1	-1	0	0	0	0	-1	/O	-0.1
1969	SD-N	138	366	39	95	22	1	14	56	45	69	.260	.352	.440	125	10	12	58	0	0	0	-13	O	-0.5
1970	SD-N	138	372	44	103	15	4	13	51	46	63	.277	.373	.444	123	10	12	64	0	0	0	-16	O	-0.8
1971	SD-N	17	17	0	2	1	0	0	2	5	5	.118	.318	.176	47	-1	-1	1	0	0	0	-1	/O	-0.1
	Cin-N	32	33	2	6	0	0	1	5	3	10	.182	.270	.273	55	-2	-2	2	0	0	0	0	/O	-0.1
	Yr	49	50	2	8	1	0	1	7	8	15	.160	.288	.240	53	-3	-3	3	0	0	0	-0		-0.2
Total	8	574	1382	148	358	60	7	51	198	156	286	.259	.346	.423	120	25	35	209	0	1	-1	-45	O	-2.2

■ MIKE FERRARO
Ferraro, Michael Dennis b: 8/18/44, Kingston, N.Y.   BR/TR, 5'11", 175 lbs.   Deb: 9/06/66   MC

YEAR	TM/L	G	AB	R	H	2B	3B	HR	RBI	BB	SO	AVG	OBP	SLG	PRO+	BR	/A	RC	SB	CS	SBR	FR	POS	TPR
1966	NY-A	10	28	4	5	0	0	0	0	3	3	.179	.281	.179	37	-2	-2	2	0	0	0	1	3	0.0
1968	NY-A	23	87	5	14	0	1	0	1	2	17	.161	.180	.184	11	-9	-9	2	0	0	0	4	3	-0.4
1969	Sea-A	5	0	0	0	0	0	0	0	1	0	.000	.200	.000	-41	-1	-1	0	0	0	0	0	H	0.0
1972	Mil-A	124	381	19	97	18	1	2	29	17	41	.255	.286	.323	83	-10	-9	29	0	5	-3	-16	*3/S	-2.6
Total	4	162	500	28	116	18	2	2	30	23	61	.232	.267	.288	67	-22	-21	33	0	5	-3	-10	3/S	-3.0

■ RICK FERRELL
Ferrell, Richard Benjamin b: 10/12/05, Durham, N.C.   BR/TR, 5'10", 160 lbs.   Deb: 4/19/29   CH

YEAR	TM/L	G	AB	R	H	2B	3B	HR	RBI	BB	SO	AVG	OBP	SLG	PRO+	BR	/A	RC	SB	CS	SBR	FR	POS	TPR
1929	StL-A	64	144	21	33	6	1	0	20	32	10	.229	.373	.285	69	-5	-6	18	1	2	-1	-0	C	-0.1
1930	StL-A	101	314	43	84	18	4	1	41	46	10	.268	.363	.360	81	-6	-8	43	1	4	-2	-10	*C	-1.0
1931	StL-A	117	386	47	118	30	4	3	57	56	12	.306	.394	.427	112	10	8	67	2	3	-1	4	*C	1.7
1932	StL-A	126	438	67	138	30	5	2	65	66	18	.315	.406	.420	108	12	8	78	5	5	-2	-2	*C	1.0
1933	StL-A	22	72	8	18	2	0	1	5	12	4	.250	.357	.319	76	-2	-2	9	2	0	1	2	C	0.1
	Bos-A	118	421	50	125	19	4	3	72	58	19	.297	.385	.382	105	4	5	66	2	2	-1	4	*C	1.3
	Yr	140	493	58	143	21	4	4	77	70	23	.290	.381	.373	100	3	3	75	4	2	0	6		1.4
1934	Bos-A	132	437	50	130	29	4	1	48	66	20	.297	.389	.389	95	3	-2	70	0	0	0	3	*C	1.2
1935	Bos-A	133	458	54	138	34	4	3	61	65	15	.301	.388	.413	100	7	2	75	5	8	-3	13	*C	1.4
1936	Bos-A	121	410	59	128	27	5	8	55	65	16	.312	.406	.461	108	10	6	80	0	1	-1	7	*C	2.0
1937	Bos-A	18	65	8	20	2	0	1	4	15	4	.308	.438	.385	105	2	1	12	0	0	0	-0	C	0.2
	Was-A	86	279	31	64	6	0	1	32	50	18	.229	.348	.262	59	-17	-15	29	1	1	-0	-6	C	-1.3
	Yr	104	344	39	84	8	0	2	36	65	22	.244	.366	.285	68	-15	-13	41	1	1	-0	-6		-1.1
1938	Was-A	135	411	55	120	24	5	1	58	75	17	.292	.401	.382	104	1	6	69	1	0	0	-5	*C	0.3
1939	Was-A	87	274	32	77	13	1	0	31	41	12	.281	.377	.336	90	-5	-2	38	1	1	-0	-4	C	0.0
1940	Was-A	103	326	35	89	18	2	0	28	47	15	.273	.365	.340	90	-6	-3	44	1	1	-0	-4	C	0.0
1941	Was-A	21	66	8	18	5	0	0	13	15	4	.273	.407	.348	107	1	1	10	1	0	0	-1	C	0.2
	StL-A	100	321	30	81	14	3	2	23	52	22	.252	.357	.333	81	-6	-8	41	2	1	0	-5	C	-0.6
	Yr	121	387	38	99	19	3	2	36	67	26	.256	.366	.336	85	-5	-6	51	3	1	0	-6		-0.4
1942	StL-A	99	273	20	61	6	1	0	26	33	13	.223	.307	.253	57	-14	-15	23	0	0	-1	9	C	0.6
1943	StL-A	74	209	12	50	7	0	0	20	34	14	.239	.348	.273	81	-3	-4	23	0	0	0	12	C	1.3
1944	Was-A	99	339	14	94	11	1	0	25	46	13	.277	.364	.316	99	-0	-2	41	2	4	-2	6	C	1.1
1945	Was-A	91	286	33	76	12	1	1	38	43	13	.266	.366	.325	110	2	5	35	2	4	-2	0	C	1.1
1947	Was-A	37	99	10	30	11	0	0	12	14	7	.303	.389	.414	127	3	4	16	0	0	0	3	C	1.0
Total	18	1884	6028	687	1692	324	45	28	734	931	277	.281	.378	.363	95	-8	-14	888	29	35	-12	25	*C	11.8

YEAR	TM/L	G	AB	R	H	2B	3B	HR	RBI	BB	SO	AVG	OBP	SLG	PRO+	BR	/A	RC	SB	CS	SBR	FR	POS	TPR

■ WES FERRELL
Ferrell, Wesley Cheek b: 2/2/08, Greensboro, N.C. d: 12/9/76, Sarasota, Fla. BR/TR, 6'2", 195 lbs. Deb: 9/09/27

YEAR	TM/L	G	AB	R	H	2B	3B	HR	RBI	BB	SO	AVG	OBP	SLG	PRO+	BR	/A	RC	SB	CS	SBR	FR	POS	TPR
1927	Cle-A	1	0	0	0	0	0	0	0	0	0	—	—	—	—	0	0	0	0	0	0	0	/P	0.0
1928	Cle-A	2	4	0	1	0	1	0	0	0	0	.250	.250	.750	152	0	0	1	0	0	0	0	/P	0.0
1929	Cle-A	47	93	12	22	5	3	1	12	6	28	.237	.283	.387	68	-4	-5	10	1	0	0	2	P	0.0
1930	Cle-A	53	118	19	35	8	3	0	14	12	15	.297	.362	.415	93	-1	-1	18	0	0	0	-4	P	0.0
1931	Cle-A	48	116	24	37	6	1	9	30	10	21	.319	.373	.621	149	9	8	27	0	0	0	5	P	0.0
1932	Cle-A	55	128	14	31	5	2	2	18	6	21	.242	.276	.359	59	-7	-9	13	0	0	0	0	P	0.0
1933	Cle-A	61	140	26	38	7	0	7	26	20	22	.271	.363	.471	114	4	3	25	0	0	0	2	PO	0.9
1934	Bos-A	34	78	12	22	4	0	4	17	7	15	.282	.341	.487	104	1	0	13	1	0	0	-2	P	0.0
1935	Bos-A	75	150	25	52	5	1	7	32	21	16	.347	.427	.533	138	11	9	35	0	0	0	2	P	0.0
1936	Bos-A	61	135	20	36	6	1	5	24	14	10	.267	.336	.437	84	-3	-4	20	0	0	0	-2	P	0.0
1937	Bos-A	18	33	7	12	2	0	1	9	7	3	.364	.475	.515	144	3	3	9	0	0	0	2	P	0.0
	Was-A	53	106	7	27	5	0	0	16	9	18	.255	.313	.302	58	-7	-6	10	0	0	0	-1	P	-0.2
	Yr	71	139	14	39	7	0	1	25	16	21	.281	.355	.353	81	-4	-4	18	0	0	0	1		-0.2
1938	Was-A	26	49	6	11	2	0	1	6	15	7	.224	.406	.327	92	-0	0	8	0	0	0	1	P	0.0
	NY-A	5	12	1	2	1	0	0	1	1	4	.167	.231	.250	20	-2	-2	1	0	0	0	1	/P	0.0
	Yr	31	61	7	13	3	0	1	7	16	11	.213	.377	.311	79	-2	-1	9	0	0	0	2		0.0
1939	NY-A	3	8	0	1	1	0	0	1	0	2	.125	.125	.250	-6	-1	-1	0	0	0	0	0	/P	0.0
1940	Bro-N	2	2	0	0	0	0	0	0	0	2	.000	.000	.000	-94	-1	-1	0				0	/P	0.0
1941	Bos-N	4	4	2	2	0	0	1	2	1	1	.500	.600	1.250	430	2	2	3	0			-0	/P	0.0
Total	15	548	1176	175	329	57	12	38	208	129	185	.280	.351	.446	99	3	-4	194	2	0		6	P/O	0.7

■ SERGIO FERRER
Ferrer, Sergio (Marrero) b: 1/29/51, Santurce, P.R. BB/TR, 5'7", 145 lbs. Deb: 4/05/74

YEAR	TM/L	G	AB	R	H	2B	3B	HR	RBI	BB	SO	AVG	OBP	SLG	PRO+	BR	/A	RC	SB	CS	SBR	FR	POS	TPR
1974	Min-A	24	57	12	16	0	2	0	0	8	6	.281	.379	.351	107	1	1	8	3	2	-0	-13	S/2	-1.1
1975	Min-A	32	81	14	20	3	1	0	2	3	11	.247	.282	.309	66	-4	-4	7	3	4	-2	1	S2/D	-0.1
1978	NY-N	37	33	8	7	0	1	0	1	4	7	.212	.316	.273	68	-1	-1	3	1	0	0	10	S/23	1.2
1979	NY-N	32	7	7	0	0	0	0	0	2	3	.000	.222	.000	-35	-1	-1	0	0	2	-1	6	3/S2	0.4
Total	4	125	178	41	43	3	4	0	3	17	27	.242	.318	.303	76	-5	-5	18	7	8	-3	4	/S23D	0.4

■ HOBE FERRIS
Ferris, Albert Sayles b: 12/7/1877, Providence, R.I. d: 3/18/38, Detroit, Mich. BR/TR, 5'8", 162 lbs. Deb: 4/26/01

YEAR	TM/L	G	AB	R	H	2B	3B	HR	RBI	BB	SO	AVG	OBP	SLG	PRO+	BR	/A	RC	SB	CS	SBR	FR	POS	TPR
1901	Bos-A	138	523	68	131	16	15	2	63	23		.250	.289	.350	79	-16	-15	59	13			9	*2/S	-1.0
1902	Bos-A	134	499	57	122	16	14	8	63	21		.244	.276	.381	80	-14	-15	58	11			27	*2	1.5
1903	*Bos-A	141	525	69	132	19	7	9	66	25		.251	.285	.366	91	-3	-7	61	11			15	*2/S	1.2
1904	Bos-A	156	563	50	120	23	10	3	63	23		.213	.244	.306	71	-16	-20	46	7			2	*2	-1.9
1905	Bos-A	142	523	51	115	24	16	6	59	23		.220	.253	.361	95	-4	-5	53	11			15	*2	1.0
1906	Bos-A	130	495	47	121	25	13	2	44	10		.244	.259	.360	95	-5	-5	50	8			9	*2/3	0.1
1907	Bos-A	150	561	41	135	25	2	4	60	10		.241	.254	.314	83	-13	-12	50	11			15	*2	0.2
1908	StL-A	148	555	54	150	26	7	2	74	14		.270	.288	.353	110	4	4	59	6			16	*3	3.3
1909	StL-A	148	556	36	120	18	5	4	58	12		.216	.232	.288	69	-25	-21	39	11			7	*32	-1.0
Total	9	1287	4800	473	1146	192	89	40	550	161		.239	.264	.341	86	-93	-96	476	89			113	*23/S	3.4

■ WILLY FETZER
Fetzer, William McKinnon b: 6/24/1884, Concord, N.C. d: 5/3/59, Butner, N.C. 5'10.5", 180 lbs. Deb: 9/04/06

YEAR	TM/L	G	AB	R	H	2B	3B	HR	RBI	BB	SO	AVG	OBP	SLG	PRO+	BR	/A	RC	SB	CS	SBR	FR	POS	TPR
1906	Phi-A	1	1	0	0	0	0	0	0	0	0	.000	.000	.000	-97	-0	-0	0	0			0	H	0.0

■ CHICK FEWSTER
Fewster, Wilson Lloyd b: 11/10/1895, Baltimore, Md. d: 4/16/45, Baltimore, Md. BR/TR, 5'11", 160 lbs. Deb: 9/19/17

YEAR	TM/L	G	AB	R	H	2B	3B	HR	RBI	BB	SO	AVG	OBP	SLG	PRO+	BR	/A	RC	SB	CS	SBR	FR	POS	TPR
1917	NY-A	11	36	2	8	0	0	0	1	5	5	.222	.317	.222	64	-1	-1	3	1			2	2	0.2
1918	NY-A	5	2	1	1	0	0	0	0	0	0	.500	.500	.500	197	0	0	0	0			0	/2	0.0
1919	NY-A	81	244	38	69	9	3	1	15	34	36	.283	.386	.357	108	5	5	36	8			8	OS/23	1.3
1920	NY-A	21	21	8	6	1	0	0	1	7	2	.286	.464	.333	110	1	1	4	0	1	-1	0	/S2	0.1
1921	*NY-A	66	207	44	58	19	0	1	19	28	43	.280	.382	.386	94	-0	-1	32	4	4	-1	-3	O2	-0.6
1922	NY-A	44	132	20	32	4	1	1	9	16	23	.242	.324	.311	65	-6	-7	14	2	4	-2	1	O/2	-0.9
	Bos-A	23	83	8	24	4	1	0	9	6	10	.289	.344	.361	85	-2	-2	11	8	3	1	4	3	0.5
	Yr	67	215	28	56	8	2	1	18	22	33	.260	.332	.330	72	-8	-9	24	10	7	-1	5		-0.4
1923	Bos-A	90	284	32	67	10	1	0	15	39	35	.236	.334	.278	62	-14	-14	26	7	14	-6	-9	2S/3	-2.3
1924	Cle-A	101	322	36	86	12	2	0	36	24	36	.267	.324	.317	65	-16	-17	32	12	12	-4	-22	23/3	-3.7
1925	Cle-A	93	294	39	73	16	1	1	38	36	25	.248	.330	.320	65	-15	-15	32	6	9	-4	-9	23/O	-2.2
1926	Bro-N	105	337	53	82	16	3	2	24	45	49	.243	.341	.326	82	-8	-7	39	9			-15	*2	-1.6
1927	Bro-N	4	1	1	0	0	0	0	0	0	0	.000	.000	.000	-99	-0	-0	0	0			0	H	0.0
Total	11	644	1963	282	506	91	12	6	167	240	264	.258	.346	.326	77	-58	-60	230	57	47		-43	2O/S3	-9.2

■ NEIL FIALA
Fiala, Neil Stephen b: 8/24/56, St.Louis, Mo. BL/TR, 6'1", 185 lbs. Deb: 9/03/81

YEAR	TM/L	G	AB	R	H	2B	3B	HR	RBI	BB	SO	AVG	OBP	SLG	PRO+	BR	/A	RC	SB	CS	SBR	FR	POS	TPR
1981	StL-N	3	3	0	0	0	0	0	0	0	1	.000	.000	.000	-97	-1	-1	0	0	0	0	0	/H	0.0
	Cin-N	2	2	1	1	0	0	0	1	0	1	.500	.500	.500	181	0	0	1	0	0	0	0	/H	0.0
	Yr	5	5	1	1	0	0	0	1	0	2	.200	.200	.200	13	-1	-1	0	0	0	0	0		0.0

■ JIM FIELD
Field, James C. b: 4/24/1863, Philadelphia, Pa. d: 5/13/53, Atlantic City, N.J 6'1", 170 lbs. Deb: 6/02/1883

YEAR	TM/L	G	AB	R	H	2B	3B	HR	RBI	BB	SO	AVG	OBP	SLG	PRO+	BR	/A	RC	SB	CS	SBR	FR	POS	TPR
1883	Col-a	76	295	31	75	10	6	1		7		.254	.272	.339	104	-2	2	28				-7	*1	-1.0
1884	Col-a	105	417	74	97	9	7	4		23		.233	.292	.317	110	1	7	40				-4	*1	-0.2
1885	Pit-a	56	209	28	50	9	1	1		13		.239	.306	.306	98	-0	0	20				-0	1	-0.3
	Bal-a	38	144	16	30	3	2	0		13		.208	.278	.257	73	-4	-4	11				1	1	-0.4
	Yr	94	353	44	80	12	3	1		26		.227	.295	.286	88	-4	-3	30				1		-0.7
1890	Roc-a	52	188	30	38	7	5	4		21		.202	.309	.356	106	-1	2	24	8			-4	1/P	-0.3
1898	Was-N	5	21	1	2	0	0	0	0	0		.095	.095	.095	-45	-4	-4	0	1			0	/1	-0.3
Total	5	332	1274	180	292	38	21	10	0	77		.229	.288	.316	99	-9	3	122	9			-14	1/P	-2.5

■ SAM FIELD
Field, Samuel Jay b: 10/12/1848, Philadelphia, Pa. d: 10/28/04, Sinking Spring, Pa BR/TR, 5'9.5", 182 lbs. Deb: 5/19/1875 M

YEAR	TM/L	G	AB	R	H	2B	3B	HR	RBI	BB	SO	AVG	OBP	SLG	PRO+	BR	/A	RC	SB	CS	SBR	FR	POS	TPR
1875	Cen-n	3	11	2	1	0	0	0		0		.091	.091	.091	-40	-1	-1	0					/CO	0.0
	Was-n	5	17	0	5	0	0	0		0		.294	.294	.294	108	0	0	2					/CO	0.0
	Yr	8	28	2	6	0	0	0		0		.214	.214	.214	51	-1	-1	1						0.0
1876	Cin-N	4	14	2	0	0	0	0	0	1	3	.000	.067	.000	-89	-3	-2	0				-3	/C2	-0.4

■ CECIL FIELDER
Fielder, Cecil Grant b: 9/21/63, Los Angeles, Cal. BR/TR, 6'3", 230 lbs. Deb: 7/20/85

YEAR	TM/L	G	AB	R	H	2B	3B	HR	RBI	BB	SO	AVG	OBP	SLG	PRO+	BR	/A	RC	SB	CS	SBR	FR	POS	TPR
1985	*Tor-A	30	74	6	23	4	0	4	16	6	16	.311	.363	.527	137	4	4	14	0	0	0	1	1	0.3
1986	Tor-A	34	83	7	13	2	0	4	13	6	27	.157	.222	.325	46	-6	-7	5	0	0	0	-0	D/13O	-0.7
1987	Tor-A	82	175	30	47	7	1	14	32	20	48	.269	.347	.560	132	8	8	32	0	1	-1	-0	D1/3	0.5
1988	Tor-A	74	174	24	40	6	1	9	23	14	53	.230	.291	.431	99	-1	-1	20	0	1	-1	0	D1/32	-0.1
1990	Det-A	159	573	104	159	25	1	**51**	**132**	90	182	.277	.380	**.592**	169	51	52	129	0	1	-1	3	*1D	4.4
Total	5	379	1079	171	282	44	3	82	216	136	326	.261	.348	.536	140	56	56	200	0	3	-2	3	1D/320	4.4

■ BRUCE FIELDS
Fields, Bruce Alan b: 10/6/60, Cleveland, Ohio BL/TR, 6', 185 lbs. Deb: 9/03/86

YEAR	TM/L	G	AB	R	H	2B	3B	HR	RBI	BB	SO	AVG	OBP	SLG	PRO+	BR	/A	RC	SB	CS	SBR	FR	POS	TPR
1986	Det-A	16	43	4	12	1	0	1	6	1	6	.279	.295	.349	75	-2	-2	4	1	1	-0	-1	O/D	-0.2
1988	Sea-A	39	67	8	18	5	0	1	5	4	11	.269	.310	.388	90	-1	-1	7	0	1	-1	-1	O/D	-0.2
1989	Sea-A	3	3	2	1	1	0	0	0	0	1	.333	.333	.667	170	0	0	1	0	0	0	0	/O	0.0
Total	3	58	113	14	31	7	0	1	11	5	18	.274	.305	.381	86	-2	-2	12	1	2	-1	-1	OD	-0.4

YEAR	TM/L	G	AB	R	H	2B	3B	HR	RBI	BB	SO	AVG	OBP	SLG	PRO+	BR	/A	RC	SB	CS	SBR	FR	POS	TPR

■ GEORGE FIELDS   Fields, George W.   b: 1851, Waterbury, Conn.   d: 9/22/33, Waterbury, Conn.   Deb: 5/02/1872

| 1872 | Man-n | 18 | 83 | 14 | 22 | 2 | 2 | 0 | | 0 | | .265 | .265 | .337 | 89 | -2 | -1 | 8 | | | | | 3/OS | 0.0 |

■ JOCKO FIELDS   Fields, John Joseph   b: 10/20/1864, Cork, Ireland   d: 10/14/50, Jersey City, N.J.   BR/TR, 5'10", 160 lbs.   Deb: 5/31/1887

1887	Pit-N	43	164	26	44	9	2	0	17	7	13	.268	.306	.348	88	-4	-2	20	7			5	OC/13P	0.4
1888	Pit-N	45	169	22	33	7	2	1	15	8	19	.195	.232	.278	69	-7	-5	13	9			-6	OC/3	-1.0
1889	Pit-N	75	289	41	90	22	5	2	43	29	30	.311	.376	.443	144	11	16	52	7			-5	OC	0.7
1890	Pit-P	126	526	101	149	18	20	9	86	57	52	.283	.357	.445	126	10	18	94	24			-18	O2C/S	0.0
1891	Pit-N	23	75	10	18	3	0	0	5	10	13	.240	.337	.280	84	-1	-1	8	1			-2	C/S	0.0
	Phi-N	8	30	4	7	2	1	0	5	4	2	.233	.324	.367	100	0	-0	4	0			-3	/C	-0.1
	Yr	31	105	14	25	5	1	0	10	14	15	.238	.333	.305	89	-1	-1	11	1			-5		-0.1
1892	NY-N	21	66	8	18	4	2	0	5	9	10	.273	.368	.394	135	3	3	11	2			-0	OC	0.3
Total	6	341	1319	212	359	65	32	12	176	124	139	.272	.338	.397	116	13	29	202	50			-30	O/C2S31P	0.3

■ JESUS FIGUEROA   Figueroa, Jesus Maria (Figueroa)   b: 2/20/57, Santo Domingo, P.R.   BL/TL, 5'10", 160 lbs.   Deb: 4/22/80

| 1980 | Chi-N | 115 | 198 | 20 | 50 | 5 | 0 | 1 | 11 | 14 | 16 | .253 | .308 | .293 | 64 | -8 | -10 | 18 | 2 | 1 | 0 | 4 | O | -0.7 |

■ SAM FILE   File, Lawrence Samuel   b: 5/18/22, Chester, Pa.   BR/TR, 5'11", 160 lbs.   Deb: 9/10/40

| 1940 | Phi-N | 7 | 13 | 0 | 1 | 0 | 0 | 0 | 1 | 0 | 1 | .077 | .077 | .077 | -60 | -3 | -3 | 0 | 0 | | | 1 | /S3 | 0.0 |

■ STEVE FILIPOWICZ   Filipowicz, Stephen Charles "Flip"   b: 6/28/21, Donora, Pa.   d: 2/21/75, Wilkes-Barre, Pa.   BR/TR, 5'8", 195 lbs.   Deb: 9/03/44

1944	NY-N	15	41	10	8	2	1	0	7	3	7	.195	.250	.293	52	-3	-3	3	0			-1	O/C	-0.4
1945	NY-N	35	112	14	23	5	0	2	16	4	13	.205	.239	.304	50	-8	-8	8	0			-5	O	-1.4
1948	Cin-N	7	26	0	9	0	1	0	3	2	1	.346	.393	.423	125	1	1	5	0			-0	/O	0.0
Total	3	57	179	24	40	7	2	2	26	9	21	.223	.265	.318	61	-10	-10	15	0			-6	/OC	-1.8

■ JACK FIMPLE   Fimple, John Joseph   b: 2/10/59, Darby, Pa.   BR/TR, 6'2", 185 lbs.   Deb: 7/30/83

1983	*LA-N	54	148	16	37	8	1	2	22	11	39	.250	.302	.358	83	-4	-4	16	1	0	0	13	C	1.2
1984	LA-N	12	26	2	5	1	0	0	3	1	6	.192	.222	.231	28	-3	-2	1	0	0	0	2	C	0.0
1986	LA-N	13	13	2	1	0	0	0	2	6	6	.077	.368	.077	32	-1	-1	1	0	0	0	1	/C12	0.0
1987	Cal-A	13	10	1	2	0	0	0	1	1	2	.200	.273	.200	29	-1	-1	1	0	0	0	1	C	0.1
Total	4	92	197	21	45	9	1	2	28	19	53	.228	.296	.315	70	-8	-8	18	1	0	0	16	/C21	1.3

■ JIM FINIGAN   Finigan, James Leroy   b: 8/19/28, Quincy, Ill.   d: 5/16/81, Quincy, Ill.   BR/TR, 5'11", 175 lbs.   Deb: 4/25/54

1954	Phi-A	136	487	57	147	25	6	7	51	64	66	.302	.383	.421	120	14	14	76	2	8	-4	2	*3	0.5
1955	KC-A	150	545	72	139	30	7	9	68	61	49	.255	.333	.385	92	-6	-7	68	1	3	-2	-7	23	-0.8
1956	KC-A	91	250	29	54	7	2	2	21	30	28	.216	.302	.284	55	-16	-16	23	3	1	0	-1	23	-1.0
1957	Det-A	64	174	20	47	4	2	0	17	23	18	.270	.359	.316	84	-2	-3	21	1	1	-0	4	3/2	0.2
1958	SF-N	23	25	3	5	2	0	0	1	3	5	.200	.310	.280	59	-1	-1	2	0	0	0	-2	/23	-0.2
1959	Bal-A	48	119	14	30	6	0	1	10	9	10	.252	.305	.328	75	-4	-4	11	1	0	0	0	3/2S	-0.2
Total	6	512	1600	195	422	74	17	19	168	190	176	.264	.344	.367	92	-16	-17	200	8	13	-5	-3	32/S	-1.5

■ BOB FINLEY   Finley, Robert Edward   b: 11/25/15, Ennis, Tex.   d: 1/2/86, W.Covina, Cal.   BR/TR, 6'1", 200 lbs.   Deb: 7/04/43

1943	Phi-N	28	81	9	21	2	0	1	7	4	10	.259	.294	.321	81	-2	-2	7	0			3	C	0.2
1944	Phi-N	94	281	18	70	11	1	1	21	12	25	.249	.292	.306	71	-12	-11	24	1			-2	C	-0.8
Total	2	122	362	27	91	13	1	2	28	16	35	.251	.292	.309	73	-14	-13	31	1			1	/C	-0.6

■ STEVE FINLEY   Finley, Steven Allen   b: 5/12/65, Union City, Tenn.   BL/TL, 6'2", 175 lbs.   Deb: 4/03/89

1989	Bal-A	81	217	35	54	5	2	2	25	15	30	.249	.300	.318	77	-7	-6	23	17	3	3	0	O/D	-0.4
1990	Bal-A	142	464	46	119	16	4	3	37	32	53	.256	.307	.328	79	-14	-13	48	22	9	1	0	*O/D	-1.2
Total	2	223	681	81	173	21	6	5	62	47	83	.254	.305	.325	79	-21	-19	70	39	12	5	0	O/D	-1.6

■ BILL FINLEY   Finley, William James   b: 10/4/1863, New York, N.Y.   d: 10/6/12, Asbury Park, N.J.   Deb: 7/12/1886

| 1886 | NY-N | 13 | 44 | 2 | 8 | 0 | 0 | 0 | 5 | 1 | 8 | .182 | .200 | .182 | 17 | -4 | -4 | 2 | 2 | | | -1 | /OC | -0.3 |

■ NEAL FINN   Finn, Cornelius Francis "Mickey"   b: 1/24/04, Brooklyn, N.Y.   d: 7/7/33, Allentown, Pa.   BR/TR, 5'11", 168 lbs.   Deb: 4/21/30

1930	Bro-N	87	273	42	76	13	0	3	30	26	18	.278	.350	.359	73	-12	-11	35	3			-6	2	-0.6
1931	Bro-N	118	413	46	113	22	2	0	45	21	42	.274	.314	.337	75	-15	-14	45	2			0	*2	-0.3
1932	Bro-N	65	189	22	45	5	2	0	14	11	15	.238	.284	.286	55	-12	-12	16	2			4	3/2S	-0.2
1933	Phi-N	51	169	15	40	4	1	0	13	10	14	.237	.287	.272	54	-8	-11	14	2			-1	2	-0.8
Total	4	321	1044	125	274	44	5	3	102	68	89	.262	.314	.323	67	-47	-48	109	9			-3	2/3S	-2.4

■ HAL FINNEY   Finney, Harold Wilson   b: 7/7/05, Lafayette, Ala.   BR/TR, 5'11", 170 lbs.   Deb: 6/24/31

1931	Pit-N	10	26	2	8	1	0	0	2	0	1	.308	.333	.346	84	-1	-1	3	1			0	/C	0.0
1932	Pit-N	31	33	14	7	3	0	0	4	3	4	.212	.297	.303	63	-2	-2	3	0			3	C	0.1
1933	Pit-N	56	133	17	31	4	1	1	18	3	19	.233	.250	.301	57	-8	-8	9	0			-2	C	-0.8
1934	Pit-N	5	0	3	0	0	0	0	0	0	0	—	1.000	—	188	0	0	0	0			0	/C	0.0
1936	Pit-N	21	35	3	0	0	0	0	3	0	8	.000	.000	.000	-98	-10	-10	0	0			1	C	-0.7
Total	5	123	227	39	46	8	1	1	27	6	32	.203	.233	.260	37	-19	-19	16	1			2	/C	-1.4

■ LOU FINNEY   Finney, Louis Klopsche   b: 8/13/10, Buffalo, Ala.   d: 4/22/66, Lafayette, Ala.   BL/TR, 6', 180 lbs.   Deb: 9/12/31

1931	Phi-A	9	24	7	9	0	1	0	3	6	1	.375	.516	.458	149	3	2	6	0	0	0	1	/O	0.3
1933	Phi-A	74	240	26	64	12	2	3	32	13	17	.267	.307	.371	78	-8	-8	27	1	3	-2	2	O	-0.8
1934	Phi-A	92	272	32	76	11	4	1	28	14	17	.279	.315	.360	77	-11	-10	31	4	3	-1	0	O1	-1.2
1935	Phi-A	109	410	45	112	11	6	0	31	18	18	.273	.307	.329	65	-22	-21	42	7	2	1	-5	O1	-2.6
1936	Phi-A	151	653	100	197	26	10	1	41	47	22	.302	.351	.377	81	-21	-19	85	7	9	-3	-5	1O	-3.5
1937	Phi-A	92	379	53	95	14	9	1	20	20	16	.251	.288	.343	59	-25	-24	36	2	5	-2	-2	1O/2	-3.3
1938	Phi-A	122	454	61	125	21	12	10	48	39	25	.275	.333	.441	94	-8	-6	65	5	8	-3	-3	1O	-1.8
1939	Phi-A	9	22	1	3	0	0	0	1	2	0	.136	.208	.136	-10	-4	-4	1	0	0	0	0	/O	-0.2
	Bos-A	95	249	43	81	18	3	1	46	24	11	.325	.385	.434	105	4	2	41	2	5	-2	-4	1O	-0.7
	Yr	104	271	44	84	18	3	1	47	26	11	.310	.370	.410	96	-0	-1	42	2	5	-2	-4		-0.9
1940	Bos-A	130	534	73	171	31	15	5	73	33	13	.320	.360	.463	107	8	5	87	5	2	-0	-2	O1	-0.3
1941	Bos-A	127	497	83	143	24	10	4	53	38	17	.288	.340	.400	93	-4	-6	66	2	5	-2	-6	O1	-1.9
1942	Bos-A	113	397	58	113	16	7	2	61	29	11	.285	.335	.383	98	0	-2	51	3	3	-1	0	O/1	-0.8
1944	Bos-A	68	251	37	72	11	2	0	32	23	7	.287	.347	.347	100	-0	0	31	1	0	0	-5	1/O	-0.7
1945	Bos-A	2	2	0	0	0	0	0	0	0	0	.000	.000	.000	-98	-1	-1	0	0	0	0	0	H	0.0
	StL-A	57	213	24	59	8	4	2	22	21	6	.277	.345	.380	105	3	1	27	0	0	0	-2	O1/3	-0.2
	Yr	59	215	24	59	8	4	2	22	21	7	.274	.342	.377	103	2	1	27	0	0	0	-2		-0.2
1946	StL-A	16	30	0	9	0	0	0	3	2	1	.300	.344	.300	77	-1	-1	3	0	0	0	1	/O	0.0
1947	Phi-N	4	4	0	0	0	0	0	0	0	0	.000	.000	.000	-99	-1	-1	0	0			0	H	0.0
Total	15	1270	4631	643	1329	203	85	31	494	329	186	.287	.336	.388	88	-88	-90	599	39	45		-29	O1/32	-17.7

■ MIKE FIORE   Fiore, Michael Gary Joseph   b: 10/11/44, Brooklyn, N.Y.   BL/TL, 6', 175 lbs.   Deb: 9/21/68

| 1968 | Bal-A | 6 | 17 | 2 | 1 | 0 | 0 | 0 | 0 | 4 | 4 | .059 | .273 | .059 | 5 | -2 | -2 | 1 | 0 | 0 | 0 | -0 | /1O | -0.2 |
| 1969 | KC-A | 107 | 339 | 53 | 93 | 14 | 1 | 12 | 35 | 84 | 63 | .274 | .421 | .428 | 137 | 22 | 21 | 66 | 4 | 4 | -1 | 12 | 1O | 2.6 |

YEAR	TM/L	G	AB	R	H	2B	3B	HR	RBI	BB	SO	AVG	OBP	SLG	PRO+	BR	/A	RC	SB	CS	SBR	FR	POS	TPR
1970	KC-A	25	72	6	13	2	0	0	4	13	24	.181	.306	.208	44	-5	-5	5	1	1	-0	1	1	-0.5
	Bos-A	41	50	5	7	0	0	0	4	8	4	.140	.259	.140	12	-6	-6	2	0	0	0	1	1/O	-0.6
	Yr	66	122	11	20	2	0	0	8	21	28	.164	.287	.180	30	-11	-11	7	1	1	-0	1		-1.1
1971	Bos-A	51	62	9	11	2	0	1	6	12	14	.177	.311	.258	58	-3	-3	5	0	3	-2	0	1	-0.5
1972	StL-N	17	10	0	1	0	0	0	1	2	3	.100	.250	.100	3	-1	-1	0	0	0	0	-0	/1O	-0.1
	SD-N	7	6	0	0	0	0	0	0	1	3	.000	.143	.000	-61	-1	-1	0	0	0	0	0	H	0.0
	Yr	24	16	0	1	0	0	0	1	3	6	.063	.211	.063	-20	-2	-2	0	0	0	0	-0		-0.1
Total	5	254	556	75	126	18	1	13	50	124	115	.227	.370	.333	97	4	3	79	5	8	-3	13	1/O	0.7

■ DAN FIROVA
Firova, Daniel Michael b: 10/16/56, Refugio, Tex. BR/TR, 6', 185 lbs. Deb: 9/01/81

YEAR	TM/L	G	AB	R	H	2B	3B	HR	RBI	BB	SO	AVG	OBP	SLG	PRO+	BR	/A	RC	SB	CS	SBR	FR	POS	TPR
1981	Sea-A	13	2	0	0	0	0	0	0	0	1	.000	.000	.000	-96	-1	-1	0	0	0	0	1	C	0.1
1982	Sea-A	3	5	0	0	0	0	0	0	0	0	.000	.000	.000	-97	-1	-1	0	0	0	0	0	/C	0.0
1988	Cle-A	1	0	0	0	0	0	0	0	0	0	—	—	—	—	0	0	0	0	0	0	0	/C	0.0
Total	3	17	7	0	0	0	0	0	0	0	1	.000	.000	.000	-97	-2	-2	0	0	0	0	1	/C	0.1

■ WILLIAM FISCHER
Fischer, William Charles b: 3/2/1891, New York, N.Y. d: 9/4/45, Richmond, Va. BL/TR, 6', 174 lbs. Deb: 6/11/13

YEAR	TM/L	G	AB	R	H	2B	3B	HR	RBI	BB	SO	AVG	OBP	SLG	PRO+	BR	/A	RC	SB	CS	SBR	FR	POS	TPR
1913	Bro-N	62	165	16	44	9	4	1	12	10	5	.267	.313	.388	97	-1	-1	19	0			-1	C	0.1
1914	Bro-N	43	105	12	27	1	2	0	8	8	12	.257	.310	.305	81	-2	-2	10	1			3	C	0.1
1915	Chi-F	105	292	30	96	15	4	4	50	24	19	.329	.384	.449	155	16	18	55	5			-4	C	1.7
1916	Chi-N	65	179	15	35	9	2	1	14	11	8	.196	.246	.285	57	-8	-10	14	2			4	C	-0.3
	Pit-N	42	113	11	29	7	1	1	6	10	3	.257	.323	.363	109	1	1	14	1			4	C	0.8
	Yr	107	292	26	64	16	3	2	20	21	11	.219	.276	.315	76	-7	-9	27	3			8		0.5
1917	Pit-N	95	245	25	70	9	2	3	25	27	19	.286	.359	.376	121	8	7	35	11			-10	C/1	0.1
Total	5	412	1099	109	301	50	15	10	115	90	66	.274	.332	.374	110	15	13	147	20			-4	C/1	2.5

■ MIKE FISCHLIN
Fischlin, Michael Thomas b: 9/13/55, Sacramento, Cal. BR/TR, 6'1", 165 lbs. Deb: 9/03/77

YEAR	TM/L	G	AB	R	H	2B	3B	HR	RBI	BB	SO	AVG	OBP	SLG	PRO+	BR	/A	RC	SB	CS	SBR	FR	POS	TPR
1977	Hou-N	13	15	0	3	0	0	0	0	0	2	.200	.200	.200	8	-2	-2	1	0	0	0	1	S	0.1
1978	Hou-N	44	86	3	10	1	0	0	0	4	9	.116	.165	.128	-19	-13	-13	2	1	0	0	-4	S	-1.3
1980	Hou-N	1	1	0	0	0	0	0	0	0	1	.000	.000	.000	-99	-0	-0	0	0	0	0	-0	/S	0.0
1981	Cle-A	22	43	3	10	1	0	0	5	3	6	.233	.283	.256	57	-2	-2	3	3	2	-0	-0	S/2	0.0
1982	Cle-A	112	276	34	74	12	1	0	21	34	36	.268	.353	.319	86	-4	-4	34	9	5	-0	-7	*S/32C	-0.1
1983	Cle-A	95	225	31	47	5	2	2	23	26	32	.209	.296	.276	56	-12	-13	22	9	2	2	21	2S/3D	1.2
1984	Cle-A	85	133	17	30	4	2	1	14	12	20	.226	.290	.308	64	-6	-6	12	2	2	-1	18	23S	1.5
1985	Cle-A	73	60	12	12	4	1	0	2	5	7	.200	.262	.300	54	-4	-4	5	0	1	-1	31	2S/13D	2.8
1986	NY-A	71	102	9	21	2	0	0	3	8	29	.206	.264	.225	35	-9	-9	6	0	1	-1	7	S2	0.1
1987	Atl-N	1	0	0	0	0	0	0	0	0	0	—	—	—	—	0	0	0	0	0	0	0	/R	0.0
Total	10	517	941	109	207	29	6	3	68	92	142	.220	.293	.273	57	-53	-53	85	24	13	-1	67	S2/31DC	4.2

■ SAM FISHBURN
Fishburn, Samuel E. b: 5/15/1893, Haverhill, Mass. d: 4/11/65, Bethlehem, Pa. BR/TR, 5'9", 157 lbs. Deb: 9/30/19

YEAR	TM/L	G	AB	R	H	2B	3B	HR	RBI	BB	SO	AVG	OBP	SLG	PRO+	BR	/A	RC	SB	CS	SBR	FR	POS	TPR
1919	StL-N	9	6	0	2	1	0	0	2	0	0	.333	.333	.500	158	0	0	1	0			1	/12	0.1

■ JOHN FISHEL
Fishel, John Alan b: 11/8/62, Fullerton, Cal. BR/TR, 5'11", 185 lbs. Deb: 7/14/88

YEAR	TM/L	G	AB	R	H	2B	3B	HR	RBI	BB	SO	AVG	OBP	SLG	PRO+	BR	/A	RC	SB	CS	SBR	FR	POS	TPR
1988	Hou-N	19	26	1	6	0	0	1	2	3	6	.231	.310	.346	92	-0	-0	3	0	0	0	-1	/O	-0.1

■ FISHER
Fisher b: Johnstown, Pa. Deb: 7/17/1884

YEAR	TM/L	G	AB	R	H	2B	3B	HR	RBI	BB	SO	AVG	OBP	SLG	PRO+	BR	/A	RC	SB	CS	SBR	FR	POS	TPR
1884	Phi-U	10	36	7	8	2	0	0			3	.222	.282	.278	97	-0	0	3	0			-2	/P1	0.0
	Wil-U	8	29	0	2	0	0	0			0	.069	.069	.069	-52	-4	-5	0	0			-1	/OS	-0.4
	Yr	18	65	7	10	2	0	0			3	.154	.191	.185	28	-5	-4	2	0			-4		-0.4
1885	Buf-N	1	4	0	0	0	0	0	0	0	0	.000	.000	.000	-97	-1	-1	0	0			0	/P	0.0
Total	2	19	69	7	10	2	0	0	0	3	0	.145	.181	.174	21	-6	-5	3				-3	/POS1	-0.4

■ GUS FISHER
Fisher, August Harris b: 10/21/1885, Pottsborough, Tex. d: 4/8/72, Portland, Ore. BL/TR, 5'10", 175 lbs. Deb: 4/18/11

YEAR	TM/L	G	AB	R	H	2B	3B	HR	RBI	BB	SO	AVG	OBP	SLG	PRO+	BR	/A	RC	SB	CS	SBR	FR	POS	TPR
1911	Cle-A	70	203	20	53	6	3	0	12	7		.261	.302	.320	73	-8	-8	21	6			9	C/1	0.8
1912	NY-A	4	10	1	1	0	0	0	0	0		.100	.100	.100	-40	-2	-2	0	0			1	/C	0.0
Total	2	74	213	21	54	6	3	0	12	7		.254	.293	.310	68	-9	-10	21	6			9	/C1	0.8

■ SHOWBOAT FISHER
Fisher, George Aloys b: 1/16/1899, Jennings, Iowa BL/TR, 5'10", 170 lbs. Deb: 4/24/23

YEAR	TM/L	G	AB	R	H	2B	3B	HR	RBI	BB	SO	AVG	OBP	SLG	PRO+	BR	/A	RC	SB	CS	SBR	FR	POS	TPR
1923	Was-A	13	23	4	6	2	0	0	2	4	3	.261	.370	.348	95	-0	-0	3	0	0	0	0	/O	0.0
1924	Was-A	15	41	7	9	1	0	0	6	6	6	.220	.319	.244	48	-3	-3	4	2	0	1	-2	O	-0.4
1930	*StL-N	92	254	49	95	18	6	8	61	25	21	.374	.432	.587	139	18	17	62	4			-2	O	0.9
1932	StL-A	18	22	2	4	0	0	0	2	2	5	.182	.250	.182	13	-3	-3	1	0	0	0	0	/O	-0.2
Total	4	138	340	62	114	21	6	8	71	37	35	.335	.402	.503	119	12	11	71	6	0		-4	/O	0.3

■ HARRY FISHER
Fisher, Harry C. b: Philadelphia, Pa. Deb: 6/07/1884

YEAR	TM/L	G	AB	R	H	2B	3B	HR	RBI	BB	SO	AVG	OBP	SLG	PRO+	BR	/A	RC	SB	CS	SBR	FR	POS	TPR
1884	KC-U	10	40	3	8	2	0	0			0	.200	.200	.250	59	-2	-1	2	0			0	/3S	0.0
	CP-U	1	3	1	2	0	0	0			1	.667	.750	.667	385	1	1	2	0			-1	/3	0.0
	Yr	11	43	4	10	2	0	0			1	.233	.250	.279	89	-1	-0	3	0			-1		0.0
	Cle-N	6	24	2	3	0	0	0	0		3	.125	.125	.125	-20	-3	-3	0				-3	/2C	-0.5
1889	Lou-a	1	2	0	1	0	0	0	0	0	0	.500	.500	.500	192	0	0	1				-0	/O	0.0
Total	2	18	69	6	14	2	0	0	0	1	3	.203	.214	.232	49	-4	-3	4	0			-4	/32OCS	-0.5

■ HARRY FISHER
Fisher, Harry Devereux b: 1/3/26, Newbury, Ont., Can. d: 9/20/81, Waterloo, Ont., Ca BL/TR, 6', 180 lbs. Deb: 9/16/51

YEAR	TM/L	G	AB	R	H	2B	3B	HR	RBI	BB	SO	AVG	OBP	SLG	PRO+	BR	/A	RC	SB	CS	SBR	FR	POS	TPR
1951	Pit-N	3	3	0	0	0	0	0	0	0	0	.000	.000	.000	-97	-1	-1	0	0	0	0	0	H	0.0
1952	Pit-N	15	15	0	5	1	0	0	1	0	3	.333	.333	.400	100	-0	-0	2	0	0	0	-0	/P	0.0
Total	2	18	18	0	5	1	0	0	1	0	3	.278	.278	.333	66	-1	-1	2	0	0	0	-0	/P	0.0

■ RED FISHER
Fisher, John Gus b: 6/22/1887, Pittsburgh, Pa. d: 1/31/40, Louisville, Ky. TR, Deb: 4/25/10

YEAR	TM/L	G	AB	R	H	2B	3B	HR	RBI	BB	SO	AVG	OBP	SLG	PRO+	BR	/A	RC	SB	CS	SBR	FR	POS	TPR
1910	StL-A	23	72	5	9	2	1	0	3	8		.125	.222	.181	28	-6	-5	4	5			-1	O	-0.7

■ NEWT FISHER
Fisher, Newton "Ike" b: 6/28/1871, Nashville, Tenn. d: 2/28/47, Norwood Park, Ill. BR/TR, 5'9.5", 171 lbs. Deb: 5/17/1898

YEAR	TM/L	G	AB	R	H	2B	3B	HR	RBI	BB	SO	AVG	OBP	SLG	PRO+	BR	/A	RC	SB	CS	SBR	FR	POS	TPR
1898	Phi-N	9	26	0	3	1	0	0	0	0		.115	.148	.154	-13	-4	-4	1	1			-1	/C3	-0.3

■ TOM FISHER
Fisher, Robert Taylor b: 11/3/1886, Nashville, Tenn. d: 8/4/63, Jacksonville, Fla. BR/TR, 5'9.5", 170 lbs. Deb: 6/03/12

YEAR	TM/L	G	AB	R	H	2B	3B	HR	RBI	BB	SO	AVG	OBP	SLG	PRO+	BR	/A	RC	SB	CS	SBR	FR	POS	TPR
1912	Bro-N	82	257	27	60	10	3	0	26	14	32	.233	.273	.296	58	-16	-15	23	7			-14	S/23	-2.1
1913	Bro-N	132	474	42	124	11	10	4	54	10	43	.262	.278	.352	77	-15	-16	49	16			-19	*S	-2.7
1914	Chi-N	15	50	5	15	2	2	0	5	3	4	.300	.340	.420	126	1	1	8	2			-1	S	0.0
1915	Chi-N	147	568	70	163	22	5	5	53	30	51	.287	.326	.370	110	6	6	69	9	20	-9	-20	*S	-2.2
1916	Cin-N	61	136	9	37	4	3	0	11	8	14	.272	.313	.346	104	0	0	17	0			-11	S/2O	-1.0
1918	StL-N	63	246	36	78	11	3	2	20	15	11	.317	.356	.411	138	9	10	37	7			19	2	3.5
1919	StL-N	3	10	0	3	1	0	0	1	0	2	.273	.273	.364	96	0	0	1	0			0	/2	0.0
Total	7	503	1742	189	480	61	26	11	170	80	157	.276	.309	.359	96	-14	-13	203	48	20		-47	S/2O3	-4.5

■ WILBUR FISHER
Fisher, Wilbur McCullough b: 7/18/1894, Greenbottom, W.Va d: 10/24/60, Welch, W.Va. BL/TR, 6', 174 lbs. Deb: 6/13/16

YEAR	TM/L	G	AB	R	H	2B	3B	HR	RBI	BB	SO	AVG	OBP	SLG	PRO+	BR	/A	RC	SB	CS	SBR	FR	POS	TPR
1916	Pit-N	1	1	0	0	0	0	0	0	0	0	.000	.000	.000	-99	-0	-0	0	0			0	H	0.0

YEAR	TM/L	G	AB	R	H	2B	3B	HR	RBI	BB	SO	AVG	OBP	SLG	PRO+	BR	/A	RC	SB	CS	SBR	FR	POS	TPR

■ CHEROKEE FISHER   Fisher, William Charles   b: 12/1845, Philadelphia, Pa.   d: 9/26/12, New York, N.Y.   BR/TR, 5'9", 164 lbs.   Deb: 5/06/1871

1871	Rok-n	25	123	24	28	3	3	1	22	3	1	.228	.246	.325	65	-6	-5	10	1				*P/S	0.0
1872	Bal-n	46	226	40	52	10	2	1			2	.230	.237	.305	63	-9	-11	17					P3O	-0.5
1873	Ath-n	51	252	50	64	4	3	1			4	.254	.266	.306	63	-10	-14	21					*O/P1	-0.5
1874	Har-n	52	242	28	54	8	0	0			0	.223	.223	.256	50	-13	-15	14					PO/3S	0.0
1875	Phi-n	41	177	26	41	2	1	0			1	.232	.236	.254	67	-5	-6	11					P/O	0.0
1876	Cin-N	35	129	12	32	1	0	0	4	0	8	.248	.248	.256	80	-4	-1	8				-3	PO/S1	0.0
1877	Chi-N	1	4	0	0	0	0	0	0	0	2	.000	.000	.000	-89	-1	-1	0				-0	/3	0.0
1878	Pro-N	1	3	0	0	0	0	0	0	0	0	.000	.000	.000	-99	-1	-1	0				0	/P	0.0
Total	5 n	215	1020	168	239	27	9	3	22	10	1	.234	.242	.287	61	-42	-51	73					P/O3S1	-1.0
Total	3	37	136	12	32	1	0	0	4	0	10	.235	.235	.243	68	-6	-3	8				-3	/PO31S	0.0

■ CARLTON FISK   Fisk, Carlton Ernest "Pudge"   b: 12/26/47, Bellows Falls, Vt.   BR/TR, 6'3", 200 lbs.   Deb: 9/18/69

1969	Bos-A	2	5	0	0	0	0	0	0	0	2	.000	.000	.000	-95	-1	-1	0	0	0	0	-1	/C	-0.2
1971	Bos-A	14	48	7	15	2	1	2	6	1	10	.313	.327	.521	128	2	2	8	0	0	0	-1	C	0.2
1972	Bos-A	131	457	74	134	28	9	22	61	52	83	.293	.370	.538	159	37	34	90	5	2	0	1	*C	4.1
1973	Bos-A	135	508	65	125	21	0	26	71	37	99	.246	.310	.441	103	4	1	69	7	2	1	5	*C/D	1.0
1974	Bos-A	52	187	36	56	12	1	11	26	24	23	.299	.385	.551	156	16	14	40	5	1	1	2	C/D	1.9
1975	*Bos-A	79	263	47	87	14	4	10	52	27	32	.331	.397	.529	147	20	18	54	4	3	-1	-5	C/D	1.4
1976	Bos-A	134	487	76	124	17	5	17	58	56	71	.255	.339	.415	107	12	4	70	12	5	1	9	*C/D	2.1
1977	Bos-A	152	536	106	169	26	3	26	102	75	85	.315	.408	.521	135	40	31	117	7	6	-2	-1	*C	3.2
1978	Bos-A	157	571	94	162	39	5	20	88	71	83	.284	.370	.475	123	28	20	103	7	2	1	11	*C/OD	3.7
1979	Bos-A	91	320	49	87	23	2	10	42	10	38	.272	.307	.450	96	-1	-3	42	3	0	1	-11	DC/O	-1.1
1980	Bos-A	131	478	73	138	25	3	18	62	36	62	.289	.355	.467	117	15	12	77	11	5	0	-9	*C/013D	0.8
1981	Chi-A	96	338	44	89	12	0	7	45	38	37	.263	.358	.361	110	5	6	45	3	2	-0	-3	*C/130	0.7
1982	Chi-A	135	476	66	127	17	3	14	65	46	60	.267	.339	.403	103	2	2	67	17	2	4	-3	*C/1	1.0
1983	*Chi-A	138	488	85	141	26	4	26	86	46	88	.289	.357	.518	133	24	22	90	9	6	-1	-1	*C/D	2.5
1984	Chi-A	102	359	54	83	20	1	21	43	26	60	.231	.292	.468	102	2	-0	49	6	0	2	-12	*C/D	-0.5
1985	Chi-A	153	543	85	129	23	1	37	107	52	81	.238	.324	.488	114	13	10	85	17	9	-0	-2	*CD	1.3
1986	Chi-A	125	457	42	101	11	0	14	63	22	92	.221	.266	.337	61	-24	-26	39	2	4	-2	-1	CO/D	-2.4
1987	Chi-A	135	454	68	116	22	1	23	71	39	72	.256	.325	.460	103	3	1	66	1	4	-2	1	*C/1OD	0.8
1988	Chi-A	76	253	37	70	8	1	19	50	37	40	.277	.380	.542	155	19	19	52	0	0	0	-6	C	1.6
1989	Chi-A	103	375	47	110	25	2	13	68	36	60	.293	.360	.475	137	16	17	61	1	0	0	-15	CD	0.6
1990	Chi-A	137	452	65	129	21	0	18	65	61	73	.285	.379	.451	134	20	21	79	7	2	1	5	*CD	3.1
Total	21	2278	8055	1220	2192	392	46	354	1231	792	1251	.272	.347	.464	118	251	203	1301	124	55	4	-36	*CD/013	25.8

■ WES FISLER   Fisler, Weston Dickson "Icicle"   b: 7/5/1841, Camden, N.J.   d: 12/25/22, Philadelphia, Pa.   5'6", 137 lbs.   Deb: 5/20/1871

1871	Ath-n	28	147	43	41	8	2	0	16	3	2	.279	.293	.361	88	-3	-2	18	6				*1/2	0.0
1872	Ath-n	47	243	50	84	14	3	0			4	.346	.356	.428	140	11	11	38					*2	0.3
1873	Ath-n	44	218	45	75	12	4	1			2	.344	.350	.450	124	9	5	35					*2/1	0.2
1874	Ath-n	37	179	26	59	12	1	0			0	.330	.330	.408	123	6	4	25					1/2	0.3
1875	Ath-n	58	267	55	74	14	3	0			4	.277	.288	.352	108	5	1	28					1/O2	0.3
1876	Phi-N	59	278	42	80	15	1	1	30	2	4	.288	.293	.360	117	4	5	30				-1	O21/S	0.3
Total	5 n	214	1054	219	333	60	13	1	16	13	2	.316	.324	.400	118	29	18	143					1/2OD	0.8

■ CHARLIE FITZBERGER   Fitzberger, Charles Casper   b: 2/13/04, Baltimore, Md.   d: 1/25/65, Baltimore, Md.   BL/TL, 6'1.5", 170 lbs.   Deb: 9/11/28

| 1928 | Bos-N | 7 | 7 | 0 | 2 | 0 | 0 | 0 | 0 | 0 | 3 | .286 | .286 | .286 | 52 | -1 | -0 | 1 | 0 | | | 0 | H | 0.0 |

■ DENNIS FITZGERALD   Fitzgerald, Dennis S.   b: 3/1865, England   d: 10/16/36, New Haven, Conn.   5'10", 160 lbs.   Deb: 4/17/1890

| 1890 | Phi-a | 2 | 8 | 0 | 2 | 0 | 0 | 0 | | 0 | | .250 | .250 | .250 | 51 | -1 | -0 | 1 | 0 | | | -2 | /S | -0.1 |

■ ED FITZGERALD   Fitzgerald, Edward Raymond   b: 5/21/24, Santa Ynez, Cal.   BR/TR, 6', 170 lbs.   Deb: 4/19/48   C

1948	Pit-N	102	262	31	70	9	3	1	35	32	37	.267	.349	.336	84	-4	-5	33	3			0	C	0.2
1949	Pit-N	75	160	16	42	7	0	2	18	8	27	.262	.302	.344	71	-6	-7	16	1			-4	C	-0.8
1950	Pit-N	6	15	1	1	1	0	0	0	0	3	.067	.067	.133	-47	-3	-3	0	0			0	/C	-0.2
1951	Pit-N	55	97	8	22	6	0	0	13	7	10	.227	.286	.289	53	-6	-6	7	1	1	-0	-2	C	-0.8
1952	Pit-N	51	73	4	17	1	0	1	7	7	15	.233	.300	.288	62	-3	-4	5	0	2	-1	-1	C/3	-0.5
1953	Pit-N	6	17	2	2	1	0	0	1	0	2	.118	.118	.176	-25	-3	-3	0	0	0	0	-1	/C	-0.3
	Was-A	88	288	23	72	13	0	3	39	19	34	.250	.299	.326	70	-13	-12	27	2	1	0	-2	C	-1.0
1954	Was-A	115	360	33	104	13	5	4	40	33	22	.289	.346	.386	108	1	3	48	0	1	-1	-17	*C	-0.9
1955	Was-A	74	236	28	56	3	1	4	19	25	23	.237	.318	.309	73	-10	-8	23	0	1	-1	-6	C	-1.1
1956	Was-A	64	148	15	45	8	0	2	12	20	16	.304	.387	.399	108	2	2	23	0	0	0	-6	C	0.5
1957	Was-A	45	125	14	34	8	0	1	13	10	9	.272	.331	.360	90	-2	-2	13	2	0	1	-8	C	-0.7
1958	Was-A	58	114	7	30	3	0	0	11	8	15	.263	.311	.289	68	-5	-5	9	0	0	0	-6	C/1	-1.0
1959	Was-A	19	62	5	12	3	0	0	5	4	8	.194	.242	.242	34	-6	-6	4	0	0	0	-1	C	-0.5
	Cle-A	49	129	12	35	6	1	0	4	12	14	.271	.343	.357	96	-1	-1	15	0	0	0	-0	C	0.2
	Yr	68	191	17	47	9	1	1	9	16	22	.246	.311	.319	76	-7	-6	19	0	0	0	-1		-0.3
Total	12	807	2086	199	542	82	10	19	217	185	235	.260	.324	.336	80	-60	-56	223	9	6		-45	C/13	-6.9

■ HOWIE FITZGERALD   Fitzgerald, Howard Chumney "Lefty"   b: 5/16/02, Eagle Lake, Tex.   d: 2/27/59, Matthews, Tex.   BL/TL, 5'11.5", 163 lbs.   Deb: 9/17/22

1922	Chi-N	10	24	3	8	1	0	0	4	3	2	.333	.407	.375	101	0	0	4	1	0	0	-2	/O	0.0
1924	Chi-N	7	19	1	3	0	0	0	2	0	2	.158	.158	.158	-15	-3	-3	0	0	0	0	-1	/O	-0.4
1926	Bos-A	31	97	11	25	2	0	0	8	5	7	.258	.294	.278	51	-7	-7	7	1	4	-2	-5	O	-1.4
Total	3	48	140	15	36	3	0	0	14	8	11	.257	.297	.279	52	-10	-10	12	2	4	-2	-7	/O	-1.8

■ MIKE FITZGERALD   Fitzgerald, Justin Howard   b: 6/22/1890, San Mateo, Cal.   d: 1/17/45, San Mateo, Cal.   BL/TR, 5'8", 160 lbs.   Deb: 6/20/11

1911	NY-A	16	37	6	10	1	0	0	6	4		.270	.341	.297	74	-1	-1	5	4			-1	/O	-0.2
1918	Phi-N	66	133	21	39	8	0	0	6	13	6	.293	.361	.353	110	3	2	18	3			-6	O	-0.7
Total	2	82	170	27	49	9	0	0	12	17	6	.288	.356	.341	102	2	1	23	7			-7	/O	-0.9

■ MATTY FITZGERALD   Fitzgerald, Matthew William   b: 8/31/1880, Albany, N.Y.   d: 9/22/49, Albany, N.Y.   TR, 6', 185 lbs.   Deb: 9/15/06

1906	NY-N	4	6	2	4	0	0	0	2	0		.667	.667	.667	313	1	1	3	1			-1	/C	0.1
1907	NY-N	7	15	1	2	1	0	0	1	0		.133	.133	.200	5	-2	-2	0	0			-1	/C	-0.2
Total	2	11	21	3	6	1	0	0	3	0		.286	.286	.333	93	-0	-0	4	1			-2	/C	-0.1

■ MIKE FITZGERALD   Fitzgerald, Michael Patrick   b: 3/28/64, Savannah, Ga.   BR/TR, 6'1", 196 lbs.   Deb: 6/23/88

| 1988 | StL-N | 13 | 46 | 4 | 9 | 1 | 0 | 0 | 1 | 0 | 9 | .196 | .213 | .217 | 23 | -5 | -5 | 2 | 0 | 0 | 0 | -1 | 1 | -0.6 |

■ MIKE FITZGERALD   Fitzgerald, Michael Roy   b: 7/13/60, Long Beach, Cal.   BR/TR, 6', 185 lbs.   Deb: 9/13/83

1983	NY-N	8	20	1	2	0	0	1	2	3	6	.100	.217	.250	29	-2	-2	1	0	0	0	2	/C	0.1
1984	NY-N	112	360	20	87	15	1	2	33	24	71	.242	.291	.306	69	-15	-15	29	1	0	0	7	*C	-0.3
1985	Mon-N	108	295	25	61	7	1	5	34	38	56	.207	.301	.288	70	-13	-11	26	5	3	-0	-6	*C	-1.2
1986	Mon-N	73	209	20	59	13	1	6	37	27	34	.282	.367	.440	123	6	7	34	3	2	-0	-7	C	0.1
1987	Mon-N	107	287	32	69	11	0	3	36	42	54	.240	.339	.310	71	-10	-11	30	3	4	-2	-1	*C/12	-0.5
1988	Mon-N	63	155	17	42	6	1	5	23	19	22	.271	.351	.419	115	4	3	23	2	2	-1	5	C/O	1.1

YEAR	TM/L	G	AB	R	H	2B	3B	HR	RBI	BB	SO	AVG	OBP	SLG	PRO+	BR	/A	RC	SB	CS	SBR	FR	POS	TPR
1989	Mon-N	100	290	33	69	18	2	7	42	35	61	.238	.324	.386	101	1	1	35	3	4	-2	-5	C/3O	0.0
1990	Mon-N	111	313	36	76	18	1	9	41	60	60	.243	.368	.393	110	6	6	51	8	1	2	-2	C/O	1.0
Total	8	682	1929	184	465	88	7	38	248	248	363	.241	.330	.353	90	-22	-22	229	25	16	-2	-7	C/O321	0.3

■ RAY FITZGERALD
Fitzgerald, Raymond Francis b: 12/5/04, Chicopee, Mass. d: 9/6/77, Westfield, Mass. BR/TR, 5'9", 168 lbs. Deb: 4/18/31

YEAR	TM/L	G	AB	R	H	2B	3B	HR	RBI	BB	SO	AVG	OBP	SLG	PRO+	BR	/A	RC	SB	CS	SBR	FR	POS	TPR
1931	Cin-N	1	1	0	0	0	0	0	0	0	0	.000	.000	.000	-99	-0	-0	0	0			0	H	0.0

■ SHAUN FITZMAURICE
Fitzmaurice, Shaun Earle b: 8/25/42, Worcester, Mass. BR/TR, 6', 180 lbs. Deb: 9/09/66

YEAR	TM/L	G	AB	R	H	2B	3B	HR	RBI	BB	SO	AVG	OBP	SLG	PRO+	BR	/A	RC	SB	CS	SBR	FR	POS	TPR
1966	NY-N	9	13	2	2	0	0	0	0	2	6	.154	.267	.154	21	-1	-1	1	1	0	0	1	/O	0.0

■ ED FITZPATRICK
Fitzpatrick, Edward Henry b: 12/9/1889, Lewiston, Pa. d: 10/23/65, Bethlehem, Pa. BR/TR, 5'8", 165 lbs. Deb: 4/17/15

YEAR	TM/L	G	AB	R	H	2B	3B	HR	RBI	BB	SO	AVG	OBP	SLG	PRO+	BR	/A	RC	SB	CS	SBR	FR	POS	TPR
1915	Bos-N	105	303	54	67	19	3	0	24	43	36	.221	.344	.304	101	1	3	36	13	8	-1	-4	2O	-0.2
1916	Bos-N	83	216	17	46	8	0	1	18	15	26	.213	.280	.264	70	-8	-7	19	5			-9	2O	-1.7
1917	Bos-N	63	178	20	45	8	4	0	17	12	22	.253	.318	.343	109	1	2	20	4			-13	2O3	-1.2
Total	3	251	697	91	158	35	7	1	59	70	84	.227	.319	.301	94	-6	-2	75	22	8		-26	2/O3	-3.1

■ TOM FITZSIMMONS
Fitzsimmons, Thomas William b: 4/6/1890, Oakland, Cal. d: 12/20/71, Oakland, Cal. BR/TR, 6'1", 190 lbs. Deb: 6/12/19

YEAR	TM/L	G	AB	R	H	2B	3B	HR	RBI	BB	SO	AVG	OBP	SLG	PRO+	BR	/A	RC	SB	CS	SBR	FR	POS	TPR
1919	Bro-N	4	4	1	0	0	0	0	0	1	2	.000	.200	.000	-36	-1	-1	0	0			-1	/3	-0.1

■ MAX FLACK
Flack, Max John b: 2/5/1890, Belleville, Ill. d: 7/31/75, Belleville, Ill. BL/TL, 5'7", 148 lbs. Deb: 4/16/14

YEAR	TM/L	G	AB	R	H	2B	3B	HR	RBI	BB	SO	AVG	OBP	SLG	PRO+	BR	/A	RC	SB	CS	SBR	FR	POS	TPR
1914	Chi-F	134	502	66	124	15	3	2	39	51	48	.247	.324	.301	85	-12	-8	64	37			-0	*O	-1.5
1915	Chi-F	141	523	88	164	20	14	3	45	40	21	.314	.365	.423	141	20	24	98	37			2	*O	2.0
1916	Chi-N	141	465	65	120	14	3	3	20	42	43	.258	.320	.320	87	-1	-7	53	24	19	-4	-5	*O	-2.3
1917	Chi-N	131	447	65	111	18	7	0	21	51	34	.248	.325	.320	91	0	-4	50	17			-3	*O	-1.1
1918	*Chi-N	123	478	74	123	17	10	4	41	56	19	.257	.343	.360	112	9	8	63	17			-2	*O	0.0
1919	Chi-N	116	469	71	138	20	4	6	35	34	13	.294	.346	.392	121	12	12	67	18			-2	*O	0.5
1920	Chi-N	135	520	85	157	30	6	4	49	52	15	.302	.373	.406	121	17	16	77	13	19	-8	-7	*O	-0.6
1921	Chi-N	133	572	80	172	31	4	6	37	32	15	.301	.342	.400	96	-4	-4	77	17	11	-2	-1	*O	-1.2
1922	Chi-N	17	54	7	12	1	0	0	6	2	4	.222	.250	.241	27	-6	-6	3	2	1	0	-2	O	-0.7
	StL-N	66	267	46	78	12	1	2	21	31	11	.292	.368	.367	95	-3	-1	37	3	5	-2	-8	O	-1.2
	Yr	83	321	53	90	13	1	2	27	33	15	.280	.349	.346	83	-9	-7	39	5	6	-2	-10		-1.9
1923	StL-N	128	505	82	147	16	9	3	28	41	16	.291	.348	.376	93	-6	-5	66	7	8	-3	-17	*O	-1.7
1924	StL-N	67	209	31	55	11	3	2	21	21	5	.263	.330	.373	90	-3	-3	25	3	5	-2	-1	O	-0.6
1925	StL-N	79	241	23	60	7	8	0	28	21	9	.249	.309	.344	65	-12	-13	26	5	3	-0	-3	O	-1.6
Total	12	1411	5252	783	1461	212	72	35	391	474	253	.278	.342	.366	101	12	10	706	200	71		-40	*O	-10.0

■ WALLY FLAGER
Flager, Walter Leonard b: 11/3/21, Chicago Heights, Ill. BL/TR, 5'11", 160 lbs. Deb: 4/17/45

YEAR	TM/L	G	AB	R	H	2B	3B	HR	RBI	BB	SO	AVG	OBP	SLG	PRO+	BR	/A	RC	SB	CS	SBR	FR	POS	TPR
1945	Cin-N	21	52	5	11	1	0	0	6	8	5	.212	.317	.231	55	-3	-3	4	0			-7	S	-0.7
	Phi-N	49	168	21	42	4	1	2	15	17	15	.250	.323	.321	82	-5	-4	18	1			1	S/2	0.2
	Yr	70	220	26	53	5	1	2	21	25	20	.241	.321	.300	75	-7	-7	23	1			-6		-0.5

■ IRA FLAGSTEAD
Flagstead, Ira James "Pete" b: 9/22/1893, Montague, Mich. d: 3/13/40, Olympia, Wash. BR/TR, 5'9", 165 lbs. Deb: 7/20/17

YEAR	TM/L	G	AB	R	H	2B	3B	HR	RBI	BB	SO	AVG	OBP	SLG	PRO+	BR	/A	RC	SB	CS	SBR	FR	POS	TPR
1917	Det-A	4	4	0	0	0	0	0	0	0	1	.000	.000	.000	-99	-1	-1	0	0			-1	/O	-0.1
1919	Det-A	97	287	43	95	22	3	5	41	35	39	.331	.416	.481	155	21	21	59	6			2	O	1.8
1920	Det-A	110	311	40	73	13	5	3	35	37	27	.235	.318	.338	76	-12	-11	35	3	4	-2	7	O	-1.1
1921	Det-A	85	259	40	79	16	2	0	31	21	21	.305	.371	.382	93	-2	-2	38	7	4	-0	-5	SO/23	0.0
1922	Det-A	44	91	21	28	5	3	3	8	14	16	.308	.411	.527	148	6	6	20	0	1	-1	-2	O	0.2
1923	Det-A	1	1	0	0	0	0	0	0	0	0	.000	.000	.000	-99	-0	-0	0	0	0	0	0	H	0.0
	Bos-A	109	382	55	119	23	4	8	53	37	26	.312	.380	.455	119	10	10	65	8	10	-4	20	*O	1.6
	Yr	110	383	55	119	23	4	8	53	37	26	.311	.379	.454	118	10	10	65	8	10	-4	20		1.6
1924	Bos-A	149	560	106	172	35	7	5	43	77	41	.307	.401	.421	112	13	13	97	10	13	-5	-1	*O	-0.3
1925	Bos-A	148	572	84	160	38	2	6	61	63	30	.280	.356	.385	88	-10	-10	81	5	6	-2	20	*O	-0.4
1926	Bos-A	98	415	65	124	31	7	3	31	36	22	.299	.363	.429	109	3	5	64	4	6	-2	9	O	0.4
1927	Bos-A	131	466	63	133	26	8	4	69	57	25	.285	.374	.401	103	2	3	71	12	2	2	11	*O	0.8
1928	Bos-A	140	510	84	148	41	4	1	39	60	23	.290	.366	.392	101	1	2	75	12	9	-2	5	*O	-0.1
1929	Bos-A	14	36	9	11	2	0	0	3	5	1	.306	.390	.361	97	-0	0	5	1	3	-2	-3	O	-0.4
	Was-A	18	39	5	7	1	0	0	9	5	4	.179	.256	.205	20	-5	-5	3	1	0	0	3	O	-0.1
	Yr	32	75	14	18	3	0	0	12	9	6	.240	.321	.280	57	-5	-5	7	2	3	-1	0		-0.5
	Pit-N	26	50	8	14	2	1	0	6	4	2	.280	.333	.360	70	-2	-2	6	1			0	/O	-0.2
1930	Pit-N	44	156	21	39	7	4	2	21	17	9	.250	.324	.385	70	-8	-8	20	1			-3	O	-1.2
Total	13	1218	4139	644	1202	262	50	40	450	467	288	.290	.370	.407	103	15	22	638	71	58		61	*O/S23	0.9

■ MARTIN FLAHERTY
Flaherty, Martin b: Worcester, Mass. BL/TL, Deb: 8/18/1881

YEAR	TM/L	G	AB	R	H	2B	3B	HR	RBI	BB	SO	AVG	OBP	SLG	PRO+	BR	/A	RC	SB	CS	SBR	FR	POS	TPR
1881	Wor-N	1	2	0	0	0	0	0	0	0	2	.000	.000	.000	-95	-0	-0	0				-0	/O	0.0

■ PAT FLAHERTY
Flaherty, Patrick Henry b: 1/31/1876, St.Louis, Mo d: 1/28/46, Chicago, Ill. 5'9", 166 lbs. Deb: 7/11/1894

YEAR	TM/L	G	AB	R	H	2B	3B	HR	RBI	BB	SO	AVG	OBP	SLG	PRO+	BR	/A	RC	SB	CS	SBR	FR	POS	TPR
1894	Lou-N	38	145	15	43	5	3	0	15	9	6	.297	.342	.372	79	-6	-4	20	2			-5	3	-0.7

■ PATSY FLAHERTY
Flaherty, Patrick Joseph b: 6/29/1876, Mansfield, Pa. d: 1/23/68, Alexandria, La. BL/TL, 5'8", 165 lbs. Deb: 9/08/1899

YEAR	TM/L	G	AB	R	H	2B	3B	HR	RBI	BB	SO	AVG	OBP	SLG	PRO+	BR	/A	RC	SB	CS	SBR	FR	POS	TPR
1899	Lou-N	7	24	3	5	1	1	0	6	3		.208	.296	.333	75	-1	-1	2	0			-1	/PO	0.0
1900	Pit-N	4	9	0	1	0	0	0	0	1		.111	.200	.111	-12	-1	-1	0	0			1	/P	0.0
1903	Chi-A	40	102	7	14	4	0	0	5	5		.137	.178	.176	8	-11	-11	4	4			3	P	0.0
1904	Chi-A	5	12	1	4	1	0	0	0	4		.333	.500	.417	203	2	2	3	0			1	/P	0.0
	Pit-N	36	104	9	22	3	4	2	19	8		.212	.268	.375	97	-0	-1	11	0			6	P/O	0.0
1905	Pit-N	30	76	7	15	4	2	0	4	3		.197	.228	.303	58	-4	-4	5	0			2	P/O	0.0
1907	Bos-N	41	115	9	22	3	2	2	11	2		.191	.205	.304	61	-6	-6	8	1			4	P/O	0.0
1908	Bos-N	32	86	8	12	0	2	0	5	6		.140	.196	.186	24	-7	-7	4	0			3	P	0.0
1910	Phi-N	2	2	0	1	0	0	0	0	0	0	.500	.500	.500	186	0	0	0	0			0	/PO	0.0
1911	Bos-N	38	94	9	27	3	2	2	20	8	11	.287	.343	.426	106	1	0	14	2			-4	O/P	-0.2
Total	9	235	624	53	123	19	13	6	70	40	11	.197	.245	.298	64	-27	-28	52	9			15	P/O	-0.2

■ AL FLAIR
Flair, Albert Dell "Broadway" b: 7/24/16, New Orleans, La. d: 7/25/88, New Orleans, La. BL/TL, 6'4", 195 lbs. Deb: 9/06/41

YEAR	TM/L	G	AB	R	H	2B	3B	HR	RBI	BB	SO	AVG	OBP	SLG	PRO+	BR	/A	RC	SB	CS	SBR	FR	POS	TPR
1941	Bos-A	10	30	3	6	2	1	0	2	1	1	.200	.226	.333	45	-2	-3	2	1	1	-0	0	/1	-0.2

■ CHARLIE FLANAGAN
Flanagan, Charles James b: 12/31/1891, Oakland, Cal. d: 1/8/30, San Francisco, Cal. BR/TR, 6', 175 lbs. Deb: 7/09/13

YEAR	TM/L	G	AB	R	H	2B	3B	HR	RBI	BB	SO	AVG	OBP	SLG	PRO+	BR	/A	RC	SB	CS	SBR	FR	POS	TPR
1913	StL-A	4	3	0	0	0	0	0	0	1	0	.000	.250	.000	-26	-0	-0	0	0			-0	/3O	0.0

■ ED FLANAGAN
Flanagan, Edward J. "Sleepy" b: 9/15/1861, Lowell, Mass. d: 11/10/26, Lowell, Mass. 6'1", 190 lbs. Deb: 4/16/1887

YEAR	TM/L	G	AB	R	H	2B	3B	HR	RBI	BB	SO	AVG	OBP	SLG	PRO+	BR	/A	RC	SB	CS	SBR	FR	POS	TPR
1887	Phi-a	19	80	12	20	5	0	1		3		.250	.286	.350	78	-2	-2	9	3			-1	1	-0.2
1889	Lou-a	23	88	11	22	7	3	0	8	7	11	.250	.305	.398	104	-0	0	11	1			-0	1	-0.1
Total	2	42	168	23	42	12	3	1	8	10	11	.250	.296	.375	91	-3	-2	20	4			-1	/1	-0.3

■ STEAMER FLANAGAN
Flanagan, James Paul b: 4/20/1881, Kingston, Pa. d: 4/21/47, Wilkes-Barre, Pa. 6'1", 185 lbs. Deb: 9/25/05

YEAR	TM/L	G	AB	R	H	2B	3B	HR	RBI	BB	SO	AVG	OBP	SLG	PRO+	BR	/A	RC	SB	CS	SBR	FR	POS	TPR
1905	Pit-N	7	25	7	7	1	1	0	3	1		.280	.308	.400	110	0	0	4	3			1	/O	0.1

YEAR	TM/L	G	AB	R	H	2B	3B	HR	RBI	BB	SO	AVG	OBP	SLG	PRO+	BR	/A	RC	SB	CS	SBR	FR	POS	TPR
JOHN FLANNERY									Flannery, John Michael		b: 1/25/57, Long Beach, Cal.		BR/TR, 6'3", 173 lbs.		Deb: 9/02/77								
1977	Chi-A	7	2	1	0	0	0	0	0	0	1	.000	.333	.000	0	-0	-0	0	0	0	0	1	/S3D	0.1
TIM FLANNERY									Flannery, Timothy Earl		b: 9/29/57, Tulsa, Okla.		BL/TR, 5'11", 175 lbs.		Deb: 9/03/79								
1979	SD-N	22	65	2	10	0	1	0	4	4	5	.154	.225	.185	14	-8	-7	3	0	0	0	2	2	-0.3
1980	SD-N	95	292	15	70	12	0	0	25	18	30	.240	.284	.281	62	-16	-14	23	2	2	-1	-4	23	-1.6
1981	SD-N	37	67	4	17	4	1	0	6	2	4	.254	.275	.343	80	-2	-2	6	1	0	0	-1	3/2	-0.2
1982	SD-N	122	379	40	100	11	7	0	30	30	32	.264	.321	.330	87	-9	-6	42	1	0	0	-24	*2/3S	-2.6
1983	SD-N	92	214	24	50	7	3	3	19	20	23	.234	.314	.336	83	-6	-5	23	2	2	-1	10	32/S	0.5
1984	*SD-N	86	128	24	35	3	3	2	10	12	17	.273	.350	.391	108	1	2	19	4	1	1	-5	23S	0.0
1985	SD-N	126	384	50	108	14	3	1	40	58	39	.281	.388	.341	107	6	7	55	2	5	-2	-19	*2/3	-1.3
1986	SD-N	134	368	48	103	11	2	3	28	54	61	.280	.379	.345	103	3	4	50	3	6	-3	-7	*23/S	-0.3
1987	SD-N	106	276	23	63	5	1	0	20	42	30	.228	.334	.254	61	-15	-13	25	2	4	-2	3	2/3S	-0.9
1988	SD-N	79	170	16	45	5	4	0	19	24	32	.265	.369	.341	107	2	3	23	3	2	-0	-4	3/2S	-0.1
1989	SD-N	73	130	9	30	5	0	0	8	13	20	.231	.301	.269	64	-6	-6	11	2	0	1	2	3/2	-0.3
Total	11	972	2473	255	631	77	25	9	209	277	293	.255	.338	.317	86	-48	-38	279	22	22	-7	-46	23/S	-7.1
ROY FLASKAMPER								Flaskamper, Raymond Harold "Flash"		b: 10/31/01, St.Louis, Mo.		d: 2/3/78, San Antonio, Tex.		BB/TR, 5'7", 140 lbs.		Deb: 8/16/27							
1927	Chi-A	26	95	12	21	5	0	0	6	3	8	.221	.260	.274	40	-9	-8	7	0	0	0	0	S	-0.5
FRANK FLEET								Fleet, Frank H.		b: 1848, New York, N.Y.		d: 6/13/1900, New York, N.Y.		Deb: 10/18/1871								
1871	Mut-n	1	6	1	2	0	0	0	1	0	0	.333	.333	.333	101	-0	0	1	0				/P	0.0
1872	Eck-n	13	54	10	13	2	0	0		0		.241	.241	.278	70	-3	-1	4					3/2O	
1873	Res-n	22	90	11	22	2	0	0		1		.244	.253	.267	57	-5	-4	6					/2SP31	-0.2
1874	Atl-n	22	95	18	22	1	0	0		2		.232	.247	.242	64	-4	-2	6					C/2O	-0.1
1875	StL-n	4	16	1	1	0	0	0		0		.063	.063	.063	-62	-2	-2	0					/P	0.0
	Atl-n	26	112	13	25	1	0	0		1		.223	.230	.232	69	-4	-2	6					2C/SP	-0.1
	Yr	30	128	14	26	1	0	0		1		.203	.209	.211	52	-7	-4	6						-0.1
Total	5 n	88	373	54	85	6	0	0		4		.228	.236	.244	60	-19	-11	23					/2CS3PO1	-0.4
ANGEL FLEITAS								Fleitas, Angel Felix Husta		b: 11/14/14, Los Abreus, Cuba		BR/TR, 5'9", 160 lbs.		Deb: 7/05/48								
1948	Was-A	15	13	1	1	0	0	0	1	3	5	.077	.250	.077	-11	-2	-2	0	0	2	-1	3	/S	0.0
LES FLEMING								Fleming, Leslie Harvey "Moe"		b: 8/7/15, Singleton, Tex.		d: 3/5/80, Cleveland, Tex.		BL/TL, 5'10", 185 lbs.		Deb: 4/22/39							
1939	Det-A	8	16	0	0	0	0	0	1	0	4	.000	.000	.000	-93	-5	-5	0	0	0	0	0	/O	-0.4
1941	Cle-A	2	8	0	2	1	0	0	2	0	0	.250	.250	.375	67	-0	-0	1	0	0	0	0	/1	0.0
1942	Cle-A	156	548	71	160	27	4	14	82	106	57	.292	.412	.432	146	32	36	105	6	8	-3	-9	*1	2.2
1945	Cle-A	42	140	18	46	10	2	3	22	11	5	.329	.382	.493	160	9	10	27	0	0	0	-3	O/1	0.5
1946	Cle-A	99	306	40	85	17	5	8	42	50	42	.278	.383	.444	140	14	16	55	1	0	0	3	1/O	1.5
1947	Cle-A	103	281	39	68	14	2	4	43	53	42	.242	.362	.349	101	1	2	40	0	0	0	4	1	0.4
1949	Pit-N	24	31	0	8	0	2	0	7	6	2	.258	.395	.387	108	1	1	5	0			-1	/1	0.0
Total	7	434	1330	168	369	69	15	29	199	226	152	.277	.386	.417	131	51	59	232	7	8		-7	1/O	4.2
TOM FLEMING								Fleming, Thomas Vincent "Sleuth"		b: 11/20/1873, Philadelphia, Pa.		d: 12/26/57, Boston, Mass.		BL/TL, 5'11", 155 lbs.		Deb: 9/19/1899						
1899	NY-N	22	77	9	16	1	1	0	4	1		.208	.218	.247	30	-7	-7	4	1			-1	O	-0.8
1902	Phi-N	5	16	2	6	0	0	0	2	1		.375	.412	.375	145	1	1	3	0			0	/O	0.1
1904	Phi-N	3	6	0	0	0	0	0	0	0		.000	.000	.000	-99	-1	-1	0	0			0	/O	0.0
Total	3	30	99	11	22	1	1	0	6	2		.222	.238	.253	41	-8	-8	7	1			-0	/O	-0.7
ART FLETCHER								Fletcher, Arthur		b: 1/5/1885, Collinsville, Ill.		d: 2/6/50, Los Angeles, Cal.		BR/TR, 5'10.5", 170 lbs.		Deb: 4/15/09		C				
1909	NY-N	33	98	7	21	0	1	0	6	1		.214	.238	.235	46	-6	-6	5	0			3	S/23	-0.2
1910	NY-N	51	125	12	28	2	1	0	13	4	9	.224	.248	.256	47	-9	-9	10	9			-5	S23	-1.2
1911	*NY-N	112	326	73	104	17	8	1	37	30	27	.319	.400	.429	128	15	13	64	20			4	S32	2.1
1912	*NY-N	129	419	64	118	17	9	1	57	16	29	.282	.330	.372	89	-6	-7	56	16			16	*S/23	2.0
1913	*NY-N	136	538	76	160	20	9	4	71	24	35	.297	.345	.390	109	6	6	80	32			-7	*S	0.8
1914	NY-N	135	514	62	147	26	8	2	79	22	37	.286	.332	.379	115	6	8	68	15			6	*S	1.9
1915	NY-N	149	562	59	143	17	7	3	74	6	36	.254	.280	.326	88	-13	-10	50	12	18	-7	34	*S	2.3
1916	NY-N	133	500	53	143	23	8	3	66	13	36	.286	.323	.382	122	8	11	68	15			20	*S	4.2
1917	*NY-N	151	557	70	145	24	5	4	56	23	28	.260	.312	.343	104	0	2	60	12			27	*S	3.5
1918	NY-N	124	468	51	123	20	2	0	47	18	26	.263	.311	.314	93	-5	-4	48	12			22	*S	2.3
1919	NY-N	127	488	54	135	20	5	3	54	9	28	.277	.300	.357	98	-3	-3	52	6			24	*S	2.8
1920	NY-N	41	171	21	44	7	2	0	24	1	15	.257	.282	.322	74	-6	-6	15	3	2	-0	-2	S	-0.6
	Phi-N	102	379	36	112	25	7	4	38	15	28	.296	.329	.430	112	7	5	52	4	6	-2	12	*S	2.1
	Yr	143	550	57	156	32	9	4	62	16	43	.284	.315	.396	100	1	-1	66	7	8	-3	10		1.5
1922	Phi-N	110	396	46	111	20	5	7	53	21	14	.280	.325	.409	80	-8	-13	53	3	2	-0	7	*S	0.0
Total	13	1533	5541	684	1534	238	77	32	675	203	348	.277	.319	.365	100	-14	-14	680	159	28		162	*S/32	22.0
DARRIN FLETCHER								Fletcher, Darrin Glen		b: 10/3/66, Elmhurst, Ill.		BL/TR, 6'2", 195 lbs.		Deb: 9/10/89							
1989	LA-N	5	8	1	4	0	0	1	2	1	0	.500	.556	.875	308	2	2	4	0	0	0	0	/C	0.3
1990	LA-N	2	1	0	0	0	0	0	0	0	1	.000	.000	.000	-99	-0	-0	0	0	0	0	0	/C	0.0
	Phi-N	9	22	3	3	1	0	0	1	1	5	.136	.174	.182	-2	-3	-3	1	0	0	0	1	/C	-0.1
	Yr	11	23	3	3	1	0	0	1	1	6	.130	.167	.174	-6	-3	-3	1	0	0	0	1		-0.1
Total	2	16	31	4	7	1	0	1	3	2	6	.226	.273	.355	74	-1	-1	5	0	0	0	1	/C	0.2
ELBIE FLETCHER								Fletcher, Elburt Preston		b: 3/18/16, Milton, Mass.		BL/TL, 6', 180 lbs.		Deb: 9/16/34							
1934	Bos-N	8	4	4	2	0	0	0	0	0	2	.500	.500	.500	182	0	0	1	1			0	/1	0.0
1935	Bos-N	39	148	12	35	7	1	0	9	7	13	.236	.271	.318	63	-9	-7	13	1			2	1	-0.5
1937	Bos-N	148	539	56	133	22	4	1	38	56	64	.247	.321	.308	79	-20	-14	56	3			1	*1	-2.0
1938	Bos-N	147	529	71	144	24	7	6	48	60	40	.272	.351	.378	112	1	8	73	5			10	*1	0.6
1939	Bos-N	35	106	14	26	2	0	0	6	19	5	.245	.365	.264	77	-3	-2	12	1			-5	1	-1.0
	Pit-N	102	370	49	112	23	4	12	71	48	28	.303	.386	.484	134	17	18	69	3			-4	*1	0.2
	Yr	137	476	63	138	25	4	12	77	67	33	.290	.383	.435	122	14	16	81	4			-9		-0.8
1940	Pit-N	147	510	94	139	22	7	16	104	119	54	.273	.418	.437	137	32	32	103	5			4	*1	2.4
1941	Pit-N	151	521	95	150	29	13	11	74	118	54	.288	.421	.457	148	38	38	111	5			9	*1	2.7
1942	Pit-N	145	506	86	146	22	5	7	57	105	60	.289	.417	.393	134	30	29	94	0			12	*1	3.0
1943	Pit-N	154	544	91	154	24	5	9	70	95	49	.283	.395	.395	124	24	22	91	1			4	*1	2.0
1946	Pit-N	148	532	72	136	25	8	4	66	111	37	.256	.384	.355	108	12	10	82	4			1	*1	0.0
1947	Pit-N	69	157	22	38	9	1	1	22	29	24	.242	.364	.331	83	-2	-3	20	2			-0	1	-0.5
1949	Bos-N	122	413	57	108	19	3	11	54	68	45	.262	.396	.402	121	12	15	72	1			0	*1	1.5
Total	12	1415	4879	723	1323	228	58	79	616	851	495	.271	.384	.390	118	133	148	796	32			34	*1	8.4
GEORGE FLETCHER								Fletcher, George H. E.		Deb: 6/21/1872												
1872	Eck-n	2	8	1	3	0	0	0		0	0	.375	.375	.375	155	0	1	1					/O	0.0

YEAR	TM/L	G	AB	R	H	2B	3B	HR	RBI	BB	SO	AVG	OBP	SLG	PRO+	BR	/A	RC	SB	CS	SBR	FR	POS	TPR

■ FRANK FLETCHER
Fletcher, Oliver Frank b: 3/6/1891, Hildreth, Ill. d: 10/7/74, St.Petersburg, Fla. BR/TR, 5'10", 165 lbs. Deb: 7/14/14

YEAR	TM/L	G	AB	R	H	2B	3B	HR	RBI	BB	SO	AVG	OBP	SLG	PRO+	BR	/A	RC	SB	CS	SBR	FR	POS	TPR
1914	Phi-N	1	1	0	0	0	0	0	0	0	1	.000	.000	.000	-94	-0	-0	0	0			0	H	0.0

■ SCOTT FLETCHER
Fletcher, Scott Brian b: 7/30/58, Fort Walton Beach Fla. BR/TR, 5'11", 168 lbs. Deb: 4/25/81

YEAR	TM/L	G	AB	R	H	2B	3B	HR	RBI	BB	SO	AVG	OBP	SLG	PRO+	BR	/A	RC	SB	CS	SBR	FR	POS	TPR
1981	Chi-N	19	46	6	10	4	0	0	1	2	4	.217	.250	.304	54	-3	-3	4	0	0	0	6	2/S3	0.4
1982	Chi-N	11	24	4	4	0	0	0	1	4	5	.167	.286	.167	29	-2	-2	2	1	0	0	-0	S	-0.1
1983	*Chi-A	114	262	42	62	16	5	3	31	29	22	.237	.317	.370	85	-4	-5	31	5	1	1	18	*S2/3D	2.0
1984	Chi-A	149	456	46	114	13	3	3	35	46	46	.250	.329	.311	75	-12	-15	51	10	4	1	-2	*S2/3	-0.3
1985	Chi-A	119	301	38	77	8	1	2	31	35	47	.256	.333	.309	74	-8	-10	31	5	5	-2	-3	3S2/D	-1.0
1986	Tex-A	147	530	82	159	34	5	3	50	47	59	.300	.361	.400	104	6	4	76	12	11	-3	-6	*S32/D	0.3
1987	Tex-A	156	588	82	169	28	4	5	63	61	66	.287	.359	.374	95	-3	-3	78	13	12	-3	5	*S	0.7
1988	Tex-A	140	515	59	142	19	4	0	47	62	34	.276	.367	.328	94	0	-1	66	8	5	-1	1	*S	0.6
1989	Tex-A	83	314	47	75	14	1	0	22	38	41	.239	.325	.290	73	-9	-10	31	1	0	0	-18	S	-2.1
	Chi-A	59	232	30	63	11	1	1	21	26	19	.272	.347	.341	97	-1	-0	29	1	1	-0	-3	2/SD	-0.1
	Yr	142	546	77	138	25	2	1	43	64	60	.253	.334	.311	83	-10	-10	60	2	1	-0	-21		-2.2
1990	Chi-A	151	509	54	123	18	3	4	56	45	63	.242	.307	.312	75	-17	-16	50	1	3	-2	-6	*2	-1.6
Total	10	1148	3777	490	998	165	27	21	358	395	406	.264	.340	.339	86	-53	-61	448	57	42	-8	-8	S2/3D	-1.2

■ ELMER FLICK
Flick, Elmer Harrison b: 1/11/1876, Bedford, Ohio d: 1/9/71, Bedford, Ohio BL/TR, 5'9", 168 lbs. Deb: 5/02/1898 H

YEAR	TM/L	G	AB	R	H	2B	3B	HR	RBI	BB	SO	AVG	OBP	SLG	PRO+	BR	/A	RC	SB	CS	SBR	FR	POS	TPR
1898	Phi-N	134	453	84	137	16	13	8	81	86		.302	.430	.448	162	37	40	100	23			7	*O	3.6
1899	Phi-N	127	485	98	166	22	11	2	98	42		.342	.407	.445	142	25	28	103	31			9	*O	2.6
1900	Phi-N	138	545	106	200	32	16	11	110	56		.367	.439	.545	175	55	56	149	35			3	*O	4.2
1901	Phi-N	138	540	112	180	32	17	8	88	52		.333	.398	.500	159	42	41	124	30			15	*O	4.0
1902	Phi-A	11	37	15	11	2	1	0	3	6		.297	.435	.405	131	2	2	9	4			-0	O	0.1
	Cle-A	110	424	70	126	20	11	2	61	47		.297	.371	.410	123	12	14	75	20			-4	*O	0.3
	Yr	121	461	85	137	22	12	2	64	53		.297	.377	.410	124	14	16	84	24			-4		0.4
1903	Cle-A	140	523	81	155	23	16	2	51	51		.296	.359	.413	136	22	23	90	24			1	*O	1.5
1904	Cle-A	150	579	97	177	31	17	6	56	51		.306	.362	.449	159	37	38	112	38			10	*O/2	4.3
1905	Cle-A	132	500	72	154	29	18	4	64	53		.308	.374	.462	165	38	37	103	35			0	*O/2	3.3
1906	Cle-A	157	624	98	194	33	22	1	62	54		.311	.366	.439	156	38	38	119	39			-11	*O/2	2.3
1907	Cle-A	147	549	78	166	15	18	3	58	64		.302	.375	.412	152	34	33	104	41			1	*O	2.8
1908	Cle-A	9	35	4	8	1	1	0	2	3		.229	.289	.314	98	-0	-0	3	0			-0	/O	0.0
1909	Cle-A	66	235	28	60	10	2	0	15	22		.255	.322	.315	97	1	-0	26	9			-2	O	-0.5
1910	Cle-A	24	68	5	18	2	1	1	7	10		.265	.359	.368	126	2	2	9	1			-3	O	-0.1
Total	13	1483	5597	948	1752	268	164	48	756	597		.313	.385	.445	150	345	352	1125	330			25	*O/2	28.4

■ LEW FLICK
Flick, Lewis Miller "Noisy" b: 2/18/15, Bristol, Tenn. BL/TL, 5'9", 155 lbs. Deb: 9/28/43

YEAR	TM/L	G	AB	R	H	2B	3B	HR	RBI	BB	SO	AVG	OBP	SLG	PRO+	BR	/A	RC	SB	CS	SBR	FR	POS	TPR
1943	Phi-A	1	5	2	3	0	0	0	0	0	0	.600	.600	.600	253	1	1	2	0	0	0	0	/O	0.1
1944	Phi-A	19	35	1	4	0	0	0	2	1	2	.114	.139	.114	-28	-6	-6	0	1	0	0	-1	/O	-0.6
Total	2	20	40	3	7	0	0	0	2	1	2	.175	.195	.175	6	-5	-5	2	1	0	0	-1	/O	-0.5

■ DON FLINN
Flinn, Don Raphael b: 11/17/1892, Bluffdale, Tex. d: 3/9/59, Waco, Tex. BR/TR, 6'1", 185 lbs. Deb: 9/02/17

YEAR	TM/L	G	AB	R	H	2B	3B	HR	RBI	BB	SO	AVG	OBP	SLG	PRO+	BR	/A	RC	SB	CS	SBR	FR	POS	TPR
1917	Pit-N	14	37	1	11	1	1	0	1	1	6	.297	.316	.378	109	0	0	4	1			1	O	0.1

■ SILVER FLINT
Flint, Frank Sylvester b: 8/3/1855, Philadelphia, Pa. d: 1/14/1892, Chicago, Ill. BR/TR, 6', 180 lbs. Deb: 5/04/1875 M

YEAR	TM/L	G	AB	R	H	2B	3B	HR	RBI	BB	SO	AVG	OBP	SLG	PRO+	BR	/A	RC	SB	CS	SBR	FR	POS	TPR
1875	RS-n	17	61	4	5	0	0	0			1	.082	.097	.082	-42	-8	-7	0					C/3	-0.5
1878	Ind-N	63	254	23	57	7	0	0	18	2	15	.224	.230	.252	67	-11	-6	15				-3	*C/O	-0.7
1879	Chi-N	79	324	46	92	22	6	1	41	6	44	.284	.297	.398	119	9	6	39				-4	*C/OM	0.1
1880	Chi-N	74	284	30	46	10	4	0	17	5	32	.162	.176	.225	33	-18	-21	12				11	*CO	-0.4
1881	Chi-N	80	306	46	95	18	0	1	34	6	39	.310	.324	.379	115	7	5	38				-10	*C/O1	-0.6
1882	Chi-N	81	331	48	83	18	8	4	44	2	50	.251	.255	.390	99	1	-1	34				-7	*CO	-0.1
1883	Chi-N	85	332	57	88	23	4	0	32	3	69	.265	.272	.358	84	-4	-7	33				-10	*CO	-1.1
1884	Chi-N	73	279	35	57	5	2	9	45	7	57	.204	.224	.333	67	-9	-13	21				0	C	-0.5
1885	*Chi-N	68	249	27	52	8	2	1	17	2	52	.209	.215	.269	49	-12	-17	15				11	C/O	0.0
1886	*Chi-N	54	173	30	35	6	2	1	13	12	36	.202	.254	.277	53	-8	-12	13	1			15	C/1	0.6
1887	Chi-N	49	187	22	50	8	6	3	21	4	28	.267	.283	.422	84	-2	-6	25	7			2	C/1	0.1
1888	Chi-N	22	77	6	14	3	0	0	3	1	21	.182	.203	.221	34	-5	-6	4	1			-2	C	-0.6
1889	Chi-N	15	56	6	13	1	0	1	9	3	18	.232	.271	.304	59	-3	-3	5	1			1	C	-0.1
Total	12	743	2852	376	682	129	34	21	294	53	461	.239	.253	.330	78	-57	-82	254	10			4	C/O1	-3.3

■ CURT FLOOD
Flood, Curtis Charles b: 1/18/38, Houston, Tex. BR/TR, 5'9", 165 lbs. Deb: 9/09/56

YEAR	TM/L	G	AB	R	H	2B	3B	HR	RBI	BB	SO	AVG	OBP	SLG	PRO+	BR	/A	RC	SB	CS	SBR	FR	POS	TPR
1956	Cin-N	5	1	0	0	0	0	0	0	0	1	.000	.000	.000	-94	-0	-0	0	0	0	0	0	H	0.0
1957	Cin-N	3	3	2	1	0	0	1	1	0	0	.333	.333	1.333	299	1	1	1	0	0	0	-1	/32	0.0
1958	StL-N	121	422	50	110	17	2	10	41	31	56	.261	.317	.382	81	-10	-12	44	2	12	-7	14	*O/3	-0.8
1959	StL-N	121	208	24	53	7	3	7	26	16	35	.255	.308	.418	86	-3	-5	26	2	1	0	5	*O/3	0.0
1960	StL-N	140	396	37	94	20	1	8	38	35	54	.237	.306	.354	73	-11	-15	41	0	3	-2	-5	*O/3	-2.7
1961	StL-N	132	335	53	108	15	5	2	21	35	33	.322	.391	.411	104	8	4	56	6	2	1	-3	*O	-0.4
1962	StL-N	151	635	99	188	30	5	12	70	42	57	.296	.349	.416	95	4	-4	92	8	6	-1	9	*O	-0.4
1963	StL-N	158	662	112	200	34	9	5	63	42	57	.302	.346	.403	105	12	6	92	17	12	-2	14	*O	1.0
1964	*StL-N	162	679	97	211	25	3	5	46	43	53	.311	.356	.378	98	7	0	90	8	11	-4	7	*O	0.0
1965	StL-N	156	617	90	191	30	3	11	83	51	50	.310	.368	.421	111	18	12	97	9	3	1	5	*O	1.3
1966	StL-N	160	626	64	167	21	5	10	78	26	50	.267	.300	.364	83	-14	-15	67	14	7	0	3	*O	-1.6
1967	*StL-N	134	514	68	172	24	1	5	50	37	46	.335	.382	.414	129	19	20	82	2	2	-1	8	*O	2.2
1968	*StL-N	150	618	71	186	17	4	5	60	33	58	.301	.345	.366	114	9	10	78	11	6	-0	14	*O	1.9
1969	StL-N	153	606	80	173	31	3	4	57	48	57	.285	.345	.366	99	9	-0	76	9	7	-2	11	*O	0.1
1971	Was-A	13	35	4	7	0	0	0	2	5	2	.200	.300	.200	47	-2	-2	2	0	1	-1	-1	O	-0.4
Total	15	1759	6357	851	1861	271	44	85	636	444	609	.293	.344	.389	99	38	-2	844	88	73	-17	79	*O/32	0.2

■ TIM FLOOD
Flood, Timothy A. b: 3/13/1877, Montgomery City, Mo. d: 6/15/29, St.Louis, Mo. BR/TR, Deb: 9/24/1899

YEAR	TM/L	G	AB	R	H	2B	3B	HR	RBI	BB	SO	AVG	OBP	SLG	PRO+	BR	/A	RC	SB	CS	SBR	FR	POS	TPR
1899	StL-N	10	31	0	9	0	0	0	3	4		.290	.371	.290	83	-0	-0	4	1			-1	2	0.0
1902	Bro-N	132	476	43	104	11	4	3	51	23		.218	.262	.277	68	-18	-18	40	8			-16	*2/O	-2.6
1903	Bro-N	89	309	27	77	15	2	0	32	15		.249	.284	.311	73	-12	-11	33	14			-9	2/SO	-1.3
Total	3	231	816	70	190	26	6	3	86	42		.233	.275	.290	70	-30	-29	77	23			-26	2/SO	-3.9

■ PAUL FLORENCE
Florence, Paul Robert "Pep" b: 4/22/1900, Chicago, Ill. d: 5/28/86, Gainesville, Fla. BB/TR, 6'1", 185 lbs. Deb: 5/22/26

YEAR	TM/L	G	AB	R	H	2B	3B	HR	RBI	BB	SO	AVG	OBP	SLG	PRO+	BR	/A	RC	SB	CS	SBR	FR	POS	TPR
1926	NY-N	76	188	19	43	4	3	2	14	23	12	.229	.322	.314	73	-7	-7	20	2			-8	C	-1.1

■ GIL FLORES
Flores, Gilberto (Garcia) b: 10/27/52, Ponce, P.R. BR/TR, 6', 185 lbs. Deb: 5/08/77

YEAR	TM/L	G	AB	R	H	2B	3B	HR	RBI	BB	SO	AVG	OBP	SLG	PRO+	BR	/A	RC	SB	CS	SBR	FR	POS	TPR
1977	Cal-A	104	342	41	95	19	4	1	26	23	39	.278	.325	.365	92	-6	-4	36	12	10	-2	-7	O/D	-1.5
1978	NY-N	11	29	8	8	0	1	0	1	3	5	.276	.344	.345	96	-0	-0	4	1	0	0	0	O	0.0
1979	NY-N	70	93	9	18	1	1	1	10	8	17	.194	.265	.258	45	-7	-7	7	2	0	1	0	O	-0.6
Total	3	185	464	58	121	20	6	2	37	34	61	.261	.314	.343	82	-13	-11	47	15	10	-2	-6	O/D	-2.1

■ DICKIE FLOWERS
Flowers, Charles Richard b: 1850, Philadelphia, Pa. d: 10/5/1892, Philadelphia, Pa. Deb: 6/03/1871

YEAR	TM/L	G	AB	R	H	2B	3B	HR	RBI	BB	SO	AVG	OBP	SLG	PRO+	BR	/A	RC	SB	CS	SBR	FR	POS	TPR
1871	Tro-n	21	105	39	33	5	4	0	18	4	0	.314	.339	.438	120	3	2	19	8				*S/P2	0.2

YEAR	TM/L	G	AB	R	H	2B	3B	HR	RBI	BB	SO	AVG	OBP	SLG	PRO+	BR	/A	RC	SB	CS	SBR	FR	POS	TPR
1872	Ath-n	3	15	1	4	0	0	0		2		.267	.353	.267	93	0	0	1					/S	0.0
Total	2 n	24	120	40	37	5	4	0		6		.308	.341	.417	117	3	2	20					/S2P	0.2

■ JAKE FLOWERS
Flowers, D'Arcy Raymond   b: 3/16/02, Cambridge, Md.   d: 12/27/62, Clearwater, Fla.   BR/TR, 5'11.5", 170 lbs.   Deb: 9/07/23   C

YEAR	TM/L	G	AB	R	H	2B	3B	HR	RBI	BB	SO	AVG	OBP	SLG	PRO+	BR	/A	RC	SB	CS	SBR	FR	POS	TPR
1923	StL-N	13	32	0	3	1	0	0	2	2	7	.094	.147	.125	-28	-6	-6	0	1	2	-1	-1	/S23	-0.6
1926	*StL-N	40	74	13	20	1	0	3	9	5	9	.270	.325	.405	92	-1	-1	10	1			1	2/1S	0.1
1927	Bro-N	67	231	26	54	5	5	2	20	21	25	.234	.300	.325	67	-11	-11	23	3			-8	S/2	-1.2
1928	Bro-N	103	339	51	93	11	6	2	44	47	30	.274	.366	.360	92	-3	-3	47	10			-6	2/S	-0.6
1929	Bro-N	46	130	16	26	6	0	1	16	22	6	.200	.316	.269	48	-11	-10	12	9			-5	2	-1.2
1930	Bro-N	89	253	37	81	18	3	2	50	21	18	.320	.372	.439	96	-2	-1	40	5			-7	2/O	0.0
1931	Bro-N	22	31	3	7	0	0	0	1	7	4	.226	.368	.226	64	-1	-1	3	1			1	/2S	-0.1
	*StL-N	45	137	19	34	11	1	2	19	9	6	.248	.295	.387	79	-4	-5	16	7			3	S2/3	0.1
	Yr	67	168	22	41	11	1	2	20	16	10	.244	.310	.357	77	-5	-6	19	8			4		0.2
1932	StL-N	67	247	35	63	11	1	2	18	31	18	.255	.341	.332	79	-5	-6	30	7			0	3/S2	0.0
1933	Bro-N	78	210	28	49	11	2	2	22	24	15	.233	.312	.333	88	-4	-3	23	13			-11	S2/3O	-1.0
1934	Cin-N	13	9	1	3	0	0	0	0	1	1	.333	.455	.333	117	0	0	2	1			0	H	0.0
Total	10	583	1693	229	433	75	18	16	201	190	139	.256	.333	.350	80	-47	-46	206	58	2		-32	2S/310	-4.3

■ BUBBA FLOYD
Floyd, Leslie Roe   b: 6/23/17, Dallas, Tex.   BR/TR, 5'11", 160 lbs.   Deb: 6/16/44

YEAR	TM/L	G	AB	R	H	2B	3B	HR	RBI	BB	SO	AVG	OBP	SLG	PRO+	BR	/A	RC	SB	CS	SBR	FR	POS	TPR
1944	Det-A	3	9	1	4	1	0	0	1	0		.444	.500	.556	191	1	1	3	0	0	0	-1	/S	0.0

■ BOBBY FLOYD
Floyd, Robert Nathan   b: 10/20/43, Hawthorne, Cal.   BR/TR, 6'1", 180 lbs.   Deb: 9/18/68

YEAR	TM/L	G	AB	R	H	2B	3B	HR	RBI	BB	SO	AVG	OBP	SLG	PRO+	BR	/A	RC	SB	CS	SBR	FR	POS	TPR
1968	Bal-A	5	9	0	1	1	0	0	1	0	3	.111	.111	.222	-1	-1	-1	0	0	0	0	2	/S	0.1
1969	Bal-A	39	84	7	17	4	0	0	1	6	17	.202	.256	.250	41	-7	-7	5	0	0	0	11	2S/3	0.6
1970	Bal-A	3	2	0	0	0	0	0	0	0	2	.000	.000	.000	-99	-1	-1	0	0	0	0	1	/S2	0.0
	KC-A	14	43	5	14	4	0	0	9	4	9	.326	.383	.419	121	1	1	7	0	1	-1	1	/S3	0.3
	Yr	17	45	5	14	4	0	0	9	4	11	.311	.367	.400	111	1	1	7	0	1	-1	1		0.3
1971	KC-A	31	66	8	10	3	0	0	2	7	21	.152	.233	.197	23	-7	-7	3	0	0	0	5	S/23	0.0
1972	KC-A	61	134	9	24	3	0	0	5	5	29	.179	.209	.201	23	-13	-13	5	1	0	0	-2	3S/2	-1.1
1973	KC-A	51	78	10	26	3	1	0	8	4	14	.333	.366	.397	107	1	1	10	1	1	-0	9	2S	1.4
1974	KC-A	10	9	1	1	0	0	0	0	2	4	.111	.273	.111	13	-1	-1	0	0	0	0	2	/23S	0.1
Total	7	214	425	40	93	18	1	0	26	28	99	.219	.267	.266	52	-26	-27	32	2	2	-1	27	/S23	1.4

■ JOHN FLUHRER
Fluhrer, John L. (a.k.a. Wm. G. Morris 1 Game In 1915)   b: 1/3/1894, Adrian, Mich.   d: 7/17/46, Columbus, Ohio   BR/TR, 5'9", 165 lbs.   Deb: 9/05/15

YEAR	TM/L	G	AB	R	H	2B	3B	HR	RBI	BB	SO	AVG	OBP	SLG	PRO+	BR	/A	RC	SB	CS	SBR	FR	POS	TPR
1915	Chi-N	6	6	0	2	0	0	0	0	1	0	.333	.429	.333	132	0	0	1	1			-0	/O	0.0

■ ED FLYNN
Flynn, Edward J.   b: 1864, Chicago, Ill.   BL, 5'9", 165 lbs.   Deb: 5/05/1887

YEAR	TM/L	G	AB	R	H	2B	3B	HR	RBI	BB	SO	AVG	OBP	SLG	PRO+	BR	/A	RC	SB	CS	SBR	FR	POS	TPR
1887	Cle-a	7	27	0	5	1	0	0		1		.185	.214	.222	24	-3	-3	2	3			-0	/3O	-0.2

■ GEORGE FLYNN
Flynn, George A. "Dibby"   b: 5/24/1871, Chicago, Ill.   d: 12/28/01, Chicago, Ill.   Deb: 4/17/1896

YEAR	TM/L	G	AB	R	H	2B	3B	HR	RBI	BB	SO	AVG	OBP	SLG	PRO+	BR	/A	RC	SB	CS	SBR	FR	POS	TPR
1896	Chi-N	29	106	15	27	1	2	0	4	11	9	.255	.336	.302	68	-4	-5	15	12			2	O	-0.3

■ JOCKO FLYNN
Flynn, John A.   b: 6/30/1864, Lawrence, Mass.   d: 12/30/07, Lawrence, Mass.   5'6.5", 143 lbs.   Deb: 5/01/1886

YEAR	TM/L	G	AB	R	H	2B	3B	HR	RBI	BB	SO	AVG	OBP	SLG	PRO+	BR	/A	RC	SB	CS	SBR	FR	POS	TPR
1886	Chi-N	57	205	40	41	6	2	4	19	18	45	.200	.265	.307	64	-6	-11	20	9			-5	PO	0.0
1887	Chi-N	1	0	0	0	0	0	0	0	0	0	—	—	—	—	0	0	0	0			-0	/O	0.0
Total	2	58	205	40	41	6	2	4	19	18	45	.200	.265	.307	64	-6	-11	20	9			-6	/PO	0.0

■ JOHN FLYNN
Flynn, John Anthony   b: 9/7/1883, Providence, R.I.   d: 3/23/35, Providence, R.I.   BR/TR, 6'0.5", 175 lbs.   Deb: 4/22/10

YEAR	TM/L	G	AB	R	H	2B	3B	HR	RBI	BB	SO	AVG	OBP	SLG	PRO+	BR	/A	RC	SB	CS	SBR	FR	POS	TPR
1910	Pit-N	96	332	32	91	10	2	6	52	30	47	.274	.336	.370	100	2	-1	44	6			-3	1	-0.4
1911	Pit-N	33	59	5	12	0	1	0	3	9	8	.203	.309	.237	52	-3	-4	4	0			1	1/O	-0.3
1912	Was-A	20	71	9	12	4	1	0	5	7		.169	.253	.254	45	-5	-5	5	2			1	1	-0.3
Total	3	149	462	46	115	14	4	6	60	46	55	.249	.320	.335	85	-7	-10	53	8			-1	1/O	-1.0

■ JOE FLYNN
Flynn, Joseph   b: Philadelphia, Pa.   Deb: 4/18/1884

YEAR	TM/L	G	AB	R	H	2B	3B	HR	RBI	BB	SO	AVG	OBP	SLG	PRO+	BR	/A	RC	SB	CS	SBR	FR	POS	TPR
1884	Phi-U	52	209	38	52	9	4	4		11		.249	.286	.388	136	6	8	24	0			-14	OC/1S	-0.4
	Bos-U	9	31	4	7	2	0	0		2		.226	.273	.290	92	-0	-0	3	0			5	/CO1	0.4
	Yr	61	240	42	59	11	4	4		13		.246	.285	.375	130	5	8	26	0			-9		0.0

■ MIKE FLYNN
Flynn, Michael E.   b: Lowell, Mass.   Deb: 8/31/1891

YEAR	TM/L	G	AB	R	H	2B	3B	HR	RBI	BB	SO	AVG	OBP	SLG	PRO+	BR	/A	RC	SB	CS	SBR	FR	POS	TPR
1891	Bos-a	1	2	0	0	0	0	0	0	0	1	.000	.000	.000	-99	-1	-0	0	0			1	/C	0.0

■ DOUG FLYNN
Flynn, Robert Douglas   b: 4/18/51, Lexington, Ky.   BR/TR, 5'11", 165 lbs.   Deb: 4/09/75

YEAR	TM/L	G	AB	R	H	2B	3B	HR	RBI	BB	SO	AVG	OBP	SLG	PRO+	BR	/A	RC	SB	CS	SBR	FR	POS	TPR
1975	Cin-N	89	127	17	34	7	0	1	20	11	13	.268	.326	.346	85	-2	-3	14	3	0	1	10	32S	1.2
1976	*Cin-N	93	219	20	62	5	2	1	20	10	24	.283	.314	.338	83	-4	-5	24	2	0	1	-3	23S	-0.3
1977	Cin-N	36	32	0	8	1	1	0	5	0	6	.250	.250	.344	56	-2	-2	3	0	0	0	7	3/2S	0.5
	NY-N	90	282	14	54	6	1	0	14	11	23	.191	.222	.220	20	-32	-31	13	1	3	-2	-13	S2/3	-3.4
	Yr	126	314	14	62	7	2	0	19	11	29	.197	.225	.232	24	-34	-33	16	1	3	-2	-6		-2.9
1978	NY-N	156	532	37	126	12	8	0	36	30	50	.237	.279	.289	61	-29	-27	40	3	5	-2	2	*2S	-1.4
1979	NY-N	157	555	35	135	19	5	4	61	17	46	.243	.266	.317	61	-33	-30	42	0	3	-2	1	*2S	-1.9
1980	NY-N	128	443	46	113	9	8	0	24	22	20	.255	.290	.312	70	-19	-18	36	2	2	-1	3	*2/S	-0.7
1981	NY-N	105	325	24	72	12	4	1	20	11	19	.222	.247	.292	53	-21	-20	20	1	2	-1	12	*2/S	-0.1
1982	Tex-A	88	270	13	57	6	2	0	19	4	14	.211	.223	.248	31	-26	-24	15	6	2	1	3	2S	-1.4
	Mon-N	58	193	13	47	6	2	0	20	4	23	.244	.259	.295	54	-12	-12	13	0	2	-1	5	2	-0.5
1983	Mon-N	143	452	44	107	18	4	0	26	19	38	.237	.268	.294	56	-28	-27	33	2	1	0	7	*2S	-1.3
1984	Mon-N	124	366	23	89	12	1	0	17	12	41	.243	.267	.281	57	-22	-21	27	0	0	0	-8	2S	-2.3
1985	Mon-N	9	6	0	1	0	0	0	0	0	0	.167	.167	.167	-7	-1	-1	0	0	0	0	-1	/2S	0.0
	Det-A	32	51	2	13	2	1	0	2	3	3	.255	.255	.333	60	-3	-3	4	0	0	0	8	2/3S	0.6
Total	11	1308	3853	288	918	115	39	7	284	151	320	.238	.267	.294	57	-234	-224	285	20	20	-6	32	2S/3	-11.0

■ CLIPPER FLYNN
Flynn, William   b: 4/29/1849, Lansingburgh, N.Y.   d: 11/11/1881, Lansingburgh, N.Y.   5'7", 140 lbs.   Deb: 5/09/1871

YEAR	TM/L	G	AB	R	H	2B	3B	HR	RBI	BB	SO	AVG	OBP	SLG	PRO+	BR	/A	RC	SB	CS	SBR	FR	POS	TPR
1871	Tro-n	29	142	43	48	6	1	0	27	4	2	.338	.356	.394	114	3	2	22	3				1/O3	0.2
1872	Oly-n	9	40	4	9	1	0	0		0		.225	.225	.250	48	-2	-2	2					/1	0.0
Total	2 n	38	182	47	57	7	1	0		4		.313	.328	.363	101	0	0	24					/1O3	0.2

■ JIM FOGARTY
Fogarty, James G.   b: 2/12/1864, San Francisco, Cal   d: 5/20/1891, Philadelphia, Pa.   BR, 5'10.5", 180 lbs.   Deb: 5/01/1884   M

YEAR	TM/L	G	AB	R	H	2B	3B	HR	RBI	BB	SO	AVG	OBP	SLG	PRO+	BR	/A	RC	SB	CS	SBR	FR	POS	TPR
1884	Phi-N	97	378	42	80	12	6	1	37	20	54	.212	.251	.283	71	-14	-11	28				1	*O3/2SP	-0.9
1885	Phi-N	111	427	49	99	13	3	0	39	30	37	.232	.282	.276	83	-8	-7	34				22	*O2/S3	1.3
1886	Phi-N	77	280	54	82	13	5	3	47	42	16	.293	.385	.407	140	15	15	57	30			-4	O2/S3P	1.1
1887	Phi-N	126	495	113	129	26	12	8	50	82	44	.261	.376	.410	114	17	11	118	102			29	*O/S32P	3.5
1888	Phi-N	121	454	72	107	14	6	1	35	53	66	.236	.325	.300	97	4	0	65	58			13	*O/3S	1.2
1889	Phi-N	128	499	107	129	15	17	3	54	65	60	.259	.352	.375	96	4	-3	103	99			18	*O/P	0.9
1890	Phi-P	91	347	71	83	17	6	4	58	59	50	.239	.364	.357	93	-1	-2	60	36			8	O/3M	0.2
Total	7	751	2880	508	709	110	55	20	320	351	327	.246	.335	.343	99	18	3	464	325			87	O/32SP	7.3

■ JOE FOGARTY   Fogarty, Joseph J.   b: San Francisco, Cal.   Deb: 9/18/1885

YEAR	TM/L	G	AB	R	H	2B	3B	HR	RBI	BB	SO	AVG	OBP	SLG	PRO+	BR	/A	RC	SB	CS	SBR	FR	POS	TPR
1885	StL-N	2	8	1	1	0	0	0	0	0	1	.125	.125	.125	-20	-1	-1	0				-0	/O	0.0

■ LEE FOHL   Fohl, Leo Alexander   b: 11/28/1876, Lowell, Ohio   d: 10/30/65, Cleveland, Ohio   BL/TR, 5'10", 175 lbs.   Deb: 8/29/02   M

YEAR	TM/L	G	AB	R	H	2B	3B	HR	RBI	BB	SO	AVG	OBP	SLG	PRO+	BR	/A	RC	SB	CS	SBR	FR	POS	TPR
1902	Pit-N	1	3	0	0	0	0	0	1	0		.000	.000	.000	-97	-1	-1	0	0			0	/C	0.0
1903	Cin-N	4	14	3	5	1	1	0	2	0		.357	.357	.571	149	1	1	3	0			0	/C	0.1
Total	2	5	17	3	5	1	1	0	3	0		.294	.294	.471	111	0	0	3	0			1	/C	0.1

■ HANK FOILES   Foiles, Henry Lee   b: 6/10/29, Richmond, Va.   BR/TR, 6', 195 lbs.   Deb: 4/21/53

YEAR	TM/L	G	AB	R	H	2B	3B	HR	RBI	BB	SO	AVG	OBP	SLG	PRO+	BR	/A	RC	SB	CS	SBR	FR	POS	TPR
1953	Cin-N	5	13	1	2	0	0	0	0	1	2	.154	.214	.154	-2	-2	-2	0	0	0	0	-1	/C	-0.1
	Cle-A	7	7	2	1	0	0	0	0	1	1	.143	.250	.143	9	-1	-1	0	0	0	0	2	/C	0.1
1955	Cle-A	62	111	13	29	9	0	1	7	17	18	.261	.359	.369	93	-0	-1	15	0	0	0	15	C	1.5
1956	Cle-A	1	0	0	0	0	0	0	0	0	0	—	—	—	—	0	0	0	0	0	0	0	/C	0.0
	Pit-N	79	222	24	47	10	2	7	25	17	56	.212	.268	.369	71	-10	-10	21	0	1	-1	-1	C	-0.9
1957	Pit-N	109	281	32	76	10	4	9	36	37	53	.270	.355	.431	113	4	5	43	1	3	-2	-5	*C	0.5
1958	Pit-N	104	264	31	54	10	2	8	30	45	53	.205	.323	.348	80	-8	-7	31	0	1	-1	8	*C	0.6
1959	Pit-N	53	80	10	18	3	0	3	4	7	16	.225	.287	.375	75	-3	-3	8	0	0	0	9	C	0.9
1960	KC-A	6	7	1	4	0	0	0	1	3	2	.571	.700	.571	246	2	2	3	0	0	0	0	C	0.2
	Cle-A	24	68	9	19	1	0	1	6	7	5	.279	.347	.338	89	-1	-1	9	0	0	0	0	C	0.1
	Det-A	26	56	5	14	3	0	0	3	1	8	.250	.263	.304	51	-4	-4	4	1	0	0	4	C	0.2
	Yr	56	131	15	37	4	0	1	10	11	15	.282	.338	.336	83	-3	-3	16	1	0	0	5		0.5
1961	Bal-A	43	124	18	34	6	0	6	19	12	27	.274	.338	.468	115	2	2	18	0	2	-1	3	C	0.4
1962	Cin-N	43	131	17	36	6	1	7	25	13	39	.275	.340	.496	118	4	3	22	0	0	0	2	C	0.5
1963	Cin-N	1	3	0	0	0	0	0	0	1	0	.000	.250	.000	-21	-0	-0	0	1	0	0	0	/C	0.0
	LA-A	41	84	8	18	1	1	4	10	8	13	.214	.290	.393	95	-1	-1	9	0	0	0	3	C	0.2
1964	LA-A	4	4	0	1	0	0	0	0	0	2	.250	.250	.250	44	-0	-0	0	0	0	0	0	H	0.0
Total	11	608	1455	171	353	59	10	46	166	170	295	.243	.323	.392	92	-20	-17	185	3	7	-3	39	C	4.2

■ CURRY FOLEY   Foley, Charles Joseph   b: 1/14/1856, Milltown, Ireland   d: 10/20/1898, Boston, Mass.   TL, 180 lbs.   Deb: 5/13/1879

YEAR	TM/L	G	AB	R	H	2B	3B	HR	RBI	BB	SO	AVG	OBP	SLG	PRO+	BR	/A	RC	SB	CS	SBR	FR	POS	TPR
1879	Bos-N	35	146	16	46	3	1	0	17	3	4	.315	.329	.349	121	4	3	17				-5	PO/1	0.0
1880	Bos-N	80	332	44	97	13	2	2	31	8	14	.292	.309	.361	130	9	10	38				-4	PO1	0.6
1881	Buf-N	83	375	58	96	20	2	1	25	7	27	.256	.270	.328	88	-6	-5	34				-4	O1P	-1.0
1882	Buf-N	84	341	51	104	16	4	3	49	12	26	.305	.329	.402	131	12	11	46				-1	*O/P	0.8
1883	Buf-N	23	111	23	30	5	3	0	6	4	12	.270	.296	.369	98	0	-0	12				-1	O/P	0.0
Total	5	305	1305	192	373	57	12	6	128	34	83	.286	.304	.362	114	19	19	148				-15	O/P1	0.4

■ MARV FOLEY   Foley, Marvis Edwin   b: 8/29/53, Stanford, Ky.   BL/TR, 6', 195 lbs.   Deb: 9/11/78

YEAR	TM/L	G	AB	R	H	2B	3B	HR	RBI	BB	SO	AVG	OBP	SLG	PRO+	BR	/A	RC	SB	CS	SBR	FR	POS	TPR
1978	Chi-A	11	34	3	12	0	0	0	6	4	6	.353	.421	.353	119	1	1	5	0	1	-1	-3	C	-0.1
1979	Chi-A	34	97	6	24	3	0	2	10	7	5	.247	.298	.340	72	-4	-4	9	0	0	0	-1	C	-0.3
1980	Chi-A	68	137	14	29	5	0	4	15	9	22	.212	.270	.336	65	-7	-7	13	0	0	0	2	C/1	-0.1
1982	Chi-A	27	36	1	4	0	0	0	1	6	4	.111	.238	.111	-0	-5	-5	1	0	0	0	5	C/31D	0.1
1984	Tex-A	63	115	13	25	2	0	6	19	15	24	.217	.313	.391	91	-1	-2	15	0	0	0	2	C/13D	0.2
Total	5	203	419	37	94	10	0	12	51	41	61	.224	.298	.334	73	-15	-16	44	0	1	-1	5	C/D13	-0.2

■ RAY FOLEY   Foley, Raymond Kirwin   b: 6/23/06, Naugatuck, Conn.   d: 3/22/80, Vero Beach, Fla.   BL/TR, 5'11", 173 lbs.   Deb: 7/04/28

YEAR	TM/L	G	AB	R	H	2B	3B	HR	RBI	BB	SO	AVG	OBP	SLG	PRO+	BR	/A	RC	SB	CS	SBR	FR	POS	TPR
1928	NY-N	2	1	1	0	0	0	0	0	1	1	.000	.500	.000	41	0	0	0				0	H	0.0

■ TOM FOLEY   Foley, Thomas J.   b: 8/16/1842, Cashel, Ireland   d: 11/3/26, Chicago, Ill.   5'9.5", 157 lbs.   Deb: 5/08/1871

YEAR	TM/L	G	AB	R	H	2B	3B	HR	RBI	BB	SO	AVG	OBP	SLG	PRO+	BR	/A	RC	SB	CS	SBR	FR	POS	TPR
1871	Chi-n	18	84	18	22	3	1	0	13	3	2	.262	.287	.321	67	-3	-5	8	1				O/C3	-0.2

■ TOM FOLEY   Foley, Thomas Michael   b: 9/9/59, Columbus, Ga.   BL/TR, 6'1", 175 lbs.   Deb: 4/09/83

YEAR	TM/L	G	AB	R	H	2B	3B	HR	RBI	BB	SO	AVG	OBP	SLG	PRO+	BR	/A	RC	SB	CS	SBR	FR	POS	TPR
1983	Cin-N	68	98	7	20	4	1	0	9	13	17	.204	.297	.265	55	-5	-6	9	1	0	0	9	S/2	0.7
1984	Cin-N	106	277	26	70	8	3	5	27	24	36	.253	.312	.357	84	-5	-6	32	3	2	-0	1	S2/3	0.4
1985	Cin-N	43	92	7	18	5	1	0	6	6	16	.196	.245	.272	42	-7	-7	7	1	0	0	3	2S/3	-0.3
	Phi-N	46	158	17	42	8	0	3	17	13	18	.266	.322	.373	91	-1	-2	18	1	3	-2	-5	S	-0.4
	Yr	89	250	24	60	13	1	3	23	19	34	.240	.294	.336	73	-8	-9	24	2	3	-1	-3		-0.7
1986	Phi-N	39	61	8	18	2	1	0	5	10	11	.295	.394	.361	106	1	1	10	2	0	1	0	S/23	0.4
	Mon-N	64	202	18	52	13	2	1	18	20	26	.257	.324	.356	88	-3	-3	24	8	3	1	-5	S23	-0.4
	Yr	103	263	26	70	15	3	1	23	30	37	.266	.341	.357	92	-2	-2	34	10	3	1	-4		0.0
1987	Mon-N	106	280	35	82	18	3	5	28	11	40	.293	.322	.432	95	-2	-3	34	6	10	-4	1	S2/3	0.1
1988	Mon-N	127	377	33	100	21	3	5	43	30	49	.265	.321	.377	95	-0	-2	41	2	7	-4	3	2S/3	0.2
1989	Mon-N	122	375	34	86	19	2	7	39	45	53	.229	.317	.347	88	-5	-5	44	2	3	-1	20	*23S/P	1.6
1990	Mon-N	73	164	11	35	2	1	0	12	12	22	.213	.267	.238	65	-13	-13	10	0	1	-1	3	S2/31	-0.6
Total	8	794	2084	196	523	100	17	26	204	184	288	.251	.313	.353	83	-40	-47	228	26	29	-10	30	S2/31P	1.7

■ WILL FOLEY   Foley, William Brown   b: 11/15/1855, Chicago, Ill.   d: 11/12/16, Chicago, Ill.   BR/TR, 5'9.5", 150 lbs.   Deb: 8/23/1875

YEAR	TM/L	G	AB	R	H	2B	3B	HR	RBI	BB	SO	AVG	OBP	SLG	PRO+	BR	/A	RC	SB	CS	SBR	FR	POS	TPR
1875	Chi-n	3	12	0	3	1	0	0		0		.250	.250	.333	99	-0	-0	0					/3	0.0
1876	Cin-N	58	221	19	50	3	2	0	9	0	14	.226	.226	.258	71	-9	-4	13				4	3C	0.0
1877	Cin-N	56	216	23	41	5	1	0	18	4	13	.190	.205	.222	39	-16	-12	10				6	*3	-0.1
1878	Mil-N	56	229	33	62	8	5	0	22	7	14	.271	.292	.349	103	2	0	24				-6	*3/C	-0.2
1879	Cin-N	56	218	22	46	5	1	0	25	2	16	.211	.218	.243	55	-11	-9	12				2	3O/2	-0.6
1881	Det-N	5	15	0	2	0	0	0	1	2	3	.133	.235	.133	18	-1	-1	0				-1	/3	-0.1
1884	CP-U	19	71	15	20	1	1	0		5		.282	.329	.324	122	2	2	8	0			-3	3	0.0
Total	6	250	970	112	221	22	10	0	75	20	60	.228	.243	.271	72	-33	-25	67	0			1	3/CO2	-1.0

■ TIM FOLI   Foli, Timothy John   b: 12/8/50, Culver City, Cal.   BR/TR, 6', 179 lbs.   Deb: 9/11/70   C

YEAR	TM/L	G	AB	R	H	2B	3B	HR	RBI	BB	SO	AVG	OBP	SLG	PRO+	BR	/A	RC	SB	CS	SBR	FR	POS	TPR
1970	NY-N	5	11	0	4	0	0	0	1	0	2	.364	.364	.364	95	-0	-0	1	0	0	0	2	/S3	0.2
1971	NY-N	97	288	32	65	12	2	0	24	18	50	.226	.274	.281	58	-16	-16	22	5	0	2	14	23S/O	0.4
1972	Mon-N	149	540	45	130	12	2	2	35	25	43	.241	.282	.281	59	-28	-29	44	11	7	-1	9	*S/2	-0.2
1973	Mon-N	126	458	37	110	11	0	2	36	28	40	.240	.285	.277	55	-27	-29	33	6	3	0	-9	*S/2O	-0.2
1974	Mon-N	121	441	41	112	10	3	0	39	28	27	.254	.303	.290	63	-19	-22	40	8	2	1	19	*S/3	1.2
1975	Mon-N	152	572	64	136	25	2	1	29	36	49	.238	.285	.294	58	-31	-33	49	13	3	2	6	*S/2	-0.8
1976	Mon-N	149	546	41	144	36	1	6	54	16	33	.264	.285	.366	80	-14	-16	52	6	5	-1	7	*S/3	0.3
1977	Mon-N	13	57	2	10	5	1	0	3	0	4	.175	.175	.298	25	-6	-6	3	0	0	0	1	S	-0.2
	SF-N	104	368	30	84	17	3	4	27	11	16	.228	.251	.323	53	-25	-25	28	2	4	-2	3	*S/23O	-0.9
	Yr	117	425	32	94	22	4	4	30	11	20	.221	.241	.320	49	-31	-31	30	2	4	-2	4		-1.1
1978	NY-N	113	413	37	106	21	1	1	27	14	30	.257	.284	.320	71	-18	-16	35	2	5	-2	-15	*S	-2.5
1979	NY-N	3	7	0	0	0	0	0	0	0	0	.000	.000	.000	-99	-2	-2	0	0	0	0	1	/S	0.0
	*Pit-N	133	525	70	153	23	1	0	65	28	14	.291	.338	.345	83	-9	-12	63	6	5	-1	-1	*S	0.0
	Yr	136	532	70	153	23	1	0	65	28	14	.288	.334	.340	81	-11	-14	62	6	5	-1	0		0.0
1980	Pit-N	127	495	61	131	22	0	3	38	19	23	.265	.300	.327	74	-17	-18	49	11	7	-1	-0	*S	-0.4
1981	Pit-N	86	316	32	78	12	2	0	20	17	20	.247	.287	.297	64	-14	-15	28	7	7	-2	-9	S	-1.9
1982	*Cal-A	150	480	46	121	14	2	3	56	14	22	.252	.276	.338	60	-26	-26	40	2	4	-2	5	*S/23	-1.0
1983	Cal-A	88	330	29	83	10	0	2	29	5	18	.252	.265	.300	56	-20	-20	25	2	3	-1	9	S3	-0.7
1984	NY-A	61	163	8	41	11	0	0	16	2	16	.252	.265	.319	63	-9	-8	13	0	0	0	7	S23/1	0.2

YEAR	TM/L	G	AB	R	H	2B	3B	HR	RBI	BB	SO	AVG	OBP	SLG	PRO+	BR	/A	RC	SB	CS	SBR	FR	POS	TPR
1985	Pit-N	19	37	1	7	0	0	0	2	4	2	.189	.268	.189	30	-3	-3	1	0	0	0	3	S	0.1
Total	16	1696	6047	576	1515	241	20	25	501	265	399	.251	.286	.309	64	-284	-297	527	81	55	-9	70	*S/2301	-6.4

■ DEE FONDY   Fondy, Dee Virgil b: 10/31/24, Slaton, Tex. BL/TL, 6'3", 195 lbs. Deb: 4/17/51

YEAR	TM/L	G	AB	R	H	2B	3B	HR	RBI	BB	SO	AVG	OBP	SLG	PRO+	BR	/A	RC	SB	CS	SBR	FR	POS	TPR
1951	Chi-N	49	170	23	46	7	2	3	20	11	20	.271	.319	.388	88	-3	-3	20	5	6	-2	-2	1	-0.8
1952	Chi-N	145	554	69	166	21	9	10	67	28	60	.300	.334	.424	108	5	4	75	13	11	-3	2	*1	-0.1
1953	Chi-N	150	595	79	184	24	11	18	78	44	106	.309	.358	.477	113	12	11	104	10	7	-1	4	*1	1.0
1954	Chi-N	141	568	77	162	30	4	9	49	35	84	.285	.328	.400	87	-10	-11	75	20	5	3	7	*1	-0.5
1955	Chi-N	150	574	69	152	23	8	17	65	35	87	.265	.309	.422	92	-8	-8	71	8	9	-3	1	*1	-2.0
1956	Chi-N	137	543	52	146	22	9	9	46	20	74	.269	.295	.392	84	-14	-13	62	9	7	-2	-3	*1	-2.4
1957	Chi-N	11	51	3	16	3	1	0	2	0	9	.314	.314	.412	94	-1	-1	5	1	2	-1	-1	1	-0.2
	Pit-N	95	323	42	101	13	2	2	35	25	59	.313	.364	.384	104	1	2	46	11	5	0	-3	1	-0.6
	Yr	106	374	45	117	16	3	2	37	25	68	.313	.357	.388	103	1	2	52	12	7	-1	-3		-0.8
1958	Cin-N	89	124	23	27	1	1	1	11	5	23	.218	.248	.266	34	-11	-12	9	7	1	2	3	1O	-1.0
Total	8	967	3502	437	1000	144	47	69	373	203	526	.286	.326	.413	95	-29	-31	467	84	53	-7	7	1/O	-6.6

■ LEW FONSECA   Fonseca, Lewis Albert b: 1/21/1899, Oakland, Cal. d: 11/26/89, Ely, Iowa BR/TR, 5'10.5", 180 lbs. Deb: 4/13/21 M

YEAR	TM/L	G	AB	R	H	2B	3B	HR	RBI	BB	SO	AVG	OBP	SLG	PRO+	BR	/A	RC	SB	CS	SBR	FR	POS	TPR
1921	Cin-N	82	297	38	82	10	3	1	41	8	13	.276	.304	.340	74	-13	-11	30	2	3	-1	-2	210	-1.4
1922	Cin-N	81	291	55	105	20	3	4	45	14	18	.361	.390	.491	128	11	11	53	7	8	-3	8	2	1.5
1923	Cin-N	65	237	33	66	11	4	3	28	9	16	.278	.310	.397	87	-6	-5	30	4	0	1	8	21	0.4
1924	Cin-N	20	57	5	13	2	1	0	9	4	4	.228	.279	.298	55	-4	-4	5	1	0	0	-2	2/1	-0.5
1925	Phi-N	126	467	78	149	30	5	7	60	21	42	.319	.352	.450	95	1	-4	74	6	2	1	-8	21	-1.7
1927	Cle-A	112	428	60	133	20	7	2	40	12	17	.311	.333	.404	90	-7	-8	53	12	4	1	-6	21	-0.7
1928	Cle-A	75	263	38	86	19	4	3	36	13	17	.327	.361	.464	114	5	5	44	4	2	0	5	13/S2	0.7
1929	Cle-A	148	566	97	209	44	15	6	103	50	23	.369	.426	.532	140	38	36	127	19	11	-1	6	*1	1.8
1930	Cle-A	40	129	20	36	9	2	0	17	7	7	.279	.316	.380	73	-5	-6	16	1	0	0	2	1/3	-0.5
1931	Cle-A	26	108	21	40	9	1	1	14	8	7	.370	.419	.500	133	6	6	22	3	2	-0	0	1	0.3
	Chi-A	121	465	65	139	26	5	2	71	32	22	.299	.348	.389	99	-4	-1	63	4	4	-1	-17	O2/13	-2.1
	Yr	147	573	86	179	35	6	3	85	40	29	.312	.361	.410	106	2	5	85	7	6	-2	-16		-1.8
1932	Chi-A	18	37	0	5	1	0	0	6	1	7	.135	.158	.162	-18	-6	-6	1	0	0	0	1	/OPM	-0.4
1933	Chi-A	23	59	8	12	2	0	2	15	7	6	.203	.288	.339	68	-3	-3	6	1	0	0	2	1M	0.0
Total	12	937	3404	518	1075	203	50	31	485	186	199	.316	.355	.432	103	14	10	524	64	36	-2	-2	120/3SP	-2.6

■ BARRY FOOTE   Foote, Barry Clifton b: 2/16/52, Smithfield, N.C. BR/TR, 6'3", 205 lbs. Deb: 9/14/73

YEAR	TM/L	G	AB	R	H	2B	3B	HR	RBI	BB	SO	AVG	OBP	SLG	PRO+	BR	/A	RC	SB	CS	SBR	FR	POS	TPR
1973	Mon-N	6	6	0	4	0	1	0	1	0	0	.667	.667	1.000	343	2	2	4	0	0	0	0	H	0.2
1974	Mon-N	125	420	44	110	23	4	11	60	35	74	.262	.323	.414	100	2	-1	52	2	1	0	9	*C	1.3
1975	Mon-N	118	387	25	75	16	1	7	30	17	48	.194	.230	.295	43	-30	-32	24	0	1	-1	11	*C	-1.8
1976	Mon-N	105	350	32	82	12	2	7	27	17	32	.234	.272	.340	70	-13	-15	31	2	1	0	7	C/31	-0.3
1977	Mon-N	15	49	4	12	3	1	2	8	4	10	.245	.302	.469	106	0	0	7	0	0	0	0	C	0.0
	Phi-N	18	32	3	7	1	0	1	3	3	6	.219	.286	.344	65	-1	-2	1	0	0	0	-1	C	-0.2
	Yr	33	81	7	19	4	1	3	11	7	16	.235	.295	.420	88	-1	-2	8	0	0	0	-0		-0.2
1978	*Phi-N	39	57	4	9	0	0	1	4	1	11	.158	.172	.211	6	-7	-7	2	0	0	0	2	C	-0.4
1979	Chi-N	132	429	47	109	26	0	16	56	34	49	.254	.316	.427	92	-1	-6	56	5	2	0	-4	*C	-0.6
1980	Chi-N	63	202	16	48	13	1	6	28	13	18	.238	.284	.401	83	-4	-5	21	1	1	-0	2	C	-0.2
1981	Chi-N	9	22	0	0	0	0	0	1	3	7	.000	.120	.000	-61	-5	-5	0	0	0	0	-1	/C	-0.5
	*NY-A	40	125	12	26	4	0	6	10	8	21	.208	.256	.384	83	-3	-3	10	0	0	0	9	C/1D	0.8
1982	NY-A	17	48	4	7	5	0	0	2	1	11	.146	.163	.250	12	-6	-6	2	0	0	0	-3	C	-0.7
Total	10	687	2127	191	489	103	10	57	230	136	287	.230	.279	.368	75	-67	-80	209	10	6	-1	31	C/D13	-2.4

■ JIM FORAN   Foran, James H. b: 1848, New York 5'6.5", 159 lbs. Deb: 5/04/1871

YEAR	TM/L	G	AB	R	H	2B	3B	HR	RBI	BB	SO	AVG	OBP	SLG	PRO+	BR	/A	RC	SB	CS	SBR	FR	POS	TPR
1871	Kek-n	19	89	21	31	1	3	1	18	2	1	.348	.363	.461	132	4	3	16	1				1/O	0.2

■ DAVY FORCE   Force, David W. "Wee Davy" or "Tom Thumb" b: 7/27/1849, New York, N.Y. d: 6/21/18, Englewood, N.J. BR/TR, 5'4", 130 lbs. Deb: 5/05/1871

YEAR	TM/L	G	AB	R	H	2B	3B	HR	RBI	BB	SO	AVG	OBP	SLG	PRO+	BR	/A	RC	SB	CS	SBR	FR	POS	TPR
1871	Oly-n	32	162	45	45	9	4	0	29	4	0	.278	.295	.383	98	-2	-0	21	8				*S/3	0.1
1872	Tro-n	25	133	40	53	7	1	0		1		.398	.403	.466	164	10	10	26					3/S	0.6
	Bal-n	19	96	29	40	3	2	0		1		.417	.423	.490	172	9	8	20					3	0.4
	Yr	44	229	69	93	10	3	0		2		.406	.411	.476	168	19	17	46						1.0
1873	Bal-n	49	234	77	85	12	3	0		9		.363	.387	.440	143	12	13	41					3S/P	0.9
1874	Chi-n	59	296	61	93	10	0	0		2		.314	.319	.348	111	4	3	34					3S/PO	0.1
1875	Ath-n	77	384	78	120	21	6	0		6		.313	.327	.398	134	19	12	51					*S	0.8
1876	Phi-N	60	284	48	66	6	0	0	17	5	3	.232	.246	.254	67	-10	-9	18				21	*S/3	1.0
	NY-N	1	3	0	0	0	0	0	0	0	0	.000	.000	.000	-99	-1	-1	0				0	/S	0.0
	Yr	61	287	48	66	6	0	0	17	5	3	.230	.243	.251	66	-10	-10	18				21		1.0
1877	StL-N	58	225	24	59	5	3	0	22	11	15	.262	.297	.311	97	-2	0	21				6	*S/3	0.7
1879	Buf-N	79	316	36	66	5	2	0	8	13	37	.209	.240	.237	57	-14	-15	18				2	*S/3	-0.6
1880	Buf-N	81	290	22	49	10	0	0	17	10	35	.169	.197	.203	35	-19	-19	12				31	2S	1.4
1881	Buf-N	75	278	21	50	9	1	0	15	11	29	.180	.211	.219	36	-20	-19	13				24	2S/O3	0.7
1882	Buf-N	73	278	39	67	10	1	1	28	12	17	.241	.272	.295	81	-5	-6	23				6	*S3/2	0.6
1883	Buf-N	96	378	40	82	11	3	0	35	12	39	.217	.241	.262	52	-21	-22	24				-3	*S3/2	-1.8
1884	Buf-N	106	403	47	83	13	3	0	36	27	41	.206	.256	.253	59	-17	-19	27				-3	*S/2	-1.0
1885	Buf-N	71	253	20	57	6	1	0	15	13	19	.225	.263	.257	67	-8	-9	18				-3	2S/3	-0.6
1886	Was-N	68	242	26	44	5	1	0	16	17	26	.182	.236	.211	39	-18	-16	14	9			17	S/23	0.0
Total	5 n	261	1305	330	436	62	16	0	29	25		.334	.347	.406	132	52	46	193	8				S3/PO	2.9
Total	10	768	2950	323	623	80	15	1	209	131	261	.211	.245	.249	58	-134	-136	189	9			97	S2/3O	0.4

■ CURT FORD   Ford, Curtis Glenn b: 10/11/60, Jackson, Miss. BL/TR, 5'10", 150 lbs. Deb: 6/22/85

YEAR	TM/L	G	AB	R	H	2B	3B	HR	RBI	BB	SO	AVG	OBP	SLG	PRO+	BR	/A	RC	SB	CS	SBR	FR	POS	TPR
1985	StL-N	11	12	2	6	2	0	0	3	4	1	.500	.625	.667	264	3	3	6	1	0	0	-1	/O	0.3
1986	StL-N	85	214	30	53	15	2	2	29	23	29	.248	.321	.364	89	-3	-3	27	13	5	1	2	O	0.0
1987	*StL-N	89	228	32	65	9	5	3	26	14	32	.285	.329	.408	92	-2	-3	28	11	8	-2	0	O	-0.6
1988	StL-N	91	128	11	25	6	0	1	18	8	26	.195	.243	.266	45	-9	-9	8	6	1	1	3	O/1	-0.6
1989	Phi-N	108	142	13	31	5	1	1	13	16	33	.218	.302	.289	70	-5	-5	12	5	3	-0	0	O/12	-0.6
1990	Phi-N	22	18	0	2	0	0	0	0	1	5	.111	.158	.111	-25	-3	-3	0	0	0	0	0	/O	-0.2
Total	6	406	742	88	182	37	8	7	89	66	126	.245	.309	.345	80	-20	-20	82	36	17	1	6	O/12	-1.7

■ DAN FORD   Ford, Darnell Glenn b: 5/19/52, Los Angeles, Cal. BR/TR, 6'1", 185 lbs. Deb: 4/12/75

YEAR	TM/L	G	AB	R	H	2B	3B	HR	RBI	BB	SO	AVG	OBP	SLG	PRO+	BR	/A	RC	SB	CS	SBR	FR	POS	TPR
1975	Min-A	130	440	72	123	21	1	15	59	30	79	.280	.333	.434	113	8	6	60	6	7	-2	-12	*O/D	-1.1
1976	Min-A	145	514	87	137	24	7	20	86	36	118	.267	.327	.457	124	16	14	75	17	6	2	-9	*O/D	0.4
1977	Min-A	144	453	66	121	25	7	11	60	41	79	.267	.341	.426	109	5	6	65	6	4	-1	-15	*O/D	-1.3
1978	Min-A	151	592	78	162	36	10	11	82	48	88	.274	.333	.424	109	8	7	80	7	7	-2	8	*O/D	1.0
1979	*Cal-A	142	569	100	165	26	5	21	101	40	86	.290	.340	.464	118	10	13	85	8	5	-1	11	*O	1.7
1980	Cal-A	65	226	22	63	11	0	7	26	19	45	.279	.340	.420	110	2	3	28	0	1	-1	-4	OD	-0.2
1981	Cal-A	97	375	53	104	14	1	15	48	23	71	.277	.328	.440	119	8	8	49	2	2	-1	-8	O	-0.2
1982	Bal-A	123	421	46	99	21	3	10	43	23	71	.235	.281	.371	78	-14	-14	43	5	2	0	-0	*O/D	-1.7
1983	*Bal-A	103	407	63	114	30	4	9	55	29	55	.280	.333	.440	113	5	6	59	9	2	2	-5	*O	0.2

YEAR	TM/L	G	AB	R	H	2B	3B	HR	RBI	BB	SO	AVG	OBP	SLG	PRO+	BR	/A	RC	SB	CS	SBR	FR	POS	TPR
1984	Bal-A	25	91	7	21	4	0	1	5	7	13	.231	.286	.308	66	-4	-4	8	1	0	0	1	O/D	-0.2
1985	Bal-A	28	75	4	14	2	0	1	1	7	17	.187	.256	.253	41	-6	-6	4	0	1	-1	0	D	-0.5
Total	11	1153	4163	598	1123	214	38	121	566	303	722	.270	.326	.427	108	38	39	556	61	37	-4	-32	*O/D	-1.9

■ ED FORD
Ford, Edward L. b: 1862, Richmond, Va. 5'9.5", 160 lbs. Deb: 10/09/1884

YEAR	TM/L	G	AB	R	H	2B	3B	HR	RBI	BB	SO	AVG	OBP	SLG	PRO+	BR	/A	RC	SB	CS	SBR	FR	POS	TPR
1884	Ric-a	2	5	0	0	0	0	0	0			.000	.000	.000	-99	-1	-1	0				1	/S1	0.0

■ HOD FORD
Ford, Horace Hills b: 7/23/1897, New Haven, Conn. d: 1/29/77, Winchester, Mass. BR/TR, 5'10", 165 lbs. Deb: 9/08/19

YEAR	TM/L	G	AB	R	H	2B	3B	HR	RBI	BB	SO	AVG	OBP	SLG	PRO+	BR	/A	RC	SB	CS	SBR	FR	POS	TPR
1919	Bos-N	10	28	4	6	0	1	0	3	2	6	.214	.290	.286	77	-1	-1	2	0			3	/S3	0.3
1920	Bos-N	88	257	16	62	12	5	1	30	18	25	.241	.296	.339	86	-6	-5	26	3	3	-1	15	2S/1	1.2
1921	Bos-N	152	555	50	155	29	5	2	61	36	49	.279	.328	.360	87	-14	-10	64	2	11	-6	16	*2S	0.4
1922	Bos-N	143	515	58	140	23	9	2	60	30	36	.272	.317	.363	78	-20	-16	61	2	1	-0	-4	*S2	-1.1
1923	Bos-N	111	380	27	103	16	7	2	50	31	30	.271	.326	.366	86	-10	-8	46	1	1	-0	-9	2S	-1.3
1924	Phi-N	145	530	58	144	27	5	3	53	27	40	.272	.308	.358	70	-17	-25	56	1	9	-5	12	*2	-2.6
1925	Bro-N	66	216	32	59	11	0	1	15	26	15	.273	.357	.338	81	-6	-5	27	0	3	-2	-0	S	-0.1
1926	Cin-N	57	197	14	55	6	1	0	18	14	12	.279	.336	.320	79	-6	-5	21	1			5	S	0.3
1927	Cin-N	115	409	45	112	16	2	1	46	33	34	.274	.331	.330	80	-12	-11	45	0			-8	*S2	-0.8
1928	Cin-N	149	506	49	122	17	4	0	54	47	31	.241	.308	.291	58	-31	-30	47	1			12	*S	0.2
1929	Cin-N	148	529	68	146	14	6	3	50	41	25	.276	.329	.342	70	-27	-23	59	8			8	*S2	0.1
1930	Cin-N	132	424	36	98	16	7	1	34	24	28	.231	.272	.309	42	-42	-38	36	2			2	S2	-1.9
1931	Cin-N	84	175	18	40	8	1	0	13	13	13	.229	.286	.286	57	-11	-10	15	0			1	S/23	-0.2
1932	StL-N	1	2	0	0	0	0	0	0	0	0	.000	.000	.000	-97	-1	-1	0	0			0	/S	0.0
	Bos-N	40	95	9	26	5	2	0	6	6	9	.274	.324	.368	89	-2	-1	12	0			-3	2S/3	0.0
	Yr	41	97	9	26	5	2	0	6	6	9	.268	.317	.361	85	-2	-2	12	0			-3		0.0
1933	Bos-N	5	15	0	1	0	0	0	1	3	1	.067	.222	.067	-16	-2	-2	0	0			5	/S	0.4
Total	15	1446	4833	484	1269	200	55	16	494	351	354	.263	.316	.337	72	-207	-191	517	21	28		55	S2/31	-5.1

■ TED FORD
Ford, Theodore Henry b: 2/7/47, Vineland, N.J. BR/TR, 5'10", 180 lbs. Deb: 4/07/70

YEAR	TM/L	G	AB	R	H	2B	3B	HR	RBI	BB	SO	AVG	OBP	SLG	PRO+	BR	/A	RC	SB	CS	SBR	FR	POS	TPR
1970	Cle-A	26	46	5	8	1	0	1	1	3	13	.174	.224	.261	32	-4	-5	3	0	0	0	2	O	-0.2
1971	Cle-A	74	196	15	38	6	0	2	14	9	34	.194	.229	.255	34	-16	-18	10	2	2	-1	4	O	-1.7
1972	Tex-A	129	429	43	101	19	1	14	50	37	80	.235	.301	.382	107	2	0	50	4	3	-1	8	*O	0.7
1973	Cle-A	11	40	3	9	0	1	0	3	2	7	.225	.262	.275	50	-3	-3	3	1	0	0	-4	O	-0.6
Total	4	240	711	66	156	26	2	17	68	51	134	.219	.275	.333	76	-23	-23	66	7	5	-1	10	O	-1.8

■ FRANK FOREMAN
Foreman, Francis Isaiah "Monkey" b: 5/1/1863, Baltimore, Md. d: 11/19/57, Baltimore, Md. BL/TL, 6', 160 lbs. Deb: 5/15/1884

YEAR	TM/L	G	AB	R	H	2B	3B	HR	RBI	BB	SO	AVG	OBP	SLG	PRO+	BR	/A	RC	SB	CS	SBR	FR	POS	TPR
1884	CP-U	3	11	0	1	0	0	0		0		.091	.091	.091	-39	-2	-2	0	0			-1	/PO	0.0
	KC-U	1	3	0	0	0	0	0		0		.000	.000	.000	-99	-1	-1	0	0			1	/P	0.0
	Yr	4	14	0	1	0	0	0		0		.071	.071	.071	-54	-2	-2	0	0			0		0.0
1885	Bal-a	3	14	4	4	0	1	0		0		.286	.286	.429	128	0	0	2				-1	/PO	0.0
1889	Bal-a	54	181	18	26	2	1	1	11	12	35	.144	.201	.182	11	-21	-21	8	7			-3	P/O	0.0
1890	Cin-N	25	75	13	10	1	3	1	7	10	13	.133	.253	.267	53	-4	-4	5	0			-2	P/O	0.0
1891	Cin-N	1	4	0	1	1	0	0	0	0	0	.250	.250	.500	117	0	0	1	0			-0	/O	0.0
	Was-a	50	153	26	34	4	5	4	19	23	35	.222	.339	.392	117	2	4	23	6			-1	P/O	0.0
1892	Was-N	11	28	5	13	2	2	1	3	3	3	.464	.516	.786	304	6	6	12	0			-1	P	0.0
	Bal-N	7	23	2	4	1	1	0	1	3	3	.174	.269	.304	72	-1	-1	2	1			0	/OP	0.0
	Yr	18	51	7	17	3	3	1	4	6	6	.333	.404	.569	196	6	6	12	1			-1		0.0
1893	NY-N	2	3	0	0	0	0	0	0	0	0	.000	.000	.000	-99	-1	-1	0	0			0	/P	0.0
1895	Cin-N	32	94	14	29	7	0	2	11	4	14	.309	.350	.447	102	1	-0	15	1			-3	P	0.0
1896	Cin-N	27	76	9	19	2	0	0	8	4	7	.250	.287	.276	47	-5	-6	7	2			-0	P	0.0
1901	Bos-A	1	4	0	0	0	0	0	0	0		.000	.000	.000	-99	-1	-1	0	0			0	/P	0.0
	Bal-A	24	80	12	26	2	2	0	10	3		.325	.349	.400	105	1	0	12	1			-3	P	0.0
	Yr	25	84	12	26	2	2	0	10	3		.310	.333	.381	96	-0	-1	12	1			-3		0.0
1902	Bal-A	2	7	1	3	1	0	0	1	0		.429	.429	.571	170	1	1	2	0			1	/P	0.0
Total	11	243	756	104	170	23	15	9	71	62	110	.225	.291	.331	76	-24	-25	89	18			-14	P/O	0.0

■ TOM FORSTER
Forster, Thomas W. b: 5/1/1859, New York, N.Y. d: 7/17/46, New York, N.Y. Deb: 8/04/1882

YEAR	TM/L	G	AB	R	H	2B	3B	HR	RBI	BB	SO	AVG	OBP	SLG	PRO+	BR	/A	RC	SB	CS	SBR	FR	POS	TPR
1882	Det-N	21	76	5	7	0	0	0	2	5	12	.092	.148	.092	-21	-10	-10	1				-7	2	-1.4
1884	Pit-a	35	126	10	28	5	0	0		7		.222	.263	.262	73	-3	-4	9				6	S/32	0.2
1885	NY-a	57	213	28	47	7	2	0		17		.221	.281	.272	85	-5	-2	17				-11	2/O	-0.9
1886	NY-a	67	251	33	49	3	2	1		20		.195	.263	.235	61	-12	-10	18	9			-7	2/OS	-1.4
Total	4	180	666	76	131	15	4	1	2	49	12	.197	.256	.236	61	-29	-25	45	9			-19	2/SO3	-3.5

■ ED FORSYTHE
Forsythe, Edward James b: 4/30/1887, Kingston, N.Y. d: 6/22/56, Hoboken, N.J. BR/TR, 5'10", 155 lbs. Deb: 10/02/15

YEAR	TM/L	G	AB	R	H	2B	3B	HR	RBI	BB	SO	AVG	OBP	SLG	PRO+	BR	/A	RC	SB	CS	SBR	FR	POS	TPR
1915	Bal-F	1	3	0	0	0	0	0	0	1	0	.000	.250	.000	-22	-0	-0	0				-0	/3	0.0

■ GEORGE FOSS
Foss, George Dueward "Deeby" b: 6/13/1897, Register, Va. d: 11/10/69, Brandon, Fla. BR/TR, 5'10.5", 170 lbs. Deb: 4/16/21

YEAR	TM/L	G	AB	R	H	2B	3B	HR	RBI	BB	SO	AVG	OBP	SLG	PRO+	BR	/A	RC	SB	CS	SBR	FR	POS	TPR
1921	Was-A	4	7	0	0	0	0	0	0	0	1	.000	.000	.000	-99	-2	-2	0	0	0	0	0	/3	-0.1

■ RAY FOSSE
Fosse, Raymond Earl b: 4/4/47, Marion, Ill. BR/TR, 6'2", 215 lbs. Deb: 9/08/67

YEAR	TM/L	G	AB	R	H	2B	3B	HR	RBI	BB	SO	AVG	OBP	SLG	PRO+	BR	/A	RC	SB	CS	SBR	FR	POS	TPR
1967	Cle-A	7	16	0	1	0	0	0	0	0	5	.063	.063	.063	-62	-3	-3	0	0	0	0	5	/C	0.3
1968	Cle-A	1	0	0	0	0	0	0	0	0	0	—	—	—	—	0	0	0	0	0	0	-0	/C	0.0
1969	Cle-A	37	116	11	20	3	0	2	9	8	29	.172	.232	.250	34	-10	-11	7	1	0	0	4	C	-0.3
1970	Cle-A	120	450	62	138	17	1	18	61	39	55	.307	.363	.469	122	16	14	74	1	5	-3	8	*C	2.1
1971	Cle-A	133	486	53	134	21	1	12	62	36	62	.276	.331	.397	97	3	-2	61	4	1	1	-3	*C/1	0.1
1972	Cle-A	134	457	42	110	20	1	10	41	45	46	.241	.313	.354	95	-1	-3	48	5	1	1	6	*C/1	0.6
1973	*Oak-A	143	492	37	126	23	2	7	52	25	62	.256	.293	.354	86	-13	-10	49	2	2	-1	1	*C/D	-0.6
1974	Oak-A	69	204	20	40	8	3	4	23	11	31	.196	.244	.324	66	-11	-9	15	1	1	-0	-2	C/D	-0.8
1975	*Oak-A	82	136	14	19	3	2	0	12	8	19	.140	.193	.191	9	-16	-16	4	0	1	-1	6	C/12	0.6
1976	Cle-A	90	276	26	83	9	1	2	30	20	20	.301	.348	.362	109	3	3	33	1	2	-1	9	C/1D	0.6
1977	Cle-A	78	238	25	63	7	1	6	27	7	26	.265	.294	.378	84	-6	-5	24	0	5	-3	9	C/1D	0.2
	Sea-A	11	34	3	12	3	0	0	5	2	2	.353	.389	.441	127	1	1	5	0	1	-1	-3	/CD	-0.1
	Yr	89	272	28	75	10	1	6	32	9	28	.276	.306	.386	90	-5	-4	28	0	6	-4	5		0.1
1979	Mil-A	19	52	6	12	3	1	0	2	3	6	.231	.286	.327	65	-3	-3	5	0	0	0	-1	C/1D	-0.2
Total	12	924	2957	299	758	117	13	61	324	203	363	.256	.308	.367	90	-40	-44	325	15	19	-7	29	C/1D2	1.1

■ POP FOSTER
Foster, Clarence Francis b: 4/8/1878, New Haven, Conn. d: 4/16/44, Princeton, N.J. BR/TR, 5'8.5", Deb: 9/13/1898

YEAR	TM/L	G	AB	R	H	2B	3B	HR	RBI	BB	SO	AVG	OBP	SLG	PRO+	BR	/A	RC	SB	CS	SBR	FR	POS	TPR
1898	NY-N	32	112	10	30	6	1	0	9	0		.268	.268	.339	78	-4	-3	10	0			-5	O3/S	-0.8
1899	NY-N	84	301	48	89	9	7	3	57	20		.296	.348	.402	112	3	4	46	7			-10	O/S3	-0.9
1900	NY-N	31	84	19	22	3	1	0	11	11		.262	.347	.321	92	-1	-0	10	0			-3	O/S2	-0.2
1901	Was-A	103	392	65	109	16	9	6	54	41		.278	.351	.411	115	7	8	62	10			-1	*O/S	0.5
	Chi-A	12	35	4	10	2	2	1	6	4		.286	.359	.543	154	2	2	7	0			-1	/O	0.1
	Yr	115	427	69	119	18	11	7	60	45		.279	.352	.422	118	9	10	69	10			-2		0.6
Total	4	262	924	146	260	36	20	10	137	76		.281	.341	.396	109	7	11	134	17			-20	O/S32	-1.3

YEAR	TM/L	G	AB	R	H	2B	3B	HR	RBI	BB	SO	AVG	OBP	SLG	PRO+	BR	/A	RC	SB	CS	SBR	FR	POS	TPR

■ EDDIE FOSTER
Foster, Edward Cunningham "Kid" b: 2/13/1887, Chicago, Ill. d: 1/15/37, Washington, D.C. BR/TR, 5'6.5", 145 lbs. Deb: 4/14/10

YEAR	TM/L	G	AB	R	H	2B	3B	HR	RBI	BB	SO	AVG	OBP	SLG	PRO+	BR	/A	RC	SB	CS	SBR	FR	POS	TPR
1910	NY-A	30	83	5	11	2	0	0	1	8		.133	.217	.157	16	-8	-8	3	2			-2	S	-1.1
1912	Was-A	154	618	98	176	34	9	2	70	53		.285	.345	.379	106	5	4	88	27			12	*3	1.3
1913	Was-A	106	409	56	101	11	5	1	41	36	31	.247	.309	.306	78	-10	-11	42	22			4	*3	-0.4
1914	Was-A	157	616	82	174	16	10	2	50	60	47	.282	.348	.351	107	8	6	79	31	18	-2	-18	*3	-1.0
1915	Was-A	154	618	75	170	25	10	0	52	48	30	.275	.329	.348	102	0	0	76	20	6	2	-5	32	0.0
1916	Was-A	158	606	75	153	18	9	1	44	68	26	.252	.332	.317	97	-3	-1	66	23	16	-3	-16	32	-1.5
1917	Was-A	143	554	66	130	16	8	0	43	46	23	.235	.293	.292	80	-15	-14	50	11			-6	32	-1.2
1918	Was-A	129	519	70	147	13	3	0	29	41	20	.283	.339	.320	101	-1	0	59	12			2	*3/2	0.3
1919	Was-A	120	478	57	126	12	5	0	26	33	21	.264	.314	.310	76	-16	-15	51	20			7	*3	0.1
1920	Bos-A	117	386	48	100	17	6	0	41	42	17	.259	.336	.334	82	-11	-9	46	10	4	1	15	32	1.2
1921	Bos-A	120	412	51	117	18	6	0	35	57	15	.284	.371	.357	89	-7	-5	58	13	7	-0	-14	32	-0.9
1922	Bos-A	48	109	11	23	3	0	0	3	9	10	.211	.277	.239	36	-10	-10	8	1	1	-0	-11	3/S	-1.7
	StL-A	37	144	29	44	4	0	0	12	20		.306	.394	.333	88	-1	-1	21	3	1	-0	-2	3	0.1
	Yr	85	253	40	67	7	0	0	15	29	18	.265	.345	.292	67	-11	-11	28	4	2	0	-12		-1.6
1923	StL-A	27	100	9	18	2	0	0	4	7	7	.180	.241	.200	16	-12	-13	6	0	0	0	-8	2/3	-1.9
Total	13	1500	5652	732	1490	191	71	6	451	528	255	.264	.329	.326	89	-80	-78	652	195	53		-41	*32/S	-6.7

■ ELMER FOSTER
Foster, Elmer Ellsworth b: 8/15/1861, Minneapolis, Minn. d: 7/22/46, Deephaven, Minn. BR/TL, Deb: 6/18/1884

YEAR	TM/L	G	AB	R	H	2B	3B	HR	RBI	BB	SO	AVG	OBP	SLG	PRO+	BR	/A	RC	SB	CS	SBR	FR	POS	TPR
1884	Phi-a	4	11	4	2	0	0	0		3		.182	.357	.182	79	0	-0	1				-1	/CO	0.0
	Phi-U	1	3	0	1	0	1	0		0		.333	.333	1.000	362	1	1	1	0			-1	/C	0.0
1886	NY-a	35	125	16	23	0	1	0		7		.184	.239	.200	41	-8	-8	7	3			-0	2O	-0.6
1888	NY-N	37	136	15	20	3	2	0	10	9	20	.147	.216	.199	35	-10	-9	9	13			-4	O/3	-1.3
1889	NY-N	2	4	2	0	0	0	0	0	3	1	.000	.429	.000	27	-0	-0	1	2			0	/O	0.0
1890	Chi-N	27	105	20	26	4	2	5	23	9	21	.248	.325	.467	127	4	3	22	18			2	O	0.4
1891	Chi-N	4	16	3	3	0	0	1	1	1	2	.188	.235	.375	79	-1	-1	2	1			-0	/O	0.0
Total	6	110	400	60	75	7	6	6	34	32	44	.188	.261	.280	69	-14	-14	42	37			-3	/O2C3	-1.5

■ GEORGE FOSTER
Foster, George Arthur b: 12/1/48, Tuscaloosa, Ala. BR/TR, 6'1.5", 180 lbs. Deb: 9/10/69

YEAR	TM/L	G	AB	R	H	2B	3B	HR	RBI	BB	SO	AVG	OBP	SLG	PRO+	BR	/A	RC	SB	CS	SBR	FR	POS	TPR
1969	SF-N	9	5	1	2	0	0	0	1	0	1	.400	.400	.400	127	0	0	1	0	0	0	0	/O	0.0
1970	SF-N	9	19	2	6	1	1	1	4	2	5	.316	.381	.632	168	2	2	4	0	0	0	0	/O	0.1
1971	SF-N	36	105	11	28	5	0	3	8	6	27	.267	.306	.400	100	-1	-0	11	0	1	-1	-1	O	-0.3
	Cin-N	104	368	39	86	18	4	10	50	23	93	.234	.291	.386	92	-6	-5	36	7	6	-2	7	*O	-0.2
	Yr	140	473	50	114	23	4	13	58	29	120	.241	.295	.389	94	-6	-5	48	7	7	-2	5		-0.5
1972	*Cin-N	59	145	15	29	4	1	2	12	5	44	.200	.232	.283	48	-11	-10	8	2	1	0	-2	O	-1.4
1973	Cin-N	17	39	6	11	3	0	4	9	4	7	.282	.349	.667	185	4	4	8	0	1	-1	0	O	0.3
1974	Cin-N	106	276	31	73	18	0	7	41	30	52	.264	.345	.406	111	3	4	38	3	2	-0	-14	O	-1.4
1975	*Cin-N	134	463	71	139	24	4	23	78	40	73	.300	.360	.518	139	24	23	82	2	1	0	13	*O/1	3.2
1976	*Cin-N	144	562	86	172	21	9	29	121	52	89	.306	.369	.530	149	37	35	111	17	3	3	8	*O/1	4.4
1977	Cin-N	158	615	124	197	31	2	52	149	61	107	.320	.386	.631	165	56	55	144	6	4	-1	13	*O	6.1
1978	Cin-N	158	604	97	170	26	7	40	120	70	138	.281	.363	.546	151	39	39	115	4	4	-1	2	*O	3.6
1979	*Cin-N	121	440	68	133	18	3	30	98	59	105	.302	.384	.561	155	34	33	95	0	2	-1	-2	*O	2.7
1980	Cin-N	144	528	79	144	21	5	25	93	75	99	.273	.364	.473	132	23	23	91	1	0	0	2	*O	2.0
1981	Cin-N	108	414	64	122	23	2	22	90	51	75	.295	.376	.519	150	28	27	81	4	0	1	4	*O	3.1
1982	NY-N	151	550	64	136	23	2	13	70	50	123	.247	.312	.367	90	-8	-8	62	1	1	-0	8	*O	-0.1
1983	NY-N	157	601	74	145	19	2	28	90	38	111	.241	.291	.419	95	-7	-6	68	1	1	-0	5	*O	-0.4
1984	NY-N	146	553	67	149	22	1	24	86	30	121	.269	.314	.443	112	6	7	73	2	2	-1	3	*O	0.4
1985	NY-N	129	452	57	119	24	1	21	77	46	87	.263	.334	.460	123	11	12	69	0	1	-1	-7	*O	0.2
1986	NY-N	72	233	28	53	6	1	13	38	21	53	.227	.291	.429	99	-2	-1	28	1	1	-0	-4	O	-0.6
	Chi-A	15	51	2	11	0	2	1	4	3	8	.216	.259	.353	63	-3	-3	4	0	0	0	1	O/D	-0.2
Total	18	1977	7023	986	1925	307	47	348	1239	666	1419	.274	.341	.480	127	229	231	1129	51	31	-3	35	*O/D1	21.5

■ LEO FOSTER
Foster, Leonard Norris b: 2/2/51, Covington, Ky. BR/TR, 5'11", 165 lbs. Deb: 7/09/71

YEAR	TM/L	G	AB	R	H	2B	3B	HR	RBI	BB	SO	AVG	OBP	SLG	PRO+	BR	/A	RC	SB	CS	SBR	FR	POS	TPR
1971	Atl-N	9	10	1	0	0	0	0	0	0	1	.000	.000	.000	-94	-3	-3	0	0	0	0	2	/S	0.0
1973	Atl-N	3	6	1	1	1	0	0	0	0	2	.167	.167	.333	33	-1	-1	0	0	0	0	-0	/S	0.0
1974	Atl-N	72	112	16	22	2	0	1	5	9	22	.196	.256	.241	38	-9	-10	7	1	2	-1	-0	S2/3O	-0.5
1976	NY-N	24	59	11	12	2	0	1	15	8	5	.203	.299	.288	71	-2	-2	6	3	0	1	1	/3S2	0.0
1977	NY-N	36	75	6	17	3	0	0	6	5	14	.227	.284	.267	51	-5	-5	6	3	1	0	-4	2/S3	-0.6
Total	5	144	262	35	52	8	0	2	26	22	44	.198	.263	.252	44	-20	-20	19	7	3	0	-2	/S23O	-1.1

■ REDDY FOSTER
Foster, Oscar E. b: 1867, Richmond, Va. d: 12/19/08, Richmond, Va. Deb: 6/03/1896

YEAR	TM/L	G	AB	R	H	2B	3B	HR	RBI	BB	SO	AVG	OBP	SLG	PRO+	BR	/A	RC	SB	CS	SBR	FR	POS	TPR
1896	NY-N	1	1	0	0	0	0	0	0	0	0	.000	.000	.000	-99	-0	-0	0	0			0	O	0.0

■ ROY FOSTER
Foster, Roy b: 7/29/45, Bixby, Miss. BR/TR, 6', 185 lbs. Deb: 4/07/70

YEAR	TM/L	G	AB	R	H	2B	3B	HR	RBI	BB	SO	AVG	OBP	SLG	PRO+	BR	/A	RC	SB	CS	SBR	FR	POS	TPR
1970	Cle-A	139	477	66	128	26	0	23	60	54	75	.268	.357	.468	120	17	14	78	3	3	-1	-9	*O	-0.1
1971	Cle-A	125	396	51	97	21	1	18	45	35	48	.245	.316	.439	103	5	1	54	6	1	1	-4	*O	-0.5
1972	Cle-A	73	143	19	32	4	0	4	13	21	23	.224	.331	.336	96	0	-0	16	0	2	-1	-4	O	-0.7
Total	3	337	1016	136	257	51	1	45	118	110	146	.253	.338	.438	110	22	14	147	9	6	-1	-18	O	-1.3

■ BOB FOTHERGILL
Fothergill, Robert Roy "Fats" b: 8/16/1897, Massillon, Ohio d: 3/20/38, Detroit, Mich. BR/TR, 5'10.5", 230 lbs. Deb: 4/18/22

YEAR	TM/L	G	AB	R	H	2B	3B	HR	RBI	BB	SO	AVG	OBP	SLG	PRO+	BR	/A	RC	SB	CS	SBR	FR	POS	TPR
1922	Det-A	42	152	20	49	12	4	0	29	8	9	.322	.356	.454	113	2	2	22	1	5	-3	-6	O	-0.9
1923	Det-A	101	241	34	76	18	2	1	49	12	19	.315	.358	.419	106	1	2	36	4	4	-1	-8	O	-1.2
1924	Det-A	54	166	28	50	8	3	0	15	5	13	.301	.326	.386	84	-5	-4	20	2	3	-1	-3	O	-1.1
1925	Det-A	71	204	38	72	14	0	2	28	6	3	.353	.377	.451	111	2	3	34	2	2	-1	-2	O	-0.4
1926	Det-A	110	387	63	142	31	7	3	73	33	23	.367	.421	.506	139	23	22	78	4	12	-6	-1	*O	0.7
1927	Det-A	143	527	93	189	38	9	9	114	47	31	.359	.413	.516	138	31	30	102	9	15	-6	-5	*O	0.8
1928	Det-A	111	347	49	110	28	10	3	63	24	19	.317	.366	.481	119	10	8	61	8	3	1	-3	O	0.1
1929	Det-A	115	277	42	98	24	9	6	62	11	11	.354	.386	.570	140	15	15	58	3	1	-0	-4	O	0.9
1930	Det-A	55	143	14	37	9	3	2	14	6	10	.259	.289	.406	72	-6	-7	16	1	1	-0	-5	O	-1.1
	Chi-A	52	135	10	40	9	0	0	24	4	8	.296	.326	.363	77	-5	-5	16	0	0	0	-3	O	-0.7
	Yr	107	278	24	77	18	3	2	38	10	18	.277	.307	.385	75	-11	-11	32	1	1	-0	-8		-1.8
1931	Chi-A	108	312	25	88	9	4	3	56	17	17	.282	.323	.365	86	-9	-6	37	2	2	-1	1	O	-0.9
1932	Chi-A	116	346	36	102	24	1	7	50	27	10	.295	.348	.431	107	0	3	51	4	4	-1	-12	O	-1.2
1933	Bos-A	28	32	1	11	1	0	0	5	2	4	.344	.382	.375	102	0	0	5	0	0	0	-0	/O	0.0
Total	12	1106	3269	453	1064	225	52	36	582	202	177	.325	.368	.459	115	58	64	537	40	52	-19	-52	O	-5.0

■ JACK FOURNIER
Fournier, Jacques Frank b: 9/29/1892, AuSable, Mich. d: 9/5/73, Tacoma, Wash. BL/TR, 6', 195 lbs. Deb: 4/13/12

YEAR	TM/L	G	AB	R	H	2B	3B	HR	RBI	BB	SO	AVG	OBP	SLG	PRO+	BR	/A	RC	SB	CS	SBR	FR	POS	TPR
1912	Chi-A	35	73	5	14	5	2	0	2	4		.192	.262	.315	67	-4	-3	6	1			3	1	0.0
1913	Chi-A	68	172	20	40	8	5	1	23	21	23	.233	.323	.355	99	-0	-0	21	9			4	1O	0.3
1914	Chi-A	109	379	44	118	14	9	6	44	31	44	.311	.368	.443	146	19	19	61	10	13	-5	5	1/O	2.1
1915	Chi-A	126	422	86	136	20	18	5	77	64	37	.322	.429	.491	170	41	39	91	21	16	-3	3	1O	3.5
1916	Chi-A	105	313	36	75	13	9	3	44	36	40	.240	.328	.367	108	3	3	44	19			-3	1/O	-0.1
1917	Chi-A	1	1	0	0	0	0	0	0	0	1	.000	.000	.000	-98	-0	-0	0	0			0	H	0.0
1918	NY-A	27	100	9	35	6	1	0	12	7	7	.350	.393	.430	145	6	5	19	7			-2	1	0.1

YEAR	TM/L	G	AB	R	H	2B	3B	HR	RBI	BB	SO	AVG	OBP	SLG	PRO+	BR	/A	RC	SB	CS	SBR	FR	POS	TPR
1920	StL-N	141	530	77	162	33	14	3	61	42	42	.306	.370	.438	136	22	24	84	26	20	-4	1	*1	2.1
1921	StL-N	149	574	103	197	27	9	16	86	56	48	.343	.409	.505	144	34	36	114	20	22	-7	-4	*1	2.1
1922	StL-N	128	404	64	119	23	9	10	61	40	21	.295	.368	.470	120	8	11	69	6	8	-3	2	*1/P	0.8
1923	Bro-N	133	515	91	181	30	13	22	102	43	28	.351	.411	.588	165	44	46	**125**	11	4	1	4	*1	**3.9**
1924	Bro-N	154	563	93	188	25	4	**27**	116	83	46	.334	.428	.536	162	48	51	133	7	5	-1	7	*1	4.9
1925	Bro-N	145	545	99	191	21	16	22	130	**86**	39	.350	.446	.569	162	50	52	141	4	6	-2	3	*1	3.5
1926	Bro-N	87	243	39	69	9	2	11	48	30	16	.284	.365	.473	126	8	9	42	0			-2	1	0.4
1927	Bos-N	122	374	55	106	18	2	10	53	44	16	.283	.368	.422	121	7	11	59	4			0	*1	0.4
Total	15	1530	5208	821	1631	252	113	136	859	587	408	.313	.392	.483	143	285	302	1010	145	94	21		*1/OP	24.0

■ BILL FOUSER　Fouser, William C.　b: 10/1855, Philadelphia, Pa.　d: 3/1/19, Philadelphia, Pa.　Deb: 4/22/1876

YEAR	TM/L	G	AB	R	H	2B	3B	HR	RBI	BB	SO	AVG	OBP	SLG	PRO+	BR	/A	RC	SB	CS	SBR	FR	POS	TPR
1876	Phi-N	21	89	11	12	0	1	0	2	0	0	.135	.135	.157	-3	-9	-9	2				3	2/O1	-0.4

■ DAVE FOUTZ　Foutz, David Luther "Scissors"　b: 9/7/1856, Carroll Co., Md.　d: 3/5/1897, Waverly, Ind.　BR/TR, 6'2", 161 lbs.　Deb: 7/29/1884　M

YEAR	TM/L	G	AB	R	H	2B	3B	HR	RBI	BB	SO	AVG	OBP	SLG	PRO+	BR	/A	RC	SB	CS	SBR	FR	POS	TPR
1884	StL-a	33	119	17	27	4	0	0		8		.227	.276	.261	76	-3	-3	9				-2	PO	0.0
1885	*StL-a	65	238	42	59	6	4	0		11		.248	.281	.307	84	-3	-5	21				6	P1/O	0.0
1886	*StL-a	102	414	66	116	18	9	3		9		.280	.297	.389	111	6	3	54	17			3	PO1	0.0
1887	*StL-a	102	423	79	151	26	13	4		23		.357	.393	.508	138	28	20	95	22			-4	OP1	1.7
1888	Bro-a	140	563	91	156	20	13	3	99	28		.277	.314	.375	124	13	14	79	35			3	O1P	1.3
1889	*Bro-a	138	553	118	152	19	8	6	113	64	23	.275	.353	.371	108	7	7	90	43			-3	*1P	-0.4
1890	*Bro-N	129	509	106	154	25	13	5	98	52	25	.303	.368	.432	135	22	22	99	42			-1	*1O/P	1.2
1891	Bro-N	130	521	87	134	26	8	2	73	40	25	.257	.313	.349	95	-4	-4	74	48			-2	*1/PS	-0.7
1892	Bro-N	61	220	33	41	5	3	1	26	14	14	.186	.235	.250	50	-14	-13	18	19			-1	OP/1	-0.9
1893	Bro-N	130	557	91	137	20	10	7	67	32	34	.246	.287	.355	75	-25	-20	70	39			-6	O1/PM	-2.2
1894	Bro-N	72	293	40	90	12	9	0	51	14	13	.307	.341	.410	88	-9	-5	47	14			-3	1/PM	-0.4
1895	Bro-N	31	115	14	34	4	1	0	21	4	2	.296	.319	.348	80	-5	-3	13	1			-5	O/1M	-0.7
1896	Bro-N	2	8	0	2	1	0	0	0	1	0	.250	.333	.375	94	-0	-0	1	0			0	/O1M	0.0
Total	13	1135	4533	784	1253	186	91	31	548	300	136	.276	.323	.378	104	13	11	670	280			-13	1OP/S	-1.1

■ FRANK FOUTZ　Foutz, Frank Hayes　b: 4/8/1877, Baltimore, Md.　d: 12/25/61, Lima, Ohio　BR/TR,　Deb: 4/26/01

YEAR	TM/L	G	AB	R	H	2B	3B	HR	RBI	BB	SO	AVG	OBP	SLG	PRO+	BR	/A	RC	SB	CS	SBR	FR	POS	TPR
1901	Bal-A	20	72	13	17	4	1	2	14	8		.236	.321	.403	97	0	-0	10	0			-0	1	0.0

■ BOOB FOWLER　Fowler, Joseph Chester "Gink"　b: 11/11/1900, Waco, Tex.　d: 10/8/88, Dallas, Tex.　BL/TR, 5'11.5", 180 lbs.　Deb: 5/06/23

YEAR	TM/L	G	AB	R	H	2B	3B	HR	RBI	BB	SO	AVG	OBP	SLG	PRO+	BR	/A	RC	SB	CS	SBR	FR	POS	TPR
1923	Cin-N	11	33	9	11	0	1	1	6	1	3	.333	.353	.485	121	1	1	6	1	0	0	-1	S	0.1
1924	Cin-N	59	129	20	43	6	1	0	9	5	15	.333	.358	.395	103	0	1	18	2	2	-1	-6	S/23	-0.3
1925	Cin-N	6	5	0	2	1	0	0	2	0	1	.400	.400	.600	155	0	0	1	0	0	0	0	H	0.0
1926	Bos-A	2	8	1	1	0	0	0	1	0	0	.125	.125	.125	-36	-2	-2	0	0	0	0	0	/3	0.0
Total	4	78	175	30	57	7	2	1	18	6	19	.326	.348	.406	102	-0	0	25	3	2	-0	-7	/S32	-0.2

■ CHARLIE FOX　Fox, Charles Francis "Irish"　b: 10/7/21, New York, N.Y.　BR/TR, 5'11", 180 lbs.　Deb: 9/24/42　MC

YEAR	TM/L	G	AB	R	H	2B	3B	HR	RBI	BB	SO	AVG	OBP	SLG	PRO+	BR	/A	RC	SB	CS	SBR	FR	POS	TPR
1942	NY-N	3	7	1	3	0	0	0	1	1	2	.429	.500	.429	172	1	1	2	0			-1	/C	0.0

■ PETE FOX　Fox, Ervin　b: 3/8/09, Evansville, Ind.　d: 7/5/66, Detroit, Mich.　BR/TR, 5'11", 165 lbs.　Deb: 4/12/33

YEAR	TM/L	G	AB	R	H	2B	3B	HR	RBI	BB	SO	AVG	OBP	SLG	PRO+	BR	/A	RC	SB	CS	SBR	FR	POS	TPR
1933	Det-A	128	535	82	154	26	13	7	57	23	38	.288	.320	.424	94	-6	-7	71	9	6	-1	-2	*O	-1.2
1934	*Det-A	128	516	101	147	31	2	2	45	49	53	.285	.351	.364	85	-11	-11	69	25	10	2	6	*O	-0.4
1935	*Det-A	131	517	116	166	38	8	15	73	45	52	.321	.382	.513	134	21	24	103	14	4	2	-2	*O	2.1
1936	Det-A	73	220	46	67	12	1	4	26	34	23	.305	.405	.423	104	3	3	39	1	3	-2	-3	O	-0.2
1937	Det-A	148	628	116	208	39	8	12	82	41	43	.331	.372	.476	110	10	8	109	12	8	-1	-2	*O	0.0
1938	Det-A	155	634	91	186	35	10	7	96	31	39	.293	.328	.413	80	-17	-22	85	16	7	1	-2	*O	-2.1
1939	Det-A	141	519	69	153	24	6	7	66	35	41	.295	.342	.405	84	-8	-14	69	23	12	-0	5	*O	-1.2
1940	*Det-A	93	350	49	101	17	4	5	48	21	30	.289	.329	.403	81	-6	-11	46	7	7	-2	-1	O	-1.9
1941	Bos-A	73	268	38	81	12	7	0	31	21	32	.302	.357	.399	98	-0	-1	41	9	2	-2	-3	O	-0.6
1942	Bos-A	77	256	42	67	15	5	3	42	20	28	.262	.323	.395	98	-0	-1	31	8	7	-2	-9	O	-1.7
1943	Bos-A	127	489	54	141	24	4	2	44	34	40	.288	.337	.366	104	3	2	62	22	8	0	-7	*O	-0.6
1944	Bos-A	121	496	70	156	37	6	1	64	27	34	.315	.354	.419	122	12	12	75	10	5	0	-5	*O	0.4
1945	Bos-A	66	208	21	51	4	1	0	20	11	18	.245	.296	.274	64	-9	-10	18	2	2	-1	-6	O	-1.9
Total	13	1461	5636	895	1678	314	75	65	694	392	471	.298	.347	.415	98	-9	-28	819	158	81	-1	-31	*O	-9.3

■ PADDY FOX　Fox, George B.　b: 12/1/1868, Pottstown, Pa.　d: 5/8/14, Philadelphia, Pa.　Deb: 7/13/1891

YEAR	TM/L	G	AB	R	H	2B	3B	HR	RBI	BB	SO	AVG	OBP	SLG	PRO+	BR	/A	RC	SB	CS	SBR	FR	POS	TPR
1891	Lou-a	6	19	1	2	0	1	0	2	2	3	.105	.261	.211	38	-1	-1	1	0			-2	/3	-0.2
1899	Pit-N	13	41	4	10	0	1	1	3	3		.244	.311	.366	88	-1	-1	5	2			1	/1C	0.1
Total	2	19	60	5	12	0	2	1	5	5	3	.200	.294	.317	72	-2	-2	6	2			-1	/13C	-0.1

■ NELLIE FOX　Fox, Jacob Nelson　b: 12/25/27, St.Thomas, Pa.　d: 12/1/75, Baltimore, Md.　BL/TR, 5'10", 160 lbs.　Deb: 6/08/47　C

YEAR	TM/L	G	AB	R	H	2B	3B	HR	RBI	BB	SO	AVG	OBP	SLG	PRO+	BR	/A	RC	SB	CS	SBR	FR	POS	TPR
1947	Phi-A	7	3	2	0	0	0	0	0	1	0	.000	.250	.000	-26	-0	-0	0	0	0	0	1	/2	0.1
1948	Phi-A	3	13	0	2	0	0	0	0	1	0	.154	.214	.154	-1	-2	-2	1	1	0	0	-1	/2	-0.2
1949	Phi-A	88	247	42	63	6	2	0	21	32	9	.255	.354	.296	75	-8	-7	28	2	2	-1	-1	2	-0.7
1950	Chi-A	130	457	45	113	12	7	0	30	35	17	.247	.304	.304	58	-31	-29	45	4	3	-1	-0	*2	-1.9
1951	Chi-A	147	604	93	189	32	12	4	55	43	11	.313	.372	.425	118	13	14	98	9	12	-5	-3	*2	1.2
1952	Chi-A	152	648	76	**192**	25	10	0	39	34	14	.296	.334	.366	91	-6	-6	80	5	5	-2	7	*2	0.6
1953	Chi-A	154	624	92	178	31	8	3	72	49	18	.285	.344	.375	91	-5	-7	81	4	5	-2	3	*2	0.2
1954	Chi-A	155	631	111	**201**	24	8	2	47	51	12	.319	.374	.391	106	9	7	93	16	9	-1	-6	*2	0.7
1955	Chi-A	154	636	100	198	28	7	6	59	38	15	.311	.366	.406	104	7	4	95	7	9	-3	**27**	*2	3.6
1956	Chi-A	154	649	109	192	20	10	4	52	44	14	.296	.350	.376	90	-8	-9	84	8	4	0	3	*2	0.5
1957	Chi-A	155	619	110	**196**	27	8	6	61	75	13	.317	.404	.415	124	24	24	109	5	6	-2	21	*2	5.2
1958	Chi-A	155	623	82	**187**	21	6	0	49	47	11	.300	.360	.353	99	-1	1	79	5	6	-2	11	*2	1.1
1959	*Chi-A	156	624	84	191	34	6	2	70	71	13	.306	.383	.389	114	13	14	97	5	6	-2	-3	*2	1.5
1960	Chi-A	150	605	85	175	24	**10**	2	59	50	13	.289	.353	.372	97	-2	-1	81	2	4	-2	12	*2	2.0
1961	Chi-A	159	606	67	152	11	5	2	51	59	12	.251	.326	.295	69	-26	-25	60	2	3	-1	-6	*2	-1.2
1962	Chi-A	157	621	79	166	27	7	2	54	38	12	.267	.317	.343	78	-19	-19	67	1	2	-1	1	*2	-0.7
1963	Chi-A	137	539	54	140	19	0	2	42	24	17	.260	.300	.306	72	-21	-20	49	0	2	-1	-8	*2	-2.0
1964	Hou-N	133	442	45	117	12	6	0	28	27	13	.265	.322	.319	86	-10	-7	47	2	2	-1	-6	*2	-0.5
1965	Hou-N	21	41	3	11	2	0	0	1	0	2	.268	.286	.317	75	-2	-1	3	0	0	0	-0	/312	-0.1
Total	19	2367	9232	1279	2663	355	112	35	790	719	216	.288	.348	.363	94	-75	-71	1197	76	80	-25	43	*2/31	9.4

■ JACK FOX　Fox, John Paul　b: 5/21/1885, Reading, Pa.　d: 6/28/63, Reading, Pa.　BR/TR, 5'10", 185 lbs.　Deb: 6/02/08

YEAR	TM/L	G	AB	R	H	2B	3B	HR	RBI	BB	SO	AVG	OBP	SLG	PRO+	BR	/A	RC	SB	CS	SBR	FR	POS	TPR
1908	Phi-A	9	30	2	6	0	0	0	0	0	0	.200	.200	.200	30	-2	-2	2	2			-1	/O	-0.3

■ BILL FOX　Fox, William Henry　b: 1/15/1872, Fiskdale, Mass.　d: 5/7/46, Minneapolis, Minn.　BB/TR, 5'10", 160 lbs.　Deb: 8/20/1897

YEAR	TM/L	G	AB	R	H	2B	3B	HR	RBI	BB	SO	AVG	OBP	SLG	PRO+	BR	/A	RC	SB	CS	SBR	FR	POS	TPR
1897	Was-N	4	14	4	4	0	0	0	0	1		.286	.333	.286	67	-1	-1	1	0			0	/S2	0.0
1901	Cin-N	43	159	9	28	2	1	0	7	4		.176	.201	.201	19	-16	-15	9	9			5	/2	-0.5
Total	2	47	173	13	32	2	1	0	7	5		.185	.212	.208	24	-17	-15	10	9			5	/2S	-0.5

■ JIMMIE FOXX　Foxx, James Emory "Beast" or "Double X"　b: 10/22/07, Sudlersville, Md.　d: 7/21/67, Miami, Fla.　BR/TR, 6', 195 lbs.　Deb: 5/01/25　H

YEAR	TM/L	G	AB	R	H	2B	3B	HR	RBI	BB	SO	AVG	OBP	SLG	PRO+	BR	/A	RC	SB	CS	SBR	FR	POS	TPR
1925	Phi-A	10	9	2	6	1	0	0	0	0	1	.667	.667	.778	249	2	2	4	0	0	0	0	/C	0.2

YEAR	TM/L	G	AB	R	H	2B	3B	HR	RBI	BB	SO	AVG	OBP	SLG	PRO+	BR	/A	RC	SB	CS	SBR	FR	POS	TPR
1926	Phi-A	26	32	8	10	2	1	0	5	1	6	.313	.333	.438	94	-0	-0	5	1	0	0	2	C/O	0.3
1927	Phi-A	61	130	23	42	6	5	3	20	14	11	.323	.393	.515	127	6	5	25	2	1	0	-2	1/C	0.2
1928	Phi-A	118	400	85	131	29	10	13	79	60	43	.327	.416	.548	147	30	29	91	3	8	-4	-2	31C	2.3
1929	*Phi-A	149	517	123	183	23	9	33	118	103	70	.354	**.463**	.625	171	63	60	154	9	7	-2	-4	*1/3	3.3
1930	*Phi-A	153	562	127	188	33	13	37	156	93	66	.335	.429	.637	159	57	53	154	7	7	-2	-2	*1	2.8
1931	*Phi-A	139	515	93	150	32	10	30	120	73	84	.291	.380	.567	138	33	28	113	4	3	-1	-3	*13/O	1.4
1932	Phi-A	154	585	**151**	213	33	9	**58**	169	116	96	**.364**	.469	**.749**	203	97	93	207	3	7	-3	-5	*13	**6.4**
1933	Phi-A	149	573	125	204	37	9	**48**	163	96	93	**.356**	.449	**.703**	199	83	82	184	2	2	-1	6	*1/S	**7.0**
1934	Phi-A	150	539	120	180	28	6	44	130	**111**	75	.334	.449	.653	188	66	70	165	11	2	2	4	*1/3	4.7
1935	Phi-A	147	535	118	185	33	7	**36**	115	114	99	.346	.461	.636	182	67	68	163	6	4	-1	6	*1C/3	5.6
1936	Bos-A	155	585	130	198	32	8	41	143	105	119	.338	.440	.631	153	57	51	168	13	4	2	1	*1O/3	2.9
1937	Bos-A	150	569	111	162	24	6	36	127	99	96	.285	.392	.538	127	27	24	123	10	8	-2	10	*1/C	1.3
1938	Bos-A	149	565	139	197	33	9	50	**175**	**119**	76	**.349**	**.462**	**.704**	180	78	74	189	5	4	-1	6	*1	**5.2**
1939	Bos-A	124	467	130	168	31	10	**35**	105	89	72	.360	**.464**	**.694**	185	66	63	150	4	3	-1	7	*1/P	**5.3**
1940	Bos-A	144	515	106	153	30	4	36	119	101	87	.297	.412	.581	148	43	39	124	4	7	-3	-1	1C/3	3.1
1941	Bos-A	135	487	87	146	27	8	19	105	93	103	.300	.412	.505	138	31	30	102	2	5	-2	7	*1/3O	2.9
1942	Bos-A	30	100	18	27	4	0	5	14	18	15	.270	.392	.460	134	6	5	20	0	0	0	6	1	1.1
	Chi-N	70	205	25	42	8	0	3	19	22	55	.205	.282	.288	69	-9	-8	16	1			-4	1/C	-1.6
1944	Chi-N	15	20	0	1	1	0	0	2	2	5	.050	.136	.100	-33	-4	-4	0	0			2	/3C	-0.1
1945	Phi-N	89	224	30	60	11	1	7	38	23	39	.268	.336	.420	112	2	3	32	0			-3	13/P	0.0
Total	20	2317	8134	1751	2646	458	125	534	1922	1452	1311	.325	.428	.609	161	803	768	2189	87	72		33	*13C/OPS	54.3

■ JOE FOY
Foy, Joseph Anthony b: 2/21/43, New York, N.Y. d: 10/12/89, Bronx, N.Y. BR/TR, 6', 215 lbs. Deb: 4/13/66

YEAR	TM/L	G	AB	R	H	2B	3B	HR	RBI	BB	SO	AVG	OBP	SLG	PRO+	BR	/A	RC	SB	CS	SBR	FR	POS	TPR
1966	Bos-A	151	554	97	145	23	8	15	63	91	80	.262	.368	.413	112	20	13	86	2	5	-2	-1	*3S	0.8
1967	*Bos-A	130	446	70	112	22	4	16	49	46	87	.251	.325	.426	111	11	7	59	8	6	-1	-10	*3/O	-0.1
1968	Bos-A	150	515	65	116	18	2	10	60	84	91	.225	.338	.326	96	4	0	64	26	8	3	3	*3/O	1.2
1969	KC-A	145	519	72	136	19	2	11	71	74	75	.262	.360	.370	104	5	5	73	37	15	2	-8	*310/S2	0.0
1970	NY-N	99	322	39	76	12	0	6	37	68	58	.236	.376	.329	90	-1	-1	45	22	13	-1	-1	3	-0.5
1971	Was-A	41	128	12	30	8	0	0	11	27	14	.234	.368	.297	96	-0	-1	16	4	1	1	4	3/2S	0.4
Total	6	716	2484	355	615	102	16	58	291	390	405	.248	.354	.372	103	38	24	343	99	48	1	-12	3/OS12	1.8

■ JULIO FRANCO
Franco, Julio Cesar (b: Julio Cesar Robles (Franco)) b: 8/23/58, Hato Mayor, D.R. BR/TR, 6', 160 lbs. Deb: 4/23/82

YEAR	TM/L	G	AB	R	H	2B	3B	HR	RBI	BB	SO	AVG	OBP	SLG	PRO+	BR	/A	RC	SB	CS	SBR	FR	POS	TPR
1982	Phi-N	16	29	3	8	1	0	0	3	2	4	.276	.323	.310	76	-1	-1	2	0	2	-1	-0	S/3	-0.1
1983	Cle-A	149	560	68	153	24	8	8	80	27	50	.273	.309	.387	87	-8	-11	61	32	12	2	-7	*S	-0.6
1984	Cle-A	160	658	82	188	22	5	3	79	43	68	.286	.335	.348	88	-9	-10	73	19	10	-0	-0	*S/D	0.1
1985	Cle-A	160	636	97	183	33	4	6	90	54	74	.288	.347	.381	100	0	1	79	13	9	-2	-22	*S/2D	-1.1
1986	Cle-A	149	599	80	183	30	5	10	74	32	66	.306	.341	.422	108	4	6	76	10	7	-1	-5	*S2/D	0.8
1987	Cle-A	128	495	86	158	24	3	8	52	57	56	.319	.393	.428	117	14	14	82	32	9	4	-24	*S/2D	0.1
1988	Cle-A	152	613	88	186	23	6	10	54	56	72	.303	.364	.409	113	14	12	90	25	11	1	-10	*2/D	1.3
1989	Tex-A	150	548	80	173	31	5	13	92	66	69	.316	.390	.462	137	30	28	95	21	3	5	-6	*2D	2.9
1990	Tex-A	157	582	96	172	27	1	11	69	82	83	.296	.384	.402	118	18	17	95	31	10	3	-2	*2/D	2.6
Total	9	1221	4720	680	1404	215	37	69	593	419	542	.297	.357	.403	108	63	56	653	183	73	11	-75	S2/D3	6.0

■ TITO FRANCONA
Francona, John Patsy b: 11/4/33, Aliquippa, Pa. BL/TL, 5'11", 190 lbs. Deb: 4/17/56

YEAR	TM/L	G	AB	R	H	2B	3B	HR	RBI	BB	SO	AVG	OBP	SLG	PRO+	BR	/A	RC	SB	CS	SBR	FR	POS	TPR
1956	Bal-A	139	445	62	115	16	4	9	57	51	60	.258	.336	.373	94	-8	-4	58	11	5	0	0	*O1	-0.9
1957	Bal-A	97	279	35	65	8	3	7	38	29	48	.233	.312	.358	88	-7	-5	31	7	3	0	-9	O/1	-1.7
1958	Chi-A	41	128	10	33	3	2	1	10	14	24	.258	.331	.336	86	-3	-2	13	2	3	-1	-3	O	-0.8
	Det-A	45	69	11	17	5	0	0	10	15	16	.246	.381	.319	88	-0	-0	9	0	0	0	-2	O/1	-0.3
	Yr	86	197	21	50	8	2	1	20	29	40	.254	.350	.330	86	-2	-3	23	2	3	-1	-5		-1.1
1959	Cle-A	122	399	68	145	17	2	20	79	35	42	.363	.419	.566	174	37	**39**	93	2	0	1	-2	O1	3.4
1960	Cle-A	147	544	84	159	**36**	2	17	79	67	67	.292	.375	.460	128	19	21	96	4	1	1	3	*O1	1.8
1961	Cle-A	155	592	87	178	30	8	16	85	56	52	.301	.365	.459	122	15	18	100	2	1	0	-2	*O1	0.9
1962	Cle-A	158	621	82	169	28	5	14	70	47	74	.272	.330	.401	99	-4	-2	84	3	2	-0	3	*1	-0.9
1963	Cle-A	142	500	57	114	29	0	10	41	47	77	.228	.297	.346	80	-14	-13	52	9	1	2	-7	*O1	-2.3
1964	Cle-A	111	270	35	67	13	2	8	24	44	46	.248	.362	.400	113	6	6	41	1	3	-2	-10	O1	-0.8
1965	StL-N	81	174	15	45	6	2	5	19	17	30	.259	.325	.402	95	1	-1	23	0	0	0	-5	O1	-0.9
1966	StL-N	83	156	14	33	4	1	4	17	7	27	.212	.250	.327	59	-9	-9	13	0	0	0	1	1/O	-1.0
1967	Phi-N	27	73	7	15	1	0	0	3	7	10	.205	.275	.219	43	-5	-5	4	0	1	-1	1	1/O	-0.5
	Atl-N	82	254	28	63	5	1	6	25	20	34	.248	.305	.346	87	-5	-4	27	1	0	0	1	1/O	-0.6
	Yr	109	327	35	78	6	1	6	28	27	44	.239	.299	.318	77	-10	-9	31	1	1	-0	2		-1.1
1968	Atl-N	122	346	32	99	13	1	2	47	51	45	.286	.378	.347	118	10	10	47	3	0	1	-8	O1	-0.1
1969	Atl-N	51	88	5	26	1	0	2	12	13	10	.295	.386	.375	114	2	2	13	0	1	-1	-1	O/1	0.0
	Oak-A	32	85	12	29	6	1	3	20	12	11	.341	.423	.541	175	8	8	21	0	0	0	-2	1/O	0.5
1970	Oak-A	32	33	2	8	0	0	1	6	6	6	.242	.375	.333	100	0	0	4	0	0	0	1	/1O	0.1
	Mil-A	52	65	4	15	3	0	0	4	6	15	.231	.296	.277	58	-4	-4	6	1	0	0	1	1	-0.2
	Yr	84	98	6	23	3	0	1	10	12	21	.235	.324	.296	73	-3	-3	10	1	0	0	1		-0.1
Total	15	1719	5121	650	1395	224	34	125	656	544	694	.272	.346	.403	108	40	55	734	46	21	1	-40	O1	-4.1

■ TERRY FRANCONA
Francona, Terry Jon b: 4/22/59, Aberdeen, S.D. BL/TL, 6'1", 190 lbs. Deb: 8/19/81

YEAR	TM/L	G	AB	R	H	2B	3B	HR	RBI	BB	SO	AVG	OBP	SLG	PRO+	BR	/A	RC	SB	CS	SBR	FR	POS	TPR
1981	*Mon-N	34	95	11	26	0	1	1	8	5	6	.274	.317	.326	82	-2	-2	11	1	0	0	0	O/1	-0.2
1982	Mon-N	46	131	14	42	3	0	0	9	8	11	.321	.360	.344	96	-0	-0	16	2	3	-1	-7	O1	-0.9
1983	Mon-N	120	230	21	59	11	1	3	22	6	20	.257	.275	.352	73	-9	-9	20	0	2	-1	0	O1	-1.3
1984	Mon-N	58	214	18	74	19	2	1	18	5	12	.346	.364	.467	138	8	9	35	0	0	0	8	1/O	1.6
1985	Mon-N	107	281	19	75	15	1	2	31	12	12	.267	.299	.349	86	-8	-6	29	5	5	-2	2	1O/3	-0.7
1986	Chi-N	86	124	13	31	3	0	2	8	6	8	.250	.283	.323	64	-5	-7	11	0	1	-1	-1	O1	-0.9
1987	Cin-N	102	207	16	47	5	0	3	12	10	12	.227	.266	.295	46	-15	-17	16	2	0	1	-1	1/O	-1.3
1988	Cle-A	62	212	24	66	8	0	1	12	5	18	.311	.327	.363	91	-2	-3	24	0	0	0	1	D/1O	-0.1
1989	Mil-A	90	233	26	54	10	1	3	23	9	20	.232	.257	.322	63	-12	-12	18	2	1	0	1	1DO/P	-1.3
1990	Mil-A	3	4	1	0	0	0	0	0	0	0	.000	.000	.000	-99	-1	-1	0	0	0	0	0	/1	0.0
Total	10	708	1731	163	474	74	6	16	143	65	119	.274	.302	.351	81	-47	-47	179	12	12	-4	11	10/DP3	-5.1

■ CHARLIE FRANK
Frank, Charles b: 5/30/1870, Mobile, Ala. d: 5/24/22, Memphis, Tenn. Deb: 8/18/1893

YEAR	TM/L	G	AB	R	H	2B	3B	HR	RBI	BB	SO	AVG	OBP	SLG	PRO+	BR	/A	RC	SB	CS	SBR	FR	POS	TPR
1893	StL-N	40	164	29	55	6	3	1	17	18	8	.335	.408	.427	124	6	6	33	8			3	O	0.6
1894	StL-N	80	319	52	89	12	7	4	42	44	13	.279	.372	.398	87	-6	-6	54	14			-2	O/1P	-0.9
Total	2	120	483	81	144	18	10	5	59	62	21	.298	.384	.408	99	0	-0	86	22			1	O/1P	-0.3

■ FRED FRANK
Frank, Frederick b: 3/11/1874, Louisa, Ky. d: 3/27/50, Ashland, Ky. Deb: 9/27/1898

YEAR	TM/L	G	AB	R	H	2B	3B	HR	RBI	BB	SO	AVG	OBP	SLG	PRO+	BR	/A	RC	SB	CS	SBR	FR	POS	TPR
1898	Cle-N	17	53	3	11	1	1	0	3	4		.208	.276	.264	58	-3	-3	4	1			3	O	0.0

■ FRANKLIN
Franklin Deb: 9/27/1884

YEAR	TM/L	G	AB	R	H	2B	3B	HR	RBI	BB	SO	AVG	OBP	SLG	PRO+	BR	/A	RC	SB	CS	SBR	FR	POS	TPR
1884	Was-U	1	3	0	0	0	0	0	0	0	0	.000	.000	.000	-99	-1	-1	0	0			0	/O	0.0

■ MOE FRANKLIN
Franklin, Murray Asher b: 4/1/14, Chicago, Ill. d: 3/16/78, Harbor City, Cal. BR/TR, 6', 175 lbs. Deb: 8/12/41

YEAR	TM/L	G	AB	R	H	2B	3B	HR	RBI	BB	SO	AVG	OBP	SLG	PRO+	BR	/A	RC	SB	CS	SBR	FR	POS	TPR
1941	Det-A	13	10	1	3	1	0	0	0	2	2	.300	.417	.400	106	0	0	2	0	0	0	-1	/S3	0.0
1942	Det-A	48	154	24	40	7	0	2	16	7	5	.260	.301	.344	75	-4	-6	16	0	0	0	-6	S/2	-0.9

YEAR	TM/L	G	AB	R	H	2B	3B	HR	RBI	BB	SO	AVG	OBP	SLG	PRO+	BR	/A	RC	SB	CS	SBR	FR	POS	TPR
Total	2	61	164	25	43	8	0	2	16	9	7	.262	.309	.348	77	-4	-6	18	0	0	0	-7	/S23	-0.9

■ HERMAN FRANKS
Franks, Herman Louis b: 1/4/14, Price, Utah BL/TR, 5'10.5", 187 lbs. Deb: 4/27/39 MC

YEAR	TM/L	G	AB	R	H	2B	3B	HR	RBI	BB	SO	AVG	OBP	SLG	PRO+	BR	/A	RC	SB	CS	SBR	FR	POS	TPR
1939	StL-N	17	17	1	1	0	0	0	3	3	3	.059	.200	.059	-26	-3	-3	0	0			3	C	0.0
1940	Bro-N	65	131	11	24	4	0	1	14	20	6	.183	.296	.237	46	-9	-10	10	2			9	C	0.1
1941	•Bro-N	57	139	10	28	7	0	1	11	14	13	.201	.275	.273	52	-8	-9	11	0			3	C/O	0.0
1947	Phi-A	8	15	2	3	0	1	0	1	4	4	.200	.368	.333	94	0	0	2	0	0	0	-1	/C	0.0
1948	Phi-A	40	98	10	22	7	1	1	14	16	11	.224	.345	.347	84	-2	-2	12	0	0	0	2	C	0.2
1949	NY-N	1	3	1	2	0	0	0	0	0	0	.667	.667	.667	259	1	1	1	0			0	/C	0.1
Total	6	188	403	35	80	18	2	3	43	57	37	.199	.302	.275	57	-21	-23	37	2	0		16	C/O	0.4

■ JOE FRAZIER
Frazier, Joseph Filmore b: 10/6/22, Liberty, N.C. BL/TR, 6', 180 lbs. Deb: 8/31/47 M

YEAR	TM/L	G	AB	R	H	2B	3B	HR	RBI	BB	SO	AVG	OBP	SLG	PRO+	BR	/A	RC	SB	CS	SBR	FR	POS	TPR
1947	Cle-A	9	14	1	1	1	0	0	0	1	1	.071	.133	.143	-24	-2	-2	0	0	0	0	-0	/O	-0.2
1954	StL-N	81	88	8	26	5	2	3	18	13	17	.295	.392	.500	129	4	4	18	0	0	0	-0	O/1	0.3
1955	StL-N	58	70	12	14	1	0	4	9	6	12	.200	.273	.386	72	-3	-3	7	0	0	0	-1	O	-0.3
1956	StL-N	14	19	1	4	2	0	1	4	3	3	.211	.318	.474	109	0	0	3	0	1	-1	-1	/O	0.0
	Cin-N	10	17	2	4	0	0	1	2	1	7	.235	.278	.412	77	-0	-1	2	0	0	0	0	/O	0.0
	Yr	24	36	3	8	2	0	2	6	4	10	.222	.300	.444	94	-0	-0	4	0	1	-1	-1		0.0
	Bal-A	45	74	7	19	6	0	1	12	11	6	.257	.360	.378	103	-0	1	10	0	0	0	1	O	0.0
Total	4	217	282	31	68	15	2	10	45	35	46	.241	.331	.415	97	-2	-1	40	0	1	-1	-1	/O1	-0.2

■ JOHNNY FREDERICK
Frederick, John Henry b: 1/26/02, Denver, Colo. d: 6/18/77, Tigard, Ore. BL/TL, 5'11", 165 lbs. Deb: 4/18/29

YEAR	TM/L	G	AB	R	H	2B	3B	HR	RBI	BB	SO	AVG	OBP	SLG	PRO+	BR	/A	RC	SB	CS	SBR	FR	POS	TPR
1929	Bro-N	148	628	127	206	52	6	24	75	39	34	.328	.372	.545	127	21	23	122	6			3	*O	1.2
1930	Bro-N	142	616	120	206	44	11	17	76	46	34	.334	.383	.524	118	16	17	120	1			10	*O	1.5
1931	Bro-N	146	611	81	165	34	8	17	71	31	46	.270	.312	.435	100	-3	-3	84	2			-4	*O	-1.3
1932	Bro-N	118	384	54	115	28	2	16	56	25	35	.299	.349	.508	130	14	15	69	1			-2	O	0.6
1933	Bro-N	147	556	65	171	22	7	7	64	36	14	.308	.355	.410	123	13	16	84	9			-6	*O	0.1
1934	Bro-N	104	307	51	91	20	1	4	35	33	13	.296	.370	.407	114	4	6	49	4			-2	O/1	0.1
Total	6	805	3102	498	954	200	35	85	377	210	176	.308	.357	.477	118	64	74	527	23			-0	O/1	2.2

■ ED FREED
Freed, Edwin Charles b: 8/22/19, Centre Valley, Pa. BR/TR, 5'6", 165 lbs. Deb: 9/11/42

YEAR	TM/L	G	AB	R	H	2B	3B	HR	RBI	BB	SO	AVG	OBP	SLG	PRO+	BR	/A	RC	SB	CS	SBR	FR	POS	TPR
1942	Phi-N	13	33	3	10	3	1	0	1	4	3	.303	.378	.455	151	2	2	6	1			0	O	0.2

■ ROGER FREED
Freed, Roger Vernon b: 6/2/46, Los Angeles, Cal. BR/TR, 6', 190 lbs. Deb: 9/18/70

YEAR	TM/L	G	AB	R	H	2B	3B	HR	RBI	BB	SO	AVG	OBP	SLG	PRO+	BR	/A	RC	SB	CS	SBR	FR	POS	TPR
1970	Bal-A	4	13	0	2	0	0	0	1	3	4	.154	.313	.154	32	-1	-1	1	0	0	0	0	/1O	0.0
1971	Phi-N	118	348	23	77	12	1	6	37	44	86	.221	.314	.313	78	-9	-9	35	0	3	-2	-7	*O/C	-2.2
1972	Phi-N	73	129	10	29	4	0	6	18	23	39	.225	.346	.395	108	2	2	18	0	1	-1	2	O	0.1
1974	Cin-N	6	6	1	2	0	0	1	3	1	1	.333	.429	.833	251	1	1	2	0	0	0	0	/1	0.1
1976	Mon-N	8	15	0	3	1	0	0	1	0	3	.200	.200	.267	30	-1	-1	1	0	0	0	0	/1O	-0.1
1977	StL-N	49	83	10	33	2	1	5	21	11	9	.398	.468	.627	194	11	11	24	0	0	0	-1	1/O	0.9
1978	StL-N	52	92	3	22	6	0	2	20	8	17	.239	.300	.370	87	-2	-2	10	1	0	0	0	1/O	-0.1
1979	StL-N	34	31	2	8	2	0	2	8	5	7	.258	.361	.516	135	2	2	6	0	0	0	0	/1	0.2
Total	8	344	717	49	176	27	2	22	109	95	166	.245	.337	.381	101	2	2	97	1	4	-2	-6	O/1C	-1.1

■ BILL FREEHAN
Freehan, William Ashley b: 11/29/41, Detroit, Mich. BR/TR, 6'3", 203 lbs. Deb: 9/26/61

YEAR	TM/L	G	AB	R	H	2B	3B	HR	RBI	BB	SO	AVG	OBP	SLG	PRO+	BR	/A	RC	SB	CS	SBR	FR	POS	TPR
1961	Det-A	4	10	1	4	0	0	0	4	1	0	.400	.455	.400	127	1	0	2	0	0	0	1	/C	0.2
1963	Det-A	100	300	37	73	12	2	9	36	39	56	.243	.334	.387	98	1	-0	40	2	0	1	-1	C1	0.0
1964	Det-A	144	520	69	156	14	8	18	80	36	68	.300	.355	.462	123	17	16	86	5	1	1	-3	*C/1	2.0
1965	Det-A	130	431	45	101	15	0	10	43	39	63	.234	.308	.339	83	-9	-10	45	4	2	0	-0	*C	0.0
1966	Det-A	136	492	47	115	22	0	12	46	40	72	.234	.295	.352	83	-10	-11	50	5	2	0	-1	*C/1	-0.5
1967	Det-A	155	517	66	146	23	1	20	74	73	71	.282	.392	.447	143	34	32	94	1	2	-1	-8	*C1	3.4
1968	•Det-A	155	540	73	142	24	2	25	84	65	64	.263	.367	.454	143	33	31	94	0	1	-1	5	*C1/O	4.5
1969	Det-A	143	489	61	128	16	3	16	49	53	55	.262	.344	.405	104	6	3	68	1	2	-1	3	*C1	1.2
1970	Det-A	117	395	44	95	17	3	16	52	52	48	.241	.335	.420	106	4	3	55	0	3	-2	-16	*C	-1.2
1971	Det-A	148	516	57	143	26	4	21	71	54	48	.277	.356	.465	126	20	18	82	2	7	-4	-13	*C/O	0.9
1972	•Det-A	111	374	51	98	18	2	10	56	48	51	.262	.355	.401	121	12	11	55	0	1	-1	-0	*C/1	1.2
1973	Det-A	110	380	33	89	10	1	6	29	40	30	.234	.325	.313	75	-9	-12	39	0	1	0	8	C/1D	-0.1
1974	Det-A	130	445	58	132	17	5	18	60	42	44	.297	.364	.479	136	23	21	77	2	0	1	-5	1C/D	1.6
1975	Det-A	120	427	42	105	17	3	14	47	32	56	.246	.308	.398	94	-2	-4	51	2	0	1	-9	*C/1	-0.9
1976	Det-A	71	237	22	64	10	1	5	27	12	27	.270	.308	.384	98	-1	-1	28	0	0	0	-2	C/1D	-0.1
Total	15	1774	6073	706	1591	241	35	200	758	626	753	.262	.342	.412	111	120	97	867	24	21	-5	-41	*C1/DO	12.2

■ JERRY FREEMAN
Freeman, Frank Ellsworth "Buck" b: 12/26/1879, Placerville, Cal. d: 9/30/52, Los Angeles, Cal. BL/TR, 6'2", 220 lbs. Deb: 4/14/08

YEAR	TM/L	G	AB	R	H	2B	3B	HR	RBI	BB	SO	AVG	OBP	SLG	PRO+	BR	/A	RC	SB	CS	SBR	FR	POS	TPR
1908	Was-A	154	531	45	134	15	5	1	45	36		.252	.300	.305	108	-1	4	50	6			-13	*1	-1.3
1909	Was-A	19	48	2	8	0	1	0	3	4		.167	.245	.208	46	-3	-3	3	3			-2	1/O	-0.4
Total	2	173	579	47	142	15	6	1	48	40		.245	.295	.297	102	-4	1	53	9			-14	1/O	-1.7

■ JOHN FREEMAN
Freeman, John Edward b: 1/24/01, Boston, Mass. d: 4/14/58, Washington, D.C. BR/TR, 5'8", 160 lbs. Deb: 6/17/27

YEAR	TM/L	G	AB	R	H	2B	3B	HR	RBI	BB	SO	AVG	OBP	SLG	PRO+	BR	/A	RC	SB	CS	SBR	FR	POS	TPR
1927	Bos-A	4	2	0	0	0	0	0	0	0	0	.000	.000	.000	-99	-1	-1	0	0	0	0	-2	/O	-0.1

■ BUCK FREEMAN
Freeman, John Frank b: 10/30/1871, Catasauqua, Pa. d: 6/25/49, Wilkes-Barre, Pa. BL/TL, 5'9", 169 lbs. Deb: 6/27/1891

YEAR	TM/L	G	AB	R	H	2B	3B	HR	RBI	BB	SO	AVG	OBP	SLG	PRO+	BR	/A	RC	SB	CS	SBR	FR	POS	TPR
1891	Was-a	5	18	1	4	1	0	0	1	2	2	.222	.300	.278	71	-1	-1	2	0			-0	/P	0.0
1898	Was-N	29	107	19	39	2	3	3	21	7		.364	.424	.523	175	10	10	25	2			1	O	0.8
1899	Was-N	155	588	107	187	19	25	25	122	23		.318	.361	.563	156	38	39	130	21			-12	*O/P	1.6
1900	Bos-N	117	418	58	126	19	13	6	65	25		.301	.355	.452	111	13	5	72	10			-11	O1	-1.2
1901	Bos-A	129	490	88	166	23	15	12	114	44		.339	.401	.520	159	37	38	113	17			-5	*1/2O	2.4
1902	Bos-A	138	564	75	174	38	19	11	121	32		.309	.352	.502	133	25	23	109	17			-0	*O	1.3
1903	•Bos-A	141	567	74	163	39	20	13	104	30		.287	.323	.496	138	28	25	96	5			-6	*O	1.0
1904	Bos-A	157	597	64	167	20	19	7	84	30		.280	.316	.412	125	20	16	83	7			-6	*O	1.0
1905	Bos-A	130	455	59	109	20	8	3	49	46		.240	.309	.338	106	4	4	53	8			-15	1O/3	-1.6
1906	Bos-A	121	392	42	98	18	9	1	30	28		.250	.300	.349	105	2	2	45	5			1	O1/3	0.0
1907	Bos-A	4	12	1	2	0	0	0	2	3		.167	.333	.417	142	1	1	2	0			0	/O	0.1
Total	11	1126	4208	588	1235	199	131	82	713	272	2	.293	.343	.462	132	177	162	729	92			-53	O1/P32	4.5

■ LA VEL FREEMAN
Freeman, La Vel Maurice b: 2/18/63, Oakland, Cal. BL/TL, 5'9", 170 lbs. Deb: 4/07/89

YEAR	TM/L	G	AB	R	H	2B	3B	HR	RBI	BB	SO	AVG	OBP	SLG	PRO+	BR	/A	RC	SB	CS	SBR	FR	POS	TPR
1989	Mil-A	2	3	1	0	0	0	0	0	0	2	.000	.000	.000	-99	-1	-1	0	0	0	0	0	/D	0.0

■ GENE FREESE
Freese, Eugene Lewis "Augie" b: 1/8/34, Wheeling, W.Va. BR/TR, 5'11", 175 lbs. Deb: 4/13/55

YEAR	TM/L	G	AB	R	H	2B	3B	HR	RBI	BB	SO	AVG	OBP	SLG	PRO+	BR	/A	RC	SB	CS	SBR	FR	POS	TPR
1955	Pit-N	134	455	69	115	21	8	14	44	34	57	.253	.310	.426	94	-6	-5	60	5	1	1	-2	32	0.0
1956	Pit-N	65	207	17	43	9	0	3	14	16	45	.208	.274	.295	54	-14	-13	18	2	1	0	-7	32	-1.8
1957	Pit-N	114	346	44	98	18	2	6	31	17	42	.283	.321	.399	95	-3	-4	44	9	4	0	-3	32O	-0.3
1958	Pit-N	17	18	1	3	0	0	1	2	1	2	.167	.211	.333	42	-2	-2	1	0	0	0	0	/3	0.0
	StL-N	62	191	28	49	11	1	6	16	10	32	.257	.294	.419	83	-4	-5	24	1	1	-0	-25	S2/3	-2.8
	Yr	79	209	29	52	11	1	7	18	11	34	.249	.286	.411	80	-6	-7	24	1	1	-0	-24		-2.8
1959	Phi-N	132	400	60	107	14	5	23	70	43	61	.268	.346	.500	120	12	11	69	8	4	0	-23	*3/2	-1.5

YEAR	TM/L	G	AB	R	H	2B	3B	HR	RBI	BB	SO	AVG	OBP	SLG	PRO+	BR	/A	RC	SB	CS	SBR	FR	POS	TPR
1960	Chi-A	127	455	60	124	32	6	17	79	29	65	.273	.318	.481	114	6	6	64	10	6	-1	0	*3	0.8
1961	*Cin-N	152	575	78	159	27	2	26	87	27	78	.277	.309	.466	101	-0	-1	77	8	2	1	-17	*3/2	-2.3
1962	Cin-N	18	42	2	6	1	0	0	1	6	8	.143	.250	.167	14	-5	-5	2	0	0	0	-2	3	-0.6
1963	Cin-N	66	217	20	53	9	1	6	26	17	42	.244	.305	.378	93	-1	-2	26	4	2	0	-6	3/O	-0.8
1964	Pit-N	99	289	33	65	13	2	9	40	19	45	.225	.273	.377	81	-8	-8	28	1	2	-1	-6	3	-1.9
1965	Pit-N	43	80	6	21	4	0	0	8	6	18	.262	.330	.313	82	-2	-2	7	0	2	-1	-1	3	-0.4
	Chi-A	17	32	2	9	0	1	1	4	5	9	.281	.378	.438	140	1	2	6	0	0	0	-3	/3	0.0
1966	Chi-A	48	106	8	22	2	0	3	10	8	20	.208	.270	.311	71	-5	-4	9	2	1	0	3	3	-0.1
	Hou-N	21	33	1	3	0	0	0	0	5	11	.091	.211	.091	-13	-5	-5	1	1	0	0	0	/32O	-0.4
Total	12	1115	3446	429	877	161	28	115	432	243	535	.254	.307	.418	94	-37	-36	434	51	26	-0	-89	32/SO	-12.1

■ GEORGE FREESE
Freese, George Walter "Bud" b: 9/12/26, Wheeling, W.Va. BR/TR, 6', 190 lbs. Deb: 4/29/53

YEAR	TM/L	G	AB	R	H	2B	3B	HR	RBI	BB	SO	AVG	OBP	SLG	PRO+	BR	/A	RC	SB	CS	SBR	FR	POS	TPR
1953	Det-A	1	1	0	0	0	0	0	0	0	0	.000	.000	.000	-99	-0	-0	0	0	0	0	0	H	0.0
1955	Pit-N	51	179	17	46	8	2	3	22	17	18	.257	.328	.374	87	-3	-3	21	1	1	-0	-8	3	-1.1
1961	Chi-N	9	7	0	2	0	0	0	1	1	4	.286	.375	.286	78	-0	-0	1	0	0	0	0	H	0.0
Total	3	61	187	17	48	8	2	3	23	18	22	.257	.329	.369	86	-4	-4	22	1	1	-0	-8	/3	-1.1

■ JIM FREGOSI
Fregosi, James Louis b: 4/4/42, San Francisco, Cal. BR/TR, 6'1", 190 lbs. Deb: 9/14/61 M

YEAR	TM/L	G	AB	R	H	2B	3B	HR	RBI	BB	SO	AVG	OBP	SLG	PRO+	BR	/A	RC	SB	CS	SBR	FR	POS	TPR
1961	LA-A	11	27	7	6	0	0	0	3	1	4	.222	.250	.222	25	-3	-3	1	0	0	0	-0	S	-0.2
1962	LA-A	58	175	15	51	3	4	3	23	18	27	.291	.358	.406	108	1	2	25	2	1	0	4	S	0.9
1963	LA-A	154	592	83	170	29	12	9	50	36	104	.287	.328	.422	115	6	10	81	2	2	-1	2	*S	1.9
1964	LA-A	147	505	86	140	22	9	18	72	72	87	.277	.372	.463	145	22	28	89	8	3	1	1	*S	3.1
1965	Cal-A	161	602	66	167	19	7	15	64	54	107	.277	.341	.407	114	9	11	85	13	5	1	6	*S	2.6
1966	Cal-A	162	611	78	154	32	7	13	67	67	89	.252	.328	.391	109	5	7	80	17	8	0	15	*S/1	3.2
1967	Cal-A	151	590	75	171	23	6	9	56	49	77	.290	.349	.395	124	14	17	82	9	6	-1	-7	*S	2.1
1968	Cal-A	159	614	77	150	21	**13**	9	49	60	101	.244	.317	.365	110	4	7	72	9	4	0	-14	*S	0.4
1969	Cal-A	161	580	78	151	22	6	12	47	93	86	.260	.364	.381	114	9	9	86	9	2	2	-16	*S	0.5
1970	Cal-A	158	601	95	167	33	5	22	82	69	92	.278	.355	.459	127	18	21	101	2	4	-1	4	*S/1	3.7
1971	Cal-A	107	347	31	81	15	1	5	33	39	61	.233	.320	.326	90	-7	-4	39	2	1	0	-9	S1/O	-0.6
1972	NY-N	101	340	31	79	15	4	5	32	38	71	.232	.311	.344	88	-6	-5	37	0	1	-1	-7	3/S1	-1.3
1973	NY-N	45	124	7	29	4	1	0	11	20	25	.234	.340	.282	75	-4	-3	12	1	2	-1	-5	S3/1O	-0.7
	Tex-A	45	157	25	42	6	2	6	16	12	31	.268	.324	.446	120	3	3	23	0	1	-1	-9	31/S	-0.6
1974	Tex-A	78	230	31	60	5	0	12	34	22	41	.261	.325	.439	121	5	5	29	0	1	-1	-1	13	0.2
1975	Tex-A	77	191	25	50	5	0	7	33	20	39	.262	.335	.398	107	2	2	24	0	1	-1	2	1D/3	0.0
1976	Tex-A	58	133	17	31	7	0	2	12	23	33	.233	.346	.331	97	1	0	17	2	0	1	0	1D/3	0.0
1977	Tex-A	13	28	4	7	1	0	1	5	3	4	.250	.323	.393	93	-0	-0	4	0	0	0	1	/1D	0.0
	Pit-N	36	56	10	16	1	1	3	16	13	10	.286	.420	.500	142	4	4	13	2	0	1	-1	1/3	0.3
1978	Pit-N	20	20	3	4	1	0	0	1	6	8	.200	.385	.250	77	-0	-0	3	0	0	0	-1	/312	-0.1
Total	18	1902	6523	844	1726	264	78	151	706	715	1097	.265	.340	.398	114	83	113	904	76	40	-1	-38	*S13/DO2	15.4

■ VERN FREIBERGER
Freiberger, Vern Donald b: 12/19/23, Detroit, Mich. BR/TL, 6'1", 170 lbs. Deb: 9/06/41

YEAR	TM/L	G	AB	R	H	2B	3B	HR	RBI	BB	SO	AVG	OBP	SLG	PRO+	BR	/A	RC	SB	CS	SBR	FR	POS	TPR
1941	Cle-A	2	8	0	1	0	0	0	1	0	2	.125	.125	.125	-35	-2	-1	0	0	0	0	1	/1	0.0

■ HOWARD FREIGAU
Freigau, Howard Earl "Ty" b: 8/1/02, Dayton, Ohio d: 7/18/32, Chattanooga, Tenn BR/TR, 5'10.5", 160 lbs. Deb: 9/13/22

YEAR	TM/L	G	AB	R	H	2B	3B	HR	RBI	BB	SO	AVG	OBP	SLG	PRO+	BR	/A	RC	SB	CS	SBR	FR	POS	TPR
1922	StL-N	3	1	0	0	0	0	0	0	0	0	.000	.000	.000	-99	-0	-0	0	0	0	0	1	/S3	0.1
1923	StL-N	113	358	30	94	18	1	1	35	25	36	.263	.314	.327	71	-16	-15	37	5	4	-1	2	S2/130	-0.5
1924	StL-N	98	376	35	101	17	6	2	39	19	24	.269	.306	.362	80	-12	-11	42	10	3	1	3	3/S	0.0
1925	StL-N	9	26	2	4	0	0	0	0	2	1	.154	.214	.154	-4	-4	-4	1	0	0	0	3	/S2	0.0
	Chi-N	117	476	77	146	22	10	8	71	30	31	.307	.349	.445	100	0	-1	73	10	6	-1	-5	3S/1	0.1
	Yr	126	502	79	150	22	10	8	71	32	32	.299	.342	.430	94	-4	-5	73	10	6	-1	-1		0.1
1926	Chi-N	140	508	51	137	27	7	3	51	43	42	.270	.327	.368	86	-10	-11	61	6			-2	*3/SO	-1.0
1927	Chi-N	30	86	12	20	5	0	0	10	9	10	.233	.313	.291	62	-4	-4	8	0			1	3	-0.1
1928	Bro-N	17	34	6	7	2	0	0	3	1	3	.206	.229	.265	29	-4	-4	2	0			-3	3/S	-0.6
	Bos-N	52	109	11	28	8	1	1	17	9	14	.257	.319	.376	86	-3	-2	13	1			-10	S2	-0.9
	Yr	69	143	17	35	10	1	1	20	10	17	.245	.299	.350	72	-7	-6	15	1			-13		-1.5
Total	7	579	1974	224	537	99	25	15	226	138	161	.272	.322	.370	82	-53	-52	238	32	13		-10	3S/210	-2.9

■ CHARLIE FRENCH
French, Charles Calvin b: 10/12/1883, Indianapolis, Ind. d: 3/30/62, Indianapolis, Ind. BL/TR, 5'6", 140 lbs. Deb: 5/23/09

YEAR	TM/L	G	AB	R	H	2B	3B	HR	RBI	BB	SO	AVG	OBP	SLG	PRO+	BR	/A	RC	SB	CS	SBR	FR	POS	TPR
1909	Bos-A	51	167	15	42	3	1	0	13	15		.251	.324	.281	90	-1	-1	18	8			-8	2S	-1.0
1910	Bos-A	9	40	4	8	1	0	0	3	1		.200	.220	.225	38	-3	-3	2	0			1	/2	-0.2
	Chi-A	45	170	17	28	1	1	0	4	10		.165	.224	.182	29	-14	-13	8	5			-14	2O	-3.4
	Yr	54	210	21	36	2	1	0	7	11		.171	.223	.190	31	-17	-16	10	5			-13		-3.6
Total	2	105	377	36	78	5	2	0	20	26		.207	.269	.231	58	-18	-18	28	13			-21	/2SO	-4.6

■ PAT FRENCH
French, Frank Alexander b: 9/22/1893, Dover, N.H. d: 7/13/69, Bath, Maine BR/TR, 6'1", 180 lbs. Deb: 7/02/17

YEAR	TM/L	G	AB	R	H	2B	3B	HR	RBI	BB	SO	AVG	OBP	SLG	PRO+	BR	/A	RC	SB	CS	SBR	FR	POS	TPR
1917	Phi-A	3	2	0	0	0	0	0	0	0	0	.000	.000	.000	-99	-0	-0	0	0			-0	/O	0.0

■ RAY FRENCH
French, Raymond Edward b: 1/9/1895, Alameda, Cal. d: 4/3/78, Alameda, Cal. BR/TR, 5'9.5", 158 lbs. Deb: 9/17/20

YEAR	TM/L	G	AB	R	H	2B	3B	HR	RBI	BB	SO	AVG	OBP	SLG	PRO+	BR	/A	RC	SB	CS	SBR	FR	POS	TPR
1920	NY-A	2	2	2	0	0	0	0	1	0	1	.000	.000	.000	-97	-1	-1	0	0	0	0	-0	/S	0.0
1923	Bro-N	43	73	14	16	2	1	0	7	4	7	.219	.269	.274	45	-6	-6	6	0	0	0	4	S	0.1
1924	Chi-A	37	112	13	20	4	0	0	11	10	13	.179	.246	.214	20	-14	-13	7	3	1	0	-2	S/2	-1.1
Total	3	82	187	29	36	6	1	0	19	14	21	.193	.252	.235	28	-20	-19	12	3	1	0	2	/S2	-1.0

■ JIM FRENCH
French, Richard James b: 8/13/41, Warren, Ohio BL/TR, 5'8", 180 lbs. Deb: 9/12/65

YEAR	TM/L	G	AB	R	H	2B	3B	HR	RBI	BB	SO	AVG	OBP	SLG	PRO+	BR	/A	RC	SB	CS	SBR	FR	POS	TPR
1965	Was-A	13	37	4	11	0	0	0	7	9	5	.297	.435	.378	135	2	2	7	1	0	0	-1	C	0.3
1966	Was-A	10	24	0	5	1	0	0	3	4	5	.208	.321	.250	67	-1	-1	2	0	1	-1	-1	C	-0.1
1967	Was-A	6	16	0	1	0	0	0	1	3	4	.063	.211	.063	-16	-2	-2	0	0	0	0	-1	/C	-0.2
1968	Was-A	59	165	9	32	5	0	1	10	19	19	.194	.281	.242	62	-8	-7	13	1	2	-1	2	C	-0.3
1969	Was-A	63	158	14	29	6	3	2	13	41	15	.184	.352	.297	88	-2	-1	20	1	0	0	8	C	1.2
1970	Was-A	69	166	20	35	3	1	1	13	38	23	.211	.358	.259	76	-4	-3	17	0	1	-1	-6	C/O	-0.8
1971	Was-A	14	41	6	6	2	0	0	4	7	7	.146	.271	.195	36	-3	-3	2	0	2	-1	-1	C	-0.4
Total	7	234	607	53	119	17	4	5	51	121	78	.196	.331	.262	74	-18	-15	61	3	6	-3	2	C/O	-0.3

■ WALT FRENCH
French, Walter Edward "Piggy" or "Fitz" b: 7/12/1899, Moorestown, N.J. d: 5/13/84, Mountain Home, Ark BL/TR, 5'7.5", 155 lbs. Deb: 9/15/23

YEAR	TM/L	G	AB	R	H	2B	3B	HR	RBI	BB	SO	AVG	OBP	SLG	PRO+	BR	/A	RC	SB	CS	SBR	FR	POS	TPR
1923	Phi-A	16	39	7	9	3	0	0	2	5	7	.231	.318	.308	64	-2	-2	4	0	1	-1	-1	O	-0.4
1925	Phi-A	67	100	20	37	9	0	0	14	1	9	.370	.376	.460	104	1	0	16	1	1	-0	0	O	0.0
1926	Phi-A	112	397	51	121	18	7	1	36	18	24	.305	.340	.393	86	-6	-9	53	2	3	-1	3	O	-1.4
1927	Phi-A	109	326	48	99	10	5	0	41	16	14	.304	.338	.365	78	-9	-11	39	9	1	2	0	O	-1.3
1928	Phi-A	48	74	9	19	4	0	0	7	2	5	.257	.286	.311	55	-5	-5	6	1	1	-0	-1	O	-0.5
1929	*Phi-A	45	45	7	12	1	0	1	9	2	3	.267	.298	.356	65	-2	-2	5	0	0	0	-3	O	-0.5
Total	6	397	981	142	297	45	12	2	109	44	62	.303	.336	.379	81	-22	-29	123	13	7	-0	-2	O	-4.2

■ BILL FRENCH
French, William b: Baltimore, Md. Deb: 4/14/1873

YEAR	TM/L	G	AB	R	H	2B	3B	HR	RBI	BB	SO	AVG	OBP	SLG	PRO+	BR	/A	RC	SB	CS	SBR	FR	POS	TPR
1873	Mar-n	5	19	3	4	0	0	0			0	.211	.211	.211	32	-2	-1	1					/1OP1	0.0

YEAR	TM/L	G	AB	R	H	2B	3B	HR	RBI	BB	SO	AVG	OBP	SLG	PRO+	BR	/A	RC	SB	CS	SBR	FR	POS	TPR

■ LONNY FREY
Frey, Linus Reinhard "Junior"   b: 8/23/10, St.Louis, Mo.   BL/TR, 5'10", 160 lbs.   Deb: 8/29/33

YEAR	TM/L	G	AB	R	H	2B	3B	HR	RBI	BB	SO	AVG	OBP	SLG	PRO+	BR	/A	RC	SB	CS	SBR	FR	POS	TPR
1933	Bro-N	34	135	25	43	5	3	0	12	13	13	.319	.378	.400	128	4	5	21	4			-14	S	-0.6
1934	Bro-N	125	490	77	139	24	5	8	57	52	54	.284	.358	.402	109	3	7	75	11			13	*S3	2.2
1935	Bro-N	131	515	88	135	35	11	11	77	66	68	.262	.352	.437	113	8	10	82	6			-4	*S/2	1.1
1936	Bro-N	148	524	63	146	29	4	4	60	71	56	.279	.369	.372	99	2	2	77	7			-32	*S2/O	-2.0
1937	Chi-N	78	198	33	55	9	3	1	22	33	15	.278	.381	.369	100	3	1	31	6			-18	S2/3O	-1.3
1938	Cin-N	124	501	76	133	26	6	4	36	49	50	.265	.331	.365	94	-6	-0	66	4			-8	*2/S	-0.2
1939	*Cin-N	125	484	95	141	27	9	11	55	72	46	.291	.387	.452	124	19	18	91	5			15	*2	3.8
1940	*Cin-N	150	563	102	150	23	6	8	54	80	48	.266	.361	.371	101	4	3	82	**22**			18	*2	3.1
1941	Cin-N	146	543	78	138	29	5	6	59	72	37	.254	.345	.359	98	-0	-0	72	16			-2	*2	0.7
1942	Cin-N	141	523	66	139	23	6	2	39	87	38	.266	.373	.344	111	10	11	75	9			5	*2	2.8
1943	Cin-N	144	586	78	154	20	8	2	43	76	56	.263	.347	.334	99	-0	1	75	7			12	*2	1.8
1946	Cin-N	111	333	46	82	10	3	3	24	63	31	.246	.368	.321	100	1	3	44	5			-3	2O	0.1
1947	Chi-N	24	43	4	9	0	0	0	3	4	6	.209	.277	.209	32	-4	-4	3	0			-2	/2	-0.4
	*NY-A	24	28	10	5	2	0	0	2	10	1	.179	.410	.250	87	0	0	5	3	0	1	3	/2	0.5
1948	NY-A	1	0	1	0	0	0	0	0	0	0	—	—	—	—	0	0	0	0	0	0	0	R	0.0
	NY-N	29	51	6	13	1	0	1	6	4	6	.255	.309	.333	73	-2	-2	6	0			-1	2	-0.1
Total	14	1535	5517	848	1482	263	69	61	549	752	525	.269	.359	.374	104	43	50	803	105	0		-17	2S/O3	11.5

■ PEPE FRIAS
Frias, Jesus Maria (Andujar)   b: 7/14/48, San De Pedro De Macoris, D.R.   BR/TR, 5'10", 159 lbs.   Deb: 4/06/73

YEAR	TM/L	G	AB	R	H	2B	3B	HR	RBI	BB	SO	AVG	OBP	SLG	PRO+	BR	/A	RC	SB	CS	SBR	FR	POS	TPR
1973	Mon-N	100	225	19	52	10	1	0	22	10	24	.231	.267	.284	51	-14	-15	16	1	3	-2	17	S2/3O	0.8
1974	Mon-N	75	112	12	24	4	1	0	7	7	10	.214	.261	.268	45	-8	-9	8	1	0	0	17	S32/O	1.3
1975	Mon-N	51	64	4	8	2	0	0	4	3	13	.125	.164	.156	-10	-10	-10	2	0	1	-1	14	S3/2	0.7
1976	Mon-N	76	113	7	28	5	0	0	8	4	14	.248	.274	.292	58	-6	-6	9	1	1	-0	14	2S/3O	1.3
1977	Mon-N	53	70	10	18	1	0	0	5	0	10	.257	.257	.271	43	-6	-5	5	1	0	0	8	2S/3	0.5
1978	Mon-N	73	15	5	4	2	1	0	5	0	3	.267	.267	.533	120	0	2	0	0	0	0	13	2/S	0.3
1979	Atl-N	140	475	41	123	18	4	1	44	20	36	.259	.292	.320	62	-22	-26	42	3	2	-0	-0	*S	-1.2
1980	Tex-A	116	227	27	55	5	1	0	10	4	23	.242	.259	.273	47	-17	-16	15	5	1	1	-16	*S/32	-2.2
	LA-N	14	9	1	2	1	0	0	0	0	0	.222	.222	.333	54	-1	-1	0	0	0	0	2	S	0.3
1981	LA-N	25	36	6	9	1	0	0	3	1	3	.250	.289	.278	64	-2	-2	3	0	0	0	-5	S/23	-0.4
Total	9	723	1346	132	323	49	8	1	108	49	136	.240	.269	.290	52	-85	-90	102	12	8	-1	64	S2/3O	2.9

■ BERNIE FRIBERG
Friberg, Bernard Albert (b: Gustaf Bernhard Friberg)   b: 8/18/1899, Manchester, N.H.   d: 12/8/58, Lynn, Mass.   BR/TR, 5'11", 178 lbs.   Deb: 8/20/19

YEAR	TM/L	G	AB	R	H	2B	3B	HR	RBI	BB	SO	AVG	OBP	SLG	PRO+	BR	/A	RC	SB	CS	SBR	FR	POS	TPR
1919	Chi-N	8	20	0	4	1	0	0	1	0	2	.200	.200	.250	35	-2	-2	1	0			0	/O	-0.1
1920	Chi-N	50	114	11	24	5	1	0	7	6	20	.211	.250	.272	49	-7	-8	8	2	2	-1	8	2O	-0.1
1922	Chi-N	97	296	51	92	8	2	0	23	37	37	.311	.391	.351	91	-1	-2	41	8	10	-4	-3	O/132	-0.9
1923	Chi-N	146	547	91	174	27	11	12	88	45	49	.318	.372	.473	122	16	16	91	13	19	-8	7	*3	1.8
1924	Chi-N	142	495	67	138	19	3	5	82	66	53	.279	.369	.360	95	-0	-1	65	19	27	-11	4	*3	0.2
1925	Chi-N	44	152	12	39	5	3	1	16	14	22	.257	.327	.349	72	-6	-6	18	0	1	-1	-4	3O/1S	-0.9
	Phi-N	91	304	41	82	12	1	5	22	39	35	.270	.353	.365	77	-7	-11	41	1	1	-0	4	23/PC	-0.6
	Yr	135	456	53	121	17	4	6	38	53	57	.265	.344	.360	75	-13	-17	59	1	2	-1	-1		-1.5
1926	Phi-N	144	478	38	128	21	3	1	51	57	77	.268	.346	.331	79	-10	-13	56	2			22	*2	1.6
1927	Phi-N	111	335	31	78	8	2	1	28	41	49	.233	.322	.278	61	-17	-17	32	3			25	*3/2	1.3
1928	Phi-N	52	94	11	19	3	0	1	7	12	16	.202	.292	.266	45	-7	-8	8	0			2	S/3201	-0.1
1929	Phi-N	128	455	74	137	21	10	7	55	49	54	.301	.370	.437	93	-0	-5	73	1			-26	SO/21	-2.1
1930	Phi-N	105	331	62	113	21	1	4	42	40	35	.341	.425	.447	104	8	4	64	1			-3	2OS/3	0.5
1931	Phi-N	103	353	33	92	19	5	1	26	33	25	.261	.324	.351	75	-9	-13	42	1			6	23/1S	-0.2
1932	Phi-N	61	154	17	37	8	2	0	14	19	23	.240	.324	.318	66	-5	-8	17	0			-1	2	-0.3
1933	Bos-A	17	41	5	13	3	0	0	9	6	1	.317	.404	.390	112	1	1	7	0	0	0	1	/23S	0.2
Total	14	1299	4169	544	1170	181	44	38	471	471	498	.281	.356	.373	87	-46	-71	564	51	60		42	32OS/1CP	0.3

■ JIM FRIDLEY
Fridley, James Riley "Big Jim"   b: 9/6/24, Philippi, W.Va.   BR/TR, 6'2", 205 lbs.   Deb: 4/15/52

YEAR	TM/L	G	AB	R	H	2B	3B	HR	RBI	BB	SO	AVG	OBP	SLG	PRO+	BR	/A	RC	SB	CS	SBR	FR	POS	TPR
1952	Cle-A	62	175	23	44	2	0	4	16	14	40	.251	.311	.331	84	-5	-4	18	3	3	-1	-3	O	-0.8
1954	Bal-A	85	240	25	59	8	5	4	36	21	41	.246	.312	.371	93	-5	-3	25	0	1	-1	-3	O	-0.7
1958	Cin-N	5	9	2	2	2	0	0	1	0	2	.222	.222	.444	67	-0	-0	1	0	0	0	-0	/O	0.0
Total	3	152	424	50	105	12	5	8	53	35	83	.248	.310	.356	89	-11	-7	44	3	4	-2	-6	O	-1.5

■ PAT FRIEL
Friel, Patrick Henry   b: 6/11/1860, Lewisburg, W.Va.   d: 1/15/24, Providence, R.I.   BB, 5'11", 170 lbs.   Deb: 7/13/1890

YEAR	TM/L	G	AB	R	H	2B	3B	HR	RBI	BB	SO	AVG	OBP	SLG	PRO+	BR	/A	RC	SB	CS	SBR	FR	POS	TPR
1890	Syr-a	62	261	51	65	8	2	3		17		.249	.302	.330	98	-4	-0	37	34			-6	O	-0.7
1891	Phi-a	2	8	2	2	1	0	0	0	0	0	.250	.250	.375	78	-0	-0	1	0			-1	/O	0.0
Total	2	64	269	53	67	9	2	3	0	17	0	.249	.301	.331	97	-5	-0	38	34			-6	/O	-0.7

■ BILL FRIEL
Friel, William Edward   b: 4/1/1876, Renovo, Pa.   d: 12/24/59, St.Louis, Mo.   BL/TR, 5'10", 215 lbs.   Deb: 5/03/01   U

YEAR	TM/L	G	AB	R	H	2B	3B	HR	RBI	BB	SO	AVG	OBP	SLG	PRO+	BR	/A	RC	SB	CS	SBR	FR	POS	TPR
1901	Mil-A	106	376	51	100	13	7	4	35	23		.266	.310	.370	94	-6	-3	50	15			-9	3O/2S	-1.1
1902	StL-A	80	267	26	64	9	2	2	20	14		.240	.280	.311	66	-13	-12	26	4			-13	O21/3SPC	-2.4
1903	StL-A	97	351	46	80	11	8	0	25	23		.228	.275	.305	78	-10	-9	32	4			-10	23/O	-1.9
Total	3	283	994	123	244	33	17	6	80	60		.245	.290	.331	81	-28	-24	109	23			-32	/2301SCP	-5.4

■ FRANK FRIEND
Friend, Frank B.   b: Washington, D.C.   d: 9/8/1897, Atlantic City, N.J   Deb: 8/02/1896

YEAR	TM/L	G	AB	R	H	2B	3B	HR	RBI	BB	SO	AVG	OBP	SLG	PRO+	BR	/A	RC	SB	CS	SBR	FR	POS	TPR
1896	Lou-N	2	5	1	1	0	0	0	0	0	1	.200	.333	.200	46	-0	-0	0	0			-0	/C	0.0

■ OWEN FRIEND
Friend, Owen Lacey "Red"   b: 3/21/27, Granite City, Ill.   BR/TR, 6'1", 180 lbs.   Deb: 10/02/49   C

YEAR	TM/L	G	AB	R	H	2B	3B	HR	RBI	BB	SO	AVG	OBP	SLG	PRO+	BR	/A	RC	SB	CS	SBR	FR	POS	TPR
1949	StL-A	2	8	1	3	0	0	0	1	0	0	.375	.375	.375	95	-0	-0	1	0	0	0	1	/2	0.1
1950	StL-A	119	372	48	88	15	2	8	50	40	68	.237	.312	.352	67	-18	-20	41	2	1	0	10	23/S	-0.3
1953	Det-A	31	96	10	17	4	0	3	10	6	9	.177	.233	.313	47	-8	-8	6	0	1	-1	4	2	-0.2
	Cle-A	34	68	7	16	2	0	2	13	5	16	.235	.288	.353	74	-3	-3	7	0	0	0	6	2/S3	0.5
	Yr	65	164	17	33	6	0	5	23	11	25	.201	.256	.329	58	-11	-10	12	0	1	-1	10		0.3
1955	Bos-A	14	42	3	11	3	0	0	2	4	11	.262	.326	.333	71	-1	-2	4	0	0	0	2	S/2	0.2
	Chi-N	6	10	0	1	0	0	0	0	0	3	.100	.100	.100	-47	-2	-2	0	0	0	0	-0	/3S	-0.2
1956	Chi-N	2	2	0	0	0	0	0	0	0	2	.000	.000	.000	-99	-1	-1	0	0	0	0	0	H	0.0
Total	5	208	598	69	136	24	2	13	76	55	109	.227	.295	.339	63	-32	-35	59	2	2	-1	23	2/3S	0.1

■ BUCK FRIERSON
Frierson, Robert Lawrence   b: 7/29/17, Chicota, Tex.   BR/TR, 6'3", 195 lbs.   Deb: 9/09/41

YEAR	TM/L	G	AB	R	H	2B	3B	HR	RBI	BB	SO	AVG	OBP	SLG	PRO+	BR	/A	RC	SB	CS	SBR	FR	POS	TPR
1941	Cle-A	5	11	2	3	1	0	0	2	1	1	.273	.333	.364	89	-0	-0	1	0	0	0	-1	/O	0.0

■ PETE FRIES
Fries, Peter Martin   b: 10/30/1857, Scranton, Pa.   d: 7/30/37, Chicago, Ill.   BL/TL, 5'8", 160 lbs.   Deb: 8/10/1883

YEAR	TM/L	G	AB	R	H	2B	3B	HR	RBI	BB	SO	AVG	OBP	SLG	PRO+	BR	/A	RC	SB	CS	SBR	FR	POS	TPR
1883	Col-a	3	10	1	3	1	0	0		1		.300	.364	.400	158	1	1	1				0	/P	0.0
1884	Ind-a	1	3	0	1	1	0	0		1		.333	.500	.667	292	1	1	1				0	/O	0.1
Total	2	4	13	1	4	2	0	0		2		.308	.400	.462	192	1	1	3				0	/PO	0.1

■ FRED FRINK
Frink, Fred Ferdinand   b: 8/25/11, Macon, Ga.   BR/TR, 6'1", 180 lbs.   Deb: 7/01/34

YEAR	TM/L	G	AB	R	H	2B	3B	HR	RBI	BB	SO	AVG	OBP	SLG	PRO+	BR	/A	RC	SB	CS	SBR	FR	POS	TPR
1934	Phi-N	2	0	0	0	0	0	0	0	0	0	—	—	—	—	0	0	0	0			0	/O	0.0

CHARLIE FRISBEE Frisbee, Charles Augustus "Bunt" b: 2/2/1874, Dows, Iowa d: 11/7/54, Alden, Iowa BB/TR, 5'9", 175 lbs. Deb: 6/22/1899

YEAR	TM/L	G	AB	R	H	2B	3B	HR	RBI	BB	SO	AVG	OBP	SLG	PRO+	BR	/A	RC	SB	CS	SBR	FR	POS	TPR
1899	Bos-N	42	152	22	50	4	2	0	20	9		.329	.374	.382	100	2	0	26	10			-2	O	-0.3
1900	NY-N	4	13	2	2	1	0	0	3	2		.154	.267	.231	42	-1	-1	1	0			-2	/O	-0.2
Total	2	46	165	24	52	5	2	0	23	11		.315	.365	.370	96	1	-1	27	10			-4	/O	-0.5

FRANKIE FRISCH Frisch, Frank Francis "The Fordham Flash" b: 9/9/1898, Bronx, N.Y. d: 3/12/73, Wilmington, Del. BB/TR, 5'11", 165 lbs. Deb: 6/14/19 MCH

YEAR	TM/L	G	AB	R	H	2B	3B	HR	RBI	BB	SO	AVG	OBP	SLG	PRO+	BR	/A	RC	SB	CS	SBR	FR	POS	TPR
1919	NY-N	54	190	21	43	3	2	2	24	4	14	.226	.242	.295	62	-9	-9	16	15			4	23/S	-0.4
1920	NY-N	110	440	57	123	10	10	4	77	20	18	.280	.311	.375	97	-3	-3	52	34	11	4	9	*3/S	1.6
1921	*NY-N	153	618	121	211	31	17	8	100	42	28	.341	.384	.485	128	25	25	118	49	13	7	4	32	3.6
1922	*NY-N	132	514	101	168	16	13	5	51	47	13	.327	.387	.438	111	10	9	87	31	17	-1	13	23/S	2.3
1923	*NY-N	151	641	116	223	32	10	12	111	46	12	.348	.395	.485	133	28	29	123	29	12	2	-8	*23	2.4
1924	*NY-N	145	603	121	198	33	15	7	69	56	24	.328	.387	.468	132	24	27	111	22	9	1	25	*2S/3	4.4
1925	NY-N	120	502	89	166	26	6	11	48	32	14	.331	.374	.472	119	11	13	87	21	12		5	32S	2.1
1926	NY-N	135	545	75	171	29	4	5	44	33	16	.314	.353	.409	106	3	4	76	23			11	*2/3	2.0
1927	StL-N	153	617	112	208	31	11	10	78	43	10	.337	.387	.472	125	25	22	109	48			49	*2/S	6.6
1928	*StL-N	141	547	107	164	29	9	10	86	64	17	.300	.374	.441	110	10	9	90	29			3	*2	1.3
1929	StL-N	138	527	93	176	40	12	5	74	53	12	.334	.397	.484	116	15	14	99	24			-4	*23/S	1.3
1930	*StL-N	133	540	121	187	46	9	10	114	55	16	.346	.407	.520	118	20	17	111	15			28	*23	5.1
1931	*StL-N	131	518	96	161	24	4	4	82	45	13	.311	.368	.396	101	5	2	78	28			16	*2	2.4
1932	StL-N	115	486	59	142	26	2	3	60	25	13	.292	.327	.372	85	-8	-10	60	18			16	23/S	1.5
1933	StL-N	147	585	74	177	32	6	4	66	48	16	.303	.358	.398	110	13	9	83	18			-3	*2SM	1.7
1934	*StL-N	140	550	74	168	30	6	3	75	45	10	.305	.359	.398	96	3	-2	79	11			5	*23M	1.6
1935	StL-N	103	354	52	104	16	2	1	55	35	16	.294	.359	.359	90	-2	-4	48	2			-8	2/3M	-0.3
1936	StL-N	93	303	40	83	10	0	1	26	36	10	.274	.353	.317	82	-6	-6	36	2			-13	23/SM	-1.2
1937	StL-N	17	32	3	7	2	0	0	4	1	0	.219	.242	.281	41	-3	-3	2	0			-1	/2M	-0.3
Total	19	2311	9112	1532	2880	466	138	105	1244	730	272	.316	.369	.432	110	159	144	1465	419	74		151	*23/S	37.7

EMIL FRISK Frisk, John Emil b: 10/15/1874, Kalkaska, Mich. d: 1/27/22, Seattle, Wash. BL/TR, 6'1", 190 lbs. Deb: 9/02/1899

YEAR	TM/L	G	AB	R	H	2B	3B	HR	RBI	BB	SO	AVG	OBP	SLG	PRO+	BR	/A	RC	SB	CS	SBR	FR	POS	TPR
1899	Cin-N	9	25	5	7	1	0	0	2	2		.280	.333	.320	80	-1	-1	3	0			-0	/P	0.0
1901	Det-A	20	48	10	15	3	0	1	7	3		.313	.365	.438	119	2	1	8	0			2	P/O	0.0
1905	StL-A	124	429	58	112	11	6	3	36	42		.261	.327	.336	119	7	9	52	7			-8	*O	-0.3
1907	StL-A	5	4	0	1	0	0	0	0	1		.250	.400	.250	111	0	0	0	0			0	H	0.0
Total	4	158	506	73	135	15	6	4	45	48		.267	.332	.344	117	8	10	63	7			-6	O/P	-0.3

HARRY FRITZ Fritz, Harry Koch "Dutchman" b: 9/30/1890, Philadelphia, Pa. d: 11/4/74, Columbus, Ohio BR/TR, 5'8", 170 lbs. Deb: 9/29/13

YEAR	TM/L	G	AB	R	H	2B	3B	HR	RBI	BB	SO	AVG	OBP	SLG	PRO+	BR	/A	RC	SB	CS	SBR	FR	POS	TPR
1913	Phi-A	5	13	1	0	0	0	0	0	2	4	.000	.188	.000	-45	-2	-2	0	0			-1	/3	-0.3
1914	Chi-F	65	174	16	37	5	1	0	13	18	18	.213	.297	.253	62	-9	-7	15	2			-9	3/S2	-1.5
1915	Chi-F	79	236	27	59	8	4	3	26	13	27	.250	.298	.356	99	-3	-1	28	4			-8	3/2S	-0.7
Total	3	149	423	44	96	13	5	3	39	33	49	.227	.294	.303	79	-14	-11	44	6			-18	3/S2	-2.5

LARRY FRITZ Fritz, Lawrence Joseph b: 2/14/49, E.Chicago, Ind. BL/TL, 6'2", 225 lbs. Deb: 5/30/75

YEAR	TM/L	G	AB	R	H	2B	3B	HR	RBI	BB	SO	AVG	OBP	SLG	PRO+	BR	/A	RC	SB	CS	SBR	FR	POS	TPR
1975	Phi-N	1	1	0	0	0	0	0	0	0	0	.000	.000	.000	-96	-0	-0	0	0	0	0	0	H	0.0

DOUG FROBEL Frobel, Douglas Steven b: 6/6/59, Ottawa, Ont., Can. BL/TR, 6'4", 196 lbs. Deb: 9/05/82

YEAR	TM/L	G	AB	R	H	2B	3B	HR	RBI	BB	SO	AVG	OBP	SLG	PRO+	BR	/A	RC	SB	CS	SBR	FR	POS	TPR
1982	Pit-N	16	34	5	7	2	0	2	3	1	11	.206	.229	.441	81	-1	-1	3	1	1	-0	0	O	0.0
1983	Pit-N	32	60	10	17	4	1	3	11	4	17	.283	.328	.533	132	2	2	9	1	1	-0	-1	O	0.1
1984	Pit-N	126	276	33	56	9	3	12	28	24	84	.203	.272	.388	83	-7	-7	27	7	5	-1	-2	*O	-1.4
1985	Pit-N	53	109	14	22	5	0	0	7	19	24	.202	.320	.248	62	-5	-5	9	4	3	-1	-2	O	-0.8
	Mon-N	12	23	3	3	1	0	1	4	2	6	.130	.200	.304	42	-2	-2	1	0	0	0	0	/O	-0.1
	Yr	65	132	17	25	6	0	1	11	21	30	.189	.301	.258	59	-7	-7	11	4	3	-1	-2		-0.9
1987	Cle-A	29	40	5	4	0	0	2	5	5	13	.100	.200	.250	18	-5	-5	2	0	0	0	-0	O/D	-0.4
Total	5	268	542	70	109	21	4	20	58	55	155	.201	.277	.365	78	-18	-18	52	13	10	-2	-5	O/D	-2.6

BEN FROELICH Froelich, William Palmer b: 11/12/1887, Pittsburgh, Pa. d: 9/1/16, Pittsburgh, Pa. TR, Deb: 7/02/09

YEAR	TM/L	G	AB	R	H	2B	3B	HR	RBI	BB	SO	AVG	OBP	SLG	PRO+	BR	/A	RC	SB	CS	SBR	FR	POS	TPR
1909	Phi-N	1	1	0	0	0	0	0	0	0		.000	.000	.000	-99	-0	-0	0	0			0	/C	0.0

JERRY FRY Fry, Jerry Ray b: 2/29/56, Salinas, Cal. BR/TR, 6', 185 lbs. Deb: 9/04/78

YEAR	TM/L	G	AB	R	H	2B	3B	HR	RBI	BB	SO	AVG	OBP	SLG	PRO+	BR	/A	RC	SB	CS	SBR	FR	POS	TPR
1978	Mon-N	4	9	0	0	0	0	0	0	1	5	.000	.100	.000	-71	-2	-2	0	0	0	0	1	/C	0.0

TRAVIS FRYMAN Fryman, David Travis b: 4/25/69, Lexington, Ky. BR/TR, 6'1", 180 lbs. Deb: 7/07/90

YEAR	TM/L	G	AB	R	H	2B	3B	HR	RBI	BB	SO	AVG	OBP	SLG	PRO+	BR	/A	RC	SB	CS	SBR	FR	POS	TPR
1990	Det-A	66	232	32	69	11	1	9	27	17	51	.297	.348	.470	127	8	8	37	3	3	-1	5	3S/D	1.3

MIKE FUENTES Fuentes, Michael Jay b: 7/11/58, Miami, Fla. BR/TR, 6'3", 190 lbs. Deb: 9/02/83

YEAR	TM/L	G	AB	R	H	2B	3B	HR	RBI	BB	SO	AVG	OBP	SLG	PRO+	BR	/A	RC	SB	CS	SBR	FR	POS	TPR
1983	Mon-N	6	4	1	1	0	0	0	0	0	2	.250	.250	.250	39	-0	-0	0	0	0	0	0	/H	0.0
1984	Mon-N	3	4	0	1	0	0	0	0	1	2	.250	.400	.250	90	-0	-0	1	0	0	0	1	/O	0.0
Total	2	9	8	1	2	0	0	0	0	1	4	.250	.333	.250	67	-0	-0	1	0	0	0	1	/O	0.0

TITO FUENTES Fuentes, Rigoberto (Peat) b: 1/4/44, Havana, Cuba BB/TR, 5'11", 175 lbs. Deb: 8/18/65

YEAR	TM/L	G	AB	R	H	2B	3B	HR	RBI	BB	SO	AVG	OBP	SLG	PRO+	BR	/A	RC	SB	CS	SBR	FR	POS	TPR
1965	SF-N	26	72	12	15	1	0	0	1	5	14	.208	.269	.222	39	-6	-6	4	0	1	-1	-7	S/23	-1.1
1966	SF-N	133	541	63	141	21	3	9	40	9	57	.261	.277	.360	73	-19	-20	53	6	3	0	-13	S2	-2.5
1967	SF-N	133	344	27	72	12	1	5	29	27	61	.209	.267	.294	61	-18	-17	26	4	3	-1	25	*2/S	1.7
1969	SF-N	67	183	28	54	4	3	1	14	15	25	.295	.352	.366	103	1	1	24	2	4	-2	-6	3S	-0.3
1970	SF-N	123	435	49	116	13	7	2	32	36	52	.267	.327	.343	81	-12	-12	49	4	5	-2	-2	2S3	-0.2
1971	*SF-N	152	630	63	172	28	6	4	52	18	46	.273	.300	.356	86	-14	-13	65	12	2	2	1	*2	-0.2
1972	SF-N	152	572	64	151	33	6	7	53	39	56	.264	.314	.379	95	-4	-5	69	16	5	2	-21	*2	-1.4
1973	SF-N	160	656	78	182	25	5	6	63	45	62	.277	.331	.358	87	-8	-11	79	12	6	0	-5	*2/3	-1.0
1974	SF-N	108	390	33	97	15	2	0	22	22	32	.249	.294	.297	63	-18	-20	33	7	3	0	-4	*2	-1.9
1975	SD-N	146	565	57	158	21	3	4	43	25	51	.280	.314	.349	89	-13	-9	58	8	8	-2	4	*2	-0.1
1976	SD-N	135	520	48	137	18	0	2	36	18	38	.263	.289	.310	76	-21	-16	45	5	3	-0	2	*2	-0.8
1977	Det-A	151	615	83	190	19	10	5	51	38	61	.309	.351	.397	98	3	-1	85	4	4	-1	4	*2/D	1.4
1978	Oak-A	13	43	5	6	1	0	0	2	1	6	.140	.159	.163	-10	-6	-6	1	0	0	0	-12	2	-1.8
Total	13	1499	5566	610	1491	211	46	45	438	298	561	.268	.309	.347	82	-135	-135	593	80	47	-4	-35	*2S/3D	-8.2

OLLIE FUHRMAN Fuhrman, Alfred George b: 7/20/1896, Jordan, Minn. d: 1/11/69, Peoria, Ill. BB/TR, 5'11", 185 lbs. Deb: 4/13/22

YEAR	TM/L	G	AB	R	H	2B	3B	HR	RBI	BB	SO	AVG	OBP	SLG	PRO+	BR	/A	RC	SB	CS	SBR	FR	POS	TPR
1922	Phi-A	6	6	1	2	1	0	0	0	0		.333	.333	.500	112	0	0	1	0	0	0	0	/C	0.0

DOT FULGHUM Fulghum, James Lavoisier b: 7/4/1900, Valdosta, Ga. d: 11/11/67, Miami, Fla. BR/TR, 5'8.5", 165 lbs. Deb: 9/15/21

YEAR	TM/L	G	AB	R	H	2B	3B	HR	RBI	BB	SO	AVG	OBP	SLG	PRO+	BR	/A	RC	SB	CS	SBR	FR	POS	TPR
1921	Phi-A	2	2	0	0	0	0	0	0	1	1	.000	.333	.000	-9	-0	-0	0	0	0	0	0	/S	0.0

NIG FULLER Fuller, Charles F. b: 3/30/1879, Toledo, Ohio d: 11/12/47, Toledo, Ohio BR/TR, Deb: 7/01/02

YEAR	TM/L	G	AB	R	H	2B	3B	HR	RBI	BB	SO	AVG	OBP	SLG	PRO+	BR	/A	RC	SB	CS	SBR	FR	POS	TPR
1902	Bro-N	3	9	0	0	0	0	0	1	0		.000	.000	.000	-99	-2	-2	0	0			-1	/C	-0.2

FRANK FULLER Fuller, Frank Edward "Rabbit" b: 1/1/1893, Detroit, Mich. d: 10/29/65, Warren, Mich. BB/TR, 5'7", 150 lbs. Deb: 4/14/15

YEAR	TM/L	G	AB	R	H	2B	3B	HR	RBI	BB	SO	AVG	OBP	SLG	PRO+	BR	/A	RC	SB	CS	SBR	FR	POS	TPR
1915	Det-A	14	32	6	5	0	0	0	2	9	7	.156	.341	.156	47	-1	-2	2	2	3	-1	-6	/2S	-0.9
1916	Det-A	20	10	2	1	0	0	0		1	1	.100	.182	.100	-15	-1	-1	1	3			3	/2S	0.2
1923	Bos-A	6	21	3	5	0	0	0	0	1	1	.238	.273	.238	35	-2	-2	1	1	1	-0	2	/2	0.0

YEAR	TM/L	G	AB	R	H	2B	3B	HR	RBI	BB	SO	AVG	OBP	SLG	PRO+	BR	/A	RC	SB	CS	SBR	FR	POS	TPR
Total	3	40	63	11	11	0	0	0	3	11	12	.175	.297	.175	35	-5	-5	4	6	4		-1	/2S	-0.7

■ HARRY FULLER
Fuller, Henry W.   b: 12/5/1862, Cincinnati, Ohio   d: 12/12/1895, Cincinnati, Ohio   Deb: 4/08/1891

YEAR	TM/L	G	AB	R	H	2B	3B	HR	RBI	BB	SO	AVG	OBP	SLG	PRO+	BR	/A	RC	SB	CS	SBR	FR	POS	TPR
1891	StL-a	1	2	0	0	0	0	0	0	0	1	.000	.000	.000	-87	-1	-1	0	0			-1	/3	0.0

■ JIM FULLER
Fuller, James Hardy   b: 11/28/50, Bethesda, Md.   BR/TR, 6'3", 215 lbs.   Deb: 9/10/73

YEAR	TM/L	G	AB	R	H	2B	3B	HR	RBI	BB	SO	AVG	OBP	SLG	PRO+	BR	/A	RC	SB	CS	SBR	FR	POS	TPR
1973	Bal-A	9	26	2	3	0	0	2	4	1	17	.115	.148	.346	36	-2	-2	1	0	0	0	1	/O1D	0.0
1974	Bal-A	64	189	17	42	11	0	7	28	8	68	.222	.265	.392	90	-4	-3	19	1	0	0	3	O/1D	-0.1
1977	Hou-N	34	100	5	16	6	0	2	9	10	45	.160	.243	.280	44	-9	-8	7	0	1	-1	3	O/1	-0.6
Total	3	107	315	24	61	17	0	11	41	19	130	.194	.249	.352	70	-15	-13	27	1	1	-0	7	/O1D	-0.7

■ JOHN FULLER
Fuller, John Edward   b: 1/29/50, Lynwood, Cal.   BL/TL, 6'2", 180 lbs.   Deb: 5/09/74

YEAR	TM/L	G	AB	R	H	2B	3B	HR	RBI	BB	SO	AVG	OBP	SLG	PRO+	BR	/A	RC	SB	CS	SBR	FR	POS	TPR
1974	Atl-N	3	3	1	1	0	0	0	0	0	0	.333	.333	.333	83	-0	-0	0	0	0	0	0	/O	0.0

■ VERN FULLER
Fuller, Vernon Gordon   b: 3/1/44, Menomonie, Wis.   BR/TR, 6'1", 170 lbs.   Deb: 9/05/64

YEAR	TM/L	G	AB	R	H	2B	3B	HR	RBI	BB	SO	AVG	OBP	SLG	PRO+	BR	/A	RC	SB	CS	SBR	FR	POS	TPR
1964	Cle-A	2	1	0	0	0	0	0	0	0	0	.000	.000	.000	-99	-0	-0	0	0	0	0	0	H	0.0
1966	Cle-A	16	47	7	11	2	1	2	2	7	6	.234	.357	.447	129	2	2	8	0	0	0	-4	2	0.0
1967	Cle-A	73	206	18	46	10	0	7	21	19	55	.223	.301	.374	98	-1	-1	24	2	3	-1	0	2/S	0.0
1968	Cle-A	97	244	14	59	8	2	0	18	24	49	.242	.320	.291	87	-3	-3	24	2	2	-1	-12	23/S	-1.3
1969	Cle-A	108	254	25	60	11	1	4	22	20	53	.236	.297	.335	74	-8	-9	24	2	1	0	9	*2/3	0.4
1970	Cle-A	29	33	3	6	2	0	1	2	3	9	.182	.250	.333	57	-2	-2	3	0	0	0	3	2/31	0.2
Total	6	325	785	67	182	33	4	14	65	73	172	.232	.307	.338	87	-12	-13	82	6	6	-2	-4	2/3S1	-0.7

■ SHORTY FULLER
Fuller, William Benjamin   b: 10/10/1867, Cincinnati, Ohio   d: 4/11/04, Cincinnati, Ohio   BR/TR,   Deb: 7/19/1888

YEAR	TM/L	G	AB	R	H	2B	3B	HR	RBI	BB	SO	AVG	OBP	SLG	PRO+	BR	/A	RC	SB	CS	SBR	FR	POS	TPR
1888	Was-N	49	170	11	31	5	2	0	12	10	14	.182	.232	.235	54	-9	-8	11	6			-6	S/2	-1.1
1889	StL-a	140	517	91	117	18	6	0	51	52	56	.226	.303	.284	62	-19	-31	57	38			0	*S	-1.7
1890	StL-a	130	526	118	146	9	9	1			73	.278	.377	.335	99	12	-1	91	60			-0	*S	0.5
1891	StL-a	137	586	107	127	15	7	2	63	67	28	.217	.301	.276	59	-23	-38	63	42			-10	*S2	-3.5
1892	NY-N	141	508	74	115	11	4	1	48	52	22	.226	.298	.270	75	-15	-14	53	37			1	*S	-0.4
1893	NY-N	130	474	78	112	14	8	0	51	60	21	.236	.325	.300	68	-21	-21	56	26			11	*S	-0.4
1894	*NY-N	93	368	81	104	14	4	2	46	52	16	.283	.374	.359	80	-11	-10	63	32			-5	*S/O32	-0.7
1895	NY-N	126	458	82	103	11	3	0	32	64	34	.225	.323	.262	55	-29	-27	45	15			34	*S	1.3
1896	NY-N	18	72	10	12	0	0	0	7	14	5	.167	.310	.167	30	-7	-6	5	4			1	S	-0.3
Total	9	964	3679	652	867	97	43	6	310	444	196	.236	.323	.290	69	-122	-156	444	260			26	S/23O	-6.3

■ CHICK FULLIS
Fullis, Charles Philip   b: 2/27/04, Girardville, Pa.   d: 3/28/46, Ashland, Pa.   BR/TR, 5'9", 170 lbs.   Deb: 4/13/28

YEAR	TM/L	G	AB	R	H	2B	3B	HR	RBI	BB	SO	AVG	OBP	SLG	PRO+	BR	/A	RC	SB	CS	SBR	FR	POS	TPR
1928	NY-N	11	1	5	0	0	0	0	0	1	1	.000	.500	.000	41	0	0	0	0			0	H	0.0
1929	NY-N	86	274	67	79	11	1	7	29	30	26	.288	.365	.412	92	-3	-3	41	7			-7	O	-1.5
1930	NY-N	13	6	2	0	0	0	0	0	0	1	.000	.000	.000	-99	-2	-2	0	1			0	/O	-0.1
1931	NY-N	89	302	61	99	15	2	3	28	23	13	.328	.383	.421	119	7	8	50	13			1	O/2	0.6
1932	NY-N	96	235	35	70	14	3	1	21	11	12	.298	.332	.396	97	-2	-1	31	1			-5	O/2	-0.9
1933	Phi-N	151	647	91	200	31	6	1	45	36	34	.309	.350	.380	96	7	-2	87	18			5	*O/3	-0.5
1934	Phi-N	28	102	8	23	6	0	0	12	10	4	.225	.301	.284	51	-6	-8	10	2			-4	O	-1.2
	*StL-N	69	199	21	52	9	1	0	26	14	11	.261	.310	.317	64	-9	-10	19	4			2	O	-1.0
	Yr	97	301	29	75	15	1	0	38	24	15	.249	.307	.306	59	-15	-18	29	6			-2		-2.2
1936	StL-N	47	89	15	25	6	1	0	6	7	11	.281	.333	.371	90	-1	-1	12	0			4	O	0.1
Total	8	590	1855	305	548	92	14	12	167	132	113	.295	.347	.380	92	-8	-19	250	46			-5	O/23	-4.5

■ CHICK FULMER
Fulmer, Charles John   b: 2/12/1851, Philadelphia, Pa.   d: 2/15/40, Philadelphia, Pa.   TR , 6', 158 lbs.   Deb: 8/23/1871   U

YEAR	TM/L	G	AB	R	H	2B	3B	HR	RBI	BB	SO	AVG	OBP	SLG	PRO+	BR	/A	RC	SB	CS	SBR	FR	POS	TPR
1871	Rok-n	16	63	11	17	1	3	0	3	5	1	.270	.324	.381	106	0	1	8	0				S/1	0.1
1872	Mut-n	36	167	28	51	2	1	1		2		.305	.314	.347	110	1	3	19					3S	0.1
1873	Phi-n	49	237	42	65	10	3	1		2		.274	.280	.354	82	-4	-6	24					*S/PC	-0.3
1874	Phi-n	57	259	49	72	5	3	0		1		.278	.281	.320	88	-3	-4	24					S3	-0.4
1875	Phi-n	69	293	50	65	5	1	0		0		.222	.222	.246	59	-11	-13	16					*S3	-1.1
1876	Lou-N	66	267	28	73	9	5	1	29	1	10	.273	.276	.356	93	2	-5	27				-3	*S	-0.7
1879	Buf-N	76	306	30	82	11	5	0	28	5	34	.268	.280	.337	100	1	-0	36				18	*2	2.2
1880	Buf-N	11	44	3	7	0	0	0	1	2	4	.159	.196	.159	21	-3	-4	1				-2	2	-0.4
1882	Cin-a	79	324	54	91	13	4	0		10		.281	.302	.346	111	6	3	35				-13	*S	-0.7
1883	Cin-a	92	361	52	93	13	5	5		13		.258	.283	.363	101	2	-1	38				-1	*S	-0.4
1884	Cin-a	31	114	13	20	2	1	0		1		.175	.183	.211	28	-8	-9	4				-10	S/O3	-1.7
	StL-a	1	5	0	0	0	0	0		0		.000	.000	.000	-96	-1	-1	0				-1	/2	-0.1
	Yr	32	119	13	20	2	1	0		1		.168	.175	.202	23	-9	-10	4				-11		-1.8
Total	5 n	227	1019	180	270	23	11	2	3	10	1	.265	.272	.315	83	-17	-19	91					S/3PC1	-1.6
Total	6	356	1421	180	366	48	20	6	58	32	48	.258	.274	.332	93	-2	-17	135				-12	S/2O3	-1.8

■ CHRIS FULMER
Fulmer, Christopher   b: 7/4/1858, Tamaqua, Pa.   d: 11/9/31, Tamaqua, Pa.   BR/TR, 5'8", 165 lbs.   Deb: 8/04/1884

YEAR	TM/L	G	AB	R	H	2B	3B	HR	RBI	BB	SO	AVG	OBP	SLG	PRO+	BR	/A	RC	SB	CS	SBR	FR	POS	TPR
1884	Was-U	48	181	39	50	9	0	0		11		.276	.318	.326	122	4	5	19	0			-3	CO/1	0.3
1886	Bal-a	80	270	54	66	9	3	1		48		.244	.363	.311	117	7	8	42	29			3	CO/P	1.3
1887	Bal-a	56	201	52	54	11	4	0		36		.269	.382	.363	118	5	7	42	35			-9	CO	0.4
1888	Bal-a	52	166	20	31	5	1	0	10	21		.187	.286	.229	70	-5	-4	14	10			-14	C/O	-1.1
1889	Bal-a	16	58	11	15	3	1	0	13	6	12	.259	.338	.345	95	-0	-0	8	2			-5	O/C	-0.4
Total	5	252	876	176	216	37	9	1	23	122	12	.247	.343	.313	108	10	15	125	76			-27	C/O1P	0.5

■ WASHINGTON FULMER
Fulmer, Washington Fayette   b: 6/15/1840, Philadelphia, Pa.   d: 12/8/07, Philadelphia, Pa.   Deb: 7/19/1875

YEAR	TM/L	G	AB	R	H	2B	3B	HR	RBI	BB	SO	AVG	OBP	SLG	PRO+	BR	/A	RC	SB	CS	SBR	FR	POS	TPR
1875	Atl-n	1	4	1	2	0	0	0		0		.500	.500	.500	284	1	1	1					/3	0.1

■ DAVE FULTZ
Fultz, David Lewis   b: 5/29/1875, Staunton, Va.   d: 10/29/59, DeLand, Fla.   BR/TR, 5'11", 170 lbs.   Deb: 7/01/1898

YEAR	TM/L	G	AB	R	H	2B	3B	HR	RBI	BB	SO	AVG	OBP	SLG	PRO+	BR	/A	RC	SB	CS	SBR	FR	POS	TPR
1898	Phi-N	19	55	7	10	2	2	0	5	6		.182	.262	.291	63	-3	-2	5	1			-1	O/2S	-0.3
1899	Phi-N	2	5	0	2	0	0	0	0	0		.400	.400	.400	127	0	0	1	1			-1	/2S	0.0
	Bal-N	57	210	31	62	3	2	0	18	13		.295	.342	.329	82	-3	-5	30	17			-6	O3/21	-1.1
	Yr	59	215	31	64	3	2	0	18	13		.298	.343	.330	83	-3	-5	31	18			-7		-1.1
1901	Phi-A	132	561	95	164	17	9	0	52	32		.292	.334	.355	89	-5	-9	82	36			-6	*O2/S	-1.4
1902	Phi-A	129	506	109	153	20	5	1	49	62		.302	.382	.368	106	10	7	94	44			-5	*O2	-0.4
1903	NY-A	79	295	39	66	12	1	0	25	25		.224	.284	.271	65	-10	-13	33	29			-2	O/3	-1.9
1904	NY-A	97	339	39	93	17	4	2	32	24		.274	.322	.366	114	7	6	49	17			3	O	0.3
1905	NY-A	129	422	49	98	13	3	0	42	39		.232	.297	.277	76	-6	-12	51	44			-6	*O	-2.6
Total	7	644	2393	369	648	84	26	3	223	201		.271	.329	.331	90	-10	-28	344	189			-24	O/23S1	-7.4

■ MARK FUNDERBURK
Funderburk, Mark Clifford   b: 5/16/57, Charlotte, N.C.   BR/TR, 6'4", 226 lbs.   Deb: 9/04/81

YEAR	TM/L	G	AB	R	H	2B	3B	HR	RBI	BB	SO	AVG	OBP	SLG	PRO+	BR	/A	RC	SB	CS	SBR	FR	POS	TPR
1981	Min-A	8	15	2	3	1	0	0	2	2	1	.200	.294	.267	59	-1	-1	1	0	0	0	0	/OD	0.0
1985	Min-A	23	70	7	22	7	1	2	13	5	12	.314	.360	.529	132	4	3	11	0	1	-1	-0	D/O1	0.2
Total	2	31	85	9	25	8	1	2	15	7	13	.294	.348	.482	120	3	2	13	0	1	-1	0	/DO1	0.2

■ LIZ FUNK
Funk, Elias Calvin   b: 10/28/04, LaCygne, Kan.   d: 1/16/68, Norman, Okla.   BL/TL, 5'8.5", 160 lbs.   Deb: 4/26/29

YEAR	TM/L	G	AB	R	H	2B	3B	HR	RBI	BB	SO	AVG	OBP	SLG	PRO+	BR	/A	RC	SB	CS	SBR	FR	POS	TPR
1929	NY-A	1	0	0	0	0	0	0	0	0	0	—	—	—		0	0	0	0	0	0	0	R	0.0
1930	Det-A	140	527	74	145	26	11	4	65	29	39	.275	.319	.389	77	-18	-20	66	12	6	0	8	*O	-1.4

YEAR	TM/L	G	AB	R	H	2B	3B	HR	RBI	BB	SO	AVG	OBP	SLG	PRO+	BR	/A	RC	SB	CS	SBR	FR	POS	TPR
1932	Chi-A	122	440	59	114	21	5	2	40	43	19	.259	.325	.343	78	-17	-13	49	17	15	-4	2	*O	-1.8
1933	Chi-A	10	9	1	2	0	0	0	0	1	0	.222	.300	.222	42	-1	-1	1	0	0	0	0	/O	0.0
Total	4	273	976	134	261	47	16	6	105	73	58	.267	.322	.367	77	-36	-33	115	29	21	-4	10	O	-3.2

■ CARL FURILLO
Furillo, Carl Anthony "Skoonj" or "The Reading Rifle"   b: 3/8/22, Stony Creek Mills, Pa.   d: 1/21/89, Stony Creek Mills, Pa.   BR/TR, 6', 190 lbs.   Deb: 4/16/46

YEAR	TM/L	G	AB	R	H	2B	3B	HR	RBI	BB	SO	AVG	OBP	SLG	PRO+	BR	/A	RC	SB	CS	SBR	FR	POS	TPR
1946	Bro-N	117	335	29	95	18	6	3	35	31	20	.284	.346	.400	110	4	4	46	6			4	*O	0.6
1947	*Bro-N	124	437	61	129	24	7	8	88	34	24	.295	.347	.437	103	3	1	62	7			-1	*O	-0.3
1948	Bro-N	108	364	55	108	20	4	4	44	43	32	.297	.374	.407	108	7	5	57	6			6	*O	0.3
1949	*Bro-N	142	549	95	177	27	10	18	106	37	29	.322	.368	.506	127	23	20	98	4			-3	*O	0.9
1950	Bro-N	153	620	99	189	30	6	18	106	41	40	.305	.353	.460	110	9	8	96	8			-3	*O	0.0
1951	Bro-N	158	667	93	197	32	4	16	91	43	33	.295	.344	.427	104	5	3	97	8	7	-2	13	*O	1.0
1952	*Bro-N	134	425	52	105	18	1	8	59	31	33	.247	.304	.351	80	-11	-12	42	1	4	-2	-2	*O	-1.9
1953	*Bro-N	132	479	82	165	38	6	21	92	34	32	.344	.393	.580	146	33	32	107	1	1	-0	-0	*O	2.5
1954	Bro-N	150	547	56	161	23	1	19	96	49	35	.294	.358	.444	104	6	4	83	2	4	-2	4	*O	0.1
1955	*Bro-N	140	523	83	164	24	3	26	95	43	43	.314	.373	.520	130	25	23	97	4	5	-2	-3	*O	1.6
1956	*Bro-N	149	523	66	151	30	0	21	83	57	41	.289	.360	.467	111	15	10	80	1	1	-0	-7	*O	-0.2
1957	Bro-N	119	395	61	121	17	4	12	66	29	33	.306	.361	.461	108	10	6	62	0	2	-1	-8	*O	-0.6
1958	LA-N	122	411	54	119	19	3	18	83	35	28	.290	.348	.482	113	9	8	64	0	2	-1	-9	*O	-0.5
1959	*LA-N	50	93	8	27	4	0	0	13	7	11	.290	.340	.333	75	-2	-3	10	0	0	0	-4	O	-0.7
1960	LA-N	8	10	1	2	0	0	0	1	0	2	.200	.200	.400	56	-1	-1	1	0	0	0	0	/O	0.0
Total	15	1806	6378	895	1910	324	56	192	1058	514	436	.299	.356	.458	112	136	107	1004	48	26		-14	*O	2.8

■ EDDIE FUSSELBACK
Fusselback, Edward L.   b: 7/17/1856, Philadelphia, Pa.   d: 4/14/26, Philadelphia, Pa.   5'6", 156 lbs.   Deb: 5/03/1882

YEAR	TM/L	G	AB	R	H	2B	3B	HR	RBI	BB	SO	AVG	OBP	SLG	PRO+	BR	/A	RC	SB	CS	SBR	FR	POS	TPR
1882	StL-a	35	136	13	31	2	0	0			5	.228	.255	.243	66	-4	-5	9				2	CO/P	-0.1
1884	Bal-U	68	303	60	86	16	3	1			3	.284	.291	.366	109	6	1	33	0			15	C/3SO	1.7
1885	Phi-a	5	19	2	6	1	0	0			0	.316	.316	.368	112	0	0	2				3	/C	0.3
1888	Lou-a	1	4	0	1	0	0	0	1	0	0	.250	.250	.250	64	-0	-0	0	0			0	/O	0.0
Total	4	109	462	75	124	19	3	1	1		8	.268	.281	.329	97	2	-4	44	0			21	/CO3SP	1.9

■ LES FUSSELMAN
Fusselman, Lester Leroy   b: 3/7/21, Pryor, Okla.   d: 5/21/70, Cleveland, Ohio   BR/TR, 6'1", 195 lbs.   Deb: 4/16/52

YEAR	TM/L	G	AB	R	H	2B	3B	HR	RBI	BB	SO	AVG	OBP	SLG	PRO+	BR	/A	RC	SB	CS	SBR	FR	POS	TPR
1952	StL-N	32	63	5	10	3	0	1	3	0	9	.159	.159	.254	13	-8	-8	2	0	0	0	4	C	-0.3
1953	StL-N	11	8	1	2	1	0	0	0	0	0	.250	.250	.375	60	-0	-0	0	0	0	0	2	C	0.2
Total	2	43	71	6	12	4	0	1	3	0	9	.169	.169	.268	18	-8	-8	3	0	0	0	5	/C	-0.1

■ GABE GABLER
Gabler, William Louis   b: 8/4/30, St.Louis, Mo.   BL/TR, 6'1", 190 lbs.   Deb: 9/16/58

YEAR	TM/L	G	AB	R	H	2B	3B	HR	RBI	BB	SO	AVG	OBP	SLG	PRO+	BR	/A	RC	SB	CS	SBR	FR	POS	TPR
1958	Chi-N	3	3	0	0	0	0	0	0	0	3	.000	.000	.000	-99	-1	-1	0	0	0	0	0	H	0.0

■ LEN GABRIELSON
Gabrielson, Leonard Gary   b: 2/14/40, Oakland, Cal.   BL/TR, 6'4", 210 lbs.   Deb: 9/09/60

YEAR	TM/L	G	AB	R	H	2B	3B	HR	RBI	BB	SO	AVG	OBP	SLG	PRO+	BR	/A	RC	SB	CS	SBR	FR	POS	TPR
1960	Mil-N	4	3	1	0	0	0	0	0	1	0	.000	.250	.000	-27	-1	-1	0	0	0	0	0	/O	0.0
1963	Mil-N	46	120	14	26	5	0	3	15	8	23	.217	.266	.333	72	-5	-4	11	1	1	-0	-2	O1/3	-0.8
1964	Mil-N	24	38	0	7	2	0	0	1	1	8	.184	.205	.237	24	-4	-4	2	1	0	0	-1	1/O	-0.4
	Chi-N	89	272	22	67	11	2	5	23	19	37	.246	.298	.357	80	-6	-7	30	9	4	0	-0	O/1	-0.9
	Yr	113	310	22	74	13	2	5	24	20	45	.239	.287	.342	74	-10	-11	32	10	4	1	-1		-1.3
1965	Chi-N	28	48	4	12	0	0	3	5	7	16	.250	.345	.438	116	1	1	7	0	2	-1	-1	O/1	-0.1
	SF-N	88	269	36	81	6	5	4	26	26	48	.301	.367	.405	114	7	6	42	4	0	1	-1	O/1	0.3
	Yr	116	317	40	93	6	5	7	31	33	64	.293	.364	.410	114	8	7	49	4	2	0	-3		0.2
1966	SF-N	94	240	27	52	7	0	4	16	21	51	.217	.280	.296	58	-13	-14	21	0	1	-1	-9	O/1	-2.6
1967	Cal-A	11	12	2	1	0	0	0	2	2	4	.083	.214	.083	-9	-2	-2	0	0	0	0	0	/O	-0.1
	LA-N	90	238	20	62	10	3	7	29	15	41	.261	.307	.416	114	1	3	30	3	1	0	-1	O	0.0
1968	LA-N	108	304	38	82	16	1	10	35	32	47	.270	.339	.428	140	11	13	44	1	1	-0	-7	O	0.2
1969	LA-N	83	178	13	48	5	1	1	18	12	25	.270	.316	.326	86	-5	-3	18	1	2	-1	-5	O/1	-1.1
1970	LA-N	43	42	1	8	2	0	0	6	1	15	.190	.209	.238	20	-5	-5	2	0	0	0	0	/O1	-0.3
Total	9	708	1764	178	446	64	12	37	176	145	315	.253	.313	.366	94	-19	-16	206	20	12	-1	-25	O/13	-5.8

■ LEN GABRIELSON
Gabrielson, Leonard Hilbourne   b: 9/8/15, Oakland, Cal.   BL/TL, 6'3", 210 lbs.   Deb: 4/21/39

YEAR	TM/L	G	AB	R	H	2B	3B	HR	RBI	BB	SO	AVG	OBP	SLG	PRO+	BR	/A	RC	SB	CS	SBR	FR	POS	TPR
1939	Phi-N	5	18	3	4	0	0	0	1	2	3	.222	.300	.222	43	-1	-1	1	0			2	/1	0.0

■ EDDIE GAEDEL
Gaedel, Edward Carl   b: 6/8/25, Chicago, Ill.   d: 6/18/61, Chicago, Ill.   BR, 3'7", 065 lbs.   Deb: 8/19/51

YEAR	TM/L	G	AB	R	H	2B	3B	HR	RBI	BB	SO	AVG	OBP	SLG	PRO+	BR	/A	RC	SB	CS	SBR	FR	POS	TPR
1951	StL-A	1	0	0	0	0	0	0	0	1	0	—	1.000	—	182	0	0	0	0	0	0	0	H	0.0

■ GARY GAETTI
Gaetti, Gary Joseph   b: 8/19/58, Centralia, Ill.   BR/TR, 6', 180 lbs.   Deb: 9/20/81

YEAR	TM/L	G	AB	R	H	2B	3B	HR	RBI	BB	SO	AVG	OBP	SLG	PRO+	BR	/A	RC	SB	CS	SBR	FR	POS	TPR
1981	Min-A	9	26	4	5	0	0	2	3	0	6	.192	.192	.423	68	-1	-1	2	0	0	0	1	/3D	0.0
1982	Min-A	145	508	59	117	25	4	25	84	37	107	.230	.286	.443	94	-4	-6	59	0	4	-2	-3	*3/SD	-1.3
1983	Min-A	157	584	81	143	30	3	21	78	54	121	.245	.313	.414	95	-2	-5	74	7	1	2	13	*3/SD	1.0
1984	Min-A	162	588	55	154	29	4	5	65	44	81	.262	.318	.350	81	-12	-15	67	11	5	0	15	*3/OS	0.2
1985	Min-A	160	560	71	138	31	4	20	63	37	89	.246	.301	.409	87	-7	-11	66	13	5	1	16	*3/O1D	0.0
1986	Min-A	157	596	91	171	34	1	34	108	52	108	.287	.350	.518	129	25	23	99	14	15	-5	19	*3/S2O	3.4
1987	*Min-A	154	584	95	150	36	2	31	109	37	92	.257	.304	.485	101	2	-1	75	10	7	-1	-4	*3/D	-0.7
1988	Min-A	133	468	66	141	29	2	28	88	36	85	.301	.358	.551	146	30	28	89	7	4	-0	-5	*3/SD	2.3
1989	Min-A	130	498	63	125	11	4	19	75	25	87	.251	.291	.404	88	-6	-10	56	6	2	1	11	*3/1D	0.2
1990	Min-A	154	577	61	132	27	5	16	85	36	101	.229	.278	.376	76	-16	-21	56	6	1	1	14	*3/1S	-0.3
Total	10	1361	4989	646	1276	252	25	201	758	358	877	.256	.310	.437	99	8	-20	643	74	44	-4	77	*3/DOS12	4.8

■ FABIAN GAFFKE
Gaffke, Fabian Sebastian   b: 8/5/13, Milwaukee, Wis.   BR/TR, 5'10", 185 lbs.   Deb: 9/09/36

YEAR	TM/L	G	AB	R	H	2B	3B	HR	RBI	BB	SO	AVG	OBP	SLG	PRO+	BR	/A	RC	SB	CS	SBR	FR	POS	TPR
1936	Bos-A	15	55	5	7	2	0	1	3	4	5	.127	.200	.218	3	-9	-9	3	0	0	0	-1	O	-0.9
1937	Bos-A	54	184	32	53	10	4	6	34	15	25	.288	.342	.484	102	1	-0	30	1	2	-1	-4	O	-0.6
1938	Bos-A	15	10	2	1	0	0	0	1	3	2	.100	.308	.100	6	-1	-1	1	0	0	0	0	/OC	0.0
1939	Bos-A	1	1	0	0	0	0	0	1	0	0	.000	.000	.000	-96	-0	-0	0	0	0	0	0	H	0.0
1941	Cle-A	4	4	0	1	0	0	0	0	2	2	.250	.500	.250	109	0	-0	1	0	0	0	0	O	0.0
1942	Cle-A	40	67	4	11	2	0	0	3	6	13	.164	.243	.194	25	-7	-6	3	1	0	0	0	O	-0.6
Total	6	129	321	43	73	14	4	7	42	30	47	.227	.297	.361	67	-16	-17	37	2	2	-1	-5	/OC	-2.1

■ PHIL GAGLIANO
Gagliano, Philip Joseph   b: 12/27/41, Memphis, Tenn.   BR/TR, 6'1", 180 lbs.   Deb: 4/16/63

YEAR	TM/L	G	AB	R	H	2B	3B	HR	RBI	BB	SO	AVG	OBP	SLG	PRO+	BR	/A	RC	SB	CS	SBR	FR	POS	TPR
1963	StL-N	10	5	1	2	0	0	0	1	1	1	.400	.500	.400	149	0	0	1	0	0	0	2	/23	0.2
1964	StL-N	40	58	5	15	4	0	1	9	3	10	.259	.295	.379	81	-1	-2	6	0	1	-1	1	2/O13	0.0
1965	StL-N	122	363	46	87	14	2	8	53	40	45	.240	.317	.355	81	-5	-9	41	2	1	0	-11	2O3	-1.9
1966	StL-N	90	213	23	54	8	2	2	15	24	29	.254	.332	.338	86	-3	-3	24	2	1	0	-3	3/1O2	-0.7
1967	*StL-N	73	217	20	48	7	0	2	21	19	26	.221	.287	.281	64	-10	-10	17	0	1	0	-13	23/1S	-2.3
1968	StL-N	53	105	13	24	4	2	0	13	7	12	.229	.283	.305	77	-3	-3	9	0	0	0	-2	23/O	-0.4
1969	StL-N	62	128	7	29	2	0	1	10	14	12	.227	.303	.266	60	-6	-6	10	0	0	0	-1	2/130	-0.7
1970	StL-N	18	32	0	6	0	0	0	2	1	6	.188	.212	.188	8	-4	-4	1	0	1	-1	-0	/312	-0.5
	Chi-N	26	40	5	6	0	0	0	5	5	5	.150	.244	.150	7	-5	-6	2	0	0	0	1	2/13	-0.2
	Yr	44	72	5	12	0	0	0	7	6	8	.167	.231	.167	8	-9	-10	3	0	1	-1	-0		-0.7
1971	Bos-A	47	68	11	22	5	0	0	13	11	5	.324	.418	.397	123	3	3	12	0	0	0	-4	O/23	0.0

YEAR	TM/L	G	AB	R	H	2B	3B	HR	RBI	BB	SO	AVG	OBP	SLG	PRO+	BR	/A	RC	SB	CS	SBR	FR	POS	TPR
1972	Bos-A	52	82	9	21	4	1	0	10	10	13	.256	.337	.329	94	0	-0	10	1	0	0	1	O/321	0.1
1973	*Cin-N	63	69	8	20	2	0	0	7	13	16	.290	.402	.319	108	1	1	10	0	0	0	-1	/321O	0.0
1974	Cin-N	46	31	2	2	0	0	0	0	15	7	.065	.370	.065	27	-2	-2	2	0	0	0	0	/213	-0.1
Total	12	702	1411	150	336	50	7	14	159	163	184	.238	.319	.313	77	-35	-41	146	5	4	-1	-31	23/01S	-6.5

■ RALPH GAGLIANO
Gagliano, Ralph Michael b: 10/8/46, Memphis, Tenn.   BL/TR, 5'11", 170 lbs. Deb: 9/21/65

YEAR	TM/L	G	AB	R	H	2B	3B	HR	RBI	BB	SO	AVG	OBP	SLG	PRO+	BR	/A	RC	SB	CS	SBR	FR	POS	TPR
1965	Cle-A	1	0	0	0	0	0	0	0	0	0	—	—	—	—	0	0	0	0	0	0	0	R	0.0

■ GREG GAGNE
Gagne, Gregory Carpenter b: 11/12/61, Fall River, Mass.   BR/TR, 5'11", 185 lbs. Deb: 6/05/83

YEAR	TM/L	G	AB	R	H	2B	3B	HR	RBI	BB	SO	AVG	OBP	SLG	PRO+	BR	/A	RC	SB	CS	SBR	FR	POS	TPR
1983	Min-A	10	27	2	3	1	0	0	3	0	6	.111	.111	.148	-28	-5	-5	1	0	0	0	-5	S	-0.9
1984	Min-A	2	0	0	0	0	0	0	0	0	0	.000	.000	.000	-96	-0	-0	0	0	0	0	0	/H	0.0
1985	Min-A	114	293	37	66	15	3	2	23	20	57	.225	.282	.317	60	-15	-17	27	10	4	1	4	*S/D	-0.3
1986	Min-A	156	472	63	118	22	6	12	54	30	108	.250	.303	.398	87	-8	-10	57	12	10	-2	-17	*S/2	-1.8
1987	*Min-A	137	437	68	116	28	7	10	40	25	84	.265	.311	.430	91	-5	-7	58	6	6	-2	18	*S/O2D	1.5
1988	Min-A	149	461	70	109	20	6	14	48	27	110	.236	.289	.397	85	-7	-9	50	15	7	0	-15	*S/O23	-1.6
1989	Min-A	149	460	69	125	29	7	9	48	17	80	.272	.301	.424	96	-1	-4	56	11	4	1	-3	*S/O	0.6
1990	Min-A	138	388	38	91	22	3	7	38	24	76	.235	.281	.361	73	-12	-16	38	8	8	-2	2	*S/O	-0.7
Total	8	855	2539	347	628	137	32	54	254	143	521	.247	.294	.390	83	-53	-67	286	62	39	-5	-15	S/O2D3	-3.2

■ ED GAGNIER
Gagnier, Edward J. b: 4/16/1883, Paris, France d: 9/13/46, Detroit, Mich.   BR/TR, 5'9", 170 lbs. Deb: 4/14/14

YEAR	TM/L	G	AB	R	H	2B	3B	HR	RBI	BB	SO	AVG	OBP	SLG	PRO+	BR	/A	RC	SB	CS	SBR	FR	POS	TPR
1914	Bro-F	94	337	22	63	12	2	0	25	13	24	.187	.219	.234	30	-31	-30	21	8			-1	S/3	-2.6
1915	Bro-F	20	50	8	13	1	0	0	4	10	5	.260	.393	.280	102	1	1	7	2			2	S/2	0.4
	Buf-F	1	2	0	0	0	0	0	0	0	0	.000	.000	.000	-98	-0	-0	0	0			0	/2	0.0
	Yr	21	52	8	13	1	0	0	4	10	5	.250	.381	.269	95	0	0	7	2			2		0.4
Total	2	115	389	30	76	13	2	0	29	23	29	.195	.244	.239	40	-30	-30	27	10			2	S/23	-2.2

■ CHICK GAGNON
Gagnon, Harold Dennis b: 9/27/1897, Millbury, Mass. d: 4/30/70, Wilmington, Del.   BR/TR, 5'7.5", 158 lbs. Deb: 6/27/22

YEAR	TM/L	G	AB	R	H	2B	3B	HR	RBI	BB	SO	AVG	OBP	SLG	PRO+	BR	/A	RC	SB	CS	SBR	FR	POS	TPR
1922	Det-A	10	4	2	1	0	0	0	0	0	2	.250	.250	.250	32	-0	-0	0	0	0	0	0	/S3	0.0
1924	Was-A	4	5	1	1	0	0	0	1	0	0	.200	.200	.200	3	-1	-1	0	0	0	0	1	/S	0.0
Total	2	14	9	3	2	0	0	0	1	0	2	.222	.222	.222	16	-1	-1	0	0	0	0	1	/S3	0.0

■ DEL GAINER
Gainer, Dellos Clinton "Sheriff" b: 11/10/1886, Montrose, W.Va. d: 1/29/47, Elkins, W.Va.   BR/TR, 6', 180 lbs. Deb: 10/02/09

YEAR	TM/L	G	AB	R	H	2B	3B	HR	RBI	BB	SO	AVG	OBP	SLG	PRO+	BR	/A	RC	SB	CS	SBR	FR	POS	TPR
1909	Det-A	2	5	0	1	0	0	0	0	0		.200	.200	.200	25	-0	-0	0	0			0	/1	0.0
1911	Det-A	70	248	32	75	11	4	2	25	20		.302	.366	.403	109	5	3	40	10			-4	1	0.1
1912	Det-A	52	179	28	43	5	6	0	20	18		.240	.320	.335	90	-3	-2	24	14			-3	1/O	-0.4
1913	Det-A	105	363	47	97	16	8	2	25	30	45	.267	.333	.372	108	2	3	46	10			-5	*1	-0.1
1914	Det-A	1	0	0	0	0	0	0	0	0	0	—	—	—	—	0	0	0	0			0	/1	0.0
	Bos-A	38	84	11	20	9	2	2	13	8	14	.238	.312	.464	133	3	3	12	2	2	-1	-3	12/O	0.0
	Yr	39	84	11	20	9	2	2	13	8	14	.238	.312	.464	133	3	3	12	2	2	-1	-3		0.0
1915	*Bos-A	82	200	30	59	5	8	1	29	21	31	.295	.371	.415	139	8	9	35	7	2	1	0	1/O	0.8
1916	*Bos-A	56	142	14	36	6	0	3	18	10	24	.254	.303	.359	98	-1	-1	18	5			1	1/2	0.1
1917	Bos-A	52	172	28	53	10	2	2	19	15	21	.308	.374	.424	145	9	9	27	1			-1	1	0.7
1919	Bos-A	47	118	9	28	6	2	0	13	13	15	.237	.318	.322	85	-3	-2	13	5			-3	1O	-0.8
1922	StL-N	43	97	19	26	7	4	2	23	14	6	.268	.360	.485	122	2	3	17	0	2	-1	0	1O	0.1
Total	10	548	1608	218	438	75	36	14	185	149	156	.272	.342	.390	113	21	24	232	54	6		-17	1/O2	0.4

■ JOE GAINES
Gaines, Arnesta Joe b: 11/22/36, Bryan, Tex.   BR/TR, 6'1", 190 lbs. Deb: 6/29/60

YEAR	TM/L	G	AB	R	H	2B	3B	HR	RBI	BB	SO	AVG	OBP	SLG	PRO+	BR	/A	RC	SB	CS	SBR	FR	POS	TPR
1960	Cin-N	11	15	2	3	0	0	0	1	0	1	.200	.200	.200	10	-2	-2	1	0	0	0	0	/O	-0.1
1961	Cin-N	5	3	2	0	0	0	0	0	2	1	.000	.400	.000	18	-0	-0	0	0	0	0	-0	/O	0.0
1962	Cin-N	64	52	12	12	3	0	1	7	8	16	.231	.333	.346	80	-1	-1	6	0	0	0	1	O	0.0
1963	Bal-A	66	126	24	36	4	1	6	20	20	39	.286	.384	.476	142	7	7	23	2	1	0	-3	O	0.3
1964	Bal-A	16	26	2	4	0	0	1	2	3	7	.154	.241	.269	42	-2	-2	2	0	0	0	0	/O	-0.1
	Hou-N	89	307	37	78	9	7	3	34	27	69	.254	.318	.397	106	0	2	39	8	2	1	-3	O	-0.1
1965	Hou-N	100	229	21	52	8	1	6	31	18	59	.227	.292	.349	86	-6	-4	24	4	1	1	-7	O	-1.2
1966	Hou-N	11	13	4	1	1	0	0	0	3	5	.077	.250	.154	17	-1	-1	1	0	0	0	-1	/O	-0.1
Total	7	362	771	104	186	25	9	21	95	81	197	.241	.317	.379	98	-6	-2	96	14	4	2	-13	O	-1.3

■ TY GAINEY
Gainey, Telmanch b: 12/25/60, Cheraw, N.C.   BL/TR, 6'1", 190 lbs. Deb: 4/24/85

YEAR	TM/L	G	AB	R	H	2B	3B	HR	RBI	BB	SO	AVG	OBP	SLG	PRO+	BR	/A	RC	SB	CS	SBR	FR	POS	TPR
1985	Hou-N	13	37	5	6	0	0	0	2	9	16	.162	.244	.162	16	-4	-4	2	0	0	0	-0	O	-0.4
1986	Hou-N	26	50	6	15	3	1	1	6	6	19	.300	.375	.460	133	2	2	9	3	1	0	1	O	0.3
1987	Hou-N	18	24	1	3	0	0	0	1	2	9	.125	.192	.125	-14	-4	-4	1	1	0	0	1	/O	-0.2
Total	3	57	111	12	24	3	1	1	7	10	37	.216	.293	.288	62	-6	-6	12	4	1	1	1	/O	-0.3

■ AUGIE GALAN
Galan, August John b: 5/25/12, Berkeley, Cal.   BB/TR, 6', 175 lbs. Deb: 4/29/34 C

YEAR	TM/L	G	AB	R	H	2B	3B	HR	RBI	BB	SO	AVG	OBP	SLG	PRO+	BR	/A	RC	SB	CS	SBR	FR	POS	TPR
1934	Chi-N	66	192	31	50	6	2	5	22	16	15	.260	.317	.391	90	-3	-3	25	4			-8	2/3S	-0.6
1935	*Chi-N	154	646	133	203	41	11	12	79	87	53	.314	.399	.467	131	32	31	133	22			4	*O	2.7
1936	Chi-N	145	575	74	152	26	4	8	81	67	50	.264	.344	.365	89	-6	-8	77	16			-0	O	-1.3
1937	Chi-N	147	611	104	154	24	10	18	78	79	48	.252	.339	.412	99	3	-1	92	23			10	*O/2S	0.3
1938	*Chi-N	110	395	52	113	16	9	6	69	49	17	.286	.368	.418	112	9	8	64	8			3	O	0.9
1939	Chi-N	148	549	104	167	36	8	6	71	75	26	.304	.392	.432	119	18	17	97	8			-6	*O	0.9
1940	Chi-N	68	209	33	48	14	2	3	22	37	23	.230	.346	.359	96	-1	-0	29	9			1	O/2	0.0
1941	Chi-N	65	120	18	25	3	0	1	13	22	10	.208	.331	.258	70	-4	-4	12	0			-2	O	-0.7
	*Bro-N	17	27	3	7	3	0	0	4	3	1	.259	.333	.370	94	-0	-0	4	0			1	/O	-0.0
	Yr	82	147	21	32	6	0	1	17	25	11	.218	.331	.279	74	-4	-4	16	0			-1		-0.7
1942	Bro-N	69	209	24	55	16	0	0	22	24	12	.263	.339	.340	97	0	-0	25	2			-2	O/12	-0.3
1943	Bro-N	139	495	83	142	26	3	9	67	103	39	.287	.412	.406	136	28	28	93	6			10	*O1	3.5
1944	Bro-N	151	547	96	174	43	9	12	93	101	23	.318	.426	.495	162	47	48	123	4			0	*O/2	3.7
1945	Bro-N	152	576	114	177	36	7	9	92	114	27	.307	.423	.441	142	37	37	116	13			-11	1O3	2.1
1946	Bro-N	99	274	53	85	22	5	3	38	68	21	.310	.451	.460	157	25	25	65	8			-6	O31	1.7
1947	Cin-N	124	392	60	123	18	2	6	61	94	19	.314	.449	.416	142	24	24	83	0			-6	*O	1.3
1948	Cin-N	54	77	18	22	3	2	2	16	26	4	.286	.471	.455	157	8	8	19	0			-3	O	0.4
1949	NY-N	22	17	0	1	1	0	0	2	5	3	.059	.273	.118	8	-2	-2	1	0			-0	/1O	-0.2
	Phi-A	12	26	4	8	2	0	0	9	9	2	.308	.486	.385	136	2	2	7	0	0	0	-1	/O	0.1
Total	16	1742	5937	1004	1706	336	74	100	830	979	393	.287	.390	.419	122	216	211	1064	123	0		-17	*O/132S	14.5

■ ANDRES GALARRAGA
Galarraga, Andres Jose (b: Andres Jose Padovani (Galarraga) b: 6/18/61, Caracas, Venez.   BR/TR, 6'3", 235 lbs. Deb: 8/23/85

YEAR	TM/L	G	AB	R	H	2B	3B	HR	RBI	BB	SO	AVG	OBP	SLG	PRO+	BR	/A	RC	SB	CS	SBR	FR	POS	TPR
1985	Mon-N	24	75	9	14	1	0	2	4	3	18	.187	.228	.280	44	-6	-6	5	1	2	-1	4	1	-0.3
1986	Mon-N	105	321	39	87	13	0	10	42	30	79	.271	.339	.405	105	2	2	43	6	5	-1	-8	*1	-1.0
1987	Mon-N	147	551	72	168	40	3	13	90	41	127	.305	.364	.459	131	13	11	88	7	10	-4	0	*1	-0.1
1988	Mon-N	157	609	99	184	42	8	29	92	39	153	.302	.354	.540	147	39	36	114	13	4	2	-4	*1	2.7
1989	Mon-N	152	572	76	147	30	1	23	85	48	158	.257	.329	.434	115	11	10	81	12	5	1	-2	*1	-0.2
1990	Mon-N	155	579	65	148	29	0	20	87	40	169	.256	.308	.409	96	-5	-4	72	10	1	2	-5	*1	-1.5
Total	6	740	2707	360	748	155	12	97	400	201	704	.276	.336	.450	115	54	49	401	49	27	-2	-15	1	-0.4

YEAR	TM/L	G	AB	R	H	2B	3B	HR	RBI	BB	SO	AVG	OBP	SLG	PRO+	BR	/A	RC	SB	CS	SBR	FR	POS	TPR

■ MILT GALATZER
Galatzer, Milton b: 5/4/07, Chicago, Il.. d: 1/29/76, San Francisco, Cal BL/TL, 5'10", 168 lbs. Deb: 6/25/33

YEAR	TM/L	G	AB	R	H	2B	3B	HR	RBI	BB	SO	AVG	OBP	SLG	PRO+	BR	/A	RC	SB	CS	SBR	FR	POS	TPR
1933	Cle-A	57	160	19	38	2	1	1	17	23	21	.237	.333	.281	61	-8	-9	16	2	3	-1	-0	O/1	-1.1
1934	Cle-A	49	196	29	53	10	2	0	15	21	8	.270	.344	.342	76	-6	-7	24	3	2	-0	-0	O	-0.7
1935	Cle-A	93	259	45	78	9	3	0	19	35	8	.301	.389	.359	93	-1	-1	38	4	5	-2	-8	O	-1.0
1936	Cle-A	49	97	12	23	4	1	0	6	13	4	.237	.333	.299	57	-6	-6	10	1	2	-1	-1	O/P1	-0.7
1939	Cin-N	3	5	0	0	0	0	0	0	0	1	.000	.000	.000	-99	-1	-1	0	0			-0	/1	-0.1
Total	5	251	717	105	192	25	7	1	57	92	46	.268	.354	.326	75	-22	-24	88	10	12		-9	O/1P	-3.6

■ ARCHIE GALBRAITH
Galbraith, Archibald Victor b: 9/22/1877, Boxford, Mass. d: 12/25/71, Northampton, Mass Deb: 8/29/02

YEAR	TM/L	G	AB	R	H	2B	3B	HR	RBI	BB	SO	AVG	OBP	SLG	PRO+	BR	/A	RC	SB	CS	SBR	FR	POS	TPR
1902	Chi-N	1	0	0	0	0	0	0	0	0		—	—	—	—	0	0	0	0			0	/3	0.0

■ AL GALLAGHER
Gallagher, Alan Mitchell Edward George Patrick Henry b: 10/19/45, San Francisco, Cal. BR/TR, 6', 180 lbs. Deb: 4/07/70

YEAR	TM/L	G	AB	R	H	2B	3B	HR	RBI	BB	SO	AVG	OBP	SLG	PRO+	BR	/A	RC	SB	CS	SBR	FR	POS	TPR
1970	SF-N	109	282	31	75	15	2	4	28	30	37	.266	.337	.376	92	-4	-3	35	2	1	0	1	3	-0.4
1971	*SF-N	136	429	47	119	18	5	5	57	40	57	.277	.342	.378	105	2	3	53	2	1	0	-16	*3	-1.3
1972	SF-N	82	233	19	52	3	1	2	18	33	39	.223	.322	.270	69	-8	-9	21	2	1	0	-3	3	-1.3
1973	SF-N	5	9	1	2	0	0	0	1	0	0	.222	.300	.222	45	-1	-1	0	0	0	0	-1	/3	-0.1
	Cal-A	110	311	16	85	6	1	0	26	35	31	.273	.349	.299	91	-5	-2	32	1	3	-2	4	3/2S	0.0
Total	4	442	1264	114	333	42	9	11	130	138	164	.263	.338	.337	91	-15	-11	142	7	6	-2	-15	3/S2	-3.1

■ SHORTY GALLAGHER
Gallagher, Charles William b: 4/30/1872, Detroit, Mich. d: 6/23/24, Detroit, Mich. Deb: 8/13/01

YEAR	TM/L	G	AB	R	H	2B	3B	HR	RBI	BB	SO	AVG	OBP	SLG	PRO+	BR	/A	RC	SB	CS	SBR	FR	POS	TPR
1901	Cle-A	2	4	0	0	0	0	0	0	0	0	.000	.000	.000	-99	-1	-1	0	0			-1	/O	-0.1

■ DAVE GALLAGHER
Gallagher, David Thomas b: 9/20/60, Trenton, N.J. BR/TR, 6' ", 180 lbs. Deb: 4/12/87

YEAR	TM/L	G	AB	R	H	2B	3B	HR	RBI	BB	SO	AVG	OBP	SLG	PRO+	BR	/A	RC	SB	CS	SBR	FR	POS	TPR
1987	Cle-A	15	36	2	4	1	1	0	1	2	5	.111	.158	.194	-7	-6	-6	1	2	0	1	3	O	-0.1
1988	Chi-A	101	347	59	105	15	3	5	31	29	40	.303	.356	.406	113	6	6	49	5	4	-1	-5	O/D	0.0
1989	Chi-A	161	601	74	160	22	2	1	46	46	79	.266	.320	.314	82	-15	-14	62	5	6	-2	-3	*O/D	-2.1
1990	Chi-A	45	75	5	21	3	1	0	5	3	9	.280	.316	.347	87	-2	-1	7	0	1	-1	3	O/D	0.0
	Bal-A	23	51	7	11	1	0	0	2	4	3	.216	.273	.235	44	-4	-4	4	1	1	-0	4	O/D	0.0
	Yr	68	126	12	32	4	1	0	7	7	12	.254	.299	.302	70	-5	-5	11	1	2	-1	7		0.0
Total	4	345	1110	147	301	42	7	6	85	84	136	.271	.324	.338	87	-20	-18	123	13	12	-3	2	O/D	-2.2

■ JIM GALLAGHER
Gallagher, James E. b: Findlay, Ohio d: 3/29/1894, Scranton, Pa. Deb: 9/04/1886

YEAR	TM/L	G	AB	R	H	2B	3B	HR	RBI	BB	SO	AVG	OBP	SLG	PRO+	BR	/A	RC	SB	CS	SBR	FR	POS	TPR
1886	Was-N	1	5	1	1	0	0	0	0	0	2	.200	.200	.200	23	-0	-0	0	0			1	/S	0.0

■ JOHN GALLAGHER
Gallagher, John Carroll b: 2/18/1892, Pittsburgh, Pa. d: 3/30/52, Norfolk, Va. BR/TR, 5'10.5", 156 lbs. Deb: 8/20/15

YEAR	TM/L	G	AB	R	H	2B	3B	HR	RBI	BB	SO	AVG	OBP	SLG	PRO+	BR	/A	RC	SB	CS	SBR	FR	POS	TPR
1915	Bal-F	40	126	11	25	4	0	0	4	5	22	.198	.229	.230	35	-10	-11	8	1			-2	2/S3	-1.2

■ JACKIE GALLAGHER
Gallagher, John Laurence b: 1/28/02, Providence, R.I. d: 9/10/84, Gladwyn, Pa. BL/TR, 5'10", 175 lbs. Deb: 8/24/23

YEAR	TM/L	G	AB	R	H	2B	3B	HR	RBI	BB	SO	AVG	OBP	SLG	PRO+	BR	/A	RC	SB	CS	SBR	FR	POS	TPR
1923	Cle-A	1	1	0	1	0	0	0	0	0	0	1.000	1.000	1.000	428	0	0	1	0	0	0	-0	/O	0.0

■ JOE GALLAGHER
Gallagher, Joseph Emmett "Muscles" b: 3/7/14, Buffalo, N.Y. BR/TR, 6'2", 210 lbs. Deb: 4/20/39

YEAR	TM/L	G	AB	R	H	2B	3B	HR	RBI	BB	SO	AVG	OBP	SLG	PRO+	BR	/A	RC	SB	CS	SBR	FR	POS	TPR
1939	NY-A	14	41	8	10	1	2	3	9	3	8	.244	.311	.439	91	-1	-1	6	1	0	0	-1	O	-0.1
	StL-A	71	266	41	75	17	2	9	40	17	42	.282	.327	.462	98	-1	-2	38	0	1	-1	1	O	-0.2
	Yr	85	307	49	85	17	3	11	49	20	50	.277	.325	.459	97	-2	-3	44	1	1	-0	1		-0.3
1940	StL-A	23	70	14	19	3	1	2	8	4	12	.271	.311	.429	88	-1	-2	9	2	0	1	-2	O	-0.3
	Bro-N	57	110	10	29	6	1	3	16	2	14	.264	.283	.418	86	-2	-3	13	1			-2	O	-0.5
Total	2	165	487	73	133	26	5	16	73	26	76	.273	.314	.446	93	-5	-7	66	4	1		-3	O	-1.1

■ GIL GALLAGHER
Gallagher, Lawrence Kirby b: 9/5/1896, Washington, D.C. d: 1/6/57, Washington, D.C. BB/TR, 5'8", 155 lbs. Deb: 9/13/22

YEAR	TM/L	G	AB	R	H	2B	3B	HR	RBI	BB	SO	AVG	OBP	SLG	PRO+	BR	/A	RC	SB	CS	SBR	FR	POS	TPR
1922	Bos-N	7	22	1	1	1	0	0	2	1	7	.045	.087	.091	-57	-5	-5	0	0	0	0	-2	/S	-0.5

■ BOB GALLAGHER
Gallagher, Robert Collins b: 7/7/48, Newton, Mass. BL/TL, 6'3", 185 lbs. Deb: 5/17/72

YEAR	TM/L	G	AB	R	H	2B	3B	HR	RBI	BB	SO	AVG	OBP	SLG	PRO+	BR	/A	RC	SB	CS	SBR	FR	POS	TPR
1972	Bos-A	7	5	0	0	0	0	0	0	0	3	.000	.000	.000	-95	-1	-1	0	0	0	0	0	H	0.0
1973	Hou-N	71	148	16	39	3	1	2	10	3	27	.264	.278	.338	70	-6	-6	13	0	1	-1	3	O/1	-0.6
1974	Hou-N	102	87	13	15	2	0	0	3	12	23	.172	.280	.195	36	-7	-7	6	1	0	0	2	O/1	-0.7
1975	NY-N	33	15	5	2	1	0	0	0	1	3	.133	.188	.200	8	-2	-2	0	0	0	0	2	O	0.0
Total	4	213	255	34	56	6	1	2	13	16	56	.220	.268	.275	52	-17	-16	20	1	1	-0	6	O/1	-1.3

■ WILLIAM GALLAGHER
Gallagher, William H. b: 1875, Lowell, Mass. Deb: 8/19/1896

YEAR	TM/L	G	AB	R	H	2B	3B	HR	RBI	BB	SO	AVG	OBP	SLG	PRO+	BR	/A	RC	SB	CS	SBR	FR	POS	TPR
1896	Phi-N	14	49	9	15	2	0	0	6	10	0	.306	.433	.347	111	1	2	8	0			-4	S	-0.1

■ BILL GALLAGHER
Gallagher, William John b: Philadelphia, Pa. TL , Deb: 5/02/1883

YEAR	TM/L	G	AB	R	H	2B	3B	HR	RBI	BB	SO	AVG	OBP	SLG	PRO+	BR	/A	RC	SB	CS	SBR	FR	POS	TPR
1883	Bal-a	16	61	9	10	3	1	0		3		.164	.203	.246	43	-4	-4	3				-2	/OPS	-0.4
	Phi-N	2	8	1	0	0	0	0	0	0	4	.000	.000	.000	-99	-2	-2	0				-0	/O	-0.1
1884	Phi-U	3	11	1	1	0	0	0	0	0		.091	.091	.091	-41	-2	-1	0	0			0	/P	0.0
Total	2	21	80	11	11	3	1	0	0	3	4	.138	.169	.200	18	-7	-7	3	0			-2	/OPS	-0.5

■ STAN GALLE
Galle, Stanley Joseph (b: Stanley Joseph Galazewski) b: 2/7/19, Milwaukee, Wis. BR/TR, 5'7", 165 lbs. Deb: 4/14/42

YEAR	TM/L	G	AB	R	H	2B	3B	HR	RBI	BB	SO	AVG	OBP	SLG	PRO+	BR	/A	RC	SB	CS	SBR	FR	POS	TPR
1942	Was-A	13	18	3	2	0	0	0	1	1	0	.111	.158	.111	-24	-3	-3	0	0	0	0	-0	/3	-0.2

■ MIKE GALLEGO
Gallego, Michael Anthon b: 10/31/60, Whittier, Cal. BR/TR, 5'8", 160 lbs. Deb: 4/11/85

YEAR	TM/L	G	AB	R	H	2B	3B	HR	RBI	BB	SO	AVG	OBP	SLG	PRO+	BR	/A	RC	SB	CS	SBR	FR	POS	TPR
1985	Oak-A	76	77	13	16	5	1	1	9	12	14	.208	.322	.338	87	-2	-1	9	1	1	-0	12	2S3	1.4
1986	Oak-A	20	37	2	10	2	0	0	4	1	6	.270	.289	.324	72	-2	-1	3	0	2	-1	9	2/3S	0.7
1987	Oak-A	72	124	18	31	6	0	2	14	12	21	.250	.321	.347	83	-4	-3	13	0	1	-1	17	23S	1.6
1988	*Oak-A	129	277	38	58	8	0	2	20	34	53	.209	.298	.260	60	-15	-14	23	2	3	-1	3	2S3	-0.4
1989	*Oak-A	133	357	45	90	14	2	3	30	35	43	.252	.329	.328	89	-6	-4	39	7	5	-1	18	S2/3D	2.1
1990	*Oak-A	140	389	36	80	13	2	3	34	35	50	.206	.278	.272	56	-23	-22	29	5	5	-2	13	2S3/OD	-0.2
Total	6	570	1261	152	285	48	5	11	111	129	187	.226	.304	.298	71	-52	-45	116	15	17	-6	72	2S/3DO	5.2

■ JIM GALLIGAN
Galligan, James M. b: 1862, Easton, Pa. d: 7/17/01, New York, N.Y. 5'10", 160 lbs. Deb: 9/02/1889

YEAR	TM/L	G	AB	R	H	2B	3B	HR	RBI	BB	SO	AVG	OBP	SLG	PRO+	BR	/A	RC	SB	CS	SBR	FR	POS	TPR
1889	Lou-a	31	120	6	20	0	2	0	7	6	17	.167	.213	.200	19	-13	-12	5	1			2	O	-0.9

■ CHICK GALLOWAY
Galloway, Clarence Edward b: 8/4/1896, Clinton, S.C. d: 11/7/69, Clinton, S.C. BR/TR, 5'8", 160 lbs. Deb: 9/09/19

YEAR	TM/L	G	AB	R	H	2B	3B	HR	RBI	BB	SO	AVG	OBP	SLG	PRO+	BR	/A	RC	SB	CS	SBR	FR	POS	TPR
1919	Phi-A	17	63	2	9	0	0	4	1	8		.143	.156	.143	-16	-10	-10	1	0			1	S	-0.7
1920	Phi-A	98	298	28	60	9	3	0	18	22	22	.201	.259	.252	35	-28	-28	21	2	2	-1	4	S/23	-1.6
1921	Phi-A	131	465	42	123	28	5	3	47	29	43	.265	.310	.366	72	-21	-21	53	12	7	-1	-22	*S3/2	-2.6
1922	Phi-A	155	571	83	185	26	9	6	69	39	38	.324	.368	.433	105	6	4	92	10	4	-1	3	*S	2.4
1923	Phi-A	134	504	64	140	18	9	2	62	37	30	.278	.327	.361	80	-15	-15	59	12	10	-2	2	*S	-0.2
1924	Phi-A	129	464	41	128	16	4	2	48	23	23	.276	.311	.341	67	-23	-23	48	11	12	-4	2	*S	-1.0
1925	Phi-A	149	481	52	116	11	4	3	71	59	28	.241	.324	.299	55	-29	-34	51	16	9	-1	-3	*S	-1.3
1926	Phi-A	133	408	37	98	13	6	0	49	31	20	.240	.295	.301	53	-27	-30	38	8	6	-1	-13	*S	-3.2
1927	Phi-A	77	181	25	48	10	4	0	22	18	9	.265	.332	.365	76	-5	-7	21	1	3	-2	5	S/3	0.2
1928	Det-A	53	148	17	39	5	2	1	17	15	3	.264	.331	.345	77	-5	-5	18	7	2	1	-4	S/31O	-0.4
Total	10	1076	3583	391	946	136	46	17	407	274	224	.264	.317	.342	69	-155	-170	401	79	55		-25	S/3201	-8.4

■ JIM GALLOWAY Galloway, James Cato "Bad News" b: 9/16/1887, Iredell, Tex. d: 5/3/50, Fort Worth, Tex. BB/TR, 6'3", 187 lbs. Deb: 8/24/12

YEAR	TM/L	G	AB	R	H	2B	3B	HR	RBI	BB	SO	AVG	OBP	SLG	PRO+	BR	/A	RC	SB	CS	SBR	FR	POS	TPR
1912	StL-N	21	54	4	10	2	0	0	4	5	8	.185	.254	.222	32	-5	-5	4	2			1	2/S	-0.3

■ JIM GALVIN Galvin, James Joseph b: 8/11/07, Somerville, Mass. d: 9/30/69, Marietta, Ga. BR/TR, 5'11.5", 180 lbs. Deb: 9/27/30

YEAR	TM/L	G	AB	R	H	2B	3B	HR	RBI	BB	SO	AVG	OBP	SLG	PRO+	BR	/A	RC	SB	CS	SBR	FR	POS	TPR
1930	Bos-A	2	2	0	0	0	0	0	0	0	0	.000	.000	.000	-99	-1	-1	0	0	0	0	0	H	0.0

■ JOHN GALVIN Galvin, John S. b: Brooklyn, N.Y. d: 4/20/04, Brooklyn, N.Y. Deb: 5/07/1872

YEAR	TM/L	G	AB	R	H	2B	3B	HR	RBI	BB	SO	AVG	OBP	SLG	PRO+	BR	/A	RC	SB	CS	SBR	FR	POS	TPR
1872	Atl-n	1	4	0	0	0	0	0		0		.000	.000	.000	-85	-1	-1	0					/2	0.0

■ JOHN GAMBLE Gamble, John Robert b: 2/10/48, Reno, Nev. BR/TR, 5'10", 165 lbs. Deb: 9/07/72

YEAR	TM/L	G	AB	R	H	2B	3B	HR	RBI	BB	SO	AVG	OBP	SLG	PRO+	BR	/A	RC	SB	CS	SBR	FR	POS	TPR
1972	Det-A	6	3	0	0	0	0	0	0	0	0	.000	.000	.000	-97	-1	-1	0	0	0	0	2	/S	0.2
1973	Det-A	7	0	1	0	0	0	0	0	0	0	—	—	—	—	0	0	0	0	0	0	0	R	0.0
Total	2	13	3	1	0	0	0	0	0	0	0	.000	.000	.000	-97	-1	-1	0	0	0	0	2	/S	0.2

■ LEE GAMBLE Gamble, Lee Jesse b: 6/28/10, Renovo, Pa. BL/TR, 6'1", 170 lbs. Deb: 9/15/35

YEAR	TM/L	G	AB	R	H	2B	3B	HR	RBI	BB	SO	AVG	OBP	SLG	PRO+	BR	/A	RC	SB	CS	SBR	FR	POS	TPR
1935	Cin-N	2	4	2	2	1	0	0	2	1	0	.500	.600	.750	269	1	1	2	1			-0	I/O	0.1
1938	Cin-N	53	75	13	24	3	1	0	5	0	6	.320	.320	.387	96	-1	-1	9	0			0	O	0.0
1939	*Cin-N	72	221	24	59	7	2	0	14	9	14	.267	.296	.317	64	-11	-11	21	5			-5	O	-1.6
1940	Cin-N	38	42	12	6	1	0	0	0	0	1	.143	.143	.167	-15	-7	-7	1	0			2	O	-0.4
Total	4	165	342	51	91	12	3	0	21	10	21	.266	.287	.319	64	-17	-17	34	6			-3	I/O	-1.9

■ OSCAR GAMBLE Gamble, Oscar Charles b: 12/20/49, Ramer, Ala. BL/TR, 5'11", 160 lbs. Deb: 8/27/69

YEAR	TM/L	G	AB	R	H	2B	3B	HR	RBI	BB	SO	AVG	OBP	SLG	PRO+	BR	/A	RC	SB	CS	SBR	FR	POS	TPR
1969	Chi-N	24	71	6	16	1	1	1	5	10	12	.225	.321	.310	69	-2	-3	7	0	2	-1	-1	O	-0.6
1970	Phi-N	88	275	31	72	12	4	1	19	27	37	.262	.330	.345	84	-7	-6	30	5	4	-1	1	O	-0.9
1971	Phi-N	92	280	24	62	11	1	6	23	21	35	.221	.278	.332	72	-11	-11	27	5	2	0	-8	O	-2.2
1972	Phi-N	74	135	17	32	5	2	1	13	19	16	.237	.335	.326	86	-2	-2	15	0	1	-1	-0	O/1	-0.4
1973	Cle-A	113	390	56	104	11	3	20	44	34	37	.267	.330	.464	120	10	9	60	3	4	-2	-3	DO	0.3
1974	Cle-A	135	454	74	132	16	4	19	59	48	51	.291	.365	.469	140	22	23	77	5	6	-2	0	*DO	2.1
1975	Cle-A	121	348	60	91	16	3	15	45	53	39	.261	.362	.454	130	14	14	58	11	5	0	0	OD	1.2
1976	*NY-A	110	340	43	79	13	1	17	57	38	38	.232	.317	.426	117	6	7	47	5	3	-0	-4	*O/D	0.0
1977	Chi-A	137	408	75	121	22	2	31	83	54	54	.297	.387	.588	162	34	35	96	1	2	-1	-2	DO	3.0
1978	SD-N	126	375	46	103	15	3	7	47	51	45	.275	.370	.387	121	8	11	57	1	2	-1	-4	*O	0.3
1979	Tex-A	64	161	27	54	6	0	8	32	37	15	.335	.462	.522	167	17	17	39	2	1	0	2	DO	1.7
	NY-A	36	113	21	44	4	1	11	32	13	13	.389	.452	.735	219	18	18	38	0	0	0	-1	O/D	1.5
	Yr	100	274	48	98	10	1	19	64	50	28	.358	.458	.609	188	35	35	79	2	1	0	1		3.2
1980	*NY-A	78	194	40	54	10	2	14	50	28	21	.278	.381	.567	159	15	15	44	2	0	1	-2	OD	1.2
1981	*NY-A	80	189	24	45	8	0	10	27	35	23	.238	.360	.439	130	3	8	31	0	2	-1	1	OD	0.7
1982	NY-A	108	316	49	86	21	2	18	57	58	47	.272	.392	.522	151	22	23	69	6	3	0	4	DO	2.6
1983	NY-A	74	180	26	47	10	2	7	26	25	23	.261	.361	.456	128	6	7	31	0	0	0	-0	OD	0.6
1984	NY-A	54	125	17	23	2	0	10	27	25	18	.184	.320	.440	112	1	2	19	1	0	0	0	DO	0.2
1985	Chi-A	70	148	20	30	5	0	4	20	34	22	.203	.355	.318	83	-2	-2	19	0	0	0	0	D	-0.1
Total	17	1584	4502	656	1195	188	31	200	666	610	546	.265	.358	.454	127	159	165	766	47	37	-8	-16	OD/1	11.2

■ DAFF GAMMONS Gammons, John Ashley b: 3/17/1876, New Bedford, Mass. d: 9/24/63, E.Greenwich, R.I. 5'11", 170 lbs. Deb: 4/23/01

YEAR	TM/L	G	AB	R	H	2B	3B	HR	RBI	BB	SO	AVG	OBP	SLG	PRO+	BR	/A	RC	SB	CS	SBR	FR	POS	TPR
1901	Bos-N	28	93	10	18	0	1	0	10	3		.194	.242	.215	32	-7	-9	7	5			-2	O/23	-1.2

■ CHICK GANDIL Gandil, Arnold b: 1/19/1887, St.Paul, Minn. d: 12/13/70, Calistoga, Cal. BR/TR, 6'1.5", 190 lbs. Deb: 4/14/10

YEAR	TM/L	G	AB	R	H	2B	3B	HR	RBI	BB	SO	AVG	OBP	SLG	PRO+	BR	/A	RC	SB	CS	SBR	FR	POS	TPR
1910	Chi-A	77	275	21	53	7	3	2	21	24		.193	.267	.262	69	-11	-9	22	12			7	1/O	0.0
1912	Was-A	117	443	59	135	20	15	2	81	27		.305	.350	.431	122	11	11	74	21			3	*1	1.5
1913	Was-A	148	550	61	175	25	8	1	72	36	33	.318	.363	.398	120	14	13	84	22			8	*1	2.2
1914	Was-A	145	526	48	136	24	10	3	75	44	44	.259	.324	.359	103	2	1	67	30	19	-2	24	*1	2.4
1915	Was-A	136	485	53	141	20	15	2	64	29	33	.291	.340	.406	122	11	11	70	20	13	-2	-0	*1	0.3
1916	Cle-A	146	533	51	138	26	9	0	72	36	48	.259	.312	.341	91	-4	-8	64	13			8	*1	-0.1
1917	*Chi-A	149	553	53	151	9	7	0	57	30	36	.273	.316	.315	91	-6	-7	58	16			-5	*1	-2.0
1918	Chi-A	114	439	49	119	18	4	0	55	27	19	.271	.319	.330	95	-3	-4	47	9			-3	*1	-1.4
1919	*Chi-A	115	441	54	128	24	7	1	60	20	20	.290	.325	.383	98	-2	-2	57	10			-4	*1	-1.6
Total	9	1147	4245	449	1176	173	78	11	557	273	233	.277	.327	.362	103	13	5	544	153	32		37	*1/O	1.3

■ BOB GANDY Gandy, Robert Brinkley "String" b: 8/25/1893, Jacksonville, Fla. d: 6/19/45, Jacksonville, Fla BR/TR, 6'3", 180 lbs. Deb: 10/05/16

YEAR	TM/L	G	AB	R	H	2B	3B	HR	RBI	BB	SO	AVG	OBP	SLG	PRO+	BR	/A	RC	SB	CS	SBR	FR	POS	TPR
1916	Phi-N	1	2	0	0	0	0	0	0	0	1	.000	.000	.000	-97	-0	-0	0				0	/O	0.0

■ BOB GANLEY Ganley, Robert Stephen b: 4/23/1875, Lowell, Mass. d: 10/9/45, Lowell, Mass. BL/TL, 5'7", 156 lbs. Deb: 9/01/05

YEAR	TM/L	G	AB	R	H	2B	3B	HR	RBI	BB	SO	AVG	OBP	SLG	PRO+	BR	/A	RC	SB	CS	SBR	FR	POS	TPR
1905	Pit-N	32	127	12	40	1	2	0	7	8		.315	.356	.354	111	2	2	19	3			-2	O	-0.2
1906	Pit-N	137	511	63	132	7	6	0	31	41		.258	.313	.295	88	-4	-7	59	19			-2	*O	-1.2
1907	Was-A	154	605	73	167	10	5	1	35	54		.276	.335	.314	119	8	13	82	40			9	*O	1.5
1908	Was-A	150	549	61	131	19	9	1	36	45		.239	.296	.311	109	0	5	63	30			4	*O	0.2
1909	Was-A	19	63	5	16	3	0	0	5	1		.254	.266	.302	83	-2	-1	6	4			-3	O	-0.5
	Phi-A	80	274	32	54	4	2	0	9	28		.197	.272	.226	56	-13	-13	24	16			7	O	-0.9
	Yr	99	337	37	70	7	2	0	14	29		.208	.270	.240	61	-14	-15	30	20			4		-1.4
Total	5	572	2129	246	540	44	24	2	123	177		.254	.311	.300	98	-9	-1	253	112			13	O	-1.1

■ BILL GANNON Gannon, William G. b: 1876, New Haven, Conn. d: 4/26/27, Fort Worth, Tex. Deb: 8/28/1898

YEAR	TM/L	G	AB	R	H	2B	3B	HR	RBI	BB	SO	AVG	OBP	SLG	PRO+	BR	/A	RC	SB	CS	SBR	FR	POS	TPR
1898	StL-N	1	3	0	0	0	0	0	0	0		.000	.000	.000	-98	-1	-1	0	0			0	/P	0.0
1901	Chi-N	15	61	2	9	0	0	0	0	1		.148	.161	.148	-9	-8	-8	2	5			-1	O	-1.0
Total	2	16	64	2	9	0	0	0	0	1		.141	.154	.141	-14	-9	-9	2	5			-1	/OP	-1.0

■ RON GANT Gant, Ronald Edwin b: 3/2/65, Victoria, Tex. BR/TR, 6' ", 172 lbs. Deb: 9/06/87

YEAR	TM/L	G	AB	R	H	2B	3B	HR	RBI	BB	SO	AVG	OBP	SLG	PRO+	BR	/A	RC	SB	CS	SBR	FR	POS	TPR
1987	Atl-N	21	83	9	22	4	0	2	9	1	11	.265	.274	.386	69	-4	-4	7	4	2	0	-0	2	-0.3
1988	Atl-N	146	563	85	146	28	8	19	60	46	118	.259	.319	.439	110	10	7	78	19	10	-0	-1	*23	0.9
1989	Atl-N	75	260	26	46	8	3	9	25	20	63	.177	.238	.335	61	-14	-14	21	9	6	-1	3	3O	-1.3
1990	Atl-N	152	575	107	174	34	3	32	84	50	86	.303	.359	.539	141	32	31	109	33	16	0	-1	*O	2.6
Total	4	394	1481	227	388	74	14	62	178	117	278	.262	.318	.456	111	25	19	215	65	34	-1	1	O2/3	1.9

■ JOE GANTENBEIN Gantenbein, Joseph Stephen "Sep" b: 8/25/16, San Francisco, Cal BL/TR, 5'9", 168 lbs. Deb: 4/20/39

YEAR	TM/L	G	AB	R	H	2B	3B	HR	RBI	BB	SO	AVG	OBP	SLG	PRO+	BR	/A	RC	SB	CS	SBR	FR	POS	TPR
1939	Phi-A	111	348	47	101	14	4	4	36	32	22	.290	.353	.388	91	-5	-4	48	1	5	-3	-34	23/S	-3.4
1940	Phi-A	75	197	21	47	6	2	4	23	11	21	.239	.282	.350	64	-11	-11	20	1	0	0	-8	3/1SO	-1.4
Total	2	186	545	68	148	20	6	8	59	43	43	.272	.328	.374	82	-17	-15	68	2	5	-2	-41	/23S10	-4.8

■ JIM GANTNER Gantner, James Elmer b: 1/5/53, Fond Du Lac, Wis. BL/TR, 6', 180 lbs. Deb: 9/03/76

YEAR	TM/L	G	AB	R	H	2B	3B	HR	RBI	BB	SO	AVG	OBP	SLG	PRO+	BR	/A	RC	SB	CS	SBR	FR	POS	TPR
1976	Mil-A	26	69	6	17	1	0	0	7	6	11	.246	.316	.261	71	-2	-2	6	1	0	0	-3	3/D	-0.5
1977	Mil-A	14	47	4	14	1	0	1	2	2	5	.298	.327	.383	93	-1	-1	6	2	1	0	1	3	0.0
1978	Mil-A	43	97	14	21	1	0	1	8	5	10	.216	.269	.258	49	-7	-7	8	2	0	1	5	23/1S	0.1
1979	Mil-A	70	208	29	59	10	3	2	22	16	17	.284	.341	.389	96	-1	-1	27	3	5	-2	4	32/SP	0.3
1980	Mil-A	132	415	47	117	21	3	4	40	30	29	.282	.332	.376	97	-4	-2	50	11	10	-3	-2	32/S	-0.2
1981	*Mil-A	107	352	35	94	14	1	2	33	29	29	.267	.328	.330	95	-4	-2	38	3	6	-3	15	*2	1.4

YEAR	TM/L	G	AB	R	H	2B	3B	HR	RBI	BB	SO	AVG	OBP	SLG	PRO+	BR	/A	RC	SB	CS	SBR	FR	POS	TPR
1982	*Mil-A	132	447	48	132	17	2	4	43	26	36	.295	.337	.369	100	-4	-0	56	6	3	0	9	*2	1.6
1983	Mil-A	161	603	85	170	23	8	11	74	38	46	.282	.331	.401	109	-0	6	79	5	6	-2	10	*2	1.8
1984	Mil-A	153	613	61	173	27	1	3	56	30	51	.282	.319	.344	87	-14	-11	64	6	5	-1	10	*2	0.5
1985	Mil-A	143	523	63	133	15	4	5	44	33	42	.254	.302	.327	73	-20	-19	49	11	8	-2	1	*23/S	-1.4
1986	Mil-A	139	497	58	136	25	1	7	38	26	50	.274	.318	.370	84	-10	-12	56	13	7	-0	-11	*2/3SD	-1.4
1987	Mil-A	81	265	37	72	14	0	4	30	19	22	.272	.332	.370	84	-5	-6	32	6	2	1	3	23/D	0.1
1988	Mil-A	155	539	67	149	28	2	0	47	34	50	.276	.323	.336	84	-11	-11	60	20	8	1	-8	*2/3	-0.8
1989	Mil-A	116	409	51	112	18	3	0	34	21	33	.274	.325	.333	86	-7	-7	45	20	6	2	9	*2/D	0.6
1990	Mil-A	88	323	36	85	8	5	0	25	29	19	.263	.328	.319	84	-7	-6	35	18	3	4	-7	2/3	-0.5
Total	15	1560	5407	641	1484	223	33	44	503	344	450	.274	.324	.352	89	-95	-80	611	127	70	-4	35	*23/SDP1	1.6

■ CHARLIE GANZEL
Ganzel, Charles William b: 6/18/1862, Waterford, Wis. d: 4/7/14, Quincy, Mass. BR/TR, 6', 161 lbs. Deb: 9/27/1884

YEAR	TM/L	G	AB	R	H	2B	3B	HR	RBI	BB	SO	AVG	OBP	SLG	PRO+	BR	/A	RC	SB	CS	SBR	FR	POS	TPR
1884	StP-U	7	23	2	5	0	0	0	0			.217	.217	.217	87	-1	0	1	0			-2	/CO	-0.1
1885	Phi-N	34	125	15	21	3	1	0	6	4	13	.168	.194	.208	31	-10	-9	5				-0	C/O	-0.5
1886	Phi-N	1	3	0	0	0	0	0	0	0	1	.000	.000	.000	-99	-1	-1	0	0			-1	/C	0.0
	Det-N	57	213	28	58	7	2	1	31	7	22	.272	.295	.338	90	-2	-3	23	5			1	C/O1	0.0
	Yr	58	216	28	58	7	2	1	31	7	23	.269	.291	.333	87	-3	-4	23	5			1		0.0
1887	*Det-N	57	227	40	59	6	5	0	20	8	2	.260	.288	.330	71	-8	-9	23	3			6	C/O13	0.2
1888	Det-N	95	386	45	96	13	5	1	46	14	15	.249	.277	.316	91	-4	-4	38	12			-2	2C/3OS1	-0.2
1889	Bos-N	73	275	30	73	3	5	1	43	15	11	.265	.308	.324	74	-8	-11	32	13			-0	CO/1S3	-0.9
1890	Bos-N	38	163	21	44	7	3	0	24	5	6	.270	.300	.350	84	-2	-4	18	1			5	CO/S2	0.1
1891	Bos-N	70	263	33	68	18	5	1	29	12	13	.259	.304	.376	89	-1	-6	33	7			3	CO	0.1
1892	*Bos-N	54	198	25	53	9	3	0	25	18	12	.268	.332	.343	97	2	-1	26	7			-7	C/O1	-0.4
1893	Bos-N	73	281	50	75	10	2	1	48	22	9	.267	.325	.327	70	-10	-14	33	6			-3	CO1	-1.1
1894	Bos-N	70	266	51	74	7	6	3	56	19	6	.278	.326	.383	67	-13	-17	34	1			-6	C/1OS2	-1.3
1895	Bos-N	80	277	38	73	2	5	1	52	24	6	.264	.325	.318	63	-13	-17	30	1			17	C/S1	0.5
1896	Bos-N	47	179	28	47	2	0	1	18	9	5	.263	.305	.291	56	-10	-12	17	2			6	C/1S	-0.1
1897	Bos-N	30	105	15	28	4	3	0	14	4		.267	.300	.362	72	-4	-5	12	2			2	C/1	-0.1
Total	14	786	2984	421	774	91	45	10	412	161	121	.259	.301	.330	75	-86	-113	325	60			19	CO/21S3	-3.6

■ BABE GANZEL
Ganzel, Foster Pirie b: 5/22/01, Malden, Mass. d: 2/6/78, Jacksonville, Fla. BR/TR, 5'10.5", 172 lbs. Deb: 9/19/27

YEAR	TM/L	G	AB	R	H	2B	3B	HR	RBI	BB	SO	AVG	OBP	SLG	PRO+	BR	/A	RC	SB	CS	SBR	FR	POS	TPR
1927	Was-A	13	48	7	21	4	2	1	13	7	3	.438	.509	.667	206	8	8	16	0	0	0	0	O	0.6
1928	Was-A	10	26	2	2	1	0	0	4	1	4	.077	.111	.115	-41	-5	-5	0	0	0	0	-1	/O	-0.6
Total	2	23	74	9	23	5	2	1	17	8	7	.311	.378	.473	122	2	2	16	0	0	0	-1	/O	0.0

■ JOHN GANZEL
Ganzel, John Henry b: 4/7/1874, Kalamazoo, Mich. d: 1/14/59, Orlando, Fla. BR/TR, 6'0.5", 195 lbs. Deb: 4/21/1898 M

YEAR	TM/L	G	AB	R	H	2B	3B	HR	RBI	BB	SO	AVG	OBP	SLG	PRO+	BR	/A	RC	SB	CS	SBR	FR	POS	TPR
1898	Pit-N	15	45	5	6	0	0	0	2	4		.133	.220	.133	4	-5	-5	1	0			-1	1	-0.5
1900	Chi-N	78	284	29	78	14	4	4	32	10		.275	.311	.394	100	-2	-1	37	5			-4	1	-0.3
1901	NY-N	138	526	42	113	13	3	2	66	20		.215	.253	.262	53	-32	-29	38	6			2	*1	-2.5
1903	NY-N	129	476	62	132	25	7	3	71	30		.277	.320	.378	104	6	2	64	9			7	*1	1.0
1904	NY-A	130	465	50	121	16	10	6	48	24		.260	.297	.376	109	6	4	58	13			-2	*1/2S	0.5
1907	Cin-N	145	531	61	135	20	**16**	2	64	29		.254	.293	.363	103	2	-0	62	9			1	*1	-0.2
1908	Cin-N	112	388	32	97	16	10	1	53	19		.250	.285	.351	108	1	2	41	6			-2	*1M	-0.2
Total	7	747	2715	281	682	104	50	18	336	136		.251	.290	.346	93	-24	-27	301	48			1	1/2S	-2.2

■ JOE GARAGIOLA
Garagiola, Joseph Henry b: 2/12/26, St.Louis, Mo. BL/TR, 6', 190 lbs. Deb: 5/26/46

YEAR	TM/L	G	AB	R	H	2B	3B	HR	RBI	BB	SO	AVG	OBP	SLG	PRO+	BR	/A	RC	SB	CS	SBR	FR	POS	TPR
1946	*StL-N	74	211	21	50	4	1	3	22	23	26	.237	.312	.308	73	-6	-7	21	0			-5	C	-1.0
1947	StL-N	77	183	20	47	10	2	5	25	40	14	.257	.398	.415	111	6	5	33	0			0	C	0.7
1948	StL-N	24	56	9	6	1	0	2	7	12	9	.107	.275	.232	36	-5	-5	5	0			2	C	-0.1
1949	StL-N	81	241	25	63	14	0	3	26	31	19	.261	.348	.357	85	-3	-4	31	0			7	C	0.5
1950	StL-N	34	88	8	28	6	1	2	20	10	7	.318	.388	.477	120	3	3	15	0			-4	C	0.0
1951	StL-N	27	72	9	14	3	2	2	9	9	7	.194	.284	.375	75	-3	-3	7	0	0	0	-2	C	-0.4
	Pit-N	72	212	24	54	8	2	9	35	32	20	.255	.358	.439	110	4	3	36	4	1	1	-8	C	-0.3
	Yr	99	284	33	68	11	4	11	44	41	27	.239	.339	.423	101	1	1	43	4	1	1	-10		-0.7
1952	Pit-N	118	344	35	94	15	4	8	54	50	24	.273	.369	.410	113	8	7	55	0	1	-1	-4	*C	0.5
1953	Pit-N	27	73	9	17	5	0	2	14	10	11	.233	.341	.384	89	-1	-1	10	1	0	0	-4	C	-0.2
	Chi-N	74	228	21	62	9	4	1	21	21	23	.272	.336	.360	80	-6	-7	27	0	0	0	1	C	-0.1
	Yr	101	301	30	79	14	4	3	35	31	34	.262	.337	.365	82	-7	-8	38	1	0	0	-4		-0.3
1954	Chi-N	63	153	16	43	5	0	5	21	28	12	.281	.405	.412	112	4	4	27	0	0	0	-7	C	-0.1
	NY-N	5	11	1	3	2	0	0	1	1	2	.273	.333	.455	102	0	0	2	0	0	0	0	/C	0.0
	Yr	68	164	17	46	7	0	5	22	29	14	.280	.401	.415	112	4	4	29	0	0	0	-7		-0.1
Total	9	676	1872	198	481	82	16	42	255	267	173	.257	.355	.385	96	2	-5	270	5	2		-23	C	-0.5

■ MIKE GARBARK
Garbark, Nathaniel Michael (b: Nathaniel Michael Garbach) b: 2/2/16, Houston, Tex. BR/TR, 6', 200 lbs. Deb: 4/18/44

YEAR	TM/L	G	AB	R	H	2B	3B	HR	RBI	BB	SO	AVG	OBP	SLG	PRO+	BR	/A	RC	SB	CS	SBR	FR	POS	TPR
1944	NY-A	89	299	23	78	9	4	1	33	25	27	.261	.320	.328	82	-6	-7	30	0	1	-1	8	C	0.6
1945	NY-A	60	176	23	38	5	3	1	26	23	12	.216	.310	.295	73	-5	-6	16	0	1	-1	3	C	0.1
Total	2	149	475	46	116	14	7	2	59	48	39	.244	.316	.316	79	-11	-13	47	0	2	-1	11	C	0.7

■ BOB GARBARK
Garbark, Robert Michael (b: Robert Michael Garbach) b: 11/13/09, Houston, Tex. d: 8/15/90, Meadville, Pa. BR/TR, 5'11", 178 lbs. Deb: 9/03/34

YEAR	TM/L	G	AB	R	H	2B	3B	HR	RBI	BB	SO	AVG	OBP	SLG	PRO+	BR	/A	RC	SB	CS	SBR	FR	POS	TPR
1934	Cle-A	5	11	1	0	0	0	0	0	1	3	.000	.083	.083	-76	-3	-3	0	0	0	0	-2	/C	-0.3
1935	Cle-A	6	18	4	6	1	0	0	4	5	1	.333	.478	.389	124	1	1	4	0	0	0	2	/C	0.3
1937	Chi-N	1	1	0	0	0	0	0	0	0	0	.000	.000	.000	-96	-0	-0	0				0	H	0.0
1938	Chi-N	23	54	2	14	0	0	0	5	1	0	.259	.273	.259	46	-4	-4	3	0			1	C/1	-0.1
1939	Chi-N	24	21	1	3	0	0	0	0	0	3	.143	.143	.143	-23	-4	-4	0				1	C	-0.1
1944	Phi-A	18	23	2	6	2	0	0	2	1	0	.261	.292	.348	83	-1	-1	2	0	0	0	-0	C	0.0
1945	Bos-A	68	199	21	52	6	0	0	17	18	10	.261	.329	.291	79	-4	-5	20	0	1	-1	-3	C	-0.3
Total		145	327	31	81	9	0	0	28	26	17	.248	.307	.275	64	-15	-15	29	0	1		-2	C/1	-0.5

■ BARBARO GARBEY
Garbey, Barbaro (Garbey) b: 12/4/56, Santiago, Cuba BR/TR, 5'10", 170 lbs. Deb: 4/03/84

YEAR	TM/L	G	AB	R	H	2B	3B	HR	RBI	BB	SO	AVG	OBP	SLG	PRO+	BR	/A	RC	SB	CS	SBR	FR	POS	TPR
1984	*Det-A	110	327	45	94	17	1	5	52	17	35	.287	.327	.391	98	-1	-1	38	6	7	-2	-4	13DO/2	-1.0
1985	Det-A	86	237	27	61	9	1	6	29	15	37	.257	.310	.380	88	-4	-4	27	3	2	-0	-1	1OD/3	-0.7
1988	Tex-A	30	62	4	12	2	0	0	5	4	11	.194	.242	.226	31	-6	-6	3	0	0	0	2	/O13D	-0.4
Total	3	226	626	76	167	28	2	11	86	36	83	.267	.312	.371	88	-11	-11	68	9	9	-3	-3	1/DO32	-2.1

■ ALEX GARBOWSKI
Garbowski, Alexander b: 6/25/25, Yonkers, N.Y BR/TR, 6'1", 185 lbs. Deb: 4/16/52

YEAR	TM/L	G	AB	R	H	2B	3B	HR	RBI	BB	SO	AVG	OBP	SLG	PRO+	BR	/A	RC	SB	CS	SBR	FR	POS	TPR
1952	Det-A	2	0	0	0	0	0	0	0			—	—	—		0	0	0	0	0	0	0	R	0.0

■ KIKO GARCIA
Garcia, Alfonso Rafael b: 10/14/53, Martinez, Cal. BR/TR, 5'11", 180 lbs. Deb: 9/11/76

YEAR	TM/L	G	AB	R	H	2B	3B	HR	RBI	BB	SO	AVG	OBP	SLG	PRO+	BR	/A	RC	SB	CS	SBR	FR	POS	TPR
1976	Bal-A	11	32	2	7	1	0	0	4			.219	.219	.406	86	-1	-1	3	2	1	0	1	S	0.1
1977	Bal-A	65	131	20	29	6	0	2	10	6	31	.221	.255	.313	58	-8	-7	9	2	3	-1	20	S/2	1.8
1978	Bal-A	79	186	17	49	6	4	0	13	7	43	.263	.290	.339	81	-6	-5	18	7	1	2	4	S/2	0.7
1979	*Bal-A	126	417	54	103	15	9	5	24	32	87	.247	.304	.362	82	-10	-11	42	11	9	-2	-17	*S2/3O	-1.5
1980	Bal-A	111	311	27	62	8	0	1	27	24	57	.199	.257	.235	36	-27	-27	18	8	4	0	2	S2/O	-1.5
1981	*Hou-N	48	136	9	37	6	1	0	15	10	16	.272	.327	.331	91	-2	-1	15	2	2	-1	3	S3/2	0.5
1982	Hou-N	34	76	5	16	5	0	1	5	3	15	.211	.241	.316	59	-4	-4	5	1	0	0	5	S/32	0.2

YEAR	TM/L	G	AB	R	H	2B	3B	HR	RBI	BB	SO	AVG	OBP	SLG	PRO+	BR	/A	RC	SB	CS	SBR	FR	POS	TPR
1983	Phi-N	84	118	22	34	7	1	2	9	9	20	.288	.344	.415	111	1	2	15	1	2	-1	19	2S3	2.4
1984	Phi-N	57	60	6	14	2	0	0	5	4	11	.233	.281	.267	54	-4	-4	4	0	0	0	5	S3/2	0.4
1985	Phi-N	4	3	0	0	0	0	0	0	0	1	.000	.000	.000	-97	-1	-1	0	0	0	0	-1	/S3	-0.1
Total	10	619	1470	162	351	56	16	12	112	95	285	.239	.287	.323	70	-66	-59	128	34	22	-3	40	S2/3O	3.0

■ **CARLOS GARCIA**   Garcia, Carlos Jesus   b: 10/15/67, Tachira, Venez.   BR/TR, 6'1", 185 lbs.   Deb: 9/20/90

YEAR	TM/L	G	AB	R	H	2B	3B	HR	RBI	BB	SO	AVG	OBP	SLG	PRO+	BR	/A	RC	SB	CS	SBR	FR	POS	TPR
1990	Pit-N	4	4	1	2	0	0	0	0	0	2	.500	.500	.500	183	0	0	1	0	0	0	1	/S	0.1

■ **DAMASO GARCIA**   Garcia, Damaso Domingo (Sanchez)   b: 2/7/55, Moca, D.R.   BR/TR, 6'1", 165 lbs.   Deb: 6/24/78

YEAR	TM/L	G	AB	R	H	2B	3B	HR	RBI	BB	SO	AVG	OBP	SLG	PRO+	BR	/A	RC	SB	CS	SBR	FR	POS	TPR
1978	NY-A	18	41	5	8	0	0	0	1	2	6	.195	.233	.195	22	-4	-4	2	1	0	0	2	2/S	0.0
1979	NY-A	11	38	3	10	1	0	0	4	0	2	.263	.263	.289	50	-3	-3	3	2	0	1	-5	S/3	-0.5
1980	Tor-A	140	543	50	151	30	7	4	46	12	55	.278	.297	.381	81	-13	-16	54	13	13	-4	16	*2/D	0.3
1981	Tor-A	64	250	24	63	8	1	1	13	9	32	.252	.278	.304	64	-11	-12	21	13	3	2	-15	2/D	-2.4
1982	Tor-A	147	597	89	185	32	3	5	42	21	44	.310	.339	.399	93	1	-6	81	54	20	4	10	*2/D	1.6
1983	Tor-A	131	525	84	161	23	6	3	38	24	34	.307	.339	.390	94	-0	-4	66	31	17	-1	-16	*2	-1.6
1984	Tor-A	152	633	79	180	32	5	5	46	16	46	.284	.312	.374	86	-10	-13	76	46	12	7	-14	*2/D	-1.3
1985	*Tor-A	146	600	70	169	25	4	8	65	15	41	.282	.304	.377	83	-13	-15	64	28	15	-1	-35	*2	-4.5
1986	Tor-A	122	424	57	119	22	0	6	46	13	32	.281	.308	.375	83	-9	-11	44	9	6	-1	-7	*2D/1	-1.2
1988	Atl-N	21	60	3	7	1	0	1	4	3	10	.117	.159	.183	-2	-8	-8	1	1	0	0	-4	2	-1.2
1989	Mon-N	80	203	26	55	9	1	3	18	15	20	.271	.321	.369	96	-1	-1	23	5	4	-1	6	2/3	0.5
Total	11	1032	3914	490	1108	183	27	36	323	130	322	.283	.311	.371	84	-72	-94	435	203	90	7	-63	2/DS31	-10.3

■ **DANNY GARCIA**   Garcia, Daniel Raphael   b: 4/29/54, Brooklyn, N.Y.   BL/TL, 6'1", 182 lbs.   Deb: 4/26/81

YEAR	TM/L	G	AB	R	H	2B	3B	HR	RBI	BB	SO	AVG	OBP	SLG	PRO+	BR	/A	RC	SB	CS	SBR	FR	POS	TPR
1981	KC-A	12	14	4	2	0	0	0	0	0	2	.143	.143	.143	-18	-2	-2	0	0	0	0	-0	/O1	-0.2

■ **LEO GARCIA**   Garcia, Leonardo Antonio (Peralt   b: 11/6/62, Santiago, D.R.   BL/TL, 5'8", 160 lbs.   Deb: 4/06/87

YEAR	TM/L	G	AB	R	H	2B	3B	HR	RBI	BB	SO	AVG	OBP	SLG	PRO+	BR	/A	RC	SB	CS	SBR	FR	POS	TPR
1987	Cin-N	31	30	8	6	0	0	1	2	4	8	.200	.294	.300	55	-2	-2	3	3	1	0	2	O	0.0
1988	Cin-N	23	28	2	4	1	0	0	0	4	5	.143	.250	.179	24	-3	-3	1	0	1	-1	0	/O	-0.3
Total	2	54	58	10	10	1	0	1	2	8	13	.172	.273	.241	41	-4	-5	4	3	2	-0	2	/O	-0.3

■ **PEDRO GARCIA**   Garcia, Pedro Modesto (Delfi)   b: 4/17/50, Guayama, P.R.   BR/TR, 5'10", 175 lbs.   Deb: 4/06/73

YEAR	TM/L	G	AB	R	H	2B	3B	HR	RBI	BB	SO	AVG	OBP	SLG	PRO+	BR	/A	RC	SB	CS	SBR	FR	POS	TPR
1973	Mil-A	160	580	67	142	32	5	15	54	40	119	.245	.299	.395	96	-6	-5	66	11	10	-3	-11	*2	-1.2
1974	Mil-A	141	452	46	90	15	4	12	54	26	67	.199	.251	.330	66	-21	-21	37	8	5	-1	-11	*2	-2.7
1975	Mil-A	98	302	40	68	15	2	6	38	18	59	.225	.273	.348	74	-11	-11	27	12	6	0	19	2/D	1.1
1976	Mil-A	41	106	12	23	7	1	1	9	4	23	.217	.259	.330	73	-4	-4	9	2	2	-1	-3	2	-0.4
	Det-A	77	227	21	45	10	2	3	20	9	40	.198	.242	.300	56	-13	-14	16	2	3	-1	-1	2	-1.1
	Yr	118	333	33	68	17	3	4	29	13	63	.204	.247	.309	61	-17	-17	25	4	5	-2	-3		-1.5
1977	Tor-A	41	130	10	27	10	1	0	9	5	21	.208	.254	.300	50	-9	-9	10	0	0	0	-2	2/D	-0.8
Total	5	558	1797	196	395	89	15	37	184	102	329	.220	.270	.348	75	-64	-64	164	35	26	-5	-8	2/D	-5.1

■ **CHICO GARCIA**   Garcia, Vinicio Uzcanga   b: 12/24/24, Verzcruz, Mexico   BR/TR, 5'8", 170 lbs.   Deb: 4/24/54

YEAR	TM/L	G	AB	R	H	2B	3B	HR	RBI	BB	SO	AVG	OBP	SLG	PRO+	BR	/A	RC	SB	CS	SBR	FR	POS	TPR
1954	Bal-A	39	62	6	7	0	2	0	5	8	3	.113	.214	.177	9	-8	-7	3	0	0	0	8	2	0.1

■ **AL GARDELLA**   Gardella, Alfred Stephan   b: 1/11/18, New York, N.Y.   BL/TL, 5'10", 172 lbs.   Deb: 5/17/45

YEAR	TM/L	G	AB	R	H	2B	3B	HR	RBI	BB	SO	AVG	OBP	SLG	PRO+	BR	/A	RC	SB	CS	SBR	FR	POS	TPR
1945	NY-N	16	26	2	2	0	0	0	1	4	3	.077	.226	.077	-14	-4	-4	1	0			-1	/1O	-0.4

■ **DANNY GARDELLA**   Gardella, Daniel Lewis   b: 2/26/20, New York, N.Y.   BL/TL, 5'7.5", 160 lbs.   Deb: 5/14/44

YEAR	TM/L	G	AB	R	H	2B	3B	HR	RBI	BB	SO	AVG	OBP	SLG	PRO+	BR	/A	RC	SB	CS	SBR	FR	POS	TPR
1944	NY-N	47	112	20	28	2	2	6	14	11	13	.250	.323	.464	120	2	2	17	0			2	O	0.2
1945	NY-N	121	430	54	117	10	1	18	71	46	55	.272	.349	.426	113	8	7	65	2			-4	O1	-0.1
1950	StL-N	1	1	0	0	0	0	0	0	0	0	.000	.000	.000	-95	-0	-0	0	0			0	H	0.0
Total	3	169	543	74	145	12	3	24	85	57	68	.267	.343	.433	114	10	9	82	2			-2	O/1	0.1

■ **RON GARDENHIRE**   Gardenhire, Ronald Clyde   b: 10/24/57, Butzbach, Germany   BR/TR, 6', 175 lbs.   Deb: 9/01/81

YEAR	TM/L	G	AB	R	H	2B	3B	HR	RBI	BB	SO	AVG	OBP	SLG	PRO+	BR	/A	RC	SB	CS	SBR	FR	POS	TPR
1981	NY-N	27	48	2	13	1	0	0	3	5	9	.271	.340	.292	82	-1	-1	5	2	2	-1	4	S/23	0.5
1982	NY-N	141	384	29	92	17	1	3	33	23	55	.240	.283	.313	67	-18	-17	32	5	6	-2	16	*S/23	0.7
1983	NY-N	17	32	1	2	0	0	0	1	1	4	.063	.091	.063	-57	-7	-7	0	0	0	0	0	S	-0.4
1984	NY-N	74	207	20	51	7	1	1	10	9	43	.246	.278	.304	64	-10	-10	17	6	1	1	-3	S2/3	-0.6
1985	NY-N	26	39	5	7	2	1	0	2	8	11	.179	.319	.282	71	-1	-1	4	0	0	0	-1	S/23	0.0
Total	5	285	710	57	165	27	3	4	49	46	122	.232	.279	.296	62	-37	-36	57	13	9	-2	16	S/23	0.2

■ **ALEX GARDNER**   Gardner, Alexander   b: 4/28/1861, Toronto, Ont., Can.   d: 6/18/26, Danvers, Mass.   Deb: 5/10/1884

YEAR	TM/L	G	AB	R	H	2B	3B	HR	RBI	BB	SO	AVG	OBP	SLG	PRO+	BR	/A	RC	SB	CS	SBR	FR	POS	TPR
1884	Was-a	1	3	0	0	0	0	0		0		.000	.000	.000	-99	-1	-1	0				0	/C	0.0

■ **ART GARDNER**   Gardner, Arthur Junior   b: 9/21/52, Madden, Miss.   BL/TL, 5'11", 175 lbs.   Deb: 9/02/75

YEAR	TM/L	G	AB	R	H	2B	3B	HR	RBI	BB	SO	AVG	OBP	SLG	PRO+	BR	/A	RC	SB	CS	SBR	FR	POS	TPR
1975	Hou-N	13	31	3	6	0	0	0	2	1	8	.194	.242	.194	24	-3	-3	1	1	0	0	-0	/O	-0.2
1977	Hou-N	66	65	7	10	0	0	0	3	3	15	.154	.203	.154	-3	-9	-9	2	0	0	0	4	/O	-0.5
1978	SF-N	7	3	2	0	0	0	0	0	0	2	.000	.000	.000	-99	-1	-1	0	0	1	-1	0	H	0.0
Total	3	86	99	12	16	0	0	0	5	4	25	.162	.210	.162	2	-13	-12	3	1	1	-0	4	/O	-0.7

■ **EARLE GARDNER**   Gardner, Earle McClurkin   b: 1/24/1884, Sparta, Ill.   d: 3/2/43, Sparta, Ill.   BR/TR, 5'11", 160 lbs.   Deb: 9/18/08

YEAR	TM/L	G	AB	R	H	2B	3B	HR	RBI	BB	SO	AVG	OBP	SLG	PRO+	BR	/A	RC	SB	CS	SBR	FR	POS	TPR
1908	NY-A	20	75	7	16	2	0	0	4	1		.213	.224	.240	52	-4	-4	4	0			4	2	0.0
1909	NY-A	22	85	12	28	4	0	0	15	3		.329	.352	.376	129	3	3	12	4			-7	2	-0.5
1910	NY-A	86	271	36	66	4	2	1	24	21		.244	.303	.284	79	-5	-7	26	9			6	2	-0.4
1911	NY-A	102	357	36	94	13	2	0	39	20		.263	.312	.311	69	-13	-16	39	14			-3	*2	-1.8
1912	NY-A	43	160	14	45	3	1	0	26	5		.281	.303	.313	72	-5	-7	18	11			-1	2	-0.8
Total	5	273	948	105	249	26	5	1	108	50		.263	.304	.304	76	-24	-31	100	38			-1	2	-3.5

■ **GID GARDNER**   Gardner, Frank Washington   b: 6/9/1859, Attleboro, Mass.   d: 8/1/14, Cambridge, Mass.   Deb: 8/23/1879

YEAR	TM/L	G	AB	R	H	2B	3B	HR	RBI	BB	SO	AVG	OBP	SLG	PRO+	BR	/A	RC	SB	CS	SBR	FR	POS	TPR
1879	Tro-N	2	6	1	1	0	0	0		0	0	.167	.167	.167	11	-1	-1	0				-0	/P	0.0
1880	Cle-N	10	32	0	6	1	1	0	4	2	4	.188	.235	.281	76	-1	-1	2				-0	/PO	0.0
1883	Bal-a	42	161	28	44	10	3	1		18		.273	.346	.391	133	7	6	22				-1	O/23P	0.6
1884	Bal-a	41	173	32	37	6	8	2		14		.214	.280	.376	111	3	2	19				4	O/1	0.5
	CP-U	38	149	22	38	10	2	0		10		.255	.302	.349	120	3	3	16	0			-1	O/3P2	0.2
	Bal-U	1	4	0	1	0	0	0		0		.250	.250	.250	63	-0	-0	0	0			0	/S	0.0
	Yr	39	153	22	39	10	2	0		10		.255	.301	.346	119	3	3	16	0			-1		0.2
1885	Bal-a	44	170	22	37	5	4	0		12		.218	.269	.294	81	-4	-3	14				4	2/O1P	0.4
1887	Ind-N	18	63	8	11	1	0	1	8	12	11	.175	.307	.238	57	-3	-3	7	7			-3	O/2	-0.4
1888	Was-N	1	3	0	1	0	0	0	0	1	1	.333	.500	.333	184	0	0	1	0			0	/S	0.1
	Phi-N	1	3	0	2	0	0	0	1	0	0	.667	.667	.667	314	1	1	0	0			-1	/2	0.0
	Was-N	1	1	0	0	0	0	0	0	0	0	.000	.000	.000	-99	-0	-0	0	0			-0	/2	0.0
	Yr	3	7	0	3	0	0	0	1	1	1	.429	.500	.429	206	1	1	2	0			-1		0.1
Total	7	199	765	113	178	33	18	4	13	69	16	.233	.298	.339	104	6	5	82	7			2	O/2P31S	1.2

■ **RAY GARDNER**   Gardner, Raymond Vincent   b: 10/25/01, Frederick, Md.   d: 5/3/68, Frederick, Md.   BR/TR, 5'8", 145 lbs.   Deb: 4/16/29

YEAR	TM/L	G	AB	R	H	2B	3B	HR	RBI	BB	SO	AVG	OBP	SLG	PRO+	BR	/A	RC	SB	CS	SBR	FR	POS	TPR
1929	Cle-A	82	256	28	67	3	2	1	24	29	16	.262	.337	.301	63	-12	-14	26	10	13	-5	8	S	-0.1
1930	Cle-A	33	13	7	1	0	0	0	1	0	0	.077	.077	.077	-59	-3	-3	0	0	1	-1	8	S/23	0.6

YEAR	TM/L	G	AB	R	H	2B	3B	HR	RBI	BB	SO	AVG	OBP	SLG	PRO+	BR	/A	RC	SB	CS	SBR	FR	POS	TPR
Total	2	115	269	35	68	3	2	1	25	29	16	.253	.326	.290	57	-15	-17	26	10	14	-5	16	S/23	0.5

■ BILLY GARDNER

Gardner, William Frederick "Shotgun" b: 7/19/27, Waterford, Conn. BR/TR, 6', 170 lbs. Deb: 4/22/54 MC

YEAR	TM/L	G	AB	R	H	2B	3B	HR	RBI	BB	SO	AVG	OBP	SLG	PRO+	BR	/A	RC	SB	CS	SBR	FR	POS	TPR
1954	NY-N	62	108	10	23	5	0	1	7	6	19	.213	.261	.287	42	-9	-9	8	0	1	-1	10	32/S	0.1
1955	NY-N	59	187	26	38	10	1	3	17	13	19	.203	.262	.316	52	-13	-13	16	0	0	0	0	S3/2	-1.1
1956	Bal-A	144	515	53	119	16	2	11	50	29	53	.231	.281	.334	67	-30	-25	45	5	5	-2	-12	*2S/3	-2.4
1957	Bal-A	154	644	79	169	36	3	6	55	53	67	.262	.326	.356	92	-12	-7	75	10	7	-1	6	*2/S	0.6
1958	Bal-A	151	560	32	126	28	2	3	33	34	53	.225	.273	.298	60	-33	-30	45	2	3	-1	-22	*2S	-4.2
1959	Bal-A	140	401	34	87	13	2	6	27	38	61	.217	.286	.304	64	-21	-20	34	2	1	0	31	*2/S3	1.6
1960	Was-A	145	592	71	152	26	5	9	56	43	76	.257	.314	.363	83	-15	-14	66	0	4	-2	-2	*2S	-0.7
1961	Min-A	45	154	13	36	9	0	1	11	10	14	.234	.280	.312	55	-9	-10	12	0	0	0	-4	2/3	-0.8
	*NY-A	41	99	11	21	5	0	1	2	6	18	.212	.278	.293	56	-7	-6	8	0	0	0	3	3/2	0.0
	Yr	86	253	24	57	14	0	2	13	16	32	.225	.279	.304	56	-16	-16	20	0	0	0	-1		-0.8
1962	NY-A	4	1	1	0	0	0	0	0	0	1	.000	.000	.000	-99	-0	-0	0	0	0	0	1	/23	0.1
	Bos-A	53	199	22	54	9	2	0	12	10	39	.271	.310	.337	72	-7	-8	20	0	1	-1	-8	2/3S	-1.3
	Yr	57	200	23	54	9	2	0	12	10	40	.270	.308	.335	71	-8	-8	20	0	1	-1	-7		-1.2
1963	Bos-A	36	84	4	16	2	1	0	1	4	19	.190	.236	.238	32	-7	-8	5	0	0	0	7	2/3	0.0
Total	10	1034	3544	356	841	159	18	41	271	246	439	.237	.293	.327	70	-164	-150	334	19	22	-8	9	2S/3	-8.1

■ LARRY GARDNER

Gardner, William Lawrence b: 5/13/1886, Enosburg Falls, Vt d: 3/11/76, St.George, Vt. BL/TR, 5'8", 165 lbs. Deb: 6/25/08

YEAR	TM/L	G	AB	R	H	2B	3B	HR	RBI	BB	SO	AVG	OBP	SLG	PRO+	BR	/A	RC	SB	CS	SBR	FR	POS	TPR
1908	Bos-A	3	10	0	3	1	0	0	1	0		.300	.300	.400	126	0	0	1	0			-3	/3	-0.2
1909	Bos-A	19	37	7	11	1	2	0	5	4		.297	.381	.432	153	2	2	7	1			-4	/3S	0.0
1910	Bos-A	113	413	55	117	12	10	2	36	41		.283	.354	.375	125	14	12	58	8			-7	*2	-0.2
1911	Bos-A	138	492	80	140	17	8	4	44	64		.285	.373	.376	110	8	8	81	27			24	32	3.1
1912	*Bos-A	143	517	88	163	24	18	3	86	56		.315	.383	.449	131	25	21	98	25			-0	*3	1.8
1913	Bos-A	131	473	64	133	17	10	0	63	47	34	.281	.347	.359	104	4	3	63	18			-16	*3	-1.0
1914	Bos-A	155	553	50	143	23	19	3	68	35	39	.259	.303	.385	107	1	1	61	16	23	-9	-0	*3	-0.4
1915	*Bos-A	127	430	51	111	14	6	1	55	39	24	.258	.327	.326	98	-3	-1	49	11	12	-4	-6	*3	-0.5
1916	*Bos-A	148	493	47	152	19	7	2	62	48	27	.308	.372	.387	128	17	17	79	12			-14	*3	1.0
1917	Bos-A	146	501	53	133	23	7	1	61	54	37	.265	.341	.345	110	6	6	66	16			-6	*3	0.7
1918	Phi-A	127	463	50	132	22	6	1	52	43	22	.285	.346	.365	113	7	7	60	9			10	*3	2.0
1919	Cle-A	139	524	67	157	29	7	2	79	39	29	.300	.352	.393	103	6	2	75	7			-6	*3	0.6
1920	*Cle-A	154	597	72	185	31	11	3	118	53	25	.310	.367	.414	103	6	3	86	3	20	-11	-2	*3	0.1
1921	Cle-A	153	586	101	187	32	14	3	120	65	16	.319	.391	.437	109	11	9	103	3	3	-1	-1	*3	1.8
1922	Cle-A	137	470	74	134	31	3	2	68	49	21	.285	.355	.377	90	-6	-6	64	9	8	-2	-5	*3	0.0
1923	Cle-A	52	79	4	20	5	1	0	12	12	7	.253	.352	.342	83	-2	-2	10	0	1	-1	3	3	0.2
1924	Cle-A	38	50	3	10	0	0	0	4	5	1	.200	.273	.200	23	-6	-6	3	0	2	-1	-4	/32	-0.8
Total	17	1923	6688	866	1931	301	129	27	934	654	282	.289	.355	.384	109	90	78	965	165	69		-37	*32/S	8.2

■ ART GARIBALDI

Garibaldi, Arthur Edward b: 8/20/07, San Francisco, Cal d: 10/19/67, Sacramento, Cal. BR/TR, 5'8", 165 lbs. Deb: 6/20/36

YEAR	TM/L	G	AB	R	H	2B	3B	HR	RBI	BB	SO	AVG	OBP	SLG	PRO+	BR	/A	RC	SB	CS	SBR	FR	POS	TPR
1936	StL-N	71	232	30	64	12	0	1	20	16	30	.276	.323	.341	79	-7	-7	26	3			-5	32	-0.6

■ DEBS GARMS

Garms, Debs C. "Tex" b: 6/26/08, Bangs, Tex. d: 12/16/84, Glen Rose, Tex. BL/TR, 5'8.5", 165 lbs. Deb: 8/10/32

YEAR	TM/L	G	AB	R	H	2B	3B	HR	RBI	BB	SO	AVG	OBP	SLG	PRO+	BR	/A	RC	SB	CS	SBR	FR	POS	TPR
1932	StL-A	34	134	20	38	7	1	1	8	17	7	.284	.364	.373	86	-1	-2	19	4	3	-1	1	O	-0.3
1933	StL-A	78	189	35	60	10	2	4	24	30	21	.317	.416	.455	123	10	8	36	2	5	-2	-1	O	0.3
1934	StL-A	91	232	25	68	14	4	0	31	27	19	.293	.372	.388	89	-1	-4	35	0	0	0	-4	O	-0.7
1935	StL-A	10	15	1	4	0	0	0	0	2	2	.267	.353	.267	59	-1	-1	2	0	0	0	-0	/O	0.0
1937	Bos-N	125	478	60	124	15	8	2	37	37	33	.259	.317	.337	85	-15	-9	54	2			-8	O3	-1.9
1938	Bos-N	117	428	62	135	19	1	0	47	34	22	.315	.371	.364	114	3	8	60	4			-6	O3/2	0.0
1939	Bos-N	132	513	68	153	24	9	2	37	39	20	.298	.350	.392	107	-1	4	73	2			-4	O3	0.0
1940	Pit-N	103	358	76	127	23	7	5	57	23	6	.355	.395	.500	147	21	22	72	3			-0	3O	2.0
1941	Pit-N	83	220	25	58	9	3	3	42	22	12	.264	.331	.373	98	-1	-1	28	0			-10	3O	-1.1
1943	*StL-N	90	249	26	64	10	2	0	22	13	8	.257	.299	.313	74	-8	-9	24	1			-5	O3/S	-1.6
1944	*StL-N	73	149	17	30	3	0	0	5	13	8	.201	.265	.221	37	-12	-12	9	0			-6	O3	-1.9
1945	StL-N	74	146	23	49	7	2	0	18	31	3	.336	.452	.411	137	10	10	30	0			-8	3O	0.1
Total	12	1010	3111	438	910	141	39	17	328	288	161	.293	.355	.379	103	6	14	442	18	8		-52	O3/S2	-5.1

■ PHIL GARNER

Garner, Philip Mason b: 4/30/49, Jefferson City, Tenn. BR/TR, 5'10", 175 lbs. Deb: 9/10/73 C

YEAR	TM/L	G	AB	R	H	2B	3B	HR	RBI	BB	SO	AVG	OBP	SLG	PRO+	BR	/A	RC	SB	CS	SBR	FR	POS	TPR
1973	Oak-A	9	5	0	0	0	0	0	0	0	0	.000	.000	.000	-99	-1	-1	0	0	0	0	1	/3	0.0
1974	Oak-A	30	28	4	5	1	0	0	1	1	5	.179	.207	.214	23	-3	-3	1	1	1	-0	4	3/S2D	0.2
1975	*Oak-A	160	488	46	120	21	5	6	54	30	65	.246	.296	.346	83	-13	-11	48	4	6	-2	-16	*2/S	-2.5
1976	Oak-A	159	555	54	145	29	12	8	74	36	71	.261	.309	.400	111	3	6	67	35	13	3	-13	*2	0.4
1977	Pit-N	153	585	99	152	35	10	17	77	55	65	.260	.326	.441	101	2	-0	84	32	9	4	1	*32S	0.8
1978	Pit-N	154	528	66	138	25	9	10	66	66	71	.261	.349	.400	104	7	4	71	27	14	-0	10	23/S	2.0
1979	*Pit-N	150	549	76	161	32	8	11	59	55	74	.293	.361	.441	112	13	10	89	17	8	0	6	23S	2.1
1980	Pit-N	151	548	62	142	27	6	5	58	46	53	.259	.319	.358	87	-8	-9	64	32	7	5	16	*2/S	2.3
1981	Pit-N	56	181	22	46	6	2	1	20	21	21	.254	.332	.326	84	-3	-3	12	9	4	6	-2	2	-0.8
	*Hou-N	31	113	13	27	3	1	0	6	15	11	.239	.328	.283	79	-3	-3	12	6	2	1	0	2	0.0
	Yr	87	294	35	73	9	3	1	26	36	32	.248	.330	.310	82	-6	-6	32	10	8	-2	-6		-0.8
1982	Hou-N	155	588	65	161	33	8	13	83	40	92	.274	.323	.423	116	4	9	78	24	13	-1	1	*23	1.6
1983	Hou-N	154	567	76	135	24	2	14	79	63	84	.238	.320	.362	94	-9	-4	68	18	12	4		*3	-0.7
1984	Hou-N	128	374	60	104	17	6	4	45	43	63	.278	.359	.388	118	6	9	53	3	2	-0	23	32	3.3
1985	Hou-N	135	463	65	124	23	10	6	51	34	72	.268	.321	.400	103	-1	1	57	4	4	-1	-9	*32	-0.8
1986	*Hou-N	107	313	43	83	14	3	9	41	30	45	.265	.331	.415	108	2	3	39	12	6	0	1	3/2	-0.2
1987	Hou-N	43	112	15	25	5	0	3	15	8	20	.223	.275	.348	66	-6	-5	11	1	0	0	2	3/2	-0.2
	LA-N	70	126	14	24	4	0	2	8	20	24	.190	.301	.270	54	-8	-8	11	5	1	1	6	32/S	0.0
	Yr	113	238	29	49	9	0	5	23	28	44	.206	.289	.307	60	-14	-13	22	6	1	1	8		-0.2
1988	SF-N	15	13	0	2	0	0	0	1	1	3	.154	.214	.154	8	-2	-1	0	0	1	-0	0	/3	-0.1
Total	16	1860	6136	780	1594	299	82	109	738	564	842	.260	.326	.389	100	-20	-8	774	225	105	4	31	23/SD	7.8

■ RALPH GARR

Garr, Ralph Allen "Road Runner" b: 12/12/45, Monroe, La. BL/TR, 5'11", 185 lbs. Deb: 9/03/68

YEAR	TM/L	G	AB	R	H	2B	3B	HR	RBI	BB	SO	AVG	OBP	SLG	PRO+	BR	/A	RC	SB	CS	SBR	FR	POS	TPR
1968	Atl-N	11	7	3	2	0	0	0	1	0	1	.286	.375	.286	100	0	0	1	1	0	0	0	H	0.0
1969	Atl-N	22	27	6	6	1	0	0	2	2	4	.222	.276	.259	50	-2	-2	2	1	1	-0	0	/O	-0.2
1970	Atl-N	37	96	18	27	3	0	0	8	5	12	.281	.317	.313	65	-4	-5	9	5	2	0	0	/O	-0.5
1971	Atl-N	154	639	101	219	24	6	9	44	30	68	.343	.374	.441	122	24	20	105	30	14	1	6	*O	2.2
1972	Atl-N	134	554	87	180	22	6	12	53	25	41	.325	.361	.430	113	16	11	87	25	9	2	-1	*O	0.5
1973	Atl-N	148	668	94	200	32	6	11	55	22	64	.299	.324	.415	96	1	-5	87	35	11	4	-1	*O	-0.8
1974	Atl-N	143	606	87	214	24	17	11	54	28	52	.353	.384	.503	141	35	32	113	26	16	-2	-5	*O	2.0
1975	Atl-N	151	625	74	174	26	11	6	31	44	50	.278	.329	.384	94	-3	-6	78	14	9	-1	3	*O	-0.9
1976	Chi-A	136	527	63	158	22	6	4	36	17	44	.300	.324	.387	107	3	3	66	14	5	-3		*O/D	0.0
1977	Chi-A	134	543	78	163	29	7	10	54	27	44	.300	.333	.435	108	4	5	77	12	7	-1	-2	*O/D	-0.1
1978	Chi-A	118	443	67	122	18	9	3	29	24	41	.275	.314	.377	93	-5	-5	51	7	5	-1	-6	*O/D	-1.4
1979	Chi-A	102	307	34	86	10	2	6	39	17	19	.280	.320	.414	96	-2	-2	39	2	4	-2	-8	OD	-1.4
	Cal-A	6	24	0	3	0	0	0	0	0	3	.125	.125	.125	-33	-4	-4	0	0	0	0	0	/D	-0.3

YEAR	TM/L	G	AB	R	H	2B	3B	HR	RBI	BB	SO	AVG	OBP	SLG	PRO+	BR	/A	RC	SB	CS	SBR	FR	POS	TPR
	Yr	108	331	34	89	10	2	9	39	17	22	.269	.307	.393	87	-7	-7	38	2	4	-2	-8		-1.7
1980	Cal-A	21	42	5	8	1	0	0	3	4	6	.190	.261	.214	33	-4	-4	2	0	0	0	-0	/OD	-0.3
Total	13	1317	5108	717	1562	212	64	75	408	246	445	.306	.340	.416	106	59	37	716	172	83	2	-19	*O/D	-1.2

■ ADRIAN GARRETT
Garrett, Henry Adrian "Pat" b: 1/3/43, Brooksville, Fla. BL/TR, 6'3", 185 lbs. Deb: 4/13/66 C

YEAR	TM/L	G	AB	R	H	2B	3B	HR	RBI	BB	SO	AVG	OBP	SLG	PRO+	BR	/A	RC	SB	CS	SBR	FR	POS	TPR
1966	Atl-N	4	3	0	0	0	0	0	0	0	2	.000	.000	.000	-99	-1	-1	0	0	0	0	0	/O	0.0
1970	Chi-N	3	3	0	0	0	0	0	0	0	3	.000	.000	.000	-89	-1	-1	0	0	0	0	0	H	0.0
1971	Oak-A	14	21	1	3	0	0	1	2	5	7	.143	.308	.286	70	-1	-1	2	0	0	0	0	/O	0.0
1972	Oak-A	14	11	0	0	0	0	0	0	1	4	.000	.083	.000	-78	-2	-2	0	0	0	0	0	/O	-0.2
1973	Chi-N	36	54	7	12	0	0	3	8	4	18	.222	.276	.389	77	-2	-2	6	1	0	0	0	/OC	0.0
1974	Chi-N	10	8	0	0	0	0	0	0	1	1	.000	.111	.000	-64	-2	-2	0	0	0	0	1	/C1O	0.0
1975	Chi-N	16	21	1	2	0	0	1	6	1	8	.095	.136	.238	2	-3	-3	1	0	0	0	1	/1	-0.1
	Cal-A	37	107	17	28	5	0	6	18	14	28	.262	.347	.477	141	4	5	20	3	0	1	0	D1/OC	0.6
1976	Cal-A	29	48	4	6	3	0	0	3	5	16	.125	.208	.188	17	-5	-5	2	0	0	0	-3	C/1D	-0.7
Total	8	163	276	30	51	8	0	11	37	31	87	.185	.267	.333	71	-12	-11	30	4	0	1	-1	/DCO1	-0.4

■ WAYNE GARRETT
Garrett, Ronald Wayne b: 12/3/47, Brooksville, Fla. BL/TR, 5'11", 175 lbs. Deb: 4/12/69

YEAR	TM/L	G	AB	R	H	2B	3B	HR	RBI	BB	SO	AVG	OBP	SLG	PRO+	BR	/A	RC	SB	CS	SBR	FR	POS	TPR
1969	*NY-N	124	400	38	87	11	3	1	39	40	75	.218	.293	.268	57	-22	-23	34	4	2	0	-13	32/S	-3.2
1970	NY-N	114	366	74	93	17	4	12	45	81	60	.254	.392	.421	118	12	12	68	5	1	1	-19	32/S	-0.2
1971	NY-N	56	202	20	43	2	0	1	11	28	31	.213	.312	.238	58	-10	-10	15	1	3	-2	-4	3/2	-1.5
1972	NY-N	111	298	41	69	13	3	2	29	70	58	.232	.378	.315	101	3	4	41	3	2	-0	2	32	0.7
1973	*NY-N	140	504	76	129	20	3	16	58	72	74	.256	.350	.403	110	6	7	74	6	5	-1	11	*3/S2	1.6
1974	NY-N	151	522	55	117	14	3	13	53	89	96	.224	.339	.337	91	-5	-4	64	4	6	-2	14	*3/S	0.5
1975	NY-N	107	274	49	73	8	3	6	34	50	45	.266	.382	.383	118	6	8	44	3	2	-0	11	3/S2	1.9
1976	NY-N	80	251	36	56	8	1	4	26	52	26	.223	.359	.311	97	-1	1	31	7	5	-1	3	32/S	0.3
	Mon-N	59	177	15	43	4	1	2	11	30	20	.243	.353	.311	86	-1	-2	21	2	2	-1	1	2/3	0.1
	Yr	139	428	51	99	12	2	6	37	82	46	.231	.356	.311	92	-2	-1	52	9	7	-2	4		0.4
1977	Mon-N	68	159	17	43	6	1	2	22	30	18	.270	.389	.358	105	2	3	24	2	2	-1	2	3/2	0.4
1978	Mon-N	49	69	6	12	0	0	1	2	8	10	.174	.260	.217	35	-6	-6	4	0	0	0	1	3	-0.5
	StL-N	33	63	11	21	4	0	1	10	11	16	.333	.432	.444	148	4	5	12	1	0	0	-2	3	0.3
	Yr	82	132	17	33	4	0	2	12	19	26	.250	.344	.326	89	-2	-1	15	1	0	0	-1		-0.2
Total	10	1092	3285	438	786	107	22	61	340	561	529	.239	.352	.341	95	-11	-5	432	38	30	-7	7	32/S	0.4

■ GIL GARRIDO
Garrido, Gil Gonzalo b: 6/26/41, Panama City, Pan. BR/TR, 5'9", 150 lbs. Deb: 4/24/64

YEAR	TM/L	G	AB	R	H	2B	3B	HR	RBI	BB	SO	AVG	OBP	SLG	PRO+	BR	/A	RC	SB	CS	SBR	FR	POS	TPR
1964	SF-N	14	25	1	2	0	0	0	1	2	7	.080	.148	.080	-33	-4	-4	0	1	0	0	-1	S	-0.3
1968	Atl-N	18	53	5	11	0	0	0	2	2	2	.208	.236	.208	34	-4	-4	3	0	0	0	3	S	0.1
1969	*Atl-N	82	227	18	50	5	1	0	10	16	11	.220	.272	.251	47	-16	-16	11	0	0	0	-11	S	-1.7
1970	Atl-N	101	367	38	97	5	4	1	19	15	16	.264	.293	.308	58	-20	-23	28	0	2	-1	-1	S2	-1.1
1971	Atl-N	79	125	8	27	3	0	0	12	15	12	.216	.300	.240	51	-7	-8	9	0	1	-1	4	S32	0.1
1972	Atl-N	40	75	11	20	1	0	0	7	11	6	.267	.368	.280	79	-1	-2	8	1	1	-0	1	2S/3	0.2
Total	6	334	872	81	207	14	5	1	51	61	54	.237	.288	.268	53	-52	-57	63	2	4	-2	-4	S/23	-2.7

■ CECIL GARRIOTT
Garriott, Virgil Cecil b: 8/15/16, Harristown, Ill. d: 2/20/90, Lake Elsinore, Cal BL/TR, 5'8", 165 lbs. Deb: 9/04/46

YEAR	TM/L	G	AB	R	H	2B	3B	HR	RBI	BB	SO	AVG	OBP	SLG	PRO+	BR	/A	RC	SB	CS	SBR	FR	POS	TPR
1946	Chi-N	6	5	1	2	0	0	0	0	0	1	.000	.167	.000	-52	-1	-1	0				0	H	0.0

■ FORD GARRISON
Garrison, Robert Ford "Rocky" or "Snapper" b: 8/29/15, Greenville, S.C. BR/TR, 5'10.5", 180 lbs. Deb: 4/22/43 C

YEAR	TM/L	G	AB	R	H	2B	3B	HR	RBI	BB	SO	AVG	OBP	SLG	PRO+	BR	/A	RC	SB	CS	SBR	FR	POS	TPR
1943	Bos-A	36	129	13	36	5	1	1	11	5	14	.279	.306	.357	92	-2	-2	13	0	1	-1	0	O	-0.2
1944	Bos-A	13	49	5	12	3	0	0	2	6	4	.245	.327	.306	82	-1	-1	6	0	0	0	-0	O	-0.1
	Phi-A	121	449	58	121	13	2	4	37	22	40	.269	.307	.334	84	-11	-10	47	10	4	1	6	*O	-0.7
	Yr	134	498	63	133	16	2	4	39	28	44	.267	.309	.331	84	-12	-11	52	10	4	1	5		-0.8
1945	Phi-A	6	23	3	7	1	0	1	6	4	3	.304	.407	.478	157	2	2	5	1	0	0	0	/O	0.2
1946	Phi-A	9	37	1	4	0	0	0	0	0	6	.108	.108	.108	-40	-7	-7	0	0	0	0	-3	/O	-1.0
Total	4	185	687	80	180	22	3	6	56	37	67	.262	.302	.329	81	-18	-18	71	11	5	0	3	O	-1.8

■ HANK GARRITY
Garrity, Francis Joseph b: 2/4/08, Boston, Mass. d: 9/1/62, Boston, Mass. BR/TR, 6'1", 185 lbs. Deb: 7/26/31

YEAR	TM/L	G	AB	R	H	2B	3B	HR	RBI	BB	SO	AVG	OBP	SLG	PRO+	BR	/A	RC	SB	CS	SBR	FR	POS	TPR
1931	Chi-A	8	14	0	3	1	0	0	2	1	2	.214	.267	.286	48	-1	-1	1	0	0	0	0	/C	0.0

■ STEVE GARVEY
Garvey, Steven Patrick b: 12/22/48, Tampa, Fla. BR/TR, 5'10", 192 lbs. Deb: 9/01/69

YEAR	TM/L	G	AB	R	H	2B	3B	HR	RBI	BB	SO	AVG	OBP	SLG	PRO+	BR	/A	RC	SB	CS	SBR	FR	POS	TPR
1969	LA-N	3	3	0	1	0	0	0	0	0	1	.333	.333	.333	94	-0	-0	0	0	0	0	0	H	0.0
1970	LA-N	34	93	8	25	5	0	1	6	6	17	.269	.313	.355	82	-3	-2	10	1	1	-0	6	3/2	0.3
1971	LA-N	81	225	27	51	12	1	7	26	21	33	.227	.293	.382	95	-4	-2	24	1	2	-1	19	3	1.7
1972	LA-N	96	294	36	79	14	2	9	30	19	36	.269	.315	.422	110	2	3	37	4	2	0	13	3/1	1.6
1973	LA-N	114	349	37	106	17	3	8	50	11	42	.304	.331	.438	116	4	6	47	0	2	-1	-8	1O	-0.7
1974	*LA-N	156	642	95	200	32	3	21	111	31	66	.312	.346	.469	132	19	22	102	5	4	-1	-13	*1	0.1
1975	LA-N	160	659	85	210	38	6	18	95	33	66	.319	.354	.476	135	22	26	106	11	2	2	-10	*1	0.9
1976	LA-N	162	631	85	200	37	4	13	80	50	69	.317	.368	.450	134	25	26	100	19	8	1	-15	*1	0.4
1977	*LA-N	162	646	91	192	25	3	33	115	38	90	.297	.337	.498	121	16	17	103	9	6	-1	-16	*1	-0.8
1978	*LA-N	162	639	89	**202**	36	9	21	113	40	70	.316	.357	.499	138	29	29	108	10	5	0	-9	*1	1.5
1979	LA-N	162	648	92	204	32	1	28	110	37	59	.315	.354	.497	131	24	25	102	3	6	-3	-2	*1	1.4
1980	LA-N	163	658	78	**200**	27	1	26	106	36	67	.304	.343	.467	126	19	20	97	6	11	-5	3	*1	1.2
1981	*LA-N	110	431	63	122	23	1	10	64	25	49	.283	.324	.411	111	3	5	54	3	5	-2	-6	*1	-0.8
1982	LA-N	162	625	66	176	35	1	16	86	20	86	.282	.305	.418	103	-2	-0	76	5	3	-0	1	*1	-0.7
1983	SD-N	100	388	76	114	22	0	14	59	29	39	.294	.348	.459	126	10	12	57	4	1	1	-11	*1	-0.2
1984	*SD-N	161	617	72	175	27	2	8	86	24	64	.284	.312	.373	92	-8	-8	64	1	2	-1	-4	*1	-1.8
1985	SD-N	162	654	80	184	34	6	17	81	35	67	.281	.321	.430	110	5	6	82	0	0	0	-8	*1	-0.6
1986	SD-N	155	557	58	142	22	0	21	81	23	72	.255	.286	.408	91	-11	-9	59	1	2	-1	-18	*1	-3.4
1987	SD-N	27	76	5	16	2	0	1	9	1	10	.211	.231	.276	35	-7	-7	4	0	0	0	0	1	-0.7
Total	19	2332	8835	1143	2599	440	43	272	1308	479	1003	.294	.333	.446	117	144	168	1233	83	62	-12	-77	*13/O2	-0.6

■ ROD GASPAR
Gaspar, Rodney Earl b: 4/3/46, Long Beach, Cal. BB/TR, 5'11", 165 lbs. Deb: 4/08/69

YEAR	TM/L	G	AB	R	H	2B	3B	HR	RBI	BB	SO	AVG	OBP	SLG	PRO+	BR	/A	RC	SB	CS	SBR	FR	POS	TPR
1969	*NY-N	118	215	26	49	6	1	1	14	25	19	.228	.314	.279	66	-9	-9	21	7	3	0	9	O	-0.4
1970	NY-N	11	14	4	0	0	0	0	0	1	4	.000	.067	.000	-80	-4	-4	0	1	0	0	1	/O	-0.1
1971	SD-N	16	17	1	2	0	0	0	2	3	3	.118	.250	.118	8	-2	-2	1	0	1	-1	0	/O	-0.2
1974	SD-N	33	14	4	3	0	0	0	1	4	3	.214	.389	.214	75	-0	-0	2	0	0	0	2	/O1	0.1
Total	4	178	260	35	54	6	1	1	17	33	29	.208	.302	.250	55	-15	-15	24	8	4	0	12	O/1	-0.6

■ TOM GASTALL
Gastall, Thomas Everett b: 6/13/32, Fall River, Mass. d: 9/20/56, Rivera Beach, Md. BR/TR, 6'2", 187 lbs. Deb: 6/21/55

YEAR	TM/L	G	AB	R	H	2B	3B	HR	RBI	BB	SO	AVG	OBP	SLG	PRO+	BR	/A	RC	SB	CS	SBR	FR	POS	TPR
1955	Bal-A	20	27	4	4	1	0	0	0	3	5	.148	.233	.185	15	-3	-3	1	0	0	0	-1	C	-0.2
1956	Bal-A	32	56	3	11	2	0	0	4	3	8	.196	.250	.232	30	-6	-5	3	0	0	0	0	/C	-0.3
Total	2	52	83	7	15	3	0	0	4	6	13	.181	.244	.217	25	-9	-8	4	0	0	0	0	/C	-0.5

■ ED GASTFIELD
Gastfield, Edward b: 8/1/1865, Chicago, Ill. d: 12/1/1899, Chicago, Ill. Deb: 8/13/1884

YEAR	TM/L	G	AB	R	H	2B	3B	HR	RBI	BB	SO	AVG	OBP	SLG	PRO+	BR	/A	RC	SB	CS	SBR	FR	POS	TPR
1884	Det-N	23	82	6	6	1	0	0	2	2	34	.073	.095	.085	-45	-13	-12	1				9	C/O1	-0.1
1885	Det-N	1	3	0	0	0	0	0	0	0	2	.000	.000	.000	-99	-1	-1	0				-0	/C	0.0
	Chi-N	1	3	0	0	0	0	0	0	0	1	.000	.000	.000	-87	-1	-1	0				2	/C	0.1

YEAR	TM/L	G	AB	R	H	2B	3B	HR	RBI	BB	SO	AVG	OBP	SLG	PRO+	BR	/A	RC	SB	CS	SBR	FR	POS	TPR
	Yr	2	6	0	0	0	0	0	0	0	3	.000	.000	.000	-93	-1	-1	0				1		0.1
Total	2	25	88	6	6	1	0	0	2	2	37	.068	.089	.080	-49	-14	-14	1				10	/C1O	0.0

■ ALEX GASTON
Gaston, Alexander Nathaniel b: 3/12/1893, New York, N.Y. d: 2/8/79, Santa Monica, Cal. BR/TR, 5'9", 170 lbs. Deb: 9/26/20

YEAR	TM/L	G	AB	R	H	2B	3B	HR	RBI	BB	SO	AVG	OBP	SLG	PRO+	BR	/A	RC	SB	CS	SBR	FR	POS	TPR
1920	NY-N	4	10	2	1	0	0	0	1	1	2	.100	.182	.100	-18	-1	-1	0	0	0	0	-1	/C	-0.2
1921	NY-N	20	22	1	5	1	1	0	3	1	9	.227	.261	.364	63	-1	-1	2	0	0	0	-0	C	0.0
1922	NY-N	16	26	1	5	0	0	0	1	0	3	.192	.192	.192	-1	-4	-4	1	1	0	0	0	C	-0.2
1923	NY-N	22	39	3	8	2	0	1	5	0	6	.205	.225	.333	46	-3	-3	3	0	0	0	-0	C	-0.1
1926	Bos-A	98	301	37	67	5	3	0	21	21	28	.223	.282	.259	43	-26	-24	24	3	0	1	-10	C	-2.5
1929	Bos-A	55	116	14	26	5	2	2	9	6	8	.224	.262	.353	58	-8	-8	11	1	0	0	-1	C	-0.3
Total	6	215	514	58	112	13	6	3	40	29	56	.218	.266	.284	45	-43	-42	41	5	0	2	-12	C	-3.3

■ CITO GASTON
Gaston, Clarence Edwin b: 3/17/44, San Antonio, Tex. BR/TR, 6'3", 190 lbs. Deb: 9/14/67 MC

YEAR	TM/L	G	AB	R	H	2B	3B	HR	RBI	BB	SO	AVG	OBP	SLG	PRO+	BR	/A	RC	SB	CS	SBR	FR	POS	TPR
1967	Atl-N	9	25	1	3	0	1	0	1	0	5	.120	.120	.200	-10	-4	-4	0	1	0	0	-1	/O	-0.4
1969	SD-N	129	391	20	90	11	7	2	28	24	117	.230	.276	.309	67	-19	-17	32	4	4	-1	1	*O	-2.4
1970	SD-N	146	584	92	186	26	9	29	93	41	142	.318	.365	.543	146	30	33	111	4	1	1	0	*O	2.7
1971	SD-N	141	518	57	118	13	9	17	61	24	121	.228	.265	.386	88	-14	-10	51	1	0	0	-6	*O	-2.1
1972	SD-N	111	379	30	102	14	0	7	44	22	76	.269	.313	.361	98	-5	-2	39	0	2	-1	-3	O	-1.1
1973	SD-N	133	476	51	119	18	4	16	57	20	88	.250	.282	.405	96	-10	-5	52	0	0	0	0	*O	-1.0
1974	SD-N	106	267	19	57	11	0	6	33	16	51	.213	.261	.322	65	-14	-13	22	0	0	0	2	O	-1.3
1975	Atl-N	64	141	17	34	4	0	6	15	17	33	.241	.323	.397	95	-0	-1	18	1	0	0	0	O/1	-0.1
1976	Atl-N	69	134	15	39	4	0	4	25	13	21	.291	.354	.410	109	3	2	18	1	0	0	-2	O/1	-0.1
1977	Atl-N	56	85	6	23	4	0	3	21	5	19	.271	.311	.424	85	-1	-2	11	1	0	0	-0	/O1	-0.2
1978	Atl-N	60	118	5	27	1	0	1	9	3	20	.229	.248	.263	38	-9	-11	7	0	0	0	-1	O/1	-1.3
	Pit-N	2	2	1	1	0	0	0	0	0	0	.500	.500	.500	172	0	0	1	0	0	0	0	/O	0.0
	Yr	62	120	6	28	1	0	1	9	3	20	.233	.252	.267	41	-9	-10	7	0	0	0	-1		-1.3
Total	11	1026	3120	314	799	106	30	91	387	185	693	.256	.300	.397	95	-43	-30	361	13	7	-0	-10	O/1	-7.3

■ JOE GATES
Gates, Joseph Daniel b: 10/3/54, Gary, Ind. BL/TR, 5'7", 175 lbs. Deb: 9/12/78

YEAR	TM/L	G	AB	R	H	2B	3B	HR	RBI	BB	SO	AVG	OBP	SLG	PRO+	BR	/A	RC	SB	CS	SBR	FR	POS	TPR
1978	Chi-A	8	24	6	6	0	0	0	1	4	6	.250	.379	.250	80	-0	-0	3	1	0	0	-2	/2	-0.1
1979	Chi-A	16	16	5	1	0	1	0	1	2	3	.063	.167	.188	-5	-2	-2	0	1	1	-0	5	/23	0.2
Total	2	24	40	11	7	0	1	0	2	6	9	.175	.298	.225	46	-3	-3	3	2	1	0	2	/23	0.1

■ MIKE GATES
Gates, Michael Grant b: 9/20/56, Culver City, Cal. BL/TR, 6', 165 lbs. Deb: 5/06/81

YEAR	TM/L	G	AB	R	H	2B	3B	HR	RBI	BB	SO	AVG	OBP	SLG	PRO+	BR	/A	RC	SB	CS	SBR	FR	POS	TPR
1981	Mon-N	1	2	1	1	0	1	0	1	0	1	.500	.500	1.500	445	1	1	2	0	0	0	-0	/2	0.0
1982	Mon-N	36	121	16	28	2	3	0	8	9	19	.231	.285	.298	62	-6	-6	11	0	0	0	-9	2	-1.4
Total	2	37	123	17	29	2	4	0	9	9	20	.236	.288	.317	68	-5	-5	12	0	0	0	-10	/2	-1.4

■ FRANK GATINS
Gatins, Frank Anthony (b: Frank Anthony Gestino) b: 3/6/1871, Johnstown, Pa. d: 11/8/11, Johnstown, Pa. Deb: 9/21/1898

YEAR	TM/L	G	AB	R	H	2B	3B	HR	RBI	BB	SO	AVG	OBP	SLG	PRO+	BR	/A	RC	SB	CS	SBR	FR	POS	TPR
1898	Was-N	17	58	6	13	2	0	0	5	3		.224	.274	.259	55	-3	-3	5	2			-8	S	-0.9
1901	Bro-N	50	197	21	45	7	2	1	21	5		.228	.251	.299	59	-10	-11	17	6			-10	3/S	-1.7
Total	2	67	255	27	58	9	2	1	26	8		.227	.257	.290	58	-13	-14	22	8			-18	/3S	-2.6

■ JIM GAUDET
Gaudet, James Jennings b: 6/3/55, New Orleans, La. BR/TR, 6', 185 lbs. Deb: 9/10/78

YEAR	TM/L	G	AB	R	H	2B	3B	HR	RBI	BB	SO	AVG	OBP	SLG	PRO+	BR	/A	RC	SB	CS	SBR	FR	POS	TPR
1978	KC-A	3	8	0	0	0	0	0	0	0	3	.000	.000	.000	-97	-2	-2	0	0	0	0	1	/C	0.0
1979	KC-A	3	6	0	1	0	0	0	0	0	0	.167	.167	.167	-10	-1	-1	0	0	0	0	0	/C	0.0
Total	2	6	14	0	1	0	0	0	0	0	3	.071	.071	.071	-59	-3	-3	0	0	0	0	1	/C	0.0

■ MIKE GAULE
Gaule, Michael John b: 8/4/1869, Baltimore, Md. d: 1/24/18, Baltimore, Md. BL/TL, 6'2". Deb: 6/15/1889

YEAR	TM/L	G	AB	R	H	2B	3B	HR	RBI	BB	SO	AVG	OBP	SLG	PRO+	BR	/A	RC	SB	CS	SBR	FR	POS	TPR
1889	Lou-a	1	2	0	0	0	0	0	0	0	1	.000	.000	.000	-99	-1	-0	0	0			-1	/O	0.0

■ DOC GAUTREAU
Gautreau, Walter Paul "Punk" b: 7/26/01, Cambridge, Mass. d: 8/23/70, Salt Lake City, Ut BR/TR, 5'4", 129 lbs. Deb: 6/22/25

YEAR	TM/L	G	AB	R	H	2B	3B	HR	RBI	BB	SO	AVG	OBP	SLG	PRO+	BR	/A	RC	SB	CS	SBR	FR	POS	TPR
1925	Phi-A	4	7	0	0	0	0	0	0	0	3	.000	.000	.000	-94	-2	-2	0	0	0	0	1	/2	0.0
	Bos-N	68	279	45	73	13	3	0	23	35	33	.262	.346	.330	81	-10	-6	33	11	7	-1	-4	2	-1.0
1926	Bos-N	79	266	36	71	9	4	0	8	35	24	.267	.356	.331	94	-4	-1	33	17			-20	2	-1.6
1927	Bos-N	87	236	38	58	12	2	0	20	25	20	.246	.321	.314	76	-9	-7	24	11			-2	2	-0.9
1928	Bos-N	23	18	3	5	0	1	0	1	4	3	.278	.409	.389	116	0	1	3	1			-0	/2S	0.0
Total	4	261	806	122	207	34	10	0	52	99	63	.257	.341	.324	83	-25	-16	94	40	7		-24	2/S	-3.5

■ SID GAUTREAUX
Gautreaux, Sidney Allen "Pudge" b: 5/4/12, Schriever, La. d: 4/19/80, Morgan City, La. BB/TR, 5'8", 190 lbs. Deb: 4/15/36

YEAR	TM/L	G	AB	R	H	2B	3B	HR	RBI	BB	SO	AVG	OBP	SLG	PRO+	BR	/A	RC	SB	CS	SBR	FR	POS	TPR
1936	Bro-N	75	71	8	19	3	0	0	16	9	7	.268	.358	.310	80	-1	-2	9	0			-1	C	-0.1
1937	Bro-N	11	10	0	1	1	0	0	2	1	1	.100	.182	.200	4	-1	-1	0	0			0	H	0.0
Total	2	86	81	8	20	4	0	0	18	10	8	.247	.337	.296	71	-3	-3	9	0			-1	/C	-0.1

■ GAVERN
Gavern Deb: 6/15/1874

YEAR	TM/L	G	AB	R	H	2B	3B	HR	RBI	BB	SO	AVG	OBP	SLG	PRO+	BR	/A	RC	SB	CS	SBR	FR	POS	TPR
1874	Atl-n	1	4	1	0	0	0	0		0		.000	.000	.000	-99	-1	-1	0					/2	0.0

■ MIKE GAZELLA
Gazella, Michael b: 10/13/1896, Olyphant, Pa. d: 9/11/78, Odessa, Tex. BR/TR, 5'7.5", 165 lbs. Deb: 7/02/23

YEAR	TM/L	G	AB	R	H	2B	3B	HR	RBI	BB	SO	AVG	OBP	SLG	PRO+	BR	/A	RC	SB	CS	SBR	FR	POS	TPR
1923	NY-A	8	13	2	1	0	0	0	1	2	3	.077	.200	.077	-25	-2	-2	0	0	0	0	-0	/S23	-0.1
1926	*NY-A	66	168	21	39	6	0	0	21	25	24	.232	.335	.268	60	-9	-9	17	2	2	-1	-4	3/S	-0.8
1927	NY-A	54	115	17	32	8	4	0	9	23	16	.278	.403	.417	117	3	3	20	4	1	1	-6	3/S	0.1
1928	NY-A	32	56	11	13	0	0	0	2	6	7	.232	.317	.232	48	-4	-4	5	2	1	0	-1	3/2S	-0.3
Total	4	160	352	51	85	14	4	0	33	56	50	.241	.350	.304	73	-13	-12	42	8	4	0	-12	3/S2	-1.1

■ DALE GEAR
Gear, Dale Dudley b: 2/2/1872, Lone Elm, Kan. d: 9/23/51, Topeka, Kan. 5'11", 165 lbs. Deb: 8/15/1896

YEAR	TM/L	G	AB	R	H	2B	3B	HR	RBI	BB	SO	AVG	OBP	SLG	PRO+	BR	/A	RC	SB	CS	SBR	FR	POS	TPR
1896	Cle-N	4	15	5	6	1	1	0	3	1	1	.400	.438	.600	165	2	1	4	0			-1	/P1	0.0
1897	Cle-N	7	24	3	4	1	0	0	2	3		.167	.286	.208	32	-2	-2	2	2			0	/O	-0.1
1901	Was-A	58	199	17	47	9	2	0	20	4		.236	.251	.302	55	-12	-12	16	2			1	OP	-0.5
Total	3	69	238	25	57	11	3	0	25	8	1	.239	.267	.311	60	-13	-13	22	4			1	/OP1	-0.6

■ GARY GEARHART
Gearhart, Lloyd William b: 8/10/23, New Lebanon, Ohio BR/TL, 5'11", 180 lbs. Deb: 4/18/47

YEAR	TM/L	G	AB	R	H	2B	3B	HR	RBI	BB	SO	AVG	OBP	SLG	PRO+	BR	/A	RC	SB	CS	SBR	FR	POS	TPR
1947	NY-N	73	179	26	44	9	0	6	17	17	30	.246	.315	.397	87	-4	-4	22	1			0	O	-0.4

■ HUCK GEARY
Geary, Eugene Francis Joseph b: 1/22/17, Buffalo, N.Y. d: 1/27/81, Cuba, N.Y. BL/TR, 5'10.5", 170 lbs. Deb: 7/17/42

YEAR	TM/L	G	AB	R	H	2B	3B	HR	RBI	BB	SO	AVG	OBP	SLG	PRO+	BR	/A	RC	SB	CS	SBR	FR	POS	TPR
1942	Pit-N	9	22	3	5	0	0	0	2	2	3	.227	.292	.227	52	-1	-1	2	0			0	/S	0.0
1943	Pit-N	46	166	17	25	4	0	1	13	18	6	.151	.234	.193	23	-16	-17	9	3			-6	S	-1.9
Total	2	55	188	20	30	4	0	1	15	20	9	.160	.240	.197	26	-17	-18	10	3			-5	/S	-1.9

■ ELMER GEDEON
Gedeon, Elmer John b: 4/15/17, Cleveland, Ohio d: 4/20/44, St.Pol, France BR/TR, 6'4", 196 lbs. Deb: 9/18/39

YEAR	TM/L	G	AB	R	H	2B	3B	HR	RBI	BB	SO	AVG	OBP	SLG	PRO+	BR	/A	RC	SB	CS	SBR	FR	POS	TPR
1939	Was-A	5	15	1	3	0	0	0	1	2	5	.200	.294	.200	31	-2	-1	1	0	0	0	1	/O	0.0

■ JOE GEDEON
Gedeon, Elmer Joseph b: 12/5/1893, Sacramento, Cal. d: 5/19/41, San Francisco, Cal BR/TR, 6', 167 lbs. Deb: 5/13/13

YEAR	TM/L	G	AB	R	H	2B	3B	HR	RBI	BB	SO	AVG	OBP	SLG	PRO+	BR	/A	RC	SB	CS	SBR	FR	POS	TPR
1913	Was-A	29	71	3	13	1	3	0	6	1	6	.183	.205	.282	41	-6	-6	4	3			2	0/32SP	-0.4
1914	Was-A	2	2	0	0	0	0	0	0	0	0	.000	.333	.000	1	-0	-0	0	0			-1	/O	-0.1
1916	NY-A	122	435	50	92	14	4	0	27	40	61	.211	.282	.262	62	-19	-20	38	14			-10	*2	-2.9
1917	NY-A	33	117	15	28	7	0	0	8	7	13	.239	.288	.299	78	-3	-3	11	4			4	2	0.3

YEAR	TM/L	G	AB	R	H	2B	3B	HR	RBI	BB	SO	AVG	OBP	SLG	PRO+	BR	/A	RC	SB	CS	SBR	FR	POS	TPR
1918	StL-A	123	441	39	94	14	3	1	41	27	29	.213	.271	.265	64	-21	-20	34	7			16	*2	0.3
1919	StL-A	120	437	57	111	13	4	0	27	50	35	.254	.340	.302	79	-9	-11	51	4			-3	*2	-0.2
1920	StL-A	153	606	95	177	33	6	0	61	55	36	.292	.355	.366	89	-7	-9	82	1	3	-2	-26	*2	-3.2
Total	7	584	2109	259	515	82	20	2	171	180	181	.244	.311	.303	75	-65	-69	220	33	3		-18	2/03SP	-6.2

■ RICH GEDMAN
Gedman, Richard Leo   b: 9/26/59, Worcester, Mass.   BL/TR, 6', 210 lbs.   Deb: 9/07/80

YEAR	TM/L	G	AB	R	H	2B	3B	HR	RBI	BB	SO	AVG	OBP	SLG	PRO+	BR	/A	RC	SB	CS	SBR	FR	POS	TPR
1980	Bos-A	9	24	2	5	0	0	0	1	0	5	.208	.208	.208	14	-3	-3	1	0	0	0	-0	/CD	-0.2
1981	Bos-A	62	205	22	59	15	0	5	26	9	31	.288	.321	.434	109	3	2	26	0	0	0	-2	C	0.3
1982	Bos-A	92	289	30	72	17	2	4	26	10	37	.249	.279	.363	71	-10	-13	25	0	1	-1	-6	C	-1.4
1983	Bos-A	81	204	21	60	16	1	2	18	15	37	.294	.345	.412	100	2	0	28	0	1	-1	-2	C	0.0
1984	Bos-A	133	449	54	121	26	4	24	72	29	72	.269	.315	.506	118	12	9	71	0	0	0	-7	*C	0.9
1985	Bos-A	144	498	66	147	30	5	18	80	50	79	.295	.363	.484	124	20	17	86	2	0	1	4	*C	2.7
1986	*Bos-A	135	462	49	119	29	0	16	65	37	61	.258	.318	.424	100	-1	-1	59	1	0	0	11	*C	1.8
1987	Bos-A	52	151	11	31	8	0	1	13	10	24	.205	.255	.278	40	-13	-13	11	0	0	0	-3	C	-1.1
1988	*Bos-A	95	299	33	69	14	0	9	39	18	49	.231	.281	.368	77	-9	-10	31	0	0	0	3	C/D	-0.3
1989	Bos-A	93	260	24	55	9	0	4	16	23	47	.212	.276	.292	57	-14	-16	20	0	1	-1	-1	C	-1.2
1990	Bos-A	10	15	3	3	0	0	0	0	5	6	.200	.429	.200	78	0	0	2	0	0	0	0	/C	0.0
	Hou-N	40	104	4	21	7	0	1	10	15	24	.202	.303	.298	67	-5	-4	10	0	0	0	7	C	0.5
Total	11	946	2960	319	762	171	12	84	366	221	472	.257	.312	.408	93	-16	-31	369	3	3	-1	3	C/D	2.0

■ COUNT GEDNEY
Gedney, Alfred W.   b: 5/10/1849, Brooklyn, N.Y.   d: 3/26/22, Hackensack, N.J.   5'9", 140 lbs.   Deb: 4/27/1872

YEAR	TM/L	G	AB	R	H	2B	3B	HR	RBI	BB	SO	AVG	OBP	SLG	PRO+	BR	/A	RC	SB	CS	SBR	FR	POS	TPR
1872	Tro-n	10	51	15	21	2	1	3		0		.412	.412	.667	223	7	7	14					/O	0.5
	Eck-n	18	72	4	11	1	0	0		0		.153	.153	.167	-2	-8	-6	2					O	-0.3
	Yr	28	123	19	32	3	1	3		0		.260	.260	.374	102	-1	1	12						0.2
1873	Mut-n	53	221	42	60	6	3	2		7		.271	.294	.353	90	-3	-2	23					*O	0.0
1874	Ath-n	54	222	49	60	6	1	1		7		.270	.293	.320	87	-1	-5	21					*O/1	-0.2
1875	Mut-n	68	266	30	54	12	4	0		2		.203	.209	.278	63	-8	-11	16					*O/P	-0.8
Total	4 n	203	832	140	206	27	9	6		16		.248	.262	.323	82	-13	-17	77					O/1P	-0.8

■ BILLY GEER
Geer, William Henry Harrison (b: George Harrison Geer)   b: 8/13/1849, Syracuse, N.Y.   TR , 5'8", 160 lbs.   Deb: 10/15/1874

YEAR	TM/L	G	AB	R	H	2B	3B	HR	RBI	BB	SO	AVG	OBP	SLG	PRO+	BR	/A	RC	SB	CS	SBR	FR	POS	TPR
1874	Mut-n	2	8	0	2	0	0	0		0		.250	.250	.250	58	-0	-0	1					/O	0.0
1875	NH-n	37	162	20	40	6	1	0		1		.247	.252	.296	104	-2	2	12					O2/S13	0.1
1878	Cin-N	61	237	31	52	13	2	0	20	10	18	.219	.251	.291	86	-5	-2	18				-4	*S/2	-0.1
1880	Wor-N	2	6	0	0	0	0	0	0	0	0	.000	.000	.000	-92	-1	-1	0				-1	/OS	-0.1
1884	Phi-U	9	36	7	9	2	1	0		4		.250	.325	.361	142	1	2	4	0			1	/S	0.2
	Bro-a	107	391	68	82	15	7	0		38		.210	.281	.284	87	-4	-4	32				17	*S/P2	1.0
1885	Lou-a	14	51	2	6	2	0	0		2		.118	.167	.157	4	-5	-5	1				2	S	-0.2
Total	2 n	39	170	20	42	6	1	0		1		.247	.251	.294	101	-2	0	13					/O2S31	0.1
Total	4	193	721	108	149	32	10	0	20	54	18	.207	.264	.279	81	-15	-11	55				15	S/2PO	0.8

■ LOU GEHRIG
Gehrig, Henry Louis "The Iron Horse"   b: 6/19/03, New York, N.Y.   d: 6/2/41, Riverdale, N.Y.   BL/TL, 6', 200 lbs.   Deb: 6/15/23   H

YEAR	TM/L	G	AB	R	H	2B	3B	HR	RBI	BB	SO	AVG	OBP	SLG	PRO+	BR	/A	RC	SB	CS	SBR	FR	POS	TPR
1923	NY-A	13	26	6	11	4	1	1	9	2	5	.423	.464	.769	217	4	4	9	0	0	0	-1	/1	0.3
1924	NY-A	10	12	2	6	1	0	0	5	1	3	.500	.538	.583	190	2	2	4	0	0	0	0	/1O	0.1
1925	NY-A	126	437	73	129	23	10	20	68	46	49	.295	.365	.531	127	14	15	85	6	3	0	-9	*1/O	0.2
1926	*NY-A	155	572	135	179	47	20	16	107	105	72	.313	.420	.549	154	44	46	137	6	5	-1	-8	*1	2.8
1927	*NY-A	155	584	149	218	52	18	47	175	109	84	.373	.474	.765	224	101	104	203	10	8	-2	-6	*1	8.2
1928	*NY-A	154	562	139	210	47	13	27	142	95	69	.374	.467	.648	197	76	79	169	4	11	-5	-8	*1	5.3
1929	NY-A	154	553	127	166	32	10	35	126	122	68	.300	.431	.584	170	52	57	146	4	4	-1	-5	*1	2.7
1930	NY-A	154	581	143	220	42	17	41	174	101	63	.379	.473	.721	207	88	93	195	12	14	-5	1	*1/O	6.3
1931	NY-A	155	619	163	211	31	15	46	184	117	56	.341	.446	.662	199	80	85	185	17	12	-2	-10	*1/O	5.4
1932	*NY-A	156	596	138	208	42	9	34	151	108	38	.349	.451	.621	184	69	73	168	4	11	-5	-6	*1	4.2
1933	NY-A	152	593	138	198	41	12	32	139	92	42	.334	.424	.605	181	60	65	151	9	13	-5	-3	*1	4.2
1934	NY-A	154	579	128	210	40	6	49	165	109	31	.363	.465	.706	213	86	92	195	9	5	-0	1	*1/S	6.0
1935	NY-A	149	535	125	176	26	10	30	119	132	38	.329	.466	.583	180	62	66	154	8	7	-2	0	*1	4.5
1936	*NY-A	155	579	167	205	37	7	49	152	130	46	.354	.478	.696	193	82	86	199	3	4	-2	1	*1	5.6
1937	*NY-A	157	569	138	200	37	9	37	159	127	49	.351	.473	.643	177	73	73	181	4	3	-1	-6	*1	4.2
1938	*NY-A	157	576	115	170	32	6	29	114	107	75	.295	.410	.523	133	30	30	131	6	1	1	-0	*1	0.8
1939	NY-A	8	28	2	4	0	0	0	1	5	1	.143	.273	.143	9	-4	-4	1	0	0	0	-1	/1	-0.4
Total	17	2164	8001	1888	2721	534	163	493	1990	1508	789	.340	.447	.632	182	918	966	2312	102	101	-30	-58	*1/OS	60.4

■ CHARLIE GEHRINGER
Gehringer, Charles Leonard "The Mechanical Man"   b: 5/11/03, Fowlerville, Mich.   BL/TR, 5'11", 180 lbs.   Deb: 9/22/24   CH

YEAR	TM/L	G	AB	R	H	2B	3B	HR	RBI	BB	SO	AVG	OBP	SLG	PRO+	BR	/A	RC	SB	CS	SBR	FR	POS	TPR
1924	Det-A	5	13	2	6	0	0	0	1	0	2	.462	.462	.462	141	1	1	2	1	1	-0	4	/2	0.4
1925	Det-A	8	18	3	3	0	0	0	0	2	0	.167	.250	.167	7	-3	-2	1	0	1	-1	4	/2	0.1
1926	Det-A	123	459	62	127	19	17	1	48	30	42	.277	.322	.399	86	-10	-11	59	9	7	-2	-10	*2/3	-1.6
1927	Det-A	133	508	110	161	29	11	4	61	52	31	.317	.383	.441	112	10	9	82	17	8	0	20	*2	3.2
1928	Det-A	154	603	108	193	29	16	6	74	69	22	.320	.395	.451	120	21	19	110	15	9	1	2	*2	2.7
1929	Det-A	155	634	131	215	45	19	13	106	64	19	.339	.405	.532	139	37	36	139	27	9	3	-3	*2	3.6
1930	Det-A	154	610	144	201	47	15	16	98	69	17	.330	.404	.534	133	33	32	130	19	15	-3	2	*2	2.9
1931	Det-A	101	383	67	119	24	5	4	53	29	15	.311	.359	.431	103	3	1	60	13	4	2	-1	2/1	0.5
1932	Det-A	152	618	112	184	44	11	19	107	68	34	.298	.370	.497	118	19	16	114	9	8	-2	-1	*2	1.8
1933	Det-A	155	628	103	204	42	6	12	105	68	27	.325	.393	.468	125	25	24	117	5	4	-1	7	*2	2.5
1934	*Det-A	154	601	134	214	50	7	11	127	99	25	.356	.450	.517	149	48	48	144	11	8	-2	7	*2	5.5
1935	*Det-A	150	610	123	201	32	8	19	108	79	16	.330	.409	.502	139	32	35	129	11	4	1	3	*2	4.1
1936	Det-A	154	641	144	227	60	12	15	116	83	13	.354	.431	.555	141	43	43	157	4	1	1	16	*2	6.0
1937	Det-A	144	564	133	209	40	1	14	96	90	25	.371	.458	.520	143	44	42	140	11	4	1	6	*2	5.6
1938	Det-A	152	568	133	174	32	5	20	107	113	21	.306	.425	.486	121	28	23	128	14	1	4	-1	*2	2.8
1939	Det-A	118	406	86	132	29	6	16	86	68	16	.325	.423	.544	135	29	24	97	4	3	-1	1	*2	2.6
1940	*Det-A	139	515	108	161	33	3	10	81	101	17	.313	.428	.447	116	26	18	111	10	0	3	-20	*2	0.8
1941	Det-A	127	436	65	96	19	4	3	46	95	26	.220	.363	.303	71	-10	-17	55	1	2	-1	-3	*2	-0.9
1942	Det-A	45	45	6	12	0	0	1	7	7	4	.267	.365	.333	90	-0	-0	6	0	0	0	1	/2	0.1
Total	19	2323	8860	1774	2839	574	146	184	1427	1186	372	.320	.404	.480	123	376	339	1781	181	89	1	34	*2/13	42.7

■ PHIL GEIER
Geier, Philip Louis "Little Phil"   b: 11/3/1875, Washington, D.C.   d: 9/25/67, Spokane, Wash.   BL/TR, 5'7", 145 lbs.   Deb: 8/17/1896

YEAR	TM/L	G	AB	R	H	2B	3B	HR	RBI	BB	SO	AVG	OBP	SLG	PRO+	BR	/A	RC	SB	CS	SBR	FR	POS	TPR
1896	Phi-N	17	56	12	13	0	0	0	6	6	7	.232	.317	.268	58	-3	-3	6	3			-2	O/2C	-0.4
1897	Phi-N	92	316	51	88	6	2	1	35	56		.278	.392	.320	94	-0	1	48	19			-7	O2/S3	-0.4
1900	Cin-N	30	113	18	29	1	4	0	10	7		.257	.300	.336	79	-4	-3	13	3			1	O/3	-0.3
1901	Phi-A	50	211	42	49	5	2	0	23	24		.232	.314	.275	63	-9	-10	21	7			-5	O/S3	-1.3
	Mil-A	11	39	4	7	1	1	0	1	5		.179	.273	.256	51	-3	-2	4	4			-1	/O3	-0.2
	Yr	61	250	46	56	6	3	0	24	29		.224	.307	.272	62	-11	-12	25	11			-6		-1.5
1904	Bos-N	149	580	70	141	17	2	1	27	56		.243	.310	.284	89	-5	-5	59	18			-3	*O/32S	-1.3
Total	5	349	1315	197	327	30	12	2	102	154	7	.249	.330	.294	82	-26	-23	151	54			-16	0/23SC	-3.9

■ GARY GEIGER
Geiger, Gary Merle   b: 4/4/37, Sand Ridge, Ill.   BL/TR, 6', 168 lbs.   Deb: 4/15/58

YEAR	TM/L	G	AB	R	H	2B	3B	HR	RBI	BB	SO	AVG	OBP	SLG	PRO+	BR	/A	RC	SB	CS	SBR	FR	POS	TPR
1958	Cle-A	91	195	28	45	3	1	1	6	27	43	.231	.333	.272	70	-7	-7	20	2	2	-1	7	O/3P	-0.2

YEAR	TM/L	G	AB	R	H	2B	3B	HR	RBI	BB	SO	AVG	OBP	SLG	PRO+	BR	/A	RC	SB	CS	SBR	FR	POS	TPR
1959	Bos-A	120	335	45	82	10	4	11	48	21	55	.245	.289	.397	83	-7	-9	38	9	3	1	-1	O	-1.3
1960	Bos-A	77	245	32	74	13	3	9	33	23	38	.302	.369	.490	126	10	9	43	2	2	-1	3	O	0.9
1961	Bos-A	140	499	82	116	21	6	18	64	87	91	.232	.351	.407	99	2	1	78	16	4	2	4	*O	0.2
1962	Bos-A	131	466	67	116	18	4	16	54	67	66	.249	.346	.408	99	2	-0	69	18	11	-1	2	*O	-0.3
1963	Bos-A	121	399	67	105	13	5	16	44	36	63	.263	.329	.441	110	7	5	59	9	4	0	8	O/1	1.1
1964	Bos-A	5	13	3	5	0	1	0	1	2	2	.385	.467	.538	170	1	1	4	0	0	0	-0	/O	0.1
1965	Bos-A	24	45	5	9	3	0	1	2	13	10	.200	.379	.333	98	1	1	7	3	0	1	1	O	0.2
1966	Atl-N	78	126	23	33	5	3	4	10	21	29	.262	.372	.444	124	5	5	22	0	1	-1	2	O	0.4
1967	Atl-N	69	117	17	19	1	1	1	5	20	35	.162	.285	.214	45	-8	-8	8	1	1	-0	-1	O	-1.0
1969	Hou-N	93	125	19	28	4	1	0	16	24	34	.224	.353	.272	79	-3	-2	14	2	1	0	1	O	-0.4
1970	Hou-N	5	4	0	1	0	0	0	0	0	0	.250	.250	.250	36	-0	-0	0	0	0	0	-0	/O	0.0
Total	12	954	2569	388	633	91	29	77	283	341	466	.246	.339	.394	98	3	-5	363	62	29	1	26	O/13P	-0.3

■ BILL GEIS

Geis, William J. (b: William J. Geiss) b: 7/15/1858, Chicago, Ill. d: 9/18/24, Chicago, Ill. 5'10", 164 lbs. Deb: 5/01/1884

YEAR	TM/L	G	AB	R	H	2B	3B	HR	RBI	BB	SO	AVG	OBP	SLG	PRO+	BR	/A	RC	SB	CS	SBR	FR	POS	TPR
1884	Det-N	75	283	23	50	11	4	2	16	6	60	.177	.194	.265	46	-18	-16	15				-7	2/O1P	-1.8

■ EMIL GEISS

Geiss, Emil August b: 3/20/1867, Chicago, Ill. d: 10/4/11, Chicago, Ill. BR , Deb: 5/18/1887

YEAR	TM/L	G	AB	R	H	2B	3B	HR	RBI	BB	SO	AVG	OBP	SLG	PRO+	BR	/A	RC	SB	CS	SBR	FR	POS	TPR
1887	Chi-N	3	12	0	1	0	0	0	0	0	7	.083	.083	.083	-47	-2	-3	0	0			-1	/21P	-0.2

■ CHARLIE GELBERT

Gelbert, Charles Magnus b: 1/26/06, Scranton, Pa. d: 1/13/67, Easton, Pa. BR/TR, 5'11", 170 lbs. Deb: 4/16/29

YEAR	TM/L	G	AB	R	H	2B	3B	HR	RBI	BB	SO	AVG	OBP	SLG	PRO+	BR	/A	RC	SB	CS	SBR	FR	POS	TPR
1929	StL-N	146	512	60	134	29	8	3	65	51	46	.262	.329	.367	71	-23	-23	62	8			7	*S	0.3
1930	*StL-N	139	513	92	156	39	11	3	72	43	41	.304	.360	.441	89	-6	-9	80	6			9	*S	1.1
1931	*StL-N	131	447	61	129	29	5	1	62	54	31	.289	.365	.383	97	2	-0	66	7			13	*S	2.3
1932	StL-N	122	455	60	122	28	9	1	45	39	30	.268	.330	.376	87	-6	-8	59	8			0	*S	0.2
1935	StL-N	62	168	24	49	7	2	2	21	17	18	.292	.357	.393	97	1	-0	25	0			5	3S/2	0.7
1936	StL-N	93	280	33	64	15	2	3	27	25	26	.229	.292	.329	67	-13	-13	25	2			8	3S/2	0.2
1937	Cin-N	43	114	12	22	4	0	1	13	15	12	.193	.287	.254	51	-8	-7	9	1			-2	S/23	-0.5
	Det-A	20	47	4	4	2	0	0	1	4	11	.085	.157	.128	-27	-9	-10	1	0	0	0	-0	S	-0.7
1939	Was-A	68	188	36	48	7	5	3	29	30	11	.255	.361	.394	100	-2	1	28	2	0	1	-4	S3/2	0.0
1940	Was-A	22	54	7	20	7	1	0	7	4	3	.370	.424	.537	157	4	4	13	0	0	0	-5	S/P2	0.0
	Bos-A	30	91	9	18	2	0	0	8	8	16	.198	.263	.220	25	-10	-10	6	0	0	0	5	3/S	-0.3
	Yr	52	145	16	38	9	1	0	15	12	19	.262	.323	.338	72	-6	-6	17	0	0	0	-1		-0.3
Total	9	876	2869	398	766	169	43	17	350	290	245	.267	.336	.374	82	-71	-76	373	34	0		36	S3/2P	3.3

■ FRANK GENINS

Genins, C. Frank "Frenchy" b: 11/2/1866, St.Louis, Mo. d: 9/30/22, St.Louis, Mo. TR , Deb: 7/05/1892

YEAR	TM/L	G	AB	R	H	2B	3B	HR	RBI	BB	SO	AVG	OBP	SLG	PRO+	BR	/A	RC	SB	CS	SBR	FR	POS	TPR
1892	Cin-N	35	110	12	20	4	0	0	7	12	12	.182	.262	.218	48	-7	-6	8	7			4	SO/3	-0.1
	StL-N	15	51	5	10	1	0	0	4	1	11	.196	.212	.216	32	-4	-4	3	3			-7	S/O	-0.9
	Yr	50	161	17	30	5	0	0	11	13	23	.186	.247	.217	43	-11	-10	11	10			-3		-1.0
1895	Pit-N	73	252	43	63	8	0	2	24	22	14	.250	.315	.306	66	-14	-11	31	19			-6	O32/S1	-1.4
1901	Cle-A	26	101	15	23	5	0	0	9	8		.228	.284	.277	60	-6	-5	10	3			1	O	-0.3
Total	3	149	514	75	116	18	0	2	44	43	37	.226	.288	.272	58	-30	-27	52	32			-8	/OS321	-2.7

■ GEORGE GENOVESE

Genovese, George Michael b: 2/22/22, Staten Island, N.Y BL/TR, 5'6.5", 160 lbs. Deb: 4/29/50

YEAR	TM/L	G	AB	R	H	2B	3B	HR	RBI	BB	SO	AVG	OBP	SLG	PRO+	BR	/A	RC	SB	CS	SBR	FR	POS	TPR
1950	Was-A	3	1	1	0	0	0	0	0	1	0	.000	.500	.000	39	0	0	0	0	0	0	0	H	0.0

■ JIM GENTILE

Gentile, James Edward "Diamond Jim" b: 6/3/34, San Francisco, Cal. BL/TL, 6'3.5", 210 lbs. Deb: 9/10/57

YEAR	TM/L	G	AB	R	H	2B	3B	HR	RBI	BB	SO	AVG	OBP	SLG	PRO+	BR	/A	RC	SB	CS	SBR	FR	POS	TPR
1957	Bro-N	4	6	1	1	0	0	1	1	1	1	.167	.286	.667	133	0	0	1	0	0	0	-0	/1	0.0
1958	LA-N	12	30	0	4	1	0	0	4	4	6	.133	.235	.167	9	-4	-4	1	0	0	0	-1	/1	-0.5
1960	Bal-A	138	384	67	112	17	0	21	98	68	72	.292	.407	.500	146	26	26	82	0	0	0	-6	*1	1.2
1961	Bal-A	148	486	96	147	25	2	46	141	96	106	.302	.428	.646	187	59	61	138	1	1	-0	3	*1	4.8
1962	Bal-A	152	545	80	137	21	1	33	87	77	100	.251	.351	.475	126	15	19	92	1	0	0	1	*1	1.0
1963	Bal-A	145	496	65	123	16	1	24	72	76	101	.248	.355	.429	121	14	15	77	1	0	0	8	*1	2.0
1964	KC-A	136	439	71	110	10	0	28	71	84	122	.251	.376	.465	128	21	20	81	0	0	0	-1	*1	1.5
1965	KC-A	38	118	14	29	5	0	10	22	9	26	.246	.305	.542	138	5	5	19	0	0	0	-1	1	0.2
	Hou-N	81	227	22	55	11	1	7	31	34	72	.242	.353	.392	118	4	6	33	0	0	0	3	1	0.6
1966	Hou-N	49	144	16	35	6	1	7	18	21	39	.243	.355	.444	129	4	6	24	0	0	0	2	1	0.6
	Cle-A	33	47	2	6	1	0	2	4	5	18	.128	.212	.277	39	-4	-4	3	0	0	0	-0	/1	-0.4
Total	9	936	2922	434	759	113	6	179	549	475	663	.260	.372	.486	136	141	150	550	3	1	0	8	1	11.0

■ SAM GENTILE

Gentile, Samuel Christopher b: 10/12/16, Charlestown, Mass. BL/TR, 5'11", 180 lbs. Deb: 4/24/43

YEAR	TM/L	G	AB	R	H	2B	3B	HR	RBI	BB	SO	AVG	OBP	SLG	PRO+	BR	/A	RC	SB	CS	SBR	FR	POS	TPR
1943	Bos-N	8	4	1	1	1	0	0	0	1	0	.250	.400	.500	162	0	0	1	0			0	H	0.0

■ HARVEY GENTRY

Gentry, Harvey William b: 5/27/26, Winston-Salem, N.C BL/TR, 6', 170 lbs. Deb: 4/14/54

YEAR	TM/L	G	AB	R	H	2B	3B	HR	RBI	BB	SO	AVG	OBP	SLG	PRO+	BR	/A	RC	SB	CS	SBR	FR	POS	TPR
1954	NY-N	5	4	0	1	0	0	0	1	1	0	.250	.400	.250	73	-0	-0	1	0	0	0	0	H	0.0

■ ALEX GEORGE

George, Alex Thomas M. b: 9/27/38, Kansas City, Mo. BL/TR, 5'11.5", 170 lbs. Deb: 9/16/55

YEAR	TM/L	G	AB	R	H	2B	3B	HR	RBI	BB	SO	AVG	OBP	SLG	PRO+	BR	/A	RC	SB	CS	SBR	FR	POS	TPR
1955	KC-A	5	10	0	1	0	0	0	0	1	7	.100	.182	.100	-22	-2	-2	0	0	0	0	-1	/S	-0.2

■ GREEK GEORGE

George, Charles Peter b: 12/25/12, Waycross, Ga. BR/TR, 6'2", 200 lbs. Deb: 6/30/35

YEAR	TM/L	G	AB	R	H	2B	3B	HR	RBI	BB	SO	AVG	OBP	SLG	PRO+	BR	/A	RC	SB	CS	SBR	FR	POS	TPR
1935	Cle-A	2	0	0	0	0	0	0	0	0	0	—	—	—	—	0	0	0	0	0	0	1	/C	0.1
1936	Cle-A	23	77	3	15	3	0	0	5	9	16	.195	.279	.234	28	-9	-9	5	0	0	0	16	C	0.8
1938	Bro-N	7	20	0	4	0	1	0	2	0	4	.200	.200	.300	35	-2	-2	1	0			2	/C	0.0
1941	Chi-N	35	64	4	10	2	0	0	6	2	10	.156	.182	.188	4	-8	-8	2	0			2	C	-0.3
1945	Phi-A	51	138	8	24	4	1	0	11	17	29	.174	.265	.217	41	-10	-10	8	0	0	0	-6	C	-1.3
Total	5	118	299	15	53	9	2	0	24	28	59	.177	.248	.221	29	-29	-29	17	0	0		14	/C	-0.7

■ BILL GEORGE

George, William M. b: 1/27/1865, Bellaire, Ohio d: 8/23/16, Wheeling, W.Va. BR/TL, 5'8", 165 lbs. Deb: 5/11/1887

YEAR	TM/L	G	AB	R	H	2B	3B	HR	RBI	BB	SO	AVG	OBP	SLG	PRO+	BR	/A	RC	SB	CS	SBR	FR	POS	TPR
1887	NY-N	13	53	6	9	0	0	0	5	1	6	.170	.185	.170	0	-7	-7	2	2			2	P/O	0.0
1888	*NY-N	9	39	7	9	1	0	1	6	0	2	.231	.231	.333	81	-1	-1	3	1			-0	/OP	0.0
1889	NY-N	3	15	1	4	0	0	0	0	0	3	.267	.267	.267	50	-1	-1	1	1			-0	/O	0.0
	Col-a	5	17	1	4	0	0	0	3	1	1	.235	.278	.235	51	-1	-1	1	1			-1	/OP	-0.1
Total	3	30	124	15	26	1	0	1	14	2	12	.210	.222	.242	37	-10	-9	8	5			-0	/PO	-0.1

■ BEN GERAGHTY

Geraghty, Benjamin Raymond b: 7/19/12, Jersey City, N.J. d: 6/18/63, Jacksonville, Fla BR/TR, 5'11", 175 lbs. Deb: 4/17/36

YEAR	TM/L	G	AB	R	H	2B	3B	HR	RBI	BB	SO	AVG	OBP	SLG	PRO+	BR	/A	RC	SB	CS	SBR	FR	POS	TPR
1936	Bro-N	51	129	11	25	4	0	0	9	8	16	.194	.241	.225	26	-13	-13	7	4			-7	S/23	-1.6
1943	Bos-N	8	1	2	0	0	0	0	0	0	0	.000	.000	.000	-99	-0	-0	0	0			2	/2S3	0.2
1944	Bos-N	11	16	3	4	0	0	0	0	1	2	.250	.294	.250	52	-1	-1	1	0			0	/23	0.0
Total	3	70	146	16	29	4	0	0	9	9	18	.199	.245	.226	28	-15	-15	8	4			-4	S23	-1.4

■ CRAIG GERBER

Gerber, Craig Stuart b: 1/8/59, Chicago, Ill. BL/TR, 6', 175 lbs. Deb: 4/11/85

YEAR	TM/L	G	AB	R	H	2B	3B	HR	RBI	BB	SO	AVG	OBP	SLG	PRO+	BR	/A	RC	SB	CS	SBR	FR	POS	TPR
1985	Cal-A	65	91	8	24	1	2	0	6	2	3	.264	.280	.319	64	-5	-5	7	0	3	-2	19	S/32D	1.5

■ WALLY GERBER

Gerber, Walter "Spooks" b: 8/18/1891, Columbus, Ohio d: 6/19/51, Columbus, Ohio BR/TR, 5'10", 152 lbs. Deb: 9/23/14

YEAR	TM/L	G	AB	R	H	2B	3B	HR	RBI	BB	SO	AVG	OBP	SLG	PRO+	BR	/A	RC	SB	CS	SBR	FR	POS	TPR
1914	Pit-N	17	54	5	13	1	1	0	5	2	8	.241	.281	.296	75	-2	-2	4	0			1	S	0.0
1915	Pit-N	56	144	8	28	2	0	0	7	9	16	.194	.252	.208	40	-10	-10	9	6	1	1	2	3S/2	-0.4
1917	StL-A	14	39	2	12	1	1	0	2	3	2	.308	.357	.385	131	1	1	6	1			-2	S/2	0.0

YEAR	TM/L	G	AB	R	H	2B	3B	HR	RBI	BB	SO	AVG	OBP	SLG	PRO+	BR	/A	RC	SB	CS	SBR	FR	POS	TPR
1918	StL-A	56	171	10	41	4	0	0	10	19	11	.240	.316	.263	77	-5	-4	15	2			-9	S	-1.0
1919	StL-A	140	462	43	105	14	6	1	37	49	36	.227	.308	.290	67	-19	-20	44	1			-8	*S	-1.7
1920	StL-A	154	584	70	163	26	2	2	60	58	32	.279	.346	.341	80	-13	-16	69	4	13	-7	7	*S	-0.1
1921	StL-A	114	436	55	121	12	9	2	48	34	19	.278	.337	.360	73	-15	-18	53	3	7	-3	-3	*S	-0.9
1922	StL-A	153	604	81	161	22	8	1	51	52	34	.267	.326	.334	70	-24	-27	69	6	4	-1	2	*S	-0.8
1923	StL-A	154	605	85	170	26	3	1	62	54	50	.281	.342	.339	75	-17	-22	72	4	6	-2	7	*S	-0.2
1924	StL-A	148	496	61	135	20	4	0	55	43	34	.272	.341	.329	69	-19	-23	58	4	5	-2	-7	*S	-1.5
1925	StL-A	72	246	29	67	13	1	0	19	26	15	.272	.344	.333	69	-10	-12	29	1	2	-1	5	S	0.3
1926	StL-A	131	411	37	111	8	0	0	42	40	29	.270	.339	.290	62	-20	-22	43	0	2	-1	3	*S	-0.9
1927	StL-A	142	438	44	98	13	9	0	45	35	25	.224	.284	.295	49	-33	-35	36	2	6	-3	9	*S/3	-1.5
1928	StL-A	6	18	1	5	1	0	0	0	1	3	.278	.316	.333	69	-1	-1	2	0	0	0	-2	/S	-0.1
	Bos-A	104	300	21	64	6	1	0	28	32	31	.213	.289	.240	41	-25	-25	24	6	1	1	34	*S	1.9
	Yr	110	318	22	69	7	1	0	28	33	34	.217	.291	.245	43	-26	-25	26	6	1	1	32		1.8
1929	Bos-A	61	91	6	15	3	1	0	5	8	12	.165	.232	.220	17	-11	-11	5	1	0	0	14	S2	0.6
Total	15	1522	5099	558	1309	172	46	7	476	465	357	.257	.323	.313	67	-222	-247	538	41	47		55	*S/23	-6.3

■ BOB GEREN
Geren, Robert Peter b: 9/22/61, San Diego, Cal. BR/TR, 6'3", 205 lbs. Deb: 5/17/88

YEAR	TM/L	G	AB	R	H	2B	3B	HR	RBI	BB	SO	AVG	OBP	SLG	PRO+	BR	/A	RC	SB	CS	SBR	FR	POS	TPR
1988	NY-A	10	10	0	1	0	0	0	0	2	3	.100	.250	.100	2	-1	-1	0	0	0	0	1	C	0.0
1989	NY-A	65	205	26	59	5	1	9	27	12	44	.288	.330	.454	120	4	5	28	0	0	0	0	C/D	0.8
1990	NY-A	110	277	21	59	7	0	8	31	13	73	.213	.261	.325	63	-14	-14	23	0	0	0	13	*C/D	0.1
Total	3	185	492	47	119	12	1	17	58	27	120	.242	.290	.374	85	-11	-11	51	0	0	0	14	C/D	0.9

■ JOE GERHARDT
Gerhardt, John Joseph "Move Up Joe" b: 2/14/1855, Washington, D.C. d: 3/11/22, Middletown, N.Y. BR/TR, 6', 160 lbs. Deb: 9/01/1873 M

YEAR	TM/L	G	AB	R	H	2B	3B	HR	RBI	BB	SO	AVG	OBP	SLG	PRO+	BR	/A	RC	SB	CS	SBR	FR	POS	TPR
1873	Was-n	13	56	6	11	2	1	0		0		.196	.196	.268	36	-4	-4	3					S	-0.2
1874	Bal-n	14	61	10	20	1	1	0		0		.328	.328	.377	125	2	2	8					S	0.0
1875	Mut-n	58	251	29	53	8	3	0		0		.211	.211	.267	61	-9	-11	15					32/S	-0.7
1876	Lou-N	65	292	33	76	10	3	2	18	3	5	.260	.268	.336	85	-0	-8	27				6	*1/2SO3	-0.1
1877	Lou-N	59	250	41	76	6	5	1	35	5	8	.304	.318	.380	101	5	-2	31				20	*2/OS1	1.8
1878	Cin-N	60	259	46	77	7	2	0	28	7	14	.297	.316	.340	127	4	8	28				5	*2	1.6
1879	Cin-N	79	313	22	62	12	3	1	39	3	19	.198	.206	.265	57	-15	-13	17				7	23/1S	0.3
1881	Det-N	80	297	35	72	13	6	0	36	7	31	.242	.260	.327	80	-6	-7	26				8	*2/3	0.3
1883	Lou-a	78	319	56	84	11	9	0		14		.263	.294	.354	117	3	7	34				20	*2M	2.4
1884	Lou-a	106	404	39	89	7	8	0		13		.220	.254	.277	79	-10	-7	29				27	*2	2.0
1885	NY-N	112	399	43	62	12	2	0	33	24	47	.155	.203	.195	30	-30	-29	16				13	*2	-0.3
1886	NY-N	123	426	44	81	11	7	0	40	22	63	.190	.230	.249	45	-28	-28	27	8			4	*2	-1.6
1887	NY-N	1	4	0	0	0	0	0	0	0	0	.000	.000	.000	-99	-1	-1	0	0			0	/3	0.0
	NY-a	85	307	40	68	13	2	0		24		.221	.280	.277	60	-17	-15	29	15			15	2/3	0.0
1890	Bro-a	99	369	34	75	10	4	2		30		.203	.270	.268	63	-18	-16	30	9			37	*2	2.1
	StL-a	37	125	15	32	0	0	1		9		.256	.321	.280	70	-3	-6	13	5			5	23M	0.0
	Yr	136	494	49	107	10	4	3		39		.217	.283	.271	65	-21	-22	43	14			42		2.1
1891	Lou-a	2	6	0	0	0	0	0	0	1	0	.000	.143	.000	-58	-1	-1	0	0			-0	/2	0.0
Total	3 n	85	368	45	84	11	5	0		0		.228	.228	.285	67	-12	-13	25	0				/3S2	-0.9
Total	12	986	3770	448	854	112	51	7	229	162	187	.227	.261	.289	72	-117	-119	308	37			167	2/13SO	8.2

■ KEN GERHART
Gerhart, Harold Kenneth b: 5/19/61, Charleston, S.C. BR/TR, 6', 190 lbs. Deb: 9/14/86

YEAR	TM/L	G	AB	R	H	2B	3B	HR	RBI	BB	SO	AVG	OBP	SLG	PRO+	BR	/A	RC	SB	CS	SBR	FR	POS	TPR
1986	Bal-A	20	69	4	16	2	0	1	7	4	18	.232	.274	.304	58	-4	-4	6	0	1	-1	-2	O	-0.6
1987	Bal-A	92	284	41	69	10	2	14	34	17	53	.243	.288	.440	92	-5	-4	35	9	2	2	-5	O	-0.8
1988	Bal-A	103	262	27	51	10	1	9	23	21	57	.195	.260	.344	69	-12	-11	24	7	3	0	-3	O/D	-1.5
Total	3	215	615	72	136	22	3	24	64	42	128	.221	.274	.384	79	-21	-19	64	16	6	1	-9	O/D	-2.9

■ GEORGE GERKEN
Gerken, George Herbert "Pickles" b: 7/28/03, Chicago, Ill. d: 10/23/77, Arcadia, Cal. BR/TR, 5'11.5", 175 lbs. Deb: 4/19/27

YEAR	TM/L	G	AB	R	H	2B	3B	HR	RBI	BB	SO	AVG	OBP	SLG	PRO+	BR	/A	RC	SB	CS	SBR	FR	POS	TPR
1927	Cle-A	6	14	1	3	0	0	0	2	1	3	.214	.267	.214	26	-2	-2	1	0	0	0	0	/O	-0.1
1928	Cle-A	38	115	16	26	7	2	0	9	12	22	.226	.305	.322	64	-6	-6	12	3	2	-0	-1	O	-0.8
Total	2	44	129	17	29	7	2	0	11	13	25	.225	.301	.310	60	-7	-8	13	3	2	-0	-1	/O	-0.9

■ JOHNNY GERLACH
Gerlach, John Glenn b: 5/11/17, Shullsburg, Wis. BR/TR, 5'9", 165 lbs. Deb: 9/03/38

YEAR	TM/L	G	AB	R	H	2B	3B	HR	RBI	BB	SO	AVG	OBP	SLG	PRO+	BR	/A	RC	SB	CS	SBR	FR	POS	TPR
1938	Chi-A	9	25	2	7	0	0	0	1	4	2	.280	.379	.280	66	-1	-1	3	0	0	0	1	/S	0.0
1939	Chi-A	3	2	0	2	0	0	0	0	0	0	1.000	1.000	1.000	402	1	1	2	0	0	0	0	/3	0.1
Total	2	12	27	2	9	0	0	0	1	4	2	.333	.419	.333	89	-0	-0	5	0	0	0	1	/S3	0.1

■ DICK GERNERT
Gernert, Richard Edward b: 9/28/28, Reading, Pa. BR/TR, 6'3", 209 lbs. Deb: 4/16/52 C

YEAR	TM/L	G	AB	R	H	2B	3B	HR	RBI	BB	SO	AVG	OBP	SLG	PRO+	BR	/A	RC	SB	CS	SBR	FR	POS	TPR
1952	Bos-A	102	367	58	89	20	2	19	67	35	83	.243	.317	.463	107	5	2	56	4	1	1	-1	1	-0.4
1953	Bos-A	139	494	73	125	15	1	21	71	88	82	.253	.371	.415	106	10	7	81	0	7	-4	-3	*1	-0.2
1954	Bos-A	14	23	2	6	2	0	0	1	6	4	.261	.414	.348	99	1	0	3	0	0	0	-1	/1	0.0
1955	Bos-A	7	20	6	4	2	0	0	1	1	5	.200	.238	.300	40	-2	-2	1	0	0	0	0	/1	-0.1
1956	Bos-A	106	306	53	89	11	0	16	68	56	57	.291	.404	.484	119	16	11	63	1	0	0	3	O1	1.0
1957	Bos-A	99	316	45	75	13	3	14	58	39	62	.237	.327	.430	99	2	-1	44	1	1	-0	0	1O	-0.1
1958	Bos-A	122	431	59	102	19	1	20	69	59	78	.237	.331	.425	100	4	-0	60	2	0	1	8	*1	0.5
1959	Bos-A	117	298	41	78	14	1	11	42	52	49	.262	.371	.426	113	9	7	47	1	2	-1	6	1O	1.1
1960	Chi-N	52	96	8	24	3	0	0	11	10	19	.250	.321	.281	67	-4	-4	8	1	0	0	3	1/O	-0.1
	Det-A	21	50	6	15	4	0	0	5	4	5	.300	.352	.440	110	1	1	8	0	0	0	-1	1/O	0.0
1961	Det-A	6	5	1	1	0	0	1	1	1	2	.200	.333	.800	187	1	1	1	0	0	0	0	H	0.1
	*Cin-N	40	63	4	19	1	0	0	7	7	9	.302	.371	.317	84	-1	-1	8	0	0	0	3	1	0.1
1962	Hou-N	10	24	1	5	0	0	0	1	5	7	.208	.345	.208	57	-1	-1	2	0	0	0	-1	/1	-0.1
Total	11	835	2493	357	632	104	8	103	402	363	462	.254	.352	.426	104	40	19	382	10	11	-4	17	1O	1.8

■ CESAR GERONIMO
Geronimo, Cesar Francisco (Zorrilla) b: 3/11/48, ElSeibo, D.R. BL/TL, 6', 165 lbs. Deb: 4/16/69

YEAR	TM/L	G	AB	R	H	2B	3B	HR	RBI	BB	SO	AVG	OBP	SLG	PRO+	BR	/A	RC	SB	CS	SBR	FR	POS	TPR
1969	Hou-N	28	8	8	2	1	0	0	0	0	3	.250	.250	.375	74	-0	-0	1	0	0	0	1	/O	0.0
1970	Hou-N	47	37	5	9	0	0	0	2	2	5	.243	.300	.243	49	-3	-2	3	0	0	0	2	O	-0.1
1971	Hou-N	94	82	13	18	2	2	1	6	5	31	.220	.264	.329	69	-4	-3	7	2	2	-1	3	O	-0.3
1972	*Cin-N	120	255	32	70	9	7	4	29	24	64	.275	.344	.412	121	5	6	34	2	7	-4	-2	*O	-1.0
1973	*Cin-N	139	324	35	68	14	3	4	33	23	74	.210	.269	.309	63	-18	-16	26	5	5	-2	-2	*O	-2.6
1974	Cin-N	150	474	73	133	17	8	7	54	46	96	.281	.347	.395	109	4	5	65	9	5	-0	19	*O	-0.1
1975	*Cin-N	148	501	69	129	25	5	6	53	48	97	.257	.327	.363	90	-6	-7	61	13	5	1	9	*O	-0.1
1976	*Cin-N	149	486	59	149	24	11	2	49	56	95	.307	.385	.414	124	19	17	82	22	5	4	5	*O	1.4
1977	Cin-N	149	492	54	131	22	4	10	52	35	89	.266	.321	.388	88	-8	-9	60	10	4	1	5	*O	-0.8
1978	Cin-N	122	296	28	67	15	1	5	27	43	67	.226	.330	.334	86	-5	-5	35	8	3	1	-4	*O	-1.2
1979	*Cin-N	123	356	38	85	17	4	4	38	37	56	.239	.314	.343	79	-10	-10	38	2	1	-0	1	*O	-1.2
1980	Cin-N	103	145	16	37	5	1	2	9	14	24	.255	.321	.331	82	-3	-3	16	2	1	0	8	O	0.1
1981	*KC-A	59	118	14	29	0	2	2	13	11	16	.246	.310	.331	85	-2	-2	13	6	1	1	-8	O	-1.0
1982	KC-A	53	119	14	32	6	3	4	23	8	16	.269	.315	.471	112	2	2	16	2	0	1	5	O/D	0.6
1983	KC-A	38	87	2	18	4	0	0	4	2	13	.207	.242	.253	36	-8	-8	5	0	1	-1	-2	*O/D	-0.6
Total	15	1522	3780	460	977	161	50	51	392	354	746	.258	.327	.368	93	-37	-36	462	82	40	1	31	*O/D	-4.9

YEAR	TM/L	G	AB	R	H	2B	3B	HR	RBI	BB	SO	AVG	OBP	SLG	PRO+	BR	/A	RC	SB	CS	SBR	FR	POS	TPR

■ LOU GERTENRICH
Gertenrich, Louis Wilhelm b: 5/4/1875, Chicago, Ill. d: 10/23/33, Chicago, Ill. 5'8", 175 lbs. Deb: 9/15/01

YEAR	TM/L	G	AB	R	H	2B	3B	HR	RBI	BB	SO	AVG	OBP	SLG	PRO+	BR	/A	RC	SB	CS	SBR	FR	POS	TPR
1901	Mil-A	2	3	1	1	0	0	0	0	0	0	.333	.333	.333	92	-0	-0	0	0			-0	/O	0.0
1903	Pit-N	1	3	0	0	0	0	0	0	0	0	.000	.000	.000	-97	-1	-1	0	0			0	/O	0.0
Total	2	3	6	1	1	0	0	0	0	0	0	.167	.167	.167	1	-1	-1	0	0			-0	/O	0.0

■ DOC GESSLER
Gessler, Harry Homer "Brownie" b: 12/23/1880, Indiana, Pa. d: 12/26/24, Indiana, Pa. BL/TR, 5'10", 180 lbs. Deb: 4/23/03 M

YEAR	TM/L	G	AB	R	H	2B	3B	HR	RBI	BB	SO	AVG	OBP	SLG	PRO+	BR	/A	RC	SB	CS	SBR	FR	POS	TPR
1903	Det-A	29	105	9	25	5	4	0	12	3		.238	.259	.362	89	-2	-2	11	1			-2	O	-0.5
	Bro-N	49	154	20	38	8	3	0	18	17		.247	.322	.338	92	-2	-1	21	9			-3	O	-0.5
1904	Bro-N	104	341	41	99	18	4	2	28	30		.290	.348	.384	131	11	12	52	13			2	O/12	1.2
1905	Bro-N	126	431	44	125	17	4	3	46	38		.290	.348	.369	125	9	13	66	26			2	*1O	0.9
1906	Bro-N	9	33	3	8	1	2	0	4	3		.242	.306	.394	130	1	1	5	3			1	/1	0.1
	*Chi-N	34	83	8	21	3	0	0	10	12		.253	.347	.289	95	1	0	10	4			-1	O/1	-0.1
	Yr	43	116	11	29	4	2	0	14	15		.250	.336	.319	103	1	1	16	7			-1		0.0
1908	Bos-A	128	435	55	134	13	14	3	63	51		.308	.381	.423	159	31	30	77	19			-7	*O	1.8
1909	Bos-A	111	396	57	115	24	1	0	46	31		.290	.354	.356	122	11	10	55	16			-1	*O	0.6
	Was-A	17	54	10	13	2	1	0	8	12		.241	.406	.315	134	3	3	9	4			-1	O/1	0.2
	Yr	128	450	67	128	26	2	0	54	43		.284	.361	.351	123	14	14	63	20			-2		0.8
1910	Was-A	145	487	58	126	17	11	2	50	62		.259	.361	.351	129	16	16	68	18			-3	*O	1.0
1911	Was-A	128	450	65	127	19	5	4	78	74		.282	.406	.373	120	16	17	80	29			-10	*O/1	-0.2
Total	8	880	2969	370	831	127	49	14	363	333		.280	.362	.370	126	94	102	454	142			-22	O1/2	4.5

■ CHARLIE GETTIG
Gettig, Charles Henry b: 12/1870, Baltimore, Md. d: 4/11/35, Baltimore, Md. 5'10", 172 lbs. Deb: 8/05/1896

YEAR	TM/L	G	AB	R	H	2B	3B	HR	RBI	BB	SO	AVG	OBP	SLG	PRO+	BR	/A	RC	SB	CS	SBR	FR	POS	TPR
1896	NY-N	6	9	3	3	1	0	0	0	0	0	.333	.333	.444	109	0	0	1	0			0	/P	0.0
1897	NY-N	22	75	8	15	6	0	0	12	6		.200	.277	.280	50	-5	-5	7	3			-8	/32OSP	-1.0
1898	NY-N	64	196	30	49	6	2	0	26	15		.250	.310	.301	80	-5	-4	20	5			-9	OP2/S31C	-0.9
1899	NY-N	34	97	7	24	3	0	0	9	7		.247	.305	.278	65	-5	-5	10	4			-3	P/3210	0.0
Total	4	126	377	48	91	16	2	0	47	28	0	.241	.302	.294	71	-15	-14	38	12			-20	/PO23S1C	-1.9

■ TOM GETTINGER
Gettinger, Thomas L. b: 1870, Mobile, Ala. BL/TL, 5'10", 180 lbs. Deb: 9/21/1889

YEAR	TM/L	G	AB	R	H	2B	3B	HR	RBI	BB	SO	AVG	OBP	SLG	PRO+	BR	/A	RC	SB	CS	SBR	FR	POS	TPR
1889	StL-a	4	16	2	7	0	0	1	2	2	1	.438	.500	.625	197	3	2	5	0			-1	/O	0.1
1890	StL-a	58	227	31	54	7	5	3		20		.238	.302	.352	83	-2	-7	27	8			-6	O	-1.3
1895	Lou-N	63	260	28	70	11	5	2	32	8	15	.269	.296	.373	78	-11	-8	31	6			-3	O/P	-1.2
Total	3	125	503	61	131	18	10	6	34	30	16	.260	.306	.373	84	-10	-13	64	14			-10	O/P	-2.4

■ JAKE GETTMAN
Gettman, Jacob John b: 10/25/1876, Frank, Russia d: 10/4/56, Denver, Colo. BB/TL, 5'11", 185 lbs. Deb: 8/20/1897

YEAR	TM/L	G	AB	R	H	2B	3B	HR	RBI	BB	SO	AVG	OBP	SLG	PRO+	BR	/A	RC	SB	CS	SBR	FR	POS	TPR
1897	Was-N	36	143	28	45	7	3	3	29	7		.315	.359	.469	120	4	4	28	8			-3	O	-0.1
1898	Was-N	142	567	75	157	16	5	5	47	29		.277	.319	.349	94	-5	-5	75	32			2	*O/1	-1.0
1899	Was-N	19	62	5	13	1	0	0	2	4		.210	.258	.226	35	-5	-5	5	4			-1	O/1	-0.6
Total	3	197	772	108	215	24	8	8	78	40		.278	.322	.361	95	-7	-7	108	44			-2	O/1	-1.7

■ GUS GETZ
Getz, Gustave "Gee-Gee" b: 8/3/1889, Pittsburgh, Pa. d: 5/28/69, Keansburg, N.J. BR/TR, 5'11", 165 lbs. Deb: 8/15/09

YEAR	TM/L	G	AB	R	H	2B	3B	HR	RBI	BB	SO	AVG	OBP	SLG	PRO+	BR	/A	RC	SB	CS	SBR	FR	POS	TPR
1909	Bos-N	40	148	6	33	2	0	0	9	1		.223	.228	.236	42	-10	-11	9	2			0	3/2S	-1.0
1910	Bos-N	54	144	14	28	0	1	0	7	6	10	.194	.232	.208	27	-13	-14	7	2			4	32/OS	-0.9
1914	Bro-N	55	210	13	52	8	1	0	20	2	15	.248	.255	.295	62	-10	-11	17	9			12	3	0.4
1915	Bro-N	130	477	39	123	10	5	2	46	8	14	.258	.275	.312	76	-14	-15	41	19	15	-3	8	*3/S	-0.5
1916	*Bro-N	40	96	9	21	1	2	0	8	0	5	.219	.219	.271	49	-6	-6	8	9			-3	3/S1	-0.9
1917	Cin-N	7	14	2	4	0	0	0	3	3	0	.286	.412	.286	121	0	0	2	0			-3	/23	-0.1
1918	Cle-A	6	15	2	2	1	0	0	4	1		.133	.350	.200	60	-0	-1	1	0			-0	/3	0.0
	Pit-N	7	10	0	2	0	0	0	0	0	1	.200	.200	.200	21	-1	-1	0	0			1	/3	0.0
Total	7	339	1114	85	265	22	9	2	93	24	46	.238	.257	.279	60	-54	-57	85	41	15		19	3/2SO1	-3.0

■ CHAPPIE GEYGAN
Geygan, James Edward b: 6/3/03, Ironton, Ohio d: 3/15/66, Columbus, Ohio BR/TR, 5'11", 170 lbs. Deb: 7/16/24

YEAR	TM/L	G	AB	R	H	2B	3B	HR	RBI	BB	SO	AVG	OBP	SLG	PRO+	BR	/A	RC	SB	CS	SBR	FR	POS	TPR
1924	Bos-A	33	82	7	21	5	2	0	4	16		.256	.307	.366	73	-4	-4	9	2	2	-1	4	S	0.3
1925	Bos-A	3	11	0	2	0	0	0	0	0	2	.182	.182	.182	-8	-2	-2	0	0	0	0	-1	/S	-0.2
1926	Bos-A	4	10	0	3	0	0	0	0	1	1	.300	.364	.300	77	-0	-0	1	0	0	0	-1	/3	0.0
Total	3	40	103	7	26	5	2	0	4	5	19	.252	.300	.340	65	-6	-6	10	2	2	-1	3	/S3	0.1

■ PATSY GHARRITY
Gharrity, Edward Patrick b: 3/13/1892, Parnell, Iowa d: 10/10/66, Beloit, Wis. BR/TR, 5'10", 170 lbs. Deb: 5/16/16 C

YEAR	TM/L	G	AB	R	H	2B	3B	HR	RBI	BB	SO	AVG	OBP	SLG	PRO+	BR	/A	RC	SB	CS	SBR	FR	POS	TPR
1916	Was-A	39	92	8	21	5	1	0	9	8	18	.228	.297	.304	83	-2	-2	9	2			-2	C1	-0.4
1917	Was-A	76	176	15	50	5	0	0	18	14	18	.284	.337	.313	99	-0	-0	20	7			1	1/CO	0.1
1918	Was-A	4	4	0	1	1	0	0	2	0	1	.250	.250	.500	129	0	0	0	0			0	H	0.0
1919	Was-A	111	347	35	94	19	4	2	43	25	39	.271	.325	.366	95	-3	-3	42	4			-5	CO/1	-0.7
1920	Was-A	131	428	51	105	18	3	3	44	37	52	.245	.307	.322	69	-21	-19	44	6	5	-1	-2	*C/1O	-1.2
1921	Was-A	121	387	62	120	19	8	7	55	45	44	.310	.386	.455	120	8	11	70	4	3	-1	-1	*C	1.2
1922	Was-A	96	273	40	70	19	6	5	45	36	30	.256	.351	.414	104	-0	2	41	3	3	-1	3	C	0.5
1923	Was-A	93	251	26	52	9	4	3	33	22	27	.207	.276	.311	57	-17	-16	23	6	2	1	1	C1	-1.2
1929	Was-A	3	2	0	0	0	0	0	0	1	2	.000	.333	.000	-7	-0	-0	0	0	0	0	0	H	0.0
1930	Was-A	2	1	0	0	0	0	0	0	0	0	.000	.000	.000	-99	-0	-0	0	0	0	0	0	/1	0.0
Total	10	676	1961	237	513	92	26	20	249	188	231	.262	.331	.366	90	-37	-27	250	32	13		-7	C1/O	-1.8

■ JOE GIANNINI
Giannini, Joseph Francis b: 9/8/1888, San Francisco, Cal d: 9/26/42, San Francisco, Cal. BL/TR, 5'8", 155 lbs. Deb: 8/07/11

YEAR	TM/L	G	AB	R	H	2B	3B	HR	RBI	BB	SO	AVG	OBP	SLG	PRO+	BR	/A	RC	SB	CS	SBR	FR	POS	TPR
1911	Bos-A	1	2	0	1	1	0	0	0	0		.500	.500	1.000	317	1	1	1	0			-0	/S	0.0

■ JOHN GIBBONS
Gibbons, John Michael b: 6/8/62, Great Falls, Mont. BR/TR, 5'11", 187 lbs. Deb: 4/11/84

YEAR	TM/L	G	AB	R	H	2B	3B	HR	RBI	BB	SO	AVG	OBP	SLG	PRO+	BR	/A	RC	SB	CS	SBR	FR	POS	TPR
1984	NY-N	10	31	1	2	0	0	0	1	3	11	.065	.171	.065	-32	-5	-5	0	0	0	0	-1	/C	-0.6
1986	NY-N	8	19	4	9	4	0	1	1	3	5	.474	.545	.842	285	5	5	8	0	0	0	1	/C	0.6
Total	2	18	50	5	11	4	0	1	2	6	16	.220	.316	.360	90	-1	-1	9	0	0	0	-0	/C	0.0

■ JAKE GIBBS
Gibbs, Jerry Dean b: 11/7/38, Grenada, Miss. BL/TR, 6', 180 lbs. Deb: 9/11/62

YEAR	TM/L	G	AB	R	H	2B	3B	HR	RBI	BB	SO	AVG	OBP	SLG	PRO+	BR	/A	RC	SB	CS	SBR	FR	POS	TPR
1962	NY-A	2	0	2	0	0	0	0	0	0		—	—	—		0	0	0	0	0	0	0	/3	0.0
1963	NY-A	4	8	1	2	0	0	0	0	0	1	.250	.250	.250	41	-1	-1	0	0	0	0	-0	/C	0.0
1964	NY-A	3	6	1	1	0	0	0	0	0	2	.167	.167	.167	-7	-1	-1	0	0	0	0	-1	/C	0.0
1965	NY-A	37	68	6	15	1	0	2	7	4	20	.221	.274	.324	70	-3	-3	7	0	0	0	2	C	0.0
1966	NY-A	62	182	19	47	6	0	3	20	19	16	.258	.328	.341	96	-1	-1	20	5	2	0	4	C	0.7
1967	NY-A	116	374	33	87	7	1	4	25	28	57	.233	.293	.289	75	-12	-11	31	7	6	-2	-1	C	-0.7
1968	NY-A	124	423	31	90	12	3	3	29	27	68	.213	.270	.277	68	-17	-16	30	9	8	-2	-5	*C	-2.0
1969	NY-A	71	219	18	49	9	2	0	18	23	30	.224	.298	.283	65	-11	-10	18	3	4	-2	8	C	0.1
1970	NY-A	49	153	23	46	9	2	8	26	7	14	.301	.335	.542	146	7	8	27	2	0	1	2	C	1.1
1971	NY-A	70	206	23	45	9	0	5	21	12	23	.218	.271	.335	76	-8	-7	18	2	2	-1	-6	C	-1.1
Total	10	538	1639	157	382	53	8	25	146	120	231	.233	.291	.321	81	-48	-41	152	28	22	-5	3	C/3	-1.9

■ CHARLIE GIBSON
Gibson, Charles Ellsworth "Gibby" b: 11/17/1879, Sharon, Pa. d: 11/22/54, Sharon, Pa. TR, 6', 160 lbs. Deb: 9/23/05

YEAR	TM/L	G	AB	R	H	2B	3B	HR	RBI	BB	SO	AVG	OBP	SLG	PRO+	BR	/A	RC	SB	CS	SBR	FR	POS	TPR
1905	StL-A	1	3	0	0	0	0	0	0	0	0	.000	.000	.000	-99	-1	-1	0	0			-0	/C	0.0

YEAR	TM/L	G	AB	R	H	2B	3B	HR	RBI	BB	SO	AVG	OBP	SLG	PRO+	BR	/A	RC	SB	CS	SBR	FR	POS	TPR
■ **CHARLIE GIBSON**					Gibson, Charles Griffin		b: 11/21/1899, Lagrange, Ga.		BR/TR, 5'8", 160 lbs.		Deb: 5/30/24													
1924	Phi-A	12	15	1	2	0	0	0	1	2	0	.133	.235	.133	-3	-2	-2	1	0	0	0	-0	C	-0.1
■ **FRANK GIBSON**					Gibson, Frank Gilbert		b: 9/27/1890, Omaha, Neb.		d: 4/27/61, Austin, Tex.		BB/TR, 6'0.5", 172 lbs.		Deb: 4/22/13										
1913	Det-A	23	57	8	8	1	0	0	2	3	9	.140	.197	.158	4	-7	-7	2	2			-6	C/O	-1.2
1921	Bos-N	63	125	14	33	5	4	2	13	3	17	.264	.292	.416	90	-3	-2	15	0	0	0	1	C	0.2
1922	Bos-N	66	164	15	49	7	2	3	20	10	27	.299	.339	.421	99	-2	-1	24	4	1	1	3	C1	0.0
1923	Bos-N	41	50	13	15	1	0	0	5	7	7	.300	.386	.320	92	-0	-0	6	0	2	-1	-2	C	-0.1
1924	Bos-N	90	229	25	71	15	6	1	30	10	23	.310	.342	.441	113	2	3	34	1	1	-0	2	C1/3	0.5
1925	Bos-N	104	316	36	88	23	5	2	50	15	28	.278	.313	.402	89	-10	-6	39	3	3	-1	-3	C/1	-0.4
1926	Bos-N	24	47	3	16	4	0	0	7	4	6	.340	.392	.426	132	1	2	8	0			1	C	0.4
1927	Bos-N	60	167	7	37	1	2	0	19	3	10	.222	.235	.251	33	-16	-15	9	2			-3	C	-1.4
Total	8	471	1155	121	317	57	19	8	146	55	127	.274	.310	.377	86	-35	-25	137	12	7		-11	C/13O	-2.0
■ **GEORGE GIBSON**					Gibson, George C. "Moon"		b: 7/22/1880, London, Ont., Can.		d: 1/25/67, London, Ont., Can.		BR/TR, 5'11.5", 190 lbs.		Deb: 7/02/05	MC								
1905	Pit-N	46	135	14	24	2	2	2	14	15		.178	.260	.267	57	-7	-7	11	2			3	C	0.1
1906	Pit-N	81	259	8	46	6	1	0	20	16		.178	.225	.208	35	-19	-20	14	1			-5	C	-2.0
1907	Pit-N	113	382	28	84	8	7	3	35	18		.220	.255	.301	75	-12	-12	32	2			-3	*C/1	-0.7
1908	Pit-N	143	486	37	111	19	4	2	45	19		.228	.257	.296	78	-13	-13	37	4			-16	*C	-2.5
1909	*Pit-N	150	510	42	135	25	9	2	52	44		.265	.326	.361	104	7	2	63	9			1	*C	1.5
1910	Pit-N	143	482	53	125	22	6	3	44	47	31	.259	.333	.349	93	-1	-4	58	7			1	*C	0.4
1911	Pit-N	100	311	32	65	12	2	0	19	29	16	.209	.281	.260	50	-20	-22	23	3			0	C	-1.4
1912	Pit-N	95	300	23	72	14	3	2	35	20	16	.240	.290	.327	69	-14	-13	28	0			-0	C	-0.7
1913	Pit-N	48	118	6	33	4	2	0	12	10	8	.280	.341	.347	101	-0	0	15	2			-8	C	-0.4
1914	Pit-N	102	274	19	78	9	5	0	30	27	27	.285	.359	.354	117	5	6	36	4			-9	*C	0.1
1915	Pit-N	120	351	28	88	15	6	1	30	31	25	.251	.313	.336	98	-1	-1	40	5	2	0	8	*C	1.5
1916	Pit-N	33	84	4	17	2	2	0	4	3	7	.202	.239	.274	57	-4	-4	6	0			7	C	0.5
1917	NY-N	35	82	1	14	3	0	0	5	7	2	.171	.236	.207	38	-6	-6	4	1			0	C	-0.3
1918	NY-N	4	2	0	1	1	0	0	0	0	0	.500	.500	1.000	360	1	1	1	0			0	/C	0.1
Total	14	1213	3776	295	893	142	49	15	345	286	132	.236	.294	.312	81	-85	-93	366	40	2		-22	*C/1	-3.8
■ **RUSS GIBSON**					Gibson, John Russell		b: 5/6/39, Fall River, Mass.		BR/TR, 6'1", 195 lbs.		Deb: 4/14/67												
1967	*Bos-A	49	138	8	28	7	0	1	15	12	31	.203	.267	.275	56	-7	-8	9	0	0	0	-7	C	-1.2
1968	Bos-A	76	231	15	52	11	1	3	20	8	38	.225	.251	.320	68	-8	-10	17	1	2	-1	2	C/1	-0.5
1969	Bos-A	85	287	21	72	9	1	3	27	15	25	.251	.290	.321	67	-12	-13	24	1	1	-0	-6	C	-1.4
1970	SF-N	24	69	3	16	6	0	0	6	7	12	.232	.303	.319	67	-3	-3	6	0	0	0	2	C	0.0
1971	SF-N	25	57	2	11	1	1	1	7	2	13	.193	.220	.298	46	-4	-4	3	0	0	0	0	C	-0.3
1972	SF-N	5	12	0	2	0	1	0	3	0	4	.167	.167	.333	38	-1	-1	0	0	0	0	-1	/C	0.0
Total	6	264	794	49	181	34	4	8	78	44	123	.228	.269	.311	64	-35	-39	60	2	3	-1	-9	C/1	-3.4
■ **KIRK GIBSON**					Gibson, Kirk Harold		b: 5/28/57, Pontiac, Mich.		BL/TL, 6'3", 215 lbs.		Deb: 9/08/79												
1979	Det-A	12	38	3	9	3	0	1	4	1	3	.237	.256	.395	70	-2	-2	3	3	3	-1	-2	O	-0.4
1980	Det-A	51	175	23	46	2	1	9	16	10	45	.263	.306	.440	100	-0	-1	22	4	7	-3	2	O/D	-0.2
1981	Det-A	83	290	41	95	11	3	9	40	18	64	.328	.371	.479	138	15	14	50	17	5	2	-3	O/D	1.2
1982	Det-A	69	266	34	74	16	2	8	35	25	41	.278	.342	.444	113	5	5	40	9	7	-2	3	O/D	0.4
1983	Det-A	128	401	60	91	12	9	15	51	53	96	.227	.323	.414	104	1	2	59	14	3	2	-3	DO	0.1
1984	*Det-A	149	531	92	150	23	10	27	91	63	103	.282	.367	.516	142	30	30	106	29	9	3	-13	*O/D	1.6
1985	Det-A	154	581	96	167	37	5	29	97	71	137	.287	.370	.518	141	32	33	118	30	4	7	-9	*O/D	2.8
1986	Det-A	119	441	84	118	11	2	28	86	68	107	.268	.374	.492	132	24	21	88	34	6	7	-12	*O/D	1.3
1987	*Det-A	128	487	95	135	25	3	24	79	71	117	.277	.375	.489	132	20	23	95	26	7	4	1	*O/D	2.3
1988	*LA-N	150	542	106	157	28	1	25	76	73	120	.290	.381	.483	151	34	36	107	31	4	7	4	*O	4.5
1989	LA-N	71	253	35	54	8	2	9	28	35	55	.213	.314	.368	96	-2	-1	31	12	3	2	-2	O	-0.1
1990	LA-N	89	315	59	82	20	0	8	38	39	65	.260	.347	.400	111	3	5	50	26	7	5	2	O	1.1
Total	12	1203	4320	728	1178	196	38	192	641	527	953	.273	.358	.469	128	157	165	769	235	60	35	-32	*OD	14.6
■ **WHITEY GIBSON**					Gibson, Leighton P.		b: 10/6/1868, Lancaster, Pa.		d: 10/11/07, Talmadge, Pa.		TR , 5'9", 178 lbs.		Deb: 5/02/1888										
1888	Phi-a	1	3	0	0	0	0	0	0	0	0	.000	.000	.000	-99	-1	-1	0	0			1	/C	0.0
■ **JOE GIEBEL**					Giebel, Joseph Henry		b: 11/30/1891, Washington, D.C.		d: 3/17/81, Silver Spring, Md.		BR/TR, 5'10.5", 175 lbs.		Deb: 9/30/13										
1913	Phi-A	1	3	0	1	0	0	0	0	0	1	.333	.333	.333	97	-0	-0	0	0			-0	/C	0.0
■ **NORM GIGON**					Gigon, Norman Phillip		b: 5/12/38, Teaneck, N.J.		BR/TR, 6', 195 lbs.		Deb: 4/12/67												
1967	Chi-N	34	70	8	12	3	1	1	6	4	14	.171	.237	.286	47	-5	-5	5	0	0	0	-2	2/O3	-0.6
■ **GUS GIL**					Gil, Tomas Gustavo (Guillen)		b: 4/19/39, Caracas, Venez.		BR/TR, 5'10", 180 lbs.		Deb: 4/11/67										
1967	Cle-A	51	96	11	11	4	0	0	5	9	18	.115	.198	.156	6	-11	-11	3	0	0	0	2	2/1	-0.7
1969	Sea-A	92	221	20	49	7	0	0	17	16	28	.222	.274	.253	49	-15	-15	16	2	0	1	1	32S	-1.1
1970	Mil-A	64	119	12	22	4	0	1	12	21	12	.185	.307	.244	53	-7	-7	10	2	0	1	3	23	0.1
1971	Mil-A	14	32	3	5	1	0	0	3	10	5	.156	.357	.188	59	-1	-1	3	1	0	0	0	/23	0.0
Total	4	221	468	46	87	16	0	1	37	56	63	.186	.274	.226	43	-34	-34	33	5	0	2	7	2/3S1	-1.7
■ **ANDY GILBERT**					Gilbert, Andrew		b: 7/18/14, Latrobe, Pa.		BR/TR, 6', 203 lbs.		Deb: 9/14/42	C										
1942	Bos-A	6	11	0	1	0	0	0	1	1	3	.091	.167	.091	-26	-2	-2	0	0	0	0	-0	/O	-0.2
1946	Bos-A	2	1	1	0	0	0	0	0	0	0	.000	.000	.000	-95	-0	-0	0	0	0	0	0	/O	0.0
Total	2	8	12	1	1	0	0	0	1	1	3	.083	.154	.083	-31	-2	-2	0	0	0	0	-0	/O	-0.2
■ **CHARLIE GILBERT**					Gilbert, Charles Mader		b: 7/8/19, New Orleans, La.		d: 8/13/83, New Orleans, La.		BL/TL, 5'9", 165 lbs.		Deb: 4/16/40									
1940	Bro-N	57	142	23	35	9	1	2	8	8	13	.246	.287	.366	74	-4	-5	16	0			5	O	-0.1
1941	Chi-N	39	86	11	24	2	1	0	12	11	6	.279	.361	.326	98	-0	0	11	0			1	O	0.0
1942	Chi-N	74	179	18	33	6	3	0	7	25	24	.184	.284	.251	60	-9	-8	14	1			3	O	-0.6
1943	Chi-N	8	20	1	3	0	0	0	0	3	3	.150	.261	.150	20	-2	-2	1	1			0	/O	-0.1
1946	Chi-N	15	13	2	1	0	0	0	1	1	4	.077	.143	.077	-38	-2	-2	0	0			1	/O	-0.1
	Phi-N	88	260	34	63	5	2	1	17	25	18	.242	.314	.288	73	-9	-8	26	3			5	O	-0.4
	Yr	103	273	36	64	5	2	1	18	26	22	.234	.306	.278	68	-12	-11	27	3			6		-0.5
1947	Phi-N	83	152	20	36	5	2	2	10	13	14	.237	.301	.336	72	-7	-6	15	1			3	O	-0.4
Total	6	364	852	109	195	27	9	5	55	86	82	.229	.302	.299	70	-34	-33	82	7			18	O	-1.7
■ **BUDDY GILBERT**					Gilbert, Drew Edward		b: 7/26/35, Knoxville, Tenn.		BL/TR, 6'3", 195 lbs.		Deb: 9/09/59										
1959	Cin-N	7	20	4	3	0	0	2	2	3	4	.150	.261	.450	82	-1	-1	3	0	0	0	1	/O	0.0
■ **TOOKIE GILBERT**					Gilbert, Harold Joseph		b: 4/4/29, New Orleans, La.		d: 6/23/67, New Orleans, La.		BL/TR, 6'2.5", 185 lbs.		Deb: 5/05/50									
1950	NY-N	113	322	40	71	12	2	4	32	43	36	.220	.314	.307	64	-16	-16	33	3			1	*1	-1.9
1953	NY-N	70	160	12	27	3	0	3	16	22	21	.169	.269	.244	34	-15	-16	12	1	0	0	1	1	-1.4
Total	2	183	482	52	98	15	2	7	48	65	57	.203	.299	.286	54	-31	-32	45	4	0		2	1	-3.3

HARRY GILBERT
Gilbert, Harry H.   b: 7/7/1868, Pottstown, Pa.   d: 12/23/09, Pottstown, Pa.   Deb: 6/23/1890

YEAR	TM/L	G	AB	R	H	2B	3B	HR	RBI	BB	SO	AVG	OBP	SLG	PRO+	BR	/A	RC	SB	CS	SBR	FR	POS	TPR
1890	Pit-N	2	8	1	2	0	0	0	0	0	3	.250	.250	.250	54	-1	-0	1	0			-1	/2	0.0

JOHN GILBERT
Gilbert, John G.   b: 1/8/1864, Pottstown, Pa.   d: 11/12/03, Pottstown, Pa.   Deb: 6/23/1890

YEAR	TM/L	G	AB	R	H	2B	3B	HR	RBI	BB	SO	AVG	OBP	SLG	PRO+	BR	/A	RC	SB	CS	SBR	FR	POS	TPR
1890	Pit-N	2	8	0	0	0	0	0	0	0	2	.000	.000	.000	-99	-2	-2	0	0			-0	/S	-0.1

JACK GILBERT
Gilbert, John Robert "Jackrabbit"   b: 9/4/1875, Rhinecliff, N.Y.   d: 7/7/41, Albany, N.Y.   Deb: 9/11/1898

YEAR	TM/L	G	AB	R	H	2B	3B	HR	RBI	BB	SO	AVG	OBP	SLG	PRO+	BR	/A	RC	SB	CS	SBR	FR	POS	TPR
1898	Was-N	2	5	0	1	0	0	0		1	1	.200	.429	.200	85	0	0	1	1			-0	/O	0.0
	NY-N	1	4	0	1	0	0	0		0	0	.250	.250	.250	47	-0	-0	1	1			-0	/O	0.0
	Yr	3	9	0	2	0	0	0		1	1	.222	.364	.222	73	-0	-0	1	2			-1		0.0
1904	Pit-N	25	87	13	21	0	0	0	3	12		.241	.333	.241	78	-1	-2	8	3			-6	O	-0.8
Total	2	28	96	13	23	0	0	0	4	13		.240	.336	.240	78	-1	-2	10	5			-6	/O	-0.8

LARRY GILBERT
Gilbert, Lawrence William   b: 12/3/1891, New Orleans, La.   d: 2/17/65, New Orleans, La.   BL/TL, 5'9", 158 lbs.   Deb: 4/14/14

YEAR	TM/L	G	AB	R	H	2B	3B	HR	RBI	BB	SO	AVG	OBP	SLG	PRO+	BR	/A	RC	SB	CS	SBR	FR	POS	TPR
1914	*Bos-N	72	224	32	60	6	1	5	25	26	34	.268	.347	.371	114	4	4	30	3			-2	O	0.0
1915	Bos-N	45	106	11	16	4	0	0	4	11	13	.151	.231	.189	29	-9	-9	6	4	1	1	-3	O	-1.2
Total	2	117	330	43	76	10	1	5	29	37	47	.230	.310	.312	88	-5	-4	35	7	1		-5	/O	-1.2

MARK GILBERT
Gilbert, Mark David   b: 8/22/56, Atlanta, Ga.   BB/TR, 6', 175 lbs.   Deb: 7/21/85

YEAR	TM/L	G	AB	R	H	2B	3B	HR	RBI	BB	SO	AVG	OBP	SLG	PRO+	BR	/A	RC	SB	CS	SBR	FR	POS	TPR
1985	Chi-A	7	22	3	6	1	0	0	3	4	5	.273	.385	.318	92	0	-0	3	0	0	0	-0	/O	0.0

PETE GILBERT
Gilbert, Peter   b: 9/6/1867, Baltic, Conn.   d: 1/1/12, Springfield, Mass.   TR, 180 lbs.   Deb: 9/06/1890

YEAR	TM/L	G	AB	R	H	2B	3B	HR	RBI	BB	SO	AVG	OBP	SLG	PRO+	BR	/A	RC	SB	CS	SBR	FR	POS	TPR
1890	Bal-a	29	100	25	28	2	1	1			10	.280	.363	.350	108	2	1	17	12			-3	3	-0.1
1891	Bal-a	139	513	81	118	15	7	3	72	37	77	.230	.317	.304	79	-12	-13	61	31			2	*3	-0.5
1892	Bal-a	4	15	0	3	0	0	0	0	1	3	.200	.250	.200	37	-1	-1	1	1			1	/3	0.0
1894	Bro-N	6	25	1	2	0	0	0	1	1	3	.080	.148	.080	-46	-6	-6	1	2			1	/23	-0.2
	Lou-N	28	108	13	33	3	1	1	14	5	4	.306	.353	.380	84	-4	-2	16	2			-6	3	-0.6
	Yr	34	133	14	35	3	1	1	15	6	7	.263	.315	.323	60	-10	-8	15	4			-5		-0.8
Total	4	206	761	120	184	20	9	5	87	54	87	.242	.321	.311	78	-21	-21	95	48			-4	3/2	-1.4

WALLY GILBERT
Gilbert, Walter John   b: 12/19/1900, Oscoda, Mich.   d: 9/7/58, Duluth, Minn.   BR/TR, 6', 180 lbs.   Deb: 8/18/28

YEAR	TM/L	G	AB	R	H	2B	3B	HR	RBI	BB	SO	AVG	OBP	SLG	PRO+	BR	/A	RC	SB	CS	SBR	FR	POS	TPR
1928	Bro-N	39	153	26	31	4	0	0	3	14	8	.203	.274	.229	33	-15	-15	10	2			-1	3	-1.4
1929	Bro-N	143	569	88	173	31	4	3	58	42	29	.304	.359	.388	87	-12	-11	79	7			7	*3	0.7
1930	Bro-N	150	623	92	183	34	5	3	67	47	33	.294	.345	.379	76	-25	-23	80	7			9	*3	-1.0
1931	Bro-N	145	552	60	147	25	6	0	46	39	38	.266	.322	.333	77	-18	-17	62	3			8	*3	0.0
1932	Cin-N	114	420	35	90	18	2	1	40	20	23	.214	.252	.274	43	-35	-33	30	2			-6	*3	-2.9
Total	5	591	2317	301	624	112	17	7	214	162	131	.269	.322	.341	71	-104	-98	261	21			17	3	-4.6

BILLY GILBERT
Gilbert, William Oliver   b: 6/21/1876, Tullytown, Pa.   d: 8/8/27, New York, N.Y.   BR/TR, 5'4", 153 lbs.   Deb: 4/25/01

YEAR	TM/L	G	AB	R	H	2B	3B	HR	RBI	BB	SO	AVG	OBP	SLG	PRO+	BR	/A	RC	SB	CS	SBR	FR	POS	TPR
1901	Mil-A	127	492	77	133	14	7	0	43	31		.270	.319	.327	85	-12	-8	61	19			-0	*2	-1.1
1902	Bal-A	129	445	74	109	12	3	2	38	45		.245	.325	.299	72	-13	-16	60	38			-5	*S	-0.8
1903	NY-N	128	413	62	104	9	0	1	40	41		.252	.319	.281	71	-13	-15	53	37			11	*2	0.3
1904	NY-N	146	478	57	121	13	3	1	54	46		.253	.319	.299	89	-3	-5	60	33			8	*2	0.7
1905	*NY-N	115	376	45	93	11	3	0	24	41		.247	.321	.293	84	-5	-6	42	11			26	*2	2.7
1906	NY-N	104	307	44	71	6	1	1	27	42		.231	.324	.267	85	-3	-4	36	22			23	2	2.1
1908	StL-N	89	276	12	59	7	0	0	10	20		.214	.267	.239	67	-11	-9	19	6			6	2	-0.3
1909	StL-N	12	29	4	5	0	0	0	1	4		.172	.333	.172	61	-1	-1	2	1			0	2	0.0
Total	8	850	2816	375	695	72	17	5	237	270		.247	.316	.290	79	-60	-64	332	167			70	2S	3.6

ROD GILBREATH
Gilbreath, Rodney Joe   b: 9/24/52, Laurel, Miss.   BR/TR, 6'2", 180 lbs.   Deb: 6/17/72

YEAR	TM/L	G	AB	R	H	2B	3B	HR	RBI	BB	SO	AVG	OBP	SLG	PRO+	BR	/A	RC	SB	CS	SBR	FR	POS	TPR
1972	Atl-N	18	38	2	9	1	0	0	1	2	10	.237	.293	.263	54	-2	-2	3	1	1	-0	3	/23	0.0
1973	Atl-N	29	74	10	21	2	1	0	2	6	10	.284	.346	.338	84	-1	-1	9	2	1	0	-0	3	-0.2
1974	Atl-N	3	6	2	2	0	0	0	0	2	1	.333	.500	.333	131	1	0	1	0	0	0	0	/2	0.1
1975	Atl-N	90	202	24	49	3	1	2	16	24	26	.243	.326	.297	71	-7	-8	21	5	5	-2	2	23/S	-0.3
1976	Atl-N	116	383	57	96	11	8	1	32	42	36	.251	.331	.329	83	-5	-8	43	7	7	-2	7	*2/3S	0.2
1977	Atl-N	128	407	47	99	15	2	8	43	45	79	.243	.322	.349	71	-11	-17	44	3	9	-5	3	*2/3	-1.1
1978	Atl-N	116	326	22	80	13	3	3	31	26	51	.245	.301	.331	69	-10	-15	32	7	6	-2	-3	32	-1.8
Total	7	500	1436	164	356	45	15	14	125	147	212	.248	.322	.329	74	-36	-51	152	25	29	-10	11	23/S	-3.1

DON GILE
Gile, Donald Loren "Bear"   b: 4/19/35, Modesto, Cal.   BR/TR, 6'6", 220 lbs.   Deb: 9/25/59

YEAR	TM/L	G	AB	R	H	2B	3B	HR	RBI	BB	SO	AVG	OBP	SLG	PRO+	BR	/A	RC	SB	CS	SBR	FR	POS	TPR
1959	Bos-A	3	10	1	2	0	0	0	1	0	2	.200	.273	.300	55	-1	-1	1	0	0	0	-0	/C	0.0
1960	Bos-A	29	51	6	9	1	1	1	4	1	13	.176	.192	.294	29	-5	-5	3	0	0	0	-1	C1	-0.5
1961	Bos-A	8	18	2	5	0	0	1	1	1	5	.278	.316	.444	98	-0	-0	3	0	0	0	-1	/1C	0.0
1962	Bos-A	18	41	3	2	0	0	1	3	3	15	.049	.133	.122	-30	-8	-8	0	0	0	0	-1	1	-0.9
Total	4	58	120	12	18	2	1	3	9	5	35	.150	.197	.258	21	-14	-14	6	0	0	0	-2	/1C	-1.4

BRIAN GILES
Giles, Brian Jeffrey   b: 4/27/60, Manhattan, Kan.   BR/TR, 6'1", 165 lbs.   Deb: 9/12/81

YEAR	TM/L	G	AB	R	H	2B	3B	HR	RBI	BB	SO	AVG	OBP	SLG	PRO+	BR	/A	RC	SB	CS	SBR	FR	POS	TPR
1981	NY-N	9	7	0	0	0	0	0	0	0	3	.000	.000	.000	-99	-2	-2	0	0	0	0	3	/2S	0.2
1982	NY-N	45	138	14	29	5	0	3	10	12	29	.210	.273	.312	64	-7	-7	13	6	1	1	15	2/S	1.2
1983	NY-N	145	400	39	98	15	0	2	27	36	77	.245	.311	.298	70	-16	-16	37	17	10	-1	15	*2S	0.5
1985	Mil-A	34	58	6	10	1	0	1	1	7	16	.172	.262	.241	39	-5	-5	4	2	1	0	8	S2/D	0.5
1986	Chi-A	9	11	0	3	0	0	0	1	0	2	.273	.273	.273	48	-1	-1	1	0	0	0	2	/2S	0.3
1990	Sea-A	45	95	19	22	6	0	4	11	15	24	.232	.336	.421	109	1	1	14	2	1	0	6	S/23	1.0
Total	6	287	709	74	162	27	0	10	50	70	151	.228	.300	.309	70	-29	-28	69	27	13	0	51	2/SD3	3.7

GEORGE GILHAM
Gilham, George Louis   b: 9/17/1899, Shamokin, Pa.   d: 4/25/37, Lansdowne, Pa.   BR/TR, 5'11", 164 lbs.   Deb: 9/24/20

YEAR	TM/L	G	AB	R	H	2B	3B	HR	RBI	BB	SO	AVG	OBP	SLG	PRO+	BR	/A	RC	SB	CS	SBR	FR	POS	TPR
1920	StL-N	1	3	0	0	0	0	0	0	0	1	.000	.000	.000	-99	-1	-1	0	0	0	0	-1	/C	0.0
1921	StL-N	1	1	0	0	0	0	0	0	0	0	.000	.000	.000	-99	-0	-0	0	0	0	0	0	H	0.0
Total	2	2	4	0	0	0	0	0	0	0	1	.000	.000	.000	-99	-1	-1	0	0	0	0	-1	/C	0.0

FRANK GILHOOLEY
Gilhooley, Frank Patrick "Flash"   b: 6/10/1892, Toledo, Ohio   d: 7/11/59, Toledo, Ohio   BL/TR, 5'8", 155 lbs.   Deb: 9/18/11

YEAR	TM/L	G	AB	R	H	2B	3B	HR	RBI	BB	SO	AVG	OBP	SLG	PRO+	BR	/A	RC	SB	CS	SBR	FR	POS	TPR
1911	StL-N	1	0	0	0	0	0	0	0	0	0	—	—	—	—	0	0	0	0			0	/O	0.0
1912	StL-N	13	49	5	11	0	0	0	2	3	8	.224	.269	.224	37	-4	-4	3	0			-2	O	-0.5
1913	NY-A	24	85	10	29	2	1	0	14	4	9	.341	.378	.388	124	2	2	14	6			-1	O	0.1
1914	NY-A	1	3	0	2	0	0	0		0	0	.667	.750	.667	327	1	1	2	0			-0	/O	0.1
1915	NY-A	1	4	0	0	0	0	0		0	0	.000	.000	.000	-99	-1	-1	0	0			-0	/O	0.0
1916	NY-A	58	223	40	62	5	3	1	10	37	17	.278	.383	.341	115	6	6	35	16			3	O	0.6
1917	NY-A	54	165	14	40	6	1	0	8	30	13	.242	.362	.291	99	1	1	19	6			-1	O	-0.2
1918	NY-A	112	427	59	118	13	5	1	23	53	24	.276	.358	.337	107	6	5	53	7			1	*O	0.0
1919	Bos-A	48	112	14	27	4	0	0	1	12	8	.241	.315	.277	95	-5	-4	10	2			-5	O	-1.1
Total	9	312	1068	142	289	30	10	2	58	140	80	.271	.357	.323	102	8	7	136	37			-5	O	-1.0

BERNARD GILKEY
Gilkey, Otis Bernard   b: 9/24/66, St.Louis, Mo.   BR/TR, 6', 170 lbs.   Deb: 9/04/90

YEAR	TM/L	G	AB	R	H	2B	3B	HR	RBI	BB	SO	AVG	OBP	SLG	PRO+	BR	/A	RC	SB	CS	SBR	FR	POS	TPR
1990	StL-N	18	64	11	19	5	2	1	3	8	5	.297	.375	.484	131	3	3	13	6	1	1	2	O	0.5

YEAR	TM/L	G	AB	R	H	2B	3B	HR	RBI	BB	SO	AVG	OBP	SLG	PRO+	BR	/A	RC	SB	CS	SBR	FR	POS	TPR
■ **BOB GILKS**								Gilks, Robert James	b: 7/2/1864, Cincinnati, Ohio	d: 8/21/44, Brunswick, Ga.		BR/TR, 5'8", 178 lbs.		Deb: 8/25/1887										
1887	Cle-a	22	83	12	26	2	0	0		3		.313	.352	.337	97	-0	-0	12	5			2	P/1O2	0.0
1888	Cle-a	119	484	59	111	14	4	1	63	7		.229	.245	.281	73	-16	-14	38	16			-1	O3/SP2	-1.6
1889	Cle-N	53	210	17	50	5	2	0	18	7	20	.238	.273	.281	57	-12	-12	18	6			-0	OS1/2	-1.1
1890	Cle-N	130	544	65	116	10	3	0	41	32	38	.213	.265	.243	51	-34	-32	40	17			0	*O/PS2	-3.0
1893	Bal-N	15	64	10	17	2	0	0	7	0	3	.266	.277	.297	53	-4	-4	6	3			3	O	-0.1
Total	5	339	1385	163	320	33	9	1	129	49	61	.231	.265	.270	62	-67	-63	115	47			4	O/3PS12	-5.8
■ **JIM GILL**				Gill, James C.	b: St.Louis, Mo.		Deb: 6/27/1889																	
1889	StL-a	2	8	2	2	1	0	0	1	1	2	.250	.333	.375	92	-0	-0	1	1			-0	/O2	0.0
■ **JOHNNY GILL**				Gill, John Wesley "Patcheye"	b: 3/27/05, Nashville, Tenn.		d: 12/26/84, Nashville, Tenn.		BL/TR, 6'2", 190 lbs.		Deb: 8/28/27												
1927	Cle-A	21	60	8	13	3	0	1	4	7	13	.217	.319	.317	65	-3	-3	6	1	1	0	-2	O	-0.5
1928	Cle-A	2	2	0	0	0	0	0	0	0	1	.000	.000	.000	-99	-1	-1	0	0	0	0	0	H	0.0
1931	Was-A	8	30	2	8	2	1	0	5	1	6	.267	.313	.400	86	-1	-1	3	0	1	-1	3	/O	0.1
1934	Was-A	13	53	7	13	3	0	2	7	2	3	.245	.286	.415	82	-2	-2	6	0	0	0	-1	O	-0.2
1935	Chi-N	3	3	2	1	1	0	0	1	0	1	.333	.333	.667	161	0	0	1	0			0	H	0.0
1936	Chi-N	71	174	20	44	8	0	7	28	13	19	.253	.309	.420	92	-2	-2	23	0			-2	O	-0.5
Total	6	118	322	39	79	17	1	10	45	23	43	.245	.306	.398	84	-8	-8	40	1	2		-2	/O	-1.1
■ **WARREN GILL**				Gill, Warren Darst "Doc"	b: 12/21/1878, Ladoga, Ind.		d: 11/26/52, Laguna Beach, Cal.		BR/TR, 6'1", 175 lbs.		Deb: 8/26/08												
1908	Pit-N	27	76	10	17	0	1	0	14	11		.224	.322	.250	85	-1	-1	8	3			-3	1	-0.4
■ **SAM GILLEN**				Gillen, Samuel (b: Samuel Gilleland)	b: 1870, Pittsburgh, Pa.		d: 5/13/05, Pittsburgh, Pa.		Deb: 8/19/1893														
1893	Pit-N	3	6	0	0	0	0	0	0	0	1	.000	.000	.000	-99	-2	-2	0	0			-0	/S	-0.1
1897	Phi-N	75	270	32	70	10	3	0	27	35		.259	.353	.319	82	-6	-5	32	2			-28	S/3	-2.7
Total	2	78	276	32	70	10	3	0	27	35	1	.254	.346	.312	78	-8	-7	32	2			-28	/S3	-2.8
■ **TOM GILLEN**				Gillen, Thomas J.	b: 5/18/1862, Philadelphia, Pa.		d: 1/26/1889, Philadelphia, Pa.		5'8", 160 lbs.		Deb: 4/18/1884												
1884	Phi-U	29	116	5	18	2	0	0		1		.155	.162	.172	14	-10	-9	3	0			2	C/O	-0.3
1886	Det-N	2	10	2	4	0	0	0	4	0	1	.400	.400	.400	140	0	0	2	0			-2	/C	0.0
Total	2	31	126	7	22	2	0	0	4	1	1	.175	.181	.190	26	-10	-8	5	0			0	/CO	-0.3
■ **CARDEN GILLENWATER**				Gillenwater, Carden Edison	b: 5/13/18, Riceville, Tenn.		BR/TR, 6'1", 175 lbs.		Deb: 9/22/40														
1940	StL-N	7	25	1	4	1	0	0	5	0	2	.160	.160	.200	-1	-3	-4	1	0			-0	/O	-0.3
1943	Bro-N	8	17	1	3	0	0	0	2	2	3	.176	.263	.176	28	-2	-2	1	0			0	/O	-0.1
1945	Bos-N	144	517	74	149	20	2	7	72	73	70	.288	.379	.375	110	10	9	75	13			19	*O	2.2
1946	Bos-N	99	224	30	51	10	1	1	14	39	27	.228	.342	.295	81	-4	-4	25	3			-3	O	-0.8
1948	Was-A	77	221	23	54	10	4	3	21	39	36	.244	.358	.367	96	-2	-1	30	4	2	0	-4	O	-0.6
Total	5	335	1004	129	261	41	7	11	114	153	138	.260	.359	.348	96	-1	-1	133	20	2		12	O	0.4
■ **JIM GILLESPIE**				Gillespie, James Wheatfield	b: Buffalo, N.Y.		Deb: 10/01/1890																	
1890	Buf-P	1	3	0	0	0	0	0	0	0	2	.000	.000	.000	-99	-1	-1	0	0			-0	/O	0.0
■ **PAUL GILLESPIE**				Gillespie, Paul Allen	b: 9/18/20, Sugar Valley, Ga.		d: 8/11/70, Anniston, Ala.		BL/TR, 6'3", 195 lbs.		Deb: 9/11/42												
1942	Chi-N	5	16	3	4	0	0	2	4	1	2	.250	.294	.625	172	1	1	3	0			-1	/C	0.0
1944	Chi-N	9	26	2	7	1	0	1	2	3	7	.269	.345	.423	116	1	1	4	0			-1	/C	0.0
1945	*Chi-N	75	163	12	47	6	0	3	25	18	9	.288	.366	.380	110	2	3	24	2			1	C/O	0.4
Total	3	89	205	17	58	7	0	6	31	22	14	.283	.358	.405	115	4	4	31	2			-1	/CO	0.4
■ **PETE GILLESPIE**				Gillespie, Peter Patrick	b: 11/30/1851, Carbondale, Pa.		d: 5/5/10, Carbondale, Pa.		BL/TR, 6'1.5", 178 lbs.		Deb: 5/01/1880												
1880	Tro-N	82	346	50	84	20	5	2	24	17	35	.243	.278	.347	105	4	2	34				6	*O	0.4
1881	Tro-N	84	348	43	96	14	3	0	41	9	24	.276	.294	.333	92	-1	-4	35				3	*O	-0.1
1882	Tro-N	74	298	46	82	5	4	2	33	9	14	.275	.296	.339	108	1	3	31				-6	*O	-0.3
1883	NY-N	98	411	64	129	23	12	1	62	9	27	.314	.329	.436	131	14	15	60				5	*O	1.9
1884	NY-N	101	413	75	109	7	4	2	44	19	35	.264	.296	.315	90	-4	-5	39				-4	*O	-0.8
1885	NY-N	102	420	67	123	17	6	0	52	15	32	.293	.317	.362	121	8	9	49				-4	*O	0.2
1886	NY-N	97	396	65	108	13	8	0	58	16	30	.273	.301	.346	95	-2	-3	48	17			-13	*O	-1.2
1887	NY-N	76	295	40	78	9	3	3	37	12	21	.264	.304	.346	86	-7	-5	43	37			-2	O/3	-0.5
Total	8	714	2927	450	809	108	45	10	351	106	218	.276	.303	.354	104	13	12	340	54			-16	O/3	-0.4
■ **JIM GILLIAM**				Gilliam, James William "Junior"	b: 10/17/28, Nashville, Tenn.		d: 10/8/78, Inglewood, Cal.		BB/TR, 5'10.5", 175 lbs.		Deb: 4/14/53	C										
1953	*Bro-N	151	605	125	168	31	**17**	6	63	100	38	.278	.383	.415	106	10	8	104	21	14	-2	3	*2	1.5
1954	Bro-N	146	607	107	171	28	8	13	52	76	30	.282	.364	.418	100	4	1	95	8	7	-2	-11	*2/O	-0.2
1955	*Bro-N	147	538	110	134	20	8	7	40	70	37	.249	.342	.355	83	-10	-12	67	15	15	-5	-10	2O	-1.8
1956	*Bro-N	153	594	102	178	23	8	6	43	95	39	.300	.400	.396	107	17	11	103	21	9	1	13	*2O	3.1
1957	Bro-N	149	617	89	154	26	4	2	37	64	31	.250	.324	.314	66	-22	-30	69	26	10	2	3	*O/2	-1.3
1958	LA-N	147	555	81	145	25	5	2	43	78	22	.261	.352	.335	81	-11	-13	71	18	11	-1	-4	O32	-1.4
1959	*LA-N	145	553	91	156	18	4	3	34	**96**	25	.282	.388	.345	91	3	-3	84	23	10	1	2	*3/2O	-0.3
1960	LA-N	151	557	96	138	20	2	5	40	96	35	.248	.361	.318	82	-5	-10	72	12	9	-2	9	*32	-0.1
1961	LA-N	144	439	74	107	26	3	4	32	79	34	.244	.359	.344	81	-5	-11	60	8	4	0	2	32O	-0.3
1962	*LA-N	160	588	83	159	24	1	4	43	93	35	.270	.372	.335	97	-3	2	81	17	7	1	-13	*23/O	0.1
1963	*LA-N	148	525	77	148	27	4	6	49	60	28	.282	.358	.383	122	10	15	76	19	5	3	-8	*23	1.8
1964	*LA-N	116	344	44	76	8	3	2	27	42	21	.228	.319	.287	78	-11	-8	32	4	4	-1	-19	32/O	-3.3
1965	*LA-N	111	372	54	104	19	4	4	39	53	31	.280	.375	.384	123	9	12	58	9	5	-0	-16	3O/2	-0.7
1966	*LA-N	88	235	30	51	9	0	1	16	34	17	.217	.316	.268	70	-10	-8	21	2	1	0	-12	3/12	-2.2
Total	14	1956	7119	1163	1889	304	71	65	558	1036	416	.265	.361	.355	92	-25	-46	992	203	111	-6	-56	*23O/1	-5.1
■ **BARNEY GILLIGAN**				Gilligan, Andrew Bernard	b: 1/3/1856, Cambridge, Mass.		d: 4/1/34, Lynn, Mass.		BR/TR, 5'6.5", 130 lbs.		Deb: 9/25/1875												
1875	Atl-n	2	8	2	2	0	0	0		0		.250	.250	.250	84	-0	-0	1					/CO	0.0
1879	Cle-N	52	205	20	35	6	2	0	11	0	13	.171	.171	.220	28	-15	-15	8				1	CO/S	-1.3
1880	Cle-N	30	99	9	17	4	3	1	13	6	12	.172	.219	.303	77	-2	-2	7				7	C/OS	0.7
1881	Pro-N	46	183	19	40	7	2	0	20	9	24	.219	.255	.279	69	-6	-6	13				-4	CS/O	-0.8
1882	Pro-N	56	201	34	45	7	6	0	26	4	26	.224	.239	.318	71	-5	-5	16				8	C/S	0.7
1883	Pro-N	74	263	34	52	13	3	0	24	26	32	.198	.270	.270	63	-10	-11	20				8	*C	0.0
1884	*Pro-N	82	294	47	72	13	2	1	38	35	41	.245	.325	.313	104	2	3	31				10	*C/31	1.7
1885	Pro-N	71	252	23	54	7	3	0	12	23	33	.214	.280	.266	80	-6	-4	19				-6	C/SO2	-0.3
1886	Was-N	81	273	23	52	9	2	0	17	39	35	.190	.292	.238	66	-11	-8	21	6			-16	CO/S3	-1.6
1887	Was-N	28	90	7	18	2	0	1	6	5	18	.200	.242	.256	42	-7	-6	6	2			-1	C/SO	-0.3
1888	Det-N	1	5	1	1	0	0	0	0	0		.200	.200	.200	29	-0	-0	0	0			0	/C	0.0
Total	10	521	1865	215	386	68	23	3	167	147	235	.207	.265	.273	71	-62	-56	141	8			7	C/OS321	-1.2
■ **GRANT GILLIS**				Gillis, Grant	b: 1/24/01, Grove Hill, Ala.		d: 2/4/81, Thomasville, Ala.		BR/TR, 5'10", 165 lbs.		Deb: 9/19/27												
1927	Was-A	10	36	8	8	3	1	0	2	2	0	.222	.263	.361	61	-2	-2	3	0	0	0	-2	S	-0.2
1928	Was-A	24	87	13	22	5	1	0	10	4	5	.253	.309	.333	69	-4	-4	9	0	1	-1	-10	S/23	-1.2

YEAR	TM/L	G	AB	R	H	2B	3B	HR	RBI	BB	SO	AVG	OBP	SLG	PRO+	BR	/A	RC	SB	CS	SBR	FR	POS	TPR
1929	Bos-A	28	73	5	18	4	0	0	11	6	8	.247	.304	.301	58	-5	-4	7	0	1	-1	-3	2	-0.7
Total	3	62	196	26	48	12	2	0	23	12	13	.245	.299	.327	63	-11	-11	19	0	2	-1	-16	/2S3	-2.1

■ JIM GILMAN
Gilman, James   Deb: 7/10/1893

YEAR	TM/L	G	AB	R	H	2B	3B	HR	RBI	BB	SO	AVG	OBP	SLG	PRO+	BR	/A	RC	SB	CS	SBR	FR	POS	TPR
1893	Cle-N	2	7	1	2	0	0	0	1	0	2	.286	.286	.286	50	-0	-1	1	0			-1	/3	0.0

■ PIT GILMAN
Gilman, Pitkin Clark   b: 3/14/1864, Laporte, Ohio   d: 8/17/50, Elyria, Ohio   BL/TL,   Deb: 9/18/1884

YEAR	TM/L	G	AB	R	H	2B	3B	HR	RBI	BB	SO	AVG	OBP	SLG	PRO+	BR	/A	RC	SB	CS	SBR	FR	POS	TPR
1884	Cle-N	2	10	0	1	0	0	0	0	0	3	.100	.100	.100	-36	-2	-2	0				0	/O	-0.1

■ GROVER GILMORE
Gilmore, Ernest Grover   b: 11/1/1888, Chicago, Ill.   d: 11/25/19, Sioux City, Iowa   BL/TR, 5'9.5", 170 lbs.   Deb: 4/18/14

YEAR	TM/L	G	AB	R	H	2B	3B	HR	RBI	BB	SO	AVG	OBP	SLG	PRO+	BR	/A	RC	SB	CS	SBR	FR	POS	TPR
1914	KC-F	139	530	91	152	25	5	1	32	37	108	.287	.337	.358	103	-1	2	76	23			3	*O	-0.1
1915	KC-F	119	411	53	117	22	15	1	47	26	50	.285	.347	.418	131	13	15	70	19			7	*O	1.7
Total	2	258	941	144	269	47	20	2	79	63	158	.286	.341	.385	115	12	17	146	42			10	O	1.6

■ JIM GILMORE
Gilmore, James   b: 5/1853, Baltimore, Md.   d: 11/18/28, Baltimore, Md.   Deb: 4/26/1875

YEAR	TM/L	G	AB	R	H	2B	3B	HR	RBI	BB	SO	AVG	OBP	SLG	PRO+	BR	/A	RC	SB	CS	SBR	FR	POS	TPR
1875	Was-n	3	12	2	3	0	0	0			0	.250	.250	.250	76	-0	-0	1					/C23	0.0

■ GILROY
Gilroy   Deb: 9/07/1874

YEAR	TM/L	G	AB	R	H	2B	3B	HR	RBI	BB	SO	AVG	OBP	SLG	PRO+	BR	/A	RC	SB	CS	SBR	FR	POS	TPR
1874	Chi-n	8	39	4	8	1	0	0			0	.205	.205	.231	38	-3	-3	2					/C	-0.1
1875	Ath-n	2	6	0	1	0	0	0			0	.167	.167	.167	14	-0	-1	0					/CO	0.0
Total	2 n	10	45	4	9	1	0	0			0	.200	.200	.222	35	-3	-3	2					/CO	-0.1

■ TINSLEY GINN
Ginn, Tinsley Rucker   b: 9/26/1891, Royston, Ga.   d: 8/30/31, Atlanta, Ga.   BL/TR, 5'9", 180 lbs.   Deb: 6/27/14

YEAR	TM/L	G	AB	R	H	2B	3B	HR	RBI	BB	SO	AVG	OBP	SLG	PRO+	BR	/A	RC	SB	CS	SBR	FR	POS	TPR
1914	Cle-A	2	1	0	0	0	0	0	0	0	0	.000	.000	.000	-96	-0	-0	0	0			0	/O	0.0

■ JOE GINSBERG
Ginsberg, Myron Nathan   b: 10/11/26, New York, N.Y.   BL/TR, 5'11", 180 lbs.   Deb: 9/15/48

YEAR	TM/L	G	AB	R	H	2B	3B	HR	RBI	BB	SO	AVG	OBP	SLG	PRO+	BR	/A	RC	SB	CS	SBR	FR	POS	TPR
1948	Det-A	11	36	7	13	0	0	0	1	3	1	.361	.410	.361	103	0	0	5	0	0	0	-2	C	0.0
1950	Det-A	36	95	12	22	6	0	0	12	11	6	.232	.318	.295	56	-6	-6	10	1	0	0	-4	C	-0.7
1951	Det-A	102	304	44	79	10	2	8	37	43	21	.260	.355	.385	100	1	0	43	0	2	-1	-1	C	0.4
1952	Det-A	113	307	29	68	13	2	6	36	51	21	.221	.338	.336	87	-4	-4	37	1	1	-0	-13	*C	-1.2
1953	Det-A	18	53	6	16	2	0	0	3	10	1	.302	.422	.340	109	1	1	9	0	0	0	0	C	0.2
	Cle-A	46	109	10	31	4	0	0	10	14	4	.284	.371	.321	91	-1	-1	14	0	0	0	-5	C	-0.4
	Yr	64	162	16	47	6	0	0	13	24	5	.290	.388	.327	97	0	1	23	0	0	0	-5		-0.2
1954	Cle-A	3	2	0	1	0	1	0	1	0	0	.500	.667	1.500	473	1	1	2	0	0	0	0	C	0.1
1956	KC-A	71	195	15	48	8	1	1	12	23	17	.246	.326	.313	69	-8	-8	19	1	1	-0	-2	C	-0.9
	Bal-A	15	28	0	2	0	0	0	2	2	4	.071	.133	.071	-48	-6	-6	0	0	0	0	-0	/C	-0.5
	Yr	86	223	15	50	8	1	1	14	25	21	.224	.302	.283	56	-14	-14	19	1	1	-0	-2		-1.4
1957	Bal-A	85	175	15	48	8	2	1	18	18	19	.274	.349	.360	100	-1	0	23	2	1	0	1	C	0.5
1958	Bal-A	61	109	4	23	1	0	3	16	13	14	.211	.306	.303	72	-5	-4	11	0	0	0	3	C	0.3
1959	Bal-A	65	166	14	30	2	0	1	14	21	13	.181	.273	.211	35	-14	-14	10	1	0	0	6	C	-0.3
1960	Bal-A	14	30	3	8	1	0	0	6	6	1	.267	.389	.300	90	-0	-0	4	0	0	0	2	C	0.2
	Chi-A	28	75	8	19	4	0	0	9	10	8	.253	.349	.307	80	-2	-2	9	1	0	0	4	C	0.4
	Yr	42	105	11	27	5	0	0	15	16	9	.257	.361	.305	83	-2	-2	13	1	0	0	6		0.6
1961	Chi-A	6	3	0	0	0	0	0	0	1	2	.000	.250	.000	-27	-1	-1	0	0	0	0	0	/C	0.0
	Bos-A	19	24	1	6	0	0	0	5	0	2	.250	.250	.250	33	-2	-2	1	0	0	0	-1	/C	-0.2
	Yr	25	27	1	6	0	0	0	5	1	4	.222	.250	.222	27	-3	-3	1	0	0	0	-1		-0.2
1962	NY-N	2	5	0	0	0	0	0	0	0	2	.000	.000	.000	-98	-1	-1	0	0	0	0	1	/C	0.0
Total	13	695	1716	168	414	59	8	20	182	226	135	.241	.334	.320	79	-48	-46	198	7	5	-1	-10	C	-2.4

■ AL GIONFRIDDO
Gionfriddo, Albert Francis   b: 3/8/22, Dysart, Pa.   BL/TL, 5'6", 165 lbs.   Deb: 9/23/44

YEAR	TM/L	G	AB	R	H	2B	3B	HR	RBI	BB	SO	AVG	OBP	SLG	PRO+	BR	/A	RC	SB	CS	SBR	FR	POS	TPR
1944	Pit-N	4	6	0	1	0	0	0	0	1	1	.167	.286	.167	28	-1	-1	0	0			0	/O	0.0
1945	Pit-N	122	409	74	116	18	9	2	42	60	22	.284	.377	.386	108	8	6	64	12			-14	*O	-1.2
1946	Pit-N	64	102	11	26	2	2	0	10	14	5	.255	.345	.314	85	-1	-2	12	1			0	O	-0.1
1947	Pit-N	1	1	0	0	0	0	0	0	0	0	.000	.000	.000	-97	-0	-0	0	0			0	H	0.0
	*Bro-N	37	62	10	11	2	1	0	6	16	11	.177	.346	.242	57	-3	-3	7	2			-1	O	-0.4
	Yr	38	63	10	11	2	1	0	6	16	11	.175	.342	.238	54	-3	-4	7	2			-1		-0.4
Total	4	228	580	95	154	22	12	2	58	91	39	.266	.366	.355	97	3	0	83	15			-15	O	-1.7

■ TOMMY GIORDANO
Giordano, Thomas Arthur "T-Bone"   b: 10/9/25, Newark, N.J.   BR/TR, 6', 175 lbs.   Deb: 9/11/53

YEAR	TM/L	G	AB	R	H	2B	3B	HR	RBI	BB	SO	AVG	OBP	SLG	PRO+	BR	/A	RC	SB	CS	SBR	FR	POS	TPR
1953	Phi-A	11	40	6	7	2	0	2	5	5	6	.175	.267	.375	69	-2	-2	4	0	1	-1	1	2	0.0

■ JOE GIRARDI
Girardi, Joseph Elliott   b: 10/14/64, Peoria, Ill.   BR/TR, 5'11", 195 lbs.   Deb: 4/04/89

YEAR	TM/L	G	AB	R	H	2B	3B	HR	RBI	BB	SO	AVG	OBP	SLG	PRO+	BR	/A	RC	SB	CS	SBR	FR	POS	TPR
1989	*Chi-N	59	157	15	39	10	0	1	14	11	26	.248	.306	.331	76	-4	-5	15	2	1	0	14	C	1.3
1990	Chi-N	133	419	36	113	24	2	1	38	17	50	.270	.303	.344	71	-13	-18	40	8	3	1	-7	*C	-1.7
Total	2	192	576	51	152	34	2	2	52	28	76	.264	.304	.340	73	-17	-23	56	10	4	1	7	C	-0.4

■ TONY GIULIANI
Giuliani, Angelo John   b: 11/24/12, St.Paul, Minn.   BR/TR, 5'11", 175 lbs.   Deb: 4/18/36

YEAR	TM/L	G	AB	R	H	2B	3B	HR	RBI	BB	SO	AVG	OBP	SLG	PRO+	BR	/A	RC	SB	CS	SBR	FR	POS	TPR
1936	StL-A	71	198	17	43	3	0	0	13	11	13	.217	.258	.232	21	-24	-25	12	0	0	0	5	C	-1.2
1937	StL-A	19	53	6	16	1	0	0	3	3	3	.302	.339	.321	67	-3	-3	6	0	0	0	0	C	0.0
1938	Was-A	46	115	10	25	4	0	0	15	8	3	.217	.268	.252	33	-12	-11	8	1	0	0	0	C	-0.8
1939	Was-A	54	172	20	43	6	2	0	18	4	7	.250	.267	.308	50	-14	-12	13	0	1	-1	2	C	-0.6
1940	Bro-N	1	1	0	0	0	0	0	0	0	0	.000	.000	.000	-94	-0	-0	0	0			0	/C	0.0
1941	Bro-N	3	2	0	0	0	0	0	0	0	0	.000	.000	.000	-96	-1	-1	0	0			1	/C	0.1
1943	Was-A	49	133	5	30	4	1	0	20	12	14	.226	.290	.271	67	-6	-5	11	0	1	-1	-0	C	-0.3
Total	7	243	674	58	157	18	3	0	69	38	40	.233	.274	.269	42	-60	-57	50	1	2		7	C	-2.8

■ JIM GLADD
Gladd, James Walter   b: 10/2/22, Ft.Gibson, Okla.   d: 11/8/77, Long Beach, Cal.   BR/TR, 6'2", 190 lbs.   Deb: 9/09/46

YEAR	TM/L	G	AB	R	H	2B	3B	HR	RBI	BB	SO	AVG	OBP	SLG	PRO+	BR	/A	RC	SB	CS	SBR	FR	POS	TPR
1946	NY-N	4	11	0	1	0	0	0	0	1	4	.091	.167	.091	-26	-2	-2	0	0			4	/C	0.2

■ DAN GLADDEN
Gladden, Clinton Daniel   b: 7/7/57, San Jose, Cal.   BR/TR, 5'11", 180 lbs.   Deb: 9/05/83

YEAR	TM/L	G	AB	R	H	2B	3B	HR	RBI	BB	SO	AVG	OBP	SLG	PRO+	BR	/A	RC	SB	CS	SBR	FR	POS	TPR
1983	SF-N	18	63	6	14	2	0	1	9	5	11	.222	.279	.302	63	-3	-3	4	4	3	-1	2	O	-0.1
1984	SF-N	86	342	71	120	17	2	4	31	33	37	.351	.411	.447	146	20	21	64	31	16	-0	6	O	2.4
1985	SF-N	142	502	64	122	15	8	7	41	40	78	.243	.308	.347	87	-12	-9	54	32	15	1	-6	*O	-1.7
1986	SF-N	102	351	55	97	16	1	4	29	39	59	.276	.357	.362	104	1	3	49	27	10	2	9	O	1.2
1987	*Min-A	121	438	69	109	21	2	8	38	38	72	.249	.313	.361	75	-14	-16	50	25	9	2	4	*O/D	-1.1
1988	Min-A	141	576	91	155	32	6	11	62	46	74	.269	.327	.403	100	2	0	78	28	8	4	12	*O/23P	1.3
1989	Min-A	121	461	69	136	23	3	8	46	23	53	.295	.335	.410	102	5	1	64	23	7	3	1	*O/PD	0.3
1990	Min-A	136	534	64	147	27	6	5	40	26	67	.275	.316	.376	87	-6	-10	60	25	9	2	7	*O/D	-0.2
Total	8	867	3267	489	900	153	28	48	296	250	451	.275	.333	.384	97	-8	-14	424	195	77	12	35	O/DP32	2.1

■ BUCK GLADMAN
Gladman, John H.   b: 1864, Washington, D.C.   Deb: 7/07/1883

YEAR	TM/L	G	AB	R	H	2B	3B	HR	RBI	BB	SO	AVG	OBP	SLG	PRO+	BR	/A	RC	SB	CS	SBR	FR	POS	TPR
1883	Phi-N	1	4	1	0	0	0	0			2	.000	.000	.000	-99	-1	-1	0				-1	/3	0.0
1884	Was-a	56	224	17	35	5	3	1			3	.156	.178	.219	35	-16	-12	9				-3	3/OS	-1.3
1886	Was-N	44	152	17	21	5	1	1	15	12	30	.138	.201	.230	33	-13	-11	8	5			-7	3	-1.4
Total	3 n	101	380	35	56	10	6	2	15	15	32	.147	.186	.221	32	-30	-24	17	5			-10	/3OS	-2.7

YEAR	TM/L	G	AB	R	H	2B	3B	HR	RBI	BB	SO	AVG	OBP	SLG	PRO+	BR	/A	RC	SB	CS	SBR	FR	POS	TPR

■ ROLAND GLADU
Gladu, Roland Edouard b: 5/10/13, Montreal, Que., Can BL/TR, 5'8.5", 185 lbs. Deb: 4/18/44

YEAR	TM/L	G	AB	R	H	2B	3B	HR	RBI	BB	SO	AVG	OBP	SLG	PRO+	BR	/A	RC	SB	CS	SBR	FR	POS	TPR
1944	Bos-N	21	66	5	16	2	1	1	7	3	8	.242	.275	.348	72	-2	-3	6	0			-4	3/O	-0.5

■ JACK GLASSCOCK
Glasscock, John Wesley "Pebbly Jack" b: 7/22/1859, Wheeling, W.Va. d: 2/24/47, Wheeling, W.Va. BR/TR, 5'8", 160 lbs. Deb: 5/01/1879 M

YEAR	TM/L	G	AB	R	H	2B	3B	HR	RBI	BB	SO	AVG	OBP	SLG	PRO+	BR	/A	RC	SB	CS	SBR	FR	POS	TPR
1879	Cle-N	80	325	31	68	9	3	0	29	6	24	.209	.224	.255	58	-14	-14	19				-6	*23	-1.1
1880	Cle-N	77	296	37	72	13	3	0	27	2	21	.243	.248	.307	89	-4	-3	23				7	*S	0.7
1881	Cle-N	85	335	49	86	9	5	0	33	15	8	.257	.289	.313	94	-4	-1	31				9	*S/2	1.3
1882	Cle-N	84	358	66	104	27	9	4	46	13	9	.291	.315	.450	147	16	18	52				24	*S/3	4.4
1883	Cle-N	96	383	67	110	19	6	0	46	13	23	.287	.311	.368	107	2	3	45				18	*S/2	2.1
1884	Cle-N	72	281	45	70	4	4	1	22	25	16	.249	.310	.302	91	-1	-3	27				27	S/2P	2.7
	Cin-U	38	172	48	72	9	5	2		8		.419	.444	.564	221	24	22	44	0			1	S/2	2.0
1885	StL-N	111	446	66	125	18	3	1	40	29	10	.280	.324	.341	123	8	12	51				19	*S/2	3.4
1886	StL-N	121	486	96	158	29	7	3	40	38	13	.325	.374	.432	154	26	31	95	38			22	*S/O	4.5
1887	Ind-N	122	483	91	142	18	7	0	40	41	8	.294	.361	.360	107	4	7	87	62			35	*S/P	3.1
1888	Ind-N	113	442	63	119	17	3	1	45	14	17	.269	.302	.328	101	1	0	60	48			11	*S/2P	1.5
1889	Ind-N	134	582	128	**205**	40	3	7	85	31	10	.352	.390	.467	138	30	28	132	57			35	*S/2PM	**5.8**
1890	NY-N	124	512	91	**172**	32	9	1	66	41	8	**.336**	.395	.439	145	29	29	113	54			20	*S	4.1
1891	NY-N	97	369	46	89	12	6	0	55	36	11	.241	.317	.306	87	-7	-5	46	29			-2	*S	-0.1
1892	StL-N	139	566	83	151	27	5	3	72	44	19	.267	.327	.348	112	4	8	75	26			6	*SM	1.9
1893	StL-N	48	195	32	56	8	1	1	26	25	3	.287	.382	.354	98	1	1	35	20			-7	S	-0.3
	Pit-N	66	293	49	100	7	11	1	74	17	4	.341	.385	.451	126	9	10	58	16			12	S	2.0
	Yr	114	488	81	156	15	12	2	100	42	7	.320	.384	.412	115	10	11	93	36			6		1.7
1894	Pit-N	86	332	46	93	10	7	1	63	31	4	.280	.349	.361	74	-14	-13	49	18			8	S	0.5
1895	Lou-N	18	74	9	25	3	1	1	6	3	1	.338	.387	.446	124	2	3	14	1			2	S/1	0.5
	Was-N	25	100	20	23	2	0	0	10	7	3	.230	.300	.250	45	-8	-8	9	3			6	S	0.0
	Yr	43	174	29	48	5	1	1	16	10	4	.276	.337	.333	78	-6	-5	21	4			9		0.5
Total	17	1736	7030	1163	2040	313	98	27	825	439	212	.290	.337	.374	114	103	124	1064	372			248	*S/231PO	38.5

■ TOMMY GLAVIANO
Glaviano, Thomas Giatano "Rabbit" b: 10/26/23, Sacramento, Cal. BR/TR, 5'9", 175 lbs. Deb: 4/19/49

YEAR	TM/L	G	AB	R	H	2B	3B	HR	RBI	BB	SO	AVG	OBP	SLG	PRO+	BR	/A	RC	SB	CS	SBR	FR	POS	TPR
1949	StL-N	87	258	32	69	16	1	6	36	41	35	.267	.380	.407	106	5	4	42	0			14	3/2	1.8
1950	StL-N	115	410	92	117	29	2	11	44	90	74	.285	.421	.446	122	21	18	85	6			6	*3/2S	2.3
1951	StL-N	54	104	20	19	4	0	1	4	26	18	.183	.356	.250	66	-4	-4	12	3	0	1	-2	O/2	-0.4
1952	StL-N	80	162	30	39	5	1	3	19	27	26	.241	.366	.340	97	0	0	21	0	0	0	4	3/2	0.6
1953	Phi-N	53	74	17	15	1	2	3	5	24	20	.203	.410	.392	111	2	2	14	2	0	1	-2	32/S	0.1
Total	5	389	1008	191	259	55	6	24	108	208	173	.257	.395	.395	108	26	21	174	11	0		20	3/2OS	4.4

■ HARRY GLEASON
Gleason, Harry Gilbert b: 3/28/1875, Camden, N.J. d: 10/21/61, Camden, N.J. TR, 5'6", 160 lbs. Deb: 9/27/01

YEAR	TM/L	G	AB	R	H	2B	3B	HR	RBI	BB	SO	AVG	OBP	SLG	PRO+	BR	/A	RC	SB	CS	SBR	FR	POS	TPR
1901	Bos-A	1	1	0	1	0	0	0	0	0		1.000	1.000	1.000	470	0	0	2	1			1	/3	0.1
1902	Bos-A	71	240	30	54	5	5	2	25	10		.225	.265	.313	59	-13	-14	23	6			-0	3O/2	-1.5
1903	Bos-A	6	13	3	2	1	0	0	2	0		.154	.154	.231	14	-1	-1	0	0			-1	/3	-0.2
1904	StL-A	46	155	10	33	7	1	0	6	4		.213	.233	.271	65	-7	-6	11	1			-2	S3/2O	-0.8
1905	StL-A	150	535	45	116	11	5	1	57	34		.217	.264	.262	72	-18	-15	46	23			-15	*3/2	-2.7
Total	5	274	944	88	206	24	11	3	90	48		.218	.258	.276	67	-39	-36	82	31			-18	3/OS2	-5.1

■ JACK GLEASON
Gleason, John Day b: 7/14/1854, St.Louis, Mo. d: 9/4/44, St.Louis, Mo. BR/TR, 170 lbs. Deb: 10/02/1877

YEAR	TM/L	G	AB	R	H	2B	3B	HR	RBI	BB	SO	AVG	OBP	SLG	PRO+	BR	/A	RC	SB	CS	SBR	FR	POS	TPR
1877	StL-N	1	4	0	1	0	0	0	0	0	1	.250	.250	.250	61	-0	-0	0				0	/O	0.0
1882	StL-a	78	331	53	84	10	1	2		**27**		.254	.310	.308	105	4	2	32				2	*3/O2	0.1
1883	StL-a	9	34	2	8	0	0	0		4		.235	.316	.235	76	-1	-1	3				0	/O3	0.0
	Lou-a	84	355	69	105	11	4	2		25		.296	.342	.366	139	12	16	46				-33	*3/S	-1.3
	Yr	93	389	71	113	11	4	2		29		.290	.340	.355	132	11	15	48				-33		-1.3
1884	StL-U	92	395	90	128	30	2	4		23		.324	.361	.441	164	28	26	64	0			-6	*3	1.9
1885	StL-N	2	7	0	1	0	0	0	0	0	1	.143	.143	.143	-8	-1	-1	0				-0	/3	0.0
1886	Phi-a	77	299	39	56	8	7	1		16		.187	.255	.271	65	-11	-12	23	8			-5	3	-1.2
Total	6	343	1425	253	383	59	14	9	0	95	2	.269	.319	.349	119	31	30	169	8			-42	3/OS2	-0.5

■ ROY GLEASON
Gleason, Roy William b: 4/9/43, Melrose Park, Ill. BB/TR, 6'5.5", 220 lbs. Deb: 9/03/63

YEAR	TM/L	G	AB	R	H	2B	3B	HR	RBI	BB	SO	AVG	OBP	SLG	PRO+	BR	/A	RC	SB	CS	SBR	FR	POS	TPR
1963	LA-N	8	1	3	1	1	0	0	0	0	0	1.000	1.000	2.000	795	1	1	2	0	0	0	0	H	0.1

■ BILL GLEASON
Gleason, William G. "Will" b: 11/12/1858, St.Louis, Mo. d: 7/21/32, St.Louis, Mo. BR/TR, 5'8", 170 lbs. Deb: 5/02/1882 U

YEAR	TM/L	G	AB	R	H	2B	3B	HR	RBI	BB	SO	AVG	OBP	SLG	PRO+	BR	/A	RC	SB	CS	SBR	FR	POS	TPR
1882	StL-a	79	347	63	100	11	6	1		6		.288	.300	.363	118	8	6	39				9	*S	1.5
1883	StL-a	98	425	81	122	21	9	2		16		.287	.313	.393	119	12	8	54				-1	*S	0.2
1884	StL-a	110	472	97	127	21	7	1		28		.269	.326	.350	119	13	10	55				-17	*S/3	-0.7
1885	*StL-a	112	472	79	119	9	5	3		29		.252	.316	.311	97	2	-2	48	19			-41	*S	-3.7
1886	*StL-a	125	524	97	141	18	5	0		43		.269	.333	.323	103	6	2	64	29			-29	*S	-1.8
1887	*StL-a	135	598	135	172	19	1	0		41		.288	.342	.323	79	-8	-20	76	23			-10	*S	-2.5
1888	Phi-a	123	499	55	112	10	2	0	61	12		.224	.256	.253	66	-19	-18	40	27			-13	*S/31	-2.3
1889	Lou-a	16	58	6	14	2	0	0	5	4	1	.241	.302	.276	68	-2	-2	5	1			-3	S	-0.2
Total	8	798	3395	613	907	111	35	7	66	179	1	.267	.314	.327	97	11	-17	380	70			-105	S/31	-9.5

■ KID GLEASON
Gleason, William J. b: 10/26/1866, Camden, N.J. d: 1/2/33, Philadelphia, Pa. BB/TR, 5'7", 158 lbs. Deb: 4/20/1888 MC

YEAR	TM/L	G	AB	R	H	2B	3B	HR	RBI	BB	SO	AVG	OBP	SLG	PRO+	BR	/A	RC	SB	CS	SBR	FR	POS	TPR
1888	Phi-N	24	83	4	17	2	0	0	5	3	16	.205	.233	.229	47	-5	-5	5	3			-3	P/O	0.0
1889	Phi-N	30	99	11	25	5	0	0	8	8	12	.253	.308	.303	67	-4	-5	11	4			-0	P/O2	0.0
1890	Phi-N	63	224	22	47	3	0	0	17	12	21	.210	.250	.223	39	-17	-18	15	10			-1	P/2	0.0
1891	Phi-N	65	214	31	53	5	2	0	17	20	17	.248	.318	.290	77	-5	-6	22	6			-6	P/OS	0.0
1892	StL-N	66	233	35	50	4	2	3	25	34	23	.215	.315	.288	88	-4	-2	24	7			4	PO/21	0.0
1893	StL-N	59	199	25	51	6	4	0	20	19	8	.256	.327	.327	75	-7	-7	22	2			-0	PO/S	0.0
1894	StL-N	9	28	3	7	0	1	0	1	2	1	.250	.300	.321	51	-2	-2	3	0			2	/P1	0.0
	*Bal-N	26	86	22	30	5	1	0	17	7	2	.349	.398	.430	97	0	0	15	1			-2	P/1	0.0
	Yr	35	114	25	37	5	2	0	18	9	3	.325	.374	.404	86	-2	-3	18	1			0		0.0
1895	*Bal-N	112	421	90	130	14	12	0	74	33	18	.309	.366	.399	96	-0	-2	70	19			-19	23/PO	-1.1
1896	NY-N	133	541	79	162	17	5	4	89	42	13	.299	.352	.372	95	-5	-3	89	46			3	*2/3O	0.3
1897	NY-N	131	540	85	172	16	4	1	106	26		.319	.353	.369	96	-5	-3	88	43			1	*2/S	0.7
1898	NY-N	150	570	78	126	8	5	0	62	39		.221	.278	.253	56	-32	-30	47	21			19	*2/S	-0.3
1899	NY-N	146	576	72	152	14	4	0	59	24		.264	.293	.302	68	-27	-24	61	29			26	*2	0.9
1900	NY-N	111	420	60	104	11	3	1	29	17		.248	.279	.295	63	-22	-20	42	23			14	*2/S	0.5
1901	Det-A	135	547	82	150	16	12	3	75	41		.274	.327	.364	89	-5	-8	79	32			6	*2	-0.7
1902	Det-A	118	441	42	109	11	4	1	38	25		.247	.292	.297	64	-20	-21	46	17			6	*2	-1.0
1903	Phi-N	106	412	65	119	19	6	1	49	23		.289	.322	.360	101	-2	0	56	12			-4	*2/O	0.1
1904	Phi-N	153	587	61	161	23	6	0	42	37		.274	.317	.334	107	2	4	73	17			1	*2/3	1.0
1905	Phi-N	155	608	95	150	17	7	1	50	45		.247	.299	.303	84	-14	-11	66	16			-8	*2	-0.9
1906	Phi-N	135	494	47	112	17	2	0	34	36		.227	.279	.249	73	-15	-15	47	17			-29	*2	-5.0
1907	Phi-N	36	126	11	18	3	0	0	6	7		.143	.188	.167	13	-12	-12	6	3			-2	2/1SO	-1.5
1908	Phi-N	2	1	0	0	0	0	0	0	0		.000	.000	.000	-97	-0	-0	0	0			0	/2O	0.0

YEAR	TM/L	G	AB	R	H	2B	3B	HR	RBI	BB	SO	AVG	OBP	SLG	PRO+	BR	/A	RC	SB	CS	SBR	FR	POS	TPR
1912	Chi-A	1	2	0	1	0	0	0	0	0	0	.500	.500	.500	192	-0	0	0	0			0	/2	0.0
Total	22	1966	7452	1020	1944	216	80	15	823	500	131	.261	.310	.317	80	-201	-189	889	328			8	*2P/OS31	-7.5

■ BILLY GLEASON
Gleason, William Patrick b: 9/6/1894, Chicago, Ill. d: 1/9/57, Holyoke, Mass. BR/TR, 5'6.5", 157 lbs. Deb: 9/25/16

YEAR	TM/L	G	AB	R	H	2B	3B	HR	RBI	BB	SO	AVG	OBP	SLG	PRO+	BR	/A	RC	SB	CS	SBR	FR	POS	TPR
1916	Pit-N	1	2	0	0	0	0	0	0	0	0	.000	.000	.000	-99	-0	-0	0	0			0	/2	0.0
1917	Pit-N	13	42	3	7	1	0	0	0	5	5	.167	.255	.190	36	-3	-3	2	1			-5	2	-0.8
1921	StL-A	26	74	6	19	0	1	0	8	6	6	.257	.329	.284	54	-4	-5	7	0	1	-1	-5	2	-0.8
Total	3	40	118	9	26	1	1	0	8	11	11	.220	.298	.246	47	-8	-9	9	1	1		-10	/2	-1.6

■ JIM GLEESON
Gleeson, James Joseph "Gee Gee" b: 3/5/12, Kansas City, Mo. BB/TR, 6'1", 191 lbs. Deb: 4/25/36 C

YEAR	TM/L	G	AB	R	H	2B	3B	HR	RBI	BB	SO	AVG	OBP	SLG	PRO+	BR	/A	RC	SB	CS	SBR	FR	POS	TPR
1936	Cle-A	41	139	26	36	9	2	4	12	18	17	.259	.344	.439	91	-2	-2	22	2	1	0	-3	O	-0.5
1939	Chi-N	111	332	43	74	19	6	4	45	39	46	.223	.308	.352	76	-11	-12	38	7			-4	O	-1.7
1940	Chi-N	129	485	76	152	39	11	5	61	54	52	.313	.389	.470	139	24	26	91	4			-1	*O	2.1
1941	Cin-N	102	301	47	70	10	0	3	34	45	30	.233	.340	.296	80	-6	-6	33	7			-9	O	-1.8
1942	Cin-N	9	20	3	4	0	0	0	2	2	2	.200	.304	.200	49	-1	-1	2	0			-0	/O	-0.1
Total	5	392	1277	195	336	77	19	16	154	158	147	.263	.350	.391	101	4	4	185	20	1		-17	O	-2.0

■ FRANK GLEICH
Gleich, Frank Elmer "Inch" b: 3/7/1894, Columbus, Ohio d: 3/27/49, Columbus, Ohio BL/TR, 5'11", 175 lbs. Deb: 9/17/19

YEAR	TM/L	G	AB	R	H	2B	3B	HR	RBI	BB	SO	AVG	OBP	SLG	PRO+	BR	/A	RC	SB	CS	SBR	FR	POS	TPR
1919	NY-A	5	4	0	1	0	0	0	1	1	0	.250	.400	.250	84	-0	-0	0				-2	/O	-0.2
1920	NY-A	24	41	6	5	0	0	0	3	6	10	.122	.234	.122	-4	-6	-6	2	0	0	0	-4	/O	-1.1
Total	2	29	45	6	6	0	0	0	4	7	10	.133	.250	.133	4	-6	-6	2	0	0		-6	/O	-1.3

■ BOB GLENALVIN
Glenalvin, Robert J. (b: Robert J. Dowling) b: 1/17/1867, Indianapolis, Ind. d: 3/24/44, Detroit, Mich. TR , Deb: 7/12/1890

YEAR	TM/L	G	AB	R	H	2B	3B	HR	RBI	BB	SO	AVG	OBP	SLG	PRO+	BR	/A	RC	SB	CS	SBR	FR	POS	TPR
1890	Chi-N	66	250	43	67	10	3	4	26	19	31	.268	.337	.380	107	3	2	43	30			-16	2	-1.0
1893	Chi-N	16	61	11	21	3	1	0	12	7	3	.344	.412	.426	127	2	3	14	7			-5	2	-0.1
Total	2	82	311	54	88	13	4	4	38	26	34	.283	.352	.389	111	6	4	57	37			-21	/2	-1.1

■ ED GLENN
Glenn, Edward C. "Mouse" b: 9/19/1860, Richmond, Va. d: 2/10/1892, Richmond, Va. BR/TR, 5'10", 160 lbs. Deb: 8/05/1884

YEAR	TM/L	G	AB	R	H	2B	3B	HR	RBI	BB	SO	AVG	OBP	SLG	PRO+	BR	/A	RC	SB	CS	SBR	FR	POS	TPR
1884	Ric-a	43	175	26	43	2	4	1		5		.246	.271	.320	96	-1	-1	16				5	O	0.3
1886	Pit-a	71	277	32	53	6	5	0		17		.191	.241	.249	55	-14	-14	22	19			0	O	-1.3
1888	KC-a	3	8	0	0	0	0	0	0	0		.000	.200	.000	-30	-1	-1	0	1			-0	/O	0.0
	Bos-N	20	65	8	10	0	2	0	3	2	8	.154	.203	.215	34	-5	-5	3	0			2	O/3	-0.2
Total	3	137	525	66	106	8	11	1	3	24	8	.202	.245	.265	64	-21	-21	40	20			7	O/3	-1.2

■ ED GLENN
Glenn, Edward D. b: 1874, Ludlow, Ky. d: 12/6/11, Ludlow, Ky. Deb: 9/07/1898

YEAR	TM/L	G	AB	R	H	2B	3B	HR	RBI	BB	SO	AVG	OBP	SLG	PRO+	BR	/A	RC	SB	CS	SBR	FR	POS	TPR
1898	Was-N	1	4	0	0	0	0	0	0	0	0	.000	.000	.000	-99	-1	-1	0	0			-1	/S	-0.1
	NY-N	2	4	1	1	0	0	0	0	0	3	.250	.571	.250	146	1	1	1	1			-2	/S	-0.1
	Yr	3	8	1	1	0	0	0	0	0	3	.125	.364	.125	45	-0	-0	1	1			-3		-0.2
1902	Chi-N	2	7	0	0	0	0	0	0	0	1	.000	.125	.000	-62	-1	-1	0	0			-1	/S	-0.2
Total	2	5	15	1	1	0	0	0	0	0	4	.067	.263	.067	0	-2	-2	1	1			-4	/S	-0.4

■ HARRY GLENN
Glenn, Harry Melville "Husky" b: 6/9/1890, Shelburn, Ind. d: 10/12/18, St.Paul, Minn. BR/TR, 6'1", 200 lbs. Deb: 4/14/15

YEAR	TM/L	G	AB	R	H	2B	3B	HR	RBI	BB	SO	AVG	OBP	SLG	PRO+	BR	/A	RC	SB	CS	SBR	FR	POS	TPR
1915	StL-N	6	16	1	5	0	0	0	1	3	0	.313	.421	.313	123	1	1	2	0			-1	/C	0.0

■ JOHN GLENN
Glenn, John b: 7/10/28, Moultrie, Ga. BR/TR, 6'3", 180 lbs. Deb: 6/16/60

YEAR	TM/L	G	AB	R	H	2B	3B	HR	RBI	BB	SO	AVG	OBP	SLG	PRO+	BR	/A	RC	SB	CS	SBR	FR	POS	TPR
1960	StL-N	32	31	4	8	0	1	0	5	0	9	.258	.258	.323	53	-2	-2	3	0	0	0	1	O	-0.1

■ JOHN GLENN
Glenn, John W. b: 1849, Rochester, N.Y. d: 11/10/1888, Sandy Hill, N.Y. BR/TR, 5'8.5", 169 lbs. Deb: 5/13/1871

YEAR	TM/L	G	AB	R	H	2B	3B	HR	RBI	BB	SO	AVG	OBP	SLG	PRO+	BR	/A	RC	SB	CS	SBR	FR	POS	TPR
1871	Oly-n	26	120	25	37	3	2	0	21	3	1	.308	.325	.367	104	-0	1	15	1				*O	0.2
1872	Oly-n	9	40	5	6	2	0	0		0		.150	.150	.200	7	-4	-4	1					/O	-0.1
	Nat-n	1	4	0	2	0	0	0		0		.500	.500	.500	179	0	0	1					/O	0.0
	Yr	10	44	5	8	2	0	0		0		.182	.182	.227	26	-4	-3	2						-0.1
1873	Was-n	39	184	41	50	9	2	1		4		.272	.287	.359	92	-3	-1	19					*1	0.0
1874	Chi-n	55	235	33	66	8	0	0		6		.281	.299	.315	95	-1	-1	23					1O	0.0
1875	Chi-n	69	303	46	75	9	0	0		5		.248	.260	.277	85	-4	-5	22					O1	-0.3
1876	Chi-N	66	276	55	84	9	2	0	32	12	6	.304	.333	.351	115	8	3	33				-2	*O1	0.1
1877	Chi-N	50	202	31	46	6	1	0	20	8	16	.228	.257	.267	58	-8	-11	14	0			0	O1	-1.0
Total	5 n	199	886	150	236	31	4	1	21	18	1	.266	.281	.314	89	-12	-9	82					1/O	-0.2
Total	2	116	478	86	130	15	3	0	52	20	22	.272	.301	.316	90	1	-8	47				-2	/O1	-0.9

■ JOE GLENN
Glenn, Joseph Charles "Gabby" (b: Joseph Charles Gurzensky) b: 11/19/08, Dickson City, Pa. d: 5/6/85, Tunkhannock, Pa. BR/TR, 5'11", 175 lbs. Deb: 9/15/32

YEAR	TM/L	G	AB	R	H	2B	3B	HR	RBI	BB	SO	AVG	OBP	SLG	PRO+	BR	/A	RC	SB	CS	SBR	FR	POS	TPR
1932	NY-A	6	16	0	2	0	0	0	0	1	5	.125	.222	.125	-8	-3	-2	1	0	0	0	-1	/C	-0.3
1933	NY-A	5	21	1	3	0	0	0	1	0	3	.143	.143	.143	-26	-4	-4	0	0	0	0	-2	/C	-0.4
1935	NY-A	17	43	7	10	4	0	0	6	4	1	.233	.298	.326	65	-3	-2	4	0	0	0	0	C	0.0
1936	NY-A	44	129	21	35	7	0	1	20	20	10	.271	.373	.349	82	-4	-3	18	1	1	-0	3	C	0.3
1937	NY-A	25	53	6	15	2	2	0	4	10	11	.283	.397	.396	100	0	0	9	0	0	0	4	C	0.5
1938	NY-A	41	123	10	32	7	2	0	25	10	14	.260	.316	.350	67	-7	-6	14	1	0	0	0	C	-0.4
1939	StL-A	88	286	29	78	13	1	4	29	31	40	.273	.344	.367	80	-8	-8	36	4	4	-1	-13	C	-1.6
1940	Bos-A	22	47	3	6	1	0	0	4	5	7	.128	.212	.149	-5	-7	-8	1	0	0	0	-0	C	-0.5
Total	8	248	718	77	181	34	5	5	89	81	91	.252	.330	.334	69	-33	-33	84	6	5	-1	-10	C	-2.4

■ NORM GLOCKSON
Glockson, Norman Stanley b: 6/15/1894, Blue Island, Ill. d: 8/5/55, Maywood, Ill. BR/TR, 6'2", 200 lbs. Deb: 9/16/14

YEAR	TM/L	G	AB	R	H	2B	3B	HR	RBI	BB	SO	AVG	OBP	SLG	PRO+	BR	/A	RC	SB	CS	SBR	FR	POS	TPR
1914	Cin-N	7	12	0	0	0	0	0	0	1	6	.000	.077	.000	-74	-3	-3	0	0			0	/C	-0.1

■ AL GLOSSOP
Glossop, Alban b: 7/23/15, Christopher, Ill. BB/TR, 6', 170 lbs. Deb: 9/23/39

YEAR	TM/L	G	AB	R	H	2B	3B	HR	RBI	BB	SO	AVG	OBP	SLG	PRO+	BR	/A	RC	SB	CS	SBR	FR	POS	TPR
1939	NY-N	10	32	3	6	0	0	1	3	4	2	.188	.278	.281	50	-2	-2	3	0			0	2	0.0
1940	NY-N	27	91	16	19	3	0	4	8	10	16	.209	.294	.374	82	-2	-2	10	1			0	2	0.0
	Bos-N	60	148	17	35	2	1	3	14	17	22	.236	.315	.324	81	-4	-3	16	1			6	23/S	0.4
	Yr	87	239	33	54	5	1	7	22	27	38	.226	.307	.343	82	-7	-6	26	2			7		0.4
1942	Phi-N	121	454	33	102	15	1	4	40	29	35	.225	.273	.289	68	-21	-19	36	3			7	*2/3	-0.2
1943	Bro-N	87	217	28	37	9	0	3	21	28	27	.171	.268	.253	51	-13	-14	17	0			-7	S23/O	-1.7
1946	Chi-N	4	10	2	0	0	0	0	0	1	3	.000	.231	.000	-32	-2	-2	0	0			-2	/2S	-0.2
Total	5	309	952	99	199	29	2	15	86	89	105	.209	.280	.291	66	-45	-42	83	5			6	2/S3O	-1.7

■ BILL GLYNN
Glynn, William Vincent b: 7/30/25, Sussex, N.J. BL/TL, 6', 190 lbs. Deb: 9/16/49

YEAR	TM/L	G	AB	R	H	2B	3B	HR	RBI	BB	SO	AVG	OBP	SLG	PRO+	BR	/A	RC	SB	CS	SBR	FR	POS	TPR
1949	Phi-N	8	10	0	2	0	0	0	1	0	3	.200	.200	.200	8	-1	-1	0	0			0	/1	0.0
1952	Cle-A	44	92	15	25	5	0	2	7	5	16	.272	.309	.391	101	-1	-0	11	1	0	0	0	1	-0.1
1953	Cle-A	147	411	60	100	14	2	5	30	44	65	.243	.324	.309	74	-16	-14	45	1	3	-2	6	*1/O	-1.2
1954	*Cle-A	111	171	19	43	3	2	5	18	12	21	.251	.301	.380	84	-4	-4	19	3	2	-0	3	1/O	-0.4
Total	4	310	684	94	170	22	4	10	56	61	105	.249	.315	.336	79	-22	-20	75	5	5		9	1/O	-1.7

■ JOHN GOCHNAUER
Gochnauer, John Peter b: 9/12/1875, Altoona, Pa. d: 9/27/29, Altoona, Pa. BR/TR, 5'9", 160 lbs. Deb: 9/29/01

YEAR	TM/L	G	AB	R	H	2B	3B	HR	RBI	BB	SO	AVG	OBP	SLG	PRO+	BR	/A	RC	SB	CS	SBR	FR	POS	TPR
1901	Bro-N	3	11	1	4	0	0	0	2	1		.364	.417	.364	126	0	0	2	1			-0	/S	0.0
1902	Cle-A	127	459	45	85	16	4	0	37	38		.185	.247	.237	38	-39	-36	31	7			-3	*S	-2.6
1903	Cle-A	134	438	48	81	16	4	0	48	48		.185	.265	.240	55	-23	-22	35	10			-22	*S	-3.9

YEAR	TM/L	G	AB	R	H	2B	3B	HR	RBI	BB	SO	AVG	OBP	SLG	PRO+	BR	/A	RC	SB	CS	SBR	FR	POS	TPR
Total	3	264	908	94	170	32	8	0	87	87		.187	.258	.240	47	-61	-58	67	18			-26	S	-6.5

■ JOHN GODAR
Godar, John Michael b: 10/25/1864, Cincinnati, Ohio d: 6/23/49, Park Ridge, Ill. 5'9", 170 lbs. Deb: 7/08/1892

| 1892 | Bal-N | 5 | 14 | 2 | 3 | 0 | 0 | 0 | 1 | 0 | | .214 | .353 | .214 | 72 | -0 | -0 | 1 | 1 | | | -0 | /O | 0.0 |

■ DANNY GODBY
Godby, Danny Ray b: 11/4/46, Logan, W.Va. BR/TR, 6', 185 lbs. Deb: 8/10/74

| 1974 | StL-N | 13 | 13 | 2 | 2 | 0 | 0 | 0 | 1 | 3 | 4 | .154 | .313 | .154 | 34 | -1 | -1 | 1 | 0 | 0 | 0 | 2 | /O | 0.0 |

■ JOE GODDARD
Goddard, Joseph Harold b: 7/23/50, Beckley, W.Va. BR/TR, 5'11", 181 lbs. Deb: 7/31/72

| 1972 | SD-N | 12 | 35 | 0 | 7 | 2 | 0 | 0 | 2 | 5 | 9 | .200 | .300 | .257 | 64 | -2 | -1 | 3 | 0 | 0 | 0 | -2 | C | -0.2 |

■ JOHN GODWIN
Godwin, John Henry "Bunny" b: 3/10/1877, E.Liverpool, Ohio d: 5/5/56, E.Liverpool, Ohio BR/TR, 6', 190 lbs. Deb: 8/14/05

1905	Bos-A	15	43	4	14	1	0	0	10	3		.326	.370	.349	129	2	1	7	3			1	/O2	0.3
1906	Bos-A	66	193	11	36	2	1	0	15	6		.187	.211	.207	32	-15	-15	11	6			2	3SO/21	-1.2
Total	2	81	236	15	50	3	1	0	25	9		.212	.241	.233	50	-13	-13	18	9			3	/3OS21	-0.9

■ ED GOEBEL
Goebel, Edwin b: 9/1/1899, Brooklyn, N.Y. d: 8/12/59, Brooklyn, N.Y. BR/TR, 5'11", 170 lbs. Deb: 5/13/22

| 1922 | Was-A | 37 | 59 | 13 | 16 | 1 | 0 | 1 | 3 | 8 | 16 | .271 | .358 | .339 | 87 | -1 | -1 | 7 | 1 | 1 | -0 | -1 | O | -0.2 |

■ BILLY GOECKEL
Goeckel, William John b: 9/3/1871, Wilkes-Barre, Pa. d: 11/1/22, Philadelphia, Pa. BL/TL, Deb: 8/10/1899

| 1899 | Phi-N | 37 | 141 | 17 | 37 | 3 | 1 | 0 | 16 | 1 | | .262 | .283 | .298 | 64 | -7 | -7 | 14 | 6 | | | -2 | 1 | -0.7 |

■ JERRY GOFF
Goff, Jerry Leroy b: 4/12/64, San Rafael, Cal. BL/TR, 6'3", 205 lbs. Deb: 5/15/90

| 1990 | Mon-N | 52 | 119 | 14 | 27 | 1 | 0 | 3 | 7 | 21 | 36 | .227 | .343 | .311 | 82 | -2 | -2 | 14 | 0 | 2 | -1 | 1 | C/13 | 0.0 |

■ CHUCK GOGGIN
Goggin, Charles Francis b: 7/7/45, Pompano Beach, Fla. BB/TR, 5'11", 175 lbs. Deb: 9/08/72

1972	Pit-N	5	7	0	2	0	0	0	0	1	1	.286	.375	.286	92	-0	-0	1	0	0	0	0	/2	0.0
1973	Pit-N	1	1	1	1	0	0	0	0	0	0	1.000	1.000	1.000	468	0	0	1	0	0	0	0	/C	0.0
	Atl-N	64	90	18	26	5	0	0	7	9	19	.289	.354	.344	88	-0	-1	11	0	1	-1	-8	2/OSC	-0.8
	Yr	65	91	19	27	5	0	0	7	9	19	.297	.360	.352	91	-0	-1	11	0	1	-1	-8		-0.8
1974	Bos-A	2	1	0	0	0	0	0	0	0	1	.000	.000	.000	-93	-0	-0	0	0	0	0	1	/2	0.0
Total	3	72	99	19	29	5	0	0	7	10	21	.293	.358	.343	90	-0	-1	13	0	1	-1	-7	/2OSC	-0.8

■ MIKE GOLDEN
Golden, Michael Henry b: 9/11/1851, Shirley, Mass. d: 1/11/29, Rockford, Ill. BR/TR, 5'8", 168 lbs. Deb: 5/05/1875

1875	Wes-n	13	46	5	6	0	0	0		0		.130	.130	.130	-9	-5	-5	1					P	0.0
	Chi-n	39	155	16	40	3	0	0		2		.258	.268	.277	88	-2	-2	12					OP/1	0.0
	Yr	52	201	21	46	3	0	0		2		.229	.236	.244	65	-7	-7	12						0.0
1878	Mil-N	55	214	16	44	6	3	0	20	3	35	.206	.217	.262	53	-10	-12	12				-3	OP/1	-1.3

■ JONAH GOLDMAN
Goldman, Jonah John b: 8/29/06, New York, N.Y. d: 8/17/80, Palm Beach, Fla. BR/TR, 5'7", 170 lbs. Deb: 9/22/28

1928	Cle-A	7	21	1	5	1	0	0	2	3	0	.238	.333	.286	63	-1	-1	2	0	0	0	0	/S	0.0
1930	Cle-A	111	306	32	74	18	0	1	44	28	25	.242	.312	.310	56	-19	-21	31	3	5	-2	21	S3	0.7
1931	Cle-A	30	62	0	8	1	0	0	3	4	6	.129	.182	.145	-12	-10	-11	2	1	1	-0	14	S	0.5
Total	3	148	389	33	87	20	0	1	49	35	31	.224	.293	.283	46	-30	-33	35	4	6	-2	35	S/3	1.2

■ GORDON GOLDSBERRY
Goldsberry, Gordon Frederick b: 8/30/27, Sacramento, Cal. BL/TL, 6', 170 lbs. Deb: 4/20/49

1949	Chi-A	39	145	25	36	3	2	1	13	18	9	.248	.331	.317	74	-6	-5	17	2	0	1	-1	1	-0.4
1950	Chi-A	82	127	19	34	8	2	2	25	26	18	.268	.392	.409	108	2	2	22	0	2	-1	5	1/O	0.3
1951	Chi-A	10	11	4	1	0	0	0	1	2	2	.091	.231	.091	-11	-2	-2	0	0	0	0	1	/1	0.0
1952	StL-A	86	227	30	52	9	3	3	17	34	37	.229	.330	.335	83	-4	-5	27	0	2	-1	-2	1/O	-1.3
Total	4	217	510	78	123	20	7	6	56	80	66	.241	.344	.343	85	-10	-9	66	2	4	-2	2	1/O	-1.4

■ WALT GOLDSBY
Goldsby, Walton Hugh b: 12/31/1861, Louisiana d: 1/11/14, Dallas, Tex. Deb: 5/28/1884

1884	StL-a	5	20	2	4	0	0	0		0		.200	.200	.200	32	-1	-2	1				-1	/O	-0.1
	Was-a	6	24	4	9	0	0	0		1		.375	.400	.375	179	1	2	4				1	/O	0.2
	Ric-a	11	40	4	9	1	0	0		1		.225	.262	.250	71	-1	-1	3				-1	/O	-0.1
	Yr	22	84	10	22	1	0	0		2		.262	.287	.274	89	-1	-1	7				-1		0.0
1886	Was-N	6	18	0	4	1	0	0	1	3	3	.222	.300	.278	81	-0	-0	2	0			-1	O	0.0
1888	Bal-a	45	165	13	39	1	1	0	14	8		.236	.288	.255	79	-4	-3	17	17			-5	O	-0.9
Total	3	73	267	23	65	3	1	0	15	12	3	.243	.289	.262	83	-5	-4	26	17			-7	/O	-0.9

■ FRED GOLDSMITH
Goldsmith, Fred Ernest b: 5/15/1852, New Haven, Conn. d: 3/28/39, Berkley, Mich. BR/TR, 6'1", 195 lbs. Deb: 10/23/1875 U

1875	NH-n	1	4	0	2	0	0	0		0		.500	.500	.500	289	1	1	1					/2	0.1
1879	Tro-N	9	38	6	9	1	0	0	2	1	3	.237	.256	.263	77	-1	-1	3				-0	/PO1	0.0
1880	Chi-N	35	142	24	37	4	2	0	15	2	15	.261	.271	.317	93	-0	-1	12				1	PO/1	0.0
1881	Chi-N	42	158	24	38	3	4	0	16	6	17	.241	.268	.310	78	-3	-4	13				6	P/O	0.0
1882	Chi-N	45	183	23	42	11	1	0	19	4	29	.230	.246	.301	71	-5	-6	14				-2	P/1	0.0
1883	Chi-N	60	235	38	52	12	3	1	1	4	35	.221	.234	.311	60	-10	-12	18				1	PO/1	0.0
1884	Chi-N	22	81	11	11	2	0	2	6	7	26	.136	.205	.235	35	-6	-7	4				-1	P/O	0.0
	Bal-a	4	14	2	2	0	0	0		2		.143	.250	.143	32	-1	-1	1				1	/P1	0.0
Total	6	217	851	128	191	33	10	3	59	26	125	.224	.247	.297	69	-27	-33	64				6	P/O1	0.0

■ WALLY GOLDSMITH
Goldsmith, Wallace b: 1849, Baltimore, Md. 5'7", 146 lbs. Deb: 5/04/1871

1871	Kek-n	19	88	8	18	1	0	0	12	4	2	.205	.239	.216	31	-7	-8	5	0				S/3C2	-0.4
1872	Oly-n	9	40	4	10	0	0	0		0		.250	.250	.250	57	-2	-2	3					/S2	0.0
1873	Mar-n	1	4	0	0	0	0	0		0		.000	.000	.000	-99	-1	-1	0					/2	0.0
1875	Wes-n	13	51	3	6	0	0	0		0		.118	.118	.118	-17	-6	-6	1					3	-0.4
Total	4 n	42	183	15	34	1	0	0		4		.186	.203	.191	21	-16	-17	8					/3S2C	-0.8

■ LONNIE GOLDSTEIN
Goldstein, Leslie Elmer b: 5/13/18, Austin, Tex. BL/TL, 6'2.5", 190 lbs. Deb: 9/11/43

1943	Cin-N	5	5	1	1	0	0	0	0	2	1	.200	.429	.200	85	0	0	0	0			-0	/1	0.0
1946	Cin-N	6	5	1	0	0	0	0	0	1	1	.000	.167	.000	-53	-1	-1	0	0			0	H	0.0
Total	2	11	10	2	1	0	0	0	0	3	2	.100	.308	.100	20	-1	-1	0	0			-0	/1	0.0

■ PURNAL GOLDY
Goldy, Purnal William b: 11/28/37, Camden, N.J. BR/TR, 6'5", 200 lbs. Deb: 4/12/62

1962	Det-A	20	70	8	16	1	1	3	12	0	12	.229	.239	.400	66	-3	-4	6	0	0	0	-1	O	-0.4
1963	Det-A	9	8	1	2	0	0	0	0	0	4	.250	.250	.250	39	-1	-1	1	0	0	0	0	H	0.0
Total	2	29	78	9	18	1	1	3	12	0	16	.231	.241	.385	64	-4	-4	6	0	0	0	-1	/O	-0.4

■ STAN GOLETZ
Goletz, Stanley "Stash" b: 5/21/18, Crescent, Ohio BL/TL, 6'3", 200 lbs. Deb: 9/09/41

| 1941 | Chi-A | 3 | 5 | 0 | 3 | 0 | 0 | 0 | 2 | 0 | 0 | .600 | .600 | .600 | 221 | 1 | 1 | 2 | 0 | 0 | 0 | 0 | H | 0.1 |

■ MIKE GOLIAT
Goliat, Mike Mitchel b: 11/5/25, Yatesboro, Pa. BR/TR, 6', 180 lbs. Deb: 8/03/49

1949	Phi-N	55	189	24	40	6	3	3	19	20	32	.212	.290	.323	66	-10	-9	17	0			-2	2/1	-0.8
1950	*Phi-N	145	483	49	113	13	6	13	64	53	75	.234	.314	.366	80	-16	-15	53	3			-18	*2	-2.7
1951	Phi-N	41	138	14	31	2	1	4	15	9	18	.225	.277	.341	66	-7	-7	13	0	1	-1	-7	2/3	-1.3
	StL-A	5	11	0	2	0	0	0	1	0	1	.182	.182	.182	-1	-2	-2	0	0	0	0	0	/2	0.0

YEAR	TM/L	G	AB	R	H	2B	3B	HR	RBI	BB	SO	AVG	OBP	SLG	PRO+	BR	/A	RC	SB	CS	SBR	FR	POS	TPR
1952	StL-A	3	4	0	0	0	0	0	0	1	1	.000	.200	.000	-40	-1	-1	0	0	0	0	1	/2	0.0
Total	4	249	825	87	186	21	10	20	99	83	127	.225	.300	.348	73	-35	-33	84	3	1		-26	2/13	-4.8

■ WALT GOLVIN
Golvin, Walter George b: 2/1/1894, Hershey, Neb. d: 6/11/73, Gardena, Cal. BL/TL, 6', 165 lbs. Deb: 4/15/22

YEAR	TM/L	G	AB	R	H	2B	3B	HR	RBI	BB	SO	AVG	OBP	SLG	PRO+	BR	/A	RC	SB	CS	SBR	FR	POS	TPR
1922	Chi-N	2	2	0	0	0	0	0	1	0	0	.000	.000	.000	-98	-1	-1	0	0	0	0	0	/1	0.0

■ CHILE GOMEZ
Gomez, Jose Luis (Rodriguez) b: 5/23/09, Villaunion, Mex. BR/TR, 5'10", 165 lbs. Deb: 7/27/35

YEAR	TM/L	G	AB	R	H	2B	3B	HR	RBI	BB	SO	AVG	OBP	SLG	PRO+	BR	/A	RC	SB	CS	SBR	FR	POS	TPR
1935	Phi-N	67	222	24	51	3	0	0	16	17	34	.230	.285	.243	39	-17	-20	15	2			12	S2	-0.3
1936	Phi-N	108	332	24	77	4	1	0	28	14	32	.232	.265	.250	36	-28	-32	22	0			18	2S	-0.6
1942	Was-A	25	73	8	14	2	2	0	6	9	7	.192	.280	.274	57	-4	-4	6	1	0	0	-1	2/3	-0.3
Total	3	200	627	56	142	9	3	0	50	40	73	.226	.274	.250	39	-49	-57	43	3	0		29	2/S3	-1.2

■ LEO GOMEZ
Gomez, Leonardo b: 3/2/67, Canovanas, P.R. BR/TR, 6', 180 lbs. Deb: 9/17/90

YEAR	TM/L	G	AB	R	H	2B	3B	HR	RBI	BB	SO	AVG	OBP	SLG	PRO+	BR	/A	RC	SB	CS	SBR	FR	POS	TPR
1990	Bal-A	12	39	3	9	0	0	1		8	7	.231	.362	.231	71	-1	-1	4	0	0	0	-2	3	-0.2

■ LUIS GOMEZ
Gomez, Luis (Sanchez) b: 8/19/51, Guadalajara, Mex. BR/TR, 5'9", 150 lbs. Deb: 4/28/74

YEAR	TM/L	G	AB	R	H	2B	3B	HR	RBI	BB	SO	AVG	OBP	SLG	PRO+	BR	/A	RC	SB	CS	SBR	FR	POS	TPR
1974	Min-A	82	168	18	35	1	0	0	3	12	16	.208	.261	.214	37	-13	-14	10	2	3	-1	18	S/2D	0.9
1975	Min-A	89	72	7	10	0	0	0	5	4	12	.139	.184	.139	-7	-10	-10	2	0	2	-1	24	S/2D	2.0
1976	Min-A	38	57	5	11	1	0	0	3	3	3	.193	.233	.211	30	-5	-5	3	1	0	-1	7	S/230D	0.4
1977	Min-A	32	65	6	16	4	2	0	11	4	9	.246	.290	.369	79	-2	-2	7	0	2	-1	4	2/S30D	0.3
1978	Tor-A	153	413	39	92	7	3	0	32	34	41	.223	.282	.254	51	-26	-27	28	2	10	-5	-10	*S	-3.0
1979	Tor-A	59	163	11	39	7	0	0	11	6	17	.239	.266	.282	48	-12	-12	11	1	0	0	2	32S	-0.5
1980	Atl-N	121	278	18	53	6	0	0	24	17	27	.191	.240	.212	26	-27	-28	13	0	4	-2	12	*S	-0.4
1981	Atl-N	35	35	4	7	0	0	0	1	6	4	.200	.317	.200	48	-2	-2	3	0	1	-1	-3	S/32P	-0.3
Total	8	609	1251	108	263	26	5	0	90	86	129	.210	.262	.239	40	-97	-100	76	6	22	-11	56	S/23DOP	-0.6

■ PRESTON GOMEZ
Gomez, Pedro (Martinez) b: 4/20/23, Preston, Cuba BR/TR, 5'11", 170 lbs. Deb: 5/05/44 MC

YEAR	TM/L	G	AB	R	H	2B	3B	HR	RBI	BB	SO	AVG	OBP	SLG	PRO+	BR	/A	RC	SB	CS	SBR	FR	POS	TPR
1944	Was-A	8	7	2	2	1	0	0	2	0	4	.286	.286	.429	107	-0	0	1	0	0	0	-1	/2S	0.0

■ RANDY GOMEZ
Gomez, Randell Scott b: 2/4/57, San Mateo, Cal. BR/TR, 5'10", 185 lbs. Deb: 8/21/84

YEAR	TM/L	G	AB	R	H	2B	3B	HR	RBI	BB	SO	AVG	OBP	SLG	PRO+	BR	/A	RC	SB	CS	SBR	FR	POS	TPR
1984	SF-N	14	30	0	5	1	0	0	0	8	3	.167	.342	.200	57	-1	-1	2	0	0	0	3	C	0.3

■ JESSE GONDER
Gonder, Jesse Lemar b: 1/20/36, Monticello, Ark. BL/TR, 5'10", 180 lbs. Deb: 9/23/60

YEAR	TM/L	G	AB	R	H	2B	3B	HR	RBI	BB	SO	AVG	OBP	SLG	PRO+	BR	/A	RC	SB	CS	SBR	FR	POS	TPR
1960	NY-A	7	7	1	2	0	0	1	3	1	1	.286	.375	.714	199	1	1	2	0	0	0	1	/C	0.2
1961	NY-A	15	12	2	4	1	0	0	3	3	1	.333	.467	.417	146	1	1	2	0	0	0	0	H	0.1
1962	Cin-N	4	4	0	0	0	0	0	0	0	3	.000	.000	.000	-97	-1	-1	0	0	0	0	0	H	0.0
1963	Cin-N	31	32	5	10	2	0	3	5	1	12	.313	.333	.656	172	3	3	7	0	0	0	2	/C	0.5
	NY-N	42	126	12	38	4	0	3	15	6	25	.302	.333	.405	110	2	1	16	1	2	-1	-13	C	-1.2
	Yr	73	158	17	48	6	0	6	20	7	37	.304	.333	.456	122	5	4	23	1	2	-1	-11		-0.7
1964	NY-N	131	341	28	92	11	1	7	35	29	65	.270	.331	.370	99	-1	-0	38	0	0	0	1	C	0.4
1965	NY-N	53	105	6	25	4	0	4	9	11	20	.238	.310	.390	100	-1	-0	11	0	0	0	-5	C	-0.3
	Mil-N	31	53	2	8	2	0	1	5	4	9	.151	.211	.245	28	-5	-5	2	0	0	0	5	C	0.0
	Yr	84	158	8	33	6	0	5	14	15	29	.209	.277	.342	75	-6	-5	13	0	0	0	0		-0.3
1966	Pit-N	59	160	13	36	3	1	7	16	12	39	.225	.287	.387	85	-3	-3	16	0	0	0	-1	C	-0.2
1967	Pit-N	22	36	4	5	1	0	0	3	5	9	.139	.279	.167	30	-3	-3	2	0	0	0	0	C	-0.1
Total	8	395	876	73	220	28	2	26	94	72	184	.251	.312	.377	94	-8	-7	97	1	2	-1	-10	C	-0.6

■ DAN GONZALES
Gonzales, Daniel David b: 9/30/53, Whittier, Cal. BL/TR, 6'1", 195 lbs. Deb: 4/07/79

YEAR	TM/L	G	AB	R	H	2B	3B	HR	RBI	BB	SO	AVG	OBP	SLG	PRO+	BR	/A	RC	SB	CS	SBR	FR	POS	TPR
1979	Det-A	7	18	1	4	1	0	0	2	0	2	.222	.222	.278	33	-2	-2	1	1	0	0	-1	/O	-0.2
1980	Det-A	2	7	1	1	0	0	0	0	0	1	.143	.143	.143	-21	-1	-1	0	0	0	0	-0	/OD	0.0
Total	2	9	25	2	5	1	0	0	2	0	3	.200	.200	.240	18	-3	-3	1	1	0	0	-1	/OD	-0.2

■ RENE GONZALES
Gonzales, Rene Adrian b: 9/3/60, Austin, Tex. BR/TR, 6'3", 180 lbs. Deb: 7/27/84

YEAR	TM/L	G	AB	R	H	2B	3B	HR	RBI	BB	SO	AVG	OBP	SLG	PRO+	BR	/A	RC	SB	CS	SBR	FR	POS	TPR
1984	Mon-N	29	30	5	7	1	0	0	2	2	5	.233	.303	.267	64	-1	-1	3	0	0	0	1	S	0.2
1986	Mon-N	11	26	1	3	0	0	0	0	2	7	.115	.179	.115	-17	-4	-4	0	0	2	-1	2	/S3	-0.3
1987	Bal-A	37	60	14	16	2	1	1	7	3	11	.267	.302	.383	82	-2	-2	7	1	0	0	6	3/2S	0.4
1988	Bal-A	92	237	13	51	6	0	2	15	13	32	.215	.265	.266	50	-16	-15	17	2	0	1	15	32/S10	0.1
1989	Bal-A	71	166	16	36	4	0	1	11	12	30	.217	.270	.259	51	-11	-10	11	5	3	-0	-1	23/S	-1.0
1990	Bal-A	67	103	13	22	3	1	1	12	12	14	.214	.296	.291	66	-5	-4	9	1	2	-1	10	23/SO	0.7
Total	6	307	622	62	135	16	2	5	47	44	99	.217	.273	.273	54	-39	-37	47	9	7	-2	31	32/SO1	0.1

■ TONY GONZALEZ
Gonzalez, Andres Antonio (Gonzalez) b: 8/28/36, Central Cunagua, Cuba BL/TR, 5'9", 170 lbs. Deb: 4/12/60

YEAR	TM/L	G	AB	R	H	2B	3B	HR	RBI	BB	SO	AVG	OBP	SLG	PRO+	BR	/A	RC	SB	CS	SBR	FR	POS	TPR
1960	Cin-N	39	99	10	21	5	1	3	14	4	27	.212	.250	.374	67	-5	-5	9	1	0	0	-1	O	-0.6
	Phi-N	78	241	27	72	17	5	6	33	11	47	.299	.337	.485	122	7	7	38	2	2	-1	5	O	0.9
	Yr	117	340	37	93	22	6	9	47	15	74	.274	.312	.453	106	2	2	47	3	2	-0	4		0.3
1961	Phi-N	126	426	58	118	16	8	12	58	49	66	.277	.360	.437	112	7	8	68	15	5	2	-8	*O	-0.4
1962	Phi-N	118	437	76	132	16	4	20	63	40	82	.302	.372	.494	134	19	20	80	17	8	0	1	*O	1.6
1963	Phi-N	155	555	78	170	36	12	4	66	53	68	.306	.375	.436	134	24	25	91	13	8	-1	-9	*O	0.8
1964	Phi-N	131	421	55	117	25	3	4	40	44	74	.278	.355	.380	108	5	6	56	0	5	-3	-3	*O	-0.3
1965	Phi-N	108	370	48	109	19	1	13	41	31	52	.295	.354	.457	112	9	13	54	3	4	-2	-11	*O	-0.1
1966	Phi-N	132	384	53	110	20	4	6	40	26	60	.286	.337	.406	105	3	3	51	2	6	-3	0	*O	-0.3
1967	Phi-N	149	508	74	172	23	9	9	59	47	58	.339	.400	.472	147	33	32	94	10	9	-2	4	*O	3.0
1968	Phi-N	121	416	45	110	13	4	3	38	40	42	.264	.339	.337	103	3	3	47	6	5	-1	-7	*O	-1.2
1969	SD-N	53	182	17	41	4	0	2	8	19	24	.225	.309	.280	69	-8	-7	16	1	0	0	2	O	-0.7
	*Atl-N	89	320	51	94	15	2	10	50	27	22	.294	.358	.447	124	10	10	51	3	1	0	3	O	0.9
	Yr	142	502	68	135	19	2	12	58	46	46	.269	.340	.386	104	2	3	66	4	1	1	4		0.2
1970	Atl-N	123	430	57	114	18	2	7	55	46	45	.265	.347	.365	86	-5	-8	54	3	5	-2	-6	*O	-2.1
	Cal-A	26	92	9	28	2	0	1	12	2	11	.304	.326	.359	92	-2	-1	10	3	2	-0	0	O	-0.2
1971	Cal-A	111	314	32	77	9	2	3	38	28	32	.245	.313	.315	84	-9	-6	30	0	1	-1	-6	O	-1.5
Total	12	1559	5195	690	1485	238	57	103	615	467	706	.286	.353	.413	114	95	100	749	79	61	-13	-36	*O	-0.2

■ DENNY GONZALEZ
Gonzalez, Denio Mariano (Manzueta) b: 7/22/63, Sabana Grande Boya, D.R. BR/TR, 5'11", 165 lbs. Deb: 8/06/84

YEAR	TM/L	G	AB	R	H	2B	3B	HR	RBI	BB	SO	AVG	OBP	SLG	PRO+	BR	/A	RC	SB	CS	SBR	FR	POS	TPR
1984	Pit-N	26	82	9	15	3	1	0	4	7	21	.183	.247	.244	38	-7	-7	4	1	1	-0	1	3S/O	-0.4
1985	Pit-N	35	124	11	28	4	0	4	12	13	27	.226	.299	.355	83	-3	-3	13	2	4	-2	-4	3O/2	-0.9
1987	Pit-N	5	7	1	0	0	0	0	0	1	2	.000	.125	.000	-63	-2	-2	0	0	0	0	-1	/S	-0.1
1988	Pit-N	24	32	5	6	1	0	0	1	6	10	.188	.316	.219	57	-2	-2	3	0	0	0	0	S/23	0.0
1989	Cle-A	8	17	3	5	1	0	0	1	0	4	.294	.333	.353	92	-0	-0	2	0	0	0	-0	/3D	0.0
Total	5	98	262	29	54	9	1	4	18	27	64	.206	.283	.294	62	-13	-13	22	3	5	-2	-4	/3SO2D	-1.4

■ EUSEBIO GONZALEZ
Gonzalez, Eusebio Miguel (Lopez) "Papo" b: 7/13/1892, Havana, Cuba d: 2/14/76, Havana, Cuba BR/TR, 5'10", 165 lbs. Deb: 7/26/18

YEAR	TM/L	G	AB	R	H	2B	3B	HR	RBI	BB	SO	AVG	OBP	SLG	PRO+	BR	/A	RC	SB	CS	SBR	FR	POS	TPR
1918	Bos-A	3	5	2	2	0	0	0	0	0	1	.400	.571	.800	319	1	1	2	0			-1	/S3	0.1

■ FERNANDO GONZALEZ
Gonzalez, Jose Fernando (Quinones) b: 6/19/50, Arecibo, P.R. BR/TR, 5'10", 165 lbs. Deb: 9/15/72

YEAR	TM/L	G	AB	R	H	2B	3B	HR	RBI	BB	SO	AVG	OBP	SLG	PRO+	BR	/A	RC	SB	CS	SBR	FR	POS	TPR
1972	Pit-N	3	2	0	0	0	0	0	0	0	2	.000	.000	.000	-99	-1	-1	0	0	0	0	0	/3	0.0
1973	Pit-N	37	49	5	11	0	1	1	5	1	11	.224	.255	.327	62	-3	-3	4	0	0	0	-1	/3	-0.3
1974	KC-A	9	21	1	3	1	0	0	2	0	4	.143	.143	.190	-5	-3	-3	1	1	0	0	0	/3D	-0.2

YEAR	TM/L	G	AB	R	H	2B	3B	HR	RBI	BB	SO	AVG	OBP	SLG	PRO+	BR	/A	RC	SB	CS	SBR	FR	POS	TPR
	NY-A	51	121	11	26	5	1	1	7	7	7	.215	.258	.298	61	-6	-6	9	0	0	0	2	2/3S	-0.1
	Yr	60	142	12	29	6	1	1	9	7	11	.204	.242	.282	51	-9	-9	9	1	0	0	3		-0.3
1977	Pit-N	80	181	17	50	10	0	4	27	13	21	.276	.325	.398	90	-2	-3	20	3	3	-1	-6	3O/2S	-0.9
1978	Pit-N	9	21	2	4	1	0	0	0	1	3	.190	.227	.238	29	-2	-2	1	0	0	0	-4	/23	-0.6
	SD-N	101	320	27	80	10	2	2	29	18	32	.250	.290	.313	74	-14	-11	29	4	4	-1	0	2	-0.6
	Yr	110	341	29	84	11	2	2	29	19	35	.246	.286	.308	71	-16	-13	30	4	4	-1	-4		-1.2
1979	SD-N	114	323	22	70	13	3	9	34	18	34	.217	.258	.359	71	-16	-14	28	0	0	0	-13	*2/3	-2.1
Total	6	404	1038	85	244	40	7	17	104	58	114	.235	.276	.336	71	-46	-42	92	8	7	-2	-22	2/3OSD	-4.8

■ JOSE GONZALEZ

Gonzalez, Jose Rafael (Gutierrez) b: 11/23/64, Puerto Plata, D.R. BR/TR, 6'2", 190 lbs. Deb: 9/02/85

YEAR	TM/L	G	AB	R	H	2B	3B	HR	RBI	BB	SO	AVG	OBP	SLG	PRO+	BR	/A	RC	SB	CS	SBR	FR	POS	TPR
1985	LA-N	23	11	6	3	2	0	0	0	1	3	.273	.333	.455	122	0	0	1	1	1	-0	1	O	0.1
1986	LA-N	57	93	15	20	5	1	2	6	7	29	.215	.270	.355	76	-4	-3	9	4	3	-1	2	O	-0.2
1987	LA-N	19	16	2	3	2	0	0	1	1	2	.188	.235	.313	45	-1	-1	2	5	0	2	3	O	0.2
1988	*LA-N	37	24	7	2	1	0	0	0	2	10	.083	.154	.125	-20	-4	-4	1	3	0	1	1	O	-0.1
1989	LA-N	95	261	31	70	11	2	3	18	23	53	.268	.327	.360	98	-1	-1	32	9	3	1	3	O	0.2
1990	LA-N	106	99	15	23	5	3	2	8	6	27	.232	.283	.404	92	-2	-1	11	3	1	0	4	O	0.0
Total	6	337	504	76	121	26	6	7	33	40	124	.240	.297	.357	86	-12	-10	56	25	8	3	15	O	0.2

■ JUAN GONZALEZ

Gonzalez, Juan Alberto (Vazquez) b: 10/20/69, Arecibo, P.R. BR/TR, 6'3", 175 lbs. Deb: 9/01/89

YEAR	TM/L	G	AB	R	H	2B	3B	HR	RBI	BB	SO	AVG	OBP	SLG	PRO+	BR	/A	RC	SB	CS	SBR	FR	POS	TPR
1989	Tex-A	24	60	6	9	3	0	1	7	6	17	.150	.227	.250	34	-5	-5	3	0	0	0	3	O	-0.2
1990	Tex-A	25	90	11	26	7	1	4	12	2	18	.289	.319	.522	129	3	3	14	0	1	-1	-1	O/D	0.1
Total	2	49	150	17	35	10	1	5	19	8	35	.233	.281	.413	91	-2	-2	17	0	1	-1	2	/OD	-0.1

■ JULIO GONZALEZ

Gonzalez, Julio Cesar (Hernandez) b: 12/25/52, Caguas, P.R. BR/TR, 5'11", 162 lbs. Deb: 4/08/77

YEAR	TM/L	G	AB	R	H	2B	3B	HR	RBI	BB	SO	AVG	OBP	SLG	PRO+	BR	/A	RC	SB	CS	SBR	FR	POS	TPR
1977	Hou-N	110	383	34	94	18	3	1	27	19	45	.245	.288	.316	68	-21	-16	34	3	3	-1	-26	S2	-3.2
1978	Hou-N	78	223	24	52	3	1	1	16	8	31	.233	.263	.269	53	-15	-13	15	6	1	1	-20	2S/3	-2.9
1979	Hou-N	68	181	16	45	5	2	0	10	5	14	.249	.280	.298	62	-11	-9	15	2	1	0	1	2S/3	-0.3
1980	Hou-N	40	52	5	6	1	0	0	1	1	8	.115	.132	.135	-28	-9	-8	1	1	0	0	3	S3/2	-0.2
1981	StL-N	20	22	2	7	1	0	1	3	1	3	.318	.348	.500	135	1	1	3	0	0	0	1	/S23	0.3
1982	StL-N	42	87	9	21	3	2	1	7	1	24	.241	.258	.356	70	-4	-4	7	1	1	-0	-1	3/2S	-0.5
1983	Det-A	12	21	0	3	1	0	0	2	1	7	.143	.182	.190	3	-3	-3	1	0	0	0	3	/S23	0.1
Total	7	370	969	90	228	32	8	4	66	36	132	.235	.269	.297	59	-61	-53	76	13	6	0	-39	2S/3	-6.7

■ LUIS GONZALEZ

Gonzalez, Luis Emilio b: 9/3/67, Tampa, Fla. BL/TR, 6'2", 180 lbs. Deb: 9/04/90

YEAR	TM/L	G	AB	R	H	2B	3B	HR	RBI	BB	SO	AVG	OBP	SLG	PRO+	BR	/A	RC	SB	CS	SBR	FR	POS	TPR
1990	Hou-N	12	21	1	4	2	0	0	0	2	5	.190	.261	.286	51	-1	-1	2	0	0	0	2	/31	0.1

■ MIKE GONZALEZ

Gonzalez, Miguel Angel (Cordero) b: 9/24/1890, Havana, Cuba d: 2/19/77, Havana, Cuba BR/TR, 6'1", 200 lbs. Deb: 9/28/12 MC

YEAR	TM/L	G	AB	R	H	2B	3B	HR	RBI	BB	SO	AVG	OBP	SLG	PRO+	BR	/A	RC	SB	CS	SBR	FR	POS	TPR
1912	Bos-N	1	2	0	0	0	0	0	0	1	1	.000	.333	.000	-5	-0	-0	0	0			1	/C	0.1
1914	Cin-N	95	176	19	41	6	0	0	10	13	16	.233	.293	.267	65	-7	-8	14	2			12	C	0.8
1915	StL-N	51	97	12	22	2	2	0	10	8	9	.227	.306	.289	80	-2	-2	9	4	2	0	4	C/1	0.3
1916	StL-N	118	331	33	79	15	4	0	29	28	18	.239	.304	.308	89	-4	-4	34	5			7	C1	0.8
1917	StL-N	106	290	28	76	8	1	1	28	22	24	.262	.316	.307	94	-3	-2	31	12			1	C1/O	0.2
1918	StL-N	117	349	33	88	13	4	3	20	39	30	.252	.327	.338	107	2	3	41	14			0	*C/O1	1.3
1919	NY-N	58	158	18	30	6	0	0	8	20	9	.190	.293	.228	58	-7	-7	11	3			-3	C/1	-0.7
1920	NY-N	11	13	1	3	0	0	0	0	3	1	.231	.375	.231	77	-0	-0	2	1	0	0	-1	/C	0.0
1921	NY-N	13	24	3	9	1	0	0	0	1	0	.375	.400	.417	116	1	1	4	0	0	0	-0	/1C	0.0
1924	StL-N	120	402	34	119	27	1	3	53	24	22	.296	.337	.391	96	-3	-2	52	1	5	-3	-7	*C	-0.9
1925	StL-N	22	71	9	22	3	0	0	4	6	2	.310	.380	.352	86	-1	-1	9	1	2	-1	4	C	0.3
	Chi-N	70	197	26	52	13	1	3	18	13	15	.264	.316	.386	77	-7	-7	24	2	1	0	1	C/1	-0.4
	Yr	92	268	35	74	16	1	3	22	19	17	.276	.333	.377	80	-8	-8	34	3	3	-1	5		-0.1
1926	Chi-N	80	253	24	63	13	3	1	23	13	17	.249	.288	.336	67	-12	-12	24	3			6	C	-0.2
1927	Chi-N	39	108	15	26	4	1	1	15	10	8	.241	.311	.324	70	-4	-5	11	1			9	C	0.6
1928	Chi-N	49	158	14	43	9	2	1	21	12	7	.272	.324	.373	83	-4	-4	19	2			8	C	0.7
1929	*Chi-N	60	167	15	40	3	0	0	18	18	14	.240	.317	.257	44	-14	-14	14	1			6	C	-0.2
1931	StL-N	15	19	1	2	0	0	0	3	0	3	.105	.105	.105	-42	-4	-4	0	0			0	C	-0.2
1932	StL-N	17	14	0	2	0	0	0	3	0	2	.143	.143	.143	-22	-2	-2	0	0			2	/C	0.0
Total	17	1042	2829	283	717	123	19	13	263	231	198	.253	.314	.324	81	-73	-71	300	52	10		48	C/1O	2.5

■ ORLANDO GONZALEZ

Gonzalez, Orlando Eugene b: 11/15/51, Havana, Cuba BL/TL, 6'2", 180 lbs. Deb: 6/07/76

YEAR	TM/L	G	AB	R	H	2B	3B	HR	RBI	BB	SO	AVG	OBP	SLG	PRO+	BR	/A	RC	SB	CS	SBR	FR	POS	TPR
1976	Cle-A	28	68	5	17	2	0	0	4	5	7	.250	.301	.279	72	-2	-2	5	1	2	-1	-0	1/OD	-0.4
1978	*Phi-N	26	26	1	5	0	0	0	0	1	1	.192	.222	.192	17	-3	-3	1	0	0	0	1	O/1	-0.2
1980	Oak-A	25	70	10	17	0	0	0	1	9	8	.243	.329	.243	64	-4	-3	6	0	2	-1	2	1/OD	-0.2
Total	3	79	164	16	39	2	0	0	5	15	16	.238	.302	.250	59	-9	-8	12	1	4	-2	2	/1OD	-0.8

■ PEDRO GONZALEZ

Gonzalez, Pedro (Olivares) b: 12/12/37, San Pedro De Macoris, D.R. BR/TR, 6', 176 lbs. Deb: 4/11/63

YEAR	TM/L	G	AB	R	H	2B	3B	HR	RBI	BB	SO	AVG	OBP	SLG	PRO+	BR	/A	RC	SB	CS	SBR	FR	POS	TPR
1963	NY-A	14	26	3	5	1	0	0	1	0	5	.192	.192	.231	18	-3	-3	1	0	1	-1	-1	/2	-0.3
1964	*NY-A	80	112	18	31	8	1	0	5	7	22	.277	.331	.366	92	-1	-1	13	3	4	-2	5	1O/32	0.1
1965	NY-A	7	5	0	2	1	0	0	0	0	2	.400	.400	.600	181	0	0	1	0	0	0	0	H	0.1
	Cle-A	116	400	38	101	14	3	5	39	18	57	.253	.290	.340	78	-12	-12	38	7	4	-0	9	*2/O3	0.2
	Yr	123	405	38	103	15	3	5	39	18	59	.254	.291	.343	79	-11	-12	39	7	4	-0	9		0.3
1966	Cle-A	110	352	21	82	9	2	2	17	15	54	.233	.268	.287	60	-18	-18	27	8	5	-1	12	*2/3O	0.1
1967	Cle-A	80	189	16	43	6	0	1	8	12	36	.228	.277	.275	63	-8	-9	13	4	6	-2	-5	2/13S	-1.5
Total	5	407	1084	99	264	39	6	8	70	52	176	.244	.283	.313	70	-42	-43	93	22	20	-5	19	2/103S	-1.3

■ CHARLIE GOOCH

Gooch, Charles Furman b: 6/5/02, Smyrna, Tenn. d: 5/30/82, Lanham, Md. BR/TR, 5'9", 170 lbs. Deb: 4/18/29

YEAR	TM/L	G	AB	R	H	2B	3B	HR	RBI	BB	SO	AVG	OBP	SLG	PRO+	BR	/A	RC	SB	CS	SBR	FR	POS	TPR
1929	Was-A	39	57	6	16	2	1	0	5	7	8	.281	.359	.351	83	-1	-1	7	0	1	-1	-1	/13S	-0.3

■ JOHNNY GOOCH

Gooch, John Beverley b: 11/9/1897, Smyrna, Tenn. d: 5/15/75, Nashville, Tenn. BB/TR, 5'11", 175 lbs. Deb: 9/09/21 C

YEAR	TM/L	G	AB	R	H	2B	3B	HR	RBI	BB	SO	AVG	OBP	SLG	PRO+	BR	/A	RC	SB	CS	SBR	FR	POS	TPR
1921	Pit-N	13	38	2	9	0	0	0	3	3	3	.237	.293	.237	41	-3	-3	3	1	0	0	3	C	0.1
1922	Pit-N	105	353	45	116	15	3	1	42	39	15	.329	.403	.397	106	6	5	59	1	1	-0	-1	*C	0.4
1923	Pit-N	66	202	16	56	10	2	1	20	17	13	.277	.336	.361	82	-4	-5	25	2	1	0	5	C	0.3
1924	Pit-N	70	224	26	65	6	5	0	25	16	12	.290	.343	.362	88	-3	-4	27	1	3	-2	-6	C	-0.9
1925	*Pit-N	79	215	24	64	8	4	0	30	20	16	.298	.357	.372	81	-4	-6	30	1	0	0	-5	C	-0.6
1926	Pit-N	86	218	19	59	15	1	1	42	20	14	.271	.340	.362	85	-3	-5	27	1			-5	C	-0.6
1927	*Pit-N	101	291	22	75	17	2	2	48	19	21	.258	.305	.351	70	-11	-13	31	0			2	C	-0.4
1928	Pit-N	31	80	7	19	2	1	0	5	3	6	.237	.265	.287	43	-7	-7	6	0			5	C	0.0
	Bro-N	42	101	9	32	1	2	0	12	7	9	.317	.361	.366	92	-1	-1	13	0			-2	C	0.0
	Yr	73	181	16	51	3	3	0	17	10	15	.282	.319	.331	70	-8	-8	19	0			3		0.0
1929	Bro-N	1	1	0	0	0	0	0	0	0	0	.000	.000	.000	-99	-0	-0	0	0			0	H	0.0
	Cin-N	92	287	22	86	13	5	0	34	24	10	.300	.356	.380	86	-8	-6	38	4			4	C	0.5
	Yr	93	288	22	86	13	5	0	34	24	10	.299	.355	.378	86	-8	-6	38	4			4		0.5
1930	Cin-N	82	276	29	67	10	3	2	30	27	15	.243	.315	.322	57	-20	-18	20	0			-5	C	-1.6
1933	Bos-A	37	77	6	14	1	1	0	2	11	7	.182	.284	.221	36	-7	-7	5	0	0	0	5	C	0.0
Total	11	805	2363	227	662	98	39	7	293	206	141	.280	.342	.355	79	-65	-69	292	11	5		-2	C	-2.8

YEAR	TM/L	G	AB	R	H	2B	3B	HR	RBI	BB	SO	AVG	OBP	SLG	PRO+	BR	/A	RC	SB	CS	SBR	FR	POS	TPR

■ LEE GOOCH   Gooch, Lee Currin b: 2/23/1890, Oxford, N.C. d: 5/18/66, Raleigh, N.C. BR/TR, 6', 190 lbs. Deb: 8/17/15

YEAR	TM/L	G	AB	R	H	2B	3B	HR	RBI	BB	SO	AVG	OBP	SLG	PRO+	BR	/A	RC	SB	CS	SBR	FR	POS	TPR
1915	Cle-A	2	2	0	1	0	0	0	0	0	0	.500	.500	.500	196	0	0	1	0			0	H	0.0
1917	Phi-A	17	59	4	17	2	0	1	8	4	10	.288	.333	.373	117	1	1	7	0			-2	O	-0.1
Total	2	19	61	4	18	2	0	1	8	4	10	.295	.338	.377	120	1	1	8	0			-2	/O	-0.1

■ GENE GOOD   Good, Eugene J. b: 12/13/1882, Roxbury, Mass. d: 8/6/47, Boston, Mass. 5'6", 130 lbs. Deb: 4/12/06

YEAR	TM/L	G	AB	R	H	2B	3B	HR	RBI	BB	SO	AVG	OBP	SLG	PRO+	BR	/A	RC	SB	CS	SBR	FR	POS	TPR
1906	Bos-N	34	119	4	18	0	0	0	0	13		.151	.235	.151	23	-10	-10	5	2			-2	O	-1.3

■ WILBUR GOOD   Good, Wilbur David "Lefty" b: 9/28/1885, Punxsutawney, Pa. d: 12/30/63, Brooksville, Fla. BL/TL, 5'6", 165 lbs. Deb: 8/18/05

YEAR	TM/L	G	AB	R	H	2B	3B	HR	RBI	BB	SO	AVG	OBP	SLG	PRO+	BR	/A	RC	SB	CS	SBR	FR	POS	TPR
1905	NY-A	5	8	2	3	0	0	0	0	0		.375	.375	.375	126	0	0	1	0			0	/P	0.0
1908	Cle-A	46	154	23	43	1	3	1	14	13		.279	.335	.344	123	4	4	20	7			-8	O	-0.6
1909	Cle-A	94	318	33	68	6	5	0	17	28		.214	.296	.264	74	-7	-9	28	13			2	O	-1.0
1910	Bos-N	23	86	15	29	5	4	0	11	6	13	.337	.394	.488	150	6	5	18	5			5	O	0.9
1911	Bos-N	43	165	21	44	9	3	0	15	12	22	.267	.316	.358	82	-3	-5	19	3			6	O	0.0
	Chi-N	58	145	27	39	5	4	2	21	11	17	.269	.329	.400	103	0	0	22	10			-1	O	-0.1
	Yr	101	310	48	83	14	7	2	36	23	39	.268	.322	.377	92	-3	-4	41	13			5		-0.1
1912	Chi-N	39	35	7	5	0	0	0	1	3	7	.143	.211	.143	-2	-5	-5	2	3			1	O	-0.3
1913	Chi-N	49	91	11	23	3	2	1	12	11	16	.253	.340	.363	100	0	0	12	5			-1	O	-0.1
1914	Chi-N	154	580	70	158	24	7	2	43	53	74	.272	.341	.348	105	4	4	77	31			-5	*O	-0.5
1915	Chi-N	128	498	66	126	18	9	2	27	34	65	.253	.300	.337	95	-3	-4	52	19	17	-5	-7	*O	-2.0
1916	Phi-N	75	136	25	34	4	3	1	15	8	13	.250	.306	.346	96	-0	-1	17	7			-0	O	-0.2
1918	Chi-A	35	148	24	37	9	4	0	11	9	16	.250	.315	.365	104	0	0	16	1			4	O	0.3
Total	11	749	2364	324	609	84	44	9	187	190	243	.258	.321	.342	97	-4	-8	285	104	17		-5	O/P	-3.6

■ BILL GOODENOUGH   Goodenough, William B. b: 1863, St.Louis, Mo. d: 5/24/05, St.Louis, Mo. 6'1", 170 lbs. Deb: 8/31/1893

YEAR	TM/L	G	AB	R	H	2B	3B	HR	RBI	BB	SO	AVG	OBP	SLG	PRO+	BR	/A	RC	SB	CS	SBR	FR	POS	TPR
1893	StL-N	10	31	4	5	1	0	0	2	3	4	.161	.297	.194	33	-3	-3	2	2			-1	O	-0.3

■ MIKE GOODFELLOW   Goodfellow, Michael J. b: 10/3/1866, Port Jervis, N.Y. d: 2/12/20, Newark, N.J. 6', 180 lbs. Deb: 6/13/1887

YEAR	TM/L	G	AB	R	H	2B	3B	HR	RBI	BB	SO	AVG	OBP	SLG	PRO+	BR	/A	RC	SB	CS	SBR	FR	POS	TPR
1887	StL-a	1	4	0	0	0	0	0		0		.000	.000	.000	-90	-1	-1	0	0			0	/C	0.0
1888	Cle-a	68	269	24	66	7	0	0	29	11		.245	.283	.271	83	-6	-5	23	7			-3	O/C1S	-0.8
Total	2	69	273	24	66	7	0	0	29	11		.242	.279	.267	80	-7	-6	23	7			-3	/OC1S	-0.8

■ IVAL GOODMAN   Goodman, Ival Richard "Goodie" b: 7/23/08, Northview, Mo. d: 11/25/84, Cincinnati, Ohio BL/TR, 5'11", 170 lbs. Deb: 4/16/35

YEAR	TM/L	G	AB	R	H	2B	3B	HR	RBI	BB	SO	AVG	OBP	SLG	PRO+	BR	/A	RC	SB	CS	SBR	FR	POS	TPR
1935	Cin-N	148	592	86	159	23	18	12	72	35	50	.269	.314	.429	101	-4	-1	83	14			5	*O	-0.1
1936	Cin-N	136	489	81	139	15	14	17	71	38	53	.284	.347	.476	128	12	16	82	6			1	*O	1.2
1937	Cin-N	147	549	86	150	25	12	12	55	55	58	.273	.347	.428	115	7	11	85	10			3	*O	0.7
1938	Cin-N	145	568	103	166	27	10	30	92	53	51	.292	.368	.533	149	33	35	116	3			3	*O	3.5
1939	*Cin-N	124	470	85	152	37	16	7	84	54	32	.323	.401	.515	144	30	30	101	2			5	*O	3.2
1940	*Cin-N	136	519	78	134	20	6	12	63	60	54	.258	.335	.389	98	-0	-1	72	9			-9	*O	-1.4
1941	Cin-N	42	149	14	40	5	2	1	12	16	15	.268	.343	.349	95	-1	-1	18	1			-2	O	-0.4
1942	Cin-N	87	226	21	55	18	1	0	15	24	32	.243	.319	.332	91	-3	-3	24	0			-2	O	-0.5
1943	Chi-N	80	225	31	72	10	5	3	45	24	20	.320	.390	.449	144	12	13	40	4			-5	O	0.6
1944	Chi-N	62	141	24	37	8	1	1	16	23	15	.262	.377	.355	107	2	2	20	0			-5	O	-0.4
Total	10	1107	3928	609	1104	188	85	95	525	382	380	.281	.352	.445	120	90	101	641	49			-5	O	6.4

■ JAKE GOODMAN   Goodman, Jacob b: 9/14/1853, Lancaster, Pa. d: 3/9/1890, Reading, Pa. Deb: 5/02/1878

YEAR	TM/L	G	AB	R	H	2B	3B	HR	RBI	BB	SO	AVG	OBP	SLG	PRO+	BR	/A	RC	SB	CS	SBR	FR	POS	TPR
1878	Mil-N	60	252	28	62	4	3	1	27	7	33	.246	.266	.298	80	-4	-6	20				-4	*1	-0.7
1882	Pit-a	10	41	5	13	2	2	0		2		.317	.349	.463	180	3	3	7				1	1	0.4
Total	2	70	293	33	75	6	5	1	27	9	33	.256	.278	.321	92	-1	-3	27				-3	/1	-0.3

■ BILLY GOODMAN   Goodman, William Dale b: 3/22/26, Concord, N.C. d: 10/1/84, Sarasota, Fla. BL/TR, 5'11", 165 lbs. Deb: 4/19/47 C

YEAR	TM/L	G	AB	R	H	2B	3B	HR	RBI	BB	SO	AVG	OBP	SLG	PRO+	BR	/A	RC	SB	CS	SBR	FR	POS	TPR
1947	Bos-A	12	11	1	2	0	0	0	1	1	2	.182	.250	.182	20	-1	-1	0	0	0	0	0	/O	0.0
1948	Bos-A	127	445	65	138	27	2	1	66	74	44	.310	.414	.387	108	12	9	75	5	3	-0	-3	*1/23	1.1
1949	Bos-A	122	443	54	132	23	3	0	56	58	21	.298	.382	.363	91	0	-4	65	2	0	1	-1	*1	-0.3
1950	Bos-A	110	424	91	150	25	3	4	68	52	25	.354	.427	.455	115	18	12	86	2	4	-2	-6	031/2S	0.2
1951	Bos-A	141	546	92	162	34	4	0	50	79	37	.297	.388	.374	97	8	1	85	7	4	-0	-5	12O/3	-0.5
1952	Bos-A	138	513	79	157	27	3	4	56	48	23	.306	.370	.394	104	9	4	80	8	2	1	21	*21/3O	3.0
1953	Bos-A	128	514	73	161	33	5	2	41	57	11	.313	.384	.409	108	11	8	87	1	4	-2	-11	*21	0.1
1954	Bos-A	127	489	71	148	25	4	1	36	51	15	.303	.371	.376	95	4	-2	70	3	3	-1	2	21O3	0.0
1955	Bos-A	149	599	100	176	31	2	0	52	99	44	.294	.397	.352	94	7	-0	90	5	5	-2	-17	*2/1O	-1.0
1956	Bos-A	105	399	61	117	22	8	2	38	40	22	.293	.358	.404	90	0	-6	59	0	3	-2	-11	2	-1.0
1957	Bos-A	18	16	1	1	1	0	0	0	2	1	.063	.167	.125	-18	-3	-3	0	0	0	0	0	H	-0.2
	Bal-A	73	263	36	81	10	3	3	33	21	18	.308	.366	.403	117	4	6	36	0	2	-1	-8	3/012S	-0.2
	Yr	91	279	37	82	11	3	3	33	23	19	.294	.354	.387	106	1	3	36	0	2	-1	-8		-0.4
1958	Chi-A	116	425	41	127	15	5	0	40	37	21	.299	.358	.358	100	-0	1	55	1	0	0	-18	*3/12S	-1.2
1959	*Chi-A	104	268	21	67	14	1	1	28	19	20	.250	.304	.321	73	-10	-10	27	3	0	1	-2	3/2	-1.1
1960	Chi-A	30	77	5	18	4	0	0	6	12	8	.234	.337	.286	71	-3	-3	7	0	0	0	3	3/2	0.1
1961	Chi-A	41	51	4	13	4	0	1	10	7	6	.255	.345	.392	98	-0	-0	7	0	0	0	-0	/312	0.0
1962	Hou-N	82	161	12	41	4	1	0	10	12	11	.255	.306	.292	66	-8	-7	14	0	0	0	-9	23/1	-1.2
Total	16	1623	5644	807	1691	299	44	19	591	669	329	.300	.377	.378	98	49	4	844	37	30	-7	-64	2130/S	-2.2

■ ED GOODSON   Goodson, James Edward b: 1/25/48, Pulaski, Va. BL/TR, 6'3", 180 lbs. Deb: 9/05/70

YEAR	TM/L	G	AB	R	H	2B	3B	HR	RBI	BB	SO	AVG	OBP	SLG	PRO+	BR	/A	RC	SB	CS	SBR	FR	POS	TPR
1970	SF-N	7	11	1	3	0	0	0	0	0	2	.273	.273	.273	47	-1	-1	1	0	0	0	0	/1	0.0
1971	SF-N	20	42	4	8	1	0	0	1	2	4	.190	.227	.214	26	-4	-4	2	0	0	0	1	1	-0.4
1972	SF-N	58	150	15	42	1	1	6	30	8	12	.280	.321	.420	107	1	1	18	0	0	0	2	1	0.1
1973	SF-N	102	384	37	116	20	1	12	53	15	44	.302	.332	.453	111	6	5	54	0	1	-1	-14	3	-1.2
1974	SF-N	98	298	25	81	15	0	6	48	18	22	.272	.320	.383	91	-2	-4	35	1	0	0	-3	1/3	-1.0
1975	SF-N	39	121	10	25	7	0	1	8	7	14	.207	.250	.289	47	-9	-9	8	0	1	-1	2	13	-0.8
	Atl-N	47	76	5	16	2	0	1	8	2	8	.211	.231	.276	39	-6	-7	4	0	0	0	0	1/3	-0.7
	Yr	86	197	15	41	9	0	2	16	9	22	.208	.243	.284	44	-15	-16	11	0	1	-1	2		-1.5
1976	LA-N	83	118	8	27	4	0	3	17	9	19	.229	.278	.339	76	-4	-4	9	0	0	0	-4	3/1O2	-0.8
1977	*LA-N	61	66	3	11	1	0	1	5	3	10	.167	.203	.227	15	-8	-8	2	0	1	-1	1	1/3	-0.7
Total	8	515	1266	108	329	51	2	30	170	63	135	.260	.298	.374	84	-27	-31	133	1	3	-2	-15	13/O2	-5.5

■ PEP GOODWIN   Goodwin, Claire Vernon b: 12/19/1891, Pocatello, Idaho d: 2/15/72, Oakland, Cal. BL/TR, 5'10.5", 160 lbs. Deb: 4/16/14

YEAR	TM/L	G	AB	R	H	2B	3B	HR	RBI	BB	SO	AVG	OBP	SLG	PRO+	BR	/A	RC	SB	CS	SBR	FR	POS	TPR
1914	KC-F	112	374	38	88	15	6	1	32	27	23	.235	.290	.316	77	-13	-11	37	4			-13	S3/1	-1.9
1915	KC-F	81	229	22	54	5	1	0	16	15	23	.236	.291	.266	68	-9	-8	22	6			-8	S2	-1.3
Total	2	193	603	60	142	20	7	1	48	42	46	.235	.291	.297	74	-23	-19	59	10			-21	S/321	-3.2

■ DANNY GOODWIN   Goodwin, Danny Kay b: 9/2/53, St.Louis, Mo. BL/TR, 6'1", 195 lbs. Deb: 9/03/75

YEAR	TM/L	G	AB	R	H	2B	3B	HR	RBI	BB	SO	AVG	OBP	SLG	PRO+	BR	/A	RC	SB	CS	SBR	FR	POS	TPR
1975	Cal-A	4	10	0	1	0	0	0	0	0	5	.100	.100	.100	-47	-2	-2	-0	0	0	0	0	/D	-0.1
1977	Cal-A	35	91	5	19	6	1	2	8	5	19	.209	.250	.330	59	-6	-5	7	0	0	0	0	D	-0.4
1978	Cal-A	24	58	9	16	5	0	2	10	10	13	.276	.382	.466	143	3	3	11	0	0	0	0	D	0.3
1979	Min-A	58	159	22	46	8	5	5	27	11	23	.289	.335	.497	117	4	3	25	0	0	0	-0	D/1	0.2
1980	Min-A	55	115	12	23	5	0	1	11	17	32	.200	.303	.270	54	-6	-7	10	0	0	0	0	D1	-0.7

YEAR	TM/L	G	AB	R	H	2B	3B	HR	RBI	BB	SO	AVG	OBP	SLG	PRO+	BR	/A	RC	SB	CS	SBR	FR	POS	TPR
1981	Min-A	59	151	18	34	6	1	2	17	16	32	.225	.299	.318	73	-4	-5	15	3	1	0	-2	1/OD	-0.8
1982	Oak-A	17	52	6	11	2	1	2	8	2	13	.212	.241	.404	77	-2	-2	4	0	0	0	0	D	-0.1
Total	7	252	636	72	150	32	8	13	81	61	137	.236	.303	.373	84	-13	-15	72	3	1	0	-2	D/1O	-1.6

■ RAY GOOLSBY
Goolsby, Raymond Daniel "Ox" b: 9/5/19, Florala, Ala. BR/TR, 6'1", 185 lbs. Deb: 4/18/46

YEAR	TM/L	G	AB	R	H	2B	3B	HR	RBI	BB	SO	AVG	OBP	SLG	PRO+	BR	/A	RC	SB	CS	SBR	FR	POS	TPR
1946	Was-A	3	4	0	0	0	0	0	0	1	1	.000	.200	.000	-43	-1	-1	0	0	0	0	-0	/O	0.0

■ GREG GOOSSEN
Goossen, Gregory Bryant b: 12/14/45, Los Angeles, Cal. BR/TR, 6'1.5", 210 lbs. Deb: 9/03/65

YEAR	TM/L	G	AB	R	H	2B	3B	HR	RBI	BB	SO	AVG	OBP	SLG	PRO+	BR	/A	RC	SB	CS	SBR	FR	POS	TPR
1965	NY-N	11	31	2	9	0	0	1	2	1	5	.290	.313	.387	99	-0	-0	4	0	0	0	-1	/C	0.0
1966	NY-N	13	32	1	6	2	0	1	5	1	11	.188	.235	.344	60	-2	-2	2	0	0	0	-4	C.	-0.5
1967	NY-N	37	69	2	11	1	0	0	3	4	26	.159	.216	.174	13	-8	-8	3	0	0	0	-1	C	-0.7
1968	NY-N	38	106	4	22	7	0	0	6	10	21	.208	.288	.274	69	-4	-4	8	0	0	0	4	1/C	0.0
1969	Sea-A	52	139	19	43	8	1	10	24	14	29	.309	.385	.597	174	13	13	30	1	1	-0	2	1/O	1.3
1970	Mil-A	21	47	3	12	3	0	1	3	10	12	.255	.407	.383	118	2	2	8	0	0	0	-1	1	0.0
	Was-A	21	36	2	8	3	0	0	1	2	8	.222	.263	.306	59	-2	-2	3	0	0	0	0	/O1	-0.1
	Yr	42	83	5	20	6	0	1	4	12	20	.241	.351	.349	96	-0	-0	11	0	0	0	-1		-0.1
Total	6	193	460	33	111	24	1	13	44	42	112	.241	.317	.383	99	-1	-1	58	1	1	-0	-1	/1CO	-0.0

■ GLEN GORBOUS
Gorbous, Glen Edward b: 7/8/30, Drumheller, Alberta, Canada d: 6/12/90, Calgary, Alberta, Canada BL/TR, 6'2", 175 lbs. Deb: 4/11/55

YEAR	TM/L	G	AB	R	H	2B	3B	HR	RBI	BB	SO	AVG	OBP	SLG	PRO+	BR	/A	RC	SB	CS	SBR	FR	POS	TPR
1955	Cin-N	8	18	2	6	3	0	0	4	3	1	.333	.429	.500	137	1	1	4	0	0	0	0	/O	0.1
	Phi-N	91	224	25	53	9	1	4	23	21	17	.237	.302	.339	71	-10	-9	22	0	3	-2	6	O	-0.5
	Yr	99	242	27	59	12	1	4	27	24	18	.244	.312	.351	77	-8	-8	25	0	3	-2	6		-0.4
1956	Phi-N	15	33	1	6	0	0	0	1	0	1	.182	.182	.182	-2	-5	-5	1	0	0	0	-1	/O	-0.6
1957	Phi-N	3	2	1	1	1	0	0	1	1	0	.500	.667	1.000	351	1	1	2	0	0	0	0	H	0.1
Total	3	117	277	29	66	13	1	4	29	25	19	.238	.301	.336	70	-12	-12	28	0	3	-2	5	/O	-0.9

■ JOE GORDON
Gordon, Joseph Lowell "Flash" b: 2/18/15, Los Angeles, Cal. d: 4/14/78, Sacramento, Cal. BR/TR, 5'10", 180 lbs. Deb: 4/18/38 MC

YEAR	TM/L	G	AB	R	H	2B	3B	HR	RBI	BB	SO	AVG	OBP	SLG	PRO+	BR	/A	RC	SB	CS	SBR	FR	POS	TPR
1938	*NY-A	127	458	83	117	24	7	25	97	56	72	.255	.340	.502	109	3	3	81	11	3	2	24	*2	2.9
1939	*NY-A	151	567	92	161	32	5	28	111	75	57	.284	.370	.506	124	17	18	103	11	10	-3	6	*2	2.5
1940	NY-A	155	616	112	173	32	10	30	103	52	57	.281	.340	.511	122	13	16	107	18	8	1	14	*2	3.6
1941	*NY-A	156	588	104	162	26	7	24	87	72	80	.276	.358	.466	118	13	14	98	10	9	-2	6	*21	2.8
1942	*NY-A	147	538	88	173	29	4	18	103	79	95	.322	.409	.491	156	39	40	108	12	6	0	4	*2	4.9
1943	*NY-A	152	543	82	135	28	5	17	69	98	75	.249	.365	.413	126	21	20	84	4	7	-3	26	*2	5.2
1946	NY-A	112	376	35	79	15	0	11	47	49	72	.210	.308	.338	79	-10	-11	38	2	5	-2	22	*2	1.8
1947	Cle-A	155	562	89	153	27	6	29	93	62	49	.272	.346	.496	136	21	23	96	7	3	0	-4	*2	2.7
1948	*Cle-A	144	550	96	154	21	4	32	124	77	68	.280	.371	.507	138	23	25	106	5	2	0	-7	*2/S	2.1
1949	Cle-A	148	541	74	136	18	3	20	84	83	33	.251	.355	.407	103	0	0	79	5	6	-2	-18	*2	-1.5
1950	Cle-A	119	368	59	87	12	1	19	57	56	44	.236	.340	.429	99	-3	-2	56	4	1	1	-18	*2	-1.0
Total	11	1566	5707	914	1530	264	52	253	975	759	702	.268	.357	.466	121	137	150	959	89	60	-9	54	*2/1S	26.0

■ MIKE GORDON
Gordon, Michael William b: 9/11/53, Leominster, Mass. BB/TR, 6'3", 215 lbs. Deb: 4/07/77

YEAR	TM/L	G	AB	R	H	2B	3B	HR	RBI	BB	SO	AVG	OBP	SLG	PRO+	BR	/A	RC	SB	CS	SBR	FR	POS	TPR
1977	Chi-N	8	23	0	1	0	0	0	2	2	8	.043	.120	.043	-49	-5	-5	0	0	0	0	-3	/C	-0.8
1978	Chi-N	4	5	0	1	0	0	0	0	3	2	.200	.556	.200	106	1	1	1	0	0	0	-0	/C	0.0
Total	2	12	28	0	2	0	0	0	2	5	10	.071	.235	.071	-11	-4	-5	1	0	0	0	-3	/C	-0.8

■ SID GORDON
Gordon, Sidney b: 8/13/17, Brooklyn, N.Y. d: 6/17/75, New York, N.Y. BR/TR, 5'10", 185 lbs. Deb: 9/11/41

YEAR	TM/L	G	AB	R	H	2B	3B	HR	RBI	BB	SO	AVG	OBP	SLG	PRO+	BR	/A	RC	SB	CS	SBR	FR	POS	TPR
1941	NY-N	9	31	4	8	1	1	0	4	6	1	.258	.378	.355	105	1	0	5	0			-1	/O	0.0
1942	NY-N	6	19	4	6	0	1	0	2	3	2	.316	.409	.421	142	1	1	3	0			1	/3	0.2
1943	NY-N	131	474	50	119	9	11	9	63	43	32	.251	.315	.373	98	-2	-2	50	2			2	31O/2	-0.3
1946	NY-N	135	450	64	132	15	4	5	45	60	27	.293	.380	.378	115	11	11	66	1			-0	*O3	0.9
1947	NY-N	130	437	57	119	19	8	13	57	50	21	.272	.347	.442	107	4	4	67	2			-3	*O/3	-0.3
1948	NY-N	142	521	100	156	24	4	30	107	74	39	.299	.390	.537	148	35	35	108	8			-5	*3O	2.5
1949	NY-N	141	489	87	139	26	2	26	90	95	37	.284	.404	.505	142	32	32	99	1			-23	*3O/1	0.9
1950	Bos-N	134	481	78	146	33	4	27	103	78	31	.304	.403	.557	160	35	40	109	2			7	*O3	4.1
1951	Bos-N	150	550	96	158	28	1	29	109	80	32	.287	.383	.500	146	28	33	103	2	0	1	-4	*O3	2.6
1952	Bos-N	144	522	69	151	22	2	25	75	77	49	.289	.384	.483	144	28	31	101	0	4	-2	-3	*O/3	2.2
1953	Mil-N	140	464	67	127	22	4	19	75	71	40	.274	.372	.461	123	12	16	82	1	1	-0	-3	*O	0.7
1954	Pit-N	131	363	38	111	12	4	12	49	67	24	.306	.414	.438	124	15	15	70	0	0	0	-9	O3	0.4
1955	Pit-N	16	47	2	8	1	0	0	1	2	6	.170	.204	.191	6	-6	-6	1	0	0	0	2	/3O	-0.3
	NY-N	66	144	19	35	6	1	7	25	25	15	.243	.355	.444	110	2	2	25	0	0	0	7	3O	0.9
	Yr	82	191	21	43	7	1	7	26	27	21	.225	.321	.382	86	-4	-4	25	0	0	0	9		0.6
Total	13	1475	4992	735	1415	220	43	202	805	731	356	.283	.377	.466	130	196	211	889	19	5		-31	O3/12	14.5

■ GEORGE GORE
Gore, George F. "Piano Legs" b: 5/3/1857, Saccarappa, Me. d: 9/16/33, Utica, N.Y. BL/TR, 5'11", 195 lbs. Deb: 5/01/1879 M

YEAR	TM/L	G	AB	R	H	2B	3B	HR	RBI	BB	SO	AVG	OBP	SLG	PRO+	BR	/A	RC	SB	CS	SBR	FR	POS	TPR
1879	Chi-N	63	266	43	70	17	4	0	32	8	30	.263	.285	.357	104	3	1	28				-3	O/1	-0.3
1880	Chi-N	77	322	70	116	23	2	2	47	21	10	.360	.399	.463	180	30	28	61				4	O/1	2.7
1881	Chi-N	73	309	86	92	18	9	1	44	27	23	.298	.354	.424	137	16	14	48				2	*O/31	1.3
1882	Chi-N	84	367	99	117	15	7	3	51	29	19	.319	.369	.422	146	22	20	59				3	*O	1.9
1883	Chi-N	92	392	105	131	30	9	2	16	27	13	.334	.377	.472	145	26	23	72				7	*O	2.8
1884	Chi-N	103	422	104	134	18	4	5	34	61	26	.318	.404	.415	145	31	25	72				0	*O	2.1
1885	*Chi-N	109	441	115	138	21	13	5	57	68	25	.313	.405	.454	154	41	30	83				-6	*O	2.0
1886	*Chi-N	118	444	150	135	20	12	6	63	102	30	.304	.434	.444	145	42	31	98	23			-5	*O	2.5
1887	NY-N	111	459	95	133	16	5	1	49	42	18	.290	.358	.353	105	2	6	74	39			-2	*O	0.4
1888	*NY-N	64	254	37	56	4	4	2	17	30	31	.220	.308	.291	95	-1	-0	27	11			-7	O	-0.7
1889	*NY-N	120	488	132	149	21	7	7	54	84	28	.305	.416	.420	135	27	27	99	28			-10	*O	1.1
1890	NY-P	93	399	132	127	26	8	10	55	77	23	.318	.432	.499	138	31	24	101	28			-12	O	0.7
1891	NY-N	130	528	103	150	22	7	2	48	74	34	.284	.379	.364	124	16	19	82	19			-6	*O	0.5
1892	NY-N	53	193	47	49	11	2	0	11	49	16	.254	.412	.332	130	10	11	35	20			1	O	0.9
	StL-N	20	73	9	15	0	1	0	4	18	6	.205	.363	.233	87	-0	0	7	2			-2	OM	-0.1
	Yr	73	266	56	64	11	3	0	15	67	22	.241	.399	.305	119	10	11	42	22			-0		0.8
Total	14	1310	5357	1327	1612	262	94	46	582	717	332	.301	.386	.411	135	297	257	945	170			-34	*O/13	17.8

■ BOB GORINSKI
Gorinski, Robert John b: 1/7/52, Latrobe, Pa. BR/TR, 6'3", 215 lbs. Deb: 4/10/77

YEAR	TM/L	G	AB	R	H	2B	3B	HR	RBI	BB	SO	AVG	OBP	SLG	PRO+	BR	/A	RC	SB	CS	SBR	FR	POS	TPR
1977	Min-A	54	118	14	23	4	1	3	22	5	29	.195	.228	.322	49	-9	-9	9	1	0	0	-2	O/D	-1.1

■ HERB GORMAN
Gorman, Herbert Allen b: 12/18/24, San Francisco, Cal d: 4/5/53, San Diego, Cal. BL/TL, 5'11", 180 lbs. Deb: 4/19/52

YEAR	TM/L	G	AB	R	H	2B	3B	HR	RBI	BB	SO	AVG	OBP	SLG	PRO+	BR	/A	RC	SB	CS	SBR	FR	POS	TPR
1952	StL-N	1	1	0	0	0	0	0	0	0	0	.000	.000	.000	-99	-0	-0	0	0	0	0	0	H	0.0

■ HOWIE GORMAN
Gorman, Howard Paul "Lefty" b: 5/14/13, Pittsburgh, Pa. d: 4/29/84, Harrisburg, Pa. BL/TL, 6'2", 160 lbs. Deb: 8/07/37

YEAR	TM/L	G	AB	R	H	2B	3B	HR	RBI	BB	SO	AVG	OBP	SLG	PRO+	BR	/A	RC	SB	CS	SBR	FR	POS	TPR
1937	Phi-N	13	19	3	4	1	0	0	1	1	1	.211	.250	.263	37	-2	-2	1	1			-2	/O	-0.3
1938	Phi-N	1	1	0	0	0	0	0	0	0	0	.000	.000	.000	-99	-0	-0	0	0			0	H	0.0
Total	2	14	20	3	4	1	0	0	1	1	1	.200	.238	.250	30	-2	-2	1	1			-2	/O	-0.3

■ JACK GORMAN
Gorman, John F. "Stooping Jack" b: 1859, St.Louis, Mo. d: 9/9/1889, St.Louis, Mo. Deb: 7/01/1883

YEAR	TM/L	G	AB	R	H	2B	3B	HR	RBI	BB	SO	AVG	OBP	SLG	PRO+	BR	/A	RC	SB	CS	SBR	FR	POS	TPR
1883	StL-a	1	4	0	0	0	0	0		0	0	.000	.000	.000	-94	-1	-1	0				0	/O	0.0

YEAR	TM/L	G	AB	R	H	2B	3B	HR	RBI	BB	SO	AVG	OBP	SLG	PRO+	BR	/A	RC	SB	CS	SBR	FR	POS	TPR
1884	KC-U	33	137	25	38	5	2	0			4	.277	.298	.343	133	2	5	14	0			-2	1/O3	0.2
	Pit-a	8	27	3	4	0	1	0			1	.148	.179	.222	31	-2	-2	1				-2	/PO3	-0.3
Total	2	42	168	28	42	5	3	0			5	.250	.272	.315	108	-1	2	15				-4	/1O3P	-0.1

■ JOHNNY GORYL
Goryl, John Albert b: 10/21/33, Cumberland, R.I. BR/TR, 5'10", 175 lbs. Deb: 9/20/57 MC

YEAR	TM/L	G	AB	R	H	2B	3B	HR	RBI	BB	SO	AVG	OBP	SLG	PRO+	BR	/A	RC	SB	CS	SBR	FR	POS	TPR
1957	Chi-N	9	38	7	8	2	0	0	1	5	9	.211	.318	.263	59	-2	-2	3	0	1	-1	-1	/3	-0.3
1958	Chi-N	83	219	27	53	9	3	4	14	27	34	.242	.331	.365	85	-5	-4	24	0	1	-1	11	32	0.8
1959	Chi-N	25	48	1	9	3	1	1	6	5	3	.188	.264	.354	63	-3	-3	4	1	1	-0	0	2/3	-0.1
1962	Min-A	37	26	6	5	0	1	2	2	2	6	.192	.250	.500	93	-0	-0	3	0	0	0	8	/2S	0.8
1963	Min-A	64	150	29	43	5	3	9	24	15	29	.287	.355	.540	144	9	9	28	0	0	0	-9	23/S	0.3
1964	Min-A	58	114	9	16	0	2	0	1	10	25	.140	.216	.175	10	-14	-14	5	1	0	0	2	23	-0.7
Total	6	276	595	79	134	19	10	16	48	64	106	.225	.306	.371	83	-15	-14	66	2	3	-1	11	2/3S	0.8

■ JIM GOSGER
Gosger, James Charles b: 11/6/42, Port Huron, Mich. BL/TL, 5'11", 185 lbs. Deb: 5/04/63

YEAR	TM/L	G	AB	R	H	2B	3B	HR	RBI	BB	SO	AVG	OBP	SLG	PRO+	BR	/A	RC	SB	CS	SBR	FR	POS	TPR
1963	Bos-A	19	16	3	1	0	0	0	0	3	5	.063	.211	.063	-19	-3	-3	0	0	0	0	1	/O	-0.1
1965	Bos-A	81	324	45	83	15	4	9	35	29	61	.256	.321	.410	100	2	0	43	3	1	0	7	O	0.5
1966	Bos-A	40	126	16	32	4	0	5	17	15	20	.254	.333	.405	101	0	0	18	0	1	-1	-1	O	-0.2
	KC-A	88	272	34	61	14	1	5	27	37	53	.224	.322	.338	93	-3	-2	32	5	3	-0	3	O	-0.2
	Yr	128	398	50	93	18	1	10	44	52	73	.234	.325	.359	96	-1	-1	50	5	4	-1	2		-0.4
1967	KC-A	134	356	31	86	14	5	5	36	53	69	.242	.340	.351	108	3	5	44	5	7	-3	2	*O	0.1
1968	Oak-A	88	150	7	27	1	1	0	5	17	21	.180	.263	.200	44	-10	-9	8	4	0	1	9	O	-0.1
1969	Sea-A	39	55	4	6	2	1	1	1	6	11	.109	.197	.236	21	-6	-6	3	2	1	0	3	O	-0.3
	NY-N	10	15	0	2	2	0	0	1	1	6	.133	.188	.267	25	-2	-2	1	0	0	0	0	/O	-0.1
1970	Mon-N	91	274	38	72	11	2	5	37	35	35	.263	.348	.372	93	-2	-2	37	5	3	-0	-1	O1	-0.7
1971	Mon-N	51	102	7	16	2	2	0	8	9	17	.157	.232	.216	27	-10	-10	5	1	1	-0	0	O/1	-1.1
1973	NY-N	38	92	9	22	2	0	0	10	9	16	.239	.307	.261	60	-5	-5	7	0	1	-1	-2	O	-0.9
1974	NY-N	26	33	3	3	0	0	0	1	0	3	.091	.167	.091	-27	-6	-5	0	0	0	0	-1	O	-0.6
Total	10	705	1815	197	411	67	16	30	177	217	316	.226	.311	.331	83	-38	-38	199	25	18	-3	20	O/1	-3.7

■ GOOSE GOSLIN
Goslin, Leon Allen b: 10/16/1900, Salem, N.J. d: 5/15/71, Bridgeton, N.J. BL/TR, 5'11.5", 185 lbs. Deb: 9/16/21 H

YEAR	TM/L	G	AB	R	H	2B	3B	HR	RBI	BB	SO	AVG	OBP	SLG	PRO+	BR	/A	RC	SB	CS	SBR	FR	POS	TPR
1921	Was-A	14	50	8	13	1	1	1	6	6	5	.260	.351	.380	91	-1	-1	7	0	0	0	0	O	-0.1
1922	Was-A	101	358	44	116	19	7	3	53	25	26	.324	.373	.441	117	6	8	58	4	4	-1	-3	O	-0.2
1923	Was-A	150	600	86	180	29	**18**	9	99	40	53	.300	.347	.453	115	5	10	95	7	2	1	7	*O	0.3
1924	•Was-A	154	579	100	199	30	17	12	**129**	68	29	.344	.421	.516	145	36	38	126	16	14	-4	5	*O	2.7
1925	•Was-A	150	601	116	201	34	**20**	18	113	53	50	.334	.394	.547	140	31	33	131	26	8	**3**	14	*O	3.3
1926	Was-A	147	568	105	201	26	15	17	108	63	38	.354	.425	.542	155	42	44	131	8	8	-2	19	*O	4.7
1927	Was-A	148	581	96	194	37	15	13	120	50	28	.334	.392	.516	136	28	29	111	21	6	3	2	*O	2.2
1928	Was-A	135	456	80	173	36	10	17	102	48	19	**.379**	.442	.614	176	49	49	125	16	3	**3**	3	*O	4.5
1929	Was-A	145	553	82	159	28	7	18	91	66	33	.288	.366	.461	111	9	8	97	10	3	1	-4	*O	0.0
1930	Was-A	47	188	34	51	11	5	7	38	19	19	.271	.344	.495	110	2	2	32	3	2	-0	-5	O	-0.4
	StL-A	101	396	81	129	25	7	30	100	48	35	.326	.400	.652	156	35	33	101	14	9	-1	12	*O	3.6
	Yr	148	584	115	180	36	12	37	138	67	54	.308	.382	.601	142	37	35	132	17	11	-2	7		3.2
1931	StL-A	151	591	114	194	42	10	24	105	80	41	.328	.412	.555	147	45	42	137	9	6	-1	5	*O	3.3
1932	StL-A	150	572	88	171	28	9	17	104	92	35	.299	.398	.469	117	22	17	110	12	9	-2	6	*O/3	1.4
1933	•Was-A	132	549	97	163	35	10	10	64	42	32	.297	.348	.452	112	7	7	87	5	2	0	2	*O	0.5
1934	•Det-A	151	614	106	187	38	7	13	100	65	38	.305	.373	.453	112	11	10	105	5	4	-1	2	*O	0.9
1935	•Det-A	147	590	88	172	34	6	9	109	56	31	.292	.355	.415	102	-2	1	88	5	4	-1	2	*O	0.1
1936	Det-A	147	572	122	180	33	8	24	125	85	50	.315	.403	.526	127	25	25	126	14	4	2	-9	*O	1.2
1937	Det-A	79	181	30	43	11	1	4	35	35	18	.238	.367	.376	86	-3	-3	27	0	1	-1	-3	O/1	-0.7
1938	Was-A	38	57	6	9	3	0	2	8	8	5	.158	.262	.316	47	-5	-5	5	0	0	0	0	O	-0.3
Total	18	2287	8656	1483	2735	500	173	248	1609	949	585	.316	.387	.500	128	341	348	1700	175	89	-1	54	*O/13	27.0

■ HOWIE GOSS
Goss, Howard Wayne b: 11/1/34, Wewoka, Okla. BR/TR, 6'4", 204 lbs. Deb: 4/10/62

YEAR	TM/L	G	AB	R	H	2B	3B	HR	RBI	BB	SO	AVG	OBP	SLG	PRO+	BR	/A	RC	SB	CS	SBR	FR	POS	TPR
1962	Pit-N	89	111	19	27	6	0	2	10	9	36	.243	.306	.351	76	-4	-4	12	5	2	0	4	O	-0.3
1963	Hou-N	133	411	37	86	18	2	9	44	31	128	.209	.265	.328	74	-16	-14	36	4	6	-2	2	*O	-2.1
Total	2	222	522	56	113	24	2	11	54	40	164	.216	.274	.333	75	-20	-17	48	9	8	-2	6	O	-2.4

■ DICK GOSSETT
Gossett, John Star b: 8/21/1891, Dennison, Ohio d: 10/6/62, Massillon, Ohio BR/TR, 5'11", 185 lbs. Deb: 4/30/13

YEAR	TM/L	G	AB	R	H	2B	3B	HR	RBI	BB	SO	AVG	OBP	SLG	PRO+	BR	/A	RC	SB	CS	SBR	FR	POS	TPR
1913	NY-A	39	105	9	17	2	0	0	9	10	22	.162	.254	.181	28	-9	-9	5	1			-4	C	-1.1
1914	NY-A	10	21	3	3	0	0	0	1	5	5	.143	.333	.143	44	-1	-1	1	0			-1	C	-0.1
Total	2	49	126	12	20	2	0	0	10	15	27	.159	.269	.175	31	-10	-10	6	1			-6	/C	-1.2

■ JULIO GOTAY
Gotay, Julio Enrique (Sanchez) b: 6/9/39, Fajardo, P.R. BR/TR, 6', 180 lbs. Deb: 8/06/60

YEAR	TM/L	G	AB	R	H	2B	3B	HR	RBI	BB	SO	AVG	OBP	SLG	PRO+	BR	/A	RC	SB	CS	SBR	FR	POS	TPR
1960	StL-N	3	8	1	3	0	0	0	0	0	2	.375	.375	.375	98	0	-0	1	1	0	0	-1	/S3	0.0
1961	StL-N	10	45	5	11	4	0	0	5	3	5	.244	.292	.333	59	-2	-3	4	0	0	0	-4	S	-0.5
1962	StL-N	127	369	47	94	12	1	2	27	27	47	.255	.316	.309	62	-16	-20	34	7	3	0	6	*S/2O3	-0.2
1963	Pit-N	4	2	0	1	0	0	0	0	0	0	.500	.500	.500	188	0	0	1	0	0	0	-1	/2	0.1
1964	Pit-N	3	2	1	1	0	0	0	0	1	0	.500	.667	.500	235	1	1	1	0	0	0	0	H	0.1
1965	Cal-A	40	77	6	19	4	0	1	3	4	9	.247	.284	.338	78	-3	-2	7	0	0	0	3	2/3S	0.2
1966	Hou-N	4	5	0	0	0	0	0	0	0	0	.000	.000	.000	-99	-1	-1	0	0	0	0	0	/3	0.0
1967	Hou-N	77	234	30	66	10	2	2	15	15	30	.282	.331	.368	103	-0	1	28	1	1	-0	-3	2S/3	0.1
1968	Hou-N	75	165	9	41	3	0	1	11	4	21	.248	.271	.285	68	-7	-6	11	1	2	-1	10	2/3	0.6
1969	Hou-N	46	81	7	21	5	0	0	9	7	13	.259	.318	.321	81	-2	-2	7	2	1	0	6	2/3	0.5
Total	10	389	988	106	257	38	3	6	70	61	127	.260	.309	.323	75	-30	-34	94	12	7	-1	17	S2/3O	0.9

■ CHARLIE GOULD
Gould, Charles Harvey b: 8/21/1847, Cincinnati, Ohio d: 4/10/17, Flushing, N.Y. BR/TR, 6', 172 lbs. Deb: 5/05/1871 M

YEAR	TM/L	G	AB	R	H	2B	3B	HR	RBI	BB	SO	AVG	OBP	SLG	PRO+	BR	/A	RC	SB	CS	SBR	FR	POS	TPR
1871	Bos-n	31	151	38	43	9	2	1	32	3	1	.285	.299	.411	98	0	-1	21	6				*1/O	0.0
1872	Bos-n	45	214	39	57	7	8	0		2		.266	.273	.374	92	-1	-3	22					*1/O	0.1
1874	Bal-n	33	142	20	31	6	0	0		3		.218	.234	.261	58	-6	-6	9					1/C	-0.4
1875	NH-n	27	109	9	29	2	1	0		1		.266	.273	.303	116	-0	2	9					1/OM	0.1
1876	Cin-N	61	258	27	65	7	0	0	11	6	11	.252	.269	.279	97	-4	1	20				1	*1/PM	0.3
1877	Cin-N	24	91	5	25	2	1	0	13	5	5	.275	.313	.319	112	0	2	9				-1	1/O	0.0
Total	4 n	136	616	106	160	24	11	2	32	9	1	.260	.270	.344	90	-7	-8	61					1/OC	-0.2
Total	2	85	349	32	90	9	1	0	24	11	16	.258	.281	.289	101	-4	3	29				1	/1PO	0.3

■ NICK GOULISH
Goulish, Nicholas Edward b: 11/13/17, Punxsutawney, Pa. d: 5/15/84, Youngstown, Ohio BL/TL, 6'1", 179 lbs. Deb: 4/19/44

YEAR	TM/L	G	AB	R	H	2B	3B	HR	RBI	BB	SO	AVG	OBP	SLG	PRO+	BR	/A	RC	SB	CS	SBR	FR	POS	TPR
1944	Phi-N	1	1	0	0	0	0	0	0	0	0	.000	.000	.000	-99	-0	-0	0	0			0	H	0.0
1945	Phi-N	13	11	4	3	0	0	0	2	1	3	.273	.333	.273	72	-0	-0	1	0			0	/O	0.0
Total	2	14	12	4	3	0	0	0	2	1	3	.250	.308	.250	58	-1	-1	1	0			0	/O	0.0

■ CLAUDE GOUZZIE
Gouzzie, Claude b: 1881, Pennsylvania d: 9/21/07, Denver, Colo. BR/TR, 5'9", 170 lbs. Deb: 7/22/03

YEAR	TM/L	G	AB	R	H	2B	3B	HR	RBI	BB	SO	AVG	OBP	SLG	PRO+	BR	/A	RC	SB	CS	SBR	FR	POS	TPR
1903	StL-A	1	0	0	0	0	0	0	0	0		.000	.000	.000	-99	-0	-0	0	0			0	/2	0.0

■ HANK GOWDY
Gowdy, Henry Morgan b: 8/24/1889, Columbus, Ohio d: 8/1/66, Columbus, Ohio BR/TR, 6'2", 182 lbs. Deb: 9/13/10 MC

YEAR	TM/L	G	AB	R	H	2B	3B	HR	RBI	BB	SO	AVG	OBP	SLG	PRO+	BR	/A	RC	SB	CS	SBR	FR	POS	TPR
1910	NY-N	7	14	1	3	1	0	0	2	2	3	.214	.313	.286	75	-0	-0	2	1			0	/1	0.0

YEAR	TM/L	G	AB	R	H	2B	3B	HR	RBI	BB	SO	AVG	OBP	SLG	PRO+	BR	/A	RC	SB	CS	SBR	FR	POS	TPR
1911	NY-N	4	4	1	1	1	0	0	0	2	0	.250	.500	.500	175	1	1	1	0			-0	/1	0.0
	Bos-N	29	97	9	28	4	2	0	16	4	19	.289	.324	.371	87	-1	-2	12	2			-1	1/C	-0.3
	Yr	33	101	10	29	5	2	0	16	6	19	.287	.333	.376	92	-0	-1	13	2			-1		-0.3
1912	Bos-N	44	96	16	26	6	1	3	10	16	13	.271	.386	.448	126	4	4	18	3			-1	C/1	0.3
1913	Bos-N	3	5	0	3	1	0	0	2	3	2	.600	.750	.800	336	2	2	3	0			-1	/C	0.1
1914	*Bos-N	128	366	42	89	17	6	3	46	48	40	.243	.337	.347	104	3	3	46	14			-6	*C/1	0.1
1915	Bos-N	118	316	27	78	15	3	2	30	41	34	.247	.339	.332	108	3	4	38	10	4	1	-0	*C	1.2
1916	Bos-N	118	349	32	88	14	1	1	34	24	33	.252	.311	.307	94	-4	-2	38	8			2	*C	0.7
1917	Bos-N	49	154	12	33	7	0	0	14	15	13	.214	.288	.260	73	-5	-4	12	2			-2	C	-0.3
1919	Bos-N	78	219	18	61	8	1	1	22	19	16	.279	.339	.338	108	1	2	26	5			4	C/1	1.3
1920	Bos-N	80	214	14	52	11	2	0	18	20	15	.243	.314	.313	84	-5	-4	23	6	1	1	10	C	1.3
1921	Bos-N	64	164	17	49	7	2	2	17	16	11	.299	.368	.402	110	1	3	26	2	0	1	-1	C	0.5
1922	Bos-N	92	221	23	70	11	1	1	27	24	13	.317	.391	.389	107	2	3	35	2	1	0	0	C/1	0.4
1923	Bos-N	23	48	5	6	1	1	0	5	15	5	.125	.354	.188	48	-3	-3	5	1	1	-0	-2	C	-0.3
	*NY-N	53	122	13	40	6	3	1	18	21	9	.328	.427	.451	133	7	7	25	2	0	1	-8	C	0.2
	Yr	76	170	18	46	7	4	1	23	36	14	.271	.404	.376	109	4	4	29	3	1	0	-10		-0.1
1924	*NY-N	87	191	25	62	9	1	4	37	26	11	.325	.411	.445	133	9	10	37	1	0	0	5	C	1.6
1925	NY-N	47	114	14	37	4	3	3	19	12	7	.325	.389	.491	128	4	5	22	0	0	0	1	C	0.7
1929	Bos-N	10	16	1	7	0	0	0	3	0	2	.438	.438	.438	122	0	1	3	0			-0	/C	0.1
1930	Bos-N	16	25	0	5	1	0	0	2	3	1	.200	.310	.240	37	-3	-2	2	0			1	C	0.0
Total	17	1050	2735	270	738	124	27	21	322	311	247	.270	.351	.358	105	15	25	372	59	7		1	C/1	7.6

■ BILLY GRABARKEWITZ
Grabarkewitz, Billy Cordell   b: 1/18/46, Lockhart, Tex.   BR/TR, 5'10", 165 lbs.   Deb: 4/22/69

YEAR	TM/L	G	AB	R	H	2B	3B	HR	RBI	BB	SO	AVG	OBP	SLG	PRO+	BR	/A	RC	SB	CS	SBR	FR	POS	TPR
1969	LA-N	34	65	4	6	1	1	0	5	4	19	.092	.145	.138	-22	-10	-10	1	1	0	0	-2	S/32	-0.9
1970	LA-N	156	529	92	153	20	8	17	84	95	149	.289	.403	.454	135	25	29	103	19	9	0	-1	3S2	3.3
1971	LA-N	44	71	9	16	5	0	0	6	19	16	.225	.389	.296	102	1	1	9	1	2	-1	4	23/S	0.6
1972	LA-N	53	144	17	24	4	0	4	16	18	53	.167	.268	.278	57	-8	-8	12	3	0	1	-4	32/S	-1.0
1973	Cal-A	61	129	27	21	6	1	3	9	28	27	.163	.316	.295	79	-4	-3	13	2	2	-1	-6	23/SOD	-0.8
	Phi-N	25	66	12	19	2	0	2	7	12	18	.288	.397	.409	121	3	2	12	3	1	0	0	2/3O	0.4
1974	Phi-N	34	30	7	4	0	0	1	2	5	10	.133	.257	.233	36	-2	-3	2	3	1	0	1	/O3	-0.1
	Chi-N	53	125	21	31	3	2	1	12	21	28	.248	.361	.328	90	-0	-1	16	1	2	-1	2	2/S3	0.3
	Yr	87	155	28	35	3	2	2	14	26	38	.226	.341	.310	80	-3	-4	18	4	3	-1	3		0.2
1975	Oak-A	6	2	0	0	0	0	0	0	0	1	.000	.000	.000	-99	-1	-1	0	0	0	0	0	/2D	0.0
Total	7	466	1161	189	274	41	12	28	141	202	321	.236	.354	.364	101	3	8	169	33	17	-0	-6	32/SOD	1.8

■ ROD GRABER
Graber, Rodney Blaine   b: 6/20/31, Marshallville, O.   BL/TL, 5'11", 175 lbs.   Deb: 9/09/58

YEAR	TM/L	G	AB	R	H	2B	3B	HR	RBI	BB	SO	AVG	OBP	SLG	PRO+	BR	/A	RC	SB	CS	SBR	FR	POS	TPR
1958	Cle-A	4	8	0	1	0	0	0	0	1	2	.125	.222	.125	-2	-1	-1	0	0	0	0	0	/O	0.0

■ JOHNNY GRABOWSKI
Grabowski, John Patrick "Nig"   b: 1/7/1900, Ware, Mass.   d: 5/23/46, Albany, N.Y.   BR/TR, 5'10", 185 lbs.   Deb: 7/11/24

YEAR	TM/L	G	AB	R	H	2B	3B	HR	RBI	BB	SO	AVG	OBP	SLG	PRO+	BR	/A	RC	SB	CS	SBR	FR	POS	TPR
1924	Chi-A	20	56	10	14	3	0	0	3	2	4	.250	.276	.304	51	-4	-4	5	0	0	0	1	C	-0.1
1925	Chi-A	21	46	5	14	4	1	0	10	2	4	.304	.333	.435	99	-1	-0	7	0	1	-1	0	C	0.0
1926	Chi-A	48	122	6	32	1	1	1	11	4	15	.262	.286	.311	58	-8	-8	11	0	1	-1	-2	C/1	-0.6
1927	*NY-A	70	195	29	54	2	4	0	25	20	15	.277	.350	.328	79	-6	-5	23	0	0	0	0	C	-0.2
1928	NY-A	75	202	21	48	7	1	1	21	10	21	.238	.274	.297	51	-15	-14	17	0	0	0	2	C	-0.6
1929	NY-A	22	59	4	12	1	0	0	2	3	6	.203	.242	.220	21	-7	-7	6	1	0	0	0	C	-0.3
1931	Det-A	40	136	9	32	7	1	1	14	6	19	.235	.268	.324	53	-9	-10	12	0	0	0	2	C	-0.4
Total	7	296	816	84	206	25	8	3	86	47	84	.252	.295	.314	60	-50	-48	76	1	2	-1	3	C/1	-2.2

■ JOE GRACE
Grace, Joseph Laverne   b: 1/5/14, Gorham, Ill.   d: 9/18/69, Murphysboro, Ill.   BL/TR, 6'1", 180 lbs.   Deb: 9/24/38

YEAR	TM/L	G	AB	R	H	2B	3B	HR	RBI	BB	SO	AVG	OBP	SLG	PRO+	BR	/A	RC	SB	CS	SBR	FR	POS	TPR
1938	StL-A	12	47	7	16	1	0	0	4	2	3	.340	.367	.362	83	-1	-1	6	0	1	-1	-2	O	-0.3
1939	StL-A	74	207	35	63	11	2	3	22	19	24	.304	.363	.420	98	-0	-1	33	3	2	-0	-1	O	-0.3
1940	StL-A	80	229	45	59	14	2	5	25	26	23	.258	.336	.402	88	-3	-4	32	2	2	-1	-7	OC	-1.3
1941	StL-A	115	362	53	112	17	4	6	60	57	31	.309	.410	.428	118	14	12	69	1	3	-2	-5	O/C	0.1
1946	StL-A	48	161	21	37	7	2	1	13	16	20	.230	.307	.317	71	-5	-6	16	1	3	-2	-1	O	-1.0
	Was-A	77	321	39	97	17	4	2	31	24	19	.302	.358	.399	118	5	7	46	1	4	-2	3	O	0.4
	Yr	125	482	60	134	24	6	3	44	40	39	.278	.341	.371	101	-1	0	61	2	7	-4	2		-0.6
1947	Was-A	78	234	25	58	9	4	3	17	35	15	.248	.348	.359	99	-0	0	31	1	2	-1	3	O	0.0
Total	6	484	1561	225	442	76	18	20	172	179	135	.283	.362	.393	102	8	7	231	9	17	-8	-9	O/C	-2.4

■ MARK GRACE
Grace, Mark Eugene   b: 6/28/64, Winston-Salem, N.C   BL/TL, 6'2", 190 lbs.   Deb: 5/02/88

YEAR	TM/L	G	AB	R	H	2B	3B	HR	RBI	BB	SO	AVG	OBP	SLG	PRO+	BR	/A	RC	SB	CS	SBR	FR	POS	TPR
1988	Chi-N	134	486	65	144	23	4	7	57	60	43	.296	.374	.403	118	16	13	74	3	3	-1	-3	*1	0.2
1989	*Chi-N	142	510	74	160	28	3	13	79	80	42	.314	.407	.457	136	34	29	96	14	7	0	13	*1	3.3
1990	Chi-N	157	589	72	182	32	1	9	82	59	54	.309	.377	.413	107	15	9	94	15	6	1	27	*1	2.9
Total	3	433	1585	211	486	83	8	29	218	199	139	.307	.386	.424	120	65	51	264	32	16	0	37	1	6.4

■ MIKE GRACE
Grace, Michael Lee   b: 6/14/56, Pontiac, Mich.   BR/TR, 6', 175 lbs.   Deb: 4/18/78

YEAR	TM/L	G	AB	R	H	2B	3B	HR	RBI	BB	SO	AVG	OBP	SLG	PRO+	BR	/A	RC	SB	CS	SBR	FR	POS	TPR
1978	Cin-N	5	3	0	0	0	0	0	0	0	2	.000	.000	.000	-99	-1	-1	0	0	0	0	1	/3	0.0

■ EARL GRACE
Grace, Robert Earl   b: 2/24/07, Barlow, Ky.   d: 12/22/80, Phoenix, Ariz.   BL/TR, 6', 175 lbs.   Deb: 4/23/29

YEAR	TM/L	G	AB	R	H	2B	3B	HR	RBI	BB	SO	AVG	OBP	SLG	PRO+	BR	/A	RC	SB	CS	SBR	FR	POS	TPR
1929	Chi-N	27	80	7	20	1	0	2	17	9	7	.250	.333	.338	67	-4	-4	9	0			3	C	0.1
1931	Chi-N	7	9	2	1	0	0	0	1	4	1	.111	.385	.111	39	-1	-1	1	0			0	/C	0.0
	Pit-N	47	150	8	42	6	1	1	20	13	5	.280	.337	.353	87	-3	-3	19	0			-1	C	-0.1
	Yr	54	159	10	43	6	1	1	21	17	6	.270	.341	.340	84	-3	-3	20	0			-1		-0.1
1932	Pit-N	115	390	41	107	17	5	8	55	14	23	.274	.305	.405	91	-7	-6	48	0			-7	*C	-0.8
1933	Pit-N	93	291	22	84	13	1	3	44	26	23	.289	.349	.371	106	3	3	40	0			0	C	0.6
1934	Pit-N	95	289	27	78	17	1	4	24	20	19	.270	.317	.377	83	-6	-7	35	0			-9	C/1	-1.2
1935	Pit-N	77	224	19	59	8	1	3	29	32	17	.263	.355	.348	87	-2	-3	27	1			2	C	-0.1
1936	Phi-N	86	221	24	55	11	0	4	32	34	20	.249	.352	.353	82	-2	-5	30	0			-5	C	-0.7
1937	Phi-N	80	223	19	47	10	1	6	29	33	15	.211	.313	.345	73	-6	-9	25	0			-3	C	-0.9
Total	8	627	1877	169	493	83	10	31	251	185	130	.263	.331	.367	86	-29	-35	235	1			-20	C/1	-3.1

■ JOHN GRADY
Grady, John J.   b: 6/18/1860, Lowell, Mass.   d: 7/15/1893, Lowell, Mass.   5'7", 150 lbs.   Deb: 5/10/1884

YEAR	TM/L	G	AB	R	H	2B	3B	HR	RBI	BB	SO	AVG	OBP	SLG	PRO+	BR	/A	RC	SB	CS	SBR	FR	POS	TPR
1884	Alt-U	9	36	6	11	3	0	0		2		.306	.342	.389	145	2	2	5	0			-1	/1O	0.0

■ MIKE GRADY
Grady, Michael William   b: 12/23/1869, Kennett Square, Pa   d: 12/3/43, Kennett Square, Pa.   BR/TR, 5'11", 190 lbs.   Deb: 4/24/1894

YEAR	TM/L	G	AB	R	H	2B	3B	HR	RBI	BB	SO	AVG	OBP	SLG	PRO+	BR	/A	RC	SB	CS	SBR	FR	POS	TPR
1894	Phi-N	60	190	45	69	13	8	0	40	14	13	.363	.427	.516	132	9	10	44	3			-11	C1/O	0.2
1895	Phi-N	46	123	21	40	3	1	1	23	14	8	.325	.407	.390	108	2	2	22	5			-10	C/O31	-0.3
1896	Phi-N	71	242	49	77	20	7	1	44	16	19	.318	.382	.471	128	9	9	49	10			-8	C/3	0.6
1897	Phi-N	4	13	1	2	0	0	0	0	1		.154	.214	.154	-1	-2	-2	0	0			0	/C	0.0
	StL-N	83	322	48	90	11	3	7	45	26		.280	.352	.398	102	0	1	49	7			-1	1/O	0.0
	Yr	87	335	49	92	11	3	7	45	27		.275	.347	.388	98	-2	-1	49	7			-0		0.0
1898	NY-N	93	287	46	85	19	5	3	49	38		.296	.399	.429	145	16	18	58	20			-1	CO/1S	1.8
1899	NY-N	86	311	47	104	18	8	2	54	29		.334	.403	.463	145	17	19	68	20			-12	C3/O1	0.8
1900	NY-N	83	251	36	55	8	4	0	27	34		.219	.322	.283	73	-9	-7	26	9			-14	C1S/302	-1.4
1901	Was-A	94	347	57	99	17	10	9	56	27		.285	.349	.470	130	12	13	63	14			6	1C/O	1.7

YEAR	TM/L	G	AB	R	H	2B	3B	HR	RBI	BB	SO	AVG	OBP	SLG	PRO+	BR	/A	RC	SB	CS	SBR	FR	POS	TPR
1904	StL-N	101	323	44	101	15	11	5	43	31		.313	.373	.474	171	23	25	62	6			-19	C1/23	1.3
1905	StL-N	100	311	41	89	20	7	4	41	33		.286	.355	.434	141	14	15	55	15			-11	C1	1.0
1906	StL-N	97	280	33	70	11	3	3	27	48		.250	.360	.343	127	9	10	38	5			-10	C1	0.4
Total	11	918	3000	486	881	155	67	35	449	311	40	.294	.371	.425	128	101	114	535	114			-90	C1/30S2	6.1

■ FRED GRAFF
Graff, Frederick Gottleib   b: 8/25/1889, Canton, Ohio   d: 10/4/79, Chattanooga, Tenn.   BR/TR, 5'10.5", 164 lbs.   Deb: 5/14/13

YEAR	TM/L	G	AB	R	H	2B	3B	HR	RBI	BB	SO	AVG	OBP	SLG	PRO+	BR	/A	RC	SB	CS	SBR	FR	POS	TPR
1913	StL-A	4	5	1	2	1	0	0	2	3	3	.400	.625	.600	266	1	1	2	0			-1	/3	0.1

■ LOUIS GRAFF
Graff, Louis George "Chappie"   b: 7/25/1866, Philadelphia, Pa.   d: 4/16/55, Bryn Mawr, Pa.   TR ,   Deb: 6/23/1890

YEAR	TM/L	G	AB	R	H	2B	3B	HR	RBI	BB	SO	AVG	OBP	SLG	PRO+	BR	/A	RC	SB	CS	SBR	FR	POS	TPR
1890	Syr-a	1	5	0	2	1	0	0		0		.400	.400	.600	218	1	1	1	0			-2	/C	0.0

■ MILT GRAFF
Graff, Milton Edward   b: 12/30/30, Jefferson Center, Pa.   BL/TR, 5'7.5", 158 lbs.   Deb: 4/16/57   C

YEAR	TM/L	G	AB	R	H	2B	3B	HR	RBI	BB	SO	AVG	OBP	SLG	PRO+	BR	/A	RC	SB	CS	SBR	FR	POS	TPR
1957	KC-A	56	155	16	28	4	3	0	10	15	10	.181	.262	.245	39	-13	-13	10	2	5	-2	1	2	-1.1
1958	KC-A	5	1	0	0	0	0	0	0	0	0	.000	.000	.000	-98	-0	-0	0	0	0	0	1	/2	0.1
Total	2	61	156	16	28	4	3	0	10	15	10	.179	.260	.244	38	-13	-14	10	2	5	-2	3	/2	-1.0

■ MOONLIGHT GRAHAM
Graham, Archibald Wright   b: 11/9/1876, Fayetteville, N.C.   d: 8/25/65, Chisolm, Minn.   5'10.5", 170 lbs.   Deb: 6/29/05

YEAR	TM/L	G	AB	R	H	2B	3B	HR	RBI	BB	SO	AVG	OBP	SLG	PRO+	BR	/A	RC	SB	CS	SBR	FR	POS	TPR
1905	NY-N	1	0	0	0	0	0	0	0	0		—	—	—		0	0	0	0			-0	/O	0.0

■ SKINNY GRAHAM
Graham, Arthur William   b: 8/12/09, Somerville, Mass.   d: 7/10/67, Cambridge, Mass.   BL/TR, 5'7", 162 lbs.   Deb: 9/14/34

YEAR	TM/L	G	AB	R	H	2B	3B	HR	RBI	BB	SO	AVG	OBP	SLG	PRO+	BR	/A	RC	SB	CS	SBR	FR	POS	TPR
1934	Bos-A	13	47	7	11	2	1	0	3	6	13	.234	.321	.319	61	-2	-3	5	2	2	-1	-1	O	-0.4
1935	Bos-A	8	10	1	3	0	0	0	1	1	3	.300	.364	.300	69	-0	-0	1	1	0	0	-0	/O	0.0
Total	2	21	57	8	14	2	1	0	4	7	16	.246	.328	.316	62	-3	-3	6	3	2	-0	-1	/O	-0.4

■ BARNEY GRAHAM
Graham, Barney   b: Philadelphia, Pa.   d: 12/31/1896, Mobile, Ala.   Deb: 9/04/1889

YEAR	TM/L	G	AB	R	H	2B	3B	HR	RBI	BB	SO	AVG	OBP	SLG	PRO+	BR	/A	RC	SB	CS	SBR	FR	POS	TPR
1889	Phi-a	4	18	0	3	0	0	0	0	0	0	.167	.167	.167	-4	-2	-2	1	0			1	/3	0.0

■ BERNIE GRAHAM
Graham, Bernard   b: 1860, Beloit, Wis.   d: 10/30/1886, Mobile, Ala.   Deb: 7/11/1884

YEAR	TM/L	G	AB	R	H	2B	3B	HR	RBI	BB	SO	AVG	OBP	SLG	PRO+	BR	/A	RC	SB	CS	SBR	FR	POS	TPR
1884	CP-U	1	5	2	1	0	0	0		0		.200	.200	.200	36	-0	-0	0	0			0	/O	0.0
	Bal-U	41	167	21	45	11	0	0		2		.269	.278	.335	96	1	-2	16	0			1	O/1	0.0
	Yr	42	172	23	46	11	0	0		2		.267	.276	.331	95	1	-2	16	0			1		0.0

■ BERT GRAHAM
Graham, Bert "B.G."   b: 4/3/1886, Tilton, Ill.   d: 6/19/71, Cottonwood, Ariz.   BB/TR, 5'11.5", 187 lbs.   Deb: 9/09/10

YEAR	TM/L	G	AB	R	H	2B	3B	HR	RBI	BB	SO	AVG	OBP	SLG	PRO+	BR	/A	RC	SB	CS	SBR	FR	POS	TPR
1910	StL-A	8	26	1	3	2	1	0	5	1		.115	.148	.269	32	-2	-2	1	0			1	/12	0.0

■ CHARLIE GRAHAM
Graham, Charles Henry   b: 4/25/1878, Santa Clara, Cal.   d: 8/29/48, San Francisco, Cal   BR/TR, 5'11", 180 lbs.   Deb: 4/16/06

YEAR	TM/L	G	AB	R	H	2B	3B	HR	RBI	BB	SO	AVG	OBP	SLG	PRO+	BR	/A	RC	SB	CS	SBR	FR	POS	TPR
1906	Bos-A	30	90	10	21	1	0	1	12	10		.233	.310	.278	86	-1	-1	8	1			7	C	0.9

■ DAN GRAHAM
Graham, Daniel Jay   b: 7/19/54, Ray, Ariz.   BL/TR, 6'1", 205 lbs.   Deb: 6/08/79

YEAR	TM/L	G	AB	R	H	2B	3B	HR	RBI	BB	SO	AVG	OBP	SLG	PRO+	BR	/A	RC	SB	CS	SBR	FR	POS	TPR
1979	Min-A	2	4	0	0	0	0	0	0	0	0	.000	.000	.000	-96	-1	-1	0	0	0	0	0	/H	0.0
1980	Bal-A	86	266	32	74	7	1	15	54	14	40	.278	.314	.481	116	4	4	40	0	0	0	1	C/3OD	0.9
1981	Bal-A	55	142	7	25	3	0	2	11	13	32	.176	.245	.239	40	-11	-11	8	0	0	0	-3	C/3D	-1.2
Total	3	143	412	39	99	10	1	17	65	27	72	.240	.287	.393	88	-8	-8	48	0	0	0	-2	C/3DO	-0.3

■ TINY GRAHAM
Graham, Dawson Francis   b: 9/9/1892, Nashville, Tenn.   d: 12/29/62, Nashville, Tenn.   BR/TR, 6'2", 185 lbs.   Deb: 8/30/14

YEAR	TM/L	G	AB	R	H	2B	3B	HR	RBI	BB	SO	AVG	OBP	SLG	PRO+	BR	/A	RC	SB	CS	SBR	FR	POS	TPR
1914	Cin-N	25	61	5	14	1	0	0	3	3	10	.230	.266	.246	51	-4	-4	4	1			-2	1	-0.5

■ PEACHES GRAHAM
Graham, George Frederick   b: 3/23/1877, Aledo, Ill.   d: 7/25/39, Long Beach, Cal.   BR/TR, 5'9", 180 lbs.   Deb: 9/14/02

YEAR	TM/L	G	AB	R	H	2B	3B	HR	RBI	BB	SO	AVG	OBP	SLG	PRO+	BR	/A	RC	SB	CS	SBR	FR	POS	TPR
1902	Cle-A	2	6	0	2	0	0	0	1	1		.333	.429	.333	120	0	0	1	0			0	/2	0.0
1903	Chi-N	1	2	0	0	0	0	0	0	0		.000	.000	.000	-99	-1	-0	0	0			0	/P	0.0
1908	Bos-N	75	215	22	59	5	0	0	22	23		.274	.345	.298	109	3	3	24	4			-3	C/2	0.4
1909	Bos-N	92	267	27	64	6	3	0	17	24		.240	.302	.285	79	-5	-7	26	7			-2	C/OS3	-0.3
1910	Bos-N	110	291	31	82	13	2	0	21	33	15	.282	.359	.340	100	2	1	38	5			-8	C/31O	-0.2
1911	Bos-N	33	88	7	24	6	1	0	12	14	5	.273	.373	.364	98	1	0	13	2			-5	C	-0.2
	Chi-N	36	71	6	17	3	0	0	8	11	8	.239	.365	.282	82	-1	-1	8	2			-5	C	-0.3
	Yr	69	159	13	41	9	1	0	20	25	13	.258	.369	.327	92	0	-1	21	4			-10		-0.5
1912	Phi-N	24	59	6	17	1	0	0	4	8	5	.288	.373	.356	94	0	-1	8	1			-1	C	0.0
Total	7	373	999	99	265	34	6	1	85	114	33	.265	.343	.314	94	-0	-5	117	21			-23	C/0231SP	-0.6

■ JACK GRAHAM
Graham, John Bernard   b: 12/24/16, Minneapolis, Minn.   BL/TL, 6'2", 200 lbs.   Deb: 4/16/46

YEAR	TM/L	G	AB	R	H	2B	3B	HR	RBI	BB	SO	AVG	OBP	SLG	PRO+	BR	/A	RC	SB	CS	SBR	FR	POS	TPR
1946	Bro-N	2	5	0	1	0	0	0	0	0	0	.200	.200	.200	14	-1	-1	0	0			0	/1	0.0
	NY-N	100	270	34	59	6	4	14	47	23	37	.219	.282	.426	99	-2	-2	32	1			-4	O/1	-0.8
	Yr	102	275	34	60	6	4	14	47	23	37	.218	.281	.422	97	-3	-3	32	1			-4		-0.8
1949	StL-A	137	500	71	119	22	1	24	79	61	62	.238	.326	.430	95	-4	-7	72	0	1	-1	-6	*1	-1.1
Total	2	239	775	105	179	28	5	38	126	84	99	.231	.310	.427	96	-7	-10	104	1	1		-10	1/O	-1.9

■ LEE GRAHAM
Graham, Lee Willard   b: 9/22/59, Summerfield, Fla.   BL/TL, 5'10", 170 lbs.   Deb: 9/03/83

YEAR	TM/L	G	AB	R	H	2B	3B	HR	RBI	BB	SO	AVG	OBP	SLG	PRO+	BR	/A	RC	SB	CS	SBR	FR	POS	TPR
1983	Bos-A	5	6	2	0	0	0	0	1	0	0	.000	.000	.000	-93	-2	-2	-0	0	1	-1	1	/O	0.0

■ ROY GRAHAM
Graham, Roy Vincent   b: 2/22/1895, San Francisco, Cal   d: 4/26/33, Manila, Phillipines   BR/TR, 5'10.5", 175 lbs.   Deb: 5/28/22

YEAR	TM/L	G	AB	R	H	2B	3B	HR	RBI	BB	SO	AVG	OBP	SLG	PRO+	BR	/A	RC	SB	CS	SBR	FR	POS	TPR
1922	Chi-A	5	3	0	0	0	0	0	0	0	0	.000	.400	.000	12	-0	-0	0	0	0	0	-0	/C	0.0
1923	Chi-A	36	82	3	16	2	0	0	6	9	6	.195	.290	.220	36	-7	-7	6	0	0	0	-7	C	-1.1
Total	2	41	85	3	16	2	0	0	6	9	6	.188	.296	.212	35	-8	-8	6	0	0	0	-7	/C	-1.1

■ WAYNE GRAHAM
Graham, Wayne Leon   b: 4/6/37, Yoakum, Tex.   BR/TR, 6', 200 lbs.   Deb: 4/10/63

YEAR	TM/L	G	AB	R	H	2B	3B	HR	RBI	BB	SO	AVG	OBP	SLG	PRO+	BR	/A	RC	SB	CS	SBR	FR	POS	TPR
1963	Phi-N	10	22	1	4	0	0	0	0	3	1	.182	.280	.182	36	-2	-2	1	0	0	0	-1	/O	-0.2
1964	NY-N	20	33	1	3	1	0	0	0	0	5	.091	.091	.121	-42	-6	-6	0	0	0	0	-2	3	-0.8
Total	2	30	55	2	7	1	0	0	0	3	6	.127	.172	.145	-9	-8	-8	2	0	0	0	-3	/3O	-1.0

■ ALEX GRAMMAS
Grammas, Alexander Peter   b: 4/3/26, Birmingham, Ala.   BR/TR, 6', 175 lbs.   Deb: 4/13/54   MC

YEAR	TM/L	G	AB	R	H	2B	3B	HR	RBI	BB	SO	AVG	OBP	SLG	PRO+	BR	/A	RC	SB	CS	SBR	FR	POS	TPR
1954	StL-N	142	401	57	106	17	4	2	29	40	29	.264	.339	.342	77	-12	-13	47	6	1	1	30	*S/3	2.7
1955	StL-N	128	366	32	88	19	2	3	25	33	36	.240	.308	.328	69	-16	-16	37	4	1	1	7	*S	-0.4
1956	StL-N	6	12	1	3	0	0	0	1	1	1	.250	.308	.250	52	-1	-1	1	0	0	0	0	/S	0.0
	Cin-N	77	140	17	34	11	0	0	16	16	18	.243	.325	.321	70	-5	-6	16	0	1	-1	4	3S/2	-0.1
	Yr	83	152	18	37	11	0	0	17	17	19	.243	.324	.316	69	-5	-7	17	0	1	-1	4		-0.1
1957	Cin-N	73	99	14	30	4	0	0	8	10	6	.303	.367	.343	86	-1	-2	11	1	3	-2	2	S2/3	0.3
1958	Cin-N	105	216	25	47	8	0	0	12	34	24	.218	.329	.255	54	-12	-14	20	2	2	-1	-2	S32	-1.1
1959	StL-N	131	368	43	99	14	2	3	30	38	26	.269	.339	.342	77	-8	-12	43	3	3	-1	12	*S	0.4
1960	StL-N	102	196	20	48	4	1	4	17	12	15	.245	.292	.337	66	-8	-10	17	0	1	-1	20	S23	1.4
1961	StL-N	89	170	23	36	10	1	0	21	19	21	.212	.295	.282	49	-11	-13	15	0	1	-1	17	S2/3	1.1
1962	StL-N	21	18	0	2	0	0	0	1	1	6	.111	.158	.111	-24	-3	-3	0	0	0	0	1	S/2	0.0
	Chi-N	23	60	3	14	3	0	0	3	2	7	.233	.270	.283	47	-4	-5	4	1	1	-0	1	S/23	-0.1
	Yr	44	78	3	16	3	0	0	4	3	13	.205	.244	.244	29	-8	-8	4	1	1	-0	3		-0.1
1963	Chi-N	16	27	1	5	0	0	0	3	0	5	.185	.185	.185	7	-3	-3	1	0	0	0	-3	S	-0.5
Total	10	913	2073	236	512	90	10	12	163	206	192	.247	.320	.317	67	-84	-96	212	17	14	-3	89	S32	3.7

YEAR	TM/L	G	AB	R	H	2B	3B	HR	RBI	BB	SO	AVG	OBP	SLG	PRO+	BR	/A	RC	SB	CS	SBR	FR	POS	TPR

■ JACK GRANEY
Graney, John Gladstone b: 6/10/1886, St.Thomas, Ont., Can. d: 4/20/78, Louisiana, Mo. BL/TL, 5'9", 180 lbs. Deb: 4/30/08

YEAR	TM/L	G	AB	R	H	2B	3B	HR	RBI	BB	SO	AVG	OBP	SLG	PRO+	BR	/A	RC	SB	CS	SBR	FR	POS	TPR
1908	Cle-A	2	0	0	0	0	0	0	0	0	0	—	—	—	—	0	0	0	0			-0	/P	0.0
1910	Cle-A	116	454	62	107	13	9	1	31	37		.236	.293	.311	88	-6	-7	46	18			1	*O	-1.2
1911	Cle-A	146	527	84	142	25	5	1	45	66		.269	.363	.342	96	0	-1	73	21			2	*O	-0.9
1912	Cle-A	78	264	44	64	13	2	0	20	50		.242	.367	.307	90	0	-1	33	9			4	*O	-0.1
1913	Cle-A	148	517	56	138	18	12	3	68	48	55	.267	.335	.366	102	3	1	69	27			2	*O	-0.5
1914	Cle-A	130	460	63	122	17	10	1	39	67	46	.265	.362	.352	111	10	8	60	20	18	-5	5	*O	0.1
1915	Cle-A	116	404	42	105	20	7	1	56	59	29	.260	.357	.351	110	7	6	51	12	15	-5	5	*O	0.0
1916	Cle-A	155	589	106	142	41	14	5	54	102	72	.241	.355	.384	115	17	13	85	10			3	*O	0.8
1917	Cle-A	146	535	87	122	29	7	3	35	**94**	49	.228	.348	.325	98	6	2	65	16			-8	*O	-1.5
1918	Cle-A	70	177	27	42	7	4	0	9	28	13	.237	.351	.322	94	2	-0	20	3			-5	O	-0.8
1919	Cle-A	128	461	79	108	22	8	1	30	**105**	39	.234	.380	.323	93	4	0	60	7			6	*O	-0.2
1920	*Cle-A	62	152	31	45	11	1	0	13	27	21	.296	.412	.382	108	4	3	27	4	2	0	-6	O	-0.6
1921	Cle-A	68	107	19	32	3	0	2	18	20	9	.299	.414	.383	103	2	2	19	1	1	-0	-9	O	-0.9
1922	Cle-A	37	58	6	9	0	0	0	2	9	12	.155	.279	.155	16	-7	-7	3	0	0	0	-1	O	-0.8
Total	14	1402	4705	706	1178	219	79	18	420	712	<u>345</u>	.250	.354	.342	100	42	18	610	148	<u>36</u>		-3	*O/P	-6.6

■ EDDIE GRANT
Grant, Edward Leslie "Harvard Eddie" b: 5/21/1883, Franklin, Mass. d: 10/5/18, Argonne Forest, France BL/TR, 5'11.5", 168 lbs. Deb: 8/04/05

YEAR	TM/L	G	AB	R	H	2B	3B	HR	RBI	BB	SO	AVG	OBP	SLG	PRO+	BR	/A	RC	SB	CS	SBR	FR	POS	TPR
1905	Cle-A	2	8	1	3	0	0	0	0	0		.375	.375	.375	139	0	1	0				-2	/2	-0.1
1907	Phi-N	74	268	26	65	4	3	0	19	10		.243	.270	.280	75	-8	-8	24	10			-2	3	-1.1
1908	Phi-N	147	598	69	146	13	8	0	32	35		.244	.286	.293	84	-9	-11	57	27			2	*3S	-0.6
1909	Phi-N	154	631	75	170	18	4	1	37	35		.269	.311	.315	94	-5	-6	71	28			1	*3	-0.1
1910	Phi-N	152	579	70	155	15	5	1	67	39	54	.268	.315	.316	81	-12	-15	67	25			-10	*3	-2.5
1911	Cin-N	136	458	49	102	12	7	1	53	51	47	.223	.301	.286	67	-22	-19	49	28			-7	*3S	-2.0
1912	Cin-N	96	255	37	61	6	1	2	20	18	27	.239	.292	.294	62	-14	-13	25	11			0	S3	-0.6
1913	Cin-N	27	94	12	20	1	0	0	9	11	10	.213	.295	.223	49	-6	-6	8	7			-4	3	-1.0
	*NY-N	27	20	8	4	1	0	0	1	2	2	.200	.273	.250	49	-1	-1	1	1			6	/32S	0.5
	Yr	54	114	20	24	2	0	0	10	13	12	.211	.291	.228	49	-7	-7	9	8			2		-0.5
1914	NY-N	88	282	34	78	7	1	0	29	23	21	.277	.333	.309	94	-3	-1	32	11			-7	3S2	-0.5
1915	NY-N	87	192	18	40	2	1	0	10	9	20	.208	.248	.229	47	-13	-12	11	5	6	-2	-5	3/21S	-1.8
Total	10	990	3385	399	844	79	30	5	277	233	<u>181</u>	.249	.299	.295	78	-93	-92	346	153	<u>6</u>		-27	3S/21	-9.8

■ JIMMY GRANT
Grant, James Charles b: 10/6/18, Racine, Wis. d: 7/8/70, Rochester, Minn. BL/TR, 5'8", 166 lbs. Deb: 9/08/42

YEAR	TM/L	G	AB	R	H	2B	3B	HR	RBI	BB	SO	AVG	OBP	SLG	PRO+	BR	/A	RC	SB	CS	SBR	FR	POS	TPR
1942	Chi-A	12	36	0	6	1	1	0	1	5	6	.167	.268	.250	47	-3	-2	3	0	0	0	1	3	-0.1
1943	Chi-A	58	197	23	51	9	2	4	22	18	34	.259	.321	.386	106	1	1	23	4	3	-1	1	3	0.2
	Cle-A	15	22	3	3	2	0	0	1	4	7	.136	.269	.227	49	-1	-1	2	0	0	0	2	/3	0.1
	Yr	73	219	26	54	11	2	4	23	22	41	.247	.315	.370	101	-0	-0	24	4	3	-1	3		0.3
1944	Cle-A	61	99	12	27	4	3	1	12	11	20	.273	.357	.404	122	2	3	16	1	0	0	-3	2/3	0.0
Total	3	146	354	38	87	16	6	5	36	38	67	.246	.322	.367	101	-1	0	43	5	3	-0	-0	/32	0.2

■ TOM GRANT
Grant, Thomas Raymond b: 5/28/57, Worcester, Mass. BL/TR, 6'2", 190 lbs. Deb: 6/17/83

YEAR	TM/L	G	AB	R	H	2B	3B	HR	RBI	BB	SO	AVG	OBP	SLG	PRO+	BR	/A	RC	SB	CS	SBR	FR	POS	TPR
1983	Chi-A	16	20	2	3	1	0	0	2	3	4	.150	.261	.200	28	-2	-2	1	0	0	0	0	O	-0.1

■ GEORGE GRANTHAM
Grantham, George Farley "Boots" b: 5/20/1900, Galena, Kan. d: 3/16/54, Kingman, Ariz. BL/TR, 5'10", 170 lbs. Deb: 9/20/22

YEAR	TM/L	G	AB	R	H	2B	3B	HR	RBI	BB	SO	AVG	OBP	SLG	PRO+	BR	/A	RC	SB	CS	SBR	FR	POS	TPR
1922	Chi-N	7	23	3	4	1	1	0	3	1	3	.174	.208	.304	30	-2	-3	2	2	0	1	-2	/3	-0.3
1923	Chi-N	152	570	81	160	36	8	8	70	71	92	.281	.360	.414	104	4	4	85	43	28	-4	1	*2	0.2
1924	Chi-N	127	469	85	148	19	6	12	60	55	63	.316	.390	.458	125	19	18	81	21	21	-6	1	*2/3	0.6
1925	*Pit-N	114	359	74	117	24	6	8	52	50	29	.326	.413	.493	122	18	14	77	14	4	2	-4	*1	0.1
1926	Pit-N	141	449	66	143	27	13	8	70	60	42	.318	.400	.490	131	25	22	88	6			-2	*1	1.4
1927	*Pit-N	151	531	96	162	33	11	8	66	74	39	.305	.396	.454	119	22	17	97	9			-24	*21	-0.9
1928	Pit-N	124	440	93	142	24	9	10	85	59	37	.323	.408	.486	128	22	20	87	9			1	*1/23	0.8
1929	Pit-N	110	349	85	107	23	10	12	90	59	38	.307	.454	.533	140	28	27	89	10			-3	2O1	2.1
1930	Pit-N	146	552	120	179	34	14	18	99	81	66	.324	.413	.534	126	25	25	121	5			-13	*2/1	2.4
1931	Pit-N	127	465	91	142	26	6	10	46	71	50	.305	.400	.452	130	21	22	89	5			-22	12	-0.3
1932	Cin-N	126	493	81	144	29	6	6	39	56	40	.292	.364	.412	112	7	9	77	4			-29	*21	-1.1
1933	Cin-N	87	260	32	53	14	3	4	28	38	21	.204	.310	.327	83	-5	-5	29	4			-11	21	-1.1
1934	NY-N	32	29	5	7	2	0	1	4	8	6	.241	.405	.414	123	1	1	6	0			0	/13	0.1
Total	13	1444	4989	912	1508	292	93	105	712	717	526	.302	.392	.461	121	185	171	927	132	<u>53</u>		-106	21/O3	4.0

■ MICKEY GRASSO
Grasso, Newton Michael b: 5/10/20, Newark, N.J. d: 10/15/75, Miami, Fla. BR/TR, 6', 195 lbs. Deb: 9/18/46

YEAR	TM/L	G	AB	R	H	2B	3B	HR	RBI	BB	SO	AVG	OBP	SLG	PRO+	BR	/A	RC	SB	CS	SBR	FR	POS	TPR
1946	NY-N	7	22	1	3	0	0	0	1	0	3	.136	.136	.136	-22	-4	-4	0	0			0	/C	-0.2
1950	Was-A	75	195	25	56	4	1	1	22	25	31	.287	.374	.333	86	-4	-3	26	1	1	-0	6	C	0.5
1951	Was-A	52	175	16	36	3	0	1	14	14	17	.206	.268	.240	39	-15	-15	10	0	0	0	-2	C	-1.2
1952	Was-A	115	361	22	78	9	0	0	27	29	36	.216	.276	.241	46	-27	-25	24	1	0	0	6	*C	-1.2
1953	Was-A	61	196	13	41	7	0	2	22	9	20	.209	.251	.276	43	-16	-16	12	0	0	0	1	C	-1.2
1954	*Cle-A	4	6	1	2	0	0	0	1	1	1	.333	.500	.833	256	1	1	3	0	0	0	0	/C	0.1
1955	NY-N	8	2	0	0	0	0	0	0	3	0	.000	.600	.000	77	0	0	0	0	0	0	0	/C	0.1
Total	7	322	957	78	216	23	1	5	87	81	108	.226	.291	.268	53	-64	-60	76	2	<u>1</u>		10	C	-3.1

■ LEW GRAULICH
Graulich, Lewis b: Camden, N.J. Deb: 9/17/1891

YEAR	TM/L	G	AB	R	H	2B	3B	HR	RBI	BB	SO	AVG	OBP	SLG	PRO+	BR	/A	RC	SB	CS	SBR	FR	POS	TPR
1891	Phi-N	7	26	2	8	0	0	0	3	1	2	.308	.333	.308	87	-0	-0	3	0			-2	/C1	-0.1

■ FRANK GRAVES
Graves, Frank M. b: 11/2/1860, Cincinnati, Ohio 6', 163 lbs. Deb: 5/10/1886

YEAR	TM/L	G	AB	R	H	2B	3B	HR	RBI	BB	SO	AVG	OBP	SLG	PRO+	BR	/A	RC	SB	CS	SBR	FR	POS	TPR
1886	StL-N	43	138	7	21	2	0	0	9	7	48	.152	.193	.167	11	-15	-13	7	11			14	C/OP	0.4

■ JOE GRAVES
Graves, Joseph Ebenezer b: 2/27/06, Marblehead, Mass. d: 12/22/80, Salem, Mass. BR/TR, 5'10", 160 lbs. Deb: 9/26/26

YEAR	TM/L	G	AB	R	H	2B	3B	HR	RBI	BB	SO	AVG	OBP	SLG	PRO+	BR	/A	RC	SB	CS	SBR	FR	POS	TPR
1926	Chi-N	2	5	0	0	0	0	0	0	0	1	.000	.000	.000	-99	-1	-1	0	0			-1	/3	-0.2

■ SID GRAVES
Graves, Samuel Sidney "Whitey" b: 11/30/01, Marblehead, Mass. d: 12/26/83, Biddeford, Maine BR/TR, 6', 170 lbs. Deb: 7/23/27

YEAR	TM/L	G	AB	R	H	2B	3B	HR	RBI	BB	SO	AVG	OBP	SLG	PRO+	BR	/A	RC	SB	CS	SBR	FR	POS	TPR
1927	Bos-N	7	20	5	5	1	1	0	2	0	1	.250	.250	.400	78	-1	-1	2	1			1	/O	0.0

■ GARY GRAY
Gray, Gary George b: 9/21/52, New Orleans, La. BR/TR, 6', 187 lbs. Deb: 6/23/77

YEAR	TM/L	G	AB	R	H	2B	3B	HR	RBI	BB	SO	AVG	OBP	SLG	PRO+	BR	/A	RC	SB	CS	SBR	FR	POS	TPR
1977	Tex-A	1	2	0	0	0	0	0	0	0	1	.000	.000	.000	-99	-1	-1	0	0	0	0	0	/O	0.0
1978	Tex-A	17	50	4	12	1	0	2	6	1	12	.240	.255	.380	76	-2	-2	5	1	0	0	0	D	-0.1
1979	Tex-A	16	42	4	10	0	0	0	1	2	8	.238	.273	.238	40	-4	-3	2	1	1	-0	0	D	-0.3
1980	Cle-A	28	54	4	8	1	0	2	4	3	13	.148	.193	.278	27	-6	-6	2	0	0	0	0	/1OD	-0.5
1981	Sea-A	69	208	27	51	7	1	13	31	4	44	.245	.259	.476	104	1	-0	22	2	0	1	0	1D/O	0.0
1982	Sea-A	80	269	26	69	14	2	7	29	24	59	.257	.322	.401	95	-1	-2	35	1	1	-0	-1	1D	-0.4
Total	6	211	625	65	150	23	3	24	71	34	137	.240	.281	.402	86	-12	-14	66	5	2	0	0	1/DO	-1.3

■ REDDY GRAY
Gray, James D. TR , Deb: 6/17/1890

YEAR	TM/L	G	AB	R	H	2B	3B	HR	RBI	BB	SO	AVG	OBP	SLG	PRO+	BR	/A	RC	SB	CS	SBR	FR	POS	TPR
1890	Pit-P	2	9	3	2	0	0	1	3	0	2	.222	.222	.556	115	-0	0	1	0			-1	/2	0.0
	Pit-N	1	3	0	0	0	0	0	0	0	1	.000	.000	.000	-99	-1	-1	0	0			-0	/S	0.0
1893	Pit-N	2	9	0	4	1	0	0	2	0	1	.444	.444	.556	171	1	1	2	0			-3	/S	-0.1
Total	2	5	21	3	6	1	0	1	5	0	4	.286	.286	.476	112	-0	0	3	0			-4	/S2	-0.1

YEAR	TM/L	G	AB	R	H	2B	3B	HR	RBI	BB	SO	AVG	OBP	SLG	PRO+	BR	/A	RC	SB	CS	SBR	FR	POS	TPR
■ **JIM GRAY**	Gray, James W. b: 8/7/1862, Pittsburgh, Pa. d: 1/31/38, Allegheny, Pa. TR, Deb: 10/09/1884																							
1884	Pit-a	1	2	0	1	0	0	0		0		.500	.500	.500	228	0	0	1				0	/3	0.0
■ **LORENZO GRAY**	Gray, Lorenzo b: 3/4/58, Mound Bayou, Miss. BR/TR, 6'1", 180 lbs. Deb: 7/08/82																							
1982	Chi-A	17	28	4	8	1	0	0	0	2	4	.286	.333	.321	81	-1	-1	3	1	0	0	-3	3	-0.3
1983	Chi-A	41	78	18	14	3	0	1	4	8	16	.179	.256	.256	40	-6	-7	5	1	0	0	2	3/D	-0.3
Total	2	58	106	22	22	4	0	1	4	10	20	.208	.276	.274	50	-7	-7	8	2	0	1	-2	/3D	-0.6
■ **MILT GRAY**	Gray, Milton Marshall b: 2/21/14, Louisville, Ky. d: 6/30/69, Quincy, Fla. BR/TR, 6'1", 170 lbs. Deb: 5/27/37																							
1937	Was-A	2	6	0	0	0	0	0	0	0	1	.000	.000	.000	-99	-2	-2	0	0	0	0	0	/C	0.0
■ **PETE GRAY**	Gray, Peter J. (b: Peter Wyshner) b: 3/6/15, Nanticoke, Pa. BL/TL, 6'1", 169 lbs. Deb: 4/17/45																							
1945	StL-A	77	234	26	51	6	2	0	13	13	11	.218	.259	.261	49	-15	-16	16	5	6	-2	5	O	-1.7
■ **DICK GRAY**	Gray, Richard Benjamin b: 7/11/31, Jefferson, Pa. BR/TR, 5'11", 165 lbs. Deb: 4/15/58																							
1958	LA-N	58	197	25	49	5	6	9	30	19	30	.249	.327	.472	105	2	1	29	1	1	-0	14	3	1.5
1959	LA-N	21	52	8	8	1	0	2	4	6	12	.154	.241	.288	38	-5	-5	4	0	0	0	-0	3	-0.5
	StL-N	36	51	9	16	1	0	1	6	6	8	.314	.386	.392	101	1	0	9	3	0	1	-8	S/32O	-0.6
	Yr	57	103	17	24	2	0	3	10	12	20	.233	.313	.340	69	-4	-5	12	3	0	1	-8		-1.1
1960	StL-N	9	5	1	0	0	0	0	1	2	2	.000	.286	.000	-13	-1	-1	0	0	0	0	1	/23	0.1
Total	3	124	305	43	73	7	6	12	41	33	52	.239	.322	.420	91	-3	-4	42	4	1	1	7	/3S2O	0.5
■ **STAN GRAY**	Gray, Stanley Oscar "Dolly" b: 12/10/1888, Ladonia, Tex. d: 10/11/64, Snyder, Tex. 6'0.5", 184 lbs. Deb: 9/17/12																							
1912	Pit-N	6	20	4	5	1	0	2		0	3	.250	.250	.350	64	-1	-1	2	0			-1	/1	-0.1
■ **CRAIG GREBECK**	Grebeck, Craig Allen b: 12/29/64, Johnstown, Pa. BR/TR, 5'8", 160 lbs. Deb: 4/13/90																							
1990	Chi-A	59	119	7	20	3	1	1	9	8	24	.168	.233	.235	32	-11	-11	7	0	0	0	7	3S/2	-0.1
■ **DAVID GREEN**	Green, David Alejandro (Casaya) b: 12/4/60, Managua, Nicaragua BR/TR, 6'3", 170 lbs. Deb: 9/04/81																							
1981	StL-N	21	34	6	5	1	0	0	2	6	5	.147	.275	.176	29	-3	-3	2	0	1	-1	2	O	-0.1
1982	*StL-N	76	166	21	47	7	1	2	23	8	29	.283	.320	.373	92	-2	-2	20	11	3	2	5	O	0.4
1983	StL-N	146	422	52	120	14	10	8	69	26	76	.284	.327	.422	106	2	2	53	34	16	1	-10	*O	-0.9
1984	StL-N	126	452	49	121	14	4	15	65	20	105	.268	.300	.416	102	-2	-1	53	17	9	-0	-2	*1O	-0.7
1985	SF-N	106	294	36	73	10	2	5	20	22	58	.248	.303	.347	85	-8	-6	28	6	5	-1	-2	1O	-1.1
1987	StL-N	14	30	4	8	2	1	1	1	2	5	.267	.313	.500	109	0	0	4	0	1	-1	-0	O/1	0.0
Total	6	489	1398	168	374	48	18	31	180	84	278	.268	.311	.394	97	-12	-9	161	68	35	-1	-7	O1	-2.4
■ **DANNY GREEN**	Green, Edward b: 11/6/1876, Burlington, N.J. d: 11/9/14, Camden, N.J. BL/TR, Deb: 8/17/1898																							
1898	Chi-N	47	188	26	59	4	3	4	27	7		.314	.342	.431	124	5	5	33	12			5	O	0.7
1899	Chi-N	117	475	90	140	12	11	6	56	35		.295	.352	.404	113	6	8	76	18			1	*O	0.2
1900	Chi-N	103	389	63	116	21	5	5	49	17		.298	.337	.416	114	4	6	66	28			0	*O	-0.1
1901	Chi-N	133	537	82	168	16	12	6	61	40		.313	.363	.421	134	20	22	96	31			8	*O	1.6
1902	Chi-A	129	481	77	150	16	11	0	62	53		.312	.389	.391	124	14	18	92	35			-3	*O	0.6
1903	Chi-A	135	499	75	154	26	7	6	62	47		.309	.368	.425	146	25	27	93	29			2	*O	2.1
1904	Chi-A	147	536	83	142	16	10	2	62	63		.265	.342	.343	124	14	16	76	28			1	*O	0.9
1905	Chi-A	112	379	56	92	13	6	0	44	53		.243	.336	.309	112	5	7	46	11			-11	*O	-0.9
Total	8	923	3484	552	1021	124	65	29	423	315		.293	.356	.391	125	92	109	577	192			3	O	5.1
■ **PUMPSIE GREEN**	Green, Elijah Jerry b: 10/27/33, Oakland, Cal. BB/TR, 6', 175 lbs. Deb: 7/21/59																							
1959	Bos-A	50	172	30	40	6	3	1	10	29	22	.233	.350	.320	81	-3	-4	22	4	2	0	4	2/S	0.2
1960	Bos-A	133	260	36	63	10	3	3	21	44	47	.242	.354	.338	85	-3	-4	32	3	4	-2	-13	2S	-1.0
1961	Bos-A	88	219	33	57	12	3	6	27	42	32	.260	.379	.425	112	6	5	38	4	2	0	-5	S/2	0.5
1962	Bos-A	56	91	12	21	2	1	2	11	11	18	.231	.314	.341	74	-3	-3	11	1	0	0	-9	2/S	-1.0
1963	NY-N	17	54	8	15	1	2	1	5	12	13	.278	.409	.426	139	3	3	9	0	2	-1	-1	3	0.2
Total	5	344	796	119	196	31	12	13	74	138	132	.246	.360	.364	94	1	-3	112	12	10	-2	-24	2S/3	-1.1
■ **GARY GREEN**	Green, Gary Allan b: 1/14/62, Pittsburgh, Pa. BR/TR, 6'3", 175 lbs. Deb: 9/14/86																							
1986	SD-N	13	33	2	7	1	0	0	2	1	11	.212	.235	.242	33	-3	-3	2	0	0	0	5	S	0.3
1989	SD-N	15	27	4	7	3	0	0		1	1	.259	.286	.370	86	-1	-1	3	0	1	-1	4	S/3	0.3
1990	Tex-A	62	88	10	19	3	0	0	8	6	18	.216	.266	.250	44	-6	-7	6	1	1	-0	21	S	1.7
Total	3	90	148	16	33	7	0	0	10	8	30	.223	.263	.270	49	-10	-10	11	1	2	-1	29	/S3	2.3
■ **GENE GREEN**	Green, Gene Leroy b: 6/26/33, Los Angeles, Cal. d: 5/23/81, St.Louis, Mo. BR/TR, 6'2.5", 200 lbs. Deb: 9/10/57																							
1957	StL-N	6	15	0	3	1	0	0	2	0	3	.200	.200	.267	23	-2	-2	1	0	0	0	-1	/O	-0.2
1958	StL-N	137	442	47	124	18	3	13	55	37	48	.281	.338	.423	96	-0	-3	56	2	1	0	8	OC	0.5
1959	StL-N	30	74	8	14	6	0	1	3	5	18	.189	.241	.311	43	-6	-6	5	0	1	0	4	OC	-0.1
1960	Bal-A	1	4	0	1	0	0	0	0	0	0	.250	.250	.250	36	-0	-0	0	0	0	0	0	/O	0.0
1961	Was-A	110	364	52	102	16	3	18	62	35	65	.280	.345	.489	122	9	10	51	0	2	-1	-19	CO	-1.0
1962	Cle-A	66	143	16	40	4	1	11	28	8	21	.280	.318	.552	133	5	5	23	0	0	0	-1	O/1	0.3
1963	Cle-A	43	78	4	16	3	0	2	7	4	22	.205	.262	.321	63	-4	-4	6	0	0	0	-2	O	-0.6
	Cin-N	15	31	3	7	1	0	1	3	0	8	.226	.250	.355	70	-1	-1	2	0	0	0	-2	/C	-0.2
Total	7	408	1151	130	307	49	7	46	160	89	185	.267	.322	.441	101	1	-0	145	2	3	-1	-12	OC/1	-1.3
■ **JIM GREEN**	Green, James R. b: Cleveland, Ohio Deb: 7/19/1884																							
1884	Was-U	10	36	4	5	1	0	0				.139	.139	.167	3	-4	-3	1	0			-0	/3O	-0.2
■ **JOE GREEN**	Green, Joseph Henry (a.k.a. Joseph Henry Greene) b: 9/17/1897, Philadelphia, Pa. d: 2/4/72, Bryn Mawr, Pa. TR, 6'2", 170 lbs. Deb: 7/02/24																							
1924	Phi-A	1	1	0	0	0	0	0	0		0	.000	.000	.000	-99	-0	-0	0	0	0	0	0	H	0.0
■ **LENNY GREEN**	Green, Leonard Charles b: 1/6/33, Detroit, Mich. BL/TL, 5'11", 170 lbs. Deb: 8/25/57																							
1957	Bal-A	19	33	2	6	1	1	1	5	1	4	.182	.206	.364	56	-2	-2	2	0	1	-1	0	O	-0.3
1958	Bal-A	69	91	10	21	4	0	0	4	9	10	.231	.300	.275	63	-5	-4	8	0	2	-1	7	O	-0.1
1959	Bal-A	27	24	3	7	0	0	1	2	1	3	.292	.346	.417	111	-0	0	4	0	0	0	1	O	0.0
	Was-A	88	190	29	46	6	1	2	15	20	15	.242	.314	.316	74	-7	-7	20	9	5	-0	0	O	-0.9
	Yr	115	214	32	53	6	1	3	17	21	18	.248	.318	.327	78	-6	-6	24	9	5	-0	1		-0.9
1960	Was-A	127	330	62	97	16	7	5	33	43	25	.294	.385	.430	121	11	11	58	21	8	2	-6	*O	0.2
1961	Min-A	156	600	92	171	28	7	9	50	81	50	.285	.376	.400	102	9	4	96	17	11	-2	-5	*O	-0.7
1962	Min-A	158	619	97	168	33	3	14	63	88	36	.271	.369	.402	104	9	6	98	8	4	0	4	*O	0.5
1963	Min-A	145	280	41	67	10	1	4	27	31	21	.239	.319	.325	80	-6	-7	32	11	5	0	3	*O	-0.8
1964	Min-A	26	15	3	0	0	0	0	0	4	6	.000	.211	.000	-35	-3	-3	0	1	0	-1	-0	*O	-0.3
	LA-A	39	92	13	23	2	0	2	4	10	8	.250	.330	.337	96	-2	-0	11	2	0	1	-0	O	0.0
	Bal-A	14	21	0	4	0	0	0	1	7	3	.190	.393	.190	69	-0	-0	2	1	0	0	2	/O	0.2
	Yr	79	128	16	27	2	0	2	5	21	17	.211	.327	.273	72	-5	-4	13	3	1	0	2		-0.1
1965	Bos-A	119	373	69	103	24	6	7	26	48	43	.276	.363	.429	117	13	10	60	8	2	1	-1	O	0.7
1966	Bos-A	85	133	16	32	6	0	1	12	15	19	.241	.327	.308	76	-2	-4	13	0	1	-1	-1	O	-0.5
1967	Det-A	58	151	22	42	8	1	1	13	9	17	.278	.319	.364	99	0	-0	17	1	1	-0	-3	O	-0.5

YEAR	TM/L	G	AB	R	H	2B	3B	HR	RBI	BB	SO	AVG	OBP	SLG	PRO+	BR	/A	RC	SB	CS	SBR	FR	POS	TPR
1968	Det-A	6	4	0	1	0	0	0	0	0	0	.250	.400	.250	97	0	0	0	0	0	0	0	/O	0.0
Total	12	1136	2956	461	788	138	27	47	253	368	260	.267	.353	.379	99	14	3	421	78	41	-1	2	O	-2.5

■ DICK GREEN
Green, Richard Larry   b: 4/21/41, Sioux City, Iowa   BR/TR, 5'10", 180 lbs.   Deb: 9/09/63

YEAR	TM/L	G	AB	R	H	2B	3B	HR	RBI	BB	SO	AVG	OBP	SLG	PRO+	BR	/A	RC	SB	CS	SBR	FR	POS	TPR
1963	KC-A	13	37	5	10	2	0	1	4	2	10	.270	.325	.405	99	0	-0	5	0	0	0	2	/S2	0.3
1964	KC-A	130	435	48	115	14	5	11	37	27	87	.264	.312	.395	92	-3	-5	52	3	3	-1	17	*2	2.4
1965	KC-A	133	474	64	110	15	1	15	55	50	110	.232	.309	.363	92	-6	-5	53	0	2	-1	-6	*2	-0.6
1966	KC-A	140	507	58	127	24	3	9	62	27	101	.250	.298	.363	92	-8	-6	54	6	1	1	-0	*2/3	0.7
1967	KC-A	122	349	26	69	12	4	5	37	30	68	.198	.261	.298	67	-16	-14	28	6	3	0	-2	32/1S	-1.5
1968	Oak-A	76	202	19	47	6	0	6	18	21	41	.233	.308	.351	104	-0	1	23	3	1	0	13	2/C3	1.8
1969	Oak-A	136	483	61	133	25	6	12	64	53	94	.275	.357	.427	123	12	14	72	2	3	-1	10	*2	2.9
1970	Oak-A	135	384	34	73	7	0	4	29	38	73	.190	.268	.240	43	-30	-29	25	3	0	1	0	*2/3C	-1.5
1971	*Oak-A	144	475	58	116	14	1	12	49	51	83	.244	.321	.354	93	-5	-4	53	1	1	-0	8	*2/S	1.0
1972	*Oak-A	26	42	1	12	1	1	0	3	3	5	.286	.348	.357	116	1	1	5	0	1	-1	2	2	0.4
1973	*Oak-A	133	332	33	87	17	0	3	42	21	63	.262	.310	.340	88	-8	-6	33	0	2	-1	-8	*2/3S3	-0.9
1974	*Oak-A	100	287	20	61	8	2	2	22	22	50	.213	.269	.275	61	-16	-14	20	2	3	-1	-5	*2	-1.6
Total	12	1288	4007	427	960	145	23	80	422	345	785	.240	.305	.347	87	-80	-67	424	26	20	-4	28	*2/3SC1	3.4

■ HANK GREENBERG
Greenberg, Henry Benjamin "Hammerin' Hank"   b: 1/1/11, New York, N.Y.   d: 9/4/86, Beverly Hills, Cal   BR/TR, 6'3.5", 210 lbs.   Deb: 9/14/30   H

YEAR	TM/L	G	AB	R	H	2B	3B	HR	RBI	BB	SO	AVG	OBP	SLG	PRO+	BR	/A	RC	SB	CS	SBR	FR	POS	TPR
1930	Det-A	1	1	0	0	0	0	0	0	0	0	.000	.000	.000	-98	-0	-0	0	0	0	0	0	H	0.0
1933	Det-A	117	449	59	135	33	3	12	87	46	78	.301	.367	.468	118	12	11	79	6	2	1	1	*1	0.3
1934	*Det-A	153	593	118	201	63	7	26	139	63	93	.339	.404	.600	156	47	47	144	9	5	-0	1	*1	1.9
1935	*Det-A	152	619	121	203	46	16	36	170	87	91	.328	.411	.628	171	57	61	161	4	3	-1	6	*1	4.6
1936	Det-A	12	46	10	16	6	2	1	16	9	6	.348	.455	.630	165	5	5	14	1	0	0	1	1	0.4
1937	Det-A	154	594	137	200	49	14	40	183	102	101	.337	.436	.668	171	67	65	178	8	3	1	5	*1	4.7
1938	Det-A	155	556	144	175	23	4	58	146	119	92	.315	.438	.683	167	66	61	172	7	5	-1	7	*1	4.0
1939	Det-A	138	500	112	156	42	7	33	112	91	95	.312	.420	.622	152	47	41	136	8	3	1	-1	*1	2.5
1940	*Det-A	148	573	129	195	50	8	41	150	93	75	.340	.433	.670	166	69	61	171	6	3	0	0	*O	4.7
1941	Det-A	19	67	12	18	5	1	2	12	16	12	.269	.410	.463	118	3	2	14	1	0	0	-3	O	-0.1
1945	*Det-A	78	270	47	84	20	2	13	60	42	40	.311	.404	.544	164	25	23	61	3	1	0	-10	*1	1.1
1946	Det-A	142	523	91	145	29	5	44	127	80	88	.277	.373	.604	160	46	42	119	5	1	1	2	*1	3.8
1947	Pit-N	125	402	71	100	13	2	25	74	104	73	.249	.408	.478	131	23	22	83	0			2	*1	1.6
Total	13	1394	5193	1051	1628	379	71	331	1276	852	844	.313	.412	.605	157	468	440	1331	58	26		11	*1O	29.5

■ AL GREENE
Greene, Altar Alphonse   b: 11/9/54, Detroit, Mich.   BL/TR, 5'11", 190 lbs.   Deb: 7/23/79

YEAR	TM/L	G	AB	R	H	2B	3B	HR	RBI	BB	SO	AVG	OBP	SLG	PRO+	BR	/A	RC	SB	CS	SBR	FR	POS	TPR
1979	Det-A	29	59	9	8	1	0	3	6	10	15	.136	.261	.305	50	-4	-4	5	0	1	-1	1	D/O	-0.3

■ JUNE GREENE
Greene, Julius Foust   b: 6/25/1899, Ramseur, N.C.   d: 3/19/74, Glendora, Cal.   BL/TR, 6'2.5", 185 lbs.   Deb: 4/20/28

YEAR	TM/L	G	AB	R	H	2B	3B	HR	RBI	BB	SO	AVG	OBP	SLG	PRO+	BR	/A	RC	SB	CS	SBR	FR	POS	TPR
1928	Phi-N	11	6	0	3	0	0	0	0	3	1	.500	.667	.500	202	1	1	2	0			0	/P	0.2
1929	Phi-N	21	19	1	4	1	0	0	0	2	4	.211	.286	.263	35	-2	-2	1	0			0	/P	0.0
Total	2	32	25	1	7	1	0	0	0	5	5	.280	.400	.320	79	-0	-1	4	0			1	/P	0.2

■ PADDY GREENE
Greene, Patrick Joseph "Patsy" (a.k.a. Patrick Foley In 1902)   b: 3/20/1875, Providence, R.I.   d: 10/20/34, Providence, R.I.   BR/TR, 5'8", 150 lbs.   Deb: 9/10/02

YEAR	TM/L	G	AB	R	H	2B	3B	HR	RBI	BB	SO	AVG	OBP	SLG	PRO+	BR	/A	RC	SB	CS	SBR	FR	POS	TPR
1902	Phi-N	19	65	6	11	1	0	0	1	2		.169	.206	.185	22	-6	-6	3	2			1	3	-0.4
1903	NY-A	4	13	1	4	1	0	0	0	0		.308	.308	.385	102	0	0	2	0			1	/3S	0.1
	Det-A	1	3	0	0	0	0	0	0	0		.000	.000	.000	-99	-1	-1	0	0			-0	/3	0.0
	Yr	5	16	1	4	1	0	0	0	0		.250	.250	.313	66	-1	-1	1	0			1		0.1
Total	2	24	81	7	15	2	0	0	1	2		.185	.214	.210	31	-6	-6	5	2			2	/3S	-0.3

■ JIM GREENGRASS
Greengrass, James Raymond   b: 10/24/27, Addison, N.Y.   BR/TR, 6'1", 200 lbs.   Deb: 9/09/52

YEAR	TM/L	G	AB	R	H	2B	3B	HR	RBI	BB	SO	AVG	OBP	SLG	PRO+	BR	/A	RC	SB	CS	SBR	FR	POS	TPR
1952	Cin-N	18	68	10	21	2	1	5	24	7	12	.309	.373	.588	163	5	5	15	0	0	0	2	O	0.7
1953	Cin-N	154	606	86	173	22	7	20	100	47	83	.285	.340	.444	102	1	1	89	6	4	-1	6	*O	0.0
1954	Cin-N	139	542	79	152	27	4	27	95	41	81	.280	.331	.494	109	7	5	82	0	3	-2	4	*O	0.2
1955	Cin-N	13	39	1	4	2	0	0	1	9	9	.103	.271	.154	16	-5	-5	2	0	0	0	2	O	-0.3
	Phi-N	94	323	43	88	20	2	12	37	33	43	.272	.342	.458	112	4	5	48	0	2	-1	1	O/3	0.0
	Yr	107	362	44	92	22	2	12	38	42	52	.254	.333	.425	100	-0	0	50	0	2	-1	3		0.0
1956	Phi-N	86	215	24	44	9	2	5	25	28	43	.205	.296	.335	71	-9	-9	20	0	0	0	-2	O	-1.2
Total	5	504	1793	243	482	82	16	69	282	165	271	.269	.332	.448	102	4	2	257	6	9	-4	12	O/3	-0.3

■ MIKE GREENWELL
Greenwell, Michael Lewis   b: 7/18/63, Louisville, Ky.   BL/TR, 6', 170 lbs.   Deb: 9/05/85

YEAR	TM/L	G	AB	R	H	2B	3B	HR	RBI	BB	SO	AVG	OBP	SLG	PRO+	BR	/A	RC	SB	CS	SBR	FR	POS	TPR
1985	Bos-A	17	31	7	10	1	0	4	8	3	4	.323	.382	.742	191	4	4	9	1	0	0	-1	O	0.3
1986	*Bos-A	31	35	4	11	2	0	0	4	5	7	.314	.400	.371	111	1	1	5	0	0	0	2	O/D	0.3
1987	Bos-A	125	412	71	135	31	6	19	89	35	40	.328	.389	.570	146	29	27	90	5	4	-1	-1	OD/C	2.2
1988	*Bos-A	158	590	86	192	39	8	22	119	87	38	.325	.420	.531	158	53	50	134	16	8	0	4	*OD	5.1
1989	Bos-A	145	578	87	178	36	0	14	95	56	44	.308	.372	.443	121	22	18	91	13	5	1	-9	*O/D	0.7
1990	*Bos-A	159	610	71	181	30	6	14	73	65	43	.297	.368	.434	118	20	16	94	8	7	-2	-2	*O	1.0
Total	6	635	2256	326	707	139	20	73	388	251	176	.313	.388	.490	135	129	116	424	43	24	-2	-8	O/DC	9.6

■ BILL GREENWOOD
Greenwood, William F.   b: 1857, Philadelphia, Pa.   d: 5/2/02, Philadelphia, Pa.   BB/TL, 5'7.5", 180 lbs.   Deb: 9/16/1882

YEAR	TM/L	G	AB	R	H	2B	3B	HR	RBI	BB	SO	AVG	OBP	SLG	PRO+	BR	/A	RC	SB	CS	SBR	FR	POS	TPR
1882	Phi-a	7	30	8	9	1	0	0		1		.300	.323	.333	109	1	0	3				-1	/O2	0.0
1884	Bro-a	92	385	52	83	8	3	3		10		.216	.237	.275	69	-13	-13	26				-8	*2/S	-1.6
1887	Bal-a	118	495	114	130	16	6	0		54		.263	.336	.319	91	-8	-3	79	71			7	*2/O	0.4
1888	Bal-a	115	409	69	78	13	1	0	29	30		.191	.256	.227	60	-18	-16	36	46			-22	2S/O	-3.1
1889	Col-a	118	414	62	93	7	10	3	49	58	71	.225	.327	.312	89	-7	-3	56	37			-3	*2	-0.3
1890	Roc-a	124	437	76	97	11	6	2		48		.222	.310	.288	85	-11	-5	53	40			2	*2/S	0.2
Total	6	574	2170	381	490	56	26	8	78	201	71	.226	.298	.287	80	-55	-40	253	194			-25	2/SO	-4.4

■ BRIAN GREER
Greer, Brian Keith   b: 5/14/59, Lynwood, Cal.   BR/TR, 6'3", 210 lbs.   Deb: 9/13/77

YEAR	TM/L	G	AB	R	H	2B	3B	HR	RBI	BB	SO	AVG	OBP	SLG	PRO+	BR	/A	RC	SB	CS	SBR	FR	POS	TPR
1977	SD-N	1	1	0	0	0	0	0	0	0	1	.000	.000	.000	-99	-0	-0	0	0	0	0	0	H	0.0
1979	SD-N	4	3	0	0	0	0	0	0	0	1	.000	.000	.000	-99	-1	-1	0	0	0	0	1	/O	0.0
Total	2	5	4	0	0	0	0	0	0	0	2	.000	.000	.000	-99	-1	-1	0	0	0	0	1	/O	0.0

■ ED GREER
Greer, Edward C.   b: 1865, Philadelphia, Pa.   d: 2/4/1890, Philadelphia, Pa.   BR,   Deb: 6/24/1885

YEAR	TM/L	G	AB	R	H	2B	3B	HR	RBI	BB	SO	AVG	OBP	SLG	PRO+	BR	/A	RC	SB	CS	SBR	FR	POS	TPR
1885	Bal-a	56	211	32	42	7	0	0		8		.199	.235	.232	51	-11	-11	12				1	OC	-0.9
1886	Bal-a	11	38	2	5	1	0	0		2		.132	.175	.158	6	-4	-4	2	4			-2	/OC	-0.5
	Phi-a	71	264	33	51	5	3	1		8		.193	.223	.246	48	-16	-16	18	12			6	O/C	-1.0
	Yr	82	302	35	56	6	3	1		10		.185	.217	.235	42	-20	-20	19	16			4		-1.5
1887	Phi-a	3	11	1	2	0	0	0		0		.182	.182	.182	3	-1	-1	1	2			0	/O	0.0
	Bro-a	91	327	49	83	13	2	2		25		.254	.318	.324	80	-8	-8	45	33			4	OC	-0.3
	Yr	94	338	50	85	13	2	2		25		.251	.314	.320	78	-9	-10	46	35			4		-0.3
Total	3	232	851	117	183	26	5	3		43		.215	.261	.268	60	-40	-41	77	51			8	O/C	-2.7

■ TOMMY GREGG
Gregg, William Thomas   b: 7/29/63, Boone, N.C.   BL/TL, 6'1", 190 lbs.   Deb: 9/14/87

YEAR	TM/L	G	AB	R	H	2B	3B	HR	RBI	BB	SO	AVG	OBP	SLG	PRO+	BR	/A	RC	SB	CS	SBR	FR	POS	TPR
1987	Pit-N	10	8	3	2	1	0	0	0	0	2	.250	.250	.375	62	-0	-0	0	0	0	0	0	/O	0.0

YEAR	TM/L	G	AB	R	H	2B	3B	HR	RBI	BB	SO	AVG	OBP	SLG	PRO+	BR	/A	RC	SB	CS	SBR	FR	POS	TPR
1988	Pit-N	14	15	4	3	1	0	1	3	1	4	.200	.250	.467	103	-0	-0	1	0	1	-1	-0	/O	0.0
	Atl-N	11	29	1	10	3	0	0	4	2	2	.345	.387	.448	132	1	1	5	0	0	0	2	/O	0.3
	Yr	25	44	5	13	4	0	1	7	3	6	.295	.340	.455	125	1	1	6	0	1	-1	2		0.3
1989	Atl-N	102	276	24	67	8	0	6	23	18	45	.243	.289	.337	76	-8	-9	26	3	4	-2	-5	O1	-2.0
1990	Atl-N	124	239	18	63	13	1	5	32	20	39	.264	.323	.389	93	-2	-2	31	4	3	-1	1	1O	-0.4
Total	4	261	567	50	145	26	1	12	62	41	92	.256	.307	.369	87	-9	-10	63	7	8	-3	-2	1O	-2.1

■ ED GREMMINGER
Gremminger, Lorenzo Edward "Battleship" b: 3/30/1874, Canton, Ohio d: 5/26/42, Canton, Ohio TR, 6'1", 200 lbs. Deb: 4/21/1895

YEAR	TM/L	G	AB	R	H	2B	3B	HR	RBI	BB	SO	AVG	OBP	SLG	PRO+	BR	/A	RC	SB	CS	SBR	FR	POS	TPR
1895	Cle-N	20	78	10	21	1	0	0	15	5	13	.269	.313	.282	53	-5	-6	7	0			-2	3	-0.5
1902	Bos-N	140	522	55	134	20	12	1	65	39		.257	.314	.347	105	3	3	61	7			3	*3	1.3
1903	Bos-N	140	511	57	135	24	9	5	56	31		.264	.306	.376	100	-4	-1	65	12			16	*3	1.5
1904	Det-A	83	309	18	66	13	3	1	28	14		.214	.248	.285	72	-11	-10	24	3			-16	3	-2.5
Total	4	383	1420	140	356	58	24	7	164	89	13	.251	.297	.340	93	-16	-14	158	22			2	3	-0.2

■ BUDDY GREMP
Gremp, Lewis Edward b: 8/5/19, Denver, Col. BR/TR, 6'1", 175 lbs. Deb: 9/13/40

YEAR	TM/L	G	AB	R	H	2B	3B	HR	RBI	BB	SO	AVG	OBP	SLG	PRO+	BR	/A	RC	SB	CS	SBR	FR	POS	TPR
1940	Bos-N	4	9	0	2	0	0	0	2	0	0	.222	.222	.222	24	-1	-1	0	0			0	/1	0.0
1941	Bos-N	37	75	7	18	3	0	0	10	5	3	.240	.287	.280	63	-4	-4	5	0			-3	1/2C	-0.8
1942	Bos-N	72	207	12	45	11	0	3	19	13	21	.217	.267	.314	71	-8	-8	17	1			1	1/3	-1.2
Total	3	113	291	19	65	14	0	3	31	18	24	.223	.271	.302	67	-13	-12	22	1			-2	/12C3	-2.0

■ REDDY GREY
Grey, Romer Carl (b: Romer Carl Gray) b: 4/8/1875, Zanesville, Ohio d: 11/9/34, Altadena, Cal. TL, 5'11", 175 lbs. Deb: 5/28/03

YEAR	TM/L	G	AB	R	H	2B	3B	HR	RBI	BB	SO	AVG	OBP	SLG	PRO+	BR	/A	RC	SB	CS	SBR	FR	POS	TPR
1903	Pit-N	1	3	1	1	0	0	0	1	1		.333	.500	.333	138	0	0	1	0			-0	/O	0.0

■ BILL GREY
Grey, William Tobin b: 4/15/1871, Philadelphia, Pa. d: 12/8/32, Philadelphia, Pa. 5'11", 175 lbs. Deb: 5/14/1890

YEAR	TM/L	G	AB	R	H	2B	3B	HR	RBI	BB	SO	AVG	OBP	SLG	PRO+	BR	/A	RC	SB	CS	SBR	FR	POS	TPR
1890	Phi-N	34	128	20	31	8	4	0	21	6	3	.242	.287	.367	90	-2	-2	15	5			-8	0/32C1	-0.8
1891	Phi-N	23	75	11	18	0	0	0	7	3	10	.240	.296	.240	57	-4	-4	6	3			-5	CO/S3	-0.7
1895	Cin-N	52	181	24	55	17	4	1	29	15	8	.304	.364	.459	109	3	2	32	4			-5	32/SCO	-0.3
1896	Cin-N	46	121	15	25	2	1	0	17	19	11	.207	.314	.240	46	-8	-10	11	6			2	2C/SO13	-0.5
1898	Pit-N	137	528	56	121	17	5	0	67	28		.229	.282	.280	65	-24	-23	44	5			-20	*3	-3.6
Total	5	292	1033	126	250	44	14	1	141	71	32	.242	.302	.315	73	-35	-37	110	23			-36	3/2COS1	-5.6

■ BOBBY GRICH
Grich, Robert Anthony b: 1/15/49, Muskegon, Mich. BR/TR, 6'2", 180 lbs. Deb: 6/29/70

YEAR	TM/L	G	AB	R	H	2B	3B	HR	RBI	BB	SO	AVG	OBP	SLG	PRO+	BR	/A	RC	SB	CS	SBR	FR	POS	TPR
1970	Bal-A	30	95	11	20	1	3	0	8	9	21	.211	.279	.284	55	-6	-6	7	1	1	-0	2	S/23	0.0
1971	Bal-A	7	30	7	9	0	0	1	6	5	8	.300	.400	.400	128	1	1	6	1	0	0	3	/S2	0.5
1972	Bal-A	133	460	66	128	21	3	12	50	53	96	.278	.362	.415	127	18	17	71	13	6	0	-25	S21/3	0.2
1973	*Bal-A	162	581	82	146	29	7	12	50	107	91	.251	.374	.387	116	15	16	92	17	9	-0	21	*2	4.3
1974	*Bal-A	160	582	92	153	29	6	19	82	90	117	.263	.380	.431	137	28	30	99	17	11	-2	9	*2	4.6
1975	Bal-A	150	524	81	136	26	4	13	57	107	88	.260	.393	.399	133	22	26	90	14	10	-2	24	*2	5.3
1976	Bal-A	144	518	93	138	31	4	13	54	86	99	.266	.374	.417	140	23	27	87	14	6	1	-1	*2/3D	3.7
1977	Cal-A	52	181	24	44	6	0	7	23	37	40	.243	.374	.392	114	4	5	27	6	6	-2	-4	S	0.5
1978	Cal-A	144	487	68	122	16	2	6	42	75	83	.251	.359	.329	98	-1	2	64	4	3	-1	0	*2	1.0
1979	*Cal-A	153	534	78	157	30	5	30	101	59	84	.294	.366	.537	145	29	32	103	1	0	0	2	*2	3.9
1980	Cal-A	150	498	60	135	22	2	14	62	84	108	.271	.381	.408	119	14	16	78	3	7	-3	3	*2/1	2.3
1981	Cal-A	100	352	56	107	14	2	**22**	61	40	71	.304	.381	**.543**	164	28	28	73	2	4	-2	10	*2	4.1
1982	*Cal-A	145	506	74	132	28	5	19	65	82	109	.261	.372	.449	124	19	19	87	3	3	-1	8	*2/D	3.3
1983	Cal-A	120	387	65	113	17	0	16	62	76	62	.292	.417	.460	142	26	26	77	2	4	-2	16	*2/S	4.3
1984	Cal-A	116	363	60	93	15	1	18	58	57	70	.256	.360	.452	124	12	13	58	2	5	-2	3	213	1.6
1985	Cal-A	144	479	74	116	17	3	13	53	81	77	.242	.355	.372	100	2	2	63	3	5	-2	15	*213/D	1.8
1986	*Cal-A	98	313	42	84	18	0	9	30	39	54	.268	.355	.412	109	4	5	45	1	3	-2	-10	21/3	-0.2
Total	17	2008	6890	1033	1833	320	47	224	864	1087	1278	.266	.373	.424	125	239	259	1129	104	83	-19	76	*2S/13D	41.2

■ TIM GRIESENBECK
Griesenbeck, Carlos Phillipe Timothy b: 12/10/1897, San Antonio, Tex. d: 3/25/53, San Antonio, Tex. BR/TR, 5'10.5", 190 lbs. Deb: 9/11/20

YEAR	TM/L	G	AB	R	H	2B	3B	HR	RBI	BB	SO	AVG	OBP	SLG	PRO+	BR	/A	RC	SB	CS	SBR	FR	POS	TPR
1920	StL-N	5	3	1	1	0	0	0	1			.333	.333	.333	95	-0	-0	0	0	0	0	0	/C	0.0

■ TOM GRIEVE
Grieve, Thomas Alan b: 3/4/48, Pittsfield, Mass. BR/TR, 6'2", 190 lbs. Deb: 7/05/70

YEAR	TM/L	G	AB	R	H	2B	3B	HR	RBI	BB	SO	AVG	OBP	SLG	PRO+	BR	/A	RC	SB	CS	SBR	FR	POS	TPR
1970	Was-A	47	116	12	23	5	1	3	10	14	38	.198	.290	.336	76	-5	-4	12	0	0	0	-5	O	-1.0
1972	Tex-A	64	142	12	29	2	1	3	11	11	39	.204	.271	.296	72	-6	-5	11	1	3	-2	-0	O	-0.8
1973	Tex-A	66	123	22	38	6	0	7	21	7	25	.309	.351	.528	151	7	7	22	1	0	0	-2	O/D	0.4
1974	Tex-A	84	259	30	66	10	4	9	32	20	48	.255	.313	.429	114	3	4	33	0	0	0	2	DO/1	0.5
1975	Tex-A	118	369	46	102	17	1	14	61	22	74	.276	.317	.442	113	4	5	48	0	2	-1	-3	OD	0.0
1976	Tex-A	149	546	57	139	23	3	20	81	35	119	.255	.304	.418	108	5	3	65	4	1	-1	-1	DO	0.2
1977	Tex-A	79	236	24	53	9	0	7	30	13	57	.225	.274	.352	68	-11	-11	23	1	0	0	-5	OD	-1.6
1978	NY-N	54	101	5	21	3	0	2	8	9	23	.208	.273	.297	61	-6	-5	8	0	1	-1	2	O/1	-0.4
1979	StL-N	9	15	1	3	1	0	0	0	4	1	.200	.368	.267	76	-0	-0	2	0	0	0	-1	/O	0.0
Total	9	670	1907	209	474	76	10	65	254	135	424	.249	.303	.401	100	-8	-6	224	7	7	-2	-12	OD/1	-2.7

■ KEN GRIFFEY
Griffey, George Kenneth Jr. b: 11/21/69, Donora, Pa. BL/TL, 6'3", 195 lbs. Deb: 4/03/89

YEAR	TM/L	G	AB	R	H	2B	3B	HR	RBI	BB	SO	AVG	OBP	SLG	PRO+	BR	/A	RC	SB	CS	SBR	FR	POS	TPR
1989	Sea-A	127	455	61	120	23	0	16	61	44	83	.264	.331	.420	107	6	4	65	16	7	1	2	*O	0.4
1990	Sea-A	155	597	91	179	28	7	22	80	63	81	.300	.369	.481	134	28	27	103	16	11	-2	-6	*O/D	1.8
Total	2	282	1052	152	299	51	7	38	141	107	164	.284	.353	.454	122	34	31	168	32	18	-1	-4	O/D	2.2

■ KEN GRIFFEY
Griffey, George Kenneth Sr. b: 4/10/50, Donora, Pa. BL/TL, 5'11", 190 lbs. Deb: 8/25/73

YEAR	TM/L	G	AB	R	H	2B	3B	HR	RBI	BB	SO	AVG	OBP	SLG	PRO+	BR	/A	RC	SB	CS	SBR	FR	POS	TPR
1973	Cin-N	25	86	19	33	5	1	3	14	6	10	.384	.424	.570	182	8	9	21	4	2	0	-5	O	0.3
1974	Cin-N	88	227	24	57	9	5	2	19	27	43	.251	.333	.361	96	-2	-1	29	9	4	0	0	O	-0.3
1975	Cin-N	132	463	95	141	15	9	4	46	67	67	.305	.394	.402	119	16	14	77	16	7	1	-9	*O	0.2
1976	Cin-N	148	562	111	189	28	9	6	74	62	65	.336	.403	.450	139	32	30	109	34	11	4	-3	*O	2.7
1977	Cin-N	154	585	117	186	35	8	12	57	69	84	.318	.390	.467	126	25	24	108	17	8	0	6	*O	2.4
1978	Cin-N	158	614	90	177	33	8	10	63	54	70	.288	.346	.417	112	9	9	93	23	5	4	2	*O	1.0
1979	Cin-N	95	380	62	120	27	4	8	32	36	39	.316	.376	.471	129	16	15	68	12	5	1	1	O	1.4
1980	Cin-N	146	544	89	160	28	10	13	85	62	77	.294	.367	.454	128	21	21	99	23	1	6	-4	*O	1.8
1981	Cin-N	101	396	65	123	21	6	2	34	39	42	.311	.374	.409	120	12	11	65	12	4	1	6	O	1.6
1982	NY-A	127	484	70	134	23	2	12	54	39	58	.277	.331	.407	103	1	2	65	10	4	1	6	*O	0.4
1983	NY-A	118	458	60	140	21	3	11	46	34	45	.306	.356	.437	121	10	13	74	6	1	1	-2	*1/OD	0.7
1984	NY-A	120	399	44	109	20	1	7	56	29	32	.273	.324	.381	98	-3	-1	49	2	2	-1	1	O1/D	-0.4
1985	NY-A	127	438	68	120	28	4	10	69	41	51	.274	.336	.425	109	4	5	63	7	7	-2	1	*O/1D	0.3
1986	NY-A	59	198	33	60	7	0	9	26	15	24	.303	.355	.475	125	6	6	31	2	2	-1	-1	O/D	0.3
	Atl-N	80	292	36	90	15	3	12	32	32	43	.308	.353	.503	126	12	10	51	12	7	-1	-4	O/1	0.4
1987	Atl-N	122	399	65	114	24	1	14	64	46	54	.286	.361	.456	109	9	6	62	4	7	-3	-4	*O1	-0.5
1988	Atl-N	69	193	21	48	5	0	2	19	17	26	.249	.310	.306	74	-5	-7	17	1	3	-2	-4	O1	-1.4
	Cin-N	25	50	5	14	1	0	2	4	2	5	.280	.308	.420	103	0	0	7	0	0	0	-0	1	0.0
	Yr	94	243	26	62	6	0	4	23	19	31	.255	.309	.329	80	-5	-6	24	1	3	-2	-4		-1.4
1989	Cin-N	106	236	26	62	8	3	8	30	29	42	.263	.346	.424	115	6	5	36	4	2	0	-7	O/1	-0.3
1990	Cin-N	46	63	6	13	2	0	1	8	2	5	.206	.242	.286	44	-5	-5	5	2	1	0	1	/1O	-0.4
	Sea-A	21	77	13	29	2	0	3	18	10	3	.377	.448	.519	168	8	7	19	0	0	0	-4	O	0.3

YEAR	TM/L	G	AB	R	H	2B	3B	HR	RBI	BB	SO	AVG	OBP	SLG	PRO+	BR	/A	RC	SB	CS	SBR	FR	POS	TPR
Total	18	2067	7144	1119	2119	357	77	151	850	706	885	.297	.361	.432	118	179	174	1142	200	83	10	-26	*O1/D	10.4

■ ALFREDO GRIFFIN
Griffin, Alfredo Claudino (b: Alfredo Claudino Baptist (Griffin))
b: 10/6/57, Santo Domingo, D.R.   BB/TR, 5'11", 160 lbs.   Deb: 9/04/76

YEAR	TM/L	G	AB	R	H	2B	3B	HR	RBI	BB	SO	AVG	OBP	SLG	PRO+	BR	/A	RC	SB	CS	SBR	FR	POS	TPR
1976	Cle-A	12	4	0	1	0	0	0	0	0	2	.250	.250	.250	47	-0	-0	0	0	1	-1	0	/SD	0.0
1977	Cle-A	14	41	5	6	1	0	0	3	3	5	.146	.205	.171	4	-5	-5	1	2	2	-1	-1	S/D	-0.5
1978	Cle-A	5	4	1	2	1	0	0	0	2	1	.500	.667	.750	301	1	1	2	0	0	0	3	/S	0.5
1979	Tor-A	153	624	81	179	22	10	2	31	40	59	.287	.335	.364	87	-10	-11	75	21	16	-3	6	*S	1.0
1980	Tor-A	155	653	63	166	26	15	2	41	24	58	.254	.285	.349	70	-25	-29	59	18	23	-8	2	*S	-2.2
1981	Tor-A	101	388	30	81	19	6	0	21	17	38	.209	.244	.289	50	-24	-27	24	8	12	-5	-19	S/32	-4.6
1982	Tor-A	162	539	57	130	20	8	1	48	22	48	.241	.271	.314	55	-30	-36	45	10	8	-2	6	*S	-1.7
1983	Tor-A	162	528	62	132	22	9	4	47	27	44	.250	.290	.348	71	-19	-23	52	8	11	-4	-4	*S/2D	-2.1
1984	Tor-A	140	419	53	101	8	2	4	30	4	33	.241	.250	.298	49	-28	-30	31	11	3	2	-5	*S2/D	-2.3
1985	Oak-A	162	614	75	166	18	7	2	64	20	50	.270	.293	.332	77	-25	-19	60	24	9	2	-15	*S	-1.9
1986	Oak-A	162	594	74	169	23	6	4	51	35	52	.285	.326	.364	95	-10	-4	71	33	16	0	-11	*S	-0.5
1987	Oak-A	144	494	69	130	23	5	3	60	28	41	.263	.308	.348	79	-19	-14	52	26	13	0	0	*S/2	-0.5
1988	*LA-N	95	316	39	63	8	3	1	27	24	30	.199	.260	.253	49	-21	-20	22	7	5	-1	2	S	-1.2
1989	LA-N	136	506	49	125	27	2	0	29	29	57	.247	.288	.308	72	-20	-19	45	10	7	-1	-7	*S	-2.0
1990	LA-N	141	461	38	97	11	3	1	35	29	65	.210	.260	.254	44	-36	-33	31	6	3	0	10	*S	-1.1
Total	15	1744	6185	696	1548	229	76	24	487	304	583	.250	.288	.324	68	-271	-269	572	184	129	-22	-32	*S/2D3	-19.1

■ DOUG GRIFFIN
Griffin, Douglas Lee   b: 6/4/47, South Gate, Cal.   BR/TR, 6', 160 lbs.   Deb: 9/11/70

YEAR	TM/L	G	AB	R	H	2B	3B	HR	RBI	BB	SO	AVG	OBP	SLG	PRO+	BR	/A	RC	SB	CS	SBR	FR	POS	TPR
1970	Cal-A	18	55	2	7	1	0	0	4	6	5	.127	.213	.145	1	-7	-7	2	0	0	0	1	2/3	-0.4
1971	Bos-A	125	483	51	118	23	2	3	27	31	45	.244	.293	.319	68	-17	-21	44	11	5	0	7	*2	-0.9
1972	Bos-A	129	470	43	122	12	1	2	35	45	48	.260	.327	.302	83	-6	-9	50	9	2	2	2	*2	0.3
1973	Bos-A	113	396	43	101	14	5	1	33	21	42	.255	.298	.323	71	-13	-16	36	7	5	-1	-14	*2	-2.7
1974	Bos-A	93	312	35	83	12	4	0	33	28	21	.266	.330	.330	85	-3	-6	32	2	8	-4	-13	2/S	-1.9
1975	*Bos-A	100	287	21	69	6	0	1	29	18	29	.240	.290	.272	55	-15	-18	22	2	2	-1	-10	2/S	-2.5
1976	Bos-A	49	127	14	24	2	0	0	4	9	14	.189	.248	.205	30	-10	-12	7	2	1	0	-1	2/D	-1.0
1977	Bos-A	5	6	0	0	0	0	0	0	0	0	.000	.000	.000	-90	-2	-2	0	0	0	0	0	/2	0.0
Total	8	632	2136	209	524	70	12	7	165	158	204	.245	.301	.299	68	-75	-92	193	33	23	-4	-27	2/3DS	-9.1

■ PUG GRIFFIN
Griffin, Francis Arthur   b: 4/24/1896, Lincoln, Neb.   d: 10/12/51, Colorado Springs, Colo.   BR/TR, 5'11.5", 187 lbs.   Deb: 7/27/17

YEAR	TM/L	G	AB	R	H	2B	3B	HR	RBI	BB	SO	AVG	OBP	SLG	PRO+	BR	/A	RC	SB	CS	SBR	FR	POS	TPR
1917	Phi-A	18	25	4	5	1	0	1	3	1	9	.200	.231	.360	81	-1	-1	2	1			1	/1	0.0
1920	NY-N	5	4	0	1	0	0	0	0	1	2	.250	.400	.250	90	0	0	0	0	0	0	0	/O	0.0
Total	2	23	29	4	6	1	0	1	3	2	11	.207	.258	.345	83	-1	-1	3	1	0		1	/1O	0.0

■ IVY GRIFFIN
Griffin, Ivy Moore   b: 12/25/1896, Tomashville, Ala.   d: 8/25/57, Gainesville, Fla.   BL/TR, 5'11", 180 lbs.   Deb: 9/09/19

YEAR	TM/L	G	AB	R	H	2B	3B	HR	RBI	BB	SO	AVG	OBP	SLG	PRO+	BR	/A	RC	SB	CS	SBR	FR	POS	TPR
1919	Phi-A	17	68	5	20	2	2	0	6	3	10	.294	.333	.382	99	-0	-0	8	0			4	1	0.2
1920	Phi-A	129	467	46	111	15	1	0	20	17	49	.238	.281	.274	47	-35	-36	37	3	3	-1	5	*1/2	-3.0
1921	Phi-A	39	103	14	33	4	2	0	13	5	6	.320	.369	.398	95	-1	-1	15	1	2	-1	-2	1	-0.3
Total	3	185	638	65	164	21	5	0	39	25	65	.257	.301	.306	60	-36	-37	60	4	5		7	1/2	-3.1

■ MIKE GRIFFIN
Griffin, Michael Joseph   b: 3/20/1865, Utica, N.Y.   d: 4/10/08, Utica, N.Y.   BL/TR, 5'7", 160 lbs.   Deb: 4/16/1887   M

YEAR	TM/L	G	AB	R	H	2B	3B	HR	RBI	BB	SO	AVG	OBP	SLG	PRO+	BR	/A	RC	SB	CS	SBR	FR	POS	TPR
1887	Bal-a	136	532	142	160	32	13	3		55		.301	.375	.427	133	19	25	123	94			-12	*O	0.7
1888	Bal-a	137	542	103	139	21	11	0	46	55		.256	.331	.336	120	12	14	77	46			7	*O	1.4
1889	Bal-a	137	531	152	148	21	14	4	48	91	29	.279	.387	.394	123	21	19	98	39			-10	*OS/2	0.5
1890	Phi-P	115	489	127	140	29	6	6	54	64	19	.286	.377	.407	109	9	7	88	30			18	*O	1.5
1891	Bro-N	134	521	106	139	36	9	3	65	57	31	.267	.340	.388	115	9	9	93	65			26	*O	2.5
1892	Bro-N	129	452	103	125	17	11	3	66	68	36	.277	.376	.383	137	19	22	86	49			13	*O/S	2.8
1893	Bro-N	95	362	85	103	21	7	6	59	59	23	.285	.396	.431	128	13	16	76	30			9	*O/2	1.7
1894	Bro-N	107	402	122	144	28	4	5	75	78	14	.358	.467	.485	142	26	32	112	39			7	*O	2.4
1895	Bro-N	131	519	140	173	38	7	4	65	93	29	.333	.444	.457	147	32	41	120	27			14	*O/S	3.5
1896	Bro-N	122	493	101	152	27	9	4	51	48	25	.308	.380	.424	121	10	15	90	23			3	*O	0.9
1897	Bro-N	134	534	136	169	25	11	2	56	81		.316	.416	.416	130	21	27	101	16			5	*O	1.9
1898	Bro-N	134	537	88	161	18	6	2	40	60		.300	.379	.367	117	14	14	82	15			10	*OM	1.4
Total	12	1511	5914	1405	1753	313	108	42	625	809	206	.296	.388	.407	126	205	241	1148	473			89	*O/S2	21.2

■ THOMAS GRIFFIN
Griffin, Thomas William   b: 1/1857, Titusville, Pa.   d: 4/17/33, Rockford, Ill.   Deb: 9/27/1884

YEAR	TM/L	G	AB	R	H	2B	3B	HR	RBI	BB	SO	AVG	OBP	SLG	PRO+	BR	/A	RC	SB	CS	SBR	FR	POS	TPR
1884	Mil-U	11	41	5	9	2	0	0		3		.220	.273	.268	154	-1	2	3	0			-1	1	0.1

■ SANDY GRIFFIN
Griffin, Tobias Charles   b: 7/19/1858, Fayetteville, N.Y.   d: 6/5/26, Fayetteville, N.Y.   5'10", 160 lbs.   Deb: 5/26/1884   M

YEAR	TM/L	G	AB	R	H	2B	3B	HR	RBI	BB	SO	AVG	OBP	SLG	PRO+	BR	/A	RC	SB	CS	SBR	FR	POS	TPR
1884	NY-N	16	62	7	11	2	0	0	6	1	19	.177	.190	.210	25	-5	-5	3				-3	O	-0.6
1890	Roc-a	107	407	85	125	28	4	5		50		.307	.388	.432	156	23	28	78	21			-19	*O/2	0.3
1891	Was-a	20	69	15	19	4	2	0	10	10	3	.275	.398	.391	135	3	4	12	2			-3	OM	0.0
1893	StL-N	23	92	9	18	1	1	0	9	16	2	.196	.315	.228	47	-6	-6	7	2			-2	O	-0.7
Total	4	166	630	116	173	35	7	5	25	77	24	.275	.361	.376	123	14	20	100	25			-26	O/2	-1.0

■ BERT GRIFFITH
Griffith, Bartholomew Joseph "Buck"   b: 3/30/1896, St.Louis, Mo.   d: 5/5/73, Bishop, Cal.   BR/TR, 5'11", 185 lbs.   Deb: 4/13/22

YEAR	TM/L	G	AB	R	H	2B	3B	HR	RBI	BB	SO	AVG	OBP	SLG	PRO+	BR	/A	RC	SB	CS	SBR	FR	POS	TPR
1922	Bro-N	106	325	45	100	22	8	2	35	5	11	.308	.322	.443	96	-4	-3	43	5	7	-3	-1	O/1	-0.9
1923	Bro-N	79	248	23	73	8	4	2	37	13	16	.294	.332	.383	91	-4	-4	31	1	2	-1	-7	O	-1.2
1924	Was-A	6	8	1	1	0	0	0	0	0	1	.125	.125	.125	-37	-2	-2	0	0	0	0	0	/O	0.0
Total	3	191	581	69	174	30	12	4	72	18	28	.299	.324	.413	92	-10	-8	74	6	9	-4	-8	O/1	-2.1

■ CLARK GRIFFITH
Griffith, Clark Calvin "The Old Fox"
b: 11/20/1869, Clear Creek, Mo.   d: 10/27/55, Washington, D.C.   BR/TR, 5'6.5", 156 lbs.   Deb: 4/11/1891   MH

YEAR	TM/L	G	AB	R	H	2B	3B	HR	RBI	BB	SO	AVG	OBP	SLG	PRO+	BR	/A	RC	SB	CS	SBR	FR	POS	TPR
1891	StL-a	27	77	11	12	1	0	1	8	8	15	.156	.253	.208	30	-6	-8	5	2			1	P	0.0
	Bos-a	10	23	6	4	1	1	1	3	6	5	.174	.367	.435	134	1	1	4	1			-1	/PO	0.0
	Yr	37	100	17	16	2	1	2	11	14	20	.160	.282	.260	52	-5	-7	8	3			-0		0.0
1893	Chi-N	4	11	1	2	0	0	0	2	0	1	.182	.182	.182	-2	-2	-2	0	0			1	/P	0.0
1894	Chi-N	46	142	27	33	5	4	0	15	23	9	.232	.339	.324	59	-8	-10	18	6			-3	P/OS	0.0
1895	Chi-N	43	144	20	46	3	0	1	27	16	9	.319	.391	.361	91	-0	-2	22	2			1	P/O	0.0
1896	Chi-N	38	135	22	36	5	2	1	16	9	7	.267	.313	.356	75	-5	-5	16	3			1	P	0.0
1897	Chi-N	46	162	27	38	8	4	0	21	18		.235	.311	.333	69	-6	-8	18	2			2	P/OS31	0.0
1898	Chi-N	38	122	15	20	2	3	0	15	13		.164	.244	.230	38	-10	-10	7	1			1	P	0.0
1899	Chi-N	39	120	15	31	5	0	0	14	14		.258	.341	.300	81	-3	-2	13	2			6	P/S	0.0
1900	Chi-N	30	95	16	24	4	1	1	7	8		.253	.311	.347	87	-2	-2	11	2			-1	P	0.0
1901	Chi-A	35	89	21	27	3	1	2	14	23		.303	.446	.427	150	7	7	18	0			1	PM	0.0
1902	Chi-A	35	92	11	20	3	0	0	8	7		.217	.273	.250	49	-6	-6	7	0			-2	P/OM	0.0
1903	NY-A	25	69	5	11	4	0	1	7	11		.159	.275	.261	59	-3	-3	6	1			-3	PM	0.0
1904	NY-A	16	42	2	6	2	0	0	1	4		.143	.217	.190	30	-3	-3	2	0			-0	PM	0.0
1905	NY-A	26	32	2	7	1	1	0	5	3		.219	.286	.313	82	-0	-0	2	0			-2	PM	0.0
1906	NY-A	17	18	0	2	0	0	0	1	3		.111	.238	.111	11	-2	-2	1	0			1	PM	0.0
1907	NY-A	5	2	0	0	0	0	0	0	0		.000	.000	.000	-93	-0	-0	0	0			0	/PM	0.0
1909	Cin-N	1	2	0	0	0	0	0	0	0		.000	.000	.000	-99	-0	-0	0	0			1	/PM	0.0

YEAR	TM/L	G	AB	R	H	2B	3B	HR	RBI	BB	SO	AVG	OBP	SLG	PRO+	BR	/A	RC	SB	CS	SBR	FR	POS	TPR
1910	Cin-N	1	0	1	0	0	0	0	0	0	0	—	—	—	—	0	0	0	0			0	RM	0.0
1912	Was-A	1	1	0	0	0	0	0	0	0	0	.000	.000	.000	-99	-0	-0	0	0			1	/P2M	0.0
1913	Was-A	1	1	0	1	1	0	0	1	0	0	1.000	1.000	2.000	758	1	1	2	0			-0	/POM	0.0
1914	Was-A	1	1	0	1	1	0	0	1	0	0	1.000	1.000	2.000	779	1	1	0	0	1	-1	0	/PM	0.0
Total	21	485	1380	202	321	49	17	8	166	166	46	.233	.317	.310	71	-48	-54	153	22	1		4	P/OS213	0.0

■ DERRELL GRIFFITH
Griffith, Robert Derrell b: 12/12/43, Anadarko, Okla. BL/TR, 6', 168 lbs. Deb: 9/26/63

YEAR	TM/L	G	AB	R	H	2B	3B	HR	RBI	BB	SO	AVG	OBP	SLG	PRO+	BR	/A	RC	SB	CS	SBR	FR	POS	TPR
1963	LA-N	1	2	0	0	0	0	0	0	0	0	.000	.000	.000	-99	-1	-0	0	0	0	0	0	/2	0.0
1964	LA-N	78	238	27	69	16	2	4	23	5	21	.290	.307	.424	112	0	2	29	5	1	1	-12	3O	-1.1
1965	LA-N	22	41	3	7	0	0	1	2	0	9	.171	.171	.244	16	-5	-4	1	0	0	0	-1	O	-0.5
1966	LA-N	23	15	3	1	0	0	0	2	2	3	.067	.176	.067	-32	-3	-2	0	0	0	0	1	/O	-0.1
Total	4	124	296	33	77	16	2	5	27	7	33	.260	.280	.378	90	-7	-5	31	5	1	1	-12	/O32	-1.7

■ TOMMY GRIFFITH
Griffith, Thomas Herman b: 10/26/1889, Prospect, Ohio d: 4/13/67, Cincinnati, Ohio BL/TR, 5'10", 175 lbs. Deb: 8/28/13

YEAR	TM/L	G	AB	R	H	2B	3B	HR	RBI	BB	SO	AVG	OBP	SLG	PRO+	BR	/A	RC	SB	CS	SBR	FR	POS	TPR
1913	Bos-N	37	127	16	32	4	1	1	12	9	8	.252	.301	.323	77	-4	-4	12	1			-1	O	-0.5
1914	Bos-N	16	48	3	5	0	0	0	1	2	6	.104	.140	.104	-27	-7	-7	1	0			4	O	-0.3
1915	Cin-N	160	583	59	179	31	16	4	85	41	34	.307	.355	.436	136	25	24	85	6	24	-13	-19	*O	-1.3
1916	Cin-N	155	595	50	158	28	7	2	61	36	37	.266	.310	.346	104	0	2	69	16			-2	*O	-0.5
1917	Cin-N	115	363	45	98	18	7	1	45	19	23	.270	.308	.366	111	0	3	41	5			1	*O	0.2
1918	Cin-N	118	427	47	113	10	4	2	48	39	30	.265	.326	.321	99	-1	-0	47	10			-3	*O	-0.9
1919	Bro-N	125	484	65	136	18	4	6	57	23	32	.281	.315	.372	104	2	1	57	8			-4	*O	-0.8
1920	*Bro-N	93	334	41	87	9	4	2	30	15	18	.260	.292	.329	76	-10	-11	32	3	3	-1	-12	*O	-3.1
1921	Bro-N	129	455	66	142	21	6	12	71	36	13	.312	.364	.464	113	11	9	77	3	3	-1	2	*O	0.4
1922	Bro-N	99	329	44	104	17	8	4	49	23	10	.316	.361	.453	110	4	4	55	7	1	2	2	O	0.4
1923	Bro-N	131	481	70	141	21	9	8	66	50	19	.293	.361	.424	109	5	7	76	8	2	1	-9	*O	-0.4
1924	Bro-N	140	482	43	121	19	5	3	67	34	19	.251	.300	.330	71	-21	-19	48	0	5	-3	-14	*O	-3.9
1925	Bro-N	7	4	2	0	0	0	0	0	3	2	.000	.429	.000	20	-0	-0	1	1	0	0	0	/O	0.0
	Chi-N	76	235	38	67	12	1	7	27	21	11	.285	.346	.434	97	-1	-1	35	2	4	-2	-4	O	-0.7
	Yr	83	239	40	67	12	1	7	27	24	13	.280	.348	.427	96	-1	-2	35	3	4	-2	-4		-0.7
Total	13	1401	4947	589	1383	208	72	52	619	351	262	.280	.328	.382	102	5	7	634	70	42		-58	*O	-11.4

■ ART GRIGGS
Griggs, Arthur Carle b: 12/10/1883, Topeka, Kan. d: 12/19/38, Los Angeles, Cal. BR/TR, 5'11", 185 lbs. Deb: 5/02/09

YEAR	TM/L	G	AB	R	H	2B	3B	HR	RBI	BB	SO	AVG	OBP	SLG	PRO+	BR	/A	RC	SB	CS	SBR	FR	POS	TPR
1909	StL-A	108	364	38	102	17	5	0	43	24		.280	.330	.354	125	6	9	46	11			-6	1O/2S	0.1
1910	StL-A	123	416	28	98	22	5	2	30	25		.236	.281	.327	96	-6	-3	40	11			-10	O21/S3	-1.9
1911	Cle-A	27	68	7	17	3	2	1	7	5		.250	.301	.397	93	-1	-1	8	1			-2	2/O31	-0.2
1912	Cle-A	89	273	29	83	16	7	0	39	33		.304	.381	.414	123	10	9	47	10			1	1	1.1
1914	Bro-F	40	112	10	32	6	1	1	15	5	11	.286	.328	.384	104	0	0	15	1			-3	1/O	-0.1
1915	Bro-F	27	38	4	11	1	0	1	2	3	7	.289	.372	.395	128	1	1	6	0			1	/1O	0.2
1918	Det-A	28	99	11	36	8	0	0	16	10	5	.364	.422	.444	168	7	8	19	2			-3	1	0.4
Total	7	442	1370	127	379	73	20	5	152	105	23	.277	.332	.370	116	18	23	181	36			-22	1/O23S	-0.4

■ DENVER GRIGSBY
Grigsby, Denver Clarence b: 3/25/01, Jackson, Ky. d: 11/10/73, Sapulpa, Okla. BL/TR, 5'9", 155 lbs. Deb: 9/01/23

YEAR	TM/L	G	AB	R	H	2B	3B	HR	RBI	BB	SO	AVG	OBP	SLG	PRO+	BR	/A	RC	SB	CS	SBR	FR	POS	TPR
1923	Chi-N	24	72	8	21	5	2	0	5	7	5	.292	.363	.417	105	1	1	10	1	3	-2	-2	O	-0.2
1924	Chi-N	124	411	58	123	18	2	3	48	31	47	.299	.357	.375	95	-1	-2	51	10	19	-8	3	*O	-0.9
1925	Chi-N	51	137	20	35	5	0	0	20	19	12	.255	.346	.292	64	-7	-7	16	1	1	-0	-1	O	-0.8
Total	3	199	620	86	179	28	4	3	73	57	64	.289	.355	.361	89	-7	-8	77	12	23	-10	1	O	-1.9

■ JOHN GRIM
Grim, John Helm b: 8/9/1867, Lebanon, Ky. d: 7/28/61, Indianapolis, Ind TR, 6'2", 175 lbs. Deb: 9/29/1888

YEAR	TM/L	G	AB	R	H	2B	3B	HR	RBI	BB	SO	AVG	OBP	SLG	PRO+	BR	/A	RC	SB	CS	SBR	FR	POS	TPR
1888	Phi-N	2	7	0	1	0	0	0	0	0	0	.143	.143	.143	-7	-1	-1	0	0			-0	/O2	0.0
1890	Roc-a	50	192	30	51	6	9	2		7		.266	.299	.422	124	2	4	29	14			-7	SC/3201P	0.0
1891	Mil-a	29	119	14	28	5	1	1	14	2	5	.235	.248	.319	53	-6	-10	10	1			3	C3/2	-0.4
1892	Lou-N	97	370	40	90	16	4	1	36	13	24	.243	.280	.316	89	-9	-5	39	18			-8	C12/OS3	-0.8
1893	Lou-N	99	415	68	111	19	8	3	54	12	16	.267	.303	.373	88	-13	-8	53	15			-5	*C/120S	-0.2
1894	Lou-N	108	410	66	122	27	7	7	70	16	15	.298	.339	.449	97	-8	-3	69	14			10	C2/13	1.2
1895	Bro-N	93	329	54	92	17	5	0	44	13	9	.280	.321	.362	84	-11	-7	42	9			-1	*C/O1	-0.1
1896	Bro-N	81	281	32	75	13	1	2	35	12	14	.267	.311	.342	78	-11	-8	33	7			-1	C/1	-0.1
1897	Bro-N	80	290	26	72	10	1	0	25	1		.248	.259	.290	49	-22	-20	23	3			5	C	-0.3
1898	Bro-N	52	178	17	50	5	1	0	11	8		.281	.323	.320	87	-3	-3	19	1			-4	C	-0.2
1899	Bro-N	15	47	3	13	1	0	0	7	1		.277	.320	.298	71	-2	-2	5	0			2	C	0.1
Total	11	706	2638	350	705	119	37	16	296	85	77	.267	.302	.359	83	-85	-61	321	82			-7	C/21S3OP	-0.7

■ ED GRIMES
Grimes, Edward Adelbert b: 9/8/05, Chicago, Ill. d: 10/5/74, Chicago, Ill. BR/TR, 5'10", 165 lbs. Deb: 4/19/31

YEAR	TM/L	G	AB	R	H	2B	3B	HR	RBI	BB	SO	AVG	OBP	SLG	PRO+	BR	/A	RC	SB	CS	SBR	FR	POS	TPR
1931	StL-A	43	57	9	15	1	2	0	5	9	3	.263	.364	.351	86	-1	-1	8	1	0	0	-2	3/2S	-0.2
1932	StL-A	31	68	7	16	0	1	0	13	6	12	.235	.297	.265	44	-5	-6	5	0	1	-1	2	3/2S	-0.2
Total	2	74	125	16	31	1	3	0	18	15	15	.248	.329	.304	63	-6	-7	14	1	1	-0	0	/32S	-0.2

■ ROY GRIMES
Grimes, Austin Roy "Bummer" b: 9/11/1893, Bergholz, Ohio d: 9/13/54, Gilford Lake, O. BR/TR, 6'1", 176 lbs. Deb: 7/31/20

YEAR	TM/L	G	AB	R	H	2B	3B	HR	RBI	BB	SO	AVG	OBP	SLG	PRO+	BR	/A	RC	SB	CS	SBR	FR	POS	TPR
1920	NY-N	26	57	5	9	1	0	0	3	3	8	.158	.200	.175	8	-7	-7	2	1	1	-0	-1	2	-0.8

■ OSCAR GRIMES
Grimes, Oscar Ray Jr. b: 4/13/15, Minerva, Ohio BR/TR, 5'11", 178 lbs. Deb: 9/28/38

YEAR	TM/L	G	AB	R	H	2B	3B	HR	RBI	BB	SO	AVG	OBP	SLG	PRO+	BR	/A	RC	SB	CS	SBR	FR	POS	TPR
1938	Cle-A	4	10	2	2	0	1	0	2	2	0	.200	.333	.400	85	-0	-0	1	0	0	0	-1	/21	0.0
1939	Cle-A	119	364	51	98	20	5	4	56	56	61	.269	.368	.385	96	-3	-1	55	8	3	1	-11	21S/3	-0.8
1940	Cle-A	11	13	3	0	0	0	0	0	0	5	.000	.000	.000	-99	-4	-4	0	0	0	2	/13	-0.1
1941	Cle-A	77	244	28	58	9	3	4	24	39	47	.238	.345	.348	88	-5	-3	34	4	0	1	-5	12/3	-0.7
1942	Cle-A	51	84	10	15	2	0	0	2	13	17	.179	.289	.202	42	-6	-6	6	3	2	-0	-3	2/31S	-0.8
1943	NY-A	9	20	4	3	0	0	0	1	3	7	.150	.261	.150	21	-2	-2	1	0	0	0	-1	/S1	-0.2
1944	NY-A	116	387	44	108	17	8	5	46	59	57	.279	.377	.403	119	13	12	67	6	0	-2	-10	3S	0.4
1945	NY-A	142	480	64	127	19	7	4	45	97	73	.265	.395	.358	114	17	14	77	7	6	-2	3	*3/1	1.9
1946	NY-A	14	39	1	8	1	0	0	4	1	7	.205	.225	.231	27	-4	-4	2	0	1	-1	0	/S2	-0.3
	Phi-N	59	191	28	50	5	0	1	20	27	29	.262	.356	.304	86	-3	-2	23	2	0	1	-12	2/3S	-0.9
	Yr	73	230	29	58	6	0	1	24	28	36	.252	.336	.291	76	-6	-6	24	2	1	0	-12		-1.2
Total	9	602	1832	235	469	73	24	18	200	297	303	.256	.363	.352	98	3	3	266	30	12	-2	-38	321/S	-1.5

■ RAY GRIMES
Grimes, Oscar Ray Sr. b: 9/11/1893, Bergholz, Ohio d: 5/25/53, Minerva, Ohio BR/TR, 5'11", 168 lbs. Deb: 9/24/20

YEAR	TM/L	G	AB	R	H	2B	3B	HR	RBI	BB	SO	AVG	OBP	SLG	PRO+	BR	/A	RC	SB	CS	SBR	FR	POS	TPR
1920	Bos-A	1	4	1	1	0	0	0	0	1		.250	.400	.250	78	-0	-0	0	0	0	0	0	/1	0.0
1921	Chi-N	147	530	91	170	38	6	6	79	70	55	.321	.406	.449	126	23	23	99	5	8	-3	-5	*1	1.1
1922	Chi-N	138	509	99	180	45	12	14	99	75	33	.354	.442	.572	157	47	46	130	7	7	-2	-2	*1	3.7
1923	Chi-N	64	216	32	71	7	2	3	36	24	17	.329	.401	.407	114	5	5	38	5	0	1	-1	1	0.2
1924	Chi-N	51	177	33	53	6	5	1	34	28	15	.299	.401	.475	133	9	9	35	4	2	1	-7	1	0.0
1926	Phi-N	32	101	13	30	5	0	3	15	6	13	.297	.343	.347	82	-2	-3	12	0			0	1	-0.2
Total	6	433	1537	269	505	101	25	27	263	204	133	.329	.413	.480	132	82	80	314	21	17		-14	1	4.8

■ CHARLIE GRIMM
Grimm, Charles John "Jolly Cholly" b: 8/25/1896, St.Louis, Mo. d: 11/15/83, Scottsdale, Ariz. BL/TL, 5'11.5", 173 lbs. Deb: 7/30/16 MC

YEAR	TM/L	G	AB	R	H	2B	3B	HR	RBI	BB	SO	AVG	OBP	SLG	PRO+	BR	/A	RC	SB	CS	SBR	FR	POS	TPR
1916	Phi-A	12	22	0	2	0	0	0	0	2	4	.091	.167	.091	-23	-3	-3	0	0			-2	/O	-0.5
1918	StL-N	50	141	11	31	7	0	0	12	6	15	.220	.262	.270	64	-6	-6	10	2			-3	1/O3	-1.0

YEAR	TM/L	G	AB	R	H	2B	3B	HR	RBI	BB	SO	AVG	OBP	SLG	PRO+	BR	/A	RC	SB	CS	SBR	FR	POS	TPR
1919	Pit-N	14	44	6	14	1	3	0	6	2	4	.318	.348	.477	141	2	2	7	1			-2	1	0.0
1920	Pit-N	148	533	38	121	13	7	2	54	30	40	.227	.273	.289	60	-26	-28	42	7	8	-3	4	*1	-3.0
1921	Pit-N	151	562	62	154	21	17	7	71	31	38	.274	.314	.409	88	-9	-11	70	6	8	-3	-6	*1	-2.3
1922	Pit-N	154	593	64	173	28	13	0	76	43	15	.292	.343	.383	86	-12	-13	76	6	10	-4	-3	*1	-2.0
1923	Pit-N	152	563	78	194	29	13	7	99	41	43	.345	.389	.480	125	22	20	102	6	9	-4	2	*1	0.8
1924	Pit-N	151	542	53	156	25	12	2	63	37	22	.288	.336	.389	92	-5	-6	70	3	6	-3	-3	*1	-1.8
1925	Chi-N	141	519	73	159	29	5	10	76	38	25	.306	.354	.439	100	0	-1	80	4	3	-1	0	*1	-1.4
1926	Chi-N	147	524	58	145	30	6	8	82	49	25	.277	.342	.403	99	-0	-1	72	3			-6	*1	-1.2
1927	Chi-N	147	543	68	169	29	6	2	74	45	21	.311	.367	.398	105	4	4	79	3			3	*1	-0.2
1928	Chi-N	147	547	67	161	25	5	5	62	39	20	.294	.342	.386	91	-8	-7	71	7			-2	*1	-2.4
1929	*Chi-N	120	463	66	138	28	3	10	91	42	25	.298	.358	.436	95	-4	-4	71	3			0	*1	-0.8
1930	Chi-N	114	429	58	124	27	2	6	66	41	26	.289	.359	.403	83	-11	-11	62	1			1	*1	-1.3
1931	Chi-N	146	531	65	176	33	11	4	66	53	29	.331	.393	.458	126	22	21	99	1			2	*1	1.1
1932	*Chi-N	149	570	66	175	42	2	7	80	35	22	.307	.349	.425	108	5	6	86	2			10	*1M	0.8
1933	Chi-N	107	384	38	95	15	2	3	37	23	15	.247	.290	.320	74	-13	-13	33	1			9	*1M	-0.5
1934	Chi-N	75	267	24	79	8	1	5	47	16	12	.296	.338	.390	96	-2	-1	34	1			1	1M	-0.6
1935	Chi-N	2	8	0	0	0	0	0	0	0	1	.000	.000	.000	-99	-2	-2	0	0			0	/1M	-0.1
1936	Chi-N	39	132	13	33	4	0	1	16	5	8	.250	.277	.303	55	-8	-9	10	0			5	1M	-0.5
Total	20	2166	7917	908	2299	394	108	79	1078	578	410	.290	.341	.397	95	-54	-63	1077	57	44		11	*1/O3	-16.9

■ MOOSE GRIMSHAW
Grimshaw, Myron Frederick b: 11/30/1875, St.Johnsville, N.Y. d: 12/11/36, Canajoharie, N.Y. BB/TR, 6'1", 173 lbs. Deb: 4/25/05

YEAR	TM/L	G	AB	R	H	2B	3B	HR	RBI	BB	SO	AVG	OBP	SLG	PRO+	BR	/A	RC	SB	CS	SBR	FR	POS	TPR
1905	Bos-A	85	285	39	68	8	2	4	35	21		.239	.291	.323	95	-1	-2	29	4			-5	1	-0.8
1906	Bos-A	110	428	46	124	16	12	0	48	23		.290	.326	.383	124	11	11	57	5			-1	*1	0.7
1907	Bos-A	64	181	19	37	7	2	0	33	16		.204	.269	.265	73	-5	-5	16	6			-7	O1/S	-1.4
Total	3	259	894	104	229	31	16	4	116	60		.256	.303	.340	105	4	4	102	15			-13	1/OS	-1.5

■ MARQUIS GRISSOM
Grissom, Marquis Deon b: 4/17/67, Atlanta, Ga. BR/TR, 5'11", 190 lbs. Deb: 8/22/89

YEAR	TM/L	G	AB	R	H	2B	3B	HR	RBI	BB	SO	AVG	OBP	SLG	PRO+	BR	/A	RC	SB	CS	SBR	FR	POS	TPR
1989	Mon-N	26	74	16	19	2	0	1	2	12	21	.257	.360	.324	96	0	0	10	1	0	0	-2	O	-0.1
1990	Mon-N	98	288	42	74	14	2	3	29	27	40	.257	.321	.351	85	-6	-6	36	22	2	5	0	O	-0.2
Total	2	124	362	58	93	16	2	4	31	39	61	.257	.329	.345	87	-6	-6	46	23	2	6	-2	O	-0.3

■ DICK GROAT
Groat, Richard Morrow b: 11/4/30, Wilkinsburg, Pa. BR/TR, 5'11.5", 180 lbs. Deb: 6/19/52

YEAR	TM/L	G	AB	R	H	2B	3B	HR	RBI	BB	SO	AVG	OBP	SLG	PRO+	BR	/A	RC	SB	CS	SBR	FR	POS	TPR
1952	Pit-N	95	384	38	109	6	1	1	29	19	27	.284	.319	.313	74	-12	-14	35	2	4	-2	1	S	-1.1
1955	Pit-N	151	521	45	139	28	2	4	51	38	26	.267	.318	.351	78	-17	-16	54	0	2	-1	15	*S	0.3
1956	Pit-N	142	520	40	142	19	3	0	37	35	25	.273	.319	.321	74	-19	-18	52	0	3	-2	0	*S/3	-0.9
1957	Pit-N	125	501	58	158	30	5	7	54	27	28	.315	.354	.437	114	7	9	74	0	1	-1	-1	*S/3	1.3
1958	Pit-N	151	584	67	175	36	9	3	66	23	32	.300	.331	.408	97	-6	-4	72	2	2	-1	3	*S	0.9
1959	Pit-N	147	593	74	163	22	7	5	51	32	35	.275	.314	.361	88	-18	-17	62	0	2	-1	3	*S	-0.9
1960	*Pit-N	138	573	85	186	26	4	2	50	39	35	.325	.372	.394	109	9	8	85	0	2	-1	11	*S	2.3
1961	Pit-N	148	596	71	164	25	6	6	55	40	44	.275	.322	.367	82	-15	-15	65	0	4	-2	9	*S/3	0.5
1962	Pit-N	161	678	76	199	34	3	2	61	31	61	.294	.327	.361	85	-15	-15	78	2	1	0	14	*S	1.4
1963	StL-N	158	631	85	201	43	11	6	73	56	58	.319	.380	.450	126	31	25	106	3	1	0	-13	*S	2.9
1964	*StL-N	161	636	70	186	35	6	1	70	44	42	.292	.338	.371	92	0	-6	78	2	3	-1	-12	*S	-0.8
1965	StL-N	153	587	55	149	26	5	0	52	56	50	.254	.320	.315	73	-15	-21	61	1	1	-0	-8	*S/3	-1.4
1966	Phi-N	155	584	58	152	21	4	2	53	40	38	.260	.313	.320	77	-18	-18	61	2	1	0	11	*S3/1	0.4
1967	Phi-N	10	26	3	3	0	0	0	1	4	4	.115	.233	.115	3	-3	-3	1	0	0	0	2	/S	0.0
	SF-N	34	70	4	12	1	1	0	4	6	7	.171	.237	.214	30	-6	-6	3	0	0	0	-8	S/2	-1.1
	Yr	44	96	7	15	1	1	0	5	10	11	.156	.236	.188	23	-9	-9	4	0	0	0	-5		-1.1
Total	14	1929	7484	829	2138	352	67	39	707	490	512	.286	.332	.366	89	-95	-110	882	14	27	-12	28	*S/321	3.8

■ HEINIE GROH
Groh, Henry Knight b: 9/18/1889, Rochester, N.Y. d: 8/22/68, Cincinnati, Ohio BR/TR, 5'8", 158 lbs. Deb: 4/12/12 M

YEAR	TM/L	G	AB	R	H	2B	3B	HR	RBI	BB	SO	AVG	OBP	SLG	PRO+	BR	/A	RC	SB	CS	SBR	FR	POS	TPR
1912	NY-N	27	48	8	13	2	1	0	3	8	7	.271	.375	.354	97	0	0	8	6			3	2/S3	0.3
1913	NY-N	4	2	0	0	0	0	0	0	0	1	.000	.000	.000	-99	-1	-1	0	0			1	/3S	0.0
	Cin-N	117	397	51	112	19	5	3	48	38	36	.282	.351	.378	109	5	5	59	24			10	*2/S	1.2
	Yr	121	399	51	112	19	5	3	48	38	37	.281	.349	.376	107	4	4	59	24			10		1.2
1914	Cin-N	139	455	59	131	18	4	2	32	64	28	.288	.391	.358	120	17	15	72	24			-7	*2/S	0.7
1915	Cin-N	160	587	72	170	32	9	3	50	50	33	.290	.354	.390	123	18	17	83	12	17	-7	11	*32	3.0
1916	Cin-N	149	553	85	149	24	14	2	28	84	34	.269	.370	.374	132	22	24	83	13			19	*32/S	5.0
1917	Cin-N	156	599	91	182	39	11	1	53	71	30	.304	.385	.411	150	33	36	96	15			8	*3/2	4.6
1918	Cin-N	126	493	86	158	28	3	1	37	54	24	.320	.395	.396	144	26	27	79	11			2	*3M	3.5
1919	*Cin-N	122	448	79	139	17	11	5	63	56	26	.310	.392	.431	151	27	29	81	21			-2	*3	3.0
1920	Cin-N	145	550	86	164	28	12	0	49	60	29	.298	.375	.393	122	17	18	81	16	19	-7	-6	*3/S	1.3
1921	Cin-N	97	357	54	118	19	6	0	48	36	17	.331	.398	.417	122	10	12	60	22	14	-2	1	3	1.1
1922	*NY-N	115	426	63	113	21	3	3	51	53	21	.265	.353	.350	81	-10	-11	55	5	6	-2	1	*3	-0.2
1923	*NY-N	123	465	91	135	22	5	4	48	60	22	.290	.379	.385	103	3	4	71	3	4	-2	4	*3	0.9
1924	*NY-N	145	559	82	157	32	3	2	46	52	29	.281	.354	.360	94	-5	-3	74	8	6	-1	3	*3	0.9
1925	NY-N	25	65	7	15	4	0	0	4	6	3	.231	.296	.292	53	-5	-4	6	0	0	0	-5	3/2	-0.7
1926	NY-N	12	35	2	8	2	0	0	3	2	3	.229	.270	.286	50	-2	-2	3	0			-1	/3	-0.2
1927	*Pit-N	14	35	2	10	1	0	0	3	2	2	.286	.324	.314	67	-1	-2	3	0			-1	3	-0.1
Total	16	1676	6074	918	1774	308	87	26	566	696	345	.292	.373	.384	119	155	164	915	180	66		40	*32/S	24.3

■ LEW GROH
Groh, Lewis Carl "Silver" b: 10/16/1883, Rochester, N.Y. d: 10/20/60, Rochester, N.Y. BR/TR, Deb: 8/02/19

YEAR	TM/L	G	AB	R	H	2B	3B	HR	RBI	BB	SO	AVG	OBP	SLG	PRO+	BR	/A	RC	SB	CS	SBR	FR	POS	TPR
1919	Phi-A	2	4	0	0	0	0	0	0	0	2	.000	.000	.000	-99	-1	-1	0	0			-0	/3	0.0

■ GEORGE GROSART
Grosart, George Albert b: 1879, Meadville, Pa. D, Apr.18, 1902 Homestead, Pa. Deb: 6/07/01

YEAR	TM/L	G	AB	R	H	2B	3B	HR	RBI	BB	SO	AVG	OBP	SLG	PRO+	BR	/A	RC	SB	CS	SBR	FR	POS	TPR
1901	Bos-N	7	26	4	3	0	0	0	1	0		.115	.115	.115	-30	-4	-5	0	0			0	/O	-0.4

■ HOWDIE GROSKLOSS
Groskloss, Howard Hoffman b: 4/9/07, Pittsburgh, Pa. BR/TR, 5'9", 176 lbs. Deb: 6/23/30

YEAR	TM/L	G	AB	R	H	2B	3B	HR	RBI	BB	SO	AVG	OBP	SLG	PRO+	BR	/A	RC	SB	CS	SBR	FR	POS	TPR
1930	Pit-N	2	3	0	1	0	0	0	1	0	0	.333	.333	.333	62	-0	-0	0	0			-1	/S	0.0
1931	Pit-N	53	161	13	45	7	2	0	20	11	16	.280	.326	.348	82	-4	-4	19	1			-1	2/S	-0.2
1932	Pit-N	17	20	1	2	0	0	0	0	0	3	.100	.100	.100	-47	-4	-4	0	0			-1	/S	-0.4
Total	3	72	184	14	48	7	2	0	21	11	19	.261	.303	.321	68	-8	-8	19	1			-3	/2S	-0.6

■ EMIL GROSS
Gross, Emil Michael b: 3/3/1858, Chicago, Ill. d: 8/24/21, Eagle River, Wis. BR/TR, 6', 190 lbs. Deb: 8/13/1879

YEAR	TM/L	G	AB	R	H	2B	3B	HR	RBI	BB	SO	AVG	OBP	SLG	PRO+	BR	/A	RC	SB	CS	SBR	FR	POS	TPR
1879	Pro-N	30	132	31	46	9	5	0	24	4	8	.348	.368	.492	183	11	11	24				-6	C	0.5
1880	Pro-N	87	347	43	90	18	3	1	34	16	15	.259	.292	.337	116	5	6	35				-19	*C	-0.6
1881	Pro-N	51	182	15	50	9	4	1	24	13	11	.275	.323	.385	124	5	5	23				-2	C/O	0.2
1883	Phi-N	57	231	39	71	25	7	1	25	12	18	.307	.342	.489	163	13	16	40				-24	C/O	-0.3
1884	CP-U	23	95	13	34	6	2	4		6		.358	.396	.589	231	13	13	23	0			0	C/O	1.1
Total	5	248	987	141	291	67	21	7	107	51	52	.295	.329	.427	149	46	52	145	0			-51	C/O	0.9

■ TURKEY GROSS
Gross, Ewell b: 2/21/1896, Mesquite, Tex. d: 1/11/36, Dallas, Tex. BR/TR, 6', 165 lbs. Deb: 4/14/25

YEAR	TM/L	G	AB	R	H	2B	3B	HR	RBI	BB	SO	AVG	OBP	SLG	PRO+	BR	/A	RC	SB	CS	SBR	FR	POS	TPR
1925	Bos-A	9	32	2	3	0	1	0	2	2	2	.094	.171	.156	-16	-6	-6	1	0	0	0	-1	/S	-0.4

YEAR	TM/L	G	AB	R	H	2B	3B	HR	RBI	BB	SO	AVG	OBP	SLG	PRO+	BR	/A	RC	SB	CS	SBR	FR	POS	TPR

■ GREG GROSS
Gross, Gregory Eugene b: 8/1/52, York, Pa. BL/TL, 5'10", 160 lbs. Deb: 9/05/73

YEAR	TM/L	G	AB	R	H	2B	3B	HR	RBI	BB	SO	AVG	OBP	SLG	PRO+	BR	/A	RC	SB	CS	SBR	FR	POS	TPR
1973	Hou-N	14	39	5	9	2	1	0	1	4	4	.231	.302	.333	76	-1	-1	4	2	1	0	0	/O	-0.1
1974	Hou-N	156	589	78	185	21	8	0	36	76	39	.314	.393	.377	121	16	19	86	12	20	-8	5	*O	1.0
1975	Hou-N	132	483	67	142	14	10	0	41	63	37	.294	.375	.364	114	6	10	69	2	2	-1	1	*O	0.7
1976	Hou-N	128	426	52	122	12	3	0	27	64	39	.286	.380	.329	112	4	9	56	2	6	-3	2	*O	0.4
1977	Chi-N	115	239	41	77	10	4	5	32	33	19	.322	.404	.460	118	12	8	45	0	1	-1	-6	O	0.0
1978	Chi-N	124	347	34	92	12	7	1	39	33	19	.265	.329	.349	80	-5	-10	41	3	1	0	-18	*O	-3.3
1979	Phi-N	111	174	21	58	6	3	0	15	29	5	.333	.429	.402	124	8	8	32	5	2	0	1	O	0.7
1980	*Phi-N	127	154	19	37	7	2	0	12	24	7	.240	.346	.312	80	-2	-3	18	1	1	-0	1	O/1	-0.6
1981	*Phi-N	83	102	14	23	6	1	0	7	15	5	.225	.325	.304	76	-2	-3	10	2	2	-1	5	O	0.0
1982	Phi-N	119	134	14	40	4	0	0	10	19	8	.299	.386	.328	99	1	1	17	4	3	-1	2	O	0.1
1983	*Phi-N	136	245	25	74	12	3	0	29	34	16	.302	.389	.376	114	6	6	36	3	5	-2	-6	*O/1	-0.3
1984	Phi-N	112	202	19	65	9	1	0	16	24	11	.322	.396	.376	116	6	6	31	1	0	0	1	O1	0.4
1985	Phi-N	93	169	21	44	5	2	0	14	32	9	.260	.378	.314	93	1	-0	22	1	0	0	-4	O/1	-0.4
1986	Phi-N	87	101	11	25	5	0	0	8	21	11	.248	.382	.297	87	-0	-1	12	1	0	0	1	O/1P	0.0
1987	Phi-N	114	133	14	38	4	1	1	12	25	12	.286	.403	.353	99	2	1	21	0	0	0	-4	O1	-0.4
1988	Phi-N	98	133	10	27	1	0	0	5	16	3	.203	.293	.211	46	-9	-9	9	0	0	0	-2	O1	-1.2
1989	Hou-N	60	75	2	15	0	0	0	4	11	6	.200	.310	.200	51	-5	-4	5	0	0	0	-2	O/1P	-0.6
Total	17	1809	3745	449	1073	130	46	7	308	523	250	.287	.375	.351	103	38	37	511	39	44	-15	-22	*O/1P	-3.6

■ WAYNE GROSS
Gross, Wayne Dale b: 1/14/52, Riverside, Cal. BL/TR, 6'2", 210 lbs. Deb: 8/21/76

YEAR	TM/L	G	AB	R	H	2B	3B	HR	RBI	BB	SO	AVG	OBP	SLG	PRO+	BR	/A	RC	SB	CS	SBR	FR	POS	TPR
1976	Oak-A	10	18	0	4	0	0	0	0	2	1	.222	.300	.222	57	-1	-1	1	0	0	0	0	/1OD	0.0
1977	Oak-A	146	485	66	113	21	1	22	63	86	84	.233	.354	.416	111	8	9	76	5	4	-1	-23	*3/1	-1.8
1978	Oak-A	118	285	18	57	10	2	7	23	40	63	.200	.309	.323	82	-8	-6	31	0	2	-1	-8	*31	-1.7
1979	Oak-A	138	442	54	99	19	1	14	50	72	62	.224	.334	.367	94	-6	-2	57	4	3	-1	-10	*31/O	-1.1
1980	Oak-A	113	366	45	103	20	3	14	61	44	39	.281	.360	.467	134	13	16	64	5	3	-0	-28	31/D	-1.2
1981	*Oak-A	82	243	29	50	7	1	10	31	34	28	.206	.308	.366	98	-2	-0	28	2	1	0	-9	31/D	-0.9
1982	Oak-A	129	386	43	97	14	0	9	41	53	50	.251	.345	.358	98	-2	0	52	3	1	0	-7	*31/D	-0.8
1983	Oak-A	137	339	34	79	18	0	12	44	36	52	.233	.312	.392	98	-4	-1	41	3	5	-2	-6	13/PD	-1.1
1984	Bal-A	127	342	53	74	9	1	22	64	68	69	.216	.348	.442	119	9	10	55	1	2	-1	-5	*3/1D	0.5
1985	Bal-A	103	217	31	51	8	0	11	18	46	48	.235	.369	.424	120	6	7	37	1	1	-0	0	3D/1	0.4
1986	Oak-A	3	2	0	0	0	0	0	0	1	0	.000	.333	.000	0	-0	-0	0	0	0	0	-0	/3	0.0
Total	11	1106	3125	373	727	126	9	121	396	482	496	.233	.339	.395	106	13	31	443	24	22	-6	-96	31/DOP	-7.7

■ JERRY GROTE
Grote, Gerald Wayne b: 10/6/42, San Antonio, Tex. BR/TR, 5'10", 185 lbs. Deb: 9/21/63

YEAR	TM/L	G	AB	R	H	2B	3B	HR	RBI	BB	SO	AVG	OBP	SLG	PRO+	BR	/A	RC	SB	CS	SBR	FR	POS	TPR
1963	Hou-N	3	5	0	1	0	0	0	1	1	3	.200	.333	.200	61	-0	-0	1	0	0	0	-1	/C	0.0
1964	Hou-N	100	298	26	54	9	3	3	24	20	75	.181	.242	.262	44	-23	-21	18	0	2	-1	2	C	-1.7
1966	NY-N	120	317	26	75	12	2	3	31	40	81	.237	.328	.315	82	-7	-7	33	4	3	-1	-0	*C/3	-0.4
1967	NY-N	120	344	25	67	8	0	4	23	14	65	.195	.228	.253	38	-28	-27	19	2	2	-1	2	*C	-2.0
1968	NY-N	124	404	29	114	18	0	3	31	44	81	.282	.357	.349	112	8	7	50	1	5	-3	6	*C	1.7
1969	*NY-N	113	365	38	92	12	3	6	40	32	59	.252	.314	.351	84	-7	-8	39	2	1	0	18	*C	1.8
1970	NY-N	126	415	38	106	14	1	2	34	36	39	.255	.316	.308	68	-18	-18	39	2	1	0	8	*C	-0.3
1971	NY-N	125	403	35	109	25	2	3	35	40	47	.270	.339	.347	96	-2	-1	44	1	4	-2	5	*C	0.4
1972	NY-N	64	205	15	43	5	1	3	21	26	27	.210	.308	.288	72	-7	-7	19	1	0	0	2	C/3O	0.0
1973	*NY-N	84	285	17	73	10	2	1	32	13	23	.256	.291	.316	69	-12	-12	24	0	0	0	8	C/3	0.1
1974	NY-N	97	319	25	82	8	1	5	36	33	33	.257	.331	.335	88	-5	-5	35	0	1	-1	-4	C	-0.5
1975	NY-N	119	386	28	114	14	5	5	39	38	23	.295	.360	.373	109	3	5	51	0	1	-1	5	*C	1.4
1976	NY-N	101	323	30	88	14	2	4	28	38	19	.272	.351	.365	110	2	4	39	1	2	-1	11	C/O	2.0
1977	NY-N	42	115	8	31	3	1	0	7	9	12	.270	.333	.313	78	-4	-3	11	0	0	0	-2	C3	-0.5
	*LA-N	18	27	3	7	0	0	0	4	2	5	.259	.310	.259	55	-2	-2	2	0	1	-1	4	C/3	0.2
	Yr	60	142	11	38	3	1	0	11	11	17	.268	.329	.303	73	-5	-5	13	0	1	-1	2		-0.3
1978	*LA-N	41	70	5	19	5	0	0	9	10	5	.271	.363	.343	98	0	0	10	0	0	0	8	C/3	0.9
1981	KC-A	22	56	4	17	3	1	1	9	3	2	.304	.350	.446	129	2	2	9	1	0	0	4	C	0.7
	LA-N	2	2	0	0	0	0	0	0	0	1	.000	.000	.000	-99	-1	-1	0	0	0	0	0	/C	0.0
Total	16	1421	4339	352	1092	160	22	39	404	399	600	.252	.318	.326	83	-102	-92	443	15	23	-9	77	*C/3O	3.8

■ JOHNNY GROTH
Groth, John Thomas b: 7/23/26, Chicago, Ill. BR/TR, 6', 182 lbs. Deb: 9/05/46

YEAR	TM/L	G	AB	R	H	2B	3B	HR	RBI	BB	SO	AVG	OBP	SLG	PRO+	BR	/A	RC	SB	CS	SBR	FR	POS	TPR
1946	Det-A	4	9	1	0	0	0	0	0	0	3	.000	.000	.000	-94	-2	-2	0	0	0	0	0	/O	-0.2
1947	Det-A	2	4	1	1	0	0	0	0	2	1	.250	.500	.250	109	0	0	0	0	0	0	0	/O	0.1
1948	Det-A	6	17	3	8	3	0	1	5	1	1	.471	.500	.824	242	3	3	7	0	0	0	1	/O	0.3
1949	Det-A	103	348	60	102	19	5	11	73	65	27	.293	.407	.471	132	17	17	66	3	7	-3	-1	O	0.9
1950	Det-A	157	566	95	173	30	8	12	85	95	27	.306	.407	.451	116	19	16	106	1	5	-3	-16	*O	-0.4
1951	Det-A	118	428	41	128	29	1	3	49	31	32	.299	.349	.393	100	-0	-1	57	1	1	-0	-5	O	-0.9
1952	Det-A	141	524	56	149	22	2	4	51	51	39	.284	.348	.357	96	-2	-3	64	2	10	-5	-7	*O	-1.9
1953	StL-A	141	557	65	141	27	4	10	57	42	53	.253	.308	.370	81	-15	-16	62	5	6	-2	12	*O	-0.9
1954	Chi-A	125	422	41	116	20	0	7	60	42	37	.275	.343	.372	93	-2	-4	49	3	9	-5	-5	*O	-1.6
1955	Chi-A	32	77	13	26	7	0	2	11	6	13	.338	.386	.506	135	4	4	15	1	0	0	3	O	0.6
	Was-A	63	183	22	40	4	5	2	17	18	18	.219	.289	.328	69	-9	-8	18	2	0	1	2	O	-0.7
	Yr	95	260	35	66	11	5	4	28	24	31	.254	.317	.381	89	-5	-5	32	3	0	1	5		-0.1
1956	KC-A	95	244	22	63	13	3	5	37	30	31	.258	.339	.398	94	-2	-2	32	1	2	-1	3	O	-0.3
1957	KC-A	55	59	10	15	0	0	0	2	7	6	.254	.333	.254	62	-3	-3	5	0	0	0	-0	O	-0.5
	Det-A	38	103	11	30	10	0	0	16	6	7	.291	.336	.388	95	-0	-1	14	0	0	0	2	O	0.0
	Yr	93	162	21	45	10	0	0	18	13	13	.278	.335	.340	83	-3	-4	19	0	0	0	2		-0.5
1958	Det-A	88	146	24	41	5	2	2	11	13	19	.281	.340	.384	92	-0	-2	18	0	1	-1	3	O	-0.3
1959	Det-A	55	102	12	24	7	1	1	10	7	14	.235	.284	.353	70	-4	-5	11	0	0	0	1	O	-0.4
1960	Det-A	25	19	3	7	1	0	0	2	6	3	.368	.455	.421	135	1	1	4	0	1	-1	1	/O	0.1
Total	15	1248	3808	480	1064	197	31	60	486	419	329	.279	.353	.395	99	4	-5	528	19	42	-20	-5	*O	-6.1

■ ROY GROVER
Grover, Roy Arthur b: 1/17/1892, Snohomish, Wash. d: 2/7/78, Milwaukie, Ore. BR/TR, 5'8", 150 lbs. Deb: 9/13/16

YEAR	TM/L	G	AB	R	H	2B	3B	HR	RBI	BB	SO	AVG	OBP	SLG	PRO+	BR	/A	RC	SB	CS	SBR	FR	POS	TPR
1916	Phi-A	20	77	8	21	1	2	0	7	6	10	.273	.325	.338	103	-0	0	11	5			-7	2	-0.6
1917	Phi-A	141	482	45	108	15	7	0	34	43	53	.224	.292	.284	77	-14	-13	46	12			5	*2	0.0
1919	Phi-A	22	56	8	13	1	0	0	2	5	6	.232	.295	.250	53	-3	-3	5	0			-6	2/3	-0.8
	Was-A	24	75	6	14	0	0	0	7	6	10	.187	.256	.187	25	-7	-7	4	2			-4	2	-0.8
	Yr	46	131	14	27	1	0	0	9	11	16	.206	.273	.214	37	-11	-11	9	2			-9		-1.6
Total	3	207	690	67	156	17	9	0	50	60	79	.226	.292	.277	71	-25	-24	66	19			-12	2/3	-2.2

■ HARVEY GRUBB
Grubb, Harvey Harrison b: 9/18/1890, Lexington, N.C. d: 1/25/70, Corpus Christi, Tex. BR/TR, 6', 165 lbs. Deb: 9/27/12

YEAR	TM/L	G	AB	R	H	2B	3B	HR	RBI	BB	SO	AVG	OBP	SLG	PRO+	BR	/A	RC	SB	CS	SBR	FR	POS	TPR
1912	Cle-A	1	0	0	0	0	0	0	0	0		—	1.000	—	187	0	0	0	0			-0	/O	0.0

■ JOHN GRUBB
Grubb, John Maywood b: 8/4/48, Richmond, Va. BL/TR, 6'3", 175 lbs. Deb: 9/10/72

YEAR	TM/L	G	AB	R	H	2B	3B	HR	RBI	BB	SO	AVG	OBP	SLG	PRO+	BR	/A	RC	SB	CS	SBR	FR	POS	TPR
1972	SD-N	7	21	4	7	1	1	0	1	1	3	.333	.364	.476	147	1	1	3	0	1	-1	1	/O	0.1
1973	SD-N	113	389	52	121	22	3	8	37	37	50	.311	.374	.445	137	14	18	66	9	3	1	3	*O/3	1.8
1974	SD-N	140	444	53	127	20	4	8	42	46	47	.286	.358	.403	118	8	10	68	4	0	1	7	*O/3	1.4
1975	SD-N	144	553	72	149	36	2	4	38	59	59	.269	.345	.363	103	-2	3	71	2	7	-4	-8	*O	-1.4

YEAR	TM/L	G	AB	R	H	2B	3B	HR	RBI	BB	SO	AVG	OBP	SLG	PRO+	BR	/A	RC	SB	CS	SBR	FR	POS	TPR
1976	SD-N	109	384	54	109	22	1	5	27	65	53	.284	.393	.385	132	14	18	62	1	2	-1	-8	O/13	0.5
1977	Cle-A	34	93	8	28	3	3	2	14	19	18	.301	.425	.462	146	6	7	18	0	3	-2	-0	O/D	0.4
1978	Cle-A	113	378	54	100	16	6	14	61	59	60	.265	.367	.450	130	15	16	66	5	1	1	1	*O	1.5
	Tex-A	21	33	8	13	3	0	1	6	11	5	.394	.545	.576	215	6	6	12	1	1	-0	1	O/D	0.7
	Yr	134	411	62	113	19	6	15	67	70	65	.275	.383	.460	137	21	22	78	6	2	1	2		2.2
1979	Tex-A	102	289	42	79	14	0	10	37	34	44	.273	.352	.426	110	4	4	43	2	4	-2	-3	O	-0.3
1980	Tex-A	110	274	40	76	12	1	9	32	42	35	.277	.377	.427	124	9	10	43	2	3	-1	-8	O/D	0.0
1981	Tex-A	67	199	26	46	9	1	3	26	23	25	.231	.317	.332	92	-3	-2	20	0	3	-2	-7	O	-1.2
1982	Tex-A	103	308	35	86	13	3	3	26	39	37	.279	.371	.370	110	3	6	44	0	3	-2	-5	OD	-0.3
1983	Det-A	57	134	20	34	5	2	4	22	28	17	.254	.390	.410	124	5	6	23	0	0	0	-2	OD	0.3
1984	*Det-A	86	176	25	47	5	0	8	17	36	36	.267	.397	.432	130	9	9	33	1	0	0	-1	OD	0.7
1985	Det-A	78	155	19	38	7	1	5	25	24	25	.245	.350	.400	106	2	2	22	0	1	-1	-1	DO	0.0
1986	Det-A	81	210	32	70	13	1	13	51	28	28	.333	.417	.590	171	21	21	54	0	1	-1	-1	DO	1.9
1987	*Det-A	59	114	9	23	6	0	2	13	15	16	.202	.295	.307	63	-7	-6	10	0	0	0	0	OD/3	-0.5
Total	16	1424	4154	553	1153	207	29	99	475	566	558	.278	.369	.413	121	105	127	658	27	33	-12	-30	*OD/13	5.6

■ FRANK GRUBE
Grube, Franklin Thomas "Hans" b: 1/7/05, Easton, Pa. d: 7/2/45, New York, N.Y. BR/TR, 5'9", 190 lbs. Deb: 5/12/31

YEAR	TM/L	G	AB	R	H	2B	3B	HR	RBI	BB	SO	AVG	OBP	SLG	PRO+	BR	/A	RC	SB	CS	SBR	FR	POS	TPR
1931	Chi-A	88	265	29	58	13	2	1	24	22	22	.219	.284	.294	55	-19	-16	23	2	2	-1	-11	C	-1.9
1932	Chi-A	93	277	36	78	16	2	0	31	33	13	.282	.362	.354	92	-5	-2	38	6	1	1	-2	C	0.2
1933	Chi-A	85	256	23	59	13	0	0	23	38	20	.230	.334	.281	67	-12	-10	27	1	1	0	-7	C	-1.2
1934	StL-A	65	170	22	49	10	0	0	11	24	11	.288	.379	.347	82	-2	-4	24	2	1	0	-1	C	0.0
1935	StL-A	3	6	3	2	1	0	0	0	0	1	.333	.333	.500	108	0	0	1	0	0	0	0	/C	0.0
	Chi-A	9	19	1	7	2	0	0	6	3	2	.368	.455	.474	137	1	1	4	0	0	0	2	/C	0.4
	Yr	12	25	4	9	3	0	0	6	3	3	.360	.429	.480	131	1	1	5	0	0	0	3		0.4
1936	Chi-A	33	93	6	15	2	1	0	11	9	15	.161	.235	.204	9	-14	-14	5	1	0	0	-2	C	-0.7
1941	StL-A	18	39	1	6	2	0	0	1	2	4	.154	.195	.205	6	-5	-6	2	0	0	0	3	C	-0.1
Total	7	394	1125	121	274	59	5	1	107	131	88	.244	.326	.308	67	-54	-51	124	12	5	1	-13	C	-3.3

■ KELLY GRUBER
Gruber, Kelly Wayne b: 2/26/62, Houston, Tex. BR/TR, 6', 180 lbs. Deb: 4/20/84

YEAR	TM/L	G	AB	R	H	2B	3B	HR	RBI	BB	SO	AVG	OBP	SLG	PRO+	BR	/A	RC	SB	CS	SBR	FR	POS	TPR
1984	Tor-A	15	16	1	1	0	0	0	2	0	5	.063	.063	.250	-18	-3	-3	0	0	0	0	2	3/OS	0.0
1985	Tor-A	5	13	0	3	0	0	0	1	0	3	.231	.231	.231	26	-1	-1	1	0	0	0	-1	/32	-0.1
1986	Tor-A	87	143	20	28	4	1	5	15	5	27	.196	.223	.343	50	-10	-11	8	2	5	-2	10	32D/OS	-0.2
1987	Tor-A	138	341	50	80	14	3	12	36	17	70	.235	.285	.399	77	-11	-12	37	12	2	2	9	*3S/2OD	0.0
1988	Tor-A	158	569	75	158	33	5	16	81	38	92	.278	.331	.438	113	9	9	79	23	5	4	26	*3/2OSD	3.9
1989	*Tor-A	135	545	83	158	24	4	18	73	30	60	.290	.330	.448	120	11	12	77	10	5	0	19	*3O/SD	3.1
1990	Tor-A	150	592	92	162	36	6	31	118	48	94	.274	.336	.512	137	24	26	101	14	2	3	-2	*3/OD	2.8
Total	7	688	2219	321	590	111	19	83	326	138	351	.266	.316	.445	109	19	20	304	61	19	7	62	3/O2SD	9.5

■ SIG GRYSKA
Gryska, Sigmund Stanley b: 11/4/15, Chicago, Ill. BR/TR, 5'11.5", 173 lbs. Deb: 9/28/38

YEAR	TM/L	G	AB	R	H	2B	3B	HR	RBI	BB	SO	AVG	OBP	SLG	PRO+	BR	/A	RC	SB	CS	SBR	FR	POS	TPR
1938	StL-A	7	21	3	10	2	1	0	4	3	3	.476	.542	.667	202	3	3	8	0	0	0	1	/S	0.4
1939	StL-A	18	49	4	13	2	0	0	8	6	10	.265	.345	.306	66	-2	-2	6	3	1	0	-4	S	-0.4
Total	2	25	70	7	23	4	1	0	12	9	13	.329	.405	.414	107	1	1	13	3	1	0	-3	/S	0.0

■ MARV GUDAT
Gudat, Marvin John b: 8/27/05, Goliad, Tex. d: 3/1/54, Los Angeles, Cal. BL/TL, 5'11", 162 lbs. Deb: 5/21/29

YEAR	TM/L	G	AB	R	H	2B	3B	HR	RBI	BB	SO	AVG	OBP	SLG	PRO+	BR	/A	RC	SB	CS	SBR	FR	POS	TPR
1929	Cin-N	9	10	0	2	0	0	0	0	0	0	.200	.200	.200	-1	-2	-1	0	0			-1	/P	0.0
1932	*Chi-N	60	94	15	24	4	1	1	15	16	10	.255	.369	.351	96	0	0	13	0			-3	O/1P	-0.3
Total	2	69	104	15	26	4	1	1	15	16	10	.250	.355	.337	87	-2	-1	14	0			-3	/O1P	-0.3

■ MIKE GUERRA
Guerra, Fermin (Romero) b: 10/11/12, Havana, Cuba BR/TR, 5'9", 150 lbs. Deb: 9/19/37

YEAR	TM/L	G	AB	R	H	2B	3B	HR	RBI	BB	SO	AVG	OBP	SLG	PRO+	BR	/A	RC	SB	CS	SBR	FR	POS	TPR
1937	Was-A	1	3	0	0	0	0	0	0	0	2	.000	.000	.000	-99	-1	-1	0	0	0	0	-0	/C	0.0
1944	Was-A	75	210	29	59	7	2	1	29	13	14	.281	.323	.348	96	-3	-1	25	8	2	1	-3	C/O	0.1
1945	Was-A	56	138	11	29	1	1	1	15	10	12	.210	.268	.254	57	-9	-7	9	4	1	1	6	C	0.3
1946	Was-A	41	83	3	21	2	1	0	4	5	6	.253	.295	.301	71	-4	-3	7	1	0	0	-1	C	-0.2
1947	Phi-A	72	209	20	45	2	2	0	18	10	15	.215	.251	.244	37	-18	-18	13	1	2	-1	2	C	-1.1
1948	Phi-A	53	142	18	30	4	2	1	23	18	13	.211	.300	.289	57	-9	-9	12	2	3	-1	2	C	-0.6
1949	Phi-A	98	298	41	79	14	1	3	31	37	26	.265	.346	.349	87	-7	-5	37	3	0	1	-2	C	-0.1
1950	Phi-A	87	252	25	71	10	4	2	26	16	12	.282	.325	.377	81	-9	-8	31	1	0	0	-6	C	-0.9
1951	Bos-A	10	32	1	5	0	0	0	2	6	5	.156	.289	.156	21	-3	-4	2	1	0	0	-1	C	-0.2
	Was-A	72	214	20	43	2	1	1	20	16	18	.201	.257	.234	34	-20	-20	13	4	4	-1	-11	C	-2.6
	Yr	82	246	21	48	2	1	1	22	22	23	.195	.261	.224	32	-23	-23	14	5	4	-1	-12		-2.8
Total	9	565	1581	168	382	42	14	9	168	131	123	.242	.300	.303	65	-81	-76	148	25	12	0	-16	C/O	-5.3

■ MARIO GUERRERO
Guerrero, Mario Miguel (Abud) b: 9/28/49, Santo Domingo, D.R. BR/TR, 5'10", 155 lbs. Deb: 4/08/73

YEAR	TM/L	G	AB	R	H	2B	3B	HR	RBI	BB	SO	AVG	OBP	SLG	PRO+	BR	/A	RC	SB	CS	SBR	FR	POS	TPR
1973	Bos-A	66	219	19	51	5	2	0	11	10	21	.233	.273	.274	51	-13	-15	16	2	2	-1	-8	S2	-1.6
1974	Bos-A	93	284	28	70	6	2	0	23	13	22	.246	.284	.282	59	-13	-16	21	3	1	0	-0	S	-0.8
1975	StL-N	64	184	17	44	9	0	0	11	10	7	.239	.286	.288	57	-10	-11	14	0	0	0	6	S	0.2
1976	Cal-A	83	268	24	76	12	0	1	18	7	12	.284	.309	.340	96	-4	-2	27	0	0	0	-12	2S/D	-0.8
1977	Cal-A	86	244	17	69	8	2	1	28	4	16	.283	.294	.344	76	-9	-8	24	0	0	0	0	SD2	-0.2
1978	Oak-A	143	505	27	139	18	4	3	38	15	35	.275	.304	.345	87	-13	-9	49	0	5	-3	-29	*S	-3.1
1979	Oak-A	46	166	12	38	5	0	0	18	6	7	.229	.256	.259	42	-14	-13	10				-4	S	-1.1
1980	Oak-A	116	381	32	91	16	2	2	23	19	32	.239	.277	.307	64	-18	-18	29	3	3	-1	-42	*S	-5.1
Total	8	697	2251	166	578	79	12	7	170	84	152	.257	.288	.312	69	-98	-91	190	8	12	-5	-89	S/2D	-12.5

■ PEDRO GUERRERO
Guerrero, Pedro b: 6/29/56, San Pedro De Macoris, D.R. BR/TR, 5'11", 176 lbs. Deb: 9/22/78

YEAR	TM/L	G	AB	R	H	2B	3B	HR	RBI	BB	SO	AVG	OBP	SLG	PRO+	BR	/A	RC	SB	CS	SBR	FR	POS	TPR
1978	LA-N	5	8	3	5	0	1	0	1	0	0	.625	.625	.875	316	2	2	4	0	0	0	0	/1	0.2
1979	LA-N	25	62	7	15	2	0	2	9	1	14	.242	.254	.371	69	-3	-3	6	2	0	1	-1	O/13	-0.3
1980	LA-N	75	183	27	59	9	1	7	31	12	31	.322	.364	.497	141	9	9	33	2	1	0	0	O2/31	1.1
1981	*LA-N	98	347	46	104	17	2	12	48	34	57	.300	.366	.464	139	15	17	54	5	9	-4	0	O3/1	1.1
1982	LA-N	150	575	87	175	27	5	32	100	65	89	.304	.380	.536	157	40	42	120	22	5	4	6	*O3	5.0
1983	*LA-N	160	584	87	174	28	6	32	103	72	110	.298	.377	.531	150	38	38	118	23	7	3	6	*3/1	4.3
1984	LA-N	144	535	85	162	29	4	16	72	49	105	.303	.362	.462	132	21	21	89	9	8	-2	-12	3O1	1.1
1985	*LA-N	137	487	99	156	22	2	33	87	83	68	.320	**.425**	**.577**	**183**	**53**	**55**	121	12	4	1	5	3O31	**6.0**
1986	LA-N	31	61	7	15	3	0	5	10	2	19	.246	.281	.541	131	1	2	9	0	0	0	-2	O/1	0.0
1987	LA-N	152	545	89	184	25	2	27	89	74	85	.338	.421	.539	156	43	45	121	9	7	-2	-4	*O1	3.2
1988	LA-N	59	215	24	64	7	1	5	35	25	33	.298	.379	.409	130	8	9	35	2	1	0	-12	31/O	-0.4
	StL-N	44	149	16	40	7	1	5	30	21	26	.268	.366	.430	126	6	6	24	2	0	1	-2	1/O	0.3
	Yr	103	364	40	104	14	2	10	65	46	59	.286	.373	.418	128	14	14	60	4	1	1	-14		-0.1
1989	StL-N	162	570	60	177	**42**	1	17	117	79	84	.311	.398	.477	145	38	36	109	2	0	1	-14	*1	1.0
1990	StL-N	136	498	42	140	31	1	13	80	44	70	.281	.341	.426	106	6	4	69	1	1	-0	-10	*1	-1.2
Total	13	1378	4819	679	1470	249	27	206	812	561	791	.305	.381	.496	144	277	282	913	91	43	2	-37	O13/2	20.8

■ OZZIE GUILLEN
Guillen, Oswaldo Jose (Barrios) b: 1/20/64, Oculare Del Tuy, Venezuela BL/TR, 5'11", 150 lbs. Deb: 4/09/85

YEAR	TM/L	G	AB	R	H	2B	3B	HR	RBI	BB	SO	AVG	OBP	SLG	PRO+	BR	/A	RC	SB	CS	SBR	FR	POS	TPR
1985	Chi-A	150	491	71	134	21	9	1	33	12	36	.273	.292	.358	74	-16	-19	50	7	4	-0	11	*S	0.3
1986	Chi-A	159	547	58	137	19	4	2	47	12	52	.250	.268	.311	55	-33	-35	43	8	4	0	14	*S/D	-1.0
1987	Chi-A	149	560	64	156	22	7	2	51	22	52	.279	.307	.354	73	-21	-22	61	25	8	3	13	*S	0.1

YEAR	TM/L	G	AB	R	H	2B	3B	HR	RBI	BB	SO	AVG	OBP	SLG	PRO+	BR	/A	RC	SB	CS	SBR	FR	POS	TPR
1988	Chi-A	156	566	58	148	16	7	0	39	25	40	.261	.295	.314	71	-22	-22	50	25	13	-0	43	*S	2.8
1989	Chi-A	155	597	63	151	20	8	1	54	15	48	.253	.271	.318	67	-28	-26	49	36	17	1	14	*S	0.1
1990	Chi-A	160	516	61	144	21	4	1	58	26	37	.279	.315	.341	85	-12	-10	52	13	17	-6	3	*S	-0.2
Total	6	929	3277	375	870	119	39	7	282	112	265	.265	.291	.332	71	-132	-134	305	114	63	-4	98	S/D	2.1

■ BOBBY GUINDON
Guindon, Robert Joseph b: 9/4/43, Brookline, Mass. BL/TL, 6'2", 185 lbs. Deb: 9/19/64

YEAR	TM/L	G	AB	R	H	2B	3B	HR	RBI	BB	SO	AVG	OBP	SLG	PRO+	BR	/A	RC	SB	CS	SBR	FR	POS	TPR
1964	Bos-A	5	8	0	1	1	0	0	0	1	4	.125	.222	.250	30	-1	-1	1	0	0	0	-0	/1O	0.0

■ BEN GUINEY
Guiney, Benjamin Franklin b: 11/16/1858, Detroit, Mich. d: 12/5/30, Detroit, Mich. BB/TR, 6', 170 lbs. Deb: 9/04/1883

YEAR	TM/L	G	AB	R	H	2B	3B	HR	RBI	BB	SO	AVG	OBP	SLG	PRO+	BR	/A	RC	SB	CS	SBR	FR	POS	TPR
1883	Det-N	1	5	1	1	0	0	0	0	0	1	.200	.200	.200	23	-0	-0	0				-1	/O	0.0
1884	Det-N	2	7	0	0	0	0	0	0	0	3	.000	.000	.000	-99	-2	-1	0				-1	/C	-0.1
Total	2	3	12	1	1	0	0	0	0	0	4	.083	.083	.083	-51	-2	-2	0				-2	/CO	-0.1

■ BEN GUINTINI
Guintini, Benjamin John b: 1/13/20, Los Banos, Cal. BR/TR, 6'1.5", 190 lbs. Deb: 4/21/46

YEAR	TM/L	G	AB	R	H	2B	3B	HR	RBI	BB	SO	AVG	OBP	SLG	PRO+	BR	/A	RC	SB	CS	SBR	FR	POS	TPR
1946	Pit-N	2	3	0	0	0	0	0	0	0	0	.000	.000	.000	-98	-1	-1	0	0			0	/O	0.0
1950	Phi-A	3	4	0	0	0	0	0	0	0	1	.000	.000	.000	-99	-1	-1	0	0	0	0	1	/O	0.0
Total	2	5	7	0	0	0	0	0	0	0	1	.000	.000	.000	-99	-2	-2	0	0	0		1	/O	0.0

■ LOU GUISTO
Guisto, Louis Joseph b: 1/16/1895, Napa, Cal. d: 10/15/89, Napa, Cal. BR/TR, 5'11", 193 lbs. Deb: 9/10/16

YEAR	TM/L	G	AB	R	H	2B	3B	HR	RBI	BB	SO	AVG	OBP	SLG	PRO+	BR	/A	RC	SB	CS	SBR	FR	POS	TPR
1916	Cle-A	6	19	2	3	0	0	0	2	4	3	.158	.304	.158	37	-1	-1	1	1			0	/1	-0.1
1917	Cle-A	73	200	9	37	4	2	0	29	25	18	.185	.282	.225	51	-10	-12	14	3			-1	1	-1.6
1921	Cle-A	2	2	0	1	0	0	0	1	0	1	.500	.500	.500	153	0	0	0	0	0	0	0	/1	0.0
1922	Cle-A	35	84	7	21	10	1	0	9	2	7	.250	.276	.393	72	-4	-4	9	0	0		1	1	-0.4
1923	Cle-A	40	144	17	26	5	0	0	18	15	15	.181	.262	.215	27	-15	-15	9	1	1	-0	1	1	-1.5
Total	5	156	449	35	88	19	3	0	59	46	44	.196	.277	.252	47	-30	-32	33	5	1		1	1	-3.6

■ BRAD GULDEN
Gulden, Bradley Lee b: 6/10/56, New Ulm, Minn. BL/TR, 5'10", 175 lbs. Deb: 9/22/78

YEAR	TM/L	G	AB	R	H	2B	3B	HR	RBI	BB	SO	AVG	OBP	SLG	PRO+	BR	/A	RC	SB	CS	SBR	FR	POS	TPR
1978	LA-N	3	4	0	0	0	0	0	0	0	2	.000	.000	.000	-99	-1	-1	0	0	0	0	1	/C	0.0
1979	NY-A	40	92	10	15	4	0	0	6	9	16	.163	.238	.207	21	-10	-10	4	0	1	-1	11	C	0.2
1980	NY-A	2	3	1	1	0	0	1	2	0	1	.333	.333	1.333	340	1	1	1	0	0	0	-0	/C	0.1
1981	Sea-A	8	16	0	3	2	0	0	1	0	2	.188	.188	.313	40	-1	-1	1	0	0	0	2	/C	0.1
1982	Mon-N	5	6	1	0	0	0	0	0	1	1	.000	.143	.000	-56	-1	-1	0	0	0	0	1	/C	0.0
1984	Cin-N	107	292	31	66	8	2	4	33	33	35	.226	.309	.308	71	-10	-11	28	2	2	-1	-3	*C	-1.2
1986	SF-N	17	22	2	2	0	0	0	1	2	5	.091	.167	.091	-28	-4	-4	0	0	0	0	-1	C	-0.4
Total	7	182	435	45	87	14	2	5	43	45	61	.200	.278	.276	53	-26	-28	35	2	3	-1	10	C	-1.2

■ TOM GULLEY
Gulley, Thomas Jefferson b: 12/25/1899, Garner, N.C. d: 11/24/66, St.Charles, Ark. BL/TR, 5'11", 178 lbs. Deb: 8/24/23

YEAR	TM/L	G	AB	R	H	2B	3B	HR	RBI	BB	SO	AVG	OBP	SLG	PRO+	BR	/A	RC	SB	CS	SBR	FR	POS	TPR
1923	Cle-A	2	3	1	1	1	0	0	0	0	0	.333	.333	.667	159	0	0	1	0	0	0	-0	/O	0.0
1924	Cle-A	8	20	4	3	0	1	0	1	3	2	.150	.261	.250	32	-2	-2	1	0	0	0	0	/O	-0.1
1926	Chi-A	16	35	5	8	3	1	0	8	5	2	.229	.325	.371	84	-1	-1	5	0	0	0	-2	O	-0.2
Total	3	26	58	10	12	4	2	0	9	8	4	.207	.303	.345	69	-3	-3	7	0	0	0	-2	/O	-0.3

■ TED GULLIC
Gullic, Theodore Jasper b: 1/2/07, Koshkonong, Mo. BR/TR, 6'2", 175 lbs. Deb: 4/15/30

YEAR	TM/L	G	AB	R	H	2B	3B	HR	RBI	BB	SO	AVG	OBP	SLG	PRO+	BR	/A	RC	SB	CS	SBR	FR	POS	TPR
1930	StL-A	92	308	39	77	7	5	4	44	27	43	.250	.310	.344	64	-16	-18	35	4	0	1	3	O/1	-1.5
1933	StL-A	104	304	34	74	18	3	5	35	15	38	.243	.281	.372	67	-14	-16	32	3	1	0	12	O31	-0.2
Total	2	196	612	73	151	25	8	9	79	42	81	.247	.296	.358	65	-30	-34	67	7	1	2	15	O/31	-1.7

■ GLENN GULLIVER
Gulliver, Glenn James b: 10/15/54, Detroit, Mich. BL/TR, 5'11", 175 lbs. Deb: 7/17/82

YEAR	TM/L	G	AB	R	H	2B	3B	HR	RBI	BB	SO	AVG	OBP	SLG	PRO+	BR	/A	RC	SB	CS	SBR	FR	POS	TPR
1982	Bal-A	50	145	24	29	7	0	1	5	37	18	.200	.363	.269	77	-3	-3	17	0	0	0	-3	3	-0.7
1983	Bal-A	23	47	5	10	3	0	0	2	9	5	.213	.339	.277	73	-1	-1	5	0	1	-1	0	3	-0.1
Total	2	73	192	29	39	10	0	1	7	46	23	.203	.357	.271	76	-4	-4	22	0	1	-1	-3	/3	-0.8

■ FRED GUNKLE
Gunkle, Frederick W. b: Dubuque, Iowa Deb: 5/17/1879

YEAR	TM/L	G	AB	R	H	2B	3B	HR	RBI	BB	SO	AVG	OBP	SLG	PRO+	BR	/A	RC	SB	CS	SBR	FR	POS	TPR
1879	Cle-N	1	3	1	0	0	0	0	0	0	1	.000	.000	.000	-99	-1	-1	0				-0	/OC	0.0

■ HY GUNNING
Gunning, Hyland b: 8/6/1888, Maplewood, N.J. d: 3/28/75, Togus, Me. BL/TR, 6'1.5", 189 lbs. Deb: 8/08/11

YEAR	TM/L	G	AB	R	H	2B	3B	HR	RBI	BB	SO	AVG	OBP	SLG	PRO+	BR	/A	RC	SB	CS	SBR	FR	POS	TPR
1911	Bos-A	4	9	0	1	0	0	0		2	2	.111	.273	.111	9	-1	-1	0	0			-1	/1	-0.1

■ TOM GUNNING
Gunning, Thomas Francis b: 3/4/1862, Newmarket, N.H. d: 3/17/31, Fall River, Mass. BR/TR, 5'10", 160 lbs. Deb: 7/26/1884 U

YEAR	TM/L	G	AB	R	H	2B	3B	HR	RBI	BB	SO	AVG	OBP	SLG	PRO+	BR	/A	RC	SB	CS	SBR	FR	POS	TPR
1884	Bos-N	12	45	4	5	1	1	0	2	1	12	.111	.130	.178	-4	-5	-5	1				-6	C	-0.9
1885	Bos-N	48	174	17	32	3	0	0	15	5	29	.184	.207	.201	34	-13	-12	7				-6	C	-1.2
1886	Bos-N	27	98	15	22	2	1	0	7	3	19	.224	.248	.265	58	-5	-5	7	3			-4	C	-0.5
1887	Phi-N	28	104	22	27	6	1	1	16	5	6	.260	.306	.365	83	-2	-3	18	18			5	C	0.5
1888	Phi-a	23	92	18	18	0	0	0	5		2	.196	.213	.196	42	-6	-6	8	14			0	C	-0.2
1889	Phi-a	8	24	3	6	0	1	1	1	0	4	.250	.250	.458	103	-0	-0	3				-2	/C	0.0
Total	6	146	537	79	110	12	4	2	46	16	70	.205	.235	.253	51	-31	-30	45	38			-12	C	-2.3

■ JOE GUNSON
Gunson, Joseph Brook b: 3/23/1863, Philadelphia, Pa. d: 11/15/42, Philadelphia, Pa. BR/TR, 5'6", 160 lbs. Deb: 6/14/1884

YEAR	TM/L	G	AB	R	H	2B	3B	HR	RBI	BB	SO	AVG	OBP	SLG	PRO+	BR	/A	RC	SB	CS	SBR	FR	POS	TPR
1884	Was-U	45	166	15	23	2	0	0		3		.139	.154	.151	3	-16	-15	4	0			11	CO	-0.1
1889	KC-a	34	122	15	24	3	1	0	12	3	17	.197	.228	.238	32	-10	-12	7	2			-7	C/O3	-1.3
1892	Bal-N	89	314	35	67	10	5	0	32	16	17	.213	.267	.277	64	-13	-14	24	2			-0	CO/12	-1.0
1893	StL-N	40	151	20	41	5	0	0	15	6	6	.272	.321	.305	68	-7	-7	15	0			3	C/O	0.0
	Cle-N	21	73	11	19	1	0	0	9	6	6	.260	.316	.274	56	-4	-5	6	0			2	C	0.0
	Yr	61	224	31	60	6	0	0	24	12	6	.268	.320	.295	64	-11	-12	22	0			5		0.0
Total	4	229	826	96	174	21	6	0	68	34	40	.211	.254	.251	49	-50	-53	57	4			8	C/O123	-2.4

■ ERNIE GUST
Gust, Ernest Herman Frank "Red" b: 1/24/1888, Bay City, Mich. d: 10/26/45, Maupin, Ore. BR/TR, 6', 170 lbs. Deb: 8/17/11

YEAR	TM/L	G	AB	R	H	2B	3B	HR	RBI	BB	SO	AVG	OBP	SLG	PRO+	BR	/A	RC	SB	CS	SBR	FR	POS	TPR
1911	StL-A	3	12	0	0	0	0	0	0	0	0	.000	.000	.000	-99	-3	-3	0	0			0	/1	-0.2

■ FRANKIE GUSTINE
Gustine, Frank William b: 2/20/20, Hoopeston, Ill. BR/TR, 6', 175 lbs. Deb: 9/13/39

YEAR	TM/L	G	AB	R	H	2B	3B	HR	RBI	BB	SO	AVG	OBP	SLG	PRO+	BR	/A	RC	SB	CS	SBR	FR	POS	TPR
1939	Pit-N	22	70	5	13	3	0	0	3	9	4	.186	.278	.229	38	-6	-6	5	0			4	3	-0.1
1940	Pit-N	133	524	59	147	32	7	1	55	35	39	.281	.328	.374	94	-5	-5	63	7			-8	*2	-0.3
1941	Pit-N	121	463	46	125	24	7	1	46	28	38	.270	.313	.359	89	-8	-8	51	5			-1	*23	-0.1
1942	Pit-N	115	388	34	89	11	4	2	35	29	27	.229	.286	.294	68	-15	-16	31	5			-10	*2/S3C	-1.8
1943	Pit-N	112	414	40	120	21	4	0	43	32	36	.290	.341	.355	98	0	-1	51	12			-5	S2/1	0.2
1944	Pit-N	127	405	42	93	18	3	2	42	33	41	.230	.288	.304	64	-18	-20	34	8			-27	*S2/3	-3.2
1945	Pit-N	128	478	67	134	27	5	2	66	37	33	.280	.335	.370	92	-3	-6	58	8			-19	*S2/C	-1.1
1946	Pit-N	131	495	60	128	23	6	8	52	40	52	.259	.318	.378	95	-3	-5	59	2			8	*2S/3	0.0
1947	Pit-N	156	616	102	183	30	6	9	67	63	65	.297	.364	.409	102	5	3	92	5			15	*3	1.3
1948	Pit-N	131	449	68	120	19	2	9	42	42	62	.267	.333	.379	90	-5	-6	56	5			9	*3	0.0
1949	Chi-N	76	261	29	59	13	4	4	27	18	22	.226	.279	.352	70	-12	-12	24	3			1	32	-0.8
1950	StL-A	9	19	1	3	1	0	0	2	3	8	.158	.273	.211	24	-2	-2	1	0	1	-1	-0	/3	-0.2
Total	12	1261	4582	553	1214	222	47	38	480	369	427	.265	.322	.359	87	-73	-83	525	60	1		-33	23S/C1	-5.3

■ BUCKY GUTH
Guth, Charles Henry b: 8/18/47, Baltimore, Md. BR/TR, 6'1", 180 lbs. Deb: 9/12/72

YEAR	TM/L	G	AB	R	H	2B	3B	HR	RBI	BB	SO	AVG	OBP	SLG	PRO+	BR	/A	RC	SB	CS	SBR	FR	POS	TPR
1972	Min-A	3	3	1	0	0	0	0	0	0	0	.000	.000	.000	-95	-1	-1	0	0	0	0	1	/S	0.0

YEAR	TM/L	G	AB	R	H	2B	3B	HR	RBI	BB	SO	AVG	OBP	SLG	PRO+	BR	/A	RC	SB	CS	SBR	FR	POS	TPR

■ CESAR GUTIERREZ
Gutierrez, Cesar Dario "Coca"   b: 1/26/43, Coro, Venez.   BR/TR, 5'9", 155 lbs.   Deb: 4/16/67

YEAR	TM/L	G	AB	R	H	2B	3B	HR	RBI	BB	SO	AVG	OBP	SLG	PRO+	BR	/A	RC	SB	CS	SBR	FR	POS	TPR
1967	SF-N	18	21	4	3	0	0	0	0	1	4	.143	.217	.143	5	-3	-3	1	1	0	0	3	S/2	0.2
1969	SF-N	15	23	4	5	1	0	0	0	6	2	.217	.379	.261	84	-0	-0	3	1	0	0	-0	/3S	0.0
	Det-A	17	49	5	12	1	0	0	0	5	3	.245	.315	.265	61	-2	-3	4	1	2	-1	1	S	0.0
1970	Det-A	135	415	40	101	11	6	0	22	18	39	.243	.276	.299	58	-24	-24	33	4	3	-1	-18	*S	-3.2
1971	Det-A	38	37	8	7	0	0	0	4	0	3	.189	.211	.189	13	-4	-4	2	0	0	0	5	S/32	0.2
Total	4	223	545	61	128	13	6	0	26	30	51	.235	.279	.281	55	-33	-33	43	7	5	-1	-9	S/32	-2.8

■ JACKIE GUTIERREZ
Gutierrez, Joaquin Fernando   b: 6/27/60, Cartagena, Columbia   BR/TR, 5'11", 175 lbs.   Deb: 9/06/83

YEAR	TM/L	G	AB	R	H	2B	3B	HR	RBI	BB	SO	AVG	OBP	SLG	PRO+	BR	/A	RC	SB	CS	SBR	FR	POS	TPR
1983	Bos-A	5	10	2	3	0	0	0	0	1	1	.300	.364	.300	79	-0	-0	1	0	1	-1	-0	/S	0.0
1984	Bos-A	151	449	55	118	12	3	2	29	15	49	.263	.287	.316	64	-20	-23	37	12	5	1	-33	*S	-4.4
1985	Bos-A	103	275	33	60	5	2	2	21	12	37	.218	.251	.273	42	-21	-23	18	10	2	2	5	S	-0.8
1986	Bal-A	61	145	8	27	3	0	0	4	3	27	.186	.208	.207	14	-17	-17	6	3	1	0	7	2/3D	-0.6
1987	Bal-A	3	1	0	0	0	0	0	0	0	0	.000	.000	.000	-99	-0	-0	0	0	0	0	0	/23	0.0
1988	Phi-N	33	77	8	19	4	0	0	9	2	9	.247	.266	.299	61	-4	-4	6	0	0	0	-2	S3	-0.4
Total	6	356	957	106	227	24	5	4	63	33	123	.237	.263	.285	50	-63	-67	67	25	9	2	-23	S/23D	-6.2

■ DON GUTTERIDGE
Gutteridge, Donald Joseph   b: 6/19/12, Pittsburg, Kan.   BR/TR, 5'10.5", 165 lbs.   Deb: 9/07/36   MC

YEAR	TM/L	G	AB	R	H	2B	3B	HR	RBI	BB	SO	AVG	OBP	SLG	PRO+	BR	/A	RC	SB	CS	SBR	FR	POS	TPR
1936	StL-N	23	91	13	29	3	4	3	16	1	14	.319	.326	.538	130	3	3	16	3			0	3	0.5
1937	StL-N	119	447	66	121	26	10	7	61	25	66	.271	.311	.421	95	-3	-5	59	12			2	*3/S	0.2
1938	StL-N	142	552	61	141	21	15	9	64	29	49	.255	.293	.397	83	-11	-15	64	14			0	3S	-1.1
1939	StL-N	148	524	71	141	27	4	7	54	27	70	.269	.309	.376	78	-14	-18	61	5			-18	*3/S	-3.1
1940	StL-N	69	108	19	29	5	0	3	14	5	15	.269	.301	.398	86	-2	-2	13	3			-1	3	-0.3
1942	StL-A	147	616	90	157	27	11	1	50	59	54	.255	.320	.339	84	-12	-13	69	16	13	-3	3	*2/3	-0.8
1943	StL-A	132	538	77	147	35	6	1	36	50	46	.273	.335	.366	103	3	2	68	10	9	-2	-31	*2	-2.7
1944	*StL-A	148	603	89	148	27	11	3	36	51	63	.245	.304	.342	80	-13	-17	67	20	8	1	-8	*2	-1.9
1945	StL-A	143	543	72	129	24	3	2	49	43	46	.238	.295	.304	70	-19	-22	51	9	6	-1	-19	*2O	-4.3
1946	*Bos-A	22	47	8	11	3	0	1	6	2	7	.234	.265	.362	70	-2	-2	5	0	0	0	-1	/23	-0.1
1947	Bos-A	54	131	20	22	2	0	2	5	17	13	.168	.264	.229	35	-11	-12	9	3	1	0	-1	23	-1.1
1948	Pit-N	4	2	0	0	0	0	0	0	0	1	.000	.000	.000	-98	-1	-1	0	0			0	H	0.0
Total	12	1151	4202	586	1075	200	64	39	391	309	444	.256	.308	.362	84	-81	-102	484	95	37		-74	23/SO	-14.7

■ DOUG GWOSDZ
Gwosdz, Douglas Wayne   b: 6/20/60, Houston, Tex.   BR/TR, 5'11", 185 lbs.   Deb: 8/17/81

YEAR	TM/L	G	AB	R	H	2B	3B	HR	RBI	BB	SO	AVG	OBP	SLG	PRO+	BR	/A	RC	SB	CS	SBR	FR	POS	TPR
1981	SD-N	16	24	1	4	2	0	0	3	3	6	.167	.259	.250	48	-2	-1	2	0	0	0	2	C	0.1
1982	SD-N	7	17	1	3	0	0	0	0	2	7	.176	.263	.176	27	-2	-2	1	0	0	0	2	/C	0.0
1983	SD-N	39	55	7	6	1	0	1	4	7	19	.109	.210	.182	10	-7	-7	2	0	0	0	2	/C	-0.3
1984	SD-N	7	8	0	2	0	0	0	1	2	5	.250	.400	.250	86	-0	-0	1	0	0	0	3	/C	0.3
Total	4	69	104	9	15	3	0	1	8	14	37	.144	.246	.202	27	-10	-10	6	0	0	0	8	/C	0.1

■ TONY GWYNN
Gwynn, Anthony Keith   b: 5/9/60, Los Angeles, Cal.   BL/TL, 5'11", 185 lbs.   Deb: 7/19/82

YEAR	TM/L	G	AB	R	H	2B	3B	HR	RBI	BB	SO	AVG	OBP	SLG	PRO+	BR	/A	RC	SB	CS	SBR	FR	POS	TPR
1982	SD-N	54	190	33	55	12	2	1	17	14	16	.289	.338	.389	109	1	2	25	8	3	1	-1	O	0.1
1983	SD-N	86	304	34	94	12	2	1	37	23	21	.309	.358	.372	106	1	3	39	7	4	-0	2	O	0.3
1984	*SD-N	158	606	88	213	21	10	5	71	59	23	.351	.411	.444	140	34	34	108	33	18	-1	11	*O	4.0
1985	SD-N	154	622	90	197	29	5	6	46	45	33	.317	.365	.408	118	13	14	88	14	11	-2	11	*O	2.0
1986	SD-N	160	642	107	211	33	7	14	59	52	35	.329	.382	.467	136	28	30	113	37	9	6	11	*O	4.9
1987	SD-N	157	589	119	218	36	13	7	54	82	35	.370	.450	.511	160	50	52	143	56	12	10	4	*O	5.8
1988	SD-N	133	521	64	163	22	5	7	70	51	40	.313	.374	.415	128	18	19	81	26	11	1	1	*O	1.9
1989	SD-N	158	604	82	203	27	7	4	62	56	30	.336	.393	.424	133	27	27	101	40	16	2	-3	*O	2.6
1990	SD-N	141	573	79	177	29	10	4	72	44	23	.309	.359	.415	111	10	9	83	17	8	0	11	*O	1.6
Total	9	1201	4651	696	1531	221	61	49	488	426	256	.329	.387	.435	130	183	191	779	238	92	16	52	*O	23.2

■ CHRIS GWYNN
Gwynn, Christopher Karlton   b: 10/13/64, Los Angeles, Cal.   BL/TL, 6' ", 200 lbs.   Deb: 8/14/87

YEAR	TM/L	G	AB	R	H	2B	3B	HR	RBI	BB	SO	AVG	OBP	SLG	PRO+	BR	/A	RC	SB	CS	SBR	FR	POS	TPR
1987	LA-N	17	32	2	7	1	0	0	2	1	7	.219	.242	.250	32	-3	-3	2	0	0	0	-1	O	-0.3
1988	LA-N	12	11	1	2	0	0	0	0	1	2	.182	.250	.182	27	-1	-1	1	0	0	0	0	/O	0.0
1989	LA-N	32	68	8	16	4	1	0	7	2	9	.235	.257	.324	66	-3	-3	6	1	0	0	-1	/O	-0.3
1990	LA-N	101	141	19	40	2	1	5	22	7	28	.284	.318	.418	107	-0	1	18	0	1	-1	-2	O	-0.2
Total	4	162	252	30	65	7	2	5	31	11	46	.258	.289	.361	82	-8	-6	26	1	1	-0	-3	/O	-0.8

■ DICK GYSELMAN
Gyselman, Richard Renald   b: 4/6/08, San Francisco, Cal.   d: 9/20/90, Seattle, Wash.   BR/TR, 6'2", 170 lbs.   Deb: 4/20/33

YEAR	TM/L	G	AB	R	H	2B	3B	HR	RBI	BB	SO	AVG	OBP	SLG	PRO+	BR	/A	RC	SB	CS	SBR	FR	POS	TPR
1933	Bos-N	58	155	10	37	6	2	0	12	7	21	.239	.272	.303	70	-7	-6	12	0			6	3/2S	0.2
1934	Bos-N	24	36	7	6	1	1	0	4	2	11	.167	.211	.250	25	-4	-4	2	0			-2	3/2	-0.3
Total	2	82	191	17	43	7	3	0	16	9	32	.225	.260	.293	61	-11	-10	14	0			4	/32S	-0.1

■ BERT HAAS
Haas, Berthold John   b: 2/8/14, Naperville, Ill.   BR/TR, 5'11", 178 lbs.   Deb: 9/09/37

YEAR	TM/L	G	AB	R	H	2B	3B	HR	RBI	BB	SO	AVG	OBP	SLG	PRO+	BR	/A	RC	SB	CS	SBR	FR	POS	TPR
1937	Bro-N	16	25	2	10	3	0	0	2	1	1	.400	.423	.520	152	2	2	5	0			-0	/O1	0.1
1938	Bro-N	1	0	0	0	0	0	0	0	0	0	—	—	—	—	0	0	0	0			0	H	0.0
1942	Cin-N	154	585	59	140	21	6	6	54	59	54	.239	.308	.326	86	-10	-10	61	6			-10	*3/1O	-2.2
1943	Cin-N	101	332	39	87	17	6	4	44	22	26	.262	.308	.386	101	-1	-1	38	6			9	13O	0.6
1946	Cin-N	140	535	57	141	24	7	3	50	33	42	.264	.310	.351	91	-10	-8	58	22			0	*1/3	-2.0
1947	Cin-N	135	482	58	138	17	7	3	67	42	27	.286	.346	.369	91	-7	-6	63	9			-8	O1	-1.8
1948	Phi-N	95	333	35	94	9	2	4	34	36	25	.282	.354	.357	95	-2	-2	42	8			-8	31	-1.0
1949	Phi-N	2	1	0	0	0	0	0	0	0	1	.000	.500	.000	47	0	0	0	0			0	H	0.0
	NY-N	54	104	12	27	2	3	1	10	5	8	.260	.294	.365	76	-4	-4	11	0			-1	13	-0.4
	Yr	56	105	12	27	2	3	1	10	6	9	.257	.297	.362	76	-4	-4	11	0			-1		-0.4
1951	Chi-A	23	43	1	7	0	1	1	2	5	4	.163	.250	.279	44	-4	-3	3	0	0	0	-0	/1O3	-0.3
Total	9	721	2440	263	644	93	32	22	263	204	188	.264	.323	.355	91	-36	-32	283	51	0		-19	13/O	-7.0

■ BRUNO HAAS
Haas, Bruno Philip "Boon"   b: 5/5/1891, Worcester, Mass.   d: 6/5/52, Sarasota, Fla.   BB/TL, 5'10", 180 lbs.   Deb: 6/23/15

YEAR	TM/L	G	AB	R	H	2B	3B	HR	RBI	BB	SO	AVG	OBP	SLG	PRO+	BR	/A	RC	SB	CS	SBR	FR	POS	TPR
1915	Phi-A	12	18	1	1	0	0	0	0	1	7	.056	.105	.056	-53	-3	-3	0				1	/PO	-0.1

■ EDDIE HAAS
Haas, George Edwin   b: 5/26/35, Paducah, Ky.   BL/TR, 5'11", 178 lbs.   Deb: 9/08/57   MC

YEAR	TM/L	G	AB	R	H	2B	3B	HR	RBI	BB	SO	AVG	OBP	SLG	PRO+	BR	/A	RC	SB	CS	SBR	FR	POS	TPR
1957	Chi-N	14	24	1	5	1	0	0	4	1	5	.208	.240	.250	32	-2	-2	2	0	0	0	-1	/O	-0.2
1958	Mil-N	9	14	2	5	0	0	0	1	2	1	.357	.438	.357	124	0	1	2	0	0	0	-0	/O	0.0
1960	Mil-N	32	32	4	7	2	0	1	5	5	14	.219	.324	.375	98	-0	-0	4	0	0	0	-0	/O	0.0
Total	3	55	70	7	17	3	0	1	10	8	20	.243	.321	.329	80	-2	-2	8	0	0	0	-1	/O	-0.2

■ MULE HAAS
Haas, George William   b: 10/15/03, Montclair, N.J.   d: 6/30/74, New Orleans, La.   BL/TR, 6'1", 175 lbs.   Deb: 8/15/25   C

YEAR	TM/L	G	AB	R	H	2B	3B	HR	RBI	BB	SO	AVG	OBP	SLG	PRO+	BR	/A	RC	SB	CS	SBR	FR	POS	TPR
1925	Pit-N	4	3	1	0	0	0	0	0	0	0	.000	.000	.000	-94	-1	-1	0	0	0	0	0	/O	0.0
1928	Phi-A	91	332	41	93	21	4	6	39	23	20	.280	.331	.422	94	-3	-4	46	2	3	-1	-3	O	-1.1
1929	*Phi-A	139	578	115	181	41	9	16	82	34	38	.313	.356	.498	113	13	10	100	2	4	-2	2	*O	0.3
1930	*Phi-A	132	532	91	159	33	7	2	68	43	33	.299	.352	.398	86	-8	-11	76	2	2	-1	12	*O	-0.3
1931	*Phi-A	102	440	82	142	29	7	8	56	30	29	.323	.366	.475	113	11	7	77	0	0	0	4	*O	0.4
1932	Phi-A	143	558	91	170	28	5	6	65	46	29	.305	.354	.405	99	3	0	89	1	0	0	-5	*O	-0.5
1933	Chi-A	146	585	97	168	33	4	1	51	65	41	.287	.360	.362	96	-5	-2	79	0	5	-3	-7	*O	-1.5
1934	Chi-A	106	351	54	94	16	3	2	22	47	22	.268	.354	.348	79	-9	-10	47	1	0	0	-5	O	-1.4

YEAR	TM/L	G	AB	R	H	2B	3B	HR	RBI	BB	SO	AVG	OBP	SLG	PRO+	BR	/A	RC	SB	CS	SBR	FR	POS	TPR
1935	Chi-A	92	327	44	95	22	1	2	40	37	17	.291	.363	.382	90	-3	-4	48	4	1	1	-0	O	-0.3
1936	Chi-A	119	408	75	116	26	2	0	46	64	29	.284	.383	.358	81	-8	-11	61	1	1	-0	-8	O/1	-1.9
1937	Chi-A	54	111	8	23	3	3	0	15	16	10	.207	.313	.288	52	-8	-8	11	1	0	0	0	1/O	-1.0
1938	Phi-A	40	78	7	16	2	0	0	12	12	10	.205	.311	.231	39	-7	-7	7	0	0	0	-1	O/1	-0.7
Total	12	1168	4303	706	1257	254	45	43	496	433	299	.292	.359	.402	93	-24	-41	642	12	16	-6	-7	*O/1	-8.0

■ EMIL HABERER
Haberer, Emil Karl　b: 2/2/1878, Cincinnati, Ohio　d: 10/19/51, Louisville, Ky.　BR/TR, 6'1", 204 lbs.　Deb: 7/09/01

YEAR	TM/L	G	AB	R	H	2B	3B	HR	RBI	BB	SO	AVG	OBP	SLG	PRO+	BR	/A	RC	SB	CS	SBR	FR	POS	TPR
1901	Cin-N	6	18	2	3	0	1	0	1		3	.167	.286	.278	70	-1	-1	1	0			-2	/31	-0.1
1903	Cin-N	5	13	1	1	0	0	0	0		2	.077	.200	.077	-17	-2	-2	0	0			-2	/C	-0.3
1909	Cin-N	5	16	1	3	1	0	0	2		0	.188	.188	.250	36	-1	-1	1	0			-2	/C	-0.2
Total	3	16	47	4	7	1	1	0	3		5	.149	.231	.213	32	-4	-4	2	0			-6	/C31	-0.6

■ IRV HACH
Hach, Irvin William "Major"　b: 6/6/1873, Louisville, Ky.　d: 8/13/36, Louisville, Ky.　Deb: 7/01/1897

YEAR	TM/L	G	AB	R	H	2B	3B	HR	RBI	BB	SO	AVG	OBP	SLG	PRO+	BR	/A	RC	SB	CS	SBR	FR	POS	TPR
1897	Lou-N	16	51	5	11	2	0	0	3		5	.216	.322	.255	57	-3	-3	5	1			-1	/23	-0.2

■ STAN HACK
Hack, Stanley Camfield "Smiling Stan"　b: 12/6/09, Sacramento, Cal.　d: 12/15/79, Dixon, Ill.　BL/TR, 6', 170 lbs.　Deb: 4/12/32　MC

YEAR	TM/L	G	AB	R	H	2B	3B	HR	RBI	BB	SO	AVG	OBP	SLG	PRO+	BR	/A	RC	SB	CS	SBR	FR	POS	TPR
1932	*Chi-N	72	178	32	42	5	6	2	19	17	16	.236	.306	.365	80	-5	-5	21	5			-5	3	-0.5
1933	Chi-N	20	60	10	21	3	1	1	2	8	3	.350	.451	.483	167	6	6	15	4			6	3	1.3
1934	Chi-N	111	402	54	116	16	6	1	21	45	42	.289	.363	.366	98	-1	0	57	11			0	*3	0.9
1935	*Chi-N	124	427	75	133	23	9	4	64	65	17	.311	.406	.436	125	19	18	83	14			11	*3/1	3.1
1936	Chi-N	149	561	102	167	27	4	6	78	89	39	.298	.396	.392	110	14	12	94	17			-12	*31	1.0
1937	Chi-N	154	582	106	173	27	6	2	63	83	42	.297	.388	.375	104	10	7	94	16			-9	*3/1	0.4
1938	*Chi-N	152	609	109	195	34	11	4	67	94	39	.320	.411	.432	128	31	28	119	16			7	*3	3.1
1939	Chi-N	156	641	112	191	28	6	8	56	65	35	.298	.364	.398	103	5	4	97	17			-7	*3	0.1
1940	Chi-N	149	603	101	191	38	6	8	40	75	24	.317	.395	.439	132	27	28	112	21			14	*3/1	4.0
1941	Chi-N	151	586	111	186	33	5	7	45	99	40	.317	.417	.427	143	34	37	114	10			-16	*3/1	2.2
1942	Chi-N	140	553	91	166	36	3	6	39	94	40	.300	.402	.409	143	30	32	100	9			-10	*3	2.4
1943	Chi-N	144	533	78	154	24	4	3	35	82	27	.289	.384	.366	119	15	16	83	5			-7	*3	0.8
1944	Chi-N	98	383	65	108	16	1	3	32	53	21	.282	.369	.352	104	4	4	53	5			2	31	0.9
1945	*Chi-N	150	597	110	193	29	7	2	43	99	30	.323	.420	.405	133	29	31	111	12			18	*3/1	4.6
1946	Chi-N	92	323	55	92	13	4	0	26	83	32	.285	.431	.350	125	16	16	56	3			-3	3	1.5
1947	Chi-N	76	240	28	65	11	2	0	12	41	19	.271	.377	.333	94	-2	-0	33	0			7	3	0.5
Total	16	1938	7278	1239	2193	363	81	57	642	1092	466	.301	.394	.397	120	231	235	1241	165			-3	*3/1	26.3

■ RICH HACKER
Hacker, Richard Warren　b: 10/6/47, Belleville, Ill.　BB/TR, 6', 160 lbs.　Deb: 7/02/71　C

YEAR	TM/L	G	AB	R	H	2B	3B	HR	RBI	BB	SO	AVG	OBP	SLG	PRO+	BR	/A	RC	SB	CS	SBR	FR	POS	TPR
1971	Mon-N	16	33	2	4	1	0	0	2	3	12	.121	.194	.152	-1	-4	-4	1	0	0	0	5	S	0.2

■ JIM HACKETT
Hackett, James Joseph "Sunny Jim"　b: 10/1/1877, Jacksonville, Ill.　d: 3/28/61, Douglas, Mich.　BR/TR, 6'2", 185 lbs.　Deb: 9/14/02

YEAR	TM/L	G	AB	R	H	2B	3B	HR	RBI	BB	SO	AVG	OBP	SLG	PRO+	BR	/A	RC	SB	CS	SBR	FR	POS	TPR
1902	StL-N	6	21	2	6	1	0	0	4	2		.286	.348	.333	117	0	0	3	1			-0	/PO	0.0
1903	StL-N	99	351	24	80	13	8	0	36	19		.228	.268	.311	68	-16	-14	31	2			-6	1/P	-2.0
Total	2	105	372	26	86	14	8	0	40	21		.231	.272	.312	71	-16	-14	34	3			-7	/1PO	-2.0

■ MERT HACKETT
Hackett, Mortimer Martin　b: 11/11/1859, Cambridge, Mass.　d: 2/22/38, Cambridge, Mass.　BR/TR, 5'10.5", 175 lbs.　Deb: 5/02/1883

YEAR	TM/L	G	AB	R	H	2B	3B	HR	RBI	BB	SO	AVG	OBP	SLG	PRO+	BR	/A	RC	SB	CS	SBR	FR	POS	TPR
1883	Bos-N	46	179	20	42	8	6	2	24	1	48	.235	.239	.380	82	-3	-4	17				-1	C/O	-0.1
1884	Bos-N	72	268	28	55	13	2	1	20	2	66	.205	.211	.280	53	-14	-14	16				6	C/3	-0.1
1885	Bos-N	34	115	9	21	7	1	0	4	2	28	.183	.197	.261	49	-7	-6	6				6	C	0.3
1886	KC-N	62	230	18	50	8	3	3	25	4	59	.217	.231	.317	61	-10	-12	18	1			-12	CO	-1.8
1887	Ind-N	42	147	12	35	6	3	2	10	7	24	.238	.282	.361	82	-4	-3	16	4			-7	C/O1	-0.4
Total	5	256	939	87	203	42	15	8	83	16	225	.216	.231	.318	65	-39	-40	73	5			-8	C/O13	-2.1

■ WALTER HACKETT
Hackett, Walter Henry　b: 8/15/1857, Cambridge, Mass.　d: 10/2/20, Cambridge, Mass.　Deb: 4/17/1884

YEAR	TM/L	G	AB	R	H	2B	3B	HR	RBI	BB	SO	AVG	OBP	SLG	PRO+	BR	/A	RC	SB	CS	SBR	FR	POS	TPR
1884	Bos-U	103	415	71	101	19	0	1		7		.243	.256	.296	88	-6	-5	32	0			12	*S	0.9
1885	Bos-N	35	125	8	23	3	0	0	9	3	22	.184	.203	.208	34	-9	-8	5				-12	2S	-1.6
Total	2	138	540	79	124	22	0	1	9	10	22	.230	.244	.276	75	-15	-14	38				1	S/2	-0.7

■ KENT HADLEY
Hadley, Kent William　b: 12/17/34, Pocatello, Idaho　BL/TL, 6'3", 190 lbs.　Deb: 9/14/58

YEAR	TM/L	G	AB	R	H	2B	3B	HR	RBI	BB	SO	AVG	OBP	SLG	PRO+	BR	/A	RC	SB	CS	SBR	FR	POS	TPR
1958	KC-A	3	11	1	2	0	0	0	0	0	4	.182	.182	.182	0	-1	-1	0	0	0	0	-1	/1	-0.1
1959	KC-A	113	288	40	73	11	1	10	39	24	74	.253	.313	.403	93	-3	-3	36	1	2	-1	-2	1	-0.5
1960	NY-A	55	64	8	13	2	0	4	11	6	19	.203	.271	.422	90	-2	-1	7	0	0	0	-0	1	-0.2
Total	3	171	363	49	88	13	1	14	50	30	97	.242	.302	.399	90	-6	-6	43	1	2	-1	-2	1	-0.8

■ BILL HAEFFNER
Haeffner, William Bernhard　b: 7/8/1894, Philadelphia, Pa.　d: 1/27/82, Springfield, Pa.　BR/TR, Deb: N/A.

YEAR	TM/L	G	AB	R	H	2B	3B	HR	RBI	BB	SO	AVG	OBP	SLG	PRO+	BR	/A	RC	SB	CS	SBR	FR	POS	TPR
1915	Phi-A	3	4	0	1	0	0	0	0	0	1	.250	.250	.250	51	-0	-0	0	0			-1	/C	0.0
1920	Pit-N	54	175	8	34	4	1	0	14	8	14	.194	.230	.229	31	-15	-16	9	1	1	-0	-4	C	-1.7
1928	NY-N	2	1	0	0	0	0	0	0	0	0	.000	.000	.000	-99	-0	-0	0	0			0	/C	0.0
Total	3	59	180	8	35	4	1	0	14	8	15	.194	.229	.228	30	-16	-16	10	1	1		-5	/C	-1.7

■ CHICK HAFEY
Hafey, Charles James　b: 2/12/03, Berkeley, Cal.　d: 7/2/73, Calistoga, Cal.　BR/TR, 6', 185 lbs.　Deb: 8/28/24　H

YEAR	TM/L	G	AB	R	H	2B	3B	HR	RBI	BB	SO	AVG	OBP	SLG	PRO+	BR	/A	RC	SB	CS	SBR	FR	POS	TPR
1924	StL-N	24	91	10	23	5	2	2	22	4	8	.253	.292	.418	90	-2	-2	11	1	0	0	-0	O	-0.1
1925	StL-N	93	358	36	108	25	2	5	57	10	29	.302	.321	.425	87	-7	-8	45	3	7	-3	-4	O	-1.6
1926	*StL-N	78	225	30	61	19	2	4	38	11	36	.271	.311	.427	93	-2	-3	29	2			-2	O	-0.7
1927	StL-N	103	346	62	114	26	5	18	63	36	41	.329	.401	.590	157	29	28	80	12			4	O	2.7
1928	*StL-N	138	520	101	175	46	6	27	111	40	53	.337	.386	.604	152	39	37	116	8			1	*O	3.2
1929	StL-N	134	517	101	175	47	9	29	125	45	42	.338	.394	.632	148	37	36	124	7			-3	*O	2.0
1930	StL-N	120	446	108	150	39	12	26	107	46	51	.336	.407	.652	146	35	33	114	12			-9	*O	1.3
1931	*StL-N	122	450	94	157	35	8	16	95	39	43	.349	.404	.569	153	36	34	105	11			-9	*O	1.9
1932	Cin-N	83	253	34	87	19	3	2	36	22	20	.344	.403	.466	137	12	13	49	4			-4	O	0.5
1933	Cin-N	144	568	77	172	34	6	7	62	40	44	.303	.353	.421	121	14	15	85	3			1	*O	0.9
1934	Cin-N	140	535	75	157	29	6	18	67	52	63	.293	.359	.471	123	15	17	93	4			-1	*O	0.9
1935	Cin-N	15	59	10	20	6	1	1	9	4	5	.339	.400	.525	151	4	4	13	1			-2	O	0.1
1937	Cin-N	89	257	39	67	11	5	9	41	23	42	.261	.324	.447	113	2	4	38	2			-0	O	0.0
Total	13	1283	4625	777	1466	341	67	164	833	372	477	.317	.372	.526	133	212	208	902	70	7		-27	*O	11.0

■ BUD HAFEY
Hafey, Daniel Albert　b: 8/6/12, Berkeley, Cal.　d: 7/27/86, Sacramento, Cal.　BR/TR, 6', 185 lbs.　Deb: 4/21/35

YEAR	TM/L	G	AB	R	H	2B	3B	HR	RBI	BB	SO	AVG	OBP	SLG	PRO+	BR	/A	RC	SB	CS	SBR	FR	POS	TPR
1935	Chi-A	2	0	1	0	0	0	0	0	0		—	—	—	—	0	0	0	0	0	0	0	R	0.0
	Pit-N	58	184	29	42	11	2	6	16	16	48	.228	.290	.408	83	-4	-5	22	0			7	O	0.0
1936	Pit-N	39	118	19	25	6	1	4	13	10	27	.212	.273	.381	73	-5	-5	12	0			2	O	-0.4
1939	Cin-N	6	13	1	2	1	0	0	1	1	4	.154	.214	.231	19	-1	-2	1	1			0	/O	-0.1
	Phi-N	18	51	3	9	1	0	0	3	3	12	.176	.222	.196	14	-6	-6	2	1			1	O/P	-0.4
	Yr	24	64	4	11	2	0	0	4	4	16	.172	.221	.203	15	-8	-8	3	2			1		-0.5
Total	3	123	366	53	78	19	3	10	33	30	91	.213	.273	.363	68	-17	-18	36	2	0		9	/OP	-0.9

■ TOM HAFEY
Hafey, Thomas Francis "Heave-O" or "The Arm"　b: 7/12/13, Berkeley, Cal.　BR/TR, 6'1", 180 lbs.　Deb: 7/21/39

YEAR	TM/L	G	AB	R	H	2B	3B	HR	RBI	BB	SO	AVG	OBP	SLG	PRO+	BR	/A	RC	SB	CS	SBR	FR	POS	TPR
1939	NY-N	70	256	37	62	10	1	6	26	10	44	.242	.271	.359	67	-12	-13	24	1			0	3	-1.0
1944	StL-A	8	14	1	5	2	0	0	2	1	4	.357	.400	.500	148	1	1	3	0	0	0	0	/O1	0.1
Total	2	78	270	38	67	12	1	6	28	11	48	.248	.278	.367	72	-11	-12	27	1	0		0	/3O1	-0.9

JOE HAGUE
Hague, Joe Clarence b: 4/25/44, Huntington, W.Va. BL/TL, 6', 195 lbs. Deb: 9/19/68

YEAR	TM/L	G	AB	R	H	2B	3B	HR	RBI	BB	SO	AVG	OBP	SLG	PRO+	BR	/A	RC	SB	CS	SBR	FR	POS	TPR
1968	StL-N	7	17	2	4	0	0	1	1	2	2	.235	.316	.412	119	0	0	2	0	0	0	-0	/O1	0.0
1969	StL-N	40	100	8	17	2	1	2	8	12	23	.170	.259	.270	48	-7	-7	7	0	2	-1	-0	O/1	-1.0
1970	StL-N	139	451	58	122	16	4	14	68	63	87	.271	.361	.417	106	6	5	69	2	1	0	-3	1O	-0.7
1971	StL-N	129	380	46	86	9	3	16	54	58	69	.226	.332	.392	100	3	1	51	0	3	-2	-1	1O	-1.0
1972	StL-N	27	76	8	18	5	1	3	11	17	18	.237	.376	.447	135	4	4	13	0	1	-1	0	1/O	0.2
	*Cin-N	69	138	17	34	7	1	4	20	20	18	.246	.342	.399	116	2	3	18	1	1	-0	0	1O	0.2
	Yr	96	214	25	52	12	2	7	31	37	36	.243	.355	.416	124	6	7	32	1	2	-1	0		0.2
1973	Cin-N	19	33	2	5	2	0	0	1	5	5	.152	.263	.212	35	-3	-3	2	1	0	0	-1	/O1	-0.3
Total	6	430	1195	141	286	41	10	40	163	177	222	.239	.339	.391	101	5	3	163	4	8	-4	-5	1O	-2.8

BILL HAGUE
Hague, William L. (b: William L. Haug) b: 1852, Philadelphia, Pa. BR/TR, 5'9", 164 lbs. Deb: 5/04/1875

YEAR	TM/L	G	AB	R	H	2B	3B	HR	RBI	BB	SO	AVG	OBP	SLG	PRO+	BR	/A	RC	SB	CS	SBR	FR	POS	TPR
1875	StL-n	62	260	24	56	2	0	0		2		.215	.221	.223	60	-12	-8	13					*3/1	-0.4
1876	Lou-N	67	294	31	78	8	0	1	22	2	10	.265	.285	.303	77	-3	-11	25				-26	*3/S	-3.4
1877	Lou-N	59	263	38	70	7	1	1	24	7	18	.266	.285	.312	75	-3	-10	24				-19	*3	-2.2
1878	Pro-N	62	250	21	51	3	0	0	25	5	34	.204	.220	.216	44	-15	-15	12				19	*3	0.7
1879	Pro-N	51	209	20	47	3	1	0	21	3	19	.225	.236	.249	61	-9	-8	13				5	3	-0.1
Total	4	239	1016	110	246	21	2	2	92	17	81	.242	.255	.273	66	-30	-44	73				-22	3/S	-5.0

DON HAHN
Hahn, Donald Antone b: 11/16/48, San Francisco, Cal. BR/TR, 6'1", 180 lbs. Deb: 4/08/69

YEAR	TM/L	G	AB	R	H	2B	3B	HR	RBI	BB	SO	AVG	OBP	SLG	PRO+	BR	/A	RC	SB	CS	SBR	FR	POS	TPR
1969	Mon-N	4	9	0	1	0	0	0	2	0	5	.111	.111	.111	-37	-2	-2	0	0	0	0	1	/O	0.0
1970	Mon-N	82	149	22	38	8	0	0	8	27	27	.255	.376	.309	86	-2	-2	21	4	2	0	0	O	-0.3
1971	NY-N	98	178	16	42	5	1	1	11	21	32	.236	.320	.292	76	-5	-5	17	2	3	-1	10	O	0.1
1972	NY-N	17	37	0	6	0	0	0	1	4	12	.162	.244	.162	18	-4	-4	2	0	0	0	-2	O	-0.6
1973	*NY-N	93	262	22	60	10	0	2	21	22	43	.229	.289	.290	62	-14	-13	22	2	1	0	-6	O	-2.4
1974	NY-N	110	323	34	81	14	1	4	28	37	34	.251	.330	.337	88	-5	-5	36	2	0	1	-5	*O	-1.3
1975	Phi-N	9	5	0	0	0	0	0	0	0	2	.000	.000	.000	-96	-1	-1	0	0	0	0	1	/O	0.0
	StL-N	7	8	3	1	0	0	0	0	1	1	.125	.222	.125	-2	-1	-1	0	0	0	0	0	/O	0.0
	SD-N	34	26	7	6	1	2	0	3	10	2	.231	.444	.423	151	2	2	5	1	0	0	2	O	0.4
	Yr	50	39	10	7	1	2	0	3	11	5	.179	.360	.308	89	-0	-0	5	1	0	0	4		0.4
Total	7	454	997	104	235	38	4	7	74	122	158	.236	.321	.303	75	-32	-30	103	11	6	-0	2	O	-4.1

DICK HAHN
Hahn, Richard Frederick b: 7/24/16, Canton, Ohio BR/TR, 5'11", 176 lbs. Deb: 9/07/40

YEAR	TM/L	G	AB	R	H	2B	3B	HR	RBI	BB	SO	AVG	OBP	SLG	PRO+	BR	/A	RC	SB	CS	SBR	FR	POS	TPR
1940	Was-A	1	3	0	0	0	0	0	0	0	0	.000	.000	.000	-99	-1	-1	0	0	0	0	0	/C	0.0

ED HAHN
Hahn, William Edgar b: 8/27/1875, Nevada, Ohio d: 11/29/41, Des Moines, Iowa BL/TR, 160 lbs. Deb: 8/31/05

YEAR	TM/L	G	AB	R	H	2B	3B	HR	RBI	BB	SO	AVG	OBP	SLG	PRO+	BR	/A	RC	SB	CS	SBR	FR	POS	TPR
1905	NY-A	43	160	32	51	5	0	0	11	25		.319	.411	.350	130	10	7	25	1			2	O	0.8
1906	NY-A	11	22	2	2	1	0	0	1	3		.091	.200	.136	6	-2	-3	1	2			-1	/O	-0.3
	*Chi-A	130	484	80	110	7	5	0	27	69		.227	.324	.262	88	-4	-3	51	19			-6	*O	-1.4
	Yr	141	506	82	112	8	5	0	28	72		.221	.318	.257	84	-7	-6	52	21			-6		-1.7
1907	Chi-A	156	592	87	151	9	7	0	45	84		.255	.348	.294	111	9	11	70	17			-5	*O	-0.2
1908	Chi-A	122	447	58	112	12	8	0	21	39		.251	.311	.313	107	3	4	47	11			-11	*O	-1.4
1909	Chi-A	76	287	30	52	6	0	0	16	31		.181	.268	.213	54	-15	-13	19	9			-7	O	-2.6
1910	Chi-A	15	53	2	6	2	0	0	1	7		.113	.217	.151	16	-5	-5	2	0			-3	O	-0.9
Total	6	553	2045	291	484	42	20	1	122	258		.237	.323	.278	95	-5	-1	214	59			-29	O	-6.0

ED HAIGH
Haigh, Edward E. b: 2/7/1867, Philadelphia, Pa. d: 2/13/53, Atlantic City, N.J Deb: 8/14/1892

YEAR	TM/L	G	AB	R	H	2B	3B	HR	RBI	BB	SO	AVG	OBP	SLG	PRO+	BR	/A	RC	SB	CS	SBR	FR	POS	TPR
1892	StL-N	1	4	0	1	0	0	0	0	0	2	.250	.250	.250	55	-0	-0	0	0			-0	/O	0.0

HINKEY HAINES
Haines, Henry Luther b: 12/23/1898, Red Lion, Pa. d: 1/9/79, Sharon Hill, Pa. BR/TR, 5'10", 170 lbs. Deb: 8/20/23

YEAR	TM/L	G	AB	R	H	2B	3B	HR	RBI	BB	SO	AVG	OBP	SLG	PRO+	BR	/A	RC	SB	CS	SBR	FR	POS	TPR
1923	*NY-A	28	25	9	4	2	0	0	3	4	5	.160	.276	.240	36	-2	-2	2	3	1	0	-3	O	-0.5

JERRY HAIRSTON
Hairston, Jerry Wayne b: 2/16/52, Birmingham, Ala. BB/TR, 5'10", 170 lbs. Deb: 7/26/73

YEAR	TM/L	G	AB	R	H	2B	3B	HR	RBI	BB	SO	AVG	OBP	SLG	PRO+	BR	/A	RC	SB	CS	SBR	FR	POS	TPR
1973	Chi-A	60	210	25	57	11	1	0	23	33	30	.271	.373	.333	97	2	1	29	0	0	0	-2	O1/D	-0.2
1974	Chi-A	45	109	8	25	7	0	0	8	13	18	.229	.311	.294	73	-3	-4	10	0	2	-1	-3	OD	-0.8
1975	Chi-A	69	219	26	62	8	0	0	23	46	23	.283	.410	.320	107	6	5	33	1	0	0	-3	O/D	0.1
1976	Chi-A	44	119	20	27	2	2	0	10	24	19	.227	.357	.277	87	-1	-1	14	1	1	0	-3	O/D	-0.4
1977	Chi-A	13	26	3	8	2	0	0	4	5	7	.308	.419	.385	121	1	1	4	0	0	0	0	O	0.1
	Pit-N	51	52	5	10	2	0	2	6	6	10	.192	.276	.346	64	-3	-3	5	0	0	0	-1	O/2	-0.3
1981	Chi-A	9	25	5	7	1	0	1	6	2	4	.280	.357	.440	131	1	1	4	0	0	0	-1	/O	0.0
1982	Chi-A	85	90	11	21	5	0	5	18	9	15	.233	.303	.456	105	0	0	12	0	0	0	5	O/D	0.4
1983	*Chi-A	101	126	17	37	9	1	5	22	23	16	.294	.403	.500	141	9	8	26	0	1	-1	-2	O/D	0.5
1984	Chi-A	115	227	41	59	13	2	5	19	41	29	.260	.375	.401	110	6	5	37	2	1	0	4	OD	0.7
1985	Chi-A	95	140	9	34	8	0	2	20	29	18	.243	.380	.343	96	1	1	20	0	0	0	0	D/O	0.1
1986	Chi-A	101	225	32	61	15	0	5	26	26	26	.271	.349	.404	101	2	1	31	0	0	0	-1	D1O	-0.1
1987	Chi-A	66	126	14	29	8	0	5	20	25	25	.230	.362	.413	102	1	1	20	0	0	0	-0	OD/1	0.0
1988	Chi-A	2	2	0	0	0	0	0	0	0	0	.000	.000	.000	-99	-1	-1	0	0	0	0	0	/H	0.0
1989	Chi-A	3	3	0	1	0	0	0	0	0	0	.333	.333	.333	91	-0	-0	0	0	0	0	0	/D	0.0
Total	14	859	1699	216	438	91	6	30	205	282	240	.258	.366	.371	103	21	15	245	4	5	-2	-7	OD/12	0.1

JOHNNY HAIRSTON
Hairston, John Louis b: 8/29/45, Birmingham, Ala. BR/TR, 6'2", 200 lbs. Deb: 9/06/69

YEAR	TM/L	G	AB	R	H	2B	3B	HR	RBI	BB	SO	AVG	OBP	SLG	PRO+	BR	/A	RC	SB	CS	SBR	FR	POS	TPR
1969	Chi-N	3	4	0	1	0	0	0	0	0	2	.250	.250	.250	36	-0	-0	0	0	0	0	-0	/CO	0.0

SAMMY HAIRSTON
Hairston, Samuel b: 1/28/20, Crawford, Miss. BR/TR, 5'10.5", 187 lbs. Deb: 7/21/51 C

YEAR	TM/L	G	AB	R	H	2B	3B	HR	RBI	BB	SO	AVG	OBP	SLG	PRO+	BR	/A	RC	SB	CS	SBR	FR	POS	TPR
1951	Chi-A	4	5	1	2	1	0	0	1	2	0	.400	.571	.600	222	1	1	2	0	0	0	-1	/C	0.0

CHET HAJDUK
Hajduk, Chester b: 7/21/18, Chicago, Ill. BR/TR, 6', 195 lbs. Deb: 4/16/41

YEAR	TM/L	G	AB	R	H	2B	3B	HR	RBI	BB	SO	AVG	OBP	SLG	PRO+	BR	/A	RC	SB	CS	SBR	FR	POS	TPR
1941	Chi-A	1	1	0	0	0	0	0	0	0	0	.000	.000	.000	-99	-0	-0	0	0	0	0	0	H	0.0

GEORGE HALAS
Halas, George Stanley b: 2/2/1895, Chicago, Ill. d: 10/31/83, Chicago, Ill. BB/TR, 6', 164 lbs. Deb: 5/06/19

YEAR	TM/L	G	AB	R	H	2B	3B	HR	RBI	BB	SO	AVG	OBP	SLG	PRO+	BR	/A	RC	SB	CS	SBR	FR	POS	TPR
1919	NY-A	12	22	0	2	0	0	0	0	0	8	.091	.091	.091	-49	-4	-4	0	0			-1	/O	-0.5

JOHN HALDEMAN
Haldeman, John Avery b: 12/2/1855, Pee Wee Valley, Ky. d: 9/17/1899, Louisville, Ky. BL/TR, 5'10", 175 lbs. Deb: 7/03/1877

YEAR	TM/L	G	AB	R	H	2B	3B	HR	RBI	BB	SO	AVG	OBP	SLG	PRO+	BR	/A	RC	SB	CS	SBR	FR	POS	TPR
1877	Lou-N	1	4	0	0	0	0	0	0	0	0	.000	.000	.000	-85	-1	-1	0				-1	/2	-0.1

ODELL HALE
Hale, Arvel Odell "Bad News" b: 8/10/08, Hosston, La. d: 6/9/80, ElDorado, Ark. BR/TR, 5'10", 175 lbs. Deb: 8/01/31

YEAR	TM/L	G	AB	R	H	2B	3B	HR	RBI	BB	SO	AVG	OBP	SLG	PRO+	BR	/A	RC	SB	CS	SBR	FR	POS	TPR
1931	Cle-A	25	92	14	26	2	4	1	5	8	8	.283	.340	.424	94	-0	-1	14	2	0	1	-4	32/S	-0.2
1933	Cle-A	98	351	49	97	19	8	10	64	30	37	.276	.333	.462	104	3	1	53	2	3	-1	3	23	0.3
1934	Cle-A	143	563	82	170	44	6	13	101	48	50	.302	.357	.471	110	8	7	91	8	12	-5	**26**	*2/3	3.1
1935	Cle-A	150	589	80	179	37	11	16	101	50	55	.304	.361	.486	115	13	11	101	15	13	-3	7	*3/2	1.5
1936	Cle-A	153	620	126	196	50	13	14	87	64	43	.316	.380	.506	116	15	14	120	8	5	0	17	*3/2	2.7
1937	Cle-A	154	561	74	150	32	4	6	82	56	41	.267	.335	.371	77	-19	-20	71	9	6	-1	26	32	1.2
1938	Cle-A	130	496	69	138	32	2	8	69	44	39	.278	.338	.399	86	-13	-12	70	8	1	2	-13	*2	-1.6
1939	Cle-A	108	253	36	79	16	2	4	48	25	18	.312	.374	.439	111	3	4	39	4	5	-2	-16	2/3	-0.9
1940	Cle-A	48	50	3	11	3	1	0	6	5	7	.220	.291	.320	60	-3	-3	5	0	0	0	-1	/3	-0.2

YEAR	TM/L	G	AB	R	H	2B	3B	HR	RBI	BB	SO	AVG	OBP	SLG	PRO+	BR	/A	RC	SB	CS	SBR	FR	POS	TPR
1941	Bos-A	12	24	5	5	2	0	1	1	3	4	.208	.296	.417	85	-1	-1	3	0	0	0	-3	/32	-0.2
	NY-N	41	102	13	20	3	0	0	9	18	13	.196	.317	.225	53	-5	-6	9	1			1	2	-0.2
Total	10	1062	3701	551	1071	240	51	73	573	353	315	.289	.352	.441	100	-1	-5	576	57	45		42	23/S	5.5

■ GEORGE HALE
Hale, George Wagner "Ducky" b: 8/3/1894, Dexter, Kan. d: 11/1/45, Wichita, Kan. BR/TR, 5'10", 160 lbs. Deb: 8/24/14

YEAR	TM/L	G	AB	R	H	2B	3B	HR	RBI	BB	SO	AVG	OBP	SLG	PRO+	BR	/A	RC	SB	CS	SBR	FR	POS	TPR
1914	StL-A	6	11	1	2	0	0	0	0	0	3	.182	.182	.182	10	-1	-1	0	0			-0	/C	0.0
1916	StL-A	4	1	0	0	0	0	0	0	0	1	.000	.500	.000	54	0	0	0	0			0	/C	0.0
1917	StL-A	38	61	4	12	2	1	0	8	10	12	.197	.310	.262	78	-2	-1	5	0			3	C	0.4
1918	StL-A	12	30	0	4	1	0	0	1	1	5	.133	.161	.167	-1	-4	-4	1	0			2	C	0.0
Total	4	60	103	5	18	3	1	0	9	11	21	.175	.261	.223	49	-6	-6	6	0			5	/C	0.4

■ JOHN HALE
Hale, John Steven b: 8/5/53, Fresno, Cal. BL/TR, 6'2", 195 lbs. Deb: 9/08/74

YEAR	TM/L	G	AB	R	H	2B	3B	HR	RBI	BB	SO	AVG	OBP	SLG	PRO+	BR	/A	RC	SB	CS	SBR	FR	POS	TPR
1974	LA-N	4	4	2	4	1	0	0	2	0	0	1.000	1.000	1.250	549	2	2	5	0	0	0	0	/O	0.2
1975	LA-N	71	204	20	43	7	0	6	22	26	51	.211	.306	.333	81	-6	-5	22	1	2	-1	1	O	-0.7
1976	LA-N	44	91	4	14	2	1	0	8	16	14	.154	.294	.198	42	-6	-6	7	4	1	1	0	O	-0.6
1977	LA-N	79	108	10	26	4	1	2	11	15	28	.241	.333	.352	84	-2	-2	14	2	1	0	1	O	-0.3
1978	Sea-A	107	211	24	36	8	0	4	22	34	64	.171	.286	.265	56	-12	-12	18	3	4	-2	2	O/D	-1.4
1979	Sea-A	54	63	6	14	3	0	2	7	12	26	.222	.347	.365	91	-0	-1	8	0	0	0	-2	O	-0.3
Total	6	359	681	66	137	25	2	14	72	103	183	.201	.310	.305	72	-25	-24	74	10	8	-2	2	O/D	-3.1

■ BOB HALE
Hale, Robert Houston b: 11/7/33, Sarasota, Fla. BL/TL, 5'10", 195 lbs. Deb: 7/04/55

YEAR	TM/L	G	AB	R	H	2B	3B	HR	RBI	BB	SO	AVG	OBP	SLG	PRO+	BR	/A	RC	SB	CS	SBR	FR	POS	TPR
1955	Bal-A	67	182	13	65	7	1	0	29	5	19	.357	.378	.407	119	3	4	25	0	2	-1	2	1	0.3
1956	Bal-A	85	207	18	49	10	1	1	24	11	10	.237	.279	.309	60	-14	-12	16	0	2	-1	-0	1	-1.4
1957	Bal-A	42	44	2	11	0	0	0	7	2	2	.250	.283	.250	50	-3	-3	2	0	0	0	-0	/1	-0.2
1958	Bal-A	19	20	2	7	2	0	0	3	2	1	.350	.409	.450	144	1	1	3	0	0	0	1	/1	0.2
1959	Bal-A	40	54	2	10	3	0	0	7	2	6	.185	.214	.241	25	-6	-5	3	0	0	0	-0	/1	-0.5
1960	Cle-A	70	70	2	21	7	0	0	12	3	6	.300	.329	.400	99	-1	-0	10	0	0	0	0	/1	0.0
1961	Cle-A	42	36	0	6	0	0	0	6	1	7	.167	.211	.167	2	-5	-5	2	0	0	0	0	H	-0.4
	NY-A	11	13	2	2	0	0	1	1	0	0	.154	.154	.385	41	-1	-1	0	0	0	0	0	/1	-0.1
	Yr	53	49	2	8	0	0	1	7	1	7	.163	.196	.224	12	-6	-6	2	0	0	0	0		-0.5
Total	7	376	626	41	171	29	2	2	89	26	51	.273	.305	.335	76	-26	-21	61	0	4	-2	2	1	-2.1

■ SAMMY HALE
Hale, Samuel Douglas b: 9/10/1896, Glen Rose, Tex. d: 9/6/74, Wheeler, Tex. BR/TR, 5'8.5", 160 lbs. Deb: 4/20/20

YEAR	TM/L	G	AB	R	H	2B	3B	HR	RBI	BB	SO	AVG	OBP	SLG	PRO+	BR	/A	RC	SB	CS	SBR	FR	POS	TPR
1920	Det-A	76	116	13	34	3	3	1	14	5	15	.293	.322	.397	92	-2	-2	15	2		1	-3	3/O2	-0.2
1921	Det-A	9	2	2	0	0	0	0	0	0	1	.000	.000	.000	-99	-1	-1	0	0	1	-1	0	H	0.0
1923	Phi-A	115	434	68	125	22	8	3	51	17	31	.288	.327	.396	89	-8	-9	57	8	3	1	-19	*3	-1.3
1924	Phi-A	80	261	41	83	14	2	2	17	17	19	.318	.367	.410	99	-0	-1	39	3	2	-0	-8	3/OS	-0.3
1925	Phi-A	110	391	62	135	30	11	8	63	17	27	.345	.376	.540	122	15	11	77	7	4	-0	-4	3/2	1.2
1926	Phi-A	111	327	49	92	22	9	4	43	13	36	.281	.311	.440	89	-5	-7	43	1	4	-2	-2	3/O	-0.4
1927	Phi-A	131	501	77	157	24	8	5	81	32	32	.313	.358	.423	97	1	-3	73	11	3	2	1	*3	0.7
1928	Phi-A	88	314	38	97	20	9	4	58	9	21	.309	.334	.468	106	2	1	49	2	0	1	12	3	1.4
1929	Phi-A	101	379	51	105	14	3	1	40	12	18	.277	.303	.338	62	-20	-22	40	6	2	1	-7	3/2	-2.1
1930	StL-A	62	190	21	52	8	1	2	25	8	18	.274	.303	.358	65	-10	-11	20	1	1	-0	-3	3	-1.0
Total	10	883	2915	422	880	157	54	30	392	130	218	.302	.336	.424	93	-27	-42	412	41	20	0	-33	3/O2S	-2.0

■ CHIP HALE
Hale, Walter William b: 12/2/64, Santa Clara, Cal. BL/TR, 5'11", 180 lbs. Deb: 8/27/89

YEAR	TM/L	G	AB	R	H	2B	3B	HR	RBI	BB	SO	AVG	OBP	SLG	PRO+	BR	/A	RC	SB	CS	SBR	FR	POS	TPR
1989	Min-A	28	67	6	14	3	0	0	4	1	6	.209	.221	.254	31	-6	-6	4	0	0	0	-3	2/3D	-0.9
1990	Min-A	1	2	0	0	0	0	0	2	0	1	.000	.000	.000	-93	-1	-1	0	0	0	0	1	/2	0.1
Total	2	29	69	6	14	3	0	0	6	1	7	.203	.214	.246	28	-6	-7	4	0	0	0	-2	/23D	-0.8

■ FRED HALEY
Haley, Fred b: Wheeling, W.Va. TR, Deb: 6/22/1880

YEAR	TM/L	G	AB	R	H	2B	3B	HR	RBI	BB	SO	AVG	OBP	SLG	PRO+	BR	/A	RC	SB	CS	SBR	FR	POS	TPR
1880	Tro-N	2	7	0	0	0	0	0	0	1	2	.000	.125	.000	-51	-1	-1	0				1	/C	0.0

■ RAY HALEY
Haley, Raymond Timothy "Pat" b: 1/23/1891, Danbury, Iowa d: 10/8/73, Bradenton, Fla. BR/TR, 5'11", 180 lbs. Deb: 4/21/15

YEAR	TM/L	G	AB	R	H	2B	3B	HR	RBI	BB	SO	AVG	OBP	SLG	PRO+	BR	/A	RC	SB	CS	SBR	FR	POS	TPR
1915	Bos-A	5	7	2	1	1	0	0	0	1	0	.143	.250	.286	62	-0	-0	1	0			1	/C	0.1
1916	Bos-A	1	1	0	0	0	0	0	0	0	1	.000	.000	.000	-99	-0	-0	0	0			0	H	0.0
	Phi-A	34	108	8	25	5	0	0	4	6	19	.231	.278	.278	70	-5	-4	8	0			6	C	0.4
	Yr	35	109	8	25	5	0	0	4	6	20	.229	.276	.275	68	-5	-4	8	0			6		0.4
1917	Phi-A	41	98	7	27	2	1	0	11	4	12	.276	.311	.316	93	-1	-1	10	2			-6	C	-0.4
Total	3	81	214	17	53	8	1	0	15	11	32	.248	.291	.294	79	-6	-6	19	2			1	/C	0.1

■ ALBERT HALL
Hall, Albert b: 3/7/58, Birmingham, Ala. BB/TR, 5'11", 155 lbs. Deb: 9/12/81

YEAR	TM/L	G	AB	R	H	2B	3B	HR	RBI	BB	SO	AVG	OBP	SLG	PRO+	BR	/A	RC	SB	CS	SBR	FR	POS	TPR
1981	Atl-N	6	2	1	0	0	0	0	0	1	1	.000	.333	.000	1	-0	-0	0	0	0	0	0	/O	0.0
1982	Atl-N	5	0	1	0	0	0	0	0	0	0	—	—	—	—	0	0	0	0	0	0	0	/R	0.0
1983	Atl-N	10	8	2	0	0	0	0	0	2	2	.000	.200	.000	-37	-2	-2	0	1	1	-0	0	O	-0.1
1984	Atl-N	87	142	25	37	6	1	1	9	10	18	.261	.309	.338	76	-3	-5	15	6	4	-1	0	O	-0.7
1985	Atl-N	54	47	5	7	0	1	0	3	9	12	.149	.286	.191	34	-4	-4	3	1	1	-0	1	O	-0.3
1986	Atl-N	16	50	6	12	2	0	0	1	5	6	.240	.309	.280	60	-2	-3	5	8	3	1	-0	O	-0.2
1987	Atl-N	92	292	54	83	20	4	3	24	38	36	.284	.370	.411	102	4	2	48	33	10	4	0	O	0.3
1988	Atl-N	85	231	27	57	7	1	1	15	21	35	.247	.315	.299	73	-6	-8	22	15	10	-2	5	O	-0.6
1989	Pit-N	20	33	4	6	2	1	0	1	3	5	.182	.250	.303	59	-2	-2	3	3	0	1	-1	O	-0.2
Total	9	375	805	125	202	37	8	5	53	89	115	.251	.309	.335	80	-16	-21	95	67	29	3	4	O	-1.8

■ AL HALL
Hall, Archibald W. b: Worcester, Mass. d: 2/10/1885, Warren, Pa. Deb: 5/01/1879

YEAR	TM/L	G	AB	R	H	2B	3B	HR	RBI	BB	SO	AVG	OBP	SLG	PRO+	BR	/A	RC	SB	CS	SBR	FR	POS	TPR
1879	Tro-N	67	306	30	79	7	3	0	14	3	13	.258	.265	.301	92	-5	-2	25				3	*O	0.0
1880	Cle-N	3	8	1	1	0	0	0	0	0	0	.125	.125	.125	-15	-1	-1	0				-1	/O	-0.1
Total	2	70	314	31	80	7	3	0	14	3	13	.255	.262	.296	90	-5	-3	25				2	/O	-0.1

■ CHARLIE HALL
Hall, Charles Walter "Doc" b: 8/24/1863, Toulon, Ill. d: 6/24/21, Tacoma, Wash. Deb: 5/03/1887

YEAR	TM/L	G	AB	R	H	2B	3B	HR	RBI	BB	SO	AVG	OBP	SLG	PRO+	BR	/A	RC	SB	CS	SBR	FR	POS	TPR
1887	NY-a	3	12	1	1	0	0	0			2	.083	.214	.083	-15	-2	-2	0	1			0	/O	0.0

■ GEORGE HALL
Hall, George William b: 3/29/1849, Stepney, England d: 6/11/23, Ridgewood, N.J. BL, 5'7", 142 lbs. Deb: 5/05/1871

YEAR	TM/L	G	AB	R	H	2B	3B	HR	RBI	BB	SO	AVG	OBP	SLG	PRO+	BR	/A	RC	SB	CS	SBR	FR	POS	TPR
1871	Oly-n	32	136	31	40	3	3	2	17	8	0	.294	.333	.404	117	2	4	19	2				*O	0.3
1872	Bal-n	53	252	69	82	14	8	1			3	.325	.333	.456	135	11	9	39					*O/1	0.8
1873	Bal-n	35	168	45	59	8	4	1			1	.351	.355	.464	140	8	8	28					O	0.6
1874	Bos-n	47	222	58	64	11	7	1			2	.288	.295	.414	117	5	3	28					*O	0.3
1875	Ath-n	77	360	71	107	12	13	5			1	.297	.299	.444	138	19	12	49					*O	1.1
1876	Phi-N	60	268	51	98	7	13	5	45	8	4	.366	.384	.545	208	29	29	57				-2	*O	2.3
1877	Lou-N	61	269	53	87	15	8	0	26	12	19	.323	.352	.439	125	14	7	43				-6	*O	0.0
Total 5 n		244	1138	274	352	48	35	10	17	15		.309	.318	.439	130	45	36	164					O/1	3.1
Total 2		121	537	104	185	22	21	5	71	20	23	.345	.368	.492	162	43	37	100				-8	O	2.3

■ IRV HALL
Hall, Irvin Gladstone b: 10/7/18, Alberton, Md. BR/TR, 5'10.5", 160 lbs. Deb: 4/20/43

YEAR	TM/L	G	AB	R	H	2B	3B	HR	RBI	BB	SO	AVG	OBP	SLG	PRO+	BR	/A	RC	SB	CS	SBR	FR	POS	TPR
1943	Phi-A	151	544	37	139	15	4	0	54	22	42	.256	.292	.298	73	-20	-19	47	10	7	-1	-11	*S/23	-3.2
1944	Phi-A	143	559	60	150	20	8	0	45	31	46	.268	.309	.333	85	-13	-12	56	2	5	-2	-5	2S/1	-1.4
1945	Phi-A	151	616	62	161	17	5	0	50	35	42	.261	.307	.305	78	-18	-17	58	3	10	-5	26	*2	0.6

YEAR	TM/L	G	AB	R	H	2B	3B	HR	RBI	BB	SO	AVG	OBP	SLG	PRO+	BR	/A	RC	SB	CS	SBR	FR	POS	TPR
1946	Phi-A	63	185	19	46	6	2	0	19	9	18	.249	.287	.303	65	-9	-9	16	1	1	-0	-4	2/S	-0.9
Total	4	508	1904	178	496	58	19	0	168	97	148	.261	.302	.311	77	-59	-57	176	16	23	-9	6	2S/13	-4.9

■ JIM HALL   Hall, James   d: 1/30/1886, Brooklyn, N.Y.   Deb: 5/20/1872

YEAR	TM/L	G	AB	R	H	2B	3B	HR	RBI	BB	SO	AVG	OBP	SLG	PRO+	BR	/A	RC	SB	CS	SBR	FR	POS	TPR
1872	Atl-n	13	56	9	16	1	1	0		1		.286	.298	.339	82	-0	-2	6					2/O	-0.2
1874	Atl-n	2	9	0	1	0	0	0		0		.111	.111	.111	-33	-1	-1	0					/2	0.0
1875	Wes-n	1	3	0	1	0	1	0		0		.333	.333	1.000	325	1	1	1					/O	0.1
Total	3 n	16	68	9	18	1	2	0		1		.265	.275	.338	79	-1	-3	7					/2O	-0.1

■ JIMMIE HALL   Hall, Jimmie Randolph   b: 3/17/38, Mt.Holly, N.C.   BL/TR, 6', 175 lbs.   Deb: 4/09/63

YEAR	TM/L	G	AB	R	H	2B	3B	HR	RBI	BB	SO	AVG	OBP	SLG	PRO+	BR	/A	RC	SB	CS	SBR	FR	POS	TPR
1963	Min-A	156	497	88	129	21	5	33	80	63	101	.260	.343	.521	136	24	23	89	3	3	-1	-0	*O	1.8
1964	Min-A	149	510	61	144	20	3	25	75	44	112	.282	.341	.480	125	16	16	83	5	2	0	6	*O	1.7
1965	*Min-A	148	522	81	149	25	4	20	86	51	79	.285	.350	.464	124	19	17	86	14	7	0	-3	*O	0.8
1966	Min-A	120	356	52	85	7	4	20	47	33	66	.239	.303	.449	106	5	2	44	1	2	-1	-0	*O	-0.2
1967	Cal-A	129	401	54	100	8	3	16	55	42	65	.249	.321	.404	117	6	8	52	4	1	1	-2	*O	0.3
1968	Cal-A	46	126	15	27	3	0	1	8	16	19	.214	.303	.262	75	-4	-3	10	1	0	0	-4	O	-0.9
	Cle-A	53	111	4	22	4	0	1	8	10	19	.198	.264	.261	61	-5	-5	8	1	0	0	2	O	-0.3
	Yr	99	237	19	49	7	0	2	16	26	38	.207	.285	.262	68	-9	-8	18	2	0	1	-2		-1.2
1969	Cle-A	4	10	1	0	0	0	0	0	2	3	.000	.167	.000	-48	-2	-2	0	1	0	0	0	/O	-0.1
	NY-A	80	212	21	50	8	5	3	26	19	34	.236	.299	.363	88	-5	-4	24	8	3	1	-6	O/1	-1.0
	Yr	84	222	22	50	8	5	3	26	21	37	.225	.292	.347	81	-7	-6	24	9	3	1	-6		-1.1
	Chi-N	11	24	1	5	1	0	0	1	1	5	.208	.240	.250	33	-2	-2	2	0	0	0	-1	/O	-0.3
1970	Chi-N	28	32	2	3	1	0	0	1	4	12	.094	.194	.125	-11	-5	-6	1	0	0	0	0	/O	-0.5
	Atl-N	39	47	7	10	2	0	2	4	2	14	.213	.245	.383	62	-3	-3	4	0	0	0	0	O	-0.3
	Yr	67	79	9	13	3	0	2	5	6	26	.165	.224	.278	31	-8	-9	5	0	0	0	1		-0.8
Total	8	963	2848	387	724	100	24	121	391	287	529	.254	.323	.434	112	46	41	402	38	18	1	-8	O/1	1.0

■ MEL HALL   Hall, Melvin   b: 9/16/60, Lyons, N.Y.   BL/TL, 6', 185 lbs.   Deb: 9/03/81

YEAR	TM/L	G	AB	R	H	2B	3B	HR	RBI	BB	SO	AVG	OBP	SLG	PRO+	BR	/A	RC	SB	CS	SBR	FR	POS	TPR
1981	Chi-N	10	11	1	1	0	0	1	2	1	4	.091	.167	.364	45	-1	-1	1	0	0	0	0	/O	0.0
1982	Chi-N	24	80	6	21	3	2	0	4	5	17	.262	.322	.350	86	-1	-2	9	0	1	-1	1	/O	0.0
1983	Chi-N	112	410	60	116	23	5	17	56	42	101	.283	.354	.488	125	16	14	71	6	6	-2	-6	*O	0.5
1984	Chi-N	48	150	25	42	11	3	4	22	12	23	.280	.333	.473	114	4	3	23	2	1	0	0	O	0.1
	Cle-A	83	257	43	66	13	1	7	30	35	55	.257	.350	.397	104	3	2	38	1	1	-0	-1	O/D	-0.1
1985	Cle-A	23	66	7	21	6	0	0	12	8	12	.318	.392	.409	121	2	2	10	0	1	-1	-0	O/D	0.1
1986	Cle-A	140	442	68	131	29	2	18	77	33	65	.296	.348	.493	128	15	16	75	6	2	1	-8	*O/D	0.5
1987	Cle-A	142	485	57	136	21	1	18	76	20	68	.280	.310	.439	95	-4	-5	63	5	4	-1	1	*OD	-0.6
1988	Cle-A	150	515	69	144	32	4	6	71	28	50	.280	.317	.392	95	-3	-4	63	7	3	0	-6	*O/D	-1.1
1989	NY-A	113	361	54	94	9	0	17	58	21	37	.260	.301	.427	104	-0	1	44	0	0	0	-4	OD	-0.4
1990	NY-A	113	360	41	93	23	2	12	46	6	46	.258	.274	.433	95	-4	-5	40	0	0	0	-5	DO	-0.9
Total	10	958	3137	431	865	170	20	100	454	211	478	.276	.324	.438	106	27	21	437	27	19	-3	-27	OD	-1.9

■ DICK HALL   Hall, Richard Wallace   b: 9/27/30, St.Louis, Mo.   BR/TR, 6'6", 200 lbs.   Deb: 4/15/52

YEAR	TM/L	G	AB	R	H	2B	3B	HR	RBI	BB	SO	AVG	OBP	SLG	PRO+	BR	/A	RC	SB	CS	SBR	FR	POS	TPR
1952	Pit-N	26	80	6	11	1	0	0	2	2	17	.138	.159	.150	-14	-12	-13	2	0	1	-1	1	O/3	-1.2
1953	Pit-N	7	24	2	4	0	0	0	1	1	3	.167	.200	.167	-3	-4	-4	1	1	1	-0	11	/2	0.7
1954	Pit-N	112	310	38	74	8	4	2	27	33	46	.239	.312	.310	64	-17	-16	29	3	0	1	4	*O	-1.3
1955	Pit-N	21	40	3	7	1	0	1	3	6	5	.175	.283	.275	50	-3	-3	3	0	0	0	-2	P/O	0.0
1956	Pit-N	33	29	5	10	0	0	0	1	5	7	.345	.441	.345	118	1	1	5	0	0	0	-1	P/1	0.0
1957	Pit-N	10	1	0	0	0	0	0	0	0	1	.000	.000	.000	-99	-0	-0	0	0	0	0	-0	/P	0.0
1959	Pit-N	2	2	0	0	0	0	0	0	0	0	.000	.000	.000	-99	-1	-1	0	0	0	0	-0	/P	0.0
1960	KC-A	32	56	5	6	0	0	0	4	4	15	.107	.167	.107	-24	-10	-10	2	1	0	0	-1	P	0.0
1961	Bal-A	30	36	4	5	0	0	0	1	3	13	.139	.205	.139	-6	-5	-5	1	0	0	0	1	P	0.0
1962	Bal-A	44	24	3	4	1	0	0	1	4	9	.167	.286	.208	37	-2	-2	2	0	0	0	-0	P	0.0
1963	Bal-A	48	28	7	13	1	0	1	4	0	8	.464	.464	.607	202	3	4	8	0	0	0	1	P	0.0
1964	Bal-A	45	16	1	2	0	0	0	3	1	3	.125	.176	.125	-14	-2	-2	0	0	0	0	0	P	0.0
1965	Bal-A	49	15	1	5	2	0	0	4	1	4	.333	.412	.467	146	1	1	3	0	0	0	-2	P	0.0
1966	Bal-A	32	12	0	2	0	0	0	2	0	5	.167	.231	.167	17	-1	-1	1	0	0	0	1	P	0.0
1967	Phi-N	48	14	1	1	0	0	0	0	0	5	.071	.071	.071	-58	-3	-3	0	0	0	0	1	P	0.0
1968	Phi-N	32	3	0	1	0	0	0	0	0	1	.333	.333	.333	101	-0	-0	0	0	0	0	-0	P	0.0
1969	*Bal-A	39	7	1	2	0	0	0	2	1	1	.286	.375	.286	86	-0	-0	1	1	0	0	-1	P	0.0
1970	*Bal-A	32	12	2	1	0	0	0	1	0	3	.083	.083	.083	-53	-2	-2	0	0	0	0	-1	P	0.0
1971	Bal-A	27	5	0	2	1	0	0	0	0	1	.400	.400	.600	182	0	0	1	0	0	0	-1	P	0.0
Total	19	669	714	79	150	15	4	4	56	61	147	.210	.274	.259	44	-57	-56	59	6	2	1	11	PO/231	-1.8

■ BOB HALL   Hall, Robert Prill   b: 12/20/1878, Baltimore, Md.   d: 12/1/50, Wellesley, Mass.   TR , 5'10", 158 lbs.   Deb: 4/18/04

YEAR	TM/L	G	AB	R	H	2B	3B	HR	RBI	BB	SO	AVG	OBP	SLG	PRO+	BR	/A	RC	SB	CS	SBR	FR	POS	TPR
1904	Phi-N	46	163	11	26	4	0	0	17	14		.160	.226	.184	30	-13	-12	8	5			-10	3S1	-2.3
1905	NY-N	1	3	1	1	0	0	0	0	0		.333	.333	.333	99	-0	-0	0	0			-0	/O	0.0
	Bro-N	56	203	21	48	4	1	2	15	11		.236	.276	.296	78	-7	-5	20	8			6	O/21	-0.1
	Yr	57	206	22	49	4	1	2	15	11		.238	.276	.296	78	-7	-5	20	8			5		-0.1
Total	2	103	369	33	75	8	1	2	32	25		.203	.254	.247	56	-20	-18	29	13			-5	/O3S12	-2.4

■ RUSS HALL   Hall, Robert Russell   b: 9/29/1871, Shelbyville, Ky.   d: 7/1/37, Los Angeles, Cal.   TL ,   Deb: 4/15/1898

YEAR	TM/L	G	AB	R	H	2B	3B	HR	RBI	BB	SO	AVG	OBP	SLG	PRO+	BR	/A	RC	SB	CS	SBR	FR	POS	TPR
1898	StL-N	39	143	13	35	2	1	0	10	7		.245	.285	.273	61	-7	-7	12	1			-14	S/3O	-1.7
1901	Cle-A	1	4	2	2	0	0	0	0	0		.500	.500	.500	188	0	0	1	0			-1	/S	0.0
Total	2	40	147	15	37	2	1	0	10	7		.252	.290	.279	64	-6	-7	13	1			-15	/S3O	-1.7

■ BILL HALL   Hall, William Lemuel   b: 7/30/28, Moultrie, Ga.   d: 1/1/86, Moultrie, Ga.   BL/TR, 5'11", 165 lbs.   Deb: 4/18/54

YEAR	TM/L	G	AB	R	H	2B	3B	HR	RBI	BB	SO	AVG	OBP	SLG	PRO+	BR	/A	RC	SB	CS	SBR	FR	POS	TPR
1954	Pit-N	5	7	0	0	0	0	0	0	0	0	.000	.000	.000	-99	-2	-2	0	0	0	0	0	/C	-0.1
1956	Pit-N	1	3	0	0	0	0	0	0	0	1	.000	.000	.000	-99	-1	-1	0	0	0	0	1	/C	0.0
1958	Pit-N	51	116	15	33	6	0	1	15	15	13	.284	.366	.362	96	-1	-0	15	0	0	0	7	C	1.0
Total	3	57	126	15	33	6	0	1	15	15	14	.262	.340	.333	81	-3	-3	15	0	0	0	8	/C	0.9

■ TOM HALLER   Haller, Thomas Frank   b: 6/23/37, Lockport, Ill.   BL/TR, 6'4", 195 lbs.   Deb: 4/11/61   C

YEAR	TM/L	G	AB	R	H	2B	3B	HR	RBI	BB	SO	AVG	OBP	SLG	PRO+	BR	/A	RC	SB	CS	SBR	FR	POS	TPR
1961	SF-N	30	62	5	9	1	0	2	8	9	23	.145	.264	.258	41	-5	-5	4	0	1	-1	2	C	-0.1
1962	*SF-N	99	272	53	71	13	1	18	55	51	59	.261	.385	.515	142	16	17	56	1	4	-2	-2	C	1.3
1963	SF-N	98	298	32	76	8	1	14	44	34	45	.255	.335	.432	120	7	8	41	4	6	-2	-3	C/O	0.4
1964	SF-N	117	388	43	98	14	3	16	48	55	51	.253	.348	.428	115	10	9	58	4	2	0	-1	*C/O	1.2
1965	SF-N	134	422	40	106	4	3	16	49	47	67	.251	.338	.389	101	3	2	56	0	0	0	-4	*C	0.2
1966	SF-N	142	471	74	113	19	2	27	67	53	74	.240	.325	.461	112	9	8	69	1	3	-2	-6	*C/1	0.3
1967	SF-N	141	455	54	114	23	5	14	49	62	61	.251	.345	.415	118	11	12	68	0	4	-2	0	*C	1.8
1968	LA-N	144	474	37	135	27	5	4	53	46	76	.285	.351	.388	132	13	17	66	1	4	-2	3	*C	2.6
1969	LA-N	134	445	46	117	18	3	6	39	48	58	.263	.337	.357	102	-2	1	55	0	3	-2	-9	*C	-0.1
1970	LA-N	112	325	47	93	16	6	10	47	32	55	.286	.354	.465	123	7	9	54	0	2	-1	3	C	0.6
1971	LA-N	84	202	23	54	5	0	5	32	25	30	.267	.354	.366	111	2	3	26	0	2	-1	4	C	0.8
1972	*Det-A	59	121	7	25	5	2	2	13	15	14	.207	.294	.331	83	-2	-3	12	0	1	-1	8	C	0.6
Total	12	1294	3935	461	1011	153	31	134	504	477	593	.257	.342	.414	114	68	77	567	14	30	-14	-17	*C/O1	9.6

YEAR	TM/L	G	AB	R	H	2B	3B	HR	RBI	BB	SO	AVG	OBP	SLG	PRO+	BR	/A	RC	SB	CS	SBR	FR	POS	TPR

■ NEWT HALLIDAY   Halliday, Newton Reese b: 6/18/1896, Chicago, Ill. d: 4/6/18, Great Lakes, Ill. BR/TR, 6'1", 175 lbs. Deb: 8/19/16

| 1916 | Pit-N | 1 | 1 | 0 | 0 | 0 | 0 | 0 | 0 | 0 | 1 | .000 | .000 | .000 | -99 | -0 | -0 | 0 | | | | 0 | /1 | 0.0 |

■ JOCKO HALLIGAN   Halligan, William E. b: 12/8/1868, Avon, N.Y. d: 2/13/45, Buffalo, N.Y. 5'9", 166 lbs. Deb: 5/13/1890

1890	Buf-P	57	211	28	53	9	2	3	33	20	19	.251	.319	.355	89	-6	-2	27	7			-3	OC	-0.4
1891	Cin-N	61	247	43	77	13	6	3	44	24	25	.312	.375	.449	141	13	12	45	5			-3	O	0.5
1892	Cin-N	26	101	14	29	4	0	2	12	12	9	.287	.363	.386	130	4	4	16	3			-1	O	0.2
	Bal-N	46	178	38	47	4	7	2	43	30	24	.264	.376	.399	132	9	8	30	8			-7	O1/C	0.0
	Yr	72	279	52	76	8	7	4	55	42	33	.272	.372	.394	132	12	12	46	11			-7		0.2
Total	3	190	737	123	206	30	15	10	132	86	77	.280	.358	.402	122	19	22	117	23			-13	O/C1	0.3

■ ED HALLINAN   Hallinan, Edward S. b: 8/23/1888, San Francisco, Cal d: 8/24/40, San Francisco, Cal BR/TR, 5'9", 168 lbs. Deb: 5/13/11

1911	StL-A	52	169	13	35	3	1	0	14	14		.207	.268	.237	43	-13	-12	11	4			-5	S2/3	-1.4
1912	StL-A	29	86	11	19	2	0	0	1	5		.221	.272	.244	50	-6	-5	7	3			-7	S	-0.9
Total	2	81	255	24	54	5	1	0	15	19		.212	.269	.239	45	-19	-18	18	7			-12	/S23	-2.3

■ JIMMY HALLINAN   Hallinan, James H. b: 5/27/1849, Ireland d: 10/28/1879, Chicago, Ill. BL/TL, 5'9", 172 lbs. Deb: 7/26/1871

1871	Kek-n	5	25	7	5	0	0	0	2	2	0	.200	.259	.200	34	-2	-2	2	1				/S	0.0
1875	Wes-n	13	51	12	14	1	1	0		0		.275	.275	.333	104	0	-0	5					S	0.0
	Mut-n	44	202	29	58	7	3	3		1		.287	.291	.396	127	7	5	24					S/3	0.3
	Yr	57	253	41	72	8	4	3		1		.285	.287	.383	123	7	5	29						0.3
1876	NY-N	54	240	45	67	7	6	2	36	2	4	.279	.285	.383	139	5	10	27				-13	*S/2O	-0.3
1877	Cin-N	16	73	18	27	1	1	0	7	1	1	.370	.378	.411	167	4	5	12				-6	2	0.0
	Chi-N	19	89	17	25	4	1	0	11	4	2	.281	.312	.348	96	1	-1	10				-3	O	-0.3
	Yr	35	162	35	52	5	2	0	18	5	3	.321	.341	.377	124	5	4	21				-9		-0.3
1878	Chi-N	16	67	14	19	3	0	0	2	5	6	.284	.333	.328	111	1	1	8				-5	O/2	-0.3
	Ind-N	3	12	0	3	2	0	0	1	0	2	.250	.250	.417	134	0	0	1				-1	/O	0.0
	Yr	19	79	14	22	5	0	0	3	5	8	.278	.321	.342	114	2	1	9				-5		-0.3
Total	2 n	62	278	48	77	8	4	3	2	3		.277	.285	.367	113	5	3	30					/S3	0.3
Total	3	108	481	94	141	17	8	2	57	12	15	.293	.310	.374	129	11	15	57				-28	/SO2	-0.9

■ BILL HALLMAN   Hallman, William Harry b: 3/15/1876, Philadelphia, Pa. d: 4/23/50, Philadelphia, Pa. BL/TL, Deb: 4/25/01

1901	Mil-A	139	549	70	135	27	6	2	47	41		.246	.301	.328	80	-17	-13	61	12			-2	*O	-1.5
1903	Chi-A	63	207	29	43	7	4	0	18	31		.208	.311	.280	84	-4	-3	22	11			2	O	-0.4
1906	Pit-N	23	89	12	24	3	1	1	6	15		.270	.375	.360	126	4	3	14	3			-0	O	0.3
1907	Pit-N	94	302	39	67	6	2	0	15	33		.222	.299	.255	74	-7	-8	31	21			-6	O	-1.9
Total	4	319	1147	150	269	43	13	3	86	120		.235	.308	.303	83	-25	-20	128	47			-6	O	-3.5

■ BILL HALLMAN   Hallman, William Wilson b: 3/31/1867, Pittsburgh, Pa. d: 9/11/20, Philadelphia, Pa. BR/TR, 5'8", 160 lbs. Deb: 4/23/1888 M

1888	Phi-N	18	63	5	13	4	1	0	6	1	12	.206	.219	.302	63	-2	-3	4	1			-6	C/2OS3	-0.8
1889	Phi-N	119	462	67	117	21	8	2	60	36	54	.253	.313	.346	79	-9	-16	58	20			6	*S2/C	-0.4
1890	Phi-P	84	356	59	95	16	7	1	37	33	24	.267	.338	.360	86	-6	-8	46	6			-8	OC23/S	-1.1
1891	Phi-a	141	587	112	166	21	13	6	69	38	56	.283	.332	.394	107	5	3	85	18			-5	*2	0.6
1892	Phi-N	138	586	106	171	27	10	2	84	32	52	.292	.335	.382	119	11	12	83	19			-24	*2	-0.9
1893	Phi-N	132	596	119	183	28	7	5	76	51	27	.307	.367	.403	107	5	5	98	22			-15	*21	-0.8
1894	Phi-N	119	505	107	156	19	7	0	66	36	15	.309	.363	.374	81	-17	-14	83	36			-19	*2	-1.9
1895	Phi-N	124	539	94	169	26	5	1	91	34	20	.314	.359	.386	94	-5	-5	82	16			5	*2/S	0.6
1896	Phi-N	120	469	82	150	21	3	2	83	45	23	.320	.382	.390	107	5	6	78	16			3	*2/P	1.1
1897	Phi-N	31	126	16	33	3	0	0	15	8		.262	.326	.286	66	-6	-5	12	1			-10	2	-1.0
	StL-N	79	298	31	66	6	2	0	26	24		.221	.288	.255	47	-22	-21	26	12			3	2/1M	-1.0
	Yr	110	424	47	99	9	2	0	41	32		.233	.300	.264	52	-28	-27	38	13			-7		-2.0
1898	Bro-N	134	509	57	124	10	7	2	63	29		.244	.291	.303	73	-18	-18	49	9			-3	*23	-1.4
1901	Cle-A	5	19	2	4	0	0	0	3	2		.211	.286	.211	42	-1	-1	1	0			-3	/S	-0.3
	Phi-N	123	445	46	82	13	5	0	38	26		.184	.236	.236	38	-34	-35	32	13			-4	23	-3.0
1902	Phi-N	73	254	14	63	8	4	0	35	14		.248	.287	.311	86	-4	-4	27	9			-6	3	-0.6
1903	Phi-N	63	198	20	42	11	2	0	17	16		.212	.271	.288	63	-10	-9	18	2			-3	23/1OS	-1.0
Total	14	1503	6012	937	1634	234	81	21	769	425	283	.272	.325	.348	86	-108	-114	783	200			-90	*23S/OC1P	-11.9

■ JIM HALPIN   Halpin, James Nathaniel b: 10/4/1863, England d: 1/4/1893, Boston, Mass. Deb: 6/15/1882

1882	Wor-N	2	8	0	0	0	0	0	0	0	2	.000	.000	.000	-98	-2	-2	0				-1	/3	-0.2
1884	Was-U	46	168	24	31	3	0	0		0	2	.185	.194	.202	35	-11	-10	7	0			-7	S/3	-1.4
1885	Det-N	15	54	3	7	2	0	0	1	1	12	.130	.145	.167	1	-6	-6	1				1	S	-0.3
Total	3	63	230	27	38	5	0	0	1	3	14	.165	.176	.187	22	-19	-18	8				-8	/S3	-1.9

■ AL HALT   Halt, Alva William b: 11/23/1890, Sandusky, Ohio d: 1/22/73, Sandusky, Ohio BR/TR, 6', 180 lbs. Deb: 5/29/14

1914	Bro-F	80	261	26	61	6	2	3	25	13	39	.234	.270	.307	65	-12	-12	26	11			-11	S/2O	-1.8
1915	Bro-F	151	524	41	131	22	7	3	64	39	79	.250	.307	.336	91	-7	-6	63	20			2	*3S	0.2
1918	Cle-A	26	69	9	12	2	0	0	1	9	12	.174	.269	.203	39	-5	-5	4	4			-1	3/2S1	-0.6
Total	3	257	854	76	204	30	9	6	90	61	130	.239	.293	.316	79	-24	-24	93	35			-9	3S/210	-2.2

■ RALPH HAM   Ham, Ralph A. b: 1850, Troy, N.Y. d: 2/13/05, Troy, N.Y. 5'8", 158 lbs. Deb: 5/06/1871

1871	Rok-n	25	113	25	28	4	0	0	12	1	7	.248	.254	.283	57	-6	-5	10	6				O/2S	-0.2
1872	Man-n	1	5	0	2	0	0	0		0		.400	.400	.400	156	0	0	1					/S	0.0
Total	2 n	26	118	25	30	4	0	0		1		.254	.261	.288	61	-6	-5	11					/O2S	-0.2

■ CHARLIE HAMBURG   Hamburg, Charles M. (b: Charles M. Hambrick) b: 11/22/1863, Louisville, Ky. d: 5/18/31, Union, N.J. 6', 175 lbs. Deb: 4/18/1890

| 1890 | *Lou-a | 133 | 485 | 93 | 132 | 22 | 2 | 3 | | 69 | | .272 | .370 | .344 | 116 | 11 | 12 | 81 | 46 | | | -1 | *O | 0.3 |

■ JIM HAMBY   Hamby, James Sanford "Cracker" b: 7/29/1897, Wilkesboro, N.C. BR/TR, 6', 170 lbs. Deb: 9/20/26

1926	NY-N	1	3	0	0	0	0	0	0	0	0	.000	.000	.000	-99	-1	-1	0	0			-1	/C	0.0
1927	NY-N	21	52	6	10	0	1	0	5	7	7	.192	.288	.231	40	-4	-4	4	1			0	C	-0.2
Total	2	22	55	6	10	0	1	0	5	7	7	.182	.274	.218	33	-5	-5	4	1			-1	/C	-0.2

■ DARRYL HAMILTON   Hamilton, Darryl Quinn b: 12/3/64, Baton Rouge, La. BL/TR, 6'1", 180 lbs. Deb: 6/03/88

1988	Mil-A	44	103	14	19	4	0	1	11	12	9	.184	.276	.252	49	-7	-7	8	7	3	0	3	O/D	-0.4
1990	Mil-A	89	156	27	46	5	0	1	18	9	12	.295	.333	.346	93	-2	-1	19	10	3	1	7	O/D	0.6
Total	2	133	259	41	65	9	0	2	29	21	21	.251	.310	.309	75	-9	-8	27	17	6	2	10	O/D	0.2

■ JEFF HAMILTON   Hamilton, Jeffrey Robert b: 3/19/64, Flint, Mich. BR/TR, 6'3", 190 lbs. Deb: 6/28/86

1986	LA-N	71	147	22	33	5	0	5	19	2	43	.224	.236	.361	66	-8	-7	12	0	0	0	11	3/S	0.3
1987	LA-N	35	83	5	18	3	0	1	7	2	22	.217	.286	.253	45	-7	-6	6	0	1	-1	9	3/S	-0.2
1988	*LA-N	111	309	34	73	14	2	6	33	10	51	.236	.269	.353	80	-10	-9	27	0	2	-1	0	*3/S1	-1.0
1989	LA-N	151	548	45	134	35	1	12	56	20	71	.245	.275	.378	86	-13	-12	55	0	0	0	-6	*3/P2S	-1.9
1990	LA-N	7	24	1	3	0	0	0	1	0	3	.125	.125	.125	-33	-4	-4	0	0	0	0	1	/3	-0.2
Total	5	375	1111	107	261	57	3	23	110	39	190	.235	.266	.354	76	-41	-38	100	0	3	-2	15	3/S2P1	-2.6

YEAR	TM/L	G	AB	R	H	2B	3B	HR	RBI	BB	SO	AVG	OBP	SLG	PRO+	BR	/A	RC	SB	CS	SBR	FR	POS	TPR

■ **TOM HAMILTON**   Hamilton, Thomas Ball "Ham" b: 9/29/25, Altoona, Kan.   d: 11/29/73, Tyler, Tex.   BL/TR, 6'4", 213 lbs.   Deb: 9/04/52

YEAR	TM/L	G	AB	R	H	2B	3B	HR	RBI	BB	SO	AVG	OBP	SLG	PRO+	BR	/A	RC	SB	CS	SBR	FR	POS	TPR
1952	Phi-A	9	10	1	2	1	0	0	1	1	1	.200	.273	.300	56	-1	-1	1	0	0	0	-0	/1	0.0
1953	Phi-A	58	56	8	11	2	0	0	5	7	11	.196	.286	.232	40	-4	-5	4	0	0	0	0	/1O	-0.4
Total	2	67	66	9	13	3	0	0	6	8	12	.197	.284	.242	42	-5	-5	5	0	0	0	-0	/1O	-0.4

■ **BILLY HAMILTON**   Hamilton, William Robert "Sliding Billy" b: 2/16/1866, Newark, N.J.   d: 12/16/40, Worcester, Mass.   BL/TR, 5'6", 165 lbs.   Deb: 7/31/1888

YEAR	TM/L	G	AB	R	H	2B	3B	HR	RBI	BB	SO	AVG	OBP	SLG	PRO+	BR	/A	RC	SB	CS	SBR	FR	POS	TPR
1888	KC-a	35	129	21	34	4	4	0	11	4		.264	.307	.357	108	2	1	20	19			-2	O	-0.2
1889	KC-a	137	534	144	161	17	12	3	77	87	41	.301	.413	.395	126	28	22	136	**111**			-7	*O	0.9
1890	Phi-N	123	496	133	161	13	9	2	49	83	37	.325	.430	.399	141	33	31	**132**	**102**			3	*O	2.7
1891	Phi-N	133	527	**141**	**179**	23	7	2	60	**102**	28	**.340**	**.453**	.421	154	**46**	**43**	**155**	**111**			5	*O	3.7
1892	Phi-N	139	554	132	183	21	7	3	53	81	29	.330	.423	.410	155	40	41	123	57			14	*O	4.6
1893	Phi-N	82	355	110	135	22	7	5	44	63	7	.380	.490	.524	172	41	41	115	43			4	O	3.4
1894	Phi-N	129	544	**192**	220	25	15	4	87	**126**	17	.404	**.523**	.528	160	61	65	206	**98**			5	*O	4.6
1895	Phi-N	123	517	**166**	201	22	6	7	74	**96**	30	.389	.490	.495	157	51	51	**177**	97			-1	*O	3.1
1896	Bos-N	131	523	152	191	24	9	3	52	**110**	29	.365	**.477**	.463	142	47	41	159	83			-11	*O	1.7
1897	*Bos-N	127	507	**152**	174	17	5	3	61	**105**		.343	.461	.414	127	34	28	130	66			-3	*O	1.3
1898	Bos-N	110	417	110	154	16	5	3	50	87		.369	**.480**	.453	**163**	45	42	120	54			-15	*O	1.8
1899	Bos-N	84	297	63	92	7	1	1	33	72		.310	.446	.350	112	15	10	56	19			-2	O	0.2
1900	Bos-N	136	520	103	173	20	5	1	47	107		.333	.449	.396	122	34	24	110	32			2	*O	1.2
1901	Bos-N	102	348	71	100	11	2	3	38	64		.287	.401	.356	113	14	9	61	20			1	O	0.0
Total	14	1591	6268	1690	2158	242	94	40	736	1187	218	.344	.455	.432	142	492	448	1701	912			-6	*O	29.0

■ **KEN HAMLIN**   Hamlin, Kenneth Lee b: 5/18/35, Detroit, Mich.   BR/TR, 5'10", 170 lbs.   Deb: 6/17/57

YEAR	TM/L	G	AB	R	H	2B	3B	HR	RBI	BB	SO	AVG	OBP	SLG	PRO+	BR	/A	RC	SB	CS	SBR	FR	POS	TPR
1957	Pit-N	2	1	0	0	0	0	0	0	0	0	.000	.000	.000	-99	-0	-0	0	0	0	0	0	/S	0.0
1959	Pit-N	3	8	1	1	0	0	0	0	2	1	.125	.300	.125	19	-1	-1	0	0	0	0	-1	/S	-0.1
1960	KC-A	140	428	51	96	10	2	2	24	44	48	.224	.298	.271	55	-26	-26	35	1	1	-0	-40	*S	-5.8
1961	LA-A	42	91	4	19	3	0	1	5	11	9	.209	.301	.275	49	-6	-7	7	0	1	-1	13	S	0.8
1962	Was-A	98	292	29	74	12	0	3	22	22	22	.253	.306	.325	70	-12	-12	28	7	7	-2	-11	S/2	-2.0
1965	Was-A	117	362	45	99	21	1	4	22	33	45	.273	.336	.370	102	0	1	47	8	2	1	-29	2S/3	-2.1
1966	Was-A	66	158	13	34	7	1	1	16	13	21	.215	.275	.291	63	-8	-7	12	1	0	0	6	2/3	0.4
Total	7	468	1340	143	323	53	4	11	89	125	146	.241	.307	.311	71	-52	-53	129	17	11	-2	-62	S2/3	-8.8

■ **STEVE HAMMOND**   Hammond, Steven Benjamin b: 5/9/57, Atlanta, Ga.   BL/TR, 6'2", 190 lbs.   Deb: 6/28/82

YEAR	TM/L	G	AB	R	H	2B	3B	HR	RBI	BB	SO	AVG	OBP	SLG	PRO+	BR	/A	RC	SB	CS	SBR	FR	POS	TPR
1982	KC-A	46	126	14	29	5	1	1	11	4	18	.230	.254	.310	54	-8	-8	8	0	1	-1	3	O/D	-0.6

■ **JACK HAMMOND**   Hammond, Walter Charles "Wobby" b: 2/26/1891, Amsterdam, N.Y.   d: 3/4/42, Kenosha, Wis.   BR/TR, 5'11", 170 lbs.   Deb: 4/15/15

YEAR	TM/L	G	AB	R	H	2B	3B	HR	RBI	BB	SO	AVG	OBP	SLG	PRO+	BR	/A	RC	SB	CS	SBR	FR	POS	TPR
1915	Cle-A	35	84	9	18	2	1	0	4	1	19	.214	.224	.262	44	-6	-6	5	0	1	-1	-8	2	-1.5
1922	Cle-A	1	4	1	1	0	0	0	0	0	0	.250	.250	.250	30	-0	-0	0	0	0	0	-1	/2	-0.1
	Pit-N	9	11	3	3	0	0	0	0	1	0	.273	.333	.273	57	-1	-1	1	0	0	0	2	/2	0.1
Total	2	45	99	13	22	2	1	0	4	2	19	.222	.238	.263	45	-7	-7	7	0	1	-1	-7	/2	-1.5

■ **GRANNY HAMNER**   Hamner, Granville Wilbur b: 4/26/27, Richmond, Va.   BR/TR, 5'10", 163 lbs.   Deb: 9/14/44

YEAR	TM/L	G	AB	R	H	2B	3B	HR	RBI	BB	SO	AVG	OBP	SLG	PRO+	BR	/A	RC	SB	CS	SBR	FR	POS	TPR
1944	Phi-N	21	77	6	19	1	0	0	5	3	7	.247	.275	.260	53	-5	-5	6	0			6	S	0.4
1945	Phi-N	14	41	3	7	2	0	0	6	1	3	.171	.190	.220	14	-5	-5	2	0			3	S	0.0
1946	Phi-N	2	7	0	1	0	0	0	0	0	3	.143	.143	.143	-19	-1	-1	0	0			-1	/S	-0.1
1947	Phi-N	2	7	1	2	0	0	0	0	1	0	.286	.375	.286	81	-0	-0	1	0			0	/S	0.0
1948	Phi-N	129	446	42	116	21	5	3	48	22	39	.260	.298	.350	76	-17	-16	45	2			-7	2S/3	-1.2
1949	Phi-N	154	662	83	174	32	5	6	53	25	47	.263	.290	.353	74	-28	-26	63	6			0	*S	-0.8
1950	*Phi-N	157	637	78	172	27	5	11	82	39	35	.270	.314	.380	83	-18	-17	74	2			-5	*S	-0.4
1951	Phi-N	150	589	61	150	23	7	9	72	29	32	.255	.290	.363	76	-22	-21	58	10	5	0	-2	*S	-1.0
1952	Phi-N	151	596	74	164	30	5	17	87	27	51	.275	.307	.428	103	-1	-0	75	7	3	0	-4	*S	0.0
1953	Phi-N	154	609	90	168	30	8	21	92	32	28	.276	.313	.455	98	-5	-4	84	2	1	0	-8	2S	-0.2
1954	Phi-N	152	596	83	178	39	11	13	89	53	44	.299	.356	.466	112	10	10	98	1	2	-1	-23	*2/S	-0.3
1955	Phi-N	104	405	57	104	12	4	5	43	41	30	.257	.327	.343	79	-12	-11	46	0	1	-1	-35	2S	-3.9
1956	Phi-N	122	401	42	90	24	3	4	42	30	42	.224	.278	.329	64	-21	-20	35	2	0	1	-12	*S2/P	-2.3
1957	Phi-N	133	502	59	114	19	5	10	62	34	42	.227	.276	.345	68	-25	-23	43	3	1	0	-39	*2/SP	-5.3
1958	Phi-N	35	133	18	40	7	3	2	18	8	16	.301	.340	.444	107	1	1	17	0	0	0	-3	32/S	0.0
1959	Phi-N	21	64	10	19	4	0	2	6	5	5	.297	.348	.453	109	1	1	9	0	1	-1	-7	S/3	-0.6
	Cle-A	27	67	4	11	1	1	1	3	1	8	.164	.176	.254	17	-8	-7	3	0	0	0	-2	S/23	-0.8
1962	KC-A	3	0	0	0	0	0	0	0	0	0	—	—	—	—	-0	-0	0	0	0	0	0	/P	0.0
Total	17	1531	5839	711	1529	272	62	104	708	351	432	.262	.304	.383	84	-157	-145	657	35	14		-138	S2/3P	-16.5

■ **GARVIN HAMNER**   Hamner, Wesley Garvin b: 3/18/24, Richmond, Va.   BR/TR, 5'11", 172 lbs.   Deb: 4/17/45

YEAR	TM/L	G	AB	R	H	2B	3B	HR	RBI	BB	SO	AVG	OBP	SLG	PRO+	BR	/A	RC	SB	CS	SBR	FR	POS	TPR
1945	Phi-N	32	101	12	20	3	0	0	5	7	9	.198	.250	.228	34	-9	-9	6	2			-4	2/S3	-0.9

■ **IKE HAMPTON**   Hampton, Isaac Bernard b: 8/22/51, Camden, S.C.   BB/TR, 6', 165 lbs.   Deb: 9/12/74

YEAR	TM/L	G	AB	R	H	2B	3B	HR	RBI	BB	SO	AVG	OBP	SLG	PRO+	BR	/A	RC	SB	CS	SBR	FR	POS	TPR
1974	NY-N	4	4	0	0	0	0	0	1	0	1	.000	.000	.000	-99	-1	-1	0	0	0	0	0	/C	0.0
1975	Cal-A	31	66	8	10	3	0	0	4	7	19	.152	.243	.197	28	-6	-6	4	0	0	0	-4	C/S3	-0.8
1976	Cal-A	3	2	0	0	0	0	0	0	0	0	.000	.000	.000	-99	-0	-0	0	0	0	0	1	/CS	0.0
1977	Cal-A	52	44	5	13	1	0	3	9	2	10	.295	.340	.523	137	2	2	7	0	0	0	1	C/D	0.4
1978	Cal-A	19	14	2	3	0	1	1	4	2	7	.214	.313	.571	149	1	1	3	1	0	0	1	C/1D	0.3
1979	Cal-A	4	5	0	2	0	0	0	0	0	1	.400	.400	.400	121	0	0	1	0	0	0	1	/1	0.1
Total	6	113	135	15	28	4	1	4	18	11	38	.207	.277	.341	75	-5	-4	14	1	0	0	-1	/CD1S3	0.0

■ **BERT HAMRIC**   Hamric, Odbert Herman b: 3/1/28, Clarksburg, W.Va.   d: 8/8/84, Springboro, Ohio   BL/TR, 6', 165 lbs.   Deb: 4/24/55

YEAR	TM/L	G	AB	R	H	2B	3B	HR	RBI	BB	SO	AVG	OBP	SLG	PRO+	BR	/A	RC	SB	CS	SBR	FR	POS	TPR
1955	Bro-N	2	1	0	0	0	0	0	0	0	1	.000	.000	.000	-97	-0	-0	0	0	0	0	0	H	0.0
1958	Bal-A	8	8	0	1	0	0	0	0	0	6	.125	.125	.125	-33	-1	-1	0	0	0	0	0	H	0.0
Total	2	10	9	0	1	0	0	0	0	0	7	.111	.111	.111	-41	-2	-2	0	0	0	0	0	H	0.0

■ **RAY HAMRICK**   Hamrick, Raymond Bernard b: 8/1/21, Nashville, Tenn.   BR/TR, 5'11.5", 160 lbs.   Deb: 8/14/43

YEAR	TM/L	G	AB	R	H	2B	3B	HR	RBI	BB	SO	AVG	OBP	SLG	PRO+	BR	/A	RC	SB	CS	SBR	FR	POS	TPR
1943	Phi-N	44	160	12	32	3	1	0	9	8	28	.200	.238	.231	37	-13	-13	9	0			-11	2S	-2.3
1944	Phi-N	74	292	22	60	10	1	1	23	23	34	.205	.268	.257	50	-20	-19	20	1			20	S	1.1
Total	2	118	452	34	92	13	2	1	32	31	62	.204	.258	.248	46	-33	-31	29	1			9	/S2	-1.2

■ **BUDDY HANCKEN**   Hancken, Morris Medlock b: 8/30/14, Birmingham, Ala.   BR/TR, 6'1", 175 lbs.   Deb: 5/14/40   C

YEAR	TM/L	G	AB	R	H	2B	3B	HR	RBI	BB	SO	AVG	OBP	SLG	PRO+	BR	/A	RC	SB	CS	SBR	FR	POS	TPR
1940	Phi-A	1	0	0	0	0	0	0	0	0	0	—	—	—	—	0	0	0	0	0	0	0	/C	0.0

■ **FRED HANCOCK**   Hancock, Fred James b: 3/28/20, Allenport, Pa.   d: 3/12/86, Clearwater, Fla.   BR/TR, 5'8", 170 lbs.   Deb: 4/26/49

YEAR	TM/L	G	AB	R	H	2B	3B	HR	RBI	BB	SO	AVG	OBP	SLG	PRO+	BR	/A	RC	SB	CS	SBR	FR	POS	TPR
1949	Chi-A	39	52	7	7	2	1	0	9	8	9	.135	.262	.212	27	-6	-5	3	0	1	-1	-3	S/3O	-0.7

■ **GARRY HANCOCK**   Hancock, Ronald Garry b: 1/23/54, Tampa, Fla.   BL/TL, 6', 175 lbs.   Deb: 7/16/78

YEAR	TM/L	G	AB	R	H	2B	3B	HR	RBI	BB	SO	AVG	OBP	SLG	PRO+	BR	/A	RC	SB	CS	SBR	FR	POS	TPR
1978	Bos-A	38	80	10	18	3	0	0	4	1	12	.225	.235	.262	36	-6	-7	5	0	0	0	3	OD	-0.4
1980	Bos-A	46	115	9	33	6	0	4	19	3	11	.287	.305	.443	97	-0	-1	14	0	3	-2	2	OD	-0.1
1981	Bos-A	26	45	4	7	3	0	0	3	2	4	.156	.191	.222	18	-5	-5	2	0	0	0	1	/OD	-0.3
1982	Bos-A	11	14	3	0	0	0	0	0	1	1	.000	.067	.000	-75	-3	-4	0	0	0	0	-1	/O	-0.3

YEAR	TM/L	G	AB	R	H	2B	3B	HR	RBI	BB	SO	AVG	OBP	SLG	PRO+	BR	/A	RC	SB	CS	SBR	FR	POS	TPR
1983	Oak-A	101	256	29	70	7	3	8	30	5	13	.273	.290	.418	98	-4	-2	30	2	0	1	2	O1/D	0.0
1984	Oak-A	51	60	2	13	2	0	0	8	0	1	.217	.217	.250	31	-6	-5	2	0	0	0	1	O/1PD	-0.4
Total	6	273	570	57	141	21	3	12	64	12	42	.247	.264	.358	71	-24	-24	53	2	3	-1	7	O/D1P	-1.5

■ MIKE HANDIBOE
Handiboe, Aloysius James "Coalyard Mike" b: 7/21/1887, Washington, D.C. d: 1/31/53, Savannah, Ga. BL/TL, 5'10", 155 lbs. Deb: 9/08/11

YEAR	TM/L	G	AB	R	H	2B	3B	HR	RBI	BB	SO	AVG	OBP	SLG	PRO+	BR	/A	RC	SB	CS	SBR	FR	POS	TPR
1911	NY-A	5	15	0	1	0	0	0	0	0	2	.067	.176	.067	-29	-3	-3	0	0			-0	/O	-0.2

■ GENE HANDLEY
Handley, Eugene Louis b: 11/25/14, Kennett, Mo. BR/TR, 5'10.5", 165 lbs. Deb: 4/16/46

YEAR	TM/L	G	AB	R	H	2B	3B	HR	RBI	BB	SO	AVG	OBP	SLG	PRO+	BR	/A	RC	SB	CS	SBR	FR	POS	TPR
1946	Phi-A	89	251	31	63	8	5	0	21	22	25	.251	.311	.323	78	-8	-7	26	8	3	1	-17	2/3S	-1.8
1947	Phi-A	36	90	10	23	2	1	0	8	10	2	.256	.330	.300	74	-3	-3	9	1	0	0	-5	23/S	-0.6
Total	2	125	341	41	86	10	6	0	29	32	27	.252	.316	.317	77	-10	-10	35	9	3	1	-22	/23S	-2.4

■ LEE HANDLEY
Handley, Lee Elmer "Jeep" b: 7/31/13, Clarion, Iowa d: 4/8/70, Pittsburgh, Pa. BR/TR, 5'7", 160 lbs. Deb: 4/15/36

YEAR	TM/L	G	AB	R	H	2B	3B	HR	RBI	BB	SO	AVG	OBP	SLG	PRO+	BR	/A	RC	SB	CS	SBR	FR	POS	TPR
1936	Cin-N	24	78	10	24	1	0	2	8	7	16	.308	.365	.397	112	1	1	12	3			-0	2/3	0.2
1937	Pit-N	127	480	59	120	21	12	3	37	37	40	.250	.305	.363	81	-14	-14	55	5			-14	*2/3	-2.2
1938	Pit-N	139	570	91	153	25	8	6	51	53	31	.268	.332	.372	93	-5	-6	72	7			9	*3	0.0
1939	Pit-N	101	376	43	107	14	5	1	42	32	16	.285	.341	.356	89	-6	-5	45	17			-10	*3	-1.2
1940	Pit-N	98	302	50	85	7	4	1	19	27	16	.281	.340	.341	89	-4	-4	37	7			1	3/2	-0.3
1941	Pit-N	124	459	59	132	18	4	0	33	35	22	.288	.338	.344	93	-4	-4	53	16			-1	*3	-0.3
1944	Pit-N	40	86	7	19	2	0	0	5	3	5	.221	.247	.244	37	-7	-7	4	1			2	23/S	-0.1
1945	Pit-N	98	312	39	93	16	2	1	32	20	16	.298	.340	.372	94	-1	-3	40	7			15	3	1.1
1946	Pit-N	116	416	43	99	8	7	1	28	29	20	.238	.289	.298	65	-19	-20	36	4			13	*3/2	-0.5
1947	Phi-N	101	277	17	70	10	3	0	42	24	18	.253	.312	.310	68	-13	-12	26	1			2	3/2S	-1.1
Total	10	968	3356	418	902	122	45	15	297	267	204	.269	.323	.345	84	-73	-73	380	68			17	32/S	-4.4

■ HARRY HANEBRINK
Hanebrink, Harry Aloysius b: 11/12/27, St.Louis, Mo. BL/TR, 6', 165 lbs. Deb: 5/03/53

YEAR	TM/L	G	AB	R	H	2B	3B	HR	RBI	BB	SO	AVG	OBP	SLG	PRO+	BR	/A	RC	SB	CS	SBR	FR	POS	TPR
1953	Mil-N	51	80	8	19	1	1	1	8	6	8	.237	.291	.313	61	-5	-4	8	1	0	0	4	2/3	0.0
1957	Mil-N	6	7	0	2	0	0	0	0	1	2	.286	.375	.286	87	-0	-0	1	0	0	0	1	/3	0.1
1958	*Mil-N	63	133	14	25	3	0	4	10	13	9	.188	.270	.301	56	-10	-8	10	0	1	-1	-1	O/3	-0.9
1959	Phi-N	57	97	10	25	3	1	1	7	2	12	.258	.273	.340	61	-5	-6	8	0	0	0	-5	2/3O	-0.9
Total	4	177	317	32	71	7	2	6	25	22	31	.224	.279	.315	60	-20	-18	27	1	1	-0	-2	/2O3	-1.7

■ FRED HANEY
Haney, Fred Girard "Pudge" b: 4/25/1898, Albuquerque, N.Mex d: 11/9/77, Beverly Hills, Cal. BR/TR, 5'6", 170 lbs. Deb: 4/18/22 MC

YEAR	TM/L	G	AB	R	H	2B	3B	HR	RBI	BB	SO	AVG	OBP	SLG	PRO+	BR	/A	RC	SB	CS	SBR	FR	POS	TPR
1922	Det-A	81	213	41	75	7	4	0	25	32	14	.352	.439	.423	129	10	11	40	3	7	-3	2	31/S	1.4
1923	Det-A	142	503	85	142	13	4	4	67	45	23	.282	.347	.348	85	-12	-10	64	12	5	1	-2	23S	0.0
1924	Det-A	86	256	54	79	11	1	1	30	39	13	.309	.400	.371	101	2	2	41	7	4	-0	4	3/S2	1.0
1925	Det-A	114	398	84	111	15	3	0	40	66	29	.279	.384	.332	84	-7	-6	58	11	1	3	-2	*3	0.1
1926	Bos-A	138	462	47	102	15	7	0	52	74	28	.221	.330	.284	63	-25	-23	50	13	6	0	6	*3	-0.3
1927	Bos-A	47	116	23	32	4	1	3	12	25	14	.276	.404	.405	113	3	3	20	4	1	1	-2	3/O	0.4
	Chi-N	4	3	0	0	0	0	0	0	0	0	.000	.000	.000	-99	-1	-1	0	0			0	H	0.0
1929	StL-N	10	26	4	3	1	1	0	2	1	2	.115	.179	.231	1	-4	-4	1	0			3	/3	0.0
Total	7	622	1977	338	544	66	21	8	228	282	123	.275	.368	.342	87	-35	-28	274	50	24		9	3/2S10	2.6

■ LARRY HANEY
Haney, Wallace Larry b: 11/19/42, Charlottesville, Va BR/TR, 6'2", 195 lbs. Deb: 7/27/66 C

YEAR	TM/L	G	AB	R	H	2B	3B	HR	RBI	BB	SO	AVG	OBP	SLG	PRO+	BR	/A	RC	SB	CS	SBR	FR	POS	TPR
1966	Bal-A	20	56	3	9	1	0	1	3	1	15	.161	.190	.232	21	-6	-6	3	0	0	0	3	C	-0.1
1967	Bal-A	58	164	13	44	11	0	3	20	6	28	.268	.294	.390	101	-0	-0	18	1	0	0	2	C	0.6
1968	Bal-A	38	89	5	21	3	1	1	5	0	19	.236	.236	.326	69	-4	-4	6	0	0	0	3	C	0.1
1969	Sea-A	22	59	3	15	3	0	2	7	6	12	.254	.323	.407	105	0	0	7	1	1	-0	-1	C	0.0
	Oak-A	53	86	8	13	4	0	2	12	7	19	.151	.223	.267	38	-8	-7	4	0	0	0	0	C	-0.3
	Yr	75	145	11	28	7	0	4	19	13	31	.193	.264	.324	66	-7	-7	11	1	1	-0	-1		-0.3
1970	Oak-A	2	2	2	0	0	0	0	0	2	1	.000	.500	.000	51	0	0	0	0	0	0	0	/C	0.0
1972	Oak-A	5	4	0	0	0	0	0	0	0	0	.000	.000	.000	-99	-1	-1	0	0	0	0	-1	/C2	-0.2
1973	Oak-A	2	2	0	1	0	0	0	0	0	0	.500	.500	.500	192	0	0	0	0	0	0	-0	/C	0.0
	StL-N	2	1	0	0	0	0	0	0	0	1	.000	.000	.000	-99	-0	-0	0	0	0	0	0	/C	0.0
1974	*Oak-A	76	121	12	20	4	0	2	3	3	18	.165	.185	.248	25	-12	-11	5	1	0	0	10	C/31	0.1
1975	Oak-A	47	26	3	5	0	0	1	2	1	4	.192	.222	.308	50	-2	-2	2	0	0	0	7	C/3	0.7
1976	Oak-A	88	177	12	40	2	0	0	10	13	26	.226	.283	.237	56	-10	-9	12	0	1	-1	10	C	0.3
1977	Mil-A	63	127	7	29	0	0	0	10	5	30	.228	.258	.244	38	-11	-11	8	0	0	0	8	C	0.0
1978	Mil-A	4	5	0	1	0	0	0	0	1	1	.200	.200	.200	13	-1	-1	0	0	0	0	-0	/C	0.0
Total	12	480	919	68	198	30	1	12	73	44	175	.215	.254	.289	57	-54	-51	66	3	2	-0	41	C/312	1.2

■ CHARLIE HANFORD
Hanford, Charles Joseph b: 6/3/1881, Tunstall, England d: 7/19/63, Trenton, N.J. BR/TR, 5'6.5", 145 lbs. Deb: 4/13/14

YEAR	TM/L	G	AB	R	H	2B	3B	HR	RBI	BB	SO	AVG	OBP	SLG	PRO+	BR	/A	RC	SB	CS	SBR	FR	POS	TPR
1914	Buf-F	155	597	83	174	28	13	13	90	32	81	.291	.332	.447	119	14	13	104	37			10	*O	1.5
1915	Chi-F	77	179	27	43	4	5	0	22	12	28	.240	.295	.318	87	-4	-3	21	10			-4	O	-0.9
Total	2	232	776	110	217	32	18	13	112	44	109	.280	.323	.418	113	10	10	125	47			6	O	0.6

■ JAY HANKINS
Hankins, Jay Nelson b: 11/7/35, St.Louis Co., Mo. BL/TR, 5'7", 170 lbs. Deb: 4/15/61

YEAR	TM/L	G	AB	R	H	2B	3B	HR	RBI	BB	SO	AVG	OBP	SLG	PRO+	BR	/A	RC	SB	CS	SBR	FR	POS	TPR
1961	KC-A	76	173	23	32	0	3	3	6	8	17	.185	.225	.272	32	-17	-17	11	2	0	1	-2	O	-2.0
1963	KC-A	10	34	2	6	0	1	1	4	0	3	.176	.176	.324	35	-3	-3	2	0	1	-1	1	/O	-0.2
Total	2	86	207	25	38	0	4	4	10	8	20	.184	.218	.280	33	-20	-20	13	2	1	0	-1	/O	-2.2

■ FRANK HANKINSON
Hankinson, Frank Edward b: 4/29/1856, New York, N.Y. d: 4/5/11, Palisades Park, N.J BR/TR, 5'11", 168 lbs. Deb: 5/01/1878

YEAR	TM/L	G	AB	R	H	2B	3B	HR	RBI	BB	SO	AVG	OBP	SLG	PRO+	BR	/A	RC	SB	CS	SBR	FR	POS	TPR
1878	Chi-N	58	240	38	64	8	3	1	27	5	36	.267	.282	.338	96	1	-2	23				8	*3/P	0.8
1879	Chi-N	44	171	14	31	4	0	0	8	2	14	.181	.191	.205	29	-12	-14	7				7	PO/3	0.0
1880	Cle-N	69	263	32	55	7	4	1	19	1	23	.209	.212	.278	66	-10	-9	16				-12	3O/P	-2.0
1881	Tro-N	85	321	34	62	15	0	1	19	10	41	.193	.218	.249	44	-19	-22	18				7	*3/S	-0.7
1883	NY-N	94	337	40	74	13	6	2	30	19	38	.220	.261	.312	74	-10	-10	28				-5	*3/O	-1.2
1884	NY-N	105	389	44	90	16	7	2	43	23	59	.231	.274	.324	85	-5	-7	35				-2	*3/O	-1.2
1885	NY-a	94	362	43	81	12	2	2			12	.224	.251	.285	77	-12	-7	26				18	*3/P	1.4
1886	NY-a	136	522	66	126	14	5	2	49			.241	.306	.299	96	-4	-0	52	10			25	*3	2.7
1887	NY-a	127	512	79	137	29	11	1	38			.268	.320	.373	99	-4	-0	68	19			8	*3	0.3
1888	KC-a	37	155	20	27	4	1	1	20	11		.174	.229	.232	47	-8	-10	9	2			-5	2/SO31	-1.2
Total	10	849	3272	410	747	122	39	13	166	170	211	.228	.267	.301	78	-85	-80	283	31			49	3/OP2S1	-1.1

■ NED HANLON
Hanlon, Edward Hugh b: 8/22/1857, Montville, Conn. d: 4/14/37, Baltimore, Md. BL/TR, 5'9.5", 170 lbs. Deb: 5/01/1880 M

YEAR	TM/L	G	AB	R	H	2B	3B	HR	RBI	BB	SO	AVG	OBP	SLG	PRO+	BR	/A	RC	SB	CS	SBR	FR	POS	TPR
1880	Cle-N	73	280	30	69	10	3	0	32	11	30	.246	.275	.304	98	-1	-0	24				-3	*O/S	-0.5
1881	Det-N	76	305	63	85	14	8	2	28	22	11	.279	.327	.397	122	10	8	41				-5	*O/S	0.1
1882	Det-N	82	347	68	80	18	6	5	38	26	25	.231	.284	.360	105	2	3	36				11	*O/2	1.1
1883	Det-N	100	413	65	100	13	2	1	40	34	44	.242	.300	.291	84	-8	-5	37				-2	*O2	-0.4
1884	Det-N	114	450	86	119	18	6	5	39	40	52	.264	.324	.364	124	9	13	55				10	*O	2.0
1885	Det-N	105	424	93	128	18	8	1	29	47	18	.302	.373	.389	146	23	23	63				1	*O	2.0
1886	Det-N	126	494	105	116	6	6	4	60	57	39	.235	.314	.296	84	-6	-9	63	50			-6	*O/2	-1.0
1887	*Det-N	118	471	79	129	13	7	4	69	30	24	.274	.320	.357	87	-6	-9	78	69			-2	*O	-0.7
1888	Det-N	109	459	64	122	8	6	3	39	15	32	.266	.295	.346	106	3	3	60	38			-7	*O	-0.5
1889	Pit-N	116	461	81	110	14	10	2	37	58	25	.239	.326	.325	93	-9	-1	68	53			-1	*OM	-0.5

YEAR	TM/L	G	AB	R	H	2B	3B	HR	RBI	BB	SO	AVG	OBP	SLG	PRO+	BR	/A	RC	SB	CS	SBR	FR	POS	TPR
1890	Pit-P	118	472	106	131	16	6	1	44	80	24	.278	.389	.343	107	3	11	90	65			-2	*OM	0.3
1891	Pit-N	119	455	87	121	12	8	0	60	48	30	.266	.341	.327	99	-0	1	71	54			0	*O/SM	-0.3
1892	Bal-N	11	43	3	7	1	1	0	2	3	3	.163	.217	.233	36	-3	-3	2	0			-0	OM	-0.3
Total	13	1267	5074	930	1317	159	79	30	517	471	357	.260	.325	.340	103	15	33	687	329			-5	*O/2S	1.3

■ **BILL HANLON**   Hanlon, William Henry "Big Bill" b: 3/16/1865, Sacramento, Cal. d: 3/18/51, Sacramento, Cal. 6', Deb: 4/16/03

YEAR	TM/L	G	AB	R	H	2B	3B	HR	RBI	BB	SO	AVG	OBP	SLG	PRO+	BR	/A	RC	SB	CS	SBR	FR	POS	TPR
1903	Chi-N	8	21	4	2	0	0	0	2	6		.095	.296	.095	16	-2	-2	1	1			0	/1	-0.1

■ **JOHN HANNA**   Hanna, John b: 11/3/1863, Philadelphia, Pa. d: 11/7/30, Philadelphia, Pa.   Deb: 5/23/1884

YEAR	TM/L	G	AB	R	H	2B	3B	HR	RBI	BB	SO	AVG	OBP	SLG	PRO+	BR	/A	RC	SB	CS	SBR	FR	POS	TPR
1884	Was-a	23	76	8	5	0	0	0		6		.066	.134	.066	-36	-10	-9	1				3	C/O	-0.4
	Ric-a	22	67	6	13	2	1	0		6		.194	.206	.254	52	-3	-3	4				4	C/S	0.2
	Yr	45	143	14	18	2	1	0		6		.126	.167	.154	7	-14	-12	4				6		-0.2

■ **TRUCK HANNAH**   Hannah, James Harrison b: 6/5/1889, Larimore, N.D. d: 4/27/82, Fountain Valley, Cal. BR/TR, 6'1", 190 lbs. Deb: 4/15/18

YEAR	TM/L	G	AB	R	H	2B	3B	HR	RBI	BB	SO	AVG	OBP	SLG	PRO+	BR	/A	RC	SB	CS	SBR	FR	POS	TPR
1918	NY-A	90	250	24	55	6	0	2	21	51	25	.220	.361	.268	88	-0	-1	26	5			3	C	1.1
1919	NY-A	75	227	14	54	8	3	1	20	22	19	.238	.313	.313	76	-7	-7	22	0			-8	C/1	-1.1
1920	NY-A	79	259	24	64	11	1	2	25	24	35	.247	.313	.320	66	-12	-13	28	2	0	1	-5	C	-1.0
Total	3	244	736	62	173	25	4	5	66	97	79	.235	.331	.300	76	-19	-21	76	7	0		-10	C/1	-1.0

■ **JACK HANNIFIN**   Hannifin, John Joseph b: 2/25/1883, Holyoke, Mass. d: 10/27/45, Northampton, Mass. BR/TR, 5'11", 167 lbs. Deb: 4/19/06

YEAR	TM/L	G	AB	R	H	2B	3B	HR	RBI	BB	SO	AVG	OBP	SLG	PRO+	BR	/A	RC	SB	CS	SBR	FR	POS	TPR
1906	Phi-A	1	1	0	1	0	0	0	0	0		1.000	1.000	1.000	517	0	0	1	0			0	H	0.0
	NY-N	10	30	4	6	0	1	0	3	2		.200	.250	.267	61	-1	-1	2	1			-1	/S32	-0.1
1907	NY-N	56	149	16	34	7	3	1	15	15		.228	.299	.336	98	0	-1	18	6			-4	13/SO	-0.4
1908	NY-N	1	2	0	0	0	0	0	0	0		.000	.000	.000	-95	-0	-0	0	0			-0	/O	0.0
	Bos-N	90	257	30	53	6	2	2	22	28		.206	.284	.268	80	-5	-5	22	7			5	32S/O	0.1
	Yr	91	259	30	53	6	2	2	22	28		.205	.282	.266	78	-6	-5	22	7			5		0.1
Total	3	158	439	50	94	13	6	3	40	45		.214	.287	.292	85	-7	-7	43	14			1	/3S120	-0.4

■ **PAT HANNIFIN**   Hannifin, Patrick James b: 1868, Nova Scotia, Canada d: 11/5/08, Springfield, Mass. Deb: 4/29/1897

YEAR	TM/L	G	AB	R	H	2B	3B	HR	RBI	BB	SO	AVG	OBP	SLG	PRO+	BR	/A	RC	SB	CS	SBR	FR	POS	TPR
1897	Bro-N	10	20	4	5	0	0	0	2	1		.250	.375	.250	73	-1	-0	3	4			2	/O2	0.1

■ **DAVE HANSEN**   Hansen, David Andrew b: 11/24/68, Long Beach, Cal. BL/TR, 6', 180 lbs. Deb: 9/16/90

YEAR	TM/L	G	AB	R	H	2B	3B	HR	RBI	BB	SO	AVG	OBP	SLG	PRO+	BR	/A	RC	SB	CS	SBR	FR	POS	TPR
1990	LA-N	5	7	0	1	0	0	0	1	0	3	.143	.143	.143	-22	-1	-1	0	0	0	0	-1	/3	-0.1

■ **DOUG HANSEN**   Hansen, Douglas William b: 12/16/28, Los Angeles, Cal. BR/TR, 6', 180 lbs. Deb: 9/04/51

YEAR	TM/L	G	AB	R	H	2B	3B	HR	RBI	BB	SO	AVG	OBP	SLG	PRO+	BR	/A	RC	SB	CS	SBR	FR	POS	TPR
1951	Cle-A	3	0	2	0	0	0	0	0	0	0	—	—	—	—	0	0	0	0	0	0	0	R	0.0

■ **BOB HANSEN**   Hansen, Robert Joseph b: 5/26/48, Boston, Mass. BL/TL, 6', 195 lbs. Deb: 5/10/74

YEAR	TM/L	G	AB	R	H	2B	3B	HR	RBI	BB	SO	AVG	OBP	SLG	PRO+	BR	/A	RC	SB	CS	SBR	FR	POS	TPR
1974	Mil-A	58	88	8	26	4	1	2	9	3	16	.295	.319	.432	115	1	1	12	2	1	0	-0	D/1	0.1
1976	Mil-A	24	61	4	10	1	0	0	4	6	8	.164	.239	.180	24	-6	-6	3	0	0	0	0	D/1	-0.5
Total	2	82	149	12	36	5	1	2	13	9	24	.242	.285	.329	78	-4	-4	15	2	1	0	-0	/D1	-0.4

■ **RON HANSEN**   Hansen, Ronald Lavern b: 4/5/38, Oxford, Neb. BR/TR, 6'3", 190 lbs. Deb: 4/15/58 C

YEAR	TM/L	G	AB	R	H	2B	3B	HR	RBI	BB	SO	AVG	OBP	SLG	PRO+	BR	/A	RC	SB	CS	SBR	FR	POS	TPR
1958	Bal-A	12	19	1	0	0	0	0	1	0	7	.000	.050	.000	-90	-5	-5	0	0	0	0	-0	S	-0.2
1959	Bal-A	2	4	0	0	0	0	0	0	1	1	.000	.200	.000	-41	-1	-1	0	0	0	0	1	/S	0.0
1960	Bal-A	153	530	72	135	22	5	22	86	69	94	.255	.343	.440	111	7	8	78	3	3	-1	6	*S	2.4
1961	Bal-A	155	533	51	132	13	2	12	51	66	96	.248	.332	.347	83	-13	-12	60	1	3	-2	12	*S/2	1.0
1962	Bal-A	71	196	12	34	7	0	3	17	30	36	.173	.289	.255	50	-14	-13	14	0	1	-1	4	S	-0.4
1963	Chi-A	144	482	55	109	17	2	13	67	78	74	.226	.334	.351	94	-3	-2	57	1	1	-0	27	*S	3.3
1964	Chi-A	158	575	85	150	25	3	20	68	73	73	.261	.350	.419	116	11	13	86	1	0		16	*S	3.1
1965	Chi-A	162	587	61	138	23	4	11	66	60	73	.235	.308	.344	91	-11	-7	60	1	1	-0	17	*S/2	1.8
1966	Chi-A	23	74	3	13	1	0	0	4	15	10	.176	.322	.189	55	-4	-3	6	0	1	-1	3	S	0.0
1967	Chi-A	157	498	35	116	20	0	8	51	64	51	.233	.320	.321	94	-5	-3	53	0	3	-2	2	*S	0.9
1968	Was-A	86	275	28	51	12	0	8	28	35	49	.185	.282	.316	84	-6	-5	23	0	0	0	2	S/3	0.2
	Chi-A	40	87	7	20	3	0	1	4	11	12	.230	.316	.299	86	-1	-1	8	0	0	0	7	3/S2	0.8
	Yr	126	362	35	71	15	0	9	32	46	61	.196	.290	.312	84	-7	-6	31	0	0	0	8		1.0
1969	Chi-A	85	185	15	48	6	1	2	22	18	25	.259	.328	.335	82	-3	-4	20	2	1	-1	-1	21/S3	-0.4
1970	NY-A	59	91	13	27	4	0	4	14	19	9	.297	.423	.473	155	7	7	20	0	1	-1	-2	S3/2	0.6
1971	NY-A	61	145	6	30	3	0	2	20	9	27	.207	.253	.269	51	-10	-9	9	0	0	0	-3	3/2S	-1.3
1972	KC-A	16	30	2	4	0	0	0	2	3	6	.133	.212	.133	4	-3	-3	1	0	0	0	3	/S32	0.0
Total	15	1384	4311	446	1007	156	17	106	501	551	643	.234	.323	.351	92	-55	-40	494	9	14	-6	92	*S/321	11.8

■ **DON HANSKI**   Hanski, Donald Thomas (b: Donald Thomas Hanyzewski) b: 2/27/16, Laporte, Ind. d: 9/2/57, Worth, Ill. BL/TL, 5'11", 180 lbs. Deb: 5/06/43

YEAR	TM/L	G	AB	R	H	2B	3B	HR	RBI	BB	SO	AVG	OBP	SLG	PRO+	BR	/A	RC	SB	CS	SBR	FR	POS	TPR
1943	Chi-A	9	21	1	5	1	0	0	2	0	5	.238	.238	.286	53	-1	-1	1	0	1	-1	-0	/1P	-0.2
1944	Chi-A	2	1	0	0	0	0	0	0	0	0	.000	.000	.000	-99	-0	-0	0	0	0	0	0	/P	0.0
Total	2	11	22	1	5	1	0	0	2	0	5	.227	.227	.273	46	-2	-2	1	0	1	-1	-0	/1P	-0.2

■ **JOE HANSON**   Hanson, Joseph b: St.Louis, Mo. TR , Deb: 7/14/13

YEAR	TM/L	G	AB	R	H	2B	3B	HR	RBI	BB	SO	AVG	OBP	SLG	PRO+	BR	/A	RC	SB	CS	SBR	FR	POS	TPR
1913	NY-A	1	2	0	0	0	0	0	0	0	0	.000	.000	.000	-99	-0	-0	0	0			-0	/C	0.0

■ **JOHN HAPPENNY**   Happenny, John Clifford "Cliff" b: 5/18/01, Waltham, Mass. d: 12/29/88, Coral Springs, Fla BR/TR, 5'11", 165 lbs. Deb: 7/02/23

YEAR	TM/L	G	AB	R	H	2B	3B	HR	RBI	BB	SO	AVG	OBP	SLG	PRO+	BR	/A	RC	SB	CS	SBR	FR	POS	TPR
1923	Chi-A	32	86	7	19	5	0	0	10	3	13	.221	.256	.279	41	-8	-7	6	0	0	0	0	2/S3	-0.4

■ **BILL HARBIDGE**   Harbidge, William Arthur "Yaller Bill" b: 3/29/1855, Philadelphia, Pa. d: 3/17/24, Philadelphia, Pa. BL/TL, 162 lbs. Deb: 5/15/1875

YEAR	TM/L	G	AB	R	H	2B	3B	HR	RBI	BB	SO	AVG	OBP	SLG	PRO+	BR	/A	RC	SB	CS	SBR	FR	POS	TPR
1875	Har-n	53	205	32	50	3	3	0		12		.244	.286	.288	94	0	-1	17					CO2/1	0.0
1876	Har-N	30	106	11	23	2	1	0	6	3	2	.217	.239	.255	59	-4	-5	7				0	C/O1	-0.2
1877	Har-N	41	167	18	37	5	2	0	8	3	6	.222	.235	.275	68	-7	-5	11				-6	C/O23	-0.8
1878	Chi-N	54	240	32	71	12	0	0	37	6	13	.296	.313	.346	109	4	2	27				-7	*C/O	-0.3
1879	Chi-N	4	18	2	2	0	0	0	1	0	5	.111	.111	.111	-25	-2	-2	0				-1	/O	-0.3
1880	Tro-N	9	27	3	10	0	1	0	2	0	3	.370	.370	.444	166	2	2	5				2	/CO	0.4
1882	Tro-N	32	123	11	23	1	1	0	13	10	17	.187	.248	.211	52	-7	-6	7				-3	O/1C	-0.8
1883	Phi-N	73	280	32	62	12	3	0	21	24	20	.221	.283	.286	81	-8	-4	23				-12	OS/2C3	-1.2
1884	Cin-U	82	341	59	95	12	5	2		25		.279	.328	.361	123	12	8	41	0			5	*O/S1	1.0
Total	8	325	1302	168	323	44	13	2	88	71	66	.248	.287	.306	92	-10	-11	120	0			-23	OC/S213	-2.2

■ **SCOTT HARDESTY**   Hardesty, Scott Durbin b: 1/26/1870, Bellville, Ohio d: 10/29/44, Fostoria, Ohio   Deb: 8/17/1899

YEAR	TM/L	G	AB	R	H	2B	3B	HR	RBI	BB	SO	AVG	OBP	SLG	PRO+	BR	/A	RC	SB	CS	SBR	FR	POS	TPR
1899	NY-N	22	72	4	16	0	0	0	4	1		.222	.243	.222	31	-7	-6	4	2			2	S/1	-0.2

■ **PAT HARDGROVE**   Hardgrove, William Henry b: 5/10/1895, Palmyra, Kan. d: 1/26/73, Jackson, Miss. BR/TR, 5'10", 158 lbs. Deb: 6/08/18

YEAR	TM/L	G	AB	R	H	2B	3B	HR	RBI	BB	SO	AVG	OBP	SLG	PRO+	BR	/A	RC	SB	CS	SBR	FR	POS	TPR
1918	Chi-A	2	2	0	0	0	0	0	0	0	0	.000	.000	.000	-99	-0	-0	0	0			0	H	0.0

■ **LOU HARDIE**   Hardie, Louis W. b: 8/24/1864, New York, N.Y. d: 3/5/29, Oakland, Cal. 5'11", 180 lbs. Deb: 5/22/1884

YEAR	TM/L	G	AB	R	H	2B	3B	HR	RBI	BB	SO	AVG	OBP	SLG	PRO+	BR	/A	RC	SB	CS	SBR	FR	POS	TPR
1884	Phi-N	3	8	0	3	0	0	0		0	2	.375	.375	.625	219	1	1	2				-1	/C	0.0
1886	Chi-N	16	51	4	9	0	0	0	3	4	10	.176	.236	.176	24	-4	-5	2	1			1	C/O3	-0.2
1890	Bos-N	47	185	17	42	8	0	3	17	18	36	.227	.296	.319	75	-5	-7	19	4			1	CO/3S1	-0.3
1891	Bal-a	15	56	7	13	0	3	0	8	8	8	.232	.328	.339	93	-0	-0	7	3			1	O	0.0

YEAR	TM/L	G	AB	R	H	2B	3B	HR	RBI	BB	SO	AVG	OBP	SLG	PRO+	BR	/A	RC	SB	CS	SBR	FR	POS	TPR
Total	4	81	300	28	67	10	3	3	21	30	56	.223	.294	.307	72	-8	-12	31	8			2	/CO31S	-0.5

■ BUD HARDIN
Hardin, William Edgar b: 6/14/22, Shelby, N.C. BR/TR, 5'10", 165 lbs. Deb: 4/15/52

YEAR	TM/L	G	AB	R	H	2B	3B	HR	RBI	BB	SO	AVG	OBP	SLG	PRO+	BR	/A	RC	SB	CS	SBR	FR	POS	TPR
1952	Chi-N	3	7	1	1	0	0	0	0	0	0	.143	.143	.143	-20	-1	-1	0	0	0	0	0	/S2	0.0

■ LOU HARDING
Harding, Louis Edward "Jumbo" b: San Francisco, Cal. 5'9.5", 213 lbs. Deb: 10/05/1886

YEAR	TM/L	G	AB	R	H	2B	3B	HR	RBI	BB	SO	AVG	OBP	SLG	PRO+	BR	/A	RC	SB	CS	SBR	FR	POS	TPR
1886	StL-a	1	3	0	1	1	0	0		0		.333	.333	.667	203	0	0	1	0			1	/C	0.1

■ CARROLL HARDY
Hardy, Carroll William b: 5/18/33, Sturgis, S.Dak. BR/TR, 6', 185 lbs. Deb: 4/15/58

YEAR	TM/L	G	AB	R	H	2B	3B	HR	RBI	BB	SO	AVG	OBP	SLG	PRO+	BR	/A	RC	SB	CS	SBR	FR	POS	TPR
1958	Cle-A	27	49	10	10	3	0	1	6	6	14	.204	.304	.327	75	-2	-2	5	1	2	-1	3	O	0.0
1959	Cle-A	32	53	12	11	1	0	0	2	3	7	.208	.250	.226	33	-5	-5	3	1	1	-0	4	O	-0.1
1960	Cle-A	29	18	7	2	1	0	0	1	2	2	.111	.200	.167	0	-3	-2	1	0	0	0	3	O	0.0
	Bos-A	73	145	26	34	5	2	2	15	17	40	.234	.315	.338	74	-5	-5	14	3	2	-0	3	O	-0.4
	Yr	102	163	33	36	6	2	2	16	19	42	.221	.302	.319	67	-7	-8	15	3	2	-0	6		-0.4
1961	Bos-A	85	281	46	74	20	2	3	36	26	53	.263	.330	.381	87	-4	-5	36	4	2	0	1	O	-0.6
1962	Bos-A	115	362	52	78	13	5	8	36	54	68	.215	.321	.345	77	-10	-12	40	3	7	-3	4	*O	-1.4
1963	Hou-N	15	44	5	10	3	0	0	3	3	7	.227	.277	.295	69	-2	-2	4	1	0	0	-0	O	-0.1
1964	Hou-N	46	157	13	29	1	1	2	12	8	30	.185	.234	.242	36	-14	-13	8	0	0	0	5	O	-0.8
1967	Min-A	11	8	1	3	0	0	1	2	1	1	.375	.444	.750	229	1	1	3	0	0	0	0	/O	0.1
Total	8	433	1117	172	251	47	10	17	113	120	222	.225	.304	.330	72	-42	-44	114	13	14	-5	23	O	-3.3

■ JACK HARDY
Hardy, John Doolittle b: 6/23/1877, Cleveland, Ohio d: 10/20/21, Cleveland, Ohio TR, 6', 185 lbs. Deb: 8/29/03

YEAR	TM/L	G	AB	R	H	2B	3B	HR	RBI	BB	SO	AVG	OBP	SLG	PRO+	BR	/A	RC	SB	CS	SBR	FR	POS	TPR
1903	Cle-A	5	19	1	3	1	0	0	1		1	.158	.200	.211	25	-2	-2	1	1			-1	/O	-0.2
1907	Chi-N	1	4	0	1	0	0	0	0		0	.250	.250	.250	55	-0	-0	0	0			1	/C	0.0
1909	Was-A	10	24	3	4	0	0	0	4		1	.167	.200	.167	17	-2	-2	1	0			-2	/C2	-0.3
1910	Was-A	7	8	1	2	0	0	0	0		0	.250	.250	.250	59	-0	0	0	0			1	/CO	0.1
Total	4	23	55	5	10	1	0	0	5		2	.182	.211	.200	29	-5	-4	2	1			-1	/CO2	-0.4

■ GARY HARGIS
Hargis, Gary Lynn b: 11/2/56, Minneapolis, Minn. BR/TR, 5'11", 165 lbs. Deb: 9/29/79

YEAR	TM/L	G	AB	R	H	2B	3B	HR	RBI	BB	SO	AVG	OBP	SLG	PRO+	BR	/A	RC	SB	CS	SBR	FR	POS	TPR
1979	Pit-N	1	0	0	0	0	0	0	0	0	0	—	—	—	—	0	0	0	0	0	0	0	/R	0.0

■ BUBBLES HARGRAVE
Hargrave, Eugene Franklin b: 7/15/1892, New Haven, Ind. d: 2/23/69, Cincinnati, Ohio BR/TR, 5'10.5", 174 lbs. Deb: 9/18/13

YEAR	TM/L	G	AB	R	H	2B	3B	HR	RBI	BB	SO	AVG	OBP	SLG	PRO+	BR	/A	RC	SB	CS	SBR	FR	POS	TPR
1913	Chi-N	3	3	0	1	0	0	0	1	0	0	.333	.333	.333	90	-0	-0	0	0			0	/C	0.0
1914	Chi-N	23	36	3	8	2	0	0	2	0	4	.222	.222	.278	48	-2	-2	2	2			-4	C	-0.5
1915	Chi-N	15	19	2	3	0	1	0	2	1	5	.158	.200	.263	40	-1	-1	1	0			-1	/C	-0.1
1921	Cin-N	93	263	28	76	17	8	1	38	12	15	.289	.327	.426	102	-1	0	36	4	2	0	-7	C	-0.1
1922	Cin-N	98	320	49	101	22	10	7	57	26	18	.316	.371	.512	128	11	12	60	7	4	-0	-9	C	0.3
1923	Cin-N	118	378	54	126	23	9	10	78	44	22	.333	.419	.521	150	27	28	84	4	5	-2	2	*C	3.2
1924	Cin-N	98	312	42	94	19	10	3	33	30	20	.301	.370	.455	122	9	10	53	2	2	-1	-1	C	0.9
1925	Cin-N	87	273	28	82	13	6	2	33	25	23	.300	.361	.414	100	-1	0	41	4	3	-1	-5	C	-0.1
1926	Cin-N	105	326	42	115	22	8	6	62	25	17	.353	.406	.525	153	22	23	67	2			-12	C	1.4
1927	Cin-N	102	305	36	94	18	3	0	35	31	18	.308	.376	.387	108	3	4	45	0			-10	C	0.0
1928	Cin-N	65	190	19	56	12	3	0	23	13	14	.295	.353	.389	95	-2	-1	26	4			2	C	0.4
1930	NY-A	45	108	11	30	7	0	0	12	10	9	.278	.339	.343	77	-4	-3	13	0	0	0	-5	C	-0.4
Total	12	852	2533	314	786	155	58	29	376	217	165	.310	.372	.452	119	60	68	429	29	16		-50	C	5.0

■ PINKY HARGRAVE
Hargrave, William Kc Kinley b: 1/31/1896, New Haven, Ind. d: 10/3/42, Ft.Wayne, Ind. BB/TR, 5'8.5", 180 lbs. Deb: 5/18/23

YEAR	TM/L	G	AB	R	H	2B	3B	HR	RBI	BB	SO	AVG	OBP	SLG	PRO+	BR	/A	RC	SB	CS	SBR	FR	POS	TPR
1923	Was-A	33	59	4	17	2	0	0	8	2	6	.288	.311	.322	70	-3	-2	6	0	0	0	-4	/3CO	-0.4
1924	Was-A	24	33	3	5	1	1	0	5	1	4	.152	.176	.242	8	-5	-5	1	0	0	0	-1	/C	-0.4
1925	Was-A	5	6	0	3	0	0	0	0	1	2	.500	.571	.500	177	1	1	2	0	0	0	1	/C	0.2
	StL-A	67	225	34	64	15	2	8	43	13	13	.284	.326	.476	97	-1	-3	35	2	0	1	-5	C	-0.2
	Yr	72	231	34	67	15	2	8	43	14	15	.290	.333	.476	99	-0	-2	37	2	0	1	-4		0.0
1926	StL-A	92	235	20	66	16	3	7	37	10	38	.281	.319	.464	98	-1	-2	35	3	0	1	-2	C	0.0
1928	Det-A	121	320	38	88	13	5	10	63	32	28	.275	.343	.441	103	1	1	50	4	1	1	-14	C	-0.5
1929	Det-A	76	185	26	61	12	0	3	26	20	24	.330	.401	.443	117	5	5	33	2	2	-1	-0	C	0.8
1930	Det-A	55	137	18	39	8	0	5	18	20	12	.285	.380	.453	108	2	2	25	2	0	1	-4	C	0.2
	Was-A	10	31	3	6	2	2	0	7	3	1	.194	.265	.484	85	-1	-1	4	1	0	0	1	/C	0.1
	Yr	65	168	21	45	10	2	6	25	23	13	.268	.359	.458	104	1	1	29	3	0	1	-3		0.3
1931	Was-A	40	80	6	26	8	0	1	19	9	12	.325	.393	.463	124	3	3	15	1	0	0	-2	C	0.3
1932	Bos-N	82	217	20	57	14	3	4	33	24	18	.263	.336	.410	103	-0	1	31	1			-4	C	0.3
1933	Bos-N	45	73	5	13	0	0	0	6	5	7	.178	.241	.178	23	-7	-7	3	1			1	C	-0.5
Total	10	650	1601	177	445	91	16	39	265	140	165	.278	.339	.428	98	-5	-7	241	17	3		-33	C/3O	-0.4

■ CHARLIE HARGREAVES
Hargreaves, Charles Russell b: 12/14/1896, Trenton, N.J. d: 5/9/79, Neptune, N.J. BR/TR, 6', 170 lbs. Deb: 7/15/23

YEAR	TM/L	G	AB	R	H	2B	3B	HR	RBI	BB	SO	AVG	OBP	SLG	PRO+	BR	/A	RC	SB	CS	SBR	FR	POS	TPR
1923	Bro-N	20	57	5	16	0	0	0	4	1	2	.281	.293	.281	54	-4	-4	5	0	0	0	-3	C	-0.5
1924	Bro-N	15	27	4	11	2	0	0	5	1	1	.407	.429	.481	148	2	2	5	0	1	-1	-1	/C	0.0
1925	Bro-N	45	83	9	23	3	1	0	13	6	1	.277	.326	.337	72	-4	-3	9	1	1	-0	1	C/1	-0.1
1926	Bro-N	85	208	14	52	13	2	2	23	19	10	.250	.316	.361	83	-6	-5	24	1			4	C	0.1
1927	Bro-N	46	133	9	38	3	1	0	11	14	7	.286	.362	.323	85	-2	-2	16	1			-1	C	0.0
1928	Bro-N	20	61	3	12	2	0	0	5	6	6	.197	.269	.230	32	-6	-6	4	1			2	C	-0.2
	Pit-N	79	260	15	74	8	2	1	32	12	9	.285	.319	.342	70	-10	-12	28	1			-6	C	-1.1
	Yr	99	321	18	86	10	2	1	37	18	15	.268	.309	.321	63	-16	-18	31	2			-4		-1.3
1929	Pit-N	102	328	33	88	12	5	1	44	16	12	.268	.306	.345	60	-20	-21	34	1			2	*C	-0.9
1930	Pit-N	11	31	4	7	1	0	0	2	2	1	.226	.273	.258	29	-4	-4	2	0			6	C	0.2
Total	8	423	1188	96	321	44	11	4	139	77	49	.270	.318	.336	69	-54	-55	126	6	2		4	C/1	-2.5

■ MIKE HARGROVE
Hargrove, Dudley Michael b: 10/26/49, Perryton, Tex. BL/TL, 6', 195 lbs. Deb: 4/07/74 C

YEAR	TM/L	G	AB	R	H	2B	3B	HR	RBI	BB	SO	AVG	OBP	SLG	PRO+	BR	/A	RC	SB	CS	SBR	FR	POS	TPR
1974	Tex-A	131	415	57	134	18	6	4	66	49	42	.323	.400	.424	141	21	23	71	0	0	0	10	1D/O	2.9
1975	Tex-A	145	519	82	157	22	2	11	62	79	66	.303	.399	.416	132	24	25	88	4	3	-1	-1	O1D	1.8
1976	Tex-A	151	541	80	155	30	1	7	58	**97**	64	.287	.401	.384	128	26	24	91	2	3	-1	1	*1/D	1.8
1977	Tex-A	153	525	98	160	28	4	18	69	103	59	.305	.424	.476	143	38	37	110	2	5	-2	-0	*1	2.5
1978	Tex-A	146	494	63	124	24	1	7	40	**107**	47	.251	.391	.346	109	12	12	73	2	5	-2	7	*1/D	1.1
1979	SD-N	52	125	15	24	5	0	0	8	25	15	.192	.327	.232	59	-7	-6	11	0	2	-1	-2	1	-1.0
	Cle-A	100	338	60	110	21	4	10	56	63	40	.325	.438	.500	152	28	28	76	2	3	-1	-5	O1/D	1.7
1980	Cle-A	160	589	86	179	22	2	11	85	111	36	.304	.421	.404	127	29	28	105	4	2	0	-5	*1	1.3
1981	Cle-A	94	322	43	102	21	0	2	49	60	16	.317	**.432**	.401	143	21	22	57	5	4	-1	6	1/D	2.5
1982	Cle-A	160	591	67	160	26	1	4	65	101	58	.271	.380	.338	100	4	4	79	2	2	-1	11	*1/D	1.1
1983	Cle-A	134	469	57	134	21	4	3	57	78	40	.286	.393	.367	107	11	8	71	0	6	-4	12	*1/D	1.1
1984	Cle-A	133	352	44	94	14	2	2	44	53	38	.267	.363	.335	93	-1	-1	43	0	2	-1	6	*1	-0.4
1985	Cle-A	107	284	31	81	14	1	1	27	39	29	.285	.372	.352	100	1	2	38	1	0	0	3	1/OD	0.0
Total	12	1666	5564	783	1614	266	28	80	686	965	550	.290	.400	.391	121	208	206	914	24	37	-15	42	*1O/D	16.4

■ TIM HARKNESS
Harkness, Thomas William b: 12/23/37, Lachine, Que., Can. BL/TL, 6'2", 182 lbs. Deb: 9/12/61

YEAR	TM/L	G	AB	R	H	2B	3B	HR	RBI	BB	SO	AVG	OBP	SLG	PRO+	BR	/A	RC	SB	CS	SBR	FR	POS	TPR
1961	LA-N	5	8	4	4	2	0	0	0	3	1	.500	.636	.750	245	2	2	5	1	0	0	0	/1	0.2
1962	LA-N	92	62	9	16	2	0	2	7	10	20	.258	.370	.387	110	1	1	10	1	0	0	1	1	0.0

YEAR	TM/L	G	AB	R	H	2B	3B	HR	RBI	BB	SO	AVG	OBP	SLG	PRO+	BR	/A	RC	SB	CS	SBR	FR	POS	TPR
1963	NY-N	123	375	35	79	12	3	10	41	36	79	.211	.292	.339	80	-9	-10	38	4	3	-1	17	*1	0.5
1964	NY-N	39	117	11	33	2	1	2	13	9	18	.282	.339	.368	101	-0	0	13	1	1	-0	4	1	0.3
Total	4	259	562	59	132	18	4	14	61	58	118	.235	.316	.356	90	-6	-6	66	7	4	-0	21	1	1.0

■ DICK HARLEY
Harley, Richard Joseph b: 9/25/1872, Philadelphia, Pa. d: 4/3/52, Philadelphia, Pa. BL/TR, 5'10.5", 165 lbs. Deb: 6/02/1897

YEAR	TM/L	G	AB	R	H	2B	3B	HR	RBI	BB	SO	AVG	OBP	SLG	PRO+	BR	/A	RC	SB	CS	SBR	FR	POS	TPR
1897	StL-N	89	330	43	96	6	4	3	35	36		.291	.379	.361	100	1	2	55	23			1	*O	-0.2
1898	StL-N	142	549	74	135	6	5	0	42	34		.246	.315	.275	70	-18	-20	53	13			9	*O	-1.7
1899	Cle-N	142	567	70	142	15	7	1	50	40		.250	.315	.307	79	-20	-13	61	15			5	*O	-1.5
1900	Cin-N	5	21	2	9	1	0	0	5	1		.429	.455	.476	164	2	2	7	4			-1	/O	0.0
1901	Cin-N	133	535	69	146	13	2	4	27	31		.273	.316	.327	95	-7	-2	71	37			-5	*O	-2.0
1902	Det-A	125	491	59	138	9	8	2	44	36		.281	.343	.344	91	-4	-5	68	20			-2	*O	-1.3
1903	Chi-N	104	386	72	89	9	1	0	33	45		.231	.311	.259	67	-16	-14	42	27			3	*O	-1.5
Total	7	740	2879	389	755	59	27	10	236	223		.262	.328	.312	84	-62	-51	357	139			10	O	-8.2

■ LARRY HARLOW
Harlow, Larry Duane b: 11/13/51, Colorado Springs, Colo. BL/TR, 6'2", 185 lbs. Deb: 9/20/75

YEAR	TM/L	G	AB	R	H	2B	3B	HR	RBI	BB	SO	AVG	OBP	SLG	PRO+	BR	/A	RC	SB	CS	SBR	FR	POS	TPR
1975	Bal-A	4	3	1	1	0	0	0	0	0	1	.333	.333	.333	95	-0	-0	0	0	0	0	0	/O	0.0
1977	Bal-A	46	48	4	10	0	1	0	0	5	8	.208	.283	.250	50	-3	-3	4	6	1	1	3	O	0.0
1978	Bal-A	147	460	67	112	25	1	8	26	55	72	.243	.326	.354	97	-5	-1	53	14	11	-2	-10	*O/P	-1.7
1979	Bal-A	38	41	5	11	1	0	0	1	7	4	.268	.375	.293	86	-1	-0	4	1	3	-2	1	O	-0.1
	*Cal-A	62	159	22	37	8	2	0	14	25	34	.233	.344	.308	80	-4	-3	18	1	3	-2	4	O	-0.2
	Yr	100	200	27	48	9	2	0	15	32	38	.240	.350	.305	81	-5	-4	22	2	6	-3	5		-0.3
1980	Cal-A	109	301	47	83	13	4	4	27	48	61	.276	.377	.385	112	6	7	45	3	2	-0	11	O/1D	1.5
1981	Cal-A	43	82	13	17	1	0	0	4	16	25	.207	.337	.220	63	-3	-3	7	1	1	-0	-2	O	-0.6
Total	6	449	1094	159	271	48	8	12	72	156	205	.248	.344	.339	94	-11	-5	132	26	21	-5	7	O/D1P	-1.1

■ BILL HARMAN
Harman, William Bell b: 1/2/19, Bridgewater, Va. BR/TR, 6'4", 200 lbs. Deb: 6/17/41

YEAR	TM/L	G	AB	R	H	2B	3B	HR	RBI	BB	SO	AVG	OBP	SLG	PRO+	BR	/A	RC	SB	CS	SBR	FR	POS	TPR
1941	Phi-N	15	14	1	1	0	0	0	0	0	3	.071	.071	.071	-62	-3	-3	0	0			-1	/PC	-0.1

■ CHUCK HARMON
Harmon, Charles Byron b: 4/23/26, Washington, Ind. BR/TR, 6'2", 175 lbs. Deb: 4/17/54

YEAR	TM/L	G	AB	R	H	2B	3B	HR	RBI	BB	SO	AVG	OBP	SLG	PRO+	BR	/A	RC	SB	CS	SBR	FR	POS	TPR
1954	Cin-N	94	286	39	68	7	3	2	25	17	27	.238	.283	.304	52	-20	-21	26	7	3	0	4	3/1	-1.5
1955	Cin-N	96	198	31	50	6	3	5	28	26	24	.253	.348	.389	90	-1	-2	27	9	9	-3	5	3O/1	0.0
1956	Cin-N	13	4	2	0	0	0	0	0	0	0	.000	.000	.000	-94	-1	-1	0	1	0	0	1	/O1	0.0
	StL-N	20	15	2	0	0	0	0	0	2	2	.000	.118	.000	-65	-4	-4	0	0	0	0	0	O/13	-0.3
	Yr	33	19	4	0	0	0	0	0	2	2	.000	.095	.000	-70	-5	-5	0	1	0	0	1		-0.3
1957	StL-N	9	3	2	1	0	1	0	1	0	1	.333	.333	1.000	236	1	1	1	1	0	0	1	/O	0.1
	Phi-N	57	86	14	22	2	1	0	5	1	4	.256	.264	.302	53	-6	-6	6	7	2	1	3	O/31	-0.2
	Yr	66	89	16	23	2	2	0	6	1	4	.258	.267	.326	60	-5	-5	7	8	2	1	4		-0.1
Total	4	289	592	90	141	15	8	7	59	46	57	.238	.298	.326	62	-31	-33	60	25	14	-1	14	3/O1	-1.9

■ TERRY HARMON
Harmon, Terry Walter b: 4/12/44, Toledo, Ohio BR/TR, 6'2", 180 lbs. Deb: 7/23/67

YEAR	TM/L	G	AB	R	H	2B	3B	HR	RBI	BB	SO	AVG	OBP	SLG	PRO+	BR	/A	RC	SB	CS	SBR	FR	POS	TPR
1967	Phi-N	2	0	0	0	0	0	0	0	0	0	—	—	—	—	0	0	0	0	0	0	0	R	0.0
1969	Phi-N	87	201	25	48	8	1	0	16	22	31	.239	.323	.289	74	-7	-6	20	1	2	-1	8	S2/3	0.8
1970	Phi-N	71	129	16	32	2	4	0	7	12	22	.248	.317	.326	75	-5	-4	14	6	3	0	-2	S2/3	0.0
1971	Phi-N	79	221	27	45	4	2	0	12	20	45	.204	.282	.240	49	-14	-14	17	3	2	-0	8	2/S31	-0.2
1972	Phi-N	73	218	35	62	8	2	2	13	29	28	.284	.373	.367	108	4	4	32	3	2	-0	-1	2S/3	0.8
1973	Phi-N	72	148	17	31	3	0	0	8	13	14	.209	.278	.230	41	-11	-12	10	1	0	0	2	2S/3	-0.5
1974	Phi-N	27	15	5	2	0	0	0	0	3	3	.133	.278	.133	17	-2	-2	1	0	0	0	3	/S2	0.2
1975	Phi-N	48	72	14	13	1	2	0	5	9	13	.181	.280	.250	46	-5	-5	5	0	0	0	1	S/23	0.0
1976	*Phi-N	42	61	12	18	4	1	0	6	3	10	.295	.328	.393	101	-0	-0	8	3	0	1	3	S2/3	0.7
1977	Phi-N	46	60	13	11	1	0	2	5	6	9	.183	.269	.300	50	-4	-4	4	0	2	-1	8	2S/3	0.6
Total	10	547	1125	164	262	31	12	4	72	117	175	.233	.312	.292	69	-43	-44	112	17	11	-2	29	2S/31	2.4

■ BRIAN HARPER
Harper, Brian David b: 10/16/59, Los Angeles, Cal. BR/TR, 6'2", 195 lbs. Deb: 9/29/79

YEAR	TM/L	G	AB	R	H	2B	3B	HR	RBI	BB	SO	AVG	OBP	SLG	PRO+	BR	/A	RC	SB	CS	SBR	FR	POS	TPR
1979	Cal-A	1	2	0	0	0	0	0	0	0	1	.000	.000	.000	-99	-1	-1	0	0	0	0	0	/H	0.0
1981	Cal-A	4	11	1	3	0	0	0	1	0	0	.273	.273	.273	58	-1	-1	1	1	0	0	-0	/OD	0.0
1982	Pit-N	20	29	4	8	1	0	2	4	1	4	.276	.300	.517	121	1	1	4	0	0	0	0	/O	0.0
1983	Pit-N	61	131	16	29	4	1	7	20	2	15	.221	.239	.427	79	-4	-5	12	0	0	0	-4	O/1	-0.9
1984	Pit-N	46	112	4	29	4	0	2	11	5	11	.259	.303	.348	82	-3	-3	11	0	0	0	-1	O/C	-0.4
1985	*StL-N	43	52	5	13	4	0	0	8	2	3	.250	.278	.327	95	-2	-2	4	0	0	0	-1	O/3C1	-0.3
1986	Det-A	19	36	2	5	1	0	0	3	3	3	.139	.205	.167	3	-5	-5	1	0	0	0	0	O/C1D	-0.4
1987	Oak-A	11	17	1	4	1	0	0	3	0	4	.235	.235	.294	42	-1	-1	1	0	0	0	0	/OD	0.0
1988	Min-A	60	166	15	49	11	1	3	20	10	12	.295	.346	.428	104	3	3	20	0	3	-2	-7	C/3D	-0.3
1989	Min-A	126	385	43	125	24	0	8	57	13	16	.325	.356	.449	118	12	9	57	2	4	-2	-14	*CD/O13	-0.2
1990	Min-A	134	479	61	141	42	3	6	54	19	27	.294	.331	.432	104	6	2	62	3	2	-0	2	*CD/31	0.6
Total	11	525	1420	152	406	92	5	28	181	55	96	.286	.321	.417	100	5	-3	173	6	9	-4	-25	CO/D31	-1.9

■ GEORGE HARPER
Harper, George Washington b: 6/24/1892, Arlington, Ky. d: 8/18/78, Magnolia, Ark. BL/TR, 5'8", 167 lbs. Deb: 4/15/16

YEAR	TM/L	G	AB	R	H	2B	3B	HR	RBI	BB	SO	AVG	OBP	SLG	PRO+	BR	/A	RC	SB	CS	SBR	FR	POS	TPR
1916	Det-A	44	56	4	9	1	0	0	3	5	8	.161	.230	.179	22	-5	-5	2	0			-4	O	-1.0
1917	Det-A	47	117	6	24	3	0	0	12	11	15	.205	.290	.231	59	-5	-5	9	2			-3	O	-1.0
1918	Det-A	69	227	19	55	5	2	0	16	18	14	.242	.301	.282	79	-7	-6	21	3			-1	O	-1.1
1922	Cin-N	128	430	67	146	22	8	2	68	35	22	.340	.397	.442	118	11	12	75	11	10	-3	-1	*O	0.4
1923	Cin-N	61	125	14	32	4	2	3	16	11	9	.256	.316	.392	88	-3	-2	15	0	2	-1	0	O	-0.4
1924	Cin-N	28	74	7	20	3	0	0	3	13	5	.270	.393	.311	92	-0	-0	10	1	3	-2	2	O	0.0
	Phi-N	109	411	68	121	26	6	16	55	38	23	.294	.361	.504	115	16	9	72	10	11	-4	2	*O	0.5
	Yr	137	485	75	141	29	6	16	58	51	28	.291	.366	.474	113	16	10	82	11	14	-5	4		0.5
1925	Phi-N	132	495	86	173	35	7	18	97	28	32	.349	.391	.558	128	28	21	105	10	8	-2	9	*O	2.3
1926	Phi-N	56	194	32	61	6	5	7	38	16	7	.314	.367	.505	126	8	8	35	6			-4	O	0.1
1927	NY-N	145	483	85	160	19	6	16	87	84	27	.331	.435	.495	149	37	37	106	7			-2	*O	2.9
1928	NY-N	19	57	11	13	1	0	2	7	10	4	.228	.353	.351	84	-1	-1	8	1			3	O	0.1
	*StL-N	99	272	41	83	8	2	17	58	51	15	.305	.418	.537	145	20	20	62	2			0	O	1.6
	Yr	118	329	52	96	9	2	19	65	61	19	.292	.407	.505	135	19	18	69	3			3		1.7
1929	Bos-N	136	457	65	133	25	5	10	68	69	27	.291	.389	.433	108	4	7	79	5			-6	*O	-0.9
Total	11	1073	3398	505	1030	158	43	91	528	389	208	.303	.380	.455	118	103	94	597	58	34		-5	O	3.5

■ TERRY HARPER
Harper, Terry Joe b: 8/19/55, Douglasville, Ga. BR/TR, 6'4", 195 lbs. Deb: 9/12/80

YEAR	TM/L	G	AB	R	H	2B	3B	HR	RBI	BB	SO	AVG	OBP	SLG	PRO+	BR	/A	RC	SB	CS	SBR	FR	POS	TPR
1980	Atl-N	21	54	3	10	2	1	0	3	6	5	.185	.279	.259	49	-3	-4	4	2	1	0	-1	O	-0.5
1981	Atl-N	40	73	9	19	1	0	2	8	11	17	.260	.357	.356	100	1	0	10	5	1	1	1	O	0.1
1982	*Atl-N	48	150	16	43	3	0	2	16	14	28	.287	.352	.347	92	-0	-1	19	7	4	-0	-0	O	-0.1
1983	Atl-N	80	201	19	53	13	1	3	26	20	43	.264	.333	.383	91	-1	-2	24	6	5	-1	-0	O	-0.4
1984	Atl-N	40	102	4	16	3	1	0	8	4	21	.157	.196	.206	12	-12	-13	3	1	1	1	3	O	-1.0
1985	Atl-N	138	492	58	130	15	2	17	72	44	76	.264	.328	.407	98	2	-1	62	9	9	-3	-7	*O	-1.4
1986	Atl-N	106	265	26	68	12	0	8	30	29	39	.257	.332	.392	94	-0	-2	30	3	6	-3	-8	O	-1.4
1987	Det-A	31	64	4	13	3	0	3	10	9	8	.203	.301	.391	85	-2	-1	8	1	0	0	0	DO	-0.2
	Pit-N	36	66	8	19	3	0	1	7	7	11	.288	.356	.379	94	-0	-0	7	0	1	-1	-1	O	-0.2
Total	8	540	1467	147	371	55	5	36	180	144	248	.253	.323	.371	88	-16	-24	167	37	28	-6	-14	O/D	-4.9

YEAR	TM/L	G	AB	R	H	2B	3B	HR	RBI	BB	SO	AVG	OBP	SLG	PRO+	BR	/A	RC	SB	CS	SBR	FR	POS	TPR

■ TOMMY HARPER
Harper, Tommy　b: 10/14/40, Oak Grove, La.　BR/TR, 5'9", 165 lbs.　Deb: 4/09/62　C

YEAR	TM/L	G	AB	R	H	2B	3B	HR	RBI	BB	SO	AVG	OBP	SLG	PRO+	BR	/A	RC	SB	CS	SBR	FR	POS	TPR
1962	Cin-N	6	23	1	4	0	0	0	1	2	6	.174	.240	.174	13	-3	-3	1	1	0	0	-1	/3	-0.3
1963	Cin-N	129	408	67	106	12	3	10	37	44	72	.260	.336	.377	102	3	2	54	12	1	3	5	*O/3	0.4
1964	Cin-N	102	317	42	77	5	2	4	22	39	56	.243	.328	.309	78	-7	-8	37	24	3	5	-0	O/3	-0.5
1965	Cin-N	159	646	126	166	28	3	18	64	78	127	.257	.342	.393	99	7	1	94	35	6	7	-2	*O/32	0.1
1966	Cin-N	149	553	85	154	22	5	5	31	57	85	.278	.349	.363	91	0	-5	74	29	10	3	2	*O	-0.5
1967	Cin-N	103	365	55	82	17	3	7	22	43	51	.225	.306	.345	77	-6	-11	42	23	8	2	8	*O	-0.5
1968	Cle-N	130	235	26	51	15	2	6	26	26	56	.217	.298	.374	104	1	1	26	11	7	-1	-18	*O/2	-2.5
1969	Sea-A	148	537	78	126	10	2	9	41	95	90	.235	.351	.311	88	-7	-5	71	73	18	11	-15	23O	-0.7
1970	Mil-A	154	604	104	179	35	4	31	82	77	107	.296	.380	.522	145	37	37	122	38	16	2	-2	*32O	3.9
1971	Mil-A	152	585	79	151	26	3	14	52	65	92	.258	.333	.385	104	2	3	82	25	3	6	-22	O3/2	-1.9
1972	Bos-A	144	556	92	141	29	2	14	49	67	104	.254	.343	.388	111	13	10	81	25	7	3	-4	*O	0.6
1973	Bos-A	147	566	92	159	23	3	17	71	61	93	.281	.352	.422	111	13	9	91	54	14	8	-1	*O/D	1.1
1974	Bos-A	118	443	66	105	15	3	5	24	46	65	.237	.313	.318	77	-10	-13	47	28	12	1	-8	OD	-2.2
1975	Cal-A	89	285	40	68	10	1	3	31	38	51	.239	.332	.312	89	-5	-3	32	19	8	1	-2	D1/O	-0.4
	*Oak-A	34	69	11	22	4	0	2	7	5	9	.319	.373	.464	139	3	3	12	7	0	2	-2	1/O3D	0.3
	Yr	123	354	51	90	14	1	5	38	43	60	.254	.340	.342	99	-2	0	44	26	8	3	-4		-0.1
1976	Bal-A	46	77	8	18	5	0	1	7	10	16	.234	.322	.338	99	-1	0	9	4	3	-1	-0	D/1O	-0.3
Total	15	1810	6269	972	1609	256	36	146	567	753	1080	.257	.340	.379	100	41	16	876	408	116	53	-61	*O3D/21	-3.1

■ TOBY HARRAH
Harrah, Colbert Dale　b: 10/26/48, Sissonville, W.Va.　BR/TR, 6', 175 lbs.　Deb: 9/05/69　C

YEAR	TM/L	G	AB	R	H	2B	3B	HR	RBI	BB	SO	AVG	OBP	SLG	PRO+	BR	/A	RC	SB	CS	SBR	FR	POS	TPR
1969	Was-A	8	1	4	0	0	0	0	0	0	0	.000	.000	.000	-99	-0	-0	0	0	0	0	0	/S	0.0
1971	Was-A	127	383	45	88	11	3	2	22	40	48	.230	.303	.290	73	-15	-13	33	10	9	-2	-7	*S/3	-0.9
1972	Tex-A	116	374	47	97	14	3	1	31	34	31	.259	.321	.321	95	-4	-2	41	16	7	1	-9	*S	0.1
1973	Tex-A	118	461	64	120	16	1	10	50	46	49	.260	.330	.364	100	-3	-0	56	10	3	1	-13	S3	-0.2
1974	Tex-A	161	573	79	149	23	2	21	74	50	65	.260	.322	.417	114	7	9	72	15	14	-4	-2	*S/3	1.6
1975	Tex-A	151	522	81	153	24	1	20	93	98	71	.293	.406	.458	145	34	34	105	23	9	2	14	*S32	6.2
1976	Tex-A	155	584	64	152	21	1	15	67	91	59	.260	.363	.377	114	15	13	82	8	5	-1	-0	*S/3D	2.3
1977	Tex-A	159	539	90	142	25	5	27	87	109	73	.263	.397	.479	136	32	31	112	27	5	5	-24	*3/S	0.9
1978	Tex-A	139	450	56	103	17	3	12	59	83	66	.229	.351	.360	100	3	3	65	31	8	5	-9	3S	0.1
1979	Cle-A	149	527	99	147	25	1	20	77	89	60	.279	.391	.444	124	21	21	98	20	9	1	-48	*3S/D	-1.9
1980	Cle-A	160	561	100	150	22	4	11	72	98	60	.267	.383	.380	109	12	11	89	17	2	4	2	*3/SD	1.7
1981	Cle-A	103	361	64	105	12	4	5	44	57	44	.291	.389	.388	126	14	14	60	12	1	3	-11	*3/SD	0.7
1982	Cle-A	162	602	100	183	29	4	25	78	84	52	.304	.400	.490	144	38	38	123	17	3	3	-19	*3/2S	2.0
1983	Cle-A	138	526	81	140	23	1	9	53	75	49	.266	.365	.365	98	4	1	73	16	10	-1	-11	*3/2D	-1.0
1984	NY-A	88	253	40	55	9	4	1	26	42	28	.217	.333	.296	79	-7	-6	27	3	0	1	3	3/2OD	0.0
1985	Tex-A	126	396	65	107	18	1	9	44	113	60	.270	.437	.389	127	23	22	80	11	4	1	-17	*2/SD	1.1
1986	Tex-A	95	289	36	63	18	2	7	41	44	53	.218	.325	.367	86	-4	-5	35	2	5	-2	-20	2	-2.1
Total	17	2155	7402	1115	1954	307	40	195	918	1153	868	.264	.368	.395	114	169	173	1152	238	94	15	-169	*3S2/DO	10.6

■ JOHN HARRELL
Harrell, John Robert　b: 11/27/47, Long Beach, Cal.　BR/TR, 6'2", 190 lbs.　Deb: 10/01/69

YEAR	TM/L	G	AB	R	H	2B	3B	HR	RBI	BB	SO	AVG	OBP	SLG	PRO+	BR	/A	RC	SB	CS	SBR	FR	POS	TPR
1969	SF-N	2	6	0	3	0	0	0	2	2	1	.500	.625	.500	223	1	1	2	0	0	0	-0	/C	0.1

■ BILLY HARRELL
Harrell, William　b: 7/18/28, Norristown, Pa.　BR/TR, 6'1.5", 180 lbs.　Deb: 9/02/55

YEAR	TM/L	G	AB	R	H	2B	3B	HR	RBI	BB	SO	AVG	OBP	SLG	PRO+	BR	/A	RC	SB	CS	SBR	FR	POS	TPR
1955	Cle-A	13	19	2	8	0	0	1	3	3	3	.421	.500	.421	144	2	2	5	1	0	-0	-0	S	0.3
1957	Cle-A	22	57	6	15	1	1	1	5	4	7	.263	.311	.368	86	-1	-1	7	3	1	0	-4	S/32	-0.3
1958	Cle-A	101	229	36	50	4	0	7	19	15	36	.218	.272	.328	66	-12	-11	22	12	2	2	-6	3S/2O	-0.5
1961	Bos-A	37	37	10	6	2	0	0	1	1	8	.162	.184	.216	6	-5	-5	1	1	0	0	7	3/S1	0.3
Total	4	173	342	54	79	7	1	8	26	23	54	.231	.283	.327	68	-16	-16	35	17	3	4	-4	/S3210	-0.2

■ BUD HARRELSON
Harrelson, Derrel McKinley　b: 6/6/44, Niles, Cal.　BB/TR, 5'11", 160 lbs.　Deb: 9/02/65　CM

YEAR	TM/L	G	AB	R	H	2B	3B	HR	RBI	BB	SO	AVG	OBP	SLG	PRO+	BR	/A	RC	SB	CS	SBR	FR	POS	TPR
1965	NY-N	19	37	3	4	1	1	0	0	2	11	.108	.154	.189	-4	-5	-5	1	0	0	0	4	S	0.1
1966	NY-N	33	99	20	22	2	4	0	4	13	23	.222	.313	.323	79	-3	-3	11	7	3	0	5	S	0.5
1967	NY-N	151	540	59	137	16	4	1	28	48	64	.254	.319	.304	80	-13	-12	54	12	13	-4	7	*S	0.8
1968	NY-N	111	402	38	88	7	3	0	14	29	68	.219	.273	.251	58	-20	-20	28	4	5	-2	-5	*S	-1.5
1969	*NY-N	123	395	42	98	11	6	0	24	54	54	.248	.341	.306	81	-7	-8	44	1	3	-2	-5	*S	0.0
1970	NY-N	157	564	72	137	18	8	1	42	95	74	.243	.355	.309	79	-13	-13	72	23	4	5	-28	*S	-1.6
1971	NY-N	142	547	55	138	16	6	0	32	53	59	.252	.321	.303	79	-15	-14	57	28	7	4	11	*S	2.1
1972	NY-N	115	418	54	90	10	4	1	24	58	57	.215	.315	.266	68	-17	-15	40	12	4	1	-11	*S	-1.2
1973	*NY-N	106	356	35	92	12	3	0	20	48	49	.258	.348	.309	85	-6	-6	42	5	1	1	-2	*S	0.7
1974	NY-N	106	331	48	75	10	0	1	13	71	39	.227	.366	.266	80	-6	-5	39	9	4	0	16	S	2.2
1975	NY-N	34	73	5	16	2	0	0	3	12	13	.219	.329	.247	65	-3	-3	7	0	0	1	5	S	0.2
1976	NY-N	118	359	34	84	12	4	1	26	63	56	.234	.351	.298	91	-4	-1	44	9	3	1	-5	*S	0.6
1977	NY-N	107	269	25	48	6	2	1	12	27	28	.178	.256	.227	32	-26	-25	17	5	4	-1	-1	S	-1.3
1978	Phi-N	71	103	16	22	1	0	0	9	18	21	.214	.331	.223	57	-5	-5	10	5	2	0	15	2S	1.4
1979	Phi-N	53	71	7	20	6	0	0	7	13	14	.282	.400	.366	107	2	1	11	3	3	-1	6	2S/3O	1.0
1980	Tex-A	87	180	26	49	6	0	1	9	29	23	.272	.373	.322	95	-1	-0	24	4	4	-1	11	S/2	1.7
Total	16	1533	4744	539	1120	136	45	7	267	633	653	.236	.324	.288	75	-142	-133	502	127	60	2	17	*S/23O	5.7

■ KEN HARRELSON
Harrelson, Kenneth Smith "Hawk"　b: 9/4/41, Woodruff, S.C.　BR/TR, 6'2", 190 lbs.　Deb: 6/09/63

YEAR	TM/L	G	AB	R	H	2B	3B	HR	RBI	BB	SO	AVG	OBP	SLG	PRO+	BR	/A	RC	SB	CS	SBR	FR	POS	TPR
1963	KC-A	79	226	16	52	10	1	6	23	23	58	.230	.301	.363	82	-5	-6	23	1	1	-0	-5	1O	-1.2
1964	KC-A	49	139	15	27	5	0	7	12	13	34	.194	.263	.381	74	-5	-5	12	0	1	-1	-1	O1	-0.8
1965	KC-A	150	483	61	115	17	3	23	66	66	112	.238	.331	.429	116	9	10	65	9	7	-2	-2	*1/O	0.0
1966	KC-A	63	210	24	47	5	0	5	22	27	59	.224	.312	.319	85	-4	-4	23	9	2	2	4	1/O	0.0
	Was-A	71	250	25	62	8	1	7	28	26	53	.248	.321	.372	100	-0	-0	30	4	1	1	-3	1	-0.4
	Yr	134	460	49	109	13	1	12	50	53	112	.237	.317	.348	93	-5	-4	53	13	3	2	1		-0.4
1967	Was-A	26	79	10	16	0	0	3	10	7	15	.203	.267	.316	75	-3	-2	6	1	0	0	1	1	-0.3
	KC-A	61	174	23	53	11	0	6	30	17	17	.305	.366	.471	151	10	10	31	8	2	1	-1	1	0.8
	*Bos-A	23	80	9	16	4	1	3	14	5	12	.200	.247	.387	79	-2	-3	7	1	1	-0	-3	O/1	-0.7
	Yr	110	333	42	85	15	1	12	54	29	44	.255	.315	.414	115	5	5	43	10	3	1	-3		-0.2
1968	Bos-A	150	535	79	147	17	4	35	109	69	90	.275	.360	.518	153	40	36	94	2	6	-3	4	*O1	3.6
1969	Bos-A	10	46	6	10	1	0	3	8	4	6	.217	.280	.435	92	-0	-1	5	0	1	-1	2	1	0.3
	Cle-A	149	519	83	115	13	4	27	84	95	96	.222	.344	.418	109	9	7	76	17	8	0	0	*O1	0.3
	Yr	159	565	89	125	14	4	30	92	99	102	.221	.339	.419	107	9	6	81	17	9	-0	2		0.3
1970	Cle-A	17	39	3	11	1	0	1	9	1	6	.282	.378	.385	106	1	1	6	0	0	1	1	1	-0.0
1971	Cle-A	52	161	20	32	2	0	5	14	24	21	.199	.303	.304	66	-6	-7	16	1	0	-1	-1	1/O	-1.0
Total	9	900	2941	374	703	94	14	131	421	382	577	.239	.328	.414	109	44	37	393	53	30	-2	-4	1O	0.3

■ ANDY HARRINGTON
Harrington, Andrew Matthew　b: 2/12/03, Mountain View, Cal　d: 1/26/79, Boise, Idaho　BR/TR, 5'11", 170 lbs.　Deb: 4/18/25

YEAR	TM/L	G	AB	R	H	2B	3B	HR	RBI	BB	SO	AVG	OBP	SLG	PRO+	BR	/A	RC	SB	CS	SBR	FR	POS	TPR
1925	Det-A	1	1	0	0	0	0	0	0	0	0	.000	.000	.000	-99	-0	-0	0	0	0	0	0	H	0.0

■ MICKEY HARRINGTON
Harrington, Charles Michael　b: 10/8/34, Hattiesburg, Miss.　BR/TR, 6'4", 205 lbs.　Deb: 7/10/63

YEAR	TM/L	G	AB	R	H	2B	3B	HR	RBI	BB	SO	AVG	OBP	SLG	PRO+	BR	/A	RC	SB	CS	SBR	FR	POS	TPR
1963	Phi-N	1	0	0	0	0	0	0	0	0	0	—	—	—	—	0	0	0	0	0	0	0	R	0.0

YEAR	TM/L	G	AB	R	H	2B	3B	HR	RBI	BB	SO	AVG	OBP	SLG	PRO+	BR	/A	RC	SB	CS	SBR	FR	POS	TPR

■ JERRY HARRINGTON Harrington, Jeremiah Peter b: 8/12/1869, Keokuk, Iowa d: 4/16/13, Keokuk, Iowa TR , 5'11", 220 lbs. Deb: 4/30/1890

YEAR	TM/L	G	AB	R	H	2B	3B	HR	RBI	BB	SO	AVG	OBP	SLG	PRO+	BR	/A	RC	SB	CS	SBR	FR	POS	TPR
1890	Cin-N	65	236	25	58	7	1	1	23	15	29	.246	.299	.297	76	-7	-7	23	4			5	C	0.3
1891	Cin-N	92	333	25	76	10	5	2	41	19	34	.228	.272	.306	69	-13	-14	30	4			-3	C/3	-0.7
1892	Cin-N	22	61	6	13	1	0	0	3	6	1	.213	.284	.230	58	-3	-3	4	0			1	C/1	0.0
1893	Lou-N	10	36	4	4	1	0	0	6	3	9	.111	.179	.139	-15	-6	-5	1	0			-3	C	-0.6
Total	4	189	666	60	151	19	6	3	73	43	73	.227	.278	.287	66	-29	-29	57	8			-0	C/13	-1.0

■ JOE HARRINGTON Harrington, Joseph C. b: 12/21/1869, Fall River, Mass. d: 9/13/33, Fall River, Mass. 5'8.5", 162 lbs. Deb: 9/10/1895

YEAR	TM/L	G	AB	R	H	2B	3B	HR	RBI	BB	SO	AVG	OBP	SLG	PRO+	BR	/A	RC	SB	CS	SBR	FR	POS	TPR
1895	Bos-N	18	65	21	18	0	2	2	13	7	5	.277	.356	.431	97	0	-1	11	3			0	2	0.1
1896	Bos-N	54	198	25	39	5	3	1	25	19	17	.197	.271	.268	41	-16	-18	15	2			-10	3/S2	-2.1
Total	2	72	263	46	57	5	5	3	38	26	22	.217	.292	.308	55	-16	-19	27	5			-10	/32S	-2.0

■ CANDY HARRIS Harris, Alonzo b: 9/17/47, Selma, Ala. BB/TR, 6', 160 lbs. Deb: 4/13/67

YEAR	TM/L	G	AB	R	H	2B	3B	HR	RBI	BB	SO	AVG	OBP	SLG	PRO+	BR	/A	RC	SB	CS	SBR	FR	POS	TPR
1967	Hou-N	6	1	0	0	0	0	0	0	0	1	.000	.000	.000	-99	-0	-0	0	0	0	0	0	H	0.0

■ SPENCER HARRIS Harris, Anthony Spencer b: 8/12/1900, Duluth, Minn. d: 7/3/82, Minneapolis, Minn. BL/TL, 5'9", 145 lbs. Deb: 4/14/25

YEAR	TM/L	G	AB	R	H	2B	3B	HR	RBI	BB	SO	AVG	OBP	SLG	PRO+	BR	/A	RC	SB	CS	SBR	FR	POS	TPR
1925	Chi-A	56	92	12	26	2	0	1	13	14	13	.283	.383	.337	89	-2	-1	12	1	3	-2	-5	O	-0.8
1926	Chi-A	80	222	36	56	11	3	2	27	20	15	.252	.317	.356	78	-8	-7	26	8	3	1	-6	O	-1.6
1929	Was-A	6	14	1	3	1	0	0	1	0	3	.214	.214	.286	27	-2	-2	1	1	0	0	-1	/O	-0.1
1930	Phi-A	22	49	4	9	1	0	0	5	5	2	.184	.259	.204	18	-6	-6	3	0	0	0	0	O	-0.5
Total	4	164	377	53	94	15	3	3	46	39	33	.249	.323	.329	70	-18	-16	43	10	6	-1	-11	O	-3.0

■ GAIL HARRIS Harris, Boyd Gail b: 10/15/31, Abingdon, Va. BL/TL, 6', 195 lbs. Deb: 6/03/55

YEAR	TM/L	G	AB	R	H	2B	3B	HR	RBI	BB	SO	AVG	OBP	SLG	PRO+	BR	/A	RC	SB	CS	SBR	FR	POS	TPR
1955	NY-N	79	263	27	61	9	0	12	36	20	46	.232	.291	.403	82	-8	-8	30	0	0	0	0	1	-1.2
1956	NY-N	12	38	2	5	0	1	1	1	3	10	.132	.233	.263	33	-4	-4	3	0	0	0	0	1	-0.3
1957	NY-N	90	225	28	54	7	3	9	31	16	28	.240	.308	.418	93	-3	-3	29	1	0	0	-2	1	-0.9
1958	Det-A	134	451	63	123	18	8	20	83	36	60	.273	.332	.481	113	11	7	70	1	2	-1	3	*1	0.5
1959	Det-A	114	349	39	77	4	3	9	39	29	49	.221	.292	.327	66	-15	-17	33	0	1	-1	3	1	-1.5
1960	Det-A	8	5	0	0	0	0	0	0	2	1	.000	.286	.000	-15	-1	-1	0	0	0	0	0	/1	0.0
Total	6	437	1331	159	320	38	15	51	190	106	194	.240	.306	.406	88	-18	-25	165	2	3	-1	4	1	-3.4

■ CHARLIE HARRIS Harris, Charles Jenkins b: 10/21/1877, Macon, Ga. d: 3/14/63, Gainesville, Fla. 5'8", 200 lbs. Deb: 5/25/1899

YEAR	TM/L	G	AB	R	H	2B	3B	HR	RBI	BB	SO	AVG	OBP	SLG	PRO+	BR	/A	RC	SB	CS	SBR	FR	POS	TPR
1899	Bal-N	30	68	16	19	3	0	0	1	3		.279	.319	.324	75	-2	-2	9	4			-5	3/O2S	-0.6

■ DAVE HARRIS Harris, David Stanley "Sheriff" b: 7/14/1900, Summerfield, N.C. d: 9/18/73, Atlanta, Ga. BR/TR, 5'11", 170 lbs. Deb: 4/14/25

YEAR	TM/L	G	AB	R	H	2B	3B	HR	RBI	BB	SO	AVG	OBP	SLG	PRO+	BR	/A	RC	SB	CS	SBR	FR	POS	TPR
1925	Bos-N	92	340	49	90	8	7	5	36	27	44	.265	.321	.374	84	-12	-8	41	6	4	-1	3	O	-0.6
1928	Bos-N	7	17	2	2	1	0	0	0	2	6	.118	.211	.176	2	-2	-2	1	0			-1	/O	-0.2
1930	Chi-A	33	86	16	21	2	1	5	13	7	22	.244	.309	.465	96	-1	-1	13	0	0	0	-0	O/2	-0.1
	Was-A	73	205	40	65	19	8	4	44	28	35	.317	.399	.546	137	12	11	45	6	3	0	1	O	0.9
	Yr	106	291	56	86	21	9	9	57	35	57	.296	.373	.522	125	10	11	57	6	3	0	1		0.8
1931	Was-A	77	231	49	72	14	8	5	50	49	38	.312	.434	.506	146	18	17	53	7	6	-2	-2	O	0.9
1932	Was-A	81	156	26	51	7	4	6	29	19	34	.327	.400	.538	143	9	10	33	4	4	-1	-0	O	0.6
1933	*Was-A	82	177	33	46	9	2	5	38	25	26	.260	.358	.418	106	1	2	28	3	1	0	-3	O/13	-0.2
1934	Was-A	97	235	28	59	14	3	2	37	39	40	.251	.358	.362	89	-4	-3	32	2	3	-1	-0	O/3	-0.4
Total	7	542	1447	243	406	74	33	32	247	196	245	.281	.368	.444	112	20	26	246	28	21		-2	O/312	0.9

■ FRANK HARRIS Harris, Frank W. b: 11/2/1858, Pittsburgh, Pa. d: 11/26/39, E.Moline, Ill. Deb: 4/17/1884

YEAR	TM/L	G	AB	R	H	2B	3B	HR	RBI	BB	SO	AVG	OBP	SLG	PRO+	BR	/A	RC	SB	CS	SBR	FR	POS	TPR
1884	Alt-U	24	95	10	25	2	1	0		3		.263	.286	.305	98	-0	-0	8	0			-0	1/O	0.0

■ BILLY HARRIS Harris, James William b: 11/24/43, Hamlet, N.C. BL/TR, 6', 175 lbs. Deb: 6/16/68

YEAR	TM/L	G	AB	R	H	2B	3B	HR	RBI	BB	SO	AVG	OBP	SLG	PRO+	BR	/A	RC	SB	CS	SBR	FR	POS	TPR
1968	Cle-A	38	94	10	20	5	1	0	3	8	22	.213	.275	.287	71	-3	-3	7	2	0	1	-1	23/S	-0.2
1969	KC-A	5	7	1	2	1	0	0	0	0	1	.286	.286	.429	97	-0	-0	1	0	0	0	-0	/2	0.0
Total	2	43	101	11	22	6	1	0	3	8	23	.218	.275	.297	73	-3	-3	8	2	0	1	-1	/23S	-0.2

■ JOHN HARRIS Harris, John Thomas b: 9/13/54, Portland, Ore. BL/TL, 6'3", 205 lbs. Deb: 9/26/79

YEAR	TM/L	G	AB	R	H	2B	3B	HR	RBI	BB	SO	AVG	OBP	SLG	PRO+	BR	/A	RC	SB	CS	SBR	FR	POS	TPR
1979	Cal-A	1	2	0	0	0	0	0	0	0	0	.000	.000	.000	-99	-1	-1	0	0	0	0	0	/1	0.0
1980	Cal-A	19	41	8	12	5	0	2	7	7	4	.293	.396	.561	163	3	4	8	0	1	-1	-0	1/O	0.2
1981	Cal-A	36	77	5	19	3	0	3	9	3	11	.247	.275	.403	93	-1	-1	7	0	0	0	-2	1O/D	-0.2
Total	3	56	120	13	31	8	0	5	16	10	15	.258	.315	.450	115	2	2	15	0	1	-1	-2	/1OD	0.0

■ JOE HARRIS Harris, Joseph "Moon" b: 5/30/1891, Coulters, Pa. d: 12/10/59, Renton, Pa. BR/TR, 5'9", 170 lbs. Deb: 6/09/14

YEAR	TM/L	G	AB	R	H	2B	3B	HR	RBI	BB	SO	AVG	OBP	SLG	PRO+	BR	/A	RC	SB	CS	SBR	FR	POS	TPR
1914	NY-A	2	1	0	0	0	0	0	0	3	1	.000	.800	.000	143	1	1	1	0			-0	/1O	0.0
1917	Cle-A	112	369	40	112	22	4	0	65	55	32	.304	.398	.385	129	19	16	59	11			10	1/O3	2.5
1919	Cle-A	62	184	30	69	16	1	1	46	33	21	.375	.472	.489	160	19	18	43	2			2	1/S	1.7
1922	Bos-A	119	408	53	129	30	9	6	54	30	15	.316	.364	.478	119	9	10	69	2	6	-3	7	O1	0.6
1923	Bos-A	142	483	82	162	28	11	13	76	52	27	.335	.406	.520	142	29	29	104	7	3	0	-2	*O/1	1.4
1924	Bos-A	133	491	82	148	36	9	3	77	81	25	.301	.406	.430	115	14	14	92	6	1	1	6	*1/O	1.4
1925	Bos-A	8	19	3	3	0	1	1	2	5	5	.158	.333	.421	90	-0	-0	3	0	0	0	-1	/1	0.0
	*Was-A	100	300	60	97	21	9	12	59	51	28	.323	.430	.573	156	25	26	76	5	3	-0	-0	1O	1.8
	Yr	108	319	64	100	21	10	13	61	56	33	.313	.424	.564	152	24	25	79	5	3	-0	-1		1.8
1926	Was-A	92	257	43	79	13	9	5	55	37	9	.307	.405	.486	135	12	13	52	2	3	-1	-3	1O	0.5
1927	*Pit-N	129	411	57	134	27	9	5	73	48	19	.326	.402	.472	125	20	16	78	0			3	*1/O	1.1
1928	Pit-N	16	23	2	9	2	1	0	2	4	2	.391	.500	.565	171	3	3	7	0			1	/1	0.3
	Bro-N	55	89	8	21	6	1	1	8	14	4	.236	.340	.360	84	-2	-2	11	0			-2	O	-0.3
	Yr	71	112	10	30	8	2	1	10	18	6	.268	.374	.402	103	1	1	17	0			-1		0.0
Total	10	970	3035	461	963	201	64	47	517	413	188	.317	.404	.472	131	150	143	595	35	16		21	1O/S3	11.0

■ LENNY HARRIS Harris, Leonard Anthony b: 10/28/64, Miami, Fla. BL/TR, 5'10", 195 lbs. Deb: 9/07/88

YEAR	TM/L	G	AB	R	H	2B	3B	HR	RBI	BB	SO	AVG	OBP	SLG	PRO+	BR	/A	RC	SB	CS	SBR	FR	POS	TPR
1988	Cin-N	16	43	7	16	1	0	0	8	5	4	.372	.438	.395	135	3	2	9	4	1	1	1	3/2	0.4
1989	Cin-N	61	188	17	42	4	0	2	11	9	20	.223	.263	.277	52	-11	-12	12	10	6	-1	1	2S3	-1.0
	LA-N	54	147	19	37	6	1	1	15	11	13	.252	.308	.327	83	-3	-3	12	4	3	-1	-7	O2/3S	-1.1
	Yr	115	335	36	79	10	1	3	26	20	33	.236	.283	.299	66	-15	-15	25	14	9	-1	-6		-2.1
1990	LA-N	137	431	61	131	16	4	2	29	29	31	.304	.349	.374	105	-0	3	55	15	10	-2	-7	32/OS	-0.2
Total	3	268	809	104	226	27	5	5	63	54	68	.279	.327	.344	90	-12	-10	88	33	20	-2	-12	3/2OS	-1.9

■ NED HARRIS Harris, Robert Ned b: 7/9/16, Ames, Iowa d: 12/18/76, W.Palm Beach, Fla. BL/TL, 5'11", 175 lbs. Deb: 4/20/41

YEAR	TM/L	G	AB	R	H	2B	3B	HR	RBI	BB	SO	AVG	OBP	SLG	PRO+	BR	/A	RC	SB	CS	SBR	FR	POS	TPR
1941	Det-A	26	61	11	13	3	1	1	4	6	13	.213	.284	.344	59	-3	-4	7	1	0	0	-3	O	-0.6
1942	Det-A	121	398	53	108	16	10	3	45	49	35	.271	.351	.430	110	9	5	63	5	4	-1	-12	*O	-1.4
1943	Det-A	114	354	43	90	14	3	6	32	47	29	.254	.343	.362	99	3	0	46	6	8	-3	-5	O	-1.0
1946	Det-A	1	1	0	0	0	0	0	0	0	0	.000	.000	.000	-94	-0	-0	0	0	0	0	0	H	0.0
Total	4	262	814	107	211	33	14	16	81	102	77	.259	.342	.393	101	9	1	115	12	12	-4	-19	O	-3.0

■ BUCKY HARRIS Harris, Stanley Raymond b: 11/8/1896, Port Jervis, N.Y. d: 11/8/77, Bethesda, Md. BR/TR, 5'9.5", 156 lbs. Deb: 8/28/19 M

YEAR	TM/L	G	AB	R	H	2B	3B	HR	RBI	BB	SO	AVG	OBP	SLG	PRO+	BR	/A	RC	SB	CS	SBR	FR	POS	TPR
1919	Was-A	8	28	0	6	2	0	0	4	1	3	.214	.267	.286	56	-2	-2	2	0			2	/2	0.1
1920	Was-A	136	506	76	152	26	6	1	68	41	36	.300	.377	.381	104	3	5	73	16	17	-5	-10	*2	-0.7

YEAR	TM/L	G	AB	R	H	2B	3B	HR	RBI	BB	SO	AVG	OBP	SLG	PRO+	BR	/A	RC	SB	CS	SBR	FR	POS	TPR
1921	Was-A	154	584	82	169	22	8	0	54	54	39	.289	.367	.354	89	-11	-7	83	29	9	3	12	*2	1.3
1922	Was-A	154	602	95	162	24	8	2	40	52	38	.269	.341	.346	84	-17	-13	75	25	11	1	26	*2	2.4
1923	Was-A	145	532	60	150	21	13	2	70	50	29	.282	.358	.382	100	-4	0	74	23	16	-3	20	*2/S	2.2
1924	*Was-A	143	544	88	146	28	9	1	58	56	41	.268	.344	.358	84	-15	-12	72	19	10	-0	-13	*2M	-1.9
1925	*Was-A	144	551	91	158	30	3	1	66	64	21	.287	.370	.358	87	-10	-9	77	14	12	-3	3	*2M	-0.1
1926	Was-A	141	537	94	152	39	9	1	63	58	41	.283	.363	.395	100	-2	0	80	16	11	-2	-11	*2M	-0.5
1927	Was-A	128	475	98	127	20	3	1	55	66	33	.267	.363	.328	81	-11	-11	59	18	3	4	1	*2M	0.0
1928	Was-A	99	358	34	73	11	5	0	28	27	26	.204	.264	.263	39	-32	-32	26	5	2	0	11	2/3OM	-1.5
1929	Det-A	7	11	3	1	0	0	0	0	2	2	.091	.231	.091	-14	-2	-2	1	1	0	0	0	/2SM	0.0
1931	Det-A	4	8	1	1	1	0	0	0	1	1	.125	.222	.250	23	-1	-1	0	0	0	0	0	/2M	0.0
Total	12	1263	4736	722	1297	224	64	9	506	472	310	.274	.352	.354	86	-104	-82	623	166	91		43	*2/SO3	1.3

■ VIC HARRIS
Harris, Victor Lanier b: 3/27/50, Los Angeles, Cal. BB/TR, 5'11", 165 lbs. Deb: 7/21/72

YEAR	TM/L	G	AB	R	H	2B	3B	HR	RBI	BB	SO	AVG	OBP	SLG	PRO+	BR	/A	RC	SB	CS	SBR	FR	POS	TPR
1972	Tex-A	61	186	8	26	5	1	0	10	12	39	.140	.192	.177	11	-20	-20	7	7	3	0	0	2/S	-1.7
1973	Tex-A	152	555	71	138	14	7	8	44	55	81	.249	.319	.342	90	-10	-7	58	13	12	-3	3	*O32	-0.9
1974	Chi-N	62	200	18	39	6	3	0	11	29	26	.195	.297	.255	53	-11	-12	18	9	3	1	-17	2	-2.6
1975	Chi-N	51	56	6	10	0	0	0	5	6	7	.179	.258	.179	22	-6	-6	3	0	0	0	1	O/32	-0.5
1976	StL-N	97	259	21	59	12	3	1	19	16	55	.228	.275	.309	65	-12	-12	21	1	2	-1	-5	2O3/S	-1.8
1977	SF-N	69	165	28	43	12	0	2	14	19	36	.261	.337	.370	90	-2	-2	22	2	1	0	-8	2S/3O	-0.7
1978	SF-N	53	100	8	15	4	0	1	11	11	24	.150	.234	.220	29	-10	-9	6	0	0	0	-6	S2/O	-1.3
1980	Mil-A	34	89	8	19	4	1	1	7	12	13	.213	.307	.315	73	-3	-3	10	4	1	1	-1	O/32	-0.3
Total	8	579	1610	168	349	57	15	13	121	160	281	.217	.289	.295	65	-75	-72	145	36	22	-2	-33	2O/3S	-9.8

■ CHUCK HARRISON
Harrison, Charles William b: 4/25/41, Abilene, Tex. BR/TR, 5'10", 185 lbs. Deb: 9/15/65

YEAR	TM/L	G	AB	R	H	2B	3B	HR	RBI	BB	SO	AVG	OBP	SLG	PRO+	BR	/A	RC	SB	CS	SBR	FR	POS	TPR
1965	Hou-N	15	45	2	9	4	0	1	9	8	9	.200	.321	.356	97	-0	-0	6	0	0	0	0	1	0.0
1966	Hou-N	119	434	52	111	23	2	9	52	37	69	.256	.317	.380	100	-4	-1	51	2	0	1	4	*1	-0.1
1967	Hou-N	70	177	13	43	7	3	2	26	13	30	.243	.295	.350	87	-4	-3	18	0	0	0	1		-0.5
1969	KC-A	75	213	18	47	5	1	3	18	16	20	.221	.278	.296	60	-11	-12	17	1	2	-1	2	1	-1.5
1971	KC-A	49	143	9	31	4	0	2	21	11	19	.217	.273	.287	59	-8	-8	12	0	0	0	0	1	-0.9
Total	5	328	1012	94	241	43	6	17	126	85	147	.238	.299	.343	83	-28	-23	104	3	2	-0	6	1	-3.0

■ BEN HARRISON
Harrison, Leo J. BR ; Deb: 9/27/01

YEAR	TM/L	G	AB	R	H	2B	3B	HR	RBI	BB	SO	AVG	OBP	SLG	PRO+	BR	/A	RC	SB	CS	SBR	FR	POS	TPR
1901	Was-A	1	2	0	0	0	0	0	0		1	.000	.333	.000	-0	-0	-0	0	0			-0	/O	0.0

■ TOM HARRISON
Harrison, Thomas James b: 1/18/45, Trail, B.C., Canada BR/TR, 6'3", 200 lbs. Deb: 5/07/65

YEAR	TM/L	G	AB	R	H	2B	3B	HR	RBI	BB	SO	AVG	OBP	SLG	PRO+	BR	/A	RC	SB	CS	SBR	FR	POS	TPR
1965	KC-A	2	0	0	0	0	0	0	0	0	0	—	—	—	—	0	0	0	0	0		0	/P	0.0

■ RIT HARRISON
Harrison, Washington Ritter b: 9/16/1849, Waterbury, Conn. d: 11/7/1888, Bridgeport, Conn. Deb: 5/20/1875

YEAR	TM/L	G	AB	R	H	2B	3B	HR	RBI	BB	SO	AVG	OBP	SLG	PRO+	BR	/A	RC	SB	CS	SBR	FR	POS	TPR
1875	NH-n	1	4	0	2	1	0	0		0		.500	.500	.750	381	1	1	2					/C	0.1

■ SAM HARSHANY
Harshany, Samuel b: 5/1/10, Madison, Ill. BR/TR, 6', 180 lbs. Deb: 9/28/37

YEAR	TM/L	G	AB	R	H	2B	3B	HR	RBI	BB	SO	AVG	OBP	SLG	PRO+	BR	/A	RC	SB	CS	SBR	FR	POS	TPR
1937	StL-A	5	11	0	1	1	0	0	0	3	0	.091	.286	.182	20	-1	-1	1	0	0	0	1	/C	0.0
1938	StL-A	11	24	2	7	0	0	0	0	3	2	.292	.370	.292	68	-1	-1	3	0	0	0	-0	C	0.0
1939	StL-A	42	145	15	35	2	0	0	15	9	8	.241	.290	.255	40	-13	-13	10	0	1	-1	-1	C	-1.1
1940	StL-A	3	1	0	0	0	0	0	0	1	0	.000	.500	.000	41	0	0	0	0	0	0	0	/C	0.0
Total	4	61	181	17	43	3	0	0	15	16	10	.238	.303	.254	43	-15	-16	14	0	1	-1	-1	/C	-1.1

■ JACK HARSHMAN
Harshman, John Elvin b: 7/12/27, San Diego, Cal. BL/TL, 6'2", 178 lbs. Deb: 9/16/48

YEAR	TM/L	G	AB	R	H	2B	3B	HR	RBI	BB	SO	AVG	OBP	SLG	PRO+	BR	/A	RC	SB	CS	SBR	FR	POS	TPR
1948	NY-N	5	8	0	2	0	0	0	1	1	3	.250	.333	.250	60	-0	-0	1	0			0	/1	0.0
1950	NY-N	9	32	3	4	0	0	2	4	3	6	.125	.200	.313	32	-3	-3	2	0			0	/1	-0.2
1952	NY-N	3	2	0	0	0	0	0	0	0	0	.000	.000	.000	-99	-1	-1	0	0	0	0	0	/P	0.0
1954	Chi-A	36	56	6	8	1	0	2	5	12	21	.143	.294	.268	53	-3	-4	5	0	0	0	-1	P/1	0.0
1955	Chi-A	32	60	6	11	1	0	2	8	9	17	.183	.290	.300	57	-4	-4	6	0	0	0	-1	P	0.0
1956	Chi-A	36	71	8	12	1	0	6	19	11	21	.169	.280	.437	86	-2	-2	10	0	0	0	-3	P	0.0
1957	Chi-A	30	45	5	10	1	0	2	5	10	17	.222	.364	.378	102	0	0	7	0	0	0	-3	P	0.0
1958	Bal-A	47	82	11	16	1	0	6	14	17	22	.195	.333	.427	114	1	2	12	0	0	0	0	P/O	0.0
1959	Bal-A	15	10	3	2	0	0	1	1	2	2	.200	.333	.500	128	0	0	2	0	0	0	1	P	0.0
	Bos-A	9	7	1	1	0	0	0	2	2	2	.143	.333	.143	34	-1	-1	1	0	0	0	-0	/P	0.0
	Cle-A	21	34	3	7	1	0	0	5	5	4	.206	.308	.235	53	-2	-2	3	0	0	0	0	P	0.0
	Yr	45	51	7	10	1	0	1	8	9	8	.196	.317	.275	65	-2	-2	5	0	0	0	1		0.0
1960	Cle-A	15	17	0	3	1	0	0	1	0	4	.176	.176	.235	11	-2	-2	1	0	0	0	-1	P	0.0
Total	10	258	424	46	76	7	0	21	65	72	119	.179	.298	.344	74	-16	-16	49	0	0		-6	P/1O	-0.2

■ BURT HART
Hart, James Burton b: 6/28/1870, Brown Co., Minn. d: 1/29/21, Sacramento, Cal. BB, 6'3", 200 lbs. Deb: 6/06/01

YEAR	TM/L	G	AB	R	H	2B	3B	HR	RBI	BB	SO	AVG	OBP	SLG	PRO+	BR	/A	RC	SB	CS	SBR	FR	POS	TPR
1901	Bal-A	58	206	33	64	3	5	0	23	20		.311	.380	.374	107	4	3	33	7			-8	1	-0.6

■ HUB HART
Hart, James Henry b: 2/2/1878, Everett, Mass. d: 10/10/60, Fort Wayne, Ind. BL/TR, 5'11", 170 lbs. Deb: 7/16/05

YEAR	TM/L	G	AB	R	H	2B	3B	HR	RBI	BB	SO	AVG	OBP	SLG	PRO+	BR	/A	RC	SB	CS	SBR	FR	POS	TPR
1905	Chi-A	11	20	3	2	0	0	0	4	3		.100	.217	.100	3	-2	-2	0	0			-1	/C	-0.2
1906	Chi-A	17	37	1	6	0	0	0	0	2		.162	.205	.162	17	-3	-3	1	0			-4	C	-0.6
1907	Chi-A	29	70	6	19	1	0	0	7	5		.271	.320	.286	99	-0	0	7	1			-4	C	-0.2
Total	3	57	127	10	27	1	0	0	11	10		.213	.270	.220	59	-6	-5	9	1			-10	/C	-1.0

■ MIKE HART
Hart, James Michael b: 12/20/51, Kalamazoo, Mich. BB/TR, 6'3", 185 lbs. Deb: 6/12/80

YEAR	TM/L	G	AB	R	H	2B	3B	HR	RBI	BB	SO	AVG	OBP	SLG	PRO+	BR	/A	RC	SB	CS	SBR	FR	POS	TPR
1980	Tex-A	5	4	1	1	0	0	0	0	1	1	.250	.400	.250	85	-0	-0	1	0	0	0	0	/O	0.0

■ JIM RAY HART
Hart, James Ray b: 10/30/41, Hookerton, N.C. BR/TR, 5'11", 185 lbs. Deb: 7/07/63

YEAR	TM/L	G	AB	R	H	2B	3B	HR	RBI	BB	SO	AVG	OBP	SLG	PRO+	BR	/A	RC	SB	CS	SBR	FR	POS	TPR
1963	SF-N	7	20	1	4	1	0	0	2	3	6	.200	.360	.250	80	-0	-0	2	0	0	0	0	/3	0.0
1964	SF-N	153	566	71	162	15	6	31	81	47	94	.286	.345	.498	132	25	23	95	5	2	0	5	*3/O	2.1
1965	SF-N	160	591	91	177	30	6	23	96	47	75	.299	.353	.487	130	25	24	98	6	4	-1	-12	*3O	0.5
1966	SF-N	156	578	88	165	23	4	33	93	48	75	.285	.344	.510	130	25	23	92	2	5	-2	-7	*3O	1.2
1967	SF-N	158	578	98	167	26	7	29	99	77	100	.289	.376	.509	153	39	40	111	1	1	-0	-14	3O	1.9
1968	SF-N	136	480	67	124	14	3	23	78	46	74	.258	.327	.444	130	17	17	66	3	1	0	-15	3O	-0.1
1969	SF-N	95	236	27	60	9	0	3	26	28	49	.254	.346	.331	92	-2	-2	27	0	0	0	-8	O/3	-1.3
1970	SF-N	76	255	30	72	12	1	8	37	30	29	.282	.365	.431	114	5	5	38	0	0	0	-17	3O	-1.3
1971	*SF-N	31	39	5	10	0	0	2	5	6	8	.256	.356	.410	118	1	1	5	0	1	-1	-1	/3O	0.0
1972	SF-N	24	79	10	24	5	0	5	8	6	10	.304	.360	.557	155	6	5	14	0	1	-1	-9	3	-0.3
1973	SF-N	5	3	0	0	0	0	0	0	3	1	.000	.500	.000	48	0	0	1	0	0	0	0	3	0.0
	NY-A	114	339	29	86	13	2	13	52	36	45	.254	.325	.419	112	3	5	42	0	2	-1	0	*D	0.3
1974	NY-A	10	19	1	1	0	0	0	0	3	7	.053	.182	.053	-31	-3	-3	0	0	0	0	0	/D	-0.2
Total	12	1125	3783	518	1052	148	29	170	578	380	573	.278	.348	.467	128	139	138	592	17	17	-5	-75	3OD	2.8

■ MIKE HART
Hart, Michael Lawrence b: 2/17/58, Milwaukee, Wis. BL/TL, 5'11", 185 lbs. Deb: 5/08/84

YEAR	TM/L	G	AB	R	H	2B	3B	HR	RBI	BB	SO	AVG	OBP	SLG	PRO+	BR	/A	RC	SB	CS	SBR	FR	POS	TPR
1984	Min-A	13	29	0	5	0	0	0	5	1	2	.172	.200	.172	4	-4	-4	1	0	1	-1	2	O	-0.2
1987	Bal-A	34	76	7	12	2	0	4	12	6	19	.158	.214	.342	47	-6	-6	5	1	4	-2	5	O	-0.3
Total	2	47	105	7	17	2	0	4	17	7	21	.162	.214	.295	35	-10	-10	5	1	5	-3	6	/O	-0.5

YEAR	TM/L	G	AB	R	H	2B	3B	HR	RBI	BB	SO	AVG	OBP	SLG	PRO+	BR	/A	RC	SB	CS	SBR	FR	POS	TPR

■ TOM HART
Hart, Thomas Henry "Bushy"   b: 6/15/1869, Canaan, N.Y.   d: 9/17/39, Gardner, Mass.   Deb: 4/15/1891

YEAR	TM/L	G	AB	R	H	2B	3B	HR	RBI	BB	SO	AVG	OBP	SLG	PRO+	BR	/A	RC	SB	CS	SBR	FR	POS	TPR
1891	Was-a	8	24	1	3	0	0	0	2	2	1	.125	.192	.125	-8	-3	-3	1	1			2	/CO	0.0

■ BILL HART
Hart, William Woodrow   b: 3/4/13, Wiconisco, Pa.   d: 7/29/68, Lykins, Pa.   BR/TR, 6', 175 lbs.   Deb: 9/18/43

YEAR	TM/L	G	AB	R	H	2B	3B	HR	RBI	BB	SO	AVG	OBP	SLG	PRO+	BR	/A	RC	SB	CS	SBR	FR	POS	TPR
1943	Bro-N	8	19	0	3	0	0	0	1	1	2	.158	.200	.158	4	-2	-2	0	0			4	/3S	0.1
1944	Bro-N	29	90	8	16	4	2	0	4	9	7	.178	.253	.267	47	-7	-6	7	1			-8	S/3	-1.0
1945	Bro-N	58	161	27	37	6	2	3	27	14	21	.230	.291	.348	78	-5	-5	17	7			-2	3/S	-0.6
Total	3	95	270	35	56	10	4	3	32	24	30	.207	.272	.307	63	-14	-14	24	8			-6	/3S	-1.5

■ CHUCK HARTENSTEIN
Hartenstein, Charles Oscar "Twiggy"   b: 5/26/42, Seguin, Tex.   BR/TR, 5'11", 165 lbs.   Deb: 9/11/65   C

YEAR	TM/L	G	AB	R	H	2B	3B	HR	RBI	BB	SO	AVG	OBP	SLG	PRO+	BR	/A	RC	SB	CS	SBR	FR	POS	TPR
1965	Chi-N	1	0	0	0	0	0	0	0	0	0	—	—	—	—	0	0	0	0	0	0	0	R	0.0
1966	Chi-N	5	0	0	0	0	0	0	0	0	0	—	—	—	—	0	0	0	0	0	0	0	/P	0.0
1967	Chi-N	45	16	0	1	0	0	0	1	0	9	.063	.063	.063	-61	-3	-3	0	0	0	0	0	P	0.0
1968	Chi-N	28	2	0	0	0	0	0	0	0	0	.000	.000	.000	-94	-0	-0	0	0	0	0	0	P	0.0
1969	Pit-N	56	14	0	1	0	0	0	0	1	8	.071	.133	.071	-42	-3	-3	0	0	0	0	2	P	0.0
1970	Pit-N	17	1	1	0	0	0	0	0	0	0	.000	.000	.000	-99	-0	-0	0	0	0	0	1	P	0.0
	StL-N	6	2	0	0	0	0	0	0	1	2	.000	.333	.000	-3	-0	-0	0	0	0	0	0	/P	0.0
	Yr	23	3	1	0	0	0	0	0	1	2	.000	.250	.000	-27	-1	-1	0	0	0	0	1		0.0
	Bos-A	17	2	0	0	0	0	0	0	1	2	.000	.333	.000	-0	-0	-0	0	0	0	0	-0	P	0.0
1977	Tor-A	13	0	0	0	0	0	0	0	0	0	—	—	—	—	0	0	0	0	0	0	0	P	0.0
Total	7	188	37	1	2	0	0	0	1	3	21	.054	.125	.054	-47	-7	-7	0	0	0	0	3	P	0.0

■ BRUCE HARTFORD
Hartford, Bruce Daniel   b: 5/14/1892, Chicago, Ill.   d: 5/25/75, Los Angeles, Cal.   BR/TR, 6'0.5", 190 lbs.   Deb: 6/03/14

YEAR	TM/L	G	AB	R	H	2B	3B	HR	RBI	BB	SO	AVG	OBP	SLG	PRO+	BR	/A	RC	SB	CS	SBR	FR	POS	TPR
1914	Cle-A	8	22	5	4	1	0	0	0	4	9	.182	.308	.227	59	-1	-1	2	0			-3	/S	-0.3

■ CHRIS HARTJE
Hartje, Christian Henry   b: 3/25/15, San Francisco, Cal   d: 6/26/46, Seattle, Wash.   BR/TR, 5'10.5", 165 lbs.   Deb: 9/09/39

YEAR	TM/L	G	AB	R	H	2B	3B	HR	RBI	BB	SO	AVG	OBP	SLG	PRO+	BR	/A	RC	SB	CS	SBR	FR	POS	TPR
1939	Bro-N	9	16	2	5	1	0	0	5	1	0	.313	.353	.375	92	-0	-0	2	0			-2	/C	-0.1

■ GROVER HARTLEY
Hartley, Grover Allen "Slick"   b: 7/2/1888, Osgood, Ind.   d: 10/19/64, Daytona Beach, Fla   BR/TR, 5'11", 175 lbs.   Deb: 5/13/11   C

YEAR	TM/L	G	AB	R	H	2B	3B	HR	RBI	BB	SO	AVG	OBP	SLG	PRO+	BR	/A	RC	SB	CS	SBR	FR	POS	TPR
1911	NY-N	11	18	1	4	2	0	0	1	1	1	.222	.263	.333	64	-1	-1	2	1			3	C	0.3
1912	NY-N	25	34	3	8	2	1	0	7	0	4	.235	.257	.353	64	-2	-2	3	2			2	C	0.2
1913	NY-N	23	19	4	6	0	0	0	0	1	2	.316	.350	.316	90	-0	-0	3	4			3	C/1	0.4
1914	StL-F	86	212	24	61	13	2	1	25	12	26	.288	.329	.382	98	1	-1	30	4			-10	C2/13O	-0.8
1915	StL-F	120	394	47	108	21	6	1	50	42	21	.274	.356	.365	108	8	5	58	10			-8	*C/1	0.0
1916	StL-A	89	222	19	50	8	0	0	12	30	24	.225	.325	.261	80	-5	-4	21	4			1	C	0.0
1917	StL-A	19	13	2	3	0	0	0	0	2	1	.231	.333	.231	75	-0	-0	1	0			1	/CS3	0.1
1924	NY-N	4	7	1	2	1	0	0	1	1	0	.286	.375	.429	118	0	0	1	1	0	0	0	/C	0.0
1925	NY-N	46	95	9	30	1	1	0	8	8	3	.316	.375	.347	89	-2	-1	13	2	0	1	5	C/1	0.5
1926	NY-N	13	21	0	1	0	0	0	0	5	0	.048	.231	.048	-22	-4	-3	0	0			0	C	-0.2
1927	Bos-A	103	244	23	67	11	0	1	31	22	14	.275	.337	.332	76	-9	-8	28	1	0	0	-12	C	-1.6
1929	Cle-A	24	33	2	9	0	1	0	8	2	1	.273	.314	.333	64	-2	-2	3	0	0	0	-3	C	-0.2
1930	Cle-A	1	4	0	3	0	0	0	1	0	0	.750	.750	.750	271	1	1	2	0	0	0	-0	/C	0.1
1934	StL-A	5	3	0	1	1	0	0	0	1	0	.333	.500	.667	183	0	0	1	0	0	0	0	/C	0.1
Total	14	569	1319	135	353	60	11	3	144	127	97	.268	.339	.337	90	-14	-16	167	29	0		-18	C/1230S	-1.1

■ CHICK HARTLEY
Hartley, Walter Scott   b: 8/22/1880, Philadelphia, Pa.   d: 7/18/48, Philadelphia, Pa.   BR/TR, 5'8", 180 lbs.   Deb: 6/04/02

YEAR	TM/L	G	AB	R	H	2B	3B	HR	RBI	BB	SO	AVG	OBP	SLG	PRO+	BR	/A	RC	SB	CS	SBR	FR	POS	TPR
1902	NY-N	1	4	0	0	0	0	0	0	0	0	.000	.000	.000	-99	-1	-1	0	0			0	/O	0.0

■ FRED HARTMAN
Hartman, Frederick Orrin "Dutch"   b: 4/25/1868, Allegheny, Pa.   d: 11/11/38, McKeesport, Pa.   BR/TR,   Deb: 7/26/1894

YEAR	TM/L	G	AB	R	H	2B	3B	HR	RBI	BB	SO	AVG	OBP	SLG	PRO+	BR	/A	RC	SB	CS	SBR	FR	POS	TPR
1894	Pit-N	49	182	41	58	4	7	2	20	16	11	.319	.389	.451	105	1	2	37	12			-4	3	-0.1
1897	StL-N	124	516	67	158	21	8	2	67	26		.306	.350	.390	99	-2	-1	79	18			-4	*3	-0.3
1898	NY-N	123	475	57	129	16	11	2	88	25		.272	.312	.364	99	-4	-1	59	11			9	*3	1.0
1899	NY-N	50	174	25	41	3	5	1	16	12		.236	.307	.328	79	-6	-5	19	2			-4	3	-0.7
1901	Chi-A	120	473	77	146	23	13	3	89	25		.309	.354	.431	122	11	13	86	31			-5	*3	0.5
1902	StL-N	114	416	30	90	10	3	0	52	14		.216	.249	.255	59	-21	-19	32	14			-4	*3/S1	-1.8
Total	6	580	2236	297	622	77	47	10	332	118	11	.278	.324	.368	97	-20	-11	311	88			-11	3/S1	-1.4

■ J C HARTMAN
Hartman, J C   b: 4/15/34, Cottonton, Ala.   BR/TR, 6', 175 lbs.   Deb: 7/21/62

YEAR	TM/L	G	AB	R	H	2B	3B	HR	RBI	BB	SO	AVG	OBP	SLG	PRO+	BR	/A	RC	SB	CS	SBR	FR	POS	TPR
1962	Hou-N	51	148	11	33	5	0	0	5	4	16	.223	.248	.257	39	-13	-12	9	1	1	-0	7	S	0.0
1963	Hou-N	39	90	2	11	1	0	0	3	2	13	.122	.151	.133	-19	-13	-13	2	1	0	0	0	S	-0.9
Total	2	90	238	13	44	6	0	0	8	6	29	.185	.211	.210	18	-27	-25	10	2	1	0	7	/S	-0.9

■ GABBY HARTNETT
Hartnett, Charles Leo   b: 12/20/1900, Woonsocket, R.I.   d: 12/20/72, Park Ridge, Ill.   BR/TR, 6'1", 195 lbs.   Deb: 4/12/22   MCH

YEAR	TM/L	G	AB	R	H	2B	3B	HR	RBI	BB	SO	AVG	OBP	SLG	PRO+	BR	/A	RC	SB	CS	SBR	FR	POS	TPR
1922	Chi-N	31	72	4	14	1	1	0	4	6	8	.194	.256	.236	27	-8	-8	5	1	0	0	5	C	-0.1
1923	Chi-N	85	231	28	62	12	2	8	39	25	22	.268	.347	.442	107	2	2	37	4	0	1	3	C1	0.6
1924	Chi-N	111	354	56	106	17	7	16	67	39	37	.299	.377	.523	137	19	18	72	10	2	2	-3	*C	1.9
1925	Chi-N	117	398	61	115	28	3	24	67	36	77	.289	.351	.555	126	14	13	75	1	5	-3	10	*C	2.4
1926	Chi-N	93	284	35	78	25	3	8	41	32	37	.275	.352	.468	118	7	7	46	0			6	C	1.5
1927	Chi-N	127	449	56	132	32	5	10	80	44	42	.294	.361	.454	117	10	10	73	2			5	*C	2.3
1928	Chi-N	120	388	61	117	26	9	14	57	65	32	.302	.404	.523	143	24	25	83	3			9	*C	3.9
1929	*Chi-N	25	22	2	6	2	1	1	9	5	5	.273	.407	.591	144	2	2	5	1			-0	/C	0.1
1930	Chi-N	141	508	84	172	31	3	37	122	55	62	.339	.404	.630	144	35	35	125	0			3	*C	3.9
1931	Chi-N	116	380	53	107	32	1	8	70	52	48	.282	.370	.434	112	9	8	64	3			2	*C	1.5
1932	*Chi-N	121	406	52	110	25	3	12	52	51	59	.271	.354	.436	112	7	7	66	0			6	*C/1	1.8
1933	Chi-N	140	490	55	135	21	4	16	88	37	51	.276	.326	.433	115	9	9	67	1			6	*C	2.1
1934	Chi-N	130	438	58	131	21	1	22	90	37	46	.299	.358	.502	136	16	17	77	0			14	*C	3.4
1935	*Chi-N	116	413	67	142	32	6	13	91	41	46	.344	.404	.545	152	30	30	91	1			14	*C	4.2
1936	Chi-N	121	424	49	130	25	6	7	64	30	36	.307	.361	.443	113	9	8	68	0			9	*C	1.9
1937	Chi-N	110	356	47	126	21	6	12	82	43	19	.354	.424	.548	156	31	29	85	0			1	*C	3.3
1938	*Chi-N	88	299	40	82	19	1	10	59	48	17	.274	.380	.445	123	12	11	53	1			-4	CM	1.0
1939	Chi-N	97	306	36	85	18	2	12	59	37	32	.278	.358	.467	118	8	8	50	0			-7	CM	0.3
1940	Chi-N	37	64	3	17	3	0	1	12	8	7	.266	.347	.359	97	-0	-0	8	0			1	C/1M	0.2
1941	NY-N	64	150	20	45	5	0	5	26	12	14	.300	.356	.433	119	4	4	22	0			-3	C	0.4
Total	20	1990	6432	867	1912	396	64	236	1179	703	697	.297	.370	.489	126	241	234	1173	28	7		77	*C/1	36.6

■ PAT HARTNETT
Hartnett, Patrick J. "Happy"   b: 10/20/1863, Boston, Mass.   d: 4/10/35, Boston, Mass.   6'1", 175 lbs.   Deb: 4/18/1890

YEAR	TM/L	G	AB	R	H	2B	3B	HR	RBI	BB	SO	AVG	OBP	SLG	PRO+	BR	/A	RC	SB	CS	SBR	FR	POS	TPR
1890	StL-a	14	53	6	10	2	1	0		6		.189	.283	.264	56	-2	-4	4	1			-1	1	-0.3

■ GREG HARTS
Harts, Gregory Rudolph   b: 4/21/50, Atlanta, Ga.   BL/TL, 6', 168 lbs.   Deb: 9/15/73

YEAR	TM/L	G	AB	R	H	2B	3B	HR	RBI	BB	SO	AVG	OBP	SLG	PRO+	BR	/A	RC	SB	CS	SBR	FR	POS	TPR
1973	NY-N	3	2	0	1	0	0	0	0	0	0	.500	.500	.500	181	0	0	1	0	0	0	0	H	0.0

■ TOPSY HARTSEL
Hartsel, Tully Frederick   b: 6/26/1874, Polk, Ohio   d: 10/14/44, Toledo, Ohio   BL/TL, 5'5", 155 lbs.   Deb: 9/14/1898

YEAR	TM/L	G	AB	R	H	2B	3B	HR	RBI	BB	SO	AVG	OBP	SLG	PRO+	BR	/A	RC	SB	CS	SBR	FR	POS	TPR
1898	Lou-N	22	71	11	23	0	0	0	9	11		.324	.422	.324	120	3	3	11	2			-2	O	0.0
1899	Lou-N	30	75	8	18	1	1	1	7	11		.240	.345	.320	85	-1	-1	9	1			-2	O	-0.3
1900	Cin-N	18	64	10	21	2	1	2	5	8		.328	.403	.484	151	4	4	16	7			-5	O	-0.1

YEAR	TM/L	G	AB	R	H	2B	3B	HR	RBI	BB	SO	AVG	OBP	SLG	PRO+	BR	/A	RC	SB	CS	SBR	FR	POS	TPR
1901	Chi-N	140	558	111	187	25	16	7	54	74		.335	.414	.475	166	44	47	130	41			-1	*O	3.1
1902	Phi-A	137	545	**109**	154	20	12	5	58	**87**		.283	.384	.391	112	16	13	103	**47**			-1	*O	0.3
1903	Phi-A	98	373	65	116	19	14	5	26	49		.311	.391	.477	155	29	27	77	13			-5	O	1.6
1904	Phi-A	147	534	79	135	17	12	2	25	75		.253	.345	.341	114	15	12	73	19			-4	*O	-0.1
1905	*Phi-A	150	538	88	148	22	8	0	28	**121**		.275	**.408**	.346	140	34	33	96	37			-7	*O	2.0
1906	Phi-A	144	533	96	136	21	9	1	30	**88**		.255	.361	.334	117	16	14	79	31			0	*O	1.0
1907	Phi-A	143	507	93	142	23	6	3	29	**106**		.280	**.405**	.367	145	34	33	87	20			-11	*O	1.5
1908	Phi-A	129	460	73	112	16	6	4	29	93		.243	.371	.330	123	21	17	62	15			-5	*O	0.7
1909	Phi-A	83	267	30	72	4	4	1	18	48		.270	.381	.326	121	10	9	35	3			-3	O	0.3
1910	*Phi-A	90	285	45	63	10	3	0	22	58		.221	.353	.277	99	2	3	32	11			-7	O	-0.8
1911	Phi-A	25	38	8	9	2	0	0	1	8		.237	.396	.289	94	0	0	5	0			1	/O	0.0
Total	14	1356	4848	826	1336	182	92	31	341	837		.276	.383	.370	130	228	214	813	247			-52	*O	9.2

■ ROY HARTSFIELD
Hartsfield, Roy Thomas "Spec" b: 10/25/25, Chattahoochee, Ga.   BR/TR, 5'9", 165 lbs.   Deb: 4/28/50   MC

YEAR	TM/L	G	AB	R	H	2B	3B	HR	RBI	BB	SO	AVG	OBP	SLG	PRO+	BR	/A	RC	SB	CS	SBR	FR	POS	TPR
1950	Bos-N	107	419	62	116	15	2	7	24	27	61	.277	.322	.372	88	-11	-8	52	7			-23	2	-2.7
1951	Bos-N	120	450	63	122	11	2	6	31	41	73	.271	.333	.344	89	-10	-6	56	7	2	1	-5	*2	-0.5
1952	Bos-N	38	107	13	28	4	3	0	4	5	12	.262	.295	.355	82	-3	-3	11	0	0	0	-6	2	-0.7
Total	3	265	976	138	266	30	7	13	59	73	146	.273	.324	.358	88	-25	-17	119	14	2		-34	2	-3.9

■ CLINT HARTUNG
Hartung, Clinton Clarence "Floppy" or "The Hondo Hurricane" b: 8/10/22, Hondo, Tex.   BR/TR, 6'5", 210 lbs.   Deb: 4/15/47

YEAR	TM/L	G	AB	R	H	2B	3B	HR	RBI	BB	SO	AVG	OBP	SLG	PRO+	BR	/A	RC	SB	CS	SBR	FR	POS	TPR
1947	NY-N	34	94	13	29	4	3	4	13	3	21	.309	.330	.543	127	3	3	16	0			-2	P/O	0.0
1948	NY-N	43	56	5	10	1	1	0	3	7	24	.179	.270	.232	37	-5	-5	4	0			0	P	0.0
1949	NY-N	38	63	7	12	0	0	4	7	4	21	.190	.239	.381	64	-4	-4	6	0			2	P	0.0
1950	NY-N	32	43	7	13	2	1	3	10	1	13	.302	.318	.605	136	2	2	8	0			2	P/O1	0.0
1951	*NY-N	21	44	4	9	1	0	0	2	1	9	.205	.222	.227	21	-5	-5	2	0	0	0	-1	O	-0.6
1952	NY-N	28	78	6	17	2	1	3	8	9	24	.218	.299	.385	88	-1	-1	10	0	0	0	-1	O	-0.2
Total	6	196	378	42	90	10	6	14	43	25	112	.238	.285	.407	84	-10	-10	46	0	0		0	P/O1	-0.8

■ ROY HARTZELL
Hartzell, Roy Allen b: 7/6/1881, Golden, Colo. d: 11/6/61, Golden, Colo.   BL/TR, 5'8.5", 155 lbs.   Deb: 4/17/06

YEAR	TM/L	G	AB	R	H	2B	3B	HR	RBI	BB	SO	AVG	OBP	SLG	PRO+	BR	/A	RC	SB	CS	SBR	FR	POS	TPR
1906	StL-A	113	404	43	86	7	0	0	24	19		.213	.248	.230	54	-22	-20	30	21			-2	*3/S2	-1.6
1907	StL-A	60	220	20	52	3	5	0	13	11		.236	.273	.295	83	-4	-4	21	7			-0	32/SO	-0.2
1908	StL-A	115	422	41	112	5	6	2	32	19		.265	.297	.320	102	1	0	48	24			-6	OS/32	-0.9
1909	StL-A	152	595	64	161	12	5	0	32	29		.271	.312	.308	103	-3	1	61	14			4	OS/2	0.3
1910	StL-A	151	542	52	118	13	5	2	30	49		.218	.290	.271	81	-15	-11	48	18			1	3SO	-0.6
1911	NY-A	144	527	67	156	17	11	3	91	63		.296	.375	.387	106	10	5	86	22			-12	*3S/O	-0.5
1912	NY-A	125	416	50	113	10	11	1	38	64		.272	.370	.356	102	6	3	63	20			-0	3OS/2	0.0
1913	NY-A	141	490	60	127	18	1	0	38	67	40	.259	.353	.300	91	-3	-3	60	26			0	203/S	-0.5
1914	NY-A	137	481	55	112	15	9	1	32	68	38	.233	.335	.308	94	-2	-2	52	22	25	-8	0	*O/2	-1.9
1915	NY-A	119	387	39	97	11	2	3	60	57	37	.251	.351	.313	99	1	1	42	7	19	-9	-3	*O/23	-1.7
1916	NY-A	33	64	12	12	1	0	0	7	9	3	.188	.297	.203	49	-3	-4	5	1			-6	O	-1.2
Total	11	1290	4548	503	1146	112	55	12	397	455	118	.252	.324	.309	93	-34	-32	514	182	44		-24	O3S2	-8.8

■ LUTHER HARVEL
Harvel, Luther Raymond "Red" b: 9/30/05, Cambria, Ill. d: 4/10/86, Kansas City, Mo.   BR/TR, 5'11", 180 lbs.   Deb: 7/31/28

YEAR	TM/L	G	AB	R	H	2B	3B	HR	RBI	BB	SO	AVG	OBP	SLG	PRO+	BR	/A	RC	SB	CS	SBR	FR	POS	TPR
1928	Cle-A	40	136	12	30	6	1	0	12	4	17	.221	.264	.279	42	-11	-12	10	1	1	-0	-1	O	-1.4

■ ERWIN HARVEY
Harvey, Ervin King "Zaza" b: 1/5/1879, Saratoga, Cal. d: 6/3/54, Santa Monica, Cal.   BL, 6', 190 lbs.   Deb: 5/03/00

YEAR	TM/L	G	AB	R	H	2B	3B	HR	RBI	BB	SO	AVG	OBP	SLG	PRO+	BR	/A	RC	SB	CS	SBR	FR	POS	TPR
1900	Chi-N	2	3	0	0	0	0	0	0	0	0	.000	.000	.000	-99	-1	-1	0	0			0	/P	0.0
1901	Chi-A	17	40	11	10	3	1	0	3	2		.250	.302	.375	91	-1	-0	5	1			2	P	0.0
	Cle-A	45	170	21	60	5	5	1	24	9		.353	.392	.459	144	8	10	38	15			2	O	0.9
	Yr	62	210	32	70	8	6	1	27	11		.333	.375	.443	133	8	9	42	16			4		0.9
1902	Cle-A	12	46	5	16	2	0	0	5	3		.348	.388	.391	123	1	1	8	1			0	O	0.1
Total	3	76	259	37	86	10	6	1	32	14		.332	.373	.429	129	8	10	50	17			4	/OP	1.0

■ ZIGGY HASBROOK
Hasbrook, Robert Lyndon "Ziggy" b: 11/21/1893, Grundy Center, Ia. d: 2/9/76, Garland, Tex.   BR/TR, 6'1", 180 lbs.   Deb: 9/06/16

YEAR	TM/L	G	AB	R	H	2B	3B	HR	RBI	BB	SO	AVG	OBP	SLG	PRO+	BR	/A	RC	SB	CS	SBR	FR	POS	TPR
1916	Chi-A	9	8	1	1	0	0	0	1	2		.125	.222	.125	4	-1	-1	0	0			1	/1	0.0
1917	Chi-A	2	1	1	0	0	0	0	0	0		.000	.000	.000	-98	-0	-0	0	0			1	/2	0.0
Total	2	11	9	2	1	0	0	0	1	2		.111	.200	.111	-6	-1	-1	0	0			1	/12	0.0

■ BILL HASELMAN
Haselman, William Joseph b: 5/25/66, Long Branch, N.J.   BR/TR, 6'3", 205 lbs.   Deb: 9/03/90

YEAR	TM/L	G	AB	R	H	2B	3B	HR	RBI	BB	SO	AVG	OBP	SLG	PRO+	BR	/A	RC	SB	CS	SBR	FR	POS	TPR
1990	Tex-A	7	13	0	2	0	0	0	3	1	5	.154	.214	.154	5	-2	-2	0	0	0	0	0	/CD	-0.1

■ DON HASENMAYER
Hasenmayer, Donald Irvin b: 4/4/27, Roslyn, Pa.   BR/TR, 5'10.5", 180 lbs.   Deb: 5/02/45

YEAR	TM/L	G	AB	R	H	2B	3B	HR	RBI	BB	SO	AVG	OBP	SLG	PRO+	BR	/A	RC	SB	CS	SBR	FR	POS	TPR
1945	Phi-N	5	18	1	2	0	0	0	1	2	1	.111	.200	.111	-13	-3	-3	1	0			3	/23	0.0
1946	Phi-N	6	12	0	1	1	0	0	0	0	2	.083	.083	.167	-31	-2	-2	0	0			2	/3	0.0
Total	2	11	30	1	3	1	0	0	1	2	3	.100	.156	.133	-19	-5	-5	1	0			5	/32	0.0

■ MICKEY HASLIN
Haslin, Michael Joseph b: 10/31/10, Wilkes-Barre, Pa.   BR/TR, 5'8", 165 lbs.   Deb: 9/07/33

YEAR	TM/L	G	AB	R	H	2B	3B	HR	RBI	BB	SO	AVG	OBP	SLG	PRO+	BR	/A	RC	SB	CS	SBR	FR	POS	TPR
1933	Phi-N	26	89	3	21	2	0	0	9	3	5	.236	.261	.258	43	-6	-7	6	1			-4	2	-0.9
1934	Phi-N	72	166	28	44	8	2	1	11	16	13	.265	.330	.355	74	-4	-7	19	1			-3	32/S	-0.4
1935	Phi-N	110	407	53	108	17	3	3	52	19	25	.265	.300	.344	66	-16	-21	42	5			-3	S3/2	-1.8
1936	Phi-N	16	64	6	22	1	1	0	6	3	8	.344	.373	.391	96	1	-0	9	0			-5	2/3	-0.3
	Bos-N	36	104	14	29	1	2	2	11	5	9	.279	.312	.385	93	-2	-1	11	0			-4	3/2	-0.3
	Yr	52	168	20	51	2	3	2	17	8	14	.304	.335	.387	95	-2	-1	20	0			-9		-0.6
1937	NY-N	27	42	8	8	1	0	0	5	9	3	.190	.333	.214	51	-2	-3	3	1			6	/S23	0.5
1938	NY-N	31	102	13	33	3	0	3	15	4	4	.324	.361	.441	119	3	2	16	0			-2	32	0.1
Total	6	318	974	125	265	33	8	9	109	59	64	.272	.316	.350	74	-27	-37	108	8			-15	S/23	-3.1

■ PETE HASNEY
Hasney, Peter James b: 5/26/1865, England d: 5/24/08, Philadelphia, Pa.   Deb: 9/13/1890

YEAR	TM/L	G	AB	R	H	2B	3B	HR	RBI	BB	SO	AVG	OBP	SLG	PRO+	BR	/A	RC	SB	CS	SBR	FR	POS	TPR
1890	Phi-a	2	7	1	1	0	0	0		1		.143	.250	.143	18	-1	-1	0	0			-1	/O	-0.1

■ BILL HASSAMAER
Hassamaer, William Louis "Roaring Bill" b: 7/26/1864, St.Louis, Mo. d: 5/29/10, St.Louis, Mo.   6', 180 lbs.   Deb: 4/19/1894

YEAR	TM/L	G	AB	R	H	2B	3B	HR	RBI	BB	SO	AVG	OBP	SLG	PRO+	BR	/A	RC	SB	CS	SBR	FR	POS	TPR
1894	Was-N	118	494	106	159	33	17	4	90	41	20	.322	.375	.482	110	4	7	98	16			4	O32/S	0.6
1895	Was-N	85	358	42	100	18	4	1	60	26	13	.279	.328	.360	80	-11	-10	46	8			-7	O/1S3	-1.8
	Lou-N	23	96	7	20	2	2	0	14	3	4	.208	.232	.271	33	-10	-9	6	0			3	1/2S	-0.3
	Yr	108	454	49	120	20	6	1	74	29	17	.264	.308	.341	71	-21	-19	52	8			-4		-2.1
1896	Lou-N	30	106	8	26	5	0	2	14	14	7	.245	.333	.349	85	-3	-2	13	1			6	1	0.4
Total	3	256	1054	163	305	58	23	7	178	84	44	.289	.342	.408	92	-20	-14	163	25			6	O/132S	-1.1

■ BUDDY HASSETT
Hassett, John Aloysius b: 9/5/11, New York, N.Y.   BL/TL, 5'11", 180 lbs.   Deb: 4/14/36

YEAR	TM/L	G	AB	R	H	2B	3B	HR	RBI	BB	SO	AVG	OBP	SLG	PRO+	BR	/A	RC	SB	CS	SBR	FR	POS	TPR
1936	Bro-N	156	635	79	197	29	11	3	82	35	17	.310	.350	.405	102	2	1	92	5			5	*1	-0.6
1937	Bro-N	137	556	71	169	31	6	1	53	20	19	.304	.334	.387	94	-4	-5	71	13			9	*1/O	-0.3
1938	Bro-N	115	335	49	98	11	6	0	40	32	19	.293	.356	.361	95	-0	-1	44	3			-1	O/1	-0.3
1939	Bos-N	147	590	72	182	15	3	2	60	29	14	.308	.342	.354	94	-10	-5	72	13			10	*1O	-0.9
1940	Bos-N	124	458	59	107	19	4	0	27	25	16	.234	.273	.293	59	-28	-24	34	4			8	10	-2.5
1941	Bos-N	118	405	59	120	29	4	1	33	36	15	.296	.354	.346	102	-1	-1	51	10			7	1	-0.5
1942	*NY-A	132	538	80	153	16	6	5	48	32	16	.284	.325	.364	95	-6	-4	65	5	5	-2	11	*1	0.3

YEAR	TM/L	G	AB	R	H	2B	3B	HR	RBI	BB	SO	AVG	OBP	SLG	PRO+	BR	/A	RC	SB	CS	SBR	FR	POS	TPR
Total	7	929	3517	469	1026	130	40	12	343	209	116	.292	.333	.362	92	-47	-38	431	53	5		49	1O	-4.8

■ RON HASSEY
Hassey, Ronald William   b: 2/27/53, Tucson, Ariz.   BL/TR, 6'2", 200 lbs.   Deb: 4/23/78

YEAR	TM/L	G	AB	R	H	2B	3B	HR	RBI	BB	SO	AVG	OBP	SLG	PRO+	BR	/A	RC	SB	CS	SBR	FR	POS	TPR
1978	Cle-A	25	74	5	15	0	0	2	9	5	7	.203	.262	.284	54	-5	-4	6	2	0	1	5	C	0.2
1979	Cle-A	75	223	20	64	14	0	4	32	19	19	.287	.343	.404	100	0	0	30	1	0	0	6	C/1	0.9
1980	Cle-A	130	390	43	124	18	4	8	65	49	51	.318	.395	.446	130	18	17	68	0	2	-1	-8	*C/1D	1.3
1981	Cle-A	61	190	8	44	4	0	1	25	17	11	.232	.301	.268	66	-8	-8	16	0	1	-1	8	C/1D	0.2
1982	Cle-A	113	323	33	81	18	0	5	34	53	32	.251	.358	.353	97	0	0	42	3	2	-0	8	*C/1D	1.4
1983	Cle-A	117	341	48	92	21	0	6	42	38	35	.270	.346	.384	97	1	-1	45	2	2	-1	-3	*C/D	0.1
1984	Cle-A	48	149	11	38	5	1	0	19	15	26	.255	.323	.302	73	-5	-5	15	1	0	0	-2	C/1D	-0.3
	Chi-N	19	33	5	11	0	0	2	5	4	6	.333	.405	.515	144	3	2	6	0	1	-1	0	/C1	0.1
1985	NY-A	92	267	31	79	16	1	13	42	28	21	.296	.369	.509	141	14	15	49	0	0	0	5	C/1D	2.2
1986	NY-A	64	191	23	57	14	0	6	29	24	16	.298	.382	.466	131	8	9	33	1	1	-0	-13	C/D	-0.1
	Chi-A	49	150	22	53	11	1	3	20	22	11	.353	.439	.500	150	12	12	32	0	0	0	1	DC	1.3
	Yr	113	341	45	110	25	1	9	49	46	27	.323	.408	.481	140	21	20	65	1	1	-0	-12		1.2
1987	Chi-A	49	145	15	31	9	0	3	12	17	11	.214	.305	.338	69	-6	-7	13	0	0	1	1	CD	-0.3
1988	*Oak-A	107	323	32	83	15	0	7	45	30	42	.257	.328	.368	98	-2	-1	39	2	0	1	0	C/D	0.4
1989	*Oak-A	97	268	29	61	12	0	5	23	24	45	.228	.294	.332	78	-9	-8	25	1	0	0	6	C/1D	0.2
1990	*Oak-A	94	254	18	54	7	0	5	22	27	29	.213	.291	.299	67	-12	-11	23	0	0	0	4	CD/1	-0.5
Total	13	1140	3321	343	887	164	7	70	424	372	362	.267	.345	.384	101	10	11	442	13	9	-2	19	C/D1	7.1

■ JOE HASSLER
Hassler, Joseph Frederick   b: 4/7/05, Ft.Smith, Ark.   d: 9/4/71, Duncan, Okla.   BR/TR, 6', 165 lbs.   Deb: 5/26/28

YEAR	TM/L	G	AB	R	H	2B	3B	HR	RBI	BB	SO	AVG	OBP	SLG	PRO+	BR	/A	RC	SB	CS	SBR	FR	POS	TPR
1928	Phi-A	28	34	5	9	2	0	0	3	2	4	.265	.306	.324	64	-2	-2	3	0	1	-1	1	S	0.1
1929	Phi-A	4	4	1	0	0	0	0	0	0	2	.000	.000	.000	-97	-1	-1	0	0	0	0	-0	/S	0.0
1930	StL-A	5	8	3	2	0	0	0	1	0	1	.250	.250	.250	26	-1	-1	0	0	0	0	1	/S	0.1
Total	3	37	46	9	11	2	0	0	4	2	7	.239	.271	.283	43	-4	-4	4	0	1	-1	2	/S	0.2

■ GENE HASSON
Hasson, Charles Eugene   b: 7/20/15, Connellsville, Pa   BL/TL, 6', 197 lbs.   Deb: 9/09/37

YEAR	TM/L	G	AB	R	H	2B	3B	HR	RBI	BB	SO	AVG	OBP	SLG	PRO+	BR	/A	RC	SB	CS	SBR	FR	POS	TPR
1937	Phi-A	28	98	12	30	6	3	6	14	13	14	.306	.387	.520	129	4	4	20	0	0	0	-2	1	0.0
1938	Phi-A	19	69	10	19	6	2	1	12	12	7	.275	.383	.464	114	1	2	13	0	0	0	-4	1	-0.3
Total	2	47	167	22	49	12	5	4	26	25	21	.293	.385	.497	123	5	6	33	0	0	0	-6	/1	-0.3

■ SCOTT HASTINGS
Hastings, Winfield Scott   b: 8/10/1847, Hillsboro, Ohio   d: 8/14/07, Sawtelle, Cal.   BR/TR, 5'8", 161 lbs.   Deb: 5/06/1871   M

YEAR	TM/L	G	AB	R	H	2B	3B	HR	RBI	BB	SO	AVG	OBP	SLG	PRO+	BR	/A	RC	SB	CS	SBR	FR	POS	TPR
1871	Rok-n	25	118	27	30	6	4	0	20	2	4	.254	.267	.373	85	-3	-2	15	11				*C/2OM	-0.1
1872	Cle-n	22	117	34	45	6	0	0			2	.385	.395	.436	164	7	9	21					C/O2M	0.6
	Bal-n	13	61	16	19	3	1	0			1	.311	.323	.393	114	1	1	8					/C2	0.0
	Yr	35	178	50	64	9	1	0			3	.360	.370	.421	146	9	9	28						0.6
1873	Bal-n	32	153	44	44	5	0	0			5	.288	.310	.320	86	-2	-2	16					CO/2	0.0
1874	Har-n	52	248	60	80	13	1	0			4	.323	.333	.383	121	7	5	32					CO/2	0.5
1875	Chi-n	65	284	43	73	9	0	0			9	.257	.280	.289	96	-1	-1	24					CO/2	0.0
1876	Lou-N	82	283	36	73	6	1	0	21	5	11	.258	.271	.286	73	-4	-12	22				-7	*O/C	-1.6
1877	Cin-N	20	71	7	10	1	0	0	3	3	6	.141	.176	.155	6	-7	-6	2				-7	C/O	-1.0
Total	5 n	209	981	224	291	42	6	0	20	23	4	.297	.313	.352	109	10	10	115					C/O2	1.0
Total	2	87	354	43	83	7	1	0	24	8	17	.234	.251	.260	61	-11	-18	24				-14	/OC	-2.6

■ MICKEY HATCHER
Hatcher, Michael Vaughn   b: 3/15/55, Cleveland, Ohio   BR/TR, 6'2", 200 lbs.   Deb: 8/03/79

YEAR	TM/L	G	AB	R	H	2B	3B	HR	RBI	BB	SO	AVG	OBP	SLG	PRO+	BR	/A	RC	SB	CS	SBR	FR	POS	TPR
1979	LA-N	33	93	9	25	4	1	1	5	7	12	.269	.327	.366	90	-1	-1	9	1	3	-2	1	O3	-0.2
1980	LA-N	57	84	4	19	2	0	1	5	2	12	.226	.244	.286	48	-6	-6	4	0	2	-1	1	O3	-0.6
1981	Min-A	99	377	36	96	23	2	3	37	15	29	.255	.287	.350	77	-9	-12	36	3	1	0	0	O/13D	-1.4
1982	Min-A	84	277	23	69	13	2	3	26	8	27	.249	.270	.343	65	-13	-14	21	0	2	-1	3	OD/3	-1.3
1983	Min-A	106	375	50	119	15	3	9	47	14	19	.317	.344	.445	111	7	5	54	2	0	1	3	OD/13	0.8
1984	Min-A	152	576	61	174	35	5	5	69	37	34	.302	.346	.406	103	6	2	78	0	1	-1	10	*OD1/3	0.7
1985	Min-A	116	444	46	125	28	0	3	49	16	23	.282	.310	.365	79	-10	-13	46	0	0	0	3	OD/1	-1.1
1986	Min-A	115	317	40	88	13	3	3	32	19	26	.278	.318	.366	84	-6	-7	36	2	1	0	-0	OD/13	-0.9
1987	LA-N	101	287	27	81	19	1	7	42	20	19	.282	.331	.429	102	-1	0	39	2	3	-1	1	31/O	-0.2
1988	*LA-N	88	191	22	56	8	0	1	25	7	7	.293	.325	.351	97	-2	-1	20	0	0	0	-1	O1/3	-0.3
1989	LA-N	94	224	18	66	9	2	2	25	13	16	.295	.336	.379	106	1	1	27	1	2	-1	-3	O3/1P	-0.3
1990	LA-N	85	132	12	28	3	1	0	13	6	22	.212	.252	.250	41	-11	-10	9	0	0	0	-3	13O	-1.4
Total	12	1130	3377	348	946	172	20	38	375	164	246	.280	.316	.377	89	-46	-56	378	11	15	-6	15	O1D3/P	-6.2

■ BILLY HATCHER
Hatcher, William Augustus   b: 10/4/60, Williams, Ariz.   BR/TR, 5'9", 175 lbs.   Deb: 9/10/84

YEAR	TM/L	G	AB	R	H	2B	3B	HR	RBI	BB	SO	AVG	OBP	SLG	PRO+	BR	/A	RC	SB	CS	SBR	FR	POS	TPR
1984	Chi-N	8	9	1	1	0	0	0	0	1	0	.111	.200	.111	-10	-1	-1	0	2	0	1	1	/O	0.0
1985	Chi-N	53	163	24	40	12	1	2	10	8	12	.245	.293	.368	75	-4	-6	14	2	4	-2	-1	O	-1.0
1986	*Hou-N	127	419	55	108	15	4	6	36	22	52	.258	.303	.356	83	-11	-10	47	38	14	3	-4	*O	-1.3
1987	Hou-N	141	564	96	167	28	3	11	63	42	70	.296	.354	.415	107	3	6	89	53	9	11	5	*O	1.5
1988	Hou-N	145	530	79	142	25	4	7	52	37	56	.268	.325	.370	103	-1	2	66	32	13	2	2	*O	0.1
1989	Hou-N	108	395	49	90	15	3	3	44	30	53	.228	.304	.304	71	-16	-15	37	22	6	3	0	*O	-1.3
	Pit-N	27	86	10	21	4	0	1	7	0	9	.244	.253	.326	67	-4	-4	7	2	1	0	-4	O	-0.8
	Yr	135	481	59	111	19	3	4	51	30	62	.231	.279	.308	70	-21	-19	44	24	7	3	-3		-2.1
1990	*Cin-N	139	504	68	139	28	5	5	25	33	42	.276	.328	.381	92	-4	-6	65	30	10	3	1	*O	-0.5
Total	7	748	2670	382	708	127	20	35	237	173	294	.265	.318	.360	91	-39	-34	325	181	57	20	1	O	-3.3

■ FRED HATFIELD
Hatfield, Fred James   b: 3/18/25, Lanett, Ala.   BL/TR, 6'1", 171 lbs.   Deb: 8/31/50   C

YEAR	TM/L	G	AB	R	H	2B	3B	HR	RBI	BB	SO	AVG	OBP	SLG	PRO+	BR	/A	RC	SB	CS	SBR	FR	POS	TPR
1950	Bos-A	10	12	3	3	0	0	0	2	3	1	.250	.400	.250	63	-0	-1	2	0	0	0	3	/3	0.2
1951	Bos-A	80	163	23	28	4	2	2	14	22	27	.172	.274	.258	40	-13	-15	13	1	0	0	21	3	0.4
1952	Bos-A	19	25	6	8	1	1	1	3	4	2	.320	.433	.560	162	3	2	4	0	3	-2	4	3	0.4
	Det-A	112	441	42	104	12	2	2	25	35	52	.236	.301	.286	63	-21	-22	38	2	2	-1	14	*3/S	-0.7
	Yr	131	466	48	112	13	3	3	28	39	54	.240	.309	.300	69	-19	-20	43	2	5	-2	18		-0.3
1953	Det-A	109	311	41	79	11	1	3	19	40	34	.254	.341	.325	81	-8	-7	36	3	5	-2	9	32/S	0.0
1954	Det-A	81	218	31	64	12	0	2	25	28	24	.294	.386	.376	112	4	5	33	4	2	0	7	23	0.0
1955	Det-A	122	413	51	96	15	3	8	33	61	49	.232	.338	.341	85	-9	-8	51	3	2	-0	-6	23S	-0.6
1956	Det-A	8	12	2	3	0	0	0	2	2	1	.250	.400	.250	75	-0	-0	2	0	0	0	-1	/2	0.0
	Chi-A	106	321	46	84	9	1	7	33	37	36	.262	.352	.361	88	-4	-5	43	1	0	0	5	*3/S	0.2
	Yr	114	333	48	87	9	1	7	35	39	37	.261	.354	.357	87	-5	-5	44	1	0	0	4		0.2
1957	Chi-A	69	114	14	23	3	0	0	8	15	20	.202	.321	.228	52	-7	-7	10	1	0	0	6	23	-0.3
1958	Cle-A	3	8	0	1	0	0	0	1	1	1	.125	.222	.125	-2	-1	-1	0	0	0	0	1	/3	0.0
	Cin-N	3	1	0	0	0	0	0	0	0	0	.000	.000	.000	-95	-0	-0	0	0	0	0	-0	/23	0.0
Total	9	722	2039	259	493	67	10	25	165	248	247	.242	.334	.321	78	-57	-58	233	15	14	-4	43	32/S	-0.4

■ GIL HATFIELD
Hatfield, Gilbert "Colonel"   b: 1/27/1855, Hoboken, N.J.   d: 5/27/21, Hoboken, N.J.   TR, 5'9.5", 168 lbs.   Deb: 9/24/1885

YEAR	TM/L	G	AB	R	H	2B	3B	HR	RBI	BB	SO	AVG	OBP	SLG	PRO+	BR	/A	RC	SB	CS	SBR	FR	POS	TPR
1885	Buf-N	11	30	1	4	1	0	0		0	11	.133	.133	.200	6	-3	-3	1				-0	/32	-0.2
1887	NY-N	2	7	2	3	1	0	0	3	0	1	.429	.429	.571	186	1	1	2	0			0	/3	0.1
1888	*NY-N	28	105	7	19	1	0	0	9	2	18	.181	.211	.190	31	-8	-8	6	8			-1	3S/O2	-0.7
1889	NY-N	32	125	21	23	2	0	1	12	9	15	.184	.250	.224	34	-11	-11	9	9			1	S/P3	-0.6
1890	NY-P	71	287	32	80	13	6	2	37	17	19	.279	.328	.387	85	-4	-8	41	12			-19	3S/PO	-1.7

YEAR	TM/L	G	AB	R	H	2B	3B	HR	RBI	BB	SO	AVG	OBP	SLG	PRO+	BR	/A	RC	SB	CS	SBR	FR	POS	TPR
1891	Was-a	134	500	83	128	11	8	1	48	50	39	.256	.335	.316	93	-6	-2	69	43			9	*S3/PO	1.1
1893	Bro-N	34	120	24	35	3	3	2	19	17	5	.292	.388	.417	122	3	4	23	9			-7	3	-0.1
1895	Lou-N	5	16	3	3	0	0	0	1	1	1	.188	.278	.188	24	-2	-2	1	0			-1	/3S	-0.1
Total	8	317	1190	173	295	31	18	6	129	96	109	.248	.315	.319	81	-30	-29	153	81			-17	S3/PO2	-2.2

■ JOHN HATFIELD
Hatfield, John Van Buskirk b: 7/20/1847, New Jersey d: 2/20/09, Long Island City, N.Y. 5'10", 165 lbs. Deb: 5/18/1871 M

YEAR	TM/L	G	AB	R	H	2B	3B	HR	RBI	BB	SO	AVG	OBP	SLG	PRO+	BR	/A	RC	SB	CS	SBR	FR	POS	TPR
1871	Mut-n	33	168	41	43	3	2	0	22	4	0	.256	.273	.298	70	-8	-4	17	10				*O/23	-0.1
1872	Mut-n	56	287	75	91	12	2	1		9		.317	.338	.383	130	7	11	38					*2	0.2
1873	Mut-n	52	256	54	76	6	7	2		3		.297	.305	.398	106	1	2	32					*32M	0.0
1874	Mut-n	63	289	46	68	12	2	0		8		.235	.256	.291	71	-8	-10	22					*O/3P1	-0.5
1875	Mut-n	2	9	2	3	1	0	0		0		.333	.333	.444	157	1	0	1					/O	0.0
1876	NY-N	1	4	0	1	0	0	0	1	0	0	.250	.250	.250	77	-0	-0	0	0				/2	0.0
Total	5 n	206	1009	218	281	34	13	3	22	24		.278	.295	.347	97	-6	-0	110					/O23P1	-0.4

■ GRADY HATTON
Hatton, Grady Edgebert b: 10/7/22, Beaumont, Tex. BL/TR, 5'8.5", 170 lbs. Deb: 4/16/46 MC

YEAR	TM/L	G	AB	R	H	2B	3B	HR	RBI	BB	SO	AVG	OBP	SLG	PRO+	BR	/A	RC	SB	CS	SBR	FR	POS	TPR
1946	Cin-N	116	436	56	118	18	3	14	69	66	53	.271	.369	.422	129	15	17	73	6			-19	*3/O	-0.1
1947	Cin-N	146	524	91	147	24	8	16	77	81	50	.281	.377	.448	119	15	15	92	7			-8	*3	0.3
1948	Cin-N	133	458	58	110	17	2	9	44	72	50	.240	.343	.345	90	-7	-5	59	7			5	*3/2SO	-0.2
1949	Cin-N	137	537	71	141	38	5	11	69	62	48	.263	.342	.413	101	1	0	79	4			-1	*3	0.1
1950	Cin-N	130	438	67	114	17	1	11	54	70	39	.260	.366	.379	96	-0	-1	67	6			-3	*3/2S	-0.3
1951	Cin-N	96	331	41	84	9	3	4	37	33	32	.254	.321	.335	76	-10	-11	48	4	2	0	4	3/O	-0.7
1952	Cin-N	128	433	48	92	14	1	9	57	66	60	.212	.319	.312	76	-13	-13	48	5	4	-1	-17	*2	-2.6
1953	Cin-N	83	159	22	37	3	1	7	22	29	24	.233	.351	.396	94	-1	-1	24	0	1	-1	-11	21/3	-1.0
1954	Cin-N	1	1	0	0	0	0	0	0	0	0	.000	.000	.000	-97	-0	-0	0	0	0	0	0	H	0.0
	Chi-A	13	30	3	5	1	0	0	3	5	3	.167	.286	.200	34	-3	-3	2	1	0	0	-1	3/1	-0.3
	Bos-A	99	302	40	85	12	3	5	33	58	25	.281	.401	.391	106	10	5	51	1	1	-0	6	3/1S	0.6
	Yr	112	332	43	90	13	3	5	36	63	28	.271	.390	.373	100	7	3	53	2	1	0	5		0.3
1955	Bos-A	126	380	48	93	11	4	4	49	76	28	.245	.371	.326	81	-3	-8	51	0	1	-1	-2	*3/2	-0.8
1956	Bos-A	5	5	0	2	0	0	0	2	0	0	.400	.400	.400	100	0	0	1	0	0	0	0	H	0.0
	StL-N	44	73	10	18	1	2	0	7	13	7	.247	.360	.315	84	-1	-1	9	1	0	0	-4	2/3	-0.3
	Bal-A	27	61	4	9	1	0	1	3	13	6	.148	.297	.213	40	-5	-5	5	0	0	0	-5	23	-0.7
1960	Chi-N	28	38	3	13	0	0	0	7	2	5	.342	.390	.342	104	0	0	5	0	0	0	-1	/2	0.0
Total	12	1312	4206	562	1068	166	33	91	533	646	430	.254	.355	.374	96	-4	-10	604	42	9		-58	32/10S	-6.0

■ ARTHUR HAUGER
Hauger, John Arthur b: 11/18/1893, Delhi, Ohio d: 8/2/44, Redwood City, Cal BL/TR, 5'11", 168 lbs. Deb: 7/17/12

YEAR	TM/L	G	AB	R	H	2B	3B	HR	RBI	BB	SO	AVG	OBP	SLG	PRO+	BR	/A	RC	SB	CS	SBR	FR	POS	TPR
1912	Cle-A	15	18	0	1	0	0	0	0	1		.056	.105	.056	-52	-4	-4	0				-1	/O	-0.5

■ ARNOLD HAUSER
Hauser, Arnold George "Peewee" or "Stub" b: 9/25/1888, Chicago, Ill. d: 5/22/66, Aurora, Ill. BR/TR, 5'6", 145 lbs. Deb: 4/21/10

YEAR	TM/L	G	AB	R	H	2B	3B	HR	RBI	BB	SO	AVG	OBP	SLG	PRO+	BR	/A	RC	SB	CS	SBR	FR	POS	TPR
1910	StL-N	119	375	37	77	7	2	1	36	49	39	.205	.312	.251	67	-15	-13	34	15			-8	*S/3	-1.7
1911	StL-N	136	515	61	124	11	8	3	46	26	67	.241	.286	.311	69	-24	-22	53	24			-15	*S/3	-3.2
1912	StL-N	133	479	73	124	14	7	1	42	39	69	.259	.319	.324	78	-16	-14	58	26			10	*S	0.8
1913	StL-N	22	45	3	13	0	3	0	9	2	2	.289	.347	.422	121	1	1	7	1			-3	/S2	-0.1
1915	Chi-F	23	54	6	11	1	0	0	4	5	7	.204	.283	.222	54	-3	-3	4	2			-3	S/3	-0.4
Total	5	433	1468	180	349	33	20	6	137	121	184	.238	.305	.300	73	-57	-52	157	68			-19	S/32	-4.6

■ JOE HAUSER
Hauser, Joseph John "Unser Choe" b: 1/12/1899, Milwaukee, Wis. BL/TL, 5'10.5", 175 lbs. Deb: 4/18/22

YEAR	TM/L	G	AB	R	H	2B	3B	HR	RBI	BB	SO	AVG	OBP	SLG	PRO+	BR	/A	RC	SB	CS	SBR	FR	POS	TPR
1922	Phi-A	111	368	61	119	21	5	9	43	30	37	.323	.378	.481	119	11	10	65	1	5	-3	-3	1	-0.2
1923	Phi-A	146	537	93	165	21	9	16	94	69	52	.307	.398	.475	127	23	22	104	6	6	-2	-3	*1	1.1
1924	Phi-A	149	562	97	162	31	8	27	115	56	52	.288	.358	.516	123	16	15	104	7	5	-1	-3	*1	0.4
1926	Phi-A	91	229	31	44	10	0	8	36	39	34	.192	.312	.341	66	-10	-12	26	1	2	-1	0	1	-1.4
1928	Phi-A	95	300	61	78	19	5	16	59	52	45	.260	.369	.517	127	13	12	60	4	2	0	-6	1	0.1
1929	Cle-A	37	48	8	12	1	1	3	9	4	8	.250	.308	.500	101	-0	-0	7	0	0	0	1	/1	0.0
Total	6	629	2044	351	580	103	28	80	356	250	228	.284	.367	.479	117	53	47	367	19	20	-6	-14	1	0.0

■ GEORGE HAUSMANN
Hausmann, George John b: 2/11/16, St.Louis, Mo. BR/TR, 5'5", 145 lbs. Deb: 4/18/44

YEAR	TM/L	G	AB	R	H	2B	3B	HR	RBI	BB	SO	AVG	OBP	SLG	PRO+	BR	/A	RC	SB	CS	SBR	FR	POS	TPR
1944	NY-N	131	466	70	124	20	4	1	30	40	25	.266	.324	.333	85	-9	-9	52	3			-7	*2	-0.3
1945	NY-N	154	623	98	174	15	8	2	45	73	46	.279	.356	.339	92	-3	-5	81	7			5	*2	1.3
1949	NY-N	16	47	5	6	0	1	0	3	7	6	.128	.241	.170	12	-6	-6	3	0			-0	2	-0.5
Total	3	301	1136	173	304	35	13	3	78	120	77	.268	.338	.329	86	-18	-19	135	10			-3	2	0.5

■ CHARLIE HAUTZ
Hautz, Charles A. b: 2/5/1852, St.Louis, Mo. d: 1/24/29, St.Louis, Mo. 5'7", 150 lbs. Deb: 5/04/1875

YEAR	TM/L	G	AB	R	H	2B	3B	HR	RBI	BB	SO	AVG	OBP	SLG	PRO+	BR	/A	RC	SB	CS	SBR	FR	POS	TPR
1875	RS-n	19	83	5	25	2	0	0		1		.301	.310	.325	133	2	3	9				1		0.2
1884	Pit-a	7	24	0	5	0	0	0		3		.208	.296	.208	69	-1	-1	2				0	/1O	0.0

■ ROY HAWES
Hawes, Roy Lee b: 7/5/26, Shiloh, Ill. BL/TL, 6'2", 190 lbs. Deb: 9/23/51

YEAR	TM/L	G	AB	R	H	2B	3B	HR	RBI	BB	SO	AVG	OBP	SLG	PRO+	BR	/A	RC	SB	CS	SBR	FR	POS	TPR
1951	Was-A	3	6	0	1	0	0	0	0	0	1	.167	.167	.167	-10	-1	-1	0	0	0	0	-0	/1	0.0

■ BILL HAWES
Hawes, William Hildreth b: 11/17/1853, Nashua, N.H. d: 6/16/40, Lowell, Mass. BR/TR, 5'10", 155 lbs. Deb: 5/01/1879

YEAR	TM/L	G	AB	R	H	2B	3B	HR	RBI	BB	SO	AVG	OBP	SLG	PRO+	BR	/A	RC	SB	CS	SBR	FR	POS	TPR
1879	Bos-N	38	155	19	31	3	3	0	9	2	13	.200	.210	.258	52	-8	-8	9				-3	O/C	-1.0
1884	Cin-U	79	349	80	97	7	4	4		5		.278	.288	.355	108	5	1	37	0			-7	O1	-0.5
Total	2	117	504	99	128	10	7	4	9	7	13	.254	.264	.325	91	-2	-7	45	0			-10	/O1C	-1.5

■ THORNY HAWKES
Hawkes, Thorndike Proctor b: 10/15/1852, Danvers, Mass. d: 2/3/29, Danvers, Mass. BR/TR, 5'8", 135 lbs. Deb: 5/01/1879

YEAR	TM/L	G	AB	R	H	2B	3B	HR	RBI	BB	SO	AVG	OBP	SLG	PRO+	BR	/A	RC	SB	CS	SBR	FR	POS	TPR
1879	Tro-N	64	250	24	52	6	1	0	20	4	14	.208	.220	.240	55	-13	-10	14				16	*2	1.1
1884	Was-a	38	151	16	42	4	2	0		4		.278	.297	.331	121	1	4	15				3	2/O	0.7
Total	2	102	401	40	94	10	3	0	20	8	14	.234	.249	.274	79	-12	-7	29				20	2/O	1.8

■ CHICKEN HAWKS
Hawks, Nelson Louis b: 2/3/1896, San Francisco, Cal. d: 5/26/73, San Rafael, Cal. BL/TL, 5'11", 167 lbs. Deb: 4/14/21

YEAR	TM/L	G	AB	R	H	2B	3B	HR	RBI	BB	SO	AVG	OBP	SLG	PRO+	BR	/A	RC	SB	CS	SBR	FR	POS	TPR
1921	NY-A	41	73	16	21	2	3	2	15	5	12	.288	.333	.479	103	0	0	11	0	1	-1	-2	O	-0.2
1925	Phi-N	105	320	52	103	15	5	5	45	32	33	.322	.387	.447	103	7	2	55	3	6	-3	0	1	-0.8
Total	2	146	393	68	124	17	8	7	60	37	45	.316	.377	.453	103	7	2	66	3	7	-3	-2	/1O	-1.0

■ HOWIE HAWORTH
Haworth, Homer Howard "Cully" b: 8/27/1893, Newberg, Ore. d: 1/28/53, Troutdale, Ore. BL/TR, 5'10.5", 165 lbs. Deb: 8/14/15

YEAR	TM/L	G	AB	R	H	2B	3B	HR	RBI	BB	SO	AVG	OBP	SLG	PRO+	BR	/A	RC	SB	CS	SBR	FR	POS	TPR
1915	Cle-A	7	7	0	1	0	0	0	1	0	0	.143	.333	.143	42	-0	-0	0	0			-1	/C	0.0

■ JACK HAYDEN
Hayden, John Francis b: 10/21/1880, Bryn Mawr, Pa. d: 8/3/42, Haverford, Pa. BR/TL, 5'9", Deb: 4/26/01

YEAR	TM/L	G	AB	R	H	2B	3B	HR	RBI	BB	SO	AVG	OBP	SLG	PRO+	BR	/A	RC	SB	CS	SBR	FR	POS	TPR
1901	Phi-A	51	211	35	56	6	4	0	17	18		.265	.323	.332	80	-4	-6	25	4			-4	O	-0.8
1906	Bos-A	85	322	22	80	6	4	1	14	17		.248	.286	.301	86	-5	-5	31	6			-1	O	-1.0
1908	Chi-N	11	45	3	9	2	0	0	2	1		.200	.217	.244	47	-3	-3	3	1			-1	O	-0.3
Total	3	147	578	60	145	14	8	1	33	36		.251	.295	.308	81	-12	-14	59	11			-5	O	-2.1

■ CHARLIE HAYES
Hayes, Charles Dewayne b: 5/29/65, Hattiesburg, Miss. BR/TR, 6', 190 lbs. Deb: 9/11/88

YEAR	TM/L	G	AB	R	H	2B	3B	HR	RBI	BB	SO	AVG	OBP	SLG	PRO+	BR	/A	RC	SB	CS	SBR	FR	POS	TPR
1988	SF-N	7	11	0	1	0	0	0	0	0	2	.091	.091	.091	-50	-2	-2	0	0	0	0	-0	/O3	-0.2
1989	SF-N	3	5	0	1	0	0	0	0	0	3	.200	.200	.200	15	-1	-1	0	0	0	0	-0	/3	0.0
	Phi-N	84	299	26	77	15	1	8	43	11	49	.258	.284	.395	92	-4	-4	32	3	1	0	10	3	0.6
	Yr	87	304	26	78	15	1	8	43	11	50	.257	.283	.391	91	-5	-5	32	3	1	0	10		0.6

YEAR	TM/L	G	AB	R	H	2B	3B	HR	RBI	BB	SO	AVG	OBP	SLG	PRO+	BR	/A	RC	SB	CS	SBR	FR	POS	TPR
1990	Phi-N	152	561	56	145	20	0	10	57	28	91	.258	.296	.348	77	-19	-18	55	4	4	-1	24	*3/12	0.8
Total	3	246	876	82	224	35	1	18	100	39	144	.256	.289	.360	80	-25	-25	88	7	5	-1	33	3/1O2	1.2

■ FRANKIE HAYES
Hayes, Frank Witman "Blimp" b: 10/13/14, Jamesburg, N.J. d: 6/22/55, Point Pleasant, N.J. BR/TR, 6', 185 lbs. Deb: 9/21/33

YEAR	TM/L	G	AB	R	H	2B	3B	HR	RBI	BB	SO	AVG	OBP	SLG	PRO+	BR	/A	RC	SB	CS	SBR	FR	POS	TPR
1933	Phi-A	3	5	0	0	0	0	0	0	0	2	.000	.000	.000	-99	-1	-1	0	0	0	0	1	/C	0.0
1934	Phi-A	92	248	24	56	10	0	6	30	20	44	.226	.286	.339	63	-15	-14	25	2	1	0	-10	C	-1.4
1936	Phi-A	144	505	39	137	25	2	10	67	46	58	.271	.335	.388	79	-19	-17	66	3	5	-2	-21	*C	-2.4
1937	Phi-A	60	188	24	49	11	1	10	38	29	34	.261	.359	.489	114	3	3	34	0	0	0	-3	C	0.4
1938	Phi-A	99	316	56	92	19	3	11	55	54	51	.291	.396	.475	120	9	10	62	2	3	-1	-16	C	-0.3
1939	Phi-A	124	431	66	122	28	5	20	83	40	55	.283	.348	.510	119	9	10	76	4	1	1	-11	*C	0.6
1940	Phi-A	136	465	73	143	23	4	16	70	61	59	.308	.389	.477	126	17	18	89	9	3	1	-12	*C/1	1.5
1941	Phi-A	126	439	66	123	27	4	12	63	62	56	.280	.369	.442	117	9	10	70	2	0	1	-10	*C	0.8
1942	Phi-A	21	63	8	15	4	0	0	5	9	8	.238	.333	.302	80	-2	-1	6	1	1	-0	-4	C	-0.2
	StL-A	56	159	14	40	6	0	2	17	28	39	.252	.364	.327	94	-0	-0	22	0	0	-0	-6	C	0.0
	Yr	77	222	22	55	10	0	2	22	37	47	.248	.355	.320	90	-2	-2	28	1	1	-0	-10		-0.2
1943	StL-A	88	250	16	47	7	0	5	30	37	36	.188	.295	.276	66	-10	-10	22	1	0	0	-9	C/1	-1.6
1944	Phi-A	155	581	62	144	18	6	13	78	57	59	.248	.315	.367	96	-5	-4	68	2	1	0	3	*C/1	1.0
1945	Phi-A	32	110	12	25	2	1	3	14	18	14	.227	.336	.345	98	-0	0	14	1	0	0	2	C	0.5
	Cle-A	119	385	39	91	15	6	6	43	53	52	.236	.335	.353	104	0	2	49	1	1	-0	2	*C	1.4
	Yr	151	495	51	116	17	7	9	57	71	66	.234	.335	.352	103	0	3	63	2	1	0	3		1.9
1946	Cle-A	51	156	11	40	12	0	3	18	21	26	.256	.345	.391	112	1	2	20	1	3	-2	-1	C	0.2
	Chi-A	53	179	15	38	6	0	2	16	29	33	.212	.322	.279	72	-7	-6	17	1	1	-0	-3	C	-0.6
	Yr	104	335	26	78	18	0	5	34	50	59	.233	.332	.331	90	-5	-3	37	2	4	-2	-4		-0.4
1947	Bos-A	5	13	0	2	0	0	0	1	0	1	.154	.154	.154	-13	-2	-2	0	0	0	0	1	/C	0.0
Total	14	1364	4493	525	1164	213	32	116	628	564	627	.259	.343	.400	100	-13	1	640	30	20	-3	-98	*C/1	-0.1

■ JACKIE HAYES
Hayes, John J. b: 6/27/1861, Brooklyn, N.Y. TR , Deb: 5/02/1882

YEAR	TM/L	G	AB	R	H	2B	3B	HR	RBI	BB	SO	AVG	OBP	SLG	PRO+	BR	/A	RC	SB	CS	SBR	FR	POS	TPR
1882	Wor-N	78	326	27	88	22	4	4	54	6	26	.270	.283	.399	113	5	4	38				-8	*OC/3S	-0.2
1883	Pit-a	85	351	41	92	23	5	3		15		.262	.292	.382	121	6	8	40				-14	CO/S12	-0.1
1884	Pit-a	33	124	11	28	6	1	0		4		.226	.256	.290	79	-3	-3	9				-2	C/1O2	-0.2
	Bro-a	16	51	4	12	3	0	0		3		.235	.278	.294	89	-1	-1	4				4	C/O	0.4
	Yr	49	175	15	40	9	1	0		7		.229	.262	.291	82	-3	-3	14				2		0.2
1885	Bro-a	42	137	10	18	3	0	0		5		.131	.179	.153	7	-14	-14	4				-2	C	-0.8
1886	Was-N	26	89	8	17	3	0	3	9	4	23	.191	.226	.326	70	-4	-3	7	0			-4	CO/2	-0.4
1887	Bal-a	8	28	2	4	3	0	0		0		.143	.143	.250	10	-3	-3	1	0			-4	/O3C	-0.5
1890	Bro-P	12	42	3	8	0	0	0	5	2	4	.190	.227	.190	13	-5	-6	2	0			-3	/OSC2	-0.6
Total	7	300	1148	106	267	63	10	10	68	39	53	.233	.260	.331	87	-18	-17	105	0			-32	CO/1S32	-2.4

■ MIKE HAYES
Hayes, Michael b: 1853, Cleveland, Ohio 5'7.5", 170 lbs. Deb: 9/09/1876

YEAR	TM/L	G	AB	R	H	2B	3B	HR	RBI	BB	SO	AVG	OBP	SLG	PRO+	BR	/A	RC	SB	CS	SBR	FR	POS	TPR
1876	NY-N	5	21	1	3	0	2	0	2	0	0	.143	.143	.333	63	-1	-1	1				0	/O	0.0

■ JACKIE HAYES
Hayes, Minter Carney b: 7/19/06, Clanton, Ala. d: 2/9/83, Birmingham, Ala. BR/TR, 5'10.5", 165 lbs. Deb: 8/05/27

YEAR	TM/L	G	AB	R	H	2B	3B	HR	RBI	BB	SO	AVG	OBP	SLG	PRO+	BR	/A	RC	SB	CS	SBR	FR	POS	TPR
1927	Was-A	10	29	2	7	0	0	0	2	1	2	.241	.267	.241	33	-3	-3	2	0	0	0	-0	/S3	-0.2
1928	Was-A	60	210	30	54	7	3	0	22	5	10	.257	.274	.319	56	-14	-14	19	3	0	1	8	2S/3	-1.1
1929	Was-A	123	424	52	117	20	3	2	57	24	29	.276	.316	.351	71	-18	-19	47	4	5	-2	3	32/S	-1.1
1930	Was-A	51	166	25	47	7	2	1	20	7	8	.283	.312	.367	71	-7	-7	18	2	3	-1	8	2/31	0.0
1931	Was-A	38	108	11	24	2	1	0	8	6	4	.222	.263	.259	38	-10	-10	8	2	0	1	-4	2/3S	-0.9
1932	Chi-A	117	475	53	122	20	5	2	54	30	28	.257	.302	.333	69	-25	-21	48	7	4	-0	1	2S3	-1.3
1933	Chi-A	138	535	65	138	23	5	2	47	55	36	.258	.331	.331	79	-18	-15	61	2	3	-1	10	*2	-0.7
1934	Chi-A	62	226	19	58	9	1	1	31	23	20	.257	.325	.319	65	-11	-12	25	3	2	-0	-8	2	-1.6
1935	Chi-A	89	329	45	88	14	0	4	45	29	15	.267	.327	.347	72	-13	-14	39	3	1	0	-6	2	-1.4
1936	Chi-A	108	417	53	130	34	3	5	84	35	25	.312	.366	.444	96	-1	-4	69	4	2	0	17	2S/3	1.8
1937	Chi-A	143	573	63	131	27	4	2	79	41	37	.229	.282	.300	47	-47	-47	49	1	6	-3	21	*2	-1.4
1938	Chi-A	62	238	40	78	21	2	1	20	24	6	.328	.389	.445	106	3	3	42	3	2	-0	-3	2	0.1
1939	Chi-A	72	269	34	67	12	3	0	23	27	10	.249	.320	.316	62	-15	-16	28	0	3	-2	5	2	-0.8
1940	Chi-A	18	41	2	8	0	1	0	1	2	11	.195	.233	.244	23	-5	-5	3	0	0	0	0	2	-0.3
Total	14	1091	4040	494	1069	196	33	20	493	309	241	.265	.318	.344	70	-184	-183	456	34	31	-8	52	2/3S1	-7.8

■ VON HAYES
Hayes, Von Francis b: 8/31/58, Stockton, Cal. BL/TR, 6'5", 185 lbs. Deb: 4/14/81

YEAR	TM/L	G	AB	R	H	2B	3B	HR	RBI	BB	SO	AVG	OBP	SLG	PRO+	BR	/A	RC	SB	CS	SBR	FR	POS	TPR
1981	Cle-A	43	109	21	28	8	2	1	17	14	10	.257	.352	.394	116	2	3	17	8	1	2	0	DO/3	0.5
1982	Cle-A	150	527	65	132	25	3	14	82	42	63	.250	.311	.389	91	-7	-7	63	32	13	2	4	*O/31	-0.5
1983	*Phi-N	124	351	45	93	9	5	6	32	36	55	.265	.338	.370	97	-1	-1	42	20	12	-1	-3	*O	-0.6
1984	Phi-N	152	561	85	164	27	6	16	67	59	84	.292	.360	.447	124	19	18	94	48	13	7	-10	*O	0.9
1985	Phi-N	152	570	76	150	30	4	13	70	61	99	.263	.334	.398	101	3	1	79	21	8	2	6	*O	0.5
1986	Phi-N	158	610	107	186	46	2	19	98	74	77	.305	.381	.480	131	30	28	111	24	12	0	1	*1O	2.4
1987	Phi-N	158	556	84	154	36	5	21	84	121	77	.277	.406	.473	128	30	27	113	16	7	1	-8	*1O	1.0
1988	Phi-N	104	367	43	100	28	2	6	45	59	59	.272	.360	.409	118	11	10	57	20	9	1	-1	1O/3	0.4
1989	Phi-N	154	540	93	140	27	2	26	78	101	103	.259	.380	.461	139	30	30	103	28	7	4	2	*O13	3.4
1990	Phi-N	129	467	70	122	14	3	17	73	87	81	.261	.382	.413	119	15	15	78	16	7	1	3	*O	1.5
Total	10	1324	4658	689	1269	250	34	139	646	644	708	.272	.363	.430	118	132	124	757	233	89	17	-8	O1/3D	9.5

■ BILL HAYES
Hayes, William Ernest b: 10/24/57, Cheverly, Md. BR/TR, 6', 195 lbs. Deb: 9/30/80

YEAR	TM/L	G	AB	R	H	2B	3B	HR	RBI	BB	SO	AVG	OBP	SLG	PRO+	BR	/A	RC	SB	CS	SBR	FR	POS	TPR
1980	Chi-N	4	9	0	2	1	0	0	0	0	3	.222	.222	.333	49	-1	-1	1	0	0	0	-0	/C	0.0
1981	Chi-N	1	0	0	0	0	0	0	0	0	0	—	—	—	—	0	0	0	0	0	0	0	/C	0.0
Total	2	5	9	0	2	1	0	0	0	0	3	.222	.222	.333	49	-1	-1	1	0	0	0	-0	/C	0.0

■ RED HAYWORTH
Hayworth, Myron Claude b: 5/14/15, High Point, N.C. BR/TR, 6'1.5", 200 lbs. Deb: 4/21/44

YEAR	TM/L	G	AB	R	H	2B	3B	HR	RBI	BB	SO	AVG	OBP	SLG	PRO+	BR	/A	RC	SB	CS	SBR	FR	POS	TPR
1944	*StL-A	90	270	20	60	11	1	1	0	0	0	.222	.222	.281	41	-21	-22	17	0	0	0	0	C	-1.6
1945	StL-A	56	160	7	31	4	0	0	17	7	6	.194	.228	.219	28	-14	-15	7	0	2	-1	3	C	-0.9
Total	2	146	430	27	91	15	1	1	17	7	6	.212	.224	.258	36	-35	-38	25	0	2	-1	4	C	-2.5

■ RAY HAYWORTH
Hayworth, Raymond Hall b: 1/29/04, High Point, N.C. BR/TR, 6', 180 lbs. Deb: 6/27/26 C

YEAR	TM/L	G	AB	R	H	2B	3B	HR	RBI	BB	SO	AVG	OBP	SLG	PRO+	BR	/A	RC	SB	CS	SBR	FR	POS	TPR
1926	Det-A	12	11	1	3	0	0	0	5	1	1	.273	.333	.273	59	-1	-1	1	0	0	0	-1	/C	0.0
1929	Det-A	14	43	5	11	0	0	0	4	3	8	.256	.304	.256	45	-3	-3	4	0	0	0	0	C	-0.1
1930	Det-A	77	227	24	63	15	4	0	22	20	19	.278	.336	.379	79	-7	-7	29	0	2	-1	-11	C	-1.1
1931	Det-A	88	273	28	70	10	3	0	25	19	27	.256	.307	.315	62	-14	-16	27	0	1	-1	4	C	-0.4
1932	Det-A	109	338	41	99	20	2	0	44	31	22	.293	.354	.382	87	-4	-6	47	1	1	-0	2	*C	0.1
1933	Det-A	134	425	37	104	14	3	1	45	35	28	.245	.302	.299	59	-24	-26	40	1	1	0	1	*C	-1.6
1934	*Det-A	54	167	20	49	5	2	0	27	16	22	.293	.355	.347	82	-4	-4	21	0	2	-1	6	C	0.5
1935	Det-A	51	175	22	54	14	2	0	22	9	14	.309	.342	.411	98	-2	-2	25	0	0	0	11	C	1.0
1936	Det-A	81	250	31	60	10	0	1	30	39	18	.240	.347	.292	59	-15	-15	28	0	0	0	-4	C	-1.0
1937	Det-A	30	78	9	21	2	0	1	8	14	15	.269	.394	.333	83	-1	-1	12	0	0	0	6	C	0.6
1938	Det-A	8	19	1	4	0	0	0	5	3	4	.211	.318	.211	33	-2	-2	1	0	1	-0	2	/C	0.0
	Bro-N	5	4	0	0	0	0	0	0	1	1	.000	.200	.000	-40	-1	-1	0	0	0	0	0	/C	0.0
1939	Bro-N	21	26	0	4	2	0	0	1	4	7	.154	.267	.231	34	-2	-3	2	0			1	C	0.0

YEAR	TM/L	G	AB	R	H	2B	3B	HR	RBI	BB	SO	AVG	OBP	SLG	PRO+	BR	/A	RC	SB	CS	SBR	FR	POS	TPR
	NY-N	5	13	1	3	0	0	0	0	0	1	.231	.231	.231	24	-1	-1	1	0			1	/C	0.0
	Yr	26	39	1	7	2	0	0	1	4	8	.179	.256	.231	31	-4	-4	2	0			0		0.0
1942	StL-A	1	1	0	1	0	0	0	0	0	0	1.000	1.000	1.000	456	0	0	1	0	0	0	0	H	0.0
1944	Bro-N	7	10	0	0	0	0	0	0	2	1	.000	.167	.000	-51	-2	-2	0	0			2	/C	0.0
1945	Bro-N	2	2	0	0	0	0	0	0	1	0	.000	.333	.000	-3	-0	-0	0	0			0	/C	0.0
Total	15	699	2062	220	546	92	16	5	238	198	188	.265	.331	.332	71	-84	-89	237	2	6		21	C	-2.0

■ DRUNGO HAZEWOOD
Hazewood, Drungo La Rue b: 9/2/59, Mobile, Ala.　BR/TR, 6'3", 210 lbs.　Deb: 9/19/80

YEAR	TM/L	G	AB	R	H	2B	3B	HR	RBI	BB	SO	AVG	OBP	SLG	PRO+	BR	/A	RC	SB	CS	SBR	FR	POS	TPR
1980	Bal-A	6	5	1	0	0	0	0	0	0	4	.000	.000	.000	-99	-1	-1	0	0	0	0	0	/O	0.0

■ BOB HAZLE
Hazle, Robert Sidney "Hurricane" b: 12/9/30, Laurens, S.C.　BL/TR, 6', 190 lbs.　Deb: 9/08/55

YEAR	TM/L	G	AB	R	H	2B	3B	HR	RBI	BB	SO	AVG	OBP	SLG	PRO+	BR	/A	RC	SB	CS	SBR	FR	POS	TPR
1955	Cin-N	6	13	0	3	0	0	0	0	0	3	.231	.231	.231	22	-1	-2	1	0	0	0	2	/O	0.0
1957	*Mil-N	41	134	26	54	12	0	7	27	18	15	.403	.477	.649	214	19	21	41	1	3	-2	-7	O	1.0
1958	Mil-N	20	56	6	10	0	0	0	5	9	4	.179	.303	.179	34	-5	-5	4	0	0	0	-1	O	-0.5
	Det-A	43	58	5	14	2	0	2	5	5	13	.241	.302	.379	80	-1	-2	7	0	0	0	-1	O	-0.3
Total	3	110	261	37	81	14	0	9	37	32	35	.310	.390	.467	135	12	13	53	1	3	-2	-8	/O	0.2

■ DOC HAZLETON
Hazleton, Willard Carpenter b: 8/28/1876, Strafford, Vt.　d: 3/17/41, Burlington, Vt.　Deb: 4/17/02

YEAR	TM/L	G	AB	R	H	2B	3B	HR	RBI	BB	SO	AVG	OBP	SLG	PRO+	BR	/A	RC	SB	CS	SBR	FR	POS	TPR
1902	StL-N	7	23	0	3	0	0	0	0	0	2	.130	.231	.130	14	-2	-2	1	0			0	/1	-0.2

■ FRAN HEALY
Healy, Francis Xavier b: 9/6/46, Holyoke, Mass.　BR/TR, 6'5", 220 lbs.　Deb: 9/03/69

YEAR	TM/L	G	AB	R	H	2B	3B	HR	RBI	BB	SO	AVG	OBP	SLG	PRO+	BR	/A	RC	SB	CS	SBR	FR	POS	TPR
1969	KC-A	6	10	0	4	1	0	0	0	0	5	.400	.400	.500	149	1	1	2	0	0	0	0	/C	0.1
1971	SF-N	47	93	10	26	3	0	2	11	15	24	.280	.380	.376	117	2	3	14	1	0	0	-2	C	0.2
1972	SF-N	45	99	12	15	4	0	1	8	13	24	.152	.257	.222	37	-8	-8	6	0	1	-1	7	C	0.2
1973	KC-A	95	279	25	77	15	2	6	34	31	56	.276	.348	.409	104	5	2	40	3	4	-2	-3	C/D	0.0
1974	KC-A	139	445	59	112	24	2	9	53	62	73	.252	.344	.375	101	5	2	59	16	8	0	-5	*C	0.2
1975	KC-A	56	188	16	48	5	2	2	18	14	19	.255	.307	.335	79	-5	-5	18	4	3	-1	-7	C/D	-1.1
1976	KC-A	8	24	2	3	0	0	0	1	4	10	.125	.250	.125	12	-3	-3	1	2	0	1	0	/CD	0.0
	NY-A	46	120	10	32	3	0	0	9	9	17	.267	.318	.292	80	-3	-3	11	3	1	0	3	C/D	0.2
	Yr	54	144	12	35	3	0	0	10	13	27	.243	.306	.264	68	-5	-5	12	5	1	1	4		0.2
1977	NY-A	27	67	10	15	5	0	0	7	6	13	.224	.288	.299	61	-4	-4	5	1	0	0	0	C	-0.2
1978	NY-A	1	1	0	0	0	0	0	0	0	1	.000	.000	.000	-99	-0	-0	0	0	0	0	0	/C	0.0
Total	9	470	1326	144	332	60	6	20	141	154	242	.250	.329	.350	90	-9	-16	158	30	17	-1	-6	C/D	-0.6

■ FRANCIS HEALY
Healy, Francis Xavier Paul b: 6/29/10, Holyoke, Mass.　BR/TR, 5'9.5", 175 lbs.　Deb: 4/29/30

YEAR	TM/L	G	AB	R	H	2B	3B	HR	RBI	BB	SO	AVG	OBP	SLG	PRO+	BR	/A	RC	SB	CS	SBR	FR	POS	TPR
1930	NY-N	7	2	2	0	0	0	0	0	0	0	.000	.000	.000	-99	-1	-1	0	0			0	/C	0.0
1931	NY-N	6	7	1	1	0	0	0	0	0	0	.143	.143	.143	-24	-1	-1	0	0			1	/C	0.0
1932	NY-N	14	32	5	8	2	0	0	4	2	8	.250	.294	.313	65	-2	-2	3	0			2	C	0.1
1934	StL-N	15	13	1	4	1	0	0	1	0	2	.308	.308	.385	79	-0	-0	1	0			1	/C3O	0.0
Total	4	42	54	9	13	3	0	0	5	2	10	.241	.268	.296	51	-4	-4	4	0			3	/CO3	0.1

■ THOMAS HEALY
Healy, Thomas Fitzgerald b: 10/30/1895, Altoona, Pa.　d: 1/15/74, Cleveland, Ohio　BR/TR, 6', 172 lbs.　Deb: 7/13/15

YEAR	TM/L	G	AB	R	H	2B	3B	HR	RBI	BB	SO	AVG	OBP	SLG	PRO+	BR	/A	RC	SB	CS	SBR	FR	POS	TPR
1915	Phi-A	23	77	11	17	1	0	0	5	6	4	.221	.310	.234	65	-3	-3	5	0	4	-2	5	3/S	0.1
1916	Phi-A	6	23	4	6	1	1	0	2	1	2	.261	.320	.391	118	0	0	3	1			-1	/3	0.0
Total	2	29	100	15	23	2	1	0	7	7	6	.230	.313	.270	77	-3	-3	8	1	4		4	/3S	0.1

■ CHARLIE HEARD
Heard, Charles b: 1/30/1872, Philadelphia, Pa.　d: 2/20/45, Philadelphia, Pa.　BR/TR, 6'2", 190 lbs.　Deb: 7/14/1890

YEAR	TM/L	G	AB	R	H	2B	3B	HR	RBI	BB	SO	AVG	OBP	SLG	PRO+	BR	/A	RC	SB	CS	SBR	FR	POS	TPR
1890	Pit-N	12	43	2	8	2	0	0	0	1	15	.186	.205	.233	32	-4	-3	2	0			-3	/OP	-0.3

■ ED HEARN
Hearn, Edmund b: 9/17/1888, Ventura, Cal.　d: 9/8/52, Sawtelle, Cal.　TR , 5'9", 160 lbs.　Deb: 6/09/10

YEAR	TM/L	G	AB	R	H	2B	3B	HR	RBI	BB	SO	AVG	OBP	SLG	PRO+	BR	/A	RC	SB	CS	SBR	FR	POS	TPR
1910	Bos-A	2	2	0	0	0	0	0	0	0	0	.000	.000	.000	-98	-0	-0	0	0			2	/S	0.1

■ ED HEARN
Hearn, Edward John b: 8/23/60, Stuart, Fla.　BR/TR, 6'3", 215 lbs.　Deb: 5/17/86

YEAR	TM/L	G	AB	R	H	2B	3B	HR	RBI	BB	SO	AVG	OBP	SLG	PRO+	BR	/A	RC	SB	CS	SBR	FR	POS	TPR
1986	NY-N	49	136	16	36	5	0	4	10	12	19	.265	.324	.390	99	-1	-0	16	0	1	-1	-6	C	-0.5
1987	KC-A	6	17	2	5	2	0	0	3	4	2	.294	.429	.412	121	1	1	3	0	0	0	-2	/C	0.0
1988	KC-A	7	18	1	4	2	0	0	1	0	1	.222	.222	.333	53	-1	-1	1	0	0	0	-0	/CD	0.0
Total	3	62	171	19	45	9	0	4	14	16	22	.263	.326	.386	97	-1	-1	20	0	1	-1	-7	/CD	-0.5

■ HUGHIE HEARNE
Hearne, Hugh Joseph b: 4/18/1873, Troy, N.Y.　d: 9/22/32, Troy, N.Y.　BR/TR, 5'8", 182 lbs.　Deb: 8/29/01

YEAR	TM/L	G	AB	R	H	2B	3B	HR	RBI	BB	SO	AVG	OBP	SLG	PRO+	BR	/A	RC	SB	CS	SBR	FR	POS	TPR
1901	Bro-N	2	5	1	2	0	0	0	3	0		.400	.400	.400	131	0	0	1	0			0	/C	0.1
1902	Bro-N	66	231	22	65	10	0	0	28	16		.281	.339	.325	106	2	2	28	3			-10	C	0.0
1903	Bro-N	26	57	8	16	3	2	0	4	3		.281	.317	.404	110	0	0	8	2			3	C/1	0.5
Total	3	94	293	31	83	13	2	0	35	19		.283	.335	.341	107	3	3	37	5			-6	/C1	0.6

■ JEFF HEARRON
Hearron, Jeffrey Vernon b: 11/19/61, Long Beach, Cal.　BR/TR, 6'1", 195 lbs.　Deb: 8/25/85

YEAR	TM/L	G	AB	R	H	2B	3B	HR	RBI	BB	SO	AVG	OBP	SLG	PRO+	BR	/A	RC	SB	CS	SBR	FR	POS	TPR
1985	*Tor-A	4	7	0	1	0	0	0	0	0	2	.143	.143	.143	-21	-1	-1	0	0	0	0	2	/C	0.0
1986	Tor-A	12	23	2	5	1	0	0	4	3	7	.217	.308	.261	55	-1	-1	2	0	0	0	1	C	0.0
Total	2	16	30	2	6	1	0	0	4	3	9	.200	.273	.233	39	-2	-3	2	0	0	0	2	/C	0.0

■ JEFF HEATH
Heath, John Geoffrey b: 4/1/15, Ft.William, Ont., Canada　d: 12/9/75, Seattle, Wash.　BL/TR, 5'11.5", 200 lbs.　Deb: 9/13/36

YEAR	TM/L	G	AB	R	H	2B	3B	HR	RBI	BB	SO	AVG	OBP	SLG	PRO+	BR	/A	RC	SB	CS	SBR	FR	POS	TPR
1936	Cle-A	12	41	6	14	3	3	1	8	3	4	.341	.386	.634	147	3	3	10	1	0	0	-2	O	0.0
1937	Cle-A	20	61	8	14	1	4	0	8	0	9	.230	.230	.377	50	-5	-5	5	0	1	-1	-1	O	-0.6
1938	Cle-A	126	502	104	172	31	18	21	112	33	55	.343	.383	.602	146	29	31	113	3	1	0	0	*O	2.8
1939	Cle-A	121	431	64	126	31	7	14	69	41	64	.292	.354	.494	119	8	10	75	8	4	0	6	*O	1.1
1940	Cle-A	100	356	55	78	16	3	14	50	40	62	.219	.298	.399	81	-12	-11	45	5	3	-0	1	O	-1.5
1941	Cle-A	151	585	89	199	32	20	24	123	50	69	.340	.396	.586	165	45	49	138	18	12	-2	-7	*O	2.9
1942	Cle-A	147	568	82	158	37	13	10	76	62	66	.278	.350	.442	130	15	19	89	9	9	-3	4	*O	1.0
1943	Cle-A	118	424	58	116	22	6	18	79	63	58	.274	.369	.481	157	25	28	79	5	8	-3	-2	*O	2.1
1944	Cle-A	60	151	20	50	5	2	5	33	18	12	.331	.402	.490	160	11	11	31	0	1	-1	0	O	1.0
1945	Cle-A	102	370	60	113	16	7	15	61	56	39	.305	.398	.508	169	29	31	80	3	1	0	-5	*O	2.3
1946	Was-A	48	166	23	47	12	3	4	27	36	36	.283	.411	.464	153	11	12	34	0	4	-2	-4	O	0.4
	StL-A	86	316	46	87	20	4	12	57	37	37	.275	.353	.478	124	12	10	56	0	2	-1	-10	O	-0.5
	Yr	134	482	69	134	32	7	16	84	73	73	.278	.374	.473	134	23	23	91	0	6	-4	-14		-0.1
1947	StL-A	141	491	81	123	20	7	27	85	88	87	.251	.366	.485	133	23	22	91	2	1	0	-1	*O	1.5
1948	Bos-N	115	364	64	116	26	5	20	76	51	46	.319	.404	.582	167	32	33	89	2			-2	O	2.3
1949	Bos-N	36	111	17	34	7	0	9	23	15	26	.306	.389	.613	174	10	10	27	0			-2	O	0.6
Total	14	1383	4937	777	1447	279	102	194	887	593	670	.293	.370	.509	140	235	254	964	56	47		-25	*O	15.4

■ KELLY HEATH
Heath, Kelly Mark b: 9/4/57, Plattsburg, N.Y.　BR/TR, 5'7", 155 lbs.　Deb: 4/20/82

YEAR	TM/L	G	AB	R	H	2B	3B	HR	RBI	BB	SO	AVG	OBP	SLG	PRO+	BR	/A	RC	SB	CS	SBR	FR	POS	TPR
1982	KC-A	1	1	0	0	0	0	0	0	0	0	.000	.000	.000	-99	-0	-0	0	0	0	0	1	/2	0.1

■ MIKE HEATH
Heath, Michael Thomas b: 2/5/55, Tampa, Fla.　BR/TR, 5'11", 180 lbs.　Deb: 6/03/78

YEAR	TM/L	G	AB	R	H	2B	3B	HR	RBI	BB	SO	AVG	OBP	SLG	PRO+	BR	/A	RC	SB	CS	SBR	FR	POS	TPR
1978	*NY-A	33	92	6	21	3	1	0	8	4	9	.228	.268	.283	56	-6	-5	7	0	0	0	2	C	-0.1
1979	Oak-A	74	258	19	66	8	0	3	27	14	18	.256	.309	.322	75	-10	-9	23	1	0	0	-4	OC/3D	-1.2
1980	Oak-A	92	305	27	74	10	2	1	33	16	28	.243	.280	.298	63	-17	-15	24	3	3	-1	17	CD/O	0.3
1981	*Oak-A	84	301	26	71	7	1	8	30	13	36	.236	.270	.346	80	-10	-8	25	3	3	-1	5	C/O	0.0

YEAR	TM/L	G	AB	R	H	2B	3B	HR	RBI	BB	SO	AVG	OBP	SLG	PRO+	BR	/A	RC	SB	CS	SBR	FR	POS	TPR
1982	Oak-A	101	318	43	77	18	4	3	39	27	36	.242	.301	.352	82	-9	-8	35	8	3	1	-6	CO/3	-0.8
1983	Oak-A	96	345	45	97	17	0	6	33	18	59	.281	.319	.383	98	-4	-2	39	3	4	-2	-9	CO/3D	-0.7
1984	Oak-A	140	475	49	118	21	5	13	64	26	72	.248	.289	.396	94	-9	-5	50	7	4	-0	-14	*CO/3S	-1.3
1985	Oak-A	138	436	71	109	18	6	13	55	41	63	.250	.316	.408	104	-3	2	53	7	7	-2	-6	*CO3	-0.1
1986	StL-N	65	190	19	39	8	1	4	25	23	36	.205	.294	.321	70	-8	-8	17	2	3	-1	-6	C/O	-1.3
	Det-A	30	98	11	26	3	0	4	11	4	17	.265	.294	.418	92	-1	-1	12	4	1	1	-2	C/3	0.0
1987	*Det-A	93	270	34	76	16	0	8	33	21	42	.281	.340	.430	107	1	2	38	1	5	-3	6	CO/13S2	1.0
1988	Det-A	86	219	24	54	7	2	5	18	18	32	.247	.307	.365	91	-4	-3	24	1	0	0	2	C/O	0.2
1989	Det-A	122	396	38	104	16	2	10	43	24	71	.263	.311	.389	98	-3	-2	44	7	1	2	0	*C/3OD	0.5
1990	Det-A	122	370	46	100	18	2	7	38	19	71	.270	.313	.386	95	-3	-3	41	7	6	-2	-1	*C/OSD	-0.2
Total	13	1276	4073	458	1032	170	26	85	457	271	590	.253	.303	.370	89	-87	-64	434	54	40	-8	-14	*CO/D31S2	-3.7

■ MICKEY HEATH
Heath, Minor Wilson b: 10/30/03, Toledo, Ohio d: 7/30/86, Dallas, Tex. BL/TL, 6', 175 lbs. Deb: 4/18/31

YEAR	TM/L	G	AB	R	H	2B	3B	HR	RBI	BB	SO	AVG	OBP	SLG	PRO+	BR	/A	RC	SB	CS	SBR	FR	POS	TPR
1931	Cin-N	7	26	2	7	0	0	0	3	2	5	.269	.321	.269	64	-1	-1	2	0			-0	/1	-0.1
1932	Cin-N	39	134	14	27	1	3	0	15	20	23	.201	.310	.254	55	-8	-8	12	0			2	1	-0.7
Total	2	46	160	16	34	1	3	0	18	22	28	.213	.311	.256	57	-10	-9	15	0			2	/1	-0.8

■ TOMMY HEATH
Heath, Thomas George b: 8/18/13, Akron, Col. d: 2/26/67, Los Gatos, Cal. BR/TR, 5'10", 185 lbs. Deb: 4/23/35

YEAR	TM/L	G	AB	R	H	2B	3B	HR	RBI	BB	SO	AVG	OBP	SLG	PRO+	BR	/A	RC	SB	CS	SBR	FR	POS	TPR
1935	StL-A	47	93	10	22	3	0	0	9	20	13	.237	.372	.269	65	-3	-4	11	0	0	0	-1	C	-0.3
1937	StL-A	17	43	4	10	0	2	1	3	10	3	.233	.377	.395	94	-0	-0	7	0	0		-0	C	0.0
1938	StL-A	70	194	22	44	13	0	2	22	35	24	.227	.345	.325	69	-9	-9	24	0	1	-1	7	C	0.0
Total	3	134	330	36	76	16	2	3	34	65	40	.230	.357	.318	71	-12	-13	42	0	1	-1	6	C	-0.3

■ BILL HEATH
Heath, William Chris b: 3/10/39, Yuba City, Cal. BL/TR, 5'8", 175 lbs. Deb: 10/03/65

YEAR	TM/L	G	AB	R	H	2B	3B	HR	RBI	BB	SO	AVG	OBP	SLG	PRO+	BR	/A	RC	SB	CS	SBR	FR	POS	TPR
1965	Chi-A	1	1	0	0	0	0	0	0	0	0	.000	.000	.000	-99	-0	-0	0	0	0	0	0	H	0.0
1966	Hou-N	55	123	12	37	6	0	0	8	9	11	.301	.353	.350	103	-0	1	15	1	0	0	-1	C	0.1
1967	Hou-N	9	11	0	1	0	0	0	0	4	3	.091	.333	.091	28	-1	-1	1	0	0	0	1	/C	-0.2
	Det-A	20	32	0	4	0	0	0	4	1	4	.125	.152	.125	-17	-5	-5	1	0	0	0	2	/C	-0.2
1969	Chi-N	27	32	1	5	0	1	0	1	12	4	.156	.386	.219	65	-0	-1	4	0	0	0	0	/C	0.0
Total	4	112	199	13	47	6	1	0	13	26	22	.236	.327	.276	73	-6	-6	20	1	0	0	1	/C	-0.1

■ CLIFF HEATHCOTE
Heathcote, Clifton Earl b: 1/24/1898, Glen Rock, Pa. d: 1/19/39, York, Pa. BL/TL, 5'10.5", 160 lbs. Deb: 6/04/18

YEAR	TM/L	G	AB	R	H	2B	3B	HR	RBI	BB	SO	AVG	OBP	SLG	PRO+	BR	/A	RC	SB	CS	SBR	FR	POS	TPR
1918	StL-N	88	348	37	90	12	3	4	32	20	40	.259	.301	.345	100	-2	-1	38	12			-8	O	-1.4
1919	StL-N	114	401	53	112	13	4	1	29	24	41	.279	.315	.339	103	-2	1	49	27			-6	*O/1	-1.0
1920	StL-N	133	489	55	139	18	8	3	56	25	31	.284	.320	.372	102	-2	0	57	21	14	-2	1	*O	-0.8
1921	StL-N	62	156	18	38	6	2	0	9	10	9	.244	.293	.308	61	-9	-9	14	7	5	-1	-2	O	-1.3
1922	StL-N	34	98	11	24	5	2	0	14	9	4	.245	.315	.337	71	-5	-4	10	0	2	-1	6	O	0.0
	Chi-N	76	243	37	68	8	7	1	34	18	15	.280	.330	.383	82	-6	-7	31	5	2	0	-0	O	-0.8
	Yr	110	341	48	92	13	9	1	48	27	19	.270	.325	.370	79	-11	-11	41	5	4	-1	6		-0.8
1923	Chi-N	117	393	48	98	14	3	1	27	25	22	.249	.298	.308	60	-23	-23	36	32	17	-1	2	*O	-2.3
1924	Chi-N	113	392	66	121	19	7	0	30	28	28	.309	.356	.393	100	1	0	51	26	24	-7	-2	*O	-1.0
1925	Chi-N	109	380	57	100	14	5	5	39	39	26	.263	.343	.366	80	-10	-11	49	15	11	-2	13	O	-0.2
1926	Chi-N	139	510	98	141	33	3	10	53	58	30	.276	.353	.412	104	4	3	74	18			13	*O	1.1
1927	Chi-N	83	228	28	67	12	4	2	25	20	16	.294	.359	.408	105	2	2	33	6			9	O	0.8
1928	Chi-N	67	137	26	39	8	0	3	18	17	12	.285	.364	.409	103	1	1	21	6			2	O	0.1
1929	*Chi-N	82	224	45	70	17	0	2	31	25	17	.313	.384	.415	98	-0	-0	36	9			3	O	-0.1
1930	Chi-N	70	150	30	39	10	1	9	18	18	15	.260	.343	.520	104	0	0	26	4			1	O	0.0
1931	Cin-N	90	252	34	65	15	6	0	28	32	16	.258	.342	.365	96	-3	-1	33	3			12	O	0.7
1932	Cin-N	8	3	3	0	0	0	0	0	0	0	.000	.000	.000	-99	-1	-1	0	0			0	H	0.0
	Phi-N	30	39	7	11	2	0	1	5	3	3	.282	.333	.410	88	-0	-1	6	0			-0	/1	0.0
	Yr	38	42	10	11	2	0	1	5	3	3	.262	.311	.381	78	-1	-1	5	0			-0		0.0
Total	15	1415	4443	653	1222	206	55	42	448	367	325	.275	.333	.375	92	-55	-50	563	191	<u>75</u>		43	*O/1	-6.2

■ RICHIE HEBNER
Hebner, Richard Joseph b: 11/26/47, Boston, Mass. BL/TR, 6'1", 195 lbs. Deb: 9/23/68 C

YEAR	TM/L	G	AB	R	H	2B	3B	HR	RBI	BB	SO	AVG	OBP	SLG	PRO+	BR	/A	RC	SB	CS	SBR	FR	POS	TPR
1968	Pit-N	2	1	0	0	0	0	0	0	0	0	.000	.000	.000	-99	-0	-0	0	0	0	0	0	H	0.0
1969	Pit-N	129	459	72	138	23	4	8	47	53	53	.301	.383	.420	127	17	18	77	4	1	1	3	3/1	2.3
1970	*Pit-N	120	420	60	122	24	8	11	46	42	48	.290	.365	.464	130	13	13	71	2	3	-1	1	*3	1.0
1971	*Pit-N	112	388	50	105	17	8	17	67	32	68	.271	.331	.487	130	13	13	62	2	2	-1	-8	*3	0.5
1972	*Pit-N	124	427	63	128	24	4	19	72	52	54	.300	.384	.508	155	29	30	85	0	0	0	-15	*3	1.5
1973	Pit-N	144	509	73	138	28	1	25	74	56	60	.271	.348	.477	130	17	19	85	0	1	-1	-14	*3	0.1
1974	*Pit-N	146	550	97	160	21	6	18	68	60	53	.291	.367	.449	132	20	22	90	0	3	-2	-6	*3	1.2
1975	*Pit-N	128	472	65	116	16	4	15	57	43	48	.246	.322	.392	98	-2	-2	61	0	1	-1	-15	*3	-1.8
1976	Pit-N	132	434	60	108	21	3	8	51	47	39	.249	.328	.366	96	-2	-2	54	1	3	-2	-9	*3	-1.5
1977	*Phi-N	118	397	67	113	17	4	18	62	61	46	.285	.384	.484	125	18	16	74	7	8	-3	2	*13/2	1.1
1978	*Phi-N	137	435	61	123	22	3	17	71	53	58	.283	.372	.464	131	19	19	74	4	7	-3	-2	*13/2	1.0
1979	NY-N	136	473	54	127	25	2	10	79	59	59	.268	.359	.393	109	5	7	71	3	1	0	-7	*3/1	-0.4
1980	Det-A	104	341	48	99	10	7	12	82	38	45	.290	.365	.466	123	12	11	57	0	3	-2	-5	13/D	0.1
1981	Det-A	78	226	19	51	6	0	8	25	28	28	.226	.314	.345	87	-3	-4	24	1	2	-1	-3	1D	-0.9
1982	Det-A	68	179	25	49	6	0	8	18	25	21	.274	.363	.441	119	5	5	30	1	1	-0	3	1D	0.6
	Pit-N	25	70	6	21	2	0	2	12	5	3	.300	.347	.414	109	1	1	11	4	0	1	-1	O/13	0.0
1983	Pit-N	78	162	23	43	4	1	5	26	17	28	.265	.339	.395	100	1	0	22	8	3	1	-5	3/1O	-0.6
1984	*Chi-N	44	81	12	27	3	0	2	8	10	15	.333	.407	.444	127	4	4	15	1	0	0	-1	3/1O	0.3
1985	Chi-N	83	120	10	26	2	0	3	22	7	15	.217	.266	.308	54	-7	-8	9	0	1	-1	0	1/3O	-0.8
Total	18	1908	6144	865	1694	273	57	203	890	687	741	.276	.356	.438	120	161	163	972	38	40	-13	-80	*31/D02	3.7

■ MIKE HECHINGER
Hechinger, Michael Vincent b: 2/14/1890, Chicago, Ill. d: 8/13/67, Chicago, Ill. BR/TR, 6', 175 lbs. Deb: 9/27/12

YEAR	TM/L	G	AB	R	H	2B	3B	HR	RBI	BB	SO	AVG	OBP	SLG	PRO+	BR	/A	RC	SB	CS	SBR	FR	POS	TPR
1912	Chi-N	2	3	0	0	0	0	0	0	0	2	.000	.400	.000	14	-0	-0	0	0			0	/C	0.0
1913	Chi-N	2	2	0	0	0	0	0	0	0	0	.000	.000	.000	-99	-1	-1	0	0			0	H	0.0
	Bro-N	9	11	1	2	1	0	0	0	0	2	.182	.182	.273	28	-1	-1	0	0			-1	/C	-0.1
	Yr	11	13	1	2	1	0	0	0	0	2	.154	.154	.231	9	-2	-2	0	0			-1		-0.1
Total	2	13	16	1	2	1	0	0	0	2	2	.125	.222	.188	16	-2	-2	0	0			-1	/C	-0.1

■ GUY HECKER
Hecker, Guy Jackson b: 4/3/1856, Youngville, Pa. d: 12/3/38, Wooster, Ohio BR/TR, 6', 190 lbs. Deb: 5/02/1882 MU

YEAR	TM/L	G	AB	R	H	2B	3B	HR	RBI	BB	SO	AVG	OBP	SLG	PRO+	BR	/A	RC	SB	CS	SBR	FR	POS	TPR
1882	Lou-a	78	340	62	94	14	4	3			5	.276	.287	.368	127	6	9	37				5	*1P/O	1.4
1883	Lou-a	79	322	56	88	6	6	1			10	.273	.295	.339	112	1	5	33				2	PO1	0.0
1884	Lou-a	78	316	53	94	14	8	4			10	.297	.323	.430	154	15	17	45				5	*P/O	0.0
1885	Lou-a	70	297	48	81	9	2	2			5	.273	.287	.337	99	-1	-1	29				3	P1/O	0.0
1886	Lou-a	84	343	76	117	14	5	4			32	.341	.402	.446	159	27	24	73	25			-4	P1O	0.0
1887	Lou-a	91	370	89	118	21	6	4			31	.319	.381	.441	129	15	14	82	48			-3	1PO	1.3
1888	Lou-a	56	211	32	48	9	2	0	29		11	.227	.285	.289	89	-3	-2	24	20				1P/O	-0.2
1889	Lou-a	81	327	42	93	17	5	1	36	18	27	.284	.333	.376	106	1	2	48	17			0	1P/O	0.0
1890	Pit-N	86	340	43	77	13	9	0	38	19	17	.226	.285	.318	88	-10	-4	35	13			2	1P/OM	-0.3
Total	9	703	2866	501	810	117	47	19	<u>103</u>	141	<u>44</u>	.283	.324	.376	120	52	65	407	123			7	P1/O	2.2

YEAR	TM/L	G	AB	R	H	2B	3B	HR	RBI	BB	SO	AVG	OBP	SLG	PRO+	BR	/A	RC	SB	CS	SBR	FR	POS	TPR

■ DANNY HEEP   Heep, Daniel William   b: 7/3/57, San Antonio, Tex.   BL/TL, 5'11", 185 lbs.   Deb: 8/31/79

YEAR	TM/L	G	AB	R	H	2B	3B	HR	RBI	BB	SO	AVG	OBP	SLG	PRO+	BR	/A	RC	SB	CS	SBR	FR	POS	TPR
1979	Hou-N	14	14	0	2	0	0	0	2	1	4	.143	.200	.143	-5	-2	-2	1	0	0	0	1	/O	0.0
1980	*Hou-N	33	87	6	24	8	0	0	6	8	9	.276	.344	.368	107	-0	1	12	0	0	0	-2	1	-0.1
1981	Hou-N	33	96	6	24	3	0	0	11	10	11	.250	.321	.281	76	-3	-3	9	0	0	0	-3	1/O	-0.6
1982	Hou-N	85	198	16	47	14	1	4	22	21	31	.237	.314	.379	100	-2	-0	23	0	2	-1	-3	O1	-0.6
1983	NY-N	115	253	30	64	12	0	8	21	29	40	.253	.332	.395	102	0	1	33	3	3	-1	-4	O1	-0.5
1984	NY-N	99	199	36	46	9	2	1	12	27	22	.231	.326	.312	81	-5	-4	20	3	1	0	0	O1	-0.5
1985	NY-N	95	271	26	76	17	0	7	42	27	27	.280	.348	.421	117	5	6	37	2	2	-1	-4	O/1	0.0
1986	*NY-N	86	195	24	55	8	2	5	33	30	31	.282	.381	.421	124	6	7	31	1	4	-2	-2	O	0.2
1987	LA-N	60	98	7	16	4	0	0	9	8	10	.163	.226	.204	16	-12	-12	4	1	0	0	0	O/1	-1.1
1988	*LA-N	95	149	14	36	2	0	0	11	22	13	.242	.343	.255	76	-4	-3	14	2	0	1	1	O1/P	-0.3
1989	Bos-A	113	320	36	96	17	0	5	49	29	26	.300	.360	.400	107	6	4	43	0	1	-1	-7	O1/D	-0.5
1990	*Bos-A	41	69	3	12	1	1	0	8	7	14	.174	.260	.217	33	-6	-6	5	0	0	0	3	O/1PD	-0.3
Total	12	869	1949	204	498	95	6	30	226	219	238	.256	.333	.357	94	-16	-12	231	12	13	-4	-19	O1/DP	-4.3

■ DON HEFFNER   Heffner, Donald Henry "Jeep"   b: 2/8/11, Rouzerville, Pa.   d: 8/1/89, Pasadena, Cal.   BR/TR, 5'10", 155 lbs.   Deb: 4/17/34   MC

YEAR	TM/L	G	AB	R	H	2B	3B	HR	RBI	BB	SO	AVG	OBP	SLG	PRO+	BR	/A	RC	SB	CS	SBR	FR	POS	TPR
1934	NY-A	72	241	29	63	8	3	0	25	25	18	.261	.331	.320	73	-11	-9	27	1	1	-0	-8	2	-1.2
1935	NY-A	10	36	3	11	3	1	0	4	8	1	.306	.375	.444	118	1	1	6	0	0	0	-1	2	0.0
1936	NY-A	19	48	7	11	2	1	0	6	6	5	.229	.315	.313	57	-3	-3	5	0	0	0	4	/32S	0.1
1937	NY-A	60	201	23	50	6	5	0	21	19	19	.249	.314	.328	62	-12	-12	20	1	4	-2	-7	2S/310	-1.5
1938	StL-A	141	473	47	116	23	3	2	69	65	53	.245	.341	.319	67	-23	-23	56	1	1	-0	-9	*2	-2.4
1939	StL-A	110	375	45	100	10	2	1	35	48	39	.267	.350	.312	69	-15	-16	41	1	7	-4	-4	S2	-1.4
1940	StL-A	126	487	52	115	23	2	3	53	39	37	.236	.295	.310	56	-31	-32	45	5	5	-2	19	*2	-0.7
1941	StL-A	110	399	48	93	14	2	0	17	38	27	.233	.303	.278	53	-26	-27	36	5	6	-2	3	*2	-1.6
1942	StL-A	19	36	2	6	2	0	0	3	1	4	.167	.189	.222	15	-4	-4	1	1	0	0	1	/21	-0.1
1943	StL-A	18	33	2	4	1	0	0	2	2	2	.121	.171	.152	-5	-4	-4	1	0	0	0	0	2/1	-0.4
	Phi-A	52	178	17	37	6	0	0	8	18	12	.208	.284	.242	55	-10	-10	13	3	2	-0	-10	2/1	-1.9
	Yr	70	211	19	41	7	0	0	10	20	14	.194	.267	.227	45	-14	-14	14	3	2	-0			-2.3
1944	Det-A	6	19	0	4	1	0	0	1	5	1	.211	.375	.263	80	-0	-0	2	0	0	0	-1	/2	0.0
Total	11	743	2526	275	610	99	19	6	248	270	218	.241	.317	.303	61	-139	-141	254	18	26	-10	-12	2/S310	-11.1

■ JIM HEGAN   Hegan, James Edward   b: 8/3/20, Lynn, Mass.   d: 6/17/84, Swampscott, Mass.   BR/TR, 6'2", 195 lbs.   Deb: 9/09/41   C

YEAR	TM/L	G	AB	R	H	2B	3B	HR	RBI	BB	SO	AVG	OBP	SLG	PRO+	BR	/A	RC	SB	CS	SBR	FR	POS	TPR
1941	Cle-A	16	47	4	15	2	0	1	5	4	7	.319	.373	.426	116	1	1	8	0	0	0	-0	C	0.1
1942	Cle-A	68	170	10	33	5	0	0	11	11	31	.194	.243	.224	34	-15	-14	9	1	3	-2	8	C	0.0
1946	Cle-A	88	271	29	64	11	5	0	17	17	44	.236	.284	.314	71	-12	-10	23	1	4	-2	9	C	0.0
1947	Cle-A	135	378	38	94	14	5	4	42	41	49	.249	.324	.344	88	-7	-6	44	3	1	-1	7	*C	1.2
1948	*Cle-A	144	472	60	117	21	6	14	61	48	74	.248	.317	.407	94	-8	-6	62	6	3	0	21	*C	2.3
1949	Cle-A	152	468	54	105	19	5	8	55	49	89	.224	.298	.338	69	-24	-22	49	1	0	0	10	*C	-0.4
1950	Cle-A	131	415	53	91	16	5	14	58	42	52	.219	.291	.383	74	-20	-18	47	1	0	0	24	*C	1.0
1951	Cle-A	133	416	60	99	17	5	6	43	38	72	.238	.302	.346	79	-16	-13	45	0	3	-2	11	*C	0.5
1952	Cle-A	112	333	39	75	17	2	4	41	29	47	.225	.287	.324	75	-14	-12	32	0	2	-1	6	*C	-0.7
1953	Cle-A	112	299	37	65	10	1	9	37	25	41	.217	.280	.348	71	-14	-13	29	1	2	-1	2	*C	-0.7
1954	*Cle-A	139	423	56	99	12	7	11	40	34	48	.234	.291	.374	80	-13	-14	43	0	1	-1	12	*C	0.5
1955	Cle-A	116	304	30	67	5	2	9	40	34	33	.220	.299	.339	69	-13	-14	31	0	1	-1	7	*C	-0.3
1956	Cle-A	122	315	42	70	15	2	6	34	49	54	.222	.327	.340	75	-11	-12	36	1	1	-0	15	*C	0.5
1957	Cle-A	58	148	14	32	7	0	4	15	16	23	.216	.293	.345	74	-6	-5	15	0	1	-1	2	C	0.0
1958	Det-A	45	130	14	25	6	0	1	7	10	32	.192	.250	.262	38	-11	-12	8	0	0	0	1	C	-1.0
	Phi-N	25	59	5	13	6	0	0	6	4	16	.220	.270	.322	57	-4	-4	5	0	0	0	4	C	0.1
1959	Phi-N	25	51	1	10	1	0	0	8	3	10	.196	.241	.216	22	-6	-6	3	0	1	-1	0	C	-0.3
	SF-N	21	30	0	4	1	0	0	0	1	10	.133	.161	.167	-13	-5	-5	1	0	1	-1	5	C	0.1
	Yr	46	81	1	14	2	0	0	8	4	20	.173	.212	.198	10	-10	-10	3	0	2	-1	5		-0.2
1960	Chi-N	24	43	4	9	2	1	1	5	1	10	.209	.244	.372	67	-2	-2	3	0	0	0	3	C	0.1
Total	17	1666	4772	550	1087	187	46	92	525	456	742	.228	.296	.344	74	-199	-187	491	15	24	-10	146	*C	3.7

■ MIKE HEGAN   Hegan, James Michael   b: 7/21/42, Cleveland, Ohio   BL/TL, 6'1", 188 lbs.   Deb: 9/13/64

YEAR	TM/L	G	AB	R	H	2B	3B	HR	RBI	BB	SO	AVG	OBP	SLG	PRO+	BR	/A	RC	SB	CS	SBR	FR	POS	TPR
1964	*NY-A	5	5	0	0	0	0	0	1	2	.000	.167	.000	-48	-1	-1	0	0	0	0	1	/1	0.0
1966	NY-A	13	39	7	8	0	1	0	2	7	11	.205	.326	.256	73	-1	-1	3	1	1	-0	0	1	-0.1
1967	NY-A	68	118	12	16	4	1	1	3	20	41	.136	.266	.212	44	-8	-7	9	7	1	2	-1	1O	-1.2
1969	Sea-A	95	267	54	78	9	6	8	37	62	61	.292	.427	.461	151	20	21	58	6	5	-1	-0	O1	1.7
1970	Mil-A	148	476	70	116	21	2	11	52	67	116	.244	.338	.366	93	-3	-3	61	9	7	-2	12	*1/O	0.0
1971	Mil-A	46	122	19	27	4	1	4	11	26	19	.221	.358	.369	107	2	2	18	1	1	-0	4	1	0.4
	*Oak-A	65	55	5	13	3	0	0	3	5	13	.236	.300	.291	69	-2	-2	5	1	0	0	2	1/O	-0.1
	Yr	111	177	24	40	7	1	4	14	31	32	.226	.341	.345	96	-0	-0	23	2	1	0	7		0.3
1972	*Oak-A	98	79	13	26	3	1	1	5	7	20	.329	.384	.430	150	4	5	14	1	0	0	2	1/O	0.0
1973	Oak-A	75	71	8	13	2	0	1	5	5	17	.183	.237	.254	40	-6	-5	4	0	0	0	-2	1/OD	-1.0
	NY-A	37	131	12	36	3	2	6	14	7	34	.275	.312	.466	121	2	3	19	0	0	0	1	1	0.1
	Yr	112	202	20	49	5	2	7	19	12	51	.243	.285	.391	93	-4	-3	22	0	0	0	-1		-0.9
1974	NY-A	18	53	3	12	2	0	2	9	5	9	.226	.317	.377	102	-0	-0	6	1	1	-0	0	1	0.0
	Mil-A	89	190	21	45	7	1	7	32	33	34	.237	.350	.395	114	4	4	27	0	4	-2	-1	D1O	0.0
	Yr	107	243	24	57	9	1	9	41	38	43	.235	.343	.391	112	4	4	33	1	5	-3	-1		0.0
1975	Mil-A	93	203	19	51	11	0	5	22	31	42	.251	.350	.379	106	2	2	28	1	1	-0	0	O1/D	0.0
1976	Mil-A	80	218	30	54	4	3	5	31	25	54	.248	.328	.362	104	1	1	27	0	0	0	-1	DO1	0.0
1977	Mil-A	35	53	8	9	0	0	2	3	10	17	.170	.313	.283	64	-2	-2	6	0	0	0	0	O/1D	-0.2
Total	12	965	2080	281	504	73	18	53	229	311	489	.242	.343	.371	103	12	15	285	28	21	-4	18	1O/D	-0.4

■ BOB HEGMAN   Hegman, Robert Hilmer   b: 2/26/58, Springfield, Minn.   BR/TR, 6'1", 180 lbs.   Deb: 8/08/85

YEAR	TM/L	G	AB	R	H	2B	3B	HR	RBI	BB	SO	AVG	OBP	SLG	PRO+	BR	/A	RC	SB	CS	SBR	FR	POS	TPR
1985	KC-A	1	0	0	0	0	0	0	0	0	0	—	—	—	—	0	0	0	0	0	0	0	/2	0.0

■ JACK HEIDEMANN   Heidemann, Jack Seale   b: 7/11/49, Brenham, Tex.   BR/TR, 6', 175 lbs.   Deb: 5/02/69

YEAR	TM/L	G	AB	R	H	2B	3B	HR	RBI	BB	SO	AVG	OBP	SLG	PRO+	BR	/A	RC	SB	CS	SBR	FR	POS	TPR
1969	Cle-A	3	3	0	0	0	0	0	0	0	2	.000	.250	.000	-24	-0	-0	0	0	0	0	1	/S	0.0
1970	Cle-A	133	445	40	94	14	2	6	37	34	88	.211	.270	.292	52	-28	-30	35	2	4	-2	-2	*S	-2.3
1971	Cle-A	81	240	16	50	7	0	0	9	12	46	.208	.252	.237	36	-19	-22	14	1	3	-2	-9	S	-2.5
1972	Cle-A	10	20	0	3	0	0	0	2	2	3	.150	.261	.150	24	-2	-2	1	0	0	0	-1	S	-0.1
1974	Cle-A	12	11	2	1	0	0	0	0	0	2	.091	.091	.091	-48	-2	-2	0	0	0	0	-1	/3S12	-0.2
	StL-N	47	70	8	19	1	0	0	3	5	10	.271	.320	.286	71	-3	-3	7	0	0	0	-10	S/3	-0.7
1975	NY-N	61	145	12	31	4	2	1	16	17	28	.214	.296	.290	66	-7	-6	13	1	0	0	-12	S/32	-1.3
1976	NY-N	5	12	0	1	0	0	0	0	0	0	.083	.083	.083	-56	-2	-2	0	0	0	0	0	/S2	-0.1
	Mil-A	69	146	11	32	1	0	2	10	7	24	.219	.255	.267	54	-9	-8	10	1	3	-2	-7	32/D	-1.5
1977	Mil-A	5	1	1	0	0	0	0	0	1	0	.000	.500	.000	50	0	0	0	0	0	0	1	/2D	0.0
Total	8	426	1093	94	231	27	4	9	75	78	203	.211	.268	.268	49	-72	-76	80	5	10	-5	-41	S/32D1	-8.6

■ EMMETT HEIDRICK   Heidrick, John Emmett "Snags"   b: 7/9/1876, Queenstown, Pa.   d: 1/20/16, Clarion, Pa.   BL/TR, 6', 185 lbs.   Deb: 9/14/1898

YEAR	TM/L	G	AB	R	H	2B	3B	HR	RBI	BB	SO	AVG	OBP	SLG	PRO+	BR	/A	RC	SB	CS	SBR	FR	POS	TPR
1898	Cle-N	19	76	10	23	2	2	0	8	3		.303	.329	.382	108	0	1	11	3			-0	O	0.0
1899	StL-N	146	591	109	194	21	14	2	82	34		.328	.368	.421	116	14	12	115	55			4	*O	0.6

YEAR	TM/L	G	AB	R	H	2B	3B	HR	RBI	BB	SO	AVG	OBP	SLG	PRO+	BR	/A	RC	SB	CS	SBR	FR	POS	TPR
1900	StL-N	85	339	51	102	6	8	2	45	18		.301	.338	.383	102	0	1	53	22			15	O	0.7
1901	StL-N	118	502	94	170	24	12	6	67	21		.339	.366	.470	152	26	29	102	32			1	*O	1.7
1902	StL-A	110	447	75	129	19	10	3	56	34		.289	.339	.396	106	3	4	70	17			2	*O/PS3	0.0
1903	StL-A	120	461	55	129	20	15	1	42	19		.280	.308	.395	115	6	7	65	19			2	*O/C	0.1
1904	StL-A	133	538	66	147	14	10	1	36	16		.273	.294	.342	110	1	4	68	35			11	*O	0.8
1908	StL-A	26	93	8	20	2	2	1	6	1		.215	.223	.312	75	-3	-3	7	3			-1	O	-0.5
Total	8	757	3047	468	914	108	73	16	342	146		.300	.333	.399	116	47	54	490	186			33	O/C3SP	3.4

■ FRANK HEIFER   Heifer, Franklin "Heck"   b: 1/18/1854, Reading, Pa.   d: 8/29/1893, Reading, Pa.   5'10.5", 175 lbs.   Deb: 6/04/1875

1875	Bos-n	11	51	11	14	0	3	0		0		.275	.275	.392	123	1	1	6					/1OP	0.1

■ CHINK HEILEMAN   Heileman, John George   b: 8/10/1872, Cincinnati, Ohio   d: 7/19/40, Cincinnati, Ohio   TR, 5'8", 155 lbs.   Deb: 7/08/01

1901	Cin-N	5	15	1	2	1	0	0	1	0		.133	.133	.200	-3	-2	-2	0	0			-1	/32	-0.2

■ HARRY HEILMANN   Heilmann, Harry Edwin "Slug"   b: 8/3/1894, San Francisco, Cal.   d: 7/9/51, Southfield, Mich.   BR/TR, 6'1", 195 lbs.   Deb: 5/16/14   CH

1914	Det-A	69	182	25	41	8	1	2	18	22	29	.225	.316	.313	86	-2	-3	18	1	8	-5	-6	O1/2	-1.6
1916	Det-A	136	451	57	127	30	11	2	73	42	40	.282	.349	.410	124	14	12	70	9			-9	O1/2	-0.1
1917	Det-A	150	556	57	156	22	11	5	86	41	54	.281	.333	.387	120	11	11	73	11			-2	*O1	0.1
1918	Det-A	79	286	34	79	10	6	5	39	35	10	.276	.359	.406	136	10	12	45	13			-4	O1/2	0.3
1919	Det-A	140	537	74	172	30	15	8	93	37	41	.320	.366	.477	139	23	25	93	7			-10	*1	0.4
1920	Det-A	145	543	66	168	28	5	9	89	39	32	.309	.358	.429	111	5	7	82	3	7	-3	-1	*1O	0.1
1921	Det-A	149	602	114	**237**	43	14	19	139	53	37	**.394**	.444	.606	167	58	59	159	2	6	-3	-11	*O/1	3.1
1922	Det-A	118	455	92	162	27	10	21	92	58	28	.356	.432	.598	172	44	46	119	8	4	0	-10	*O/1	2.5
1923	Det-A	144	524	121	211	44	11	18	115	74	40	**.403**	.481	.632	195	71	72	159	8	7	-2	2	*O1	5.7
1924	Det-A	153	570	107	197	**45**	16	10	114	78	41	.346	.428	.533	149	40	42	134	13	5	1	9	*O/1	3.7
1925	Det-A	150	573	97	225	40	11	13	134	67	27	**.393**	.457	.569	161	**52**	**54**	149	6	6	-2	-3	*O	3.3
1926	Det-A	141	502	90	184	41	8	9	103	67	19	.367	.445	.534	152	42	41	120	6	7	-2	-1	*O	2.6
1927	Det-A	141	505	106	201	50	9	14	120	72	16	**.398**	.475	.616	179	62	61	142	11	5	0	-8	*O	4.2
1928	Det-A	151	558	83	183	38	10	14	107	57	45	.328	.390	.507	132	27	26	112	7	3	0	1	*O1	1.8
1929	Det-A	125	453	86	156	41	7	15	120	50	39	.344	.412	.565	148	33	32	104	5	6	-2	-6	*O/1	1.8
1930	Cin-N	142	459	79	153	43	6	19	91	64	50	.333	.416	.577	144	28	32	109	2			15	*O1	3.3
1932	Cin-N	15	31	3	8	2	0	0	6	0	2	.258	.258	.323	57	-2	-2	3	0			-0	/1	-0.2
Total	17	2148	7787	1291	2660	542	151	183	1539	856	550	.342	.410	.520	148	517	527	1690	112	<u>64</u>		-44	*O1/2	31.0

■ VAL HEIM   Heim, Val Raymond   b: 11/4/20, Plymouth, Wis.   BL/TR, 5'11", 170 lbs.   Deb: 8/31/42

1942	Chi-A	13	45	6	9	1	1	0	7	5	3	.200	.294	.267	60	-2	-2	4	1	0	0	-2	O	-0.4

■ BUD HEINE   Heine, William Henry   b: 9/22/1900, Elmira, N.Y.   d: 9/2/76, Ft.Lauderdale, Fla   BL/TR, 5'8", 145 lbs.   Deb: 10/01/21

1921	NY-N	1	2	0	0	0	0	0	0	0	0	.000	.000	.000	-99	-1	-1	0	0	0	0	0	/2	0.0

■ TOM HEINTZELMAN   Heintzelman, Thomas Kenneth   b: 11/3/46, St.Charles, Mo.   BR/TR, 6'1", 180 lbs.   Deb: 8/12/73

1973	StL-N	23	29	5	9	0	0	0	3	3	3	.310	.375	.310	92	-0	-0	3	0	0	0	1	/2	0.1
1974	StL-N	38	74	10	17	4	0	1	6	9	14	.230	.313	.324	79	-2	-2	8	0	0	0	0	2/3S	0.0
1977	SF-N	2	2	0	0	0	0	0	0	0	0	.000	.000	.000	-99	-1	-1	0	0	0	0	0	H	0.0
1978	SF-N	27	35	2	8	1	0	2	6	2	5	.229	.270	.429	96	-1	-0	4	0	0	0	2	/231	0.2
Total	4	90	140	17	34	5	0	3	12	14	22	.243	.312	.343	84	-3	-3	16	0	0	0	4	/231S	0.3

■ JACK HEINZMAN   Heinzman, John Peter   b: 9/27/1863, New Albany, Ind.   d: 11/10/14, Louisville, Ky.   BR/TR,   Deb: 10/02/1886

1886	Lou-a	1	5	1	0	0	0	0	0	0		.000	.000	.000	-99	-1	-1	0	0			0	/1	0.0

■ BOB HEISE   Heise, Robert Lowell   b: 5/12/47, San Antonio, Tex.   BR/TR, 6', 175 lbs.   Deb: 9/12/67

1967	NY-N	16	62	7	20	4	0	0	3	3	1	.323	.354	.387	114	1	1	8	0	1	-1	2	2/S3	0.3
1968	NY-N	6	23	3	5	0	0	0	1	1	1	.217	.250	.217	41	-2	-2	1	0	0	0	-5	/S2	-0.6
1969	NY-N	4	10	1	3	1	0	0	0	3	2	.300	.462	.400	140	1	1	2	0	0	0	-2	/S	0.0
1970	SF-N	67	154	15	36	5	1	1	22	5	13	.234	.258	.299	49	-11	-11	11	0	1	-1	-1	S2/3	-0.5
1971	SF-N	13	11	2	0	0	0	0	0	0	1	.000	.000	.000	-99	-3	-3	0	0	0	0	0	/S32	-0.1
	Mil-A	68	189	10	48	7	0	0	7	7	15	.254	.281	.291	63	-10	-9	14	1	1	-0	5	S3/2O	0.3
1972	Mil-A	95	271	23	72	10	1	0	12	12	14	.266	.302	.310	84	-6	-6	25	1	1	-0	-3	23/S	-0.4
1973	Mil-A	49	98	8	20	2	0	0	4	4	4	.204	.235	.224	31	-9	-9	5	1	0	0	-1	S/312D	-0.5
1974	StL-N	3	7	0	1	0	0	0	0	0	0	.143	.143	.143	-20	-1	-1	0	0	0	0	2	/2	0.1
	Cal-A	29	75	7	20	7	0	0	6	5	10	.267	.313	.360	99	-1	-0	8	0	1	-1	2	2/3S	0.2
1975	Bos-A	63	126	12	27	3	0	0	21	4	6	.214	.250	.238	35	-10	-11	8	0	0	0	11	32/S1	0.1
1976	Bos-A	32	56	5	15	2	0	0	5	1	2	.268	.293	.304	67	-2	-2	5	0	1	-1	2	3/S2	0.0
1977	KC-A	54	62	11	16	2	1	0	5	2	8	.258	.292	.323	67	-3	-3	6	0	1	-1	10	2S3/1	1.0
Total	11	499	1144	104	283	43	3	1	86	47	77	.247	.281	.293	63	-55	-56	92	3	7	-3	24	S23/1DO	-0.1

■ AL HEIST   Heist, Alfred Michael   b: 10/5/27, Brooklyn, N.Y.   BR/TR, 6'2", 185 lbs.   Deb: 7/17/60   C

1960	Chi-N	41	102	11	28	5	3	1	6	10	12	.275	.339	.412	106	1	1	14	3	1	0	3	O	0.3
1961	Chi-N	109	321	48	82	14	3	7	37	39	51	.255	.338	.383	90	-4	-4	42	3	3	-1	-4	O	-1.4
1962	Hou-N	27	72	4	16	1	0	0	3	3	9	.222	.263	.236	38	-6	-6	4	0	0	0	1	O	-0.5
Total	3	177	495	63	126	20	6	8	46	52	72	.255	.328	.368	86	-10	-9	60	6	4	-1	-1	O	-1.6

■ HEINIE HEITMULLER   Heitmuller, William Frederick   b: 1883, San Francisco, Cal.   d: 10/8/12, Los Angeles, Cal.   6'2", 215 lbs.   Deb: 4/26/09

1909	Phi-A	64	210	36	60	9	8	0	15	18		.286	.351	.405	136	9	8	32	7			-1	O	0.6
1910	Phi-A	31	111	11	27	2	2	0	7	7		.243	.288	.297	84	-2	-2	11	6			-1	O	-0.4
Total	2	95	321	47	87	11	10	0	22	25		.271	.330	.368	118	7	6	43	13			-2	/O	0.2

■ WOODIE HELD   Held, Woodson George   b: 3/25/32, Sacramento, Cal.   BR/TR, 5'10.5", 167 lbs.   Deb: 9/05/54

1954	NY-A	4	3	2	0	0	0	0	0	2	1	.000	.400	.000	17	-0	-0	0	0	0	0	-1	/S3	0.0
1957	NY-A	1	1	0	0	0	0	0	0	0	0	.000	.000	.000	-99	-0	-0	0	0	0	0	0	H	0.0
	KC-A	92	326	48	78	14	3	20	50	37	81	.239	.322	.485	116	7	6	52	4	0	1	12	O	1.4
	Yr	93	327	48	78	14	3	20	50	37	81	.239	.322	.483	115	6	6	52	4	0	1	12		1.4
1958	KC-A	47	131	13	28	2	0	4	16	10	28	.214	.280	.321	64	-6	-7	11	0	1	-1	2	O/3S	-0.7
	Cle-A	67	144	12	28	4	1	3	17	15	36	.194	.288	.299	64	-7	-7	12	1	2	-1	7	OS/3	-0.1
	Yr	114	275	25	56	6	1	7	33	25	64	.204	.284	.309	64	-14	-14	23	1	3	-2	8		-0.8
1959	Cle-A	143	525	82	132	19	3	29	71	46	118	.251	.314	.465	115	6	8	74	1	2	-1	-7	*S3/O2	0.8
1960	Cle-A	109	376	45	97	15	1	21	67	44	73	.258	.344	.471	122	9	10	62	0	1	-1	9	*S	2.7
1961	Cle-A	146	509	67	136	23	5	23	78	69	111	.267	.358	.468	122	13	15	85	0	0	0	-14	*S	1.1
1962	Cle-A	139	466	55	116	12	2	19	58	73	107	.249	.364	.406	110	6	8	72	5	1	1	-14	*S/3O	0.3
1963	Cle-A	133	416	61	103	19	4	17	61	61	96	.248	.355	.435	121	12	13	66	2	2	-1	-0	2O/S3	1.9
1964	Cle-A	118	364	50	86	13	0	18	49	43	88	.236	.329	.420	107	3	4	51	1	0	0	4	2O3	0.7
1965	Was-A	122	332	46	82	16	2	16	54	49	74	.247	.349	.452	128	12	13	53	0	0	0	-2	*O/32S	0.7
1966	Bal-A	56	82	6	17	3	1	1	7	7	30	.207	.309	.305	78	-2	-2	9	0	0	0	-3	O/2S3	-0.4
1967	Bal-A	26	41	4	6	3	0	1	6	6	12	.146	.286	.293	72	-1	-1	4	0	0	0	1	3OS/2	0.0
	Cal-A	58	141	15	31	3	0	4	17	18	41	.220	.317	.326	94	-1	-1	14	0	2	-1	-1	3OS/2	-0.2

YEAR	TM/L	G	AB	R	H	2B	3B	HR	RBI	BB	SO	AVG	OBP	SLG	PRO+	BR	/A	RC	SB	CS	SBR	FR	POS	TPR
	Yr	84	182	19	37	6	0	5	23	24	53	.203	.310	.319	88	-3	-2	18	0	2	-1	-0		-0.2
1968	Cal-A	33	45	4	5	1	0	0	0	5	15	.111	.231	.133	13	-5	-4	2	0	0	0	-2	/2S3O	-0.6
	Chi-A	40	54	5	9	1	0	0	2	5	14	.167	.250	.185	33	-4	-4	3	0	0	0	2	O/32	-0.3
	Yr	73	99	9	14	2	0	0	2	10	29	.141	.241	.162	24	-9	-9	5	0	0	0	-1		-0.9
1969	Chi-A	56	63	9	9	2	0	3	6	13	19	.143	.299	.317	69	-2	-3	7	0	0	0	2	O/S32	-0.2
Total	14	1390	4019	524	963	150	22	179	559	508	944	.240	.333	.421	109	38	47	578	14	11	-2	-7	SO23	7.9

■ HANK HELF

Helf, Henry Hartz b: 8/26/13, Austin, Tex. d: 10/27/84, Austin, Tex. BR/TR, 6'1", 196 lbs. Deb: 5/05/38

YEAR	TM/L	G	AB	R	H	2B	3B	HR	RBI	BB	SO	AVG	OBP	SLG	PRO+	BR	/A	RC	SB	CS	SBR	FR	POS	TPR
1938	Cle-A	6	13	1	1	0	0	0	1	1	1	.077	.143	.077	-44	-3	-3	0	0	0	0	0	/C	-0.1
1940	Cle-A	1	1	0	0	0	0	0	0	0	0	.000	.000	.000	-99	-0	-0	0	0	0	0	0	/C	0.0
1946	StL-A	71	182	17	35	11	0	6	21	9	40	.192	.234	.352	59	-10	-11	14	0	1	-1	12	C	0.3
Total	3	78	196	18	36	11	0	6	22	10	41	.184	.227	.332	51	-14	-14	14	0	1	-1	12	/C	0.2

■ TY HELFRICH

Helfrich, Emory Wilbur b: 10/9/1890, Pleasantville, N.J. d: 3/18/55, Pleasantville, N.J BR/TR, 5'10", 178 lbs. Deb: 6/30/15

YEAR	TM/L	G	AB	R	H	2B	3B	HR	RBI	BB	SO	AVG	OBP	SLG	PRO+	BR	/A	RC	SB	CS	SBR	FR	POS	TPR
1915	Bro-F	43	104	12	25	6	0	0	5	15	21	.240	.336	.298	89	-1	-1	12	2	·		-4	2/O	-0.4

■ HELLINGS

Hellings b: Philadelphia, Pa. Deb: 7/19/1875

YEAR	TM/L	G	AB	R	H	2B	3B	HR	RBI	BB	SO	AVG	OBP	SLG	PRO+	BR	/A	RC	SB	CS	SBR	FR	POS	TPR
1875	Atl-n	1	4	0	1	0	0	0		0		.250	.250	.250	84	-0	-0	0					/2	0.0

■ TONY HELLMAN

Hellman, Anthony J. b: 1861, Cincinnati, Ohio d: 3/29/1898, Cincinnati, Ohio Deb: 10/10/1886

YEAR	TM/L	G	AB	R	H	2B	3B	HR	RBI	BB	SO	AVG	OBP	SLG	PRO+	BR	/A	RC	SB	CS	SBR	FR	POS	TPR
1886	Bal-a	1	3	0	0	0	0	0		0		.000	.000	.000	-99	-1	-1	0	0			2	/C	0.1

■ TOMMY HELMS

Helms, Tommy Vann b: 5/5/41, Charlotte, N.C. BR/TR, 5'10", 165 lbs. Deb: 9/23/64 MC

YEAR	TM/L	G	AB	R	H	2B	3B	HR	RBI	BB	SO	AVG	OBP	SLG	PRO+	BR	/A	RC	SB	CS	SBR	FR	POS	TPR
1964	Cin-N	2	1	0	0	0	0	0	0	0	1	.000	.000	.000	-97	-0	-0	0	0	0	0	0	H	0.0
1965	Cin-N	21	42	4	16	2	2	0	6	3	7	.381	.435	.524	158	4	4	10	1	0	0	-2	/S32	0.3
1966	Cin-N	138	542	72	154	23	1	9	49	24	31	.284	.317	.380	85	-6	-11	61	3	4	-2	-13	*32	-2.7
1967	Cin-N	137	497	40	136	27	4	2	35	24	41	.274	.307	.356	80	-7	-14	49	5	10	-5	-9	2S	-1.7
1968	Cin-N	127	507	35	146	28	2	2	47	12	27	.288	.307	.363	94	-1	-4	53	5	6	-2	8	*2/S3	1.0
1969	Cin-N	126	480	38	129	18	1	1	40	18	33	.269	.297	.317	68	-18	-21	39	4	6	-2	-3	*2/S	-1.6
1970	*Cin-N	150	575	42	136	21	1	1	45	21	33	.237	.263	.282	46	-44	-44	39	2	2	-1	1	*2S	-2.5
1971	Cin-N	150	547	40	141	26	1	3	52	26	33	.258	.293	.325	76	-19	-17	48	3	4	-2	14	*2	0.3
1972	Hou-N	139	518	45	134	20	5	5	60	24	27	.259	.297	.346	84	-13	-12	52	4	3	-1	27	*2	2.5
1973	Hou-N	146	543	44	156	28	2	4	61	32	21	.287	.327	.368	93	-6	-6	63	1	1	-0	-1	*2	-0.2
1974	Hou-N	137	452	32	126	21	1	5	50	23	27	.279	.315	.363	93	-7	-5	48	5	4	-1	-11	*2	-1.0
1975	Hou-N	64	135	7	28	2	0	0	14	10	8	.207	.267	.222	40	-11	-10	8	0	0	0	-0	2/3S	-0.8
1976	Pit-N	62	87	10	24	5	1	1	14	13	10	.276	.357	.391	111	2	1	13	0	0	0	2	32/S	0.4
1977	Pit-N	15	12	0	0	0	0	0	0	0	3	.000	.000	.000	-97	-3	-3	0	0	0	0	0	H	-0.2
	Bos-A	21	59	5	16	2	0	1	5	4	4	.271	.328	.356	77	-1	-2	7	0	0	0	-2	D/32	-0.3
Total	14	1435	4997	414	1342	223	21	34	477	231	301	.269	.303	.342	79	-132	-145	491	33	40	-14	11	*23/SD	-6.5

■ HEINIE HELTZEL

Heltzel, William Wade b: 12/21/13, York, Pa. BR/TR, 5'10", 150 lbs. Deb: 7/27/43

YEAR	TM/L	G	AB	R	H	2B	3B	HR	RBI	BB	SO	AVG	OBP	SLG	PRO+	BR	/A	RC	SB	CS	SBR	FR	POS	TPR
1943	Bos-N	29	86	6	13	3	0	0	5	7	13	.151	.215	.186	17	-9	-9	4	0			-2	3	-1.2
1944	Phi-N	11	22	1	4	1	0	0	0	2	3	.182	.280	.227	45	-2	-1	1	0			-2	S	-0.1
Total	2	40	108	7	17	4	0	0	5	9	16	.157	.229	.194	23	-11	-11	5	0			-5	/3S	-1.3

■ ED HEMINGWAY

Hemingway, Edson Marshall b: 5/8/1893, Sheridan, Mich. d: 7/5/69, Grand Rapids, Mich BB/TR, 5'11.5", 165 lbs. Deb: 9/17/14

YEAR	TM/L	G	AB	R	H	2B	3B	HR	RBI	BB	SO	AVG	OBP	SLG	PRO+	BR	/A	RC	SB	CS	SBR	FR	POS	TPR
1914	StL-A	3	5	0	0	0	0	0	0	0	1	.000	.167	.000	-51	-1	-1	0	1			0	/3	0.0
1917	NY-N	7	25	3	8	1	1	0	1	2	1	.320	.370	.440	153	1	1	4	2			1	/3	0.3
1918	Phi-N	33	108	7	23	4	1	0	12	7	9	.213	.267	.269	59	-5	-6	9	4			2	2/31	-0.2
Total	3	43	138	10	31	5	2	0	13	10	11	.225	.282	.290	71	-4	-5	14	7			3	/231	0.1

■ SCOTT HEMOND

Hemond, Scott Mathew b: 11/18/65, Taunton, Mass. BR/TR, 6', 205 lbs. Deb: 9/09/89

YEAR	TM/L	G	AB	R	H	2B	3B	HR	RBI	BB	SO	AVG	OBP	SLG	PRO+	BR	/A	RC	SB	CS	SBR	FR	POS	TPR
1989	Oak-A	4	0	2	0	0	0	0	0	0	0	—	—	—	—	0	0	0	0	0	0	0	R	0.0
1990	Oak-A	7	13	0	2	0	0	0	1	0	5	.154	.154	.154	-14	-2	-2	0	0	0	0	-1	/32	-0.2
Total	2	11	13	2	2	0	0	0	1	0	5	.154	.154	.154	-14	-2	-2	0	0	0	0	-1	/32	-0.2

■ DUCKY HEMP

Hemp, William H. b: 12/27/1867, St.Louis, Mo. d: 3/6/23, St.Louis, Mo. Deb: 10/06/1887

YEAR	TM/L	G	AB	R	H	2B	3B	HR	RBI	BB	SO	AVG	OBP	SLG	PRO+	BR	/A	RC	SB	CS	SBR	FR	POS	TPR
1887	Lou-a	1	3	1	1	0	0	0		0	1	.333	.500	.667	223	1	1	1	0			-1	/O	0.0
1890	Pit-N	21	81	9	19	0	2	0	4	8	12	.235	.311	.284	86	-2	-1	8	3			1	O	0.0
	Syr-a	9	33	1	5	1	0	0		0		.152	.152	.182	-1	-4	-4	1	1			2	/O	-0.1
Total	2	31	117	11	25	2	2	0	4	9	12	.214	.276	.265	67	-6	-4	10	4			2	/O	-0.1

■ CHARLIE HEMPHILL

Hemphill, Charles Judson "Eagle Eye" b: 4/20/1876, Greenville, Mich. d: 6/22/53, Detroit, Mich. BL/TL, 5'9", 160 lbs. Deb: 6/27/1899

YEAR	TM/L	G	AB	R	H	2B	3B	HR	RBI	BB	SO	AVG	OBP	SLG	PRO+	BR	/A	RC	SB	CS	SBR	FR	POS	TPR
1899	StL-N	11	37	4	9	0	0	1	3	6		.243	.364	.324	90	-0	-0	4	0			-2	O	-0.2
	Cle-N	55	202	23	56	3	5	2	23	6		.277	.298	.371	92	-5	-3	24	3			-8	O	-1.2
	Yr	66	239	27	65	3	5	3	26	12		.272	.310	.364	92	-5	-3	29	3			-10		-1.4
1901	Bos-A	136	545	71	142	10	10	3	62	39		.261	.312	.332	82	-14	-12	63	11			-3	*O	-1.5
1902	Cle-A	25	94	14	25	2	0	0	11	5		.266	.303	.287	66	-4	-4	10	4			-1	O	-0.4
	StL-A	103	416	67	132	14	11	6	58	44		.317	.383	.447	133	18	19	83	23			-3	*O/2	0.9
	Yr	128	510	81	157	16	11	6	69	49		.308	.369	.418	122	14	15	91	27			-3		0.5
1903	StL-A	105	383	36	94	6	3	3	29	23		.245	.288	.300	81	-10	-8	40	16			2	*O	-1.2
1904	StL-A	114	438	47	112	13	2	2	45	35		.256	.311	.308	105	-0	3	52	23			-2	*O/2	-0.5
1906	StL-A	154	585	90	169	19	12	4	62	43		.289	.338	.383	133	18	21	91	33			1	*O	1.7
1907	StL-A	153	603	66	156	20	9	0	38	51		.259	.317	.322	106	4	5	70	14			-2	*O	-0.6
1908	NY-A	142	505	62	150	12	9	0	44	59		.297	.371	.356	138	24	23	82	42			-1	*O	1.6
1909	NY-A	73	181	23	44	5	1	0	10	32		.243	.357	.282	101	2	2	22	10			-1	O	0.0
1910	NY-A	102	351	49	84	9	4	0	21	55		.239	.350	.288	95	3	0	42	19			-2	O	-0.6
1911	NY-A	69	201	32	57	4	2	1	15	37		.284	.397	.338	99	4	2	31	9			-7	O	-0.9
Total	11	1242	4541	580	1230	117	68	22	421	435		.271	.336	.341	107	40	47	612	207			-28	*O/2	-2.9

■ FRANK HEMPHILL

Hemphill, Frank Vernon b: 5/13/1878, Greenville, Mich. d: 11/16/50, Chicago, Ill. BR/TR, 5'11", 165 lbs. Deb: 4/17/06

YEAR	TM/L	G	AB	R	H	2B	3B	HR	RBI	BB	SO	AVG	OBP	SLG	PRO+	BR	/A	RC	SB	CS	SBR	FR	POS	TPR
1906	Chi-A	13	40	0	3	0	0	0	2	9		.075	.245	.075	3	-4	-4	1	1			1	O	-0.3
1909	Was-A	1	3	0	0	0	0	0	0	0		.000	.000	.000	-99	-1	-1	0	0			0	/O	0.0
Total	2	14	43	0	3	0	0	0	2	9		.070	.231	.070	-3	-5	-5	1	1			1	/O	-0.3

■ ROLLIE HEMSLEY

Hemsley, Ralston Burdett b: 6/24/07, Syracuse, Ohio d: 7/31/72, Washington, D.C. BR/TR, 5'10", 170 lbs. Deb: 4/13/28 C

YEAR	TM/L	G	AB	R	H	2B	3B	HR	RBI	BB	SO	AVG	OBP	SLG	PRO+	BR	/A	RC	SB	CS	SBR	FR	POS	TPR
1928	Pit-N	50	133	14	36	2	3	0	18	4	10	.271	.292	.331	60	-7	-8	12	1			1	C	-0.3
1929	Pit-N	88	235	31	68	13	7	0	37	11	22	.289	.321	.404	77	-8	-9	29	1			8	C	0.5
1930	Pit-N	104	324	45	82	19	6	2	45	22	21	.253	.301	.367	60	-21	-22	35	3			3	C	-1.1
1931	Pit-N	10	35	3	6	3	0	0	1	3	3	.171	.237	.257	43	-3	-3	2	0			1	/C	-0.1
	Chi-N	66	204	28	63	17	4	3	31	17	30	.309	.362	.475	121	6	6	36	4			6	C	1.4
	Yr	76	239	31	69	20	4	3	32	20	33	.289	.344	.444	109	3	3	37	4			7		1.3
1932	*Chi-N	60	151	27	36	10	3	4	20	10	16	.238	.286	.424	89	-3	-3	19	2			2	C/O	0.1
1933	Cin-N	49	116	9	22	8	0	0	7	6	8	.190	.230	.259	40	-9	-9	6	0			5	C	-0.2
	StL-A	32	95	7	23	2	1	1	15	11	12	.242	.321	.316	65	-4	-5	10	0	0	0	-3	C	-0.5
1934	StL-A	123	431	47	133	31	7	2	52	29	37	.309	.355	.427	93	-0	-5	66	6	2	1	24	*C/O	2.7

YEAR	TM/L	G	AB	R	H	2B	3B	HR	RBI	BB	SO	AVG	OBP	SLG	PRO+	BR	/A	RC	SB	CS	SBR	FR	POS	TPR
1935	StL-A	144	504	57	146	32	7	0	48	44	41	.290	.349	.381	85	-8	-12	69	3	2	-0	9	*C	0.1
1936	StL-A	116	377	43	99	24	2	2	39	46	30	.263	.343	.353	70	-16	-18	47	2	3	-1	-11	*C	-1.7
1937	StL-A	100	334	30	74	12	3	3	28	25	29	.222	.276	.302	45	-29	-29	29	0	0	0	-6	C/1	-2.5
1938	Cle-A	66	203	27	60	11	3	2	28	23	14	.296	.367	.409	96	-2	-1	31	1	1	-0	15	*C	1.3
1939	Cle-A	107	395	58	104	17	4	4	36	26	26	.263	.309	.342	69	-21	-19	41	2	4	-2	6	*C	-0.6
1940	Cle-A	119	416	46	111	20	5	4	42	22	25	.267	.304	.368	75	-17	-16	45	1	3	-2	8	*C	0.0
1941	Cle-A	98	288	29	69	10	5	2	24	18	19	.240	.284	.330	65	-16	-15	27	2	0	1	8	*C	-1.0
1942	Cin-N	36	115	7	13	1	2	0	7	4	11	.113	.143	.157	-12	-16	-16	3	0			11	C	-0.4
	NY-A	31	85	12	25	3	1	0	15	5	9	.294	.333	.353	95	-1	-1	10	1	0	0	1	C	0.4
1943	NY-A	62	180	12	43	6	3	2	24	13	9	.239	.290	.339	83	-4	-4	15	0	1	-1	2	C	0.0
1944	NY-A	81	284	23	76	12	5	2	26	9	13	.268	.290	.366	84	-6	-7	25	0	2	-1	-3	C	-0.5
1946	Phi-N	49	139	7	31	4	1	0	11	9	10	.223	.270	.266	54	-9	-8	10	0			11	C	0.5
1947	Phi-N	2	3	0	1	0	0	0	1	0	0	.333	.333	.333	80	-0	-0	0	0			-0	/C	0.0
Total	19	1593	5047	562	1321	257	72	31	555	357	395	.262	.311	.360	74	-196	-204	571	29	18		87	*C/O1	-1.9

■ SOLLY HEMUS

Hemus, Solomon Joseph   b: 4/17/23, Phoenix, Ariz.   BL/TR, 5'9", 165 lbs.   Deb: 4/27/49   MC

YEAR	TM/L	G	AB	R	H	2B	3B	HR	RBI	BB	SO	AVG	OBP	SLG	PRO+	BR	/A	RC	SB	CS	SBR	FR	POS	TPR
1949	StL-N	20	33	8	11	1	0	0	2	7	3	.333	.450	.364	115	2	1	6	0			2	2	0.4
1950	StL-N	11	15	1	2	1	0	0	0	2	4	.133	.235	.200	15	-2	-2	1	0			1	/3	0.0
1951	StL-N	120	420	68	118	18	9	2	32	75	31	.281	.395	.381	109	9	9	70	7	7	-2	13	*S2	2.9
1952	StL-N	151	570	105	153	28	8	15	52	96	55	.268	.392	.425	126	25	24	103	1	5	-3	4	*S/3	3.1
1953	StL-N	154	585	110	163	32	11	14	61	86	40	.279	.382	.443	114	15	15	107	2	1	0	7	*S/2	3.2
1954	StL-N	124	214	43	65	15	3	2	27	55	27	.304	.456	.430	131	14	14	50	5	1	1	-20	S32	0.0
1955	StL-N	96	206	36	50	10	2	5	21	27	22	.243	.336	.383	91	-3	-2	28	1	1	-0	-4	32/S	-0.5
1956	StL-N	8	5	1	1	0	0	0	2	1	1	.200	.429	.200	77	-0	-0	1	0	0	0	0	H	0.0
	Phi-N	78	187	24	54	10	4	5	24	28	21	.289	.401	.465	134	10	10	36	1	1	-0	-25	2/3	-1.0
	Yr	86	192	25	55	10	4	5	26	29	22	.286	.402	.458	133	10	10	36	1	1	-0	-25		-1.0
1957	Phi-N	70	108	8	20	6	1	0	5	20	8	.185	.323	.259	61	-6	-5	8	1	1	-0	-3	2	-0.6
1958	Phi-N	105	334	53	95	14	3	8	36	51	34	.284	.392	.416	116	9	10	59	3	1	0	-14	2/3	0.1
1959	StL-N	24	17	2	4	2	0	0	1	8	2	.235	.500	.353	124	2	1	4	0	0	0	1	/23M	0.2
Total	11	961	2694	459	736	137	41	51	263	456	248	.273	.390	.411	115	74	75	472	21	18		-37	S2/3	7.8

■ DAVE HENDERSON

Henderson, David Lee   b: 7/21/58, Merced, Cal.   BR/TR, 6'2", 210 lbs.   Deb: 4/09/81

YEAR	TM/L	G	AB	R	H	2B	3B	HR	RBI	BB	SO	AVG	OBP	SLG	PRO+	BR	/A	RC	SB	CS	SBR	FR	POS	TPR
1981	Sea-A	59	126	17	21	3	0	6	13	16	24	.167	.266	.333	69	-5	-5	11	2	1	0	5	O	-0.1
1982	Sea-A	104	324	47	82	17	1	14	48	36	67	.253	.328	.441	106	4	2	46	2	5	-2	4	*O	0.0
1983	Sea-A	137	484	50	130	24	5	17	55	28	93	.269	.310	.444	101	2	-1	67	9	3	1	3	*O/D	0.2
1984	Sea-A	112	350	42	98	23	0	14	43	19	56	.280	.321	.466	116	6	6	51	5	5	-2	2	OD	0.4
1985	Sea-A	139	502	70	121	28	2	14	68	48	104	.241	.311	.388	90	-7	-7	60	6	1	-1	-6	O	-1.4
1986	Sea-A	103	337	51	93	19	4	14	44	37	95	.276	.351	.481	123	11	10	57	1	3	-2	8	OD	1.4
	*Bos-A	36	51	8	10	3	0	1	3	2	15	.196	.226	.314	45	-4	-4	4	1	0	0	5	O	0.1
	Yr	139	388	59	103	22	4	15	47	39	110	.265	.336	.459	113	7	6	60	2	3	-1	13		1.5
1987	Bos-A	75	184	30	43	10	0	8	25	22	48	.234	.316	.418	90	-2	-3	25	1	1	-0	-4	O/D	-0.8
	SF-N	15	21	2	5	2	0	0	1	8	5	.238	.448	.333	117	1	1	5	2	0	1	0	/O	0.2
1988	*Oak-A	146	507	100	154	38	1	24	94	47	92	.304	.367	.525	152	31	33	94	2	4	-2	0	*O	2.7
1989	*Oak-A	152	579	77	145	24	3	15	80	54	131	.250	.318	.380	99	-4	-1	69	8	5	-1	0	*O/D	-0.3
1990	*Oak-A	127	450	65	122	28	0	20	63	40	105	.271	.332	.467	125	11	13	71	3	1	0	3	*O/D	1.5
Total	10	1205	3915	559	1024	219	16	147	537	357	835	.262	.326	.438	110	43	45	559	42	29	-5	19	*O/D	3.9

■ KEN HENDERSON

Henderson, Kenneth Joseph   b: 6/15/46, Carroll, Iowa   BB/TR, 6'2", 180 lbs.   Deb: 4/23/65

YEAR	TM/L	G	AB	R	H	2B	3B	HR	RBI	BB	SO	AVG	OBP	SLG	PRO+	BR	/A	RC	SB	CS	SBR	FR	POS	TPR
1965	SF-N	63	73	10	14	1	1	0	7	9	19	.192	.280	.233	45	-5	-5	4	1	1	-0	5	O	-0.2
1966	SF-N	11	29	4	9	1	1	1	1	2	3	.310	.375	.517	141	2	2	6	0	0	0	-1	O	0.0
1967	SF-N	65	179	15	34	3	0	4	14	19	52	.190	.275	.274	58	-10	-9	14	0	1	-1	-1	O	-1.4
1968	SF-N	3	3	1	1	0	0	0	0	2	1	.333	.600	.333	186	1	1	1	0	0	0	0	/O	0.1
1969	SF-N	113	374	42	84	14	4	6	44	42	64	.225	.311	.332	82	-10	-9	39	6	4	-1	-2	*O/3	-1.8
1970	SF-N	148	554	104	163	35	3	17	88	87	78	.294	.395	.460	130	25	25	106	20	3	4	5	*O	2.7
1971	*SF-N	141	504	80	133	26	6	15	65	84	76	.264	.372	.429	128	19	20	86	18	3	4	-4	O/1	1.6
1972	SF-N	130	439	60	113	21	2	18	51	38	66	.257	.319	.437	112	6	6	61	14	7	0	8	*O	0.8
1973	Chi-A	73	262	32	68	13	0	6	32	27	49	.260	.331	.378	96	-0	-1	30	3	4	-2	-1	OD	-0.4
1974	Chi-A	162	602	76	176	35	5	20	95	66	112	.292	.364	.467	134	29	27	100	12	7	-1	6	*O	2.9
1975	Chi-A	140	513	65	129	20	3	9	53	74	65	.251	.350	.355	98	2	1	64	5	3	-0	20	*O/D	1.7
1976	Atl-N	133	435	52	114	19	0	13	61	62	68	.262	.355	.395	106	8	5	60	5	7	-3	-7	*O	-0.9
1977	Tex-A	75	244	23	63	14	0	5	23	18	37	.258	.317	.377	87	-4	-4	28	2	1	0	-8	O/D	-1.4
1978	NY-N	7	22	2	5	2	0	1	4	4	4	.227	.346	.455	127	1	1	3	0	1	-1	0	/O	0.0
	Cin-N	64	144	10	24	6	1	3	19	23	32	.167	.281	.285	59	-8	-8	11	0	0	0	-1	O	-1.0
	Yr	71	166	12	29	8	1	4	23	27	36	.175	.290	.307	67	-7	-7	14	0	1	-1	-1		-1.0
1979	Cin-N	10	13	1	3	1	0	0	2	0	2	.231	.231	.308	45	-1	-1	1	0	0	0	-0	/O	0.0
	Chi-N	62	81	11	19	2	0	2	8	15	16	.235	.361	.333	83	-0	-1	11	0	0	0	-3	O	-0.4
	Yr	72	94	12	22	3	0	2	10	15	18	.234	.345	.330	79	-1	-2	12	0	0	0	-3		-0.4
1980	Chi-N	44	82	7	16	3	0	2	9	17	19	.195	.333	.305	74	-2	-3	9	0	0	0	-0	O	-0.3
Total	16	1444	4553	595	1168	216	26	122	576	589	763	.257	.346	.396	106	53	45	634	86	42		15	*O/D31	2.0

■ RICKEY HENDERSON

Henderson, Rickey Henley   b: 12/25/58, Chicago, Ill.   BR/TL, 5'10", 180 lbs.   Deb: 6/24/79

YEAR	TM/L	G	AB	R	H	2B	3B	HR	RBI	BB	SO	AVG	OBP	SLG	PRO+	BR	/A	RC	SB	CS	SBR	FR	POS	TPR
1979	Oak-A	89	351	49	96	13	3	1	26	34	39	.274	.341	.336	88	-7	-5	44	33	11	3	6	O	0.2
1980	Oak-A	158	591	111	179	22	4	9	53	117	54	.303	.422	.399	136	29	34	120	100	26	14	17	*O	6.2
1981	*Oak-A	108	423	89	135	18	7	6	35	64	68	.319	.411	.437	152	27	29	81	56	22	4	18	*O	5.0
1982	Oak-A	149	536	119	143	24	4	10	51	116	94	.267	.399	.382	121	17	21	99	130	42	14	7	*O/D	3.6
1983	Oak-A	145	513	105	150	25	7	9	48	103	80	.292	.415	.421	139	27	31	109	108	19	21	8	*O/D	5.7
1984	Oak-A	142	502	113	147	27	4	16	58	86	81	.293	.401	.458	147	29	33	103	66	18	9	6	*O/D	4.4
1985	NY-A	143	547	146	172	28	5	24	72	99	65	.314	.422	.516	159	45	47	138	80	10	18	11	*O/D	7.1
1986	NY-A	153	608	130	160	31	5	28	74	89	81	.263	.359	.469	125	20	21	112	87	18	15	5	*O/D	3.7
1987	NY-A	95	358	78	104	17	3	17	37	80	52	.291	.423	.497	144	26	26	84	41	8	8	4	OD	3.4
1988	NY-A	140	554	118	169	30	2	6	50	82	54	.305	.397	.399	125	21	22	107	93	13	20	6	*O/D	4.5
1989	NY-A	65	235	41	58	13	1	3	22	56	29	.247	.394	.349	112	6	7	40	25	8	3	1	O	1.0
	*Oak-A	85	306	72	90	13	2	9	35	70	39	.294	.429	.438	150	22	24	70	52	6	12	3	O/D	3.8
	Yr	150	541	113	148	26	3	12	57	126	68	.274	.413	.399	133	29	31	110	77	14	15	5		4.8
1990	*Oak-A	136	489	119	159	33	3	28	61	97	60	.325	.441	.577	188	58	59	137	65	10	14	6	*OD	7.7
Total	12	1608	6013	1290	1762	294	50	166	622	1093	796	.293	.405	.441	139	320	351	1246	936	211	154	98	*O/D	56.3

■ STEVE HENDERSON

Henderson, Stephen Curtis   b: 11/18/52, Houston, Tex.   BR/TR, 6'2", 190 lbs.   Deb: 6/16/77

YEAR	TM/L	G	AB	R	H	2B	3B	HR	RBI	BB	SO	AVG	OBP	SLG	PRO+	BR	/A	RC	SB	CS	SBR	FR	POS	TPR
1977	NY-N	99	350	67	104	16	6	12	65	43	79	.297	.376	.480	134	14	16	61	6	3	0	0	O	1.3
1978	NY-N	157	587	83	156	30	9	10	65	60	109	.266	.380	.399	108	3	6	74	13	7	-0	6	*O	0.6
1979	NY-N	98	350	42	107	16	8	5	39	38	58	.306	.380	.440	128	12	13	59	13	5	1	4	O	1.6
1980	NY-N	143	513	75	149	17	8	8	58	62	90	.290	.370	.402	119	12	10	75	23	12	-0	5	*O	1.4
1981	Chi-N	82	287	32	84	9	5	5	35	42	61	.293	.387	.411	121	11	10	45	5	7	-3	-11	O	-0.6
1982	Chi-N	92	257	23	60	12	4	2	29	22	64	.233	.294	.335	73	-9	-9	25	6	5	-1	-3	O	-1.4

YEAR	TM/L	G	AB	R	H	2B	3B	HR	RBI	BB	SO	AVG	OBP	SLG	PRO+	BR	/A	RC	SB	CS	SBR	FR	POS	TPR
1983	Sea-A	121	436	50	128	32	3	10	54	44	82	.294	.358	.450	116	12	10	66	10	14	-5	-2	*O/D	0.1
1984	Sea-A	109	325	42	85	12	3	10	35	38	62	.262	.341	.409	108	3	4	45	2	4	-2	-4	OD	-0.3
1985	Oak-A	85	193	25	58	8	3	3	31	18	34	.301	.360	.420	122	4	5	27	0	0	0	-5	O/D	0.0
1986	Oak-A	11	26	2	2	1	0	0	3	0	5	.077	.077	.115	-52	-5	-5	-0	0	0	0	-1	/OD	-0.5
1987	Oak-A	46	114	14	33	7	0	3	9	12	19	.289	.357	.430	115	1	2	16	0	0	0	-3	O/D	0.0
1988	Hou-N	42	46	4	10	2	0	0	5	7	14	.217	.321	.261	72	-2	-1	4	1	1	-0	1	/O1	0.0
Total	12	1085	3484	459	976	162	49	68	428	386	677	.280	.354	.413	113	58	65	497	79	58	-11	-12	O/D1	2.2

■ GEORGE HENDRICK

Hendrick, George Andrew b: 10/18/49, Los Angeles, Cal. BR/TR, 6'3", 195 lbs. Deb: 6/04/71

YEAR	TM/L	G	AB	R	H	2B	3B	HR	RBI	BB	SO	AVG	OBP	SLG	PRO+	BR	/A	RC	SB	CS	SBR	FR	POS	TPR
1971	Oak-A	42	114	8	27	4	1	0	8	3	20	.237	.256	.289	55	-7	-7	7	0	1	-1	-1	O	-1.0
1972	*Oak-A	58	121	10	22	1	1	4	15	3	22	.182	.208	.306	54	-8	-7	7	3	2	-0	1	O	-0.8
1973	Cle-A	113	440	64	118	18	0	21	61	25	71	.268	.310	.452	111	5	4	58	7	6	-2	-5	*O	-0.4
1974	Cle-A	139	495	65	138	23	1	19	67	33	73	.279	.325	.444	121	11	11	66	6	4	-1	0	*O/D	0.7
1975	Cle-A	145	561	82	145	21	2	24	86	40	78	.258	.308	.431	107	3	3	65	6	7	-2	4	*O	0.1
1976	Cle-A	149	551	72	146	20	3	25	81	51	82	.265	.327	.448	127	16	17	77	4	4	-1	-11	*O/D	0.1
1977	SD-N	152	541	75	168	25	2	23	81	61	74	.311	.382	.492	148	25	32	102	11	6	-0	8	*O	3.5
1978	SD-N	36	111	9	27	4	0	3	8	12	16	.243	.317	.360	96	-2	-1	13	1	1	-0	2	O	0.0
	StL-N	102	382	55	110	27	1	17	67	28	44	.288	.340	.497	133	14	15	63	1	0	-0	1	*O	1.3
	Yr	138	493	64	137	31	1	20	75	40	60	.278	.335	.467	126	13	14	76	2	1	0	3		1.3
1979	StL-N	140	493	67	148	27	1	16	75	49	62	.300	.353	.456	121	15	14	78	2	3	-1	7	*O	1.6
1980	StL-N	150	572	73	173	33	2	25	109	32	67	.302	.344	.498	128	22	20	94	6	1	1	4	*O	2.0
1981	StL-N	101	394	67	112	19	3	18	61	41	44	.284	.358	.485	134	18	17	67	4	2	0	-12	*O	0.3
1982	*StL-N	136	515	65	145	20	5	19	104	37	80	.282	.331	.450	115	10	9	74	3	2	-0	-8	*O	0.0
1983	StL-N	144	529	73	168	33	3	18	97	51	76	.318	.380	.493	140	28	28	96	3	4	-2	-1	1O	2.1
1984	StL-N	120	441	57	122	28	1	9	69	32	75	.277	.327	.406	108	2	3	55	0	2	-1	-5	*O/1	-0.6
1985	Pit-N	69	256	23	59	15	0	2	25	18	42	.230	.281	.313	66	-12	-12	21	1	0	0	1	O	-1.2
	Cal-A	16	41	5	5	1	0	2	6	4	8	.122	.200	.293	33	-4	-4	1	0	0	0	-0	O/D	-0.4
1986	*Cal-A	102	283	45	77	13	1	14	47	26	41	.272	.335	.473	119	6	7	42	1	1	-0	-0	O/1D	0.3
1987	Cal-A	65	162	14	39	10	0	5	25	14	18	.241	.301	.395	85	-4	-4	17	0	0	0	-3	O/1D	-0.7
1988	Cal-A	69	127	12	31	1	0	3	19	7	20	.244	.289	.323	73	-5	-5	12	0	1	-1	2	O1/D	-0.3
Total	18	2048	7129	941	1980	343	27	267	1111	567	1013	.278	.333	.446	117	134	144	1015	59	47	-11	-18	*O1/D	6.6

■ HARVEY HENDRICK

Hendrick, Harvey "Gink" b: 11/9/1897, Mason, Tenn. d: 10/29/41, Covington, Tenn. BL/TR, 6'2", 190 lbs. Deb: 8/20/23

YEAR	TM/L	G	AB	R	H	2B	3B	HR	RBI	BB	SO	AVG	OBP	SLG	PRO+	BR	/A	RC	SB	CS	SBR	FR	POS	TPR
1923	*NY-A	37	66	9	18	3	1	3	12	2	8	.273	.294	.485	101	-0	-1	10	3	0	1	-2	O	-0.2
1924	NY-A	40	76	7	20	0	0	1	11	2	7	.263	.291	.303	53	-5	-5	7	1	0	0	-0	O	-0.5
1925	Cle-A	25	28	2	8	1	2	0	9	3	5	.286	.355	.464	106	0	0	5	0	0	0	0	/1	0.0
1927	Bro-N	128	458	55	142	18	11	4	50	24	40	.310	.350	.424	106	3	3	66	29			-6	O1/2	-0.8
1928	Bro-N	126	425	83	135	15	10	11	59	54	34	.318	.397	.478	129	18	19	80	16			4	3O	2.3
1929	Bro-N	110	384	69	136	25	6	14	82	31	20	.354	.404	.560	139	21	22	84	14			0	O1/3S	1.6
1930	Bro-N	68	167	29	43	10	1	5	28	20	19	.257	.344	.419	84	-5	-4	24	2			-2	O/1	-0.8
1931	Bro-N	1	1	0	0	0	0	0	0	0	0	.000	.000	.000	-99	-0	-0	0	0			0	H	0.0
	Cin-N	137	530	74	167	32	9	1	75	53	40	.315	.379	.415	121	11	15	87	3			-5	*1	0.0
	Yr	138	531	74	167	32	9	1	75	53	40	.315	.379	.414	120	11	15	87	3			-5		0.0
1932	StL-N	28	72	8	18	2	0	1	5	5	9	.250	.299	.319	64	-3	-4	7	0			-2	3/O	-0.4
	Cin-N	94	398	56	120	30	3	4	40	23	29	.302	.341	.422	107	2	4	58	3			-4	1	-0.8
	Yr	122	470	64	138	32	3	5	45	28	38	.294	.335	.406	100	-1	-0	65	3			-6		-0.8
1933	Chi-N	69	189	30	55	13	3	4	23	13	17	.291	.346	.455	128	6	6	31	4			-1	1/O3	0.4
1934	Phi-N	59	116	12	34	8	0	0	19	9	15	.293	.344	.362	79	-2	-4	15	0			-4	O/13	-0.7
Total	11	922	2910	434	896	157	46	48	413	239	243	.308	.364	.443	113	46	52	473	75	0		-21	103/S2	0.5

■ ELLIE HENDRICKS

Hendricks, Elrod Jerome b: 12/22/40, Charlotte Amalie, V.I. BL/TR, 6'1", 175 lbs. Deb: 4/13/68 C

YEAR	TM/L	G	AB	R	H	2B	3B	HR	RBI	BB	SO	AVG	OBP	SLG	PRO+	BR	/A	RC	SB	CS	SBR	FR	POS	TPR
1968	Bal-A	79	183	19	37	8	1	7	23	19	51	.202	.281	.372	96	-1	-1	19	0	0	0	-4	C	-0.2
1969	*Bal-A	105	295	36	72	5	0	12	38	39	44	.244	.336	.383	100	1	0	40	0	1	-1	5	C/1	1.0
1970	*Bal-A	106	322	32	78	9	0	12	41	33	44	.242	.320	.382	92	-3	-4	41	1	0	0	-7	C	-0.8
1971	*Bal-A	101	316	33	79	14	1	9	42	39	38	.250	.336	.386	105	2	2	41	0	0	0	-6	C/1	-0.8
1972	Bal-A	33	84	6	13	4	0	0	4	12	19	.155	.260	.202	38	-6	-6	5	0	1	-1	1	C	-0.5
	Chi-N	17	43	7	5	1	0	2	6	13	8	.116	.321	.279	65	-1	-2	4	0	1	-1	1	C	0.0
	Yr	54	132	8	23	2	0	4	9	10	23	.174	.232	.280	52	-9	-8	9	0	1	-1	-4		-1.1
1973	Bal-A	41	101	9	18	5	1	3	15	10	22	.178	.259	.337	67	-5	-5	9	0	0	0	4	C/D	0.0
1974	*Bal-A	66	159	18	33	8	2	3	8	17	25	.208	.288	.340	83	-4	-4	16	0	0	0	0	C/1D	-0.1
1975	Bal-A	85	223	32	48	8	2	8	38	34	40	.215	.322	.377	103	-1	1	28	0	1	-1	-1	C	0.2
1976	Bal-A	28	79	2	11	1	0	1	4	7	13	.139	.209	.190	19	-8	-8	3	0	1	-1	-5	C	-1.2
	*NY-A	26	53	6	12	1	0	3	5	3	10	.226	.268	.415	99	-0	-0	6	0	0	0	1	C	0.1
	Yr	54	132	8	23	2	0	4	9	10	23	.174	.232	.280	52	-9	-8	9	0	1	-1	-4		-1.1
1977	NY-A	10	11	1	3	1	0	1	5	0	2	.273	.273	.636	140	0	0	2	0	0	0	0	/C	0.1
1978	Bal-A	13	18	4	6	1	0	1	1	3	3	.333	.429	.556	186	2	2	4	0	0	0	0	/CPD	0.2
1979	Bal-A	1	1	0	0	0	0	0	0	0	0	.000	.000	.000	-99	-0	-0	0	0	0	0	-0	/C	0.0
Total	12	711	1888	205	415	66	7	62	230	229	319	.220	.308	.361	90	-26	-23	218	1	5	-3	-10	C/1DP	-1.2

■ JACK HENDRICKS

Hendricks, John Charles b: 4/9/1875, Joliet, Ill. d: 5/13/43, Chicago, Ill. BL/TL, 5'11.5", 160 lbs. Deb: 6/12/02 M

YEAR	TM/L	G	AB	R	H	2B	3B	HR	RBI	BB	SO	AVG	OBP	SLG	PRO+	BR	/A	RC	SB	CS	SBR	FR	POS	TPR
1902	NY-N	8	26	1	6	2	0	0	0	2		.231	.286	.308	86	-0	-0	3	2			0	/O	0.0
	Chi-N	2	7	0	4	0	1	0	0			.571	.571	.857	354	2	2	3	0			0	/O	0.2
	Yr	10	33	1	10	2	1	0	0	2		.303	.343	.424	140	1	1	6	2			1		0.2
1903	Was-A	32	112	10	20	1	3	0	4	13		.179	.264	.241	53	-6	-6	9	3			-4	O	-1.2
Total	2	42	145	11	30	3	4	0	4	15		.207	.281	.283	71	-4	-5	16	5			-3	/O	-1.0

■ TIM HENDRYX

Hendryx, Timothy Green b: 1/31/1891, Leroy, Ill. d: 8/14/57, Corpus Christi, Tex. BR/TR, 5'9", 170 lbs. Deb: 9/28/11

YEAR	TM/L	G	AB	R	H	2B	3B	HR	RBI	BB	SO	AVG	OBP	SLG	PRO+	BR	/A	RC	SB	CS	SBR	FR	POS	TPR
1911	Cle-A	3	7	0	2	0	0	0	0	0		.286	.286	.286	59	-0	-0	1	0			-1	/3	0.0
1912	Cle-A	23	70	9	17	2	4	1	14	8		.243	.329	.429	112	1	1	11	3			-2	O	-0.1
1915	NY-A	13	40	4	8	2	0	0	1	4	2	.200	.289	.250	61	-2	-2	2	0	3	-2	1	O	-0.3
1916	NY-A	15	62	10	18	7	1	0	5	8	6	.290	.380	.435	142	3	3	12	4			-1	O	0.1
1917	NY-A	125	393	43	98	14	7	5	44	62	45	.249	.359	.359	118	11	10	53	6			5	*O	0.9
1918	StL-A	88	219	22	61	14	3	0	33	37	35	.279	.388	.370	133	9	10	34	5			-9	O	-0.1
1920	Bos-A	99	363	45	119	21	5	0	73	42	27	.328	.400	.413	121	10	12	60	7	9	-3	-10	O	-0.9
1921	Bos-A	49	137	10	33	8	2	0	22	24	13	.241	.362	.328	79	-4	-3	18	1	1	-0	-4	O	-1.0
Total	8	415	1291	152	356	68	22	6	192	185	128	.276	.372	.376	115	28	31	191	26	13		-21	O/3	-1.4

■ DAVE HENGEL

Hengel, David Lee b: 12/18/61, Oakland, Cal. BR/TR, 6', 185 lbs. Deb: 9/03/86

YEAR	TM/L	G	AB	R	H	2B	3B	HR	RBI	BB	SO	AVG	OBP	SLG	PRO+	BR	/A	RC	SB	CS	SBR	FR	POS	TPR
1986	Sea-A	21	63	3	12	1	0	1	6	1	13	.190	.215	.254	27	-6	-6	3	0	0	0	1	D/O	-0.5
1987	Sea-A	10	19	2	6	0	0	1	4	0	4	.316	.316	.474	100	0	-0	2	0	0	0	-0	/OD	0.0
1988	Sea-A	26	60	3	10	1	0	2	7	1	15	.167	.180	.283	27	-6	-6	3	0	0	0	0	/OD	-0.5
1989	Cle-A	12	25	2	3	1	0	0	1	2	4	.120	.185	.160	-2	-3	-3	1	0	0	0	1	/OD	-0.2
Total	4	69	167	10	31	3	0	4	18	4	36	.186	.209	.275	31	-16	-16	9	0	0	0	1	/OD	-1.2

YEAR	TM/L	G	AB	R	H	2B	3B	HR	RBI	BB	SO	AVG	OBP	SLG	PRO+	BR	/A	RC	SB	CS	SBR	FR	POS	TPR

■ MOXIE HENGLE   Hengle, Emery J.   b: 10/7/1857, Chicago, Ill.   d: 12/11/24, Forest River, Ill.   BR , 5'8", 144 lbs.   Deb: 4/20/1884

1884	CP-U	19	74	9	15	2	1	0			3	.203	.234	.257	66	-3	-2	5	0			-7	2	-0.8
	StP-U	9	33	2	5	1	1	0			0	.152	.152	.242	58	-2	0	1	0			1	/2	0.1
	Yr	28	107	11	20	3	2	0			3	.187	.209	.252	65	-5	-2	6	0			-6		-0.7
1885	Buf-N	7	26	2	4	0	0	0	0	1	2	.154	.185	.154	10	-2	-3	1				-3	/2O	-0.4
Total	2	35	133	13	24	3	2	0	0	4	2	.180	.204	.233	52	-7	-5	7				-9	/2O	-1.1

■ GAIL HENLEY   Henley, Gail Curtice   b: 10/15/28, Wichita, Kan.   BL/TR, 5'9", 180 lbs.   Deb: 4/13/54

| 1954 | Pit-N | 14 | 30 | 7 | 9 | 1 | 0 | 1 | 2 | 4 | 4 | .300 | .382 | .433 | 114 | 1 | 1 | 5 | 0 | 0 | 0 | -0 | /O | 0.0 |

■ BUTCH HENLINE   Henline, Walter John   b: 12/20/1894, Ft.Wayne, Ind.   d: 10/9/57, Sarasota, Fla.   BR/TR, 5'10", 175 lbs.   Deb: 4/13/21   U

1921	NY-N	1	1	0	0	0	0	0	0	0	1	.000	.000	.000	-99	-0	-0	0	0	0	0	0	H	0.0
	Phi-N	33	111	8	34	2	0	0	8	2	6	.306	.319	.324	65	-5	-6	11	1	0	0	9	C	0.5
	Yr	34	112	8	34	2	0	0	8	2	7	.304	.316	.321	64	-5	-6	11	1	0	0	9		0.5
1922	Phi-N	125	430	57	136	20	4	14	64	36	33	.316	.380	.479	110	13	7	79	2	2	-1	2	*C	0.8
1923	Phi-N	111	330	45	107	14	3	7	46	37	33	.324	.407	.448	112	14	8	62	7	5	-1	-16	C/O	-0.2
1924	Phi-N	115	289	41	82	18	4	5	35	27	15	.284	.361	.426	98	4	-0	45	1	2	-1	-1	C/O	0.0
1925	Phi-N	93	263	43	80	12	5	8	48	24	16	.304	.380	.479	108	7	4	49	3	1	0	-3	C/O	0.4
1926	Phi-N	99	283	32	80	14	1	2	30	21	18	.283	.339	.360	84	-4	-6	35	1			-9	C/1O	-1.2
1927	Bro-N	67	177	12	47	10	3	1	18	17	10	.266	.337	.373	90	-2	-3	22	1			1	C	0.2
1928	Bro-N	55	132	12	28	3	1	2	8	17	8	.212	.302	.295	58	-8	-8	12	2			-4	C	-0.8
1929	Bro-N	27	62	5	15	2	0	1	7	9	9	.242	.338	.323	66	-3	-3	7	0			0	C	0.0
1930	Chi-A	3	8	1	1	0	0	0	2	0	3	.125	.125	.125	-38	-2	-2	0	0	0	0	0	/C	0.0
1931	Chi-A	11	15	2	1	1	0	0	2	2	4	.067	.176	.133	-19	-3	-3	-2	0	0	0	1	/C	-0.1
Total	11	740	2101	258	611	96	21	40	268	192	156	.291	.361	.414	96	10	-12	324	18	10		-20	C/O1	-0.4

■ LES HENNESSEY   Hennessey, Lester Baker   b: 12/12/1893, Lynn, Mass.   d: 11/20/76, New York, N.Y.   BR/TR, 6', 190 lbs.   Deb: 6/04/13

| 1913 | Det-A | 14 | 22 | 2 | 3 | 0 | 0 | 0 | 0 | 3 | 6 | .136 | .240 | .136 | 11 | -2 | -2 | 1 | 2 | | | -2 | 2 | -0.4 |

■ FRITZ HENRICH   Henrich, Frank Wilde   b: 5/8/1899, Cincinnati, Ohio   d: 5/1/59, Philadelphia, Pa.   BL/TL, 5'10", 160 lbs.   Deb: 4/21/24

| 1924 | Phi-N | 36 | 90 | 4 | 19 | 4 | 0 | 0 | 4 | 2 | 12 | .211 | .228 | .256 | 26 | -9 | -10 | 5 | 0 | 0 | 0 | -1 | O | -1.1 |

■ BOBBY HENRICH   Henrich, Robert Edward   b: 12/24/38, Lawrence, Kan.   BR/TR, 6'1", 185 lbs.   Deb: 5/03/57

1957	Cin-N	29	10	8	2	0	0	0	1	1	4	.200	.273	.200	28	-1	-1	1	0	0	0	3	/SO32	0.2
1958	Cin-N	5	3	2	0	0	0	0	0	0	2	.000	.000	.000	-95	-1	-1	0	0	0	0	1	/S	0.0
1959	Cin-N	14	3	3	0	0	0	0	0	0	1	.000	.000	.000	-97	-1	-1	0	0	0	0	3	/S3	0.2
Total	3	48	16	13	2	0	0	0	1	1	7	.125	.176	.125	-17	-3	-3	1	0	0	0	6	/SO32	0.4

■ TOMMY HENRICH   Henrich, Thomas David "The Clutch" or "Old Reliable"   b: 2/20/13, Massillon, Ohio   BL/TL, 6', 180 lbs.   Deb: 5/11/37   C

1937	NY-A	67	206	39	66	14	5	8	42	35	17	.320	.419	.553	142	14	14	50	4	0	1	-5	O	0.7
1938	*NY-A	131	471	109	127	24	7	22	91	92	32	.270	.391	.490	120	15	15	96	6	2	1	-1	*O	1.3
1939	NY-A	99	347	64	96	18	4	9	57	51	23	.277	.371	.429	106	3	3	60	7	0	2	1	O/1	0.3
1940	NY-A	90	293	57	90	28	5	10	53	48	30	.307	.408	.539	149	20	21	68	1	2	-1	-3	O/1	1.2
1941	*NY-A	144	538	106	149	27	5	31	85	81	40	.277	.377	.519	137	26	27	113	3	1	0	-2	*O	1.6
1942	NY-A	127	483	77	129	30	5	13	67	58	42	.267	.352	.431	122	12	13	79	4	4	-1	-3	*O/1	0.0
1946	NY-A	150	565	92	142	25	4	19	83	87	63	.251	.358	.411	113	12	11	92	5	2	0	-0	*O	0.3
1947	*NY-A	142	550	109	158	35	13	16	98	71	54	.287	.372	.485	139	26	27	104	3	2	-0	4	*O/1	2.6
1948	NY-A	146	588	138	181	42	14	25	100	76	42	.308	.391	.554	151	39	40	130	2	3	-1	-7	*O1	3.3
1949	*NY-A	115	411	90	118	20	3	24	85	86	34	.287	.416	.526	148	30	30	98	2	2	-1	-7	O1	2.0
1950	NY-A	73	151	20	41	6	8	6	34	27	6	.272	.382	.536	137	7	7	30	0	1	-1	-5	1	0.0
Total	11	1284	4603	901	1297	269	73	183	795	712	383	.282	.382	.491	132	203	209	922	37	19	-0	-24	*O1	13.3

■ OLAF HENRIKSEN   Henriksen, Olaf "Swede"   b: 4/26/1888, Kirkerup, Denmark   d: 10/17/62, Norwood, Mass.   BL/TL, 5'7.5", 158 lbs.   Deb: 8/11/11

1911	Bos-A	27	93	17	34	2	0	0	8	14		.366	.449	.409	141	6	6	19	4			0	O	0.4
1912	*Bos-A	44	56	20	18	3	1	0	8	14		.321	.457	.411	142	5	4	11	0			-2	O	0.1
1913	Bos-A	31	40	8	15	1	0	0	2	7	5	.375	.468	.400	151	3	3	8	3			-1	/O	0.2
1914	Bos-A	63	95	16	25	2	1	1	5	22	12	.263	.407	.337	124	4	4	14	5	4	-1	-5	O	-0.3
1915	*Bos-A	73	92	9	18	2	2	0	13	18	7	.196	.333	.261	80	-2	-1	8	1	5	-3	-4	O	-0.9
1916	Bos-A	68	99	13	20	2	2	0	11	19	15	.202	.331	.263	78	-2	-2	10	2			-4	O	-0.7
1917	Bos-A	15	12	1	1	0	0	0	1	3	4	.083	.267	.083	7	-1	-1	0	0			0	H	0.0
Total	7	321	487	84	131	12	7	1	48	97	43	.269	.392	.329	112	13	13	70	15	9		-16	O	-1.2

■ SNAKE HENRY   Henry, Frederick Marshall   b: 7/19/1895, Waynesville, N.C.   d: 10/12/87, Wendell, N.C.   BL/TL, 6', 170 lbs.   Deb: 9/15/22

1922	Bos-N	18	66	5	13	4	1	0	5	2	8	.197	.221	.288	32	-7	-7	4	2	2	-1	1	1	-0.5
1923	Bos-N	11	9	1	1	0	0	0	2	1	1	.111	.200	.111	-17	-2	-1	0	0	0	0	0	H	0.0
Total	2	29	75	6	14	4	1	0	7	3	9	.187	.218	.267	26	-9	-8	4	2	2	-1	1	/1	-0.5

■ GEORGE HENRY   Henry, George Washington   b: 8/10/1863, Philadelphia, Pa.   d: 12/30/34, Lynn, Mass.   BR/TR, 5'9", 180 lbs.   Deb: 4/27/1893

| 1893 | Cin-N | 21 | 83 | 11 | 23 | 3 | 0 | 0 | 13 | 11 | 12 | .277 | .375 | .313 | 84 | -1 | -1 | 11 | 2 | | | 5 | O | 0.2 |

■ JOHN HENRY   Henry, John Michael   b: 9/2/1863, Springfield, Mass.   d: 6/11/39, Hartford, Conn.   Deb: 8/13/1884

1884	Cle-N	9	26	2	4	0	0	0	0	0	12	.154	.154	.154	-3	-3	-3	1				1	/PO	0.0
1885	Bal-a	10	34	4	9	3	0	0		1		.265	.286	.353	105	0	0	4				2	/PO	0.0
1886	Was-N	4	14	3	5	0	0	0	0	0	3	.357	.357	.357	125	0	0	2	0			-0	/P	0.0
1890	NY-N	37	144	19	35	6	0	0	16	7	12	.243	.283	.285	67	-6	-6	15	12			-3	O	-0.8
Total	4	60	218	28	53	9	0	0	16	8	27	.243	.273	.284	68	-9	-9	21	12			-0	/OP	-0.8

■ JOHN HENRY   Henry, John Park "Bull"   b: 12/26/1889, Amherst, Mass.   d: 11/24/41, Fort Huachuca, Ariz.   BR/TR, 6', 180 lbs.   Deb: 7/08/10

1910	Was-A	29	87	2	13	1	1	0	5	2		.149	.169	.184	11	-9	-9	3	2			2	C1	-0.4
1911	Was-A	85	261	24	53	5	0	0	21	25		.203	.273	.222	39	-21	-20	18	8			12	C1	-0.1
1912	Was-A	66	191	23	37	4	1	0	9	31		.194	.309	.225	53	-10	-11	16	10			8	C	0.4
1913	Was-A	96	273	26	61	8	4	1	26	30	43	.223	.309	.293	75	-8	-8	26	5			4	C	0.3
1914	Was-A	92	261	22	44	7	4	0	20	37	47	.169	.274	.226	49	-15	-16	19	7	3	0	6	C	-0.3
1915	Was-A	95	277	20	61	9	2	1	22	36	28	.220	.323	.278	79	-6	-6	29	10	2	2	4	C	0.7
1916	Was-A	117	305	28	76	12	3	0	46	49	40	.249	.364	.308	104	3	4	40	12			-3	*C	0.6
1917	Was-A	65	163	10	31	6	0	0	18	24	16	.190	.302	.227	62	-7	-6	12	1			1	C	0.0
1918	Bos-N	43	102	6	21	2	0	0	4	10	15	.206	.283	.225	58	-5	-5	6	0			1	C	0.0
Total	9	688	1920	161	397	54	15	2	171	244	189	.207	.303	.254	65	-78	-77	169	55	5		34	C/1	1.2

■ RON HENRY   Henry, Ronald Baxter   b: 8/7/36, Chester, Pa.   BR/TR, 6'1", 180 lbs.   Deb: 4/15/61

1961	Min-A	20	28	1	4	0	0	0	3	2	7	.143	.200	.143	-6	-4	-4	0	0	0	0	-1	/C1	-0.4
1964	Min-A	22	41	4	5	1	1	2	5	2	17	.122	.163	.341	36	-4	-4	2	0	0	0	-0	C	-0.3
Total	2	42	69	5	9	1	1	2	8	4	24	.130	.178	.261	18	-8	-8	3	0	0	0	-1	/C1	-0.7

YEAR	TM/L	G	AB	R	H	2B	3B	HR	RBI	BB	SO	AVG	OBP	SLG	PRO+	BR	/A	RC	SB	CS	SBR	FR	POS	TPR

■ BABE HERMAN   Herman, Floyd Caves b: 6/26/03, Buffalo, N.Y. d: 11/27/87, Glendale, Cal. BL/TL, 6'4", 190 lbs. Deb: 4/14/26 C

YEAR	TM/L	G	AB	R	H	2B	3B	HR	RBI	BB	SO	AVG	OBP	SLG	PRO+	BR	/A	RC	SB	CS	SBR	FR	POS	TPR
1926	Bro-N	137	496	64	158	35	11	11	81	44	53	.319	.375	.500	136	22	23	91	8			2	*1O	1.9
1927	Bro-N	130	412	65	112	26	9	14	73	39	41	.272	.336	.481	116	8	8	65	4			1	*1/O	0.1
1928	Bro-N	134	486	64	165	37	6	12	91	38	36	.340	.390	.514	136	23	24	94	1			-7	*O	1.2
1929	Bro-N	146	569	105	217	42	13	21	113	55	45	.381	.436	.612	160	50	51	146	21			-13	*O/1	2.3
1930	Bro-N	153	614	143	241	48	11	35	130	66	56	.393	.455	.678	171	69	70	183	18			-16	*O	3.8
1931	Bro-N	151	610	93	191	43	16	18	97	50	65	.313	.365	.525	138	29	30	118	17			3	*O	2.5
1932	Cin-N	148	577	87	188	38	19	16	87	60	45	.326	.389	.541	152	38	40	124	7			15	*O	4.4
1933	Chi-N	137	508	77	147	36	12	16	93	50	57	.289	.353	.502	142	26	26	90	6			-6	*O	1.3
1934	Chi-N	125	467	65	142	34	5	14	84	35	71	.304	.353	.488	125	14	15	81	1			-11	*O/1	-0.1
1935	Pit-N	26	81	8	19	8	1	0	7	3	10	.235	.271	.358	65	-4	-4	7	0			-3	O/1	-0.7
	Cin-N	92	349	44	117	23	5	10	58	35	25	.335	.396	.516	147	21	23	75	5			-2	O1	1.6
	Yr	118	430	52	136	31	6	10	65	38	35	.316	.373	.486	131	17	18	80	5			-6		0.9
1936	Cin-N	119	380	59	106	25	2	13	71	39	36	.279	.348	.458	123	7	11	61	4			-8	O/1	0.0
1937	Det-A	17	20	2	6	3	0	0	3	1	6	.300	.364	.450	102	0	0	4	2	0	1	-0	/O	0.0
1945	Bro-N	37	34	6	9	1	0	1	9	5	7	.265	.359	.382	107	0	0	5	0			0	/O	0.0
Total	13	1552	5603	882	1818	399	110	181	997	520	553	.324	.383	.532	141	304	318	1143	94	0		-46	*O1	18.3

■ BILLY HERMAN   Herman, William Jennings Bryan b: 7/7/09, New Albany, Ind. BR/TR, 5'11", 180 lbs. Deb: 8/29/31 MCH

YEAR	TM/L	G	AB	R	H	2B	3B	HR	RBI	BB	SO	AVG	OBP	SLG	PRO+	BR	/A	RC	SB	CS	SBR	FR	POS	TPR
1931	Chi-N	25	98	14	32	7	0	0	16	13	6	.327	.405	.398	115	3	3	17	2			3	2	0.6
1932	*Chi-N	154	656	102	206	42	7	1	51	40	33	.314	.358	.404	105	5	6	97	14			17	*2	3.3
1933	Chi-N	153	619	82	173	35	2	0	44	45	34	.279	.332	.342	93	-5	-5	70	5			29	*2	3.7
1934	Chi-N	113	456	79	138	21	6	3	42	34	31	.303	.355	.395	102	1	2	66	6			16	*2	2.8
1935	*Chi-N	154	666	113	227	57	6	7	83	42	29	.341	.383	.476	128	27	26	121	6			19	*2	5.5
1936	Chi-N	153	632	101	211	57	7	5	93	59	30	.334	.392	.470	128	28	26	118	5			15	*2	4.9
1937	Chi-N	138	564	106	189	35	11	8	65	56	22	.335	.396	.479	131	29	26	112	2			19	*2	4.9
1938	*Chi-N	152	624	86	173	34	7	1	56	59	31	.277	.342	.359	90	-5	-7	76	3			25	*2	2.8
1939	Chi-N	156	623	111	191	34	18	7	70	66	31	.307	.378	.453	120	20	18	104	9			-3	*2	2.1
1940	Chi-N	135	558	77	163	24	4	5	57	47	30	.292	.347	.376	101	0	1	72	1			19	*2	2.9
1941	Chi-N	11	36	4	7	0	1	0	0	9	5	.194	.356	.250	75	-1	-1	4	0			-5	2	-0.4
	*Bro-N	133	536	77	156	30	4	3	41	58	38	.291	.361	.379	104	7	4	75	1			-27	*2	-1.4
	Yr	144	572	81	163	30	5	3	41	67	43	.285	.361	.371	103	6	4	79	1			-32		-1.8
1942	Bro-N	155	571	76	146	34	2	2	65	72	52	.256	.339	.333	95	-1	-2	68	6			-11	*2/1	-0.1
1943	Bro-N	153	585	76	193	41	2	2	100	66	26	.330	.398	.417	135	28	28	97	4			-17	*23	1.5
1946	Bro-N	47	184	24	53	8	4	0	28	26	10	.288	.376	.375	112	4	4	26	2			-2	32	0.3
	Bos-N	75	252	32	77	23	1	3	22	43	13	.306	.409	.440	139	15	15	47	1			-16	21/3	-0.1
	Yr	122	436	56	130	31	5	3	50	69	23	.298	.395	.413	128	19	18	73	3			-17		0.2
1947	Pit-N	15	47	3	10	4	0	0	6	2	7	.213	.245	.298	42	-4	-4	3	0			-9	2/1M	-1.1
Total	15	1922	7707	1163	2345	486	82	47	839	737	428	.304	.367	.407	112	151	141	1173	67			72	*2/31	32.2

■ AL HERMANN   Hermann, Albert Bartel b: 3/28/1899, Milltown, N.J. d: 8/20/80, Lewes, Del. BR/TR, 6', 180 lbs. Deb: 7/17/23

YEAR	TM/L	G	AB	R	H	2B	3B	HR	RBI	BB	SO	AVG	OBP	SLG	PRO+	BR	/A	RC	SB	CS	SBR	FR	POS	TPR
1923	Bos-N	31	93	2	22	4	0	0	11	0	7	.237	.237	.280	37	-9	-8	6	3	2	-0	-6	2/31	-1.3
1924	Bos-N	1	1	0	0	0	0	0	0	0	1	.000	.000	.000	-99	-0	-0	0	0	0	0	0	H	0.0
Total	2	32	94	2	22	4	0	0	11	0	8	.234	.234	.277	36	-9	-8	6	3	2	-0	-6	/231	-1.3

■ GENE HERMANSKI   Hermanski, Eugene Victor b: 5/11/20, Pittsfield, Mass. BL/TR, 5'11.5", 185 lbs. Deb: 8/15/43

YEAR	TM/L	G	AB	R	H	2B	3B	HR	RBI	BB	SO	AVG	OBP	SLG	PRO+	BR	/A	RC	SB	CS	SBR	FR	POS	TPR
1943	Bro-N	18	60	6	18	2	1	0	12	11	7	.300	.417	.367	127	3	3	10	1			2	O	0.5
1946	Bro-N	64	110	15	22	2	2	0	8	17	10	.200	.313	.255	61	-5	-5	9	2			-3	O	-0.9
1947	*Bro-N	79	189	36	52	7	1	7	39	28	7	.275	.377	.434	111	5	4	33	5			-0	O	0.1
1948	Bro-N	133	400	63	116	22	7	15	60	64	46	.290	.391	.493	133	22	20	81	15			-1	*O	1.0
1949	*Bro-N	87	224	48	67	12	3	8	42	47	21	.299	.431	.487	140	17	15	50	12			-4	O	0.7
1950	Bro-N	94	289	36	86	17	3	7	34	36	26	.298	.381	.450	115	8	7	50	2			5	O	0.9
1951	Bro-N	31	80	8	20	4	0	1	5	10	12	.250	.333	.338	79	-2	-2	9	0	2	-1	1	O	-0.2
	Chi-N	75	231	28	65	12	1	3	20	35	30	.281	.385	.381	105	4	3	37	3	0	1	0	O	0.3
	Yr	106	311	36	85	16	1	4	25	45	42	.273	.372	.370	98	2	1	46	3	2	-0	1		0.1
1952	Chi-N	99	275	28	70	6	0	4	34	29	32	.255	.330	.320	80	-6	-6	32	2	0	1	1	O	-0.7
1953	Chi-N	18	40	1	6	1	0	0	1	4	7	.150	.227	.175	7	-5	-6	2	1	0	0	-1	O	-0.6
	Pit-N	41	62	7	11	0	0	1	4	8	14	.177	.282	.226	35	-6	-6	4	0	0	0	-0	O	-0.5
	Yr	59	102	8	17	1	0	1	5	12	21	.167	.261	.206	24	-11	-11	6	1	0	0	-1		-1.1
Total	9	739	1960	276	533	85	18	46	259	289	212	.272	.372	.404	107	33	27	316	43	2		-1	O	0.6

■ REMY HERMOSO   Hermoso, Angel Remigio b: 10/1/46, Carabobo, Venezuela BR/TR, 5'8", 155 lbs. Deb: 9/14/67

YEAR	TM/L	G	AB	R	H	2B	3B	HR	RBI	BB	SO	AVG	OBP	SLG	PRO+	BR	/A	RC	SB	CS	SBR	FR	POS	TPR
1967	Atl-N	11	26	3	8	0	0	0	0	2	4	.308	.357	.308	93	-0	-0	3	1	0	0	1	/S2	0.2
1969	Mon-N	28	74	6	12	0	0	0	3	5	10	.162	.225	.162	10	-9	-9	3	3	1	0	4	2/S	-0.2
1970	Mon-N	4	1	1	0	0	0	0	0	0	0	.000	.000	.000	-99	-0	-0	0	0	0	0	0	/23	0.0
1974	Cle-A	48	122	15	27	3	1	0	5	7	7	.221	.264	.262	52	-8	-7	9	2	2	-1	7	2	0.1
Total	4	91	223	25	47	3	1	0	8	14	21	.211	.261	.233	42	-17	-17	15	6	3	0	12	/2S3	0.1

■ CARLOS HERNANDEZ   Hernandez, Carlos Alberto b: 5/24/67, San Felix, Venez. BR/TR, 5'11", 185 lbs. Deb: 4/20/90

YEAR	TM/L	G	AB	R	H	2B	3B	HR	RBI	BB	SO	AVG	OBP	SLG	PRO+	BR	/A	RC	SB	CS	SBR	FR	POS	TPR
1990	LA-N	10	20	2	4	1	0	0	1	0	2	.200	.200	.250	24	-2	-2	1	0	0	0	1	C	0.0

■ ENZO HERNANDEZ   Hernandez, Enzo Octavio b: 2/12/49, Valle De Guanape, Venez. BR/TR, 5'8", 155 lbs. Deb: 4/17/71

YEAR	TM/L	G	AB	R	H	2B	3B	HR	RBI	BB	SO	AVG	OBP	SLG	PRO+	BR	/A	RC	SB	CS	SBR	FR	POS	TPR
1971	SD-N	143	549	58	122	9	3	0	12	54	34	.222	.295	.250	60	-31	-26	46	21	5	3	-11	*S	-1.5
1972	SD-N	114	329	33	64	11	2	1	15	22	25	.195	.245	.249	44	-26	-23	23	24	3	5	6	*S/O	0.1
1973	SD-N	70	247	26	55	2	1	0	9	17	14	.223	.273	.239	47	-19	-16	17	15	4	2	-1	S	-0.5
1974	SD-N	147	512	55	119	19	2	0	34	38	36	.232	.285	.277	60	-29	-26	45	37	10	5	-8	*S	-1.2
1975	SD-N	116	344	37	75	12	2	0	19	26	25	.218	.277	.265	54	-23	-20	28	20	4	8	4	*S	0.5
1976	SD-N	113	340	31	87	13	3	1	24	32	16	.256	.320	.321	89	-8	-7	36	12	7	-1	4	*S	0.9
1977	SD-N	7	3	1	0	0	0	0	0	0	0	.000	.000	.000	-99	-1	-1	0	0	0	0	2	/S	0.2
1978	LA-N	4	3	0	0	0	0	0	0	0	1	.000	.000	.000	-99	-1	-1	0	0	0	0	0	/S	0.0
Total	8	714	2327	241	522	66	13	2	113	189	151	.224	.284	.266	59	-136	-118	196	129	33	19	0	S/O	-1.5

■ JACKIE HERNANDEZ   Hernandez, Jacinto (Zulueta) b: 9/11/40, Central Tinguaro, Cuba BR/TR, 5'11", 165 lbs. Deb: 9/14/65

YEAR	TM/L	G	AB	R	H	2B	3B	HR	RBI	BB	SO	AVG	OBP	SLG	PRO+	BR	/A	RC	SB	CS	SBR	FR	POS	TPR
1965	Cal-A	6	6	2	2	1	0	0	1	0	1	.333	.333	.500	137	0	0	1	0	0	0	-0	/S3	0.0
1966	Cal-A	58	23	19	1	0	0	0	2	1	4	.043	.083	.043	-64	-5	-5	0	1	1	-0	16	3/2SO	1.3
1967	Min-A	29	28	1	4	0	0	0	3	0	6	.143	.143	.143	-14	-4	-4	1	0	0	0	6	S3	0.3
1968	Min-A	83	199	13	35	3	0	2	17	9	52	.176	.219	.221	32	-16	-17	10	5	2	0	9	S/1	-0.2
1969	KC-A	145	504	54	112	14	2	4	40	38	111	.222	.279	.282	57	-29	-29	42	17	7	1	-15	*S	-3.8
1970	KC-A	83	238	14	55	4	1	2	10	15	50	.231	.282	.282	56	-14	-14	18	1	3	-2	-5	S	-1.4
1971	*Pit-N	88	233	30	48	7	3	3	26	17	45	.206	.260	.300	59	-13	-13	18	0	2	-1	12	S/3	0.8
1972	Pit-N	72	176	12	33	7	1	1	14	9	43	.188	.227	.256	38	-15	-14	10	0	0	0	17	S/3	1.1
1973	Pit-N	54	73	8	18	1	2	0	8	4	12	.247	.286	.315	68	-3	-3	6	0	0	0	17	S	2.1
Total	9	618	1480	153	308	37	9	12	121	93	324	.208	.258	.270	49	-99	-99	106	25	15	-1	56	S/32O1	0.2

KEITH HERNANDEZ
Hernandez, Keith b: 10/20/53, San Francisco, Cal. BL/TL, 6', 180 lbs. Deb: 8/30/74

YEAR	TM/L	G	AB	R	H	2B	3B	HR	RBI	BB	SO	AVG	OBP	SLG	PRO+	BR	/A	RC	SB	CS	SBR	FR	POS	TPR
1974	StL-N	14	34	3	10	1	2	0	2	7	8	.294	.415	.441	141	2	2	7	0	0	0	-2	/1	0.0
1975	StL-N	64	188	20	47	8	2	3	20	17	26	.250	.312	.362	84	-4	-4	20	0	1	-1	3	1	-0.5
1976	StL-N	129	374	54	108	21	5	7	46	49	61	.289	.376	.428	126	14	14	61	4	2	0	16	*1	2.6
1977	StL-N	161	560	90	163	41	4	15	91	79	88	.291	.380	.459	126	20	22	95	7	7	-2	5	*1	1.6
1978	StL-N	159	542	90	138	32	4	11	64	82	68	.255	.355	.389	109	7	8	78	13	5	1	3	*1	0.7
1979	StL-N	161	610	**116**	210	**48**	11	11	105	80	78	**.344**	**.421**	.513	152	47	46	**135**	11	6	-0	19	*1	**5.8**
1980	StL-N	159	595	**111**	191	39	8	16	99	86	73	.321	**.410**	.494	147	43	41	122	14	8	-1	5	*1	3.9
1981	StL-N	103	376	65	115	27	4	8	48	61	45	.306	.405	.463	142	25	23	73	12	5	1	6	1/O	2.8
1982	*StL-N	160	579	79	173	33	6	7	94	100	67	.299	.404	.413	128	27	26	101	19	11	-1	7	*1/O	2.5
1983	StL-N	55	218	34	62	15	4	3	26	24	30	.284	.355	.431	117	5	5	34	1	1	-0	3	1	0.5
	NY-N	95	320	43	98	8	3	9	37	64	42	.306	.425	.434	140	20	21	64	8	4	0	11	1	2.7
	Yr	150	538	77	160	23	7	12	63	88	72	.297	.398	.433	131	25	26	98	9	5	-0	14		3.2
1984	NY-N	154	550	83	171	31	0	15	94	97	89	.311	.415	.449	145	35	37	108	2	3	-1	18	*1	5.0
1985	NY-N	158	593	87	183	34	4	10	91	77	59	.309	.390	.430	132	25	27	100	3	3	-1	16	*1	3.8
1986	*NY-N	149	551	94	171	34	1	13	83	**94**	69	.310	.414	.446	141	32	34	106	2	1	0	18	*1	4.8
1987	NY-N	154	587	87	170	28	2	18	89	81	104	.290	.379	.436	122	15	19	98	0	2	-1	18	*1	2.6
1988	*NY-N	95	348	43	96	16	0	11	55	31	57	.276	.337	.417	121	7	8	47	2	1	0	8	1	1.2
1989	NY-N	75	215	18	50	8	0	4	19	27	39	.233	.324	.326	90	-3	-2	23	0	3	-2	-1	1	-1.0
1990	Cle-A	43	130	7	26	2	0	1	8	14	17	.200	.283	.238	46	-9	-9	9	0	0	0	-2	1	-1.3
Total	17	2088	7370	1124	2182	426	60	162	1071	1070	1012	.296	.388	.436	129	310	318	1282	98	63	-8	149	*1/O	37.7

LEONARDO HERNANDEZ
Hernandez, Leonardo Jesus b: 11/6/59, Santa Lucia, Venz. BR/TR, 5'11", 170 lbs. Deb: 9/19/82

YEAR	TM/L	G	AB	R	H	2B	3B	HR	RBI	BB	SO	AVG	OBP	SLG	PRO+	BR	/A	RC	SB	CS	SBR	FR	POS	TPR
1982	Bal-A	2	2	0	0	0	0	0	0	0	2	.000	.000	.000	-99	-1	-1	0	0	0	0	0	/H	0.0
1983	Bal-A	64	203	21	50	6	1	6	26	12	19	.246	.288	.374	82	-6	-5	21	1	0	0	-11	3	-1.6
1985	Bal-A	12	21	0	1	0	0	0	0	0	4	.048	.048	.048	-76	-5	-5	-0	0	0	0	-0	/1OD	-0.4
1986	NY-A	7	22	2	5	2	0	1	4	1	8	.227	.261	.455	91	-0	-0	3	0	0	0	-1	/32	0.0
Total	4	85	248	23	56	8	1	7	30	13	33	.226	.264	.351	69	-12	-11	24	1	0	0	-12	/3D201	-2.0

PEDRO HERNANDEZ
Hernandez, Pedro Julio (b: Pedro Julio Montas (Hernandez)) b: 4/4/59, LaRomana, D.R. BR/TR, 6'1", 160 lbs. Deb: 9/08/79

YEAR	TM/L	G	AB	R	H	2B	3B	HR	RBI	BB	SO	AVG	OBP	SLG	PRO+	BR	/A	RC	SB	CS	SBR	FR	POS	TPR
1979	Tor-A	3	0	1	0	0	0	0	0	0	0	—	—	—		0	0	0	0	0	0	0	/R	0.0
1982	Tor-A	8	9	1	0	0	0	0	0	0	3	.000	.000	.000	-92	-2	-3	0	0	0	0	-0	/3OD	-0.2
Total	2	11	9	2	0	0	0	0	0	0	3	.000	.000	.000	-92	-2	-3	0	0	0	0	-0	/D3O	-0.2

TOBY HERNANDEZ
Hernandez, Rafael Tobias (Alvarado) b: 11/30/58, Calabozo, Venz. BR/TR, 6'1", 160 lbs. Deb: 6/22/84

YEAR	TM/L	G	AB	R	H	2B	3B	HR	RBI	BB	SO	AVG	OBP	SLG	PRO+	BR	/A	RC	SB	CS	SBR	FR	POS	TPR
1984	Tor-A	3	2	1	1	0	0	0	0	0	0	.500	.500	.500	171	0	0	1	0	0	0	-0	/C	0.0

RUDY HERNANDEZ
Hernandez, Rodolfo (Acosta) b: 10/18/51, Enpalme, Mexico BR/TR, 5'9", 150 lbs. Deb: 9/06/72

YEAR	TM/L	G	AB	R	H	2B	3B	HR	RBI	BB	SO	AVG	OBP	SLG	PRO+	BR	/A	RC	SB	CS	SBR	FR	POS	TPR
1972	Chi-A	8	21	0	4	0	0	0	1	0	3	.190	.190	.190	13	-2	-2	1	0	0	0	1	/S	0.0

CHICO HERNANDEZ
Hernandez, Salvador Jose (Ramos) b: 1/3/16, Havana, Cuba d: 1/3/86, Havana, Cuba BR/TR, 6', 195 lbs. Deb: 4/16/42

YEAR	TM/L	G	AB	R	H	2B	3B	HR	RBI	BB	SO	AVG	OBP	SLG	PRO+	BR	/A	RC	SB	CS	SBR	FR	POS	TPR
1942	Chi-N	47	118	6	27	5	0	0	7	11	13	.229	.295	.271	69	-5	-4	10	0			-2	C	-0.5
1943	Chi-N	43	126	10	34	4	0	0	9	9	9	.270	.324	.302	82	-3	-3	12	0			-1	C	-0.2
Total	2	90	244	16	61	9	0	0	16	20	22	.250	.309	.287	76	-8	-7	22	0			-3	/C	-0.7

LARRY HERNDON
Herndon, Larry Darnell b: 11/3/53, Sunflower, Miss. BR/TR, 6'3", 190 lbs. Deb: 9/04/74

YEAR	TM/L	G	AB	R	H	2B	3B	HR	RBI	BB	SO	AVG	OBP	SLG	PRO+	BR	/A	RC	SB	CS	SBR	FR	POS	TPR
1974	StL-N	12	1	3	1	0	0	0	0	0	0	1.000	1.000	1.000	465	0	0	1	0	0	0	1	/O	0.2
1976	SF-N	115	337	42	97	11	3	2	23	23	45	.288	.337	.356	94	-1	-3	40	12	10	-2	-11	*O	-2.1
1977	SF-N	49	109	13	26	4	3	1	5	5	20	.239	.278	.358	69	-5	-5	20	4	2	0	6	O	0.0
1978	SF-N	151	471	52	122	15	9	1	32	35	71	.259	.312	.335	84	-12	-10	48	13	8	-1	-3	*O	-1.9
1979	SF-N	132	354	35	91	14	5	7	36	29	70	.257	.315	.384	96	-5	-2	43	8	6	-1	-5	*O	-1.1
1980	SF-N	139	493	54	127	17	11	8	49	19	91	.258	.287	.385	88	-11	-10	50	8	8	-2	-1	*O	-1.8
1981	SF-N	96	364	48	105	15	8	5	41	20	55	.288	.327	.415	111	3	4	46	15	6	1	5	O	0.8
1982	Det-A	157	614	92	179	21	13	23	88	38	92	.292	.334	.480	120	15	15	90	12	9	-2	1	*O/D	0.9
1983	Det-A	153	603	88	182	28	9	20	92	46	95	.302	.354	.478	130	21	23	97	9	3	1	-3	*OD	1.9
1984	*Det-A	125	407	52	114	18	5	7	43	32	63	.280	.336	.400	103	1	2	55	6	2	1	-8	*O/D	-0.9
1985	Det-A	137	442	45	108	12	7	12	37	33	79	.244	.298	.385	86	-10	-9	50	2	1	0	-1	*O	-1.1
1986	Det-A	106	283	33	70	13	1	8	37	27	40	.247	.315	.385	90	-4	-4	36	2	1	0	-1	OD	-0.6
1987	*Det-A	89	225	32	73	13	2	9	47	23	35	.324	.387	.520	144	12	14	42	1	0	0	-0	OD	1.2
1988	Det-A	76	174	16	39	5	4	0	20	23	37	.224	.318	.322	83	-4	-3	17	0	1	-1	0	DO	-0.3
Total	14	1537	4877	605	1334	186	76	107	550	353	793	.274	.325	.409	103	1	12	624	92	57	-7	-20	*OD	-4.8

TOM HERNON
Hernon, Thomas H. b: 11/4/1866, E.Bridgewater, Mass d: 2/4/02, New Bedford, Mass. BR/TR, Deb: 9/13/1897

YEAR	TM/L	G	AB	R	H	2B	3B	HR	RBI	BB	SO	AVG	OBP	SLG	PRO+	BR	/A	RC	SB	CS	SBR	FR	POS	TPR
1897	Chi-N	4	16	2	1	0	0	0	2		0	.063	.063	.063	-64	-4	-4	0	1			0	/O	-0.3

ED HERR
Herr, Edward Joseph b: 5/18/1862, St.Louis, Mo. d: 7/18/43, St.Louis, Mo. BR/TR, 5'9.5", 179 lbs. Deb: 4/16/1887

YEAR	TM/L	G	AB	R	H	2B	3B	HR	RBI	BB	SO	AVG	OBP	SLG	PRO+	BR	/A	RC	SB	CS	SBR	FR	POS	TPR
1887	Cle-a	11	44	6	12	2	0	0			6	.273	.360	.318	95	-0	0	6	2			-3	3	-0.2
1888	*StL-a	43	172	21	46	7	1	3	43	11		.267	.323	.372	113	5	2	24	9			-9	SO/3	-0.4
1890	StL-a	12	41	5	9	2	1	0			5	.220	.347	.317	86	0	-1	5	2			-7	/2O3	-0.6
Total	3	66	257	32	67	11	2	3	43		22	.261	.333	.354	105	5	1	35	13			-18	/S3O2	-1.2

TOM HERR
Herr, Thomas Mitchell b: 4/4/56, Lancaster, Pa. BB/TR, 6', 175 lbs. Deb: 8/13/79

YEAR	TM/L	G	AB	R	H	2B	3B	HR	RBI	BB	SO	AVG	OBP	SLG	PRO+	BR	/A	RC	SB	CS	SBR	FR	POS	TPR
1979	StL-N	14	10	4	2	0	0	0	1	2	2	.200	.333	.200	49	-1	-1	1	1	0	0	6	/2	0.6
1980	StL-N	76	222	29	55	12	5	0	15	16	21	.248	.301	.347	78	-6	-7	22	9	2	2	2	2S	0.2
1981	StL-N	103	411	50	110	14	9	0	46	39	30	.268	.333	.345	90	-4	-5	49	23	7	3	4	*2	1.0
1982	*StL-N	135	493	83	131	19	4	0	36	57	56	.266	.344	.320	86	-7	-7	59	25	12	6	4	*2	0.2
1983	StL-N	89	313	43	101	14	4	2	31	43	27	.323	.406	.412	127	13	13	53	6	8	-3	-18	2	-0.4
1984	StL-N	145	558	67	154	23	2	4	49	49	56	.276	.337	.346	94	-5	-3	66	13	7	-0	-1	*2	0.0
1985	*StL-N	159	596	97	180	38	3	8	110	80	55	.302	.386	.416	126	22	23	107	31	3	8	-31	*2	0.0
1986	StL-N	152	559	48	141	30	4	2	61	73	75	.252	.344	.331	88	-8	-7	69	22	8	2	-22	*2	-2.6
1987	*StL-N	141	510	73	134	29	0	2	83	68	62	.263	.353	.331	81	-11	-12	65	19	4	3	-17	*2	-2.2
1988	StL-N	15	50	4	13	0	0	1	3	11	4	.260	.393	.320	106	1	1	8	3	0	1	-6	2	-0.3
	Min-A	86	304	42	80	16	0	1	21	40	47	.263	.349	.326	88	-3	-4	36	10	3	1	-8	2/SD	-0.5
1989	Phi-N	151	561	65	161	25	6	2	37	54	63	.287	.353	.364	105	5	5	73	10	7	2	2	*2	0.8
1990	Phi-N	119	447	39	118	21	3	4	50	36	47	.264	.322	.351	85	-9	-9	51	7	1	2	-3	*2	-0.9
	NY-N	27	100	9	25	5	0	1	10	14	11	.250	.342	.330	88	-2	-1	12	0	0	0	-5	2	-0.6
	Yr	146	547	48	143	26	3	5	60	50	58	.261	.326	.347	86	-11	-10	64	7	1	2	-8		-1.5
Total	12	1412	5134	653	1405	246	40	27	553	582	556	.274	.350	.353	96	-12	-14	670	179	62	17	-93	*2/SD	-4.7

JOSE HERRERA
Herrera, Jose Concepcion (Ontiveros) "Loco" b: 4/8/42, San Lorenzo, Venez. BR/TR, 5'8", 165 lbs. Deb: 6/03/67

YEAR	TM/L	G	AB	R	H	2B	3B	HR	RBI	BB	SO	AVG	OBP	SLG	PRO+	BR	/A	RC	SB	CS	SBR	FR	POS	TPR
1967	Hou-N	5	4	0	1	0	0	0	1	0	1	.250	.250	.250	45	-0	-0	0	0	0	0	0	H	0.0
1968	Hou-N	27	100	9	24	5	0	0		4	12	.240	.269	.290	69	-4	-4	7	0	2	-1	-3	O/2	-0.9
1969	Mon-N	47	126	7	36	5	0	2	12	3	14	.286	.302	.373	88	-2	-2	13	1	2	-1	-1	O/23	-0.5
1970	Mon-N	1	1	0	0	0	0	0	0	0	1	.000	.000	.000	-99	-0	-0	0	0	0	0	0	H	0.0
Total	4	80	231	16	61	10	0	2	20	7	28	.264	.286	.333	79	-7	-7	21	1	4	-2	-4	/O23	-1.4

■ PANCHO HERRERA
Herrera, Juan Francisco (Willavicencio) b: 6/16/34, Santiago, Cuba   BR/TR, 6'3", 220 lbs.   Deb: 4/15/58

YEAR	TM/L	G	AB	R	H	2B	3B	HR	RBI	BB	SO	AVG	OBP	SLG	PRO+	BR	/A	RC	SB	CS	SBR	FR	POS	TPR
1958	Phi-N	29	63	5	17	3		1	6	7	15	.270	.352	.365	92	-1	-1	8	1	2	-1	2	31	0.0
1960	Phi-N	145	512	61	144	26	6	17	71	51	136	.281	.352	.455	119	13	13	78	2	3	-1	10	*12	1.8
1961	Phi-N	126	400	56	103	17	2	13	51	55	120	.257	.353	.408	102	2	2	58	5	1	1	6	*1	0.2
Total	3	300	975	122	264	46	8	31	128	113	271	.271	.352	.430	110	14	15	145	8	6	-1	18	1/23	2.0

■ MIKE HERRERA
Herrera, Ramon b: 12/19/1897, Havana, Cuba   d: 2/3/78, Havana, Cuba   BR/TR, 5'6", 147 lbs.   Deb: 9/22/25

YEAR	TM/L	G	AB	R	H	2B	3B	HR	RBI	BB	SO	AVG	OBP	SLG	PRO+	BR	/A	RC	SB	CS	SBR	FR	POS	TPR
1925	Bos-A	10	39	2	15	0	0	0	8	2	2	.385	.415	.385	104	0	0	6	1	0	0	3	2	0.4
1926	Bos-A	74	237	20	61	14	1	0	19	15	13	.257	.304	.325	66	-13	-12	23	0	5	-3	5	23/S	-0.5
Total	2	84	276	22	76	14	1	0	27	17	15	.275	.320	.333	72	-12	-11	29	1	5	-3	8	/23S	-0.1

■ LEFTY HERRING
Herring, Silas Clarke b: 3/4/1880, Philadelphia, Pa.   d: 2/11/65, Massapequa, N.Y.   BL/TL, 5'11", 160 lbs.   Deb: 5/16/1899

YEAR	TM/L	G	AB	R	H	2B	3B	HR	RBI	BB	SO	AVG	OBP	SLG	PRO+	BR	/A	RC	SB	CS	SBR	FR	POS	TPR
1899	Was-N	2	1	1	1	0	0	0	0		1	1.000	1.000	1.000	462	1	1	1	0			0	/P	0.0
1904	Was-A	15	46	3	8	1	0	0	2		7	.174	.283	.196	56	-2	-2	3	0			1	1/O	-0.1
Total	2	17	47	4	9	1	0	0	2		8	.191	.309	.213	69	-1	-1	4	0			1	/1OP	-0.1

■ ED HERRMANN
Herrmann, Edward Martin b: 8/27/46, San Diego, Cal.   BL/TR, 6'1", 195 lbs.   Deb: 9/01/67

YEAR	TM/L	G	AB	R	H	2B	3B	HR	RBI	BB	SO	AVG	OBP	SLG	PRO+	BR	/A	RC	SB	CS	SBR	FR	POS	TPR
1967	Chi-A	2	3	1	2	1	0		1	1	0	.667	.750	1.000	429	1	1	2	0	0	0	1	/C	0.3
1969	Chi-A	102	290	31	67	8	0	8	31	30	35	.231	.320	.341	81	-6	-7	32	0	2	-1	-1	C	-0.3
1970	Chi-A	96	297	42	84	9	0	19	52	31	41	.283	.356	.505	130	13	12	54	0	1	-1	6	C	1.9
1971	Chi-A	101	294	32	63	6	0	11	35	44	48	.214	.321	.347	86	-4	-5	33	2	0	1	10	C	1.1
1972	Chi-A	116	354	23	88	9	0	10	40	43	37	.249	.337	.359	105	4	3	41	0	0	0	2	*C	0.7
1973	Chi-A	119	379	42	85	17	1	10	39	31	55	.224	.295	.354	79	-10	-11	37	2	4	-2	8	*C/D	-0.2
1974	Chi-A	107	367	32	95	13	1	10	39	16	49	.259	.290	.381	90	-5	-6	37	1	0	0	4	*C	0.2
1975	NY-A	80	200	16	51	9	2	6	30	16	23	.255	.310	.410	105	-0	1	24	0	0	0	7	DC	0.9
1976	Cal-A	29	46	5	8	3	0	2	8	7	8	.174	.283	.370	96	-1	-0	5	0	0	0	-5	C	-0.4
	Hou-N	79	265	14	54	8	0	3	25	22	40	.204	.275	.268	60	-16	-13	20	0	0	0	1	C	-0.8
1977	Hou-N	56	158	7	46	7	0	1	17	15	18	.291	.356	.354	100	-1	0	20	1	1	-0	10	C	0.9
1978	Hou-N	16	36	1	4	1	0	0	0	3	3	.111	.179	.139	-11	-5	-5	1	0	0	0	-0	C	-0.5
	Mon-N	19	40	1	7	1	0	0	3	1	4	.175	.195	.200	11	-5	-5	1	0	0	0	-1	C	-0.5
	Yr	35	76	2	11	2	0	0	3	4	7	.145	.188	.171	1	-10	-10	2	0	0	0	-2		-1.0
Total	11	922	2729	247	654	92	4	80	320	260	361	.240	.312	.364	91	-33	-35	308	6	8	-3	41	C/D	3.3

■ RICK HERRSCHER
Herrscher, Richard Franklin b: 11/3/36, St.Louis, Mo.   BR/TR, 6'2.5", 187 lbs.   Deb: 8/01/62

YEAR	TM/L	G	AB	R	H	2B	3B	HR	RBI	BB	SO	AVG	OBP	SLG	PRO+	BR	/A	RC	SB	CS	SBR	FR	POS	TPR
1962	NY-N	35	50	5	11	3	0	1	6	5	11	.220	.291	.340	68	-2	-2	5	0	0	0	3	1/3OS	0.1

■ JOHN HERRNSTEIN
Herrnstein, John Ellett b: 5/31/38, Hampton, Va.   BL/TL, 6'3", 215 lbs.   Deb: 9/15/62

YEAR	TM/L	G	AB	R	H	2B	3B	HR	RBI	BB	SO	AVG	OBP	SLG	PRO+	BR	/A	RC	SB	CS	SBR	FR	POS	TPR
1962	Phi-N	6	5	0	1	0	0	0	1	1	3	.200	.333	.200	48	-0	-0	0	0	0	0	0	/O	0.0
1963	Phi-N	15	12	1	2	0	0	1	1	1	5	.167	.231	.417	83	-0	-0	1	0	0	0	0	/O1	0.0
1964	Phi-N	125	303	38	71	12	4	6	25	22	67	.234	.291	.360	83	-7	-7	31	1	2	-1	-8	O1	-2.0
1965	Phi-N	63	85	8	17	2	0	1	5	2	18	.200	.227	.259	37	-7	-7	4	0	0	0	1	1O	-0.7
1966	Phi-N	4	10	0	1	0	0	0	1	0	7	.100	.100	.100	-44	-2	-2	0	0	0	0	-0	/O	-0.1
	Chi-N	9	17	3	3	0	0	0	0	3	6	.176	.300	.176	36	-1	-1	1	0	0	0	-1	/1O	-0.2
	Atl-N	17	18	2	4	0	0	0	1	0	7	.222	.222	.222	24	-2	-2	1	0	0	0	0	/O	-0.1
	Yr	30	45	5	8	0	0	0	2	3	22	.178	.229	.178	15	-5	-5	2	0	0	0	-1		-0.4
Total	5	239	450	52	99	14	4	8	34	29	115	.220	.272	.322	67	-20	-20	39	1	2	-1	-8	/O1	-3.1

■ EARL HERSH
Hersh, Earl Walter b: 5/21/32, Ebbvale, Md.   BL/TL, 6', 205 lbs.   Deb: 9/04/56

YEAR	TM/L	G	AB	R	H	2B	3B	HR	RBI	BB	SO	AVG	OBP	SLG	PRO+	BR	/A	RC	SB	CS	SBR	FR	POS	TPR
1956	Mil-N	7	13	0	3	3	0	0	0	0	5	.231	.231	.462	85	-0	-0	1	0	0	0	-1	/O	-0.1

■ MIKE HERSHBERGER
Hershberger, Norman Michael b: 10/9/39, Massillon, Ohio   BR/TR, 5'10", 175 lbs.   Deb: 9/05/61

YEAR	TM/L	G	AB	R	H	2B	3B	HR	RBI	BB	SO	AVG	OBP	SLG	PRO+	BR	/A	RC	SB	CS	SBR	FR	POS	TPR
1961	Chi-A	15	55	9	17	3	0	0	5	2	2	.309	.333	.364	88	-1	-1	6	1	1	-0	1	O	0.0
1962	Chi-A	148	427	54	112	14	2	4	46	37	36	.262	.325	.333	78	-13	-13	43	10	6	-1	-4	*O	-2.1
1963	Chi-A	135	476	64	133	26	2	3	45	39	39	.279	.339	.361	98	-2	-1	60	9	3	1	5	*O	0.2
1964	Chi-A	141	452	55	104	15	3	2	31	48	47	.230	.310	.290	70	-18	-17	42	8	6	-1	2	*O	-2.2
1965	KC-A	150	494	43	114	15	5	5	48	37	42	.231	.291	.312	72	-18	-18	42	7	3	0	5	*O	-1.8
1966	KC-A	146	538	55	136	27	7	2	57	47	37	.253	.316	.340	92	-7	-5	58	13	5	1	9	*O	-0.1
1967	KC-A	142	480	55	122	25	1	1	49	38	40	.254	.318	.317	91	-6	-5	49	10	3	1	6	*O	-0.1
1968	Oak-A	99	246	23	67	9	2	5	32	21	22	.272	.332	.386	123	5	6	32	8	3	1	-5	O	-0.1
1969	Oak-A	51	129	11	26	2	0	1	10	10	15	.202	.259	.240	42	-10	-10	8	1	2	-1	-4	O	-1.5
1970	Mil-A	49	98	7	23	5	0	1	6	10	8	.235	.306	.316	71	-4	-4	9	1	2	-1	-3	O	-0.8
1971	Chi-A	74	177	22	46	9	0	2	15	30	23	.260	.379	.345	103	3	2	25	6	2	1	-2	O	0.0
Total	11	1150	3572	398	900	150	22	26	344	319	311	.252	.319	.328	85	-72	-64	374	74	36	1	12	*O	-8.4

■ WILLARD HERSHBERGER
Hershberger, Willard McKee "Bill" b: 5/28/10, Lemon Cove, Cal.   d: 8/3/40, Boston, Mass.   BR/TR, 5'10.5", 167 lbs.   Deb: 4/19/38

YEAR	TM/L	G	AB	R	H	2B	3B	HR	RBI	BB	SO	AVG	OBP	SLG	PRO+	BR	/A	RC	SB	CS	SBR	FR	POS	TPR
1938	Cin-N	49	105	12	29	3	1	0	12	5	6	.276	.315	.324	78	-3	-3	11	1			-1	C/2	-0.1
1939	*Cin-N	63	174	23	60	9	2	0	32	9	4	.345	.384	.420	115	4	4	27	1			-2	C	0.4
1940	Cin-N	48	123	6	38	4	2	0	26	6	6	.309	.351	.374	99	0	-0	15	0			-2	C	0.0
Total	3	160	402	41	127	16	5	0	70	20	16	.316	.356	.381	101	1	1	53	2			-4	C/2	0.3

■ NEAL HERTWECK
Hertweck, Neal Charles b: 11/22/31, St.Louis, Mo.   BL/TL, 6'1.5", 175 lbs.   Deb: 9/27/52

YEAR	TM/L	G	AB	R	H	2B	3B	HR	RBI	BB	SO	AVG	OBP	SLG	PRO+	BR	/A	RC	SB	CS	SBR	FR	POS	TPR
1952	StL-N	2	6	0	0	0	0	0	0		1	1	.000	.143	.000	-57	-1	-1	0	0	0	0	0	/1	-0.1

■ STEVE HERTZ
Hertz, Stephen Allan b: 2/26/45, Fairfield, Ohio   BR/TR, 6'1", 195 lbs.   Deb: 4/21/64

YEAR	TM/L	G	AB	R	H	2B	3B	HR	RBI	BB	SO	AVG	OBP	SLG	PRO+	BR	/A	RC	SB	CS	SBR	FR	POS	TPR
1964	Hou-N	5	4	2	0	0	0	0	0	0	3	.000	.000	.000	-99	-1	-1	0	0	0	0	0	/3	0.0

■ BUCK HERZOG
Herzog, Charles Lincoln b: 7/9/1885, Baltimore, Md.   d: 9/4/53, Baltimore, Md.   BR/TR, 5'11", 160 lbs.   Deb: 4/17/08   M

YEAR	TM/L	G	AB	R	H	2B	3B	HR	RBI	BB	SO	AVG	OBP	SLG	PRO+	BR	/A	RC	SB	CS	SBR	FR	POS	TPR
1908	NY-N	64	160	38	48	6	2	0	11	36		.300	.429	.363	149	13	12	33	16			1	2S/3O	1.4
1909	NY-N	42	130	16	24	2	0	0	8	13		.185	.264	.200	43	-8	-8	7	2			-2	O/23S	-1.2
1910	Bos-N	106	380	51	95	20	3	3	32	30	34	.250	.329	.342	92	-2	-4	48	13			4	*3	0.0
1911	Bos-N	79	294	53	91	19	5	5	41	33	21	.310	.398	.459	129	16	12	65	26			8	S/3	2.3
	*NY-N	69	247	37	66	14	4	1	26	14	19	.267	.325	.368	91	-3	-4	36	22			10	3/2S	0.8
	Yr	148	541	90	157	33	9	6	67	47	40	.290	.365	.418	112	13	9	100	48			18	3/2S	3.1
1912	*NY-N	140	482	72	127	20	9	2	47	57	34	.263	.350	.355	90	-4	-6	73	37			19	*3	1.4
1913	*NY-N	96	290	46	83	15	3	3	31	22	12	.286	.349	.390	110	4	4	45	23			3	3/2	0.8
1914	Cin-N	138	498	54	140	14	8	1	40	42	27	.281	.348	.347	104	5	3	72	46			31	*S/1M	4.1
1915	Cin-N	155	579	61	153	14	10	1	42	34	21	.264	.314	.328	93	-4	-5	66	35	16	1	31	*S/1M	3.3
1916	Cin-N	79	281	30	75	14	2	1	24	21	12	.267	.329	.342	109	2	3	33	15	12	-3	-2	S3/OM	0.5
	NY-N	77	280	40	73	10	4	0	25	22	24	.261	.326	.325	106	2	2	31	19	16	-4	14	23/S	2.0
	Yr	156	561	70	148	24	6	1	49	43	36	.264	.327	.333	107	3	5	64	34	28	-7	12		2.5
1917	*NY-N	114	417	69	98	10	8	2	31	31	36	.235	.308	.312	93	-4	-3	43	12			-8	*2	-0.4
1918	Bos-N	118	473	57	108	12	6	0	26	29	28	.228	.280	.279	74	-16	-14	39	10			4	21/S	-0.6
1919	Bos-N	73	275	27	77	8	5	1	25	13	11	.280	.327	.356	110	2	3	36	16			-14	2/1	-0.9
	Chi-N	52	193	15	53	4	4	0	17	10	7	.275	.336	.337	102	1	1	25	12			-11	2	-0.8
	Yr	125	468	42	130	12	9	1	42	23	18	.278	.331	.348	106	3	4	61	28			-24		-1.7

YEAR	TM/L	G	AB	R	H	2B	3B	HR	RBI	BB	SO	AVG	OBP	SLG	PRO+	BR	/A	RC	SB	CS	SBR	FR	POS	TPR
1920	Chi-N	91	305	39	59	9	2	0	19	20	21	.193	.261	.236	43	-22	-22	20	8	9	-3	-6	23/1	-3.1
Total	13	1493	5284	705	1370	191	75	20	445	427	307	.259	.328	.335	95	-20	-27	672	312	53		79	23S/01	9.2

■ WHITEY HERZOG
Herzog, Dorrel Norman Elvert   b: 11/9/31, New Athens, Ill.   BL/TL, 5'11", 182 lbs.   Deb: 4/17/56   MC

YEAR	TM/L	G	AB	R	H	2B	3B	HR	RBI	BB	SO	AVG	OBP	SLG	PRO+	BR	/A	RC	SB	CS	SBR	FR	POS	TPR
1956	Was-A	117	421	49	103	13	7	4	35	35	74	.245	.303	.337	69	-20	-20	44	8	5	-1	7	*O/1	-1.7
1957	Was-A	36	78	7	13	3	0	0	4	13	12	.167	.301	.205	41	-6	-6	6	1	2	-1	0	O	-0.7
1958	Was-A	8	5	0	0	0	0	0	0	1	5	.000	.167	.000	-51	-1	-1	0	0	0	0	0	O	0.0
	KC-A	88	96	11	23	1	2	0	9	16	21	.240	.348	.292	77	-2	-2	10	0	3	-2	1	O1	-0.6
	Yr	96	101	11	23	1	2	0	9	17	26	.228	.339	.277	71	-3	-3	10	0	3	-2	1		-0.6
1959	KC-A	38	123	25	36	7	1	1	9	34	23	.293	.446	.390	129	8	7	25	1	0		0	O/1	0.6
1960	KC-A	83	252	43	67	10	2	8	38	40	32	.266	.366	.417	111	5	5	39	0	1	-1	-2	O/1	0.0
1961	Bal-A	113	323	39	94	11	6	5	35	50	41	.291	.388	.409	115	8	9	53	1	4	-2	-12	O	-0.8
1962	Bal-A	99	263	34	70	13	1	7	35	41	36	.266	.371	.403	114	4	6	41	2	3	-1	-1	O	0.1
1963	Det-A	52	53	5	8	2	1	0	7	11	17	.151	.308	.226	51	-3	-3	5	0	0		-1	/1O	-0.4
Total	8	634	1614	213	414	60	20	25	172	241	261	.257	.356	.365	95	-8	-6	222	13	18	-7	-7	O/1	-3.5

■ OTTO HESS
Hess, Otto C.   b: 10/10/1878, Berne, Switzerland   d: 2/25/26, Tucson, Ariz.   BL/TL, 6'1", 170 lbs.   Deb: 8/03/02

YEAR	TM/L	G	AB	R	H	2B	3B	HR	RBI	BB	SO	AVG	OBP	SLG	PRO+	BR	/A	RC	SB	CS	SBR	FR	POS	TPR
1902	Cle-A	7	14	2	1	0	0	0	1	2		.071	.188	.071	-26	-2	-2	0	0			1	/P	0.0
1904	Cle-A	34	100	4	12	2	1	0	5	3		.120	.146	.160	-2	-11	-11	2	0			-0	PO	0.0
1905	Cle-A	54	173	15	44	8	1	2	13	7		.254	.283	.347	100	-0	-0	18	2			2	OP	0.5
1906	Cle-A	53	154	13	31	5	2	0	11	2		.201	.212	.260	49	-9	-9	9	1			-4	P/O	0.0
1907	Cle-A	19	30	4	4	0	0	0	0	4		.133	.235	.133	19	-2	-3	1	1			-1	P/O	0.0
1908	Cle-A	9	14	0	0	0	0	0	0	1		.000	.067	.000	-77	-3	-3	0	0			-1	/PO	-0.2
1912	Bos-N	33	94	10	23	4	4	0	10	0	26	.245	.245	.372	66	-5	-5	9	0			-3	P	0.0
1913	Bos-N	35	83	9	26	0	1	2	11	7	15	.313	.367	.410	119	2	2	12	0			1	P	0.0
1914	Bos-N	31	47	5	11	1	0	1	6	1	11	.234	.250	.319	69	-2	-2	4	0			2	P/1	0.2
1915	Bos-N	5	5	1	2	1	0	0	1	0	2	.400	.400	.600	210	1	1	1	0			0	/P1	0.0
Total	10	280	714	63	154	21	9	5	58	27	54	.216	.244	.291	63	-32	-32	57	4			-3	P/O1	0.5

■ TOM HESS
Hess, Thomas (b: Thomas Heslin)   b: 8/15/1875, Brooklyn, N.Y.   d: 12/15/45, Albany, N.Y.   Deb: 6/06/1892

YEAR	TM/L	G	AB	R	H	2B	3B	HR	RBI	BB	SO	AVG	OBP	SLG	PRO+	BR	/A	RC	SB	CS	SBR	FR	POS	TPR
1892	Bal-N	1	2	0	0	0	0	0	0	0	0	.000	.000	.000	-97	-0	-0	0	0			0	/C	0.0

■ GUS HETLING
Hetling, August Julius   b: 11/21/1885, St.Louis, Mo.   d: 10/13/62, Wichita, Kan.   BR/TR, 5'10", 165 lbs.   Deb: 10/06/06

YEAR	TM/L	G	AB	R	H	2B	3B	HR	RBI	BB	SO	AVG	OBP	SLG	PRO+	BR	/A	RC	SB	CS	SBR	FR	POS	TPR
1906	Det-A	2	7	0	1	0	0	0	0	0		.143	.143	.143	-9	-1	-1	0				-0	/3	0.0

■ GEORGE HEUBEL
Heubel, George A.   b: 1849, Paterson, N.J.   d: 1/22/1896, Philadelphia, Pa.   5'11.5", 178 lbs.   Deb: 5/20/1871

YEAR	TM/L	G	AB	R	H	2B	3B	HR	RBI	BB	SO	AVG	OBP	SLG	PRO+	BR	/A	RC	SB	CS	SBR	FR	POS	TPR
1871	Ath-n	17	75	18	23	4	2	0	13	2	0	.307	.325	.413	111	1	1	11	1				O/1	0.1
1872	Oly-n	5	23	2	3	1	0	0		0		.130	.130	.174	-8	-3	-3	1					/O	-0.1
1876	NY-N	1	4	0	0	0	0	0	0	0	0	.000	.000	.000	-99	-1	-0	0				-0	/1	0.0
Total	2 n	22	98	20	26	5	2	0	13	2		.265	.280	.357	86	-2	-1	11					/O1	0.0

■ JOHNNY HEVING
Heving, John Aloysius   b: 4/29/1896, Covington, Ky.   d: 12/24/68, Salisbury, N.C.   BR/TR, 6', 175 lbs.   Deb: 9/24/20

YEAR	TM/L	G	AB	R	H	2B	3B	HR	RBI	BB	SO	AVG	OBP	SLG	PRO+	BR	/A	RC	SB	CS	SBR	FR	POS	TPR
1920	StL-A	1	1	0	0	0	0	0	0	0	0	.000	.000	.000	-97	-0	-0	0	0	0	0	0	H	0.0
1924	Bos-A	45	109	15	31	5	1	0	11	10	7	.284	.345	.349	79	-3	-3	14	0	0	0	3	C	0.2
1925	Bos-A	45	119	14	20	7	0	0	6	12	7	.168	.244	.227	20	-15	-15	7	0	1	-1	2	C	-1.0
1928	Bos-A	82	158	11	41	7	2	0	11	11	10	.259	.308	.329	69	-8	-7	16	1	1	-0	-4	C	-0.6
1929	Bos-A	76	188	26	60	4	3	0	23	8	7	.319	.354	.372	89	-3	-3	24	1	2	-1	5	C	0.6
1930	Bos-A	75	220	15	61	5	3	0	17	11	14	.277	.312	.327	65	-12	-11	23	2	0	1	-4	C	-0.7
1931	*Phi-A	42	113	8	27	3	2	1	12	6	8	.239	.277	.327	55	-7	-8	10	0	0	0	3	C	-0.1
1932	Phi-A	33	77	14	21	6	1	0	10	7	6	.273	.333	.377	81	-2	-2	10	0	0	0	-1	C	-0.1
Total	8	399	985	103	261	37	12	1	90	65	59	.265	.312	.330	66	-51	-50	104	4	4	-1	5	C	-1.6

■ MIKE HEYDON
Heydon, Michael Edward "Ed"   b: 7/15/1874, Missouri   d: 10/13/13, Indianapolis, Ind.   BL/TR, 6',   Deb: 10/12/1898

YEAR	TM/L	G	AB	R	H	2B	3B	HR	RBI	BB	SO	AVG	OBP	SLG	PRO+	BR	/A	RC	SB	CS	SBR	FR	POS	TPR
1898	Bal-N	3	9	2	1	0	0	0	1	0		.111	.333	.111	31	-1	-1	0				-1	/C	0.0
1899	Was-N	3	3	0	0	0	0	0	0	0	2	.000	.400	.000	17	-0	-0	0	0			0	/C	0.0
1901	StL-N	16	43	2	9	1	1	0	6	5		.209	.292	.349	92	-1	-0	5	2			-2	C/O	0.0
1904	Chi-A	4	10	0	1	1	0	0	1	1		.100	.182	.200	23	-1	-1	0				2	/C	0.1
1905	Was-A	77	245	20	47	7	4	1	26	21		.192	.256	.265	70	-9	-8	19	5			11	C	1.2
1906	Was-A	49	145	14	23	7	1	0	10	14		.159	.233	.221	46	-9	-8	8	2			-1	C	-0.5
1907	Was-A	62	164	14	30	3	0	0	9	25		.183	.291	.201	64	-6	-5	11	3			-7	C	-0.7
Total	7	214	619	52	111	19	6	2	53	70		.179	.264	.239	63	-26	-23	44	12			2	C/O	0.1

■ JACK HIATT
Hiatt, Jack E   b: 7/27/42, Bakersfield, Cal.   BR/TR, 6'2", 190 lbs.   Deb: 9/07/64   C

YEAR	TM/L	G	AB	R	H	2B	3B	HR	RBI	BB	SO	AVG	OBP	SLG	PRO+	BR	/A	RC	SB	CS	SBR	FR	POS	TPR
1964	LA-A	9	16	2	6	0	0	0	2	2	3	.375	.444	.375	145	1	1	3	0	0	0	-1	/C1	0.0
1965	SF-N	40	67	5	19	4	0	1	7	12	14	.284	.392	.388	118	2	2	10	0	0	0	-1	C/1	0.1
1966	SF-N	18	23	2	7	2	0	0	1	4	5	.304	.407	.391	120	1	1	4	0	0	0	1	/1	0.2
1967	SF-N	73	153	24	42	6	0	6	26	27	37	.275	.387	.431	136	8	8	27	0	0	0	-2	1/CO	0.5
1968	SF-N	90	224	14	52	10	2	4	34	41	61	.232	.353	.348	111	5	5	29	0	0	0	-1	C1	0.6
1969	SF-N	69	194	19	38	4	0	3	34	48	58	.196	.355	.325	93	-0	0	25	0	0	0	-0	C/1	0.3
1970	Mon-N	17	43	4	14	2	0	0	7	14	14	.326	.491	.372	135	3	3	9	0	0	0	-3	C/1	0.0
	Chi-N	66	178	19	43	12	1	2	22	31	48	.242	.354	.354	81	-2	-5	23	0	0	0	5	C/1	0.3
	Yr	83	221	23	57	14	1	2	29	45	62	.258	.383	.357	91	2	-1	33	0	0	0	2		0.3
1971	Hou-N	69	174	16	48	8	1	1	16	35	39	.276	.403	.351	118	6	6	28	0	1	-1	-1	C/1	0.6
1972	Hou-N	10	25	2	5	3	0	0	0	5	5	.200	.333	.320	88	-0	-0	3	0	0	0	-3	C	-0.2
	Cal-A	22	45	4	13	0	1	1	5	5	11	.289	.360	.400	133	1	2	7	0	0	0	-8	C/1	-0.7
Total	9	483	1142	110	287	51	5	22	154	224	295	.251	.376	.363	109	25	23	168	0	1	-1	-15	C/1O	1.7

■ JIM HIBBS
Hibbs, James Kerr   b: 9/10/44, Klamath Falls, Ore.   BR/TR, 6', 190 lbs.   Deb: 4/12/67

YEAR	TM/L	G	AB	R	H	2B	3B	HR	RBI	BB	SO	AVG	OBP	SLG	PRO+	BR	/A	RC	SB	CS	SBR	FR	POS	TPR
1967	Cal-A	3	3	0	0	0	0	0	0	0	2	.000	.000	.000	-99	-1	-1	0	0	0	0	0	H	0.0

■ EDDIE HICKEY
Hickey, Edward A.   b: 8/18/1872, Cleveland, Ohio   d: 3/25/41, Tacoma, Wash.   Deb: 9/03/01

YEAR	TM/L	G	AB	R	H	2B	3B	HR	RBI	BB	SO	AVG	OBP	SLG	PRO+	BR	/A	RC	SB	CS	SBR	FR	POS	TPR
1901	Chi-N	10	37	4	6	0	0	0	3	2		.162	.225	.162	15	-4	-4	2	1			-1	3	-0.4

■ MIKE HICKEY
Hickey, Michael Francis   b: 12/25/1871, Chicopee, Mass.   d: 6/11/18, Springfield, Mass   BR/TR, 5'10.5", 150 lbs.   Deb: 9/14/1899

YEAR	TM/L	G	AB	R	H	2B	3B	HR	RBI	BB	SO	AVG	OBP	SLG	PRO+	BR	/A	RC	SB	CS	SBR	FR	POS	TPR
1899	Bos-N	1	3	0	1	0	0	0	0	0		.333	.333	.333	78	-0	-0	0				1	/2	0.1

■ CHARLIE HICKMAN
Hickman, Charles Taylor "Cheerful Charlie" or "Piano Legs"   b: 3/4/1876, Taylortown, Dunkard Township, Pa.   d: 4/19/34, Morgantown, W.Va.   BR/TR, 5'11.5", 215 lbs.   Deb: 9/08/1897

YEAR	TM/L	G	AB	R	H	2B	3B	HR	RBI	BB	SO	AVG	OBP	SLG	PRO+	BR	/A	RC	SB	CS	SBR	FR	POS	TPR
1897	*Bos-N	2	3	1	2	0	0	1	2	0		.667	.667	1.667	479	2	2	3	0			0	/P	0.0
1898	Bos-N	19	58	4	15	2	0	0	7	1		.259	.283	.293	64	-2	-3	5	0			-1	/O1P	-0.2
1899	Bos-N	19	63	15	25	2	7	0	15	2		.397	.433	.651	181	8	7	19	1			-2	P/O1	0.0
1900	NY-N	127	473	65	148	19	17	9	91	17		.313	.351	.482	138	18	21	86	10			-5	*3/O	1.5
1901	NY-N	112	406	44	113	20	6	4	62	15		.278	.311	.387	108	1	3	65	6			-6	OS3/P21	-0.3
1902	Bos-A	28	108	13	32	5	2	3	19	6		.296	.339	.463	119	3	2	18	1			1	O	0.1
	Cle-A	102	426	61	161	31	11	8	94	12		.378	.399	.559	172	35	37	101	8			-7	1/2P	3.0
	Yr	130	534	74	193	36	13	11	110	15		.361	.387	.539	161	38	39	118	9			-6		3.1

YEAR	TM/L	G	AB	R	H	2B	3B	HR	RBI	BB	SO	AVG	OBP	SLG	PRO+	BR	/A	RC	SB	CS	SBR	FR	POS	TPR
1903	Cle-A	131	522	64	154	31	11	12	97	17		.295	.317	.466	137	19	21	84	14			-7	*1/2	1.5
1904	Cle-A	86	337	34	97	22	10	4	45	13		.288	.314	.448	143	14	15	52	9			-0	21/O	1.7
	Det-A	42	144	18	35	6	6	2	22	11		.243	.297	.410	128	4	4	19	3			-2	1	0.3
	Yr	128	481	52	132	28	16	6	67	24		.274	.309	.437	139	18	19	71	12			-3		2.0
1905	Det-A	59	213	21	47	12	3	2	20	12		.221	.262	.333	90	-3	-3	21	3			3	O1	-0.2
	Was-A	88	360	48	112	25	9	2	46	9		.311	.328	.447	153	17	18	56	3			7	2/1	2.7
	Yr	147	573	69	159	37	12	4	66	21		.277	.303	.405	129	14	15	75	6			9		2.5
1906	Was-A	120	451	53	128	25	5	9	57	14		.284	.305	.421	135	12	15	63	9			-1	O1/32	1.0
1907	Was-A	60	198	20	55	9	4	1	23	14		.278	.325	.379	137	5	7	26	4			-3	1O/2P	0.3
	Chi-A	21	23	1	6	2	0	0	1	4		.261	.370	.348	136	1	1	3	0			-1	/O	0.0
	Yr	81	221	21	61	11	4	1	24	18		.276	.331	.376	136	6	8	30	4			-4		0.3
1908	Cle-A	65	197	16	46	6	1	2	16	9		.234	.267	.305	87	-3	-3	16	2			-0	O1/2	-0.5
Total	12	1081	3982	478	1176	217	92	59	614	153		.295	.325	.440	134	130	143	624	72			-26	1023/PS	10.9

■ JIM HICKMAN   Hickman, David James b: 5/19/1894, Johnson City, Tenn d: 12/30/58, Brooklyn, N.Y. BR/TR, 5'7.5", 170 lbs. Deb: 9/17/15

YEAR	TM/L	G	AB	R	H	2B	3B	HR	RBI	BB	SO	AVG	OBP	SLG	PRO+	BR	/A	RC	SB	CS	SBR	FR	POS	TPR
1915	Bal-F	20	81	7	17	4	1	1	7	4	14	.210	.256	.321	68	-3	-4	8	5			4	O	0.0
1916	Bro-N	9	5	3	1	0	0	0	0	2	0	.200	.429	.200	94	0	0	1	1			0	/O	0.0
1917	Bro-N	114	370	46	81	15	4	6	36	17	66	.219	.253	.330	76	-11	-12	33	14			2	*O	-1.4
1918	Bro-N	53	167	14	39	4	7	1	16	8	31	.234	.281	.359	95	-2	-2	17	5			-2	O	-0.6
1919	Bro-N	57	104	14	20	3	1	0	11	6	17	.192	.236	.240	43	-7	-7	6	2			1	O	-0.7
Total	5	253	727	84	158	26	13	8	70	37	128	.217	.259	.322	75	-23	-24	65	27			5	O	-2.7

■ JIM HICKMAN   Hickman, James Lucius b: 5/10/37, Henning, Tenn. BR/TR, 6'3", 192 lbs. Deb: 4/14/62

YEAR	TM/L	G	AB	R	H	2B	3B	HR	RBI	BB	SO	AVG	OBP	SLG	PRO+	BR	/A	RC	SB	CS	SBR	FR	POS	TPR
1962	NY-N	140	392	54	96	18	2	13	46	47	96	.245	.330	.401	94	-3	-4	52	4	4	-1	-9	*O	-2.0
1963	NY-N	146	494	53	113	21	6	17	51	44	120	.229	.293	.399	96	-3	-4	56	0	5	-3	-6	O3	-1.7
1964	NY-N	139	409	48	105	14	1	11	57	36	90	.257	.320	.377	98	-2	-1	48	0	1	-1	-4	*O/3	-0.9
1965	NY-N	141	369	32	87	18	0	15	40	27	76	.236	.291	.407	98	-4	-2	42	3	1	0	0	O13	-0.6
1966	NY-N	58	160	15	38	7	0	4	16	13	34	.237	.299	.356	83	-4	-4	17	2	1	0	5	O1	-0.6
1967	LA-N	65	98	7	16	6	1	0	10	14	28	.163	.268	.245	52	-6	-6	6	1	1	-0	3	O/13P	-0.4
1968	Chi-N	75	188	22	42	6	3	5	23	18	38	.223	.295	.367	91	-1	-2	20	1	1	-0	-1	O	-0.7
1969	Chi-N	134	338	38	80	11	2	21	54	47	74	.237	.330	.467	107	9	3	52	2	1	0	-13	*O	-1.6
1970	Chi-N	149	514	102	162	33	4	32	115	93	99	.315	.421	.582	148	50	41	129	0	1	-1	3	O1	3.3
1971	Chi-N	117	383	50	98	13	2	19	60	50	61	.256	.346	.449	108	12	5	58	0	1	-1	-5	O1	-0.6
1972	Chi-N	115	368	65	100	15	2	17	64	52	64	.272	.365	.462	121	17	12	66	3	1	0	7	1O	1.4
1973	Chi-N	92	201	27	49	1	2	3	20	42	42	.244	.374	.313	86	-0	-2	25	1	1	-0	1	1O	-0.4
1974	StL-N	50	60	5	16	0	0	2	4	8	10	.267	.353	.367	102	0	0	7	0	0	0	1	1/3	0.1
Total	13	1421	3974	518	1002	163	25	159	560	491	832	.252	.337	.426	106	64	38	578	17	19	-6	-18	O1/3P	-4.1

■ BUDDY HICKS   Hicks, Clarence Walter b: 2/15/27, Belvedere, Cal. BB/TR, 5'10", 170 lbs. Deb: 4/17/56

YEAR	TM/L	G	AB	R	H	2B	3B	HR	RBI	BB	SO	AVG	OBP	SLG	PRO+	BR	/A	RC	SB	CS	SBR	FR	POS	TPR
1956	Det-A	26	47	5	10	2	0	0	5	3	2	.213	.260	.255	36	-4	-4	3	0	1	-1	-1	S/23	-0.3

■ JIM HICKS   Hicks, James Edward b: 5/18/40, East Chicago, Ind. BR/TR, 6'3", 205 lbs. Deb: 10/02/64

YEAR	TM/L	G	AB	R	H	2B	3B	HR	RBI	BB	SO	AVG	OBP	SLG	PRO+	BR	/A	RC	SB	CS	SBR	FR	POS	TPR
1964	Chi-A	2	0	0	0	0	0	0	0	0	0	—	—	—		0	0	0	0	0	0	0	R	0.0
1965	Chi-A	13	19	2	5	1	0	1	2	0	9	.263	.263	.474	112	-0	0	2	0	0	0	-1	/O	0.0
1966	Chi-A	18	26	3	5	0	1	0	1	1	5	.192	.222	.269	43	-2	-2	1	0	0	0	-2	O/1	-0.4
1969	StL-N	19	44	5	8	0	2	1	3	4	14	.182	.250	.341	64	-2	-2	4	0	0	0	2	O	0.0
	Cal-A	37	48	6	4	0	0	3	8	13	18	.083	.279	.271	57	-3	-3	4	0	1	-1	-1	O/1	-0.5
1970	Cal-A	4	4	0	1	0	0	0	0	0	2	.250	.250	.250	40	-0	-0	0	0	0	0	0	H	0.0
Total	5	93	141	16	23	1	3	5	14	18	48	.163	.258	.319	64	-8	-7	12	0	1	-1	-2	/O1	-0.9

■ NAT HICKS   Hicks, Nathaniel Woodhull b: 4/19/1845, Hempstead, N.Y. d: 4/21/07, Hoboken, N.J. BR/TR, 6'1", 186 lbs. Deb: 4/22/1872 M

YEAR	TM/L	G	AB	R	H	2B	3B	HR	RBI	BB	SO	AVG	OBP	SLG	PRO+	BR	/A	RC	SB	CS	SBR	FR	POS	TPR
1872	Mut-n	56	266	55	81	12	2	0		5		.305	.317	.365	117	3	7	32					*C/O	0.3
1873	Mut-n	28	122	12	29	2	2	1		6		.238	.273	.311	72	-4	-4	11					C	-0.1
1874	Phi-n	58	264	50	74	8	2	0		5		.280	.294	.326	94	-1	-2	26					*C/O	0.0
1875	Mut-n	62	269	32	67	11	2	0		2		.249	.255	.305	87	-2	-4	21					*C/OM	-0.2
1876	NY-N	45	188	20	44	4	1	0	15	3	4	.234	.246	.266	81	-6	-2	13				-8	C	-0.6
1877	Cin-N	8	32	3	6	0	0	0	3	1	2	.188	.212	.188	30	-3	-2	1				-0	/C	-0.1
Total	4 n	204	921	149	251	33	8	1		18		.273	.286	.329	95	-4	-4	89					C/O	0.0
Total	2	53	220	23	50	4	1	0	18	4	6	.227	.241	.255	73	-8	-4	14				-8	/C	-0.7

■ JOE HICKS   Hicks, William Joseph b: 4/7/33, Ivy, Va. BL/TR, 6', 180 lbs. Deb: 9/18/59

YEAR	TM/L	G	AB	R	H	2B	3B	HR	RBI	BB	SO	AVG	OBP	SLG	PRO+	BR	/A	RC	SB	CS	SBR	FR	POS	TPR
1959	Chi-A	6	7	0	3	0	0	0	0	1	1	.429	.500	.429	160	1	1	1	0	1	-1	1	/O	0.1
1960	Chi-A	36	47	3	9	1	0	0	2	6	3	.191	.296	.213	40	-4	-3	3	0	1	-1	-1	/O	-0.5
1961	Was-A	12	29	2	5	0	0	1	1	0	4	.172	.172	.276	18	-3	-3	1	0	1	-1	1	/O	-0.2
1962	Was-A	102	174	20	39	4	2	6	14	15	34	.224	.286	.374	76	-6	-6	19	3	1	0	1	O	-0.6
1963	NY-N	56	159	16	36	6	1	5	22	7	31	.226	.272	.371	82	-4	-4	16	0	2	-1	1	O	-0.6
Total	5	212	416	41	92	11	3	12	39	29	73	.221	.278	.349	72	-17	-17	40	3	6	-3	2	O	-1.8

■ MAHLON HIGBEE   Higbee, Mahlon Jesse b: 8/16/01, Louisville, Ky. d: 4/7/68, DePauw, Ind. 5'11", 165 lbs. Deb: 9/27/22

YEAR	TM/L	G	AB	R	H	2B	3B	HR	RBI	BB	SO	AVG	OBP	SLG	PRO+	BR	/A	RC	SB	CS	SBR	FR	POS	TPR
1922	NY-N	3	10	2	4	0	0	1	5	0	2	.400	.400	.700	177	1	1	3	0	0	0	-1	/O	0.0

■ HIGBY   Higby Deb: 9/18/1872

YEAR	TM/L	G	AB	R	H	2B	3B	HR	RBI	BB	SO	AVG	OBP	SLG	PRO+	BR	/A	RC	SB	CS	SBR	FR	POS	TPR
1872	Atl-n	1	4	0	0	0	0	0		0		.000	.000	.000	-85	-1	-1	0					/O	0.0

■ BILL HIGDON   Higdon, William Travis b: 4/27/24, Camp Hill, Ala. d: 8/30/86, Pascagoula, Miss. BL/TR, 6'1", 193 lbs. Deb: 9/10/49

YEAR	TM/L	G	AB	R	H	2B	3B	HR	RBI	BB	SO	AVG	OBP	SLG	PRO+	BR	/A	RC	SB	CS	SBR	FR	POS	TPR
1949	Chi-A	11	23	3	7	3	0	0	1	6	3	.304	.448	.435	139	1	2	6	1	0	0	-0	/O	0.1

■ MARK HIGGINS   Higgins, Mark Douglas b: 7/9/63, Miami, Fla. BR/TR, 6'2", 210 lbs. Deb: 9/07/89

YEAR	TM/L	G	AB	R	H	2B	3B	HR	RBI	BB	SO	AVG	OBP	SLG	PRO+	BR	/A	RC	SB	CS	SBR	FR	POS	TPR
1989	Cle-A	6	10	1	1	0	0	0	0	1	6	.100	.182	.100	-18	-2	-2	0	0	0	0	1	/1	0.0

■ MIKE HIGGINS   Higgins, Michael Franklin "Pinky" b: 5/27/09, Red Oak, Tex. d: 3/21/69, Dallas, Tex. BR/TR, 6'1", 185 lbs. Deb: 6/25/30 M

YEAR	TM/L	G	AB	R	H	2B	3B	HR	RBI	BB	SO	AVG	OBP	SLG	PRO+	BR	/A	RC	SB	CS	SBR	FR	POS	TPR
1930	Phi-A	14	24	1	6	2	0	0	0	4	5	.250	.357	.333	73	-1	-1	3	0	0	0	-2	/32S	-0.2
1933	Phi-A	152	567	85	178	35	11	13	99	61	53	.314	.383	.483	127	22	22	104	2	7	-4	-6	*3	2.2
1934	Phi-A	144	543	89	179	37	6	16	90	56	70	.330	.392	.508	136	24	27	110	9	3	1	-19	*3	0.8
1935	Phi-A	133	524	69	155	32	4	23	94	42	62	.296	.350	.504	120	12	12	93	6	2	1	-14	*3	0.0
1936	Phi-A	146	550	89	159	32	2	12	80	67	61	.289	.366	.420	96	-6	-4	87	7	4	-0	-14	*3	-1.4
1937	Bos-A	153	570	88	172	33	5	9	106	76	51	.302	.385	.425	100	5	1	95	2	6	-3	-16	*3	-1.3
1938	Bos-A	139	524	77	159	29	5	5	106	71	55	.303	.388	.406	95	1	-3	85	10	9	-2	-10	*3	-0.9
1939	Det-A	132	489	57	135	23	2	8	76	56	41	.276	.353	.380	81	-9	-14	66	7	4	-0	-11	*3	-2.5
1940	*Det-A	131	480	70	130	24	3	13	76	61	31	.271	.357	.415	91	-0	-7	73	4	2	0	-11	*3	-0.9
1941	Det-A	147	540	79	161	28	3	11	73	67	45	.298	.378	.422	101	10	2	86	5	4	1	1	*3	1.0
1942	Det-A	143	499	65	133	34	2	11	79	72	21	.267	.362	.409	108	12	7	72	3	7	-3	-13	*3	-0.8
1943	Det-A	138	523	62	145	20	1	10	84	57	31	.277	.349	.377	104	8	4	68	2	5	-2	-7	*3	-0.3
1944	Det-A	148	543	79	161	32	4	7	76	81	34	.297	.392	.409	122	23	19	91	4	4	-1	-7	*3	1.1
1946	Det-A	18	60	2	13	3	1	0	8	5	6	.217	.277	.300	58	-3	-4	5	0	1	-1	-2	3	-0.4

YEAR	TM/L	G	AB	R	H	2B	3B	HR	RBI	BB	SO	AVG	OBP	SLG	PRO+	BR	/A	RC	SB	CS	SBR	FR	POS	TPR
	*Bos-A	64	200	18	55	11	1	2	28	24	24	.275	.356	.370	97	1	-0	26	0	2	-1	0	3	0.4
	Yr	82	260	20	68	14	2	2	36	29	30	.262	.338	.354	88	-2	-4	30	0	3	-2	-2		0.0
Total	14	1802	6636	930	1941	375	50	140	1075	800	590	.292	.370	.427	105	100	62	1065	61	60	-18	-130	*3/2S	-3.1

■ **BOB HIGGINS** Higgins, Robert Stone b: 9/23/1886, Fayetteville, Tenn. d: 5/25/41, Chattanooga, Tenn. BR/TR, 5'8", 176 lbs. Deb: 9/13/09

YEAR	TM/L	G	AB	R	H	2B	3B	HR	RBI	BB	SO	AVG	OBP	SLG	PRO+	BR	/A	RC	SB	CS	SBR	FR	POS	TPR
1909	Cle-A	8	23	0	2	0	0	0	0	0		.087	.087	.087	-43	-4	-4	0	0				3 /C	0.0
1911	Bro-N	4	10	1	3	0	0	0	2	1	0	.300	.364	.300	90	-0	-0	1	1				0 /C3	0.0
1912	Bro-N	1	2	0	0	0	0	0	0	0	1	.000	.000	.000	-99	-1	-1	0	0				-0 /C	0.0
Total	3	13	35	1	5	0	0	0	2	1	1	.143	.167	.143	-6	-4	-4	2	1				3 /C3	0.0

■ **BILL HIGGINS** Higgins, William Edward b: 9/8/1861, Wilmington, Del. d: 4/25/19, Wilmington, Del. TR , Deb: 8/09/1888

YEAR	TM/L	G	AB	R	H	2B	3B	HR	RBI	BB	SO	AVG	OBP	SLG	PRO+	BR	/A	RC	SB	CS	SBR	FR	POS	TPR
1888	Bos-N	14	54	5	10	1	0	0	4	1	3	.185	.200	.204	30	-4	-4	2	1				5 2	0.2
1890	StL-a	67	258	39	65	6	2	0		24		.252	.316	.291	71	-6	-12	27	7				13 2	0.4
	Syr-a	1	4	1	1	1	0	0		0		.250	.250	.500	136	0	0	1	0				1 /2	0.1
	Yr	68	262	40	66	7	2	0		24		.252	.315	.294	72	-6	-11	27	7				14	0.5
Total	2	82	316	45	76	8	2	0	4	25	3	.241	.296	.278	66	-10	-16	29	8				20 /2	0.7

■ **ANDY HIGH** High, Andrew Aird "Handy Andy" b: 11/21/1897, Ava, Ill. d: 2/22/81, Toledo, Ohio BL/TR, 5'6", 155 lbs. Deb: 4/12/22 C

YEAR	TM/L	G	AB	R	H	2B	3B	HR	RBI	BB	SO	AVG	OBP	SLG	PRO+	BR	/A	RC	SB	CS	SBR	FR	POS	TPR
1922	Bro-N	153	579	82	164	27	10	6	65	59	26	.283	.354	.396	94	-6	-5	80	3	12	-6	-5	*3S/2	-0.3
1923	Bro-N	123	426	51	115	23	9	3	37	47	13	.270	.344	.387	95	-4	-3	60	4	1	1	-9	3S/2	-0.4
1924	Bro-N	144	582	98	191	26	13	6	61	57	16	.328	.390	.448	128	21	23	102	3	6	-3	-10	*2S/3	0.4
1925	Bro-N	44	115	11	23	4	1	0	6	14	5	.200	.287	.252	40	-10	-10	9	0	1	-1	-5	23/S	-1.3
	Bos-N	60	219	31	63	11	1	4	28	24	2	.288	.361	.402	104	-1	1	32	3	5	-2	-9	3/2	-0.5
	Yr	104	334	42	86	15	2	4	34	38	7	.257	.335	.350	80	-12	-9	40	3	6	-3	-14		-1.8
1926	Bos-N	130	476	55	141	17	10	2	66	39	9	.296	.351	.387	108	-1	5	64	4			-6	32	0.2
1927	Bos-N	113	384	59	116	15	9	4	46	26	11	.302	.350	.419	114	2	6	55	4			-20	3/2S	-0.8
1928	*StL-N	111	368	58	105	14	3	6	37	37	10	.285	.355	.389	93	-3	-3	51	2			-19	32	-2.0
1929	StL-N	146	603	95	178	32	4	10	63	38	18	.295	.340	.411	84	-15	-16	82	7			-19	*32	-2.2
1930	*StL-N	72	215	34	60	12	2	2	29	23	6	.279	.349	.381	74	-8	-9	29	1			-7	3/2	-1.2
1931	*StL-N	63	131	20	35	6	1	0	19	24	4	.267	.389	.328	91	-0	0	19	0			-4	32	-0.2
1932	Cin-N	84	191	16	36	4	2	0	12	23	6	.188	.276	.230	39	-16	-15	14	1			-10	32	-2.0
1933	Cin-N	24	43	4	9	2	0	1	6	5	1	.209	.292	.326	77	-1	-1	4	0			1	3/2	0.0
1934	Phi-N	47	68	4	14	2	0	0	7	9	3	.206	.299	.235	40	-5	-6	4	1			-2	3/2	-0.6
Total	13	1314	4400	618	1250	195	65	44	482	425	130	.284	.350	.388	94	-47	-33	603	33	25		-123	32/S	-10.9

■ **CHARLIE HIGH** High, Charles Edwin b: 12/1/1898, Ava, Ill. d: 9/11/60, Oak Grove, Ore. BL/TR, 5'9", 170 lbs. Deb: 9/05/19

YEAR	TM/L	G	AB	R	H	2B	3B	HR	RBI	BB	SO	AVG	OBP	SLG	PRO+	BR	/A	RC	SB	CS	SBR	FR	POS	TPR
1919	Phi-A	11	29	2	2	0	0	0	1	3	4	.069	.182	.069	-28	-5	-5	1	2			-0	/O	-0.5
1920	Phi-A	17	65	7	20	2	1	1	6	3	6	.308	.375	.415	108	1	1	10	0	2	-1	-1	O	-0.1
Total	2	28	94	9	22	2	1	1	7	6	10	.234	.314	.309	68	-4	-4	11	2	2		-1	/O	-0.6

■ **HUGH HIGH** High, Hugh Jenken "Bunny" b: 10/24/1887, Pottstown, Pa. d: 11/16/62, St.Louis, Mo. BL/TL, 5'7.5", 155 lbs. Deb: 4/11/13

YEAR	TM/L	G	AB	R	H	2B	3B	HR	RBI	BB	SO	AVG	OBP	SLG	PRO+	BR	/A	RC	SB	CS	SBR	FR	POS	TPR
1913	Det-A	87	183	18	42	6	1	0	16	28	24	.230	.335	.273	80	-4	-4	18	6			1	O	-0.5
1914	Det-A	84	184	25	49	5	3	0	17	26	21	.266	.363	.326	104	3	2	24	7	6	-2	-7	O	-1.0
1915	NY-A	119	427	51	110	19	7	1	43	62	47	.258	.356	.342	109	6	6	56	22	13	-1	-1	*O	-0.1
1916	NY-A	116	377	44	99	13	4	1	28	47	44	.263	.349	.326	101	2	1	51	13			-1	*O	-0.6
1917	NY-A	103	365	37	86	11	6	1	19	48	31	.236	.329	.307	93	-1	-2	39	8			0	*O	-0.8
1918	NY-A	7	10	1	0	0	0	0	0	1	1	.000	.091	.000	-71	-2	-2	0	0			0	/O	-0.1
Total	6	516	1546	176	386	54	21	3	123	212	168	.250	.345	.318	98	4	2	189	56	19		-8	O	-3.1

■ **DICK HIGHAM** Higham, Richard b: 1852, England d: 3/18/05, Chicago, Ill. BL/TR, Deb: 6/01/1871 MU

YEAR	TM/L	G	AB	R	H	2B	3B	HR	RBI	BB	SO	AVG	OBP	SLG	PRO+	BR	/A	RC	SB	CS	SBR	FR	POS	TPR
1871	Mut-n	21	94	21	34	3	1	0	9	2	0	.362	.375	.415	139	3	5	16	3				2/OC3	0.3
1872	Bal-n	50	244	72	85	9	2	2		2		.348	.354	.426	133	11	8	38					CO/21	0.5
1873	Mut-n	49	245	57	77	6	7	0		2		.314	.320	.396	110	3	3	32					O2C/3	0.2
1874	Mut-n	65	331	58	87	13	4	1		4		.263	.272	.335	89	-3	-5	31					*CO/2M	-0.1
1875	Chi-n	42	204	44	49	3	3	0		0		.240	.240	.284	80	-4	-4	14					C2/O	-0.2
	Mut-n	15	64	12	25	5	0	0		0		.391	.391	.469	185	6	5	12					/C2O1	0.4
	Yr	57	268	56	74	8	3	0		0		.276	.276	.328	106	2	1	25						0.2
1876	Har-N	67	312	59	102	21	2	0	35	2	7	.327	.331	.407	134	14	10	43				-3	*OC/S2	0.6
1878	Pro-N	62	281	60	90	22	1	1	29	5	16	.320	.332	.416	145	13	13	40				1	*O/C	0.8
1880	Tro-N	1	5	1	1	0	0	0	0	0	0	.200	.200	.200	34	-0	-0	0				-2	/OC	-0.1
Total	5 n	242	1182	264	357	39	17	3	9	10		.302	.308	.371	110	15	13	143					C/0213	1.1
Total	3	130	598	120	193	43	3	1	64	7	23	.323	.331	.410	138	26	23	83				-5	O/C2S	1.3

■ **JOHN HILAND** Hiland, John William b: 1861, Philadelphia, Pa. d: 4/10/01, Philadelphia, Pa. TL , Deb: 8/20/1885

YEAR	TM/L	G	AB	R	H	2B	3B	HR	RBI	BB	SO	AVG	OBP	SLG	PRO+	BR	/A	RC	SB	CS	SBR	FR	POS	TPR
1885	Phi-N	3	9	0	0	0	0	0	0	0	4	.000	.000	.000	-99	-2	-2	0				-2	/2	-0.3

■ **GEORGE HILDEBRAND** Hildebrand, George Albert b: 9/6/1878, San Francisco, Cal d: 5/30/60, Woodland Hills, Cal. 5'8", 170 lbs. Deb: 4/17/02 U

YEAR	TM/L	G	AB	R	H	2B	3B	HR	RBI	BB	SO	AVG	OBP	SLG	PRO+	BR	/A	RC	SB	CS	SBR	FR	POS	TPR
1902	Bro-N	11	41	3	9	1	0	0	5	3		.220	.289	.244	66	-1	-1	3	0			2	O	0.0

■ **PALMER HILDEBRAND** Hildebrand, Palmer Marion "Pete" b: 12/23/1884, Shauck, Ohio d: 1/25/60, N.Canton, Ohio BR/TR, 5'10", 170 lbs. Deb: 5/14/13

YEAR	TM/L	G	AB	R	H	2B	3B	HR	RBI	BB	SO	AVG	OBP	SLG	PRO+	BR	/A	RC	SB	CS	SBR	FR	POS	TPR
1913	StL-N	26	55	3	9	2	0	0	1	1	10	.164	.207	.200	17	-6	-6	2	1			1	C/O	-0.3

■ **R. E. HILDEBRAND** Hildebrand, R. E. Deb: 8/29/02

YEAR	TM/L	G	AB	R	H	2B	3B	HR	RBI	BB	SO	AVG	OBP	SLG	PRO+	BR	/A	RC	SB	CS	SBR	FR	POS	TPR
1902	Chi-N	1	4	1	0	0	0	0	0	0	1	.000	.200	.000	-37	-1	-1	0	0			-0	/O	0.0

■ **BELDEN HILL** Hill, Belden L. b: 8/24/1864, Kewanee, Ill. d: 10/22/34, Cedar Rapids, Iowa BR/TR, 6', Deb: 8/27/1890

YEAR	TM/L	G	AB	R	H	2B	3B	HR	RBI	BB	SO	AVG	OBP	SLG	PRO+	BR	/A	RC	SB	CS	SBR	FR	POS	TPR
1890	Bal-a	9	30	3	5	2	0	0		3		.167	.306	.233	59	-1	-1	4	6			1	/3	0.0

■ **DON HILL** Hill, Donald Earl b: 11/12/60, Pomona, Cal. BB/TR, 5'10", 160 lbs. Deb: 7/25/83

YEAR	TM/L	G	AB	R	H	2B	3B	HR	RBI	BB	SO	AVG	OBP	SLG	PRO+	BR	/A	RC	SB	CS	SBR	FR	POS	TPR
1983	Oak-A	53	158	20	42	7	0	2	15	4	21	.266	.284	.348	77	-6	-5	15	1	1	-0	-0	S	-0.2
1984	Oak-A	73	174	21	40	6	0	2	16	5	12	.230	.251	.299	55	-12	-10	13	1	1	-0	-12	S/23D	-1.6
1985	Oak-A	123	393	45	112	13	2	3	48	23	33	.285	.325	.351	92	-8	-4	45	9	4	0	-41	*2	-3.9
1986	Oak-A	108	339	37	96	16	2	4	29	23	38	.283	.329	.378	99	-4	-4	41	5	2	0	-12	23/SD	-0.8
1987	Chi-A	111	410	57	98	14	6	9	46	30	35	.239	.293	.368	72	-16	-17	43	1	0	0	-29	23/D	-3.8
1988	Chi-A	83	221	17	48	6	1	2	20	26	32	.217	.300	.281	64	-10	-10	20	3	1	0	-11	23/D	-1.6
1990	Cal-A	103	352	36	93	18	2	3	32	29	27	.264	.322	.352	88	-5	-6	39	1	2	-1	4	2S3/1PD	0.2
Total	7	654	2047	233	529	80	13	25	206	140	198	.258	.307	.347	81	-61	-53	216	21	11	-0	-101	2S3/D1P	-11.7

■ **GLENALLEN HILL** Hill, Glenallen b: 3/22/65, Santa Cruz, Cal. BR/TR, 6'3", 210 lbs. Deb: 9/01/89

YEAR	TM/L	G	AB	R	H	2B	3B	HR	RBI	BB	SO	AVG	OBP	SLG	PRO+	BR	/A	RC	SB	CS	SBR	FR	POS	TPR
1989	Tor-A	19	52	4	15	0	0	1	7	3	12	.288	.327	.346	92	-1	-1	6	2	1	0	-0	O/D	0.0
1990	Tor-A	84	260	47	60	11	3	12	32	18	62	.231	.281	.435	99	-2	-2	31	8	3	1	-0	OD	-0.1
Total	2	103	312	51	75	11	3	13	39	21	74	.240	.288	.420	98	-3	-2	37	10	4	1	-1	/OD	-0.1

■ **HERMAN HILL** Hill, Herman Alexander b: 10/12/45, Tuskegee, Ala. d: 12/14/70, Valencia, Venez. BL/TR, 6'2", 190 lbs. Deb: 9/02/69

YEAR	TM/L	G	AB	R	H	2B	3B	HR	RBI	BB	SO	AVG	OBP	SLG	PRO+	BR	/A	RC	SB	CS	SBR	FR	POS	TPR
1969	Min-A	16	2	4	0	0	0	0	0	0	1	.000	.000	.000	-98	-1	-1	-1	1	2	-1	0	/O	-0.1
1970	Min-A	27	22	8	2	0	0	0	0	0	6	.091	.091	.091	-49	-4	-4	0	0	0	0	3	O	-0.1

YEAR	TM/L	G	AB	R	H	2B	3B	HR	RBI	BB	SO	AVG	OBP	SLG	PRO+	BR	/A	RC	SB	CS	SBR	FR	POS	TPR
Total	2	43	24	12	2	0	0	0	0	0	7	.083	.083	.083	-53	-5	-5	-0	1	2	-1	3	/O	-0.2

■ HUGH HILL
Hill, Hugh Ellis b: 7/21/1879, Ringgold, Ga. d: 9/6/58, Cincinnati, Ohio BL/TR, 5'11.5", 168 lbs. Deb: 5/01/03

YEAR	TM/L	G	AB	R	H	2B	3B	HR	RBI	BB	SO	AVG	OBP	SLG	PRO+	BR	/A	RC	SB	CS	SBR	FR	POS	TPR
1903	Cle-A	1	1	0	0	0	0	0	0	0	0	.000	.000	.000	-99	-0	-0	0	0			0	H	0.0
1904	StL-N	23	93	13	21	2	1	3	4	2		.226	.242	.366	92	-2	-1	9	3			0	/O	-0.1
Total	2	24	94	13	21	2	1	3	4	2		.223	.240	.362	90	-2	-1	9	3			0	/O	-0.1

■ HUNTER HILL
Hill, Hunter Benjamin b: 6/21/1879, Austin, Tex. d: 2/22/59, Austin, Tex. BR/TR, Deb: 7/01/03

YEAR	TM/L	G	AB	R	H	2B	3B	HR	RBI	BB	SO	AVG	OBP	SLG	PRO+	BR	/A	RC	SB	CS	SBR	FR	POS	TPR
1903	StL-A	86	317	30	77	11	3	0	25	8		.243	.262	.297	71	-12	-11	27	2			-1	3	-1.3
1904	StL-A	58	219	19	47	3	0	0	14	6		.215	.236	.228	52	-12	-11	14	4			-16	3/O	-2.8
	Was-A	77	290	18	57	6	1	0	17	11		.197	.226	.224	45	-18	-17	19	10			-6	3/O	-2.3
	Yr	135	509	37	104	9	1	0	31	17		.204	.230	.226	48	-30	-28	33	14			-22		-5.1
1905	Was-A	104	374	37	78	12	1	1	24	32		.209	.271	.254	72	-12	-11	34	10			-1	*3	-0.8
Total	3	325	1200	104	259	32	5	1	80	57		.216	.251	.253	61	-55	-50	94	26			-24	3/O	-7.2

■ JESSE HILL
Hill, Jesse Terrill b: 1/20/07, Yates, Mo. BR/TR, 5'9", 165 lbs. Deb: 4/17/35

YEAR	TM/L	G	AB	R	H	2B	3B	HR	RBI	BB	SO	AVG	OBP	SLG	PRO+	BR	/A	RC	SB	CS	SBR	FR	POS	TPR
1935	NY-A	107	392	69	115	20	3	4	33	42	32	.293	.362	.390	100	-3	0	58	14	4	2	3	O	0.4
1936	Was-A	85	233	50	71	19	5	0	34	29	23	.305	.384	.429	106	1	3	42	11	0	3	-8	O	-0.2
1937	Was-A	33	92	24	20	2	1	1	4	13	16	.217	.314	.293	57	-6	-6	9	2	1	0	3	O	-0.2
	Phi-A	70	242	32	71	12	3	1	37	31	20	.293	.374	.380	92	-3	-2	38	16	3	3	-8	O	-0.8
	Yr	103	334	56	91	14	4	2	41	44	36	.272	.357	.356	82	-9	-8	47	18	4	3	-5		-1.0
Total	3	295	959	175	277	53	12	6	108	115	91	.289	.366	.388	95	-11	-5	147	43	8	8	-9	O	-0.8

■ MARC HILL
Hill, Marc Kevin b: 2/18/52, Elsberry, Mo. BR/TR, 6'3", 205 lbs. Deb: 9/28/73 C

YEAR	TM/L	G	AB	R	H	2B	3B	HR	RBI	BB	SO	AVG	OBP	SLG	PRO+	BR	/A	RC	SB	CS	SBR	FR	POS	TPR
1973	StL-N	1	3	0	0	0	0	0	0	0	1	.000	.000	.000	-99	-1	-1	0	0	0	0	0	/C	0.0
1974	StL-N	10	21	2	5	1	0	0	2	4	5	.238	.360	.286	83	-0	-0	2	0	0	0	3	/C	0.3
1975	SF-N	72	182	14	39	4	0	5	23	25	27	.214	.309	.319	71	-6	-7	18	0	0	0	0	C/3	-0.4
1976	SF-N	54	131	11	24	5	0	3	15	10	19	.183	.246	.290	50	-9	-9	9	0	1	-1	0	C/1	-0.6
1977	SF-N	108	320	28	80	10	0	9	50	34	34	.250	.322	.366	84	-7	-7	36	0	1	-1	-4	*C	-1.2
1978	SF-N	117	358	20	87	15	1	3	36	45	39	.243	.329	.316	84	-8	-6	36	1	2	-1	-1	*C/1	-0.5
1979	SF-N	63	169	20	35	3	0	3	15	26	25	.207	.313	.278	67	-8	-7	15	0	1	-1	-6	C/1	-1.1
1980	SF-N	17	41	1	7	2	0	0	0	1	7	.171	.190	.220	14	-5	-5	2	0	0	0	2	C	-0.2
	Sea-A	29	70	8	16	2	1	2	9	3	10	.229	.260	.371	70	-3	-3	6	0	0	0	-1	C	-0.2
1981	Chi-A	16	6	0	0	0	0	0	0	0	1	.000	.000	.000	-99	-2	-1	0	0	0	0	1	C/13	0.0
1982	Chi-A	53	88	9	23	2	0	3	13	6	13	.261	.316	.386	92	-1	-1	10	0	0	0	4	C/13	0.6
1983	Chi-A	58	133	11	30	6	0	1	11	9	24	.226	.275	.293	54	-8	-9	10	0	1	-1	5	C/1D	-0.1
1984	Chi-A	77	193	15	45	10	1	5	20	9	26	.233	.275	.373	74	-6	-7	16	0	1	-1	-0	C/1	-0.3
1985	Chi-A	40	75	5	10	2	0	0	4	12	9	.133	.253	.160	16	-8	-9	4	0	0	0	7	C/3	0.0
1986	Chi-A	22	19	2	3	0	0	0	0	1	3	.158	.238	.158	10	-2	-2	1	0	0	0	7	C	0.6
Total	14	737	1809	146	404	62	3	34	198	185	243	.223	.298	.317	69	-75	-75	165	1	7	-4	18	C/13D	-3.1

■ OLIVER HILL
Hill, Oliver Clinton b: 10/16/12, Powder Springs, Ga d: 9/20/70, Decatur, Ga. BL/TR, 5'11", 178 lbs. Deb: 4/19/39

YEAR	TM/L	G	AB	R	H	2B	3B	HR	RBI	BB	SO	AVG	OBP	SLG	PRO+	BR	/A	RC	SB	CS	SBR	FR	POS	TPR
1939	Bos-N	2	2	1	1	1	0	0	0	0	0	.500	.500	1.000	317	1	1	1	0			0	H	0.1

■ HOMER HILLEBRAND
Hillebrand, Homer Hiller Henry "Doc" b: 10/10/1879, Freeport, Ill. d: 1/20/74, Elsinore, Cal. 5'8", 165 lbs. Deb: 4/24/05

YEAR	TM/L	G	AB	R	H	2B	3B	HR	RBI	BB	SO	AVG	OBP	SLG	PRO+	BR	/A	RC	SB	CS	SBR	FR	POS	TPR
1905	Pit-N	39	110	9	26	3	2	0	7	6		.236	.276	.300	72	-4	-4	10	1			-3	1P/OC	-0.5
1906	Pit-N	7	21	1	5	1	0	0	3	1		.238	.273	.286	73	-1	-1	2	0			1	/P	0.0
1908	Pit-N	1	0	0	0	0	0	0	0	0		—	—	—	—	0	0	0	0			0	/P	0.0
Total	3	47	131	10	31	4	2	0	10	7		.237	.275	.298	72	-4	-5	12	1			-2	/P1OC	-0.5

■ CHUCK HILLER
Hiller, Charles Joseph b: 10/1/34, Johnsburg, Ill. BL/TR, 5'11", 170 lbs. Deb: 4/11/61 C

YEAR	TM/L	G	AB	R	H	2B	3B	HR	RBI	BB	SO	AVG	OBP	SLG	PRO+	BR	/A	RC	SB	CS	SBR	FR	POS	TPR
1961	SF-N	70	240	38	57	12	1	2	12	32	30	.237	.330	.321	76	-8	-7	28	4	4	-1	-14	2	-1.4
1962	*SF-N	161	602	94	166	22	2	3	48	55	49	.276	.344	.334	84	-13	-11	71	5	4	-1	-18	*2	-1.5
1963	SF-N	111	417	44	93	10	2	6	33	20	23	.223	.262	.300	62	-21	-20	31	3	2	-0	-15	*2	-3.1
1964	SF-N	80	205	21	37	8	1	1	17	17	23	.180	.247	.244	38	-16	-17	13	1	1	-0	2	2/3	-1.0
1965	SF-N	7	7	1	1	0	0	1	1	0	1	.143	.143	.571	88	-0	-0	0	0	0	0	-1	/2	0.0
	NY-N	100	286	24	68	11	1	5	21	14	24	.238	.276	.336	74	-11	-10	25	1	1	-0	-12	2/O3	-1.8
	Yr	107	293	25	69	11	1	6	22	14	25	.235	.273	.341	74	-11	-10	26	1	1	-0	-12		-1.8
1966	NY-N	108	254	25	71	8	2	2	14	15	22	.280	.332	.350	92	-3	-2	31	0	0	0	10	23/O	1.1
1967	NY-N	25	54	0	5	3	0	0	3	2	11	.093	.125	.148	-22	-9	-8	1	0	0	0	2	2	-0.5
	Phi-N	31	43	4	13	1	0	0	2	2	4	.302	.333	.326	88	-1	-1	4	0	2	-1	-3	/2	-0.3
	Yr	56	97	4	18	4	0	0	5	4	15	.186	.218	.227	27	-9	-9	4	0	2	-1	-0		-0.8
1968	Pit-N	11	13	2	5	1	0	0	1	0	0	.385	.385	.462	155	1	1	2	0	0	0	-0	/2	0.1
Total	8	704	2121	253	516	76	9	20	152	157	187	.243	.301	.316	72	-81	-77	206	14	14	-4	-48	2/3O	-8.4

■ HOB HILLER
Hiller, Harvey Max b: 5/12/1893, E.Mauch Chunk, Pa. d: 12/27/56, Leighton, Pa. BR/TR, 5'8", 162 lbs. Deb: 4/22/20

YEAR	TM/L	G	AB	R	H	2B	3B	HR	RBI	BB	SO	AVG	OBP	SLG	PRO+	BR	/A	RC	SB	CS	SBR	FR	POS	TPR
1920	Bos-A	17	29	4	5	1	1	0	2	2	5	.172	.226	.276	34	-3	-3	1	0	3	-2	1	/3S2O	-0.2
1921	Bos-A	1	1	0	0	0	0	0	0	0	0	.000	.000	.000	-99	-0	-0	0	0	0	0	0	H	0.0
Total	2	18	30	4	5	1	1	0	2	2	5	.167	.219	.267	29	-3	-3	1	0	3	-2	1	/3S2O	-0.2

■ ED HILLEY
Hilley, Edward Garfield "Whitey" b: 6/17/1879, Cleveland, Ohio d: 11/14/56, Cleveland, Ohio BR/TR, 5'10.5", 170 lbs. Deb: 9/29/03

YEAR	TM/L	G	AB	R	H	2B	3B	HR	RBI	BB	SO	AVG	OBP	SLG	PRO+	BR	/A	RC	SB	CS	SBR	FR	POS	TPR
1903	Phi-A	1	3	1	1	0	0	0	0	1		.333	.500	.333	150	0	0	1	0			0	/3	0.0

■ MACK HILLIS
Hillis, Malcolm David b: 7/23/01, Cambridge, Mass. d: 6/16/61, Cambridge, Mass. BR/TR, 5'10", 165 lbs. Deb: 9/13/24

YEAR	TM/L	G	AB	R	H	2B	3B	HR	RBI	BB	SO	AVG	OBP	SLG	PRO+	BR	/A	RC	SB	CS	SBR	FR	POS	TPR
1924	NY-A	1	1	1	0	0	0	0	0	0	0	.000	.000	.000	-99	-0	-0	0	0	0	0	0	/2	0.0
1928	Pit-N	11	36	6	9	2	3	1	7	0	6	.250	.250	.556	101	-0	-0	5	1			-1	/23	-0.1
Total	2	12	37	7	9	2	3	1	7	0	6	.243	.243	.541	96	-0	-1	5	1	0		-1	/23	-0.1

■ PAT HILLY
Hilly, William Edward (b: William Edward Hilgerink) b: 2/24/1887, Fostoria, Ohio d: 7/25/53, Eureka, Mo. BR/TR, 5'11", 180 lbs. Deb: 5/07/14

YEAR	TM/L	G	AB	R	H	2B	3B	HR	RBI	BB	SO	AVG	OBP	SLG	PRO+	BR	/A	RC	SB	CS	SBR	FR	POS	TPR
1914	Phi-N	8	10	2	3	0	0	0	1	1	5	.300	.364	.300	92	0	-0	1	0			0	/O	0.0

■ CHARLIE HILSEY
Hilsey, Charles T. b: 3/23/1864, Philadelphia, Pa. d: 10/31/18, Philadelphia, Pa. 5'7", 180 lbs. Deb: 9/27/1883

YEAR	TM/L	G	AB	R	H	2B	3B	HR	RBI	BB	SO	AVG	OBP	SLG	PRO+	BR	/A	RC	SB	CS	SBR	FR	POS	TPR
1883	Phi-N	3	10	0	1	0	0	0	1	0	4	.100	.100	.100	-43	-2	-1	0				-0	/P	0.0
1884	Phi-a	6	24	5	5	1	1	0		0		.208	.208	.333	71	-1	-1	2				-0	/OP	0.0
Total	2	9	34	5	6	1	1	0	1	0	4	.176	.176	.265	39	-2	-2	2				-1	/PO	0.0

■ DAVE HILTON
Hilton, John David b: 9/15/50, Uvalde, Tex. BR/TR, 5'11", 191 lbs. Deb: 9/10/72 C

YEAR	TM/L	G	AB	R	H	2B	3B	HR	RBI	BB	SO	AVG	OBP	SLG	PRO+	BR	/A	RC	SB	CS	SBR	FR	POS	TPR
1972	SD-N	13	47	2	10	2	1	0	5	3	6	.213	.260	.298	63	-3	-2	4	1	0	0	-3	3	-0.4
1973	SD-N	70	234	21	46	9	0	5	16	19	35	.197	.260	.299	59	-15	-13	18	2	1	0	-4	32	-1.7
1974	SD-N	74	217	17	52	8	2	1	12	13	28	.240	.283	.309	68	-10	-9	17	3	5	-2	-5	32	-1.6
1975	SD-N	4	8	0	0	0	0	0	0	0	0	.000	.000	.000	-99	-2	-2	0	0	0	0	1	/3	0.0
Total	4	161	506	40	108	19	3	6	33	35	69	.213	.266	.298	61	-30	-26	40	6	6	-2	-10	3/2	-3.7

■ JACK HIMES
Himes, John Herb b: 9/22/1878, Bryan, Ohio d: 12/16/49, Joliet, Ill. BL/TR, 6'2", 180 lbs. Deb: 9/18/05

YEAR	TM/L	G	AB	R	H	2B	3B	HR	RBI	BB	SO	AVG	OBP	SLG	PRO+	BR	/A	RC	SB	CS	SBR	FR	POS	TPR
1905	StL-N	12	41	3	6	0	0	0	0	1		.146	.167	.146	-6	-5	-5	1	0			-1	O	-0.6
1906	StL-N	40	155	10	42	5	2	0	14	7		.271	.302	.329	103	-1	0	18	4			5	O	0.4

YEAR	TM/L	G	AB	R	H	2B	3B	HR	RBI	BB	SO	AVG	OBP	SLG	PRO+	BR	/A	RC	SB	CS	SBR	FR	POS	TPR
Total	2	52	196	13	48	5	2	0	14	8		.245	.275	.291	79	-6	-5	19	4			4	/O	-0.2

■ HARRY HINCHMAN
Hinchman, Harry Sibley b: 8/4/1878, Philadelphia, Pa. d: 1/19/33, Toledo, Ohio BB/TR, 5'11", 165 lbs. Deb: 7/29/07

YEAR	TM/L	G	AB	R	H	2B	3B	HR	RBI	BB	SO	AVG	OBP	SLG	PRO+	BR	/A	RC	SB	CS	SBR	FR	POS	TPR
1907	Cle-A	15	51	3	11	3	1	0	9	5		.216	.286	.314	92	-0	-0	6	2			4	2	0.4

■ BILL HINCHMAN
Hinchman, William White b: 4/4/1883, Philadelphia, Pa. d: 2/21/63, Columbus, Ohio BR/TR, 5'11", 190 lbs. Deb: 9/24/05 C

YEAR	TM/L	G	AB	R	H	2B	3B	HR	RBI	BB	SO	AVG	OBP	SLG	PRO+	BR	/A	RC	SB	CS	SBR	FR	POS	TPR
1905	Cin-N	17	51	10	13	4	1	0	10	13		.255	.406	.373	122	3	2	10	4			-2	O/31	0.0
1906	Cin-N	18	54	7	11	1	1	0	1	8		.204	.306	.259	75	-1	-1	5	2			1	O	0.0
1907	Cle-A	152	514	62	117	19	9	1	50	47		.228	.292	.305	92	-4	-4	54	15			-5	*O/12	-1.8
1908	Cle-A	137	464	55	107	23	8	6	59	38		.231	.289	.353	110	5	5	50	9			-6	OS/1	-0.4
1909	Cle-A	139	457	57	118	20	13	2	53	41		.258	.331	.372	117	11	9	64	22			1	*O/S	0.6
1915	Pit-N	156	577	72	177	33	14	5	77	48	75	.307	.368	.438	146	30	31	94	17	17	-5	-3	*O	2.0
1916	Pit-N	152	555	64	175	18	16	4	76	54	61	.315	.378	.427	146	31	31	96	10			-9	*O1	1.8
1917	Pit-N	69	244	27	46	5	5	2	29	33	27	.189	.288	.275	70	-7	-8	20	5			-1	O1	-1.2
1918	Pit-N	50	111	10	26	5	2	0	13	15	8	.234	.336	.315	96	0	-0	12	1			-1	O/1	-0.3
1920	Pit-N	18	16	0	3	0	0	0	1	1	3	.188	.278	.188	34	-1	-1	1	0	0	0	0	H	0.0
Total	10	908	3043	364	793	128	69	20	369	298	174	.261	.331	.368	117	67	62	404	85	17		-25	O/1S32	0.7

■ HUNKEY HINES
Hines, Henry Fred b: 9/29/1867, Elgin, Ill. d: 1/2/28, Rockford, Ill. BR/TR, 5'7", 165 lbs. Deb: 5/16/1895

YEAR	TM/L	G	AB	R	H	2B	3B	HR	RBI	BB	SO	AVG	OBP	SLG	PRO+	BR	/A	RC	SB	CS	SBR	FR	POS	TPR
1895	Bro-N	2	8	3	2	0	0	0	1	2	0	.250	.400	.250	78	-0	-0	1	0			0	/O	0.0

■ MIKE HINES
Hines, Michael P. b: 9/ 862, Reland d: 3/14/10, New Bedford, Mass. BR/TL, 5'10", 176 lbs. Deb: 5/01/1883

YEAR	TM/L	G	AB	R	H	2B	3B	HR	RBI	BB	SO	AVG	OBP	SLG	PRO+	BR	/A	RC	SB	CS	SBR	FR	POS	TPR
1883	Bos-N	63	231	38	52	13	1	0	16	7	36	.225	.248	.290	61	-10	-11	17				17	C/O	0.8
1884	Bos-N	35	132	16	23	3	0	0	3	3	24	.174	.193	.197	23	-11	-11	5				8	C	0.0
1885	Bos-N	14	56	11	13	4	0	0	4	4	5	.232	.283	.304	93	-1	-0	5				-3	O	-0.3
	Bro-a	3	13	1	1	0	1	0		0		.077	.077	.231	-5	-1	-2	0				0	/C	0.0
	Pro-N	1	3	0	0	0	0	0	0	0	2	.000	.000	.000	-99	-1	-1	0				0	/C	0.0
1888	Bos-N	4	16	3	2	0	1	0	2	2	0	.125	.222	.250	51	-1	-1	1	0			-0	/OC	0.0
Total	4	120	451	69	91	20	3	0	25	16	67	.202	.229	.259	51	-25	-25	28	0			22	/CO	0.5

■ PAUL HINES
Hines, Paul A. b: 3/1/1852, Washington, D.C. d: 7/10/35, Hyattsville, Md. BR/TR, 5'9.5", 173 lbs. Deb: 4/20/1872

YEAR	TM/L	G	AB	R	H	2B	3B	HR	RBI	BB	SO	AVG	OBP	SLG	PRO+	BR	/A	RC	SB	CS	SBR	FR	POS	TPR
1872	Nat-n	11	50	10	12	1	1	0		0		.240	.240	.300	56	-2	-4	4					1/3	-0.1
1873	Was-n	39	181	33	60	11	2	2		1		.331	.335	.448	132	6	7	28					*O/2C	0.6
1874	Chi-n	59	270	47	81	12	1	0		4		.300	.310	.352	109	3	3	30					*O2/S	0.2
1875	Chi-n	69	308	45	97	13	4	0		1		.315	.317	.383	140	12	12	38					O2	0.9
1876	Chi-N	64	305	62	101	21	3	2	59	1	3	.331	.333	.439	139	17	11	46				3	*O/2	1.2
1877	Chi-N	60	261	44	73	11	7	0	23	1	8	.280	.282	.375	94	1	-3	28				-7	*O2	-0.9
1878	Pro-N	62	257	42	92	13	4	4	50	2	10	.358	.363	.486	178	20	20	47				2	*O/S	1.6
1879	Pro-N	85	409	81	146	25	10	2	52	8	16	.357	.369	.482	181	33	34	75				5	*O	3.3
1880	Pro-N	85	374	64	115	20	2	3	35	13	17	.307	.331	.396	150	17	19	50				6	*O/21	2.0
1881	Pro-N	80	361	65	103	27	5	2	31	13	12	.285	.310	.404	125	9	10	46				-1	*O/21	0.7
1882	Pro-N	84	379	73	117	28	10	4	34	10	14	.309	.326	.467	151	21	21	59				-1	*O/1	1.6
1883	Pro-N	97	442	94	132	32	4	4	45	18	23	.299	.326	.416	120	12	10	61				3	*O/1	1.3
1884	*Pro-N	114	490	94	148	36	10	3	41	44	28	.302	.360	.435	152	28	29	78				-1	*O/1P	2.4
1885	Pro-N	98	411	63	111	20	4	1	35	19	18	.270	.302	.345	113	4	6	44				2	*O/1S32	0.4
1886	Was-N	121	487	80	152	30	8	9	56	35	21	.312	.358	.462	157	27	31	90	21			1	*O31/S2	2.9
1887	Was-N	123	478	83	147	32	5	10	72	48	24	.308	.380	.458	141	23	27	103	46			-17	*O/12S	0.8
1888	Ind-N	133	513	84	144	26	3	4	58	41	45	.281	.343	.366	126	18	16	77	31			-8	*O/1S	0.6
1889	Ind-N	121	486	77	148	27	1	6	72	49	22	.305	.374	.401	116	13	11	88	34			4	*1O	0.5
1890	Pit-N	31	121	11	22	1	0	0	9	11	7	.182	.256	.190	36	-10	-8	8	6			2	1O	-0.5
	Bos-N	69	273	41	72	12	3	2	48	32	20	.264	.350	.352	99	3	-1	38	9			-12	O/1	-1.2
	Yr	100	394	52	94	13	3	2	57	43	27	.239	.321	.302	82	-7	-8	44	15			-10		-1.7
1891	Was-a	54	206	25	58	7	5	0	31	21	16	.282	.376	.364	120	5	6	31	6			-3	O/1	0.1
Total	4 n	178	809	135	250	37	8	2		6		.309	.314	.382	121	19	18	100	0				0/21SC3	1.6
Total	16	1481	6253	1083	1881	368	84	56	751	366	304	.301	.343	.413	134	239	241	970	153			-22	*O1/23SP	16.8

■ GORDIE HINKLE
Hinkle, Daniel Gordon b: 4/3/05, Toronto, Ohio d: 3/19/72, Houston, Tex. BR/TR, 6', 185 lbs. Deb: 4/19/34

YEAR	TM/L	G	AB	R	H	2B	3B	HR	RBI	BB	SO	AVG	OBP	SLG	PRO+	BR	/A	RC	SB	CS	SBR	FR	POS	TPR
1934	Bos-A	27	75	7	13	6	1	0	9	7	23	.173	.244	.280	33	-8	-8	5	0	0	0	4	C	0.0

■ GEORGE HINSHAW
Hinshaw, George Addison b: 10/23/59, Los Angeles, Cal. BR/TR, 6', 185 lbs. Deb: 9/19/82

YEAR	TM/L	G	AB	R	H	2B	3B	HR	RBI	BB	SO	AVG	OBP	SLG	PRO+	BR	/A	RC	SB	CS	SBR	FR	POS	TPR
1982	SD-N	6	15	1	4	0	0	0	1	3	5	.267	.389	.267	91	-0	0	2	0	0	0	1	/O	0.0
1983	SD-N	7	16	1	7	1	0	0	4	0	4	.438	.438	.500	165	1	1	4	1	0	0	-0	/3	0.1
Total	2	13	31	2	11	1	0	0	5	3	9	.355	.412	.387	129	1	1	5	1	0	0	0	/O3	0.1

■ PAUL HINSON
Hinson, James Paul b: 5/9/04, Van Leer, Tenn. d: 9/23/60, Muskogee, Okla. BR/TR, 5'10", 150 lbs. Deb: 4/19/28

YEAR	TM/L	G	AB	R	H	2B	3B	HR	RBI	BB	SO	AVG	OBP	SLG	PRO+	BR	/A	RC	SB	CS	SBR	FR	POS	TPR
1928	Bos-A	3	0	1	0	0	0	0		0	0	—	—	—		0	0	0	0	0	0	0	R	0.0

■ CHUCK HINTON
Hinton, Charles Edward b: 5/3/34, Rocky Mount, N.C. BR/TR, 6'1", 180 lbs. Deb: 5/14/61

YEAR	TM/L	G	AB	R	H	2B	3B	HR	RBI	BB	SO	AVG	OBP	SLG	PRO+	BR	/A	RC	SB	CS	SBR	FR	POS	TPR
1961	Was-A	106	339	51	88	13	5	6	34	40	81	.260	.339	.381	93	-4	-3	47	22	5	4	-2	O	-0.4
1962	Was-A	151	542	73	168	25	6	17	75	47	66	.310	.365	.472	124	17	18	92	28	10	2	-6	*O2/S	1.0
1963	Was-A	150	566	80	152	20	12	15	55	64	79	.269	.344	.426	115	11	11	84	25	9	2	1	*O3/1S	1.1
1964	Was-A	138	514	71	141	25	7	11	53	57	77	.274	.348	.414	112	8	8	71	17	6	2	5	*O/3	1.0
1965	Cle-A	133	431	59	110	17	6	18	54	53	65	.255	.338	.448	120	12	11	68	17	3	3	-5	O12/3	0.7
1966	Cle-A	123	348	46	89	9	3	12	50	35	66	.256	.326	.402	108	3	3	45	10	6	-1	2	*O/12	0.1
1967	Cle-A	147	498	50	122	19	3	10	37	43	100	.245	.306	.355	94	-3	-4	53	6	8	-3	1	*O/2	-1.0
1968	Cal-A	116	267	28	52	10	3	7	23	24	61	.195	.261	.333	82	-7	-6	22	3	1	0	1	1O3/2	-0.8
1969	Cle-A	94	121	18	31	3	2	3	19	8	22	.256	.308	.388	91	-1	-2	15	2	0	1	-1	O3	-0.2
1970	Cle-A	107	195	24	62	4	0	9	29	25	34	.318	.395	.477	133	11	10	37	0	2	-1	-2	10/C23	0.4
1971	Cle-A	88	147	13	33	7	0	5	14	20	34	.224	.317	.374	87	-1	-2	18	0	0	0	-4	10/C	-0.8
Total	11	1353	3968	518	1048	152	47	113	443	416	685	.264	.335	.412	108	46	45	553	130	50	9	-10	O1/23CS	1.1

■ JOHN HINTON
Hinton, John Robert "Red" b: 6/20/1876, Pittsburg, Pa. d: 7/19/20, Braddock, Pa. BR/TR, 6', 200 lbs. Deb: 6/03/01

YEAR	TM/L	G	AB	R	H	2B	3B	HR	RBI	BB	SO	AVG	OBP	SLG	PRO+	BR	/A	RC	SB	CS	SBR	FR	POS	TPR
1901	Bos-N	4	13	0	1	0	0	0	0	2		.077	.200	.077	-15	-2	-2	0	0			-2	/3	-0.2

■ TOMMY HINZO
Hinzo, Thomas Lee b: 6/18/64, San Diego, Cal. BB/TR, 5'10", 170 lbs. Deb: 7/16/87

YEAR	TM/L	G	AB	R	H	2B	3B	HR	RBI	BB	SO	AVG	OBP	SLG	PRO+	BR	/A	RC	SB	CS	SBR	FR	POS	TPR
1987	Cle-A	67	257	31	68	9	3	3	21	10	47	.265	.297	.358	72	-10	-10	26	9	4	0	-4	2	-0.7
1989	Cle-A	18	17	4	0	0	0	0	0	2	6	.000	.105	.000	-67	-4	-4	0	1	2	-1	0	/2SD	-0.3
Total	2	85	274	35	68	9	3	3	21	12	53	.248	.285	.336	64	-14	-14	26	10	6	-1	-3	/2DS	-1.0

■ GENE HISER
Hiser, Gene Taylor b: 12/11/48, Baltimore, Md. BL/TL, 5'11", 175 lbs. Deb: 8/20/71

YEAR	TM/L	G	AB	R	H	2B	3B	HR	RBI	BB	SO	AVG	OBP	SLG	PRO+	BR	/A	RC	SB	CS	SBR	FR	POS	TPR
1971	Chi-N	17	29	4	6	0	0	0	1	4	8	.207	.303	.241	41	-2	-2	2	1	0	0	1	/O	-0.1
1972	Chi-N	32	46	2	9	0	0	0	4	6	8	.196	.288	.196	36	-3	-4	3	1	0	0	2	O	-0.2
1973	Chi-N	100	109	15	19	3	0	1	6	11	17	.174	.256	.229	33	-9	-10	7	4	5	-2	-1	O	-1.6
1974	Chi-N	12	17	2	4	1	0	0	1	0	3	.235	.235	.294	46	-1	-1	1	0	0	0	0	/O	0.0
1975	Chi-N	45	62	11	15	3	0	0	6	11	7	.242	.356	.290	77	-1	-1	7	0	1	-1	-0	O/1	-0.2
Total	5	206	263	34	53	7	0	1	18	32	43	.202	.291	.240	46	-17	-20	20	6	6	-2	2	O/1	-2.1

■ LARRY HISLE
Hisle, Larry Eugene b: 5/5/47, Portsmouth, Ohio BR/TR, 6'2", 193 lbs. Deb: 4/10/68

YEAR	TM/L	G	AB	R	H	2B	3B	HR	RBI	BB	SO	AVG	OBP	SLG	PRO+	BR	/A	RC	SB	CS	SBR	FR	POS	TPR
1968	Phi-N	7	11	1	4	1	0	0	1	1	4	.364	.417	.455	161	1	1	2	0	0	0	1	/O	0.1
1969	Phi-N	145	482	75	128	23	5	20	56	48	152	.266	.338	.459	125	13	14	75	18	8	1	6	*O	1.3
1970	Phi-N	126	405	52	83	22	4	10	44	53	139	.205	.302	.353	77	-15	-13	44	5	5	-2	0	*O	-1.9
1971	Phi-N	36	76	7	15	3	0	0	3	6	22	.197	.256	.237	40	-6	-6	4	1	0	0	2	O	-0.3
1973	Min-A	143	545	88	148	25	6	15	64	64	128	.272	.352	.422	113	13	10	82	11	4	1	13	*O	2.1
1974	Min-A	143	510	68	146	20	7	19	79	48	112	.286	.357	.465	130	22	20	83	12	6	0	-2	*O	1.4
1975	Min-A	80	255	37	80	9	2	11	51	27	39	.314	.382	.494	143	15	15	50	17	3	3	0	OD	1.7
1976	Min-A	155	581	81	158	19	5	14	96	56	93	.272	.340	.394	111	11	8	77	31	18	-2	11	*O	1.5
1977	Min-A	141	546	95	165	36	3	28	119	56	106	.302	.373	.533	146	32	33	107	21	10	0	-12	*O/D	1.7
1978	Mil-A	142	520	96	151	24	0	34	115	67	90	.290	.377	.533	153	36	36	103	10	6	-1	-8	OD	2.5
1979	Mil-A	26	96	18	27	7	0	3	14	11	19	.281	.355	.448	115	2	2	15	1	0	0	0	DO	0.2
1980	Mil-A	17	60	16	17	0	0	6	16	14	7	.283	.427	.583	180	7	7	16	1	1	-0	0	DO	0.6
1981	Mil-A	27	87	11	20	4	0	4	11	6	17	.230	.295	.414	108	-0	1	11	0	0	0	0	D	0.1
1982	Mil-A	9	31	7	4	0	0	2	5	5	13	.129	.250	.323	60	-2	-2	2	0	0	0	0	/D	-0.1
Total	14	1197	4205	652	1146	193	32	166	674	462	941	.273	.350	.452	123	129	126	671	128	61	2	10	*OD	10.9

■ JIM HITCHCOCK
Hitchcock, James Franklin b: 6/28/11, Inverness, Ala. d: 6/23/59, Montgomery, Ala. BR/TR, 5'11", 175 lbs. Deb: 8/24/38

YEAR	TM/L	G	AB	R	H	2B	3B	HR	RBI	BB	SO	AVG	OBP	SLG	PRO+	BR	/A	RC	SB	CS	SBR	FR	POS	TPR
1938	Bos-N	28	76	2	13	0	0	0	7	2	11	.171	.192	.171	1	-10	-9	2	1			-2	S/3	-0.9

■ BILLY HITCHCOCK
Hitchcock, William Clyde b: 7/31/16, Inverness, Ala. BR/TR, 6'1.5", 185 lbs. Deb: 4/14/42 MC

YEAR	TM/L	G	AB	R	H	2B	3B	HR	RBI	BB	SO	AVG	OBP	SLG	PRO+	BR	/A	RC	SB	CS	SBR	FR	POS	TPR
1942	Det-A	85	280	27	59	8	1	0	29	26	21	.211	.280	.246	45	-19	-22	20	2	2	-1	-3	S/3	-2.1
1946	Det-A	3	3	0	0	0	0	0	0	1	0	.000	.250	.000	-25	-0	-1	0	0	0	0	0	/2	0.0
	Was-A	98	354	27	75	8	3	0	25	26	52	.212	.268	.251	48	-26	-23	23	2	4	-2	-3	S3	-2.5
	Yr	101	357	27	75	8	3	0	25	27	52	.210	.268	.249	48	-26	-24	23	2	4	-2	-3		-2.5
1947	StL-A	80	275	25	61	2	2	1	28	21	34	.222	.277	.255	47	-19	-20	20	3	0	1	11	23/S1	-0.5
1948	Bos-A	49	124	15	37	3	2	1	20	7	9	.298	.341	.379	87	-2	-3	16	0	0	0	6	23	0.3
1949	Bos-A	55	147	22	30	6	1	0	9	17	11	.204	.291	.259	43	-12	-13	11	2	3	-1	-8	1/2	-2.1
1950	Phi-A	115	399	35	109	22	5	1	54	45	32	.273	.347	.361	83	-11	-10	45	3	1	0	-2	*2/S	-0.4
1951	Phi-A	77	222	27	68	10	4	1	36	21	23	.306	.371	.401	107	3	2	36	2	0	1	7	32/1	0.9
1952	Phi-A	119	407	45	100	8	4	1	56	39	45	.246	.318	.292	66	-15	-19	40	1	1	-0	-0	*31	-2.0
1953	Det-A	22	38	8	8	0	0	0	3	3	3	.211	.268	.211	31	-4	-4	2	0	0	0	-3	3/2S	-0.3
Total	9	703	2249	231	547	67	22	5	257	206	230	.243	.310	.299	65	-105	-110	212	15	11	-2	8	32S/1	-8.7

■ MYRIL HOAG
Hoag, Myril Oliver b: 3/9/08, Davis, Cal. d: 7/28/71, High Springs, Fla BR/TR, 5'11", 180 lbs. Deb: 4/15/31

YEAR	TM/L	G	AB	R	H	2B	3B	HR	RBI	BB	SO	AVG	OBP	SLG	PRO+	BR	/A	RC	SB	CS	SBR	FR	POS	TPR
1931	NY-A	44	28	6	4	2	0	0	3	1	8	.143	.172	.214	1	-4	-4	1	0	0	0	-7	O/3	-1.0
1932	*NY-A	46	54	18	20	5	0	1	7	7	13	.370	.443	.519	156	4	4	12	1	1	-0	1	O/1	0.4
1934	NY-A	97	251	45	67	8	2	3	34	21	21	.267	.324	.351	79	-10	-8	28	1	3	-2	5	O	-0.4
1935	NY-A	48	110	13	28	4	1	1	13	12	19	.255	.328	.336	76	-4	-4	13	4	2	0	2	O/3	-0.1
1936	NY-A	45	156	23	47	9	4	3	34	7	16	.301	.343	.468	102	-1	-0	25	3	1	0	-1	O	-0.1
1937	*NY-A	106	362	48	109	19	8	3	46	33	33	.301	.364	.423	97	-1	-2	55	4	7	-3	-5	O	-1.1
1938	*NY-A	85	267	28	74	14	3	0	48	25	31	.277	.344	.352	75	-10	-10	33	4	3	-1	-3	O	-1.1
1939	StL-A	129	482	58	142	23	4	10	75	24	35	.295	.329	.421	89	-8	-10	62	9	5	-0	-3	*O/P	-1.5
1940	StL-A	76	191	20	50	11	0	3	26	13	30	.262	.309	.366	73	-8	-8	22	2	0	1	-5	O	-1.4
1941	StL-A	1	1	0	0	0	0	0	0	0	0	.000	.000	.000	-97	-0	-0	0	0	0	0	0	H	0.0
	Chi-A	106	380	30	97	13	3	1	44	27	29	.255	.306	.313	65	-20	-19	34	6	10	-4	-3	O	-3.2
	Yr	107	381	30	97	13	3	1	44	27	29	.255	.306	.312	65	-20	-19	34	6	10	-4	-3		-3.2
1942	Chi-A	113	412	47	99	18	2	2	37	36	21	.240	.301	.308	73	-16	-15	38	17	8	0	-4	*O	-2.7
1944	Chi-A	17	48	5	11	1	0	0	4	10	1	.229	.362	.250	77	-1	-1	5	1	3	-2	-2	O	-0.2
	Cle-A	67	277	33	79	9	3	1	27	25	23	.285	.347	.350	103	0	1	35	6	4	-1	4	O	0.3
	Yr	84	325	38	90	10	3	1	31	35	24	.277	.349	.335	99	-1	-0	39	7	7	-2	4		0.1
1945	Cle-A	40	128	10	27	5	3	0	3	11	18	.211	.279	.297	70	-6	-5	11	1	2	-1	-6	O/P	-0.6
Total	13	1020	3147	384	854	141	33	28	401	252	298	.271	.328	.364	83	-85	-79	374	59	49	-12	-18	O/P31	-12.7

■ DON HOAK
Hoak, Donald Albert "Tiger" b: 2/5/28, Roulette, Pa. d: 10/9/69, Pittsburgh, Pa. BR/TR, 6'1", 170 lbs. Deb: 4/18/54 C

YEAR	TM/L	G	AB	R	H	2B	3B	HR	RBI	BB	SO	AVG	OBP	SLG	PRO+	BR	/A	RC	SB	CS	SBR	FR	POS	TPR
1954	Bro-N	88	261	41	64	9	5	5	26	25	39	.245	.321	.398	83	-6	-7	33	8	3	1	4	3	-0.1
1955	*Bro-N	94	279	50	67	13	3	5	19	46	50	.240	.350	.362	87	-3	-4	36	9	5	-0	17	3	1.2
1956	Chi-N	121	424	51	91	18	4	5	37	41	46	.215	.285	.311	61	-24	-23	40	8	3	1	-18	*3	-4.2
1957	Cin-N	149	529	78	155	39	2	19	89	74	54	.293	.384	.482	122	24	20	94	8	15	-7	-0	*3/2	1.6
1958	Cin-N	114	417	51	109	30	0	6	50	43	36	.261	.333	.376	83	-7	-10	50	6	8	-3	4	*3/S	-0.8
1959	Pit-N	155	564	60	166	29	3	8	65	71	75	.294	.377	.399	108	8	9	86	9	2	2	9	*3	1.5
1960	*Pit-N	155	553	97	156	24	9	16	79	74	74	.282	.368	.445	120	17	17	90	3	2	0	-3	*3	1.9
1961	Pit-N	145	503	72	150	27	7	12	61	73	53	.298	.390	.451	122	18	18	90	4	2	0	-3	*3	0.8
1962	Pit-N	121	411	63	99	14	8	5	48	49	49	.241	.323	.350	81	-11	-11	44	4	2	0	-2	*3	-1.0
1963	Phi-N	115	377	35	87	11	3	6	24	27	52	.231	.284	.324	75	-12	-12	32	5	5	-2	6	*3	-0.6
1964	Phi-N	6	4	0	0	0	0	0	0	0	2	.000	.000	.000	-99	-1	-1	0	0	0	0	0	H	0.0
Total	11	1263	4322	598	1144	214	44	89	498	523	530	.265	.347	.396	98	4	-4	597	64	47	-9	21	*3/S2	0.3

■ BILL HOBBS
Hobbs, William Lee "Smokey" b: 5/7/1893, Grant's Lick, Ky. d: 1/5/45, Hamilton, Ohio BR/TR, 5'9.5", 155 lbs. Deb: 8/09/13

YEAR	TM/L	G	AB	R	H	2B	3B	HR	RBI	BB	SO	AVG	OBP	SLG	PRO+	BR	/A	RC	SB	CS	SBR	FR	POS	TPR
1913	Cin-N	4	4	0	0	0	0	0	0	0	3	.000	.000	.000	-99	-1	-1	0	0			1	/23	0.0
1916	Cin-N	6	11	1	2	1	0	0	1	2	0	.182	.308	.273	81	-0	-0	1	1			6	/S	0.6
Total	2	10	15	1	2	1	0	0	1	2	3	.133	.235	.200	32	-1	-1	1	1			6	/S32	0.6

■ DOC HOBLITZEL
Hoblitzel, Richard Carleton (b: Richard Carleton Hoblitzell) b: 10/26/1888, Waverly, W.Va. d: 11/14/62, Parkersburg, W.Va. BR/TR, 6', 172 lbs. Deb: 9/05/08

YEAR	TM/L	G	AB	R	H	2B	3B	HR	RBI	BB	SO	AVG	OBP	SLG	PRO+	BR	/A	RC	SB	CS	SBR	FR	POS	TPR
1908	Cin-N	32	114	8	29	3	2	0	8	7		.254	.298	.316	101	-0	-0	11	2			2	1	0.1
1909	Cin-N	142	517	59	159	23	11	4	67	44		.308	.364	.418	144	24	25	86	17			-3	*1	2.1
1910	Cin-N	155	611	85	170	24	13	4	70	47	32	.278	.332	.380	112	4	7	85	28			-8	*1/2	-0.1
1911	Cin-N	158	622	81	180	19	13	11	91	42	44	.289	.342	.415	116	7	10	98	32			2	*1	0.6
1912	Cin-N	148	558	73	164	32	12	2	85	48	28	.294	.352	.405	110	4	7	88	23			2	*1	0.2
1913	Cin-N	137	502	59	143	23	7	3	62	35	26	.285	.334	.376	103	1	1	67	18			-5	*1	-1.0
1914	Cin-N	78	248	31	52	8	7	0	26	26	26	.210	.287	.298	72	-8	-9	24	7			-4	*1	-1.5
	Bos-A	69	229	31	73	10	3	0	33	19	21	.319	.386	.389	133	9	9	35	12	12	-4	-5	1	0.1
1915	*Bos-A	124	399	54	113	15	12	2	61	38	26	.283	.351	.396	128	11	12	57	9	14	-6	-1	*1	0.0
1916	*Bos-A	130	417	57	108	17	1	0	39	47	28	.259	.338	.305	93	-2	-3	50	10			-1	*1	-0.6
1917	Bos-A	120	420	49	108	19	7	1	47	46	22	.257	.336	.343	108	4	4	53	12			-8	*1	-0.8
1918	Bos-A	25	69	4	11	1	0	0	4	9	4	.159	.266	.174	33	-5	-5	4	3			1	1	-0.5
Total	11	1318	4706	591	1310	194	88	27	593	407	256	.278	.340	.374	111	49	59	658	173	26		-28	*1/2	-1.4

■ BUTCH HOBSON
Hobson, Clell Lavern b: 8/17/51, Tuscaloosa, Ala. BR/TR, 6'1", 193 lbs. Deb: 9/07/75

YEAR	TM/L	G	AB	R	H	2B	3B	HR	RBI	BB	SO	AVG	OBP	SLG	PRO+	BR	/A	RC	SB	CS	SBR	FR	POS	TPR
1975	Bos-A	2	4	0	1	0	0	0	0	0	2	.250	.250	.250	38	-0	-0	0	0	0	0	1	/3	0.0
1976	Bos-A	76	269	34	63	7	5	8	34	15	62	.234	.275	.387	82	-4	-8	26	0	1	-1	-7	3	-1.6
1977	Bos-A	159	593	77	157	33	5	30	112	27	162	.265	.301	.489	100	6	-3	80	5	4	-1	-28	*3	-3.4
1978	Bos-A	147	512	65	128	26	2	17	80	50	122	.250	.317	.408	92	1	-6	65	1	0	0	-14	*3D	-2.0

YEAR	TM/L	G	AB	R	H	2B	3B	HR	RBI	BB	SO	AVG	OBP	SLG	PRO+	BR	/A	RC	SB	CS	SBR	FR	POS	TPR
1979	Bos-A	146	528	74	138	26	7	28	93	30	78	.261	.301	.496	105	5	1	70	3	2	-0	-21	*3/2	-1.6
1980	Bos-A	93	324	35	74	6	0	11	39	25	69	.228	.284	.349	69	-13	-15	30	1	1	-0	-9	3D	-2.3
1981	Cal-A	85	268	27	63	7	4	4	36	35	60	.235	.326	.336	91	-2	-2	31	1	1	-0	-11	3/D	-1.4
1982	NY-A	30	58	2	10	2	0	0	3	1	14	.172	.186	.207	8	-7	-7	2	0	0	0	-0	D1	-0.7
Total	8	738	2556	314	634	107	23	98	397	183	569	.248	.300	.423	91	-15	-40	305	11	9	-2	-89	3/D12	-13.0

■ ED HOCK

Hock, Edward Francis   b: 3/27/1899, Franklin Furnace, Ohio   d: 11/21/63, Portsmouth, Ohio   BL/TL, 5'10.5", 165 lbs.   Deb: 7/08/20

YEAR	TM/L	G	AB	R	H	2B	3B	HR	RBI	BB	SO	AVG	OBP	SLG	PRO+	BR	/A	RC	SB	CS	SBR	FR	POS	TPR
1920	StL-N	1	0	0	0	0	0	0	0	0	0	—	—	—	—	0	0	0	0	0	0	0	/O	0.0
1923	Cin-N	2	0	0	0	0	0	0	0	0	0	—	—	—	—	0	0	0	0	0	0	0	R	0.0
1924	Cin-N	16	10	7	1	0	0	0	0	0	2	.100	.182	.100	-23	-2	-2	0	0	0	0	2	/O	0.0
Total	3	19	10	7	1	0	0	0	0	0	2	.100	.182	.100	-23	-2	-2	0	0	0	0	2	/O	0.0

■ ORIS HOCKETT

Hockett, Oris Leon "Brown"   b: 9/29/09, Amboy, Ind.   d: 3/23/69, Torrance, Cal.   BL/TR, 5'9", 182 lbs.   Deb: 9/04/38

YEAR	TM/L	G	AB	R	H	2B	3B	HR	RBI	BB	SO	AVG	OBP	SLG	PRO+	BR	/A	RC	SB	CS	SBR	FR	POS	TPR
1938	Bro-N	21	70	8	23	5	1	1	8	4	9	.329	.365	.471	126	3	2	13	0			-3	O	0.0
1939	Bro-N	9	13	3	3	0	0	0	1	1	1	.231	.286	.231	39	-1	-1	1	0			0	/O	0.0
1941	Cle-A	2	6	0	2	0	0	0	1	2	0	.333	.500	.333	131	0	0	1	0	0	0	-1	/O	0.0
1942	Cle-A	148	601	85	150	22	7	7	48	45	45	.250	.305	.344	88	-15	-11	63	12	12	-4	-4	*O	-2.9
1943	Cle-A	141	601	70	166	33	4	2	51	45	45	.276	.331	.354	107	-0	4	69	13	18	-7	-3	*O	-1.0
1944	Cle-A	124	457	47	132	29	5	1	50	35	27	.289	.339	.381	110	3	5	59	8	9	-3	-11	*O	-1.2
1945	Chi-A	106	417	46	122	23	4	2	55	27	30	.293	.340	.381	114	4	5	52	10	9	-2	-1	*O	-0.2
Total	7	551	2165	259	598	112	21	13	214	159	157	.276	.329	.365	103	-7	4	258	43	<u>48</u>		-21	O	-5.3

■ JOHNNY HODAPP

Hodapp, Urban John   b: 9/26/05, Cincinnati, Ohio   d: 6/14/80, Cincinnati, Ohio   BR/TR, 6', 185 lbs.   Deb: 8/19/25

YEAR	TM/L	G	AB	R	H	2B	3B	HR	RBI	BB	SO	AVG	OBP	SLG	PRO+	BR	/A	RC	SB	CS	SBR	FR	POS	TPR
1925	Cle-A	37	130	12	31	5	1	0	14	11	7	.238	.298	.292	50	-10	-10	12	2	2	-1	3	3	-0.4
1926	Cle-A	3	5	0	1	0	0	0	0	0	1	.200	.200	.200	4	-1	-1	0	0	0	0	-1	/3	0.0
1927	Cle-A	79	240	25	73	15	3	5	40	14	23	.304	.343	.454	105	1	1	35	2	2	-1	1	3/1	0.5
1928	Cle-A	116	449	51	145	31	6	2	73	20	20	.323	.352	.432	104	2	2	68	2	1	0	-2	*31	0.0
1929	Cle-A	90	294	30	96	12	7	4	51	15	14	.327	.361	.456	105	3	2	47	3	3	-1	5	2	0.7
1930	Cle-A	154	635	111	**225**	51	8	9	121	32	29	.354	.386	.502	119	21	18	120	6	5	-1	12	*2	2.7
1931	Cle-A	122	468	71	138	19	4	2	56	27	23	.295	.336	.365	80	-11	-14	56	1	5	-3	16	*2	0.6
1932	Cle-A	7	16	2	2	1	0	0	0	0	2	.125	.125	.188	-19	-3	-3	0	0	0	0	-2	/2	-0.4
	Chi-A	68	176	21	40	8	0	3	20	11	3	.227	.273	.324	58	-12	-11	16	1	0	0	-5	O/23	-1.4
	Yr	75	192	23	42	9	0	3	20	11	5	.219	.261	.313	51	-15	-14	16	1	0	0	-7		-1.8
1933	Bos-A	115	413	55	129	27	5	3	54	33	14	.312	.365	.424	109	5	5	64	1	1	-0	3	*21	0.5
Total	9	791	2826	378	880	169	34	28	429	163	136	.311	.350	.425	98	-4	-12	419	18	19	-6	30	23/O1	2.8

■ MEL HODERLEIN

Hoderlein, Melvin Anthony   b: 6/24/23, Mt.Carmel, Ohio   BB/TR, 5'10", 185 lbs.   Deb: 8/16/51

YEAR	TM/L	G	AB	R	H	2B	3B	HR	RBI	BB	SO	AVG	OBP	SLG	PRO+	BR	/A	RC	SB	CS	SBR	FR	POS	TPR
1951	Bos-A	9	14	1	5	1	1	0	1	6	2	.357	.550	.571	185	3	2	4	0	1	-1	1	/23	0.3
1952	Was-A	72	208	16	56	8	2	0	17	18	22	.269	.333	.327	87	-4	-3	20	2	0	1	-1	2	-0.1
1953	Was-A	23	47	5	9	0	0	0	5	6	9	.191	.283	.191	31	-4	-4	3	0	0	0	-3	2/S	-0.6
1954	Was-A	14	25	0	4	1	0	0	1	1	4	.160	.192	.200	8	-3	-3	1	0	0	0	1	/S2	0.0
Total	4	118	294	22	74	10	3	0	24	31	37	.252	.327	.306	78	-9	-8	28	2	1	0	-2	/2S3	-0.4

■ CHARLIE HODES

Hodes, Charles   b: 1848, New York, N.Y.   d: 2/14/1875, Brooklyn, N.Y.   5'11.5", 175 lbs.   Deb: 5/08/1871

YEAR	TM/L	G	AB	R	H	2B	3B	HR	RBI	BB	SO	AVG	OBP	SLG	PRO+	BR	/A	RC	SB	CS	SBR	FR	POS	TPR
1871	Chi-n	28	130	32	36	4	1	2	25	7	0	.277	.314	.369	86	-1	-4	16	3				C/3OS	-0.3
1872	Tro-n	13	65	17	15	5	0	0		1		.231	.242	.308	67	-2	-3	5					/SOC3	-0.1
1874	Atl-n	22	82	8	13	2	1	0		0		.159	.159	.207	17	-7	-6	3					O/2	-0.3
Total	3 n	63	277	57	64	11	2	2		8		.231	.253	.307	66	-10	-12	24					/OC3S2	-0.7

■ BERT HODGE

Hodge, Edward Burton   b: 5/25/17, Knoxville, Tenn.   BL/TR, 5'11", 170 lbs.   Deb: 4/14/42

YEAR	TM/L	G	AB	R	H	2B	3B	HR	RBI	BB	SO	AVG	OBP	SLG	PRO+	BR	/A	RC	SB	CS	SBR	FR	POS	TPR
1942	Phi-N	8	11	0	2	0	0	0	0	1	0	.182	.250	.182	29	-1	-1	0	0			-0	/3	-0.1

■ GOMER HODGE

Hodge, Harold Morris   b: 4/3/44, Rutherfordton, N.C.   BB/TR, 6'2", 185 lbs.   Deb: 4/06/71

YEAR	TM/L	G	AB	R	H	2B	3B	HR	RBI	BB	SO	AVG	OBP	SLG	PRO+	BR	/A	RC	SB	CS	SBR	FR	POS	TPR
1971	Cle-A	80	83	3	17	3	0	1	9	4	19	.205	.258	.277	47	-5	-6	6	0	0	0	-2	/132	-0.8

■ GIL HODGES

Hodges, Gilbert Raymond (b: Gilbert Ray Hodge)   b: 4/4/24, Princeton, Ind.   d: 4/2/72, West Palm Beach, Fla   BR/TR, 6'1.5", 200 lbs.   Deb: 10/03/43   M

YEAR	TM/L	G	AB	R	H	2B	3B	HR	RBI	BB	SO	AVG	OBP	SLG	PRO+	BR	/A	RC	SB	CS	SBR	FR	POS	TPR
1943	Bro-N	1	2	0	0	0	0	0	0	1	2	.000	.333	.000	0	-0	-0	0	1			0	/3	0.0
1947	*Bro-N	28	77	9	12	3	1	1	7	14	19	.156	.286	.260	44	-6	-6	6	0			-2	C	-0.7
1948	Bro-N	134	481	48	120	18	5	11	70	43	61	.249	.311	.376	82	-11	-13	56	7			-0	1C	-1.0
1949	*Bro-N	156	596	94	170	23	4	23	115	66	64	.285	.360	.453	112	14	11	99	10			-4	*1	0.6
1950	Bro-N	153	561	98	159	26	2	32	113	73	73	.283	.367	.508	125	22	20	105	6			1	*1	1.4
1951	Bro-N	158	582	118	156	25	3	40	103	93	99	.268	.374	.527	137	32	31	119	9	7	-2	7	*1	3.3
1952	*Bro-N	153	508	87	129	27	1	32	102	107	90	.254	.386	.500	142	32	32	106	2	4	-2	5	*1	3.0
1953	Bro-N	141	520	101	157	22	7	31	122	75	84	.302	.393	.550	139	33	31	119	1	4	-2	8	*1O	3.2
1954	Bro-N	154	579	106	176	23	5	42	130	74	84	.304	.384	.579	142	38	36	128	3	3	-1	9	*1	3.7
1955	*Bro-N	150	546	75	158	24	5	27	102	80	91	.289	.383	.500	128	26	24	105	2	1	0	3	*1O	1.6
1956	*Bro-N	153	550	86	146	29	4	32	87	76	91	.265	.355	.507	119	22	16	97	3	3	-1	2	*1O/C	1.0
1957	Bro-N	150	579	94	173	28	7	27	98	63	91	.299	.370	.511	122	27	20	109	5	3	-0	2	*1/32	0.8
1958	LA-N	141	475	68	123	15	1	22	64	52	87	.259	.332	.434	98	0	-2	67	8	2	1	2	*13/OC	-0.6
1959	*LA-N	124	413	57	114	19	2	25	80	58	92	.276	.369	.513	123	19	15	77	3	2	-0	0	*1/3	0.6
1960	LA-N	101	197	22	39	8	1	8	30	26	37	.198	.295	.371	76	-5	-7	22	0	1	-1	1	13	-1.0
1961	LA-N	109	215	25	52	4	0	8	31	24	43	.242	.318	.372	76	-5	-8	26	3	1	0	0	*1	-1.2
1962	NY-N	54	127	15	32	1	0	9	17	15	27	.252	.331	.472	111	2	2	19	0	0	0	3	1	0.4
1963	NY-N	11	22	2	5	0	0	0	3	3	2	.227	.320	.227	60	-1	-1	2	0	0	0	2	1	0.1
Total	18	2071	7030	1105	1921	295	48	370	1274	943	1137	.273	.361	.487	119	238	200	1261	63	<u>31</u>		40	*1/OC32	15.2

■ RON HODGES

Hodges, Ronald Wray   b: 6/22/49, Rocky Mount, Va.   BL/TR, 6'1", 185 lbs.   Deb: 6/13/73

YEAR	TM/L	G	AB	R	H	2B	3B	HR	RBI	BB	SO	AVG	OBP	SLG	PRO+	BR	/A	RC	SB	CS	SBR	FR	POS	TPR
1973	*NY-N	45	127	5	33	2	0	1	18	11	19	.260	.319	.299	73	-5	-4	11	0	1	-1	2	C	0.0
1974	NY-N	59	136	16	30	4	0	4	14	19	11	.221	.316	.338	84	-3	-3	15	0	0	0	-1	C	-0.1
1975	NY-N	9	34	3	7	1	0	2	4	1	6	.206	.229	.412	79	-1	-1	3	0	0	0	0	/C	0.0
1976	NY-N	56	155	21	35	6	0	4	24	27	16	.226	.341	.342	100	1	1	19	2	0	1	-9	C	-0.5
1977	NY-N	66	117	6	31	4	0	1	5	9	17	.265	.317	.325	76	-4	-4	12	0	2	-1	0	C	-0.4
1978	NY-N	47	102	4	26	4	1	0	7	10	11	.255	.327	.314	83	-3	-2	10	1	2	-1	7	C	0.5
1979	NY-N	59	86	4	14	4	0	0	5	19	16	.163	.314	.209	47	-6	-5	7	0	0	0	1	C	-0.3
1980	NY-N	36	42	4	10	2	0	0	5	10	13	.238	.385	.286	92	0	0	5	1	1	-0	4	/C	0.4
1981	NY-N	35	43	5	13	2	0	1	6	5	8	.302	.375	.419	127	1	2	7	1	0	0	-1	/C	0.1
1982	NY-N	80	228	26	56	12	1	5	27	41	40	.246	.361	.373	106	3	3	32	4	3	-1	1	C	0.2
1983	NY-N	110	250	20	65	12	0	1	21	49	42	.260	.385	.308	95	1	1	31	0	3	-2	-11	C	-0.8
1984	NY-N	64	106	5	22	3	0	1	11	23	18	.208	.354	.264	77	-2	-2	11	1	1	-0	-0	C	-0.1
Total	12	666	1426	119	342	56	2	19	147	224	217	.240	.345	.322	88	-19	-15	165	10	13	-5	-9	C	-1.0

■ RALPH HODGIN

Hodgin, Elmer Ralph   b: 2/10/16, Greensboro, N.C.   BL/TR, 5'10", 167 lbs.   Deb: 4/19/39

YEAR	TM/L	G	AB	R	H	2B	3B	HR	RBI	BB	SO	AVG	OBP	SLG	PRO+	BR	/A	RC	SB	CS	SBR	FR	POS	TPR
1939	Bos-N	32	48	4	10	1	0	0	4	3	4	.208	.255	.229	33	-5	-4	2	0			-0	/O	-0.4
1943	Chi-A	117	407	52	128	22	8	1	50	20	24	.314	.356	.415	125	12	12	59	3	5	-2	-6	3O	0.3

YEAR	TM/L	G	AB	R	H	2B	3B	HR	RBI	BB	SO	AVG	OBP	SLG	PRO+	BR	/A	RC	SB	CS	SBR	FR	POS	TPR
1944	Chi-A	121	465	56	137	25	7	1	51	21	14	.295	.333	.385	106	2	2	60	3	1	0	10	3O	1.2
1946	Chi-A	87	258	32	65	10	1	0	25	19	6	.252	.308	.298	73	-10	-9	23	0	1	-1	-6	O	-1.9
1947	Chi-A	59	180	26	53	10	3	1	24	13	4	.294	.352	.400	113	2	3	25	1	0	0	-1	O	0.0
1948	Chi-A	114	331	28	88	11	5	1	34	21	11	.266	.310	.338	75	-14	-12	33	0	3	-2	0	O	-1.5
Total	6	530	1689	198	481	79	24	4	188	97	63	.285	.330	.367	98	-13	-9	203	7	10		-3	O3	-2.3

■ PAUL HODGSON   Hodgson, Paul Joseph Denis   b: 4/14/60, Montreal, Que., Can.   BR/TR, 6'2", 190 lbs.   Deb: 8/31/80

YEAR	TM/L	G	AB	R	H	2B	3B	HR	RBI	BB	SO	AVG	OBP	SLG	PRO+	BR	/A	RC	SB	CS	SBR	FR	POS	TPR
1980	Tor-A	20	41	5	9	0	1	1	5	3	12	.220	.273	.341	64	-2	-2	3	0	1	-1	1	O/D	-0.1

■ ART HOELSKOETTER   Hoelskoetter, Arthur "Holley" or "Hoss" (a.k.a. Arthur H. Hostetter)   b: 9/30/1882, St.Louis, Mo.   d: 8/3/54, St.Louis, Mo.   BR/TR, 6'2",   Deb: 9/10/05

YEAR	TM/L	G	AB	R	H	2B	3B	HR	RBI	BB	SO	AVG	OBP	SLG	PRO+	BR	/A	RC	SB	CS	SBR	FR	POS	TPR
1905	StL-N	24	83	7	20	2	1	0	5	3		.241	.267	.289	70	-3	-3	7	1			1	3/2P	0.0
1906	StL-N	94	317	21	71	6	3	0	14	4		.224	.234	.262	58	-17	-15	21	2			-5	3SPO/2	-2.1
1907	StL-N	119	397	21	98	6	3	2	28	27		.247	.295	.292	89	-7	-5	38	5			10	21/COP3	0.6
1908	StL-N	62	155	10	36	7	1	0	6	6		.232	.261	.290	82	-4	-3	12	1			1	C/312	0.0
Total	4	299	952	59	225	21	8	2	53	40		.236	.267	.282	76	-31	-27	78	9			6	/23C1OSP	-1.5

■ JACK HOEY   Hoey, John Bernard   b: 11/10/1881, Watertown, Mass.   d: 11/14/47, Waterbury, Conn.   BL/TL, 5'9", 185 lbs.   Deb: 6/27/06

YEAR	TM/L	G	AB	R	H	2B	3B	HR	RBI	BB	SO	AVG	OBP	SLG	PRO+	BR	/A	RC	SB	CS	SBR	FR	POS	TPR
1906	Bos-A	94	361	27	88	8	4	0	24	14		.244	.272	.288	77	-10	-10	33	10			-7	O	-2.2
1907	Bos-A	39	96	7	21	2	1	0	8	1		.219	.272	.260	57	-5	-5	6	2			-5	O	-1.2
1908	Bos-A	13	43	5	7	0	0	0	3	0		.163	.163	.163	7	-4	-4	1	1			0	O	-0.5
Total	3	146	500	39	116	10	5	0	35	15		.232	.254	.272	67	-19	-19	41	13			-13	O	-3.9

■ STEW HOFFERTH   Hofferth, Stewart Edward   b: 1/27/13, Logansport, Ind.   BR/TR, 6'2", 195 lbs.   Deb: 4/19/44

YEAR	TM/L	G	AB	R	H	2B	3B	HR	RBI	BB	SO	AVG	OBP	SLG	PRO+	BR	/A	RC	SB	CS	SBR	FR	POS	TPR
1944	Bos-N	66	180	14	36	8	0	1	26	11	5	.200	.246	.261	41	-14	-15	10	0			0	C	-1.2
1945	Bos-N	50	170	13	40	2	0	3	15	14	11	.235	.297	.300	66	-8	-8	15	1			6	C	0.0
1946	Bos-N	20	58	3	12	1	1	0	10	3	6	.207	.246	.259	43	-4	-5	4	0			-1	C	-0.5
Total	3	136	408	30	88	11	1	4	51	28	22	.216	.268	.277	52	-26	-27	30	1			5	C	-1.7

■ DUTCH HOFFMAN   Hoffman, Clarence Casper "Red"   b: 1/28/04, Freeburg, Ill.   d: 12/6/62, Belleville, Ill.   BR/TR, 6', 175 lbs.   Deb: 4/23/29

YEAR	TM/L	G	AB	R	H	2B	3B	HR	RBI	BB	SO	AVG	OBP	SLG	PRO+	BR	/A	RC	SB	CS	SBR	FR	POS	TPR
1929	Chi-A	107	337	27	87	16	5	3	37	24	28	.258	.307	.362	73	-15	-14	38	6	3	0	-1	O	-1.7

■ DANNY HOFFMAN   Hoffman, Daniel John   b: 3/2/1880, Canaan, Conn.   d: 3/14/22, Manchester, Conn.   BL/TL, 5'9", 175 lbs.   Deb: 4/20/03

YEAR	TM/L	G	AB	R	H	2B	3B	HR	RBI	BB	SO	AVG	OBP	SLG	PRO+	BR	/A	RC	SB	CS	SBR	FR	POS	TPR
1903	Phi-A	74	248	29	61	5	7	2	22	6		.246	.264	.347	80	-5	-7	26	7			0	O/P	-1.0
1904	Phi-A	53	204	31	61	7	5	3	24	5		.299	.316	.426	129	7	6	32	9			0	O	0.4
1905	*Phi-A	120	459	66	120	10	10	1	35	33		.261	.311	.333	105	3	2	65	46			-2	*O	-0.5
1906	Phi-A	7	22	4	5	0	0	0	0	3		.227	.320	.227	72	-0	-1	3	1			1	/O	0.0
	NY-A	100	320	34	82	10	6	0	23	27		.256	.314	.325	93	1	-3	45	32			-9	O	-1.6
	Yr	107	342	38	87	10	6	0	23	30		.254	.315	.319	91	1	-3	47	33			-8		-1.6
1907	NY-A	136	517	81	131	10	3	5	46	42		.253	.309	.313	93	1	-4	62	30			8	*O	-0.3
1908	StL-A	99	363	41	91	9	7	1	25	23		.251	.295	.322	102	1	1	39	17			11	O	0.7
1909	StL-A	110	387	44	104	6	7	2	26	41		.269	.349	.336	125	9	12	53	24			2	*O	1.0
1910	StL-A	106	380	20	90	11	5	0	27	34		.237	.306	.292	93	-5	-2	38	16			0	*O	-0.7
1911	StL-A	24	81	11	17	3	2	0	7	12		.210	.326	.296	77	-3	-2	9	3			3	O	0.0
Total	9	829	2981	361	762	71	52	14	235	226		.256	.311	.328	101	8	3	371	185			14	O/P	-2.0

■ TEX HOFFMAN   Hoffman, Edward Adolph   b: 11/30/1893, San Antonio, Tex.   d: 5/19/47, New Orleans, La.   BL/TR, 5'9", 195 lbs.   Deb: 7/11/15

YEAR	TM/L	G	AB	R	H	2B	3B	HR	RBI	BB	SO	AVG	OBP	SLG	PRO+	BR	/A	RC	SB	CS	SBR	FR	POS	TPR
1915	Cle-A	9	13	1	2	0	0	0	2	1	5	.154	.214	.154	10	-1	-1	1	0			-2	/3	-0.2

■ GLENN HOFFMAN   Hoffman, Glenn Edward   b: 7/7/58, Orange, Cal.   BR/TR, 6'1", 175 lbs.   Deb: 4/12/80

YEAR	TM/L	G	AB	R	H	2B	3B	HR	RBI	BB	SO	AVG	OBP	SLG	PRO+	BR	/A	RC	SB	CS	SBR	FR	POS	TPR
1980	Bos-A	114	312	37	89	15	4	4	42	19	41	.285	.330	.397	94	-1	-3	39	2	4	-2	0	*3/S2	-0.4
1981	Bos-A	78	242	28	56	10	0	1	20	12	25	.231	.271	.285	57	-12	-14	18	0	1	-1	5	S/3	-0.3
1982	Bos-A	150	469	53	98	23	2	7	49	30	69	.209	.264	.311	54	-28	-31	35	0	4	-2	13	*S	-0.7
1983	Bos-A	143	473	56	123	24	1	4	41	30	76	.260	.307	.340	73	-14	-19	51	1	1	-0	-6	*S	-1.6
1984	Bos-A	64	74	8	14	4	0	0	4	5	10	.189	.241	.243	33	-7	-7	4	0	1	-1	5	S/32	0.2
1985	Bos-A	96	279	40	77	17	2	6	34	25	40	.276	.346	.416	103	3	2	40	2	2	-1	-1	S/23	0.7
1986	Bos-A	12	23	1	5	2	0	0	1	2	3	.217	.280	.304	59	-1	-1	2	0	0	0	-2	S/3	-0.2
1987	Bos-A	21	55	5	11	3	0	0	6	3	9	.200	.267	.255	38	-5	-5	4	0	0	0	0	S/32	-0.1
	LA-N	40	132	10	29	5	0	0	10	7	23	.220	.270	.258	42	-11	-11	9	0	1	-1	1	S	-0.4
1989	Cal-A	48	104	9	22	3	0	1	3	3	13	.212	.241	.269	44	-8	-8	6	0	2	-1	6	S3/21D	0.0
Total	9	766	2163	247	524	106	9	23	210	136	309	.242	.293	.331	68	-84	-97	207	5	16	-8	25	S3/2D1	-2.8

■ IZZY HOFFMAN   Hoffman, Harry C.   b: 1/5/1875, Bridgeport, N.J.   d: 11/13/42, Philadelphia, Pa.   BL/TL,   Deb: 4/14/04

YEAR	TM/L	G	AB	R	H	2B	3B	HR	RBI	BB	SO	AVG	OBP	SLG	PRO+	BR	/A	RC	SB	CS	SBR	FR	POS	TPR
1904	Was-A	10	30	1	3	1	0	0	1	2		.100	.156	.133	-7	-4	-3	1	0			1	/O	-0.3
1907	Bos-N	19	86	17	24	3	1	0	3	6		.279	.326	.337	110	1	1	10	2			-1	O	0.0
Total	2	29	116	18	27	4	1	0	4	8		.233	.282	.284	80	-3	-3	11	2			-1	/O	-0.3

■ JOHN HOFFMAN   Hoffman, John Edward "Pork Chop"   b: 10/31/43, Aberdeen, S.D.   BL/TL, 6', 190 lbs.   Deb: 7/30/64

YEAR	TM/L	G	AB	R	H	2B	3B	HR	RBI	BB	SO	AVG	OBP	SLG	PRO+	BR	/A	RC	SB	CS	SBR	FR	POS	TPR
1964	Hou-N	6	15	1	1	0	0	0	0	1	7	.067	.125	.067	-47	-3	-3	0	0	0	0	-2	/C	-0.4
1965	Hou-N	2	6	1	2	0	0	0	1	0	3	.333	.333	.333	95	-0	-0	1	0	0	0	-1	/C	0.0
Total	2	8	21	2	3	0	0	0	1	1	10	.143	.182	.143	-8	-3	-3	1	0	0	0	-2	/C	-0.4

■ LARRY HOFFMAN   Hoffman, Lawrence Charles   b: 7/18/1878, Chicago, Ill.   d: 12/29/48, Chicago, Ill.   BR/TR,   Deb: 7/09/01

YEAR	TM/L	G	AB	R	H	2B	3B	HR	RBI	BB	SO	AVG	OBP	SLG	PRO+	BR	/A	RC	SB	CS	SBR	FR	POS	TPR
1901	Chi-N	6	22	2	7	1	0	0	6	0		.318	.348	.364	113	0	0	3	1			-2	/32	0.0

■ HICKEY HOFFMAN   Hoffman, Otto Charles   b: 10/27/1856, Cleveland, Ohio   d: 10/27/15, Peoria, Ill.   Deb: 5/10/1879

YEAR	TM/L	G	AB	R	H	2B	3B	HR	RBI	BB	SO	AVG	OBP	SLG	PRO+	BR	/A	RC	SB	CS	SBR	FR	POS	TPR
1879	Cle-N	2	6	0	0	0	0	0	0	0	3	.000	.000	.000	-99	-1	-1	0				2	/CO	0.1

■ RAY HOFFMAN   Hoffman, Raymond Lamont   b: 6/14/17, Detroit, Mich.   BL/TR, 6'0.5", 175 lbs.   Deb: 8/30/42

YEAR	TM/L	G	AB	R	H	2B	3B	HR	RBI	BB	SO	AVG	OBP	SLG	PRO+	BR	/A	RC	SB	CS	SBR	FR	POS	TPR
1942	Was-A	7	19	2	1	0	0	0	2	1	1	.053	.100	.053	-57	-4	-4	0	0	0	0	2	/3	-0.1

■ JESSE HOFFMEISTER   Hoffmeister, Jesse H.   b: Toledo, Ohio   Deb: 7/24/1897

YEAR	TM/L	G	AB	R	H	2B	3B	HR	RBI	BB	SO	AVG	OBP	SLG	PRO+	BR	/A	RC	SB	CS	SBR	FR	POS	TPR
1897	Pit-N	48	188	33	58	6	9	3	36	8		.309	.337	.484	122	3	5	33	6			-13	3	-0.6

■ SOLLY HOFMAN   Hofman, Arthur Frederick "Circus Solly"   b: 10/29/1882, St.Louis, Mo.   d: 3/10/56, St.Louis, Mo.   BR/TR, 6', 160 lbs.   Deb: 7/28/03

YEAR	TM/L	G	AB	R	H	2B	3B	HR	RBI	BB	SO	AVG	OBP	SLG	PRO+	BR	/A	RC	SB	CS	SBR	FR	POS	TPR
1903	Pit-N	3	2	0	0	0	0	0	0	0		.000	.000	.000	-97	-1	-1	0	0			-1	/O	-0.1
1904	Chi-N	7	26	7	7	0	0	1	4	1		.269	.296	.385	111	0	0	4	2			0	/OS	0.0
1905	Chi-N	86	287	43	68	14	4	1	38	20		.237	.287	.324	81	-6	-7	33	15			3	2/1S30	0.0
1906	*Chi-N	64	195	30	50	2	3	2	20	20		.256	.326	.328	100	2	0	26	13			-1	O1/2S3	-0.1
1907	Chi-N	134	470	67	126	11	3	1	36	41		.268	.327	.311	96	2	-2	62	29			4	OS1/32	0.1
1908	*Chi-N	120	411	55	100	15	5	2	42	33		.243	.300	.319	95	-0	-2	45	15			5	O12/3	0.2
1909	Chi-N	153	527	60	150	21	4	2	58	53		.285	.351	.351	115	11	10	74	20			5	*O	1.2
1910	*Chi-N	136	477	83	155	24	16	3	86	65	34	.325	.406	.461	154	32	33	102	29			3	*O1/3	3.2
1911	Chi-N	143	512	66	129	17	2	2	70	66	40	.252	.341	.305	81	-11	-11	65	30			-9	*O1	-2.4
1912	Chi-N	36	125	28	34	11	0	0	18	22	13	.272	.385	.360	105	2	2	19	5			4	O/1	0.5
	Pit-N	17	53	7	15	4	1	0	2	5	6	.283	.345	.396	104	0	0	7	0			3	O	0.3

YEAR	TM/L	G	AB	R	H	2B	3B	HR	RBI	BB	SO	AVG	OBP	SLG	PRO+	BR	/A	RC	SB	CS	SBR	FR	POS	TPR
	Yr	53	178	35	49	15	1	0	20	27	19	.275	.374	.371	105	2	2	26	5			7		0.8
1913	Pit-N	28	83	11	19	5	2	0	7	8	6	.229	.297	.337	84	-2	-2	9	3			1	O	0.1
1914	Bro-F	147	515	65	148	25	12	5	83	54	41	.287	.357	.412	121	13	14	91	34			5	*21O/S	2.0
1915	Buf-F	109	346	29	81	10	6	0	27	30	28	.234	.295	.298	74	-10	-11	36	12			1	O1/32S	-1.4
1916	NY-A	6	27	0	8	1	1	0	2	1	1	.296	.321	.407	116	0	0	4	1			2	/O	0.2
	Chi-N	5	16	2	5	2	1	0	2	2	2	.313	.389	.563	172	2	1	4	0			0	/O	0.2
Total	14	1194	4072	554	1095	162	60	19	495	421	171	.269	.338	.352	104	34	25	581	208			25	O21/S3	3.9

■ BOBBY HOFMAN
Hofman, Robert George b: 10/5/25, St.Louis, Mo. BR/TR, 5'10", 160 lbs. Deb: 4/19/49 C

YEAR	TM/L	G	AB	R	H	2B	3B	HR	RBI	BB	SO	AVG	OBP	SLG	PRO+	BR	/A	RC	SB	CS	SBR	FR	POS	TPR
1949	NY-N	19	48	4	10	0	0	0	3	5	6	.208	.296	.208	38	-4	-4	3	0			0	2	-0.3
1952	NY-N	32	63	11	18	2	2	2	4	8	10	.286	.375	.476	134	3	3	11	0	0	0	3	2/31	0.7
1953	NY-N	74	169	21	45	7	2	12	34	12	23	.266	.315	.544	117	4	3	27	1	1	-0	2	32	0.4
1954	NY-N	71	125	12	28	5	0	8	30	17	15	.224	.322	.456	99	-0	-1	19	0	0	0	-4	12/3	-0.3
1955	NY-N	96	207	32	55	7	2	10	28	22	31	.266	.339	.464	110	3	3	30	0	2	-1	-5	1C2/3	-0.3
1956	NY-N	47	56	1	10	1	0	0	2	6	8	.179	.270	.196	28	-6	-5	3	0	0	0	1	/C312	-0.3
1957	NY-N	2	2	0	0	0	0	0	0	0	1	.000	.000	.000	-99	-1	-1	0	0	0	0	0	/H	0.0
Total	7	341	670	81	166	22	6	32	101	70	94	.248	.323	.442	100	-1	-2	93	1	3		-3	/213C	-0.1

■ FRED HOFMANN
Hofmann, Fred "Bootnose" b: 6/10/1894, St.Louis, Mo. d: 11/19/64, St.Helena, Cal. BR/TR, 5'11.5", 175 lbs. Deb: 9/26/19 C

YEAR	TM/L	G	AB	R	H	2B	3B	HR	RBI	BB	SO	AVG	OBP	SLG	PRO+	BR	/A	RC	SB	CS	SBR	FR	POS	TPR
1919	NY-A	1	1	0	0	0	0	0	0	0	0	.000	.000	.000	-99	-0	-0	0	0			0	/C	0.0
1920	NY-A	15	24	3	7	0	0	0	1	1	2	.292	.346	.292	68	-1	-1	2	0			-4	C	-0.3
1921	NY-A	23	62	7	11	1	1	1	5	5	13	.177	.250	.274	33	-6	-7	4	0	0	0	0	C/1	-0.5
1922	NY-A	37	91	13	27	5	3	2	10	9	12	.297	.360	.484	116	2	2	16	0	0	0	-3	C	0.0
1923	*NY-A	72	238	24	69	10	4	3	26	18	27	.290	.350	.403	96	-1	-2	34	2	1	0	-2	C	0.1
1924	NY-A	62	166	17	29	6	1	1	11	12	15	.175	.239	.241	24	-19	-19	10	2	1	0	3	C	-1.2
1925	NY-A	3	2	0	0	0	0	0	0	0	0	.000	.000	.000	-99	-1	-1	0	0	0	0	0	/C	0.0
1927	Bos-A	87	217	20	59	19	1	0	24	21	26	.272	.342	.369	86	-5	-4	28	2	0	1	-2	C	-0.1
1928	Bos-A	78	199	14	45	8	1	0	16	11	25	.226	.270	.276	45	-16	-16	15	0	1	-1	4	C	-0.6
Total	9	378	1000	98	247	49	11	7	93	77	120	.247	.308	.339	68	-48	-48	110	6	3		-3	C/1	-2.6

■ HARRY HOGAN
Hogan, Harry S. b: 11/1/1875, Syracuse, N.Y. d: 1/24/34, Syracuse, N.Y. Deb: 8/13/01

YEAR	TM/L	G	AB	R	H	2B	3B	HR	RBI	BB	SO	AVG	OBP	SLG	PRO+	BR	/A	RC	SB	CS	SBR	FR	POS	TPR
1901	Cle-A	1	4	0	0	0	0	0	0	0		.000	.000	.000	-99	-1	-1	0	0			-0	/O	0.0

■ SHANTY HOGAN
Hogan, James Francis b: 3/21/06, Somerville, Mass. d: 4/7/67, Boston, Mass. BR/TR, 6'1", 240 lbs. Deb: 6/23/25

YEAR	TM/L	G	AB	R	H	2B	3B	HR	RBI	BB	SO	AVG	OBP	SLG	PRO+	BR	/A	RC	SB	CS	SBR	FR	POS	TPR
1925	Bos-N	9	21	2	6	1	1	0	3	1	3	.286	.318	.429	97	-0	-0	3	0	0	0	-1	/O	0.0
1926	Bos-N	4	14	1	4	1	1	0	5	0	0	.286	.286	.500	119	0	0	2	0			1	C	0.1
1927	Bos-N	71	229	24	66	17	1	3	32	9	23	.288	.324	.410	104	-2	0	29	2			1	C	0.5
1928	NY-N	131	411	48	137	25	2	10	71	42	25	.333	.406	.477	129	19	19	79	0			-10	*C	1.6
1929	NY-N	102	317	19	95	13	0	5	45	25	22	.300	.362	.388	86	-6	-6	44	1			-4	C	-0.2
1930	NY-N	122	389	60	132	26	2	13	75	21	24	.339	.378	.517	116	8	9	73	2			-3	C	0.9
1931	NY-N	123	396	42	119	17	1	12	65	29	29	.301	.354	.439	115	6	8	63	1			-1	*C	1.2
1932	NY-N	140	502	36	144	18	2	8	77	26	22	.287	.323	.378	90	-9	-7	62	0			-8	*C	-0.9
1933	Bos-N	96	328	15	83	7	0	3	30	13	9	.253	.288	.302	75	-13	-10	25	0			-1	C	-0.8
1934	Bos-N	92	279	20	73	5	2	4	34	16	13	.262	.316	.337	81	-10	-7	27	0			-3	C	-0.6
1935	Bos-N	59	163	9	49	8	0	2	25	21	8	.301	.394	.387	120	4	5	27	0			-5	C	0.1
1936	Was-A	19	65	8	21	4	0	1	7	11	2	.323	.421	.431	117	2	2	12	0	1	-1	2	C	0.4
1937	Was-A	21	66	4	10	4	0	0	5	6	8	.152	.222	.212	10	-9	-9	3	0	1	-1	2	C	-0.5
Total	13	989	3180	288	939	146	12	61	474	220	188	.295	.348	.406	101	-12	3	449	6	2		-29	C/O	1.8

■ KENNY HOGAN
Hogan, Kenneth Sylvester b: 10/9/02, Cleveland, Ohio d: 1/2/80, Cleveland, Ohio BL/TR, 5'9", 145 lbs. Deb: 10/02/21

YEAR	TM/L	G	AB	R	H	2B	3B	HR	RBI	BB	SO	AVG	OBP	SLG	PRO+	BR	/A	RC	SB	CS	SBR	FR	POS	TPR
1921	Cin-N	1	2	0	0	0	0	0	0	0	1	.000	.000	.000	-99	-1	-1	0	0	0	0	0	/O	0.0
1923	Cle-A	1	0	0	0	0	0	0	0	0	0	—	—	—	—	0	0	0	0	0	0	0	R	0.0
1924	Cle-A	2	1	0	0	0	0	0	0	0	0	.000	.000	.000	-99	-0	-0	0	0	0	0	0	H	0.0
Total	3	4	3	0	0	0	0	0	0	0	1	.000	.000	.000	-99	-1	-1	0	0	0	0	0	/O	0.0

■ MARTY HOGAN
Hogan, Martin F. b: 10/15/1869, Wensbury, England d: 8/15/23, Youngstown, Ohio 5'8", 145 lbs. Deb: 8/06/1894

YEAR	TM/L	G	AB	R	H	2B	3B	HR	RBI	BB	SO	AVG	OBP	SLG	PRO+	BR	/A	RC	SB	CS	SBR	FR	POS	TPR
1894	Cin-N	6	23	4	3	0	0	0	3	1	4	.130	.167	.130	-26	-5	-5	1	2			-0	/O	-0.3
	StL-N	29	100	11	28	3	4	0	13	3	13	.280	.308	.390	69	-5	-5	15	7			-1	O	-0.6
	Yr	35	123	15	31	3	4	0	16	4	17	.252	.281	.341	50	-10	-10	15	9			-1		-0.9
1895	StL-N	5	18	2	3	1	0	0	2	3	0	.167	.286	.222	34	-2	-2	2	2			1	/O	0.0
Total	2	40	141	17	34	4	4	0	18	7	17	.241	.282	.326	49	-12	-12	17	11			-1	/O	-0.9

■ EDDIE HOGAN
Hogan, Robert Edward b: 4/1860, St.Louis, Mo. BR, 5'7", 153 lbs. Deb: 7/05/1882

YEAR	TM/L	G	AB	R	H	2B	3B	HR	RBI	BB	SO	AVG	OBP	SLG	PRO+	BR	/A	RC	SB	CS	SBR	FR	POS	TPR
1882	StL-a	1	3	1	1	0	0	0		0		.333	.333	.333	121	0	0	0				-0	/P	0.0
1884	Mil-U	11	37	6	3	1	0	0		7		.081	.227	.108	31	-3	0	1	0			7	O	0.6
1887	NY-a	32	120	22	24	6	1	0		30		.200	.373	.267	86	-1	0	17	12			-7	O/S3	-0.5
1888	Cle-a	78	269	60	61	16	6	0	24	50		.227	.368	.331	131	12	13	45	30			-5	O	0.5
Total	4	122	429	89	89	23	7	0	24	87		.207	.357	.294	112	8	13	63	42			-5	O/S3P	0.6

■ WILLIE HOGAN
Hogan, William Henry "Happy" b: 9/14/1884, N.San Juan, Cal. d: 9/28/74, San Jose, Cal. BR/TR, 5'10", 175 lbs. Deb: 4/12/11

YEAR	TM/L	G	AB	R	H	2B	3B	HR	RBI	BB	SO	AVG	OBP	SLG	PRO+	BR	/A	RC	SB	CS	SBR	FR	POS	TPR
1911	Phi-A	7	19	1	2	1	0	0	2	0		.105	.105	.158	-28	-3	-3	0	0			0	/O	-0.3
	StL-A	123	443	53	115	17	8	2	62	43		.260	.328	.348	92	-7	-5	57	18			13	*O/1	0.0
	Yr	130	462	54	117	18	8	2	64	43		.253	.320	.340	87	-10	-8	56	18			13		-0.3
1912	StL-A	108	360	32	77	10	2	1	36	34		.214	.284	.261	58	-20	-19	32	17			11	*O	-1.3
Total	2	238	822	86	194	28	10	3	100	77		.236	.304	.305	75	-31	-26	89	35			24	O/1	-1.6

■ BERT HOGG
Hogg, Wilbert George "Sonny" b: 4/21/13, Detroit, Mich. d: 11/5/73, Detroit, Mich. BR/TR, 5'11.5", 162 lbs. Deb: 6/01/34

YEAR	TM/L	G	AB	R	H	2B	3B	HR	RBI	BB	SO	AVG	OBP	SLG	PRO+	BR	/A	RC	SB	CS	SBR	FR	POS	TPR
1934	Bro-N	2	1	0	0	0	0	0	0	0	0	.000	.000	.000	-99	-0	-0	0	0			0	/3	0.0

■ GEORGE HOGRIEVER
Hogriever, George C. b: 3/17/1869, Cincinnati, Ohio d: 1/26/61, Appleton, Wis. BR/TR, 5'8", 160 lbs. Deb: 4/24/1895

YEAR	TM/L	G	AB	R	H	2B	3B	HR	RBI	BB	SO	AVG	OBP	SLG	PRO+	BR	/A	RC	SB	CS	SBR	FR	POS	TPR
1895	Cin-N	69	239	61	65	8	7	2	34	36	17	.272	.374	.389	95	1	-1	51	41			2	O/2	-0.3
1901	Mil-A	54	221	25	52	10	2	0	16	30		.235	.329	.299	81	-6	-4	25	7			2	O	-0.2
Total	2	123	460	86	117	18	9	2	50	66	17	.254	.353	.346	89	-5	-5	76	48			4	O/2	-0.5

■ BILL HOHMAN
Hohman, William Henry b: 11/27/03, Brooklyn, Md. d: 10/29/68, Baltimore, Md. BR/TR, 6', 178 lbs. Deb: 8/24/27

YEAR	TM/L	G	AB	R	H	2B	3B	HR	RBI	BB	SO	AVG	OBP	SLG	PRO+	BR	/A	RC	SB	CS	SBR	FR	POS	TPR
1927	Phi-N	7	18	1	5	0	0	0	2	3		.278	.350	.278	69	-1	-1	2	0			0	/O	0.0

■ EDDIE HOHNHORST
Hohnhorst, Edward Hicks b: 1/31/1885, Kentucky d: 3/28/16, Covington, Ky. BL/TL, 6'1", 175 lbs. Deb: 9/14/10

YEAR	TM/L	G	AB	R	H	2B	3B	HR	RBI	BB	SO	AVG	OBP	SLG	PRO+	BR	/A	RC	SB	CS	SBR	FR	POS	TPR
1910	Cle-A	17	62	8	20	3	1	0	6	4		.323	.364	.403	138	3	3	10	3			-1	1	0.2
1912	Cle-A	15	54	5	11	1	0	0	2	2		.204	.232	.222	29	-5	-5	4	5			-1	1	-0.5
Total	2	32	116	13	31	4	1	0	8	6		.267	.303	.319	85	-2	-3	14	8			-2	/1	-0.3

■ CHRIS HOILES
Hoiles, Christopher Allen b: 3/20/65, Bowling Green, O. BR/TR, 6', 195 lbs. Deb: 4/25/89

YEAR	TM/L	G	AB	R	H	2B	3B	HR	RBI	BB	SO	AVG	OBP	SLG	PRO+	BR	/A	RC	SB	CS	SBR	FR	POS	TPR
1989	Bal-A	6	9	0	1	1	0	0	1	1	3	.111	.200	.222	19	-1	-1	0	0	0	0	1	/CD	0.0
1990	Bal-A	23	63	7	12	3	0	1	6	5	12	.190	.250	.286	51	-4	-4	5	0	0	0	-1	/C1D	-0.4
Total	2	29	72	7	13	4	0	1	7	6	15	.181	.244	.278	47	-5	-5	5	0	0	0	1	/DC1	-0.4

YEAR	TM/L	G	AB	R	H	2B	3B	HR	RBI	BB	SO	AVG	OBP	SLG	PRO+	BR	/A	RC	SB	CS	SBR	FR	POS	TPR

■ BILL HOLBERT   Holbert, William H. b: 3/14/1855, Baltimore, Md. d: 3/1/35, Laurel, Md.   BR/TR,   Deb: 9/05/1876   MU

YEAR	TM/L	G	AB	R	H	2B	3B	HR	RBI	BB	SO	AVG	OBP	SLG	PRO+	BR	/A	RC	SB	CS	SBR	FR	POS	TPR
1876	Lou-N	12	43	3	11	0	0	0	5	0	3	.256	.256	.256	60	-1	-2	3				7	C	0.4
1878	Mil-N	45	173	10	32	2	0	0	12	3	14	.185	.199	.197	28	-13	-14	7				6	OC	-0.9
1879	Syr-N	59	229	11	46	0	0	0	21	1	20	.201	.204	.201	38	-16	-12	10				-2	*C/O	-1.3
	Tro-N	4	15	1	4	0	0	0	2	0	1	.267	.267	.267	82	-0	-0	1				1	/CM	0.1
	Yr	63	244	12	50	0	0	0	23	1	21	.205	.208	.205	41	-16	-12	11				-1		-1.2
1880	Tro-N	60	212	18	40	5	1	0	8	9	18	.189	.222	.222	48	-10	-12	11				8	*C/O	0.0
1881	Tro-N	46	180	16	49	3	0	0	14	3	13	.272	.284	.289	77	-4	-5	15				4	C/O	-0.1
1882	Tro-N	71	251	24	46	5	0	0	23	11	22	.183	.218	.203	38	-17	-16	11				15	*C3/O	0.3
1883	NY-a	73	299	26	71	9	1	0		1		.237	.240	.274	63	-11	-13	20				27	*C/O2	1.7
1884	*NY-a	65	255	28	53	5	0	0		7		.208	.235	.227	55	-12	-11	14				14	C/OS	0.7
1885	NY-a	56	202	13	35	3	0	0		8		.173	.205	.188	29	-16	-14	8				10	CO/3	0.2
1886	NY-a	48	171	8	35	4	2	0		6		.205	.232	.251	55	-9	-8	11	4			17	C/OS	1.0
1887	NY-a	69	255	20	58	4	3	0		7		.227	.248	.267	47	-19	-17	20	12			-3	C/1S2	-0.7
1888	Bro-a	15	50	4	6	1	0	0	1	2		.120	.170	.140	1	-5	-5	1	0			1	C	-0.2
Total	12	623	2335	182	486	41	7	0	86	58	91	.208	.228	.232	48	-135	-130	133	16			104	C/O31S2	1.2

■ SAMMY HOLBROOK   Holbrook, James Marbury b: 7/17/10, Meridian, Miss.   BR/TR, 5'11", 189 lbs.   Deb: 4/25/35

YEAR	TM/L	G	AB	R	H	2B	3B	HR	RBI	BB	SO	AVG	OBP	SLG	PRO+	BR	/A	RC	SB	CS	SBR	FR	POS	TPR
1935	Was-A	52	135	20	35	2	2	2	25	30	16	.259	.408	.348	101	1	2	22	0	0	0	-11	C	-0.6

■ JOE HOLDEN   Holden, Joseph Francis "Socks" b: 6/4/13, St.Clair, Pa.   BL/TR, 5'8", 175 lbs.   Deb: 6/14/34

YEAR	TM/L	G	AB	R	H	2B	3B	HR	RBI	BB	SO	AVG	OBP	SLG	PRO+	BR	/A	RC	SB	CS	SBR	FR	POS	TPR
1934	Phi-N	10	14	1	1	0	0	0	0	0	2	.071	.071	.071	-54	-3	-3	0	0			2	/C	0.0
1935	Phi-N	6	9	0	1	0	0	0	0	0	3	.111	.111	.111	-36	-2	-2	-0	1			-0	/C	-0.1
1936	Phi-N	1	1	0	0	0	0	0	0	0	0	.000	.000	.000	-91	-0	-0	0	0			0	H	0.0
Total	3	17	24	1	2	0	0	0	0	0	5	.083	.083	.083	-49	-5	-6	-0	1			2	/C	-0.1

■ BILL HOLDEN   Holden, William Paul b: 9/7/1889, Birmingham, Ala. d: 9/14/71, Pensacola, Fla.   BR/TR, 6', 170 lbs.   Deb: 9/11/13

YEAR	TM/L	G	AB	R	H	2B	3B	HR	RBI	BB	SO	AVG	OBP	SLG	PRO+	BR	/A	RC	SB	CS	SBR	FR	POS	TPR
1913	NY-A	18	53	6	16	3	1	0	8	8	5	.302	.393	.396	131	2	2	9	0			3	O	0.4
1914	NY-A	50	165	12	30	3	2	0	12	16	26	.182	.254	.224	44	-11	-11	9	2	4	-2	-1	O	-1.8
	Cin-N	11	28	2	6	0	0	0	1	3	5	.214	.290	.214	49	-2	-2	2	0			-0	O	-0.2
Total	2	79	246	20	52	6	3	0	21	27	36	.211	.289	.260	64	-11	-11	20	2	4		1	/O	-1.6

■ JIM HOLDSWORTH   Holdsworth, James "Long Jim" b: 7/14/1850, New York, N.Y. d: 3/22/18, New York, N.Y.   BR/TR,   Deb: 5/14/1872

YEAR	TM/L	G	AB	R	H	2B	3B	HR	RBI	BB	SO	AVG	OBP	SLG	PRO+	BR	/A	RC	SB	CS	SBR	FR	POS	TPR
1872	Cle-n	22	111	19	33	5	1	0		1		.297	.304	.360	110	0	2	12					*S	0.1
	Eck-n	2	7	1	2	0	0	0		0		.286	.286	.286	90	-0	0	1					/S	0.0
	Yr	24	118	20	35	5	1	0		1		.297	.303	.356	109	0	2	13						0.1
1873	Mut-n	53	229	46	72	6	8	0		0		.314	.314	.410	112	3	3	30					*S	0.2
1874	Phi-n	57	286	60	97	8	9	0		1		.339	.341	.430	139	13	12	43					3S/O	0.7
1875	Mut-n	71	325	45	91	11	1	0		1		.280	.282	.320	102	2	-1	30					OS	0.0
1876	NY-N	52	241	23	64	3	2	0	19	1	2	.266	.269	.295	101	-3	2	20				-0	*O/2	0.0
1877	Har-N	55	260	26	66	5	2	0	20	2	8	.254	.260	.288	81	-8	-4	20				-5	*O	-0.9
1882	Tro-N	1	3	0	0	0	0	0	0	0	1	.000	.000	.000	-99	-1	-1	0				1	/O	0.0
1884	Ind-a	5	18	1	2	0	0	0		0	2	.111	.200	.111	6	-2	-2	0				1	/O	0.0
Total	4 n	205	958	171	295	30	19	0		3		.308	.310	.379	116	19	16	116					S/O3	1.0
Total	4	113	522	50	132	8	4	0	39	5	11	.253	.260	.284	86	-14	-5	40				-3	O/2	-0.9

■ WALTER HOLKE   Holke, Walter Henry "Union Man" b: 12/25/1892, St.Louis, Mo. d: 10/12/54, St.Louis, Mo.   BB/TL, 6'1.5", 185 lbs.   Deb: 10/06/14   C

YEAR	TM/L	G	AB	R	H	2B	3B	HR	RBI	BB	SO	AVG	OBP	SLG	PRO+	BR	/A	RC	SB	CS	SBR	FR	POS	TPR
1914	NY-N	2	6	0	2	0	0	0	0	0	0	.333	.333	.333	102	-0	-0	1	0			0	/1	0.0
1916	*NY-N	34	111	16	39	4	2	0	13	6	16	.351	.390	.423	158	6	7	22	10			0	1	0.6
1917	*NY-N	153	527	55	146	12	7	2	55	34	54	.277	.327	.338	107	3	4	61	13			-5	*1	-0.2
1918	NY-N	88	326	38	82	17	4	1	27	10	26	.252	.276	.337	88	-6	-6	32	10			5	1	-0.2
1919	Bos-N	137	518	48	151	14	6	0	48	21	25	.292	.325	.342	105	0	2	63	19			6	*1	0.8
1920	Bos-N	144	551	53	162	15	11	3	64	28	31	.294	.329	.377	107	1	4	66	4	11	-5	-2	*1	-0.5
1921	Bos-N	150	579	60	151	15	10	3	63	17	41	.261	.284	.337	67	-31	-27	53	8	11	-4	3	*1	-3.1
1922	Bos-N	105	395	35	115	9	4	0	46	14	23	.291	.317	.334	71	-19	-16	40	6	8	-3	-4	*1	-2.2
1923	Phi-N	147	562	64	175	31	4	7	70	16	37	.311	.330	.418	86	-5	-13	74	7	9	-3	-1	*1/P	-2.6
1924	Phi-N	148	563	60	169	23	6	6	64	25	33	.300	.330	.394	83	-6	-15	70	3	8	-4	4	*1	-2.0
1925	Phi-N	39	86	11	21	5	0	1	17	3	6	.244	.270	.337	50	-6	-7	8	0	0	0	1	1	-0.7
	Cin-N	65	232	24	65	8	4	1	20	17	12	.280	.329	.362	78	-8	-7	28	1	3	-2	1	1	-1.2
	Yr	104	318	35	86	13	4	2	37	20	18	.270	.314	.355	69	-14	-15	35	1	3	-2	2		-1.9
Total	11	1212	4456	464	1278	153	58	24	487	191	304	.287	.318	.363	89	-71	-74	517	81	50		8	*1/P	-11.3

■ BILL HOLLAHAN   Hollahan, William James "Happy" b: 11/22/1896, New York, N.Y. d: 11/27/65, New York, N.Y.   BR/TR, 5'8", 165 lbs.   Deb: 9/27/20

YEAR	TM/L	G	AB	R	H	2B	3B	HR	RBI	BB	SO	AVG	OBP	SLG	PRO+	BR	/A	RC	SB	CS	SBR	FR	POS	TPR
1920	Was-A	3	4	0	1	0	0	0	1	1	2	.250	.400	.250	77	-0	-0	1	0	0	0	0	/3	0.1

■ DUTCH HOLLAND   Holland, Robert Clyde b: 10/12/03, Middlesex, N.C. d: 6/16/67, Lumberton, N.C.   BR/TR, 6'1", 190 lbs.   Deb: 8/16/32

YEAR	TM/L	G	AB	R	H	2B	3B	HR	RBI	BB	SO	AVG	OBP	SLG	PRO+	BR	/A	RC	SB	CS	SBR	FR	POS	TPR
1932	Bos-N	39	156	15	46	11	1	1	18	12	20	.295	.345	.397	103	-0	1	22	0			-1	O	-0.2
1933	Bos-N	13	31	3	8	3	0	0	3	3	8	.258	.324	.355	102	-0	0	4	1			-1	/O	-0.1
1934	Cle-A	50	128	19	32	12	1	2	13	13	11	.250	.319	.406	85	-3	-3	17	0	0	0	-4	O	-0.6
Total	3	102	315	37	86	26	2	3	34	28	39	.273	.332	.397	95	-3	-3	43	1	0		-7	/O	-0.9

■ WILL HOLLAND   Holland, Willard A. b: Georgetown, Del. d: 7/19/30, Philadelphia, Pa.   5'10", 180 lbs.   Deb: 7/10/1889

YEAR	TM/L	G	AB	R	H	2B	3B	HR	RBI	BB	SO	AVG	OBP	SLG	PRO+	BR	/A	RC	SB	CS	SBR	FR	POS	TPR
1889	Bal-a	40	143	13	27	1	2	0	16	9	28	.189	.247	.224	35	-12	-12	9	4			-15	S/O	-2.0

■ GARY HOLLE   Holle, Gary Charles b: 8/11/54, Albany, N.Y.   BR/TL, 6'6", 210 lbs.   Deb: 6/02/79

YEAR	TM/L	G	AB	R	H	2B	3B	HR	RBI	BB	SO	AVG	OBP	SLG	PRO+	BR	/A	RC	SB	CS	SBR	FR	POS	TPR
1979	Tex-A	5	6	0	1	1	0	0	0	0	0	.167	.286	.333	67	-0	-0	1	0	0	0	-0	/1	0.0

■ BUG HOLLIDAY   Holliday, James Wear b: 2/8/1867, St.Louis, Mo. d: 2/15/10, Cincinnati, Ohio   BR/TR, 5'11", 151 lbs.   Deb: 4/17/1889   U

YEAR	TM/L	G	AB	R	H	2B	3B	HR	RBI	BB	SO	AVG	OBP	SLG	PRO+	BR	/A	RC	SB	CS	SBR	FR	POS	TPR
1889	Cin-a	135	563	107	181	28	7	19	104	43	59	.321	.372	.497	145	33	30	124	46			-7	*O	1.5
1890	Cin-N	131	518	93	140	18	14	4	75	49	36	.270	.341	.382	114	8	9	87	50			-3	*O	0.3
1891	Cin-N	111	442	74	141	21	10	9	84	37	28	.319	.376	.473	148	26	25	92	30			-8	*O	1.0
1892	Cin-N	152	602	114	176	23	16	13	91	57	39	.292	.355	.449	147	30	31	114	43			-4	*O/P	2.1
1893	Cin-N	126	500	108	155	24	10	5	89	73	22	.310	.401	.428	119	18	16	101	32			-10	*O/1	0.0
1894	Cin-N	121	511	119	190	24	7	13	119	40	20	.372	.420	.523	123	23	19	127	29			0	*O/1	0.8
1895	Cin-N	32	127	25	38	9	2	0	20	10	3	.299	.350	.402	92	-1	-2	20	6			-4	O	-0.4
1896	Cin-N	29	84	17	27	4	0	0	8	9	4	.321	.394	.369	97	1	-0	13	1			-2	O/1SP	-0.1
1897	Cin-N	61	195	50	61	9	4	2	20	27		.313	.399	.431	114	7	5	37	6			-7	O/S21	-0.3
1898	Cin-N	30	106	21	25	2	1	0	7	14		.236	.325	.274	70	-3	-4	11	5			-2	O	-0.6
Total	10	928	3648	728	1134	162	71	65	617	359	211	.311	.376	.448	127	141	128	727	248			-45	O/1S2P	4.1

■ HOLLY HOLLINGSHEAD   Hollingshead, John Samuel (a.k.a. Samuel John Holly)
b: 1/17/1853, Washington, D.C. d: 10/6/26, Washington, D.C.   Deb: 4/20/1872   M

YEAR	TM/L	G	AB	R	H	2B	3B	HR	RBI	BB	SO	AVG	OBP	SLG	PRO+	BR	/A	RC	SB	CS	SBR	FR	POS	TPR
1872	Nat-n	9	46	12	15	0	1	0		1		.326	.340	.370	102	1	-1	6					/2	0.0
1873	Was-n	30	134	25	35	1	3	0		0		.261	.261	.313	70	-5	-4	11					O/2	-0.1
1875	Was-n	19	81	7	20	0	2	0		0		.247	.247	.296	90	-1	-1	6					OM	0.0

YEAR	TM/L	G	AB	R	H	2B	3B	HR	RBI	BB	SO	AVG	OBP	SLG	PRO+	BR	/A	RC	SB	CS	SBR	FR	POS	TPR
Total	3 n	58	261	44	70	1	6	0		1		.268	.271	.318	82	-5	-6	23					/O2	-0.1

■ DAVE HOLLINS
Hollins, David Michaels b: 5/25/66, Buffalo, N.Y. BB/TR, 6'1", 195 lbs. Deb: 4/12/90

YEAR	TM/L	G	AB	R	H	2B	3B	HR	RBI	BB	SO	AVG	OBP	SLG	PRO+	BR	/A	RC	SB	CS	SBR	FR	POS	TPR
1990	Phi-N	72	114	14	21	0	0	5	15	10	28	.184	.256	.316	57	-7	-7	10	0	0	0	-1	3/1	-0.7

■ STAN HOLLMIG
Hollmig, Stanley Ernest "Hondo" b: 1/2/26, Fredericksburg, Tex d: 12/4/81, San Antonio, Tex. BR/TR, 6'2.5", 190 lbs. Deb: 4/19/49

YEAR	TM/L	G	AB	R	H	2B	3B	HR	RBI	BB	SO	AVG	OBP	SLG	PRO+	BR	/A	RC	SB	CS	SBR	FR	POS	TPR
1949	Phi-N	81	251	28	64	11	6	2	26	20	43	.255	.315	.371	85	-6	-5	28	1			-9	O	-1.7
1950	Phi-N	11	12	1	3	2	0	0	1	0	3	.250	.250	.417	73	-1	-1	1	0			0	/O	0.0
1951	Phi-N	2	2	0	0	0	0	0	0	0	0	.000	.000	.000	-99	-1	-1	0	0	0	0	0	H	0.0
Total	3	94	265	29	67	13	6	2	27	20	46	.253	.310	.370	84	-7	-6	29	1	0		-9	/O	-1.7

■ CHARLIE HOLLOCHER
Hollocher, Charles Jacob b: 6/11/1896, St.Louis, Mo. d: 8/14/40, Frontenac, Mo. BL/TR, 5'7", 154 lbs. Deb: 4/16/18

YEAR	TM/L	G	AB	R	H	2B	3B	HR	RBI	BB	SO	AVG	OBP	SLG	PRO+	BR	/A	RC	SB	CS	SBR	FR	POS	TPR
1918	*Chi-N	131	509	72	161	23	6	2	38	47	30	.316	.379	.397	133	23	22	85	26			-19	*S	0.6
1919	Chi-N	115	430	51	116	14	5	3	26	44	19	.270	.347	.347	108	6	6	57	16			6	*S	1.7
1920	Chi-N	80	301	53	96	17	2	0	22	41	15	.319	.406	.389	126	13	13	49	20	14	-2	9	S	2.4
1921	Chi-N	140	558	71	161	28	8	3	37	43	13	.289	.342	.384	91	-6	-6	70	5	16	-8	3	*S	0.2
1922	Chi-N	152	592	90	201	37	8	3	69	58	5	.340	.403	.444	116	18	16	100	19	29	-12	-5	*S	0.8
1923	Chi-N	66	260	46	89	14	2	1	28	26	5	.342	.410	.423	120	9	9	44	9	10	-3	-9	S	0.2
1924	Chi-N	76	286	28	70	12	4	2	21	18	7	.245	.292	.336	67	-13	-14	26	4	11	-5	4	S	-0.9
Total	7	760	2936	411	894	145	35	14	241	277	94	.304	.370	.392	110	50	45	432	99	80		-13	S	5.0

■ ED HOLLY
Holly, Edward William (b: Edward William Ruthlavy) b: 7/6/1879, Chicago, Ill. d: 11/27/73, Williamsport, Pa. BR/TR, 5'10", 165 lbs. Deb: 7/18/06

YEAR	TM/L	G	AB	R	H	2B	3B	HR	RBI	BB	SO	AVG	OBP	SLG	PRO+	BR	/A	RC	SB	CS	SBR	FR	POS	TPR
1906	StL-N	10	34	1	2	0	0	0	7	5		.059	.179	.059	-25	-5	-5	0	0			-3	S	-0.7
1907	StL-N	150	545	55	125	18	3	1	40	36		.229	.277	.279	79	-15	-13	50	16			12	*S/2	0.5
1914	Pit-F	100	350	28	86	9	4	0	26	17	52	.246	.281	.294	65	-16	-16	35	14			-2	S/O2	-1.2
1915	Pit-F	16	42	8	11	2	0	0	5	5	6	.262	.354	.310	98	-0	0	6	3			-4	S/3	-0.3
Total	4	276	971	92	224	29	7	1	78	63	58	.231	.278	.278	71	-36	-33	92	33			2	S/23O	-1.7

■ WATTIE HOLM
Holm, Roscoe Albert b: 12/28/01, Peterson, Iowa d: 5/19/50, Everly, Iowa BR/TR, 5'9.5", 160 lbs. Deb: 4/15/24

YEAR	TM/L	G	AB	R	H	2B	3B	HR	RBI	BB	SO	AVG	OBP	SLG	PRO+	BR	/A	RC	SB	CS	SBR	FR	POS	TPR
1924	StL-N	81	293	40	86	10	4	0	23	8	16	.294	.317	.355	81	-9	-8	32	1	4	-2	0	O/C3	-1.0
1925	StL-N	13	58	10	12	1	1	0	2	3	1	.207	.246	.259	28	-6	-6	4	1	0	0	2	O	-0.3
1926	*StL-N	55	144	18	41	5	1	0	21	18	14	.285	.364	.333	85	-2	-2	18	3			-3	O	-0.6
1927	StL-N	110	419	55	120	27	8	3	66	24	29	.286	.327	.411	93	-3	-5	54	4			-7	O/3	-1.5
1928	*StL-N	102	386	61	107	24	6	3	47	32	17	.277	.334	.394	88	-6	-7	50	1			-10	3/O	-1.5
1929	StL-N	64	176	21	41	5	6	0	14	12	8	.233	.282	.330	50	-14	-14	16	1			4	O/3	-1.2
1932	StL-N	11	17	2	3	1	0	0	1	3	1	.176	.333	.235	55	-1	-1	2	0			0	/O	0.0
Total	7	436	1493	207	410	73	26	6	174	100	86	.275	.322	.370	81	-41	-44	176	11	4		-14	O/3C	-6.1

■ BILLY HOLM
Holm, William Frederick Henry b: 7/21/12, Chicago, Ill. d: 7/27/77, East Chicago, Ind BR/TR, 5'10.5", 168 lbs. Deb: 9/24/43

YEAR	TM/L	G	AB	R	H	2B	3B	HR	RBI	BB	SO	AVG	OBP	SLG	PRO+	BR	/A	RC	SB	CS	SBR	FR	POS	TPR
1943	Chi-N	7	15	0	1	0	0	0		2	4	.067	.176	.067	-29	-2	-2	0				1	/C	0.0
1944	Chi-N	54	132	10	18	2	0	0	6	16	19	.136	.235	.152	10	-15	-15	6	1			-2	C	-1.4
1945	Bos-A	58	135	12	25	2	1	0	9	23	17	.185	.317	.215	54	-7	-7	11	1	1	-0	-3	C	-0.6
Total	3	119	282	22	44	4	1	0	15	41	40	.156	.272	.177	30	-24	-25	17	2	1		-4	C	-2.0

■ GARY HOLMAN
Holman, Gary Richard b: 1/25/44, Long Beach, Cal. BL/TL, 6'1", 200 lbs. Deb: 6/26/68

YEAR	TM/L	G	AB	R	H	2B	3B	HR	RBI	BB	SO	AVG	OBP	SLG	PRO+	BR	/A	RC	SB	CS	SBR	FR	POS	TPR
1968	Was-A	75	85	10	25	5	1	0	7	13	15	.294	.388	.376	137	4	4	13	0	0	0	2	1O	0.5
1969	Was-A	41	31	1	5	1	0	0	2	4	7	.161	.257	.194	29	-3	-3	2	0	0	0	-0	1/O	-0.3
Total	2	116	116	11	30	6	1	0	9	17	22	.259	.353	.328	107	1	1	15	0	0	0	2	/1O	0.2

■ FRED HOLMES
Holmes, Frederick C. b: 7/1/1878, Chicago, Ill. d: 2/13/56, Norwood Park, Ill. TR, Deb: 8/23/03

YEAR	TM/L	G	AB	R	H	2B	3B	HR	RBI	BB	SO	AVG	OBP	SLG	PRO+	BR	/A	RC	SB	CS	SBR	FR	POS	TPR
1903	NY-A	1	0	0	0	0	0	0	0	1		—	1.000	—	213	0	0	0	0			-0	/1	0.0
1904	Chi-N	1	3	1	1	1	0	0	0	0	1	.333	.333	.667	208	0	0	1	0			0	/C	0.0
Total	2	2	3	1	1	1	0	0	0	1	.333	.500	.667	258	1	1	1	0			-0	/C1	0.0

■ DUCKY HOLMES
Holmes, Howard Elbert b: 7/8/1883, Dayton, Ohio d: 9/18/45, Dayton, Ohio BR/TR, 5'10", 160 lbs. Deb: 4/18/06

YEAR	TM/L	G	AB	R	H	2B	3B	HR	RBI	BB	SO	AVG	OBP	SLG	PRO+	BR	/A	RC	SB	CS	SBR	FR	POS	TPR
1906	StL-N	9	27	2	5	0	0	0	2	2		.185	.241	.185	36	-2	-2	1	0			0	/C	0.0

■ DUCKY HOLMES
Holmes, James William b: 1/28/1869, Des Moines, Iowa d: 8/6/32, Truro, Iowa BL/TR, 5'6", 170 lbs. Deb: 8/08/1895

YEAR	TM/L	G	AB	R	H	2B	3B	HR	RBI	BB	SO	AVG	OBP	SLG	PRO+	BR	/A	RC	SB	CS	SBR	FR	POS	TPR
1895	Lou-N	40	161	33	60	10	2	3	20	12	9	.373	.426	.516	154	11	12	40	9			-11	O/S3P	0.0
1896	Lou-N	47	141	22	38	3	2	0	18	13	5	.270	.360	.319	85	-3	-2	20	8			-7	O/PS2	-0.8
1897	Lou-N	2	4	0	0	0	0	0	0	0	1	.000	.200	.000	-45	-1	-1	0	0			1	/S	0.0
	NY-N	79	306	51	82	8	6	1	44	18		.268	.317	.343	78	-10	-9	44	30			-7	O/S	-1.8
	Yr	81	310	51	82	8	6	1	44	19		.265	.315	.339	77	-11	-10	44	30			-6		-1.8
1898	StL-N	23	101	9	24	1	1	0	2	2		.238	.260	.267	52	-6	-6	8	4			2	O	-0.4
	Bal-N	113	442	54	126	10	9	1	64	23		.285	.333	.355	98	-0	-1	62	25			3	*O	-0.4
	Yr	136	543	63	150	11	10	1	64	25		.276	.320	.339	89	-6	-8	70	29			6		-0.8
1899	Bal-N	138	553	80	177	31	7	4	66	39		.320	.381	.423	118	17	18	111	50			6	*O	0.9
1901	Det-A	131	537	90	158	28	10	4	62	37		.294	.347	.406	105	7	7	91	35			-2	*O	0.0
1902	Det-A	92	362	50	93	15	4	2	33	28		.257	.321	.337	82	-7	-8	46	16			6	O	-0.7
1903	Was-A	21	71	13	16	3	1	1	8	5		.225	.276	.338	84	-1	-1	10	10			1	O/32	0.0
	Chi-A	86	344	53	96	7	5	0	18	25		.279	.328	.328	104	0	2	48	25			2	O/3	0.0
	Yr	107	415	66	112	10	6	1	26	30		.270	.319	.330	100	-1	1	58	35			3		0.0
1904	Chi-A	68	251	42	78	11	9	1	19	14		.311	.347	.438	156	13	14	45	13			2	O	1.4
1905	Chi-A	92	328	42	66	15	2	0	22	19		.201	.245	.259	55	-14	-13	27	11			-1	O	-1.9
Total	10	932	3601	539	1014	142	58	17	374	236	14	.282	.335	.367	101	6	4	552	236			-5	O/3SP2	-3.7

■ TOMMY HOLMES
Holmes, Thomas Francis "Kelly" b: 3/29/17, Brooklyn, N.Y. BL/TL, 5'10", 180 lbs. Deb: 4/14/42 M

YEAR	TM/L	G	AB	R	H	2B	3B	HR	RBI	BB	SO	AVG	OBP	SLG	PRO+	BR	/A	RC	SB	CS	SBR	FR	POS	TPR
1942	Bos-N	141	558	56	155	24	4	4	41	64	10	.278	.353	.357	110	7	7	76	2			9	*O	1.4
1943	Bos-N	152	629	75	170	33	10	5	41	58	20	.270	.334	.378	107	4	5	82	7			2	*O	0.1
1944	Bos-N	155	631	93	195	42	6	13	73	61	11	.309	.372	.456	127	26	23	110	4			3	*O	1.4
1945	Bos-N	154	636	125	224	47	6	28	117	70	9	.352	.420	.577	175	63	62	156	15			-1	*O	5.3
1946	Bos-N	149	568	80	176	35	6	6	79	58	14	.310	.377	.424	126	20	19	91	7			4	*O	2.1
1947	Bos-N	150	618	90	191	33	3	9	53	44	16	.309	.360	.416	108	4	6	91	3			4	*O	0.5
1948	*Bos-N	139	585	85	190	35	7	6	61	46	20	.325	.375	.439	122	16	17	94	1			-3	*O	0.4
1949	Bos-N	117	380	47	101	20	4	8	59	44	9	.266	.337	.403	103	-2	1	51	1			-1	*O	-0.5
1950	Bos-N	105	322	44	96	20	1	9	51	33	8	.298	.370	.450	122	7	10	53	0			-4	*O	0.3
1951	Bos-N	27	29	1	5	2	0	0	5	3	4	.172	.250	.241	35	-3	-2	2	0	0	0	-1	/OM	-0.2
1952	*Bro-N	31	36	2	4	1	0	0	1	4	4	.111	.200	.139	-4	-5	-5	1	0	0	0		/O	-0.4
Total	11	1320	4992	698	1507	292	47	88	581	480	122	.302	.366	.432	122	138	145	809	40	0		12	*O	10.4

■ RED HOLT
Holt, James Emmett Madison b: 7/25/1894, Dayton, Tenn. d: 2/2/61, Birmingham, Ala. BL/TL, 5'11", 175 lbs. Deb: 9/05/25

YEAR	TM/L	G	AB	R	H	2B	3B	HR	RBI	BB	SO	AVG	OBP	SLG	PRO+	BR	/A	RC	SB	CS	SBR	FR	POS	TPR
1925	Phi-A	27	88	13	24	7	0	1	8	12	9	.273	.360	.386	84	-1	-2	13	0	0	0	0	1	-0.1

■ JIM HOLT
Holt, James William b: 5/27/44, Graham, N.C. BL/TR, 6', 180 lbs. Deb: 4/17/68

YEAR	TM/L	G	AB	R	H	2B	3B	HR	RBI	BB	SO	AVG	OBP	SLG	PRO+	BR	/A	RC	SB	CS	SBR	FR	POS	TPR
1968	Min-A	70	106	9	22	2	1	0	8	4	20	.208	.236	.245	44	-7	-7	5	0	1	-1	0	O/1	-1.0
1969	Min-A	12	14	3	5	0	0	1	2	0	4	.357	.357	.571	153	1	1	3	0	0	0	-0	/O1	0.0

YEAR	TM/L	G	AB	R	H	2B	3B	HR	RBI	BB	SO	AVG	OBP	SLG	PRO+	BR	/A	RC	SB	CS	SBR	FR	POS	TPR
1970	*Min-A	142	319	37	85	9	3	3	40	17	32	.266	.304	.342	77	-10	-11	32	3	1	0	-11	*O/1	-2.7
1971	Min-A	126	340	35	88	11	3	1	29	16	28	.259	.294	.318	71	-12	-13	30	5	1	1	-6	*O/1	-2.3
1972	Min-A	10	27	6	12	1	0	1	6	0	1	.444	.444	.593	197	3	3	6	0	0	0	0	/O1	0.3
1973	Min-A	132	441	52	131	25	3	11	58	29	43	.297	.343	.442	115	10	8	63	0	3	-2	-3	*O1	-0.1
1974	Min-A	79	197	24	50	11	0	0	16	14	16	.254	.307	.310	75	-6	-6	18	0	0	0	5	1/O	-0.4
	*Oak-A	30	42	1	6	0	0	0	0	1	9	.143	.182	.143	-6	-6	-5	1	0	0	0	1	1/D	-0.4
	Yr	109	239	25	56	11	0	0	16	15	25	.234	.285	.280	62	-11	-11	19	0	0	0	6		-0.8
1975	*Oak-A	102	123	7	27	3	0	2	16	11	11	.220	.294	.293	68	-5	-5	10	0	0	0	2	1/OCD	-0.6
1976	Oak-A	4	7	0	2	2	0	0	2	1	2	.286	.375	.571	182	1	1	2	0	0	0	0	/D	0.1
Total	9	707	1616	174	428	64	10	19	177	93	166	.265	.308	.352	84	-31	-35	170	8	6	-1	-12	O1/DC	-7.1

■ ROGER HOLT   Holt, Roger Boyd b: 4/8/56, Daytona Beach, Fla.   BB/TR, 5'11", 165 lbs.   Deb: 10/04/80

YEAR	TM/L	G	AB	R	H	2B	3B	HR	RBI	BB	SO	AVG	OBP	SLG	PRO+	BR	/A	RC	SB	CS	SBR	FR	POS	TPR
1980	NY-A	2	6	0	1	0	0	0	1	1	2	.167	.286	.167	28	-1	-1	0	0	0	0	1	/2	0.0

■ MARTY HONAN   Honan, Martin Weldon b: 1870, Chicago, Ill. d: 8/20/08, Chicago, Ill.   Deb: 10/03/1890

YEAR	TM/L	G	AB	R	H	2B	3B	HR	RBI	BB	SO	AVG	OBP	SLG	PRO+	BR	/A	RC	SB	CS	SBR	FR	POS	TPR
1890	Chi-N	1	3	0	0	0	0	0	1	0	2	.000	.000	.000	-96	-1	-1	0	0			0	/C	0.0
1891	Chi-N	1	12	1	2	0	1	0	3	1	3	.167	.231	.333	65	-1	-1	1	0			3	/C	0.2
Total	2	6	15	1	2	0	1	0	4	1	5	.133	.188	.267	33	-1	-1	1	0			3	/C	0.2

■ ABIE HOOD   Hood, Albie Larrison b: 1/31/03, Sanford, N.C. d: 10/14/88, Chesapeake, Va.   BL/TR, 5'7", 152 lbs.   Deb: 7/15/25

YEAR	TM/L	G	AB	R	H	2B	3B	HR	RBI	BB	SO	AVG	OBP	SLG	PRO+	BR	/A	RC	SB	CS	SBR	FR	POS	TPR
1925	Bos-N	5	21	2	6	2	0	1	2	1	0	.286	.318	.524	122	0	0	3	0	0	0	-4	/2	-0.2

■ WALLY HOOD   Hood, Wallace James Sr. b: 2/9/1895, Whittier, Cal. d: 5/2/65, Hollywood, Cal.   BR/TR, 5'11.5", 160 lbs.   Deb: 4/15/20

YEAR	TM/L	G	AB	R	H	2B	3B	HR	RBI	BB	SO	AVG	OBP	SLG	PRO+	BR	/A	RC	SB	CS	SBR	FR	POS	TPR
1920	Bro-N	7	14	4	2	1	0	0	1	4	4	.143	.333	.214	58	-1	-1	2	2	0	1	2	/O	0.1
	Pit-N	2	1	1	0	0	0	0	0	1	0	.000	.500	.000	50	0	0	0	1	0	0	0	H	0.0
	Yr	9	15	5	2	1	0	0	1	5	4	.133	.360	.200	59	-0	-1	2	3	0	1	2		0.1
1921	Bro-N	56	65	16	17	1	2	1	4	9	14	.262	.360	.385	94	-0	-0	9	2	2	-1	-5	O	-0.6
1922	Bro-N	2	0	2	0	0	0	0	0	0	0	—	—	—	—	0	0	0	0	0	0	0	R	0.0
Total	3	67	80	23	19	2	2	1	5	14	18	.237	.358	.350	88	-1	-0	11	5	2	0	-3	/O	-0.5

■ ALEX HOOKS   Hooks, Alexander Marcus b: 8/29/06, Edgewood, Tex.   BL/TL, 6'1", 183 lbs.   Deb: 4/17/35

YEAR	TM/L	G	AB	R	H	2B	3B	HR	RBI	BB	SO	AVG	OBP	SLG	PRO+	BR	/A	RC	SB	CS	SBR	FR	POS	TPR
1935	Phi-A	15	44	4	10	3	0	0	4	3	10	.227	.277	.295	48	-3	-3	4	0	0	0	0	1	-0.3

■ HARRY HOOPER   Hooper, Harry Bartholomew b: 8/24/1887, Bell Station, Cal. d: 12/18/74, Santa Cruz, Cal.   BL/TR, 5'10", 168 lbs.   Deb: 4/16/09   H

YEAR	TM/L	G	AB	R	H	2B	3B	HR	RBI	BB	SO	AVG	OBP	SLG	PRO+	BR	/A	RC	SB	CS	SBR	FR	POS	TPR
1909	Bos-A	81	255	29	72	3	4	0	12	16		.282	.337	.325	107	3	2	33	15			4	O	0.4
1910	Bos-A	155	584	81	156	9	10	2	27	62		.267	.346	.327	108	9	7	82	40			11	*O	1.2
1911	Bos-A	130	524	93	163	20	6	4	45	73		.311	.399	.395	123	18	19	98	38			6	*O	1.4
1912	*Bos-A	147	590	98	143	20	12	2	53	66		.242	.327	.327	83	-10	-14	73	29			2	*O	-2.0
1913	Bos-A	148	586	100	169	29	12	4	40	60	51	.288	.359	.399	119	16	14	89	26			9	*O/P	1.6
1914	Bos-A	142	530	85	137	23	15	1	41	58	47	.258	.336	.364	110	6	6	73	19	14	-3	11	*O	0.7
1915	*Bos-A	149	566	90	133	20	13	2	51	89	36	.235	.342	.327	103	2	4	66	22	20	-5	11	*O	0.2
1916	*Bos-A	151	575	75	156	20	11	1	37	80	35	.271	.361	.350	113	11	11	80	27	11	2	8	*O	1.3
1917	Bos-A	151	559	89	143	21	11	3	45	80	41	.256	.355	.349	116	12	13	76	21			-1	*O	0.3
1918	*Bos-A	126	474	81	137	26	13	1	44	75	25	.289	.391	.405	143	25	26	82	24			0	*O	2.2
1919	Bos-A	128	491	76	131	25	6	3	49	79	28	.267	.374	.360	113	7	11	72	23			10	*O	1.2
1920	Bos-A	139	536	91	167	30	17	7	53	88	27	.312	.411	.470	139	28	31	104	16	18	-6	7	*O	1.9
1921	Chi-A	108	419	74	137	26	5	8	58	55	21	.327	.406	.470	125	16	16	82	13	7	-0	-3	*O	0.4
1922	Chi-A	152	602	111	183	35	8	11	80	68	33	.304	.379	.444	114	13	13	102	16	12	-2	7	*O	0.6
1923	Chi-A	145	576	87	166	32	4	10	65	68	22	.288	.370	.410	106	5	6	88	18	18	-5	-4	*O	-1.5
1924	Chi-A	130	476	107	156	27	8	10	62	65	26	.328	.413	.481	134	22	25	95	16	13	-3	11	*O	2.1
1925	Chi-A	127	442	62	117	23	5	6	55	54	21	.265	.351	.380	90	-10	-6	62	12	8	-1	4	*O	-1.3
Total	17	2309	8785	1429	2466	389	160	75	817	1136	412	.281	.368	.387	114	174	185	1349	375	121		91	*O/P	10.7

■ MIKE HOOPER   Hooper, Michael H. b: 2/7/1850, Baltimore, Md. d: 12/1/17, Baltimore, Md.   5'6", 165 lbs.   Deb: 6/27/1873

YEAR	TM/L	G	AB	R	H	2B	3B	HR	RBI	BB	SO	AVG	OBP	SLG	PRO+	BR	/A	RC	SB	CS	SBR	FR	POS	TPR
1873	Mar-n	3	14	3	3	0	0	0		0		.214	.214	.214	35	-1	-1	1					/CO	0.0

■ CHARLIE HOOVER   Hoover, Charles E. b: 9/21/1865, Mound City, Ill.   TR ,   Deb: 10/09/1888

YEAR	TM/L	G	AB	R	H	2B	3B	HR	RBI	BB	SO	AVG	OBP	SLG	PRO+	BR	/A	RC	SB	CS	SBR	FR	POS	TPR
1888	KC-a	3	10	0	3	0	0	0	1	0		.300	.300	.300	90	-0	-0	1	0			0	/C	0.0
1889	KC-a	71	258	44	64	2	5	1	25	29	38	.248	.329	.306	79	-5	-7	30	9			-3	C/3O	-0.2
Total	2	74	268	44	67	2	5	1	26	29	38	.250	.328	.306	79	-5	-8	31	9			-3	/C3O	-0.2

■ JOE HOOVER   Hoover, Robert Joseph b: 4/15/15, Brawley, Tex. d: 9/2/65, Los Angeles, Cal.   BR/TR, 5'11", 175 lbs.   Deb: 4/21/43

YEAR	TM/L	G	AB	R	H	2B	3B	HR	RBI	BB	SO	AVG	OBP	SLG	PRO+	BR	/A	RC	SB	CS	SBR	FR	POS	TPR
1943	Det-A	144	575	78	140	15	8	4	38	36	101	.243	.289	.318	72	-18	-23	54	6	5	-1	-6	*S	-3.0
1944	Det-A	120	441	67	104	20	2	0	29	35	66	.236	.291	.290	66	-17	-20	40	7	10	-4	15	*S/2	-0.1
1945	*Det-A	74	222	33	57	10	5	1	17	21	35	.257	.324	.360	92	-1	-2	28	6	2	1	-7	S	-0.5
Total	3	338	1238	178	301	45	15	5	84	92	202	.243	.300	.316	73	-36	-45	122	19	17	-5	3	S/2	-3.6

■ BUSTER HOOVER   Hoover, William J. b: 1863, Philadelphia, Pa.   BR/TR, 6'1", 178 lbs.   Deb: 4/17/1884

YEAR	TM/L	G	AB	R	H	2B	3B	HR	RBI	BB	SO	AVG	OBP	SLG	PRO+	BR	/A	RC	SB	CS	SBR	FR	POS	TPR
1884	Phi-U	63	275	76	100	20	8	0		12		.364	.390	.495	213	27	30	54	0			-1	OS/123	2.5
	Phi-N	10	42	6	8	1	0	1	4	4	9	.190	.261	.286	75	-1	-1	3				-2	O	-0.1
1886	Bal-a	40	157	25	34	2	6	0		16		.217	.297	.306	93	-1	-1	19	15			-1	O	-0.2
1892	Cin-N	14	51	7	9	0	0	0	2	5	4	.176	.250	.176	31	-4	-4	3	1			1	O	-0.2
Total	3	127	525	114	151	23	14	1	6	37	13	.288	.337	.390	143	20	25	79	16			-3	O/S213	2.0

■ DON HOPKINS   Hopkins, Donald b: 1/9/52, West Point, Miss.   BL/TR, 6', 175 lbs.   Deb: 4/08/75

YEAR	TM/L	G	AB	R	H	2B	3B	HR	RBI	BB	SO	AVG	OBP	SLG	PRO+	BR	/A	RC	SB	CS	SBR	FR	POS	TPR
1975	*Oak-A	82	6	25	1	0	0	0	0	2	0	.167	.375	.167	59	-0	-0	-9	21	9	1	1	D/OR	0.2
1976	Oak-A	3	0	0	0	0	0	0	0	0	0	—	—	—	—	0	0	0	0	1	-1	0	R	0.0
Total	2	85	6	25	1	0	0	0	0	2	0	.167	.375	.167	59	-0	-0	-9	21	10	0	1	/DO	0.2

■ GAIL HOPKINS   Hopkins, Gail Eason b: 2/19/43, Tulsa, Okla.   BL/TR, 5'10", 198 lbs.   Deb: 6/29/68

YEAR	TM/L	G	AB	R	H	2B	3B	HR	RBI	BB	SO	AVG	OBP	SLG	PRO+	BR	/A	RC	SB	CS	SBR	FR	POS	TPR
1968	Chi-A	29	37	4	8	2	0	2	6	3	.216	.326	.270	81	-1	-1	4	0	0	0	-2	/1	-0.3
1969	Chi-A	124	373	52	99	13	3	8	46	50	28	.265	.354	.381	100	4	1	51	2	1	0	-3	*1	-0.9
1970	Chi-A	116	287	32	82	8	1	6	29	28	19	.286	.348	.383	99	-1	-0	39	0	0	0	-2	1/C	-0.5
1971	KC-A	103	295	35	82	16	1	9	47	37	13	.278	.366	.431	126	10	10	47	3	1	0	3	1	1.0
1972	KC-A	53	71	1	15	2	0	0	5	7	4	.211	.282	.239	56	-4	-4	5	0	0	0	-1	1/3	-0.6
1973	KC-A	74	138	17	34	6	1	2	16	29	15	.246	.385	.348	100	3	1	18	1	2	-1	0	D1	0.0
1974	LA-N	15	18	1	4	0	0	0	3	1	.222	.333	.222	60	-1	-1	1	0	0	0	1	/C1	0.0
Total	7	514	1219	142	324	47	6	25	145	160	83	.266	.355	.376	103	13	8	165	6	4	-1	-5	1/DC3	-1.3

■ BUCK HOPKINS   Hopkins, John Winton "Sis" b: 1/3/1883, Grafton, Va. d: 10/2/29, Phoebus, Va.   BR/TR, 5'10", 165 lbs.   Deb: 7/22/07

YEAR	TM/L	G	AB	R	H	2B	3B	HR	RBI	BB	SO	AVG	OBP	SLG	PRO+	BR	/A	RC	SB	CS	SBR	FR	POS	TPR
1907	StL-N	15	44	7	6	3	0	0	3	10		.136	.296	.205	61	-2	-1	3				-4	O	-0.6

■ MARTY HOPKINS   Hopkins, Meredith Hilliard b: 2/22/07, Wolfe City, Tex. d: 11/20/63, Dallas, Tex.   BR/TR, 5'11", 175 lbs.   Deb: 4/17/34

YEAR	TM/L	G	AB	R	H	2B	3B	HR	RBI	BB	SO	AVG	OBP	SLG	PRO+	BR	/A	RC	SB	CS	SBR	FR	POS	TPR
1934	Phi-N	10	25	6	3	2	0	0	3	7	5	.120	.313	.200	36	-2	-2	2	0			-1	/3	-0.1
	Chi-A	67	210	22	45	8	1	0	28	42	26	.214	.348	.276	61	-10	-11	23	0	3	-2	4	3	-0.7
1935	Chi-A	59	144	20	32	3	0	2	17	36	23	.222	.378	.285	72	-4	-5	19	1	0	0	-7	3/2	-1.0

YEAR	TM/L	G	AB	R	H	2B	3B	HR	RBI	BB	SO	AVG	OBP	SLG	PRO+	BR	/A	RC	SB	CS	SBR	FR	POS	TPR
Total	2	136	379	48	80	12	0	4	48	85	54	.211	.357	.274	63	-16	-18	44	1	3̲		-3	3/2	-1.8

■ MIKE HOPKINS   Hopkins, Michael Joseph "Skinner"   b: 11/1/1872, Glasgow, Scotland   d: 2/5/52, Pittsburgh, Pa.   BR/TR, 5'8", 160 lbs.   Deb: 8/24/02

YEAR	TM/L	G	AB	R	H	2B	3B	HR	RBI	BB	SO	AVG	OBP	SLG	PRO+	BR	/A	RC	SB	CS	SBR	FR	POS	TPR
1902	Pit-N	1	2	0	2	1	0	0	0	0	0	1.000	1.000	1.500	653	1	1	3	0			0	/C	0.2

■ JOHNNY HOPP   Hopp, John Leonard "Hippity"   b: 7/18/16, Hastings, Neb.   BL/TL, 5'10", 170 lbs.   Deb: 9/18/39   C

YEAR	TM/L	G	AB	R	H	2B	3B	HR	RBI	BB	SO	AVG	OBP	SLG	PRO+	BR	/A	RC	SB	CS	SBR	FR	POS	TPR
1939	StL-N	6	4	1	2	1	0	0	2	1	1	.500	.600	.750	246	1	1	2	0			0	/1	0.1
1940	StL-N	80	152	24	41	7	4	1	14	9	21	.270	.315	.388	88	-2	-3	18	3			5	O1	0.0
1941	StL-N	134	445	83	135	25	11	4	50	50	63	.303	.378	.436	121	17	14	77	15			1	O1	0.5
1942	*StL-N	95	314	41	81	16	7	3	37	36	40	.258	.334	.382	102	4	1	43	14			-3	1	-0.9
1943	*StL-N	91	241	33	54	10	2	2	25	24	22	.224	.297	.307	71	-8	-9	24	8			2	O1	-1.0
1944	*StL-N	139	527	106	177	35	9	11	72	58	47	.336	.404	.499	150	37	36	110	15			-12	*O/1	1.3
1945	StL-N	124	446	67	129	22	8	3	44	49	24	.289	.363	.395	108	7	6	68	14			1	*O1	0.1
1946	Bos-N	129	445	71	148	23	8	3	48	34	34	.333	.386	.440	133	20	19	77	21			1	1O	1.4
1947	Bos-N	134	430	74	124	20	2	2	32	58	30	.288	.376	.358	98	-0	1	62	13			-9	*O	-1.2
1948	Pit-N	120	392	64	109	15	12	1	31	40	25	.278	.345	.385	95	-1	-2	53	5			5	O1	-0.3
1949	Pit-N	20	55	5	12	3	1	0	3	7	3	.218	.306	.309	64	-3	-3	5	0			-1	/O1	-0.3
	Bro-N	8	14	0	0	0	0	0	0	0	3	.000	.000	.000	-96	-4	-4	0	0			1	/O1	-0.2
	Pit-N	85	316	50	106	11	4	5	36	30	26	.335	.393	.443	121	11	10	56	9			-1	1/O	0.8
	Yr	113	385	55	118	14	5	5	39	37	32	.306	.367	.408	105	5	3	59	9			-1		0.3
1950	Pit-N	106	318	51	108	24	5	8	47	43	17	.340	.420	.522	141	22	21	71	7			-6	1/O	1.1
	*NY-A	19	27	9	9	2	1	1	8	8	1	.333	.486	.593	180	3	4	8	0	1	-1	0	1/O	0.2
1951	*NY-A	46	63	10	13	1	0	2	4	9	11	.206	.306	.317	71	-3	-2	7	2	0	1	-1	1	-0.3
1952	NY-A	15	25	4	4	0	0	0	2	2	3	.160	.250	.160	17	-3	-3	1	2	0	1	1	1	-0.1
	Det-A	42	46	5	10	1	0	0	3	6	7	.217	.308	.239	53	-3	-3	4	0	0	0	-1	/O1	-0.3
	Yr	57	71	9	14	1	0	0	5	8	10	.197	.287	.211	41	-5	-5	5	2	0	1	-0		-0.4
Total	14	1393	4260	698	1262	216	74	46	458	464	378	.296	.368	.414	113	96	82	685	128	1̲		-19	O1	0.9

■ SHAGS HORAN   Horan, Joseph Patrick   b: 9/6/1895, St.Louis, Mo.   d: 2/13/69, Torrance, Cal.   BR/TR, 5'10", 170 lbs.   Deb: 7/14/24

YEAR	TM/L	G	AB	R	H	2B	3B	HR	RBI	BB	SO	AVG	OBP	SLG	PRO+	BR	/A	RC	SB	CS	SBR	FR	POS	TPR
1924	NY-A	22	31	4	9	1	0	0	7	1	5	.290	.313	.323	64	-2	-2	3	0	0	0	-4	O	-0.5

■ SAM HORN   Horn, Samuel Lee   b: 11/2/63, Dallas, Tex.   BL/TL, 6'5", 215 lbs.   Deb: 7/25/87

YEAR	TM/L	G	AB	R	H	2B	3B	HR	RBI	BB	SO	AVG	OBP	SLG	PRO+	BR	/A	RC	SB	CS	SBR	FR	POS	TPR
1987	Bos-A	46	158	31	44	7	0	14	34	17	55	.278	.356	.589	141	10	9	32	0	1	-1	0	D	0.8
1988	Bos-A	24	61	4	9	0	0	2	8	11	20	.148	.278	.246	46	-4	-4	5	0	0	0	0	D	-0.4
1989	Bos-A	33	54	1	8	2	0	0	4	8	16	.148	.258	.185	25	-5	-6	2	0	0	0	0	D/1	-0.5
1990	Bal-A	79	246	30	61	13	0	14	45	32	62	.248	.335	.472	110	6	7	38	0	0	0	-0	D1	0.7
Total	4	182	519	66	122	22	0	30	91	68	153	.235	.326	.451	110	7	7	76	0	1	-1	-0	D/1	0.6

■ BOB HORNER   Horner, James Robert   b: 8/6/57, Junction City, Kan.   BR/TR, 6'1", 195 lbs.   Deb: 6/16/78

YEAR	TM/L	G	AB	R	H	2B	3B	HR	RBI	BB	SO	AVG	OBP	SLG	PRO+	BR	/A	RC	SB	CS	SBR	FR	POS	TPR
1978	Atl-N	89	323	50	86	17	1	23	63	24	42	.266	.321	.539	123	13	9	54	0	0	0	6	3	1.5
1979	Atl-N	121	487	66	153	15	1	33	98	22	74	.314	.348	.552	132	25	21	89	0	2	-1	-6	31	0.8
1980	Atl-N	124	463	81	124	15	1	35	89	27	50	.268	.310	.529	126	15	14	70	3	1	0	5	*3/1	1.9
1981	Atl-N	79	300	42	83	10	0	15	42	32	39	.277	.348	.460	125	10	9	47	2	3	-1	-15	3	-1.1
1982	*Atl-N	140	499	85	130	24	0	32	97	66	75	.261	.351	.501	131	23	21	86	3	5	-2	-17	*3	0.0
1983	Atl-N	104	386	75	117	25	1	20	68	50	63	.303	.384	.528	140	26	23	76	4	2	0	-13	*3/1	0.6
1984	Atl-N	32	113	15	31	8	0	3	19	14	17	.274	.354	.425	110	3	2	17	0	0	0	-1	3	0.1
1985	Atl-N	130	483	61	129	25	3	27	89	50	57	.267	.337	.499	123	18	15	77	1	1	-0	-10	13	0.2
1986	Atl-N	141	517	70	141	22	0	27	87	52	72	.273	.342	.472	116	14	11	79	1	4	-2	2	*1	0.6
1988	StL-N	60	206	15	53	9	1	3	33	32	23	.257	.360	.354	105	3	2	26	0	0	0	-1	1	0.0
Total	10	1020	3777	560	1047	169	8	218	685	369	512	.277	.344	.499	125	151	126	621	14	18	-7	-50	31	4.6

■ ROGERS HORNSBY   Hornsby, Rogers "Rajah"   b: 4/27/1896, Winters, Tex.   d: 1/5/63, Chicago, Ill.   BR/TR, 5'11", 175 lbs.   Deb: 9/10/15   MCH

YEAR	TM/L	G	AB	R	H	2B	3B	HR	RBI	BB	SO	AVG	OBP	SLG	PRO+	BR	/A	RC	SB	CS	SBR	FR	POS	TPR
1915	StL-N	18	57	5	14	2	0	0	4	2	6	.246	.271	.281	67	-2	-2	4	0	2	-1	1	S	-0.2
1916	StL-N	139	495	63	155	17	15	6	65	40	63	.313	.369	.444	150	28	28	88	17			-2	3S1/2	3.3
1917	StL-N	145	523	86	171	24	**17**	8	66	45	34	.327	.385	**.484**	170	40	41	100	17			21	*S	7.0
1918	StL-N	115	416	51	117	19	11	5	60	40	43	.281	.349	.416	138	16	17	60	8			11	*S/O	3.3
1919	StL-N	138	512	68	163	15	9	8	71	48	41	.318	.384	.430	154	29	32	87	17			2	3S2/1	3.9
1920	StL-N	149	589	96	**218**	**44**	20	9	**94**	60	50	**.370**	**.431**	.559	190	63	65	138	12	15	-5	11	*2	7.7
1921	StL-N	154	592	**131**	**235**	**44**	18	21	**126**	60	48	**.397**	**.458**	.639	191	74	76	169	13	13	-4	-3	*2/OS31	6.7
1922	StL-N	154	623	141	**250**	**46**	14	**42**	**152**	65	50	**.401**	**.459**	**.722**	210	90	94	**200**	17	12	-2	-7	*2	7.6
1923	StL-N	107	424	89	163	32	10	17	83	55	29	**.384**	**.459**	.627	188	52	53	120	3	7	-3	-17	21	3.2
1924	StL-N	143	536	121	**227**	43	14	25	94	**89**	32	**.424**	**.507**	**.696**	223	94	96	186	5	12	-6	-4	*2	7.5
1925	StL-N	138	504	133	203	41	10	**39**	**143**	83	39	**.403**	**.489**	**.756**	208	87	85	187	5	3	-0	-20	*2M	**5.8**
1926	*StL-N	134	527	96	167	34	5	11	93	61	39	.317	.388	.463	123	21	19	94	3			-29	*2M	-0.3
1927	NY-N	155	568	**133**	205	32	9	26	125	**86**	38	.361	.448	.586	176	63	63	148	9			3	*2	6.1
1928	Bos-N	140	486	99	188	42	7	21	94	**107**	41	**.387**	**.498**	.632	204	72	76	154	5			-23	*2M	5.2
1929	*Chi-N	156	602	**156**	229	47	8	39	149	87	65	.380	.459	.679	178	74	74	183	2			1	*2	7.0
1930	Chi-N	42	104	15	32	5	1	2	18	12	12	.308	.385	.433	96	-0	-0	17	0			-3	2M	0.0
1931	Chi-N	100	357	64	118	37	1	16	90	56	23	.331	.421	.574	162	34	33	90	1			-15	23M	2.2
1932	Chi-N	19	58	10	13	0	0	1	7	10	4	.224	.357	.310	82	-1	-1	7	0			-4	O/3M	-0.4
1933	StL-N	46	83	9	27	6	0	2	21	12	6	.325	.423	.470	147	7	6	17	1			-7	2	0.0
	StL-A	11	9	2	3	1	0	1	2	2	1	.333	.455	.778	208	2	1	3	0	0	0	0	HM	0.1
1934	StL-A	24	23	2	7	2	0	1	11	7	4	.304	.484	.522	147	3	2	7	0	0	0	1	/3OM	0.3
1935	StL-A	10	24	1	5	3	0	0	3	3	6	.208	.296	.333	60	-1	-2	2	0	0	0	0	/123M	-0.1
1936	StL-A	2	5	1	2	0	0	0	2	1	0	.400	.500	.400	121	0	0	1	0	0	0	-0	/1M	0.0
1937	StL-A	20	56	1	18	3	0	1	11	7	5	.321	.397	.429	107	1	1	9	0	0	0	-4	2M	0.0
Total	23	2259	8173	1579	2930	541	169	301	1584	1038	679	.358	.434	.577	176	844	859	2074	135	64̲		-89	*2S3/10	75.8

■ JOE HORNUNG   Hornung, Michael Joseph "Ubbo Ubbo"   b: 6/12/1857, Carthage, N.Y.   d: 10/30/31, Howard Beach, N.Y.   BR/TR, 5'8.5", 164 lbs.   Deb: 5/01/1879   U

YEAR	TM/L	G	AB	R	H	2B	3B	HR	RBI	BB	SO	AVG	OBP	SLG	PRO+	BR	/A	RC	SB	CS	SBR	FR	POS	TPR
1879	Buf-N	78	319	46	85	18	7	0	38	2	27	.266	.271	.367	105	2	1	33				-2	*O/1	-0.2
1880	Buf-N	85	342	47	91	8	11	1	42	8	29	.266	.283	.363	115	6	5	36				-1	*O1/2P	0.1
1881	Bos-N	83	324	40	78	12	8	2	25	5	25	.241	.252	.346	90	-5	-3	29				11	*O	0.6
1882	Bos-N	85	388	67	117	14	11	1	50	2	25	.302	.305	.402	124	10	10	49				10	*O/1	1.7
1883	Bos-N	98	446	**107**	124	25	13	8	66	8	54	.278	.291	.446	117	10	8	59				6	*O/3	1.4
1884	Bos-N	115	518	119	139	27	10	7	51	17	80	.268	.292	.400	116	8	9	62				3	*O/1	0.9
1885	Bos-N	25	109	14	22	4	1	1	7	1	20	.202	.209	.284	61	-5	-5	7				-3	O	-0.7
1886	Bos-N	94	424	67	109	12	2	2	40	10	62	.257	.274	.309	80	-12	-10	41	16			6	*O	-0.1
1887	Bos-N	98	437	85	118	10	6	5	49	17	28	.270	.302	.355	83	-10	-10	61	41			13	*O	0.3
1888	Bos-N	107	431	61	103	11	7	3	53	16	39	.239	.269	.318	87	-6	-7	46	29			-8	*O	-1.5
1889	Bal-a	135	533	73	122	13	9	1	78	22	72	.229	.269	.293	60	-27	-29	52	34			11	*O/3	-1.8
1890	NY-N	120	513	62	122	18	5	0	65	12	37	.238	.258	.292	62	-26	-26	50	39			-4	O1/3S	-2.9
Total	12	1123	4784	788	1230	172	90	31	564	120	498	.257	.277	.350	92	-56	-56	524	159			44	*O/132SP	-2.2

■ TONY HORTON   Horton, Anthony Darrin   b: 12/6/44, Santa Monica, Cal.   BR/TR, 6'3", 210 lbs.   Deb: 7/31/64

YEAR	TM/L	G	AB	R	H	2B	3B	HR	RBI	BB	SO	AVG	OBP	SLG	PRO+	BR	/A	RC	SB	CS	SBR	FR	POS	TPR
1964	Bos-A	36	126	9	28	5	0	1	8	3	20	.222	.240	.286	44	-9	-10	7	0	0	0	-1	O/1	-1.2

YEAR	TM/L	G	AB	R	H	2B	3B	HR	RBI	BB	SO	AVG	OBP	SLG	PRO+	BR	/A	RC	SB	CS	SBR	FR	POS	TPR
1965	Bos-A	60	163	23	48	8	1	7	23	18	36	.294	.365	.485	131	8	7	29	0	2	-1	-0	1	0.4
1966	Bos-A	6	22	0	3	0	0	0	2	0	5	.136	.136	.136	-19	-3	-4	0	0	0	0	1	/1	-0.2
1967	Bos-A	21	39	2	12	3	0	0	9	0	5	.308	.308	.385	96	0	-0	4	0	0	0	-1	/1	-0.1
	Cle-A	106	363	35	102	13	4	10	44	18	52	.281	.322	.421	117	7	7	48	3	0	1	-5	1	-0.4
	Yr	127	402	37	114	16	4	10	53	18	57	.284	.321	.418	114	7	6	52	3	0	1	-6		-0.5
1968	Cle-A	133	477	57	119	29	3	14	59	34	56	.249	.304	.411	117	7	8	59	3	1	0	-3	*1	0.0
1969	Cle-A	159	625	77	174	25	4	27	93	37	91	.278	.321	.461	113	10	8	85	3	3	-1	-0	*1	-0.3
1970	Cle-A	115	413	48	111	19	3	17	59	30	54	.269	.324	.453	107	5	3	55	3	2	-0	3	*1	0.0
Total	7	636	2228	251	597	102	15	76	297	140	319	.268	.315	.430	109	26	19	287	12	8	-1	-7	1/O	-1.8

■ WILLIE HORTON
Horton, Willie Watterson b: 10/18/42, Arno, Va. BR/TR, 5'11", 209 lbs. Deb: 9/10/63 C

YEAR	TM/L	G	AB	R	H	2B	3B	HR	RBI	BB	SO	AVG	OBP	SLG	PRO+	BR	/A	RC	SB	CS	SBR	FR	POS	TPR
1963	Det-A	15	43	6	14	2	1	1	4	0	8	.326	.326	.488	120	1	1	7	2	0	1	-1	/O	0.0
1964	Det-A	25	80	6	13	1	3	1	10	11	20	.162	.272	.287	55	-5	-5	7	0	0	0	-3	O	-0.8
1965	Det-A	143	512	69	140	20	2	29	104	48	101	.273	.343	.490	132	22	21	81	5	9	-4	3	*O/3	1.6
1966	Det-A	146	526	72	138	22	6	27	100	44	103	.262	.323	.481	125	17	16	80	1	1	-0	-4	*O	0.6
1967	Det-A	122	401	47	110	20	3	19	67	36	80	.274	.340	.481	137	19	18	64	0	0	0	-6	*O	0.9
1968	*Det-A	143	512	68	146	20	2	36	85	49	110	.285	.357	.543	165	41	40	95	0	3	-2	-5	*O	3.1
1969	Det-A	141	508	66	133	17	1	28	91	52	93	.262	.334	.465	116	13	10	78	3	3	-1	6	*O	1.2
1970	Det-A	96	371	53	113	18	2	17	69	28	43	.305	.357	.501	133	16	16	65	0	1	-1	-2	O	0.9
1971	Det-A	119	450	64	130	25	1	22	72	37	75	.289	.352	.496	133	21	19	73	1	5	-3	-13	*O	0.0
1972	*Det-A	108	333	44	77	9	5	11	36	27	42	.231	.295	.387	99	-0	-1	37	0	0	0	-8	O	-1.3
1973	Det-A	111	411	42	130	19	3	17	53	23	57	.316	.363	.501	132	21	18	69	1	4	-2	-13	*O/D	0.0
1974	Det-A	72	238	32	71	8	1	15	47	21	36	.298	.363	.529	149	16	15	44	0	1	-1	-7	O/D	0.6
1975	Det-A	159	615	62	169	18	1	25	92	44	109	.275	.323	.421	104	5	2	79	1	2	-1	0	*D	0.1
1976	Det-A	114	401	40	105	17	0	14	56	49	63	.262	.345	.409	116	10	8	55	0	0	0	0	*D	0.9
1977	Det-A	1	4	0	1	0	0	0	0	0	0	.250	.250	.250	35	-0	-0	0	0	0	0	-0	/O	0.0
	Tex-A	139	519	55	150	23	3	15	75	42	117	.289	.342	.432	108	6	6	73	2	3	-1	-2	*DO	0.2
	Yr	140	523	55	151	23	3	15	75	42	117	.289	.342	.430	108	6	5	73	2	3	-1	-2		0.2
1978	Cle-A	50	169	15	42	7	0	5	22	15	25	.249	.314	.379	95	-2	-1	19	3	0	1	0	D	0.0
	Oak-A	32	102	11	32	8	0	3	19	9	15	.314	.369	.480	145	5	6	18	0	1	-1	-1	D/O	0.4
	Tor-A	33	122	12	25	6	0	3	19	4	29	.205	.230	.328	54	-8	-8	8	0	0	0	-0	D	-0.7
	Yr	115	393	38	99	21	0	11	60	28	69	.252	.303	.389	95	-4	-4	44	3	1	0	-1		-0.3
1979	Sea-A	162	646	77	180	19	5	29	106	42	112	.279	.327	.458	107	6	5	91	1	1	-0	0	*D	0.4
1980	Sea-A	97	335	32	74	10	1	8	36	39	70	.221	.310	.328	74	-11	-12	35	0	4	-2	0	D	-1.3
Total	18	2028	7298	873	1993	284	40	325	1163	620	1313	.273	.335	.457	119	194	171	1077	20	38	-17	-56	*OD/3	6.8

■ TIM HOSLEY
Hosley, Timothy Kenneth b: 5/10/47, Spartanburg, S.C. BR/TR, 5'11", 185 lbs. Deb: 9/08/70

YEAR	TM/L	G	AB	R	H	2B	3B	HR	RBI	BB	SO	AVG	OBP	SLG	PRO+	BR	/A	RC	SB	CS	SBR	FR	POS	TPR
1970	Det-A	7	12	1	2	0	0	0	2	0	6	.167	.167	.417	55	-1	-1	1	0	0	0	2	/C	0.1
1971	Det-A	7	16	2	3	0	0	2	6	0	1	.188	.188	.563	102	-0	-0	1	0	0	0	-0	/C1	0.0
1973	Oak-A	13	14	3	3	0	0	0	2	2	3	.214	.313	.214	53	-1	-1	1	0	0	0	-1	C	-0.1
1974	Oak-A	11	7	3	2	0	0	0	1	1	2	.286	.375	.286	99	-0	0	1	0	0	0	-1	/C1	0.1
1975	Chi-N	62	141	22	36	7	0	6	20	27	25	.255	.382	.433	120	6	5	24	1	1	-0	-1	C	0.5
1976	Oak-A	37	55	4	9	2	0	1	4	8	12	.164	.270	.255	56	-3	-3	4	0	0	0	-1	C	-0.1
	Chi-N	1	1	0	0	0	0	0	0	0	0	.000	.000	.000	-92	-0	-0	0	0	0	0	0	H	0.0
1977	Oak-A	39	78	5	15	0	0	1	10	16	13	.192	.337	.231	59	-4	-4	7	0	0	0	3	CD/1	0.0
1978	Oak-A	13	23	1	7	2	0	0	3	1	6	.304	.360	.391	117	0	1	3	0	0	0	1	/CD	0.1
1981	Oak-A	18	21	2	2	0	0	1	5	2	5	.095	.174	.238	19	-2	-2	1	0	0	0	-0	/1D	-0.2
Total	9	208	368	43	79	11	0	12	53	57	73	.215	.326	.342	87	-5	-5	44	1	1	-0	1	C/D1	0.4

■ CHUCK HOSTETLER
Hostetler, Charles Cloyd b: 9/22/03, McClellandtown, Pa. d: 2/18/71, Fort Collins, Colo BL/TR, 6', 175 lbs. Deb: 4/18/44

YEAR	TM/L	G	AB	R	H	2B	3B	HR	RBI	BB	SO	AVG	OBP	SLG	PRO+	BR	/A	RC	SB	CS	SBR	FR	POS	TPR
1944	Det-A	90	265	42	79	9	2	0	20	21	31	.298	.350	.347	94	0	-2	33	4	4	-1	-4	O	-0.8
1945	*Det-A	42	44	3	7	3	0	0	2	7	8	.159	.275	.227	43	-3	-3	3	0	0	0	-1	/O	-0.4
Total	2	132	309	45	86	12	2	0	22	28	39	.278	.338	.330	87	-3	-5	36	4	4	-1	-4	/O	-1.2

■ DAVE HOSTETLER
Hostetler, David Alan b: 3/27/56, Pasadena, Cal. BR/TR, 6'4", 215 lbs. Deb: 9/15/81

YEAR	TM/L	G	AB	R	H	2B	3B	HR	RBI	BB	SO	AVG	OBP	SLG	PRO+	BR	/A	RC	SB	CS	SBR	FR	POS	TPR
1981	Mon-N	5	6	1	3	0	0	1	1	0	2	.500	.500	1.000	314	2	2	3	0	0	0	-0	/1	0.1
1982	Tex-A	113	418	53	97	12	3	22	67	42	113	.232	.304	.433	105	-1	1	52	2	2	-1	-11	*1/D	-1.2
1983	Tex-A	94	304	31	67	9	2	11	46	42	103	.220	.325	.372	93	-3	-2	36	0	2	-1	-0	D/1	-0.3
1984	Tex-A	37	82	7	18	2	1	3	10	13	27	.220	.326	.378	91	-0	-1	9	0	0	0	1	1D	0.0
1988	Pit-N	6	8	0	2	0	0	0	0	0	3	.250	.250	.250	45	-1	-1	1	0	0	0	0	/1C	0.0
Total	5	255	818	92	187	23	6	37	124	97	248	.229	.315	.407	100	-4	-1	101	2	4	-2	-10	1D/C	-1.4

■ PETE HOTALING
Hotaling, Peter James "Monkey" b: 12/16/1856, Mohawk, N.Y. d: 7/3/28, Cleveland, Ohio BR/TR, 5'8", 166 lbs. Deb: 5/01/1879

YEAR	TM/L	G	AB	R	H	2B	3B	HR	RBI	BB	SO	AVG	OBP	SLG	PRO+	BR	/A	RC	SB	CS	SBR	FR	POS	TPR
1879	Cin-N	81	369	64	103	20	9	1	27	12	17	.279	.302	.390	133	10	13	45				0	*O/C23	1.0
1880	Cle-N	78	325	40	78	17	8	0	41	10	30	.240	.263	.342	105	1	2	30				-4	*O/C	-0.4
1881	Wor-N	77	317	51	98	15	3	1	35	18	12	.309	.346	.385	123	11	8	43				-1	*O/C	0.6
1882	Bos-N	84	378	64	98	16	5	0	28	16	21	.259	.289	.328	97	-1	-1	37				1	*O	0.0
1883	Cle-N	100	417	54	108	20	8	0	30	12	31	.259	.280	.345	90	-6	-5	41				-2	*O	-0.3
1884	Cle-N	102	408	69	99	16	6	3	27	28	50	.243	.291	.333	93	-2	-2	41				-3	*O/2	-0.6
1885	Bro-a	94	370	73	95	9	5	1		49		.257	.350	.316	114	9	8	42				0	*O	0.3
1887	Cle-a	126	505	108	151	28	13	3		53		.299	.373	.424	128	17	20	98	43			1	*O	1.3
1888	Cle-a	98	403	67	101	7	6	0	55	26		.251	.307	.298	100	-0	1	49	35			-9	*O/C	-1.0
Total	9	840	3492	590	931	148	63	9	243	224	161	.267	.314	.353	109	39	42	426	78			-17	O/C23	0.9

■ KEN HOTTMAN
Hottman, Kenneth Roger b: 5/7/48, Stockton, Cal. BR/TR, 5'11", 190 lbs. Deb: 9/11/71

YEAR	TM/L	G	AB	R	H	2B	3B	HR	RBI	BB	SO	AVG	OBP	SLG	PRO+	BR	/A	RC	SB	CS	SBR	FR	POS	TPR
1971	Chi-A	6	16	1	2	0	0	0	0	1	2	.125	.176	.125	-13	-2	-2	0	0	0	0	-1	/O	-0.3

■ SADIE HOUCK
Houck, Sargent Perry b: 1856, Washington, D.C. d: 5/26/19, Washington, D.C. BR/TR, 5'7", 151 lbs. Deb: 5/01/1879

YEAR	TM/L	G	AB	R	H	2B	3B	HR	RBI	BB	SO	AVG	OBP	SLG	PRO+	BR	/A	RC	SB	CS	SBR	FR	POS	TPR
1879	Bos-N	80	356	69	95	24	9	2	49	4	11	.267	.275	.402	117	7	6	40				-8	OS	-0.1
1880	Bos-N	12	47	2	7	0	0	0	2	0	6	.149	.149	.149	1	-5	-4	1				-1	O	-0.5
	Pro-N	49	184	27	37	7	7	1	22	3	6	.201	.214	.332	85	-3	-3	13				-1	O	-0.4
	Yr	61	231	29	44	7	7	1	24	3	12	.190	.201	.294	68	-8	-7	14				-2		-0.9
1881	Det-N	75	308	43	86	16	6	1	36	6	6	.279	.293	.380	106	3	1	35				1	*S	0.7
1883	Det-N	101	416	52	105	18	12	0	40	9	18	.252	.268	.353	91	-7	-4	40				4	*S	0.4
1884	Phi-a	108	472	93	140	19	14	0		7		.297	.318	.396	126	17	12	61	23				*S/2	3.0
1885	Phi-a	93	388	74	99	10	9	0		10		.255	.286	.327	91	-2	-5	37	22				*S	1.5
1886	Bal-a	61	260	29	50	8	1	0		4		.192	.216	.231	42	-17	-16	19	25			-5	S/2O	-1.6
	Was-N	52	195	14	42	3	0	0	14	2	28	.215	.223	.231	41	-14	-13	11	4			-1	S/2	-1.2
1887	NY-a	10	33	3	5	1	0	0		3		.152	.243	.182	22	-3	-2	2	4				S/2	0.2
Total	8	641	2659	406	666	106	58	4	163	48	75	.250	.269	.338	92	-25	-29	261	31			38	SO/2	1.9

■ RALPH HOUK
Houk, Ralph George "Major" b: 8/9/19, Lawrence, Kan. BR/TR, 5'11", 193 lbs. Deb: 4/26/47 MC

YEAR	TM/L	G	AB	R	H	2B	3B	HR	RBI	BB	SO	AVG	OBP	SLG	PRO+	BR	/A	RC	SB	CS	SBR	FR	POS	TPR
1947	*NY-A	41	92	7	25	3	1	0	12	11	5	.272	.350	.326	89	-1	-1	11	0	0	0	2	C	0.4
1948	NY-A	14	29	3	8	2	0	0	3	0	0	.276	.276	.345	65	-2	-2	3	0	0	0	4	C	0.4
1949	NY-A	5	7	0	4	0	0	0	1	0	1	.571	.571	.571	203	1	1	2	0	0	0	-0	/C	0.1

YEAR	TM/L	G	AB	R	H	2B	3B	HR	RBI	BB	SO	AVG	OBP	SLG	PRO+	BR	/A	RC	SB	CS	SBR	FR	POS	TPR
1950	NY-A	10	9	0	1	1	0	0	1	0	2	.111	.111	.222	-17	-2	-2	0	0	0	0	0	/C	0.0
1951	NY-A	3	5	0	1	0	0	0	2	0	1	.200	.200	.200	9	-1	-1	0	0	0	0	-1	/C	0.0
1952	*NY-A	9	6	0	2	0	0	0	0	1	0	.333	.429	.333	121	0	0	1	0	0	0	0	/C	0.1
1953	NY-A	8	9	2	2	0	0	0	1	0	1	.222	.222	.222	21	-1	-1	0	0	0	0	-0	/C	0.0
1954	NY-A	1	1	0	0	0	0	0	0	0	0	.000	.000	.000	-99	-0	-0	0	0	0	0	0	H	0.0
Total	8	91	158	12	43	6	1	0	20	12	10	.272	.324	.323	78	-5	-5	18	0	0	0	6	/C	1.0

■ FRANK HOUSE
House, Henry Franklin "Pig"   b: 2/18/30, Bessemer, Ala.   BL/TR, 6'1.5", 190 lbs.   Deb: 7/21/50

YEAR	TM/L	G	AB	R	H	2B	3B	HR	RBI	BB	SO	AVG	OBP	SLG	PRO+	BR	/A	RC	SB	CS	SBR	FR	POS	TPR
1950	Det-A	5	5	1	2	1	0	0	0	0	1	.400	.400	.600	148	0	0	1	0	0	0	0	/C	0.1
1951	Det-A	18	41	3	9	2	0	1	4	6	2	.220	.319	.341	78	-1	-1	4	1	1	-0	1	C	0.1
1954	Det-A	114	352	35	88	12	1	9	38	31	34	.250	.313	.366	87	-8	-7	41	2	1	0	-1	*C	-0.2
1955	Det-A	102	328	37	85	11	1	15	53	22	25	.259	.312	.436	102	-2	-1	45	0	0	0	1	C	0.3
1956	Det-A	94	321	44	77	6	2	10	44	21	19	.240	.293	.364	72	-14	-14	31	1	1	-0	-7	C	-1.8
1957	Det-A	106	348	31	90	9	0	7	36	35	26	.259	.328	.345	82	-7	-8	38	1	1	-0	8	C	0.4
1958	KC-A	76	202	16	51	6	3	4	24	12	13	.252	.298	.371	81	-5	-6	20	1	0	0	-7	C	-1.1
1959	KC-A	98	347	32	82	14	3	1	30	20	23	.236	.282	.303	59	-19	-20	27	0	3	-2	-9	C	-2.5
1960	Cin-N	23	28	0	5	2	0	0	3	0	2	.179	.179	.250	16	-3	-3	1	0	0	0	1	/C	-0.1
1961	Det-A	17	22	3	5	1	1	0	3	4	2	.227	.346	.364	87	-0	-0	3	0	0	0	-1	C	0.0
Total	10	653	1994	202	494	64	11	47	235	151	147	.248	.304	.362	80	-59	-60	210	6	7	-2	-12	C	-4.8

■ CHARLIE HOUSEHOLDER
Householder, Charles F.   b: 1856, Harrisburg, Pa.   5'7", 150 lbs.   Deb: 4/20/1884

YEAR	TM/L	G	AB	R	H	2B	3B	HR	RBI	BB	SO	AVG	OBP	SLG	PRO+	BR	/A	RC	SB	CS	SBR	FR	POS	TPR
1884	CP-U	83	310	32	74	12	5	1	12			.239	.267	.319	98	-1	-0	27	0			-6	3O/SP	-0.5

■ CHARLIE HOUSEHOLDER
Householder, Charles W.   b: 1856, Harrisburg, Pa.   d: 12/26/08, Harrisburg, Pa.   BL/TL, 5'11", 158 lbs.   Deb: 5/02/1882

YEAR	TM/L	G	AB	R	H	2B	3B	HR	RBI	BB	SO	AVG	OBP	SLG	PRO+	BR	/A	RC	SB	CS	SBR	FR	POS	TPR
1882	Bal-a	74	307	42	78	10	7	1	4			.254	.264	.342	111	0	4	28				4	*1/C	0.6
1884	Bro-a	76	273	28	66	15	3	3	12			.242	.279	.352	106	2	2	27				-1	1C/O2	0.1
Total	2	150	580	70	144	25	10	4	16			.248	.271	.347	109	3	6	56				2	1/CO2	0.7

■ ED HOUSEHOLDER
Householder, Edward H.   b: 10/12/1869, Pittsburgh, Pa.   d: 7/3/24, Los Angeles, Cal.   Deb: 4/17/03

YEAR	TM/L	G	AB	R	H	2B	3B	HR	RBI	BB	SO	AVG	OBP	SLG	PRO+	BR	/A	RC	SB	CS	SBR	FR	POS	TPR
1903	Bro-N	12	43	5	9	0	0	0	9		2	.209	.244	.209	32	-4	-4	3	3			1	O	-0.2

■ PAUL HOUSEHOLDER
Householder, Paul Wesley   b: 9/4/58, Columbus, Ohio   BB/TR, 6', 180 lbs.   Deb: 8/26/80

YEAR	TM/L	G	AB	R	H	2B	3B	HR	RBI	BB	SO	AVG	OBP	SLG	PRO+	BR	/A	RC	SB	CS	SBR	FR	POS	TPR
1980	Cin-N	20	45	3	11	1	1	0	7	1	13	.244	.261	.311	59	-3	-3	4	1	0	0	0	O	-0.2
1981	Cin-N	23	69	12	19	4	0	2	9	10	16	.275	.367	.420	121	2	2	11	3	1	0	-1	O	0.1
1982	Cin-N	138	417	40	88	11	5	9	34	30	77	.211	.267	.326	64	-20	-21	35	17	11	-2	3	*O	-2.2
1983	Cin-N	123	380	40	97	24	4	6	43	44	60	.255	.336	.387	96	-0	-2	48	12	12	-4	2	*O	-0.5
1984	Cin-N	14	12	3	1	1	0	0	0	3	3	.083	.267	.167	23	-1	-1	1	1	1	-0	1	O	0.0
	StL-N	13	14	1	2	0	0	0	0	0	3	.143	.143	.143	-20	-2	-2	0	0	0	0	-0	/O	-0.2
	Yr	27	26	4	3	1	0	0	0	3	6	.115	.207	.154	3	-3	-3	1	1	1	-0	1		-0.2
1985	Mil-A	95	299	41	77	15	0	11	34	27	60	.258	.321	.418	101	-0	-0	40	1	2	-1	2	O/D	0.0
1986	Mil-A	26	78	4	17	3	1	1	16	7	16	.218	.291	.321	64	-4	-4	7	1	2	-1	-1	O/D	-0.5
1987	Hou-N	14	12	2	1	1	0	0	1	4	2	.083	.313	.167	33	-1	-1	1	0	0	0	-0	/O	-0.1
Total	8	466	1326	146	313	60	11	29	144	126	250	.236	.305	.363	83	-29	-31	146	36	29	-7	5	O/D	-3.6

■ JOHN HOUSEMAN
Houseman, John Franklin   b: 1/10/1870, Holland   d: 11/4/22, Chicago, Ill.   160 lbs.   Deb: 9/11/1894

YEAR	TM/L	G	AB	R	H	2B	3B	HR	RBI	BB	SO	AVG	OBP	SLG	PRO+	BR	/A	RC	SB	CS	SBR	FR	POS	TPR
1894	Chi-N	4	15	5	6	3	1	0	4	5	3	.400	.571	.733	204	3	3	8	2			0	/S2	0.2
1897	StL-N	80	278	34	68	6	6	0	21	28		.245	.329	.309	73	-11	-10	34	16			-4	2O/S3	-1.0
Total	2	84	293	39	74	9	7	0	25	33	3	.253	.344	.331	81	-7	-7	42	18			-4	/2OS3	-0.8

■ BEN HOUSER
Houser, Benjamin Franklin   b: 11/30/1883, Shenandoah, Pa.   d: 1/15/52, Augusta, Maine   BL/TL, 6'1", 185 lbs.   Deb: 5/02/10

YEAR	TM/L	G	AB	R	H	2B	3B	HR	RBI	BB	SO	AVG	OBP	SLG	PRO+	BR	/A	RC	SB	CS	SBR	FR	POS	TPR
1910	Phi-A	34	69	9	13	3	2	0	7	7		.188	.263	.290	74	-2	-2	5	0			-0	1	-0.1
1911	Bos-N	20	71	11	18	1	0	1	9	8	6	.254	.329	.310	73	-2	-3	8	2			0	1	-0.2
1912	Bos-N	108	332	38	95	17	3	8	52	22	29	.286	.332	.428	105	2	1	47	1			-3	1	-0.4
Total	3	162	472	58	126	21	5	9	68	37	35	.267	.322	.390	96	-2	-4	60	3			-3	1	-0.7

■ LEFTY HOUTZ
Houtz, Fred Fritz   b: 9/4/1875, Connersville, Ind.   d: 2/15/59, Wapakoneta, Ohio   BL/TL, 5'10", 170 lbs.   Deb: 7/23/1899

YEAR	TM/L	G	AB	R	H	2B	3B	HR	RBI	BB	SO	AVG	OBP	SLG	PRO+	BR	/A	RC	SB	CS	SBR	FR	POS	TPR
1899	Cin-N	5	17	1	4	0	1	0	0	4		.235	.381	.353	103	0	0	3	1			4	/O	0.4

■ STEVE HOVLEY
Hovley, Stephen Eugene   b: 12/18/44, Ventura, Cal.   BL/TL, 5'10", 188 lbs.   Deb: 6/26/69

YEAR	TM/L	G	AB	R	H	2B	3B	HR	RBI	BB	SO	AVG	OBP	SLG	PRO+	BR	/A	RC	SB	CS	SBR	FR	POS	TPR
1969	Sea-A	91	329	41	91	14	3	3	20	30	34	.277	.339	.365	98	-1	-1	43	10	4	1	8	O	0.6
1970	Mil-A	40	135	17	38	9	0	0	16	17	11	.281	.366	.348	97	0	0	18	5	1	1	-2	O	-0.2
	Oak-A	72	100	8	19	1	0	0	1	5	11	.190	.229	.200	20	-11	-11	5	3	0	1	4	O	-0.6
	Yr	112	235	25	57	10	0	0	17	22	22	.243	.310	.285	67	-11	-10	22	8	1	2	3		-0.8
1971	Oak-A	24	27	3	3	2	0	0	3	7	9	.111	.314	.185	45	-2	-2	3	2	0	1	1	O	0.0
1972	KC-A	105	196	24	53	5	1	3	24	24	29	.270	.353	.352	111	3	3	26	3	3	-1	4	O	0.5
1973	KC-A	104	232	29	59	8	1	2	24	33	34	.254	.347	.323	83	-2	-4	28	6	4	-1	1	OD	-0.5
Total	5	436	1019	122	263	39	5	8	88	116	128	.258	.336	.330	88	-13	-14	122	29	12	2	17	O/D	-0.2

■ DAVE HOWARD
Howard, David Austin "Del"   b: 5/1/1889, Washington, D.C.   d: 1/26/56, Dallas, Tex.   BR/TR, 5'11", 165 lbs.   Deb: 5/08/12

YEAR	TM/L	G	AB	R	H	2B	3B	HR	RBI	BB	SO	AVG	OBP	SLG	PRO+	BR	/A	RC	SB	CS	SBR	FR	POS	TPR
1912	Was-A	1	0	1	0	0	0	0	0	0		—	—	—	—	0	0	0	0			0	R	0.0
1915	Bro-F	24	36	5	8	1	0	0	1	1	8	.222	.243	.250	46	-2	-2	2	0			3	2/OS3	0.1
Total	2	25	36	6	8	1	0	0	1	1	8	.222	.243	.250	46	-2	-2	2	0			3	/2O3S	0.1

■ DOUG HOWARD
Howard, Douglas Lynn   b: 2/6/48, Salt Lake City, Utah   BR/TR, 6'3", 185 lbs.   Deb: 9/06/72

YEAR	TM/L	G	AB	R	H	2B	3B	HR	RBI	BB	SO	AVG	OBP	SLG	PRO+	BR	/A	RC	SB	CS	SBR	FR	POS	TPR
1972	Cal-A	11	38	4	10	1	0	0	2	1	3	.263	.300	.289	81	-1	-1	3	0	0	0	-1	/O13	-0.2
1973	Cal-A	8	21	2	2	0	0	0	1	1	6	.095	.136	.095	-37	-4	-3	0	0	0	0	-1	/O13	-0.4
1974	Cal-A	22	39	5	9	0	1	0	5	2	1	.231	.268	.282	62	-2	-2	2	1	0	0	1	/O1D	-0.1
1975	StL-N	17	29	1	6	0	0	1	1	0	7	.207	.207	.310	41	-2	-2	2	0	0	0	1	/1	-0.1
1976	Cle-A	39	90	7	19	4	0	0	13	3	13	.211	.245	.256	47	-6	-6	5	1	1	-0	2	1/OD	-0.5
Total	5	97	217	19	46	5	1	1	22	7	30	.212	.243	.258	46	-15	-15	13	2	1	0	2	/1OD3	-1.3

■ ELSTON HOWARD
Howard, Elston Gene   b: 2/23/29, St.Louis, Mo.   d: 12/14/80, New York, N.Y.   BR/TR, 6'2", 196 lbs.   Deb: 4/14/55   C

YEAR	TM/L	G	AB	R	H	2B	3B	HR	RBI	BB	SO	AVG	OBP	SLG	PRO+	BR	/A	RC	SB	CS	SBR	FR	POS	TPR
1955	*NY-A	97	279	33	81	8	7	10	43	20	36	.290	.340	.477	120	5	6	45	0	0	0	2	O/C	0.5
1956	*NY-A	98	290	35	76	8	3	5	34	21	30	.262	.314	.362	81	-10	-8	30	0	1	-1	-2	OC	-1.2
1957	*NY-A	110	356	33	90	13	4	8	44	16	43	.253	.285	.379	81	-11	-10	31	2	5	-2	-8	OC/1	-2.4
1958	*NY-A	103	376	45	118	19	5	11	66	22	60	.314	.352	.479	131	12	14	60	1	1	-0	-0	CO/1	1.2
1959	NY-A	125	443	59	121	24	6	18	73	20	57	.273	.309	.476	116	5	7	61	0	1	-1	-2	1CO	0.5
1960	NY-A	107	323	29	79	11	3	6	39	28	43	.245	.305	.353	82	-11	-8	35	3	0	1	2	C/O	0.0
1961	*NY-A	129	446	64	155	17	5	21	77	28	65	.348	.390	.549	156	29	32	94	0	3	-2	7	*C/1	3.4
1962	*NY-A	136	494	63	138	23	5	21	91	31	76	.279	.323	.474	115	6	8	69	1	1	-0	-2	*C	1.3
1963	*NY-A	135	487	75	140	21	6	28	85	35	68	.287	.343	.528	141	24	25	83	0	0	0	-4	*C	2.3
1964	*NY-A	150	550	63	172	27	3	15	84	48	73	.313	.373	.455	127	22	21	93	1	1	-0	9	*C	3.6
1965	NY-A	110	391	38	91	15	1	9	45	24	65	.233	.278	.345	77	-13	-12	34	0	0	0	-6	C/1O	-1.2
1966	NY-A	126	410	38	105	19	2	6	35	37	65	.256	.319	.350	97	-3	-1	40	0	0	0	-4	*C1	0.0
1967	NY-A	66	199	13	39	6	0	3	17	12	36	.196	.249	.271	56	-12	-11	13	0	0	0	-1	C/1	-0.9
	*Bos-A	42	116	9	17	3	0	1	11	9	24	.147	.214	.198	21	-11	-12	5	0	0	0	2	C	-0.7

YEAR	TM/L	G	AB	R	H	2B	3B	HR	RBI	BB	SO	AVG	OBP	SLG	PRO+	BR	/A	RC	SB	CS	SBR	FR	POS	TPR
	Yr	108	315	22	56	9	0	4	28	21	60	.178	.236	.244	42	-23	-23	17	0	0	0	1		-1.6
1968	Bos-A	71	203	22	49	4	0	5	18	22	45	.241	.319	.335	92	-0	-2	21	1	1	-0	-4	C	-0.2
Total	14	1605	5363	619	1471	218	50	167	762	373	786	.274	.325	.427	108	34	47	718	9	14	-6	-11	*CO/1	6.2

■ FRANK HOWARD

Howard, Frank Oliver "Hondo" or "The Capital Punisher" b: 8/8/36, Columbus, Ohio BR/TR, 6'7", 255 lbs. Deb: 9/10/58 MC

YEAR	TM/L	G	AB	R	H	2B	3B	HR	RBI	BB	SO	AVG	OBP	SLG	PRO+	BR	/A	RC	SB	CS	SBR	FR	POS	TPR
1958	LA-N	8	29	3	7	1	0	1	2	1	11	.241	.267	.379	66	-1	-1	3	0	0	0	-0	/O	-0.1
1959	LA-N	9	21	2	3	0	1	1	6	2	9	.143	.217	.381	52	-1	-2	2	0	0	0	-0	/O	-0.1
1960	LA-N	117	448	54	120	15	2	23	77	32	108	.268	.321	.464	105	6	3	66	0	1	-1	-4	*O/1	-0.5
1961	LA-N	92	267	36	79	10	2	15	45	21	50	.296	.349	.517	116	9	6	44	0	1	-1	-5	O/1	-0.3
1962	LA-N	141	493	80	146	25	6	31	119	39	108	.296	.349	.560	148	25	29	90	1	0	0	3	*O	2.5
1963	*LA-N	123	417	58	114	16	1	28	64	33	116	.273	.333	.518	151	21	24	70	1	2	-1	-2	*O	1.6
1964	LA-N	134	433	60	98	13	2	24	69	51	113	.226	.308	.432	114	3	7	56	1	0	0	-8	*O	-0.4
1965	Was-A	149	516	53	149	22	6	21	84	55	112	.289	.360	.477	138	24	25	90	0	0	0	-9	*O	1.1
1966	Was-A	146	493	52	137	19	4	18	71	53	104	.278	.349	.442	127	16	17	74	1	1	-0	-8	*O	0.4
1967	Was-A	149	519	71	133	20	2	36	89	60	155	.256	.339	.511	154	30	32	88	0	1	-1	-11	*O/1	1.7
1968	Was-A	158	598	79	164	28	3	**44**	106	54	141	.274	.340	**.552**	172	45	47	110	0	0	0	-1	*O1	4.4
1969	Was-A	161	592	111	175	17	2	48	111	102	96	.296	.402	.574	180	57	61	132	1	0	0	-21	*O1	3.4
1970	Was-A	161	566	90	160	15	1	**44**	**126**	**132**	125	.283	.420	.546	173	54	58	130	1	2	-1	-15	*O1	3.5
1971	Was-A	153	549	60	153	25	2	26	83	77	121	.279	.369	.474	146	27	31	89	1	0	0	-3	*O1	2.4
1972	Tex-A	95	287	28	70	9	0	9	31	42	55	.244	.342	.369	117	5	6	34	1	0	0	-6	1O	-0.6
	Det-A	14	33	1	8	1	0	1	7	4	8	.242	.324	.364	101	0	0	4	0	0	0	-0	1/O	0.0
	Yr	109	320	29	78	10	0	10	38	46	63	.244	.341	.369	115	5	6	39	1	0	0	-6		-0.6
1973	Det-A	85	227	26	58	9	1	12	29	24	28	.256	.327	.463	113	5	3	30	0	1	-1	-0	D/1	0.2
Total	16	1895	6488	864	1774	245	35	382	1119	782	1460	.273	.355	.499	143	324	344	1110	8	9	-3	-89	*O1/D	19.2

■ DEL HOWARD

Howard, George Elmer b: 12/24/1877, Kenney, Ill. d: 12/24/56, Seattle, Wash. BL/TR, 6', 180 lbs. Deb: 4/15/05

YEAR	TM/L	G	AB	R	H	2B	3B	HR	RBI	BB	SO	AVG	OBP	SLG	PRO+	BR	/A	RC	SB	CS	SBR	FR	POS	TPR
1905	Pit-N	123	435	56	127	18	5	2	63	27		.292	.333	.370	109	6	4	63	19			-7	1O/P	-0.8
1906	Bos-N	147	545	46	142	19	8	1	54	26		.261	.294	.330	99	-4	-2	61	17			-12	O2S/1	-1.6
1907	Bos-N	50	187	20	51	4	2	1	13	11		.273	.313	.332	104	1	1	23	11			-3	O/2	-0.3
	*Chi-N	51	148	10	34	2	2	0	13	6		.230	.260	.270	64	-6	-7	11	3			-4	1/O	-1.2
	Yr	101	335	30	85	6	4	1	26	17		.254	.290	.304	85	-5	-6	34	14			-6		-1.5
1908	*Chi-N	96	315	42	88	7	3	1	26	23		.279	.328	.330	108	4	3	38	11			-5	O/1	-0.3
1909	Chi-N	69	203	25	40	4	2	1	24	18		.197	.282	.251	64	-8	-8	17	6			0	1	-0.9
Total	5	536	1833	199	482	54	22	6	193	111		.263	.307	.326	97	-7	-9	214	67			-30	O1/2SP	-5.1

■ IVON HOWARD

Howard, Ivon Chester b: 10/12/1882, Kenney, Ill. d: 3/30/67, Medford, Ore. BB/TR, 5'10", 170 lbs. Deb: 4/25/14

YEAR	TM/L	G	AB	R	H	2B	3B	HR	RBI	BB	SO	AVG	OBP	SLG	PRO+	BR	/A	RC	SB	CS	SBR	FR	POS	TPR
1914	StL-A	81	209	21	51	6	2	0	20	28	42	.244	.342	.292	94	-1	-0	23	14	10	-2	-7	31/OS	-0.9
1915	StL-A	113	324	43	90	10	7	2	43	43	48	.278	.368	.370	126	9	11	50	29	12	2	5	130/2S	1.5
1916	Cle-A	81	246	20	46	11	5	0	23	30	34	.187	.298	.272	68	-8	-10	24	9			7	2/1	0.0
1917	Cle-A	27	39	7	4	0	0	0	0	3	5	.103	.167	.103	-17	-5	-6	1	1			2	/32O	-0.3
Total	4	302	818	91	191	27	14	2	86	104	129	.233	.331	.308	92	-6	-5	98	53	22		6	/1230S	0.3

■ LARRY HOWARD

Howard, Lawrence Rayford b: 6/6/45, Columbus, Ohio BR/TR, 6'3", 200 lbs. Deb: 8/09/70

YEAR	TM/L	G	AB	R	H	2B	3B	HR	RBI	BB	SO	AVG	OBP	SLG	PRO+	BR	/A	RC	SB	CS	SBR	FR	POS	TPR
1970	Hou-N	31	88	11	27	6	0	2	16	10	23	.307	.378	.443	124	2	3	15	0	0	0	-5	C/1O	0.0
1971	Hou-N	24	64	6	15	3	0	2	14	3	17	.234	.269	.375	83	-2	-2	6	0	1	-1	3	C	0.1
1972	Hou-N	54	157	16	35	7	0	2	13	17	30	.223	.299	.306	74	-6	-5	14	0	0	0	1	C/O	-0.1
1973	Hou-N	20	48	3	8	3	0	0	4	5	12	.167	.245	.229	32	-4	-4	3	0	0	0	-1	C	-0.4
	Atl-N	4	8	0	1	0	0	0	0	2	3	.125	.300	.125	20	-1	-1	0	0	0	0	-0	/C	0.0
	Yr	24	56	3	9	3	0	0	4	7	15	.161	.254	.214	31	-5	-5	3	0	0	0	-1		-0.4
Total	4	133	365	36	86	19	0	6	47	37	85	.236	.306	.337	81	-10	-9	37	0	1	-1	-3	C/O1	-0.4

■ MIKE HOWARD

Howard, Michael Fredric b: 4/2/58, Seattle, Wash. BB/TR, 6'2", 185 lbs. Deb: 9/12/81

YEAR	TM/L	G	AB	R	H	2B	3B	HR	RBI	BB	SO	AVG	OBP	SLG	PRO+	BR	/A	RC	SB	CS	SBR	FR	POS	TPR
1981	NY-N	14	24	4	4	1	0	0	3	4	6	.167	.286	.208	43	-2	-2	2	2	0	1	2	O	0.0
1982	NY-N	33	39	5	7	0	0	1	3	6	7	.179	.304	.256	59	-2	-2	4	2	0	1	4	O/2	0.2
1983	NY-N	1	3	0	1	0	0	0	1	0	1	.333	.333	.333	86	-0	-0	0	0	0	0	0	/O	0.0
Total	3	48	66	9	12	1	0	1	7	10	14	.182	.299	.242	54	-4	-4	6	4	0	1	5	/O2	0.2

■ PAUL HOWARD

Howard, Paul Joseph "Del" b: 5/20/1884, Boston, Mass. d: 8/29/68, Miami, Fla. BR/TR, 5'8", 170 lbs. Deb: 9/16/09

YEAR	TM/L	G	AB	R	H	2B	3B	HR	RBI	BB	SO	AVG	OBP	SLG	PRO+	BR	/A	RC	SB	CS	SBR	FR	POS	TPR
1909	Bos-A	6	15	2	3	1	0	0	2	3		.200	.368	.267	99	0	0	2	0			-1	/O	0.0

■ STEVE HOWARD

Howard, Steven Bernard b: 12/7/63, Oakland, Cal. BR/TR, 6'2", 205 lbs. Deb: 6/16/90

YEAR	TM/L	G	AB	R	H	2B	3B	HR	RBI	BB	SO	AVG	OBP	SLG	PRO+	BR	/A	RC	SB	CS	SBR	FR	POS	TPR
1990	Oak-A	21	52	5	12	4	0	1	4		17	.231	.286	.308	68	-2	-2	5	0	0	0	-1	O/D	-0.2

■ TOM HOWARD

Howard, Thomas Sylvester b: 12/11/64, Middletown, Ohio BB/TR, 6', 200 lbs. Deb: 7/03/90

YEAR	TM/L	G	AB	R	H	2B	3B	HR	RBI	BB	SO	AVG	OBP	SLG	PRO+	BR	/A	RC	SB	CS	SBR	FR	POS	TPR
1990	SD-N	20	44	4	12	2	0	0	0	0	11	.273	.273	.318	61	-2	-2	3	0	1	-1	-1	O	-0.3

■ WILBUR HOWARD

Howard, Wilbur Leon b: 1/8/49, Lowell, N.C. BB/TR, 6'2", 170 lbs. Deb: 9/04/73

YEAR	TM/L	G	AB	R	H	2B	3B	HR	RBI	BB	SO	AVG	OBP	SLG	PRO+	BR	/A	RC	SB	CS	SBR	FR	POS	TPR
1973	Mil-A	16	39	3	8	0	0	1	2		10	.205	.244	.205	28	-4	-4	2	0	1	-1	3	O/D	-0.1
1974	Hou-N	64	111	19	24	4	0	2	5	5	18	.216	.250	.306	57	-7	-6	7	4	5	-2	4	O	-0.6
1975	Hou-N	121	392	62	111	16	8	0	21	21	67	.283	.325	.365	98	-5	-2	49	32	11	3	4	O	0.1
1976	Hou-N	94	191	26	42	7	2	1	18	7	28	.220	.247	.293	58	-12	-10	12	7	5	-1	1	O/2	-1.2
1977	Hou-N	87	187	22	48	6	0	2	13	5	30	.257	.276	.321	65	-11	-9	17	11	1	3	2	O/2	-0.5
1978	Hou-N	84	148	17	34	4	1	1	13	5	22	.230	.269	.291	61	-9	-7	12	6	2	1	1	O/C2	-0.6
Total	6	466	1068	149	267	37	11	6	71	45	175	.250	.284	.322	73	-48	-39	98	60	25	3	14	O/2CD	-2.9

■ JIM HOWARTH

Howarth, James Eugene b: 3/7/47, Biloxi, Miss. BL/TL, 5'11", 175 lbs. Deb: 9/05/71

YEAR	TM/L	G	AB	R	H	2B	3B	HR	RBI	BB	SO	AVG	OBP	SLG	PRO+	BR	/A	RC	SB	CS	SBR	FR	POS	TPR
1971	SF-N	7	13	3	3	1	0	0	2	3	3	.231	.375	.308	97	0	0	2	0	0	0	0	/O	0.0
1972	SF-N	74	119	16	28	4	0	1	7	16	18	.235	.326	.294	76	-3	-3	12	3	2	-0	-1	O/1	-0.6
1973	SF-N	65	90	8	18	1	1	0	7	7	8	.200	.258	.233	36	-8	-8	6	0	0	0	2	O/1	-0.7
1974	SF-N	6	4	0	0	0	0	0	0	0	0	.000	.000	.000	-96	-1	-1	0	0	0	0	0	/O	0.0
Total	4	152	226	27	49	6	1	1	16	26	29	.217	.298	.265	58	-12	-12	19	3	2	-0	2	/O1	-1.3

■ ART HOWE

Howe, Arthur Henry b: 12/15/46, Pittsburgh, Pa. BR/TR, 6'2", 190 lbs. Deb: 7/10/74 MC

YEAR	TM/L	G	AB	R	H	2B	3B	HR	RBI	BB	SO	AVG	OBP	SLG	PRO+	BR	/A	RC	SB	CS	SBR	FR	POS	TPR
1974	*Pit-N	29	74	10	18	4	1	1	5	9	13	.243	.325	.365	96	-0		9	0	0	0	4	3/S	0.3
1975	Pit-N	63	146	13	25	9	0	1	10	15	15	.171	.248	.253	40	-12	-12	9	1	0	0	3	3/S	-0.8
1976	Hou-N	21	29	0	4	1	0	0	0	6	6	.138	.286	.172	35	-2	-2	2	0	0	0	2	/32	0.0
1977	Hou-N	125	413	44	109	23	7	8	58	41	60	.264	.338	.412	110	-0	5	57	0	1	-1	-6	23S	1.7
1978	Hou-N	119	420	46	123	33	3	7	55	34	41	.293	.347	.436	127	9	13	60	2	3	-1	-4	*23/1	1.5
1979	Hou-N	118	355	32	88	15	2	6	33	36	37	.248	.319	.352	88	-8	-6	41	3	1	0	6	23/1	0.2
1980	*Hou-N	110	321	34	91	12	5	10	46	34	29	.283	.354	.445	132	9	12	50	1	0	0	1	13/S2	1.1
1981	*Hou-N	103	361	43	107	22	4	3	36	41	23	.296	.368	.404	125	10	12	53	1	3	-2	3	3/1	1.1
1982	Hou-N	110	365	29	87	15	1	5	38	41	45	.238	.317	.326	87	-9	-6	38	2	0	1	8	31	0.0
1984	StL-N	89	139	17	30	5	0	2	12	18	18	.216	.306	.295	71	-5	-5	12	0	2	-1	8	31/2S	0.2
1985	StL-N	4	3	0	0	0	0	0	0	0	0	.000	.000	.000	-99	-1	-1	0	0	0	0	0	/13	0.0
Total	11	891	2626	268	682	139	23	43	293	275	287	.260	.332	.379	103	-11	10	330	10	10	-3	38	321/S	5.3

YEAR	TM/L	G	AB	R	H	2B	3B	HR	RBI	BB	SO	AVG	OBP	SLG	PRO+	BR	/A	RC	SB	CS	SBR	FR	POS	TPR

■ SHORTY HOWE   Howe, John   b: New York, N.Y.   Deb: 6/17/1890

YEAR	TM/L	G	AB	R	H	2B	3B	HR	RBI	BB	SO	AVG	OBP	SLG	PRO+	BR	/A	RC	SB	CS	SBR	FR	POS	TPR
1890	NY-N	19	64	4	11	0	0	0	4	3	2	.172	.221	.172	16	-7	-7	3	3			3	2/3	-0.2
1893	NY-N	1	5	1	3	0	0	0	2	0	0	.600	.600	.600	221	1	1	2	1			-1	/3	0.0
Total	2	20	69	5	14	0	0	0	6	3	2	.203	.247	.203	32	-6	-6	6	4			2	/23	-0.2

■ HARRY HOWELL   Howell, Henry Harry   b: 11/14/1876, New Jersey   d: 5/22/56, Spokane, Wash.   BR/TR, 5'9″,   Deb: 10/10/1898   U

YEAR	TM/L	G	AB	R	H	2B	3B	HR	RBI	BB	SO	AVG	OBP	SLG	PRO+	BR	/A	RC	SB	CS	SBR	FR	POS	TPR
1898	Bro-N	8	8	1	2	0	0	0	1	1		.250	.333	.250	71	-0	-0	1	0			-0	/P	0.0
1899	Bal-N	28	82	4	12	2	2	0	3	3		.146	.195	.220	14	-10	-10	4	0			1	P	0.0
1900	*Bro-N	22	42	6	12	2	0	1	6	6		.286	.375	.405	111	1	1	7	1			1	P	0.0
1901	Bal-A	53	188	26	41	10	5	2	26	5		.218	.242	.356	63	-9	-10	18	6			-4	P/OS12	0.0
1902	Bal-A	96	347	42	93	16	11	2	42	18		.268	.310	.395	92	-3	-5	47	7			-9	P203S/1	-0.6
1903	NY-A	40	106	14	23	3	2	1	12	5		.217	.252	.311	66	-4	-5	9	1			1	P/3S12	0.0
1904	StL-A	36	113	9	25	5	2	1	6	4		.221	.248	.327	88	-2	-2	10	0			9	P	0.0
1905	StL-A	42	135	9	26	6	2	1	10	3		.193	.210	.289	63	-6	-6	8	0			17	P/O	0.0
1906	StL-A	35	103	5	13	3	1	0	6	6		.126	.174	.175	11	-10	-10	4	2			7	P	0.0
1907	StL-A	44	114	12	27	5	1	1	7	7		.237	.281	.325	95	-1	-1	12	2			9	P/O	0.0
1908	StL-A	41	120	10	22	7	0	1	9	4		.183	.210	.267	56	-6	-6	6	0			1	P	0.0
1909	StL-A	18	34	5	6	1	0	0	3	2		.176	.222	.206	38	-3	-2	2	0			1	P/3O	0.0
1910	StL-A	1	2	0	0	0	0	0	0	0		.000	.000	.000	-99	-0	-0	0	0			0	/P	0.0
Total	13	458	1394	143	302	60	26	10	131	64		.217	.254	.319	69	-53	-56	128	19			33	P/O32S1	-0.6

■ DIXIE HOWELL   Howell, Homer Elliott   b: 4/24/19, Louisville, Ky.   BR/TR, 5'11.5″, 190 lbs.   Deb: 5/06/47

YEAR	TM/L	G	AB	R	H	2B	3B	HR	RBI	BB	SO	AVG	OBP	SLG	PRO+	BR	/A	RC	SB	CS	SBR	FR	POS	TPR
1947	Pit-N	76	214	23	59	11	0	4	25	27	34	.276	.357	.383	94	-1	-1	31	1			-1	C	0.0
1949	Cin-N	64	172	17	42	6	1	2	18	8	21	.244	.286	.326	63	-9	-9	15	0			6	C	-0.1
1950	Cin-N	82	224	30	50	9	1	2	22	32	31	.223	.326	.299	65	-11	-11	23	0			-4	C	-1.1
1951	Cin-N	77	207	22	52	6	1	2	18	15	34	.251	.302	.319	66	-10	-10	20	0	2	-1	4	C	-0.6
1952	Cin-N	17	37	4	7	1	1	2	4	3	9	.189	.250	.432	86	-1	-1	3	0	0	0	1	C	0.0
1953	Bro-N	1	1	0	0	0	0	0	0	0	1	.000	.000	.000	-98	-0	-0	0	0	0	0	0	H	0.0
1955	Bro-N	16	42	2	11	4	0	0	5	1	7	.262	.279	.357	66	-2	-2	4	0	0	0	-1	C	-0.2
1956	Bro-N	7	13	0	3	2	0	0	1	1	3	.231	.286	.385	72	-0	-1	2	0	0	0	-0	/C	0.0
Total	8	340	910	98	224	39	4	12	93	87	140	.246	.315	.337	73	-34	-35	98	1	2		3	C	-2.0

■ JACK HOWELL   Howell, Jack Robert   b: 8/18/61, Tucson, Ariz.   BL/TR, 6', 180 lbs.   Deb: 5/20/85

YEAR	TM/L	G	AB	R	H	2B	3B	HR	RBI	BB	SO	AVG	OBP	SLG	PRO+	BR	/A	RC	SB	CS	SBR	FR	POS	TPR
1985	Cal-A	43	137	19	27	4	0	5	18	16	33	.197	.281	.336	68	-6	-6	14	1	1	-0	-1	3	-0.8
1986	*Cal-A	63	151	26	41	14	2	4	21	19	28	.272	.353	.470	123	5	5	27	2	0	1	0	3/OD	0.4
1987	Cal-A	138	449	64	110	18	5	23	64	57	118	.245	.333	.461	111	4	7	70	4	3	-1	-10	O32	-0.4
1988	Cal-A	154	500	59	127	32	2	16	63	46	130	.254	.324	.422	110	4	6	67	2	6	-3	-20	*3/O	-1.6
1989	Cal-A	144	474	56	108	19	4	20	52	52	125	.228	.308	.411	103	-0	1	60	0	3	-2	22	*3/O	2.1
1990	Cal-A	105	316	35	72	19	1	8	33	46	61	.228	.328	.370	95	-2	-2	42	3	0	1	7	*3/1S	0.7
Total	6	647	2027	259	485	106	14	76	251	236	495	.239	.322	.418	104	5	10	279	12	13	-4	-2	30/2DS1	0.4

■ RED HOWELL   Howell, Murray Donald "Porky"   b: 1/29/09, Atlanta, Ga.   d: 10/1/50, Travelers Rest, S.C   BR/TR, 6', 215 lbs.   Deb: 4/24/41

YEAR	TM/L	G	AB	R	H	2B	3B	HR	RBI	BB	SO	AVG	OBP	SLG	PRO+	BR	/A	RC	SB	CS	SBR	FR	POS	TPR
1941	Cle-A	11	7	0	2	0	0	0	2	4	2	.286	.545	.286	132	1	1	2	0	0	0	0	H	0.1

■ ROY HOWELL   Howell, Roy Lee   b: 12/18/53, Lompoc, Cal.   BL/TR, 6'1″, 190 lbs.   Deb: 9/09/74

YEAR	TM/L	G	AB	R	H	2B	3B	HR	RBI	BB	SO	AVG	OBP	SLG	PRO+	BR	/A	RC	SB	CS	SBR	FR	POS	TPR
1974	Tex-A	13	44	2	11	1	0	1	3	2	10	.250	.283	.341	81	-1	-1	4	0	0	0	-2	3	-0.2
1975	Tex-A	125	383	43	96	15	2	10	51	39	79	.251	.325	.379	99	-1	-1	48	2	2	-1	-6	*3/D	-0.5
1976	Tex-A	140	491	55	124	28	2	8	53	30	106	.253	.297	.367	92	-5	-7	51	1	0	0	-8	*3/D	-1.3
1977	Tex-A	7	17	0	0	0	0	0	0	2	4	.000	.105	.000	-68	-4	-4	0	0	0	0	-0	/O13D	-0.4
	Tor-A	96	364	41	115	17	1	10	44	42	76	.316	.388	.451	126	15	14	61	4	1	1	-7	3/D	0.6
	Yr	103	381	41	115	17	1	10	44	44	80	.302	.376	.430	117	11	10	60	4	1	1	-7		0.2
1978	Tor-A	140	551	67	149	28	3	8	61	44	78	.270	.326	.376	95	-3	-4	67	0	1	-1	11	*3/OD	0.5
1979	Tor-A	138	511	60	126	28	4	15	72	42	91	.247	.311	.405	90	-7	-8	62	1	4	-2	2	*3/D	-0.5
1980	Tor-A	142	528	51	142	28	9	10	57	50	92	.269	.338	.413	100	3	3	74	0	0	0	-17	*3/D	-1.7
1981	*Mil-A	76	244	37	58	13	1	6	33	23	39	.238	.309	.373	101	-2	-0	28	0	0	0	-5	3D/1O	-0.4
1982	*Mil-A	98	300	31	78	11	2	4	38	21	39	.260	.308	.350	86	-8	-6	33	0	2	-1	-0	D/1O	-0.6
1983	Mil-A	69	194	23	54	9	6	4	25	15	29	.278	.330	.448	121	3	5	27	1	3	-2	1	D/1	0.4
1984	Mil-A	68	164	12	38	5	1	4	17	8	32	.232	.284	.348	77	-6	-5	14	0	1	-1	1	3/1D	-0.3
Total	11	1112	3791	422	991	183	31	80	454	318	675	.261	.322	.389	97	-16	-16	470	9	14	-6	-31	3D/1O	-4.4

■ BILL HOWERTON   Howerton, William Ray "Hopalong"   b: 12/12/21, Lompoc, Cal.   BL/TR, 5'11″, 185 lbs.   Deb: 9/11/49

YEAR	TM/L	G	AB	R	H	2B	3B	HR	RBI	BB	SO	AVG	OBP	SLG	PRO+	BR	/A	RC	SB	CS	SBR	FR	POS	TPR
1949	StL-N	9	13	1	4	1	0	0	1	0	2	.308	.308	.385	81	-0	-0	2	0			0	/O	0.0
1950	StL-N	110	313	50	88	20	8	10	59	47	60	.281	.375	.492	120	12	10	61	0			-4	O	0.2
1951	StL-N	24	65	10	17	4	1	1	4	10	12	.262	.360	.400	104	1	1	9	0	1	-1	0	O	0.0
	Pit-N	80	219	29	60	12	2	11	37	26	44	.274	.351	.498	122	7	7	37	1	0	0	-5	O/3	0.0
	Yr	104	284	39	77	16	3	12	41	36	56	.271	.353	.475	118	8	7	47	1	1	-0	-5		0.0
1952	Pit-N	13	25	3	8	1	1	0	4	6	5	.320	.452	.440	144	2	2	5	0	0	0	0	/O3	0.0
	NY-N	11	15	2	1	1	0	0	1	3	2	.067	.222	.133	1	-2	-2	1	0	0	0	/O	-0.1
	Yr	24	40	5	9	2	1	0	5	9	7	.225	.367	.325	92	0	-0	5	0	0	0	-2		-0.1
Total	4	247	650	95	178	39	12	22	106	92	125	.274	.364	.472	117	20	16	115	1	1		-11	O/3	0.1

■ DANN HOWITT   Howitt, Dann Paul John   b: 2/13/64, Battle Creek, Mich.   BL/TR, 6'5″, 205 lbs.   Deb: 9/15/89

YEAR	TM/L	G	AB	R	H	2B	3B	HR	RBI	BB	SO	AVG	OBP	SLG	PRO+	BR	/A	RC	SB	CS	SBR	FR	POS	TPR
1989	Oak-A	3	3	0	0	0	0	0	0	0	2	.000	.000	.000	-99	-1	-1	0	0	0	0	-0	/1O	0.0
1990	Oak-A	14	22	3	3	0	1	0	1	3	12	.136	.240	.227	32	-2	-2	1	0	0	0	1	O/13	-0.1
Total	2	17	25	3	3	0	1	0	1	3	14	.120	.214	.200	17	-3	-3	1	0	0	0	1	/O13	-0.1

■ DAN HOWLEY   Howley, Daniel Philip "Howling Dan" or "Dapper Dan"   b: 10/16/1885, E.Weymouth, Mass.   d: 3/10/44, E.Weymouth, Mass.   TR , 6', 187 lbs.   Deb: 5/15/13   MC

YEAR	TM/L	G	AB	R	H	2B	3B	HR	RBI	BB	SO	AVG	OBP	SLG	PRO+	BR	/A	RC	SB	CS	SBR	FR	POS	TPR
1913	Phi-N	26	32	5	4	2	0	0	2	4	4	.125	.222	.188	17	-3	-4	2	1			1	C	0.0

■ DICK HOWSER   Howser, Richard Dalton   b: 5/14/36, Miami, Fla.   d: 6/17/87, Kansas City, Mo.   BR/TR, 5'8″, 155 lbs.   Deb: 4/11/61   MC

YEAR	TM/L	G	AB	R	H	2B	3B	HR	RBI	BB	SO	AVG	OBP	SLG	PRO+	BR	/A	RC	SB	CS	SBR	FR	POS	TPR
1961	KC-A	158	611	108	171	29	6	3	45	92	38	.280	.379	.362	99	3	3	95	37	9	6	-17	*S	0.2
1962	KC-A	83	286	53	68	8	3	6	34	38	8	.238	.329	.350	80	-6	-8	37	19	2	5	-8	S	-0.6
1963	KC-A	15	41	4	8	0	0	0	1	7	3	.195	.313	.195	44	-3	-3	3	0	0	0	-4	S	-0.6
	Cle-A	49	162	25	40	5	0	1	10	22	18	.247	.337	.296	80	-4	-4	17	9	3	1	-17	S	-1.7
	Yr	64	203	29	48	5	0	1	11	29	21	.236	.332	.276	72	-6	-6	21	9	3	1	-20		-2.3
1964	Cle-A	162	637	101	163	23	4	3	52	76	39	.256	.337	.319	84	-12	-11	74	20	7	2	3	*S	-0.5
1965	Cle-A	107	307	47	72	8	2	1	6	57	25	.235	.356	.283	83	-4	-4	38	17	4	3	-6	S2	-0.2
1966	Cle-A	67	140	18	32	9	1	2	4	15	23	.229	.303	.350	87	-2	-2	14	2	4	-2	-7	2S	-0.7
1967	NY-A	63	149	18	40	6	0	0	10	25	15	.268	.381	.309	110	3	3	19	1	4	-2	-6	23/S	-0.4
1968	NY-A	85	150	24	23	2	1	0	3	35	17	.153	.321	.180	57	-6	-6	11	0	1	-1	5	2/3S	0.0
Total	8	789	2483	398	617	90	17	16	165	367	186	.248	.348	.318	87	-32	-32	308	105	34	11	-55	S/23	-4.5

■ DUMMY HOY   Hoy, William Ellsworth   b: 5/23/1862, Houckstown, Ohio   d: 12/15/61, Cincinnati, Ohio   BL/TR, 5'4″, 148 lbs.   Deb: 4/20/1888

YEAR	TM/L	G	AB	R	H	2B	3B	HR	RBI	BB	SO	AVG	OBP	SLG	PRO+	BR	/A	RC	SB	CS	SBR	FR	POS	TPR
1888	Was-N	136	503	77	138	10	8	2	29	69	48	.274	.374	.338	139	21	26	97	82			5	*O	2.8

YEAR	TM/L	G	AB	R	H	2B	3B	HR	RBI	BB	SO	AVG	OBP	SLG	PRO+	BR	/A	RC	SB	CS	SBR	FR	POS	TPR
1889	Was-N	127	507	98	139	11	6	0	39	75	30	.274	.374	.320	103	2	7	76	35			-6	*O	-0.2
1890	Buf-P	122	493	107	147	17	8	1	53	94	36	.298	.418	.371	124	16	24	95	39			6	*O/2	1.9
1891	StL-a	141	567	136	165	14	5	5	66	**119**	25	.291	.424	.360	111	29	13	114	59			-1	*O	0.6
1892	Was-N	152	593	108	166	19	8	3	75	86	23	.280	.375	.354	126	20	22	104	60			-12	*O	0.4
1893	Was-N	130	564	106	138	12	6	0	45	66	9	.245	.337	.287	70	-23	-20	73	48			-1	*O	-2.1
1894	Cin-N	126	495	114	148	22	13	5	70	87	18	.299	.416	.426	101	8	4	101	27			3	*O	-0.1
1895	Cin-N	107	429	93	119	21	12	3	55	52	8	.277	.352	.403	96	0	-3	83	50			-3	*O	-1.2
1896	Cin-N	121	443	120	132	23	7	4	57	65	13	.298	.403	.409	109	14	8	95	50			5	*O	0.4
1897	Cin-N	128	497	87	145	24	6	2	42	54		.292	.371	.376	94	2	-4	85	37			7	*O	-0.5
1898	Lou-N	148	582	104	177	15	16	6	66	49		.304	.367	.416	129	20	22	105	37			6	*O	1.7
1899	Lou-N	154	633	116	194	17	13	5	49	61		.306	.374	.398	114	14	14	109	32			-6	*O	-0.1
1901	Chi-A	132	527	112	155	28	11	2	60	**86**		.294	.405	.400	130	23	26	101	27			2	*O	2.3
1902	Cin-N	72	279	48	81	15	2	2	20	41		.290	.389	.380	128	15	12	48	11			-5	O	0.1
Total	14	1796	7112	1426	2044	248	121	40	726	1004	210	.287	.385	.373	111	160	149	1286	594			-0	*O/2	6.0

■ KENT HRBEK

Hrbek, Kent Alan b: 5/21/60, Minneapolis, Minn. BL/TR, 6'4", 200 lbs. Deb: 8/24/81

YEAR	TM/L	G	AB	R	H	2B	3B	HR	RBI	BB	SO	AVG	OBP	SLG	PRO+	BR	/A	RC	SB	CS	SBR	FR	POS	TPR
1981	Min-A	24	67	5	16	5	0	1	7	5	9	.239	.301	.358	84	-1	-2	8	0	0	0	-1	1/D	-0.2
1982	Min-A	140	532	82	160	21	4	23	92	54	80	.301	.365	.485	128	22	21	91	3	1	0	-0	*1/D	1.7
1983	Min-A	141	515	75	153	41	5	16	84	57	71	.297	.370	.489	130	24	22	91	4	6	-2	-2	*1/D	1.1
1984	Min-A	149	559	80	174	31	3	27	107	65	87	.311	.387	.522	142	37	34	110	1	1	-0	-6	*1/D	1.8
1985	Min-A	158	593	78	165	31	2	21	93	67	87	.278	.353	.444	110	14	9	93	1	1	-0	1	*1/D	0.0
1986	Min-A	149	550	85	147	27	1	29	91	71	81	.267	.357	.478	122	19	17	93	2	2	-1	-2	*1/D	0.5
1987	*Min-A	143	477	85	136	20	1	34	90	84	60	.285	.392	.545	140	32	30	103	5	2	0	-10	*1/D	0.7
1988	Min-A	143	510	75	159	31	0	25	76	67	54	.312	.392	.520	149	37	35	104	0	3	-2	-6	*1/D	2.1
1989	Min-A	109	375	59	102	17	0	25	84	53	35	.272	.364	.517	136	22	19	73	3	0	1	1	1/D	1.5
1990	Min-A	143	492	61	141	26	0	22	79	69	45	.287	.382	.474	129	26	22	89	5	2	0	1	*1/D/3	1.4
Total	10	1299	4670	685	1353	250	16	223	803	592	609	.290	.372	.493	130	234	207	854	24	18	-4	-25	*1/D3	10.6

■ WALT HRINIAK

Hriniak, Walter John b: 5/22/43, Natick, Mass. BL/TR, 5'11", 180 lbs. Deb: 9/10/68 C

YEAR	TM/L	G	AB	R	H	2B	3B	HR	RBI	BB	SO	AVG	OBP	SLG	PRO+	BR	/A	RC	SB	CS	SBR	FR	POS	TPR
1968	Atl-N	9	26	0	9	0	0	0	3	0	3	.346	.346	.346	108	0	0	3	0	0	0	3	/C	0.4
1969	Atl-N	7	7	0	1	0	0	0	0	2	1	.143	.333	.143	38	-0	-0	0	0	0	0	-1	/C	0.0
	SD-N	31	66	4	15	0	0	0	1	8	11	.227	.329	.227	61	-3	-3	5	0	0	0	-2	C	-0.2
	Yr	38	73	4	16	0	0	0	1	10	12	.219	.329	.219	58	-4	-3	6	0	0	0	-2		-0.2
Total	2	47	99	4	25	0	0	0	4	10	15	.253	.333	.253	71	-4	-3	9	0	0	0	1	/C	0.2

■ AL HUBBARD

Hubbard, Allen (Player Under Name Of Al West For 1 Game In 1883) b: 12/9/1860, Westfield, Mass. d: 12/14/30, Newton, Mass. Deb: 9/13/1883

YEAR	TM/L	G	AB	R	H	2B	3B	HR	RBI	BB	SO	AVG	OBP	SLG	PRO+	BR	/A	RC	SB	CS	SBR	FR	POS	TPR
1883	Phi-a	2	6	2	2	0	0	0		1		.333	.429	.333	137	0	0	1				0	/SC	0.0

■ GLENN HUBBARD

Hubbard, Glenn Dee b: 9/25/57, Hahn Afb, Germany BR/TR, 5'9", 150 lbs. Deb: 7/14/78

YEAR	TM/L	G	AB	R	H	2B	3B	HR	RBI	BB	SO	AVG	OBP	SLG	PRO+	BR	/A	RC	SB	CS	SBR	FR	POS	TPR
1978	Atl-N	44	163	15	42	4	0	2	13	10	20	.258	.309	.319	68	-5	-7	17	2	1	0	3	2	-0.1
1979	Atl-N	97	325	34	75	12	0	3	29	27	43	.231	.292	.295	56	-17	-20	28	0	6	-4	5	2	-1.3
1980	Atl-N	117	431	55	107	21	3	9	43	49	69	.248	.325	.374	91	-3	-5	53	7	5	-1	19	*2	2.2
1981	Atl-N	99	361	39	85	13	5	6	33	33	59	.235	.303	.349	82	-8	-9	39	4	2	0	-4	2	-0.5
1982	*Atl-N	145	532	75	132	25	1	9	59	59	62	.248	.327	.350	86	-7	-10	65	4	3	-1	20	*2	1.7
1983	Atl-N	148	517	65	136	24	6	12	70	55	71	.263	.339	.402	97	3	-2	69	3	8	-4	21	*2	2.1
1984	Atl-N	120	397	53	93	27	2	9	43	55	61	.234	.333	.380	93	1	-3	53	4	1	1	20	*2	2.1
1985	Atl-N	142	439	51	102	21	0	5	39	56	54	.232	.325	.314	75	-11	-14	47	3	4	-1	62	*2	4.9
1986	Atl-N	143	408	42	94	16	1	4	36	66	74	.230	.343	.304	76	-9	-12	47	3	2	0	41	*2	3.1
1987	Atl-N	141	443	69	117	33	2	5	38	77	57	.264	.380	.381	98	5	2	67	1	1	-0	28	*2	3.1
1988	*Oak-A	105	294	35	75	12	2	3	33	33	50	.255	.336	.340	93	-3	-2	34	1	3	-2	4	*2/D	0.7
1989	Oak-A	53	131	12	26	6	0	3	12	19	20	.198	.300	.313	76	-4	-4	13	2	0	1	10	2/D	0.8
Total	12	1354	4441	545	1084	214	22	70	448	539	640	.244	.330	.349	85	-59	-85	530	35	35	-11	228	*2/D	18.8

■ KEN HUBBS

Hubbs, Kenneth Douglas b: 12/23/41, Riverside, Cal. d: 2/13/64, Provo, Utah BR/TR, 6'2", 175 lbs. Deb: 9/10/61

YEAR	TM/L	G	AB	R	H	2B	3B	HR	RBI	BB	SO	AVG	OBP	SLG	PRO+	BR	/A	RC	SB	CS	SBR	FR	POS	TPR
1961	Chi-N	10	28	4	5	1	1	1	2	0	8	.179	.179	.393	46	-2	-2	2	0	0	0	-2	/2	-0.2
1962	Chi-N	160	661	90	172	24	9	5	49	35	129	.260	.300	.346	71	-26	-29	64	3	7	-3	4	*2	-1.2
1963	Chi-N	154	566	54	133	19	3	8	47	39	93	.235	.287	.322	71	-18	-22	48	8	9	-3	20	*2	0.5
Total	3	324	1255	148	310	44	13	14	98	74	230	.247	.292	.336	70	-46	-53	114	11	16	-6	23	2	-0.9

■ CLARENCE HUBER

Huber, Clarence Bill "Gilly" b: 10/27/1896, Tyler, Tex. d: 2/22/65, Laredo, Tex. BR/TR, 5'10", 165 lbs. Deb: 9/17/20

YEAR	TM/L	G	AB	R	H	2B	3B	HR	RBI	BB	SO	AVG	OBP	SLG	PRO+	BR	/A	RC	SB	CS	SBR	FR	POS	TPR
1920	Det-A	11	42	4	9	2	1	0	5	0	5	.214	.214	.310	39	-4	-4	3	0	0	0	2	3	0.0
1921	Det-A	1	0	0	0	0	0	0	0	0	0	—	—	—	—	0	0	0	0	0	0	0	/3	0.0
1925	Phi-N	124	436	46	124	28	5	5	54	17	33	.284	.311	.406	75	-13	-18	53	3	5	-2	-9	*3	-1.9
1926	Phi-N	118	376	45	92	17	7	1	34	42	29	.245	.324	.335	74	-11	-14	42	9			8	*3	-0.4
Total	4	254	854	95	225	47	13	6	93	59	67	.263	.313	.370	73	-28	-36	97	12	5		2	3	-2.3

■ OTTO HUBER

Huber, Otto b: 3/12/14, Garfield, N.J. d: 4/9/89, Passaic, N.J. BR/TR, 5'10", 165 lbs. Deb: 6/10/39

YEAR	TM/L	G	AB	R	H	2B	3B	HR	RBI	BB	SO	AVG	OBP	SLG	PRO+	BR	/A	RC	SB	CS	SBR	FR	POS	TPR
1939	Bos-N	11	22	2	6	1	0	0	3	0	1	.273	.273	.318	63	-1	-1	2	0			-0	/23	0.0

■ DAVE HUDGENS

Hudgens, David Mark b: 12/5/56, Oroville, Cal. BL/TL, 6'2", 210 lbs. Deb: 9/04/83

YEAR	TM/L	G	AB	R	H	2B	3B	HR	RBI	BB	SO	AVG	OBP	SLG	PRO+	BR	/A	RC	SB	CS	SBR	FR	POS	TPR
1983	Oak-A	6	7	0	1	0	0	0	0	0	3	.143	.143	.143	-22	-1	-1	0	0	0	0	0	/1D	0.0

■ JIMMY HUDGENS

Hudgens, James Price b: 8/24/02, Newburg, Mo. d: 8/26/55, St.Louis, Mo. BB/TR, 6', 180 lbs. Deb: 9/14/23

YEAR	TM/L	G	AB	R	H	2B	3B	HR	RBI	BB	SO	AVG	OBP	SLG	PRO+	BR	/A	RC	SB	CS	SBR	FR	POS	TPR
1923	StL-N	6	12	2	3	1	0	0	0	3	3	.250	.400	.333	97	0	0	2	0	0	0	1	/12	0.1
1925	Cin-N	3	7	0	3	1	1	0	0	1	1	.429	.500	.857	245	1	1	3	0	0	0	0	/1	0.1
1926	Cin-N	17	20	2	5	1	0	0	1	1	0	.250	.286	.300	59	-1	-1	2	0			0	/1	0.0
Total	3	26	39	4	11	3	1	0	1	5	4	.282	.364	.410	107	0	0	7	0	0		1	/12	0.2

■ REX HUDLER

Hudler, Rex Allen b: 9/2/60, Tempe, Ariz. BR/TR, 6'1", 180 lbs. Deb: 9/09/84

YEAR	TM/L	G	AB	R	H	2B	3B	HR	RBI	BB	SO	AVG	OBP	SLG	PRO+	BR	/A	RC	SB	CS	SBR	FR	POS	TPR
1984	NY-A	9	7	2	1	1	0	0	0	1	5	.143	.333	.286	76	-0	-0	1	0	0	0	0	/2	0.0
1985	NY-A	20	51	4	8	0	1	0	1	1	9	.157	.173	.196	1	-7	-7	2	0	1	-1	7	2/1S	0.0
1986	Bal-A	14	1	1	0	0	0	0	0	0	0	.000	.000	.000	-99	-0	-0	0	1	0	0	1	2/3	0.2
1988	Mon-N	77	216	38	59	14	2	4	14	10	34	.273	.305	.412	100	0	-1	28	29	7	5	-0	2S/O	0.7
1989	Mon-N	92	155	21	38	7	0	6	13	6	23	.245	.284	.406	92	-2	-2	17	15	4	2	-9	2OS	-0.8
1990	Mon-N	4	3	1	1	0	0	0	0	0	1	.333	.333	.333	84	-0	-0	0	0	0	0	0	/H	0.0
	StL-N	89	217	30	61	11	2	7	22	12	31	.281	.325	.447	107	2	2	29	18	10	-1	3	O2/13S	0.3
	Yr	93	220	31	62	11	2	7	22	12	32	.282	.325	.445	107	2	2	30	18	10	-1	3		0.3
Total	6	305	650	97	168	33	5	17	50	30	103	.258	.295	.403	92	-7	-9	78	63	22	6	2	2/OS31	0.4

■ JOHNNY HUDSON

Hudson, John Wilson "Mr. Chips" b: 6/30/12, Bryan, Tex. d: 11/7/70, Bryan, Tex. BR/TR, 5'10", 160 lbs. Deb: 6/20/36

YEAR	TM/L	G	AB	R	H	2B	3B	HR	RBI	BB	SO	AVG	OBP	SLG	PRO+	BR	/A	RC	SB	CS	SBR	FR	POS	TPR
1936	Bro-N	6	12	1	2	0	0	0	0	2	1	.167	.286	.167	24	-1	-1	1	0			-1	/S2	-0.1
1937	Bro-N	13	27	3	5	4	0	0	2	3	9	.185	.267	.333	61	-1	-2	2	0			-4	S/2	-0.4
1938	Bro-N	135	498	59	130	21	5	2	37	39	76	.261	.315	.335	77	-14	-16	51	7			-4	*2/S	-0.9
1939	Bro-N	109	343	46	87	17	3	2	32	30	36	.254	.317	.338	74	-11	-13	36	5			-18	S2/3	-2.5
1940	Bro-N	85	179	13	39	4	3	0	19	9	26	.218	.255	.274	43	-13	-15	12	2			0	S2/3	-0.8

YEAR	TM/L	G	AB	R	H	2B	3B	HR	RBI	BB	SO	AVG	OBP	SLG	PRO+	BR	/A	RC	SB	CS	SBR	FR	POS	TPR
1941	Chi-N	50	99	8	20	4	0	0	6	3	15	.202	.225	.242	33	-9	-9	5	3			-1	S23	-0.6
1945	NY-N	28	11	8	0	0	0	0	0	1	1	.000	.083	.000	-75	-3	-3	0	0			5	/32	0.2
Total	7	426	1169	138	283	50	11	4	96	87	164	.242	.296	.314	65	-53	-57	107	17			-22	2S/3	-5.1

■ FRANK HUELSMAN
Huelsman, Frank Elmer   b: 6/5/1874, St.Louis, Mo.   d: 6/9/59, Affton, Mo.   BR/TR, 6'2", 210 lbs.   Deb: 10/03/1897

YEAR	TM/L	G	AB	R	H	2B	3B	HR	RBI	BB	SO	AVG	OBP	SLG	PRO+	BR	/A	RC	SB	CS	SBR	FR	POS	TPR
1897	StL-N	2	7	0	2	1	0	0	0	0		.286	.286	.429	91	-0	-0	1	0			-1	/O	0.0
1904	Chi-A	3	6	0	1	1	0	0	0	0		.167	.167	.333	60	-0	-0	0	0			-1	/O	0.0
	Det-A	4	18	1	6	1	0	0	4	1		.333	.368	.389	147	1	1	3	1			-1	/O	0.0
	Chi-A	1	1	0	0	0	0	0	0	0		.000	.000	.000	-99	-0	-0	0	0			0	H	0.0
	StL-A	20	68	6	15	2	1	0	1	6		.221	.284	.279	86	-1	-1	6	0			-3	O	-0.5
	Was-A	84	303	21	75	19	4	2	30	24		.248	.303	.356	112	3	4	36	6			-3	O	-0.4
	Yr	112	396	28	97	23	5	2	35	31		.245	.300	.343	108	2	3	44	7			-7		-0.9
1905	Was-A	121	421	48	114	28	8	3	62	31		.271	.321	.397	135	13	15	59	11			-9	*O	0.0
Total	3	235	824	76	213	52	13	5	97	62		.258	.310	.371	121	15	18	105	18			-17	O	-0.9

■ MIKE HUFF
Huff, Michael Kale   b: 8/11/63, Honolulu, Hawaii   BR/TR, 6'1", 180 lbs.   Deb: 8/07/89

YEAR	TM/L	G	AB	R	H	2B	3B	HR	RBI	BB	SO	AVG	OBP	SLG	PRO+	BR	/A	RC	SB	CS	SBR	FR	POS	TPR
1989	LA-N	12	25	4	5	1	0	1	2	3	6	.200	.310	.360	93	-0	-0	3	0	1	-1	1	/O	0.0

■ BEN HUFFMAN
Huffman, Benjamin Franklin   b: 6/26/14, Rileyville, Va.   BL/TR, 5'11.5", 175 lbs.   Deb: 4/23/37

YEAR	TM/L	G	AB	R	H	2B	3B	HR	RBI	BB	SO	AVG	OBP	SLG	PRO+	BR	/A	RC	SB	CS	SBR	FR	POS	TPR
1937	StL-A	76	176	18	48	9	0	1	24	10	7	.273	.323	.341	67	-9	-9	20	1	0	0	-8	C	-1.1

■ ED HUG
Hug, Edward Ambrose   b: 7/14/1880, Fayetteville, O.   d: 5/11/53, Cincinnati, Ohio   BR/TR,   Deb: 7/06/03

YEAR	TM/L	G	AB	R	H	2B	3B	HR	RBI	BB	SO	AVG	OBP	SLG	PRO+	BR	/A	RC	SB	CS	SBR	FR	POS	TPR
1903	Bro-N	1	0	0	0	0	0	0	0	1		—	1.000	—	205	0	0	0	0			0	/C	0.0

■ MILLER HUGGINS
Huggins, Miller James "Hug" or "Mighty Mite"
b: 3/27/1879, Cincinnati, Ohio   d: 9/25/29, New York, N.Y.   BB/TR, 5'6.5", 140 lbs.   Deb: 4/15/04   MH

YEAR	TM/L	G	AB	R	H	2B	3B	HR	RBI	BB	SO	AVG	OBP	SLG	PRO+	BR	/A	RC	SB	CS	SBR	FR	POS	TPR
1904	Cin-N	140	491	96	129	12	7	2	30	88		.263	.375	.328	110	16	10	69	13			1	*2	1.6
1905	Cin-N	149	564	117	154	11	8	1	38	103		.273	.385	.326	104	16	8	85	27			36	*2	5.4
1906	Cin-N	146	545	81	159	11	7	0	26	71		.292	.373	.338	119	18	15	89	41			22	*2	4.0
1907	Cin-N	156	561	64	139	12	4	1	31	83		.248	.345	.289	97	4	2	71	28			0	*2	0.5
1908	Cin-N	135	498	65	119	14	5	0	23	58		.239	.318	.287	98	-0	1	57	30			4	*2	0.4
1909	Cin-N	57	159	18	34	3	1	0	6	28		.214	.335	.245	81	-2	-2	17	11			4	23	0.2
1910	StL-N	151	547	101	145	15	6	1	36	116	46	.265	.399	.320	114	14	17	85	34			3	*2	2.4
1911	StL-N	138	509	106	133	19	2	1	24	96	52	.261	.385	.312	99	3	5	76	37			11	*2	1.2
1912	StL-N	120	431	82	131	15	4	0	29	87	31	.304	.422	.357	117	14	16	80	35			-7	*2	0.5
1913	StL-N	121	382	74	109	12	0	0	27	92	49	.285	.432	.317	117	16	17	62	23			0	*2M	1.4
1914	StL-N	148	509	85	134	17	4	1	24	105	63	.263	.396	.318	115	15	16	75	32			-4	*2M	1.1
1915	StL-N	107	353	57	85	5	2	2	24	74	68	.241	.377	.283	101	5	5	40	13	12	-3	4	*2M	0.7
1916	StL-N	18	9	2	3	0	0	0	0	2	3	.333	.500	.333	159	1	1	2	0			4	/2M	0.6
Total	13	1586	5558	948	1474	146	50	9	318	1003	312	.265	.381	.314	108	121	111	809	324	12		77	*2/3	20.0

■ ED HUGHES
Hughes, Edward J.   b: 10/5/1880, Chicago, Ill.   d: 10/11/27, McHenry, Ill.   6'1", 180 lbs.   Deb: 8/29/02

YEAR	TM/L	G	AB	R	H	2B	3B	HR	RBI	BB	SO	AVG	OBP	SLG	PRO+	BR	/A	RC	SB	CS	SBR	FR	POS	TPR
1902	Chi-A	1	4	0	1	0	0	0	0	0		.250	.250	.250	42	-0	-0	0	0			0	/C	0.0
1905	Bos-A	6	14	2	3	0	0	0	2	0		.214	.214	.214	37	-1	-1	1	0			-2	/P	0.0
1906	Bos-A	2	3	0	0	0	0	0	0	0		.000	.000	.000	-99	-1	-1	0	0			0	/P	0.0
Total	3	9	21	2	4	0	0	0	2	0		.190	.190	.190	19	-2	-2	1	0			-1	/PC	0.0

■ JOE HUGHES
Hughes, Joseph Thompson   b: 2/21/1880, Pardo, Pa.   d: 3/13/51, Cleveland, Ohio   BR/TR, 5'10", 165 lbs.   Deb: 8/30/02

YEAR	TM/L	G	AB	R	H	2B	3B	HR	RBI	BB	SO	AVG	OBP	SLG	PRO+	BR	/A	RC	SB	CS	SBR	FR	POS	TPR
1902	Chi-N	1	3	0	0	0	0	0	0	0		.000	.000	.000	-99	-1	-1	0	0			-0	/O	0.0

■ KEITH HUGHES
Hughes, Keith Wills   b: 9/12/63, Bryn Mawr, Pa.   BL/TL, 6'3"; 210 lbs.   Deb: 5/19/87

YEAR	TM/L	G	AB	R	H	2B	3B	HR	RBI	BB	SO	AVG	OBP	SLG	PRO+	BR	/A	RC	SB	CS	SBR	FR	POS	TPR
1987	NY-A	4	4	0	0	0	0	0	0	0	2	.000	.000	.000	-99	-1	-1	0	0	0	0	0	/H	0.0
	Phi-N	37	76	8	20	2	0	0	10	7	11	.263	.333	.289	65	-3	-4	8	0	0	0	-2	O	-0.6
1988	Bal-A	41	108	10	21	4	2	2	14	16	27	.194	.298	.324	76	-4	-3	11	1	0	0	0	O/D	-0.2
1990	NY-N	8	9	0	0	0	0	0	0	0	4	.000	.000	.000	-99	-2	-2	0	0	0	0	0	/O	-0.1
Total	3	90	197	18	41	6	2	2	24	23	44	.208	.294	.289	61	-10	-10	19	1	0	0	-1	/OD	-0.9

■ ROY HUGHES
Hughes, Roy John "Jeep" or "Sage"   b: 1/11/11, Cincinnati, Ohio   BR/TR, 5'10.5", 167 lbs.   Deb: 4/16/35

YEAR	TM/L	G	AB	R	H	2B	3B	HR	RBI	BB	SO	AVG	OBP	SLG	PRO+	BR	/A	RC	SB	CS	SBR	FR	POS	TPR
1935	Cle-A	82	266	40	78	15	3	0	14	18	17	.293	.340	.372	83	-6	-7	35	13	3	2	-1	2S/3	-0.2
1936	Cle-A	152	638	112	188	35	9	0	63	57	40	.295	.356	.378	81	-18	-19	88	20	9	1	5	*2	-0.2
1937	Cle-A	104	346	57	96	12	6	1	40	40	22	.277	.352	.355	78	-11	-11	45	11	6	-0	12	32	0.4
1938	StL-A	58	96	16	27	3	0	2	13	12	11	.281	.361	.375	85	-2	-2	14	3	0	1	4	2/3S	0.4
1939	StL-A	17	23	6	2	0	0	0	1	4	4	.087	.222	.087	-18	-4	-4	1	0	0	0	0	/2S	0.0
	Phi-N	65	237	22	54	5	1	1	16	21	18	.228	.291	.270	53	-16	-15	18	4			0	2	-1.1
1940	Phi-N	1	0	0	0	0	0	0	0	0	0	—	—	—	—	0	0	0				-0	/2	0.0
1944	Chi-N	126	478	86	137	16	6	1	28	35	30	.287	.337	.351	94	-4	-3	58	16			11	3S	1.8
1945	*Chi-N	69	222	34	58	8	1	0	8	16	18	.261	.311	.306	73	-8	-8	22	6			-8	S2/31	-0.9
1946	Phi-N	89	276	23	65	11	1	0	22	19	15	.236	.287	.283	64	-14	-13	23	7			-12	S3/21	-2.3
Total	9	763	2582	396	705	105	27	5	205	222	175	.273	.332	.340	78	-83	-82	305	80	18		12	23S/1	-2.3

■ TERRY HUGHES
Hughes, Terry Wayne   b: 5/13/49, Spartanburg, S.C.   BR/TR, 6'1", 185 lbs.   Deb: 9/02/70

YEAR	TM/L	G	AB	R	H	2B	3B	HR	RBI	BB	SO	AVG	OBP	SLG	PRO+	BR	/A	RC	SB	CS	SBR	FR	POS	TPR
1970	Chi-N	2	3	0	1	0	0	0	0	0	0	.333	.333	.333	71	-0	-0	0	0	0	0	0	/3O	0.0
1973	StL-N	11	14	1	3	1	0	0	1	1	4	.214	.267	.286	53	-1	-1	1	0	0	0	0	/31	0.0
1974	Bos-A	41	69	5	14	2	0	1	6	6	18	.203	.286	.275	58	-3	-4	6	0	0	0	4	3/D	0.0
Total	3	54	86	6	18	3	0	1	7	7	22	.209	.284	.279	58	-4	-5	7	0	0	0	4	/3D1O	0.0

■ TOM HUGHES
Hughes, Thomas Franklin   b: 8/6/07, Emmet, Ark.   BL/TR, 6'1", 190 lbs.   Deb: 9/09/30

YEAR	TM/L	G	AB	R	H	2B	3B	HR	RBI	BB	SO	AVG	OBP	SLG	PRO+	BR	/A	RC	SB	CS	SBR	FR	POS	TPR
1930	Det-A	17	59	8	22	2	3	0	5	4	8	.373	.413	.508	130	3	3	12	0	1	-1	-3	O	-0.1

■ BILL HUGHES
Hughes, William R.   b: 11/25/1866, Bladensville, Ill.   d: 8/25/43, Santa Ana, Cal.   BL/TL,   Deb: 9/28/1884

YEAR	TM/L	G	AB	R	H	2B	3B	HR	RBI	BB	SO	AVG	OBP	SLG	PRO+	BR	/A	RC	SB	CS	SBR	FR	POS	TPR
1884	Was-U	14	49	5	6	0	0	0		2		.122	.157	.122	-5	-5	-5	1	0			0	/1O	-0.3
1885	Phi-a	4	16	3	3	1	1	0		1		.188	.278	.375	101	0	0	2				-0	/OP	0.0
Total	2	18	65	8	9	1	1	0		3		.138	.188	.185	25	-5	-5	3				-0	/1OP	-0.3

■ EMIL HUHN
Huhn, Emil Hugo "Hap"   b: 3/10/1892, North Vernon, Ind.   d: 9/5/25, Camden, S.C.   BR/TR, 6', 180 lbs.   Deb: 4/10/15

YEAR	TM/L	G	AB	R	H	2B	3B	HR	RBI	BB	SO	AVG	OBP	SLG	PRO+	BR	/A	RC	SB	CS	SBR	FR	POS	TPR
1915	New-F	124	415	34	94	18	1	1	41	28	40	.227	.279	.282	70	-18	-15	39	13			-6	*1C	-2.0
1916	Cin-N	37	94	4	24	3	2	0	3	2	11	.255	.271	.330	86	-2	-2	8	0			1	C1/O	0.0
1917	Cin-N	23	51	2	10	1	2	0	3	2	5	.196	.226	.294	62	-3	-2	3	1			-2	C/1	-0.3
Total	3	184	560	40	128	22	5	1	47	32	56	.229	.273	.291	72	-22	-19	51	14			-6	1/CO	-2.3

■ TIM HULETT
Hulett, Timothy Craig   b: 1/12/60, Springfield, Ill.   BR/TR, 6', 185 lbs.   Deb: 9/15/83

YEAR	TM/L	G	AB	R	H	2B	3B	HR	RBI	BB	SO	AVG	OBP	SLG	PRO+	BR	/A	RC	SB	CS	SBR	FR	POS	TPR
1983	Chi-A	6	5	0	1	0	0	0	0	0	0	.200	.200	.200	10	-1	-1	0	1	0	0	2	/2	0.2
1984	Chi-A	8	7	1	0	0	0	0	0	1	4	.000	.125	.000	-59	-2	-2	0	1	0	0	4	/32	0.3
1985	Chi-A	141	395	52	106	19	4	5	37	30	81	.268	.326	.375	88	-5	-7	48	6	4	1	8	*32/O	-0.1
1986	Chi-A	150	520	53	120	16	5	17	44	21	91	.231	.262	.379	70	-22	-24	49	4	5	-1	-6	32	-2.6
1987	Chi-A	68	240	20	52	10	0	7	28	10	41	.217	.248	.346	54	-16	-17	19	0	2	-1	-3	3/2	-1.9

YEAR	TM/L	G	AB	R	H	2B	3B	HR	RBI	BB	SO	AVG	OBP	SLG	PRO+	BR	/A	RC	SB	CS	SBR	FR	POS	TPR
1989	Bal-A	33	97	12	27	5	0	3	18	10	17	.278	.346	.423	119	2	2	14	0	0	0	-5	23	-0.1
1990	Bal-A	53	153	16	39	7	1	3	16	15	41	.255	.321	.373	96	-1	-1	19	1	0	0	6	32/D	0.6
Total	7	459	1417	154	345	57	10	35	143	87	275	.243	.290	.372	77	-44	-48	149	13	7	-0	7	32/DO	-3.6

■ BILLY HULEN
Hulen, William Franklin b: 3/12/1870, Dixon, Cal. d: 10/2/47, Santa Rosa, Cal. BL/TL, 5'8", 148 lbs. Deb: 5/02/1896

YEAR	TM/L	G	AB	R	H	2B	3B	HR	RBI	BB	SO	AVG	OBP	SLG	PRO+	BR	/A	RC	SB	CS	SBR	FR	POS	TPR
1896	Phi-N	88	339	87	90	18	7	0	38	55	20	.265	.368	.360	95	-1	-0	55	23			-21	SO/2	-1.7
1899	Was-N	19	68	10	10	1	0	0	3	10		.147	.256	.162	18	-7	-7	4	5			-4	S	-0.9
Total	2	107	407	97	100	19	7	0	41	65	20	.246	.350	.327	83	-8	-7	59	28			-25	/SO2	-2.6

■ RUDY HULSWITT
Hulswitt, Rudolph Edward b: 2/23/1877, Newport, Ky. d: 1/16/50, Louisville, Ky. BR/TR, 5'8.5", 165 lbs. Deb: 6/16/1899 C

YEAR	TM/L	G	AB	R	H	2B	3B	HR	RBI	BB	SO	AVG	OBP	SLG	PRO+	BR	/A	RC	SB	CS	SBR	FR	POS	TPR
1899	Lou-N	1	0	0	0	0	0	0	0	0		—	—	—	—	0	0	0	0			-1	/S	0.0
1902	Phi-N	128	497	59	135	11	7	0	38	30		.272	.314	.322	98	-1	-1	56	12			8	*S/3	1.3
1903	Phi-N	138	519	56	128	22	9	1	58	28		.247	.285	.329	79	-17	-14	54	10			-3	*S	-0.8
1904	Phi-N	113	406	36	99	11	4	1	36	16		.244	.273	.298	81	-11	-9	37	8			-13	*S	-2.2
1908	Cin-N	119	386	27	88	5	7	1	28	30		.228	.284	.285	86	-7	-6	33	7			-6	*S/2	-1.5
1909	StL-N	82	289	21	81	8	3	0	29	19		.280	.329	.329	111	1	3	33	7			-5	S2	-0.1
1910	StL-N	63	133	9	33	7	2	0	14	13	10	.248	.320	.331	93	-2	-1	15	5			-12	S/2	-1.2
Total	7	644	2230	208	564	64	32	3	203	136	10	.253	.297	.314	90	-36	-28	230	49			-32	S/23	-4.5

■ JOHN HUMMEL
Hummel, John Edwin "Silent John" b: 4/4/1883, Bloomsburg, Pa. d: 5/18/59, Springfield, Mass. BR/TR, 5'11", 160 lbs. Deb: 9/12/05

YEAR	TM/L	G	AB	R	H	2B	3B	HR	RBI	BB	SO	AVG	OBP	SLG	PRO+	BR	/A	RC	SB	CS	SBR	FR	POS	TPR
1905	Bro-N	30	109	19	29	3	4	0	7	9		.266	.322	.367	116	1	2	16	6			0	2	0.4
1906	Bro-N	97	286	20	57	6	4	1	21	36		.199	.289	.259	79	-8	-6	25	10			1	2O1	-0.5
1907	Bro-N	107	342	41	80	12	3	3	31	26		.234	.288	.313	98	-4	-1	36	8			13	2O1/S	1.2
1908	Bro-N	154	594	51	143	11	12	4	41	34		.241	.282	.320	98	-5	-3	58	20			8	O2/S1	0.5
1909	Bro-N	146	542	54	152	15	9	4	52	22		.280	.311	.363	113	3	5	67	16			-16	12SO	-1.3
1910	Bro-N	153	578	67	141	21	13	5	74	57	81	.244	.314	.351	97	-6	-4	69	21			-14	*2	-1.4
1911	Bro-N	137	477	54	129	21	11	5	58	67	66	.270	.360	.392	115	7	10	73	16			-5	*2/1S	0.2
1912	Bro-N	122	411	55	116	21	7	5	54	49	55	.282	.359	.404	113	5	7	62	7			-13	2O1	-0.8
1913	Bro-N	67	198	20	48	7	7	2	24	13	23	.242	.292	.379	88	-3	-4	22	4			-0	OS/12	-0.3
1914	Bro-N	73	208	25	55	8	9	0	20	16	25	.264	.317	.389	107	2	1	26	5			0	1O/2S	0.0
1915	Bro-N	53	100	6	23	2	3	0	8	6	11	.230	.274	.310	75	-3	-3	9	1	1	-0	-2	O1/S	-0.7
1918	NY-A	22	61	9	18	1	2	0	4	11	8	.295	.411	.377	135	3	3	10	3			-3	O/12	0.0
Total	12	1161	3906	421	991	128	84	29	394	346	269	.254	.315	.352	103	-8	8	473	117	1		-31	2O1/S	-2.7

■ AL HUMPHREY
Humphrey, Albert b: 2/28/1886, Ashtabula, Ohio d: 5/13/61, Ashtabula, Ohio BL/TR, 5'11", 180 lbs. Deb: 9/01/11

YEAR	TM/L	G	AB	R	H	2B	3B	HR	RBI	BB	SO	AVG	OBP	SLG	PRO+	BR	/A	RC	SB	CS	SBR	FR	POS	TPR
1911	Bro-N	8	27	4	5	0	0	0	0	3	7	.185	.267	.185	29	-3	-2	2	0			-2	/O	-0.4

■ TERRY HUMPHREY
Humphrey, Terryal Gene b: 8/4/49, Chickasha, Okla. BR/TR, 6'3", 185 lbs. Deb: 9/05/71

YEAR	TM/L	G	AB	R	H	2B	3B	HR	RBI	BB	SO	AVG	OBP	SLG	PRO+	BR	/A	RC	SB	CS	SBR	FR	POS	TPR
1971	Mon-N	9	26	1	5	1	0	0	1	0	4	.192	.192	.231	19	-3	-3	1	0	0	0	2	/C	0.0
1972	Mon-N	69	215	13	40	8	0	1	9	16	38	.186	.249	.237	38	-17	-18	12	4	1	1	-3	C	-1.7
1973	Mon-N	43	90	5	15	2	0	1	9	5	16	.167	.211	.222	19	-10	-10	4	0	1	-1	5	C	-0.3
1974	Mon-N	20	52	3	10	3	0	0	3	4	9	.192	.250	.250	38	-4	-5	4	0	0	0	6	C	0.2
1975	Det-A	18	41	0	10	0	0	0	1	2	6	.244	.279	.244	47	-3	-3	3	0	0	0	1	C	-0.1
1976	Cal-A	71	196	17	48	10	0	1	19	13	30	.245	.308	.311	87	-4	-3	18	0	1	-1	1	C	0.0
1977	Cal-A	123	304	17	69	11	0	2	34	21	58	.227	.286	.283	58	-18	-17	24	1	1	-0	-1	*C	-1.4
1978	Cal-A	53	114	11	25	4	1	1	9	6	12	.219	.270	.298	62	-6	-6	9	0	1	-1	11	C/23	0.6
1979	Cal-A	9	17	2	1	0	0	0	0	1	2	.059	.111	.059	-55	-4	-4	0	0	0	0	6	/C	0.3
Total	9	415	1055	69	223	39	1	6	85	68	175	.211	.268	.267	51	-69	-67	75	5	5	-2	28	C/32	-2.4

■ JOHN HUMPHRIES
Humphries, John Henry b: 11/12/1861, N.Gower, Ont., Can. d: 11/29/33, Salinas, Cal. TL , 6', 185 lbs. Deb: 7/07/1883

YEAR	TM/L	G	AB	R	H	2B	3B	HR	RBI	BB	SO	AVG	OBP	SLG	PRO+	BR	/A	RC	SB	CS	SBR	FR	POS	TPR
1883	NY-N	29	107	5	12	1	0	0	4	1	22	.112	.120	.121	-26	-16	-15	2				-2	CO	-1.3
1884	Was-a	49	193	23	34	2	0	0		9		.176	.217	.187	39	-13	-10	8				-6	CO/1	-1.1
	NY-N	20	64	6	6	0	0	0	2	9	19	.094	.205	.094	-2	-7	-7	1				12	C	0.5
Total	2	98	364	34	52	3	0	0	6	19	41	.143	.188	.151	10	-36	-33	11				4	/CO1	-1.9

■ RANDY HUNDLEY
Hundley, Cecil Randolph b: 6/1/42, Martinsville, Va. BR/TR, 5'11", 170 lbs. Deb: 9/27/64 C

YEAR	TM/L	G	AB	R	H	2B	3B	HR	RBI	BB	SO	AVG	OBP	SLG	PRO+	BR	/A	RC	SB	CS	SBR	FR	POS	TPR
1964	SF-N	2	1	1	0	0	0	0	0	0	1	.000	.000	.000	-98	-0	-0	0	0	0	0	0	/C	0.0
1965	SF-N	6	15	0	1	0	0	0	0	0	4	.067	.067	.067	-61	-3	-3	0	0	0	0	4	/C	0.1
1966	Chi-N	149	526	50	124	22	3	19	63	35	113	.236	.287	.397	87	-10	-10	58	1	3	-2	-11	*C	-1.9
1967	Chi-N	152	539	68	144	25	3	14	60	44	75	.267	.325	.403	102	4	2	68	2	4	-2	-14	*C	-0.5
1968	Chi-N	160	553	41	125	18	4	7	65	39	69	.226	.282	.311	73	-15	-19	46	1	0	0	-15	*C	-3.1
1969	Chi-N	151	522	67	133	15	1	18	64	61	90	.255	.336	.391	91	2	-6	69	2	3	-1	10	*C	1.3
1970	Chi-N	73	250	13	61	5	0	7	36	16	52	.244	.289	.348	62	-11	-15	25	0	1	-1	-1	*C	-1.2
1971	Chi-N	9	21	1	7	1	0	0	2	0	2	.333	.333	.381	89	-0	-0	3	0	0	0	3	/C	0.2
1972	Chi-N	114	357	23	78	12	0	5	30	22	62	.218	.264	.294	53	-20	-24	25	1	0	0	7	*C	-1.1
1973	Chi-N	124	368	35	83	11	1	10	43	30	51	.226	.284	.342	68	-14	-17	33	5	6	-2	9	*C	-0.2
1974	Min-A	32	88	2	17	2	0	0	3	4	12	.193	.228	.216	27	-8	-8	4	0	0	0	1	C	-0.6
1975	SD-N	74	180	7	37	5	1	2	14	19	29	.206	.285	.278	60	-10	-9	14	0	0	0	-0	C	-0.7
1976	Chi-N	13	18	3	3	2	0	0	1	1	4	.167	.211	.278	35	-2	-2	1	0	0	0	-0	/C	-0.1
1977	Chi-N	2	4	0	0	0	0	0	0	0	1	.000	.000	.000	-90	-1	-1	0	0	0	0	1	/C	0.0
Total	14	1061	3442	311	813	118	13	82	381	271	565	.236	.294	.350	76	-87	-114	346	12	17	-7	-7	*C	-7.8

■ TODD HUNDLEY
Hundley, Todd Randolph b: 5/27/69, Martinsville, Va. BB/TR, 5'11", 170 lbs. Deb: 5/18/90

YEAR	TM/L	G	AB	R	H	2B	3B	HR	RBI	BB	SO	AVG	OBP	SLG	PRO+	BR	/A	RC	SB	CS	SBR	FR	POS	TPR
1990	NY-N	36	67	8	14	6	0	0	2	6	18	.209	.274	.299	59	-4	-4	6	0	0	0	3	C	0.1

■ BERNIE HUNGLING
Hungling, Bernard Herman "Bud" b: 3/5/1896, Dayton, Ohio d: 3/30/68, Dayton, Ohio BR/TR, 6'2", 180 lbs. Deb: 4/14/22

YEAR	TM/L	G	AB	R	H	2B	3B	HR	RBI	BB	SO	AVG	OBP	SLG	PRO+	BR	/A	RC	SB	CS	SBR	FR	POS	TPR
1922	Bro-N	39	102	9	23	1	2	1	13	6	20	.225	.269	.304	48	-8	-8	9	2	0	1	1	C	-0.5
1923	Bro-N	2	4	0	0	0	0	0	0	0	2	.000	.000	.000	-99	-1	-1	0	0	1	-1	-1	C	-0.1
1930	StL-A	10	31	4	10	2	0	0	2	5	3	.323	.417	.387	102	1	0	5	0	1	-1	-4	C	-0.2
Total	3	51	137	13	33	3	2	1	15	11	25	.241	.297	.314	57	-9	-9	14	2	2	-1	-3	/C	-0.8

■ BILL HUNNEFIELD
Hunnefield, William Fenton "Wild Bill" b: 1/5/1899, Dedham, Mass. d: 8/28/76, Nantucket, Mass. BB/TR, 5'10", 165 lbs. Deb: 4/17/26

YEAR	TM/L	G	AB	R	H	2B	3B	HR	RBI	BB	SO	AVG	OBP	SLG	PRO+	BR	/A	RC	SB	CS	SBR	FR	POS	TPR
1926	Chi-A	131	470	81	129	26	4	3	48	37	28	.274	.329	.366	84	-14	-11	59	24	9	2	-8	S32	-0.7
1927	Chi-A	112	365	45	104	25	1	2	36	25	24	.285	.332	.375	85	-9	-8	40	13	13	-4	-20	S2/3	-2.3
1928	Chi-A	94	333	42	98	8	3	2	24	26	24	.294	.351	.354	87	-6	-6	43	16	6	1	-12	2/S3	-1.1
1929	Chi-A	47	127	13	23	5	0	0	9	7	3	.181	.224	.220	15	-16	-16	7	5	2	0	-4	2/3S	-1.7
1930	Chi-A	31	81	11	22	2	0	1	5	4	10	.272	.314	.333	67	-4	-4	9	1	1	-0	-10	S/1	-1.1
1931	Cle-A	21	71	13	17	4	1	0	4	9	4	.239	.325	.324	67	-3	-3	8	3	1	0	-9	S/2	-0.9
	Bos-N	11	21	2	6	0	0	0	1	0	2	.286	.286	.286	56	-1	-1	2	0			2	/32	0.1
	NY-N	64	196	23	53	5	0	1	17	9	16	.270	.302	.311	67	-9	-9	19	3			-5	2/S	-1.0
	Yr	75	217	25	59	5	0	1	18	9	18	.272	.301	.309	66	-11	-10	20	3			-3		-0.9
Total	6	511	1664	230	452	75	9	9	144	117	111	.272	.322	.344	76	-64	-59	187	65	32		-67	S2/31	-8.7

■ RANDY HUNT
Hunt, James Randall b: 1/3/60, Prattville, Ala. BR/TR, 6', 185 lbs. Deb: 6/04/85

YEAR	TM/L	G	AB	R	H	2B	3B	HR	RBI	BB	SO	AVG	OBP	SLG	PRO+	BR	/A	RC	SB	CS	SBR	FR	POS	TPR
1985	StL-N	14	19	1	3	0	0	0	1	0	5	.158	.158	.158	-12	-3	-3	0	0	1	-1	1	C	-0.1

YEAR	TM/L	G	AB	R	H	2B	3B	HR	RBI	BB	SO	AVG	OBP	SLG	PRO+	BR	/A	RC	SB	CS	SBR	FR	POS	TPR
1986	Mon-N	21	48	4	10	0	0	2	5	5	16	.208	.283	.333	70	-2	-2	4	0	0	0	7	C	0.5
Total	2	35	67	5	13	0	0	2	6	5	21	.194	.250	.284	48	-5	-5	4	0	1	-1	8	/C	0.4

■ KEN HUNT
Hunt, Kenneth Lawrence b: 7/13/34, Grand Forks, N.Dak   BR/TR, 6'1", 205 lbs.   Deb: 9/10/59

YEAR	TM/L	G	AB	R	H	2B	3B	HR	RBI	BB	SO	AVG	OBP	SLG	PRO+	BR	/A	RC	SB	CS	SBR	FR	POS	TPR
1959	NY-A	6	12	2	4	1	0	0	1	0	3	.333	.333	.417	108	0	0	2	0	0	0	0	/O	0.0
1960	NY-A	25	22	4	6	2	0	0	1	4	4	.273	.407	.364	117	1	1	4	0	0	0	1	O	0.1
1961	LA-A	149	479	70	122	29	3	25	84	49	120	.255	.329	.484	103	8	1	76	8	2	1	-12	*O/2	-1.3
1962	LA-A	13	11	4	2	0	0	1	1	1	5	.182	.250	.455	88	-0	-0	1	1	0	0	-0	/1	0.0
1963	LA-A	59	142	17	26	6	1	5	16	15	49	.183	.261	.345	72	-6	-5	12	0	1	-1	-3	O	-1.0
	Was-A	7	20	1	4	0	0	1	4	2	6	.200	.273	.350	73	-1	-1	1	0	0	0	0	/O	0.0
	Yr	66	162	18	30	6	1	6	20	17	55	.185	.263	.346	73	-7	-6	14	0	1	-1	-3		-1.0
1964	Was-A	51	96	9	13	4	0	1	4	14	35	.135	.245	.208	28	-9	-9	5	0	1	-1	4	O	-0.7
Total	6	310	782	107	177	42	4	33	111	85	222	.226	.306	.417	89	-8	-14	101	9	4	0	-9	O/12	-2.9

■ JOEL HUNT
Hunt, Oliver Joel "Jodie" b: 10/11/05, Texico, N.Mex.   d: 7/24/78, Teague, Tex.   BR/TR, 5'10", 165 lbs.   Deb: 4/27/31

YEAR	TM/L	G	AB	R	H	2B	3B	HR	RBI	BB	SO	AVG	OBP	SLG	PRO+	BR	/A	RC	SB	CS	SBR	FR	POS	TPR
1931	StL-N	4	1	2	0	0	0	0	0	0	1	.000	.000	.000	-96	-0	-0	0	0			0	/O	0.0
1932	StL-N	12	21	0	4	1	0	0	3	4	3	.190	.320	.238	51	-1	-1	2	0			0	/O	0.0
Total	2	16	22	2	4	1	0	0	3	4	4	.182	.308	.227	45	-2	-2	2	0			0	/O	0.0

■ DICK HUNT
Hunt, Richard M. b: 1847, New York   d: 11/20/1895, Brooklyn, N.Y.   5'9", 145 lbs.   Deb: 5/07/1872

YEAR	TM/L	G	AB	R	H	2B	3B	HR	RBI	BB	SO	AVG	OBP	SLG	PRO+	BR	/A	RC	SB	CS	SBR	FR	POS	TPR
1872	Eck-n	11	48	11	15	4	0	0		1		.313	.327	.396	143	1	3	6					/O2	0.2

■ RON HUNT
Hunt, Ronald Kenneth b: 2/23/41, St.Louis, Mo.   BR/TR, 6', 186 lbs.   Deb: 4/16/63

YEAR	TM/L	G	AB	R	H	2B	3B	HR	RBI	BB	SO	AVG	OBP	SLG	PRO+	BR	/A	RC	SB	CS	SBR	FR	POS	TPR
1963	NY-N	143	533	64	145	28	4	10	42	40	50	.272	.338	.396	109	8	7	71	5	4	-1	2	*2/3	1.8
1964	NY-N	127	475	59	144	19	6	6	42	29	30	.303	.357	.406	117	10	11	66	6	2	1	-8	*23	1.3
1965	NY-N	57	196	21	47	12	1	1	10	14	19	.240	.310	.327	82	-5	-4	18	2	7	-6	-5	2/3	-1.0
1966	NY-N	132	479	63	138	19	2	3	33	41	34	.288	.358	.355	101	1	2	61	8	10	-4	7	*2/S3	1.4
1967	LA-N	110	388	44	102	17	3	3	33	39	24	.263	.346	.345	107	1	4	48	2	1	0	-16	2/3	-0.6
1968	SF-N	148	529	79	132	19	0	2	28	78	41	.250	.372	.297	103	7	7	66	6	6	-2	-17	*2	-0.3
1969	SF-N	128	478	72	125	23	3	3	41	51	47	.262	.363	.341	100	2	3	66	9	2	2	-9	*2/3	0.5
1970	SF-N	117	367	70	103	17	1	6	41	44	29	.281	.396	.381	111	8	9	59	1	2	-1	-28	23	-1.0
1971	Mon-N	152	520	89	145	20	3	5	38	58	41	.279	.403	.358	116	18	17	85	5	7	-3	-9	*23	1.2
1972	Mon-N	129	443	56	112	20	0	0	18	51	29	.253	.363	.298	88	-2	-3	55	9	2	3	-7	*2/3	0.0
1973	Mon-N	113	401	61	124	14	0	0	18	52	19	.309	.419	.344	110	12	11	63	10	7	-1	-21	*23	-0.8
1974	Mon-N	115	403	66	108	15	0	0	26	55	17	.268	.375	.305	87	-1	-4	51	2	5	-2	-14	32/S	-2.0
	StL-N	12	23	1	4	0	0	0	0	3	2	.174	.321	.174	42	-2	-2	2	0	0	0	-1	/2	-0.2
	Yr	127	426	67	112	15	0	0	26	58	19	.263	.372	.298	85	-3	-5	53	2	5	-2	-15		-2.2
Total	12	1483	5235	745	1429	223	23	39	370	555	382	.273	.369	.347	104	56	58	711	65	55	-14	-125	*23/S	0.3

■ EDDIE HUNTER
Hunter, Edison Franklin b: 2/6/05, Bellevue, Ky.   d: 3/14/67, Collrain Turnpike Ohio   BR/TR, 5'7.5", 150 lbs.   Deb: 8/05/33

YEAR	TM/L	G	AB	R	H	2B	3B	HR	RBI	BB	SO	AVG	OBP	SLG	PRO+	BR	/A	RC	SB	CS	SBR	FR	POS	TPR
1933	Cin-N	1	0	0	0	0	0	0	0	0	0	—	—	—	—	0	0	0	0			0	/3	0.0

■ NEWT HUNTER
Hunter, Frederick Creighton b: 1/5/1880, Chillicothe, Ohio   d: 10/26/63, Columbus, Ohio   BR/TR, 6', 180 lbs.   Deb: 4/12/11   C

YEAR	TM/L	G	AB	R	H	2B	3B	HR	RBI	BB	SO	AVG	OBP	SLG	PRO+	BR	/A	RC	SB	CS	SBR	FR	POS	TPR
1911	Pit-N	65	209	35	53	10	6	2	24	25	43	.254	.345	.388	101	1	0	31	9			-2	1	-0.3

■ GEORGE HUNTER
Hunter, George Henry b: 7/8/1887, Buffalo, N.Y.   d: 1/11/68, Harrisburg, Pa.   BB , 5'8.5", 165 lbs.   Deb: 5/04/09

YEAR	TM/L	G	AB	R	H	2B	3B	HR	RBI	BB	SO	AVG	OBP	SLG	PRO+	BR	/A	RC	SB	CS	SBR	FR	POS	TPR
1909	Bro-N	44	123	8	28	7	0	0	8	9		.228	.286	.285	80	-3	-3	10	1			-4	OP	-0.4
1910	Bro-N	1	0	0	0	0	0	0	0	0	0	—	—	—	—	0	0	0	0			0	/O	0.0
Total	2	45	123	8	28	7	0	0	8	9	0	.228	.286	.285	80	-3	-3	10	1			-4	/OP	-0.4

■ BILLY HUNTER
Hunter, Gordon William b: 6/4/28, Punxsutawney, Pa.   BR/TR, 6', 180 lbs.   Deb: 4/14/53   MC

YEAR	TM/L	G	AB	R	H	2B	3B	HR	RBI	BB	SO	AVG	OBP	SLG	PRO+	BR	/A	RC	SB	CS	SBR	FR	POS	TPR
1953	StL-A	154	567	50	124	18	1	1	37	24	45	.219	.253	.259	38	-49	-50	37	3	1	0	15	*S	-2.4
1954	Bal-A	125	411	28	100	9	5	2	27	21	38	.243	.283	.304	66	-23	-19	33	5	4	-1	1	*S	-0.8
1955	NY-A	98	255	14	58	7	1	3	20	15	18	.227	.270	.298	54	-17	-17	20	9	2	2	1	S	-0.3
1956	NY-A	39	75	8	21	3	4	0	11	2	4	.280	.299	.427	93	-2	-1	8	0	1	-1	10	S/3	1.0
1957	KC-A	116	319	39	61	10	4	8	29	27	43	.191	.261	.323	58	-19	-20	27	1	2	-1	-5	2S3	-1.9
1958	KC-A	22	58	6	9	1	1	2	11	5	7	.155	.222	.310	44	-5	-5	4	1	1	-0	-3	S/23	-0.5
	Cle-A	76	190	21	37	10	2	0	9	17	37	.195	.264	.268	48	-14	-13	14	4	1	1	1	S/3	0.0
	Yr	98	248	27	46	11	3	2	20	22	44	.185	.255	.278	47	-18	-18	18	5	2	0	-1		-0.5
Total	6	630	1875	166	410	58	18	16	144	111	192	.219	.265	.294	53	-128	-125	144	23	12	-0	19	S/23	-4.9

■ BUDDY HUNTER
Hunter, Harold James b: 8/9/47, Omaha, Neb.   BR/TR, 5'10", 170 lbs.   Deb: 7/01/71

YEAR	TM/L	G	AB	R	H	2B	3B	HR	RBI	BB	SO	AVG	OBP	SLG	PRO+	BR	/A	RC	SB	CS	SBR	FR	POS	TPR
1971	Bos-A	8	9	2	2	1	0	0	0	2	1	.222	.364	.333	92	0	-0	1	0	0	0	1	/2	0.2
1973	Bos-A	13	7	3	3	1	0	0	2	3	1	.429	.636	.571	229	2	2	3	0	0	0	4	/32D	0.6
1975	Bos-A	1	1	0	0	0	0	0	0	0	0	.000	.000	.000	-92	-0	-0	0	0	0	0	0	/2	0.0
Total	3	22	17	5	5	2	0	0	2	5	2	.294	.478	.412	144	2	2	5	0	0	0	5	/23D	0.8

■ HERB HUNTER
Hunter, Herbert Harrison b: 12/25/1896, Boston, Mass.   d: 7/25/70, Orlando, Fla.   BL/TR, 6'0.5", 165 lbs.   Deb: 4/29/16

YEAR	TM/L	G	AB	R	H	2B	3B	HR	RBI	BB	SO	AVG	OBP	SLG	PRO+	BR	/A	RC	SB	CS	SBR	FR	POS	TPR
1916	NY-N	21	28	3	7	0	0	1	4	0	5	.250	.250	.357	90	-1	-0	3	0			0	/31	0.0
	Chi-N	2	4	0	0	0	0	0	0	0	0	.000	.000	.000	-90	-1	-1	0	0			0	/3	0.0
	Yr	23	32	3	7	0	0	1	4	0	5	.219	.219	.313	65	-2	-1	2	0			1		0.0
1917	Chi-N	3	3	0	0	0	0	0	0	0	0	.000	.000	.000	-93	-1	-1	0	0			0	/23	0.0
1920	Bos-A	4	12	2	1	0	0	0	0	1	1	.083	.154	.083	-38	-2	-2	0	0	0	0	-0	/O	-0.2
1921	StL-N	9	2	3	0	0	0	0	0	1	0	.000	.333	.000	-4	-0	-0	-0	0	3	-2	0	/1	-0.1
Total	4	39	49	8	8	0	0	1	4	2	6	.163	.196	.224	24	-5	-5	3	0	3		1	/3O12	-0.3

■ LEM HUNTER
Hunter, Robert Lemuel b: 1/16/1863, Warren, Ohio   d: 11/9/56, W.Lafayette, Ohio   Deb: 9/01/1883

YEAR	TM/L	G	AB	R	H	2B	3B	HR	RBI	BB	SO	AVG	OBP	SLG	PRO+	BR	/A	RC	SB	CS	SBR	FR	POS	TPR
1883	Cle-N	1	4	1	1	0	0	0	0	0	0	.250	.250	.250	53	-0	0	0				-0	/OP	0.0

■ BILL HUNTER
Hunter, William Ellsworth b: 7/8/1887, Buffalo, N.Y.   d: 4/10/34, Buffalo, N.Y.   BL/TL, 5'7.5", 155 lbs.   Deb: 8/06/12

YEAR	TM/L	G	AB	R	H	2B	3B	HR	RBI	BB	SO	AVG	OBP	SLG	PRO+	BR	/A	RC	SB	CS	SBR	FR	POS	TPR
1912	Cle-A	21	55	6	9	2	0	0	2	10		.164	.303	.200	43	-4	-4	4	0			-0	O	-0.4

■ BILL HUNTER
Hunter, William Robert b: St.Thomas, Ont., Can.   5'7.5", 160 lbs.   Deb: 5/02/1884

YEAR	TM/L	G	AB	R	H	2B	3B	HR	RBI	BB	SO	AVG	OBP	SLG	PRO+	BR	/A	RC	SB	CS	SBR	FR	POS	TPR
1884	Lou-a	2	7	1	1	0	0	0				.143	.143	.143	-5	-1	-1	0				-2	/C	-0.2

■ STEVE HUNTZ
Huntz, Stephen Michael b: 12/3/45, Cleveland, Ohio   BB/TR, 6'1", 204 lbs.   Deb: 9/19/67

YEAR	TM/L	G	AB	R	H	2B	3B	HR	RBI	BB	SO	AVG	OBP	SLG	PRO+	BR	/A	RC	SB	CS	SBR	FR	POS	TPR
1967	StL-N	3	6	1	1	0	0	0	1	0	1	.167	.286	.167	33	-0	-0	0	0	0	0	-1	/2	-0.1
1969	StL-N	71	139	13	27	4	0	3	13	27	34	.194	.325	.288	73	-4	-4	13	0	0	0	-5	S2/3	-0.2
1970	SD-N	106	352	54	77	8	0	11	37	66	69	.219	.344	.335	86	-7	-5	44	0	3	-2	-12	S3	-1.3
1971	Chi-A	35	86	10	18	3	1	2	6	7	9	.209	.269	.337	69	-4	-4	8	1	0	-0	0	2/3S	-0.2
1975	SD-N	22	53	3	8	4	0	0	4	7	8	.151	.250	.226	35	-5	-4	3	0	0	0	1	3/2	-0.2
Total	5	237	636	81	131	19	1	16	60	108	122	.206	.322	.314	76	-20	-18	70	1	3	-2	-18	S/32	-2.0

■ DAVE HUPPERT
Huppert, David Blain b: 4/1/57, Southgate, Cal.   BR/TR, 6'1", 190 lbs.   Deb: 9/15/83

YEAR	TM/L	G	AB	R	H	2B	3B	HR	RBI	BB	SO	AVG	OBP	SLG	PRO+	BR	/A	RC	SB	CS	SBR	FR	POS	TPR
1983	Bal-A	2	0	0	0	0	0	0	0	0	0	—	—	—	—	0	0	0	0	0	0	0	/C	0.0
1985	Mil-A	15	21	1	1	0	0	0	0	2	7	.048	.130	.048	-49	-4	-4	0	0	0	0	3	C	0.0

1000 HUPPERT-HUTTON Player Register

YEAR	TM/L	G	AB	R	H	2B	3B	HR	RBI	BB	SO	AVG	OBP	SLG	PRO+	BR	/A	RC	SB	CS	SBR	FR	POS	TPR
Total	2	17	21	1	1	0	0	0	0	2	7	.048	.130	.048	-49	-4	-4	0	0	0	0	3	/C	0.0

■ CLINT HURDLE Hurdle, Clinton Merrick b: 7/30/57, Big Rapids, Mich.   BL/TR, 6'3", 195 lbs.   Deb: 9/18/77

YEAR	TM/L	G	AB	R	H	2B	3B	HR	RBI	BB	SO	AVG	OBP	SLG	PRO+	BR	/A	RC	SB	CS	SBR	FR	POS	TPR
1977	KC-A	9	26	5	8	0	0	2	7	2	7	.308	.357	.538	139	1	1	5	0	0	0	0	/O	0.1
1978	*KC-A	133	417	48	110	25	5	7	56	56	84	.264	.352	.398	108	7	5	61	1	3	-2	-9	O1/3D	-0.8
1979	KC-A	59	171	16	41	10	3	3	30	28	24	.240	.350	.386	96	0	-0	24	0	1	-1	-1	O/3D	-0.3
1980	*KC-A	130	395	50	116	31	2	10	60	34	61	.294	.353	.458	119	11	10	62	0	0	0	-11	*O	-0.2
1981	*KC-A	28	76	12	25	3	1	4	15	13	10	.329	.427	.553	182	8	8	18	0	0	0	0	O	0.8
1982	Cin-N	19	34	2	7	1	0	0	1	2	6	.206	.270	.235	42	-3	-3	2	0	1	-1	1	O	-0.2
1983	NY-N	13	33	3	6	2	0	0	2	2	10	.182	.229	.242	31	-3	-3	2	0	0	0	-1	/3O	-0.4
1985	NY-N	43	82	7	16	4	0	3	7	13	20	.195	.313	.354	88	-1	-1	9	0	1	-1	-1	CO	-0.1
1986	StL-N	78	154	18	30	5	1	3	15	26	38	.195	.315	.299	71	-6	-6	16	0	0	0	1	1O/C3	-0.6
1987	NY-N	3	3	1	1	0	0	0	0	0	1	.333	.333	.333	82	-0	-0	0	0	0	0	0	/1	0.0
Total	10	515	1391	162	360	81	12	32	193	176	261	.259	.345	.403	106	14	12	199	1	6	-3	-21	O/1C3D	-1.7

■ JERRY HURLEY Hurley, Jeremiah Joseph b: 6/15/1863, Boston, Mass.   d: 9/17/50, Boston, Mass.   TR, 6', 190 lbs.   Deb: 5/01/1889

YEAR	TM/L	G	AB	R	H	2B	3B	HR	RBI	BB	SO	AVG	OBP	SLG	PRO+	BR	/A	RC	SB	CS	SBR	FR	POS	TPR
1889	Bos-N	1	4	0	0	0	0	0	0	0	0	.000	.000	.000	-94	-1	-1	0	0			-1	/OC	-0.1
1890	Pit-P	8	22	5	6	1	0	0	2	2	5	.273	.333	.318	83	-1	-0	2	0			-3	/CO	-0.1
1891	Cin-a	24	66	10	14	3	2	0	6	12	13	.212	.333	.318	82	-1	-2	8	2			-4	C/O1	-0.3
Total	3	33	92	15	20	4	2	0	8	14	18	.217	.321	.304	75	-2	-3	10	2			-7	/CO1	-0.5

■ JERRY HURLEY Hurley, Jeremiah b: 4/1875, New York, N.Y.   d: 12/27/19, New York, N.Y.   BR/TR,   Deb: 9/23/01

YEAR	TM/L	G	AB	R	H	2B	3B	HR	RBI	BB	SO	AVG	OBP	SLG	PRO+	BR	/A	RC	SB	CS	SBR	FR	POS	TPR
1901	Cin-N	9	21	1	1	0	0	0	0	1		.048	.130	.048	-50	-4	-4	0	0	1		1	/C	-0.1
1907	Bro-N	1	2	0	0	0	0	0	0	0	1	.000	.333	.000	8	-0	-0	0	0	0		0	/C	0.0
Total	2	10	23	1	1	0	0	0	0	0	2	.043	.154	.043	-43	-4	-4	0	1			1	/C	-0.1

■ DICK HURLEY Hurley, William H. b: 1847, Honesdale, Pa.   5'7", 160 lbs.   Deb: 4/18/1872

YEAR	TM/L	G	AB	R	H	2B	3B	HR	RBI	BB	SO	AVG	OBP	SLG	PRO+	BR	/A	RC	SB	CS	SBR	FR	POS	TPR
1872	Oly-n	2	7	0	0	0	0	0		0		.000	.000	.000	-99	-2	-2	0					/O	0.0

■ DON HURST Hurst, Frank O'Donnell b: 8/12/05, Maysville, Ky.   d: 12/6/52, Los Angeles, Cal.   BL/TL, 6', 215 lbs.   Deb: 5/13/28

YEAR	TM/L	G	AB	R	H	2B	3B	HR	RBI	BB	SO	AVG	OBP	SLG	PRO+	BR	/A	RC	SB	CS	SBR	FR	POS	TPR
1928	Phi-N	107	396	73	113	23	4	19	64	68	40	.285	.391	.508	129	20	18	80	3			4	*1	1.0
1929	Phi-N	154	589	100	179	29	4	31	125	80	36	.304	.390	.525	117	22	16	120	10			5	*1	1.2
1930	Phi-N	119	391	78	128	19	3	17	78	46	22	.327	.401	.522	113	14	9	81	6			-2	1/O	0.2
1931	Phi-N	137	489	63	149	37	5	11	91	64	28	.305	.386	.468	119	21	15	93	8			11	*1	1.6
1932	Phi-N	150	579	109	196	41	4	24	**143**	65	27	.339	.412	.547	139	46	37	134	10			-2	*1	2.6
1933	Phi-N	147	550	58	147	27	8	8	76	48	32	.267	.327	.389	92	3	-6	72	3			7	*1	0.0
1934	Phi-N	40	130	16	34	9	0	2	21	12	7	.262	.324	.377	77	-2	-5	17	1			-1	1	-0.7
	Chi-N	51	151	13	30	5	0	3	12	8	18	.199	.239	.291	42	-13	-12	10	0			-2	1	-1.8
	Yr	91	281	29	64	14	0	5	33	20	25	.228	.279	.331	60	-15	-17	27	1			-3		-2.5
Total	7	905	3275	510	976	190	28	115	610	391	210	.298	.375	.478	113	110	72	606	41			20	1/O	4.1

■ JEFF HUSON Huson, Jeffrey Kent b: 8/15/64, Scottsdale, Ariz.   BL/TR, 6'3", 180 lbs.   Deb: 9/02/88

YEAR	TM/L	G	AB	R	H	2B	3B	HR	RBI	BB	SO	AVG	OBP	SLG	PRO+	BR	/A	RC	SB	CS	SBR	FR	POS	TPR
1988	Mon-N	20	42	7	13	2	0	0	3	4	3	.310	.370	.357	105	1	0	5	2	1	0	1	S/23O	0.3
1989	Mon-N	32	74	1	12	5	0	0	2	6	6	.162	.225	.230	30	-7	-7	3	3	0	1	4	S/23	0.0
1990	Tex-A	145	396	57	95	12	2	0	28	46	54	.240	.322	.280	69	-15	-15	39	12	4	1	-12	*S32	-1.8
Total	3	197	512	65	120	19	2	0	33	56	63	.234	.312	.279	66	-21	-22	47	17	5	2	-7	S/32O	-1.5

■ CARL HUSTA Husta, Carl Lawrence "Sox" b: 4/8/02, Egg Harbor, N.J.   d: 11/6/51, Kingston, N.Y.   BR/TR, 5'11", 176 lbs.   Deb: 9/24/25

YEAR	TM/L	G	AB	R	H	2B	3B	HR	RBI	BB	SO	AVG	OBP	SLG	PRO+	BR	/A	RC	SB	CS	SBR	FR	POS	TPR
1925	Phi-A	6	22	2	3	0	0	0	2	3	3	.136	.208	.136	-11	-4	-4	1	0	0	0	2	/S	0.0

■ HARRY HUSTON Huston, Harry Emanuel Kress b: 10/14/1883, Bellefontaine, O.   d: 10/13/69, Blackwell, Okla.   TR, 5'9", 168 lbs.   Deb: 9/03/06

YEAR	TM/L	G	AB	R	H	2B	3B	HR	RBI	BB	SO	AVG	OBP	SLG	PRO+	BR	/A	RC	SB	CS	SBR	FR	POS	TPR
1906	Phi-N	2	4	0	0	0	0	0	0	1		.000	.200	.000	-36	-1	-1	0	0			-0	/C	0.0

■ WARREN HUSTON Huston, Warren Llewellyn b: 10/31/13, Newtonville, Mass.   BR/TR, 6', 170 lbs.   Deb: 6/24/37

YEAR	TM/L	G	AB	R	H	2B	3B	HR	RBI	BB	SO	AVG	OBP	SLG	PRO+	BR	/A	RC	SB	CS	SBR	FR	POS	TPR
1937	Phi-A	38	54	5	7	3	0	0	3	2	9	.130	.161	.185	-13	-10	-9	1	0	1	-1	8	2S/3	0.0
1944	Bos-N	33	55	7	11	1	0	0	1	8	5	.200	.313	.218	49	-3	-3	4	0			3	3/2S	0.2
Total	2	71	109	12	18	4	0	0	4	10	14	.165	.242	.202	19	-13	-13	5	0	1		11	/32S	0.2

■ JOE HUTCHESON Hutcheson, Joseph Johnson "Slug" or "Poodles" b: 2/5/05, Springtown, Tex.   BL/TR, 6'2", 200 lbs.   Deb: 7/08/33

YEAR	TM/L	G	AB	R	H	2B	3B	HR	RBI	BB	SO	AVG	OBP	SLG	PRO+	BR	/A	RC	SB	CS	SBR	FR	POS	TPR
1933	Bro-N	55	184	19	43	4	1	6	21	15	13	.234	.295	.364	91	-3	-2	20	1			0	O	-0.4

■ ED HUTCHINSON Hutchinson, Edwin Forrest b: 5/19/1867, Pittsburgh, Pa.   d: 7/19/34, Colfax, Cal.   BL, 5'11", 175 lbs.   Deb: 6/17/1890

YEAR	TM/L	G	AB	R	H	2B	3B	HR	RBI	BB	SO	AVG	OBP	SLG	PRO+	BR	/A	RC	SB	CS	SBR	FR	POS	TPR
1890	Chi-N	4	17	0	1	1	0	0	0	0	0	.059	.059	.118	-47	-3	-3	0	0			6	/2	0.2

■ FRED HUTCHINSON Hutchinson, Frederick Charles b: 8/12/19, Seattle, Wash.   d: 11/12/64, Bradenton, Fla.   BL/TR, 6'2", 190 lbs.   Deb: 5/02/39 M

YEAR	TM/L	G	AB	R	H	2B	3B	HR	RBI	BB	SO	AVG	OBP	SLG	PRO+	BR	/A	RC	SB	CS	SBR	FR	POS	TPR
1939	Det-A	13	34	5	13	1	0	0	6	2	0	.382	.417	.412	105	1	0	5	0	0	0	0	P	0.0
1940	*Det-A	17	30	1	8	1	0	0	2	0	0	.267	.267	.300	43	-2	-3	2	0	0	0	0	P	0.0
1941	Det-A	2	2	0	0	0	0	0	0	0	2	.000	.000	.000	-91	-1	-1	0	0	0	0	0	H	0.0
1946	Det-A	40	89	11	28	4	0	0	13	6	1	.315	.358	.360	95	0	-0	12	0	0	0	3	P	0.0
1947	Det-A	56	106	8	32	5	2	2	15	6	6	.302	.339	.443	113	2	1	15	2	0	1	2	P	0.0
1948	Det-A	76	112	11	23	1	0	1	12	23	9	.205	.341	.241	55	-6	-7	11	3	0	1	3	P	0.1
1949	Det-A	38	73	12	18	2	1	0	7	8	5	.247	.329	.301	67	-3	-3	7	1	0	0	2	P	0.0
1950	Det-A	44	95	15	31	7	0	0	20	12	3	.326	.407	.400	104	2	1	17	0	0	0	3	P	0.0
1951	Det-A	47	85	7	16	2	0	0	7	7	4	.188	.250	.212	26	-9	-9	5	0	1	-1	3	P	0.0
1952	Det-A	17	18	0	1	0	0	0	0	3	0	.056	.190	.056	-29	-3	-3	0	0	0	0	2	PM	0.0
1953	Det-A	4	6	1	1	0	0	1	1	0	0	.167	.167	.667	118	0	0	1	0	0	0	-0	/P1M	0.0
Total	11	354	650	71	171	23	3	4	83	67	30	.263	.334	.326	75	-20	-23	76	6	1	1	17	P/1	0.1

■ ROY HUTSON Hutson, Roy Lee b: 2/27/02, Luray, Mo.   d: 5/20/57, LaMesa, Cal.   BL/TR, 5'9", 165 lbs.   Deb: 9/20/25

YEAR	TM/L	G	AB	R	H	2B	3B	HR	RBI	BB	SO	AVG	OBP	SLG	PRO+	BR	/A	RC	SB	CS	SBR	FR	POS	TPR
1925	Bro-N	7	8	1	4	0	0	0	1	1		.500	.556	.500	177	1	1	2	0	0	0	0	/O	0.1

■ JIM HUTTO Hutto, James Neamon b: 10/17/47, Norfolk, Va.   BR/TR, 5'11", 195 lbs.   Deb: 4/17/70

YEAR	TM/L	G	AB	R	H	2B	3B	HR	RBI	BB	SO	AVG	OBP	SLG	PRO+	BR	/A	RC	SB	CS	SBR	FR	POS	TPR
1970	Phi-N	57	92	7	17	2	0	3	12	5	20	.185	.227	.304	42	-8	-8	6	0	0	0	-1	O1/C3	-1.0
1975	Bal-A	4	5	0	0	0	0	0	0	0	2	.000	.000	.000	-99	-1	-1	0	0	0	0	0	/C	0.0
Total	2	61	97	7	17	2	0	3	12	5	22	.175	.216	.289	35	-9	-9	6	0	0	0	-1	/O1C3	-1.0

■ TOM HUTTON Hutton, Thomas George b: 4/20/46, Los Angeles, Cal.   BL/TL, 5'11", 180 lbs.   Deb: 9/16/66

YEAR	TM/L	G	AB	R	H	2B	3B	HR	RBI	BB	SO	AVG	OBP	SLG	PRO+	BR	/A	RC	SB	CS	SBR	FR	POS	TPR
1966	LA-N	3	2	0	0	0	0	0	0	0	0	.000	.000	.000	-99	-1	-1	0	0	0	0	0	/1	0.0
1969	LA-N	16	48	2	13	0	0	0	4	5	7	.271	.340	.271	78	-2	-1	5	0	0	0	4	1	0.2
1972	Phi-N	134	381	40	99	16	2	4	38	56	24	.260	.355	.344	97	1	0	47	5	8	-3	0	1O	-1.1
1973	Phi-N	106	247	31	65	11	0	5	29	32	31	.263	.348	.368	96	0	-1	31	3	1	0	4	1	0.1
1974	Phi-N	96	208	32	50	6	3	4	33	30	13	.240	.336	.356	90	-1	-2	25	2	2	-1	-2	1O	-0.8
1975	Phi-N	113	165	24	41	6	0	3	24	27	10	.248	.354	.339	90	-1	-2	19	2	5	-2	5	1O	-0.3
1976	*Phi-N	95	124	15	25	5	1	1	13	27	11	.202	.344	.282	77	-2	-3	13	1	2	-1	4	1/O	-0.2
1977	*Phi-N	107	81	12	25	3	0	2	11	12	10	.309	.398	.420	114	3	2	13	1	1	-0	3	1/O	0.1
1978	Tor-A	64	173	19	44	9	0	2	9	19	11	.254	.328	.341	87	-2	-3	19	1	2	-1	-8	O/1	-1.3

YEAR	TM/L	G	AB	R	H	2B	3B	HR	RBI	BB	SO	AVG	OBP	SLG	PRO+	BR	/A	RC	SB	CS	SBR	FR	POS	TPR
	Mon-N	39	59	4	12	3	0	0	5	10	5	.203	.319	.254	63	-3	-3	5	0	0	0	-1	1/O	-0.4
1979	Mon-N	86	83	14	21	2	1	1	13	10	7	.253	.333	.337	84	-2	-2	9	0	0	0	3	1/O	0.0
1980	Mon-N	62	55	2	12	2	0	0	5	4	10	.218	.271	.255	47	-4	-4	4	0	0	0	-0	/1OP	-0.4
1981	Mon-N	31	29	1	3	0	0	0	2	2	1	.103	.161	.103	-23	-5	-5	1	0	0	0	0	/1O	-0.4
Total	12	952	1655	196	410	63	7	22	186	234	140	.248	.341	.334	87	-18	-22	190	15	21	-8	13	1O/P	-4.5

■ HAM HYATT
Hyatt, Robert Hamilton b: 11/1/1884, Buncombe Co., N.C. d: 9/11/63, Liberty Lake, Wash. BL/TR, 6'1", 185 lbs. Deb: 4/15/09

YEAR	TM/L	G	AB	R	H	2B	3B	HR	RBI	BB	SO	AVG	OBP	SLG	PRO+	BR	/A	RC	SB	CS	SBR	FR	POS	TPR
1909	*Pit-N	49	67	9	20	3	4	0	7	3		.299	.329	.463	134	3	2	10	1			3	/O1	0.6
1910	Pit-N	74	175	19	46	5	6	1	30	8	14	.263	.306	.377	94	-1	-2	20	3			-1	1/O	-0.3
1912	Pit-N	46	97	13	28	3	1	0	22	6	8	.289	.330	.340	85	-2	-2	11	2			-3	O/1	-0.5
1913	Pit-N	63	81	8	27	6	2	4	16	3	8	.333	.372	.605	184	7	8	18	0			-1	/1O	0.7
1914	Pit-N	74	79	2	17	3	1	1	15	7	14	.215	.295	.316	86	-2	-1	7	1			-1	/1C	-0.2
1915	StL-N	106	295	23	79	8	9	2	46	28	24	.268	.337	.376	116	6	6	38	3	3	-1	-5	1O	-0.3
1918	NY-N	53	131	11	30	8	0	2	10	8	8	.229	.273	.336	82	-3	-4	12	1			-1	O/1	-0.6
Total	7	465	925	85	247	36	23	10	146	63	76	.267	.321	.388	108	7	6	117	11	3		-9	1/OC	-0.6

■ JIM HYNDMAN
Hyndman, James William b: 1864, Kingston, Pa. Deb: 7/23/1886

YEAR	TM/L	G	AB	R	H	2B	3B	HR	RBI	BB	SO	AVG	OBP	SLG	PRO+	BR	/A	RC	SB	CS	SBR	FR	POS	TPR
1886	Phi-a	1	4	0	0	0	0	0		0	0	.000	.000	.000	-99	-1	-1	0	0			0	/OP	0.0

■ PAT HYNES
Hynes, Patrick J. b: 3/12/1884, St.Louis, Mo. d: 3/12/07, St.Louis, Mo. TL , Deb: 9/27/03

YEAR	TM/L	G	AB	R	H	2B	3B	HR	RBI	BB	SO	AVG	OBP	SLG	PRO+	BR	/A	RC	SB	CS	SBR	FR	POS	TPR
1903	StL-N	1	3	0	0	0	0	0		0		.000	.000	.000	-99	-1	-1	0	0			-0	/P	0.0
1904	StL-A	66	254	23	60	7	3	0	15	3		.236	.245	.287	74	-9	-7	20	3			-11	O/P	-2.4
Total	2	67	257	23	60	7	3	0	15	3		.233	.242	.284	72	-10	-8	20	3			-12	/OP	-2.4

■ PETE INCAVIGLIA
Incaviglia, Peter Joseph b: 4/2/64, Pebble Beach, Cal. BR/TR, 6'1", 225 lbs. Deb: 4/08/86

YEAR	TM/L	G	AB	R	H	2B	3B	HR	RBI	BB	SO	AVG	OBP	SLG	PRO+	BR	/A	RC	SB	CS	SBR	FR	POS	TPR
1986	Tex-A	153	540	82	135	21	2	30	88	55	185	.250	.324	.463	108	7	5	82	3	2	-0	-16	*OD	-1.2
1987	Tex-A	139	509	85	138	26	4	27	80	48	168	.271	.335	.497	116	11	11	85	9	3	1	-8	*O/D	0.0
1988	Tex-A	116	418	59	104	19	3	22	54	39	153	.249	.323	.467	116	9	8	63	6	4	-1	-0	OD	0.5
1989	Tex-A	133	453	48	107	27	4	21	81	32	136	.236	.295	.453	106	3	2	56	5	7	-3	-5	*O/D	-0.7
1990	Tex-A	153	529	59	123	27	0	24	85	45	146	.233	.304	.420	98	-1	-3	63	3	4	-2	3	*O/D	-0.1
Total	5	694	2449	333	607	120	13	124	388	219	788	.248	.317	.459	109	29	23	349	26	20	-4	-26	O/D	-1.5

■ ALEXIS INFANTE
Infante, Fermin Alexis (Carpio) b: 12/4/61, Barquisimeto, Venez. BR/TR, 5'10", 175 lbs. Deb: 9/27/87

YEAR	TM/L	G	AB	R	H	2B	3B	HR	RBI	BB	SO	AVG	OBP	SLG	PRO+	BR	/A	RC	SB	CS	SBR	FR	POS	TPR
1987	Tor-A	1	0	0	0	0	0	0	0	0	0	—	—	—	—	0	0	0	0	0	0	0	/R	0.0
1988	Tor-A	19	15	7	3	0	0	0	0	2	4	.200	.294	.200	41	-1	-1	1	0	0	0	1	/3SD	0.0
1989	Tor-A	20	12	1	2	0	0	0	0	0	1	.167	.167	.167	-6	-2	-2	0	1	0	0	4	/S32	0.4
1990	Atl-N	20	28	3	1	1	0	0	0	0	7	.036	.069	.071	-60	-6	-6	0	0	0	0	4	2/3S	-0.1
Total	4	60	55	11	6	1	0	0	0	2	12	.109	.155	.127	-20	-9	-9	1	1	0	0	9	/3S2D	0.3

■ SCOTTY INGERTON
Ingerton, William John b: 4/19/1886, Peninsula, Ohio d: 6/15/56, Cleveland, Ohio BR/TR, 6'1", 172 lbs. Deb: 4/12/11

YEAR	TM/L	G	AB	R	H	2B	3B	HR	RBI	BB	SO	AVG	OBP	SLG	PRO+	BR	/A	RC	SB	CS	SBR	FR	POS	TPR
1911	Bos-N	136	521	63	130	24	4	5	61	39	68	.250	.304	.340	74	-15	-21	55	6			18	3O12/S	-0.2

■ CHARLIE INGRAHAM
Ingraham, Charles b: 4/1860, Illinois 5'11", 170 lbs. Deb: 7/04/1883

YEAR	TM/L	G	AB	R	H	2B	3B	HR	RBI	BB	SO	AVG	OBP	SLG	PRO+	BR	/A	RC	SB	CS	SBR	FR	POS	TPR
1883	Bal-a	1	4	0	1	0	0	0		0		.250	.250	.250	60	-0	-0	0				0	/C	0.0

■ MEL INGRAM
Ingram, Melvin David b: 7/4/04, Asheville, N.C. d: 10/28/79, Medford, Ore. BR/TR, 5'11.5", 175 lbs. Deb: 7/24/29

YEAR	TM/L	G	AB	R	H	2B	3B	HR	RBI	BB	SO	AVG	OBP	SLG	PRO+	BR	/A	RC	SB	CS	SBR	FR	POS	TPR
1929	Pit-N	3	0	1	0	0	0	0	0	0	0	—	—	—	—	0	0	0	0			0	R	0.0

■ DANE IORG
Iorg, Dane Charles b: 5/11/50, Eureka, Cal. BL/TR, 6', 180 lbs. Deb: 4/09/77

YEAR	TM/L	G	AB	R	H	2B	3B	HR	RBI	BB	SO	AVG	OBP	SLG	PRO+	BR	/A	RC	SB	CS	SBR	FR	POS	TPR
1977	Phi-N	12	30	3	5	1	0	0	2	1	3	.167	.194	.200	6	-4	-4	1	0	0	0	0	/1	-0.4
	StL-N	30	32	2	10	1	0	0	4	5	4	.313	.405	.344	105	0	1	4	0	1	-1	-0	/O	0.0
	Yr	42	62	5	15	2	0	0	6	6	7	.242	.309	.274	58	-4	-4	5	0	1	-1	-0		-0.4
1978	StL-N	35	85	6	23	4	1	0	4	4	10	.271	.303	.341	81	-2	-2	8	0	0	0	1	O	-0.1
1979	StL-N	79	179	12	52	11	1	1	21	12	28	.291	.339	.380	95	-1	-1	22	1	2	-1	-3	O1	-0.7
1980	StL-N	105	251	33	76	23	1	3	36	20	34	.303	.354	.438	116	6	6	38	1	1	-0	-6	O/13	-0.3
1981	StL-N	75	217	23	71	11	2	2	39	7	9	.327	.348	.424	115	4	4	30	2	0	1	-9	O/13	-0.6
1982	*StL-N	102	238	17	70	14	1	0	34	23	23	.294	.356	.361	100	1	1	28	1	1	0	-3	O1/3	-0.4
1983	StL-N	58	116	6	31	9	1	0	11	10	11	.267	.331	.362	92	-1	-1	13	1	0	0	-2	O1	-0.3
1984	StL-N	15	28	3	4	2	0	0	3	2	6	.143	.200	.214	17	-3	-3	1	0	0	0	-1	/1O	-0.3
	*KC-A	78	235	27	60	16	2	5	30	13	15	.255	.294	.404	90	-3	-4	26	0	1	-1	-3	1O/3D	-1.0
1985	*KC-A	64	130	7	29	9	1	1	21	8	16	.223	.268	.323	63	-7	-7	10	0	1	-1	1	O/13D	-0.6
1986	SD-N	90	106	10	24	2	1	2	11	2	21	.226	.241	.321	55	-7	-7	8	0	0	0	-3	1/3OP	-0.8
Total	10	743	1647	149	455	103	11	14	216	107	180	.276	.321	.378	92	-17	-19	190	5	7	-3	-26	O1/3DP	-5.5

■ GARTH IORG
Iorg, Garth Ray b: 10/12/54, Arcata, Cal. BR/TR, 5'11", 170 lbs. Deb: 4/09/78

YEAR	TM/L	G	AB	R	H	2B	3B	HR	RBI	BB	SO	AVG	OBP	SLG	PRO+	BR	/A	RC	SB	CS	SBR	FR	POS	TPR
1978	Tor-A	19	49	3	8	0	0	0	3	3	4	.163	.226	.163	11	-6	-6	2	0	0	0	4	2	0.0
1980	Tor-A	80	222	24	55	10	1	2	14	12	39	.248	.286	.329	65	-10	-11	20	2	1	0	11	2301/SD	0.1
1981	Tor-A	70	215	17	52	11	0	0	10	7	31	.242	.269	.293	58	-11	-12	16	2	3	-1	-1	23/S1D	-1.2
1982	Tor-A	129	417	45	119	20	5	1	36	12	38	.285	.312	.365	78	-9	-14	47	3	2	-0	-4	*32/D	-1.8
1983	Tor-A	122	375	40	103	22	5	2	39	13	45	.275	.301	.376	80	-8	-11	41	7	0	2	-3	32/S	-1.0
1984	Tor-A	121	247	24	56	10	3	1	25	5	16	.227	.245	.304	49	-17	-18	16	1	3	-2	1	*3/2SD	-1.5
1985	*Tor-A	131	288	33	90	22	1	7	37	21	26	.313	.359	.469	122	9	8	45	3	6	-3	11	*32	1.3
1986	Tor-A	137	327	30	85	19	1	3	44	20	47	.260	.305	.352	76	-10	-11	35	3	0	1	-15	32/S	-2.3
1987	Tor-A	122	310	35	65	11	0	4	30	21	52	.210	.264	.284	45	-24	-25	23	2	2	-1	-13	23/D	-3.0
Total	9	931	2450	251	633	125	16	20	238	114	298	.258	.294	.347	72	-85	-100	244	23	17	-3	-9	32/O1DS	-9.4

■ HAPPY IOTT
Iott, Frederick "Happy Jack" or "Biddo" (b: Frederick Hoyot) b: 7/7/1876, Houlton, Me. d: 2/17/41, Island Falls, Me. BR/TR, 5'10", 175 lbs. Deb: 9/16/03

YEAR	TM/L	G	AB	R	H	2B	3B	HR	RBI	BB	SO	AVG	OBP	SLG	PRO+	BR	/A	RC	SB	CS	SBR	FR	POS	TPR
1903	Cle-A	3	10	1	2	0	0	0	0	0	2	.200	.333	.200	66	-0	-0	1	1			-0	/O	0.0

■ HAL IRELAN
Irelan, Harold "Grump" b: 8/5/1890, Burnettsville, Ind. d: 7/16/44, Carmel, Ind. BB/TR, 5'7", 165 lbs. Deb: 4/23/14

YEAR	TM/L	G	AB	R	H	2B	3B	HR	RBI	BB	SO	AVG	OBP	SLG	PRO+	BR	/A	RC	SB	CS	SBR	FR	POS	TPR
1914	Phi-N	67	165	16	39	8	0	1	16	21	22	.236	.326	.303	82	-2	-3	17	3			11	2/S13	0.8

■ TIM IRELAND
Ireland, Timothy Neal b: 3/14/53, Oakland, Cal. BR/TR, 6', 180 lbs. Deb: 9/20/81

YEAR	TM/L	G	AB	R	H	2B	3B	HR	RBI	BB	SO	AVG	OBP	SLG	PRO+	BR	/A	RC	SB	CS	SBR	FR	POS	TPR
1981	KC-A	4	0	1	0	0	0	0	0	0	0	—	—	—	—	0	0	0	0	1	-1	0	/1	0.0
1982	KC-A	7	7	2	1	0	0	0	0	1	1	.143	.250	.143	11	-1	-1	0	0	0	0	1	/2O3	0.0
Total	2	11	7	3	1	0	0	0	0	1	1	.143	.250	.143	11	-1	-1	0	0	1	-1	1	/21O3	0.0

■ MONTE IRVIN
Irvin, Monford b: 2/25/19, Columbia, Ala. BR/TR, 6'1", 195 lbs. Deb: 7/08/49 H

YEAR	TM/L	G	AB	R	H	2B	3B	HR	RBI	BB	SO	AVG	OBP	SLG	PRO+	BR	/A	RC	SB	CS	SBR	FR	POS	TPR
1949	NY-N	36	76	7	17	3	2	0	7	17	11	.224	.366	.316	84	-1	-1	10	0			1	O/13	0.0
1950	NY-N	110	374	61	112	19	5	15	66	52	41	.299	.392	.497	131	18	18	76	3			3	1O/3	1.6
1951	*NY-N	151	558	94	174	19	11	24	121	89	44	.312	.415	.514	147	41	40	127	12	2	2	11	*O1	4.8
1952	NY-N	46	126	10	39	2	1	4	21	10	11	.310	.365	.437	120	4	3	20	0			-4	O	-0.1
1953	NY-N	124	444	72	146	21	5	21	97	55	34	.329	.406	.541	142	29	28	96	2	0	1	6	*O	2.9
1954	*NY-N	135	432	62	113	13	3	19	64	70	23	.262	.367	.438	108	6	6	69	7	4	-0	3	*O/13	0.4
1955	NY-N	51	150	16	38	7	1	1	17	17	15	.253	.341	.333	80	-4	-4	18	3	0	1	2	O	0.0

YEAR	TM/L	G	AB	R	H	2B	3B	HR	RBI	BB	SO	AVG	OBP	SLG	PRO+	BR	/A	RC	SB	CS	SBR	FR	POS	TPR
1956	Chi-N	111	339	44	92	13	3	15	50	41	41	.271	.350	.460	118	7	8	53	1	0	0	7	O	1.2
Total	8	764	2499	366	731	97	31	99	443	351	220	.293	.385	.475	126	101	99	468	28	7		30	O1/3	10.8

■ ED IRVIN
Irvin, William Edward b: 1882, Philadelphia, Pa. d: 2/18/16, Philadelphia, Pa. TR, Deb: 5/18/12

YEAR	TM/L	G	AB	R	H	2B	3B	HR	RBI	BB	SO	AVG	OBP	SLG	PRO+	BR	/A	RC	SB	CS	SBR	FR	POS	TPR
1912	Det-A	1	3	0	2	0	2	0	0	0		.667	.667	2.000	675	2	2	4	0			-1	/3	0.1

■ ARTHUR IRWIN
Irwin, Arthur Albert "Doc" or "Sandy" b: 2/14/1858, Toronto, Ont., Can. d: 7/16/21, Atlantic Ocean BL/TR, 5'8.5", 158 lbs. Deb: 5/01/1880 MU

YEAR	TM/L	G	AB	R	H	2B	3B	HR	RBI	BB	SO	AVG	OBP	SLG	PRO+	BR	/A	RC	SB	CS	SBR	FR	POS	TPR
1880	Wor-N	85	352	53	91	19	4	1	35	11	27	.259	.281	.344	102	4	-0	35				31	*S/3C	3.3
1881	Wor-N	50	206	27	55	8	2	0	24	7	4	.267	.291	.325	88	-1	-3	20				-8	S	-0.6
1882	Wor-N	84	333	30	73	12	4	0	30	14	34	.219	.251	.279	68	-11	-12	24				21	3S	1.1
1883	Pro-N	98	406	67	116	22	7	0	44	12	38	.286	.306	.374	103	2	1	48				-7	*S/2	-0.1
1884	*Pro-N	102	404	73	97	14	3	2	44	28	52	.240	.289	.304	89	-6	-4	36				-4	*S/P	0.1
1885	Pro-N	59	218	16	39	2	1	0	14	14	29	.179	.228	.197	40	-14	-13	10				4	S/32	-0.5
1886	Phi-N	101	373	51	87	6	6	0	34	35	39	.233	.299	.282	77	-9	-10	40	24			4	*S/3	-0.6
1887	Phi-N	100	374	65	95	14	8	2	56	48	26	.254	.344	.350	90	-1	-5	53	19			-9	*S	-1.4
1888	Phi-N	125	448	51	98	12	4	0	28	33	56	.219	.277	.263	71	-11	-15	39	19			11	*S/2	0.0
1889	Phi-N	18	73	9	16	5	0	0	10	6	6	.219	.278	.288	55	-4	-5	8	6			-6	*S	-0.8
	Was-N	85	313	49	73	10	5	0	32	42	37	.233	.326	.297	81	-9	-6	34	9			11	S/P2M	0.8
	Yr	103	386	58	89	15	5	0	42	48	43	.231	.317	.295	76	-13	-10	42	15			5		0.0
1890	Bos-P	96	354	60	92	17	1	0	45	57	29	.260	.364	.314	78	-6	-11	47	16			3	*S	-0.1
1891	Bos-a	6	17	1	2	0	0	0	0	2	1	.118	.286	.118	19	-2	-2	1	0			-1	/SM	-0.1
1894	Phi-N	1	0	0	0	0	0	0	0	0	0	—	—	—	—	0	0	0	0			0	/SM	0.0
Total	13	1010	3871	552	934	141	45	5	396	309	378	.241	.299	.305	82	-68	-84	394	93			48	S/32PC	1.1

■ CHARLIE IRWIN
Irwin, Charles Edwin b: 2/15/1869, Clinton, Ill. d: 9/21/25, Chicago, Ill. BL/TR, 5'10", 160 lbs. Deb: 9/03/1893

YEAR	TM/L	G	AB	R	H	2B	3B	HR	RBI	BB	SO	AVG	OBP	SLG	PRO+	BR	/A	RC	SB	CS	SBR	FR	POS	TPR
1893	Chi-N	21	82	14	25	6	2	0	13	10	1	.305	.394	.427	122	3	3	16	4			-1	S	0.2
1894	Chi-N	128	498	84	144	24	9	8	95	63	23	.289	.379	.422	90	-4	-9	95	35			-11	3S	-1.3
1895	Chi-N	3	10	4	2	0	0	0	0	2	1	.200	.333	.200	39	-1	-1	1	0			-2	/S	-0.1
1896	Cin-N	127	476	77	141	16	6	1	67	26	17	.296	.338	.361	81	-9	-15	70	31			7	*3	-0.1
1897	Cin-N	134	505	89	146	26	6	0	74	47		.289	.359	.364	88	-3	-9	78	27			-6	*3	-1.2
1898	Cin-N	136	501	77	120	14	5	3	55	31		.240	.293	.305	69	-17	-22	51	18			13	*3	-0.4
1899	Cin-N	90	314	42	73	4	8	1	52	26		.232	.295	.306	66	-14	-15	37	26			-13	3/S21	-2.4
1900	Cin-N	87	333	59	91	15	6	1	44	14		.273	.309	.363	89	-6	-5	41	9			-11	3S/O2	-1.2
1901	Cin-N	67	260	25	62	12	2	0	25	14		.238	.285	.300	77	-9	-7	27	13			4	3	0.2
	Bro-N	65	242	25	52	13	2	0	20	14		.215	.269	.285	61	-11	-12	21	4			-2	3	-0.9
	Yr	132	502	50	114	25	4	0	45	28		.227	.277	.293	69	-20	-19	48	17			3		-0.7
1902	Bro-N	131	458	59	125	14	0	2	45	28		.273	.341	.344	104	4	4	57	13			-10	*3/S	0.0
Total	10	989	3679	555	981	144	46	16	488	286	42	.267	.328	.344	83	-68	-88	493	180			-31	3S/O21	-7.2

■ JOHN IRWIN
Irwin, John b: 7/21/1861, Toronto, Ont., Can d: 2/28/34, Boston, Mass. BL/TR, 5'10", 168 lbs. Deb: 5/31/1882

YEAR	TM/L	G	AB	R	H	2B	3B	HR	RBI	BB	SO	AVG	OBP	SLG	PRO+	BR	/A	RC	SB	CS	SBR	FR	POS	TPR
1882	Wor-N	1	4	0	0	0	0	0	0	0	0	.000	.000	.000	-98	-1	-1	0				-1	/1	-0.1
1884	Bos-U	105	432	81	101	22	6	1		15		.234	.260	.319	96	-2	-1	37	0			4	*3	0.4
1886	Phi-a	3	13	4	3	1	0	0		0		.231	.231	.308	69	-0	-1	1	0			-1	/S3	0.0
1887	Was-N	8	31	6	11	2	0	2	3	6		.355	.429	.613	198	4	4	11	6			-2	/S3	0.1
1888	Was-N	37	126	14	28	5	2	0	8	5	18	.222	.263	.294	84	-3	-2	14	15			-2	S3	-0.2
1889	Was-N	58	228	42	66	11	4	0	25	25	14	.289	.370	.373	116	4	6	36	10			0	3	0.8
1890	Buf-P	77	308	62	72	11	4	0	34	43	19	.234	.335	.295	77	-11	-6	37	18			4	31/2	0.1
1891	Bos-a	19	72	6	16	2	2	0	15	6	9	.222	.282	.306	71	-3	-3	8	6			0	O/3S	-0.2
	Lou-a	14	55	7	15	1	1	0	7	5	6	.273	.344	.327	96	-0	-0	7	1			-7	3	-0.5
	Yr	33	127	13	31	3	3	0	22	11	15	.244	.309	.315	82	-3	-3	15	7			-6		-0.7
Total	8	322	1269	222	312	55	19	3	92	102	74	.246	.308	.326	94	-14	-4	151	56			-4	3/SO12	0.4

■ TOMMY IRWIN
Irwin, Thomas Andrew b: 12/20/12, Altoona, Pa. BR/TR, 5'11", 165 lbs. Deb: 10/01/38

YEAR	TM/L	G	AB	R	H	2B	3B	HR	RBI	BB	SO	AVG	OBP	SLG	PRO+	BR	/A	RC	SB	CS	SBR	FR	POS	TPR
1938	Cle-A	3	9	1	1	0	0	0	0	3	1	.111	.333	.111	16	-1	-1	1	0	0	0	0	/S	0.0

■ WALT IRWIN
Irwin, Walter Kingsley b: 9/23/1897, Henrietta, Pa. d: 8/18/76, Spring Lake, Mich. BR/TR, 5'10.5", 170 lbs. Deb: 4/24/21

YEAR	TM/L	G	AB	R	H	2B	3B	HR	RBI	BB	SO	AVG	OBP	SLG	PRO+	BR	/A	RC	SB	CS	SBR	FR	POS	TPR
1921	StL-N	4	1	1	0	0	0	0	0	0	0	.000	.000	.000	-99	-0	-0	0	0	0	0	0	H	0.0

■ ORLANDO ISALES
Isales, Orlando (Pizarro) b: 12/22/59, Santurce, P.R. BR/TR, 5'9", 175 lbs. Deb: 9/11/80

YEAR	TM/L	G	AB	R	H	2B	3B	HR	RBI	BB	SO	AVG	OBP	SLG	PRO+	BR	/A	RC	SB	CS	SBR	FR	POS	TPR
1980	Phi-N	3	5	1	2	0	1	0	3	1	0	.400	.500	.800	244	1	1	2	0	0	0	0	/O	0.1

■ FRANK ISBELL
Isbell, William Frank "Bald Eagle" b: 8/21/1875, Delevan, N.Y. d: 7/15/41, Wichita, Kan. BL/TR, 5'11", 190 lbs. Deb: 5/01/1898

YEAR	TM/L	G	AB	R	H	2B	3B	HR	RBI	BB	SO	AVG	OBP	SLG	PRO+	BR	/A	RC	SB	CS	SBR	FR	POS	TPR
1898	Chi-N	45	159	17	37	4	0	8		3		.233	.252	.258	48	-11	-11	11	3			-7	OP/32S	-1.5
1901	Chi-A	137	556	93	143	15	8	3	70	36		.257	.311	.329	81	-15	-13	76	52			14	*1/2PS3	-0.4
1902	Chi-A	137	515	62	130	14	4	4	59	14		.252	.276	.318	69	-24	-21	59	38			10	*1/SPC	-0.7
1903	Chi-A	138	546	52	132	25	9	2	59	12		.242	.258	.332	81	-16	-13	57	26			7	*13/2SO	-0.4
1904	Chi-A	96	314	27	66	10	3	1	34	16		.210	.248	.271	69	-12	-11	28	19			0	12/OS	-0.9
1905	Chi-A	94	341	55	101	21	11	2	45	15		.296	.326	.440	151	15	17	57	15			-2	2O/1S	1.4
1906	*Chi-A	143	549	71	153	18	11	0	57	30		.279	.316	.352	114	6	8	78	37			-22	*2O/PC	-1.9
1907	Chi-A	125	486	60	118	19	7	0	41	22		.243	.276	.311	92	-7	-5	51	22			9	*2/OPS	0.4
1908	Chi-A	84	320	31	79	15	3	1	49	19		.247	.289	.322	102	-0	0	35	18			2	12	0.0
1909	Chi-A	120	433	33	97	17	6	0	33	23		.224	.265	.291	79	-13	-11	40	23			1	*1/O2	-1.1
Total	10	1119	4219	501	1056	158	62	13	455	190		.250	.285	.326	89	-76	-59	493	253			13	12O/3PSC	-5.1

■ MIKE IVIE
Ivie, Michael Wilson b: 8/8/52, Atlanta, Ga. BR/TR, 6'3", 205 lbs. Deb: 9/04/71

YEAR	TM/L	G	AB	R	H	2B	3B	HR	RBI	BB	SO	AVG	OBP	SLG	PRO+	BR	/A	RC	SB	CS	SBR	FR	POS	TPR
1971	SD-N	6	17	0	8	0	0	0	3	1	1	.471	.526	.471	198	2	2	3	0	0	0	-2	/C	0.0
1974	SD-N	12	34	1	3	0	0	1	3	2	8	.088	.139	.176	-13	-5	-5	1	0	0	0	0	1	-0.5
1975	SD-N	111	377	36	94	16	2	8	46	20	63	.249	.294	.366	88	-10	-7	37	4	4	-1	-5	13/C	-1.9
1976	SD-N	140	405	51	118	19	5	7	70	30	41	.291	.348	.415	126	8	12	56	6	6	-2	1	*1/C3	0.5
1977	SD-N	134	489	66	133	29	2	9	66	39	57	.272	.328	.395	104	-5	1	64	3	2	-0	7	*13	-0.9
1978	SF-N	117	318	34	98	14	3	11	55	27	45	.308	.366	.475	139	14	15	55	3	0	1	-9	1O	0.4
1979	SF-N	133	402	58	115	18	3	27	89	47	80	.286	.362	.547	155	24	27	79	5	1	-3	1O/32		2.0
1980	SF-N	79	286	21	69	16	1	4	25	19	40	.241	.289	.346	78	-9	-9	27	1	2	-1	-6	1	-2.0
1981	SF-N	7	17	1	5	2	0	0	3	0	1	.294	.294	.412	100	-0	-0	2	0	0	0	1	/1	0.0
	Hou-N	19	42	2	10	3	0	0	6	2	11	.238	.273	.310	68	-2	-2	3	0	1	-1	2	1	0.0
	Yr	26	59	3	15	5	0	0	9	2	12	.254	.279	.339	78	-2	-2	5	0	1	-1	3		0.0
1982	Hou-N	7	6	0	2	0	0	0	0	1	0	.333	.429	.333	125	0	0	1	0	0	0	0	/H	0.0
	Det-A	80	259	35	60	12	1	14	38	24	51	.232	.302	.448	102	0	0	35	0	0	0	0	D	0.0
1983	Det-A	12	42	4	9	4	0	0	7	2	4	.214	.250	.310	54	-3	-3	0	0	0	0	-0	1	-0.2
Total	11	857	2694	309	724	133	17	81	411	214	402	.269	.326	.421	112	13	32	366	22	16	-3	-27	1/3DOC2	-2.6

■ HANK IZQUIERDO
Izquierdo, Enrique Roberto (Valdes) b: 3/20/31, Matanzas, Cuba BR/TR, 5'11", 175 lbs. Deb: 8/09/67

YEAR	TM/L	G	AB	R	H	2B	3B	HR	RBI	BB	SO	AVG	OBP	SLG	PRO+	BR	/A	RC	SB	CS	SBR	FR	POS	TPR
1967	Min-A	16	26	4	7	2	0	0	2	1	2	.269	.296	.346	83	-0	-1	3	0	0	0	4	C	0.4

YEAR	TM/L	G	AB	R	H	2B	3B	HR	RBI	BB	SO	AVG	OBP	SLG	PRO+	BR	/A	RC	SB	CS	SBR	FR	POS	TPR

■ RAY JABLONSKI
Jablonski, Raymond Leo "Jabbo" b: 12/17/26, Chicago, Ill. d: 11/25/85, Chicago, Ill. BR/TR, 5'10", 175 lbs. Deb: 4/14/53

YEAR	TM/L	G	AB	R	H	2B	3B	HR	RBI	BB	SO	AVG	OBP	SLG	PRO+	BR	/A	RC	SB	CS	SBR	FR	POS	TPR
1953	StL-N	157	604	64	162	23	5	21	112	34	61	.268	.308	.427	89	-11	-11	77	2	1	-1	-16	*3	-3.1
1954	StL-N	152	611	80	181	33	3	12	104	49	42	.296	.350	.419	99	-1	-1	88	9	4	0	-7	*3/1	-0.6
1955	Cin-N	74	221	28	53	9	0	9	28	13	35	.240	.291	.403	77	-6	-8	25	0	1	-1	-10	3O	-1.9
1956	Cin-N	130	407	42	104	25	1	15	66	37	57	.256	.328	.432	96	1	-2	54	2	4	-2	-25	*3/2	-3.0
1957	NY-N	107	305	37	88	15	1	9	57	31	47	.289	.354	.433	110	5	5	46	0	2	-1	-2	3/1O	0.2
1958	SF-N	82	230	28	53	15	1	12	46	17	50	.230	.289	.461	97	-3	-2	27	2	0	1	-7	3	-0.8
1959	StL-N	60	87	11	22	4	0	3	14	8	19	.253	.316	.402	84	-1	-2	11	1	0	0	-3	3/S	-0.5
	KC-A	25	65	4	17	1	0	2	8	3	11	.262	.294	.369	79	-2	-2	7	0	0	0	-3	3	-0.4
1960	KC-A	21	32	3	7	1	0	0	3	4	8	.219	.306	.250	52	-2	-2	3	0	0	0	0	/3	-0.1
Total	8	808	2562	297	687	126	11	83	438	196	330	.268	.324	.423	94	-21	-26	338	16	13	-3	-74	3/O1S2	-10.2

■ FRED JACKLITSCH
Jacklitsch, Frederick Lawrence b: 5/24/1876, Brooklyn, N.Y. d: 7/18/37, Brooklyn, N.Y. BR/TR, 5'9", 180 lbs. Deb: 6/06/00

YEAR	TM/L	G	AB	R	H	2B	3B	HR	RBI	BB	SO	AVG	OBP	SLG	PRO+	BR	/A	RC	SB	CS	SBR	FR	POS	TPR
1900	Phi-N	5	11	0	2	1	0	0	3	0		.182	.182	.273	26	-1	-1	1	0			-2	/C	-0.1
1901	Phi-N	33	120	14	30	4	3	0	24	12		.250	.323	.333	91	-1	-1	14	2			0	C/3	0.3
1902	Phi-N	38	114	8	23	4	0	0	8	9		.202	.278	.237	61	-5	-5	8	2			-7	C/O	-0.9
1903	Bro-N	60	176	31	47	8	3	1	21	33		.267	.383	.364	119	5	6	27	4			-9	C/2O	0.1
1904	Bro-N	26	77	8	18	3	1	0	8	7		.234	.298	.299	88	-1	-1	9	7			-7	1/2C	-0.7
1905	NY-A	1	3	1	0	0	0	0	1	1		.000	.250	.000	-15	-0	-0	0	0			-0	/C	0.0
1907	Phi-N	73	202	19	43	7	0	0	17	27		.213	.306	.248	77	-5	-4	18	7			10	C/1O	1.2
1908	Phi-N	37	86	6	19	3	0	0	7	14		.221	.330	.256	87	-0	-1	9	3			3	C	0.5
1909	Phi-N	20	32	6	10	1	1	0	1	10		.313	.476	.406	173	4	4	7	1			-2	C/2	0.3
1910	Phi-N	25	51	7	10	3	0	0	2	5	9	.196	.268	.255	51	-3	-3	3	0			5	C/123	0.3
1914	Bal-F	122	337	40	93	21	4	2	48	52	66	.276	.376	.380	113	9	8	53	7			-32	*C	-1.9
1915	Bal-F	49	135	20	32	9	0	2	13	31	25	.237	.387	.348	115	5	4	20	2			-20	C/S	-1.5
1917	Bos-N	1	0	0	0	0	0	0	0	0	0	—	—	—				0	0			-0	/C	0.0
Total	13	490	1344	160	327	64	12	5	153	201	100	.243	.345	.320	98	7	5	168	35			-59	C/1203S	-2.4

■ CHARLIE JACKSON
Jackson, Charles Herbert "Lefty" b: 2/7/1894, Granite City, Ill. d: 5/27/68, Radford, Va. BL/TL, 5'9", 150 lbs. Deb: 8/20/15

YEAR	TM/L	G	AB	R	H	2B	3B	HR	RBI	BB	SO	AVG	OBP	SLG	PRO+	BR	/A	RC	SB	CS	SBR	FR	POS	TPR
1915	Chi-A	1	1	0	0	0	0	0	0	0	1	.000	.000	.000	-97	-0	-0	0	0			0	H	0.0
1917	Pit-N	41	121	7	29	3	2	0	1	10	22	.240	.303	.298	82	-2	-2	12	4			1	O	-0.2
Total	2	42	122	7	29	3	2	0	1	10	23	.238	.301	.295	80	-2	-3	12	4			1	/O	-0.2

■ CHUCK JACKSON
Jackson, Charles Leo b: 3/19/63, Seattle, Wash. BR/TR, 6' ", 185 lbs. Deb: 5/26/87

YEAR	TM/L	G	AB	R	H	2B	3B	HR	RBI	BB	SO	AVG	OBP	SLG	PRO+	BR	/A	RC	SB	CS	SBR	FR	POS	TPR
1987	Hou-N	35	71	3	15	3	0	1	6	7	19	.211	.282	.296	55	-5	-4	6	1	1	-0	3	3O/S	-0.1
1988	Hou-N	46	83	7	19	5	1	1	8	7	16	.229	.289	.349	86	-2	-2	8	1	1	-0	3	3/SO	0.1
Total	2	81	154	10	34	8	1	2	14	14	35	.221	.286	.325	71	-7	-6	14	2	2	-1	6	/3OS	0.0

■ DARRIN JACKSON
Jackson, Darrin Jay b: 8/22/62, Los Angeles, Cal. BR/TR, 6'1", 170 lbs. Deb: 6/17/85

YEAR	TM/L	G	AB	R	H	2B	3B	HR	RBI	BB	SO	AVG	OBP	SLG	PRO+	BR	/A	RC	SB	CS	SBR	FR	POS	TPR
1985	Chi-N	5	11	0	1	0	0	0	0	0	3	.091	.091	.091	-44	-2	-2	0	0	0	0	0	/O	-0.1
1987	Chi-N	7	5	2	4	1	0	0	0	0	0	.800	.800	1.000	359	2	2	4	0	0	0	0	/O	0.2
1988	Chi-N	100	188	29	50	11	3	6	20	5	28	.266	.289	.452	105	1	0	24	4	1	1	5	O	0.4
1989	Chi-N	45	83	7	19	4	0	1	8	6	17	.229	.281	.313	65	-3	-4	7	1	2	-1	5	O	0.0
	SD-N	25	87	10	18	3	0	3	12	7	17	.207	.266	.345	73	-3	-3	7	0	2	-1	3	O	-0.1
	Yr	70	170	17	37	7	0	4	20	13	34	.218	.273	.329	68	-7	-7	14	1	4	-2	8		-0.1
1990	SD-N	58	113	10	29	3	0	3	9	5	24	.257	.288	.363	77	-4	-4	12	3	0	1	2	O	-0.2
Total	5	240	487	58	121	22	3	13	49	23	89	.248	.284	.386	85	-9	-11	54	8	5	-1	14	O	0.2

■ GEORGE JACKSON
Jackson, George Christopher "Hickory" b: 10/14/1882, Springfield, Mo. d: 11/25/72, Cleburne, Tex. BR/TR, 6'0.5", 180 lbs. Deb: 8/02/11

YEAR	TM/L	G	AB	R	H	2B	3B	HR	RBI	BB	SO	AVG	OBP	SLG	PRO+	BR	/A	RC	SB	CS	SBR	FR	POS	TPR
1911	Bos-N	39	147	28	51	11	2	0	25	12	21	.347	.404	.449	128	8	6	31	12			-3	O	0.2
1912	Bos-N	110	397	55	104	13	5	4	48	38	72	.262	.342	.350	88	-5	-6	55	22			5	*O	-0.4
1913	Bos-N	3	10	2	3	0	0	0	0	0	2	.300	.300	.300	70	-0	-0	1	0			1	/O	0.0
Total	3	152	554	85	158	24	7	4	73	50	95	.285	.357	.375	98	2	-1	87	34			3	O	-0.2

■ HENRY JACKSON
Jackson, Henry Everett b: 6/23/1861, Union City, Ind. d: 9/14/32, Chicago, Ill. BR/TR, 6'2", 185 lbs. Deb: 9/13/1887

YEAR	TM/L	G	AB	R	H	2B	3B	HR	RBI	BB	SO	AVG	OBP	SLG	PRO+	BR	/A	RC	SB	CS	SBR	FR	POS	TPR
1887	Ind-N	10	38	1	10	1	0	0	3	0	12	.263	.263	.289	57	-2	-2	4	2			-1	1	-0.3

■ JIM JACKSON
Jackson, James Benner b: 11/28/1877, Philadelphia, Pa. d: 10/9/55, Philadelphia, Pa. BR/TR, Deb: 4/26/01

YEAR	TM/L	G	AB	R	H	2B	3B	HR	RBI	BB	SO	AVG	OBP	SLG	PRO+	BR	/A	RC	SB	CS	SBR	FR	POS	TPR
1901	Bal-A	99	364	42	91	17	3	2	50	20		.250	.291	.330	70	-13	-15	41	11			3	O	-1.2
1902	NY-N	35	110	14	20	5	1	0	13	15		.182	.280	.245	65	-4	-4	10	6			-2	O	-0.9
1905	Cle-A	109	426	59	109	12	4	2	31	34		.256	.311	.317	100	1	0	49	15			4	*O/3	0.0
1906	Cle-A	105	374	44	80	13	2	0	38	38		.214	.286	.259	74	-10	-10	38	25			-6	*O	-2.1
Total	4	348	1274	159	300	47	10	4	132	107		.235	.295	.297	81	-27	-29	137	57			-1	O/3	-4.2

■ JOE JACKSON
Jackson, Joseph Jefferson "Shoeless Joe" b: 7/16/1889, Pickens Co., S.C. d: 12/5/51, Greenville, S.C. BL/TR, 6'1", 200 lbs. Deb: 8/25/08

YEAR	TM/L	G	AB	R	H	2B	3B	HR	RBI	BB	SO	AVG	OBP	SLG	PRO+	BR	/A	RC	SB	CS	SBR	FR	POS	TPR
1908	Phi-A	5	23	0	3	0	0	0	3	0		.130	.130	.130	-13	-3	-3	0	0			-0	/O	-0.3
1909	Phi-A	5	17	3	3	0	0	0	3	1		.176	.222	.176	26	-1	-1	1	0			0	/O	-0.1
1910	Cle-A	20	75	15	29	2	5	1	11	8		.387	.446	.587	220	10	10	21	4			1	O	1.1
1911	Cle-A	147	571	126	233	45	19	7	83	56		.408	.468	.590	192	72	71	175	41			8	*O	6.5
1912	Cle-A	154	572	121	226	44	26	3	90	54		.395	.458	.579	190	70	68	166	35			12	*O	6.9
1913	Cle-A	148	528	109	197	39	17	7	71	80	26	.373	.460	.551	190	66	64	140	26			2	*O	6.0
1914	Cle-A	122	453	61	153	22	13	3	53	41	34	.338	.399	.464	153	32	30	86	22	15	-2	2	*O	2.4
1915	Cle-A	83	303	42	99	16	9	3	45	28	11	.327	.389	.469	154	20	19	54	10	10	-3	-3	O1	0.9
	Chi-A	45	158	21	43	4	5	2	36	24	12	.272	.378	.399	129	7	6	23	6	10	-4	-2	O	-0.1
	Yr	128	461	63	142	20	14	5	81	52	23	.308	.385	.445	145	27	25	77	16	20	-7	-5		0.8
1916	Chi-A	155	592	91	202	40	21	3	78	46	25	.341	.393	.495	165	45	44	119	24	14	-1	-1	*O	3.6
1917	*Chi-A	146	538	91	162	20	17	5	75	57	25	.301	.375	.429	142	29	27	89	13			9	*O	3.1
1918	Chi-A	17	65	9	23	2	2	1	20	8	1	.354	.425	.492	175	6	6	15	3			-0	O	0.5
1919	*Chi-A	139	516	79	181	31	14	7	96	60	10	.351	.422	.506	159	42	41	111	9			-4	*O	2.8
1920	Chi-A	146	570	105	218	42	20	12	121	56	14	.382	.444	.589	169	52	58	145	9	12	-5	-1	*O	3.9
Total	13	1332	4981	873	1772	307	168	54	785	519	158	.356	.423	.517	169	452	440	1146	202	61		23	*O/1	37.2

■ KEN JACKSON
Jackson, Kenneth Bernard b: 8/21/63, Shreveport, La. BR/TR, 5'9", 170 lbs. Deb: 9/12/87

YEAR	TM/L	G	AB	R	H	2B	3B	HR	RBI	BB	SO	AVG	OBP	SLG	PRO+	BR	/A	RC	SB	CS	SBR	FR	POS	TPR
1987	Phi-N	8	16	1	4	2	0	0	2	1	4	.250	.333	.375	85	-0	-0	2	0	0	0	-1	/S	0.0

■ LOU JACKSON
Jackson, Louis Clarence b: 7/26/35, Riverton, La. d: 5/27/69, Tokyo, Japan BL/TR, 5'10", 168 lbs. Deb: 7/23/58

YEAR	TM/L	G	AB	R	H	2B	3B	HR	RBI	BB	SO	AVG	OBP	SLG	PRO+	BR	/A	RC	SB	CS	SBR	FR	POS	TPR
1958	Chi-N	24	35	5	6	2	1	1	6	1	9	.171	.194	.371	46	-3	-3	2	0	1	-1	-1	O	-0.4
1959	Chi-N	6	4	2	1	0	0	0	1	0	2	.250	.250	.250	34	-0	-0	0	0	0	0	0	H	0.0
1964	Bal-A	4	8	0	3	0	0	0	0	0	2	.375	.375	.375	110	-0	0	1	0	0	0	0	/O	0.0
Total	3	34	47	7	10	2	1	1	7	1	13	.213	.229	.362	55	-3	-3	3	0	1	-1	-1	/O	-0.4

■ RANDY JACKSON
Jackson, Ransom Joseph "Handsome Ransom" b: 2/10/26, Little Rock, Ark. BR/TR, 6'1.5", 180 lbs. Deb: 5/02/50

YEAR	TM/L	G	AB	R	H	2B	3B	HR	RBI	BB	SO	AVG	OBP	SLG	PRO+	BR	/A	RC	SB	CS	SBR	FR	POS	TPR
1950	Chi-N	34	111	13	25	4	3	3	6	7	25	.225	.271	.396	74	-5	-5	11	4			-4	3	-0.8
1951	Chi-N	145	557	78	153	24	6	16	76	47	44	.275	.332	.425	101	1	-1	77	14	3	2	8	*3	0.9
1952	Chi-N	116	379	44	88	8	5	9	34	27	42	.232	.285	.351	75	-13	-14	36	6	5	-1	-2	*3/O	-1.5

YEAR	TM/L	G	AB	R	H	2B	3B	HR	RBI	BB	SO	AVG	OBP	SLG	PRO+	BR	/A	RC	SB	CS	SBR	FR	POS	TPR
1953	Chi-N	139	498	61	142	22	8	19	66	42	61	.285	.341	.476	108	6	5	77	8	4	0	3	*3	0.4
1954	Chi-N	126	484	77	132	17	6	19	67	44	55	.273	.336	.450	102	1	0	74	2	1	0	-0	*3	0.1
1955	Chi-N	138	499	73	132	13	7	21	70	58	58	.265	.342	.445	107	5	5	75	0	2	-1	-13	*3	-0.9
1956	*Bro-N	101	307	37	84	15	7	8	53	28	38	.274	.338	.446	101	4	0	43	2	1	0	21	3	2.1
1957	Bro-N	48	131	7	26	1	0	2	16	9	20	.198	.250	.252	32	-12	-13	8	0	0	0	-2	3	-1.5
1958	LA-N	35	65	8	12	3	0	1	4	5	10	.185	.243	.277	36	-6	-6	4	0	0	0	7	3	0.1
	Cle-A	29	91	7	22	3	1	4	13	3	18	.242	.266	.429	90	-2	-2	9	0	0	0	5	3	0.5
1959	Cle-A	3	7	0	1	0	0	0	0	0	1	.143	.143	.143	-22	-1	-1	0	0	0	0	-1	/3	-0.1
	Chi-N	41	74	7	18	5	1	1	10	11	10	.243	.341	.378	92	-1	-1	9	0	0	0	-2	3/O	-0.2
Total	10	955	3203	412	835	115	44	103	415	281	382	.261	.322	.421	94	-24	-32	422	36	16		19	3/O	-1.0

■ REGGIE JACKSON
Jackson, Reginald Martinez b: 5/18/46, Wyncote, Pa. BL/TL, 6', 195 lbs. Deb: 6/09/67

YEAR	TM/L	G	AB	R	H	2B	3B	HR	RBI	BB	SO	AVG	OBP	SLG	PRO+	BR	/A	RC	SB	CS	SBR	FR	POS	TPR
1967	KC-A	35	118	13	21	4	4	1	6	10	46	.178	.271	.305	72	-4	-4	10	1	1	-0	-3	O	-0.8
1968	Oak-A	154	553	82	138	13	6	29	74	50	171	.250	.317	.452	138	19	22	83	14	4	2	7	*O	2.8
1969	Oak-A	152	549	123	151	36	3	47	118	114	142	.275	.410	.608	190	62	65	144	13	5	1	2	*O	6.6
1970	Oak-A	149	426	57	101	21	2	23	66	75	135	.237	.361	.458	129	15	17	70	26	17	-2	-4	*O	0.5
1971	*Oak-A	150	567	87	157	29	3	32	80	63	161	.277	.355	.508	145	30	31	103	16	10	-1	6	*O	3.3
1972	*Oak-A	135	499	72	132	25	2	25	75	59	125	.265	.352	.473	152	26	29	84	9	8	-2	6	*O	3.3
1973	*Oak-A	151	539	99	158	28	2	32	117	76	111	.293	.387	.531	165	41	44	112	22	8	2	-2	*O/D	4.0
1974	*Oak-A	148	506	90	146	25	1	29	93	86	105	.289	.396	.514	171	41	45	109	25	5	5	6	*OD	5.3
1975	*Oak-A	157	593	91	150	39	3	36	104	67	133	.253	.332	.511	138	25	27	100	17	8	0	4	*O/D	2.8
1976	Bal-A	134	498	84	138	27	2	27	91	54	108	.277	.353	.502	158	29	33	86	28	7	4	2	*OD	3.8
1977	*NY-A	146	525	93	150	39	2	32	110	74	129	.286	.377	.550	151	36	36	116	17	3	3	-7	*OD	2.8
1978	*NY-A	139	511	82	140	13	5	27	97	58	133	.274	.358	.477	136	22	24	87	14	11	-2	-0	*OD	1.9
1979	NY-A	131	465	78	138	24	2	29	89	65	107	.297	.385	.544	151	31	33	93	9	8	-2	3	*O/D	2.8
1980	*NY-A	143	514	94	154	22	4	41	111	83	122	.300	.399	.597	172	49	50	125	1	2	-1	-8	OD	3.9
1981	*NY-A	94	334	33	79	17	1	15	54	46	82	.237	.331	.428	119	7	8	47	0	3	-2	-3	OD	0.2
1982	*Cal-A	153	530	92	146	17	1	39	101	85	156	.275	.378	.532	147	35	35	107	4	5	-2	-23	*O/D	0.6
1983	Cal-A	116	397	43	77	14	1	14	49	52	140	.194	.294	.340	74	-14	-14	42	0	2	-1	-4	DO	-1.9
1984	Cal-A	143	525	67	117	17	2	25	81	55	141	.223	.300	.406	94	-6	-5	64	8	4	0	0	*D/O	-0.4
1985	Cal-A	143	460	64	116	27	0	27	85	78	138	.252	.362	.487	130	20	20	79	1	2	-1	-10	OD	0.8
1986	*Cal-A	132	419	65	101	12	2	18	58	92	115	.241	.381	.408	116	12	13	68	1	1	-0	0	*D/O	1.2
1987	Oak-A	115	336	42	74	14	1	15	43	33	97	.220	.298	.402	89	-9	-6	42	2	1	0	-1	DO	-0.6
Total	21	2820	9864	1551	2584	463	49	563	1702	1375	2597	.262	.358	.490	140	466	503	1772	228	115	-1	-26	*OD	42.9

■ SONNY JACKSON
Jackson, Roland Thomas b: 7/9/44, Washington, D.C. BL/TR, 5'9", 150 lbs. Deb: 9/27/63 C

YEAR	TM/L	G	AB	R	H	2B	3B	HR	RBI	BB	SO	AVG	OBP	SLG	PRO+	BR	/A	RC	SB	CS	SBR	FR	POS	TPR
1963	Hou-N	1	3	0	0	0	0	0	0	0	1	.000	.000	.000	-99	-1	-1	0	0	0	0	1	/S	0.0
1964	Hou-N	9	23	3	8	1	0	0	1	2	3	.348	.400	.391	131	1	1	4	1	0	0	-3	/S	-0.1
1965	Hou-N	10	23	1	3	0	0	0	0	1	1	.130	.167	.130	-16	-3	-3	0	1	1	-0	-1	/S3	-0.3
1966	Hou-N	150	596	80	174	6	5	3	25	42	53	.292	.342	.334	95	-8	-3	74	49	14	6	-13	*S	0.3
1967	Hou-N	129	520	67	123	18	3	0	25	36	45	.237	.286	.283	66	-24	-22	42	22	9	1	-8	*S	-1.5
1968	Atl-N	105	358	37	81	8	2	1	19	25	35	.226	.282	.268	66	-14	-14	27	16	6	1	-17	S	-2.1
1969	*Atl-N	98	318	41	76	3	5	1	27	35	33	.239	.318	.289	71	-11	-11	32	12	7	-1	-22	S	-2.4
1970	Atl-N	103	328	60	85	14	3	0	20	45	27	.259	.350	.320	76	-7	-10	41	11	4	1	-23	S	-2.0
1971	Atl-N	149	547	58	141	20	5	2	25	35	45	.258	.304	.324	73	-16	-20	54	7	6	-2	-3	*O	-3.2
1972	Atl-N	60	126	20	30	6	3	0	8	7	9	.238	.278	.333	67	-5	-6	11	1	0	0	-3	SO/3	-0.6
1973	Atl-N	117	206	29	43	5	2	0	12	22	13	.209	.288	.252	47	-13	-15	17	6	3	0	-1	OS	-1.4
1974	Atl-N	5	7	0	3	0	0	0	0	0	0	.429	.429	.429	134	0	0	1	0	1	-1	0	/O	0.0
Total	12	936	3055	396	767	81	28	7	162	250	265	.251	.310	.303	73	-102	-105	301	126	51	7	-93	SO/3	-13.3

■ RON JACKSON
Jackson, Ronald Harris b: 10/22/33, Kalamazoo, Mich. BR/TR, 6'7", 225 lbs. Deb: 6/15/54

YEAR	TM/L	G	AB	R	H	2B	3B	HR	RBI	BB	SO	AVG	OBP	SLG	PRO+	BR	/A	RC	SB	CS	SBR	FR	POS	TPR
1954	Chi-A	40	93	10	26	4	0	4	10	6	20	.280	.337	.452	111	1	1	14	2	1	0	-2	1	-0.1
1955	Chi-A	40	74	10	15	1	1	2	7	8	22	.203	.280	.324	61	-4	-4	7	1	0	0	-1	1	-0.6
1956	Chi-A	22	56	7	12	3	0	1	4	10	13	.214	.333	.321	73	-2	-2	6	1	0	0	-1	1	-0.1
1957	Chi-A	13	60	4	19	3	0	2	8	1	12	.317	.338	.467	114	1	1	9	0	0	0	-1	1	0.0
1958	Chi-A	61	146	19	34	4	0	7	21	18	46	.233	.325	.404	101	-0	-0	20	2	0	1	-2	1	-0.1
1959	Chi-A	10	14	3	3	1	0	1	2	1	0	.214	.313	.500	121	0	0	2	0	0	0	-0	/1	0.0
1960	Bos-A	10	31	1	7	2	0	0	2	1	6	.226	.250	.290	44	-2	-3	2	0	0	0	0	/1	-0.2
Total	7	196	474	54	116	18	1	17	52	45	119	.245	.317	.395	92	-6	-7	60	6	1	1	-6	1	-1.1

■ RON JACKSON
Jackson, Ronnie Damien b: 5/9/53, Birmingham, Ala. BR/TR, 6', 200 lbs. Deb: 9/12/75

YEAR	TM/L	G	AB	R	H	2B	3B	HR	RBI	BB	SO	AVG	OBP	SLG	PRO+	BR	/A	RC	SB	CS	SBR	FR	POS	TPR
1975	Cal-A	13	39	2	9	2	0	0	2	2	10	.231	.268	.282	60	-2	-2	3	1	1	-0	-0	/O3D	-0.2
1976	Cal-A	127	410	44	93	18	3	8	40	30	38	.227	.291	.344	91	-8	-5	40	5	4	-1	2	*3/2OD	-0.2
1977	Cal-A	106	292	38	71	15	2	8	28	24	42	.243	.303	.390	91	-6	-4	34	3	2	-0	3	13D/OS	-0.3
1978	Cal-A	105	387	49	115	18	6	6	57	16	31	.297	.340	.421	117	6	8	53	2	3	-1	-3	13/OD	0.0
1979	Min-A	159	583	85	158	40	6	14	68	51	59	.271	.339	.429	102	4	1	84	3	1	0	11	*1/S3O	0.4
1980	Min-A	131	396	48	105	29	3	5	42	28	41	.265	.319	.391	87	-4	-8	43	1	8	-5	2	*1O/3D	-1.7
1981	Min-A	54	175	17	46	9	0	4	28	10	15	.263	.306	.383	91	-1	-2	20	2	2	-1	0	1/O3D	-0.3
	Det-A	31	95	12	27	8	1	1	12	8	11	.284	.340	.421	114	2	2	15	4	1	1	-0	1	0.1
	Yr	85	270	29	73	17	1	5	40	18	26	.270	.318	.396	99	1	-1	34	6	3	0			-0.2
1982	*Cal-A	53	142	15	47	6	0	2	19	10	12	.331	.383	.415	119	4	4	22	0	1	-1	0	1/3	0.3
1983	Cal-A	102	348	41	80	16	1	8	39	27	33	.230	.291	.351	76	-12	-11	34	2	2	-1	5	31DO	-0.8
1984	Cal-A	33	91	5	15	2	1	0	5	7	13	.165	.224	.209	21	-10	-10	4	0	0	0	-1	1/3O	-1.0
	Bal-A	12	28	0	8	2	0	0	2	0	4	.286	.286	.357	78	-1	-1	2	0	2	-1	1	3	0.0
	Yr	45	119	5	23	4	1	0	7	7	17	.193	.238	.244	34	-11	-11	6	0	2	-1	1		-1.0
Total	10	926	2986	356	774	165	22	56	342	213	329	.259	.316	.385	94	-27	-28	355	23	27	-9	23	13/OD2S	-3.7

■ SAM JACKSON
Jackson, Samuel b: 3/24/1849, Ripon, England d: 8/4/1893, Chilton Springs, N.Y. BR/TR, 5'5.5", 160 lbs. Deb: 5/16/1871

YEAR	TM/L	G	AB	R	H	2B	3B	HR	RBI	BB	SO	AVG	OBP	SLG	PRO+	BR	/A	RC	SB	CS	SBR	FR	POS	TPR
1871	Bos-n	16	76	17	17	5	3	0	11	1	4	.224	.234	.368	67	-3	-4	7	0				2/O	-0.1
1872	Atl-n	3	12	0	2	1	0	0			0	.167	.167	.250	23	-1	-1	1					/O	0.0
Total	2 n	19	88	17	19	6	3	0			1	.216	.225	.352	61	-4	-5	7					/2O	-0.1

■ TRAVIS JACKSON
Jackson, Travis Calvin "Stonewall" b: 11/2/03, Waldo, Ark. d: 7/27/87, Waldo, Ark. BR/TR, 5'10.5", 160 lbs. Deb: 9/27/22 CH

YEAR	TM/L	G	AB	R	H	2B	3B	HR	RBI	BB	SO	AVG	OBP	SLG	PRO+	BR	/A	RC	SB	CS	SBR	FR	POS	TPR
1922	NY-N	3	8	1	0	0	0	0	0	0	0	.000	.000	.000	-99	-2	-2	0	0	0	0	0	/S	-0.1
1923	NY-N	96	327	45	90	12	7	4	37	22	40	.275	.321	.391	88	-7	-6	41	3	3	-1	-3	S3/2	-0.3
1924	*NY-N	151	596	81	180	26	8	11	76	21	56	.302	.326	.428	103	-1	1	80	6	7	-2	-0	*S	1.0
1925	NY-N	112	411	51	117	15	2	9	59	24	43	.285	.327	.397	87	-10	-8	54	8	3	1	5	*S	0.6
1926	NY-N	111	385	64	126	24	8	8	51	20	26	.327	.360	.494	130	14	14	66	2			0	*S	2.2
1927	NY-N	127	469	67	149	29	4	14	98	32	30	.318	.363	.486	126	15	15	80	8			28	*S/3	5.3
1928	NY-N	150	537	73	145	35	6	14	77	56	46	.270	.339	.436	101	-0	-1	79	8			28	*S	4.6
1929	NY-N	149	551	92	162	21	12	21	94	64	56	.294	.369	.490	111	3	8	98	10	3		19	*S	4.3
1930	NY-N	116	431	70	146	28	8	13	82	32	25	.339	.386	.529	121	12	14	85	6			11	*S	3.1
1931	NY-N	145	555	65	172	26	10	5	71	36	23	.310	.353	.420	110	5	7	83	13			10	*S	2.8
1932	NY-N	52	195	23	50	17	1	4	38	13	16	.256	.310	.415	95	-2	-2	26	1			-4	S	-0.1

YEAR	TM/L	G	AB	R	H	2B	3B	HR	RBI	BB	SO	AVG	OBP	SLG	PRO+	BR	/A	RC	SB	CS	SBR	FR	POS	TPR
1933	*NY-N	53	122	11	30	5	0	0	12	8	11	.246	.292	.287	67	-5	-5	10	2			7	S3	0.4
1934	NY-N	137	523	75	140	26	7	16	101	37	71	.268	.316	.436	102	-2	-0	71	1			12	*S/3	1.4
1935	NY-N	128	511	74	154	20	12	9	80	29	64	.301	.340	.440	110	5	6	76	3			-7	*3	0.4
1936	*NY-N	126	465	41	107	8	1	7	53	18	56	.230	.260	.297	50	-33	-33	36	0			-1	*3/S	-2.3
Total	15	1656	6086	833	1768	291	86	135	929	412	565	.291	.337	.433	102	-5	8	883	71	13		105	*S3/O2	23.3

■ BO JACKSON
Jackson, Vincent Edward   b: 11/30/62, Bessemer, Ala.   BR/TR, 6'1", 220 lbs.   Deb: 9/02/86

YEAR	TM/L	G	AB	R	H	2B	3B	HR	RBI	BB	SO	AVG	OBP	SLG	PRO+	BR	/A	RC	SB	CS	SBR	FR	POS	TPR
1986	KC-A	25	82	9	17	2	1	2	9	7	34	.207	.286	.329	66	-4	-4	8	3	1	0	-3	O/D	-0.6
1987	KC-A	116	396	46	93	17	2	22	53	30	158	.235	.297	.455	93	-4	-5	55	10	4	1	-8	*O/D	-1.3
1988	KC-A	124	439	63	108	16	4	25	68	25	146	.246	.288	.472	108	3	2	59	27	6	5	3	*O/D	0.8
1989	KC-A	135	515	86	132	15	6	32	105	39	172	.256	.312	.495	125	14	14	77	26	9	2	4	*OD	1.8
1990	KC-A	111	405	74	110	16	1	28	78	44	128	.272	.346	.523	143	20	21	70	15	9	-1	1	OD	2.0
Total	5	511	1837	278	460	66	14	109	313	145	638	.250	.310	.480	115	29	29	270	81	29	7	-3	O/D	2.7

■ BILL JACKSON
Jackson, William Riley   b: 4/4/1881, Pittsburgh, Pa.   d: 9/24/58, Peoria, Ill.   BL/TL, 5'11.5", 160 lbs.   Deb: 4/30/14

YEAR	TM/L	G	AB	R	H	2B	3B	HR	RBI	BB	SO	AVG	OBP	SLG	PRO+	BR	/A	RC	SB	CS	SBR	FR	POS	TPR
1914	Chi-F	26	25	2	1	0	0	0	1	3	5	.040	.143	.040	-49	-5	-5	0	0			0	/O1	-0.4
1915	Chi-F	50	98	15	16	1	0	1	12	14	15	.163	.268	.204	43	-7	-6	7	3			0	1/O	-0.5
Total	2	76	123	17	17	1	0	1	13	17	20	.138	.243	.171	24	-12	-11	7	3			0	/1O	-0.9

■ SPOOK JACOBS
Jacobs, Forrest Vandergrift   b: 11/4/25, Cheswold, Del.   BR/TR, 5'8.5", 155 lbs.   Deb: 4/13/54

YEAR	TM/L	G	AB	R	H	2B	3B	HR	RBI	BB	SO	AVG	OBP	SLG	PRO+	BR	/A	RC	SB	CS	SBR	FR	POS	TPR
1954	Phi-A	132	508	63	131	11	1	0	26	60	22	.258	.336	.283	71	-18	-18	55	17	3	3	-19	*2	-2.9
1955	KC-A	13	23	7	6	0	0	0	1	3	0	.261	.370	.261	71	-1	-1	2	1	2	-1	-3	/2	-0.3
1956	KC-A	32	97	13	21	3	0	0	5	15	5	.216	.321	.247	52	-6	-6	8	4	1	1	-3	2	-0.6
	Pit-N	11	37	4	6	2	0	0	1	2	5	.162	.225	.216	20	-4	-4	2	0	2	-1	-4	2	-0.8
Total	3	188	665	87	164	16	1	0	33	80	32	.247	.329	.274	65	-29	-30	67	22	8	2	-29	2	-4.6

■ JAKE JACOBS
Jacobs, Lamar Gary   b: 6/9/37, Youngstown, Ohio   BR/TR, 6', 175 lbs.   Deb: 9/13/60

YEAR	TM/L	G	AB	R	H	2B	3B	HR	RBI	BB	SO	AVG	OBP	SLG	PRO+	BR	/A	RC	SB	CS	SBR	FR	POS	TPR
1960	Was-A	6	2	0	0	0	0	0	0	0	0	.000	.000	.000	-99	-1	-1	0	0	0	0	0	H	0.0
1961	Min-A	4	8	0	2	0	0	0	0	0	2	.250	.250	.250	32	-1	-1	1	0	0	0	-0	/O	0.0
Total	2	10	10	0	2	0	0	0	0	0	2	.200	.200	.200	7	-1	-1	1	0	0	0	-0	/O	0.0

■ MIKE JACOBS
Jacobs, Morris Elmore   b: 1877,   d: 3/21/49, Louisville, Ky.   Deb: 7/16/02

YEAR	TM/L	G	AB	R	H	2B	3B	HR	RBI	BB	SO	AVG	OBP	SLG	PRO+	BR	/A	RC	SB	CS	SBR	FR	POS	TPR
1902	Chi-N	5	19	1	4	0	0	0	2	0		.211	.211	.211	32	-2	-1	1	0			-2	/S	-0.2

■ OTTO JACOBS
Jacobs, Otto Albert   b: 4/19/1889, Chicago, Ill.   d: 11/19/55, Chicago, Ill.   BR/TR, 5'9", 180 lbs.   Deb: 6/13/18

YEAR	TM/L	G	AB	R	H	2B	3B	HR	RBI	BB	SO	AVG	OBP	SLG	PRO+	BR	/A	RC	SB	CS	SBR	FR	POS	TPR
1918	Chi-A	29	73	4	15	3	1	0	3	5	8	.205	.256	.274	59	-4	-4	5	0			-3	C	-0.5

■ RAY JACOBS
Jacobs, Raymond F.   b: 1/2/02, Salt Lake City, Utah   d: 4/5/52, Los Angeles, Cal.   BR/TR, 6', 160 lbs.   Deb: 4/20/28

YEAR	TM/L	G	AB	R	H	2B	3B	HR	RBI	BB	SO	AVG	OBP	SLG	PRO+	BR	/A	RC	SB	CS	SBR	FR	POS	TPR
1928	Chi-N	2	0	0	0	0	0	0	0	0	1	.000	.000	.000	-99	-1	-1	0	0			0	H	0.0

■ MERWIN JACOBSON
Jacobson, Merwin John William "Jake"   b: 3/7/1894, New Britain, Conn.   d: 1/13/78, Baltimore, Md.   BL/TL, 5'11.5", 165 lbs.   Deb: 9/08/15

YEAR	TM/L	G	AB	R	H	2B	3B	HR	RBI	BB	SO	AVG	OBP	SLG	PRO+	BR	/A	RC	SB	CS	SBR	FR	POS	TPR
1915	NY-N	8	24	0	2	0	0	0	1	1	5	.083	.120	.083	-40	-4	-4	0	0			0	/O	-0.4
1916	Chi-N	4	13	2	3	0	0	0	0	1	4	.231	.286	.231	54	-1	-1	1	2			0	/O	0.0
1926	Bro-N	110	288	41	71	9	2	0	23	36	24	.247	.330	.292	70	-12	-11	29	5			4	O	-0.9
1927	Bro-N	11	6	4	0	0	0	0	1	0	1	.000	.000	.000	-99	-2	-2	0	0			0	/O	0.0
Total	4	133	331	47	76	9	2	0	24	38	34	.230	.309	.269	59	-18	-17	31	7			4	/O	-1.3

■ BABY DOLL JACOBSON
Jacobson, William Chester   b: 8/16/1890, Cable, Ill.   d: 1/16/77, Orion, Ill.   BR/TR, 6'3", 215 lbs.   Deb: 4/14/15

YEAR	TM/L	G	AB	R	H	2B	3B	HR	RBI	BB	SO	AVG	OBP	SLG	PRO+	BR	/A	RC	SB	CS	SBR	FR	POS	TPR
1915	Det-A	37	65	5	14	6	2	0	4	5	14	.215	.282	.369	90	-1	-1	6	0	2	-1	-2	1/O	-0.5
	StL-A	34	115	13	24	6	1	1	9	10	26	.209	.295	.304	82	-3	-3	10	3	3	-1	-1	O	-0.6
	Yr	71	180	18	38	12	3	1	13	15	40	.211	.290	.328	84	-4	-4	17	3	5	-2	-4		-1.1
1917	StL-A	148	529	53	131	23	7	4	55	31	67	.248	.294	.340	97	-6	-6	53	10			6	*O1	-0.6
1919	StL-A	120	455	70	147	31	8	4	51	24	47	.323	.362	.453	125	15	14	75	9			1	*O/1	0.7
1920	StL-A	154	609	97	216	34	14	9	122	46	37	.355	.402	.501	134	32	30	121	11	7	-1	11	*O/1	2.5
1921	StL-A	151	599	90	211	38	14	5	90	42	30	.352	.398	.487	118	22	17	114	8	8	-2	5	*O1	0.7
1922	StL-A	145	555	88	176	22	16	9	102	46	36	.317	.379	.463	114	15	12	100	19	6	2	4	*O/1	0.7
1923	StL-A	147	592	76	183	29	6	8	81	29	27	.309	.343	.419	95	-2	-6	84	6		-2	8	*O	-1.3
1924	StL-A	152	579	103	184	41	12	19	97	35	45	.318	.361	.528	124	19	14	107	6	3		16	*O	1.5
1925	StL-A	142	540	103	184	30	9	15	76	45	26	.341	.392	.513	122	21	17	105	8	11	-4	1	*O	0.2
1926	StL-A	50	182	18	52	15	1	2	21	9	14	.286	.319	.412	86	-4	-5	23	1	2	-1	-6	O	-1.4
	Bos-A	98	394	44	120	36	1	6	69	22	22	.305	.344	.447	109	1	3	61	4	1	1	-8	O	-1.1
	Yr	148	576	62	172	51	2	8	90	31	36	.299	.337	.436	101	-2	-2	84	5	3	-0	-14		-2.5
1927	Bos-A	45	155	11	38	9	3	0	24	5	12	.245	.278	.342	61	-10	-9	14	1	0	0	1	O	-0.9
	Cle-A	32	103	13	26	5	0	0	13	6	4	.252	.300	.301	56	-7	-7	9	0	0	0	-1	O	-0.8
	Phi-A	17	35	3	8	3	0	1	5	0	3	.229	.229	.400	57	-2	-3	3	0	0	0	-5	O	-0.7
	Yr	94	293	27	72	17	3	1	42	11	19	.246	.280	.334	59	-19	-19	27	1	0	0	-5		-2.4
Total	11	1472	5507	787	1714	328	94	83	819	355	410	.311	.357	.450	111	91	69	886	86	54		29	*O/1	-1.6

■ BROOK JACOBY
Jacoby, Brook Wallace   b: 11/23/59, Philadelphia, Pa.   BR/TR, 5'11", 175 lbs.   Deb: 9/13/81

YEAR	TM/L	G	AB	R	H	2B	3B	HR	RBI	BB	SO	AVG	OBP	SLG	PRO+	BR	/A	RC	SB	CS	SBR	FR	POS	TPR
1981	Atl-N	11	10	0	2	0	0	0	1	0	3	.200	.200	.200	13	-1	-1	0	0	0	0	2	/3	0.1
1983	Atl-N	4	8	0	0	0	0	0	0	0	1	.000	.000	.000	-93	-2	-2	0	0	0	0	-1	/3	-0.2
1984	Cle-A	126	439	64	116	19	3	7	40	32	73	.264	.319	.369	88	-6	-7	50	3	2	-0	-20	*3/S	-2.5
1985	Cle-A	161	606	72	166	26	3	20	87	48	120	.274	.327	.426	105	3	3	81	2	3	-1	-8	*3/2	-1.0
1986	Cle-A	158	583	83	168	30	4	17	80	56	137	.288	.351	.441	116	11	12	88	2	1	0	-13	*3	-0.3
1987	Cle-A	155	540	73	162	26	4	32	69	75	73	.300	.388	.541	147	34	33	110	2	3	-1	-7	*3/1D	2.2
1988	Cle-A	152	552	59	133	25	0	9	49	48	101	.241	.303	.335	76	-16	-18	55	2	3	-1	1	*3	-1.7
1989	Cle-A	147	519	49	141	26	5	13	64	62	90	.272	.353	.416	114	12	10	75	2	5	-2	-10	*3/D	-0.1
1990	Cle-A	155	553	77	162	24	4	14	75	63	58	.293	.367	.427	119	17	15	83	1	4	-2	-12	31	-0.2
Total	9	1069	3810	477	1050	176	23	112	465	384	656	.276	.344	.422	109	51	47	542	14	21	-8	-66	3/1D2S	-3.7

■ HARRY JACOBY
Jacoby, Harry   b: Philadelphia, Pa.   Deb: 5/02/1882

YEAR	TM/L	G	AB	R	H	2B	3B	HR	RBI	BB	SO	AVG	OBP	SLG	PRO+	BR	/A	RC	SB	CS	SBR	FR	POS	TPR
1882	Bal-a	31	121	17	21	1	1	1		7		.174	.219	.223	53	-6	-5	6				8	3O	0.2
1885	Bal-a	11	43	4	6	2	0	0		2		.140	.178	.186	17	-4	-4	1				-8	2	-1.0
Total	2	42	164	21	27	3	1	1		9		.165	.208	.213	43	-10	-9	8				0	/3O2	-0.8

■ ART JAHN
Jahn, Arthur Charles   b: 12/2/1895, Struble, Iowa   d: 1/9/48, Little Rock, Ark.   BR/TR, 6', 180 lbs.   Deb: 7/02/25

YEAR	TM/L	G	AB	R	H	2B	3B	HR	RBI	BB	SO	AVG	OBP	SLG	PRO+	BR	/A	RC	SB	CS	SBR	FR	POS	TPR
1925	Chi-N	58	226	30	68	10	8	0	37	11	20	.301	.336	.416	90	-3	-4	31	2	2	-1	-2	O	-0.6
1928	NY-N	10	29	7	8	1	0	1	7	2	5	.276	.323	.414	91	-0	-0	4	0			1	/O	0.0
	Phi-N	36	94	8	21	4	0	0	11	4	11	.223	.270	.266	39	-8	-9	7	0			-2	O	-1.0
	Yr	46	123	15	29	5	0	1	18	6	16	.236	.282	.301	51	-9	-9	10	0			-1		-1.0
Total	2	104	349	45	97	15	8	1	55	17	36	.278	.317	.375	76	-12	-13	41	2	2		-2	/O	-1.6

■ ART JAMES
James, Arthur   b: 8/2/52, Detroit, Mich.   BL/TL, 6', 170 lbs.   Deb: 4/10/75

YEAR	TM/L	G	AB	R	H	2B	3B	HR	RBI	BB	SO	AVG	OBP	SLG	PRO+	BR	/A	RC	SB	CS	SBR	FR	POS	TPR
1975	Det-A	11	40	2	9	2	0	0	1	1	3	.225	.244	.275	44	-3	-3	2	1	2	-1	0	O	-0.3

YEAR	TM/L	G	AB	R	H	2B	3B	HR	RBI	BB	SO	AVG	OBP	SLG	PRO+	BR	/A	RC	SB	CS	SBR	FR	POS	TPR

■ BERT JAMES
James, Berton Hulon "Jesse" b: 7/7/1886, Coopertown, Tenn. d: 1/2/59, Adairville, Ky. BL/TR, 5'11", 175 lbs. Deb: 9/18/09

YEAR	TM/L	G	AB	R	H	2B	3B	HR	RBI	BB	SO	AVG	OBP	SLG	PRO+	BR	/A	RC	SB	CS	SBR	FR	POS	TPR
1909	StL-N	6	21	1	6	0	0	0	0	4		.286	.400	.286	120	1	1	3	1			0	/O	0.1

■ CHARLIE JAMES
James, Charles Wesley b: 12/22/37, St.Louis, Mo. BR/TR, 6'1", 195 lbs. Deb: 8/02/60

YEAR	TM/L	G	AB	R	H	2B	3B	HR	RBI	BB	SO	AVG	OBP	SLG	PRO+	BR	/A	RC	SB	CS	SBR	FR	POS	TPR
1960	StL-N	43	50	5	9	1	0	2	5	1	12	.180	.196	.320	35	-4	-5	3	0	0	0	-0	O	-0.5
1961	StL-N	108	349	43	89	19	2	4	44	15	59	.255	.292	.355	64	-15	-19	34	2	2	-1	-4	O	-2.9
1962	StL-N	129	388	50	107	13	4	8	59	10	58	.276	.301	.392	77	-9	-14	42	3	4	-2	-9	*O	-3.0
1963	StL-N	116	347	34	93	14	2	10	45	10	64	.268	.292	.406	91	-2	-5	37	2	1	0	-3	*O	-1.3
1964	*StL-N	88	233	24	52	9	1	5	17	11	58	.223	.261	.335	61	-11	-13	19	0	0	0	-5	O	-2.0
1965	Cin-N	26	39	2	8	0	0	0	2	1	9	.205	.225	.205	21	-4	-4	1	0	0	0	-0	/O	-0.4
Total	6	510	1406	158	358	56	9	29	172	48	260	.255	.284	.369	71	-45	-60	137	7	7	-2	-21	O	-10.1

■ CLEO JAMES
James, Cleo Joel b: 8/31/40, Clarksdale, Miss. BR/TR, 5'10", 176 lbs. Deb: 4/15/68

YEAR	TM/L	G	AB	R	H	2B	3B	HR	RBI	BB	SO	AVG	OBP	SLG	PRO+	BR	/A	RC	SB	CS	SBR	FR	POS	TPR
1968	LA-N	10	10	2	2	1	0	0	0	0	6	.200	.200	.300	52	-1	-1	1	0	0	0	0	/O	0.0
1970	Chi-N	100	176	33	37	7	2	3	14	17	24	.210	.298	.324	59	-8	-11	18	5	0	2	7	O	-0.5
1971	Chi-N	54	150	25	43	7	0	2	13	10	16	.287	.355	.373	93	2	-1	21	6	2	1	2	O/3	0.0
1973	Chi-N	44	45	9	5	0	0	0	0	1	6	.111	.130	.111	-30	-8	-8	1	5	0	2	2	O	-0.5
Total	4	208	381	69	87	15	2	5	27	28	52	.228	.300	.318	63	-15	-21	40	16	2	4	12	O/3	-1.0

■ DION JAMES
James, Dion b: 11/9/62, Philadelphia, Pa. BL/TL, 6'1", 170 lbs. Deb: 9/16/83

YEAR	TM/L	G	AB	R	H	2B	3B	HR	RBI	BB	SO	AVG	OBP	SLG	PRO+	BR	/A	RC	SB	CS	SBR	FR	POS	TPR
1983	Mil-A	11	20	1	2	0	0	0	1	2	2	.100	.182	.100	-22	-3	-3	1	1	0	0	1	/OD	-0.1
1984	Mil-A	128	387	52	114	19	5	1	30	32	41	.295	.353	.377	106	2	4	50	10	10	-3	1	*O	-0.1
1985	Mil-A	18	49	5	11	1	0	0	3	6	6	.224	.309	.245	54	-3	-3	4	0	0	0	-1	O/D	-0.3
1987	Atl-N	134	494	80	154	37	6	10	61	70	63	.312	.399	.472	124	23	20	95	10	8	-2	-6	*O	0.6
1988	Atl-N	132	386	46	99	17	5	3	30	58	59	.256	.355	.350	98	3	1	48	9	9	-3	-5	*O	-1.0
1989	Atl-N	63	170	15	44	7	0	1	11	25	23	.259	.357	.318	92	-0	-1	20	1	3	-2	-0	O/1	-0.3
	Cle-A	71	245	26	75	11	0	4	29	24	26	.306	.368	.400	114	6	5	35	1	4	-2	-3	OD/1	0.0
1990	Cle-A	87	248	28	68	15	2	1	22	27	23	.274	.348	.363	97	0	-0	31	5	3	-0	-4	1OD	-0.7
Total	7	644	1999	253	567	107	18	20	187	244	243	.284	.364	.385	106	28	23	284	37	37	-11	-17	O/1D	-1.9

■ CHRIS JAMES
James, Donald Chris b: 10/4/62, Rusk, Tex. BR/TR, 6'1", 195 lbs. Deb: 4/23/86

YEAR	TM/L	G	AB	R	H	2B	3B	HR	RBI	BB	SO	AVG	OBP	SLG	PRO+	BR	/A	RC	SB	CS	SBR	FR	POS	TPR
1986	Phi-N	16	46	5	13	3	0	1	5	1	13	.283	.298	.413	91	-1	-1	5	0	0	0	-1	O	-0.1
1987	Phi-N	115	358	48	105	20	6	17	54	27	67	.293	.346	.525	123	12	11	66	3	1	0	-2	*O	0.4
1988	Phi-N	150	566	57	137	24	1	19	66	31	73	.242	.285	.389	90	-8	-9	59	7	4	-0	2	*O/3	-1.1
1989	Phi-N	45	179	14	37	4	0	2	19	4	23	.207	.224	.263	39	-14	-14	8	3	1	0	-3	O3	-1.9
	SD-N	87	303	41	80	13	2	11	46	22	45	.264	.316	.429	111	3	3	38	2	1	0	-4	O/3	0.0
	Yr	132	482	55	117	17	2	13	65	26	68	.243	.283	.367	84	-11	-11	45	5	2	0	-7		-1.9
1990	Cle-A	140	528	62	158	32	4	12	70	31	71	.299	.343	.443	116	12	11	78	4	3	-1	0	*DO	1.0
Total	5	553	1980	227	530	96	13	62	260	116	292	.268	.311	.423	102	5	1	255	19	10	-0	-8	OD/3	-1.7

■ SKIP JAMES
James, Philip Robert b: 10/21/49, Elmhurst, Ill. BL/TL, 6', 185 lbs. Deb: 9/12/77

YEAR	TM/L	G	AB	R	H	2B	3B	HR	RBI	BB	SO	AVG	OBP	SLG	PRO+	BR	/A	RC	SB	CS	SBR	FR	POS	TPR
1977	SF-N	10	15	3	4	1	0	0	3	2	3	.267	.353	.333	86	-0	-0	2	0	0	0	1	/1	0.0
1978	SF-N	41	21	5	2	1	0	0	3	4	5	.095	.240	.143	10	-3	-2	1	1	0	0	2	1	0.0
Total	2	51	36	8	6	2	0	0	6	6	8	.167	.286	.222	42	-3	-3	2	1	0	0	3	/1	0.0

■ BERNIE JAMES
James, Robert Byrne b: 9/2/05, Angleton, Tex. BB/TR, 5'9.5", 150 lbs. Deb: 5/06/29

YEAR	TM/L	G	AB	R	H	2B	3B	HR	RBI	BB	SO	AVG	OBP	SLG	PRO+	BR	/A	RC	SB	CS	SBR	FR	POS	TPR
1929	Bos-N	46	101	12	31	3	2	0	9	9	13	.307	.369	.376	89	-2	-1	14	3			-9	2/O	-0.8
1930	Bos-N	8	11	1	2	1	0	0	1	0	1	.182	.182	.273	8	-2	-2	1	0			0	/2	0.0
1933	NY-N	60	125	22	28	2	1	1	10	8	12	.224	.271	.280	58	-7	-7	10	5			2	2/S3	-0.1
Total	3	114	237	35	61	6	3	1	20	17	26	.257	.310	.321	70	-11	-10	25	8			-6	/2S3O	-0.9

■ CHARLIE JAMIESON
Jamieson, Charles Devine "Cuckoo" b: 2/7/1893, Paterson, N.J. d: 10/27/69, Paterson, N.J. BL/TL, 5'8.5", 165 lbs. Deb: 9/20/15

YEAR	TM/L	G	AB	R	H	2B	3B	HR	RBI	BB	SO	AVG	OBP	SLG	PRO+	BR	/A	RC	SB	CS	SBR	FR	POS	TPR
1915	Was-A	17	68	9	19	3	2	0	7	6	9	.279	.338	.382	115	1	1	9	0			4	O	0.4
1916	Was-A	64	145	16	36	4	0	0	13	18	18	.248	.331	.276	84	-3	-2	16	5			-4	O/1P	-0.8
1917	Was-A	20	35	4	6	2	0	0	2	6	5	.171	.293	.229	60	-2	-1	2	0			-2	/OP	-0.4
	Phi-A	85	345	41	92	6	2	0	27	37	36	.267	.341	.296	96	-1	-1	36	8			-2	O	-0.8
	Yr	105	380	45	98	8	2	0	29	43	41	.258	.336	.289	92	-3	-2	38	8			-4		-1.2
1918	Phi-A	110	416	50	84	11	2	0	11	54	30	.202	.297	.238	61	-18	-19	30	11			0	*O/P	-2.5
1919	Cle-A	26	17	3	6	2	1	0	2	0	2	.353	.353	.588	153	1	1	4	2			-1	/PO	0.0
1920	*Cle-A	108	370	69	118	17	7	1	40	41	26	.319	.388	.411	108	7	6	58	7	9	-5	-2	O/1	-0.9
1921	Cle-A	140	536	94	166	33	10	3	46	67	27	.310	.387	.414	103	5	4	89	8	4	0	-6	*O	-1.2
1922	Cle-A	145	567	87	183	29	11	3	57	54	22	.323	.388	.429	112	11	11	96	15	8	-0	-1	*O/P	0.0
1923	Cle-A	152	644	130	222	36	12	2	51	80	37	.345	.422	.447	129	30	30	125	19	12	-2	8	*O	2.1
1924	Cle-A	143	594	98	213	34	8	3	54	47	15	.359	.407	.458	121	20	19	111	21	11	-0	4	*O	1.2
1925	Cle-A	138	557	109	165	24	5	4	42	72	26	.296	.380	.379	92	-4	-5	81	14	18	-7	7	*O	-1.4
1926	Cle-A	143	555	89	166	33	7	2	45	53	22	.299	.361	.395	96	-2	-3	80	9	8	-2	-0	*O	-1.5
1927	Cle-A	127	489	73	151	23	6	0	36	64	14	.309	.394	.380	101	4	4	72	7	9	-3	5	*O	-0.2
1928	Cle-A	112	433	63	133	18	4	1	37	56	20	.307	.388	.374	100	3	2	63	3	12	-6	20	*O	0.9
1929	Cle-A	102	364	56	106	22	1	0	26	50	21	.291	.378	.357	87	-3	-5	48	2	13	-7	-2	*O	-1.6
1930	Cle-A	103	366	64	110	22	1	1	52	36	20	.301	.368	.374	85	-5	-7	53	5	2	0	-5	O	-1.4
1931	Cle-A	28	43	7	13	2	1	0	4	5	1	.302	.375	.395	97	0	-0	6	1	1	-0	-2	/O	-0.1
1932	Cle-A	16	16	0	1	1	0	0	0	2	3	.063	.211	.125	-10	-3	-3	1	0	0	0	1	/O	-0.1
Total	18	1779	6560	1062	1990	322	80	18	552	748	345	.303	.378	.385	101	43	32	980	132	107		21	*O/P1	-8.3

■ VIC JANOWICZ
Janowicz, Victor Felix b: 2/26/30, Elyria, Ohio BR/TR, 5'9", 185 lbs. Deb: 5/31/53

YEAR	TM/L	G	AB	R	H	2B	3B	HR	RBI	BB	SO	AVG	OBP	SLG	PRO+	BR	/A	RC	SB	CS	SBR	FR	POS	TPR
1953	Pit-N	42	123	10	31	3	1	2	8	5	31	.252	.287	.341	63	-7	-7	11	0	1	-1	-11	C	-1.5
1954	Pit-N	41	73	10	11	3	0	0	2	7	23	.151	.235	.192	13	-9	-9	4	0	0	0	1	3/O	-0.7
Total	2	83	196	20	42	6	1	2	10	12	54	.214	.267	.286	44	-16	-16	15	0	1	-1	-10	/C3O	-2.2

■ RAY JANSEN
Jansen, Raymond William b: 1/16/1889, St.Louis, Mo. d: 3/19/34, St.Louis, Mo. BR/TR, 5'11", 155 lbs. Deb: 9/30/10

YEAR	TM/L	G	AB	R	H	2B	3B	HR	RBI	BB	SO	AVG	OBP	SLG	PRO+	BR	/A	RC	SB	CS	SBR	FR	POS	TPR
1910	StL-A	1	5	0	4	0	0	0	0	0		.800	.800	.800	428	2	2	3	0			0	/3	0.2

■ HEINIE JANTZEN
Jantzen, Walter C. b: 4/9/1890, Chicago, Ill. d: 4/1/48, Hines, Ill. BR/TR, 5'11.5", 170 lbs. Deb: 6/29/12

YEAR	TM/L	G	AB	R	H	2B	3B	HR	RBI	BB	SO	AVG	OBP	SLG	PRO+	BR	/A	RC	SB	CS	SBR	FR	POS	TPR
1912	StL-A	31	119	10	22	0	1	1	8	4		.185	.218	.227	28	-11	-11	6	3			3	O	-0.9

■ HAL JANVRIN
Janvrin, Harold Chandler "Childe Harold" b: 8/27/1892, Haverhill, Mass. d: 3/1/62, Boston, Mass. BR/TR, 5'11.5", 168 lbs. Deb: 7/09/11

YEAR	TM/L	G	AB	R	H	2B	3B	HR	RBI	BB	SO	AVG	OBP	SLG	PRO+	BR	/A	RC	SB	CS	SBR	FR	POS	TPR
1911	Bos-A	9	27	2	4	1	0	0	1	3		.148	.258	.185	25	-3	-3	1	0			-2	/31	-0.4
1913	Bos-A	87	276	18	57	5	1	3	25	23	27	.207	.272	.264	56	-15	-16	24	17			-10	S3/21	-2.3
1914	Bos-A	145	492	65	117	18	6	1	51	38	50	.238	.296	.305	81	-12	-12	48	29	20	-4	-22	21S/3	-3.9
1915	*Bos-A	99	316	41	85	9	1	0	37	14	27	.269	.317	.304	88	-6	-5	31	8	14	-6	-20	S3/2	-2.5
1916	*Bos-A	117	310	32	69	11	4	0	26	32	32	.223	.299	.284	75	-9	-9	31	6			-19	S2/13	-2.4
1917	Bos-A	55	127	21	25	3	0	0	8	11	13	.197	.266	.220	49	-8	-7	9	2			1	2S/1	-0.3
1919	Was-A	61	208	17	37	4	1	1	13	19	17	.178	.253	.221	34	-18	-18	13	8			-27	2/S	-4.2
	StL-N	7	14	1	3	1	0	0	1	2	2	.214	.313	.286	86	-0	-0	1	0			-1	/2S3	-0.1
1920	StL-N	87	270	33	74	8	4	1	28	17	19	.274	.317	.344	93	-4	-2	29	5	6	-2	-2	S1O/2	-0.6

YEAR	TM/L	G	AB	R	H	2B	3B	HR	RBI	BB	SO	AVG	OBP	SLG	PRO+	BR	/A	RC	SB	CS	SBR	FR	POS	TPR
1921	StL-N	18	32	5	9	1	0	0	5	1	0	.281	.303	.313	65	-2	-2	3	1	0	0	0	/12	0.0
	Bro-N	44	92	8	18	4	0	0	14	7	6	.196	.253	.239	30	-9	-10	6	3	1	0	-4	S2/130	-1.1
	Yr	62	124	13	27	5	0	0	19	8	6	.218	.265	.258	38	-11	-11	9	4	1	1	-4		-1.1
1922	Bro-N	30	57	7	17	3	1	0	1	4	4	.298	.344	.386	89	-1	-1	8	0	0	0	-3	2/S310	-0.3
Total	10	759	2221	250	515	68	18	6	210	171	197	.232	.292	.287	70	-87	-85	205	79	41		-108	S21/30	-18.1

■ ROY JARVIS Jarvis, Leroy Gilbert b: 6/27/26, Shawnee, Okla. BR/TR, 5'9", 160 lbs. Deb: 4/30/44

YEAR	TM/L	G	AB	R	H	2B	3B	HR	RBI	BB	SO	AVG	OBP	SLG	PRO+	BR	/A	RC	SB	CS	SBR	FR	POS	TPR
1944	Bro-N	1	1	0	0	0	0	0	0	0	1	.000	.000	.000	-99	-0	-0	0	0			0	/C	0.0
1946	Pit-N	2	4	0	1	0	0	0	0	1	1	.250	.400	.250	84	0	-0	1	0			-0	/C	0.0
1947	Pit-N	18	45	4	7	1	0	1	4	6	5	.156	.255	.244	32	-4	-5	3	0			-0	C	-0.4
Total	3	21	50	4	8	1	0	1	4	7	7	.160	.263	.240	34	-5	-5	3				-1	/C	-0.4

■ PAUL JATA Jata, Paul b: 9/4/49, Astoria, N.Y. BR/TR, 6'1", 190 lbs. Deb: 4/19/72

YEAR	TM/L	G	AB	R	H	2B	3B	HR	RBI	BB	SO	AVG	OBP	SLG	PRO+	BR	/A	RC	SB	CS	SBR	FR	POS	TPR
1972	Det-A	32	74	8	17	2	0	0	3	7	14	.230	.296	.257	64	-3	-3	6	0	1	-1	-0	1O/C	-0.6

■ AL JAVIER Javier, Ignacio Alfred (b: Ignacio Alfredo Wilkes (Javier)) b: 2/4/54, San Pedro De Macoris, D.R. BR/TR, 5'11", 170 lbs. Deb: 9/09/76

YEAR	TM/L	G	AB	R	H	2B	3B	HR	RBI	BB	SO	AVG	OBP	SLG	PRO+	BR	/A	RC	SB	CS	SBR	FR	POS	TPR
1976	Hou-N	8	24	1	5	0	0	0	2		5	.208	.269	.208	41	-2	-2	1	0	0	0	-1	/O	-0.3

■ JULIAN JAVIER Javier, Manuel Julian (Liranzo) b: 8/9/36, San Francisco De Macoris, D.R. BR/TR, 6'1", 175 lbs. Deb: 5/28/60

YEAR	TM/L	G	AB	R	H	2B	3B	HR	RBI	BB	SO	AVG	OBP	SLG	PRO+	BR	/A	RC	SB	CS	SBR	FR	POS	TPR
1960	StL-N	119	451	55	107	19	8	4	21	21	72	.237	.273	.341	62	-21	-26	43	19	4	3	5	*2	-0.7
1961	StL-N	113	445	58	124	14	3	2	41	30	51	.279	.327	.337	70	-14	-14	51	11	4	1	-0	*2	-0.5
1962	StL-N	155	598	97	157	25	5	7	39	47	73	.263	.317	.356	73	-16	-24	70	26	9	2	1	*2/S	-0.6
1963	StL-N	161	609	82	160	27	9	9	46	24	86	.263	.297	.356	86	-6	-12	68	18	10	-1	-14	*2	-1.7
1964	*StL-N	155	535	66	129	19	5	12	65	30	82	.241	.283	.363	74	-15	-20	52	9	7	-2	-7	*2	-1.6
1965	StL-N	77	229	34	52	6	4	2	23	8	44	.227	.262	.314	56	-12	-14	17	5	5	-2	-6	2	-1.8
1966	StL-N	147	460	52	105	13	5	7	31	26	63	.228	.271	.324	64	-22	-22	40	11	5	0	2	*2	-1.0
1967	*StL-N	140	520	68	146	16	3	14	64	25	92	.281	.315	.404	106	2	2	63	6	7	-2	-19	*2	-1.0
1968	*StL-N	139	519	54	135	25	4	4	52	24	61	.260	.294	.347	93	-6	-5	52	10	3	1	-24	*2	-2.3
1969	StL-N	143	493	59	139	28	2	10	42	40	74	.282	.337	.408	107	4	4	67	8	4	0	-18	*2	-0.1
1970	StL-N	139	513	62	129	16	3	2	42	24	70	.251	.286	.306	58	-30	-31	42	6	4	-1	13	*2	-0.3
1971	StL-N	90	259	32	67	6	4	3	28	9	33	.259	.289	.347	76	-8	-9	25	5	1	1	2	2/3	-0.2
1972	*Cin-N	44	91	3	19	2	0	2	12	6	11	.209	.258	.297	61	-5	-5	7	1	0	0	-2	3/21	-0.6
Total	13	1622	5722	722	1469	216	55	78	506	314	812	.257	.298	.355	78	-149	-182	597	135	63	3	-67	*2/3S1	-12.4

■ STAN JAVIER Javier, Stanley Julian Antonio (De Javier) b: 1/9/64, San Francisco De Macoris, D.R. BB/TR, 6', 185 lbs. Deb: 4/15/84

YEAR	TM/L	G	AB	R	H	2B	3B	HR	RBI	BB	SO	AVG	OBP	SLG	PRO+	BR	/A	RC	SB	CS	SBR	FR	POS	TPR
1984	NY-A	7	7	1	1	0	0	0	0	0	1	.143	.143	.143	-22	-1	-1	0	0	0	0	0	/O	0.0
1986	Oak-A	59	114	13	23	8	0	0	8	16	27	.202	.305	.272	63	-6	-5	11	8	0	2	10	O/D	0.6
1987	Oak-A	81	151	22	28	3	1	2	9	19	33	.185	.276	.258	46	-12	-11	12	3	2	-0	7	O/1D	-0.5
1988	*Oak-A	125	397	49	102	13	3	2	35	32	63	.257	.316	.320	81	-11	-9	42	20	1	5	-0	*O/1D	-0.5
1989	*Oak-A	112	310	42	77	12	3	1	28	31	45	.248	.319	.316	82	-8	-6	33	12	2	2	-1	*O/12	-0.6
1990	Oak-A	19	33	4	8	0	2	0	3	3	6	.242	.306	.364	89	-1	-1	4	0	0	0	1	O/D	0.0
	LA-N	104	276	56	84	9	4	3	24	37	44	.304	.387	.399	123	7	9	44	15	7	0	-2	O	0.5
Total	6	507	1288	187	323	45	13	8	107	138	219	.251	.325	.325	84	-32	-24	147	58	12	10	13	O/1D2	-0.5

■ TEX JEANES Jeanes, Ernest Lee b: 12/19/1900, Maypearl, Tex. d: 4/5/73, Longview, Tex. BR/TR, 6', 176 lbs. Deb: 4/20/21

YEAR	TM/L	G	AB	R	H	2B	3B	HR	RBI	BB	SO	AVG	OBP	SLG	PRO+	BR	/A	RC	SB	CS	SBR	FR	POS	TPR
1921	Cle-A	5	3	2	2	1	0	0	4	1	0	.667	.750	1.000	338	1	1	2	0	0	0	-1	/O	0.0
1922	Cle-A	1	1	0	0	0	0	0	0	1	0	.000	.500	.000	39	0	0	0	0	0	0	-0	/PO	0.0
1925	Was-A	15	19	2	5	1	0	1	4	3	2	.263	.364	.474	113	0	0	4	1	0	0	-5	O	-0.4
1926	Was-A	21	30	6	7	2	0	0	3	0	3	.233	.233	.300	39	-3	-3	2	0	0	0	-3	O	-0.6
1927	NY-N	11	20	5	6	0	0	0	0	2	2	.300	.364	.300	79	-0	-0	2	0			2	/OP	0.1
Total	5	53	73	15	20	4	0	1	11	7	7	.274	.338	.370	85	-2	-2	10	1	0		-8	/OP	-0.9

■ HAL JEFFCOAT Jeffcoat, Harold Bentley b: 9/6/24, W.Columbia, S.C. BR/TR, 5'10.5", 185 lbs. Deb: 4/20/48

YEAR	TM/L	G	AB	R	H	2B	3B	HR	RBI	BB	SO	AVG	OBP	SLG	PRO+	BR	/A	RC	SB	CS	SBR	FR	POS	TPR
1948	Chi-N	134	473	53	132	16	4	4	42	24	68	.279	.315	.355	85	-13	-11	54	8			4	*O	-1.4
1949	Chi-N	108	363	43	89	18	6	2	26	20	48	.245	.286	.344	70	-17	-16	36	12			8	*O	-1.2
1950	Chi-N	66	179	21	42	13	1	2	18	6	23	.235	.259	.352	60	-11	-11	13	7			-0	O	-1.2
1951	Chi-N	113	278	44	76	20	2	4	27	16	23	.273	.315	.403	90	-4	-5	35	8	4	0	1	O	-0.5
1952	Chi-N	102	297	29	65	17	2	4	30	15	40	.219	.259	.330	61	-16	-16	22	7	2	1	2	O	-1.5
1953	Chi-N	106	183	22	43	3	1	4	22	21	26	.235	.314	.328	66	-9	-9	20	5	0	2	15	*O	0.3
1954	Chi-N	56	31	13	8	2	1	1	6	1	7	.258	.281	.484	94	-0	-0	4	2	0	1	1	P/O	0.0
1955	Chi-N	52	23	3	4	0	0	1	1	2	9	.174	.240	.304	43	-2	-2	1	0	0	0	1	P	0.0
1956	Cin-N	49	54	5	8	2	0	0	5	3	20	.148	.193	.185	2	-7	-8	2	0	1	-1	4	P	0.0
1957	Cin-N	53	69	13	14	3	1	4	11	5	20	.203	.267	.449	82	-2	-2	8	0	0	0	-0	P	0.0
1958	Cin-N	50	9	2	5	0	0	0	0	1	2	.556	.600	.556	198	2	1	3	0	0	0	2	P/O	0.0
1959	Cin-N	17	1	1	1	1	0	0	0	0	0	1.000	1.000	2.000	655	1	1	2	0	0	0	0	P	0.0
	StL-N	12	3	0	0	0	0	0	0	0	3	.000	.000	.000	-94	-1	-1	0	0	0	0	0	P	0.0
	Yr	29	4	1	1	1	0	0	0	0	3	.250	.250	.500	90	-0	-0	1	0	0	0	0		0.0
Total	12	918	1963	249	487	95	18	26	188	114	289	.248	.291	.355	73	-79	-78	200	49	7		38	OP	-5.5

■ GREGG JEFFERIES Jefferies, Gregory Scott b: 8/1/67, Burlingame, Cal. BB/TR, 5'11", 175 lbs. Deb: 9/06/87

YEAR	TM/L	G	AB	R	H	2B	3B	HR	RBI	BB	SO	AVG	OBP	SLG	PRO+	BR	/A	RC	SB	CS	SBR	FR	POS	TPR
1987	NY-N	6	6	0	3	1	0	0	2	0	0	.500	.500	.667	217	1	1	2	0	0	0	0	/H	0.1
1988	*NY-N	29	109	19	35	8	2	6	17	8	10	.321	.368	.596	181	10	10	24	5	1	1	-3	32	0.9
1989	NY-N	141	508	72	131	28	2	12	56	39	46	.258	.317	.392	107	0	3	61	21	6	3	-31	*23	-2.5
1990	NY-N	153	604	96	171	**40**	3	15	68	46	40	.283	.339	.434	114	8	10	89	11	2	2	-9	*23	0.4
Total	4	329	1227	187	340	77	7	33	143	93	96	.277	.333	.432	117	19	24	177	37	9	6	-44	2/3	-1.1

■ STAN JEFFERSON Jefferson, Stanley b: 12/4/62, New York, N.Y. BB/TR, 5'11", 175 lbs. Deb: 9/07/86

YEAR	TM/L	G	AB	R	H	2B	3B	HR	RBI	BB	SO	AVG	OBP	SLG	PRO+	BR	/A	RC	SB	CS	SBR	FR	POS	TPR
1986	NY-N	14	24	6	5	1	0	1	3	2	8	.208	.296	.375	86	-1	-0	3	0	0	0	1	/O	0.0
1987	SD-N	116	422	59	97	8	7	8	29	39	92	.230	.298	.339	71	-19	-17	45	34	11	4	-3	*O	-2.0
1988	SD-N	49	111	16	16	1	2	1	4	4	22	.144	.215	.216	25	-11	-11	6	5	1	1	-4	O	-1.2
1989	NY-A	10	12	1	1	0	0	0	1	0	4	.083	.083	.083	-54	-2	-2	0	1	1	-0	-0	/OD	-0.2
	Bal-A	35	127	19	33	7	0	4	20	4	22	.260	.288	.409	97	-1	-1	15	9	3	1	2	O/D	0.2
	Yr	45	139	20	34	7	0	4	21	4	26	.245	.271	.381	84	-4	-3	14	10	4	1	2		0.3
1990	Bal-A	10	19	1	0	0	0	0	0	2	8	.000	.095	.000	-73	-4	-4	0	1	0	0	0	/OD	-0.3
	Cle-A	49	98	21	27	8	0	2	10	8	18	.276	.343	.418	110	1	1	14	8	4	0	5	O/D	0.6
	Yr	59	117	22	27	8	0	2	10	10	26	.231	.302	.350	81	-3	-3	13	9	4	0	5		0.3
Total	5	283	813	123	179	25	9	16	67	64	174	.220	.283	.332	69	-38	-35	82	58	20	5	4	O/D	-2.9

■ IRV JEFFRIES Jeffries, Irvine Franklin b: 9/10/05, Louisville, Ky. d: 6/8/82, Louisville, Ky. BR/TR, 5'10", 175 lbs. Deb: 4/30/30

YEAR	TM/L	G	AB	R	H	2B	3B	HR	RBI	BB	SO	AVG	OBP	SLG	PRO+	BR	/A	RC	SB	CS	SBR	FR	POS	TPR
1930	Chi-A	40	97	14	23	3	0	2	11	3	2	.237	.275	.330	54	-7	-7	9	1	2	-1	-3	3S	-0.7
1931	Chi-A	79	223	29	50	10	0	2	16	14	9	.224	.270	.296	52	-17	-15	19	3	0	1	2	3/2SO	-0.6
1934	Phi-N	56	175	28	43	6	0	4	19	15	10	.246	.305	.349	66	-6	-9	18	2			4	2/3	0.0
Total	3	175	495	71	116	19	0	8	46	32	21	.234	.284	.321	58	-30	-31	46	6	2		3	/32SO	-1.3

YEAR	TM/L	G	AB	R	H	2B	3B	HR	RBI	BB	SO	AVG	OBP	SLG	PRO+	BR	/A	RC	SB	CS	SBR	FR	POS	TPR

■ CHRIS JELIC　Jelic, Christopher John b: 12/16/63, Bethlehem, Pa. BR/TR, 5'11", 180 lbs. Deb: 9/30/90

| 1990 | NY-N | 4 | 11 | 2 | 1 | 0 | 0 | 1 | 1 | 0 | 3 | .091 | .091 | .364 | 19 | -1 | -1 | 0 | 0 | 0 | 0 | -1 | /O | -0.2 |

■ FRANK JELINICH　Jelinich, Frank Anthony "Jelly" b: 9/3/19, San Jose, Cal. BR/TR, 6'2", 198 lbs. Deb: 9/06/41

| 1941 | Chi-N | 4 | 8 | 0 | 1 | 0 | 0 | 0 | 2 | 1 | 2 | .125 | .222 | .125 | -1 | -1 | -1 | 0 | 0 | | | -1 | /O | -0.1 |

■ GREG JELKS　Jelks, Gregory Dion b: 8/16/61, Cherokee, Ala. BR/TR, 6'2", 190 lbs. Deb: 8/20/87

| 1987 | Phi-N | 10 | 11 | 2 | 1 | 1 | 0 | 0 | 0 | 3 | 4 | .091 | .286 | .182 | 26 | -1 | -1 | 1 | 0 | 0 | 0 | 0 | /31O | 0.0 |

■ STEVE JELTZ　Jeltz, Larry Steven b: 5/28/59, Paris, France BB/TR, 5'11", 180 lbs. Deb: 7/17/83

1983	Phi-N	13	8	0	1	0	1	0	1	1	2	.125	.222	.375	63	-0	-0	0	0	0	0	1	/2S3	0.0
1984	Phi-N	28	68	7	14	0	1	1	7	7	11	.206	.280	.279	57	-4	-4	5	2	1	0	11	S/3	1.1
1985	Phi-N	89	196	17	37	4	1	0	12	26	55	.189	.284	.219	41	-14	-15	13	1	1	-0	6	S	-0.2
1986	Phi-N	145	439	44	96	11	4	0	36	65	97	.219	.321	.262	60	-20	-22	40	6	3	0	-2	*S	-1.0
1987	Phi-N	114	293	37	68	9	6	0	12	39	54	.232	.324	.304	66	-13	-14	28	1	2	-1	4	*S/O	0.2
1988	Phi-N	148	379	39	71	11	4	0	27	59	58	.187	.297	.237	54	-20	-21	29	3	0	1	-1	*S	-1.1
1989	Phi-N	116	263	28	64	7	3	4	25	45	44	.243	.356	.338	99	1	1	34	4	2	0	1	S32/O	0.7
1990	KC-A	74	103	11	16	4	0	0	10	6	21	.155	.202	.194	12	-12	-12	4	1	1	-0	13	2SO/3D	0.4
Total	8	727	1749	183	367	46	20	5	130	248	342	.210	.309	.268	61	-83	-88	153	18	10	-1	33	S/230D	0.1

■ JOHN JENKINS　Jenkins, John Robert b: 7/7/1896, Bosworth, Mo. d: 8/3/68, Columbia, Mo. BR/TR, 5'8", 160 lbs. Deb: 8/05/22

| 1922 | Chi-A | 5 | 3 | 0 | 0 | 0 | 0 | 0 | 1 | 0 | 2 | .000 | .000 | .000 | -99 | -1 | -1 | 0 | 0 | 0 | 0 | -0 | /2S | 0.0 |

■ JOE JENKINS　Jenkins, Joseph Daniel b: 10/12/1890, Shelbyville, Tenn. d: 6/21/74, Fresno, Cal. BR/TR, 5'11", 170 lbs. Deb: 4/30/14

1914	StL-A	19	32	0	4	1	1	0	0	1	11	.125	.152	.219	12	-4	-3	1	2			-4	/C	-0.6
1917	Chi-A	10	9	0	1	0	0	0	2	0	5	.111	.111	.111	-32	-1	-1	0	0			0	/C	-0.1
1919	Chi-A	11	19	0	3	1	0	0	1	1	1	.158	.200	.211	15	-2	-2	1	1			-1	/C	-0.3
Total	3	40	60	0	8	2	1	0	3	2	17	.133	.161	.200	6	-7	-7	2	3			-6	/C	-1.0

■ TOM JENKINS　Jenkins, Thomas Griffith "Tut" b: 4/10/1898, Camden, Ala. d: 5/3/79, Weymouth, Mass. BL/TR, 6'1.5", 174 lbs. Deb: 9/15/25

1925	Bos-A	15	64	9	19	2	1	0	5	3	4	.297	.338	.359	77	-2	-2	8	0	0	0	-2	O	-0.4
1926	Bos-A	21	50	3	9	1	1	0	6	3	7	.180	.226	.240	22	-6	-6	3	0	0	0	-1	O	-0.7
	Phi-A	6	23	3	4	2	0	0	0	0	2	.174	.174	.261	12	-3	-3	1	0	0	0	0	/O	-0.3
	Yr	27	73	6	13	3	1	0	6	3	9	.178	.211	.247	19	-9	-9	4	0	0	0	-1		-1.0
1929	StL-A	21	22	1	4	0	1	0	0	4	8	.182	.308	.273	49	-2	-2	2	0	0	0	-1	/O	-0.2
1930	StL-A	2	8	1	2	1	1	0	3	0	1	.250	.250	.625	110	-0	0	1	0	0	0	0	/O	0.0
1931	StL-A	81	230	20	61	7	2	3	25	17	25	.265	.316	.352	73	-8	-10	25	1	3	-2	-4	O	-1.6
1932	StL-A	25	62	5	20	1	0	0	5	1	6	.323	.333	.339	70	-2	-3	7	0	0	0	1	O	-0.1
Total	6	171	459	42	119	14	6	3	44	28	53	.259	.303	.336	64	-23	-25	47	1	3	-2	-6	O	-3.3

■ ALAMAZOO JENNINGS　Jennings, Alfred Gorden b: 11/30/1850, Newport, Ky. d: 11/2/1894, Cincinnati, Ohio BR , Deb: 8/15/1878 U

| 1878 | Mil-N | 1 | 2 | 0 | 0 | 0 | 0 | 0 | 0 | 1 | 0 | .000 | .333 | .000 | 16 | -0 | -0 | 0 | | | | -0 | /C | 0.0 |

■ HUGHIE JENNINGS　Jennings, Hugh Ambrose "Ee-Yah" b: 4/2/1869, Pittston, Pa. d: 2/1/28, Scranton, Pa. BR/TR, 5'8.5", 165 lbs. Deb: 6/01/1891 MCH

1891	Lou-a	90	360	53	105	10	8	1	58	17	36	.292	.339	.372	108	2	3	51	12			7	S1/3	1.0
1892	Lou-N	152	594	65	132	16	4	2	61	30	30	.222	.270	.273	71	-25	-18	53	28			15	*S	0.4
1893	Lou-N	23	88	6	12	3	0	0	9	3	3	.136	.174	.170	-8	-14	-12	3	0			6	S	-0.4
	Bal-N	16	55	6	14	0	0	1	6	4	3	.255	.339	.309	73	-2	-2	6	0			-2	S/O	-0.2
	Yr	39	143	12	26	3	0	1	15	7	6	.182	.240	.224	26	-15	-14	8	0			4		-0.6
1894	*Bal-N	128	501	134	168	28	16	4	109	37	17	.335	.411	.479	111	14	9	117	37			33	*S	3.7
1895	*Bal-N	131	529	159	204	41	7	4	125	24	17	.386	.444	.512	145	39	37	148	53			36	*S	6.5
1896	*Bal-N	130	521	125	209	27	9	0	121	19	11	.401	.472	.488	154	46	44	157	70			34	*S	6.6
1897	*Bal-N	117	439	133	156	26	9	2	79	42		.355	.463	.469	149	37	37	126	60			27	*S	5.6
1898	Bal-N	143	534	135	175	25	11	1	87	78		.328	.454	.421	152	46	44	118	28			0	*S2/O	4.7
1899	Bro-N	16	41	7	7	0	2	0	6	9		.171	.346	.268	70	-1	-1	5	4			-6	S/1	-0.5
	Bal-N	2	8	2	3	0	2	0	2	0		.375	.375	.875	229	1	1	3	0			-1	/2	0.0
	Bro-N	51	175	35	57	3	8	0	34	13		.326	.424	.434	136	11	10	39	14			-0	1/2S	0.9
	Yr	69	224	44	67	3	12	0	42	22		.299	.408	.420	127	11	10	47	18			-7		0.4
1900	*Bro-N	115	441	61	120	18	6	1	69	31		.272	.335	.347	86	-5	-9	63	31			6	*1/2	-0.1
1901	Phi-N	82	302	38	79	21	2	1	39	25		.262	.338	.354	101	2	1	43	13			-3	1/2S	0.3
1902	Phi-N	78	290	32	79	13	4	1	32	14		.272	.328	.355	113	4	4	38	8			1	1/S2	0.3
1903	Bro-N	6	17	2	4	0	0	0	1	1		.235	.278	.235	50	-1	-1	1	1			-0	/O	0.0
1907	Det-A	1	4	0	1	1	0	0	0	0		.250	.250	.500	135	0	0	1	0			-1	/2SM	0.0
1909	Det-A	2	4	1	2	0	0	0	2	0		.500	.500	.500	207	0	0	1	0			0	/1M	0.1
1912	Det-A	1	1	0	0	0	0	0	0	0		.000	.000	.000	-99	-0	-0	0	0			0	HM	0.0
1918	Det-A	1	0	0	0	0	0	0	0	0	0	—	—	—	-99	0	0	0	0			0	/1M	0.0
Total	17	1285	4904	994	1527	232	88	18	840	347	117	.311	.389	.406	119	155	147	971	359			152	S1/203	28.6

■ DOUG JENNINGS　Jennings, James Douglas b: 9/30/64, Atlanta, Ga. BL/TL, 5'10", 175 lbs. Deb: 4/08/88

1988	Oak-A	71	101	9	21	6	0	1	15	21	28	.208	.355	.297	88	-1	-1	12	0	1	-1	0	O1/D	-0.1
1989	Oak-A	4	4	0	0	0	0	0	0	0	2	.000	.000	.000	-99	-1	-1	0	0	0	0	0	/O	0.0
1990	*Oak-A	64	156	19	30	7	2	2	14	17	48	.192	.280	.301	64	-8	-7	14	0	3	-2	-3	O/1D	-1.2
Total	3	139	261	28	51	13	2	3	29	38	78	.195	.307	.295	72	-10	-9	26	0	4	-2	-3	/O1D	-1.3

■ BILL JENNINGS　Jennings, William Lee b: 9/28/25, St.Louis, Mo. BR/TR, 6'2", 175 lbs. Deb: 7/19/51

| 1951 | StL-A | 64 | 195 | 20 | 35 | 10 | 2 | 0 | 13 | 26 | 42 | .179 | .276 | .251 | 42 | -15 | -16 | 15 | 1 | 0 | 0 | -5 | S | -1.6 |

■ WOODY JENSEN　Jensen, Forrest Docenus b: 8/11/07, Bremerton, Wash. BL/TL, 5'10.5", 160 lbs. Deb: 4/20/31

1931	Pit-N	73	267	43	65	5	4	3	17	10	18	.243	.276	.326	62	-15	-15	25	4			0	O	-1.7
1932	Pit-N	7	5	2	0	0	0	0	0	0	2	.000	.000	.000	-99	-1	-1	0	0			0	/O	0.0
1933	Pit-N	70	196	29	58	7	3	0	15	8	2	.296	.330	.362	98	-1	-1	25	1			-2	O	-0.4
1934	Pit-N	88	283	34	82	13	4	0	27	4	13	.290	.304	.364	76	-9	-10	30	2			-1	O	-1.3
1935	Pit-N	143	627	97	203	28	7	8	62	15	14	.324	.344	.429	103	4	2	90	9			-6	*O	-0.9
1936	Pit-N	153	696	98	197	34	10	10	58	16	19	.283	.305	.404	87	-13	-15	84	2			-1	*O	-2.1
1937	Pit-N	124	509	77	142	23	9	5	45	15	29	.279	.301	.389	86	-11	-11	58	2			-1	*O	-1.6
1938	Pit-N	68	125	12	25	4	0	0	10	1	3	.200	.213	.232	22	-13	-13	6	0			-3	O	-1.7
1939	Pit-N	12	12	0	2	0	0	0	1	0	0	.167	.167	.167	-10	-2	-2	0	0			1	/O	0.0
Total	9	738	2720	392	774	114	37	26	235	69	100	.285	.307	.382	84	-61	-66	318	20			-13	O	-9.7

■ JACKIE JENSEN　Jensen, Jack Eugene b: 3/9/27, San Francisco, Cal. d: 7/14/82, Charlottesville, Va. BR/TR, 5'11", 190 lbs. Deb: 4/18/50

1950	*NY-A	45	70	13	12	2	2	1	5	7	8	.171	.247	.300	41	-7	-7	5	4	0	1	0	O	-0.4
1951	NY-A	56	168	30	50	8	1	8	25	18	18	.298	.369	.500	138	7	8	34	8	2	1	5	O	1.2
1952	NY-A	7	19	3	2	1	1	0	2	4	4	.105	.261	.263	49	-1	-1	1	1	0	0	-1	/O	-0.1
	Was-A	144	570	80	163	29	5	10	80	63	40	.286	.360	.407	117	10	13	86	17	6	2	3	*O	1.3
	Yr	151	589	83	165	30	6	10	82	67	44	.280	.357	.402	115	9	11	88	18	6	2	2		1.2

YEAR	TM/L	G	AB	R	H	2B	3B	HR	RBI	BB	SO	AVG	OBP	SLG	PRO+	BR	/A	RC	SB	CS	SBR	FR	POS	TPR
1953	Was-A	147	552	87	147	32	8	10	84	73	51	.266	.357	.408	109	5	7	82	18	8	1	-6	*O	-0.1
1954	Bos-A	152	580	92	160	25	7	25	117	79	52	.276	.365	.472	115	21	13	94	**22**	7	2	-15	*O	-0.2
1955	Bos-A	152	574	95	158	27	6	26	**116**	89	63	.275	.375	.479	118	23	16	102	16	7	1	-2	*O	0.7
1956	Bos-A	151	578	80	182	23	**11**	20	97	89	43	.315	.407	.497	123	33	23	116	11	3	2	-2	*O	1.5
1957	Bos-A	145	544	82	153	29	2	23	103	75	66	.281	.370	.469	121	21	17	91	8	5	-1	0	*O	0.9
1958	Bos-A	154	548	83	157	31	0	35	**122**	99	65	.286	.398	.535	144	43	38	120	9	4	0	3	*O	3.2
1959	Bos-A	148	535	101	148	31	0	28	**112**	88	67	.277	.379	.492	131	28	25	100	20	5	3	11	*O	3.1
1961	Bos-A	137	498	64	131	21	2	13	66	66	69	.263	.353	.392	96	0	-2	68	9	8	-2	9	*O	0.0
Total	11	1438	5236	810	1463	259	45	199	929	750	546	.279	.372	.460	119	184	151	900	143	55	10	5	*O	11.1

■ DAN JESSEE
Jessee, Daniel Edward   b: 2/22/01, Olive Hill, Ky.   d: 4/30/70, Venice, Fla.   BL/TR, 5'10", 165 lbs.   Deb: 8/14/29

YEAR	TM/L	G	AB	R	H	2B	3B	HR	RBI	BB	SO	AVG	OBP	SLG	PRO+	BR	/A	RC	SB	CS	SBR	FR	POS	TPR
1929	Cle-A	1	0	0	0	0	0	0	0	0	0	—	—	—	—	0	0	0	0	0	0	0	R	0.0

■ GARRY JESTADT
Jestadt, Garry Arthur   b: 3/19/47, Chicago, Ill.   BR/TR, 6'2", 188 lbs.   Deb: 9/17/69

YEAR	TM/L	G	AB	R	H	2B	3B	HR	RBI	BB	SO	AVG	OBP	SLG	PRO+	BR	/A	RC	SB	CS	SBR	FR	POS	TPR
1969	Mon-N	6	6	1	0	0	0	0	1	0	0	.000	.000	.000	-99	-2	-2	0	0	0	0	-0	/S	-0.1
1971	Chi-N	3	3	0	0	0	0	0	0	0	0	.000	.000	.000	-87	-1	-1	0	0	0	0	0	/3	0.0
	SD-N	75	189	17	55	13	0	0	13	11	24	.291	.330	.360	102	1	0	19	1	3	-2	11	32/S	1.1
	Yr	78	192	17	55	13	0	0	13	11	24	.286	.325	.354	98	-2	-1	19	1	3	-2	11		1.1
1972	SD-N	92	256	15	63	5	1	6	22	13	21	.246	.283	.344	83	-8	-6	24	0	0	0	-17	23/S	-2.1
Total	3	176	454	33	118	18	1	6	36	24	45	.260	.297	.344	87	-12	-8	44	1	3	-2	-6	/32S	-1.1

■ JOHNNY JETER
Jeter, John   b: 10/24/44, Shreveport, La.   BR/TR, 6'1", 180 lbs.   Deb: 6/14/69

YEAR	TM/L	G	AB	R	H	2B	3B	HR	RBI	BB	SO	AVG	OBP	SLG	PRO+	BR	/A	RC	SB	CS	SBR	FR	POS	TPR
1969	Pit-N	28	29	7	9	1	1	1	6	3	15	.310	.375	.517	151	2	2	6	1	1	-0	1	O	0.1
1970	*Pit-N	85	126	27	30	3	2	2	12	13	34	.238	.314	.341	77	-4	-4	13	9	5	-0	1	O	-0.5
1971	SD-N	18	75	8	24	4	0	1	3	2	16	.320	.338	.413	120	1	1	11	2	0	1	4	O	0.6
1972	SD-N	110	326	25	72	4	3	7	21	18	92	.221	.266	.316	70	-16	-13	25	11	5	0	-3	O	-2.1
1973	Chi-A	89	300	38	72	14	4	7	26	9	74	.240	.262	.383	77	-9	-11	28	4	3	-1	-9	O/D	-2.2
1974	Cle-A	6	17	3	6	1	0	0	1	1	6	.353	.389	.412	132	1	1	2	1	2	-1	-1	/O	-0.1
Total	6	336	873	108	213	27	10	18	69	46	237	.244	.284	.360	82	-26	-24	85	28	16	-1	-7	O/D	-4.2

■ SAM JETHROE
Jethroe, Samuel "Jet"   b: 1/20/22, E.St.Louis, Ill.   BB/TR, 6'1", 178 lbs.   Deb: 4/18/50

YEAR	TM/L	G	AB	R	H	2B	3B	HR	RBI	BB	SO	AVG	OBP	SLG	PRO+	BR	/A	RC	SB	CS	SBR	FR	POS	TPR
1950	Bos-N	141	582	100	159	28	8	18	58	52	93	.273	.338	.442	110	2	7	89	**35**			4	*O	0.6
1951	Bos-N	148	572	101	160	29	10	18	65	57	88	.280	.356	.460	127	14	19	103	**35**	5	**8**	-0	*O	2.2
1952	Bos-N	151	608	79	141	23	7	13	58	68	112	.232	.318	.357	90	-11	-8	76	28	9	3	2	*O	-0.6
1954	Pit-N	2	1	0	0	0	0	0	0	0	0	.000	.000	.000	-99	-0	-0	0	0	0	0	0	/O	0.0
Total	4	442	1763	280	460	80	25	49	181	177	293	.261	.337	.418	108	5	18	267	98	<u>14</u>		6	O	2.2

■ NAT JEWETT
Jewett, Nathan W.   b: 12/25/1842, New York, N.Y.   d: 2/23/14, Bronx, N.Y.   5'6", 137 lbs.   Deb: 7/04/1872

YEAR	TM/L	G	AB	R	H	2B	3B	HR	RBI	BB	SO	AVG	OBP	SLG	PRO+	BR	/A	RC	SB	CS	SBR	FR	POS	TPR
1872	Eck-n	2	8	1	1	0	0	0		0		.125	.125	.125	-27	-1	-1	0					/C	0.0

■ HOUSTON JIMENEZ
Jimenez, Alfonso (Gonzalez)   b: 10/30/57, Navojoa, Sonora, Mex   BR/TR, 5'8", 144 lbs.   Deb: 6/13/83

YEAR	TM/L	G	AB	R	H	2B	3B	HR	RBI	BB	SO	AVG	OBP	SLG	PRO+	BR	/A	RC	SB	CS	SBR	FR	POS	TPR
1983	Min-A	36	86	5	15	5	1	0	9	4	11	.174	.211	.256	27	-9	-9	5	0	1	-1	4	S	-0.3
1984	Min-A	108	298	28	60	11	1	0	19	15	34	.201	.240	.245	33	-26	-28	17	0	1	-1	-5	*S	-2.5
1987	Pit-N	5	6	0	0	0	0	0	0	0	2	.000	.143	.000	-58	-1	-1	0	0	0	0	1	/2S	0.0
1988	Cle-A	9	21	1	1	0	0	0	1	0	2	.048	.048	.048	-71	-5	-5	0	0	0	0	6	/2S	0.1
Total	4	158	411	34	76	16	2	0	29	20	49	.185	.223	.234	25	-41	-43	21	0	2	-1	7	S/2	-2.7

■ ELVIO JIMENEZ
Jimenez, Felix Elvio (Rivera)   b: 1/6/40, San Pedro De Macoris, D.R.   BR/TR, 5'9", 170 lbs.   Deb: 10/04/64

YEAR	TM/L	G	AB	R	H	2B	3B	HR	RBI	BB	SO	AVG	OBP	SLG	PRO+	BR	/A	RC	SB	CS	SBR	FR	POS	TPR
1964	NY-A	1	6	0	2	0	0	0	0	0	0	.333	.333	.333	85	-0	-0	1	0	0	0	0	/O	0.0

■ MANNY JIMENEZ
Jimenez, Manuel Emilio (Rivera)   b: 11/19/38, San Pedro De Macoris, D.R.   BL/TR, 6'1", 185 lbs.   Deb: 4/11/62

YEAR	TM/L	G	AB	R	H	2B	3B	HR	RBI	BB	SO	AVG	OBP	SLG	PRO+	BR	/A	RC	SB	CS	SBR	FR	POS	TPR
1962	KC-A	139	479	48	144	24	2	11	69	31	34	.301	.357	.428	107	7	5	72	0	1	-1	-7	*O	-0.7
1963	KC-A	60	157	12	44	9	0	0	15	16	14	.280	.365	.338	95	-0	0	19	0	1	-1	-1	O	-0.2
1964	KC-A	95	204	19	46	7	0	12	38	15	24	.225	.295	.436	97	-1	-1	21	0	0	0	-5	O	-0.8
1966	KC-A	13	35	1	4	0	1	0	1	6	4	.114	.244	.171	22	-3	-3	2	0	0	0	-2	O	-0.5
1967	Pit-N	50	56	3	14	2	0	2	10	1	4	.250	.276	.393	89	-1	-1	5	0	0	0	-1	/O	-0.1
1968	Pit-N	66	66	7	20	1	1	1	11	6	15	.303	.403	.394	142	4	4	11	0	0	0	-1	/O	0.3
1969	Chi-N	6	6	0	1	0	0	0	0	0	2	.167	.167	.167	-6	-1	-1	0	0	0	0	0	H	0.0
Total	7	429	1003	90	273	43	4	26	144	75	97	.272	.339	.401	101	5	2	130	0	2	-1	-16	O	-2.0

■ TOMMY JOHNS
Johns, Thomas Pearce   b: 9/7/1851, Baltimore, Md.   d: 4/13/27, Baltimore, Md.   Deb: 5/14/1873

YEAR	TM/L	G	AB	R	H	2B	3B	HR	RBI	BB	SO	AVG	OBP	SLG	PRO+	BR	/A	RC	SB	CS	SBR	FR	POS	TPR
1873	Mar-n	1	4	0	0	0	0	0		0		.000	.000	.000	-99	-1	-1	0					/O	0.0

■ PETE JOHNS
Johns, William R.   b: 1/17/1889, Cleveland, Ohio   d: 8/9/64, Cleveland, Ohio   BR/TR, 5'10", 165 lbs.   Deb: 8/25/15

YEAR	TM/L	G	AB	R	H	2B	3B	HR	RBI	BB	SO	AVG	OBP	SLG	PRO+	BR	/A	RC	SB	CS	SBR	FR	POS	TPR
1915	Chi-A	28	100	7	21	2	1	0	11	8	11	.210	.275	.250	56	-5	-6	6	2	7	-4	4	3	-0.4
1918	StL-A	46	89	5	16	1	1	0	11	4	6	.180	.215	.213	30	-8	-8	4	0			-1	1/S3O2	-0.9
Total	2	74	189	12	37	3	2	0	22	12	17	.196	.248	.233	44	-13	-13	10	2	<u>7</u>		3	/31OS2	-1.3

■ ABBIE JOHNSON
Johnson, Albert J.   b: 7/26/1872, Sweden   d: 5/2/24, Oak Forest, Ill.   Deb: 9/01/1896

YEAR	TM/L	G	AB	R	H	2B	3B	HR	RBI	BB	SO	AVG	OBP	SLG	PRO+	BR	/A	RC	SB	CS	SBR	FR	POS	TPR
1896	Lou-N	25	87	10	20	2	1	0	14	4	6	.230	.264	.276	46	-7	-6	6	0			-4	2	-0.8
1897	Lou-N	48	161	16	39	6	1	0	23	13		.242	.303	.292	61	-9	-8	15	2			-10	2S	-1.2
Total	2	73	248	26	59	8	2	0	37	17	<u>6</u>	.238	.289	.286	56	-16	-15	22	2			-14	/2S	-2.0

■ ALEX JOHNSON
Johnson, Alexander   b: 12/7/42, Helena, Ark.   BR/TR, 6', 205 lbs.   Deb: 7/25/64

YEAR	TM/L	G	AB	R	H	2B	3B	HR	RBI	BB	SO	AVG	OBP	SLG	PRO+	BR	/A	RC	SB	CS	SBR	FR	POS	TPR
1964	Phi-N	43	109	18	33	7	1	4	18	6	26	.303	.345	.495	135	5	5	18	1	2	-1	-0	O	0.3
1965	Phi-N	97	262	27	77	9	3	8	28	15	60	.294	.337	.443	120	6	6	37	4	4	-1	-2	O	0.1
1966	StL-N	25	86	7	16	0	1	2	6	5	18	.186	.231	.279	41	-7	-7	4	1	1	-0	-3	O	-1.1
1967	StL-N	81	175	20	39	9	2	1	12	9	26	.223	.273	.314	68	-7	-7	15	6	3	0	7	O	-0.2
1968	Cin-N	149	603	79	188	32	6	2	58	26	71	.312	.343	.395	114	14	11	77	16	6	1	-5	*O	0.0
1969	Cin-N	139	523	86	165	18	4	17	88	25	69	.315	.357	.463	122	18	15	82	11	8	-2	-9	*O	-0.2
1970	Cal-A	156	614	85	202	26	6	14	86	35	68	**.329**	.372	.459	133	22	25	99	17	2	4	-3	*O	1.9
1971	Cal-A	65	242	19	63	8	0	2	21	15	34	.260	.309	.318	84	-7	-5	22	5	2	0	-12	O	-1.9
1972	Cle-A	108	356	31	85	10	1	8	37	22	40	.239	.285	.340	83	-7	-8	30	6	8	-3	-12	O	-2.9
1973	Tex-A	158	624	62	179	26	3	8	68	32	82	.287	.324	.377	101	-4	-1	72	10	5	0	-1	*DO	-0.2
1974	Tex-A	114	453	57	132	14	3	4	41	28	59	.291	.338	.362	104	1	2	52	20	9	1	-4	OD	-0.3
	NY-A	10	28	3	6	1	0	1	2	0	3	.214	.214	.357	64	-1	-1	2	0	0	0	0	/OD	-0.1
	Yr	124	481	60	138	15	3	5	43	28	62	.287	.331	.362	102	-1	1	54	20	9	1	-4		-0.4
1975	NY-A	52	119	15	31	5	1	1	15	7	21	.261	.302	.345	85	-3	-3	11	2	3	-1	0	D/O	-0.3
1976	Det-A	125	429	41	115	15	2	6	45	19	49	.268	.302	.354	88	-5	-8	41	14	10	-2	-6	OD	-1.8
Total	13	1322	4623	550	1331	180	33	78	525	244	626	.288	.329	.392	105	23	24	563	113	63	-4	-49	OD	-6.7

■ TONY JOHNSON
Johnson, Anthony Clair   b: 6/23/56, Memphis, Tenn.   BR/TR, 6'3", 145 lbs.   Deb: 9/28/81

YEAR	TM/L	G	AB	R	H	2B	3B	HR	RBI	BB	SO	AVG	OBP	SLG	PRO+	BR	/A	RC	SB	CS	SBR	FR	POS	TPR
1981	Mon-N	2	1	0	0	0	0	0	0	0	0	.000	.000	.000	-99	-0	-0	0	0	0	0	0	/O	0.0
1982	Tor-A	70	98	17	23	2	1	3	14	11	26	.235	.312	.367	79	-2	-3	7	3	13	-7	4	OD	-0.6
Total	2	72	99	17	23	2	1	3	14	11	26	.232	.309	.364	77	-3	-3	7	3	13	-7	4	/OD	-0.6

YEAR	TM/L	G	AB	R	H	2B	3B	HR	RBI	BB	SO	AVG	OBP	SLG	PRO+	BR	/A	RC	SB	CS	SBR	FR	POS	TPR

■ BOB JOHNSON   Johnson, Bobby Earl b: 7/31/59, Dallas, Tex.   BR/TR, 6'3", 195 lbs.   Deb: 9/01/81

YEAR	TM/L	G	AB	R	H	2B	3B	HR	RBI	BB	SO	AVG	OBP	SLG	PRO+	BR	/A	RC	SB	CS	SBR	FR	POS	TPR
1981	Tex-A	6	18	2	5	0	0	2	4	1	3	.278	.316	.611	171	1	1	3	0	0	0	-1	/C1	0.1
1982	Tex-A	20	56	4	7	2	0	2	7	3	22	.125	.183	.268	23	-6	-6	2	0	1	-1	1	C/1	-0.4
1983	Tex-A	72	175	18	37	6	1	5	16	16	55	.211	.281	.343	72	-7	-7	16	3	0	1	3	C1	0.0
Total	3	98	249	24	49	8	1	9	27	20	80	.197	.262	.345	68	-12	-11	21	3	1	0	4	/C1	-0.3

■ CALEB JOHNSON   Johnson, Caleb Clark b: 5/23/1844, Fulton, Ill.   d: 3/7/25, Sterling, Ill.   Deb: 5/24/1871

YEAR	TM/L	G	AB	R	H	2B	3B	HR	RBI	BB	SO	AVG	OBP	SLG	PRO+	BR	/A	RC	SB	CS	SBR	FR	POS	TPR
1871	Cle-n	16	67	10	15	1	0	0	7	0	1	.224	.224	.239	35	-6	-5	4	1				/2OS	-0.2

■ CHARLIE JOHNSON   Johnson, Charles Cleveland "Home Run" b: 3/12/1885, Slatington, Pa.   d: 8/28/40, Marcus Hook, Pa.   5'9", 150 lbs.   Deb: 9/21/08

YEAR	TM/L	G	AB	R	H	2B	3B	HR	RBI	BB	SO	AVG	OBP	SLG	PRO+	BR	/A	RC	SB	CS	SBR	FR	POS	TPR
1908	Phi-N	6	16	2	4	0	1	0	2	1		.250	.294	.375	112	0	0	2	0			-0	/O	0.0

■ CLIFF JOHNSON   Johnson, Clifford b: 7/22/47, San Antonio, Tex.   BR/TR, 6'4", 215 lbs.   Deb: 9/13/72

YEAR	TM/L	G	AB	R	H	2B	3B	HR	RBI	BB	SO	AVG	OBP	SLG	PRO+	BR	/A	RC	SB	CS	SBR	FR	POS	TPR
1972	Hou-N	5	4	0	1	0	0	0	0	2	0	.250	.500	.250	121	0	0	1	0	0	0	0	/C	0.1
1973	Hou-N	7	20	6	6	2	0	2	6	1	7	.300	.364	.700	189	2	2	5	0	0	0	-0	/1	0.2
1974	Hou-N	83	171	26	39	4	1	10	29	33	45	.228	.362	.439	129	6	7	28	0	1	-1	-3	C1	0.3
1975	Hou-N	122	340	52	94	16	1	20	65	46	64	.276	.371	.506	152	19	22	65	1	0	0	-12	1C/O	0.9
1976	Hou-N	108	318	36	72	21	2	10	49	62	59	.226	.359	.399	126	8	12	48	0	0	0	-11	CO1	0.2
1977	Hou-N	51	144	22	43	8	0	10	23	23	30	.299	.409	.563	173	12	14	35	0	1	-1	-1	O1	1.1
	NY-A	56	142	24	42	8	0	12	31	20	23	.296	.405	.606	173	14	15	36	0	1	-1	3	DC1	1.6
1978	NY-A	76	174	20	32	9	1	6	19	30	32	.184	.307	.351	87	-3	-3	19	0	0	0	1	DC/1	-0.1
1979	NY-A	28	64	11	17	6	0	2	6	10	7	.266	.365	.453	122	2	2	11	0	0	0	0	D/C	0.2
	Cle-A	72	240	37	65	10	0	18	61	24	39	.271	.349	.538	135	11	11	45	2	0	1	-0	D/C	1.1
	Yr	100	304	48	82	16	0	20	67	34	46	.270	.353	.520	132	13	13	57	2	0	1	0		1.3
1980	Cle-A	54	174	25	40	3	1	6	28	25	30	.230	.327	.362	88	-2	-3	19	0	1	-1	0	D	-0.2
	Chi-N	68	196	28	46	8	0	10	34	29	35	.235	.336	.429	104	3	1	29	0	0	0	-6	1/OC	-0.6
1981	Oak-A	84	273	40	71	8	0	17	59	28	60	.260	.336	.476	138	10	12	44	5	3	-0	-1	D/1	1.1
1982	Oak-A	73	214	19	51	10	0	7	31	26	41	.238	.326	.383	98	-2	-0	27	1	2	-1	1	D1	0.0
1983	Tor-A	142	407	59	108	23	1	22	76	67	69	.265	.376	.489	128	21	18	76	0	1	-1	-1	*D/1	1.7
1984	Tor-A	127	359	51	109	23	1	16	61	50	62	.304	.393	.507	142	24	22	72	0	1	-1	-1	*D/1	2.1
1985	Tex-A	82	296	31	76	17	1	12	56	31	44	.257	.333	.443	109	4	3	45	0	0	0	0	D	0.3
	Tor-A	24	73	4	20	0	0	1	10	9	15	.274	.354	.315	83	-1	-1	9	0	0	0	-0	D/1	-0.1
	Yr	106	369	35	96	17	1	13	66	40	59	.260	.337	.417	104	3	2	54	0	0	0	-0		0.2
1986	Tor-A	107	336	48	84	12	1	15	55	52	57	.250	.357	.426	109	7	5	52	0	1	-1	0	D/1	0.5
Total	15	1369	3945	539	1016	188	10	196	699	568	719	.258	.358	.459	125	135	139	667	9	12	-5	-30	D1C/O	10.4

■ DARRELL JOHNSON   Johnson, Darrell Dean b: 8/25/28, Horace, Neb.   BR/TR, 6'1", 180 lbs.   Deb: 4/20/52   MC

YEAR	TM/L	G	AB	R	H	2B	3B	HR	RBI	BB	SO	AVG	OBP	SLG	PRO+	BR	/A	RC	SB	CS	SBR	FR	POS	TPR
1952	StL-A	29	78	9	22	2	1	0	9	11	4	.282	.371	.333	94	0	-0	10	0	0	0	1	C	0.2
	Chi-A	22	37	3	4	0	0	1	5	9		.108	.214	.108	-8	-5	-5	1	1	0	0	4	C	0.0
	Yr	51	115	12	26	2	1	0	10	16	13	.226	.321	.261	62	-5	-6	11	1	0	0	5		0.2
1957	NY-A	21	46	4	10	1	0	1	8	3	10	.217	.280	.304	61	-3	-3	4	0	0	0	4	C	0.3
1958	NY-A	5	16	1	4	0	0	0	0	0	2	.250	.250	.250	39	-1	-1	1	0	0	0	1	/C	0.0
1960	StL-N	8	2	0	0	0	0	0	0	1	0	.000	.333	.000	1	-0	-0	0	0	0	0	1	/C	0.1
1961	Phi-N	21	61	4	14	1	0	0	3	3	8	.230	.277	.246	41	-5	-5	4	0	0	0	3	C	0.0
	*Cin-N	20	54	3	17	2	0	1	6	1	2	.315	.327	.407	92	-1	-1	7	0	0	0	4	C	0.5
	Yr	41	115	7	31	3	0	1	9	4	10	.270	.300	.322	65	-6	-6	11	0	0	0	7		0.5
1962	Cin-N	2	4	0	0	0	0	0	0	2	0	.000	.333	.000	-2	-0	-1	0	0	0	0	2	/C	0.1
	Bal-N	6	22	0	4	0	0	0	1	0	4	.182	.182	.182	-2	-3	-3	1	0	0	0	-0	/C	-0.2
Total	6	134	320	24	75	6	1	2	28	26	39	.234	.296	.278	57	-19	-19	28	1	0	0	20	C	1.0

■ DAVE JOHNSON   Johnson, David Allen b: 1/30/43, Orlando, Fla.   BR/TR, 6'1", 170 lbs.   Deb: 4/13/65   M

YEAR	TM/L	G	AB	R	H	2B	3B	HR	RBI	BB	SO	AVG	OBP	SLG	PRO+	BR	/A	RC	SB	CS	SBR	FR	POS	TPR
1965	Bal-A	20	47	5	8	3	0	0	1	5	6	.170	.250	.234	38	-4	-4	3	3	0	1	3	/32S	0.0
1966	*Bal-A	131	501	47	129	20	3	7	56	31	64	.257	.302	.351	88	-9	-8	52	3	4	-2	2	*2/S	0.4
1967	Bal-A	148	510	62	126	30	3	10	64	59	82	.247	.330	.376	109	6	6	63	4	5	-2	0	*2/3	1.0
1968	Bal-A	145	504	50	122	24	4	9	56	44	80	.242	.309	.359	102	1	1	53	7	3	0	4	*2S	1.3
1969	*Bal-A	142	511	52	143	34	1	7	57	57	68	.280	.356	.391	108	7	6	70	3	4	-2	-3	*2/S	0.7
1970	*Bal-A	149	530	68	149	27	1	10	53	66	68	.281	.361	.392	106	7	6	77	2	1	0	1	*2/S	2.2
1971	*Bal-A	142	510	67	144	26	1	18	72	51	55	.282	.353	.443	125	16	16	79	3	1	0	-1	*2	2.3
1972	Bal-A	118	376	31	83	22	3	5	32	52	64	.221	.322	.335	93	-1	-2	41	1	1	-0	10	*2	1.6
1973	Atl-N	157	559	84	151	25	0	43	99	81	93	.270	.371	.546	140	38	33	116	5	3	-0	-3	*2	3.6
1974	Atl-N	136	454	56	114	18	0	15	62	75	59	.251	.361	.390	105	8	5	64	1	2	-1	7	12	1.2
1975	Atl-N	1	1	0	1	1	0	0	0	1	0	1.000	1.000	2.000	691	1	1	2	0	0	0	0	H	0.1
1977	*Phi-N	78	156	23	50	9	1	8	36	23	20	.321	.414	.545	148	13	12	35	1	1	-0	-2	1/23	0.8
1978	Phi-N	44	89	14	17	2	0	2	14	10	19	.191	.287	.281	59	-5	-5	8	0	0	0	-6	2/31	-1.0
	Chi-N	24	49	5	15	1	1	2	6	5	9	.306	.393	.490	130	3	2	10	0	0	0	-3	3	0.0
	Yr	68	138	19	32	3	1	4	20	15	28	.232	.325	.355	86	-2	-2	17	0	0	0	-9		-1.0
Total	13	1435	4797	564	1252	242	18	136	609	559	675	.261	.343	.404	110	80	70	673	33	25	-5	10	*21/S3	14.2

■ DERON JOHNSON   Johnson, Deron Roger b: 7/17/38, San Diego, Cal.   BR/TR, 6'2", 200 lbs.   Deb: 9/20/60   C

YEAR	TM/L	G	AB	R	H	2B	3B	HR	RBI	BB	SO	AVG	OBP	SLG	PRO+	BR	/A	RC	SB	CS	SBR	FR	POS	TPR
1960	NY-A	6	4	0	2	1	0	0	0	0	0	.500	.500	.750	247	1	1	2	0	0	0	0	/3	0.1
1961	NY-A	13	19	1	2	0	0	0	2	2	5	.105	.190	.105	-20	-3	-3	0	0	0	0	2	/3	0.0
	KC-A	83	283	31	61	11	3	8	42	14	44	.216	.255	.360	62	-16	-16	24	0	1	-1	1	O3/1	-1.7
	Yr	96	302	32	63	11	3	8	44	16	49	.209	.251	.344	58	-19	-19	23	0	1	-1	3		-1.7
1962	KC-A	17	19	1	2	1	0	0	0	3	8	.105	.227	.158	6	-3	-3	1	0	0	0	-1	/13O	-0.3
1964	Cin-N	140	477	63	130	24	4	21	79	37	98	.273	.322	.472	118	13	11	71	4	3	-1	3	*1O/3	0.9
1965	Cin-N	159	616	92	177	30	7	32	130	52	97	.287	.345	.515	129	30	25	105	0	4	-2	-12	*3	0.4
1966	Cin-N	142	505	75	130	25	3	24	81	39	87	.257	.313	.461	103	7	2	70	1	2	-1	-13	*O13	-1.9
1967	Cin-N	108	361	39	81	18	1	13	53	22	104	.224	.287	.388	78	-7	-12	36	0	1	-1	-3	13	-2.1
1968	Atl-N	127	342	29	71	11	0	8	33	35	79	.208	.287	.316	81	-8	-8	31	0	1	-1	-3	13	-1.8
1969	Phi-N	138	475	51	121	19	4	17	80	60	111	.255	.338	.419	114	7	8	66	4	2	0	-15	O31	-1.1
1970	Phi-N	159	574	66	147	28	3	27	93	72	132	.256	.338	.456	114	8	10	89	0	0	0	-11	*1/3	-1.3
1971	Phi-N	158	582	74	154	29	0	34	95	72	146	.265	.348	.490	135	26	26	96	0	3	-1	-4	*13	1.1
1972	Phi-N	96	230	19	49	4	1	9	31	26	69	.213	.301	.357	84	-4	-5	24	0	1	-1	-4	1	-1.4
1973	Phi-N	12	36	3	6	2	0	1	5	5	10	.167	.286	.306	62	-2	-2	3	0	0	0	-0	1	-0.2
	*Oak-A	131	464	61	114	14	2	19	81	50	116	.246	.332	.407	113	4	7	63	0	1	-1	-3	*D1	1.0
1974	Oak-A	50	174	16	34	1	2	7	23	11	37	.195	.243	.345	72	-8	-7	13	1	0	0	-2	1D	-1.0
	Mil-A	49	152	14	23	3	0	6	18	21	41	.151	.254	.289	56	-9	-9	11	1	0	0	-0	D/1	-0.8
	Bos-A	11	25	0	3	0	0	0	2	0	6	.120	.120	.120	-29	-4	-4	0	0	0	0	0	/D	-0.4
	Yr	110	351	30	60	4	2	13	43	32	84	.171	.240	.305	57	-21	-20	25	2	0	1	-3		-2.2
1975	Chi-A	148	555	66	129	25	1	18	72	48	117	.232	.295	.378	88	-9	-10	58	0	1	-1	-4	D1	-1.8
	Bos-A	3	10	2	6	0	0	1	3	2	0	.600	.667	.900	313	3	3	6	0	0	0	-0	/1D	0.3
	Yr	151	565	68	135	25	1	19	75	50	117	.239	.302	.388	92	-6	-7	63	0	1	-1	-5		-1.5
1976	Bos-A	15	38	3	5	1	1	0	5	5	11	.132	.233	.211	27	-3	-4	2	0	0	0	-0	/1D	-0.4
Total	16	1765	5941	706	1447	247	33	245	923	585	1318	.244	.313	.420	103	22	10	772	11	18	-8	-69	13DO	-13.1

YEAR	TM/L	G	AB	R	H	2B	3B	HR	RBI	BB	SO	AVG	OBP	SLG	PRO+	BR	/A	RC	SB	CS	SBR	FR	POS	TPR

■ DON JOHNSON Johnson, Donald Spore "Pep" b: 12/7/11, Chicago, Ill. BR/TR, 6', 170 lbs. Deb: 9/26/43

YEAR	TM/L	G	AB	R	H	2B	3B	HR	RBI	BB	SO	AVG	OBP	SLG	PRO+	BR	/A	RC	SB	CS	SBR	FR	POS	TPR
1943	Chi-N	10	42	5	8	2	0	0	1	2	4	.190	.227	.238	35	-4	-4	2	0			3	2	0.0
1944	Chi-N	154	608	50	169	37	1	2	71	28	48	.278	.311	.352	87	-12	-12	65	8			1	*2	0.4
1945	*Chi-N	138	557	94	168	23	2	2	58	32	34	.302	.343	.361	98	-4	-2	70	9			10	*2	1.9
1946	Chi-N	83	314	37	76	10	1	1	19	26	39	.242	.306	.290	71	-12	-12	29	6			-10	2	-1.9
1947	Chi-N	120	402	33	104	17	2	3	26	24	45	.259	.302	.333	71	-18	-16	41	2			-4	*2/3	-0.8
1948	Chi-N	6	12	0	3	0	0	0	0	0	1	.250	.250	.250	37	-1	-1	1	1			-1	/23	-0.1
Total	6	511	1935	219	528	89	6	8	175	112	171	.273	.315	.337	83	-51	-46	208	26			-1	2/3	-0.5

■ ED JOHNSON Johnson, Edwin Cyril b: 3/31/1899, Morganfield, Ky. d: 7/3/75, Morganfield, Ky. BL/TR, 5'9", 160 lbs. Deb: 9/26/20

YEAR	TM/L	G	AB	R	H	2B	3B	HR	RBI	BB	SO	AVG	OBP	SLG	PRO+	BR	/A	RC	SB	CS	SBR	FR	POS	TPR
1920	Was-A	4	13	1	3	0	0	0	2	3	2	.231	.375	.231	65	-1	-0	1	0	0	0	-0	/O	0.0

■ ELMER JOHNSON Johnson, Elmer Ellsworth "Hickory" b: 6/12/1884, Beard, Ind. d: 10/31/66, Hollywood, Fla. BR/TR, 5'9", 185 lbs. Deb: 4/24/14

YEAR	TM/L	G	AB	R	H	2B	3B	HR	RBI	BB	SO	AVG	OBP	SLG	PRO+	BR	/A	RC	SB	CS	SBR	FR	POS	TPR
1914	NY-N	11	12	0	2	1	0	0	0	1	3	.167	.231	.250	44	-1	-1	1	0			-1	C	-0.1

■ ERNIE JOHNSON Johnson, Ernest Rudolph b: 4/29/1888, Chicago, Ill. d: 5/1/52, Monrovia, Cal. BL/TR, 5'9", 151 lbs. Deb: 8/05/12

YEAR	TM/L	G	AB	R	H	2B	3B	HR	RBI	BB	SO	AVG	OBP	SLG	PRO+	BR	/A	RC	SB	CS	SBR	FR	POS	TPR
1912	Chi-A	21	42	7	11	0	1	0	5	1		.262	.279	.310	70	-2	-2	4	0			3	S	0.3
1915	StL-F	152	512	58	123	18	10	3	67	46	35	.240	.305	.355	90	-4	-7	69	32			18	*S	2.3
1916	StL-A	74	236	29	54	9	3	0	19	30	23	.229	.323	.292	89	-4	-2	27	13			-8	S3	-0.5
1917	StL-A	80	199	28	49	6	2	2	20	12	16	.246	.296	.327	93	-3	-2	23	13			11	S23	1.3
1918	StL-A	29	34	7	9	1	0	0	0	0	2	.265	.286	.294	77	-1	-1	4	4			-2	S/3	-0.2
1921	Chi-A	142	613	93	181	28	7	1	51	29	24	.295	.328	.369	78	-21	-20	73	22	13	-1	18	*S	1.3
1922	Chi-A	144	603	85	153	17	3	0	56	40	30	.254	.304	.292	56	-38	-38	54	21	18	-5	3	*S	-2.2
1923	Chi-A	12	53	5	10	2	0	0	1	3	5	.189	.246	.226	25	-6	-6	3	2	1	0	-0	S	-0.4
	*NY-A	19	38	6	17	1	1	1	8	1	1	.447	.462	.605	176	4	4	10	0	0	0	-1	S/3	0.5
	Yr	31	91	11	27	3	1	1	9	4	6	.297	.333	.385	88	-2	-2	12	2	1	0	-1		0.1
1924	NY-A	64	119	24	42	4	8	3	12	11	7	.353	.412	.597	158	10	10	26	1	6	-3	-1	S/3	0.6
1925	NY-A	76	170	30	48	5	1	5	17	8	10	.282	.315	.412	85	-5	-5	22	6	3	0	-9	2S/3	-0.7
Total	10	813	2619	372	697	91	36	19	256	181	153	.266	.317	.350	82	-71	-69	315	114	41		31	S/23	2.3

■ FRANK JOHNSON Johnson, Frank Herbert b: 7/22/42, El Paso, Tex. BR/TR, 6'1", 155 lbs. Deb: 9/07/66

YEAR	TM/L	G	AB	R	H	2B	3B	HR	RBI	BB	SO	AVG	OBP	SLG	PRO+	BR	/A	RC	SB	CS	SBR	FR	POS	TPR
1966	SF-N	15	32	2	7	0	0	0	2	7	.219	.265	.219	35	-3	-3	2	0	1	-1	-0	O	-0.4
1967	SF-N	8	10	3	3	0	0	0	0	1	2	.300	.364	.300	93	-0	-0	1	0	0	0	1	/O	0.1
1968	SF-N	67	174	11	33	2	0	1	7	12	23	.190	.246	.218	40	-12	-12	10	1	0	0	4	3/OS2	-0.1
1969	SF-N	7	10	2	1	0	0	0	0	0	1	.100	.100	.100	-45	-2	-2	0	0	0	0	-0	/O	-0.1
1970	SF-N	67	161	25	44	1	2	3	31	19	18	.273	.357	.360	94	-1	-1	18	1	1	-0	-0	O1	-0.4
1971	SF-N	32	49	4	4	1	0	0	5	3	9	.082	.135	.102	-33	-8	-8	1	0	0	0	-2	/1O	-1.1
Total	6	196	436	47	92	4	2	4	43	37	60	.211	.277	.257	52	-27	-26	31	2	2	-1	3	/013S2	-2.7

■ HOWARD JOHNSON Johnson, Howard Michael b: 11/29/60, Clearwater, Fla. BB/TR, 5'11", 178 lbs. Deb: 4/14/82

YEAR	TM/L	G	AB	R	H	2B	3B	HR	RBI	BB	SO	AVG	OBP	SLG	PRO+	BR	/A	RC	SB	CS	SBR	FR	POS	TPR
1982	Det-A	54	155	23	49	5	0	4	14	16	30	.316	.384	.426	122	5	5	25	7	4	-0	-4	3D/O	0.0
1983	Det-A	27	66	11	14	0	0	3	5	7	10	.212	.297	.348	79	-2	-2	7	0	0	0	-6	3/D	-0.7
1984	*Det-A	116	355	43	88	14	1	12	50	40	67	.248	.326	.394	99	-1	-0	46	10	6	-1	-17	*3/S10D	-1.5
1985	NY-N	126	389	38	94	18	4	11	46	34	78	.242	.303	.393	96	-4	-3	45	6	4	-1	-12	*3S/SO	-1.5
1986	*NY-N	88	220	30	54	14	0	10	39	31	64	.245	.341	.445	119	4	5	36	8	1	2	-2	3S/O	0.8
1987	NY-N	157	554	93	147	22	1	36	99	83	113	.265	.366	.504	135	22	26	106	32	10	4	-17	*3S/O	1.5
1988	*NY-N	148	495	85	114	21	1	24	68	86	104	.230	.348	.422	126	14	17	78	23	7	3	-14	*3S	1.0
1989	NY-N	153	571	104	164	41	3	36	101	77	126	.287	.373	.559	171	46	49	127	41	8	8	-33	*3S	2.6
1990	NY-N	154	590	89	144	37	3	23	90	69	100	.244	.323	.434	109	4	6	87	34	8	5	-5	3S	1.6
Total	9	1023	3395	516	868	172	13	159	512	443	692	.256	.344	.454	124	89	103	558	161	48	20	-109	3S/DO1	3.8

■ SPUD JOHNSON Johnson, John Ralph b: 1860, Canada BL/TL, 5'9", 175 lbs. Deb: 4/18/1889

YEAR	TM/L	G	AB	R	H	2B	3B	HR	RBI	BB	SO	AVG	OBP	SLG	PRO+	BR	/A	RC	SB	CS	SBR	FR	POS	TPR
1889	Col-a	116	459	91	130	14	10	2	79	39	47	.283	.355	.370	114	6	10	74	34			-11	O3/1S	-0.2
1890	Col-a	135	538	106	186	23	18	1		48		.346	.409	.461	171	39	45	122	43			-16	*O	2.0
1891	Cle-N	80	327	49	84	8	3	1	46	22	23	.257	.319	.309	82	-6	-8	38	16			-5	O/1	-1.4
Total	3	331	1324	246	400	45	31	4	125	109	70	.302	.368	.392	128	40	48	235	93			-32	O/31S	0.4

■ LANCE JOHNSON Johnson, Kenneth Lance b: 7/6/63, Cincinnati, Ohio BL/TL, 5'10", 160 lbs. Deb: 7/10/87

YEAR	TM/L	G	AB	R	H	2B	3B	HR	RBI	BB	SO	AVG	OBP	SLG	PRO+	BR	/A	RC	SB	CS	SBR	FR	POS	TPR
1987	*StL-N	33	59	4	13	2	1	0	7	4	6	.220	.270	.288	47	-4	-5	5	6	1	1	-1	O	-0.5
1988	Chi-A	33	124	11	23	4	1	0	6	6	11	.185	.223	.234	28	-12	-12	7	6	2	1	-3	O/D	-1.5
1989	Chi-A	50	180	28	54	8	2	0	16	17	24	.300	.360	.367	108	2	2	27	16	3	3	-1	O/D	0.3
1990	Chi-A	151	541	76	154	18	9	1	51	33	45	.285	.327	.357	93	-7	-5	59	36	22	-2	-6	*O/D	-1.5
Total	4	267	904	119	244	32	13	1	80	60	86	.270	.316	.337	84	-21	-19	98	64	28	2	-12	O/D	-3.2

■ LAMAR JOHNSON Johnson, Lamar b: 9/2/50, Bessemer, Ala. BR/TR, 6'2", 215 lbs. Deb: 5/18/74

YEAR	TM/L	G	AB	R	H	2B	3B	HR	RBI	BB	SO	AVG	OBP	SLG	PRO+	BR	/A	RC	SB	CS	SBR	FR	POS	TPR
1974	Chi-A	10	29	1	10	0	0	0	2	0	3	.345	.345	.345	97	-0	-0	2	0	0	0	-0	/1D	0.0
1975	Chi-A	8	30	2	6	3	0	1	1	1	5	.200	.226	.400	73	-1	-1	3	0	0	0	-1	/1D	-0.2
1976	Chi-A	82	222	29	71	11	1	4	33	19	37	.320	.379	.432	136	10	10	34	2	1	0	-0	D1/O	0.9
1977	Chi-A	118	374	52	113	12	5	18	65	24	53	.302	.344	.505	128	13	13	59	1	1	-0	1	D1	1.2
1978	Chi-A	148	498	52	136	23	2	8	72	43	46	.273	.333	.376	98	-1	-1	59	6	5	-1	2	*1D	-0.4
1979	Chi-A	133	479	60	148	29	1	12	74	41	56	.309	.366	.449	118	12	12	73	8	2	1	-1	1D	0.8
1980	Chi-A	147	541	51	150	26	3	13	81	47	53	.277	.335	.409	103	2	2	71	2	3	-1	2	1D	-0.1
1981	Chi-A	41	134	10	37	7	0	1	15	5	14	.276	.302	.351	89	-2	-2	12	0	2	-1	-0	1/D	-0.4
1982	Tex-A	105	324	37	84	11	0	7	38	31	40	.259	.326	.358	92	-5	-3	35	3	5	-2	-1	D1	-0.6
Total	9	792	2631	294	755	122	12	64	381	211	307	.287	.342	.415	109	28	30	349	22	19	-5	2	1D/O	1.2

■ LARRY JOHNSON Johnson, Larry Doby b: 8/17/50, Cleveland, Ohio BR/TR, 6', 185 lbs. Deb: 10/03/72

YEAR	TM/L	G	AB	R	H	2B	3B	HR	RBI	BB	SO	AVG	OBP	SLG	PRO+	BR	/A	RC	SB	CS	SBR	FR	POS	TPR
1972	Cle-A	1	2	0	1	0	0	0	0	0	1	.500	.500	.500	192	0	0	1	0	0	0	0	/C	0.1
1974	Cle-A	1	0	1	0	0	0	0	0	0	0	—	—	—	—	0	0	0	0	0	0	0	R	0.0
1975	Mon-N	1	3	0	1	1	0	0	1	1	1	.333	.500	.667	212	1	1	1	0	0	0	0	/C	0.0
1976	Mon-N	6	13	0	2	1	0	0	0	0	2	.154	.154	.231	8	-2	-2	1	0	0	0	1	/C	0.0
1978	Chi-A	3	8	0	1	0	0	0	0	1	4	.125	.222	.125	0	-1	-1	0	0	0	0	-0	/CD	-0.1
Total	5	12	26	1	5	2	0	0	1	2	8	.192	.250	.269	46	-2	-2	2	0	0	0	1	/CD	0.0

■ LOU JOHNSON Johnson, Louis Brown "Slick" b: 9/22/34, Lexington, Ky. BR/TR, 5'11", 170 lbs. Deb: 4/17/60

YEAR	TM/L	G	AB	R	H	2B	3B	HR	RBI	BB	SO	AVG	OBP	SLG	PRO+	BR	/A	RC	SB	CS	SBR	FR	POS	TPR
1960	Chi-N	34	68	6	14	2	1	0	1	5	19	.206	.270	.265	48	-5	-5	5	3	1	0	4	O	0.0
1961	LA-A	1	0	0	0	0	0	0	0	0	0	—	—	—	—	0	0	0	0	0	0	0	/O	0.0
1962	Mil-N	61	117	22	33	4	5	2	13	11	27	.282	.349	.453	116	2	3	20	6	1	1	0	O	0.1
1965	*LA-N	131	468	57	121	24	1	12	58	24	81	.259	.317	.391	105	-1	2	58	15	6	1	-7	*O	-0.7
1966	*LA-N	152	526	71	143	20	2	17	73	21	75	.272	.317	.414	110	0	5	63	8	10	-4	2	*O	0.0
1967	LA-N	104	330	39	89	14	1	11	41	24	52	.270	.332	.418	124	6	9	44	4	3	-1	-1	O	0.4
1968	Chi-N	62	205	14	50	14	3	1	14	6	23	.244	.289	.356	87	-2	-4	20	4	1	0	-6	O	-1.3
	Cle-A	65	202	25	52	11	1	5	23	9	24	.257	.302	.396	112	2	2	24	6	1	1	0	O	0.1
1969	Cal-A	67	133	10	27	8	0	0	9	10	19	.203	.274	.263	53	-9	-8	10	5	1	1	-2	O	-0.9
Total	8	677	2049	244	529	97	14	48	232	110	320	.258	.313	.389	103	-7	4	244	50	24	1	-8	O	-2.3

YEAR	TM/L	G	AB	R	H	2B	3B	HR	RBI	BB	SO	AVG	OBP	SLG	PRO+	BR	/A	RC	SB	CS	SBR	FR	POS	TPR

■ OTIS JOHNSON Johnson, Otis L. b: 11/5/1883, Fowler, Ind. d: 11/9/15, Johnson City, N.Y. BB/TR, 5'9", 185 lbs. Deb: 4/12/11

YEAR	TM/L	G	AB	R	H	2B	3B	HR	RBI	BB	SO	AVG	OBP	SLG	PRO+	BR	/A	RC	SB	CS	SBR	FR	POS	TPR
1911	NY-A	71	209	21	49	9	6	3	36	39		.234	.363	.378	100	3	1	34	12			-9	S2/3	-0.3

■ PAUL JOHNSON Johnson, Paul Oscar b: 9/2/1896, N.Grosvenordale, Conn. d: 2/14/73, McAllen, Tex. BR/TR, 5'8", 160 lbs. Deb: 9/13/20

YEAR	TM/L	G	AB	R	H	2B	3B	HR	RBI	BB	SO	AVG	OBP	SLG	PRO+	BR	/A	RC	SB	CS	SBR	FR	POS	TPR
1920	Phi-A	18	72	6	15	0	0	0	5	4	8	.208	.250	.208	22	-8	-8	4	1	1	-0	-3	O	-1.2
1921	Phi-A	48	127	17	40	6	2	1	10	9	17	.315	.360	.417	97	-1	-1	18	0	2	-1	-4	O	-0.7
Total	2	66	199	23	55	6	2	1	15	13	25	.276	.321	.342	71	-8	-9	22	1	3	-2	-7	/O	-1.9

■ RANDY JOHNSON Johnson, Randall Glenn b: 6/10/56, Escondido, Cal. BR/TR, 6'1", 190 lbs. Deb: 4/27/82

YEAR	TM/L	G	AB	R	H	2B	3B	HR	RBI	BB	SO	AVG	OBP	SLG	PRO+	BR	/A	RC	SB	CS	SBR	FR	POS	TPR
1982	Atl-N	27	46	5	11	5	0	0	6	6	4	.239	.352	.348	93	0	-0	6	0	1	-1	5	2/3	0.5
1983	Atl-N	86	144	22	36	3	0	1	17	20	27	.250	.345	.292	73	-3	-5	15	1	3	-2	10	3/2	0.2
1984	Atl-N	91	294	28	82	13	0	5	30	21	21	.279	.329	.374	91	-1	-4	35	4	7	-3	5	3	-0.1
Total	3	204	484	55	129	21	0	6	53	47	52	.267	.336	.347	85	-5	-9	56	5	11	-5	20	3/2	0.6

■ RANDY JOHNSON Johnson, Randall Stuart b: 8/15/58, Miami, Fla. BL/TL, 6'2", 195 lbs. Deb: 7/05/80

YEAR	TM/L	G	AB	R	H	2B	3B	HR	RBI	BB	SO	AVG	OBP	SLG	PRO+	BR	/A	RC	SB	CS	SBR	FR	POS	TPR
1980	Chi-A	12	20	0	4	0	0	0	3	2	4	.200	.304	.200	41	-2	-1	2	0	0	0	-0	/1OD	-0.1
1982	Min-A	89	234	26	58	10	0	10	33	30	46	.248	.331	.419	102	2	1	34	0	0	0	0	D/O	0.1
Total	2	101	254	26	62	10	0	10	36	32	50	.244	.331	.402	98	-0	-1	36	0	0	0	0	/DO1	0.0

■ FOOTER JOHNSON Johnson, Richard Allan "Treads" b: 2/15/32, Dayton, Ohio BL/TL, 5'11", 175 lbs. Deb: 6/22/58

YEAR	TM/L	G	AB	R	H	2B	3B	HR	RBI	BB	SO	AVG	OBP	SLG	PRO+	BR	/A	RC	SB	CS	SBR	FR	POS	TPR
1958	Chi-N	8	5	1	0	0	0	0	0	0	1	.000	.000	.000	-99	-1	-1	0	0	0	0	0	H	0.00

■ BOB JOHNSON Johnson, Robert Lee "Indian Bob" b: 11/26/06, Pryor, Okla. d: 7/6/82, Tacoma, Wash. BR/TR, 6', 180 lbs. Deb: 4/12/33

YEAR	TM/L	G	AB	R	H	2B	3B	HR	RBI	BB	SO	AVG	OBP	SLG	PRO+	BR	/A	RC	SB	CS	SBR	FR	POS	TPR
1933	Phi-A	142	535	103	155	44	4	21	93	85	74	.290	.387	.505	133	27	26	109	8	3	1	2	*O	2.2
1934	Phi-A	141	547	111	168	26	6	34	92	58	60	.307	.375	.563	144	29	31	114	12	8	-1	11	*O	3.5
1935	Phi-A	147	582	103	174	29	5	28	109	78	76	.299	.384	.510	130	25	25	116	2	4	-2	6	*O	2.6
1936	Phi-A	153	566	91	165	29	14	25	121	88	71	.292	.389	.525	126	20	22	118	6	6	-2	-1	*O2/1	1.5
1937	Phi-A	138	477	91	146	32	6	25	108	98	65	.306	.425	.556	148	35	36	117	9	7	-2	10	*O/2	3.6
1938	Phi-A	152	563	114	176	27	9	30	113	87	73	.313	.406	.552	142	33	35	128	9	8	-2	4	*O/23	3.3
1939	Phi-A	150	544	115	184	30	9	23	114	99	59	.338	.440	.553	156	46	48	138	15	5	2	9	*O/2	4.9
1940	Phi-A	138	512	93	137	25	4	31	103	83	64	.268	.374	.514	130	21	22	100	8	2	1	6	*O	1.9
1941	Phi-A	149	552	98	152	30	8	22	107	95	75	.275	.385	.478	130	22	24	106	6	4	-1	6	*O1	2.1
1942	Phi-A	149	550	78	160	35	7	13	80	82	61	.291	.384	.451	135	26	26	99	3	2	-0	7	*O	2.3
1943	Was-A	117	438	65	116	22	8	7	63	64	50	.265	.362	.400	127	14	15	67	11	5	0	9	O31	2.3
1944	Bos-A	144	525	106	170	40	8	17	106	95	67	.324	.431	.528	175	53	54	124	2	7	-4	5	*O	5.2
1945	Bos-A	143	529	71	148	27	7	12	74	63	56	.280	.358	.425	124	17	16	83	5	3	-0	1	*O	1.2
Total	13	1863	6920	1239	2051	396	95	288	1283	1075	851	.296	.393	.506	139	366	381	1418	96	64	-10	74	*O/123	36.6

■ BOB JOHNSON Johnson, Robert Wallace b: 3/4/36, Omaha, Neb. BR/TR, 5'10", 175 lbs. Deb: 4/19/60

YEAR	TM/L	G	AB	R	H	2B	3B	HR	RBI	BB	SO	AVG	OBP	SLG	PRO+	BR	/A	RC	SB	CS	SBR	FR	POS	TPR
1960	KC-A	76	146	12	30	4	0	1	9	19	23	.205	.301	.253	51	-9	-10	11	2	0	1	12	S23	0.7
1961	Was-A	61	224	27	66	13	1	6	28	19	26	.295	.352	.442	113	3	4	32	4	2	0	-2	S/23	0.6
1962	Was-A	135	466	58	134	20	2	12	43	32	50	.288	.335	.416	102	-0	0	59	9	6	-1	-4	3S/2O	0.0
1963	Bal-A	82	254	34	75	10	0	8	32	18	35	.295	.347	.429	119	5	6	39	5	1	1	-2	2/1S3	0.9
1964	Bal-A	93	210	18	52	8	2	3	29	9	37	.248	.282	.348	74	-8	-8	19	0	0	0	-12	S12/30	-1.8
1965	Bal-A	87	273	36	66	13	2	5	27	15	34	.242	.284	.359	80	-7	-8	26	1	0	0	-10	1S3/2	-1.8
1966	Bal-A	71	157	13	34	5	0	1	10	12	24	.217	.276	.268	58	-9	-8	11	0	1	-1	1	21/3	-0.7
1967	Bal-A	4	3	1	1	0	0	0	0	1	1	.333	.500	.333	152	0	0	1	0	0	0	0	H	0.0
	NY-N	90	230	26	80	8	3	5	27	12	29	.348	.380	.474	145	12	13	39	1	1	-0	-7	21S/3	0.9
1968	Cin-N	16	15	2	4	0	0	0	1	1	2	.267	.313	.267	71	-0	-1	1	0	0	0	-1	/S1	0.0
	Atl-N	59	187	15	49	5	1	0	11	10	20	.262	.299	.299	80	-4	-5	16	0	0	0	0	3/2	-0.4
	Yr	75	202	17	53	5	1	0	12	11	22	.262	.300	.297	79	-5	-5	17	0	0	0	-0		-0.4
1969	StL-N	19	29	1	6	0	0	1	2	2	4	.207	.258	.310	58	-2	-2	2	0	0	0	-1	/31	-0.2
	Oak-A	51	67	5	23	1	0	1	9	3	4	.343	.380	.403	125	2	2	11	0	0	0	0	/12	0.2
1970	Oak-A	30	46	6	8	1	0	1	2	3	2	.174	.240	.261	39	-4	-4	3	2	1	0	1	/31	-0.2
Total	11	874	2307	254	628	88	11	44	230	156	291	.272	.321	.377	95	-21	-19	269	24	12	0	-25	S231/O	-1.8

■ RON JOHNSON Johnson, Ronald David b: 3/23/56, Long Beach, Cal. BR/TR, 6'3", 215 lbs. Deb: 9/12/82

YEAR	TM/L	G	AB	R	H	2B	3B	HR	RBI	BB	SO	AVG	OBP	SLG	PRO+	BR	/A	RC	SB	CS	SBR	FR	POS	TPR
1982	KC-A	8	14	2	4	2	0	0	4	3	3	.286	.444	.429	141	1	1	3	0	0	0	-0	/1	0.0
1983	KC-A	9	27	2	7	0	0	0	1	3	1	.259	.333	.259	66	-1	-1	3	0	0	0	-1	/1C	-0.2
1984	Mon-N	5	5	0	1	0	0	0	1	0	2	.200	.200	.200	13	-1	-1	0	0	0	0	-0	/1O	0.0
Total	3	22	46	4	12	2	0	0	2	7	6	.261	.358	.304	85	-1	-1	6	0	0	0	-2	/1CO	-0.2

■ RONDIN JOHNSON Johnson, Rondin Allen b: 12/16/58, Bremerton, Wash. BB/TR, 5'10", 160 lbs. Deb: 9/03/86

YEAR	TM/L	G	AB	R	H	2B	3B	HR	RBI	BB	SO	AVG	OBP	SLG	PRO+	BR	/A	RC	SB	CS	SBR	FR	POS	TPR
1986	KC-A	11	31	1	8	0	1	0	2	0	3	.258	.258	.323	56	-2	-2	3	0	0	0	4	2	0.2

■ ROY JOHNSON Johnson, Roy Cleveland b: 2/23/03, Pryor, Okla. d: 9/10/73, Tacoma, Wash. BL/TR, 5'9", 175 lbs. Deb: 4/18/29

YEAR	TM/L	G	AB	R	H	2B	3B	HR	RBI	BB	SO	AVG	OBP	SLG	PRO+	BR	/A	RC	SB	CS	SBR	FR	POS	TPR
1929	Det-A	148	640	128	201	45	14	10	69	67	60	.314	.379	.475	118	17	17	114	20	15	-3	14	*O	2.0
1930	Det-A	125	462	84	127	30	13	2	35	40	46	.275	.333	.409	85	-10	-11	63	17	10	-1	4	*O	-1.0
1931	Det-A	151	621	107	173	37	19	8	55	72	51	.279	.355	.438	104	6	3	96	33	21	-3	15	*O	0.6
1932	Det-A	49	195	33	49	14	2	3	22	20	26	.251	.324	.390	81	-5	-6	26	7	2	1	-3	O	-0.9
	Bos-A	94	349	70	104	24	4	11	47	44	41	.298	.378	.484	125	11	13	66	13	4	2	-6	O	0.5
	Yr	143	544	103	153	38	6	14	69	64	67	.281	.359	.450	109	6	7	91	20	6	2	-9		-0.4
1933	Bos-A	133	483	88	151	30	7	10	95	55	36	.313	.387	.466	126	18	19	88	13	10	-2	3	*O	1.4
1934	Bos-A	143	569	85	182	43	10	7	119	54	36	.320	.379	.467	109	14	8	102	11	5	0	-3	*O	0.3
1935	Bos-A	145	553	70	174	33	9	2	66	74	34	.315	.398	.423	105	13	7	95	11	12	-4	-0	*O	0.2
1936	*NY-A	63	147	21	39	8	2	1	19	21	14	.265	.361	.367	83	-4	-3	21	3	1	0	3	O	-0.4
1937	NY-A	12	51	5	15	3	0	0	6	3	2	.294	.333	.353	73	-2	-2	6	1	0	0	-3	O	-0.4
	Bos-N	85	260	24	72	8	3	3	22	38	29	.277	.369	.365	110	1	5	37	5			-4	O/3	-0.2
1938	Bos-N	7	29	2	5	0	0	1	1	5		.172	.294	.172	4	-4	-3	1	1			-2	/O	-0.5
Total	10	1155	4359	717	1292	275	83	58	556	489	380	.296	.369	.437	107	55	45	715	135	80		14	*O/3	1.6

■ ROY JOHNSON Johnson, Roy Edward b: 6/27/59, Parkin, Ark. BL/TL, 6'4", 205 lbs. Deb: 7/03/82

YEAR	TM/L	G	AB	R	H	2B	3B	HR	RBI	BB	SO	AVG	OBP	SLG	PRO+	BR	/A	RC	SB	CS	SBR	FR	POS	TPR
1982	Mon-N	17	32	2	7	2	0	0	2	1	6	.219	.242	.281	45	-2	-2	2	0	0	0	1	O	-0.1
1984	Mon-N	16	33	2	5	2	0	1	2	7	10	.152	.300	.303	73	-1	-1	4	1	0	0	-1	O	-0.1
1985	Mon-N	3	5	0	0	0	0	0	0	0	3	.000	.000	.000	-99	-1	-1	0	0	0	0	0	/O	0.0
Total	3	36	70	4	12	4	0	1	4	8	19	.171	.256	.271	49	-5	-5	6	1	0	0	-0	/O	-0.2

■ STAN JOHNSON Johnson, Stanley Lucius b: 2/12/37, Dallas, Tex. BL/TL, 5'10", 180 lbs. Deb: 9/18/60

YEAR	TM/L	G	AB	R	H	2B	3B	HR	RBI	BB	SO	AVG	OBP	SLG	PRO+	BR	/A	RC	SB	CS	SBR	FR	POS	TPR
1960	Chi-A	5	6	1	1	0	0	1	1	0	1	.167	.167	.667	116	0	0	0	0	1	-1	0	/O	0.0
1961	KC-A	3	3	1	0	0	0	0	0	2	1	.000	.400	.000	17	-0	-0	0	0	0	0	0	/O	0.0
Total	2	8	9	2	1	0	0	1	1	2	2	.111	.273	.444	90	-0	-0	0	0	1	-1	0	/O	0.0

■ TIM JOHNSON Johnson, Timothy Evald b: 7/22/49, Grand Forks, N.D. BL/TR, 6'1", 170 lbs. Deb: 4/24/73

YEAR	TM/L	G	AB	R	H	2B	3B	HR	RBI	BB	SO	AVG	OBP	SLG	PRO+	BR	/A	RC	SB	CS	SBR	FR	POS	TPR
1973	Mil-A	136	465	39	99	10	2	0	32	29	93	.213	.261	.243	44	-35	-34	30	6	3	0	-18	*S	-3.4
1974	Mil-A	93	245	25	60	7	7	0	25	11	48	.245	.280	.331	76	-8	-8	23	4	3	-1	-1	S2/30D	-0.3

YEAR	TM/L	G	AB	R	H	2B	3B	HR	RBI	BB	SO	AVG	OBP	SLG	PRO+	BR	/A	RC	SB	CS	SBR	FR	POS	TPR
1975	Mil-A	38	85	6	12	1	0	0	2	6	17	.141	.198	.153	0	-11	-11	3	3	0	1	1	23S/1D	-0.7
1976	Mil-A	105	273	25	75	4	3	0	14	19	32	.275	.327	.311	89	-4	-3	28	4	1	1	-18	*23/1S	-1.5
1977	Mil-A	30	33	5	2	1	0	0	2	5	10	.061	.184	.091	-22	-6	-6	1	1	0	0	3	2/S30D	0.0
1978	Mil-A	3	3	1	0	0	0	0	0	2	0	.000	.400	.000	22	-0	-0	0	0	0	0	-1	/S	0.0
	Tor-A	68	79	9	19	2	0	0	3	8	16	.241	.318	.266	65	-3	-3	7	0	1	-1	5	S2	0.6
	Yr	71	82	10	19	2	0	0	3	10	16	.232	.323	.256	63	-3	-4	8	0	1	-1	4		0.6
1979	Tor-A	43	86	6	16	2	1	0	6	8	15	.186	.255	.233	32	-8	-8	5	0	1	-1	5	2/31	-0.2
Total	7	516	1269	116	283	27	13	0	84	88	231	.223	.276	.265	55	-76	-74	98	18	9	0	-24	S2/1D0	-5.5

■ WALLACE JOHNSON

Johnson, Wallace Darnell b: 12/25/56, Gary, Ind. BB/TR, 6', 173 lbs. Deb: 9/08/81

YEAR	TM/L	G	AB	R	H	2B	3B	HR	RBI	BB	SO	AVG	OBP	SLG	PRO+	BR	/A	RC	SB	CS	SBR	FR	POS	TPR
1981	*Mon-N	11	9	1	2	0	1	0	3	1	1	.222	.300	.444	108	0	0	0	1	1	-0	1	/2	0.1
1982	Mon-N	36	57	5	11	0	2	0	2	5	5	.193	.258	.263	45	-4	-4	4	4	1	1	-6	2	-0.8
1983	Mon-N	3	2	1	1	0	0	0	0	1	0	.500	.667	.500	229	1	1	1	1	0	0	0	/H	0.1
	SF-N	7	8	0	1	0	0	0	1	0	0	.125	.125	.125	-32	-1	-1	0	0	0	0	1	/2	0.0
	Yr	10	10	1	2	0	0	0	1	1	0	.200	.273	.200	34	-1	-1	1	1	0	0	1		0.1
1984	Mon-N	17	24	3	5	0	0	0	4	5	4	.208	.345	.208	61	-1	-1	2	0	0	0	0	/1	0.0
1986	Mon-N	61	127	13	36	3	1	1	10	7	9	.283	.321	.346	85	-3	-3	14	6	3	0	-0	1	-0.3
1987	Mon-N	75	85	7	21	5	0	1	14	7	6	.247	.304	.341	69	-4	-4	10	5	0	2	-1	/1	-0.3
1988	Mon-N	86	94	7	29	5	1	0	3	12	15	.309	.387	.383	116	3	3	14	1	0	2	1	1/2	0.2
1989	Mon-N	85	114	9	31	3	1	2	17	7	12	.272	.314	.368	93	-1	-1	13	1	0	0	-1	1	-0.3
1990	Mon-N	47	49	6	8	1	0	1	5	7	6	.163	.281	.245	46	-4	-3	4	1	0	0	-1	/1	-0.4
Total	9	428	569	52	145	17	6	5	59	52	58	.255	.318	.332	80	-14	-15	63	19	7	2	-7	/12	-1.7

■ WALTER JOHNSON

Johnson, Walter Perry "Barney" or "The Big Train"
b: 11/6/1887, Humboldt, Kan. d: 12/10/46, Washington, D.C. BR/TR, 6'1", 200 lbs. Deb: 8/02/07 MH

YEAR	TM/L	G	AB	R	H	2B	3B	HR	RBI	BB	SO	AVG	OBP	SLG	PRO+	BR	/A	RC	SB	CS	SBR	FR	POS	TPR
1907	Was-A	14	36	3	4	0	0	0	1	1		.111	.135	.167	-3	-4	-4	1	0			-3	P	0.0
1908	Was-A	36	79	7	13	3	2	0	5	6		.165	.224	.253	62	-4	-3	5	0			-5	P	0.0
1909	Was-A	40	101	6	13	3	0	1	6	1		.129	.137	.188	3	-11	-11	2	0			-3	P	0.0
1910	Was-A	45	137	14	24	6	1	2	12	4		.175	.199	.277	51	-9	-8	7	2			-4	P	0.0
1911	Was-A	42	128	18	30	5	3	1	15	0		.234	.234	.344	62	-8	-7	10	1			3	P	0.0
1912	Was-A	55	144	16	38	6	4	2	20	7		.264	.298	.403	99	-1	-1	18	2			-1	P	0.0
1913	Was-A	54	134	12	35	5	6	2	14	5	14	.261	.293	.433	109	1	0	16	2			-2	P/O	0.0
1914	Was-A	55	136	23	30	4	1	3	16	10	27	.221	.274	.331	80	-4	-4	13	2	1	0	1	P/O	0.0
1915	Was-A	64	147	14	34	7	4	2	17	8	34	.231	.276	.374	94	-2	-2	15	0	2	-1	-0	P/O	0.0
1916	Was-A	58	142	13	32	2	4	1	7	11	28	.225	.286	.317	83	-4	-3	13	0			-6	P	0.0
1917	Was-A	57	130	15	33	12	1	0	15	9	30	.254	.312	.362	107	0	1	14	1			-1	P	0.0
1918	Was-A	65	150	10	40	4	4	1	18	9	18	.267	.321	.367	109	1	1	18	2			-4	P/O	0.0
1919	Was-A	56	125	13	24	1	3	1	8	12	17	.192	.263	.272	51	-8	-8	9	1			-1	P/O	0.0
1920	Was-A	33	64	6	17	1	3	1	7	3	10	.266	.299	.422	92	-1	-1	8	0	0	0	-2	P	0.0
1921	Was-A	38	111	10	30	7	0	0	10	6	14	.270	.308	.333	67	-6	-5	11	0	0	0	-4	P	0.0
1922	Was-A	43	108	8	22	3	0	1	15	2	12	.204	.218	.259	25	-12	-12	6	0	0	0	0	P	0.0
1923	Was-A	42	93	11	18	3	3	0	13	4	15	.194	.227	.290	37	-9	-8	6	0	0	0	-2	P	0.0
1924	*Was-A	39	113	18	32	9	0	1	14	3	11	.283	.308	.389	82	-4	-4	13	0	0	0	-2	P	0.0
1925	*Was-A	36	97	12	42	6	1	2	20	3	6	.433	.455	.577	164	9	9	24	0	1	-1	-4	P	0.0
1926	Was-A	35	103	6	20	5	0	1	12	3	11	.194	.217	.272	28	-11	-11	6	0	0	0	-5	P	0.0
1927	Was-A	26	46	6	16	2	0	2	10	3	4	.348	.388	.522	136	2	2	9	0	0	0	0	P	0.0
Total	21	933	2324	241	547	94	41	24	255	110	251	.235	.273	.342	76	-86	-80	228	13	4		-44	P/O	0.0

■ BILL JOHNSON

Johnson, William Lawrence b: 10/18/1892, Chicago, Ill. d: 11/3/50, Los Angeles, Cal. BL/TR, 5'11", 170 lbs. Deb: 9/22/16

YEAR	TM/L	G	AB	R	H	2B	3B	HR	RBI	BB	SO	AVG	OBP	SLG	PRO+	BR	/A	RC	SB	CS	SBR	FR	POS	TPR
1916	Phi-A	4	15	1	4	1	0	0	1	0	4	.267	.267	.333	84	-0	-0	1	0			-1	/O	-0.1
1917	Phi-A	48	109	7	19	2	2	1	8	8	14	.174	.237	.257	51	-7	-7	8	4			-3	O	-1.2
Total	2	52	124	8	23	3	2	1	9	8	18	.185	.241	.266	55	-7	-7	9	4			-4	/O	-1.3

■ BILL JOHNSON

Johnson, William Russell "Bull" b: 8/30/18, Montclair, N.J. BR/TR, 5'10", 180 lbs. Deb: 4/22/43

YEAR	TM/L	G	AB	R	H	2B	3B	HR	RBI	BB	SO	AVG	OBP	SLG	PRO+	BR	/A	RC	SB	CS	SBR	FR	POS	TPR
1943	*NY-A	155	592	70	166	24	6	5	94	53	30	.280	.344	.367	107	6	5	71	3	5	-2	12	*3	1.8
1946	NY-A	85	296	51	77	14	5	4	35	31	42	.260	.334	.382	98	-0	-1	40	1	0	0	7	3	1.3
1947	*NY-A	132	494	67	141	19	8	10	95	44	43	.285	.351	.417	114	8	8	69	1	2	-1	-17	*3	-0.6
1948	NY-A	127	446	59	131	20	6	12	64	41	30	.294	.358	.446	114	7	7	68	0	0	0	6	*3	0.9
1949	*NY-A	113	329	48	82	11	3	8	56	48	44	.249	.348	.374	91	-4	-4	43	1	0	0	-2	31/2	-0.5
1950	*NY-A	108	327	44	85	16	2	6	40	42	30	.260	.346	.376	87	-8	-6	43	1	0	0	-1	*3/1	-0.9
1951	NY-A	15	40	5	12	3	0	0	4	7	0	.300	.404	.375	116	1	1	6	0	1	-1	-3	*3	-0.2
	StL-N	124	442	52	116	23	1	14	64	46	49	.262	.340	.414	101	1	1	63	5	3	-0	11	*3	1.1
1952	StL-N	94	282	23	71	10	2	2	34	34	21	.252	.339	.323	84	-5	-5	32	1	0	0	2	3	0.0
1953	StL-N	11	5	0	1	1	0	0	1	1	1	.200	.333	.400	90	-0	-0	1	0	0	0	2	3	0.2
Total	9	964	3253	419	882	141	33	61	487	347	290	.271	.346	.391	102	5	6	437	13	11	-3	18	3/12	3.1

■ BILL JOHNSON

Johnson, William F. "Sleepy Bill" b: 9/1862, New Jersey d: 21, BL/TL, 140 lbs. Deb: 6/27/1884

YEAR	TM/L	G	AB	R	H	2B	3B	HR	RBI	BB	SO	AVG	OBP	SLG	PRO+	BR	/A	RC	SB	CS	SBR	FR	POS	TPR
1884	Phi-U	1	4	0	0	0	0	0		0		.000	.000	.000	-99	-1	-1	0	0			-0	/O	0.0
1887	Ind-N	11	42	3	8	0	0	0	3	0	6	.190	.209	.190	13	-5	-5	3	5			-2	O	-0.5
1890	Bal-a	24	95	15	28	2	3	0		7		.295	.350	.379	112	2	1	16	8			2	O	0.2
1891	Bal-a	129	480	101	130	13	14	2	79	89	55	.271	.389	.369	119	16	15	83	32			6	*O	1.3
1892	Bal-N	4	15	2	2	0	0	0	2	2	0	.133	.235	.133	13	-1	-2	0	0			-1	/O	-0.2
Total	5	169	636	121	168	15	17	2	84	98	61	.264	.368	.351	108	11	10	102	45			5	O	0.8

■ GREGORY JOHNSTON

Johnston, Gregory Bernard b: 2/12/55, Los Angeles, Cal. BL/TL, 6', 175 lbs. Deb: 7/27/79

YEAR	TM/L	G	AB	R	H	2B	3B	HR	RBI	BB	SO	AVG	OBP	SLG	PRO+	BR	/A	RC	SB	CS	SBR	FR	POS	TPR
1979	SF-N	42	74	5	15	2	0	1	7	2	17	.203	.224	.270	37	-7	-6	4	0	0	0	0	O	-0.6
1980	Min-A	14	27	3	5	3	0	0	1	2	4	.185	.241	.296	43	-2	-2	1	0	0	0	1	O	-0.1
1981	Min-A	7	16	2	2	0	0	0	0	2	5	.125	.222	.125	2	-2	-2	1	0	0	0	1	/O	0.0
Total	3	63	117	10	22	5	0	1	8	6	26	.188	.228	.256	33	-11	-11	6	0	0	0	2	/O	-0.7

■ JIMMY JOHNSTON

Johnston, James Harle b: 12/10/1889, Cleveland, Tenn. d: 2/14/67, Chattanooga, Tenn. BR/TR, 5'10", 160 lbs. Deb: 5/03/11 C

YEAR	TM/L	G	AB	R	H	2B	3B	HR	RBI	BB	SO	AVG	OBP	SLG	PRO+	BR	/A	RC	SB	CS	SBR	FR	POS	TPR
1911	Chi-A	1	2	0	0	0	0	0	2	0		.000	.000	.000	-99	-1	-1	0	0			-0	/O	0.0
1914	Chi-N	50	101	9	23	3	2	1	8	4	9	.228	.264	.327	76	-3	-3	9	3			8	O/2	0.4
1916	*Bro-N	118	425	58	107	13	8	1	26	35	38	.252	.313	.327	94	-1	-3	44	22	19	-5	8	*O	-0.2
1917	Bro-N	103	330	33	89	10	4	0	25	23	28	.270	.321	.324	96	-1	-2	39	16			1	O1/S23	-0.3
1918	Bro-N	123	484	54	136	16	8	0	27	33	31	.281	.328	.347	106	3	3	59	22			7	O1/32	0.5
1919	Bro-N	117	405	56	114	11	4	1	23	29	26	.281	.334	.336	100	1	0	48	11			-4	2O/1S	-0.1
1920	*Bro-N	155	635	87	185	17	12	1	52	43	23	.291	.338	.361	98	1	-2	77	19	15	-3	-5	*3/OS	-0.3
1921	Bro-N	152	624	104	203	41	14	5	56	45	26	.325	.372	.460	115	16	14	105	28	16	-1	8	*3/S	2.1
1922	Bro-N	138	567	110	181	20	7	4	49	38	17	.319	.364	.400	98	-2	-3	83	18	9	0	7	2S3	1.0
1923	Bro-N	151	625	111	203	29	11	4	60	53	15	.325	.378	.426	115	11	13	100	16	13	-3	20	2S3	3.4
1924	Bro-N	86	315	51	94	11	2	2	29	27	10	.298	.356	.365	97	-2	-1	41	5	6	-2	-3	S3/1O	0.0
1925	Bro-N	123	431	63	128	13	3	2	43	45	15	.297	.369	.355	88	-7	-6	59	7	5	-1	-22	3O/1S	-2.3
1926	Bos-N	23	57	7	14	1	0	1	5	10	3	.246	.358	.316	91	-1	-0	7	2			-3	3/2O	-0.2

YEAR	TM/L	G	AB	R	H	2B	3B	HR	RBI	BB	SO	AVG	OBP	SLG	PRO+	BR	/A	RC	SB	CS	SBR	FR	POS	TPR
	NY-N	37	69	11	16	0	0	0	5	6	5	.232	.293	.232	43	-5	-5	5	0			-4	O	-0.9
	Yr	60	126	18	30	1	0	1	10	16	8	.238	.324	.270	64	-6	-6	11	2			-7		-1.1
Total	13	1377	5070	754	1493	185	75	22	410	391	246	.294	.347	.374	100	9	8	676	169	83		16	302S/1	3.1

■ JOHNNY JOHNSTON   Johnston, John Thomas b: 3/28/1890, Longview, Tex. d: 3/7/40, San Diego, Cal. BL/TR, 5'11", 172 lbs. Deb: 4/10/13

YEAR	TM/L	G	AB	R	H	2B	3B	HR	RBI	BB	SO	AVG	OBP	SLG	PRO+	BR	/A	RC	SB	CS	SBR	FR	POS	TPR
1913	StL-A	111	380	37	85	14	4	2	27	42	51	.224	.308	.297	79	-11	-9	38	11			12	*O	-0.2

■ REX JOHNSTON   Johnston, Rex David b: 11/8/37, Colton, Cal. BB/TR, 6'1.5", 202 lbs. Deb: 4/15/64

YEAR	TM/L	G	AB	R	H	2B	3B	HR	RBI	BB	SO	AVG	OBP	SLG	PRO+	BR	/A	RC	SB	CS	SBR	FR	POS	TPR
1964	Pit-N	14	7	1	0	0	0	0	0	3	0	.000	.300	.000	-7	-1	-1	0	0	0	0	0	/O	0.0

■ DICK JOHNSTON   Johnston, Richard Frederick b: 4/6/1863, Kingston, N.Y. d: 4/4/34, Detroit, Mich. BR/TR, 5'8", 155 lbs. Deb: 8/12/1884

YEAR	TM/L	G	AB	R	H	2B	3B	HR	RBI	BB	SO	AVG	OBP	SLG	PRO+	BR	/A	RC	SB	CS	SBR	FR	POS	TPR
1884	Ric-a	39	146	23	41	5	5	2		2		.281	.291	.425	135	5	5	18				9	O/S	1.2
1885	Bos-N	26	111	17	26	6	3	1	23	0	15	.234	.234	.369	96	-1	-1	10				1	O	0.0
1886	Bos-N	109	413	48	99	18	9	1	57	3	70	.240	.245	.334	78	-13	-11	37	11			15	*O	0.5
1887	Bos-N	127	507	87	131	13	20	5	77	16	35	.258	.281	.393	86	-10	-10	72	52			22	*O	1.0
1888	Bos-N	135	585	102	173	31	18	12	68	15	33	.296	.314	.472	148	30	29	100	35			5	*O	3.2
1889	Bos-N	132	539	80	123	16	4	5	67	41	60	.228	.285	.301	61	-25	-31	57	34			-8	*O	-3.7
1890	Bos-P	2	9	0	1	0	0	0	0	0	1	.111	.111	.111	-37	-2	-2	0	0			0	/O	-0.1
	NY-P	77	306	37	74	9	7	1	43	18	25	.242	.288	.327	60	-16	-20	32	7			3	O/S	-1.6
	Yr	79	315	37	75	9	7	1	43	18	26	.238	.284	.321	58	-17	-22	31	7			3		-1.7
1891	Cin-a	99	376	59	83	11	2	6	51	38	44	.221	.301	.309	71	-11	-17	39	12			-1	*O	-1.8
Total	8	746	2992	453	751	109	68	33	386	133	283	.251	.285	.366	88	-44	-58	367	151			46	O/S	-1.3

■ DOC JOHNSTON   Johnston, Wheeler Roger b: 9/9/1887, Cleveland, Tenn. d: 2/17/61, Chattanooga, Tenn. BL/TL, 6', 170 lbs. Deb: 10/03/09

YEAR	TM/L	G	AB	R	H	2B	3B	HR	RBI	BB	SO	AVG	OBP	SLG	PRO+	BR	/A	RC	SB	CS	SBR	FR	POS	TPR
1909	Cin-N	3	10	1	0	0	0	0	1	0		.000	.000	.000	-99	-2	-2	-0	0			0	/1	-0.1
1912	Cle-A	43	164	22	46	7	4	1	11	11		.280	.326	.390	101	0	-0	23	8			-2	1	-0.1
1913	Cle-A	133	530	74	135	19	12	2	39	35	65	.255	.309	.347	89	-7	-9	60	19			-1	*1	-0.9
1914	Cle-A	103	340	43	83	15	1	0	23	28	46	.244	.311	.294	79	-7	-9	34	14	9	-1	-7	1/O	-1.8
1915	Pit-N	147	543	71	144	19	12	5	64	38	40	.265	.328	.372	113	7	8	72	26	17	-2	-12	*1	-1.4
1916	Pit-N	114	404	33	86	10	10	0	39	20	42	.213	.262	.287	68	-15	-16	37	17			-2	*1	-2.5
1918	Cle-A	74	273	30	62	12	2	0	25	26	19	.227	.301	.286	70	-8	-10	27	12			-3	1	-1.9
1919	Cle-A	102	331	42	101	17	3	1	33	25	18	.305	.359	.384	102	4	1	53	21			-3	1	-0.9
1920	*Cle-A	147	535	68	156	24	10	2	71	28	32	.292	.333	.385	87	-9	-11	69	13	6	0	-1	*1	-1.0
1921	Cle-A	118	384	53	114	20	7	2	46	29	15	.297	.353	.401	90	-5	-6	53	2	9	-5	-1	*1	-1.1
1922	Phi-A	71	260	41	65	11	7	1	29	24	15	.250	.316	.358	73	-10	-11	30	7	6	-2	-5	1	-2.1
Total	11	1055	3774	478	992	154	68	14	381	264	292	.263	.319	.351	88	-51	-65	457	139	47		-36	*1/O	-13.8

■ FRED JOHNSTON   Johnston, Wilfred Ivy b: 7/9/1900, Pineville, N.C. d: 7/14/59, Tyler, Tex. BR/TR, 5'11.5", 170 lbs. Deb: 6/29/24

YEAR	TM/L	G	AB	R	H	2B	3B	HR	RBI	BB	SO	AVG	OBP	SLG	PRO+	BR	/A	RC	SB	CS	SBR	FR	POS	TPR
1924	Bro-N	4	4	1	1	0	0	0	0	0	1	.250	.250	.250	35	-0	-0	0	0	0	0	0	/23	0.0

■ JAY JOHNSTONE   Johnstone, John William b: 11/20/45, Manchester, Conn. BL/TR, 6'1", 175 lbs. Deb: 7/30/66

YEAR	TM/L	G	AB	R	H	2B	3B	HR	RBI	BB	SO	AVG	OBP	SLG	PRO+	BR	/A	RC	SB	CS	SBR	FR	POS	TPR
1966	Cal-A	61	254	35	67	12	4	3	17	11	36	.264	.297	.378	95	-3	-2	28	3	3	-1	-5	O	-1.0
1967	Cal-A	79	230	18	48	7	1	2	10	5	37	.209	.226	.274	49	-16	-15	13	3	2	-0	6	O	-1.1
1968	Cal-A	41	115	11	30	4	1	0	3	7	15	.261	.303	.313	90	-2	-1	12	2	1	0	3	O	0.0
1969	Cal-A	148	540	64	146	20	5	10	59	38	75	.270	.324	.381	102	-3	-3	65	3	9	-5	5	*O	-0.2
1970	Cal-A	119	320	34	76	10	5	11	39	24	53	.237	.293	.403	93	-5	-4	37	1	0	0	-5	*O	-1.2
1971	Chi-A	124	388	53	101	14	1	16	40	38	50	.260	.331	.425	109	6	4	56	10	5	0	-4	O	-0.3
1972	Chi-A	113	261	27	49	9	0	4	17	25	42	.188	.259	.268	56	-14	-14	19	2	1	0	5	O	-1.3
1973	Oak-A	23	28	1	3	1	0	0	3	2	4	.107	.167	.143	-13	-4	-4	1	0	1	-1	-0	/O2D	-0.4
1974	Phi-N	64	200	30	59	10	4	6	30	24	28	.295	.371	.475	130	9	8	35	5	5	-2	-5	O	0.9
1975	Phi-N	122	350	50	115	19	2	7	54	42	39	.329	.401	.454	132	18	16	64	7	3	0	-4	*O	0.9
1976	*Phi-N	129	440	62	140	38	4	5	53	41	39	.318	.379	.457	132	21	19	75	5	5	-2	6	*O/1	2.0
1977	*Phi-N	112	363	64	103	18	4	15	59	38	38	.284	.355	.479	116	11	8	59	3	7	-3	0	O1	0.1
1978	Phi-N	35	56	3	10	2	0	0	4	6	9	.179	.258	.214	33	-5	-5	3	0	2	-1	1	/1O	-0.5
	*NY-A	36	65	6	17	0	0	1	6	4	1	.262	.333	.308	83	-1	-1	7	0	1	-1	0	O/D	-0.1
1979	NY-A	23	48	7	10	1	0	1	7	2	7	.208	.240	.292	44	-4	-4	4	1	0	0	1	O	-0.3
	SD-N	75	201	10	59	8	2	0	32	18	21	.294	.352	.353	99	-2	-0	24	1	3	-2	-1	O1	-0.4
1980	LA-N	109	251	31	77	15	2	2	20	24	29	.307	.372	.406	119	6	7	39	3	2	-0	0	O	0.4
1981	*LA-N	61	83	8	17	3	0	3	6	7	13	.205	.267	.349	76	-3	-3	7	0	1	-1	1	O/1	-0.2
1982	LA-N	21	13	1	1	1	0	0	2	5	2	.077	.333	.154	41	-1	-1	1	0	0	0	0	H	0.0
	Chi-N	98	269	39	67	13	1	10	43	40	41	.249	.346	.416	109	5	4	40	0	2	-1	1	O	0.3
	Yr	119	282	40	68	14	1	10	45	45	43	.241	.346	.404	107	4	3	41	0	2	-1	1		0.3
1983	Chi-N	86	140	16	36	7	0	6	22	20	24	.257	.362	.436	115	4	3	22	1	1	-0	1	O	0.1
1984	Chi-N	52	73	8	21	2	2	0	3	7	18	.288	.350	.370	94	0	-0	9	0	0	0	-2	O	-0.2
1985	*LA-N	17	15	0	2	1	0	0	2	1	2	.133	.188	.200	9	-2	-2	0	0	0	0	0	H	-0.1
Total	20	1748	4703	578	1254	215	38	102	531	429	623	.267	.331	.394	103	15	14	618	50	54	-17	3	*O/1D2	-3.5

■ STAN JOK   Jok, Stanley Edward "Tucker" b: 5/3/26, Buffalo, N.Y. d: 3/6/72, Buffalo, N.Y. BR/TR, 6', 190 lbs. Deb: 4/13/54

YEAR	TM/L	G	AB	R	H	2B	3B	HR	RBI	BB	SO	AVG	OBP	SLG	PRO+	BR	/A	RC	SB	CS	SBR	FR	POS	TPR
1954	Phi-N	3	3	0	0	0	0	0	0	0	2	.000	.000	.000	-99	-1	-1	0	0	0	0	0	H	0.0
	Chi-A	3	12	1	2	0	0	0	2	1	2	.167	.231	.167	10	-1	-2	0	0	0	0	0	/3	-0.1
1955	Chi-A	6	4	3	1	0	0	1	2	1	1	.250	.400	1.000	260	1	1	2	0	0	0	1	/3O	0.2
Total	2	12	19	4	3	0	0	1	4	2	5	.158	.238	.316	47	-1	-2	2	0	0	0	1	/3O	0.1

■ SMEAD JOLLEY   Jolley, Smead Powell "Guinea" or "Smudge" b: 1/14/02, Wesson, Ark. BL/TR, 6'3.5", 210 lbs. Deb: 4/17/30

YEAR	TM/L	G	AB	R	H	2B	3B	HR	RBI	BB	SO	AVG	OBP	SLG	PRO+	BR	/A	RC	SB	CS	SBR	FR	POS	TPR
1930	Chi-A	152	616	76	193	38	12	16	114	28	52	.313	.346	.492	114	7	10	103	3	1	0	-3	*O	0.1
1931	Chi-A	54	110	5	33	11	0	3	28	7	4	.300	.353	.482	125	2	3	19	0	0	0	-5	O	-0.2
1932	Chi-A	12	42	3	15	3	0	0	7	3	0	.357	.413	.429	127	1	2	8	1	0	0	-3	O	0.0
	Bos-A	137	531	57	164	27	5	18	99	27	29	.309	.345	.480	115	7	9	85	0	5	-3	-7	*O/C	-0.5
	Yr	149	573	60	179	30	5	18	106	30	29	.312	.350	.476	116	8	10	93	1	5	-3	-10		-0.5
1933	Bos-A	118	411	47	116	32	4	9	65	24	20	.282	.325	.445	103	-1	0	59	1	1	-0	-6	*O	-0.8
Total	4	473	1710	188	521	111	21	46	313	89	105	.305	.343	.475	112	17	24	274	5	7	-3	-23	O/C	-1.4

■ JONES   Jones   Deb: 5/14/1873

YEAR	TM/L	G	AB	R	H	2B	3B	HR	RBI	BB	SO	AVG	OBP	SLG	PRO+	BR	/A	RC	SB	CS	SBR	FR	POS	TPR
1873	Mar-n	1	4	0	3	1	0	0		0		.750	.750	1.000	534	1	2	3					/O	0.1
1874	Bal-n	2	7	0	1	0	0	0		0		.143	.143	.143	-9	-1	-1	0					/CO	0.0
Total	2 n	3	11	0	4	1	0	0		0		.364	.364	.455	166	1	1	3					/OC	0.1

■ JONES   Jones b: Johnstown, Pa. Deb: 7/14/1884

YEAR	TM/L	G	AB	R	H	2B	3B	HR	RBI	BB	SO	AVG	OBP	SLG	PRO+	BR	/A	RC	SB	CS	SBR	FR	POS	TPR
1884	Was-a	4	17	2	5	0	0	0		1		.294	.333	.294	124	0	0	2				0	/O	0.0

■ CHARLIE JONES   Jones, Charles C. "Casey" b: 6/2/1876, Butler, Pa. d: 4/2/47, Two Harbors, Minn. BR/TR, 6'1", Deb: 5/03/01

YEAR	TM/L	G	AB	R	H	2B	3B	HR	RBI	BB	SO	AVG	OBP	SLG	PRO+	BR	/A	RC	SB	CS	SBR	FR	POS	TPR
1901	Bos-A	10	41	6	6	2	0	0	6	1		.146	.167	.195	1	-5	-5	2	2			-2	O	-0.6
1904	Chi-A	5	17	2	4	0	1	0	1	1		.235	.278	.353	105	-0	0	2	0			1	/O	0.1
1905	Was-A	142	544	68	113	18	4	2	41	31		.208	.250	.267	68	-21	-19	44	24			16	*O	-0.9
1906	Was-A	131	497	56	120	11	11	3	42	24		.241	.276	.326	95	-7	-4	57	34			8	*O/2	0.0

YEAR	TM/L	G	AB	R	H	2B	3B	HR	RBI	BB	SO	AVG	OBP	SLG	PRO+	BR	/A	RC	SB	CS	SBR	FR	POS	TPR
1907	Was-A	121	437	48	116	14	10	0	37	22		.265	.301	.343	116	3	6	56	26			-1	*O/21S	0.0
1908	StL-A	74	263	37	61	11	2	0	17	14		.232	.271	.289	83	-5	-5	24	14			-1	O	-1.0
Total	6	483	1799	217	420	56	28	5	144	93		.233	.271	.304	88	-35	-26	185	100			21	O/21S	-2.4

■ CHARLIE JONES
Jones, Charles F. b: New York, N.Y. Deb: 6/28/1884

YEAR	TM/L	G	AB	R	H	2B	3B	HR	RBI	BB	SO	AVG	OBP	SLG	PRO+	BR	/A	RC	SB	CS	SBR	FR	POS	TPR
1884	Bro-a	25	90	10	16	1	0	0		5		.178	.221	.189	37	-6	-6	4				-7	23/O	-1.1
1885	NY-a	1	4	0	1	0	0	0		0		.250	.250	.250	66	-0	-0	0				1	/3	0.1
Total	2	26	94	10	17	1	0	0		5		.181	.222	.191	38	-6	-6	4				-6	/23O	-1.0

■ CHARLEY JONES
Jones, Charles Wesley "Baby" (b: Benjamin Wesley Rippay) b: 4/30/1850, Alamance Co., N.C. BR/TR, 5'11.5", 202 lbs. Deb: 5/04/1875 U

YEAR	TM/L	G	AB	R	H	2B	3B	HR	RBI	BB	SO	AVG	OBP	SLG	PRO+	BR	/A	RC	SB	CS	SBR	FR	POS	TPR
1875	Wes-n	12	47	5	13	2	4	0		0		.277	.277	.489	151	3	2	7					O	0.2
	Har-n	1	4	1	0	0	0	0		0		.000	.000	.000	-95	-1	-1	0					/O	0.0
	Yr	13	51	6	13	2	4	0		0		.255	.255	.451	132	2	1	6					O	0.2
1876	Cin-N	64	276	40	79	17	4	4	38	7	17	.286	.304	.420	162	11	17	36				1	*O	1.5
1877	Cin-N	17	69	16	21	3	3	1	10	4	8	.304	.342	.478	175	4	6	12				1	1/O	0.5
	Chi-N	2	8	1	3	1	0	0	2	1	0	.375	.444	.500	176	1	1	2				1	/O	0.1
	Cin-N	38	163	36	51	8	7	1	26	10	17	.313	.353	.466	175	10	13	27				10	O	1.9
	Yr	57	240	53	75	12	10	2	38	15	25	.313	.353	.471	175	16	19	41				12		**2.5**
1878	Cin-N	61	261	50	81	11	7	3	39	4	17	.310	.321	.441	163	13	16	38				6	*O	1.6
1879	Bos-N	83	355	**85**	112	22	10	9	**62**	**29**	38	.315	.367	.510	181	33	32	68				12	*O	3.7
1880	Bos-N	66	280	44	84	15	3	5	37	11	27	.300	.326	.429	159	15	16	40				-5	*O	0.9
1883	Cin-a	90	391	84	115	15	12	10	20			.294	.328	.471	145	23	19	62				2	*O	1.9
1884	Cin-a	112	472	117	148	19	17	7	37			.314	**.376**	.470	170	40	37	85				3	*O	3.5
1885	Cin-a	112	487	108	157	19	17	5	21			.322	.362	.462	159	31	32	83				12	*O	3.3
1886	Cin-a	127	500	87	135	22	10	6	61			.270	.356	.390	132	22	20	72	3			3	*O	1.6
1887	Cin-a	41	153	28	48	7	4	2	19			.314	.400	.451	137	9	8	31	7			-0	O	0.5
	NY-a	62	247	30	63	11	3	3	12			.255	.306	.360	91	-5	-3	30	8			4	O/P1	0.5
	Yr	103	400	58	111	18	7	5	31			.278	.343	.395	110	4	6	61	15			4		0.5
1888	KC-a	6	25	2	4	0	1	0	5	1		.160	.192	.240	38	-2	-2	1	1			-1	/O	-0.2
Total	11	881	3687	728	1101	170	98	56	219	237	124	.299	.347	.443	152	208	212	589	19			49	O/1P	20.8

■ CHRIS JONES
Jones, Christopher Dale b: 7/13/57, Los Angeles, Cal. BL/TL, 6', 183 lbs. Deb: 6/08/85

YEAR	TM/L	G	AB	R	H	2B	3B	HR	RBI	BB	SO	AVG	OBP	SLG	PRO+	BR	/A	RC	SB	CS	SBR	FR	POS	TPR
1985	Hou-N	31	25	0	5	0	0	0	1	3	7	.200	.286	.200	39	-2	-2	2	0	0	0	2	O	0.0
1986	SF-N	3	1	0	0	0	0	0	0	0	0	.000	.000	.000	-99	-0	-0	0	1	0	0	0	/H	0.0
Total	2	34	26	0	5	0	0	0	1	3	7	.192	.276	.192	34	-2	-2	2	1	0	0	2	/O	0.0

■ CLARENCE JONES
Jones, Clarence Woodrow b: 11/7/41, Zanesville, Ohio BL/TL, 6'2", 185 lbs. Deb: 4/20/67 C

YEAR	TM/L	G	AB	R	H	2B	3B	HR	RBI	BB	SO	AVG	OBP	SLG	PRO+	BR	/A	RC	SB	CS	SBR	FR	POS	TPR
1967	Chi-N	53	135	13	34	7	0	2	16	14	33	.252	.322	.348	88	-1	-2	16	0	0	0	-4	O1	-0.7
1968	Chi-N	5	2	0	0	0	0	0	0	2	1	.000	.500	.000	56	0	0	0	0	0	0	0	/1	0.0
Total	2	58	137	13	34	7	0	2	16	16	34	.248	.327	.343	88	-1	-2	16	0	0	0	-4	/O1	-0.7

■ CLEON JONES
Jones, Cleon Joseph b: 8/4/42, Plateau, Ala. BR/TL, 6', 185 lbs. Deb: 9/14/63

YEAR	TM/L	G	AB	R	H	2B	3B	HR	RBI	BB	SO	AVG	OBP	SLG	PRO+	BR	/A	RC	SB	CS	SBR	FR	POS	TPR
1963	NY-N	6	15	1	2	0	0	0	1	0	4	.133	.133	.133	-23	-2	-2	0	0	0	0	-0	/O	-0.2
1965	NY-N	30	74	2	11	1	0	1	9	2	23	.149	.171	.203	5	-9	-9	3	1	0	0	1	O	-0.8
1966	NY-N	139	495	74	136	16	4	8	57	30	62	.275	.320	.372	94	-6	-4	57	16	8	0	-3	*O	-1.0
1967	NY-N	129	411	46	101	10	5	5	30	19	57	.246	.286	.331	77	-13	-12	39	12	2	2	-6	*O	-2.3
1968	NY-N	147	509	63	151	29	4	14	55	31	98	.297	.343	.452	136	22	21	77	23	12	-0	-7	*O	0.8
1969	*NY-N	137	483	92	164	25	4	12	75	64	60	.340	.424	.482	150	37	36	100	16	8	0	-0	*O1	2.8
1970	NY-N	134	506	71	140	25	8	10	63	57	87	.277	.356	.417	106	5	5	71	12	3	2	5	*O	0.5
1971	NY-N	136	505	63	161	24	6	14	69	53	87	.319	.386	.473	144	28	29	92	6	5	-1	-1	*O	2.4
1972	NY-N	106	375	39	92	15	1	5	52	30	83	.245	.308	.331	84	-9	-8	36	1	6	-3	0	O1	-1.7
1973	*NY-N	92	339	48	88	13	0	11	48	28	51	.260	.322	.395	99	-2	-1	41	1	1	-0	-1	O	-0.6
1974	NY-N	124	461	62	130	23	1	13	60	38	79	.282	.345	.421	115	7	8	66	3	3	-1	-2	*O	0.1
1975	NY-N	21	50	2	12	1	0	0	2	3	6	.240	.283	.260	54	-3	-3	4	0	0	0	-3	O	-0.6
1976	Chi-A	12	40	2	8	1	0	0	3	5	5	.200	.304	.225	56	-2	-2	3	0	0	0	-2	/OD	-0.3
Total	13	1213	4263	565	1196	183	33	93	524	360	702	.281	.342	.404	111	53	57	589	91	48	-2	-18	*O/1D	-0.9

■ COBE JONES
Jones, Coburn Dyas b: 8/21/07, Denver, Colo. d: 6/3/69, Denver, Colo. BB/TR, 5'7", 155 lbs. Deb: 9/27/28

YEAR	TM/L	G	AB	R	H	2B	3B	HR	RBI	BB	SO	AVG	OBP	SLG	PRO+	BR	/A	RC	SB	CS	SBR	FR	POS	TPR
1928	Pit-N	1	2	0	1	0	0	0	0	0	0	.500	.500	.500	156	0	0	0	0			-0	/S	0.0
1929	Pit-N	25	63	6	16	5	1	0	4	1	5	.254	.266	.365	53	-5	-5	6	1			-8	S	-0.9
Total	2	26	65	6	17	5	1	0	4	1	5	.262	.273	.369	56	-5	-5	6	1			-8	/S	-0.9

■ DARRYL JONES
Jones, Darryl Lee b: 6/5/51, Meadville, Pa. BR/TR, 5'10", 175 lbs. Deb: 6/06/79

YEAR	TM/L	G	AB	R	H	2B	3B	HR	RBI	BB	SO	AVG	OBP	SLG	PRO+	BR	/A	RC	SB	CS	SBR	FR	POS	TPR
1979	NY-A	18	47	6	12	5	1	0	6	2	7	.255	.286	.404	86	-1	-1	5	0	0	0	0	D/O	0.0

■ DAVY JONES
Jones, David Jefferson "Kangaroo" b: 6/30/1880, Cambria, Wis. d: 3/31/72, Mankato, Minn. BL/TR, 5'10", 165 lbs. Deb: 9/15/01

YEAR	TM/L	G	AB	R	H	2B	3B	HR	RBI	BB	SO	AVG	OBP	SLG	PRO+	BR	/A	RC	SB	CS	SBR	FR	POS	TPR
1901	Mil-A	14	52	12	9	0	0	3	5	11		.173	.328	.346	94	-0	-0	7	4			1	O	0.1
1902	StL-A	15	49	4	11	1	1	0	3	6		.224	.321	.286	72	-2	-2	6	5			5	O	0.2
	Chi-N	64	243	41	74	12	3	0	14	38		.305	.399	.379	147	14	15	44	12			-1	O	1.0
1903	Chi-N	130	497	64	140	18	3	1	62	53		.282	.351	.336	101	0	2	67	15			0	*O	-0.4
1904	Chi-N	98	336	44	82	11	5	3	39	41		.244	.326	.333	106	3	3	43	14			-10	O	-1.0
1906	Det-A	84	323	41	84	12	2	0	24	41		.260	.343	.310	104	4	3	43	21			4	O	0.5
1907	*Det-A	126	491	101	134	10	6	0	27	60		.273	.352	.318	112	11	9	69	30			13	*O	1.7
1908	*Det-A	56	121	17	25	2	1	0	10	13		.207	.284	.240	70	-3	-4	11	11			2	O	-0.3
1909	*Det-A	69	204	44	57	2	2	0	10	28		.279	.369	.309	110	5	4	28	12			-2	O	0.0
1910	Det-A	113	377	77	100	6	6	0	24	51		.265	.362	.313	104	7	4	52	25			1	*O	0.1
1911	Det-A	98	341	78	93	10	2	0	19	41		.273	.354	.302	80	-6	-8	45	25			-1	O	-1.6
1912	Det-A	99	316	54	93	5	2	0	24	38		.294	.370	.323	102	1	2	44	16			-1	O	-0.3
1913	Chi-A	12	21	2	6	0	0	0	0	9		.286	.500	.286	132	2	2	1	1			-1	/O	0.1
1914	Pit-F	97	352	58	96	9	8	2	24	42	16	.273	.355	.361	106	4	4	54	15			8	O	0.7
1915	Pit-F	14	49	6	16	0	1	0	4	6	0	.327	.400	.367	129	2	2	8	1			-1	O	0.1
Total	14	1089	3772	643	1020	98	40	9	289	478	16	.270	.355	.325	104	43	38	524	207			18	*O	0.9

■ FIELDER JONES
Jones, Fielder Allison b: 8/13/1871, Shinglehouse, Pa. d: 3/13/34, Portland, Ore. BL/TR, 5'11", 180 lbs. Deb: 4/18/1896 M

YEAR	TM/L	G	AB	R	H	2B	3B	HR	RBI	BB	SO	AVG	OBP	SLG	PRO+	BR	/A	RC	SB	CS	SBR	FR	POS	TPR
1896	Bro-N	104	395	82	140	10	8	3	46	48	15	.354	.427	.443	140	20	24	84	18			-4	*O	1.1
1897	Bro-N	135	548	134	172	15	10	1	49	61		.314	.392	.383	114	9	14	104	48			4	*O	0.7
1898	Bro-N	146	596	89	181	15	9	1	69	46		.304	.362	.364	111	9	10	94	36			-7	*O/S	-0.5
1899	Bro-N	102	365	75	104	8	2	2	38	54		.285	.390	.334	100	5	3	56	18			-3	O	-0.5
1900	*Bro-N	136	552	106	171	26	4	4	54	57		.310	.378	.393	109	13	9	97	33			0	*O	0.1
1901	Chi-A	133	521	120	162	16	3	2	65	84		.311	.411	.365	122	19	21	99	38			1	*O	1.8
1902	Chi-A	135	532	98	171	16	5	0	54	57		.321	.394	.370	120	14	17	96	33			13	*O	2.0
1903	Chi-A	136	530	71	152	18	5	0	47	45		.287	.345	.340	113	7	10	74	21			0	*O	0.1
1904	Chi-A	149	547	72	133	14	5	3	42	53		.243	.310	.303	100	-1	2	65	25			5	*OM	-0.2
1905	Chi-A	153	568	91	139	17	12	2	38	73		.245	.331	.327	116	9	12	72	20			7	*OM	1.3
1906	*Chi-A	144	496	77	114	22	4	2	34	83		.230	.340	.302	106	6	8	66	26			8	*OM	1.1

YEAR	TM/L	G	AB	R	H	2B	3B	HR	RBI	BB	SO	AVG	OBP	SLG	PRO+	BR	/A	RC	SB	CS	SBR	FR	POS	TPR
1907	Chi-A	154	559	72	146	18	1	0	47	67		.261	.340	.297	109	6	9	69	17			2	*OM	0.2
1908	Chi-A	149	529	92	134	11	7	1	50	86		.253	.358	.306	121	15	16	70	26			-1	*OM	0.8
1914	StL-F	5	3	0	1	0	0	0	0	1	0	.333	.500	.333	134	0	0	1	0			0	HM	0.0
1915	StL-F	7	6	1	0	0	0	0	0	0	0	.000	.000	.000	-95	-1	-1	0	0			-1	/OM	-0.2
Total	15	1788	6747	1180	1920	206	75	21	631	817	15	.285	.366	.347	114	130	152	1045	359			25	*O/S	7.5

■ FRANK JONES
Jones, Frank M. b: 8/25/1858, Princeton, Ill. d: 2/4/36, Marietta, Ohio   Deb: 7/02/1884

YEAR	TM/L	G	AB	R	H	2B	3B	HR	RBI	BB	SO	AVG	OBP	SLG	PRO+	BR	/A	RC	SB	CS	SBR	FR	POS	TPR
1884	Det-N	2	6	1	2	0	0	0	0	0	0	.333	.333	.333	117	0	0	1				0	/SO	0.0

■ DEACON JONES
Jones, Grover William b: 4/18/34, White Plains, N.Y. BL/TR, 5'10", 185 lbs.   Deb: 9/08/62 C

YEAR	TM/L	G	AB	R	H	2B	3B	HR	RBI	BB	SO	AVG	OBP	SLG	PRO+	BR	/A	RC	SB	CS	SBR	FR	POS	TPR
1962	Chi-A	18	28	3	9	2	0	0	8	4	6	.321	.406	.393	117	1	1	5	0	0	0	-0	/1	0.0
1963	Chi-A	17	16	4	3	0	1	1	2	2	2	.188	.316	.500	127	0	1	2	0	0	0	0	/1	0.1
1966	Chi-A	5	5	0	2	0	0	0	0	0	0	.400	.400	.400	140	0	0	1	0	0	0	0	H	0.0
Total	3	40	49	7	14	2	1	1	10	6	8	.286	.375	.429	122	2	2	8	0	0	0	0	/1	0.1

■ HAL JONES
Jones, Harold Marion b: 4/9/36, Louisiana, Mo. BR/TR, 6'2", 194 lbs. Deb: 9/15/61

YEAR	TM/L	G	AB	R	H	2B	3B	HR	RBI	BB	SO	AVG	OBP	SLG	PRO+	BR	/A	RC	SB	CS	SBR	FR	POS	TPR
1961	Cle-A	12	35	2	6	0	0	2	4	2	12	.171	.216	.343	48	-3	-3	2	0	0	0	-1	1	-0.4
1962	Cle-A	5	16	2	5	1	0	0	1	0	4	.313	.353	.375	99	-0	-0	2	0	0	0	0	/1	0.0
Total	2	17	51	4	11	1	0	2	5	2	16	.216	.259	.353	64	-3	-3	5	0	0	0	-1	/1	-0.4

■ HENRY JONES
Jones, Henry M. "Baldy" b: Cadillac, Mich.   Deb: 8/20/1884

YEAR	TM/L	G	AB	R	H	2B	3B	HR	RBI	BB	SO	AVG	OBP	SLG	PRO+	BR	/A	RC	SB	CS	SBR	FR	POS	TPR
1884	Det-N	34	129	23	27	3	1	0	3	16	19	.209	.297	.248	78	-3	-2	10				-2	2O/S	-0.2
1890	Pit-N	5	9	0	2	0	0	0	0	0	0	.222	.222	.222	35	-1	-1	1	1			-1	/P	0.0
Total	2	39	138	23	29	3	1	0	3	16	19	.210	.292	.246	75	-4	-3	10	1			-2	/2OSP	-0.2

■ HOWIE JONES
Jones, Howard "Cotton" (b: Howard Painter) b: 3/1/1897, Irwin, Pa. d: 7/15/72, Jeanette, Pa. BL/TL, 5'11", 165 lbs. Deb: 9/05/21

YEAR	TM/L	G	AB	R	H	2B	3B	HR	RBI	BB	SO	AVG	OBP	SLG	PRO+	BR	/A	RC	SB	CS	SBR	FR	POS	TPR
1921	StL-N	3	2	0	0	0	0	0	0	0	1	.000	.000	.000	-99	-1	-1	0	0	0	0	0	/O	0.0

■ DALTON JONES
Jones, James Dalton b: 12/10/43, McComb, Miss. BL/TR, 6'1", 180 lbs. Deb: 4/17/64

YEAR	TM/L	G	AB	R	H	2B	3B	HR	RBI	BB	SO	AVG	OBP	SLG	PRO+	BR	/A	RC	SB	CS	SBR	FR	POS	TPR
1964	Bos-A	118	374	37	86	16	4	6	39	22	38	.230	.275	.342	67	-15	-18	36	6	3	0	-8	2/S3	-1.7
1965	Bos-A	112	367	41	99	13	5	5	37	28	45	.270	.325	.373	92	-1	-4	46	8	1	2	-3	3/2	-0.3
1966	Bos-A	115	252	26	59	11	5	4	23	22	27	.234	.303	.365	83	-3	-6	27	1	2	-1	-15	2/3	-1.6
1967	*Bos-A	89	159	18	46	6	2	3	25	11	23	.289	.335	.409	110	3	2	21	0	1	-1	-4	32/1	-0.1
1968	Bos-A	111	354	38	83	13	0	5	29	17	53	.234	.272	.314	72	-10	-13	28	1	1	-0	-5	12/3	-2.2
1969	Bos-A	111	336	50	74	18	3	3	33	39	36	.220	.305	.318	71	-11	-13	34	1	1	-0	-1	1/32	-2.0
1970	Det-A	89	191	29	42	7	0	6	21	33	33	.220	.338	.351	90	-2	-2	24	1	1	-0	-3	231	-0.2
1971	Det-A	83	138	15	35	5	0	5	11	9	21	.254	.304	.399	94	-1	-1	15	1	3	-2	-5	O3/12	-0.9
1972	Det-A	7	7	0	0	0	0	0	0	0	2	.000	.000	.000	-97	-2	-2	0	0	0	0	0	H	-0.1
	Tex-A	72	151	14	24	2	0	4	19	10	31	.159	.211	.252	39	-12	-11	8	1	0	0	-7	32/1O	-1.8
	Yr	79	158	14	24	2	0	4	19	10	33	.152	.202	.241	33	-14	-13	8	1	0	0	-7		-1.9
Total	9	907	2329	268	548	91	19	41	237	191	309	.235	.296	.343	79	-54	-68	240	20	13	-2	-51	231/OS	-10.9

■ JAKE JONES
Jones, James Murrell b: 11/23/20, Epps, La. BR/TR, 6'3", 197 lbs. Deb: 9/20/41

YEAR	TM/L	G	AB	R	H	2B	3B	HR	RBI	BB	SO	AVG	OBP	SLG	PRO+	BR	/A	RC	SB	CS	SBR	FR	POS	TPR
1941	Chi-A	3	11	0	0	0	0	0	0	0	4	.000	.000	.000	-99	-3	-3	0	0	0	0	-1	/1	-0.3
1942	Chi-A	7	20	2	3	1	0	0	0	2	2	.150	.227	.200	21	-2	-2	1	1	0	0	-1	/1	-0.2
1946	Chi-A	24	79	10	21	5	1	3	13	2	13	.266	.284	.468	112	0	0	10	0	0	0	-3	1	-0.3
1947	Chi-A	45	171	15	41	7	1	3	20	13	25	.240	.297	.345	81	-5	-5	18	1	0	0	-1	1	-0.5
	Bos-A	109	404	50	95	14	3	16	76	41	60	.235	.310	.403	91	-3	-7	52	5	4	-1	-2	*1	-1.2
	Yr	154	575	65	136	21	4	19	96	54	85	.237	.306	.386	88	-9	-11	70	6	4	-1	-3		-1.7
1948	Bos-A	36	105	3	21	4	0	1	8	11	26	.200	.276	.267	43	-8	-9	8	1	0	0	2	1	-0.4
Total	5	224	790	80	181	31	5	23	117	69	130	.229	.294	.368	80	-22	-25	88	8	4	0	-5	1	-2.9

■ JIM JONES
Jones, James Tilford "Sheriff" b: 12/25/1876, London, Ky. d: 5/6/53, London, Ky. TR, 5'10", 162 lbs. Deb: 6/29/1897

YEAR	TM/L	G	AB	R	H	2B	3B	HR	RBI	BB	SO	AVG	OBP	SLG	PRO+	BR	/A	RC	SB	CS	SBR	FR	POS	TPR
1897	Lou-N	2	4	2	1	1	0	0	0	1		.250	.400	.500	144	0	0	1	0			-0	/P	0.0
1901	NY-N	21	91	10	19	4	3	0	5	4		.209	.242	.319	66	-4	-4	8	2			1	O/P	-0.4
1902	NY-N	67	249	16	59	11	1	0	19	13		.237	.275	.289	76	-7	-7	23	7			-1	O	-1.3
Total	3	90	344	28	79	16	4	0	24	18		.230	.268	.299	75	-11	-11	31	9			0	/OP	-1.7

■ JEFF JONES
Jones, Jeffrey Raymond b: 10/22/57, Philadelphia, Pa. BR/TR, 6'2", 200 lbs. Deb: 4/04/83

YEAR	TM/L	G	AB	R	H	2B	3B	HR	RBI	BB	SO	AVG	OBP	SLG	PRO+	BR	/A	RC	SB	CS	SBR	FR	POS	TPR
1983	Cin-N	16	44	6	10	3	0	0	5	11	13	.227	.393	.295	90	0	0	7	2	0	1	0	O/1	0.1

■ BINKY JONES
Jones, John Joseph b: 7/11/1899, St.Louis, Mo. d: 5/13/61, St.Louis, Mo. BR/TR, 5'9", 154 lbs. Deb: 4/15/24

YEAR	TM/L	G	AB	R	H	2B	3B	HR	RBI	BB	SO	AVG	OBP	SLG	PRO+	BR	/A	RC	SB	CS	SBR	FR	POS	TPR
1924	Bro-N	10	37	0	4	1	0	0	2	0	3	.108	.108	.135	-36	-7	-7	1	0	0	0	-1	S	-0.6

■ JOHN JONES
Jones, John William "Skins" b: 5/13/01, Coatesville, Pa. d: 11/3/56, Baltimore, Md. BL/TL, 5'11", 185 lbs. Deb: 9/26/23

YEAR	TM/L	G	AB	R	H	2B	3B	HR	RBI	BB	SO	AVG	OBP	SLG	PRO+	BR	/A	RC	SB	CS	SBR	FR	POS	TPR
1923	Phi-A	1	4	0	1	0	0	0	1	0	1	.250	.250	.250	31	-0	-0	0	0	0	0	0	/O	0.0
1932	Phi-A	4	6	0	1	0	0	0	0	0	3	.167	.167	.167	-13	-1	-1	0	0	0	0	0	/O	0.0
Total	2	5	10	0	2	0	0	0	1	0	4	.200	.200	.200	4	-1	-1	0	0	0	0	0	/O	0.0

■ LYNN JONES
Jones, Lynn Morris b: 1/1/53, Meadville, Pa. BR/TR, 5'9", 175 lbs. Deb: 4/13/79

YEAR	TM/L	G	AB	R	H	2B	3B	HR	RBI	BB	SO	AVG	OBP	SLG	PRO+	BR	/A	RC	SB	CS	SBR	FR	POS	TPR
1979	Det-A	95	213	33	63	8	6	0	26	17	22	.296	.351	.390	96	0	-1	28	9	6	-1	1	O	-0.3
1980	Det-A	30	55	9	14	2	2	0	6	10	5	.255	.369	.364	99	0	0	8	1	0	0	1	O/D	0.1
1981	Det-A	71	174	19	45	5	0	2	19	18	10	.259	.332	.322	86	-2	-3	18	1	2	-1	-1	O/D	-0.5
1982	Det-A	58	139	15	31	3	1	0	14	7	14	.223	.260	.259	43	-11	-11	9	2	2	-1	1	O/D	-1.2
1983	Det-A	49	64	9	17	1	2	0	6	3	6	.266	.299	.344	78	-2	-2	7	1	0	0	2	O/D	0.0
1984	*KC-A	47	103	11	31	6	0	1	10	4	9	.301	.333	.388	98	-0	-0	11	1	3	-2	-5	O	-0.7
1985	*KC-A	110	152	12	32	7	0	0	9	8	15	.211	.264	.257	43	-12	-12	10	0	1	-1	5	*O/D	-0.7
1986	KC-A	67	47	1	6	2	0	0	1	6	5	.128	.226	.170	10	-6	-6	2	0	0	0	3	O/2D	-0.4
Total	8	527	947	109	239	34	5	7	91	73	86	.252	.310	.321	73	-32	-34	92	13	14	-5	8	O/D2	-3.7

■ MACK JONES
Jones, Mack "Mack The Knife" b: 11/6/38, Alanta, Ga. BL/TR, 6'1", 180 lbs. Deb: 7/13/61

YEAR	TM/L	G	AB	R	H	2B	3B	HR	RBI	BB	SO	AVG	OBP	SLG	PRO+	BR	/A	RC	SB	CS	SBR	FR	POS	TPR
1961	Mil-N	28	104	13	24	3	2	0	12	12	28	.231	.322	.298	70	-5	-4	10	4	4	-1	-2	O	-0.8
1962	Mil-N	91	333	51	85	17	4	10	36	44	100	.255	.354	.420	110	4	5	52	5	1	1	-6	O	-0.4
1963	Mil-N	93	228	36	50	11	4	3	22	26	59	.219	.318	.342	91	-2	-2	26	8	4	0	-11	O	-1.8
1965	Mil-N	143	504	78	132	18	7	31	75	29	122	.262	.314	.510	127	16	16	81	8	2	1	-11	*O	0.2
1966	Atl-N	118	417	60	110	14	1	23	66	39	85	.264	.338	.468	120	12	11	65	16	10	-1	-6	*O/1	0.0
1967	Atl-N	140	454	72	115	23	4	17	50	64	108	.253	.357	.434	127	16	17	73	10	6	-1	-3	*O	0.8
1968	Cin-N	103	234	40	59	9	1	10	34	28	46	.252	.345	.427	123	9	8	34	2	3	-1	-5	O	-0.1
1969	Mon-N	135	455	73	123	23	5	22	79	67	110	.270	.382	.488	142	27	27	85	6	7	-2	-1	*O	1.7
1970	Mon-N	108	271	51	65	11	3	14	52	59	74	.240	.399	.458	129	14	14	56	5	3	-0	-7	O	0.2
1971	Mon-N	43	91	11	15	3	0	3	9	15	24	.165	.296	.297	68	-4	-4	9	1	0	0	-2	O	-0.6
Total	10	1002	3091	485	778	132	31	133	415	383	756	.252	.349	.444	120	87	87	492	65	40	-5	-55	O/1	-0.8

■ RED JONES
Jones, Maurice Morris b: 11/2/14, Timpson, Tex. d: 6/30/75, Lincoln, Cal. BL/TR, 6'3", 190 lbs. Deb: 4/16/40

YEAR	TM/L	G	AB	R	H	2B	3B	HR	RBI	BB	SO	AVG	OBP	SLG	PRO+	BR	/A	RC	SB	CS	SBR	FR	POS	TPR
1940	StL-N	12	11	0	1	0	0	0	1	1	2	.091	.167	.091	-26	-2	-2	0	0			0	/O	-0.1

YEAR	TM/L	G	AB	R	H	2B	3B	HR	RBI	BB	SO	AVG	OBP	SLG	PRO+	BR	/A	RC	SB	CS	SBR	FR	POS	TPR

■ RICKY JONES   Jones, Ricky Miron   b: 6/4/58, Tupelo, Miss.   BR/TR, 6'3", 186 lbs.   Deb: 9/03/86

YEAR	TM/L	G	AB	R	H	2B	3B	HR	RBI	BB	SO	AVG	OBP	SLG	PRO+	BR	/A	RC	SB	CS	SBR	FR	POS	TPR
1986	Bal-A	16	33	2	6	2	0	0	4	6	8	.182	.308	.242	53	-2	-2	3	0	0	0	7	2/3	0.5

■ BOB JONES   Jones, Robert Oliver   b: 10/11/49, Elkton, Md.   BL/TL, 6'2", 195 lbs.   Deb: 10/01/74

YEAR	TM/L	G	AB	R	H	2B	3B	HR	RBI	BB	SO	AVG	OBP	SLG	PRO+	BR	/A	RC	SB	CS	SBR	FR	POS	TPR
1974	Tex-A	2	5	0	0	0	0	0	0	0	1	.000	.000	.000	-99	-1	-1	0	0	0	0	0	/O	0.0
1975	Tex-A	9	11	2	1	0	0	0	0	3	3	.091	.286	.091	11	-1	-1	1	0	0	0	0	/OD	0.0
1976	Cal-A	78	166	22	35	6	0	6	17	14	30	.211	.276	.355	90	-4	-2	16	3	0	1	3	O/D	0.0
1977	Cal-A	14	17	3	3	0	0	1	3	4	5	.176	.333	.353	91	-0	-0	2	0	0	0	0	/D	0.0
1981	Tex-A	10	34	4	9	1	0	3	7	1	7	.265	.286	.559	146	1	2	5	0	1	-1	3	O	0.4
1983	Tex-A	41	72	5	16	4	0	1	11	5	17	.222	.291	.319	69	-3	-3	6	0	2	-1	1	OD/1	-0.3
1984	Tex-A	64	143	14	37	4	0	4	22	10	19	.259	.312	.371	85	-2	-3	17	1	1	-0	0	O1/D	-0.4
1985	Tex-A	83	134	14	30	2	0	5	23	11	30	.224	.288	.351	73	-5	-5	14	1	0	0	-1	OD/1	-0.6
1986	Tex-A	13	21	1	2	0	0	0	3	2	5	.095	.174	.095	-24	-4	-4	0	0	0	0	0	/O1	-0.3
Total	9	314	603	65	133	17	0	20	86	50	117	.221	.286	.348	78	-19	-18	62	5	4	-1	6	O/D1	-1.2

■ BOB JONES   Jones, Robert Walter "Ducky"   b: 12/2/1889, Clayton, Cal.   d: 8/30/64, San Diego, Cal.   BL/TR, 6', 170 lbs.   Deb: 4/11/17

YEAR	TM/L	G	AB	R	H	2B	3B	HR	RBI	BB	SO	AVG	OBP	SLG	PRO+	BR	/A	RC	SB	CS	SBR	FR	POS	TPR
1917	Det-A	46	77	16	12	1	2	0	2	4	8	.156	.198	.221	28	-7	-7	4	3			-1	2/3	-0.6
1918	Det-A	74	287	43	79	14	4	0	21	17	16	.275	.320	.352	107	-0	1	34	7			-8	3/1O	-0.7
1919	Det-A	127	439	37	114	18	6	1	57	34	39	.260	.314	.335	84	-11	-9	50	11			-24	*3	-2.5
1920	Det-A	81	265	35	66	6	3	1	18	22	13	.249	.309	.306	65	-14	-13	26	3	4	-2	-5	3/2S	-1.3
1921	Det-A	141	554	82	168	23	9	1	72	37	24	.303	.348	.383	87	-12	-11	73	8	9	-3	10	*3	0.7
1922	Det-A	124	455	65	117	10	6	3	44	36	18	.257	.314	.325	69	-22	-20	48	8	6	-1	11	*3	0.2
1923	Det-A	100	372	51	93	15	4	1	40	29	13	.250	.306	.320	66	-19	-18	38	7	6	-2	5	3	-0.2
1924	Det-A	110	393	52	107	27	4	0	47	20	20	.272	.308	.361	73	-18	-17	43	1	5	-3	-2	*3	-1.1
1925	Det-A	50	148	18	35	6	0	0	15	9	5	.236	.280	.277	42	-13	-13	12	1	1	-0	9	3	0.0
Total	9	853	2990	399	791	120	38	7	316	208	156	.265	.314	.337	75	-115	-107	327	49	31		-4	3/21SO	-5.5

■ RON JONES   Jones, Ronald Glen   b: 6/11/64, Seguin, Tex.   BL/TR, 5'10", 195 lbs.   Deb: 8/26/88

YEAR	TM/L	G	AB	R	H	2B	3B	HR	RBI	BB	SO	AVG	OBP	SLG	PRO+	BR	/A	RC	SB	CS	SBR	FR	POS	TPR
1988	Phi-N	33	124	15	36	6	1	8	26	2	14	.290	.302	.548	136	5	5	20	0	0	0	1	O	0.5
1989	Phi-N	12	31	7	9	0	0	2	4	9	1	.290	.450	.484	167	3	3	7	1	0	0	2	O	0.6
1990	Phi-N	24	58	5	16	2	0	3	7	9	9	.276	.373	.466	130	2	2	10	0	1	-1	-1	O	0.0
Total	3	69	213	27	61	8	1	13	37	20	24	.286	.348	.516	140	11	11	37	1	1	-0	1	/O	1.1

■ ROSS JONES   Jones, Ross A.   b: 1/14/60, Miami, Fla.   BR/TR, 6'2", 185 lbs.   Deb: 4/02/84

YEAR	TM/L	G	AB	R	H	2B	3B	HR	RBI	BB	SO	AVG	OBP	SLG	PRO+	BR	/A	RC	SB	CS	SBR	FR	POS	TPR
1984	NY-N	17	10	2	1	0	0	0	1	3	4	.100	.308	.200	46	-1	-1	1	0	0	0	1	/S23	0.1
1986	Sea-A	11	21	0	2	0	0	0	0	0	4	.095	.095	.095	-48	-4	-4	0	0	1	-1	1	/S23D	-0.2
1987	KC-A	39	114	10	29	4	2	0	10	5	15	.254	.292	.325	62	-6	-6	10	1	0	0	1	S/2	-0.2
Total	3	67	145	12	32	5	2	0	11	8	23	.221	.266	.283	46	-11	-11	11	1	1	-0	3	/S23D	-0.3

■ RUPPERT JONES   Jones, Ruppert Sanderson   b: 3/12/55, Dallas, Tex.   BL/TL, 5'10", 170 lbs.   Deb: 8/01/76

YEAR	TM/L	G	AB	R	H	2B	3B	HR	RBI	BB	SO	AVG	OBP	SLG	PRO+	BR	/A	RC	SB	CS	SBR	FR	POS	TPR
1976	KC-A	28	51	9	11	1	1	1	7	3	16	.216	.259	.333	72	-2	-2	4	0	2	-1	-0	O/D	-0.3
1977	Sea-A	160	597	85	157	26	8	24	76	55	120	.263	.327	.454	111	7	8	89	13	9	-2	13	*O/D	1.5
1978	Sea-A	129	472	48	111	24	3	6	46	55	85	.235	.315	.337	84	-10	-10	51	22	6	3	12	*O	0.2
1979	Sea-A	162	622	109	166	29	9	21	78	85	78	.267	.358	.444	113	14	12	99	33	12	3	8	*O	1.6
1980	NY-A	83	328	38	73	11	3	9	42	34	50	.223	.301	.357	81	-9	-9	36	18	8	1	6	O	-0.3
1981	SD-N	105	397	42	99	34	4	4	39	43	66	.249	.323	.370	104	-2	1	47	7	9	-3	6	*O	0.1
1982	SD-N	116	424	69	120	20	2	12	61	62	90	.283	.376	.425	130	15	18	69	18	15	-4	2	*O	1.5
1983	SD-N	133	335	42	78	12	3	12	49	35	58	.233	.305	.394	96	-4	-3	37	11	11	-3	-8	*O/1	-1.6
1984	*Det-A	79	215	26	61	12	1	12	37	21	47	.284	.347	.516	136	10	10	36	2	4	-2	5	O/D	1.1
1985	Cal-A	125	389	66	90	17	2	21	67	57	82	.231	.330	.447	111	5	6	60	7	4	-0	12	OD	1.6
1986	*Cal-A	126	393	73	90	21	3	17	49	64	87	.229	.341	.427	109	5	5	60	10	3	1	-10	*O	-0.5
1987	Cal-A	85	192	25	47	8	2	8	28	20	38	.245	.316	.432	99	-1	-1	26	2	1	0	-6	O/D	-0.7
Total	12	1331	4415	643	1103	215	38	147	579	534	817	.250	.332	.416	106	27	37	614	143	84	-8	40	*O/D1	4.2

■ JACK JONES   Jones, Ryerson L. "Ri" or "Angel Sleeves"   b: Cincinnati, Ohio   TR ,   Deb: 8/13/1883

YEAR	TM/L	G	AB	R	H	2B	3B	HR	RBI	BB	SO	AVG	OBP	SLG	PRO+	BR	/A	RC	SB	CS	SBR	FR	POS	TPR
1883	Lou-a	2	7	1	0	0	0	0		0		.000	.000	.000	-99	-1	-1	0				-1	/OS	-0.1
1884	Cin-U	69	272	36	71	5	1	2		12		.261	.292	.309	96	1	-2	25	0			2	S23	0.0
Total	2	71	279	37	71	5	1	2		12		.254	.285	.301	91	-0	-4	25	0			1	/S23O	-0.1

■ TOM JONES   Jones, Thomas   b: 1/22/1877, Honesdale, Pa.   d: 6/21/23, Danville, Pa.   BR/TR, 6'1", 195 lbs.   Deb: 8/25/02

YEAR	TM/L	G	AB	R	H	2B	3B	HR	RBI	BB	SO	AVG	OBP	SLG	PRO+	BR	/A	RC	SB	CS	SBR	FR	POS	TPR
1902	Bal-A	37	159	22	45	8	4	0	14	2		.283	.292	.384	84	-3	-4	19	1			-2	1/2	-0.4
1904	StL-A	156	625	52	152	15	10	2	68	15		.243	.261	.309	87	-14	-10	57	16			0	*12/O	-0.6
1905	StL-A	135	504	44	122	16	2	0	48	30		.242	.285	.282	86	-10	-7	46	5			7	*1	-0.2
1906	StL-A	144	539	51	136	22	6	0	30	24		.252	.284	.315	93	-7	-5	62	27			11	*1	0.2
1907	StL-A	155	549	53	137	17	3	0	34	34		.250	.293	.291	89	-7	-7	59	24			2	*1	-0.7
1908	StL-A	155	549	43	135	14	2	1	50	30		.246	.285	.284	87	-8	-8	51	18			-2	*1	-1.4
1909	StL-A	97	337	30	84	9	3	0	29	18		.249	.299	.294	94	-5	-2	34	13			7	1/3	0.5
	*Det-A	44	153	13	43	9	0	0	18	5		.281	.317	.340	103	1	0	20	9			2	1	0.3
	Yr	141	490	43	127	18	3	0	47	23		.259	.305	.308	97	-4	-2	54	22			9		0.8
1910	Det-A	135	432	32	110	12	4	1	45	35		.255	.325	.308	92	-0	-4	53	22			-4	*1	-0.2
Total	8	1058	3847	341	964	122	34	4	336	193		.251	.290	.303	90	-53	-46	400	135			23	*1/2O3	-2.5

■ TRACY JONES   Jones, Tracy Donald   b: 3/31/61, Hawthorne, Cal.   BR/TR, 6'3", 180 lbs.   Deb: 4/07/86

YEAR	TM/L	G	AB	R	H	2B	3B	HR	RBI	BB	SO	AVG	OBP	SLG	PRO+	BR	/A	RC	SB	CS	SBR	FR	POS	TPR
1986	Cin-N	46	86	16	30	3	0	2	10	9	5	.349	.411	.453	132	5	4	17	7	1	2	1	O/1	0.6
1987	Cin-N	117	359	53	104	17	3	10	44	23	40	.290	.338	.437	99	1	-1	52	31	8	5	-1	O	0.0
1988	Cin-N	37	83	9	19	1	0	1	9	8	6	.229	.304	.277	65	-3	-4	8	9	0	3	-1	O	-0.2
	Mon-N	53	141	20	47	5	1	2	15	12	12	.333	.390	.426	128	6	6	23	9	6	-1	-4	O	0.0
	Yr	90	224	29	66	6	1	3	24	20	18	.295	.358	.371	105	3	2	31	18	6	2	-5		-0.2
1989	SF-N	40	97	5	18	4	0	0	5	5	14	.186	.233	.227	33	-9	-8	4	2	1	0	-4	O	-1.3
	Det-A	46	158	17	41	10	0	3	26	16	16	.259	.331	.380	102	0	1	21	1	1	0	-4	O/D	-0.4
1990	Det-A	50	118	15	27	4	1	4	9	6	13	.229	.283	.381	85	-3	-3	12	1	1	-0	0	OD	-0.2
	Sea-A	25	86	8	26	4	0	2	15	3	12	.302	.341	.419	110	1	1	11	0	1	-1	-2	O/D	-0.1
	Yr	75	204	23	53	8	1	6	24	9	25	.260	.307	.397	96	-2	-2	23	1	2	-1	-2		-0.3
Total	5	414	1128	143	312	48	5	24	140	82	118	.277	.332	.392	98	-1	-4	149	60	19	7	-14	O/D1	-1.6

■ NIPPY JONES   Jones, Vernal Leroy   b: 6/29/25, Los Angeles, Cal.   BR/TR, 6'1", 185 lbs.   Deb: 6/08/46

YEAR	TM/L	G	AB	R	H	2B	3B	HR	RBI	BB	SO	AVG	OBP	SLG	PRO+	BR	/A	RC	SB	CS	SBR	FR	POS	TPR
1946	*StL-N	16	12	3	4	0	0	0	1	2	2	.333	.429	.333	113	0	0	1	0			1	/2	0.1
1947	StL-N	23	73	6	18	4	0	1	5	2	10	.247	.267	.342	58	-4	-5	6	0			-1	2/O	-0.3
1948	StL-N	132	481	58	122	21	9	10	81	36	45	.254	.307	.397	84	-9	-12	52	2			-9	*1	-2.1
1949	StL-N	110	380	51	114	20	2	8	62	16	20	.300	.330	.426	97	-0	-3	50	1			-8	1	-1.0
1950	StL-N	13	26	0	6	1	0	0	6	3	1	.231	.310	.269	52	-2	-2	2	0			-0	/1	-0.2
1951	StL-N	80	300	20	79	12	0	3	41	9	13	.263	.287	.333	66	-15	-15	25	1	2	-1	-1	1	-1.7
1952	Phi-N	8	30	3	5	0	0	1	5	0	4	.167	.167	.267	19	-3	-3	1	0	0	0	0	/1	-0.2
1957	*Mil-N	30	79	5	21	2	1	2	8	3	7	.266	.293	.392	88	-2	-1	9	0	0	0	-0	1/O	-0.3
Total	8	412	1381	146	369	60	12	25	209	71	102	.267	.304	.382	81	-35	-41	147	4	2		-18	1/2O	-5.7

■ BILL JONES
Jones, William b: Syracuse, N.Y. Deb: 5/17/1882

YEAR	TM/L	G	AB	R	H	2B	3B	HR	RBI	BB	SO	AVG	OBP	SLG	PRO+	BR	/A	RC	SB	CS	SBR	FR	POS	TPR
1882	Bal-a	4	15	1	1	0	0	0	0			.067	.067	.067	-59	-2	-2	0				0	/OC	-0.1
1884	Phi-U	4	14	2	2	0	0	0			1	.143	.200	.143	19	-1	-1	0	0			1	/CO	0.1
Total	2	8	29	3	3	0	0	0			1	.103	.133	.103	-21	-3	-3	0	0			2	/CO	0.0

■ BILL JONES
Jones, William Dennis "Midget" b: 4/8/1887, Hartland, N.B., Can. d: 10/10/46, Boston, Mass. BL/TR, 5'6.5", 157 lbs. Deb: 6/20/11

YEAR	TM/L	G	AB	R	H	2B	3B	HR	RBI	BB	SO	AVG	OBP	SLG	PRO+	BR	/A	RC	SB	CS	SBR	FR	POS	TPR
1911	Bos-N	24	51	6	11	2	1	0	3	15	7	.216	.394	.294	87	0	-0	6	1			1	O	0.0
1912	Bos-N	3	2	0	1	0	0	0	2	0	1	.500	.500	.500	171	0	0	0				0	H	0.0
Total	2	27	53	6	12	2	1	0	5	15	8	.226	.397	.302	89	1	-0	7	1			1	/O	0.0

■ TEX JONES
Jones, William Roderick b: 8/4/1885, Marion, Kan. d: 2/26/38, Wichita, Kan. BR/TR, 6', 192 lbs. Deb: 4/13/11

YEAR	TM/L	G	AB	R	H	2B	3B	HR	RBI	BB	SO	AVG	OBP	SLG	PRO+	BR	/A	RC	SB	CS	SBR	FR	POS	TPR
1911	Chi-A	9	31	4	6	1	0	0	4	3		.194	.265	.226	39	-3	-3	2	1			3	/1	0.1

■ TIM JONES
Jones, William Timothy b: 12/1/62, Sumter, S.C. BL/TR, 5'10", 172 lbs. Deb: 7/26/88

YEAR	TM/L	G	AB	R	H	2B	3B	HR	RBI	BB	SO	AVG	OBP	SLG	PRO+	BR	/A	RC	SB	CS	SBR	FR	POS	TPR
1988	StL-N	31	52	2	14	0	0	0	3	4	10	.269	.321	.269	70	-2	-2	5	4	1	1	5	/S23	0.5
1989	StL-N	42	75	11	22	6	0	0	7	7	8	.293	.361	.373	107	1	1	10	1	0	0	-2	2S/3CO	0.0
1990	StL-N	67	128	9	28	7	1	1	12	12	20	.219	.291	.313	64	-6	-6	12	3	4	-2	2	S2/3P	-0.2
Total	3	140	255	22	64	13	1	1	22	23	38	.251	.318	.322	78	-7	-7	27	8	5	-1	5	/S23POC	0.3

■ PUDDIN' HEAD JONES
Jones, Willie Edward b: 8/16/25, Dillon, S.C. d: 10/18/83, Cincinnati, Ohio BR/TR, 6'1", 188 lbs. Deb: 9/10/47

YEAR	TM/L	G	AB	R	H	2B	3B	HR	RBI	BB	SO	AVG	OBP	SLG	PRO+	BR	/A	RC	SB	CS	SBR	FR	POS	TPR
1947	Phi-N	18	62	5	14	0	1	0	10	7	0	.226	.304	.258	53	-4	-4	5	2			2	3	-0.1
1948	Phi-N	17	60	9	20	2	0	2	9	3	5	.333	.365	.467	126	2	2	9	0			2	3	0.4
1949	Phi-N	149	532	71	130	35	1	19	77	65	66	.244	.328	.421	102	-1	-1	71	3			-4	*3	-0.1
1950	*Phi-N	157	610	100	163	28	6	25	88	61	40	.267	.337	.456	108	4	5	93	5			-6	*3	0.0
1951	Phi-N	148	564	79	161	28	5	22	81	60	47	.285	.358	.470	123	16	17	100	6	2	1	-8	*3	0.8
1952	Phi-N	147	541	60	135	12	3	18	72	53	36	.250	.323	.383	96	-4	-3	68	5	3	-0	4	*3	0.4
1953	Phi-N	149	481	61	108	16	2	19	70	85	45	.225	.342	.385	90	-7	-6	69	1	1	-0	-3	*3	-1.2
1954	Phi-N	142	535	64	145	28	3	12	56	61	54	.271	.346	.402	94	-4	-4	77	4	1	1	-2	*3	-0.4
1955	Phi-N	146	516	65	133	20	3	16	81	77	51	.258	.357	.401	103	2	4	77	6	2	1	-13	*3	-0.9
1956	Phi-N	149	520	88	144	20	4	17	78	92	45	.277	.387	.429	121	17	18	89	5	4	-1	1	*3	1.8
1957	Phi-N	133	440	58	96	19	2	9	47	61	41	.218	.313	.332	76	-16	-14	47	1	0	-0	-7	*3	-1.8
1958	Phi-N	118	398	52	108	15	1	14	60	49	45	.271	.354	.420	105	3	3	60	1	2	-1	-13	*3/1	-1.0
1959	Phi-N	47	160	23	43	9	1	7	24	19	14	.269	.346	.469	113	3	3	26	0	0	0	-3	3	-0.1
	Cle-A	11	18	1	4	1	0	0	1	1	3	.222	.263	.278	51	-1	-1	1	0	0	0	2	/3	0.1
	Cin-N	72	233	33	58	12	1	7	31	28	26	.249	.332	.399	91	-2	-3	30	0	2	-1	-3	3	-0.8
1960	Cin-N	79	149	16	40	7	0	3	27	31	16	.268	.394	.376	110	4	4	25	1	0	0	-3	3/2	0.0
1961	Cin-N	9	7	1	0	0	0	0	0	2	3	.000	.222	.000	-34	-1	-1	0	0	0	0	-0	/3	-0.1
Total	15	1691	5826	786	1502	252	33	190	812	755	541	.258	.345	.410	102	10	20	845	40	17		-54	*3/21	-3.0

■ BUBBER JONNARD
Jonnard, Clarence James b: 11/23/1897, Nashville, Tenn. d: 8/23/77, New York, N.Y. BR/TR, 6'1", 185 lbs. Deb: 10/01/20 C

YEAR	TM/L	G	AB	R	H	2B	3B	HR	RBI	BB	SO	AVG	OBP	SLG	PRO+	BR	/A	RC	SB	CS	SBR	FR	POS	TPR
1920	Chi-A	2	5	0	0	0	0	0	0	0	1	.000	.000	.000	-99	-1	-1	0	0			0	/C	0.0
1922	Pit-N	10	21	4	5	0	1	0	2	2	4	.238	.304	.333	64	-1	-1	2	0	0	0	2	C	0.1
1926	Phi-N	19	34	3	4	1	0	0	2	3	4	.118	.189	.147	-8	-5	-5	1	0			0	C	-0.4
1927	Phi-N	53	143	18	42	6	0	0	14	7	7	.294	.327	.336	77	-4	-5	15	0			-9	C	-1.0
1929	StL-N	18	31	1	3	0	0	0	2	0	6	.097	.097	.097	-51	-7	-7	0	0			1	C	-0.3
1935	Phi-N	1	1	0	0	0	0	0	0	0	0	.000	.000	.000	-91	-0	-0	0	0			0	/C	0.0
Total	6	103	235	26	54	7	1	0	20	12	23	.230	.267	.268	41	-20	-20	19	0	0		-6	/C	-1.6

■ EDDIE JOOST
Joost, Edwin David b: 6/5/16, San Francisco, Cal BR/TR, 6', 175 lbs. Deb: 9/11/36 M

YEAR	TM/L	G	AB	R	H	2B	3B	HR	RBI	BB	SO	AVG	OBP	SLG	PRO+	BR	/A	RC	SB	CS	SBR	FR	POS	TPR
1936	Cin-N	13	26	1	4	1	0	0	1	2	5	.154	.214	.192	11	-3	-3	1	0			-1	/S2	-0.3
1937	Cin-N	6	12	0	1	0	0	0	0	0	0	.083	.083	.083	-57	-3	-2	0	0			0	/2	-0.1
1939	Cin-N	42	143	23	36	6	3	0	14	12	15	.252	.310	.336	73	-5	-5	15	1			-3	2/S	-0.6
1940	*Cin-N	88	278	24	60	7	2	1	24	32	40	.216	.301	.266	57	-15	-16	24	4			-0	S/23	-0.7
1941	Cin-N	152	537	67	136	25	4	4	40	69	59	.253	.340	.337	91	-5	-5	66	9			-6	*S/213	-0.1
1942	Cin-N	142	562	65	126	30	3	6	41	62	57	.224	.307	.320	84	-11	-11	59	9			-10	*S2	-1.1
1943	Bos-N	124	421	34	78	16	3	2	20	68	80	.185	.299	.252	61	-20	-19	35	5			13	32/S	-0.5
1945	Bos-N	35	141	16	35	7	1	0	9	13	7	.248	.312	.312	73	-5	-5	14	0			-7	23	-1.0
1947	Phi-A	151	540	76	111	22	3	13	64	114	110	.206	.348	.330	87	-5	-6	73	6	6	-2	-3	*S	-1.1
1948	Phi-A	135	509	99	127	22	2	16	55	119	87	.250	.393	.395	110	11	11	91	2	4	-2	5	*S	1.4
1949	Phi-A	144	525	128	138	25	3	23	81	149	80	.263	.429	.453	138	32	35	119	2	1	0	8	*S	4.2
1950	Phi-A	131	476	79	111	12	3	18	58	103	68	.233	.373	.384	96	-2	-1	77	5	1	1	-7	*S	0.0
1951	Phi-A	140	553	107	160	28	5	19	78	106	70	.289	.409	.461	132	30	29	115	10	8	-2	4	*S	3.8
1952	Phi-A	146	540	94	132	26	3	20	75	122	94	.244	.388	.415	116	21	17	98	5	8	-3		*S	1.5
1953	Phi-A	51	177	39	44	6	0	6	15	45	24	.249	.401	.384	109	5	4	32	3	2	-0	-6	S	0.2
1954	Phi-A	19	47	7	17	3	0	1	9	10	10	.362	.474	.489	163	5	5	10	0	1	-1	-3	/S32M	0.2
1955	Bos-A	55	119	15	23	2	0	5	17	17	21	.193	.299	.336	65	-5	-7	13	0	0	0	5	S2/3	0.2
Total	17	1574	5606	874	1339	238	35	134	601	1043	827	.239	.361	.366	99	25	19	842	61	31		-19	*S2/31	6.2

■ DUTCH JORDAN
Jordan, Adolf Otto b: 1/5/1880, Pittsburgh, Pa. d: 12/23/72, W.Allegheny, Pa. BR/TR, 5'10", 185 lbs. Deb: 4/25/03

YEAR	TM/L	G	AB	R	H	2B	3B	HR	RBI	BB	SO	AVG	OBP	SLG	PRO+	BR	/A	RC	SB	CS	SBR	FR	POS	TPR
1903	Bro-N	78	267	27	63	11	1	0	21	19		.236	.287	.285	67	-12	-11	26	9			-13	23/O1	-2.0
1904	Bro-N	87	252	21	45	10	2	0	19	13		.179	.219	.234	42	-17	-16	17	7			-17	23/1	-3.3
Total	2	165	519	48	108	21	3	0	40	32		.208	.254	.260	55	-29	-27	42	16			-31	2/31O	-5.3

■ BUCK JORDAN
Jordan, Baxter Byerly b: 1/16/07, Cooleemee, N.C. BL/TR, 6', 170 lbs. Deb: 9/15/27

YEAR	TM/L	G	AB	R	H	2B	3B	HR	RBI	BB	SO	AVG	OBP	SLG	PRO+	BR	/A	RC	SB	CS	SBR	FR	POS	TPR
1927	NY-N	5	5	0	1	0	0	0	0	0	3	.200	.200	.200	7	-1	-1	0	0			0	H	0.0
1929	NY-N	2	2	1	1	1	0	0	0	0	0	.500	.500	1.000	262	0	0	1	0			0	/1	0.0
1931	Was-A	9	18	3	4	2	0	0	1	1	3	.222	.263	.333	56	-1	-1	2	0	0	0	-1	/1	-0.2
1932	Bos-N	49	212	27	68	12	3	2	29	4	5	.321	.333	.434	109	1	2	30	1			-1	1	-0.1
1933	Bos-N	152	588	77	168	29	9	4	46	34	22	.286	.327	.386	112	2	7	74	4			-3	*1	-0.3
1934	Bos-N	124	489	68	152	26	9	3	58	35	19	.311	.358	.413	114	4	9	74	3			-3	*1	-0.3
1935	Bos-N	130	470	62	131	24	5	5	35	19	17	.279	.307	.383	91	-11	-6	54	3			1	1/3O	-0.6
1936	Bos-N	138	555	81	179	27	5	3	66	45	22	.323	.375	.405	118	9	14	83	2			1	*1	0.3
1937	Bos-N	8	8	1	2	0	0	0	0	0	0	.250	.250	.250	40	-1	-1	0	0			0	H	0.0
	Cin-N	98	316	45	89	14	3	1	28	25	14	.282	.334	.354	92	-5	-3	39	6			-2	1	-0.8
	Yr	106	324	46	91	14	3	1	28	25	14	.281	.332	.352	91	-6	-4	39	6			-2		-0.8
1938	Cin-N	9	7	0	2	0	0	0	0	2	0	.286	.444	.286	107	0	0	1	0			-3	H	-0.8
	Phi-N	87	310	31	93	18	1	0	18	17	4	.300	.336	.365	95	-3	-2	38	1			-3	31	-0.8
	Yr	96	317	31	95	18	1	0	18	19	4	.300	.339	.363	96	-3	-2	39	1			-3		-0.8
Total	10	811	2980	396	890	153	35	17	281	182	109	.299	.340	.391	106	-6	18	397	20	0		-11	1/3O	-2.5

■ SLATS JORDAN
Jordan, Clarence Veasey b: 9/26/1879, Baltimore, Md. d: 12/7/53, Catonsville, Md. BL/TL, 6'1", 190 lbs. Deb: 9/28/01

YEAR	TM/L	G	AB	R	H	2B	3B	HR	RBI	BB	SO	AVG	OBP	SLG	PRO+	BR	/A	RC	SB	CS	SBR	FR	POS	TPR
1901	Bal-A	1	3	0	0	0	0	0	0			.000	.000	.000	-96	-1	-1	0	0			-0	/O	0.0
1902	Bal-A	1	4	0	0	0	0	0	0			.000	.000	.000	-96	-1	-1	0	0			-0	/O	-0.1
Total	2	2	7	0	0	0	0	0	0			.000	.000	.000	-96	-2	-2	0	0			-1	/O1	-0.1

YEAR	TM/L	G	AB	R	H	2B	3B	HR	RBI	BB	SO	AVG	OBP	SLG	PRO+	BR	/A	RC	SB	CS	SBR	FR	POS	TPR

■ JIMMY JORDAN
Jordan, James William "Lord" b: 1/13/08, Tucapau, S.C. d: 12/4/57, Gastonia, N.C. BR/TR, 5'9", 157 lbs. Deb: 4/20/33

YEAR	TM/L	G	AB	R	H	2B	3B	HR	RBI	BB	SO	AVG	OBP	SLG	PRO+	BR	/A	RC	SB	CS	SBR	FR	POS	TPR
1933	Bro-N	70	211	16	54	12	1	0	17	4	6	.256	.270	.322	71	-9	-8	18	3			12	S2	0.8
1934	Bro-N	97	369	34	98	17	2	0	43	9	32	.266	.285	.322	66	-20	-17	33	1			-13	S2/3	-2.3
1935	Bro-N	94	295	26	82	7	0	0	30	9	17	.278	.302	.302	64	-15	-14	27	3			27	2S/3	1.7
1936	Bro-N	115	398	26	93	15	1	2	28	15	21	.234	.262	.291	48	-29	-29	31	1			-17	2/S3	-3.8
Total	4	376	1273	102	327	51	4	2	118	37	76	.257	.279	.308	60	-73	-69	108	8			8	2S/3	-3.6

■ MIKE JORDAN
Jordan, Michael Henry "Mitty" b: 2/7/1863, Lawrence, Mass. d: 9/25/40, Lawrence, Mass. Deb: 8/21/1890

YEAR	TM/L	G	AB	R	H	2B	3B	HR	RBI	BB	SO	AVG	OBP	SLG	PRO+	BR	/A	RC	SB	CS	SBR	FR	POS	TPR
1890	Pit-N	37	125	8	12	1	0	0	6	15	19	.096	.210	.104	-7	-16	-14	4	5			2	O	-1.0

■ RICKY JORDAN
Jordan, Paul Scott b: 5/26/65, Richmond, Cal. BR/TR, 6'5", 210 lbs. Deb: 7/17/88

YEAR	TM/L	G	AB	R	H	2B	3B	HR	RBI	BB	SO	AVG	OBP	SLG	PRO+	BR	/A	RC	SB	CS	SBR	FR	POS	TPR
1988	Phi-N	69	273	41	84	15	1	11	43	7	39	.308	.325	.491	128	9	9	41	1	1	-0	-5	1	0.0
1989	Phi-N	144	523	63	149	22	3	12	75	23	62	.285	.321	.407	107	3	3	62	4	3	-1	-11	*1	-2.0
1990	Phi-N	92	324	32	78	21	0	5	44	13	39	.241	.281	.352	73	-13	-12	30	2	0	1	-8	1	-2.4
Total	3	305	1120	136	311	58	4	28	162	43	140	.278	.310	.412	102	0	-0	134	7	4	-0	-24	1	-4.4

■ SCOTT JORDAN
Jordan, Scott Allan b: 5/27/63, Waco, Tex. BR/TR, 6', 175 lbs. Deb: 9/02/88

YEAR	TM/L	G	AB	R	H	2B	3B	HR	RBI	BB	SO	AVG	OBP	SLG	PRO+	BR	/A	RC	SB	CS	SBR	FR	POS	TPR
1988	Cle-A	7	9	0	1	0	0	0	1	0	3	.111	.111	.111	-37	-2	-2	0	0	0	0	1	/O	0.0

■ TOM JORDAN
Jordan, Thomas Jefferson b: 9/5/19, Lawton, Okla. BR/TR, 6'1.5", 195 lbs. Deb: 9/04/44

YEAR	TM/L	G	AB	R	H	2B	3B	HR	RBI	BB	SO	AVG	OBP	SLG	PRO+	BR	/A	RC	SB	CS	SBR	FR	POS	TPR
1944	Chi-A	14	45	2	12	1	1	0	3	1	0	.267	.283	.333	77	-2	-2	4	0	0	0	-1	C	-0.1
1946	Chi-A	10	15	1	4	2	1	0	0	0	1	.267	.267	.533	124	0	0	1	0	0	0	1	/C	0.1
	Cle-A	14	35	2	7	1	0	1	3	3	1	.200	.263	.314	65	-2	-2	2	1	1	-0	-6	C	-0.7
	Yr	24	50	3	11	3	1	1	3	3	2	.220	.264	.380	83	-2	-1	3	1	1	-0	-5		-0.6
1948	StL-A	1	1	0	0	0	0	0	0	0	0	.000	.000	.000	-97	-0	-0	0	0	0	0	0	H	0.0
Total	3	39	96	5	23	4	2	1	6	4	2	.240	.270	.354	78	-4	-3	7	1	1	-0	-6	/C	-0.7

■ TIM JORDAN
Jordan, Timothy Joseph b: 2/14/1879, New York, N.Y. d: 9/13/49, Bronx, N.Y. BL/TL, 6'1", 170 lbs. Deb: 8/10/01

YEAR	TM/L	G	AB	R	H	2B	3B	HR	RBI	BB	SO	AVG	OBP	SLG	PRO+	BR	/A	RC	SB	CS	SBR	FR	POS	TPR
1901	Was-A	6	20	2	4	1	0	0	2	3		.200	.304	.250	58	-1	-1	2	0			-1	/1	-0.1
1903	NY-A	2	8	2	1	0	0	0	0	0		.125	.125	.125	-23	-1	-1	0	0			-1	/1	-0.1
1906	Bro-N	129	450	67	118	20	8	12	78	59		.262	.348	.422	154	22	26	75	16			-9	*1	1.2
1907	Bro-N	147	485	43	133	15	8	4	53	74		.274	.370	.363	144	20	25	73	10			-6	*1	1.8
1908	Bro-N	148	515	58	127	18	5	12	60	59		.247	.324	.371	129	14	16	64	9			-15	*1	-0.2
1909	Bro-N	103	330	47	90	20	3	3	36	59		.273	.386	.379	142	17	18	54	13			-9	1	0.9
1910	Bro-N	5	5	1	1	0	0	1	3	0	2	.200	.200	.800	195	0	0	1	0			0	H	0.0
Total	7	540	1813	220	474	74	24	32	232	254	2	.261	.353	.382	140	71	83	268	48			-40	1	3.5

■ ART JORGENS
Jorgens, Arndt Ludwig b: 5/18/05, Modum, Norway d: 3/1/80, Wilmette, Ill. BR/TR, 5'9", 160 lbs. Deb: 4/26/29

YEAR	TM/L	G	AB	R	H	2B	3B	HR	RBI	BB	SO	AVG	OBP	SLG	PRO+	BR	/A	RC	SB	CS	SBR	FR	POS	TPR
1929	NY-A	18	34	6	11	3	0	0	4	6	7	.324	.425	.412	125	1	2	6	0	2	-1	0	C	0.2
1930	NY-A	16	30	7	11	3	0	0	1	2	4	.367	.406	.467	126	1	1	6	0	0	0	0	C	0.3
1931	NY-A	46	100	12	27	1	2	0	14	9	3	.270	.330	.320	76	-4	-3	11	0	1	-1	-1	C	-0.1
1932	NY-A	56	151	13	33	7	1	2	19	14	11	.219	.285	.318	59	-10	-9	14	0	0	0	0	C	-0.4
1933	NY-A	21	50	9	11	3	0	2	13	12	3	.220	.371	.400	111	1	1	8	1	0	0	2	C	0.4
1934	NY-A	58	183	14	38	6	1	0	20	23	24	.208	.296	.251	45	-15	-14	15	2	0	1	6	C	0.0
1935	NY-A	36	84	6	20	2	0	0	8	12	10	.238	.333	.262	59	-5	-4	8	0	0	0	6	C	0.2
1936	NY-A	31	66	5	18	3	1	0	5	2	3	.273	.294	.348	60	-5	-4	7	0	0	0	3	C	0.1
1937	NY-A	13	23	3	3	1	0	0	3	2	5	.130	.200	.174	-5	-4	-4	1	0	0	0	0	C	-0.2
1938	NY-A	9	17	3	4	2	0	0	2	3	3	.235	.350	.353	77	-1	-1	2	0	0	0	0	/C	0.0
1939	NY-A	3	0	1	0	0	0	0	0	0	0	—	—	—	—	0	0	0	0	0	0	1	/C	0.1
Total	11	307	738	79	176	31.	5	4	89	85	73	.238	.317	.310	66	-41	-35	78	3	3	-1	18	C	0.6

■ PINKY JORGENSEN
Jorgensen, Carl b: 11/21/14, Laton, Cal. BR/TR, 6'1", 195 lbs. Deb: 9/14/37

YEAR	TM/L	G	AB	R	H	2B	3B	HR	RBI	BB	SO	AVG	OBP	SLG	PRO+	BR	/A	RC	SB	CS	SBR	FR	POS	TPR
1937	Cin-N	6	14	1	4	0	0	0	1	1	2	.286	.333	.286	73	-1	-0	2	0			0	/O	0.0

■ SPIDER JORGENSEN
Jorgensen, John Donald b: 11/3/19, Folsom, Cal. BL/TR, 5'9", 155 lbs. Deb: 4/15/47

YEAR	TM/L	G	AB	R	H	2B	3B	HR	RBI	BB	SO	AVG	OBP	SLG	PRO+	BR	/A	RC	SB	CS	SBR	FR	POS	TPR
1947	*Bro-N	129	441	57	121	29	8	5	67	58	45	.274	.360	.410	100	3	1	69	4			-5	*3	-0.7
1948	Bro-N	31	90	15	27	6	2	1	13	16	13	.300	.411	.444	127	5	4	18	1			-6	3	-0.2
1949	*Bro-N	53	134	15	36	5	1	1	14	23	13	.269	.376	.343	90	-0	-1	19	0			-5	3	-0.4
1950	Bro-N	2	2	0	0	0	0	0	1	1	0	.000	.333	.000	-4	-0	-0	0	0			0	/3	0.0
	NY-N	24	37	5	5	0	0	0	4	5	2	.135	.238	.135	1	-5	-5	2	0			1	/3	-0.3
	Yr	26	39	5	5	0	0	0	5	6	2	.128	.244	.128	1	-6	-6	2	0			1		-0.3
1951	NY-N	28	51	5	12	0	0	2	8	3	2	.235	.291	.353	72	-2	-2	6	0	0	0	-2	O/3	-0.4
Total	5	267	755	97	201	40	11	9	107	106	75	.266	.359	.384	95	-0	-4	114	5	0		-17	3/O	-2.0

■ MIKE JORGENSEN
Jorgensen, Michael b: 8/16/48, Passaic, N.J. BL/TL, 6', 195 lbs. Deb: 9/10/68

YEAR	TM/L	G	AB	R	H	2B	3B	HR	RBI	BB	SO	AVG	OBP	SLG	PRO+	BR	/A	RC	SB	CS	SBR	FR	POS	TPR
1968	NY-N	8	14	0	2	1	0	0	0	0	4	.143	.143	.214	6	-2	-2	0	0	0	0	-0	/1	-0.1
1970	NY-N	76	87	15	17	3	1	3	4	10	23	.195	.278	.356	69	-4	-4	9	2	2	-1	4	1O	-0.5
1971	NY-N	45	118	16	26	1	1	5	11	11	24	.220	.303	.373	92	-2	-1	12	1	2	-1	-0	O/1	-0.3
1972	Mon-N	113	372	48	86	12	3	13	47	53	75	.231	.333	.384	102	2	2	47	12	13	-4	3	1O	-0.6
1973	Mon-N	138	413	49	95	16	2	9	47	64	49	.230	.338	.344	86	-5	-7	52	16	7	1	6	*1O	-0.6
1974	Mon-N	131	287	45	89	16	1	11	59	70	39	.310	.448	.488	153	28	26	68	3	5	-2	7	1O	2.6
1975	Mon-N	144	445	58	116	18	0	18	67	79	75	.261	.380	.422	117	16	13	76	3	3	-1	5	*1/O	1.0
1976	Mon-N	125	343	36	87	13	0	6	23	52	48	.254	.352	.344	94	1	-1	45	7	1	2	4	1O	0.0
1977	Mon-N	19	20	3	4	1	0	0	0	3	4	.200	.304	.250	52	-1	-1	2	0	0	0	-1	/1	0.0
	Oak-A	66	203	18	50	4	1	8	32	25	44	.246	.335	.394	99	-0	-0	28	3	2	-0	1	1O/D	-0.2
1978	Tex-A	96	97	20	19	3	0	1	9	18	10	.196	.322	.258	65	-4	-4	9	3	1	0	8	1/OD	-0.4
1979	Tex-A	90	157	21	35	7	0	6	16	14	29	.223	.295	.382	82	-4	-4	17	0	2	-1	4	1O	-0.4
1980	NY-N	119	321	43	82	11	0	7	43	46	55	.255	.349	.355	100	-0	1	39	0	3	-2	0	1O	-0.5
1981	NY-N	86	122	8	25	5	2	3	15	12	24	.205	.276	.352	79	-4	-4	13	0	1	1	1	1O	-0.3
1982	NY-N	120	114	16	29	6	0	2	14	21	24	.254	.370	.360	106	2	2	17	2	0	1	-1	1O	-0.1
1983	NY-N	38	24	5	6	3	0	1	3	2	4	.250	.333	.500	129	1	1	3	0	1	1	1	1	0.0
	Atl-N	57	48	5	12	1	0	1	8	8	8	.250	.357	.333	86	-0	-1	6	0	0	0	1	1/O	0.0
	Yr	95	72	10	18	4	0	2	11	10	12	.250	.349	.389	100	1	0	10	0	1	-1	1		0.0
1984	Atl-N	31	26	4	7	1	0	0	5	3	6	.269	.345	.308	79	-0	-1	3	0	1	-1	-0	/1O	-0.1
	StL-N	59	98	5	24	4	2	1	12	10	17	.245	.315	.357	91	-2	-1	11	0	0	0	2	1	0.0
	Yr	90	124	9	31	5	2	1	17	13	23	.250	.321	.347	87	-2	-2	14	0	1	-1	2		-0.1
1985	*StL-N	72	112	14	22	6	0	0	11	31	27	.196	.375	.250	79	-1	-1	13	2	1	0	-1	1O/O	-0.4
Total	17	1633	3421	429	833	132	13	95	426	532	589	.243	.349	.373	100	19	12	470	58	44	-9	42	*1O/D	-0.5

■ TERRY JORGENSEN
Jorgensen, Terry Allen b: 9/2/66, Kewaunee, Wis. BR/TR, 6'4", 208 lbs. Deb: 9/10/89

YEAR	TM/L	G	AB	R	H	2B	3B	HR	RBI	BB	SO	AVG	OBP	SLG	PRO+	BR	/A	RC	SB	CS	SBR	FR	POS	TPR
1989	Min-A	10	23	1	4	1	0	0	2	4	5	.174	.296	.217	44	-2	-2	2	0	0	0	3	/3	0.1

■ FELIX JOSE
Jose, Domingo Felix Andujar (b: Domingo Felix Andujar (Jose)) b: 5/2/65, Santo Domingo, D.R. BB/TR, 6'1", 190 lbs. Deb: 9/02/88

YEAR	TM/L	G	AB	R	H	2B	3B	HR	RBI	BB	SO	AVG	OBP	SLG	PRO+	BR	/A	RC	SB	CS	SBR	FR	POS	TPR
1988	Oak-A	8	6	2	2	1	0	0	1	0	1	.333	.333	.500	135	0	0	1	1	0	0	1	/O	0.2
1989	Oak-A	20	57	3	11	2	0	0	5	4	13	.193	.246	.228	36	-5	-5	3	0	1	-1	1	O	-0.4

YEAR	TM/L	G	AB	R	H	2B	3B	HR	RBI	BB	SO	AVG	OBP	SLG	PRO+	BR	/A	RC	SB	CS	SBR	FR	POS	TPR
1990	Oak-A	101	341	42	90	12	0	8	39	16	65	.264	.307	.370	91	-6	-5	38	8	2	1	3	O/D	0.0
	StL-N	25	85	12	23	4	1	3	13	8	16	.271	.333	.447	110	1	1	12	4	4	-1	-2	O	-0.3
Total	3	154	489	59	126	19	1	11	58	28	95	.258	.305	.368	89	-9	-8	54	13	7	-0	3	O/D	-0.5

■ RICK JOSEPH
Joseph, Ricardo Emelindo b: 8/24/39, San Pedro De Macoris, D.R. d: 9/8/79, Santiago, D.R. BR/TR, 6'1", 192 lbs. Deb: 6/18/64

YEAR	TM/L	G	AB	R	H	2B	3B	HR	RBI	BB	SO	AVG	OBP	SLG	PRO+	BR	/A	RC	SB	CS	SBR	FR	POS	TPR
1964	KC-A	17	54	3	12	2	0	0	1	3	11	.222	.263	.259	45	-4	-4	3	0	1	-1	-2	1/3	-0.6
1967	Phi-N	17	41	4	9	2	0	1	5	4	10	.220	.289	.341	79	-1	-1	4	0	0	0	1	1	0.0
1968	Phi-N	66	155	20	34	5	0	3	12	16	35	.219	.297	.310	82	-3	-3	14	0	1	-1	1	13/O	-0.4
1969	Phi-N	99	264	35	72	15	0	6	37	22	57	.273	.331	.398	106	1	2	34	2	1	0	7	31/2	0.8
1970	Phi-N	71	119	7	27	2	1	3	10	6	28	.227	.264	.336	61	-7	-7	9	0	0	0	-4	O1/3	-1.2
Total	5	270	633	69	154	26	1	13	65	51	141	.243	.302	.349	85	-14	-13	66	2	3	-1	3	/31O2	-1.4

■ DUANE JOSEPHSON
Josephson, Duane Charles b: 6/3/42, New Hampton, Iowa BR/TR, 6', 190 lbs. Deb: 9/15/65

YEAR	TM/L	G	AB	R	H	2B	3B	HR	RBI	BB	SO	AVG	OBP	SLG	PRO+	BR	/A	RC	SB	CS	SBR	FR	POS	TPR
1965	Chi-A	4	9	2	1	0	0	0	0	2	4	.111	.273	.111	14	-1	-1	0	0	0	0	1	/C	0.0
1966	Chi-A	11	38	3	9	1	0	0	3	3	3	.237	.293	.263	65	-2	-2	3	0	0	0	3	C	0.2
1967	Chi-A	62	189	11	45	5	1	1	9	6	24	.238	.262	.291	65	-9	-8	13	0	3	-2	-5	C	-1.2
1968	Chi-A	128	434	35	107	16	6	6	45	18	52	.247	.286	.353	92	-5	-5	41	2	4	-2	11	*C	1.1
1969	Chi-A	52	162	19	39	6	2	1	20	13	17	.241	.301	.321	71	-6	-7	16	0	0	0	0	C	-0.3
1970	Chi-A	96	285	28	90	12	1	4	41	24	28	.316	.375	.407	111	6	5	42	0	1	-1	-10	C	-0.3
1971	Bos-A	91	306	38	75	14	1	10	39	22	35	.245	.296	.395	88	-3	-6	31	2	0	1	-5	C	-0.5
1972	Bos-A	26	82	11	22	4	1	1	7	4	11	.268	.310	.378	99	0	-0	7	0	2	-1	-1	1/C	-0.4
Total	8	470	1505	147	388	58	12	23	164	92	174	.258	.305	.358	89	-19	-23	153	4	10	-5	-6	C/1	-1.4

■ VON JOSHUA
Joshua, Von Everett b: 5/1/48, Oakland, Cal. BL/TL, 5'10", 170 lbs. Deb: 9/02/69

YEAR	TM/L	G	AB	R	H	2B	3B	HR	RBI	BB	SO	AVG	OBP	SLG	PRO+	BR	/A	RC	SB	CS	SBR	FR	POS	TPR
1969	LA-N	14	8	2	2	0	0	0	0	0	2	.250	.250	.250	43	-1	-1	1	1	0	0	0	/O	0.0
1970	LA-N	72	109	23	29	1	3	1	8	6	24	.266	.304	.358	80	-4	-3	12	2	2	-1	1	O	-0.4
1971	LA-N	11	7	2	0	0	0	0	0	0	1	.000	.000	.000	-99	-2	-2	0	0	0	0	1	/O	0.0
1973	LA-N	75	159	19	40	4	1	2	17	8	29	.252	.292	.327	74	-6	-6	16	7	2	1	-2	O	-0.8
1974	*LA-N	81	124	11	29	5	1	1	16	7	17	.234	.280	.315	69	-6	-5	10	3	2	-0	-3	O	-1.0
1975	SF-N	129	507	75	161	25	10	7	43	32	75	.318	.359	.448	118	14	12	81	20	10	3	3	*O	1.1
1976	SF-N	42	156	13	41	5	2	0	2	4	20	.263	.281	.321	68	-6	-7	13	1	3	-2	-2	O	-1.2
	Mil-A	107	423	44	113	13	5	5	28	18	58	.267	.297	.357	93	-6	-5	42	8	10	-4	0	*O/D	-1.0
1977	Mil-A	144	536	58	140	25	7	9	49	21	74	.261	.289	.384	82	-15	-15	53	12	9	-2	-13	*O	-3.4
1979	LA-N	94	142	22	40	7	1	3	14	7	23	.282	.315	.408	97	-1	-1	17	1	1	-0	0	O	-0.1
1980	SD-N	53	63	8	15	2	1	2	7	5	15	.238	.294	.397	97	-1	-1	7	0	1	-1	1	O/1	-0.1
Total	10	822	2234	277	610	87	31	30	184	108	338	.273	.307	.380	91	-33	-32	250	55	40	-8	-13	O/1D	-6.8

■ TED JOURDAN
Jourdan, Theodore Charles b: 9/5/1895, New Orleans, La. d: 9/23/61, New Orleans, La. BL/TL, 6', 175 lbs. Deb: 9/18/16

YEAR	TM/L	G	AB	R	H	2B	3B	HR	RBI	BB	SO	AVG	OBP	SLG	PRO+	BR	/A	RC	SB	CS	SBR	FR	POS	TPR
1916	Chi-A	3	2	0	0	0	0	0	0	1	1	.000	.333	.000	1	-0	-0	1	2			0	H	0.0
1917	Chi-A	17	34	2	5	0	1	0	2	1	3	.147	.171	.206	15	-4	-4	1	0			-0	1	-0.4
1918	Chi-A	7	10	1	1	0	0	0	1	0	0	.100	.100	.100	-39	-2	-2	0	0			-0	/1	-0.1
1920	Chi-A	48	150	16	36	5	2	0	8	17	17	.240	.337	.300	70	-6	-6	17	3	2	-0	-4	1	-0.9
Total	4	75	196	19	42	5	3	0	11	19	21	.214	.300	.270	56	-11	-11	18	5	2		-4	/1	-1.4

■ POP JOY
Joy, Aloysius C. b: 6/11/1860, Washington, D.C. d: 6/28/37, Washington, D.C. Deb: 6/03/1884

YEAR	TM/L	G	AB	R	H	2B	3B	HR	RBI	BB	SO	AVG	OBP	SLG	PRO+	BR	/A	RC	SB	CS	SBR	FR	POS	TPR
1884	Was-U	36	130	12	28	0	0	0		2		.215	.227	.215	52	-7	-6	7	0			0	1	-0.5

■ JOYCE
Joyce Deb: 8/14/1886

YEAR	TM/L	G	AB	R	H	2B	3B	HR	RBI	BB	SO	AVG	OBP	SLG	PRO+	BR	/A	RC	SB	CS	SBR	FR	POS	TPR
1886	Was-N	1	0	0	0	0	0	0	0	0		—	—	—	—	0	0	0	0			-0	/O	0.0

■ BILL JOYCE
Joyce, William Michael "Scrappy Bill" b: 9/21/1865, St.Louis, Mo. d: 5/8/41, St.Louis, Mo. BL/TR, 5'11", 185 lbs. Deb: 4/19/1890 M

YEAR	TM/L	G	AB	R	H	2B	3B	HR	RBI	BB	SO	AVG	OBP	SLG	PRO+	BR	/A	RC	SB	CS	SBR	FR	POS	TPR
1890	Bro-P	133	489	121	123	18	18	1	78	123	77	.252	.413	.368	105	15	9	95	43			-11	*3	0.6
1891	Bos-a	65	243	76	75	9	15	3	51	63	27	.309	.460	.506	183	29	30	75	36			-1	3/1	2.6
1892	Bro-N	97	372	89	91	15	12	6	45	82	55	.245	.392	.398	147	23	25	69	23			-19	3/O	1.1
1894	Was-N	99	355	103	126	25	14	17	89	87	33	.355	.496	.648	182	48	51	128	21			-3	*3	3.5
1895	Was-N	126	474	110	148	25	13	17	95	96	54	.312	.442	.527	154	40	42	126	29			-8	*3	2.8
1896	Was-N	81	310	85	97	16	10	8	51	67	20	.313	.454	.506	155	29	29	88	32			-7	32	2.1
	NY-N	49	165	36	61	9	2	5	43	34	14	.370	.500	.539	182	21	22	52	13			0	3M	2.1
	Yr	130	475	121	158	25	12	13	94	101	34	.333	.470	.518	165	50	51	140	45			-6		4.2
1897	NY-N	109	388	109	118	15	13	3	64	78		.304	.441	.433	138	25	27	91	33			-1	*3/1M	2.2
1898	NY-N	145	508	91	131	20	9	10	91	88		.258	.385	.392	130	21	24	92	34			8	*13/2M	3.0
Total	8	904	3304	820	970	152	106	70	607	718	280	.294	.435	.467	147	251	257	815	264			-40	31/2O	20.0

■ WALLY JOYNER
Joyner, Wallace Keith b: 6/16/62, Atlanta, Ga. BL/TL, 6'2", 185 lbs. Deb: 4/08/86

YEAR	TM/L	G	AB	R	H	2B	3B	HR	RBI	BB	SO	AVG	OBP	SLG	PRO+	BR	/A	RC	SB	CS	SBR	FR	POS	TPR
1986	*Cal-A	154	593	82	172	27	3	22	100	57	58	.290	.354	.457	120	15	16	96	5	2	0	9	*1	1.5
1987	Cal-A	149	564	100	161	33	1	34	117	72	64	.285	.371	.528	140	28	31	111	8	2	1	-7	*1	1.1
1988	Cal-A	158	597	81	176	31	2	13	85	55	51	.295	.359	.419	120	14	16	89	8	2	1	11	*1	1.9
1989	Cal-A	159	593	78	167	30	2	16	79	46	58	.282	.340	.420	115	9	11	82	3	2	-0	-4	*1	-0.3
1990	Cal-A	83	310	35	83	15	0	8	41	41	34	.268	.355	.394	109	5	4	43	2	1	0	2	1	0.0
Total	5	703	2657	376	759	136	8	93	422	271	265	.286	.356	.448	122	72	79	421	26	9	2	11	1	4.2

■ FRANK JUDE
Jude, Frank b: 1884, Libby, Minn. d: 5/4/61, Brownsville, Tex. BR/TR, 5'7", 150 lbs. Deb: 7/09/06

YEAR	TM/L	G	AB	R	H	2B	3B	HR	RBI	BB	SO	AVG	OBP	SLG	PRO+	BR	/A	RC	SB	CS	SBR	FR	POS	TPR
1906	Cin-N	80	308	31	64	6	4	1	31	16		.208	.247	.263	58	-14	-16	23	7			-2	O	-2.2

■ JOE JUDGE
Judge, Joseph Ignatius b: 5/25/1894, Brooklyn, N.Y. d: 3/11/63, Washington, D.C. BL/TL, 5'8.5", 155 lbs. Deb: 9/20/15 C

YEAR	TM/L	G	AB	R	H	2B	3B	HR	RBI	BB	SO	AVG	OBP	SLG	PRO+	BR	/A	RC	SB	CS	SBR	FR	POS	TPR
1915	Was-A	12	41	7	17	2	0	0	9	4	6	.415	.500	.463	187	5	5	10	2	3	-1	-1	1/O	0.2
1916	Was-A	103	336	42	74	10	8	0	28	54	44	.220	.333	.298	92	-3	-2	40	18			4	*1	0.0
1917	Was-A	102	393	62	112	15	15	2	30	50	40	.285	.369	.415	141	18	19	63	17			-1	*1	1.5
1918	Was-A	130	502	56	131	23	7	1	46	49	32	.261	.332	.341	105	1	1	63	20			2	*1	-0.3
1919	Was-A	135	521	83	150	33	12	2	31	81	35	.288	.386	.409	124	18	19	87	23			-4	*1	0.5
1920	Was-A	126	493	103	164	19	15	5	51	65	34	.333	.416	.462	136	26	27	96	12	12	-4	-8	*1	1.5
1921	Was-A	153	622	87	187	26	11	6	72	68	35	.301	.372	.412	105	1	1	100	21	6	3	-3	*1	0.3
1922	Was-A	148	591	84	174	32	15	10	81	50	20	.294	.355	.450	114	6	10	91	5	15	-8	3	*1	-0.5
1923	Was-A	113	405	56	127	24	6	2	63	58	20	.314	.404	.417	123	12	15	72	11	7	-1	8	*1	1.7
1924	*Was-A	140	516	71	167	38	9	3	79	53	21	.324	.393	.450	121	13	16	93	13	8	-1	-2	*1	0.5
1925	*Was-A	112	376	65	118	31	5	6	66	55	21	.314	.406	.487	128	15	16	73	7	12	-5	3	*1	1.1
1926	Was-A	134	453	70	132	25	11	7	92	53	25	.291	.367	.442	113	6	8	75	7	5	-1	10	*1	1.1
1927	Was-A	137	522	68	161	29	11	2	71	45	22	.308	.366	.418	104	2	3	77	10	5	0	-6	*1	-0.7
1928	Was-A	153	542	78	166	31	10	8	93	80	19	.306	.396	.417	105	14	14	96	16	4	2	1	*1	0.8
1929	Was-A	143	543	83	171	35	8	6	71	73	33	.315	.397	.442	115	15	14	100	3	5	-1	3	*1	-0.2
1930	Was-A	126	442	83	144	29	11	10	80	60	29	.326	.410	.509	131	22	22	95	13	6	0	2	*1	1.0
1931	Was-A	35	74	11	21	3	0	0	9	8	8	.284	.354	.324	79	-2	-2	9	0	0	0	1		-0.1
1932	Was-A	82	291	45	75	16	3	3	29	37	19	.258	.343	.364	84	-7	-6	38	3	3	-1	1		-1.2
1933	Bro-N	42	112	7	24	2	1	0	9	7	10	.214	.261	.250	48	-8	-7	7	0	1		0	1	-0.7
	Bos-A	35	108	20	32	8	1	0	22	13	4	.296	.372	.389	103	1	1	16	2	1	0	-0	1	-0.1

YEAR	TM/L	G	AB	R	H	2B	3B	HR	RBI	BB	SO	AVG	OBP	SLG	PRO+	BR	/A	RC	SB	CS	SBR	FR	POS	TPR
1934	Bos-A	10	15	3	5	2	0	0	2	2	1	.333	.412	.467	118	1	0	3	0	0	0	0	/1	0.0
Total	20	2171	7898	1184	2352	433	159	71	1034	965	478	.298	.378	.420	115	157	180	1304	213	92		14	*1/O	6.4

■ WALLY JUDNICH
Judnich, Walter Franklin   b: 1/24/17, San Francisco, Cal   d: 7/12/71, Glendale, Cal.   BL/TL, 6'1", 205 lbs.   Deb: 4/16/40

YEAR	TM/L	G	AB	R	H	2B	3B	HR	RBI	BB	SO	AVG	OBP	SLG	PRO+	BR	/A	RC	SB	CS	SBR	FR	POS	TPR
1940	StL-A	137	519	97	157	27	7	24	89	54	71	.303	.368	.520	125	20	18	102	8	5	-1	-2	*O	0.6
1941	StL-A	146	546	90	155	40	6	14	83	80	45	.284	.377	.456	116	16	13	98	5	5	-2	-0	*O	0.3
1942	StL-A	132	457	78	143	22	6	17	82	74	41	.313	.413	.499	153	35	34	101	3	2	-0	-4	*O	2.2
1946	StL-A	142	511	60	134	23	4	15	72	60	54	.262	.340	.411	104	6	3	74	0	4	-2	8	*O	0.1
1947	StL-A	144	500	58	129	24	3	18	64	60	62	.258	.338	.426	109	6	5	75	2	5	-2	-5	*1O	-0.6
1948	*Cle-A	79	218	36	56	13	3	2	29	56	23	.257	.411	.372	112	6	6	38	2	3	-1	-4	O1	0.1
1949	Pit-N	10	35	5	8	1	0	0	1	1	2	.229	.250	.257	35	-3	-3	2	0			1	/O	-0.1
Total	7	790	2786	424	782	150	29	90	420	385	298	.281	.369	.452	119	85	77	491	20	24		-6	O1	2.6

■ LYLE JUDY
Judy, Lyle Leroy "Punch"   b: 11/15/13, Lawrenceville, Ill   BR/TR, 5'10", 150 lbs.   Deb: 9/17/35

YEAR	TM/L	G	AB	R	H	2B	3B	HR	RBI	BB	SO	AVG	OBP	SLG	PRO+	BR	/A	RC	SB	CS	SBR	FR	POS	TPR
1935	StL-N	8	11	2	0	0	0	0	0	2	2	.000	.154	.000	-53	-2	-2	0	2			1	/2	-0.1

■ RED JUELICH
Juelich, John Samuel   b: 9/20/16, St.Louis, Mo.   d: 12/25/70, St.Louis, Mo.   BR/TR, 5'11.5", 170 lbs.   Deb: 5/30/39

YEAR	TM/L	G	AB	R	H	2B	3B	HR	RBI	BB	SO	AVG	OBP	SLG	PRO+	BR	/A	RC	SB	CS	SBR	FR	POS	TPR
1939	Pit-N	17	46	5	11	0	2	0	4	2	4	.239	.271	.326	61	-3	-3	3	0			-5	2/3	-0.7

■ GEORGE JUMONVILLE
Jumonville, George Benedict   b: 5/16/17, Mobile, Ala.   BR/TR, 6', 175 lbs.   Deb: 9/13/40

YEAR	TM/L	G	AB	R	H	2B	3B	HR	RBI	BB	SO	AVG	OBP	SLG	PRO+	BR	/A	RC	SB	CS	SBR	FR	POS	TPR
1940	Phi-N	11	34	0	3	0	0	0	0	1	6	.088	.139	.088	-38	-6	-6	0	0			-4	S/3	-0.9
1941	Phi-N	6	7	1	3	0	0	1	2	0	0	.429	.429	.857	266	1	1	3	0			1	/2S	0.2
Total	2	17	41	1	6	0	0	1	2	1	6	.146	.186	.220	12	-5	-5	3	0			-3	/S23	-0.7

■ ED JURAK
Jurak, Edward James   b: 10/24/57, Los Angeles, Cal.   BR/TR, 6'2", 185 lbs.   Deb: 6/30/82

YEAR	TM/L	G	AB	R	H	2B	3B	HR	RBI	BB	SO	AVG	OBP	SLG	PRO+	BR	/A	RC	SB	CS	SBR	FR	POS	TPR
1982	Bos-A	12	21	3	7	0	0	0	7	2	4	.333	.391	.333	96	0	-0	3	0	0	0	2	3/O	0.2
1983	Bos-A	75	159	19	44	8	4	0	18	18	25	.277	.354	.377	95	1	-1	21	1	2	-1	9	S13/2D	0.9
1984	Bos-A	47	66	6	16	3	1	1	7	12	12	.242	.359	.364	96	0	0	9	0	2	-1	5	12/3S	0.3
1985	Bos-A	26	13	4	3	0	0	0	0	1	3	.231	.286	.231	42	-1	-1	1	0	0	0	4	/3S10D	0.3
1988	Oak-A	3	1	1	0	0	0	0	0	0	0	.000	.000	.000	-99	-0	-0	0	0	0	0	-0	/3D	0.0
1989	SF-N	30	42	2	10	0	0	0	1	5	5	.238	.319	.238	63	-2	-2	3	0	0	0	-1	/S3201	-0.2
Total	6	193	302	35	80	11	5	1	33	38	49	.265	.349	.344	88	-2	-4	37	1	4	-2	18	/S312DO	1.5

■ BILLY JURGES
Jurges, William Frederick   b: 5/9/08, Bronx, N.Y.   BR/TR, 5'11", 175 lbs.   Deb: 5/04/31   MC

YEAR	TM/L	G	AB	R	H	2B	3B	HR	RBI	BB	SO	AVG	OBP	SLG	PRO+	BR	/A	RC	SB	CS	SBR	FR	POS	TPR
1931	Chi-N	88	293	34	59	15	5	0	23	25	41	.201	.264	.287	47	-22	-22	24	2			11	32/S	-0.5
1932	*Chi-N	115	396	40	100	24	4	2	52	19	26	.253	.288	.348	71	-17	-16	41	1			32	*S/3	2.4
1933	Chi-N	143	487	49	131	17	6	5	50	26	39	.269	.313	.359	92	-6	-6	52	3			20	*S	2.5
1934	Chi-N	100	358	43	88	15	2	8	33	19	34	.246	.289	.366	76	-14	-13	37	1			14	*S	0.3
1935	*Chi-N	146	519	69	125	33	1	1	59	42	39	.241	.304	.314	66	-24	-24	50	3			30	*S	1.2
1936	Chi-N	118	429	51	120	25	1	1	42	23	25	.280	.321	.350	79	-12	-13	46	4			17	*S	1.0
1937	Chi-N	129	450	53	134	18	10	1	65	42	41	.298	.365	.389	101	4	2	66	2			-7	*S	0.4
1938	*Chi-N	137	465	53	114	18	3	1	47	58	53	.245	.335	.303	75	-13	-15	48	3			-0	*S	-0.4
1939	NY-N	138	543	84	155	21	11	6	63	47	34	.285	.349	.398	99	0	-0	71	3			15	*S	2.3
1940	NY-N	63	214	23	54	3	3	2	36	25	14	.252	.347	.322	85	-3	-3	23	2			-1	S	0.2
1941	NY-N	134	471	50	138	25	2	5	61	47	36	.293	.361	.386	108	7	6	66	0			7	*S	2.5
1942	NY-N	127	464	45	119	7	1	2	30	43	42	.256	.324	.289	79	-11	-11	42	1			7	*S	0.5
1943	NY-N	136	481	46	110	8	2	4	29	53	38	.229	.310	.279	70	-17	-17	44	2			1	S3	-0.7
1944	NY-N	85	246	28	52	2	1	1	23	23	20	.211	.279	.240	47	-17	-17	17	4			-0	3S/2	-1.2
1945	NY-N	61	176	22	57	3	1	3	24	24	11	.324	.405	.403	123	7	7	30	2			2	3/S	0.8
1946	Chi-N	82	221	26	49	9	2	0	17	43	28	.222	.351	.281	82	-4	-3	24	3			-3	S/32	0.0
1947	Chi-N	14	40	5	8	2	0	1	2	9	9	.200	.347	.325	83	-1	-1	5	0			-4	S	-0.2
Total	17	1816	6253	721	1613	245	55	43	656	568	530	.258	.325	.335	82	-140	-147	686	36			141	*S3/2	11.1

■ JOE JUST
Just, Joseph Erwin (b: Joseph Erwin Juszczak)   b: 1/8/16, Milwaukee, Wis.   BR/TR, 5'11", 185 lbs.   Deb: 5/13/44

YEAR	TM/L	G	AB	R	H	2B	3B	HR	RBI	BB	SO	AVG	OBP	SLG	PRO+	BR	/A	RC	SB	CS	SBR	FR	POS	TPR
1944	Cin-N	11	11	0	2	0	0	0	0	2	2	.182	.250	.182	24	-1	-1	0	0			0	C	0.0
1945	Cin-N	14	34	2	5	0	0	0	2	4	7	.147	.237	.147	8	-4	-4	1	0			-2	C	-0.5
Total	2	25	45	2	7	0	0	0	2	4	9	.156	.240	.156	12	-5	-5	2	0			-1	/C	-0.5

■ DAVE JUSTICE
Justice, David Christopher   b: 4/14/66, Cincinnati, Ohio   BL/TL, 6'3", 195 lbs.   Deb: 5/24/89

YEAR	TM/L	G	AB	R	H	2B	3B	HR	RBI	BB	SO	AVG	OBP	SLG	PRO+	BR	/A	RC	SB	CS	SBR	FR	POS	TPR
1989	Atl-N	16	51	7	12	3	0	1	3	3	9	.235	.291	.353	81	-1	-1	5	2	1	0	-1	O	-0.2
1990	Atl-N	127	439	76	124	23	2	28	78	64	92	.282	.374	.535	145	28	27	92	11	6	-0	-6	1O	1.6
Total	2	143	490	83	136	26	2	29	81	67	101	.278	.366	.516	138	27	26	97	13	7	-0	-7	/O1	1.4

■ SKIP JUTZE
Jutze, Alfred Henry   b: 5/28/46, Queens, N.Y.   BR/TR, 5'11", 190 lbs.   Deb: 9/01/72

YEAR	TM/L	G	AB	R	H	2B	3B	HR	RBI	BB	SO	AVG	OBP	SLG	PRO+	BR	/A	RC	SB	CS	SBR	FR	POS	TPR
1972	StL-N	21	71	1	17	2	0	0	5	1	16	.239	.250	.268	48	-5	-5	4	0	1	-1	0	C	-0.4
1973	Hou-N	90	278	18	62	6	0	0	18	19	37	.223	.275	.245	45	-20	-20	17	0	1	-1	-6	C	-2.2
1974	Hou-N	8	13	0	3	0	0	0	1	1	1	.231	.286	.231	48	-1	-1	1	0	0	0	-0	/C	0.0
1975	Hou-N	51	93	9	21	2	0	0	6	2	4	.226	.242	.247	39	-8	-7	6	1	0	0	4	C	-0.1
1976	Hou-N	42	92	7	14	2	3	0	6	4	16	.152	.188	.239	22	-10	-9	4	0	0	0	3	C	-0.3
1977	Sea-A	42	109	10	24	2	0	3	15	7	12	.220	.267	.321	60	-6	-6	8	0	4	-2	-2	C	-0.9
Total	6	254	656	45	141	14	3	3	51	34	86	.215	.255	.259	44	-50	-48	39	1	6	-3	-1	C	-3.9

■ HERB JUUL
Juul, Herbert Victor   b: 2/2/1886, Chicago, Ill.   d: 11/14/28, Chicago, Ill.   BL/TL, 5'11", 150 lbs.   Deb: 7/11/11

YEAR	TM/L	G	AB	R	H	2B	3B	HR	RBI	BB	SO	AVG	OBP	SLG	PRO+	BR	/A	RC	SB	CS	SBR	FR	POS	TPR
1911	Cin-N	2	2	0	0	0	0	0	0	0	0	.000	.000	.000	-99	-1	-1	0	0			-0	/P	0.0

■ JIM KAAT
Kaat, James Lee   b: 11/7/38, Zeeland, Mich.   BL/TL, 6'4.5", 205 lbs.   Deb: 8/02/59   C

YEAR	TM/L	G	AB	R	H	2B	3B	HR	RBI	BB	SO	AVG	OBP	SLG	PRO+	BR	/A	RC	SB	CS	SBR	FR	POS	TPR
1959	Was-A	3	1	0	0	0	0	0	0	0	1	.000	.000	.000	-99	-0	-0	0	0	0	0	0	/P	0.0
1960	Was-A	13	14	0	2	0	0	0	0	0	6	.143	.143	.143	-23	-2	-2	0	0	0	0	0	P	0.0
1961	Min-A	47	63	10	15	3	1	0	1	4	13	.238	.294	.317	60	-3	-4	6	0	0	0	3	P	0.2
1962	Min-A	48	100	9	18	3	1	1	10	8	40	.180	.241	.260	33	-9	-10	7	0	0	0	4	P	0.2
1963	Min-A	36	61	2	8	1	0	1	8	2	19	.131	.185	.197	7	-8	-8	2	0	0	0	4	P	0.2
1964	Min-A	46	83	11	14	1	0	3	11	11	31	.169	.266	.289	54	-5	-5	7	0	0	0	3	P	0.2
1965	*Min-A	56	93	6	23	4	0	1	9	3	29	.247	.271	.323	65	-4	-5	9	2	0	1	4	P	0.2
1966	Min-A	47	118	12	23	2	1	2	13	5	41	.195	.228	.280	42	-8	-9	8	0	0	0	1	P	0.0
1967	Min-A	45	99	7	17	3	1	1	4	7	26	.172	.226	.253	38	-7	-8	6	0	0	0	1	P	0.0
1968	Min-A	36	77	7	12	0	0	0	5	2	18	.156	.177	.195	12	-8	-8	2	0	0	0	3	P	0.0
1969	Min-A	43	87	8	18	8	0	2	10	4	20	.207	.239	.368	69	-4	-4	8	0	0	0	-3	P	0.0
1970	*Min-A	56	76	17	15	1	0	1	8	6	20	.197	.265	.250	42	-6	-6	5	0	0	0	2	P	0.0
1971	Min-A	54	93	6	15	3	0	0	5	2	16	.161	.179	.194	5	-12	-12	4	0	0	0	1	P	0.0
1972	Min-A	24	45	3	13	3	0	2	4	1	16	.289	.304	.489	127	1	1	6	0	1	-1	-0	P	0.0
1973	Min-A	31	0	0	0	0	0	0	0	0	0	—	—	—		0	0	0	0	0	0	-1	P	0.0
	Chi-A	7	0	0	0	0	0	0	0	0	0	—	—	—		0	0	0	0	0	0	-1	/P	0.0
	Yr	38	0	1	0	0	0	0	0	0	0	—	—	—		0	0	0	0	0	0	-1		0.0
1974	Chi-A	42	1	0	0	0	0	0	0	0	0	.000	.000	.000	-98	-0	-0	0	0	0	0	-1	P	0.0
1975	Chi-A	43	0	0	0	0	0	0	0	0	0					0	0	0	0	0	0	-1	P	0.0

YEAR	TM/L	G	AB	R	H	2B	3B	HR	RBI	BB	SO	AVG	OBP	SLG	PRO+	BR	/A	RC	SB	CS	SBR	FR	POS	TPR
1976	*Phi-N	42	79	4	14	3	1	1	8	2	24	.177	.198	.278	33	-7	-7	5	0	0	0	-2	P	0.0
1977	Phi-N	36	53	4	10	3	0	0	2	2	12	.189	.218	.245	23	-6	-6	3	0	0	0	-1	P	0.0
1978	Phi-N	26	48	4	7	1	0	0	4	0	15	.146	.163	.167	-8	-7	-7	1	0	0	0	-1	P	0.0
1979	Phi-N	3	1	0	0	0	0	0	0	0	1	.000	.500	.000	47	0	0	0	0	0	0	0	/P	0.0
	NY-A	40	0	0	0	0	0	0	0	0	0	—	—	—	—	0	0	0	0	0	0	-1	P	0.0
1980	NY-A	4	0	0	0	0	0	0	0	0	0	—	—	—	—	0	0	0	0	0	0	1	/P	0.0
	StL-N	49	35	4	5	1	0	1	2	2	13	.143	.189	.257	23	-4	-4	2	1	0	0	-1	P	0.0
1981	StL-N	41	8	2	3	1	0	0	2	1	0	.375	.444	.500	163	1	1	2	0	0	0	1	P	0.0
1982	*StL-N	62	12	0	0	0	0	0	0	1	4	.000	.077	.000	-76	-3	-3	0	0	0	0	1	P	0.0
1983	StL-N	24	4	0	0	0	0	0	0	0	2	.000	.000	.000	-99	-1	-1	0	0	0	0	0	P	0.0
Total	25	1004	1251	117	232	44	5	16	106	63	367	.185	.229	.267	38	-102	-108	83	5	1	1	12	P	0.0

■ JACK KADING Kading, John Frederick b: 11/17/1884, Waukesha, Wis. d: 6/2/64, Chicago, Ill. 6'3", 190 lbs. Deb: 9/12/10

YEAR	TM/L	G	AB	R	H	2B	3B	HR	RBI	BB	SO	AVG	OBP	SLG	PRO+	BR	/A	RC	SB	CS	SBR	FR	POS	TPR
1910	Pit-N	8	23	5	7	2	1	0	4	4	5	.304	.407	.478	149	2	2	5	0			1	/1	0.3
1914	Chi-F	3	3	0	0	0	0	0	0	0	0	.000	.000	.000	-99	-1	-1	0	0			0	H	0.0
Total	2	11	26	5	7	2	1	0	4	4	5	.269	.367	.423	124	1	1	5	0			1	/1	0.3

■ JAKE KAFORA Kafora, Frank Jacob "Tomatoes" b: 10/16/1888, Chicago, Ill. d: 3/23/28, Chicago, Ill. BR/TR, 6', 180 lbs. Deb: 10/05/13

YEAR	TM/L	G	AB	R	H	2B	3B	HR	RBI	BB	SO	AVG	OBP	SLG	PRO+	BR	/A	RC	SB	CS	SBR	FR	POS	TPR
1913	Pit-N	1	1	1	0	0	0	0	0	0	1	.000	.500	.000	52	0	0	0	0			-0	/C	0.0
1914	Pit-N	21	23	2	3	0	0	0	0	0	6	.130	.200	.130	-1	-3	-3	1	0			-1	C	-0.3
Total	2	22	24	3	3	0	0	0	0	0	7	.125	.222	.125	4	-3	-3	1	0			-2	/C	-0.3

■ IKE KAHDOT Kahdot, Isaac Leonard "Chief" b: 10/22/01, Georgetown, Okla. BR/TR, 5'5.5", 145 lbs. Deb: 9/05/22

YEAR	TM/L	G	AB	R	H	2B	3B	HR	RBI	BB	SO	AVG	OBP	SLG	PRO+	BR	/A	RC	SB	CS	SBR	FR	POS	TPR
1922	Cle-A	4	2	0	0	0	0	0	0	0	1	.000	.000	.000	-99	-1	-1	0	0	0	0	1	/3	0.0

■ NICK KAHL Kahl, Nicholas Alexander b: 4/10/1879, Coulterville, Ill. d: 7/13/59, Sparta, Ill. BR/TR, 5'9", 185 lbs. Deb: 5/02/05

YEAR	TM/L	G	AB	R	H	2B	3B	HR	RBI	BB	SO	AVG	OBP	SLG	PRO+	BR	/A	RC	SB	CS	SBR	FR	POS	TPR
1905	Cle-A	40	135	16	29	4	1	0	21	4		.215	.237	.259	58	-6	-6	9	1			0	2/SO	-0.6

■ BOB KAHLE Kahle, Robert Wayne b: 11/23/15, Newcastle, Ind. d: 12/16/88, Inglewood, Cal. BR/TR, 6', 170 lbs. Deb: 4/21/38

YEAR	TM/L	G	AB	R	H	2B	3B	HR	RBI	BB	SO	AVG	OBP	SLG	PRO+	BR	/A	RC	SB	CS	SBR	FR	POS	TPR
1938	Bos-N	8	3	2	1	0	0	0	0	0	0	.333	.333	.333	93	-0	-0	0	0			0	H	0.0

■ OWEN KAHN Kahn, Owen Earle "Jack" b: 6/5/05, Richmond, Va. d: 1/17/81, Richmond, Va. BR/TR, 5'11", 160 lbs. Deb: 5/24/30

YEAR	TM/L	G	AB	R	H	2B	3B	HR	RBI	BB	SO	AVG	OBP	SLG	PRO+	BR	/A	RC	SB	CS	SBR	FR	POS	TPR
1930	Bos-N	1	0	1	0	0	0	0	0	0	0	—	—	—	—	0	0	0	0			0	R	0.0

■ MIKE KAHOE Kahoe, Michael Joseph b: 9/3/1873, Yellow Springs, O. d: 5/14/49, Akron, Ohio BR/TR, 6', 185 lbs. Deb: 9/22/1895

YEAR	TM/L	G	AB	R	H	2B	3B	HR	RBI	BB	SO	AVG	OBP	SLG	PRO+	BR	/A	RC	SB	CS	SBR	FR	POS	TPR
1895	Cin-N	3	4	0	0	0	0	0	0	0	0	.000	.000	.000	-96	-1	-1	0	0			-1	/C	0.0
1899	Cin-N	14	42	2	7	1	1	0	4	0		.167	.167	.238	11	-5	-5	2	1			5	C	0.0
1900	Cin-N	52	175	18	33	3	3	1	9	4		.189	.215	.257	32	-16	-16	11	3			7	C/S	-0.3
1901	Cin-N	4	13	0	4	0	0	0	0	1		.308	.357	.308	103	-0	-0	1	0			-1	/C	0.0
	Chi-N	67	237	21	53	12	2	1	21	8		.224	.249	.304	64	-12	-11	20	5			11	C/1	0.8
	Yr	71	250	21	57	12	2	1	21	9		.228	.255	.304	66	-12	-11	22	5			10		0.8
1902	Chi-N	7	18	0	4	1	0	0	2	0		.222	.222	.278	57	-1	-1	1	0			-0	/C3S	
	StL-A	55	197	21	48	9	2	2	28	6		.244	.270	.340	71	-8	-8	20	4			0	C	-0.2
1903	StL-A	77	244	26	46	7	5	0	23	11		.189	.224	.258	47	-16	-15	15	1			-4	C/O	-1.0
1904	StL-A	72	236	9	51	6	1	0	12	8		.216	.242	.250	61	-11	-10	17	4			2	C	0.0
1905	Phi-N	16	51	2	13	2	0	0	4	1		.255	.269	.294	72	-2	-2	5	1			-0	C	0.0
1907	Chi-N	5	10	0	4	0	0	0	1	0		.400	.400	.400	144	1	0	2	0			-1	/C1	0.0
	Was-A	17	47	3	9	1	0	0	1	0		.191	.191	.213	33	-4	-3	2	0			1	C	0.0
1908	Was-A	17	27	1	5	1	0	0	0	0		.185	.185	.222	37	-2	-2	1	0			5	C	0.4
1909	Was-A	4	8	0	1	0	0	0	0	0		.125	.125	.125	-22	-1	-1	0	2			-0	/C	0.0
Total	11	410	1309	103	278	43	14	4	105	39	0	.212	.237	.276	54	-79	-74	97	21			23	C/103S	-0.3

■ AL KAISER Kaiser, Alfred Edward "Deerfoot" b: 8/3/1886, Cincinnati, Ohio d: 4/11/69, Cincinnati, Ohio BR/TR, 5'9", 165 lbs. Deb: 4/18/11

YEAR	TM/L	G	AB	R	H	2B	3B	HR	RBI	BB	SO	AVG	OBP	SLG	PRO+	BR	/A	RC	SB	CS	SBR	FR	POS	TPR
1911	Chi-N	26	84	16	21	0	5	0	7	7	12	.250	.308	.369	89	-2	-2	11	6			-2	O	-0.3
	Bos-N	66	197	20	40	5	2	2	15	10	26	.203	.249	.279	44	-14	-17	15	4			-1	O	-1.9
	Yr	92	281	36	61	5	7	2	22	17	38	.217	.267	.306	57	-16	-18	26	10			-3		-2.2
1912	Bos-N	4	13	0	0	0	0	0	0	0	3	.000	.000	.000	-98	-4	-4	-0	0			1	/O	-0.2
1914	Ind-F	59	187	22	43	10	0	1	16	17	41	.230	.301	.299	65	-6	-9	20	6			-3	O/1	-1.4
Total	3	155	481	58	104	15	7	3	38	34	82	.216	.274	.295	56	-26	-31	46	16			-5	O/1	-3.8

■ JOHN KALAHAN Kalahan, John Joseph b: 9/30/1878, Philadelphia, Pa. d: 6/20/52, Philadelphia, Pa. TR, 6', 165 lbs. Deb: 9/29/03

YEAR	TM/L	G	AB	R	H	2B	3B	HR	RBI	BB	SO	AVG	OBP	SLG	PRO+	BR	/A	RC	SB	CS	SBR	FR	POS	TPR
1903	Phi-A	1	5	0	0	0	0	0	0	0	0	.000	.000	.000	-96	-1	-1	0	0			-1	/C	-0.1

■ CHARLIE KALBFUS Kalbfus, Charles Henry "Skinny" b: 12/28/1864, Washington, D.C. d: 11/18/41, Washington, D.C. BR/TR, 5'11", 145 lbs. Deb: 4/18/1884

YEAR	TM/L	G	AB	R	H	2B	3B	HR	RBI	BB	SO	AVG	OBP	SLG	PRO+	BR	/A	RC	SB	CS	SBR	FR	POS	TPR
1884	Was-U	1	5	1	1	0	0	0	0	0	0	.200	.200	.200	37	-0	-0	0	0			-0	/O	0.0

■ FRANK KALIN Kalin, Frank Bruno "Fats" (b: Frank Bruno Kalinkiewicz) b: 10/3/17, Steubenville, Ohio d: 1/12/75, Weirton, W.Va. BR/TR, 6', 200 lbs. Deb: 9/25/40

YEAR	TM/L	G	AB	R	H	2B	3B	HR	RBI	BB	SO	AVG	OBP	SLG	PRO+	BR	/A	RC	SB	CS	SBR	FR	POS	TPR
1940	Pit-N	3	3	0	0	0	0	0	1	2	0	.000	.400	.000	19	-0	-0	0	0			-0	/O	0.0
1943	Chi-A	4	4	0	0	0	0	0	0	0	0	.000	.000	.000	-99	-1	-1	0	0	0	0	0	H	0.0
Total	2	7	7	0	0	0	0	0	1	2	0	.000	.222	.000	-34	-1	-1	0	0	0		-0	/O	0.0

■ AL KALINE Kaline, Albert William b: 12/19/34, Baltimore, Md. BR/TR, 6'1.5", 175 lbs. Deb: 6/25/53 H

YEAR	TM/L	G	AB	R	H	2B	3B	HR	RBI	BB	SO	AVG	OBP	SLG	PRO+	BR	/A	RC	SB	CS	SBR	FR	POS	TPR
1953	Det-A	30	28	9	7	0	0	0	2	1	5	.250	.300	.357	78	-1	-1	3	1	0	0	1	O	0.0
1954	Det-A	138	504	42	139	18	3	4	43	22	45	.276	.306	.347	80	-16	-15	48	9	5	-0	5	*O	-1.3
1955	Det-A	152	588	121	**200**	24	8	27	102	82	57	**.340**	.425	.546	163	50	52	135	6	8	-3	4	*O	4.4
1956	Det-A	153	617	96	194	32	10	27	128	70	55	.314	.385	.530	139	33	33	129	7	1	2	16	*O	4.2
1957	Det-A	149	577	83	170	29	4	23	90	43	38	.295	.347	.478	120	17	15	92	11	9	-2	11	*O	1.5
1958	Det-A	146	543	84	170	34	7	16	85	54	47	.313	.377	.490	127	27	22	96	7	4	-0	**22**	*O	3.5
1959	Det-A	136	511	86	167	19	2	27	94	72	42	.327	.414	**.530**	149	42	38	114	10	4	1	4	*O	3.6
1960	Det-A	147	551	77	153	29	4	15	68	65	47	.278	.357	.426	108	9	7	84	19	4	3	3	*O	0.7
1961	Det-A	153	586	116	190	**41**	7	19	82	66	42	.324	.396	.515	138	35	33	121	14	1	4	18	*O/3	4.8
1962	Det-A	100	398	78	121	16	6	29	94	47	39	.304	.379	.593	152	31	29	85	4	0	1	10	*O	3.6
1963	Det-A	145	551	89	172	24	3	27	101	54	48	.312	.378	.514	142	34	32	105	6	4	-1	-4	*O	2.4
1964	Det-A	146	525	77	154	31	5	17	68	75	51	.293	.385	.469	134	27	26	97	4	1	1	9	*O	3.1
1965	Det-A	125	399	72	112	18	2	18	72	72	49	.281	.391	.471	142	25	24	77	6	0	2	-2	*O/3	2.1
1966	Det-A	142	479	85	138	29	1	29	88	81	66	.288	.396	.534	161	42	41	105	5	5	-2	-1	*O	3.5
1967	Det-A	131	458	94	141	28	2	25	78	83	47	.308	.415	.541	176	48	47	104	8	2	1	6	*O	5.4
1968	*Det-A	102	327	49	94	14	1	10	53	55	39	.287	.395	.428	145	22	21	59	6	4	-1	-3	O1	1.4
1969	Det-A	131	456	74	124	17	0	21	69	54	61	.272	.350	.447	117	13	10	71	1	2	-1	-3	*O/1	0.3
1970	Det-A	131	467	64	130	24	4	16	71	77	49	.278	.382	.450	127	20	19	79	2	2	-1	-2	O1	1.1
1971	Det-A	133	405	69	119	19	2	15	54	82	57	.294	.421	.462	144	31	29	81	4	6	-2	-9	*O/1	1.4
1972	*Det-A	106	278	46	87	11	2	10	32	28	33	.313	.380	.470	148	17	18	48	1	0	0	-5	O1	1.0
1973	Det-A	91	310	40	79	13	0	10	45	29	28	.255	.325	.394	95	0	-2	39	4	1	1	-6	O1	-1.1
1974	Det-A	147	558	71	146	28	2	13	64	65	75	.262	.340	.389	105	7	5	75	2	2	-1	0	*D	0.4
Total	22	2834	10116	1622	3007	498	75	399	1583	1277	1020	.297	.379	.480	134	513	481	1846	137	65	2	74	*OD1/3	46.0

YEAR	TM/L	G	AB	R	H	2B	3B	HR	RBI	BB	SO	AVG	OBP	SLG	PRO+	BR	/A	RC	SB	CS	SBR	FR	POS	TPR

■ WILLIE KAMM
Kamm, William Edward b: 2/2/1900, San Francisco, Cal. d: 12/21/88, Belmont, Cal. BR/TR, 5'10.5", 170 lbs. Deb: 4/18/23

YEAR	TM/L	G	AB	R	H	2B	3B	HR	RBI	BB	SO	AVG	OBP	SLG	PRO+	BR	/A	RC	SB	CS	SBR	FR	POS	TPR
1923	Chi-A	149	544	57	159	39	9	6	87	62	82	.292	.366	.430	110	7	8	86	17	13	-3	8	*3	2.9
1924	Chi-A	147	528	58	134	28	6	6	93	64	59	.254	.337	.364	83	-16	-13	68	9	8	-2	8	*3	0.4
1925	Chi-A	152	509	82	142	32	4	6	83	90	36	.279	.391	.393	105	2	7	83	11	13	-5	-0	*3	1.0
1926	Chi-A	143	480	63	141	24	10	0	62	77	24	.294	.396	.385	108	6	9	80	14	4	2	14	*3	3.5
1927	Chi-A	148	540	85	146	32	13	0	59	70	18	.270	.354	.378	92	-7	-5	71	7	9	-3	1	*3	0.2
1928	Chi-A	155	552	70	170	30	12	1	84	73	22	.308	.391	.411	112	11	12	93	17	9	-0	-3	*3	1.1
1929	Chi-A	147	523	72	140	33	6	3	63	75	23	.268	.363	.371	90	-7	-6	76	13	4	2	4	*3	0.8
1930	Chi-A	112	331	49	89	21	6	3	47	51	20	.269	.368	.396	97	-2	-0	51	5	4	-1	15	*3	1.6
1931	Chi-A	18	59	9	15	4	1	0	9	7	6	.254	.333	.356	86	-2	-1	7	1	1	-0	2	3	0.2
	Cle-A	114	410	68	121	31	4	0	66	64	13	.295	.392	.390	100	6	3	66	13	9	-2	1	*3	0.8
	Yr	132	469	77	136	35	5	0	75	71	19	.290	.384	.386	99	5	2	73	14	10	-2	3		1.0
1932	Cle-A	148	524	76	150	34	9	3	83	75	36	.286	.379	.403	96	4	-1	85	6	3	0	7	*3	1.4
1933	Cle-A	133	447	59	126	17	2	1	47	54	27	.282	.359	.336	81	-8	-11	58	7	3	0	1	*3	0.0
1934	Cle-A	121	386	52	104	23	3	0	42	62	38	.269	.372	.345	84	-6	-7	55	7	1	2	11	*3	0.5
1935	Cle-A	6	18	2	6	0	0	0	1	0	1	.333	.333	.333	72	-1	-1	2	0	1	-1	-2	/3	-0.2
Total	13	1693	5851	802	1643	348	85	29	826	824	405	.281	.372	.384	97	-12	-7	881	127	82	-11	66	*3	14.2

■ ALEX KAMPOURIS
Kampouris, Alexis William b: 11/13/12, Sacramento, Cal. BR/TR, 5'8", 155 lbs. Deb: 7/31/34

YEAR	TM/L	G	AB	R	H	2B	3B	HR	RBI	BB	SO	AVG	OBP	SLG	PRO+	BR	/A	RC	SB	CS	SBR	FR	POS	TPR
1934	Cin-N	19	66	6	13	1	0	0	3	3	18	.197	.254	.212	27	-7	-7	4	2			-1	2	-0.5
1935	Cin-N	148	499	46	123	26	5	7	62	32	84	.246	.295	.361	77	-18	-16	55	8			-1	*2/S	-0.4
1936	Cin-N	122	355	43	85	10	4	5	46	24	46	.239	.289	.332	72	-17	-14	35	3			28	*2/O	2.1
1937	Cin-N	146	458	62	114	21	4	17	71	60	65	.249	.342	.424	112	4	8	67	2			3	*2	1.7
1938	Cin-N	21	74	13	19	1	0	2	7	10	13	.257	.353	.351	97	-0	-0	9	0			0	2	0.2
	NY-N	82	268	35	66	9	1	5	37	27	50	.246	.318	.343	81	-7	-7	30	0			13	2	1.2
	Yr	103	342	48	85	10	1	7	44	37	63	.249	.325	.345	84	-7	-7	39	0			14		1.4
1939	NY-N	74	201	23	50	12	2	5	29	30	41	.249	.349	.403	101	1	1	29	0			10	23	1.3
1941	Bro-N	16	51	8	16	4	2	2	9	11	8	.314	.444	.588	181	6	6	15	0			0	2	0.7
1942	Bro-N	10	21	3	5	2	1	0	3	0	4	.238	.238	.429	92	-0	-0	2	0			2	/2	0.3
1943	Bro-N	19	44	9	10	4	1	0	4	17	6	.227	.452	.364	136	4	4	9	0			-1	2	0.3
	Was-A	51	145	24	30	4	0	2	13	30	25	.207	.361	.276	91	-1	0	19	7	1	2	-3	32/O	0.0
Total	9	708	2182	272	531	94	20	45	284	244	360	.243	.325	.367	91	-34	-26	272	22	1		51	2/3SO	6.9

■ FRANK KANE
Kane, Francis Thomas "Sugar" b: 3/9/1895, Whitman, Mass. d: 12/2/62, Brockton, Mass. BL/TR, 5'11.5", 175 lbs. Deb: 9/13/15

YEAR	TM/L	G	AB	R	H	2B	3B	HR	RBI	BB	SO	AVG	OBP	SLG	PRO+	BR	/A	RC	SB	CS	SBR	FR	POS	TPR
1915	Bro-F	3	10	2	2	0	1	0	2	0	0	.200	.200	.400	76	-0	-0	1	0			1	/O	0.0
1919	NY-A	1	1	0	0	0	0	0	0	0	0	.000	.000	.000	-99	-0	-0	0	0			0	H	0.0
Total	2	4	11	2	2	0	1	0	2	0	0	.182	.182	.364	59	-1	-1	1	0			1	/O	0.0

■ JIM KANE
Kane, James Joseph "Shamus" b: 11/27/1881, Scranton, Pa. d: 10/2/47, Omaha, Neb. BL/TL, 6'2", 225 lbs. Deb: 4/21/08

YEAR	TM/L	G	AB	R	H	2B	3B	HR	RBI	BB	SO	AVG	OBP	SLG	PRO+	BR	/A	RC	SB	CS	SBR	FR	POS	TPR
1908	Pit-N	55	145	16	35	3	3	0	22	12		.241	.299	.303	95	-1	-1	15	5			-2	1	-0.3

■ JOHN KANE
Kane, John Francis b: 9/24/1882, Chicago, Ill. d: 1/28/34, St.Anthony, Idaho BR/TR, 5'6", 138 lbs. Deb: 4/11/07

YEAR	TM/L	G	AB	R	H	2B	3B	HR	RBI	BB	SO	AVG	OBP	SLG	PRO+	BR	/A	RC	SB	CS	SBR	FR	POS	TPR
1907	Cin-N	79	262	40	65	9	4	3	19	22		.248	.306	.347	102	2	0	37	20			-1	O3/S2	-0.1
1908	Cin-N	130	455	61	97	11	7	3	23	43		.213	.281	.288	86	-8	-6	46	30			4	*O/2	-0.3
1909	Chi-N	20	45	6	4	1	0	0	5	2		.089	.146	.111	-20	-6	-6	1	1			3	/OS32	-0.3
1910	*Chi-N	32	62	11	15	0	0	1	12	9	10	.242	.338	.290	84	-1	-1	7	2			-2	O/23S	-0.3
Total	4	261	824	118	181	21	11	7	59	76	10	.220	.286	.297	85	-14	-13	91	53			5	O/32S	-1.0

■ JOHN KANE
Kane, John Francis b: 2/19/1900, Chicago, Ill. d: 7/25/56, Chicago, Ill. BB/TR, 5'10.5", 162 lbs. Deb: 9/03/25

YEAR	TM/L	G	AB	R	H	2B	3B	HR	RBI	BB	SO	AVG	OBP	SLG	PRO+	BR	/A	RC	SB	CS	SBR	FR	POS	TPR
1925	Chi-A	14	56	6	10	1	0	0	3	0	3	.179	.193	.196	-1	-9	-8	2	0	0	0	1	/S2	-0.4

■ TOM KANE
Kane, Thomas Joseph "Sugar" b: 12/15/06, Chicago, Ill. d: 11/26/73, Chicago, Ill. BR/TR, 5'10.5", 160 lbs. Deb: 8/03/38

YEAR	TM/L	G	AB	R	H	2B	3B	HR	RBI	BB	SO	AVG	OBP	SLG	PRO+	BR	/A	RC	SB	CS	SBR	FR	POS	TPR
1938	Bos-N	2	2	0	0	0	0	0	0	2	0	.000	.500	.000	53	0	0	0	0			-1	/2	0.0

■ JERRY KANE
Kane, William b: 1867, Collinsville, Ill. BR/TR, 6', 175 lbs. Deb: 5/02/1890

YEAR	TM/L	G	AB	R	H	2B	3B	HR	RBI	BB	SO	AVG	OBP	SLG	PRO+	BR	/A	RC	SB	CS	SBR	FR	POS	TPR
1890	StL-a	8	25	3	5	0	0	0	0	0	0	.200	.259	.200	33	-2	-2	1	0			-0	/1C	-0.1

■ ROD KANEHL
Kanehl, Roderick Edwin "Hot Rod" b: 4/1/34, Wichita, Kan. BR/TR, 6'1", 180 lbs. Deb: 4/15/62

YEAR	TM/L	G	AB	R	H	2B	3B	HR	RBI	BB	SO	AVG	OBP	SLG	PRO+	BR	/A	RC	SB	CS	SBR	FR	POS	TPR
1962	NY-N	133	351	52	87	10	2	4	27	23	36	.248	.296	.322	65	-17	-18	32	8	6	-1	18	230/1S	0.4
1963	NY-N	109	191	26	46	6	0	1	9	5	26	.241	.268	.288	59	-10	-10	13	6	3	0	4	O32/1	-0.8
1964	NY-N	98	254	25	59	7	1	1	11	7	18	.232	.256	.280	52	-17	-16	19	3	1	0	21	2O3/1	0.7
Total	3	340	796	103	192	23	3	6	47	35	80	.241	.277	.300	60	-43	-44	64	17	10	-1	43	2O/31S	0.3

■ HEINIE KAPPEL
Kappel, Henry b: 1862, Philadelphia, Pa. d: 8/27/05, Philadelphia, Pa. BR/TR, 5'8", 160 lbs. Deb: 5/22/1887

YEAR	TM/L	G	AB	R	H	2B	3B	HR	RBI	BB	SO	AVG	OBP	SLG	PRO+	BR	/A	RC	SB	CS	SBR	FR	POS	TPR
1887	Cin-a	23	78	11	22	3	2	0		2		.282	.309	.372	90	-1	-1	10	3			-3	/3O2S	-0.3
1888	Cin-a	36	143	18	37	4	4	1	15	2		.259	.274	.364	102	0	-0	20	20			-12	S2/3	-0.9
1889	Col-a	46	173	25	47	7	5	3	21	21	28	.272	.354	.422	129	5	7	30	10			-2	S3	0.5
Total	3	105	394	54	106	14	11	4	36	25	28	.269	.318	.391	111	4	5	60	33			-17	/S32O	-0.7

■ JOE KAPPEL
Kappel, Joseph b: 4/27/1857, Philadelphia, Pa. d: 7/8/29, Philadelphia, Pa. BR , 5'11", 175 lbs. Deb: 5/26/1884

YEAR	TM/L	G	AB	R	H	2B	3B	HR	RBI	BB	SO	AVG	OBP	SLG	PRO+	BR	/A	RC	SB	CS	SBR	FR	POS	TPR
1884	Phi-N	4	15	1	1	0	0	0	0	0	2	.067	.067	.067	-61	-3	-3	0				0	/C	-0.1
1890	Phi-a	56	208	29	50	8	1	1		20		.240	.310	.303	85	-4	-3	24	12			-5	OS3/C2	-0.6
Total	2	60	223	30	51	8	1	1	0	20	2	.229	.295	.287	76	-7	-6	24	12			-4	/OS3C2	-0.7

■ RON KARKOVICE
Karkovice, Ronald Joseph b: 8/8/63, Union, N.J. BR/TR, 6'1", 210 lbs. Deb: 8/17/86

YEAR	TM/L	G	AB	R	H	2B	3B	HR	RBI	BB	SO	AVG	OBP	SLG	PRO+	BR	/A	RC	SB	CS	SBR	FR	POS	TPR
1986	Chi-A	37	97	13	24	7	0	4	13	9	37	.247	.318	.443	101	0	-0	13	1	0	0	15	C	1.6
1987	Chi-A	39	85	7	6	0	0	2	7	7	40	.071	.160	.141	-19	-15	-15	2	3	0	1	10	C/D	0.0
1988	Chi-A	46	115	10	20	4	0	3	9	7	30	.174	.228	.287	43	-9	-9	8	4	2	0	8	C	0.1
1989	Chi-A	71	182	21	48	9	2	3	24	10	56	.264	.309	.385	97	-2	-1	23	0	0	0	17	C/D	1.9
1990	Chi-A	68	183	30	45	10	0	6	20	16	52	.246	.310	.399	99	-1	-1	24	2	0	1	6	C/D	0.8
Total	5	261	662	81	143	30	2	18	73	49	215	.216	.277	.349	73	-26	-26	70	10	2	2	56	C/D	4.4

■ BILL KARLON
Karlon, William John "Hank" b: 1/21/09, Palmer, Mass. d: 12/7/64, Ware, Mass. BR/TR, 6'1", 190 lbs. Deb: 4/28/30

YEAR	TM/L	G	AB	R	H	2B	3B	HR	RBI	BB	SO	AVG	OBP	SLG	PRO+	BR	/A	RC	SB	CS	SBR	FR	POS	TPR
1930	NY-A	2	5	0	0	0	0	0	0	0	1	.000	.000	.000	-99	-2	-1	0	0	0	0	-0	/O	-0.1

■ MARTY KAROW
Karow, Martin Gregory (b: Martin Gregory Karowsky) b: 7/18/04, Braddock, Pa. d: 4/27/86, Bryan, Texas BR/TR, 5'10.5", 170 lbs. Deb: 6/21/27

YEAR	TM/L	G	AB	R	H	2B	3B	HR	RBI	BB	SO	AVG	OBP	SLG	PRO+	BR	/A	RC	SB	CS	SBR	FR	POS	TPR
1927	Bos-A	6	10	0	2	1	0	0	0	0	2	.200	.200	.300	29	-1	-1	0	0	0	0	1	/S3	0.0

■ JOHN KARST
Karst, John Gottlieb "King" b: 10/15/1893, Philadelphia, Pa. d: 5/21/76, Cape May Court House, N.J. TR , 5'11.5", 175 lbs. Deb: 10/06/15

YEAR	TM/L	G	AB	R	H	2B	3B	HR	RBI	BB	SO	AVG	OBP	SLG	PRO+	BR	/A	RC	SB	CS	SBR	FR	POS	TPR
1915	Bro-N	1	0	0	0	0	0	0	0	0	0	—	—	—	—	—	—	0	0	0	0	0	/3	0.0

■ EDDIE KASKO
Kasko, Edward Michael b: 6/27/32, Linden, N.J. BR/TR, 6', 180 lbs. Deb: 4/18/57 M

YEAR	TM/L	G	AB	R	H	2B	3B	HR	RBI	BB	SO	AVG	OBP	SLG	PRO+	BR	/A	RC	SB	CS	SBR	FR	POS	TPR
1957	StL-N	134	479	59	131	16	5	1	35	33	53	.273	.320	.334	75	-16	-17	52	6	1	1	-7	*3S/2	-1.9
1958	StL-N	104	259	20	57	8	1	2	22	21	25	.220	.279	.282	47	-19	-20	19	1	2	-1	6	S2/3	-0.8
1959	Cin-N	118	329	39	93	14	1	2	31	14	38	.283	.312	.350	74	-11	-13	35	2	2	-1	12	S3/2	0.1
1960	Cin-N	126	479	56	140	21	1	6	51	46	37	.292	.362	.378	101	3	2	66	9	9	-3	0	32S	0.2

YEAR	TM/L	G	AB	R	H	2B	3B	HR	RBI	BB	SO	AVG	OBP	SLG	PRO+	BR	/A	RC	SB	CS	SBR	FR	POS	TPR
1961	*Cin-N	126	469	64	127	22	1	2	27	32	36	.271	.323	.335	74	-16	-17	52	4	3	-1	-18	*S3/2	-2.4
1962	Cin-N	134	533	74	148	26	2	4	41	35	44	.278	.328	.356	81	-12	-14	59	3	3	-1	-8	*3S	-1.7
1963	Cin-N	76	199	25	48	9	0	3	10	21	29	.241	.314	.332	83	-3	-4	21	0	2	-1	-1	3S/2	-0.4
1964	Hou-N	133	448	45	109	16	1	0	22	37	52	.243	.302	.283	70	-19	-16	38	4	6	-2	-10	*S/3	0.0
1965	Hou-N	68	215	18	53	7	1	1	10	11	20	.247	.296	.302	74	-9	-7	17	1	3	-2	-10	S/3	-1.2
1966	Bos-A	58	136	11	29	7	0	1	12	15	19	.213	.291	.287	61	-6	-7	11	1	0	0	8	S3/2	0.2
Total	10	1077	3546	411	935	146	13	22	261	265	353	.264	.318	.331	76	-108	-113	370	31	31	-9	-8	S3/2	-7.9

■ RAY KATT   Katt, Raymond Frederick b: 5/9/27, New Braunfels, Tex. BR/TR, 6'2", 190 lbs. Deb: 9/16/52 C

YEAR	TM/L	G	AB	R	H	2B	3B	HR	RBI	BB	SO	AVG	OBP	SLG	PRO+	BR	/A	RC	SB	CS	SBR	FR	POS	TPR
1952	NY-N	9	27	4	6	0	0	0	1	1	5	.222	.250	.222	32	-2	-2	1	0	0	0	1	/C	0.0
1953	NY-N	8	29	2	5	1	0	0	1	1	3	.172	.200	.207	6	-4	-4	1	0	0	0	-1	/C	-0.3
1954	NY-N	86	200	26	51	7	1	9	33	19	29	.255	.320	.435	94	-2	-2	28	1	0	0	-5	C	-0.4
1955	NY-N	124	326	27	70	7	2	7	28	22	38	.215	.269	.313	54	-22	-22	25	0	0	0	-6	*C	-2.4
1956	NY-N	37	101	10	23	4	0	7	14	6	16	.228	.278	.475	98	-1	-1	13	0	1	-1	1	C	0.0
	StL-N	47	158	11	41	4	0	6	20	6	24	.259	.291	.399	83	-4	-4	18	0	1	-1	-2	C	-0.5
	Yr	84	259	21	64	8	0	13	34	12	40	.247	.286	.429	89	-5	-5	31	0	2	-1	-1		-0.5
1957	NY-N	72	165	11	38	3	1	2	17	15	35	.230	.302	.297	62	-9	-9	15	1	0	0	-6	C	-1.0
1958	StL-N	19	41	1	7	1	0	1	4	4	6	.171	.244	.268	34	-4	-4	2	0	0	0	0	C	-0.2
1959	StL-N	15	24	0	7	2	0	0	2	0	8	.292	.292	.375	71	-1	-1	2	0	0	0	-0	C	0.0
Total	8	417	1071	92	248	29	4	32	120	74	164	.232	.285	.356	69	-49	-49	105	2	2	-1	-18	C	-4.8

■ BENNY KAUFF   Kauff, Benjamin Michael b: 1/5/1890, Pomeroy, Ohio d: 11/17/61, Columbus, Ohio BL/TL, 5'8", 157 lbs. Deb: 4/20/12

YEAR	TM/L	G	AB	R	H	2B	3B	HR	RBI	BB	SO	AVG	OBP	SLG	PRO+	BR	/A	RC	SB	CS	SBR	FR	POS	TPR
1912	NY-A	5	11	4	3	0	0	0	2	3		.273	.429	.273	96	0	0	2	1			-1	/O	0.0
1914	Ind-F	154	571	120	211	44	13	8	95	72	55	.370	.447	.534	163	62	53	175	75			16	*O	6.2
1915	Bro-F	136	483	92	165	23	11	12	83	85	50	.342	.446	.509	184	53	54	138	55			15	*O	6.5
1916	NY-N	154	552	71	146	22	15	9	74	68	65	.264	.348	.408	139	21	25	81	40	26	-4	-3	*O	1.4
1917	*NY-N	153	559	89	172	22	4	5	68	59	54	.308	.379	.388	140	25	27	91	30			-9	*O	1.5
1918	NY-N	67	270	41	85	19	4	2	39	16	30	.315	.355	.437	144	12	13	43	9			-3	O	0.6
1919	NY-N	135	491	73	136	27	7	10	67	39	45	.277	.334	.422	128	15	15	72	21			-7	*O	0.3
1920	NY-N	55	157	31	43	12	3	3	26	25	14	.274	.380	.446	138	8	8	26	3	7	-3	6	O	0.8
Total	8	859	3094	521	961	169	57	49	454	367	313	.311	.389	.450	150	197	195	628	234	33		12	O	17.3

■ DICK KAUFFMAN   Kauffman, Howard Richard b: 6/22/1888, E.Lewisburg, Pa. d: 4/16/48, Mifflinburg, Pa. BB/TR, 6'3", 190 lbs. Deb: 9/17/14

YEAR	TM/L	G	AB	R	H	2B	3B	HR	RBI	BB	SO	AVG	OBP	SLG	PRO+	BR	/A	RC	SB	CS	SBR	FR	POS	TPR
1914	StL-A	7	15	1	4	1	0	0	3		3	.267	.267	.333	83	-0	-0	1	0			-1	/1	-0.1
1915	StL-A	37	124	9	32	8	2	0	14	5	27	.258	.298	.355	99	-1	-1	12	0	3	-2	-1	1/O	-0.4
Total	2	44	139	10	36	9	2	0	16	5	30	.259	.295	.353	97	-2	-2	14	0	3		-2	/1O	-0.5

■ TONY KAUFMANN   Kaufmann, Anthony Charles b: 12/16/1900, Chicago, Ill. d: 6/4/82, Elgin, Ill. BR/TR, 5'11", 165 lbs. Deb: 9/23/21 C

YEAR	TM/L	G	AB	R	H	2B	3B	HR	RBI	BB	SO	AVG	OBP	SLG	PRO+	BR	/A	RC	SB	CS	SBR	FR	POS	TPR
1921	Chi-N	2	5	0	2	1	0	0	0	0	1	.400	.400	.600	161	0	0	1	0	0	0	-0	/P	0.0
1922	Chi-N	38	45	4	9	2	1	1	4	2	14	.200	.234	.356	49	-4	-4	4	0	0	0	-1	P	0.0
1923	Chi-N	33	74	10	16	2	0	2	10	7	17	.216	.284	.324	60	-4	-4	7	0	0	0	-1	P	0.0
1924	Chi-N	35	76	6	24	5	0	1	14	3	10	.316	.342	.421	102	0	0	11	0	0	0	-2	P	0.0
1925	Chi-N	31	78	8	15	7	0	2	13	2	17	.192	.213	.359	42	-7	-7	6	0	0	0	0	P	0.0
1926	Chi-N	30	60	9	15	2	0	1	7	2	10	.250	.274	.333	62	-3	-3	5	1			-1	P	0.0
1927	Chi-N	9	16	2	5	0	1	0	8	4	4	.313	.450	.500	154	1	1	4	0			2	/P	0.0
	Phi-N	8	7	1	1	0	0	1	0	0	1	.143	.143	.571	83	-0	-0	1	0			-0	/PO	0.0
	StL-N	1	0	0	0	0	0	0	0	0	0	—	—	—	—	0	0	0	0			0	/P	0.0
	Yr	18	23	3	6	0	1	0	2	8	4	5	.261	.370	.522	136	1	1	4	0			1		0.0
1928	StL-N	5	0	0	0	0	0	0	0	0	0	—	—	—	—	0	0	0	0			0	/P	0.0
1929	NY-N	39	32	18	1	0	0	0	1	6	4	.031	.184	.031	-43	-7	-7	1	3			3	O	-0.4
1930	StL-N	2	3	1	1	0	0	0	0	1	1	.333	.500	.333	103	0	0	1	0			-0	/P	0.0
1931	StL-N	20	18	1	2	0	0	0	0	1	3	.111	.158	.111	-26	-3	-3	0	0			0	P/O	0.0
1935	StL-N	7	0	2	0	0	0	0	0	0	0	—	—	—	—	0	0	0	0			0	/P	0.1
Total	12	260	414	62	91	19	1	9	57	28	82	.220	.269	.336	57	-27	-28	40	4	0		-0	P/O	-0.3

■ CHARLIE KAVANAGH   Kavanagh, Charles Hugh "Silk" b: 6/9/1893, Chicago, Ill. d: 9/6/73, Reedsburg, Wis. BR/TR, 5'9", 165 lbs. Deb: 6/11/14

YEAR	TM/L	G	AB	R	H	2B	3B	HR	RBI	BB	SO	AVG	OBP	SLG	PRO+	BR	/A	RC	SB	CS	SBR	FR	POS	TPR
1914	Chi-A	6	5	0	1	0	0	0	0	0	2	.200	.333	.200	62	-0	-0	0	0			0	H	0.0

■ LEO KAVANAGH   Kavanagh, Leo Daniel b: 8/9/1894, Chicago, Ill. d: 8/10/50, Chicago, Ill. BR/TR, 5'9", 180 lbs. Deb: 4/22/14

YEAR	TM/L	G	AB	R	H	2B	3B	HR	RBI	BB	SO	AVG	OBP	SLG	PRO+	BR	/A	RC	SB	CS	SBR	FR	POS	TPR
1914	Chi-F	5	11	0	3	0	0	0	1	1	0	.273	.333	.273	79	-0	-0	1	0			-1	/S	0.0

■ MARTY KAVANAGH   Kavanagh, Martin Joseph b: 6/13/1891, Harrison, N.J. d: 7/28/60, Eloise, Mich. BR/TR, 6', 187 lbs. Deb: 4/18/14

YEAR	TM/L	G	AB	R	H	2B	3B	HR	RBI	BB	SO	AVG	OBP	SLG	PRO+	BR	/A	RC	SB	CS	SBR	FR	POS	TPR
1914	Det-A	128	439	60	109	21	6	4	35	41	42	.248	.318	.351	98	-0	-2	51	16	14	-4	-7	*2/1	-1.3
1915	Det-A	113	332	55	98	14	13	3	49	42	44	.295	.378	.443	139	18	16	56	8	8	-2	-15	12/SO3	-0.3
1916	Det-A	58	78	6	11	4	0	0	5	9	15	.141	.239	.192	29	-7	-7	4	0			0	O/23	-0.7
	Cle-A	19	44	4	11	2	1	1	10	2	5	.250	.283	.409	102	-0	-0	5	0			-0	/213	-0.7
	Yr	77	122	10	22	6	1	1	15	11	20	.180	.254	.270	55	-7	-7	9	0			-0		-0.7
1917	Cle-A	14	14	1	0	0	0	0	0	3	2	.000	.176	.000	-43	-2	-2	0	0			0	/O	-0.2
1918	Cle-A	13	38	4	8	2	0	0	6	7	7	.211	.348	.263	77	-0	-1	4	1			-1	1	-0.2
	StL-N	12	44	6	8	1	0	1	8	3	1	.182	.234	.273	56	-2	-2	3	1			-2	/O2	-0.5
	Det-A	13	44	2	12	3	0	0	9	11	6	.273	.418	.341	135	2	3	6	0			-1	1	0.0
Total	5	370	1033	138	257	47	20	9	122	118	122	.249	.330	.359	103	8	4	129	26	22		-26	2/103S	-3.2

■ KAVANAUGH   Kavanaugh Deb: 9/11/1872

YEAR	TM/L	G	AB	R	H	2B	3B	HR	RBI	BB	SO	AVG	OBP	SLG	PRO+	BR	/A	RC	SB	CS	SBR	FR	POS	TPR
1872	Eck-n	5	22	3	6	1	0	0		0		.273	.273	.318	96	-0	-0	2					/1O	0.0

■ BILL KAY   Kay, Walter Brocton "King Bill" b: 2/14/1878, New Castle, Va. d: 12/3/45, Roanoke, Va. BL/TR, 6'2", 180 lbs. Deb: 8/12/07

YEAR	TM/L	G	AB	R	H	2B	3B	HR	RBI	BB	SO	AVG	OBP	SLG	PRO+	BR	/A	RC	SB	CS	SBR	FR	POS	TPR
1907	Was-A	25	60	8	20	1	1	0	7	0		.333	.333	.383	141	2	2	8	0			0	O	0.2

■ EDDIE KAZAK   Kazak, Edward Terrance (b: Edward Terrance Tkaczuk) b: 7/18/20, Steubenville, O. BR/TR, 6', 175 lbs. Deb: 9/29/48

YEAR	TM/L	G	AB	R	H	2B	3B	HR	RBI	BB	SO	AVG	OBP	SLG	PRO+	BR	/A	RC	SB	CS	SBR	FR	POS	TPR
1948	StL-N	6	22	1	6	3	0	0	2	0	2	.273	.273	.409	78	-1	-1	2	0			1	/3	0.0
1949	StL-N	92	326	43	99	15	3	6	42	29	17	.304	.362	.423	105	5	3	49	0			-4	3/2	0.0
1950	StL-N	93	207	21	53	2	2	5	23	18	19	.256	.319	.357	74	-7	-8	23	0			1	3	-0.6
1951	StL-N	11	33	2	6	2	0	0	4	5	5	.182	.289	.242	44	-2	-3	3	0	0	0	-1	3	-0.3
1952	StL-N	3	2	1	0	0	0	0	0	0	0	.000	.000	.000	-99	-1	-1	0	0	0	0	0	/3	-0.3
	Cin-N	13	15	1	1	0	1	0	0	0	2	.067	.067	.200	-29	-3	-3	0	0	0	0	-1	/31	-0.2
	Yr	16	17	2	1	0	1	0	0	0	2	.059	.059	.176	-37	-3	-3	0	0	0	0	-0		-0.2
Total	5	218	605	69	165	22	6	11	71	52	45	.273	.332	.383	87	-9	-12	77	0	0		-3	3/21	-1.1

■ TED KAZANSKI   Kazanski, Theodore Stanley b: 1/25/34, Hamtramck, Mich. BR/TR, 6'1", 175 lbs. Deb: 6/25/53

YEAR	TM/L	G	AB	R	H	2B	3B	HR	RBI	BB	SO	AVG	OBP	SLG	PRO+	BR	/A	RC	SB	CS	SBR	FR	POS	TPR
1953	Phi-N	95	360	39	78	17	5	2	27	26	53	.217	.275	.308	52	-26	-25	31	1	1	-0	-19	S	-3.6
1954	Phi-N	39	104	7	14	2	0	1	8	4	14	.135	.167	.183	-9	-17	-17	2	0	1	-1	-7	S	-2.1
1955	Phi-N	9	12	1	1	0	0	1	1	1	1	.083	.154	.333	25	-1	-1	1	0	0	0	1	/S3	0.0
1956	Phi-N	117	379	35	80	11	1	4	34	20	41	.211	.253	.277	43	-31	-30	25	0	2	-1	-10	*2/S	-3.2
1957	Phi-N	62	185	15	49	7	1	3	11	17	20	.265	.327	.362	88	-4	-3	21	1	1	-0	-3	32/S	-0.3

YEAR	TM/L	G	AB	R	H	2B	3B	HR	RBI	BB	SO	AVG	OBP	SLG	PRO+	BR	/A	RC	SB	CS	SBR	FR	POS	TPR
1958	Phi-N	95	289	21	66	12	2	3	35	22	34	.228	.292	.315	62	-16	-16	25	2	3	-1	-13	2S3	-2.4
Total	6	417	1329	118	288	49	9	14	116	90	163	.217	.270	.299	51	-95	-92	105	4	8	-4	-51	2S/3	-11.6

■ BOB KEARNEY Kearney, Robert Henry b: 10/3/56, San Antonio, Tex. BR/TR, 6', 190 lbs. Deb: 9/25/79

YEAR	TM/L	G	AB	R	H	2B	3B	HR	RBI	BB	SO	AVG	OBP	SLG	PRO+	BR	/A	RC	SB	CS	SBR	FR	POS	TPR
1979	SF-N	2	0	0	0	0	0	0	0	1	0	—	1.000	—	211	0	0	0	0	0	0	0	/C	0.0
1981	Oak-A	1	0	0	0	0	0	0	0	0	0	—	—	—	—	0	0	0	0	0	0	0	/C	0.0
1982	Oak-A	22	71	7	12	3	0	0	5	3	10	.169	.224	.211	21	-8	-7	4	0	0	0	4	C	-0.1
1983	Oak-A	108	298	33	76	11	0	8	32	21	50	.255	.313	.372	93	-5	-3	32	1	4	-2	6	*C/D	0.6
1984	Sea-A	133	431	39	97	24	1	7	43	18	72	.225	.259	.334	64	-22	-22	36	7	5	-1	5	*C	-0.8
1985	Sea-A	108	305	24	74	14	1	6	27	11	59	.243	.278	.354	71	-12	-13	29	1	1	-0	7	*C	-0.1
1986	Sea-A	81	204	23	49	10	0	6	25	12	35	.240	.282	.377	77	-7	-7	20	0	2	-1	14	C	1.0
1987	Sea-A	24	47	5	8	4	1	0	1	1	9	.170	.188	.298	25	-5	-5	3	0	0	0	5	C	0.2
Total	8	479	1356	131	316	66	3	27	133	67	235	.233	.275	.346	70	-59	-56	123	9	12	-5	41	C/D	0.8

■ TEDDY KEARNS Kearns, Edward Joseph b: 1/1/1900, Trenton, N.J. d: 12/21/49, Trenton, N.J. BR/TR, 5'11", 180 lbs. Deb: 9/18/24

YEAR	TM/L	G	AB	R	H	2B	3B	HR	RBI	BB	SO	AVG	OBP	SLG	PRO+	BR	/A	RC	SB	CS	SBR	FR	POS	TPR
1924	Chi-N	4	16	0	4	0	1	0	1	1	1	.250	.294	.375	77	-1	-1	2	0	0	0	0	/1	0.0
1925	Chi-N	3	2	0	1	0	0	0	0	0	0	.500	.500	.500	154	0	0	0	0	0	0	0	/1	0.0
Total	2	7	18	0	5	0	1	0	1	1	1	.278	.316	.389	86	-0	-0	2	0	0	0	0	/1	0.0

■ TOM KEARNS Kearns, Thomas J. "Dasher" b: 11/9/1859, Rochester, N.Y. d: 12/7/38, Buffalo, N.Y. TR, 5'7", 160 lbs. Deb: 8/26/1880

YEAR	TM/L	G	AB	R	H	2B	3B	HR	RBI	BB	SO	AVG	OBP	SLG	PRO+	BR	/A	RC	SB	CS	SBR	FR	POS	TPR
1880	Buf-N	2	7	0	0	0	0	0	0	0	0	.000	.000	.000	-98	-1	-1	0				-1	/C	-0.1
1882	Det-N	4	13	2	4	2	0	0	1	0	4	.308	.308	.462	143	1	1	2				-3	/2	-0.1
1884	Det-N	21	79	9	16	0	1	0	7	2	10	.203	.222	.228	45	-5	-4	4				-10	2	-1.2
Total	3	27	99	11	20	2	1	0	8	2	14	.202	.218	.242	48	-6	-5	6				-13	/2C	-1.4

■ EDDIE KEARSE Kearse, Edward Paul "Truck" b: 2/23/16, San Francisco, Cal d: 7/15/68, Eureka, Cal. BR/TR, 6'1", 195 lbs. Deb: 6/13/42

YEAR	TM/L	G	AB	R	H	2B	3B	HR	RBI	BB	SO	AVG	OBP	SLG	PRO+	BR	/A	RC	SB	CS	SBR	FR	POS	TPR
1942	NY-A	11	26	2	5	0	0	0	2	3	1	.192	.276	.192	34	-2	-2	2	1	0	0	3	C	0.3

■ CHICK KEATING Keating, Walter Francis b: 8/8/1891, Philadelphia, Pa. d: 7/13/59, Philadelphia, Pa. BR/TR, 5'9.5", 155 lbs. Deb: 9/26/13

YEAR	TM/L	G	AB	R	H	2B	3B	HR	RBI	BB	SO	AVG	OBP	SLG	PRO+	BR	/A	RC	SB	CS	SBR	FR	POS	TPR
1913	Chi-N	2	5	0	1	1	0	0	0	0	1	.200	.200	.400	69	-0	-0	0	0			-1	/S	0.0
1914	Chi-N	20	30	3	3	0	1	0	0	6	9	.100	.250	.167	25	-3	-3	1	0			0	S	-0.1
1915	Chi-N	4	8	1	0	0	0	0	0	0	3	.000	.000	.000	-99	-2	-2	0	1			-0	/S	0.0
1926	Phi-N	4	2	0	0	0	0	0	0	0	0	.000	.000	.000	-95	-1	-1	0	0			-0	/2S3	0.0
Total	4	30	45	4	4	1	1	0	0	6	13	.089	.196	.156	4	-5	-5	2	1			-1	/S23	-0.2

■ GREG KEATLEY Keatley, Gregory Steven b: 9/12/53, Princeton, W.Va. BR/TR, 6'2", 200 lbs. Deb: 9/27/81

YEAR	TM/L	G	AB	R	H	2B	3B	HR	RBI	BB	SO	AVG	OBP	SLG	PRO+	BR	/A	RC	SB	CS	SBR	FR	POS	TPR
1981	KC-A	2	0	0	0	0	0	0	0	0	0	—	—	—	—	0	0	0	0	0	0	0	/C	0.0

■ PAT KEEDY Keedy, Charles Patrick b: 1/10/58, Birmingham, Ala. BR/TR, 6'4", 205 lbs. Deb: 9/10/85

YEAR	TM/L	G	AB	R	H	2B	3B	HR	RBI	BB	SO	AVG	OBP	SLG	PRO+	BR	/A	RC	SB	CS	SBR	FR	POS	TPR
1985	Cal-A	3	4	1	2	1	0	1	1	0	0	.500	.500	1.500	424	2	2	2	0	1	-1	-0	/3O	0.0
1987	Chi-A	17	41	6	7	1	0	2	2	2	14	.171	.209	.341	42	-4	-4	3	1	0	0	4	3/12SOD	0.1
1989	Cle-A	9	14	3	3	2	0	0	1	2	5	.214	.313	.357	87	-0	-0	2	0	0	0	1	/O31SD	0.1
Total	3	29	59	10	12	4	0	3	4	4	19	.203	.254	.424	77	-2	-2	6	1	1	-0	4	/3O1DS2	0.1

■ WILLIE KEELER Keeler, William Henry "Wee Willie" b: 3/3/1872, Brooklyn, N.Y. d: 1/1/23, Brooklyn, N.Y. BL/TL, 5'4.5", 140 lbs. Deb: 9/30/1892 H

YEAR	TM/L	G	AB	R	H	2B	3B	HR	RBI	BB	SO	AVG	OBP	SLG	PRO+	BR	/A	RC	SB	CS	SBR	FR	POS	TPR
1892	NY-N	14	53	7	17	3	0	0	6	3	3	.321	.368	.377	130	2	2	9	5			-3	3	0.0
1893	NY-N	7	24	5	8	2	1	1	7	5	1	.333	.448	.625	186	3	3	8	3			-5	/O2S	-0.1
	Bro-N	20	80	14	25	1	1	1	9	4	4	.313	.353	.387	103	-0	0	12	2			-1	3/O	0.0
	Yr	27	104	19	33	3	2	2	16	9	5	.317	.377	.442	123	3	3	20	5			-6		-0.1
1894	*Bal-N	129	590	165	219	27	22	5	94	40	6	.371	.427	.517	123	28	23	148	32			3	*O/2	1.3
1895	*Bal-N	131	565	162	213	24	15	4	78	37	12	.377	.429	.494	136	34	31	143	47			-1	*O	1.5
1896	*Bal-N	126	544	153	210	22	13	4	82	37		.386	.432	.496	145	37	35	149	67			6	*O	2.7
1897	*Bal-N	129	564	145	239	27	19	0	74	35		.424	.464	.539	167	54	54	175	64			-2	*O	3.6
1898	Bal-N	129	561	126	216	7	2	1	44	31		.385	.420	.410	139	30	29	111	28			0	*O/3	2.0
1899	Bro-N	141	570	140	216	12	13	1	61	37		.379	.425	.451	140	34	33	132	45			-2	*O	1.9
1900	*Bro-N	136	563	106	204	13	12	4	68	30		.362	.398	.449	128	27	22	120	41			5	*O/2	1.4
1901	Bro-N	136	595	123	202	18	12	2	43	21		.339	.366	.420	127	21	19	105	23			-5	*O3/2	0.1
1902	Bro-N	133	559	86	186	20	5	0	38	21		.333	.365	.386	133	21	21	91	19			2	*O	1.4
1903	NY-A	132	512	95	160	14	7	0	32	32		.313	.353	.367	111	12	8	80	24			-9	*O/3	-0.9
1904	NY-A	143	543	78	186	14	8	2	40	35		.343	.382	.409	146	32	29	98	21			-3	*O	1.9
1905	NY-A	149	560	81	169	14	4	4	38	43		.302	.352	.363	116	18	11	85	19			-4	*O2/3	0.1
1906	NY-A	152	592	96	180	9	3	2	33	40		.304	.348	.340	107	12	5	84	23			-2	*O	-0.2
1907	NY-A	107	423	50	99	5	2	0	17	15		.234	.260	.255	61	-16	-20	34	7			-2	*O	-3.1
1908	NY-A	91	323	38	85	3	1	1	14	31		.263	.328	.288	102	2	2	37	14			-1	O	-0.3
1909	NY-A	99	360	44	95	7	5	1	32	24		.264	.327	.319	104	2	2	44	10			-5	O	-0.7
1910	NY-N	19	10	5	3	0	0	0	0	3	1	.300	.462	.300	123	1	1	2	1			1	/O	0.1
Total	19	2123	8591	1719	2932	242	145	33	810	524	36	.341	.385	.415	127	354	309	1667	495			-28	*O/32S	12.7

■ BOB KEELY Keely, Robert William b: 8/22/09, St.Louis, Mo. BR/TR, 6', 175 lbs. Deb: 7/25/44 C

YEAR	TM/L	G	AB	R	H	2B	3B	HR	RBI	BB	SO	AVG	OBP	SLG	PRO+	BR	/A	RC	SB	CS	SBR	FR	POS	TPR
1944	StL-N	1	0	0	0	0	0	0	0	0	0	—	—	—	—	0	0	0	0			0	/C	0.0
1945	StL-N	1	1	0	0	0	0	0	0	0	0	.000	.000	.000	-98	-0	-0	0	0			0	/C	0.0
Total	2	2	1	0	0	0	0	0	0	0	0	.000	.000	.000	-98	-0	-0	0	0			0	/C	0.0

■ BILL KEEN Keen, William Brown "Buster" b: 8/16/1892, Oglethorpe, Ga. d: 7/16/47, South Point, Ohio BR/TR, 6', 181 lbs. Deb: 8/08/11

YEAR	TM/L	G	AB	R	H	2B	3B	HR	RBI	BB	SO	AVG	OBP	SLG	PRO+	BR	/A	RC	SB	CS	SBR	FR	POS	TPR
1911	Pit-N	6	7	0	0	0	0	0	0	1	4	.000	.125	.000	-62	-2	-2	0				0	/1	-0.1

■ JIM KEENAN Keenan, James W. b: 2/10/1858, New Haven, Conn. d: 9/21/26, Cincinnati, Ohio BR/TR, 5'10", 186 lbs. Deb: 5/17/1875

YEAR	TM/L	G	AB	R	H	2B	3B	HR	RBI	BB	SO	AVG	OBP	SLG	PRO+	BR	/A	RC	SB	CS	SBR	FR	POS	TPR
1875	NH-n	4	13	1	1	0	0	0		0		.077	.077	.077	-55	-2	-2	0					/3C	0.0
1880	Buf-N	2	7	1	1	0	0	0	0	1	1	.143	.250	.143	36	-0	-0	0				3	/C	0.3
1882	Pit-a	25	96	10	21	7	0	1		1		.219	.227	.323	87	-2	-1	7				1	C/OS	0.0
1884	Ind-a	68	249	36	73	14	4	3		16		.293	.343	.418	156	14	15	37				-6	C/1OSP	1.2
1885	Cin-a	36	132	16	35	2	2	1		8		.265	.307	.333	103	1	0	14				-4	C/1P	0.1
1886	Cin-a	44	148	31	40	4	3	3		18		.270	.357	.399	135	7	6	22	0			-2	C/O31P	0.5
1887	Cin-a	47	174	19	44	4	1	0		11		.253	.301	.287	65	-8	-8	18	7			7	C/1	0.4
1888	Cin-a	85	313	38	73	9	8	1	40	22		.233	.294	.323	96	0	-2	33	9			-1	C1	0.3
1889	Cin-a	87	300	52	86	10	11	6	60	48	35	.287	.395	.453	140	18	17	62	18			-2	C1/3	1.7
1890	Cin-a	54	202	21	28	4	2	3	19	19	36	.139	.216	.223	30	-18	-18	11	5			4	C/1O3	-0.9
1891	Cin-N	75	252	30	51	7	5	4	33	33	39	.202	.302	.317	82	-5	-6	25	2			-3	1C/3	-0.5
Total	10	523	1873	254	452	61	36	22	152	177	111	.241	.314	.348	101	7	3	229	41			-2	C1/O3PS	3.1

■ GEORGE KEERL Keerl, George Henry b: 4/10/1847, Baltimore, Md. d: 9/13/23, Menominee, Mich. 5'7", 145 lbs. Deb: 5/05/1875

YEAR	TM/L	G	AB	R	H	2B	3B	HR	RBI	BB	SO	AVG	OBP	SLG	PRO+	BR	/A	RC	SB	CS	SBR	FR	POS	TPR
1875	Chi-n	6	23	2	3	0	0	0		0		.130	.130	.130	-9	-2	-2	0					/2	-0.1

■ JIM KEESEY Keesey, James Ward b: 10/27/02, Perryville, Md. d: 9/5/51, Boise, Idaho BR/TR, 6'0.5", 170 lbs. Deb: 9/06/25

YEAR	TM/L	G	AB	R	H	2B	3B	HR	RBI	BB	SO	AVG	OBP	SLG	PRO+	BR	/A	RC	SB	CS	SBR	FR	POS	TPR
1925	Phi-A	5	5	1	2	0	0	0	1	0	2	.400	.400	.400	97	0	-0	1	0	0	0	0	/1	0.0
1930	Phi-A	11	12	2	3	1	0	0	2	1	2	.250	.308	.333	60	-1	-1	1	0	0	0	-0	/1	0.0

YEAR	TM/L	G	AB	R	H	2B	3B	HR	RBI	BB	SO	AVG	OBP	SLG	PRO+	BR	/A	RC	SB	CS	SBR	FR	POS	TPR
Total	2	16	17	3	5	1	0	0	3	1	4	.294	.333	.353	71	-1	-1	2	0	0	0	-0	/1	0.0

■ BILL KEISTER
Keister, William Hoffman "Wagon Tongue" b: 8/17/1874, Baltimore, Md. d: 8/19/24, Baltimore, Md.   BL/TR, 5'5.5", 168 lbs.   Deb: 5/20/1896

YEAR	TM/L	G	AB	R	H	2B	3B	HR	RBI	BB	SO	AVG	OBP	SLG	PRO+	BR	/A	RC	SB	CS	SBR	FR	POS	TPR
1896	Bal-N	15	58	8	14	3	0	0	5	3	5	.241	.302	.293	58	-3	-4	6	4			-4	/23	-0.6
1898	Bos-N	10	30	5	5	2	0	0	4	0		.167	.167	.233	15	-3	-3	1	0			1	/S2O	-0.1
1899	Bal-N	136	523	96	172	22	16	3	73	16		.329	.368	.449	120	17	13	101	33			-30	S2/O	-0.7
1900	StL-N	126	497	78	149	26	10	1	72	25		.300	.346	.398	108	5	5	82	32			-24	*2/S3	-1.0
1901	Bal-A	115	442	78	145	20	21	2	93	18		.328	.367	.482	130	20	17	89	24			-23	*S	0.1
1902	Was-A	119	483	82	145	33	9	9	90	14		.300	.329	.462	118	10	10	85	27			-4	O23/S	0.3
1903	Phi-N	100	400	53	128	27	7	3	63	14		.320	.343	.445	130	11	13	67	11			3	*O	1.0
Total	7	621	2433	400	758	133	63	18	400	90	5	.312	.347	.440	118	56	51	432	131			-80	S2O/3	-1.0

■ MICKEY KELIHER
Keliher, Maurice Michael b: 1/11/1890, Washington, D.C. d: 9/7/30, Washington, D.C.   BL/TL, 6', 175 lbs.   Deb: 9/09/11

YEAR	TM/L	G	AB	R	H	2B	3B	HR	RBI	BB	SO	AVG	OBP	SLG	PRO+	BR	/A	RC	SB	CS	SBR	FR	POS	TPR
1911	Pit-N	3	7	0	0	0	0	0	0	0	5	.000	.000	.000	-96	-2	-2	0	0			0	/1	-0.1
1912	Pit-N	2	0	1	0	0	0	0	0	0	0	—	—	—	—	0	0	0	0			0	R	0.0
Total	2	5	7	1	0	0	0	0	0	0	5	.000	.000	.000	-96	-2	-2	0	0			0	/1	-0.1

■ SKEETER KELL
Kell, Everett Lee b: 10/11/29, Swifton, Ark.   BR/TR, 5'9", 160 lbs.   Deb: 4/19/52

YEAR	TM/L	G	AB	R	H	2B	3B	HR	RBI	BB	SO	AVG	OBP	SLG	PRO+	BR	/A	RC	SB	CS	SBR	FR	POS	TPR
1952	Phi-A	75	213	24	47	8	3	0	17	14	18	.221	.275	.286	53	-13	-14	18	5	1	1	-5	2	-1.5

■ GEORGE KELL
Kell, George Clyde b: 8/23/22, Swifton, Ark.   BR/TR, 5'9", 175 lbs.   Deb: 9/28/43   H

YEAR	TM/L	G	AB	R	H	2B	3B	HR	RBI	BB	SO	AVG	OBP	SLG	PRO+	BR	/A	RC	SB	CS	SBR	FR	POS	TPR
1943	Phi-A	1	5	1	1	0	1	0	1	0	0	.200	.200	.600	131	0	0	1	0	0	0	0	/3	0.0
1944	Phi-A	139	514	51	138	15	3	0	44	22	23	.268	.300	.309	75	-18	-17	43	5	2	0	-5	*3	-2.2
1945	Phi-A	147	567	50	154	30	3	4	56	27	15	.272	.306	.356	92	-8	-8	61	2	0	1	22	*3	1.9
1946	Phi-A	26	87	3	26	6	1	0	11	10	6	.299	.378	.391	116	2	2	14	0	0	0	3	3	0.7
	Det-A	105	434	67	142	19	9	4	41	30	14	.327	.371	.440	119	14	11	71	3	2	-0	5	*3/1	2.5
	Yr	131	521	70	168	25	10	4	52	40	20	.322	.372	.432	118	16	13	85	3	2	-0	8		3.2
1947	Det-A	152	588	75	188	29	5	5	93	61	16	.320	.387	.412	118	18	16	95	9	11	-4	18	*3	3.4
1948	Det-A	92	368	47	112	24	3	2	44	33	15	.304	.369	.402	102	3	1	56	2	2	-1	-8	*3	-1.0
1949	Det-A	134	522	97	179	38	9	3	59	71	13	.343	.424	.467	136	28	28	106	7	5	-1	1	*3	2.7
1950	Det-A	157	641	114	218	56	6	8	101	66	18	.340	.403	.484	122	25	22	123	3	3	-1	-3	*3	1.1
1951	Det-A	147	598	92	191	36	3	2	59	61	18	.319	.386	.400	112	12	12	97	10	3	1	9	*3	1.6
1952	Det-A	39	152	11	45	8	0	1	17	15	13	.296	.359	.368	102	1	1	21	0	1	-1	-2	3	-0.1
	Bos-A	75	276	41	88	15	2	6	40	31	10	.319	.390	.453	124	13	10	48	0	1	-1	-6	3	0.3
	Yr	114	428	52	133	23	2	7	57	46	23	.311	.379	.423	117	13	11	69	0	2	-1	-8		0.2
1953	Bos-A	134	460	68	141	41	2	12	73	52	22	.307	.383	.483	126	21	18	88	5	2	0	-12	*3/O	0.0
1954	Bos-A	26	93	15	24	3	0	0	10	15	3	.258	.361	.290	72	-2	-3	11	0	0	-0	-3	3	-0.7
	Chi-A	71	233	25	66	10	0	5	48	18	12	.283	.335	.391	95	-1	-2	30	1	1	-0	-11	13/O	-1.6
	Yr	97	326	40	90	13	0	5	58	33	15	.276	.343	.362	88	-3	-5	41	1	1	-0	-14		-2.3
1955	Chi-A	128	429	44	134	24	1	8	81	51	36	.312	.393	.429	118	14	12	75	2	2	-1	-18	*31/O	-0.5
1956	Chi-A	21	80	7	25	5	0	1	11	8	6	.313	.375	.412	106	1	1	12	0	0	-1	-4	3/1	-0.2
	Bal-A	102	345	45	90	17	2	8	37	25	31	.261	.316	.391	93	-8	-4	42	0	1	-1	-7	3/12	-0.9
	Yr	123	425	52	115	22	2	9	48	33	37	.271	.328	.395	96	-7	-4	54	0	1	-1	-11		-1.1
1957	Bal-A	99	310	28	92	9	0	9	44	25	16	.297	.353	.413	116	4	6	44	2	0	1	-4	31	0.4
Total	15	1795	6702	881	2054	385	50	78	870	621	287	.306	.368	.414	111	118	106	1038	51	36	-6	-25	*3/1O2	7.4

■ DUKE KELLEHER
Kelleher, Albert Aloysius b: 9/30/1893, New York, N.Y. d: 9/28/47, Staten Island, N.Y.   TR ,   Deb: 8/18/16

YEAR	TM/L	G	AB	R	H	2B	3B	HR	RBI	BB	SO	AVG	OBP	SLG	PRO+	BR	/A	RC	SB	CS	SBR	FR	POS	TPR
1916	NY-N	1	0	0	0	0	0	0	0	0	0	—	—	—	—	0	0	0	0			0	/C	0.0

■ FRANKIE KELLEHER
Kelleher, Francis Eugene b: 8/22/16, San Francisco, Cal. d: 4/13/79, Stockton, Cal.   BR/TR, 6'1", 195 lbs.   Deb: 7/18/42

YEAR	TM/L	G	AB	R	H	2B	3B	HR	RBI	BB	SO	AVG	OBP	SLG	PRO+	BR	/A	RC	SB	CS	SBR	FR	POS	TPR
1942	Cin-N	38	110	13	20	3	1	3	12	16	20	.182	.286	.309	74	-4	-4	10	0			-0	O	-0.4
1943	Cin-N	9	10	1	0	0	0	0	0	2	0	.000	.167	.000	-51	-2	-2	0	0			0	/O	-0.1
Total	2	47	120	14	20	3	1	3	12	18	20	.167	.275	.283	64	-6	-5	10	0			-0	/O	-0.5

■ JOHN KELLEHER
Kelleher, John Patrick b: 9/13/1893, Brookline, Mass. d: 8/21/60, Brighton, Mass.   BR/TR, 5'11", 150 lbs.   Deb: 7/31/12

YEAR	TM/L	G	AB	R	H	2B	3B	HR	RBI	BB	SO	AVG	OBP	SLG	PRO+	BR	/A	RC	SB	CS	SBR	FR	POS	TPR
1912	StL-N	8	12	0	4	1	0	0	1	0	2	.333	.333	.417	107	0	0	2	0			1	/3	0.1
1916	Bro-N	2	3	0	0	0	0	0	0	0	0	.000	.000	.000	-97	-1	-1	0	0			-1	/S3	-0.1
1921	Chi-N	95	301	31	93	11	7	4	47	16	16	.309	.346	.432	104	2	2	44	2	5	-2	3	321S/O	0.3
1922	Chi-N	63	193	23	50	7	1	0	20	15	14	.259	.316	.306	60	-11	-11	18	5	7	-3	4	3/S1	-0.5
1923	Chi-N	66	193	27	59	10	0	6	21	14	9	.306	.353	.451	110	3	2	29	2	4	-2	-7	1S3/2	-0.5
1924	Bos-N	1	1	0	0	0	0	0	0	0	1	.000	.000	.000	-99	-0	-0	0	0	0	0	0	H	0.0
Total	6	235	703	81	206	29	8	10	89	45	42	.293	.337	.400	92	-8	-8	93	9	16		0	/312SO	-0.7

■ MICK KELLEHER
Kelleher, Michael Dennis b: 7/25/47, Seattle, Wash.   BR/TR, 5'9", 176 lbs.   Deb: 9/01/72   C

YEAR	TM/L	G	AB	R	H	2B	3B	HR	RBI	BB	SO	AVG	OBP	SLG	PRO+	BR	/A	RC	SB	CS	SBR	FR	POS	TPR
1972	StL-N	23	63	5	10	2	1	0	1	6	15	.159	.232	.222	30	-6	-6	4	0	0	0	5	S	0.2
1973	StL-N	43	38	4	7	2	0	0	2	4	11	.184	.279	.237	44	-3	-3	3	0	0	0	9	S	1.2
1974	Hou-N	19	57	4	9	2	0	0	2	5	10	.158	.226	.158	9	-7	-7	2	1	1	-0	4	S	0.0
1975	StL-N	7	4	0	0	0	0	0	0	0	1	.000	.000	.000	-97	-1	-1	0	0	0	0	2	/S	0.1
1976	Chi-N	124	337	28	77	12	1	0	22	15	32	.228	.266	.270	48	-21	-25	22	0	4	-2	12	*S3/2	-0.5
1977	Chi-N	63	122	14	28	5	2	0	11	9	12	.230	.288	.303	53	-7	-9	10	0	0	0	18	2S/3	1.4
1978	Chi-N	68	95	8	24	1	0	0	6	7	11	.253	.304	.263	53	-5	-6	7	4	1	1	18	32S	1.4
1979	Chi-N	73	142	14	36	4	1	0	10	7	9	.254	.298	.296	57	-7	-9	13	2	0	1	22	32S	1.6
1980	Chi-N	105	96	12	14	1	1	0	4	9	17	.146	.219	.177	11	-11	-12	3	1	3	-2	25	23S	1.8
1981	Det-A	61	77	10	17	4	0	0	6	7	10	.221	.286	.273	59	-4	-4	6	0	0	0	6	32/S	0.3
1982	Det-A	2	1	0	0	0	0	0	0	0	0	.000	.000	.000	-99	-0	-0	0	0	0	0	-0	/23	0.0
	Cal-A	34	49	9	8	1	0	0	1	5	5	.163	.255	.184	23	-5	-5	2	1	1	-0	7	S/3	0.4
	Yr	36	50	9	8	1	0	0	1	5	5	.160	.250	.180	20	-5	-5	2	1	1	-0	7		0.4
Total	11	622	1081	108	230	32	6	0	65	74	133	.213	.268	.253	43	-77	-86	72	9	10	-3	128	S32	7.9

■ CHARLIE KELLER
Keller, Charles Ernest "King Kong" b: 9/12/16, Middletown, Md. d: 5/23/90, Frederick, Md.   BL/TR, 5'10", 185 lbs.   Deb: 4/22/39

YEAR	TM/L	G	AB	R	H	2B	3B	HR	RBI	BB	SO	AVG	OBP	SLG	PRO+	BR	/A	RC	SB	CS	SBR	FR	POS	TPR
1939	*NY-A	111	398	87	133	21	6	11	83	81	49	.334	.447	.500	144	29	30	97	6	3	0	-5	*O	2.0
1940	*NY-A	138	500	102	143	18	15	21	93	106	65	.286	.411	.508	142	30	33	114	8	2	1	0	*O	2.3
1941	*NY-A	140	507	102	151	24	10	33	122	102	65	.298	.416	.580	163	46	47	134	6	4	-1	3	*O	3.9
1942	*NY-A	152	544	106	159	24	9	26	108	114	61	.292	.417	.513	164	47	48	131	14	2	3	1	*O	4.2
1943	*NY-A	141	512	97	139	15	11	31	86	106	65	.271	.396	.525	167	46	45	116	7	5	-1	4	*O	4.7
1945	NY-A	44	163	26	49	7	4	10	34	31	21	.301	.412	.577	178	17	17	41	0	2	-1	2	O	1.6
1946	NY-A	150	538	98	148	29	10	30	101	113	101	.275	.405	.533	158	46	45	127	1	4	-2	-2	*O	3.4
1947	NY-A	45	151	36	36	6	1	13	36	41	18	.238	.404	.550	165	14	14	37	0	0	0	-4	O	0.8
1948	NY-A	83	247	41	66	15	2	6	44	41	25	.267	.372	.417	111	4	4	40	1	1	-0	-7	O	-0.4
1949	NY-A	60	116	17	29	4	1	3	16	25	15	.250	.392	.379	104	2	2	20	0	2	-1	-6	O	-0.3
1950	Det-A	50	51	7	16	1	3	2	16	13	6	.314	.453	.569	155	5	5	15	0	0	0	-0	/O	0.4
1951	Det-A	54	62	6	16	2	0	3	21	19	11	.258	.419	.435	117	2	2	11	0	0	0	-0	/O	0.2
1952	NY-A	2	1	0	0	0	0	0	0	0	0	.000	.000	.000	-99	-0	-0	0	0	0	0	0	/O	0.0
Total	13	1170	3790	725	1085	166	72	189	760	784	499	.286	.410	.518	152	287	291	883	45	23	-0	-13	*O	22.8

YEAR	TM/L	G	AB	R	H	2B	3B	HR	RBI	BB	SO	AVG	OBP	SLG	PRO+	BR	/A	RC	SB	CS	SBR	FR	POS	TPR
■ **HAL KELLER**		Keller, Harold Kefauver b: 7/7/27, Middletown, Md.										BL/TR, 6'1", 200 lbs.		Deb: 9/13/49										
1949	Was-A	3	3	1	1	0	0	0	0	0	0	.333	.333	.333	78	-0	-0	0	0	0	0	0	H	0.0
1950	Was-A	11	28	1	6	3	0	1	5	2	2	.214	.267	.429	79	-1	-1	3	0	0	0	-1	/C	-0.1
1952	Was-A	11	23	2	4	2	0	0	0	1	1	.174	.208	.261	31	-2	-2	1	0	0	0	-0	C	-0.1
Total	3	25	54	4	11	5	0	1	5	3	3	.204	.246	.352	60	-4	-3	5	0	0	0	-2	/C	-0.2
■ **FRANK KELLERT**		Kellert, Frank William b: 7/6/24, Oklahoma City, Okla.										d: 11/19/76, Oklahoma City, Okla.		BR/TR, 6'2.5", 185 lbs.		Deb: 4/18/53								
1953	StL-A	2	4	0	0	0	0	0	0	0	0	.000	.000	.000	-98	-1	-1	0	0	0	0	-0	/1	0.0
1954	Bal-A	10	34	3	7	2	0	0	1	5	4	.206	.308	.265	62	-2	-2	3	0	0	0	-1	/1	-0.2
1955	*Bro-N	39	80	12	26	4	2	4	19	9	10	.325	.393	.575	149	6	6	18	0	1	-1	-0	1	0.3
1956	Chi-N	71	129	10	24	3	1	4	17	12	22	.186	.255	.318	54	-9	-8	9	0	0	0	3	1	-0.6
Total	4	122	247	25	57	9	3	8	37	26	36	.231	.304	.389	85	-6	-5	30	0	1	-1	1	/1	-0.5
■ **RED KELLETT**		Kellett, Donald Stafford b: 7/15/09, Brooklyn, N.Y.										d: 11/5/70, Ft.Lauderdale, Fla.		BR/TR, 6', 185 lbs.		Deb: 7/02/34								
1934	Bos-A	9	9	0	0	0	0	0	0	1	5	.000	.100	.000	-68	-2	-2	0	0	0	0	1	/S23	0.0
■ **JOE KELLEY**		Kelley, Joseph James b: 12/9/1871, Cambridge, Mass.										d: 8/14/43, Baltimore, Md.		BR/TR, 5'11", 190 lbs.		Deb: 7/27/1891 MCH								
1891	Bos-N	12	45	7	11	1	1	0	3	2	7	.244	.277	.311	65	-2	-2	4				-1	O	-0.2
1892	Pit-N	56	205	26	49	7	7	0	28	17	21	.239	.297	.341	94	-2	-2	24	8			2	O	-0.1
	Bal-N	10	33	3	7	0	0	0	4	4	7	.212	.316	.212	60	-1	-1	3	2			-3	O	-0.3
	Yr	66	238	29	56	7	7	0	32	21	28	.235	.300	.324	89	-3	-3	27	10			-1		-0.4
1893	Bal-N	125	502	120	153	27	16	9	76	77	44	.305	.401	.476	132	26	24	112	33			7	*O	2.1
1894	*Bal-N	129	507	165	199	48	20	6	111	107	36	.393	.502	.602	160	62	57	181	46			2	*O	3.8
1895	*Bal-N	131	518	148	189	26	19	10	134	77	29	.365	.456	.546	156	49	46	158	54			12	*O	3.8
1896	*Bal-N	131	519	148	189	31	19	8	100	91	19	.364	.469	.543	167	56	55	**178**	**87**			4	*O	4.2
1897	*Bal-N	131	505	113	183	31	9	5	118	70		.362	.447	.489	150	39	39	133	44			-2	*O/S3	2.3
1898	Bal-N	124	464	71	149	18	15	2	110	56		.321	.398	.438	140	26	25	93	24			1	*O/3	1.7
1899	Bro-N	143	538	108	175	21	14	6	93	70		.325	.410	.450	136	30	29	115	31			8	*O	2.4
1900	*Bro-N	121	454	90	145	23	17	6	91	53		.319	.395	.485	137	28	23	100	26			0	O13	1.6
1901	Bro-N	120	492	77	151	22	12	4	65	40		.307	.360	.425	126	18	16	84	18			6	*1/3	2.3
1902	Bal-A	60	222	50	69	17	7	1	34	34		.311	.402	.464	136	13	12	48	12			0	O/31	0.8
	Cin-N	40	156	24	50	9	2	1	12	15		.321	.380	.423	137	9	7	27	3			3	O2/3SM	1.0
1903	Cin-N	105	383	85	121	22	4	3	45	51		.316	.396	.418	121	19	12	73	18			-7	OS2/31M	0.3
1904	Cin-N	123	449	75	126	21	13	0	63	49		.281	.351	.385	119	16	11	70	15			0	*1/O2M	0.6
1905	Cin-N	90	321	43	89	7	6	1	37	27		.277	.333	.346	94	2	-2	42	8			-3	O/1M	-1.1
1906	Cin-N	129	465	43	106	19	11	1	53	44		.228	.295	.323	90	-3	-6	51	9			-5	*O/1S3	-1.4
1908	Bos-N	73	228	25	59	8	2	2	17	27		.259	.337	.338	120	5	6	28	5			-4	O1M	0.1
Total	17	1853	7006	1421	2220	358	194	65	1194	911	163	.317	.400	.451	134	391	349	1522	443			22	*O1/32S	23.9
■ **MIKE KELLEY**		Kelley, Michael Joseph b: 12/2/1876, Otter River, Mass.										d: 6/6/55, Minneapolis, Minn.		BR/TR, 6', 210 lbs.		Deb: 7/15/1899								
1899	Lou-N	76	282	48	68	11	2	0	33	21		.241	.305	.326	75	-9	-9	32	10			-0	1	-0.7
■ **FRANK KELLIHER**		Kelliher, Francis Mortimer "Yucka" b: 5/23/1899, Somerville, Mass.										d: 3/4/56, Somerville, Mass.		BL/TL, 5'9.5", 175 lbs.		Deb: 9/19/19								
1919	Was-A	1	1	0	0	0	0	0	0	0	0	.000	.000	.000	-99	-0	-0	0	0			0	H	0.0
■ **NATE KELLOGG**		Kellogg, Nathaniel Monroe b: 9/28/1858, Rochester, Iowa										d: 15, 5'9", 175 lbs.		Deb: 8/27/1885										
1885	Det-N	5	17	4	2	1	0	0	0	1	5	.118	.167	.176	11	-2	-2	1				-2	/S	-0.2
■ **BILL KELLOGG**		Kellogg, William Dearstyne b: 5/25/1884, Albany, N.Y.										d: 12/12/71, Baltimore, Md.		BR/TR, 5'10", 153 lbs.		Deb: 4/14/14								
1914	Cin-N	71	126	14	22	0	1	0	7	14	28	.175	.262	.190	34	-10	-10	8	7			0	12/O3	-1.1
■ **RED KELLY**		Kelly, Albert Michael b: 11/15/1884, Union, Ill.										d: 2/4/61, Zephyr Hills, Fla.		TR, 5'11.5", 165 lbs.		Deb: 6/18/10								
1910	Chi-A	14	45	6	7	0	1	0	1	7		.156	.296	.200	58	-2	-2	3	0			-1	O	-0.2
■ **CHARLIE KELLY**		Kelly, Charles H.				Deb: 6/14/1883																		
1883	Phi-N	2	7	1	1	0	1	0	0	0	3	.143	.143	.429	71	-0	-0	0				0	/3	0.0
1886	Phi-a	1	3	0	0	0	0	0	0	0		.000	.000	.000	-99	-1	-1	0	0			-1	/S	-0.1
Total	2	3	10	1	1	0	1	0	0	0	3	.100	.100	.300	19	-1	-1	0				-1	/3S	-0.1
■ **PAT KELLY**		Kelly, Dale Patrick b: 8/27/55, Santa Maria, Cal.										BR/TR, 6'3", 210 lbs.		Deb: 5/28/80										
1980	Tor-A	3	7	1	2	0	0	0	0	0	4	.286	.286	.286	55	-0	-0	1	0	0	0	1	/C	0.1
■ **GEORGE KELLY**		Kelly, George Lange "Highpockets" b: 9/10/1895, San Francisco, Cal.										d: 10/13/84, Burlingame, Cal.		BR/TR, 6'4", 190 lbs.		Deb: 8/18/15 CH								
1915	NY-N	17	38	2	6	0	0	1	4	1	9	.158	.179	.237	27	-3	-3	1	0	1	-1	-2	1O	-0.4
1916	NY-N	49	76	4	12	2	1	0	3	6	24	.158	.220	.211	34	-6	-6	4	1			-2	1O/3	-0.9
1917	NY-N	11	7	0	0	0	0	0	0	0	3	.000	.000	.000	-99	-2	-2	0				1	/OP12	0.0
	Pit-N	8	23	2	2	0	1	0	0	1	9	.087	.125	.174	-9	-3	-3	0	0			-1	/1	-0.4
	Yr	19	30	2	2	0	1	0	0	1	12	.067	.097	.133	-30	-5	-5	0	0			0		-0.4
1919	NY-N	32	107	12	31	6	2	1	14	3	15	.290	.315	.411	119	2	2	14	1			-3	1	0.0
1920	NY-N	155	590	69	157	22	11	11	**94**	41	92	.266	.320	.397	106	3	4	71	6	16	-8	4	*1	-0.1
1921	*NY-N	149	587	95	181	42	9	**23**	122	40	73	.308	.356	.528	131	23	23	104	4	12	-6	12	*1	2.5
1922	*NY-N	151	592	96	194	33	8	17	107	30	65	.328	.363	.497	119	15	14	106	12	3	2	10	*1	2.2
1923	*NY-N	145	560	82	172	23	5	16	103	47	64	.307	.362	.452	115	10	11	92	14	7	0	-6	*1	-0.4
1924	*NY-N	144	571	91	185	37	9	21	**136**	38	52	.324	.371	.531	143	29	31	112	7	2	1	-1	*1O/23	2.5
1925	NY-N	147	586	87	181	29	3	20	99	35	54	.309	.350	.471	112	5	6	96	5	2	0	18	*21O	2.0
1926	NY-N	136	499	70	151	24	4	13	80	36	52	.303	.352	.445	115	8	9	76	4			8	*12	1.3
1927	Cin-N	61	222	27	60	16	4	5	21	11	23	.270	.308	.446	103	-1	-0	29	1			-2	12/O	-0.5
1928	Cin-N	116	402	46	119	33	7	3	58	28	35	.296	.345	.435	104	1	2	59	2			8	1O	-0.1
1929	Cin-N	147	577	73	169	45	9	5	103	33	61	.293	.332	.428	91	-13	-9	79	7			4	*1	-1.0
1930	Cin-N	51	188	18	54	10	1	5	35	7	20	.287	.313	.431	81	-7	-6	24	1			2	1	-0.5
	Chi-N	39	166	22	55	6	1	3	19	7	16	.331	.362	.434	91	-2	-2	25	0			4	1	0.0
	Yr	90	354	40	109	16	2	8	54	14	36	.308	.336	.432	86	-10	-8	49	1			5		-0.5
1932	Bro-N	64	202	23	49	9	1	4	22	22	27	.243	.317	.356	82	-5	-5	24	0			-2	1/O	-0.9
Total	16	1622	5993	819	1778	337	76	148	1020	386	694	.297	.342	.452	110	53	68	918	65	<u>43</u>		54	*12/O3P	5.3
■ **PAT KELLY**		Kelly, Harold Patrick b: 7/30/44, Philadelphia, Pa.										BL/TL, 6'1", 185 lbs.		Deb: 9/06/67										
1967	Min-A	8	1	1	0	0	0	0	0	0	1	.000	.000	.000	-93	-0	-0	0	0	0	0	0	H	0.0
1968	Min-A	12	35	2	4	2	0	1	2	3	10	.114	.205	.257	37	-3	-3	1	0	2	-1	1	O	-0.3
1969	KC-A	112	417	61	110	20	4	8	32	49	70	.264	.348	.388	105	4	3	61	40	13	4	4	*O	0.9
1970	KC-A	136	452	56	106	16	1	6	38	76	105	.235	.347	.314	84	-8	-8	55	34	16	1	7	*O	-0.4
1971	Chi-A	67	213	32	62	6	3	3	22	36	29	.291	.390	.390	119	8	7	34	14	9	1	-0	O	0.5
1972	Chi-A	119	402	57	105	14	7	5	24	55	69	.261	.356	.368	113	9	8	59	32	9	4	-4	*O	0.7
1973	Chi-A	144	550	77	154	24	5	1	44	65	91	.280	.358	.347	96	2	-1	67	KELLY 15	-2		-4	*O/D	-1.0
1974	Chi-A	122	424	60	119	16	3	4	21	46	58	.281	.354	.361	103	4	3	54	18	11	-1	-5	DO	-0.4
1975	Chi-A	133	471	73	129	21	7	9	45	58	69	.274	.356	.406	113	10	9	67	18	10	-1	-6	*OD	0.0

YEAR	TM/L	G	AB	R	H	2B	3B	HR	RBI	BB	SO	AVG	OBP	SLG	PRO+	BR	/A	RC	SB	CS	SBR	FR	POS	TPR
1976	Chi-A	107	311	42	79	20	3	5	34	45	45	.254	.354	.386	116	7	7	44	15	7	0	-2	DO	0.5
1977	Bal-A	120	360	50	92	13	0	10	49	53	75	.256	.357	.375	106	1	5	53	25	7	3	-12	*O/D	-0.7
1978	Bal-A	100	274	38	75	12	1	11	40	34	58	.274	.358	.445	133	9	11	41	10	8	-2	-9	O/D	-0.1
1979	*Bal-A	68	153	25	44	11	0	9	25	20	25	.288	.374	.536	147	9	10	30	4	5	-2	-2	OD	0.5
1980	Bal-A	89	200	38	52	10	1	3	26	34	54	.260	.368	.365	102	2	2	31	16	2	4	0	OD	0.5
1981	Cle-A	48	75	8	16	4	0	1	16	14	9	.213	.337	.307	88	-1	-1	7	2	4	-2	0	D/O	-0.2
Total	15	1385	4338	620	1147	189	35	76	418	588	768	.264	.356	.377	107	54	54	604	250	118	4	-31	OD	0.4

■ JIM KELLY   Kelly, James Robert (Also Played Under Real Name Of Robert John Taggert In 1918) b: 2/1/1884, Bloomfield, N.J. d: 4/10/61, Kingsport, Tenn. BL/TR, 5'10.5", 180 lbs. Deb: 4/26/14

YEAR	TM/L	G	AB	R	H	2B	3B	HR	RBI	BB	SO	AVG	OBP	SLG	PRO+	BR	/A	RC	SB	CS	SBR	FR	POS	TPR
1914	Pit-N	32	44	4	10	2	1	0	3	2	3	.227	.261	.318	75	-2	-1	4	0			0	/O	0.0
1915	Pit-F	148	524	68	154	12	17	4	50	35	46	.294	.340	.405	121	12	12	89	38			14	*O	2.0
1918	Bos-N	35	146	19	48	1	4	0	4	9	9	.329	.376	.390	140	6	7	22	4			-1	O	0.4
Total	3	215	714	91	212	15	22	4	57	46	58	.297	.343	.396	122	16	17	115	42			13	O	2.4

■ TOM KELLY   Kelly, Jay Thomas b: 8/15/50, Graceville, Minn. BL/TL, 5'11", 188 lbs. Deb: 5/11/75 M

YEAR	TM/L	G	AB	R	H	2B	3B	HR	RBI	BB	SO	AVG	OBP	SLG	PRO+	BR	/A	RC	SB	CS	SBR	FR	POS	TPR
1975	Min-A	49	127	11	23	5	0	1	11	15	22	.181	.268	.244	44	-9	-9	9	0	0	0	2	1/O	-1.0

■ JOHN KELLY   Kelly, John B. b: 3/13/1879, Clifton Heights, Pa. d: 3/19/44, Baltimore, Md. 5'9", 165 lbs. Deb: 4/11/07

YEAR	TM/L	G	AB	R	H	2B	3B	HR	RBI	BB	SO	AVG	OBP	SLG	PRO+	BR	/A	RC	SB	CS	SBR	FR	POS	TPR
1907	StL-N	53	197	12	37	5	0	0	6		13	.188	.238	.213	44	-13	-12	13	7			-1	O	-1.6

■ JOHN KELLY   Kelly, John Francis "Honest John" or "Father" b: 3/3/1859, Paterson, N.J. d: 4/13/08, Paterson, N.J. BR/TR, 6', 185 lbs. Deb: 5/01/1882

YEAR	TM/L	G	AB	R	H	2B	3B	HR	RBI	BB	SO	AVG	OBP	SLG	PRO+	BR	/A	RC	SB	CS	SBR	FR	POS	TPR
1882	Cle-N	30	104	6	14	2	0		5	1	24	.135	.143	.154	-5	-12	-11	2				-9	C	-1.6
1883	Bal-a	48	202	18	46	9	2	0		3		.228	.239	.292	68	-7	-8	14				-11	CO	-1.2
	Phi-N	1	3	0	0	0	0	0	0	0	0	.000	.000	.000	-99	-1	-1	0				1	/O	0.0
1884	Cin-U	38	142	23	40	5	1	1		6		.282	.311	.352	115	3	2	16	0			0	C/O	0.4
	Was-U	4	14	1	5	1	0	0		0		.357	.357	.429	170	1	1	2	0			0	/CO	0.1
	Yr	42	156	24	45	6	1	1		6		.288	.315	.359	119	4	3	18	0			1		0.5
Total	3	121	465	48	105	17	3	1	5	10	26	.226	.242	.282	69	-15	-17	35	0			-19	C/O	-2.3

■ KICK KELLY   Kelly, John O. "Diamond John" b: 10/31/1856, New York, N.Y. d: 3/27/26, Malba, N.Y. 6'0.5", 185 lbs. Deb: 5/01/1879 MU

YEAR	TM/L	G	AB	R	H	2B	3B	HR	RBI	BB	SO	AVG	OBP	SLG	PRO+	BR	/A	RC	SB	CS	SBR	FR	POS	TPR
1879	Syr-N	10	36	4	4	1	0	0	2	0	6	.111	.111	.139	-20	-4	-4	1				-1	/C1	-0.4
	Tro-N	6	22	1	5	0	0	0	0	0	1	.227	.227	.227	54	-1	-1	1				-1	/CO3	-0.1
	Yr	16	58	5	9	1	0	0	2	0	7	.155	.155	.172	9	-6	-5	2				-2		-0.5

■ JOE KELLY   Kelly, Joseph Henry b: 9/23/1886, Weir City, Kan. d: 8/16/77, St.Joseph, Mo. BR/TR, 5'10", 175 lbs. Deb: 4/14/14

YEAR	TM/L	G	AB	R	H	2B	3B	HR	RBI	BB	SO	AVG	OBP	SLG	PRO+	BR	/A	RC	SB	CS	SBR	FR	POS	TPR
1914	Pit-N	141	508	47	113	19	9	1	48	39	59	.222	.283	.301	77	-17	-14	48	21			-3	*O	-2.3
1916	Chi-N	54	169	18	43	7	1	2	15	9	16	.254	.296	.343	87	-1	-3	20	10			2	O	-0.2
1917	Bos-N	116	445	41	99	9	8	3	36	26	45	.222	.268	.299	78	-14	-12	40	21			14	*O	0.0
1918	Bos-N	47	155	20	36	2	4	0	15	6	12	.232	.265	.297	74	-6	-5	14	12			0	O	-0.7
1919	Bos-N	18	64	3	9	1	0	0	3	0	11	.141	.154	.156	-7	-8	-8	2	2			-0	O	-0.9
Total	5	376	1341	129	300	38	22	6	117	80	143	.224	.272	.298	75	-46	-42	123	66			13	O	-4.1

■ JOE KELLY   Kelly, Joseph James b: 4/23/1900, New York, N.Y. d: 11/24/67, Lynbrook, N.Y. BL/TL, 6', 180 lbs. Deb: 4/13/26

YEAR	TM/L	G	AB	R	H	2B	3B	HR	RBI	BB	SO	AVG	OBP	SLG	PRO+	BR	/A	RC	SB	CS	SBR	FR	POS	TPR
1926	Chi-N	65	176	16	59	15	3	0	32	7	11	.335	.361	.455	117	4	4	27	0			-6	O	-0.3
1928	Chi-N	32	52	3	11	1	0	1	7	1	3	.212	.255	.288	42	-5	-4	4	0			0	1	-0.4
Total	2	97	228	19	70	16	3	1	39	8	14	.307	.336	.417	100	-1	-1	31	0			-6	/O1	-0.7

■ KING KELLY   Kelly, Michael Joseph b: 12/31/1857, Troy, N.Y. d: 11/8/1894, Boston, Mass. BR/TR, 5'10", 170 lbs. Deb: 5/01/1878 MH

YEAR	TM/L	G	AB	R	H	2B	3B	HR	RBI	BB	SO	AVG	OBP	SLG	PRO+	BR	/A	RC	SB	CS	SBR	FR	POS	TPR
1878	Cin-N	60	237	29	67	7	1	0	27	7	7	.283	.303	.321	116	1	4	24				9	*OC/3	0.9
1879	Cin-N	77	345	78	120	20	12	2	47	8	14	.348	.363	.493	188	28	31	63				15	3OC/2	**4.0**
1880	Chi-N	84	344	72	100	17	9	1	60	12	22	.291	.315	.401	133	14	11	45				-2	*OC3/S2P	0.8
1881	Chi-N	82	353	84	114	**27**	3	2	55	16	14	.323	.352	.433	139	18	16	55				-2	*OC/3	1.2
1882	Chi-N	84	377	81	115	**37**	4	1	55	10	27	.305	.323	.432	134	16	13	54				-2	SOC/31	1.4
1883	Chi-N	98	428	92	109	28	10	3	61	16	35	.255	.282	.388	95	0	-4	48				2	*OC/23P	0.2
1884	Chi-N	108	452	**120**	160	28	5	13	95	46	24	**.354**	**.414**	.524	178	49	43	100				-5	OCS3/1P	3.5
1885	*Chi-N	107	438	**124**	126	24	7	9	75	46	24	.288	.355	.436	135	27	18	70				4	OC/231	2.1
1886	*Chi-N	118	451	**155**	175	32	11	4	79	83	33	**.388**	**.483**	.534	181	64	53	146	53			2	OC/132S	5.1
1887	Bos-N	116	484	120	156	34	11	8	63	55	40	.322	.393	.488	145	30	30	129	84			-11	O2C/PS3M	2.1
1888	Bos-N	107	440	85	140	22	11	9	71	31	39	.318	.368	.480	168	34	33	101	56			-3	CO	3.1
1889	Bos-N	125	507	120	149	**41**	5	9	78	65	40	.294	.376	.448	124	22	16	114	68			-9	*OC	2.1
1890	Bos-P	89	340	83	111	18	6	4	66	52	22	.326	.419	.450	126	18	14	88	51			-4	CS/O13PM	1.1
1891	Cin-a	82	283	56	84	15	7	1	53	51	28	.297	.408	.410	126	16	11	58	22			13	C/3O21PS	2.3
	Bos-a	4	15	2	4	0	0	1	4	0	2	.267	.267	.467	113	0	0	2	1			-1	/C	0.0
	Yr	86	298	58	88	15	7	2	57	51	30	.295	.402	.413	126	16	11	60	23			12		2.3
	Bos-N	16	52	7	12	1	0	0	5	6	10	.231	.322	.250	62	-2	-3	6	6			-5	C/O	-0.6
1892	*Bos-N	78	281	40	53	7	0	2	41	39	31	.189	.287	.235	55	-12	-16	27	24			2	C/O31P	-0.9
1893	NY-N	20	67	9	18	1	0	0	15	6	5	.269	.329	.284	65	-3	-3	7	3			-1	C/O	-0.1
Total	16	1455	5894	1357	1813	359	102	69	950	549	417	.308	.368	.438	137	321	267	1135	368			1	OC/3S21P	26.5

■ SPEED KELLY   Kelly, R B b: 8/12/1884, Brian, Ohio d: 5/6/49, Goshen, Ind. BR/TR, 6'2", 185 lbs. Deb: 7/13/09

YEAR	TM/L	G	AB	R	H	2B	3B	HR	RBI	BB	SO	AVG	OBP	SLG	PRO+	BR	/A	RC	SB	CS	SBR	FR	POS	TPR
1909	Was-A	17	42	3	6	2	1	0	1	3		.143	.200	.238	40	-3	-3	2	1			-1	3/2O	-0.3

■ ROBERTO KELLY   Kelly, Roberto Conrado (Gray) b: 10/1/64, Panama City, Pan. BR/TR, 6'2", 180 lbs. Deb: 7/29/87

YEAR	TM/L	G	AB	R	H	2B	3B	HR	RBI	BB	SO	AVG	OBP	SLG	PRO+	BR	/A	RC	SB	CS	SBR	FR	POS	TPR
1987	NY-A	23	52	12	14	3	0	1	5		15	.269	.333	.385	91	-1	-1	7	9	3	1	2	O/D	0.2
1988	NY-A	38	77	9	19	4	1	1	7	3	15	.247	.275	.364	78	-3	-2	8	5	2	0	6	O/D	0.3
1989	NY-A	137	441	65	133	18	3	9	48	41	89	.302	.369	.417	123	13	14	70	35	12	3	3	*O	1.8
1990	NY-A	162	641	85	183	32	4	15	61	33	148	.285	.324	.418	106	4	3	87	42	17	2	3	*O	0.6
Total	4	360	1211	171	349	57	8	26	123	82	267	.288	.338	.413	109	13	14	172	91	34	7	12	O/D	2.9

■ VAN KELLY   Kelly, Van Howard b: 3/18/46, Charlotte, N.C. BL/TR, 5'11", 180 lbs. Deb: 6/13/69

YEAR	TM/L	G	AB	R	H	2B	3B	HR	RBI	BB	SO	AVG	OBP	SLG	PRO+	BR	/A	RC	SB	CS	SBR	FR	POS	TPR
1969	SD-N	73	209	16	51	7	1	3	15	12	24	.244	.285	.330	75	-8	-7	19	0	1	-1	-3	32	-1.0
1970	SD-N	38	89	9	15	3	0	1	9	15	21	.169	.288	.236	44	-7	-7	7	0	1	-1	1	3/2	-0.6
Total	2	111	298	25	66	10	1	4	24	27	45	.221	.286	.302	65	-15	-14	26	0	2	-1	-2	/32	-1.6

■ BILL KELLY   Kelly, William Henry "Big Bill" b: 12/28/1898, Syracuse, N.Y. d: 4/8/90, Syracuse, N.Y. BR/TR, 6', 190 lbs. Deb: 9/06/20

YEAR	TM/L	G	AB	R	H	2B	3B	HR	RBI	BB	SO	AVG	OBP	SLG	PRO+	BR	/A	RC	SB	CS	SBR	FR	POS	TPR
1920	Phi-A	9	13	0	3	1	0	0	0	0	0	.231	.231	.308	41	-1	-1	1	0	0	0	0	/1	0.0
1928	Phi-N	23	71	6	12	1	1	0	5	7	20	.169	.244	.211	19	-8	-9	4	0			1	1	-0.9
Total	2	32	84	6	15	2	1	0	5	7	22	.179	.242	.226	22	-9	-10	5	0	0	0	2	/1	-0.9

■ BILL KELLY   Kelly, William J. b: New York, N.Y. Deb: 5/04/1871

YEAR	TM/L	G	AB	R	H	2B	3B	HR	RBI	BB	SO	AVG	OBP	SLG	PRO+	BR	/A	RC	SB	CS	SBR	FR	POS	TPR
1871	Kek-n	18	67	16	15	1	1	0	7	6	1	.224	.288	.269	60	-3	-3	5	0				O/1	-0.1

■ BILLY KELLY   Kelly, William Joseph b: 5/1/1886, Baltimore, Md. d: 6/3/40, Detroit, Mich. BR/TR, 6'0.5", 183 lbs. Deb: 5/02/10

YEAR	TM/L	G	AB	R	H	2B	3B	HR	RBI	BB	SO	AVG	OBP	SLG	PRO+	BR	/A	RC	SB	CS	SBR	FR	POS	TPR
1910	StL-N	2	2	1	0	0	0	0	0	0	0	.000	.333	.000	-1	-0	-0	0	0			0	/C	0.0
1911	Pit-N	6	8	0	1	0	0	0	0	0	2	.125	.125	.125	-29	-1	-1	0	0			1	/C	0.0

YEAR	TM/L	G	AB	R	H	2B	3B	HR	RBI	BB	SO	AVG	OBP	SLG	PRO+	BR	/A	RC	SB	CS	SBR	FR	POS	TPR
1912	Pit-N	48	132	20	42	3	2	1	11	2	16	.318	.328	.394	99	-1	-1	20	8			-9	C	-0.7
1913	Pit-N	48	82	11	22	2	2	0	9	2	12	.268	.302	.341	87	-2	-1	8	1			5	C	0.6
Total	4	104	224	32	65	5	4	1	20	5	30	.290	.312	.362	89	-5	-4	28	9			-4	/C	-0.1

■ BILLY KELSEY
Kelsey, George William b: 8/24/1881, Covington, Ohio d: 4/25/68, Springfield, Ohio BR/TR, 5'10", 150 lbs. Deb: 10/04/07

YEAR	TM/L	G	AB	R	H	2B	3B	HR	RBI	BB	SO	AVG	OBP	SLG	PRO+	BR	/A	RC	SB	CS	SBR	FR	POS	TPR
1907	Pit-N	2	5	1	2	0	0	0	0	0		.400	.400	.400	151	0	0	1	0			0	/C	0.0

■ KEN KELTNER
Keltner, Kenneth Frederick "Butch" b: 10/31/16, Milwaukee, Wis. BR/TR, 6', 190 lbs. Deb: 10/02/37

YEAR	TM/L	G	AB	R	H	2B	3B	HR	RBI	BB	SO	AVG	OBP	SLG	PRO+	BR	/A	RC	SB	CS	SBR	FR	POS	TPR
1937	Cle-A	1	1	0	0	0	0	0	1	0	0	.000	.000	.000	-99	-0	-0	0	0	0	0	0	/3	0.0
1938	Cle-A	149	576	86	159	31	9	26	113	33	75	.276	.319	.497	103	-4	-2	90	4	3	-1	-10	*3	-0.6
1939	Cle-A	154	587	84	191	35	11	13	97	51	41	.325	.379	.489	125	17	20	105	6	6	-2	6	*3	1.9
1940	Cle-A	149	543	67	138	24	10	15	77	51	56	.254	.322	.418	93	-9	-7	75	10	5	0	-5	*3	-0.3
1941	Cle-A	149	581	83	156	31	13	23	84	51	56	.269	.330	.485	119	8	11	95	2	2	-1	23	*3	3.9
1942	Cle-A	152	624	72	179	34	4	6	78	20	36	.287	.312	.383	101	-7	-3	72	4	3	-1	16	*3	1.5
1943	Cle-A	110	427	47	111	31	3	4	39	36	20	.260	.317	.375	109	-0	3	50	2	2	-1	6	*3	1.0
1944	Cle-A	149	573	74	169	41	9	13	91	53	29	.295	.355	.466	139	23	25	91	4	3	-1	15	*3	4.0
1946	Cle-A	116	398	47	96	17	1	13	45	30	38	.241	.294	.387	95	-7	-4	42	0	3	-2	-2	*3	0.0
1947	Cle-A	151	541	49	139	29	3	11	76	59	45	.257	.331	.383	101	-2	-0	72	5	4	-1	-9	*3	-0.6
1948	*Cle-A	153	558	91	166	24	4	31	119	89	52	.297	.395	.522	146	33	35	116	2	1	0	0	*3	2.8
1949	Cle-A	80	246	35	57	9	2	8	30	38	26	.232	.335	.382	91	-4	-4	32	0	1	-1	-1	3	-0.5
1950	Bos-A	13	28	2	9	2	0	0	2	3	6	.321	.387	.393	91	0	-0	4	0	0	0	-1	/3	-0.1
Total	13	1526	5683	737	1570	308	69	163	852	514	480	.276	.338	.441	113	46	74	843	39	33	-8	36	*3/1	13.0

■ JOHN KELTY
Kelty, John James "Chief" b: 1867, Jersey City, N.J. 5'10", 175 lbs. Deb: 4/19/1890

YEAR	TM/L	G	AB	R	H	2B	3B	HR	RBI	BB	SO	AVG	OBP	SLG	PRO+	BR	/A	RC	SB	CS	SBR	FR	POS	TPR
1890	Pit-N	59	207	24	49	10	2	1	27	22	42	.237	.322	.319	101	-2	1	25	10			-4	O	-0.2

■ BILL KEMMER
Kemmer, William E. b: 2/1878, Texas BR, 6'2", Deb: 6/03/1895

YEAR	TM/L	G	AB	R	H	2B	3B	HR	RBI	BB	SO	AVG	OBP	SLG	PRO+	BR	/A	RC	SB	CS	SBR	FR	POS	TPR
1895	Lou-N	11	38	5	7	0	0	1	3	2	4	.184	.225	.263	29	-4	-4	2	0			3	/31	0.0

■ RUDY KEMMLER
Kemmler, Rudolph (b: Rudolph Kemler) b: 1860, Chicago, Ill. d: 6/20/09, Chicago, Ill. BR/TR, Deb: 7/26/1879

YEAR	TM/L	G	AB	R	H	2B	3B	HR	RBI	BB	SO	AVG	OBP	SLG	PRO+	BR	/A	RC	SB	CS	SBR	FR	POS	TPR
1879	Pro-N	2	7	0	1	0	0	0	0	0	1	.143	.143	.143	-6	-1	-1	0				2	/C	0.1
1881	Cle-N	1	3	0	0	0	0	0	0	0	1	.000	.000	.000	-99	-1	-1	0				1	/C	0.0
1882	Cin-a	3	11	0	1	1	0	0		0		.091	.091	.182	-10	-1	-1	0				-1	/CO	-0.1
	Pit-a	24	99	7	25	4	0	0			1	.253	.260	.293	90	-1	-1	8				0	C/O	0.0
	Yr	27	110	7	26	5	0	0			1	.236	.243	.282	79	-3	-2	8				-1		-0.1
1883	Col-a	84	318	27	66	6	2	0		13		.208	.239	.239	59	-16	-12	19				-7	*C/O	-1.0
1884	Col-a	61	211	28	42	3	3	0		15		.199	.252	.242	70	-8	-5	13				-21	C/1O	-1.9
1885	Pit-a	18	64	2	13	2	1	0			2	.203	.239	.266	62	-3	-3	4				-2	C	-0.1
1886	StL-a	35	123	13	17	2	0	0			8	.138	.197	.154	11	-12	-13	4	0			3	C/1	-0.6
1889	Col-a	8	26	2	3	0	0	0	0	3	3	.115	.207	.115	-6	-3	-3	1	0			2	/C	0.0
Total	8	236	862	79	168	18	6	0	0	42	5	.195	.234	.230	53	-46	-39	48	0			-23	C/1O	-3.6

■ STEVE KEMP
Kemp, Steven F b: 8/7/54, San Angelo, Tex. BL/TL, 6', 195 lbs. Deb: 4/07/77

YEAR	TM/L	G	AB	R	H	2B	3B	HR	RBI	BB	SO	AVG	OBP	SLG	PRO+	BR	/A	RC	SB	CS	SBR	FR	POS	TPR
1977	Det-A	151	552	75	142	29	4	18	88	71	93	.257	.347	.422	103	7	3	83	3	3	-1	-9	*O	-1.0
1978	Det-A	159	582	75	161	18	4	15	79	97	87	.277	.381	.399	116	18	16	94	2	3	-1	-6	*O	0.5
1979	Det-A	134	490	88	156	26	3	26	105	68	70	.318	.404	.543	148	37	35	106	5	6	-2	2	*OD	2.9
1980	Det-A	135	508	88	149	23	3	21	101	69	64	.293	.382	.474	130	24	23	89	5	1	1	3	OD	2.4
1981	Det-A	105	372	52	103	18	4	9	49	70	48	.277	.393	.419	129	19	17	64	9	3	1	0	OD	1.7
1982	Chi-A	160	591	90	166	23	1	19	98	89	83	.286	.384	.428	123	21	21	99	7	7	-2	-12	*O/D	0.2
1983	NY-A	109	373	53	90	17	3	12	49	41	37	.241	.320	.399	100	-2	-0	45	1	0	0	0	*O/D	0.0
1984	NY-A	94	313	37	91	12	1	7	41	40	54	.291	.373	.403	119	7	9	47	4	1	1	-9	OD	-0.1
1985	Pit-N	92	236	19	59	13	2	2	21	25	54	.250	.322	.347	88	-4	-4	27	1	0	0	-4	O	-0.8
1986	Pit-N	13	16	1	3	0	0	1	1	4	6	.188	.350	.375	98	0	0	2	1	0	0	1	/O	0.1
1988	Tex-A	16	36	2	8	0	0	0	2	2	9	.222	.263	.222	36	-3	-3	2	1	0	0	0	/O1D	-0.2
Total	11	1168	4058	581	1128	179	25	130	634	576	605	.278	.370	.431	119	126	118	658	39	24	-3	-35	*O/D1	5.7

■ FRED KENDALL
Kendall, Fred Lyn b: 1/31/49, Torrance, Cal. BR/TR, 6'1", 185 lbs. Deb: 9/08/69

YEAR	TM/L	G	AB	R	H	2B	3B	HR	RBI	BB	SO	AVG	OBP	SLG	PRO+	BR	/A	RC	SB	CS	SBR	FR	POS	TPR
1969	SD-N	10	26	2	4	0	0	0	0	2	5	.154	.214	.154	5	-3	-3	1	0	0	0	-0	/C	-0.2
1970	SD-N	4	9	0	0	0	0	0	1	0	0	.000	.000	.000	-99	-4	-2	0	0	0	0	-1	/C1O	-0.3
1971	SD-N	49	111	2	19	1	0	1	7	7	16	.171	.220	.207	23	-11	-11	5	1	0	0	0	C/13	-0.9
1972	SD-N	91	273	18	59	3	4	6	18	11	42	.216	.249	.322	66	-15	-12	21	0	0	0	2	C/1	-0.5
1973	SD-N	145	507	39	143	22	3	10	59	30	35	.282	.323	.396	107	-2	3	61	3	1	0	-18	*C	-0.6
1974	SD-N	141	424	32	98	15	2	8	45	49	33	.231	.311	.333	84	-11	-9	43	0	1	-1	-25	*C	-3.0
1975	SD-N	103	286	16	57	12	1	0	24	26	28	.199	.266	.248	46	-22	-20	18	0	1	-1	-9	C	-2.7
1976	SD-N	146	456	30	112	17	0	2	39	36	42	.246	.305	.296	77	-17	-13	39	1	1	-0	-21	*C	-2.7
1977	Cle-A	103	317	18	79	13	1	3	39	16	27	.249	.287	.325	69	-15	-13	29	0	1	-1	-13	*C/D	-2.4
1978	Bos-A	20	41	3	8	1	0	0	4	1	2	.195	.214	.220	20	-4	-5	2	0	0	0	3	1/CD	-0.1
1979	SD-N	46	102	8	17	2	0	1	6	11	7	.167	.248	.216	29	-10	-9	5	0	0	0	4	C/1	-0.3
1980	SD-N	19	24	2	7	0	0	0	2	0	3	.292	.292	.292	67	-1	-1	2	0	0	0	0	C/1	0.0
Total	12	877	2576	170	603	86	11	31	244	189	240	.234	.288	.312	72	-114	-96	225	5	5	-2	-76	C/1D3O	-13.7

■ AL KENDERS
Kenders, Albert Daniel George b: 4/4/37, Barrington, N.J. BR/TR, 6', 185 lbs. Deb: 8/14/61

YEAR	TM/L	G	AB	R	H	2B	3B	HR	RBI	BB	SO	AVG	OBP	SLG	PRO+	BR	/A	RC	SB	CS	SBR	FR	POS	TPR
1961	Phi-N	10	23	0	4	0	0	0	1	1	0	.174	.208	.217	13	-3	-3	1	0	0	0	-1	C	-0.2

■ EDDIE KENNA
Kenna, Edward Aloysius "Scrap Iron" b: 9/30/1897, San Francisco, Cal. d: 8/21/72, San Francisco, Cal BR/TR, 5'7.5", 150 lbs. Deb: 6/02/28

YEAR	TM/L	G	AB	R	H	2B	3B	HR	RBI	BB	SO	AVG	OBP	SLG	PRO+	BR	/A	RC	SB	CS	SBR	FR	POS	TPR
1928	Was-A	41	118	14	35	4	2	1	20	14	8	.297	.376	.390	102	1	1	16	1	5	-3	-2	C	-0.1

■ ED KENNEDY
Kennedy, Edward b: 4/1/1856, Carbondale, Pa. d: 5/20/05, New York, N.Y. Deb: 5/02/1883

YEAR	TM/L	G	AB	R	H	2B	3B	HR	RBI	BB	SO	AVG	OBP	SLG	PRO+	BR	/A	RC	SB	CS	SBR	FR	POS	TPR
1883	NY-a	94	356	57	78	6	7	2		17		.219	.255	.292	73	-9	-11	27				-7	*O	-1.5
1884	*NY-a	103	378	49	72	6	2	1		16		.190	.225	.225	51	-20	-18	20				6	*O/S2C	-1.1
1885	NY-a	96	349	35	71	8	4	2		12		.203	.238	.266	67	-15	-11	23				2	*O	-1.2
1886	Bro-a	6	22	1	4	0	0	0		2		.182	.250	.182	37	-1	-2	1	1			-1	/O	-0.1
Total	4	299	1105	142	225	20	13	5		47		.204	.239	.259	63	-45	-42	71	1			-0	O/C2S	-3.9

■ JIM KENNEDY
Kennedy, James Earl b: 11/1/46, Tulsa, Okla. BL/TR, 5'9", 160 lbs. Deb: 6/14/70

YEAR	TM/L	G	AB	R	H	2B	3B	HR	RBI	BB	SO	AVG	OBP	SLG	PRO+	BR	/A	RC	SB	CS	SBR	FR	POS	TPR
1970	StL-N	12	24	1	3	0	0	0	0	0	0	.125	.125	.125	-32	-4	-5	0	0	0	0	1	/S2	-0.1

■ JOHN KENNEDY
Kennedy, John Edward b: 5/29/41, Chicago, Ill. BR/TR, 6', 185 lbs. Deb: 9/05/62

YEAR	TM/L	G	AB	R	H	2B	3B	HR	RBI	BB	SO	AVG	OBP	SLG	PRO+	BR	/A	RC	SB	CS	SBR	FR	POS	TPR
1962	Was-A	14	42	6	11	0	1	1	2	2	7	.262	.295	.381	81	-1	-1	5	0	1	-1	0	/S3	0.0
1963	Was-A	36	62	3	11	1	1	0	4	6	22	.177	.261	.226	38	-5	-5	4	2	0	1	6	3/S	0.0
1964	Was-A	148	482	55	111	16	4	7	35	29	119	.230	.281	.324	68	-21	-21	41	3	3	-1	9	*3S/2	-1.1
1965	*LA-N	104	105	12	18	3	0	1	5	8	33	.171	.243	.229	36	-9	-8	6	1	0	0	11	3/S	0.1
1966	*LA-N	125	274	15	55	9	2	3	24	10	64	.201	.242	.281	49	-20	-18	18	1	2	-1	13	3S2	-0.3
1967	NY-A	78	179	22	35	4	0	1	17	17	35	.196	.269	.235	52	-11	-10	12	2	1	0	7	S3/2	0.0
1969	Sea-A	61	128	18	30	3	1	4	14	14	25	.234	.315	.367	92	-2	-2	16	4	0	1	-4	S3	-0.2
1970	Mil-A	25	55	8	14	2	0	2	6	5	9	.255	.317	.400	96	-0	-0	6	0	1	-1	-1	2/3S1	0.0

YEAR	TM/L	G	AB	R	H	2B	3B	HR	RBI	BB	SO	AVG	OBP	SLG	PRO+	BR	/A	RC	SB	CS	SBR	FR	POS	TPR
	Bos-A	43	129	15	33	7	1	4	17	6	14	.256	.294	.419	88	-2	-3	16	0	0	0	3	3/2	0.0
	Yr	68	184	23	47	9	1	6	23	11	23	.255	.301	.413	91	-2	-3	22	0	1	-1	1		0.0
1971	Bos-A	74	272	41	75	12	5	5	22	14	42	.276	.321	.412	99	1	-1	36	1	1	-0	-18	2S/3	-1.4
1972	Bos-A	71	212	22	52	11	1	2	22	18	40	.245	.313	.335	88	-2	-3	23	0	1	-1	-6	2S3	-0.4
1973	Bos-A	67	155	17	28	9	1	1	16	12	45	.181	.249	.271	44	-11	-12	11	0	0	0	18	23/D	0.7
1974	Bos-A	10	15	3	2	0	0	1	1	1	6	.133	.188	.333	44	-1	-1	0	0	0	0	-0	/23	0.0
Total	12	856	2110	237	475	77	17	32	185	142	461	.225	.282	.323	70	-84	-85	193	14	10	-2	38	3S2/D1	-2.5

■ **JOHN KENNEDY**   Kennedy, John Irvin   b: 11/23/34, Sumter, S.C.   BR/TR, 5'10", 175 lbs.   Deb: 4/22/57

YEAR	TM/L	G	AB	R	H	2B	3B	HR	RBI	BB	SO	AVG	OBP	SLG	PRO+	BR	/A	RC	SB	CS	SBR	FR	POS	TPR
1957	Phi-N	5	2	1	0	0	0	0	0	0	1	.000	.000	.000	-99	-1	-1	0	0	0	0	1	/3	0.0

■ **JUNIOR KENNEDY**   Kennedy, Junior Raymond   b: 8/9/50, Fort Gibson, Okla.   BR/TR, 5'11", 175 lbs.   Deb: 8/09/74

YEAR	TM/L	G	AB	R	H	2B	3B	HR	RBI	BB	SO	AVG	OBP	SLG	PRO+	BR	/A	RC	SB	CS	SBR	FR	POS	TPR
1974	Cin-N	22	19	2	3	0	0	0	0	6	4	.158	.360	.158	49	-1	-1	1	0	0	0	-1	2/3	0.0
1978	Cin-N	89	157	22	40	2	2	0	11	31	28	.255	.381	.293	91	-0	-0	20	4	1	1	13	2/3	1.8
1979	Cin-N	83	220	29	60	7	0	1	17	28	31	.273	.355	.318	85	-3	-4	26	4	3	-1	-0	2/S3	0.0
1980	Cin-N	104	337	31	88	16	3	1	34	36	34	.261	.332	.335	87	-5	-5	39	3	1	0	2	*2	0.4
1981	Cin-N	27	44	5	11	1	0	0	5	1	5	.250	.267	.273	52	-3	-3	3	0	0	0	2	2/3	0.0
1982	Chi-N	105	242	22	53	3	1	2	25	21	34	.219	.281	.264	52	-15	-16	17	1	4	-2	13	2S/3	0.1
1983	Chi-N	17	22	3	3	0	0	0	3	1	6	.136	.174	.136	-12	-3	-3	0	0	0	0	2	/23S	0.0
Total	7	447	1041	114	258	29	6	4	95	124	142	.248	.328	.299	75	-31	-32	107	12	9	-2	30	2/S3	2.3

■ **DOC KENNEDY**   Kennedy, Michael Joseph   b: 8/11/1853, Brooklyn, N.Y.   d: 5/23/20, Grove, N.Y.   BR/TR,   Deb: 5/01/1879

YEAR	TM/L	G	AB	R	H	2B	3B	HR	RBI	BB	SO	AVG	OBP	SLG	PRO+	BR	/A	RC	SB	CS	SBR	FR	POS	TPR
1879	Cle-N	49	193	19	56	8	2	1	18	2	10	.290	.297	.368	119	3	4	22				-0	C/1	0.3
1880	Cle-N	66	250	26	50	10	1	0	18	5	12	.200	.216	.248	58	-11	-10	14				-5	*C/O	-0.9
1881	Cle-N	39	150	19	47	7	1	0	15	5	13	.313	.335	.373	129	4	5	19				4	C/O3	0.8
1882	Cle-N	1	3	0	1	0	0	0	0	1	0	.333	.500	.333	180	0	0	1				3	/C	0.3
1883	Buf-N	5	19	3	6	0	0	0	2	2	2	.316	.381	.316	113	0	0	2				-1	/O1	0.0
Total	5	160	615	67	160	25	4	1	53	15	37	.260	.278	.319	98	-3	-1	57				1	C/O13	0.5

■ **RAY KENNEDY**   Kennedy, Raymond Lincoln   b: 5/19/1895, Pittsburgh, Pa.   d: 1/18/69, Casselberry, Fla.   BR/TR, 5'9", 165 lbs.   Deb: 9/08/16

YEAR	TM/L	G	AB	R	H	2B	3B	HR	RBI	BB	SO	AVG	OBP	SLG	PRO+	BR	/A	RC	SB	CS	SBR	FR	POS	TPR
1916	StL-A	1	1	0	0	0	0	0	0	0	0	.000	.000	.000	-99	-0	-0	0	0			0	H	0.0

■ **BOB KENNEDY**   Kennedy, Robert Daniel   b: 8/18/20, Chicago, Ill.   BR/TR, 6'2", 193 lbs.   Deb: 9/14/39   MC

YEAR	TM/L	G	AB	R	H	2B	3B	HR	RBI	BB	SO	AVG	OBP	SLG	PRO+	BR	/A	RC	SB	CS	SBR	FR	POS	TPR
1939	Chi-A	3	8	0	2	0	0	0	1	0	0	.250	.250	.250	27	-1	-1	0	0	0	0	-1	/3	-0.1
1940	Chi-A	154	606	74	153	23	3	3	52	42	58	.252	.301	.315	59	-36	-37	55	3	7	-3	-3	*3	-3.2
1941	Chi-A	76	257	16	53	9	3	1	29	17	23	.206	.255	.276	41	-22	-22	19	5	3	-0	3	3	-1.4
1942	Chi-A	113	412	37	95	18	5	0	38	22	41	.231	.270	.299	61	-23	-22	31	11	7	-1	5	3O	-1.8
1946	Chi-A	113	411	43	106	13	5	5	34	24	42	.258	.300	.350	85	-11	-9	40	6	8	-3	5	O3	-0.9
1947	Chi-A	115	428	47	112	19	3	6	48	18	38	.262	.291	.362	84	-13	-11	42	3	4	-2	-5	*O/3	-2.2
1948	Chi-A	30	113	4	28	8	1	0	14	4	17	.248	.274	.336	64	-7	-6	9	0	2	-1	-1	O	-0.9
	*Cle-A	66	73	10	22	3	2	0	5	4	6	.301	.338	.397	98	-1	-1	10	0	0	0	2	O/21	0.0
	Yr	96	186	14	50	11	3	0	19	8	23	.269	.299	.360	77	-7	-7	18	0	2	-1	1		-0.9
1949	Cle-A	121	424	49	117	23	5	9	57	37	40	.276	.334	.417	100	-3	-2	57	5	5	-2	-0	O3	-0.7
1950	Cle-A	146	540	79	157	27	5	9	54	53	31	.291	.355	.409	99	-5	-2	79	3	4	-2	1	*O	-0.4
1951	Cle-A	108	321	30	79	15	4	7	29	34	33	.246	.320	.383	95	-5	-3	38	4	2	0	-7	*O	-1.3
1952	Cle-A	22	40	6	12	3	1	0	12	9	5	.300	.429	.425	148	3	3	9	1	0	0	3	O/3	0.6
1953	Cle-A	100	161	22	38	5	0	3	22	19	11	.236	.320	.323	76	-5	-5	16	0	2	-1	-0	O	-0.9
1954	Cle-A	1	0	0	0	0	0	0	0	0	0	—	—	—	—	0	0	0	0	0	0	0	/O	0.0
	Bal-A	106	323	37	81	13	2	6	45	28	43	.251	.311	.359	90	-8	-5	33	2	1	0	-6	3O	-1.5
	Yr	107	323	37	81	13	2	6	45	28	43	.251	.311	.359	90	-8	-5	33	2	1	0	-6		-1.5
1955	Bal-A	26	70	10	10	1	0	0	5	10	10	.143	.250	.157	12	-9	-8	3	0	1	-1	-1	O/13	-1.0
	Chi-A	83	214	28	65	10	2	9	43	16	16	.304	.352	.495	122	7	6	35	0	2	-1	-8	3O/1	-0.3
	Yr	109	284	38	75	11	2	9	48	26	26	.264	.326	.412	97	-2	-2	35	0	3	-2	-9		-1.3
1956	Chi-A	8	13	0	1	0	0	0	0	2	4	.077	.200	.077	-24	-2	-2	0	0	0	0	-1	/3	-0.2
	Det-A	69	177	17	41	5	0	4	22	24	19	.232	.330	.328	74	-6	-6	18	2	2	-1	-2	O3	-0.9
	Yr	77	190	17	42	5	0	4	22	26	23	.221	.321	.311	67	-9	-9	18	2	2	-1	-2		-1.1
1957	Chi-A	4	2	0	0	0	0	0	0	0	0	.000	.000	.000	-99	-1	-1	0	0	0	0	0	H	0.0
	Bro-N	19	31	5	4	1	0	1	4	1	5	.129	.156	.258	8	-4	-4	1	0	0	0	-2	/O3	-0.6
Total	16	1483	4624	514	1176	196	41	63	514	364	443	.254	.310	.355	80	-153	-139	495	45	50	-17	-20	O3/12	-17.7

■ **SNAPPER KENNEDY**   Kennedy, Sherman Montgomery   b: 11/1/1878, Conneaut, Ohio   d: 8/15/45, Pasadena, Tex.   BB/TR, 5'10", 165 lbs.   Deb: 5/01/02

YEAR	TM/L	G	AB	R	H	2B	3B	HR	RBI	BB	SO	AVG	OBP	SLG	PRO+	BR	/A	RC	SB	CS	SBR	FR	POS	TPR
1902	Chi-N	1	5	0	0	0	0	0	0	0	0	.000	.000	.000	-99	-1	-1	0				1	/O	0.0

■ **TERRY KENNEDY**   Kennedy, Terrence Edward   b: 6/4/56, Euclid, Ohio   BL/TR, 6'3", 220 lbs.   Deb: 9/04/78

YEAR	TM/L	G	AB	R	H	2B	3B	HR	RBI	BB	SO	AVG	OBP	SLG	PRO+	BR	/A	RC	SB	CS	SBR	FR	POS	TPR
1978	StL-N	10	29	0	5	0	0	0	2	4	3	.172	.273	.172	27	-3	-3	1	0	0	0	0	C	-0.1
1979	StL-N	33	109	11	31	7	0	2	17	6	20	.284	.322	.404	96	-1	-1	14	0	0	0	-4	C	-0.4
1980	StL-N	84	248	28	63	12	3	4	34	28	34	.254	.330	.375	93	-1	-2	30	0	0	0	-3	CO	-0.5
1981	SD-N	101	382	32	115	24	1	2	41	22	53	.301	.342	.385	114	3	6	49	0	2	-1	-8	*C	-0.2
1982	SD-N	153	562	75	166	42	1	21	97	26	91	.295	.332	.486	133	17	20	90	1	0	0	-19	*C1	0.3
1983	SD-N	149	549	47	156	27	2	17	98	51	89	.284	.347	.434	119	11	13	81	1	3	-2	-10	*C/1	0.6
1984	*SD-N	148	530	54	127	16	1	14	57	33	99	.240	.287	.353	79	-16	-16	50	1	2	-1	-15	*C	-2.8
1985	SD-N	143	532	54	139	27	1	10	74	31	102	.261	.302	.372	89	-10	-9	55	0	0	0	-1	*C/1	-0.5
1986	SD-N	141	432	46	114	22	1	12	57	37	74	.264	.325	.403	102	-1	0	54	0	3	-2	-0	*C	0.1
1987	Bal-A	143	512	51	128	13	1	18	62	35	112	.250	.299	.385	82	-16	-14	57	1	0	0	-19	*C	-1.9
1988	Bal-A	85	265	20	60	10	0	3	16	15	53	.226	.270	.298	61	-15	-14	19	0	0	0	-8	C	-1.8
1989	*SF-N	125	355	19	85	15	0	5	34	35	56	.239	.308	.324	83	-9	-7	35	1	3	-2	-4	*C/1	-0.4
1990	SF-N	107	303	25	84	22	0	2	26	31	38	.277	.344	.370	98	-1	-1	38	1	2	-1	-12	*C	-0.8
Total	13	1422	4808	462	1273	237	11	110	615	354	824	.265	.317	.387	97	-41	-27	572	6	15	-7	-102	*C/O1	-8.4

■ **ED KENNEDY**   Kennedy, William Edward   b: 4/5/1861, Bellevue, Ky.   d: 12/22/12, Cheyenne, Wyoming   BR/TR, 5'7", 160 lbs.   Deb: 5/17/1884

YEAR	TM/L	G	AB	R	H	2B	3B	HR	RBI	BB	SO	AVG	OBP	SLG	PRO+	BR	/A	RC	SB	CS	SBR	FR	POS	TPR
1884	Cin-U	13	48	6	10	1	1			0	1	.208	.224	.271	62	-2	-2	3	0			0	/3SO	0.0

■ **JERRY KENNEY**   Kenney, Gerald T   b: 6/30/45, St.Louis, Mo.   BL/TR, 6'1", 170 lbs.   Deb: 9/05/67

YEAR	TM/L	G	AB	R	H	2B	3B	HR	RBI	BB	SO	AVG	OBP	SLG	PRO+	BR	/A	RC	SB	CS	SBR	FR	POS	TPR
1967	NY-A	20	58	4	18	2	0	1	5	10	8	.310	.412	.397	145	3	4	11	2	1	0	-4	S	0.1
1969	NY-A	130	447	49	115	14	2	2	34	48	36	.257	.331	.311	83	-11	-9	47	25	14	-1	10	3OS	0.2
1970	NY-A	140	404	46	78	10	7	4	35	52	44	.193	.285	.282	60	-23	-21	34	20	6	2	15	*3/2	-0.2
1971	NY-A	120	325	50	85	10	3	0	20	56	38	.262	.372	.311	101	1	3	40	9	8	-2	11	*3/S1	0.9
1972	NY-A	50	119	16	25	2	0	0	7	16	13	.210	.304	.227	62	-5	-5	8	3	0	1	5	S/3	0.6
1973	Cle-A	5	16	0	4	0	1	0	2	2	0	.250	.333	.375	97	-0	-0	2	0	0	0	-2	/2	-0.1
Total	6	465	1369	165	325	38	13	7	103	184	139	.237	.329	.299	82	-36	-28	142	59	29	0	36	3/SO21	1.5

■ **JOHN KENNEY**   Kenney, John   Deb: 5/02/1872

YEAR	TM/L	G	AB	R	H	2B	3B	HR	RBI	BB	SO	AVG	OBP	SLG	PRO+	BR	/A	RC	SB	CS	SBR	FR	POS	TPR
1872	Atl-n	5	19	0	0	0	0	0	0			.000	.000	.000	-85	-4	-5	0					/2O	-0.3

YEAR	TM/L	G	AB	R	H	2B	3B	HR	RBI	BB	SO	AVG	OBP	SLG	PRO+	BR	/A	RC	SB	CS	SBR	FR	POS	TPR

■ DICK KENWORTHY
Kenworthy, Richard Lee b: 4/1/41, Red Oak, Iowa   BR/TR, 5'9", 170 lbs.   Deb: 9/08/62

YEAR	TM/L	G	AB	R	H	2B	3B	HR	RBI	BB	SO	AVG	OBP	SLG	PRO+	BR	/A	RC	SB	CS	SBR	FR	POS	TPR
1962	Chi-A	3	4	0	0	0	0	0	0	0	3	.000	.000	.000	-99	-1	-1	0	0	0	0	1	/2	0.0
1964	Chi-A	2	2	0	0	0	0	0	0	0	1	.000	.000	.000	-99	-1	-1	0	0	0	0	0	H	0.0
1965	Chi-A	3	1	0	0	0	0	0	0	1	0	.000	.667	.000	113	0	0	0	0	0	0	0	H	0.0
1966	Chi-A	9	25	1	5	0	0	0	0	0	0	.200	.200	.200	16	-3	-3	1	0	0	0	-3	/3	-0.5
1967	Chi-A	50	97	9	22	4	1	4	11	4	17	.227	.265	.412	101	-1	-0	9	0	2	-1	1	3	-0.1
1968	Chi-A	58	122	2	27	2	0	0	2	5	21	.221	.252	.238	49	-7	-8	7	0	1	-1	5	3	-0.1
Total	6	125	251	12	54	6	1	4	13	10	42	.215	.251	.295	63	-12	-12	18	0	3	-2	5	/32	-0.6

■ DUKE KENWORTHY
Kenworthy, William Jennings "Iron Duke" b: 7/4/1886, Cambridge, Ohio   d: 9/21/50, Eureka, Cal.   BB/TR, 5'7", 165 lbs.   Deb: 8/28/12

YEAR	TM/L	G	AB	R	H	2B	3B	HR	RBI	BB	SO	AVG	OBP	SLG	PRO+	BR	/A	RC	SB	CS	SBR	FR	POS	TPR
1912	Was-A	12	38	6	9	1	0	0	2	2		.237	.293	.263	59	-2	-2	4	3			-0	O	-0.2
1914	KC-F	146	545	93	173	40	14	15	91	36	44	.317	.372	.525	162	36	39	124	37			21	*2	6.2
1915	KC-F	122	396	59	118	30	7	3	52	28	32	.298	.355	.432	138	15	17	71	20			-7	*2/O	1.1
1917	StL-A	5	10	1	1	0	0	0	1	1	1	.100	.182	.100	-14	-1	-1	0	1			1	/2	0.0
Total	4	285	989	159	301	71	21	18	146	67	77	.304	.360	.473	146	48	53	200	61			14	2/O	7.1

■ JOE KEOUGH
Keough, Joseph William b: 1/7/46, Pomona, Cal.   BL/TL, 6', 185 lbs.   Deb: 8/07/68

YEAR	TM/L	G	AB	R	H	2B	3B	HR	RBI	BB	SO	AVG	OBP	SLG	PRO+	BR	/A	RC	SB	CS	SBR	FR	POS	TPR
1968	Oak-A	34	98	7	21	2	1	2	18	8	11	.214	.274	.316	82	-3	-2	9	1	0	0	-1	O/1	-0.3
1969	KC-A	70	166	17	31	2	0	0	7	13	13	.187	.254	.199	28	-16	-16	10	5	2	0	0	O/1	-1.6
1970	KC-A	57	183	28	59	6	2	4	21	23	18	.322	.398	.443	132	8	8	32	1	1	-0	-1	O1	0.5
1971	KC-A	110	351	34	87	14	2	3	30	35	26	.248	.318	.325	83	-8	-7	34	0	6	-4	-8	*O	-2.3
1972	KC-A	56	64	8	14	2	0	0	5	8	7	.219	.324	.250	73	-2	-2	6	2	0	1	-0	O	-0.1
1973	Chi-A	5	1	1	0	0	0	0	0	0	0	.000	.000	.000	-97	-0	-0	0	0	0	0	0	H	0.0
Total	6	332	863	95	212	26	5	9	81	87	75	.246	.318	.319	82	-20	-19	90	9	9	-3	-10	O/1	-3.8

■ MARTY KEOUGH
Keough, Richard Martin b: 4/14/35, Oakland, Cal.   BL/TL, 6', 180 lbs.   Deb: 4/21/56

YEAR	TM/L	G	AB	R	H	2B	3B	HR	RBI	BB	SO	AVG	OBP	SLG	PRO+	BR	/A	RC	SB	CS	SBR	FR	POS	TPR
1956	Bos-A	3	2	1	0	0	0	0	1	1	0	.000	.333	.000	-5	-0	-0	0	0	0	0	0	H	0.0
1957	Bos-A	9	17	1	1	0	0	0	0	4	3	.059	.238	.059	-14	-3	-3	0	0	0	0	1	/O	-0.1
1958	Bos-A	68	118	21	26	3	3	1	9	7	29	.220	.264	.322	57	-7	-8	10	1	1	-0	-2	O/1	-1.1
1959	Bos-A	96	251	40	61	13	5	7	27	26	40	.243	.321	.418	97	0	-1	35	3	1	0	-4	O/1	-0.8
1960	Bos-A	38	105	15	26	6	1	1	9	8	8	.248	.301	.352	73	-4	-4	11	2	2	-2	2	O	-0.3
	Cle-A	65	149	19	37	5	0	3	11	9	23	.248	.296	.342	74	-6	-5	15	2	3	-1	-1	O	-0.8
	Yr	103	254	34	63	11	1	4	20	17	31	.248	.298	.346	74	-10	-9	26	4	5	-2	2		-1.1
1961	Was-A	135	390	59	97	18	9	9	34	32	60	.249	.309	.410	92	-6	-6	50	12	5	1	1	*O1	-0.7
1962	Cin-N	111	230	34	64	8	2	7	27	21	31	.278	.349	.422	102	2	1	35	3	1	0	3	O1	0.0
1963	Cin-N	95	172	21	39	8	2	6	21	25	37	.227	.338	.401	109	3	3	24	1	4	-2	1	1O	0.0
1964	Cin-N	109	276	29	71	9	1	4	28	22	58	.257	.314	.395	95	-1	-2	35	1	2	-1	-1	O/1	-0.6
1965	Cin-N	62	43	14	5	0	0	0	3	3	14	.116	.191	.116	-10	-6	-7	1	0	0	0	1	1/O	-0.7
1966	Atl-N	17	17	1	1	0	0	0	1	1	6	.059	.111	.059	-50	-3	-3	0	0	0	0	-1	/1O	-0.4
	Chi-N	33	26	3	6	1	0	0	5	5	9	.231	.375	.269	82	-0	-0	3	1	0	0	0	/O	0.0
	Yr	50	43	4	7	1	0	0	6	6	15	.163	.280	.186	32	-4	-4	3	1	0	0	-1		-0.4
Total	11	841	1796	256	434	71	23	43	176	164	318	.242	.311	.379	86	-31	-36	220	26	19	-4	0	O1	-5.5

◨ JOHN KERINS
Kerins, John Nelson b: 7/15/1858, Indianapolis, Ind   d: 9/8/19, Louisville, Ky.   BR/TR, 5'10", 177 lbs.   Deb: 5/01/1884 MU

YEAR	TM/L	G	AB	R	H	2B	3B	HR	RBI	BB	SO	AVG	OBP	SLG	PRO+	BR	/A	RC	SB	CS	SBR	FR	POS	TPR
1884	Ind-a	94	364	58	78	10	3	6		6		.214	.229	.308	78	-9	-8	26				7	*1/CO3	-0.4
1885	Lou-a	112	456	65	111	9	16	3		20		.243	.281	.353	102	1	1	46				4	*1C/O3	0.0
1886	Lou-a	120	487	113	131	19	9	4		66		.269	.360	.370	124	19	14	76	26			41	C1/OS	4.9
1887	Lou-a	112	476	101	140	18	19	5		38		.294	.349	.443	120	13	11	93	49			25	1C/O	3.2
1888	Lou-a	83	319	38	75	11	4	2	41	25		.235	.297	.313	101	-0	-1	35	16			3	OC/132M	0.5
1889	Lou-a	2	9	2	3	1	0	0	3	0	1	.333	.333	.444	125	0	0	1	0			-1	/OC	0.0
	Bal-a	16	53	7	15	2	0	0	12	2	4	.283	.321	.321	84	-1	-1	6	2			-2	/1COS	-0.2
	Yr	18	62	9	18	3	0	0	15	2	5	.290	.323	.339	89	-1	-1	8	2			-2		-0.2
1890	StL-a	18	63	8	8	2	0	0		8		.127	.225	.159	13	-6	-8	3	2			1	1/CM	-0.5
Total	7	557	2227	392	561	72	51	20	56	165	5	.252	.308	.357	105	16	11	287	95			78	1C/O3S2	7.5

■ ORIE KERLIN
Kerlin, Orie Milton "Cy" b: 1/23/1891, Summerfield, La.   d: 10/29/74, Shreveport, La.   BL/TL, 5'7", 149 lbs.   Deb: 6/06/15

YEAR	TM/L	G	AB	R	H	2B	3B	HR	RBI	BB	SO	AVG	OBP	SLG	PRO+	BR	/A	RC	SB	CS	SBR	FR	POS	TPR
1915	Pit-F	3	1	0	0	0	0	0	0	0	0	.000	.000	.000	-99	-0	-0	0	0			0	/C	0.0

■ BILL KERN
Kern, William George b: 2/28/33, Coplay, Pa.   BR/TR, 6'2", 184 lbs.   Deb: 9/19/62

YEAR	TM/L	G	AB	R	H	2B	3B	HR	RBI	BB	SO	AVG	OBP	SLG	PRO+	BR	/A	RC	SB	CS	SBR	FR	POS	TPR
1962	KC-A	8	16	1	4	0	0	1	1	0	3	.250	.250	.438	78	-1	-1	2	0	0	0	1	/O	0.0

■ JOE KERNAN
Kernan, Joseph b: Baltimore, Md.   Deb: 4/14/1873

YEAR	TM/L	G	AB	R	H	2B	3B	HR	RBI	BB	SO	AVG	OBP	SLG	PRO+	BR	/A	RC	SB	CS	SBR	FR	POS	TPR
1873	Mar-n	2	9	1	3	0	0	0				.333	.333	.333	126	-0	0	1					/2O	0.0

■ GEORGE KERNEK
Kernek, George Boyd b: 1/12/40, Holdenville, Okla.   BL/TL, 6'3", 170 lbs.   Deb: 9/05/65

YEAR	TM/L	G	AB	R	H	2B	3B	HR	RBI	BB	SO	AVG	OBP	SLG	PRO+	BR	/A	RC	SB	CS	SBR	FR	POS	TPR
1965	StL-N	10	31	6	9	3	1	0	3	2	4	.290	.333	.452	109	1	0	5	0	0	0	0	/1	0.0
1966	StL-N	20	50	5	12	0	1	0	3	4	9	.240	.309	.280	65	-2	-2	5	1	0	0	0	1	-0.2
Total	2	30	81	11	21	3	2	0	6	6	13	.259	.318	.346	82	-2	-2	9	1	0	0	0	/1	-0.2

■ DAN KERNS
Kerns, Daniel P. b: Philadelphia, Pa.   Deb: 10/01/20

YEAR	TM/L	G	AB	R	H	2B	3B	HR	RBI	BB	SO	AVG	OBP	SLG	PRO+	BR	/A	RC	SB	CS	SBR	FR	POS	TPR
1920	Phi-A	1	1	0	0	0	0	0	0	0	0	.000	.000	.000	-99	-0	-0	0	0	0	0	0	H	0.0

■ RUSS KERNS
Kerns, Russell Eldon b: 11/10/20, Fremont, Ohio   BL/TR, 6', 188 lbs.   Deb: 8/18/45

YEAR	TM/L	G	AB	R	H	2B	3B	HR	RBI	BB	SO	AVG	OBP	SLG	PRO+	BR	/A	RC	SB	CS	SBR	FR	POS	TPR
1945	Det-A	1	1	0	0	0	0	0	0	0	0	.000	.000	.000	-94	-0	-0	0	0	0	0	0	H	0.0

■ JOHN KERR
Kerr, John Francis b: 11/26/1898, San Francisco, Cal   BR/TR, 5'8", 158 lbs.   Deb: 5/01/23

YEAR	TM/L	G	AB	R	H	2B	3B	HR	RBI	BB	SO	AVG	OBP	SLG	PRO+	BR	/A	RC	SB	CS	SBR	FR	POS	TPR
1923	Det-A	19	42	4	9	1	0	0	1	4	5	.214	.283	.238	39	-4	-4	3	0	0	0	4	S	0.2
1924	Det-A	17	11	3	3	0	0	0	1	0	0	.273	.273	.273	42	-1	-1	1	0	0	0	-0	/3O	0.0
1929	Chi-A	127	419	50	108	20	4	1	39	31	24	.258	.310	.332	66	-22	-21	44	9	7	-2	24	*2/S	0.4
1930	Chi-A	70	266	37	77	11	6	3	27	21	23	.289	.351	.410	95	-3	-2	39	4	2	0	2	2S	0.1
1931	Chi-A	128	444	51	119	17	2	2	50	35	22	.268	.324	.329	77	-18	-14	50	9	3	1	8	*2/3S	0.2
1932	Was-A	51	132	14	36	6	1	0	15	13	3	.273	.338	.333	75	-5	-4	15	3	2	-0	-1	2S/3	-0.2
1933	*Was-A	28	40	5	8	0	0	0	0	3	2	.200	.256	.200	22	-4	-4	2	0	0	0	3	2S/3	0.0
1934	Was-A	31	103	8	28	4	0	0	12	8	13	.272	.324	.311	67	-5	-5	11	1	1	-0	10	32	0.5
Total	8	471	1457	172	388	59	13	6	145	115	92	.266	.323	.337	73	-62	-55	165	26	15	-1	48	2/S3O	1.2

■ DOC KERR
Kerr, John Jonas b: 1/17/1882, Del Roy, Ohio   d: 6/9/37, Baltimore, Md.   BB/TR, 5'10.5", 190 lbs.   Deb: 4/22/14

YEAR	TM/L	G	AB	R	H	2B	3B	HR	RBI	BB	SO	AVG	OBP	SLG	PRO+	BR	/A	RC	SB	CS	SBR	FR	POS	TPR
1914	Pit-F	42	71	3	17	4	2	1	7	10	13	.239	.333	.394	109	1	1	10	0			-4	C	-0.1
	Bal-F	14	34	4	9	1	1	0	1	1	6	.265	.286	.353	80	-1	-1	4	1			1	C/1	0.1
	Yr	56	105	7	26	5	3	1	8	11	19	.248	.319	.381	100	-0	-0	14	1			-2		0.0
1915	Bal-F	3	6	1	2	0	0	0	0	1	0	.333	.429	.333	123	0	0	1	0			-1	/C1	0.0
Total	2	59	111	8	28	5	3	1	8	12	19	.252	.325	.378	101	0	0	14	1			-4	/C1	0.0

■ BUDDY KERR
Kerr, John Joseph b: 11/6/22, Astoria, N.Y.   BR/TR, 6'2", 175 lbs.   Deb: 9/08/43

YEAR	TM/L	G	AB	R	H	2B	3B	HR	RBI	BB	SO	AVG	OBP	SLG	PRO+	BR	/A	RC	SB	CS	SBR	FR	POS	TPR
1943	NY-N	27	98	14	28	3	0	2	12	8	5	.286	.352	.378	110	1	1	13	1			5	S	0.9

YEAR	TM/L	G	AB	R	H	2B	3B	HR	RBI	BB	SO	AVG	OBP	SLG	PRO+	BR	/A	RC	SB	CS	SBR	FR	POS	TPR
1944	NY-N	150	548	68	146	31	4	9	63	37	32	.266	.316	.387	97	-3	-3	65	14			17	*S	3.3
1945	NY-N	149	546	53	136	20	3	4	40	41	34	.249	.304	.319	72	-20	-21	54	5			28	*S	2.2
1946	NY-N	145	497	50	124	20	3	6	40	53	31	.249	.324	.338	87	-8	-8	57	7			6	*S3	0.8
1947	NY-N	138	547	73	157	23	5	7	49	36	49	.287	.331	.386	89	-9	-9	69	2			12	*S	1.3
1948	NY-N	144	496	41	119	16	4	0	46	56	36	.240	.317	.288	64	-23	-24	48	9			3	*S	-0.4
1949	NY-N	90	220	16	46	4	0	0	19	21	23	.209	.284	.227	39	-19	-18	16	0			6	S	-0.2
1950	Bos-N	155	507	45	115	24	6	2	46	50	50	.227	.296	.310	64	-30	-25	45	0			2	*S	-0.6
1951	Bos-N	69	172	18	32	4	0	1	18	22	20	.186	.282	.227	41	-14	-13	13	0	0	0	13	S/2	0.6
Total	9	1067	3631	378	903	145	25	31	333	324	280	.249	.312	.328	76	-124	-120	380	38	0		92	*S/32	7.9

■ MEL KERR Kerr, John Melville b: 5/22/03, Souris, Man., Can. d: 8/9/80, Vero Beach, Fla. BL/TL, 5'11.5", 155 lbs. Deb: 9/16/25 C

YEAR	TM/L	G	AB	R	H	2B	3B	HR	RBI	BB	SO	AVG	OBP	SLG	PRO+	BR	/A	RC	SB	CS	SBR	FR	POS	TPR
1925	Chi-N	1	0	1	0	0	0	0	0	0	0	—	—	—	—	0	0	0	0	0	0	0	R	0.0

■ DAN KERWIN Kerwin, Daniel Patrick (b: Daniel Patrick Kervin) b: 7/9/1879, Philadelphia, Pa. d: 7/13/60, Philadelphia, Pa. BL/TL, 5'9", 164 lbs. Deb: 9/27/03

YEAR	TM/L	G	AB	R	H	2B	3B	HR	RBI	BB	SO	AVG	OBP	SLG	PRO+	BR	/A	RC	SB	CS	SBR	FR	POS	TPR
1903	Cin-N	2	6	1	4	1	0	0	1	2		.667	.750	.833	320	2	2	4	0			-1	/O	0.1

■ DON KESSINGER Kessinger, Donald Eulon b: 7/17/42, Forrest City, Ark. BB/TR, 6'1", 170 lbs. Deb: 9/07/64 M

YEAR	TM/L	G	AB	R	H	2B	3B	HR	RBI	BB	SO	AVG	OBP	SLG	PRO+	BR	/A	RC	SB	CS	SBR	FR	POS	TPR
1964	Chi-N	4	12	1	2	0	0	0	0	0	1	.167	.167	.167	-6	-2	-2	0	0	0	0	-1	/S	-0.2
1965	Chi-N	106	309	19	62	4	3	0	14	20	44	.201	.254	.233	37	-25	-26	18	1	2	-1	21	*S	0.6
1966	Chi-N	150	533	50	146	8	2	1	43	26	46	.274	.308	.302	70	-21	-21	49	13	7	-0	-10	*S	-2.0
1967	Chi-N	145	580	61	134	10	7	0	42	33	80	.231	.277	.272	55	-31	-34	43	6	13	-6	-3	*S	-2.9
1968	Chi-N	160	655	63	157	14	7	1	32	38	86	.240	.283	.287	67	-22	-27	54	9	9	-3	18	*S	0.9
1969	Chi-N	158	664	109	181	38	6	4	53	61	70	.273	.335	.366	85	-3	-13	84	11	8	-2	25	*S	2.9
1970	Chi-N	154	631	100	168	21	14	1	39	66	59	.266	.338	.349	75	-13	-23	76	12	6	0	9	*S	0.5
1971	Chi-N	155	617	77	159	18	6	2	38	52	54	.258	.318	.316	70	-15	-25	63	15	8	-0	4	*S	0.0
1972	Chi-N	149	577	77	158	20	6	1	39	67	44	.274	.351	.334	87	-1	-8	70	8	7	-2	8	*S	1.6
1973	Chi-N	160	577	52	151	22	3	0	43	57	44	.262	.328	.310	72	-16	-21	57	6	6	-2	17	*S	1.6
1974	Chi-N	153	599	83	155	20	7	1	42	62	54	.259	.332	.321	80	-12	-15	64	7	7	-2	2	*S	0.1
1975	Chi-N	154	601	77	146	26	10	0	46	68	47	.243	.321	.319	75	-17	-20	66	4	7	-3	-2	*S3	-0.9
1976	StL-N	145	502	55	120	22	6	1	40	61	51	.239	.323	.313	80	-11	-12	53	3	0	1	-4	*S2/3	-0.2
1977	StL-N	59	134	14	32	4	0	0	7	14	26	.239	.311	.269	58	-8	-7	12	0	0	1	2	S2/3	-0.1
	Chi-A	39	119	12	28	3	2	0	11	13	7	.235	.311	.294	66	-5	-5	11	2	1	0	-4	S2/3	-0.5
1978	Chi-A	131	431	35	110	18	1	1	31	36	34	.255	.313	.309	75	-14	-14	41	2	4	-2	-19	*S/2	-2.4
1979	Chi-A	56	110	14	22	6	0	1	7	10	12	.200	.267	.282	48	-8	-8	8	1	0	0	-0	S/12	-0.1
Total	16	2078	7651	899	1931	254	80	14	527	684	759	.252	.316	.312	72	-225	-283	769	100	85	-21	62	*S/231	-1.0

■ HENRY KESSLER Kessler, Henry "Lucky" b: 1847, Brooklyn, N.Y. d: 1/9/1900, Franklin, Pa. BR/TR, 5'10", 144 lbs. Deb: 8/04/1873

YEAR	TM/L	G	AB	R	H	2B	3B	HR	RBI	BB	SO	AVG	OBP	SLG	PRO+	BR	/A	RC	SB	CS	SBR	FR	POS	TPR
1873	Atl-n	1	5	0	1	0	0			0		.200	.200	.200	20	-0	-0	0					/1	0.0
1874	Atl-n	14	57	8	16	2	0	0		0		.281	.281	.316	101	-1	1	5					/C2O3	0.1
1875	Atl-n	25	104	17	26	2	0	0		1		.250	.257	.269	94	-2	0	7					S/OC2	0.0
1876	Cin-N	59	248	26	64	5	0	0	11	7	10	.258	.278	.278	100	-3	2	20				-9	SO	-0.6
1877	Cin-N	6	20	0	2	0	0	0	0	2	1	.100	.182	.100	-10	-2	-2	0				-5	/C1	-0.5
Total	3 n	40	166	25	43	4	0	0		1		.259	.263	.283	94	-3	0	13					/SCO231	0.1
Total	2	65	268	26	66	5	0	0	11	9	11	.246	.271	.265	91	-6	0	20				-14	/SOC1	-1.1

■ FRED KETCHUM Ketchum, Frederick L. b: 7/27/1875, Elmira, N.Y. d: 3/12/08, Cortland, N.Y. BL/TR, Deb: 9/12/1899

YEAR	TM/L	G	AB	R	H	2B	3B	HR	RBI	BB	SO	AVG	OBP	SLG	PRO+	BR	/A	RC	SB	CS	SBR	FR	POS	TPR
1899	Lou-N	15	61	13	18	1	0	0	5	5	0	.295	.306	.311	72	-2	-2	7	2			-4	O	-0.6
1901	Phi-A	5	22	5	5	0	0	0	2	0		.227	.227	.227	26	-2	-2	1	0			-1	/O	-0.2
Total	2	20	83	18	23	1	0	0	7	0		.277	.286	.289	60	-4	-5	8	2			-5	/O	-0.8

■ PHIL KETTER Ketter, Philip b: Hutchinson, Kan. TR , Deb: 5/23/12

YEAR	TM/L	G	AB	R	H	2B	3B	HR	RBI	BB	SO	AVG	OBP	SLG	PRO+	BR	/A	RC	SB	CS	SBR	FR	POS	TPR
1912	StL-A	2	6	1	2	0	0	0	0	0		.333	.333	.333	94	-0	-0	1	0			-1	/C	0.0

■ SAM KHALIFA Khalifa, Sam b: 12/5/63, Fontana, Cal. BR/TR, 5'11", 170 lbs. Deb: 6/25/85

YEAR	TM/L	G	AB	R	H	2B	3B	HR	RBI	BB	SO	AVG	OBP	SLG	PRO+	BR	/A	RC	SB	CS	SBR	FR	POS	TPR
1985	Pit-N	95	320	30	76	14	3	2	31	34	56	.237	.311	.319	77	-10	-9	32	5	2	0	13	S	1.2
1986	Pit-N	64	151	9	28	6	0	0	4	19	28	.185	.276	.225	39	-12	-12	9	0	2	-1	14	S/2	0.6
1987	Pit-N	5	17	1	3	0	0	0	2	0	2	.176	.176	.176	-6	-3	-3	1	0	0	0	-4	/S	-0.6
Total	3	164	488	39	107	20	3	2	37	53	86	.219	.296	.285	62	-24	-24	41	5	4	-1	22	S/2	1.2

■ HOD KIBBIE Kibbie, Horace Kent b: 7/18/03, Ft.Worth, Tex. d: 10/19/75, Ft.Worth, Tex. BR/TR, 5'10", 150 lbs. Deb: 6/13/25

YEAR	TM/L	G	AB	R	H	2B	3B	HR	RBI	BB	SO	AVG	OBP	SLG	PRO+	BR	/A	RC	SB	CS	SBR	FR	POS	TPR
1925	Bos-N	11	41	5	11	2	0	0	2	5	6	.268	.348	.317	78	-2	-1	5	0	0	0	-0	/2S	0.0

■ JACK KIBBLE Kibble, John Westly "Happy" b: 1/2/1892, Seatonville, Ill. d: 12/13/69, Roundup, Mont. BB/TR, 5'9.5", 154 lbs. Deb: 9/10/12

YEAR	TM/L	G	AB	R	H	2B	3B	HR	RBI	BB	SO	AVG	OBP	SLG	PRO+	BR	/A	RC	SB	CS	SBR	FR	POS	TPR
1912	Cle-A	5	8	1	0	0	0	0	0	0		.000	.111	.000	-65	-2	-2	0	0			4	/32	0.2

■ STEVE KIEFER Kiefer, Steven George b: 10/18/60, Chicago, Ill. BR/TR, 6'1", 175 lbs. Deb: 9/03/84

YEAR	TM/L	G	AB	R	H	2B	3B	HR	RBI	BB	SO	AVG	OBP	SLG	PRO+	BR	/A	RC	SB	CS	SBR	FR	POS	TPR
1984	Oak-A	23	40	7	7	1	2	0	2	2	10	.175	.214	.300	43	-3	-3	3	2	1	0	1	S/3D	0.0
1985	Oak-A	40	66	8	13	1	1	1	10	1	18	.197	.209	.288	37	-6	-5	4	0	0	0	3	3/D	-0.3
1986	Mil-A	2	6	0	0	0	0	0	0	0	4	.000	.000	.000	-97	-2	-2	0	0	0	0	3	/S	0.1
1987	Mil-A	28	99	17	20	4	0	5	17	7	28	.202	.262	.394	69	-5	-5	10	0	0	0	-4	3/2	-0.8
1988	Mil-A	7	10	2	3	1	0	1	1	2	3	.300	.462	.700	219	2	2	4	0	0	0	-1	/23	0.1
1989	NY-A	5	8	0	1	0	0	0	0	0	5	.125	.125	.125	-30	-1	-1	0	0	0	0	-1	/3	-0.2
Total	6	105	229	34	44	7	3	7	30	12	68	.192	.239	.341	56	-15	-15	20	2	1	0	0	/3S2D	-1.1

■ BILL KIENZLE Kienzle, William H. b: Philadelphia, Pa. BL/TL, Deb: 9/15/1882

YEAR	TM/L	G	AB	R	H	2B	3B	HR	RBI	BB	SO	AVG	OBP	SLG	PRO+	BR	/A	RC	SB	CS	SBR	FR	POS	TPR
1882	Phi-a	9	33	8	11	3	2	0		5		.333	.421	.545	200	4	4	8				-1	/O	0.3
1884	Phi-U	67	299	76	76	13	8	0		21		.254	.303	.351	130	7	10	33	0			-2	O	0.6
Total	2	76	332	84	87	16	10	0		26		.262	.316	.370	139	11	14	40	0			-3	/O	0.9

■ PETE KILDUFF Kilduff, Peter John b: 4/4/1893, Weir City, Kan. d: 2/14/30, Pittsburg, Kan. BR/TR, 5'7", 155 lbs. Deb: 4/18/17

YEAR	TM/L	G	AB	R	H	2B	3B	HR	RBI	BB	SO	AVG	OBP	SLG	PRO+	BR	/A	RC	SB	CS	SBR	FR	POS	TPR
1917	NY-N	31	78	12	16	3	0	1	12	4	11	.205	.253	.282	66	-3	-3	6	2			-2	2/S3	-0.3
	Chi-N	56	202	23	56	9	5	0	15	12	19	.277	.324	.371	105	3	1	27	11			-14	S/2	-1.3
	Yr	87	280	35	72	12	5	1	27	16	30	.257	.304	.346	96	-1	-2	32	13			-16		-1.6
1918	Chi-N	30	93	7	19	2	2	0	13	7	7	.204	.267	.269	62	-4	-4	8	1			-3	2	-0.5
1919	Chi-N	31	88	5	24	4	2	0	8	10	5	.273	.360	.364	117	2	2	12	1			-4	3/2S	0.0
	Bro-N	32	73	9	22	3	1	0	8	12	11	.301	.407	.370	132	4	4	13	5			-4	3/2	0.0
	Yr	63	161	14	46	7	3	0	16	22	16	.286	.382	.366	124	6	6	24	6			-8		0.0
1920	*Bro-N	141	478	62	130	26	8	0	58	58	43	.272	.351	.360	101	4	4	61	2	9	-5	8	*2/3	0.9
1921	Bro-N	107	372	45	107	15	10	3	45	31	36	.288	.344	.406	94	-1	-3	52	6	6	-2	13	*2/3	0.8
Total	5	428	1384	163	374	62	28	4	159	134	132	.270	.338	.364	98	4	-1	178	28	15		-6	2/S3	-0.4

■ JOHN KILEY Kiley, John Frederick b: 7/1/1859, S.Dedham, Mass. d: 12/18/40, Norwood, Mass. BL/TL, Deb: 5/01/1884

YEAR	TM/L	G	AB	R	H	2B	3B	HR	RBI	BB	SO	AVG	OBP	SLG	PRO+	BR	/A	RC	SB	CS	SBR	FR	POS	TPR
1884	Was-a	14	56	9	12	2	2	0		3		.214	.267	.321	106	-0	1	5				-4	O	-0.2
1891	Bos-N	1	2	0	0	0	0	0	0	1	1	.000	.500	.000	47	0	0	0	0			0	/P	0.0
Total	2	15	58	9	12	2	2	0	0	4	1	.207	.281	.310	105	-0	1	5	0			-3	/OP	-0.2

YEAR	TM/L	G	AB	R	H	2B	3B	HR	RBI	BB	SO	AVG	OBP	SLG	PRO+	BR	/A	RC	SB	CS	SBR	FR	POS	TPR

■ **PAT KILHULLEN**   Kilhullen, Joseph Isadore   b: 8/10/1890, Carbondale, Pa.   d: 11/2/22, Oakland, Cal.   BR/TR, 5'9", 175 lbs.   Deb: 6/10/14

| 1914 | Pit-N | 1 | 1 | 0 | 0 | 0 | 0 | 0 | 0 | 0 | 0 | .000 | .000 | .000 | -99 | -0 | -0 | 0 | 0 | | | 0 | /C | 0.0 |

■ **HARMON KILLEBREW**   Killebrew, Harmon Clayton "Killer"   b: 6/29/36, Payette, Idaho   BR/TR, 6', 195 lbs.   Deb: 6/23/54   H

1954	Was-A	9	13	1	4	1	0	0	3	2	3	.308	.400	.385	122	0	0	2	0	0	0	-2	/2	-0.1
1955	Was-A	38	80	12	16	1	0	4	7	9	31	.200	.281	.363	76	-4	-3	8	0	0	0	5	3/2	0.3
1956	Was-A	44	99	10	22	2	0	5	13	10	39	.222	.294	.394	80	-3	-3	11	0	0	0	-0	3/2	-0.2
1957	Was-A	9	31	4	9	2	0	2	5	2	8	.290	.333	.548	139	1	1	6	0	0	0	-1	/32	0.1
1958	Was-A	13	31	2	6	0	0	0	2	0	12	.194	.219	.194	15	-4	-4	1	0	0	0	0	/3	-0.2
1959	Was-A	153	546	98	132	20	2	42	105	90	116	.242	.356	.516	137	27	27	103	3	2	-0	-7	*3/O	1.8
1960	Was-A	124	442	84	122	19	1	31	80	71	106	.276	.377	.534	145	27	27	91	1	0	0	-9	13	1.5
1961	Min-A	150	541	94	156	20	7	46	122	107	109	.288	.409	.606	159	53	49	138	1	2	-1	-9	*13/O	2.9
1962	Min-A	155	552	85	134	21	1	48	126	106	142	.243	.369	.545	137	33	30	113	1	2	-1	-13	*O/1	1.0
1963	Min-A	142	515	88	133	18	0	45	96	72	105	.258	.353	.555	147	33	32	99	0	0	0	-8	*O	2.0
1964	Min-A	158	577	95	156	11	1	49	111	93	135	.270	.379	.548	153	43	43	122	0	0	0	-13	*O	2.5
1965	*Min-A	113	401	78	108	16	1	25	75	72	69	.269	.386	.501	144	28	26	79	0	0	0	-7	13/O	1.6
1966	Min-A	162	569	89	160	27	1	39	110	103	98	.281	.393	.538	155	50	45	122	0	2	-1	-15	*31O	2.6
1967	Min-A	163	547	105	147	24	1	44	113	131	111	.269	.413	.558	170	62	57	131	1	0	0	-7	*1/3	4.1
1968	Min-A	100	295	40	62	7	2	17	40	70	70	.210	.365	.420	131	16	14	46	0	0	0	4	13	1.7
1969	*Min-A	162	555	106	153	20	2	49	140	145	84	.276	.430	.584	177	66	64	146	8	2	1	-21	*31	4.1
1970	*Min-A	157	527	96	143	20	1	41	113	128	84	.271	.416	.546	161	50	49	116	0	3	-2	-29	*31	1.7
1971	Min-A	147	500	61	127	19	1	28	119	114	96	.254	.393	.464	137	31	29	92	3	2	-0	-15	13	0.8
1972	Min-A	139	433	53	100	13	2	26	74	94	91	.231	.369	.450	136	26	23	73	0	1	-1	11	*1	2.3
1973	Min-A	69	248	29	60	9	1	5	32	41	59	.242	.352	.347	94	0	-1	31	0	0	0	8	1/D	0.3
1974	Min-A	122	333	28	74	7	0	13	54	45	61	.222	.315	.360	90	-2	-4	37	0	0	0	5	D1	0.0
1975	KC-A	106	312	25	62	13	0	14	44	54	70	.199	.319	.375	93	-2	-3	39	1	2	-1	-1	D/1	-0.4
Total	22	2435	8147	1283	2086	290	24	573	1584	1559	1699	.256	.379	.509	142	532	500	1609	19	18	-5	-124	13OD/2	30.4

■ **RED KILLEFER**   Killefer, Wade Hampton   b: 4/13/1884, Bloomingdale, Mich   d: 9/4/58, Los Angeles, Cal.   BR/TR, 5'9", 175 lbs.   Deb: 9/16/07

1907	Det-A	1	4	0	0	0	0	0	0	0		.000	.000	.000	-97	-1	-1	0	0			0	/O	0.0
1908	Det-A	28	75	9	16	1	0	0	11	3		.213	.244	.227	53	-4	-4	5	4			-5	2/S3	-1.0
1909	Det-A	23	61	6	17	2	2	1	4	3		.279	.343	.426	137	3	3	9	2			-1	2/O	0.0
	Was-A	40	121	11	21	1	0	0	5	13		.174	.265	.182	43	-8	-7	7	4			-2	O/3C2S	-1.0
	Yr	63	182	17	38	3	2	1	9	16		.209	.291	.264	76	-5	-4	16	6			-4		-0.9
1910	Was-A	106	345	35	79	17	1	0	24	29		.229	.318	.284	93	-3	-1	39	17			-4	20	-1.2
1914	Cin-N	42	141	16	39	6	1	0	12	20	18	.277	.386	.333	111	4	3	22	11			-6	O/23	-0.3
1915	Cin-N	155	555	75	151	25	11	1	41	38	33	.272	.340	.362	110	9	8	69	12	18	-7	-4	*O/1	-0.8
1916	Cin-N	70	234	29	57	9	1	1	18	21	8	.244	.327	.303	96	-1	-0	26	7			0	O	-0.1
	NY-N	2	1	0	1	0	0	0	1	1	0	1.000	1.000	1.000	544	1	1	1	0			0	H	0.1
	Yr	72	235	29	58	9	1	1	19	22	8	.247	.332	.306	99	0	1	27	7			0		0.0
Total	7	467	1537	181	381	61	16	3	116	128	59	.248	.327	.314	98	0	1	179	57	18		-22	O2/3SC1	-4.2

■ **BILL KILLEFER**   Killefer, William Lavier "   b: 10/10/1887, Bloomingdale, Mich   d: 7/3/60, Elsmere, Del.   BR/TR, 5'10.5", 200 lbs.   Deb: 9/13/09   MC

1909	StL-A	11	29	0	4	0	0	0	1	0		.138	.138	.138	-14	-4	-4	1	2			2	C	0.0
1910	StL-A	74	193	14	24	2	2	0	7	12		.124	.184	.155	7	-21	-19	6	0			13	C	0.1
1911	Phi-N	6	16	3	3	0	0	0	2	0	2	.188	.188	.188	5	-2	-2	1	0			2	/C	0.0
1912	Phi-N	85	268	18	60	6	3	1	21	4	14	.224	.241	.280	40	-22	-24	20	6			17	C	-0.2
1913	Phi-N	120	360	25	88	14	3	0	24	4	17	.244	.255	.300	56	-20	-22	27	2			17	*C/1	0.2
1914	Phi-N	98	299	27	70	10	1	0	27	8	17	.234	.261	.274	56	-16	-18	22	3			16	C	0.2
1915	*Phi-N	105	320	26	76	9	2	0	24	18	14	.237	.287	.278	70	-11	-11	26	5	3	-0	14	*C	0.9
1916	Phi-N	97	286	22	62	5	4	3	27	8	14	.217	.246	.294	63	-12	-13	22	2			-0	C	-0.9
1917	Phi-N	125	409	28	112	12	0	0	31	15	21	.274	.306	.303	84	-6	-8	38	4			9	*C/O	0.7
1918	*Chi-N	104	331	30	77	10	3	0	22	17	10	.233	.276	.281	68	-12	-13	27	5			9	*C	0.5
1919	Chi-N	103	315	17	90	10	2	0	22	15	8	.286	.322	.330	96	-1	-2	35	5			16	*C	2.3
1920	Chi-N	62	191	16	42	7	1	0	16	8	5	.220	.280	.267	56	-10	-11	15	2	2	-1	18	C	1.1
1921	Chi-N	45	133	11	43	1	0	0	16	4	4	.323	.357	.331	83	-3	-3	15	3	3	-1	-1	CM	-0.1
Total	13	1035	3150	237	751	86	21	4	240	113	126	.238	.273	.283	63	-141	-150	255	39	8		130	*C/O1	4.8

■ **GENE KIMBALL**   Kimball, Eugene Boynton   b: 8/31/1850, Rochester, N.Y.   d: 8/2/1882, Rochester, N.Y.   5'10", 160 lbs.   Deb: 5/04/1871

| 1871 | Cle-n | 29 | 131 | 18 | 25 | 1 | 0 | 0 | 9 | 3 | 2 | .191 | .209 | .198 | 19 | -13 | -12 | 7 | 5 | | | | 2/SO | -0.6 |

■ **DICK KIMBLE**   Kimble, Richard Lewis   b: 7/27/15, Buchtel, Ohio   BL/TR, 5'9", 160 lbs.   Deb: 8/20/45

| 1945 | Was-A | 20 | 49 | 5 | 12 | 1 | 1 | 0 | 1 | 5 | 2 | .245 | .315 | .306 | 88 | -1 | -1 | 5 | 0 | 0 | 0 | -3 | S | -0.2 |

■ **BRUCE KIMM**   Kimm, Bruce Edward   b: 6/29/51, Cedar Rapids, Iowa   BR/TR, 5'11", 175 lbs.   Deb: 5/04/76   C

1976	Det-A	63	152	13	40	8	0	1	6	15	20	.263	.329	.336	91	-1	-2	17	4	3	-1	6	C/D	0.6
1977	Det-A	14	25	2	2	1	0	0	1	0	4	.080	.115	.120	-34	-5	-5	0	0	1	-1	7	C/D	0.1
1979	Chi-N	9	11	0	1	0	0	0	0	0	0	.091	.091	.091	-46	-2	-2	0	0	1	-1	2	/C	0.0
1980	Chi-A	100	251	20	61	10	1	0	19	17	26	.243	.291	.291	60	-14	-13	19	1	3	-2	-2	C	-1.1
Total	4	186	439	35	104	19	1	1	26	32	50	.237	.290	.292	62	-21	-22	37	5	8	-3	13	C/D	-0.4

■ **WALLY KIMMICK**   Kimmick, Walter Lyons   b: 5/30/1897, Turtle Creek, Pa.   d: 7/21/89, Boswell, Pa.   BR/TR, 5'11", 174 lbs.   Deb: 9/13/19

1919	StL-N	2	1	1	0	0	0	0	0	1	0	.000	.500	.000	61	0	0	0	1			0	/S	0.0
1921	Cin-N	3	6	0	1	0	0	0	1	0	1	.167	.167	.167	-12	-1	-1	0	0	0	0	-0	/3	0.0
1922	Cin-N	39	89	11	22	2	1	0	12	3	12	.247	.272	.292	46	-7	-7	7	0	0	0	2	S/23	-0.2
1923	Cin-N	29	80	11	18	2	1	0	6	5	15	.225	.271	.275	45	-6	-6	7	3	0	1	8	2/3S	0.3
1925	Phi-N	70	141	16	43	3	2	1	10	22	26	.305	.399	.376	91	-1	-1	21	0	3	-2	-3	S32	-0.1
1926	Phi-N	20	28	0	6	2	1	0	2	3	7	.214	.290	.357	70	-1	-1	3	0			-2	/1S32	-0.2
Total	6	163	345	39	90	9	5	1	31	34	61	.261	.327	.325	67	-15	-16	39	4	3		4	/S231	-0.2

■ **JERRY KINDALL**   Kindall, Gerald Donald "Slim"   b: 5/27/35, St.Paul, Minn.   BR/TR, 6'2.5", 175 lbs.   Deb: 7/01/56

1956	Chi-N	32	55	7	9	1	1	0	6	0	17	.164	.246	.218	27	-6	-6	3	1	0	0	2	S	-0.1
1957	Chi-N	72	181	18	29	3	0	6	12	8	48	.160	.196	.276	25	-19	-19	9	1	0	0	-4	23/S	-2.0
1958	Chi-N	3	6	0	1	1	0	0	0	0	3	.167	.167	.333	29	-1	-1	0	0	0	0	1	/2	0.1
1960	Chi-N	89	246	17	59	16	2	2	23	5	52	.240	.255	.346	63	-13	-13	19	4	3	-1	14	2/S	0.8
1961	Chi-N	96	310	37	75	22	3	9	44	18	89	.242	.288	.419	84	-8	-8	36	2	2	-1	7	2S	0.9
1962	Cle-A	154	530	51	123	21	4	13	55	45	107	.232	.292	.349	74	-22	-20	53	4	3	-1	21	*2	1.1
1963	Cle-A	86	234	27	48	4	1	5	20	20	71	.205	.268	.295	58	-13	-13	19	3	1	0	3	S2/1	-0.4
1964	Cle-A	23	25	5	9	1	0	2	2	2	7	.360	.407	.640	188	3	3	6	0	0	0	3	1	0.5
	Min-A	62	128	8	19	2	0	1	6	7	44	.148	.199	.188	8	-16	-16	3	0	0	0	5	2/S1	-0.5
	Yr	85	153	13	28	3	0	3	8	9	51	.183	.233	.261	37	-13	-13	9	0	0	0	8		0.0
1965	Min-A	125	342	41	67	12	1	6	36	36	97	.196	.278	.289	59	-17	-19	29	2	2	-1	-1	*23/S	-1.4
Total	9	742	2057	211	439	83	9	44	198	145	535	.213	.268	.327	62	-112	-111	180	17	11	-2	50	2S/31	-1.0

YEAR	TM/L	G	AB	R	H	2B	3B	HR	RBI	BB	SO	AVG	OBP	SLG	PRO+	BR	/A	RC	SB	CS	SBR	FR	POS	TPR

■ RALPH KINER
Kiner, Ralph McPherran b: 10/27/22, Santa Rita, N.Mex.   BR/TR, 6'2", 195 lbs.   Deb: 4/16/46 H

YEAR	TM/L	G	AB	R	H	2B	3B	HR	RBI	BB	SO	AVG	OBP	SLG	PRO+	BR	/A	RC	SB	CS	SBR	FR	POS	TPR
1946	Pit-N	144	502	63	124	17	3	23	81	74	109	.247	.345	.430	116	12	11	75	3			3	*O	1.1
1947	Pit-N	152	565	118	177	23	4	51	127	98	81	.313	.417	.639	172	61	59	154	1			9	*O	6.0
1948	Pit-N	156	555	104	147	19	5	40	123	112	61	.265	.391	.533	145	39	37	120	1			-9	*O	1.7
1949	Pit-N	152	549	116	170	19	5	54	127	117	61	.310	.432	.658	183	70	68	163	6			-4	*O	5.4
1950	Pit-N	150	547	112	149	21	6	47	118	122	79	.272	.408	.590	154	49	46	133	2			-1	*O	3.8
1951	Pit-N	151	531	124	164	31	6	42	109	137	57	.309	.452	.627	182	71	69	165	2	1	0	-6	O1	5.7
1952	Pit-N	149	516	90	126	17	2	37	87	110	77	.244	.384	.500	140	33	31	111	3	0	1	-11	*O	1.8
1953	Pit-N	41	148	27	40	6	1	7	29	25	21	.270	.383	.466	121	5	5	30	1	0	0	-2	O	0.1
	Chi-N	117	414	73	117	14	2	28	87	75	67	.283	.394	.529	135	24	23	91	1	1	-0	-5	*O	1.2
	Yr	158	562	100	157	20	3	35	116	100	88	.279	.391	.512	131	29	28	120	2	1	0	-8		1.3
1954	Chi-N	147	557	88	159	36	5	22	73	76	90	.285	.373	.487	121	18	17	101	2	0	1	-2	*O	1.1
1955	Cle-A	113	321	56	78	13	0	18	54	65	46	.243	.370	.452	116	10	8	57	0	0	0	-7	O	-0.2
Total	10	1472	5205	971	1451	216	39	369	1015	1011	749	.279	.398	.548	148	391	373	1201	22	2		-36	*O/1	27.7

■ CHICK KING
King, Charles Gilbert b: 11/10/30, Paris, Tenn.   BR/TR, 6'2", 190 lbs.   Deb: 8/27/54

YEAR	TM/L	G	AB	R	H	2B	3B	HR	RBI	BB	SO	AVG	OBP	SLG	PRO+	BR	/A	RC	SB	CS	SBR	FR	POS	TPR
1954	Det-A	11	28	4	6	0	0	0	3	3	8	.214	.290	.286	59	-2	-2	2	0	0	0	2	/O	0.0
1955	Det-A	7	21	3	5	0	0	0	0	1	2	.238	.273	.238	39	-2	-2	1	0	0	0	-0	/O	-0.1
1956	Det-A	7	9	0	2	0	0	0	0	1	4	.222	.300	.222	40	-1	-1	1	0	0	0	-0	/O	0.0
1958	Chi-N	8	8	1	2	0	0	0	1	3	1	.250	.455	.250	95	0	0	1	0	0	0	0	/O	0.0
1959	Chi-N	7	3	3	0	0	0	0	0	0	1	.000	.000	.000	-99	-1	-1	0	0	0	0	1	/O	0.0
	StL-N	5	7	0	3	0	0	0	1	0	2	.429	.429	.429	121	0	0	1	0	0	0	1	/O	0.1
	Yr	12	10	3	3	0	0	0	1	0	3	.300	.300	.300	59	-1	-1	1	0	0	0	1		0.1
Total	5	45	76	11	18	0	1	0	5	8	18	.237	.310	.263	56	-5	-4	7	0	0	0	3	/O	0.0

■ LEE KING
King, Edward Lee b: 3/28/1894, Waltham, Mass. d: 9/7/38, Newton Centre, Mass.   BR/TR, 5'10", 160 lbs.   Deb: 6/24/16

YEAR	TM/L	G	AB	R	H	2B	3B	HR	RBI	BB	SO	AVG	OBP	SLG	PRO+	BR	/A	RC	SB	CS	SBR	FR	POS	TPR
1916	Phi-A	42	144	13	27	1	2	0	8	7	15	.188	.230	.222	38	-11	-11	9	4			-10	OS/32	-2.3
1919	Bos-N	2	1	0	0	0	0	0	0	0	0	.000	.000	.000	-99	-0	-0	0	0			0	H	0.0
Total	2	44	145	13	27	1	2	0	8	7	15	.186	.229	.221	37	-12	-11	9	4			-10	/OS32	-2.3

■ HAL KING
King, Harold b: 2/1/44, Oviedo, Fla.   BL/TR, 6'1", 200 lbs.   Deb: 9/06/67

YEAR	TM/L	G	AB	R	H	2B	3B	HR	RBI	BB	SO	AVG	OBP	SLG	PRO+	BR	/A	RC	SB	CS	SBR	FR	POS	TPR
1967	Hou-N	15	44	2	11	1	0	2	6	2	9	.250	.283	.364	87	-1	-1	5	0	0	0	-2	C	-0.1
1968	Hou-N	27	55	4	8	2	1	0	2	7	16	.145	.242	.218	40	-4	-4	3	0	0	0	-3	C	-0.7
1970	Atl-N	89	204	29	53	8	0	11	30	32	41	.260	.366	.461	113	6	4	35	1	0	0	-10	C	-0.2
1971	Atl-N	86	198	14	41	9	0	5	19	29	43	.207	.320	.328	79	-4	-5	20	0	0	0	-1	C	-0.4
1972	Tex-A	50	122	12	22	5	0	4	12	25	35	.180	.333	.320	99	0	1	14	0	0	0	-7	C	-0.6
1973	*Cin-N	35	43	5	8	0	0	4	10	6	10	.186	.286	.465	110	0	0	6	0	0	0	-1	/C	0.0
1974	Cin-N	20	17	1	3	1	0	0	3	3	4	.176	.300	.235	52	-1	-1	1	0	0	0	0	/C	0.0
Total	7	322	683	67	146	26	3	24	82	104	158	.214	.325	.366	93	-3	-5	85	1	0	0	-23	C	-2.0

■ JIM KING
King, James Hubert b: 8/27/32, Elkins, Ark.   BL/TR, 6', 185 lbs.   Deb: 4/17/55

YEAR	TM/L	G	AB	R	H	2B	3B	HR	RBI	BB	SO	AVG	OBP	SLG	PRO+	BR	/A	RC	SB	CS	SBR	FR	POS	TPR
1955	Chi-N	113	301	43	77	12	3	11	45	24	39	.256	.315	.425	95	-3	-3	41	2	1	0	4	O	0.0
1956	Chi-N	118	317	32	79	13	2	15	54	30	40	.249	.316	.445	103	0	1	44	1	2	-1	8	O	0.5
1957	StL-N	22	35	1	11	0	0	0	2	4	2	.314	.385	.314	89	-0	-0	4	0	0	0	-1	O	-0.1
1958	SF-N	34	56	8	12	2	1	2	8	10	8	.214	.343	.393	96	-0	-0	8	0	1	-1	-2	O	-0.2
1961	Was-A	110	263	43	71	12	1	11	46	38	45	.270	.366	.449	118	7	7	46	4	0	1	-1	O/C	0.4
1962	Was-A	132	333	39	81	15	0	11	35	55	37	.243	.355	.387	101	1	2	49	4	2	0	1	*O	0.0
1963	Was-A	136	459	61	106	16	5	24	62	45	43	.231	.301	.444	106	2	2	60	3	0	1	-1	*O	-0.1
1964	Was-A	134	415	46	100	15	1	18	56	55	65	.241	.337	.412	108	4	5	60	3	1	0	7	O	0.7
1965	Was-A	120	258	46	55	10	2	14	49	44	50	.213	.339	.430	119	6	7	38	1	0	0	2	O	0.6
1966	Was-A	117	310	41	77	14	2	10	30	38	41	.248	.330	.403	111	4	4	41	4	0	1	-2	O	0.1
1967	Was-A	47	100	10	21	2	2	1	12	15	13	.210	.331	.300	91	-1	-1	11	1	1	-0	-2	O/C	-0.3
	Chi-A	23	50	2	6	1	0	0	2	4	16	.120	.185	.140	-3	-6	-6	1	0	0	0	-2	O	-0.8
	Cle-A	19	21	2	3	0	0	0	0	1	2	.143	.182	.143	-3	-3	-3	1	0	0	0	-0	/O	-0.2
	Yr	89	171	14	30	3	2	1	14	20	31	.175	.273	.234	53	-10	-9	12	1	1	-0	-3		-1.3
Total	11	1125	2918	374	699	112	19	117	401	363	401	.240	.328	.411	104	11	15	406	23	8	2	11	O/C	0.6

■ JEFF KING
King, Jeffrey Wayne b: 12/26/64, Marion, Ind.   BR/TR, 6'1", 175 lbs.   Deb: 6/02/89

YEAR	TM/L	G	AB	R	H	2B	3B	HR	RBI	BB	SO	AVG	OBP	SLG	PRO+	BR	/A	RC	SB	CS	SBR	FR	POS	TPR
1989	Pit-N	75	215	31	42	13	3	5	19	20	34	.195	.270	.353	80	-7	-6	21	4	2	0	-2	13/2S	-1.1
1990	*Pit-N	127	371	46	91	17	1	14	53	21	50	.245	.288	.410	93	-7	-5	40	3	3	-1	16	*3/1	1.4
Total	2	202	586	77	133	30	4	19	72	41	84	.227	.281	.389	88	-14	-11	61	7	5	-1	15	3/12S	0.3

■ LEE KING
King, Lee b: 12/26/1892, Hundred, W.Va. d: 9/16/67, Shinnstown, W.Va.   BR/TR, 5'8", 160 lbs.   Deb: 9/20/16

YEAR	TM/L	G	AB	R	H	2B	3B	HR	RBI	BB	SO	AVG	OBP	SLG	PRO+	BR	/A	RC	SB	CS	SBR	FR	POS	TPR
1916	Pit-N	8	18	0	2	0	0	0	1	0	7	.111	.111	.111	-31	-3	-3	0	0			-1	/O	-0.4
1917	Pit-N	111	381	32	95	14	5	1	35	15	58	.249	.281	.320	81	-8	-9	35	8			4	*O	-0.8
1918	Pit-N	36	112	9	26	3	2	1	11	11	15	.232	.301	.321	87	-1	-2	11	3			-6	O	-1.0
1919	NY-N	21	20	5	2	1	0	0	1	1	6	.100	.143	.150	-12	-3	-3	0	0			0	O	-0.3
1920	NY-N	93	261	32	72	11	4	7	42	21	38	.276	.335	.429	120	6	6	36	3	7	-3	-13	O	-1.6
1921	NY-N	39	94	17	21	4	2	0	7	13	6	.223	.324	.309	68	-4	-4	10	0	2	-1	1	O/1	-0.5
	Phi-N	64	216	25	58	19	4	4	32	8	37	.269	.298	.449	88	-3	-5	27	1	4	-2	-2	O	-1.1
	Yr	103	310	42	79	23	6	4	39	21	43	.255	.306	.406	83	-7	-9	37	1	6	-3	-2		-1.6
1922	Phi-N	19	53	8	12	5	1	2	13	8	6	.226	.328	.472	95	-0	-1	9	0	0	0	0	O	0.0
	NY-N	20	34	6	6	3	0	0	2	5	7	.176	.282	.265	41	-3	-3	3	1	0	0	0	/1O	-0.1
	Yr	39	87	14	18	8	1	2	15	13	8	.207	.310	.391	76	-3	-4	11	1	0	0	1		-0.1
Total	7	411	1189	134	294	60	18	15	144	82	175	.247	.299	.366	87	-19	-23	131	16	13		-17	O/1	-5.8

■ LYNN KING
King, Lynn Paul "Dig" b: 11/28/07, Villisca, Iowa d: 5/11/72, Atlantic, Iowa   BL/TR, 5'9", 165 lbs.   Deb: 9/21/35

YEAR	TM/L	G	AB	R	H	2B	3B	HR	RBI	BB	SO	AVG	OBP	SLG	PRO+	BR	/A	RC	SB	CS	SBR	FR	POS	TPR
1935	StL-N	8	22	6	4	0	0	0	4	1	.182	.308	.182	34	-2	-2	1	2			2	/O	0.0
1936	StL-N	78	100	12	19	2	1	0	10	9	14	.190	.257	.230	32	-9	-9	6	2			5	O	-0.5
1939	StL-N	89	85	10	20	2	0	0	11	15	3	.235	.350	.259	62	-3	-4	9	2			5	O	0.0
Total	3	175	207	28	43	4	1	0	21	28	18	.208	.302	.237	45	-15	-16	16	6			12	/O	-0.5

■ MART KING
King, Marshal Ney b: 12/1849, Troy, N.Y. d: 10/19/11, Troy, N.Y.   5'9.5", 176 lbs.   Deb: 5/08/1871

YEAR	TM/L	G	AB	R	H	2B	3B	HR	RBI	BB	SO	AVG	OBP	SLG	PRO+	BR	/A	RC	SB	CS	SBR	FR	POS	TPR
1871	Chi-n	20	101	23	21	1	0	2	16	8	1	.208	.266	.277	51	-5	-8	9	5				O/CS	-0.4
1872	Tro-n	3	11	0	0	0	0	0	0			.000	.000	.000	-99	-2	-3	0					O	-0.1
Total	2 n	23	112	23	21	1	0	2		8		.188	.242	.250	39	-8	-11	9					/OCS	-0.5

■ SAM KING
King, Samuel Warren b: 5/17/1852, Peabody, Mass. d: 8/11/22, Peabody, Mass.   TL, 6',   Deb: 5/01/1884

YEAR	TM/L	G	AB	R	H	2B	3B	HR	RBI	BB	SO	AVG	OBP	SLG	PRO+	BR	/A	RC	SB	CS	SBR	FR	POS	TPR
1884	Was-a	12	45	3	8	2	0	0		1		.178	.213	.222	50	-3	-2	2				-1	1	-0.3

■ STEVE KING
King, Stephen F. b: 1844, Troy, N.Y. d: 7/8/1895, Troy, N.Y.   5'9", 175 lbs.   Deb: 5/09/1871

YEAR	TM/L	G	AB	R	H	2B	3B	HR	RBI	BB	SO	AVG	OBP	SLG	PRO+	BR	/A	RC	SB	CS	SBR	FR	POS	TPR
1871	Tro-n	29	144	45	57	10	6	0	34	1	1	.396	.400	.549	167	12	12	34	3				*O	0.8
1872	Tro-n	25	129	33	40	9	1	0		1		.310	.315	.395	116	2	2	16					O	0.2
Total	2 n	54	273	78	97	19	7	0		2		.355	.360	.476	144	15	14	50					/O	1.0

YEAR	TM/L	G	AB	R	H	2B	3B	HR	RBI	BB	SO	AVG	OBP	SLG	PRO+	BR	/A	RC	SB	CS	SBR	FR	POS	TPR

■ WES KINGDON
Kingdon, Westcott William b: 7/4/1900, Los Angeles, Cal. d: 4/19/75, Capistrano, Cal. BR/TR, 5'8", 148 lbs. Deb: 6/12/32

| 1932 | Was-A | 18 | 34 | 10 | 11 | 3 | 1 | 0 | 3 | 5 | 2 | .324 | .410 | .471 | 129 | 2 | 2 | 7 | 0 | 0 | 0 | -2 | /3S | 0.1 |

■ MIKE KINGERY
Kingery, Michael Scott b: 3/29/61, St.James, Minn. BL/TL, 6', 180 lbs. Deb: 7/07/86

1986	KC-A	62	209	25	54	8	5	3	14	12	30	.258	.299	.388	83	-5	-5	23	7	3	0	-6	O	-1.1
1987	Sea-A	120	354	38	99	25	4	9	52	27	43	.280	.334	.449	100	2	-0	51	7	9	-3	7	*O/D	0.1
1988	Sea-A	57	123	21	25	6	0	1	9	19	23	.203	.315	.276	64	-5	-6	12	3	1	0	3	O1	-0.2
1989	Sea-A	31	76	14	17	3	0	2	6	7	14	.224	.289	.342	75	-2	-3	7	1	1	-0	5	O	0.1
1990	SF-N	105	207	24	61	7	1	0	24	12	19	.295	.336	.338	87	-4	-3	25	6	1	1	-13	O	-1.8
Total	5	375	969	122	256	49	10	15	105	77	129	.264	.321	.382	88	-14	-17	120	24	15	-2	-3	O/1D	-2.9

■ DAVE KINGMAN
Kingman, David Arthur b: 12/21/48, Pendleton, Ore. BR/TR, 6'6", 210 lbs. Deb: 7/30/71

1971	*SF-N	41	115	17	32	10	2	6	24	9	35	.278	.336	.557	151	7	7	22	5	0	2	-3	1O	0.4
1972	SF-N	135	472	65	106	17	4	29	83	51	140	.225	.306	.462	114	8	7	67	16	6	1	2	31O	0.5
1973	SF-N	112	305	54	62	10	1	24	55	41	122	.203	.302	.479	109	4	2	42	8	5	-1	3	31/P	0.2
1974	SF-N	121	350	41	78	18	2	18	55	37	125	.223	.303	.440	101	1	-1	44	8	8	-2	2	13/O	-0.6
1975	NY-N	134	502	65	116	22	1	36	88	34	153	.231	.285	.494	119	4	7	66	7	5	-1	2	O13	0.2
1976	NY-N	123	474	70	113	14	1	37	86	28	135	.238	.288	.506	130	10	13	65	7	4	-0	2	*O1	1.0
1977	NY-N	58	211	22	44	7	0	9	28	13	66	.209	.264	.370	71	-10	-9	20	3	2	-0	-4	O1	-1.5
	SD-N	56	168	16	40	9	0	11	39	12	48	.238	.297	.488	119	1	3	23	2	3	-1	0	O1/3	0.0
	Yr	114	379	38	84	16	0	20	67	25	114	.222	.279	.422	92	-10	-6	43	5	5	-2	-3		-1.5
	Cal-A	10	36	4	7	2	0	2	4	1	16	.194	.237	.417	77	-1	-1	4	0	0	0	-0	/1O	-0.1
	NY-A	8	24	5	6	2	0	4	7	2	13	.250	.333	.833	208	3	3	6	0	1	-1	0	/D	0.3
	Yr	18	60	9	13	4	0	6	11	3	29	.217	.277	.583	131	2	2	9	0	1	-1	-0		0.2
1978	Chi-N	119	395	65	105	17	4	28	79	39	111	.266	.341	.542	128	21	15	73	3	4	-2	-6	*O/1	0.4
1979	Chi-N	145	532	97	153	19	5	48	115	45	131	.288	.348	.613	143	38	32	112	4	2	-0	-2	*O	2.6
1980	Chi-N	81	255	31	71	8	0	18	57	21	44	.278	.333	.522	126	11	8	40	2	2	-1	-1	O/1	0.4
1981	NY-N	100	353	40	78	11	3	22	59	55	105	.221	.328	.456	122	9	10	54	6	0	2	-7	1O	0.1
1982	NY-N	149	535	80	109	9	1	37	99	59	156	.204	.288	.432	99	-3	-3	67	4	0	1	-14	*1	-2.4
1983	NY-N	100	248	25	49	7	0	13	29	22	57	.198	.266	.383	79	-9	-8	26	2	1	0	-4	1/O	-1.5
1984	Oak-A	147	549	68	147	23	1	35	118	44	119	.268	.329	.505	136	18	23	91	2	1	0	-2	*D/1	2.0
1985	Oak-A	158	592	66	141	16	0	30	91	62	114	.238	.313	.417	105	-3	3	75	3	2	-0	-1	*D/1	0.1
1986	Oak-A	144	561	70	118	19	0	35	94	33	126	.210	.258	.431	90	-16	-10	57	3	3	-1	-1	*D/1	-1.1
Total	16	1941	6677	901	1575	240	25	442	1210	608	1816	.236	.305	.478	115	91	100	955	85	49	-4	-33	O1D3/P	1.0

■ HARRY KINGMAN
Kingman, Henry Lees b: 4/3/1892, Tientsin, China d: 12/27/82, Oakland, Cal. BL/TL, 6'1.5", 165 lbs. Deb: 7/01/14

| 1914 | NY-A | 4 | 3 | 0 | 0 | 0 | 0 | 0 | 0 | 1 | 2 | .000 | .250 | .000 | -24 | -0 | -0 | 0 | 0 | | | 0 | /1 | 0.0 |

■ WALT KINLOCK
Kinlock, Walter b: 1878, St.Joseph, Mo. Deb: 8/01/1895

| 1895 | StL-N | 1 | 3 | 0 | 1 | 0 | 0 | 0 | 0 | 0 | 2 | .333 | .333 | .333 | 75 | -0 | -0 | 0 | 0 | | | 1 | /3 | 0.0 |

■ BOB KINSELLA
Kinsella, Robert Francis "Red" b: 1/5/1899, Springfield, Ill. d: 12/30/51, Los Angeles, Cal. BL/TR, 5'9.5", 165 lbs. Deb: 9/20/19

1919	NY-N	3	9	1	2	0	0	0	0	0	3	.222	.222	.222	34	-1	-1	1	1			-1	/O	-0.1
1920	NY-N	1	3	0	1	0	0	0	1	0	2	.333	.333	.333	93	-0	-0	0	0	0	0	-0	/O	0.0
Total	2	4	12	1	3	0	0	0	1	0	5	.250	.250	.250	49	-1	-1	1	1	0		-1	/O	-0.1

■ KINSLER
Kinsler b: Staten Island, N.Y. Deb: 6/08/1893

| 1893 | NY-N | 1 | 3 | 1 | 0 | 0 | 0 | 0 | 0 | 1 | 1 | .000 | .250 | .000 | -30 | -1 | -1 | 0 | 0 | | | -0 | /O | 0.0 |

■ TOM KINSLOW
Kinslow, Thomas F. b: 1/12/1866, Washington, D.C. d: 2/22/01, Washington, D.C. BR/TR, 5'10", 160 lbs. Deb: 6/04/1886

1886	Was-N	3	8	1	2	0	0	0	1	0	1	.250	.250	.250	56	-0	-0	1	0			0	/C	0.0
1887	NY-a	2	6	0	0	0	0	0	0			.000	.000	.000	-99	-2	-2	0	0			0	/C	0.0
1890	Bro-P	64	242	30	64	11	6	4	46	10	22	.264	.299	.409	85	-5	-8	31	2			9	C	0.3
1891	Bro-N	61	228	22	54	6	0	0	33	9	22	.237	.266	.263	56	-13	-13	17	3			-9	C	-1.4
1892	Bro-N	66	246	37	75	6	11	2	40	13	16	.305	.342	.443	144	10	11	40	4			5	C	1.8
1893	Bro-N	78	312	38	76	8	4	4	45	11	13	.244	.272	.333	65	-18	-16	30	4			-2	C/O	-0.8
1894	Bro-N	62	223	39	68	5	6	2	41	20	11	.305	.362	.408	94	-5	-2	35	4			-8	C/1	-0.2
1895	Pit-N	19	62	10	14	2	0	0	5	2	2	.226	.250	.258	34	-6	-6	4	1			-1	C	-0.3
1896	Lou-N	8	25	4	7	0	1	0	7	1	5	.280	.308	.360	80	-1	-1	3	0			-1	/C1	0.0
1898	Was-N	3	9	0	1	0	0	0	0	0		.111	.111	.111	-36	-2	-2	0	0			-1	/C1	-0.1
	StL-N	14	53	5	15	2	1	0	4	1		.283	.309	.358	91	-1	-1	6	0			1	C	0.1
	Yr	17	62	5	16	2	1	0	4	1		.258	.281	.323	74	-2	-2	6	0			0		0.0
Total	10	380	1414	186	376	40	29	12	222	67	92	.266	.301	.361	83	-42	-36	167	18			-7	C/1O	-0.6

■ WALT KINZIE
Kinzie, Walter Harris b: 3/1858, Kansas d: 11/5/09, Chicago, Ill. BR , 5'10.5", 161 lbs. Deb: 7/17/1882

1882	Det-N	13	53	5	5	0	1	0	2	0	8	.094	.094	.132	-28	-7	-7	1				-4	S	-0.8
1884	Chi-N	19	82	4	13	3	0	2	8	0	13	.159	.159	.268	29	-6	-7	4				-2	S/3	-0.7
	StL-a	2	9	0	1	0	0	0	0			.111	.111	.111	-25	-1	-1	0				-3	/2	-0.3
Total	2	34	144	9	19	3	1	2	10	0	21	.132	.132	.208	6	-15	-16	4				-9	/S23	-1.8

■ ED KIPPERT
Kippert, Edward August "Kickapoo" b: 1/3/1880, Detroit, Mich. d: 6/3/60, Detroit, Mich. BR/TR, 5'10.5", 180 lbs. Deb: 4/14/14

| 1914 | Cin-N | 2 | 2 | 0 | 0 | 0 | 0 | 0 | 0 | 0 | 0 | .000 | .000 | .000 | -97 | -0 | -0 | 0 | 0 | | | 0 | /O | 0.0 |

■ JIM KIRBY
Kirby, James Herschel b: 5/5/23, Nashville, Tenn. BR/TR, 5'11", 175 lbs. Deb: 5/01/49

| 1949 | Chi-N | 3 | 2 | 0 | 1 | 0 | 0 | 0 | 0 | 0 | 0 | .500 | .500 | .500 | 174 | 0 | 0 | 1 | 0 | | | 0 | H | 0.0 |

■ LA RUE KIRBY
Kirby, La Rue b: 12/30/1889, Eureka, Mich. d: 6/10/61, Lansing, Mich. BB/TR, 6', 185 lbs. Deb: 8/07/12

1912	NY-N	3	5	1	1	1	0	0	0	0	0	.200	.200	.400	60	-0	-0	0	0			0	/P	0.0
1914	StL-F	52	195	21	48	6	3	2	18	14	30	.246	.303	.338	79	-4	-6	22	5			2	O	-0.6
1915	StL-F	61	178	15	38	7	2	0	16	17	31	.213	.282	.275	62	-8	-9	16	3			-3	O/P	-1.4
Total	3	116	378	37	87	14	5	2	34	31	61	.230	.292	.310	71	-12	-15	39	8			-1	O/P	-2.0

■ TOM KIRK
Kirk, Thomas Daniel b: 9/27/27, Philadelphia, Pa. d: 8/1/74, Philadelphia, Pa. BL/TL, 5'10.5", 182 lbs. Deb: 6/24/47

| 1947 | Phi-A | 1 | 1 | 0 | 0 | 0 | 0 | 0 | 0 | 0 | 0 | .000 | .000 | .000 | -98 | -0 | -0 | 0 | 0 | 0 | 0 | 0 | H | 0.0 |

■ JAY KIRKE
Kirke, Judson Fabian b: 6/16/1888, Fleischmann's, N.Y d: 8/31/68, New Orleans, La. BL/TR, 6', 195 lbs. Deb: 9/28/10

1910	Det-A	8	25	3	5	1	0	0	3	1		.200	.231	.240	44	-2	-2	2	1			-3	/2O	-0.5
1911	Bos-N	20	89	9	32	5	5	0	12	2	6	.360	.380	.528	142	6	5	19	3			-1	O/12S3	0.3
1912	Bos-N	103	359	53	115	11	4	4	62	9	46	.320	.339	.407	102	0	-1	51	7			2	O3/S1	0.1
1913	Bos-N	18	38	3	9	2	0	0	3	1	6	.237	.293	.289	65	-2	-2	3	0			3	O	0.1
1914	Cle-A	67	242	18	66	10	2	1	25	7	30	.273	.296	.343	89	-4	-5	23	5	10	-5	0	O1	-1.2
1915	Cle-A	87	339	35	105	19	2	2	40	14	21	.310	.346	.395	120	7	7	47	5	6	-2	-1	1	0.2
1918	NY-N	17	56	1	14	1	0	0	3	1	3	.250	.263	.268	63	-3	-2	4	0			1	1	-0.2
Total	7	320	1148	122	346	49	13	7	148	35	112	.301	.328	.385	103	4	0	149	21	16		2	O1/32S	-1.5

YEAR	TM/L	G	AB	R	H	2B	3B	HR	RBI	BB	SO	AVG	OBP	SLG	PRO+	BR	/A	RC	SB	CS	SBR	FR	POS	TPR

■ WILLIE KIRKLAND   Kirkland, Willie Charles   b: 2/17/34, Siluria, Ala.   BL/TR, 6′1″, 206 lbs.   Deb: 4/15/58

YEAR	TM/L	G	AB	R	H	2B	3B	HR	RBI	BB	SO	AVG	OBP	SLG	PRO+	BR	/A	RC	SB	CS	SBR	FR	POS	TPR
1958	SF-N	122	418	48	108	25	6	14	56	43	69	.258	.335	.447	107	2	4	64	3	2	-0	-3	*O	-0.3
1959	SF-N	126	463	64	126	22	3	22	68	42	84	.272	.337	.475	116	8	9	75	5	3	-0	0	*O	0.7
1960	SF-N	146	515	59	130	21	10	21	65	44	86	.252	.316	.454	115	4	8	74	12	7	-1	3	*O	0.6
1961	Cle-A	146	525	84	136	22	5	27	95	48	77	.259	.322	.474	113	5	7	84	7	0	2	6	*O	1.0
1962	Cle-A	137	419	56	84	9	1	21	72	43	62	.200	.275	.377	76	-17	-15	44	9	1	2	2	*O	-1.5
1963	Cle-A	127	427	51	98	13	2	15	47	45	99	.230	.304	.375	90	-6	-6	50	8	2	1	9	*O	-0.3
1964	Bal-A	66	150	14	30	5	0	3	22	17	26	.200	.286	.293	62	-8	-8	14	3	2	-0	6	O	-0.3
	Was-A	32	102	8	22	6	0	5	13	6	30	.216	.259	.422	86	-2	-2	11	0	0	-0	-5	O	-0.8
	Yr	98	252	22	52	11	0	8	35	23	56	.206	.275	.345	72	-10	-10	25	3	2	-0	2		-1.1
1965	Was-A	123	312	38	72	9	1	14	54	19	65	.231	.275	.401	91	-5	-5	33	3	2	-0	1	O	-0.8
1966	Was-A	124	163	21	31	2	1	6	17	16	50	.190	.263	.422	68	-7	-7	14	2	0	1	0	O	-0.9
Total	9	1149	3494	443	837	134	29	148	509	323	648	.240	.307	.422	99	-26	-16	463	52	19	4	20	O	-2.3

■ ED KIRKPATRICK   Kirkpatrick, Edgar Leon   b: 10/8/44, Spokane, Wash.   BL/TR, 5′11.5″, 195 lbs.   Deb: 9/13/62

YEAR	TM/L	G	AB	R	H	2B	3B	HR	RBI	BB	SO	AVG	OBP	SLG	PRO+	BR	/A	RC	SB	CS	SBR	FR	POS	TPR
1962	LA-A	3	6	0	0	0	0	0	0	0	2	.000	.000	.000	-99	-2	-2	0	0	0	0	1	/C	0.0
1963	LA-A	34	77	4	15	5	0	2	7	6	19	.195	.262	.338	71	-4	-3	7	1	0	0	0	CO	-0.2
1964	LA-A	75	219	20	53	13	3	2	22	23	30	.242	.320	.356	97	-3	-1	24	2	2	-1	-5	O	-0.8
1965	Cal-A	19	73	8	19	5	0	3	8	3	9	.260	.289	.452	110	0	1	8	1	2	-1	-0	O	0.0
1966	Cal-A	117	312	31	60	7	4	9	44	51	67	.192	.315	.327	87	-5	-4	35	7	4	-0	-9	*O/1	-1.8
1967	Cal-A	3	8	0	0	0	0	0	0	0	2	.000	.000	.000	-99	-2	-2	0	0	0	0	-2	/CO	-0.4
1968	Cal-A	89	161	23	37	4	0	1	15	25	32	.230	.337	.273	90	-2	-1	16	1	3	-2	-3	O/C1	-0.8
1969	KC-A	120	315	40	81	11	4	14	49	43	42	.257	.352	.451	122	10	9	52	3	5	-2	7	O/C132	1.3
1970	KC-A	134	424	59	97	17	2	18	62	55	65	.229	.319	.406	98	-1	-1	54	4	4	-1	-7	CO1	-0.9
1971	KC-A	120	365	46	80	12	1	9	46	48	60	.219	.313	.332	83	-8	-7	37	3	4	-2	1	OC	-0.6
1972	KC-A	113	364	43	100	15	1	9	43	51	50	.275	.368	.396	128	14	14	55	3	5	-2	-4	*C/1	0.9
1973	KC-A	126	429	61	113	24	3	6	45	46	48	.263	.336	.375	93	0	-4	52	3	7	-3	-7	*OC/D	-1.7
1974	*Pit-N	116	271	32	67	9	0	6	38	51	30	.247	.370	.347	105	3	4	37	1	2	-1	-3	1O/C	-0.2
1975	*Pit-N	89	144	15	34	5	0	5	16	18	22	.236	.321	.375	93	-2	-1	17	1	0	0	-1	1O	-0.3
1976	Pit-N	83	146	14	34	9	0	0	16	14	15	.233	.300	.295	69	-6	-6	13	1	0	0	0	1/O3	-0.6
1977	Pit-N	21	28	5	4	2	0	1	4	8	6	.143	.333	.321	75	-1	-1	3	1	0	0	-0	1/O3	0.0
	Tex-A	20	48	2	9	1	0	0	3	4	11	.188	.250	.208	26	-5	-5	3	2	0	1	0	/O1CD	-0.3
	Mil-A	29	77	8	21	4	0	0	6	10	8	.273	.364	.325	89	-1	-1	10	0	1	-1	-2	O/3D	-0.3
	Yr	49	125	10	30	5	0	0	9	14	19	.240	.321	.280	65	-5	-6	12	2	1	0	-2		-0.6
Total	16	1311	3467	411	824	143	18	85	424	456	518	.238	.330	.363	97	-13	-11	424	34	39	-13	-32	OC1/D32	-6.7

■ ENOS KIRKPATRICK   Kirkpatrick, Enos Claire   b: 12/8/1885, Pittsburgh, Pa.   d: 4/14/64, Pittsburgh, Pa.   BR/TR, 5′10″, 175 lbs.   Deb: 8/24/12

YEAR	TM/L	G	AB	R	H	2B	3B	HR	RBI	BB	SO	AVG	OBP	SLG	PRO+	BR	/A	RC	SB	CS	SBR	FR	POS	TPR
1912	Bro-N	32	94	13	18	1	1	0	6	9	15	.191	.269	.223	37	-8	-8	7	5			6	3/S	-0.1
1913	Bro-N	48	89	13	22	4	1	1	5	3	18	.247	.287	.348	79	-2	-3	10	5			-1	S/123	-0.3
1914	Bal-F	55	174	22	44	7	2	2	16	18	30	.253	.330	.351	92	-1	-2	24	10			-4	3S/O1	-0.4
1915	Bal-F	68	171	22	41	8	2	0	19	24	15	.240	.337	.310	89	-1	-2	23	12			-3	32/1S	-0.2
Total	4	203	528	70	125	20	6	3	46	54	78	.237	.315	.314	79	-13	-14	65	32			-2	/3S210	-1.0

■ JOE KIRRENE   Kirrene, Joseph John   b: 10/4/31, San Francisco, Cal.   BR/TR, 6′2″, 195 lbs.   Deb: 10/01/50

YEAR	TM/L	G	AB	R	H	2B	3B	HR	RBI	BB	SO	AVG	OBP	SLG	PRO+	BR	/A	RC	SB	CS	SBR	FR	POS	TPR
1950	Chi-A	1	4	0	1	0	0	0	0	1		.250	.250	.250	29	-0	-0	0	0	0	0	-0	/3	0.0
1954	Chi-A	9	23	4	7	1	0	0	4	5	2	.304	.448	.348	116	1	1	4	1	0	0	-2	/3	0.0
Total	2	10	27	4	8	1	0	0	4	5	3	.296	.424	.333	105	1	1	4	1	0	0	-3	/3	0.0

■ ERNIE KISH   Kish, Ernest Alexander   b: 2/6/18, Washington, D.C.   BL/TR, 5′9.5″, 170 lbs.   Deb: 7/29/45

YEAR	TM/L	G	AB	R	H	2B	3B	HR	RBI	BB	SO	AVG	OBP	SLG	PRO+	BR	/A	RC	SB	CS	SBR	FR	POS	TPR
1945	Phi-A	43	110	10	27	5	1	0	10	9	9	.245	.320	.309	83	-2	-2	11	0	3	-2	-2	O	-0.7

■ BILL KISSINGER   Kissinger, William Francis "Shang"   b: 8/15/1871, Dayton, Ky.   d: 4/20/29, Cincinnati, Ohio   BR/TR, 185 lbs.   Deb: 5/30/1895

YEAR	TM/L	G	AB	R	H	2B	3B	HR	RBI	BB	SO	AVG	OBP	SLG	PRO+	BR	/A	RC	SB	CS	SBR	FR	POS	TPR
1895	Bal-N	2	5	1	1	0	0	0	0	0	1	.200	.200	.200	4	-1	-1	0	0			0	/P	0.0
	StL-N	33	97	8	24	6	1	0	8	0	11	.247	.247	.330	50	-8	-7	8	1			-4	P/SO3	0.0
	Yr	35	102	9	25	6	1	0	8	0	12	.245	.245	.324	48	-8	-8	9	1			-4		0.0
1896	StL-N	23	73	8	22	4	0	0	12	0	4	.301	.301	.356	78	-3	-2	8	0			0	P/O3	0.0
1897	StL-N	14	39	7	13	3	2	0	6	3		.333	.381	.513	140	2	2	8	0			-1	/OP	0.1
Total	3	72	214	24	60	13	3	0	26	3	16	.280	.290	.369	75	-9	-8	24	1			-5	/POS3	0.1

■ CHRIS KITSOS   Kitsos, Christopher Anestos   b: 2/11/28, New York, N.Y.   BB/TR, 5′9″, 165 lbs.   Deb: 4/21/54

YEAR	TM/L	G	AB	R	H	2B	3B	HR	RBI	BB	SO	AVG	OBP	SLG	PRO+	BR	/A	RC	SB	CS	SBR	FR	POS	TPR
1954	Chi-N	1	0	0	0	0	0	0	0	0	0	—	—	—	—	0	0	0	0	0	0	0	/S	0.0

■ RON KITTLE   Kittle, Ronald Dale   b: 1/5/58, Gary, Indiana   BR/TR, 6′4″, 200 lbs.   Deb: 9/02/82

YEAR	TM/L	G	AB	R	H	2B	3B	HR	RBI	BB	SO	AVG	OBP	SLG	PRO+	BR	/A	RC	SB	CS	SBR	FR	POS	TPR
1982	Chi-A	20	29	3	7	2	0	1	7	3	12	.241	.313	.414	97	-0	-0	4	0	0	0	1	/OD	0.0
1983	*Chi-A	145	520	75	132	19	3	35	100	39	150	.254	.316	.504	117	13	11	81	8	3	1	-13	*O/D	-0.3
1984	Chi-A	139	466	67	100	15	0	32	74	49	137	.215	.298	.453	100	1	-2	62	3	6	-3	-1	*O/D	-0.9
1985	Chi-A	116	379	51	87	12	0	26	58	31	92	.230	.296	.467	101	1	-1	48	1	4	-2	-2	OD	-0.4
1986	Chi-A	86	296	34	63	11	0	17	48	28	87	.213	.287	.422	87	-5	-6	34	2	1	0	1	DO	-0.5
	NY-A	30	80	8	19	2	0	4	12	7	23	.237	.299	.412	92	-1	-1	11	2	0	1	0	D/O	0.0
	Yr	116	376	42	82	13	0	21	60	35	110	.218	.290	.420	89	-6	-7	45	4	1	1	1		-0.5
1987	NY-A	59	159	21	44	5	0	12	28	10	36	.277	.324	.535	123	4	3	26	0	1	-1	1	D/O	0.4
1988	Cle-A	75	225	31	58	8	0	18	43	16	65	.258	.329	.533	134	10	9	42	0	0	0	0	D	1.0
1989	Chi-A	51	169	26	51	10	0	11	37	22	42	.302	.385	.556	166	14	14	37	0	1	-1	-3	1D/O	0.9
1990	Chi-A	83	277	29	68	14	0	16	43	24	77	.245	.313	.469	118	5	5	41	0	0	0	-4	D1	-0.5
	Bal-A	22	61	4	10	2	0	2	3	2	14	.164	.203	.295	39	-5	-5	3	0	0	0	-0	D/1	-0.5
	Yr	105	338	33	78	16	0	18	46	26	91	.231	.293	.438	104	-1	0	43	0	0	0	-4		-0.5
Total	9	826	2661	349	639	100	3	174	453	231	735	.240	.309	.476	111	37	30	388	16	16	-5	-22	OD/1	-0.3

■ MALACHI KITTRIDGE   Kittridge, Malachi Jedediah "Jedediah"   b: 10/12/1869, Clinton, Mass.   d: 6/23/28, Gary, Ind.   BR/TR, 5′7″, 170 lbs.   Deb: 4/19/1890   M

YEAR	TM/L	G	AB	R	H	2B	3B	HR	RBI	BB	SO	AVG	OBP	SLG	PRO+	BR	/A	RC	SB	CS	SBR	FR	POS	TPR
1890	Chi-N	96	333	46	67	8	3	3	35	39	53	.201	.287	.270	62	-14	-17	29	7			0	*C	-0.8
1891	Chi-N	79	296	26	62	8	5	2	27	17	28	.209	.252	.291	60	-16	-15	23	4			-1	C	-0.8
1892	Chi-N	69	229	19	41	5	0	0	10	11	27	.179	.217	.201	27	-20	-20	11	2			13	C	-0.2
1893	Chi-N	70	255	32	59	9	5	2	30	17	15	.231	.279	.329	64	-14	-13	25	3			4	C	-0.2
1894	Chi-N	51	168	36	53	8	2	0	23	26	20	.315	.407	.387	89	-0	-2	28	2			3	C	0.4
1895	Chi-N	60	212	30	48	6	3	3	29	16	9	.226	.284	.325	55	-13	-16	22	6			-2	C	-0.9
1896	Chi-N	65	215	17	48	4	1	0	19	14	14	.223	.274	.265	42	-17	-19	18	6			0	C/P	-1.0
1897	Chi-N	79	262	25	53	5	1	0	30	22		.202	.264	.271	41	-21	-23	22	9			2	C	-0.8
1898	Lou-N	86	287	27	70	8	5	1	30	15		.244	.281	.317	75	-10	-10	29	9			-11	C	-1.3
1899	Lou-N	45	129	11	26	2	1	0	12	26		.202	.340	.233	61	-6	-6	11	3			8	C	0.4
	Was-N	44	133	14	20	3	0	0	11	10		.150	.215	.173	9	-16	-16	6	2			5	C	-0.6
	Yr	89	262	25	46	5	1	0	23	36		.176	.278	.202	35	-22	-22	17	5			13		-0.2
1901	Bos-N	114	381	24	96	14	0	2	40	32		.252	.312	.304	74	-8	-13	39	2			10	*C	1.0
1902	Bos-N	80	255	18	60	7	0	2	30	24		.235	.304	.286	83	-4	-4	25	4			4	C	0.7
1903	Bos-N	32	99	10	21	2	0	0	6	11		.212	.291	.232	54	-6	-5	8	5			5	C	0.2

YEAR	TM/L	G	AB	R	H	2B	3B	HR	RBI	BB	SO	AVG	OBP	SLG	PRO+	BR	/A	RC	SB	CS	SBR	FR	POS	TPR
	Was-A	60	192	8	41	4	1	0	16	10		.214	.252	.245	50	-11	-11	13	1			-4	C	-0.8
1904	Was-A	81	265	11	64	7	0	0	24	8		.242	.264	.268	71	-9	-8	21	2			0	CM	0.0
1905	Was-A	77	238	16	39	8	0	0	14	15		.164	.213	.197	33	-18	-17	12	1			3	C	-0.5
1906	Was-A	22	68	5	13	0	0	0	3	1		.191	.203	.191	26	-6	-5	3	0			-2	C	-0.6
	Cle-A	5	10	0	1	0	0	0	0	0		.100	.100	.100	-37	-2	-2	0	0			-0	/C	-0.1
	Yr	27	78	5	14	0	0	0	3	1		.179	.190	.179	18	-7	-7	3	0			-3		-0.7
Total	16	1215	4027	375	882	108	31	17	390	314	166	.219	.277	.274	58	-212	-222	343	64			34	*C/P	-5.9

■ **BOBBY KLAUS**   Klaus, Robert Francis b: 12/27/37, Spring Grove, Ill. BR/TR, 5'10", 170 lbs. Deb: 4/21/64

YEAR	TM/L	G	AB	R	H	2B	3B	HR	RBI	BB	SO	AVG	OBP	SLG	PRO+	BR	/A	RC	SB	CS	SBR	FR	POS	TPR
1964	Cin-N	40	93	10	17	5	1	2	6	4	13	.183	.216	.323	48	-6	-7	7	1	0	0	4	23/S	-0.1
	NY-N	56	209	25	51	8	3	2	11	25	30	.244	.325	.340	90	-3	-2	24	3	4	-2	-3	23/S	-0.5
	Yr	96	302	35	68	13	4	4	17	29	43	.225	.293	.334	76	-9	-9	30	4	4	-1	1		-0.6
1965	NY-N	119	288	30	55	12	0	2	12	45	49	.191	.302	.253	61	-15	-13	24	1	6	-3	15	2S3	0.5
Total	2	215	590	65	123	25	4	6	29	74	92	.208	.298	.295	69	-24	-23	54	5	10	-5	16	2/3S	-0.1

■ **BILLY KLAUS**   Klaus, William Joseph b: 12/9/28, Fox Lake, Ill. BL/TR, 5'9", 160 lbs. Deb: 4/16/52

YEAR	TM/L	G	AB	R	H	2B	3B	HR	RBI	BB	SO	AVG	OBP	SLG	PRO+	BR	/A	RC	SB	CS	SBR	FR	POS	TPR
1952	Bos-N	7	4	3	0	0	0	0	0	1	1	.000	.200	.000	-42	-1	-1	0	0	0	0	-1	/S	-0.1
1953	Mil-N	2	2	1	0	0	0	0	1	0	0	.000	.000	.000	-99	-1	-1	0	0	0	0	0	H	0.0
1955	Bos-A	135	541	83	153	26	2	7	60	60	44	.283	.354	.377	89	-2	-8	78	6	0	2	-7	*S/3	0.0
1956	Bos-A	135	520	91	141	29	5	7	59	90	43	.271	.380	.387	92	5	-4	83	1	0	0	-4	*3S	-0.2
1957	Bos-A	127	477	76	120	18	4	10	42	55	53	.252	.329	.369	85	-6	-10	59	2	0	1	11	*S	1.2
1958	Bos-A	61	88	5	14	4	0	1	7	5	16	.159	.204	.239	20	-10	-10	4	0	0	0	-6	S	-1.2
1959	Bal-A	104	321	33	80	11	0	3	25	51	38	.249	.352	.312	86	-5	-4	37	2	4	-2	-12	S3/2	-1.3
1960	Bal-A	46	43	8	9	2	0	1	6	9	9	.209	.346	.326	84	-1	-1	5	0	0	0	8	2S/3	1.0
1961	Was-A	91	251	26	57	8	2	7	30	30	34	.227	.314	.359	81	-7	-7	30	2	2	-1	-4	3S/2O	-0.6
1962	Phi-N	102	248	30	51	8	2	4	20	29	43	.206	.291	.302	61	-14	-13	23	1	1	-0	-6	3S2	-1.3
1963	Phi-N	11	18	1	1	0	0	0	0	1	4	.056	.105	.056	-53	-3	-3	0	0	0	0	-2	/S3	-0.4
Total	11	821	2513	357	626	106	15	40	250	331	285	.249	.337	.351	82	-45	-62	320	14	7	0	-23	S3/2O	-2.9

■ **OLLIE KLEE**   Klee, Ollie Chester "Babe" b: 5/20/1900, Piqua, Ohio d: 2/9/77, Toledo, Ohio BL/TL, 5'9.5", 160 lbs. Deb: 8/10/25

YEAR	TM/L	G	AB	R	H	2B	3B	HR	RBI	BB	SO	AVG	OBP	SLG	PRO+	BR	/A	RC	SB	CS	SBR	FR	POS	TPR
1925	Cin-N	3	1	0	0	0	0	0	0	0	1	.000	.000	.000	-99	-0	-0	0	0	0	0	0	/O	0.0

■ **CHUCK KLEIN**   Klein, Charles Herbert b: 10/7/04, Indianapolis, Ind. d: 3/28/58, Indianapolis, Ind. BL/TR, 6', 185 lbs. Deb: 7/30/28 CH

YEAR	TM/L	G	AB	R	H	2B	3B	HR	RBI	BB	SO	AVG	OBP	SLG	PRO+	BR	/A	RC	SB	CS	SBR	FR	POS	TPR
1928	Phi-N	64	253	41	91	14	4	11	34	14	22	.360	.396	.577	146	18	16	55	0			1	O	1.4
1929	Phi-N	149	616	126	219	45	6	**43**	145	54	61	.356	.407	.657	149	53	47	158	5			4	*O	3.4
1930	Phi-N	156	648	**158**	250	**59**	8	40	170	54	50	.386	.436	.687	155	67	60	186	4			**28**	*O	**6.6**
1931	Phi-N	148	594	**121**	200	34	10	31	**121**	59	49	.337	.398	.584	149	**49**	**43**	140	7			-4	*O	3.0
1932	Phi-N	154	650	**152**	**226**	50	15	**38**	137	60	49	.348	.404	**.646**	158	**68**	58	171	20			8	*O	**5.4**
1933	Phi-N	152	606	101	**223**	44	7	28	**120**	56	36	**.368**	**.422**	**.602**	168	**69**	60	162	15			8	*O	**6.1**
1934	Chi-N	115	435	78	131	27	2	20	80	47	38	.301	.372	.510	136	20	22	86	3			-4	*O	1.2
1935	*Chi-N	119	434	71	127	14	4	21	73	41	42	.293	.355	.488	123	14	14	76	4			-3	*O	0.6
1936	Chi-N	29	109	19	32	5	0	5	18	16	14	.294	.384	.477	128	5	5	21	0			-0	O	0.3
	Phi-N	117	492	83	152	30	7	20	86	33	45	.309	.352	.520	120	20	13	92	6			-10	*O	-0.1
	Yr	146	601	102	184	35	7	25	104	49	59	.306	.358	.512	122	25	18	114	6			-10		0.2
1937	Phi-N	115	406	74	132	20	2	15	57	39	21	.325	.386	.495	127	21	17	81	3			-5	*O	0.7
1938	Phi-N	129	458	53	113	22	2	8	61	38	30	.247	.304	.356	83	-12	-11	52	7			-4	*O	-1.6
1939	Phi-N	25	47	8	9	2	1	1	9	10	4	.191	.333	.340	84	-1	-1	6	1			-0	O/1	-0.1
	Pit-N	85	270	37	81	16	4	11	47	26	17	.300	.361	.511	134	11	12	50	1			-4	O	0.7
	Yr	110	317	45	90	18	5	12	56	36	21	.284	.357	.486	127	10	11	57	2			-4		0.6
1940	Phi-N	116	354	39	77	16	2	7	37	44	30	.218	.304	.333	79	-12	-10	37	2			-5	O	-1.8
1941	Phi-N	50	73	6	9	0	0	1	3	10	6	.123	.229	.164	12	-8	-8	3	0			-1	O	-0.9
1942	Phi-N	14	14	0	1	0	0	0	0	0	2	.071	.071	.071	-61	-3	-3	0	0			0	H	-0.2
1943	Phi-N	12	20	0	2	0	0	0	3	0	3	.100	.100	.100	-44	-4	-4	0	1			-1	/O	-0.5
1944	Phi-N	4	7	1	1	0	0	0	0	0	2	.143	.143	.143	-42	-1	-1	0	0			1	/O	0.0
Total	17	1753	6486	1168	2076	398	74	300	1201	601	521	.320	.379	.543	135	375	330	1378	79			8	*O/1	24.2

■ **LOU KLEIN**   Klein, Louis Frank b: 10/22/18, New Orleans, La. d: 6/20/76, Metaire, La. BR/TR, 5'11", 167 lbs. Deb: 4/21/43 MC

YEAR	TM/L	G	AB	R	H	2B	3B	HR	RBI	BB	SO	AVG	OBP	SLG	PRO+	BR	/A	RC	SB	CS	SBR	FR	POS	TPR
1943	*StL-N	154	627	91	180	28	14	7	62	50	70	.287	.342	.410	112	12	9	91	9			-19	*2S	-0.1
1945	StL-N	19	57	12	13	4	1	1	6	14	9	.228	.389	.386	113	2	2	10	0			-0	/SO32	0.2
1946	StL-N	23	93	12	18	3	0	1	4	9	7	.194	.265	.258	47	-6	-7	7	1			-3	2	-0.9
1949	StL-N	58	114	25	25	6	0	2	12	22	20	.219	.355	.325	80	-2	-3	15	0			-4	S/23	-0.3
1951	Cle-A	2	2	0	0	0	0	0	0	0	1	.000	.000	.000	-99	-1	-1	0	0	0	0	0	H	0.0
	Phi-A	49	144	22	33	7	0	5	17	10	12	.229	.279	.382	76	-5	-6	15	0	0	0	-4	2	-0.7
	Yr	51	146	22	33	7	0	5	17	10	13	.226	.276	.377	74	-6	-6	15	0	0	0	-4		-0.7
Total	5	305	1037	162	269	48	15	16	101	105	119	.259	.330	.381	97	-1	-5	139	10	0		-30	2/S3O	-1.8

■ **RED KLEINOW**   Kleinow, John Peter b: 7/20/1879, Milwaukee, Wis. d: 10/9/29, New York, N.Y. BR/TR, 5'10", 165 lbs. Deb: 5/03/04

YEAR	TM/L	G	AB	R	H	2B	3B	HR	RBI	BB	SO	AVG	OBP	SLG	PRO+	BR	/A	RC	SB	CS	SBR	FR	POS	TPR
1904	NY-A	68	209	12	43	8	4	0	16	15		.206	.259	.282	70	-6	-7	17	4			-7	C/3O	-0.7
1905	NY-A	88	253	23	56	6	3	1	24	20		.221	.278	.281	71	-6	-9	23	7			-7	C/1	-0.8
1906	NY-A	96	268	30	59	9	3	0	31	24		.220	.284	.276	70	-6	-10	26	8			0	C/1	-0.1
1907	NY-A	90	269	30	71	6	4	0	26	24		.264	.324	.316	98	2	-0	31	5			-13	C/1	-0.5
1908	NY-A	96	279	16	47	3	2	1	13	22		.168	.229	.204	42	-17	-17	14	5			-5	C/2	-1.5
1909	NY-A	78	206	24	47	11	4	0	15	25		.228	.315	.320	100	1	0	23	7			-3	C	0.4
1910	NY-A	6	12	2	5	0	0	0	2	1		.417	.462	.417	166	1	1	3	2			0	C	0.2
	Bos-A	50	147	9	22	1	0	1	8	20		.150	.251	.177	34	-11	-11	7	3			5	C	0.0
	Yr	56	159	11	27	1	0	1	10	21		.170	.267	.195	44	-9	-10	9	5			5		0.2
1911	Bos-A	8	14	0	3	0	0	0	0	2		.214	.313	.214	48	-1	-1	1	1			0	/C	0.0
	Phi-N	4	8	0	1	1	0	0	0	0	1	.125	.125	.250	4	-1	-1	0	0			0	/C	0.0
Total	8	584	1665	146	354	45	20	3	135	153	1	.213	.279	.269	71	-44	-54	146	42			-30	C/1230	-3.0

■ **JAY KLEVEN**   Kleven, Jay Allen b: 12/2/49, Oakland, Cal. BR/TR, 6'2", 190 lbs. Deb: 6/20/76

YEAR	TM/L	G	AB	R	H	2B	3B	HR	RBI	BB	SO	AVG	OBP	SLG	PRO+	BR	/A	RC	SB	CS	SBR	FR	POS	TPR
1976	NY-N	2	5	0	1	0	0	0	2	0	1	.200	.200	.200	15	-1	-1	0	0	0	0	0	/C	0.0

■ **LOU KLIMCHOCK**   Klimchock, Louis Stephen b: 10/15/39, Hostetter, Pa. BL/TR, 5'11", 180 lbs. Deb: 9/27/58

YEAR	TM/L	G	AB	R	H	2B	3B	HR	RBI	BB	SO	AVG	OBP	SLG	PRO+	BR	/A	RC	SB	CS	SBR	FR	POS	TPR
1958	KC-A	2	10	2	2	0	0	1	1	0	1	.200	.200	.500	84	-0	-0	1	0	0	0	-1	/2	0.0
1959	KC-A	17	66	10	18	1	0	4	13	1	6	.273	.284	.470	101	-0	-0	8	0	0	0	-3	2	-0.2
1960	KC-A	10	10	0	3	0	0	0	0	0	0	.300	.300	.300	62	-1	-1	1	0	0	0	0	/2	0.0
1961	KC-A	57	121	8	26	4	1	1	16	5	13	.215	.246	.289	42	-10	-10	9	0	0	0	-5	1/O32	-1.5
1962	Mil-N	8	8	0	0	0	0	0	0	0	2	.000	.000	.000	-99	-2	-2	0	0	0	0	0	H	-0.1
1963	Was-A	9	14	1	2	0	0	0	2	0	1	.143	.143	.143	-20	-2	-2	0	0	0	0	1	/2	0.0
	Mil-N	24	46	6	9	1	0	0	1	0	12	.196	.196	.217	19	-5	-5	2	0	1	-1	0	1	-0.5
1964	Mil-N	10	21	3	7	2	0	0	2	1	2	.333	.364	.429	121	1	1	3	0	0	0	-3	/32	-0.1
1965	Mil-N	34	39	3	3	0	0	0	3	2	8	.077	.122	.077	-42	-7	-7	0	0	0	0	1	/1	-0.6
1966	NY-N	5	5	0	0	0	0	0	0	0	3	.000	.000	.000	-99	-1	-1	0	0	0	0	0	H	0.0
1968	Cle-A	11	15	0	2	0	0	0	3	1	0	.133	.188	.133	-2	-2	-2	0	0	0	0	-3	/312	-0.4

YEAR	TM/L	G	AB	R	H	2B	3B	HR	RBI	BB	SO	AVG	OBP	SLG	PRO+	BR	/A	RC	SB	CS	SBR	FR	POS	TPR
1969	Cle-A	90	258	26	74	13	2	6	26	18	14	.287	.333	.422	107	3	2	36	0	0	0	-16	32/C	-1.2
1970	Cle-A	41	56	5	9	0	0	1	2	3	9	.161	.217	.214	18	-6	-7	3	0	0	0	-1	/12	-0.6
Total	12	318	669	64	155	21	3	13	69	31	71	.232	.267	.330	63	-33	-35	63	0	1	-1	-30	/3210C	-5.2

■ BOBBY KLINE
Kline, John Robert b: 1/27/29, St.Petersburg, Fla BR/TR, 6', 179 lbs. Deb: 4/11/55

YEAR	TM/L	G	AB	R	H	2B	3B	HR	RBI	BB	SO	AVG	OBP	SLG	PRO+	BR	/A	RC	SB	CS	SBR	FR	POS	TPR
1955	Was-A	77	140	12	31	5	0	0	9	11	27	.221	.288	.257	50	-10	-9	11	0	0	0	13	S/23P	1.1

■ JOHNNY KLING
Kling, John "Noisy" b: 2/25/1875, Kansas City, Mo. d: 1/31/47, Kansas City, Mo. BR/TR, 5'9.5", 160 lbs. Deb: 9/11/00 M

YEAR	TM/L	G	AB	R	H	2B	3B	HR	RBI	BB	SO	AVG	OBP	SLG	PRO+	BR	/A	RC	SB	CS	SBR	FR	POS	TPR
1900	Chi-N	15	51	8	15	3	1	0	7	2		.294	.321	.392	102	-0	0	7	0			-3	C	0.0
1901	Chi-N	74	256	26	70	6	3	0	21	9		.273	.301	.320	85	-6	-5	28	8			-11	C/1O	-0.6
1902	Chi-N	114	431	49	123	19	3	0	57	29		.285	.330	.343	113	5	6	60	24			6	*C/S	2.4
1903	Chi-N	132	491	67	146	29	13	3	68	22		.297	.327	.428	120	8	10	79	23			-0	*C	1.9
1904	Chi-N	123	452	41	110	18	0	2	46	16		.243	.269	.296	76	-13	-13	41	7			-10	*CO/1	-1.5
1905	Chi-N	111	380	26	83	8	6	1	52	28		.218	.272	.279	64	-16	-17	35	13			0	*C/O1	-0.6
1906	*Chi-N	107	343	45	107	15	8	2	46	23		.312	.355	.420	136	16	14	58	14			3	C/O	2.7
1907	*Chi-N	104	334	44	95	15	8	1	43	27		.284	.338	.386	121	10	8	48	9			4	C/1	2.2
1908	*Chi-N	126	424	51	117	23	5	4	59	21		.276	.310	.382	118	9	7	54	16			0	*C/O1	1.5
1910	*Chi-N	91	297	31	80	17	2	2	32	37	27	.269	.354	.360	109	4	4	39	3			-5	C	0.3
1911	Chi-N	27	80	8	14	3	2	1	5	8	14	.175	.250	.300	53	-5	-5	6	1			5	C	0.1
	Bos-N	75	241	32	54	8	1	2	24	29	29	.224	.310	.290	63	-10	-13	22	0			-4	C/3	-1.1
	Yr	102	321	40	68	11	3	3	29	38	43	.212	.295	.293	61	-15	-18	28	1			0		-1.0
1912	Bos-N	81	252	26	80	10	3	2	30	15	30	.317	.356	.405	106	2	2	37	3			5	CM	1.0
1913	Cin-N	80	209	20	57	7	6	0	23	14	14	.273	.318	.364	95	-2	-2	24	2			10	CM	1.2
Total	13	1260	4241	474	1151	181	61	20	513	281	114	.271	.317	.357	101	2	-4	538	123			-1	*C/O13S	9.5

■ RUDY KLING
Kling, Rudolph A. b: 3/23/1870, St.Louis, Mo. d: 3/14/37, St.Louis, Mo. TR , 5'10", 178 lbs. Deb: 9/21/02

YEAR	TM/L	G	AB	R	H	2B	3B	HR	RBI	BB	SO	AVG	OBP	SLG	PRO+	BR	/A	RC	SB	CS	SBR	FR	POS	TPR
1902	StL-N	4	10	1	2	0	0	0	0	4		.200	.429	.200	101	0	0	2	1			-2	/S	0.0

■ JOE KLINGER
Klinger, Joseph John b: 8/2/02, Canonsburg, Pa. d: 7/31/60, Little Rock, Ark. BR/TR, 6', 190 lbs. Deb: 9/13/27

YEAR	TM/L	G	AB	R	H	2B	3B	HR	RBI	BB	SO	AVG	OBP	SLG	PRO+	BR	/A	RC	SB	CS	SBR	FR	POS	TPR
1927	NY-N	3	5	0	2	0	0	0	0	0	2	.400	.400	.400	115	0	0	1	0			0	/O	0.0
1930	Chi-A	4	8	0	3	0	0	0	1	0	0	.375	.375	.375	94	-0	-0	1	0	0	0	-1	/C1	0.0
Total	2	7	13	0	5	0	0	0	1	0	2	.385	.385	.385	102	0	0	2	0	0		-0	/1CO	0.0

■ NAP KLOZA
Kloza, John Clarence b: 9/7/03, Poland d: 6/11/62, Milwaukee, Wis. BR/TR, 5'11", 180 lbs. Deb: 8/16/31

YEAR	TM/L	G	AB	R	H	2B	3B	HR	RBI	BB	SO	AVG	OBP	SLG	PRO+	BR	/A	RC	SB	CS	SBR	FR	POS	TPR
1931	StL-A	3	7	1	1	0	0	0	1		4	.143	.250	.143	5	-1	-1	0	0	0	0	-0	/O	0.0
1932	StL-A	19	13	4	2	0	1	0	2	4	4	.154	.353	.308	69	-0	-1	2	0	0	0	-0	/O	0.0
Total	2	22	20	5	3	0	1	0	2	5	8	.150	.320	.250	48	-1	-2	2	0	0	0	0	/O	0.0

■ JOE KLUGMANN
Klugmann, Joe b: 3/26/1895, St.Louis, Mo. d: 7/18/51, Moberly, Mo. BR/TR, 5'11", 175 lbs. Deb: 9/23/21

YEAR	TM/L	G	AB	R	H	2B	3B	HR	RBI	BB	SO	AVG	OBP	SLG	PRO+	BR	/A	RC	SB	CS	SBR	FR	POS	TPR
1921	Chi-N	6	21	3	6	0	0	0	2	1	2	.286	.348	.286	69	-1	-1	2	0	1	-1	0	/2	0.0
1922	Chi-N	2	2	0	0	0	0	0	0	0	0	.000	.000	.000	-98	-1	-1	0	0	0	0	1	/2	0.0
1924	Bro-N	31	79	7	13	2	1	0	3	2	9	.165	.185	.215	7	-10	-10	3	0	0	0	-1	2/S	-1.2
1925	Cle-A	38	85	12	28	9	2	0	12	8	4	.329	.387	.482	119	2	2	16	3	1	0	-3	2/13	0.1
Total	4	77	187	22	47	11	3	0	17	11	15	.251	.296	.342	67	-9	-9	21	3	2	-0	-3	/213S	-1.1

■ ELMER KLUMPP
Klumpp, Elmer Edward b: 8/26/06, St.Louis, Mo. BR/TR, 6', 184 lbs. Deb: 4/17/34

YEAR	TM/L	G	AB	R	H	2B	3B	HR	RBI	BB	SO	AVG	OBP	SLG	PRO+	BR	/A	RC	SB	CS	SBR	FR	POS	TPR
1934	Was-A	12	15	2	2	0	0	0	0	0	1	.133	.188	.133	-17	-3	-3	0	0	0	0	-0	C	-0.1
1937	Bro-N	5	11	0	1	0	0	0	2	1		.091	.167	.091	-28	-2	-2	0	0			1	/C	0.0
Total	2	17	26	2	3	0	0	0	2	1	5	.115	.179	.115	-21	-5	-4	1	0	0		0	/C	-0.1

■ BILLY KLUSMAN
Klusman, William F. b: 3/24/1865, Cincinnati, Ohio d: 6/24/07, Cincinnati, Ohio BR/TR, 5'10.5", 185 lbs. Deb: 6/21/1888

YEAR	TM/L	G	AB	R	H	2B	3B	HR	RBI	BB	SO	AVG	OBP	SLG	PRO+	BR	/A	RC	SB	CS	SBR	FR	POS	TPR
1888	Bos-N	28	107	9	18	4	0	2	11	5	13	.168	.205	.262	49	-6	-6	7	3			-9	2	-1.3
1890	StL-a	15	65	9	18	4	1	1		1		.277	.288	.415	96	0	-1	8	1			-3	2	-0.2
Total	2	43	172	18	36	8	1	3	11	6	13	.209	.236	.320	68	-6	-7	15	4			-12	/2	-1.5

■ TED KLUSZEWSKI
Kluszewski, Theodore Bernard "Big Klu" b: 9/10/24, Argo, Ill. d: 3/29/88, Cincinnati, Ohio BL/TL, 6'2", 225 lbs. Deb: 4/18/47 C

YEAR	TM/L	G	AB	R	H	2B	3B	HR	RBI	BB	SO	AVG	OBP	SLG	PRO+	BR	/A	RC	SB	CS	SBR	FR	POS	TPR
1947	Cin-N	9	10	1	1	0	0	0	2	1	2	.100	.182	.100	-23	-2	-2	0	0			-0	/1	-0.1
1948	Cin-N	113	379	49	104	23	4	12	57	18	32	.274	.307	.451	107	-1	1	48	1			1	1	0.2
1949	Cin-N	136	531	63	164	26	2	8	68	19	24	.309	.333	.411	97	-3	-3	70	3			-6	*1	-0.9
1950	Cin-N	134	538	76	165	37	0	25	111	33	28	.307	.348	.515	123	16	16	89	3			-11	*1	0.0
1951	Cin-N	154	607	74	157	35	2	13	77	35	33	.259	.301	.387	83	-15	-17	69	6	2	1	-6	*1	-2.5
1952	Cin-N	135	497	62	159	24	11	16	86	47	28	.320	.383	.509	146	30	30	97	3	3	-1	-10	*1	1.5
1953	Cin-N	149	570	97	180	25	0	40	108	55	34	.316	.380	.570	142	35	34	126	2	0	1	-17	*1	1.4
1954	Cin-N	149	573	104	187	28	3	**49**	**141**	78	35	.326	.410	.642	165	57	55	151	0	2	-1	-4	*1	4.3
1955	Cin-N	153	612	116	**192**	25	0	47	113	66	40	.314	.384	.585	144	45	40	136	1	1	-0	-9	*1	1.9
1956	Cin-N	138	517	91	156	14	1	35	102	49	31	.302	.366	.536	130	27	23	99	1	0	0	-5	*1	1.3
1957	Cin-N	69	127	12	34	7	0	6	21	5	5	.268	.301	.465	95	-0	-1	17	0	0	0	0	1	-0.2
1958	Pit-N	100	301	29	88	13	4	4	37	26	16	.292	.351	.402	101	-0	-1	41	0	0	0	-5	1	-0.8
1959	Pit-N	60	122	11	32	10	1	2	17	5	14	.262	.291	.410	85	-3	-3	14	0	0	0	-1	1	-0.4
	*Chi-A	31	101	11	30	2	1	2	10	9	10	.297	.355	.396	107	1	1	13	0	1	-1	-2	1	-0.1
1960	Chi-A	81	181	20	53	9	0	5	39	22	10	.293	.369	.425	116	4	4	29	0	1	-1	-2	1	0.0
1961	LA-A	107	263	32	64	12	0	15	39	24	23	.243	.307	.460	91	-1	-4	37	0	0	0	-5	1	-1.4
Total	15	1718	5929	848	1766	290	29	279	1028	492	365	.298	.354	.498	122	190	175	1036	20	10		-81	*1	4.2

■ MICKEY KLUTTS
Klutts, Gene Ellis b: 9/20/54, Montebello, Cal. BR/TR, 5'11", 170 lbs. Deb: 7/07/76

YEAR	TM/L	G	AB	R	H	2B	3B	HR	RBI	BB	SO	AVG	OBP	SLG	PRO+	BR	/A	RC	SB	CS	SBR	FR	POS	TPR
1976	NY-A	2	3	0	0	0	0	0	0	0	1	.000	.000	.000	-99	-1	-1	0	0	0	0	0	/S	0.0
1977	NY-A	5	15	3	4	1	0	1	4	2	1	.267	.389	.533	150	1	1	3	0	1	-1	2	/3S	0.3
1978	NY-A	1	2	1	2	1	0	0	0	0	0	1.000	1.000	1.500	608	2	2	3	0	0	0	0	/3	0.2
1979	Oak-A	24	73	3	14	2	1	1	4	7	20	.192	.262	.288	51	-5	-5	5	0	1	-1	-4	S/23	-0.7
1980	Oak-A	75	197	20	53	14	0	4	21	13	41	.269	.314	.401	102	-2	-0	22	1	4	-2	-6	3/S2D	-0.7
1981	*Oak-A	15	46	9	17	0	0	5	11	2	9	.370	.396	.696	220	6	6	13	0	0	0	-5	3	0.1
1982	Oak-A	55	157	10	28	8	0	0	14	9	18	.178	.229	.229	26	-16	-15	8	0	0	0	-3	3	-1.8
1983	Tor-A	22	43	3	11	0	0	3	5	1	11	.256	.289	.465	98	0	-0	5	0	1	-1	-2	3/D	-0.2
Total	8	199	536	49	129	26	1	14	59	34	101	.241	.290	.371	84	-16	-12	60	1	7	-4	-17	3/S2D	-2.8

■ CLYDE KLUTTZ
Kluttz, Clyde Franklin b: 12/12/17, Rockwell, N.C. d: 5/12/79, Salisbury, N.C. BR/TR, 6', 193 lbs. Deb: 4/20/42

YEAR	TM/L	G	AB	R	H	2B	3B	HR	RBI	BB	SO	AVG	OBP	SLG	PRO+	BR	/A	RC	SB	CS	SBR	FR	POS	TPR
1942	Bos-N	72	210	21	56	10	1	1	31	7	13	.267	.294	.338	86	-5	-4	20	0			0	C	-0.2
1943	Bos-N	66	207	13	51	7	0	0	20	15	9	.246	.297	.280	68	-9	-8	17	0			2	C	-0.4
1944	Bos-N	81	229	20	64	12	2	2	19	13	14	.279	.318	.376	91	-2	-3	28	0			4	C	0.3
1945	Bos-N	25	81	9	24	4	1	0	10	2	6	.296	.313	.370	89	-1	-1	8	0			-0	C	-0.1
	NY-N	73	222	25	62	14	0	4	21	15	10	.279	.331	.396	100	-0	-2	29	1			-6	C	-0.5
	Yr	98	303	34	86	18	1	4	31	17	16	.284	.326	.389	97	-2	-2	37	1			-6		-0.6
1946	NY-N	5	8	0	3	0	0	0	1	0	1	.375	.375	.375	112	0	0	1	0			-0	/C	0.0
	StL-N	52	136	8	36	7	0	0	14	10	10	.265	.315	.316	76	-4	-4	14	0			2	C	-0.1
	Yr	57	144	8	39	7	0	0	15	10	11	.271	.318	.319	78	-4	-4	15	0			1		-0.1

YEAR	TM/L	G	AB	R	H	2B	3B	HR	RBI	BB	SO	AVG	OBP	SLG	PRO+	BR	/A	RC	SB	CS	SBR	FR	POS	TPR
1947	Pit-N	73	232	26	70	9	2	6	42	17	18	.302	.355	.435	106	3	2	37	1			3	C	0.6
1948	Pit-N	94	271	26	60	12	2	4	20	20	19	.221	.275	.325	61	-15	-16	25	3			0	C	-0.8
1951	StL-A	4	4	2	2	1	0	0	1	1	0	.500	.600	.750	256	1	1	2	0	0	0	1	/C	0.2
	Was-A	53	159	15	49	9	0	1	22	20	8	.308	.389	.384	111	3	3	26	0	0	0	-7	C	0.0
	Yr	57	163	17	51	10	0	1	23	21	8	.313	.395	.393	115	4	4	27	0	0	0	-6		0.2
1952	Was-A	58	144	7	33	5	0	1	11	12	11	.229	.293	.285	63	-8	-7	11	0	0	0	-1	C	-0.4
Total	9	656	1903	172	510	90	8	19	212	132	119	.268	.318	.354	86	-37	-39	218	5	0		-4	C	-1.4

■ OTTO KNABE
Knabe, Franz Otto "Dutch"   b: 6/12/1884, Carrick, Pa.   d: 5/17/61, Philadelphia, Pa.   BR/TR, 5'8", 175 lbs.   Deb: 10/03/05   M

YEAR	TM/L	G	AB	R	H	2B	3B	HR	RBI	BB	SO	AVG	OBP	SLG	PRO+	BR	/A	RC	SB	CS	SBR	FR	POS	TPR
1905	Pit-N	3	10	0	3	1	0	0	2	3		.300	.462	.400	156	1	1	2	0			0	/3	0.2
1907	Phi-N	129	444	67	113	16	9	1	34	52		.255	.333	.338	114	7	8	62	18			1	*2/O	1.2
1908	Phi-N	151	555	63	121	26	8	0	27	49		.218	.281	.294	83	-9	-11	56	27			11	*2	0.0
1909	Phi-N	113	402	40	94	13	3	0	34	35		.234	.308	.281	82	-7	-8	39	9			8	*2/O	0.0
1910	Phi-N	137	510	73	133	18	6	1	44	47	42	.261	.327	.325	87	-6	-8	62	15			14	*2	0.9
1911	Phi-N	142	528	99	125	15	6	1	42	94	35	.237	.352	.294	80	-10	-11	64	23			4	*2	-0.9
1912	Phi-N	126	426	56	120	11	4	0	46	55	20	.282	.366	.326	85	-4	-7	57	16			1	*2	-1.0
1913	Phi-N	148	571	70	150	25	7	2	53	45	26	.263	.320	.342	85	-8	-11	68	14			12	*2	-0.3
1914	Bal-F	147	469	45	106	26	2	2	42	53	28	.226	.307	.303	73	-14	-16	51	10			1	*2M	-1.3
1915	Bal-F	103	320	38	81	16	2	1	25	37	16	.253	.334	.325	93	-1	-2	40	7			7	2/OM	0.6
1916	Pit-N	28	89	4	17	3	1	0	9	6	6	.191	.258	.247	55	-5	-5	7	1			-0	2	-0.4
	Chi-N	51	145	17	40	8	0	0	7	9	18	.276	.327	.331	92	-0	-1	17	3			6	2/S3O	0.6
	Yr	79	234	21	57	11	1	0	16	15	24	.244	.300	.299	79	-4	-6	24	4			5		0.2
Total	11	1278	4469	572	1103	178	48	8	365	485	191	.247	.324	.313	86	-55	-72	526	143			64	*2/O3S	-0.4

■ COTTON KNAUPP
Knaupp, Henry Antone   b: 8/13/1889, San Antonio, Tex.   d: 7/6/67, New Orleans, La.   BR/TR, 5'9", 165 lbs.   Deb: 8/30/10

YEAR	TM/L	G	AB	R	H	2B	3B	HR	RBI	BB	SO	AVG	OBP	SLG	PRO+	BR	/A	RC	SB	CS	SBR	FR	POS	TPR
1910	Cle-A	18	59	3	14	3	1	0	11	8		.237	.338	.322	105	1	1	7	1			-8	S	-0.8
1911	Cle-A	13	39	2	4	1	0	0	0	0		.103	.103	.128	-35	-7	-7	1	3			2	S	-0.3
Total	2	31	98	5	18	4	1	0	11	8		.184	.252	.245	48	-6	-7	8	4			-6	/S	-1.1

■ ALAN KNICELY
Knicely, Alan Lee   b: 5/19/55, Harrisonburg, Va.   BR/TR, 6', 190 lbs.   Deb: 8/12/79

YEAR	TM/L	G	AB	R	H	2B	3B	HR	RBI	BB	SO	AVG	OBP	SLG	PRO+	BR	/A	RC	SB	CS	SBR	FR	POS	TPR
1979	Hou-N	7	6	0	0	0	0	0	0	2	3	.000	.250	.000	-27	-1	-1	0	0	0	0	-2	/C3	-0.2
1980	Hou-N	1	1	0	0	0	0	0	0	0	1	.000	.000	.000	-99	-0	-0	0	0	0	0	0	/H	0.0
1981	Hou-N	3	7	2	4	0	0	2	2	0	1	.571	.571	1.429	477	3	3	6	0	0	0	0	/CO	0.3
1982	Hou-N	59	133	10	25	2	0	2	12	14	30	.188	.270	.248	50	-9	-8	9	0	1	-1	-7	CO3	-1.6
1983	Cin-N	59	98	11	22	3	0	2	10	16	28	.224	.333	.316	78	-2	-3	9	0	2	-1	-1	C/O1	-0.3
1984	Cin-N	10	29	0	4	0	0	0	5	3	6	.138	.219	.138	2	-4	-4	1	0	0	0	0	/1C	-0.3
1985	Cin-N	48	158	17	40	9	0	5	26	16	34	.253	.326	.405	98	1	-0	20	0	0	0	-14	C	-1.2
	Phi-N	7	7	0	0	0	0	0	0	0	4	.000	.000	.000	-97	-2	-2	0	0	0	0	0	/1	-0.1
	Yr	55	165	17	40	9	0	5	26	16	38	.242	.313	.388	91	-1	-2	19	0	0	0	-14		-1.3
1986	StL-N	34	82	8	16	3	0	1	6	17	21	.195	.333	.268	68	-3	-3	9	1	1	-0	-1	1/C	-0.4
Total	8	228	521	48	111	17	0	12	61	68	128	.213	.306	.315	73	-18	-18	53	1	4	-2	-23	C/1O3	-3.8

■ AUSTIN KNICKERBOCKER
Knickerbocker, Austin Jay   b: 10/15/18, Bangall, N.Y.   BR/TR, 5'11", 185 lbs.   Deb: 4/19/47

YEAR	TM/L	G	AB	R	H	2B	3B	HR	RBI	BB	SO	AVG	OBP	SLG	PRO+	BR	/A	RC	SB	CS	SBR	FR	POS	TPR
1947	Phi-A	21	48	8	12	3	2	0	3	4		.250	.294	.396	89	-1	-1	5	0	1	-1	1	O	0.0

■ BILL KNICKERBOCKER
Knickerbocker, William Hart   b: 12/29/11, Los Angeles, Cal.   d: 9/8/63, Sebastopol, Cal.   BR/TR, 5'11", 170 lbs.   Deb: 4/12/33

YEAR	TM/L	G	AB	R	H	2B	3B	HR	RBI	BB	SO	AVG	OBP	SLG	PRO+	BR	/A	RC	SB	CS	SBR	FR	POS	TPR
1933	Cle-A	80	279	20	63	16	3	2	32	11	30	.226	.255	.326	51	-20	-21	22	1	4	-2	2	S	-1.4
1934	Cle-A	146	593	82	188	32	5	4	67	25	40	.317	.347	.408	93	-6	-8	82	6	6	-2	-7	*S	-0.5
1935	Cle-A	132	540	77	161	34	5	0	55	27	31	.298	.332	.380	82	-14	-15	64	2	12	-7	9	*S	-0.5
1936	Cle-A	155	618	81	182	35	3	8	73	56	30	.294	.354	.400	85	-14	-15	85	5	14	-7	-1	*S	-1.0
1937	StL-A	121	491	53	128	29	5	4	61	30	32	.261	.303	.365	67	-26	-26	55	3	2	-0	-13	*S/2	-2.9
1938	NY-A	46	128	15	32	8	3	1	21	11	10	.250	.309	.383	73	-6	-6	16	0	0	0	-2	2/S	-0.5
1939	NY-A	6	13	2	2	1	0	0	1	0	0	.154	.154	.231	-3	-2	-2	0	0	0	0	2	/2S	0.0
1940	NY-A	45	124	17	30	8	1	1	10	14	8	.242	.333	.347	80	-4	-3	15	1	1	-0	2	S3	-0.2
1941	Chi-A	89	343	51	84	23	2	7	29	41	27	.245	.329	.385	89	-6	-6	46	6	5	-1	-17	2	-1.4
1942	Phi-A	87·	289	25	73	12	0	1	19	29	30	.253	.323	.304	77	-8	-8	28	1	2	-1	-12	2/S	-1.8
Total	10	907	3418	423	943	198	27	28	368	244	238	.276	.326	.374	79	-107	-110	413	25	46	-20	-41	S2/3	-10.2

■ LON KNIGHT
Knight, Alonzo P.   b: 6/16/1853, Philadelphia, Pa.   d: 4/23/32, Philadelphia, Pa.   BR/TR, 5'11.5", 165 lbs.   Deb: 9/04/1875   MU

YEAR	TM/L	G	AB	R	H	2B	3B	HR	RBI	BB	SO	AVG	OBP	SLG	PRO+	BR	/A	RC	SB	CS	SBR	FR	POS	TPR
1875	Ath-n	13	47	4	6	2	0	0		0		.128	.128	.170	2	-4	-5	1					P	0.0
1876	Phi-N	55	240	32	60	9	3	0	24	2	2	.250	.256	.313	89	-3	-3	20				-6	P1/O2	0.0
1880	Wor-N	49	201	31	48	11	3	0	21	5	8	.239	.257	.323	88	-1	-3	17				4	O	0.0
1881	Det-N	83	340	67	92	16	3	1	52	23	21	.271	.317	.344	104	4	2	38				-1	*O/21	0.0
1882	Det-N	86	347	39	72	12	6	0	24	16	21	.207	.242	.277	66	-13	-13	24				-1	*O/1	-1.3
1883	Phi-a	97	429	98	108	23	9	1		21		.252	.287	.354	97	3	-3	45				0	*O/32M	-0.1
1884	Phi-a	108	448	94	131	18	12	1		10		.271	.287	.364	106	6	2	52				11	*O/P1M	1.0
1885	Phi-a	29	119	17	25	1	1	0		9		.210	.271	.235	60	-4	-6	8				4	O/P	-0.1
	Pro-N	25	81	8	13	1	0	0	8	11	17	.160	.261	.173	44	-5	-4	4				2	O/P	-0.1
Total	7	532	2241	386	549	91	37	3	129	97	69	.245	.277	.323	90	-13	-28	207				14	O/P123	-0.6

■ RAY KNIGHT
Knight, Charles Ray   b: 12/28/52, Albany, Ga.   BR/TR, 6'1", 185 lbs.   Deb: 9/10/74

YEAR	TM/L	G	AB	R	H	2B	3B	HR	RBI	BB	SO	AVG	OBP	SLG	PRO+	BR	/A	RC	SB	CS	SBR	FR	POS	TPR
1974	Cin-N	14	11	1	2	1	0	0	2	1	2	.182	.250	.273	47	-1	-1	1	0	0	0	1	3	0.0
1977	Cin-N	80	92	8	24	5	1	1	13	9	16	.261	.327	.370	85	-2	-2	12	1	1	-0	5	32/OS	0.4
1978	Cin-N	83	65	7	13	3	0	1	4	3	13	.200	.235	.292	47	-5	-5	3	0	0	0	6	3/201S	0.1
1979	*Cin-N	150	551	64	175	37	4	10	79	38	57	.318	.365	.454	121	16	16	85	4	4	-1	-16	*3	-0.7
1980	Cin-N	162	618	71	163	39	7	14	78	36	62	.264	.309	.417	101	-1	-1	72	1	2	-1	-15	*3	-1.8
1981	Cin-N	106	386	43	100	23	1	6	34	33	51	.259	.324	.370	95	-2	-3	42	2	4	-2	-13	*3	-2.4
1982	Hou-N	158	609	72	179	36	6	6	70	48	58	.294	.350	.402	119	8	14	83	2	5	-2	-2	13	0.3
1983	Hou-N	145	507	43	154	36	4	9	70	42	60	.304	.362	.444	130	15	19	77	3	5	-2	-10	*1	0.0
1984	Hou-N	88	278	15	62	10	0	2	29	14	30	.223	.263	.281	67	-18	-15	20	0	3	-2	-2	31	-2.1
	NY-N	27	93	13	26	4	0	1	6	7	13	.280	.337	.355	96	-1	-0	11	0	0	0	-4	3/1	-0.4
	Yr	115	371	28	88	14	0	3	35	21	43	.237	.282	.299	67	-18	-16	31	0	3	-2	-6		-2.5
1985	NY-N	90	271	22	59	12	0	6	36	13	32	.218	.256	.328	64	-14	-13	18	1	1	-0	-10	3/21	-2.5
1986	*NY-N	137	486	51	145	24	2	11	76	40	63	.298	.357	.424	118	9	11	70	2	1	-0	-11	*3/1	-0.2
1987	Bal-A	150	563	46	144	24	0	14	65	39	90	.256	.311	.373	82	-16	-14	63	0	0	0	10	*3D/1	-0.5
1988	Det-A	105	299	34	65	12	2	3	33	20	30	.217	.273	.301	63	-16	-14	23	1	1	-0	-2	1D3/O	-2.0
Total	13	1495	4829	490	1311	266	27	84	595	343	579	.271	.325	.390	99	-26	-10	579	14	25	-11	-65	*31/D2OS	-11.8

■ JOHN KNIGHT
Knight, John Wesley "Schoolboy"   b: 10/6/1885, Philadelphia, Pa.   d: 12/19/65, Walnut Creek, Cal.   BR/TR, 6'2.5", 180 lbs.   Deb: 4/14/05

YEAR	TM/L	G	AB	R	H	2B	3B	HR	RBI	BB	SO	AVG	OBP	SLG	PRO+	BR	/A	RC	SB	CS	SBR	FR	POS	TPR
1905	Phi-A	88	325	28	66	12	1	3	29	19		.203	.225	.255	58	-15	-16	23	4			-28	S/3	-4.6
1906	Phi-A	74	253	29	49	7	2	3	20	19		.194	.250	.273	63	-10	-11	20	6			3	3/2	-0.5
1907	Phi-A	40	139	6	29	7	1	0	12	10		.209	.262	.273	71	-4	-5	11	-0			3		-0.2
	Bos-A	98	360	31	78	9	3	2	29	19		.217	.256	.275	72	-12	-12	28	8			8	3/2	0.2
	Yr	138	499	37	107	16	4	2	41	29		.214	.258	.275	71	-16	-16	39	8			9		0.0
1909	NY-A	116	360	46	85	8	5	0	40	37		.236	.311	.286	88	-4	-4	38	15			1	S12	-0.1

YEAR	TM/L	G	AB	R	H	2B	3B	HR	RBI	BB	SO	AVG	OBP	SLG	PRO+	BR	/A	RC	SB	CS	SBR	FR	POS	TPR
1910	NY-A	117	414	58	129	25	4	3	45	34		.312	.372	.413	138	21	19	72	23			-1	S1/230	2.2
1911	NY-A	132	470	69	126	16	7	3	62	42		.268	.342	.351	88	-4	-8	63	18			3	S12/3	0.3
1912	Was-A	32	93	10	15	2	1	0	9	16		.161	.284	.204	40	-7	-7	7	4			-5	2/1	-1.1
1913	NY-A	70	250	24	59	10	0	0	24	25	27	.236	.310	.276	72	-8	-9	23	7			8	12	0.0
Total	8	767	2664	301	636	96	24	14	270	211	27	.239	.300	.309	84	-43	-52	285	86			-13	S312/O	-3.8

■ JOE KNIGHT
Knight, Jonas William "Quiet Joe"
b: 9/28/1859, Point Stanley, Ont., Canada d: 10/18/38, St.Thomas, Ont., Can. BL/TL, 5'11", 185 lbs. Deb: 5/16/1884

YEAR	TM/L	G	AB	R	H	2B	3B	HR	RBI	BB	SO	AVG	OBP	SLG	PRO+	BR	/A	RC	SB	CS	SBR	FR	POS	TPR
1884	Phi-N	6	24	2	6	3	0	0	2	0	2	.250	.250	.375	98	-0	-0	2				0	/P	0.0
1890	Cin-N	127	481	67	150	26	8	4	67	38	31	.312	.367	.424	133	19	19	83	17			-8	*O	0.8
Total	2	133	505	69	156	29	8	4	69	38	33	.309	.362	.422	132	19	19	85	17			-8	O/P	0.8

■ PETE KNISELY
Knisely, Peter Cole b: 8/11/1887, Waynesburg, Pa. d: 7/1/48, Brownsville, Pa. BR/TR, 5'9", 185 lbs. Deb: 9/04/12

YEAR	TM/L	G	AB	R	H	2B	3B	HR	RBI	BB	SO	AVG	OBP	SLG	PRO+	BR	/A	RC	SB	CS	SBR	FR	POS	TPR
1912	Cin-N	21	67	10	22	7	3	0	7	4	5	.328	.375	.522	148	4	4	14	3			-2	O/2S	0.1
1913	Chi-N	2	2	0	0	0	0	0	0	0	1	.000	.000	.000	-99	-1	-1	0	0			0	H	0.0
1914	Chi-N	37	69	5	9	0	1	0	5	5	6	.130	.200	.159	7	-8	-8	2	0			3	O	-0.4
1915	Chi-N	64	134	12	33	9	0	0	17	15	18	.246	.331	.313	95	-0	-0	14	1	2	-1	-4	O/2	-0.6
Total	4	124	272	27	64	16	4	0	29	24	30	.235	.307	.324	86	-5	-5	30	4	2		-3	/O2S	-0.9

■ MIKE KNODE
Knode, Kenneth Thomson b: 11/8/1895, Westminster, Md. d: 12/20/80, South Bend, Ind. BR/TR, 5'10", 160 lbs. Deb: 6/28/20

YEAR	TM/L	G	AB	R	H	2B	3B	HR	RBI	BB	SO	AVG	OBP	SLG	PRO+	BR	/A	RC	SB	CS	SBR	FR	POS	TPR
1920	StL-N	42	65	11	15	1	1	0	12	5	6	.231	.306	.277	71	-2	-2	6	0	1	-1	0	/O2S3	-0.2

■ RAY KNODE
Knode, Robert Troxell "Bob" b: 1/28/01, Westminster, Md. d: 4/13/82, Battle Creek, Mich BL/TL, 5'10", 160 lbs. Deb: 6/30/23

YEAR	TM/L	G	AB	R	H	2B	3B	HR	RBI	BB	SO	AVG	OBP	SLG	PRO+	BR	/A	RC	SB	CS	SBR	FR	POS	TPR
1923	Cle-A	22	38	7	11	0	0	2	4	2	4	.289	.325	.447	102	-0	-0	6	1	0	0	0	1	0.0
1924	Cle-A	11	37	6	9	1	0	0	4	3	0	.243	.300	.270	47	-3	-3	3	2	1	0	1	1	-0.1
1925	Cle-A	45	108	13	27	5	0	0	11	10	4	.250	.314	.296	55	-7	-7	10	3	3	-1	1	1	-0.7
1926	Cle-A	31	24	6	8	1	1	0	4	3	4	.333	.407	.458	124	1	1	5	0	0	0	1	1	0.1
Total	4	109	207	32	55	7	1	2	23	18	12	.266	.324	.338	70	-9	-9	24	6	4	-1	2	/1	-0.7

■ PUNCH KNOLL
Knoll, Charles Elmer b: 10/7/1881, Evansville, Ind. d: 2/8/60, Evansville, Ind. BR/TR, 5'7.5", 170 lbs. Deb: 4/27/05

YEAR	TM/L	G	AB	R	H	2B	3B	HR	RBI	BB	SO	AVG	OBP	SLG	PRO+	BR	/A	RC	SB	CS	SBR	FR	POS	TPR
1905	Was-A	79	244	24	52	10	5	0	29	9		.213	.241	.295	74	-8	-7	20	3			2	O/C1	-0.7

■ BOBBY KNOOP
Knoop, Robert Frank b: 10/18/38, Sioux City, Iowa BR/TR, 6'1", 170 lbs. Deb: 4/13/64 C

YEAR	TM/L	G	AB	R	H	2B	3B	HR	RBI	BB	SO	AVG	OBP	SLG	PRO+	BR	/A	RC	SB	CS	SBR	FR	POS	TPR
1964	LA-A	162	486	42	105	8	1	7	38	46	109	.216	.291	.280	66	-26	-20	39	3	2	-0	**37**	*2	3.5
1965	Cal-A	142	465	47	125	24	4	7	43	31	101	.269	.315	.383	99	-2	-1	56	3	2	-0	13	*2	2.0
1966	Cal-A	161	590	54	137	18	11	17	72	43	144	.232	.285	.386	94	-8	-6	61	1	5	-3	17	*2	2.3
1967	Cal-A	159	511	51	125	18	5	9	38	44	136	.245	.306	.352	98	-4	-2	54	2	2	-1	1	*2	0.4
1968	Cal-A	152	494	48	123	20	4	3	39	35	128	.249	.303	.324	93	-6	-4	47	3	2	-0	16	*2	1.9
1969	Cal-A	27	71	5	14	1	0	1	6	13	16	.197	.321	.254	66	-3	-3	6	1	3	-2	2	2	-0.1
	Chi-A	104	345	34	79	14	1	6	41	35	68	.229	.304	.328	73	-11	-13	34	2	0	1	23	*2	1.5
	Yr	131	416	39	93	15	1	7	47	48	84	.224	.307	.315	72	-14	-16	40	3	3	-1	25		1.4
1970	Chi-A	130	402	34	92	13	2	5	36	34	79	.229	.292	.308	63	-19	-21	37	0	1	-1	**35**	*2	2.7
1971	KC-A	72	161	14	33	8	1	1	11	15	36	.205	.273	.286	59	-9	-9	12	1	0	0	-1	2/3	-0.7
1972	KC-A	44	97	8	23	5	0	0	7	9	16	.237	.302	.289	77	-3	-3	8	0	0	0	8	2/3	0.8
Total	9	1153	3622	337	856	129	29	56	331	305	833	.236	.298	.334	83	-91	-81	353	16	17	-5	150	*2/3	14.3

■ GEORGE KNOTHE
Knothe, George Bertram b: 1/12/1898, Bayonne, N.J. d: 7/3/81, Dover, N.J. BR/TR, 5'10", 165 lbs. Deb: 4/25/32

YEAR	TM/L	G	AB	R	H	2B	3B	HR	RBI	BB	SO	AVG	OBP	SLG	PRO+	BR	/A	RC	SB	CS	SBR	FR	POS	TPR
1932	Phi-N	6	12	2	1	1	0	0	0	0	0	.083	.083	.167	-31	-2	-2	0	0			-1	/2	-0.2

■ FRITZ KNOTHE
Knothe, Wilfred Edgar b: 5/1/03, Passaic, N.J. d: 3/27/63, Passaic, N.J. BR/TR, 5'10.5", 180 lbs. Deb: 4/12/32

YEAR	TM/L	G	AB	R	H	2B	3B	HR	RBI	BB	SO	AVG	OBP	SLG	PRO+	BR	/A	RC	SB	CS	SBR	FR	POS	TPR
1932	Bos-N	89	344	45	82	19	1	1	36	39	37	.238	.318	.308	72	-14	-12	36	5			-3	3	-0.7
1933	Bos-N	44	158	15	36	5	2	1	6	13	25	.228	.291	.304	76	-6	-5	15	1			-6	3/S	-0.9
	Phi-N	41	113	10	17	2	0	0	11	6	19	.150	.193	.168	3	-14	-16	3	2			15	3/2	0.0
	Yr	85	271	25	53	7	2	1	17	19	44	.196	.251	.247	42	-20	-21	17	3			8		-0.9
Total	2	174	615	70	135	26	3	2	53	58	81	.220	.289	.281	59	-34	-32	55	8			5	3/S2	-1.6

■ JOE KNOTTS
Knotts, Joseph Steven b: 3/3/1884, Greensboro, N.C. d: 9/15/50, Philadelphia, Pa. BR/TR, Deb: 9/18/07

YEAR	TM/L	G	AB	R	H	2B	3B	HR	RBI	BB	SO	AVG	OBP	SLG	PRO+	BR	/A	RC	SB	CS	SBR	FR	POS	TPR
1907	Bos-N	3	8	0	0	0	0	0	0	0	1	.000	.111	.000	-65	-1	-1	0	0			0	/C	-0.1

■ ED KNOUFF
Knouff, Edward "Fred" b: 1867, Philadelphia, Pa. d: 9/14/1900, Philadelphia, Pa. BR/TR, 210 lbs. Deb: 7/01/1885

YEAR	TM/L	G	AB	R	H	2B	3B	HR	RBI	BB	SO	AVG	OBP	SLG	PRO+	BR	/A	RC	SB	CS	SBR	FR	POS	TPR
1885	Phi-a	14	48	5	9	0	0	0		2		.188	.220	.188	30	-4	-4	2				1	P/O	0.0
1886	Bal-a	1	3	0	0	0	0	0		0		.000	.250	.000	-18	-0	-0	0	0			1	/P	0.0
1887	Bal-a	9	31	4	9	0	0	0		1		.290	.313	.290	75	-1	-1	3	1			-1	/PO	0.0
	StL-a	15	56	4	10	1	2	0		1		.179	.207	.268	30	-5	-6	3	1			-2	/OP	-0.5
	Yr	24	87	8	19	1	2	0		2		.218	.244	.276	44	-6	-7	7	2			-3		-0.5
1888	StL-a	9	31	1	3	0	0	0	1	3		.097	.200	.097	-2	-3	-4	1	1			-1	/P	0.0
	Cle-a	2	6	0	1	0	0	0	0	1		.167	.286	.333	104	0	0	1	0			1	/P2	0.0
	Yr	11	37	1	4	1	0	0	1	4		.108	.214	.135	14	-3	-4	1	1			-1		0.0
1889	Phi-a	3	12	2	3	1	0	0	2	1	1	.250	.308	.333	86	-0	-0	2	1			-0	/P	0.0
Total	5	53	187	16	35	3	2	0	3	9	1	.187	.236	.225	37	-14	-15	12	4			-3	/PO2	-0.5

■ JAKE KNOWDELL
Knowdell, Jacob Augustus b: 7/27/1840, Brooklyn, N.Y. 5'7.5", 148 lbs. Deb: 6/20/1874

YEAR	TM/L	G	AB	R	H	2B	3B	HR	RBI	BB	SO	AVG	OBP	SLG	PRO+	BR	/A	RC	SB	CS	SBR	FR	POS	TPR
1874	Atl-n	23	84	8	12	1	1	0		2		.143	.163	.179	10	-8	-8	3					C/O	-0.3
1875	Atl-n	43	161	17	32	3	0	0		2		.199	.209	.217	55	-8	-5	7					C/SO	-0.3
1878	Mil-N	4	14	2	3	1	0	0	2	0	3	.214	.214	.286	59	-1	-1	1				-1	/COS	0.0
Total	2 n	66	245	25	44	4	1	0		4		.180	.193	.204	38	-16	-11	10					/CSO	-0.6

■ JIMMY KNOWLES
Knowles, James "Darby" b: 1859, Toronto, Ont., Canada 5'9", 160 lbs. Deb: 5/02/1884

YEAR	TM/L	G	AB	R	H	2B	3B	HR	RBI	BB	SO	AVG	OBP	SLG	PRO+	BR	/A	RC	SB	CS	SBR	FR	POS	TPR
1884	Pit-a	46	182	19	42	5	7	0		5		.231	.259	.335	93	-1	-1	16				-0	1	-0.3
	Bro-a	41	153	19	36	5	1	1		3		.235	.255	.301	82	-3	-3	12				1	13	-0.2
	Yr	87	335	38	78	10	8	1		8		.233	.257	.319	88	-4	-4	28				1		-0.5
1886	Was-N	115	443	43	94	16	11	3	35	15	73	.212	.238	.318	72	-18	-14	39	20			26	23	1.5
1887	NY-a	16	60	12	15	1	1	0		1		.250	.262	.300	61	-3	-3	6	6			-3	2/3	-0.4
1890	Roc-a	123	491	83	138	12	8	5		59		.281	.359	.369	127	11	17	87	55			7	*3	2.0
1892	NY-N	16	59	9	9	1	0	0	7	6	8	.153	.231	.169	23	-5	-5	3	2			-4	3/S	-0.7
Total	5	357	1388	185	334	40	28	9	42	89	81	.241	.288	.329	93	-19	-9	164	83			27	3/21S	1.9

■ ANDY KNOX
Knox, Andrew Jackson "Dasher" b: 1/6/1864, Philadelphia, Pa. d: 9/14/40, Philadelphia, Pa. BR/TR, Deb: 9/19/1890

YEAR	TM/L	G	AB	R	H	2B	3B	HR	RBI	BB	SO	AVG	OBP	SLG	PRO+	BR	/A	RC	SB	CS	SBR	FR	POS	TPR
1890	Phi-a	21	75	6	19	3	0	0		9		.253	.333	.293	90	-1	-1	9	5			-1	1	-0.2

■ CLIFF KNOX
Knox, Clifford Hiram "Bud" b: 1/7/02, Coalville, Iowa d: 9/24/65, Oskaloosa, Iowa BB/TR, 5'11.5", 178 lbs. Deb: 7/01/24

YEAR	TM/L	G	AB	R	H	2B	3B	HR	RBI	BB	SO	AVG	OBP	SLG	PRO+	BR	/A	RC	SB	CS	SBR	FR	POS	TPR
1924	Pit-N	6	18	1	4	0	0	0	2	2	0	.222	.300	.222	41	-1	-1	1	0	0	0	3	/C	0.1

■ JOHN KNOX
Knox, John Clinton b: 7/26/48, Newark, N.J. BL/TR, 6', 170 lbs. Deb: 8/01/72

YEAR	TM/L	G	AB	R	H	2B	3B	HR	RBI	BB	SO	AVG	OBP	SLG	PRO+	BR	/A	RC	SB	CS	SBR	FR	POS	TPR
1972	*Det-A	14	13	1	1	1	0	0	0	1	2	.077	.143	.154	-11	-2	-2	0	0	0	0	4	/2	0.2
1973	Det-A	12	32	1	9	1	0	0	3	3	3	.281	.343	.313	80	-1	-1	4	1	1	-0	-3	/2	-0.3

(upper-right margin, rotated fragment, partly cut off: "1042 … YEAR … 1952 1953 Tot…")

YEAR	TM/L	G	AB	R	H	2B	3B	HR	RBI	BB	SO	AVG	OBP	SLG	PRO+	BR	/A	RC	SB	CS	FR	/A	Pos	TPR
1974	Det-A	55	88	11	27	1	1	0	6	6	13	.307	.351	.341	96	0	-0	9	5					
1975	Det-A	43	86	8	23	1	0	0	2	10	9	.267	.344	.279	74	-2	-3	8	1					
Total	4	124	219	21	60	4	1	0	11	20	27	.274	.335	.301	79	-4	-5	21	7					

■ NICK KOBACK
Koback, Nicholas Nicholie b: 7/19/35, Hartford, Conn. BR/TR, 6', 187 lbs. Deb: 7/29/53

YEAR	TM/L	G	AB	R	H	2B	3B	HR	RBI	BB	SO	AVG	OBP	SLG	PRO+	BR	/A	RC	SB	CS	FR	/A	Pos	TPR
1953	Pit-N	7	16	1	2	0	1	0	0	1	4	.125	.176	.250	10	-2	-2	0	0	0	0			
1954	Pit-N	4	10	0	0	0	0	0	0	0	8	.000	.000	.000	-99	-3	-3	0	0	0	0	0	/C	
1955	Pit-N	5	7	0	2	0	0	0	0	0	1	.286	.286	.286	53	-0	-0	1	0	0	0	0	/C	
Total	3	16	33	1	4	0	1	0	0	1	13	.121	.147	.182	-15	-6	-6	1	0	0	0	-2	/C	-0.5

■ BARNEY KOCH
Koch, Barnett b: 3/23/23, Campbell, Neb. d: 6/6/87, Tacoma, Wash. BR/TR, 5'8", 140 lbs. Deb: 7/23/44

YEAR	TM/L	G	AB	R	H	2B	3B	HR	RBI	BB	SO	AVG	OBP	SLG	PRO+	BR	/A	RC	SB	CS	FR	/A	Pos	TPR
1944	Bro-N	33	96	11	21	2	0	0	1	3	9	.219	.242	.240	37	-8	-8	6	0			-6	2/S	-1.0

■ BRAD KOCHER
Kocher, Bradley Wilson b: 1/16/1888, White Haven, Pa. d: 1/13/65, White Haven, Pa. BR/TR, 5'11", 188 lbs. Deb: 4/24/12

YEAR	TM/L	G	AB	R	H	2B	3B	HR	RBI	BB	SO	AVG	OBP	SLG	PRO+	BR	/A	RC	SB	CS	FR	/A	Pos	TPR
1912	Det-A	29	63	5	13	3	1	0	9	2		.206	.231	.286	49	-5	-4	4	0			-3	C	-0.4
1915	NY-N	4	11	3	5	0	1	0	2	0	1	.455	.455	.636	243	2	2	3	0			-1	/C	0.1
1916	NY-N	34	65	1	7	2	0	0	1	2	10	.108	.134	.138	-17	-9	-9	1	0			-6	C	-1.5
Total	3	67	139	9	25	5	2	0	12	4	11	.180	.203	.245	34	-12	-11	9	0			-9	/C	-1.8

■ PETE KOEGEL
Koegel, Peter John b: 7/31/47, Mineola, N.Y. BR/TR, 6'6.5", 230 lbs. Deb: 9/01/70

YEAR	TM/L	G	AB	R	H	2B	3B	HR	RBI	BB	SO	AVG	OBP	SLG	PRO+	BR	/A	RC	SB	CS	FR	/A	Pos	TPR
1970	Mil-A	7	8	2	2	0	0	1	1	1	3	.250	.333	.625	157	1	1	2	0	0	0	0	/O	0.0
1971	Mil-A	2	3	0	0	0	0	0	0	2	2	.000	.400	.000	22	-0	-0	0	0	0	0	-0	/1	0.0
	Phi-N	12	26	1	6	1	0	0	3	2	7	.231	.286	.269	58	-1	-1	2	0	0	0	-0	/CO	-0.1
1972	Phi-N	41	49	3	7	2	0	0	1	6	16	.143	.236	.184	20	-5	-5	2	0	0	0	-2	/1C3O	-0.7
Total	3	62	86	6	15	3	0	1	5	11	28	.174	.268	.244	45	-6	-6	6	0	0	0	-2	/C13O	-0.8

■ BEN KOEHLER
Koehler, Benard James b: 1/26/1877, Schoerndorn, Germany d: 5/21/61, South Bend, Ind. BR/TR, 5'10.5", 175 lbs. Deb: 4/23/05

YEAR	TM/L	G	AB	R	H	2B	3B	HR	RBI	BB	SO	AVG	OBP	SLG	PRO+	BR	/A	RC	SB	CS	FR	/A	Pos	TPR
1905	StL-A	142	536	55	127	14	6	2	47	32		.237	.280	.297	90	-9	-6	53	22			6	*O1/2	-0.7
1906	StL-A	66	186	27	41	1	1	0	15	24		.220	.310	.237	77	-4	-4	18	9			-4	O/2S3	-1.0
Total	2	208	722	82	168	15	7	2	62	56		.233	.288	.281	86	-14	-10	71	31			2	O/213S	-1.7

■ PIP KOEHLER
Koehler, Horace Levering b: 1/16/02, Gilbert, Pa. d: 12/8/86, Tacoma, Wash. BR/TR, 5'10", 165 lbs. Deb: 4/22/25

YEAR	TM/L	G	AB	R	H	2B	3B	HR	RBI	BB	SO	AVG	OBP	SLG	PRO+	BR	/A	RC	SB	CS	FR	/A	Pos	TPR
1925	NY-N	12	2	1	0	0	0	0	0	0	1	.000	.000	.000	-99	-1	-1	0	0	0	0	2	/O	0.1

■ LEN KOENECKE
Koenecke, Leonard George b: 1/18/04, Baraboo, Wis. d: 9/17/35, Toronto, Ont., Can BL/TR, 5'11", 180 lbs. Deb: 4/12/32

YEAR	TM/L	G	AB	R	H	2B	3B	HR	RBI	BB	SO	AVG	OBP	SLG	PRO+	BR	/A	RC	SB	CS	FR	/A	Pos	TPR
1932	NY-N	42	137	33	35	5	0	4	14	11	13	.255	.320	.380	89	-2	-2	17	3			-7	O	-1.0
1934	Bro-N	123	460	79	147	31	7	14	73	70	38	.320	.411	.509	152	31	34	103	8			-1	*O	2.6
1935	Bro-N	100	325	43	92	13	2	4	27	43	45	.283	.369	.372	102	1	2	49	0			-8	O	-0.8
Total	3	265	922	155	274	49	9	22	114	124	96	.297	.383	.441	125	30	34	169	11			-15	O	0.8

■ MARK KOENIG
Koenig, Mark Anthony b: 7/19/02, San Francisco, Cal BB/TR, 6', 180 lbs. Deb: 9/08/25

YEAR	TM/L	G	AB	R	H	2B	3B	HR	RBI	BB	SO	AVG	OBP	SLG	PRO+	BR	/A	RC	SB	CS	FR	/A	Pos	TPR
1925	NY-A	28	110	14	23	6	1	0	4	5	4	.209	.243	.282	34	-12	-11	7	0	1	-1	-3	S	-0.9
1926	*NY-A	147	617	93	167	26	8	5	62	43	37	.271	.319	.363	79	-22	-20	72	4	3	-1	-0	*S	-0.9
1927	*NY-A	123	526	99	150	20	11	3	62	25	21	.285	.320	.382	84	-16	-13	62	3	2	-0	14	*S	1.0
1928	*NY-A	132	533	89	170	19	10	4	63	32	19	.319	.360	.415	106	2	4	78	3	5	-2	-20	*S	-0.5
1929	NY-A	116	373	44	109	27	5	3	41	23	17	.292	.335	.416	99	-5	-2	52	1	1	-0	-13	S3/2	-0.6
1930	NY-A	21	74	9	17	5	0	0	9	6	5	.230	.296	.297	53	-5	-5	7	0	0	0	2	S	
	Det-A	76	267	37	64	9	2	1	16	20	15	.240	.295	.300	50	-20	-21	25	2	0	1	-14	S/P3O	-2.4
	Yr	97	341	46	81	14	2	1	25	26	20	.238	.295	.299	51	-25	-25	32	2	0	1	-13		-2.4
1931	Det-A	106	364	33	92	24	4	1	39	14	12	.253	.282	.349	63	-19	-21	36	8	2	1	-23	2S/P	-3.3
1932	*Chi-N	33	102	15	36	5	1	3	11	3	5	.353	.377	.510	137	5	5	19	0			10	S	1.7
1933	Chi-N	80	218	32	62	12	1	3	25	15	9	.284	.330	.390	105	1	1	28	5			5	3S/2	0.9
1934	Cin-N	151	633	60	172	26	6	1	67	15	24	.272	.289	.336	68	-30	-28	59	5			6	3S2/1	-1.3
1935	NY-N	107	396	40	112	12	0	3	37	13	18	.283	.306	.336	74	-15	-15	39	0			-11	2S3	-1.7
1936	*NY-N	42	58	7	16	4	0	1	7	8	4	.276	.373	.397	109	1	1	10	0			-1	S/23	0.1
Total	12	1162	4271	572	1190	195	49	28	443	222	190	.279	.316	.367	81	-135	-125	495	31	14		-49	S32/P10	-7.9

■ HENRY KOHLER
Kohler, Henry C. b: 5/5/1852, Baltimore, Md. d: 8/27/34, Baltimore, Md. Deb: 7/12/1871

YEAR	TM/L	G	AB	R	H	2B	3B	HR	RBI	BB	SO	AVG	OBP	SLG	PRO+	BR	/A	RC	SB	CS	FR	/A	Pos	TPR
1871	Kek-n	3	12	0	2	1	0	0	1	0	0	.167	.167	.250	17	-1	-1	1	0				/13	0.0
1873	Mar-n	6	26	2	3	3	0	0	0	0	0	.115	.115	.231	-1	-3	-2	1					/3C	0.0
1874	Bal-n	2	4	0	0	0	0	0	0	0	0	.000	.000	.000	-99	-1	-1	0					/1	0.0
Total	3 n	11	42	2	5	4	0	0				.119	.119	.214	-5	-5	-4	1					/31C	0.0

■ DICK KOKOS
Kokos, Richard Jerome (b: Richard Jerome Kokoszka) b: 2/28/28, Chicago, Ill. d: 4/9/86, Chicago, Ill. BL/TL, 5'8.5", 170 lbs. Deb: 7/08/48

YEAR	TM/L	G	AB	R	H	2B	3B	HR	RBI	BB	SO	AVG	OBP	SLG	PRO+	BR	/A	RC	SB	CS	FR	/A	Pos	TPR
1948	StL-A	71	258	40	77	15	3	4	40	28	32	.298	.374	.426	110	4	4	44	4	3	-1	-5	O	-0.3
1949	StL-A	143	501	80	131	28	1	23	77	66	91	.261	.351	.459	109	7	4	86	3	5	-2	2	*O	0.8
1950	StL-A	143	490	77	128	27	5	18	67	88	73	.261	.375	.447	106	7	4	87	8	8	-2	9	*O	0.8
1953	StL-A	107	299	44	72	12	0	13	38	56	53	.241	.361	.411	106	4	3	47	0	5	-3	-4	/O	-0.5
1954	Bal-A	11	10	1	2	0	0	1	1	4	3	.200	.429	.500	166	1	1	2	0	0	0	0	/O	0.1
Total	5	475	1558	239	410	82	9	59	223	242	252	.263	.365	.441	108	24	17	266	15	21	-8	2	O	0.1

■ GARY KOLB
Kolb, Gary Alan b: 3/13/40, Rock Falls, Ill. BL/TR, 6', 194 lbs. Deb: 9/07/60

YEAR	TM/L	G	AB	R	H	2B	3B	HR	RBI	BB	SO	AVG	OBP	SLG	PRO+	BR	/A	RC	SB	CS	FR	/A	Pos	TPR
1960	StL-N	9	3	1	0	0	0	0	0	0	0	.000	.000	.000	-92	-1	-1	0	0	0	0	1	/O	0.0
1962	StL-N	6	14	1	5	0	0	0	0	1	3	.357	.400	.357	96	0	-0	2	0	0	0	0	/O	0.0
1963	StL-N	75	96	23	26	1	5	3	10	12	26	.271	.407	.479	141	8	7	21	2	1	0	0	O/C3	0.4
1964	Mil-N	36	64	7	12	1	0	0	2	6	10	.188	.257	.203	31	-6	-6	4	3	2	-0	-3	O/32C	-0.9
1965	Mil-N	24	27	3	7	1	0	0	1	1	6	.259	.286	.259	54	-2	-2	2	0	0	0	1	O	-0.1
	NY-N	40	90	8	15	2	0	1	7	3	28	.167	.194	.222	17	-10	-10	4	3	0	1	2	O/13	-0.8
	Yr	64	117	11	22	2	0	1	8	4	34	.188	.215	.231	26	-11	-11	5	3	0	1	2		-0.9
1968	Pit-N	74	119	16	26	4	1	2	6	11	17	.218	.285	.319	82	-3	-3	11	2	1	0	0	OC/32	-0.3
1969	Pit-N	29	37	4	3	1	0	0	3	2	14	.081	.128	.108	-34	-7	-6	1	0	0	0	1	/C	-0.5
Total	7	293	450	63	94	9	6	6	29	46	104	.209	.282	.296	65	-19	-20	43	10	4	1	2	O/C321	-2.2

■ DON KOLLOWAY
Kolloway, Donald Martin "Butch" or "Cab" b: 8/4/18, Posen, Ill. BR/TR, 6'3", 200 lbs. Deb: 9/16/40

YEAR	TM/L	G	AB	R	H	2B	3B	HR	RBI	BB	SO	AVG	OBP	SLG	PRO+	BR	/A	RC	SB	CS	FR	/A	Pos	TPR
1940	Chi-A	10	40	5	9	1	0	0	3	0	3	.225	.225	.250	23	-5	-5	2	1	0	0	-2	2	-0.4
1941	Chi-A	71	280	33	76	8	3	3	24	6	12	.271	.292	.354	71	-13	-12	27	11	4	1	-7	2/1	-1.2
1942	Chi-A	147	601	72	164	**40**	4	3	60	30	39	.273	.311	.368	92	-10	-8	66	16	14	-4	-9	*21	-1.7
1943	Chi-A	85	348	29	75	14	4	1	33	9	30	.216	.235	.287	53	-22	-22	22	11	7	-1	-1	2	-2.1
1946	Chi-A	123	482	45	135	23	4	3	53	9	29	.280	.293	.363	86	-13	-11	52	14	6	1	3	23	0.3
1947	Chi-A	124	485	49	135	25	4	2	35	17	34	.278	.303	.359	87	-13	-10	48	11	4	1	5	21/3	0.0
1948	Chi-A	119	417	60	114	14	0	4	38	18	18	.273	.303	.369	81	-15	-13	44	2	4	-2	11	23	-0.2
1949	Chi-A	4	4	0	0	0	0	0	0	0	1	.000	.000	.000	-99	-1	-1	0	0	0	0	0	/3	0.0
	Det-A	126	483	71	142	19	3	2	47	49	25	.294	.361	.358	91	-6	-6	62	7	7	-2	-21	21/3	-2.6
	Yr	130	487	71	142	19	3	2	47	49	26	.292	.359	.355	89	-7	-7	61	7	7	-2	-21		-2.6
1950	Det-A	125	467	55	135	20	4	6	62	29	28	.289	.331	.388	81	-13	-15	57	1	3	-2	3	*1/2	-1.7
1951	Det-A	78	212	28	54	7	0	1	17	15	12	.255	.307	.302	65	-10	-10	19	2	3	-1	6	1	-0.6

M/L	G	AB	R	H	2B	3B	HR	RBI	BB	SO	AVG	OBP	SLG	PRO+	BR	/A	RC	SB	CS	SBR	FR	POS	TPR
Det-A	65	173	19	42	9	0	2	21	7	19	.243	.280	.329	69	-8	-8	15	0	2	-1	-1	1/2	-1.1
Phi-A	2	1	0	0	0	0	0	0	0	0	.000	.000	.000	-96	-0	-0	0	0	0	0	0	/3	0.0
12	1079	3993	466	1081	180	30	29	393	189	251	.271	.305	.353	80	-128	-122	413	76	54	-10	-12	21/3	-11.3

■ KARL KOLSETH
Kolseth, Karl Dickey "Koley" b: 12/25/1892, Cambridge, Mass. d: 5/3/56, Cumberland, Md. BL/TR, 6', 182 lbs. Deb: 9/30/15

Year	M/L	G	AB	R	H	2B	3B	HR	RBI	BB	SO	AVG	OBP	SLG	PRO+	BR	/A	RC	SB	CS	SBR	FR	POS	TPR
1915	Bal-F	6	23	1	6	1	1	0	1	1	0	.261	.292	.391	98	-0	-0	3	0			-1	/1	-0.1

■ FRED KOMMERS
Kommers, Frederick Raymond "Bugs" b: 3/31/1886, Chicago, Ill. d: 6/14/43, Chicago, Ill. BL/TR, 6', 175 lbs. Deb: 6/25/13

Year	M/L	G	AB	R	H	2B	3B	HR	RBI	BB	SO	AVG	OBP	SLG	PRO+	BR	/A	RC	SB	CS	SBR	FR	POS	TPR
1913	Pit-N	40	155	14	36	5	4	0	22	10	29	.232	.279	.316	73	-6	-6	13	1			-2	O	-0.8
1914	StL-F	76	244	33	75	9	8	3	41	24	36	.307	.376	.447	128	11	9	46	7			-2	O	0.4
	Bal-F	16	42	5	9	1	0	1	1	7	7	.214	.340	.310	84	-0	-1	5	0			-2	O	-0.3
	Yr	92	286	38	84	10	8	4	42	31	43	.294	.371	.427	122	11	9	50	7			-4		0.1
Total	2	132	441	52	120	15	12	4	64	41	72	.272	.340	.388	106	4	3	64	8			-6	O	-0.7

■ BRAD KOMMINSK
Komminsk, Brad Lynn b: 4/4/61, Lima, Ohio BR/TR, 6'2", 202 lbs. Deb: 9/28/83

Year	M/L	G	AB	R	H	2B	3B	HR	RBI	BB	SO	AVG	OBP	SLG	PRO+	BR	/A	RC	SB	CS	SBR	FR	POS	TPR
1983	Atl-N	19	36	2	8	2	0	0	4	5	7	.222	.317	.278	62	-2	-2	3	0	0	0	0	O	-0.1
1984	Atl-N	90	301	37	61	10	0	8	36	29	77	.203	.277	.316	62	-14	-16	27	18	8	1	-5	O	-2.4
1985	Atl-N	106	300	52	68	12	3	4	21	38	71	.227	.316	.327	75	-8	-10	32	10	8	-2	-8	O	-2.2
1986	Atl-N	5	5	1	2	0	0	0	1	0	1	.400	.400	.400	115	0	0	0	0	1	-1	0	/3O	0.0
1987	Mil-A	7	15	0	1	0	0	0	0	1	1	.067	.125	.067	-46	-3	-3	0	1	0	0	1	/OD	-0.1
1989	Cle-A	71	198	27	47	8	2	8	33	24	55	.237	.323	.419	106	2	1	28	8	2	1	7	O	0.9
1990	SF-N	8	5	2	1	0	0	0	0	1	2	.200	.333	.200	51	-0	-0	0	0	0	0	0	/O	0.0
	Bal-A	46	101	18	24	4	0	3	8	14	29	.238	.342	.366	100	0	0	13	1	1	-0	2	O/D	0.1
Total	7	352	961	139	212	36	5	23	103	112	249	.221	.306	.340	77	-24	-30	104	38	20	-1	-3	O/D3	-3.8

■ ED KONETCHY
Konetchy, Edward Joseph "Big Ed" b: 9/3/1885, Lacrosse, Wis. d: 5/27/47, Ft.Worth, Tex. BR/TR, 6'2.5", 195 lbs. Deb: 6/29/07

Year	M/L	G	AB	R	H	2B	3B	HR	RBI	BB	SO	AVG	OBP	SLG	PRO+	BR	/A	RC	SB	CS	SBR	FR	POS	TPR
1907	StL-N	91	331	34	83	11	8	3	30	26		.251	.305	.360	114	3	4	43	13			4	1	0.7
1908	StL-N	154	545	46	135	19	12	3	50	38		.248	.297	.354	115	5	7	62	16			11	*1	1.6
1909	StL-N	152	576	88	165	23	14	4	80	65		.286	.366	.396	145	25	29	92	25			5	*1	3.4
1910	StL-N	144	520	87	157	23	16	3	78	78	59	.302	.397	.425	145	28	31	94	18			8	*1/P	3.9
1911	StL-N	158	571	90	165	38	13	6	88	81	63	.289	.384	.433	132	23	25	105	27			-6	*1	1.3
1912	StL-N	143	538	81	169	26	13	8	82	62	66	.314	.389	.455	134	23	25	105	25			6	*1/O	2.4
1913	StL-N	140	504	75	139	18	17	7	68	53	41	.276	.353	.427	124	14	15	82	27			7	*1/P	1.6
1914	Pit-N	154	563	56	140	23	9	4	51	32	48	.249	.291	.343	92	-10	-7	61	20			5	*1	-0.5
1915	Pit-F	152	576	79	181	31	18	10	93	41	52	.314	.363	.483	150	33	33	115	27			0	*1	3.7
1916	Bos-N	158	566	76	147	29	13	3	70	43	46	.260	.320	.373	117	8	10	74	13			9	*1	1.4
1917	Bos-N	130	474	56	129	19	13	2	54	36	40	.272	.330	.380	125	9	12	62	16			2	*1	1.4
1918	Bos-N	119	437	33	103	15	5	2	56	32	35	.236	.291	.307	86	-9	-7	40	5			-2	*1/OP	-1.3
1919	Bro-N	132	486	46	145	24	9	1	47	29	39	.298	.342	.391	117	11	10	68	14			7	*1	1.6
1920	*Bro-N	131	497	62	153	22	12	5	63	33	18	.308	.352	.431	120	14	13	75	3	2	-0	1	*1	1.2
1921	Bro-N	55	197	25	53	6	5	3	23	19	21	.269	.336	.396	90	-2	-3	26	3	3	-1	-1	1	-0.5
	Phi-N	72	268	38	86	17	4	8	59	21	17	.321	.379	.504	122	12	9	52	3	0	1	6	1	1.3
	Yr	127	465	63	139	23	9	11	82	40	38	.299	.361	.458	109	10	6	78	6	3	0	4		0.8
Total	15	2085	7649	972	2150	344	181	75	992	689	545	.281	.345	.403	123	186	206	1157	255	5		59	*1/OP	23.2

■ MIKE KONNICK
Konnick, Michael Aloysius b: 1/13/1889, Glen Lyon, Pa. d: 7/9/71, Wilkes-Barre, Pa. BR/TR, 5'9", 180 lbs. Deb: 10/03/09

Year	M/L	G	AB	R	H	2B	3B	HR	RBI	BB	SO	AVG	OBP	SLG	PRO+	BR	/A	RC	SB	CS	SBR	FR	POS	TPR
1909	Cin-N	2	5	0	2	1	0	0	1	0		.400	.400	.600	211	1	1	1	0			-1	/C	0.0
1910	Cin-N	1	3	0	0	0	0	0	0	1	0	.000	.250	.000	-27	-0	-0	0	0			-1	/S	0.0
Total	2	3	8	0	2	1	0	0	1	1	0	.250	.333	.375	117	0	0	1	0			-1	/CS	0.0

■ BRUCE KONOPKA
Konopka, Bruno Bruce b: 9/16/19, Hammond, Ind. BL/TL, 6'2", 190 lbs. Deb: 6/07/42

Year	M/L	G	AB	R	H	2B	3B	HR	RBI	BB	SO	AVG	OBP	SLG	PRO+	BR	/A	RC	SB	CS	SBR	FR	POS	TPR
1942	Phi-A	5	10	2	3	0	0	0	1	1	0	.300	.364	.300	88	-0	-0	1	0	0	0	-0	/1	0.0
1943	Phi-A	2	2	0	0	0	0	0	0	0	1	.000	.000	.000	-99	-0	-0	0	0	0	0	0	H	0.0
1946	Phi-A	38	93	7	22	4	1	0	9	4	8	.237	.268	.301	59	-5	-5	7	0	0	0	2	1/O	-0.4
Total	3	45	105	9	25	4	1	0	10	5	9	.238	.273	.295	59	-6	-6	8	0	0	0	2	/1O	-0.4

■ HARRY KOONS
Koons, Henry M. b: 1863, Philadelphia, Pa. BR/TR, 5'8", 174 lbs. Deb: 4/17/1884

Year	M/L	G	AB	R	H	2B	3B	HR	RBI	BB	SO	AVG	OBP	SLG	PRO+	BR	/A	RC	SB	CS	SBR	FR	POS	TPR
1884	Alt-U	21	78	8	18	2	1	0			2	.231	.250	.282	78	-2	-2	6	0			5	3/C	0.3
	CP-U	1	3	0	0	0	0	0			0	.000	.000	.000	-99	-1	-1	0	0			0	/3	0.0
	Yr	22	81	8	18	2	1	0			2	.222	.241	.272	72	-2	-2	5	0			5		0.3

■ GEORGE KOPACZ
Kopacz, George Felix "Sonny" b: 2/26/41, Chicago, Ill. BL/TL, 6'1", 195 lbs. Deb: 9/18/66

Year	M/L	G	AB	R	H	2B	3B	HR	RBI	BB	SO	AVG	OBP	SLG	PRO+	BR	/A	RC	SB	CS	SBR	FR	POS	TPR
1966	Atl-N	6	9	1	0	0	0	0	0	1	5	.000	.100	.000	-68	-2	-2	0	0	0	0	-0	/1	-0.2
1970	Pit-N	10	16	1	3	0	0	0	0	0	5	.188	.188	.188	1	-2	-2	1	0	0	0	-1	/1	-0.2
Total	2	16	25	2	3	0	0	0	0	1	10	.120	.154	.120	-25	-4	-4	1	0	0	0	-1	/1	-0.4

■ WALLY KOPF
Kopf, Walter Henry b: 7/10/1899, Stonington, Conn. d: 4/30/79, Hamilton Co., Ohio BB/TR, 5'11", 168 lbs. Deb: 10/01/21

Year	M/L	G	AB	R	H	2B	3B	HR	RBI	BB	SO	AVG	OBP	SLG	PRO+	BR	/A	RC	SB	CS	SBR	FR	POS	TPR
1921	NY-N	2	3	0	1	0	0	0	0	1	1	.333	.500	.333	125	0	0	1	0	0	0	2	/3	0.2

■ LARRY KOPF
Kopf, William Lorenz (a.k.a. Fred Brady In 1913) b: 11/3/1890, Bristol, Conn. d: 10/15/86, Anderson Twp., O. BB/TR, 5'9", 160 lbs. Deb: 9/09/13

Year	M/L	G	AB	R	H	2B	3B	HR	RBI	BB	SO	AVG	OBP	SLG	PRO+	BR	/A	RC	SB	CS	SBR	FR	POS	TPR
1913	Cle-A	5	9	1	2	0	0	0	1	0	0	.222	.222	.222	29	-1	-1	0	0			2	/23	0.2
1914	Phi-A	37	69	8	13	2	2	0	12	8	14	.188	.300	.275	76	-2	-2	8	6			1	S/32	0.3
1915	Phi-A	118	386	39	87	10	2	1	33	41	45	.225	.314	.269	77	-11	-10	33	5	9	-4	-8	S3/2	-1.3
1916	Cin-N	11	40	2	11	2	0	0	5	1	8	.275	.293	.325	92	-1	-1	4	1			-2	S	-0.2
1917	Cin-N	148	573	81	146	19	8	2	26	28	48	.255	.297	.326	95	-7	-4	59	17			-11	*S	-1.5
1919	*Cin-N	135	503	51	136	18	5	0	58	28	27	.270	.313	.326	95	-5	-3	54	18			-34	*S	-3.6
1920	Cin-N	126	458	56	112	15	6	0	59	35	24	.245	.305	.303	76	-14	-13	43	14	13	-4	-32	*S/23O	-4.6
1921	Cin-N	107	367	36	80	8	3	1	25	43	20	.218	.310	.264	56	-23	-21	30	3	14	-8	-15	S/23O	-3.3
1922	Bos-N	126	466	59	124	8	6	3	37	45	22	.266	.332	.298	67	-24	-21	48	8	9	-3	-14	2S3	-3.3
1923	Bos-N	39	138	15	38	3	1	0	10	13	6	.275	.338	.312	75	-5	-4	15	0	3	-2	-8	S/2	-0.9
Total	10	852	3009	348	749	83	30	5	266	242	214	.249	.312	.301	78	-92	-80	295	72	48		-120	S/23O	-18.2

■ MERLIN KOPP
Kopp, Merlin Henry "Manny" b: 1/2/1892, Toledo, Ohio d: 5/6/60, Sacramento, Cal. BB/TR, 5'8", 158 lbs. Deb: 8/02/15

Year	M/L	G	AB	R	H	2B	3B	HR	RBI	BB	SO	AVG	OBP	SLG	PRO+	BR	/A	RC	SB	CS	SBR	FR	POS	TPR
1915	Was-A	16	32	2	8	0	0	0		5	7	.250	.351	.250	80	-1	-1	3	1			-1	/O	-0.1
1918	Phi-A	96	363	60	85	7	7	0	18	42	55	.234	.320	.292	84	-6	-6	40	22			12	O	0.1
1919	Phi-A	75	235	34	53	2	4	1	12	42	43	.226	.348	.281	77	-5	-6	27	16			-2	O	-1.2
Total	3	187	630	96	146	9	11	1	30	89	105	.232	.332	.286	81	-12	-13	70	39			9	O	-1.2

■ JOE KOPPE
Koppe, Joseph (b: Joseph Kopchia) b: 10/19/30, Detroit, Mich. BR/TR, 5'10", 165 lbs. Deb: 8/09/58

Year	M/L	G	AB	R	H	2B	3B	HR	RBI	BB	SO	AVG	OBP	SLG	PRO+	BR	/A	RC	SB	CS	SBR	FR	POS	TPR
1958	Mil-N	16	9	3	4	0	0	0	0	1	1	.444	.500	.444	167	1	1	2	0	0	0	6	/S	0.7
1959	Phi-N	126	422	68	110	18	7	7	28	49	80	.261	.329	.386	88	-6	-7	54	7	7	-2	5	*S2	0.1
1960	Phi-N	58	170	13	29	6	1	0	13	23	47	.171	.273	.235	41	-14	-14	12	2	3	-0	-12	S/3	-2.4
1961	Phi-N	6	3	1	0	0	0	0	0	0	0	.000	.000	.000	-99	-1	-1	0	0	0	0	0	/S	0.0
	LA-A	91	338	46	85	12	2	5	40	45	77	.251	.341	.343	75	-7	-12	42	3	3	-1	-5	S/23	-1.1
1962	LA-A	128	375	47	85	16	0	4	40	73	84	.227	.356	.301	81	-8	-7	45	2	1	0	4	*S/23	0.5
1963	LA-A	76	143	11	30	4	1	1	12	9	30	.210	.261	.273	53	-10	-9	10	0	0	0	8	S32/O	0.1

YEAR	TM/L	G	AB	R	H	2B	3B	HR	RBI	BB	SO	AVG	OBP	SLG	PRO+	BR	/A	RC	SB	CS	SBR	FR	POS	TPR
1964	LA-A	54	113	10	29	4	1	0	6	14	16	.257	.339	.310	91	-2	-1	13	0	0	0	15	S2/3	1.6
1965	Cal-A	23	33	3	7	1	0	1	2	3	10	.212	.278	.333	75	-1	-1	3	0	0	0	9	2/S3	0.9
Total	8	578	1606	202	379	61	12	19	141	209	345	.236	.327	.324	76	-48	-50	181	16	13	-3	30	S/23O	0.4

■ GEORGE KOPSHAW
Kopshaw, George Karl   b: 7/5/1895, Passaic, N.J.   d: 12/26/34, Lynchburg, Va.   BR/TR, 5'11.5", 176 lbs.   Deb: 8/04/23

YEAR	TM/L	G	AB	R	H	2B	3B	HR	RBI	BB	SO	AVG	OBP	SLG	PRO+	BR	/A	RC	SB	CS	SBR	FR	POS	TPR
1923	StL-N	2	5	1	1	1	0	0	0	0	1	.200	.200	.400	56	-0	-0	0	0	0	0	-1	/C	0.0

■ STEVE KORCHECK
Korcheck, Stephen Joseph "Hoss"   b: 8/11/32, McClellandtown, Pa.   BR/TR, 6'1", 205 lbs.   Deb: 9/06/54

YEAR	TM/L	G	AB	R	H	2B	3B	HR	RBI	BB	SO	AVG	OBP	SLG	PRO+	BR	/A	RC	SB	CS	SBR	FR	POS	TPR
1954	Was-A	2	7	0	1	0	0	0	0	0	2	.143	.143	.143	-23	-1	-1	0	0	0	0	-1	/C	-0.1
1955	Was-A	13	36	3	10	2	0	0	2	0	5	.278	.297	.333	73	-2	-1	4	0	0	0	2	C	0.1
1958	Was-A	21	51	6	4	2	1	0	1	1	16	.078	.096	.157	-32	-9	-9	1	0	0	0	1	C	-0.8
1959	Was-A	22	51	3	8	2	0	0	4	5	13	.157	.232	.196	19	-6	-6	3	0	0	0	6	C	0.1
Total	4	58	145	12	23	6	1	0	7	6	36	.159	.197	.214	13	-18	-17	7	0	0	0	7	/C	-0.7

■ ART KORES
Kores, Arthur Emil "Dutch"   b: 7/22/1886, Milwaukee, Wis.   d: 3/26/74, Milwaukee, Wis.   BR/TR, 5'9", 167 lbs.   Deb: 7/24/15

YEAR	TM/L	G	AB	R	H	2B	3B	HR	RBI	BB	SO	AVG	OBP	SLG	PRO+	BR	/A	RC	SB	CS	SBR	FR	POS	TPR
1915	StL-F	60	201	18	47	9	2	1	22	21	13	.234	.306	.313	79	-4	-5	24	6			19	3	1.6

■ ANDY KOSCO
Kosco, Andrew John   b: 10/5/41, Youngstown, Ohio   BR/TR, 6'3", 205 lbs.   Deb: 8/13/65

YEAR	TM/L	G	AB	R	H	2B	3B	HR	RBI	BB	SO	AVG	OBP	SLG	PRO+	BR	/A	RC	SB	CS	SBR	FR	POS	TPR
1965	Min-A	23	55	3	13	4	0	1	6	1	15	.236	.250	.364	69	-2	-2	5	0	0	0	1	O/1	-0.1
1966	Min-A	57	158	11	35	5	0	2	13	7	31	.222	.255	.291	53	-9	-10	11	0	1	-1	-1	O/1	-1.4
1967	Min-A	9	28	4	4	1	0	0	4	2	4	.143	.200	.179	12	-3	-3	1	0	0	0	-1	/O	-0.4
1968	NY-A	131	466	47	112	19	1	15	59	16	71	.240	.270	.382	99	-4	-3	45	2	2	-1	-6	O1	-1.6
1969	LA-N	120	424	51	105	13	2	19	74	21	66	.248	.285	.422	103	-5	-4	46	0	1	-1	-7	*O/1	-1.5
1970	LA-N	74	224	21	51	12	0	8	27	1	40	.228	.231	.388	66	-13	-12	17	1	1	-0	-1	O/1	-1.5
1971	Mil-A	98	264	27	60	6	2	10	39	24	57	.227	.292	.379	90	-5	-4	28	1	3	-2	-3	O13	-1.2
1972	Cal-A	49	142	15	34	4	2	6	13	5	23	.239	.270	.423	110	-0	1	15	1	0	0	-2	O	-0.1
	Bos-A	17	47	5	10	2	1	3	6	2	9	.213	.260	.489	113	1	0	4	0	0	0	-0	O	0.0
	Yr	66	189	20	44	6	3	9	19	7	32	.233	.268	.439	111	1	1	19	1	0	0	-2		-0.1
1973	*Cin-N	47	118	17	33	7	0	9	21	13	26	.280	.351	.568	159	7	8	22	0	0	0	-4	O/1	0.3
1974	Cin-N	33	37	3	7	2	0	0	5	7	8	.189	.318	.243	59	-2	-2	3	0	0	0	-2	/3O	-0.3
Total	10	658	1963	204	464	75	8	73	267	99	350	.236	.275	.394	92	-34	-28	197	5	8	-3	-25	O/13	-7.8

■ CLEM KOSHOREK
Koshorek, Clement John "Scooter"   b: 6/20/26, Royal Oak, Mich.   BR/TR, 5'6", 165 lbs.   Deb: 4/15/52

YEAR	TM/L	G	AB	R	H	2B	3B	HR	RBI	BB	SO	AVG	OBP	SLG	PRO+	BR	/A	RC	SB	CS	SBR	FR	POS	TPR
1952	Pit-N	98	322	27	84	17	0	0	15	26	39	.261	.320	.314	74	-10	-11	33	4	7	-3	1	S23	-1.0
1953	Pit-N	1	1	0	0	0	0	0	0	0	1	.000	.000	.000	-99	-0	-0	0	0	0	0	0	H	0.0
Total	2	99	323	27	84	17	0	0	15	26	40	.260	.319	.313	74	-10	-11	33	4	7	-3	1	/S23	-1.0

■ MIKE KOSMAN
Kosman, Michael Thomas   b: 12/10/17, Hamtramck, Mich.   BR/TR, 5'9", 160 lbs.   Deb: 4/20/44

YEAR	TM/L	G	AB	R	H	2B	3B	HR	RBI	BB	SO	AVG	OBP	SLG	PRO+	BR	/A	RC	SB	CS	SBR	FR	POS	TPR
1944	Cin-N	1	0	0	0	0	0	0	0	0	0	—	—	—	—	0	0	0	0			0	R	0.0

■ FRED KOSTER
Koster, Frederick Charles "Fritz"   b: 12/21/05, Louisville, Ky.   d: 4/24/79, St.Matthews, Ky.   BL/TL, 5'10.5", 165 lbs.   Deb: 4/27/31

YEAR	TM/L	G	AB	R	H	2B	3B	HR	RBI	BB	SO	AVG	OBP	SLG	PRO+	BR	/A	RC	SB	CS	SBR	FR	POS	TPR
1931	Phi-N	76	151	21	34	2	2	0	8	14	21	.225	.291	.265	47	-10	-12	13	4			1	O	-1.2

■ FRANK KOSTRO
Kostro, Frank Jerry   b: 8/4/37, Windber, Pa.   BR/TR, 6'2", 190 lbs.   Deb: 9/02/62

YEAR	TM/L	G	AB	R	H	2B	3B	HR	RBI	BB	SO	AVG	OBP	SLG	PRO+	BR	/A	RC	SB	CS	SBR	FR	POS	TPR
1962	Det-A	16	41	5	11	3	0	0	3	1	6	.268	.286	.341	66	-2	-2	4	0	0	0	1	3	0.0
1963	Det-A	31	52	4	12	1	0	0	0	9	13	.231	.344	.250	67	-2	-2	5	0	0	0	-0	/31O	-0.2
	LA-A	43	99	6	22	2	1	2	10	6	17	.222	.267	.323	68	-5	-4	8	0	0	0	-2	3/1O	-0.5
	Yr	74	151	10	34	3	1	2	10	15	30	.225	.295	.298	68	-6	-6	13	0	0	0	-2		-0.7
1964	Min-A	59	103	10	28	5	0	3	12	4	21	.272	.306	.408	96	-1	-1	12	0	0	0	-3	3/2O1	-0.2
1965	Min-A	20	31	2	5	2	0	0	1	4	5	.161	.257	.226	37	-2	-3	2	0	0	0	0	/23O	-0.1
1967	Min-A	32	31	4	10	0	0	0	2	3	2	.323	.382	.323	102	1	0	3	0	0	0	-1	/O3	0.0
1968	Min-A	63	108	9	26	4	1	0	9	6	20	.241	.281	.296	71	-3	-4	9	0	0	0	-0	O/1	-0.5
1969	Min-A	2	2	0	0	0	0	0	0	0	1	.000	.000	.000	-98	-1	-1	0	0	0	0	0	H	0.0
Total	7	266	467	40	114	17	2	5	37	33	85	.244	.295	.321	74	-15	-16	44	0	0	0	-5	/3O21	-1.5

■ ERNIE KOY
Koy, Ernest Anyz "Chief"   b: 9/17/09, Sealy, Tex.   BR/TR, 6', 200 lbs.   Deb: 4/19/38

YEAR	TM/L	G	AB	R	H	2B	3B	HR	RBI	BB	SO	AVG	OBP	SLG	PRO+	BR	/A	RC	SB	CS	SBR	FR	POS	TPR
1938	Bro-N	142	521	78	156	29	13	11	76	38	76	.299	.352	.468	121	15	14	87	15			-11	*O/3	0.0
1939	Bro-N	125	425	57	118	37	5	8	67	39	64	.278	.338	.445	105	4	2	63	11			-2	*O	-0.1
1940	Bro-N	24	48	9	11	2	1	1	8	3	3	.229	.275	.375	73	-2	-2	5	1			-0	O	-0.2
	StL-N	93	348	44	108	19	5	8	52	28	59	.310	.368	.463	121	13	10	60	12			-3	O	0.4
	Yr	117	396	53	119	21	6	9	60	31	62	.301	.357	.452	115	11	8	65	13			-3		0.2
1941	StL-N	13	40	5	8	1	0	2	4	1	8	.200	.220	.375	61	-2	-2	3	0			-1	O	-0.3
	Cin-N	67	204	24	51	11	2	2	27	14	22	.250	.301	.353	84	-5	-5	22	1			-3	O	-0.9
	Yr	80	244	29	59	12	2	4	31	15	30	.242	.288	.357	80	-7	-7	25	1			-4		-1.2
1942	Cin-N	3	2	0	0	0	0	0	0	0	2	.000	.000	.000	-99	-0	-0	0	0			0	H	0.0
	Phi-N	91	258	21	63	9	3	4	26	14	50	.244	.283	.349	89	-6	-5	25	0			1	O	-0.5
	Yr	94	260	21	63	9	3	4	26	14	52	.242	.281	.346	87	-7	-5	25	0			1		-0.5
Total	5	558	1846	238	515	108	29	36	260	137	284	.279	.332	.427	107	18	12	266	40			-19	O/3	-1.6

■ AL KOZAR
Kozar, Albert Kenneth   b: 7/5/22, McKees Rocks, Pa.   BR/TR, 5'9.5", 173 lbs.   Deb: 4/19/48

YEAR	TM/L	G	AB	R	H	2B	3B	HR	RBI	BB	SO	AVG	OBP	SLG	PRO+	BR	/A	RC	SB	CS	SBR	FR	POS	TPR
1948	Was-A	150	577	61	144	25	8	1	58	66	52	.250	.327	.326	76	-22	-19	63	4	2	0	-21	*2	-3.5
1949	Was-A	105	350	46	94	15	2	4	31	25	23	.269	.321	.357	81	-12	-11	41	2	1	0	-7	*2	-1.5
1950	Was-A	20	55	7	11	1	0	0	3	5	8	.200	.267	.218	27	-6	-6	3	0	0	0	-0	2	-0.4
	Chi-A	10	10	4	3	0	0	1	2	0	3	.300	.300	.600	129	0	0	1	0	0	0	3	/23	0.3
	Yr	30	65	11	14	1	0	1	5	5	11	.215	.271	.277	42	-6	-6	5	0	0	0	2		-0.1
Total	3	285	992	118	252	41	10	6	94	96	86	.254	.321	.334	76	-39	-35	108	6	3	0	-26	2/3	-5.1

■ JOE KRACHER
Kracher, Joseph Peter "Jug"   b: 11/4/15, Philadelphia, Pa.   d: 12/24/81, San Angelo, Tex.   BR/TR, 5'11", 185 lbs.   Deb: 9/17/39

YEAR	TM/L	G	AB	R	H	2B	3B	HR	RBI	BB	SO	AVG	OBP	SLG	PRO+	BR	/A	RC	SB	CS	SBR	FR	POS	TPR
1939	Phi-N	5	5	1	1	0	0	0	0	2	1	.200	.429	.200	76	-0	-0	1	0			-1	/C	0.0

■ CLARENCE KRAFT
Kraft, Clarence Otto "Big Boy"   b: 6/9/1887, Evansville, Ind.   d: 3/26/58, Fort Worth, Tex.   BR/TR, 6', 190 lbs.   Deb: 5/01/14

YEAR	TM/L	G	AB	R	H	2B	3B	HR	RBI	BB	SO	AVG	OBP	SLG	PRO+	BR	/A	RC	SB	CS	SBR	FR	POS	TPR
1914	Bos-N	3	3	0	1	0	0	0	0	0	0	.333	.333	.333	99	-0	-0	0	0			0	/1	0.0

■ ED KRANEPOOL
Kranepool, Edward Emil   b: 11/8/44, New York, N.Y.   BL/TL, 6'3", 205 lbs.   Deb: 9/22/62

YEAR	TM/L	G	AB	R	H	2B	3B	HR	RBI	BB	SO	AVG	OBP	SLG	PRO+	BR	/A	RC	SB	CS	SBR	FR	POS	TPR
1962	NY-N	3	6	0	1	1	0	0	0	0	1	.167	.167	.333	30	-1	-1	0	0	0	0	1	/1	0.0
1963	NY-N	86	273	22	57	12	2	2	14	18	50	.209	.258	.289	56	-15	-16	19	4	2	0	-2	O1	-2.2
1964	NY-N	119	420	47	108	19	4	10	45	32	50	.257	.313	.393	100	-2	-1	51	0	1	-1	4	*1/O	-1.0
1965	NY-N	153	525	44	133	24	4	10	53	39	71	.253	.307	.371	94	-7	-5	57	1	4	-2	-1	*1	-1.3
1966	NY-N	146	464	51	118	15	2	16	57	41	66	.254	.319	.399	100	-1	-0	60	1	1	-0	4	*1O	-0.3
1967	NY-N	141	469	37	126	17	1	10	54	37	51	.269	.323	.393	100	-1	-0	53	0	4	-2	4	*1	-0.4
1968	NY-N	127	373	29	86	13	1	3	20	19	39	.231	.272	.295	70	-14	-14	29	0	3	-2	3	*1/O	-1.8
1969	*NY-N	112	353	36	84	9	2	11	49	37	32	.238	.310	.368	88	-5	-6	39	3	2	-0	5	*1/O	-1.2
1970	NY-N	43	47	2	8	0	0	0	3	5	2	.170	.250	.170	15	-6	-6	0	0	0	0	0	/1	-0.5
1971	NY-N	122	421	61	118	20	4	14	58	38	33	.280	.341	.447	123	11	12	63	0	4	-2	-1	1O	-0.9
1972	NY-N	122	327	28	88	15	1	8	34	34	35	.269	.340	.394	111	4	5	42	1	0	0	-0	*1/O	-0.2
1973	*NY-N	100	284	28	68	12	2	1	35	30	28	.239	.312	.306	73	-10	-10	28	1	0	0	-0	1O	-1.3

YEAR	TM/L	G	AB	R	H	2B	3B	HR	RBI	BB	SO	AVG	OBP	SLG	PRO+	BR	/A	RC	SB	CS	SBR	FR	POS	TPR
1974	NY-N	94	217	20	65	11	1	4	24	18	14	.300	.353	.415	116	4	4	32	1	1	0	-5	O1	-0.3
1975	NY-N	106	325	42	105	16	0	4	43	27	21	.323	.375	.409	123	8	10	47	1	1	-0	0	1/O	0.5
1976	NY-N	123	415	47	121	17	1	10	49	35	38	.292	.347	.410	121	7	10	58	1	0	0	-6	1O	0.0
1977	NY-N	108	281	28	79	17	0	10	40	23	20	.281	.336	.448	113	3	4	38	1	4	-2	2	O1	0.0
1978	NY-N	66	81	7	17	2	0	3	19	8	12	.210	.289	.346	79	-3	-2	7	0	0	0	0	O/1	-0.2
1979	NY-N	82	155	7	36	5	0	2	17	13	18	.232	.296	.303	66	-8	-7	13	0	1	-1	-1	1/O	-0.7
Total	18	1853	5436	536	1418	225	25	118	614	454	581	.261	.319	.377	97	-36	-22	638	15	27	-12	11	*1O	-9.9

■ CHARLIE KRAUSE   Krause, Charles b: 10/2/1873, Detroit, Mich. d: 3/30/48, Eloise, Mich. TR , Deb: 7/27/01

YEAR	TM/L	G	AB	R	H	2B	3B	HR	RBI	BB	SO	AVG	OBP	SLG	PRO+	BR	/A	RC	SB	CS	SBR	FR	POS	TPR
1901	Cin-N	1	4	0	1	0	0	0	0	0		.250	.250	.250	50	-0	-0	0	0			0	/2	0.0

■ DANNY KRAVITZ   Kravitz, Daniel "Dusty" or "Beak" b: 12/21/30, Lopez, Pa. BL/TR, 5'11", 195 lbs. Deb: 4/17/56

YEAR	TM/L	G	AB	R	H	2B	3B	HR	RBI	BB	SO	AVG	OBP	SLG	PRO+	BR	/A	RC	SB	CS	SBR	FR	POS	TPR
1956	Pit-N	32	68	6	18	2	2	2	10	5	9	.265	.315	.441	103	-0	0	9	1	1	-0	1	C/3	0.2
1957	Pit-N	19	41	2	6	1	0	0	4	2	10	.146	.186	.171	-3	-6	-6	1	0	0	0	0	C	-0.4
1958	Pit-N	45	100	9	24	3	2	1	5	11	10	.240	.315	.340	76	-4	-3	10	0	0	0	-6	C	-0.7
1959	Pit-N	52	162	18	41	9	1	3	21	5	14	.253	.275	.377	72	-7	-7	16	0	1	-1	-1	C	-0.5
1960	Pit-N	8	6	0	0	0	0	0	0	1	2	.000	.143	.000	-57	-1	-1	0	0	0	0	0	/C	0.0
	KC-A	59	175	17	41	7	2	4	14	11	19	.234	.280	.366	73	-7	-7	16	0	0	0	-3	C	-0.7
Total	5	215	552	52	130	22	7	10	54	35	64	.236	.281	.355	70	-25	-24	53	1	2	-1	-8	C/3	-2.1

■ MIKE KREEVICH   Kreevich, Michael Andreas b: 6/10/08, Mt.Olive, Ill. BR/TR, 5'7.5", 168 lbs. Deb: 9/07/31

YEAR	TM/L	G	AB	R	H	2B	3B	HR	RBI	BB	SO	AVG	OBP	SLG	PRO+	BR	/A	RC	SB	CS	SBR	FR	POS	TPR
1931	Chi-N	5	12	0	2	0	0	0	0	0	6	.167	.167	.167	-10	-2	-2	0	1			1	/O	-0.1
1935	Chi-A	6	23	3	10	2	0	0	2	1	0	.435	.458	.522	149	2	2	5	1	1	-0	-2	/3	0.0
1936	Chi-A	137	550	99	169	32	11	5	69	61	46	.307	.378	.433	96	0	-3	93	10	5	0	6	*O	0.0
1937	Chi-A	144	583	94	176	29	16	12	73	43	45	.302	.350	.468	104	2	2	97	10	1	2	5	*O	0.4
1938	Chi-A	129	489	73	145	26	12	6	73	55	23	.297	.371	.436	99	1	-1	82	13	5	1	1	*O	0.1
1939	Chi-A	145	541	85	175	30	8	5	77	59	40	.323	.390	.436	108	10	8	93	23	10	1	11	*O/3	1.4
1940	Chi-A	144	582	86	154	27	10	8	55	34	49	.265	.305	.387	77	-20	-21	66	15	7	0	11	*O	-1.8
1941	Chi-A	121	436	44	101	16	8	0	37	35	26	.232	.289	.305	58	-27	-27	40	17	5	2	-2	*O	-3.2
1942	Phi-A	116	444	57	113	19	1	1	30	47	31	.255	.326	.309	79	-12	-11	46	7	9	-3	3	*O	-1.9
1943	StL-A	60	161	24	41	6	0	0	10	26	13	.255	.358	.292	89	-1	-1	20	4	1	1	10	O	0.9
1944	*StL-A	105	402	55	121	15	6	5	44	27	24	.301	.348	.405	108	7	4	56	3	3	-1	12	*O	1.3
1945	StL-A	84	295	34	70	11	1	2	21	37	27	.237	.322	.302	78	-6	-8	31	4	1	1	2	O	-0.9
	Was-A	45	158	22	44	8	2	1	23	21	9	.278	.363	.373	124	3	5	22	7	5	-1	-1	O	0.1
	Yr	129	453	56	114	19	3	3	44	58	36	.252	.337	.327	92	-3	-3	53	11	6	-0	1		-0.8
Total	12	1241	4676	676	1321	221	75	45	514	446	339	.283	.346	.391	92	-43	-54	651	115	53		56	*O/3	-3.7

■ CHARLIE KREHMEYER   Krehmeyer, Charles L. b: 7/5/1863, St.Louis, Mo. d: 2/10/26, St.Louis, Mo. BL/TL, Deb: 7/08/1884

YEAR	TM/L	G	AB	R	H	2B	3B	HR	RBI	BB	SO	AVG	OBP	SLG	PRO+	BR	/A	RC	SB	CS	SBR	FR	POS	TPR
1884	StL-a	21	70	3	16	0	1	0			2	.229	.250	.257	66	-2	-3	5				-5	O/C1	-0.6
1885	Lou-a	7	31	4	7	1	1	0			1	.226	.250	.323	82	-1	-1	3				-0	/CO1	0.0
	StL-N	1	3	0	0	0	0	0	0		2	.000	.000	.000	-99	-1	-1	0				-1	/C	0.0
Total	2	29	104	7	23	1	2	0	0	3	2	.221	.243	.269	66	-4	-4	7				-6	/OC1	-0.6

■ MICKEY KREITNER   Kreitner, Albert Joseph b: 10/10/22, Nashville, Tenn. BR/TR, 6'3", 190 lbs. Deb: 9/28/43

YEAR	TM/L	G	AB	R	H	2B	3B	HR	RBI	BB	SO	AVG	OBP	SLG	PRO+	BR	/A	RC	SB	CS	SBR	FR	POS	TPR
1943	Chi-N	3	8	0	3	0	0	0	2	1	2	.375	.444	.375	140	0	0	1	0			-0	/C	0.0
1944	Chi-N	39	85	3	13	2	0	0	1	8	16	.153	.234	.176	17	-9	-9	4	0			-1	C	-0.8
Total	2	42	93	3	16	2	0	0	3	9	18	.172	.252	.194	27	-9	-9	6	0			-1	/C	-0.8

■ RALPH KREITZ   Kreitz, Ralph Wesley "Red" b: 11/13/1885, Plum Creek, Neb. d: 7/20/41, Portland, Ore. BR/TR, 5'9.5", 175 lbs. Deb: 8/01/11

YEAR	TM/L	G	AB	R	H	2B	3B	HR	RBI	BB	SO	AVG	OBP	SLG	PRO+	BR	/A	RC	SB	CS	SBR	FR	POS	TPR
1911	Chi-A	7	17	0	4	1	0	0		0	2	.235	.316	.294	73	-1	-1	2	0			-2	/C	-0.1

■ JIMMY KREMERS   Kremers, James Edward b: 10/8/65, Little Rock, Ark. BL/TR, 6'3", 205 lbs. Deb: 6/05/90

YEAR	TM/L	G	AB	R	H	2B	3B	HR	RBI	BB	SO	AVG	OBP	SLG	PRO+	BR	/A	RC	SB	CS	SBR	FR	POS	TPR
1990	Atl-N	29	73	7	8	1	1	1	2	6	27	.110	.177	.192	1	-10	-10	3	0	0	0	-3	C	-1.2

■ WAYNE KRENCHICKI   Krenchicki, Wayne Richard b: 9/17/54, Trenton, N.J. BL/TR, 6'1", 180 lbs. Deb: 6/15/79

YEAR	TM/L	G	AB	R	H	2B	3B	HR	RBI	BB	SO	AVG	OBP	SLG	PRO+	BR	/A	RC	SB	CS	SBR	FR	POS	TPR
1979	Bal-A	16	21	1	4	1	0	0	0	0	0	.190	.190	.238	15	-2	-2	1	0	0	0	1	/32	0.0
1980	Bal-A	9	14	1	2	0	0	0	0	1	3	.143	.200	.143	-4	-2	-2	0	0	0	0	0	/S2D	0.0
1981	Bal-A	33	56	7	12	4	0	0	6	4	9	.214	.267	.286	59	-3	-3	4	0	0	0	4	S/23D	0.3
1982	Cin-N	94	187	19	53	6	1	2	21	13	23	.283	.330	.358	91	-2	-2	22	5	3	-0	7	3/2	0.4
1983	Cin-N	51	77	6	21	2	0	0	11	8	4	.273	.349	.299	78	-2	-2	8	0	0	0	3	3/2	-0.1
	Det-A	59	133	18	37	7	0	1	16	11	27	.278	.338	.353	93	-1	-1	17	0	0	0	-7	3/2S1	-0.7
1984	Cin-N	97	181	18	54	9	2	6	22	19	23	.298	.366	.470	127	8	7	30	0	1	-1	3	3/12	0.9
1985	Cin-N	90	173	16	47	9	0	4	25	28	20	.272	.373	.393	109	4	3	27	0	0	0	8	3/2	0.8
1986	Mon-N	101	221	21	53	6	2	2	23	22	32	.240	.309	.312	72	-8	-8	22	2	4	-2	2	13/2O	-1.0
Total	8	550	1063	107	283	44	5	15	124	106	141	.266	.334	.359	92	-9	-11	131	7	8	-3	15	3/12SDO	0.6

■ CHUCK KRESS   Kress, Charles Steven b: 12/9/21, Philadelphia, Pa. BL/TL, 6', 190 lbs. Deb: 4/16/47

YEAR	TM/L	G	AB	R	H	2B	3B	HR	RBI	BB	SO	AVG	OBP	SLG	PRO+	BR	/A	RC	SB	CS	SBR	FR	POS	TPR
1947	Cin-N	11	27	4	4	0	0	0	0	6	4	.148	.303	.148	23	-3	-3	2	0			1	/1	-0.1
1949	Cin-N	27	29	3	6	3	0	0	3	3	5	.207	.281	.310	58	-2	-2	2	0			0	1	-0.1
	Chi-A	97	353	45	98	17	6	1	44	39	44	.278	.349	.368	93	-5	-4	47	6	7	-2	-0	1	-0.4
1950	Chi-A	3	8	0	0	0	0	0	0	0	2	.000	.000	.000	-99	-2	-2	-0	0	0	0	0	/1	-0.1
1954	Det-A	24	37	4	7	0	1	0	3	1	4	.189	.211	.243	24	-4	-4	2	0	1	-1	0	/1O	-0.4
	Bro-N	13	12	1	1	0	0	0	2	0	0	.083	.083	.083	-55	-3	-3	0	0	0	0	-0	/1	-0.2
Total	4	175	466	57	116	20	7	1	52	49	59	.249	.320	.328	74	-19	-17	53	6	8		1	1/O	-1.3

■ RED KRESS   Kress, Ralph b: 1/2/07, Columbia, Cal. d: 11/29/62, Los Angeles, Cal. BR/TR, 5'11.5", 165 lbs. Deb: 9/24/27 C

YEAR	TM/L	G	AB	R	H	2B	3B	HR	RBI	BB	SO	AVG	OBP	SLG	PRO+	BR	/A	RC	SB	CS	SBR	FR	POS	TPR
1927	StL-A	7	23	3	7	2	1	1	3	3	3	.304	.385	.609	150	2	2	5	0	0	0	1	/S	0.3
1928	StL-A	150	560	78	153	26	10	3	81	48	70	.273	.332	.371	82	-13	-15	71	5	4	-1	-16	*S	-1.7
1929	StL-A	147	557	82	170	38	4	9	107	52	54	.305	.366	.436	102	4	1	88	5	8	-3	-2	*S	0.9
1930	StL-A	154	614	94	192	43	8	16	112	50	56	.313	.366	.487	110	12	9	105	3	12	-6	-12	*S3	0.4
1931	StL-A	150	605	87	188	46	8	16	114	46	48	.311	.360	.493	118	17	14	101	3	16	-9	-10	3OS1	0.0
1932	StL-A	14	52	2	9	0	1	2	9	4	6	.173	.232	.327	41	-5	-5	4	1	1	-0	2	3	-0.1
	Chi-A	135	515	83	147	42	4	9	57	47	36	.285	.346	.435	108	-0	5	79	6	3	0	9	OS3/1	1.5
	Yr	149	567	85	156	42	5	11	66	51	42	.275	.336	.425	101	-5	-0	82	7	4	0	12		1.4
1933	Chi-A	129	467	47	116	20	5	10	78	37	40	.248	.306	.377	83	-15	-12	54	4	4	-1	-4	*1/O	-2.4
1934	Chi-A	8	14	3	4	0	0	0	1	3	3	.286	.412	.286	80	-0	-0	2	0	0	0	-4	/2	-0.3
	Was-A	56	171	18	39	4	3	4	24	17	19	.228	.298	.357	71	-9	-8	19	3	0	1	-0	10/2S3	-1.1
	Yr	64	185	21	43	4	3	4	25	20	22	.232	.307	.351	72	-9	-8	21	3	0	1	-4		-1.4
1935	Was-A	84	252	32	75	13	4	2	42	25	16	.298	.361	.405	101	-1	-0	37	3	3	-1	17	S/1PO2	1.8
1936	Was-A	109	391	51	111	20	6	8	51	39	25	.284	.349	.427	96	-7	-3	60	6	0	2	9	S2/1	1.2
1938	StL-A	150	566	74	171	33	3	7	79	69	47	.302	.378	.408	97	-2	-1	90	5	4	-1	-15	*S	-0.6
1939	StL-A	13	43	5	12	1	0	0	8	6	2	.279	.367	.302	72	-1	-2	4	1	0	0	-3	S	-0.3
	Det-A	51	157	19	38	7	0	1	22	17	16	.242	.316	.306	55	-9	-11	15	2	1	0	2	S2/3	-0.5
	Yr	64	200	24	50	8	0	1	30	23	18	.250	.327	.305	59	-11	-13	19	3	1	0	-1		-0.7
1940	Det-A	33	99	13	22	3	1	1	11	10	12	.222	.294	.303	50	-7	-8	8	0	0	0	9	3S	0.3

YEAR	TM/L	G	AB	R	H	2B	3B	HR	RBI	BB	SO	AVG	OBP	SLG	PRO+	BR	/A	RC	SB	CS	SBR	FR	POS	TPR
1946	NY-N	1	1	0	0	0	0	0	0	1	0	.000	.500	.000	48	0	0	0	0			1	/P	0.0
Total	14	1391	5087	691	1454	298	58	89	799	474	453	.286	.347	.420	96	-32	-35	742	47	56		-15	S310/2P	-0.5

■ **CHAD KREUTER**   Kreuter, Chad Michael   b: 8/26/64, Greenbrae, Cal.   BB/TR, 6'2", 190 lbs.   Deb: 9/14/88

YEAR	TM/L	G	AB	R	H	2B	3B	HR	RBI	BB	SO	AVG	OBP	SLG	PRO+	BR	/A	RC	SB	CS	SBR	FR	POS	TPR
1988	Tex-A	16	51	3	14	2	1	1	5	7	13	.275	.362	.412	113	1	1	8	0	0	0	2	C	0.3
1989	Tex-A	87	158	16	24	3	0	5	9	27	40	.152	.276	.266	52	-10	-10	13	0	1	-1	15	C	0.8
1990	Tex-A	22	22	2	1	1	0	0	2	8	9	.045	.300	.091	14	-2	-2	1	0	0	0	-2	C	-0.3
Total	3	125	231	21	39	6	1	6	16	42	62	.169	.297	.281	62	-11	-11	22	0	1	-1	15	C	0.8

■ **PAUL KRICHELL**   Krichell, Paul Bernard   b: 12/19/1882, New York, N.Y.   d: 6/4/57, New York, N.Y.   BR/TR, 5'7", 150 lbs.   Deb: 5/12/11

YEAR	TM/L	G	AB	R	H	2B	3B	HR	RBI	BB	SO	AVG	OBP	SLG	PRO+	BR	/A	RC	SB	CS	SBR	FR	POS	TPR
1911	StL-A	28	82	6	19	3	0	0	8	4		.232	.276	.268	54	-5	-5	7	2			-2	C	-0.3
1912	StL-A	59	161	19	35	6	0	0	8	19		.217	.304	.255	62	-8	-7	13	2			-2	C	-0.2
Total	2	87	243	25	54	9	0	0	16	23		.222	.295	.259	60	-13	-12	20	4			-3	/C	-0.5

■ **BILL KRIEG**   Krieg, William Frederick   b: 1/29/1859, Petersburg, Ill.   d: 3/25/30, Chillicothe, Ill.   BR/TR, 5'8", 180 lbs.   Deb: 4/20/1884

YEAR	TM/L	G	AB	R	H	2B	3B	HR	RBI	BB	SO	AVG	OBP	SLG	PRO+	BR	/A	RC	SB	CS	SBR	FR	POS	TPR
1884	CP-U	71	279	35	69	15	4	0		11		.247	.276	.330	105	1	1	26	0			15	CO/S1	1.7
1885	Chi-N	1	3	0	0	0	0	0	0	0	2	.000	.000	.000	-87	-1	-1	0				2	/O	0.1
	Bro-a	17	60	7	9	4	0	1		2		.150	.177	.267	40	-4	-4	3				-4	C/1	-0.5
1886	Was-N	27	98	11	25	6	3	1	15	3	12	.255	.277	.408	113	0	1	12	2			-1	1	-0.4
1887	Was-N	25	95	9	24	4	1	2	17	7	5	.253	.311	.379	97	-1	-0	12	2			-2	1/O	-0.3
Total	4	141	535	62	127	29	8	4	32	23	19	.237	.270	.344	96	-4	-2	53	4			11	/C1OS	0.6

■ **KRIEGER**   Krieger   Deb: 7/28/1884

YEAR	TM/L	G	AB	R	H	2B	3B	HR	RBI	BB	SO	AVG	OBP	SLG	PRO+	BR	/A	RC	SB	CS	SBR	FR	POS	TPR
1884	KC-U	1	3	0	0	0	0	0		0		.000	.000	.000	-99	-1	-1	0	0			-0	/OP	0.0

■ **JOHN KRONER**   Kroner, John Harold   b: 11/13/08, St.Louis, Mo.   d: 8/26/68, St.Louis, Mo.   BR/TR, 6', 185 lbs.   Deb: 9/29/35

YEAR	TM/L	G	AB	R	H	2B	3B	HR	RBI	BB	SO	AVG	OBP	SLG	PRO+	BR	/A	RC	SB	CS	SBR	FR	POS	TPR
1935	Bos-A	2	4	1	1	0	0	0	0	1	1	.250	.400	.250	67	-0	-0	1	0	0	0	-1	/3	0.0
1936	Bos-A	84	298	40	87	17	8	4	62	26	24	.292	.349	.443	89	-4	-6	46	2	3	-1	-1	23S/O	-0.3
1937	Cle-A	86	283	29	67	14	1	2	26	22	25	.237	.292	.314	52	-21	-21	27	1	1	-0	-3	23	-1.6
1938	Cle-A	51	117	13	29	16	0	1	17	19	6	.248	.353	.410	92	-2	-1	18	0	1	-1	12	2/13S	0.9
Total	4	223	702	83	184	47	9	7	105	68	56	.262	.327	.385	75	-26	-29	91	3	5	-2	7	2/3S10	-1.0

■ **MIKE KRSNICH**   Krsnich, Michael   b: 9/24/31, W.Allis, Wis.   BR/TR, 6'1", 190 lbs.   Deb: 4/23/60

YEAR	TM/L	G	AB	R	H	2B	3B	HR	RBI	BB	SO	AVG	OBP	SLG	PRO+	BR	/A	RC	SB	CS	SBR	FR	POS	TPR
1960	Mil-N	4	9	0	3	1	0	0	2	0	0	.333	.333	.444	120	0	0	1	0	0	0	0	/O	0.0
1962	Mil-N	11	12	0	1	1	0	0	2	0	4	.083	.083	.167	-36	-2	-2	0	0	0	0	0	/O13	-0.1
Total	2	15	21	0	4	2	0	0	4	0	4	.190	.190	.286	28	-2	-2	1	0	0	0	0	/O31	-0.1

■ **ROCKY KRSNICH**   Krsnich, Rocco Peter   b: 8/5/27, W.Allis, Wis.   BR/TR, 6'1", 174 lbs.   Deb: 9/13/49

YEAR	TM/L	G	AB	R	H	2B	3B	HR	RBI	BB	SO	AVG	OBP	SLG	PRO+	BR	/A	RC	SB	CS	SBR	FR	POS	TPR
1949	Chi-A	16	55	7	12	3	1	1	9	6	4	.218	.295	.364	76	-2	-2	6	0	1	-1	4	3	0.1
1952	Chi-A	40	91	11	21	7	2	1	15	12	9	.231	.327	.385	97	-0	-0	11	0	0	0	10	3	1.0
1953	Chi-A	64	129	9	26	8	0	1	14	12	11	.202	.270	.287	49	-9	-10	10	0	2	-1	9	3	-0.4
Total	3	120	275	27	59	18	3	3	38	30	24	.215	.294	.335	70	-12	-12	27	0	3	-2	23	3	0.7

■ **OTTO KRUEGER**   Krueger, Arthur William "Oom Paul"   b: 9/17/1876, Chicago, Ill.   d: 2/20/61, St.Louis, Mo.   BR/TR, 5'7", 165 lbs.   Deb: 9/16/1899

YEAR	TM/L	G	AB	R	H	2B	3B	HR	RBI	BB	SO	AVG	OBP	SLG	PRO+	BR	/A	RC	SB	CS	SBR	FR	POS	TPR
1899	Cle-N	13	44	4	10	1	0	0	2	8		.227	.358	.250	76	-1	-1	4	1			-2	/3S2	-0.2
1900	StL-N	12	35	8	14	3	2	1	3	10		.400	.543	.686	244	8	8	13	0			-4	2	0.4
1901	StL-N	142	520	77	143	16	12	2	79	50		.275	.341	.363	112	5	9	74	19			-9	*3	0.9
1902	StL-N	128	467	55	124	7	8	0	46	29		.266	.314	.315	100	-2	-0	53	14			1	*S3	0.7
1903	Pit-N	80	256	42	63	6	8	1	28	21		.246	.303	.344	83	-5	-6	30	5			-5	SO3/2	-0.9
1904	Pit-N	86	268	34	52	6	2	1	26	29		.194	.273	.243	60	-11	-12	22	8			-5	OS3	-1.8
1905	Phi-N	46	114	10	21	1	1	0	12	13		.184	.268	.211	47	-7	-7	7	1			-9	S/O3	-1.6
Total	7	507	1704	230	427	40	33	5	196	160		.251	.318	.322	94	-14	-9	204	48			-33	S3/O2	-2.5

■ **ERNIE KRUEGER**   Krueger, Ernest George   b: 12/27/1890, Chicago, Ill.   d: 4/22/76, Waukegan, Ill.   BR/TR, 5'10.5", 185 lbs.   Deb: 8/04/13

YEAR	TM/L	G	AB	R	H	2B	3B	HR	RBI	BB	SO	AVG	OBP	SLG	PRO+	BR	/A	RC	SB	CS	SBR	FR	POS	TPR
1913	Cle-A	5	6	0	0	0	0	0	0	0	2	.000	.000	.000	-97	-1	-2	0	0			-0	/C	-0.1
1915	NY-A	10	29	3	5	1	0	0	0	0	5	.172	.200	.207	22	-3	-3	1	0	1	-1	-3	/C	-0.6
1917	NY-N	8	10	0	0	0	0	0	0	0	4	.000	.000	.000	-99	-2	-2	0	0			-2	/C	-0.3
	Bro-N	31	81	10	22	2	2	1	6	5	7	.272	.330	.383	115	2	1	10	1			1	C	0.4
	Yr	39	91	10	22	2	2	1	6	5	11	.242	.296	.341	94	-1	-1	9	1			-1		0.1
1918	Bro-N	30	87	4	25	4	2	0	7	4	9	.287	.319	.379	113	1	1	10	2			6	C	1.0
1919	Bro-N	80	226	24	56	7	4	5	36	19	25	.248	.312	.381	105	2	1	27	4			7	C	1.3
1920	*Bro-N	52	146	21	42	4	2	1	17	16	13	.288	.358	.363	104	2	1	20	2	0	1	-4	C	0.2
1921	Bro-N	65	163	18	43	11	4	3	20	14	12	.264	.322	.436	95	-1	-2	23	2	2	-1	-2	C	0.0
1925	Cin-N	37	88	7	27	4	0	1	7	6	8	.307	.351	.386	90	-1	-1	11	1	2	-1	-4	C	-0.3
Total	8	318	836	87	220	33	14	11	93	64	85	.263	.319	.376	97	-3	-4	102	12	5		-1	C	1.6

■ **CHRIS KRUG**   Krug, Everett Ben   b: 12/25/39, Los Angeles, Cal.   BR/TR, 6'4", 200 lbs.   Deb: 5/30/65

YEAR	TM/L	G	AB	R	H	2B	3B	HR	RBI	BB	SO	AVG	OBP	SLG	PRO+	BR	/A	RC	SB	CS	SBR	FR	POS	TPR
1965	Chi-N	60	169	16	34	5	0	5	24	13	52	.201	.262	.320	61	-8	-9	12	0	1	-1	1	C	-0.6
1966	Chi-N	11	28	1	6	1	0	0	1	1	8	.214	.241	.250	36	-2	-2	2	0	0	0	3	C	0.1
1969	SD-N	8	17	0	1	0	0	0	0	1	6	.059	.111	.059	-53	-3	-3	0	0	0	0	-0	/C	-0.3
Total	3	79	214	17	41	6	0	5	25	15	66	.192	.248	.290	50	-14	-15	14	0	1	-1	3	/C	-0.8

■ **GENE KRUG**   Krug, Gary Eugene   b: 2/12/55, Garden City, Kan.   BL/TL, 6'4", 225 lbs.   Deb: 4/29/81

YEAR	TM/L	G	AB	R	H	2B	3B	HR	RBI	BB	SO	AVG	OBP	SLG	PRO+	BR	/A	RC	SB	CS	SBR	FR	POS	TPR
1981	Chi-N	7	5	0	2	0	0	0	0	1	1	.400	.500	.400	151	0	0	1	0	0	0	0	/H	0.0

■ **HENRY KRUG**   Krug, Henry Charles   b: 12/4/1876, San Francisco, Cal.   d: 1/14/08, San Francisco, Cal   TR ,   Deb: 7/26/02

YEAR	TM/L	G	AB	R	H	2B	3B	HR	RBI	BB	SO	AVG	OBP	SLG	PRO+	BR	/A	RC	SB	CS	SBR	FR	POS	TPR
1902	Phi-N	53	198	20	45	3	3	0	14	7		.227	.264	.273	67	-8	-8	16	2			-6	O2/S3	-1.4

■ **MARTY KRUG**   Krug, Martin John   b: 9/10/1888, Coblenz, Germany   d: 6/27/66, Glendale, Cal.   BR/TR, 5'9", 165 lbs.   Deb: 5/29/12

YEAR	TM/L	G	AB	R	H	2B	3B	HR	RBI	BB	SO	AVG	OBP	SLG	PRO+	BR	/A	RC	SB	CS	SBR	FR	POS	TPR
1912	Bos-A	24	39	6	12	2	1	0	7	5		.308	.386	.410	122	1	1	7	2			-2	/S2	0.0
1922	Chi-N	127	450	67	124	23	4	4	60	43	43	.276	.343	.371	82	-10	-12	58	7	9	-3	-5	*32/S	-1.1
Total	2	151	489	73	136	25	5	4	67	48	43	.278	.346	.374	85	-9	-10	65	9	9		-7	3/2S	-1.1

■ **ART KRUGER**   Kruger, Arthur T.   b: 3/16/1881, San Antonio, Tex.   d: 11/28/49, Hondo, Cal.   BR/TR, 6', 185 lbs.   Deb: 4/11/07

YEAR	TM/L	G	AB	R	H	2B	3B	HR	RBI	BB	SO	AVG	OBP	SLG	PRO+	BR	/A	RC	SB	CS	SBR	FR	POS	TPR
1907	Cin-N	100	317	25	74	10	9	0	28	18		.233	.275	.322	85	-5	-6	33	10			0	O	-1.0
1910	Cle-A	47	168	14	26	4	2	0	10	15		.155	.237	.202	37	-12	-12	11	10			2	O	-1.3
	Bos-N	1	0	0	0	0	0	0	0	0	0	.000	.000	.000	-96	-0	-0	0	0			0	H	0.0
	Cle-A	15	55	5	12	2	1	0	4	5		.218	.295	.291	82	-1	-1	5	2			2	O	0.0
1914	KC-F	122	441	45	114	24	7	4	47	23	59	.259	.297	.372	95	-7	-4	55	11			-7	*O	-1.7
1915	KC-F	80	240	24	57	9	2	2	16	12	29	.237	.277	.317	79	-8	-7	24	5			0	O	-0.9
Total	4	365	1222	113	283	49	21	6	115	73	88	.232	.278	.321	80	-33	-31	128	38			-2	O	-4.9

■ **JOHN KRUK**   Kruk, John Martin   b: 2/9/61, Charleston, W.Va.   BL/TL, 5'10", 170 lbs.   Deb: 4/07/86

YEAR	TM/L	G	AB	R	H	2B	3B	HR	RBI	BB	SO	AVG	OBP	SLG	PRO+	BR	/A	RC	SB	CS	SBR	FR	POS	TPR
1986	SD-N	122	278	33	86	16	2	4	38	45	58	.309	.406	.424	132	13	14	47	2	4	-2	-6	O/1	0.4
1987	SD-N	138	447	72	140	14	2	20	91	73	93	.313	.410	.488	142	26	28	92	18	10	-1	4	*1O	2.4
1988	SD-N	120	378	54	91	17	1	9	44	80	68	.241	.373	.362	114	9	10	56	5	3	-0	-4	1O	0.1

YEAR	TM/L	G	AB	R	H	2B	3B	HR	RBI	BB	SO	AVG	OBP	SLG	PRO+	BR	/A	RC	SB	CS	SBR	FR	POS	TPR
1989	SD-N	31	76	7	14	0	0	3	6	17	14	.184	.333	.303	83	-1	-1	8	0	0	0	1	O	0.0
	Phi-N	81	281	46	93	13	6	5	38	27	39	.331	.390	.473	146	17	17	53	3	0	1	-6	O/1	1.0
	Yr	112	357	53	107	13	6	8	44	44	53	.300	.377	.437	132	15	15	59	3	0	1	-5		1.0
1990	Phi-N	142	443	52	129	25	8	7	67	69	70	.291	.387	.431	125	17	17	75	10	5	0	-7	O1	0.4
Total	5	634	1903	264	553	85	19	48	284	311	342	.291	.390	.431	129	80	84	330	38	22	-2	-18	O1	4.3

■ DICK KRYHOSKI
Kryhoski, Richard David b: 3/24/25, Leonia, N.J. BL/TL, 6'2", 182 lbs. Deb: 4/19/49

YEAR	TM/L	G	AB	R	H	2B	3B	HR	RBI	BB	SO	AVG	OBP	SLG	PRO+	BR	/A	RC	SB	CS	SBR	FR	POS	TPR
1949	NY-A	54	177	18	52	10	3	1	27	9	17	.294	.335	.401	94	-2	-2	22	2	4	-2	-1	1	-0.3
1950	Det-A	53	169	20	37	10	0	4	19	8	11	.219	.258	.349	53	-13	-13	15	0	1	-1	-0	1	-1.5
1951	Det-A	119	421	58	121	19	4	12	57	28	29	.287	.335	.437	107	3	2	60	1	2	-1	3	*1	0.2
1952	StL-A	111	342	38	83	13	1	11	42	23	42	.243	.296	.383	86	-7	-8	39	2	0	1	-5	1	-1.7
1953	StL-A	104	338	35	94	18	4	16	50	26	33	.278	.333	.497	119	8	7	52	0	5	-3	5	1	0.8
1954	Bal-A	100	300	32	78	13	2	1	34	19	24	.260	.308	.327	80	-11	-8	29	0	0	0	3	1	-0.6
1955	KC-A	28	47	2	10	2	0	0	2	6	7	.213	.302	.255	50	-3	-3	4	0	1	-1	0	1	-0.4
Total	7	569	1794	203	475	85	14	45	231	119	163	.265	.315	.403	93	-25	-25	221	5	13	-6	6	1	-3.5

■ TONY KUBEK
Kubek, Anthony Christopher b: 10/12/36, Milwaukee, Wis. BL/TR, 6'3", 190 lbs. Deb: 4/20/57

YEAR	TM/L	G	AB	R	H	2B	3B	HR	RBI	BB	SO	AVG	OBP	SLG	PRO+	BR	/A	RC	SB	CS	SBR	FR	POS	TPR
1957	*NY-A	127	431	56	128	21	3	3	39	24	48	.297	.338	.381	98	-3	-2	56	6	6	-2	1	OS3/2	-0.1
1958	*NY-A	138	559	66	148	21	1	2	48	25	57	.265	.297	.317	72	-24	-21	52	5	4	-1	20	*S/O12	1.7
1959	NY-A	132	512	67	143	25	7	6	51	24	46	.279	.314	.391	95	-6	-4	60	3	3	-1	5	SO3/2	0.3
1960	*NY-A	147	568	77	155	25	3	14	62	31	42	.273	.314	.401	98	-8	-4	70	3	0	1	3	*SO	0.9
1961	*NY-A	153	617	84	170	38	6	8	46	27	60	.276	.307	.395	91	-14	-10	74	1	3	-2	13	*S	1.2
1962	NY-A	45	169	28	53	6	1	4	17	12	17	.314	.359	.432	115	3	3	26	2	1	0	5	S/O	1.0
1963	*NY-A	135	557	72	143	21	3	7	44	28	68	.257	.295	.343	79	-17	-16	57	4	2	0	10	*S/O	0.1
1964	NY-A	106	415	46	95	16	3	8	31	26	55	.229	.276	.340	69	-17	-18	39	4	1	1	4	S	-1.3
1965	NY-A	109	339	26	74	5	3	5	35	20	48	.218	.262	.295	58	-19	-19	25	1	3	-2	-8	S/O1	-2.6
Total	9	1092	4167	522	1109	178	30	57	373	217	441	.266	.305	.364	85	-104	-90	459	29	23	-5	53	SO/321	1.2

■ TED KUBIAK
Kubiak, Theodore Rodger b: 5/12/42, New Brunswick, N.J. BB/TR, 6', 175 lbs. Deb: 4/14/67

YEAR	TM/L	G	AB	R	H	2B	3B	HR	RBI	BB	SO	AVG	OBP	SLG	PRO+	BR	/A	RC	SB	CS	SBR	FR	POS	TPR
1967	KC-A	53	102	6	16	2	1	0	5	12	20	.157	.246	.196	33	-8	-8	5	0	0	0	-3	S2/3	-0.9
1968	Oak-A	48	120	10	30	5	2	0	8	8	18	.250	.308	.325	96	-1	-1	12	1	1	-0	-3	2S	-0.2
1969	Oak-A	92	305	38	76	9	1	2	27	25	35	.249	.308	.305	75	-11	-10	29	2	0	1	-0	S2	-0.6
1970	Mil-A	158	540	63	136	9	6	4	41	72	51	.252	.340	.313	81	-12	-12	56	4	9	-4	-17	2S	-1.8
1971	Mil-A	89	260	26	59	6	5	3	17	41	31	.227	.332	.323	87	-4	-3	28	0	5	-3	-3	2S	-0.2
	StL-N	32	72	8	18	3	2	1	10	11	12	.250	.349	.389	105	1	1	11	1	0	0	-4	S2	0.0
1972	Tex-A	46	116	5	26	3	0	0	7	12	12	.224	.302	.250	69	-5	-4	8	0	1	-1	-3	2S/3	-0.4
	*Oak-A	51	94	14	17	4	1	0	8	9	11	.181	.252	.245	51	-6	-5	6	0	0	0	2	2/3	0.0
	Yr	97	210	19	43	7	1	0	15	21	23	.205	.280	.248	61	-10	-9	15	0	1	-1	-0		-0.4
1973	*Oak-A	106	182	15	40	6	1	3	17	12	19	.220	.268	.313	67	-9	-8	15	1	1	-0	6	2S/3	0.5
1974	Oak-A	99	220	22	46	3	0	0	18	18	15	.209	.269	.223	46	-16	-14	12	1	1	-0	-9	2S3/D	-1.9
1975	Oak-A	20	28	2	7	1	0	0	4	2	2	.250	.300	.286	68	-1	-1	2	0	0	0	2	/S32	0.2
	SD-N	87	196	13	44	5	0	0	14	24	18	.224	.309	.250	60	-11	-9	16	3	1	0	-7	32/1	-0.7
1976	SD-N	96	212	16	50	5	2	0	26	25	28	.236	.316	.278	76	-8	-6	18	0	3	-2	-9	32/S1	-1.6
Total	10	977	2447	238	565	61	21	13	202	271	272	.231	.309	.289	73	-91	-81	219	13	22	-9	-38	2S3/1D	-7.6

■ JACK KUBISZYN
Kubiszyn, John Henry b: 12/19/36, Buffalo, N.Y. BR/TR, 5'11", 170 lbs. Deb: 4/23/61

YEAR	TM/L	G	AB	R	H	2B	3B	HR	RBI	BB	SO	AVG	OBP	SLG	PRO+	BR	/A	RC	SB	CS	SBR	FR	POS	TPR
1961	Cle-A	25	42	4	9	0	0	0	0	2	5	.214	.250	.214	26	-4	-4	2	0	0	0	3	/3S2	0.0
1962	Cle-A	25	59	3	10	2	0	1	2	5	7	.169	.234	.254	32	-6	-6	4	0	0	0	2	S/3	-0.1
Total	2	50	101	7	19	2	0	1	2	7	12	.188	.241	.238	30	-10	-10	6	0	0	0	5	/S32	-0.1

■ GIL KUBSKI
Kubski, Gilbert Thomas b: 10/12/54, Longview, Tex. BL/TR, 6'3", 185 lbs. Deb: 9/02/80

YEAR	TM/L	G	AB	R	H	2B	3B	HR	RBI	BB	SO	AVG	OBP	SLG	PRO+	BR	/A	RC	SB	CS	SBR	FR	POS	TPR
1980	Cal-A	22	63	11	16	3	0	0	6	6	10	.254	.319	.302	73	-2	-2	6	1	1	-0	1	O	-0.1

■ STEVE KUCZEK
Kuczek, Stanislaw Leo b: 12/28/24, Amsterdam, N.Y. BR/TR, 6', 160 lbs. Deb: 9/29/49

YEAR	TM/L	G	AB	R	H	2B	3B	HR	RBI	BB	SO	AVG	OBP	SLG	PRO+	BR	/A	RC	SB	CS	SBR	FR	POS	TPR
1949	Bos-N	1	1	0	1	1	0	0	0	0	0	1.000	1.000	2.000	723	1	1	2	0			0	H	0.1

■ BILL KUEHNE
Kuehne, William J. (b: William J. Knelme) b: 10/24/1858, Leipzig, Germany d: 10/27/21, Sulphur Springs, O BR/TR, 185 lbs. Deb: 5/01/1883

YEAR	TM/L	G	AB	R	H	2B	3B	HR	RBI	BB	SO	AVG	OBP	SLG	PRO+	BR	/A	RC	SB	CS	SBR	FR	POS	TPR
1883	Col-a	95	374	38	85	8	14	1			2	.227	.231	.332	86	-9	-4	29				-5	*32/SO	-0.6
1884	Col-a	110	415	48	98	13	16	5			9	.236	.254	.381	116	3	7	41				11	*3	1.8
1885	Pit-a	104	411	54	93	9	19	0			15	.226	.257	.341	91	-5	-4	37				-1	*3/S	0.0
1886	Pit-a	117	481	73	98	16	17	1			19	.204	.237	.314	74	-16	-16	43	26			-1	O31	-1.4
1887	Pit-N	102	402	68	120	18	15	1	41	14	39	.299	.324	.425	115	3	7	62	17			-11	*S/31O	-0.6
1888	Pit-N	138	524	60	123	22	11	3	62	9	68	.235	.256	.336	95	-8	-3	54	34			0	3S	0.2
1889	Pit-N	97	390	43	96	20	5	5	57	9	36	.246	.263	.362	83	-15	-9	42	15			3	30/2S1	0.0
1890	Pit-P	126	528	66	126	21	12	5	73	28	37	.239	.277	.352	75	-25	-18	59	21			6	*3	-0.1
1891	Col-a	68	261	32	56	9	0	2	22	10	22	.215	.244	.272	52	-18	-15	23	21			-2	3	-1.2
	Lou-a	41	159	28	44	3	1	1	18	8	13	.277	.315	.327	87	-3	-3	20	10		3	3		0.1
	Yr	109	420	60	100	12	1	3	40	18	35	.238	.271	.293	66	-21	-18	43	31			1		-1.1
1892	Lou-N	76	287	22	48	4	5	0	36	13	36	.167	.203	.216	30	-25	-22	14	6			-3	3	-1.8
	StL-N	6	24	1	4	1	0	0	0	0	3	.167	.200	.208	26	-2	-2	1	1			0	/3S	0.0
	Cin-N	6	24	3	5	1	0	1	4	1	5	.208	.240	.375	88	-1	-1	2	0			2	/32	0.1
	StL-N	1	4	0	0	0	0	0	0	0	1	.000	.000	.000	-99	-1	-1	0	0			1	/3	0.0
	Yr	89	339	26	57	6	5	1	40	14	45	.168	.203	.224	33	-29	-25	17	7			-0		-1.7
Total	10	1087	4284	536	996	145	115	25	313	137	260	.232	.258	.338	84	-122	-83	428	151			3	3S/O21	-3.5

■ HARVEY KUENN
Kuenn, Harvey Edward b: 12/4/30, W.Allis, Wis. d: 2/28/88, Peoria, Ariz. BR/TR, 6'2", 187 lbs. Deb: 9/06/52 MC

YEAR	TM/L	G	AB	R	H	2B	3B	HR	RBI	BB	SO	AVG	OBP	SLG	PRO+	BR	/A	RC	SB	CS	SBR	FR	POS	TPR
1952	Det-A	19	80	2	26	2	2	0	8	2	1	.325	.349	.400	107	1	1	10	2	1	0	2	S	0.4
1953	Det-A	155	679	94	209	33	7	2	48	50	31	.308	.356	.386	101	0	1	96	6	5	-1	-20	*S	-0.8
1954	Det-A	155	656	81	201	28	6	5	48	29	13	.306	.351	.390	100	-3	-1	80	9	9	-3	1	*S	1.2
1955	Det-A	145	620	101	190	38	5	8	62	40	27	.306	.349	.423	109	4	6	92	8	3	1	-28	*S	-0.5
1956	Det-A	146	591	96	196	32	7	12	88	55	34	.332	.391	.470	126	23	22	109	9	5	-0	-19	*S/O	1.5
1957	Det-A	151	624	74	173	30	6	9	44	47	28	.277	.328	.388	92	-5	-7	75	5	8	-3	-49	*S3/1	-5.0
1958	Det-A	139	561	73	179	39	3	8	54	51	34	.319	.376	.442	116	19	14	89	5	10	-5	11	*O	1.2
1959	Det-A	139	561	99	198	42	7	9	71	48	37	.353	.405	.501	140	36	32	117	7	2	1	-11	*O	2.5
1960	Cle-A	126	474	65	146	24	0	9	54	55	25	.308	.381	.416	119	11	13	77	3	0	1	-0	*O/3	0.9
1961	SF-N	131	471	60	125	22	4	5	46	47	34	.265	.330	.361	87	-10	-8	55	5	4	-1	-8	*O/S	-2.2
1962	*SF-N	130	487	73	148	23	5	10	68	49	37	.304	.369	.433	116	10	12	77	3	6	-3	-14	*O3	-0.9
1963	SF-N	120	417	61	121	13	2	6	31	44	38	.290	.361	.374	113	8	8	57	2	1	0	-28	O3	-2.4
1964	SF-N	111	351	42	92	16	2	4	22	35	32	.262	.331	.353	91	-3	-4	42	0	1	-1	-13	O1/3	-2.0
1965	SF-N	23	59	4	14	0	0	0	6	10	3	.237	.357	.237	69	-2	-2	6	3	1	0	-3	O/1	-0.3
	Chi-N	54	120	11	26	5	0	0	6	22	13	.217	.338	.258	69	-4	-4	12	1	0	0	-3	O/1	-0.8
	Yr	77	179	15	40	5	0	0	12	32	16	.223	.344	.251	69	-5	-6	18	4	1	1	-4		-1.1
1966	Chi-N	3	3	0	1	0	0	0	0	0	0	.333	.333	.333	85	-0	-0	0	0	0	0	0	/O	0.0
	Phi-N	86	159	15	47	9	0	0	15	10	16	.296	.337	.352	92	-2	-2	18	0	0	0	-4	O1/3	-0.7
	Yr	89	162	15	48	9	0	0	15	10	17	.296	.337	.352	92	-2	-2	19	0	0	0	-4		-0.7

YEAR	TM/L	G	AB	R	H	2B	3B	HR	RBI	BB	SO	AVG	OBP	SLG	PRO+	BR	/A	RC	SB	CS	SBR	FR	POS	TPR
Total	15	1833	6913	951	2092	356	56	87	671	594	404	.303	.359	.408	108	85	82	1013	68	56	-13	-173	OS3/1	-7.9

■ JOE KUHEL
Kuhel, Joseph Anthony   b: 6/25/06, Cleveland, Ohio   d: 2/26/84, Kansas City, Kan.   BL/TL, 6', 180 lbs.   Deb: 7/31/30   M

YEAR	TM/L	G	AB	R	H	2B	3B	HR	RBI	BB	SO	AVG	OBP	SLG	PRO+	BR	/A	RC	SB	CS	SBR	FR	POS	TPR
1930	Was-A	18	63	9	18	3	3	0	17	5	6	.286	.348	.429	95	-0	-1	10	1	0	0	-1	1	-0.1
1931	Was-A	139	524	70	141	34	8	8	85	47	45	.269	.335	.410	94	-5	-5	73	7	5	-1	-7	*1	-2.4
1932	Was-A	101	347	52	101	21	5	4	52	32	19	.291	.353	.415	99	-1	-0	52	5	2	0	-2	1	-0.9
1933	*Was-A	153	602	89	194	34	10	11	107	59	48	.322	.385	.467	126	21	22	110	17	8	0	-7	*1	0.4
1934	Was-A	63	263	49	76	12	3	3	25	30	14	.289	.364	.392	99	-2	-0	37	2	7	-4	-4	1	-1.7
1935	Was-A	151	633	99	165	25	9	2	74	78	44	.261	.345	.338	80	-20	-17	78	5	4	-1	0	*1	-3.0
1936	Was-A	149	588	107	189	42	8	16	118	64	30	.321	.392	.502	126	17	22	117	15	7	0	-2	*1	0.0
1937	Was-A	136	547	73	155	24	11	6	61	63	39	.283	.357	.400	95	-8	-4	81	6	3	0	3	*1	-1.5
1938	Chi-A	117	412	67	110	27	4	8	51	72	35	.267	.376	.410	95	-1	-2	67	9	7	-2	-7	*1	-2.3
1939	Chi-A	139	546	107	164	24	9	15	56	64	51	.300	.376	.460	110	10	8	99	18	5	2	-4	*1	-0.5
1940	Chi-A	155	603	111	169	28	8	27	94	87	59	.280	.374	.488	120	19	18	116	12	5	1	-5	*1	0.6
1941	Chi-A	153	600	99	150	39	5	12	63	70	55	.250	.331	.392	92	-9	-8	81	20	5	3	-1	*1	-0.9
1942	Chi-A	115	413	60	103	14	4	4	52	60	22	.249	.347	.332	94	-3	-2	54	22	9	1	-4	*1	-0.6
1943	Chi-A	153	531	55	113	21	1	5	46	76	45	.213	.319	.284	77	-13	-13	54	14	8	-1	1	*1	-1.8
1944	Was-A	139	518	90	144	26	7	4	51	68	40	.278	.364	.378	117	10	13	75	11	6	-0	-2	*1	0.2
1945	Was-A	142	533	73	152	29	13	2	75	79	31	.285	.378	.400	137	19	25	88	10	5	0	-6	*1	1.5
1946	Was-A	14	20	2	3	0	0	0	2	5	2	.150	.320	.150	36	-2	-1	1	0	0	0	0	/1	-0.1
	Chi-A	64	238	24	65	9	3	4	20	21	24	.273	.335	.387	105	0	1	30	4	4	-1	-2	1	-0.5
	Yr	78	258	26	68	9	3	4	22	26	26	.264	.333	.368	100	-1	-0	32	4	4	-1	-1		-0.6
1947	Chi-A	3	3	0	0	0	0	0	0	0	3	.000	.000	.000	-99	-1	-1	0	0	0	0	0	H	0.0
Total	18	2104	7984	1236	2212	412	111	131	1049	980	612	.277	.359	.406	104	33	54	1223	178	90	-1	-46	*1	-13.6

■ KENNY KUHN
Kuhn, Kenneth Harold   b: 3/20/37, Louisville, Ky.   BR/TR, 5'10.5", 175 lbs.   Deb: 7/07/55

YEAR	TM/L	G	AB	R	H	2B	3B	HR	RBI	BB	SO	AVG	OBP	SLG	PRO+	BR	/A	RC	SB	CS	SBR	FR	POS	TPR
1955	Cle-A	4	6	0	2	0	0	0	0	1	0	.333	.429	.333	103	0	0	1	1	0	0	-2	/S	0.0
1956	Cle-A	27	22	7	6	1	0	0	2	0	4	.273	.273	.318	54	-1	-2	2	0	1	-1	2	S/2	0.2
1957	Cle-A	40	53	5	9	0	0	0	5	4	9	.170	.228	.170	10	-6	-6	2	0	0	0	-3	2/3S	-0.8
Total	3	71	81	12	17	1	0	0	7	5	13	.210	.256	.222	30	-8	-8	5	1	1	-0	-2	/S23	-0.6

■ WALT KUHN
Kuhn, Walter Charles "Red"   b: 2/2/1884, Fresno, Cal.   d: 6/14/35, Fresno, Cal.   BR/TR, 5'7", 162 lbs.   Deb: 4/18/12

YEAR	TM/L	G	AB	R	H	2B	3B	HR	RBI	BB	SO	AVG	OBP	SLG	PRO+	BR	/A	RC	SB	CS	SBR	FR	POS	TPR
1912	Chi-A	76	178	16	36	7	0	0	10	20		.202	.286	.242	53	-11	-10	14	5			9	C/2	0.6
1913	Chi-A	26	50	5	8	1	0	0	5	13	8	.160	.333	.180	52	-2	-2	3	1			-2	C	-0.1
1914	Chi-A	17	40	4	11	1	0	0	0	8	11	.275	.396	.300	111	1	1	5	2	3	-1	-1	C	0.0
Total	3	119	268	25	55	9	0	0	15	41	19	.205	.313	.239	62	-12	-11	22	8	3		6	C/2	0.5

■ CHARLIE KUHNS
Kuhns, Charles B.   b: 10/27/1877, Freeport, Pa.   d: 7/15/22, Pittsburgh, Pa.   5'9", 160 lbs.   Deb: 6/04/1897

YEAR	TM/L	G	AB	R	H	2B	3B	HR	RBI	BB	SO	AVG	OBP	SLG	PRO+	BR	/A	RC	SB	CS	SBR	FR	POS	TPR
1897	Pit-N	1	3	0	0	0	0	0	0	1		.000	.250	.000	-30	-1	-1	0	0			0	/3	0.0
1899	Bos-N	7	18	2	5	0	0	0	3	2		.278	.350	.278	69	-0	-1	2	0			-1	/S3	-0.1
Total	2	8	21	2	5	0	0	0	3	3		.238	.333	.238	55	-1	-1	2	0			-1	/S3	-0.1

■ DUANE KUIPER
Kuiper, Duane Eugene   b: 6/19/50, Racine, Wis.   BL/TR, 6', 175 lbs.   Deb: 9/09/74

YEAR	TM/L	G	AB	R	H	2B	3B	HR	RBI	BB	SO	AVG	OBP	SLG	PRO+	BR	/A	RC	SB	CS	SBR	FR	POS	TPR
1974	Cle-A	10	22	7	11	2	0	0	4	2	2	.500	.542	.591	228	4	4	6	1	1	-0	1	/2	0.5
1975	Cle-A	90	346	42	101	11	1	0	25	30	26	.292	.362	.329	97	-0	-0	39	19	18	-5	-14	2/D	-1.6
1976	Cle-A	135	506	47	133	13	6	0	37	30	42	.263	.305	.312	82	-12	-11	43	10	17	-7	20	*2/1D	0.9
1977	Cle-A	148	610	62	169	15	8	1	50	37	55	.277	.326	.333	83	-16	-14	66	11	11	-3	2	*2	-0.2
1978	Cle-A	149	547	52	155	18	6	0	43	19	35	.283	.312	.338	84	-13	-12	54	4	9	-4	-19	*2	-2.7
1979	Cle-A	140	479	46	122	9	5	0	39	37	27	.255	.313	.294	65	-23	-23	41	4	9	-4	-4	*2	-2.4
1980	Cle-A	42	149	10	42	5	0	0	9	13	8	.282	.340	.315	80	-4	-4	17	0	1	-1	-8	2	-0.9
1981	Cle-A	72	206	15	53	6	0	0	14	8	13	.257	.285	.286	66	-9	-9	17	1	1	-0	-6	2	-1.2
1982	SF-N	107	218	26	61	9	1	0	17	32	24	.280	.377	.330	100	1	1	28	2	2	-1	-7	2	-0.3
1983	SF-N	72	176	14	44	2	2	0	14	27	13	.250	.356	.284	82	-4	-3	18	0	1	-1	-8	2	-0.9
1984	SF-N	83	115	8	23	1	0	0	11	12	10	.200	.276	.209	39	-9	-9	7	0	1	-1	6	2/1	-0.2
1985	SF-N	9	5	0	3	0	0	0	0	1	0	.600	.667	.600	270	1	1	2	0	0	0	0	/H	0.1
Total	12	1057	3379	329	917	91	29	1	263	248	255	.271	.326	.316	81	-83	-78	340	52	71	-27	-36	2/1D	-8.9

■ JEFF KUNKEL
Kunkel, Jeffrey William   b: 3/25/62, W.Palm Beach, Fla.   BR/TR, 6'2", 180 lbs.   Deb: 7/23/84

YEAR	TM/L	G	AB	R	H	2B	3B	HR	RBI	BB	SO	AVG	OBP	SLG	PRO+	BR	/A	RC	SB	CS	SBR	FR	POS	TPR
1984	Tex-A	50	142	13	29	2	3	3	7	2	35	.204	.221	.324	47	-10	-11	9	4	3	-1	-1	S/D	-0.8
1985	Tex-A	2	4	1	1	0	0	0	0	0	3	.250	.250	.250	37	-0	-0	0	0	0	0	1	/S	0.0
1986	Tex-A	8	13	3	3	0	0	1	2	0	2	.231	.231	.462	81	-0	-0	1	0	0	0	-0	/SD	0.0
1987	Tex-A	15	32	1	7	0	0	1	2	0	10	.219	.242	.313	46	-3	-3	2	0	1	-1	3	2/301SD	0.0
1988	Tex-A	55	154	14	35	8	3	2	15	4	35	.227	.252	.357	67	-7	-7	12	0	1	-1	9	2S3/OPD	0.4
1989	Tex-A	108	293	39	79	21	2	8	29	20	75	.270	.323	.437	110	4	3	41	3	2	-0	10	SO/23PD	1.3
1990	Tex-A	99	200	17	34	11	1	3	17	11	66	.170	.221	.280	38	-17	-17	11	2	1	0	10	S32/O	-0.1
Total	7	337	838	88	188	42	9	18	72	37	226	.224	.264	.360	71	-33	-35	77	9	8	-2	27	S/203DP1	0.8

■ RUSTY KUNTZ
Kuntz, Russell Jay   b: 2/4/55, Orange, Cal.   BR/TR, 6'3", 190 lbs.   Deb: 9/01/79   C

YEAR	TM/L	G	AB	R	H	2B	3B	HR	RBI	BB	SO	AVG	OBP	SLG	PRO+	BR	/A	RC	SB	CS	SBR	FR	POS	TPR
1979	Chi-A	5	11	0	1	0	0	0	0	2	6	.091	.231	.091	-9	-2	-2	0	0	0	0	2	/O	0.0
1980	Chi-A	36	62	5	14	4	0	0	3	5	13	.226	.284	.290	58	-4	-4	5	1	0	0	2	O	-0.1
1981	Chi-A	67	55	15	14	2	0	0	4	6	8	.255	.339	.291	85	-1	-1	6	1	0	0	8	O/D	0.7
1982	Chi-A	21	26	4	5	1	0	0	3	2	8	.192	.250	.231	33	-2	-2	1	0	0	0	0	O	-0.2
1983	Chi-A	28	42	6	11	1	0	0	1	6	13	.262	.354	.286	76	-1	-1	5	1	0	0	2	O/D	0.1
	Min-A	31	100	13	19	3	0	3	5	12	28	.190	.277	.310	59	-5	-6	8	0	0	0	2	O	-0.4
	Yr	59	142	19	30	4	0	3	6	18	41	.211	.300	.303	64	-6	-7	13	1	0	0	4		-0.3
1984	*Det-A	84	140	32	40	12	0	2	22	25	28	.286	.398	.414	126	6	6	25	2	2	-1	1	OD	0.4
1985	Det-A	5	5	0	0	0	0	0	0	2	2	.000	.286	.000	-13	-1	-1	0	0	1	-1	-0	/1D	-0.1
Total	7	277	441	75	104	23	0	5	38	60	106	.236	.330	.322	81	-10	-10	50	5	3	-0	16	O/D1	0.4

■ WHITEY KUROWSKI
Kurowski, George John   b: 4/19/18, Reading, Pa.   BR/TR, 5'11", 193 lbs.   Deb: 9/23/41

YEAR	TM/L	G	AB	R	H	2B	3B	HR	RBI	BB	SO	AVG	OBP	SLG	PRO+	BR	/A	RC	SB	CS	SBR	FR	POS	TPR
1941	StL-N	5	9	1	3	2	0	0	2	0	2	.333	.400	.556	157	1	1	2	0			-1	/3	0.0
1942	*StL-N	115	366	51	93	17	3	9	42	33	60	.254	.326	.391	102	4	0	48	7			9	*3/SO	1.0
1943	StL-N	139	522	69	150	24	8	13	70	31	54	.287	.330	.439	116	11	9	74	3			9	*3/S	1.0
1944	*StL-N	149	555	95	150	25	7	20	87	58	40	.270	.341	.449	119	14	13	85	2			4	*3/2S	2.5
1945	StL-N	133	511	84	165	27	3	21	102	45	45	.323	.383	.511	144	31	29	100	1			2	*3/S	2.9
1946	*StL-N	142	519	76	156	32	5	14	89	72	47	.301	.391	.462	136	29	26	97	2			0	*3	2.9
1947	StL-N	146	513	108	159	27	6	27	104	87	56	.310	.420	.544	148	42	39	118	4			-14	*3	2.0
1948	StL-N	77	220	34	47	8	0	2	33	42	28	.214	.352	.277	68	-7	-8	25	0			-11	3	-2.0
1949	StL-N	10	14	0	2	0	0	0	0	1	6	.143	.200	.143	4	-2	-1	0	0			-0	/3	-0.2
Total	9	916	3229	518	925	162	32	106	529	369	332	.286	.366	.455	124	123	106	551	19			-10	3/S2O	10.1

■ CRAIG KUSICK
Kusick, Craig Robert   b: 9/30/48, Milwaukee, Wis.   BR/TR, 6'3", 210 lbs.   Deb: 9/08/73

YEAR	TM/L	G	AB	R	H	2B	3B	HR	RBI	BB	SO	AVG	OBP	SLG	PRO+	BR	/A	RC	SB	CS	SBR	FR	POS	TPR
1973	Min-A	15	48	4	12	2	0	4	7	7	9	.250	.357	.292	98	-1	-1	6	0	0	0	0	1/OD	0.0
1974	Min-A	76	201	36	48	7	1	8	26	35	36	.239	.354	.403	113	5	4	30	0	0	0	3	1	0.4
1975	Min-A	57	156	14	37	8	0	6	27	21	23	.237	.346	.404	109	3	2	23	0	0	0	1	1	0.0

YEAR	TM/L	G	AB	R	H	2B	3B	HR	RBI	BB	SO	AVG	OBP	SLG	PRO+	BR	/A	RC	SB	CS	SBR	FR	POS	TPR
1976	Min-A	109	266	33	69	13	0	11	36	35	44	.259	.348	.432	124	9	8	43	5	1	1	3	D1	1.2
1977	Min-A	115	268	34	68	12	0	12	45	49	60	.254	.375	.433	121	9	9	43	3	1	0	-1	D1	0.7
1978	Min-A	77	191	23	33	3	2	4	20	37	38	.173	.310	.272	64	-8	-8	17	3	2	-0	2	D1/O	-0.7
1979	Min-A	24	54	8	13	4	0	3	6	3	11	.241	.281	.481	97	-0	-1	7	0	0	0	0	D/1	0.0
	Tor-A	24	54	3	11	1	0	2	7	7	7	.204	.306	.333	72	-2	-2	6	0	0	0	1	1/PD	-0.1
	Yr	48	108	11	24	5	0	5	13	10	18	.222	.294	.407	85	-2	-3	13	0	0	0	1		-0.1
Total	7	497	1238	155	291	50	3	46	171	194	228	.235	.345	.392	105	15	12	174	11	4	1	9	1D/OP	1.5

■ ART KUSNYER   Kusnyer, Arthur William b: 12/19/45, Akron, Ohio   BR/TR, 6'2", 197 lbs.   Deb: 9/21/70 C

YEAR	TM/L	G	AB	R	H	2B	3B	HR	RBI	BB	SO	AVG	OBP	SLG	PRO+	BR	/A	RC	SB	CS	SBR	FR	POS	TPR
1970	Chi-A	4	10	0	1	0	0	0	0	0	4	.100	.100	.100	-43	-2	-2	0	0	0	0	1	/C	0.0
1971	Cal-A	6	13	0	2	0	0	0	0	0	3	.154	.154	.154	-14	-2	-2	0	0	0	0	0	/C	0.0
1972	Cal-A	64	179	13	37	2	1	2	13	16	33	.207	.276	.263	64	-9	-7	14	0	0	0	-1	C	-0.8
1973	Cal-A	41	64	5	8	2	0	0	3	2	12	.125	.152	.156	-14	-10	-9	1	0	1	-1	1	C	-0.7
1976	Mil-A	15	34	2	4	1	0	0	3	1	5	.118	.167	.147	-8	-5	-5	1	1	0	0	-0	C	-0.3
1978	KC-A	9	13	1	3	1	0	1	2	2	4	.231	.333	.538	138	1	1	3	0	0	0	3	/C	0.4
Total	6	139	313	21	55	6	1	3	21	21	61	.176	.232	.230	37	-26	-24	19	1	1	-0	5	C	-1.4

■ JUL KUSTUS   Kustus, Joseph J. "Joe" or "Kul" b: 9/5/1882, Detroit, Mich.   d: 4/27/16, Eloise, Mich.   BR/TR, 5'10", Deb: 4/17/09

YEAR	TM/L	G	AB	R	H	2B	3B	HR	RBI	BB	SO	AVG	OBP	SLG	PRO+	BR	/A	RC	SB	CS	SBR	FR	POS	TPR
1909	Bro-N	53	173	12	25	5	1	1	11	11		.145	.204	.191	23	-16	-15	9	9			1	O	-1.7

■ RANDY KUTCHER   Kutcher, Randy Scott b: 4/20/60, Anchorage, Alaska   BR/TR, 5'11", 170 lbs.   Deb: 6/19/86

YEAR	TM/L	G	AB	R	H	2B	3B	HR	RBI	BB	SO	AVG	OBP	SLG	PRO+	BR	/A	RC	SB	CS	SBR	FR	POS	TPR
1986	SF-N	71	186	28	44	9	1	7	16	11	41	.237	.279	.409	92	-4	-3	20	6	5	-1	2	OS/32	-0.1
1987	SF-N	14	16	7	3	1	1	0	1	1	5	.188	.235	.375	61	-1	-1	2	1	0	0	2	/O23S	0.1
1988	Bos-A	19	12	2	2	1	0	0	0	0	2	.167	.167	.250	14	-1	-1	0	0	1	-1	1	/O3D	0.1
1989	Bos-A	77	160	28	36	10	3	2	18	11	46	.225	.275	.363	74	-5	-6	15	3	0	1	6	O/3CD	0.0
1990	*Bos-A	63	74	18	17	4	1	1	5	13	18	.230	.345	.351	91	-0	-1	9	3	3	-1	11	O3/2D	1.0
Total	5	244	448	83	102	25	6	10	40	36	112	.228	.285	.377	82	-12	-12	46	13	9	-2	24	O/3DS2C	1.1

■ JOE KUTINA   Kutina, Joseph Peter b: 1/16/1885, Chicago, Ill.   d: 4/13/45, Chicago, Ill.   BR/TR, 6'2", 205 lbs.   Deb: 9/06/11

YEAR	TM/L	G	AB	R	H	2B	3B	HR	RBI	BB	SO	AVG	OBP	SLG	PRO+	BR	/A	RC	SB	CS	SBR	FR	POS	TPR
1911	StL-A	26	101	12	26	6	2	3	15	2		.257	.279	.446	105	-1	0	13	2			-1	1	0.0
1912	StL-A	69	205	18	42	9	3	1	18	13		.205	.262	.293	61	-12	-11	16	0			-3	1/O	-1.2
Total	2	95	306	30	68	15	5	4	33	15		.222	.268	.343	76	-12	-11	28	2			-3	/1O	-1.2

■ AL KVASNAK   Kvasnak, Alexander b: 1/11/21, Sagamore, Pa.   BR/TR, 6'1", 170 lbs.   Deb: 4/15/42

YEAR	TM/L	G	AB	R	H	2B	3B	HR	RBI	BB	SO	AVG	OBP	SLG	PRO+	BR	/A	RC	SB	CS	SBR	FR	POS	TPR
1942	Was-A	5	11	3	2	0	0	0	0	2	1	.182	.308	.182	40	-1	-1	1	0	0	0	-0	/O	0.0

■ ANDY KYLE   Kyle, Andrew Ewing b: 10/29/1889, Toronto, Ont., Can.   d: 9/6/71, Toronto, Ont., Can.   BL/TL, 5'8", 160 lbs.   Deb: 9/07/12

YEAR	TM/L	G	AB	R	H	2B	3B	HR	RBI	BB	SO	AVG	OBP	SLG	PRO+	BR	/A	RC	SB	CS	SBR	FR	POS	TPR
1912	Cin-N	9	21	3	7	1	0	0	4	4	2	.333	.440	.381	129	1	1	4	0			1	/O	0.2

■ CHET LAABS   Laabs, Chester Peter b: 4/30/12, Milwaukee, Wis.   d: 1/26/83, Warren, Mich.   BR/TR, 5'8", 175 lbs.   Deb: 5/05/37

YEAR	TM/L	G	AB	R	H	2B	3B	HR	RBI	BB	SO	AVG	OBP	SLG	PRO+	BR	/A	RC	SB	CS	SBR	FR	POS	TPR
1937	Det-A	72	242	31	58	13	5	8	37	24	66	.240	.308	.434	83	-7	-8	33	6	2	1	-2	O	-1.0
1938	Det-A	64	211	26	50	7	3	7	37	15	52	.237	.288	.398	66	-11	-13	24	3	2	-0	3	O	-0.9
1939	Det-A	5	16	1	5	1	1	0	2	2	0	.313	.389	.500	117	1	0	3	0	0	0	1	/O	0.1
	StL-A	95	317	52	95	20	5	10	62	33	62	.300	.368	.489	115	7	6	57	4	1	1	-4	O	0.0
	Yr	100	333	53	100	21	6	10	64	35	62	.300	.369	.489	115	8	7	60	4	1	1	-3		0.1
1940	StL-A	105	218	32	59	11	5	10	40	34	59	.271	.372	.505	122	8	7	43	3	3	-1	-5	O	-0.2
1941	StL-A	118	392	64	109	23	6	15	59	51	59	.278	.361	.482	117	11	9	71	5	2	0	-2	*O	0.1
1942	StL-A	144	520	90	143	21	7	27	99	88	88	.275	.380	.498	144	32	31	103	0	3	-2	-2	*O	1.8
1943	StL-A	151	580	83	145	27	7	17	85	73	105	.250	.338	.409	115	12	11	82	5	7	-3	6	*O	1.0
1944	*StL-A	66	201	28	47	10	2	5	23	29	33	.234	.330	.378	96	1	-1	27	3	1	0	-3	O	-0.4
1945	StL-A	35	109	15	26	4	3	1	8	16	17	.239	.352	.358	101	1	1	15	0	0	0	-2	O	-0.2
1946	StL-A	80	264	40	69	13	0	16	52	20	50	.261	.316	.492	117	6	5	38	3	1	0	0	O	0.1
1947	Phi-A	15	32	5	7	1	0	1	5	4	4	.219	.306	.344	79	-1	-1	4	0	0	0	1	/O	0.0
Total	11	950	3102	467	813	151	44	117	509	389	595	.262	.346	.452	113	60	48	501	32	22	-4	-9	O	0.4

■ COCO LABOY   Laboy, Jose Alberto b: 7/3/39, Ponce, P.R.   BR/TR, 5'10", 165 lbs.   Deb: 4/08/69

YEAR	TM/L	G	AB	R	H	2B	3B	HR	RBI	BB	SO	AVG	OBP	SLG	PRO+	BR	/A	RC	SB	CS	SBR	FR	POS	TPR
1969	Mon-N	157	562	53	145	29	1	18	83	40	96	.258	.312	.409	100	-1	-1	70	0	2	-1	4	*3	0.2
1970	Mon-N	137	432	37	86	26	1	5	53	31	81	.199	.256	.299	48	-33	-32	31	0	2	-1	-4	*3/2	-4.1
1971	Mon-N	76	151	10	38	4	0	1	14	11	19	.252	.302	.298	70	-6	-6	13	0	1	-1	1	3/2	-0.4
1972	Mon-N	28	69	6	18	2	0	3	14	10	16	.261	.354	.420	117	2	2	11	0	0	0	-2	3/2S	0.0
1973	Mon-N	22	33	2	4	1	0	1	2	5	8	.121	.237	.242	32	-3	-3	2	0	0	0	1	3/2	-0.2
Total	5	420	1247	108	291	62	2	28	166	97	220	.233	.292	.354	77	-41	-41	127	0	5	-3	0	*3/2S	-4.5

■ CANDY LaCHANCE   LaChance, George Joseph b: 2/15/1870, Waterbury, Conn.   d: 8/18/32, Waterville, Conn.   BB/TR, 6'1", 183 lbs.   Deb: 8/15/1893

YEAR	TM/L	G	AB	R	H	2B	3B	HR	RBI	BB	SO	AVG	OBP	SLG	PRO+	BR	/A	RC	SB	CS	SBR	FR	POS	TPR
1893	Bro-N	11	35	1	6	1	0	0	6	2	12	.171	.237	.200	19	-4	-4	2	0			-6	/CO	-0.7
1894	Bro-N	68	257	48	83	13	6	5	52	16	32	.323	.365	.494	115	2	2	55	20			-9	1C/O	0.0
1895	Bro-N	127	536	99	167	22	8	8	108	29	48	.312	.356	.427	112	2	9	97	37			-6	*1/O	0.5
1896	Bro-N	89	348	60	99	10	13	7	58	23	32	.284	.331	.448	112	1	5	59	17			-3	*1	0.3
1897	Bro-N	126	520	86	160	28	16	4	90	15		.308	.333	.446	113	3	7	88	26			-4	*1	0.1
1898	Bro-N	136	526	61	130	23	7	5	65	31		.247	.299	.346	87	-10	-9	63	23			-20	1SO	-2.5
1899	Bal-N	125	472	65	145	23	10	1	75	21		.307	.340	.405	104	5	1	80	31			-7	*1	-0.2
1901	Cle-A	133	548	81	166	22	9	1	75	7		.303	.315	.381	98	-5	-2	72	11			-3	*1	-0.9
1902	Bos-A	138	541	60	151	13	4	6	56	18		.279	.309	.351	82	-12	-14	64	8			-11	*1	-2.2
1903	*Bos-A	141	522	60	134	22	6	1	53	28		.257	.295	.328	84	-7	-11	58	12			-11	*1	-2.1
1904	Bos-A	157	573	55	130	19	5	1	47	23		.227	.257	.283	68	-18	-21	47	7			-13	*1	-3.4
1905	Bos-A	12	41	1	6	1	0	0	5	6		.146	.255	.171	37	-3	-3	2	0			-0	1	-0.3
Total	12	1263	4919	678	1377	197	86	39	690	219	124	.280	.316	.379	95	-47	-36	686	192			-92	*1/SOC	-11.4

■ RENE LACHEMANN   Lachemann, Rene George b: 5/4/45, Los Angeles, Cal.   BR/TR, 6', 198 lbs.   Deb: 5/04/65 MC

YEAR	TM/L	G	AB	R	H	2B	3B	HR	RBI	BB	SO	AVG	OBP	SLG	PRO+	BR	/A	RC	SB	CS	SBR	FR	POS	TPR
1965	KC-A	92	216	20	49	7	1	9	29	12	57	.227	.268	.394	87	-5	-5	22	0	0	0	1	C	0.2
1966	KC-A	7	5	0	1	1	0	0	0	0	1	.200	.200	.400	70	-0	-0	0	0	0	0	1	/C	0.1
1968	Oak-A	19	60	3	9	1	0	0	4	1	11	.150	.177	.167	5	-7	-7	2	0	0	0	-6	C	-1.4
Total	3	118	281	23	59	9	1	9	33	13	69	.210	.247	.345	70	-12	-11	24	0	0	0	-4	/C	-1.1

■ PETE LaCOCK   LaCock, Ralph Pierre b: 1/17/52, Burbank, Cal.   BL/TL, 6'2", 200 lbs.   Deb: 9/06/72

YEAR	TM/L	G	AB	R	H	2B	3B	HR	RBI	BB	SO	AVG	OBP	SLG	PRO+	BR	/A	RC	SB	CS	SBR	FR	POS	TPR
1972	Chi-N	5	6	3	3	0	0	0	4	0	1	.500	.500	.500	167	1	1	2	1	0	0	-0	/O	0.1
1973	Chi-N	11	16	1	4	1	0	0	3	1	2	.250	.294	.313	63	-1	-1	2	0	0	0	1	/O	0.0
1974	Chi-N	35	110	9	20	4	1	1	8	12	16	.182	.268	.264	47	-7	-8	8	0	0	0	2	O1	-0.7
1975	Chi-N	106	249	30	57	8	1	6	30	37	27	.229	.329	.341	82	-4	-6	27	0	2	-1	5	1O	-0.5
1976	Chi-N	106	244	34	54	9	2	8	28	42	37	.221	.338	.373	93	1	-2	31	1	4	-2	-2	1O	-0.8
1977	*KC-A	88	218	25	66	12	1	3	29	15	26	.303	.360	.408	105	2	2	31	2	1	0	1	1DO	0.2
1978	*KC-A	118	322	44	95	21	2	5	48	21	27	.295	.338	.419	109	4	3	44	1	0	0	-6	*1	-0.6
1979	KC-A	132	408	49	113	25	4	3	56	37	26	.277	.339	.380	92	-3	-5	50	2	1	0	2	*1D	-0.8
1980	*KC-A	114	156	14	32	6	0	1	18	17	10	.205	.287	.263	51	-10	-10	11	1	0	0	2	1O	-1.3
Total	9	715	1729	214	444	86	11	27	224	182	171	.257	.329	.366	89	-18	-25	206	8	8	-2	6	1O/D	-4.4

YEAR	TM/L	G	AB	R	H	2B	3B	HR	RBI	BB	SO	AVG	OBP	SLG	PRO+	BR	/A	RC	SB	CS	SBR	FR	POS	TPR
■ LEON LACY			Lacy, Leondaus b: 4/10/48, Longview, Tex. BR/TR, 6'1", 175 lbs. Deb: 6/30/72																					
1972	LA-N	60	243	34	63	7	3	0	12	19	37	.259	.313	.313	80	-7	-6	24	5	3	-0	-8	2	-1.0
1973	LA-N	57	135	14	28	2	0	0	8	15	34	.207	.287	.222	45	-10	-9	9	2	3	-1	-1	2	-0.9
1974	*LA-N	48	78	13	22	6	0	0	8	2	14	.282	.300	.359	87	-2	-2	9	2	0	1	2	2/3	0.3
1975	LA-N	101	306	44	96	11	5	7	40	22	29	.314	.360	.451	129	9	11	44	5	9	-4	-6	2O/S	0.1
1976	Atl-N	50	180	25	49	4	2	3	20	6	12	.272	.299	.367	83	-3	-5	18	2	2	-1	-9	2/O3	-1.2
	LA-N	53	158	17	42	7	1	0	14	16	13	.266	.333	.323	88	-2	-2	16	1	2	-1	1	O/32	-0.3
	Yr	103	338	42	91	11	3	3	34	22	25	.269	.316	.346	86	-6	-6	34	3	4	-2	-8		-1.5
1977	*LA-N	75	169	28	45	7	0	6	21	10	21	.266	.307	.414	92	-2	-2	22	4	0	1	-5	O23	-0.5
1978	*LA-N	103	245	29	64	16	4	13	40	27	30	.261	.337	.518	136	11	11	42	7	4	-0	-4	O2/3S	0.6
1979	Pit-N	84	182	17	45	9	3	5	15	22	36	.247	.332	.412	97	0	-1	27	6	1	1	-5	O/2	-0.5
1980	Pit-N	109	278	45	93	20	4	7	33	28	33	.335	.399	.511	150	20	19	57	18	9	0	5	O/3	2.1
1981	Pit-N	78	213	31	57	11	4	2	10	11	29	.268	.307	.385	92	-2	-3	28	24	3	5	0	O/3	0.1
1982	Pit-N	121	359	66	112	16	3	5	31	32	57	.312	.370	.415	116	10	8	56	40	15	3	-4	*O/3	0.5
1983	Pit-N	108	288	40	87	12	3	4	13	22	36	.302	.352	.406	107	4	3	42	31	13	2	-4	O	-0.1
1984	Pit-N	138	474	66	152	26	3	12	70	32	61	.321	.364	.464	131	18	18	77	21	11	-0	13	*O/2	2.8
1985	Bal-A	121	492	69	144	22	4	9	48	39	95	.293	.347	.409	109	4	6	70	10	3	1	0	*O/D	0.6
1986	Bal-A	130	491	77	141	18	0	11	47	37	71	.287	.337	.391	99	-2	-1	62	4	6	-2	2	*O/D	-0.3
1987	Bal-A	87	258	35	63	13	3	7	28	32	49	.244	.328	.399	94	-3	-2	34	3	2	-0	2	O/D	-0.1
Total	16	1523	4549	650	1303	207	42	91	458	372	657	.286	.342	.410	108	42	44	637	185	86	4	-22	*O2/3DS	2.2
■ GUY LACY			Lacy, Osceola Guy b: 6/12/1897, Cleveland, Tenn. d: 11/19/53, Cleveland, Tenn. BR/TR, 5'11.5", 170 lbs. Deb: 5/17/26																					
1926	Cle-A	13	24	2	4	0	0	1	2	2	2	.167	.259	.292	43	-2	-2	2	0	0	0	1	2/3	0.0
■ HI LADD			Ladd, Arthur Clifford b: 2/9/1870, Willimantic, Conn. d: 5/7/48, Cranston, R.I. 6'4", 180 lbs. Deb: 7/12/1898																					
1898	Pit-N	1	1	0	0	0	0	0	0	0		.000	.000	.000	-99	-0	-0	0	0			0		0.0
	Bos-N	1	4	1	1	0	0	0	0	0		.250	.250	.250	43	-0	-0	0	0			0	/O	0.0
	Yr	2	5	1	1	0	0	0	0	0		.200	.200	.200	16	-1	-1	0	0			0		0.0
■ STEVE LADEW			Ladew, Stephen b: St.Louis, Mo. Deb: 9/27/1889																					
1889	KC-a	2	4	0	0	0	0	0	0	0	3	.000	.000	.000	-95	-1	-1	0	0			-0	/OP	0.0
■ JOE LAFATA			Lafata, Joseph Joseph b: 8/3/21, Detroit, Mich. BL/TL, 6', 163 lbs. Deb: 4/17/47																					
1947	NY-N	62	95	13	21	1	0	2	18	15	18	.221	.333	.295	68	-4	-4	10	1			1	O/1	-0.3
1948	NY-N	1	1	0	0	0	0	0	0	0	1	.000	.000	.000	-99	-0	-0	0	0			0	H	0.0
1949	NY-N	64	140	18	33	2	2	3	16	9	23	.236	.282	.343	67	-7	-7	14	1			-4	1	-1.0
Total	3	127	236	31	54	3	2	5	34	24	42	.229	.303	.322	67	-11	-11	24	2			-4	/1O	-1.3
■ FLIP LAFFERTY			Lafferty, Frank Bernard b: 5/4/1854, Scranton, Pa. d: 2/8/10, Wilmington, Del. TR , Deb: 9/15/1876																					
1876	Phi-N	1	3	0	0	0	0	0	0	0	0	.000	.000	.000	-99	-1	-1	0				0	/P	0.0
1877	Lou-N	4	17	2	1	1	0	0	0	0	4	.059	.059	.118	-39	-3	-3	0				-1	O	-0.3
Total	2	5	20	2	1	1	0	0	0	0	4	.050	.050	.100	-46	-3	-4	0				-1	/OP	-0.3
■ TY LaFOREST			LaForest, Byron Joseph b: 4/18/17, Edmunston, N.B., Canada d: 5/5/47, Arlington, Mass. BR/TR, 5'9", 165 lbs. Deb: 8/04/45																					
1945	Bos-A	52	204	25	51	7	4	2	16	10	35	.250	.285	.353	83	-5	-5	19	4	4	-1	1	3/O	-0.4
■ ROGER LaFRANCOIS			LaFrancois, Roger Victor b: 8/2/54, Norwich, Conn. BL/TR, 6'2", 215 lbs. Deb: 5/27/82																					
1982	Bos-A	8	10	1	4	1	0	0	1	0	0	.400	.400	.500	137	1	1	2	0	0	0	-0	/C	0.1
■ MIKE LAGA			Laga, Michael Russell b: 6/14/60, Ridgewood, N.J. BL/TL, 6'2", 210 lbs. Deb: 9/01/82																					
1982	Det-A	27	88	6	23	9	0	3	11	4	23	.261	.293	.466	104	0	0	12	1	0	0	-2	1/D	-0.1
1983	Det-A	12	21	2	4	0	0	0	2	1	9	.190	.227	.190	17	-2	-2	1	0	0	0	0	/1D	-0.1
1984	Det-A	9	11	1	6	0	0	0	1	1	2	.545	.583	.545	216	2	2	4	0	0	0	0	/1D	0.2
1985	Det-A	9	36	3	6	1	0	2	6	0	9	.167	.167	.361	40	-3	-3	2	0	0	0	-0	1/D	-0.2
1986	Det-A	15	45	6	9	1	0	3	8	5	13	.200	.280	.422	88	-1	-1	6	0	0	0	-0	1/D	-0.1
	StL-N	18	46	7	10	4	0	3	8	5	18	.217	.308	.500	122	1	1	7	0	0	0	2	1	0.3
1987	StL-N	17	29	4	4	1	0	1	4	2	7	.138	.194	.276	22	-3	-3	1	0	0	0	1	1	-0.3
1988	StL-N	41	100	5	13	0	0	1	4	2	21	.130	.147	.160	-12	-14	-14	2	0	0	0	1	1	-1.6
1989	SF-N	17	20	1	4	1	0	1	7	1	6	.200	.238	.400	82	-1	-1	2	0	0	0	0	/1	0.0
1990	SF-N	23	27	4	5	1	0	2	4	1	7	.185	.241	.444	85	-1	-1	3	0	0	0	1	1	0.0
Total	9	188	423	39	84	18	0	16	55	22	115	.199	.242	.355	63	-23	-22	39	1	0	0	3	1/D	-1.9
■ JOE LAHOUD			Lahoud, Joseph Michael b: 4/14/47, Danbury, Conn. BL/TL, 6'1", 198 lbs. Deb: 4/10/68																					
1968	Bos-A	29	78	5	15	1	0	1	6	16	16	.192	.330	.244	71	-2	-2	7	0	2	-1	-4	O	-0.8
1969	Bos-A	101	218	32	41	5	0	9	21	40	43	.188	.317	.335	78	-5	-6	26	2	1	0	-4	O/1	-1.1
1970	Bos-A	17	49	6	12	1	0	2	5	7	6	.245	.339	.388	93	0	-0	7	0	0	0	2	O	0.1
1971	Bos-A	107	256	39	55	9	3	14	32	40	45	.215	.330	.438	108	5	3	38	2	2	-1	2	O	0.2
1972	Mil-A	111	316	35	75	9	3	12	34	45	54	.237	.332	.399	119	7	7	41	3	4	-2	-3	O	0.1
1973	Mil-A	96	225	29	46	9	0	5	26	27	36	.204	.304	.311	75	-8	-7	20	5	5	-2	4	DO	-0.5
1974	Cal-A	127	325	46	88	16	3	13	44	47	57	.271	.368	.458	145	16	18	55	4	5	-2	-10	*OD	0.4
1975	Cal-A	76	192	21	41	6	2	6	33	48	33	.214	.373	.359	116	4	6	30	2	1	0	-1	DO	0.4
1976	Cal-A	42	96	8	17	4	0	4	4	18	16	.177	.319	.219	63	-4	-3	8	0	0	0	-2	O/D	-0.5
	Tex-A	38	89	10	20	3	1	1	5	10	16	.225	.303	.315	79	-2	-2	8	1	0	0	0	D/O	-0.1
	Yr	80	185	18	37	7	1	1	9	28	32	.200	.312	.265	72	-6	-6	16	1	0	0	-2		-0.6
1977	*KC-A	34	65	8	17	5	0	2	8	11	16	.262	.368	.431	116	2	2	11	1	0	0	0	O/D	0.1
1978	KC-A	13	16	0	2	0	0	0	0	0	1	.125	.125	.125	-29	-3	-3	0	0	0	0	0	/OD	-0.2
Total	11	791	1925	239	429	68	12	65	218	309	339	.223	.335	.372	103	11	13	252	20	20	-6	-16	OD/1	-1.9
■ DICK LAJESKIE			Lajeskie, Richard Edward b: 1/8/26, Passaic, N.J. d: 8/15/76, Ramsey, N.J. BR/TR, 5'11", 175 lbs. Deb: 9/10/46																					
1946	NY-N	6	10	3	2	0	0	0	3	2	.200		.429	.200	81	0	0	1	0			5	/2	0.5
■ NAP LAJOIE			Lajoie, Napoleon "Larry" b: 9/5/1874, Woonsocket, R.I. d: 2/7/59, Daytona Beach, Fla. BR/TR, 6'1", 195 lbs. Deb: 8/12/1896 MH																					
1896	Phi-N	39	175	36	57	12	7	4	42	1	11	.326	.330	.543	131	6	6	34	7			-3	1	0.3
1897	Phi-N	127	545	107	197	40	23	9	127	15		.361	.392	**.569**	158	38	40	132	20			-6	*1O/3	2.7
1898	Phi-N	147	608	113	197	43	11	6	**127**	21		.324	.354	.461	142	24	28	111	25			-1	*2/1	3.0
1899	Phi-N	77	312	70	118	19	9	6	70	12		.378	.419	.554	175	28	29	80	13			23	2/O	4.9
1900	Phi-N	102	451	95	152	33	12	7	92	10		.337	.362	.510	143	23	23	94	22			30	*2/3	5.2
1901	Phi-A	131	544	**145**	**232**	48	14	**14**	125	24		**.426**	**.462**	**.643**	198	75	72	179	27			29	*2S	8.4
1902	Phi-A	1	4	0	1	0	0	0	1	0		.250	.250	.250	38	-0	-0	1	1			-0	2	-0.0
	Cle-A	86	348	81	132	35	5	7	64	19		.379	.421	.569	182	34	36	94	19			30	2	6.2
	Yr	87	352	81	133	35	5	7	65	19		.378	.419	.565	180	33	35	95	20			**30**		6.2
1903	Cle-A	125	485	90	167	41	11	7	93	24		**.344**	.375	**.518**	171	38	39	106	21			40	*2/13	8.1
1904	Cle-A	140	553	92	208	49	15	6	102	27		.376	**.405**	**.552**	205	61	62	139	29			-0	2S/1	6.8
1905	Cle-A	65	249	29	82	12	2	2	41	17		.329	.372	.418	151	14	14	44	11			9	2/1M	2.4
1906	Cle-A	152	602	88	214	48	9	0	91	30		.355	.386	.465	171	44	45	120	20			32	*23/SM	8.0

YEAR	TM/L	G	AB	R	H	2B	3B	HR	RBI	BB	SO	AVG	OBP	SLG	PRO+	BR	/A	RC	SB	CS	SBR	FR	POS	TPR
1907	Cle-A	137	509	53	152	30	6	2	63	30		.299	.338	.393	134	18	18	79	24			45	*2/1M	6.7
1908	Cle-A	157	581	77	168	32	6	2	74	47		.289	.342	.375	135	22	22	81	15			49	*2/1M	7.5
1909	Cle-A	128	469	56	152	33	7	1	47	35		.324	.378	.431	149	29	27	81	13			19	*2/1M	4.7
1910	Cle-A	159	591	94	227	51	7	4	76	60		.384	.445	.514	198	68	67	147	26			17	*21	8.0
1911	Cle-A	90	315	36	115	20	1	2	60	26		.365	.420	.454	142	19	18	65	13			-7	12	1.2
1912	Cle-A	117	448	66	165	34	4	0	90	28		.368	.414	.462	146	29	27	93	18			5	21	3.0
1913	Cle-A	137	465	66	156	25	2	1	68	33	17	.335	.398	.404	131	21	19	79	17			9	*2	2.7
1914	Cle-A	121	419	37	108	14	3	0	50	32	15	.258	.313	.305	83	-7	-9	41	14	15	-5	6	21	-0.8
1915	Phi-A	129	490	40	137	24	5	1	61	11	16	.280	.301	.355	99	-5	-4	55	10	6	-1	14	*2S/13	1.0
1916	Phi-A	113	426	33	105	14	4	2	35	14	26	.246	.272	.312	79	-15	-13	42	15			30	*2/1O	2.2
Total	21	2480	9589	1504	3242	657	163	83	1599	516	85	.338	.378	.467	151	564	567	1895	380	21		370	*21/SO3	92.2

■ EDDIE LAKE   Lake, Edward Erving "Sparky" b: 3/18/16, Antioch, Cal. BR/TR, 5'7", 159 lbs. Deb: 9/26/39

YEAR	TM/L	G	AB	R	H	2B	3B	HR	RBI	BB	SO	AVG	OBP	SLG	PRO+	BR	/A	RC	SB	CS	SBR	FR	POS	TPR
1939	StL-N	2	4	0	1	0	0	0	0	1	0	.250	.400	.250	74	-0	-0	1	0			-1	/S	0.0
1940	StL-N	32	66	12	14	3	0	2	7	12	17	.212	.342	.348	86	-1	-1	8	1			-7	2/S	-0.5
1941	StL-N	45	76	9	8	2	0	0	0	15	22	.105	.253	.132	10	-9	-9	3	3			6	S3/2	-0.1
1943	Bos-A	75	216	26	43	10	0	3	16	47	35	.199	.345	.287	84	-2	-2	24	3	6	-3	3	S	-0.1
1944	Bos-A	57	126	21	26	5	0	0	8	23	22	.206	.329	.246	66	-5	-4	13	5	2	0	-5	S/P23	-0.5
1945	Bos-A	133	473	81	132	27	1	11	51	106	37	.279	.412	.410	136	29	27	89	9	7	-2	19	*S/2	5.3
1946	Det-A	155	587	105	149	24	1	8	31	103	69	.254	.369	.339	93	3	-2	83	15	9	-1	-21	*S	-2.2
1947	Det-A	158	602	96	127	19	6	12	46	120	54	.211	.343	.322	83	-9	-11	74	11	10	-3	-29	*S	-4.5
1948	Det-A	64	198	51	52	6	0	2	18	57	20	.263	.427	.323	99	4	3	33	3	3	-1	-3	23	0.0
1949	Det-A	94	240	38	47	9	1	1	15	61	33	.196	.359	.254	63	-10	-10	26	2	8	-4	-10	S23	-2.2
1950	Det-A	20	7	3	0	0	0	0	0	1	3	.000	.125	.000	-64	-2	-2	0	0	0	0	0	/S3	-0.1
Total	11	835	2595	442	599	105	9	39	193	546	312	.231	.366	.323	91	-1	-11	354	52	45		-47	S/23P	-4.9

■ FRED LAKE   Lake, Frederick Lovett b: 10/16/1866, Nova Scotia, Can. d: 11/24/31, Boston, Mass.   Deb: 5/07/1891 M

YEAR	TM/L	G	AB	R	H	2B	3B	HR	RBI	BB	SO	AVG	OBP	SLG	PRO+	BR	/A	RC	SB	CS	SBR	FR	POS	TPR
1891	Bos-N	5	7	1	1	0	0	0	0	2	4	.143	.333	.143	38	-0	-1	0	0			-0	/CO	0.0
1894	Lou-N	16	42	8	12	2	0	1	10	11	6	.286	.474	.405	124	2	3	9	2			-4	/2SC	0.0
1897	*Bos-N	19	62	2	15	4	0	0	5	1		.242	.254	.306	46	-5	-5	5	2			-1	C	-0.2
1898	Pit-N	5	13	1	1	0	0	0	1	2		.077	.200	.077	-19	-2	-2	0	0			0	/1	-0.1
1910	Bos-N	3	1	0	0	0	0	0	0	1	0	.000	.500	.000	46	0	0	0	0			0	HM	0.0
Total	5	48	125	12	29	6	0	1	16	17	10	.232	.342	.304	70	-5	-5	15	4			-5	/C2S1O	-0.3

■ STEVE LAKE   Lake, Steven Michael b: 3/14/57, Inglewood, Cal. BR/TR, 6'1", 180 lbs. Deb: 4/09/83

YEAR	TM/L	G	AB	R	H	2B	3B	HR	RBI	BB	SO	AVG	OBP	SLG	PRO+	BR	/A	RC	SB	CS	SBR	FR	POS	TPR
1983	Chi-N	38	85	9	22	4	1	1	7	2	6	.259	.284	.365	75	-3	-3	7	0	0	0	4	C	0.2
1984	*Chi-N	25	54	4	12	4	0	2	7	0	7	.222	.236	.407	71	-2	-2	5	0	0	0	0	C	-0.1
1985	Chi-N	58	119	5	18	2	0	1	11	3	21	.151	.179	.193	4	-15	-17	4	1	0	0	6	C	-0.8
1986	Chi-N	10	19	4	8	1	0	0	4	1	2	.421	.450	.474	144	1	1	4	0	0	0	-0	C	0.1
	StL-N	26	49	4	12	1	0	2	10	2	5	.245	.275	.388	81	-1	-1	5	0	0	0	1	C	0.0
	Yr	36	68	8	20	2	0	2	14	3	7	.294	.324	.412	100	-0	-0	8	0	0	0	1		0.1
1987	*StL-N	74	179	19	45	7	2	2	19	10	18	.251	.291	.346	67	-8	-9	18	0	0	0	-2	C	-0.6
1988	StL-N	36	54	5	15	3	0	1	4	3	15	.278	.339	.389	107	1	1	8	0	0	0	-1	C	0.1
1989	Phi-N	58	155	9	39	5	1	2	14	12	20	.252	.305	.335	83	-3	-3	15	0	0	0	3	C	0.3
1990	Phi-N	29	80	4	20	2	0	0	6	3	12	.250	.286	.275	55	-5	-5	6	0	0	0	4	C	0.0
Total	8	354	794	63	191	29	4	11	82	36	106	.241	.279	.329	65	-36	-39	72	1	0	0	14	C	-0.8

■ AL LAKEMAN   Lakeman, Albert Wesley "Moose" b: 12/31/18, Cincinnati, Ohio d: 5/25/76, Spartanburg, S.C. BR/TR, 6'2", 195 lbs. Deb: 4/19/42 C

YEAR	TM/L	G	AB	R	H	2B	3B	HR	RBI	BB	SO	AVG	OBP	SLG	PRO+	BR	/A	RC	SB	CS	SBR	FR	POS	TPR
1942	Cin-N	20	38	0	6	1	0	0	2	3	10	.158	.238	.184	24	-4	-4	2	0			2	C	0.0
1943	Cin-N	22	55	5	14	2	1	0	6	3	11	.255	.293	.327	80	-2	-2	5	0			-1	C	-0.1
1944	Cin-N	1	1	0	0	0	0	0	0	0	1	.000	.000	.000	-99	-0	-0	0	0			0	H	0.0
1945	Cin-N	76	258	22	66	9	4	8	31	17	45	.256	.304	.415	101	-2	-1	31	0			-10	C	-0.9
1946	Cin-N	23	30	0	4	0	0	0	4	2	7	.133	.188	.133	-9	-4	-4	1	0			-0	/C	-0.4
1947	Cin-N	2	2	0	0	0	0	0	0	0	0	.000	.000	.000	-99	-1	-1	0	0			0	H	0.0
	Phi-N	55	182	11	29	3	0	6	19	5	39	.159	.186	.275	22	-21	-20	9	0			-4	1C	-2.5
	Yr	57	184	11	29	3	0	6	19	5	40	.158	.184	.272	20	-22	-21	9	0			-4		-2.5
1948	Phi-N	32	68	2	11	2	0	1	4	5	22	.162	.219	.235	23	-7	-7	4	0			-2	C/P	-0.6
1949	Bos-N	3	6	0	1	0	0	0	0	1	0	.167	.286	.167	26	-1	-1	0	0			1	/1	0.0
1954	Det-A	5	6	0	0	0	0	0	0	0	1	.000	.000	.000	-99	-2	-2	0	0	0	0	1	/C	0.0
Total	9	239	646	40	131	17	5	15	66	36	137	.203	.248	.314	55	-43	-41	51	0	0		-14	C/1P	-4.5

■ DAN LALLY   Lally, Daniel J. b: 8/12/1867, Jersey City, N.J. d: 4/14/36, Milwaukee, Wis. BR/TR, 5'11.5", 210 lbs. Deb: 8/19/1891

YEAR	TM/L	G	AB	R	H	2B	3B	HR	RBI	BB	SO	AVG	OBP	SLG	PRO+	BR	/A	RC	SB	CS	SBR	FR	POS	TPR
1891	Pit-N	41	143	24	32	6	2	1	17	16	20	.224	.319	.315	89	-2	-1	15	0			-6	O	-0.8
1897	StL-N	87	355	56	99	15	5	2	42	9		.279	.310	.366	82	-11	-10	45	12			2	O/1	-1.1
Total	2	128	498	80	131	21	7	3	59	25	20	.263	.313	.351	84	-13	-11	60	12			-4	O/1	-1.9

■ RAY LAMANNO   Lamanno, Raymond Simond b: 11/17/19, Oakland, Cal. BR/TR, 6', 185 lbs. Deb: 9/11/41

YEAR	TM/L	G	AB	R	H	2B	3B	HR	RBI	BB	SO	AVG	OBP	SLG	PRO+	BR	/A	RC	SB	CS	SBR	FR	POS	TPR
1941	Cin-N	1	0	0	0	0	0	0	0	0	0	—	1.000	—	197	0	0	0	0			0	/C	0.0
1942	Cin-N	111	371	40	98	12	2	12	43	31	54	.264	.324	.404	113	5	5	46	0			-10	*C	-0.2
1946	Cin-N	85	239	18	58	12	0	1	30	11	26	.243	.285	.305	70	-11	-10	20	0			2	C	-0.6
1947	Cin-N	118	413	33	106	21	3	5	50	28	39	.257	.307	.358	77	-15	-14	46	0			8	*C	-0.3
1948	Cin-N	127	385	31	93	12	0	0	27	48	32	.242	.329	.273	67	-18	-16	35	2			-12	*C	-1.8
Total	5	442	1408	122	355	57	5	18	150	118	151	.252	.314	.338	82	-38	-35	147	2			-12	C	-2.9

■ BILL LAMAR   Lamar, William Harmong "Good Time Bill" b: 3/21/1897, Rockville, Md. d: 5/24/70, Rockport, Mass. BL/TR, 6'1", 185 lbs. Deb: 9/19/17

YEAR	TM/L	G	AB	R	H	2B	3B	HR	RBI	BB	SO	AVG	OBP	SLG	PRO+	BR	/A	RC	SB	CS	SBR	FR	POS	TPR
1917	NY-A	11	41	2	10	0	0	0	3	0	2	.244	.244	.244	48	-3	-3	3	1			0	O	-0.2
1918	NY-A	28	110	12	25	3	0	0	2	6	2	.227	.267	.255	56	-6	-6	8	2			-2	O	-1.0
1919	NY-A	11	16	1	3	1	0	0	0	2	1	.188	.278	.250	48	-1	-1	1	1			-1	/O1	-0.1
	Bos-A	48	148	18	43	5	1	0	14	5	9	.291	.314	.338	88	-4	-3	16	3			-2	O	-0.7
	Yr	59	164	19	46	6	1	0	14	7	10	.280	.310	.329	83	-5	-4	18	4			-3		-0.8
1920	*Bro-N	24	44	5	12	4	0	0	4	0	1	.273	.273	.364	79	-1	-1	4	0	0	0	-1	O	-0.2
1921	Bro-N	3	3	2	1	0	0	0	0	0	0	.333	.333	.333	74	-0	-0	0	0	0	0	0	/O	0.0
1924	Phi-A	87	367	68	121	22	5	7	48	18	25	.330	.361	.474	113	6	5	60	8	8	-2	4	O	0.0
1925	Phi-A	138	568	85	202	39	8	3	77	21	17	.356	.379	.468	107	10	5	97	2	6	-3	-3	*O	-0.4
1926	Phi-A	116	419	62	119	17	6	5	50	18	15	.284	.315	.389	78	-12	-15	50	4	5	-2	-3	*O	-2.7
1927	Phi-A	84	324	48	97	23	3	4	47	16	10	.299	.334	.417	91	-3	-6	41	4	8	-4	-3	O	-1.6
Total	9	550	2040	303	633	114	23	19	245	86	78	.310	.339	.417	94	-14	-24	280	25	27		-3	O/1	-6.9

■ LYMAN LAMB   Lamb, Lyman Raymond b: 3/17/1895, Lincoln, Neb. d: 10/5/55, Fayetteville, Ark. BR/TR, 5'7", 150 lbs. Deb: 9/14/20

YEAR	TM/L	G	AB	R	H	2B	3B	HR	RBI	BB	SO	AVG	OBP	SLG	PRO+	BR	/A	RC	SB	CS	SBR	FR	POS	TPR
1920	StL-A	9	24	4	9	2	0	0	4	0	0	.375	.375	.458	116	1	0	2	0	0	1	-2	/O	0.0
1921	StL-A	45	134	18	34	9	2	1	17	4	12	.254	.281	.373	62	-8	-9	14	2	0	0	-9	3/2O	-1.4
Total	2	54	158	22	43	11	2	1	21	4	19	.272	.294	.386	70	-7	-8	19	2	0	1	-10	/3O2	-1.4

■ PETE LAMERE   Lamere, Pierre b: 12/1873, New York d: 10/24/31, Brooklyn, N.Y. TR, Deb: 9/10/02

YEAR	TM/L	G	AB	R	H	2B	3B	HR	RBI	BB	SO	AVG	OBP	SLG	PRO+	BR	/A	RC	SB	CS	SBR	FR	POS	TPR
1902	Chi-N	2	9	2	2	0	0	0	0	0	0	.222	.222	.222	40	-1	-1	0	0			0	/C	0.0

YEAR	TM/L	G	AB	R	H	2B	3B	HR	RBI	BB	SO	AVG	OBP	SLG	PRO+	BR	/A	RC	SB	CS	SBR	FR	POS	TPR
1907	Cin-N	1	2	0	0	0	0	0	0	0	0	.000	.000	.000	-96	-0	-0	0	0			-0	/C	0.0
Total	2	3	11	2	2	0	0	0	0	0	0	.182	.182	.182	14	-1	-1	0	0			-0	/C	0.0

■ GENE LAMONT
Lamont, Gene William b: 12/25/46, Rockford, Ill. BL/TR, 6'1", 195 lbs. Deb: 9/02/70 C

YEAR	TM/L	G	AB	R	H	2B	3B	HR	RBI	BB	SO	AVG	OBP	SLG	PRO+	BR	/A	RC	SB	CS	SBR	FR	POS	TPR
1970	Det-A	15	44	3	13	3	1	1	4	2	9	.295	.340	.477	122	1	1	7	0	0	0	2	C	0.3
1971	Det-A	7	15	2	1	0	0	0	1	0	5	.067	.067	.067	-60	-3	-3	0	0	0	0	3	/C	0.0
1972	Det-A	1	0	0	0	0	0	0	0	0	0	—	—	—	—	0	0	0	0	0	0	0	/C	0.0
1974	Det-A	60	92	9	20	4	0	3	8	7	19	.217	.273	.359	78	-3	-3	9	0	0	0	7	C	0.6
1975	Det-A	4	8	1	3	1	0	0	1	0	2	.375	.375	.500	139	0	0	2	1	0	0	1	/C	0.2
Total	5	87	159	15	37	8	1	4	14	9	35	.233	.278	.371	80	-4	-5	18	1	0	0	12	/C	1.1

■ BOBBY LaMOTTE
LaMotte, Robert Eugene b: 2/15/1898, Savannah, Ga. d: 11/2/70, Chatham, Ga. BR/TR, 5'11", 160 lbs. Deb: 9/01/20

YEAR	TM/L	G	AB	R	H	2B	3B	HR	RBI	BB	SO	AVG	OBP	SLG	PRO+	BR	/A	RC	SB	CS	SBR	FR	POS	TPR
1920	Was-A	4	3	0	0	0	0	0	0	1	1	.000	.250	.000	-31	-1	-1	0	0	0	0	0	/S3	0.0
1921	Was-A	16	41	5	8	0	0	0	2	5	0	.195	.283	.195	25	-5	-4	3	0	0	0	2	S	0.0
1922	Was-A	68	214	22	54	10	2	1	23	15	21	.252	.307	.332	70	-11	-9	23	6	1	1	8	3/S	0.7
1925	StL-A	97	356	61	97	20	4	2	51	34	22	.272	.338	.368	75	-12	-14	45	5	5	-2	2	S/3	0.0
1926	StL-A	36	79	11	16	4	3	0	9	11	6	.203	.300	.329	61	-4	-5	9	0	0	0	-2	S/3	-0.3
Total	5	221	693	99	175	34	9	3	85	66	50	.253	.320	.341	69	-32	-33	80	11	6	-0	10	S/3	0.4

■ KEITH LAMPARD
Lampard, Christopher Keith b: 12/20/45, Warrington, England BL/TR, 6'2", 197 lbs. Deb: 9/15/69

YEAR	TM/L	G	AB	R	H	2B	3B	HR	RBI	BB	SO	AVG	OBP	SLG	PRO+	BR	/A	RC	SB	CS	SBR	FR	POS	TPR
1969	Hou-N	9	12	2	3	0	0	1	2	0	3	.250	.250	.500	108	-0	0	2	0	0	0	1	/O	0.1
1970	Hou-N	53	72	8	17	8	1	0	5	5	24	.236	.295	.375	82	-2	-2	7	0	0	0	1	O/1	-0.1
Total	2	62	84	10	20	8	1	1	7	5	27	.238	.289	.393	85	-2	-2	9	0	0	0	2	/O1	0.0

■ TOM LAMPKIN
Lampkin, Thomas Michael b: 3/4/64, Cincinnati, Ohio BL/TR, 5'11", 180 lbs. Deb: 9/10/88

YEAR	TM/L	G	AB	R	H	2B	3B	HR	RBI	BB	SO	AVG	OBP	SLG	PRO+	BR	/A	RC	SB	CS	SBR	FR	POS	TPR
1988	Cle-A	4	4	0	0	0	0	0	0	1	0	.000	.200	.000	-38	-1	-1	0	0	0	0	-1	/C	-0.1
1990	SD-N	26	63	4	14	0	1	1	4	4	9	.222	.269	.302	56	-4	-4	4	0	1	-1	1	C	-0.2
Total	2	30	67	4	14	0	1	1	4	5	9	.209	.264	.284	50	-5	-5	4	0	1	-1	0	/C	-0.3

■ RICK LANCELLOTTI
Lancellotti, Richard Anthony b: 7/5/56, Providence, R.I. BL/TL, 6'3", 195 lbs. Deb: 8/27/82

YEAR	TM/L	G	AB	R	H	2B	3B	HR	RBI	BB	SO	AVG	OBP	SLG	PRO+	BR	/A	RC	SB	CS	SBR	FR	POS	TPR
1982	SD-N	17	39	2	7	2	0	0	4	2	8	.179	.220	.231	28	-4	-4	2	0	0	0	-1	/1O	-0.5
1986	SF-N	15	18	2	4	0	0	2	6	0	7	.222	.222	.556	113	-0	0	2	0	0	0	0	/1O	0.0
1990	Bos-A	4	8	0	0	0	0	0	1	0	3	.000	.000	.000	-96	-2	-2	0	0	0	0	0	/1	-0.1
Total	3	36	65	4	11	2	0	2	11	2	18	.169	.194	.292	35	-6	-6	4	0	0	0	-1	/1O	-0.6

■ GROVER LAND
Land, Grover Cleveland b: 9/22/1884, Frankfort, Ky. d: 7/22/58, Phoenix, Ariz. BR/TR, 6', 190 lbs. Deb: 9/02/08 C

YEAR	TM/L	G	AB	R	H	2B	3B	HR	RBI	BB	SO	AVG	OBP	SLG	PRO+	BR	/A	RC	SB	CS	SBR	FR	POS	TPR
1908	Cle-A	8	16	1	3	0	0	0	2	0		.188	.188	.188	23	-1	-1	1	0			-1	/C	-0.1
1910	Cle-A	34	111	4	23	0	0	0	7	2		.207	.228	.207	36	-8	-8	6	1			6	C	0.1
1911	Cle-A	35	107	5	15	1	2	0	10	3		.140	.164	.187	-2	-15	-15	3	2			1	C/1	-0.9
1913	Cle-A	17	47	3	11	1	0	0	9	4	1	.234	.321	.255	67	-2	-2	4	1			0	C	0.0
1914	Bro-F	102	335	24	92	6	2	0	29	12	23	.275	.306	.304	76	-11	-10	35	7			-29	C	-3.7
1915	Bro-F	96	290	25	75	13	2	0	22	6	20	.259	.279	.317	77	-9	-9	28	3			-28	C	-3.7
Total	6	292	906	62	219	21	6	0	79	27	44	.242	.270	.278	60	-46	-46	77	14			-51	C/1	-8.3

■ DOC LAND
Land, William Gilbert (b: Doc Burrell Land) b: 5/14/03, Bennsville, Miss. d: 4/14/86, Livingston, Ala. BL/TL, 5'11", 165 lbs. Deb: 10/06/29

YEAR	TM/L	G	AB	R	H	2B	3B	HR	RBI	BB	SO	AVG	OBP	SLG	PRO+	BR	/A	RC	SB	CS	SBR	FR	POS	TPR
1929	Was-A	1	3	0	0	0	0	0	0	0	1	.000	.250	.000	-30	-1	-1	0	0			-0	/O	0.0

■ KEN LANDENBERGER
Landenberger, Kenneth Henry "Red" b: 7/29/28, Lyndhurst, Ohio d: 7/28/60, Cleveland, Ohio BL/TL, 6'3", 200 lbs. Deb: 9/20/52

YEAR	TM/L	G	AB	R	H	2B	3B	HR	RBI	BB	SO	AVG	OBP	SLG	PRO+	BR	/A	RC	SB	CS	SBR	FR	POS	TPR
1952	Chi-A	2	5	0	1	0	0	0	0	0	2	.200	.200	.200	11	-1	-1	0	0	0	0	0	/1	0.0

■ RAFAEL LANDESTOY
Landestoy, Rafael Silvialdo (Santana) b: 5/28/53, Bani, D.R. BB/TR, 5'10", 165 lbs. Deb: 8/27/77 C

YEAR	TM/L	G	AB	R	H	2B	3B	HR	RBI	BB	SO	AVG	OBP	SLG	PRO+	BR	/A	RC	SB	CS	SBR	FR	POS	TPR
1977	*LA-N	15	18	6	5	0	0	0	0	3	2	.278	.381	.278	80	-0	-0	2	2	0	1	3	/2S	0.4
1978	Hou-N	59	218	18	58	5	1	0	9	8	23	.266	.292	.298	70	-10	-8	19	7	4	-0	-13	S/O2	-1.8
1979	Hou-N	129	282	33	76	9	6	0	30	29	24	.270	.340	.344	92	-4	-2	36	13	4	2	-2	*2/S	0.5
1980	*Hou-N	149	393	42	97	13	8	1	27	31	37	.247	.307	.328	84	-12	-8	41	23	12	-0	-6	2S/3	-0.1
1981	Hou-N	35	74	6	11	1	1	0	4	16	9	.149	.300	.189	43	-5	-5	5	4	1	1	-4	2	-0.6
	Cin-N	12	11	2	2	0	0	0	1	1	0	.182	.250	.182	24	-1	-1	0	1	0	0	-0	/2	0.0
	Yr	47	85	8	13	1	1	0	5	17	9	.153	.294	.188	40	-6	-6	5	5	1	1	-4		-0.6
1982	Cin-N	73	111	11	21	3	0	1	9	8	14	.189	.250	.243	38	-9	-9	6	2	0	1	5	32/OS	-0.3
1983	Cin-N	7	5	0	0	0	0	0	0	0	0	.000	.000	.000	-97	-1	-1	0	0	0	0	-1	/130	-0.1
	*LA-N	64	64	6	11	1	1	1	1	3	8	.172	.209	.266	31	-6	-6	3	0	2	-1	5	230/S	-0.1
	Yr	71	69	6	11	1	1	1	1	3	8	.159	.194	.246	21	-7	-7	3	0	2	-1	4		-0.2
1984	LA-N	53	54	10	10	0	0	1	2	1	6	.185	.200	.241	24	-6	-5	2	2	1	0	3	23/O	-0.2
Total	8	596	1230	134	291	32	17	4	83	100	123	.237	.297	.300	70	-55	-47	115	54	24	2	-11	2S/301	-2.3

■ JIM LANDIS
Landis, James Henry b: 3/9/34, Fresno, Cal. BR/TR, 6'1", 180 lbs. Deb: 4/16/57

YEAR	TM/L	G	AB	R	H	2B	3B	HR	RBI	BB	SO	AVG	OBP	SLG	PRO+	BR	/A	RC	SB	CS	SBR	FR	POS	TPR
1957	Chi-A	96	274	38	58	11	3	2	16	45	61	.212	.329	.296	72	-9	-10	31	14	4	2	6	*O	-0.6
1958	Chi-A	142	523	72	145	23	7	15	64	52	80	.277	.352	.434	117	11	12	82	19	7	2	1	*O	0.6
1959	*Chi-A	149	515	78	140	26	7	5	60	78	68	.272	.376	.379	109	8	9	81	20	9	1	9	*O	1.2
1960	Chi-A	148	494	89	125	25	6	10	49	80	84	.253	.367	.389	106	5	6	78	23	6	3	6	*O	1.0
1961	Chi-A	140	534	87	151	18	8	22	85	65	71	.283	.365	.470	123	16	17	95	19	5	3	13	*O	2.7
1962	Chi-A	149	534	82	122	21	6	15	61	80	105	.228	.339	.375	92	-5	-5	73	19	7	2	3	*O	-0.5
1963	Chi-A	133	396	56	89	6	6	13	45	47	75	.225	.316	.369	93	-4	-3	48	8	6	-1	-6	*O	-1.5
1964	Chi-A	106	298	30	62	8	4	1	18	36	64	.208	.306	.272	64	-14	-13	28	5	0	2	-10	*O	-2.6
1965	KC-A	118	364	46	87	15	1	3	36	57	84	.239	.347	.310	90	-4	-3	42	8	3	1	2	*O	-0.4
1966	Cle-A	85	158	23	35	5	1	3	14	20	25	.222	.317	.323	84	-3	-3	17	2	1	0	2	*O	-0.3
1967	Det-A	25	48	4	10	0	0	2	4	7	12	.208	.309	.333	87	-1	-1	5	0	2	-1	1	O	-0.1
	Bos-A	5	7	1	1	0	0	1	1	1	3	.143	.250	.571	126	0	0	1	0	0	0	0	/O	0.0
	Yr	30	55	5	11	0	0	3	5	8	15	.200	.302	.364	92	-0	-0	6	0	2	-1			-0.1
	Hou-N	50	143	19	36	11	1	1	14	20	35	.252	.348	.364	107	1	2	20	2	1	0	-1	O	0.0
Total	11	1346	4288	625	1061	169	50	93	467	588	767	.247	.346	.375	100	3	10	602	139	51	11	26	*O	-0.5

■ KEN LANDREAUX
Landreaux, Kenneth Francis b: 12/22/54, Los Angeles, Cal. BL/TR, 5'10", 165 lbs. Deb: 9/11/77

YEAR	TM/L	G	AB	R	H	2B	3B	HR	RBI	BB	SO	AVG	OBP	SLG	PRO+	BR	/A	RC	SB	CS	SBR	FR	POS	TPR
1977	Cal-A	23	76	6	19	5	1	0	5	5	15	.250	.296	.342	76	-3	-2	8	1	1	-0	6	O	0.3
1978	Cal-A	93	260	37	58	7	5	5	23	20	20	.223	.284	.346	79	-9	-7	25	7	3	0	0	O/D	-0.8
1979	Min-A	151	564	81	172	27	5	15	83	37	57	.305	.352	.450	110	11	8	88	10	3	1	-20	*O	-1.5
1980	Min-A	129	484	56	136	23	11	7	62	39	42	.281	.337	.417	98	3	-1	65	8	6	-1	-18	*O/D	-2.2
1981	*LA-N	99	390	48	98	16	4	7	41	25	42	.251	.298	.367	91	-7	-6	44	18	4	3	-8	O	-1.3
1982	LA-N	129	461	71	131	23	7	7	50	39	54	.284	.345	.410	113	6	8	68	31	10	3	-4	*O	0.6
1983	*LA-N	141	481	63	135	25	3	17	66	34	52	.281	.331	.451	115	8	8	70	30	11	2	-8	*O	0.0
1984	LA-N	134	438	39	110	11	5	11	47	29	35	.251	.299	.374	89	-8	-7	47	10	9	-2	-22	*O	-3.8
1985	*LA-N	147	482	70	129	26	2	12	50	33	37	.268	.316	.405	103	-1	1	61	15	5	2	-15	*O	-1.6
1986	LA-N	103	283	34	74	13	2	4	29	22	24	.261	.317	.364	94	-5	-3	32	10	6	-0	-2	O	-0.5
1987	LA-N	115	182	17	37	4	0	6	23	16	28	.203	.271	.324	58	-12	-11	16	5	3	-0	2	O	-1.1
Total	11	1264	4101	522	1099	180	45	91	479	299	421	.268	.321	.400	99	-16	-13	524	145	60	8	-87	*O/D	-11.9

YEAR	TM/L	G	AB	R	H	2B	3B	HR	RBI	BB	SO	AVG	OBP	SLG	PRO+	BR	/A	RC	SB	CS	SBR	FR	POS	TPR

■ HOBIE LANDRITH
Landrith, Hobert Neal   b: 3/16/30, Decatur, Ill.   BL/TR, 5'10", 170 lbs.   Deb: 7/30/50   C

YEAR	TM/L	G	AB	R	H	2B	3B	HR	RBI	BB	SO	AVG	OBP	SLG	PRO+	BR	/A	RC	SB	CS	SBR	FR	POS	TPR
1950	Cin-N	4	14	1	3	0	0	0	1	2	1	.214	.313	.214	41	-1	-1	1	0			-1	/C	-0.1
1951	Cin-N	4	13	3	5	1	0	0	0	1	1	.385	.429	.462	137	1	1	3	0	0	0	1	/C	0.2
1952	Cin-N	15	50	1	13	4	0	0	4	0	4	.260	.260	.340	65	-2	-2	4	0	1	-1	0	C	-0.2
1953	Cin-N	52	154	15	37	3	1	3	16	12	8	.240	.299	.331	64	-8	-8	16	2	0	1	0	C	-0.4
1954	Cin-N	48	81	12	16	0	0	5	14	18	9	.198	.343	.383	86	-1	-1	12	1	0	0	4	C	0.4
1955	Cin-N	43	87	9	22	3	0	4	7	10	14	.253	.330	.425	93	-0	-1	12	0	1	-1	3	C	0.2
1956	Chi-N	111	312	22	69	10	3	4	32	39	38	.221	.310	.311	69	-14	-13	32	0	2	-1	-2	C	-1.3
1957	StL-N	75	214	18	52	6	0	3	26	25	27	.243	.322	.313	70	-8	-9	22	1	2	-1	5	C	0.0
1958	StL-N	70	144	9	31	4	0	3	13	26	21	.215	.335	.306	68	-5	-6	16	0	1	-1	2	C	-0.1
1959	SF-N	109	283	30	71	14	0	3	29	43	23	.251	.350	.332	85	-6	-5	34	0	4	-2	6	*C	0.5
1960	SF-N	71	190	18	46	10	0	1	20	23	11	.242	.324	.311	79	-6	-5	20	1	1	-0	-5	C	-0.6
1961	SF-N	43	71	11	17	4	0	2	10	12	7	.239	.349	.380	97	-0	-0	9	0	0	0	1	C	0.4
1962	NY-N	23	45	6	13	3	0	1	7	8	3	.289	.396	.422	118	2	1	8	0	0	0	-0	C	0.1
	Bal-A	60	167	18	37	4	1	4	17	19	9	.222	.305	.329	74	-7	-6	17	0	0	0	5	C	0.2
1963	Bal-A	2	1	0	0	0	0	0	0	0	0	.000	.000	.000	-99	-0	-0	0	0	0	0	0	/C	0.0
	Was-A	42	103	6	18	3	0	1	7	15	12	.175	.280	.233	46	-7	-7	7	0	0	0	2	C	-0.4
	Yr	44	104	6	18	3	0	1	7	15	12	.173	.277	.231	44	-7	-7	7	0	0	0	2		-0.4
Total	14	772	1929	179	450	69	5	34	203	253	188	.233	.323	.327	75	-64	-62	213	5	12		21	C	-1.1

■ DON LANDRUM
Landrum, Donald Leroy   b: 2/16/36, Santa Rosa, Cal.   BL/TR, 6', 180 lbs.   Deb: 9/28/57

YEAR	TM/L	G	AB	R	H	2B	3B	HR	RBI	BB	SO	AVG	OBP	SLG	PRO+	BR	/A	RC	SB	CS	SBR	FR	POS	TPR
1957	Phi-N	2	7	1	1	0	0	0	2	1	1	.143	.333	.286	71	-0	-0	1	0	0	0	1	/O	0.0
1960	StL-N	13	49	7	12	0	1	2	3	4	6	.245	.315	.408	88	-0	-1	7	3	0	1	1	O	0.1
1961	StL-N	28	66	5	11	2	0	1	3	5	14	.167	.225	.242	22	-7	-8	4	1	0	0	3	O/2	-0.5
1962	StL-N	32	35	11	11	0	0	0	3	4	2	.314	.385	.314	82	-0	-1	5	2	0	1	0	O	-0.1
	Chi-N	83	238	29	67	5	2	1	15	30	31	.282	.369	.332	87	-2	-3	33	9	2	2	1	O	-0.3
	Yr	115	273	40	78	5	2	1	18	34	33	.286	.371	.330	85	-2	-4	38	11	2	2	1		-0.4
1963	Chi-N	84	227	27	55	4	1	1	10	13	42	.242	.295	.282	64	-9	-11	19	6	3	0	-1	O	-1.5
1964	Chi-N	11	11	2	0	0	0	0	0	1	2	.000	.083	.000	-71	-3	-3	0	0	0	0	1	/O	-0.1
1965	Chi-N	131	425	60	96	20	4	6	34	36	84	.226	.301	.334	77	-12	-13	45	14	8	-1	-4	*O	-2.2
1966	SF-N	72	102	9	19	4	0	1	7	9	18	.186	.259	.255	42	-8	-8	7	1	1	-0	5	O	-0.4
Total	8	456	1160	151	272	36	8	12	75	104	200	.234	.308	.310	69	-41	-47	121	36	14	2	6	O/2	-5.0

■ JESSE LANDRUM
Landrum, Jesse Glenn   b: 7/31/12, Crockett, Tex.   d: 6/27/83, Beaumont, Tex.   BR/TR, 5'11.5", 175 lbs.   Deb: 4/26/38

YEAR	TM/L	G	AB	R	H	2B	3B	HR	RBI	BB	SO	AVG	OBP	SLG	PRO+	BR	/A	RC	SB	CS	SBR	FR	POS	TPR
1938	Chi-A	4	6	0	0	0	0	0	1	0	2	.000	.000	.000	-98	-2	-2	0	0	0	0	-1	/2	-0.1

■ TITO LANDRUM
Landrum, Terry Lee   b: 10/25/54, Joplin, Mo.   BR/TR, 5'11", 175 lbs.   Deb: 7/23/80

YEAR	TM/L	G	AB	R	H	2B	3B	HR	RBI	BB	SO	AVG	OBP	SLG	PRO+	BR	/A	RC	SB	CS	SBR	FR	POS	TPR
1980	StL-N	35	77	6	19	2	2	0	7	6	17	.247	.310	.325	75	-2	-3	7	3	2	-0	-1	O	-0.5
1981	StL-N	81	119	13	31	5	4	0	10	6	14	.261	.302	.370	87	-2	-2	13	4	2	0	4	O	0.0
1982	StL-N	79	72	12	20	3	0	2	14	8	18	.278	.358	.403	111	1	1	11	0	1	-1	5	O	0.5
1983	StL-N	6	5	0	1	0	1	0	0	1	2	.200	.333	.600	154	0	0	1	1	0	0	-0	/O	0.0
	*Bal-A	26	42	8	13	2	0	1	4	1	11	.310	.326	.429	108	0	0	5	0	2	-1	2	O	0.0
1984	StL-N	105	173	21	47	9	1	3	26	10	27	.272	.311	.387	98	-1	-1	18	3	4	-2	-0	O	-0.5
1985	*StL-N	85	161	21	45	8	2	4	21	19	30	.280	.356	.429	119	4	4	24	1	4	-2	1	O	0.2
1986	StL-N	96	205	24	43	7	1	2	17	20	41	.210	.283	.283	57	-12	-12	17	3	1	0	7	O	-0.6
1987	StL-N	30	50	5	10	1	0	0	6	7	14	.200	.298	.220	39	-4	-4	3	1	1	-0	3	O/1	-0.1
	LA-N	51	67	8	16	3	0	1	4	3	16	.239	.282	.328	63	-4	-4	6	1	1	-0	1	O	-0.3
	Yr	81	117	13	26	4	0	1	10	10	30	.222	.289	.282	53	-8	-8	10	2	2	-1	5		-0.4
1988	Bal-A	13	24	2	3	0	1	0	2	4	6	.125	.250	.208	31	-2	-2	2	0	0	0	0	O/D	-0.1
Total	9	607	995	120	248	40	12	13	111	85	196	.249	.312	.353	84	-22	-21	106	17	18	-6	21	O/D1	-1.4

■ CHAPPY LANE
Lane, George M.   b: Pittsburgh, Pa.   Deb: 5/16/1882

YEAR	TM/L	G	AB	R	H	2B	3B	HR	RBI	BB	SO	AVG	OBP	SLG	PRO+	BR	/A	RC	SB	CS	SBR	FR	POS	TPR
1882	Pit-a	57	214	26	38	8	2	3			5	.178	.196	.276	60	-9	-8	12				6	1O/C	-0.1
1884	Tol-a	57	215	26	49	9	5	1			2	.228	.242	.330	84	-3	-4	18				3	1/O3C	-0.2
Total	2	114	429	52	87	17	7	4			7	.203	.219	.303	73	-12	-12	29				10	/1OC3	-0.3

■ HUNTER LANE
Lane, James Hunter "Dodo"   b: 7/20/1900, Pulaski, Tenn.   BR/TR, 5'11", 165 lbs.   Deb: 5/13/24

YEAR	TM/L	G	AB	R	H	2B	3B	HR	RBI	BB	SO	AVG	OBP	SLG	PRO+	BR	/A	RC	SB	CS	SBR	FR	POS	TPR
1924	Bos-N	7	15	0	1	0	0	0	1	1	1	.067	.125	.067	-49	-3	-3	0	0	0	0	-1	/32	-0.3

■ MARVIN LANE
Lane, Marvin   b: 1/18/50, Sandersville, Ga.   BR/TR, 5'11", 180 lbs.   Deb: 9/04/71

YEAR	TM/L	G	AB	R	H	2B	3B	HR	RBI	BB	SO	AVG	OBP	SLG	PRO+	BR	/A	RC	SB	CS	SBR	FR	POS	TPR
1971	Det-A	8	14	0	2	0	0	0	1	1	3	.143	.200	.143	-1	-2	-2	0	0	0	0	-0	/O	-0.2
1972	Det-A	8	6	2	0	0	0	0	0	0	2	.000	.000	.000	-97	-1	-1	0	0	0	0	1	/O	0.0
1973	Det-A	6	8	2	2	0	0	1	2	2	2	.250	.400	.625	173	1	1	2	0	0	0	1	/O	0.1
1974	Det-A	50	103	16	24	4	1	2	9	19	24	.233	.352	.350	99	1	0	14	2	0	1	4	O/D	0.4
1976	Det-A	18	48	3	9	1	0	0	5	6	11	.188	.278	.208	42	-3	-3	3	0	0	0	-3	O	-0.6
Total	5	90	179	23	37	5	1	3	17	28	42	.207	.314	.296	74	-5	-6	19	2	0	1	3	/OD	-0.3

■ DICK LANE
Lane, Richard Harrison   b: 6/28/27, Highland Park, Mich.   BR/TR, 5'11", 178 lbs.   Deb: 6/20/49

YEAR	TM/L	G	AB	R	H	2B	3B	HR	RBI	BB	SO	AVG	OBP	SLG	PRO+	BR	/A	RC	SB	CS	SBR	FR	POS	TPR
1949	Chi-A	12	42	4	5	0	0	0	4	5	3	.119	.213	.119	-11	-7	-7	1	0	1	-1	1	O	-0.5

■ DON LANG
Lang, Donald Charles   b: 3/15/15, Selma, Cal.   BR/TR, 6', 175 lbs.   Deb: 7/04/38

YEAR	TM/L	G	AB	R	H	2B	3B	HR	RBI	BB	SO	AVG	OBP	SLG	PRO+	BR	/A	RC	SB	CS	SBR	FR	POS	TPR
1938	Cin-N	21	50	5	13	3	1	1	11	2	7	.260	.288	.420	95	-1	-1	5	0			2	3/2S	0.1
1948	StL-N	117	323	30	87	14	1	4	31	47	38	.269	.364	.356	90	-1	-3	46	2			9	3/2	0.4
Total	2	138	373	35	100	17	2	5	42	49	45	.268	.355	.365	91	-1	-4	51	2			10	3/2S	0.5

■ BILL LANGE
Lange, William Alexander "Little Eva"   b: 6/6/1871, San Francisco, Cal   d: 7/23/50, San Francisco, Cal.   BR/TR, 6'1.5", 190 lbs.   Deb: 4/27/1893

YEAR	TM/L	G	AB	R	H	2B	3B	HR	RBI	BB	SO	AVG	OBP	SLG	PRO+	BR	/A	RC	SB	CS	SBR	FR	POS	TPR
1893	Chi-N	117	469	92	132	8	7	8	88	52	20	.281	.358	.380	100	-1	1	83	47			3	20/3SC	0.2
1894	Chi-N	111	442	84	145	16	9	6	90	56	18	.328	.405	.446	101	6	1	109	65			4	*O/S3	-0.1
1895	Chi-N	123	478	120	186	27	16	10	98	55	24	.389	.454	.575	157	48	42	160	67			10	*O	1.9
1896	Chi-N	122	469	114	153	21	16	4	92	65	24	.326	.414	.465	129	24	21	128	84			10	O/C	1.9
1897	Chi-N	118	479	119	163	24	14	5	83	48		.340	.406	.480	131	25	22	126	**73**			2	*O	1.3
1898	Chi-N	113	442	79	141	16	11	5	69	36		.319	.377	.430	137	20	20	83	22			10	*O/1	2.2
1899	Chi-N	107	416	81	135	21	7	1	58	38		.325	.382	.416	125	13	14	84	41			12	O1	1.8
Total	7	811	3195	689	1055	133	80	39	578	350	86	.330	.401	.459	126	136	122	773	399			51	O/21S3C	10.7

■ SAM LANGFORD
Langford, Elton J.   b: 5/21/1900, Briggs, Tex.   BL/TR, 6', 180 lbs.   Deb: 4/13/26

YEAR	TM/L	G	AB	R	H	2B	3B	HR	RBI	BB	SO	AVG	OBP	SLG	PRO+	BR	/A	RC	SB	CS	SBR	FR	POS	TPR
1926	Bos-A	1	1	1	0	0	0	0	0	0	0	.000	.000	.000	-99	-0	-0	0	0	0	0	0	H	0.0
1927	Cle-A	20	67	10	18	5	0	1	7	5	7	.269	.347	.388	90	-1	-1	9	0	1	-1	-2	O	-0.4
1928	Cle-A	110	427	50	118	17	8	4	50	21	35	.276	.312	.382	81	-13	-13	49	3	6	-3	-8	*O	-2.9
Total	3	131	495	61	136	22	8	5	57	26	42	.275	.316	.382	81	-14	-14	58	3	7	-3	-10	O	-3.3

■ BOB LANGSFORD
Langsford, Robert William (b: Robert Hugo Lankswert)   b: 8/5/1865, Louisville, Ky.   d: 1/10/07, Louisville, Ky.   BR/TR,   Deb: 6/18/1899

YEAR	TM/L	G	AB	R	H	2B	3B	HR	RBI	BB	SO	AVG	OBP	SLG	PRO+	BR	/A	RC	SB	CS	SBR	FR	POS	TPR
1899	Lou-N	1	4	0	0	0	0	0	0	0		.000	.000	.000	-99	-1	-1	0	0			-0	/S	0.0

YEAR	TM/L	G	AB	R	H	2B	3B	HR	RBI	BB	SO	AVG	OBP	SLG	PRO+	BR	/A	RC	SB	CS	SBR	FR	POS	TPR

■ HAL LANIER　　Lanier, Harold Clifton　b: 7/4/42, Denton, N.C.　BR/TR, 6'2", 180 lbs.　Deb: 6/18/64　MC

YEAR	TM/L	G	AB	R	H	2B	3B	HR	RBI	BB	SO	AVG	OBP	SLG	PRO+	BR	/A	RC	SB	CS	SBR	FR	POS	TPR
1964	SF-N	98	383	40	105	16	3	2	28	5	44	.274	.284	.347	75	-12	-13	34	2	1	0	10	2/S	0.5
1965	SF-N	159	522	41	118	15	9	0	39	21	67	.226	.256	.289	52	-33	-34	34	2	1	0	-5	*2/S	-3.2
1966	SF-N	149	459	37	106	14	2	3	37	16	49	.231	.257	.290	50	-30	-31	30	1	0	0	28	*2S	0.8
1967	SF-N	151	525	37	112	16	3	0	42	16	61	.213	.239	.255	42	-40	-39	29	2	2	-1	29	*S2	0.8
1968	SF-N	151	486	37	100	14	1	0	27	12	57	.206	.225	.239	39	-36	-36	23	2	2	-1	14	*S	-0.4
1969	SF-N	150	495	37	113	9	1	0	35	25	68	.228	.265	.251	46	-36	-35	31	0	1	-1	**29**	*S	1.1
1970	•SF-N	134	438	33	101	13	1	2	41	21	41	.231	.266	.279	47	-34	-33	28	1	2	-1	13	*S/21	-0.2
1971	•SF-N	109	206	21	48	8	0	1	13	15	26	.233	.285	.286	63	-10	-10	16	0	0	0	5	32/S1	-0.2
1972	NY-A	60	103	5	22	3	0	0	6	2	13	.214	.236	.243	44	-7	-7	5	1	2	-1	9	3/S2	0.4
1973	NY-A	35	86	9	18	3	0	0	5	3	10	.209	.244	.244	39	-7	-7	5	0	0	0	0	S/23	-0.2
Total	10	1196	3703	297	843	111	20	8	273	136	436	.228	.256	.275	50	-244	-245	236	11	11	-3	131	S23/1	-0.8

■ RIMP LANIER　　Lanier, Lorenzo　b: 10/19/48, Tuskegee, Ala.　BL/TR, 5'8", 150 lbs.　Deb: 9/11/71

YEAR	TM/L	G	AB	R	H	2B	3B	HR	RBI	BB	SO	AVG	OBP	SLG	PRO+	BR	/A	RC	SB	CS	SBR	FR	POS	TPR
1971	Pit-N	6	4	0	0	0	0	0	0	0	1	.000	.200	.000	-39	-1	-1	0	0	0	0	0	H	0.0

■ RAY LANKFORD　　Lankford, Raymond Lewis　b: 6/5/67, Modesto, Cal.　BL/TL, 5'11", 180 lbs.　Deb: 8/21/90

YEAR	TM/L	G	AB	R	H	2B	3B	HR	RBI	BB	SO	AVG	OBP	SLG	PRO+	BR	/A	RC	SB	CS	SBR	FR	POS	TPR
1990	StL-N	39	126	12	36	10	1	3	12	13	27	.286	.353	.452	116	3	3	21	8	2	1	3	O	0.6

■ RED LANNING　　Lanning, Lester Alfred　b: 5/13/1895, Harvard, Ill.　d: 6/13/62, Bristol, Conn.　BL/TL, 5'9", 165 lbs.　Deb: 6/20/16

YEAR	TM/L	G	AB	R	H	2B	3B	HR	RBI	BB	SO	AVG	OBP	SLG	PRO+	BR	/A	RC	SB	CS	SBR	FR	POS	TPR
1916	Phi-A	19	33	5	6	2	0	0	1	10	9	.182	.372	.242	89	0	0	3	0			-3	/OP	-0.2

■ CARNEY LANSFORD　　Lansford, Carney Ray　b: 2/7/57, San Jose, Cal.　BR/TR, 6'2", 195 lbs.　Deb: 4/08/78

YEAR	TM/L	G	AB	R	H	2B	3B	HR	RBI	BB	SO	AVG	OBP	SLG	PRO+	BR	/A	RC	SB	CS	SBR	FR	POS	TPR
1978	Cal-A	121	453	63	133	23	2	8	52	31	67	.294	.344	.406	115	6	8	65	20	9	1	-26	*3/SD	-1.8
1979	•Cal-A	157	654	114	188	30	5	19	79	39	115	.287	.330	.436	108	3	6	91	20	8	1	-24	*3	-1.3
1980	Cal-A	151	602	87	157	27	3	15	80	50	93	.261	.317	.390	95	-7	-5	75	14	5	1	-24	*3	-2.7
1981	Bos-A	102	399	61	134	23	3	4	52	34	28	**.336**	.391	.439	131	20	17	68	15	10	-2	-0	3D	1.6
1982	Bos-A	128	482	65	145	28	4	11	63	46	48	.301	.364	.444	114	14	10	76	9	4	0	-13	*3D	-0.3
1983	Oak-A	80	299	43	92	16	2	10	45	22	33	.308	.361	.475	136	11	13	47	3	8	-4	-6	3/S	0.4
1984	Oak-A	151	597	70	179	31	5	14	74	40	62	.300	.347	.439	124	12	17	90	9	3	1	-8	*3	1.3
1985	Oak-A	98	401	51	111	18	2	13	46	18	27	.277	.314	.429	109	-0	4	53	2	3	-1	-31	3	-3.2
1986	Oak-A	151	591	80	168	16	4	19	72	39	51	.284	.334	.421	112	3	8	80	16	7	1	-18	*31/2D	-1.4
1987	Oak-A	151	554	89	160	27	4	19	76	60	44	.289	.368	.455	125	14	19	96	27	8	3	-3	*31/D	1.5
1988	•Oak-A	150	556	80	155	20	2	7	57	35	35	.279	.329	.360	96	-5	-3	65	29	8	4	-13	*3/12D	-1.1
1989	•Oak-A	148	551	81	185	28	2	2	52	51	25	.336	.401	.405	132	22	25	88	37	15	2	-26	*31/D	0.0
1990	•Oak-A	134	507	58	136	15	1	3	50	45	50	.268	.335	.320	86	-10	-8	54	16	14	-4	-21	*3/1D	-3.1
Total	13	1722	6646	942	1943	302	39	144	798	510	678	.292	.348	.415	113	83	113	946	217	102	4	-211	*31/DS2	-10.1

■ JODY LANSFORD　　Lansford, Joseph Dale　b: 1/15/61, San Jose, Cal.　BR/TR, 6'5", 225 lbs.　Deb: 7/31/82

YEAR	TM/L	G	AB	R	H	2B	3B	HR	RBI	BB	SO	AVG	OBP	SLG	PRO+	BR	/A	RC	SB	CS	SBR	FR	POS	TPR
1982	SD-N	13	22	6	4	0	0	0	3	6	4	.182	.357	.182	58	-1	-1	2	0	1	-1	-1	/1	-0.2
1983	SD-N	12	8	1	2	0	0	1	2	0	3	.250	.250	.625	140	0	0	1	0	0	0	0	/1	0.0
Total	2	25	30	7	6	0	0	1	5	6	7	.200	.333	.300	82	-1	-1	3	0	1	-1	-1	/1	-0.2

■ PETE LAPAN　　Lapan, Peter Nelson　b: 6/25/1891, Easthampton, Mass　d: 1/5/53, Norwalk, Cal.　BR/TR, 5'7", 165 lbs.　Deb: 9/16/22

YEAR	TM/L	G	AB	R	H	2B	3B	HR	RBI	BB	SO	AVG	OBP	SLG	PRO+	BR	/A	RC	SB	CS	SBR	FR	POS	TPR
1922	Was-A	11	34	7	11	1	0	1	6	3	4	.324	.378	.441	119	1	1	6	1	0	0	0	C	0.1
1923	Was-A	2	2	0	0	0	0	0	0	0	0	.000	.000	.000	-99	-1	-1	0	0	0	0	0	H	0.0
Total	2	13	36	7	11	1	0	1	6	3	4	.306	.359	.417	107	0	0	6	1	0	0	0	/C	0.1

■ RALPH LaPOINTE　　LaPointe, Ralph Robert　b: 1/8/22, Winooski, Vt.　d: 9/13/67, Burlington, Vt.　BR/TR, 5'11", 185 lbs.　Deb: 4/15/47

YEAR	TM/L	G	AB	R	H	2B	3B	HR	RBI	BB	SO	AVG	OBP	SLG	PRO+	BR	/A	RC	SB	CS	SBR	FR	POS	TPR
1947	Phi-N	56	211	33	65	7	0	1	15	17	15	.308	.362	.355	95	-2	-1	29	8			-10	S	-0.6
1948	StL-N	87	222	27	50	3	0	0	15	18	19	.225	.283	.239	40	-17	-19	16	1			8	2S/3	-0.4
Total	2	143	433	60	115	10	0	1	30	35	34	.266	.322	.296	66	-19	-20	45	9			-2	/S23	-1.0

■ FRANK LaPORTE　　LaPorte, Frank Breyfogle "Pot"　b: 2/6/1880, Uhrichsville, Ohio　d: 9/25/39, Newcomerstown, O.　BR/TR, 5'8", 175 lbs.　Deb: 9/29/05

YEAR	TM/L	G	AB	R	H	2B	3B	HR	RBI	BB	SO	AVG	OBP	SLG	PRO+	BR	/A	RC	SB	CS	SBR	FR	POS	TPR
1905	NY-A	11	40	4	16	1	0	1	12	1		.400	.415	.500	173	4	3	9	1			-3	2	0.0
1906	NY-A	123	454	60	120	23	9	2	54	22		.264	.298	.368	100	4	-1	55	10			-5	*3/2O	0.2
1907	NY-A	130	470	56	127	20	11	0	48	27		.270	.310	.360	107	7	3	58	10			-10	3O/1	-0.7
1908	Bos-A	62	156	14	37	1	3	0	15	12		.237	.292	.282	86	-2	-2	14	3			10	23/O	0.8
	NY-A	39	145	7	38	3	4	1	15	8		.262	.301	.359	115	2	2	16	3			-3	2O	-0.2
	Yr	101	301	21	75	4	7	1	30	20		.249	.296	.319	100	0	-0	30	6			6		0.6
1909	NY-A	89	309	35	92	19	3	0	31	18		.298	.340	.379	126	9	8	41	5			-15	2	-0.9
1910	NY-A	124	432	43	114	14	6	2	67	33		.264	.321	.338	100	3	-0	52	16			-10	2O3	-1.6
1911	StL-A	136	507	71	159	37	12	2	82	34		.314	.361	.446	130	15	18	83	4			-6	*2/3	1.1
1912	StL-A	80	266	32	83	11	4	1	38	20		.312	.367	.395	122	6	7	41	7			-3	2O	0.2
	Was-A	40	136	13	42	9	1	0	17	12		.309	.365	.390	115	3	3	20	3			3	2	0.5
	Yr	120	402	45	125	20	5	1	55	32		.311	.366	.393	120	9	10	62	10			0		0.7
1913	Was-A	79	242	25	61	5	4	0	18	17	16	.252	.309	.306	78	-6	-7	25	10			3	32O	-0.4
1914	Ind-F	133	505	86	157	27	12	4	**107**	36	36	.311	.361	.436	115	17	10	89	15			6	*2	1.9
1915	New-F	148	550	55	139	28	10	2	56	48	33	.253	.314	.351	102	-3	1	69	14			5	*2	0.8
Total	11	1194	4212	501	1185	198	79	15	560	288	<u>85</u>	.281	.330	.377	110	58	45	572	101			-28	23O/1	1.7

■ JACK LAPP　　Lapp, John Walker　b: 9/10/1884, Frazer, Pa.　d: 2/6/20, Philadelphia, Pa.　BL/TR, 5'8",　Deb: 9/11/08

YEAR	TM/L	G	AB	R	H	2B	3B	HR	RBI	BB	SO	AVG	OBP	SLG	PRO+	BR	/A	RC	SB	CS	SBR	FR	POS	TPR
1908	Phi-A	13	35	4	5	0	1	0	1	5		.143	.250	.200	45	-2	-2	2	0			-1	C	-0.1
1909	Phi-A	21	56	8	19	3	1	0	10	3		.339	.373	.429	150	3	3	9	1			2	C	0.7
1910	•Phi-A	71	192	18	45	4	3	0	17	20		.234	.310	.286	88	-3	-2	17	0			7	C	1.2
1911	•Phi-A	68	167	35	59	10	3	1	26	24		.353	.435	.467	154	12	13	36	4			-7	C/1	1.3
1912	Phi-A	91	281	26	82	15	6	1	35	19		.292	.337	.399	114	3	4	38	3			-14	C	-0.1
1913	•Phi-A	82	238	23	54	4	4	1	20	37	26	.227	.336	.290	85	-4	-3	23	1			-14	C/1	-1.2
1914	•Phi-A	69	199	22	46	7	2	0	19	31	14	.231	.338	.286	91	-2	-1	20	1	4	-2	-7	C	-0.5
1915	Phi-A	112	312	26	85	16	5	2	31	30	29	.272	.340	.375	117	5	6	43	5	2	0	-4	C1	0.9
1916	Chi-A	40	101	6	21	0	1	0	7	8	10	.208	.266	.228	48	-6	-6	7	1			-0	C	-0.5
Total	9	567	1581	168	416	59	26	5	166	177	<u>79</u>	.263	.340	.343	104	6	11	194	16	<u>6</u>		-39	C/1	1.7

■ NORM LARKER　　Larker, Norman Howard John　b: 12/27/30, Beaver Meadows, Pa.　BL/TL, 6', 185 lbs.　Deb: 4/15/58

YEAR	TM/L	G	AB	R	H	2B	3B	HR	RBI	BB	SO	AVG	OBP	SLG	PRO+	BR	/A	RC	SB	CS	SBR	FR	POS	TPR
1958	LA-N	99	253	32	70	16	5	4	29	29	21	.277	.358	.427	103	3	2	38	1	1	-0	-5	O1	-0.6
1959	•LA-N	108	311	37	90	14	1	8	49	26	25	.289	.348	.418	96	1	-2	43	0	1	-1	4	1O	-0.1
1960	LA-N	133	440	56	142	26	3	5	78	36	24	.323	.375	.430	112	12	9	71	1	0	0	4	*1/O	0.7
1961	LA-N	97	282	29	76	16	1	5	38	24	22	.270	.329	.387	82	-4	-8	34	0	0	0	2	1/O	-1.0
1962	Hou-N	147	506	58	133	19	5	9	63	70	47	.263	.360	.374	105	0	5	71	1	1	-0	7	*1/O	0.7
1963	Mil-N	64	147	15	26	6	0	1	14	24	24	.177	.301	.238	58	-7	-7	12	0	2	-1	3	1	-0.6
	SF-N	19	14	0	1	0	0	0	0	2	2	.071	.188	.071	-22	-2	-2	0	0	0	0	0	1	-0.2
	Yr	83	161	15	27	6	0	1	14	26	26	.168	.291	.224	51	-10	-9	12	0	2	-1	3		-0.8
Total	6	667	1953	227	538	97	15	32	271	211	165	.275	.351	.390	97	-3	-3	269	3	5	-2	14	1/O	-1.1

YEAR	TM/L	G	AB	R	H	2B	3B	HR	RBI	BB	SO	AVG	OBP	SLG	PRO+	BR	/A	RC	SB	CS	SBR	FR	POS	TPR

■ BARRY LARKIN
Larkin, Barry Louis b: 4/28/64, Cincinnati, Ohio BR/TR, 6', 185 lbs. Deb: 8/13/86

1986	Cin-N	41	159	27	45	4	3	3	19	9	21	.283	.321	.403	94	-1	-1	22	8	0	2	-0	S/2	0.4
1987	Cin-N	125	439	64	107	16	2	12	43	36	52	.244	.308	.371	76	-14	-16	52	21	6	3	-0	*S	0.0
1988	Cin-N	151	588	91	174	32	5	12	56	41	24	.296	.350	.429	118	16	14	94	40	7	8	10	*S	4.4
1989	Cin-N	97	325	47	111	14	4	4	36	20	23	.342	.383	.446	132	15	14	54	10	5	0	16	S	3.7
1990	*Cin-N	158	614	85	185	25	6	7	67	49	49	.301	.360	.396	105	7	5	91	30	5	6	20	*S	4.5
Total	5	572	2125	314	622	91	20	38	221	155	169	.293	.347	.408	105	24	15	312	109	23	19	45	S/2	13.0

■ ED LARKIN
Larkin, Edward Francis b: 7/1/1885, Wyalusing, Pa. d: 3/28/34, Wyalusing, Pa. BR/TR, 5'8", Deb: 10/02/09

1909	Phi-A	2	6	0	1	0	0	0	1	1		.167	.286	.167	42	-0	-0	0	0			-1	/C	-0.1

■ GENE LARKIN
Larkin, Eugene Thomas b: 10/24/62, Flushing, N.Y. BB/TR, 6'3", 195 lbs. Deb: 5/21/87

1987	*Min-A	85	233	23	62	11	2	4	28	25	31	.266	.342	.382	89	-2	-4	30	1	4	-2	-2	D1	-0.9
1988	Min-A	149	505	56	135	30	2	8	70	68	55	.267	.371	.382	108	10	8	75	3	2	-0	-5	D1	-1.0
1989	Min-A	136	446	61	119	25	1	6	46	54	57	.267	.358	.368	98	5	1	60	5	2	0	-6	1DO	-1.0
1990	Min-A	119	401	46	108	26	4	5	42	42	55	.269	.346	.392	99	4	-0	56	5	3	-0	-4	OD1	-0.6
Total	4	489	1585	186	424	92	9	23	186	189	198	.268	.357	.380	100	16	5	221	14	11	-2	-16	D1/O	-2.5

■ TERRY LARKIN
Larkin, Frank S. d: 9/16/1894, Brooklyn, N.Y. BR/TR, Deb: 5/20/1876

1876	NY-N	1	4	0	0	0	0	0	0	0	0	.000	.000	.000	-99	-1	-1	0				0	/P	0.0
1877	Har-N	58	228	28	52	6	5	1	18	5	23	.228	.245	.311	83	-7	-3	18				-1	*P/32	0.0
1878	Chi-N	58	226	33	65	9	4	0	32	17	17	.288	.337	.363	122	8	6	28				-3	*P/O3	0.0
1879	Chi-N	60	228	26	50	12	2	0	18	8	24	.219	.246	.289	71	-6	-8	17				-6	*P/O	0.0
1880	Tro-N	6	20	1	3	1	0	0	1	3	4	.150	.261	.200	56	-1	-1	1				0	/POS	0.0
1884	Was-U	17	70	11	17	0	0	0		4		.243	.284	.243	82	-1	-1	5	0			-4	3	-0.3
	Ric-a	40	139	17	28	1	4	0		9		.201	.265	.266	77	-3	-3	10				0	2	-0.1
Total	6	240	915	116	215	29	15	1	69	46	68	.235	.274	.303	88	-10	-10	79				-14	P/23OS	-0.4

■ HENRY LARKIN
Larkin, Henry E. "Ted" b: 1/12/1860, Reading, Pa. d: 1/31/42, Reading, Pa. BR/TR, 5'10", 175 lbs. Deb: 5/01/1884 M

1884	Phi-a	85	326	59	90	21	9	3		15		.276	.324	.423	136	16	12	46				-7	*O/2	0.4
1885	Phi-a	108	453	114	149	37	14	8		26		.329	.372	.525	174	42	37	91				12	*O	3.8
1886	Phi-a	139	565	133	180	36	16	2		59		.319	.390	.450	163	43	42	114	32			5	*O	3.6
1887	Phi-a	126	497	105	154	22	12	3		48		.310	.380	.421	125	18	18	96	37			3	O12	1.4
1888	Phi-a	135	546	92	147	28	12	7	101	33		.269	.326	.403	137	21	22	80	20			-8	*12	0.6
1889	Phi-a	133	516	105	164	23	12	3	74	83	41	.318	.428	.426	148	36	37	101	11			-4	*1/32	1.8
1890	Cle-P	125	506	93	168	32	15	5	112	65	18	.332	.420	.484	156	33	41	108	5			-8	*1/OM	1.6
1891	Phi-a	133	526	94	147	27	14	10	93	66	56	.279	.376	.441	133	25	22	90	2			-5	*1O	0.9
1892	Was-N	119	464	76	130	13	7	8	96	39	21	.280	.346	.390	128	13	15	72	21			1	*1/O	0.7
1893	Was-N	81	319	54	101	20	3	4	73	50	5	.317	.422	.436	134	16	18	61	1			-9	1	0.7
Total	10	1184	4718	925	1430	259	114	53	549	484	141	.303	.380	.440	144	262	264	858	129			-20	1O/23	15.5

■ BOB LARMORE
Larmore, Robert McKahan "Red" b: 12/6/1896, Anderson, Ind. d: 1/15/64, St.Louis, Mo. BR/TR, 5'10.5", 185 lbs. Deb: 5/14/18

1918	StL-N	4	7	0	2	0	0	0	1	0	2	.286	.286	.286	77	-0	-0	1	0			-0	/S	0.0

■ SAM LaROQUE
LaRoque, Samuel H. J. b: 2/26/1864, St.Mathias, Que., Canada TR, 5'11", 190 lbs. Deb: 7/30/1888

1888	Det-N	2	9	1	4	0	0	0	2	1	1	.444	.500	.444	207	1	1	2	0			0	/2	0.1
1890	Pit-N	111	434	59	105	20	4	1	40	35	29	.242	.316	.313	97	-7	1	53	27			-9	2S/1O	-0.5
1891	Pit-N	1	4	0	0	0	0	0	0	0	1	.000	.000	.000	-99	-1	-1	0	0			0	/3	0.0
	Lou-a	10	35	6	11	2	1	1	8	5	8	.314	.429	.514	175	3	4	8	1			-3	2/1	0.1
Total	3	124	482	66	120	22	5	2	50	41	39	.249	.326	.328	104	-4	4	63	28			-12	/2S13O	-0.3

■ VIC LaROSE
LaRose, Victor Raymond b: 12/23/44, Los Angeles, Cal. BR/TR, 5'11", 180 lbs. Deb: 9/13/68

1968	Chi-N	4	2	0	0	0	0	0	0	0	1	.000	.333	.000	6	-0	-0	0	0	0	0	1	/2S	0.1

■ HARRY LaROSS
LaRoss, Harry Raymond "Spike" b: 1/2/1888, Easton, Pa. d: 3/22/54, Chicago, Ill. 5'11.5", 170 lbs. Deb: 6/24/14

1914	Cin-N	22	48	7	11	1	0	0	5	2	10	.229	.260	.250	50	-3	-3	4	4			-2	O	-0.6

■ SWEDE LARSEN
Larsen, Erling Adeli b: 11/15/13, Jersey City, N.J. BR/TR, 5'11", 170 lbs. Deb: 6/17/36

1936	Bos-N	3	1	0	0	0	0	0	0	0	0	.000	.000	.000	-99	-0	-0	0				-0	/2	0.0

■ TONY LaRUSSA
LaRussa, Anthony b: 10/4/44, Tampa, Fla. BR/TR, 6', 175 lbs. Deb: 5/10/63 MC

1963	KC-A	34	44	4	11	1	0	0	1	7	12	.250	.353	.318	86	-0	-1	6	0	0	0	2	S/2	0.3
1968	Oak-A	5	3	0	1	0	0	0	0	0	0	.333	.333	.333	108	-0	0	0	0	0	0	0	H	0.0
1969	Oak-A	8	8	0	0	0	0	0	0	0	1	.000	.000	.000	-99	-2	-2	0	0	0	0	0	H	-0.1
1970	Oak-A	52	106	6	21	4	1	0	6	15	19	.198	.303	.255	57	-6	-6	9	0	0	0	-1	2	-0.1
1971	Oak-A	23	8	3	0	0	0	0	0	0	4	.000	.000	.000	-99	-2	-2	0	0	0	0	5	/2S3	0.4
	Atl-N	9	7	1	2	0	0	0	0	1	1	.286	.375	.286	84	-0	-0	0	0	0	0	0	/2	0.1
1973	Chi-N	1	0	1	0	0	0	0	0	0	0	—	—	—	—	0	0	0	0	0	0	0	R	0.0
Total	6	132	176	15	35	5	2	0	7	23	37	.199	.295	.250	54	-11	-10	16	0	0	0	7	/2S3	0.6

■ AL LARY
Lary, Alfred Allen b: 9/26/29, Northport, Ala. BR/TR, 6'3", 185 lbs. Deb: 9/06/54

1954	Chi-N	2	2	0	1	0	0	0	0	0	1	.500	.500	.500	160	0	0	1	0	0	0	0	/P	0.0
1955	Chi-N	4	0	1	0	0	0	0	0	0	0	—	—	—	—	0	0	0	0	0	0	0	R	0.0
1962	Chi-N	23	6	1	1	0	0	0	0	2	1	.167	.375	.167	49	-0	-0	1	0	0	0	-0	P	0.0
Total	3	29	8	2	2	0	0	0	0	2	2	.250	.400	.250	75	-0	-0	1	0	0	0	0	/P	0.0

■ LYN LARY
Lary, Lynford Hobart "Broadway" b: 1/28/06, Armona, Cal. d: 1/9/73, Downey, Cal. BR/TR, 6', 165 lbs. Deb: 5/11/29

1929	NY-A	80	236	48	73	9	2	6	26	24	15	.309	.380	.428	115	3	5	40	4	1	1	5	3S/2	1.4
1930	NY-A	117	464	93	134	20	8	3	52	45	40	.289	.357	.386	92	-7	-4	68	14	2	3	-8	*S	0.2
1931	NY-A	155	610	100	171	35	9	10	107	88	54	.280	.376	.416	115	9	14	99	13	10	-2	9	*S	3.3
1932	NY-A	91	280	56	65	14	4	3	39	52	28	.232	.358	.343	87	-6	-4	39	9	3	1	2	S/1230	0.5
1933	NY-A	52	127	25	28	3	3	0	13	28	17	.220	.361	.291	79	-4	-2	16	2	1	0	2	3S/1O	0.3
1934	NY-A	1	0	0	0	0	0	0	0	1	0	—	1.000	—	189	-0	0	0	0	0	0	-0	/1	0.0
	Bos-A	129	419	58	101	20	4	2	54	66	51	.241	.344	.322	68	-16	-20	52	12	5	1	-5	*S	-1.3
	Yr	130	419	58	101	20	4	2	54	67	51	.241	.346	.322	68	-15	-20	52	12	5	1	-5		-1.3
1935	Was-A	39	103	8	20	4	0	0	7	12	10	.194	.278	.233	35	-10	-10	8	3	0	1	-4	S	-0.9
	StL-A	93	371	78	107	25	7	2	35	64	43	.288	.393	.410	104	7	4	68	25	4	5	13	S	2.5
	Yr	132	474	86	127	29	7	2	42	76	53	.268	.371	.371	90	-3	-5	74	28	4	6	9		1.6
1936	StL-A	155	619	112	179	30	6	2	52	117	54	.289	.404	.367	89	-3	-6	105	37	9	6	-3	*S	0.6
1937	Cle-A	156	644	110	187	46	7	8	77	88	64	.290	.374	.421	100	2	2	107	18	8	1	6	*S	1.5
1938	Cle-A	141	568	94	152	36	4	3	51	88	65	.268	.366	.361	84	-13	-12	82	23	6	3	-0	*S	0.0
1939	Cle-A	3	2	0	0	0	0	0	0	0	1	.000	.000	.000	-99	-1	-1	0	0	0	0	-1	/S	0.0
	Bro-N	29	31	7	5	1	1	0	1	12	6	.161	.409	.258	80	0	-0	5	1			1	S/3	0.2
	StL-N	34	75	11	14	3	0	1	10	28	15	.187	.330	.227	49	-4	-5	6	1			-5	S/3	-0.8
	Yr	63	106	18	19	4	1	1	11	40	21	.179	.356	.236	59	-4	-5	11	2			-4		-0.6

YEAR	TM/L	G	AB	R	H	2B	3B	HR	RBI	BB	SO	AVG	OBP	SLG	PRO+	BR	/A	RC	SB	CS	SBR	FR	POS	TPR
1940	StL-A	27	54	5	3	1	1	0	3	4	7	.056	.136	.111	-35	-11	-11	1	0	0	0	1	S/2	-0.8
Total	12	1302	4603	805	1239	247	56	38	526	705	470	.269	.369	.372	90	-53	-48	696	162	49		13	*S/3120	6.7

■ DON LASSETTER
Lassetter, Donald O'Neal   b: 3/27/33, Newnan, Ga.   BR/TR, 6'3", 200 lbs.   Deb: 9/21/57

YEAR	TM/L	G	AB	R	H	2B	3B	HR	RBI	BB	SO	AVG	OBP	SLG	PRO+	BR	/A	RC	SB	CS	SBR	FR	POS	TPR
1957	StL-N	4	13	2	2	0	1	0	0	1	3	.154	.214	.308	37	-1	-1	0	0	0	0	0	/O	0.0

■ JUICE LATHAM
Latham, George Warren "Jumbo"   b: 9/6/1852, Utica, N.Y.   d: 5/26/14, Utica, N.Y.   BR/TR, 5'8", 240 lbs.   Deb: 4/19/1875   M

YEAR	TM/L	G	AB	R	H	2B	3B	HR	RBI	BB	SO	AVG	OBP	SLG	PRO+	BR	/A	RC	SB	CS	SBR	FR	POS	TPR
1875	Bos-n	16	77	23	21	4	1	0		0		.273	.273	.351	110	1	1	8					1	0.0
	NH-n	20	76	6	15	1	0	0		0		.197	.197	.211	48	-4	-3	3					1/S3M	-0.2
	Yr	36	153	29	36	5	1	0		0		.235	.235	.281	83	-3	-2	10						-0.2
1877	Lou-N	59	278	42	81	10	6	0	22	5	6	.291	.304	.371	94	3	-4	32				2	*1	-0.4
1882	Phi-a	74	323	47	92	10	2	0		10		.285	.306	.328	102	5	-1	33				-0	*1M	-0.1
1883	Lou-a	88	368	60	92	7	6	0		12		.250	.274	.302	92	-6	-2	31				-3	*12/S	-0.8
1884	Lou-a	77	308	31	52	3	3	0		8		.169	.197	.198	33	-22	-20	12				3	*1/3	-1.9
Total	4	298	1277	180	317	30	17	0	22	35	6	.248	.270	.298	82	-20	-26	109				1	1/2S3	-3.2

■ ARLIE LATHAM
Latham, Walter Arlington "The Freshest Man On Earth"
b: 3/15/1860, W.Lebanon, N.H.   d: 11/29/52, Garden City, N.Y.   BR/TR, 5'8", 150 lbs.   Deb: 7/05/1880   MUC

YEAR	TM/L	G	AB	R	H	2B	3B	HR	RBI	BB	SO	AVG	OBP	SLG	PRO+	BR	/A	RC	SB	CS	SBR	FR	POS	TPR
1880	Buf-N	22	79	9	10	3	1	0	3	1	8	.127	.138	.190	10	-7	-7	2				-1	SO/C	-0.7
1883	StL-a	98	406	86	96	12	7	0		18		.236	.269	.300	78	-7	-11	34				22	*3/C	1.1
1884	StL-a	110	474	115	130	17	12	1		19		.274	.311	.367	119	12	9	55				40	*3/C	4.5
1885	*StL-a	110	485	84	100	15	3	1		18		.206	.242	.256	57	-21	-25	31				2	*3/C	-1.4
1886	*StL-a	134	578	152	174	23	8	1		55		.301	.368	.374	129	24	20	104	60			0	*3/2	2.2
1887	*StL-a	136	627	163	198	35	10	2		45		.316	.366	.413	108	16	4	146	129			2	*3/2C	0.2
1888	*StL-a	133	570	119	151	19	5	2	31	43		.265	.325	.326	101	9	-1	98	109			3	*3/S	0.2
1889	StL-a	118	512	110	126	13	3	4	49	42	30	.246	.317	.307	71	-12	-24	73	69			11	*3/2	-1.0
1890	Chi-P	52	214	47	49	7	2	1	20	22	22	.229	.310	.294	61	-11	-12	30	32			3	3	-0.4
	Cin-N	41	164	35	41	6	2	0	15	23	18	.250	.346	.311	94	-0	-0	25	20			6	3	0.6
1891	Cin-N	135	533	119	145	20	10	7	53	74	35	.272	.372	.386	122	18	17	112	87			21	*3/C	3.8
1892	Cin-N	152	622	111	148	20	4	0	44	60	54	.238	.310	.283	82	-13	-11	77	66			-4	*3/2O	-0.5
1893	Cin-N	127	531	101	150	18	6	2	49	62	20	.282	.368	.350	91	-3	-5	92	57			-11	*3	-1.2
1894	Cin-N	129	524	129	164	23	6	4	60	60	24	.313	.393	.403	90	-3	-7	109	59			-10	*3/2	-1.4
1895	Cin-N	112	460	93	143	14	6	2	69	42	25	.311	.375	.380	93	-1	-4	86	48			-15	*3/12	-1.4
1896	StL-N	8	35	3	7	0	0	0	5	4	3	.200	.282	.200	31	-3	-3	3	2			-1	/3M	-0.2
1899	Was-N	6	6	1	1	0	0	0	0	1		.167	.286	.167	28	-1	-1	0	0			-0	/O2	0.0
1909	NY-N	4	2	1	0	0	0	0	0	0		.000	.000	.000	-99	-0	-0	-0	1			1	/2	0.0
Total	17	1627	6822	1478	1833	245	85	27	398	589	239	.269	.334	.341	93	-5	-63	1076	739			66	*3/2SOC	4.4

■ CHICK LATHERS
Lathers, Charles Ten Eyck   b: 10/22/1888, Detroit, Mich.   d: 7/26/71, Petoskey, Mich.   BL/TR, 6', 180 lbs.   Deb: 5/01/10

YEAR	TM/L	G	AB	R	H	2B	3B	HR	RBI	BB	SO	AVG	OBP	SLG	PRO+	BR	/A	RC	SB	CS	SBR	FR	POS	TPR
1910	Det-A	41	82	4	19	2	0	0	3	8		.232	.300	.256	70	-2	-3	6	0			5	3/2S	0.2
1911	Det-A	29	45	5	10	1	0	0	4	5		.222	.314	.244	54	-2	-3	4	0			-3	/23S1	-0.4
Total	2	70	127	9	29	3	0	0	7	13		.228	.305	.252	64	-5	-6	10	0			2	/32S1	-0.2

■ TACKS LATIMER
Latimer, Clifford Wesley   b: 11/30/1877, Loveland, Ohio   d: 4/24/36, Loveland, Ohio   TR , 6', 160 lbs.   Deb: 10/01/1898

YEAR	TM/L	G	AB	R	H	2B	3B	HR	RBI	BB	SO	AVG	OBP	SLG	PRO+	BR	/A	RC	SB	CS	SBR	FR	POS	TPR
1898	NY-N	5	17	1	5	1	0	0	1	0		.294	.294	.353	90	-0	-0	2	0			0	/CO	0.0
1899	Lou-N	9	29	3	8	1	0	0	4	2		.276	.323	.310	76	-1	-1	3	1			2	/C1	0.2
1900	Pit-N	4	12	1	4	1	0	0	2	0		.333	.333	.417	108	0	0	2	0			0	/C	0.1
1901	Bal-A	1	4	0	1	0	0	0	0	0		.250	.250	.250	39	-0	-0	0	0			-0	/C	0.0
1902	Bro-N	8	24	0	1	0	0	0	0	0		.042	.042	.042	-74	-5	-5	0	0			-0	/C	-0.4
Total	5	27	86	5	19	3	0	0	7	2		.221	.239	.256	43	-6	-6	7	1			2	/CO1	-0.1

■ CHARLIE LAU
Lau, Charles Richard   b: 4/12/33, Romulus, Mich.   d: 3/18/84, Key Colony Beach, Fla.   BL/TR, 6', 190 lbs.   Deb: 9/12/56   C

YEAR	TM/L	G	AB	R	H	2B	3B	HR	RBI	BB	SO	AVG	OBP	SLG	PRO+	BR	/A	RC	SB	CS	SBR	FR	POS	TPR
1956	Det-A	3	9	1	2	0	0	0	0	0	1	.222	.222	.222	18	-1	-1	0	0	0	0	1	/C	0.0
1958	Det-A	30	68	8	10	1	2	0	6	12	15	.147	.293	.221	41	-5	-6	5	0	0	0	1	C	-0.4
1959	Det-A	2	6	0	1	0	0	0	0	0	2	.167	.167	.167	-8	-1	-1	0	0	0	0	1	/C	0.0
1960	Mil-N	21	53	4	10	2	0	0	2	6	10	.189	.271	.226	41	-4	-4	4	0	0	0	5	C	0.2
1961	Mil-N	28	82	3	17	5	0	0	5	14	11	.207	.330	.268	65	-4	-3	8	1	1	-0	-3	C	-0.4
	Bal-A	17	47	3	8	0	0	1	4	1	3	.170	.188	.234	12	-6	-6	2	0	0	0	5	C	0.0
1962	Bal-A	81	197	21	58	11	2	6	37	7	11	.294	.322	.462	114	1	3	29	1	0	0	-4	C	0.2
1963	Bal-A	29	48	4	9	0	0	0	6	1	5	.188	.204	.229	22	-5	-5	2	0	0	0	1	/C	-0.3
	KC-A	62	187	15	55	11	0	3	26	14	17	.294	.343	.401	104	2	1	24	1	0	0	-10	C	-0.8
	Yr	91	235	19	64	13	0	3	32	15	22	.272	.316	.366	89	-3	-4	25	1	0	0	-9		-1.1
1964	KC-A	43	118	11	32	7	1	2	9	10	18	.271	.328	.398	98	-0	-0	16	0	0	0	-7	C	-0.5
	Bal-A	62	158	16	41	15	1	1	14	17	27	.259	.335	.386	100	0	0	20	0	0	0	-3	C	0.0
	Yr	105	276	27	73	22	2	3	23	27	45	.264	.332	.391	99	-0	-0	36	0	0	0	-10		-0.5
1965	Bal-A	68	132	15	39	5	2	2	18	17	18	.295	.376	.409	120	4	4	20	0	0	0	-7	C	0.0
1966	Bal-A	18	12	1	6	2	1	0	5	4	1	.500	.625	.833	320	4	4	7	0	0	0	0	H	0.4
1967	Bal-A	11	8	0	1	1	0	0	3	2	2	.125	.300	.250	65	-0	-0	1	0	0	0	0	H	0.0
	Atl-N	52	45	3	9	1	0	1	5	4	9	.200	.265	.289	59	-2	-2	3	0	0	0	0	H	-0.2
Total	11	527	1170	105	298	63	9	16	140	109	150	.255	.321	.365	89	-17	-17	141	3	1	0	-21	C	-1.8

■ BILLY LAUDER
Lauder, William   b: 2/23/1874, New York, N.Y.   d: 5/20/33, Norwalk, Conn.   BR/TR, 5'10", 160 lbs.   Deb: 6/25/1898   C

YEAR	TM/L	G	AB	R	H	2B	3B	HR	RBI	BB	SO	AVG	OBP	SLG	PRO+	BR	/A	RC	SB	CS	SBR	FR	POS	TPR
1898	Phi-N	97	361	42	95	14	7	2	67	19		.263	.300	.357	94	-5	-3	42	6			-16	3	-1.5
1899	Phi-N	151	583	74	156	17	6	3	90	34		.268	.310	.333	81	-17	-14	66	15			-14	*3	-2.5
1901	Phi-A	2	8	1	1	0	0	0	0	0		.125	.125	.125	-29	-1	-1	0	0			1	/3	0.0
1902	NY-N	125	482	41	114	20	1	1	44	10		.237	.252	.288	69	-19	-18	41	19			3	*3/O	-1.0
1903	NY-N	108	395	52	111	13	0	0	53	14		.281	.306	.314	76	-11	-13	47	19			-6	*3	-1.8
Total	5	483	1829	210	477	64	14	6	254	77		.261	.291	.321	79	-54	-50	196	59			-33	3/O	-6.8

■ TIM LAUDNER
Laudner, Timothy Jon   b: 6/7/58, Mason City, Iowa   BR/TR, 6'3", 212 lbs.   Deb: 8/28/81

YEAR	TM/L	G	AB	R	H	2B	3B	HR	RBI	BB	SO	AVG	OBP	SLG	PRO+	BR	/A	RC	SB	CS	SBR	FR	POS	TPR
1981	Min-A	14	43	4	7	2	0	2	5	3	17	.163	.234	.349	62	-2	-2	4	0	0	0	-0	C/D	-0.1
1982	Min-A	93	306	37	78	19	1	7	33	34	74	.255	.329	.392	95	-1	-2	39	0	2	-1	-15	C	-1.3
1983	Min-A	62	168	20	31	9	0	6	18	15	49	.185	.251	.339	60	-9	-10	15	0	0	0	5	C	-0.1
1984	Min-A	87	262	31	54	16	1	10	35	18	78	.206	.260	.389	73	-9	-11	26	0	0	0	8	C/D	0.3
1985	Min-A	72	164	16	39	5	0	7	19	12	45	.238	.294	.396	82	-3	-5	19	0	1	-1	-5	C/1	-0.6
1986	Min-A	76	193	21	47	10	0	10	29	24	56	.244	.336	.451	109	3	2	30	1	0	0	-15	C	-0.7
1987	*Min-A	113	288	30	55	7	1	16	43	23	80	.191	.253	.389	65	-15	-16	29	1	0	0	-7	*C/1D	-1.4
1988	Min-A	117	375	38	94	18	1	13	54	36	89	.251	.318	.408	99	0	-1	46	0	0	0	-0	*C/1D	0.3
1989	Min-A	100	239	24	53	11	1	6	27	25	65	.222	.295	.351	76	-6	-8	25	1	0	0	-0	CD1	-0.5
Total	9	734	2038	221	458	97	5	77	263	190	553	.225	.293	.391	83	-42	-52	233	3	3	-1	-29	C/D1	-4.1

■ CHUCK LAUER
Lauer, John Charles   b: 1865, Pittsburgh, Pa.   TR ,   Deb: 7/17/1884

YEAR	TM/L	G	AB	R	H	2B	3B	HR	RBI	BB	SO	AVG	OBP	SLG	PRO+	BR	/A	RC	SB	CS	SBR	FR	POS	TPR
1884	Pit-a	13	44	5	5	0	0	0		0		.114	.114	.114	-24	-6	-6	1				-1	O/P1	-0.6
1889	Pit-N	4	16	2	3	0	0	0	1	0	5	.188	.188	.188	6	-2	-2	1	0			1	/CO	0.0
1890	Chi-N	2	8	1	2	1	0	0	2	0	0	.250	.250	.375	80	-0	-0	1	0			1	/C	0.0

YEAR	TM/L	G	AB	R	H	2B	3B	HR	RBI	BB	SO	AVG	OBP	SLG	PRO+	BR	/A	RC	SB	CS	SBR	FR	POS	TPR
Total	3	19	68	8	10	1	0	0	3	0	5	.147	.147	.162	-3	-8	-8	2	0			0	/OCP1	-0.6

■ BEN LAUGHLIN   Laughlin, Benjamin   Deb: 4/28/1873

YEAR	TM/L	G	AB	R	H	2B	3B	HR	RBI	BB	SO	AVG	OBP	SLG	PRO+	BR	/A	RC	SB	CS	SBR	FR	POS	TPR
1873	Res-n	12	50	3	12	1	0	0			0	.240	.240	.260	51	-3	-2	3					2/13	-0.1

■ BILL LAUTERBORN   Lauterborn, William Bernard   b: 6/9/1879, Hornell, N.Y.   d: 4/19/65, Andover, N.Y.   BR/TR, 5'6", 140 lbs.   Deb: 9/20/04

YEAR	TM/L	G	AB	R	H	2B	3B	HR	RBI	BB	SO	AVG	OBP	SLG	PRO+	BR	/A	RC	SB	CS	SBR	FR	POS	TPR
1904	Bos-N	20	69	7	19	2	0	0	2	1		.275	.286	.304	87	-1	-1	7	1			-3	2	-0.3
1905	Bos-N	67	200	11	37	1	1	0	9	12		.185	.231	.200	31	-17	-16	10	1			-7	32/SO	-2.0
Total	2	87	269	18	56	3	1	0	11	13		.208	.245	.227	45	-18	-17	17	2			-10	/23SO	-2.3

■ COOKIE LAVAGETTO   Lavagetto, Harry Arthur   b: 12/1/12, Oakland, Cal.   d: 8/10/90, Orinda, Cal.   BR/TR, 6', 170 lbs.   Deb: 4/17/34   MC

YEAR	TM/L	G	AB	R	H	2B	3B	HR	RBI	BB	SO	AVG	OBP	SLG	PRO+	BR	/A	RC	SB	CS	SBR	FR	POS	TPR
1934	Pit-N	87	304	41	67	16	3	3	46	32	39	.220	.295	.322	64	-15	-16	31	6			-14	2	-2.0
1935	Pit-N	78	231	27	67	9	4	0	19	18	15	.290	.341	.364	87	-3	-4	29	1			-11	23	-1.0
1936	Pit-N	60	197	21	48	15	2	2	26	15	13	.244	.300	.371	78	-6	-7	22	0			-1	23/S	-0.3
1937	Bro-N	149	503	64	142	26	6	8	70	74	41	.282	.375	.406	110	11	9	79	13			-7	*23	0.9
1938	Bro-N	137	487	68	133	34	6	6	79	68	31	.273	.364	.405	109	9	7	76	15			-11	*3/2	-0.6
1939	Bro-N	153	587	93	176	28	5	10	87	78	30	.300	.387	.416	112	15	12	95	14			-5	*3	1.2
1940	Bro-N	118	448	56	115	21	3	4	43	70	32	.257	.361	.344	90	-0	-4	59	4			-14	*3	-1.8
1941	*Bro-N	132	441	75	122	24	7	1	78	80	21	.277	.388	.370	109	12	9	69	7			-20	*3	-0.9
1946	Bro-N	88	242	36	57	9	1	3	27	38	17	.236	.339	.318	86	-3	-3	28	3			-5	3	-0.7
1947	*Bro-N	41	69	6	18	1	0	3	11	12	5	.261	.370	.406	102	1	0	11	0			3	3/1	0.3
Total	10	1043	3509	487	945	183	37	40	486	485	244	.269	.360	.377	98	20	5	500	63			-84	32/1S	-4.9

■ MIKE LaVALLIERE   LaValliere, Michael Eugene   b: 8/18/60, Charlotte, N.C.   BL/TR, 5'10", 180 lbs.   Deb: 9/09/84

YEAR	TM/L	G	AB	R	H	2B	3B	HR	RBI	BB	SO	AVG	OBP	SLG	PRO+	BR	/A	RC	SB	CS	SBR	FR	POS	TPR
1984	Phi-N	6	7	0	0	0	0	0	0	2	2	.000	.222	.000	-32	-1	-1	0	0	0	0	2	/C	0.1
1985	StL-N	12	34	2	5	1	0	0	6	7	3	.147	.293	.176	34	-3	-3	2	0	0	0	-2	C	-0.3
1986	StL-N	110	303	18	71	10	2	3	30	36	37	.234	.318	.310	74	-10	-10	31	0	1	-1	1	*C	-0.7
1987	Pit-N	121	340	33	102	19	0	1	36	43	32	.300	.380	.365	98	1	1	50	0	0	0	6	*C	1.6
1988	Pit-N	120	352	24	92	18	0	2	47	50	34	.261	.356	.330	99	1	2	43	3	2	-0	-1	*C	0.6
1989	Pit-N	68	190	15	60	10	0	2	23	29	24	.316	.406	.400	136	9	10	31	0	2	-1	-7	C	0.6
1990	*Pit-N	96	279	27	72	15	0	3	31	44	20	.258	.363	.344	100	-0	1	36	0	3	-2	1	C	0.5
Total	7	533	1505	119	402	73	2	11	173	211	152	.267	.359	.340	96	-3	0	193	3	8	-4	-0	C	2.4

■ DOC LAVAN   Lavan, John Leonard   b: 10/28/1890, Grand Rapids, Mich   d: 5/29/52, Detroit, Mich.   BR/TR, 5'8.5", 151 lbs.   Deb: 6/22/13

YEAR	TM/L	G	AB	R	H	2B	3B	HR	RBI	BB	SO	AVG	OBP	SLG	PRO+	BR	/A	RC	SB	CS	SBR	FR	POS	TPR
1913	StL-A	46	149	8	21	2	1	0	4	10	46	.141	.210	.168	11	-17	-16	6	3			-5	S	-1.8
	Phi-A	5	14	1	1	0	1	0	1	0	0	.071	.071	.214	-17	-2	-2	0	0			0	/S	-0.1
	Yr	51	163	9	22	2	2	0	5	10	46	.135	.199	.172	9	-19	-18	6	3			-4		-1.9
1914	StL-A	75	239	21	63	7	4	1	21	17	39	.264	.318	.339	101	-1	-0	24	6	12	-5	-12	S	-1.1
1915	StL-A	157	514	44	112	17	7	1	48	42	83	.218	.281	.284	72	-21	-18	42	13	19	-8	5	*S	-0.6
1916	StL-A	110	343	32	81	13	1	0	19	32	38	.236	.305	.280	80	-10	-8	32	7			34	*S	3.7
1917	StL-A	118	355	19	85	8	5	0	30	19	34	.239	.284	.290	78	-11	-10	30	5			12	*S/2	0.7
1918	Was-A	117	464	44	129	17	2	0	45	14	21	.278	.302	.323	90	-8	-7	47	12			-10	*S/O	-1.0
1919	StL-N	100	356	25	86	12	2	1	25	11	30	.242	.264	.295	72	-14	-12	28	4			9	S	0.1
1920	StL-N	142	516	52	149	21	10	1	63	19	38	.289	.318	.374	102	-2	-0	58	11	14	-5	16	*S	1.9
1921	StL-N	150	560	58	145	23	11	2	82	23	30	.259	.291	.350	70	-26	-24	56	7	7	-2	19	*S	0.6
1922	StL-N	89	264	24	60	8	1	0	27	13	10	.227	.271	.265	41	-24	-22	20	3	1	0	15	S/3	-0.1
1923	StL-N	50	111	10	22	6	0	1	12	9	7	.198	.264	.279	44	-9	-9	8	0	3	-2	1	S/312	-0.5
1924	StL-N	4	6	0	0	0	0	0	0	0	0	.000	.000	.000	-99	-2	-2	0	0	0	0	2	/2S	0.0
Total	12	1163	3891	338	954	134	45	7	377	209	376	.245	.288	.308	75	-147	-131	351	71	56		85	*S/2310	1.8

■ ART LaVIGNE   LaVigne, Arthur David   b: 1/26/1885, Worcester, Mass.   d: 7/18/50, Worcester, Mass.   BR/TR, 5'10", 162 lbs.   Deb: 4/24/14

YEAR	TM/L	G	AB	R	H	2B	3B	HR	RBI	BB	SO	AVG	OBP	SLG	PRO+	BR	/A	RC	SB	CS	SBR	FR	POS	TPR
1914	Buf-F	51	90	10	14	2	0	0	4	7	25	.156	.216	.178	13	-10	-10	4	0			6	C/1	-0.2

■ JOHNNY LAVIN   Lavin, John   b: Bay City, Mich.   5'11", 175 lbs.   Deb: 9/10/1884

YEAR	TM/L	G	AB	R	H	2B	3B	HR	RBI	BB	SO	AVG	OBP	SLG	PRO+	BR	/A	RC	SB	CS	SBR	FR	POS	TPR
1884	StL-a	16	52	9	11	2	0	0			3	.212	.268	.250	70	-1	-2	4				-3	O	-0.4

■ RUDY LAW   Law, Rudy Karl   b: 10/7/56, Waco, Tex.   BL/TL, 6'1", 165 lbs.   Deb: 9/12/78

YEAR	TM/L	G	AB	R	H	2B	3B	HR	RBI	BB	SO	AVG	OBP	SLG	PRO+	BR	/A	RC	SB	CS	SBR	FR	POS	TPR
1978	LA-N	11	12	2	3	0	0	0	1	1	2	.250	.308	.250	58	-1	-1	1	3	1	0	-0	/O	0.0
1980	LA-N	128	388	55	101	5	4	1	23	23	27	.260	.307	.302	72	-15	-14	39	40	13	4	-7	*O	-2.2
1982	Chi-A	121	336	55	107	15	8	3	32	23	41	.318	.362	.438	118	8	8	55	36	10	5	-10	O/D	0.0
1983	*Chi-A	141	501	95	142	20	7	3	34	42	36	.283	.341	.369	92	-2	-5	74	77	12	16	-8	*O/D	0.1
1984	Chi-A	136	487	68	122	14	7	6	37	39	42	.251	.310	.345	77	-12	-15	50	29	17	-2	-10	*O	-3.0
1985	Chi-A	125	390	62	101	21	6	4	36	27	40	.259	.312	.374	84	-7	-9	49	29	6	5	-1	*O/D	-0.5
1986	KC-A	87	307	42	80	26	5	1	36	29	22	.261	.328	.388	92	-2	-3	40	14	6	1	-4	O/D	-0.8
Total	7	749	2421	379	656	101	37	18	199	184	210	.271	.326	.366	88	-32	-39	308	228	65	29	-41	O/D	-6.4

■ VANCE LAW   Law, Vance Aaron   b: 10/1/56, Boise, Idaho   BR/TR, 6'2", 185 lbs.   Deb: 6/01/80

YEAR	TM/L	G	AB	R	H	2B	3B	HR	RBI	BB	SO	AVG	OBP	SLG	PRO+	BR	/A	RC	SB	CS	SBR	FR	POS	TPR
1980	Pit-N	25	74	11	17	2	2	0	3	3	7	.230	.260	.311	58	-4	-4	6	2	0	1	-3	2/S3	-0.5
1981	Pit-N	30	67	1	9	0	1	0	3	2	15	.134	.159	.164	-8	-9	-10	1	1	1	-0	5	2/S3	-0.3
1982	Chi-A	114	359	40	101	20	1	5	54	26	46	.281	.332	.384	96	-2	-2	45	4	2	0	-13	S32/O	-0.7
1983	*Chi-A	145	408	55	99	21	5	4	42	51	56	.243	.328	.348	83	-7	-9	49	3	1	0	5	*3/2SOD	-0.2
1984	Chi-A	151	481	60	121	18	2	17	59	41	75	.252	.312	.403	92	-3	-6	59	4	1	1	-14	*32/OS	-1.6
1985	Mon-N	147	519	75	138	30	6	10	52	86	96	.266	.372	.405	124	14	18	82	6	5	-1	-0	*213/O	1.8
1986	Mon-N	112	360	37	81	17	2	5	44	37	66	.225	.299	.325	73	-14	-13	34	3	5	-2	18	213/PO	0.3
1987	Mon-N	133	436	52	119	27	1	12	56	51	62	.273	.349	.422	100	2	0	65	8	5	-1	-9	*231/P	-0.7
1988	Chi-N	151	556	73	163	29	2	11	78	55	79	.293	.360	.412	116	16	13	80	1	4	-2	-11	*3/O	0.0
1989	*Chi-N	130	408	38	96	22	3	7	42	38	73	.235	.300	.355	81	-7	-11	43	2	2	-1	-18	*3/O	-3.2
Total	10	1138	3668	442	944	186	25	71	433	390	575	.257	.330	.380	95	-14	-23	465	34	26	-5	-41	32S/10PD	-5.1

■ GARLAND LAWING   Lawing, Garland Frederick "Knobby" "Knobby"   b: 8/29/19, Gastonia, N.C.   BR/TR, 6'1", 180 lbs.   Deb: 5/29/46

YEAR	TM/L	G	AB	R	H	2B	3B	HR	RBI	BB	SO	AVG	OBP	SLG	PRO+	BR	/A	RC	SB	CS	SBR	FR	POS	TPR
1946	Cin-N	2	3	0	0	0	0	0	0	0	2	.000	.000	.000	-99	-1	-1	0	0			0	/O	0.0
	NY-N	8	12	2	2	0	0	0	0	0	3	.167	.167	.167	-5	-2	-2	0	0			0	/O	-0.1
	Yr	10	15	2	2	0	0	0	0	0	5	.133	.133	.133	-24	-2	-2	0	0			0		-0.1

■ TOM LAWLESS   Lawless, Thomas James   b: 12/19/56, Erie, Pa.   BR/TR, 5'11", 170 lbs.   Deb: 7/15/82

YEAR	TM/L	G	AB	R	H	2B	3B	HR	RBI	BB	SO	AVG	OBP	SLG	PRO+	BR	/A	RC	SB	CS	SBR	FR	POS	TPR
1982	Cin-N	49	165	19	35	6	0	0	4	9	30	.212	.253	.248	40	-13	-13	10	16	5	2	7	2	-0.2
1984	Cin-N	43	80	10	20	2	0	1	2	8	12	.250	.318	.313	74	-2	-3	8	6	3	0	-3	2/3	-0.4
	Mon-N	11	17	1	3	1	0	0	0	0	4	.176	.176	.235	15	-2	-2	0	1	0	0	0	/2	-0.0
	Yr	54	97	11	23	3	0	1	2	8	16	.237	.295	.299	66	-4	-4	8	7	3	0	-3		-0.4
1985	*StL-N	47	58	8	12	3	1	0	8	5	4	.207	.270	.293	58	-3	-3	5	2	1	0	9	32	0.6
1986	StL-N	46	39	5	11	1	0	0	3	2	8	.282	.317	.308	74	-1	-1	5	8	1	2	3	3/2O	0.3
1987	*StL-N	19	25	5	2	1	0	0	0	3	5	.080	.179	.120	-19	-4	-4	1	2	0	1	-1	/23O	-0.3
1988	StL-N	54	65	9	10	2	1	1	3	7	14	.154	.236	.262	42	-5	-5	5	6	0	2	2	3/O21	0.0
1989	Tor-A	59	70	20	16	1	0	0	3	7	12	.229	.299	.243	55	-4	-4	7	12	1	3	6	O3D/2C	0.5
1990	Tor-A	15	12	1	1	0	0	0	1	0	1	.083	.083	.083	-54	-2	-2	-0	0	2	-1	3	/3O2D	0.0

YEAR	TM/L	G	AB	R	H	2B	3B	HR	RBI	BB	SO	AVG	OBP	SLG	PRO+	BR	/A	RC	SB	CS	SBR	FR	POS	TPR
Total	8	343	531	78	110	17	2	2	24	41	85	.207	.264	.258	46	-38	-38	41	53	13	8	27	2/30DC1	0.5

■ MIKE LAWLOR
Lawlor, Michael H. b: 3/11/1854, Troy, N.Y. d: 8/3/18, Troy, N.Y. TR , 6′, 180 lbs. Deb: 5/27/1880

YEAR	TM/L	G	AB	R	H	2B	3B	HR	RBI	BB	SO	AVG	OBP	SLG	PRO+	BR	/A	RC	SB	CS	SBR	FR	POS	TPR
1880	Tro-N	4	9	1	1	0	0	0	0	1	1	.111	.200	.111	8	-1	-1	0				4	/C	0.3
1884	Was-U	2	7	0	0	0	0	0		0		.000	.000	.000	-99	-1	-1	0	0			1	/C	0.0
Total	2	6	16	1	1	0	0	0	0	1	1	.063	.118	.063	-37	-2	-2	0	0			5	/C	0.3

■ JIM LAWRENCE
Lawrence, James Ross b: 2/12/39, Hamilton, Ont., Can. BL/TR, 6′1″, 185 lbs. Deb: 5/30/63

YEAR	TM/L	G	AB	R	H	2B	3B	HR	RBI	BB	SO	AVG	OBP	SLG	PRO+	BR	/A	RC	SB	CS	SBR	FR	POS	TPR
1963	Cle-A	2	0	0	0	0	0	0	0	0	0	—	—	—	—	0	0	0	0	0	0	0	/C	0.0

■ BILL LAWRENCE
Lawrence, William Henry b: 3/11/06, San Mateo, Cal. BR/TR, 6′4″, 194 lbs. Deb: 4/13/32

YEAR	TM/L	G	AB	R	H	2B	3B	HR	RBI	BB	SO	AVG	OBP	SLG	PRO+	BR	/A	RC	SB	CS	SBR	FR	POS	TPR
1932	Det-A	25	46	10	10	1	0	0	3	5	5	.217	.294	.239	38	-4	-4	3	0	2	-1	4	O	-0.1

■ OTIS LAWRY
Lawry, Otis Carroll "Rabbit" b: 11/1/1893, Fairfield, Me. d: 10/23/65, China, Maine BL/TR, 5′8″, 133 lbs. Deb: 6/28/16

YEAR	TM/L	G	AB	R	H	2B	3B	HR	RBI	BB	SO	AVG	OBP	SLG	PRO+	BR	/A	RC	SB	CS	SBR	FR	POS	TPR
1916	Phi-A	41	123	10	25	0	0	0	4	9	21	.203	.263	.203	42	-9	-8	8	4			-10	2/O	-1.9
1917	Phi-A	30	55	7	9	1	0	0	1	2	9	.164	.193	.182	15	-6	-6	2	1			-3	2/O	-0.8
Total	2	71	178	17	34	1	0	0	5	11	30	.191	.242	.197	34	-14	-14	10	5			-13	/2O	-2.7

■ MARCUS LAWTON
Lawton, Marcus Dwayne b: 8/18/65, Gulfport, Miss. BB/TR, 6′1″, 160 lbs. Deb: 8/11/89

YEAR	TM/L	G	AB	R	H	2B	3B	HR	RBI	BB	SO	AVG	OBP	SLG	PRO+	BR	/A	RC	SB	CS	SBR	FR	POS	TPR
1989	NY-A	10	14	1	3	0	0	0	0	0	3	.214	.214	.214	21	-1	-1	1	1	0	0	0	/OD	0.0

■ GENE LAYDEN
Layden, Eugene Francis b: 3/14/1894, Pittsburgh, Pa. d: 12/12/84, Pittsburgh, Pa. BL/TL, 5′10″, 160 lbs. Deb: 7/29/15

YEAR	TM/L	G	AB	R	H	2B	3B	HR	RBI	BB	SO	AVG	OBP	SLG	PRO+	BR	/A	RC	SB	CS	SBR	FR	POS	TPR
1915	NY-A	3	7	2	2	0	0	0	0	0	1	.286	.286	.286	71	-0	-0	0	0	1	-1	-1	/O	-0.1

■ PETE LAYDON
Laydon, Peter John b: 12/30/19, Dallas, Tex. d: 7/18/82, Edna, Tex. BR/TR, 5′11″, 185 lbs. Deb: 4/28/48

YEAR	TM/L	G	AB	R	H	2B	3B	HR	RBI	BB	SO	AVG	OBP	SLG	PRO+	BR	/A	RC	SB	CS	SBR	FR	POS	TPR
1948	StL-A	41	104	11	26	2	1	0	4	6	10	.250	.297	.288	55	-7	-7	9	4	2	0	4	O	-0.3

■ HERMAN LAYNE
Layne, Herman b: 2/13/01, New Haven, W.Va. d: 8/27/73, Gallipolis, Ohio BR/TR, 5′11″, 165 lbs. Deb: 4/16/27

YEAR	TM/L	G	AB	R	H	2B	3B	HR	RBI	BB	SO	AVG	OBP	SLG	PRO+	BR	/A	RC	SB	CS	SBR	FR	POS	TPR
1927	Pit-N	11	6	3	0	0	0	0	0	1	0	.000	.143	.000	-55	-1	-1	0	0			0	/O	0.0

■ HILLIS LAYNE
Layne, Ivoria Hillis "Tony" b: 2/23/18, Whitwell, Tenn. BL/TR, 6′, 170 lbs. Deb: 9/16/41

YEAR	TM/L	G	AB	R	H	2B	3B	HR	RBI	BB	SO	AVG	OBP	SLG	PRO+	BR	/A	RC	SB	CS	SBR	FR	POS	TPR
1941	Was-A	13	50	8	14	2	0	0	6	4	5	.280	.333	.320	77	-2	-2	5	1	1	-0	0	3	0.0
1944	Was-A	33	87	6	17	2	0	0	8	6	10	.195	.263	.218	40	-7	-6	6	2	0	1	1	3/2	-0.4
1945	Was-A	61	147	23	44	5	4	1	14	10	7	.299	.352	.408	132	3	5	20	0	1	-1	-5	3	0.0
Total	3	107	284	37	75	9	4	1	28	20	22	.264	.321	.335	92	-5	-3	30	3	2	-0	-3	/32	-0.4

■ LES LAYTON
Layton, Lester Lee b: 11/18/21, Nardin, Okla. BR/TR, 6′, 165 lbs. Deb: 4/24/48

YEAR	TM/L	G	AB	R	H	2B	3B	HR	RBI	BB	SO	AVG	OBP	SLG	PRO+	BR	/A	RC	SB	CS	SBR	FR	POS	TPR
1948	NY-N	63	91	14	21	4	4	2	12	6	21	.231	.286	.429	90	-2	-2	11	1			1	O	-0.1

■ JOHNNY LAZOR
Lazor, John Paul b: 9/9/12, Taylor, Wash. BL/TR, 5′9.5″, 180 lbs. Deb: 4/22/43

YEAR	TM/L	G	AB	R	H	2B	3B	HR	RBI	BB	SO	AVG	OBP	SLG	PRO+	BR	/A	RC	SB	CS	SBR	FR	POS	TPR
1943	Bos-A	83	208	21	47	10	2	0	13	21	25	.226	.297	.293	72	-7	-7	18	5	6	-2	6	O	-0.5
1944	Bos-A	16	24	0	2	1	0	0	0	1	0	.083	.120	.125	-30	-4	-4	0	0	0	0	1	/OC	-0.2
1945	Bos-A	101	335	35	104	19	2	5	45	18	17	.310	.346	.424	120	8	7	50	3	2	-0	-10	O	-0.5
1946	Bos-A	23	29	1	4	0	0	1	4	2	11	.138	.194	.241	20	-3	-3	1	0	0	0	0	/O	-0.3
Total	4	223	596	57	157	30	4	6	62	42	53	.263	.312	.357	92	-6	-8	70	8	8	-2	-3	O/C	-1.5

■ TONY LAZZERI
Lazzeri, Anthony Michael "Poosh 'Em Up Tony"
b: 12/6/03, San Francisco, Cal. d: 8/6/46, San Francisco, Cal. BR/TR, 5′11.5″, 170 lbs. Deb: 4/13/26 C

YEAR	TM/L	G	AB	R	H	2B	3B	HR	RBI	BB	SO	AVG	OBP	SLG	PRO+	BR	/A	RC	SB	CS	SBR	FR	POS	TPR
1926	*NY-A	155	589	79	162	28	14	18	114	54	96	.275	.338	.462	109	3	4	93	16	7	1	-20	*2/S3	-0.7
1927	*NY-A	153	570	92	176	29	8	18	102	69	82	.309	.383	.482	127	19	22	98	22	14	-2	5	*2S/3	3.1
1928	*NY-A	116	404	62	134	30	11	10	82	43	50	.332	.397	.535	148	24	26	87	15	5	2	-11	*2	2.2
1929	NY-A	147	545	101	193	37	11	18	106	68	45	.354	.429	.561	164	44	49	130	9	10	-3	-4	*2	4.2
1930	NY-A	143	571	109	173	34	15	9	121	60	62	.303	.372	.462	115	9	13	100	4	4	-1	6	23/S10	1.9
1931	NY-A	135	484	67	129	27	7	8	83	79	80	.267	.371	.401	109	4	8	76	18	9	0	-3	23	1.1
1932	*NY-A	142	510	79	153	28	16	15	113	82	64	.300	.399	.506	140	26	30	104	11	11	-3	6	*2/3	3.6
1933	NY-A	139	523	94	154	22	12	18	104	73	62	.294	.383	.486	137	22	26	100	15	7	0	-14	*2	1.0
1934	NY-A	123	438	59	117	24	6	14	67	71	64	.267	.369	.445	117	6	11	77	11	1	3	-13	23	0.4
1935	NY-A	130	477	72	130	18	6	13	83	63	64	.273	.361	.417	107	1	5	75	11	5	0	-21	*2/S	-0.9
1936	*NY-A	150	537	82	154	29	6	14	109	97	65	.287	.397	.441	110	8	11	100	8	5	-1	-32	*2/S	-0.9
1937	*NY-A	126	446	56	109	21	3	14	70	71	76	.244	.348	.399	87	-8	-9	67	7	1	2	-8	*2	-0.2
1938	*Chi-N	54	120	21	32	5	0	5	23	22	30	.267	.380	.433	120	4	4	20	0			-8	S/32O	-0.1
1939	Bro-N	14	39	6	11	2	0	3	6	10	7	.282	.451	.564	165	5	4	11	1			0	2/3	0.5
	NY-N	13	44	7	13	0	0	1	8	7	6	.295	.392	.364	103	1	1	6	0			-3	3	0.0
	Yr	27	83	13	24	2	0	4	14	17	13	.289	.422	.458	133	5	5	17	1			-2		0.5
Total	14	1740	6297	986	1840	334	115	178	1191	869	864	.292	.380	.467	122	166	205	1146	148	79		-117	*23/SO1	15.2

■ FREDDY LEACH
Leach, Frederick b: 11/23/1897, Springfield, Mo. d: 12/10/81, Hagerman, Idaho BL/TR, 5′11″, 183 lbs. Deb: 5/24/23

YEAR	TM/L	G	AB	R	H	2B	3B	HR	RBI	BB	SO	AVG	OBP	SLG	PRO+	BR	/A	RC	SB	CS	SBR	FR	POS	TPR
1923	Phi-N	52	104	5	27	4	0	1	16	3	14	.260	.280	.327	54	-6	-8	9	1	2	-1	-3	O	-1.1
1924	Phi-N	8	28	6	13	2	1	2	7	2	1	.464	.500	.821	221	6	5	11	0	0	0	-1	/O	0.4
1925	Phi-N	65	292	47	91	15	4	5	28	5	21	.312	.323	.442	86	-4	-7	40	1	2	-1	-4	O	-1.2
1926	Phi-N	129	492	73	162	29	7	11	71	16	33	.329	.352	.484	117	13	10	79	6			3	*O	0.9
1927	Phi-N	140	536	69	164	30	4	12	83	21	32	.306	.342	.444	108	5	4	78	2			10	*O	0.8
1928	Phi-N	145	588	83	179	36	11	13	96	30	30	.304	.342	.469	107	6	4	91	4			13	*O1	0.9
1929	NY-N	113	411	74	119	22	6	8	47	17	14	.290	.324	.431	85	-11	-11	55	10			-21	O	-3.6
1930	NY-N	126	544	90	178	19	13	13	71	22	25	.327	.361	.482	104	0	2	91	3			-10	*O	-1.4
1931	NY-N	129	515	75	159	30	5	6	61	29	9	.309	.348	.421	108	4	5	76	4			-8	*O	-0.8
1932	Bos-N	84	223	21	55	9	2	1	29	18	10	.247	.306	.318	71	-10	-9	23	1			-1	O	-1.3
Total	10	991	3733	543	1147	196	53	72	509	163	189	.307	.341	.446	101	4	-4	553	32	4		-22	O/1	-6.4

■ RICK LEACH
Leach, Richard Max b: 5/4/57, Ann Arbor, Mich. BL/TL, 6′1″, 180 lbs. Deb: 4/30/81

YEAR	TM/L	G	AB	R	H	2B	3B	HR	RBI	BB	SO	AVG	OBP	SLG	PRO+	BR	/A	RC	SB	CS	SBR	FR	POS	TPR
1981	Det-A	54	83	9	16	3	1	1	11	16	15	.193	.323	.289	75	-2	-2	7	0	1	-1	1	1O/D	-0.2
1982	Det-A	82	218	23	52	7	2	3	12	21	29	.239	.305	.330	74	-7	-8	24	4	0	1	-0	1O/D	-0.7
1983	Det-A	99	242	22	60	17	0	3	26	19	21	.248	.305	.355	83	-6	-5	25	2	2	-1	4	1O/D	-0.4
1984	Tor-A	65	88	11	23	6	2	0	7	8	14	.261	.323	.375	89	-1	-1	10	0	0	0	5	O1/PD	0.2
1985	Tor-A	16	35	2	7	1	0	0	1	3	9	.200	.263	.257	42	-3	-3	3	0	0	0	0	1/O	-0.2
1986	Tor-A	110	246	35	76	14	1	5	39	13	24	.309	.344	.435	108	3	2	35	0	0	0	-2	DO/1	-0.1
1987	Tor-A	98	195	26	55	13	1	3	25	25	25	.282	.372	.405	104	2	2	30	0	1	-1	-1	OD/1	-0.1
1988	Tor-A	87	199	21	55	13	1	0	23	18	27	.276	.336	.352	93	-2	-2	22	0	1	-1	1	OD/1	-0.2
1989	Tex-A	110	239	32	65	14	1	1	23	32	33	.272	.360	.351	100	1	1	31	2	1	0	0	DO/1	0.0
1990	SF-N	78	174	24	51	13	0	2	16	21	20	.293	.372	.402	114	4	4	27	0	2	-1	0	O/1	0.1
Total	10	799	1719	205	460	100	10	18	183	176	217	.268	.338	.369	94	-10	-12	214	8	8	-2	7	O1D/P	-1.5

■ TOMMY LEACH
Leach, Thomas William b: 11/4/1877, French Creek, N.Y. d: 9/29/69, Haines City, Fla. BR/TR, 5′6.5″, 150 lbs. Deb: 9/28/1898

YEAR	TM/L	G	AB	R	H	2B	3B	HR	RBI	BB	SO	AVG	OBP	SLG	PRO+	BR	/A	RC	SB	CS	SBR	FR	POS	TPR
1898	Lou-N	3	10	0	1	0	0	0	0	0		.100	.100	.100	-43	-2	-2	0	0			-0	/32	-0.1
1899	Lou-N	106	406	75	117	10	6	5	57	37		.288	.349	.379	102	1	2	62	19			1	3S/2	0.3
1900	*Pit-N	51	160	20	34	1	2	1	16	21		.213	.304	.262	59	-8	-8	16	8			1	3/S2O	-0.5

YEAR	TM/L	G	AB	R	H	2B	3B	HR	RBI	BB	SO	AVG	OBP	SLG	PRO+	BR	/A	RC	SB	CS	SBR	FR	POS	TPR
1901	Pit-N	98	374	64	114	12	13	2	44	20		.305	.342	.422	120	10	9	62	16			9	3/S	2.2
1902	Pit-N	135	514	97	143	14	22	6	85	45		.278	.341	.426	134	22	20	87	25			13	*3	4.0
1903	*Pit-N	127	507	97	151	16	17	7	87	40		.298	.349	.438	122	15	13	89	22			7	*3	2.0
1904	Pit-N	146	579	92	149	15	12	2	56	45		.257	.311	.335	99	1	-1	70	23			36	*3	4.3
1905	Pit-N	131	499	71	128	10	14	2	53	37		.257	.308	.345	94	-3	-4	62	17			11	O3/2S	0.6
1906	Pit-N	133	476	66	136	10	7	1	39	33		.286	.332	.342	108	6	4	65	21			2	3O/S	0.3
1907	Pit-N	149	547	102	166	19	12	4	43	40		.303	.351	.404	137	23	22	98	43			11	*O3/S2	3.2
1908	Pit-N	152	583	93	151	24	16	5	41	54		.259	.322	.381	126	16	16	79	24			-4	*3/O	1.9
1909	*Pit-N	151	587	126	153	29	8	6	43	66		.261	.337	.368	110	13	7	83	27			3	*O3	0.7
1910	Pit-N	135	529	83	143	24	5	4	52	38	62	.270	.319	.357	92	-4	-7	66	18			5	*O/S2	-0.6
1911	Pit-N	108	386	60	92	12	6	3	43	46	50	.238	.323	.324	78	-10	-12	46	19			5	OS/3	-0.8
1912	Pit-N	28	97	24	29	4	2	0	19	12	9	.299	.376	.381	109	1	1	16	6			4	O	0.4
	Chi-N	82	265	50	64	10	3	2	32	55	20	.242	.378	.325	93	0	0	38	14			5	O/3	0.2
	Yr	110	362	74	93	14	5	2	51	67	29	.257	.377	.340	97	1	2	54	20			8		0.6
1913	Chi-N	131	456	99	131	23	10	6	32	77	44	.287	.391	.421	132	21	21	80	21			-0	*O/3	1.9
1914	Chi-N	153	577	80	152	24	9	7	46	79	50	.263	.353	.373	116	13	13	80	16			3	*O3	1.3
1915	Cin-N	107	335	42	75	7	5	0	17	56	38	.224	.338	.275	85	-3	-4	34	20	14	-2	3	O	-0.5
1918	Pit-N	30	72	14	14	2	3	0	5	19	5	.194	.363	.306	101	1	1	9	2			-1	O/S	-0.1
Total	19	2156	7959	1355	2143	266	172	63	810	820	278	.269	.339	.370	109	116	92	1138	361	14		110	*O3/S2	20.7

■ DAN LEAHY
Leahy, Daniel C. b: 8/8/1870, Knoxville, Tenn. d: 12/30/03, Knoxville, Tenn. Deb: 9/02/1896

YEAR	TM/L	G	AB	R	H	2B	3B	HR	RBI	BB	SO	AVG	OBP	SLG	PRO+	BR	/A	RC	SB	CS	SBR	FR	POS	TPR
1896	Phi-N	2	6	0	2	1	0	0	1	1	2	.333	.429	.500	148	0	0	1	0			1	/S	0.1

■ TOM LEAHY
Leahy, Thomas Joseph b: 6/2/1869, New Haven, Conn. d: 6/11/51, New Haven, Conn. TR, 168 lbs. Deb: 5/18/1897

YEAR	TM/L	G	AB	R	H	2B	3B	HR	RBI	BB	SO	AVG	OBP	SLG	PRO+	BR	/A	RC	SB	CS	SBR	FR	POS	TPR
1897	Pit-N	24	92	10	24	3	3	0	12	7		.261	.320	.359	84	-3	-2	12	3			-2	O/C3	-0.3
	Was-N	19	52	12	20	2	1	0	7	9		.385	.529	.462	167	7	7	16	6			-3	O/32C	0.2
	Yr	43	144	22	44	5	4	0	19	16		.306	.405	.396	117	4	5	27	9			-6		-0.1
1898	Was-N	15	55	10	10	2	0	0	5	8		.182	.297	.218	51	-3	-3	5	6			0	3/2	-0.2
1901	Mil-A	33	99	18	24	6	2	0	10	11		.242	.348	.343	99	-0	1	13	3			-3	C/O2	0.0
	Phi-A	5	15	1	5	1	0	0	1	1		.333	.375	.400	112	0	0	2	0			-0	/OCS	0.0
	Yr	38	114	19	29	7	2	0	11	12		.254	.351	.351	101	0	1	16	3			-4		0.0
1905	StL-N	35	97	3	22	1	3	0	7	8		.227	.286	.299	79	-3	-2	9	0			-9	C	-0.8
Total	4	131	410	54	105	15	9	0	42	44		.256	.348	.337	95	-2	-0	58	18			-18	/CO32S	-1.1

■ FRED LEAR
Lear, Frederick Francis "King" b: 4/7/1894, New York, N.Y. d: 10/13/55, E.Orange, N.J. BR/TR, 6'0.5", 180 lbs. Deb: 6/07/15

YEAR	TM/L	G	AB	R	H	2B	3B	HR	RBI	BB	SO	AVG	OBP	SLG	PRO+	BR	/A	RC	SB	CS	SBR	FR	POS	TPR
1915	Phi-A	2	2	0	0	0	0	0	0	0	2	.000	.000	.000	-99	-0	-0	0	0			-0	/3	0.0
1918	Chi-N	2	1	0	0	0	0	0	0	1	0	.000	.500	.000	56	0	0	0	0			0	H	0.0
1919	Chi-N	40	76	8	17	3	1	1	11	8	11	.224	.306	.329	90	-1	-1	8	2			-2	/12S	-0.2
1920	NY-N	31	87	12	22	0	1	1	7	8	15	.253	.323	.310	83	-2	-2	9	0	2	-1	-2	3/2	-0.3
Total	4	75	166	20	39	3	2	2	18	17	28	.235	.314	.313	84	-3	-3	17	2	2		-5	/321S	-0.5

■ BILL LEARD
Leard, William Wallace "Wild Bill" b: 10/14/1885, Oneida, N.Y. d: 1/15/70, San Francisco, Cal TR, 5'10", 155 lbs. Deb: 7/21/17

YEAR	TM/L	G	AB	R	H	2B	3B	HR	RBI	BB	SO	AVG	OBP	SLG	PRO+	BR	/A	RC	SB	CS	SBR	FR	POS	TPR
1917	Bro-N	3	3	0	0	0	0	0	0	0	1	.000	.000	.000	-97	-1	-1	0	0			0	/2	0.0

■ JACK LEARY
Leary, John J. b: 1858, New Haven, Conn. TL, 5'11", 186 lbs. Deb: 8/21/1880

YEAR	TM/L	G	AB	R	H	2B	3B	HR	RBI	BB	SO	AVG	OBP	SLG	PRO+	BR	/A	RC	SB	CS	SBR	FR	POS	TPR
1880	Bos-N	1	3	1	0	0	0	0	0	1	0	.000	.250	.000	-7	-0	-0	0				0	/OP	0.0
1881	Det-N	3	11	2	3	1	1	0	4	1	1	.273	.333	.545	165	1	1	2				0	/OP	0.0
1882	Pit-a	60	257	32	75	7	3	1			5	.292	.305	.354	128	5	7	28				-14	3O/P12	-0.6
	Bal-a	4	18	3	4	1	0	0			0	.222	.222	.278	73	-1	-0	1				-0	/PO	0.0
	Yr	64	275	35	79	8	3	1			5	.287	.300	.349	124	5	7	30				-14		-0.6
1883	Lou-a	40	165	16	31	1	3	3			2	.188	.198	.285	58	-8	-6	10				-1	S	-0.7
	Bal-a	3	11	1	2	0	2	0			0	.182	.182	.545	122	0	0	1				-1	/2	0.0
	Yr	43	176	17	33	1	5	3			2	.188	.197	.301	62	-8	-6	11				-2		-0.7
1884	Alt-U	8	33	1	3	0	0	0			1	.091	.118	.091	-28	-4	-4	0	0			-2	/OP3	-0.4
	CP-U	10	40	0	7	1	0	0			0	.175	.175	.200	27	-3	-3	1	0			1	/23OP	-0.1
	Yr	18	73	1	10	1	0	0			1	.137	.149	.151	1	-7	-7	2	0			-1		-0.5
Total	5	129	538	56	125	11	9	4	4	10	1	.232	.246	.309	87	-10	-6	44	0			-16	/SO3P21	-1.8

■ JOHN LEARY
Leary, John Louis "Jack" b: 5/2/1891, Waltham, Mass. d: 8/18/61, Waltham, Mass. BR/TR, 5'11.5", 180 lbs. Deb: 4/14/14

YEAR	TM/L	G	AB	R	H	2B	3B	HR	RBI	BB	SO	AVG	OBP	SLG	PRO+	BR	/A	RC	SB	CS	SBR	FR	POS	TPR
1914	StL-A	144	533	35	141	28	7	0	45	10	71	.265	.282	.343	91	-11	-9	49	9	15	-6	-4	*1C	-1.9
1915	StL-A	75	227	19	55	10	0	0	15	5	36	.242	.268	.286	68	-10	-9	17	2	4	-2	-2	1C	-1.5
Total	2	219	760	54	196	38	7	0	60	15	107	.258	.278	.326	85	-21	-18	66	11	19	-8	-7	1/C	-3.4

■ HAL LEATHERS
Leathers, Harold Langford "Chuck" b: 12/2/1898, Selma, Cal. d: 4/12/77, Modesto, Cal. BL/TR, 5'8", 152 lbs. Deb: 9/13/20

YEAR	TM/L	G	AB	R	H	2B	3B	HR	RBI	BB	SO	AVG	OBP	SLG	PRO+	BR	/A	RC	SB	CS	SBR	FR	POS	TPR
1920	Chi-N	9	23	3	7	1	0	1	1	1	1	.304	.333	.478	129	1	1	4	1	0	0	-1	/S2	0.1

■ EMIL LEBER
Leber, Emil Bohmiel b: 5/15/1881, Cleveland, Ohio d: 11/6/24, Cleveland, Ohio TR, 5'11", 170 lbs. Deb: 9/02/05

YEAR	TM/L	G	AB	R	H	2B	3B	HR	RBI	BB	SO	AVG	OBP	SLG	PRO+	BR	/A	RC	SB	CS	SBR	FR	POS	TPR
1905	Cle-A	2	6	1	0	0	0	0	0		1	.000	.143	.000	-52	-1	-1	0	0			-0	/3	0.0

■ BEVO LeBOURVEAU
LeBourveau, De Witt Wiley b: 8/24/1894, Dana, Cal. d: 12/9/47, Nevada City, Cal. BL/TR, 5'11", 175 lbs. Deb: 9/09/19

YEAR	TM/L	G	AB	R	H	2B	3B	HR	RBI	BB	SO	AVG	OBP	SLG	PRO+	BR	/A	RC	SB	CS	SBR	FR	POS	TPR
1919	Phi-N	17	63	4	17	0	0	0		10	8	.270	.370	.270	88	0	-0	7	2			2	O	0.1
1920	Phi-N	84	261	29	67	7	2	3	12	11	36	.257	.295	.333	76	-7	-8	26	9	6	-1	4	O	-1.0
1921	Phi-N	93	281	42	83	12	5	6	35	29	51	.295	.361	.438	102	4	1	44	4	5	-2	-10	O	-1.3
1922	Phi-N	74	167	24	45	8	3	2	20	24	29	.269	.368	.389	87	-1	-3	24	0	3	-2	-3	O	-0.8
1929	Phi-A	12	16	1	5	0	1	0	2	5	1	.313	.476	.438	132	1	1	3	0	1	-1	0	/O	0.0
Total	5	280	788	100	217	27	11	11	69	79	125	.275	.345	.379	91	-2	-9	104	15	15		-7	O	-3.0

■ MIKE LEDWITH
Ledwith, Michael b: Brooklyn, N.Y. d: 1/2/29, Bronx, N.Y. Deb: 8/19/1874

YEAR	TM/L	G	AB	R	H	2B	3B	HR	RBI	BB	SO	AVG	OBP	SLG	PRO+	BR	/A	RC	SB	CS	SBR	FR	POS	TPR
1874	Atl-n	1	4	1	1	0	0	0		0		.250	.250	.250	68	-0	-0	0					/C	0.0

■ CLIFF LEE
Lee, Clifford Walker b: 8/4/1896, Lexington, Neb. d: 8/25/80, Denver, Colo. BR/TR, 6'1", 175 lbs. Deb: 5/15/19

YEAR	TM/L	G	AB	R	H	2B	3B	HR	RBI	BB	SO	AVG	OBP	SLG	PRO+	BR	/A	RC	SB	CS	SBR	FR	POS	TPR
1919	Pit-N	42	112	5	22	2	4	0	2	6	8	.196	.237	.286	55	-6	-7	8	2			-10	C/O	-1.6
1920	Pit-N	37	76	9	18	2	2	0	8	4	14	.237	.275	.316	67	-3	-3	6	0	1	-1	1	C/O	-0.1
1921	Phi-N	88	286	31	88	14	4	4	29	13	34	.308	.338	.427	94	-0	-3	41	5	2	0	-5	1O/C	-0.9
1922	Phi-N	122	422	65	136	29	6	17	77	32	43	.322	.371	.540	121	18	13	83	2	3	-1	-6	O1/3	0.1
1923	Phi-N	107	355	54	114	20	4	11	47	20	39	.321	.357	.493	110	10	4	61	3	3	-1	-7	O1	-0.7
1924	Phi-N	21	56	4	14	3	2	1	7	2	5	.250	.276	.429	77	-1	-2	6	0	1	-1	1	O/1	-0.2
	Cin-N	6	6	1	2	1	0	0	2	0	2	.333	.333	.500	122	0	0	1	0	0	0	0	/O	0.0
	Yr	27	62	5	16	4	2	1	9	2	7	.258	.281	.435	82	-1	-2	7	0	1	-1	1		-0.2
1925	Cle-A	77	230	43	74	15	6	4	42	21	33	.322	.378	.491	118	6	6	43	2	1	0	-3	O	-0.2
1926	Cle-A	21	40	4	7	1	0	1	2	6	8	.175	.280	.275	45	-3	-3	3	0	0	0	0	/OC	-0.3
Total	8	521	1583	216	475	87	28	38	216	104	186	.300	.344	.462	103	20	5	252	14	11		-30	O/1C3	-3.9

■ DUD LEE
Lee, Ernest Dudley (a.k.a. Ernest Dudley In 1920-21) b: 8/22/1899, Denver, Colo. d: 1/7/71, Denver, Colo. BL/TR, 5'9", 150 lbs. Deb: 10/03/20

YEAR	TM/L	G	AB	R	H	2B	3B	HR	RBI	BB	SO	AVG	OBP	SLG	PRO+	BR	/A	RC	SB	CS	SBR	FR	POS	TPR
1920	StL-A	1	2	2	2	0	0	0	1	0	0	1.000	1.000	1.000	418	1	1	2	1	0	0	-1	/S	0.0
1921	StL-A	72	180	18	30	4	2	0	11	14	34	.167	.235	.211	14	-24	-25	10	1	1	-0	5	S2/3	-1.3

YEAR	TM/L	G	AB	R	H	2B	3B	HR	RBI	BB	SO	AVG	OBP	SLG	PRO+	BR	/A	RC	SB	CS	SBR	FR	POS	TPR
1924	Bos-A	94	288	36	73	9	4	0	29	40	17	.253	.350	.313	72	-11	-11	35	8	4	0	-8	S	-0.8
1925	Bos-A	84	255	22	57	7	3	0	19	34	19	.224	.315	.275	51	-19	-19	24	2	3	-1	17	S	0.8
1926	Bos-A	2	7	2	1	0	0	0	0	0	0	.143	.250	.143	4	-1	-1	0	0			-1	/S	-0.1
Total	5	253	732	80	163	20	9	0	60	88	70	.223	.311	.275	50	-53	-55	71	12	8	-1	12	S/23	-1.4

■ HAL LEE
Lee, Harold Burnham "Sheriff"   b: 2/15/05, Ludlow, Miss.   d: 9/4/89, Pascagoula, Miss.   BR/TR, 5'11", 180 lbs.   Deb: 4/19/30

YEAR	TM/L	G	AB	R	H	2B	3B	HR	RBI	BB	SO	AVG	OBP	SLG	PRO+	BR	/A	RC	SB	CS	SBR	FR	POS	TPR
1930	Bro-N	22	37	5	6	0	0	1	4	4	5	.162	.244	.243	19	-5	-5	2	0			-0	O	-0.5
1931	Phi-N	44	131	13	29	10	0	2	12	10	18	.221	.282	.344	62	-6	-8	13	0			1	O	-0.8
1932	Phi-N	149	595	76	180	42	10	18	85	36	45	.303	.343	.497	110	17	8	102	6			7	*O	0.5
1933	Phi-N	46	167	25	48	12	2	0	12	18	13	.287	.360	.383	100	3	1	24	1			-0	O	-0.1
	Bos-N	88	312	32	69	15	9	1	28	18	26	.221	.266	.337	77	-12	-9	29	1			1	O	-1.3
	Yr	134	479	57	117	27	11	1	40	36	39	.244	.300	.353	87	-9	-9	53	2			1		-1.4
1934	Bos-N	139	521	70	152	23	6	8	79	47	43	.292	.353	.405	111	2	7	76	3			0	*O/2	0.2
1935	Bos-N	112	422	49	128	18	6	0	39	18	25	.303	.333	.374	98	-6	-2	51	0			3	*O	-0.2
1936	Bos-N	152	565	46	143	24	7	3	64	52	50	.253	.318	.336	82	-18	-13	59	4			-7	*O	-2.6
Total	7	752	2750	316	755	144	40	33	323	203	225	.275	.326	.392	95	-25	-21	357	15			5	O/2	-4.8

■ LEONIDAS LEE
Lee, Leonidas Pyrrhus (b: Leonidas Pyrrhus Funkhouser)   b: 12/13/1860, St.Louis, Mo.   d: 6/11/12, Hendersonville, N.C.   Deb: 7/17/1877

YEAR	TM/L	G	AB	R	H	2B	3B	HR	RBI	BB	SO	AVG	OBP	SLG	PRO+	BR	/A	RC	SB	CS	SBR	FR	POS	TPR
1877	StL-N	4	18	0	5	1	0	0	0	0	1	.278	.278	.333	97	-0	-0	2				-2	/OS	-0.1

■ LERON LEE
Lee, Leron   b: 3/4/48, Bakersfield, Cal.   BL/TR, 6', 196 lbs.   Deb: 9/05/69

YEAR	TM/L	G	AB	R	H	2B	3B	HR	RBI	BB	SO	AVG	OBP	SLG	PRO+	BR	/A	RC	SB	CS	SBR	FR	POS	TPR
1969	StL-N	7	23	3	5	1	0	0	0	3	8	.217	.308	.261	60	-1	-1	2	0	0	0	-0	/O	-0.1
1970	StL-N	121	264	28	60	13	1	6	23	24	66	.227	.294	.352	71	-11	-11	28	5	1	1	-6	O	-1.9
1971	StL-N	25	28	3	5	1	0	1	2	4	12	.179	.281	.321	68	-1	-1	2	0	1	-1	-1	/O	-0.2
	SD-N	79	256	29	70	20	2	4	21	18	45	.273	.321	.414	115	2	4	32	4	5	-2	-9	O	-0.9
	Yr	104	284	32	75	21	2	5	23	22	57	.264	.317	.405	108	1	2	34	4	6	-2	-10		-1.1
1972	SD-N	101	370	50	111	23	7	12	47	29	58	.300	.356	.497	151	18	21	62	2	5	-2	2	O	1.7
1973	SD-N	118	333	36	79	7	2	3	30	33	61	.237	.308	.297	74	-14	-10	31	4	0	1	-2	O	-1.5
1974	Cle-A	79	232	18	54	13	0	5	25	15	42	.233	.279	.353	82	-6	-6	21	3	2	-0	-0	O/D	-0.8
1975	Cle-A	13	23	3	3	1	0	0	0	2	5	.130	.231	.174	16	-3	-3	1	1	0	0	0	/OD	-0.1
	LA-N	48	43	2	11	4	0	0	2	3	9	.256	.304	.349	85	-1	-1	5	0	0	0	0	O	0.0
1976	LA-N	23	45	1	6	0	1	0	2	2	9	.133	.170	.178	-1	-6	-6	1	0	0	0	-2	O	-0.8
Total	8	614	1617	173	404	83	13	31	152	133	315	.250	.309	.375	95	-23	-15	185	19	14	-3	-18	O/D	-4.6

■ MANNY LEE
Lee, Manuel Lora (b: Manuel Lora (Lee))   b: 6/17/65, San Pedro De Macoris, D.R.   BB/TR, 5'10", 145 lbs.   Deb: 4/10/85

YEAR	TM/L	G	AB	R	H	2B	3B	HR	RBI	BB	SO	AVG	OBP	SLG	PRO+	BR	/A	RC	SB	CS	SBR	FR	POS	TPR
1985	*Tor-A	64	40	9	8	0	0	0	2	9	9	.200	.238	.200	21	-4	-4	1	1	4	-2	20	2/S3D	1.5
1986	Tor-A	35	78	8	16	0	1	1	7	4	10	.205	.244	.269	39	-7	-7	4	0	1	-1	4	2/S/3	-0.1
1987	Tor-A	56	121	14	31	2	3	1	11	6	13	.256	.291	.347	67	-6	-6	13	2	0	1	10	2S/D	1.0
1988	Tor-A	116	381	38	111	16	3	2	38	26	64	.291	.337	.365	96	-2	-2	44	3	3	-1	12	2S/3D	1.4
1989	*Tor-A	99	300	27	78	9	2	3	34	20	60	.260	.306	.333	82	-8	-7	30	4	2	0	-1	2S3D/O	-0.5
1990	Tor-A	117	391	45	95	12	4	6	41	26	90	.243	.290	.340	77	-13	-12	38	3	1	0	-9	*2/S	-1.5
Total	6	487	1311	141	339	39	13	13	131	84	246	.259	.303	.338	78	-39	-39	129	13	11	-3	35	2/S3DO	1.8

■ TERRY LEE
Lee, Terry James   b: 3/13/62, San Francisco, Cal.   BR/TR, 6'5", 215 lbs.   Deb: 9/03/90

YEAR	TM/L	G	AB	R	H	2B	3B	HR	RBI	BB	SO	AVG	OBP	SLG	PRO+	BR	/A	RC	SB	CS	SBR	FR	POS	TPR
1990	Cin-N	12	19	1	4	1	0	0	3	2	2	.211	.286	.263	51	-1	-1	1	0	0	0	0	/1	0.0

■ BILLY LEE
Lee, William Joseph   b: 1/9/1892, Bayonne, N.J.   d: 1/6/84, West Hazelton, Pa.   BR/TR, 5'9", 165 lbs.   Deb: 4/15/15

YEAR	TM/L	G	AB	R	H	2B	3B	HR	RBI	BB	SO	AVG	OBP	SLG	PRO+	BR	/A	RC	SB	CS	SBR	FR	POS	TPR
1915	StL-A	18	59	2	11	1	0	0	4	6	5	.186	.262	.203	41	-4	-4	3	1	1	-0	2	O/3	-0.2
1916	StL-A	7	11	1	2	0	0	0	0	1	1	.182	.250	.182	31	-1	-1	1	0			-1	/O	-0.1
Total	2	25	70	3	13	1	0	0	4	7	6	.186	.260	.200	39	-5	-5	4	1	1		2	/O3	-0.3

■ WATTY LEE
Lee, Wyatt Arnold   b: 8/12/1879, Lynch's Station, Va.   d: 3/6/36, Washington, D.C.   TL, 5'10.5", 171 lbs.   Deb: 4/30/01

YEAR	TM/L	G	AB	R	H	2B	3B	HR	RBI	BB	SO	AVG	OBP	SLG	PRO+	BR	/A	RC	SB	CS	SBR	FR	POS	TPR
1901	Was-A	43	129	15	33	6	3	0	12	7		.256	.299	.349	82	-3	-3	14	0			0	P/O	0.0
1902	Was-A	109	391	61	100	21	5	4	45	33		.256	.320	.366	91	-4	-5	50	8			0	OP	-0.6
1903	Was-A	75	231	17	48	8	4	0	13	18		.208	.265	.277	63	-10	-10	19	5			7	OP	-0.1
1904	Pit-N	8	12	1	4	0	1	0	0	0		.333	.333	.500	154	1	1	2	0			0	/P	0.0
Total	4	235	763	94	185	35	13	4	70	58		.242	.300	.338	82	-17	-17	86	13			8	O/P	-0.7

■ GENE LEEK
Leek, Eugene Harold   b: 7/15/36, San Diego, Cal.   BR/TR, 6', 185 lbs.   Deb: 4/22/59

YEAR	TM/L	G	AB	R	H	2B	3B	HR	RBI	BB	SO	AVG	OBP	SLG	PRO+	BR	/A	RC	SB	CS	SBR	FR	POS	TPR
1959	Cle-A	13	36	7	8	3	0	1	5	2	7	.222	.263	.389	80	-1	-1	4	0	0	0	-2	3/S	-0.2
1961	LA-A	57	199	16	45	9	1	5	20	7	54	.226	.260	.357	57	-11	-14	16	0	1	-1	18	3/SO	0.7
1962	LA-A	7	14	0	2	0	0	0	0	0	6	.143	.143	.143	-24	-2	-2	0	0	0	0	0	/3	-0.1
Total	3	77	249	23	55	12	1	6	25	9	67	.221	.254	.349	55	-15	-17	20	0	1	-1	17	/3SO	0.4

■ DAVE LEEPER
Leeper, David Dale   b: 10/30/59, Santa Ana, Cal.   BL/TL, 5'11", 170 lbs.   Deb: 9/10/84

YEAR	TM/L	G	AB	R	H	2B	3B	HR	RBI	BB	SO	AVG	OBP	SLG	PRO+	BR	/A	RC	SB	CS	SBR	FR	POS	TPR
1984	KC-A	4	6	1	0	0	0	0	0	0	1	.000	.000	.000	-99	-2	-2	0	0	0	0	1	/OD	0.0
1985	KC-A	15	34	1	3	0	0	0	4	1	3	.088	.114	.088	-43	-7	-7	0	0	0	0	-2	/O	-0.8
Total	2	19	40	2	3	0	0	0	4	1	4	.075	.098	.075	-52	-8	-8	0	0	0	0	-1	/OD	-0.8

■ GEORGE LEES
Lees, George Edward   b: 2/2/1895, Bethlehem, Pa.   d: 1/2/80, Harrisburg, Pa.   BR/TR, 5'9", 150 lbs.   Deb: 5/07/21

YEAR	TM/L	G	AB	R	H	2B	3B	HR	RBI	BB	SO	AVG	OBP	SLG	PRO+	BR	/A	RC	SB	CS	SBR	FR	POS	TPR
1921	Chi-A	20	42	3	9	2	0	0	4	0	3	.214	.214	.262	21	-5	-5	2	0	1	-1	-2	C	-0.6

■ JIM LEFEBVRE
Lefebvre, James Kenneth   b: 1/7/42, Inglewood, Cal.   BB/TR, 6', 180 lbs.   Deb: 4/12/65   MC

YEAR	TM/L	G	AB	R	H	2B	3B	HR	RBI	BB	SO	AVG	OBP	SLG	PRO+	BR	/A	RC	SB	CS	SBR	FR	POS	TPR
1965	*LA-N	157	544	57	136	21	4	12	69	71	92	.250	.339	.369	106	1	5	71	3	5	-2	-12	*2	0.0
1966	*LA-N	152	544	69	149	23	3	24	74	48	72	.274	.336	.460	128	13	18	84	1	1	-0	-11	*23	1.5
1967	LA-N	136	494	51	129	18	5	8	50	44	64	.261	.325	.366	106	-1	3	57	1	5	-3	6	32/1	0.3
1968	LA-N	84	286	23	69	12	1	5	31	26	55	.241	.307	.343	102	-2	0	31	0	0	0	-10	23/O1	-0.7
1969	LA-N	95	275	29	65	15	2	4	44	48	37	.236	.352	.349	104	0	3	35	2	1	0	1	32/1	0.7
1970	LA-N	109	314	33	79	15	1	4	44	29	42	.252	.317	.344	81	-10	-8	34	1	1	-0	-4	23/1	-0.5
1971	LA-N	119	388	40	95	14	2	12	68	39	55	.245	.317	.384	104	-1	1	44	0	2	-1	-16	*2/3	-1.2
1972	LA-N	70	169	11	34	8	0	5	24	17	30	.201	.274	.337	75	-6	-6	16	0	0	0	-1	23	-0.4
Total	8	922	3014	313	756	126	18	74	404	322	447	.251	.326	.378	105	-7	17	372	8	15	-7	-47	23/1O	-0.3

■ JOE LEFEBVRE
Lefebvre, Joseph Henry   b: 2/22/56, Concord, N.H.   BL/TR, 5'10", 170 lbs.   Deb: 5/22/80

YEAR	TM/L	G	AB	R	H	2B	3B	HR	RBI	BB	SO	AVG	OBP	SLG	PRO+	BR	/A	RC	SB	CS	SBR	FR	POS	TPR
1980	*NY-A	74	150	26	34	1	1	8	21	27	30	.227	.345	.407	107	1	2	21	0	0	0	-4	O	-0.3
1981	SD-N	86	246	31	63	13	4	8	31	35	33	.256	.353	.439	133	8	10	35	6	4	-1	-1	O	0.7
1982	SD-N	102	239	25	57	9	0	4	21	18	50	.238	.295	.326	78	-9	-7	24	0	0	0	-2	3O/C	-1.0
1983	SD-N	18	20	1	5	0	0	0	1	2	3	.250	.318	.250	61	-1	-1	2	0	0	0	0	/O3C	0.0
	*Phi-N	101	258	34	80	20	8	8	38	31	46	.310	.390	.543	158	19	20	53	5	3	-0	-1	O/3C	1.2
	Yr	119	278	35	85	20	8	8	39	33	49	.306	.385	.522	151	18	19	54	5	3	-0	-6		1.2
1984	Phi-N	52	160	22	40	9	0	3	18	23	37	.250	.351	.363	99	1	1	20	0	2	-1	-1	O/3	-0.3
1986	Phi-N	14	18	0	2	0	0	0	0	4	5	.111	.238	.111	-1	-2	-2	0	0	0	0	O	-0.2
Total	6	447	1091	139	281	52	13	31	130	139	204	.258	.346	.414	115	18	22	155	11	9	-2	-15	O/3C	0.1

■ BILL LeFEBVRE
LeFebvre, Wilfrid Henry "Lefty"   b: 11/11/15, Natick, R.I.   BL/TL, 5'11.5", 180 lbs.   Deb: 6/10/38

YEAR	TM/L	G	AB	R	H	2B	3B	HR	RBI	BB	SO	AVG	OBP	SLG	PRO+	BR	/A	RC	SB	CS	SBR	FR	POS	TPR
1938	Bos-A	1	1	1	1	0	0	1	1	0	0	1.000	1.000	4.000	1048	1	1	4	0	0	0	-0	/P	0.0

YEAR	TM/L	G	AB	R	H	2B	3B	HR	RBI	BB	SO	AVG	OBP	SLG	PRO+	BR	/A	RC	SB	CS	SBR	FR	POS	TPR
1939	Bos-A	7	10	3	3	0	0	0	1	2	2	.300	.417	.300	83	-0	-0	1	0	0	0	-0	/P	0.0
1943	Was-A	7	14	0	4	3	0	0	1	1	0	.286	.333	.500	148	1	1	2	0	0	0	0	/P	0.0
1944	Was-A	60	62	4	16	2	2	0	8	12	9	.258	.378	.355	115	1	2	9	0	0	0	-0	P/1	0.5
Total	4	75	87	8	24	5	2	1	11	15	11	.276	.382	.414	129	3	4	17	0	0	0	-1	/P1	0.5

■ AL LEFEVRE
Lefevre, Alfredo Modesto b: 9/16/1898, New York, N.Y. d: 1/21/82, Glen Cove, N.Y. BR/TR, 5′10.5″, 160 lbs. Deb: 6/28/20

YEAR	TM/L	G	AB	R	H	2B	3B	HR	RBI	BB	SO	AVG	OBP	SLG	PRO+	BR	/A	RC	SB	CS	SBR	FR	POS	TPR
1920	NY-N	17	27	5	4	0	1	0	0	0	13	.148	.148	.222	5	-3	-3	1	0	0	0	3	/S23	0.0

■ WADE LEFLER
Lefler, Wade Hampton b: 6/5/1896, Cooleemee, N.C. d: 3/6/81, Hickory, N.C. BL , 5′11″, 162 lbs. Deb: 4/16/24

YEAR	TM/L	G	AB	R	H	2B	3B	HR	RBI	BB	SO	AVG	OBP	SLG	PRO+	BR	/A	RC	SB	CS	SBR	FR	POS	TPR
1924	Bos-N	1	1	0	0	0	0	0	0	0	1	.000	.000	.000	-99	-0	-0	0	0	0	0	0	H	0.0
	Was-A	5	8	0	5	3	0	0	4	0	0	.625	.625	1.000	325	2	2	5	0	0	0	0	/O	0.2

■ RON LeFLORE
LeFlore, Ronald b: 6/16/48, Detroit, Mich. BR/TR, 6′, 200 lbs. Deb: 8/01/74

YEAR	TM/L	G	AB	R	H	2B	3B	HR	RBI	BB	SO	AVG	OBP	SLG	PRO+	BR	/A	RC	SB	CS	SBR	FR	POS	TPR
1974	Det-A	59	254	37	66	8	1	2	13	13	58	.260	.304	.323	78	-7	-8	26	23	9	2	8	O	0.1
1975	Det-A	136	550	66	142	13	6	8	37	33	139	.258	.303	.347	80	-13	-16	57	28	20	-4	2	*O	-2.1
1976	Det-A	135	544	93	172	23	8	4	39	51	111	.316	.377	.410	125	21	19	86	58	20	5	10	*O/D	3.3
1977	Det-A	154	652	100	212	30	10	16	57	37	121	.325	.365	.475	121	23	19	110	39	19	0	-7	*O	0.7
1978	Det-A	155	666	126	198	30	3	12	62	65	104	.297	.363	.405	113	15	13	105	68	16	11	-2	*O	1.8
1979	Det-A	148	600	110	180	22	10	9	57	52	95	.300	.356	.415	104	6	4	94	78	14	15	-0	*OD	1.3
1980	Mon-N	139	521	95	134	21	11	4	39	62	99	.257	.337	.363	95	-2	-2	76	97	19	18	-2	*O	0.9
1981	Chi-A	82	337	46	83	10	4	0	24	28	70	.246	.306	.300	77	-10	-10	32	36	11	4	-1	O	-0.8
1982	Chi-A	91	334	58	96	15	4	4	25	22	91	.287	.331	.392	98	-1	-1	42	28	14	0	-2	O/D	-0.5
Total	9	1099	4458	731	1283	172	57	59	353	363	888	.288	.344	.392	103	33	17	628	455	142	51	6	*O/D	4.7

■ LOU LEGETT
Legett, Louis Alfred "Doc" b: 6/1/01, New Orleans, La. d: 3/6/88, New Orleans, La. BR/TR, 5′10″, 166 lbs. Deb: 5/08/29

YEAR	TM/L	G	AB	R	H	2B	3B	HR	RBI	BB	SO	AVG	OBP	SLG	PRO+	BR	/A	RC	SB	CS	SBR	FR	POS	TPR
1929	Bos-N	39	81	7	13	2	0	0	6	3	18	.160	.190	.185	-7	-14	-13	3	2			-1	C	-1.0
1933	Bos-A	8	5	1	1	1	0	0	1	0	0	.200	.200	.400	56	-0	-0	0	0	0	0	1	/C	0.1
1934	Bos-A	19	38	4	11	0	0	0	1	2	4	.289	.325	.289	56	-2	-3	4	0	0	0	-0	O	0.0
1935	Bos-A	2	0	1	0	0	0	0	0	0	0	—	—	—	—	0	0	0	0	0	0	0	R	0.0
Total	4	68	124	13	25	3	0	0	8	5	22	.202	.233	.226	16	-16	-16	7	2	0		0	/C	-0.9

■ GREG LEGG
Legg, Gregory Lynn b: 4/21/60, San Jose, Cal. BR/TR, 6′1″, 185 lbs. Deb: 4/18/86

YEAR	TM/L	G	AB	R	H	2B	3B	HR	RBI	BB	SO	AVG	OBP	SLG	PRO+	BR	/A	RC	SB	CS	SBR	FR	POS	TPR
1986	Phi-N	11	20	2	9	1	0	0	1	0	3	.450	.450	.500	156	2	2	5	0	0	0	2	/2S	0.4
1987	Phi-N	3	2	1	0	0	0	0	0	0	0	.000	.000	.000	-97	-1	-1	0	0	0	0	-0	/2S3	0.0
Total	2	14	22	3	9	1	0	0	1	0	3	.409	.409	.455	132	1	1	5	0	0	0	2	/2S3	0.4

■ MIKE LEHANE
Lehane, Michael Patrick b: Rhode Island BR , 6′1.5″, 180 lbs. Deb: 4/26/1884

YEAR	TM/L	G	AB	R	H	2B	3B	HR	RBI	BB	SO	AVG	OBP	SLG	PRO+	BR	/A	RC	SB	CS	SBR	FR	POS	TPR
1884	Was-U	3	12	1	4	2	0	0		0		.333	.333	.500	184	1	1	2	0			-1	/SO3	0.0
1890	Col-a	140	512	54	108	19	5	0		43		.211	.275	.268	66	-24	-19	42	13			10	*1	-1.1
1891	Col-a	137	511	59	110	12	7	1	52	34	77	.215	.268	.272	60	-29	-24	43	16			7	*1	-2.0
Total	3	280	1035	114	222	33	12	1	52	77	77	.214	.272	.272	65	-52	-42	87	29			16	1/S3O	-3.1

■ PAUL LEHNER
Lehner, Paul Eugene "Peanuts" or "Gulliver" b: 7/1/20, Dolomite, Ala. d: 12/27/67, Birmingham, Ala. BL/TL, 5′9″, 160 lbs. Deb: 9/10/46

YEAR	TM/L	G	AB	R	H	2B	3B	HR	RBI	BB	SO	AVG	OBP	SLG	PRO+	BR	/A	RC	SB	CS	SBR	FR	POS	TPR
1946	StL-A	16	45	6	10	1	2	0	5	1	5	.222	.239	.333	56	-3	-3	4	0	0	0	-1	O	-0.4
1947	StL-A	135	483	59	120	25	9	7	48	28	29	.248	.294	.381	85	-11	-12	50	5	5	-2	-10	*O	-3.0
1948	StL-A	103	333	23	92	15	4	2	46	30	19	.276	.336	.363	84	-7	-8	40	0	2	-1	-10	O/1	-2.1
1949	StL-A	104	297	25	68	13	0	3	37	16	20	.229	.271	.303	50	-22	-23	22	0	2	-1	3	O1	-2.1
1950	Phi-A	114	427	48	132	17	5	9	52	32	33	.309	.357	.436	104	0	1	66	1	1	-0	7	*O	0.5
1951	Phi-A	9	28	1	4	1	0	0	1	1	1	.143	.172	.179	-5	-4	-4	0	0	0	0	1	/O	-0.3
	Chi-A	23	72	9	15	3	1	0	3	10	4	.208	.305	.278	60	-4	-4	7	0	0	0	1	O	-0.2
	StL-A	21	67	2	9	5	0	1	2	6	5	.134	.205	.254	23	-8	-8	3	0	1	-1	0	O	-0.8
	Cle-A	12	13	2	3	0	0	0	1	1	2	.231	.286	.231	43	-1	-1	1	0	0	0	-0	/O	0.0
	Yr	65	180	14	31	9	1	1	7	18	12	.172	.247	.250	35	-17	-17	11	0	1	-1	2		-1.3
1952	Bos-A	3	3	0	2	0	0	0	2	2	0	.667	.800	.667	288	1	1	2	0	0	0	0	/O	0.1
Total	7	540	1768	175	455	80	21	22	197	127	118	.257	.309	.364	78	-58	-61	196	6	11	-5	-9	O/1	-8.3

■ CLARENCE LEHR
Lehr, Clarence Emanuel "King" b: 5/16/1886, Escanaba, Mich. d: 1/31/48, Detroit, Mich. TR , 5′11″, 165 lbs. Deb: 5/18/11

YEAR	TM/L	G	AB	R	H	2B	3B	HR	RBI	BB	SO	AVG	OBP	SLG	PRO+	BR	/A	RC	SB	CS	SBR	FR	POS	TPR
1911	Phi-N	23	27	2	4	0	0	0	2	0	7	.148	.148	.148	-17	-4	-4	1	0			1	/O2S	-0.3

■ HANK LEIBER
Leiber, Henry Edward b: 1/17/11, Phoenix, Ariz. BR/TR, 6′1.5″, 205 lbs. Deb: 4/16/33

YEAR	TM/L	G	AB	R	H	2B	3B	HR	RBI	BB	SO	AVG	OBP	SLG	PRO+	BR	/A	RC	SB	CS	SBR	FR	POS	TPR
1933	NY-N	6	10	1	2	0	0	0	0	0	2	.200	.200	.200	15	-1	-1	0	0			1	/O	0.0
1934	NY-N	63	187	17	45	5	3	2	25	4	13	.241	.257	.332	58	-12	-11	15	1			0	O	-1.3
1935	NY-N	154	613	110	203	37	4	22	107	48	29	.331	.389	.512	143	34	36	121	1			-17	*O	1.1
1936	*NY-N	101	337	44	94	19	7	9	67	37	41	.279	.352	.457	118	7	8	57	1			-4	O/1	0.0
1937	*NY-N	51	184	24	54	7	3	4	32	15	27	.293	.347	.429	108	2	2	26	1			-5	O	-0.5
1938	NY-N	98	360	50	97	18	4	12	65	31	45	.269	.327	.442	109	4	3	54	0			-10	O	-0.8
1939	Chi-N	112	365	65	113	16	1	24	88	59	42	.310	.411	.556	155	30	30	83	1			0	O	2.8
1940	Chi-N	117	440	68	133	24	2	17	86	45	68	.302	.371	.482	136	20	21	80	1			-3	*O1	1.3
1941	Chi-N	53	162	20	35	5	0	7	25	16	25	.216	.291	.377	90	-3	-3	18	0			-3	O1	-0.8
1942	NY-N	58	147	11	32	6	0	4	23	19	27	.218	.315	.340	91	-1	-1	15	0			2	O/P	0.0
Total	10	813	2805	410	808	137	24	101	518	274	319	.288	.356	.462	122	80	83	469	5			-40	O/1P	1.8

■ NEMO LEIBOLD
Leibold, Harry Loran b: 2/17/1892, Butler, Ind. d: 2/4/77, Detroit, Mich. BL/TR, 6′6.5″, 157 lbs. Deb: 4/12/13

YEAR	TM/L	G	AB	R	H	2B	3B	HR	RBI	BB	SO	AVG	OBP	SLG	PRO+	BR	/A	RC	SB	CS	SBR	FR	POS	TPR
1913	Cle-A	93	286	37	74	11	6	0	12	21	43	.259	.309	.339	87	-4	-5	33	16			-0	O	-1.0
1914	Cle-A	115	402	46	106	13	3	0	32	54	56	.264	.354	.311	96	2	0	45	12	14	-5	9	*O	-0.1
1915	Cle-A	57	207	28	53	5	4	0	4	24	16	.256	.339	.319	95	-0	-1	24	5	3	-0	9	O	0.6
	Chi-A	36	74	10	17	1	0	0	11	15	11	.230	.360	.243	78	-1	-1	8	1	3	-2	5	O	0.1
	Yr	93	281	38	70	6	4	0	15	39	27	.249	.345	.299	91	-1	-2	31	6	6	-2	14		0.7
1916	Chi-A	45	82	5	20	1	2	0	13	7	7	.244	.303	.305	82	-2	-2	10	7			-4	O	-0.8
1917	*Chi-A	125	428	59	101	12	6	0	29	74	34	.236	.350	.292	94	1	0	50	27			-0	*O	-0.8
1918	Chi-A	116	440	57	110	14	7	0	31	63	32	.250	.344	.314	97	1	0	50	13			8	*O	0.3
1919	*Chi-A	122	434	81	131	18	2	0	26	72	30	.302	.404	.353	113	12	12	67	17			7	*O	1.0
1920	Chi-A	108	413	61	91	16	3	1	28	55	30	.220	.316	.281	59	-23	-23	37	7	15	-7	6	*O	-3.2
1921	Bos-A	123	467	88	143	26	6	0	31	41	27	.306	.363	.388	94	-5	-4	67	13	7	-0	4	*O	-0.7
1922	Bos-A	81	271	42	70	8	1	1	18	41	14	.258	.360	.306	76	-8	-8	31	1	6	-3	6	O	-0.9
1923	Bos-A	12	18	1	2	0	0	0	0	1	2	.111	.158	.111	-28	-3	-3	0	0	1	-1	-3	O	-0.7
	Was-A	95	315	68	96	13	4	1	22	53	16	.305	.408	.381	114	7	9	53	7	5	-1	1	O	0.2
	Yr	107	333	69	98	13	4	1	22	54	18	.294	.396	.366	106	3	5	52	7	6	-2	-1		-0.5
1924	*Was-A	84	246	41	72	6	4	0	20	42	10	.293	.398	.350	97	-0	1	37	6	5	-1	-3	O	-0.7
1925	*Was-A	56	84	14	23	1	1	0	7	8	7	.274	.337	.310	66	-4	-4	9	1	0	0	-6	O/3	-1.1
Total	13	1268	4167	638	1109	145	49	3	284	571	335	.266	.357	.327	91	-30	-30	523	133	59		38	*O/3	-7.8

■ ELMER LEIFER
Leifer, Elmer Edwin b: 5/23/1893, Clarington, Ohio d: 9/26/48, Everett, Wash. BL/TR, 5′9.5″, 170 lbs. Deb: 9/07/21

YEAR	TM/L	G	AB	R	H	2B	3B	HR	RBI	BB	SO	AVG	OBP	SLG	PRO+	BR	/A	RC	SB	CS	SBR	FR	POS	TPR
1921	Chi-A	9	10	0	3	1	0	0	0	0	4	.300	.300	.300	54	-1	-1	1	0	0	0	-1	/3O	0.0

YEAR	TM/L	G	AB	R	H	2B	3B	HR	RBI	BB	SO	AVG	OBP	SLG	PRO+	BR	/A	RC	SB	CS	SBR	FR	POS	TPR

■ **JOHN LEIGHTON** Leighton, John Atkinson b: 10/4/1861, Peabody, Mass. d: 10/31/56, Lynn, Mass. 5'11", 170 lbs. Deb: 7/12/1890

| 1890 | Syr-a | 7 | 27 | 6 | 8 | 2 | 0 | 0 | | 3 | | .296 | .367 | .370 | 133 | 1 | 1 | 5 | 2 | | | -0 | /O | 0.0 |

■ **BILL LEINHAUSER** Leinhauser, William Charles b: 11/4/1893, Philadelphia, Pa. d: 4/14/78, Elkins Park, Pa. 5'10", 150 lbs. Deb: 5/18/12

| 1912 | Det-A | 1 | 4 | 0 | 0 | 0 | 0 | 0 | 0 | 0 | | .000 | .000 | .000 | -99 | -1 | -1 | 0 | 0 | | | 0 | /O | 0.0 |

■ **ED LEIP** Leip, Edgar Ellsworth b: 11/29/10, Trenton, N.J. d: 11/24/83, Zephyrhills, Fla. BR/TR, 5'9", 160 lbs. Deb: 9/16/39

1939	Was-A	9	32	4	11	1	0	0	2	2	4	.344	.382	.375	102	-0	-0	4	0	1	-1	-1	/2	0.0
1940	Pit-N	3	5	2	1	0	0	0	0	0	0	.200	.200	.200	11	-1	-1	0	0			-0	/2	0.0
1941	Pit-N	15	25	1	5	0	2	0	3	1	2	.200	.231	.360	65	-1	-1	1	1			2	/23	0.1
1942	Pit-N	3	0	0	0	0	0	0	0	0	0	—	—	—	—	0	0	0	0			0	R	0.0
Total	4	30	62	7	17	1	2	0	5	3	6	.274	.308	.355	80	-2	-2	6	1	1		1	/23	0.1

■ **SCOTT LEIUS** Leius, Scott Thomas b: 9/24/65, Yonkers, N.Y. BR/TR, 6'3", 180 lbs. Deb: 9/03/90

| 1990 | Min-A | 14 | 25 | 4 | 6 | 1 | 0 | 1 | 4 | 2 | 2 | .240 | .296 | .400 | 87 | -0 | -1 | 2 | 0 | 0 | 0 | 3 | S/3 | 0.4 |

■ **FRANK LEJA** Leja, Frank John b: 2/7/36, Holyoke, Mass. BL/TL, 6'4", 205 lbs. Deb: 5/01/54

1954	NY-A	12	5	2	1	0	0	0	0	0	1	.200	.200	.200	10	-1	-1	0	0	0	0	0	/1	0.0
1955	NY-A	7	2	1	0	0	0	0	0	0	1	.000	.000	.000	-99	-1	-1	0	0	0	0	0	/1	0.0
1962	LA-A	7	16	0	0	0	0	0	0	1	6	.000	.059	.000	-85	-4	-4	0	0	0	0	-0	/1	-0.4
Total	3	26	23	3	1	0	0	0	0	1	8	.043	.083	.043	-67	-5	-5	0	0	0	0	0	/1	-0.4

■ **LARRY LeJEUNE** LeJeune, Sheldon Aldenbert b: 7/22/1885, Chicago, Ill. d: 4/21/52, Eloise, Mich. 6', 185 lbs. Deb: 5/10/11

1911	Bro-N	6	19	2	3	0	0	0	2	2	8	.158	.238	.158	12	-2	-2	1	2			-1	/O	-0.3
1915	Pit-N	18	65	4	11	0	1	0	2	2	7	.169	.206	.200	23	-6	-6	3	4	3	-1	4	O	-0.3
Total	2	24	84	6	14	0	1	0	4	4	15	.167	.213	.190	21	-8	-8	4	6	3		2	/O	-0.6

■ **DON LeJOHN** LeJohn, Donald Everett b: 5/13/34, Daisytown, Pa. BR/TR, 5'10", 175 lbs. Deb: 6/30/65

| 1965 | *LA-N | 34 | 78 | 2 | 20 | 2 | 0 | 0 | 7 | 5 | 13 | .256 | .301 | .282 | 70 | -3 | -3 | 6 | 0 | 1 | -1 | 1 | 3 | -0.3 |

■ **JACK LELIVELT** Lelivelt, John Frank b: 11/14/1885, Chicago, Ill. d: 1/20/41, Seattle, Wash. BL/TL, 5'11", 175 lbs. Deb: 6/24/09

1909	Was-A	91	318	25	93	8	6	0	24	19		.292	.334	.355	124	6	7	40	8			8	O	1.3
1910	Was-A	110	347	40	92	10	3	0	33	40		.265	.343	.311	109	3	5	45	20			4	O/1	0.6
1911	Was-A	72	225	29	72	12	4	0	22	22		.320	.386	.409	124	7	7	38	7			4	O/1	0.7
1912	NY-A	36	149	12	54	6	7	2	23	4		.362	.383	.537	153	11	9	32	7			0	O	0.7
1913	NY-A	18	28	2	6	0	1	0	4	2	2	.214	.267	.286	61	-1	-1	2	1			1	O	0.0
	Cle-A	23	23	0	9	2	0	0	7	0	3	.391	.391	.478	150	1	1	4	1			-0	/O	0.1
	Yr	41	51	2	15	2	1	0	11	2	5	.294	.321	.373	101	-0	-0	6	2			1		0.1
1914	Cle-A	34	64	6	21	5	1	0	13	2	10	.328	.348	.438	131	2	2	9	2	3	-1	-3	O/1	-0.2
Total	6	384	1154	114	347	43	22	2	126	89	15	.301	.353	.381	124	29	31	171	46	3		15	O/1	3.2

■ **JOHNNIE LeMASTER** LeMaster, Johnnie Lee b: 6/19/54, Portsmouth, Ohio BR/TR, 6'2", 165 lbs. Deb: 9/02/75

1975	SF-N	22	74	4	14	4	0	2	9	4	15	.189	.241	.324	53	-5	-5	6	2	1	0	-1	S	-0.2
1976	SF-N	33	100	9	21	3	2	0	9	2	21	.210	.225	.280	42	-8	-8	6	2	0	1	11	S	0.6
1977	SF-N	68	134	13	20	5	1	0	8	13	27	.149	.224	.201	15	-16	-16	7	2	1	0	7	S/3	0.0
1978	SF-N	101	272	23	64	18	3	1	14	21	45	.235	.293	.335	78	-9	-8	26	6	6	-2	2	S/2	0.0
1979	SF-N	108	343	42	87	11	2	3	29	23	55	.254	.304	.324	77	-13	-11	34	9	5	-0	-0	*S	0.0
1980	SF-N	135	405	33	87	16	6	3	31	25	57	.215	.260	.306	59	-24	-22	32	0	1	-1	-14	*S	-2.2
1981	SF-N	104	324	27	82	9	1	0	28	24	46	.253	.307	.287	70	-13	-12	26	3	7	-3	-8	*S	-1.2
1982	SF-N	130	436	34	94	14	1	2	30	31	78	.216	.268	.266	50	-29	-29	30	13	4	2	-8	*S	-2.6
1983	SF-N	141	534	81	128	16	1	6	30	60	96	.240	.319	.307	77	-17	-15	57	39	19	0	-22	*S	-2.5
1984	SF-N	132	451	46	98	13	2	4	32	31	97	.217	.268	.282	56	-27	-26	36	17	5	2	4	*S	-0.5
1985	SF-N	12	16	1	0	0	0	0	0	1	5	.000	.059	.000	-86	-4	-4	0	0	0	0	-1	S	-0.3
	Cle-A	11	20	0	3	0	0	0	2	0	6	.150	.150	.150	-18	-3	-3	0	0	1	-1	2	S	0.0
	Pit-N	22	58	4	9	0	0	1	6	5	12	.155	.222	.207	21	-6	-6	3	1	0	0	13	S	0.9
1987	Oak-A	20	24	3	2	0	0	0	1	1	4	.083	.120	.083	-5	-5	-5	0	0	1	-1	5	/3S2D	0.0
Total	12	1039	3191	320	709	109	19	22	229	241	564	.222	.278	.289	60	-180	-170	263	94	51	-2	-9	S/32D	-8.0

■ **STEVE LEMBO** Lembo, Stephen Neal b: 11/13/26, Brooklyn, N.Y. d: 12/4/89, Flushing, N.Y. BR/TR, 6'1", 185 lbs. Deb: 9/16/50

1950	Bro-N	5	6	0	1	0	0	0	0	1		.167	.286	.167	22	-1	-1	0	0			2	/C	0.2
1952	Bro-N	2	5	0	1	0	0	0	1	0	1	.200	.200	.200	11	-1	-1	0	0	0	0	0	/C	0.0
Total	2	7	11	0	2	0	0	0	1	1	1	.182	.250	.182	18	-1	-1	0	0	0		3	/C	0.2

■ **MARK LEMKE** Lemke, Mark Alan b: 8/13/65, Utica, N.Y. BB/TR, 5'10", 167 lbs. Deb: 9/17/88

1988	Atl-N	16	58	8	13	4	0	0	2	4	5	.224	.274	.293	60	-3	-3		0	2	-1	4	2	0.0
1989	Atl-N	14	55	4	10	2	1	2	10	5	7	.182	.250	.364	72	-2	-2	5	0	1	-1	-2	2	-0.4
1990	Atl-N	102	239	22	54	13	0	0	21	21	22	.226	.288	.280	56	-14	-14	19	0	1	-1	23	32/S	1.0
Total	3	132	352	34	77	19	1	2	33	30	34	.219	.280	.295	59	-19	-20	28	0	4	-2	26	/23S	0.6

■ **CHET LEMON** Lemon, Chester Earl b: 2/12/55, Jackson, Miss. BR/TR, 6', 190 lbs. Deb: 9/09/75

1975	Chi-A	9	35	2	9	2	0	0	1	2	6	.257	.297	.314	72	-1	-1	4	1	0	0	-3	/3OD	-0.4
1976	Chi-A	132	451	46	111	15	5	4	38	28	65	.246	.300	.328	83	-9	-10	44	13	7	-0	6	*O	-0.7
1977	Chi-A	150	553	99	151	38	4	19	67	52	88	.273	.347	.459	118	13	13	89	8	7	-2	27	*O	3.3
1978	Chi-A	105	357	51	107	24	6	13	55	39	46	.300	.381	.510	147	23	23	65	5	9	-4	10	OD	2.6
1979	Chi-A	148	556	79	177	**44**	2	17	86	56	68	.318	.394	.496	138	31	31	104	7	11	-5	3	*O	2.3
1980	Chi-A	147	514	76	150	32	6	11	51	71	56	.292	.390	.442	128	22	22	90	6	6	-2	-2	*O/2D	1.5
1981	Chi-A	94	328	50	99	23	6	9	50	33	48	.302	.388	.491	155	22	23	60	6	8	-3	-1	O	1.7
1982	Det-A	125	436	75	116	20	1	19	52	56	69	.266	.369	.447	122	15	15	72	1	4	-2	-0	*O/D	0.8
1983	Det-A	145	491	78	125	21	5	24	69	54	70	.255	.352	.464	111	16	16	79	0	7	-4	6	*O	1.7
1984	*Det-A	141	509	77	146	34	6	20	76	51	83	.287	.360	.495	135	23	23	86	5	5	-2	7	*O/D	2.5
1985	Det-A	145	517	69	137	28	4	18	68	45	93	.265	.336	.439	111	7	7	78	0	2	-1	4	*O	0.8
1986	Det-A	126	403	45	101	21	3	12	53	39	53	.251	.329	.407	99	-1	-0	52	2	1	0	-3	*O	-0.5
1987	*Det-A	146	470	75	130	30	3	20	75	70	82	.277	.380	.481	132	19	22	86	0	0	0	-1	*O	1.7
1988	Det-A	144	512	67	135	29	4	17	64	59	65	.264	.348	.436	123	13	15	75	1	2	-1	0	*O	1.2
1989	Det-A	127	414	45	98	19	2	7	47	46	71	.237	.325	.343	90	-6	-4	47	1	5	-3	-8	*OD	-1.7
1990	Det-A	104	322	39	83	16	4	5	32	48	61	.258	.361	.379	108	4	5	59	3	2	0	3	OD	0.7
Total	16	1988	6868	973	1875	396	61	215	884	749	1024	.273	.357	.442	121	191	201	1078	58	76	-28	45	*O/D32	17.5

■ **JIM LEMON** Lemon, James Robert b: 3/23/28, Covington, Va. BR/TR, 6'4", 200 lbs. Deb: 8/20/50 MC

1950	Cle-A	12	34	4	6	1	0	1	1	3	12	.176	.243	.294	38	-3	-3	2	0	0	0	-1	O	-0.3
1953	Cle-A	16	46	5	8	1	0	1	5	3	15	.174	.224	.261	32	-5	-4	3	0	0	0	-1	O/1	-0.5
1954	Was-A	37	128	12	30	2	3	2	13	9	34	.234	.285	.344	76	-5	-5	10	0	0	0	-5	O	-1.0
1955	Was-A	10	25	3	5	2	0	1	3	3	4	.200	.286	.400	88	-1	-1	3	0	0	0	-1	/O	-0.1
1956	Was-A	146	538	77	146	21	**11**	27	96	65	138	.271	.352	.502	123	16	16	94	2	4	-2	5	*O	1.2
1957	Was-A	137	518	58	147	23	6	17	64	49	94	.284	.349	.450	118	11	12	77	1	7	-4	-8	*O/1	-0.7

YEAR	TM/L	G	AB	R	H	2B	3B	HR	RBI	BB	SO	AVG	OBP	SLG	PRO+	BR	/A	RC	SB	CS	SBR	FR	POS	TPR
1958	Was-A	142	501	65	123	15	9	26	75	50	120	.246	.315	.467	114	7	8	71	2	4	-2	-1	*O	-0.3
1959	Was-A	147	531	73	148	18	3	33	100	46	99	.279	.337	.510	130	19	19	91	5	2	0	-2	*O	1.1
1960	Was-A	148	528	81	142	10	1	38	100	67	114	.269	.359	.508	133	22	23	99	2	0	1	-3	*O	1.5
1961	Min-A	129	423	57	109	26	1	14	52	44	98	.258	.333	.423	95	-0	-3	59	1	1	-0	-11	*O	-1.8
1962	Min-A	12	17	1	3	0	0	1	5	3	4	.176	.300	.353	72	-1	-1	2	0	0	0	-1	/O	-0.1
1963	Min-A	7	17	0	2	0	0	0	1	1	5	.118	.167	.118	-18	-3	-3	0	0	0	0	-1	/O	-0.3
	Phi-N	31	59	6	16	2	0	2	6	8	18	.271	.358	.407	121	2	2	9	0	0	0	-0	O	0.1
	Chi-A	36	80	4	16	0	1	1	8	12	32	.200	.304	.262	62	-4	-4	7	0	0	0	-3	1	-0.7
Total	12	1010	3445	446	901	121	35	164	529	363	787	.262	.335	.460	114	55	57	530	13	18	-7	-34	O/1	-1.9

■ BOB LEMON

Lemon, Robert Granville b: 9/22/20, San Bernardino, Cal. BL/TR, 6', 180 lbs. Deb: 9/09/41 MCH

YEAR	TM/L	G	AB	R	H	2B	3B	HR	RBI	BB	SO	AVG	OBP	SLG	PRO+	BR	/A	RC	SB	CS	SBR	FR	POS	TPR
1941	Cle-A	5	4	0	1	0	0	0	0	0	1	.250	.250	.250	34	-0	-0	0	0	0	0	0	/3	0.0
1942	Cle-A	5	5	0	0	0	0	0	0	0	3	.000	.000	.000	-99	-1	-1	0	0	0	0	0	/3	0.0
1946	Cle-A	55	89	9	16	3	0	1	4	7	18	.180	.240	.247	39	-8	-7	6	0	1	-1	6	PO	0.0
1947	Cle-A	47	56	11	18	4	3	2	5	6	9	.321	.387	.607	179	5	5	14	0	0	0	5	P/O	0.0
1948	*Cle-A	52	119	20	34	9	0	5	21	8	23	.286	.331	.487	119	2	2	20	0	0	0	8	P	0.0
1949	Cle-A	46	108	17	29	6	2	7	19	10	20	.269	.331	.556	135	4	4	21	0	0	0	6	P	0.0
1950	Cle-A	72	136	21	37	9	1	6	26	13	25	.272	.340	.485	113	1	2	24	0	0	0	4	P	0.0
1951	Cle-A	56	102	11	21	4	1	3	13	9	22	.206	.270	.353	72	-5	-4	10	0	0	0	4	P	0.0
1952	Cle-A	54	124	14	28	5	0	2	9	4	21	.226	.250	.315	60	-8	-7	10	0	0	0	7	P	0.0
1953	Cle-A	51	112	12	26	9	1	2	17	7	20	.232	.277	.384	79	-4	-4	13	2	0	1	8	P	0.0
1954	*Cle-A	40	98	11	21	4	1	2	10	6	24	.214	.260	.337	61	-5	-6	9	0	0	0	4	P	0.0
1955	Cle-A	49	78	11	19	0	0	1	9	13	16	.244	.352	.282	69	-3	-3	9	0	0	0	3	P	0.0
1956	Cle-A	43	93	8	18	0	0	5	12	9	21	.194	.272	.355	63	-5	-5	10	0	0	0	5	P	0.0
1957	Cle-A	25	46	2	3	1	0	1	1	0	4	.065	.065	.152	-43	-9	-9	0	0	0	0	3	P	0.0
1958	Cle-A	15	13	1	3	0	0	0	1	1	4	.231	.286	.231	45	-1	-1	1	0	0	0	1	P	0.0
Total	15	615	1183	148	274	54	9	37	147	93	241	.232	.289	.386	82	-38	-35	147	2	1	0	64	P/O3	0.0

■ DON LENHARDT

Lenhardt, Donald Eugene "Footsie" b: 10/4/22, Alton, Ill. BR/TR, 6'3", 190 lbs. Deb: 4/18/50 C

YEAR	TM/L	G	AB	R	H	2B	3B	HR	RBI	BB	SO	AVG	OBP	SLG	PRO+	BR	/A	RC	SB	CS	SBR	FR	POS	TPR
1950	StL-A	139	480	75	131	22	6	22	81	90	94	.273	.390	.481	118	16	14	98	3	2	-0	-11	1O3	-0.2
1951	StL-A	31	103	9	27	3	0	5	18	6	13	.262	.303	.437	95	-1	-1	14	1	0	0	-2	O/1	-0.3
	Chi-A	64	199	23	53	9	1	10	45	24	25	.266	.351	.472	124	5	6	35	1	1	-0	-3	O/1	0.1
	Yr	95	302	32	80	12	1	15	63	30	38	.265	.335	.460	114	4	4	49	2	1	-0	-5		-0.2
1952	Bos-A	30	105	18	31	4	0	7	24	15	18	.295	.383	.533	142	7	6	21	0	1	-1	-4	O	0.1
	Det-A	45	144	18	27	2	1	3	13	28	18	.188	.320	.278	67	-6	-6	14	0	1	-1	2	O	-0.5
	StL-A	18	48	5	13	4	1	1	5	4	8	.271	.327	.458	114	1	1	7	0	0	0	0	O/1	0.1
	Yr	93	297	41	71	10	2	11	42	47	44	.239	.343	.397	102	2	1	42	0	2	-1	-2		-0.3
1953	StL-A	97	303	37	96	15	0	10	35	41	41	.317	.400	.465	131	15	14	58	1	2	-1	-4	O/3	0.7
1954	Bal-A	13	33	2	5	1	0	0	1	3	9	.152	.222	.182	12	-4	-4	1	0	0	0	-0	/O1	-0.3
	Bos-A	44	66	5	18	4	0	3	17	3	9	.273	.314	.470	101	1	-0	9	0	0	0	-2	O/3	-0.1
	Yr	57	99	7	23	5	0	3	18	6	18	.232	.283	.374	74	-3	-4	10	0	0	0	-2		-0.4
Total	5	481	1481	192	401	64	9	61	239	214	235	.271	.365	.450	114	34	29	258	6	7	-2	-23	O/13	-0.4

■ BOB LENNON

Lennon, Robert Albert "Arch" b: 9/15/28, Brooklyn, N.Y. BL/TL, 6', 200 lbs. Deb: 9/09/54

YEAR	TM/L	G	AB	R	H	2B	3B	HR	RBI	BB	SO	AVG	OBP	SLG	PRO+	BR	/A	RC	SB	CS	SBR	FR	POS	TPR
1954	NY-N	3	3	0	0	0	0	0	0	0	0	.000	.000	.000	-99	-1	-1	0	0	0	0	0	H	0.0
1956	NY-N	26	55	3	10	1	0	0	1	4	17	.182	.237	.200	19	-6	-6	3	0	0	0	-1	O	-0.7
1957	Chi-N	9	21	2	3	1	0	1	3	1	9	.143	.182	.333	35	-2	-2	1	0	0	0	-1	/O	-0.2
Total	3	38	79	5	13	2	0	1	4	5	26	.165	.214	.228	19	-9	-9	4	0	0	0	-2	/O	-0.9

■ BILL LENNON

Lennon, William F. b: 1848, Brooklyn, N.Y. 5'7", 145 lbs. Deb: 5/04/1871 M

YEAR	TM/L	G	AB	R	H	2B	3B	HR	RBI	BB	SO	AVG	OBP	SLG	PRO+	BR	/A	RC	SB	CS	SBR	FR	POS	TPR
1871	Kek-n	12	48	5	11	3	0	0	5	1	0	.229	.245	.292	52	-3	-3	4	1				CM	-0.1
1872	Nat-n	11	55	11	12	2	0	0		0		.218	.218	.255	39	-3	-5	3					C	-0.3
1873	Mar-n	5	20	2	4	1	0	0		0		.200	.200	.250	41	-2	-1	1					/1/C3	0.0
Total	3 n	28	123	18	27	6	0	0		1		.220	.226	.268	44	-8	-9	8					/C13	-0.4

■ ED LENNOX

Lennox, James Edgar "Eggie" b: 11/3/1885, Camden, N.J. d: 10/26/39, Camden, N.J. BR/TR, 5'10", 174 lbs. Deb: 8/08/06

YEAR	TM/L	G	AB	R	H	2B	3B	HR	RBI	BB	SO	AVG	OBP	SLG	PRO+	BR	/A	RC	SB	CS	SBR	FR	POS	TPR
1906	Phi-A	6	17	1	1	1	0	0	0	1		.059	.111	.118	-27	-2	-3	0	0			5	/3	0.3
1909	Bro-N	126	435	33	114	18	9	2	44	47		.262	.337	.359	120	8	10	56	11			-4	*3	0.9
1910	Bro-N	110	367	19	95	19	4	3	32	36	39	.259	.333	.357	104	0	2	46	7			-15	*3	-1.3
1912	Chi-N	27	81	13	19	4	1	1	16	12	10	.235	.347	.346	90	-1	-1	11	1			-5	*3	-0.5
1914	Pit-F	124	430	71	134	25	10	11	84	71	38	.312	.414	.493	160	35	36	100	19			-15	*3	2.3
1915	Pit-F	55	53	1	16	3	1	1	9	7	12	.302	.383	.453	148	3	3	10	0			2	/3	0.6
Total	6	448	1383	138	379	70	25	18	185	174	99	.274	.361	.400	127	43	47	222	38			-33	3	2.3

■ JIM LENTINE

Lentine, James Matthew b: 7/16/54, Los Angeles, Cal. BR/TR, 6', 175 lbs. Deb: 9/03/78

YEAR	TM/L	G	AB	R	H	2B	3B	HR	RBI	BB	SO	AVG	OBP	SLG	PRO+	BR	/A	RC	SB	CS	SBR	FR	POS	TPR
1978	StL-N	8	11	1	2	0	0	0	1	0	0	.182	.250	.182	23	-1	-1	1	1	0	0	0	/O	0.0
1979	StL-N	11	23	2	9	1	0	0	1	3	6	.391	.462	.435	145	2	2	5	0	1	-1	1	/O	0.2
1980	StL-N	9	10	1	1	0	0	0	1	0	2	.100	.100	.100	-43	-2	-2	0	0	0	0	0	/O	-0.1
	Det-A	67	161	19	42	8	1	1	17	28	30	.261	.377	.342	96	1	0	23	2	1	0	2	O/D	0.1
Total	3	95	205	23	54	9	1	1	20	31	38	.263	.368	.332	92	-0	-1	28	3	2	-0	3	/OD	0.2

■ EDDIE LEON

Leon, Eduardo Antonio b: 8/11/46, Tucson, Ariz. BR/TR, 6', 170 lbs. Deb: 9/09/68

YEAR	TM/L	G	AB	R	H	2B	3B	HR	RBI	BB	SO	AVG	OBP	SLG	PRO+	BR	/A	RC	SB	CS	SBR	FR	POS	TPR
1968	Cle-A	6	1	0	0	0	0	0	0	0	1	.000	.000	.000	-99	-0	-0	0	0	0	0	3	/S	0.3
1969	Cle-A	64	213	20	51	6	0	3	19	19	37	.239	.302	.310	69	-8	-9	20	2	2	-1	9	S	0.2
1970	Cle-A	152	549	58	136	20	4	10	56	47	89	.248	.309	.353	78	-14	-17	61	1	2	-1	8	*2S/3	0.6
1971	Cle-A	131	429	35	112	12	2	4	35	34	69	.261	.317	.326	76	-10	-14	41	3	5	-2	0	*2S	-0.9
1972	Cle-A	89	225	14	45	2	1	4	16	20	47	.200	.268	.271	59	-11	-12	15	0	2	-1	-1	2S	-0.8
1973	Chi-A	127	399	37	91	10	3	3	30	34	103	.228	.294	.291	63	-18	-20	34	1	5	-3	-2	*S/2	-0.8
1974	Chi-A	31	46	1	5	1	0	0	3	2	12	.109	.146	.130	-20	-7	-7	1	0	0	0	8	S/23D	0.3
1975	NY-A	1	0	0	0	0	0	0	0	0	0	—	—	—	-99	-0	-0	0	0	0	0	0	/S	0.0
Total	8	601	1862	165	440	51	10	24	159	156	358	.236	.298	.313	69	-68	-79	171	7	16	-8	25	S2/3D	-1.1

■ ANDY LEONARD

Leonard, Andrew Jackson b: 6/1/1846, County Cavan, Ireland d: 8/21/03, Roxbury, Mass. BR/TR, 5'7", 168 lbs. Deb: 5/05/1871

YEAR	TM/L	G	AB	R	H	2B	3B	HR	RBI	BB	SO	AVG	OBP	SLG	PRO+	BR	/A	RC	SB	CS	SBR	FR	POS	TPR
1871	Oly-n	31	148	33	43	8	3	0	30	0	3	.291	.305	.385	102	-1	1	22	14				*2O/S	0.1
1872	Bos-n	46	243	59	84	8	2	2		0		.346	.346	.420	128	9	6	36					*O/32	0.5
1873	Bos-n	58	303	81	95	12	6	0		2		.314	.318	.393	100	-3	-3	39					*O2/S	-0.1
1874	Bos-n	71	340	68	109	18	4	0		2		.321	.325	.397	122	10	7	45					*OS/2	0.5
1875	Bos-n	80	394	87	127	14	6	1		1		.322	.324	.396	143	18	16	52					*O/S32	1.4
1876	Bos-N	64	303	53	85	10	2	0	27	4	6	.281	.290	.327	103	1	1	29				-1	O2	0.0
1877	Bos-N	58	277	46	78	5	0	0	27	5	5	.287	.300	.305	88	-3	-4	25				-4	OS	-0.7
1878	Bos-N	60	262	41	68	8	5	0	16	3	19	.260	.268	.328	88	-2	-4	24				-7	*O	-1.5
1880	Cin-N	33	133	15	28	3	0	1	17	8	11	.211	.255	.256	75	-3	-3	9				-11	S3	-1.2
Total	5 n	286	1428	328	458	60	21	3	30	8	1	.321	.325	.398	121	39	27	194					O/2S3	2.4
Total	4	215	970	155	259	26	7	1	87	20	41	.267	.282	.311	91	-6	-11	87				-23	O/S23	-3.4

YEAR	TM/L	G	AB	R	H	2B	3B	HR	RBI	BB	SO	AVG	OBP	SLG	PRO+	BR	/A	RC	SB	CS	SBR	FR	POS	TPR
■ JEFFREY LEONARD						Leonard, Jeffrey		b: 9/22/55, Philadelphia, Pa.			BR/TR, 6'2", 200 lbs.		Deb: 9/02/77										
1977	LA-N	11	10	1	3	0	1	0	2	1	4	.300	.364	.500	130	0	0	1	0	0	0	0	O	0.0
1978	Hou-N	8	26	2	10	2	0	0	4	1	2	.385	.407	.462	154	1	2	5	0	1	-1	1	/O	0.2
1979	Hou-N	134	411	47	119	15	5	0	47	46	68	.290	.364	.350	102	-1	2	53	23	10	1	-4	*O	-0.3
1980	*Hou-N	88	216	29	46	7	5	3	20	19	46	.213	.277	.333	75	-9	-7	19	4	1	1	0	O1	-0.9
1981	Hou-N	7	18	1	3	1	1	0	3	0	4	.167	.167	.333	41	-2	-1	1	1	0	0	-0	/1O	-0.1
	SF-N	37	127	20	39	11	3	4	26	12	21	.307	.371	.535	158	9	9	23	4	2	0	3	O/1	1.2
	Yr	44	145	21	42	12	4	4	29	12	25	.290	.348	.510	145	7	8	24	5	2	0	3		1.1
1982	SF-N	80	278	32	72	16	1	9	49	19	65	.259	.311	.421	103	0	0	34	18	5	2	-5	O/1	-0.2
1983	SF-N	139	516	74	144	17	7	21	87	35	116	.279	.326	.461	120	9	11	77	26	7	4	6	*O	1.9
1984	SF-N	136	514	76	155	27	2	21	86	47	123	.302	.360	.484	140	23	25	87	17	7	1	4	*O	2.6
1985	SF-N	133	507	49	122	20	3	17	62	21	107	.241	.272	.393	88	-13	-10	47	11	6	-0	-4	*O	-1.8
1986	SF-N	89	341	48	95	11	3	6	42	20	62	.279	.324	.381	99	-3	-1	44	16	3	3	-4	O	-0.3
1987	*SF-N	131	503	70	141	29	4	19	63	21	68	.280	.312	.467	108	-0	3	66	16	7	1	-9	*O	-1.0
1988	SF-N	44	160	12	41	8	1	2	20	9	24	.256	.296	.356	90	-3	-2	15	7	5	-1	-4	O	-0.9
	Mil-A	94	374	45	88	19	0	8	44	16	68	.235	.272	.350	72	-14	-15	34	10	4	1	-0	O/D	-1.5
1989	Sea-A	150	566	69	144	20	1	24	93	38	125	.254	.307	.420	100	1	-2	72	6	1	1	-0	*DO	-0.2
1990	Sea-A	134	478	39	120	20	0	10	75	37	97	.251	.309	.356	84	-10	-10	49	4	2	0	-11	OD	-2.2
Total	14	1415	5045	614	1342	223	37	144	723	342	1000	.266	.316	.411	103	-11	4	627	163	61	12	-27	*OD/1	-3.3
■ JOE LEONARD						Leonard, Joseph Howard		b: 11/15/1894, W.Chicago, Ill.			d: 5/1/20, Washington, D.C.		BL/TR, 5'7.5", 156 lbs.		Deb: 5/07/14								
1914	Pit-N	53	126	17	25	2	2	0	4	12	21	.198	.268	.246	56	-7	-7	10	4			-8	3/S	-1.4
1916	Cle-A	3	2	1	0	0	0	0	0	0	1	.000	.000	.000	-94	-0	-0	0	0			0	/2	0.0
	Was-A	42	168	20	46	7	0	0	14	22	23	.274	.358	.315	105	1	2	20	4			-7	3	-0.4
	Yr	45	170	21	46	7	0	0	14	22	24	.271	.354	.312	102	1	1	20	4			-7		-0.4
1917	Was-A	99	297	30	57	6	7	0	23	45	40	.192	.302	.259	72	-9	-9	25	6			-2	31/SO	-0.9
1919	Was-A	71	198	26	51	8	3	2	20	20	28	.258	.329	.359	94	-2	-2	23	3			-9	23/1O	-0.6
1920	Was-A	1	0	0	0	0	0	0	0	0	0	—	—	—	—	0	0	0	0	0	0	0	R	0.0
Total	5	269	791	94	179	23	12	2	61	99	113	.226	.315	.293	82	-17	-16	78	17	0		-27	3/210S	-3.3
■ MARK LEONARD						Leonard, Mark David		b: 8/14/64, Mountain View, Cal.			BL/TR, 6'1", 195 lbs.		Deb: 7/21/90										
1990	SF-N	11	17	3	3	1	0	1	2	3	8	.176	.300	.412	95	-0	-0	2	0	0	0	0	/O	0.0
■ JOHN LEOVICH						Leovich, John Joseph		b: 5/5/18, Portland, Ore.			BR/TR, 6'0.5", 200 lbs.		Deb: 5/01/41										
1941	Phi-A	1	2	0	1	1	0	0	0	0	0	.500	.500	1.000	296	0	1	0	0	0	0	0	/C	0.1
■ TED LEPCIO						Lepcio, Thaddeus Stanley		b: 7/28/30, Utica, N.Y.			BR/TR, 5'10", 177 lbs.		Deb: 4/15/52										
1952	Bos-A	84	274	34	72	17	2	5	26	24	41	.263	.329	.394	93	-0	-3	37	3	3	-1	8	23/S	0.7
1953	Bos-A	66	161	17	38	4	2	4	11	17	24	.236	.313	.360	77	-4	-6	18	0	0	0	17	2S3	1.4
1954	Bos-A	116	398	42	102	19	4	8	45	42	62	.256	.332	.384	86	-3	-8	51	3	4	-2	16	23S	1.0
1955	Bos-A	51	134	19	31	9	0	6	15	12	36	.231	.313	.433	91	-1	-2	18	1	1	-0	6	3	0.4
1956	Bos-A	83	284	34	74	10	0	15	51	30	77	.261	.338	.454	96	2	-3	44	1	3	-2	7	23	0.8
1957	Bos-A	79	232	24	56	10	2	9	37	29	61	.241	.328	.418	97	1	-1	32	0	0	0	9	2	1.1
1958	Bos-A	50	136	10	27	3	0	6	14	12	47	.199	.268	.353	65	-6	-7	13	0	1	-1	-3	2	-0.7
1959	Bos-A	3	3	1	1	1	0	0	1	0	2	.333	.333	.667	160	0	0	1	0	0	0	0	/2	0.0
	Det-A	76	215	25	60	8	0	7	24	17	49	.279	.332	.414	98	1	-1	28	2	0	1	-6	S23	-0.1
	Yr	79	218	26	61	9	0	7	25	17	51	.280	.332	.417	99	1	-1	29	2	0	1	-6		-0.1
1960	Phi-N	69	141	16	32	7	0	2	8	17	41	.227	.319	.319	75	-4	-4	14	0	3	-2	-5	3S/2	-1.0
1961	Chi-A	5	2	0	0	0	0	0	0	1	0	.000	.333	.000	-2	-0	-0	0	0	0	0	/3	0.0
	Min-A	47	112	11	19	3	1	7	19	8	31	.170	.231	.402	62	-6	-7	10	1	0	0	2	32/S	0.0
	Yr	52	114	11	19	3	1	7	19	9	31	.167	.234	.395	62	-7	-7	10	1	0	0	2		0.0
Total	10	729	2092	233	512	91	11	69	251	209	471	.245	.319	.398	87	-22	-42	266	11	15	-6	52	23/S	3.6
■ PETE LePINE						LePine, Louis Joseph		b: 9/5/1876, Montreal, Que., Can			d: 12/3/49, Woonsocket, R.I.		BL/TL,		Deb: 7/21/02								
1902	Det-A	30	96	8	20	3	2	1	19	8		.208	.276	.313	63	-5	-5	9				-1	O/1	-0.6
■ DON LEPPERT						Leppert, Don Eugene "Tiger"		b: 11/20/30, Memphis, Tenn.			BL/TR, 5'8", 175 lbs.		Deb: 4/11/55										
1955	Bal-A	40	70	6	8	0	1	0	2	9	10	.114	.215	.143	-2	-10	-9	2	1	1	-0	-7	2	-1.4
■ DON LEPPERT						Leppert, Donald George		b: 10/19/31, Indianapolis, Ind.			BR/TR, 6'2", 220 lbs.		Deb: 6/18/61	C								
1961	Pit-N	22	60	6	16	2	1	3	5	1	11	.267	.279	.483	97	-1	-1	5	0	0	0	1	C	0.2
1962	Pit-N	45	139	14	37	6	1	3	18	12	21	.266	.329	.388	92	-2	-2	16	0	1	-1	4	C	0.3
1963	Was-A	73	211	20	50	11	0	6	24	20	29	.237	.306	.374	90	-3	-3	23	0	0	0	-7	C	-0.9
1964	Was-A	50	122	6	19	3	0	3	12	11	32	.156	.226	.254	33	-11	-11	7	0	0	0	1	C	-0.8
Total	4	190	532	46	122	22	2	15	59	44	93	.229	.291	.363	78	-16	-16	51	0	1	-1	-1	C	-1.2
■ DUTCH LERCHEN						Lerchen, Bertram Roe		b: 4/4/1889, Detroit, Mich.			d: 1/7/62, Detroit, Mich.		TR , 5'8", 160 lbs.		Deb: 8/14/10								
1910	Bos-A	6	15	1	0	0	0	0	0	0	1	.000	.063	.000	-78	-3	-3	0				-3	/S	-0.7
■ GEORGE LERCHEN						Lerchen, George Edward		b: 12/1/22, Detroit, Mich.			BB/TR, 5'11", 175 lbs.		Deb: 4/15/52										
1952	Det-A	14	32	1	5	1	0	1	3	7	10	.156	.308	.281	64	-1	-1	3	1	0	0	-1	/O	-0.1
1953	Cin-N	22	17	2	5	1	0	0	2	5	6	.294	.455	.353	113	1	1	3	0	0	0	0	/O	0.1
Total	2	36	49	3	10	2	0	1	5	12	16	.204	.361	.306	82	-1	-1	7	1	0	0	-1	/O	0.0
■ WALT LERIAN						Lerian, Walter Irvin "Peck"		b: 2/10/03, Baltimore, Md.			d: 10/22/29, Baltimore, Md.		BR/TR, 5'11", 170 lbs.		Deb: 4/16/28								
1928	Phi-N	96	239	28	65	16	2	2	25	41	29	.272	.385	.381	97	2	1	37	1			-3	C	0.2
1929	Phi-N	105	273	28	61	13	2	7	25	53	37	.223	.354	.363	73	-9	-12	37	0			1	*C	-0.1
Total	2	201	512	56	126	29	4	9	50	94	66	.246	.368	.371	84	-7	-11	74	1			-2	C	0.1
■ ROY LESLIE						Leslie, Roy Reid		b: 8/23/1894, Bailey, Tex.			d: 4/9/72, Sherman, Tex.		BR/TR, 6'1", 175 lbs.		Deb: 9/06/17								
1917	Chi-N	7	19	1	4	0	0	0	1	1	5	.211	.250	.211	39	-1	-1	1	1			0	/1	-0.1
1919	StL-N	12	24	2	5	1	0	0	4	4	3	.208	.321	.250	78	-1	-0	2	0			-0	/1	0.0
1922	Phi-N	141	513	44	139	23	2	6	50	37	49	.271	.320	.359	68	-20	-26	58	3	7	-3	-4	*1	-3.3
Total	3	160	556	47	148	24	2	6	55	42	57	.266	.318	.349	68	-21	-28	61	4	7		-4	1	-3.4
■ SAM LESLIE						Leslie, Samuel Andrew "Sambo"		b: 7/26/05, Moss Point, Miss.			d: 1/21/79, Pascagoula, Miss.		BL/TL, 6', 192 lbs.		Deb: 10/06/29								
1929	NY-N	1	1	0	0	0	0	0	1	0	0	.000	.000	.000	-99	-0	-0	0	0			0	/O	0.0
1930	NY-N	2	2	0	1	0	0	0	0	0	1	.500	.500	.500	146	0	0	0	0			0	H	0.0
1931	NY-N	53	53	11	16	4	0	3	5	1	2	.302	.315	.547	131	2	2	9	3			0	/1	0.1
1932	NY-N	77	75	5	22	4	0	1	15	2	5	.293	.329	.387	94	-1	-1	10	0			-0	/1	0.0
1933	NY-N	40	137	21	44	12	3	3	27	12	9	.321	.380	.518	157	9	10	27	0			-0	1	0.9
	Bro-N	96	364	41	104	11	4	5	46	23	14	.286	.340	.379	110	3	4	45	1			-6	1	-0.3
	Yr	136	501	62	148	23	7	8	73	35	23	.295	.351	.417	123	12	14	71	1			-6		0.6
1934	Bro-N	146	546	75	181	29	6	9	102	69	34	.332	.409	.456	138	27	31	108	5			5	*1	2.3
1935	Bro-N	142	520	72	160	30	7	5	93	55	19	.308	.379	.421	117	12	14	87	4			-0	*1	1.1

YEAR	TM/L	G	AB	R	H	2B	3B	HR	RBI	BB	SO	AVG	OBP	SLG	PRO+	BR	/A	RC	SB	CS	SBR	FR	POS	TPR
1936	*NY-N	117	417	49	123	19	5	6	54	23	16	.295	.335	.408	100	-1	-1	55	0			0	1	-0.8
1937	*NY-N	72	191	25	59	7	2	3	30	20	12	.309	.380	.414	114	5	4	30		3	1		1	0.5
1938	NY-N	76	154	12	39	7	1	1	16	11	6	.253	.307	.331	75	-5	-5	16	0			-2	1	-1.0
Total	10	822	2460	311	749	123	28	36	389	216	118	.304	.366	.421	117	50	58	385	14			-1	1/O	2.8

■ CHARLIE LETCHAS
Letchas, Charlie b: 10/3/15, Thomasville, Ga.   BR/TR, 5'10", 150 lbs.   Deb: 9/16/39

YEAR	TM/L	G	AB	R	H	2B	3B	HR	RBI	BB	SO	AVG	OBP	SLG	PRO+	BR	/A	RC	SB	CS	SBR	FR	POS	TPR
1939	Phi-N	12	44	2	10	2	0	1	3	1	2	.227	.244	.341	57	-3	-3	3	0			-1	2	-0.2
1941	Was-A	2	8	0	1	0	0	0	1	1	1	.125	.222	.125	-6	-1	-1	0	0	0	0	-1	/2	-0.1
1944	Phi-N	116	396	29	94	8	0	0	33	32	27	.237	.298	.258	59	-22	-20	30	0			6	23S	-0.3
1946	Phi-N	6	13	1	3	0	0	0	0	1	1	.231	.286	.231	49	-1	-1	1	0			1	/2	0.0
Total	4	136	461	32	108	10	0	1	37	35	31	.234	.291	.262	58	-27	-25	35	0	0		5	/23S	-0.6

■ TOM LETCHER
Letcher, Thomas F. b: 1868, Grand Rapids, Mich.   Deb: 9/27/1891

YEAR	TM/L	G	AB	R	H	2B	3B	HR	RBI	BB	SO	AVG	OBP	SLG	PRO+	BR	/A	RC	SB	CS	SBR	FR	POS	TPR
1891	Mil-a	6	21	3	4	1	0	0	2	0	1	.190	.190	.238	20	-2	-3	1	1			0	/O	-0.1

■ LEUTZ
Leutz   Deb: 5/07/1872

YEAR	TM/L	G	AB	R	H	2B	3B	HR	RBI	BB	SO	AVG	OBP	SLG	PRO+	BR	/A	RC	SB	CS	SBR	FR	POS	TPR
1872	Eck-n	4	13	2	1	0	0	0		0		.077	.077	.077	-62	-2	-2	0					/C	0.0

■ JESSE LEVAN
Levan, Jesse Roy b: 7/15/26, Reading, Pa.   BL/TR, 6', 172 lbs.   Deb: 9/27/47

YEAR	TM/L	G	AB	R	H	2B	3B	HR	RBI	BB	SO	AVG	OBP	SLG	PRO+	BR	/A	RC	SB	CS	SBR	FR	POS	TPR
1947	Phi-N	2	9	3	4	0	0	0	1	0	0	.444	.444	.444	142	0	1	2	0			-1	/O	0.0
1954	Was-A	7	10	1	3	0	0	0	0	0	0	.300	.300	.300	68	-0	-0	1	0	0	0	0	/31	0.0
1955	Was-A	16	16	1	3	0	0	1	4	0	2	.188	.188	.375	51	-1	-1	1	0	0	0	0	H	0.0
Total	3	25	35	5	10	0	0	1	5	0	2	.286	.286	.371	80	-1	-1	3	0	0		-1	/3O1	0.0

■ JIM LEVEY
Levey, James Julius b: 9/13/06, Pittsburgh, Pa.   d: 3/14/70, Dallas, Tex.   BB/TR, 5'10.5", 154 lbs.   Deb: 9/17/30

YEAR	TM/L	G	AB	R	H	2B	3B	HR	RBI	BB	SO	AVG	OBP	SLG	PRO+	BR	/A	RC	SB	CS	SBR	FR	POS	TPR
1930	StL-A	8	37	7	9	2	0	0	3	3	2	.243	.300	.297	50	-3	-3	3	0	0	0	2	/S	0.0
1931	StL-A	139	498	53	104	19	2	5	38	35	83	.209	.264	.285	43	-41	-44	38	13	8	-1	-10	*S	-3.8
1932	StL-A	152	568	59	159	30	8	4	63	21	48	.280	.310	.382	74	-19	-24	66	6	4	-1	-18	*S	-2.9
1933	StL-A	141	529	43	103	10	4	2	36	26	68	.195	.237	.240	25	-56	-61	30	4	6	-2	-6	*S	-5.5
Total	4	440	1632	162	375	61	14	11	140	85	201	.230	.272	.305	48	-119	-131	138	23	18	-4	-32	S	-12.2

■ CHARLIE LEVIS
Levis, Charles H. b: 6/21/1860, St.Louis, Mo.   d: 10/16/26, St.Louis, Mo.   Deb: 4/17/1884

YEAR	TM/L	G	AB	R	H	2B	3B	HR	RBI	BB	SO	AVG	OBP	SLG	PRO+	BR	/A	RC	SB	CS	SBR	FR	POS	TPR
1884	Bal-U	87	373	59	85	11	4	6		3		.228	.234	.327	80	-5	-11	29	0			-0	*1	-1.0
	Was-U	1	3	0	0	0	0	0		0		.000	.000	.000	-99	-1	-1	0	0			0	/1	0.0
	Yr	88	376	59	85	11	4	6		3		.226	.232	.324	78	-6	-12	29	0			-0	/1	-1.0
	Ind-a	3	10	0	2	0	0	0		0		.200	.200	.200	34	-1	-1	0				0	/1	0.0
1885	Bal-a	1	4	2	1	0	0	0		0		.250	.400	.250	114	0	0	0				-0	/1	0.0
Total	2	92	390	61	88	11	4	6		3		.226	.234	.321	78	-6	-12	30				0	/1	-1.0

■ ED LEVY
Levy, Edward Clarence (b: Edward Clarence Whitner) b: 10/28/16, Birmingham, Ala.   BR/TR, 6'5.5", 190 lbs.   Deb: 4/16/40

YEAR	TM/L	G	AB	R	H	2B	3B	HR	RBI	BB	SO	AVG	OBP	SLG	PRO+	BR	/A	RC	SB	CS	SBR	FR	POS	TPR
1940	Phi-N	1	1	0	0	0	0	0	0	0	0	.000	.000	.000	-99	-0	-0	0	0			0	H	0.0
1942	NY-A	13	41	5	5	0	0	0	3	4	5	.122	.200	.122	-9	-6	-6	1	1	0	0	2	1	-0.3
1944	NY-A	40	153	12	37	11	2	4	29	6	19	.242	.270	.418	92	-2	-3	17	1	1	-0	-3	O	-0.7
Total	3	54	195	17	42	11	2	4	32	10	24	.215	.254	.354	70	-8	-9	18	2	1		-1	/O1	-1.0

■ LEWIS
Lewis b: Brooklyn, N.Y.   Deb: 7/12/1890

YEAR	TM/L	G	AB	R	H	2B	3B	HR	RBI	BB	SO	AVG	OBP	SLG	PRO+	BR	/A	RC	SB	CS	SBR	FR	POS	TPR
1890	Buf-P	1	5	1	1	0	0	0	0	0	0	.200	.200	.200	9	-1	-1	0	0			0	/OP	0.0

■ ALLAN LEWIS
Lewis, Allan Sydney "The Panamanian Express" b: 12/12/41, Colon, Panama   BB/TR, 6', 170 lbs.   Deb: 4/11/67

YEAR	TM/L	G	AB	R	H	2B	3B	HR	RBI	BB	SO	AVG	OBP	SLG	PRO+	BR	/A	RC	SB	CS	SBR	FR	POS	TPR
1967	KC-A	34	6	7	1	0	0	0	0	0	3	.167	.167	.167	-1	-1	-1	-6	14	5	1	0	H	0.1
1968	Oak-A	26	4	9	1	0	0	0	0	1	0	.250	.400	.250	105	0	0	-2	8	4	0	0	/O	0.0
1969	Oak-A	12	1	2	0	0	0	0	0	0	0	.000	.000	.000	-99	-0	-0	0	0	0	0	0	H	0.0
1970	Oak-A	25	8	8	2	0	0	1	1	0	0	.250	.250	.625	139	0	0	1	7	1	2	2	/O	0.4
1972	*Oak-A	24	10	5	2	1	0	0	2	0	1	.200	.200	.300	50	-1	-1	-1	8	3	1	3	/O	0.3
1973	*Oak-A	35	0	16	0	0	0	0	0	0	0	—	—	—	—	0	0	0	7	4	-0	0	/OD	0.0
Total	6	156	29	47	6	1	0	1	3	1	4	.207	.233	.345	69	-1	-1	-7	44	17	3	5	/OD	0.8

■ DARREN LEWIS
Lewis, Darren Joel b: 8/28/67, Berkeley, Cal.   BR/TR, 6', 180 lbs.   Deb: 8/21/90

YEAR	TM/L	G	AB	R	H	2B	3B	HR	RBI	BB	SO	AVG	OBP	SLG	PRO+	BR	/A	RC	SB	CS	SBR	FR	POS	TPR
1990	Oak-A	25	35	4	8	0	0	0	1	7	4	.229	.372	.229	74	-1	-1	4	2	0	1	2	O/D	0.1

■ FRED LEWIS
Lewis, Frederick Miller b: 10/13/1858, Buffalo, N.Y.   d: 6/5/45, Utica, N.Y.   BB/TR, 5'10.5", 194 lbs.   Deb: 7/02/1881

YEAR	TM/L	G	AB	R	H	2B	3B	HR	RBI	BB	SO	AVG	OBP	SLG	PRO+	BR	/A	RC	SB	CS	SBR	FR	POS	TPR
1881	Bos-N	27	114	17	25	6	0	0	9	7	5	.219	.264	.272	72	-4	-3	8				-2	O	-0.4
1883	Phi-N	38	160	21	40	7	0	0	18	4	13	.250	.268	.294	78	-5	-3	13				-1	O	-0.2
	StL-a	49	209	37	63	8	4	1		1		.301	.305	.392	116	5	3	26				-0	O	0.3
1884	StL-a	73	300	59	97	25	3	0		16		.323	.366	.427	155	20	18	48				3	O	1.8
	StL-U	8	30	6	9	1	0	0		3		.300	.364	.333	132	1	1	4	0			-1	/O	0.0
1885	StL-N	45	181	12	53	9	0	1	27	9	10	.293	.326	.359	130	4	6	22				5	O	0.9
1886	Cin-a	77	324	72	103	14	6	2		20		.318	.365	.417	143	17	15	53	8			-2	O/3	1.0
Total	5	317	1318	224	390	70	13	4	54	60	28	.296	.330	.378	126	37	37	174	8			2	O/3	3.4

■ DUFFY LEWIS
Lewis, George Edward b: 4/18/1888, San Francisco, Cal   d: 6/17/79, Salem, N.H.   BL/TL, 5'10.5", 165 lbs.   Deb: 4/16/10   C

YEAR	TM/L	G	AB	R	H	2B	3B	HR	RBI	BB	SO	AVG	OBP	SLG	PRO+	BR	/A	RC	SB	CS	SBR	FR	POS	TPR
1910	Bos-A	151	541	64	153	29	7	8	68	32		.283	.328	.407	127	16	14	76	10			10	*O	1.9
1911	Bos-A	130	469	64	144	32	4	7	86	25		.307	.355	.437	122	11	12	77	11			5	*O	0.7
1912	*Bos-A	154	581	85	165	36	9	6	109	52		.284	.346	.408	110	10	6	86	9			6	*O	0.3
1913	Bos-A	149	551	54	164	31	12	0	90	30	55	.298	.336	.397	112	8	6	77	12			11	*O/P3	1.0
1914	Bos-A	146	510	53	142	37	9	2	79	57	41	.278	.357	.398	127	16	16	70	22	31	-12	-2	*O	-0.6
1915	*Bos-A	152	557	69	162	31	7	2	76	45	63	.291	.348	.382	122	11	13	80	14	7	0	-7	*O	-0.1
1916	*Bos-A	152	563	56	151	29	5	1	56	33	56	.268	.313	.343	97	-4	-4	68	16			-1	*O	-1.4
1917	Bos-A	150	553	55	167	29	9	1	65	29	54	.302	.342	.392	125	14	14	77	8			4	*O	1.0
1919	NY-A	141	559	67	152	23	4	7	89	17	42	.272	.293	.365	84	-14	-15	61	8			-6	*O	-3.1
1920	NY-A	107	365	34	99	8	1	4	61	24	32	.271	.320	.332	70	-14	-16	38	2	8	-4	-2	O	-3.0
1921	Was-A	27	102	11	19	4	1	0	14	8	10	.186	.252	.245	29	-11	-11	7	1	1	-0	-2	O	-1.4
Total	11	1459	5351	612	1518	289	68	38	793	352	353	.284	.333	.384	108	42	36	716	113	47		16	*O/3P	-4.7

■ JACK LEWIS
Lewis, John David b: 2/12/1884, Pittsburgh, Pa.   d: 2/25/56, Steubenville, Ohio   BR/TR, 5'8", 158 lbs.   Deb: 9/16/11

YEAR	TM/L	G	AB	R	H	2B	3B	HR	RBI	BB	SO	AVG	OBP	SLG	PRO+	BR	/A	RC	SB	CS	SBR	FR	POS	TPR
1911	Bos-A	18	59	7	16	0	0	0	6	7		.271	.368	.271	80	-1	-1	7	2			-2	2	-0.2
1914	Pit-F	117	394	32	92	14	5	1	48	17	46	.234	.276	.302	66	-18	-18	39	9			9	*2/S	-0.6
1915	Pit-F	82	231	24	61	6	5	0	26	8	31	.264	.292	.333	85	-5	-5	26	7			-2	2S/013	-0.5
Total	3	217	684	63	169	20	10	1	80	32	77	.247	.290	.310	74	-24	-23	72	18			6	2/SO13	-1.3

■ BUDDY LEWIS
Lewis, John Kelly b: 8/10/16, Gastonia, N.C.   BL/TR, 6'1", 175 lbs.   Deb: 9/16/35

YEAR	TM/L	G	AB	R	H	2B	3B	HR	RBI	BB	SO	AVG	OBP	SLG	PRO+	BR	/A	RC	SB	CS	SBR	FR	POS	TPR
1935	Was-A	8	28	0	3	0	0	0	2	0	5	.107	.107	.107	-46	-6	-6	0	0	0	0	0	/3	-0.5
1936	Was-A	143	601	100	175	21	13	6	67	47	46	.291	.347	.399	89	-16	-11	83	6	6	-2	5	*3	-0.5
1937	Was-A	156	668	107	210	32	6	10	79	52	44	.314	.367	.425	104	-1	3	105	11	5	0	-19	*3	-1.1
1938	Was-A	151	656	122	194	35	9	12	91	58	35	.296	.354	.431	103	-6	1	101	17	9	-0	-0	*3	0.5
1939	Was-A	140	536	87	171	23	16	10	75	72	27	.319	.402	.478	134	20	27	106	10	9	-2	14	*3	3.2

YEAR	TM/L	G	AB	R	H	2B	3B	HR	RBI	BB	SO	AVG	OBP	SLG	PRO+	BR	/A	RC	SB	CS	SBR	FR	POS	TPR
1940	Was-A	148	600	101	190	38	10	6	63	74	36	.317	.393	.443	124	16	22	109	15	10	-2	-3	*O3	1.0
1941	Was-A	149	569	97	169	29	11	9	72	82	30	.297	.386	.434	122	15	19	99	10	7	-1	1	O3	1.4
1945	Was-A	69	258	42	86	14	7	2	37	37	15	.333	.423	.465	172	20	23	54	1	2	-1	2	O	2.2
1946	Was-A	150	582	82	170	28	13	7	45	59	26	.292	.359	.421	125	13	17	92	5	3	-0	2	*O	1.2
1947	Was-A	140	506	67	132	15	4	6	48	51	27	.261	.330	.342	89	-9	-7	56	6	6	-2	-2	*O	-1.6
1949	Was-A	95	257	25	63	14	4	3	28	41	12	.245	.355	.366	93	-3	-2	36	2	2	-1	-3	O	-0.7
Total	11	1349	5261	830	1563	249	93	71	607	573	303	.297	.368	.420	112	44	85	841	83	59	-11	-4	3O	5.1

■ JOHNNY LEWIS
Lewis, Johnny Joe   b: 8/10/39, Greenville, Ala.   BL/TR, 6'1", 189 lbs.   Deb: 4/14/64   C

YEAR	TM/L	G	AB	R	H	2B	3B	HR	RBI	BB	SO	AVG	OBP	SLG	PRO+	BR	/A	RC	SB	CS	SBR	FR	POS	TPR
1964	StL-N	40	94	10	22	2	2	2	7	13	23	.234	.327	.362	86	-1	-2	11	2	2	-1	2	O	0.0
1965	NY-N	148	477	64	117	15	3	15	45	59	117	.245	.332	.384	105	1	3	61	4	7	-3	-6	*O	-0.9
1966	NY-N	65	166	21	32	6	1	5	20	21	43	.193	.283	.331	72	-7	-6	17	2	0	1	-2	O	-0.8
1967	NY-N	13	34	2	4	1	0	0	2	2	11	.118	.167	.147	-10	-5	-5	1	0	0	0	0	O	-0.4
Total	4	266	771	97	175	24	6	22	74	95	194	.227	.314	.359	90	-11	-9	91	8	9	-3	-4	O	-2.1

■ PHIL LEWIS
Lewis, Philip   b: 10/7/1883, Pittsburgh, Pa.   d: 8/8/59, Port Wentworth, Ga.   BR/TR, 6', 195 lbs.   Deb: 4/14/05

YEAR	TM/L	G	AB	R	H	2B	3B	HR	RBI	BB	SO	AVG	OBP	SLG	PRO+	BR	/A	RC	SB	CS	SBR	FR	POS	TPR
1905	Bro-N	118	433	32	110	9	2	3	33	16		.254	.281	.305	82	-13	-9	44	16			-6	*S	-1.3
1906	Bro-N	136	452	40	110	8	4	0	37	43		.243	.309	.279	93	-7	-3	47	14			-22	*S	-1.9
1907	Bro-N	136	475	52	118	11	1	0	30	23		.248	.283	.276	84	-13	-9	45	16			-20	*S	-2.6
1908	Bro-N	118	415	22	91	5	6	1	30	13		.219	.243	.267	67	-17	-15	29	9			-7	*S	-2.7
Total	4		508	1775	146	429	33	13	4	130	95	.242	.280	.282	82	-49	-36	165	55		-55	S	-8.5

■ BILL LEWIS
Lewis, William Henry "Buddy"   b: 10/15/04, Ripley, Tenn.   d: 10/24/77, Memphis, Tenn.   BR/TR, 5'9", 165 lbs.   Deb: 6/03/33

YEAR	TM/L	G	AB	R	H	2B	3B	HR	RBI	BB	SO	AVG	OBP	SLG	PRO+	BR	/A	RC	SB	CS	SBR	FR	POS	TPR
1933	StL-N	15	35	8	14	1	0	1	8	2	3	.400	.432	.514	161	3	3	8	0			1	/C	0.4
1935	Bos-N	6	4	1	0	0	0	0	0	1	1	.000	.200	.000	-45	-1	-1	0	0			0	/C	0.0
1936	Bos-N	29	62	11	19	2	0	0	3	12	7	.306	.419	.339	113	1	2	10	0			-4	C	0.0
Total	3	50	101	20	33	3	0	1	11	15	11	.327	.414	.386	124	4	4	19	0			-3	/C	0.4

■ JIM LEYRITZ
Leyritz, James Joseph   b: 12/27/63, Lakewood, Ohio   BR/TR, 6', 190 lbs.   Deb: 6/08/90

YEAR	TM/L	G	AB	R	H	2B	3B	HR	RBI	BB	SO	AVG	OBP	SLG	PRO+	BR	/A	RC	SB	CS	SBR	FR	POS	TPR
1990	NY-A	92	303	28	78	13	1	5	25	27	51	.257	.332	.356	92	-3	-3	34	2	3	-1	-18	3OC	-2.1

■ CARLOS LEZCANO
Lezcano, Carlos Manuel (Rubio)   b: 9/30/55, Arecibo, P.R.   BR/TR, 6'2", 185 lbs.   Deb: 4/10/80

YEAR	TM/L	G	AB	R	H	2B	3B	HR	RBI	BB	SO	AVG	OBP	SLG	PRO+	BR	/A	RC	SB	CS	SBR	FR	POS	TPR
1980	Chi-N	42	88	15	18	4	1	3	12	11	29	.205	.300	.375	81	-2	-2	9	1	2	-1	4	O	0.0
1981	Chi-N	7	14	1	1	0	0	0	2	0	4	.071	.071	.071	-57	-3	-3	0	0	0	0	0	/O	-0.2
Total	2	49	102	16	19	4	1	3	14	11	33	.186	.272	.333	64	-4	-5	9	1	2	-1	4	/O	-0.2

■ SIXTO LEZCANO
Lezcano, Sixto Joaquin (Curras)   b: 11/28/53, Arecibo, P.R.   BR/TR, 5'10", 165 lbs.   Deb: 9/10/74

YEAR	TM/L	G	AB	R	H	2B	3B	HR	RBI	BB	SO	AVG	OBP	SLG	PRO+	BR	/A	RC	SB	CS	SBR	FR	POS	TPR
1974	Mil-A	15	54	5	13	2	0	2	9	4	9	.241	.293	.389	95	-1	-0	6	1	1	-0	1	O	0.0
1975	Mil-A	134	429	55	106	19	3	11	43	46	93	.247	.326	.382	99	-0	-1	51	5	5	-2	-17	*O/D	-2.2
1976	Mil-A	145	513	53	146	19	5	7	56	51	112	.285	.352	.382	117	10	11	70	14	10	-2	7	*O/D	1.5
1977	Mil-A	109	400	50	109	21	4	21	49	52	78	.273	.359	.503	132	17	18	72	6	5	-1	8	*O	2.0
1978	Mil-A	132	442	62	129	21	4	15	61	64	83	.292	.383	.459	135	22	22	81	3	3	-1	6	*O/D	2.4
1979	Mil-A	138	473	84	152	29	3	28	101	77	74	.321	.420	.573	165	45	45	115	4	3	-1	0	*O	3.7
1980	Mil-A	112	411	51	94	19	3	18	55	39	75	.229	.300	.421	98	-4	-2	53	1	1	-0	-1	*O/D	-0.5
1981	StL-N	72	214	26	57	8	2	5	28	40	40	.266	.382	.393	117	7	6	33	0	1	-1	-7	O	-0.3
1982	SD-N	138	470	73	136	26	6	16	84	78	69	.289	.393	.472	149	28	31	90	2	1	0	10	*O	4.1
1983	SD-N	97	317	41	74	11	2	8	49	47	66	.233	.334	.356	95	-3	-2	39	0	0	0	1	O	-0.1
	*Phi-N	18	39	8	11	1	0	0	7	5	9	.282	.364	.308	89	-0	-0	5	1	0	0	1	O	0.0
	Yr	115	356	49	85	12	2	8	56	52	75	.239	.337	.351	94	-3	-2	45	1	0	0	2		-0.1
1984	Phi-N	109	256	36	71	6	2	14	40	38	43	.277	.371	.480	135	13	13	44	0	1	-1	-4	O	0.5
1985	Pit-N	72	116	16	24	2	0	3	9	35	17	.207	.395	.302	98	2	2	16	0	0	0	-1	O	0.0
Total	12	1291	4134	560	1122	184	34	148	591	576	768	.271	.363	.440	125	136	142	675	37	31	-8	4	*O/D	11.1

■ STEVE LIBBY
Libby, Stephen Augustus   b: 12/8/1853, Scarborough, Me.   6'1.5", 168 lbs.   Deb: 5/10/1879

YEAR	TM/L	G	AB	R	H	2B	3B	HR	RBI	BB	SO	AVG	OBP	SLG	PRO+	BR	/A	RC	SB	CS	SBR	FR	POS	TPR
1879	Buf-N	1	2	0	0	0	0	0	0	0	1	.000	.000	.000	-98	-0	-0	0				0	/1	0.0

■ AL LIBKE
Libke, Albert Walter   b: 9/12/18, Tacoma, Wash.   BL/TR, 6'4", 215 lbs.   Deb: 4/19/45

YEAR	TM/L	G	AB	R	H	2B	3B	HR	RBI	BB	SO	AVG	OBP	SLG	PRO+	BR	/A	RC	SB	CS	SBR	FR	POS	TPR
1945	Cin-N	130	449	41	127	23	5	4	53	34	62	.283	.336	.383	102	-1	0	59	6			0	*O/P1	-0.3
1946	Cin-N	124	431	32	109	22	1	5	42	43	50	.253	.322	.343	92	-7	-5	46	0			-8	*O/P	-1.5
Total	2	254	880	73	236	45	6	9	95	77	112	.268	.329	.364	97	-7	-4	105	6			-8	O/P1	-1.8

■ FRANKIE LIBRAN
Libran, Francisco (Rosas)   b: 5/6/48, Mayaguez, P.R.   BR/TR, 6', 168 lbs.   Deb: 9/03/69

YEAR	TM/L	G	AB	R	H	2B	3B	HR	RBI	BB	SO	AVG	OBP	SLG	PRO+	BR	/A	RC	SB	CS	SBR	FR	POS	TPR
1969	SD-N	10	10	1	1	1	0	0	1	1	2	.100	.182	.200	7	-1	-1	0	0	0	0	1	/S	0.1

■ JOHN LICKERT
Lickert, John Wilbur   b: 4/4/60, Pittsburgh, Pa.   BR/TR, 5'11", 175 lbs.   Deb: 9/19/81

YEAR	TM/L	G	AB	R	H	2B	3B	HR	RBI	BB	SO	AVG	OBP	SLG	PRO+	BR	/A	RC	SB	CS	SBR	FR	POS	TPR
1981	Bos-A	1	0	0	0	0	0	0	0	0	0	—	—	—	—	0	0	0	0	0	0	0	/C	0.0

■ DAVE LIDDELL
Liddell, David Alexander   b: 6/15/66, Los Angeles, Cal.   BR/TR, 6', 190 lbs.   Deb: 6/03/90

YEAR	TM/L	G	AB	R	H	2B	3B	HR	RBI	BB	SO	AVG	OBP	SLG	PRO+	BR	/A	RC	SB	CS	SBR	FR	POS	TPR
1990	NY-N	1	1	1	1	0	0	0	0	0	0	1.000	1.000	1.000	463	0	0	1	0	0	0	-0	/C	0.0

■ FRED LIESE
Liese, Frederick Richard   b: 10/7/1885, Wisconsin   d: 6/30/67, Los Angeles, Cal.   TL ,   Deb: 4/14/10

YEAR	TM/L	G	AB	R	H	2B	3B	HR	RBI	BB	SO	AVG	OBP	SLG	PRO+	BR	/A	RC	SB	CS	SBR	FR	POS	TPR
1910	Bos-N	5	4	0	0	0	0	0	0	1	2	.000	.200	.000	-39	-1	-1	0	0			0	H	0.0

■ GENE LILLARD
Lillard, Robert Eugene   b: 11/12/13, Santa Barbara, Cal   BR/TR, 5'10.5", 178 lbs.   Deb: 5/08/36

YEAR	TM/L	G	AB	R	H	2B	3B	HR	RBI	BB	SO	AVG	OBP	SLG	PRO+	BR	/A	RC	SB	CS	SBR	FR	POS	TPR
1936	Chi-N	19	34	6	7	1	0	0	2	3	8	.206	.270	.235	36	-3	-3	2	0			-1	/S3	-0.2
1939	Chi-N	23	10	3	1	0	0	0	0	6	3	.100	.438	.100	51	-0	-0	1	0			0	P	0.0
1940	StL-N	2	0	0	0	0	0	0	0	0	0	—	—	—	—	0	0	0	0			0	/P	0.0
Total	3	44	44	9	8	1	0	0	2	9	11	.182	.321	.205	43	-3	-3	3	0			-1	/PS3	-0.2

■ BILL LILLARD
Lillard, William Beverly   b: 1/10/18, Goleta, Cal.   BR/TR, 5'10", 170 lbs.   Deb: 9/11/39

YEAR	TM/L	G	AB	R	H	2B	3B	HR	RBI	BB	SO	AVG	OBP	SLG	PRO+	BR	/A	RC	SB	CS	SBR	FR	POS	TPR
1939	Phi-A	7	19	4	6	1	0	0	1	3	1	.316	.409	.368	102	0	0	3	0	0	0	2	/S	0.3
1940	Phi-A	73	206	26	49	8	2	1	21	28	28	.238	.332	.311	69	-9	-9	23	0	1	-1	-18	S/2	-2.0
Total	2	80	225	30	55	9	2	1	22	31	29	.244	.339	.316	72	-9	-8	27	0	1	-1	-16	/S2	-1.7

■ JIM LILLIE
Lillie, James J. "Grasshopper"   b: 1862, New Haven, Conn.   d: 11/9/1890, Kansas City, Mo.   Deb: 5/17/1883

YEAR	TM/L	G	AB	R	H	2B	3B	HR	RBI	BB	SO	AVG	OBP	SLG	PRO+	BR	/A	RC	SB	CS	SBR	FR	POS	TPR
1883	Buf-N	50	201	25	47	7	3	1	29	1	31	.234	.238	.313	64	-8	-9	15				-7	O/PCS32	-1.2
1884	Buf-N	114	471	68	105	12	5	3	53	5	71	.223	.231	.289	61	-20	-22	32				15	*O/P	-0.6
1885	Buf-N	112	430	49	107	13	3	2	30	6	39	.249	.259	.307	80	-9	-11	35				-0	*O/S1	-1.3
1886	KC-N	114	416	37	73	9	0	0	22	11	80	.175	.197	.197	19	-39	-43	19	13			10	*O/P	-2.8
Total	4	390	1518	179	332	41	11	6	134	23	221	.219	.230	.272	54	-77	-85	102	13			17	O/PSC123	-5.9

■ BOB LILLIS
Lillis, Robert Perry   b: 6/2/30, Altadena, Cal.   BR/TR, 5'11", 160 lbs.   Deb: 8/30/58   MC

YEAR	TM/L	G	AB	R	H	2B	3B	HR	RBI	BB	SO	AVG	OBP	SLG	PRO+	BR	/A	RC	SB	CS	SBR	FR	POS	TPR
1958	LA-N	20	69	10	27	3	1	1	5	4	2	.391	.432	.507	143	5	5	14	1	2	-1	-3	S	0.2
1959	LA-N	30	48	7	11	2	0	0	2	3	4	.229	.275	.271	43	-4	-4	4	0	0	0	8	S	0.5
1960	LA-N	48	60	6	16	4	0	0	6	2	6	.267	.290	.333	66	-3	-3	6	2	0	1	15	S3/2	1.3
1961	LA-N	19	9	0	1	0	0	0	1	1	1	.111	.200	.111	-13	-1	-2	0	0	0	0	1	3/2S	0.0

YEAR	TM/L	G	AB	R	H	2B	3B	HR	RBI	BB	SO	AVG	OBP	SLG	PRO+	BR	/A	RC	SB	CS	SBR	FR	POS	TPR
	StL-N	86	230	24	50	4	0	0	21	7	13	.217	.247	.235	26	-23	-26	12	3	3	-1	2	S2	-1.6
	Yr	105	239	24	51	4	0	0	22	8	14	.213	.245	.230	25	-25	-28	12	3	3	-1	3		-1.6
1962	Hou-N	129	457	38	114	12	4	1	30	28	23	.249	.293	.300	64	-26	-22	40	7	3	0	9	S2/3	0.0
1963	Hou-N	147	469	31	93	13	1	1	19	15	35	.198	.230	.237	37	-39	-36	24	3	4	-2	-5	*S2/3	-3.2
1964	Hou-N	109	332	31	89	11	2	0	17	11	10	.268	.292	.313	75	-13	-11	27	4	9	-4	1	2S3	-0.7
1965	Hou-N	124	408	34	90	12	1	0	20	20	10	.221	.267	.255	51	-28	-24	27	2	2	-1	-12	*S/32	-2.7
1966	Hou-N	68	164	14	38	6	0	0	11	7	4	.232	.263	.268	52	-11	-10	10	1	1	-0	-9	2S/3	-1.6
1967	Hou-N	37	82	3	20	1	0	0	5	1	8	.244	.253	.256	48	-6	-5	4	0	1	-1	3	S/23	-1.6
Total	10	817	2328	198	549	68	9	3	137	99	116	.236	.271	.277	54	-149	-139	167	23	25	-8	9	S2/3	-7.8

■ LOU LIMMER   Limmer, Louis b: 3/10/25, New York, N.Y. BL/TL, 6'2", 190 lbs. Deb: 4/22/51

YEAR	TM/L	G	AB	R	H	2B	3B	HR	RBI	BB	SO	AVG	OBP	SLG	PRO+	BR	/A	RC	SB	CS	SBR	FR	POS	TPR
1951	Phi-A	94	214	25	34	9	1	5	30	28	40	.159	.256	.280	44	-17	-18	17	1	0	0	2	1	-1.5
1954	Phi-A	115	316	41	73	10	3	14	32	35	37	.231	.308	.415	96	-3	-3	40	2	3	-1	2	1	-0.3
Total	2	209	530	66	107	19	4	19	62	63	77	.202	.287	.360	75	-20	-21	57	3	3	-1	4	1	-1.8

■ RUFINO LINARES   Linares, Rufino (b: Rufino De La Cruz (Linares)) b: 2/28/51, San Pedro De Macoris, D.R. BR/TR, 6', 170 lbs. Deb: 4/10/81

YEAR	TM/L	G	AB	R	H	2B	3B	HR	RBI	BB	SO	AVG	OBP	SLG	PRO+	BR	/A	RC	SB	CS	SBR	FR	POS	TPR
1981	Atl-N	78	253	27	67	9	2	5	25	9	28	.265	.290	.375	85	-5	-6	23	8	4	0	1	O	-0.6
1982	Atl-N	77	191	28	57	7	1	2	17	7	29	.298	.327	.377	92	-1	-2	20	5	2	0	2	O	0.0
1984	Atl-N	34	58	4	12	3	0	1	10	6	12	.207	.281	.310	62	-3	-3	5	0	0	0	0	O	-0.2
1985	Cal-A	18	43	7	11	2	0	3	11	2	5	.256	.289	.512	114	1	1	6	2	0	1	0	D/O	0.1
Total	4	207	545	66	147	21	3	11	63	24	74	.270	.302	.380	88	-8	-10	55	15	6	1	3	O/D	-0.7

■ CARL LIND   Lind, Henry Carl "Hooks" b: 9/19/03, New Orleans, La. d: 8/2/46, New York, N.Y. BR/TR, 6', 160 lbs. Deb: 9/14/27

YEAR	TM/L	G	AB	R	H	2B	3B	HR	RBI	BB	SO	AVG	OBP	SLG	PRO+	BR	/A	RC	SB	CS	SBR	FR	POS	TPR
1927	Cle-A	12	37	2	5	0	0	0	1	5	7	.135	.256	.135	4	-5	-5	2	1	0	0	2	2/S	-0.1
1928	Cle-A	154	650	102	191	42	4	1	54	36	48	.294	.331	.375	84	-15	-15	80	8	7	-2	4	*2	-0.4
1929	Cle-A	66	225	19	54	8	1	0	13	13	17	.240	.282	.284	44	-18	-19	18	0	2	-1	16	2/3	-0.2
1930	Cle-A	24	69	8	17	3	0	0	6	3	7	.246	.278	.290	43	-6	-6	5	0	1	-1	11	S/2	0.5
Total	4	256	981	131	267	53	5	1	74	57	79	.272	.313	.339	69	-44	-46	106	9	10	-3	33	2/S3	-0.2

■ JACK LIND   Lind, Jackson Hugh b: 6/8/46, Denver, Col. BB/TR, 6', 170 lbs. Deb: 9/10/74

YEAR	TM/L	G	AB	R	H	2B	3B	HR	RBI	BB	SO	AVG	OBP	SLG	PRO+	BR	/A	RC	SB	CS	SBR	FR	POS	TPR
1974	Mil-A	9	17	4	4	1	0	0	1	3	2	.235	.350	.353	103	0	0	2	0	0	0	-0	/S2	0.1
1975	Mil-A	17	20	1	1	0	0	0	0	2	12	.050	.136	.050	-45	-4	-4	0	1	0	0	5	/S31	0.2
Total	2	26	37	5	5	2	0	0	1	5	14	.135	.238	.189	23	-4	-4	2	1	0	0	5	/S321	0.3

■ JOSE LIND   Lind, Jose (Salgado) b: 5/1/64, Toabaja, P.R. BR/TR, 5'11", 155 lbs. Deb: 8/28/87

YEAR	TM/L	G	AB	R	H	2B	3B	HR	RBI	BB	SO	AVG	OBP	SLG	PRO+	BR	/A	RC	SB	CS	SBR	FR	POS	TPR
1987	Pit-N	35	143	21	46	8	4	0	11	8	12	.322	.358	.434	108	2	2	21	2	1	0	6	2	0.8
1988	Pit-N	154	611	82	160	24	4	2	49	42	75	.262	.309	.324	83	-14	-13	63	15	4	2	3	*2	-0.3
1989	Pit-N	153	578	52	134	21	3	2	48	39	64	.232	.283	.289	66	-27	-25	49	15	1	4	-14	*2	-3.5
1990	*Pit-N	152	514	46	134	28	5	1	48	35	52	.261	.309	.340	82	-15	-13	51	8	0	2	17	*2	0.8
Total	4	494	1846	201	474	81	16	5	156	124	203	.257	.305	.326	80	-55	-49	183	40	6	8	12	2	-2.2

■ EM LINDBECK   Lindbeck, Emerit Desmond b: 8/27/35, Kewanee, Ill. BL/TR, 6', 185 lbs. Deb: 4/22/60

YEAR	TM/L	G	AB	R	H	2B	3B	HR	RBI	BB	SO	AVG	OBP	SLG	PRO+	BR	/A	RC	SB	CS	SBR	FR	POS	TPR
1960	Det-A	2	1	0	0	0	0	0	0	0	1	.000	.500	.000	46	0	0	0	0	0	0	0	H	0.0

■ JOHNNY LINDELL   Lindell, John Harlan b: 8/30/16, Greeley, Colo. d: 8/27/85, Newport Beach, Cal. BR/TR, 6'4.5", 217 lbs. Deb: 4/18/41

YEAR	TM/L	G	AB	R	H	2B	3B	HR	RBI	BB	SO	AVG	OBP	SLG	PRO+	BR	/A	RC	SB	CS	SBR	FR	POS	TPR
1941	NY-A	1	1	0	0	0	0	0	0	0	0	.000	.000	.000	-99	-0	-0	0	0	0	0	0	H	0.0
1942	NY-A	27	24	1	6	1	0	0	4	0	5	.250	.250	.292	53	-2	-2	2	0	0	0	-0	P	0.0
1943	*NY-A	122	441	53	108	17	12	4	51	51	55	.245	.329	.365	102	1	1	53	2	5	-2	0	*O	-0.4
1944	NY-A	149	594	91	178	33	16	18	103	44	56	.300	.351	.500	137	29	26	102	5	4	-1	7	*O	2.9
1945	NY-A	41	159	26	45	6	3	1	20	17	10	.283	.363	.377	110	3	2	23	2	1	0	1	O	0.2
1946	NY-A	102	332	41	86	10	5	10	40	32	47	.259	.328	.410	104	1	1	44	4	1	1	1	O1	-0.1
1947	*NY-A	127	476	66	131	18	7	11	67	32	70	.275	.322	.412	104	-0	-0	61	1	2	-1	-5	*O	-1.0
1948	NY-A	88	309	58	98	17	2	13	55	35	50	.317	.387	.511	139	15	16	62	0	0	0	2	O	1.4
1949	*NY-A	78	211	33	51	10	0	6	27	35	27	.242	.350	.374	92	-3	-3	29	3	0	1	-2	O	-0.4
1950	NY-A	7	21	2	4	0	0	0	2	4	2	.190	.320	.190	34	-2	-1	1	0	0	0	-2	/O	-0.3
	StL-N	36	113	16	21	5	2	5	16	15	24	.186	.287	.398	74	-4	-5	12	0	0	0	-2	O	-0.7
1953	Pit-N	58	91	11	26	6	1	4	15	16	15	.286	.404	.505	136	5	5	18	0	0	0	2	P/1	1.0
	Phi-N	11	18	3	7	1	0	0	2	6	2	.389	.542	.444	162	2	2	5	0	0	0	-1	/PO	0.2
	Yr	69	109	14	33	7	1	4	17	22	17	.303	.429	.495	141	7	8	24	0	0	0	1		1.2
1954	Phi-N	7	5	0	1	0	0	0	2	3	3	.200	.429	.200	70	-0	-0	1	0	0	0	0	H	0.0
Total	12	854	2795	401	762	124	48	72	404	289	366	.273	.344	.429	113	47	44	412	17	13		-0	O/P1	2.8

■ JIM LINDEMAN   Lindeman, James William b: 1/10/62, Evanston, Ill. BR/TR, 6'1", 200 lbs. Deb: 9/03/86

YEAR	TM/L	G	AB	R	H	2B	3B	HR	RBI	BB	SO	AVG	OBP	SLG	PRO+	BR	/A	RC	SB	CS	SBR	FR	POS	TPR
1986	StL-N	19	55	7	14	1	0	0	6	2	10	.255	.281	.327	68	-3	-2	4	1	1	-0	-1	1/3O	-0.3
1987	*StL-N	75	207	20	43	13	0	8	28	11	56	.208	.258	.386	67	-10	-11	20	3	1	0	1	O1	-1.2
1988	StL-N	17	43	3	9	1	0	2	7	2	9	.209	.244	.372	74	-2	-2	4	0	0	0	-1	O/1	-0.2
1989	StL-N	73	45	8	5	1	0	0	2	3	18	.111	.167	.133	-13	-7	-7	1	0	0	0	2	1/O	-0.8
1990	Det-A	12	32	5	7	1	0	2	8	2	13	.219	.265	.438	94	-0	-0	4	0	0	0	-0	D/1O	0.0
Total	5	196	382	43	78	17	0	13	51	20	106	.204	.249	.351	61	-22	-22	33	4	2	0	1	/1OD3	-2.5

■ BOB LINDEMANN   Lindemann, John Frederick Mann b: 6/5/1881, Philadelphia, Pa. d: 12/19/51, Williamsport, Pa. BB/TR, 6', 175 lbs. Deb: 8/28/01

YEAR	TM/L	G	AB	R	H	2B	3B	HR	RBI	BB	SO	AVG	OBP	SLG	PRO+	BR	/A	RC	SB	CS	SBR	FR	POS	TPR
1901	Phi-A	3	9	0	1	0	0	0	0	0		.111	.111	.111	-36	-2	-2	0	0			-0	/O	-0.1

■ WALT LINDEN   Linden, Walter Charles b: 3/27/24, Chicago, Ill. BR/TR, 6'1", 190 lbs. Deb: 4/30/50

YEAR	TM/L	G	AB	R	H	2B	3B	HR	RBI	BB	SO	AVG	OBP	SLG	PRO+	BR	/A	RC	SB	CS	SBR	FR	POS	TPR
1950	Bos-N	3	5	0	2	1	0	0	1	0	1	.400	.500	.600	201	1	1	2	0			-1	/C	0.0

■ CHRIS LINDSAY   Lindsay, Christian Haller "Pinky" or "The Crab" b: 7/24/1878, Baker's Yard, Moon Township, Beaver County, Pa d: 1/25/41, Cleveland, Ohio BR/TR, 6', 190 lbs. Deb: 7/06/05

YEAR	TM/L	G	AB	R	H	2B	3B	HR	RBI	BB	SO	AVG	OBP	SLG	PRO+	BR	/A	RC	SB	CS	SBR	FR	POS	TPR
1905	Det-A	88	329	38	88	14	1	0	31	18		.267	.305	.316	99	-0	-1	37	10			-0	1	-0.2
1906	Det-A	141	499	59	112	16	2	0	33	45		.224	.289	.265	73	-13	-14	48	18			-7	*12/3	-2.8
Total	2	229	828	97	200	30	3	0	64	63		.242	.295	.285	83	-13	-15	85	28			-8	1/23	-3.0

■ BILL LINDSAY   Lindsay, William Gibbons b: 2/24/1881, Madison, N.C. d: 7/14/63, Greensboro, N.C. BL/TR, 5'10.5", 165 lbs. Deb: 6/21/11

YEAR	TM/L	G	AB	R	H	2B	3B	HR	RBI	BB	SO	AVG	OBP	SLG	PRO+	BR	/A	RC	SB	CS	SBR	FR	POS	TPR
1911	Cle-A	19	66	6	16	2	0	0	5	1		.242	.265	.273	49	-5	-5	5	2			2	3/2	-0.1

■ BILL LINDSEY   Lindsey, William Donald b: 4/12/60, Staten Island, N.Y. BR/TR, 6'3", 195 lbs. Deb: 7/18/87

YEAR	TM/L	G	AB	R	H	2B	3B	HR	RBI	BB	SO	AVG	OBP	SLG	PRO+	BR	/A	RC	SB	CS	SBR	FR	POS	TPR
1987	Chi-A	9	16	2	3	0	0	0	1	0	3	.188	.188	.188	-0	-2	-2	0	0	0	0	2	/C	0.0

■ CHUCK LINDSTROM   Lindstrom, Charles William b: 9/7/36, Chicago, Ill. BR/TR, 5'11", 175 lbs. Deb: 9/28/58

YEAR	TM/L	G	AB	R	H	2B	3B	HR	RBI	BB	SO	AVG	OBP	SLG	PRO+	BR	/A	RC	SB	CS	SBR	FR	POS	TPR
1958	Chi-A	1	1	1	1	0	1	0	1	1	0	1.000	1.000	3.000	975	1	1	3	0	0	0	0	/C	0.1

■ FREDDY LINDSTROM   Lindstrom, Frederick Charles (b: Frederick Anthony Lindstrom) b: 11/21/05, Chicago, Ill. d: 10/4/81, Chicago, Ill. BR/TR, 5'11", 170 lbs. Deb: 4/15/24 H

YEAR	TM/L	G	AB	R	H	2B	3B	HR	RBI	BB	SO	AVG	OBP	SLG	PRO+	BR	/A	RC	SB	CS	SBR	FR	POS	TPR
1924	NY-N	52	79	19	20	3	1	0	4	6	10	.253	.314	.316	71	-3	-3	8	3	1	0	7	23	0.3
1925	NY-N	104	356	43	102	15	12	4	33	22	20	.287	.332	.430	97	-5	-3	48	5	9	-4	-1	3/2S	0.0
1926	NY-N	140	543	90	164	19	9	9	76	39	21	.302	.351	.420	108	4	5	78	11			-3	*3/O	0.4
1927	NY-N	138	562	107	172	36	8	7	58	40	40	.306	.354	.436	111	8	8	85	10			1	3O	1.1

YEAR	TM/L	G	AB	R	H	2B	3B	HR	RBI	BB	SO	AVG	OBP	SLG	PRO+	BR	/A	RC	SB	CS	SBR	FR	POS	TPR
1928	NY-N	153	646	99	**231**	39	9	14	107	25	21	.358	.383	.511	131	28	27	120	15			15	*3	4.3
1929	NY-N	130	549	99	175	23	6	15	91	30	28	.319	.354	.464	101	-1	-0	87	10			7	*3	1.5
1930	NY-N	148	609	127	231	39	7	22	106	48	33	.379	.425	.575	142	38	40	143	15			6	*3	4.2
1931	NY-N	78	303	38	91	12	6	5	36	26	12	.300	.356	.429	113	4	5	47	5			-7	O/2	-0.5
1932	NY-N	144	595	83	161	26	5	15	92	27	28	.271	.303	.407	91	-10	-9	74	6			-6	*O3	-2.1
1933	Pit-N	138	538	70	167	39	10	5	55	33	22	.310	.350	.448	127	17	17	86	1			8	*O	1.8
1934	Pit-N	97	383	59	111	24	4	4	49	23	21	.290	.333	.405	94	-2	-3	51	1			-2	O	-0.9
1935	Chi-N	90	342	49	94	22	4	3	62	10	13	.275	.297	.389	82	-9	-9	37	1			-0	O3	-1.0
1936	Bro-N	26	106	12	28	4	0	0	10	5	7	.264	.297	.302	61	-6	-6	9	1			0	O	-0.6
Total	13	1438	5611	895	1747	301	81	103	779	334	276	.311	.351	.449	110	64	70	873	84	10		25	3O/2S	8.5

■ **CARL LINHART**   Linhart, Carl James   b: 12/14/29, Zborov, Czech.   BL/TR, 5'11", 184 lbs.   Deb: 8/02/52

YEAR	TM/L	G	AB	R	H	2B	3B	HR	RBI	BB	SO	AVG	OBP	SLG	PRO+	BR	/A	RC	SB	CS	SBR	FR	POS	TPR
1952	Det-A	3	2	0	0	0	0	0	0	0	0	.000	.000	.000	-99	-1	-1	0	0	0	0	0	H	0.0

■ **BOB LINTON**   Linton, Claud Clarence   b: 4/18/03, Emerson, Ark.   d: 4/3/80, Destin, Fla.   BL/TR, 6', 185 lbs.   Deb: 4/26/29

YEAR	TM/L	G	AB	R	H	2B	3B	HR	RBI	BB	SO	AVG	OBP	SLG	PRO+	BR	/A	RC	SB	CS	SBR	FR	POS	TPR
1929	Pit-N	17	18	0	2	0	0	0	1	1	2	.111	.158	.111	-31	-4	-4	0	0			0	/C	-0.2

■ **LARRY LINTZ**   Lintz, Larry   b: 10/10/49, Martinez, Cal.   BB/TR, 5'9", 150 lbs.   Deb: 7/14/73

YEAR	TM/L	G	AB	R	H	2B	3B	HR	RBI	BB	SO	AVG	OBP	SLG	PRO+	BR	/A	RC	SB	CS	SBR	FR	POS	TPR
1973	Mon-N	52	116	20	29	1	0	0	3	17	18	.250	.351	.259	69	-4	-4	14	12	4	1	2	2S	0.2
1974	Mon-N	113	319	60	76	10	1	0	20	44	50	.238	.334	.276	68	-10	-13	40	50	7	11	-13	2S/3	-0.7
1975	Mon-N	46	132	18	26	0	0	0	3	23	18	.197	.316	.197	43	-9	-10	10	17	9	-0	-6	2/S	-1.4
	StL-N	27	18	6	5	1	0	0	1	3	2	.278	.381	.333	96	0	0	3	4	0	1	9	/2S	1.1
	Yr	73	150	24	31	1	0	0	4	26	20	.207	.324	.213	49	-9	-10	13	21	9	1	3		-0.3
1976	Oak-A	68	1	21	0	0	0	0	0	2	0	.000	.667	.000	111	0	0	-39	31	11	3	2	D/2O	0.6
1977	Oak-A	41	30	11	4	1	0	0	0	8	13	.133	.333	.167	42	-2	-2	3	13	5	1	11	2/S3D	1.2
1978	Cle-A	3	0	1	0	0	0	0	0	0	0	—	—	—	—	0	0	0	1	2	-1	0	R	0.0
Total	6	350	616	137	140	13	1	0	27	97	101	.227	.336	.252	63	-24	-28	32	128	38	16	5	2/SD03	1.0

■ **PHIL LINZ**   Linz, Philip Francis   b: 6/4/39, Baltimore, Md.   BR/TR, 6'1", 180 lbs.   Deb: 4/13/62

YEAR	TM/L	G	AB	R	H	2B	3B	HR	RBI	BB	SO	AVG	OBP	SLG	PRO+	BR	/A	RC	SB	CS	SBR	FR	POS	TPR
1962	NY-A	71	129	28	37	8	0	1	14	6	17	.287	.319	.372	88	-3	-2	15	6	2	1	-2	S/32O	-0.1
1963	*NY-A	72	186	22	50	9	0	2	12	15	18	.269	.330	.349	91	-2	-2	19	1	6	-3	2	S3O/2	-0.1
1964	*NY-A	112	368	63	92	21	3	5	25	43	61	.250	.332	.364	92	-3	-3	45	3	4	-2	13	S3/2O	0.9
1965	NY-A	99	285	37	59	12	1	2	16	30	33	.207	.283	.277	60	-15	-15	24	2	1	0	10	S3O2	0.0
1966	Phi-N	40	70	4	14	3	0	0	6	2	14	.200	.222	.243	29	-7	-7	3	0	0	0	1	3/S2	-0.5
1967	Phi-N	23	18	4	4	2	0	1	5	2	1	.222	.300	.500	124	0	0	2	0	0	0	-1	/S3	0.0
	NY-N	24	58	8	12	2	0	0	1	4	10	.207	.270	.241	48	-4	-4	4	0	0	0	-2	2/S3O	-0.4
	Yr	47	76	12	16	4	0	1	6	6	11	.211	.277	.303	66	-3	-3	6	0	0	0	-3		-0.4
1968	NY-N	78	258	19	54	7	0	0	17	10	41	.209	.244	.236	45	-17	-17	14	1	0	0	-12	2	-2.8
Total	7	519	1372	185	322	64	4	11	96	112	195	.235	.296	.311	72	-49	-49	126	13	13	-4	9	S2/3O	-3.0

■ **JOHNNY LIPON**   Lipon, John Joseph "Skids"   b: 11/10/22, Martin's Ferry, O.   BR/TR, 6', 175 lbs.   Deb: 8/16/42   MC

YEAR	TM/L	G	AB	R	H	2B	3B	HR	RBI	BB	SO	AVG	OBP	SLG	PRO+	BR	/A	RC	SB	CS	SBR	FR	POS	TPR
1942	Det-A	34	131	5	25	2	0	0	9	7	7	.191	.232	.206	22	-13	-15	6	1	3	-2	7	S	-0.6
1946	Det-A	14	20	4	6	0	0	0	1	5	3	.300	.440	.300	103	1	1	3	0	0	0	3	/S3	0.4
1948	Det-A	121	458	65	133	18	8	5	52	68	22	.290	.384	.397	105	7	5	75	4	4	-1	-11	*S/23	-0.6
1949	Det-A	127	439	57	110	14	6	3	59	75	24	.251	.362	.330	84	-8	-8	55	2	4	-2	4	*S	-0.5
1950	Det-A	147	601	104	176	27	6	2	63	81	26	.293	.378	.368	89	-5	-8	87	9	6	-1	9	*S	0.6
1951	Det-A	129	487	56	129	15	1	0	38	49	27	.265	.335	.300	72	-17	-18	52	7	6	-2	-13	*S	-2.3
1952	Det-A	39	136	17	30	4	2	0	12	16	6	.221	.303	.279	62	-7	-7	12	3	1	0	-2	S	-0.6
	Bos-A	79	234	25	48	8	1	0	18	32	20	.205	.301	.248	50	-14	-16	20	1	1	-0	14	S/3	0.2
	Yr	118	370	42	78	12	3	0	30	48	26	.211	.301	.259	54	-21	-23	33	4	2	0	12		-0.4
1953	Bos-A	60	145	18	31	7	0	0	13	14	16	.214	.283	.262	46	-10	-11	11	1	0	0	4	S	-0.2
	StL-A	7	9	0	2	0	0	0	1	0	1	.222	.222	.222	20	-1	-1	0	0	0	0	-1	/32	-0.1
	Yr	67	154	18	33	7	0	0	14	14	17	.214	.280	.260	44	-11	-12	12	1	0	0	3		-0.3
1954	Cin-N	1	1	0	0	0	0	0	0	0	0	.000	.000	.000	-97	-0	-0	0	0	0	0	0	H	0.0
Total	9	758	2661	351	690	95	24	10	266	347	152	.259	.346	.324	77	-69	-79	323	28	25	-7	13	S/32	-3.7

■ **NIG LIPSCOMB**   Lipscomb, Gerard   b: 2/24/11, Rutherfordton, N.C   d: 2/27/78, Huntersville, N.C.   BR/TR, 6', 175 lbs.   Deb: 4/23/37

YEAR	TM/L	G	AB	R	H	2B	3B	HR	RBI	BB	SO	AVG	OBP	SLG	PRO+	BR	/A	RC	SB	CS	SBR	FR	POS	TPR
1937	StL-A	36	96	11	31	9	1	0	8	11	10	.323	.398	.438	110	2	2	17	0	0	0	2	2/P3	0.6

■ **BOB LIPSKI**   Lipski, Robert Peter   b: 7/7/38, Scranton, Pa.   BL/TR, 6'1", 180 lbs.   Deb: 4/28/63

YEAR	TM/L	G	AB	R	H	2B	3B	HR	RBI	BB	SO	AVG	OBP	SLG	PRO+	BR	/A	RC	SB	CS	SBR	FR	POS	TPR
1963	Cle-A	2	1	0	0	0	0	0	0	0	1	.000	.000	.000	-99	-0	-0	0	0	0	0	0	/C	0.0

■ **NELSON LIRIANO**   Liriano, Nelson Arturo (Bonilla)   b: 6/3/64, Santo Domingo, D.R.   BB/TR, 5'10", 165 lbs.   Deb: 8/25/87

YEAR	TM/L	G	AB	R	H	2B	3B	HR	RBI	BB	SO	AVG	OBP	SLG	PRO+	BR	/A	RC	SB	CS	SBR	FR	POS	TPR
1987	Tor-A	37	158	29	38	6	2	1	10	16	22	.241	.310	.342	71	-6	-7	18	13	2	3	3	2	0.2
1988	Tor-A	99	276	36	73	6	2	3	23	11	40	.264	.298	.333	76	-9	-9	27	12	5	1	-13	2D/3	-1.6
1989	*Tor-A	132	418	51	110	26	3	5	53	43	51	.263	.335	.376	102	0	1	53	16	7	1	-18	*2/D	-1.4
1990	Tor-A	50	170	16	36	7	2	1	15	16	20	.212	.283	.294	63	-9	-8	13	3	5	-2	-12	2	-2.0
	Min-A	53	185	30	47	5	7	0	13	22	24	.254	.333	.357	87	-1	-3	23	5	2	0	-15	2/SD	-1.5
	Yr	103	355	46	83	12	9	1	28	38	44	.234	.310	.327	76	-10	-11	36	8	7	-2	-27		-3.5
Total	4	371	1207	162	304	50	16	11	114	108	157	.252	.316	.347	84	-25	-26	135	49	21	2	-56	2/DS3	-6.3

■ **JOE LIS**   Lis, Joseph Anthony   b: 8/15/46, Somerville, N.J.   BR/TR, 6', 175 lbs.   Deb: 9/05/70

YEAR	TM/L	G	AB	R	H	2B	3B	HR	RBI	BB	SO	AVG	OBP	SLG	PRO+	BR	/A	RC	SB	CS	SBR	FR	POS	TPR
1970	Phi-N	13	37	1	7	2	0	1	4	5	11	.189	.286	.324	65	-2	-2	4	0	0	0	-1	/O	-0.2
1971	Phi-N	59	123	16	26	6	0	6	10	16	43	.211	.312	.407	102	0	0	16	0	1	-1	-4	/O	-0.5
1972	Phi-N	62	140	13	34	6	0	6	18	30	34	.243	.380	.414	122	6	5	24	0	1	-1	1	1O	0.3
1973	Min-A	103	253	37	62	11	1	9	25	28	66	.245	.327	.403	101	1	0	31	0	1	-1	-0	1/D	-0.6
1974	Min-A	24	41	5	8	0	0	0	3	5	12	.195	.298	.195	42	-3	-3	3	0	0	0	-0	1	-0.3
	Cle-A	57	109	15	22	3	0	6	16	14	30	.202	.293	.394	97	-1	-1	12	1	0	0	-0	1/3OD	-0.1
	Yr	81	150	20	30	3	0	6	19	19	42	.200	.294	.340	82	-3	-4	14	1	0	0	-1		-0.4
1975	Cle-A	9	13	4	4	2	0	2	8	3	3	.308	.471	.923	286	3	3	6	0	0	0	0	/1D	0.3
1976	Cle-A	20	51	4	16	1	0	2	7	8	8	.314	.407	.451	153	4	4	10	0	0	0	-0	1/D	0.3
1977	Sea-A	9	13	1	3	0	0	0	1	1	2	.231	.286	.231	43	-1	-1	0	0	0	0	-0	/1C	-0.1
Total	8	356	780	96	182	31	1	32	92	110	209	.233	.334	.399	105	8	6	106	1	3	-2	-5	1/OD3C	-0.9

■ **RICK LISI**   Lisi, Riccardo Patrick Emilio   b: 3/17/56, Halifax, N.S., Can.   BR/TR, 6', 175 lbs.   Deb: 5/09/81

YEAR	TM/L	G	AB	R	H	2B	3B	HR	RBI	BB	SO	AVG	OBP	SLG	PRO+	BR	/A	RC	SB	CS	SBR	FR	POS	TPR
1981	Tex-A	9	16	6	5	0	0	0	1	4	0	.313	.450	.313	130	1	1	2	0	1	-1	-1	/O	0.0

■ **PETE LISTER**   Lister, Morris Elmer   b: 7/21/1881, Savanna, Ill.   d: 3/27/47, St.Petersburg, Fla   BR/TR,   Deb: 9/14/07

YEAR	TM/L	G	AB	R	H	2B	3B	HR	RBI	BB	SO	AVG	OBP	SLG	PRO+	BR	/A	RC	SB	CS	SBR	FR	POS	TPR
1907	Cle-A	22	65	5	18	2	0	0	4		3	.277	.309	.308	98	-0	-0	7	2			-1	1	-0.1

■ **SCOTT LITTLE**   Little, Dennis Scott   b: 1/19/63, E.St.Louis, Ill.   BR/TR, 6', 198 lbs.   Deb: 7/27/89

YEAR	TM/L	G	AB	R	H	2B	3B	HR	RBI	BB	SO	AVG	OBP	SLG	PRO+	BR	/A	RC	SB	CS	SBR	FR	POS	TPR
1989	Pit-N	3	4	0	1	0	0	0	0	0	1	.250	.250	.250	45	-0	-0	0	0	0	0	1	/O	0.1

■ **HARRY LITTLE**   Little, Harry A.   b: St.Louis, Mo.   TR,   Deb: 7/16/1877

YEAR	TM/L	G	AB	R	H	2B	3B	HR	RBI	BB	SO	AVG	OBP	SLG	PRO+	BR	/A	RC	SB	CS	SBR	FR	POS	TPR
1877	StL-N	3	12	2	2	0	0	0	0	1	6	.167	.231	.167	29	-1	-1	0				-0	/O	0.0
	Lou-N	1	3	0	0	0	0	0	0	1	1	.000	.250	.000	-13	-0	-0	0				0	/2	0.0

YEAR	TM/L	G	AB	R	H	2B	3B	HR	RBI	BB	SO	AVG	OBP	SLG	PRO+	BR	/A	RC	SB	CS	SBR	FR	POS	TPR
	Yr	4	15	2	2	0	0	0	0	2	7	.133	.235	.133	19	-1	-1	0				0		0.0

■ BRYAN LITTLE
Little, Richard Bryan "Twig" b: 10/8/59, Houston, Tex.   BB/TR, 5'10", 160 lbs.   Deb: 7/29/82

YEAR	TM/L	G	AB	R	H	2B	3B	HR	RBI	BB	SO	AVG	OBP	SLG	PRO+	BR	/A	RC	SB	CS	SBR	FR	POS	TPR
1982	Mon-N	29	42	6	9	0	0	0	3	4	6	.214	.283	.214	40	-3	-3	3	2	1	0	-2	2S	-0.3
1983	Mon-N	106	350	48	91	15	3	1	36	50	22	.260	.356	.329	91	-3	-2	42	4	5	-2	-32	S2	-2.9
1984	Mon-N	85	266	31	65	11	1	0	9	34	19	.244	.332	.293	81	-7	-6	28	2	3	-1	-21	2/S	-2.7
1985	Chi-A	73	188	35	47	9	1	2	27	26	21	.250	.350	.340	87	-2	-3	24	0	1	-1	-6	2/3S	-0.6
1986	Chi-A	20	35	3	6	1	0	0	2	4	4	.171	.256	.200	25	-4	-4	2	0	0	0	0	2/3S	-0.1
	NY-A	14	41	3	8	1	0	0	0	2	7	.195	.233	.220	24	-4	-4	2	0	0	0	5	2	0.2
	Yr	34	76	6	14	2	0	0	2	6	11	.184	.244	.211	25	-8	-8	4	0	0	0	6		0.1
Total	5	327	922	126	226	37	5	3	77	120	79	.245	.336	.306	80	-22	-22	100	8	10	-4	-56	2/S3	-6.4

■ JACK LITTLE
Little, William Arthur b: 3/12/1891, Mart, Tex.   d: 7/27/61, Dallas, Tex.   BR/TR, 5'11", 175 lbs.   Deb: 7/02/12

YEAR	TM/L	G	AB	R	H	2B	3B	HR	RBI	BB	SO	AVG	OBP	SLG	PRO+	BR	/A	RC	SB	CS	SBR	FR	POS	TPR
1912	NY-A	3	12	2	3	0	0	0	0	1		.250	.357	.250	70	-0	-0	2	2			1	/O	0.0

■ DENNIS LITTLEJOHN
Littlejohn, Dennis Gerald b: 10/4/54, Santa Monica, Cal.   BR/TR, 6'2", 200 lbs.   Deb: 7/09/78

YEAR	TM/L	G	AB	R	H	2B	3B	HR	RBI	BB	SO	AVG	OBP	SLG	PRO+	BR	/A	RC	SB	CS	SBR	FR	POS	TPR
1978	SF-N	2	0	0	0	0	0	0	0	0	0	—	—	—	—	0	0	0	0	0	0	0	/C	0.0
1979	SF-N	63	193	15	38	6	1	1	13	21	46	.197	.276	.254	49	-14	-13	14	0	0	0	6	C	-0.5
1980	SF-N	13	29	2	7	1	0	0	2	7	7	.241	.389	.276	91	-0	-0	4	0	0	0	2	C	0.2
Total	3	78	222	17	45	7	1	1	15	28	53	.203	.292	.257	55	-14	-13	18	0	0	0	7	/C	-0.3

■ LARRY LITTLETON
Littleton, Larry Marvin b: 4/3/54, Charlotte, N.C.   BR/TR, 6'1", 185 lbs.   Deb: 4/12/81

YEAR	TM/L	G	AB	R	H	2B	3B	HR	RBI	BB	SO	AVG	OBP	SLG	PRO+	BR	/A	RC	SB	CS	SBR	FR	POS	TPR
1981	Cle-A	26	23	2	0	0	0	0	1	3	6	.000	.115	.000	-65	-5	-5	0	0	0	0	-1	O	-0.6

■ GREG LITTON
Litton, Jon Gregory b: 7/13/64, New Orleans, La.   BR/TR, 6', 175 lbs.   Deb: 5/02/89

YEAR	TM/L	G	AB	R	H	2B	3B	HR	RBI	BB	SO	AVG	OBP	SLG	PRO+	BR	/A	RC	SB	CS	SBR	FR	POS	TPR
1989	*SF-N	71	143	12	36	5	3	4	17	7	29	.252	.291	.413	102	-1	-0	16	0	2	-1	-3	32/SOC	-0.4
1990	SF-N	93	204	17	50	9	1	1	24	11	45	.245	.287	.314	66	-10	-9	18	1	0	0	-5	O2/S3	-1.4
Total	2	164	347	29	86	14	4	5	41	18	74	.248	.289	.354	80	-10	-10	34	1	2	-1	-8	/O32SC	-1.8

■ JACK LITTRELL
Littrell, Jack Napier b: 1/22/29, Louisville, Ky.   BR/TR, 6', 179 lbs.   Deb: 4/19/52

YEAR	TM/L	G	AB	R	H	2B	3B	HR	RBI	BB	SO	AVG	OBP	SLG	PRO+	BR	/A	RC	SB	CS	SBR	FR	POS	TPR
1952	Phi-A	4	2	0	0	0	0	0	0	1	2	.000	.333	.000	-2	-0	-0	0	0	0	0	0	/S3	0.0
1954	Phi-A	9	30	7	9	2	0	1	3	6	3	.300	.417	.467	141	2	2	6	1	0	0	-1	/S	0.2
1955	KC-A	37	70	7	14	0	1	0	1	4	12	.200	.243	.229	27	-7	-7	4	0	0	0	0	S/12	-0.4
1957	Chi-N	61	153	8	29	4	2	1	13	9	43	.190	.235	.261	34	-15	-14	10	0	0	0	1	S/23	-1.0
Total	4	111	255	22	52	6	3	2	17	20	60	.204	.262	.275	45	-20	-20	20	1	0	0	1	/S213	-1.2

■ DANNY LITWHILER
Litwhiler, Daniel Webster b: 8/31/16, Ringtown, Pa.   BR/TR, 5'10.5", 198 lbs.   Deb: 4/25/40   C

YEAR	TM/L	G	AB	R	H	2B	3B	HR	RBI	BB	SO	AVG	OBP	SLG	PRO+	BR	/A	RC	SB	CS	SBR	FR	POS	TPR
1940	Phi-N	36	142	10	49	2	2	5	17	3	13	.345	.363	.493	139	6	7	25	1			-0	O	0.5
1941	Phi-N	151	590	72	180	29	6	18	66	39	43	.305	.350	.466	134	20	22	93	1			15	*O	3.2
1942	Phi-N	151	591	59	160	25	9	9	56	27	42	.271	.310	.389	109	1	4	68	2			1	*O	0.1
1943	Phi-N	36	139	12	36	6	0	5	17	11	14	.259	.313	.410	113	1	1	18	1			3	O	0.3
	*StL-N	80	258	40	72	14	3	7	31	19	31	.279	.333	.438	117	6	5	38	1			-0	O	0.2
	Yr	116	397	63	108	20	3	12	48	30	45	.272	.326	.428	115	7	6	56	2			3		0.5
1944	*StL-N	140	492	53	130	25	5	15	82	37	56	.264	.328	.427	109	6	5	69	2			-4	*O	-0.9
1946	StL-N	6	5	0	0	0	0	0	0	1	1	.000	.167	.000	-49	-1	-1	0	0			0	H	0.0
	Bos-N	79	247	29	72	12	2	8	38	19	23	.291	.347	.453	125	7	7	39	1			-4	O/3	0.2
	Yr	85	252	29	72	12	2	8	38	20	24	.286	.343	.444	121	6	6	39	1			-4		0.2
1947	Bos-N	91	226	38	59	5	2	7	31	25	43	.261	.337	.394	96	-2	-1	30	1			-2	O	-0.5
1948	Bos-N	13	33	0	9	2	0	0	6	4	2	.273	.385	.333	97	0	0	5	0			1	/O	0.1
	Cin-N	106	338	51	93	19	2	14	44	48	41	.275	.365	.467	128	11	13	56	0			-1	O3	0.5
	Yr	119	371	51	102	21	2	14	50	52	43	.275	.367	.456	125	11	13	61	1			1		0.6
1949	Cin-N	102	292	35	85	18	1	11	48	44	42	.291	.384	.473	127	12	12	56	0			-4	O/3	0.3
1950	Cin-N	54	112	15	29	4	0	6	12	20	21	.259	.371	.455	116	3	3	19	0			-3	O	0.0
1951	Cin-N	12	29	3	8	1	0	2	3	2	5	.276	.323	.517	120	1	1	5	0			-1	/O	0.0
Total	11	1057	3494	428	982	162	32	107	451	299	377	.281	.342	.438	119	71	77	521	11	0	0	1	O/3	4.0

■ PADDY LIVINGSTON
Livingston, Patrick Joseph b: 1/14/1880, Cleveland, Ohio   d: 9/19/77, Cleveland, Ohio   BR/TR, 5'8", 197 lbs.   Deb: 9/02/01

YEAR	TM/L	G	AB	R	H	2B	3B	HR	RBI	BB	SO	AVG	OBP	SLG	PRO+	BR	/A	RC	SB	CS	SBR	FR	POS	TPR
1901	Cle-A	1	2	0	0	0	0	0	0	0		.000	.333	.000	-0	-0	-0	0	0			-0	/C	0.0
1906	Cin-N	50	139	8	22	1	4	0	8	12		.158	.225	.223	39	-9	-10	8	0			2	C	-0.3
1909	Phi-A	64	175	15	41	6	4	0	15	15		.234	.323	.314	99	1	0	20	4			9	C	1.6
1910	Phi-A	37	120	11	25	4	3	0	9	6		.208	.264	.292	75	-4	-4	10	2			4	C	0.5
1911	Phi-A	27	71	9	17	4	0	0	8	7		.239	.316	.296	72	-3	-2	7	1			4	C	0.5
1912	Cle-A	20	47	5	11	2	1	0	3	1		.234	.280	.319	69	-2	-2	4	0			-0	C	0.0
1917	StL-N	7	20	0	4	0	0	0	2	0	1	.200	.200	.200	23	-2	-2	1	2			1	/C	0.0
Total	7	206	574	48	120	17	12	0	45	41	1	.209	.279	.280	71	-19	-20	49	9			20	C	2.3

■ MICKEY LIVINGSTON
Livingston, Thompson Orville b: 11/15/14, Newberry, S.C.   d: 4/3/83, Newberry, S.C.   BR/TR, 6'1.5", 185 lbs.   Deb: 9/17/38

YEAR	TM/L	G	AB	R	H	2B	3B	HR	RBI	BB	SO	AVG	OBP	SLG	PRO+	BR	/A	RC	SB	CS	SBR	FR	POS	TPR
1938	Was-A	2	4	0	3	2	0	0	1	0		.750	.750	1.250	421	2	2	4	0	0	0	-1	/C	0.1
1941	Phi-N	95	207	16	42	6	1	0	18	20	38	.203	.276	.242	49	-14	-13	13	2			0	C/1	-0.6
1942	Phi-N	89	239	20	49	6	1	2	22	25	20	.205	.283	.264	64	-12	-10	19	0			-6	C/1	-1.5
1943	Phi-N	84	265	25	66	9	2	3	18	19	18	.249	.304	.332	87	-6	-5	27	1			-2	C/1	-0.2
	Chi-N	36	111	11	29	5	1	4	16	12	8	.261	.333	.432	122	3	3	14	1			-5	C/1	0.0
	Yr	120	376	36	95	14	3	7	34	31	26	.253	.313	.362	98	-3	-2	41	2			-7		-0.2
1945	*Chi-N	71	224	19	57	4	2	2	23	19	6	.254	.324	.317	80	-6	-6	23	2			-1	C/1	-0.4
1946	Chi-N	66	176	14	45	14	0	0	20	20	19	.256	.338	.369	103	0	1	23	0			2	C	0.4
1947	Chi-N	19	33	2	7	2	0	0	3	1	5	.212	.235	.273	36	-3	-3	2	0			-0	/C	-0.2
	NY-N	5	6	0	1	0	0	0	0	1	2	.167	.286	.167	23	-1	-1	0	0			0	/C	0.0
	Yr	24	39	2	8	2	0	0	3	2	7	.205	.244	.256	34	-4	-4	3	0			-0		-0.2
1948	NY-N	45	99	9	21	4	1	2	12	21	11	.212	.350	.333	85	-1	-1	13	1			-1	C	0.1
1949	NY-N	19	57	6	17	2	0	4	12	2	14	.298	.333	.544	132	2	2	10	0			-1	C	0.1
	Bos-N	28	64	6	15	2	1	0	6	3	5	.234	.290	.297	61	-4	-3	6	0			1	C	-0.1
	Yr	47	121	12	32	4	1	4	18	5	13	.264	.310	.413	95	-2	-1	15	0			-1		0.0
1951	Bro-N	2	5	0	2	0	0	0	2	1	0	.400	.500	.400	142	0	0	1	0	0	0	-0	/C	0.0
Total	10	561	1490	128	354	56	9	19	153	144	141	.238	.310	.326	82	-40	-35	154	7	0		-14	C/1	-2.3

■ ABEL LIZOTTE
Lizotte, Abel b: 4/13/1870, Lewiston, Me.   d: 12/4/26, Wilkes-Barre, Pa.   Deb: 9/17/1896

YEAR	TM/L	G	AB	R	H	2B	3B	HR	RBI	BB	SO	AVG	OBP	SLG	PRO+	BR	/A	RC	SB	CS	SBR	FR	POS	TPR
1896	Pit-N	7	29	3	3	0	0	0	3	2	2	.103	.161	.103	-30	-5	-5	1	1			1	/1	-0.3

■ WINSTON LLENAS
Llenas, Winston Enriquillo (Davila) b: 9/23/43, Santiago, D.R.   BR/TR, 5'10", 165 lbs.   Deb: 8/15/68   C

YEAR	TM/L	G	AB	R	H	2B	3B	HR	RBI	BB	SO	AVG	OBP	SLG	PRO+	BR	/A	RC	SB	CS	SBR	FR	POS	TPR
1968	Cal-A	16	39	5	5	1	0	0	1	2	5	.128	.190	.154	6	-4	-4	1	0	0	0	-3	/3	-0.7
1969	Cal-A	34	47	5	8	2	0	0	0	2	10	.170	.204	.213	18	-5	-5	2	0	0	0	-2	/3	-0.6
1972	Cal-A	44	64	3	17	3	0	0	7	3	8	.266	.299	.313	87	-1	-1	5	0	0	0	-1	3/2O	-0.1
1973	Cal-A	78	130	16	35	1	0	1	25	10	16	.269	.326	.300	84	-4	-2	13	0	0	0	-3	23/OD	-0.4
1974	Cal-A	72	138	16	36	6	0	2	17	11	19	.261	.315	.348	96	-2	-1	15	0	0	0	-4	O2D/3	-0.4
1975	Cal-A	56	113	6	21	4	0	0	11	9	11	.186	.252	.221	37	-10	-9	6	0	1	-1	5	20/13D	-0.4

YEAR	TM/L	G	AB	R	H	2B	3B	HR	RBI	BB	SO	AVG	OBP	SLG	PRO+	BR	/A	RC	SB	CS	SBR	FR	POS	TPR
Total	6	300	531	50	122	17	0	3	61	38	69	.230	.284	.279	66	-26	-22	42	0	1	-1	-8	/203D1	-2.6

■ MIKE LOAN
Loan, William Joseph   b: 9/27/1894, Philadelphia, Pa.   d: 11/21/66, Springfield, Pa.   TR , 5'11", 185 lbs.   Deb: 9/18/12

YEAR	TM/L	G	AB	R	H	2B	3B	HR	RBI	BB	SO	AVG	OBP	SLG	PRO+	BR	/A	RC	SB	CS	SBR	FR	POS	TPR
1912	Phi-N	1	2	1	1	0	0	0	0	0	0	.500	.500	.500	163	0	0	0	0			-1	/C	0.0

■ BOB LOANE
Loane, Robert Kenneth   b: 8/6/14, Berkeley, Cal.   BR/TR, 6', 190 lbs.   Deb: 7/29/39

YEAR	TM/L	G	AB	R	H	2B	3B	HR	RBI	BB	SO	AVG	OBP	SLG	PRO+	BR	/A	RC	SB	CS	SBR	FR	POS	TPR
1939	Was-A	3	9	2	0	0	0	0	1	4	4	.000	.308	.000	-16	-1	-1	0	0	0	0	2	/O	0.0
1940	Bos-N	13	22	4	5	3	0	0	1	2	5	.227	.292	.364	84	-1	-0	3	2			3	O	0.2
Total	2	16	31	6	5	3	0	0	2	6	9	.161	.297	.258	54	-2	-2	3	2	0		5	/O	0.2

■ FRANK LOBERT
Lobert, Frank John   b: 11/26/1883, Williamsport, Pa.   d: 5/29/32, Pittsburgh, Pa.   TR , 6', 180 lbs.   Deb: 6/06/14

YEAR	TM/L	G	AB	R	H	2B	3B	HR	RBI	BB	SO	AVG	OBP	SLG	PRO+	BR	/A	RC	SB	CS	SBR	FR	POS	TPR
1914	Bal-F	11	30	3	6	0	1	0	2	0	0	.200	.200	.267	32	-3	-3	2	0			-1	/32	-0.3

■ HANS LOBERT
Lobert, John Bernard "Honus"   b: 10/18/1881, Wilmington, Del.   d: 9/14/68, Philadelphia, Pa.   BR/TR, 5'9", 170 lbs.   Deb: 9/21/03   MC

YEAR	TM/L	G	AB	R	H	2B	3B	HR	RBI	BB	SO	AVG	OBP	SLG	PRO+	BR	/A	RC	SB	CS	SBR	FR	POS	TPR
1903	Pit-N	5	13	1	1	1	0	0	0	1		.077	.143	.154	-14	-2	-2	1	1			-1	/32S	-0.2
1905	Chi-N	14	46	7	9	2	0	0	1	3		.196	.245	.239	44	-3	-3	4	4			0	3/O	-0.2
1906	Cin-N	79	268	39	83	5	5	0	19	19		.310	.355	.366	122	8	7	44	20			-11	3S2/O	-0.4
1907	Cin-N	148	537	61	132	9	12	1	41	37		.246	.294	.313	88	-5	-8	63	30			-17	*S/3	-2.1
1908	Cin-N	155	570	71	167	17	18	4	63	46		.293	.346	.407	147	26	28	96	47			-26	3SO	0.4
1909	Cin-N	122	425	50	90	13	5	4	52	48		.212	.304	.294	86	-7	-6	47	30			-15	*3	-2.0
1910	Cin-N	93	314	43	97	6	6	3	40	30	9	.309	.369	.395	128	9	11	61	41			-2	3	1.0
1911	Phi-N	147	541	94	154	20	9	9	72	66	31	.285	.368	.405	115	12	11	97	40			-17	*3	0.9
1912	Phi-N	65	257	37	84	12	5	2	33	19	13	.327	.373	.436	113	7	5	46	13			-13	3	-0.7
1913	Phi-N	150	573	98	172	28	11	7	55	42	34	.300	.353	.424	117	15	12	96	41			-17	*3/S2	-0.6
1914	Phi-N	135	505	83	139	24	5	1	52	49	32	.275	.343	.349	99	4	0	69	31			-25	*3/S	-2.1
1915	NY-N	106	386	46	97	18	4	0	38	25	24	.251	.304	.319	94	-6	-3	38	14	15	-5	-5	*3	-0.9
1916	NY-N	48	76	6	17	3	2	0	11	5	8	.224	.272	.316	84	-2	-1	8	2			2	3	0.1
1917	NY-N	50	52	4	10	1	0	1	5	5	5	.192	.276	.269	70	-2	-2	4	2			2	3	0.0
Total	14	1317	4563	640	1252	159	82	32	482	395	156	.274	.336	.366	109	54	47	675	316	15		-145	3S/O2	-7.7

■ HARRY LOCHHEAD
Lochhead, Robert Henry   b: 3/29/1876, Stockton, Cal.   d: 8/22/09, Stockton, Cal.   TR ,   Deb: 4/16/1899

YEAR	TM/L	G	AB	R	H	2B	3B	HR	RBI	BB	SO	AVG	OBP	SLG	PRO+	BR	/A	RC	SB	CS	SBR	FR	POS	TPR
1899	Cle-N	148	541	52	129	7	1	1	43	21		.238	.280	.261	55	-35	-29	47	23			2	*S/2P	-1.6
1901	Det-A	1	4	2	2	0	0	0	0	0		.500	.600	.500	202	1	1	1	0			0	/S	0.1
	Phi-A	9	34	3	3	0	0	0	2	3		.088	.162	.088	-27	-6	-6	0	0			-8	/S	-1.2
	Yr	10	38	5	5	0	0	0	2	3		.132	.214	.132	-1	-5	-5	1	0			-8		-1.1
Total	2	158	579	57	134	7	1	1	45	24		.231	.275	.252	50	-40	-35	49	23			-6	S/P2	-2.7

■ DON LOCK
Lock, Don Wilson   b: 7/27/36, Wichita, Kan.   BR/TR, 6'2", 195 lbs.   Deb: 7/17/62

YEAR	TM/L	G	AB	R	H	2B	3B	HR	RBI	BB	SO	AVG	OBP	SLG	PRO+	BR	/A	RC	SB	CS	SBR	FR	POS	TPR
1962	Was-A	71	225	30	57	6	2	12	37	30	63	.253	.341	.458	114	4	4	33	4	5	-2	1	O	0.1
1963	Was-A	149	531	71	134	20	1	27	82	70	151	.252	.342	.446	119	14	14	83	7	3	0	9	*O	1.9
1964	Was-A	152	512	73	127	17	4	28	80	79	137	.248	.350	.461	124	17	17	84	4	2	0	7	*O	1.9
1965	Was-A	143	418	52	90	15	1	16	39	57	115	.215	.317	.371	96	-2	-2	48	1	3	-2	-3	*O	-1.1
1966	Was-A	138	386	52	90	13	1	16	48	57	126	.233	.335	.396	110	5	6	51	2	6	-3	3	*O	0.1
1967	Phi-N	112	313	46	79	13	1	14	51	43	98	.252	.352	.435	123	10	10	50	9	5	-0	5	O	1.1
1968	Phi-N	99	248	27	52	7	2	8	34	26	64	.210	.285	.351	90	-3	-3	24	3	4	-2	3	O	-0.6
1969	Phi-N	4	4	0	0	0	0	0	0	0	1	.000	.000	.000	-99	-1	-1	0	0	0	0	0	/O	0.0
	Bos-A	53	58	8	13	1	0	1	2	11	21	.224	.348	.293	77	-1	-1	6	0	1	-1	1	O/1	-0.2
Total	8	921	2695	359	642	92	12	122	373	373	776	.238	.334	.417	111	42	43	379	30	29	-8	26	O/1	3.2

■ MARSHALL LOCKE
Locke, Marshall   b: Indianapolis, Ind.   Deb: 1884

YEAR	TM/L	G	AB	R	H	2B	3B	HR	RBI	BB	SO	AVG	OBP	SLG	PRO+	BR	/A	RC	SB	CS	SBR	FR	POS	TPR
1884	Ind-a	7	29	5	7	0	1	0		0		.241	.241	.310	84	-1	-0	2				-1	/O	0.0

■ GENE LOCKLEAR
Locklear, Gene   b: 7/19/49, Lumberton, N.C.   BL/TR, 5'10", 165 lbs.   Deb: 4/05/73

YEAR	TM/L	G	AB	R	H	2B	3B	HR	RBI	BB	SO	AVG	OBP	SLG	PRO+	BR	/A	RC	SB	CS	SBR	FR	POS	TPR
1973	Cin-N	29	26	6	5	0	0	0	2	5		.192	.276	.192	34	-2	-2	1	0	0	0	-0	/O	-0.1
	SD-N	67	154	20	37	6	1	3	25	21	22	.240	.331	.351	97	-2	-0	19	9	4	0	-0	O	-0.1
	Yr	96	180	26	42	6	1	3	25	23	27	.233	.324	.328	87	-4	-3	20	9	4	0	0		-0.2
1974	SD-N	39	74	7	20	3	2	1	3	4	12	.270	.308	.405	103	-0	-0	9	0	1	-1	-1	O	-0.1
1975	SD-N	100	237	31	76	11	1	5	27	22	26	.321	.381	.439	135	9	10	40	4	2	0	-4	O	0.5
1976	SD-N	43	67	9	15	3	0	0	8	4	15	.224	.268	.269	57	-4	-4	5	0	0	0	-1	O	-0.5
	NY-A	13	32	2	7	1	0	0	1	2	7	.219	.265	.250	52	-2	-2	2	0	0	0	0	/OD	-0.1
1977	NY-A	1	5	1	3	0	0	0	2	0	0	.600	.600	.600	231	1	1	2	0	0	0	-0	/O	0.0
Total	5	292	595	76	163	24	4	9	66	55	87	.274	.337	.373	105	-1	3	78	13	7	-0	-6	O/D	-0.4

■ STU LOCKLIN
Locklin, Stuart Carlton   b: 7/22/28, Appleton, Wis.   BL/TL, 6'1.5", 190 lbs.   Deb: 6/23/55

YEAR	TM/L	G	AB	R	H	2B	3B	HR	RBI	BB	SO	AVG	OBP	SLG	PRO+	BR	/A	RC	SB	CS	SBR	FR	POS	TPR
1955	Cle-A	16	18	4	3	1	0	0	3	4	.167	.286	.222	37	-2	-2	1	0	0	0	-1	/O	-0.2
1956	Cle-A	9	6	0	1	0	0	0	0	1	.167	.167	.167	-12	-1	-1	0	0	0	0	0	/O	0.0
Total	2	25	24	4	4	1	0	0	3	5	.167	.259	.208	26	-2	-2	1	0	0	0	-0	/O	-0.2

■ WHITEY LOCKMAN
Lockman, Carroll Walter   b: 7/25/26, Lowell, N.C.   BL/TR, 6'1", 175 lbs.   Deb: 7/05/45   MC

YEAR	TM/L	G	AB	R	H	2B	3B	HR	RBI	BB	SO	AVG	OBP	SLG	PRO+	BR	/A	RC	SB	CS	SBR	FR	POS	TPR
1945	NY-N	32	129	16	44	9	0	3	18	13	10	.341	.410	.481	145	8	8	27	1			-2	O	0.4
1947	NY-N	2	2	0	1	0	0	0	1	0	0	.500	.500	.500	165	0	0	1	0			0	H	0.0
1948	NY-N	146	584	117	167	24	10	18	59	68	63	.286	.361	.454	119	15	15	101	8			-2	*O	0.2
1949	NY-N	151	617	97	186	32	7	11	65	62	31	.301	.368	.429	113	12	12	101	12			1	*O	0.5
1950	NY-N	129	532	72	157	28	5	6	52	42	29	.295	.349	.400	96	-3	-3	76	1			12	*O	0.4
1951	*NY-N	153	614	85	173	27	7	12	73	50	32	.282	.339	.407	99	-1	-1	83	4	5	-2	1	*1O	-0.5
1952	NY-N	154	606	99	176	17	4	13	58	67	52	.290	.363	.396	110	10	9	92	2	4	-2	2	*1	0.4
1953	NY-N	150	607	85	179	22	4	9	61	52	36	.295	.351	.389	91	-6	-7	87	3	4	-2	5	*1O	-0.7
1954	*NY-N	148	570	73	143	17	3	16	60	59	31	.251	.321	.375	80	-16	-17	73	2	2	-1	-8	*1/O	-3.0
1955	NY-N	147	576	76	157	19	0	15	49	39	34	.273	.322	.384	86	-12	-12	72	3	3	-1	-5	O1	-2.3
1956	NY-N	48	169	13	46	7	1	1	10	16	17	.272	.335	.343	83	-4	-4	20	2	2	-1	-3	O/1	-0.9
	StL-N	70	193	14	48	0	2	0	10	18	8	.249	.313	.269	59	-11	-11	17	2	2	-1	-4	O/1	-1.7
	Yr	118	362	27	94	7	3	1	20	34	25	.260	.323	.304	70	-14	-14	37	2	4	-2	-7		-2.6
1957	NY-N	133	456	51	113	9	4	7	30	39	19	.248	.310	.331	73	-17	-17	48	5	5	-2	-3	*1O	-3.2
1958	SF-N	92	122	15	29	5	0	2	7	13	8	.238	.311	.328	71	-5	-5	14	0	0	0	-4	O2/1	-0.9
1959	Bal-A	38	69	7	15	1	1	0	2	8	4	.217	.299	.261	56	-4	-4	6	0	0	0	-3	1/2O	-0.6
	Cin-N	52	84	10	22	5	1	0	7	4	6	.262	.295	.345	68	-4	-4	9	0	0	0	0	1/23O	-0.4
1960	Cin-N	21	10	6	2	0	0	0	1	2	3	.200	.385	.500	138	0	0	1	0	0	0	0	/1	0.1
Total	15	1666	5940	836	1658	222	49	114	563	552	383	.279	.342	.391	95	-36	-40	826	43	27		-13	1O/23	-12.2

■ SKIP LOCKWOOD
Lockwood, Claude Edward   b: 8/17/46, Boston, Mass.   BR/TR, 6'1", 175 lbs.   Deb: 4/23/65

YEAR	TM/L	G	AB	R	H	2B	3B	HR	RBI	BB	SO	AVG	OBP	SLG	PRO+	BR	/A	RC	SB	CS	SBR	FR	POS	TPR
1965	KC-A	42	33	4	4	0	0	0	0	7	11	.121	.293	.121	23	-3	-3	2	0	0	0	2	/3	0.0
1969	Sea-A	6	7	0	0	0	0	0	0	0	2	.000	.000	.000	-99	-2	-2	0	0	0	0	1	/P	0.0
1970	Mil-A	27	53	2	12	1	0	1	2	1	11	.226	.241	.302	48	-4	-4	2	0	0	0	-1	P	0.0
1971	Mil-A	36	62	2	5	1	0	0	4	5	20	.081	.149	.145	-17	-10	-9	2	0	0	0	-3	P	0.0
1972	Mil-A	31	53	3	7	1	0	0	0	3	12	.132	.193	.132	-2	-7	-6	2	0	1	-1	-3	P	0.0

YEAR	TM/L	G	AB	R	H	2B	3B	HR	RBI	BB	SO	AVG	OBP	SLG	PRO+	BR	/A	RC	SB	CS	SBR	FR	POS	TPR
1973	Mil-A	37	0	0	0	0	0	0	0	0	0	—	—	—	—	0	0	0	0	0	0	-0	P	0.0
1974	Cal-A	37	0	0	0	0	0	0	0	0	0	—	—	—	—	0	0	0	0	0	0	0	P	0.0
1975	NY-N	24	6	0	1	0	0	0	1	0	0	.167	.167	.167	-8	-1	-1	0	0	0	0	-1	P	0.0
1976	NY-N	56	18	2	6	1	0	0	2	2	3	.333	.400	.389	132	1	1	3	0	1	-1	-1	P	0.0
1977	NY-N	63	15	1	3	0	0	0	1	0	1	.200	.200	.200	8	-2	-2	1	0	0	0	-2	P	0.0
1978	NY-N	57	11	1	2	1	0	1	1	0	5	.182	.182	.545	100	-0	-0	1	0	0	0	-2	P	0.0
1979	NY-N	28	2	0	0	0	0	0	0	0	1	.000	.000	.000	-99	-1	-1	0	0	0	0	-1	P	0.0
1980	Bos-A	24	0	0	0	0	0	0	0	0	0	—	—	—	—	0	0	0	0	0	0	-1	P	0.0
Total	13	468	260	15	40	4	0	3	11	18	66	.154	.214	.204	19	-28	-27	14	0	2	-1	-11	P/3	0.0

■ MILO LOCKWOOD

Lockwood, Milo Hathaway b: 4/7/1858, Solon, Ohio d: 10/9/1897, Economy, Pa. 5'10", 160 lbs. Deb: 4/17/1884

YEAR	TM/L	G	AB	R	H	2B	3B	HR	RBI	BB	SO	AVG	OBP	SLG	PRO+	BR	/A	RC	SB	CS	SBR	FR	POS	TPR
1884	Was-U	20	67	9	14	1	0	0			8	.209	.293	.224	80	-1	-1	5	0			2	OP/3	0.0

■ DARIO LODIGIANI

Lodigiani, Dario Antonio b: 6/6/16, San Francisco, Cal BR/TR, 5'8", 150 lbs. Deb: 4/18/38 C

YEAR	TM/L	G	AB	R	H	2B	3B	HR	RBI	BB	SO	AVG	OBP	SLG	PRO+	BR	/A	RC	SB	CS	SBR	FR	POS	TPR
1938	Phi-A	93	325	36	91	15	1	6	44	34	25	.280	.361	.388	90	-6	-5	48	3	0	1	-6	23	-0.5
1939	Phi-A	121	393	46	102	22	4	6	44	42	18	.260	.337	.382	85	-10	-9	52	2	0	1	2	32	-0.6
1940	Phi-A	1	1	0	0	0	0	0	0	0	0	.000	.000	.000	-99	-0	-0	0	0	0	0	0	H	0.0
1941	Chi-A	87	322	39	77	19	2	4	40	31	19	.239	.316	.348	76	-12	-11	34	0	4	-2	6	3	-0.2
1942	Chi-A	59	168	9	47	7	0	0	15	18	10	.280	.353	.321	92	-2	-1	19	3	4	-2	6	3/2	0.4
1946	Chi-A	44	155	12	38	8	0	0	13	16	14	.245	.324	.297	77	-5	-4	17	4	0	1	-5	3	-0.3
Total	6	405	1364	142	355	71	7	16	156	141	86	.260	.338	.358	84	-34	-30	170	12	8	-1	3	32	-1.2

■ GEORGE LOEPP

Loepp, George Herbert b: 9/11/01, Detroit, Mich. d: 9/4/67, Los Angeles, Cal. BR/TR, 5'11", 170 lbs. Deb: 8/29/28

YEAR	TM/L	G	AB	R	H	2B	3B	HR	RBI	BB	SO	AVG	OBP	SLG	PRO+	BR	/A	RC	SB	CS	SBR	FR	POS	TPR
1928	Bos-A	15	51	6	9	3	1	0	3	5	12	.176	.250	.275	38	-5	-5	4	0	0	0	-0	O	-0.5
1930	Was-A	50	134	23	37	7	1	0	14	20	9	.276	.382	.343	85	-2	-2	18	0	4	-2	-5	O	-1.0
Total	2	65	185	29	46	10	2	0	17	25	21	.249	.347	.324	73	-7	-7	22	0	4	-2	-6	/O	-1.5

■ DICK LOFTUS

Loftus, Richard Joseph b: 3/7/01, Concord, Mass. d: 1/21/72, Concord, Mass. BL/TR, 6', 155 lbs. Deb: 4/20/24

YEAR	TM/L	G	AB	R	H	2B	3B	HR	RBI	BB	SO	AVG	OBP	SLG	PRO+	BR	/A	RC	SB	CS	SBR	FR	POS	TPR
1924	Bro-N	46	81	18	22	6	0	0	8	7	2	.272	.330	.346	84	-2	-2	10	1	0	0	2	O/1	0.0
1925	Bro-N	51	131	16	31	6	0	0	13	5	5	.237	.275	.282	44	-11	-11	11	2	0	1	3	O	-0.6
Total	2	97	212	34	53	12	0	0	21	12	7	.250	.296	.307	59	-13	-12	20	3	0	1	6	/O1	-0.6

■ TOM LOFTUS

Loftus, Thomas Joseph b: 11/15/1856, St.Louis, Mo. d: 4/16/10, Dubuque, Iowa 168 lbs. Deb: 8/17/1877 M

YEAR	TM/L	G	AB	R	H	2B	3B	HR	RBI	BB	SO	AVG	OBP	SLG	PRO+	BR	/A	RC	SB	CS	SBR	FR	POS	TPR
1877	StL-N	3	11	2	2	0	0	0	0	0	1	.182	.182	.182	16	-1	-1	0				2	/O	0.0
1883	StL-a	6	22	1	4	0	0	0	0	2		.182	.250	.182	39	-1	-2	1				0	/O	0.0
Total	2	9	33	3	6	0	0	0	0	2	1	.182	.229	.182	32	-2	-2	1				2	/O	0.0

■ JOHNNY LOGAN

Logan, John "Yatcha" b: 3/23/27, Endicott, N.Y. BR/TR, 5'11", 175 lbs. Deb: 4/17/51

YEAR	TM/L	G	AB	R	H	2B	3B	HR	RBI	BB	SO	AVG	OBP	SLG	PRO+	BR	/A	RC	SB	CS	SBR	FR	POS	TPR
1951	Bos-N	62	169	14	37	7	1	0	16	18	13	.219	.298	.272	59	-11	-9	14	0	0	0	4	S	0.0
1952	Bos-N	117	456	56	129	21	3	4	42	31	33	.283	.334	.368	98	-3	-1	57	1	2	-1	18	*S	1.9
1953	Mil-N	150	611	100	167	27	8	11	73	41	33	.273	.326	.398	93	-12	-6	80	2	2	-1	21	*S	2.4
1954	Mil-N	154	560	66	154	17	7	8	66	51	51	.275	.342	.373	92	-11	-6	73	2	0	1	14	*S	1.8
1955	Mil-N	154	595	95	177	37	5	13	83	58	58	.297	.364	.442	118	11	15	96	3	3	-1	8	*S	2.6
1956	Mil-N	148	545	69	153	27	5	15	46	46	49	.281	.342	.431	113	5	9	81	3	0	1	3	*S	2.3
1957	*Mil-N	129	494	59	135	19	7	10	49	31	49	.273	.321	.401	100	-6	-1	62	5	0	2	24	*S	2.9
1958	*Mil-N	145	530	54	120	20	0	11	53	40	57	.226	.287	.326	68	-29	-24	51	1	2	-1	10	*S	-0.3
1959	Mil-N	138	470	59	137	17	0	13	50	72	45	.291	.372	.411	118	7	12	71	1	3	-2	-3	*S	1.3
1960	Mil-N	136	482	52	118	14	4	7	42	43	40	.245	.309	.334	82	-16	-11	50	1	1	0	2	*S	-0.4
1961	Mil-N	18	19	2	2	1	0	0	1	1	3	.105	.150	.158	-19	-3	-3	0	0	0	0	-0	/S	-0.2
	Pit-N	27	52	5	12	4	0	0	5	4	8	.231	.286	.308	57	-3	-3	0	0	0	0	0	/3S	-0.1
	Yr	45	71	5	14	5	0	0	6	5	11	.197	.250	.268	38	-6	-6	4	0	0	0	0		-0.3
1962	Pit-N	44	80	7	24	3	0	1	12	7	6	.300	.356	.375	90	-0	-0	10	0	0	0	2	3	0.2
1963	Pit-N	81	181	15	42	2	1	0	9	23	27	.232	.325	.254	69	-6	-6	15	0	0	0	2	S/3	0.0
Total	13	1503	5244	651	1407	216	41	93	547	451	472	.268	.331	.378	95	-77	-35	665	19	13	-2	105	*S/3	14.4

■ PETE LOHMAN

Lohman, George F. b: 10/21/1864, Lake Elmo, Minn. d: 11/21/28, Los Angeles, Cal. Deb: 5/11/1891

YEAR	TM/L	G	AB	R	H	2B	3B	HR	RBI	BB	SO	AVG	OBP	SLG	PRO+	BR	/A	RC	SB	CS	SBR	FR	POS	TPR
1891	Was-a	32	109	18	21	1	4	1	11	16	17	.193	.302	.303	79	-3	-2	11	1			-3	C/O3S2	-0.3

■ HOWARD LOHR

Lohr, Howard Sylvester b: 6/3/1892, Philadelphia, Pa. d: 6/9/77, Philadelphia, Pa. BR/TR, 6', 165 lbs. Deb: 6/17/14

YEAR	TM/L	G	AB	R	H	2B	3B	HR	RBI	BB	SO	AVG	OBP	SLG	PRO+	BR	/A	RC	SB	CS	SBR	FR	POS	TPR
1914	Cin-N	18	47	6	10	1	1	0	7	0	8	.213	.213	.277	44	-3	-3	3	2			-0	O	-0.4
1916	Cle-A	3	7	0	1	0	0	0	1	0	1	.143	.143	.143	-13	-1	-1	0	1			-1	/O	-0.1
Total	2	21	54	6	11	1	1	0	8	0	9	.204	.204	.259	36	-4	-5	3	3			-1	/O	-0.5

■ JACK LOHRKE

Lohrke, Jack Wayne "Lucky" b: 2/25/24, Los Angeles, Cal. BR/TR, 6', 180 lbs. Deb: 4/18/47

YEAR	TM/L	G	AB	R	H	2B	3B	HR	RBI	BB	SO	AVG	OBP	SLG	PRO+	BR	/A	RC	SB	CS	SBR	FR	POS	TPR
1947	NY-N	112	329	44	79	12	4	11	35	46	29	.240	.337	.401	95	-2	-3	45	3			-2	*3	-0.7
1948	NY-N	97	280	35	70	15	1	5	31	30	30	.250	.323	.364	85	-6	-6	33	3			-2	32	-0.5
1949	NY-N	55	180	32	48	11	4	5	22	16	12	.267	.333	.456	110	2	2	27	3			4	23S	0.8
1950	NY-N	30	43	4	8	0	0	0	4	4	4	.186	.255	.186	18	-5	-5	2	0			0	3/2	-0.4
1951	*NY-N	23	40	3	8	0	0	1	3	10	2	.200	.360	.275	73	-1	-1	4	0	0	0	-1	3/S	-0.1
1952	Phi-N	25	29	4	6	0	0	0	1	4	3	.207	.303	.207	44	-2	-2	2	0	0	0	0	/S32	0.0
1953	Phi-N	12	13	3	2	0	0	0	0	1	2	.154	.214	.154	-2	-2	-2	0	0	0	0	1	/2S3	0.0
Total	7	354	914	125	221	38	9	22	96	111	86	.242	.327	.375	87	-16	-17	114	9	0		2	3/2S	-0.9

■ ALBERTO LOIS

Lois, Alberto (b: Alberto Louis (Pie)) b: 5/6/56, Hato Mayor, D.R. BR/TR, 5'9", 175 lbs. Deb: 9/08/78

YEAR	TM/L	G	AB	R	H	2B	3B	HR	RBI	BB	SO	AVG	OBP	SLG	PRO+	BR	/A	RC	SB	CS	SBR	FR	POS	TPR
1978	Pit-N	3	4	0	1	0	1	0	0	0	1	.250	.250	.750	163	0	0	1	0	0	0	1	/O	0.1
1979	Pit-N	11	0	6	0	0	0	0	0	0	0	—	—	—	—	0	0	0	1	1	-0	0	/R	0.0
Total	2	14	4	6	1	0	1	0	0	0	1	.250	.250	.750	163	0	0	1	1	1	-0	1	/O	0.1

■ RON LOLICH

Lolich, Ronald John b: 9/19/46, Portland, Ore. BR/TR, 6'1", 185 lbs. Deb: 7/18/71

YEAR	TM/L	G	AB	R	H	2B	3B	HR	RBI	BB	SO	AVG	OBP	SLG	PRO+	BR	/A	RC	SB	CS	SBR	FR	POS	TPR
1971	Chi-A	2	8	0	1	1	0	0	0	0	2	.125	.125	.250	4	-1	-1	0	0	0	0	-1	/O	-0.1
1972	Cle-A	24	80	4	15	1	0	2	8	4	20	.188	.226	.275	47	-5	-5	5	0	0	0	-1	O	-0.7
1973	Cle-A	61	140	16	32	7	0	2	15	7	27	.229	.265	.321	63	-7	-7	11	0	2	-1	-2	OD	-1.0
Total	3	87	228	20	48	9	0	4	23	11	49	.211	.247	.303	56	-13	-14	16	0	2	-1	-3	/OD	-1.8

■ SHERM LOLLAR

Lollar, John Sherman b: 8/23/24, Durham, Ark. d: 9/24/77, Springfield, Mo. BR/TR, 6'1", 185 lbs. Deb: 4/20/46 C

YEAR	TM/L	G	AB	R	H	2B	3B	HR	RBI	BB	SO	AVG	OBP	SLG	PRO+	BR	/A	RC	SB	CS	SBR	FR	POS	TPR
1946	Cle-A	28	62	7	15	6	0	1	9	5	9	.242	.299	.387	97	-1	-1	7	0	1	-1	-3	C	-0.3
1947	*NY-A	11	32	4	7	0	1	1	6	1	5	.219	.242	.375	71	-2	-1	4	0	1	-1	1	/C	0.0
1948	NY-A	22	38	0	8	0	0	0	4	1	6	.211	.231	.211	18	-4	-4	1	0	0	0	1	C	-0.1
1949	StL-A	109	284	28	74	9	1	8	49	32	22	.261	.340	.384	88	-4	-6	38	0	1	-1	-3	C	-0.4
1950	StL-A	126	396	55	111	22	3	13	65	64	25	.280	.391	.449	110	10	7	74	2	0	1	-5	C	0.6
1951	StL-A	98	310	44	78	21	0	8	44	43	26	.252	.350	.397	99	1	-0	41	1	0	0	-2	C/3	0.4
1952	Chi-A	132	375	35	90	15	0	13	50	54	34	.240	.354	.384	104	4	3	53	1	0	0	-3	*C	0.7
1953	Chi-A	111	334	46	96	19	0	8	54	47	29	.287	.388	.416	114	10	8	59	1	0	0	-3	*C/1	1.0
1954	Chi-A	107	316	31	77	13	0	7	34	37	28	.244	.336	.351	85	-5	-6	39	0	1	-1	-3	*C	-0.4
1955	Chi-A	138	426	67	111	13	1	16	61	68	34	.261	.375	.408	108	8	6	68	2	2	-1	9	*C	1.9
1956	Chi-A	136	450	55	132	28	2	11	75	53	34	.293	.387	.438	116	13	12	76	2	0	1	3	*C	1.6

YEAR	TM/L	G	AB	R	H	2B	3B	HR	RBI	BB	SO	AVG	OBP	SLG	PRO+	BR	/A	RC	SB	CS	SBR	FR	POS	TPR
1957	Chi-A	101	351	33	90	11	2	11	70	35	24	.256	.346	.393	101	1	1	50	2	0	1	-2	C	0.4
1958	Chi-A	127	421	53	115	16	0	20	84	57	37	.273	.370	.454	128	16	17	72	2	1	0	0	*C	1.8
1959	*Chi-A	140	505	63	134	22	3	22	84	55	49	.265	.348	.451	119	12	13	73	4	3	-1	9	*C1	2.8
1960	Chi-A	129	421	43	106	23	0	7	46	42	39	.252	.331	.356	87	-8	-7	47	2	0	1	-4	*C	-0.2
1961	Chi-A	116	337	38	95	10	1	7	41	37	22	.282	.363	.380	100	0	1	48	0	0	0	-11	*C	-1.0
1962	Chi-A	84	220	17	59	12	0	2	26	32	23	.268	.369	.350	95	-0	-0	29	1	0	0	-9	C	-0.4
1963	Chi-A	35	73	4	17	4	0	0	6	8	7	.233	.317	.288	72	-3	-2	7	0	0	0	-2	C/1	-0.4
Total	18	1752	5351	623	1415	244	14	155	808	671	453	.264	.359	.402	104	47	40	782	20	10	0	-28	*C/13	8.0

■ DOUG LOMAN

Loman, Douglas Edward b: 5/9/58, Bakersfield, Cal. BL/TL, 5'11", 185 lbs. Deb: 9/03/84

YEAR	TM/L	G	AB	R	H	2B	3B	HR	RBI	BB	SO	AVG	OBP	SLG	PRO+	BR	/A	RC	SB	CS	SBR	FR	POS	TPR
1984	Mil-A	23	76	13	21	4	0	2	12	15	7	.276	.402	.408	130	3	4	13	0	2	-1	1	O	0.3
1985	Mil-A	24	66	10	14	3	2	0	7	1	12	.212	.224	.318	47	-5	-5	5	0	0	0	3	O	-0.1
Total	2	47	142	23	35	7	2	2	19	16	19	.246	.327	.366	93	-2	-1	18	0	2	-1	4	/O	0.2

■ ERNIE LOMBARDI

Lombardi, Ernesto Natali "Schnozz" or "Bocci" b: 4/6/08, Oakland, Cal. d: 9/26/77, Santa Cruz, Cal. BR/TR, 6'3", 230 lbs. Deb: 4/15/31 H

YEAR	TM/L	G	AB	R	H	2B	3B	HR	RBI	BB	SO	AVG	OBP	SLG	PRO+	BR	/A	RC	SB	CS	SBR	FR	POS	TPR
1931	Bro-N	73	182	20	54	7	1	4	23	12	12	.297	.340	.412	102	0	0	26	1			3	C	0.5
1932	Cin-N	118	413	43	125	22	9	11	68	41	19	.303	.371	.479	131	16	18	76	0			-9	*C	1.2
1933	Cin-N	107	350	30	99	21	1	4	47	16	17	.283	.322	.383	102	-0	0	36	2			-15	C	-1.1
1934	Cin-N	132	417	42	127	19	4	9	62	16	22	.305	.335	.434	107	2	3	53	0			-3	C	0.3
1935	Cin-N	120	332	36	114	23	3	12	64	16	6	.343	.379	.539	148	19	21	65	0			-5	C	1.5
1936	Cin-N	121	387	42	129	23	2	12	68	19	16	.333	.375	.496	142	17	20	69	1			-13	*C	1.0
1937	Cin-N	120	368	41	123	22	1	9	59	14	17	.334	.362	.473	132	12	14	60	1			-16	C	0.1
1938	*Cin-N	129	489	60	167	30	1	19	95	40	14	.342	.391	.524	154	32	34	91	0			-3	*C	3.5
1939	*Cin-N	130	450	43	129	26	2	20	85	35	19	.287	.342	.487	120	11	11	67	0			5	*C	1.9
1940	*Cin-N	109	376	50	120	22	0	14	74	31	14	.319	.382	.489	137	20	19	66	0			-4	*C	2.0
1941	Cin-N	117	398	33	105	12	1	10	60	36	14	.264	.325	.374	96	-2	-2	45	1			1	*C	1.0
1942	Bos-N	105	309	32	102	14	0	11	46	37	12	.330	.403	.482	162	23	24	56	1			-15	C	1.0
1943	NY-N	104	295	19	90	7	0	10	51	16	11	.305	.347	.431	123	8	8	38	1			-13	C	-0.2
1944	NY-N	117	373	37	95	13	0	10	58	33	25	.255	.317	.370	93	-4	-4	38	0			-14	*C	-1.3
1945	NY-N	115	368	46	113	7	1	19	70	43	11	.307	.387	.486	140	21	20	69	0			3	C	2.4
1946	NY-N	88	238	19	69	4	1	12	39	18	24	.290	.347	.466	129	8	8	37	0			1	C	1.1
1947	NY-N	48	110	8	31	5	0	4	21	7	9	.282	.325	.436	100	-0	-0	15	0			-3	C	-0.2
Total	17	1853	5855	601	1792	277	27	190	990	430	262	.306	.358	.460	126	180	191	907	8			-100	*C	14.7

■ PHIL LOMBARDI

Lombardi, Phillip Andrew b: 2/20/63, Abilene, Tex. BR/TR, 6'2", 200 lbs. Deb: 4/26/86

YEAR	TM/L	G	AB	R	H	2B	3B	HR	RBI	BB	SO	AVG	OBP	SLG	PRO+	BR	/A	RC	SB	CS	SBR	FR	POS	TPR
1986	NY-A	20	36	6	10	3	0	2	6	4	7	.278	.366	.528	141	2	2	6	0	0	0	0	/OC	0.2
1987	NY-A	5	8	0	1	0	0	0	0	0	2	.125	.125	.125	-34	-2	-1	0	0	0	0	-0	/C	-0.1
1989	NY-N	18	48	4	11	1	0	1	3	5	8	.229	.302	.313	80	-1	-1	4	0	0	0	-1	C/1	0.0
Total	3	43	92	10	22	4	0	3	9	9	17	.239	.314	.380	95	-1	-1	11	0	0	0	-1	/CO1	0.1

■ STEVE LOMBARDOZZI

Lombardozzi, Stephen Paul b: 4/26/60, Malden, Mass. BR/TR, 6', 175 lbs. Deb: 7/12/85

YEAR	TM/L	G	AB	R	H	2B	3B	HR	RBI	BB	SO	AVG	OBP	SLG	PRO+	BR	/A	RC	SB	CS	SBR	FR	POS	TPR
1985	Min-A	28	54	10	20	4	1	0	6	6	6	.370	.433	.481	142	4	4	12	3	2	-0	11	2	1.5
1986	Min-A	156	453	53	103	20	5	8	33	52	76	.227	.308	.347	76	-14	-15	50	3	1	0	-3	*2	-0.8
1987	*Min-A	136	432	51	103	19	3	8	38	33	66	.238	.299	.352	69	-18	-20	46	5	1	1	-1	*2	-0.8
1988	Min-A	103	287	34	60	15	2	3	27	35	48	.209	.299	.307	68	-11	-12	28	2	5	-2	-7	2S/3	-1.4
1989	Hou-N	21	37	5	8	3	1	1	3	4	9	.216	.293	.432	109	0	0	5	0	0	0	0	2/3	0.1
1990	Hou-N	2	1	0	0	0	0	0	0	1	1	.000	.500	.000	51	0	0	0	0	0	0	0	/H	0.0
Total	6	446	1264	153	294	61	12	20	107	131	206	.233	.308	.347	76	-38	-43	141	13	9	-2	1	2/S3	-1.4

■ WALTER LONERGAN

Lonergan, Walter E. b: 9/22/1885, Boston, Mass. d: 1/23/58, Lexington, Mass. BR/TR, 5'7", 156 lbs. Deb: 8/17/11

YEAR	TM/L	G	AB	R	H	2B	3B	HR	RBI	BB	SO	AVG	OBP	SLG	PRO+	BR	/A	RC	SB	CS	SBR	FR	POS	TPR
1911	Bos-A	10	26	2	7	0	0	0	1	1		.269	.296	.269	59	-1	-1	3	1			-0	/2S3	-0.1

■ DAN LONG

Long, Daniel W. b: 8/27/1867, Boston, Mass. d: 4/30/29, Sausalito, Cal. Deb: 8/29/1888

YEAR	TM/L	G	AB	R	H	2B	3B	HR	RBI	BB	SO	AVG	OBP	SLG	PRO+	BR	/A	RC	SB	CS	SBR	FR	POS	TPR
1888	Lou-a	1	2	0	0	0	0	0		0	1	.000	.333	.000	14	-0	-0	0	0			-0	/O	0.0
1890	Bal-a	21	77	19	12	0	0	0		0	14	.156	.301	.156	36	-5	-6	9	16			-1	O	-0.6
Total	2	22	79	19	12	0	0	0		0	15	.152	.302	.152	35	-5	-6	9	16			-1	/O	-0.6

■ HERMAN LONG

Long, Herman C. "Germany" or "Flying Dutchman" b: 4/13/1866, Chicago, Ill. d: 9/17/09, Denver, Colo. BL/TR, 5'8.5", 160 lbs. Deb: 4/17/1889

YEAR	TM/L	G	AB	R	H	2B	3B	HR	RBI	BB	SO	AVG	OBP	SLG	PRO+	BR	/A	RC	SB	CS	SBR	FR	POS	TPR
1889	KC-a	136	574	137	158	32	6	3	60	64	63	.275	.358	.368	103	8	2	110	89			32	*S/2O	3.7
1890	Bos-N	101	431	95	108	15	3	8	52	40	34	.251	.320	.355	91	-1	-7	66	49			11	*S	0.2
1891	Bos-N	139	577	129	163	21	11	10	76	80	51	.282	.377	.414	119	26	15	116	60			15	*S	3.2
1892	*Bos-N	151	646	115	181	33	6	6	78	44	36	.280	.334	.378	107	12	3	103	57			14	*SO/3	2.2
1893	Bos-N	128	552	149	159	22	6	6	58	73	32	.288	.376	.382	96	5	-3	96	38			16	*S/2	1.3
1894	Bos-N	104	475	137	154	28	11	12	79	35	17	.324	.375	.505	104	8	0	102	24			4	*S/O2	0.6
1895	Bos-N	124	535	109	169	23	10	9	75	31	12	.316	.357	.447	100	5	-3	100	35			-7	*S/2	0.0
1896	Bos-N	120	501	105	172	26	8	6	100	26	16	.343	.382	.463	117	16	11	105	36			10	*S	1.8
1897	*Bos-N	107	450	89	145	32	7	3	69	23		.322	.358	.444	107	7	3	81	22			-2	*S/O	0.2
1898	Bos-N	144	589	99	156	21	10	6	99	39		.265	.311	.365	91	-5	-9	75	20			2	*S/2	0.0
1899	Bos-N	145	578	91	153	30	8	6	100	45		.265	.321	.375	85	-6	-15	78	20			-9	*S/1	-1.4
1900	Bos-N	125	486	80	127	19	4	12	66	44		.261	.324	.391	88	-1	-10	72	26			-6	*S	-0.2
1901	Bos-N	138	518	54	112	14	6	3	68	25		.216	.254	.284	53	-28	-34	45	20			-3	*S	-2.9
1902	Bos-N	120	439	40	101	11	0	2	44	31		.230	.269	.269	71	-14	-15	42	24			23	*S2	1.4
1903	NY-A	22	80	6	15	3	0	0	8	2		.188	.207	.225	29	-7	-7	5	3			-4	S	-1.0
	Det-A	69	239	21	53	12	0	0	23	10		.222	.253	.272	61	-12	-11	21	11			2	S2	-0.6
	Yr	91	319	27	68	15	0	0	31	12		.213	.242	.260	52	-18	-18	25	14			-2		-1.6
1904	Phi-N	1	4	0	1	0	0	0	0	0		.250	.250	.250	58	-0	-0	0	0			1	/2	0.1
Total	16	1874	7674	1456	2127	342	96	92	1055	612	261	.277	.335	.383	95	13	-79	1217	534			97	*S/2013	8.6

■ JIMMIE LONG

Long, James Albert b: 6/29/1898, Ft.Dodge, Iowa d: 9/14/70, Ft.Dodge, Iowa BR/TR, 5'11", 160 lbs. Deb: 9/12/22

YEAR	TM/L	G	AB	R	H	2B	3B	HR	RBI	BB	SO	AVG	OBP	SLG	PRO+	BR	/A	RC	SB	CS	SBR	FR	POS	TPR
1922	Chi-A	3	3	0	0	0	0	0	0	1	0	.000	.250	.000	-30	-1	-1	0	0	0	0	-1	/C	0.0

■ JIM LONG

Long, James M. b: 11/15/1862, Louisville, Ky. d: 12/12/32, Louisville, Ky. Deb: 8/09/1891

YEAR	TM/L	G	AB	R	H	2B	3B	HR	RBI	BB	SO	AVG	OBP	SLG	PRO+	BR	/A	RC	SB	CS	SBR	FR	POS	TPR
1891	Lou-a	6	25	5	6	0	0	0	4	3	6	.240	.367	.240	78	-0	-0	3	1			1	/O	0.0
1893	Bal-N	55	226	31	48	8	1	2	25	16	27	.212	.276	.283	49	-16	-17	25	23			-1	O	-1.6
Total	2	61	251	36	54	8	1	2	29	19	33	.215	.286	.279	52	-17	-17	27	24			-0	/O	-1.6

■ JEOFF LONG

Long, Jeoffrey Keith b: 10/9/41, Covington, Ky. BR/TR, 6'1", 200 lbs. Deb: 7/31/63

YEAR	TM/L	G	AB	R	H	2B	3B	HR	RBI	BB	SO	AVG	OBP	SLG	PRO+	BR	/A	RC	SB	CS	SBR	FR	POS	TPR
1963	StL-N	5	5	0	1	0	0	0	0	0	1	.200	.200	.200	14	-1	-1	0	0	0	0	0	H	0.0
1964	StL-N	28	43	5	10	1	0	1	4	6	18	.233	.340	.326	81	-0	-1	5	0	0	0	-1	/O1	-0.2
	Chi-A	23	35	0	5	0	0	0	5	4	15	.143	.231	.143	-4	-4	-4	1	0	0	0	0	/1O	-0.4
Total	2	56	83	5	16	1	0	1	9	10	34	.193	.287	.241	48	-5	-6	7	0	0	0	-1	/O1	-0.6

■ DALE LONG

Long, Richard Dale b: 2/6/26, Springfield, Mo. BL/TL, 6'4", 205 lbs. Deb: 4/21/51 C

YEAR	TM/L	G	AB	R	H	2B	3B	HR	RBI	BB	SO	AVG	OBP	SLG	PRO+	BR	/A	RC	SB	CS	SBR	FR	POS	TPR
1951	Pit-N	10	12	1	2	0	0	1	1	0	3	.167	.167	.417	50	-1	-1	1	0	0	0	-0	/1	0.0
	StL-A	34	105	11	25	5	1	2	11	10	22	.238	.310	.362	79	-3	-3	13	0	0	0	-0	1/O	-0.3

YEAR	TM/L	G	AB	R	H	2B	3B	HR	RBI	BB	SO	AVG	OBP	SLG	PRO+	BR	/A	RC	SB	CS	SBR	FR	POS	TPR
1955	Pit-N	131	419	59	122	19	13	16	79	48	72	.291	.365	.513	132	18	18	76	0	1	-1	6	*1	1.5
1956	Pit-N	148	517	64	136	20	7	27	91	54	85	.263	.333	.485	119	11	12	83	1	0	0	-3	*1	0.4
1957	Pit-N	7	22	0	4	1	0	0	5	4	10	.182	.308	.227	48	-2	-1	2	0	0	0	0	/1	-0.1
	Chi-N	123	397	55	121	19	0	21	62	52	63	.305	.387	.511	141	22	23	79	1	1	-0	-1	*1	1.2
	Yr	130	419	55	125	20	0	21	67	56	73	.298	.382	.496	136	21	22	80	1	1	-0	-1		1.1
1958	Chi-N	142	480	68	130	26	4	20	75	66	64	.271	.361	.467	119	12	13	80	2	0	1	-1	*1/C	0.4
1959	Chi-N	110	296	34	70	10	3	14	37	31	53	.236	.309	.432	96	-3	-3	39	0	0	0	-2	1	-1.0
1960	SF-N	37	54	4	9	0	0	3	6	7	7	.167	.262	.333	66	-3	-3	4	0	0	0	0	1	-0.2
	*NY-A	26	41	6	15	3	1	3	10	5	6	.366	.435	.707	216	6	6	12	0	0	0	-0	1	0.5
1961	Was-A	123	377	52	94	20	4	17	49	39	41	.249	.321	.459	107	2	3	56	0	0	0	-7	1	-1.3
1962	Was-A	67	191	17	46	8	0	4	24	18	22	.241	.310	.346	77	-6	-6	20	5	1	1	0	1	-0.8
	*NY-A	41	94	12	28	4	0	4	17	18	9	.298	.411	.468	140	5	6	19	1	0	0	1	1	0.5
	Yr	108	285	29	74	12	0	8	41	36	31	.260	.345	.386	98	-1	-0	39	6	1	1	1		-0.3
1963	NY-A	14	15	1	3	0	0	0	3	0	0	.200	.250	.200	28	-1	-1	1	0	0	0	-0	/1	-0.1
Total	10	1013	3020	384	805	135	33	132	467	353	460	.267	.345	.464	116	57	63	485	10	3	1	-8	1/CO	0.7

■ TOM LONG
Long, Thomas Augustus b: 6/1/1890, Mitchum, Ala. d: 6/15/72, Mobile, Ala. BR/TR, 5'10.5", 165 lbs. Deb: 9/11/11

YEAR	TM/L	G	AB	R	H	2B	3B	HR	RBI	BB	SO	AVG	OBP	SLG	PRO+	BR	/A	RC	SB	CS	SBR	FR	POS	TPR
1911	Was-A	14	48	1	11	3	0	0	5	1		.229	.245	.292	50	-3	-3	4	4			-2	O	-0.6
1912	Was-A	1	1	0	0	0	0	0	0	0		.000	.000	.000	-99	-0	-0	0	0			0	H	0.0
1915	StL-N	140	507	61	149	21	25	2	61	31	50	.294	.339	.446	137	20	20	77	19	15	-3	-2	*O	1.2
1916	StL-N	119	403	37	118	11	10	1	33	10	43	.293	.312	.377	112	4	4	48	21	14	-2	-12	*O	-1.5
1917	StL-N	144	530	49	123	12	14	3	41	37	44	.232	.285	.325	89	-9	-7	52	21			-25	*O	-4.2
Total	5	418	1489	148	401	47	49	6	140	79	137	.269	.309	.379	110	11	13	182	65	29		-42	O	-5.1

■ JOE LONNETT
Lonnett, Joseph Paul b: 2/7/27, Beaver Falls, Pa. BR/TR, 5'10", 180 lbs. Deb: 4/22/56 C

YEAR	TM/L	G	AB	R	H	2B	3B	HR	RBI	BB	SO	AVG	OBP	SLG	PRO+	BR	/A	RC	SB	CS	SBR	FR	POS	TPR
1956	Phi-N	16	22	2	4	0	0	0	0	2	7	.182	.250	.182	19	-2	-2	1	0	0	0	0	/C	-0.1
1957	Phi-N	67	160	12	27	5	0	5	15	22	39	.169	.273	.294	54	-11	-10	14	0	0	0	5	C	-0.1
1958	Phi-N	17	50	0	7	2	0	0	2	2	11	.140	.173	.180	-6	-8	-8	2	0	0	0	2	C	-0.4
1959	Phi-N	43	93	8	16	1	0	1	10	14	17	.172	.287	.215	36	-8	-8	6	0	1	-1	-6	C	-1.2
Total	4	143	325	22	54	8	0	6	27	40	74	.166	.262	.246	37	-29	-29	22	0	1	-1	1	C	-1.8

■ BRUCE LOOK
Look, Bruce Michael b: 6/9/43, Lansing, Mich. BL/TR, 5'11", 183 lbs. Deb: 4/17/68

YEAR	TM/L	G	AB	R	H	2B	3B	HR	RBI	BB	SO	AVG	OBP	SLG	PRO+	BR	/A	RC	SB	CS	SBR	FR	POS	TPR
1968	Min-A	59	118	7	29	4	0	0	9	20	24	.246	.355	.280	90	0	-1	12	0	1	-1	2	C	0.3

■ DEAN LOOK
Look, Dean Zachary b: 7/23/37, Lansing, Mich. BR/TR, 5'11", 185 lbs. Deb: 9/22/61

YEAR	TM/L	G	AB	R	H	2B	3B	HR	RBI	BB	SO	AVG	OBP	SLG	PRO+	BR	/A	RC	SB	CS	SBR	FR	POS	TPR
1961	Chi-A	3	6	0	0	0	0	0	0	0	1	.000	.000	.000	-99	-2	-2	0	0	0	0	-0	/O	-0.1

■ STAN LOPATA
Lopata, Stanley Edward "Stash" b: 9/12/25, Delray, Mich. BR/TR, 6'2", 210 lbs. Deb: 9/19/48

YEAR	TM/L	G	AB	R	H	2B	3B	HR	RBI	BB	SO	AVG	OBP	SLG	PRO+	BR	/A	RC	SB	CS	SBR	FR	POS	TPR
1948	Phi-N	6	15	2	2	1	0	0	2	0	4	.133	.133	.200	-11	-2	-2	0	0			0	/C	-0.1
1949	Phi-N	83	240	31	65	9	2	8	27	21	44	.271	.330	.425	104	-0	1	33	1			-3	C	0.0
1950	*Phi-N	58	129	10	27	2	2	1	11	22	25	.209	.325	.279	61	-7	-7	12	1			0	C	-0.4
1951	Phi-N	3	5	0	0	0	0	0	0	0	0	.000	.000	.000	-99	-1	-1	0	0	0	0	0	/C	0.0
1952	Phi-N	57	179	25	49	9	1	4	27	36	33	.274	.395	.402	123	7	7	31	1	1	-0	6	C	1.4
1953	Phi-N	81	234	34	56	12	3	8	31	28	39	.239	.321	.419	91	-3	-3	35	3	1	0	4	C	0.6
1954	Phi-N	86	259	42	75	14	5	14	42	33	37	.290	.372	.544	136	13	13	50	1	3	-2	8	C/1	2.1
1955	Phi-N	99	303	49	82	9	3	22	58	58	62	.271	.391	.538	146	20	21	64	4	1	1	4	C1	2.5
1956	Phi-N	146	535	96	143	33	7	32	95	75	93	.267	.358	.535	138	27	28	100	5	2	0	-19	*C1	1.0
1957	Phi-N	116	388	50	92	18	2	18	67	56	81	.237	.335	.433	108	3	4	56	2	2	-1	-9	*C	0.0
1958	Phi-N	86	258	36	64	9	0	9	33	60	63	.248	.394	.388	109	6	6	39	0	1	-1	-7	C	0.2
1959	Mil-N	25	48	0	5	0	0	0	4	3	13	.104	.157	.104	-31	-9	-8	1	0	0	0	-2	C/1	-1.0
1960	Mil-N	7	8	0	1	0	0	0	0	1	3	.125	.222	.125	-2	-1	-1	0	0	0	0	1	/C	0.0
Total	13	853	2601	375	661	116	25	116	397	393	497	.254	.354	.452	115	50	56	422	18	11		-15	C/1	6.3

■ DAVEY LOPES
Lopes, David Earl b: 5/3/45, E.Providence, R.I. BR/TR, 5'9", 170 lbs. Deb: 9/22/72 C

YEAR	TM/L	G	AB	R	H	2B	3B	HR	RBI	BB	SO	AVG	OBP	SLG	PRO+	BR	/A	RC	SB	CS	SBR	FR	POS	TPR
1972	LA-N	11	42	6	9	4	0	0	1	7	6	.214	.327	.310	84	-1	-1	5	4	0	1	-2	2	0.0
1973	LA-N	142	535	77	147	13	5	6	37	62	77	.275	.355	.351	101	-1	2	69	36	16	1	-12	*2/OS3	-0.3
1974	*LA-N	145	530	95	141	26	3	10	35	66	71	.266	.352	.383	110	5	7	77	59	18	7	-22	*2	0.0
1975	LA-N	155	618	108	162	24	6	8	41	91	93	.262	.359	.359	104	2	5	97	77	12	16	-21	*2OS	0.7
1976	LA-N	117	427	72	103	17	7	4	20	56	49	.241	.335	.342	94	-3	-2	58	63	10	13	-19	*2O	-0.4
1977	*LA-N	134	502	85	142	19	5	11	53	73	69	.283	.376	.406	110	9	9	87	47	12	7	8	*2	3.2
1978	*LA-N	151	587	93	163	25	4	17	58	71	70	.278	.356	.421	117	13	13	97	45	4	11	3	*2/O	3.9
1979	LA-N	153	582	109	154	20	6	28	73	97	88	.265	.373	.464	129	23	25	113	44	4	11	-34	*2	1.1
1980	LA-N	141	553	79	139	15	3	10	49	58	71	.251	.324	.344	88	-9	-8	65	23	7	3	-16	*2	-1.2
1981	*LA-N	58	214	35	44	2	0	5	17	22	35	.206	.289	.285	66	-10	-9	20	20	2	5	-4	2	-0.4
1982	Oak-A	128	450	58	109	19	3	11	42	40	51	.242	.305	.371	89	-10	-7	49	28	12	1	-17	*2/O	-1.6
1983	Oak-A	147	494	64	137	13	4	17	67	51	61	.277	.347	.423	118	8	11	76	22	4	4	-33	*2D/O3	-1.3
1984	Oak-A	72	230	32	59	11	1	9	36	31	36	.257	.347	.430	122	5	7	36	12	0	4	-9	O2/3D	0.1
	*Chi-N	16	17	5	4	1	0	0	0	6	5	.235	.435	.294	99	1	0	4	3	0	1	-0	/O2	0.1
1985	Chi-N	99	275	52	78	11	0	11	44	46	37	.284	.386	.444	118	13	9	52	47	4	12	-9	O/32	1.0
1986	Chi-N	59	157	38	47	8	2	6	22	31	16	.299	.421	.490	140	12	11	34	17	6	2	-3	3O	0.9
	*Hou-N	37	98	11	23	2	1	1	13	12	9	.235	.318	.306	75	-3	-3	10	8	2	1	4	O/3	0.2
	Yr	96	255	49	70	10	3	7	35	43	25	.275	.383	.420	117	9	8	43	25	8	3	1		1.1
1987	Hou-N	47	43	4	10	2	0	1	6	13	8	.233	.411	.349	108	1	1	7	2	1	0	-0	/O	0.2
Total	16	1812	6354	1023	1671	232	50	155	614	833	852	.263	.351	.388	107	54	71	955	557	114	99	-184	*20/3DS	6.1

■ AL LOPEZ
Lopez, Alfonso Ramon b: 8/20/08, Tampa, Fla. BR/TR, 5'11", 165 lbs. Deb: 9/27/28 MH

YEAR	TM/L	G	AB	R	H	2B	3B	HR	RBI	BB	SO	AVG	OBP	SLG	PRO+	BR	/A	RC	SB	CS	SBR	FR	POS	TPR
1928	Bro-N	3	12	0	0	0	0	0	0	0	0	.000	.000	.000	-99	-3	-3	0	0			-2	/C	-0.4
1930	Bro-N	128	421	60	130	20	4	6	57	33	35	.309	.362	.418	89	-8	-7	62	3			4	*C	0.3
1931	Bro-N	111	360	38	97	13	4	0	40	28	33	.269	.324	.328	76	-12	-11	40	1			-8	*C	-1.3
1932	Bro-N	126	404	44	111	18	6	1	43	34	35	.275	.331	.356	87	-8	-7	50	3			-3	*C	-0.4
1933	Bro-N	126	372	39	112	11	4	3	41	21	39	.301	.338	.376	108	2	4	47	10			18	*C/2	2.7
1934	Bro-N	140	439	58	120	23	2	7	54	49	44	.273	.349	.383	101	-2	1	60	2			-7	*C/23	0.0
1935	Bro-N	128	379	50	95	12	4	3	39	35	36	.251	.316	.327	75	-14	-13	41	2			5	*C	-0.7
1936	Bos-N	128	426	46	103	12	5	7	50	41	41	.242	.311	.343	81	-14	-11	45	1			2	*C/1	0.2
1937	Bos-N	105	334	31	68	11	3	8	38	35	57	.204	.281	.269	55	-23	-19	25	3			7	*C	-0.7
1938	Bos-N	71	210	19	63	6	1	1	14	11	24	.267	.305	.314	78	-9	-7	22	5			3	C	0.0
1939	Bos-N	131	412	32	104	22	1	8	49	40	45	.252	.319	.369	91	-9	-6	49	1			2	*C	0.0
1940	Bos-N	36	119	20	35	3	1	2	17	6	8	.294	.328	.387	102	-1	0	15	1			2	C	0.3
	Pit-N	59	174	15	45	6	2	1	24	13	13	.259	.310	.333	78	-5	-5	17	5			3	C	0.1
	Yr	95	293	35	80	9	3	3	41	19	21	.273	.317	.355	87	-6	-5	31	6			5		0.4
1941	Pit-N	114	317	33	84	9	1	5	43	31	23	.265	.330	.347	91	-4	-3	36	0			-1	*C	0.6
1942	Pit-N	103	289	17	74	8	2	1	26	34	17	.256	.338	.308	88	-3	-4	31	0			5	C	0.4
1943	Pit-N	118	372	40	98	9	4	1	39	44	25	.263	.341	.317	88	-5	-5	43	2			8	*C/3	0.8
1944	Pit-N	115	331	27	76	12	1	1	34	34	24	.230	.303	.281	62	-15	-16	29	4			5	*C	-0.5

YEAR	TM/L	G	AB	R	H	2B	3B	HR	RBI	BB	SO	AVG	OBP	SLG	PRO+	BR	/A	RC	SB	CS	SBR	FR	POS	TPR
1945	Pit-N	91	243	22	53	8	0	0	18	35	12	.218	.317	.251	57	-12	-14	21	1			8	C	-0.3
1946	Pit-N	56	150	13	46	2	0	1	12	23	14	.307	.399	.340	108	3	3	21	1			0	C	0.5
1947	Cle-A	61	126	9	33	1	0	0	14	9	13	.262	.311	.270	64	-6	-6	11	1	1	-0	-0	C	-0.1
Total	19	1950	5916	613	1547	206	43	51	652	556	538	.261	.326	.337	83	-147	-128	664	46	1		59	*C/321	1.5

■ **ART LOPEZ**   Lopez, Arturo (Rodriguez)   b: 6/8/37, Mayaguez, P.R.   BL/TL, 5'9", 170 lbs.   Deb: 4/12/65

YEAR	TM/L	G	AB	R	H	2B	3B	HR	RBI	BB	SO	AVG	OBP	SLG	PRO+	BR	/A	RC	SB	CS	SBR	FR	POS	TPR
1965	NY-A	38	49	5	7	0	0	0	0	1	6	.143	.160	.143	-13	-7	-7	1	0	0	0	2	O	-0.6

■ **CARLOS LOPEZ**   Lopez, Carlos Antonio (Morales)   b: 9/27/50, Mazatlan, Mexico   BR/TR, 6', 190 lbs.   Deb: 9/17/76

YEAR	TM/L	G	AB	R	H	2B	3B	HR	RBI	BB	SO	AVG	OBP	SLG	PRO+	BR	/A	RC	SB	CS	SBR	FR	POS	TPR
1976	Cal-A	9	10	1	0	0	0	0	0	2	3	.000	.167	.000	-52	-2	-2	0	2	0	1	0	/OD	0.0
1977	Sea-A	99	297	39	84	18	1	8	34	14	61	.283	.322	.431	104	1	1	44	16	4	2	3	O/D	0.4
1978	Bal-A	129	193	21	46	6	0	4	20	9	34	.238	.276	.332	75	-8	-7	15	5	7	-3	-16	*O/D	-2.8
Total	3	237	500	61	130	24	1	12	54	25	98	.260	.301	.384	90	-9	-7	59	23	11	0	-12	O/D	-2.4

■ **HECTOR LOPEZ**   Lopez, Hector Headley (Swainson)   b: 7/9/29, Colon, Panama   BR/TR, 5'11", 182 lbs.   Deb: 5/12/55

YEAR	TM/L	G	AB	R	H	2B	3B	HR	RBI	BB	SO	AVG	OBP	SLG	PRO+	BR	/A	RC	SB	CS	SBR	FR	POS	TPR
1955	KC-A	128	483	50	140	15	2	15	68	33	58	.290	.339	.422	103	1	0	65	1	4	-2	15	32	1.7
1956	KC-A	151	561	91	153	27	3	18	69	63	73	.273	.349	.428	104	3	2	83	4	5	-2	2	*3O/2S	0.5
1957	KC-A	121	391	51	115	19	4	11	35	41	66	.294	.361	.448	118	10	10	61	1	6	-3	5	*3/2O	1.3
1958	KC-A	151	564	84	147	28	4	17	73	49	61	.261	.322	.415	99	-0	-1	70	2	2	-1	6	23/SO	1.3
1959	KC-A	35	135	22	38	10	3	6	24	8	23	.281	.326	.533	129	5	5	24	1	0	0	-12	2	-0.5
	NY-A	112	406	60	115	16	2	16	69	28	54	.283	.339	.451	119	7	9	61	3	1	0	-8	3O	0.0
	Yr	147	541	82	153	26	5	22	93	36	77	.283	.336	.471	122	12	14	85	4	1	1	-19		-0.5
1960	*NY-A	131	408	66	116	14	6	9	42	46	64	.284	.362	.414	116	6	9	63	1	1	-0	-1	*O/23	0.4
1961	*NY-A	93	243	27	54	7	2	3	22	24	38	.222	.295	.305	64	-14	-12	22	1	0	0	2	O	-1.1
1962	*NY-A	106	335	45	92	19	1	6	48	33	53	.275	.340	.391	99	-2	-0	41	0	1	-1	2	O/23	-0.1
1963	*NY-A	130	433	54	108	13	4	14	52	35	71	.249	.306	.395	95	-4	-3	50	1	2	-1	-7	*O/2	-1.5
1964	*NY-A	127	285	34	74	9	3	10	34	24	54	.260	.319	.418	101	1	0	37	1	1	-0	-2	*O/3	-0.6
1965	NY-A	111	283	25	74	12	2	7	39	26	61	.261	.326	.392	104	1	1	34	0	0	0	-7	O/1	-0.9
1966	NY-A	54	117	14	25	4	1	4	16	8	20	.214	.270	.368	84	-3	-3	11	0	0	0	-2	O	-0.6
Total	12	1450	4644	623	1251	193	37	136	591	418	696	.269	.333	.415	104	12	17	622	16	23	-9	-8	O32/S1	-0.1

■ **LUIS LOPEZ**   Lopez, Luis Antonio   b: 9/1/64, Brooklyn, N.Y.   BR/TR, 6'1", 190 lbs.   Deb: 9/14/90

YEAR	TM/L	G	AB	R	H	2B	3B	HR	RBI	BB	SO	AVG	OBP	SLG	PRO+	BR	/A	RC	SB	CS	SBR	FR	POS	TPR
1990	LA-N	6	6	0	0	0	0	0	0	0	2	.000	.000	.000	-99	-2	-2	0	0	0	0	0	/1	-0.1

■ **BRIS LORD**   Lord, Bristol Robotham "The Human Eyeball"   b: 9/21/1883, Upland, Pa.   d: 11/13/64, Annapolis, Md.   BR/TR, 5'9", 185 lbs.   Deb: 4/21/05

YEAR	TM/L	G	AB	R	H	2B	3B	HR	RBI	BB	SO	AVG	OBP	SLG	PRO+	BR	/A	RC	SB	CS	SBR	FR	POS	TPR
1905	*Phi-A	66	238	38	57	14	0	0	13	14		.239	.282	.298	85	-4	-4	23	3			0	O	-0.7
1906	Phi-A	118	434	50	101	13	7	1	44	27		.233	.278	.302	81	-9	-10	44	12			-2	*O	-1.7
1907	Phi-A	57	170	12	31	3	0	1	11	14		.182	.245	.218	48	-9	-10	11	2			-2	O/P	-1.5
1909	Cle-A	69	249	26	67	7	3	1	25	8		.269	.295	.333	94	-1	-2	27	10			5	O	0.0
1910	Cle-A	58	210	23	46	8	7	0	17	12		.219	.268	.324	84	-4	-5	19	4			4	O	-0.3
	*Phi-A	70	279	53	78	13	11	1	20	23		.280	.337	.416	137	10	11	41	6			4	O	1.2
	Yr	128	489	76	124	21	18	1	37	35		.254	.307	.376	114	6	6	60	10			7		0.9
1911	*Phi-A	134	574	92	178	37	11	3	55	35		.310	.355	.429	120	12	13	92	15			8	*O	1.0
1912	Phi-A	97	378	63	90	12	9	0	25	34		.238	.309	.317	82	-10	-8	42	15			-1	O	-1.4
1913	Bos-N	73	235	22	59	12	1	6	26	8	22	.251	.276	.387	86	-5	-5	25	7			-10	O	-1.7
Total	8	742	2767	379	707	119	49	13	236	175	22	.256	.303	.348	95	-20	-21	324	74			7	O/P	-5.1

■ **HARRY LORD**   Lord, Harry Donald   b: 3/8/1882, Porter, Me.   d: 8/9/48, Westbrook, Maine   BL/TR, 5'10.5", 165 lbs.   Deb: 9/25/07   M

YEAR	TM/L	G	AB	R	H	2B	3B	HR	RBI	BB	SO	AVG	OBP	SLG	PRO+	BR	/A	RC	SB	CS	SBR	FR	POS	TPR
1907	Bos-A	10	38	4	6	1	0	0	3	1		.158	.179	.184	17	-3	-3	2	1			0	3	-0.2
1908	Bos-A	145	560	61	145	15	6	2	37	22		.259	.287	.318	96	-2	-4	59	23			-9	*3	-0.3
1909	Bos-A	136	534	86	166	12	7	0	31	20		.311	.345	.360	120	13	11	79	36			-7	*3	1.1
1910	Bos-A	77	288	25	72	5	5	1	32	14		.250	.294	.313	88	-4	-5	32	17			-5	3/S	-0.7
	Chi-A	44	165	26	49	6	3	0	10	14		.297	.352	.370	131	5	6	27	17			-11	3	-0.3
	Yr	121	453	51	121	11	8	1	42	28		.267	.315	.333	103	1	1	59	34			-15		-1.0
1911	Chi-A	141	561	103	180	18	18	3	61	32		.321	.364	.433	126	15	17	104	43			-17	*3	0.1
1912	Chi-A	151	570	81	152	19	12	5	54	52		.267	.333	.368	104	-0	2	80	28			-27	*3O	-2.9
1913	Chi-A	150	547	62	144	18	12	1	42	45	39	.263	.327	.346	98	-3	-2	68	24			-31	*3	-3.1
1914	Chi-A	21	69	8	13	1	1	1	3	5	3	.188	.243	.275	57	-4	-4	5	2	2	-1	-6	3/OM	-1.0
1915	Buf-F	97	359	50	97	12	4	1	21	21	15	.270	.311	.345	92	-3	-4	45	15			-14	3/OM	-1.7
Total	9	972	3691	506	1024	107	70	14	294	226	57	.277	.324	.356	105	12	14	501	206	2		-125	3/OS	-9.0

■ **CARLTON LORD**   Lord, William Carlton   b: 1/7/1900, Philadelphia, Pa.   d: 8/15/47, Chester, Pa.   BR/TR, 5'11", 170 lbs.   Deb: 7/12/23

YEAR	TM/L	G	AB	R	H	2B	3B	HR	RBI	BB	SO	AVG	OBP	SLG	PRO+	BR	/A	RC	SB	CS	SBR	FR	POS	TPR
1923	Phi-N	17	47	3	11	2	0	0	2	2	3	.234	.265	.277	39	-4	-5	3	0	1	-1	-1	3	-0.4

■ **SCOTT LOUCKS**   Loucks, Scott Gregory   b: 11/11/56, Anchorage, Alaska   BR/TR, 6', 178 lbs.   Deb: 9/01/80

YEAR	TM/L	G	AB	R	H	2B	3B	HR	RBI	BB	SO	AVG	OBP	SLG	PRO+	BR	/A	RC	SB	CS	SBR	FR	POS	TPR
1980	Hou-N	8	3	4	1	0	0	0	0	0	2	.333	.333	.333	94	-0	-0	0	0	0	0	0	/O	0.0
1981	Hou-N	10	7	2	4	0	0	0	0	1	3	.571	.625	.571	254	1	1	3	1	0	0	1	/O	0.2
1982	Hou-N	44	49	6	11	2	0	0	3	3	17	.224	.269	.265	54	-3	-3	4	4	1	1	5	O	0.3
1983	Hou-N	7	14	2	3	0	0	0	1	0	1	.214	.267	.214	37	-1	-1	1	2	2	1	2	/O	0.0
1985	Pit-N	4	7	1	2	2	0	0	1	2	2	.286	.444	.571	184	1	1	2	0	0	0	-1	/O	0.0
Total	5	73	80	15	21	4	0	0	4	7	28	.262	.322	.313	83	-2	-2	10	7	3	0	8	/O	0.5

■ **BALDY LOUDEN**   Louden, William P.   b: 8/27/1885, Piedmont, W.Va.   d: 12/8/35, Piedmont, W.Va.   BR/TR, 5'11", 175 lbs.   Deb: 9/13/07

YEAR	TM/L	G	AB	R	H	2B	3B	HR	RBI	BB	SO	AVG	OBP	SLG	PRO+	BR	/A	RC	SB	CS	SBR	FR	POS	TPR
1907	NY-A	4	9	4	1	0	0	0	0	2		.111	.273	.111	23	-1	-1	1	1			1	/3	0.0
1912	Det-A	122	403	57	97	12	4	1	36	58		.241	.352	.298	89	-5	-3	53	28			23	23/S	1.8
1913	Det-A	76	191	28	46	4	5	0	23	24	22	.241	.344	.314	94	-1	-1	23	6			0	23/SO	0.0
1914	Buf-F	126	431	73	135	11	4	6	63	52	41	.313	.391	.399	124	17	15	85	35			-18	*S	0.6
1915	Buf-F	141	469	67	132	18	5	4	48	64	45	.281	.372	.367	117	13	12	80	30			13	2S3	3.1
1916	Cin-N	134	439	38	96	16	4	1	32	54	54	.219	.313	.280	85	-7	-6	42	12			17	*2S	1.7
Total	6	603	1942	267	507	61	22	12	202	254	162	.261	.355	.334	103	17	18	284	112			36	2S/3O	7.2

■ **CHARLIE LOUDENSLAGER**   Loudenslager, Charles Edward   b: 5/21/1881, Baltimore, Md.   d: 10/31/33, Baltimore, Md.   TR , 5'9", 186 lbs.   Deb: 4/15/04

YEAR	TM/L	G	AB	R	H	2B	3B	HR	RBI	BB	SO	AVG	OBP	SLG	PRO+	BR	/A	RC	SB	CS	SBR	FR	POS	TPR
1904	Bro-N	1	2	0	0	0	0	0	0	0		.000	.000	.000	-99	-0	-0	0				-1	/2	0.0

■ **BILL LOUGHLIN**   Loughlin, William H.   b: Baltimore, Md.   Deb: 5/08/1883

YEAR	TM/L	G	AB	R	H	2B	3B	HR	RBI	BB	SO	AVG	OBP	SLG	PRO+	BR	/A	RC	SB	CS	SBR	FR	POS	TPR
1883	Bal-a	1	5	0	2	0	0	0	0			.400	.400	.400	154	0	0	1				-0	/O	0.0

■ **LOUGHRAN**   Loughran   b: New York, N.Y.   Deb: 6/06/1884

YEAR	TM/L	G	AB	R	H	2B	3B	HR	RBI	BB	SO	AVG	OBP	SLG	PRO+	BR	/A	RC	SB	CS	SBR	FR	POS	TPR
1884	NY-N	9	29	4	3	1	1	0	3	1	11	.103	.278	.207	54	-1	-1	2				-1	/CO	-0.1

■ **TOM LOVELACE**   Lovelace, Thomas Rivers   b: 10/19/1897, Wolfe City, Tex.   d: 7/12/79, Dallas, Tex.   BR/TR, 5'11", 170 lbs.   Deb: 9/23/22

YEAR	TM/L	G	AB	R	H	2B	3B	HR	RBI	BB	SO	AVG	OBP	SLG	PRO+	BR	/A	RC	SB	CS	SBR	FR	POS	TPR
1922	Pit-N	1	1	0	0	0	0	0	0	0	0	.000	.000	.000	-99	-0	-0	0	0	0	0	0	H	0.0

■ **LEN LOVETT**   Lovett, Leonard Walker   b: 7/17/1852, Lancaster Co., Pa.   d: 11/18/22, Newark, Del.   BR/TR,   Deb: 8/04/1873

YEAR	TM/L	G	AB	R	H	2B	3B	HR	RBI	BB	SO	AVG	OBP	SLG	PRO+	BR	/A	RC	SB	CS	SBR	FR	POS	TPR
1873	Res-n	1	5	1	2	0	0	0	0			.400	.400	.400	148	0	0	1					/P	0.0
1875	Cen-n	6	21	2	5	1	0	0		1		.238	.273	.286	102	-0	0	2					/O	0.0

YEAR	TM/L	G	AB	R	H	2B	3B	HR	RBI	BB	SO	AVG	OBP	SLG	PRO+	BR	/A	RC	SB	CS	SBR	FR	POS	TPR
Total	2 n	7	26	3	7	1	0	0			1	.269	.296	.308	112	0	0	2					/OP	0.0

■ MEM LOVETT
Lovett, Merritt Marwood b: 6/15/12, Chicago, Ill. BR/TR, 5'9.5", 165 lbs. Deb: 9/04/33

YEAR	TM/L	G	AB	R	H	2B	3B	HR	RBI	BB	SO	AVG	OBP	SLG	PRO+	BR	/A	RC	SB	CS	SBR	FR	POS	TPR
1933	Chi-A	1	1	0	0	0	0	0	0	0	0	.000	.000	.000	-99	-0	-0	0	0	0	0	0	H	0.0

■ JAY LOVIGLIO
Loviglio, John Paul b: 5/30/56, Freeport, N.Y. BR/TR, 5'9", 160 lbs. Deb: 9/02/80

YEAR	TM/L	G	AB	R	H	2B	3B	HR	RBI	BB	SO	AVG	OBP	SLG	PRO+	BR	/A	RC	SB	CS	SBR	FR	POS	TPR
1980	Phi-N	16	5	7	0	0	0	0	0	1	0	.000	.167	.000	-47	-1	-1	-0	1	2	-1	7	/2	0.5
1981	Chi-A	14	15	5	4	0	0	0	2	1	1	.267	.313	.267	70	-1	-1	0	2	2	-1	5	/32D	0.4
1982	Chi-A	15	31	5	6	0	0	0	2	1	4	.194	.219	.194	14	-4	-4	1	2	1	0	11	2/D	0.8
1983	Chi-N	1	1	0	0	0	0	0	0	0	0	.000	.000	.000	-95	-0	-0	0	0	0	0	0	/H	0.0
Total	4	46	52	17	10	0	0	0	4	3	6	.192	.236	.192	21	-5	-5	2	5	5	-2	22	/2D3	1.7

■ JOE LOVITTO
Lovitto, Joseph b: 1/6/51, San Pedro, Cal. BB/TR, 6', 185 lbs. Deb: 4/15/72

YEAR	TM/L	G	AB	R	H	2B	3B	HR	RBI	BB	SO	AVG	OBP	SLG	PRO+	BR	/A	RC	SB	CS	SBR	FR	POS	TPR
1972	Tex-A	117	330	23	74	9	1	1	19	37	54	.224	.306	.267	75	-11	-9	27	13	11	-3	9	*O	-0.5
1973	Tex-A	26	44	3	6	1	0	0	0	5	7	.136	.224	.159	10	-5	-5	2	1	0	0	2	3/O	-0.2
1974	Tex-A	113	283	27	63	9	3	2	26	25	36	.223	.286	.297	69	-12	-11	21	6	8	-3	-14	*O/1	-3.2
1975	Tex-A	50	106	17	22	3	0	1	8	13	16	.208	.294	.264	59	-6	-5	9	2	2	-1	2	O/1CD	-0.4
Total	4	306	763	70	165	22	4	4	53	80	113	.216	.292	.271	67	-33	-30	59	22	21	-6	-0	O/31DC	-4.3

■ TONY LOVULLO
Lovullo, Salvatore Anthony b: 7/25/65, Santa Monica, Cal. BB/TR, 6'1", 185 lbs. Deb: 9/10/88

YEAR	TM/L	G	AB	R	H	2B	3B	HR	RBI	BB	SO	AVG	OBP	SLG	PRO+	BR	/A	RC	SB	CS	SBR	FR	POS	TPR
1988	Det-A	12	21	2	8	1	1	1	2	1	2	.381	.409	.667	204	3	3	5	0	0	0	-0	/23	0.3
1989	Det-A	29	87	8	10	2	0	1	4	14	20	.115	.238	.172	18	-9	-9	4	0	0	0	-3	13	-1.3
Total	2	41	108	10	18	3	1	2	6	15	22	.167	.268	.269	53	-7	-6	9	0	0	0	-3	/132	-1.0

■ FLETCHER LOW
Low, Fletcher b: 4/7/1893, Essex, Mass. d: 6/6/73, Hanover, N.H. BR/TR, 5'10.5", 175 lbs. Deb: 10/07/15

YEAR	TM/L	G	AB	R	H	2B	3B	HR	RBI	BB	SO	AVG	OBP	SLG	PRO+	BR	/A	RC	SB	CS	SBR	FR	POS	TPR
1915	Bos-N	1	4	1	1	0	1	0	1	0	0	.250	.250	.750	207	0	0	1	0			-0	/3	0.0

■ CHARLIE LOWE
Lowe, Charles b: Baltimore, Md. Deb: 9/28/1872

YEAR	TM/L	G	AB	R	H	2B	3B	HR	RBI	BB	SO	AVG	OBP	SLG	PRO+	BR	/A	RC	SB	CS	SBR	FR	POS	TPR
1872	Atl-n	7	32	1	5	0	0	0			0	.156	.156	.156	-3	-4	-5	1					/2	-0.3

■ DICK LOWE
Lowe, Richard Alvern b: 1/28/1854, Evansville, Wis. d: 6/28/22, Janesville, Wis. Deb: 6/26/1884

YEAR	TM/L	G	AB	R	H	2B	3B	HR	RBI	BB	SO	AVG	OBP	SLG	PRO+	BR	/A	RC	SB	CS	SBR	FR	POS	TPR
1884	Det-N	1	3	0	1	0	0	0	0	0	1	.333	.333	.333	117	0	0	0				-2	/C	-0.1

■ BOBBY LOWE
Lowe, Robert Lincoln "Link" b: 7/10/1868, Pittsburg, Pa. d: 12/8/51, Detroit, Mich. BR/TR, 5'10", 150 lbs. Deb: 4/19/1890 M

YEAR	TM/L	G	AB	R	H	2B	3B	HR	RBI	BB	SO	AVG	OBP	SLG	PRO+	BR	/A	RC	SB	CS	SBR	FR	POS	TPR
1890	Bos-N	52	207	35	58	13	2	2	21	26	32	.280	.366	.391	114	6	4	36	15			-8	SO3	-0.3
1891	Bos-N	125	497	92	129	19	5	6	74	53	54	.260	.342	.354	94	4	-5	77	43			-6	*02/S3P	-1.4
1892	*Bos-N	124	475	79	115	16	7	3	57	37	46	.242	.308	.324	85	-4	-10	60	36			14	O3S2	0.1
1893	Bos-N	126	526	130	157	19	5	14	89	55	29	.298	.369	.433	106	10	3	95	22			1	*2/S	0.3
1894	Bos-N	133	613	158	212	34	11	17	115	50	25	.346	.401	.520	113	21	11	140	23			-6	*2/S3	1.0
1895	Bos-N	99	412	101	122	12	7	7	62	40	16	.296	.370	.410	95	2	-4	73	24			15	*2	1.4
1896	Bos-N	73	305	59	98	11	4	2	48	20	11	.321	.371	.403	100	3	-0	52	15			24	2	2.2
1897	*Bos-N	123	499	87	154	24	8	5	106	32		.309	.355	.419	100	4	-1	82	16			-4	*2	0.4
1898	Bos-N	147	559	65	152	11	7	4	94	29		.272	.311	.338	84	-9	-13	64	12			17	*2/S	0.9
1899	Bos-N	152	559	81	152	5	9	4	88	35		.272	.316	.335	74	-15	-23	66	17			3	*2/S	-0.9
1900	Bos-N	127	474	65	132	11	5	3	71	26		.278	.323	.342	76	-9	-18	59	15			-7	*2	-1.6
1901	Bos-N	129	491	47	125	11	1	3	47	17		.255	.284	.299	65	-18	-24	50	22			-5	*32	-2.0
1902	Chi-N	119	472	41	116	13	3	0	31	11		.246	.270	.286	76	-15	-14	43	16			26	*2/3	2.1
1903	Chi-N	32	105	14	28	5	3	0	15	4		.267	.294	.371	93	-2	-1	14	5			4	2/13	0.4
1904	Pit-N	1	1	0	0	0	0	0	0	0		.000	.000	.000	-97	-0	-0	0	0			0	H	0.0
	Det-A	140	506	47	105	14	6	0	40	17		.208	.233	.259	59	-24	-23	36	15			-0	*2M	-2.4
1905	Det-A	58	181	17	35	7	2	0	9	13		.193	.247	.254	60	-8	-8	14	3			-1	O3/2S1	-0.9
1906	Det-A	41	145	11	30	3	0	1	12	4		.207	.228	.248	49	-8	-9	9	3			8	S2/3	0.0
1907	Det-A	17	37	2	9	2	0	0	5	4		.243	.317	.297	95	0	-0	4	0			-4	3/OS	-0.3
Total	18	1818	7064	1131	1929	230	85	71	984	473	213	.273	.324	.360	88	-62	-136	974	302			69	*203/S1P	-1.0

■ JOHN LOWENSTEIN
Lowenstein, John Lee b: 1/27/47, Wolf Point, Mont. BL/TR, 6', 175 lbs. Deb: 9/02/70

YEAR	TM/L	G	AB	R	H	2B	3B	HR	RBI	BB	SO	AVG	OBP	SLG	PRO+	BR	/A	RC	SB	CS	SBR	FR	POS	TPR
1970	Cle-A	17	43	5	11	3	1	1	6	1	9	.256	.273	.442	89	-1	-1	5	1	0	0	4	2/3OS	0.4
1971	Cle-A	58	140	15	26	5	0	4	9	16	28	.186	.269	.307	58	-7	-8	11	1	5	-3	-2	2O/S	-1.2
1972	Cle-A	68	151	16	32	8	1	6	21	20	43	.212	.304	.397	104	1	1	18	2	4	-2	3	O/1	0.0
1973	Cle-A	98	305	42	89	16	1	6	40	23	41	.292	.341	.410	109	4	3	41	5	3	-0	-9	02/31D	-0.5
1974	Cle-A	140	508	65	123	14	2	8	48	53	85	.242	.316	.325	85	-9	-9	55	36	17	1	-4	*O31/2	-1.5
1975	Cle-A	91	265	37	64	5	1	12	33	28	28	.242	.314	.404	102	0	0	32	15	10	-2	-3	OD/32	-0.5
1976	Cle-A	93	229	33	47	8	2	2	14	25	35	.205	.283	.284	67	-9	-9	18	11	8	-2	1	OD/1	-1.2
1977	Cle-A	81	149	24	36	6	1	4	12	21	29	.242	.335	.376	97	-1	-0	16	1	8	-5	2	O/1	-0.3
1978	Tex-A	77	176	28	39	8	3	5	21	37	29	.222	.363	.386	110	4	4	29	16	3	-5	3DO		0.1
1979	*Bal-A	97	197	33	50	8	2	11	34	30	37	.254	.355	.482	128	7	8	36	16	4	2	4	O/13D	1.1
1980	Bal-A	104	196	38	61	8	0	4	27	32	29	.311	.408	.413	127	8	9	36	7	3	0	2	O/D	0.9
1981	Bal-A	83	189	19	47	7	0	6	20	22	32	.249	.330	.381	105	1	1	22	7	6	-2		O/D	-0.3
1982	*Bal-A	122	322	69	103	15	2	24	66	54	59	.320	.419	.602	177	35	35	81	7	6	-2	-4	*O	2.5
1983	*Bal-A	122	310	52	87	13	2	15	60	49	55	.281	.381	.481	138	16	17	61	2	1	0	-11	*O/2D	0.4
1984	Bal-A	105	270	34	64	13	0	8	28	33	54	.237	.322	.374	91	-3	-2	34	1	0	0	1	OD/1	-0.2
1985	Bal-A	12	26	0	2	0	0	0	2	3	3	.077	.143	.077	-39	-5	-5	0	0	0	0	0	/OD	-0.4
Total	16	1368	3476	510	881	137	18	116	441	446	596	.253	.340	.403	108	41	43	496	128	78	-8	-24	OD/321S	-0.7

■ PEANUTS LOWREY
Lowrey, Harry Lee b: 8/27/18, Culver City, Cal. d: 7/2/86, Inglewood, Cal. BR/TR, 5'8.5", 170 lbs. Deb: 4/14/42 C

YEAR	TM/L	G	AB	R	H	2B	3B	HR	RBI	BB	SO	AVG	OBP	SLG	PRO+	BR	/A	RC	SB	CS	SBR	FR	POS	TPR
1942	Chi-N	27	58	4	11	0	0	1	4	4	4	.190	.242	.241	43	-4	-4	4				4	O	0.0
1943	Chi-N	130	480	59	140	25	12	1	63	35	24	.292	.340	.400	115	7	8	64	13			10	*OS/2	1.6
1945	*Chi-N	143	523	72	148	22	7	7	89	48	27	.283	.343	.392	106	2	4	73	11			3	*O/S	0.1
1946	Chi-N	144	540	75	139	24	5	4	54	56	22	.257	.328	.343	92	-7	-5	63	10			3	*O3	-0.4
1947	Chi-N	115	448	56	126	17	5	5	37	38	26	.281	.339	.375	93	-7	-5	58	2			9	3O/2	0.1
1948	Chi-N	129	435	47	128	12	3	2	54	34	31	.294	.347	.349	93	-6	-4	52	2			3	*O/32S	-0.8
1949	Chi-N	38	111	18	30	5	0	2	10	9	8	.270	.325	.369	88	-2	-2	13	3			-3	O/3	-0.6
	Cin-N	89	309	48	85	16	2	2	25	37	11	.275	.354	.359	91	-3	-3	39	1			7	O	0.0
	Yr	127	420	66	115	21	2	4	35	46	19	.274	.347	.362	90	-5	-5	52	4			3		-0.6
1950	Cin-N	91	264	34	60	14	0	1	11	36	7	.227	.320	.292	62	-14	-14	25	0			2	O/2	-1.3
	StL-N	17	56	10	15	0	0	1	4	6	1	.268	.349	.321	74	-2	-2	7	0			2	/23O	-0.0
	Yr	108	320	44	75	14	0	2	15	42	8	.234	.325	.297	64	-15	-16	31	0			4		-1.3
1951	StL-N	114	370	52	112	19	5	5	40	35	12	.303	.366	.422	111	6	6	57	0	1	-1	-5	O3/2	-0.1
1952	StL-N	132	374	48	107	18	2	1	48	34	13	.286	.352	.353	96	-1	-1	48	3	2	-0	-8	*O/3	-1.2
1953	StL-N	104	182	26	49	9	2	5	27	15	21	.269	.325	.423	93	-2	-2	24	1	0	0	-6	O2/3	-0.7
1954	StL-N	74	61	6	7	1	2	0	6	8	3	.115	.229	.197	12	-8	-8	3	0	0	0	-0	O	-0.8
1955	Phi-N	54	106	9	20	4	0	0	8	7	10	.189	.239	.226	25	-11	-11	5	2	0	1	-2	O/21	-0.1
Total	13	1401	4317	564	1177	186	45	37	479	403	226	.273	.336	.362	92	-52	-44	533	48	3		17	O3/2S1	-5.3

YEAR	TM/L	G	AB	R	H	2B	3B	HR	RBI	BB	SO	AVG	OBP	SLG	PRO+	BR	/A	RC	SB	CS	SBR	FR	POS	TPR

■ DWIGHT LOWRY   Lowry, Dwight (b: Dwight Lowery)   b: 10/23/57, Lumberton, N.C.   BL/TR, 6'3", 210 lbs.   Deb: 4/03/84

1984	Det-A	32	45	8	11	2	0	2	7	3	11	.244	.292	.422	95	-0	-0	5	0	0	0	4	C	0.6
1986	Det-A	56	150	21	46	4	0	3	18	17	19	.307	.392	.393	115	4	4	24	0	0	0	-1	C/1O	0.6
1987	Det-A	13	25	0	5	2	0	0	1	0	6	.200	.200	.280	27	-3	-3	1	0	0	0	1	C/1	0.0
1988	Min-A	7	7	0	0	0	0	0	0	0	2	.000	.000	.000	-97	-2	-2	0	0	0	0	2	/CD	0.0
Total	4	108	227	29	62	8	0	5	26	20	38	.273	.343	.374	96	-1	-1	30	0	0	0	6	C/D1O	1.2

■ JOHN LOWRY   Lowry, John D.   b: Baltimore, Md.   Deb: 6/12/1875

1875	Was-n	6	21	2	3	0	0	0		0	1	.143	.182	.143	14	-2	-2	1					/O	0.0

■ WILLIE LOZADO   Lozado, William   b: 5/12/59, New York, N.Y.   BR/TR, 6', 166 lbs.   Deb: 7/16/84

1984	Mil-A	43	107	15	29	8	2	1	20	12	23	.271	.345	.411	113	1	2	15	0	3	-2	-1	3/S2D	0.0

■ STEVE LUBRATICH   Lubratich, Steven George   b: 5/1/55, Oakland, Cal.   BR/TR, 6', 170 lbs.   Deb: 9/27/81

1981	Cal-A	7	21	2	3	1	0	0	1	0	2	.143	.143	.190	-5	-3	-3	0	1	0	0	2	/3	0.0
1983	Cal-A	57	156	12	34	9	0	0	7	4	17	.218	.237	.276	41	-13	-12	10	0	1	-1	15	S32	0.4
Total	2	64	177	14	37	10	0	0	8	4	19	.209	.227	.266	36	-15	-15	10	1	1	-0	17	/3S2	0.4

■ HAL LUBY   Luby, Hugh Max   b: 6/13/13, Blackfoot, Idaho   d: 5/4/86, Eugene, Oregon   BR/TR, 5'10", 185 lbs.   Deb: 9/10/36

1936	Phi-A	9	38	3	7	1	0	0	3	0	7	.184	.205	.211	3	-6	-6	2	2	0	1	-4	/2	-0.7
1944	NY-N	111	323	30	82	10	2	0	35	52	15	.254	.364	.316	93	-1	-1	40	2			16	32/1	2.4
Total	2	120	361	33	89	11	2	2	38	52	22	.247	.349	.305	83	-7	-6	42	4	0		12	/321	1.7

■ JOHNNY LUCADELLO   Lucadello, John   b: 2/22/19, Thurber, Tex.   BB/TR, 5'11", 160 lbs.   Deb: 9/24/38

1938	StL-A	7	20	1	3	1	0	0	0	0	0	.150	.150	.200	-13	-4	-4	1	0	0	0	-1	/3	-0.3
1939	StL-A	9	30	0	7	2	0	0	4	2	4	.233	.281	.300	48	-2	-2	3	0	0	0	-4	/2	-0.5
1940	StL-A	17	63	15	20	4	2	2	10	6	4	.317	.394	.540	137	4	3	15	1	0	0	0	2	0.5
1941	StL-A	107	351	58	98	22	4	2	31	48	23	.279	.366	.382	95	-0	-2	54	5	2	0	-16	2S/3O	-0.9
1946	StL-A	87	210	21	52	7	1	1	15	36	20	.248	.358	.305	82	-2	-4	26	0	1	-1	-7	32	-0.6
1947	NY-A	12	12	0	1	0	0	0	0	1	5	.083	.154	.083	-33	-2	-2	0	0	0	0	-2	/2	-0.3
Total	6	239	686	95	181	36	7	5	60	93	56	.264	.353	.359	88	-7	-10	98	6	3	0	-29	2/3SO	-2.1

■ RED LUCAS   Lucas, Charles Frederick "The Nashville Narcissus"   b: 4/28/02, Columbia, Tenn.   d: 7/9/86, Nashville, Tenn.   BL/TR, 5'9.5", 170 lbs.   Deb: 4/19/23

1923	NY-N	3	2	0	0	0	0	0	0	0	1	.000	.000	.000	-99	-1	-1	0	0	0	0	0	/P	0.0
1924	Bos-N	33	33	5	11	1	0	0	5	1	4	.333	.353	.364	96	-0	-0	4	0	0	0	1	P/3	0.0
1925	Bos-N	6	20	1	3	0	0	0	2	2	4	.150	.227	.150	-2	-3	-3	1	0	0	0	0	/2	-0.2
1926	Cin-N	66	76	15	23	4	4	0	14	10	13	.303	.384	.461	130	3	3	13	0			-1	P/2	0.0
1927	Cin-N	80	150	14	47	5	2	0	28	12	10	.313	.368	.373	102	0	1	21	0			-5	P/2SO	0.2
1928	Cin-N	39	73	8	23	2	1	0	7	4	6	.315	.351	.370	90	-1	-1	9	0			0	P	0.0
1929	Cin-N	76	140	15	41	6	0	0	13	13	15	.293	.353	.336	75	-6	-5	17	1			0	P	0.2
1930	Cin-N	80	113	18	38	4	1	2	19	17	4	.336	.423	.442	115	3	4	22	0			-2	P	0.6
1931	Cin-N	97	153	15	43	4	0	0	17	12	9	.281	.333	.307	78	-5	-4	17	0			1	P	0.2
1932	Cin-N	76	150	13	43	11	2	0	19	10	9	.287	.335	.387	97	-1	-1	20	0			0	P	0.4
1933	Cin-N	75	122	14	35	6	1	1	15	12	6	.287	.356	.377	111	2	2	17	0			0	P	0.7
1934	Pit-N	68	105	11	23	5	1	0	8	6	16	.219	.261	.286	45	-8	-8	8	1			-2	P	-0.5
1935	Pit-N	47	66	6	21	6	0	0	10	7	11	.318	.392	.409	112	2	1	11	0			-0	P	0.4
1936	Pit-N	69	108	11	26	4	1	0	14	8	17	.241	.293	.296	58	-6	-6	9	0			-0	P	-0.2
1937	Pit-N	59	82	8	22	3	0	0	17	7	6	.268	.326	.305	72	-3	-3	8	0			-1	P	0.0
1938	Pit-N	33	46	1	5	0	0	0	2	3	2	.109	.163	.109	-24	-8	-8	1	0			-1	P	-0.5
Total	16	907	1439	155	404	61	13	3	190	124	133	.281	.340	.347	84	-33	-29	177	2	0		-10	P/2S3O	1.3

■ FRED LUCAS   Lucas, Frederick Warrington "Fritz"   b: 1/19/03, Vineland, N.J.   d: 3/11/87, Cambridge, Md.   BR/TR, 5'10", 165 lbs.   Deb: 7/15/35

1935	Phi-N	20	34	1	9	0	0	0	3	6		.265	.324	.265	55	-2	-2	3	0			0	O	-0.2

■ JOHNNY LUCAS   Lucas, John Charles "Buster"   b: 2/10/03, Glen Carbon, Ill.   d: 10/31/70, Maryville, Ill.   BR/TL, 5'10", 186 lbs.   Deb: 4/15/31

1931	Bos-A	3	2	0	0	0	0	0	0	0	1	.000	.000	.000	-99	-1	-1	0	0	0	0	-1	/O	-0.1
1932	Bos-A	1	1	0	0	0	0	0	0	0	0	.000	.000	.000	-99	-0	-0	0	0	0	0	0	H	0.0
Total	2	4	3	0	0	0	0	0	0	0	1	.000	.000	.000	-99	-1	-1	0	0	0	0	-1	/O	-0.1

■ FRANK LUCE   Luce, Frank Edward   b: 12/6/1896, Spencer, Ohio   d: 2/3/42, Milwaukee, Wis.   BL/TR, 5'11", 180 lbs.   Deb: 9/17/23

1923	Pit-N	9	12	2	6	0	0	0	3	2	2	.500	.571	.500	181	2	2	4	2	1	0	-0	/O	0.1

■ JOE LUCEY   Lucey, Joseph Earl "Scootch"   b: 3/27/1897, Holyoke, Mass.   d: 7/30/80, Holyoke, Mass.   BR/TR, 6', 168 lbs.   Deb: 7/06/20

1920	NY-A	3	3	0	0	0	0	0	0	0	0	.000	.000	.000	-97	-1	-1	0	0	0	0	0	/2S	0.0
1925	Bos-A	10	15	0	2	0	0	0	0	0	4	.133	.133	.133	-32	-3	-3	0	0	0	0	-1	/PS	0.0
Total	2	13	18	0	2	0	0	0	0	0	4	.111	.111	.111	-43	-4	-4	0	0	0	0	-0	/PS2	0.0

■ FRED LUDERUS   Luderus, Frederick William   b: 9/12/1885, Milwaukee, Wis.   d: 1/4/61, Milwaukee, Wis.   BL/TR, 5'11.5", 185 lbs.   Deb: 9/23/09

1909	Chi-N	11	37	8	11	1	1	1	9	3		.297	.366	.459	152	2	2	6	0			-1	1	0.1
1910	Chi-N	24	54	5	11	1	1	0	3	4	3	.204	.259	.259	52	-3	-3	4	0			-0	1	-0.3
	Phi-N	21	68	10	20	5	2	0	14	9	5	.294	.385	.426	132	3	3	12	2			1	1	0.4
	Yr	45	122	15	31	6	3	0	17	13	8	.254	.331	.352	98	-0	-0	15	2			0		0.1
1911	Phi-N	146	551	69	166	24	11	16	99	40	76	.301	.353	.472	128	19	18	93	6			-2	*1	1.1
1912	Phi-N	148	572	77	147	31	5	10	69	44	65	.257	.318	.381	85	-9	-14	70	8			10	*1	-0.9
1913	Phi-N	155	588	67	154	32	7	18	86	34	51	.262	.304	.432	105	3	1	75	5			1	*1	-0.5
1914	Phi-N	121	443	55	110	16	5	12	55	33	31	.248	.308	.388	100	2	-1	51	2			1	*1	-0.1
1915	*Phi-N	141	499	55	157	36	7	7	62	42	36	.315	.376	.457	150	30	30	87	9	7	-2	10	*1	3.4
1916	Phi-N	146	508	52	143	26	3	5	53	41	32	.281	.341	.374	115	12	10	69	8			-2	*1	0.2
1917	Phi-N	154	522	57	136	24	4	5	72	65	35	.261	.349	.351	110	11	9	64	5			5	*1	1.3
1918	Phi-N	125	468	54	135	23	2	1	67	42	33	.288	.351	.378	115	13	9	61	4			7	*1	1.4
1919	Phi-N	138	509	60	149	30	6	5	49	54	48	.293	.365	.405	123	20	16	75	6			10	*1	2.6
1920	Phi-N	16	32	1	5	2	0	0	4	3	6	.156	.229	.219	28	-3	-3	2	0	1	-1	0	/1	-0.3
Total	12	1346	4851	570	1344	251	54	84	642	414	421	.277	.340	.403	113	101	75	669	55	8		40	*1	8.4

■ BILL LUDWIG   Ludwig, William Lawrence   b: 5/27/1882, Louisville, Ky.   d: 9/5/47, Louisville, Ky.   TR ,   Deb: 4/16/08

1908	StL-N	66	187	15	34	2	2	0	8	16		.182	.246	.214	51	-10	-9	11	3			-3	C	-1.0

■ ROY LUEBBE   Luebbe, Roy John   b: 9/17/1900, Parkersburg, Iowa   d: 8/21/85, Papillion, Neb.   BB/TR, 6', 175 lbs.   Deb: 8/22/25

1925	NY-A	8	15	1	0	0	0	0	3	2	6	.000	.118	.000	-69	-4	-4	0	0	0	0	2	/C	-0.1

■ HENRY LUFF   Luff, Henry T.   b: 9/14/1856, Philadelphia, Pa.   d: 10/11/16, Philadelphia, Pa.   5'11", 175 lbs.   Deb: 4/21/1875

1875	NH-n	38	165	15	46	11	3	2		0		.279	.279	.418	161	6	10	20					3/PO	1.0
1882	Det-N	3	11	1	3	2	0	0	1	0		.273	.273	.455	129	0	0	1				-1	/2O	0.0
	Cin-a	28	120	16	28	2	2	0			2	.233	.246	.283	74	-3	-4	9				-2	1/O	-0.5
1883	Lou-a	6	23	1	4	0	0	0		0		.174	.174	.174	13	-2	-2	1				-1	/1O	-0.2
1884	Phi-U	26	111	9	30	4	2	0		4		.270	.296	.342	124	2	3	12	0			-3	O/132	0.0

YEAR	TM/L	G	AB	R	H	2B	3B	HR	RBI	BB	SO	AVG	OBP	SLG	PRO+	BR	/A	RC	SB	CS	SBR	FR	POS	TPR
	KC-U	5	19	0	1	0	0	0			1	.053	.100	.053	-54	-3	-2	0	0			-4	/3O	-0.5
Yr		31	130	9	31	4	2	0			5	.238	.267	.300	100	-1	1	11	0			-7		-0.5
Total	3	68	284	27	66	8	4	0	1	7	0	.232	.251	.289	82	-6	-5	22	0			-11	/1O32	-1.2

■ EDDIE LUKON
Lukon, Edward Paul "Mongoose" b: 8/5/20, Burgettstown, Pa.　BL/TL, 5'10", 168 lbs.　Deb: 8/06/41

YEAR	TM/L	G	AB	R	H	2B	3B	HR	RBI	BB	SO	AVG	OBP	SLG	PRO+	BR	/A	RC	SB	CS	SBR	FR	POS	TPR
1941	Cin-N	23	86	6	23	3	0	0	3	6	6	.267	.315	.302	74	-3	-3	8	1			0	O	-0.3
1945	Cin-N	2	8	1	1	0	0	0	0	0	1	.125	.125	.125	-31	-1	-1	0	0			0	/O	0.0
1946	Cin-N	102	312	31	78	8	8	12	34	26	29	.250	.310	.442	116	3	4	43	3			1	O	0.4
1947	Cin-N	86	200	26	41	6	1	11	33	28	36	.205	.306	.410	89	-4	-4	26	0			0	O	-0.5
Total	4	213	606	64	143	17	9	23	70	60	72	.236	.307	.408	99	-5	-4	77	4			1	O	-0.4

■ MIKE LUM
Lum, Michael Ken-Wai b: 10/27/45, Honolulu, Hawaii　BL/TL, 6', 180 lbs.　Deb: 9/12/67　C

YEAR	TM/L	G	AB	R	H	2B	3B	HR	RBI	BB	SO	AVG	OBP	SLG	PRO+	BR	/A	RC	SB	CS	SBR	FR	POS	TPR
1967	Atl-N	9	26	1	6	0	0	0	1	1	4	.231	.259	.231	42	-2	-2	1	0	1	-1	1	/O	-0.1
1968	Atl-N	122	232	22	52	7	3	3	21	14	35	.224	.280	.319	79	-6	-6	19	3	5	-2	-11	O	-2.7
1969	*Atl-N	121	168	20	45	8	0	1	22	16	18	.268	.332	.333	86	-3	-3	18	0	0	0	10	O	0.2
1970	Atl-N	123	291	25	74	17	2	7	28	17	43	.254	.307	.399	83	-6	-8	36	3	2	-0	6	O	-0.6
1971	Atl-N	145	454	56	122	14	1	13	55	47	43	.269	.344	.390	101	5	2	61	0	3	-2	10	*O/1	0.6
1972	Atl-N	123	369	40	84	14	2	9	38	50	52	.228	.325	.350	84	-3	-7	43	1	4	-2	5	*O/1	-0.9
1973	Atl-N	138	513	74	151	26	6	16	82	41	89	.294	.354	.462	116	16	11	84	2	5	-2	-3	1O	0.0
1974	Atl-N	106	361	50	84	11	2	11	50	45	49	.233	.321	.366	88	-4	-6	42	0	2	-1	-6	1O	-1.8
1975	Atl-N	124	364	32	83	8	2	8	36	39	38	.228	.303	.327	72	-13	-14	34	2	4	-2	-1	1O	-2.2
1976	*Cin-N	84	136	15	31	5	1	3	20	22	24	.228	.340	.346	93	-0	-1	17	0	1	-1	-4	O	-0.6
1977	Cin-N	81	125	14	20	1	0	5	16	9	33	.160	.222	.288	35	-12	-12	8	2	0	1	-1	O/1	-1.3
1978	Cin-N	86	146	15	39	7	1	6	23	22	18	.267	.363	.452	126	5	5	24	0	0	0	5	O/1	0.8
1979	Atl-N	111	217	27	54	6	0	6	27	18	34	.249	.306	.359	75	-6	-8	22	0	2	-1	2	1/O	-0.9
1980	Atl-N	93	83	7	17	3	0	0	5	18	19	.205	.347	.241	65	-3	-3	8	0	0	0	1	O1	-0.2
1981	Atl-N	10	11	1	1	0	0	0	0	2	2	.091	.231	.091	-6	-1	-2	0	0	0	0	0	O	-0.1
	Chi-N	41	58	5	14	1	0	2	7	5	5	.241	.313	.362	87	-1	-1	7	0	0	0	-2	O/1	-0.3
Yr		51	69	6	15	1	0	2	7	7	7	.217	.299	.319	72	-2	-3	7	0	0	0	-2		-0.4
Total	15	1517	3554	404	877	128	20	90	431	366	506	.247	.322	.370	89	-34	-55	426	13	29	-14	13	O1	-10.1

■ HARRY LUMLEY
Lumley, Harry G "Judge" b: 9/29/1880, Forest City, Pa.　d: 5/22/38, Binghamton, N.Y.　BL/TL, 5'10", 183 lbs.　Deb: 4/14/04　M

YEAR	TM/L	G	AB	R	H	2B	3B	HR	RBI	BB	SO	AVG	OBP	SLG	PRO+	BR	/A	RC	SB	CS	SBR	FR	POS	TPR
1904	Bro-N	150	577	79	161	23	18	9	78	41		.279	.327	.428	138	21	23	94	30			4	*O	2.2
1905	Bro-N	130	505	50	148	19	10	7	47	36		.293	.340	.412	136	15	19	82	22			-1	*O	0.9
1906	Bro-N	133	484	72	157	23	12	9	61	48		.324	.385	.477	186	38	43	107	35			1	*O	4.5
1907	Bro-N	127	454	47	121	23	11	9	66	31		.267	.313	.425	145	15	19	70	18			-4	*O	1.2
1908	Bro-N	127	440	36	95	13	12	4	39	29		.216	.264	.327	94	-6	-4	39	4			-5	*O	-1.1
1909	Bro-N	55	172	13	43	8	3	0	14	16		.250	.314	.331	104	-0	1	19	1			2	OM	0.1
1910	Bro-N	8	21	3	3	0	0	0	0	3	6	.143	.280	.143	25	-2	-2	1	0			-1	/O	-0.2
Total	7	730	2653	300	728	109	66	38	305	204	6	.274	.326	.408	137	81	99	411	110			-5	O	7.6

■ JERRY LUMPE
Lumpe, Jerry Dean b: 6/2/33, Lincoln, Mo.　BL/TR, 6'2", 185 lbs.　Deb: 4/17/56　C

YEAR	TM/L	G	AB	R	H	2B	3B	HR	RBI	BB	SO	AVG	OBP	SLG	PRO+	BR	/A	RC	SB	CS	SBR	FR	POS	TPR
1956	NY-A	20	62	12	16	3	0	0	4	5	11	.258	.313	.306	66	-3	-3	6	1	1	-0	3	S/3	0.2
1957	*NY-A	40	103	15	35	6	2	0	11	9	13	.340	.393	.437	128	4	4	18	2	2	-1	-2	3/S	0.3
1958	*NY-A	81	232	34	59	8	4	3	32	23	21	.254	.324	.362	92	-3	-2	26	1	2	-1	4	3/S	0.4
1959	NY-A	18	45	2	10	0	0	0	2	6	7	.222	.314	.222	52	-3	-3	3	0	0	0	2	3/S2	-0.1
	KC-A	108	403	47	98	11	5	3	28	41	32	.243	.313	.318	72	-14	-15	41	2	1	-0	-10	2S/3	-1.8
Yr		126	448	49	108	11	5	3	30	47	39	.241	.313	.308	70	-17	-18	44	2	1	0	-8		-1.8
1960	KC-A	146	574	69	156	19	3	8	53	48	49	.272	.328	.357	85	-12	-12	67	1	1	-0	-7	*2S	-0.9
1961	KC-A	148	569	81	167	29	9	3	54	48	39	.293	.351	.392	98	-1	-1	79	1	0	0	16	*2	3.2
1962	KC-A	156	641	89	193	34	10	10	83	44	38	.301	.346	.432	105	6	8	94	0	2	-1	-4	*2/S	1.0
1963	KC-A	157	595	75	161	26	7	5	59	58	44	.271	.335	.363	92	-3	-5	74	3	2	-0	2	*2	0.8
1964	Det-A	158	624	75	160	21	6	6	46	50	61	.256	.314	.338	80	-15	-16	67	2	1	-0	-21	*2	-2.2
1965	Det-A	145	502	72	129	15	3	4	39	56	34	.257	.335	.323	87	-7	-7	58	7	0	2	-18	*2	-1.6
1966	Det-A	113	385	30	89	14	3	1	26	24	44	.231	.276	.291	62	-18	-19	31	0	3	-2	-6	2	-1.9
1967	Det-A	81	177	19	41	4	0	4	17	16	18	.232	.295	.322	80	-4	-4	17	0	0	0	-3	2/3	-0.5
Total	12	1371	4912	620	1314	190	52	47	454	428	411	.268	.327	.356	87	-73	-81	581	20	15	-3	-43	*23S	-3.0

■ DON LUND
Lund, Donald Andrew b: 5/18/23, Detroit, Mich.　BR/TR, 6', 200 lbs.　Deb: 7/03/45　C

YEAR	TM/L	G	AB	R	H	2B	3B	HR	RBI	BB	SO	AVG	OBP	SLG	PRO+	BR	/A	RC	SB	CS	SBR	FR	POS	TPR
1945	Bro-N	4	3	0	0	0	0	0	0	1	1	.000	.250	.000	-27	-0	-0	0	0			0	H	0.0
1947	Bro-N	11	20	5	6	2	0	2	5	3	7	.300	.391	.700	178	2	2	6	0			0	/O	0.2
1948	Bro-N	27	69	9	13	4	0	1	5	5	16	.188	.243	.290	42	-6	-6	5	1			1	O	-0.6
	StL-A	63	161	21	40	7	4	3	25	10	17	.248	.305	.398	84	-4	-5	21	0	0	0	-3	O	-0.8
1949	Det-A	2	2	0	0	0	0	0	0	0	1	.000	.000	.000	-99	-1	-1	0	0	0	0	0	H	0.0
1952	Det-A	8	23	1	7	0	0	0	1	3	3	.304	.385	.304	93	-0	-0	3	0	1	-1	-0	/O	0.0
1953	Det-A	131	421	51	108	21	4	9	47	39	65	.257	.323	.390	93	-6	-5	53	3	3	-1	8	*O	0.0
1954	Det-A	35	54	4	7	2	0	0	3	4	3	.130	.190	.167	-2	-8	-8	2	1	0	0	0	O	-0.7
Total	7	281	753	91	181	36	8	15	86	65	113	.240	.305	.369	81	-22	-22	89	5	4		7	O	-1.9

■ GORDY LUND
Lund, Gordon Thomas b: 2/23/41, Iron Mountain, Mich.　BR/TR, 5'11", 170 lbs.　Deb: 8/01/67

YEAR	TM/L	G	AB	R	H	2B	3B	HR	RBI	BB	SO	AVG	OBP	SLG	PRO+	BR	/A	RC	SB	CS	SBR	FR	POS	TPR
1967	Cle-A	3	8	1	2	1	0	0	0	0	2	.250	.250	.375	82	-0	-0	1	0	0	0	-1	/S	-0.1
1969	Sea-A	20	38	4	10	0	0	0	1	5	7	.263	.349	.263	75	-1	-1	4	1	1	-0	-1	S/23	0.0
Total	2	23	46	5	12	1	0	0	1	5	9	.261	.333	.283	76	-1	-1	5	1	1	-0	-2	/S32	-0.1

■ TOM LUNDSTEDT
Lundstedt, Thomas Robert b: 4/10/49, Davenport, Iowa　BB/TR, 6'4", 195 lbs.　Deb: 8/31/73

YEAR	TM/L	G	AB	R	H	2B	3B	HR	RBI	BB	SO	AVG	OBP	SLG	PRO+	BR	/A	RC	SB	CS	SBR	FR	POS	TPR
1973	Chi-N	4	5	0	0	0	0	0	0	0	1	.000	.000	.000	-93	-1	-1	0	0	0	0	1	/C	0.0
1974	Chi-N	22	32	1	3	0	0	0	0	5	7	.094	.216	.094	-11	-5	-5	1	0	0	0	2	C	-0.1
1975	Min-A	18	28	2	3	0	0	0	1	4	5	.107	.219	.107	-5	-4	-4	1	0	0	0	3	C/D	0.0
Total	3	44	65	3	6	0	0	0	1	9	13	.092	.203	.092	-14	-10	-10	2	0	0	0	5	/CD	-0.1

■ HARRY LUNTE
Lunte, Harry August b: 9/15/1892, St.Louis, Mo.　d: 7/27/65, St.Louis, Mo.　BR/TR, 5'11.5", 165 lbs.　Deb: 5/19/19

YEAR	TM/L	G	AB	R	H	2B	3B	HR	RBI	BB	SO	AVG	OBP	SLG	PRO+	BR	/A	RC	SB	CS	SBR	FR	POS	TPR
1919	Cle-A	26	77	2	15	2	0	0	2	1	7	.195	.215	.221	21	-8	-9	4	0			-2	S	-0.8
1920	*Cle-A	23	71	6	14	0	0	0	7	5	6	.197	.250	.197	19	-8	-8	3	0	1	-1	3	S/2	-0.3
Total	2	49	148	8	29	2	0	0	9	6	13	.196	.232	.209	20	-16	-17	7	0	1		1	/S2	-1.1

■ TONY LUPIEN
Lupien, Ulysses John b: 4/23/17, Chelmsford, Mass.　BL/TL, 5'10.5", 185 lbs.　Deb: 9/12/40

YEAR	TM/L	G	AB	R	H	2B	3B	HR	RBI	BB	SO	AVG	OBP	SLG	PRO+	BR	/A	RC	SB	CS	SBR	FR	POS	TPR
1940	Bos-A	10	19	5	9	3	2	0	4	1	1	.474	.500	.842	232	4	4	8	0	0	0	0	/1	0.3
1942	Bos-A	128	463	63	130	25	7	3	70	50	20	.281	.351	.384	103	4	2	65	10	12	-4	-7	*1	-1.0
1943	Bos-A	154	608	65	155	21	9	4	47	54	23	.255	.317	.339	90	-7	-8	70	16	9	-1	4	*1	-0.9
1944	Phi-N	153	597	82	169	23	9	5	52	56	29	.283	.347	.377	107	3	6	82	18			1	*1	-0.5
1945	Phi-N	15	54	1	17	1	0	0	3	6	0	.315	.383	.333	103	0	1	8	2			3	1	0.3
1948	Chi-A	154	617	69	152	19	3	6	54	74	38	.246	.327	.316	74	-25	-22	71	11	7	-1	-4	*1	-1.8
Total	6	614	2358	285	632	92	30	18	230	241	111	.268	.337	.355	94	-20	-18	304	57	28	-1	-3	1	-3.6

YEAR	TM/L	G	AB	R	H	2B	3B	HR	RBI	BB	SO	AVG	OBP	SLG	PRO+	BR	/A	RC	SB	CS	SBR	FR	POS	TPR

■ AL LUPLOW
Luplow, Alvin David b: 3/13/39, Saginaw, Mich. BL/TR, 5'10", 175 lbs. Deb: 9/16/61

1961	Cle-A	5	18	0	1	0	0	0	0	2	6	.056	.150	.056	-44	-4	-4	0	0	0	0	1	/O	-0.1
1962	Cle-A	97	318	54	88	15	3	14	45	36	44	.277	.361	.475	127	10	12	57	1	0	0	-1	O	0.7
1963	Cle-A	100	295	34	69	6	2	7	27	33	62	.234	.317	.339	85	-6	-5	32	4	4	-1	3	O	-0.6
1964	Cle-A	19	18	1	2	0	0	0	1	1	8	.111	.158	.111	-24	-3	-3	0	0	0	0	1	/O	-0.2
1965	Cle-A	53	45	3	6	2	0	1	4	3	14	.133	.188	.244	22	-5	-5	2	0	1	-1	1	/O	-0.4
1966	NY-N	111	334	31	84	9	1	7	31	38	46	.251	.332	.347	91	-4	-3	37	2	6	-3	-7	*O	-1.6
1967	NY-N	41	112	11	23	1	0	3	9	8	19	.205	.264	.295	61	-6	-6	9	0	0	0	-1	O	-0.7
	Pit-N	55	103	13	19	1	0	1	8	6	14	.184	.236	.223	32	-9	-9	6	1	0	0	3	O	-0.6
	Yr	96	215	24	42	2	0	4	17	14	33	.195	.251	.260	47	-15	-15	14	1	0	0	3		-1.3
Total	7	481	1243	147	292	34	6	33	125	127	213	.235	.312	.352	85	-26	-23	142	8	11	-4	-1	O	-3.5

■ SCOTT LUSADER
Lusader, Scott Edward b: 9/30/64, Chicago, Ill. BL/TL, 5'10", 165 lbs. Deb: 9/01/87

1987	Det-A	23	47	8	15	3	1	1	8	5	7	.319	.385	.489	135	2	2	9	1	0	0	-0	O/D	0.2
1988	Det-A	16	16	3	1	0	0	1	3	1	4	.063	.118	.250	-0	-2	-2	0	0	0	0	1	/O	-0.1
1989	Det-A	40	103	15	26	4	0	1	8	9	21	.252	.313	.320	81	-3	-3	11	3	0	1	-2	O/D	-0.4
1990	Det-A	45	87	13	21	2	0	2	16	12	8	.241	.333	.333	87	-1	-1	10	0	0	0	-2	O	-0.2
Total	4	124	253	39	63	9	1	5	35	27	40	.249	.321	.352	89	-4	-3	31	4	0	1	-4	O/D	-0.5

■ ERNIE LUSH
Lush, Ernest Benjamin b: 10/31/1884, Bridgeport, Conn. d: 2/26/37, Detroit, Mich. BR/TL, Deb: 4/20/10

1910	StL-N	1	4	0	0	0	0	0	0	1	1	.000	.200	.000	-42	-1	-1	0	0			-0	/O	0.0

■ JOHNNY LUSH
Lush, John Charles b: 10/8/1885, Williamsport, Pa. d: 11/18/46, Beverly Hills, Cal BL/TL, 5'9.5", 165 lbs. Deb: 4/22/04

1904	Phi-N	106	369	39	102	22	3	2	42	27		.276	.326	.369	121	7	8	50	12			-10	1O/P	-0.4
1905	Phi-N	6	16	3	5	0	0	0	1	1		.313	.353	.313	105	-0	0	2	0			-1	1OP	0.0
1906	Phi-N	76	212	28	56	7	1	0	15	14		.264	.310	.307	94	-2	-2	23	6			3	PO/1	1.0
1907	Phi-N	17	40	5	8	1	1	0	5	1		.200	.220	.275	57	-2	-2	3	1			0	/PO	0.0
	StL-N	27	82	6	23	2	3	0	5	5		.280	.322	.378	125	2	2	12	4			-3	P/O	0.0
	Yr	44	122	11	31	3	4	0	10	6		.254	.289	.344	103	-0	-0	14	5			-3		0.0
1908	StL-N	45	89	7	15	2	0	0	2	7		.169	.229	.191	38	-6	-6	4	1			1	P	0.0
1909	StL-N	45	92	11	22	5	0	0	14	6		.239	.293	.293	87	-2	-1	8	2			-1	P/O	0.0
1910	StL-N	47	93	8	21	1	3	0	10	8	11	.226	.287	.301	74	-4	-3	8	2			-1	P	0.0
Total	7	369	993	107	252	40	11	2	94	69	11	.254	.303	.322	98	-7	-3	110	28			-12	P/O1	0.6

■ BILLY LUSH
Lush, William Lucas b: 11/10/1873, Bridgeport, Conn. d: 8/28/51, Hawthorne, N.Y. BB/TR, 5'8", 165 lbs. Deb: 9/03/1895

1895	Was-N	5	18	2	6	0	0	0	2	2	1	.333	.400	.333	94	-0	-0	2	0			-1	/O	0.0
1896	Was-N	97	352	74	87	9	11	4	45	66	49	.247	.369	.369	97	0	1	60	28			-2	*O/2	-0.6
1897	Was-N	3	12	1	0	0	0	0	0	2		.000	.143	.000	-60	-3	-3	0	0			1	/O	-0.1
1901	Bos-N	7	27	2	5	1	1	0	3	3		.185	.267	.296	59	-1	-2	2	0			3	/O	0.0
1902	Bos-N	120	413	68	92	8	1	2	19	76		.223	.346	.262	89	-0	-1	51	30			11	*O/3	0.2
1903	Det-A	119	423	71	116	18	14	1	33	70		.274	.377	.390	137	20	22	76	14			11	*O3/2S	2.7
1904	Cle-A	138	477	76	123	13	8	1	50	72		.258	.355	.325	119	13	14	65	12			3	*O	0.9
Total	7	489	1722	294	429	49	35	8	152	291	50	.249	.359	.332	108	29	31	256	84			24	O/32S	3.1

■ CHARLIE LUSKEY
Luskey, Charles Melton b: 4/6/1876, Washington, D.C. d: 12/20/62, Bethesda, Md. 5'7", 165 lbs. Deb: 9/12/01

1901	Was-A	11	41	8	8	3	1	0	3	2		.195	.233	.317	54	-3	-3	3	0			-1	/OC	-0.3

■ LUKE LUTENBERG
Lutenberg, Charles William b: 10/4/1864, Quincy, Ill. d: 12/24/38, Quincy, Ill. BR, 6'2", 225 lbs. Deb: 7/07/1894

1894	Lou-N	69	250	42	48	10	4	0	23	23	21	.192	.284	.264	36	-27	-24	20	4			1	1/2	-1.6

■ LYLE LUTTRELL
Luttrell, Lyle Kenneth b: 2/22/30, Bloomington, Ill. d: 7/11/84, Chattanooga, Tenn BR/TR, 6', 180 lbs. Deb: 5/15/56

1956	Was-A	38	122	17	23	5	3	2	9	8	19	.189	.256	.328	53	-9	-9	9	5	1	1	-6	S	-1.0
1957	Was-A	19	45	4	9	4	0	0	5	3	8	.200	.250	.289	47	-3	-3	3	0	0	0	-5	S	-0.7
Total	2	57	167	21	32	9	3	2	14	11	27	.192	.254	.317	52	-12	-12	12	5	1	1	-12	/S	-1.7

■ RED LUTZ
Lutz, Louis William b: 12/17/1898, Cincinnati, Ohio d: 2/22/84, Cincinnati, Ohio BR/TR, 5'10", 170 lbs. Deb: 5/31/22

1922	Cin-N	1	1	0	1	1	0	0	0	0	0	1.000	1.000	2.000	669	1	1	2	0	0	0	0	/C	0.1

■ JOE LUTZ
Lutz, Rollin Joseph b: 2/18/25, Keokuk, Iowa BL/TL, 6', 195 lbs. Deb: 4/17/51 C

1951	StL-A	14	36	7	6	0	1	0	2	6	9	.167	.286	.222	38	-3	-3	3	0	0	0	-1	1	-0.3

■ RUBE LUTZKE
Lutzke, Walter John b: 11/17/1897, Milwaukee, Wis. d: 3/6/38, Granville, Wis. BR/TR, 5'11", 175 lbs. Deb: 4/18/23

1923	Cle-A	143	511	71	131	20	6	3	65	59	57	.256	.338	.337	78	-16	-16	62	10	6	-1	20	*3	2.1
1924	Cle-A	106	341	37	83	18	3	0	42	38	46	.243	.328	.314	65	-17	-17	39	4	0	1	19	*3/2	1.1
1925	Cle-A	81	238	31	52	9	0	1	16	26	29	.218	.295	.269	44	-20	-21	20	2	4	-2	-0	32	-1.6
1926	Cle-A	142	475	42	124	28	6	0	59	34	35	.261	.313	.345	71	-21	-21	53	6	3	0	-1	*3	-0.8
1927	Cle-A	100	311	35	78	12	3	0	41	22	29	.251	.307	.309	60	-18	-19	30	2	1	0	6	3	-0.5
Total	5	572	1876	216	468	87	18	4	223	179	196	.249	.319	.321	66	-92	-93	204	24	14	-1	45	3/2	0.3

■ GREG LUZINSKI
Luzinski, Gregory Michael b: 11/22/50, Chicago, Ill. BR/TR, 6'1", 220 lbs. Deb: 9/09/70

1970	Phi-N	8	12	0	2	0	0	0	0	3	5	.167	.333	.167	39	-1	-1	1	0	1	-1	1	/1	0.0
1971	Phi-N	28	100	13	30	8	0	3	15	12	32	.300	.386	.470	141	6	6	19	2	0	1	6	1	1.1
1972	Phi-N	150	563	66	158	33	5	18	68	42	114	.281	.334	.453	119	14	13	81	0	4	-2	-2	*O/1	0.1
1973	Phi-N	161	610	76	174	26	4	29	97	51	135	.285	.347	.484	125	21	19	101	3	3	-1	-9	*O	0.2
1974	Phi-N	85	302	29	82	14	1	7	48	29	76	.272	.335	.394	99	1	-0	40	3	0	1	-2	*O	-0.4
1975	Phi-N	161	596	85	179	35	3	34	120	89	151	.300	.398	.540	152	47	44	128	3	6	-3	-11	*O	2.6
1976	*Phi-N	149	533	74	162	28	1	21	95	50	107	.304	.375	.478	137	28	26	96	1	2	-1	-16	*O	0.5
1977	*Phi-N	149	554	99	171	35	3	39	130	80	140	.309	.399	.594	155	49	45	132	3	2	-0	-15	*O	2.5
1978	Phi-N	155	540	85	143	32	2	35	101	100	135	.265	.390	.526	152	41	40	114	8	7	-2	-16	*O	1.8
1979	Phi-N	137	452	47	114	23	1	18	81	56	103	.252	.347	.427	107	7	5	68	3	3	-1	-21	*O	-2.1
1980	*Phi-N	106	368	44	84	19	1	19	56	60	100	.228	.346	.440	112	9	7	60	3	0	-1	-18	*O	-1.4
1981	Chi-A	104	378	55	100	15	1	21	62	58	80	.265	.367	.476	144	25	22	67	0	0	0	0	*D	2.3
1982	Chi-A	159	583	87	170	37	1	18	102	89	120	.292	.391	.451	130	27	27	103	1	1	-0	0	*D	2.7
1983	*Chi-A	144	502	73	128	26	1	32	95	70	117	.255	.358	.502	129	24	21	93	2	1	0	0	*D/1	2.1
1984	Chi-A	125	412	47	98	13	0	13	58	56	80	.238	.333	.364	89	-3	-5	52	5	1	1	0	*D	-0.4
Total	15	1821	6505	880	1795	344	24	307	1128	845	1495	.276	.366	.478	129	291	269	1154	37	31	-8	-102	*OD/1	11.6

■ JERRY LYNCH
Lynch, Gerald Thomas b: 7/17/30, Bay City, Mich. BL/TR, 6'1", 185 lbs. Deb: 4/15/54

1954	Pit-N	98	284	27	68	4	5	8	36	20	43	.239	.292	.373	73	-12	-12	29	2	2	-1	-4	O	-1.8
1955	Pit-N	88	282	43	80	18	6	5	28	22	33	.284	.336	.443	106	1	2	40	2	2	-1	-4	O/C	-0.3
1956	Pit-N	19	19	1	3	0	1	0	0	1	4	.158	.200	.263	24	-2	-2	1	0	0	0	0	/O	-0.1
1957	Cin-N	67	124	11	32	4	1	4	17	6	18	.258	.292	.403	79	-3	-4	15	0	0	0	0	O/C	-0.6
1958	Cin-N	122	420	58	131	20	5	16	68	18	54	.312	.340	.498	112	10	7	67	1	4	-2	-10	*O	-0.8
1959	Cin-N	117	379	49	102	16	3	17	58	29	50	.269	.323	.462	103	2	1	56	2	0	1	-1	O	0.0
1960	Cin-N	102	159	23	46	8	2	6	27	16	25	.289	.358	.478	124	6	5	28	0	0	0	-4	O	0.0

YEAR	TM/L	G	AB	R	H	2B	3B	HR	RBI	BB	SO	AVG	OBP	SLG	PRO+	BR	/A	RC	SB	CS	SBR	FR	POS	TPR
1961	*Cin-N	96	181	33	57	13	2	13	50	27	25	.315	.407	.624	166	18	18	46	2	2	-1	-6	O	0.9
1962	Cin-N	114	288	41	81	15	4	12	57	24	38	.281	.339	.486	115	7	5	46	3	3	-1	-5	O	-0.3
1963	Cin-N	22	32	5	8	3	0	2	9	1	5	.250	.294	.531	129	1	1	5	0	1	-1	-1	O	0.0
	Pit-N	88	237	26	63	6	3	10	36	22	28	.266	.331	.443	120	6	6	34	0	1	-1	-9	O	-0.7
	Yr	110	269	31	71	9	3	12	45	23	33	.264	.327	.454	121	7	7	39	0	1	-1	-10		-0.7
1964	Pit-N	114	297	35	81	14	2	16	66	26	57	.273	.333	.495	130	11	11	48	0	1	-1	-17	O	-0.9
1965	Pit-N	73	121	7	34	1	0	5	16	8	26	.281	.331	.413	108	1	1	14	0	2	-1	-3	O	-0.3
1966	Pit-N	64	56	5	12	1	0	1	6	4	10	.214	.267	.286	54	-3	-3	4	0	0	0	1	/O	-0.2
Total	13	1184	2879	364	798	123	34	115	470	224	416	.277	.331	.463	110	42	35	434	12	17	-7	-65	O/C	-5.1

■ HENRY LYNCH

Lynch, Henry W. b: 4/8/1866, Worcester, Mass. d: 11/23/25, Worcester, Mass. 5'7", 143 lbs. Deb: 9/21/1893

YEAR	TM/L	G	AB	R	H	2B	3B	HR	RBI	BB	SO	AVG	OBP	SLG	PRO+	BR	/A	RC	SB	CS	SBR	FR	POS	TPR
1893	Chi-N	4	14	0	3	2	0	0	2	1	1	.214	.267	.357	68	-1	-1	1	0			-1	/O	0.0

■ DANNY LYNCH

Lynch, Matt Dan "Dummy" b: 2/7/27, Dallas, Tex. d: 6/30/78, Plano, Tex. BR/TR, 5'11", 174 lbs. Deb: 9/14/48

YEAR	TM/L	G	AB	R	H	2B	3B	HR	RBI	BB	SO	AVG	OBP	SLG	PRO+	BR	/A	RC	SB	CS	SBR	FR	POS	TPR
1948	Chi-N	7	7	3	2	0	0	1	1	1	1	.286	.375	.714	197	1	1	2	0			0	/2	0.1

■ MIKE LYNCH

Lynch, Michael Joseph b: 9/10/1875, St.Paul, Minn. d: 4/1/47, Jennings Lodge, Ore TR, 6'2", 170 lbs. Deb: 4/24/02

YEAR	TM/L	G	AB	R	H	2B	3B	HR	RBI	BB	SO	AVG	OBP	SLG	PRO+	BR	/A	RC	SB	CS	SBR	FR	POS	TPR
1902	Chi-N	7	28	4	4	0	0	0	0	2		.143	.200	.143	7	-3	-3	1	0			-1	/O	-0.3

■ TOM LYNCH

Lynch, Thomas James b: 4/3/1860, Bennington, Vt. d: 3/28/55, Cohoes, N.Y. BL/TR, 5'10.5", 170 lbs. Deb: 8/18/1884 U

YEAR	TM/L	G	AB	R	H	2B	3B	HR	RBI	BB	SO	AVG	OBP	SLG	PRO+	BR	/A	RC	SB	CS	SBR	FR	POS	TPR
1884	Wil-U	16	58	6	16	3	1	0			5	.276	.333	.362	131	2	2	7	0			-3	/CO1	0.0
	Phi-N	13	48	7	15	4	2	0	3	4	5	.313	.365	.479	171	3	4	9				-1	/CO	0.3
1885	Phi-N	13	53	7	10	3	0	0	1	10	3	.189	.317	.245	86	-0	-0	4				2	O	0.2
Total	2	42	159	20	41	10	3	0	4	19	8	.258	.337	.358	128	5	6	20				-2	/OC1	0.5

■ WALT LYNCH

Lynch, Walter Edward "Jabber" b: 4/15/1897, Buffalo, N.Y. d: 12/21/76, Daytona Beach, Fla TR, 6', 176 lbs. Deb: 7/08/22

YEAR	TM/L	G	AB	R	H	2B	3B	HR	RBI	BB	SO	AVG	OBP	SLG	PRO+	BR	/A	RC	SB	CS	SBR	FR	POS	TPR
1922	Bos-A	3	2	1	1	0	0	0	0	0	0	.500	.500	.500	163	0	0	0	0	0	0	0	/C	0.0

■ BYRD LYNN

Lynn, Byrd "Birdie" b: 3/13/1889, Unionville, Ill. d: 2/5/40, Napa, Cal. BR/TR, 5'11", 165 lbs. Deb: 4/16/16

YEAR	TM/L	G	AB	R	H	2B	3B	HR	RBI	BB	SO	AVG	OBP	SLG	PRO+	BR	/A	RC	SB	CS	SBR	FR	POS	TPR
1916	Chi-A	31	40	4	9	1	0	0	3	4	7	.225	.311	.250	68	-1	-1	4	2			9	C	0.8
1917	*Chi-A	35	72	7	16	2	0	0	5	7	11	.222	.300	.250	67	-3	-3	6	1			-2	C	-0.2
1918	Chi-A	5	8	0	2	0	0	0	0	2	1	.250	.400	.250	95	0	0	1	0			-1	/C	0.0
1919	*Chi-A	29	66	4	15	4	0	0	4	4	9	.227	.271	.288	57	-4	-4	5	0			1	C	-0.1
1920	Chi-A	16	25	0	8	2	1	0	3	1	3	.320	.346	.480	117	0	0	4	0	0	0	-1	C	0.1
Total	5	116	211	15	50	9	1	0	15	18	31	.237	.303	.289	72	-7	-8	20	3	0		6	/C	0.6

■ FRED LYNN

Lynn, Fredric Michael b: 2/3/52, Chicago, Ill. BL/TL, 6'1", 185 lbs. Deb: 9/05/74

YEAR	TM/L	G	AB	R	H	2B	3B	HR	RBI	BB	SO	AVG	OBP	SLG	PRO+	BR	/A	RC	SB	CS	SBR	FR	POS	TPR
1974	Bos-A	15	43	5	18	2	2	2	10	6	6	.419	.500	.698	226	8	8	16	0	0	0	-0	O/D	0.7
1975	*Bos-A	145	528	103	175	47	7	21	105	62	90	.331	.405	.566	158	49	44	120	10	5	0	9	*O	4.9
1976	Bos-A	132	507	76	159	32	8	10	65	48	67	.314	.374	.467	130	28	20	88	14	9	-1	8	*O/D	2.6
1977	Bos-A	129	497	81	129	29	5	18	76	51	63	.260	.332	.447	98	6	-2	72	2	3	-1	1	*O/D	-0.5
1978	Bos-A	150	541	75	161	33	3	22	82	75	50	.298	.384	.492	131	33	25	103	3	6	-3	3	*O	2.2
1979	Bos-A	147	531	116	177	42	1	39	122	82	79	.333	.426	.637	173	62	58	147	2	2	-1	5	*O	5.0
1980	Bos-A	110	415	67	125	32	3	12	61	58	39	.301	.387	.480	129	21	19	80	12	0	4	5	*O	2.5
1981	Cal-A	76	256	28	56	8	1	5	31	38	42	.219	.327	.316	86	-4	-4	27	1	2	-1	-1	O	-0.7
1982	*Cal-A	138	472	89	141	38	1	21	86	58	72	.299	.379	.517	143	28	28	91	7	8	-3	-9	*O	1.2
1983	Cal-A	117	437	56	119	20	3	22	74	55	83	.272	.356	.483	130	17	18	76	2	2	-1	-6	*O/D	1.0
1984	Cal-A	142	517	84	140	28	4	23	79	77	97	.271	.367	.474	132	23	23	90	2	2	-1	8	*O	2.6
1985	Bal-A	124	448	59	118	12	1	23	68	53	100	.263	.343	.449	118	9	11	70	7	3	0	-5	*O	0.4
1986	Bal-A	112	397	67	114	13	1	23	67	53	59	.287	.374	.499	137	20	20	69	2	2	-1	-9	*O	0.8
1987	Bal-A	111	396	49	100	24	0	23	60	39	72	.253	.321	.487	113	5	6	58	3	7	-3	-5	*O/D	-0.3
1988	Bal-A	87	301	37	76	13	1	18	37	28	66	.252	.316	.482	123	7	8	44	2	2	-1	-4	O/D	0.2
	Det-A	27	90	9	20	1	0	7	19	5	16	.222	.271	.467	106	-0	0	11	0	0	0	-1	O	0.0
	Yr	114	391	46	96	14	1	25	56	33	82	.246	.306	.478	120	7	8	55	2	2	-1	-5		0.2
1989	Det-A	117	353	44	85	11	1	11	46	47	71	.241	.332	.371	100	-0	1	46	1	1	-0	-3	OD	-0.3
1990	SD-N	90	196	18	47	3	1	6	23	22	44	.240	.320	.357	85	-4	-4	24	2	0	1	-3	O	-0.7
Total	17	1969	6925	1063	1960	388	43	306	1111	857	1116	.283	.364	.484	129	309	279	1233	72	54	-11	-12	*O/D	21.6

■ JERRY LYNN

Lynn, Jerome Edward b: 4/14/16, Scranton, Pa. d: 9/25/72, Scranton, Pa. BR/TR, 5'10", 164 lbs. Deb: 9/19/37

YEAR	TM/L	G	AB	R	H	2B	3B	HR	RBI	BB	SO	AVG	OBP	SLG	PRO+	BR	/A	RC	SB	CS	SBR	FR	POS	TPR
1937	Was-A	1	3	0	2	1	0	0	0	0	0	.667	.667	1.000	329	1	1	2	0	0	0	1	/2	0.2

■ RUSS LYON

Lyon, Russell Mayo b: 6/26/13, Ball Ground, Ga. BR/TR, 6'1", 230 lbs. Deb: 4/21/44

YEAR	TM/L	G	AB	R	H	2B	3B	HR	RBI	BB	SO	AVG	OBP	SLG	PRO+	BR	/A	RC	SB	CS	SBR	FR	POS	TPR
1944	Cle-A	7	11	1	2	0	0	0	1	1	1	.182	.250	.182	25	-1	-1	0	0	0	0	0	/C	0.0

■ BARRY LYONS

Lyons, Barry Stephen b: 6/3/60, Biloxi, Miss. BR/TR, 6'1", 205 lbs. Deb: 4/19/86

YEAR	TM/L	G	AB	R	H	2B	3B	HR	RBI	BB	SO	AVG	OBP	SLG	PRO+	BR	/A	RC	SB	CS	SBR	FR	POS	TPR
1986	NY-N	6	9	1	0	0	0	0	2	1	2	.000	.100	.000	-72	-2	-2	0	0	0	0	0	/C	-0.1
1987	NY-N	53	130	15	33	4	1	4	24	8	24	.254	.307	.392	88	-3	-2	16	0	0	0	1	C	0.2
1988	NY-N	50	91	5	21	7	1	0	11	3	12	.231	.255	.330	70	-4	-4	7	0	0	0	-2	C/1	-0.3
1989	NY-N	79	235	15	58	13	0	3	27	11	28	.247	.286	.340	82	-7	-6	21	0	1	-1	1	C	0.0
1990	NY-N	24	80	8	19	0	0	2	7	2	9	.237	.265	.313	60	-5	-4	6	0	0	0	3	C	0.0
	LA-N	3	5	1	1	0	0	1	2	0	1	.200	.200	.800	171	0	0	1	0	0	0	-1	/C	0.0
	Yr	27	85	9	20	0	0	3	9	2	10	.235	.261	.341	66	-4	-4	7	0	0	0	3		0.0
Total	5	215	550	45	132	24	2	10	73	25	76	.240	.279	.345	77	-21	-18	51	0	1	-1	3	C/1	-0.2

■ DENNY LYONS

Lyons, Dennis Patrick Aloysius b: 3/12/1866, Cincinnati, Ohio d: 1/2/29, W.Covington, Ky. BR/TR, 5'10", 185 lbs. Deb: 9/18/1885

YEAR	TM/L	G	AB	R	H	2B	3B	HR	RBI	BB	SO	AVG	OBP	SLG	PRO+	BR	/A	RC	SB	CS	SBR	FR	POS	TPR
1885	Pro-N	4	16	3	2	1	0	0	1	0	3	.125	.125	.188	-0	-2	-2	0				-0	/3	-0.1
1886	Phi-a	32	123	22	26	3	1	0			8	.211	.281	.252	69	-4	-4	11	7			-6	3	-0.7
1887	Phi-a	137	570	120	209	43	14	6		47		.367	.421	.523	165	48	48	160	73			-5	*3	3.1
1888	Phi-a	111	456	93	135	22	5	6	83	41		.296	.363	.406	151	26	26	83	39			-13	*3	1.2
1889	Phi-a	131	510	135	168	36	4	9	82	79	44	.329	.426	.469	160	41	42	109	10			9	*3	4.3
1890	Phi-a	88	339	79	120	29	5	7		57		.354	.458	.531	200	42	44	94	21			9	3	4.4
1891	StL-a	120	451	124	142	24	3	11	84	88	58	.315	.445	.455	140	41	29	98	9			-6	*3	2.2
1892	NY-N	108	389	71	100	16	7	8	51	59	36	.257	.359	.396	132	15	16	61	11			-5	*3	1.6
1893	Pit-N	131	490	103	150	19	16	3	105	97	21	.306	.430	.429	133	26	28	101	19			5	*3	2.8
1894	Pit-N	71	254	51	82	14	4	4	50	42	12	.323	.427	.457	116	8	8	57	14			7	3	1.1
1895	StL-N	33	129	24	38	6	0	2	25	14	5	.295	.372	.388	100	0	0	20	3			-4	3	-0.2
1896	Pit-N	118	436	77	134	25	6	4	71	67	25	.307	.406	.420	125	15	18	81	13			-15	*3	0.8
1897	Pit-N	37	131	22	27	6	4	2	17	22		.206	.346	.359	92	-2	-1	18	5			-0	1/3	0.0
Total	13	1121	4294	932	1333	244	69	62	569	621	212	.310	.407	.443	141	256	254	894	224			-26	*3/1	20.5

■ ED LYONS

Lyons, Edward Hoyte "Mouse" b: 5/12/23, Winston-Salem, N.C BR/TR, 5'9", 165 lbs. Deb: 9/15/47 C

YEAR	TM/L	G	AB	R	H	2B	3B	HR	RBI	BB	SO	AVG	OBP	SLG	PRO+	BR	/A	RC	SB	CS	SBR	FR	POS	TPR
1947	Was-A	7	26	2	4	0	0	0	2	1		.154	.214	.154	3	-3	-3	1	0	0	0	4	/2	0.1

■ HARRY LYONS

Lyons, Harry P. b: 3/25/1866, Chester, Pa. d: 6/30/12, Mauricetown, N.J. BR/TR, 5'10.5", 157 lbs. Deb: 8/29/1887

YEAR	TM/L	G	AB	R	H	2B	3B	HR	RBI	BB	SO	AVG	OBP	SLG	PRO+	BR	/A	RC	SB	CS	SBR	FR	POS	TPR
1887	Phi-N	1	4	0	0	0	0	0	0	1	0	.000	.200	.000	-37	-1	-1	0	0			-0	/O	0.0
	*StL-a	2	8	2	1	0	0	0			0	.125	.125	.125	-27	-1	-1	0	2			1	/2O	0.0

YEAR	TM/L	G	AB	R	H	2B	3B	HR	RBI	BB	SO	AVG	OBP	SLG	PRO+	BR	/A	RC	SB	CS	SBR	FR	POS	TPR
1888	*StL-a	123	499	66	97	10	5	4	63	20		.194	.230	.259	53	-23	-31	39	36			6	*O/3S2	-2.6
1889	NY-N	5	20	1	2	0	1	0	2	2	0	.100	.182	.200	7	-3	-3	1	0			-1	/O	-0.3
1890	Roc-a	133	584	83	152	11	11	3		27		.260	.294	.332	94	-12	-5	73	47			11	*O/3CP	0.0
1892	NY-N	96	411	67	98	5	2	0	53	33	29	.238	.297	.260	72	-14	-13	40	25			3	O	-1.2
1893	NY-N	47	187	27	51	5	2	0	21	14	6	.273	.323	.321	73	-7	-7	23	10			2	O	-0.5
Total	6	407	1713	246	401	31	21	7	139	97	35	.234	.277	.289	71	-60	-60	176	120			21	O/32PCS	-4.6

■ **PAT LYONS**   Lyons, Patrick Jerry b: 1860, Canada d: 1/20/14, Springfield, Ohio TR, Deb: 7/21/1890

YEAR	TM/L	G	AB	R	H	2B	3B	HR	RBI	BB	SO	AVG	OBP	SLG	PRO+	BR	/A	RC	SB	CS	SBR	FR	POS	TPR
1890	Cle-N	11	38	2	2	1	0	0	1	4	4	.053	.143	.079	-35	-6	-6	0	0			-5	2	-0.9

■ **STEVE LYONS**   Lyons, Stephen John b: 6/3/60, Tacoma, Wash. BL/TR, 6'3", 190 lbs. Deb: 4/15/85

YEAR	TM/L	G	AB	R	H	2B	3B	HR	RBI	BB	SO	AVG	OBP	SLG	PRO+	BR	/A	RC	SB	CS	SBR	FR	POS	TPR
1985	Bos-A	133	371	52	98	14	3	5	30	32	64	.264	.324	.358	83	-6	-8	44	12	9	-2	-14	*O/3SD	-2.5
1986	Bos-A	59	124	20	31	7	2	1	14	12	23	.250	.316	.363	84	-3	-3	13	2	3	-1	6	O	0.1
	Chi-A	42	123	10	25	2	1	0	6	7	24	.203	.252	.236	53	-11	-12	7	2	3	-1	1	O/31D	-1.1
	Yr	101	247	30	56	9	3	1	20	19	47	.227	.285	.300	58	-14	-14	21	4	6	-2	8		-1.0
1987	Chi-A	76	193	26	54	11	1	1	19	12	37	.280	.322	.363	79	-5	-6	22	3	1	0	13	3O/2D	0.6
1988	Chi-A	146	472	59	127	28	3	5	45	32	59	.269	.317	.373	93	-5	-5	57	1	2	-1	10	*30/2C1	0.4
1989	Chi-A	140	443	51	117	21	3	2	50	35	68	.264	.319	.339	88	-8	-7	50	9	6	-1	-5	2130/SC	-1.3
1990	Chi-A	94	146	22	28	6	1	1	11	10	41	.192	.248	.267	45	-11	-11	11	1	0	0	1	12/O3SDP	-1.2
Total	6	690	1872	240	480	89	14	15	175	140	316	.256	.310	.343	80	-50	-51	204	30	24	-5	13	O31/2DSC	-5.0

■ **TERRY LYONS**   Lyons, Terence Hilbert b: 12/14/08, New Holland, Ohio d: 9/9/59, Dayton, Ohio BR/TR, 6'0.5", 165 lbs. Deb: 4/19/29

YEAR	TM/L	G	AB	R	H	2B	3B	HR	RBI	BB	SO	AVG	OBP	SLG	PRO+	BR	/A	RC	SB	CS	SBR	FR	POS	TPR
1929	Phi-N	1	0	0	0	0	0	0	0	0	0	—	—	—	—	0	0	0	0			0	/1	0.0

■ **TED LYONS**   Lyons, Theodore Amar b: 12/28/1900, Lake Charles, La. d: 7/25/86, Sulphur, La. BB/TR, 5'11", 200 lbs. Deb: 7/02/23 MCH

YEAR	TM/L	G	AB	R	H	2B	3B	HR	RBI	BB	SO	AVG	OBP	SLG	PRO+	BR	/A	RC	SB	CS	SBR	FR	POS	TPR
1923	Chi-A	9	5	0	1	0	0	0	1	1	3	.200	.333	.200	43	-0	-0	0	0	0	0	1	/P	0.0
1924	Chi-A	41	77	10	17	0	1	0	6	5	13	.221	.277	.247	37	-7	-7	6	0	0	0	-2	P	0.0
1925	Chi-A	43	97	6	18	3	0	0	7	3	13	.186	.218	.216	11	-13	-13	5	0	0	0	2	P	0.0
1926	Chi-A	41	104	7	22	1	1	0	3	1	10	.212	.219	.240	20	-12	-12	6	0	0	0	4	P	0.0
1927	Chi-A	41	110	16	28	6	2	1	9	6	17	.255	.293	.373	74	-5	-5	12	0	0	0	1	P	0.0
1928	Chi-A	49	91	10	23	2	0	0	8	1	9	.253	.261	.275	41	-8	-8	7	0	0	0	2	P	0.0
1929	Chi-A	40	91	7	20	4	0	0	11	9	13	.220	.290	.264	44	-8	-7	8	0	0	0	2	P/O	0.0
1930	Chi-A	57	122	20	38	6	3	1	15	2	18	.311	.323	.434	93	-2	-2	17	0	0	0	4	P	0.0
1931	Chi-A	42	33	6	5	0	0	0	3	2	1	.152	.200	.152	-7	-5	-5	1	0	0	0	-0	P	0.0
1932	Chi-A	49	73	11	19	2	1	1	10	4	10	.260	.308	.356	76	-3	-2	8	0	0	0	-1	P	0.0
1933	Chi-A	51	91	11	26	2	1	1	11	4	6	.286	.316	.363	83	-3	-2	10	0	1	-1	0	P	0.0
1934	Chi-A	50	97	9	20	4	0	1	16	3	19	.206	.245	.278	34	-10	-10	7	0	0	0	2	P	0.0
1935	Chi-A	29	82	5	18	4	0	0	6	3	4	.220	.256	.268	35	-8	-8	6	0	0	0	-1	P	0.0
1936	Chi-A	26	70	2	11	0	0	0	5	5	12	.157	.213	.157	-7	-12	-12	3	0	0	0	2	P	0.0
1937	Chi-A	23	57	6	12	0	0	0	3	9	14	.211	.318	.211	36	-5	-5	5	0	0	0	1	P	0.0
1938	Chi-A	24	72	9	14	2	0	0	4	2	9	.194	.216	.222	10	-10	-10	4	0	0	0	2	P	0.0
1939	Chi-A	21	61	5	18	3	0	0	8	5	7	.295	.348	.344	76	-2	-2	8	0	0	0	-1	P	0.0
1940	Chi-A	22	75	4	18	4	0	0	7	2	7	.240	.260	.293	43	-6	-6	5	0	0	0	-2	P	0.0
1941	Chi-A	22	74	8	20	2	0	0	6	2	6	.270	.289	.297	56	-5	-5	6	0	0	0	1	P	0.0
1942	Chi-A	20	67	10	16	4	0	0	10	3	7	.239	.282	.299	65	-3	-3	6	0	0	0	1	P	0.0
1946	Chi-A	5	14	0	0	0	0	0	0	1	3	.000	.067	.000	-83	-3	-3	0	0	0	0	0	/PM	0.0
Total	21	705	1563	162	364	49	9	5	149	73	201	.233	.270	.285	44	-132	-129	128	0	1	-1	16	P/O	0.0

■ **BILL LYONS**   Lyons, William Allen b: 4/26/58, Alton, Ill. BR/TR, 6'1", 175 lbs. Deb: 7/20/83

YEAR	TM/L	G	AB	R	H	2B	3B	HR	RBI	BB	SO	AVG	OBP	SLG	PRO+	BR	/A	RC	SB	CS	SBR	FR	POS	TPR
1983	StL-N	42	60	3	10	1	1	0	3	1	11	.167	.180	.217	10	-7	-7	2	3	2	-0	2	2/3S	-0.4
1984	StL-N	46	73	13	16	3	0	0	3	9	13	.219	.305	.260	62	-4	-3	7	3	1	0	14	2S/3	1.3
Total	2	88	133	16	26	4	1	0	6	10	24	.195	.252	.241	39	-11	-11	9	6	3	0	16	/2S3	0.9

■ **DAD LYTLE**   Lytle, Edward Benson "Pop" b: 3/10/1862, Racine, Wis. d: 12/21/50, Long Beach, Cal. 5'11", 160 lbs. Deb: 8/11/1890

YEAR	TM/L	G	AB	R	H	2B	3B	HR	RBI	BB	SO	AVG	OBP	SLG	PRO+	BR	/A	RC	SB	CS	SBR	FR	POS	TPR
1890	Chi-N	1	4	1	0	0	0	0	0	0	1	.000	.000	.000	-96	-1	-1	0	0			1	/O	0.0
	Pit-N	15	55	2	8	1	0	0	0	8	9	.145	.254	.164	27	-5	-4	2	0			-6	/2O	-0.8
	Yr	16	59	3	8	1	0	0	0	8	10	.136	.239	.153	18	-6	-5	2	0			-5		-0.8

■ **JIM LYTTLE**   Lyttle, James Lawrence b: 5/20/46, Hamilton, Ohio BL/TR, 6', 180 lbs. Deb: 5/17/69

YEAR	TM/L	G	AB	R	H	2B	3B	HR	RBI	BB	SO	AVG	OBP	SLG	PRO+	BR	/A	RC	SB	CS	SBR	FR	POS	TPR
1969	NY-A	28	83	7	15	4	0	0	4	4	19	.181	.218	.229	26	-8	-8	4	1	2	-1	3	O	-0.6
1970	NY-A	87	126	20	39	7	1	3	14	10	26	.310	.360	.452	129	4	4	18	3	6	-3	4	O	0.2
1971	NY-A	49	86	7	17	5	0	1	7	8	18	.198	.274	.291	64	-5	-4	6	0	2	-1	1	O	-0.5
1972	Chi-A	44	82	8	19	5	2	0	5	1	28	.232	.241	.341	70	-3	-3	7	0	1	-1	1	O	-0.3
1973	Mon-N	49	116	12	30	5	1	4	19	9	14	.259	.312	.422	98	-0	-1	14	0	2	-1	4	O	0.0
1974	Mon-N	25	9	1	3	0	0	0	2	1	3	.333	.400	.333	101	0	0	1	0	0	0	2	O	0.1
1975	Mon-N	44	55	7	15	4	0	0	6	13	6	.273	.412	.345	107	2	1	9	0	1	-1	-1	O	0.0
1976	Mon-N	42	85	6	23	4	1	1	8	7	13	.271	.326	.376	95	-0	-1	10	0	1	0	1	O	0.0
	LA-N	23	68	3	15	3	0	0	5	8	12	.221	.303	.265	63	-3	-3	6	0	1	-1	5	O	0.1
	Yr	65	153	9	38	7	1	1	13	15	25	.248	.315	.327	81	-3	-4	16	0	1	-1	6		0.1
Total	8	391	710	71	176	37	5	9	70	61	139	.248	.308	.352	86	-14	-14	75	4	15	-8	20	O	-1.0

■ **KEVIN MAAS**   Maas, Kevin Christian b: 1/20/65, Castro Valley, Cal. BL/TL, 6'3", 195 lbs. Deb: 6/29/90

YEAR	TM/L	G	AB	R	H	2B	3B	HR	RBI	BB	SO	AVG	OBP	SLG	PRO+	BR	/A	RC	SB	CS	SBR	FR	POS	TPR
1990	NY-A	79	254	42	64	9	0	21	41	43	76	.252	.367	.535	149	17	17	52	1	2	-1	-3	1D	0.9

■ **HARVEY MacDONALD**   MacDonald, Harvey Forsyth b: 5/18/1898, New York, N.Y. d: 10/4/65, Manoa, Pa. BL/TL, 5'11", 170 lbs. Deb: 6/12/28

YEAR	TM/L	G	AB	R	H	2B	3B	HR	RBI	BB	SO	AVG	OBP	SLG	PRO+	BR	/A	RC	SB	CS	SBR	FR	POS	TPR
1928	Phi-N	13	16	0	4	0	0	0	2	2	3	.250	.333	.250	53	-1	-1	1	0			-0	/O	0.0

■ **MACEY**   Macey b: Columbus, Ohio Deb: 10/02/1890

YEAR	TM/L	G	AB	R	H	2B	3B	HR	RBI	BB	SO	AVG	OBP	SLG	PRO+	BR	/A	RC	SB	CS	SBR	FR	POS	TPR
1890	Phi-a	1	1	1							0	.000	.000	.000	-99	-0	-0	0	0			0	/C	0.0

■ **MIKE MACFARLANE**   Macfarlane, Michael Andrew b: 4/12/64, Stockton, Cal. BR/TR, 6', 195 lbs. Deb: 7/23/87

YEAR	TM/L	G	AB	R	H	2B	3B	HR	RBI	BB	SO	AVG	OBP	SLG	PRO+	BR	/A	RC	SB	CS	SBR	FR	POS	TPR
1987	KC-A	8	19	0	4	1	0	0	3	2	2	.211	.286	.263	46	-1	-1	1	0	0	0	-1	/C	-0.1
1988	KC-A	70	211	25	56	15	0	4	26	21	37	.265	.335	.393	102	1	1	28	0	0	0	-14	C	-1.0
1989	KC-A	69	157	13	35	6	0	2	19	7	27	.223	.265	.299	59	-9	-9	11	0	0	0	4	C/D	-0.1
1990	KC-A	124	400	37	102	24	4	6	58	25	69	.255	.310	.380	94	-5	-4	47	1	0	0	-20	*C/D	-2.0
Total	4	271	787	75	197	46	4	12	106	55	135	.250	.308	.365	88	-14	-13	87	1	0	0	-32	C/D	-3.2

■ **ED MacGAMWELL**   MacGamwell, Edward M. b: 1/10/1879, Buffalo, N.Y. d: 5/26/24, Albany, N.Y. BL/TL, Deb: 4/14/05

YEAR	TM/L	G	AB	R	H	2B	3B	HR	RBI	BB	SO	AVG	OBP	SLG	PRO+	BR	/A	RC	SB	CS	SBR	FR	POS	TPR
1905	Bro-N	4	16	0	4	0	0	0	0	0	0	.250	.294	.250	70	-1	-1	1	0			-1	/1	0.0

■ **KEN MACHA**   Macha, Kenneth Edward b: 9/29/50, Monroeville, Pa. BR/TR, 6'2", 215 lbs. Deb: 9/14/74 C

YEAR	TM/L	G	AB	R	H	2B	3B	HR	RBI	BB	SO	AVG	OBP	SLG	PRO+	BR	/A	RC	SB	CS	SBR	FR	POS	TPR
1974	Pit-N	5	5	1	3	1	0	0	1	0	0	.600	.600	.800	300	1	1	2	0	0	0	0	/C	0.1
1977	Pit-N	35	95	2	26	4	0	0	11	6	17	.274	.317	.316	68	-4	-4	8	1	1	-0	-3	31/O	-0.8
1978	Pit-N	29	52	5	11	1	1	0	5	12	10	.212	.359	.269	75	-1	-1	6	2	0	1	-3	3	-0.3
1979	Mon-N	25	36	8	10	3	1	0	4	2	9	.278	.333	.417	104	0	0	4	0	0	0	2	3/1OC	0.2
1980	Mon-N	49	107	10	31	5	1	1	8	11	17	.290	.361	.383	108	1	1	13	0	2	-1	-5	3/1CO	-0.4

YEAR	TM/L	G	AB	R	H	2B	3B	HR	RBI	BB	SO	AVG	OBP	SLG	PRO+	BR	/A	RC	SB	CS	SBR	FR	POS	TPR
1981	Tor-A	37	85	4	17	2	0	0	6	8	15	.200	.269	.224	41	-6	-7	5	1	1	-0	-1	31/CD	-0.8
Total	6	180	380	30	98	16	3	1	35	39	68	.258	.330	.324	80	-8	-9	39	4	4	-1	-10	3/10CD	-2.0

■ MIKE MACHA
Macha, Michael William b: 2/17/54, Victoria, Tex.   BR/TR, 5'11", 180 lbs.   Deb: 4/20/79

YEAR	TM/L	G	AB	R	H	2B	3B	HR	RBI	BB	SO	AVG	OBP	SLG	PRO+	BR	/A	RC	SB	CS	SBR	FR	POS	TPR
1979	Atl-N	6	13	2	2	0	0	0	1	1	5	.154	.214	.154	2	-2	-2	0	0	0	0	0	/3	-0.1
1980	Tor-A	5	8	0	0	0	0	0	0	0	1	.000	.000	.000	-96	-2	-2	0	0	0	0	1	/3C	-0.1
Total	2	11	21	2	2	0	0	0	1	1	6	.095	.136	.095	-33	-4	-4	0	0	0	0	1	/3C	-0.2

■ DAVE MACHEMER
Machemer, David Ritchie b: 5/24/51, St.Joseph, Mo.   BR/TR, 5'11.5", 180 lbs.   Deb: 6/21/78

YEAR	TM/L	G	AB	R	H	2B	3B	HR	RBI	BB	SO	AVG	OBP	SLG	PRO+	BR	/A	RC	SB	CS	SBR	FR	POS	TPR
1978	Cal-A	10	22	6	6	1	0	1	2	2	1	.273	.333	.455	124	1	1	3	0	1	-1	-2	/23S	-0.1
1979	Det-A	19	26	8	5	1	0	0	2	3	2	.192	.276	.231	37	-2	-2	1	0	3	-2	4	2/O	0.0
Total	2	29	48	14	11	2	0	1	4	5	3	.229	.302	.333	74	-2	-2	4	0	4	-2	2	/23OS	-0.1

■ CONNIE MACK
Mack, Cornelius Alexander "The Tall Tactician" (b: Cornelius Alexander McGillicuddy)
b: 12/22/1862, E.Brookfield, Mass d: 2/8/56, Germantown, Pa.   BR/TR, 6'1", 150 lbs.   Deb: 9/11/1886 MH

YEAR	TM/L	G	AB	R	H	2B	3B	HR	RBI	BB	SO	AVG	OBP	SLG	PRO+	BR	/A	RC	SB	CS	SBR	FR	POS	TPR
1886	Was-N	10	36	4	13	2	1	0	5	0	2	.361	.361	.472	161	2	2	6	0			9	C	1.0
1887	Was-N	82	314	35	63	6	1	0	20	8	17	.201	.228	.226	29	-30	-27	23	26			6	C/O2	-0.9
1888	Was-N	85	300	49	56	5	6	3	29	17	18	.187	.249	.273	72	-10	-8	29	31			4	C/OS1	0.2
1889	Was-N	98	386	51	113	16	1	0	42	15	12	.293	.333	.339	95	-5	-2	54	26			7	CO1	0.2
1890	Buf-P	123	503	95	134	15	12	0	53	47	13	.266	.353	.344	96	-7	1	68	16			-14	*C/O1	-0.6
1891	Pit-N	75	280	43	60	10	0	0	29	19	11	.214	.286	.250	60	-14	-13	22	4			10	C/1	0.3
1892	Pit-N	97	346	39	84	9	4	1	31	21	22	.243	.298	.301	82	-7	-7	35	11			24	C/O1	2.0
1893	Pit-N	37	133	22	38	3	1	0	15	10	9	.286	.358	.323	85	-3	-2	17	4			5	C	0.5
1894	Pit-N	69	228	32	57	7	1	1	21	20	14	.250	.321	.303	53	-17	-17	25	8			6	CM	-0.2
1895	Pit-N	14	49	12	15	2	0	0	4	7	1	.306	.404	.347	102	0	1	7	1			-2	C/1M	0.0
1896	Pit-N	33	120	9	26	4	1	0	16	5	8	.217	.248	.267	39	-11	-10	8	0			1	1/CM	-0.6
Total	11	723	2695	391	659	79	28	5	265	169	127	.245	.305	.300	74	-102	-82	295	127			56	C/102S	1.7

■ DENNY MACK
Mack, Dennis Joseph (b: Dennis Joseph McGee) b: 1851, Easton, Pa. d: 4/10/1888, Wilkes-Barre, Pa.   BR/TR, 5'7", 164 lbs.   Deb: 5/06/1871 MU

YEAR	TM/L	G	AB	R	H	2B	3B	HR	RBI	BB	SO	AVG	OBP	SLG	PRO+	BR	/A	RC	SB	CS	SBR	FR	POS	TPR
1871	Rok-n	25	122	34	30	7	1	0	17	8	7	.246	.292	.320	79	-4	-2	15	12				*2/PS	0.0
1872	Ath-n	47	205	68	59	9	1	0	23			.288	.360	.341	116	5	5	26					1S	0.6
1873	Phi-n	48	204	55	60	5	0	0	16			.294	.345	.319	93	0	-2	23					*1/O2S	0.0
1874	Phi-n	56	248	48	51	7	4	0	1			.206	.209	.266	48	-13	-15	14					*1	-1.1
1876	StL-N	48	180	32	39	5	0	1	7	11	5	.217	.262	.261	79	-4	-3	13				-8	S/2O	-0.9
1880	Buf-N	17	59	5	12	0	0	0	3	5	7	.203	.266	.203	60	-2	-2	3				-1	S/2	-0.2
1882	Lou-a	72	264	41	48	3	1	0	16			.182	.229	.201	49	-14	-12	12				-3	S2/OM	-1.0
1883	Pit-a	60	224	26	44	5	3	0	13			.196	.241	.246	60	-10	-9	14				4	S1/2	-0.5
Total	4 n	176	779	205	200	28	6	0	17	48	7	.257	.300	.308	84	-12	-14	78					1/S20P	-0.5
Total	4	197	727	104	143	13	4	1	10	45	12	.197	.244	.230	61	-31	-25	42				-8	S/21O	-2.7

■ EARLE MACK
Mack, Earle Thaddeus (b: Earle Thaddeus McGillicuddy)
b: 2/1/1890, Spencer, Mass. d: 2/4/67, Upper Darby Township, Pa.   BL/TR, 5'8", 140 lbs.   Deb: 10/05/10 MC

YEAR	TM/L	G	AB	R	H	2B	3B	HR	RBI	BB	SO	AVG	OBP	SLG	PRO+	BR	/A	RC	SB	CS	SBR	FR	POS	TPR
1910	Phi-A	1	4	0	2	0	1	0	0	0		.500	.500	1.000	372	1	1	2				-0	/C	0.1
1911	Phi-A	2	4	0	0	0	0	0	0	0		.000	.000	.000	-99	-1	-1	0	0			0	/3	0.0
1914	Phi-A	2	8	0	0	0	0	0	1	0	0	.000	.000	.000	-99	-2	-2	0	1			0	/1	-0.1
Total	3	5	16	0	2	0	1	0	1	0	0	.125	.125	.250	11	-2	-2	2	1			-0	/13C	0.0

■ REDDY MACK
Mack, Joseph (b: Joseph McNamara) b: 5/2/1866, Ireland d: 12/30/16, Newport, Ky.   Deb: 9/16/1885

YEAR	TM/L	G	AB	R	H	2B	3B	HR	RBI	BB	SO	AVG	OBP	SLG	PRO+	BR	/A	RC	SB	CS	SBR	FR	POS	TPR
1885	Lou-a	11	41	7	10	1	0	0			2	.244	.295	.268	82	-1	-1	3				0	2	0.0
1886	Lou-a	137	483	82	118	23	11	1			68	.244	.342	.344	111	12	7	63	13			6	*2	1.1
1887	Lou-a	128	478	117	147	23	8	1			83	.308	.415	.395	127	23	22	90	22			5	*2	2.2
1888	Lou-a	112	446	77	97	13	5	3	34	52		.217	.320	.289	101	2	4	48	18			4	*2	1.0
1889	Bal-a	136	519	84	125	24	7	1	87	60	69	.241	.329	.320	86	-7	-9	64	23			-11	*2/O	-1.4
1890	Bal-a	26	95	14	27	3	5	0		10		.284	.370	.421	130	4	4	18	7			1	2	0.4
Total	6	550	2062	381	524	87	36	6	121	275	69	.254	.352	.340	107	34	26	286	83			5	2/O	3.3

■ JOE MACK
Mack, Joe John (b: Joseph John Maciarz) b: 1/4/12, Chicago, Ill.   BB/TL, 5'11.5", 185 lbs.   Deb: 4/17/45

YEAR	TM/L	G	AB	R	H	2B	3B	HR	RBI	BB	SO	AVG	OBP	SLG	PRO+	BR	/A	RC	SB	CS	SBR	FR	POS	TPR
1945	Bos-N	66	260	30	60	13	1	3	44	34	39	.231	.320	.323	79	-7	-7	29	1			0	1	-0.9

■ RAY MACK
Mack, Raymond James (b: Raymond James Mickovsky) b: 8/31/16, Cleveland, Ohio d: 5/7/69, Bucyrus, Ohio BR/TR, 6', 200 lbs.   Deb: 9/09/38

YEAR	TM/L	G	AB	R	H	2B	3B	HR	RBI	BB	SO	AVG	OBP	SLG	PRO+	BR	/A	RC	SB	CS	SBR	FR	POS	TPR
1938	Cle-A	2	6	2	2	0	1	0	2	0	1	.333	.333	.667	147	0	0	1	0	0	0	2	/2	0.2
1939	Cle-A	36	112	12	17	4	1	1	6	12	19	.152	.240	.232	22	-14	-13	6	0	2	-1	2	2/3	-0.9
1940	Cle-A	146	530	60	150	21	5	12	69	51	77	.283	.346	.409	98	-4	-2	76	4	2	0	-9	*2	-0.2
1941	Cle-A	145	500	54	114	22	4	9	44	54	69	.228	.303	.342	74	-22	-19	55	8	4	0	-5	*2	-0.9
1942	Cle-A	143	481	48	108	14	6	2	45	41	51	.225	.288	.291	67	-24	-20	42	9	3	1	-4	*2	-1.8
1943	Cle-A	153	545	56	120	25	2	2	62	47	61	.220	.285	.312	79	-19	-15	49	8	3	1	-2	*2	-1.0
1944	Cle-A	83	284	24	66	15	3	0	29	28	45	.232	.301	.306	77	-10	-8	28	4	1	1	10	2	0.5
1946	Cle-A	61	171	13	35	6	2	1	9	23	27	.205	.299	.281	67	-8	-7	16	2	2	-1	1	2	0.0
1947	NY-A	1	0	0	0	0	0	0	0	0	0	—				0	0	0	0	0	0	0	R	0.0
	Chi-N	21	78	9	17	6	0	2	12	5	15	.218	.274	.372	73	-4	-3	7	0			7	2	0.6
Total	9	791	2707	273	629	113	24	34	278	261	365	.232	.301	.330	76	-103	-87	281	35	17		3	2/3	-3.5

■ SHANE MACK
Mack, Shane Lee b: 12/7/63, Los Angeles, Cal.   BR/TR, 6' ", 185 lbs.   Deb: 5/25/87

YEAR	TM/L	G	AB	R	H	2B	3B	HR	RBI	BB	SO	AVG	OBP	SLG	PRO+	BR	/A	RC	SB	CS	SBR	FR	POS	TPR
1987	SD-N	105	238	28	57	11	3	4	25	18	47	.239	.301	.361	77	-9	-8	22	4	6	-2	-6	O	-1.9
1988	SD-N	56	119	13	29	3	0	0	12	14	21	.244	.338	.269	78	-3	-3	13	5	1	1	9	O	0.6
1990	Min-A	125	313	50	102	10	4	8	44	29	69	.326	.392	.460	128	16	13	58	13	4	2	3	*O/D	1.7
Total	3	286	670	91	188	24	7	12	81	61	137	.281	.350	.391	102	4	3	92	22	11	0	6	O/D	0.4

■ PETE MACKANIN
Mackanin, Peter b: 8/1/51, Chicago, Ill.   BR/TR, 6'2", 190 lbs.   Deb: 7/03/73

YEAR	TM/L	G	AB	R	H	2B	3B	HR	RBI	BB	SO	AVG	OBP	SLG	PRO+	BR	/A	RC	SB	CS	SBR	FR	POS	TPR
1973	Tex-A	44	90	3	9	2	0	0	2	0	26	.100	.147	.122	-24	-15	-14	2	0	0	0	2	S3	-0.8
1974	Tex-A	6	6	0	1	0	1	0	0	0	2	.167	.167	.500	88	-0	-0	1	0	0	0	2	/S	0.2
1975	Mon-N	130	448	59	101	19	6	12	44	31	99	.225	.279	.375	77	-14	-16	46	11	5	0	18	*2/S3	0.8
1976	Mon-N	114	380	36	85	15	2	8	33	15	66	.224	.257	.337	65	-17	-19	31	6	2	1	-2	*2/3SO	-1.6
1977	Mon-N	55	85	9	19	2	2	1	6	4	17	.224	.258	.329	58	-5	-5	7	3	1	0	4	/2S3O	0.1
1978	Phi-N	5	8	0	2	0	0	0	0	1	2	.250	.250	.250	40	-1	-1	1	0	0	0	0	/13	0.0
1979	Phi-N	13	9	2	1	0	0	0	2	1	2	.111	.200	.444	69	-0	-0	1	0	0	0	3	/2S3	0.3
1980	Min-A	108	319	31	85	18	0	4	35	14	34	.266	.297	.361	74	-10	-12	33	6	2	1	16	2S/13D	1.0
1981	Min-A	77	225	21	52	7	1	4	18	7	40	.231	.258	.324	63	-10	-12	18	1	2	-1	-3	2S1/3D	-1.3
Total	9	548	1570	161	355	63	12	30	141	76	290	.226	.265	.339	66	-72	-80	138	27	12	1	40	2S/31DO	-1.3

■ ERIC MacKENZIE
MacKenzie, Eric Hugh b: 8/29/32, Glendon, Alt., Can.   BL/TR, 6', 185 lbs.   Deb: 4/23/55

YEAR	TM/L	G	AB	R	H	2B	3B	HR	RBI	BB	SO	AVG	OBP	SLG	PRO+	BR	/A	RC	SB	CS	SBR	FR	POS	TPR
1955	KC-A	1	1	0	0	0	0	0	0	0	0	.000	.000	.000	-99	-0	-0	0	0	0	0	0	/C	0.0

■ GORDON MacKENZIE
MacKenzie, Henry Gordon b: 7/9/37, St.Petersburg, Fla   BR/TR, 5'11", 175 lbs.   Deb: 8/13/61 C

YEAR	TM/L	G	AB	R	H	2B	3B	HR	RBI	BB	SO	AVG	OBP	SLG	PRO+	BR	/A	RC	SB	CS	SBR	FR	POS	TPR
1961	KC-A	11	24	1	3	0	0	0	1	1	6	.125	.160	.125	-23	-4	-4	0	0	0	0	-1	/C	-0.4

YEAR	TM/L	G	AB	R	H	2B	3B	HR	RBI	BB	SO	AVG	OBP	SLG	PRO+	BR	/A	RC	SB	CS	SBR	FR	POS	TPR

■ FELIX MACKIEWICZ Mackiewicz, Felix Thaddeus b: 11/20/17, Chicago, Ill. BR/TR, 6'2", 195 lbs. Deb: 9/07/41

1941	Phi-A	5	14	3	4	0	1	0	0	1	0	.286	.333	.429	103	-0	0	2	0	0	0	-1	/O	0.0
1942	Phi-A	6	14	3	3	2	0	0	2	0	4	.214	.214	.357	59	-1	-1	1	0	0	0	1	/O	0.0
1943	Phi-A	9	16	1	1	0	0	0	0	2	8	.063	.167	.063	-32	-3	-3	0	0	0	0	0	/O	-0.2
1945	Cle-A	120	359	42	98	14	7	2	37	44	41	.273	.356	.368	115	5	7	47	5	5	-2	3	*O	0.4
1946	Cle-A	78	258	35	67	15	4	0	16	16	32	.260	.305	.349	88	-7	-5	28	5	1	1	4	O	-0.2
1947	Cle-A	2	5	0	0	0	0	0	0	0	2	.000	.000	.000	-99	-1	-1	-0	0	0	0	0	/O	0.0
	Was-A	3	6	1	1	1	0	0	0	0	1	.167	.167	.333	38	-1	-1	-0	0	0	0	-0	/O	0.0
	Yr	5	11	1	1	1	0	0	0	0	3	.091	.091	.182	-26	-2	-2	-0	0	0	0	0		0.0
Total	6	223	672	85	174	32	12	2	55	63	88	.259	.325	.351	97	-7	-3	79	10	6	-1	8	O	0.0

■ STEVE MACKO Macko, Steven Joseph b: 9/6/54, Burlington, Iowa d: 11/15/81, Arlington, Tex. BL/TR, 5'10", 160 lbs. Deb: 8/18/79

1979	Chi-N	19	40	2	9	1	0	0	3	4	8	.225	.295	.250	46	-3	-3	3	0	0	0	4	2/3	0.2
1980	Chi-N	6	20	2	6	2	0	0	2	0	3	.300	.300	.400	87	-0	-0	2	0	0	0	1	/S32	0.1
Total	2	25	60	4	15	3	0	0	5	4	11	.250	.297	.300	59	-3	-4	6	0	0	0	6	/23S	0.3

■ MAX MACON Macon, Max Cullen b: 10/14/15, Pensacola, Fla. d: 8/5/89, Jupiter, Fla. BL/TL, 6'3", 175 lbs. Deb: 4/21/38

1938	StL-N	46	36	5	11	0	0	0	3	2	4	.306	.342	.306	75	-1	-1	4	0			1	P/O	0.0
1940	Bro-N	2	1	0	1	0	0	0	0	0	0	1.000	1.000	1.000	427	0	0	1	0			0	/P	0.0
1942	Bro-N	26	43	4	12	2	1	0	1	2	4	.279	.311	.372	98	-0	-0	5	1			-0	P	0.0
1943	Bro-N	45	55	7	9	0	0	0	6	0	1	.164	.164	.164	-5	-7	-7	1	1			0	P/1	0.0
1944	Bos-N	106	366	38	100	15	3	3	36	12	23	.273	.296	.355	79	-9	-11	38	7			-2	1O/P	-2.0
1947	Bos-N	1	1	0	0	0	0	0	0	0	0	.000	.000	.000	-99	-0	-0	0	0			0	/P	0.0
Total	6	226	502	54	133	17	4	3	46	16	32	.265	.288	.333	72	-18	-20	49	9			-0	/P1O	-2.0

■ WADDY MacPHEE MacPhee, Walter Scott b: 12/23/1899, Brooklyn, N.Y. d: 1/20/80, Charlotte, N.C. BR/TR, 5'8", 140 lbs. Deb: 9/27/22

| 1922 | NY-N | 2 | 7 | 2 | 2 | 0 | 1 | 0 | 0 | 1 | 0 | .286 | .375 | .571 | 140 | 0 | 0 | 2 | 0 | 0 | 0 | 1 | /3 | 0.1 |

■ JIMMY MACULLAR Macullar, James F. "Little Mac" b: 1/16/1855, Boston, Mass. d: 4/8/24, Baltimore, Md. BR/TL, Deb: 5/05/1879 MU

1879	Syr-N	64	246	24	52	9	6	0	13	3	27	.211	.221	.248	61	-12	-8	14				1	SO/23M	-0.4
1882	Cin-a	79	299	44	70	6	6	0		14		.234	.268	.294	84	-3	-6	24				-0	*O	-0.6
1883	Cin-a	14	48	4	8	2	0	0		4		.167	.231	.208	40	-3	-3	2				-3	O/S	-0.5
1884	Bal-a	107	360	73	73	16	6	4	36			.203	.290	.314	96	1	-1	34				1	*S	-0.1
1885	Bal-a	100	320	52	61	7	6	3	49			.191	.306	.278	89	-2	-1	28				0	*S/O	0.0
1886	Bal-a	85	268	49	55	7	1	0	49			.205	.332	.239	84	-3	-2	30	23			-9	S/O2P	-0.5
Total	6	449	1541	246	319	47	19	7	13	155	27	.207	.285	.276	84	-21	-21	131	23			-11	SO/2P3	-2.1

■ GENE MADDEN Madden, Eugene b: 6/5/1890, Elm Grove, W.Va. d: 4/6/49, Utica, N.Y. BL/TR, 5'10", 155 lbs. Deb: 4/20/16

| 1916 | Pit-N | 1 | 1 | 0 | 0 | 0 | 0 | 0 | 0 | 0 | 0 | .000 | .000 | .000 | -99 | -0 | -0 | 0 | 0 | | | 0 | H | 0.0 |

■ FRANK MADDEN Madden, Francis A. "Red" b: 10/17/1892, Pittsburgh, Pa. d: 4/30/52, Pittsburgh, Pa. Deb: 7/04/14

| 1914 | Pit-F | 2 | 2 | 0 | 1 | 0 | 0 | 0 | 1 | 0 | 0 | .500 | .500 | .500 | 189 | 0 | 0 | 1 | 0 | | | 0 | /C | 0.0 |

■ BUNNY MADDEN Madden, Thomas Francis b: 9/14/1882, Boston, Mass. d: 1/20/54, Cambridge, Mass. BR/TR, 5'10", 190 lbs. Deb: 6/03/09

1909	Bos-A	10	17	0	4	0	0	0	1	0		.235	.235	.235	48	-1	-1	1	0			1	/C	0.1
1910	Bos-A	14	35	4	13	3	0	0	4	3		.371	.436	.457	175	3	3	7	0			-3	C	0.2
1911	Bos-A	4	15	2	3	0	0	0	2	2		.200	.294	.200	39	-1	-1	1	0			-2	/C	-0.2
	Phi-N	28	76	4	21	1	1	0	4	0	13	.276	.276	.316	65	-4	-4	6	0			3	C	0.1
Total	3	56	143	10	41	4	1	0	11	5	13	.287	.315	.329	87	-3	-3	15	0			-1	/C	0.2

■ TOMMY MADDEN Madden, Thomas Joseph b: 7/31/1883, Philadelphia, Pa. d: 7/26/30, Philadelphia, Pa. BL/TL, 5'11", 160 lbs. Deb: 9/10/06

1906	Bos-N	4	15	1	4	0	0	0	0	0	1	.267	.313	.267	85	-0	-0	1	0			-0	/O	0.0
1910	NY-A	1	1	0	0	0	0	0	0	0	0	.000	.000	.000	-95	-0	-0	0	0			-0	H	0.0
Total	2	5	16	1	4	0	0	0	0	0	1	.250	.294	.250	73	-1	-0	1	0			-1	/O	0.0

■ CLARENCE MADDERN Maddern, Clarence James b: 9/26/21, Bisbee, Ariz. d: 8/9/86, Tucson, Ariz. BR/TR, 6'1", 185 lbs. Deb: 9/19/46

1946	Chi-N	3	3	0	0	0	0	0	0	0	0	.000	.250	.000	-27	-0	-0	0	0			0	/O	0.0
1948	Chi-N	80	214	16	54	12	1	4	27	10	25	.252	.301	.374	85	-6	-5	25	0			-0	O	-0.8
1949	Chi-N	10	9	1	3	0	0	1	2	2	0	.333	.455	.667	202	1	1	3	0			0	/1	0.2
1951	Cle-A	11	12	0	2	0	0	0	0	0	1	.167	.167	.167	-10	-2	-2	0	0	0	0	1	/O1	-0.1
Total	4	104	238	17	59	12	1	5	29	12	26	.248	.301	.370	84	-7	-6	28	0	0	0	1	/O1	-0.7

■ ELLIOTT MADDOX Maddox, Elliott b: 12/21/47, East Orange, N.J. BR/TR, 5'11", 180 lbs. Deb: 4/07/70

1970	Det-A	109	258	30	64	13	4	3	24	30	42	.248	.333	.364	92	-2	-3	31	2	3	-1	3	3OS/2	0.0
1971	Was-A	128	258	38	56	8	2	1	18	51	42	.217	.346	.275	83	-5	-4	28	10	4	1	-5	*O3	-1.1
1972	Tex-A	98	294	40	74	7	2	0	10	49	53	.252	.362	.289	100	1	2	34	20	10	0	-1	O	-0.1
1973	Tex-A	100	172	24	41	1	0	1	17	29	28	.238	.358	.262	80	-4	-3	18	5	4	-1	-3	O/3D	-0.8
1974	NY-A	137	466	75	141	26	2	3	45	69	48	.303	.397	.386	130	19	21	74	6	5	-1	5	*O/23	2.2
1975	NY-A	55	218	36	67	10	3	1	23	21	24	.307	.386	.394	124	7	8	33	9	3	1	6	O/2	1.4
1976	*NY-A	18	46	4	10	2	0	0	3	4	3	.217	.280	.261	60	-2	-2	4	0	1	-1	1	O/D	-0.1
1977	Bal-A	49	107	14	28	7	0	2	9	13	9	.262	.363	.383	110	1	2	14	2	2	-1	4	O/3	0.4
1978	NY-N	119	389	43	100	18	2	2	39	71	38	.257	.374	.329	102	2	4	50	2	11	-6	-2	O3/1	-0.6
1979	NY-N	86	224	21	60	13	0	1	12	20	27	.268	.336	.339	88	-4	-3	26	3	2	-0	5	O3	0.0
1980	NY-N	130	411	35	101	16	1	4	34	52	44	.246	.339	.319	87	-7	-5	44	1	9	-5	-1	*3/O1	-1.2
Total	11	1029	2843	360	742	121	16	18	234	409	358	.261	.361	.334	100	5	17	357	60	54	-14	14	O3/S21D	0.1

■ GARRY MADDOX Maddox, Garry Lee b: 9/1/49, Cincinnati, Ohio BR/TR, 6'3", 175 lbs. Deb: 4/25/72

1972	SF-N	125	458	62	122	26	7	12	58	14	97	.266	.294	.432	103	0	-1	57	13	6	0	-4	*O	-1.0
1973	SF-N	144	587	81	187	30	10	11	76	24	73	.319	.352	.460	118	16	14	94	24	10	1	3	*O	1.2
1974	SF-N	135	538	74	153	31	3	8	50	29	64	.284	.325	.398	97	-1	-4	68	21	9	1	3	*O	-0.4
1975	SF-N	17	52	4	7	1	0	1	4	6	3	.135	.237	.212	24	-5	-6	3	1	1	-0	4	O	-0.2
	Phi-N	99	374	50	109	25	8	4	46	36	54	.291	.361	.433	115	10	8	64	24	3	5	15	O	2.6
	Yr	116	426	54	116	26	8	5	50	42	57	.272	.346	.406	104	4	2	65	25	4	5	19		2.4
1976	*Phi-N	146	531	75	175	37	6	6	68	42	59	.330	.383	.456	133	26	24	92	29	12	2	18	*O	3.9
1977	*Phi-N	139	571	85	167	27	10	14	74	24	58	.292	.326	.448	101	2	-1	84	22	6	3	7	*O	0.5
1978	*Phi-N	155	598	62	172	34	3	11	68	39	89	.288	.333	.410	106	4	3	83	33	7	6	14	*O	1.8
1979	Phi-N	148	548	70	154	28	6	13	61	17	71	.281	.308	.425	95	-4	-6	68	26	13	0	20	*O	1.1
1980	*Phi-N	143	549	59	142	31	3	11	73	18	52	.259	.282	.386	80	-13	-16	58	25	5	5	5	*O	-1.2
1981	Phi-N	94	323	37	85	7	1	5	40	17	42	.263	.302	.337	78	-8	-10	33	9	4	0	4	O	-0.8
1982	Phi-N	119	412	39	117	27	2	8	61	12	32	.284	.304	.417	98	-2	-3	47	7	5	-1	2	*O	-0.2
1983	*Phi-N	97	324	27	89	14	2	4	32	17	31	.275	.313	.367	89	-6	-5	34	7	6	-2	-5	O	-1.3
1984	Phi-N	77	241	29	68	11	0	5	19	13	29	.282	.319	.390	97	-1	-2	30	7	4	-2	6	O	0.2
1985	Phi-N	105	218	22	52	8	1	4	23	13	26	.239	.284	.339	72	-8	-9	21	4	2	0	-9	O	-2.0
1986	Phi-N	6	7	1	3	0	0	0	1	2	1	.429	.556	.429	169	1	1	2	0	1	-1	-0	/O	0.0
Total	15	1749	6331	777	1802	337	62	117	754	323	781	.285	.323	.413	100	12	-11	838	248	92	19	83	*O	4.2

YEAR	TM/L	G	AB	R	H	2B	3B	HR	RBI	BB	SO	AVG	OBP	SLG	PRO+	BR	/A	RC	SB	CS	SBR	FR	POS	TPR

■ JERRY MADDOX   Maddox, Jerry Glenn   b: 7/28/53, Whittier, Cal.   BR/TR, 6'2", 200 lbs.   Deb: 6/03/78

YEAR	TM/L	G	AB	R	H	2B	3B	HR	RBI	BB	SO	AVG	OBP	SLG	PRO+	BR	/A	RC	SB	CS	SBR	FR	POS	TPR
1978	Atl-N	7	14	1	3	0	0	0	1	1	2	.214	.267	.214	32	-1	-1	1	0	0	0	-0	/3	-0.1

■ ART MADISON   Madison, Arthur   b: 1/14/1872, Clarksburg, Mass.   d: 1/27/33, N.Adams, Mass.   BR/TR, 5'9", 165 lbs.   Deb: 9/09/1895

YEAR	TM/L	G	AB	R	H	2B	3B	HR	RBI	BB	SO	AVG	OBP	SLG	PRO+	BR	/A	RC	SB	CS	SBR	FR	POS	TPR
1895	Phi-N	11	34	6	12	3	0	0	8	1	1	.353	.371	.441	111	0	0	7	4			-1	/S23	0.0
1899	Pit-N	42	118	20	32	2	4	0	19	11		.271	.338	.356	93	-1	-1	15	1			-6	2S/3	-0.3
Total	2	53	152	26	44	5	4	0	27	12	1	.289	.345	.375	97	-1	-0	22	5			-6	/2S3	-0.3

■ SCOTTI MADISON   Madison, Charles Scott   b: 9/12/59, Pensacola, Fla.   BB/TR, 5'11", 185 lbs.   Deb: 7/06/85

YEAR	TM/L	G	AB	R	H	2B	3B	HR	RBI	BB	SO	AVG	OBP	SLG	PRO+	BR	/A	RC	SB	CS	SBR	FR	POS	TPR
1985	Det-A	6	11	0	0	0	0	0	1	2	0	.000	.154	.000	-54	-2	-2	0	0	0	0	0	/CD	-0.1
1986	Det-A	2	7	0	0	0	0	0	1	0	3	.000	.000	.000	-99	-2	-2	0	0	0	0	-0	/3D	-0.2
1987	KC-A	7	15	4	4	3	0	0	0	1	5	.267	.313	.467	100	0	-0	2	0	0	0	-1	/1C	-0.1
1988	KC-A	16	35	4	6	2	0	0	2	4	5	.171	.256	.229	37	-3	-3	2	1	0	0	-1	/CO1D	-0.3
1989	Cin-N	40	98	13	17	7	0	1	7	8	9	.173	.243	.276	46	-7	-7	6	0	1	-1	2	3	-0.5
Total	5	71	166	21	27	12	0	1	11	15	22	.163	.236	.253	37	-14	-14	11	1	1	-0	-1	/3DC10	-1.2

■ ED MADJESKI   Madjeski, Edward William (b: Edward William Majewski)   b: 7/24/09, Far Rockaway, N.Y   BR/TR, 5'11", 178 lbs.   Deb: 5/02/32

YEAR	TM/L	G	AB	R	H	2B	3B	HR	RBI	BB	SO	AVG	OBP	SLG	PRO+	BR	/A	RC	SB	CS	SBR	FR	POS	TPR
1932	Phi-A	17	35	4	8	0	0	0	3	3	6	.229	.289	.229	35	-3	-3	2	0	0	0	2	/C	0.0
1933	Phi-A	51	142	17	40	4	0	0	17	4	21	.282	.301	.310	62	-8	-8	13	0	0	0	-4	C	-0.8
1934	Phi-A	8	8	1	3	1	0	0	2	0	1	.375	.375	.500	129	0	0	1	0	0	0	-0	/C	0.0
	Chi-A	85	281	36	62	14	2	5	32	14	31	.221	.260	.338	52	-21	-22	25	2	0	1	3	C	-0.9
	Yr	93	289	37	65	15	2	5	34	14	32	.225	.263	.343	54	-21	-22	26	2	0	1	3		-0.9
1937	NY-N	5	15	0	3	0	0	0	2	0	2	.200	.200	.200	9	-2	-2	1	0			-2	/C	-0.3
Total	4	166	481	58	116	19	2	5	56	21	61	.241	.274	.320	53	-33	-35	43	2	0		-1	C	-2.0

■ BILL MADLOCK   Madlock, Bill   b: 1/2/51, Memphis, Tenn.   BR/TR, 5'11", 180 lbs.   Deb: 9/07/73

YEAR	TM/L	G	AB	R	H	2B	3B	HR	RBI	BB	SO	AVG	OBP	SLG	PRO+	BR	/A	RC	SB	CS	SBR	FR	POS	TPR
1973	Tex-A	21	77	16	27	5	3	1	5	7	9	.351	.412	.532	171	7	7	17	3	2	-0	-6	3	0.1
1974	Chi-N	128	453	65	142	21	5	9	54	42	39	.313	.378	.442	124	17	15	72	11	7	-1	-12	*3	0.0
1975	Chi-N	130	514	77	182	29	7	7	64	42	34	**.354**	.406	.479	139	31	28	98	9	7	-2	-11	*3	1.6
1976	Chi-N	142	514	68	174	36	1	15	84	56	27	**.339**	.415	.500	146	41	35	100	15	11	-2	-20	*3	1.2
1977	SF-N	140	533	70	161	28	1	12	46	43	33	.302	.361	.426	111	8	8	73	13	10	-2	-17	*3/2	-1.1
1978	SF-N	122	447	76	138	26	3	15	44	48	39	.309	.380	.481	145	23	25	84	16	5	2	-24	*2/1	1.1
1979	SF-N	69	249	37	65	9	2	7	41	18	19	.261	.311	.398	99	-3	-1	31	11	3	2	-13	2/1	-0.9
	*Pit-N	85	311	48	102	17	3	7	44	34	22	.328	.396	.469	129	16	14	55	21	8	2	-6	3	0.6
	Yr	154	560	85	167	26	5	14	85	52	41	.298	.359	.438	117	12	13	86	32	11	3	-20		-0.3
1980	Pit-N	137	494	62	137	22	4	10	53	45	33	.277	.343	.399	105	4	3	64	16	10	-1	-17	*31	-1.6
1981	Pit-N	82	279	35	95	23	1	6	45	34	17	.341	.418	.495	153	22	21	59	18	6	2	-4	3	1.6
1982	Pit-N	154	568	92	181	33	3	19	95	48	39	.319	.376	.488	136	29	27	103	18	6	2	-6	*3/1	2.1
1983	Pit-N	130	473	68	153	21	0	12	68	49	24	**.323**	.389	.444	127	20	19	78	3	4	-2	-13	*3	0.0
1984	Pit-N	103	403	38	102	16	0	4	44	26	29	.253	.300	.323	75	-14	-14	38	3	1	0	-8	3/1	-2.2
1985	Pit-N	110	399	49	100	23	1	10	41	39	42	.251	.325	.388	100	-1	-0	49	3	3	-1	-15	31	-1.7
	*LA-N	34	114	20	41	4	0	2	15	10	11	.360	.425	.447	149	7	8	23	7	1	2	3	3	1.3
	Yr	144	513	69	141	27	1	12	56	49	53	.275	.347	.402	110	6	7	71	10	4	1	-13		-0.4
1986	LA-N	111	379	38	106	17	0	10	60	30	43	.280	.341	.404	112	2	5	52	3	3	-1	-8	*3/1	-0.6
1987	LA-N	21	61	5	11	1	0	3	7	6	5	.180	.265	.344	61	-4	-3	5	0	0	0	-4	3/1	-0.7
	*Det-A	87	326	56	91	17	0	14	50	28	45	.279	.354	.460	119	7	9	52	4	3	-1	-2	D1/3	0.3
Total	15	1806	6594	920	2008	348	34	163	860	605	510	.305	.369	.442	123	213	206	1053	174	90	-2	-184	*32/D1	1.1

■ SAL MADRID   Madrid, Salvador   b: 6/9/20, ElPaso, Tex.   d: 2/24/77, Ft.Wayne, Ind.   BR/TR, 5'9", 165 lbs.   Deb: 9/17/47

YEAR	TM/L	G	AB	R	H	2B	3B	HR	RBI	BB	SO	AVG	OBP	SLG	PRO+	BR	/A	RC	SB	CS	SBR	FR	POS	TPR
1947	Chi-N	8	24	0	3	1	0	0	1	1	6	.125	.160	.167	-14	-4	-4	1	0			4	/S	0.0

■ DAVE MAGADAN   Magadan, David Joseph   b: 9/30/62, Tampa, Fla.   BL/TR, 6'3", 190 lbs.   Deb: 9/07/86

YEAR	TM/L	G	AB	R	H	2B	3B	HR	RBI	BB	SO	AVG	OBP	SLG	PRO+	BR	/A	RC	SB	CS	SBR	FR	POS	TPR
1986	NY-N	10	18	3	8	0	0	0	3	3	1	.444	.524	.444	175	2	2	4	0	0	0	1	/1	0.3
1987	NY-N	85	192	21	61	13	1	3	24	22	22	.318	.388	.443	126	6	7	33	0	0	0	3	31	0.9
1988	*NY-N	112	314	39	87	15	0	1	35	60	39	.277	.396	.334	117	8	10	45	0	1	-1	-1	13	0.5
1989	NY-N	127	374	47	107	22	3	4	41	49	37	.286	.370	.393	124	10	12	58	1	0	0	3	13	0.9
1990	NY-N	144	451	74	148	28	6	6	72	74	55	.328	**.425**	.457	146	30	31	91	2	1	0	3	*13	2.9
Total	5	478	1349	184	411	78	10	14	175	208	154	.305	.399	.408	131	56	63	232	3	2	-0	8	13	5.5

■ LEE MAGEE   Magee, Leo Christopher (b: Leopold Christopher Hoernschemeyer)   b: 6/4/1889, Cincinnati, Ohio   d: 3/14/66, Columbus, Ohio   BB/TR, 5'11", 165 lbs.   Deb: 7/04/11   M

YEAR	TM/L	G	AB	R	H	2B	3B	HR	RBI	BB	SO	AVG	OBP	SLG	PRO+	BR	/A	RC	SB	CS	SBR	FR	POS	TPR
1911	StL-N	26	69	9	18	1	1	0	8	8	8	.261	.338	.304	82	-2	-1	8	4			-2	2/S	-0.3
1912	StL-N	128	458	60	133	13	8	0	40	39	29	.290	.347	.354	94	-5	-3	63	16			10	O2/1S	0.3
1913	StL-N	137	531	54	142	13	7	2	31	34	30	.267	.314	.330	85	-11	-11	61	23			18	*O2/1S	0.6
1914	StL-N	142	529	59	150	23	4	2	40	42	24	.284	.337	.353	107	3	4	74	36			-0	*O1/2	0.0
1915	Bro-F	121	452	87	146	19	10	4	49	22	19	.323	.356	.436	135	17	17	86	34			-1	*2/1M	1.9
1916	NY-A	131	510	57	131	18	4	3	45	50	31	.257	.324	.325	93	-3	-4	56	29	25	-6	5	*O/2	-1.4
1917	NY-A	51	173	17	38	4	1	0	8	13	18	.220	.278	.254	62	-8	-8	14	3			-8	O	-2.0
	StL-A	36	112	11	19	1	0	0	4	6	6	.170	.212	.179	20	-11	-10	5	3			6	3/21O	-0.3
	Yr	87	285	28	57	5	1	0	12	19	24	.200	.252	.225	46	-19	-18	19	6			-2		-2.3
1918	Cin-N	119	459	61	133	22	13	0	28	28	19	.290	.331	.394	123	10	11	65	19			9	*2/3	2.9
1919	Bro-N	45	181	16	43	7	2	0	7	5	8	.238	.262	.298	67	-7	-8	16	5			-1	2/3	-0.7
	Chi-N	79	267	36	78	12	4	1	17	19	16	.292	.339	.378	115	5	5	38	14			-5	OS3/2	-0.1
	Yr	124	448	52	121	19	6	1	24	23	24	.270	.309	.346	96	-2	-3	53	19			-6		-0.9
Total	9	1015	3741	467	1031	133	54	12	277	265	208	.276	.325	.350	99	-12	-8	486	186	25		31	O2/13S	0.9

■ SHERRY MAGEE   Magee, Sherwood Robert   b: 8/6/1884, Clarendon, Pa.   d: 3/13/29, Philadelphia, Pa.   BR/TR, 5'11", 179 lbs.   Deb: 6/29/04   U

YEAR	TM/L	G	AB	R	H	2B	3B	HR	RBI	BB	SO	AVG	OBP	SLG	PRO+	BR	/A	RC	SB	CS	SBR	FR	POS	TPR
1904	Phi-N	95	364	51	101	15	12	3	57	14		.277	.304	.409	126	7	9	51	11			5	O/1	1.0
1905	Phi-N	155	603	100	180	24	17	5	98	44		.299	.346	.420	135	21	23	108	48			11	*O	2.4
1906	Phi-N	154	563	77	159	36	8	6	67	52		.282	.343	.407	136	22	22	101	55			11	*O	3.3
1907	Phi-N	140	503	75	165	28	12	4	**85**	53		.328	.392	.455	171	39	39	111	46			7	*O	4.6
1908	Phi-N	143	508	79	144	30	16	2	57	49		.283	.346	.417	141	25	24	87	40			2	*O	2.7
1909	Phi-N	143	522	60	141	33	14	2	66	43		.270	.339	.398	128	16	16	83	38			-6	*O	0.6
1910	Phi-N	154	519	**110**	172	39	17	6	**123**	94	36	**.331**	.445	.507	172	55	53	139	49			-8	*O	4.1
1911	Phi-N	121	445	79	128	32	5	15	94	49	33	.288	.366	.483	135	20	19	86	22			5	*O	2.1
1912	Phi-N	132	464	79	142	25	9	6	66	55	54	.306	.388	.438	118	17	13	91	30			-8	*O/1	0.1
1913	Phi-N	138	470	92	144	36	6	11	70	38	36	.306	.369	.479	136	24	21	89	23			-7	*O/1	1.3
1914	Phi-N	146	544	96	**171**	**39**	11	15	**103**	55	42	.314	.380	**.509**	154	41	37	110	25			7	OS1/2	4.5
1915	Bos-N	156	571	72	160	34	12	2	87	54	39	.280	.350	.392	130	17	20	82	15	12	-3	9	*O1	2.3
1916	Bos-N	122	419	44	101	17	5	3	54	44	52	.241	.322	.327	104	1	3	50	10			-5	*O/1S	-0.6
1917	Bos-N	72	246	24	63	8	4	1	29	13	25	.256	.302	.333	100	-2	-0	27	7			2	O/1	0.0
	Cin-N	45	137	17	44	8	4	0	23	16	7	.321	.400	.438	164	10	10	25	4			4	O/1	1.4
	Yr	117	383	41	107	16	8	1	52	29	30	.279	.338	.371	124	8	10	51	11			6		1.4
1918	Cin-N	115	400	46	119	15	13	2	**76**	37	18	.298	.370	.415	142	19	20	64	14			-5	1O/2	1.3

YEAR	TM/L	G	AB	R	H	2B	3B	HR	RBI	BB	SO	AVG	OBP	SLG	PRO+	BR	/A	RC	SB	CS	SBR	FR	POS	TPR
1919	*Cin-N	56	163	11	35	6	1	0	21	26	19	.215	.337	.264	84	-2	-2	16	4			-4	O/23	-0.8
Total	16	2087	7441	1112	2169	425	166	83	1176	736	359	.291	.361	.427	137	329	327	1319	441	12		19	*O1/S23	30.3

■ **HARL MAGGERT**　Maggert, Harl Vestin b: 2/13/1883, Cromwell, Ind. d: 1/7/63, Fresno, Cal. BL/TR, 5'8", 155 lbs. Deb: 9/04/07

YEAR	TM/L	G	AB	R	H	2B	3B	HR	RBI	BB	SO	AVG	OBP	SLG	PRO+	BR	/A	RC	SB	CS	SBR	FR	POS	TPR
1907	Pit-N	3	6	1	0	0	0	0	0	0	2	.000	.250	.000	-19	-1	-1	0	1			0	/O	0.0
1912	Phi-A	74	242	39	62	8	6	1	13	36		.256	.357	.351	107	2	3	34	10			-6	O	-0.6
Total	2	77	248	40	62	8	6	1	13	38		.250	.354	.343	104	1	2	34	11			-6	/O	-0.6

■ **HARL MAGGERT**　Maggert, Harl Warren b: 5/4/14, Los Angeles, Cal. d: 7/10/86, Citrus Heights, Cal. BR/TR, 6', 190 lbs. Deb: 4/19/38

YEAR	TM/L	G	AB	R	H	2B	3B	HR	RBI	BB	SO	AVG	OBP	SLG	PRO+	BR	/A	RC	SB	CS	SBR	FR	POS	TPR
1938	Bos-N	66	89	12	25	3	0	3	19	10	20	.281	.354	.416	123	1	2	13	0			1	O/3	0.3

■ **STUBBY MAGNER**　Magner, Edmund Burke b: 2/20/1888, Kalamazoo, Mich. d: 9/6/56, Chillicother, Ohio BR/TR, 5'3", 135 lbs. Deb: 7/12/11

YEAR	TM/L	G	AB	R	H	2B	3B	HR	RBI	BB	SO	AVG	OBP	SLG	PRO+	BR	/A	RC	SB	CS	SBR	FR	POS	TPR
1911	NY-A	13	33	3	7	0	0	0	4	4		.212	.297	.212	40	-2	-3	3	1			-0	/S2	-0.2

■ **JOHN MAGNER**　Magner, John T. b: 1855, St.Louis, Mo.　Deb: 7/14/1879 U

YEAR	TM/L	G	AB	R	H	2B	3B	HR	RBI	BB	SO	AVG	OBP	SLG	PRO+	BR	/A	RC	SB	CS	SBR	FR	POS	TPR
1879	Cin-N	1	4	0	0	0	0	0		0	1	.000	.000	.000	-99	-1	-1	0				-0	/O	0.0

■ **GEORGE MAGOON**　Magoon, George Henry "Maggie" or "Topsy"
b: 3/27/1875, St.Albans, Maine d: 12/6/43, Rochester, N.H. BR/TR, 5'10", 160 lbs. Deb: 6/29/1898

YEAR	TM/L	G	AB	R	H	2B	3B	HR	RBI	BB	SO	AVG	OBP	SLG	PRO+	BR	/A	RC	SB	CS	SBR	FR	POS	TPR
1898	Bro-N	93	343	35	77	7	0	1	39	30		.224	.293	.254	59	-17	-17	28	7			13	S	0.1
1899	Bal-N	62	207	26	53	8	3	0	31	26		.256	.353	.324	84	-2	-4	27	7			6	S	0.5
	Chi-N	59	189	24	43	5	1	0	21	24		.228	.333	.265	69	-7	-6	19	5			7	S	0.4
	Yr	121	396	50	96	13	4	0	52	50		.242	.344	.295	77	-9	-10	45	12			13		0.9
1901	Cin-N	127	460	47	116	16	7	1	53	52		.252	.329	.324	98	-3	1	56	15			-20	*S2	-1.1
1902	Cin-N	45	162	29	44	9	2	0	23	13		.272	.344	.352	107	4	2	24	7			4	2/S	0.8
1903	Cin-N	42	139	6	30	6	0	0	9	19		.216	.310	.259	58	-6	-8	13	2			5	2/3	0.0
	Chi-A	94	334	32	76	11	3	0	25	30		.228	.291	.278	77	-10	-8	30	4			-21	2	-2.8
Total	5	522	1834	199	439	62	16	2	201	194		.239	.319	.294	80	-41	-40	197	47			-7	S2/3	-2.1

■ **TOM MAGRANN**　Magrann, Thomas Joseph b: 12/9/63, Hollywood, Fla. BR/TR, 6'3", 177 lbs. Deb: 9/07/89

YEAR	TM/L	G	AB	R	H	2B	3B	HR	RBI	BB	SO	AVG	OBP	SLG	PRO+	BR	/A	RC	SB	CS	SBR	FR	POS	TPR
1989	Cle-A	9	10	0	0	0	0	0	0	0	4	.000	.000	.000	-98	-3	-3	0	0	0	0	3	/C	0.1

■ **FREDDIE MAGUIRE**　Maguire, Frederick Edward b: 5/10/1889, Roxbury, Mass. d: 11/3/61, Boston, Mass. BR/TR, 5'11", 155 lbs. Deb: 9/22/22

YEAR	TM/L	G	AB	R	H	2B	3B	HR	RBI	BB	SO	AVG	OBP	SLG	PRO+	BR	/A	RC	SB	CS	SBR	FR	POS	TPR
1922	NY-N	5	12	4	4	0	0	0	1	0	1	.333	.333	.333	72	-0	-0	1	1	0	0	2	/2	0.1
1923	*NY-N	41	30	11	6	1	0	0	2	2	4	.200	.250	.233	29	-3	-3	2	1	0	0	12	2/3	0.9
1928	Chi-N	140	574	67	160	24	7	1	41	25	38	.279	.312	.350	74	-23	-22	62	6			51	*2	2.9
1929	Bos-N	138	496	54	125	26	8	0	41	19	40	.252	.284	.337	55	-37	-34	46	8			8	*2/S	-1.9
1930	Bos-N	146	516	54	138	21	5	0	52	20	22	.267	.297	.328	53	-41	-38	49	4			-3	*2	-2.1
1931	Bos-N	148	492	36	112	18	2	0	26	16	26	.228	.259	.272	44	-39	-37	37	3			9	*2	-2.1
Total	6	618	2120	226	545	90	22	1	163	82	131	.257	.289	.322	57	-144	-135	197	23	0		77	2/S3	-2.2

■ **JACK MAGUIRE**　Maguire, Jack b: 2/5/25, St.Louis, Mo. BR/TR, 5'11", 165 lbs. Deb: 4/18/50

YEAR	TM/L	G	AB	R	H	2B	3B	HR	RBI	BB	SO	AVG	OBP	SLG	PRO+	BR	/A	RC	SB	CS	SBR	FR	POS	TPR
1950	NY-N	29	40	3	7	2	0	0	3	3	13	.175	.233	.225	21	-5	-5	2	0			3	/O1	-0.1
1951	NY-N	16	20	6	8	1	1	1	4	2	2	.400	.455	.700	204	3	3	7	0	0	0	1	/O	0.4
	Pit-N	8	5	1	0	0	0	0	0	1	0	.000	.167	.000	-50	-1	-1	0	0	0	0	1	/23	0.0
	Yr	24	25	7	8	1	1	1	4	3	2	.320	.393	.560	151	2	2	6	0	0	0	2		0.4
	StL-A	41	127	15	31	2	1	1	14	12	21	.244	.309	.299	63	-6	-7	12	1	0	0	-1	O/32	-0.8
Total	2	94	192	25	46	5	2	2	21	18	36	.240	.305	.318	66	-9	-9	20	1	0		4	/O321	-0.5

■ **JIM MAHADY**　Mahady, James Bernard b: 4/22/01, Cortland, N.Y. d: 8/9/36, Cortland, N.Y. BR/TR, 5'11", 170 lbs. Deb: 10/02/21

YEAR	TM/L	G	AB	R	H	2B	3B	HR	RBI	BB	SO	AVG	OBP	SLG	PRO+	BR	/A	RC	SB	CS	SBR	FR	POS	TPR
1921	NY-N	1	0	0	0	0	0	0	0	0	0					0	0	0	0	0	0	0	/2	0.0

■ **ART MAHAN**　Mahan, Arthur Leo b: 6/8/13, Somerville, Mass. BL/TL, 5'11", 178 lbs. Deb: 4/30/40

YEAR	TM/L	G	AB	R	H	2B	3B	HR	RBI	BB	SO	AVG	OBP	SLG	PRO+	BR	/A	RC	SB	CS	SBR	FR	POS	TPR
1940	Phi-N	146	544	55	133	24	5	2	39	40	37	.244	.297	.318	73	-22	-20	52	4			4	*1/P	-2.8

■ **FRANK MAHAR**　Mahar, Frank Edward b: 12/4/1878, Natick, Mass. d: 12/5/61, Somerville, Mass. TR, 5'10.5", Deb: 8/29/02

YEAR	TM/L	G	AB	R	H	2B	3B	HR	RBI	BB	SO	AVG	OBP	SLG	PRO+	BR	/A	RC	SB	CS	SBR	FR	POS	TPR
1902	Phi-N	1	1	0	0	0	0	0	0	0		.000	.000	.000	-99	-0	-0	0	0			0	H	0.0

■ **BILLY MAHARG**　Maharg, William Joseph b: 3/19/1881, Philadelphia, Pa. d: 11/20/53, Philadelphia, Pa. BR/TR, 5'4.5", Deb: 5/18/12

YEAR	TM/L	G	AB	R	H	2B	3B	HR	RBI	BB	SO	AVG	OBP	SLG	PRO+	BR	/A	RC	SB	CS	SBR	FR	POS	TPR
1912	Det-A	1	1	0	0	0	0	0	0	0		.000	.000	.000	-99	-0	-0	0	0			1	/3	0.0
1916	Phi-N	1	1	0	0	0	0	0	0	0	0	.000	.000	.000	-97	-0	-0	0	0			0	/O	0.0
Total	2	2	2	0	0	0	0	0	0	0	0	.000	.000	.000	-99	-0	-0	0	0			1	/O3	30.0

■ **TOM MAHER**　Maher, Thomas Francis b: 7/6/1870, Philadelphia, Pa. d: 8/25/29, Philadelphia, Pa.　Deb: 4/24/02

YEAR	TM/L	G	AB	R	H	2B	3B	HR	RBI	BB	SO	AVG	OBP	SLG	PRO+	BR	/A	RC	SB	CS	SBR	FR	POS	TPR
1902	Phi-N	1	0	0	0	0	0	0	0	0		—	—	—	—	0	0	0	0			0	R	0.0

■ **GREG MAHLBERG**　Mahlberg, Gregory John b: 8/8/52, Milwaukee, Wis. BR/TR, 5'10", 180 lbs. Deb: 9/24/78

YEAR	TM/L	G	AB	R	H	2B	3B	HR	RBI	BB	SO	AVG	OBP	SLG	PRO+	BR	/A	RC	SB	CS	SBR	FR	POS	TPR
1978	Tex-A	1	1	0	0	0	0	0	0	0	0	.000	.000	.000	-99	-0	-0	0	0	0	0	0	/C	0.0
1979	Tex-A	7	17	2	2	0	0	1	1	2	4	.118	.211	.294	35	-2	-2	1	0	0	0	-2	/C	-0.2
Total	2	8	18	2	2	0	0	1	1	2	4	.111	.200	.278	28	-2	-2	1	0	0	0	-2	/C	-0.2

■ **DAN MAHONEY**　Mahoney, Daniel J. b: 3/20/1864, Springfield, Mass. d: 2/1/04, Springfield, Mass. BR/TR, 5'9.5", 165 lbs. Deb: 8/20/1892

YEAR	TM/L	G	AB	R	H	2B	3B	HR	RBI	BB	SO	AVG	OBP	SLG	PRO+	BR	/A	RC	SB	CS	SBR	FR	POS	TPR
1892	Cin-N	5	21	1	4	0	1	0	1	1	4	.190	.227	.286	57	-1	-1	1	0			2	/C	0.1
1895	Was-N	6	12	2	2	0	0	0	1	0		.167	.167	.167	-13	-2	-2	0	0			-0	/C1	-0.1
Total	2	11	33	3	6	0	1	0	2	1	4	.182	.206	.242	29	-3	-3	2	0			2	/C1	0.0

■ **DANNY MAHONEY**　Mahoney, Daniel Joseph b: 9/6/1888, Haverhill, Mass. d: 9/28/60, Utica, N.Y. 5'6.5", 145 lbs. Deb: 5/15/11

YEAR	TM/L	G	AB	R	H	2B	3B	HR	RBI	BB	SO	AVG	OBP	SLG	PRO+	BR	/A	RC	SB	CS	SBR	FR	POS	TPR
1911	Cin-N	1	0	0	0	0	0	0	0	0	0	—	—	—	—	0	0	0	0			0	R	0.0

■ **MIKE MAHONEY**　Mahoney, George W. "Big Mike" b: 12/5/1873, Boston, Mass. d: 1/3/40, Boston, Mass. BR , 6'4", 220 lbs. Deb: 5/18/1897

YEAR	TM/L	G	AB	R	H	2B	3B	HR	RBI	BB	SO	AVG	OBP	SLG	PRO+	BR	/A	RC	SB	CS	SBR	FR	POS	TPR
1897	Bos-N	2	2	1	1	0	0	0	1	0		.500	.500	.500	158	0	0	1	0			0	/CP	0.0
1898	StL-N	2	7	0	0	0	0	0	0	0		.000	.000	.000	-98	-2	-2	0	0			-0	/1	-0.1
Total	2	4	9	1	1	0	0	0	1	0		.111	.111	.111	-36	-2	-2	1	0			-0	/1PC	-0.1

■ **JIM MAHONEY**　Mahoney, James Thomas "Moe" b: 5/26/34, Englewood, N.J. BR/TR, 6', 175 lbs. Deb: 7/28/59 C

YEAR	TM/L	G	AB	R	H	2B	3B	HR	RBI	BB	SO	AVG	OBP	SLG	PRO+	BR	/A	RC	SB	CS	SBR	FR	POS	TPR
1959	Bos-A	31	23	10	3	0	0	1	4	3	7	.130	.231	.261	33	-2	-2	2	0	0	0	10	S	1.0
1961	Was-A	43	108	10	26	0	1	0	6	5	23	.241	.274	.259	44	-9	-8	7	1	2	-1	12	S/2	0.5
1962	Cle-A	41	74	12	18	4	0	3	5	3	14	.243	.273	.419	86	-2	-2	8	0	0	0	8	S/23	0.8
1965	Hou-N	5	5	0	1	0	0	0	0	0	3	.200	.200	.200	14	-1	-1	0	0	0	0	0	/S	0.0
Total	4	120	210	32	48	4	1	4	15	11	47	.229	.267	.314	57	-13	-13	17	1	2	-1	31	/S23	2.3

■ **BOB MAIER**　Maier, Robert Phillip b: 9/5/15, Dunellen, N.J. BR/TR, 5'8", 180 lbs. Deb: 4/17/45

YEAR	TM/L	G	AB	R	H	2B	3B	HR	RBI	BB	SO	AVG	OBP	SLG	PRO+	BR	/A	RC	SB	CS	SBR	FR	POS	TPR
1945	*Det-A	132	486	58	128	25	7	1	34	38	32	.263	.317	.350	88	-5	-8	52	7	11	-5	-11	*3/O	-2.2

■ **EMIL MAILHO**　Mailho, Emil Pierre "Lefty" b: 12/16/09, Berkeley, Cal. BL/TL, 5'10", 165 lbs. Deb: 4/14/36

YEAR	TM/L	G	AB	R	H	2B	3B	HR	RBI	BB	SO	AVG	OBP	SLG	PRO+	BR	/A	RC	SB	CS	SBR	FR	POS	TPR
1936	Phi-A	21	18	5	1	0	0	0	0	5	3	.056	.261	.056	-18	-3	-3	1	0	0	0	0	/O	-0.2

YEAR	TM/L	G	AB	R	H	2B	3B	HR	RBI	BB	SO	AVG	OBP	SLG	PRO+	BR	/A	RC	SB	CS	SBR	FR	POS	TPR

■ CHARLIE MAISEL — Maisel, Charles Louis b: 4/21/1894, Catonsville, Md. d: 8/25/53, Baltimore, Md. BR/TR, 6', Deb: 10/02/15

YEAR	TM/L	G	AB	R	H	2B	3B	HR	RBI	BB	SO	AVG	OBP	SLG	PRO+	BR	/A	RC	SB	CS	SBR	FR	POS	TPR
1915	Bal-F	1	4	0	0	0	0	0	0	0	0	.000	.000	.000	-97	-1	-1	0	0			0	/C	0.0

■ FRITZ MAISEL — Maisel, Frederick Charles "Flash" b: 12/23/1889, Catonsville, Md. d: 4/22/67, Baltimore, Md. BR/TR, 5'7.5", 170 lbs. Deb: 8/11/13

YEAR	TM/L	G	AB	R	H	2B	3B	HR	RBI	BB	SO	AVG	OBP	SLG	PRO+	BR	/A	RC	SB	CS	SBR	FR	POS	TPR
1913	NY-A	51	187	33	48	4	3	0	12	34	20	.257	.371	.310	99	2	1	29	25			-5	3	-0.2
1914	NY-A	150	548	78	131	23	9	2	47	76	69	.239	.334	.325	98	-0	0	74	74	17	12	-18	*3	-0.2
1915	NY-A	135	530	77	149	16	6	4	46	48	35	.281	.342	.357	109	5	5	76	51	12	8	-9	*3	1.1
1916	NY-A	53	158	18	36	5	0	0	7	20	18	.228	.318	.259	72	-4	-5	15	4			-5	O3/2	-1.1
1917	NY-A	113	404	46	80	4	4	0	20	36	18	.198	.267	.228	51	-23	-24	32	29			-1	*2/3	-2.0
1918	StL-A	90	284	43	66	4	2	0	16	46	17	.232	.341	.261	84	-4	-3	31	11			-4	3/O	-0.7
Total	6	592	2111	295	510	56	24	6	148	260	177	.242	.327	.299	88	-25	-25	258	194	29		-43	32/O	-3.1

■ GEORGE MAISEL — Maisel, George John b: 3/12/1892, Catonsville, Md. d: 11/20/68, Baltimore, Md. BR/TR, 5'10.5", 180 lbs. Deb: 5/01/13

YEAR	TM/L	G	AB	R	H	2B	3B	HR	RBI	BB	SO	AVG	OBP	SLG	PRO+	BR	/A	RC	SB	CS	SBR	FR	POS	TPR
1913	StL-A	11	18	2	3	2	0	0	1	1	7	.167	.211	.278	44	-1	-1	1	0			-2	/O	-0.3
1916	Det-A	8	5	2	0	0	0	0	0	0	0	.000	.000	.000	-97	-1	-1	0	0			2	/3	0.1
1921	Chi-N	111	393	54	122	7	2	0	43	11	13	.310	.334	.338	78	-12	-12	45	17	7	1	-4	*O	-1.9
1922	Chi-N	38	84	9	16	1	1	0	6	8	2	.190	.261	.226	26	-9	-9	5	1	3	-2	1	O	-1.0
Total	4	168	500	67	141	10	3	0	50	20	24	.282	.314	.314	66	-23	-24	51	18	10		-3	O/3	-3.1

■ HANK MAJESKI — Majeski, Henry "Heeney" b: 12/13/16, Staten Island, N.Y. BR/TR, 5'9", 174 lbs. Deb: 5/17/39

YEAR	TM/L	G	AB	R	H	2B	3B	HR	RBI	BB	SO	AVG	OBP	SLG	PRO+	BR	/A	RC	SB	CS	SBR	FR	POS	TPR
1939	Bos-N	106	367	35	100	16	1	7	54	18	30	.272	.310	.379	91	-9	-6	41	2			12	3	0.9
1940	Bos-N	3	3	0	0	0	0	0	0	0	0	.000	.000	.000	-99	-1	-1	0	0			0	H	0.0
1941	Bos-N	19	55	5	8	5	0	0	3	1	13	.145	.161	.236	11	-7	-6	2	0			1	3	-0.5
1946	NY-A	8	12	1	1	0	1	0	0	0	0	.083	.083	.250	-9	-2	-2	0	0			-1	/3	-0.1
	Phi-A	78	264	25	66	14	3	1	25	26	13	.250	.320	.337	84	-6	-6	29	3	2	-0	8	3	0.8
	Yr	86	276	26	67	14	4	1	25	26	16	.243	.310	.333	80	-8	-7	29	3	2	-0	8		0.7
1947	Phi-A	141	479	54	134	26	5	8	72	53	31	.280	.358	.405	110	8	6	70	1	0	0	7	*3/S2	1.7
1948	Phi-A	148	590	88	183	41	4	12	120	48	48	.310	.368	.454	118	13	13	98	2	1	0	1	*3/S	0.9
1949	Phi-A	114	448	62	124	26	5	9	67	29	23	.277	.326	.417	100	-5	-3	58	0	1	-1	-4	*3	-0.7
1950	Chi-A	122	414	47	128	18	2	6	46	42	34	.309	.377	.406	103	1	2	62	1	4	-2	10	*3	0.6
1951	Chi-A	12	35	4	9	4	0	0	6	1	0	.257	.278	.371	76	-1	-1	3	0	0	0	-0	/3	-0.1
	Phi-A	89	323	41	92	19	4	5	42	35	24	.285	.358	.415	106	4	3	48	1	2	-1	14	3	1.2
	Yr	101	358	45	101	23	4	5	48	36	24	.282	.351	.411	104	2	2	52	1	2	-1	14		1.1
1952	Phi-A	34	117	14	30	2	2	0	20	19	10	.256	.365	.359	96	1	-0	15	0	1	-1	4	3	0.4
	Cle-A	36	54	7	16	2	0	0	9	7	7	.296	.377	.333	106	0	1	6	0	0	-0	-0	3/2	0.1
	Yr	70	171	21	46	4	2	0	29	26	17	.269	.369	.351	101	1	1	21	0	1	-1	4		0.5
1953	Cle-A	50	50	6	15	1	0	2	12	3	8	.300	.352	.440	116	1	1	8	0	0	0	-2	2/3O	0.0
1954	*Cle-A	57	121	10	34	4	0	3	17	7	14	.281	.320	.388	92	-1	-2	14	0	0	0	4	23	0.3
1955	Cle-A	36	48	3	9	2	0	2	6	8	3	.188	.328	.354	80	-1	-1	6	0	0	0	-2	/32	-0.2
	Bal-A	16	41	2	7	1	0	0	2	2	4	.171	.209	.195	10	-5	-5	2	0	0	0	-3	/32	-0.7
	Yr	52	89	5	16	3	0	2	8	10	7	.180	.277	.281	50	-6	-6	7	0	0	0	-5		-0.9
Total	13	1069	3421	404	956	181	27	57	501	299	260	.279	.342	.398	100	-11	-7	462	10	11		50	3/2SO	4.6

■ CHARLIE MALAY — Malay, Charles Francis b: 6/13/1879, Brooklyn, N.Y. d: 9/18/49, Brooklyn, N.Y. BB/TR, 5'11.5", 175 lbs. Deb: 4/24/05

YEAR	TM/L	G	AB	R	H	2B	3B	HR	RBI	BB	SO	AVG	OBP	SLG	PRO+	BR	/A	RC	SB	CS	SBR	FR	POS	TPR
1905	Bro-N	102	349	33	88	7	2	1	31	22		.252	.296	.292	84	-9	-6	37	13			-9	2O/S	-1.3

■ JOE MALAY — Malay, Joseph Charles b: 10/25/05, Brooklyn, N.Y. d: 3/19/89, Bridgeport, Conn. BL/TL, 6', 175 lbs. Deb: 9/07/33

YEAR	TM/L	G	AB	R	H	2B	3B	HR	RBI	BB	SO	AVG	OBP	SLG	PRO+	BR	/A	RC	SB	CS	SBR	FR	POS	TPR
1933	NY-N	8	24	0	3	0	0	0	2	0	0	.125	.125	.125	-29	-4	-4	0	0			2	/1	-0.2
1935	NY-N	1	1	0	1	0	0	0	0	0	0	1.000	1.000	1.000	447	0	0	1	0			0	H	0.0
Total	2	9	25	0	4	0	0	0	2	0	0	.160	.160	.160	-9	-3	-3	1	0			2	/1	-0.2

■ CANDY MALDONADO — Maldonado, Candido (Guadarrama) b: 9/5/60, Humacao, P.R. BR/TR, 6', 185 lbs. Deb: 9/07/81

YEAR	TM/L	G	AB	R	H	2B	3B	HR	RBI	BB	SO	AVG	OBP	SLG	PRO+	BR	/A	RC	SB	CS	SBR	FR	POS	TPR
1981	LA-N	11	12	0	1	0	0	0	0	0	5	.083	.083	.083	-55	-2	-2	0	0	0	0	0	/O	-0.1
1982	LA-N	6	4	0	0	0	0	0	0	1	2	.000	.200	.000	-41	-1	-1	0	0	0	0	1	/O	0.0
1983	*LA-N	42	62	5	12	1	1	1	6	5	14	.194	.254	.290	51	-4	-4	5	0	0	0	-1	O	-0.5
1984	LA-N	116	254	25	68	14	0	5	28	19	29	.268	.321	.382	98	-1	-1	30	0	3	-2	-15	*O/3	-2.2
1985	*LA-N	121	213	20	48	7	1	5	19	19	40	.225	.289	.338	77	-7	-7	21	1	1	-0	4	*O	-0.5
1986	SF-N	133	405	49	102	31	3	18	85	20	77	.252	.292	.477	114	2	4	51	4	4	-1	-2	*O/3	0.2
1987	*SF-N	118	442	69	129	28	4	20	85	34	78	.292	.351	.509	131	14	17	75	8	8	-2	-8	*O	0.2
1988	SF-N	142	499	53	127	23	1	12	68	37	89	.255	.315	.377	102	-2	1	57	6	5	-1	-8	*O	-1.2
1989	*SF-N	129	345	39	75	23	0	9	41	37	69	.217	.299	.362	91	-6	-4	38	4	1	1	-11	*O	-1.7
1990	Cle-A	155	590	76	161	32	2	22	95	49	134	.273	.334	.446	114	11	10	85	3	5	-2	6	*OD	1.2
Total	10	973	2826	336	723	159	12	92	427	221	537	.256	.315	.418	105	4	13	362	26	27	-8	-35	O/D3	-4.8

■ JIM MALER — Maler, James Michael b: 8/16/58, New York, N.Y. BR/TR, 6'4", 230 lbs. Deb: 9/03/81

YEAR	TM/L	G	AB	R	H	2B	3B	HR	RBI	BB	SO	AVG	OBP	SLG	PRO+	BR	/A	RC	SB	CS	SBR	FR	POS	TPR
1981	Sea-A	12	23	1	8	1	0	0	2	2	4	.348	.423	.391	131	1	1	4	1	0	0	0	/1D	0.1
1982	Sea-A	64	221	18	50	8	3	4	26	12	35	.226	.275	.344	67	-10	-11	21	0	0	0	2	1/D	-0.9
1983	Sea-A	26	66	5	12	1	0	1	3	5	11	.182	.260	.242	38	-5	-6	3	0	3	-2	0	1/D	-0.7
Total	3	102	310	24	70	10	3	5	31	19	47	.226	.284	.326	65	-14	-15	28	1	3	-2	3	/1D	-1.5

■ TONY MALINOSKY — Malinosky, Anthony Francis b: 10/5/09, Collinsville, Ill. BR/TR, 5'10.5", 165 lbs. Deb: 4/26/37

YEAR	TM/L	G	AB	R	H	2B	3B	HR	RBI	BB	SO	AVG	OBP	SLG	PRO+	BR	/A	RC	SB	CS	SBR	FR	POS	TPR
1937	Bro-N	35	79	7	18	2	0	0	3	9	11	.228	.307	.253	53	-5	-5	7	0			-9	3S	-1.2

■ BOBBY MALKMUS — Malkmus, Robert Edward b: 7/4/31, Newark, N.J. BR/TR, 5'9", 175 lbs. Deb: 6/01/57

YEAR	TM/L	G	AB	R	H	2B	3B	HR	RBI	BB	SO	AVG	OBP	SLG	PRO+	BR	/A	RC	SB	CS	SBR	FR	POS	TPR
1957	Mil-N	13	22	6	2	0	1	0	0	3	3	.091	.200	.182	4	-3	-3	1	0	0	0	4	/2	0.1
1958	Was-A	41	70	5	13	2	1	0	3	4	15	.186	.230	.243	31	-7	-7	3	0	0	0	8	2/3S	0.3
1959	Was-A	6	0	0	0	0	0	0	0	0	0	—	—	—	—	0	0	0	0	0	0	0	R	0.0
1960	Phi-N	79	133	16	28	4	1	1	12	11	28	.211	.271	.278	51	-9	-9	10	2	2	-1	7	S23	0.0
1961	Phi-N	121	342	39	79	8	2	7	31	20	43	.231	.277	.327	61	-20	-19	30	1	3	-2	16	2S3	0.5
1962	Phi-N	8	5	3	1	1	0	0	0	0	1	.200	.200	.400	58	-0	-0	0	0	0	0	3	/S	0.3
Total	6	268	572	69	123	15	5	8	46	38	90	.215	.266	.301	53	-39	-38	45	3	5	-2	37	2/S3	1.2

■ JERRY MALLETT — Mallett, Gerald Gordon b: 9/18/35, Bonne Terre, Mo. BR/TR, 6'5", 208 lbs. Deb: 9/19/59

YEAR	TM/L	G	AB	R	H	2B	3B	HR	RBI	BB	SO	AVG	OBP	SLG	PRO+	BR	/A	RC	SB	CS	SBR	FR	POS	TPR
1959	Bos-A	4	15	1	4	0	0	0	1	1	3	.267	.313	.267	58	-1	-1	1	0	0	0	3	/O	0.2

■ LES MALLON — Mallon, Leslie Clyde b: 11/21/05, Sweetwater, Tex. Deceased BR/TR, 5'8", 160 lbs. Deb: 4/14/31

YEAR	TM/L	G	AB	R	H	2B	3B	HR	RBI	BB	SO	AVG	OBP	SLG	PRO+	BR	/A	RC	SB	CS	SBR	FR	POS	TPR
1931	Phi-N	122	375	41	116	19	2	1	45	29	40	.309	.359	.379	91	-0	-4	53	0			6	2/1S3	0.6
1932	Phi-N	103	347	44	90	16	0	5	33	28	28	.259	.318	.349	71	-10	-15	40	1			-31	2/3	-3.9
1934	Bos-N	42	166	23	49	6	1	0	18	15	12	.295	.354	.343	95	-2	-1	20	0			-4	2	0.0
1935	Bos-N	116	412	48	113	24	2	2	25	28	37	.274	.322	.357	89	-10	-6	47	3			-13	23/O	-1.1
Total	4	383	1300	156	368	65	5	8	119	100	117	.283	.336	.359	85	-23	-26	161	4			-42	2/31SO	-4.4

■ BEN MALLONEE — Mallonee, Howard Bennett "Lefty" b: 3/31/1894, Baltimore, Md. d: 2/19/78, Baltimore, Md. BL/TL, 5'6", 150 lbs. Deb: 9/14/21

YEAR	TM/L	G	AB	R	H	2B	3B	HR	RBI	BB	SO	AVG	OBP	SLG	PRO+	BR	/A	RC	SB	CS	SBR	FR	POS	TPR
1921	Phi-A	7	25	2	6	1	0	0	4	1	2	.240	.269	.280	40	-2	-2	2	1	0	0	0	/O	-0.1

YEAR	TM/L	G	AB	R	H	2B	3B	HR	RBI	BB	SO	AVG	OBP	SLG	PRO+	BR	/A	RC	SB	CS	SBR	FR	POS	TPR
■ **JULE MALLONEE**			Mallonee, Julius Norris		b: 4/4/1900, Charlotte, N.C.			d: 12/26/34, Charlotte, N.C.		BL/TR, 6'2", 180 lbs.		Deb: 8/04/25												
1925	Chi-A	2	3	1	0	0	0	0	0	1	0	.000	.250	.000	-34	-1	-1	0	0	0	0	-0	/O	0.0
■ **JIM MALLORY**			Mallory, James Baugh "Sunny Jim"		b: 9/1/18, Lawrenceville, Va.			BR/TR, 6'1", 170 lbs.		Deb: 9/08/40														
1940	Was-A	4	12	2	2	0	0	0	0	1	1	.167	.231	.167	5	-2	-2	1	0	0	0	1	/O	0.0
1945	StL-N	13	43	3	10	2	0	0	5	0	2	.233	.233	.279	41	-3	-4	3	0			0	O	-0.3
	NY-N	37	94	10	28	1	0	0	9	6	7	.298	.340	.309	80	-2	-2	10	1			0	O	-0.2
	Yr	50	137	13	38	3	0	0	14	6	9	.277	.308	.299	68	-6	-6	13	1			0		-0.5
Total	2	54	149	15	40	3	0	0	14	7	10	.268	.301	.289	63	-7	-8	14	1	0		1	/O	-0.5
■ **SHELDON MALLORY**			Mallory, Sheldon		b: 7/16/53, Argo, Ill.			BL/TL, 6'2", 175 lbs.		Deb: 4/10/77														
1977	Oak-A	64	126	19	27	4	1	0	5	11	18	.214	.293	.262	53	-8	-8	11	12	5	1	3	O/1D	-0.5
■ **HARRY MALMBERG**			Malmberg, Harry William "Swede"		b: 7/31/26, Fairfield, Ala.			d: 10/29/76, San Francisco, Cal		BR/TR, 6'1", 170 lbs.		Deb: 4/12/55 C											
1955	Det-A	67	208	25	45	5	2	0	19	29	19	.216	.312	.260	56	-13	-12	17	0	1	-1	6	2	-0.1
■ **EDDIE MALONE**			Malone, Edward Russell		b: 6/16/20, Chicago, Ill.			BR/TR, 5'10", 175 lbs.		Deb: 7/17/49														
1949	Chi-A	55	170	17	46	7	2	1	16	29	19	.271	.377	.353	97	-1	0	25	2	1	0	-4	C	0.0
1950	Chi-A	31	71	2	16	2	0	0	10	10	8	.225	.321	.254	50	-5	-5	5	0	0	0	2	C	-0.1
Total	2	86	241	19	62	9	2	1	26	39	27	.257	.361	.324	83	-6	-5	30	2	1	0	-2	/C	-0.1
■ **FERGY MALONE**			Malone, Ferguson G.		b: 1842, Ireland			d: 1/1/05, Seattle, Wash.		BR/TL, 5'8", 156 lbs.		Deb: 6/03/1871 MU											
1871	Ath-n	27	134	33	46	7	1	1	33	9	4	.343	.385	.433	136	6	7	26	9				*C	0.4
1872	Ath-n	41	213	46	61	6	2	0		4		.286	.300	.333	94	-1	-1	22					C1	0.0
1873	Phi-n	53	257	59	75	9	3	0	14			.292	.328	.350	96	0	-2	30					*C/S	0.0
1874	Chi-n	47	222	32	55	5	0	0		5		.248	.264	.270	77	-0	-7	16					*CM	-0.3
1875	Phi-n	29	122	15	28	2	1	0		1		.230	.236	.262	69	-3	-4	8					1/CO	-0.3
1876	Phi-N	22	96	14	22	2	0	0	6	0	1	.229	.229	.250	60	-4	-4	6				0	C/OS	-0.1
1884	Phi-U	1	4	0	1	0	0	0		0		.250	.250	.250	75	-0	-0	0	0			-0	/CM	0.0
Total	5 n	197	948	185	265	29	7	1	33	33	4	.280	.304	.328	93	-5	-8	102	9				C/1OS	-0.2
Total	2	23	100	14	23	2	0	0	6	0	1	.230	.230	.250	61	-4	-4	6				0	/COS	-0.1
■ **LEW MALONE**			Malone, Lewis Aloysius		b: 3/13/1897, Baltimore, Md.			d: 2/17/72, Brooklyn, N.Y.		BR/TR, 5'11", 175 lbs.		Deb: 5/31/15											
1915	Phi-A	76	201	17	41	4	4	1	17	21	40	.204	.283	.279	70	-8	-7	18	7	1	2	-4	23/OS	-1.0
1916	Phi-A	5	4	1	0	0	0	0	0	1	2	.000	.200	.000	-41	-1	-1	0	0			-0	/S	0.0
1917	Bro-N	1	0	1	0	0	0	0	0	0	0	—	—	—		0	0	0	0			0	R	0.0
1919	Bro-N	51	162	9	33	7	3	0	11	6	18	.204	.232	.284	54	-9	-10	11	1			-6	3/2S	-1.7
Total	4	133	367	28	74	11	7	1	28	28	60	.202	.260	.278	62	-18	-18	29	8	1		-11	/32SO	-2.7
■ **JOHN MALONEY**			Maloney, John		d: 7/21/1890,			Deb: 9/15/1876																
1876	NY-N	2	7	1	2	0	0	0	2	0	1	.286	.286	.571	206	1	1	1				-0	/O	0.0
1877	Har-N	1	4	0	1	0	0	0	0	0	0	.250	.250	.250	65	-0	-0	0				-1	/O	0.0
Total	2	3	11	1	3	0	0	1	0	2	0	1	.273	.273	.455	152	0	1	1				-1	/O	0.0
■ **PAT MALONEY**			Maloney, Patrick William		b: 1/19/1888, Grosvenordale, Conn.			d: 6/27/79, Pawtucket, R.I.		6', 150 lbs.		Deb: 6/19/12											
1912	NY-A	25	79	9	17	1	0	0	4	6		.215	.279	.228	43	-5	-6	6	3			3	O	-0.3
■ **BILLY MALONEY**			Maloney, William Alphonse		b: 6/5/1878, Lewiston, Me.			d: 9/2/60, Breckenridge, Tex.		BL/TR, 5'10", 177 lbs.		Deb: 5/02/01											
1901	Mil-A	86	290	42	85	3	4	0	22	7		.293	.323	.331	88	-6	-4	37	11			9	C/O	1.0
1902	StL-A	30	112	8	23	3	0	0	11	6		.205	.258	.232	38	-9	-9	7	0			-4	O/C	-1.2
	Cin-N	27	89	13	22	4	0	1	7	2		.247	.272	.326	79	-2	-3	11	8			-3	O/C	-0.5
1905	Chi-N	145	558	78	145	17	14	2	56	43		.260	.313	.351	96	-1	-3	83	59			2	*O	-1.1
1906	Bro-N	151	566	71	125	15	7	0	32	49		.221	.283	.272	81	-16	-11	58	38			11	*O	-0.2
1907	Bro-N	144	502	51	115	7	10	0	32	31		.229	.274	.283	83	-14	-10	50	25			5	*O	-1.0
1908	Bro-N	113	359	31	70	5	7	3	17	24		.195	.245	.273	71	-13	-12	27	14			4	*O/C	-0.9
Total	6	696	2476	294	585	54	42	6	177	162		.236	.286	.299	82	-61	-52	272	155			26	O/C	-3.9
■ **FRANK MALZONE**			Malzone, Frank James		b: 2/28/30, Bronx, N.Y.			BR/TR, 5'10", 180 lbs.		Deb: 9/17/55													
1955	Bos-A	6	20	2	7	1	0	0	1	1	3	.350	.381	.400	101	0	0	3	0	0	0	2	/3	0.2
1956	Bos-A	27	103	15	17	3	1	2	11	9	8	.165	.232	.272	29	-10	-12	6	1	0	0	1	3	-0.9
1957	Bos-A	153	634	82	185	31	5	15	103	31	41	.292	.326	.427	98	2	-3	85	2	1	0	14	*3	1.5
1958	Bos-A	155	627	76	185	30	2	15	87	33	53	.295	.334	.421	100	4	-1	82	1	3	-2	17	*3	2.1
1959	Bos-A	154	604	90	169	34	2	19	92	42	58	.280	.328	.437	103	5	2	85	6	0	2	8	*3	1.0
1960	Bos-A	152	595	60	161	30	2	14	79	36	42	.271	.317	.398	89	-8	-10	70	2	3	-1	8	*3	-0.1
1961	Bos-A	151	590	74	157	21	4	14	87	44	49	.266	.318	.386	85	-11	-13	68	1	3	-2	-5	*3	-1.0
1962	Bos-A	156	619	74	175	20	3	21	95	35	43	.283	.321	.426	96	-2	-5	80	0	1	-1	5	*3	0.1
1963	Bos-A	151	580	66	169	25	2	15	71	31	45	.291	.331	.419	105	6	3	73	0	2	-1	4	*3	0.7
1964	Bos-A	148	537	62	142	19	0	13	56	37	43	.264	.314	.372	86	-7	-10	64	0	0	0	-0	*3	-0.8
1965	Bos-A	106	364	40	87	20	0	3	34	28	38	.239	.295	.319	70	-12	-15	31	1	1	-0	-3	3	-1.8
1966	Cal-A	82	155	6	32	5	0	2	12	10	11	.206	.255	.277	54	-9	-9	10	0	0	0	-1	3	-1.1
Total	12	1441	5428	647	1486	239	21	133	728	337	434	.274	.318	.399	91	-44	-73	656	14	14	-4	48	*3	-0.1
■ **GUS MANCUSO**			Mancuso, August Rodney "Blackie"		b: 12/5/05, Galveston, Tex.			d: 10/26/84, Houston, Tex.		BR/TR, 5'10", 185 lbs.		Deb: 4/30/28 C										
1928	StL-N	11	38	2	7	1	0	3	0	5	.184	.184	.237	9	-5	-5	2	0			4	C	0.0
1930	*StL-N	76	227	39	83	17	2	7	59	18	16	.366	.415	.551	127	11	10	50	1			1	C	1.3
1931	*StL-N	67	187	13	49	16	1	1	23	18	13	.262	.327	.374	85	-3	-4	24	2			6	C	0.5
1932	StL-N	103	310	25	88	23	1	5	43	30	15	.284	.347	.413	100	2	1	46	0			7	C	1.1
1933	*NY-N	144	481	39	127	17	2	6	56	48	21	.264	.331	.345	95	-3	-2	56	0			3	*C	0.6
1934	NY-N	122	383	32	94	14	0	7	46	27	19	.245	.295	.337	70	-17	-16	39	0			7	*C	-0.4
1935	NY-N	128	447	33	133	18	2	5	56	30	16	.298	.342	.380	95	-4	-3	57	1			-5	*C	-0.7
1936	*NY-N	139	519	55	156	31	3	9	63	39	28	.301	.351	.405	104	2	3	73	0			5	*C	1.1
1937	*NY-N	86	287	30	80	17	1	4	39	17	20	.279	.319	.387	90	-4	-5	36	1			15	C	1.3
1938	NY-N	52	158	19	55	8	0	2	15	17	13	.348	.411	.437	132	8	8	29	0			4	C	1.3
1939	Chi-N	80	251	17	58	10	0	2	17	24	19	.231	.298	.295	59	-14	-15	23	0			5	C	-0.7
1940	Bro-N	60	144	16	33	8	0	0	16	13	7	.229	.293	.285	56	-8	-9	12	0			4	C	0.0
1941	StL-N	106	328	25	75	13	1	2	37	37	19	.229	.309	.293	66	-12	-15	31	0			10	*C	0.5
1942	StL-N	5	13	0	1	0	0	0	1	0	0	.077	.077	.077	-51	-3	-3	0	0			-1	/C	-0.3
	NY-N	39	109	4	21	1	1	0	8	14	7	.193	.285	.220	48	-7	-7	7	1			3	C	-0.3
	Yr	44	122	4	22	1	1	0	9	14	7	.180	.265	.205	38	-9	-9	7	1			2		-0.6
1943	NY-N	94	252	11	50	5	0	2	20	28	16	.198	.284	.242	52	-15	-15	17	0			-0	C	-1.2
1944	NY-N	78	195	15	49	4	1	1	25	30	20	.251	.351	.297	84	-3	-3	22	0			4	C	0.5
1945	Phi-N	70	176	11	35	5	0	0	16	28	10	.199	.309	.227	52	-11	-10	13	2			1	C	-0.7
Total	17	1460	4505	386	1194	197	16	53	543	418	264	.265	.328	.351	85	-85	-90	536	8			75	*C	3.9

FRANK MANCUSO — Mancuso, Frank Octavius b: 5/23/18, Houston, Tex. BR/TR, 6', 195 lbs. Deb: 4/18/44

YEAR	TM/L	G	AB	R	H	2B	3B	HR	RBI	BB	SO	AVG	OBP	SLG	PRO+	BR	/A	RC	SB	CS	SBR	FR	POS	TPR
1944	*StL-A	88	244	19	50	11	0	1	24	20	32	.205	.271	.262	50	-15	-17	17	1	0	0	-7	C	-1.7
1945	StL-A	119	365	39	98	13	3	1	38	46	44	.268	.354	.329	94	1	-1	43	0	2	-1	-7	*C	0.0
1946	StL-A	87	262	22	63	8	3	3	23	30	31	.240	.323	.328	78	-6	-7	29	1	0	0	-17	C	-2.1
1947	Was-A	43	131	5	30	5	1	0	13	5	11	.229	.257	.282	51	-9	-9	8	0	0	0	-4	C	-0.9
Total	4	337	1002	85	241	37	7	5	98	101	118	.241	.314	.306	74	-29	-34	96	2	2	-1	-34	C	-4.7

CARL MANDA — Manda, Carl Alan b: 11/16/1888, Little River, Kan. d: 3/9/83, Artesia, N.Mex. BR/TR, 5'10", 170 lbs. Deb: 9/11/14

YEAR	TM/L	G	AB	R	H	2B	3B	HR	RBI	BB	SO	AVG	OBP	SLG	PRO+	BR	/A	RC	SB	CS	SBR	FR	POS	TPR
1914	Chi-A	9	15	2	4	0	0	0	1	3	3	.267	.389	.267	99	0	0	2	1			4	/2	0.5

JIM MANGAN — Mangan, James Daniel b: 9/24/29, San Francisco, Cal BR/TR, 5'10", 190 lbs. Deb: 4/16/52

YEAR	TM/L	G	AB	R	H	2B	3B	HR	RBI	BB	SO	AVG	OBP	SLG	PRO+	BR	/A	RC	SB	CS	SBR	FR	POS	TPR
1952	Pit-N	11	13	1	2	0	0	0	2	1	3	.154	.214	.154	4	-2	-2	0	0	0	0	-1	/C	-0.2
1954	Pit-N	14	26	2	5	0	0	0	2	4	9	.192	.300	.192	32	-3	-2	2	0	0	0	0	/C	-0.1
1956	NY-N	20	20	2	2	0	0	0	1	4	6	.100	.250	.100	-1	-3	-3	1	0	0	0	0	C	-0.1
Total	3	45	59	5	9	0	0	0	5	9	18	.153	.265	.153	15	-7	-7	3	0	0	0	-1	/C	-0.4

ANGEL MANGUAL — Mangual, Angel Luis (Guilbe) b: 3/19/47, Juana Diaz, P.R. BR/TR, 5'10", 178 lbs. Deb: 9/15/69

YEAR	TM/L	G	AB	R	H	2B	3B	HR	RBI	BB	SO	AVG	OBP	SLG	PRO+	BR	/A	RC	SB	CS	SBR	FR	POS	TPR
1969	Pit-N	6	4	1	1	1	0	0				.250	.250	.500	108	-0	-0	1	0	0	0	-0	/O	0.0
1971	*Oak-A	94	287	32	82	8	1	4	30	17	27	.286	.326	.362	97	-2	-2	31	1	4	-2	3	O	-0.2
1972	*Oak-A	91	272	19	67	13	2	5	32	14	48	.246	.286	.364	97	-3	-2	26	0	1	-1	-3	O	-0.7
1973	*Oak-A	74	192	20	43	4	1	3	13	8	34	.224	.259	.302	61	-11	-10	15	1	1	-0	1	OD/12	-1.1
1974	*Oak-A	115	365	37	85	14	4	9	43	17	59	.233	.267	.367	87	-10	-8	36	3	0	1	0	OD/3	-0.8
1975	Oak-A	62	109	13	24	3	0	1	6	3	18	.220	.241	.275	47	-8	-8	7	0	1	-1	2	OD	-0.7
1976	Oak-A	8	12	0	2	1	0	0	1	0	1	.167	.167	.250	22	-1	-1	0	0	1	-1	0	/O	-0.1
Total	7	450	1241	122	304	44	8	22	125	59	187	.245	.280	.346	83	-36	-30	116	5	8	-3	0	O/D132	-3.6

PEPE MANGUAL — Mangual, Jose Manuel (Guilbe) b: 5/23/52, Ponce, P.R. BR/TR, 5'10", 157 lbs. Deb: 9/06/72

YEAR	TM/L	G	AB	R	H	2B	3B	HR	RBI	BB	SO	AVG	OBP	SLG	PRO+	BR	/A	RC	SB	CS	SBR	FR	POS	TPR
1972	Mon-N	8	11	2	3	0	0	0		1	5	.273	.333	.273	73	-0	-0	1	0	1	-1	-0	/O	-0.1
1973	Mon-N	33	62	9	11	2	1	3	7	6	18	.177	.250	.387	71	-3	-3	5	2	4	-2	-1	O	-0.6
1974	Mon-N	23	61	10	19	3	0	0	4	5	15	.311	.364	.361	98	-0	-0	10	5	0	2	-3	O	-0.2
1975	Mon-N	140	514	84	126	16	2	9	45	74	115	.245	.345	.337	86	-5	-8	65	33	11	3	-8	*O	-1.8
1976	Mon-N	66	215	34	56	9	1	3	16	50	49	.260	.404	.353	112	8	6	37	17	7	1	-3	O	0.2
	NY-N	41	102	15	19	5	2	1	9	10	32	.186	.259	.304	63	-6	-5	9	7	3	0	2	O	-0.3
	Yr	107	317	49	75	14	3	4	25	60	81	.237	.361	.338	99	2	2	46	24	10	1	-1		-0.1
1977	NY-N	8	7	1	1	0	0	0	2	1	4	.143	.250	.143	9	-1	-1	0	0	0	0	0	/O	0.0
Total	6	319	972	155	235	35	6	16	83	147	238	.242	.345	.340	89	-7	-11	127	64	26	4	-13	O	-2.8

GEORGE MANGUS — Mangus, George Graham b: 5/22/1890, Red Creek, N.Y. d: 8/10/33, Rutland, Mass. BL/TR, 5'11.5", 165 lbs. Deb: 8/20/12

YEAR	TM/L	G	AB	R	H	2B	3B	HR	RBI	BB	SO	AVG	OBP	SLG	PRO+	BR	/A	RC	SB	CS	SBR	FR	POS	TPR
1912	Phi-N	10	25	2	5	3	0	0	3	1	6	.200	.231	.320	47	-2	-2	2	0			-1	/O	-0.3

CLYDE MANION — Manion, Clyde Jennings "Pete" b: 10/30/1896, Jefferson City, Mo d: 9/4/67, Detroit, Mich. BR/TR, 5'11", 175 lbs. Deb: 5/05/20

YEAR	TM/L	G	AB	R	H	2B	3B	HR	RBI	BB	SO	AVG	OBP	SLG	PRO+	BR	/A	RC	SB	CS	SBR	FR	POS	TPR
1920	Det-A	32	80	4	22	4	1	0	8	4	7	.275	.318	.350	79	-3	-2	9	0	0	0	-2	C	-0.1
1921	Det-A	12	10	0	2	0	0	0	2	2	2	.200	.385	.200	53	-1	-1	1	0	0	0	1	/C	0.0
1922	Det-A	42	69	9	19	4	1	0	12	4	6	.275	.315	.362	79	-3	-3	8	0	1	-1	-3	C/1	-0.4
1923	Det-A	23	22	0	3	0	0	0	2	2	2	.136	.208	.136	-8	-3	-3	1	0	0	0	-0	/C1	-0.2
1924	Det-A	14	13	1	3	0	0	0	2	1	1	.231	.286	.231	35	-1	-1	1	0	0	0	-1	/C1	-0.1
1926	Det-A	75	176	15	35	4	0	0	14	24	16	.199	.295	.222	36	-16	-16	13	1	1	-0	0	C	-1.1
1927	Det-A	1	0	0	0	0	0	0	0	1	0	—	1.000	—	174	0	0	0	0	0	0	0	H	0.0
1928	StL-A	76	243	25	55	5	1	2	31	15	18	.226	.274	.280	44	-19	-20	20	3	0	1	11	C	-0.2
1929	StL-A	35	111	16	27	2	0	0	11	15	3	.243	.333	.261	53	-7	-8	11	1	0	0	4	C	0.0
1930	StL-A	57	148	12	32	1	0	1	11	24	17	.216	.326	.243	45	-11	-12	13	0	0	-1	11	C	0.3
1932	Cin-N	49	135	7	28	4	0	0	12	14	16	.207	.282	.237	43	-11	-10	10	0			4	C	-0.4
1933	Cin-N	36	84	3	14	1	0	0	3	8	7	.167	.239	.179	21	-8	-8	4	0			4	C	-0.2
1934	Cin-N	25	54	4	10	0	0	0	4	4	7	.185	.241	.185	16	-6	-6	3	0			3	C	-0.2
Total	13	477	1145	96	250	25	3	3	112	118	102	.218	.293	.253	45	-89	-90	94	5	3		33	C/1	-2.6

PHIL MANKOWSKI — Mankowski, Philip Anthony b: 1/9/53, Buffalo, N.Y. BL/TR, 6', 180 lbs. Deb: 8/30/76

YEAR	TM/L	G	AB	R	H	2B	3B	HR	RBI	BB	SO	AVG	OBP	SLG	PRO+	BR	/A	RC	SB	CS	SBR	FR	POS	TPR
1976	Det-A	24	85	9	23	2	1	1	4	4	8	.271	.303	.353	88	-1	-1	8	0	0	0	2	3	0.1
1977	Det-A	94	286	21	79	7	3	3	27	16	41	.276	.319	.353	79	-7	-9	32	1	2	-1	13	3/2	0.1
1978	Det-A	88	222	28	61	8	4	0	20	22	28	.275	.346	.365	97	0	-0	26	2	3	-1	8	3/D	0.6
1979	Det-A	42	99	11	22	4	0	0	8	10	16	.222	.294	.263	50	-7	-7	8	0	0	0	-1	3	-0.6
1980	NY-N	8	12	1	2	1	0	0	1	2	4	.167	.286	.250	52	-1	-1	1	0	0	0	-1	/3	-0.1
1982	NY-N	13	35	2	8	1	0	0	4	1	6	.229	.257	.257	42	-3	-3	2	0	1	-1	-0	3	-0.3
Total	6	269	739	72	195	23	4	8	64	55	103	.264	.318	.338	79	-17	-21	76	3	6	-3	21	3/D2	-0.2

CHARLIE MANLOVE — Manlove, Charles Henry "Chick" b: 10/8/1862, Philadelphia, Pa. d: 2/12/52, Altoona, Pa. BR/TR, 5'9", 165 lbs. Deb: 5/31/1884

YEAR	TM/L	G	AB	R	H	2B	3B	HR	RBI	BB	SO	AVG	OBP	SLG	PRO+	BR	/A	RC	SB	CS	SBR	FR	POS	TPR
1884	Alt-U	2	7	1	3	0	0	0		0		.429	.429	.429	188	1	1	1	0			-2	/CO	0.0
	NY-N	3	10	0	0	0	0	0		0	4	.000	.000	.000	-98	-2	-2	0				1	/CO	0.0

GARTH MANN — Mann, Ben Garth "Red" b: 11/16/15, Brandon, Tex. BR/TR, 6', 155 lbs. Deb: 5/14/44

YEAR	TM/L	G	AB	R	H	2B	3B	HR	RBI	BB	SO	AVG	OBP	SLG	PRO+	BR	/A	RC	SB	CS	SBR	FR	POS	TPR
1944	Chi-N	1	0	1	0	0	0	0	0	0	0	—	—	—	—	0	0	0	0			0	R	0.0

FRED MANN — Mann, Fred J. b: 4/1/1858, Sutton, Vt. d: 4/6/16, Springfield, Mass. BL, 5'10.5", 178 lbs. Deb: 5/01/1882

YEAR	TM/L	G	AB	R	H	2B	3B	HR	RBI	BB	SO	AVG	OBP	SLG	PRO+	BR	/A	RC	SB	CS	SBR	FR	POS	TPR
1882	Wor-N	19	77	12	18	5	0	0	7	2	15	.234	.253	.299	74	-2	-2	6				-6	3/1	-0.7
	Phi-a	29	121	13	28	7	4	0	4			.231	.256	.355	93	0	-2	11				-10	3	-1.1
1883	Col-a	96	394	61	98	18	13	1	18			.249	.282	.368	117	3	8	42				-2	*O/13S	0.5
1884	Col-a	99	366	70	101	12	18	7	25			.276	.341	.464	178	25	30	59				-6	*O/2	2.1
1885	Pit-a	99	391	60	99	17	6	0	31			.253	.318	.327	108	4	5	42				-8	*O/3	-0.6
1886	Pit-a	116	440	85	110	16	14	2	45			.250	.335	.364	121	11	12	64	26			-3	*O	0.4
1887	Cle-a	64	259	45	80	15	7	2	23			.309	.385	.444	137	12	13	55	25			1	O	1.0
	Phi-a	55	229	42	63	14	6	0	15			.275	.336	.389	104	1	1	36	16			-4	O	-0.3
	Yr	119	488	87	143	29	13	2	38			.293	.362	.418	121	13	14	91	41			-3		0.7
Total	6	577	2277	388	597	104	68	12	7	163	15	.262	.323	.383	123	55	65	315	67			-38	0/312S	1.3

JOHNNY MANN — Mann, John Leo b: 2/4/1898, Fontanet, Ind. d: 3/31/77, Terre Haute, Ind. BR/TR, 5'11", 160 lbs. Deb: 4/18/28

YEAR	TM/L	G	AB	R	H	2B	3B	HR	RBI	BB	SO	AVG	OBP	SLG	PRO+	BR	/A	RC	SB	CS	SBR	FR	POS	TPR
1928	Chi-A	6	6	0	2	0	0	0	1	1	0	.333	.429	.333	104	0	0	1	0	0	0	0	/3	0.0

KELLY MANN — Mann, Kelly John b: 8/17/67, Santa Monica, Cal. BR/TR, 6'3", 215 lbs. Deb: 9/04/89

YEAR	TM/L	G	AB	R	H	2B	3B	HR	RBI	BB	SO	AVG	OBP	SLG	PRO+	BR	/A	RC	SB	CS	SBR	FR	POS	TPR
1989	Atl-N	7	24	1	5	1	0	0	1	0	6	.208	.240	.292	50	-2	-2	1	0	0	0	2	/C	0.1
1990	Atl-N	11	28	2	4	1	0	1	2	0	6	.143	.143	.286	15	-3	-3	1	0	0	0	-0	C	-0.3
Total	2	18	52	3	9	2	0	1	3	0	12	.173	.189	.288	31	-5	-5	2	0	0	0	2	/C	-0.2

LES MANN — Mann, Leslie "Major" b: 11/18/1893, Lincoln, Neb. d: 1/14/62, Pasadena, Cal. BR/TR, 5'9", 172 lbs. Deb: 4/30/13

YEAR	TM/L	G	AB	R	H	2B	3B	HR	RBI	BB	SO	AVG	OBP	SLG	PRO+	BR	/A	RC	SB	CS	SBR	FR	POS	TPR
1913	Bos-N	120	407	54	103	24	7	3	51	18	73	.253	.291	.369	86	-8	-9	43	7			-6	*O	-1.6
1914	*Bos-N	126	389	44	96	16	11	4	40	24	50	.247	.292	.375	99	-3	-2	43	9			6	*O	0.0

YEAR	TM/L	G	AB	R	H	2B	3B	HR	RBI	BB	SO	AVG	OBP	SLG	PRO+	BR	/A	RC	SB	CS	SBR	FR	POS	TPR
1915	Chi-F	135	470	75	144	12	19	4	58	36	40	.306	.357	.438	143	19	22	83	18			5	*O/S	2.2
1916	Chi-N	127	415	46	113	13	9	2	29	19	31	.272	.307	.361	95	1	-3	48	11	7	-1	-6	*O	-1.4
1917	Chi-N	117	444	63	121	19	10	1	44	27	46	.273	.316	.367	101	4	0	54	14			3	*O	0.0
1918	*Chi-N	129	489	69	141	27	7	2	55	38	45	.288	.342	.384	119	12	11	70	21			-5	*O	0.0
1919	Chi-N	80	299	31	68	8	8	1	22	11	29	.227	.257	.318	72	-11	-11	26	12			2	O	-1.3
	Bos-N	40	145	15	41	6	4	3	20	9	14	.283	.329	.441	136	5	5	22	7			2	O	0.6
	Yr	120	444	46	109	14	12	4	42	20	43	.245	.281	.358	92	-6	-5	48	19			4		-0.7
1920	Bos-N	115	424	48	117	7	8	3	32	38	42	.276	.341	.351	104	0	2	52	7	7	-2	1	*O	-0.4
1921	StL-N	97	256	57	84	12	7	7	30	23	28	.328	.390	.512	140	13	14	50	5	5	-2	-4	O	0.5
1922	StL-N	84	147	42	51	14	1	2	20	16	12	.347	.415	.497	141	8	9	30	0	1	-1	3	O	0.8
1923	StL-N	38	89	20	33	5	2	5	11	9	5	.371	.434	.640	184	10	10	25	0	0	0	1	O	0.9
	Cin-N	8	1	1	0	0	0	0	0	0	0	.000	.000	.000	-99	-0	-0	0	0	0	0	0	H	0.0
	Yr	46	90	21	33	5	2	5	11	9	5	.367	.430	.633	181	10	10	25	0	0	0	1		0.9
1924	Bos-N	32	102	13	28	7	4	0	10	8	10	.275	.333	.422	106	-0	1	15	1	0	0	2	O	0.2
1925	Bos-N	60	184	27	63	11	4	2	20	5	11	.342	.373	.478	127	4	6	33	6	1	1	4	O	0.9
1926	Bos-N	50	129	23	39	8	2	1	20	9	9	.302	.348	.419	116	1	2	18	5			2	O	0.3
1927	Bos-N	29	66	8	17	3	1	0	6	8	3	.258	.338	.333	87	-2	-1	8	2			1	O	0.0
	NY-N	29	67	13	22	4	1	2	10	8	7	.328	.400	.507	142	4	4	13	2			-1	O	0.2
	Yr	58	133	21	39	7	2	2	16	16	10	.293	.369	.421	116	2	3	21	4			0		0.2
1928	NY-N	82	193	29	51	7	1	2	25	18	9	.264	.330	.342	76	-7	-7	22	2			-5	O	-1.3
Total	16	1498	4716	678	1332	203	106	44	503	324	464	.282	.332	.398	110	51	54	656	129	21		5	*O/S	0.6

■ JIM MANNING

Manning, James H.   b: 1/31/1862, Fall River, Mass.   d: 10/22/29, Edinburg, Tex.   TR , 157 lbs.   Deb: 5/16/1884 M

YEAR	TM/L	G	AB	R	H	2B	3B	HR	RBI	BB	SO	AVG	OBP	SLG	PRO+	BR	/A	RC	SB	CS	SBR	FR	POS	TPR
1884	Bos-N	89	345	52	83	8	6	2	35	19	47	.241	.280	.316	88	-5	-5	31				-0	O/S23	-0.3
1885	Bos-N	84	306	34	63	8	9	2	27	19	36	.206	.252	.310	84	-6	-5	25				6	*O/S	-0.3
	Det-N	20	78	15	21	4	0	1	9	4	10	.269	.305	.359	114	1	1	9				-6	S	-0.3
	Yr	104	384	49	84	12	9	3	36	23	46	.219	.263	.320	91	-5	-4	33				-0		-0.3
1886	Det-N	26	97	14	18	2	3	0	7	6	10	.186	.233	.268	51	-6	-6	8	7			-1	O/S	-0.5
1887	Det-N	13	52	5	10	1	0	0	3	5	4	.192	.276	.212	37	-4	-4	4	3			-5	O/S	-0.7
1889	KC-a	132	506	68	103	16	7	3	68	54	61	.204	.297	.281	63	-21	-26	61	58			-10	O2/S3	-3.1
Total	5	364	1384	188	298	39	25	8	149	107	168	.215	.278	.297	74	-41	-44	137	68			-16	O/2S3	-4.9

■ JACK MANNING

Manning, John E.   b: 12/20/1853, Braintree, Mass.   d: 8/15/29, Boston, Mass.   BR/TR, 5'8.5", 158 lbs.   Deb: 4/23/1873 M

YEAR	TM/L	G	AB	R	H	2B	3B	HR	RBI	BB	SO	AVG	OBP	SLG	PRO+	BR	/A	RC	SB	CS	SBR	FR	POS	TPR
1873	Bos-n	32	158	29	42	5	2	0			2	.266	.275	.323	69	-5	-7	14					1/O	-0.4
1874	Bal-n	42	168	33	59	10	1	0			3	.351	.363	.423	150	9	9	26					P2/S	0.0
	Har-n	1	5	1	1	0	0	0			0	.200	.200	.200	26	-0	-0	0					/3	0.0
	Yr	43	173	34	60	10	1	0			3	.347	.358	.416	146	9	9	26						0.0
1875	Bos-n	77	343	71	94	8	2	1			2	.274	.278	.318	102	2	-0	31					*OP13	0.3
1876	Bos-N	70	288	52	76	13	0	2	25	7	5	.264	.281	.330	101	1	0	27				-6	*OP/S2	-0.3
1877	Cin-N	57	252	47	80	16	7	0	36	5	6	.317	.331	.437	157	11	15	37				-12	S1OP/2	0.4
1878	Bos-N	60	248	41	63	10	1	0	23	10	16	.254	.283	.302	86	-2	-4	22				-15	*O/P	-2.2
1880	Cin-N	48	190	20	41	6	3	2	17	7	15	.216	.244	.311	87	-3	-2	15				-3	O/1	-0.6
1881	Buf-N	1	4	0	0	0	0	0	0	0	0	.000	.000	.000	-99	-0	-0	0				0	/O	0.0
1883	Phi-N	98	420	60	112	31	5	0	37	20	37	.267	.300	.364	110	0	6	47				9	*O	1.5
1884	Phi-N	104	424	71	115	29	4	5	52	40	67	.271	.334	.394	134	14	17	57				-3	*O	1.2
1885	Phi-N	107	445	61	114	24	4	3	40	37	27	.256	.313	.348	116	7	9	50				-7	*O	0.0
1886	Bal-a	137	556	78	124	18	7	1			50	.223	.291	.286	85	-10	-8	55	24			-10	*O	-1.8
Total	3 n	152	674	134	196	23	5	1			7	.291	.298	.344	104	6	1	72	0				/OP12S3	-0.1
Total	9	682	2824	430	725	147	31	13	230	176	173	.257	.301	.345	109	19	33	310	24			-45	O/PS12	-1.8

■ RICK MANNING

Manning, Richard Eugene   b: 9/2/54, Niagara Falls, N.Y.   BL/TR, 6'1", 180 lbs.   Deb: 5/23/75

YEAR	TM/L	G	AB	R	H	2B	3B	HR	RBI	BB	SO	AVG	OBP	SLG	PRO+	BR	/A	RC	SB	CS	SBR	FR	POS	TPR
1975	Cle-A	120	480	69	137	16	5	3	35	44	62	.285	.348	.358	100	1	1	60	19	11	-1	10	*O/D	0.7
1976	Cle-A	138	552	73	161	24	7	6	43	41	75	.292	.341	.393	116	9	10	72	16	10	-1	16	*O	2.3
1977	Cle-A	68	252	33	57	7	3	5	18	21	35	.226	.286	.337	71	-11	-10	24	9	5	-0	1	O	-1.0
1978	Cle-A	148	566	65	149	27	3	3	50	38	62	.263	.311	.337	83	-13	-13	57	12	12	-4	10	O	-1.9
1979	Cle-A	144	560	67	145	12	2	3	51	55	48	.259	.326	.304	71	-21	-22	59	30	8	4	10	O	-1.2
1980	Cle-A	140	471	55	110	17	4	3	52	63	66	.234	.326	.306	74	-15	-15	49	12	6	0	4	O	-1.3
1981	Cle-A	103	360	47	88	15	3	4	33	40	57	.244	.320	.336	90	-4	-4	44	25	3	.6	10	*O	1.0
1982	Cle-A	152	562	71	152	18	2	8	44	54	60	.270	.334	.352	89	-8	-7	66	12	8	-1	-1	*O	-1.4
1983	Cle-A	50	194	20	54	6	0	1	10	12	22	.278	.320	.325	75	-6	-7	20	7	3	0	3	O	-0.3
	Mil-A	108	375	40	86	14	4	3	33	26	40	.229	.281	.312	68	-19	-15	33	11	2	2	2	*O	-1.1
	Yr	158	569	60	140	20	4	4	43	38	62	.246	.294	.316	71	-25	-22	53	18	5	2	5		-1.4
1984	Mil-A	119	341	53	85	10	5	7	31	34	32	.249	.319	.370	94	-5	-3	39	5	7	-3	-21	*O/D	-3.0
1985	Mil-A	79	216	19	47	9	1	2	18	14	19	.218	.265	.296	54	-14	-14	18	1	0	0	4	O/D	-1.0
1986	Mil-A	89	205	31	52	7	3	6	27	17	20	.254	.314	.434	98	-0	-1	27	5	3	-0	-4	O/D	-0.6
1987	Mil-A	97	114	21	26	7	1	0	13	12	18	.228	.302	.307	60	-6	-7	11	4	0	1	2	O/D	-0.3
Total	13	1555	5248	664	1349	189	43	56	458	471	616	.257	.319	.341	84	-112	-106	580	168	78	4	37	*O/D	-9.1

■ TIM MANNING

Manning, Timothy Edward   b: 12/3/1853, Henley-On-The- Thames, England   d: 6/11/34, Oak Park, Ill.   BR/TR, 5'10", 170 lbs.   Deb: 5/01/1882

YEAR	TM/L	G	AB	R	H	2B	3B	HR	RBI	BB	SO	AVG	OBP	SLG	PRO+	BR	/A	RC	SB	CS	SBR	FR	POS	TPR
1882	Pro-N	21	76	7	8	0	0	0	8	5	13	.105	.160	.105	-13	-9	-9	1				-9	S/C	-1.4
1883	Bal-a	35	121	23	26	5	0	0			14	.215	.296	.256	77	-2	-3	9				3	2	0.1
1884	Bal-a	91	341	49	70	14	5	2			26	.205	.275	.293	85	-3	-5	28				-2	*2	-0.4
1885	Bal-a	43	157	17	32	8	1	0			10	.204	.265	.268	72	-5	-4	11				3	2/3	0.0
	Pro-N	10	35	3	2	1	0	0	0	1	11	.057	.083	.086	-47	-5	-5	0				-3	S	-0.7
Total	4	200	730	99	138	28	6	2	8	56	24	.189	.256	.252	65	-25	-27	51				-8	2/SC3	-2.4

■ DON MANNO

Manno, Donald D.   b: 5/15/15, Williamsport, Pa.   BR/TR, 6'1", 190 lbs.   Deb: 9/22/40

YEAR	TM/L	G	AB	R	H	2B	3B	HR	RBI	BB	SO	AVG	OBP	SLG	PRO+	BR	/A	RC	SB	CS	SBR	FR	POS	TPR
1940	Bos-N	3	7	1	2	0	0	0	4	0	2	.286	.286	.714	177	1	1	1	0			0	/O	0.1
1941	Bos-N	22	30	2	5	1	0	0	4	3	7	.167	.242	.200	27	-3	-3	1				-1	/O31	-0.3
Total	2	25	37	3	7	1	0	0	8	3	9	.189	.250	.297	56	-2	-2	3	0			-0	/O31	-0.2

■ FRED MANRIQUE

Manrique, Fred Eloy (Reyes)   b: 5/11/61, Edo Bolivar, Venez.   BR/TR, 6'1", 175 lbs.   Deb: 8/23/81

YEAR	TM/L	G	AB	R	H	2B	3B	HR	RBI	BB	SO	AVG	OBP	SLG	PRO+	BR	/A	RC	SB	CS	SBR	FR	POS	TPR
1981	Tor-A	14	28	1	4	0	0	0	1	0	12	.143	.172	.143	-8	-4	-4	1	0	1	-1	3	S/3D	0.0
1984	Tor-A	10	9	0	3	0	0	0	1	0	1	.333	.333	.333	82	-0	-0	1	0	0	0	3	/2D	0.3
1985	Mon-N	9	13	5	4	1	1	1	1	1	3	.308	.357	.769	219	2	2	4	0	0	0	2	/2S3	0.4
1986	StL-N	13	17	2	3	0	0	1	1	1	1	.176	.222	.353	57	-1	-1	1	1	0	0	-1	/32	-0.1
1987	Chi-A	115	298	30	77	13	3	4	29	19	69	.258	.305	.362	74	-10	-11	33	5	3	-0	19	2S/D	1.5
1988	Chi-A	140	345	43	81	10	6	5	37	21	54	.235	.285	.342	75	-12	-12	33	6	5	-1	12	*2S/D	0.8
1989	Chi-A	65	187	23	56	13	1	2	30	8	30	.299	.335	.412	112	2	2	23	0	4	-2	-5	2/S3	-0.3
	Tex-A	54	191	23	55	12	0	2	22	9	33	.288	.320	.382	96	-1	-1	24	4	1	1	-11	S2/3	-1.1
	Yr	119	378	46	111	25	1	4	52	17	63	.294	.327	.397	104	1	1	46	4	5	-2	-16		-1.1
1990	Min-A	69	228	22	54	10	0	5	29	4	35	.237	.256	.346	63	-11	-13	18	2	0	1	-10	2/D	-1.8
Total	8	489	1316	149	337	59	11	20	151	63	238	.256	.295	.363	80	-36	-38	137	18	14	-3	11	2/S3D	0.0

YEAR	TM/L	G	AB	R	H	2B	3B	HR	RBI	BB	SO	AVG	OBP	SLG	PRO+	BR	/A	RC	SB	CS	SBR	FR	POS	TPR

■ JOHN MANSELL Mansell, John b: 1861, Auburn, N.Y. d: 2/20/25, Romulus, N.Y. BL, Deb: 5/09/1882

1882	Phi-a	31	126	17	30	3	1	0		4		.238	.262	.278	73	-2	-4	9				-4	O	-0.7

■ MIKE MANSELL Mansell, Michael R. b: 1/15/1858, Auburn, N.Y. d: 12/4/02, Auburn, N.Y. BL, Deb: 5/01/1879

1879	Syr-N	67	242	24	52	4	2	1	13	5	45	.215	.231	.260	69	-10	-6	15				15	*O	0.7
1880	Cin-N	53	187	22	36	6	2	2	12	4	37	.193	.209	.278	64	-7	-7	11				12	O	0.3
1882	Pit-a	79	347	59	96	18	16	2		7		.277	.291	.438	150	14	17	45				3	*O	1.7
1883	Pit-a	96	412	90	106	12	13	3		25		.257	.300	.371	120	7	10	47				4	*O	1.2
1884	Pit-a	27	100	15	14	0	3	1		7		.140	.204	.230	42	-6	-6	5				-1	O	-0.6
	Phi-a	20	70	6	14	1	1	0		5		.200	.253	.243	61	-2	-3	4				-1	O	-0.3
	Ric-a	29	113	21	34	2	5	0		8		.301	.363	.407	156	7	7	17				-5	O	0.2
	Yr	76	283	42	62	3	9	1		20		.219	.280	.304	91	-1	-2	25				-7		-0.7
Total	5	371	1471	237	352	43	42	9		25	61	82	.239	.271	.344	106	3	12	145				26	O	3.2

■ TOM MANSELL Mansell, Thomas E. "Brick" b: 1/1/1855, Auburn, N.Y. d: 10/6/34, Auburn, N.Y. BL/TL, 5'8", 160 lbs. Deb: 5/01/1879

1879	Tro-N	40	177	29	43	6	0	0	11	3	9	.243	.256	.277	81	-5	-3	13				-6	O	-0.8
	Syr-N	1	4	0	1	0	0	0	0	0	0	.250	.250	.250	74	-0	-0	0				0	/O	0.0
	Yr	41	181	29	44	6	0	0	11	3	9	.243	.255	.276	81	-5	-3	13				-6		-0.8
1883	Det-N	34	131	22	29	4	1	0	10	8	13	.221	.266	.267	66	-6	-5	10				-2	O/P	-0.4
	StL-a	28	112	23	45	8	1	0		7		.402	.437	.491	187	12	11	25				-5	O	0.5
1884	Cin-a	65	266	49	66	4	6	0		15		.248	.301	.308	97	1	-1	25				-11	O	-1.0
	Col-a	23	77	9	15	1	3	0		6		.195	.262	.286	88	-1	-0	6				-4	O	-0.3
	Yr	88	343	58	81	5	9	0		21		.236	.292	.303	96	-0	-1	31				-14		-1.3
Total	3	191	767	132	199	23	11	0	21	39	22	.259	.300	.318	101	2	2	78				-28	O/P	-2.0

■ FELIX MANTILLA Mantilla, Felix (Lamela) b: 7/29/34, Isabela, P.R. BR/TR, 6', 160 lbs. Deb: 6/21/56

1956	Mil-N	35	53	9	15	1	1	0	3	1	8	.283	.309	.340	79	-2	-2	5	0	1	-1	9	S/3	0.8
1957	*Mil-N	71	182	28	43	9	1	4	21	14	34	.236	.298	.363	82	-6	-5	20	2	0	1	7	S2/3O	0.5
1958	*Mil-N	85	226	37	50	5	1	7	19	20	20	.221	.285	.345	72	-11	-9	22	2	0	1	-1	O2/S3	-0.8
1959	Mil-N	103	251	26	54	5	0	3	19	16	31	.215	.268	.271	48	-20	-17	18	6	1	1	6	2S/3O	-0.4
1960	Mil-N	63	148	21	38	7	0	3	11	7	16	.257	.295	.365	86	-4	-3	16	3	1	0	-10	2S/O	-0.9
1961	Mil-N	45	93	13	20	3	0	1	5	10	16	.215	.298	.280	58	-6	-5	8	1	1	-0	-3	S2O/3	-0.5
1962	NY-N	141	466	54	128	17	4	11	59	37	51	.275	.335	.399	94	-3	-4	62	3	1	1	-7	3S2	-0.4
1963	Bos-A	66	178	27	56	8	0	6	15	20	14	.315	.384	.461	131	9	8	31	2	1	0	-5	SO/2	0.5
1964	Bos-A	133	425	69	123	20	1	30	64	41	46	.289	.357	.553	142	27	24	81	0	1	-1	-5	O2/3S	2.3
1965	Bos-A	150	534	60	147	17	2	18	92	79	84	.275	.377	.416	118	20	16	83	7	3	0	-21	*2O/1	0.1
1966	Hou-N	77	151	16	33	5	0	6	22	11	32	.219	.280	.371	85	-4	-3	15	1	0	0	-3	13/2O	-0.4
Total	11	969	2707	360	707	97	10	89	330	256	352	.261	.331	.403	100	-1	1	361	27	10	2	-31	2SO3/1	0.8

■ MICKEY MANTLE Mantle, Mickey Charles "The Commerce Comet" b: 10/20/31, Spavinaw, Okla. BB/TR, 5'11.5", 195 lbs. Deb: 4/17/51 CH

1951	*NY-A	96	341	61	91	11	5	13	65	43	74	.267	.349	.443	117	5	7	55	8	7	-2	-15	O	-1.2
1952	*NY-A	142	549	94	171	37	7	23	87	75	111	.311	.394	.530	166	40	44	123	4	1	1	-7	*O/3	3.5
1953	*NY-A	127	461	105	136	24	3	21	92	79	90	.295	.398	.497	145	27	29	100	8	4	0	-4	*O/S	2.2
1954	NY-A	146	543	129	163	17	12	27	102	102	107	.300	.411	.525	160	43	45	127	5	2	0	-5	*O/S2	3.8
1955	*NY-A	147	517	121	158	25	11	37	99	113	97	.306	.433	.611	181	59	60	148	8	1	2	3	*O/S	5.7
1956	*NY-A	150	533	132	188	22	5	52	130	112	99	.353	.467	.705	213	83	86	188	10	1	2	2	*O	7.9
1957	*NY-A	144	474	121	173	28	6	34	94	146	75	.365	.515	.665	223	89	90	178	16	3	3	-7	*O	7.8
1958	*NY-A	150	519	127	158	21	1	42	97	129	120	.304	.445	.592	189	64	67	147	18	3	4	-4	*O	5.7
1959	NY-A	144	541	104	154	23	4	31	75	93	126	.285	.392	.514	152	36	38	117	21	3	5	2	*O	3.8
1960	*NY-A	153	527	119	145	17	6	40	94	111	125	.275	.402	.558	166	44	48	125	14	3	2	-8	*O	3.7
1961	*NY-A	153	514	132	163	16	6	54	128	126	112	.317	.452	.687	210	76	80	174	12	1	3	-3	*O	7.2
1962	*NY-A	123	377	96	121	15	1	30	89	122	78	.321	.488	.605	198	57	59	126	9	0	3	-13	*O	4.4
1963	*NY-A	65	172	40	54	8	0	15	35	40	32	.314	.443	.622	197	23	24	49	2	1	0	-1	O	2.2
1964	*NY-A	143	465	92	141	25	2	35	111	99	102	.303	.426	.591	177	53	52	121	6	3	0	-24	*O	2.4
1965	NY-A	122	361	44	92	12	1	19	46	73	76	.255	.380	.452	136	19	19	64	4	1	1	-6	*O	1.0
1966	NY-A	108	333	40	96	12	1	23	56	57	76	.288	.392	.538	171	29	30	71	1	1	-0	-10	O	1.7
1967	NY-A	144	440	63	108	17	0	22	55	107	113	.245	.394	.434	150	29	31	82	1	1	-0	-0	*1	2.2
1968	NY-A	144	435	57	103	14	1	18	54	106	97	.237	.387	.398	143	25	27	74	6	2	1	-2	*1	2.2
Total	18	2401	8102	1677	2415	344	72	536	1509	1733	1710	.298	.423	.557	173	803	838	2069	153	38	23	-102	*O1/S23	66.2

■ JEFF MANTO Manto, Jeffrey Paul b: 8/23/64, Bristol, Pa. BR/TR, 6'3", 210 lbs. Deb: 6/07/90

| 1990 | Cle-A | 30 | 76 | 12 | 17 | 5 | 1 | 2 | 14 | 21 | 18 | .224 | .392 | .395 | 119 | 3 | 3 | 13 | 0 | 1 | -1 | 1 | 1/3 | 0.2 |

■ CHARLIE MANUEL Manuel, Charles Fuqua b: 1/4/44, North Fork, W.Va. BL/TR, 6'4", 195 lbs. Deb: 4/08/69 C

1969	*Min-A	83	164	14	34	6	0	2	24	28	33	.207	.323	.280	69	-6	-6	16	1	0	0	-4	O	-1.0
1970	*Min-A	59	64	4	12	0	0	1	7	6	17	.188	.268	.234	39	-5	-5	4	0	0	0	-1	O	-0.6
1971	Min-A	18	16	1	2	1	0	0	1	1	8	.125	.176	.188	3	-2	-2	1	0	0	0	0	/O	-0.1
1972	Min-A	63	122	6	25	5	0	1	8	4	16	.205	.236	.270	48	-8	-8	8	0	0	0	0	O	-0.9
1974	LA-N	4	3	0	1	0	0	0	1	1	0	.333	.500	.333	142	0	0	1	0	0	0	0	H	0.0
1975	LA-N	15	15	0	2	0	0	0	2	0	3	.133	.133	.133	-27	-3	-2	0	0	0	0	0	H	-0.2
Total	6	242	384	25	76	12	0	4	43	40	77	.198	.277	.260	52	-23	-24	30	1	0	0	-5	/O	-2.8

■ JERRY MANUEL Manuel, Jerry b: 12/23/53, Hahira, Ga. BB/TR, 6', 165 lbs. Deb: 9/18/75

1975	Det-A	6	18	0	1	0	0	0	0	0	4	.056	.056	.056	-66	-4	-4	0	0	0	0	-4	/2	-0.7
1976	Det-A	54	43	4	6	1	0	0	2	3	9	.140	.213	.163	11	-5	-5	2	1	0	0	12	2/SD	1.0
1980	Mon-N	7	6	0	0	0	0	0	0	0	2	.000	.000	.000	-99	-2	-2	0	0	0	0	3	/S	0.2
1981	*Mon-N	27	55	10	11	5	0	3	10	6	11	.200	.279	.455	104	0	-0	7	0	0	0	-0	2/S	0.1
1982	SD-N	2	5	0	1	0	0	1	1	0	0	.200	.333	.600	165	0	0	1	0	0	0	-1	/2S3	0.0
Total	5	96	127	14	19	6	1	3	13	12	26	.150	.217	.283	42	-10	-10	10	1	0	0	9	/2S3D	0.6

■ FRANK MANUSH Manush, Frank Benjamin b: 9/18/1883, Tuscumbia, Ala. d: 1/5/65, Laguna Beach, Cal. BR/TR, 5'10.5", 175 lbs. Deb: 8/31/08

| 1908 | Phi-A | 23 | 77 | 6 | 12 | 2 | 1 | 0 | 0 | 2 | | .156 | .177 | .208 | 25 | -6 | -7 | 3 | 2 | | | -5 | 3/2 | -1.1 |

■ HEINIE MANUSH Manush, Henry Emmett b: 7/20/01, Tuscumbia, Ala. d: 5/12/71, Sarasota, Fla. BL/TL, 6'1", 200 lbs. Deb: 4/20/23 CH

1923	Det-A	109	308	59	103	20	5	4	54	20	21	.334	.406	.471	133	14	15	59	3	5	-2	-4	O	0.1
1924	Det-A	120	422	83	122	24	8	9	68	27	30	.289	.355	.448	108	2	3	69	14	5	1	-6	*O/1	-0.8
1925	Det-A	99	278	46	84	14	3	5	47	24	21	.302	.362	.428	101	-1	0	44	8	3	1	-5	O	-0.9
1926	Det-A	136	498	95	188	35	8	14	86	31	28	.378	.421	.564	153	38	37	116	11	5	0	-4	*O	2.4
1927	Det-A	151	593	102	177	31	18	6	90	47	29	.298	.354	.442	104	3	2	88	12	8	-1	-3	*O	-1.0
1928	StL-A	154	638	104	241	47	20	13	108	39	14	.378	.414	.575	153	50	48	150	17	5	2	2	*O	4.1
1929	StL-A	142	574	85	204	45	10	6	81	43	24	.355	.401	.500	126	26	23	113	9	8	-2	-2	*O	1.2
1930	StL-A	49	198	26	65	16	4	2	29	5	7	.328	.345	.480	103	1	0	32	1	3	1	0	O	0.1
	Was-A	88	356	74	129	33	8	7	65	26	17	.362	.406	.559	141	22	22	79	4	3	-1	-2	O	1.4
	Yr	137	554	100	194	49	12	9	94	31	24	.350	.385	.531	128	23	22	111	5	4	-0	1		1.5
1931	Was-A	146	616	110	189	41	11	6	70	36	27	.307	.351	.438	106	4	4	94	3	3	-1	-10	*O	-1.4

YEAR	TM/L	G	AB	R	H	2B	3B	HR	RBI	BB	SO	AVG	OBP	SLG	PRO+	BR	/A	RC	SB	CS	SBR	FR	POS	TPR
1932	Was-A	149	625	121	214	41	14	14	116	36	29	.342	.383	.520	133	27	28	124	7	2	1	-3	*O	1.9
1933	*Was-A	153	658	115	221	32	17	5	95	36	18	.336	.372	.459	120	17	18	111	6	4	-1	-2	*O	0.9
1934	Was-A	137	556	88	194	42	11	11	89	36	23	.349	.392	.523	140	26	29	113	7	3	0	1	*O	2.6
1935	Was-A	119	479	68	131	26	9	4	56	35	17	.273	.328	.390	88	-12	-9	62	2	0	1	4	*O	-0.4
1936	Bos-A	82	313	43	91	15	5	0	45	17	11	.291	.329	.371	87	-2	-2	37	1	3	-2	-13	*O	-2.9
1937	Bro-N	132	466	57	155	25	7	4	73	40	24	.333	.389	.442	123	17	16	84	6			-15	*O	-0.4
1938	Bro-N	17	51	9	12	3	1	0	6	5	4	.235	.304	.333	73	-2	-2	5	1			1	O	0.0
	Pit-N	15	13	2	4	1	1	0	4	2	0	.308	.400	.538	155	1	1	3	0			0	H	0.1
	Yr	32	64	11	16	4	2	0	10	7	4	.250	.324	.375	90	-1	-1	7	1			1		0.1
1939	Pit-N	10	12	0	0	0	0	0	1	1	1	.000	.077	.000	-79	-3	-3	0	0			-0	/O	-0.2
Total	17	2008	7654	1287	2524	491	160	110	1183	506	345	.330	.377	.479	121	218	215	1383	114	58		-58	*O/1	6.8

■ KIRT MANWARING
Manwaring, Kirt Dean　b: 7/15/65, Elmira, N.Y.　BR/TR, 6'1", 195 lbs.　Deb: 9/15/87

YEAR	TM/L	G	AB	R	H	2B	3B	HR	RBI	BB	SO	AVG	OBP	SLG	PRO+	BR	/A	RC	SB	CS	SBR	FR	POS	TPR
1987	SF-N	6	7	0	1	0	0	0	0	0	1	.143	.250	.143	8	-1	-1	0	0	0	0	-1	/C	0.0
1988	SF-N	40	116	12	29	7	0	1	15	2	21	.250	.281	.336	80	-4	-3	11	0	1	-1	-1	C	-0.2
1989	*SF-N	85	200	14	42	4	2	0	18	11	28	.210	.265	.250	49	-13	-13	13	2	1	0	0	C	-0.6
1990	SF-N	8	13	0	2	0	1	0	1	0	3	.154	.154	.308	24	-1	-1	1	0	0	0	2	/C	0.1
Total	4	139	336	26	74	11	3	1	34	13	53	.220	.266	.280	58	-19	-18	25	2	2	-1	0	C	-0.7

■ CLIFF MAPES
Mapes, Clifford Franklin　b: 3/13/22, Sutherland, Neb.　BL/TR, 6'3", 205 lbs.　Deb: 4/20/48

YEAR	TM/L	G	AB	R	H	2B	3B	HR	RBI	BB	SO	AVG	OBP	SLG	PRO+	BR	/A	RC	SB	CS	SBR	FR	POS	TPR
1948	NY-A	53	88	19	22	11	1	1	12	6	13	.250	.298	.432	94	-2	-2	11	1	1	-0	4	O	0.1
1949	*NY-A	111	304	56	75	13	3	7	38	58	50	.247	.369	.378	98	0	0	49	6	0	2	5	*O	0.4
1950	*NY-A	108	356	60	88	14	6	12	61	47	61	.247	.338	.421	96	-5	-3	49	1	6	-3	-5	*O	-1.2
1951	NY-A	45	51	6	11	3	1	2	8	4	14	.216	.273	.431	92	-1	-1	6	0	0	0	-0	O	-0.1
	StL-A	56	201	32	55	7	2	7	30	26	33	.274	.360	.433	110	4	3	32	0	1	-1	-3	O	-0.1
	Yr	101	252	38	66	10	3	9	38	30	47	.262	.343	.433	109	2	2	38	0	1	-1	-3		-0.2
1952	Det-A	86	193	26	38	7	0	9	23	27	42	.197	.295	.373	84	-4	-5	23	0	1	-1	-4	O	-1.0
Total	5	459	1193	199	289	55	13	38	172	168	213	.242	.338	.406	97	-8	-7	169	8	9	-3	-3	O	-1.9

■ HOWARD MAPLE
Maple, Howard Albert "Mape"　b: 7/20/03, Adrian, Mo.　d: 11/9/70, Portland, Ore.　BL/TR, 5'7", 175 lbs.　Deb: 5/19/32

YEAR	TM/L	G	AB	R	H	2B	3B	HR	RBI	BB	SO	AVG	OBP	SLG	PRO+	BR	/A	RC	SB	CS	SBR	FR	POS	TPR
1932	Was-A	44	41	6	10	0	1	0	7	7	7	.244	.367	.293	74	-1	-1	5	0	0	0	-3	C	-0.1

■ GEORGE MAPPES
Mappes, George Richard "Dick"　b: 12/25/1865, St.Louis, Mo.　d: 2/20/34, St.Louis, Mo.　Deb: 9/23/1885

YEAR	TM/L	G	AB	R	H	2B	3B	HR	RBI	BB	SO	AVG	OBP	SLG	PRO+	BR	/A	RC	SB	CS	SBR	FR	POS	TPR
1885	Bal-a	6	19	2	4	0	1	0			1	.211	.250	.316	81	-0	-0	2				-2	/2	-0.1
1886	StL-N	6	14	1	2	0	0	0	0	1	5	.143	.200	.143	6	-2	-1	0	0			-1	/C32	-0.1
Total	2	12	33	3	6	0	1	0	0	2	5	.182	.229	.242	49	-2	-2	2	0			-3	/2C3	-0.2

■ RABBIT MARANVILLE
Maranville, Walter James Vincent　b: 11/11/1891, Springfield, Mass.　d: 1/5/54, New York, N.Y.　BR/TR, 5'5", 155 lbs.　Deb: 9/10/12　MH

YEAR	TM/L	G	AB	R	H	2B	3B	HR	RBI	BB	SO	AVG	OBP	SLG	PRO+	BR	/A	RC	SB	CS	SBR	FR	POS	TPR
1912	Bos-N	26	86	8	18	2	0	0	8	9	14	.209	.292	.233	44	-6	-7	7	1			5	S	0.1
1913	Bos-N	143	571	68	141	13	8	2	48	68	62	.247	.330	.308	81	-11	-12	64	25			15	*S	1.2
1914	*Bos-N	156	586	74	144	23	6	4	78	45	56	.246	.306	.326	88	-9	-9	66	28			52	*S	5.1
1915	Bos-N	149	509	51	124	23	6	2	43	45	65	.244	.308	.324	96	-5	-3	55	18	12	-2	21	*S	2.2
1916	Bos-N	155	604	79	142	16	13	4	38	50	69	.235	.296	.325	94	-7	-4	64	32	15	1	22	*S	2.9
1917	Bos-N	142	561	69	146	19	13	3	43	40	47	.260	.312	.357	111	2	6	67	27			14	*S	2.4
1918	Bos-N	11	38	3	12	0	1	0	3	4	0	.316	.381	.368	135	1	2	5	0			2	S	0.4
1919	Bos-N	131	480	44	128	18	10	5	43	36	23	.267	.319	.377	113	5	7	59	12			29	*S	4.4
1920	Bos-N	134	493	48	131	19	15	1	43	28	24	.266	.305	.371	98	-5	-3	54	14	11	-2	14	*S	1.7
1921	Pit-N	153	612	90	180	25	12	1	70	47	38	.294	.347	.379	90	-6	-8	82	25	12	0	-11	*S	-0.3
1922	Pit-N	155	672	115	198	26	15	0	63	61	43	.295	.355	.378	88	-10	-11	92	24	13	-1	11	*S2	0.8
1923	Pit-N	141	581	78	161	19	9	1	41	42	34	.277	.327	.346	76	-18	-20	66	14	11	-2	12	*S	0.2
1924	Pit-N	152	594	62	158	33	20	2	71	35	53	.266	.307	.399	86	-12	-13	70	18	14	-3	4	*2	-2.0
1925	Chi-N	75	266	37	62	10	3	0	23	29	20	.233	.308	.293	54	-18	-18	25	6	5	-1	4	SM	-0.8
1926	Bro-N	78	234	32	55	8	5	0	24	26	24	.235	.312	.312	69	-10	-10	23	7			10	S2	0.5
1927	StL-N	9	29	0	7	1	0	0	0	2	2	.241	.290	.276	51	-2	-2	2	0			3	/S	0.2
1928	*StL-N	112	366	40	88	14	10	1	34	36	27	.240	.310	.342	69	-16	-17	39	3			-5	*S/2	-0.6
1929	Bos-N	146	560	87	159	26	10	0	55	47	33	.284	.344	.366	79	-21	-17	70	13			20	*S/2	2.0
1930	Bos-N	142	558	85	157	26	8	2	43	48	23	.281	.344	.367	75	-25	-21	70	9			-13	*S/3	-1.8
1931	Bos-N	145	562	69	146	22	5	0	33	56	34	.260	.329	.317	77	-19	-16	63	9			-24	*S2	-2.8
1932	Bos-N	149	571	67	134	20	4	0	37	46	28	.235	.295	.284	59	-34	-31	51	4			6	*2	-1.4
1933	Bos-N	143	478	46	104	15	4	0	38	36	34	.218	.274	.266	59	-28	-23	35	2			-26	*2	-4.2
1935	Bos-N	23	67	3	10	2	0	0	5	3	3	.149	.186	.179	-2	-10	-9	2	0			-5	2	-1.1
Total	23	2670	10078	1255	2605	380	177	28	884	839	756	.258	.318	.340	82	-263	-240	1132	291	93		159	*S2/3	9.1

■ JOHNNY MARCUM
Marcum, John Alfred "Footsie"　b: 9/9/09, Campbellsburg, Ky.　d: 9/10/84, Louisville, Ky.　BL/TR, 5'11", 197 lbs.　Deb: 9/07/33

YEAR	TM/L	G	AB	R	H	2B	3B	HR	RBI	BB	SO	AVG	OBP	SLG	PRO+	BR	/A	RC	SB	CS	SBR	FR	POS	TPR
1933	Phi-A	5	12	2	2	0	0	0	0	2	1	.167	.286	.167	22	-1	-1	1	0	0	0	0	/P	0.0
1934	Phi-A	58	112	10	30	4	0	1	13	3	5	.268	.287	.330	61	-7	-7	10	0	1	-1	-0	P	0.0
1935	Phi-A	64	119	13	37	2	1	2	17	9	5	.311	.359	.395	96	-1	-1	17	0	0	0	-3	P	0.0
1936	Bos-A	48	88	6	18	3	0	2	7	3	5	.205	.231	.307	30	-10	-11	6	0	0	0	0	P	0.0
1937	Bos-A	51	86	12	23	8	0	0	13	7	4	.267	.323	.360	69	-4	-4	10	0	0	0	2	P	0.0
1938	Bos-A	19	37	3	5	0	0	0	3	6	9	.135	.256	.135	1	-6	-6	2	0	0	0	-1	P	0.0
1939	StL-A	16	22	3	10	1	0	0	5	1	2	.455	.478	.500	147	2	2	5	0	0	0	-0	P	0.0
	Chi-A	38	57	7	16	0	0	0	12	5	1	.281	.339	.281	58	-3	-3	6	0	0	0	-1	P	0.0
	Yr	54	79	10	26	1	0	0	17	6	3	.329	.376	.342	83	-1	-2	10	0	0	0	-1		0.0
Total	7	299	533	56	141	18	1	5	70	36	32	.265	.311	.330	62	-30	-31	57	0	1	-1	-2	P	0.0

■ RED MARION
Marion, John Wyeth　b: 3/14/14, Richburg, S.C.　d: 3/13/75, San Jose, Cal.　BR/TR, 6'2", 175 lbs.　Deb: 9/16/35

YEAR	TM/L	G	AB	R	H	2B	3B	HR	RBI	BB	SO	AVG	OBP	SLG	PRO+	BR	/A	RC	SB	CS	SBR	FR	POS	TPR
1935	Was-A	4	11	1	2	1	0	1	1	0	2	.182	.182	.545	85	-0	-0	1	0	0	0	0	/O	0.0
1943	Was-A	14	17	2	3	0	0	0	1	3	1	.176	.300	.176	42	-1	-1	1	0	0	0	0	/O	0.0
Total	2	18	28	3	5	1	0	1	2	3	3	.179	.258	.321	63	-2	-1	2	0	0	0	0	/O	0.0

■ MARTY MARION
Marion, Martin Whitford "Slats" or "The Octopus"　b: 12/1/17, Richburg, S.C.　BR/TR, 6'2", 170 lbs.　Deb: 4/16/40　MC

YEAR	TM/L	G	AB	R	H	2B	3B	HR	RBI	BB	SO	AVG	OBP	SLG	PRO+	BR	/A	RC	SB	CS	SBR	FR	POS	TPR
1940	StL-N	125	435	44	121	18	1	3	46	21	34	.278	.311	.345	76	-12	-15	45	9			-6	*S	-0.8
1941	StL-N	155	547	50	138	22	3	3	58	42	48	.252	.308	.320	72	-17	-21	56	8			7	*S	0.0
1942	*StL-N	147	485	66	134	38	5	0	54	48	50	.276	.343	.375	102	6	2	64	8			7	*S	2.1
1943	*StL-N	129	418	38	117	15	3	1	52	32	37	.280	.334	.337	90	-3	-5	49	1			25	*S	3.4
1944	StL-N	144	506	50	135	26	2	6	63	43	50	.267	.324	.362	91	-5	-6	61	1			5	*S	1.7
1945	StL-N	123	430	63	119	27	5	1	59	39	39	.277	.340	.370	95	-2	-3	56	2			-2	*S	0.7
1946	*StL-N	146	498	51	116	29	4	3	46	59	53	.233	.318	.325	79	-11	-14	55	1			19	*S	1.6
1947	StL-N	149	540	57	147	19	6	4	74	49	58	.272	.334	.352	79	-13	-17	63	3			20	*S	1.4
1948	StL-N	144	567	70	143	26	4	4	43	37	54	.252	.298	.333	67	-24	-28	59	1			-1	*S	-1.2
1949	StL-N	134	515	61	140	31	2	5	70	37	42	.272	.323	.369	81	-11	-14	59	0			17	*S	1.7
1950	StL-N	106	372	36	92	10	2	4	40	44	55	.247	.327	.317	67	-15	-18	39	1			-1	*S	-0.8
1952	StL-A	67	186	16	46	11	0	2	19	19	17	.247	.320	.339	84	-4	-5	20	0	2	-1	-7	SM	-0.9
1953	StL-A	3	7	0	0	0	0	0	0	0	0	.000	.000	.000	-98	-1	-1	0	0	0	0	-1	/3M	-0.3
Total	13	1572	5506	602	1448	272	37	36	624	470	537	.263	.323	.345	81	-113	-145	623	35	2		92	*S/3	9.7

YEAR	TM/L	G	AB	R	H	2B	3B	HR	RBI	BB	SO	AVG	OBP	SLG	PRO+	BR	/A	RC	SB	CS	SBR	FR	POS	TPR

■ ROGER MARIS   Maris, Roger Eugene (b: Roger Eugene Maras)   b: 9/10/34, Hibbing, Minn.   d: 12/14/85, Houston, Tex.   BL/TR, 6′, 197 lbs.   Deb: 4/16/57

YEAR	TM/L	G	AB	R	H	2B	3B	HR	RBI	BB	SO	AVG	OBP	SLG	PRO+	BR	/A	RC	SB	CS	SBR	FR	POS	TPR
1957	Cle-A	116	358	61	84	9	5	14	51	60	79	.235	.346	.405	106	3	3	53	8	4	0	-0	*O	-0.2
1958	Cle-A	51	182	26	41	5	1	9	27	17	33	.225	.291	.412	94	-3	-2	23	4	2	0	4	O	0.0
	KC-A	99	401	61	99	14	3	19	53	28	52	.247	.299	.439	99	-1	-2	54	0	0	0	2	O	-0.6
	Yr	150	583	87	140	19	4	28	80	45	85	.240	.297	.431	97	-4	-4	77	4	2	0	6		-0.6
1959	KC-A	122	433	69	118	21	7	16	72	58	53	.273	.362	.464	123	15	14	76	2	1	0	3	*O	1.1
1960	*NY-A	136	499	98	141	18	7	39	**112**	70	65	.283	.374	**.581**	164	36	40	111	2	2	-1	2	*O	3.6
1961	*NY-A	161	590	**132**	159	16	4	**61**	**142**	94	67	.269	.376	.620	170	50	54	138	0	0	0	-10	*O	3.7
1962	*NY-A	157	590	92	151	34	1	33	100	87	78	.256	.357	.485	128	20	23	107	1	0	0	2	*O	1.9
1963	*NY-A	90	312	53	84	14	1	23	53	35	40	.269	.347	.542	146	18	18	61	1	0	0	1	O	1.7
1964	*NY-A	141	513	86	144	12	2	26	71	62	78	.281	.365	.464	127	21	20	91	3	0	1	1	*O	1.6
1965	NY-A	46	155	22	37	7	0	8	27	29	29	.239	.359	.439	126	6	6	25	0	0	0	-5	O	0.0
1966	NY-A	119	348	37	81	9	2	13	43	36	60	.233	.310	.382	101	-1	0	41	0	0	0	-10	O	-1.4
1967	*StL-N	125	410	64	107	18	7	9	55	52	61	.261	.350	.405	117	9	10	59	0	0	0	2	*O	0.7
1968	*StL-N	100	310	25	79	18	2	5	45	24	38	.255	.310	.374	106	1	2	37	0	0	0	2	O	0.0
Total	12	1463	5101	826	1325	195	42	275	851	652	733	.260	.348	.476	128	174	185	878	21	9	1	-7	*O	12.1

■ GENE MARKLAND   Markland, Cleneth Eugene "Mousey"   b: 12/26/19, Detroit, Mich.   BR/TR, 5′10″, 160 lbs.   Deb: 4/25/50

YEAR	TM/L	G	AB	R	H	2B	3B	HR	RBI	BB	SO	AVG	OBP	SLG	PRO+	BR	/A	RC	SB	CS	SBR	FR	POS	TPR
1950	Phi-A	5	8	2	1	0	0	0	3	0	1	.125	.364	.125	30	-1	-1	1	0	0	0	0	/2	0.0

■ HAL MARNIE   Marnie, Harry Sylvester   b: 7/6/18, Philadelphia, Pa.   BR/TR, 6′1″, 178 lbs.   Deb: 9/15/40

YEAR	TM/L	G	AB	R	H	2B	3B	HR	RBI	BB	SO	AVG	OBP	SLG	PRO+	BR	/A	RC	SB	CS	SBR	FR	POS	TPR
1940	Phi-N	11	34	4	6	0	0	0	4	4	2	.176	.263	.176	24	-3	-3	2	0			6	2	0.3
1941	Phi-N	61	158	12	38	3	3	0	11	13	25	.241	.298	.297	71	-7	-6	13	0			5	2S/3	0.3
1942	Phi-N	24	30	3	5	0	0	0	0	1	2	.167	.194	.167	6	-4	-3	1	1			8	2/S3	0.6
Total	3	96	222	19	49	3	3	0	15	18	29	.221	.279	.261	55	-14	-13	16	1			19	/2S3	1.2

■ FRED MAROLEWSKI   Marolewski, Fred Daniel "Fritz"   b: 10/6/28, Chicago, Ill.   BR/TR, 6′2.5″, 205 lbs.   Deb: 9/19/53

YEAR	TM/L	G	AB	R	H	2B	3B	HR	RBI	BB	SO	AVG	OBP	SLG	PRO+	BR	/A	RC	SB	CS	SBR	FR	POS	TPR
1953	StL-N	1	0	0	0	0	0	0	0	0	0	—	—	—	0	0	0	0	0	0	0	0	/1	0.0

■ OLLIE MARQUARDT   Marquardt, Albert Ludwig   b: 9/22/02, Toledo, Ohio   d: 2/7/68, Fort Clinton, Ohio   BR/TR, 5′9″, 156 lbs.   Deb: 4/14/31

YEAR	TM/L	G	AB	R	H	2B	3B	HR	RBI	BB	SO	AVG	OBP	SLG	PRO+	BR	/A	RC	SB	CS	SBR	FR	POS	TPR
1931	Bos-A	17	39	4	7	1	0	0	2	3	4	.179	.238	.205	18	-5	-4	2	0	1	-1	-3	2/S3	-0.5

■ GONZALO MARQUEZ   Marquez, Gonzalo Enrique (Moya)   b: 3/31/46, Carupano, Venez.   d: 12/20/84, Valencia, Venez.   BL/TL, 5′11″, 180 lbs.   Deb: 8/11/72

YEAR	TM/L	G	AB	R	H	2B	3B	HR	RBI	BB	SO	AVG	OBP	SLG	PRO+	BR	/A	RC	SB	CS	SBR	FR	POS	TPR
1972	*Oak-A	23	21	2	8	0	0	0	4	3	4	.381	.480	.381	167	2	2	4	1	1	-0	0	/1	0.2
1973	Oak-A	23	25	1	6	1	0	0	2	0	4	.240	.240	.280	49	-2	-2	1	0	0	0	-1	/21OD	-0.2
	Chi-N	19	58	5	13	2	0	1	4	3	4	.224	.274	.310	57	-3	-4	5	0	0	0	2	1	-0.1
1974	Chi-N	11	11	1	0	0	0	0	0	1	2	.000	.083	.000	-72	-3	-3	0	0	0	0	1	1	-0.2
Total	3	76	115	9	27	3	0	1	10	7	14	.235	.290	.287	62	-6	-6	11	1	1	-0	2	/12DO	-0.3

■ LUIS MARQUEZ   Marquez, Luis Angel (Sanchez) "Canena"   b: 10/28/25, Aguadilla, P.R.   d: 3/1/88, Aguadilla, P.R.   BR/TR, 5′10.5″, 174 lbs.   Deb: 4/18/51

YEAR	TM/L	G	AB	R	H	2B	3B	HR	RBI	BB	SO	AVG	OBP	SLG	PRO+	BR	/A	RC	SB	CS	SBR	FR	POS	TPR
1951	Bos-N	68	122	19	24	5	1	0	11	10	20	.197	.274	.254	46	-10	-9	9	4	4	-1	7	O	-0.3
1954	Chi-N	17	12	2	1	0	0	0	0	2	4	.083	.214	.083	-19	-2	-2	1	3	0	1	2	O	0.0
	Pit-N	14	9	3	1	0	0	0	0	4	0	.111	.385	.111	37	-1	-1	1	0	0	0	0	/O	0.0
	Yr	31	21	5	2	0	0	0	0	6	4	.095	.296	.095	7	-3	-3	2	3	0	1	2	O	0.0
Total	2	99	143	24	26	5	1	0	11	16	24	.182	.278	.231	40	-12	-11	10	7	4	-0	9	/O	-0.3

■ BOB MARQUIS   Marquis, Robert Rudolph   b: 12/23/24, Oklahoma City, Okla.   BL/TL, 6′1″, 170 lbs.   Deb: 4/17/53

YEAR	TM/L	G	AB	R	H	2B	3B	HR	RBI	BB	SO	AVG	OBP	SLG	PRO+	BR	/A	RC	SB	CS	SBR	FR	POS	TPR
1953	Cin-N	40	44	9	12	1	1	2	3	4	11	.273	.333	.477	107	0	0	8	0	0	0	1	O	0.1

■ ROGER MARQUIS   Marquis, Roger Julian "Noonie"   b: 4/5/37, Holyoke, Mass.   BL/TL, 6′, 190 lbs.   Deb: 9/25/55

YEAR	TM/L	G	AB	R	H	2B	3B	HR	RBI	BB	SO	AVG	OBP	SLG	PRO+	BR	/A	RC	SB	CS	SBR	FR	POS	TPR
1955	Bal-A	1	1	0	0	0	0	0	0	0	0	.000	.000	.000	-99	-0	-0	0	0	0	0	0	/O	0.0

■ LEFTY MARR   Marr, Charles W.   b: 9/19/1862, Cincinnati, Ohio   d: 1/11/12, New Britain, Conn.   BL/TL,   Deb: 10/03/1886

YEAR	TM/L	G	AB	R	H	2B	3B	HR	RBI	BB	SO	AVG	OBP	SLG	PRO+	BR	/A	RC	SB	CS	SBR	FR	POS	TPR
1886	Cin-a	8	29	2	8	1	1	0		1		.276	.323	.379	118	1	1	4	1			-1	/O	0.0
1889	Col-a	139	546	110	167	26	**15**	1	75	87	32	.306	.407	.414	144	30	35	106	29			12	3OS/1C	3.9
1890	Cin-N	130	527	91	158	17	12	1	73	46	29	.300	.363	.383	120	13	14	91	44			-12	O3/S	0.3
1891	Cin-N	72	286	32	74	9	7	0	32	25	15	.259	.323	.339	94	-2	-2	37	16			-10	O	-1.3
	Cin-a	14	57	9	11	1	0	0	4	7	4	.193	.281	.211	40	-4	-5	4	2			-0	O	-0.4
Total	4	363	1445	244	418	54	35	2	**184**	166	<u>80</u>	.289	.368	.379	120	38	42	243	92			-10	O3/S1C	2.5

■ WILLIAM MARRIOTT   Marriott, William Earl   b: 4/18/1893, Pratt, Kan.   d: 8/11/69, Berkeley, Cal.   BL/TR, 6′, 170 lbs.   Deb: 9/06/17

YEAR	TM/L	G	AB	R	H	2B	3B	HR	RBI	BB	SO	AVG	OBP	SLG	PRO+	BR	/A	RC	SB	CS	SBR	FR	POS	TPR
1917	Chi-N	3	6	0	0	0	0	0	0	0	1	.000	.000	.000	-93	-1	-1	0	0			-0	/O	-0.1
1920	Chi-N	14	43	7	12	4	2	0	5	6	5	.279	.367	.465	135	2	2	7	1	1	-0	-4	2	-0.1
1921	Chi-N	30	38	3	12	1	1	0	7	4	1	.316	.381	.395	105	0	0	6	0	1	-1	-1	/2S3O	0.0
1925	Bos-N	103	370	37	99	9	1	1	40	28	26	.268	.322	.305	67	-21	-16	36	3	8	-4	3	3/2	-1.0
1926	Bro-N	109	360	39	96	13	9	3	42	17	20	.267	.303	.378	84	-10	-9	40	12			-7	*3	-1.4
1927	Bro-N	6	9	0	1	0	1	0	1	2	2	.111	.273	.333	61	-1	-1	1	0			1	/3	0.0
Total	6	265	826	86	220	27	14	4	95	57	55	.266	.317	.347	78	-30	-25	90	16	<u>10</u>		-8	3/2OS	-2.6

■ ARMANDO MARSANS   Marsans, Armando   b: 10/3/1887, Matanzas, Cuba   d: 9/3/60, Havana, Cuba   BR/TR, 5′10″, 157 lbs.   Deb: 7/04/11

YEAR	TM/L	G	AB	R	H	2B	3B	HR	RBI	BB	SO	AVG	OBP	SLG	PRO+	BR	/A	RC	SB	CS	SBR	FR	POS	TPR
1911	Cin-N	58	138	17	36	2	2	0	11	15	11	.261	.346	.304	86	-3	-2	18	11			-4	O/13	-0.6
1912	Cin-N	110	416	59	132	19	7	1	38	20	17	.317	.353	.404	110	3	4	70	35			-3	O/1	-0.1
1913	Cin-N	118	435	49	129	7	6	0	38	17	25	.297	.327	.340	91	-6	-5	57	37			-11	O1/3S	-1.9
1914	Cin-N	36	124	16	37	3	0	0	22	14	6	.298	.374	.323	105	2	1	19	13			-1	O	0.0
	StL-F	9	40	5	14	0	2	0	3	0		.350	.395	.450	135	2	2	9	4			0	/2S	0.2
1915	StL-F	36	124	16	22	3	0	0	6	14	5	.177	.261	.202	36	-9	-10	9	5			3	O	-0.9
1916	StL-A	151	528	51	134	12	1	1	60	57	41	.254	.333	.286	91	-7	-4	58	46	26	-2	5	*O	-1.0
1917	StL-A	75	257	31	59	12	0	0	20	20	6	.230	.285	.276	74	-9	-8	23	11			-4	O/32	-1.7
	NY-A	25	88	10	20	4	0	0	15	8	3	.227	.292	.273	72	-3	-3	9	6			3	O	-0.0
	Yr	100	345	41	79	16	0	0	35	28	9	.229	.287	.275	73	-12	-11	31	17			-1		-1.7
1918	NY-A	37	123	13	29	5	1	0	9	5	3	.236	.266	.293	67	-5	-5	10	3			-6	O	-1.4
Total	8	655	2273	267	612	67	19	2	221	173	117	.269	.325	.318	89	-35	-30	283	171	<u>26</u>		-17	O/123S	-7.4

■ FRED MARSH   Marsh, Fred Francis   b: 1/5/24, Valley Falls, Kan.   BR/TR, 5′10″, 180 lbs.   Deb: 4/19/49

YEAR	TM/L	G	AB	R	H	2B	3B	HR	RBI	BB	SO	AVG	OBP	SLG	PRO+	BR	/A	RC	SB	CS	SBR	FR	POS	TPR
1949	Cle-A	1	0	0	0	0	0	0	0	0	0	—	—	—		0	0	0	0	0	0	0	R	0.0
1951	StL-A	130	445	44	108	21	4	4	43	36	56	.243	.299	.335	69	-19	-20	45	4	4	-1	3	*3/S2	-2.1
1952	StL-A	11	24	3	5	1	0	0	1	5	4	.208	.345	.250	65	-1	-1	2	0	1	-0	2	/2S	0.1
	Was-A	9	24	1	1	0	0	0	1	1	4	.042	.080	.042	-68	-5	-5	0	0	0	0	2	/2O	-0.7
	StL-A	76	223	25	64	8	1	2	26	22	29	.287	.351	.359	95	-0	-1	29	3	2	-0	-15	S3	-1.3
	Yr	96	271	29	70	9	1	2	28	28	37	.258	.328	.321	79	-7	-7	29	3	3	-1	-15		-1.9
1953	Chi-A	67	95	22	19	1	0	2	2	13	26	.200	.303	.274	55	-6	-6	8	3	3	-2	-11	3S/12	0.0
1954	Chi-A	62	98	21	30	5	2	0	4	9	16	.306	.364	.398	105	1	1	14	4	2	0	**18**	3/S1O	1.7
1955	Bal-A	89	303	35	66	7	1	2	19	35	33	.218	.301	.267	58	-19	-17	25	1	2	-1	-15	23S	-2.5
1956	Bal-A	20	24	2	3	0	0	0	0	4	3	.125	.250	.125	29	-3	-3	1	1	0	0	0	/S32	0.0
Total	7	465	1236	148	296	43	8	10	96	125	171	.239	.310	.311	69	-52	-53	125	13	14	-5	-2	3S/210	-4.8

YEAR	TM/L	G	AB	R	H	2B	3B	HR	RBI	BB	SO	AVG	OBP	SLG	PRO+	BR	/A	RC	SB	CS	SBR	FR	POS	TPR

■ CHARLIE MARSHALL
Marshall, Charles Anthony (b: Charles Anthony Marczlewicz) b: 8/28/19, Wilmington, Del. BR/TR, 5'10.5", 178 lbs. Deb: 6/14/41

| 1941 | StL-N | 1 | 0 | 0 | 0 | 0 | 0 | 0 | 0 | 0 | 0 | — | — | — | | 0 | 0 | 0 | 0 | | | 0 | /C | 0.0 |

■ DAVE MARSHALL
Marshall, David Lewis b: 1/14/43, Artesia, Cal. BL/TR, 6'1", 182 lbs. Deb: 9/07/67

1967	SF-N	1	0	0	0	0	0	0	0	0	0	—	—	—		0	0	0	0	0	0	0	R	0.0
1968	SF-N	76	174	17	46	5	1	1	16	20	37	.264	.344	.322	101	1	1	21	2	1	0	-4	O	-0.6
1969	SF-N	110	267	32	62	7	1	2	33	40	68	.232	.343	.288	80	-6	-5	28	1	8	-5	-7	O	-2.2
1970	NY-N	92	189	21	46	10	1	6	29	17	43	.243	.306	.402	88	-4	-4	23	4	1	1	0	O	-0.4
1971	NY-N	100	214	28	51	9	1	3	21	26	54	.238	.326	.332	88	-3	-3	24	3	1	0	-2	O	-0.7
1972	NY-N	72	156	21	39	5	0	4	11	22	28	.250	.346	.359	103	1	1	19	3	3	-1	-2	O	-0.3
1973	SD-N	39	49	4	14	5	0	0	4	8	9	.286	.397	.388	128	2	2	7	0	1	-1	-0	/O	0.1
Total	7	490	1049	123	258	41	4	16	114	133	239	.246	.336	.338	92	-10	-8	123	13	15	-5	-15	O	-4.1

■ ED MARSHALL
Marshall, Edward Herbert b: 6/4/06, New Albany, Miss. BR/TR, 5'11", 150 lbs. Deb: 9/28/29

1929	NY-N	5	15	6	6	2	0	0	2	1	0	.400	.438	.533	140	1	1	3	0			-2	/2	0.0
1930	NY-N	78	223	33	69	5	3	0	21	13	9	.309	.350	.359	73	-10	-9	27	0			-3	S2/3	-0.4
1931	NY-N	68	194	15	39	6	2	0	10	8	8	.201	.233	.253	31	-19	-18	12	1			4	2S/3	-1.1
1932	NY-N	68	226	18	56	8	1	0	28	6	11	.248	.270	.292	52	-15	-15	18	1			-2	S	-1.1
Total	4	219	658	72	170	21	6	0	61	28	28	.258	.291	.309	56	-43	-41	61	2			-4	S/23	-2.6

■ JOE MARSHALL
Marshall, Joseph Hanley "Home Run Joe" b: 2/19/1876, Audubon, Minn. d: 9/11/31, Santa Monica, Cal BR/TR, Deb: 9/07/03

1903	Pit-N	10	23	2	6	1	2	0	2	0		.261	.261	.478	107	0	-0	3	0			-4	/SO2	-0.3
1906	StL-N	33	95	2	15	1	2	0	7	6		.158	.208	.211	33	-7	-7	4	0			-1	O/1	-0.9
Total	2	43	118	4	21	2	4	0	9	6		.178	.218	.263	50	-7	-7	7	0			-5	/O1S2	-1.2

■ KEITH MARSHALL
Marshall, Keith Alan b: 7/2/51, San Francisco, Cal. BR/TR, 6'2", 175 lbs. Deb: 4/07/73

| 1973 | KC-A | 8 | 9 | 0 | 2 | 1 | 0 | 0 | 3 | 1 | 4 | .222 | .300 | .333 | 73 | -0 | -0 | 1 | 0 | 0 | 0 | 0 | /O | 0.0 |

■ MIKE MARSHALL
Marshall, Michael Allen b: 1/12/60, Libertyville, Ill. BR/TR, 6'5", 215 lbs. Deb: 9/07/81

1981	*LA-N	14	25	2	5	3	0	0	1	1	4	.200	.259	.320	66	-1	-1	2	0	0	0	-1	/13O	-0.2
1982	LA-N	49	95	10	23	3	0	5	9	13	23	.242	.339	.432	117	2	2	15	2	0	1	-2	O1	0.0
1983	*LA-N	140	465	47	132	17	1	17	65	43	127	.284	.351	.434	117	10	10	72	7	3	0	-12	*O1	-0.4
1984	LA-N	134	495	68	127	27	0	21	65	40	93	.257	.316	.438	111	5	6	66	4	3	-1	-1	*O1	0.0
1985	*LA-N	135	518	72	152	27	2	28	95	37	137	.293	.344	.515	141	23	25	87	3	10	-5	-5	*O/1	1.3
1986	LA-N	103	330	47	77	11	0	19	53	27	90	.233	.299	.439	109	-1	2	42	4	4	-1	-4	O	-0.5
1987	LA-N	104	402	45	118	19	0	16	72	18	79	.294	.330	.460	109	3	4	55	0	5	-3	-8	*O	-1.1
1988	*LA-N	144	542	63	150	27	2	20	82	24	93	.277	.316	.445	120	9	11	71	4	1	1	-4	O1	0.2
1989	LA-N	105	377	41	98	21	1	11	42	33	78	.260	.328	.408	111	4	5	49	2	5	-2	-6	*O	-0.5
1990	NY-N	53	163	24	39	8	1	6	27	7	40	.239	.280	.411	91	-3	-3	18	0	2	-1	-0	1/O	0.3
	*Bos-A	30	112	10	32	6	1	4	12	4	26	.286	.316	.464	110	2	1	16	0	0	0	3	D/1O	0.3
Total	10	1011	3524	429	953	169	8	147	523	247	790	.270	.325	.448	116	53	63	492	26	33	-12	-41	O1/D3	-1.5

■ MAX MARSHALL
Marshall, Milo Max b: 9/18/13, Shenandoah, Iowa BL/TR, 6'1", 180 lbs. Deb: 5/10/42

1942	Cin-N	131	530	49	135	17	6	7	43	34	38	.255	.301	.349	90	-8	-8	56	4			-8	*O	-1.9
1943	Cin-N	132	508	55	120	11	8	4	39	34	52	.236	.287	.313	74	-18	-17	47	8			-7	*O	-3.1
1944	Cin-N	66	229	36	56	13	2	4	23	21	10	.245	.308	.371	94	-3	-2	27	3			-2	O	-0.8
Total	3	329	1267	140	311	41	16	15	105	89	100	.245	.297	.339	84	-30	-28	131	15			-16	O	-5.8

■ JIM MARSHALL
Marshall, Rufus James b: 5/25/31, Danville, Ill. BL/TL, 6'1", 190 lbs. Deb: 4/15/58 MC

1958	Bal-A	85	191	17	41	4	3	5	19	18	30	.215	.282	.346	76	-8	-6	18	3	2	-0	-2	1/O	-1.0
	Chi-N	26	81	12	22	2	0	5	11	12	13	.272	.372	.481	126	3	3	16	1	0	0	-1	1O	0.1
1959	Chi-N	108	294	39	74	10	1	11	40	33	39	.252	.327	.405	95	-3	-2	39	0	1	-1	2	1/O	-0.5
1960	SF-N	75	118	19	28	2	2	2	13	17	24	.237	.333	.339	90	-2	-1	13	0	1	-1	-3	1/O	-0.5
1961	SF-N	44	36	5	8	0	0	1	7	3	8	.222	.282	.306	58	-2	-2	3	0	0	0	0	/1O	-0.1
1962	NY-N	17	32	6	11	1	0	3	4	3	6	.344	.400	.656	175	3	3	9	0	0	0	0	/1O	0.3
	Pit-N	55	100	13	22	5	1	2	12	15	19	.220	.322	.350	80	-3	-3	12	1	0	0	1	1	-0.1
	Yr	72	132	19	33	6	1	5	16	18	25	.250	.340	.424	103	1	1	20	1	0	0	1		0.2
Total	5	410	852	111	206	24	7	29	106	101	139	.242	.323	.388	93	-11	-8	111	5	4	-1	-2	1/O	-1.8

■ WILLARD MARSHALL
Marshall, Willard Warren b: 2/8/21, Richmond, Va. BL/TR, 6'1", 205 lbs. Deb: 4/14/42

1942	NY-N	116	401	41	103	9	2	11	59	26	20	.257	.307	.372	98	-2	-2	46	1			-4	*O	-0.9
1946	NY-N	131	510	63	144	18	3	13	48	33	29	.282	.327	.406	107	3	3	65	3			-7	*O	-0.6
1947	NY-N	155	587	102	171	19	6	36	107	67	30	.291	.366	.528	134	27	27	113	3			6	*O	2.6
1948	NY-N	143	537	72	146	21	8	14	86	64	34	.272	.350	.419	107	6	5	80	2			-2	*O	-0.7
1949	NY-N	141	499	81	153	19	3	12	70	78	20	.307	.401	.429	123	19	19	90	4			-1	*O	1.0
1950	Bos-N	105	298	38	70	10	2	5	40	36	5	.235	.319	.332	77	-12	-9	32	1			1	O	-1.0
1951	Bos-N	136	469	65	132	24	7	11	62	48	18	.281	.351	.433	118	6	10	69	0	3	-2	-10	*O	-0.5
1952	Bos-N	21	66	5	15	4	1	2	11	4	4	.227	.271	.409	89	-2	-1	7	0	0	0	0	O	-0.1
	Cin-N	107	397	52	106	23	1	8	46	37	21	.267	.333	.390	100	-0	-0	53	0	1	-1	1	*O	-0.2
	Yr	128	463	57	121	27	2	10	57	41	25	.261	.324	.393	99	-2	-1	59	0	1	-1	1		-0.3
1953	Cin-N	122	357	51	95	14	6	17	62	41	28	.266	.342	.482	111	5	5	59	0	0	0	3	O	0.4
1954	Chi-A	47	71	7	18	2	0	1	7	11	9	.254	.354	.324	84	-1	-1	9	0	0	0	-3	O	-0.4
1955	Chi-A	22	41	6	7	0	0	0	6	13	1	.171	.370	.171	48	-2	-2	4	0	0	0	-1	O	-0.3
Total	11	1246	4233	583	1160	163	39	130	604	458	219	.274	.347	.423	109	47	52	625	14	4		-18	*O	-0.7

■ BILL MARSHALL
Marshall, William Henry b: 2/14/11, Dorchester, Mass. d: 5/5/77, Sacramento, Cal. BR/TR, 5'8.5", 156 lbs. Deb: 6/20/31

1931	Bos-A	1	0	1	0	0	0	0	0	0	0	—	—	—		0	0	0	0	0	0	0	R	0.0
1934	Cin-N	6	8	0	1	0	0	0	0	0	2	.125	.125	.125	-34	-1	-1	0	0	0	0	1	/2	0.0
Total	2	7	8	1	1	0	0	0	0	0	2	.125	.125	.125	-34	-1	-1	0	0	0	0	1	/2	0.0

■ DOC MARSHALL
Marshall, William Riddle b: 9/22/1875, Butler, Pa. d: 12/11/59, Clinton, Ill. BR/TR, 6', 185 lbs. Deb: 4/15/04

1904	Phi-N	8	20	1	2	0	0	0	0	0		.100	.100	.100	-39	-3	-3	0	0			2	/C	0.0
	NY-N	1	0	0	0	0	0	0	0	0		—	—	—		0	0	0	0			0	/C	0.0
	Bos-N	13	43	3	9	0	1	0	2	2		.209	.244	.256	58	-2	-2	3	2			1	C/O	0.0
	NY-N	10	17	3	6	1	0	0	2	1		.353	.389	.412	144	1	1	3	0			2	/CO2	0.3
	Yr	32	80	7	17	1	1	0	5	3		.213	.241	.250	54	-4	-4	5	2			5		0.3
1906	NY-N	38	102	8	17	3	2	0	7	7		.167	.220	.235	43	-7	-7	7	7			-2	OC/1	-0.8
	StL-N	39	123	6	34	4	1	0	10	6		.276	.310	.325	104	-0	-0	13	1			10	C	1.4
	Yr	77	225	14	51	7	3	0	17	13		.227	.269	.284	75	-7	-7	20	8			8		0.6
1907	StL-N	84	268	19	54	8	2	2	18	12		.201	.236	.269	62	-13	-12	18	2			6	C	0.0
1908	StL-N	6	14	0	1	0	0	0	1	0		.071	.071	.071	-57	-2	-2	0	0			2	/C	0.0
	Chi-N	12	20	4	6	0	1	0	3	0		.300	.300	.400	120	0	0	2	0			5	/CO	0.6
	Yr	18	34	4	7	0	1	0	4	0		.206	.206	.265	51	-2	-2	2	0			7		0.6
1909	Bro-N	50	149	7	30	7	1	0	10	6		.201	.232	.262	55	-9	-8	9	3			-6	C/O	-1.0
Total	5	261	756	51	159	23	8	2	54	34		.210	.244	.270	63	-35	-33	57	15			20	C/O12	0.5

YEAR	TM/L	G	AB	R	H	2B	3B	HR	RBI	BB	SO	AVG	OBP	SLG	PRO+	BR	/A	RC	SB	CS	SBR	FR	POS	TPR

■ **DOC MARTEL**   Martel, Leon Alphonse "Marty"   b: 1/29/1883, Weymouth, Mass.   d: 10/11/47, Washington, D.C.   TR , 6′, 185 lbs.   Deb: 7/06/09

YEAR	TM/L	G	AB	R	H	2B	3B	HR	RBI	BB	SO	AVG	OBP	SLG	PRO+	BR	/A	RC	SB	CS	SBR	FR	POS	TPR
1909	Phi-N	24	41	1	11	3	1	0	7	4		.268	.333	.390	123	1	1	5	0			5	C	0.8
1910	Bos-N	10	31	0	4	0	0	0	1	2	3	.129	.182	.129	-9	-4	-4	1	0			0	1	-0.4
Total	2	34	72	1	15	3	1	0	8	6	3	.208	.269	.278	64	-3	-3	6	0			5	/C1	0.4

■ **AL MARTIN**   Martin, Albert (a.k.a. Albert May In 1872)   Deb: 5/07/1872

YEAR	TM/L	G	AB	R	H	2B	3B	HR	RBI	BB	SO	AVG	OBP	SLG	PRO+	BR	/A	RC	SB	CS	SBR	FR	POS	TPR
1872	Eck-n	4	18	2	5	0	0	0		0		.278	.278	.278	84	-1	-0	1					/2	0.0
1874	Atl-n	7	30	1	4	0	0	0		0		.133	.133	.133	-17	-4	-3	1					/2O	-0.1
1875	Atl-n	6	26	1	3	0	0	0		0		.115	.115	.115	-23	-3	-2	0					/O	-0.1
Total	3 n	17	74	4	12	0	0	0		0		.162	.162	.162	6	-7	-6	2					/2O	-0.2

■ **BILLY MARTIN**   Martin, Alfred Manuel   b: 5/16/28, Berkeley, Cal.   d: 12/25/89, Johnson City, N.Y.   BR/TR, 5′11.5″, 165 lbs.   Deb: 4/18/50   MC

YEAR	TM/L	G	AB	R	H	2B	3B	HR	RBI	BB	SO	AVG	OBP	SLG	PRO+	BR	/A	RC	SB	CS	SBR	FR	POS	TPR
1950	NY-A	34	36	10	9	1	0	1	8	3	3	.250	.308	.361	73	-2	-2	4	0	0	0	-1	2/3	0.0
1951	*NY-A	51	58	10	15	1	2	0	2	4	9	.259	.328	.345	85	-1	-1	5	0	1	-1	16	2/S3O	1.5
1952	*NY-A	109	363	32	97	13	3	3	33	22	31	.267	.323	.344	91	-7	-5	40	3	6	-3	18	*2	1.6
1953	*NY-A	149	587	72	151	24	6	15	75	43	56	.257	.314	.395	94	-9	-7	70	6	7	-2	-1	*2S	0.0
1955	*NY-A	20	70	8	21	2	0	1	9	7	9	.300	.364	.371	100	-0	-0	9	1	2	-1	1	2/S	0.2
1956	*NY-A	121	458	76	121	24	5	9	49	30	56	.264	.314	.397	90	-10	-8	57	7	3	0	-14	*23	-1.3
1957	NY-A	43	145	12	35	5	2	1	12	3	14	.241	.262	.324	60	-8	-8	11	2	1	0	-3	23	-0.9
	KC-A	73	265	33	68	9	3	9	27	12	20	.257	.296	.415	91	-4	-4	32	7	1	2	-20	23/S	-2.0
	Yr	116	410	45	103	14	5	10	39	15	34	.251	.284	.383	80	-12	-13	42	9	2	2	-23		-2.9
1958	Det-A	131	498	56	127	19	1	7	42	16	62	.255	.282	.339	65	-21	-25	44	5	3	-0	-18	S3	-3.0
1959	Cle-A	73	242	37	63	7	0	9	24	8	18	.260	.292	.401	92	-5	-4	27	0	2	-1	-11	2/3	-1.3
1960	Cin-N	103	317	34	78	17	1	3	16	27	34	.246	.305	.334	74	-11	-11	30	0	1	-1	-13	2	-1.7
1961	Mil-N	6	6	1	0	0	0	0	0	0	1	.000	.000	.000	-99	-2	-2	0	0	0	0	0	H	-0.1
	Min-A	108	374	44	92	15	5	6	36	13	42	.246	.277	.361	65	-17	-20	35	3	2	-0	-15	*2/S	-2.2
Total	11	1021	3419	425	877	137	28	64	333	188	355	.257	.301	.369	81	-98	-97	364	34	29	-7	-60	2S/3O	-9.2

■ **PHONNEY MARTIN**   Martin, Alphonse Case   b: 8/4/1845, New York, N.Y.   d: 5/24/33, Hollis, N.Y.   5′7″, 148 lbs.   Deb: 4/26/1872

YEAR	TM/L	G	AB	R	H	2B	3B	HR	RBI	BB	SO	AVG	OBP	SLG	PRO+	BR	/A	RC	SB	CS	SBR	FR	POS	TPR
1872	Tro-n	25	120	27	34	3	1	0		0		.283	.283	.325	86	-2	-2	11					O/P	0.0
	Eck-n	18	79	12	14	0	0	0		1		.177	.188	.177	15	-8	-5	3					P/O	0.0
	Yr	43	199	39	48	3	1	0		1		.241	.245	.266	61	-10	-7	13						0.0
1873	Mut-n	31	136	12	30	2	0	0		0		.221	.221	.235	34	-11	-11	7					O/P	-0.5
Total	2 n	74	335	51	78	5	1	0		1		.233	.235	.254	49	-20	-18	21					/OP	-0.5

■ **BABE MARTIN**   Martin, Boris Michael (b: Boris Michael Martinovich)   b: 3/28/20, Seattle, Wash.   BR/TR, 5′11.5″, 194 lbs.   Deb: 9/25/44

YEAR	TM/L	G	AB	R	H	2B	3B	HR	RBI	BB	SO	AVG	OBP	SLG	PRO+	BR	/A	RC	SB	CS	SBR	FR	POS	TPR
1944	StL-A	2	4	0	3	1	0	0	1	0	0	.750	.750	1.000	376	1	1	3	0	0	0	-0	/O	0.1
1945	StL-A	54	185	13	37	5	2	2	16	11	24	.200	.245	.281	50	-12	-13	12	0	1	-1	6	O/1	-0.9
1946	StL-A	3	9	0	2	0	0	0	1	1	2	.222	.300	.222	45	-1	-1	1	0	0	0	1	/C	0.0
1948	Bos-A	4	4	0	2	0	0	0	0	0	1	.500	.500	.500	158	0	0	1	0	0	0	0	/C	0.0
1949	Bos-A	2	2	0	0	0	0	0	0	0	0	.000	.000	.000	-93	-1	-1	0	0	0	0	0	/C	0.0
1953	StL-A	4	2	0	0	0	0	0	0	1	0	.000	.333	.000	-4	-0	-0	0	0	0	0	0	/C	0.0
Total	6	69	206	13	44	6	2	2	18	13	27	.214	.260	.291	56	-11	-13	17	0	1	-1	7	/O1C	-0.8

■ **FRANK MARTIN**   Martin, Frank   b: 1877, Chicago, Ill.   Deb: 6/30/1897

YEAR	TM/L	G	AB	R	H	2B	3B	HR	RBI	BB	SO	AVG	OBP	SLG	PRO+	BR	/A	RC	SB	CS	SBR	FR	POS	TPR
1897	Lou-N	2	8	1	2	0	0	0	0	0		.250	.250	.250	35	-1	-1	1	0			0	/2	0.0
1898	Chi-N	1	4	0	0	0	0	0	0	0		.000	.000	.000	-99	-1	-1	0	0			0	/2	0.0
1899	NY-N	17	54	5	14	2	0	0	1	2		.259	.298	.296	68	-2	-2	5	0			2	3	0.0
Total	3	20	66	6	16	2	0	0	1	2		.242	.275	.273	54	-4	-4	5	0			3	/32	0.0

■ **HERSH MARTIN**   Martin, Hershel Ray   b: 9/19/09, Birmingham, Ala.   d: 11/17/80, Cuba, Mo.   BB/TR, 6′2″, 190 lbs.   Deb: 4/23/37

YEAR	TM/L	G	AB	R	H	2B	3B	HR	RBI	BB	SO	AVG	OBP	SLG	PRO+	BR	/A	RC	SB	CS	SBR	FR	POS	TPR
1937	Phi-N	141	579	102	164	35	7	8	49	69	66	.283	.362	.409	101	8	2	92	11			-1	*O	-0.4
1938	Phi-N	120	466	58	139	36	6	3	39	34	48	.298	.347	.421	113	6	8	67	8			-3	*O	0.3
1939	Phi-N	111	393	59	111	28	5	1	22	42	27	.282	.355	.387	102	0	2	56	4			7	O	0.7
1940	Phi-N	33	83	10	21	6	1	0	5	9	9	.253	.326	.349	90	-1	-1	10	1			1	O	0.0
1944	NY-A	85	328	49	99	12	4	9	47	34	26	.302	.371	.454	128	14	12	57	5	2	0	3	O	1.4
1945	NY-A	117	408	53	109	18	6	7	53	65	31	.267	.368	.392	115	12	10	66	4	1	1	1	*O	0.8
Total	6	607	2257	331	643	135	29	28	215	253	207	.285	.359	.408	109	38	32	350	33	3		10	O	2.8

■ **JERRY MARTIN**   Martin, Jerry Lindsey   b: 5/11/49, Columbia, S.C.   BR/TR, 6′1″, 195 lbs.   Deb: 9/07/74

YEAR	TM/L	G	AB	R	H	2B	3B	HR	RBI	BB	SO	AVG	OBP	SLG	PRO+	BR	/A	RC	SB	CS	SBR	FR	POS	TPR
1974	Phi-N	13	14	2	3	1	0	1	1	1	5	.214	.267	.286	52	-1	-1	1	0	0	0	-0	O	-0.1
1975	Phi-N	57	113	15	24	7	1	2	11	11	16	.212	.288	.345	72	-4	-5	11	2	2	-1	7	O	0.0
1976	*Phi-N	130	121	30	30	7	0	2	15	7	28	.248	.289	.355	80	-3	-4	11	3	2	-0	3	*O/1	-0.4
1977	*Phi-N	116	215	34	56	16	3	6	28	18	42	.260	.329	.447	101	1	0	31	6	4	-1	4	*O/1	-0.2
1978	*Phi-N	128	266	40	72	13	4	9	36	28	65	.271	.342	.451	119	7	6	42	9	5	-0	4	*O	0.6
1979	Chi-N	150	534	74	145	34	3	19	73	38	85	.272	.323	.453	100	5	-1	74	2	4	-2	-9	*O	-1.5
1980	Chi-N	141	494	57	112	22	2	23	73	38	107	.227	.285	.419	88	-6	-10	57	8	3	1	-13	*O	-2.9
1981	SF-N	72	241	23	58	5	3	4	25	21	52	.241	.309	.336	85	-5	-5	24	6	2	1	-6	O	-1.2
1982	KC-A	147	519	52	138	22	1	15	65	38	138	.266	.318	.399	95	-4	-4	66	1	1	-0	1	*O/D	-0.6
1983	KC-A	13	44	4	14	2	0	2	13	1	7	.318	.333	.500	125	1	1	8	1	0	0	-3	O	-0.1
1984	NY-N	51	91	6	14	1	0	3	5	6	29	.154	.206	.264	32	-9	-8	4	0	0	0	2	O/1	-0.7
Total	11	1018	2652	337	666	130	17	85	345	207	574	.251	.309	.409	93	-17	-29	329	38	23	-2	-13	O/1D	-7.1

■ **JACK MARTIN**   Martin, John Christopher   b: 4/19/1887, Plainfield, N.J.   d: 7/4/80, Plainfield, N.J.   BR/TR, 5′9″, 159 lbs.   Deb: 4/25/12

YEAR	TM/L	G	AB	R	H	2B	3B	HR	RBI	BB	SO	AVG	OBP	SLG	PRO+	BR	/A	RC	SB	CS	SBR	FR	POS	TPR
1912	NY-A	71	231	30	52	6	1	0	17	37		.225	.347	.260	70	-6	-8	26	14			4	S/32	0.2
1914	Bos-N	33	85	10	18	2	0	0	5	6	7	.212	.264	.235	49	-5	-5	5	0			0	3/12	-0.4
	Phi-N	83	292	26	74	5	3	0	21	27	29	.253	.319	.291	77	-6	-8	29	6			-3	S	-0.8
	Yr	116	377	36	92	7	3	0	26	33	36	.244	.307	.279	71	-11	-13	34	6			-3		-1.2
Total	2	187	608	66	144	13	4	0	43	70	36	.237	.323	.271	71	-17	-21	61	20			1	S/321	-1.0

■ **PEPPER MARTIN**   Martin, John Leonard Roosevelt "The Wild Horse Of The Osage"   b: 2/29/04, Temple, Okla.   d: 3/5/65, McAlester, Okla.   BR/TR, 5′8″, 170 lbs.   Deb: 4/16/28   C

YEAR	TM/L	G	AB	R	H	2B	3B	HR	RBI	BB	SO	AVG	OBP	SLG	PRO+	BR	/A	RC	SB	CS	SBR	FR	POS	TPR
1928	*StL-N	39	13	11	4	0	0	0	0	0		.308	.400	.308	86	-0	-0	2	2			3	/O	0.3
1930	StL-N	6	1	5	0	0	0	0	0	0	0	.000	.000	.000	-97	-0	-0	0	0			0	H	0.0
1931	*StL-N	123	413	68	124	32	8	7	75	30	40	.300	.351	.467	114	9	7	69	16			-4	*O	-0.1
1932	StL-N	85	323	47	77	19	6	4	34	30	31	.238	.305	.372	79	-9	-10	38	9			-5	O3	-1.7
1933	StL-N	145	599	**122**	189	36	12	8	57	67	46	.316	.387	.456	133	32	29	111	**26**			-3	*3	3.1
1934	*StL-N	110	454	74	131	25	11	5	49	32	41	.289	.337	.425	96	1	-3	69	23			-5	*3/P	0.1
1935	StL-N	135	539	121	161	41	6	9	54	33	58	.299	.341	.447	106	7	4	84	20			-14	*3O	-0.6
1936	StL-N	143	572	121	177	36	11	11	76	58	66	.309	.373	.469	126	20	20	103	23			-11	*O3/P	0.4
1937	StL-N	98	339	60	103	27	8	5	38	33	50	.304	.366	.475	124	12	11	62	9			11	O/3	1.9
1938	StL-N	91	346	34	79	18	2	2	38	18	34	.228	.340	.398	97	-1	-1	38	4			-1	O3	-0.3
1939	StL-N	88	281	48	86	17	7	3	37	30	35	.306	.375	.441	113	8	6	47	6			-3	O3	0.3
1940	StL-N	86	228	28	72	15	4	3	39	22	24	.316	.378	.456	122	9	8	41	6			3	O/3	0.8
1944	StL-N	40	86	15	24	4	0	2	4	15	11	.279	.386	.395	118	3	3	14	2			-0	O	0.0

YEAR	TM/L	G	AB	R	H	2B	3B	HR	RBI	BB	SO	AVG	OBP	SLG	PRO+	BR	/A	RC	SB	CS	SBR	FR	POS	TPR
Total	13	1189	4117	754	1227	270	75	59	501	369	438	.298	.358	.443	112	93	73	679	146			-29	O3/P	4.2

■ J.C. MARTIN
Martin, Joseph Clifton   b: 12/13/36, Axton, Va.   BL/TR, 6'2", 188 lbs.   Deb: 9/10/59   C

YEAR	TM/L	G	AB	R	H	2B	3B	HR	RBI	BB	SO	AVG	OBP	SLG	PRO+	BR	/A	RC	SB	CS	SBR	FR	POS	TPR
1959	Chi-A	3	4	0	1	0	0	0	1	0	1	.250	.250	.250	38	-0	-0	0	0	0	0	0	/3	0.0
1960	Chi-A	7	20	0	2	1	0	0	2	0	6	.100	.100	.150	-34	-4	-4	0	0	0	0	-0	/31	-0.3
1961	Chi-A	110	274	26	63	8	3	5	32	21	31	.230	.290	.336	68	-13	-13	27	1	2	-1	10	13	-0.7
1962	Chi-A	18	26	0	2	0	0	0	2	0	3	.077	.077	.077	-59	-6	-6	0	0	0	0	-0	/C13	-0.5
1963	Chi-A	105	259	25	53	11	1	5	28	26	35	.205	.280	.313	67	-12	-11	24	0	0	0	15	C/13	0.5
1964	Chi-A	122	294	23	58	10	1	4	22	16	30	.197	.244	.279	46	-22	-21	20	0	0	0	11	*C	-0.5
1965	Chi-A	119	230	21	60	12	0	2	21	24	29	.261	.336	.339	98	-2	-0	28	2	1	0	6	*C/13	1.4
1966	Chi-A	67	157	13	40	5	3	2	20	14	24	.255	.320	.363	103	-1	0	18	0	0	0	0	C	0.4
1967	Chi-A	101	252	22	59	12	1	4	22	30	41	.234	.318	.337	97	-2	-0	27	4	4	-1	5	C/1	1.0
1968	NY-N	78	244	20	55	9	2	3	31	21	31	.225	.300	.316	84	-4	-4	24	0	0	0	-2	C1	-0.4
1969	*NY-N	66	177	12	37	5	1	4	21	12	32	.209	.259	.316	59	-10	-10	14	0	0	0	-6	C/1	-1.4
1970	Chi-N	40	77	11	12	1	0	1	4	20	11	.156	.337	.208	44	-5	-6	6	0	0	0	2	C/1	-0.2
1971	Chi-N	47	125	13	33	5	0	2	17	12	16	.264	.338	.352	84	-0	-3	15	1	1	-0	3	C/O	0.1
1972	Chi-N	25	50	3	12	3	0	0	7	5	9	.240	.309	.300	67	-2	-2	4	1	0	0	-3	C	-0.4
Total	14	908	2189	189	487	82	12	32	230	201	299	.222	.293	.315	72	-82	-80	207	9	8	-2	41	C/13O	-1.0

■ MIKE MARTIN
Martin, Joseph Michael   b: 12/3/58, Portland, Ore.   BL/TR, 6'2", 193 lbs.   Deb: 8/15/86

YEAR	TM/L	G	AB	R	H	2B	3B	HR	RBI	BB	SO	AVG	OBP	SLG	PRO+	BR	/A	RC	SB	CS	SBR	FR	POS	TPR
1986	Chi-N	8	13	1	1	1	0	0	2	4	.077	.200	.154	-1	-2	-2	0	0	0	0	0	/C	-0.1

■ JOE MARTIN
Martin, Joseph Samuel "Silent Joe"   b: 1/1/1876, Hollidaysburg, Pa.   d: 5/25/64, Altoona, Pa.   BL/TR, 5'9.5", 155 lbs.   Deb: 4/28/03

YEAR	TM/L	G	AB	R	H	2B	3B	HR	RBI	BB	SO	AVG	OBP	SLG	PRO+	BR	/A	RC	SB	CS	SBR	FR	POS	TPR
1903	Was-A	35	119	11	27	4	5	0	7	5		.227	.258	.345	79	-3	-3	12	2			-4	23/O	-0.7
	StL-A	44	173	18	37	6	4	0	7	6		.214	.240	.295	63	-8	-8	13	0			-3	O/23	-1.2
	Yr	79	292	29	64	10	9	0	14	11		.219	.248	.315	70	-11	-11	25	2			-7		-1.9

■ JOE MARTIN
Martin, Stuart McGuire   b: 11/17/13, Rich Square, N.C.   BL/TR, 6', 155 lbs.   Deb: 4/14/36

YEAR	TM/L	G	AB	R	H	2B	3B	HR	RBI	BB	SO	AVG	OBP	SLG	PRO+	BR	/A	RC	SB	CS	SBR	FR	POS	TPR
1936	StL-N	92	332	63	99	21	4	6	41	29	27	.298	.356	.440	114	6	6	53	17			-13	2/S	-0.1
1937	StL-N	90	223	34	58	6	1	1	17	32	18	.260	.353	.309	80	-5	-5	26	3			-6	2/1S	-0.8
1938	StL-N	114	417	54	116	26	2	1	27	30	28	.278	.328	.357	84	-7	-10	52	4			-9	2	-1.1
1939	StL-N	120	425	60	114	26	7	3	30	33	40	.268	.325	.384	85	-7	-10	54	4			-3	*2/1	-0.8
1940	StL-N	112	369	45	88	12	6	4	32	33	35	.238	.301	.336	71	-12	-15	39	4			-25	32	-3.9
1941	Pit-N	88	233	37	71	13	2	0	19	10	17	.305	.341	.378	103	0	1	29	2			-4	2/31	0.0
1942	Pit-N	42	120	16	27	4	2	1	12	8	10	.225	.273	.317	71	-4	-5	11	1			-11	2/1S	-1.4
1943	Chi-N	64	118	13	26	4	0	0	5	15	10	.220	.308	.254	64	-5	-5	10	1			2	2/31	-0.2
Total	8	722	2237	322	599	112	24	16	183	190	185	.268	.327	.361	86	-33	-43	273	36			-69	2/31S	-8.3

■ GENE MARTIN
Martin, Thomas Eugene   b: 1/12/47, Americus, Ga.   BL/TR, 6'0.5", 190 lbs.   Deb: 7/28/68

YEAR	TM/L	G	AB	R	H	2B	3B	HR	RBI	BB	SO	AVG	OBP	SLG	PRO+	BR	/A	RC	SB	CS	SBR	FR	POS	TPR
1968	Was-A	9	11	1	4	1	0	1	1	0	1	.364	.364	.727	232	1	2	2	0	0	0	0	/O	0.2

■ BILLY MARTIN
Martin, William Lloyd   b: 2/13/1894, Washington, D.C.   d: 9/14/49, Arlington, Va.   BR/TR, 5'8.5", 170 lbs.   Deb: 10/06/14

YEAR	TM/L	G	AB	R	H	2B	3B	HR	RBI	BB	SO	AVG	OBP	SLG	PRO+	BR	/A	RC	SB	CS	SBR	FR	POS	TPR
1914	Bos-N	1	3	0	0	0	0	0	0	0	0	.000	.000	.000	-99	-1	-1	0	0			-1	/S	-0.1

■ JOE MARTIN
Martin, William Joseph "Smokey Joe"   b: 8/28/11, Seymour, Mo.   d: 9/28/60, Buffalo, N.Y.   BR/TR, 5'11.5", 181 lbs.   Deb: 5/05/36

YEAR	TM/L	G	AB	R	H	2B	3B	HR	RBI	BB	SO	AVG	OBP	SLG	PRO+	BR	/A	RC	SB	CS	SBR	FR	POS	TPR
1936	NY-N	7	15	0	4	1	0	0	2	0	4	.267	.313	.333	75	-1	-1	1	0			1	/3	0.1
1938	Chi-A	1	0	0	0	0	0	0	0	0	0	—	—	—		0	0	0	0	0	0	0	R	0.0
Total	2	8	15	0	4	1	0	0	2	0	4	.267	.313	.333	75	-1	-1	1	0	0		1	/3	0.1

■ CARLOS MARTINEZ
Martinez, Carlos Alberto Escobar (b: Carlos Alberto Escobar (Martinez))   b: 8/11/64, LaGuaira, Venez.   BR/TR, 6'5", 175 lbs.   Deb: 9/02/88

YEAR	TM/L	G	AB	R	H	2B	3B	HR	RBI	BB	SO	AVG	OBP	SLG	PRO+	BR	/A	RC	SB	CS	SBR	FR	POS	TPR
1988	Chi-A	17	55	3	9	1	0	0	0	0	12	.164	.164	.182	-3	-7	-7	2	1	0	0	3	3/D	-0.4
1989	Chi-A	109	350	44	105	22	0	5	32	21	57	.300	.341	.406	112	4	5	45	4	1	1	-6	310/D	-0.2
1990	Chi-A	92	272	18	61	6	5	4	24	10	40	.224	.252	.327	62	-15	-14	19	0	4	-2	-5	1/OD	-2.8
Total	3	218	677	67	175	29	5	9	56	31	109	.258	.292	.356	83	-18	-17	66	5	5	-2	-8	1/3OD	-3.4

■ CARMELO MARTINEZ
Martinez, Carmelo (Salgado)   b: 7/28/60, Dorado, P.R.   BR/TR, 6'1", 190 lbs.   Deb: 8/22/83

YEAR	TM/L	G	AB	R	H	2B	3B	HR	RBI	BB	SO	AVG	OBP	SLG	PRO+	BR	/A	RC	SB	CS	SBR	FR	POS	TPR
1983	Chi-N	29	89	8	23	3	0	6	16	4	19	.258	.290	.494	108	1	1	12	0	0	0	-0	1/3O	0.0
1984	*SD-N	149	488	64	122	28	2	13	66	68	82	.250	.346	.395	108	6	6	70	1	3	-2	13	*O/1	1.3
1985	SD-N	150	514	64	130	28	1	21	72	87	82	.253	.364	.434	124	17	18	84	0	4	-2	3	*O/1	1.6
1986	SD-N	113	244	28	58	10	0	9	25	35	46	.238	.336	.389	101	0	1	31	1	1	-0	-2	O1/3	-0.3
1987	SD-N	139	447	59	122	21	2	15	70	70	82	.273	.375	.430	117	10	12	73	5	5	-2	-4	O1	0.0
1988	SD-N	121	365	48	86	12	0	18	65	35	57	.236	.303	.416	106	1	2	44	1	1	-0	8	O1	0.6
1989	SD-N	111	267	23	59	12	2	6	39	32	54	.221	.304	.348	86	-5	-5	27	0	0	0	0	O1	-0.8
1990	Phi-N	71	198	23	48	8	0	8	31	29	37	.242	.339	.404	104	1	1	28	2	1	0	-1	1O	-0.2
	*Pit-N	12	19	3	4	1	0	2	4	1	5	.211	.250	.579	126	0	0	3	0	0	0	1	/1O	0.1
	Yr	83	217	26	52	9	0	10	35	30	42	.240	.332	.419	106	2	2	32	2	1	0	-0		-0.1
Total	8	895	2631	320	652	123	7	98	388	361	464	.248	.341	.412	110	32	37	372	10	15	-6	17	O1/3	2.3

■ TINO MARTINEZ
Martinez, Constantino   b: 12/7/67, Tampa, Fla.   BL/TR, 6'2", 205 lbs.   Deb: 8/20/90

YEAR	TM/L	G	AB	R	H	2B	3B	HR	RBI	BB	SO	AVG	OBP	SLG	PRO+	BR	/A	RC	SB	CS	SBR	FR	POS	TPR
1990	Sea-A	24	68	4	15	4	0	0	5	9	9	.221	.312	.279	66	-3	-3	7	0	0	0	1	1	-0.4

■ DAVE MARTINEZ
Martinez, David   b: 9/26/64, New York, N.Y.   BL/TL, 5'10", 150 lbs.   Deb: 6/15/86

YEAR	TM/L	G	AB	R	H	2B	3B	HR	RBI	BB	SO	AVG	OBP	SLG	PRO+	BR	/A	RC	SB	CS	SBR	FR	POS	TPR
1986	Chi-N	53	108	13	15	1	1	1	7	6	22	.139	.191	.194	6	-14	-15	4	4	2	0	5	O	-1.0
1987	Chi-N	142	459	70	134	18	8	8	36	57	96	.292	.373	.418	105	7	5	75	16	8	0	-1	*O	-0.1
1988	Chi-N	75	256	27	65	10	1	4	34	21	46	.254	.315	.348	86	-3	-4	29	7	3	0	2	O	-0.4
	Mon-N	63	191	24	49	3	5	2	12	17	48	.257	.317	.356	89	-2	-3	23	16	6	1	2	O	0.0
	Yr	138	447	51	114	13	6	6	46	38	94	.255	.316	.351	87	-5	-7	52	23	9	2	4		-0.4
1989	Mon-N	126	361	41	99	16	7	3	27	27	57	.274	.325	.382	100	0	-0	49	23	4	5	-17	*O	-1.4
1990	Mon-N	118	391	60	109	13	5	11	39	24	48	.279	.322	.422	104	1	1	49	13	11	-3	-2	*O/P	-0.7
Total	5	577	1766	235	471	61	27	29	155	152	317	.267	.327	.381	93	-10	-16	230	79	34	3	-11	O/P	-3.6

■ EDGAR MARTINEZ
Martinez, Edgar   b: 1/2/63, New York, N.Y.   BR/TR, 6' ", 175 lbs.   Deb: 9/12/87

YEAR	TM/L	G	AB	R	H	2B	3B	HR	RBI	BB	SO	AVG	OBP	SLG	PRO+	BR	/A	RC	SB	CS	SBR	FR	POS	TPR
1987	Sea-A	13	43	6	16	5	2	0	5	2	5	.372	.413	.581	152	4	3	11	0	0	0	1	3/D	0.4
1988	Sea-A	14	32	0	9	4	0	0	5	4	7	.281	.361	.406	110	1	1	5	0	0	0	-4	3	-0.3
1989	Sea-A	65	171	20	41	5	0	2	20	17	26	.240	.319	.304	74	-5	-6	18	2	1	0	-6	3	-1.1
1990	Sea-A	144	487	71	147	27	2	11	49	74	62	.302	.399	.433	119	24	24	86	1	4	-2	-1	*3/D	2.2
Total	4	236	733	97	213	41	4	13	79	97	100	.291	.380	.411	119	24	22	119	3	5	-2	-10	3/D	1.2

■ TONY MARTINEZ
Martinez, Gabriel Antonio (Diaz)   b: 3/18/41, Perico, Cuba   BR/TR, 5'10", 165 lbs.   Deb: 4/09/63

YEAR	TM/L	G	AB	R	H	2B	3B	HR	RBI	BB	SO	AVG	OBP	SLG	PRO+	BR	/A	RC	SB	CS	SBR	FR	POS	TPR
1963	Cle-A	43	141	10	22	4	0	0	8	5	18	.156	.185	.184	4	-18	-18	4	1	1	-0	-6	S	-2.3
1964	Cle-A	9	14	1	3	1	0	0	2	0	2	.214	.214	.286	38	-1	-1	0	0	1	-1	4	/2S	0.3
1965	Cle-A	4	3	0	0	0	0	0	0	0	0	.000	.000	.000	-99	-0	-0	0	0	0	0	0	H	0.0
1966	Cle-A	17	17	2	5	0	0	0	0	1	6	.294	.333	.294	82	-0	-0	2	1	1	0	-1	/S2	0.1
Total	4	73	175	13	30	5	0	0	10	6	26	.171	.199	.200	13	-20	-20	6	2	3	-1	-1	/S2	-1.9

YEAR	TM/L	G	AB	R	H	2B	3B	HR	RBI	BB	SO	AVG	OBP	SLG	PRO+	BR	/A	RC	SB	CS	SBR	FR	POS	TPR

■ BUCK MARTINEZ
Martinez, John Albert b: 11/7/48, Redding, Cal. BR/TR, 5'10", 190 lbs. Deb: 6/18/69

YEAR	TM/L	G	AB	R	H	2B	3B	HR	RBI	BB	SO	AVG	OBP	SLG	PRO+	BR	/A	RC	SB	CS	SBR	FR	POS	TPR
1969	KC-A	72	205	14	47	6	1	4	23	8	25	.229	.258	.327	62	-11	-11	16	0	0	0	-1	C/O	-0.8
1970	KC-A	6	9	1	1	0	0	0	0	2	1	.111	.273	.111	10	-1	-1	0	0	0	0	1	/C	0.0
1971	KC-A	22	46	3	7	2	0	0	1	5	9	.152	.235	.196	23	-5	-5	2	0	1	-1	2	C	-0.1
1973	KC-A	14	32	2	8	1	0	1	6	4	5	.250	.333	.375	92	-0	-0	4	0	0	0	-1	C	0.0
1974	KC-A	43	107	10	23	3	1	1	8	14	19	.215	.317	.290	71	-3	-4	11	0	1	-1	1	C	-0.1
1975	KC-A	80	226	15	51	9	2	3	23	21	28	.226	.294	.323	72	-8	-8	22	1	0	0	1	C	-0.4
1976	*KC-A	95	267	24	61	13	3	5	34	16	45	.228	.272	.356	82	-7	-7	27	0	0	0	5	C	0.2
1977	KC-A	29	80	3	18	4	0	1	9	3	12	.225	.253	.313	53	-5	-5	6	0	1	-1	3	C	-0.2
1978	Mil-A	89	256	26	56	10	1	1	20	14	42	.219	.259	.277	51	-17	-17	19	1	1	-0	-3	C	-1.8
1979	Mil-A	69	196	17	53	8	0	4	26	8	25	.270	.299	.372	80	-6	-6	21	0	1	-1	-2	C/P	-0.5
1980	Mil-A	76	219	16	49	9	0	3	17	12	33	.224	.267	.306	58	-13	-12	18	1	0	0	10	C	0.2
1981	Tor-A	45	128	13	29	8	1	4	21	11	16	.227	.293	.398	92	-1	-2	14	1	0	0	1	C	0.2
1982	Tor-A	96	260	26	63	17	0	10	37	24	34	.242	.306	.423	90	-1	-4	31	1	1	-0	6	C	0.6
1983	Tor-A	88	221	27	56	14	0	10	33	29	39	.253	.340	.452	109	5	3	33	0	1	-1	-3	C	0.3
1984	Tor-A	102	232	24	51	13	1	5	37	29	49	.220	.312	.349	80	-5	-6	27	0	3	-2	-4	C/D	-0.6
1985	Tor-A	42	99	11	16	3	0	4	14	10	12	.162	.245	.313	50	-7	-7	8	0	0	0	4	C	-0.1
1986	Tor-A	81	160	13	29	8	0	2	12	20	25	.181	.272	.269	47	-11	-12	12	0	0	0	-2	C/D	-0.8
Total	17	1049	2743	245	618	128	10	58	321	230	419	.225	.287	.343	73	-96	-105	272	5	10	-5	17	*C/DPO	-3.9

■ JOSE MARTINEZ
Martinez, Jose (Azcuiz) b: 7/26/41, Cardenas, Cuba BR/TR, 5'10", 190 lbs. Deb: 6/18/69 C

YEAR	TM/L	G	AB	R	H	2B	3B	HR	RBI	BB	SO	AVG	OBP	SLG	PRO+	BR	/A	RC	SB	CS	SBR	FR	POS	TPR
1969	Pit-N	77	168	20	45	6	0	1	16	9	32	.268	.309	.321	78	-5	-5	15	1	3	-2	10	2S/3O	0.9
1970	Pit-N	19	20	1	1	0	0	0	0	1	5	.050	.095	.050	-61	-5	-4	0	0	0	0	3	/32S	0.0
Total	2	96	188	21	46	6	0	1	16	10	37	.245	.286	.293	63	-10	-9	16	1	3	-2	13	/2S3O	0.9

■ MARTY MARTINEZ
Martinez, Orlando (Oliva) b: 8/23/41, Havana, Cuba BB/TR, 6', 170 lbs. Deb: 5/02/62 MC

YEAR	TM/L	G	AB	R	H	2B	3B	HR	RBI	BB	SO	AVG	OBP	SLG	PRO+	BR	/A	RC	SB	CS	SBR	FR	POS	TPR
1962	Min-A	37	18	13	3	0	1	0	3	3	4	.167	.286	.278	51	-1	-1	2	0	0	0	13	S/3	1.2
1967	Atl-N	44	73	14	21	2	1	0	5	11	11	.288	.388	.342	112	2	2	10	0	1	-1	4	S/2C31	0.9
1968	Atl-N	113	356	34	82	5	3	0	12	29	28	.230	.292	.261	67	-14	-14	27	6	6	-2	4	S32C	-1.3
1969	Hou-N	78	198	14	61	5	4	0	15	10	21	.308	.341	.374	102	-0	0	24	0	0	0	-8	OS3/CP2	-0.6
1970	Hou-N	75	150	12	33	3	0	0	12	9	22	.220	.264	.240	38	-13	-13	9	0	0	0	-5	S3/C2	-1.3
1971	Hou-N	32	62	4	16	3	1	0	4	3	6	.258	.292	.339	80	-2	-2	5	1	0	0	1	/2S13	0.0
1972	StL-N	9	7	0	3	0	0	0	2	0	1	.429	.429	.429	146	0	0	1	0	0	0	0	/S23	0.1
	Oak-A	22	40	3	5	0	0	0	1	3	6	.125	.186	.125	-7	-5	-5	1	0	0	0	3	2/S3	0.0
	Tex-A	26	41	3	6	1	1	0	3	2	8	.146	.186	.220	21	-4	-4	1	0	1	-1	-1	/S32	-0.5
	Yr	48	81	6	11	1	1	0	4	5	14	.136	.186	.173	8	-9	-9	2	0	1	-1	2		-0.5
Total	7	436	945	97	230	19	11	0	57	70	107	.243	.298	.287	70	-37	-36	82	7	8	-3	2	S/32CO1P	-1.5

■ HECTOR MARTINEZ
Martinez, Rodolfo Hector (Santos) b: 5/11/39, Las Villas, Cuba BR/TR, 5'10", 160 lbs. Deb: 9/30/62

YEAR	TM/L	G	AB	R	H	2B	3B	HR	RBI	BB	SO	AVG	OBP	SLG	PRO+	BR	/A	RC	SB	CS	SBR	FR	POS	TPR
1962	KC-A	1	1	0	0	0	0	0	0	0	1	.000	.000	.000	-97	-0	-0	0	0	0	0	0	H	0.0
1963	KC-A	6	14	2	4	0	0	1	3	1	3	.286	.375	.500	137	1	1	2	0	1	-1	0	/O	0.0
Total	2	7	15	2	4	0	0	1	3	1	4	.267	.353	.467	122	1	0	2	0	1	-1	0	/O	0.0

■ TED MARTINEZ
Martinez, Teodoro Noel (Encarnacion) b: 12/10/47, Central Barahona, D.R. BR/TR, 6', 165 lbs. Deb: 7/18/70

YEAR	TM/L	G	AB	R	H	2B	3B	HR	RBI	BB	SO	AVG	OBP	SLG	PRO+	BR	/A	RC	SB	CS	SBR	FR	POS	TPR
1970	NY-N	4	16	0	1	0	0	0	0	0	3	.063	.063	.063	-66	-4	-4	0	0	0	0	1	/2S	-0.2
1971	NY-N	38	125	16	36	5	2	1	10	4	22	.288	.326	.384	102	-0	0	17	6	0	2	-7	S2/3O	-0.1
1972	NY-N	103	330	22	74	5	5	1	19	12	49	.224	.254	.279	52	-21	-20	21	7	4	-0	1	2SO/3	-1.3
1973	*NY-N	92	263	34	67	11	0	1	14	13	38	.255	.295	.308	68	-12	-11	22	3	5	-2	-2	SO3/2	-1.0
1974	NY-N	116	334	32	73	15	7	2	43	14	40	.219	.250	.323	61	-19	-19	23	3	2	-0	15	S32O	0.4
1975	StL-N	16	21	1	4	2	0	0	2	0	2	.190	.190	.286	30	-2	-2	1	0	0	0	0	/O2S3	-0.1
	*Oak-A	86	87	7	15	0	0	0	3	2	9	.172	.200	.172	6	-11	-10	3	1	1	-0	4	S23	0.0
1977	LA-N	67	137	21	41	6	1	1	10	2	20	.299	.309	.380	84	-3	-3	15	3	4	-2	14	2S3	1.3
1978	LA-N	54	55	13	14	1	0	1	5	4	14	.255	.317	.327	80	-1	-1	6	3	2	-0	10	S32	1.1
1979	LA-N	81	112	19	30	5	1	0	2	3	16	.268	.293	.330	71	-5	-5	10	3	2	-0	-0	3S2	-0.2
Total	9	657	1480	165	355	50	16	7	108	55	213	.240	.271	.309	62	-78	-76	118	29	20	-3	36	S2/3O	-0.1

■ JOE MARTY
Marty, Joseph Anton b: 9/1/13, Sacramento, Cal. d: 10/4/84, Sacramento, Cal. BR/TR, 6', 182 lbs. Deb: 4/22/37

YEAR	TM/L	G	AB	R	H	2B	3B	HR	RBI	BB	SO	AVG	OBP	SLG	PRO+	BR	/A	RC	SB	CS	SBR	FR	POS	TPR
1937	Chi-N	88	290	41	84	17	2	5	44	28	30	.290	.356	.414	104	4	2	41	3			-5	O	-0.6
1938	*Chi-N	76	235	32	57	8	3	7	35	18	26	.243	.305	.391	88	-4	-5	27	0			3	O	-0.2
1939	Chi-N	23	76	6	10	1	0	2	10	4	13	.132	.175	.224	6	-10	-10	2	2			-1	O	-1.1
	Phi-N	91	299	32	76	12	6	9	44	24	27	.254	.310	.425	98	-3	-2	38	1			5	O/P	0.2
	Yr	114	375	38	86	13	6	11	54	28	40	.229	.283	.384	79	-13	-12	38	3			4		-0.9
1940	Phi-N	123	455	52	123	21	8	13	50	17	50	.270	.298	.437	105	-2	0	54	2			-0	*O	-0.3
1941	Phi-N	137	477	60	128	19	3	8	39	51	41	.268	.344	.371	105	1	4	63	6			-10	*O	-1.1
Total	5	538	1832	223	478	78	22	44	222	142	187	.261	.318	.400	97	-14	-11	225	14			-8	O/P	-3.1

■ BOB MARTYN
Martyn, Robert Gordon b: 8/15/30, Weiser, Idaho BL/TR, 6', 176 lbs. Deb: 6/18/57

YEAR	TM/L	G	AB	R	H	2B	3B	HR	RBI	BB	SO	AVG	OBP	SLG	PRO+	BR	/A	RC	SB	CS	SBR	FR	POS	TPR
1957	KC-A	58	131	10	35	2	4	1	12	11	20	.267	.324	.366	87	-2	-2	15	1	3	-2	1	O	-0.5
1958	KC-A	95	226	25	59	10	7	2	23	26	36	.261	.337	.394	99	0	-0	30	1	4	-2	0	O	-0.6
1959	KC-A	1	1	0	0	0	0	0	0	0	0	.000	.000	.000	-98	-0	-0	0	0	0	0	0	R	0.0
Total	3	154	358	35	94	12	11	3	35	37	56	.263	.332	.383	94	-2	-3	45	2	7	-4	1	O	-1.1

■ GARY MARTZ
Martz, Gary Arthur b: 1/10/51, Spokane, Wash. BR/TR, 6'4", 210 lbs. Deb: 7/08/75

YEAR	TM/L	G	AB	R	H	2B	3B	HR	RBI	BB	SO	AVG	OBP	SLG	PRO+	BR	/A	RC	SB	CS	SBR	FR	POS	TPR
1975	KC-A	1	0	0	0	0	0	0	0	0	0	.000	.000	.000	-97	-0	-0	0	0	0	0	0	/O	0.0

■ JOHN MARZANO
Marzano, John Robert b: 2/14/63, Philadelphia, Pa. BR/TR, 5'11", 185 lbs. Deb: 7/31/87

YEAR	TM/L	G	AB	R	H	2B	3B	HR	RBI	BB	SO	AVG	OBP	SLG	PRO+	BR	/A	RC	SB	CS	SBR	FR	POS	TPR
1987	Bos-A	52	168	20	41	11	0	5	24	7	41	.244	.287	.399	77	-5	-6	19	0	1	-1	1	C	0.0
1988	Bos-A	10	29	3	4	1	0	0	1	1	3	.138	.167	.172	-5	-4	-4	1	0	0	0	5	C	0.2
1989	Bos-A	7	18	5	8	3	0	0	3	0	2	.444	.444	.778	224	3	3	5	0	0	0	-0	/C	0.3
1990	Bos-A	32	83	8	20	4	0	0	6	5	10	.241	.283	.289	58	-4	-5	7	0	1	-1	4	C	0.0
Total	4	101	298	36	73	19	0	6	34	13	56	.245	.283	.369	73	-11	-12	32	0	2	-1	11	C	0.5

■ CLYDE MASHORE
Mashore, Clyde Wayne b: 5/29/45, Concord, Cal. BR/TR, 6', 182 lbs. Deb: 7/11/69

YEAR	TM/L	G	AB	R	H	2B	3B	HR	RBI	BB	SO	AVG	OBP	SLG	PRO+	BR	/A	RC	SB	CS	SBR	FR	POS	TPR
1969	Cin-N	2	1	1	0	0	0	0	0	0	0	.000	.000	.000	-95	-0	-0	0	0	0	0	0	H	0.0
1970	Mon-N	13	25	2	4	0	0	1	3	4	11	.160	.276	.280	49	-2	-2	2	0	0	0	-0	O	-0.2
1971	Mon-N	66	114	20	22	5	0	1	7	10	22	.193	.258	.263	48	-8	-8	8	1	0	0	-0	O/3	-0.9
1972	Mon-N	93	176	23	40	7	1	3	23	14	41	.227	.284	.330	73	-6	-7	18	6	1	1	-2	O	-1.1
1973	Mon-N	67	103	12	21	3	0	3	14	15	28	.204	.305	.320	71	-4	-4	11	4	3	-1	4	O/2	-0.2
Total	5	241	419	58	87	15	1	8	47	43	102	.208	.281	.305	64	-20	-21	38	11	4	1	1	O/23	-2.4

■ PHIL MASI
Masi, Philip Samuel b: 1/6/17, Chicago, Ill. d: 3/29/90, Mt.Prospect, Ill. BR/TR, 5'10", 177 lbs. Deb: 4/23/39

YEAR	TM/L	G	AB	R	H	2B	3B	HR	RBI	BB	SO	AVG	OBP	SLG	PRO+	BR	/A	RC	SB	CS	SBR	FR	POS	TPR
1939	Bos-N	46	114	14	29	7	2	1	14	9	15	.254	.315	.377	92	-3	-3	13	0			-2	C	-0.2
1940	Bos-N	63	138	11	27	4	1	1	14	14	14	.196	.270	.261	50	-10	-9	9	0			-1	C	-0.7
1941	Bos-N	87	180	17	40	8	2	3	18	16	13	.222	.286	.339	79	-6	-5	18	4			-7	C	-0.3
1942	Bos-N	57	87	14	19	3	1	0	9	12	4	.218	.313	.276	74	-3	-2	8	2			4	C/O	0.2

YEAR	TM/L	G	AB	R	H	2B	3B	HR	RBI	BB	SO	AVG	OBP	SLG	PRO+	BR	/A	RC	SB	CS	SBR	FR	POS	TPR
1943	Bos-N	80	238	27	65	9	1	2	28	27	20	.273	.347	.345	102	1	1	28	7			-7	C	-0.2
1944	Bos-N	89	251	33	69	13	5	3	23	31	20	.275	.355	.402	108	4	3	37	4			-1	C1/3	0.5
1945	Bos-N	114	371	55	101	25	4	7	46	42	32	.272	.348	.418	112	6	5	54	9			0	C/1	0.7
1946	Bos-N	133	397	52	106	17	5	3	62	55	41	.267	.358	.358	102	3	2	53	5			-5	*C	0.0
1947	Bos-N	126	411	54	125	22	4	9	50	47	27	.304	.377	.443	120	10	12	69	7			-7	*C	0.7
1948	*Bos-N	113	376	43	95	19	0	5	44	35	26	.253	.318	.343	80	-11	-10	40	2			0	*C	-0.1
1949	Bos-N	37	105	13	22	2	0	0	6	14	10	.210	.303	.229	47	-8	-7	7	1			-2	C	-0.7
	Pit-N	48	135	16	37	6	1	2	13	17	16	.274	.355	.378	94	-0	-1	18	1			-2	C/1	0.0
	Yr	85	240	29	59	8	1	2	19	31	26	.246	.332	.313	74	-8	-8	25	2			-4		-0.7
1950	Chi-A	122	377	38	105	17	2	7	55	49	36	.279	.366	.390	96	-3	-2	54	2	1	0	-1	*C	0.2
1951	Chi-A	84	225	24	61	11	2	4	28	32	27	.271	.367	.391	107	2	3	34	1	0	0	-0	C	0.8
1952	Chi-A	30	63	9	16	1	1	0	7	10	10	.254	.356	.302	84	-1	-1	8	0	0	0	1	C	0.1
Total	14	1229	3468	420	917	164	31	47	417	410	311	.264	.344	.370	97	-19	-13	450	45	1		-29	*C/1O3	1.0

■ HARRY MASKREY
Maskrey, Harry H.   b: 12/21/1861, Mercer, Pa.   d: 8/17/30, Mercer, Pa.   Deb: 9/21/1882

YEAR	TM/L	G	AB	R	H	2B	3B	HR	RBI	BB	SO	AVG	OBP	SLG	PRO+	BR	/A	RC	SB	CS	SBR	FR	POS	TPR
1882	Lou-a	1	4	0	0	0	0	0	0		0	.000	.000	.000	-99	-1	-1	0				-1	/O	0.0

■ LEECH MASKREY
Maskrey, Samuel Leech   b: 2/11/1854, Mercer, Pa.   d: 4/1/22, Mercer, Pa.   BR/TR, 5'8", 150 lbs.   Deb: 5/02/1882

YEAR	TM/L	G	AB	R	H	2B	3B	HR	RBI	BB	SO	AVG	OBP	SLG	PRO+	BR	/A	RC	SB	CS	SBR	FR	POS	TPR
1882	Lou-a	76	288	30	65	14	2	0			9	.226	.249	.288	86	-6	-3	21				-0	*O/2	-0.3
1883	Lou-a	96	361	50	73	13	8	1			10	.202	.224	.291	70	-14	-10	24				9	*O/S	0.0
1884	Lou-a	105	412	48	103	13	4	0			17	.250	.281	.301	97	-3	-0	36				2	*O/3S	0.0
1885	Lou-a	109	423	54	97	8	11	1			19	.229	.269	.307	84	-7	-7	36				-3	*O/3	-1.4
1886	Lou-a	5	19	1	3	1	0	0			1	.158	.200	.211	28	-2	-2	1	0			-1	/O	-0.2
	Cin-a	27	98	7	19	3	1	0			5	.194	.240	.245	52	-5	-6	7	4			1	O/3	-0.4
	Yr	32	117	8	22	4	1	0			6	.188	.234	.239	48	-7	-7	8	4			-0		-0.6
Total	5	418	1601	190	360	52	26	2			61	.225	.256	.294	82	-37	-28	125	4			8	O/3S2	-2.3

■ CHARLIE MASON
Mason, Charles E.   b: 6/25/1853, New Orleans, La.   d: 10/21/36, Philadelphia, Pa.   TR,   Deb: 4/26/1875   M

YEAR	TM/L	G	AB	R	H	2B	3B	HR	RBI	BB	SO	AVG	OBP	SLG	PRO+	BR	/A	RC	SB	CS	SBR	FR	POS	TPR
1875	Cen-n	12	47	5	11	1	0	0			0	.234	.234	.255	75	-1	-1	3					/O1	0.0
	Was-n	8	34	2	3	0	0	0			0	.088	.088	.088	-40	-5	-4	0					/OP	-0.3
	Yr	20	81	7	14	1	0	0			0	.173	.173	.185	25	-6	-5	3						-0.3
1883	Phi-a	1	2	0	1	0	0	0			0	.500	.500	.500	206	0	0	1				-0	/O	0.0

■ DON MASON
Mason, Donald Stetson   b: 12/20/44, Boston, Mass.   BL/TR, 5'11", 160 lbs.   Deb: 4/14/66

YEAR	TM/L	G	AB	R	H	2B	3B	HR	RBI	BB	SO	AVG	OBP	SLG	PRO+	BR	/A	RC	SB	CS	SBR	FR	POS	TPR
1966	SF-N	42	25	8	3	0	0	1	1	0	2	.120	.120	.240	-3	-3	-4	1	0	1	-1	9	/2	0.5
1967	SF-N	4	3	0	0	0	0	0	0	0	0	.000	.000	.000	-99	-1	-1	0	0	0	0	1	/2	0.0
1968	SF-N	10	19	3	3	0	0	0	1	1	4	.158	.200	.158	9	-2	-2	1	1	1	-0	-1	/2S3	-0.2
1969	SF-N	104	250	43	57	4	2	0	13	36	29	.228	.325	.260	67	-10	-10	24	1	5	-3	10	23/S	0.2
1970	SF-N	46	36	4	5	0	0	0	1	5	7	.139	.244	.139	5	-5	-5	1	0	0	0	2	2	0.0
1971	SD-N	113	344	43	73	12	1	2	11	27	35	.212	.270	.270	57	-21	-18	24	6	4	-1	-12	2/3	-2.8
1972	SD-N	9	11	1	2	0	0	0	0	1	1	.182	.250	.182	26	-1	-1	1	0	0	0	-0	/2	0.0
1973	SD-N	8	8	0	0	0	0	0	0	0	2	.000	.000	.000	-99	-2	-2	0	0	0	0	1	/2	0.0
Total	8	336	696	102	143	16	3	3	27	70	80	.205	.278	.250	52	-45	-42	50	8	11	-4	8	2/3S	-2.3

■ JIM MASON
Mason, James Percy   b: 8/14/50, Mobile, Ala.   BL/TR, 6'2", 185 lbs.   Deb: 9/26/71

YEAR	TM/L	G	AB	R	H	2B	3B	HR	RBI	BB	SO	AVG	OBP	SLG	PRO+	BR	/A	RC	SB	CS	SBR	FR	POS	TPR
1971	Was-A	3	9	0	3	0	0	0	0	1	3	.333	.400	.333	116	0	0	1	0	0	0	2	/S	0.3
1972	Tex-A	46	147	10	29	3	0	0	10	9	39	.197	.248	.218	41	-11	-10	8	0	0	0	-6	S3	-1.3
1973	Tex-A	92	238	23	49	7	2	3	19	23	48	.206	.276	.290	62	-13	-12	20	0	1	-1	9	S2/3	0.7
1974	NY-A	152	440	41	110	18	6	5	37	35	87	.250	.305	.352	91	-7	-5	48	1	2	-1	-4	*S	0.1
1975	NY-A	94	223	17	34	3	2	2	16	22	49	.152	.229	.211	26	-22	-21	10	0	2	-1	-10	S/2	-2.4
1976	*NY-A	93	217	17	39	7	1	1	14	9	37	.180	.212	.235	31	-19	-19	11	0	0	0	7	S	-0.6
1977	Tor-A	22	79	10	13	3	0	0	2	7	10	.165	.233	.203	20	-9	-9	4	1	1	-0	-5	S	-1.1
	Tex-A	36	55	9	12	3	0	1	7	6	10	.218	.295	.327	69	-2	-2	6	0	0	0	7	S/3D	0.8
	Yr	58	134	19	25	6	0	1	9	13	20	.187	.259	.254	40	-11	-11	9	1	1	-0	3		-0.3
1978	Tex-A	55	105	10	20	4	0	0	3	5	17	.190	.227	.229	28	-10	-10	6	0	0	0	1	S3/2D	-0.5
1979	Mon-N	40	71	3	13	5	1	0	6	7	16	.183	.256	.282	47	-5	-4	4	0	2	-1	0	S/3	-0.2
Total	9	633	1584	140	322	53	12	12	114	124	316	.203	.262	.275	54	-98	-93	117	2	8	-4	2	S/32D	-4.2

■ GORDON MASSA
Massa, Gordon Richard "Moose" or "Duke"   b: 9/2/35, Cincinnati, Ohio   BL/TR, 6'3", 210 lbs.   Deb: 9/24/57

YEAR	TM/L	G	AB	R	H	2B	3B	HR	RBI	BB	SO	AVG	OBP	SLG	PRO+	BR	/A	RC	SB	CS	SBR	FR	POS	TPR
1957	Chi-N	6	15	2	7	1	0	0	3	4	3	.467	.579	.533	205	3	3	5	0	0	0	-3	/C	0.0
1958	Chi-N	2	2	0	0	0	0	0	0	0	2	.000	.000	.000	-99	-1	-1	0	0	0	0	0	H	0.0
Total	2	8	17	2	7	1	0	0	3	4	5	.412	.524	.471	172	2	2	5	0	0	0	-3	/C	0.0

■ RED MASSEY
Massey, Roy Hardee "Roy" or "Red"   b: 10/9/1890, Sevierville, Tenn.   d: 6/23/54, Atlanta, Ga.   BL/TR, 5'11", 170 lbs.   Deb: 4/16/18

YEAR	TM/L	G	AB	R	H	2B	3B	HR	RBI	BB	SO	AVG	OBP	SLG	PRO+	BR	/A	RC	SB	CS	SBR	FR	POS	TPR
1918	Bos-N	66	203	20	59	6	2	0	18	23	20	.291	.363	.340	120	4	5	25	1			1	O/31S	0.5

■ BILL MASSEY
Massey, William Harry "Big Bill"   b: 1/1871, Philadelphia, Pa.   d: 10/9/40, Manila, Philippines   BR, 5'11", 168 lbs.   Deb: 9/18/1894

YEAR	TM/L	G	AB	R	H	2B	3B	HR	RBI	BB	SO	AVG	OBP	SLG	PRO+	BR	/A	RC	SB	CS	SBR	FR	POS	TPR
1894	Cin-N	13	53	7	15	3	0	0	5	3	2	.283	.321	.340	59	-3	-4	6	0			-1	1/23	-0.3

■ MIKE MASSEY
Massey, William Herbert   b: 9/28/1893, Galveston, Tex.   d: 10/17/71, Shreveport, La.   BB/TR, 6', 195 lbs.   Deb: 4/12/17

YEAR	TM/L	G	AB	R	H	2B	3B	HR	RBI	BB	SO	AVG	OBP	SLG	PRO+	BR	/A	RC	SB	CS	SBR	FR	POS	TPR
1917	Bos-N	31	91	12	18	0	0	0	2	15	15	.198	.318	.198	63	-3	-3	7	2			-8	2	-1.0

■ VICTOR MATA
Mata, Victor Jose (Abreu)   b: 6/17/61, Santiago, D.R.   BR/TR, 6'1", 165 lbs.   Deb: 7/22/84

YEAR	TM/L	G	AB	R	H	2B	3B	HR	RBI	BB	SO	AVG	OBP	SLG	PRO+	BR	/A	RC	SB	CS	SBR	FR	POS	TPR
1984	NY-A	30	70	8	23	5	0	1	6	0	12	.329	.338	.443	119	1	1	10	1	1	-0	-0	O	0.0
1985	NY-A	6	7	1	1	0	0	0	0	0	0	.143	.143	.143	-22	-1	-1	0	0	0	0	-0	/O	-0.1
Total	2	36	77	9	24	5	0	1	6	0	12	.312	.321	.416	106	-0	0	10	1	1	-0	-0	/O	-0.1

■ TOMMY MATCHICK
Matchick, John Thomas   b: 9/7/43, Hazleton, Pa.   BL/TR, 6'1", 173 lbs.   Deb: 9/02/67

YEAR	TM/L	G	AB	R	H	2B	3B	HR	RBI	BB	SO	AVG	OBP	SLG	PRO+	BR	/A	RC	SB	CS	SBR	FR	POS	TPR
1967	Det-A	8	6	1	1	0	0	0	0	0	2	.167	.167	.167	-1	-1	-1	0	0	0	0	1	/S	0.0
1968	*Det-A	80	227	18	46	6	2	3	14	10	46	.203	.249	.286	60	-11	-11	16	0	2	-1	-13	S2/1	-2.5
1969	Det-A	94	298	25	72	11	2	0	32	15	51	.242	.278	.292	57	-16	-18	23	3	0	-1	-7	23/S1	-2.2
1970	Bos-A	10	14	2	1	0	0	0	0	2	2	.071	.188	.071	-24	-2	-3	0	0	1	-1	-1	/32S	-0.3
	KC-A	55	158	11	31	3	2	0	11	5	23	.196	.226	.241	29	-15	-15	7	0	0	0	13	S2/3	0.2
	Yr	65	172	13	32	3	2	0	11	7	25	.186	.222	.227	24	-18	-18	7	0	1	-1	12		-0.1
1971	Mil-A	42	114	6	25	1	0	1	7	7	23	.219	.264	.254	48	-8	-8	8	3	2	-0	1	3/2	-0.8
1972	Bal-A	3	9	0	2	0	0	0	0	0	1	.222	.222	.222	32	-1	-1	0	0	1	-1	-0	/3	-0.1
Total	6	292	826	63	178	21	6	4	64	39	148	.215	.255	.270	49	-54	-56	54	6	6	-2	-7	S/321	-5.7

■ JOE MATHES
Mathes, Joseph John   b: 7/28/1891, Milwaukee, Wis.   d: 12/21/78, St.Louis, Mo.   BB/TR, 6'0.5", 180 lbs.   Deb: 9/19/12

YEAR	TM/L	G	AB	R	H	2B	3B	HR	RBI	BB	SO	AVG	OBP	SLG	PRO+	BR	/A	RC	SB	CS	SBR	FR	POS	TPR
1912	Phi-A	4	14	0	2	0	0	0	0	0		.143	.200	.143	-2	-2	-2	0	0			-1	/3	-0.2
1914	StL-F	26	85	10	25	3	0	0	6	9	11	.294	.362	.329	94	0	-0	11	1			-4	2	-0.3
1916	Bos-N	2	0	0	0	0	0	0	0	0	0	—	—	—	—	0	0	0	0			-1	/2	0.0
Total	3	32	99	10	27	3	0	0	6	9	11	.273	.339	.303	81	-2	-2	11	1			-5	/23	-0.5

■ EDDIE MATHEWS
Mathews, Edwin Lee   b: 10/13/31, Texarkana, Tex.   BL/TR, 6'1", 190 lbs.   Deb: 4/15/52   MCH

YEAR	TM/L	G	AB	R	H	2B	3B	HR	RBI	BB	SO	AVG	OBP	SLG	PRO+	BR	/A	RC	SB	CS	SBR	FR	POS	TPR
1952	Bos-N	145	528	80	128	23	5	25	58	59	115	.242	.320	.447	114	6	8	78	6	4	-1	-10	*3	0.2

YEAR	TM/L	G	AB	R	H	2B	3B	HR	RBI	BB	SO	AVG	OBP	SLG	PRO+	BR	/A	RC	SB	CS	SBR	FR	POS	TPR
1953	Mil-N	157	579	110	175	31	8	47	135	99	83	.302	.406	.627	175	55	60	157	1	3	-2	3	*3	5.3
1954	Mil-N	138	476	96	138	21	4	40	103	113	61	.290	.428	.603	177	49	53	131	10	3	1	-2	*3O	5.1
1955	Mil-N	141	499	108	144	23	5	41	101	109	98	.289	.417	.601	175	50	54	131	3	4	-2	-4	*3	4.6
1956	Mil-N	151	552	103	150	21	2	37	95	91	86	.272	.388	.518	146	30	34	114	0	2		-12	*3	2.3
1957	*Mil-N	148	572	109	167	28	9	32	94	90	79	.292	.388	.540	157	38	44	126	3	1	0	-2	*3	4.5
1958	*Mil-N	149	546	97	137	18	1	31	77	85	85	.251	.354	.458	123	11	17	94	5	0	2	5	*3	2.4
1959	Mil-N	148	594	118	182	16	8	46	114	80	71	.306	.391	.593	172	48	55	143	2	1	0	3	*3	5.3
1960	Mil-N	153	548	108	152	19	7	39	124	111	113	.277	.401	.551	170	46	52	128	7	3	0	-13	*3	3.7
1961	Mil-N	152	572	103	175	23	6	32	91	93	95	.306	.405	.535	156	40	45	128	12	7	-1	-6	*3	3.1
1962	Mil-N	152	536	106	142	25	6	29	90	101	90	.265	.383	.496	138	28	30	106	4	2	0	2	*3/1	3.4
1963	Mil-N	158	547	82	144	27	4	23	84	124	119	.263	.400	.453	147	37	38	106	3	4	-2	13	*3O	5.1
1964	Mil-N	141	502	83	117	19	1	23	74	85	100	.233	.345	.412	112	10	9	75	2	2	-1	-4	*3/1	0.3
1965	Mil-N	156	546	77	137	23	0	32	95	73	110	.251	.342	.469	125	19	18	89	1	0	0	9	*3	2.3
1966	Atl-N	134	452	72	113	21	4	16	53	63	82	.250	.342	.420	109	7	6	67	1	1	-0	-2	*3	0.2
1967	Hou-N	101	328	39	78	13	2	10	38	48	65	.238	.337	.381	109	3	4	43	2	4	-2	-4	13	-0.6
	Det-A	36	108	14	25	3	0	6	19	15	23	.231	.336	.426	121	3	3	17	0	0	0	-2	31	0.1
1968	*Det-A	31	52	4	11	0	0	3	8	5	12	.212	.281	.385	97	-0	-0	6	0	0	0	-0	/13	0.0
Total	17	2391	8537	1509	2315	354	72	512	1453	1444	1487	.271	.378	.509	145	480	531	1738	68	39	-3	-21	*31/O	47.3

■ NELSON MATHEWS

Mathews, Nelson Elmer b: 7/21/41, Columbia, Ill. BR/TR, 6'4", 195 lbs. Deb: 9/09/60

YEAR	TM/L	G	AB	R	H	2B	3B	HR	RBI	BB	SO	AVG	OBP	SLG	PRO+	BR	/A	RC	SB	CS	SBR	FR	POS	TPR
1960	Chi-N	3	8	1	2	0	0	0	0	0	2	.250	.250	.250	38	-1	-1	1	0	0	0	0	/O	0.0
1961	Chi-N	3	9	0	1	0	0	0	0	0	2	.111	.111	.111	-40	-2	-2	0	0	0	0	0	/O	-0.1
1962	Chi-N	15	49	5	15	2	0	2	13	5	4	.306	.393	.469	126	2	2	8	3	3	-1	-1	O	0.0
1963	Chi-N	61	155	12	24	3	2	4	10	16	48	.155	.234	.277	44	-11	-12	9	3	4	-2	2	O	-1.4
1964	KC-A	157	573	58	137	27	5	14	60	43	143	.239	.293	.377	82	-13	-15	59	2	3	-1	1	*O	-2.2
1965	KC-A	67	184	17	39	7	7	2	15	24	49	.212	.303	.359	89	-3	-3	20	0	2	-1	-0	O	-0.6
Total	6	306	978	93	218	39	14	22	98	88	248	.223	.289	.359	78	-27	-29	96	8	12	-5	2	O	-4.3

■ BOBBY MATHEWS

Mathews, Robert T. b: 11/21/1851, Baltimore, Md. d: 4/17/1898, Baltimore, Md. BR/TR, 5'5.5", 140 lbs. Deb: 5/04/1871 U

YEAR	TM/L	G	AB	R	H	2B	3B	HR	RBI	BB	SO	AVG	OBP	SLG	PRO+	BR	/A	RC	SB	CS	SBR	FR	POS	TPR
1871	Kek-n	19	89	15	24	3	1	0	10	2	0	.270	.286	.326	74	-3	-3	9	2				P	0.0
1872	Bal-n	50	221	35	50	2	1	0			4	.226	.240	.244	47	-13	-15	13					*P/O3	0.0
1873	Mut-n	52	223	40	43	4	3	0			9	.193	.224	.238	36	-17	-17	12					*P/O	0.0
1874	Mut-n	65	297	47	70	8	1	0			4	.236	.246	.269	62	-12	-13	20					*P	0.0
1875	Mut-n	70	268	23	47	5	2	0			4	.175	.175	.209	31	-17	-20	10					*P	0.0
1876	NY-N	56	218	19	40	4	1	0	9	3	2	.183	.195	.211	40	-14	-10	9				-3	P/O	0.0
1877	Cin-N	15	59	5	10	0	0	0	0	1	2	.169	.183	.169	13	-6	-5	2				-2	P/OS	0.0
1879	Pro-N	43	173	25	35	2	0	1	10	7	12	.202	.233	.231	55	-8	-8	10				-5	PO/3	0.0
1881	Pro-N	16	57	6	11	1	0	0	4	5	6	.193	.258	.211	50	-3	-3	3				-2	P/O	0.0
	Bos-N	19	71	2	12	2	0	0	4	0	5	.169	.169	.197	15	-7	-6	2				-2	O/P	-0.7
	Yr	35	128	8	23	3	0	0	8	5	11	.180	.211	.203	32	-10	-9	6				-4		-0.7
1882	Bos-N	45	169	17	38	6	0	0	13	8	18	.225	.260	.260	67	-6	-6	12				-10	PO/S	0.0
1883	Phi-a	45	167	15	31	2	0	0			4	.186	.205	.198	28	-13	-15	7				-3	P/O	0.0
1884	Phi-a	49	184	26	34	5	1	0			7	.185	.215	.223	42	-11	-12	9				-2	P/O	0.0
1885	Phi-a	48	179	22	30	3	0	0			10	.168	.212	.184	26	-14	-16	7				-1	P/O	0.0
1886	Phi-a	24	88	16	21	3	0	0			3	.239	.264	.273	69	-3	-3	7	1			-0	P/O	0.0
1887	Phi-a	7	25	5	5	0	0	0			4	.200	.310	.200	46	-2	-2	2	0			1	/P	0.0
Total	5 n	256	1098	160	234	22	8	0		10	19	.213	.226	.248	47	-62	-68	65	2				P/O3	0.0
Total	10	367	1390	158	267	28	2	1	40	52	45	.192	.221	.217	42	-86	-85	69	1			-29	P/O3S	-0.7

■ JIMMY MATHISON

Mathison, James I. b: 11/1878, Baltimore, Md. d: 7/4/11, Baltimore, Md. TR, Deb: 8/29/02

YEAR	TM/L	G	AB	R	H	2B	3B	HR	RBI	BB	SO	AVG	OBP	SLG	PRO+	BR	/A	RC	SB	CS	SBR	FR	POS	TPR
1902	Bal-A	29	91	12	24	2	1	0	7		9	.264	.374	.308	88	-0	-1	12	2			-1	3/S	-0.2

■ JOHN MATIAS

Matias, John Roy b: 8/15/44, Honolulu, Hawaii BL/TL, 5'11", 170 lbs. Deb: 4/07/70

YEAR	TM/L	G	AB	R	H	2B	3B	HR	RBI	BB	SO	AVG	OBP	SLG	PRO+	BR	/A	RC	SB	CS	SBR	FR	POS	TPR
1970	Chi-A	58	117	7	22	0	2	6		3	22	.188	.215	.256	28	-11	-12	6	1	0	0	-0	O1	-1.3

■ C. V. MATTERSON

Matterson, C. V. b: Ohio Deb: 6/13/1884

YEAR	TM/L	G	AB	R	H	2B	3B	HR	RBI	BB	SO	AVG	OBP	SLG	PRO+	BR	/A	RC	SB	CS	SBR	FR	POS	TPR
1884	StL-U	1	4	0	0	0	0	0		0		.000	.000	.000	-97	-1	-1	0	0			-1	/OP	0.0

■ GARY MATTHEWS

Matthews, Gary Nathaniel b: 7/5/50, San Fernando, Cal. BR/TR, 6'2", 185 lbs. Deb: 9/06/72

YEAR	TM/L	G	AB	R	H	2B	3B	HR	RBI	BB	SO	AVG	OBP	SLG	PRO+	BR	/A	RC	SB	CS	SBR	FR	POS	TPR
1972	SF-N	20	62	11	18	1	1	4	14	7	13	.290	.362	.532	149	4	4	11	0	1	-1	-2	O	0.1
1973	SF-N	148	540	74	162	22	10	12	58	58	83	.300	.369	.444	119	18	15	90	17	5	2	-0	*O	1.1
1974	SF-N	154	561	87	161	27	6	16	82	70	69	.287	.369	.442	120	20	17	90	11	9	-2	-3	*O	0.6
1975	SF-N	116	425	67	119	22	3	12	58	65	53	.280	.378	.431	119	15	13	71	13	4	2	6	*O	1.6
1976	SF-N	156	587	79	164	28	4	20	84	75	94	.279	.362	.443	124	21	19	98	12	5	1	-12	*O	0.3
1977	Atl-N	148	555	89	157	25	5	17	64	67	90	.283	.362	.438	101	11	3	89	22	8	2	-1	*O	-0.1
1978	Atl-N	129	474	75	135	20	5	18	62	61	92	.285	.369	.462	118	20	13	78	8	7	-2	-1	*O	0.6
1979	Atl-N	156	631	97	192	34	5	27	90	60	75	.304	.365	.502	125	28	23	118	18	6	2	1	*O	2.2
1980	Atl-N	155	571	79	159	17	3	19	75	42	93	.278	.328	.419	104	4	2	76	11	3	2	-9	*O	-1.1
1981	*Phi-N	101	359	62	108	21	3	9	67	59	42	.301	.404	.451	136	22	20	71	15	2	3	-2	*O	1.9
1982	Phi-N	162	616	89	173	31	1	19	83	66	87	.281	.352	.427	114	14	12	91	21	4	4	-2	*O	1.3
1983	*Phi-N	132	446	66	115	18	2	10	50	69	81	.258	.357	.374	104	3	4	62	13	9	-2	-5	*O	-0.4
1984	*Chi-N	147	491	101	143	21	2	14	82	103	97	.291	.417	.428	126	30	24	96	17	8	0	-12	*O	0.8
1985	Chi-N	97	298	45	70	12	0	13	40	59	64	.235	.365	.406	104	8	4	47	2	0	1	-7	O	-0.4
1986	Chi-N	123	370	49	96	16	1	21	46	60	59	.259	.363	.478	121	15	12	63	3	2	-0	-15	*O	-0.4
1987	Chi-N	44	42	3	11	3	0	0	8	4	11	.262	.326	.333	72	-1	-2	4	0	0	0	0	/O	-0.1
	Sea-A	45	119	10	28	1	0	3	15	15	22	.235	.321	.319	67	-5	-6	11	0	1	-1	0	D	-0.5
Total	16	2033	7147	1083	2011	319	51	234	978	940	1125	.281	.367	.439	116	229	178	1167	183	74	11	-64	*O/D	7.5

■ BOB MATTHEWS

Matthews, Robert b: Camden, N.J. Deb: 9/25/1891

YEAR	TM/L	G	AB	R	H	2B	3B	HR	RBI	BB	SO	AVG	OBP	SLG	PRO+	BR	/A	RC	SB	CS	SBR	FR	POS	TPR
1891	Phi-a	1	3	1	1	0	0	0		0		.333	.600	.333	168	1	1	1	0			-0	/O	0.0

■ WID MATTHEWS

Matthews, Wid Curry "Matty" b: 10/20/1896, Raleigh, Ill d: 10/5/65, Hollywood, Cal. BL/TL, 5'8.5", 155 lbs. Deb: 4/18/23

YEAR	TM/L	G	AB	R	H	2B	3B	HR	RBI	BB	SO	AVG	OBP	SLG	PRO+	BR	/A	RC	SB	CS	SBR	FR	POS	TPR
1923	Phi-A	129	485	52	133	11	6	1	25	50	27	.274	.343	.328	76	-15	-16	54	16	17	-5	-8	*O	-3.9
1924	Was-A	53	169	25	51	10	4	0	13	11	4	.302	.355	.408	100	-1	-0	23	3	8	-4	5	O	-0.1
1925	Was-A	10	9	2	4	0	0	0	1	0	1	.444	.444	.444	129	0	0	2	0	0	0	-0	/O	0.0
Total	3	192	663	79	188	21	10	1	39	61	32	.284	.348	.350	83	-16	-16	79	19	25	-9	-3	O	-4.0

■ STEVE MATTHIAS

Matthias, Stephen J. b: 1860, Mitchellville, Md. 5'8", 160 lbs. Deb: 4/20/1884

YEAR	TM/L	G	AB	R	H	2B	3B	HR	RBI	BB	SO	AVG	OBP	SLG	PRO+	BR	/A	RC	SB	CS	SBR	FR	POS	TPR
1884	CP-U	37	142	24	39	7	1	0		9		.275	.299	.338	116	2	2	15	0			2	S/O	0.5

■ BOBBY MATTICK

Mattick, Robert James b: 12/5/15, Sioux City, Iowa BR/TR, 5'11", 178 lbs. Deb: 5/05/38 M

YEAR	TM/L	G	AB	R	H	2B	3B	HR	RBI	BB	SO	AVG	OBP	SLG	PRO+	BR	/A	RC	SB	CS	SBR	FR	POS	TPR
1938	Chi-N	1	1	0	0	0	0	0	1	0	0	1.000	1.000	1.000	439	0	0	1	0			0	/S	0.1
1939	Chi-N	51	178	16	51	12	1	0	23	6	19	.287	.314	.365	80	-5	-5	20	1			7	S	0.5
1940	Chi-N	128	441	30	96	15	0	0	33	19	33	.218	.250	.252	39	-37	-36	27	5			10	*S/3	-1.3
1941	Cin-N	20	60	8	11	3	0	0	7	8	7	.183	.279	.233	45	-4	-4	4	1			-1	S/32	-0.4

YEAR	TM/L	G	AB	R	H	2B	3B	HR	RBI	BB	SO	AVG	OBP	SLG	PRO+	BR	/A	RC	SB	CS	SBR	FR	POS	TPR
1942	Cin-N	6	10	0	2	1	0	0	0	0	1	.200	.200	.300	45	-1	-1	1	0			1	/S	0.1
Total	5	206	690	54	161	31	1	0	64	33	60	.233	.269	.281	52	-46	-45	53	7			17	S/32	-1.0

■ WALLY MATTICK
Mattick, Walter Joseph "Chink"   b: 3/12/1887, St.Louis, Mo.   d: 11/5/68, Los Altos, Cal.   BR/TR, 5'10", 180 lbs.   Deb: 4/11/12

YEAR	TM/L	G	AB	R	H	2B	3B	HR	RBI	BB	SO	AVG	OBP	SLG	PRO+	BR	/A	RC	SB	CS	SBR	FR	POS	TPR
1912	Chi-A	90	285	45	74	7	9	1	35	27		.260	.334	.358	101	-1	0	40	15			-3	O	-0.7
1913	Chi-A	71	207	15	39	8	1	0	11	18	16	.188	.253	.237	44	-15	-15	14	3			2	O	-1.7
1918	StL-N	8	14	0	2	0	0	0	1	2	3	.143	.333	.143	49	-1	-1	1	0			0	/O	0.0
Total	3	169	506	60	115	15	10	1	47	47	19	.227	.302	.302	77	-16	-15	54	18			-1	O	-2.4

■ MIKE MATTIMORE
Mattimore, Michael Joseph   b: 1859, Renovo, Pa.   d: 4/28/31, Butte, Mont.   BL/TL, 5'8.5", 160 lbs.   Deb: 5/03/1887

YEAR	TM/L	G	AB	R	H	2B	3B	HR	RBI	BB	SO	AVG	OBP	SLG	PRO+	BR	/A	RC	SB	CS	SBR	FR	POS	TPR
1887	NY-N	8	32	5	8	1	0	0	4	0	6	.250	.250	.281	51	-2	-2	3	1			-1	/PO	0.0
1888	Phi-a	41	142	22	38	6	5	0	12	12		.268	.333	.380	133	5	5	24	16			5	PO	0.0
1889	Phi-a	23	73	10	17	1	2	1	8	9	7	.233	.333	.342	96	-0	-0	11	6			-3	O/1P	-0.2
	KC-a	19	75	6	12	1	1	0	5	3	16	.160	.192	.200	12	-8	-9	3	0			-1	O/P	-0.9
	Yr	42	148	16	29	2	3	1	13	12	23	.196	.265	.270	53	-9	-9	13	6			-4		-1.1
1890	Bro-a	33	129	14	17	1	1	0		16		.132	.238	.155	18	-13	-12	8	11			-5	PO	0.0
Total	4	124	451	57	92	10	9	1	29	40	29	.204	.278	.273	67	-19	-18	48	34			-5	/OP1	-1.1

■ DON MATTINGLY
Mattingly, Donald Arthur   b: 4/20/61, Evansville, Ind.   BL/TL, 6', 175 lbs.   Deb: 9/08/82

YEAR	TM/L	G	AB	R	H	2B	3B	HR	RBI	BB	SO	AVG	OBP	SLG	PRO+	BR	/A	RC	SB	CS	SBR	FR	POS	TPR
1982	NY-A	7	12	0	2	0	0	0	1	0	1	.167	.167	.167	-8	-2	-2	0	0	0	0	2	/O1	0.0
1983	NY-A	91	279	34	79	15	4	4	32	21	31	.283	.336	.409	108	1	3	37	0	0	0	-7	O1/2	-0.6
1984	NY-A	153	603	91	**207**	**44**	2	23	110	41	33	**.343**	.386	.537	**159**	41	44	120	1	1	-0	12	*1O	4.6
1985	NY-A	159	652	107	211	**48**	3	35	**145**	56	41	.324	.379	.567	159	48	50	136	2	2	-1	-11	*1	2.7
1986	NY-A	162	677	117	**238**	**53**	2	31	113	53	35	.352	.399	**.573**	163	56	57	150	0	0	0	-7	*1/3D	3.8
1987	NY-A	141	569	93	186	38	2	30	115	51	38	.327	.383	.559	147	36	37	115	1	4	-2	-4	*1/D	1.7
1988	NY-A	144	599	94	186	37	0	18	88	41	29	.311	.358	.462	129	21	22	96	1	0	0	-3	*1/OD	1.0
1989	NY-A	158	631	79	191	37	2	23	113	51	30	.303	.356	.477	134	26	27	104	3	0	1	-5	*1D/O	1.3
1990	NY-A	102	394	40	101	16	0	5	42	28	20	.256	.311	.335	80	-10	-10	39	1	0	0	6	1D/O	-1.0
Total	9	1117	4416	655	1401	288	15	169	759	342	258	.317	.368	.504	140	217	227	798	9	7	-2	-18	*1/OD32	13.5

■ RALPH MATTIS
Mattis, Ralph "Matty"   b: 8/24/1890, Roxborough, Pa.   d: 9/13/60, Williamsport, Pa.   BR/TR, 5'11", 172 lbs.   Deb: 4/22/14

YEAR	TM/L	G	AB	R	H	2B	3B	HR	RBI	BB	SO	AVG	OBP	SLG	PRO+	BR	/A	RC	SB	CS	SBR	FR	POS	TPR
1914	Pit-F	36	85	14	21	4	1	0	8	9	11	.247	.326	.318	86	-1	-1	10	2			2	O	0.0

■ CLOY MATTOX
Mattox, Cloy Mitchell "Monk"   b: 11/24/02, Leesville, Va.   d: 8/3/85, Danville, Va.   BL/TR, 5'8", 168 lbs.   Deb: 9/01/29

YEAR	TM/L	G	AB	R	H	2B	3B	HR	RBI	BB	SO	AVG	OBP	SLG	PRO+	BR	/A	RC	SB	CS	SBR	FR	POS	TPR
1929	Phi-A	3	6	0	1	0	0	0	0	1	1	.167	.286	.167	19	-1	-1	0	0	0	0	-0	/C	0.0

■ JIM MATTOX
Mattox, James Powell   b: 12/17/1896, Leesville, Va.   d: 10/12/73, Myrtle Beach, S.C.   BL/TR, 5'9.5", 168 lbs.   Deb: 4/30/22

YEAR	TM/L	G	AB	R	H	2B	3B	HR	RBI	BB	SO	AVG	OBP	SLG	PRO+	BR	/A	RC	SB	CS	SBR	FR	POS	TPR
1922	Pit-N	29	51	11	15	1	1	0	3	1	3	.294	.308	.353	69	-2	-2	5	0	0	0	2	C	0.0
1923	Pit-N	22	32	4	6	1	1	0	1	0	5	.188	.235	.281	35	-3	-3	2	0	0	0	1	/C	-0.1
Total	2	51	83	15	21	2	2	0	4	1	8	.253	.279	.325	56	-5	-6	8	0	0	0	2	/C	-0.1

■ LEN MATUSZEK
Matuszek, Leonard James   b: 9/27/54, Toledo, Ohio   BL/TR, 6'2", 190 lbs.   Deb: 9/03/81

YEAR	TM/L	G	AB	R	H	2B	3B	HR	RBI	BB	SO	AVG	OBP	SLG	PRO+	BR	/A	RC	SB	CS	SBR	FR	POS	TPR
1981	Phi-N	13	11	1	3	1	0	0	1	3	1	.273	.429	.364	121	1	1	2	0	1	-1	2	/13	0.1
1982	Phi-N	25	39	1	3	1	0	0	3	1	10	.077	.122	.103	-36	-7	-7	0	0	1	-1	-2	/31	-1.0
1983	Phi-N	28	80	12	22	6	1	4	16	4	14	.275	.310	.525	129	2	2	12	0	1	-1	-1	1	0.0
1984	Phi-N	101	262	40	65	17	1	12	43	39	54	.248	.354	.458	125	10	9	43	4	3	-1	1	1/O	1.0
1985	Tor-A	62	151	23	32	6	2	2	15	11	24	.212	.265	.318	57	-9	-9	12	2	1	0	0	D/1	-0.8
	*LA-N	43	63	10	14	2	1	3	13	8	14	.222	.319	.429	111	1	1	9	0	1	-1	-1	O1/3	0.0
1986	LA-N	91	199	26	52	7	0	9	28	21	47	.261	.335	.432	118	2	4	29	2	2	-1	-1	O1	0.1
1987	LA-N	16	15	0	1	0	0	0	0	1	4	.067	.125	.067	-49	-3	-3	0	0	0	0	0	/1	-0.2
Total	7	379	820	113	192	40	5	30	119	88	168	.234	.314	.405	99	-3	-3	107	8	10	-4	2	1/OD3	-0.8

■ GENE MAUCH
Mauch, Gene William "Skip"   b: 11/18/25, Salina, Kan.   BR/TR, 5'10", 165 lbs.   Deb: 4/18/44   M

YEAR	TM/L	G	AB	R	H	2B	3B	HR	RBI	BB	SO	AVG	OBP	SLG	PRO+	BR	/A	RC	SB	CS	SBR	FR	POS	TPR
1944	Bro-N	5	15	2	2	1	0	0	2	2	3	.133	.235	.200	24	-2	-1	1	0			-2	/S	-0.2
1947	Pit-N	16	30	8	9	0	0	0	1	7	6	.300	.432	.300	95	-0	0	5	0			-2	/2S	0.0
1948	Bro-N	12	13	1	2	0	0	0	0	1	4	.154	.214	.154	1	-2	-2	1	0			1	/2S	0.0
	Chi-N	53	138	18	28	3	2	1	7	26	10	.203	.329	.275	68	-6	-5	15	1			-6	2S	-0.7
	Yr	65	151	19	30	3	2	1	7	27	14	.199	.320	.265	62	-8	-7	15	1			-5		-0.7
1949	Chi-N	72	150	15	37	6	2	1	7	21	15	.247	.339	.333	83	-4	-3	17	3			12	2S/3	1.1
1950	Bos-N	48	121	17	28	5	0	1	15	14	9	.231	.316	.298	67	-6	-5	11	1			-1	2/3S	-0.4
1951	Bos-N	19	20	5	2	0	0	0	1	7	4	.100	.333	.100	24	-2	-2	1	0	0	0	-0	S/32	0.0
1952	StL-N	7	3	0	0	0	0	0	0	1	2	.000	.250	.000	-25	-0	-0	0	0	0	0	0	/S	0.0
1956	Bos-A	7	25	4	8	0	0	0	1	3	3	.320	.393	.320	80	-0	-1	3	0	0	0	-2	/2	-0.1
1957	Bos-A	65	222	23	60	10	3	2	28	22	26	.270	.339	.369	88	-2	-3	27	1	0	0	-10	2	-0.9
Total	9	304	737	93	176	25	7	5	62	104	82	.239	.335	.312	75	-23	-23	80	6	0		-9	2/S3	-1.2

■ AL MAUL
Maul, Albert Joseph "Smiling Al"   b: 10/9/1865, Philadelphia, Pa.   d: 5/3/58, Philadelphia, Pa.   BR/TR, 6', 175 lbs.   Deb: 6/20/1884

YEAR	TM/L	G	AB	R	H	2B	3B	HR	RBI	BB	SO	AVG	OBP	SLG	PRO+	BR	/A	RC	SB	CS	SBR	FR	POS	TPR
1884	Phi-U	1	4	0	0	0	0	0		0		.000	.000	.000	-99	-1	-1	0	0			-0	/P	0.0
1887	Phi-N	16	56	15	17	2	2	1	4	15	10	.304	.451	.464	148	5	5	14	5			2	/OP1	0.6
1888	Pit-N	74	259	21	54	9	4	0	31	21	45	.208	.276	.274	84	-6	-3	23	9			1	1O/P	-0.5
1889	Pit-N	68	257	37	71	6	6	4	44	29	41	.276	.356	.393	123	4	8	43	18			11	O/P	1.6
1890	Pit-P	45	162	31	42	6	2	0	21	22	12	.259	.344	.321	88	-4	-1	20	5			4	PO/S	0.0
1891	Pit-N	47	149	15	28	2	4	0	14	20	28	.188	.284	.255	61	-7	-7	12	4			-2	O/P	-0.7
1893	Was-N	44	134	10	34	8	4	0	12	33	14	.254	.405	.373	112	3	4	21	1			1	P/O	0.0
1894	Was-N	41	124	23	30	3	3	2	20	14	11	.242	.352	.363	77	-5	-4	17	1			3	PO	0.0
1895	Was-N	22	72	9	18	5	2	0	16	6	7	.250	.308	.375	78	-3	-2	9	0			1	P/O	0.0
1896	Was-N	8	28	6	8	1	1	0	5	3	2	.286	.355	.393	99	-0	-0	4	0			-1	/P	0.0
1897	Was-N	1	1	0	0	0	0	0	0	0		.000	.000	.000	-99	-0	-0	0	0			-0	/P	0.0
	Bal-N	2	3	0	1	0	0	0	0	0		.333	.333	.333	78	-0	-0	0	0			-0	/P	0.0
	Yr	3	4	0	1	0	0	0	0	0		.250	.250	.250	34	-0	-0	0	0			0		0.0
1898	Bal-N	29	93	21	19	3	2	0	10	16		.204	.333	.280	77	-2	-2	9	1			-4	P/O	0.0
1899	Bro-N	4	11	2	3	0	0	0	0	1		.273	.333	.273	68	-0	-0	1	0			0	/P	0.0
1900	Phi-N	5	15	2	3	0	0	0	1	2		.200	.294	.200	40	-1	-1	1	0			0	/P	0.0
1901	NY-N	3	8	1	3	0	0	0	1	0		.375	.375	.375	125	0	0	1	0			1	/P	0.0
Total	15	410	1376	193	331	45	30	7	179	182	170	.241	.336	.332	93	-16	-5	176	44			16	PO/1S	1.0

■ MARK MAULDIN
Mauldin, Marshall Reese   b: 11/5/14, Atlanta, Ga.   d: 9/2/90, Union City, Ga.   BR/TR, 5'11", 170 lbs.   Deb: 9/10/34

YEAR	TM/L	G	AB	R	H	2B	3B	HR	RBI	BB	SO	AVG	OBP	SLG	PRO+	BR	/A	RC	SB	CS	SBR	FR	POS	TPR
1934	Chi-A	10	38	3	10	2	0	1	3	0	3	.263	.263	.395	66	-2	-2	4	0	0	0	-0	3	-0.1

■ CARMEN MAURO
Mauro, Carmen Louis   b: 11/10/26, St.Paul, Minn.   BL/TR, 6', 167 lbs.   Deb: 10/01/48

YEAR	TM/L	G	AB	R	H	2B	3B	HR	RBI	BB	SO	AVG	OBP	SLG	PRO+	BR	/A	RC	SB	CS	SBR	FR	POS	TPR
1948	Chi-N	3	5	2	1	0	0	1	1	2	2	.200	.429	.800	235	1	1	2	0			1	/O	0.1
1950	Chi-N	62	185	19	42	4	3	1	10	13	31	.227	.285	.297	54	-13	-12	16	3			-5	O	-1.8
1951	Chi-N	13	29	3	5	1	0	0	3	2	6	.172	.250	.207	24	-3	-3	2	0	0	0	1	/O	-0.2
1953	Bro-N	8	9	1	0	0	0	0	0	0	4	.000	.000	.000	-98	-3	-3	0	0	0	0	0	/O	-0.2
	Was-A	17	23	1	4	0	1	0	2	1	3	.174	.208	.261	27	-2	-2	1	0	0	0	1	/O	0.0

YEAR	TM/L	G	AB	R	H	2B	3B	HR	RBI	BB	SO	AVG	OBP	SLG	PRO+	BR	/A	RC	SB	CS	SBR	FR	POS	TPR
	Phi-A	64	165	14	44	4	4	0	17	19	21	.267	.342	.339	81	-3	-4	18	3	4	-2	6	O/3	0.0
	Yr	81	188	15	48	4	5	0	19	20	24	.255	.327	.330	76	-6	-6	20	3	4	-2	7		0.0
Total	4	167	416	40	96	9	8	2	33	37	65	.231	.298	.305	61	-23	-23	39	6	4		3	O/3	-2.1

■ BOB MAVIS   Mavis, Robert Henry   b: 4/8/18, Milwaukee, Wis.   BL/TR, 5'7", 160 lbs.   Deb: 9/17/49

YEAR	TM/L	G	AB	R	H	2B	3B	HR	RBI	BB	SO	AVG	OBP	SLG	PRO+	BR	/A	RC	SB	CS	SBR	FR	POS	TPR
1949	Det-A	1	0	0	0	0	0	0	0	0	0	—	—	—	—	0	0	0	0	0	0	0	R	0.0

■ DAL MAXVILL   Maxvill, Charles Dallan   b: 2/18/39, Granite City, Ill.   BR/TR, 5'11", 157 lbs.   Deb: 6/10/62   C

YEAR	TM/L	G	AB	R	H	2B	3B	HR	RBI	BB	SO	AVG	OBP	SLG	PRO+	BR	/A	RC	SB	CS	SBR	FR	POS	TPR
1962	StL-N	79	189	20	42	3	1	1	18	17	39	.222	.290	.265	46	-13	-15	15	1	2	-1	-2	S/3	-1.0
1963	StL-N	53	51	12	12	2	0	0	3	6	11	.235	.316	.275	66	-2	-2	5	0	0	0	7	S/23	0.8
1964	*StL-N	37	26	4	6	0	0	0	4	0	7	.231	.231	.231	28	-2	-3	2	1	0	0	6	2S/3O	0.6
1965	StL-N	68	89	10	12	2	2	0	10	7	15	.135	.206	.202	14	-10	-11	4	0	0	0	13	2S	0.6
1966	StL-N	134	394	25	96	14	3	0	24	37	61	.244	.312	.294	69	-15	-15	36	3	0	1	24	*S/2O	2.1
1967	*StL-N	152	476	37	108	14	4	1	41	48	66	.227	.299	.279	67	-20	-19	39	0	2	-1	3	*S/2	0.0
1968	*StL-N	151	459	51	116	8	5	1	24	52	71	.253	.330	.298	91	-4	-3	46	0	2	-1	-9	*S	0.5
1969	StL-N	132	372	27	65	10	2	2	32	44	52	.175	.264	.228	39	-30	-30	23	1	1	-0	21	*S	0.7
1970	StL-N	152	399	35	80	5	2	0	28	51	56	.201	.291	.223	39	-33	-34	29	0	0	0	38	*S2	2.3
1971	StL-N	142	356	31	80	10	1	0	24	43	45	.225	.310	.258	60	-16	-18	28	1	2	-1	29	*S	3.1
1972	StL-N	105	276	22	61	6	1	1	23	31	47	.221	.300	.261	61	-14	-13	21	0	1	-1	9	S2	0.8
	*Oak-A	27	36	2	9	1	0	0	1	1	11	.250	.270	.278	67	-2	-1	3	0	1	-1	4	2/S	0.4
1973	Oak-A	29	19	0	4	0	0	0	1	1	3	.211	.250	.211	33	-2	-2	1	0	0	0	4	S2/3	0.5
	Pit-N	74	217	19	41	4	3	0	17	22	40	.189	.264	.235	40	-18	-17	14	0	0	0	4	S	-0.2
1974	Pit-N	8	22	3	4	0	0	0	0	2	4	.182	.250	.182	23	-2	-2	1	0	0	0	1	/S	0.0
	*Oak-A	60	52	3	10	0	0	0	2	8	10	.192	.300	.192	47	-3	-3	4	0	0	0	9	2S/3	0.9
1975	Oak-A	20	10	1	2	0	0	0	0	0	0	.200	.200	.200	14	-1	-1	0	0	0	0	2	S/2	0.3
Total	14	1423	3443	302	748	79	24	6	252	370	538	.217	.295	.259	57	-186	-190	270	7	11	-5	161	*S2/3O	12.4

■ CHARLIE MAXWELL   Maxwell, Charles Richard "Smokey"   b: 4/8/27, Lawton, Mich.   BL/TL, 5'11", 185 lbs.   Deb: 9/20/50

YEAR	TM/L	G	AB	R	H	2B	3B	HR	RBI	BB	SO	AVG	OBP	SLG	PRO+	BR	/A	RC	SB	CS	SBR	FR	POS	TPR
1950	Bos-A	3	8	1	0	0	0	0	0	1	3	.000	.111	.000	-63	-2	-2	0	0	0	0	0	/O	-0.1
1951	Bos-A	49	80	8	15	1	0	3	12	9	18	.188	.270	.313	52	-5	-6	7	0	1	-1	-2	O	-0.8
1952	Bos-A	8	15	0	1	1	0	0	0	3	11	.067	.222	.133	0	-2	-2	1	0	0	0	2	/1O	-0.3
1954	Bos-A	74	104	9	26	4	1	0	5	12	21	.250	.328	.308	67	-3	-5	11	3	0	1	-2	O	-0.6
1955	Bal-A	4	4	0	0	0	0	0	0	0	1	.000	.000	.000	-99	-1	-1	0	0	0	0	0	H	0.0
	Det-A	55	109	19	29	7	1	7	18	8	20	.266	.328	.541	134	4	4	19	0	0	0	3	O/1	0.5
	Yr	59	113	19	29	7	1	7	18	8	21	.257	.317	.522	126	3	3	19	0	0	0	3		0.5
1956	Det-A	141	500	96	163	14	3	28	87	79	74	.326	.420	.534	150	38	37	118	1	1	-0	6	*O	3.5
1957	Det-A	138	492	75	136	23	4	24	82	76	84	.276	.379	.482	130	24	22	94	3	2	-0	9	*O	2.3
1958	Det-A	131	397	56	108	14	4	13	65	64	54	.272	.373	.426	111	12	8	68	6	1	1	-5	*O1	-0.3
1959	Det-A	145	518	81	130	12	2	31	95	81	91	.251	.359	.461	117	17	14	89	0	2	-1	7	*O	1.2
1960	Det-A	134	482	70	114	16	5	24	81	58	75	.237	.326	.440	102	2	1	73	5	0	2	5	*O	0.3
1961	Det-A	79	131	11	30	4	2	5	18	20	24	.229	.336	.405	94	-1	-1	19	0	0	0	1	O	0.0
1962	Det-A	30	67	5	13	2	0	1	9	8	10	.194	.280	.269	47	-5	-5	5	0	0	0	-1	O/1	-0.6
	Chi-A	69	206	30	61	8	3	9	43	34	32	.296	.396	.495	139	12	12	42	0	0	0	-2	O/1	0.8
	Yr	99	273	35	74	10	3	10	52	42	42	.271	.368	.440	115	7	7	46	0	0	0	-3		0.2
1963	Chi-A	71	130	17	30	4	2	3	17	31	27	.231	.379	.362	111	3	3	20	0	0	0	-4	O1	-0.1
1964	Chi-A	2	2	0	0	0	0	0	0	0	0	.000	.000	.000	-99	-1	-1	0	0	0	0	0	H	0.0
Total	14	1133	3245	478	856	110	26	148	532	484	545	.264	.363	.451	116	92	78	566	18	7	1	18	O/1	6.1

■ CARLOS MAY   May, Carlos   b: 5/17/48, Birmingham, Ala.   BL/TR, 5'11", 200 lbs.   Deb: 9/06/68

YEAR	TM/L	G	AB	R	H	2B	3B	HR	RBI	BB	SO	AVG	OBP	SLG	PRO+	BR	/A	RC	SB	CS	SBR	FR	POS	TPR
1968	Chi-A	17	67	4	12	1	0	0	3	3	15	.179	.214	.194	24	-6	-6	3	0	0	0	-3	O	-1.1
1969	Chi-A	100	367	62	103	18	2	18	62	58	66	.281	.387	.488	137	22	20	69	1	4	-2	-3	*O	1.3
1970	Chi-A	150	555	83	158	28	4	12	68	79	96	.285	.377	.414	114	16	13	84	12	5	1	-6	*O/1	0.1
1971	Chi-A	141	500	64	147	21	7	7	70	62	61	.294	.379	.406	119	16	14	77	16	7	1	-5	*1/O	0.3
1972	Chi-A	148	523	83	161	26	3	12	68	79	70	.308	.408	.438	149	37	36	96	23	14	-2	-6	*O/1	2.7
1973	Chi-A	149	553	62	148	20	0	20	96	53	73	.268	.337	.412	106	7	5	75	8	6	-1	-2	DO/1	0.0
1974	Chi-A	149	551	66	137	19	2	8	58	46	76	.249	.308	.334	82	-11	-13	56	8	9	-3	-2	*OD	-2.1
1975	Chi-A	128	454	55	123	19	2	8	53	67	46	.271	.375	.374	111	10	9	66	12	7	-1	-0	1OD	0.4
1976	Chi-A	20	63	7	11	2	0	0	3	9	5	.175	.278	.206	43	-4	-4	5	4	0	1	-1	D/O	-0.3
	*NY-A	87	288	38	80	11	2	3	40	34	32	.278	.364	.361	114	6	6	39	1	1	-0	-1	D/O1	0.5
	Yr	107	351	45	91	13	2	3	43	43	37	.259	.348	.333	101	2	2	44	5	1	1	-1		0.2
1977	NY-A	65	181	21	41	7	1	2	16	17	24	.227	.296	.309	66	-9	-8	16	0	0	0	-0	D/O	-0.7
	Cal-A	11	18	0	6	0	0	0	1	5	1	.333	.478	.333	131	1	1	3	0	0	0	0	/1D	0.1
	Yr	76	199	21	47	7	1	2	17	22	25	.236	.315	.312	73	-7	-7	19	0	0	0	0		-0.6
Total	10	1165	4120	545	1127	172	23	90	536	512	565	.274	.360	.392	111	85	73	589	85	53	-6	-28	OD1	1.2

■ DAVE MAY   May, David La France   b: 12/23/43, New Castle, Del.   BL/TR, 5'10.5", 186 lbs.   Deb: 7/28/67

YEAR	TM/L	G	AB	R	H	2B	3B	HR	RBI	BB	SO	AVG	OBP	SLG	PRO+	BR	/A	RC	SB	CS	SBR	FR	POS	TPR
1967	Bal-A	36	85	12	20	1	1	1	7	6	13	.235	.286	.306	75	-3	-3	8	0	0	0	-1	O	-0.4
1968	Bal-A	84	152	15	29	6	3	0	7	19	27	.191	.285	.270	69	-5	-5	11	3	3	-1	-2	O	-1.1
1969	*Bal-A	78	120	8	29	6	0	3	10	9	23	.242	.305	.367	86	-2	-2	12	2	1	0	2	O	-0.1
1970	Bal-A	25	31	6	6	0	1	1	6	4	4	.194	.286	.355	75	-1	-1	2	0	0	0	-1	/O	-0.2
	Mil-A	101	342	36	82	8	1	7	31	44	56	.240	.330	.330	82	-7	-8	37	8	6	-1	15	O	0.2
	Yr	126	373	42	88	8	2	8	37	48	60	.236	.326	.332	81	-8	-9	40	8	6	-1	15		0.0
1971	Mil-A	144	501	74	139	20	3	16	65	50	59	.277	.347	.425	119	11	12	70	15	9	-1	6	*O	1.3
1972	Mil-A	143	500	49	119	20	2	9	45	47	56	.238	.307	.340	94	-5	-4	49	11	13	-5	10	*O	-0.1
1973	Mil-A	156	624	96	189	23	4	25	93	44	78	.303	.354	.473	134	24	25	100	6	7	-2	1	*O/D	2.0
1974	Mil-A	135	477	56	108	15	1	10	42	28	73	.226	.274	.325	72	-18	-18	41	4	3	-1	-14	*O/D	-3.7
1975	Atl-N	82	203	28	56	8	0	12	40	25	27	.276	.361	.493	130	9	8	36	1	1	-0	-1	O	0.5
1976	Atl-N	105	214	27	46	5	3	3	23	26	31	.215	.303	.308	69	-7	-9	21	5	1	1	0	O	-0.9
1977	Tex-A	120	340	46	82	14	1	7	42	32	43	.241	.314	.350	80	-9	-9	38	4	3	-1	-7	*O/D	-2.0
1978	Mil-A	39	77	9	15	4	0	2	11	9	10	.195	.284	.325	74	-3	-3	7	0	0	0	1	O/D	-0.1
	Pit-N	5	4	0	0	0	0	0	0	1	1	.000	.200	.000	-38	-1	-1	0	1	0	0	0	H	0.0
Total	12	1253	3670	462	920	130	20	96	422	344	501	.251	.320	.375	97	-17	-17	435	60	47	-10	9	*O/D	-4.6

■ DERRICK MAY   May, Derrick Brant   b: 7/14/68, Rochester, N.Y.   BL/TR, 6'4", 210 lbs.   Deb: 9/06/90

YEAR	TM/L	G	AB	R	H	2B	3B	HR	RBI	BB	SO	AVG	OBP	SLG	PRO+	BR	/A	RC	SB	CS	SBR	FR	POS	TPR
1990	Chi-N	17	61	8	15	3	0	1	11	2	7	.246	.270	.344	62	-3	-3	6	1	0	0	0	O	-0.3

■ JERRY MAY   May, Jerry Lee   b: 12/14/43, Staunton, Va.   BR/TR, 6'2", 190 lbs.   Deb: 9/19/64

YEAR	TM/L	G	AB	R	H	2B	3B	HR	RBI	BB	SO	AVG	OBP	SLG	PRO+	BR	/A	RC	SB	CS	SBR	FR	POS	TPR
1964	Pit-N	11	31	1	8	0	0	0	3	3	9	.258	.324	.258	66	-1	-1	3	0	0	0	5	C	0.4
1965	Pit-N	4	2	0	1	0	0	0	1	0	0	.500	.500	.500	182	0	0	1	0	0	0	-0	/C	0.0
1966	Pit-N	42	52	6	13	4	0	1	2	2	15	.250	.291	.385	86	-1	-1	6	0	1	-1	9	C	0.8
1967	Pit-N	110	325	23	88	13	2	3	22	36	55	.271	.349	.351	100	1	1	37	0	0	0	-1	*C	0.7
1968	Pit-N	137	416	26	91	15	2	1	33	41	48	.219	.293	.272	72	-14	-13	33	0	0	0	3	*C	-0.5
1969	Pit-N	62	190	21	44	8	0	7	23	9	53	.232	.274	.384	84	-5	-5	20	1	1	-0	-5	C	-0.6
1970	Pit-N	51	139	13	29	4	2	1	16	21	25	.209	.317	.288	65	-7	-6	13	0	0	0	13	C	0.8

YEAR	TM/L	G	AB	R	H	2B	3B	HR	RBI	BB	SO	AVG	OBP	SLG	PRO+	BR	/A	RC	SB	CS	SBR	FR	POS	TPR
1971	KC-A	71	218	16	55	13	2	1	24	27	37	.252	.335	.344	93	-2	-1	25	0	0	0	-0	C	0.2
1972	KC-A	53	116	10	22	5	1	1	4	14	13	.190	.277	.276	65	-5	-5	9	0	0	0	-1	C	-0.5
1973	KC-A	11	30	4	4	1	1	0	2	3	5	.133	.235	.233	30	-3	-3	2	0	0	0	-1	C	-0.3
	NY-N	4	8	0	2	0	0	0	0	1	1	.250	.333	.250	65	-0	-0	1	0	0	0	-1	/C	0.0
Total	10	556	1527	120	357	63	10	15	130	157	293	.234	.310	.318	81	-36	-35	148	1	2	-1	20	C	1.0

■ LEE MAY
May, Lee Andrew   b: 3/23/43, Birmingham, Ala.   BR/TR, 6'3", 195 lbs.   Deb: 9/01/65   C

YEAR	TM/L	G	AB	R	H	2B	3B	HR	RBI	BB	SO	AVG	OBP	SLG	PRO+	BR	/A	RC	SB	CS	SBR	FR	POS	TPR
1965	Cin-N	5	4	1	0	0	0	0	0	0	1	.000	.000	.000	-94	-1	-1	0	0	0	0	0	H	0.0
1966	Cin-N	25	75	14	25	5	1	2	10	0	14	.333	.333	.507	119	3	2	12	0	1	-1	-1	1	0.0
1967	Cin-N	127	438	54	116	29	2	12	57	19	80	.265	.310	.422	97	3	-2	53	4	8	-4	1	1O	-1.1
1968	Cin-N	146	559	78	162	32	1	22	80	34	100	.290	.337	.469	132	25	22	79	4	7	-3	1	*1O	1.5
1969	Cin-N	158	607	85	169	32	3	38	110	45	142	.278	.334	.529	132	28	24	104	5	4	-1	1	*1/O	1.1
1970	*Cin-N	153	605	78	153	34	2	34	94	38	125	.253	.299	.484	106	2	1	81	1	1	-0	0	*1	-1.1
1971	Cin-N	147	553	85	154	17	3	39	98	42	135	.278	.334	.532	145	27	28	96	3	0	1	-7	*1	1.2
1972	Hou-N	148	592	87	168	31	2	29	98	52	145	.284	.344	.490	137	25	26	97	3	1	0	-2	*1	1.5
1973	Hou-N	148	545	65	147	24	3	28	105	34	122	.270	.315	.479	117	10	10	78	1	1	-0	-3	*1	0.0
1974	Hou-N	152	556	59	149	26	0	24	85	17	97	.268	.298	.444	110	1	3	71	1	0	0	1	*1	-0.1
1975	Bal-A	146	580	67	152	28	3	20	99	36	91	.262	.311	.424	113	2	7	68	1	2	-1	3	*1/D	0.0
1976	Bal-A	148	530	61	137	17	4	25	**109**	41	104	.258	.315	.447	130	12	16	73	4	1	1	0	1D	1.2
1977	Bal-A	150	585	75	148	16	2	27	99	38	119	.253	.299	.426	101	-6	-6	68	2	2	-1	-7	*1D	-1.4
1978	Bal-A	148	556	56	137	16	1	25	80	31	110	.246	.287	.414	101	-6	-2	61	5	2	0	-0	*D/1	-0.1
1979	*Bal-A	124	456	59	116	15	0	19	69	28	100	.254	.299	.412	93	-8	-6	50	3	4	-2	-1	*D/1	-0.7
1980	Bal-A	78	222	20	54	10	2	7	31	15	53	.243	.291	.401	88	-4	-4	23	2	0	1	-0	D/1	-0.4
1981	*KC-A	26	55	3	16	3	0	0	8	3	14	.291	.328	.345	95	-0	-0	5	0	1	-1	-1	/1D	-0.1
1982	KC-A	42	91	12	28	5	2	3	12	14	18	.308	.400	.505	147	6	6	20	0	0	0	-2	1/D	0.3
Total	18	2071	7609	959	2031	340	31	354	1244	487	1570	.267	.315	.459	116	117	129	1039	39	35	-9	-17	*1D/O	1.8

■ PINKY MAY
May, Merrill Glend   b: 1/18/11, Laconia, Ind.   BR/TR, 5'11.5", 165 lbs.   Deb: 4/21/39

YEAR	TM/L	G	AB	R	H	2B	3B	HR	RBI	BB	SO	AVG	OBP	SLG	PRO+	BR	/A	RC	SB	CS	SBR	FR	POS	TPR
1939	Phi-N	135	464	49	133	27	3	2	62	41	20	.287	.346	.371	95	-4	-3	59	4			8	*3	0.9
1940	Phi-N	136	501	59	147	24	2	1	48	58	33	.293	.371	.355	105	3	6	69	2			13	*3/S	1.7
1941	Phi-N	142	490	46	131	17	4	0	39	55	30	.267	.344	.318	91	-7	-4	54	2			**25**	*3	2.2
1942	Phi-N	115	345	25	82	15	0	0	18	51	17	.238	.338	.281	86	-6	-4	36	3			17	*3	1.4
1943	Phi-N	137	415	31	117	19	2	1	48	56	21	.282	.369	.345	111	6	7	53	2			11	*3	1.9
Total	5	665	2215	210	610	102	11	4	215	261	121	.275	.354	.337	98	-8	2	270	13			74	3/S	8.1

■ MILT MAY
May, Milton Scott   b: 8/1/50, Gary, Ind.   BL/TR, 6', 190 lbs.   Deb: 9/08/70   C

YEAR	TM/L	G	AB	R	H	2B	3B	HR	RBI	BB	SO	AVG	OBP	SLG	PRO+	BR	/A	RC	SB	CS	SBR	FR	POS	TPR
1970	Pit-N	5	4	1	2	1	0	0	2	0	0	.500	.600	.750	265	1	1	2	0	0	0	0	H	0.1
1971	*Pit-N	49	126	15	35	1	0	6	25	9	16	.278	.326	.429	113	2	2	16	0	0	0	3	C	0.6
1972	*Pit-N	57	139	12	39	10	0	0	14	10	13	.281	.329	.353	96	-1	-1	16	0	0	0	4	C	0.6
1973	Pit-N	101	283	29	76	8	1	7	31	34	26	.269	.351	.402	105	1	2	36	0	1	-1	-7	C	0.0
1974	Hou-N	127	405	47	117	17	4	7	54	39	33	.289	.353	.402	116	6	8	57	0	1	-1	2	*C	1.4
1975	Hou-N	111	386	29	93	15	1	4	52	26	41	.241	.289	.316	73	-17	-14	35	1	2	-1	2	*C	-0.8
1976	Det-A	6	25	2	7	1	0	0	1	0	1	.280	.280	.320	73	-1	-1	2	0	0	0	1	/C	0.0
1977	Det-A	115	397	32	99	9	3	12	46	26	31	.249	.296	.378	78	-11	-13	42	0	0	0	-6	*C	-1.5
1978	Det-A	105	352	24	88	9	0	10	37	27	26	.250	.307	.361	85	-6	-8	37	0	0	0	1	C	-0.3
1979	Det-A	6	11	1	3	2	0	0	3	1	1	.273	.333	.455	107	0	0	1	0	0	0	1	/C	0.1
	Chi-A	65	202	23	51	13	0	7	28	14	27	.252	.307	.421	94	-2	-2	26	0	0	0	2	C	0.2
	Yr	71	213	24	54	15	0	7	31	15	28	.254	.309	.423	95	-2	-2	28	0	0	0	3		0.3
1980	SF-N	111	358	27	93	16	2	6	50	25	40	.260	.310	.366	90	-6	-5	38	0	1	-1	-5	*C	-0.8
1981	SF-N	97	316	20	98	17	0	2	33	34	29	.310	.377	.383	118	8	8	44	1	4	-2	-1	C	0.7
1982	SF-N	114	395	29	104	19	0	9	39	28	38	.263	.312	.380	93	-5	-4	47	0	1	-1	-2	*C	-0.5
1983	SF-N	66	186	18	46	6	0	6	20	21	23	.247	.324	.376	96	-2	-1	21	2	2	-1	-2	C	-0.1
	Pit-N	7	12	0	3	0	0	0	0	1	1	.250	.308	.250	55	-1	-1	1	0	0	0	2	/C	0.1
	Yr	73	198	18	49	6	0	6	20	22	24	.247	.323	.369	94	-2	-2	23	2	2	-1	-1		0.0
1984	Pit-N	50	96	4	17	3	0	1	8	10	15	.177	.255	.240	40	-8	-8	6	0	1	-1	4	C	-0.2
Total	15	1192	3693	313	971	147	11	77	443	305	361	.263	.321	.371	93	-41	-37	426	4	13	-7	0	*C	-0.4

■ JOHN MAYBERRY
Mayberry, John Claiborn   b: 2/18/49, Detroit, Mich.   BL/TL, 6'3", 215 lbs.   Deb: 9/10/68   C

YEAR	TM/L	G	AB	R	H	2B	3B	HR	RBI	BB	SO	AVG	OBP	SLG	PRO+	BR	/A	RC	SB	CS	SBR	FR	POS	TPR
1968	Hou-N	4	9	0	0	0	0	0	0	0	2	.000	.100	.000	-69	-2	-2	0	0	0	0	-0	/1	-0.2
1969	Hou-N	5	5	0	0	0	0	0	0	0	1	.000	.200	.000	-41	-1	-1	0	0	0	0	0	H	0.0
1970	Hou-N	50	148	23	32	3	2	5	14	21	33	.216	.322	.365	87	-3	-3	17	1	1	-0	3	1	-0.3
1971	Hou-N	46	137	16	25	0	1	7	14	13	32	.182	.263	.350	74	-5	-5	13	0	0	0	-3	1	-1.0
1972	KC-A	149	503	65	150	24	3	25	100	78	74	.298	.396	.507	168	43	43	101	0	2	-1	-0	*1	3.1
1973	KC-A	152	510	87	142	20	2	26	100	**122**	79	.278	**.420**	.478	141	41	36	113	3	0	1	-5	*1/D	2.3
1974	KC-A	126	427	63	100	13	1	22	69	77	72	.234	.359	.424	118	15	12	70	4	2	0	-2	*1D	0.5
1975	KC-A	156	554	95	161	38	1	34	106	**119**	73	.291	.419	.547	**167**	**56**	54	135	5	3	-0	3	*1D	4.9
1976	*KC-A	161	594	76	138	22	2	13	95	82	73	.232	.327	.342	95	-1	-2	70	3	2	-0	-3	*1/D	-1.3
1977	*KC-A	153	543	73	125	22	1	23	82	83	86	.230	.340	.401	100	2	1	76	1	3	-2	-6	*1/D	-1.3
1978	Tor-A	152	515	51	129	15	2	22	70	60	57	.250	.333	.416	107	6	5	71	1	2	-1	-15	*1/D	-1.7
1979	Tor-A	137	464	61	127	22	1	21	74	69	60	.274	.374	.462	122	17	16	82	1	1	-0	-9	*1	0.0
1980	Tor-A	149	501	62	124	19	2	30	82	77	80	.248	.351	.473	118	16	13	86	0	0	0	-4	*1/D	0.2
1981	Tor-A	94	290	34	72	6	1	17	43	44	45	.248	.363	.452	125	13	11	49	1	1	-0	-6	1D	0.2
1982	Tor-A	17	33	7	9	0	0	2	3	7	5	.273	.415	.455	127	2	2	7	0	0	0	-0	D/1	0.1
	NY-A	69	215	20	45	7	0	8	27	28	38	.209	.315	.353	84	-5	-4	24	0	0	0	-4	1/D	-0.9
	Yr	86	248	27	54	7	0	10	30	35	43	.218	.329	.367	90	-3	-3	31	0	0	0	-4		-0.8
Total	15	1620	5447	733	1379	211	19	255	879	881	810	.253	.363	.439	122	195	177	913	20	17	-4	-50	*1/D	4.4

■ LEE MAYE
Maye, Arthur Lee   b: 12/11/34, Tuscaloosa, Ala.   BL/TR, 6'2", 190 lbs.   Deb: 7/17/59

YEAR	TM/L	G	AB	R	H	2B	3B	HR	RBI	BB	SO	AVG	OBP	SLG	PRO+	BR	/A	RC	SB	CS	SBR	FR	POS	TPR
1959	Mil-N	51	140	17	42	5	1	4	16	7	26	.300	.338	.436	114	1	2	20	2	2	-1	2	O	0.3
1960	Mil-N	41	83	14	25	6	0	0	2	7	21	.301	.363	.373	110	0	1	12	5	0	2	-2	O	0.1
1961	Mil-N	110	373	68	101	11	5	14	41	36	50	.271	.340	.440	112	2	5	60	10	1	2	-4	O	0.0
1962	Mil-N	99	349	40	85	10	0	10	41	25	58	.244	.296	.358	77	-13	-12	39	9	3	1	5	O	-1.0
1963	Mil-N	124	442	67	120	22	7	11	34	36	54	.271	.331	.448	118	9	10	65	14	2	3	5	*O	1.2
1964	Mil-N	153	588	96	179	**44**	5	10	74	34	54	.304	.343	.447	121	16	16	86	5	10	-5	5	*O/3	1.2
1965	Mil-N	15	53	8	16	2	0	2	7	2	6	.302	.339	.453	120	1	1	8	0	0	0	1	O	0.0
	Hou-N	108	415	38	104	17	7	3	36	20	37	.251	.287	.347	83	-13	-10	40	1	5	-3	-2	*O	-1.8
	Yr	123	468	46	120	19	7	5	43	22	43	.256	.293	.359	88	-11	-8	48	1	5	-3	-1		-1.6
1966	Hou-N	115	358	38	103	12	4	9	36	20	26	.288	.325	.419	113	2	5	47	4	3	-1	-6	O	-0.4
1967	Cle-A	115	297	43	77	20	4	9	27	26	47	.259	.321	.444	123	8	8	43	3	3	-1	-6	O/2	-0.1
1968	Cle-A	109	299	20	84	13	2	4	26	15	24	.281	.317	.324	112	3	3	36	0	0	0	-2	O/1	-0.1
1969	Cle-A	43	108	9	27	5	0	1	15	8	15	.250	.308	.324	74	-3	-4	11	1	0	0	0	O	-0.3
	Was-A	71	238	41	69	9	3	9	26	20	25	.290	.345	.466	132	7	9	35	1	3	-2	-7	O	-0.1
	Yr	114	346	50	96	14	3	10	41	28	40	.277	.333	.422	112	4	9	46	2	3	-1	-7		-0.4
1970	Was-A	96	255	28	67	12	1	7	30	21	32	.263	.321	.400	103	-1	0	33	4	2	0	-8	O/3	-1.1

YEAR	TM/L	G	AB	R	H	2B	3B	HR	RBI	BB	SO	AVG	OBP	SLG	PRO+	BR	/A	RC	SB	CS	SBR	FR	POS	TPR
	Chi-A	6	6	0	1	0	0	0	1	0	1	.167	.167	.167	-8	-1	-1	0	0	0	0	0	H	0.0
	Yr	102	261	28	68	12	1	7	31	21	33	.261	.318	.395	100	-2	-1	33	4	2	0	-8		-1.1
1971	Chi-A	32	44	6	9	2	0	1	7	5	7	.205	.286	.318	69	-2	-2	4	0	0	0	0	O	-0.1
Total	13	1288	4048	533	1109	190	39	94	419	282	481	.274	.324	.410	108	17	32	539	59	34	-3	-18	*O/312	-2.0

■ **ED MAYER**   Mayer, Edward H.   b: 8/16/1866, Marshall, Ill.   d: 5/18/13, Chicago, Ill.   5'8.5", 155 lbs.   Deb: 4/19/1890

YEAR	TM/L	G	AB	R	H	2B	3B	HR	RBI	BB	SO	AVG	OBP	SLG	PRO+	BR	/A	RC	SB	CS	SBR	FR	POS	TPR
1890	Phi-N	117	484	49	117	25	5	1	70	22	36	.242	.286	.320	77	-14	-16	51	20			-7	*3	-1.5
1891	Phi-N	68	268	24	50	2	4	0	31	14	29	.187	.238	.224	35	-21	-22	16	7			-6	3O/S2	-2.5
Total	2	185	752	73	167	27	9	1	101	36	65	.222	.269	.286	62	-36	-38	68	27			-13	3/OS2	-4.0

■ **SAM MAYER**   Mayer, Samuel Frankel (b: Samuel Frankel Erskine)   b: 2/28/1893, Atlanta, Ga.   d: 7/1/62, Atlanta, Ga.   BR/TL, 5'10", 164 lbs.   Deb: 9/14/15

YEAR	TM/L	G	AB	R	H	2B	3B	HR	RBI	BB	SO	AVG	OBP	SLG	PRO+	BR	/A	RC	SB	CS	SBR	FR	POS	TPR
1915	Was-A	11	29	5	7	0	0	1	4	4	2	.241	.333	.345	102	0	0	3	1	2	-1	0	/OP1	0.0

■ **WALLY MAYER**   Mayer, Walter A.   b: 7/8/1890, Cincinnati, Ohio   d: 11/18/51, Minneapolis, Minn.   BR/TR, 5'11", 168 lbs.   Deb: 9/28/11

YEAR	TM/L	G	AB	R	H	2B	3B	HR	RBI	BB	SO	AVG	OBP	SLG	PRO+	BR	/A	RC	SB	CS	SBR	FR	POS	TPR
1911	Chi-A	1	3	0	0	0	0	0	0	0	2	.000	.400	.000	16	-0	-0	0	0			-0	/C	0.0
1912	Chi-A	9	9	1	0	0	0	0	0	0	1	.000	.100	.000	-73	-2	-2	0	0			0	/C	0.0
1914	Chi-A	40	85	7	14	3	1	0	5	14	23	.165	.290	.224	55	-4	-4	6	1	1	-0	5	C/3	0.3
1915	Chi-A	22	54	3	12	3	1	0	5	5	8	.222	.288	.315	78	-1	-2	5	0	2	-1	-1	C	-0.1
1917	Bos-A	4	12	2	2	0	0	0	0	5	2	.167	.412	.167	78	0	1	0	0			2	/C	0.2
1918	Bos-A	26	49	7	11	4	0	0	5	7	7	.224	.321	.306	91	-1	-0	5	0			-0	C	0.1
1919	StL-A	30	62	2	14	4	1	0	5	8	11	.226	.314	.323	77	-2	-2	7	0			6	C	0.5
Total	7	132	274	22	53	14	3	0	20	42	51	.193	.303	.266	68	-10	-10	23	1	3		11	C/3	1.0

■ **PADDY MAYES**   Mayes, Adair Bushyhead   b: 3/17/1885, Locust Grove, Okla   d: 5/28/62, Fayetteville, Ark.   BL/TR, 5'11", 160 lbs.   Deb: 6/11/11

YEAR	TM/L	G	AB	R	H	2B	3B	HR	RBI	BB	SO	AVG	OBP	SLG	PRO+	BR	/A	RC	SB	CS	SBR	FR	POS	TPR
1911	Phi-N	5	5	1	0	0	0	0	0	1	2	.000	.286	.000	-17	-1	-1	0	0			-0	/O	0.0

■ **BUSTER MAYNARD**   Maynard, James Walter   b: 3/25/13, Henderson, S.C.   d: 9/7/77, Durham, N.C.   BR/TR, 5'11", 170 lbs.   Deb: 9/17/40

YEAR	TM/L	G	AB	R	H	2B	3B	HR	RBI	BB	SO	AVG	OBP	SLG	PRO+	BR	/A	RC	SB	CS	SBR	FR	POS	TPR
1940	NY-N	7	29	6	8	2	2	1	2	2	6	.276	.323	.586	145	2	2	6	0			-1	/O	0.0
1942	NY-N	89	190	17	47	4	1	4	32	19	19	.247	.319	.342	93	-2	-2	20	3			10	O3/2	0.7
1943	NY-N	121	393	43	81	8	2	9	32	24	27	.206	.252	.305	60	-21	-21	30	3			-4	O3	-3.0
1946	NY-N	7	4	2	0	0	0	0	0	1	1	.000	.200	.000	-41	-1	-1	0	0			0	/O	0.0
Total	4	224	616	68	136	14	5	14	66	46	53	.221	.276	.328	74	-22	-22	56	6			5	O/32	-2.3

■ **CHICK MAYNARD**   Maynard, Le Roy Evans   b: 11/2/1896, Turners Falls, Mass   d: 1/31/57, Bangor, Maine   TR, 5'9", 150 lbs.   Deb: 6/27/22

YEAR	TM/L	G	AB	R	H	2B	3B	HR	RBI	BB	SO	AVG	OBP	SLG	PRO+	BR	/A	RC	SB	CS	SBR	FR	POS	TPR
1922	Bos-A	12	24	1	3	0	0	0	3	2		.125	.222	.125	-8	-4	-4	1	0	1	-1	-2	S	-0.4

■ **BRENT MAYNE**   Mayne, Brent Danem   b: 4/19/68, Loma Linda, Cal.   BL/TR, 6'1", 195 lbs.   Deb: 9/18/90

YEAR	TM/L	G	AB	R	H	2B	3B	HR	RBI	BB	SO	AVG	OBP	SLG	PRO+	BR	/A	RC	SB	CS	SBR	FR	POS	TPR
1990	KC-A	5	13	2	3	0	0	0	1	3	3	.231	.375	.231	75	0	-0	1	0	1	-1	1	/C	0.0

■ **EDDIE MAYO**   Mayo, Edward Joseph "Hotshot" (b: Edward Joseph Mayoski)   b: 4/15/10, Holyoke, Mass.   BL/TR, 5'11", 178 lbs.   Deb: 5/29/36   C

YEAR	TM/L	G	AB	R	H	2B	3B	HR	RBI	BB	SO	AVG	OBP	SLG	PRO+	BR	/A	RC	SB	CS	SBR	FR	POS	TPR
1936	*NY-N	46	141	11	28	4	1	1	8	11	12	.199	.257	.262	40	-12	-12	10	0			5	3	-0.3
1937	Bos-N	65	172	19	39	6	1	1	18	15	20	.227	.293	.291	65	-10	-8	15	1			-4	3	-0.8
1938	Bos-N	8	14	2	3	0	0	1	4	1	0	.214	.267	.429	98	-0	-0	1	0			2	/3S	0.1
1943	Phi-A	128	471	49	103	10	1	0	28	34	32	.219	.278	.244	54	-27	-27	36	2	0	1	-2	*3	-2.9
1944	Det-A	154	607	76	151	18	3	5	63	57	23	.249	.317	.313	76	-15	-19	62	9	13	-5	29	*2S	1.1
1945	*Det-A	134	501	71	143	24	3	10	54	47	29	.285	.347	.405	111	10	7	72	7	7	-2	18	*2	2.5
1946	Det-A	51	202	21	51	9	2	0	22	14	12	.252	.301	.312	68	-8	-9	19	6	2	1	-11	2	-1.5
1947	Det-A	142	535	66	149	28	4	6	48	48	28	.279	.338	.379	96	-1	-3	67	3	7	-3	-23	*2	-2.3
1948	Det-A	106	370	35	92	20	1	2	42	30	19	.249	.310	.324	67	-17	-18	35	1	9	-5	-9	23	-3.0
Total	9	834	3013	350	759	119	16	26	287	257	175	.252	.313	.328	78	-79	-89	316	29	38	3	23/S		-7.1

■ **JACKIE MAYO**   Mayo, John Lewis   b: 7/26/25, Litchfield, Ill.   BL/TR, 6'1", 190 lbs.   Deb: 9/19/48

YEAR	TM/L	G	AB	R	H	2B	3B	HR	RBI	BB	SO	AVG	OBP	SLG	PRO+	BR	/A	RC	SB	CS	SBR	FR	POS	TPR
1948	Phi-N	12	35	7	8	2	1	0	3	7	7	.229	.386	.343	101	0	0	6	1			1	O	0.1
1949	Phi-N	45	39	3	5	0	0	0	2	4	5	.128	.209	.128	-8	-6	-6	1	0			2	O	-0.4
1950	*Phi-N	18	36	1	8	3	0	0	3	2	5	.222	.263	.306	50	-3	-3	3	0			0	O	-0.2
1951	Phi-N	9	7	1	1	0	0	0	0	0	0	.143	.143	.143	-23	-1	-1	0	0	0	0	0	/O	0.0
1952	Phi-N	50	119	13	29	5	0	1	4	12	17	.244	.313	.311	74	-4	-4	11	1	3	-2	4	O/1	-0.2
1953	Phi-N	5	4	0	0	0	0	0	0	0	1	.000	.000	.000	-99	-1	-1	0	0			0	/O	0.0
Total	6	139	240	25	51	10	1	1	12	25	35	.213	.292	.275	56	-15	-14	21	2	3		7	/O1	-0.7

■ **WILLIE MAYS**   Mays, Willie Howard "Say Hey"   b: 5/6/31, Westfield, Ala.   BR/TR, 5'10.5", 170 lbs.   Deb: 5/25/51   CH

YEAR	TM/L	G	AB	R	H	2B	3B	HR	RBI	BB	SO	AVG	OBP	SLG	PRO+	BR	/A	RC	SB	CS	SBR	FR	POS	TPR
1951	*NY-N	121	464	59	127	22	5	20	68	57	60	.274	.356	.472	120	13	13	80	7	4	-0	5	*O	1.4
1952	NY-N	34	127	17	30	2	4	4	23	16	17	.236	.326	.409	102	0	0	18	4	1	1	9	O	0.9
1954	*NY-N	151	565	119	195	33	13	41	110	66	57	.345	.415	.667	176	62	61	155	8	5	-1	11	*O	6.5
1955	NY-N	152	580	123	185	18	13	51	127	79	60	.319	.404	.659	176	62	62	157	24	4	5	14	*O	7.6
1956	NY-N	152	578	101	171	27	8	36	84	68	65	.296	.371	.557	146	36	36	118	40	10	6	8	*O	4.5
1957	NY-N	152	585	112	195	26	20	35	97	76	62	.333	.407	.626	174	61	61	145	38	19	0	5	*O	6.1
1958	SF-N	152	600	121	208	33	11	29	96	78	56	.347	.423	.583	167	55	57	152	31	6	6	10	*O	6.7
1959	SF-N	151	575	125	180	43	5	34	104	65	58	.313	.385	.583	157	43	44	131	27	4	6	0	*O	4.8
1960	SF-N	153	595	107	190	29	12	29	103	61	70	.319	.386	.555	164	44	48	124	25	10	2	8	*O	5.3
1961	SF-N	154	572	129	176	32	3	40	123	81	77	.308	.395	.584	162	46	49	130	18	9	0	4	*O	4.3
1962	*SF-N	162	621	130	189	36	5	49	141	78	85	.304	.385	.615	167	55	55	146	18	2	4	7	*O	5.6
1963	SF-N	157	596	115	187	32	7	38	103	66	83	.314	.384	.582	176	56	57	131	8	3	1	8	*O/S	6.0
1964	SF-N	157	578	121	171	21	9	47	111	82	72	.296	.384	.607	171	57	55	136	19	5	3	8	*O/1S3	6.3
1965	SF-N	157	558	118	177	21	3	52	112	76	71	.317	.399	.645	184	65	63	143	9	4	0	10	*O	7.1
1966	SF-N	152	552	99	159	29	4	37	103	70	81	.288	.370	.556	149	39	37	113	5	1	1	5	*O	4.0
1967	SF-N	141	486	83	128	22	2	22	70	51	92	.263	.336	.453	125	14	15	74	6	0	2	-5	*O	0.7
1968	SF-N	148	498	84	144	20	5	23	79	67	81	.289	.376	.488	158	36	36	91	12	6	0	-3	*O/1	2.9
1969	SF-N	117	403	64	114	17	3	13	58	49	71	.283	.365	.437	126	13	14	66	6	2	1	-12	*O/1	-0.3
1970	SF-N	139	478	94	139	15	2	28	83	79	90	.291	.395	.506	141	28	29	101	5	2	0	-2	*O/1	2.2
1971	*SF-N	136	417	82	113	24	5	18	61	112	123	.271	.429	.482	160	38	38	98	23	3	5	-6	O1	3.3
1972	SF-N	19	49	8	9	2	0	0	3	17	5	.184	.394	.224	79	-0	-0	6	3	0	1	-1	O	0.0
	NY-N	69	195	27	52	9	1	8	19	43	43	.267	.402	.446	144	12	13	35	1	5	-3	2	O1	1.0
	Yr	88	244	35	61	11	1	8	22	60	48	.250	.400	.402	131	12	13	41	4	5	-2	1		1.0
1973	*NY-N	66	209	24	44	10	0	6	25	27	47	.211	.304	.344	81	-6	-5	22	1	0	0	0	O1	-0.7
Total	22	2992	10881	2062	3283	523	140	660	1903	1464	1526	.302	.387	.557	157	827	838	2372	338	103	40	86	*O/1S3	86.2

■ **BILL MAZEROSKI**   Mazeroski, William Stanley "Maz"   b: 9/5/36, Wheeling, W.Va.   BR/TR, 5'11.5", 183 lbs.   Deb: 7/07/56   C

YEAR	TM/L	G	AB	R	H	2B	3B	HR	RBI	BB	SO	AVG	OBP	SLG	PRO+	BR	/A	RC	SB	CS	SBR	FR	POS	TPR
1956	Pit-N	81	255	30	62	8	5	3	14	18	24	.243	.293	.318	66	-13	-12	24	0	0	0	11	2	0.6
1957	Pit-N	148	526	59	149	27	7	8	54	27	49	.283	.319	.407	96	-6	-4	68	3	3	-1	4	*2	1.1
1958	Pit-N	152	567	69	156	24	6	19	68	25	71	.275	.309	.439	98	-6	-4	73	1	3	-1	19	*2	2.3
1959	Pit-N	135	493	50	119	15	6	7	59	29	54	.241	.282	.339	66	-25	-24	44	1	3	-2	-9	*2	-2.4
1960	*Pit-N	151	538	58	147	21	5	11	64	40	50	.273	.325	.392	95	-4	-4	68	4	0	1	25	*2	3.6
1961	Pit-N	152	558	71	148	21	2	13	59	26	55	.265	.302	.380	79	-17	-17	62	2	1	0	31	*2	3.1
1962	Pit-N	159	572	55	155	24	9	14	81	37	47	.271	.318	.418	95	-5	-5	71	0	3	-2	41	*2	4.8

YEAR	TM/L	G	AB	R	H	2B	3B	HR	RBI	BB	SO	AVG	OBP	SLG	PRO+	BR	/A	RC	SB	CS	SBR	FR	POS	TPR
1963	Pit-N	142	534	43	131	22	3	8	52	32	46	.245	.288	.343	80	-14	-14	50	2	0	1	**57**	*2	5.5
1964	Pit-N	162	601	66	161	22	8	10	64	29	52	.268	.302	.381	91	-8	-8	63	1	1	-0	**34**	*2	4.0
1965	Pit-N	130	494	52	134	17	1	6	54	18	34	.271	.300	.346	81	-13	-13	47	2	1	0	26	*2	2.0
1966	Pit-N	162	621	56	163	22	7	16	82	31	62	.262	.299	.398	91	-8	-8	69	4	3	-1	**41**	*2	4.4
1967	Pit-N	163	639	62	167	25	3	9	77	30	55	.261	.294	.352	84	-14	-14	62	1	2	-1	17	*2	1.3
1968	Pit-N	143	506	36	127	18	2	3	42	38	38	.251	.306	.312	87	-8	-8	45	3	4	-2	26	*2	2.8
1969	Pit-N	67	227	13	52	7	1	3	25	22	16	.229	.303	.308	73	-8	-8	21	1	1	-0	14	2	1.1
1970	*Pit-N	112	367	29	84	14	0	7	39	27	40	.229	.285	.324	64	-20	-19	34	2	0	1	24	*2	1.7
1971	*Pit-N	70	193	17	49	3	1	1	16	15	8	.254	.308	.295	72	-7	-7	18	0	0	0	-1	2/3	-0.5
1972	*Pit-N	34	64	3	12	4	0	0	3	3	5	.188	.224	.250	35	-6	-5	3	0	0	0	3	2/3	0.0
Total	17	2163	7755	769	2016	294	62	138	853	447	706	.260	.302	.367	84	-180	-174	824	27	23	-6	362	*2/3	35.4

■ MEL MAZZERA
Mazzera, Melvin Leonard "Mike" b: 1/31/14, Stockton, Cal. BL/TL, 5'11", 180 lbs. Deb: 9/09/35

YEAR	TM/L	G	AB	R	H	2B	3B	HR	RBI	BB	SO	AVG	OBP	SLG	PRO+	BR	/A	RC	SB	CS	SBR	FR	POS	TPR
1935	StL-A	12	30	4	7	2	0	1	2	4	9	.233	.324	.400	82	-1	-1	4	0	0	0	0	O	0.0
1937	StL-A	7	7	1	2	2	0	0	0	0	2	.286	.286	.571	110	0	0	1	0	0	0	0	H	0.0
1938	StL-A	86	204	33	57	8	2	6	29	12	25	.279	.329	.426	88	-5	-5	29	1	1	-0	0	O	-0.3
1939	StL-A	33	110	21	33	5	2	3	0	0	0	.300	.300	.464	91	-2	-2	15	0	0	0	-0	O	-0.2
1940	Phi-N	69	156	16	37	5	4	0	13	19	15	.237	.320	.321	80	-5	-4	16	1			-2	O/1	-0.7
Total	5	207	507	75	136	22	8	10	44	35	51	.268	.319	.402	87	-12	-11	65	2	1		-1	O/1	-1.2

■ LEE MAZZILLI
Mazzilli, Lee Louis b: 3/25/55, New York, N.Y. BB/TR, 6'1", 180 lbs. Deb: 9/07/76

YEAR	TM/L	G	AB	R	H	2B	3B	HR	RBI	BB	SO	AVG	OBP	SLG	PRO+	BR	/A	RC	SB	CS	SBR	FR	POS	TPR
1976	NY-N	24	77	9	15	2	0	2	7	14	10	.195	.326	.299	83	-2	-1	8	5	4	-1	3	O	0.0
1977	NY-N	159	537	66	134	24	3	6	46	72	72	.250	.342	.339	87	-11	-8	66	22	15	-2	3	*O	-1.1
1978	NY-N	148	542	78	148	28	5	16	61	69	82	.273	.356	.432	124	14	17	85	20	13	-2	8	*O	1.8
1979	NY-N	158	597	78	181	34	4	15	79	93	74	.303	.397	.449	135	28	31	115	34	12	3	1	*O1	3.1
1980	NY-N	152	578	82	162	31	4	16	76	82	92	.280	.373	.431	127	20	22	98	41	15	3	-3	1O	1.6
1981	NY-N	95	324	36	74	14	5	6	34	46	53	.228	.328	.358	96	-2	-1	41	17	7	1	2	O	0.0
1982	Tex-A	58	195	23	47	8	0	4	17	28	26	.241	.339	.344	93	-2	-1	24	11	6	-0	-3	OD	-0.4
	NY-A	37	128	20	34	2	0	6	17	15	15	.266	.347	.422	112	2	2	19	2	3	-1	-3	1/OD	-0.2
	Yr	95	323	43	81	10	0	10	34	43	41	.251	.342	.375	100	-1	1	42	13	9	-2	-6		-0.6
1983	Pit-N	109	246	37	59	9	0	5	24	49	43	.240	.370	.337	95	1	0	34	15	5	2	1	O/1	0.2
1984	Pit-N	111	266	37	63	11	1	4	21	40	42	.237	.339	.331	89	-3	-3	33	8	1	2	-11	O/1	-1.5
1985	Pit-N	92	117	20	33	8	0	1	9	29	17	.282	.425	.376	127	6	6	21	4	1	1	-1	1/O	0.5
1986	Pit-N	61	93	18	21	2	1	1	8	26	25	.226	.395	.301	93	1	1	13	3	3	-1	-3	O/1	-0.3
	*NY-N	39	58	10	16	3	0	2	7	12	11	.276	.417	.431	138	3	4	11	1	1	-0	-1	O/1	0.2
	Yr	100	151	28	37	5	1	3	15	38	36	.245	.403	.351	109	4	4	24	4	4	-1	-3		-0.1
1987	NY-N	88	124	26	38	8	1	3	24	21	14	.306	.407	.460	136	6	7	24	5	3	-0	-2	O1	0.3
1988	*NY-N	68	116	9	17	2	0	0	12	12	16	.147	.233	.164	16	-12	-12	5	4	1	1	-2	O1	-1.5
1989	NY-N	48	60	10	11	2	0	2	7	17	19	.183	.364	.317	101	0	1	9	3	0	1	-2	O/1	0.0
	*Tor-A	28	66	12	15	3	0	4	11	17	16	.227	.400	.455	143	4	5	14	2	0	1	-0	D/1O	0.4
Total	14	1475	4124	571	1068	191	24	93	460	642	627	.259	.361	.385	109	54	69	618	197	90	5	-12	O1/D	3.1

■ JIMMY McALEER
McAleer, James Robert "Loafer" b: 7/10/1864, Youngstown, Ohio d: 4/29/31, Youngstown, Ohio BR/TR, 6', 175 lbs. Deb: 4/24/1889 M

YEAR	TM/L	G	AB	R	H	2B	3B	HR	RBI	BB	SO	AVG	OBP	SLG	PRO+	BR	/A	RC	SB	CS	SBR	FR	POS	TPR
1889	Cle-N	110	447	66	105	6	6	1	35	30	49	.235	.289	.282	62	-23	-21	48	37			8	*O	-1.5
1890	Cle-P	86	341	58	91	8	7	1	42	37	33	.267	.340	.340	91	-7	-2	48	21			11	O	0.4
1891	Cle-N	136	565	97	134	16	11	1	61	49	47	.237	.304	.310	77	-14	-17	70	51			5	*O	-1.6
1892	*Cle-N	149	571	92	136	26	7	4	70	63	54	.238	.318	.329	94	-1	-4	74	40			12	*O	0.2
1893	Cle-N	91	350	63	83	5	1	2	41	35	21	.237	.314	.274	55	-20	-24	41	32			4	*O	-1.9
1894	Cle-N	64	253	36	73	15	1	2	40	13	17	.289	.331	.379	70	-12	-14	37	14			3	O	-1.0
1895	*Cle-N	131	528	84	143	17	2	0	68	38	37	.271	.327	.311	63	-25	-30	66	32			3	*O	-3.1
1896	*Cle-N	116	455	70	131	16	4	1	54	47	32	.288	.361	.347	84	-5	-10	67	24			7	*O	-0.8
1897	Cle-N	24	91	6	20	2	0	0	10	7		.220	.283	.242	39	-7	-8	8	4			-1	O	-0.8
1898	Cle-N	106	366	47	87	3	0	0	48	46		.238	.331	.246	69	-12	-11	33	7			3	*O/2	-1.3
1901	Cle-A	3	7	0	1	0	0	0	0	0		.143	.143	.143	-21	-1	-1	0	0			-1	/OP3M	0.0
1902	StL-A	2	3	0	2	0	0	0	0	0		.667	.667	.667	278	1	1	1	0			-1	/OM	0.0
1907	StL-A	2	0	0	0	0	0	0	0	0		—	—	—	—	0	0	0	0			0	RM	0.0
Total	13	1020	3977	619	1006	114	39	12	469	365	290	.253	.322	.310	74	-127	-143	494	262			53	*O/23P	-11.4

■ JACK McALEESE
McAleese, John James b: 1877, Sharon, Pa. d: 11/15/50, New York, N.Y. TR, 5'8", Deb: 8/10/01

YEAR	TM/L	G	AB	R	H	2B	3B	HR	RBI	BB	SO	AVG	OBP	SLG	PRO+	BR	/A	RC	SB	CS	SBR	FR	POS	TPR
1901	Chi-A	1	1	0	0	0	0	0	0	0		.000	.000	.000	-99	-0	-0	0	0			0	/P	0.0
1909	StL-A	85	267	33	57	7	0	0	12	32		.213	.318	.240	82	-5	-3	26	18			-3	O/3	-0.9
Total	2	86	268	33	57	7	0	0	12	32		.213	.317	.239	82	-6	-3	26	18			-3	/O3P	-0.9

■ BILL McALLESTER
McAllester, William Lusk b: 12/29/1889, Chattanooga, Tenn. d: 3/3/70, Chattanooga, Tenn. BR/TR, 5'11.5", 170 lbs. Deb: 5/02/13

YEAR	TM/L	G	AB	R	H	2B	3B	HR	RBI	BB	SO	AVG	OBP	SLG	PRO+	BR	/A	RC	SB	CS	SBR	FR	POS	TPR
1913	StL-A	49	85	3	13	4	0	0	6	11	12	.153	.250	.200	33	-7	-7	5	2	1		-4	C	-0.7

■ SPORT McALLISTER
McAllister, Lewis William b: 7/23/1874, Austin, Miss. d: 7/17/62, Wyandotte, Mich. BB/TR, 5'11", 180 lbs. Deb: 8/07/1896

YEAR	TM/L	G	AB	R	H	2B	3B	HR	RBI	BB	SO	AVG	OBP	SLG	PRO+	BR	/A	RC	SB	CS	SBR	FR	POS	TPR
1896	Cle-N	8	27	2	6	2	0	0	1	0	2	.222	.250	.296	43	-2	-2	2	1			-6	/OCP	-0.7
1897	Cle-N	43	137	23	30	5	1	0	11	12		.219	.287	.270	47	-10	-11	12	3			-6	O/SP1C2	-1.5
1898	Cle-N	17	57	8	13	3	1	0	9	5		.228	.290	.316	77	-2	-2	5	0			1	/PO	0.0
1899	Cle-N	113	418	29	99	6	8	1	31	19		.237	.273	.297	63	-24	-19	36	5			-15	OC/31SP2	-3.3
1901	Det-A	90	306	45	92	9	4	3	57	15		.301	.344	.386	99	2	-1	49	17			-20	C103/S	-1.6
1902	Det-A	21	67	8	14	1	0	1	8	2		.209	.243	.269	42	-5	-5	5	0			1	/1S2C3O	-0.3
	Bal-A	3	11	0	1	0	0	0	1	1		.091	.167	.091	-25	-2	-2	0	0			-0	/21	-0.1
	Det-A	45	162	11	34	4	2	0	24	3		.210	.229	.259	36	-14	-14	10	1			-1	10/C3S	-1.3
	Yr	69	240	19	49	5	2	1	33	6		.204	.230	.254	34	-21	-21	15	1			0		-1.7
1903	Det-A	78	265	31	69	8	2	0	22	10		.260	.287	.306	82	-6	-6	26	5			-7	SC/O31	-0.8
Total	7	418	1450	157	358	38	18	5	164	67	2	.247	.285	.308	68	-63	-62	145	32			-53	O/C1S3P2	-9.6

■ JIM McANANY
McAnany, James b: 9/4/36, Los Angeles, Cal. BR/TR, 5'10", 196 lbs. Deb: 9/19/58

YEAR	TM/L	G	AB	R	H	2B	3B	HR	RBI	BB	SO	AVG	OBP	SLG	PRO+	BR	/A	RC	SB	CS	SBR	FR	POS	TPR
1958	Chi-A	5	13	0	0	0	0	0	0	0	5	.000	.000	.000	-99	-3	-3	0	0	0	0	1	/O	-0.2
1959	*Chi-A	67	210	22	58	9	3	0	27	19	26	.276	.339	.348	90	-3	-2	26	2	1	0	-3	O	-0.8
1960	Chi-A	3	2	0	0	0	0	0	0	0	0	.000	.000	.000	-99	-1	-1	0	0	0	0	0	H	0.0
1961	Chi-N	11	10	1	3	1	0	0	0	1	3	.300	.364	.400	101	0	0	1	0	0	0	0	/O	0.0
1962	Chi-N	7	6	0	0	0	0	0	0	1	2	.000	.143	.000	-56	-1	-1	0	0	0	0	0	H	0.0
Total	5	93	241	23	61	10	3	0	27	21	38	.253	.316	.320	75	-8	-8	27	2	1	0	-2	/O	-1.0

■ BUB McATEE
McAtee, Michael James "Butch" b: 3/1845, Troy, N.Y. d: 10/18/1876, Troy, N.Y. 5'9", 160 lbs. Deb: 5/08/1871

YEAR	TM/L	G	AB	R	H	2B	3B	HR	RBI	BB	SO	AVG	OBP	SLG	PRO+	BR	/A	RC	SB	CS	SBR	FR	POS	TPR
1871	Chi-n	26	135	34	37	8	2	0	10	5	2	.274	.300	.363	81	-2	-5	17	5				*1	-0.3
1872	Tro-n	25	130	30	29	4	1	0		1		.223	.223	.269	52	-7	-7	8					1	-0.2
Total	2 n	51	265	64	66	12	3	0		6		.249	.266	.317	68	-9	-13	25					/1	-0.5

■ IKE McAULEY
McAuley, James Earl b: 8/19/1891, Wichita, Kan. d: 4/6/28, Des Moines, Iowa BR/TR, 5'9.5", 150 lbs. Deb: 9/10/14

YEAR	TM/L	G	AB	R	H	2B	3B	HR	RBI	BB	SO	AVG	OBP	SLG	PRO+	BR	/A	RC	SB	CS	SBR	FR	POS	TPR
1914	Pit-N	15	24	3	3	0	0	0	0	0	8	.125	.125	.125	-27	-4	-4	0	0			1	/S32	-0.2
1915	Pit-N	5	15	0	2	1	0	0	0	0	6	.133	.133	.200	0	-2	-2	0	0			-3	/S	-0.4

YEAR	TM/L	G	AB	R	H	2B	3B	HR	RBI	BB	SO	AVG	OBP	SLG	PRO+	BR	/A	RC	SB	CS	SBR	FR	POS	TPR
1916	Pit-N	4	8	1	2	0	0	0	1	0	1	.250	.250	.250	53	-0	-0	1	0			1	/S	0.0
1917	StL-N	3	7	0	2	0	0	0	1	0	1	.286	.286	.286	78	-0	-0	1	0			-2	/S	-0.2
1925	Chi-N	37	125	10	35	7	2	0	11	11	12	.280	.343	.368	80	-3	-4	17	1	0	0	-8	S	-0.7
Total	5	64	179	14	44	8	2	0	13	11	28	.246	.293	.313	62	-9	-10	19	1	0		-12	/S32	-1.5

■ GENE McAULIFFE

McAuliffe, Eugene Leo   b: 2/28/1872, Randolph, Mass.   d: 4/29/53, Randolph, Mass.   TR, 6'1", 180 lbs.   Deb: 8/17/04

YEAR	TM/L	G	AB	R	H	2B	3B	HR	RBI	BB	SO	AVG	OBP	SLG	PRO+	BR	/A	RC	SB	CS	SBR	FR	POS	TPR
1904	Bos-N	1	2	0	1	0	0	0	0	0	0	.500	.500	.500	220	-0	0	1	0			-0	/C	0.0

■ DICK McAULIFFE

McAuliffe, Richard John   b: 11/29/39, Hartford, Conn.   BL/TR, 5'11", 176 lbs.   Deb: 9/17/60

YEAR	TM/L	G	AB	R	H	2B	3B	HR	RBI	BB	SO	AVG	OBP	SLG	PRO+	BR	/A	RC	SB	CS	SBR	FR	POS	TPR
1960	Det-A	8	27	2	7	0	1	0	1	2	6	.259	.310	.333	72	-1	-1	3	0	0	0	1	/S	0.1
1961	Det-A	80	285	36	73	12	4	6	33	24	39	.256	.323	.389	87	-5	-6	36	2	3	-1	-28	S3	-3.0
1962	Det-A	139	471	50	124	20	5	12	63	64	76	.263	.351	.403	99	2	0	68	4	2	0	-20	23S	-1.3
1963	Det-A	150	568	77	149	18	6	13	61	64	75	.262	.337	.384	98	2	-0	75	11	5	0	-24	*S2	-1.7
1964	Det-A	162	557	85	134	18	7	24	66	77	96	.241	.336	.427	109	8	7	81	8	5	-1	-8	*S	0.0
1965	Det-A	113	404	61	105	13	6	15	54	49	62	.260	.343	.433	118	10	10	60	6	9	-4	-15	*S	-0.4
1966	Det-A	124	430	83	118	16	8	23	56	66	80	.274	.375	.509	148	29	28	83	5	7	-3	-10	*S3	2.2
1967	Det-A	153	557	92	133	16	7	22	65	105	118	.239	.366	.411	126	24	22	93	6	5	-1	-14	*2S	1.5
1968	*Det-A	151	570	95	142	24	10	16	56	82	99	.249	.346	.411	125	21	19	87	8	7	-2	-19	*2/S	0.3
1969	Det-A	74	271	49	71	10	5	11	33	47	41	.262	.371	.458	125	12	10	48	2	5	-2	0	2	1.1
1970	Det-A	146	530	73	124	21	1	12	50	101	62	.234	.360	.345	95	-0	-0	74	5	6	-2	-6	2S3	0.5
1971	Det-A	128	477	67	99	16	6	18	57	53	67	.208	.293	.379	86	-8	-10	55	4	1	1	7	*2/S	0.4
1972	*Det-A	122	408	47	98	16	3	8	30	59	59	.240	.339	.353	103	4	3	53	0	0	0	-7	*2/S3	0.3
1973	Det-A	106	343	39	94	18	1	12	47	49	52	.274	.366	.437	118	12	9	57	0	4	-2	5	*2/SD	1.7
1974	Bos-A	100	272	32	57	13	1	5	24	39	40	.210	.311	.320	76	-6	-8	28	2	0	1	-8	23/SD	-1.2
1975	Bos-A	7	15	0	2	0	0	0	1	1	2	.133	.188	.133	-7	-2	-2	0	0	0	0	-2	/3	-0.3
Total	16	1763	6185	888	1530	231	71	197	697	882	974	.247	.344	.403	108	104	81	899	63	59	-17	-148	2S3/D	0.2

■ GEORGE McAVOY

McAvoy, George H.   Deb: 7/17/14

YEAR	TM/L	G	AB	R	H	2B	3B	HR	RBI	BB	SO	AVG	OBP	SLG	PRO+	BR	/A	RC	SB	CS	SBR	FR	POS	TPR
1914	Phi-N	1	1	0	0	0	0	0	0	0	0	.000	.000	.000	-94	-0	-0	0	0			0	H	0.0

■ WICKEY McAVOY

McAvoy, James Eugene   b: 10/22/1894, Rochester, N.Y.   d: 7/5/73, Rochester, N.Y.   BR/TR, 5'11", 172 lbs.   Deb: 9/29/13

YEAR	TM/L	G	AB	R	H	2B	3B	HR	RBI	BB	SO	AVG	OBP	SLG	PRO+	BR	/A	RC	SB	CS	SBR	FR	POS	TPR
1913	Phi-A	4	9	0	1	0	0	0	0	0	4	.111	.200	.111	-9	-1	-1	0	0			1	/C	0.0
1914	Phi-A	8	16	1	2	0	1	0	0	0	4	.125	.125	.250	13	-2	-2	1	0			1	/C	0.0
1915	Phi-A	68	184	12	35	7	2	0	6	11	32	.190	.236	.250	47	-13	-12	11	0	2	-1	5	C	-0.3
1917	Phi-A	10	24	1	6	1	0	1	4	0	3	.250	.250	.417	105	-0	-0	2	0			3	/C	0.4
1918	Phi-A	83	271	14	66	5	3	0	32	13	23	.244	.283	.284	70	-10	-10	23	5			5	C/P1O	0.1
1919	Phi-A	62	170	10	24	5	2	0	11	14	21	.141	.207	.194	13	-20	-20	7	1			-3	C	-2.0
Total	6	235	674	38	134	18	8	1	53	38	87	.199	.245	.254	47	-46	-46	43	6	2		12	C/O1P	-1.8

■ ALGIE McBRIDE

McBride, Algernon Griggs   b: 5/23/1869, Washington, D.C.   d: 1/10/56, Georgetown, Ohio   BL/TL, 5'9", 152 lbs.   Deb: 5/12/1896

YEAR	TM/L	G	AB	R	H	2B	3B	HR	RBI	BB	SO	AVG	OBP	SLG	PRO+	BR	/A	RC	SB	CS	SBR	FR	POS	TPR
1896	Chi-N	9	29	2	7	1	1	1	7	7	3	.241	.389	.448	118	1	1	5	0			0	/O	0.0
1898	Cin-N	120	486	94	147	14	12	2	43	51		.302	.380	.393	116	17	12	81	16			7	*O	1.1
1899	Cin-N	64	251	57	87	12	5	1	23	30		.347	.431	.446	141	17	16	52	5			-2	O	0.8
1900	Cin-N	112	436	59	120	15	8	4	59	25		.275	.317	.374	95	-5	-3	57	12			-9	*O	-2.0
1901	Cin-N	30	123	19	29	7	0	2	18	7		.236	.282	.341	88	-3	-2	12	0			-2	O	-0.6
	NY-N	68	264	27	74	11	0	2	29	12		.280	.312	.345	96	-3	-2	31	3			-3	O	-1.1
	Yr	98	387	46	103	18	0	4	47	19		.266	.302	.344	93	-6	-3	43	3			-6		-1.7
Total	5	403	1589	258	464	60	26	12	179	132	3	.292	.354	.385	110	24	22	237	36			-9	O	-1.8

■ BAKE McBRIDE

McBride, Arnold Ray   b: 2/3/49, Fulton, Mo.   BL/TR, 6'2", 190 lbs.   Deb: 7/26/73

YEAR	TM/L	G	AB	R	H	2B	3B	HR	RBI	BB	SO	AVG	OBP	SLG	PRO+	BR	/A	RC	SB	CS	SBR	FR	POS	TPR
1973	StL-N	40	63	8	19	3	0	0	5	4	10	.302	.362	.349	98	0	0	8	0	1	-1	3	O	0.2
1974	StL-N	150	559	81	173	19	5	6	56	43	57	.309	.372	.394	115	12	12	85	30	11	2	9	*O	1.9
1975	StL-N	116	413	70	124	10	9	5	36	34	52	.300	.355	.404	107	5	4	62	26	8	3	15	*O	1.9
1976	StL-N	72	272	40	91	13	4	3	24	18	28	.335	.389	.445	135	13	13	48	10	5	0	9	O	2.0
1977	StL-N	43	122	21	32	5	1	4	20	7	19	.262	.302	.418	93	-2	-2	16	9	3	1	-3	O	-0.4
	*Phi-N	85	280	55	95	20	5	11	41	25	25	.339	.399	.564	149	21	20	67	27	4	6	-0	O	2.3
	Yr	128	402	76	127	25	6	15	61	32	44	.316	.371	.520	133	20	18	81	36	7	7	-3		1.9
1978	*Phi-N	122	472	68	127	20	4	10	49	28	68	.269	.317	.392	96	-3	-3	63	28	3	7	2	*O	0.0
1979	Phi-N	151	582	82	163	16	12	12	60	41	77	.280	.332	.411	98	0	-2	79	25	14	-1	15	*O	0.8
1980	*Phi-N	137	554	68	171	33	10	9	87	26	58	.309	.345	.453	115	14	11	79	13	10	-2	2	*O	0.5
1981	*Phi-N	58	221	26	60	17	1	2	21	11	25	.271	.306	.385	91	-2	-3	25	5	0	2	-9	O	-1.3
1982	Cle-A	27	85	8	31	3	3	0	13	2	12	.365	.379	.471	132	3	4	14	2	2	-1	-3	O	0.0
1983	Cle-A	70	230	21	67	8	1	1	18	9	26	.291	.321	.348	81	-5	-6	24	8	2	1	-2	OD	-0.6
Total	11	1071	3853	548	1153	167	55	63	430	248	457	.299	.348	.420	109	57	46	570	183	63	17	39	O/D	7.3

■ GEORGE McBRIDE

McBride, George Florian   b: 11/20/1880, Milwaukee, Wis.   d: 7/2/73, Milwaukee, Wis.   BR/TR, 5'11", 170 lbs.   Deb: 9/12/01   MC

YEAR	TM/L	G	AB	R	H	2B	3B	HR	RBI	BB	SO	AVG	OBP	SLG	PRO+	BR	/A	RC	SB	CS	SBR	FR	POS	TPR
1901	Mil-A	3	12	0	2	0	0	0	0	1		.167	.231	.167	13	-1	-1	0	0			-1	/S	-0.1
1905	Pit-N	27	87	9	19	4	0	0	7	6		.218	.269	.264	59	-4	-4	7	2			-4	3/S	-0.7
	StL-N	81	281	22	61	1	2	2	34	14		.217	.254	.256	56	-16	-15	22	10			-2	S/1	-1.5
	Yr	108	368	31	80	5	2	2	41	20		.217	.258	.258	56	-20	-19	29	12			-6		-2.2
1906	StL-N	90	313	24	53	8	2	0	13	17		.169	.212	.208	34	-24	-23	16	5			9	S	-1.0
1908	Was-A	155	518	47	120	10	6	0	34	41		.232	.288	.274	93	-8	-3	44	12			33	*S	3.8
1909	Was-A	156	504	38	118	16	0	0	34	36		.234	.294	.266	81	-12	-10	46	17			11	*S	0.5
1910	Was-A	154	514	54	118	19	4	1	55	61		.230	.321	.288	95	-4	-1	53	11			27	*S	3.1
1911	Was-A	154	557	58	131	11	4	0	59	52		.235	.312	.269	64	-27	-25	52	15			24	*S	1.3
1912	Was-A	152	521	56	118	13	7	1	52	38		.226	.288	.284	63	-25	-25	48	17			31	*S	2.0
1913	Was-A	150	499	52	107	18	7	1	52	43	46	.214	.286	.285	66	-21	-22	43	12			11	*S	0.2
1914	Was-A	156	503	49	102	12	4	0	24	43	70	.203	.274	.243	54	-27	-29	36	12	14	-5	12	*S	-0.7
1915	Was-A	146	476	54	97	8	6	1	30	29	60	.204	.251	.252	50	-30	-30	34	10	5	0	9	*S	-0.8
1916	Was-A	139	466	36	106	15	4	1	36	23	58	.227	.271	.283	68	-20	-19	41	8			13	*S	0.5
1917	Was-A	50	141	6	27	3	0	0	9	10	17	.191	.265	.213	46	-9	-9	9	1			-1	S/32	-0.8
1918	Was-A	18	53	2	7	0	0	0	1	0	11	.132	.132	.132	-21	-8	-8	1	1			2	S/2	-0.4
1919	Was-A	15	40	3	8	1	1	0	4	3	6	.200	.256	.275	49	-3	-3	3	0			1	S	0.0
1920	Was-A	13	41	6	9	1	0	0	3	2	3	.220	.256	.244	34	-4	-4	3	0	0	0	-3	S	-0.5
Total	16	1659	5526	516	1203	140	47	7	447	419	271	.218	.280	.264	65	-243	-231	459	133	19		171	*S/321	4.9

■ JOHN McBRIDE

McBride, John F.   Deb: 10/12/1890

YEAR	TM/L	G	AB	R	H	2B	3B	HR	RBI	BB	SO	AVG	OBP	SLG	PRO+	BR	/A	RC	SB	CS	SBR	FR	POS	TPR
1890	Phi-a	1	2	0	0	0	0	0		0		.000	.000	.000	-99	-0	-0	0	0			1	/O	0.0

■ TOM McBRIDE

McBride, Thomas Raymond   b: 11/2/14, Bonham, Tex.   BR/TR, 6'0.5", 188 lbs.   Deb: 4/23/43

YEAR	TM/L	G	AB	R	H	2B	3B	HR	RBI	BB	SO	AVG	OBP	SLG	PRO+	BR	/A	RC	SB	CS	SBR	FR	POS	TPR
1943	Bos-A	26	96	11	23	3	1	0	7	7	3	.240	.291	.292	70	-4	-4	7	2	0	1	1	O	-0.2
1944	Bos-A	71	216	29	53	7	3	0	24	8	13	.245	.276	.306	67	-10	-10	18	4	0	1	5	O/1	-0.5
1945	Bos-A	100	344	38	105	11	7	1	47	26	17	.305	.354	.387	112	6	5	47	2	2	-1	5	O1	0.6
1946	*Bos-A	61	153	21	46	5	2	0	19	9	6	.301	.340	.359	90	-1	-2	18	0	1	-1	-3	O	-0.8
1947	Bos-A	2	5	0	1	0	0	0	0	0	0	.200	.200	.200	11	-1	-1	0	0	0	0	1	/O	0.0

YEAR	TM/L	G	AB	R	H	2B	3B	HR	RBI	BB	SO	AVG	OBP	SLG	PRO+	BR	/A	RC	SB	CS	SBR	FR	POS	TPR
	Was-A	56	166	19	45	4	2	0	15	15	9	.271	.331	.319	84	-4	-3	17	3	1	0	-1	O/3	-0.5
	Yr	58	171	19	46	4	2	0	15	15	9	.269	.328	.316	81	-5	-4	17	3	1	0	0		-0.5
1948	Was-A	92	206	22	53	9	1	1	29	28	15	.257	.346	.325	81	-6	-5	23	2	2	-1	2	O	-0.5
Total	6	408	1186	140	326	39	16	2	141	93	63	.275	.328	.340	88	-19	-19	130	13	6	0	8	O/13	-1.9

■ SWAT McCABE
McCabe, James Arthur b: 11/20/1881, Towanda, Pa. d: 12/9/44, Bristol, Conn. BL/TR, 5'10", Deb: 9/23/09

YEAR	TM/L	G	AB	R	H	2B	3B	HR	RBI	BB	SO	AVG	OBP	SLG	PRO+	BR	/A	RC	SB	CS	SBR	FR	POS	TPR
1909	Cin-N	3	11	2	6	1	0	0	0	0		.545	.545	.636	269	2	2	4	1			-1	/O	0.1
1910	Cin-N	13	35	3	9	1	0	0	5	1	2	.257	.297	.286	73	-1	-1	3	0			1	/O	0.0
Total	2	16	46	5	15	2	0	0	5	1	2	.326	.354	.370	118	1	1	7	1			-0	/O	0.1

■ JOE McCABE
McCabe, Joseph Robert b: 8/27/38, Indianapolis, Ind. BR/TR, 6', 190 lbs. Deb: 4/18/64

YEAR	TM/L	G	AB	R	H	2B	3B	HR	RBI	BB	SO	AVG	OBP	SLG	PRO+	BR	/A	RC	SB	CS	SBR	FR	POS	TPR
1964	Min-A	14	19	1	3	0	0	0	2	0	8	.158	.158	.158	-12	-3	-3	1	0	0	0	0	C	-0.1
1965	Was-A	14	27	1	5	0	0	1	5	4	13	.185	.290	.296	68	-1	-1	3	1	0	0	-3	C	-0.2
Total	2	28	46	2	8	0	0	1	7	4	21	.174	.240	.239	36	-4	-4	3	1	0	0	-2	/C	-0.3

■ BILL McCABE
McCabe, William Francis b: 10/28/1892, Chicago, Ill. d: 9/2/66, Chicago, Ill. BB/TR, 5'9.5", 180 lbs. Deb: 4/16/18

YEAR	TM/L	G	AB	R	H	2B	3B	HR	RBI	BB	SO	AVG	OBP	SLG	PRO+	BR	/A	RC	SB	CS	SBR	FR	POS	TPR
1918	*Chi-N	29	45	9	8	0	1	0	5	4	7	.178	.245	.222	42	-3	-3	3	2			6	2/O	0.4
1919	Chi-N	33	84	8	13	3	1	0	5	9	15	.155	.253	.214	41	-6	-6	5	3			-1	O/S3	-0.8
1920	Chi-N	3	2	1	1	0	0	0	0	0	0	.500	.500	.500	184	0	0	0	0	0	0	0	H	0.0
	*Bro-N	41	68	10	10	0	0	0	3	2	6	.147	.171	.147	-8	-9	-10	2	1	2	-1	5	S/O23	-0.5
	Yr	44	70	11	11	0	0	0	3	2	6	.157	.181	.157	-2	-9	-9	2	1	2	-1	5		-0.5
Total	3	106	199	28	32	3	2	0	13	15	28	.161	.227	.196	26	-18	-18	10	6	2		9	/OS23	-0.9

■ HARRY McCAFFERY
McCaffery, Harry Charles b: 11/25/1858, St.Louis, Mo. d: 4/19/28, St.Louis, Mo. BR/TR, 5'10.5", 185 lbs. Deb: 6/15/1882 U

YEAR	TM/L	G	AB	R	H	2B	3B	HR	RBI	BB	SO	AVG	OBP	SLG	PRO+	BR	/A	RC	SB	CS	SBR	FR	POS	TPR
1882	Lou-a	1	4	1	1	0	0	0		0		.250	.250	.250	74	-0	-0	0				-1	/2	0.0
	StL-a	38	153	23	42	8	6	0		3		.275	.288	.405	127	5	4	18				4	O/231	0.7
	Yr	39	157	24	43	8	6	0		3		.274	.287	.401	125	5	4	19				3	O/2	0.7
1883	StL-a	5	18	0	1	0	0	0		1		.056	.105	.056	-44	-3	-3	0				1	/O	-0.1
1885	Cin-a	1	5	0	0	0	0	0		0		.000	.000	.000	-98	-1	-1	0				-0	/P	0.0
Total	3	45	180	24	44	8	6	0		4		.244	.261	.356	101	1	-0	19				4	/O23P1	0.6

■ SPARROW McCAFFREY
McCaffrey, Charles P. b: 1868, Philadelphia, Pa. d: 4/29/1894, Philadelphia, Pa. 120 lbs. Deb: 8/13/1889

YEAR	TM/L	G	AB	R	H	2B	3B	HR	RBI	BB	SO	AVG	OBP	SLG	PRO+	BR	/A	RC	SB	CS	SBR	FR	POS	TPR
1889	Col-a	2	1	1	1	0	0	0	1	0	1.000	1.000	1.000	501	1	1	0				0	/C	0.1

■ BRIAN McCALL
McCall, Brian Allen "Bam" b: 1/25/43, Kentfield, Cal. BL/TL, 5'10", 170 lbs. Deb: 9/18/62

YEAR	TM/L	G	AB	R	H	2B	3B	HR	RBI	BB	SO	AVG	OBP	SLG	PRO+	BR	/A	RC	SB	CS	SBR	FR	POS	TPR
1962	Chi-A	4	8	2	3	0	0	2	3	0	2	.375	.375	1.125	287	2	2	3	0	0	0	0	/O	0.2
1963	Chi-A	3	7	1	0	0	0	0	0	1	2	.000	.125	.000	-62	-2	-2	0	0	0	0	0	/O	-0.1
Total	2	7	15	3	3	0	0	2	3	1	4	.200	.250	.600	126	0	0	3	0	0	0	0	/O	0.1

■ JACK McCANDLESS
McCandless, Scott Cook b: 5/5/1891, Pittsburgh, Pa. d: 8/17/61, Pittsburgh, Pa. BL/TR, 6', 170 lbs. Deb: 9/10/14

YEAR	TM/L	G	AB	R	H	2B	3B	HR	RBI	BB	SO	AVG	OBP	SLG	PRO+	BR	/A	RC	SB	CS	SBR	FR	POS	TPR
1914	Bal-F	11	31	5	8	0	1	0	1	3	0	.258	.343	.290	88	-0	-0	4	0			-0	/O	0.0
1915	Bal-F	117	406	47	87	6	7	5	34	41	99	.214	.296	.300	74	-11	-13	41	9			3	*O	-1.5
Total	2	128	437	52	95	6	8	5	35	44	99	.217	.299	.302	75	-12	-13	44	9			3	O	-1.5

■ EMMETT McCANN
McCann, Robert Emmett b: 3/4/02, Philadelphia, Pa. d: 4/15/37, Philadelphia, Pa. BR/TR, 5'11", 150 lbs. Deb: 4/19/20

YEAR	TM/L	G	AB	R	H	2B	3B	HR	RBI	BB	SO	AVG	OBP	SLG	PRO+	BR	/A	RC	SB	CS	SBR	FR	POS	TPR
1920	Phi-A	13	34	4	9	1	1	0	3	3	1	.265	.342	.353	84	-1	-1	4	0	1	-1	-0	S	0.0
1921	Phi-A	52	157	15	35	5	0	0	15	4	6	.223	.242	.255	27	-17	-18	10	2	1	0	-0	S/321	-1.1
1926	Bos-A	6	3	0	0	0	0	0	0	1	1	.000	.250	.000	-32	-1	-1	0	0	0	0	-0	/S3	0.0
Total	3	71	194	19	44	6	1	0	18	8	8	.227	.261	.268	36	-19	-19	14	2	2	-1	-1	/S321	-1.1

■ ROGER McCARDELL
McCardell, Roger Morton b: 8/29/32, Gorsuch Mills, Md. BR/TR, 6', 200 lbs. Deb: 5/08/59

YEAR	TM/L	G	AB	R	H	2B	3B	HR	RBI	BB	SO	AVG	OBP	SLG	PRO+	BR	/A	RC	SB	CS	SBR	FR	POS	TPR
1959	SF-N	4	4	0	0	0	0	0	0	0	0	.000	.000	.000	-99	-1	-1	0	0	0	0	0	/C	0.0

■ BILL McCARREN
McCarren, William Joseph b: 11/4/1895, Fortenia, Pa. d: 9/11/83, Denver, Colo. BR/TR, 5'11.5", 170 lbs. Deb: 5/04/23

YEAR	TM/L	G	AB	R	H	2B	3B	HR	RBI	BB	SO	AVG	OBP	SLG	PRO+	BR	/A	RC	SB	CS	SBR	FR	POS	TPR
1923	Bro-N	69	216	28	53	10	1	3	27	22	39	.245	.326	.343	79	-7	-6	25	0	1	-1	-2	3/O	-0.6

■ ALEX McCARTHY
McCarthy, Alexander George b: 5/12/1888, Chicago, Ill. d: 3/12/78, Salisbury, Md. BR/TR, 5'9", 150 lbs. Deb: 10/07/10

YEAR	TM/L	G	AB	R	H	2B	3B	HR	RBI	BB	SO	AVG	OBP	SLG	PRO+	BR	/A	RC	SB	CS	SBR	FR	POS	TPR
1910	Pit-N	3	12	1	1	0	1	0	0	0	2	.083	.083	.250	-3	-2	-2	0	0			0	/S	-0.1
1911	Pit-N	50	150	18	36	5	1	2	31	14	24	.240	.305	.327	74	-5	-6	16	4			-0	S2/3O	-0.4
1912	Pit-N	111	401	53	111	12	4	1	41	30	26	.277	.332	.334	84	-10	-9	48	8			3	*2/3	-0.8
1913	Pit-N	31	74	7	15	5	0	0	10	7	7	.203	.298	.270	66	-3	-3	7	1			-2	S3/2	-0.4
1914	Pit-N	57	173	14	26	0	1	1	14	6	17	.150	.192	.179	11	-19	-18	6	2			11	32/S	-0.5
1915	Pit-N	21	49	3	10	0	1	0	3	5	10	.204	.291	.245	64	-2	-2	4	1	2	-1	1	/2S31	-0.2
	Chi-N	23	72	4	19	3	0	1	6	5	7	.264	.329	.347	105	0	0	8	2	3	-1	11	23/S	1.2
	Yr	44	121	7	29	3	1	1	9	10	17	.240	.313	.306	88	-2	-1	12	3	5	-2	12		1.1
1916	Chi-N	37	107	10	26	2	3	0	6	11	7	.243	.341	.318	93	1	-0	12	1			-2	2/S	-0.1
	Pit-N	50	146	11	29	3	0	0	3	15	10	.199	.282	.219	54	-7	-7	11	3			-5	S/23	-1.1
	Yr	87	253	21	55	5	3	0	9	26	17	.217	.308	.261	72	-6	-8	24	4			-7		-1.2
1917	Pit-N	49	151	15	33	4	0	0	8	11	13	.219	.276	.245	58	-7	-7	11	1			7	32/S	0.0
Total	8	432	1335	136	306	34	11	5	122	104	123	.229	.295	.282	67	-53	-54	124	23	5		23	2S3/10	-2.3

■ JERRY McCARTHY
McCarthy, Jerome Francis b: 5/23/23, Brooklyn, N.Y. d: 10/3/65, Oceanside, N.Y. BL/TL, 6'1", 205 lbs. Deb: 6/19/48

YEAR	TM/L	G	AB	R	H	2B	3B	HR	RBI	BB	SO	AVG	OBP	SLG	PRO+	BR	/A	RC	SB	CS	SBR	FR	POS	TPR
1948	StL-A	2	3	0	1	0	0	0	0	0	0	.333	.333	.333	76	-0	-0	0	0	0	0	-1	/1	0.0

■ JACK McCARTHY
McCarthy, John Arthur b: 3/26/1869, Gilbertville, Mass. d: 9/11/31, Chicago, Ill. BL/TL, 5'9", 155 lbs. Deb: 8/03/1893

YEAR	TM/L	G	AB	R	H	2B	3B	HR	RBI	BB	SO	AVG	OBP	SLG	PRO+	BR	/A	RC	SB	CS	SBR	FR	POS	TPR
1893	Cin-N	49	195	28	55	8	3	0	22	22	7	.282	.355	.354	88	-2	-3	27	6			-1	O/1	-0.4
1894	Cin-N	40	167	29	45	9	1	0	21	17	6	.269	.348	.335	64	-9	-10	21	3			2	O1	-0.6
1898	Pit-N	137	537	75	155	13	12	4	78	34		.289	.334	.380	109	4	5	72	7			4	*O	0.0
1899	Pit-N	138	560	108	171	22	17	3	67	39		.305	.355	.421	115	11	11	96	28			-5	*O	-0.2
1900	Chi-N	124	503	68	148	16	7	0	48	24		.294	.329	.354	94	-6	-4	67	22			-1	*O	-1.3
1901	Cle-A	86	343	60	110	14	7	0	32	30		.321	.380	.402	124	10	12	60	9			-0	O	0.9
1902	Cle-A	95	359	45	102	31	5	0	41	24		.284	.329	.398	107	1	3	54	12			-5	O	-0.7
1903	Cle-A	108	415	47	110	20	8	0	43	19		.265	.297	.352	98	-2	-1	51	15			-3	*O	-1.1
	Chi-N	24	101	11	28	5	0	0	14	4		.277	.305	.327	84	-3	-2	13	8			-3	O	-0.5
1904	Chi-N	115	432	36	114	14	2	0	51	23		.264	.301	.306	89	-5	-5	47	14			-5	*O	-1.5
1905	Chi-N	59	170	16	47	4	3	0	14	10		.276	.317	.335	93	-1	-2	22	8			2	O/1	-0.2
1906	Bro-N	91	322	23	98	13	1	0	35	20		.304	.345	.351	129	7	9	44	9			2	O	1.0
1907	Bro-N	25	91	4	20	2	0	0	8	2		.220	.237	.242	56	-5	-4	7	4			-4	O	-1.0
Total	12	1091	4195	550	1203	171	66	7	474	268	13	.287	.332	.364	102	-2	9	582	145			-16	*O/1	-5.6

■ JOHNNY McCARTHY
McCarthy, John Joseph b: 1/7/10, Chicago, Ill. d: 9/13/73, Mundelein, Ill. BL/TL, 6'1.5", 185 lbs. Deb: 9/02/34

YEAR	TM/L	G	AB	R	H	2B	3B	HR	RBI	BB	SO	AVG	OBP	SLG	PRO+	BR	/A	RC	SB	CS	SBR	FR	POS	TPR
1934	Bro-N	17	39	7	7	2	0	1	5	2	2	.179	.220	.308	42	-3	-3	3	0			1	1	-0.2
1935	Bro-N	22	48	9	12	1	1	0	4	2	9	.250	.280	.313	60	-3	-3	4	1			-3	1	-0.5
1936	NY-N	4	16	1	7	0	0	1	2	0	1	.438	.438	.625	185	2	2	4	1			1	/1	0.3
1937	*NY-N	114	420	53	117	19	3	10	65	24	37	.279	.322	.410	96	-2	-3	56	2			2	*1	-0.6
1938	NY-N	134	470	55	128	13	4	8	59	39	28	.272	.329	.368	91	-5	-6	60	3			-3	*1	-1.9

YEAR	TM/L	G	AB	R	H	2B	3B	HR	RBI	BB	SO	AVG	OBP	SLG	PRO+	BR	/A	RC	SB	CS	SBR	FR	POS	TPR
1939	NY-N	50	80	12	21	6	1	1	11	3	8	.262	.298	.400	85	-2	-2	9	0			-2	1/OP	-0.4
1940	NY-N	51	67	6	16	4	0	0	5	2	8	.239	.261	.299	53	-4	-4	4	0			1	/1	-0.3
1941	NY-N	14	40	1	13	3	0	0	12	3	0	.325	.372	.400	115	1	1	6	0			1	/1O	0.0
1943	Bos-N	78	313	32	95	24	6	2	33	10	19	.304	.327	.438	122	6	7	41	1			1	1	0.4
1946	Bos-N	2	7	0	1	0	0	0	1	2	0	.143	.333	.143	37	-0	-0	1	0			-1	/1	0.0
1948	NY-N	56	57	6	15	0	1	2	12	3	2	.263	.300	.404	88	-1	-1	7	0			-0	/1	-0.1
Total	11	542	1557	182	432	72	16	25	209	90	114	.277	.319	.392	95	-13	-14	194	8			-2	1/OP	-3.3

■ JOE McCARTHY
McCarthy, Joseph N. b: 12/25/1881, Syracuse, N.Y. d: 1/12/37, Syracuse, N.Y. TR , Deb: 9/27/05

YEAR	TM/L	G	AB	R	H	2B	3B	HR	RBI	BB	SO	AVG	OBP	SLG	PRO+	BR	/A	RC	SB	CS	SBR	FR	POS	TPR
1905	NY-A	1	2	0	0	0	0	0	0	0		.000	.000	.000	-90	-0	-0	0	0			0	/C	0.0
1906	StL-N	15	37	3	9	2	0	0	2	2		.243	.282	.297	86	-1	-1	3	0			0	C	0.1
Total	2	16	39	3	9	2	0	0	2	2		.231	.268	.282	76	-1	-1	3	0			0	/C	0.1

■ TOMMY McCARTHY
McCarthy, Thomas Francis Michael b: 7/24/1863, Boston, Mass. d: 8/5/22, Boston, Mass. BR/TR, 5'7", 170 lbs. Deb: 7/10/1884   MH

YEAR	TM/L	G	AB	R	H	2B	3B	HR	RBI	BB	SO	AVG	OBP	SLG	PRO+	BR	/A	RC	SB	CS	SBR	FR	POS	TPR
1884	Bos-U	53	209	37	45	2	2	0		6		.215	.237	.244	64	-8	-7	12	0			-1	O/P	-0.7
1885	Bos-N	40	148	16	27	2	0	0	11	5	25	.182	.209	.196	33	-11	-10	6				3	O	-0.7
1886	Phi-N	8	27	6	5	2	1	0	3	2	3	.185	.241	.333	73	-1	-1	2	1			-1	/OP	-0.1
1887	Phi-N	18	70	7	13	4	0	0	6	2	5	.186	.219	.243	28	-7	-7	7	15			-8	/O2S3	-1.2
1888	*StL-a	131	511	107	140	20	3	1	68	38		.274	.328	.331	103	9	0	88	93			30	*O/P	2.3
1889	StL-a	140	604	136	176	24	7	2	63	46	26	.291	.348	.364	93	4	-9	99	57			14	*O/2P	0.0
1890	StL-a	133	548	137	192	28	9	6		66		.350	.430	.467	147	**48**	35	**150**	83			7	*O3/2M	3.2
1891	StL-a	136	578	127	179	21	6	8	95	50	19	.310	.375	.408	110	20	5	105	37			-1	*O2S/3P	0.1
1892	*Bos-N	152	603	119	146	19	5	4	63	93	29	.242	.347	.310	93	4	-4	85	53			2	*O	-0.6
1893	Bos-N	116	462	107	160	28	6	5	111	64	10	.346	.429	.465	130	28	21	115	46			3	*O/2S	1.6
1894	Bos-N	127	539	118	188	21	8	13	126	59	17	.349	.419	.490	111	19	10	132	43			11	*O/S2P	1.0
1895	Bos-N	117	452	90	131	13	2	2	73	72	12	.290	.391	.341	85	-2	-9	69	18			-10	*O/2	-2.1
1896	Bro-N	104	377	62	94	8	4	3	47	34	11	.249	.316	.316	73	-17	-13	46	22			-2	*O	-1.8
Total	13	1275	5128	1069	1496	192	53	44	<u>666</u>	537	<u>163</u>	.292	.364	.376	102	87	11	916	468			47	*O/23SP	1.0

■ BILL McCARTHY
McCarthy, William John b: Boston, Mass. d: 2/4/28, Washington, D.C. TR , Deb: 6/05/05

YEAR	TM/L	G	AB	R	H	2B	3B	HR	RBI	BB	SO	AVG	OBP	SLG	PRO+	BR	/A	RC	SB	CS	SBR	FR	POS	TPR
1905	Bos-N	1	3	0	0	0	0	0	0	0	0	.000	.000	.000	-99	-1	-1	0	0			-0	/C	0.0
1907	Cin-N	3	8	1	1	0	0	0	0	0	0	.125	.125	.125	-20	-1	-1	0	0			0	/C	0.0
Total	2	4	11	1	1	0	0	0	0	0	0	.091	.091	.091	-42	-2	-2	0	0			-0	/C	0.0

■ FRANK McCARTON
McCarton, Francis b: 10/6/1854, Middleton, Conn. d: 6/17/07, New York, N.Y. Deb: 4/26/1872

YEAR	TM/L	G	AB	R	H	2B	3B	HR	RBI	BB	SO	AVG	OBP	SLG	PRO+	BR	/A	RC	SB	CS	SBR	FR	POS	TPR
1872	Man-n	19	83	19	31	5	0	0		1		.373	.381	.434	159	5	6	14					O	0.5

■ LEW McCARTY
McCarty, George Lewis b: 11/17/1888, Milton, Pa. d: 6/9/30, Reading, Pa. BR/TR, 5'11.5", 192 lbs. Deb: 8/30/13

YEAR	TM/L	G	AB	R	H	2B	3B	HR	RBI	BB	SO	AVG	OBP	SLG	PRO+	BR	/A	RC	SB	CS	SBR	FR	POS	TPR
1913	Bro-N	9	26	1	6	0	0	0	2	2	2	.231	.286	.231	47	-2	-2	2	0			1	/C	0.0
1914	Bro-N	90	284	20	72	14	2	1	30	14	22	.254	.293	.327	83	-6	-7	27	1			0	C	-0.3
1915	Bro-N	84	276	19	66	9	4	0	19	7	23	.239	.261	.301	68	-11	-11	23	7	4	-0	-9	C	-1.6
1916	Bro-N	55	150	17	47	6	1	0	13	14	16	.313	.383	.367	127	6	6	24	4			-4	C1	0.2
	NY-N	25	68	6	27	3	4	0	9	7	9	.397	.453	.559	222	9	9	18	0			-0	C	1.1
	Yr	80	218	23	74	9	5	0	22	21	25	.339	.405	.427	155	15	15	41	4			-4		1.3
1917	*NY-N	56	162	15	40	3	2	2	19	14	6	.247	.311	.327	99	-1	-0	16	1			-4	C	0.0
1918	NY-N	86	257	16	69	7	3	0	24	17	13	.268	.321	.319	97	-1	-1	27	3			-7	C	-0.1
1919	NY-N	85	210	17	59	5	4	2	21	18	15	.281	.341	.371	115	4	4	27	4			-8	C	0.0
1920	NY-N	36	38	2	5	0	0	0	0	4	2	.132	.214	.132	1	-5	-5	1	2	0	1	2	/C	-0.1
	StL-N	5	7	0	2	0	0	0	0	5	0	.286	.583	.286	160	1	1	2	0	0	0	-0	/C	0.1
	Yr	41	45	2	7	0	0	0	0	9	2	.156	.296	.156	33	-4	-3	3	2	0	1	2		0.0
1921	StL-N	1	1	0	0	0	0	0	0	0	1	.000	.000	.000	-99	-0	-0	0	0	0	0	0	H	0.0
Total	9	532	1479	113	393	47	20	5	137	102	109	.266	.318	.335	97	-6	-6	167	20	<u>4</u>		-28	C/1	-0.7

■ TIM McCARVER
McCarver, James Timothy b: 10/16/41, Memphis, Tenn. BL/TR, 6', 183 lbs. Deb: 9/10/59

YEAR	TM/L	G	AB	R	H	2B	3B	HR	RBI	BB	SO	AVG	OBP	SLG	PRO+	BR	/A	RC	SB	CS	SBR	FR	POS	TPR
1959	StL-N	8	24	3	4	1	0	0	2	2	1	.167	.231	.208	17	-3	-3	1	0	0	0	-1	/C	-0.3
1960	StL-N	10	10	3	2	0	0	0	0	0	2	.200	.200	.200	9	-1	-1	0	0	0	0	-0	/C	-0.1
1961	StL-N	22	67	5	16	2	1	1	6	0	5	.239	.239	.343	47	-5	-5	5	0	0	0	-2	C	-0.5
1963	StL-N	127	405	39	117	12	7	4	51	27	43	.289	.336	.383	97	3	-1	53	5	2	0	1	*C	0.4
1964	*StL-N	143	465	53	134	19	3	9	52	40	44	.288	.346	.400	101	6	1	64	2	0	1	-9	*C	-0.2
1965	StL-N	113	409	48	113	17	2	11	48	31	26	.276	.329	.408	97	3	3	55	5	1	1	-3	*C	0.0
1966	StL-N	150	543	50	149	19	**13**	12	68	36	38	.274	.322	.424	105	3	3	71	9	6	-1	-5	*C	0.0
1967	*StL-N	138	471	68	139	26	3	14	69	54	32	.295	.374	.452	137	22	23	78	8	8	-2	2	*C	3.2
1968	*StL-N	128	434	35	110	15	6	5	48	26	31	.253	.297	.350	95	-4	-4	44	4	3	-1	3	*C	0.3
1969	StL-N	138	515	46	134	27	3	7	51	49	26	.260	.327	.365	93	-4	-5	60	4	9	-4	9	*C	0.9
1970	Phi-N	44	164	16	47	11	1	4	14	14	10	.287	.346	.439	112	2	2	24	2	0	-1	-0	C	0.3
1971	Phi-N	134	474	51	132	20	5	8	46	43	26	.278	.342	.392	107	4	4	62	5	3	-0	-7	*C	0.0
1972	Phi-N	45	152	14	36	8	0	2	14	17	15	.237	.322	.329	83	-3	-3	17	1	2	-1	-3	C	-0.4
	Mon-N	77	239	19	60	5	1	5	20	19	14	.251	.309	.343	84	-5	-5	24	4	4	-1	1	CO/3	-0.3
	Yr	122	391	33	96	13	1	7	34	36	29	.246	.314	.338	83	-7	-8	40	5	6	-2	-2		-0.7
1973	StL-N	130	331	30	88	16	4	3	49	38	31	.266	.345	.366	97	-1	-1	44	2	0	1	-6	1C	-0.8
1974	StL-N	74	106	13	23	0	1	0	11	22	6	.217	.366	.236	72	-3	-3	11	0	1	-1	-1	C/1	-0.2
	Bos-A	11	28	3	7	1	0	0	1	4	1	.250	.344	.286	77	-0	-1	3	1	0	0	1	/CD	0.1
1975	Bos-A	12	21	1	8	2	1	0	3	1	3	.381	.409	.571	161	2	2	5	0	0	0	-0	/C	0.2
	Phi-N	47	59	6	15	2	0	1	7	14	7	.254	.397	.339	102	1	1	9	0	0	0	1	C/1	0.2
1976	*Phi-N	90	155	26	43	11	2	3	29	35	14	.277	.414	.432	136	10	9	31	2	1	0	5	C/1	1.7
1977	*Phi-N	93	169	28	54	13	2	6	30	28	11	.320	.422	.527	146	14	13	37	3	5	-2	1	C/1	1.1
1978	*Phi-N	90	146	18	36	9	1	1	14	28	24	.247	.375	.342	101	2	2	20	2	2	-1	1	C1	0.3
1979	Phi-N	79	137	13	33	5	1	1	12	19	12	.241	.338	.314	76	-3	-4	14	2	0	1	3	C/O	0.0
1980	Phi-N	6	5	2	1	1	0	0	2	1	0	.200	.333	.400	98	-0	-0	0	0	0	0	-0	/1	0.0
Total	21	1909	5529	590	1501	242	57	97	645	548	422	.271	.340	.388	102	41	24	735	61	49	-11	-10	*C1/O3D	6.0

■ AL McCAULEY
McCauley, Allen A. b: 3/4/1863, Indianapolis, Ind. d: 8/24/17, Wayne Twnshp., Ind BL/TL, 6', 180 lbs. Deb: 6/21/1884

YEAR	TM/L	G	AB	R	H	2B	3B	HR	RBI	BB	SO	AVG	OBP	SLG	PRO+	BR	/A	RC	SB	CS	SBR	FR	POS	TPR
1884	Ind-a	17	53	6	10	1	0	0		12		.189	.358	.226	102	1	1	4				0	P/1O	0.0
1890	Phi-N	112	418	63	102	25	7	1	42	57	38	.244	.346	.344	101	3	2	54	8			-6	*1	-1.0
1891	Was-a	59	206	36	58	5	8	1	31	30	13	.282	.378	.398	131	7	9	35	9			-1	1	0.4
Total	3	188	677	106	170	30	16	2	<u>73</u>	99	<u>51</u>	.251	.357	.352	110	12	12	94	17			-7	1/PO	-0.6

■ JIM McCAULEY
McCauley, James A. b: 3/24/1863, Stanley, N.Y. d: 9/14/30, Canandaiqua.N.Y. BL/TR, 6', 180 lbs. Deb: 9/17/1884

YEAR	TM/L	G	AB	R	H	2B	3B	HR	RBI	BB	SO	AVG	OBP	SLG	PRO+	BR	/A	RC	SB	CS	SBR	FR	POS	TPR
1884	StL-a	1	2	0	0	0	0	0		0		.000	.000	.000	-96	-0	-0	0				1	/C	0.1
1885	Buf-N	24	84	4	15	2	1	0	7	11	12	.179	.274	.226	61	-3	-3	5				1	C/O	0.0
	Chi-N	3	6	1	1	0	0	0	0	2	3	.167	.375	.167	70	0	-0	0				-2	/CO	-0.1
	Yr	27	90	5	16	2	1	0	7	13	15	.178	.282	.222	62	-3	-4	6				-1		-0.1
1886	Bro-a	11	30	5	7	1	0	0		11		.233	.439	.267	124	2	2	5	2			1	C	0.3
Total	3	39	122	10	23	3	1	0	<u>7</u>	24	<u>15</u>	.189	.322	.230	77	-1	-2	10	2			0	/CO	0.3

YEAR	TM/L	G	AB	R	H	2B	3B	HR	RBI	BB	SO	AVG	OBP	SLG	PRO+	BR	/A	RC	SB	CS	SBR	FR	POS	TPR

■ PAT McCAULEY   McCauley, Patrick M.   b: 6/10/1870, Ware, Mass.   d: 1/23/17, Newark, N.J.   TR ,   Deb: 9/05/1893

YEAR	TM/L	G	AB	R	H	2B	3B	HR	RBI	BB	SO	AVG	OBP	SLG	PRO+	BR	/A	RC	SB	CS	SBR	FR	POS	TPR
1893	StL-N	5	16	0	1	0	0	0	0	0	1	.063	.063	.063	-66	-4	-4	0	0			1	/C	-0.1
1896	Was-N	26	84	14	21	3	0	3	11	7	8	.250	.315	.393	88	-2	-2	12	3			2	C/O	0.2
1903	NY-A	6	19	0	1	0	0	0	1	0		.053	.053	.053	-64	-4	-4	0	0			-2	/C	-0.4
Total	3	37	119	14	23	3	0	3	12	7	9	.193	.244	.294	45	-9	-9	12	3			1	/CO	-0.3

■ BILL McCAULEY   McCauley, William H.   b: 12/20/1869, Washington, D.C.   d: 1/27/26, Washington, D.C.   Deb: 8/31/1895

YEAR	TM/L	G	AB	R	H	2B	3B	HR	RBI	BB	SO	AVG	OBP	SLG	PRO+	BR	/A	RC	SB	CS	SBR	FR	POS	TPR
1895	Was-N	1	2	0	0	0	0	0	0	0	0	.000	.000	.000	-99	-1	-1	0	0			0	/S	0.0

■ HARRY McCHESNEY   McChesney, Harry Vincent "Pud"   b: 6/1/1880, Pittsburgh, Pa.   d: 8/11/60, Pittsburgh, Pa.   BR/TR, 5'9", 165 lbs.   Deb: 9/17/04

YEAR	TM/L	G	AB	R	H	2B	3B	HR	RBI	BB	SO	AVG	OBP	SLG	PRO+	BR	/A	RC	SB	CS	SBR	FR	POS	TPR
1904	Chi-N	22	88	9	23	6	2	0	11	4		.261	.293	.375	108	0	0	11	2			-2	O	-0.2

■ PETE McCLANAHAN   McClanahan, Robert Hugh   b: 10/24/06, Coldspring, Tex.   d: 10/28/87, Mont Belvieu, Tex.   BR/TR, 5'9", 170 lbs.   Deb: 4/24/31

YEAR	TM/L	G	AB	R	H	2B	3B	HR	RBI	BB	SO	AVG	OBP	SLG	PRO+	BR	/A	RC	SB	CS	SBR	FR	POS	TPR
1931	Pit-N	7	4	2	2	0	0	0	2	0	0	.500	.667	.500	220	1	1	2	0			0	H	0.1

■ HARVEY McCLELLAN   McClellan, Harvey McDowell "Little Mac"   b: 12/22/1894, Cynthiana, Ky.   d: 11/6/25, Cynthiana, Ky.   BR/TR, 5'9.5", 143 lbs.   Deb: 5/31/19

YEAR	TM/L	G	AB	R	H	2B	3B	HR	RBI	BB	SO	AVG	OBP	SLG	PRO+	BR	/A	RC	SB	CS	SBR	FR	POS	TPR
1919	Chi-A	7	12	2	4	0	0	0	1	1	1	.333	.385	.333	102	0	0	1	0			1	/3S	0.1
1920	Chi-A	10	18	4	6	1	1	0	5	4	1	.333	.455	.500	153	2	2	5	2	0	1	-3	/S3	0.0
1921	Chi-A	63	196	20	35	4	1	1	14	14	18	.179	.237	.224	18	-24	-24	11	2	3	-1	18	2SO/3	-0.4
1922	Chi-A	91	301	28	68	17	3	2	28	16	32	.226	.272	.322	55	-21	-21	27	3	2	-0	-4	3/S2O	-1.6
1923	Chi-A	141	550	67	129	29	3	1	41	27	44	.235	.270	.304	52	-41	-40	45	14	11	-2	-18	*S/2	-4.4
1924	Chi-A	32	85	9	15	3	0	0	9	6	7	.176	.239	.212	17	-11	-10	5	2	0	1	3	S/23O	-0.3
Total	6	344	1162	130	257	54	8	4	98	68	103	.221	.267	.292	46	-95	-93	95	23	16		-4	S/32O	-6.6

■ BILL McCLELLAN   McClellan, William Henry   b: 3/22/1856, Chicago, Ill.   d: 7/3/29, Chicago, Ill.   BL/TL, 156 lbs.   Deb: 5/20/1878

YEAR	TM/L	G	AB	R	H	2B	3B	HR	RBI	BB	SO	AVG	OBP	SLG	PRO+	BR	/A	RC	SB	CS	SBR	FR	POS	TPR
1878	Chi-N	48	205	26	46	6	1	0	29	2	13	.224	.232	.263	59	-8	-10	13				-8	*2/SO	-1.3
1881	Pro-N	68	259	30	43	3	1	0	16	15	21	.166	.212	.185	26	-21	-21	10				-7	SO/2	-2.2
1883	Phi-N	80	326	42	75	21	4	1	33	19	18	.230	.272	.328	89	-7	-2	30				5	*S/O3	0.6
1884	Phi-N	111	450	71	116	13	2	3	33	28	43	.258	.301	.316	99	-3	-1	44				-13	*S/O	-0.1
1885	Bro-a	112	464	85	124	22	7	0		28		.267	.317	.345	111	7	6	52				-5	32	0.6
1886	Bro-a	141	595	131	152	33	9	1		56		.255	.322	.346	110	8	7	82	43			-7	*2	0.0
1887	Bro-a	136	548	109	144	24	6	1		80		.263	.363	.334	96	2	0	94	70			-22	*2	-1.7
1888	Bro-a	74	278	33	57	7	3	0	21	40		.205	.307	.252	83	-3	-3	26	13			-7	2O	-0.8
	Cle-a	22	72	6	16	0	0	0	5	6		.222	.282	.222	67	-3	-2	6	6			-3	O/2S	-0.5
	Yr	96	350	39	73	7	3	0	26	46		.209	.302	.246	80	-6	-5	33	19			-10		-1.3
Total	8	792	3197	533	773	129	33	6	137	274	95	.242	.305	.308	91	-28	-24	358	132			-67	2S/3O	-5.4

■ LLOYD McCLENDON   McClendon, Lloyd Glenn   b: 1/11/59, Gary, Ind.   BR/TR, 5'10", 190 lbs.   Deb: 4/06/87

YEAR	TM/L	G	AB	R	H	2B	3B	HR	RBI	BB	SO	AVG	OBP	SLG	PRO+	BR	/A	RC	SB	CS	SBR	FR	POS	TPR
1987	Cin-N	45	72	8	15	5	0	2	13	4	15	.208	.250	.444	57	-4	-5	7	1	0	0	-1	C/13O	-0.4
1988	Cin-N	72	137	9	30	4	0	3	14	15	22	.219	.305	.314	75	-4	-4	13	4	0	1	-1	CO1/3	-0.4
1989	*Chi-N	92	259	47	74	12	1	12	40	37	31	.286	.377	.479	133	15	13	48	6	4	-1	-7	O1/3C	0.2
1990	Chi-N	49	107	5	17	3	0	1	10	14	21	.159	.256	.215	28	-10	-11	6	1	0	0	2	O/C1	-1.0
	Pit-N	4	3	1	1	0	0	1	2	0	1	.333	.333	1.333	350	1	1	1	0	0	0	0	/O	0.1
	Yr	53	110	6	18	3	0	2	12	14	22	.164	.258	.245	36	-9	-10	8	1	0	0	2		-0.9
Total	4	262	578	70	137	24	1	19	79	70	90	.237	.323	.381	91	-2	-7	76	12	4	1	-8	/O1C3	-1.5

■ JEFF McCLESKEY   McCleskey, Jefferson Lamar   b: 11/6/1891, Americus, Ga.   d: 5/11/71, Americus, Ga.   BL/TR, 5'11", 160 lbs.   Deb: 9/08/13

YEAR	TM/L	G	AB	R	H	2B	3B	HR	RBI	BB	SO	AVG	OBP	SLG	PRO+	BR	/A	RC	SB	CS	SBR	FR	POS	TPR
1913	Bos-N	2	3	0	0	0	0	0	0	1	0	.000	.250	.000	-25	-0	-0	0	0			-0	/3	0.0

■ MC CLOSKEY   McCloskey   b: Brooklyn, N.Y.   Deb: 5/25/1875

YEAR	TM/L	G	AB	R	H	2B	3B	HR	RBI	BB	SO	AVG	OBP	SLG	PRO+	BR	/A	RC	SB	CS	SBR	FR	POS	TPR
1875	Was-n	11	40	1	7	0	0	0		1		.175	.195	.175	30	-3	-2	1					C	-0.1

■ BILL McCLOSKEY   McCloskey, William George   b: 5/1854, Pennsylvania   5'8", 155 lbs.   Deb: 8/18/1884

YEAR	TM/L	G	AB	R	H	2B	3B	HR	RBI	BB	SO	AVG	OBP	SLG	PRO+	BR	/A	RC	SB	CS	SBR	FR	POS	TPR
1884	Wil-U	9	30	0	3	0	0	0		0		.100	.100	.100	-31	-4	-4	0	0			3	/OC	0.0

■ HALL McCLURE   McClure, Harold Murray "Mac"   b: 8/8/1859, Lewisburg, Pa.   d: 3/1/19, Lewisburg, Pa.   TR , 6', 165 lbs.   Deb: 5/10/1882

YEAR	TM/L	G	AB	R	H	2B	3B	HR	RBI	BB	SO	AVG	OBP	SLG	PRO+	BR	/A	RC	SB	CS	SBR	FR	POS	TPR
1882	Bos-N	2	6	1	2	0	0	0	0	0	1	.333	.333	.333	115	0	0	1				-0	/O	0.0

■ LARRY McCLURE   McClure, Lawrence Ledwith   b: 10/3/1885, Wayne, W.Va.   d: 8/31/49, Huntington, W.Va.   BR , 5'6.5", 130 lbs.   Deb: 7/26/10

YEAR	TM/L	G	AB	R	H	2B	3B	HR	RBI	BB	SO	AVG	OBP	SLG	PRO+	BR	/A	RC	SB	CS	SBR	FR	POS	TPR
1910	NY-A	1	1	0	0	0	0	0	0	0	0	.000	.000	.000	-95	-0	-0	0	0			0	/O	0.0

■ AMBY McCONNELL   McConnell, Ambrose Moses   b: 4/29/1883, N.Pownal, Vt.   d: 5/20/42, Utica, N.Y.   BL/TR, 5'7", 150 lbs.   Deb: 4/17/08

YEAR	TM/L	G	AB	R	H	2B	3B	HR	RBI	BB	SO	AVG	OBP	SLG	PRO+	BR	/A	RC	SB	CS	SBR	FR	POS	TPR
1908	Bos-A	140	502	77	140	10	6	2	43	38		.279	.330	.335	115	10	9	65	31			-19	*2/S	-1.5
1909	Bos-A	121	453	61	108	7	8	0	36	34		.238	.300	.289	84	-7	-8	47	26			14	*2	0.4
1910	Bos-A	11	35	6	6	0	0	0	1	5		.171	.310	.171	50	-2	-2	3	4			-1	2	-0.3
	Chi-A	33	120	13	33	2	3	0	5	7		.275	.320	.342	112	1	1	14	4			-1	2	0.0
	Yr	44	155	19	39	2	3	0	6	12		.252	.318	.303	97	-1	-0	17	8			-1		-0.3
1911	Chi-A	104	396	45	111	11	5	1	34	23		.280	.331	.341	90	-7	-5	47	7			-6	*2	-1.1
Total	4	409	1506	202	398	30	22	3	119	107		.264	.320	.319	97	-4	-5	176	72			-13	2/S	-2.5

■ GEORGE McCONNELL   McConnell, George Neely "Slats"   b: 9/16/1877, Shelbyville, Tenn.   d: 5/10/64, Chattanooga, Tenn.   BR/TR, 6'3", 190 lbs.   Deb: 4/13/09

YEAR	TM/L	G	AB	R	H	2B	3B	HR	RBI	BB	SO	AVG	OBP	SLG	PRO+	BR	/A	RC	SB	CS	SBR	FR	POS	TPR
1909	NY-A	13	43	4	9	0	1	0	5	1		.209	.227	.256	52	-2	-2	3	1			2	1/P	0.0
1912	NY-A	42	91	11	27	4	2	0	8	4		.297	.333	.385	99	0	-0	11	0			5	P/1	0.0
1913	NY-A	39	67	4	12	2	0	0	2	0	11	.179	.179	.209	13	-7	-7	3	0			5	P/1	0.0
1914	Chi-N	1	2	0	0	0	0	0	0	0	1	.000	.000	.000	-99	-0	-0	0	0			0	/P	0.0
1915	Chi-F	53	125	14	31	6	2	1	18	0	16	.248	.254	.352	83	-4	-3	12	2			2	P	0.0
1916	Chi-N	28	57	2	9	0	0	0	0	2	4	.158	.200	.158	10	-6	-7	2	0			1	P	0.0
Total	6	176	385	35	88	12	5	1	33	7	32	.229	.248	.294	60	-20	-21	31	3			15	P/1	0.0

■ SAM McCONNELL   McConnell, Samuel Faulkner   b: 6/8/1895, Philadelphia, Pa.   d: 6/27/81, Phoenixville, Pa.   BL/TR, 5'6.5", 150 lbs.   Deb: 4/19/15

YEAR	TM/L	G	AB	R	H	2B	3B	HR	RBI	BB	SO	AVG	OBP	SLG	PRO+	BR	/A	RC	SB	CS	SBR	FR	POS	TPR
1915	Phi-A	6	11	1	2	1	0	0	1	3		.182	.250	.273	58	-1	-1	1				2	/3	0.1

■ DON McCORMACK   McCormack, Donald Ross   b: 9/18/55, Omak, Wash.   BR/TR, 6'3", 205 lbs.   Deb: 9/30/80

YEAR	TM/L	G	AB	R	H	2B	3B	HR	RBI	BB	SO	AVG	OBP	SLG	PRO+	BR	/A	RC	SB	CS	SBR	FR	POS	TPR
1980	Phi-N	2	1	0	1	0	0	0	0	0	0	1.000	1.000	1.000	436	0	0	1	0	0	0	1	/C	0.1
1981	Phi-N	3	4	0	1	0	0	0	0	0	1	.250	.250	.250	40	-0	-0	0	0	0	0	0	/C	0.0
Total	2	5	5	0	2	0	0	0	0	0	1	.400	.400	.400	121	0	0	1	0	0	0	1	/C	0.1

■ FRANK McCORMICK   McCormick, Frank Andrew "Buck"   b: 6/9/11, New York, N.Y.   d: 11/21/82, Manhassett, N.Y.   BR/TR, 6'4", 205 lbs.   Deb: 9/11/34   C

YEAR	TM/L	G	AB	R	H	2B	3B	HR	RBI	BB	SO	AVG	OBP	SLG	PRO+	BR	/A	RC	SB	CS	SBR	FR	POS	TPR
1934	Cin-N	12	16	1	5	2	1	0	5	0	1	.313	.313	.563	132	1	1	2	0			-0	/1	0.0
1937	Cin-N	24	83	5	27	5	0	0	9	2	4	.325	.341	.386	102	-0	0	9	1			1	1/2O	0.0
1938	Cin-N	151	640	89	209	40	4	5	106	18	17	.327	.348	.425	115	8	10	93	1			-3	*1	-0.5
1939	Cin-N	156	630	99	209	41	4	18	128	40	16	.332	.374	.495	131	26	26	110	1			2	*1	0.9
1940	*Cin-N	155	618	93	191	44	3	19	127	52	26	.309	.367	.482	131	26	26	104	2			1	*1	1.2
1941	Cin-N	154	603	77	162	31	5	17	97	40	13	.269	.318	.421	107	3	3	76	2			1	*1	-1.8
1942	Cin-N	145	564	58	156	24	0	13	89	45	18	.277	.332	.388	111	6	6	72	1			6	*1	0.1
1943	Cin-N	126	472	56	143	28	0	8	56	29	15	.303	.345	.413	120	10	10	67	2			4	*1	0.9

YEAR	TM/L	G	AB	R	H	2B	3B	HR	RBI	BB	SO	AVG	OBP	SLG	PRO+	BR	/A	RC	SB	CS	SBR	FR	POS	TPR
1944	Cin-N	153	581	85	177	37	3	20	102	57	17	.305	.371	.482	144	29	31	101	7			12	*1	3.2
1945	Cin-N	152	580	68	160	33	0	10	81	56	22	.276	.345	.384	105	2	3	75	6			5	*1	0.3
1946	Phi-N	135	504	46	143	20	2	11	66	36	21	.284	.333	.397	110	3	4	66	2			4	*1	-0.2
1947	Phi-N	15	40	7	9	2	0	1	8	3	2	.225	.279	.350	69	-2	-2	3	0			-1	1	-0.3
	Bos-N	81	212	24	75	18	2	2	43	11	8	.354	.386	.486	133	9	9	37	2			-1	1	0.5
	Yr	96	252	31	84	20	2	3	51	14	10	.333	.368	.464	123	6	7	40	2			-2		0.2
1948	*Bos-N	75	180	14	45	9	2	4	34	10	9	.250	.289	.389	84	-5	-5	19	0			3	1	-0.2
Total	13	1534	5723	722	1711	334	26	128	951	399	189	.299	.348	.434	118	115	124	834	27			32	*1/2O	4.1

■ MOOSE McCORMICK
McCormick, Harry Elwood b: 2/28/1881, Philadelphia, Pa. d: 7/9/62, Lewisburg, Pa. TL, 5'11", 180 lbs. Deb: 4/14/04

YEAR	TM/L	G	AB	R	H	2B	3B	HR	RBI	BB	SO	AVG	OBP	SLG	PRO+	BR	/A	RC	SB	CS	SBR	FR	POS	TPR
1904	NY-N	59	203	28	54	9	5	1	26	13		.266	.310	.374	108	3	2	28	13			-5	O	-0.4
	Pit-N	66	238	25	69	10	6	2	23	13		.290	.327	.408	125	7	6	35	6			-6	O	-0.1
	Yr	125	441	53	123	19	11	3	49	26		.279	.319	.392	117	10	8	64	19			-10		-0.5
1908	Phi-N	11	22	0	2	0	0	0	2	2		.091	.167	.091	-16	-3	-3	0	0			0	/O	-0.3
	NY-N	73	252	31	76	16	3	0	32	4		.302	.313	.389	120	6	5	32	6			-11	O	-0.7
	Yr	84	274	31	78	16	3	0	34	6		.285	.300	.365	109	3	2	31	6			-11		-1.0
1909	NY-N	110	413	68	120	21	8	3	27	49		.291	.373	.402	138	20	19	63	4			-14	*O	0.2
1912	*NY-N	42	39	4	13	4	1	0	8	6	9	.333	.422	.487	144	3	3	8	1			-1	/O1	0.1
1913	*NY-N	57	80	9	22	2	3	0	15	5	13	.275	.318	.375	97	-0	-1	9	0			-1	O	-0.1
Total	5	418	1247	165	356	62	26	6	133	92	22	.285	.337	.391	122	35	31	176	30			-37	O/1	-1.3

■ JIM McCORMICK
McCormick, James Ambrose b: 11/2/1868, Spencer, Mass. d: 2/1/48, Saco, Maine BR/TR, 6'1", 160 lbs. Deb: 9/10/1892

YEAR	TM/L	G	AB	R	H	2B	3B	HR	RBI	BB	SO	AVG	OBP	SLG	PRO+	BR	/A	RC	SB	CS	SBR	FR	POS	TPR
1892	StL-N	3	11	0	0	0	0	0	0	1	5	.000	.083	.000	-78	-2	-2	0	0			-0	/23	-0.1

■ JERRY McCORMICK
McCormick, John b: Philadelphia, Pa. d: 9/19/05, Philadelphia, Pa. Deb: 5/01/1883

YEAR	TM/L	G	AB	R	H	2B	3B	HR	RBI	BB	SO	AVG	OBP	SLG	PRO+	BR	/A	RC	SB	CS	SBR	FR	POS	TPR
1883	Bal-a	93	389	40	102	16	6	0			2	.262	.266	.334	89	-4	-6	35				1	*3	-0.3
1884	Phi-U	67	295	41	84	12	2	0			4	.285	.294	.339	123	4	7	30	0			14	3/2OSP	1.9
	Was-U	42	157	23	34	8	2	0			1	.217	.222	.293	75	-5	-4	10	0			-6	3/S	-0.7
	Yr	109	452	64	118	20	4	0			5	.261	.269	.323	106	-1	3	40	0			8		1.2
Total	2	202	841	104	220	36	10	0			7	.262	.268	.328	98	-5	-2	76	0			9	3/SO2P	0.9

■ MIKE McCORMICK
McCormick, Michael J. "Kid" or "Dude" b: 1883, Jersey City, N.J. d: 11/18/53, Jersey City, N.J. BR/TR, 5'9", Deb: 4/14/04

YEAR	TM/L	G	AB	R	H	2B	3B	HR	RBI	BB	SO	AVG	OBP	SLG	PRO+	BR	/A	RC	SB	CS	SBR	FR	POS	TPR
1904	Bro-N	105	347	28	64	5	4	0	27	43		.184	.274	.222	57	-16	-15	29				-3	*3/2	-1.4

■ MIKE McCORMICK
McCormick, Myron Winthrop b: 5/6/17, Angels Camp, Cal. d: 4/14/76, Ventura, Cal. BR/TR, 6', 195 lbs. Deb: 4/16/40

YEAR	TM/L	G	AB	R	H	2B	3B	HR	RBI	BB	SO	AVG	OBP	SLG	PRO+	BR	/A	RC	SB	CS	SBR	FR	POS	TPR
1940	*Cin-N	110	417	48	125	20	0	1	30	13	36	.300	.326	.355	87	-7	-8	48	8			10	*O	-0.1
1941	Cin-N	110	369	52	106	17	3	4	31	30	24	.287	.341	.382	103	1	1	48	4			7	*O	0.4
1942	Cin-N	40	135	18	32	2	3	1	11	13	7	.237	.304	.319	82	-3	-3	13	0			2	O	-0.1
1943	Cin-N	4	15	0	2	0	0	0	0	2	0	.133	.235	.133	8	-2	-2	1	0			-0	/O	-0.2
1946	Cin-N	23	74	10	16	2	0	0	5	8	4	.216	.293	.243	55	-4	-4	6	0			1	O	-0.3
	Bos-N	59	164	23	43	6	2	1	16	11	7	.262	.309	.341	83	-4	-4	18	0			2	O	-0.2
	Yr	82	238	33	59	8	2	1	21	19	11	.248	.304	.311	75	-8	-8	23	0			3		-0.5
1947	Bos-N	92	284	42	81	13	7	3	36	20	21	.285	.332	.412	99	-2	-1	37	1			-2	O	-0.5
1948	*Bos-N	115	343	45	104	22	7	1	39	32	34	.303	.363	.417	112	5	6	52	1			-1	*O	-0.2
1949	*Bro-N	55	139	17	29	5	1	2	14	14	12	.209	.281	.302	54	-9	-9	12	1			-1	O	-1.2
1950	NY-N	4	4	0	0	0	0	0	0	0	2	.000	.000	.000	-99	-1	-1	0	0			0	H	0.0
	Chi-A	55	138	16	32	4	3	0	10	16	6	.232	.312	.304	60	-9	-8	12	0	1	-1	6	O	-0.3
1951	Was-A	81	243	31	70	9	3	1	23	29	20	.288	.364	.362	98	-0	0	30	1	2	-1	0	O	-0.2
Total	10	748	2325	302	640	100	29	14	215	188	173	.275	.330	.361	90	-35	-33	277	16	3		24	O	-2.9

■ BARRY McCORMICK
McCormick, William J. b: 12/25/1874, Maysville, Ky. d: 1/28/56, Cincinnati, Ohio TR, 5'9", Deb: 9/25/1895 U

YEAR	TM/L	G	AB	R	H	2B	3B	HR	RBI	BB	SO	AVG	OBP	SLG	PRO+	BR	/A	RC	SB	CS	SBR	FR	POS	TPR
1895	Lou-N	3	12	2	3	0	1	0	0	0	0	.250	.250	.417	76	-1	-0	2	1			-1	/S2	0.0
1896	Chi-N	45	168	22	37	3	1	1	23	14	30	.220	.280	.268	45	-13	-14	16	9			-6	3/S2O	-1.4
1897	Chi-N	101	419	87	112	8	10	2	55	33		.267	.324	.348	77	-12	-15	63	44			-3	3S/2	-1.4
1898	Chi-N	137	530	76	131	15	9	2	78	47		.247	.314	.321	85	-10	-10	60	15			4	*3/S2	-0.2
1899	Chi-N	102	376	48	97	15	2	2	52	25		.258	.311	.324	79	-12	-10	43	14			4	2/S	0.0
1900	Chi-N	110	379	35	83	13	5	3	48	38		.219	.292	.303	69	-17	-15	37	8			-8	S3/2	-1.1
1901	Chi-N	115	427	45	100	15	6	1	32	31		.234	.286	.304	76	-14	-12	42	12			0	*S/3	-0.5
1902	StL-A	139	504	55	124	14	4	3	51	37		.246	.304	.308	72	-19	-18	53	10			-12	*3/2O	-3.1
1903	StL-A	61	207	13	45	6	1	1	16	18		.217	.280	.271	69	-8	-7	18	5			-4	23/S	-1.0
	Was-A	63	219	14	47	10	2	0	23	10		.215	.249	.279	58	-11	-11	16	3			8	2	-0.1
	Yr	124	426	27	92	16	3	1	39	28		.216	.264	.275	64	-18	-18	34	8			5		-1.1
1904	Was-A	113	404	36	88	11	1	0	39	27		.218	.267	.250	67	-15	-14	31	9			-1	*2	-1.5
Total	10	989	3645	433	867	110	42	15	417	280	30	.238	.295	.303	72	-130	-126	381	130			-17	32S/O	-10.3

■ BARNEY McCOSKY
McCosky, William Barney b: 4/11/18, Coal Run, Pa. BL/TR, 6'1", 184 lbs. Deb: 4/18/39

YEAR	TM/L	G	AB	R	H	2B	3B	HR	RBI	BB	SO	AVG	OBP	SLG	PRO+	BR	/A	RC	SB	CS	SBR	FR	POS	TPR
1939	Det-A	147	611	120	190	33	14	4	58	70	45	.311	.384	.430	100	8	1	108	20	4	4	4	*O	0.4
1940	*Det-A	143	589	123	200	39	19	4	57	67	41	.340	.408	.491	120	29	21	123	13	9	-2	-2	*O	0.7
1941	Det-A	127	494	80	160	25	8	3	55	61	33	.324	.401	.425	108	15	8	92	8	3	1	0	*O	0.2
1942	Det-A	154	600	75	176	28	11	7	50	68	37	.293	.365	.412	109	15	9	94	11	5	0	5	*O	0.4
1946	Det-A	25	91	11	18	5	0	1	11	17	9	.198	.324	.286	67	-3	-4	10	0	0	0	0	O	-0.4
	Phi-A	92	308	33	109	17	4	1	34	43	13	.354	.433	.445	146	21	21	63	2	2	-1	-6	O	1.1
	Yr	117	399	44	127	22	4	2	45	60	22	.318	.407	.409	127	18	17	72	2	2	-1	-6		0.7
1947	Phi-A	137	546	77	179	22	7	1	52	57	29	.328	.395	.399	119	17	16	92	1	4	-2	9	*O	1.8
1948	Phi-A	135	515	95	168	21	5	0	46	68	22	.326	.405	.386	111	11	11	86	1	3	-2	-4	*O	0.0
1950	Phi-A	66	179	19	43	10	1	0	11	22	12	.240	.323	.307	63	-10	-10	19	0	0	0	-7	O	-1.5
1951	Phi-A	12	27	4	8	2	0	1	1	3	4	.296	.367	.481	125	1	1	5	0	0	0	-0	/O	0.0
	Cin-N	25	50	2	16	2	1	1	11	4	2	.320	.370	.460	120	1	1	9	0	0	0	-2	O	0.0
	Cle-A	31	61	8	13	3	0	0	2	8	5	.213	.304	.262	57	-4	-3	5	1	0	0	-1	O	-0.3
1952	Cle-A	54	80	14	17	4	1	1	6	8	5	.213	.284	.325	74	-3	-3	7	1	1	-0	-3	O	-0.6
1953	Cle-A	22	21	3	4	3	0	0	3	1	4	.190	.227	.333	51	-2	-2	2	0	0	0	0	H	-0.1
Total	11	1170	4172	664	1301	214	71	24	397	497	261	.312	.386	.414	109	96	68	715	58	31	-1	-5	*O	1.7

■ WILLIE McCOVEY
McCovey, Willie Lee "Stretch" b: 1/10/38, Mobile, Ala. BL/TL, 6'4", 198 lbs. Deb: 7/30/59 H

YEAR	TM/L	G	AB	R	H	2B	3B	HR	RBI	BB	SO	AVG	OBP	SLG	PRO+	BR	/A	RC	SB	CS	SBR	FR	POS	TPR
1959	SF-N	52	192	32	68	9	5	13	38	22	35	.354	.431	.656	189	23	24	53	2			-2	1	1.9
1960	SF-N	101	260	37	62	15	3	13	51	45	53	.238	.351	.469	130	8	10	45	1	1	-0	-3	1	0.3
1961	SF-N	106	328	59	89	12	3	18	50	37	60	.271	.354	.491	126	10	11	56	1	2	-1	-1	1	0.4
1962	*SF-N	91	229	41	67	6	1	20	54	29	39	.293	.372	.590	156	17	17	48	3	3	-1	-2	O1	1.0
1963	SF-N	152	564	103	158	19	5	44	102	50	119	.280	.350	.566	161	41	42	111	1	1	-0	-6	*O1	3.0
1964	SF-N	130	364	55	80	14	1	18	54	61	73	.220	.340	.412	108	6	5	53	2	1	0	-9	*O1	-0.6
1965	SF-N	160	540	93	149	17	4	39	92	88	118	.276	.383	.539	152	42	40	115	0	4	-2	0	*1	3.1
1966	SF-N	150	502	85	148	26	6	36	96	76	100	.295	.386	.586	163	47	45	119	2	1	-1	-3	*1	3.6
1967	SF-N	135	456	73	126	17	4	31	91	71	110	.276	.381	.535	162	36	37	94	3	3	-1	1	*1	3.3
1968	SF-N	148	523	81	153	16	4	36	105	72	71	.293	.383	.545	176	49	49	110	4	2	0	3	*1	5.1
1969	SF-N	149	491	101	157	26	2	45	126	121	66	.320	.458	.656	212	76	77	151	0	0	0	-5	*1	6.1

YEAR	TM/L	G	AB	R	H	2B	3B	HR	RBI	BB	SO	AVG	OBP	SLG	PRO+	BR	/A	RC	SB	CS	SBR	FR	POS	TPR
1970	SF-N	152	495	98	143	39	2	39	126	137	75	.289	.446	.612	183	62	63	140	0	0	0	13	*1	6.1
1971	*SF-N	105	329	45	91	13	0	18	70	64	57	.277	.401	.480	151	23	24	65	0	2	-1	-2	1	1.5
1972	SF-N	81	263	30	56	8	0	14	35	38	45	.213	.317	.403	102	1	1	35	0	0	0	-5	1	-0.9
1973	SF-N	130	383	52	102	14	3	29	75	105	78	.266	.425	.546	161	39	37	95	1	0	0	1	*1	3.3
1974	SD-N	128	344	53	87	19	1	22	63	96	76	.253	.417	.506	164	30	32	79	1	0	0	-6	*1	2.3
1975	SD-N	122	413	43	104	17	0	23	68	57	80	.252	.347	.460	130	12	15	66	1	0	0	-0	*1	0.9
1976	SD-N	71	202	20	41	9	0	7	36	21	39	.203	.281	.351	86	-6	-4	20	0	0	0	5	1	-0.1
	Oak-A	11	24	0	5	0	0	0	0	3	4	.208	.296	.208	52	-1	-1	2	0	0	0	0	/D	0.0
1977	SF-N	141	478	54	134	21	0	28	86	67	106	.280	.369	.500	131	21	21	86	3	0	1	-7	*1	0.8
1978	SF-N	108	351	32	80	19	2	12	64	36	57	.228	.300	.396	97	-4	-3	40	1	0	0	-4	1	-0.9
1979	SF-N	117	353	34	88	9	0	15	57	36	70	.249	.321	.402	103	-2	1	45	0	2	-1	-1	1	-0.5
1980	SF-N	48	113	8	23	8	0	1	16	13	23	.204	.291	.301	67	-5	-5	10	0	0	0	-2	1	-0.8
Total	22	2588	8197	1229	2211	353	46	521	1555	1345	1550	.270	.377	.515	148	524	538	1638	26	22	-5	-35	*1O/D	38.9

■ ART McCOY
McCoy, Arthur Gray b: 1865, Danville, Pa. d: 3/22/04, Danville, Pa. 168 lbs. Deb: 7/08/1889

YEAR	TM/L	G	AB	R	H	2B	3B	HR	RBI	BB	SO	AVG	OBP	SLG	PRO+	BR	/A	RC	SB	CS	SBR	FR	POS	TPR
1889	Was-N	2	6	0	0	0	0	0	0	2	1	.000	.250	.000	-28	-1	-1	0	0			-2	/2	-0.1

■ BENNY McCOY
McCoy, Benjamin Jenison b: 11/9/15, Jenison, Mich. BL/TR, 5'9", 170 lbs. Deb: 9/14/38

YEAR	TM/L	G	AB	R	H	2B	3B	HR	RBI	BB	SO	AVG	OBP	SLG	PRO+	BR	/A	RC	SB	CS	SBR	FR	POS	TPR
1938	Det-A	7	15	2	3	1	0	0	1	2	2	.200	.250	.267	28	-2	-2	1	0	0	0	2	/23	0.1
1939	Det-A	55	192	38	58	13	6	1	33	29	26	.302	.394	.448	107	5	3	35	3	1	0	-2	2S	0.4
1940	Phi-A	134	490	56	126	26	5	7	62	65	44	.257	.345	.373	88	-9	-8	65	2	2	-1	-16	*2/3	-1.6
1941	Phi-A	141	517	86	140	12	7	8	61	95	50	.271	.384	.368	102	3	5	80	3	3	-1	-13	*2	0.3
Total	4	337	1214	182	327	52	18	16	156	190	122	.269	.369	.381	97	-3	-2	182	8	6	-1	-28	2/S3	-0.8

■ TOMMY McCRAW
McCraw, Tommy Lee b: 11/21/40, Malvern, Ark. BL/TL, 6', 183 lbs. Deb: 6/04/63 C

YEAR	TM/L	G	AB	R	H	2B	3B	HR	RBI	BB	SO	AVG	OBP	SLG	PRO+	BR	/A	RC	SB	CS	SBR	FR	POS	TPR
1963	Chi-A	102	280	38	71	11	3	6	33	21	46	.254	.313	.379	94	-3	-2	34	15	4	2	-3	1	-0.6
1964	Chi-A	125	368	47	96	11	5	6	36	32	65	.261	.327	.367	95	-3	-2	46	15	7	0	-4	1O	-0.9
1965	Chi-A	133	273	38	65	12	1	5	21	25	48	.238	.309	.344	91	-5	-3	28	12	7	-1	0	1O	-1.0
1966	Chi-A	151	389	49	89	16	4	5	48	29	40	.229	.291	.329	83	-11	-8	37	20	11	-1	-8	*1O	-2.4
1967	Chi-A	125	453	55	107	18	3	11	45	33	55	.236	.290	.362	95	-6	-4	46	24	10	1	12	*1/O	0.0
1968	Chi-A	136	477	51	112	16	12	9	44	36	58	.235	.295	.375	101	0	-0	53	20	5	3	0	*1	-0.3
1969	Chi-A	93	240	21	62	12	2	2	25	21	24	.258	.326	.350	85	-3	-5	26	1	3	-2	-7	1O	-1.7
1970	Chi-A	129	332	39	73	11	2	6	31	21	50	.220	.275	.319	61	-17	-19	31	12	3	-2	-2	1O	-2.4
1971	Was-A	122	207	33	44	6	4	7	25	19	24	.213	.294	.382	96	-3	-2	23	3	3	-1	-4	O1	-1.0
1972	Cle-A	129	391	43	101	13	5	7	33	44	47	.258	.335	.371	106	5	4	47	12	10	-2	0	O1	-0.4
1973	Cal-A	99	264	25	70	7	0	3	24	30	42	.265	.345	.326	97	-3	-0	32	3	2	-0	0	O1/D	0.0
1974	Cal-A	56	119	21	34	8	0	3	17	12	13	.286	.351	.429	131	4	4	18	2	1	0	2	1O/D	0.5
	Cle-A	45	112	17	34	8	0	3	17	5	11	.304	.339	.455	128	3	4	16	0	1	-1	2	1/O	0.4
	Yr	101	231	38	68	16	0	6	34	17	24	.294	.345	.442	130	7	8	33	2	2	-1	5		0.9
1975	Cle-A	23	51	7	14	1	1	2	5	7	7	.275	.362	.451	129	2	2	9	4	1	1	-1	1/O	0.0
Total	13	1468	3956	484	972	150	42	75	404	332	544	.246	.311	.362	94	-40	-32	446	143	68	2	-10	1O/D	-9.8

■ RODNEY McCRAY
McCray, Rodney Duncan b: 9/13/63, Detroit, Mich. BR/TR, 5'10", 175 lbs. Deb: 4/30/90

YEAR	TM/L	G	AB	R	H	2B	3B	HR	RBI	BB	SO	AVG	OBP	SLG	PRO+	BR	/A	RC	SB	CS	SBR	FR	POS	TPR
1990	Chi-A	32	6	8	0	0	0	0	0	1	4	.000	.143	.000	-58	-1	-1	0	6	0	2	2	O/D	0.2

■ FRANK McCREA
McCrea, Francis William b: 9/6/1896, Jersey City, N.J. d: 2/25/81, Dover, N.J. BR/TR, 5'9", 155 lbs. Deb: 9/26/25

YEAR	TM/L	G	AB	R	H	2B	3B	HR	RBI	BB	SO	AVG	OBP	SLG	PRO+	BR	/A	RC	SB	CS	SBR	FR	POS	TPR
1925	Cle-A	1	5	1	1	0	0	0	0	0	0	.200	.200	.200	2	-1	-1	0	0	0	0	-0	/C	0.0

■ JUDGE McCREDIE
McCredie, Walter Henry b: 11/29/1876, Manchester, Iowa d: 7/29/34, Portland, Ore. BL/TR, 6'2", 195 lbs. Deb: 4/20/03

YEAR	TM/L	G	AB	R	H	2B	3B	HR	RBI	BB	SO	AVG	OBP	SLG	PRO+	BR	/A	RC	SB	CS	SBR	FR	POS	TPR
1903	Bro-N	56	213	40	69	5	0	0	20	24		.324	.392	.347	117	5	6	34	10			-4	O	0.0

■ TOM McCREERY
McCreery, Thomas Livingston b: 10/19/1874, Beaver, Pa. d: 7/3/41, Beaver, Pa. BB, 5'11", 180 lbs. Deb: 6/08/1895

YEAR	TM/L	G	AB	R	H	2B	3B	HR	RBI	BB	SO	AVG	OBP	SLG	PRO+	BR	/A	RC	SB	CS	SBR	FR	POS	TPR
1895	Lou-N	31	108	18	35	3	1	0	10	8	15	.324	.376	.370	101	-0	1	17	3			-6	O/PS31	-0.3
1896	Lou-N	115	441	87	155	23	21	7	65	42	58	.351	.409	.546	159	32	35	112	26			1	*O/2P	2.4
1897	Lou-N	89	338	55	96	5	6	4	40	38		.284	.356	.370	97	-2	-0	50	13			-5	*O	-1.0
	NY-N	49	177	36	53	8	5	1	27	22		.299	.380	.418	116	4	5	35	15			-1	O/2	0.0
	Yr	138	515	91	149	13	11	5	67	60		.289	.365	.386	104	2	4	85	28			-6		-1.0
1898	NY-N	35	121	15	24	4	3	1	17	19		.198	.307	.306	81	-3	-2	13	3			-5	O	-0.8
	Pit-N	53	190	33	59	5	7	2	20	26		.311	.394	.442	145	11	11	35	3			-1	O	0.7
	Yr	88	311	48	83	9	10	3	37	45		.267	.360	.389	120	8	9	47	6			-6		-0.1
1899	Pit-N	118	455	76	147	21	9	2	64	47		.323	.389	.422	125	16	17	81	11			-8	O/S2	0.3
1900	Pit-N	43	132	20	29	4	3	1	13	16		.220	.304	.318	73	-4	-5	14	2			2	O/P	-0.4
1901	Bro-N	91	335	47	97	11	14	3	53	32		.290	.351	.433	126	12	11	57	13			4	O/1S	0.6
1902	Bro-N	112	430	49	105	8	4	4	57	29		.244	.295	.309	88	-6	-6	46	16			-1	*1/O	-1.2
1903	Bro-N	40	141	13	37	5	2	0	10	20		.262	.354	.326	99	0	1	19	5			-2	O	-0.2
	Bos-N	23	83	15	18	2	1	1	10	9		.217	.293	.301	74	-3	-3	9	6			0	O	-0.2
	Yr	63	224	28	55	7	3	1	20	29		.246	.332	.317	90	-3	-3	28	11			-2		-0.4
Total	9	799	2951	464	855	99	76	26	386	308	73	.290	.358	.401	115	56	64	487	116			-21	O1/S2P3	-0.1

■ FRANK McCUE
McCue, Frank Aloysius b: 10/4/1898, Chicago, Ill. d: 7/5/53, Chicago, Ill. BB/TR, 5'9", 150 lbs. Deb: 9/15/22

YEAR	TM/L	G	AB	R	H	2B	3B	HR	RBI	BB	SO	AVG	OBP	SLG	PRO+	BR	/A	RC	SB	CS	SBR	FR	POS	TPR
1922	Phi-A	2	5	0	0	0	0	0	0	0	0	.000	.000	.000	-97	-1	-1	0	0	0	0	0	/3	0.0

■ CLYDE McCULLOUGH
McCullough, Clyde Edward b: 3/4/17, Nashville, Tenn. d: 9/18/82, San Francisco, Cal. BR/TR, 5'11.5", 180 lbs. Deb: 4/28/40 C

YEAR	TM/L	G	AB	R	H	2B	3B	HR	RBI	BB	SO	AVG	OBP	SLG	PRO+	BR	/A	RC	SB	CS	SBR	FR	POS	TPR
1940	Chi-N	9	26	4	4	1	0	0	1	5	5	.154	.290	.192	36	-2	-2	2	0			2	/C	0.1
1941	Chi-N	125	418	41	95	9	2	9	53	34	67	.227	.289	.323	75	-16	-14	39	5			-8	*C	-1.0
1942	Chi-N	109	337	39	95	22	1	5	31	25	47	.282	.331	.398	117	4	6	43	7			-2	C	0.7
1943	Chi-N	87	266	20	63	5	2	2	23	24	33	.237	.302	.293	73	-9	-9	24	6			-14	C	-2.0
1946	Chi-N	95	307	38	88	18	5	4	34	22	39	.287	.338	.417	116	4	5	42	2			-2	C	0.6
1947	Chi-N	86	234	25	59	12	4	3	30	20	20	.252	.314	.376	86	-6	-5	27	1			6	C	0.3
1948	Chi-N	69	172	10	36	4	2	1	7	15	25	.209	.273	.273	50	-12	-12	12	0			5	C	-0.2
1949	Pit-N	91	241	30	57	9	3	4	21	24	30	.237	.316	.349	76	-7	-8	28	1			7	C	0.2
1950	Pit-N	103	279	28	71	16	4	9	34	31	35	.254	.340	.405	92	-2	-3	40	3			-9	*C	-0.8
1951	Pit-N	92	259	26	77	9	2	8	39	27	31	.297	.366	.440	113	6	5	40	2	0	1	6	C	1.5
1952	Pit-N	66	172	10	40	5	1	1	15	10	18	.233	.283	.291	58	-9	-10	14	0	1	-1	6	C/1	-0.2
1953	Chi-N	77	229	21	59	3	2	6	23	15	23	.258	.303	.367	72	-9	-10	24	0	0	0	-4	C	-0.8
1954	Chi-N	31	81	9	21	7	0	3	17	5	5	.259	.310	.457	96	-1	-1	12	0	0	0	-1	C/3	0.0
1955	Chi-N	44	81	7	16	0	0	2	10	8	15	.198	.278	.198	29	-8	-8	5	0	0	0	7	C	0.0
1956	Chi-N	14	19	0	4	1	0	0	1	0	5	.211	.211	.263	27	-2	-2	1	0	0	0	1	/C	0.0
Total	15	1098	3121	308	785	121	28	52	339	265	398	.252	.314	.358	85	-70	-68	352	27	1		5	C/31	-1.6

■ HARRY McCURDY
McCurdy, Harry Henry "Hank" b: 9/15/1899, Stevens Point, Wis. d: 7/21/72, Houston, Tex. BL/TR, 5'11", 187 lbs. Deb: 7/04/22

YEAR	TM/L	G	AB	R	H	2B	3B	HR	RBI	BB	SO	AVG	OBP	SLG	PRO+	BR	/A	RC	SB	CS	SBR	FR	POS	TPR
1922	StL-N	13	27	3	8	2	2	0	5	1	1	.296	.321	.519	119	0	0	4	0	0	0	-1	/C1	0.0
1923	StL-N	67	185	17	49	11	2	0	15	11	11	.265	.308	.346	73	-8	-7	20	3	1	0	7	C	-1.0
1926	Chi-A	44	86	16	28	7	2	1	11	6	10	.326	.370	.488	127	2	3	15	0	1	-1	-4	C/1	0.0
1927	Chi-A	86	262	34	75	19	3	1	27	32	24	.286	.366	.393	99	-1	0	37	6	4	-1	-3	C	0.0

YEAR	TM/L	G	AB	R	H	2B	3B	HR	RBI	BB	SO	AVG	OBP	SLG	PRO+	BR	/A	RC	SB	CS	SBR	FR	POS	TPR
1928	Chi-A	49	103	12	27	10	0	2	13	8	15	.262	.315	.417	92	-2	-2	13	1	3	-2	-3	C	-0.3
1930	Phi-N	80	148	23	49	6	2	1	25	15	12	.331	.393	.419	90	-0	-2	24	0			-6	C	-0.4
1931	Phi-N	66	150	21	43	9	0	1	25	23	16	.287	.382	.367	95	1	-0	23	2			-1	C	0.0
1932	Phi-N	62	136	13	32	6	1	1	14	17	13	.235	.325	.316	65	-5	-7	15	0			-1	C	-0.5
1933	Phi-N	73	54	9	15	1	0	2	12	16	6	.278	.451	.407	130	5	4	12	0			0	/C	0.4
1934	Cin-N	3	6	0	0	0	0	0	1	0	0	.000	.000	.000	-99	-2	-2	0	0			1	/1	0.0
Total	10	543	1157	148	326	71	12	9	148	129	108	.282	.355	.387	92	-8	-12	163	12	9		-25	C/1	-1.8

■ RED McDERMOTT
McDermott, Frank A. b: 11/12/1889, Philadelphia, Pa. d: 9/11/64, Philadelphia, Pa. BR/TR, 5'6", 150 lbs. Deb: 8/06/12

YEAR	TM/L	G	AB	R	H	2B	3B	HR	RBI	BB	SO	AVG	OBP	SLG	PRO+	BR	/A	RC	SB	CS	SBR	FR	POS	TPR
1912	Det-A	5	15	2	4	1	0	0	0	0		.267	.313	.333	87	-0	-0	2	1			-0	/O	0.0

■ JOE McDERMOTT
McDermott, Joseph Deb: 5/04/1871

YEAR	TM/L	G	AB	R	H	2B	3B	HR	RBI	BB	SO	AVG	OBP	SLG	PRO+	BR	/A	RC	SB	CS	SBR	FR	POS	TPR
1871	Kek-n	2	8	3	2	0	0	0	1	1	1	.250	.333	.250	69	-0	-0	1	1				/O	0.0
1872	Eck-n	7	33	3	9	3	0	0			1	.273	.294	.364	119	0	1	4					/P	0.0
Total	2 n	9	41	6	11	3	0	0			2	.268	.302	.341	107	0	1	5					/PO	0.0

■ MICKEY McDERMOTT
McDermott, Maurice Joseph "Maury" b: 8/29/28, Poughkeepsie, N.Y. BL/TL, 6'2", 170 lbs. Deb: 4/24/48 C

YEAR	TM/L	G	AB	R	H	2B	3B	HR	RBI	BB	SO	AVG	OBP	SLG	PRO+	BR	/A	RC	SB	CS	SBR	FR	POS	TPR
1948	Bos-A	7	8	2	3	1	0	0	0	0	0	.375	.375	.500	125	0	0	2	0	0	0	1	/P	0.0
1949	Bos-A	12	33	3	7	3	0	0	6	3	6	.212	.278	.303	50	-2	-3	3	0	0	0	-0	P	0.0
1950	Bos-A	39	44	11	16	5	0	0	12	9	3	.364	.472	.477	131	3	3	11	0	0	0	0	P	0.0
1951	Bos-A	43	66	8	18	1	1	1	6	3	14	.273	.314	.364	76	-2	-3	7	0	1	-1	1	P	0.0
1952	Bos-A	36	62	10	14	1	1	1	7	4	11	.226	.273	.323	60	-3	-4	6	0	0	0	-1	P	0.0
1953	Bos-A	45	93	9	28	8	0	1	13	2	13	.301	.316	.419	92	-1	-1	12	0	1	-1	1	P	0.0
1954	Was-A	54	95	7	19	3	0	0	4	7	12	.200	.255	.232	36	-9	-8	5	0	0	0	0	P	0.0
1955	Was-A	70	95	10	25	4	0	1	10	6	16	.263	.314	.337	79	-3	-3	11	1	0	0	0	P	0.2
1956	*NY-A	46	52	4	11	0	0	1	4	8	13	.212	.317	.269	58	-3	-3	4	0	0	0	-0	P	0.0
1957	KC-A	58	49	6	12	1	0	4	7	9	16	.245	.362	.510	133	2	2	9	0	0	0	1	P/1	0.7
1958	Det-A	4	3	0	1	0	0	0	1	0	2	.333	.333	.333	78	-0	-0	0	0	0	0	-0	/P	0.0
1961	StL-N	22	14	1	1	1	0	0	3	0	4	.071	.071	.143	-41	-3	-3	0	0	0	0	-0	/P	0.0
	KC-A	7	5	0	1	1	0	0	1	1	2	.200	.333	.400	95	-0	-0	1	0	0	0	-0	/P	0.0
Total	12	443	619	71	156	29	2	9	74	52	112	.252	.312	.349	76	-20	-22	69	1	2	-1	2	P/1	0.9

■ TERRY McDERMOTT
McDermott, Terrence Michael b: 3/20/51, Rockville Cen., N.Y. BR/TR, 6'3", 205 lbs. Deb: 9/12/72

YEAR	TM/L	G	AB	R	H	2B	3B	HR	RBI	BB	SO	AVG	OBP	SLG	PRO+	BR	/A	RC	SB	CS	SBR	FR	POS	TPR
1972	LA-N	9	23	2	3	0	0	0	2		8	.130	.200	.130	-5	-3	-3	1	0	0	0	-0	/1	-0.3

■ SANDY McDERMOTT
McDermott, Thomas Nathaniel b: 3/15/1856, Zanesville, Ohio d: 11/23/22, Mansfield, Ohio Deb: 6/18/1885

YEAR	TM/L	G	AB	R	H	2B	3B	HR	RBI	BB	SO	AVG	OBP	SLG	PRO+	BR	/A	RC	SB	CS	SBR	FR	POS	TPR
1885	Bal-a	1	0	0	0	0	0	0	0			—	—	—	—	0	0	0				0	/2	0.0

■ MC DONALD
McDonald Deb: 5/18/1872

YEAR	TM/L	G	AB	R	H	2B	3B	HR	RBI	BB	SO	AVG	OBP	SLG	PRO+	BR	/A	RC	SB	CS	SBR	FR	POS	TPR
1872	Eck-n	1	4	0	0	0	0	0	0			.000	.000	.000	-99	-1	-1	0					/S	0.0

■ TEX McDONALD
McDonald, Charles E. (b: Charles C. Crabtree) b: 1/31/1891, Farmersville, Tex. d: 3/31/43, Houston, Tex. BL/TR, 5'10", 160 lbs. Deb: 4/11/12

YEAR	TM/L	G	AB	R	H	2B	3B	HR	RBI	BB	SO	AVG	OBP	SLG	PRO+	BR	/A	RC	SB	CS	SBR	FR	POS	TPR
1912	Cin-N	61	140	16	36	3	4	1	15	13	24	.257	.329	.357	90	-2	-2	18	5			-9	S	-0.5
1913	Cin-N	11	10	1	3	0	0	0	2	0	1	.300	.300	.300	72	-0	-0	1	0			0	/S	0.0
	Bos-N	62	145	24	52	4	4	0	18	15	17	.359	.422	.441	144	9	9	28	4			-2	3/2O	0.7
	Yr	73	155	25	55	4	4	0	20	15	18	.355	.415	.432	140	9	9	29	4			-2		0.7
1914	Pit-F	67	223	27	71	16	7	3	29	13	23	.318	.361	.493	145	11	12	44	9			-3	O2/S	0.8
	Buf-F	69	250	32	74	13	6	3	32	20	26	.296	.353	.432	121	7	7	44	11			-3	O2	0.1
	Yr	136	473	59	145	29	13	6	61	33	49	.307	.357	.461	132	19	18	88	20			-6		0.9
1915	Buf-F	87	251	31	68	9	6	3	39	27	34	.271	.346	.426	125	8	8	40	5			-7	O	-0.1
Total	4	357	1019	131	304	45	27	13	135	88	125	.298	.359	.434	126	34	33	175	34			-23	O/S23	1.0

■ JACK McDONALD
McDonald, Daniel b: 1847, Brooklyn, N.Y. d: 11/23/1880, Brooklyn, N.Y. Deb: 5/02/1872

YEAR	TM/L	G	AB	R	H	2B	3B	HR	RBI	BB	SO	AVG	OBP	SLG	PRO+	BR	/A	RC	SB	CS	SBR	FR	POS	TPR
1872	Atl-n	15	61	9	15	4	1	0			0	.246	.246	.344	68	-1	-4	5					O	-0.1

■ DAVE McDONALD
McDonald, David Bruce b: 5/20/43, New Albany, Ind. BL/TR, 6'3", 215 lbs. Deb: 9/15/69

YEAR	TM/L	G	AB	R	H	2B	3B	HR	RBI	BB	SO	AVG	OBP	SLG	PRO+	BR	/A	RC	SB	CS	SBR	FR	POS	TPR
1969	NY-A	9	23	0	5	1	0	0	2	2	5	.217	.280	.261	54	-1	-1	2	0	1	-1	-1	/1	-0.2
1971	Mon-N	24	39	3	4	2	0	1	4	4	14	.103	.186	.231	17	-4	-4	1	0	0	0	-0	/1O	-0.5
Total	2	33	62	3	9	3	0	1	6	6	19	.145	.221	.242	31	-6	-6	3	0	1	-1	-1	/1O	-0.7

■ ED McDONALD
McDonald, Edward C. b: 10/28/1886, Albany, N.Y. d: 3/11/46, Albany, N.Y. BR/TR, 6', 180 lbs. Deb: 8/05/11

YEAR	TM/L	G	AB	R	H	2B	3B	HR	RBI	BB	SO	AVG	OBP	SLG	PRO+	BR	/A	RC	SB	CS	SBR	FR	POS	TPR
1911	Bos-N	54	175	28	36	7	3	1	21	40	39	.206	.359	.297	78	-2	-4	23	11			-6	3/S	-0.7
1912	Bos-N	121	459	70	119	23	6	2	34	70	91	.259	.363	.349	94	-1	-2	65	22			-1	*3	-0.2
1913	Chi-N	1	0	0	0	0	0	0	0	0	0	—	—	—	—	0	0	0	0			0	R	0.0
Total	3	176	634	98	155	30	9	3	55	110	130	.244	.362	.334	89	-3	-6	88	33			-7	3/S	-0.9

■ JIM McDONALD
McDonald, James b: Philadelphia, Pa. BR/TR, 6', 180 lbs. Deb: 6/02/02

YEAR	TM/L	G	AB	R	H	2B	3B	HR	RBI	BB	SO	AVG	OBP	SLG	PRO+	BR	/A	RC	SB	CS	SBR	FR	POS	TPR
1902	NY-N	2	9	0	3	0	0	0	1	0		.333	.333	.333	109	0	0	1	0			-0	/O	0.0

■ JIM McDONALD
McDonald, James A. b: 8/6/1860, San Francisco, Cal. d: 9/14/14, San Francisco, Cal. Deb: 10/02/1884

YEAR	TM/L	G	AB	R	H	2B	3B	HR	RBI	BB	SO	AVG	OBP	SLG	PRO+	BR	/A	RC	SB	CS	SBR	FR	POS	TPR
1884	Was-U	2	6	0	1	0	0	0	0			.167	.167	.167	13	-1	-0	0	0			-0	/CO	0.0
	Pit-a	38	145	11	23	3	0	0			2	.159	.170	.179	15	-13	-13	5				-6	3O/2	-1.7
1885	Buf-a	5	14	0	0	0	0	0	0		4	.000	.000	.000	-97	-3	-3	0				2	/SO	0.0
Total	2	45	165	11	24	3	0	0		2	4	.145	.156	.164	6	-16	-17	5				-5	/30S2C	-1.7

■ JOE McDONALD
McDonald, Malcolm Joseph b: 4/9/1888, Texas d: 5/30/63, Baytown, Tex. BR/TR, 5'11", 175 lbs. Deb: 9/06/10

YEAR	TM/L	G	AB	R	H	2B	3B	HR	RBI	BB	SO	AVG	OBP	SLG	PRO+	BR	/A	RC	SB	CS	SBR	FR	POS	TPR
1910	StL-A	10	32	4	5	0	0	0	1	1		.156	.182	.156	6	-3	-3	1	0			-3	3	-0.6

■ JIM McDONNELL
McDonnell, James William "Mack" b: 8/15/22, Gagetown, Mich. BL/TR, 5'11", 165 lbs. Deb: 9/23/43

YEAR	TM/L	G	AB	R	H	2B	3B	HR	RBI	BB	SO	AVG	OBP	SLG	PRO+	BR	/A	RC	SB	CS	SBR	FR	POS	TPR
1943	Cle-A	2	1	1	0	0	0	0	0	2	1	.000	.667	.000	108	0	0	0	0	0	0	-0	/C	0.0
1944	Cle-A	20	43	5	10	0	0	0	4	4	3	.233	.298	.233	55	-3	-2	3	0	0	0	-2	C	-0.3
1945	Cle-A	28	51	3	10	2	0	0	8	2	4	.196	.226	.235	36	-4	-4	3	0	0	0	8	C	0.6
Total	3	50	95	9	20	2	0	0	12	8	8	.211	.272	.232	48	-7	-6	6	0	0	0	6	/C	0.3

■ ED McDONOUGH
McDonough, Edward Sebastian b: 9/11/1886, Elgin, Ill. d: 9/2/26, Elgin, Ill. BR/TR, 6', 160 lbs. Deb: 8/03/09

YEAR	TM/L	G	AB	R	H	2B	3B	HR	RBI	BB	SO	AVG	OBP	SLG	PRO+	BR	/A	RC	SB	CS	SBR	FR	POS	TPR
1909	Phi-N	1	1	0	0	0	0	0	0	0		.000	.000	.000	-99	-0	-0	0	0			0	/C	0.0
1910	Phi-N	5	9	1	1	0	0	0	0	0	1	.111	.111	.111	-34	-2	-2	0	0			-1	/C	-0.1
Total	2	6	10	1	1	0	0	0	0	0	1	.100	.100	.100	-40	-2	-2	0	0			-1	/C	-0.1

■ GIL McDOUGALD
McDougald, Gilbert James b: 5/19/28, San Francisco, Cal BR/TR, 6', 175 lbs. Deb: 4/20/51

YEAR	TM/L	G	AB	R	H	2B	3B	HR	RBI	BB	SO	AVG	OBP	SLG	PRO+	BR	/A	RC	SB	CS	SBR	FR	POS	TPR
1951	*NY-A	131	402	72	123	23	4	14	63	56	54	.306	.396	.488	143	22	24	81	14	5	1	-16	32	0.8
1952	*NY-A	152	555	65	146	16	5	11	78	57	73	.263	.336	.369	102	-3	1	71	6	5	-1	12	*32	1.4
1953	*NY-A	141	541	82	154	27	7	10	83	60	65	.285	.361	.416	113	7	10	85	3	4	-2	6	*32	0.9
1954	NY-A	126	394	66	102	22	2	12	48	62	64	.259	.367	.416	118	9	10	64	3	4	-2	1	23	1.2
1955	*NY-A	141	533	79	152	10	8	13	53	65	77	.285	.365	.407	109	6	7	83	6	4	-1	19	*23	3.3
1956	*NY-A	120	438	79	136	13	3	13	56	68	59	.311	.407	.443	128	18	20	82	3	8	-4	3	S2/3	2.8

YEAR	TM/L	G	AB	R	H	2B	3B	HR	RBI	BB	SO	AVG	OBP	SLG	PRO+	BR	/A	RC	SB	CS	SBR	FR	POS	TPR
1957	*NY-A	141	539	87	156	25	9	13	62	59	71	.289	.364	.442	121	14	15	86	2	5	-2	15	*S2/3	4.0
1958	*NY-A	138	503	69	126	19	1	14	65	59	75	.250	.333	.376	98	-3	-1	64	6	2	1	-3	*2S	0.7
1959	NY-A	127	434	44	109	16	8	4	34	35	40	.251	.311	.353	85	-11	-9	46	0	3	-2	8	2S3	0.3
1960	*NY-A	119	337	54	87	16	4	8	34	38	45	.258	.339	.401	105	-0	2	47	2	4	-2	-3	32	0.2
Total	10	1336	4676	697	1291	187	51	112	576	559	623	.276	.358	.410	112	58	79	708	45	44	-13	42	23S	15.6

■ ODDIBE McDOWELL
McDowell, Oddibe b: 8/25/62, Hollywood, Fla. BL/TL, 5'9", 165 lbs. Deb: 5/19/85

YEAR	TM/L	G	AB	R	H	2B	3B	HR	RBI	BB	SO	AVG	OBP	SLG	PRO+	BR	/A	RC	SB	CS	SBR	FR	POS	TPR
1985	Tex-A	111	406	63	97	14	5	18	42	36	85	.239	.306	.431	98	-1	-2	55	25	7	3	5	*O/D	0.5
1986	Tex-A	154	572	105	152	24	7	18	49	65	112	.266	.342	.427	105	6	4	83	33	15	1	-4	*O/D	-0.2
1987	Tex-A	128	407	65	98	26	4	14	52	51	99	.241	.325	.428	97	-2	-2	61	24	2	6	-5	*O	-0.2
1988	Tex-A	120	437	55	108	19	5	6	37	41	89	.247	.315	.355	85	-7	-9	53	33	10	4	-8	*O/D	-1.4
1989	Cle-A	69	239	33	53	5	2	3	22	25	36	.222	.298	.297	67	-10	-10	23	12	5	1	-4	O/D	-1.4
	Atl-N	76	280	56	85	18	4	7	24	27	37	.304	.365	.471	134	13	12	49	15	10	-2	1	O	1.2
1990	Atl-N	113	305	47	74	14	0	7	25	21	53	.243	.296	.357	77	-9	-10	34	13	2	3	-5	O	-1.4
Total	6	771	2646	424	667	120	27	73	251	266	511	.252	.322	.401	96	-10	-16	357	155	51	16	-20	O/D	-2.9

■ PRYOR McELVEEN
McElveen, Pryor Mynatt "Humpty" b: 11/5/1883, Atlanta, Ga. d: 10/27/51, Pleasant Hill, Tenn. TR, 5'10", 168 lbs. Deb: 4/26/09

YEAR	TM/L	G	AB	R	H	2B	3B	HR	RBI	BB	SO	AVG	OBP	SLG	PRO+	BR	/A	RC	SB	CS	SBR	FR	POS	TPR
1909	Bro-N	81	258	22	51	8	1	3	25	14		.198	.242	.271	61	-13	-12	18	6			-5	30S/12	-1.7
1910	Bro-N	74	213	19	48	8	3	1	26	22	47	.225	.307	.305	81	-6	-5	22	6			-5	3/S2C	-0.9
1911	Bro-N	16	31	1	6	0	0	0	5	0	3	.194	.194	.194	9	-4	-4	1	0			-1	/2S	-0.4
Total	3	171	502	42	105	16	4	4	56	36	50	.209	.268	.281	67	-23	-21	41	12			-10	/3S201C	-3.0

■ LEE McELWEE
McElwee, Leland Stanford b: 5/23/1894, LaMesa, Cal. d: 2/8/57, Union, Maine BR/TR, 5'10.5", 160 lbs. Deb: 7/03/16

YEAR	TM/L	G	AB	R	H	2B	3B	HR	RBI	BB	SO	AVG	OBP	SLG	PRO+	BR	/A	RC	SB	CS	SBR	FR	POS	TPR
1916	Phi-A	54	155	9	41	3	0	0	10	8	17	.265	.301	.284	79	-5	-4	14	0			-2	3/021S	-0.5

■ FRANK McELYEA
McElyea, Frank b: 8/4/18, Carmi, Ill. BR/TR, 6'6", 221 lbs. Deb: 9/10/42

YEAR	TM/L	G	AB	R	H	2B	3B	HR	RBI	BB	SO	AVG	OBP	SLG	PRO+	BR	/A	RC	SB	CS	SBR	FR	POS	TPR
1942	Bos-N	7	4	2	0	0	0	0	0	0	0	.000	.000	.000	-99	-1	-1	0	0			1	/O	0.0

■ GUY McFADDEN
McFadden, Guy G. b: 1873, Topeka, Kan. Deb: 8/24/1895

YEAR	TM/L	G	AB	R	H	2B	3B	HR	RBI	BB	SO	AVG	OBP	SLG	PRO+	BR	/A	RC	SB	CS	SBR	FR	POS	TPR
1895	StL-N	4	14	1	3	0	0	0	2	0	2	.214	.214	.214	12	-2	-2	1	0			-1	/1	-0.1

■ LEON McFADDEN
McFadden, Leon b: 4/26/44, Little Rock, Ark. BR/TR, 6'2", 195 lbs. Deb: 9/06/68

YEAR	TM/L	G	AB	R	H	2B	3B	HR	RBI	BB	SO	AVG	OBP	SLG	PRO+	BR	/A	RC	SB	CS	SBR	FR	POS	TPR
1968	Hou-N	16	47	2	13	1	0	0	1	6	10	.277	.358	.298	101	0	0	6	1	0	0	-1	S	0.2
1969	Hou-N	44	74	3	13	2	0	0	3	4	9	.176	.218	.203	19	-8	-8	3	1	2	-1	-1	O/S	-0.9
1970	Hou-N	2	0	0	0	0	0	0	0	0	0	—	—	—	—	0	0	0	0	0	0	0	R	0.0
Total	3	62	121	5	26	3	0	0	4	10	19	.215	.275	.240	50	-8	-8	9	2	2	-1	-1	/SO	-0.7

■ ALEX McFARLAN
McFarlan, Alexander Shepherd b: 11/11/1866, Kentucky d: 3/2/39, Peewee Valley, Ky. Deb: 6/19/1892

YEAR	TM/L	G	AB	R	H	2B	3B	HR	RBI	BB	SO	AVG	OBP	SLG	PRO+	BR	/A	RC	SB	CS	SBR	FR	POS	TPR
1892	Lou-N	14	42	2	7	0	0	0	1	8	11	.167	.300	.167	47	-2	-2	2	1			-3	O/2	-0.4

■ CHRIS McFARLAND
McFarland, Christopher b: 8/17/1861, Fall River, Mass. d: 5/24/18, New Bedford, Mass. 5'9", 170 lbs. Deb: 4/19/1884

YEAR	TM/L	G	AB	R	H	2B	3B	HR	RBI	BB	SO	AVG	OBP	SLG	PRO+	BR	/A	RC	SB	CS	SBR	FR	POS	TPR
1884	Bal-U	3	14	2	3	1	0	0		0		.214	.214	.286	61	-0	-1	1	0			-1	/OP	-0.1

■ ED McFARLAND
McFarland, Edward William b: 8/3/1874, Cleveland, Ohio d: 11/28/59, Cleveland, Ohio BR/TR, 5'10", 180 lbs. Deb: 7/07/1893

YEAR	TM/L	G	AB	R	H	2B	3B	HR	RBI	BB	SO	AVG	OBP	SLG	PRO+	BR	/A	RC	SB	CS	SBR	FR	POS	TPR
1893	Cle-N	8	22	5	9	2	1	0	6	1	2	.409	.458	.591	170	2	2	6	0			-3	/O3C	0.0
1896	StL-N	83	290	48	70	13	4	3	36	15	17	.241	.281	.345	69	-15	-13	31	7			8	C/O	0.2
1897	StL-N	31	107	14	35	5	2	1	17	8		.327	.374	.439	119	2	3	19	2			3	C/1O2	0.7
	Phi-N	38	130	18	29	3	5	1	16	14		.223	.308	.346	76	-5	-4	15	2			0	C	0.1
	Yr	69	237	32	64	8	7	2	33	22		.270	.337	.388	95	-2	-1	33	4			3		0.8
1898	Phi-N	121	429	65	121	21	5	3	71	44		.282	.352	.375	116	7	9	59	4			-1	*C	1.5
1899	Phi-N	96	324	59	108	22	9	2	57	36		.333	.403	.475	149	19	21	67	9			17	C	3.9
1900	Phi-N	94	344	50	105	14	8	0	38	29		.305	.364	.392	112	6	6	54	9			-2	C/3	1.1
1901	Phi-N	74	295	33	84	14	2	1	32	18		.285	.326	.356	98	-0	-1	39	11			2	C	1.0
1902	Chi-A	75	246	29	56	9	2	1	25	19		.228	.291	.293	66	-12	-10	25	8			2	C/O1	-0.2
1903	Chi-A	61	201	15	42	7	2	1	19	14		.209	.260	.279	66	-9	-8	16	3			-0	C/1	0.0
1904	Chi-A	50	160	22	44	11	3	0	20	17		.275	.345	.381	137	6	6	23	2			-11	C	0.1
1905	Chi-A	80	250	24	70	13	4	0	31	23		.280	.341	.364	131	7	9	34	5			6	C	2.3
1906	*Chi-A	12	23	0	4	1	0	0	3	3		.174	.269	.217	56	-1	-1	2	0			-1	/C	0.0
1907	Chi-A	52	138	11	39	9	1	0	8	12		.283	.340	.362	130	4	5	19	3			-1	C	0.8
1908	Bos-A	19	48	5	10	2	1	0	4	1		.208	.224	.292	67	-2	-2	3	0			3	C	0.3
Total	14	894	3007	398	826	146	49	13	383	254	19	.275	.334	.369	106	11	23	412	65			22	C/0132	11.8

■ HERM McFARLAND
McFarland, Hermas Walter b: 3/11/1870, Des Moines, Iowa d: 9/21/35, Richmond, Va. BL/TR, 5'6", 150 lbs. Deb: 4/21/1896

YEAR	TM/L	G	AB	R	H	2B	3B	HR	RBI	BB	SO	AVG	OBP	SLG	PRO+	BR	/A	RC	SB	CS	SBR	FR	POS	TPR
1896	Lou-N	30	110	11	21	4	1	1	12	9	14	.191	.252	.273	41	-10	-9	9	4			-3	O/C	-1.1
1898	Cin-N	19	64	10	18	1	3	0	11	7		.281	.361	.391	110	2	1	10	3			-2	O	-0.1
1901	Chi-A	132	473	83	130	21	9	4	59	75		.275	.385	.383	119	14	16	86	33			5	*O	1.7
1902	Chi-A	7	27	5	5	0	0	0	4	2		.185	.241	.185	22	-3	-3	1	1			-0	/O	-0.2
	Bal-A	61	242	54	78	19	6	3	36	36		.322	.420	.488	147	19	17	55	10			6	O	1.8
	Yr	68	269	59	83	19	6	3	40	38		.309	.404	.457	136	16	15	56	11			6		1.6
1903	NY-A	103	362	41	88	16	9	5	45	46		.243	.328	.378	107	7	4	52	13			-3	*O	-0.5
Total	5	352	1278	204	340	61	28	13	167	175	14	.266	.361	.388	112	29	26	214	64			3	O/C	1.6

■ HOWIE McFARLAND
McFarland, Howard Alexander b: 3/7/11, ElReno, Okla. BR/TR, 6', 175 lbs. Deb: 7/16/45

YEAR	TM/L	G	AB	R	H	2B	3B	HR	RBI	BB	SO	AVG	OBP	SLG	PRO+	BR	/A	RC	SB	CS	SBR	FR	POS	TPR
1945	Was-A	6	11	0	1	0	0	0	2	0	3	.091	.091	.091	-52	-2	-2	0	0	0	0	0	/O	-0.1

■ ORLANDO McFARLANE
McFarlane, Orlando Dejesus (Quesada) b: 6/28/38, Oriente, Cuba BR/TR, 6', 180 lbs. Deb: 4/23/62

YEAR	TM/L	G	AB	R	H	2B	3B	HR	RBI	BB	SO	AVG	OBP	SLG	PRO+	BR	/A	RC	SB	CS	SBR	FR	POS	TPR
1962	Pit-N	8	23	0	2	0	0	0	1	1	4	.087	.125	.087	-42	-5	-5	0	0	0	0	2	/C	-0.1
1964	Pit-N	37	78	5	19	5	0	0	1	4	27	.244	.280	.308	66	-4	-4	7	0	0	0	-6	C/O	-0.8
1966	Det-A	49	138	16	35	7	0	5	13	9	46	.254	.304	.413	102	0	0	17	0	0	0	-2	C	0.0
1967	Cal-A	12	22	0	5	0	0	0	3	1	7	.227	.261	.227	47	-1	-1	1	0	0	0	-1	/C	-0.1
1968	Cal-A	18	31	1	9	0	0	0	2	5	9	.290	.389	.290	112	1	1	4	0	0	0	-0	/C	0.1
Total	5	124	292	22	70	12	0	5	20	20	93	.240	.291	.332	78	-9	-9	29	0	0	0	-6	/CO	-0.9

■ PATSY McGAFFIGAN
McGaffigan, Mark Andrew b: 9/12/1888, Carlyle, Ill. d: 12/22/40, Carlyle, Ill. BR/TR, 5'8", 140 lbs. Deb: 4/16/17

YEAR	TM/L	G	AB	R	H	2B	3B	HR	RBI	BB	SO	AVG	OBP	SLG	PRO+	BR	/A	RC	SB	CS	SBR	FR	POS	TPR
1917	Phi-N	19	60	5	10	1	0	0	6	0	7	.167	.167	.183	7	-7	-7	2	1			-0	S/O	-0.7
1918	Phi-N	54	192	17	39	3	2	1	8	16	23	.203	.268	.255	56	-9	-10	14	3			-12	2/S	-2.1
Total	2	73	252	22	49	4	2	1	14	16	30	.194	.245	.238	45	-16	-17	17	4			-12	/2SO	-2.8

■ EDDIE McGAH
McGah, Edward Joseph b: 9/30/21, Oakland, Cal. BR/TR, 6', 183 lbs. Deb: 4/26/46

YEAR	TM/L	G	AB	R	H	2B	3B	HR	RBI	BB	SO	AVG	OBP	SLG	PRO+	BR	/A	RC	SB	CS	SBR	FR	POS	TPR
1946	Bos-A	15	37	2	8	1	0	1	1	7	7	.216	.341	.297	75	-1	-1	5	0	0	0	-2	C	-0.2
1947	Bos-A	9	14	1	0	0	0	0	2	3	0	.000	.176	.000	-45	-3	-3	0	0	0	0	2	/C	0.0
Total	2	24	51	3	8	1	0	1	3	10	7	.157	.295	.216	41	-4	-4	5	0	0	0	0	/C	-0.2

■ DAN McGANN
McGann, Dennis Lawrence "Cap" b: 7/15/1871, Shelbyville, Ky. d: 12/13/10, Louisville, Ky. BB/TR, 6', 190 lbs. Deb: 5/02/1895

YEAR	TM/L	G	AB	R	H	2B	3B	HR	RBI	BB	SO	AVG	OBP	SLG	PRO+	BR	/A	RC	SB	CS	SBR	FR	POS	TPR
1895	Lou-N	20	73	9	21	5	2	0	9	8	6	.288	.358	.411	107	-0	1	13	6			-3	/S3O	0.0
1896	Bos-N	43	171	25	55	6	7	2	30	12	10	.322	.383	.474	120	6	5	33	2			-17	2	-0.9

YEAR	TM/L	G	AB	R	H	2B	3B	HR	RBI	BB	SO	AVG	OBP	SLG	PRO+	BR	/A	RC	SB	CS	SBR	FR	POS	TPR
1898	Bal-N	145	535	99	161	18	8	5	106	53		.301	.404	.393	129	26	24	101	33			2	*1	2.4
1899	Bro-N	63	214	49	52	11	4	2	32	21		.243	.362	.360	99	2	1	35	16			2	1	0.3
	Was-N	76	280	65	96	9	8	5	58	14		.343	.410	.486	150	19	19	62	11			2	1	2.0
	Yr	139	494	114	148	20	12	7	90	35		.300	.389	.431	127	20	20	96	27			4		2.3
1900	StL-N	121	444	79	132	10	9	4	58	32		.297	.368	.387	112	8	8	75	26			-1	*1/2	0.7
1901	StL-N	103	423	73	115	15	9	6	56	16		.272	.313	.392	111	2	5	59	17			-3	*1	0.2
1902	Bal-A	68	250	40	79	10	8	0	42	19		.316	.380	.420	118	8	7	49	17			3	1	1.0
	NY-N	61	227	25	68	5	7	0	21	12		.300	.351	.383	130	7	8	36	12			2	1	0.7
1903	NY-N	129	482	75	130	21	6	3	50	32		.270	.315	.357	90	-5	-8	70	36			-0	*1	-1.0
1904	NY-N	141	517	81	148	22	6	6	71	36		.286	.333	.387	119	14	11	85	42			3	*1	0.8
1905	*NY-N	136	491	88	147	23	14	5	75	55		.299	.370	.434	139	25	24	91	22			4	*1	2.2
1906	NY-N	134	451	62	107	14	8	0	37	60		.237	.327	.304	97	1	-0	59	30			3	*1	-0.1
1907	NY-N	81	262	29	78	9	1	2	36	29		.298	.368	.363	127	10	9	40	9			5	1	1.4
1908	Bos-N	135	475	52	114	8	5	2	55	38		.240	.296	.291	91	-5	-4	44	9			5	*1/2	-0.2
Total	13	1456	5295	851	1503	186	102	42	736	437	16	.284	.352	.381	115	118	109	851	288			7	*1/2S30	9.5

■ CHIPPY McGARR
McGarr, James B.   b: 5/10/1863, Worcester, Mass.   d: 6/6/04, Worcester, Mass.   BR/TR,   Deb: 7/11/1884   U

YEAR	TM/L	G	AB	R	H	2B	3B	HR	RBI	BB	SO	AVG	OBP	SLG	PRO+	BR	/A	RC	SB	CS	SBR	FR	POS	TPR
1884	CP-U	19	70	10	11	2	0	0		0		.157	.157	.186	16	-6	-6	2	0			-6	2/O	-1.0
1886	Phi-a	71	267	41	71	9	3	2		9		.266	.295	.345	101	-0	-1	33	17			1	S	0.3
1887	Phi-a	137	536	93	158	23	6	1		23		.295	.326	.366	95	-4	-4	94	84			-1	*S	-0.5
1888	StL-a	34	132	17	31	1	0	0	13	6		.235	.268	.242	60	-5	-7	16	25			-2	2/S	-0.7
1889	KC-a	25	108	22	31	3	0	0	16	6	11	.287	.330	.315	81	-2	-3	16	12			-2	3/O2S	-0.3
	Bal-a	3	7	1	1	0	0	0	0	1	1	.143	.250	.143	14	-1	-1	0	0			-2	/S	-0.1
	Yr	28	115	23	32	3	0	0	16	7	12	.278	.325	.304	77	-3	-4	16	12			-4		-0.4
1890	Bos-N	121	487	68	115	12	7	1	51	34	38	.236	.291	.296	68	-17	-23	55	39			-2	*3/SO	-1.7
1893	Cle-N	63	249	38	77	12	0	0	28	20	15	.309	.363	.357	88	-2	-5	42	24			0	3	-0.2
1894	Cle-N	128	523	94	144	24	6	2	74	28	29	.275	.316	.356	61	-32	-36	70	31			-7	*3	-3.4
1895	*Cle-N	112	419	85	111	14	2	2	59	34	33	.265	.322	.322	64	-19	-24	51	19			-5	*3/2	-2.1
1896	*Cle-N	113	455	68	122	16	4	1	53	22	30	.268	.302	.327	64	-22	-26	51	16			-6	*3/C	-2.2
Total	10	826	3253	537	872	116	28	9	294	183	157	.268	.310	.329	73	-109	-134	429	267			-32	3S/2OC	-11.9

■ JIM McGARR
McGarr, James Vincent "Reds"   b: 11/9/1888, Philadelphia, Pa.   d: 7/21/81, Miami, Fla.   5'9.5", 170 lbs.   Deb: 5/18/12

YEAR	TM/L	G	AB	R	H	2B	3B	HR	RBI	BB	SO	AVG	OBP	SLG	PRO+	BR	/A	RC	SB	CS	SBR	FR	POS	TPR
1912	Det-A	1	4	0	0	0	0	0	0	0		.000	.000	.000	-99	-1	-1	0	0			-0	/2	-0.1

■ DAN McGARVEY
McGarvey, Daniel Francis   b: 12/2/1887, Philadelphia, Pa.   d: 3/7/47, Philadelphia, Pa.   Deb: 5/18/12

YEAR	TM/L	G	AB	R	H	2B	3B	HR	RBI	BB	SO	AVG	OBP	SLG	PRO+	BR	/A	RC	SB	CS	SBR	FR	POS	TPR
1912	Det-A	1	3	0	0	0	0	0	0	1		.000	.400	.000	18	-0	-0	0	0			0	/O	0.0

■ JACK McGEACHEY
McGeachey, John Charles   b: 5/23/1864, Clinton, Mass.   d: 4/5/30, Cambridge, Mass.   BR , 5'8", 165 lbs.   Deb: 6/17/1886

YEAR	TM/L	G	AB	R	H	2B	3B	HR	RBI	BB	SO	AVG	OBP	SLG	PRO+	BR	/A	RC	SB	CS	SBR	FR	POS	TPR
1886	Det-N	6	27	3	9	0	1	0	4	0	3	.333	.333	.407	121	1	1	4	2			-1	/O	0.0
	StL-N	59	226	31	46	12	3	2	24	1		.204	.207	.310	59	-12	-10	17	8			2	O/23	-0.5
	Yr	65	253	34	55	12	4	2	28	1	40	.217	.220	.320	66	-12	-10	21	10			1		-0.5
1887	Ind-N	99	405	49	109	17	3	1	56	5	16	.269	.280	.333	74	-16	-14	46	27			4	*O/3P	-0.6
1888	Ind-N	118	452	45	99	15	2	0	30	5	21	.219	.231	.261	57	-21	-22	40	49			4	*O/SP	-1.8
1889	Ind-N	131	532	83	142	32	1	2	63	9	39	.267	.282	.342	74	-19	-21	63	37			8	*O/P	-1.4
1890	Bro-P	104	443	84	108	24	4	1	65	19	12	.244	.278	.323	58	-25	-30	47	21			-1	*O	-2.8
1891	Phi-a	50	201	24	46	4	3	2	13	6	12	.229	.255	.308	61	-10	-11	19	9			2	O	-0.9
	Bos-a	41	178	26	45	2	1	1	21	12	8	.253	.304	.292	74	-6	-6	20	11			-4	O	-0.9
	Yr	91	379	50	91	6	4	3	34	18	20	.240	.278	.301	67	-17	-17	38	20			-2		-1.8
Total	6	608	2464	345	604	106	18	9	276	57	148	.245	.265	.314	66	-110	-113	255	164			15	O/P32S	-8.9

■ MIKE McGEARY
McGeary, Michael Henry   b: 1851, Philadelphia, Pa.   BR/TR, 5'7", 138 lbs.   Deb: 5/09/1871   M

YEAR	TM/L	G	AB	R	H	2B	3B	HR	RBI	BB	SO	AVG	OBP	SLG	PRO+	BR	/A	RC	SB	CS	SBR	FR	POS	TPR
1871	Tro-n	29	148	42	39	4	0	0	12	6	0	.264	.292	.291	67	-6	-6	19	20				*C/S	-0.4
1872	Ath-n	47	226	68	81	9	2	0		1		.358	.361	.416	138	10	10	35					CS/O	0.6
1873	Ath-n	52	275	62	81	9	1	0		1		.295	.297	.335	79	-5	-9	28					*SC	-0.6
1874	Ath-n	54	270	61	87	11	2	0		2		.322	.327	.378	114	7	3	34					SC/O	0.1
1875	Phi-n	68	309	71	89	6	2	0		1		.288	.290	.320	107	3	1	29					32S/OCM	0.1
1876	StL-N	61	276	48	72	3	0	0	30	2	1	.261	.266	.272	84	-6	-4	20	6				*2/CO3	0.3
1877	StL-N	57	258	35	65	3	2	0	20	2	6	.252	.258	.279	73	-9	-7	19	7				23	0.2
1879	Pro-N	85	374	62	103	7	2	0	35	5	13	.275	.285	.305	96	-2	-1	33	1				*23	0.6
1880	Pro-N	18	59	5	8	0	0	0	1	0	6	.136	.136	.136	-8	-6	-6	1	3				3/2SM	-0.2
	Cle-N	31	111	14	28	2	1	0	6	4	3	.252	.278	.288	94	-1	-1	9	-4				3/O	-0.4
	Yr	49	170	19	36	2	1	0	7	4	9	.212	.230	.235	60	-7	-7	9				-1		-0.6
1881	Cle-N	11	41	1	9	0	0	0	5	0	6	.220	.220	.220	41	-3	-3	2				-7	3M	-0.7
1882	Det-N	34	133	14	19	4	1	0	2	2	20	.143	.188	.188	10	-13	-13	4				8	S/2	-0.2
Total	5 n	250	1228	304	377	39	7	0	12	11		.307	.313	.350	102	9	-2	145					S/C32O	-0.2
Total	6	297	1252	179	304	19	6	0	99	15	55	.243	.252	.268	72	-40	-34	89				14	2/3SCO	-0.2

■ DAN McGEE
McGee, Daniel Aloysius   b: 9/29/13, New York, N.Y.   BR/TR, 5'8.5", 152 lbs.   Deb: 7/14/34

YEAR	TM/L	G	AB	R	H	2B	3B	HR	RBI	BB	SO	AVG	OBP	SLG	PRO+	BR	/A	RC	SB	CS	SBR	FR	POS	TPR
1934	Bos-N	7	22	2	3	0	0	0	1	3	6	.136	.240	.136	4	-3	-3	1	0			3	/S	0.0

■ FRANK McGEE
McGee, Francis De Sales   b: 4/28/1899, Columbus, Ohio   d: 1/30/34, Columbus, Ohio   BR/TR, 5'11.5", 175 lbs.   Deb: 9/19/25

YEAR	TM/L	G	AB	R	H	2B	3B	HR	RBI	BB	SO	AVG	OBP	SLG	PRO+	BR	/A	RC	SB	CS	SBR	FR	POS	TPR
1925	Was-A	2	3	0	0	0	0	0	0	0	1	.000	.000	.000	-99	-1	-1	0	0	0	0	0	/1	0.0

■ PAT McGEE
McGee, Patrick   b: Philadelphia, Pa.   d: 6/21/1889, New York, N.Y.   Deb: 9/24/1874

YEAR	TM/L	G	AB	R	H	2B	3B	HR	RBI	BB	SO	AVG	OBP	SLG	PRO+	BR	/A	RC	SB	CS	SBR	FR	POS	TPR
1874	Atl-n	16	65	4	11	2	0	0		0		.169	.169	.200	19	-6	-4	2					O/S2	-0.2
1875	Mut-n	25	94	4	16	3	0	0		0		.170	.170	.202	27	-6	-7	3					O	-0.5
	Atl-n	18	63	3	9	4	1	0		1		.143	.156	.238	39	-4	-3	2					O/2	-0.1
	Yr	43	157	7	25	7	1	0		1		.159	.165	.217	31	-10	-10	6						-0.6
Total	2 n	59	222	11	36	9	1	0		1		.162	.166	.212	28	-16	-14	8					/O2S	-0.8

■ WILLIE McGEE
McGee, Willie Dean   b: 11/2/58, San Francisco, Cal.   BB/TR, 6'1", 175 lbs.   Deb: 5/10/82

YEAR	TM/L	G	AB	R	H	2B	3B	HR	RBI	BB	SO	AVG	OBP	SLG	PRO+	BR	/A	RC	SB	CS	SBR	FR	POS	TPR
1982	*StL-N	123	422	43	125	12	8	4	56	12	58	.296	.319	.391	97	-2	-3	49	24	12	0	-15	*O	-2.0
1983	StL-N	147	601	75	172	22	8	5	75	26	98	.286	.316	.374	90	-2	-9	73	39	8	7	1	*O	-0.3
1984	StL-N	145	571	82	166	19	11	6	50	29	80	.291	.326	.394	104	-0	2	74	43	10	7	5	*O	0.9
1985	*StL-N	152	612	114	216	26	18	10	82	34	86	.353	.387	.503	148	37	37	123	56	16	7	5	*O	4.7
1986	StL-N	124	497	65	127	22	7	7	48	37	82	.256	.308	.370	87	-10	-9	53	19	16	-4	10	*O	-0.5
1987	*StL-N	153	620	76	177	37	11	11	105	24	90	.285	.314	.434	94	-6	-7	77	16	4	2	1	*O/S	-0.9
1988	StL-N	137	562	73	164	24	6	3	50	32	84	.292	.331	.372	100	1	0	72	41	6	9	4	*O	1.0
1989	StL-N	58	199	23	47	10	2	3	17	10	34	.236	.276	.352	76	-6	-7	18	8	6	-1	-1	*O	-0.7
1990	StL-N	125	501	76	168	32	5	3	62	38	86	.335	.383	.437	122	17	16	85	28	9	3	8	*O	2.4
	*Oak-A	29	113	23	31	3	2	0	15	10	18	.274	.333	.336	90	-2	-1	13	3	0	1	1	O/D	0.0
Total	9	1193	4698	650	1393	207	78	52	560	252	716	.297	.334	.407	104	20	19	638	277	87	31	20	*O/DS	4.6

■ DAN McGEEHAN
McGeehan, Daniel De Sales   b: 6/7/1885, Jeddo, Pa.   d: 7/12/55, Hazleton, Pa.   BR/TR, 5'6", 135 lbs.   Deb: 4/22/11

YEAR	TM/L	G	AB	R	H	2B	3B	HR	RBI	BB	SO	AVG	OBP	SLG	PRO+	BR	/A	RC	SB	CS	SBR	FR	POS	TPR
1911	StL-N	3	9	0	2	0	0	0	1	0	1	.222	.222	.222	25	-1	-1	0	0			-1	/2	-0.1

YEAR	TM/L	G	AB	R	H	2B	3B	HR	RBI	BB	SO	AVG	OBP	SLG	PRO+	BR	/A	RC	SB	CS	SBR	FR	POS	TPR

■ ED McGHEE
McGhee, Warren Edward   b: 9/29/24, Perry, Ark.   d: 2/13/86, Memphis, Tenn.   BR/TR, 5'11", 170 lbs.   Deb: 9/20/50

YEAR	TM/L	G	AB	R	H	2B	3B	HR	RBI	BB	SO	AVG	OBP	SLG	PRO+	BR	/A	RC	SB	CS	SBR	FR	POS	TPR
1950	Chi-A	3	6	0	1	0	1	0	0	0	1	.167	.167	.500	67	-0	-0	1	0	0	0	-0	/O	0.0
1953	Phi-A	104	358	36	94	11	4	1	29	32	43	.263	.328	.324	74	-11	-13	38	4	3	-1	3	O	-1.2
1954	Phi-A	21	53	5	11	2	0	2	9	4	8	.208	.263	.358	69	-3	-3	5	0	1	-1	2	O	-0.1
	Chi-A	42	75	12	17	1	0	0	5	12	8	.227	.333	.240	57	-4	-4	7	5	0	2	3	O	0.0
	Yr	63	128	17	28	3	0	2	14	16	16	.219	.306	.289	62	-6	-7	12	5	1	1	5		-0.1
1955	Chi-A	26	13	6	1	0	0	0	0	6	1	.077	.368	.077	24	-1	-1	1	2	1	0	1	O	0.0
Total	4	196	505	59	124	14	5	3	43	54	61	.246	.322	.311	70	-19	-21	51	11	5	0	9	O	-1.3

■ BILL McGHEE
McGhee, William Mac "Fibber"   b: 9/5/08, Shawmut, Ala.   BL/TL, 5'10.5", 185 lbs.   Deb: 7/05/44

YEAR	TM/L	G	AB	R	H	2B	3B	HR	RBI	BB	SO	AVG	OBP	SLG	PRO+	BR	/A	RC	SB	CS	SBR	FR	POS	TPR
1944	Phi-A	77	287	27	83	12	0	1	19	21	20	.289	.338	.341	96	-2	-2	32	2	1	0	-0	1	-0.6
1945	Phi-A	93	250	24	63	6	1	0	19	24	16	.252	.320	.284	76	-7	-7	24	3	2	-0	-6	O/1	-1.6
Total	2	170	537	51	146	18	1	1	38	45	36	.272	.329	.315	87	-9	-9	57	5	3	-0	-6	/1O	-2.2

■ BILL McGILVRAY
McGilvray, William Alexander "Big Bill"   b: 4/29/1883, Portland, Ore.   d: 5/23/52, Denver, Colo.   6', 160 lbs.   Deb: 4/17/08

YEAR	TM/L	G	AB	R	H	2B	3B	HR	RBI	BB	SO	AVG	OBP	SLG	PRO+	BR	/A	RC	SB	CS	SBR	FR	POS	TPR
1908	Cin-N	2	2	0	0	0	0	0	0	0	0	.000	.000	.000	-99	-0	-0	0	0			0	H	0.0

■ TIM McGINLEY
McGinley, Timothy S.   b: Philadelphia, Pa.   d: 11/2/1899, Oakland, Cal.   5'9.5", 155 lbs.   Deb: 4/30/1875

YEAR	TM/L	G	AB	R	H	2B	3B	HR	RBI	BB	SO	AVG	OBP	SLG	PRO+	BR	/A	RC	SB	CS	SBR	FR	POS	TPR
1875	Cen-n	13	51	5	13	1	1	0		1		.255	.269	.314	110	0	1	4					C/O	0.1
	NH-n	32	130	13	36	3	1	0		1		.277	.282	.315	124	1	4	12					C	0.4
	Yr	45	181	18	49	4	2	0		2		.271	.279	.315	120	1	4	16						0.5
1876	Bos-N	9	40	5	6	0	0	0	2	0	1	.150	.150	.150	0	-4	-4	1				-2	/OC	-0.5

■ FRANK McGINN
McGinn, Frank J.   b: Cincinnati, Ohio   d: 11/19/1897, Cincinnati, Ohio   Deb: 6/09/1890

YEAR	TM/L	G	AB	R	H	2B	3B	HR	RBI	BB	SO	AVG	OBP	SLG	PRO+	BR	/A	RC	SB	CS	SBR	FR	POS	TPR
1890	Pit-N	1	4	0	0	0	0	0	0	0	2	.000	.000	.000	-99	-1	-1	0	0			-0	/O	0.0

■ JOHN McGLONE
McGlone, John T.   b: 1864, Brooklyn, N.Y.   d: 11/24/27, Brooklyn, N.Y.   Deb: 10/07/1886

YEAR	TM/L	G	AB	R	H	2B	3B	HR	RBI	BB	SO	AVG	OBP	SLG	PRO+	BR	/A	RC	SB	CS	SBR	FR	POS	TPR
1886	Was-N	4	15	2	1	0	0	0	1	0	3	.067	.067	.067	-63	-3	-3	0	0			-1	/3	-0.3
1887	Cle-a	21	79	14	20	2	1	0		7		.253	.337	.304	84	-2	-1	13	15			1	3	0.0
1888	Cle-a	55	203	22	37	1	3	1	22	16		.182	.249	.232	58	-9	-8	19	26			-6	3/O	-1.3
Total	3	80	297	38	58	3	4	1	23	23	3	.195	.265	.242	60	-14	-12	32	41			-7	/3O	-1.6

■ ART McGOVERN
McGovern, Arthur John   b: 2/27/1882, St.John, N.B., Can.   d: 11/14/15, Thornton, R.I.   160 lbs.   Deb: 4/21/05

YEAR	TM/L	G	AB	R	H	2B	3B	HR	RBI	BB	SO	AVG	OBP	SLG	PRO+	BR	/A	RC	SB	CS	SBR	FR	POS	TPR
1905	Bos-A	15	44	1	5	1	0	0	1	4		.114	.188	.136	4	-5	-5	1	0			-3	C	-0.6

■ BEAUTY McGOWAN
McGowan, Frank Bernard   b: 11/8/01, Branford, Conn.   d: 5/6/82, Hamden, Conn.   BL/TR, 5'11", 190 lbs.   Deb: 4/12/22

YEAR	TM/L	G	AB	R	H	2B	3B	HR	RBI	BB	SO	AVG	OBP	SLG	PRO+	BR	/A	RC	SB	CS	SBR	FR	POS	TPR
1922	Phi-A	99	300	36	69	10	5	1	20	40	46	.230	.323	.307	63	-15	-16	32	6	5	-1	9	O	-1.4
1923	Phi-A	95	287	41	73	9	1	1	19	36	25	.254	.340	.303	69	-12	-12	32	4	3	-1	-0	O	-1.9
1928	StL-A	47	168	35	61	13	4	2	18	16	15	.363	.425	.524	143	12	11	38	2	1	0	-1	O	0.7
1929	StL-A	125	441	62	112	26	6	2	51	61	34	.254	.346	.354	78	-12	-14	58	5	2	0	7	*O	-1.1
1937	Bos-N	9	12	0	1	0	0	0	0	1	2	.083	.154	.083	-37	-2	-2	0	0			-0	/O	-0.2
Total	5	375	1208	174	316	58	16	6	108	154	122	.262	.347	.351	80	-29	-34	160	17	11		14	O	-3.9

■ JOHN McGRAW
McGraw, John Joseph "Mugsy" or "Little Napoleon"
b: 4/7/1873, Truxton, N.Y.   d: 2/25/34, New Rochelle, N.Y.   BL/TR, 5'7", 155 lbs.   Deb: 8/26/1891   MH

YEAR	TM/L	G	AB	R	H	2B	3B	HR	RBI	BB	SO	AVG	OBP	SLG	PRO+	BR	/A	RC	SB	CS	SBR	FR	POS	TPR
1891	Bal-a	33	115	17	31	3	5	0	14	12	17	.270	.359	.383	114	2	2	18	4			-15	S/O2	-0.9
1892	Bal-N	79	286	41	77	13	2	1	26	32	21	.269	.355	.339	109	5	4	41	15			1	O2/S3	0.4
1893	Bal-N	127	480	123	154	9	10	5	64	101	11	.321	.454	.412	131	31	29	110	38			-23	*SO	0.7
1894	*Bal-N	124	512	156	174	18	14	1	92	91	12	.340	.451	.436	112	20	15	139	78			-1	*3/2	0.9
1895	*Bal-N	96	388	110	143	13	6	2	48	60	9	.369	.459	.448	133	26	23	111	61			9	*3/2	2.7
1896	*Bal-N	23	77	20	25	2	2	0	14	11	4	.325	.422	.403	119	3	3	19	13			-2	3/1	0.1
1897	*Bal-N	106	391	90	127	15	3	0	48	99		.325	.471	.379	129	25	25	93	44			-13	*3	1.1
1898	Bal-N	143	515	143	176	8	10	0	53	112		.342	.475	.396	151	47	46	120	43			-12	*3/O	3.4
1899	Bal-N	117	399	140	156	13	3	1	33	124		.391	.547	.446	169	58	54	141	73			2	*3M	5.0
1900	StL-N	99	334	84	115	10	4	2	33	85		.344	.502	.416	159	37	37	86	29			-8	*3	2.7
1901	Bal-A	73	232	71	81	14	9	0	28	61		.349	.508	.487	172	32	30	72	24			-18	3M	0.9
1902	Bal-A	20	63	14	18	3	2	1	3	17		.286	.458	.444	147	6	6	16	5			-7	3M	-0.2
	NY-N	35	107	13	25	0	0	0	5	26		.234	.397	.234	98	2	2	13	7			-2	SM	0.2
1903	NY-N	12	11	2	3	0	0	0	1	1		.273	.333	.273	73	-0	-0	1	1			-2	/2OS3	-0.2
1904	NY-N	5	12	0	4	0	0	0	0	3		.333	.467	.333	145	1	1	2	0			3	/2SM	0.4
1905	NY-N	3	0	0	0	0	0	0	0	0		—	—	—	—	0	0	0	1			-0	/OM	0.0
1906	NY-N	4	2	0	0	0	0	0	0	1		.000	.333	.000	6	-0	-0	0	0			0	/3M	0.0
Total	16	1099	3924	1024	1309	121	70	13	462	836	74	.334	.465	.410	137	295	277	981	436			-87	3S/O21	17.2

■ FRED McGRIFF
McGriff, Frederick Stanley   b: 10/31/63, Tampa, Fla.   BL/TL, 6'3", 200 lbs.   Deb: 5/17/86

YEAR	TM/L	G	AB	R	H	2B	3B	HR	RBI	BB	SO	AVG	OBP	SLG	PRO+	BR	/A	RC	SB	CS	SBR	FR	POS	TPR
1986	Tor-A	3	5	1	1	0	0	0	0	0	2	.200	.200	.200	9	-1	-1	0	0	0	0	0	/1D	0.0
1987	Tor-A	107	295	58	73	16	0	20	43	60	104	.247	.376	.505	128	14	13	60	3	2	-0	-1	D1	1.0
1988	Tor-A	154	536	100	151	35	4	34	82	79	149	.282	.378	.552	156	41	41	113	6	1	1	-5	*1	2.7
1989	*Tor-A	161	551	98	148	27	3	36	92	119	132	.269	.402	.525	162	47	48	121	7	4	-0	-1	*1/D	3.6
1990	Tor-A	153	557	91	167	21	1	35	88	94	108	.300	.403	.530	162	46	47	124	5	3	-0	9	*1/D	4.5
Total	5	578	1944	348	540	99	8	125	305	352	495	.278	.391	.530	155	147	148	417	21	10	0	1	1D	11.8

■ TERRY McGRIFF
McGriff, Terence Roy   b: 9/23/63, Fort Pierce, Fla.   BR/TR, 6'2", 190 lbs.   Deb: 7/11/87

YEAR	TM/L	G	AB	R	H	2B	3B	HR	RBI	BB	SO	AVG	OBP	SLG	PRO+	BR	/A	RC	SB	CS	SBR	FR	POS	TPR
1987	Cin-N	34	89	6	20	3	0	2	11	8	17	.225	.289	.326	60	-5	-5	8	0	0	0	4	C	0.1
1988	Cin-N	35	96	9	19	3	0	1	4	12	31	.198	.287	.260	56	-5	-5	7	1	0	0	3	C	0.0
1989	Cin-N	6	11	1	3	0	0	0	2	2	3	.273	.385	.273	88	-0	-0	1	0	0	0	0	/C	0.1
1990	Cin-N	2	4	0	0	0	0	0	0	0	1	.000	.000	.000	-98	-1	-1	0	0	0	0	1	/C	0.0
	Hou-N	4	5	0	0	0	0	0	0	0	0	.000	.000	.000	-99	-1	-1	0	0	0	0	0	/C	0.0
	Yr	6	9	0	0	0	0	0	0	0	1	.000	.000	.000	-99	-2	-2	0	0	0	0	1		0.0
Total	4	81	205	16	42	6	0	3	17	22	52	.205	.282	.278	53	-12	-13	17	1	0	0	8	/C	0.2

■ MARK McGRILLIS
McGrillis, Mark A.   b: 10/22/1872, Philadelphia, Pa.   d: 5/16/35, Philadelphia, Pa.   Deb: 9/17/1892

YEAR	TM/L	G	AB	R	H	2B	3B	HR	RBI	BB	SO	AVG	OBP	SLG	PRO+	BR	/A	RC	SB	CS	SBR	FR	POS	TPR
1892	StL-N	1	3	0	0	0	0	0	0	0	1	.000	.000	.000	-99	-1	-1	0	0			0	/3	0.0

■ JOE McGUCKIN
McGuckin, Joseph W.   b: 1862, Paterson, N.J.   d: 12/31/03, Yonkers, N.Y.   Deb: 8/27/1890

YEAR	TM/L	G	AB	R	H	2B	3B	HR	RBI	BB	SO	AVG	OBP	SLG	PRO+	BR	/A	RC	SB	CS	SBR	FR	POS	TPR
1890	Bal-a	11	37	2	4	0	0	0		6		.108	.250	.108	7	-4	-4	2	3			3	O	-0.1

■ JOHN McGUINNESS
McGuinness, John James   b: 1857, Ireland   d: 12/19/16, Binghamton, N.Y.   Deb: 5/06/1876

YEAR	TM/L	G	AB	R	H	2B	3B	HR	RBI	BB	SO	AVG	OBP	SLG	PRO+	BR	/A	RC	SB	CS	SBR	FR	POS	TPR
1876	NY-N	1	4	0	0	0	0	0	0	0	0	.000	.000	.000	-99	-1	-1	0				-1	/2C	-0.1
1879	Syr-N	12	51	7	15	1	1	0	4	0	6	.294	.294	.353	126	1	1	5				-0	1	0.0
1884	Phi-U	53	220	25	52	8	1	0		5		.236	.253	.282	87	-4	-2	16	0			-0	1/2S	-0.2
Total	3	66	275	32	67	9	2	0	4	5	6	.244	.257	.291	91	-5	-1	22	0			-2	/12SC	-0.3

■ JIM McGUIRE
McGuire, James A.   b: 2/4/1875, Dunkirk, N.Y.   d: 1/26/17, Buffalo, N.Y.   TR ,   Deb: 9/10/01

YEAR	TM/L	G	AB	R	H	2B	3B	HR	RBI	BB	SO	AVG	OBP	SLG	PRO+	BR	/A	RC	SB	CS	SBR	FR	POS	TPR
1901	Cle-A	18	69	4	16	2	0	0	3	0		.232	.232	.261	39	-6	-5	4	0			1	S	-0.2

YEAR	TM/L	G	AB	R	H	2B	3B	HR	RBI	BB	SO	AVG	OBP	SLG	PRO+	BR	/A	RC	SB	CS	SBR	FR	POS	TPR

■ DEACON McGUIRE   McGuire, James Thomas b: 11/18/1863, Youngstown, Ohio d: 10/31/36, Albion, Mich. BR/TR, 6'1", 185 lbs. Deb: 6/21/1884 MC

YEAR	TM/L	G	AB	R	H	2B	3B	HR	RBI	BB	SO	AVG	OBP	SLG	PRO+	BR	/A	RC	SB	CS	SBR	FR	POS	TPR
1884	Tol-a	45	151	12	28	7	0	1		5		.185	.217	.252	52	-7	-8	8				-5	C/OS	-0.8
1885	Det-N	34	121	11	23	4	2	0	9	5	23	.190	.222	.256	54	-6	-6	7				12	C/O	0.8
1886	Phi-N	50	167	25	33	7	1	2	18	19	25	.198	.280	.287	72	-5	-5	14	2			-7	C/O	-0.7
1887	Phi-N	41	150	22	46	6	6	2	23	11	8	.307	.362	.467	123	6	5	27	3			-0	C	0.7
1888	Phi-N	12	51	7	17	4	2	0	11	4	9	.333	.382	.490	170	4	4	10	0			-5	C/3	0.0
	Det-N	3	13	0	0	0	0	0	0	0	4	.000	.000	.000	-99	-3	-3	0	0			-2	/C	-0.4
	Yr	15	64	7	17	4	2	0	11	4	13	.266	.309	.391	119	2	1	8	0			-6		-0.4
	Cle-a	26	94	15	24	1	3	1	13	7		.255	.333	.362	129	3	3	12	2			0	C/1O	0.4
1890	Roc-a	87	331	46	99	16	4	4		21		.299	.356	.408	138	10	14	52	8			5	C1/OP	2.3
1891	Was-a	114	413	55	125	22	10	3	66	43	34	.303	.382	.426	141	18	22	73	10			-12	*CO/31	1.0
1892	Was-N	97	315	46	73	14	4	4	43	61	48	.232	.360	.340	117	8	9	42	7			-1	C/1O	1.1
1893	Was-N	63	237	29	62	14	3	1	26	26	12	.262	.342	.359	90	-4	-3	31	3			-5	C1	-0.1
1894	Was-N	104	425	67	130	18	6	6	78	33	19	.306	.366	.419	93	-7	-4	71	11			-1	*C	0.4
1895	Was-N	132	533	89	179	30	8	10	97	40	18	.336	.388	.478	126	18	20	108	16			10	*C/S	3.3
1896	Was-N	108	389	60	125	25	3	2	70	30	14	.321	.379	.416	112	7	7	68	12			-2	*C/1	1.1
1897	Was-N	93	327	51	112	17	7	4	53	21		.343	.386	.474	129	13	13	65	9			7	C/1	2.5
1898	Was-N	131	489	59	131	18	3	1	57	24		.268	.310	.323	84	-10	-10	53	10			3	C1M	0.0
1899	Was-N	59	199	25	54	3	1	1	12	16		.271	.335	.312	81	-5	-4	22	3			-5	C/1	-0.5
	Bro-N	46	157	22	50	12	4	0	23	12		.318	.385	.446	128	7	6	29	4			2	C	1.0
	Yr	105	356	47	104	15	5	1	35	28		.292	.357	.371	102	2	2	51	7			-3		0.5
1900	*Bro-N	71	241	20	69	15	2	0	34	19		.286	.341	.365	92	-1	-3	31	2			-8	C	-0.3
1901	Bro-N	85	301	28	89	16	4	0	40	18		.296	.338	.375	106	3	2	41	4			-5	C/1	0.7
1902	Det-A	73	229	27	52	14	1	2	23	24		.227	.300	.323	73	-8	-8	23	3			-6	C	-0.7
1903	Det-A	72	248	15	62	12	1	0	21	19		.250	.303	.306	88	-4	-3	25	3			-6	C/1	0.0
1904	NY-A	101	322	17	67	12	2	0	20	27		.208	.269	.258	66	-11	-12	24	2			14	C/1	1.3
1905	NY-A	72	228	9	50	7	2	0	33	18		.219	.276	.268	67	-6	-9	19	3			-6	C	-0.8
1906	NY-A	51	144	11	43	5	0	0	14	12		.299	.353	.333	106	3	2	18	3			-1	C/1	0.4
1907	NY-A	1	0	1	0	0	0	0	0	0		.000	.000	.000	-93	-0	-0	0	0			1	/C	0.1
	Bos-A	6	4	1	3	0	0	1	1	0		.750	.750	1.500	625	2	2	5	0			0	HM	0.2
	Yr	7	5	1	3	0	0	1	1	0		.600	.600	1.200	474	2	2	4	0			1		0.3
1908	Bos-A	1	1	0	0	0	0	0	0	0		.000	.000	.000	-97	-0	-0	0	0			0	HM	0.0
	Cle-A	1	4	0	1	1	0	0	2	0		.250	.250	.500	144	0	0	0	0			-0	/1	0.0
	Yr	2	5	0	1	1	0	0	2	0		.200	.200	.400	94	-0	-0	0	0			-0		0.0
1910	Cle-A	1	3	0	1	0	0	0	0	0		.333	.500	.333	159	0	0	0	0			-1	/CM	0.0
1912	Det-A	1	2	1	1	0	0	0	0	0		.500	.500	.500	192	0	0	0	0			0	/C	0.1
Total	26	1781	6290	770	1749	300	79	45	787	515	214	.278	.339	.372	103	27	30	880	117			-22	*C/103SP	13.1

■ MICKEY McGUIRE   McGuire, M C Adolphus b: 1/18/41, Dayton, Ohio BR/TR, 5'10", 170 lbs. Deb: 9/07/62

YEAR	TM/L	G	AB	R	H	2B	3B	HR	RBI	BB	SO	AVG	OBP	SLG	PRO+	BR	/A	RC	SB	CS	SBR	FR	POS	TPR
1962	Bal-A	6	4	0	0	0	0	0	0	0	0	.000	.000	.000	-99	-1	-1	0	0	0	0	0	/S	0.0
1967	Bal-A	10	17	2	4	0	0	0	2	0	2	.235	.235	.235	40	-1	-1	1	0	0	0	-2	/2	-0.3
Total	2	16	21	2	4	0	0	0	2	0	2	.190	.190	.190	11	-2	-2	1	0	0	0	-2	/S2	-0.3

■ BILL McGUIRE   McGuire, William Patrick b: 2/14/64, Omaha, Neb. BR/TR, 6'3", 205 lbs. Deb: 8/02/88

YEAR	TM/L	G	AB	R	H	2B	3B	HR	RBI	BB	SO	AVG	OBP	SLG	PRO+	BR	/A	RC	SB	CS	SBR	FR	POS	TPR
1988	Sea-A	9	16	1	3	0	0	0	2	3	2	.188	.316	.188	43	-1	-1	1	0	0	0	0	/C	0.0
1989	Sea-A	14	28	2	5	0	0	1	4	2	6	.179	.233	.286	44	-2	-2	1	0	0	0	5	C	0.3
Total	2	23	44	3	8	0	0	1	6	5	8	.182	.265	.250	44	-3	-3	3	0	0	0	5	/C	0.3

■ BILL McGUNNIGLE   McGunnigle, William Henry "Gunner" b: 1/1/1855, Boston, Mass. d: 3/9/1899, Brockton, Mass. BR/TR, 5'9", 155 lbs. Deb: 5/02/1879 M

YEAR	TM/L	G	AB	R	H	2B	3B	HR	RBI	BB	SO	AVG	OBP	SLG	PRO+	BR	/A	RC	SB	CS	SBR	FR	POS	TPR
1879	Buf-N	47	171	22	30	0	1	0	5	5	24	.175	.199	.187	27	-13	-13	7				0	OP	-1.0
1880	Buf-N	7	22	0	4	0	0	0	1	0	4	.182	.182	.182	23	-2	-2	1				-1	/PO	0.0
	Wor-N	1	4	0	0	0	0	0	0	0	2	.000	.000	.000	-92	-1	-1	0				-0	/O	0.0
	Yr	8	26	0	4	0	0	0	1	0	6	.154	.154	.154	5	-2	-3	1				-1		0.0
1882	Cle-N	1	5	2	1	0	0	0	0	0	1	.200	.200	.200	30	-0	-0	0				-0	/O	0.0
Total	3	56	202	24	35	0	1	0	6	5	31	.173	.193	.183	25	-16	-16	7				-1	/OP	-1.0

■ MARK McGWIRE   McGwire, Mark David b: 10/1/63, Pomona, Cal. BR/TR, 6'5", 215 lbs. Deb: 8/22/86

YEAR	TM/L	G	AB	R	H	2B	3B	HR	RBI	BB	SO	AVG	OBP	SLG	PRO+	BR	/A	RC	SB	CS	SBR	FR	POS	TPR
1986	Oak-A	18	53	10	10	1	0	3	9	4	18	.189	.259	.377	76	-2	-2	5	0	1	-1	-3	3	-0.4
1987	Oak-A	151	557	97	161	28	4	**49**	118	71	131	.289	.374	**.618**	168	44	50	131	1	1	-0	-6	*1/3O	2.8
1988	*Oak-A	155	550	87	143	22	1	32	99	76	117	.260	.354	.478	135	23	25	93	0	0	-0	-8	*1/O	0.9
1989	Oak-A	143	490	74	113	17	0	33	95	83	94	.231	.345	.467	132	18	20	76	1	1	-0	7	*1/D	1.8
1990	*Oak-A	156	523	87	123	16	0	39	108	**110**	116	.235	.375	.489	144	30	32	101	2	1	0	-5	*1/D	1.7
Total	5	623	2173	355	550	84	5	156	429	344	476	.253	.360	.512	144	113	126	407	4	4	-1	-14	1/3DO	6.8

■ JIM McHALE   McHale, James Bernard "J.B." b: 12/17/1875, Miners Mills, Pa. d: 6/17/59, Los Angeles, Cal. BR/TR, 5'11", 165 lbs. Deb: 4/14/08

YEAR	TM/L	G	AB	R	H	2B	3B	HR	RBI	BB	SO	AVG	OBP	SLG	PRO+	BR	/A	RC	SB	CS	SBR	FR	POS	TPR
1908	Bos-A	21	67	9	15	2	2	0	7	4		.224	.268	.313	88	-1	-1	7	4			-1	O	-0.3

■ JOHN McHALE   McHale, John Joseph b: 9/21/21, Detroit, Mich. BL/TR, 6', 200 lbs. Deb: 5/28/43

YEAR	TM/L	G	AB	R	H	2B	3B	HR	RBI	BB	SO	AVG	OBP	SLG	PRO+	BR	/A	RC	SB	CS	SBR	FR	POS	TPR
1943	Det-A	4	3	0	0	0	0	0	0	1	1	.000	.250	.000	-23	-0	-0	0	0	0	0	0	H	0.0
1944	Det-A	1	1	0	0	0	0	0	0	0	0	.000	.000	.000	-95	-0	-0	0	0	0	0	0	H	0.0
1945	*Det-A	19	14	0	2	0	0	0	1	1	4	.143	.250	.143	14	-1	-2	1	0	0	0	0	/1	0.0
1947	Det-A	39	95	10	20	1	0	3	11	7	24	.211	.265	.316	59	-5	-6	8	1	1	-0	-1	1	-0.7
1948	Det-A	1	1	0	0	0	0	0	0	0	0	.000	.000	.000	-97	-0	-0	0	0	0	0	0	H	0.0
Total	5	64	114	10	22	1	0	3	12	9	29	.193	.258	.281	49	-8	-8	9	1	1	-0	-0	/1	-0.7

■ BOB McHALE   McHale, Robert Emmet "Rabbit" b: 2/25/1872, Michigan Bluff, Cal. d: 6/9/52, Sacramento, Cal. Deb: 5/09/1898

YEAR	TM/L	G	AB	R	H	2B	3B	HR	RBI	BB	SO	AVG	OBP	SLG	PRO+	BR	/A	RC	SB	CS	SBR	FR	POS	TPR
1898	Was-N	11	33	5	6	2	0	0	7	1		.182	.270	.242	49	-2	-2	2	1			-1	/OS1	-0.3

■ AUSTIN McHENRY   McHenry, Austin Bush "Mac" b: 9/22/1895, Wrightsville, O. d: 11/27/22, Jefferson, Ohio BR/TR, 5'11", 152 lbs. Deb: 6/22/18

YEAR	TM/L	G	AB	R	H	2B	3B	HR	RBI	BB	SO	AVG	OBP	SLG	PRO+	BR	/A	RC	SB	CS	SBR	FR	POS	TPR
1918	StL-N	80	272	32	71	12	6	1	29	21	24	.261	.319	.360	111	2	3	33	8			0	O	0.0
1919	StL-N	110	371	41	106	19	11	1	47	19	57	.286	.322	.404	125	7	9	49	7			4	*O	1.0
1920	StL-N	137	504	66	142	19	11	10	65	25	73	.282	.316	.423	115	5	7	64	8	11	-4	10	*O	0.5
1921	StL-N	152	574	92	201	37	8	17	102	38	48	.350	.393	.531	145	33	35	111	10	20	-9	7	*O	2.5
1922	StL-N	64	238	31	72	18	3	5	43	14	27	.303	.344	.466	112	2	3	37	2	2	-1	5	O	0.5
Total	5	543	1959	262	592	105	39	34	286	117	229	.302	.343	.448	126	49	58	294	35	33		26	O	4.5

■ VANCE McHENRY   McHenry, Vance Loren b: 7/10/56, Chico, Cal. BR/TR, 5'9", 165 lbs. Deb: 8/13/81

YEAR	TM/L	G	AB	R	H	2B	3B	HR	RBI	BB	SO	AVG	OBP	SLG	PRO+	BR	/A	RC	SB	CS	SBR	FR	POS	TPR
1981	Sea-A	15	18	3	4	0	0	0	2	1	1	.222	.263	.222	39	-1	-1	1	0	0	0	3	S/D	0.3
1982	Sea-A	3	1	0	0	0	0	0	0	0	0	.000	.000	.000	-97	-0	-0	0	0	0	0	-0	/SD	0.0
Total	2	18	19	3	4	0	0	0	2	1	1	.211	.250	.211	32	-2	-2	1	0	0	0	3	/SD	0.3

■ IRISH McILVEEN   McIlveen, Henry Cooke b: 7/27/1880, Belfast, Ireland d: 10/18/60, Lorain, Ohio TL, 5'11.5", 180 lbs. Deb: 7/10/06

YEAR	TM/L	G	AB	R	H	2B	3B	HR	RBI	BB	SO	AVG	OBP	SLG	PRO+	BR	/A	RC	SB	CS	SBR	FR	POS	TPR
1906	Pit-N	5	5	1	2	0	0	0	0	0		.400	.400	.400	146	0	0	1	0			0	/P	0.1
1908	NY-A	44	169	17	36	3	3	0	8	14		.213	.273	.266	77	-4	-4	14	6			0	O	-0.6
1909	NY-A	4	3	0	0	0	0	0	0	0	1	.000	.250	.000	-20	-0	-0	0	0			0	H	0.0

YEAR	TM/L	G	AB	R	H	2B	3B	HR	RBI	BB	SO	AVG	OBP	SLG	PRO+	BR	/A	RC	SB	CS	SBR	FR	POS	TPR
Total	3	53	177	18	38	3	3	0	8	15		.215	.276	.266	77	-4	-4	15	6			0	/OP	-0.5

■ STUFFY McINNIS
McInnis, John Phalen "Jack" b: 9/19/1890, Gloucester, Mass.   d: 2/16/60, Ipswich, Mass.   BR/TR, 5'9.5", 162 lbs.   Deb: 4/12/09 M

YEAR	TM/L	G	AB	R	H	2B	3B	HR	RBI	BB	SO	AVG	OBP	SLG	PRO+	BR	/A	RC	SB	CS	SBR	FR	POS	TPR
1909	Phi-A	19	46	4	11	0	0	1	4	2		.239	.286	.304	85	-1	-1	4	0			4	S	0.4
1910	Phi-A	38	73	10	22	2	4	0	12	7		.301	.363	.438	152	4	4	12	3			-5	S/23O	0.0
1911	*Phi-A	126	468	76	150	20	10	3	77	25		.321	.361	.425	121	10	12	80	23			-14	1S	0.2
1912	Phi-A	153	568	83	186	25	13	3	101	24		.327	.384	.433	139	24	27	105	27			3	*1	3.2
1913	*Phi-A	148	543	79	176	30	4	4	90	45	31	.324	.382	.416	137	23	24	91	16			-1	*1	2.4
1914	*Phi-A	149	576	74	181	12	8	1	95	19	27	.314	.341	.368	117	7	9	76	25	19	-4	0	*1	0.6
1915	Phi-A	119	456	44	143	14	4	0	49	14	17	.314	.337	.362	112	3	4	57	8	8	-2	5	*1	0.2
1916	Phi-A	140	512	42	151	25	3	1	60	25	19	.295	.331	.361	113	3	6	67	7			7	*1	1.1
1917	Phi-A	150	567	50	172	19	4	0	44	33	19	.303	.342	.351	113	6	7	72	18			2	*1	0.3
1918	*Bos-A	117	423	40	115	11	5	0	56	19	10	.272	.306	.322	91	-7	-6	46	10			4	13	-0.7
1919	Bos-A	120	440	32	134	12	5	1	58	23	11	.305	.341	.361	103	-2	1	57	8			3	*1	0.5
1920	Bos-A	148	559	50	166	21	3	2	71	18	19	.297	.321	.356	83	-17	-14	62	6	11	-5	-1	*1	-1.9
1921	Bos-A	152	584	72	179	31	10	0	76	21	9	.307	.335	.394	88	-14	-12	76	2	4	-2	4	*1	-0.9
1922	Cle-A	142	537	58	164	28	7	1	78	15	5	.305	.325	.389	85	-13	-13	66	1	5	-3	-5	*1	-3.1
1923	Bos-N	154	607	70	191	23	9	2	95	26	12	.315	.343	.392	97	-6	-3	80	7	8	-3	4	*1	-1.1
1924	Bos-N	146	581	57	169	23	7	1	59	15	6	.291	.311	.360	83	-18	-14	65	9	3	1	7	*1	-1.2
1925	*Pit-N	59	155	19	57	10	4	0	24	17	1	.368	.437	.484	126	9	7	33	1	1	-0	1	1	0.4
1926	Pit-N	47	127	12	38	6	1	0	13	7	3	.299	.336	.362	83	-2	-3	15	1			-1	1	-0.4
1927	Phi-N	1	0	0	0	0	0	0	0	0	0	—	—	—	—	0	0	0	0			0	/1M	0.0
Total	19	2128	7822	872	2405	312	101	20	1062	380	189	.307	.343	.381	105	9	35	1065	172	59		17	*1/S320	-1.0

■ TIM McINTOSH
McIntosh, Timothy Allen b: 3/21/65, Minneapolis, Minn.   BR/TR, 5'11", 195 lbs.   Deb: 9/03/90

YEAR	TM/L	G	AB	R	H	2B	3B	HR	RBI	BB	SO	AVG	OBP	SLG	PRO+	BR	/A	RC	SB	CS	SBR	FR	POS	TPR
1990	Mil-A	5	5	1	1	0	0	1	1	0	2	.200	.200	.800	173	0	0	1	0	0	0	0	/C	0.1

■ MATTY McINTYRE
McIntyre, Matthew W. b: 6/12/1880, Stonington, Conn.   d: 4/2/20, Detroit, Mich.   BL/TL, 5'11", 175 lbs.   Deb: 7/03/01

YEAR	TM/L	G	AB	R	H	2B	3B	HR	RBI	BB	SO	AVG	OBP	SLG	PRO+	BR	/A	RC	SB	CS	SBR	FR	POS	TPR
1901	Phi-A	82	308	38	85	12	4	0	46	30		.276	.344	.341	88	-2	-4	42	11			-3	O	-0.6
1904	Det-A	152	578	74	146	11	10	2	46	44		.253	.305	.317	102	-0	2	64	11			12	*O	0.5
1905	Det-A	131	495	59	130	21	5	0	30	48		.263	.328	.325	109	6	6	58	9			16	*O	1.7
1906	Det-A	133	493	63	128	19	11	0	39	56		.260	.335	.343	111	9	8	69	29			12	*O	1.6
1907	Det-A	20	81	6	23	1	1	0	9	7		.284	.341	.321	109	1	1	10	3			3	O	0.3
1908	*Det-A	151	569	105	168	24	13	0	28	83		.295	.385	.383	146	36	33	91	20			15	*O	4.6
1909	*Det-A	125	476	65	116	18	9	1	34	54		.244	.325	.326	101	4	2	54	13			0	*O	-0.2
1910	Det-A	83	305	40	72	15	5	0	25	39		.236	.323	.318	94	1	-1	32	4			4	O	-0.1
1911	Chi-A	146	569	102	184	19	11	1	52	64		.323	.397	.401	127	19	22	96	17			-2	*O	0.8
1912	Chi-A	49	84	10	14	0	0	0	10	14		.167	.300	.167	36	-6	-6	5	3			-1	O	-0.8
Total	10	1072	3958	562	1066	140	69	4	319	439		.269	.344	.343	111	68	62	522	120			57	*O	7.8

■ OTTO McIVOR
McIvor, Edward Otto b: 7/26/1884, Greenville, Tex.   d: 5/4/54, Dallas, Tex.   BB/TL, 5'11.5", 175 lbs.   Deb: 4/18/11

YEAR	TM/L	G	AB	R	H	2B	3B	HR	RBI	BB	SO	AVG	OBP	SLG	PRO+	BR	/A	RC	SB	CS	SBR	FR	POS	TPR
1911	StL-N	30	62	11	14	2	1	1	9	9	14	.226	.333	.339	91	-1	-1	7	0			-2	O	-0.2

■ DAVE McKAY
McKay, David Lawrence b: 3/14/50, Vancouver, B.C., Can   BB/TR, 6'1", 195 lbs.   Deb: 8/22/75 C

YEAR	TM/L	G	AB	R	H	2B	3B	HR	RBI	BB	SO	AVG	OBP	SLG	PRO+	BR	/A	RC	SB	CS	SBR	FR	POS	TPR
1975	Min-A	33	125	8	32	4	1	2	16	6	14	.256	.295	.352	81	-3	-3	12	1	1	-0	1	3	-0.1
1976	Min-A	45	138	8	28	2	0	0	8	9	27	.203	.272	.217	43	-9	-10	8	1	2	-1	-2	3/SD	-1.2
1977	Tor-A	95	274	18	54	4	3	3	22	7	51	.197	.223	.266	32	-26	-26	15	2	1	0	7	23S/D	-1.4
1978	Tor-A	145	504	59	120	20	8	7	45	20	91	.238	.269	.351	71	-19	-21	43	4	4	-1	-6	*2/S3D	-2.0
1979	Tor-A	47	156	19	34	9	0	0	12	7	19	.218	.256	.276	43	-12	-13	10	1	1	-0	6	2/3	-0.4
1980	Oak-A	123	295	29	72	16	1	1	29	10	57	.244	.283	.315	68	-15	-12	27	1	1	-0	-8	23S	-1.6
1981	*Oak-A	79	224	25	59	11	1	4	21	16	43	.263	.318	.375	104	-0	1	27	4	1	1	-5	32/S	-0.2
1982	Oak-A	78	212	25	42	4	1	4	17	11	35	.198	.238	.283	44	-17	-16	16	6	1	1	-3	23/S	-1.4
Total	8	645	1928	191	441	70	15	21	170	86	337	.229	.268	.313	62	-102	-100	157	20	12	-1	-10	23/SD	-8.3

■ ED McKEAN
McKean, Edwin John "Mack" b: 6/6/1864, Grafton, Ohio   d: 8/16/19, Cleveland, Ohio   BR/TR, 5'9", 160 lbs.   Deb: 4/16/1887

YEAR	TM/L	G	AB	R	H	2B	3B	HR	RBI	BB	SO	AVG	OBP	SLG	PRO+	BR	/A	RC	SB	CS	SBR	FR	POS	TPR
1887	Cle-a	132	539	97	154	16	13	2		60		.286	.358	.375	109	6	9	102	76			-8	*S/2O	0.0
1888	Cle-a	131	548	94	164	21	15	6	68	28		.299	.340	.425	152	28	30	99	52			3	SO/23	3.1
1889	Cle-N	123	500	88	159	22	8	4	75	42	25	.318	.375	.418	126	15	17	94	35			5	*S/2	2.3
1890	Cle-N	136	530	95	157	15	14	7	61	87	25	.296	.401	.417	144	31	32	100	23			-15	*S/2	1.4
1891	Cle-N	141	603	115	170	13	12	6	69	64	19	.282	.352	.373	109	11	7	86	14			-12	*S	0.1
1892	*Cle-N	129	531	76	139	14	10	0	93	49	28	.262	.325	.326	95	-0	-3	64	19			-45	*S	-3.8
1893	Cle-N	125	545	103	169	29	24	4	133	50	14	.310	.372	.473	119	18	12	105	16			-4	*S	1.0
1894	Cle-N	130	554	116	198	30	15	8	122	49	12	.357	.408	.509	118	20	16	133	33			-21	*S	0.1
1895	*Cle-N	131	565	131	193	32	17	8	119	45	25	.342	.397	.501	125	26	20	120	12			-19	*S	0.9
1896	*Cle-N	133	571	100	193	29	12	7	112	45	9	.338	.388	.468	120	21	16	111	13			-33	*S	-1.3
1897	Cle-N	125	523	83	143	21	14	2	78	40		.273	.330	.379	84	-9	-14	72	15			-30	*S	-3.4
1898	Cle-N	151	604	89	172	23	1	9	94	56		.285	.346	.371	110	7	8	83	11			-36	*S	-1.8
1899	StL-N	67	277	40	72	7	3	3	40	20		.260	.310	.339	78	-8	-9	31	4			-17	S12	-1.9
Total	13	1654	6890	1227	2083	272	158	66	1070	635	157	.302	.364	.416	116	166	141	1201	323			-230	*S/O213	-3.3

■ BILL McKECHNIE
McKechnie, William Boyd "Deacon" b: 8/7/1886, Wilkinsburg, Pa.   d: 10/29/65, Bradenton, Fla.   BB/TR, 5'10", 160 lbs.   Deb: 9/08/07 MCH

YEAR	TM/L	G	AB	R	H	2B	3B	HR	RBI	BB	SO	AVG	OBP	SLG	PRO+	BR	/A	RC	SB	CS	SBR	FR	POS	TPR
1907	Pit-N	3	8	0	1	0	0	0	0	0		.125	.125	.125	-21	-1	-1	0	0			-0	/32	-0.1
1910	Pit-N	71	212	23	46	1	2	0	12	11	23	.217	.256	.241	42	-15	-17	14	4			8	2S/31	-1.0
1911	Pit-N	104	321	40	73	8	7	2	37	28	18	.227	.293	.315	68	-13	-15	34	9			-0	12S/3	-1.6
1912	Pit-N	24	73	8	18	0	1	0	4	4	5	.247	.286	.274	54	-5	-5	6	2			2	3/S21	-0.2
1913	Bos-N	1	4	1	0	0	0	0	0	0	1	.000	.200	.000	-39	-1	-1	0	0			0	/O	0.0
	NY-A	45	112	7	15	0	0	0	8	8	17	.134	.198	.134	-2	-14	-14	3	2			5	2/S3	-0.9
1914	Ind-F	149	570	107	173	24	6	2	38	53	36	.304	.368	.377	103	11	3	103	47			23	*3	3.0
1915	New-F	127	451	49	113	22	5	1	43	41	31	.251	.316	.328	96	-5	-2	59	28			2	*3/OM	0.3
1916	NY-N	71	260	22	64	9	1	0	17	7	20	.246	.268	.288	75	-9	-8	22	7			-3	3	-1.1
	Cin-N	37	130	4	36	3	0	0	10	3	12	.277	.293	.300	84	-3	-3	13	4			-4	3M	-0.6
	Yr	108	390	26	100	12	1	0	27	10	32	.256	.277	.292	78	-12	-11	36	11			-7		-1.7
1917	Cin-N	48	134	11	34	3	1	0	15	7	7	.254	.296	.291	84	-3	-3	12	5			-7	2S/3	-0.8
1918	Pit-N	126	435	34	111	13	9	2	43	24	22	.255	.297	.340	91	-4	-6	47	12			-1	*3	-0.4
1920	Pit-N	40	133	13	29	3	1	0	13	4	7	.218	.241	.278	47	-9	-9	9	7	4	-0	-1	3S/21	-0.9
Total	11	846	2843	319	713	86	33	8	240	190	199	.251	.301	.313	79	-71	-79	324	127	4		23	32/1SO	-4.0

■ FRANK McKEE
McKee, Frank b: Philadelphia, Pa.   Deb: 6/11/1884

YEAR	TM/L	G	AB	R	H	2B	3B	HR	RBI	BB	SO	AVG	OBP	SLG	PRO+	BR	/A	RC	SB	CS	SBR	FR	POS	TPR
1884	Was-U	4	17	2	3	0	0	0		1		.176	.222	.176	38	-1	-1	1	0			-1	/O3C	-0.1

■ RED McKEE
McKee, Raymond Ellis b: 7/20/1890, Shawnee, Ohio   d: 8/5/72, Saginaw, Mich.   BL/TR, 5'11", 180 lbs.   Deb: 4/19/13

YEAR	TM/L	G	AB	R	H	2B	3B	HR	RBI	BB	SO	AVG	OBP	SLG	PRO+	BR	/A	RC	SB	CS	SBR	FR	POS	TPR
1913	Det-A	68	187	18	53	3	4	1	20	21	21	.283	.359	.358	112	3	3	27	7			-4	C	0.4
1914	Det-A	34	64	7	12	1	1	0	8	4	8	.188	.243	.234	71	-1	-2	5	1	2	-1	-6	C	-0.6
1915	Det-A	55	106	10	29	5	0	1	17	13	16	.274	.353	.349	105	1	1	14	1			-6	C	-0.2
1916	Det-A	32	76	3	16	1	2	0	4	6	11	.211	.268	.276	61	-4	-4	6	0			-5	C	-0.7

YEAR	TM/L	G	AB	R	H	2B	3B	HR	RBI	BB	SO	AVG	OBP	SLG	PRO+	BR	/A	RC	SB	CS	SBR	FR	POS	TPR
Total	4	189	433	38	110	10	7	2	49	54	64	.254	.339	.323	95	-1	-2	52	9	2		-21	C	-1.1

■ JIM McKEEVER
McKeever, James b: 4/19/1861, St.John's, Newfoundland, Can. d: 8/19/1897, Boston, Mass.   Deb: 4/17/1884

YEAR	TM/L	G	AB	R	H	2B	3B	HR	RBI	BB	SO	AVG	OBP	SLG	PRO+	BR	/A	RC	SB	CS	SBR	FR	POS	TPR
1884	Bos-U	16	66	13	9	0	0	0		0		.136	.136	.136	-8	-7	-7	1	0			-4	C/O	-0.8

■ JOHN McKELVEY
McKelvey, John Wellington b: 8/27/1847, Rochester, N.Y. d: 5/31/44, Rochester, N.Y. 5'7.5", 175 lbs.   Deb: 4/21/1875

YEAR	TM/L	G	AB	R	H	2B	3B	HR	RBI	BB	SO	AVG	OBP	SLG	PRO+	BR	/A	RC	SB	CS	SBR	FR	POS	TPR
1875	NH-n	43	187	26	43	4	1	0		4		.230	.246	.262	89	-1	-0	12					O/3	0.1

■ RUSS McKELVY
McKelvy, Russell Errett b: 9/8/1856, Meadville, Pa. d: 10/19/15, Omaha, Neb. BR/TR   Deb: 5/01/1878

YEAR	TM/L	G	AB	R	H	2B	3B	HR	RBI	BB	SO	AVG	OBP	SLG	PRO+	BR	/A	RC	SB	CS	SBR	FR	POS	TPR
1878	Ind-N	63	253	33	57	4	3	2	36	5	38	.225	.240	.289	84	-7	-2	18				5	*O/P	-0.1
1882	Pit-a	1	4	0	0	0	0	0		0		.000	.000	.000	-99	-1	-1	0				-0	/O	0.0
Total	2	64	257	33	57	4	3	2	36	5	38	.222	.237	.284	81	-8	-3	18				5	/OP	-0.1

■ ED McKENNA
McKenna, Edward J. b: St.Louis, Mo.   Deb: 7/29/1874

YEAR	TM/L	G	AB	R	H	2B	3B	HR	RBI	BB	SO	AVG	OBP	SLG	PRO+	BR	/A	RC	SB	CS	SBR	FR	POS	TPR
1874	Phi-n	1	4	0	0	0	0	0		0		.000	.000	.000	-97	-1	-1	0					/1	0.0
1877	StL-N	1	5	0	1	0	0	0	0	0	1	.200	.200	.200	28	-0	-0	0				-0	/O	0.0
1884	Was-U	32	117	19	22	1	0	0		4		.188	.215	.197	41	-7	-6	5	0			-11	CO/3	-1.3
Total	2	33	122	19	23	1	0	0	0	4	1	.189	.214	.197	41	-7	-7	5	0			-11	/CO3	-1.3

■ DAVE McKEOUGH
McKeough, David J. b: 12/1/1863, Utica, N.Y. d: 7/11/01, Utica, N.Y. 5'7", 158 lbs.   Deb: 4/22/1890

YEAR	TM/L	G	AB	R	H	2B	3B	HR	RBI	BB	SO	AVG	OBP	SLG	PRO+	BR	/A	RC	SB	CS	SBR	FR	POS	TPR
1890	Roc-a	62	218	38	49	5	0	0		29		.225	.316	.248	74	-7	-5	22	14			-6	CS/23	-0.3
1891	Phi-a	15	54	4	14	1	1	0	3	8	6	.259	.355	.315	92	-0	-0	6	0			-4	C/S	-0.2
Total	2	77	272	42	63	6	1	0	3	37	6	.232	.324	.261	78	-8	-5	28	14			-10	/CS23	-0.5

■ RICH McKINNEY
McKinney, Charles Richard b: 11/22/46, Piqua, Ohio BR/TR, 5'11", 185 lbs.   Deb: 6/26/70

YEAR	TM/L	G	AB	R	H	2B	3B	HR	RBI	BB	SO	AVG	OBP	SLG	PRO+	BR	/A	RC	SB	CS	SBR	FR	POS	TPR
1970	Chi-A	43	119	12	20	5	0	4	17	11	25	.168	.244	.311	50	-8	-9	8	3	2	-0	2	3S	-0.5
1971	Chi-A	114	369	35	100	11	2	8	46	35	37	.271	.337	.377	99	1	-0	46	0	0	0	-10	2O/3	-0.8
1972	NY-A	37	121	10	26	2	0	1	7	7	13	.215	.258	.256	55	-7	-7	7	1	0	0	-2	3	-0.8
1973	Oak-A	48	65	9	16	3	0	1	7	7	4	.246	.319	.338	90	-1	-1	6	0	0	0	0	3/2OD	0.0
1974	Oak-A	5	7	0	1	0	0	0	0	0	0	.143	.143	.143	-19	-1	-1	0	0	0	0	-2	/2	-0.2
1975	Oak-A	8	7	0	1	0	0	0	2	1	2	.143	.250	.143	14	-1	-1	0	0	0	0	0	/1D	0.0
1977	Oak-A	86	198	13	35	7	0	6	21	16	43	.177	.238	.303	47	-15	-15	12	0	1	-1	-2	1D/302	-1.9
Total	7	341	886	79	199	28	2	20	100	77	124	.225	.289	.328	73	-32	-33	80	4	3	-1	-15	/3210DS	-4.2

■ BOB McKINNEY
McKinney, Robert Francis b: 10/4/1875, McSherrystown, Pa. d: 8/19/46, Hanover, Pa. BR/TR, 5'7", 165 lbs.   Deb: 7/23/01

YEAR	TM/L	G	AB	R	H	2B	3B	HR	RBI	BB	SO	AVG	OBP	SLG	PRO+	BR	/A	RC	SB	CS	SBR	FR	POS	TPR
1901	Phi-A	2	2	0	0	0	0	0	0	0		.000	.000	.000	-96	-1	-1	0	0			-1	/23	-0.1

■ ALEX McKINNON
McKinnon, Alexander J. b: 8/14/1856, Boston, Mass. d: 7/24/1887, Charlestown, Mass BR , 5'11.5",   Deb: 5/01/1884   M

YEAR	TM/L	G	AB	R	H	2B	3B	HR	RBI	BB	SO	AVG	OBP	SLG	PRO+	BR	/A	RC	SB	CS	SBR	FR	POS	TPR
1884	NY-N	116	470	66	128	21	12	4	73	8	62	.272	.285	.394	108	5	3	54				-2	*1	-0.9
1885	StL-N	100	411	42	121	21	6	1	44	8	31	.294	.308	.382	130	9	12	50				-2	*1M	-0.5
1886	StL-N	122	491	75	148	24	7	8	72	21	23	.301	.330	.428	138	16	20	74	10			-5	*1/O	-0.5
1887	Pit-N	48	200	26	68	16	4	1	30	8	9	.340	.365	.475	142	8	10	38	6			3	1	0.5
Total	4	386	1572	209	465	82	29	14	219	45	125	.296	.315	.412	127	37	46	216	16			-6	1/O	-1.4

■ JIM McKNIGHT
McKnight, James Arthur b: 6/1/36, Bee Branch, Ark. BR/TR, 6'1", 185 lbs.   Deb: 9/22/60

YEAR	TM/L	G	AB	R	H	2B	3B	HR	RBI	BB	SO	AVG	OBP	SLG	PRO+	BR	/A	RC	SB	CS	SBR	FR	POS	TPR
1960	Chi-N	3	6	0	2	0	0	0	1	0	1	.333	.333	.333	84	-0	-0	1	0	0	0	-2	/2O	-0.1
1962	Chi-N	60	85	6	19	0	1	0	5	2	13	.224	.241	.247	30	-8	-9	4	0	0	0	3	/3O2	-0.4
Total	2	63	91	6	21	0	1	0	6	2	14	.231	.247	.253	34	-8	-9	5	0	0	0	2	/3O2	-0.5

■ JEFF McKNIGHT
McKnight, Jefferson Alan b: 2/18/63, Conway, Ark. BB/TR, 6', 170 lbs.   Deb: 6/06/89

YEAR	TM/L	G	AB	R	H	2B	3B	HR	RBI	BB	SO	AVG	OBP	SLG	PRO+	BR	/A	RC	SB	CS	SBR	FR	POS	TPR
1989	NY-N	6	12	2	3	0	0	0		2	1	.250	.357	.250	80	-0	-0	1	0	0	0	-3	/213S	-0.2
1990	Bal-A	29	75	11	15	2	0	1	4	5	17	.200	.259	.267	48	-5	-5	6	0	0	0	-1	1/O2SD	-0.6
Total	2	35	87	13	18	2	0	1	4	7	18	.207	.274	.264	53	-6	-5	7	0	0	0	-4	/12OSD3	-0.8

■ ED McLANE
McLane, Edward Cameron b: 8/20/1881, Weston, Mass. 5'10", 179 lbs.   Deb: 10/06/07

YEAR	TM/L	G	AB	R	H	2B	3B	HR	RBI	BB	SO	AVG	OBP	SLG	PRO+	BR	/A	RC	SB	CS	SBR	FR	POS	TPR
1907	Bro-N	1	2	0	0	0	0	0	0	0		.000	.000	.000	-99	-0	-0	0				-1	/O	0.0

■ ART McLARNEY
McLarney, Arthur James b: 12/20/08, Ft.Worden, Wash. d: 12/20/84, Seattle, Wash. BB/TR, 6', 168 lbs.   Deb: 8/23/32

YEAR	TM/L	G	AB	R	H	2B	3B	HR	RBI	BB	SO	AVG	OBP	SLG	PRO+	BR	/A	RC	SB	CS	SBR	FR	POS	TPR
1932	NY-N	9	23	2	3	1	0	0	3	1	3	.130	.167	.174	-8	-3	-3	1				-1	/S	-0.3

■ POLLY McLARRY
McLarry, Howard Zell b: 3/25/1891, Leonard, Tex. d: 11/4/71, Bonham, Tex. 6', 185 lbs.   Deb: 9/02/12

YEAR	TM/L	G	AB	R	H	2B	3B	HR	RBI	BB	SO	AVG	OBP	SLG	PRO+	BR	/A	RC	SB	CS	SBR	FR	POS	TPR
1912	Chi-A	2	2	0	0	0	0	0	0	0		.000	.000	.000	-99	-1	-0	0	0			0	H	0.0
1915	Chi-N	68	127	16	25	3	0	1	12	14	20	.197	.277	.244	58	-6	-6	9	2	2	-1	3	21	-0.4
Total	2	70	129	16	25	3	0	1	12	14	20	.194	.273	.240	56	-7	-7	9	2	2		3	/21	-0.4

■ BARNEY McLAUGHLIN
McLaughlin, Bernard b: 1857, Ireland d: 2/13/21, Lowell, Mass. BR/TR,   Deb: 8/02/1884

YEAR	TM/L	G	AB	R	H	2B	3B	HR	RBI	BB	SO	AVG	OBP	SLG	PRO+	BR	/A	RC	SB	CS	SBR	FR	POS	TPR
1884	KC-U	42	162	15	37	7	3	0		9		.228	.269	.309	109	-1	3	14	0			-3	O2/PS	0.0
1887	Phi-N	50	205	26	45	8	3	1	26	11	27	.220	.263	.302	55	-12	-14	17	2			-11	2	-1.8
1890	Syr-a	86	329	43	87	8	1	2		47		.264	.360	.313	112	2	8	43	13			-12	S	0.0
Total	3	178	696	84	169	23	7	3	26	67	27	.243	.312	.309	92	-10	-3	74	15			-26	/S2OP	-1.8

■ FRANK McLAUGHLIN
McLaughlin, Francis Edward b: 6/19/1856, Lowell, Mass. d: 4/5/17, Lowell, Mass. BR/TR, 5'9", 160 lbs.   Deb: 8/09/1882

YEAR	TM/L	G	AB	R	H	2B	3B	HR	RBI	BB	SO	AVG	OBP	SLG	PRO+	BR	/A	RC	SB	CS	SBR	FR	POS	TPR
1882	Wor-N	15	55	7	12	0	2	1	4	0	11	.218	.218	.345	76	-1	-2	4				-3	S/O	-0.2
1883	Pit-a	29	114	15	25	2	0	1		6		.219	.258	.263	72	-4	-3	8				-1	S/O2P	-0.3
1884	Cin-U	16	67	10	16	4	1	2		2		.239	.261	.418	117	2	1	7	0			-6	S	-0.4
	CP-U	15	67	11	16	4	1	0		1		.239	.250	.328	95	-0	-0	6	0			6	2/SO	0.4
	KC-U	32	123	17	28	11	0	1		9		.228	.280	.341	126	1	4	12	0			-9	20/3SP	-0.4
	Yr	63	257	38	60	19	2	3		12		.233	.268	.358	115	3	5	25	0			-10		-0.4
Total	3	107	426	60	97	21	4	5	4	18	11	.228	.259	.331	98	-3	-0	37	0			-14	/S2O3P	-0.9

■ KID McLAUGHLIN
McLaughlin, James Anson "Sunshine" b: 4/12/1888, Randolph, N.Y. d: 11/13/34, Allegheny, N.Y. BL/TR, 5'8.5", 158 lbs.   Deb: 6/30/14

YEAR	TM/L	G	AB	R	H	2B	3B	HR	RBI	BB	SO	AVG	OBP	SLG	PRO+	BR	/A	RC	SB	CS	SBR	FR	POS	TPR
1914	Cin-N	3	2	1	0	0	0	0		0	4	.000	.000	.000	-97	-0	-0	0				0	/O	0.0

■ JIM McLAUGHLIN
McLaughlin, James C. b: 1860, Cleveland, Ohio d: 11/16/1895, Cleveland, Ohio TL ,   Deb: 5/03/1884

YEAR	TM/L	G	AB	R	H	2B	3B	HR	RBI	BB	SO	AVG	OBP	SLG	PRO+	BR	/A	RC	SB	CS	SBR	FR	POS	TPR
1884	Was-U	10	37	3	7	3	0	0		0		.189	.189	.270	56	-2	-2	2	0			-3	/S3	-0.3
	Bal-a	5	22	3	5	1	1	0		0		.227	.227	.364	88	-0	-0	2				2	/PO	0.0

■ JIM McLAUGHLIN
McLaughlin, James Robert b: 1/3/02, St.Louis, Mo. d: 12/18/68, Mount Vernon, Ill. BR/TR, 5'8.5", 168 lbs.   Deb: 4/18/32

YEAR	TM/L	G	AB	R	H	2B	3B	HR	RBI	BB	SO	AVG	OBP	SLG	PRO+	BR	/A	RC	SB	CS	SBR	FR	POS	TPR
1932	StL-A	1	1	0	0	0	0	0	1	0	0	.000	.000	.000	-95	-0	-0	0	0	0	0	0	/3	0.0

■ TOM McLAUGHLIN
McLaughlin, Thomas b: 3/28/1860, Louisville, Ky. d: 7/21/21, Louisville, Ky.   Deb: 7/17/1883

YEAR	TM/L	G	AB	R	H	2B	3B	HR	RBI	BB	SO	AVG	OBP	SLG	PRO+	BR	/A	RC	SB	CS	SBR	FR	POS	TPR
1883	Lou-a	42	146	16	28	1	2	0		5		.192	.219	.226	47	-9	-7	7				4	SO/132	-0.3
1884	Lou-a	98	335	41	67	11	6	0		22		.200	.262	.269	80	-8	-5	24	19			10	*S/32	1.0
1885	Lou-a	112	411	49	87	13	9	2		15		.212	.245	.302	74	-12	-12	31	1			-5	*2S	-0.5
1886	NY-a	74	250	27	34	3	1	0		26		.136	.220	.156	21	-22	-20	12	13			7	S2/O	-0.8
1891	Was-a	14	41	9	11	0	1	0	3	7	6	.268	.400	.317	114	1	1	7	3			0	S	0.2
Total	5	340	1183	142	227	28	19	2	3	75	6	.192	.247	.253	63	-50	-43	81	16			30	S2/O31	-0.4

RALPH McLAURIN — McLaurin, Ralph Edgar b: 5/23/1885, Kissimmee, Fla. d: 2/11/43, McColl, S.C. Deb: 9/05/08

YEAR	TM/L	G	AB	R	H	2B	3B	HR	RBI	BB	SO	AVG	OBP	SLG	PRO+	BR	/A	RC	SB	CS	SBR	FR	POS	TPR
1908	StL-N	8	22	2	5	0	0	0	0	0	0	.227	.227	.227	49	-1	-1	1	0			-0	/O	-0.1

LARRY McLEAN — McLean, John Bannerman b: 7/18/1881, Cambridge, Mass. d: 3/24/21, Boston, Mass. BR/TR, 6'5", 228 lbs. Deb: 4/26/01

YEAR	TM/L	G	AB	R	H	2B	3B	HR	RBI	BB	SO	AVG	OBP	SLG	PRO+	BR	/A	RC	SB	CS	SBR	FR	POS	TPR
1901	Bos-A	9	19	4	4	1	0	0	2	0		.211	.211	.263	33	-2	-2	1	0			0	/1	0.0
1903	Chi-N	1	4	0	0	0	0	0	1	1		.000	.200	.000	-41	-1	-1	0	0			-0	/C	0.0
1904	StL-N	27	84	5	14	2	1	0	4	4		.167	.205	.214	32	-7	-6	4	1			-2	C	-0.6
1906	Cin-N	12	35	3	7	2	0	0	2	4		.200	.282	.257	67	-1	-1	3	0			-1	C	0.0
1907	Cin-N	113	374	35	108	9	9	0	54	13		.289	.313	.361	108	4	2	45	4			-3	C1	0.7
1908	Cin-N	99	309	24	67	9	4	1	28	15		.217	.253	.282	74	-10	-9	22	2			-6	C1	-1.3
1909	Cin-N	95	324	26	83	12	2	2	36	21		.256	.307	.324	97	-2	-2	33	1			-5	C	0.0
1910	Cin-N	127	423	27	126	14	7	2	71	26	23	.298	.340	.378	114	4	6	55	4			-4	*C	0.8
1911	Cin-N	107	328	24	94	7	2	0	34	20	18	.287	.330	.320	85	-8	-6	34	1			7	C	0.8
1912	Cin-N	102	333	17	81	15	1	1	27	18	15	.243	.284	.303	63	-19	-17	28	1			-3	C	-1.4
1913	StL-N	48	152	7	41	9	0	0	12	6	9	.270	.297	.329	80	-4	-4	14	0			-6	C	-0.7
	*NY-N	30	75	3	24	4	0	0	9	4	4	.320	.354	.373	107	1	1	10	1			-3	C	0.0
	Yr	78	227	10	65	13	0	0	21	10	13	.286	.316	.344	89	-4	-4	23	1			-9		-0.7
1914	NY-N	79	154	8	40	6	0	0	14	4	9	.260	.283	.299	76	-5	-5	13	4			-4	C	-0.6
1915	NY-N	13	33	0	5	0	0	0	4	0	1	.152	.152	.152	-9	-4	-4	1	0			2	C	-0.1
Total	13	862	2647	183	694	90	26	6	298	136	79	.262	.300	.323	86	-55	-49	263	20			-28	C/1	-2.4

MARK McLEMORE — McLemore, Mark Tremell b: 10/4/64, San Diego, Cal. BB/TR, 5'11", 175 lbs. Deb: 9/13/86

YEAR	TM/L	G	AB	R	H	2B	3B	HR	RBI	BB	SO	AVG	OBP	SLG	PRO+	BR	/A	RC	SB	CS	SBR	FR	POS	TPR
1986	Cal-A	5	4	0	0	0	0	0	1	2		.000	.200	.000	-40	-1	-1	0	0	1	-1	4	/2	0.2
1987	Cal-A	138	433	61	102	13	3	3	41	48	72	.236	.312	.300	66	-22	-20	45	25	8	3	-5	*2/SD	-1.0
1988	Cal-A	77	233	38	56	11	2	2	16	25	28	.240	.314	.330	83	-6	-5	24	13	7	-0	4	2/3D	0.2
1989	Cal-A	32	103	12	25	3	1	0	14	7	19	.243	.297	.291	68	-4	-4	10	6	1	1	4	2/D	0.1
1990	Cal-A	20	48	4	7	2	0	0	2	4	9	.146	.212	.188	12	-6	-6	2	1	0	0	-2	/2S	-0.6
	Cle-A	8	12	2	2	0	0	0	0	0	6	.167	.167	.167	-6	-2	-2	0	0	0	0	2	/32	0.1
	Yr	28	60	6	9	2	0	0	2	4	15	.150	.203	.183	9	-7	-7	2	1	0	0	0		-0.5
Total	5	280	833	117	192	29	6	5	73	85	136	.230	.303	.298	66	-40	-37	81	45	17	3	6	2/S3D	-1.0

RALPH McLEOD — McLeod, Ralph Alton b: 10/19/16, N.Quincy, Mass. BL/TL, 6', 170 lbs. Deb: 9/14/38

YEAR	TM/L	G	AB	R	H	2B	3B	HR	RBI	BB	SO	AVG	OBP	SLG	PRO+	BR	/A	RC	SB	CS	SBR	FR	POS	TPR
1938	Bos-N	6	7	1	2	1	0	0	0	0	2	.286	.286	.429	105	-0	-0	0	0			0	/O	0.0

JIM McLEOD — McLeod, Soule James b: 9/12/08, Jones, La. d: 8/3/81, Little Rock, Ark. BR/TR, 6', 187 lbs. Deb: 5/22/30

YEAR	TM/L	G	AB	R	H	2B	3B	HR	RBI	BB	SO	AVG	OBP	SLG	PRO+	BR	/A	RC	SB	CS	SBR	FR	POS	TPR
1930	Was-A	18	34	3	9	1	0	0	1	1	5	.265	.306	.294	53	-2	-2	3	1	1	-0	-0	3/S	-0.1
1932	Was-A	7	0	1	0	0	0	0	0	1	0	—	1.000	—	183	0	0	0	0	0	0	3	/S	0.3
1933	Phi-N	67	232	20	45	6	1	0	15	12	25	.194	.237	.228	30	-20	-23	13	1			-6	3/S	-2.9
Total	3	92	266	24	54	7	1	0	16	14	30	.203	.248	.237	33	-22	-25	16	2	1		-4	/3S	-2.7

JACK McMAHON — McMahon, John Henry b: 10/15/1869, Waterbury, Conn. d: 12/30/1894, Bridgeport, Conn. BR/TL, 5'10", 165 lbs. Deb: 8/08/1892

YEAR	TM/L	G	AB	R	H	2B	3B	HR	RBI	BB	SO	AVG	OBP	SLG	PRO+	BR	/A	RC	SB	CS	SBR	FR	POS	TPR
1892	NY-N	40	147	21	33	5	7	1	24	10	9	.224	.278	.374	100	-1	-1	17	3			-2	1/C	-0.4
1893	NY-N	11	30	5	10	2	1	0	4	2	0	.333	.375	.467	125	1	1	5	0			-0	C	0.1
Total	2	51	177	26	43	7	8	1	28	12	9	.243	.295	.390	105	-0	-0	22	3			-2	/1C	-0.3

FRANK McMANUS — McManus, Francis E. b: 9/21/1875, Lawrence, Mass. d: 9/1/23, Syracuse, N.Y. TR, 5'10", Deb: 9/14/1899

YEAR	TM/L	G	AB	R	H	2B	3B	HR	RBI	BB	SO	AVG	OBP	SLG	PRO+	BR	/A	RC	SB	CS	SBR	FR	POS	TPR
1899	Was-N	7	21	3	8	1	0	0	2	2		.381	.435	.429	142	1	1	5	3			0	/C	0.2
1903	Bro-N	2	7	0	0	0	0	0	0	0		.000	.000	.000	-99	-2	-2	0	0			1	/C	0.0
1904	Det-A	1	0	0	0	0	0	0	0	0		—	—	—		0	0	0	0			0	/C	0.0
	NY-A	4	7	0	0	0	0	0	0	0		.000	.000	.000	-96	-2	-2	0	0			-1	/C	-0.2
	Yr	5	7	0	0	0	0	0	0	0		.000	.000	.000	-97	-2	-2	0	0			-1		-0.2
Total	3	14	35	3	8	1	0	0	2	2		.229	.270	.257	52	-2	-2	5	3			-1	/C	0.0

JIM McMANUS — McManus, James Michael b: 7/20/36, Brookline, Mass. BL/TL, 6'4", 215 lbs. Deb: 9/21/60

YEAR	TM/L	G	AB	R	H	2B	3B	HR	RBI	BB	SO	AVG	OBP	SLG	PRO+	BR	/A	RC	SB	CS	SBR	FR	POS	TPR
1960	KC-A	5	13	3	4	0	0	1	2	1	2	.308	.357	.538	138	1	1	2	0	0	0	-0	/1	0.0

MARTY McMANUS — McManus, Martin Joseph b: 3/14/1900, Chicago, Ill. d: 2/18/66, St.Louis, Mo. BR/TR, 5'10.5", 160 lbs. Deb: 9/26/20 M

YEAR	TM/L	G	AB	R	H	2B	3B	HR	RBI	BB	SO	AVG	OBP	SLG	PRO+	BR	/A	RC	SB	CS	SBR	FR	POS	TPR
1920	StL-A	1	3	0	1	0	1	0	1	0	0	.333	.333	1.000	237	1	1	1	0	0	0	-0	/3	0.0
1921	StL-A	121	412	49	107	19	8	3	64	27	30	.260	.308	.367	68	-19	-22	48	5	3	-0	-11	23/1S	-2.6
1922	StL-A	154	606	88	189	34	11	11	109	38	41	.312	.358	.459	108	9	6	99	9	6	-1	3	*2/1	1.8
1923	StL-A	154	582	86	180	35	10	15	94	49	50	.309	.367	.481	116	16	12	102	14	10	-2	-1	*21	1.2
1924	StL-A	123	442	71	147	23	5	5	80	55	40	.333	.409	.441	112	14	10	82	13	9	-2	7	*2	1.7
1925	StL-A	154	587	108	169	44	8	13	90	73	69	.288	.371	.457	104	7	3	99	5	11	-5	4	*2/O	0.7
1926	StL-A	149	549	102	156	30	10	9	68	55	62	.284	.350	.424	97	-0	-4	82	5	7	-3	15	32/1	1.7
1927	Det-A	108	369	60	99	19	7	9	69	34	38	.268	.332	.431	95	-3	-4	49	8	7	-2	-2	S23/1	0.0
1928	Det-A	139	500	78	144	37	5	8	73	51	32	.288	.355	.430	104	3	2	75	11	13	-5	0	31/S	-0.2
1929	Det-A	154	599	99	168	32	8	18	90	60	52	.280	.347	.451	103	2	2	93	16	11	-2	8	*3/S	1.6
1930	Det-A	132	484	74	155	40	4	9	89	59	28	.320	.396	.475	118	16	14	95	23	8	2	6	*3/S1	2.4
1931	Det-A	107	362	39	98	17	3	3	53	49	22	.271	.361	.359	87	-4	-6	50	7	3	0	13	32/1	1.2
	Bos-A	17	62	8	18	4	0	1	9	8	1	.290	.371	.403	110	0	1	9	1	1	-0	8	3/2	0.9
	Yr	124	424	47	116	21	3	4	62	57	23	.274	.362	.366	90	-4	-5	59	8	4	0	21		2.1
1932	Bos-A	93	302	39	71	19	4	5	24	36	30	.235	.317	.374	80	-10	-9	37	1	2	-1	6	23/S1M	0.5
1933	Bos-A	106	366	51	104	30	4	3	36	49	21	.284	.369	.413	108	4	5	59	3	0	1	-5	32/1M	0.5
1934	Bos-N	119	435	56	120	18	0	8	47	32	42	.276	.330	.372	95	-7	-3	53	5			-5	23	0.2
Total	15	1831	6660	1008	1926	401	88	120	996	675	558	.289	.357	.430	101	29	7	1033	126	91		45	23/1SO	11.1

JIMMY McMATH — McMath, Jimmy Lee b: 8/10/49, Tuscaloosa, Ala. BL/TL, 6'1.5", 195 lbs. Deb: 9/07/68

YEAR	TM/L	G	AB	R	H	2B	3B	HR	RBI	BB	SO	AVG	OBP	SLG	PRO+	BR	/A	RC	SB	CS	SBR	FR	POS	TPR
1968	Chi-N	6	14	0	2	0	0	0	2	0	6	.143	.143	.143	-13	-2	-2	0	0	0	0	0	/O	-0.2

GEORGE McMILLAN — McMillan, George A. "Reddy" b: Evansville, Ind. 5'8", 175 lbs. Deb: 8/11/1890

YEAR	TM/L	G	AB	R	H	2B	3B	HR	RBI	BB	SO	AVG	OBP	SLG	PRO+	BR	/A	RC	SB	CS	SBR	FR	POS	TPR
1890	NY-N	10	35	4	5	0	0	0	1	7	4	.143	.286	.143	28	-3	-3	2	1			-2	O	-0.4

NORM McMILLAN — McMillan, Norman Alexis "Bub" b: 10/5/1895, Latta, S.C. d: 9/28/69, Marion, S.C. BR/TR, 6', 175 lbs. Deb: 4/12/22

YEAR	TM/L	G	AB	R	H	2B	3B	HR	RBI	BB	SO	AVG	OBP	SLG	PRO+	BR	/A	RC	SB	CS	SBR	FR	POS	TPR
1922	*NY-A	33	78	7	20	1	2	0	11	6	10	.256	.310	.321	63	-4	-4	8	4	1	1	-8	O/3	-1.2
1923	Bos-A	131	459	37	116	24	5	0	42	28	44	.253	.299	.327	64	-24	-25	46	13	5	1	12	32S	0.0
1924	StL-A	76	201	25	56	12	2	0	27	12	17	.279	.332	.358	73	-7	-9	24	6	4	-1	-3	23/S1	-0.8
1928	Chi-N	49	123	11	27	2	2	1	12	13	19	.220	.299	.293	56	-8	-8	11	0			-1	23	-0.7
1929	*Chi-N	124	495	77	134	35	5	5	55	36	43	.271	.324	.392	76	-19	-19	62	13			6	*3	-0.3
Total	5	413	1356	157	353	74	16	6	147	95	133	.260	.313	.352	69	-62	-65	152	36	10	3	3/2SO1	-3.0

ROY McMILLAN — McMillan, Roy David b: 7/17/30, Bonham, Tex. BR/TR, 5'11", 170 lbs. Deb: 4/17/51 MC

YEAR	TM/L	G	AB	R	H	2B	3B	HR	RBI	BB	SO	AVG	OBP	SLG	PRO+	BR	/A	RC	SB	CS	SBR	FR	POS	TPR
1951	Cin-N	85	199	21	42	4	0	0	8	17	26	.211	.273	.246	40	-16	-17	15	0	0	0	5	S3/2	-0.6
1952	Cin-N	154	540	60	132	32	2	7	57	45	81	.244	.306	.350	82	-14	-14	57	4	5	-2	11	*S	0.0
1953	Cin-N	155	557	51	130	15	4	5	43	43	52	.233	.290	.302	54	-37	-38	49	2	4	-2	14	*S	-1.2
1954	Cin-N	154	588	86	147	21	2	4	42	47	54	.250	.311	.313	61	-31	-34	61	4	2	0	6	*S	-1.7

YEAR	TM/L	G	AB	R	H	2B	3B	HR	RBI	BB	SO	AVG	OBP	SLG	PRO+	BR	/A	RC	SB	CS	SBR	FR	POS	TPR
1955	Cin-N	151	470	50	126	21	2	1	37	66	33	.268	.366	.328	81	-7	-10	60	4	4	-1	17	*S	0.9
1956	Cin-N	150	479	51	126	16	7	3	62	76	54	.263	.370	.344	88	-1	-5	64	4	3	-1	30	*S	3.5
1957	Cin-N	151	448	50	122	25	5	1	55	66	44	.272	.373	.357	91	1	-3	64	5	1	1	-8	*S	-0.3
1958	Cin-N	145	393	48	90	18	3	1	25	47	33	.229	.313	.298	60	-20	-23	38	5	2	0	-4	*S	-0.8
1959	Cin-N	79	246	38	65	14	2	9	24	27	27	.264	.347	.447	106	3	2	35	0	2	-1	-7	S	-0.2
1960	Cin-N	124	399	42	94	12	2	10	42	35	40	.236	.304	.351	77	-12	-13	43	2	0	1	-13	*S2	-2.0
1961	Mil-N	154	505	42	111	16	0	7	48	61	86	.220	.309	.293	65	-27	-23	46	2	4	-2	-0	*S	-0.9
1962	Mil-N	137	468	66	115	13	0	12	41	60	53	.246	.338	.350	87	-9	-7	57	2	2	-1	1	*S	0.6
1963	Mil-N	100	320	35	80	10	1	4	29	17	25	.250	.292	.325	78	-9	-9	29	1	5	-3	7	S	0.5
1964	Mil-N	8	13	1	4	0	0	0	2	0	2	.308	.308	.308	73	-0	-0	1	1	0	0	-1	/S	0.0
	NY-N	113	379	30	80	8	2	1	25	14	16	.211	.247	.251	42	-30	-29	20	3	1	0	1	*S	-2.0
	Yr	121	392	31	84	8	2	1	27	14	18	.214	.249	.253	43	-30	-29	22	4	1	1	0	*S	-2.0
1965	NY-N	157	528	44	128	19	2	1	42	24	60	.242	.281	.292	64	-27	-25	44	1	0	0	-4	*S	-1.1
1966	NY-N	76	220	24	47	9	1	1	12	20	25	.214	.285	.277	59	-12	-12	18	1	1	-0	6	S	0.0
Total	16	2093	6752	739	1639	253	35	68	594	665	711	.243	.316	.321	72	-249	-258	702	41	36	-9	68	*S/32	-5.3

■ TOM McMILLAN
McMillan, Thomas Erwin b: 9/13/51, Richmond, Va. BR/TR, 5'9", 165 lbs. Deb: 9/17/77

YEAR	TM/L	G	AB	R	H	2B	3B	HR	RBI	BB	SO	AVG	OBP	SLG	PRO+	BR	/A	RC	SB	CS	SBR	FR	POS	TPR
1977	Sea-A	2	5	0	0	0	0	0	0	0	0	.000	.000	.000	-99	-1	-1	0	0	0	0	-0	/S	-0.1

■ TOMMY McMILLAN
McMillan, Thomas Law "Rebel" b: 4/18/1888, Pittston, Pa. d: 7/15/66, Orlando, Fla. BR/TR, 5'5", 130 lbs. Deb: 8/19/08

YEAR	TM/L	G	AB	R	H	2B	3B	HR	RBI	BB	SO	AVG	OBP	SLG	PRO+	BR	/A	RC	SB	CS	SBR	FR	POS	TPR
1908	Bro-N	43	147	9	35	3	0	0	3	9		.238	.282	.259	78	-4	-3	12	5			-5	SO	-1.0
1909	Bro-N	108	373	18	79	15	1	0	24	20		.212	.254	.257	61	-19	-17	26	11			-10	*S/23	-2.8
1910	Bro-N	23	74	2	13	1	0	0	2	6	10	.176	.237	.189	26	-7	-7	4	4			-1	S	-0.7
	Cin-N	82	248	20	46	0	3	0	13	31	23	.185	.281	.210	46	-17	-15	18	7			10	S	-0.2
	Yr	105	322	22	59	1	3	0	15	37	33	.183	.271	.205	41	-24	-22	22	11			8		-0.9
1912	NY-A	41	149	24	34	2	0	0	12	15		.228	.303	.242	53	-8	-9	17	18			-4	S	-0.8
Total	4	297	991	73	207	21	4	0	54	81	33	.209	.271	.238	55	-55	-52	77	45			-10	S/O23	-5.5

■ HUGH McMULLEN
McMullen, Hugh Raphael b: 12/16/01, LaCygne, Kan. d: 5/23/86, Whittier, Cal. BB/TR, 6'1", 180 lbs. Deb: 9/19/25

YEAR	TM/L	G	AB	R	H	2B	3B	HR	RBI	BB	SO	AVG	OBP	SLG	PRO+	BR	/A	RC	SB	CS	SBR	FR	POS	TPR
1925	NY-N	5	15	1	2	1	0	0	0	0	3	.133	.133	.200	-17	-3	-3	0	0	0	0	-2	/C	-0.3
1926	NY-N	57	91	5	17	2	0	0	6	2	18	.187	.204	.209	11	-11	-11	4	1			0	C	-0.8
1928	Was-A	1	1	0	0	0	0	0	0	0	1	.000	.000	.000	-99	-0	-0	0	0	0	0	0	H	0.0
1929	Cin-N	1	1	0	0	0	0	0	0	0	0	.000	.000	.000	-99	-0	-0	0	0			0	/C	0.0
Total	4	64	108	6	19	3	0	0	6	2	22	.176	.191	.204	5	-15	-14	4	1	0		-1	/C	-1.1

■ KEN McMULLEN
McMullen, Kenneth Lee b: 6/1/42, Oxnard, Cal. BR/TR, 6'3", 190 lbs. Deb: 9/17/62

YEAR	TM/L	G	AB	R	H	2B	3B	HR	RBI	BB	SO	AVG	OBP	SLG	PRO+	BR	/A	RC	SB	CS	SBR	FR	POS	TPR
1962	LA-N	6	11	0	3	0	0	0	0	0	3	.273	.273	.273	50	-1	-1	1	0	0	0	-0	/O	0.0
1963	LA-N	79	233	16	55	9	0	5	28	20	46	.236	.299	.339	89	-5	-3	22	1	2	-1	7	3/2O	0.3
1964	LA-N	24	67	3	14	0	0	1	2	3	7	.209	.243	.254	43	-5	-5	3	0	1	-1	-2	1/3O	-0.8
1965	Was-A	150	555	75	146	18	6	18	54	47	90	.263	.325	.414	110	6	7	74	2	0	1	5	*3/O1	1.4
1966	Was-A	147	524	48	122	19	4	13	54	44	89	.233	.292	.359	87	-10	-9	53	3	1	-0	-0	*3/1O	-1.4
1967	Was-A	146	563	73	138	22	2	16	67	46	84	.245	.303	.377	104	-1	1	62	5	3	-0	12	*3	1.8
1968	Was-A	151	557	66	138	11	2	20	62	63	66	.248	.327	.382	118	10	12	70	1	3	-2	5	*3S	2.3
1969	Was-A	158	562	83	153	25	2	19	87	70	103	.272	.354	.425	123	13	16	86	4	5	-2	13	*3	3.1
1970	Was-A	15	59	5	12	2	0	0	3	5	10	.203	.266	.237	42	-5	-4	4	0	0	0	6	3	0.1
	Cal-A	124	422	50	98	9	3	14	61	59	81	.232	.331	.367	96	-4	-2	52	1	0	0	9	*3	0.8
	Yr	139	481	55	110	11	3	14	64	64	91	.229	.323	.351	89	-9	-6	55	1	0	0	15		0.9
1971	Cal-A	160	593	63	148	19	2	21	68	53	74	.250	.314	.395	107	-1	3	71	1	1	-0	-1	*3	-0.2
1972	Cal-A	137	472	36	127	18	1	9	34	48	59	.269	.337	.369	116	6	9	58	1	2	-1	2	*3	1.6
1973	LA-N	42	85	6	21	5	0	5	18	6	13	.247	.297	.482	118	1	1	12	0	0	0	5	3	0.5
1974	•LA-N	44	60	5	15	1	0	3	12	2	12	.250	.274	.417	95	-1	-1	7	0	0	0	-1	/32	-0.1
1975	LA-N	39	46	4	11	1	1	2	14	7	12	.239	.340	.435	119	1	1	7	0	0	0	1	3/1	0.2
1976	Oak-A	98	186	20	41	6	2	5	23	22	33	.220	.306	.355	97	-2	-1	20	1	1	-0	-0	31D/O2	-0.2
1977	Mil-A	63	136	15	31	7	1	3	19	15	33	.228	.305	.404	91	-2	-2	16	0	0	0	2	D1/3	0.0
Total	16	1583	5131	568	1273	172	26	156	606	510	815	.248	.318	.383	105	-1	23	617	20	19	-5	63	*3/1DOS2	9.4

■ FRED McMULLIN
McMullin, Frederick William b: 10/13/1891, Scammon, Kan. d: 11/21/52, Los Angeles, Cal. BR/TR, 5'11", 170 lbs. Deb: 8/27/14

YEAR	TM/L	G	AB	R	H	2B	3B	HR	RBI	BB	SO	AVG	OBP	SLG	PRO+	BR	/A	RC	SB	CS	SBR	FR	POS	TPR
1914	Det-A	1	1	0	0	0	0	0	0	0	1	.000	.000	.000	-97	-0	-0	0				0	/S	0.0
1916	Chi-A	68	187	8	48	3	0	0	10	19	30	.257	.332	.273	81	-4	-4	22	9			-4	3/S2	-0.4
1917	•Chi-A	59	194	35	46	2	1	0	12	27	17	.237	.339	.258	81	-3	-3	22	9			-13	3/S	-1.5
1918	Chi-A	70	235	32	65	7	0	1	16	25	26	.277	.356	.319	103	2	2	30	7			-2	3/2	0.6
1919	•Chi-A	60	170	31	50	8	4	0	19	11	18	.294	.355	.388	108	2	2	25	4			-0	3/2	0.6
1920	•Chi-A	46	127	14	25	1	4	0	13	9	13	.197	.255	.268	39	-11	-11	9	1	1	-0	-5	3/2S	-1.3
Total	6	304	914	120	234	21	9	1	70	91	105	.256	.333	.302	85	-14	-15	108	30	1		-23	3/2S	-2.6

■ JOHN McMULLIN
McMullin, John F. "Lefty" b: 1848, Philadelphia, Pa. d: 4/11/1881, Philadelphia, Pa. BL/TL, 5'9", 160 lbs. Deb: 5/09/1871

YEAR	TM/L	G	AB	R	H	2B	3B	HR	RBI	BB	SO	AVG	OBP	SLG	PRO+	BR	/A	RC	SB	CS	SBR	FR	POS	TPR
1871	Tro-n	29	136	38	38	0	5	0	32	8	6	.279	.319	.353	92	-1	-1	19	11				*P	0.0
1872	Mut-n	54	237	48	60	7	1	0	11			.253	.286	.291	83	-6	-2	20					*O/P	0.0
1873	Ath-n	51	222	54	60	8	1	0	8			.270	.296	.315	74	-5	-9	21					*O/P	-0.4
1874	Ath-n	55	262	61	89	10	2	2	7			.340	.357	.416	134	13	9	41					*O/C	0.8
1875	Phi-n	54	223	34	56	9	4	2	5			.251	.268	.354	109	3	2	22					*O/P	0.2
Total	5 n	243	1080	235	303	34	13	4	39			.281	.306	.347	100	4	-2	122					O/PC	0.6

■ CARL McNABB
McNabb, Carl Mac "Skinny" b: 1/25/17, Stevenson, Ala. BR/TR, 5'9", 155 lbs. Deb: 4/20/45

YEAR	TM/L	G	AB	R	H	2B	3B	HR	RBI	BB	SO	AVG	OBP	SLG	PRO+	BR	/A	RC	SB	CS	SBR	FR	POS	TPR
1945	Det-A	1	1	0	0	0	0	0	0	0	1	.000	.000	.000	-94	-0	-0	0	0	0	0	0	H	0.0

■ ERIC McNAIR
McNair, Donald Eric "Boob" b: 4/12/09, Meridian, Miss. d: 3/11/49, Meridian, Miss. BR/TR, 5'8", 160 lbs. Deb: 9/20/29

YEAR	TM/L	G	AB	R	H	2B	3B	HR	RBI	BB	SO	AVG	OBP	SLG	PRO+	BR	/A	RC	SB	CS	SBR	FR	POS	TPR
1929	Phi-A	4	8	2	4	1	0	0	3	0	0	.500	.500	.625	181	1	1	3	1	0	0	0	/S	0.1
1930	•Phi-A	78	237	27	63	12	2	0	34	9	19	.266	.296	.333	57	-15	-16	23	5	2	0	-7	S3/2O	-1.6
1931	•Phi-A	79	280	41	76	10	1	5	33	11	19	.271	.306	.368	72	-10	-13	30	1	4	-2	-6	32S	-1.4
1932	Phi-A	135	554	87	158	47	3	18	95	28	29	.285	.323	.478	101	1	-2	84	8	4	0	-7	*S	0.1
1933	Phi-A	89	310	57	81	15	4	7	48	15	32	.261	.302	.403	85	-8	-8	38	2	1	0	-2	S2	-0.6
1934	Phi-A	151	599	80	168	20	4	17	82	46	35	.280	.321	.412	91	-13	-10	77	7	8	-3	4	*S	0.2
1935	Bos-A	137	526	55	142	22	2	4	57	35	33	.270	.319	.342	72	-23	-22	57	3	7	-3	-21	*S3/1	-3.7
1936	Bos-A	128	494	68	141	36	2	4	74	27	34	.285	.329	.391	73	-19	-23	63	3	3	-1	-12	S23	-2.4
1937	Bos-A	126	455	60	133	29	4	12	76	30	33	.292	.340	.453	94	-3	-6	69	10	7	-1	-6	*2/S31	-0.1
1938	Bos-A	46	96	9	15	1	1	0	7	3	6	.156	.182	.188	-7	-16	-17	3	0	1	-1	3	S2/3	-1.1
1939	Chi-A	129	479	62	155	18	5	7	82	38	41	.324	.375	.426	102	3	1	74	17	9	-0	4	*32/S	0.4
1940	Chi-A	66	251	26	57	13	1	7	31	12	46	.227	.265	.371	62	-15	-15	21	1	7	-4	-17	2/3	-3.1
1941	Det-A	23	59	5	11	1	0	0	3	4	4	.186	.250	.203	19	-7	-7	2	0	0	0	-2	3/S	-0.8
1942	Det-A	26	68	5	11	2	0	1	4	3	5	.162	.197	.235	20	-7	-8	2	0	1	-1	-7	S	-1.5
	Phi-A	34	103	8	25	2	0	0	4	11	5	.243	.316	.262	46	-5	-5	9	1	0	0	-6	S/2	-0.8
	Yr	60	171	13	36	4	0	1	8	14	10	.211	.270	.251	46	-12	-13	11	1	1	-0	-13		-2.3
Total	14	1251	4519	592	1240	229	29	82	633	261	328	.274	.318	.392	80	-135	-150	556	59	54	-15	-82	S23/10	-16.3

YEAR	TM/L	G	AB	R	H	2B	3B	HR	RBI	BB	SO	AVG	OBP	SLG	PRO+	BR	/A	RC	SB	CS	SBR	FR	POS	TPR

■ MIKE McNALLY
McNally, Michael Joseph "Minooka Mike"   b: 9/9/1892, Minooka, Pa.   d: 5/29/65, Bethlehem, Pa.   BR/TR, 5'11", 150 lbs.   Deb: 4/21/15

1915	Bos-A	23	53	7	8	0	1	0	0	3	7	.151	.196	.189	16	-6	-5	2	0	2	-1	1	3/2	-0.5
1916	*Bos-A	87	135	28	23	0	0	0	9	10	19	.170	.228	.170	20	-13	-13	8	9			7	23/SO	-0.4
1917	Bos-A	42	50	9	15	1	0	0	2	6	3	.300	.375	.320	113	1	1	8	3			6	3/S2	0.9
1919	Bos-A	33	42	10	11	4	0	0	6	1	2	.262	.279	.357	83	-1	-1	5	4			9	S3/2	1.0
1920	Bos-A	93	312	42	80	5	1	0	23	31	24	.256	.326	.279	64	-16	-14	30	13	10	-2	-9	2/S1	-2.2
1921	*NY-A	71	215	36	56	4	2	1	24	14	15	.260	.306	.312	57	-14	-14	20	5	6	-2	18	32	0.5
1922	*NY-A	52	143	20	36	2	2	0	18	16	14	.252	.331	.294	63	-7	-8	16	2	0	1	0	3/2S1	-0.2
1923	NY-A	30	38	5	8	0	0	0	1	3	4	.211	.268	.211	27	-4	-4	3	2	0	1	0	S/32	0.0
1924	NY-A	49	69	11	17	0	0	0	2	7	5	.246	.316	.246	46	-5	-5	6	1	1	-0	10	23/S	0.6
1925	Was-A	12	21	1	3	0	0	0	0	1	4	.143	.182	.143	-17	-4	-4	1	0	0	0	1	/3S2	-0.1
Total	10	492	1078	169	257	16	6	1	85	92	97	.238	.299	.267	54	-69	-68	98	39	19		42	23/S10	-0.4

■ GEORGE McNAMARA
McNamara, George Francis   b: 1/11/01, Chicago, Ill.   d: 6/12/90, Hinsdale, Ill.   BL/TR, 6', 175 lbs.   Deb: 9/28/22

1922	Was-A	3	11	3	3	0	0	0	1	1	2	.273	.333	.273	63	-1	-1	1	0	0	0	-1	/O	0.0

■ DINNY McNAMARA
McNamara, John Raymond   b: 9/16/05, Lexington, Mass.   d: 12/20/63, Arlington, Mass.   BL/TR, 5'9", 165 lbs.   Deb: 7/02/27

1927	Bos-N	11	9	3	0	0	0	0	0	0	3	.000	.000	.000	-99	-3	-2	0	0			2	/O	0.0
1928	Bos-N	9	4	2	1	0	0	0	0	0	1	.250	.250	.250	33	-0	-0	0	0			2	/O	0.1
Total	2	20	13	5	1	0	0	0	0	0	4	.077	.077	.077	-63	-3	-3	0	0			3	/O	0.1

■ BOB McNAMARA
McNamara, Robert Maxey   b: 9/19/16, Denver, Colo.   BR/TR, 5'10", 170 lbs.   Deb: 5/27/39

1939	Phi-A	9	9	0	2	1	0	0	3	1	1	.222	.300	.333	63	-1	-1	1	0	0	0	0	/3S12	0.0

■ TOM McNAMARA
McNamara, Thomas Henry   b: 11/5/1895, Roxbury, Mass.   d: 5/5/74, Danvers, Mass.   BR , 6'2", 200 lbs.   Deb: 6/25/22

1922	Pit-N	1	1	0	0	0	0	0	0	0	0	.000	.000	.000	-99	-0	-0	0	0	0	0	0	H	0.0

■ RUSTY McNEALY
McNealy, Robert Lee   b: 8/12/58, Sacramento, Cal.   BL/TL, 5'8", 160 lbs.   Deb: 9/04/83

1983	Oak-A	15	4	5	0	0	0	0	0	0	0	.000	.000	.000	-99	-1	-1	0	0	1	-1	1	/OD	0.0

■ EARL McNEELY
McNeely, George Earl   b: 5/12/1898, Sacramento, Cal.   d: 7/16/71, Sacramento, Cal.   BR/TR, 5'9", 155 lbs.   Deb: 8/09/24   C

1924	*Was-A	43	179	31	59	5	6	0	15	5	21	.330	.355	.425	104	-0	0	27	3	1	0	-1	O	-0.3
1925	*Was-A	122	385	76	110	14	2	3	37	48	54	.286	.378	.356	89	-6	-6	53	14	16	-5	-2	*O/1	-2.0
1926	Was-A	124	442	84	134	20	12	0	48	44	28	.303	.373	.403	105	2	3	70	18	6	2	0	*O	-0.2
1927	Was-A	73	185	40	51	10	4	0	16	11	13	.276	.320	.373	80	-6	-6	20	11	4	1	-7	O/1	-1.3
1928	StL-A	127	496	66	117	27	7	0	44	37	39	.236	.299	.319	61	-27	-29	49	8	6	-1	7	*O	-2.8
1929	StL-A	69	230	27	56	8	1	1	18	7	13	.243	.272	.300	45	-18	-20	19	2	1	0	-6	O	-2.7
1930	StL-A	76	235	33	64	19	1	0	20	22	14	.272	.340	.362	75	-8	-9	30	8	3	1	-7	O1	-1.7
1931	StL-A	49	102	12	23	4	0	0	15	9	5	.225	.288	.265	45	-8	-8	8	4	4	-1	-5	O/1	-1.5
Total	8	683	2254	369	614	107	33	4	213	183	187	.272	.335	.354	78	-71	-73	275	68	41	-4	-21	O/1	-12.5

■ NORM McNEIL
McNeil, Norman Francis   b: 10/22/1892, Chicago, Ill.   d: 4/11/42, Buffalo, N.Y.   BR/TR, 5'11", 180 lbs.   Deb: 6/21/19

1919	Bos-A	5	9	0	3	0	0	0	1	1	0	.333	.400	.333	113	0	0	1	0			-2	/C	0.0

■ JERRY McNERTNEY
McNertney, Gerald Edward   b: 8/7/36, Boone, Iowa   BR/TR, 6', 180 lbs.   Deb: 4/16/64   C

1964	Chi-A	73	186	16	40	5	0	3	23	19	24	.215	.298	.290	66	-9	-8	16	0	0	0	8	C	0.3
1966	Chi-A	44	59	3	13	0	0	0	1	7	6	.220	.303	.220	57	-3	-3	4	1	1	-0	6	C	0.5
1967	Chi-A	56	123	8	28	6	0	3	13	6	14	.228	.275	.350	87	-3	-2	11	0	0	0	14	C	1.6
1968	Chi-A	74	169	18	37	4	1	3	18	18	29	.219	.302	.308	84	-3	-3	17	0	0	0	14	C/1	1.6
1969	Sea-A	128	410	39	99	18	1	8	55	29	63	.241	.292	.349	80	-13	-12	40	1	0	0	1	*C	-0.2
1970	Mil-A	111	296	27	72	11	1	6	22	22	33	.243	.304	.348	79	-9	-9	27	1	4	-2	-9	C1	-1.9
1971	StL-N	56	128	15	37	4	2	4	22	12	14	.289	.350	.445	119	4	3	19	0	0	0	-2	C	0.2
1972	StL-N	39	48	3	10	3	1	0	9	6	16	.208	.296	.313	74	-2	-2	5	0	0	0	2	C	0.1
1973	Pit-N	9	4	0	1	0	0	0	0	0	0	.250	.250	.250	40	-0	-0	0	0	0	0	1	/C	0.1
Total	9	590	1423	129	337	51	6	27	163	119	199	.237	.301	.338	81	-37	-35	140	3	5	-2	34	C/1	2.3

■ PAT McNULTY
McNulty, Patrick Howard   b: 2/27/1899, Cleveland, Ohio   d: 5/4/63, Hollywood, Cal.   BL/TR, 5'11", 160 lbs.   Deb: 9/05/22

1922	Cle-A	22	59	10	16	2	1	0	5	9	5	.271	.368	.339	85	-1	-1	8	4	1	1	-3	O	-0.4
1924	Cle-A	101	291	46	78	13	5	0	26	33	22	.268	.347	.347	78	-9	-9	36	10	8	-2	-4	O	-1.9
1925	Cle-A	118	373	70	117	18	2	6	43	47	23	.314	.392	.421	105	5	4	63	7	7	-2	-1	*O	-0.8
1926	Cle-A	48	56	3	14	2	1	0	6	5	9	.250	.311	.321	65	-3	-3	6	0	1	-1	-2	/O	-0.5
1927	Cle-A	19	41	3	13	1	0	0	4	4	3	.317	.378	.341	87	-1	-1	5	1	2	-1	-0	O	-0.2
Total	5	308	820	132	238	36	9	6	84	98	62	.290	.368	.378	91	-9	-10	118	22	19	-5	-11	O	-3.8

■ BILL McNULTY
McNulty, William Francis   b: 8/29/46, Sacramento, Cal.   BR/TR, 6'4", 205 lbs.   Deb: 7/09/69

1969	Oak-A	5	17	0	0	0	0	0	0	0	10	.000	.000	.000	-99	-4	-4	0	0	0	0	2	/O	-0.2
1972	Oak-A	4	10	0	1	0	0	0	0	2	1	.100	.250	.100	7	-1	-1	0	0	0	0	-2	/3	-0.2
Total	2	9	27	0	1	0	0	0	0	2	11	.037	.103	.037	-61	-6	-5	0	0	0	0	-0	/O3	-0.4

■ BID McPHEE
McPhee, John Alexander   b: 11/1/1859, Massena, N.Y.   d: 1/3/43, San Diego, Cal.   BR/TR, 5'8", 152 lbs.   Deb: 5/02/1882   M

1882	Cin-a	78	311	43	71	8	7	1		11		.228	.255	.309	84	-3	-6	25				-1	*2	-0.1
1883	Cin-a	96	367	61	90	10	10	2		18		.245	.281	.343	94	0	-3	36				3	*2	0.1
1884	Cin-a	112	450	107	125	8	7	5		27		.278	.327	.360	121	14	10	54				16	*2	2.6
1885	Cin-a	110	431	78	114	12	4	0		19		.265	.306	.311	96	-1	-2	42				6	*2	0.8
1886	Cin-a	140	560	139	150	23	12	8		59		.268	.343	.395	129	21	19	92	40			31	*2	4.2
1887	Cin-a	129	540	137	156	20	19	2		55		.289	.360	.407	114	12	10	116	95			26	*2	3.0
1888	Cin-a	111	458	88	110	12	10	4	51	43		.240	.312	.336	106	6	3	67	54			31	*2	3.4
1889	Cin-a	135	540	109	145	25	7	5	57	60	29	.269	.346	.369	103	5	2	93	63			41	*2/3	3.8
1890	Cin-N	132	528	125	135	16	22	3	39	82	26	.256	.362	.386	121	16	16	96	55			30	*2	4.4
1891	Cin-N	138	562	107	144	14	16	6	38	74	35	.256	.345	.370	109	8	8	85	33			23	*2	3.1
1892	Cin-N	144	573	111	157	19	12	4	60	84	48	.274	.373	.370	129	22	23	98	44			25	*2	4.5
1893	Cin-N	127	491	101	138	17	11	3	68	94	20	.281	.401	.379	107	11	9	87	25			34	*2	3.4
1894	Cin-N	126	474	107	144	21	9	5	88	90	23	.304	.420	.418	101	7	3	99	33			31	*2	3.2
1895	Cin-N	115	432	107	129	24	12	1	75	73	30	.299	.409	.417	111	13	10	88	30			15	*2	2.5
1896	Cin-N	117	433	81	132	18	7	1	87	51	18	.305	.391	.386	101	7	2	86	48			6	*2	0.9
1897	Cin-N	81	282	45	85	13	7	1	39	35		.301	.382	.408	104	5	2	49	9			13	2	1.9
1898	Cin-N	133	486	72	121	26	9	1	60	66		.249	.341	.346	93	1	-4	66	21			-12	*2/O	-0.9
1899	Cin-N	111	373	60	104	17	7	1	65	40		.279	.349	.370	101	3	1	57	18			-4	*2/O	0.3
Total	18	2135	8291	1678	2250	303	188	53	727	981	229	.271	.354	.372	108	147	103	1337	568			315	*2/O3	41.1

■ MART McQUAID
McQuaid, Mortimer Martin   b: 6/28/1861, Chicago, Ill.   d: 3/5/28, Chicago, Ill.   Deb: 8/15/1891

1891	StL-a	4	11	1	4	2	0	0	1	0	1	.364	.364	.545	141	1	0	3	1			-1	/2O	0.0
1898	Was-N	1	4	0	0	0	0	0	0	0	0	.000	.000	.000	-99	-1	-1	0	0			-1	/O	-0.1
Total	2	5	15	1	4	2	0	0	1	0	1	.267	.267	.400	83	-0	-1	3	1			-1	/2O	-0.1

YEAR	TM/L	G	AB	R	H	2B	3B	HR	RBI	BB	SO	AVG	OBP	SLG	PRO+	BR	/A	RC	SB	CS	SBR	FR	POS	TPR

■ JERRY McQUAIG   McQuaig, Gerald Joseph b: 1/31/12, Douglas, Ga.   BR/TR, 5'11", 183 lbs.   Deb: 8/25/34

| 1934 | Phi-A | 7 | 16 | 2 | 1 | 0 | 0 | 0 | 1 | 2 | 4 | .063 | .167 | .063 | -40 | -3 | -3 | 0 | 0 | 0 | 0 | -0 | /O | -0.3 |

■ MOX McQUERY   McQuery, William Thomas b: 6/28/1861, Garrard Co., Ky.   d: 6/12/1900, Covington, Ky.   6'4",   Deb: 8/20/1884

1884	Cin-U	35	132	31	37	5	0	2		8		.280	.321	.364	122	4	3	16	0			1	1	0.3
1885	Det-N	70	278	34	76	15	4	3	30	8	29	.273	.294	.388	119	5	5	33				5	1/O	-0.1
1886	KC-N	122	449	62	111	27	4	4	38	36	44	.247	.303	.352	93	-1	-5	50	4			1	*1	-2.3
1890	Syr-a	122	461	64	142	17	6	2		53		.308	.383	.384	143	18	25	80	26			-1	*1	1.7
1891	Was-a	68	261	40	63	9	4	2	37	18	19	.241	.305	.330	88	-6	-4	28	3			1	1	-0.4
Total	5	417	1581	231	429	73	18	13	105	123	92	.271	.327	.365	113	21	24	206	33			7	1/O	-0.8

■ GLENN McQUILLEN   McQuillen, Glenn Richard "Red" b: 4/19/15, Strasburg, Va.   d: 6/8/89, Gardenville, Md.   BR/TR, 6', 198 lbs.   Deb: 6/16/38

1938	StL-A	43	116	14	33	4	0	0	13	6	4	.284	.308	.319	57	-8	-8	11	0	1	-1	1	O	-0.6
1941	StL-A	7	21	4	7	2	1	0	3	1	2	.333	.364	.524	128	1	1	3	0	1	-1	0	/O	0.0
1942	StL-A	100	339	40	96	15	12	3	47	10	17	.283	.306	.425	103	-0	-1	37	1	1	-0	-5	O	-1.1
1946	StL-A	59	166	24	40	3	3	1	12	19	18	.241	.319	.313	73	-5	-6	16	0	2	-1	0	O	-0.9
1947	StL-A	1	1	0	0	0	0	0	0	0	0	.000	.000	.000	-98	-0	-0	0	0	0	0	0	H	0.0
Total	5	210	643	82	176	24	16	4	75	34	49	.274	.311	.379	87	-12	-14	67	1	5	-3	-4	O	-2.6

■ GEORGE McQUINN   McQuinn, George Hartley b: 5/29/10, Arlington, Va.   d: 12/24/78, Alexandria, Va.   BL/TL, 5'11", 165 lbs.   Deb: 4/14/36

1936	Cin-N	38	134	5	27	3	4	0	13	10	22	.201	.262	.284	50	-10	-9	11	0			1	1	-1.1
1938	StL-A	148	602	100	195	42	7	12	82	58	49	.324	.384	.477	115	13	13	110	4	5	-2	-0	*1	-0.8
1939	StL-A	154	617	101	195	37	13	20	94	65	42	.316	.383	.515	125	24	22	122	6	5	-1	10	*1	1.5
1940	StL-A	151	594	78	166	39	10	16	84	57	58	.279	.343	.460	104	4	2	95	3	3	-1	10	*1	0.4
1941	StL-A	130	495	93	147	28	4	18	80	74	30	.297	.388	.479	124	21	18	96	5	4	-1	8	*1	2.1
1942	StL-A	145	554	86	145	32	5	12	78	60	77	.262	.335	.403	105	4	3	78	1	1	-0	1	*1	0.2
1943	StL-A	125	449	53	109	19	2	12	74	56	65	.243	.327	.374	103	2	1	58	4	3	-1	2	*1	0.0
1944	*StL-A	146	516	83	129	26	3	11	72	85	74	.250	.357	.376	103	8	4	79	4	3	-1	-5	*1	-1.0
1945	StL-A	139	483	69	134	31	3	7	61	65	51	.277	.364	.398	115	14	11	75	1	1	-0	4	*1	1.1
1946	Phi-A	136	484	47	109	23	6	3	35	64	62	.225	.317	.316	78	-14	-14	54	4	2	0	3	*1	-1.8
1947	*NY-A	144	517	84	157	24	3	13	80	78	66	.304	.395	.437	132	23	24	97	0	2	-1	-1	*1	1.8
1948	NY-A	94	302	33	75	11	4	11	41	40	38	.248	.336	.421	102	-1	-0	45	0	2	-1	-1	1	0.2
Total	12	1550	5747	832	1588	315	64	135	794	712	634	.276	.357	.424	109	88	76	920	32	31		32	*1	2.6

■ BRIAN McRAE   McRae, Brian Wesley b: 8/27/67, Bradenton, Fla.   BB/TR, 6', 175 lbs.   Deb: 8/07/90

| 1990 | KC-A | 46 | 168 | 21 | 48 | 8 | 3 | 2 | 23 | 9 | 29 | .286 | .322 | .405 | 104 | 0 | 1 | 20 | 4 | 3 | -1 | 3 | O | 0.3 |

■ HAL McRAE   McRae, Harold Abraham b: 7/10/45, Avon Park, Fla.   BR/TR, 5'11", 180 lbs.   Deb: 7/11/68   C

1968	Cin-N	17	51	1	10	1	0	0	2	4	14	.196	.255	.216	40	-3	-4	2	1	1	-0	-4	2	-0.7
1970	*Cin-N	70	165	18	41	6	1	8	23	15	23	.248	.315	.442	100	-0	-1	21	0	2	-1	-5	O/32	-0.8
1971	Cin-N	99	337	39	89	24	2	9	34	11	35	.264	.291	.427	103	-1	-0	39	3	2	-1	-3	O	-0.6
1972	*Cin-N	61	97	9	27	4	0	5	26	2	10	.278	.307	.474	126	2	2	12	0	0	0	-4	O3	-0.2
1973	KC-A	106	338	36	79	18	3	9	50	34	38	.234	.315	.385	89	-2	-5	41	2	2	-1	-5	OD/3	-1.2
1974	KC-A	148	539	71	167	36	4	15	88	54	68	.310	.378	.475	136	30	27	95	11	8	-2	-1	DO/3	2.4
1975	KC-A	126	480	58	147	38	6	5	71	47	47	.306	.373	.442	126	19	17	75	11	8	-2	-6	*OD/3	0.7
1976	*KC-A	149	527	75	175	34	5	8	73	64	43	.332	.412	.461	154	39	38	101	22	12	-1	-2	*DO	3.6
1977	*KC-A	162	641	104	191	54	11	21	92	59	43	.298	.369	.515	137	33	32	119	18	14	-3	-1	*DO	2.6
1978	*KC-A	156	623	90	170	39	5	16	72	51	62	.273	.334	.429	110	10	8	87	17	8	0	0	*DO	0.9
1979	KC-A	101	393	55	113	32	4	10	74	38	46	.288	.356	.466	117	11	10	66	5	4	-1	0	*D	0.8
1980	*KC-A	124	489	73	145	39	5	14	83	29	56	.297	.346	.483	123	15	15	79	10	2	2	-1	*DO	1.5
1981	*KC-A	101	389	38	106	23	2	7	36	34	33	.272	.334	.396	111	5	5	49	3	4	-2	-1	DO	0.3
1982	KC-A	159	613	91	189	46	8	27	133	55	61	.308	.370	.542	146	38	38	123	4	4	-1	-0	*D/O	3.6
1983	KC-A	157	589	84	183	41	6	12	82	50	68	.311	.374	.462	128	24	23	98	2	3	-1	0	*D	2.2
1984	*KC-A	106	317	30	96	13	4	3	42	34	47	.303	.372	.397	112	7	6	45	0	3	-2	0	*D	0.4
1985	*KC-A	112	320	41	83	19	0	14	70	44	45	.259	.351	.450	117	8	8	49	0	1	-1	0	*D	0.7
1986	KC-A	112	278	22	70	14	0	7	37	18	39	.252	.300	.378	81	-7	-8	29	0	0	0	0	D	-0.7
1987	KC-A	18	32	5	10	3	0	1	9	5	1	.313	.405	.500	135	2	2	6	0	0	0	0	/D	0.2
Total	19	2084	7218	940	2091	484	66	191	1097	648	779	.290	.355	.454	122	227	213	1138	109	78	-14	-31	*DO/32	15.7

■ McREMER   McRemer   Deb: 6/20/1884

| 1884 | Was-U | 1 | 3 | 0 | 0 | 0 | 0 | 0 | | 0 | | .000 | .000 | .000 | -99 | -1 | -1 | 0 | 0 | | | 0 | /O | 0.0 |

■ KEVIN McREYNOLDS   McReynolds, Walter Kevin b: 10/16/59, Little Rock, Ark.   BR/TR, 6', 205 lbs.   Deb: 6/02/83

1983	SD-N	39	140	15	31	3	1	4	14	12	29	.221	.283	.343	75	-5	-5	14	2	1	0	3	O	-0.2
1984	*SD-N	147	525	68	146	26	6	20	75	34	69	.278	.322	.465	119	11	11	72	3	6	-3	13	*O	1.6
1985	SD-N	152	564	61	132	24	4	15	75	43	81	.234	.292	.371	85	-13	-12	59	4	0	1	16	*O	0.1
1986	SD-N	158	560	89	161	31	6	26	96	66	83	.287	.364	.504	140	27	29	103	8	6	-1	0	*O	2.6
1987	NY-N	151	590	86	163	32	5	29	95	39	70	.276	.322	.495	119	8	12	93	14	1	4	2	*O	1.1
1988	*NY-N	147	552	82	159	30	2	27	99	38	56	.288	.338	.496	144	24	27	97	21	0	6	6	*O	3.7
1989	NY-N	148	545	74	148	25	3	22	85	46	74	.272	.329	.450	127	13	16	80	15	7	0	9	*O	2.5
1990	NY-N	147	521	75	140	23	1	24	82	71	61	.269	.358	.455	125	16	17	88	9	2	2	1	*O	1.6
Total	8	1089	3997	550	1080	194	28	167	621	349	523	.270	.331	.458	121	81	95	605	76	23	9	50	*O	13.0

■ PETE McSHANNIC   McShannic, Peter Robert b: 3/20/1864, Pittsburgh, Pa.   d: 11/30/46, Toledo, Ohio   BB, 5'7", 190 lbs.   Deb: 9/15/1888

| 1888 | Pit-N | 26 | 98 | 5 | 19 | 1 | 0 | 0 | 5 | 1 | 9 | .194 | .218 | .204 | 40 | -7 | -6 | 5 | 3 | | | 0 | 3 | -0.4 |

■ TRICK McSORLEY   McSorley, John Bernard b: 12/6/1858, St.Louis, Mo.   d: 2/9/36, St.Louis, Mo.   TR, 5'4", 142 lbs.   Deb: 5/06/1875

1875	RS-n	15	52	4	11	0	0	0		0		.212	.212	.212	52	-3	-2	2					/3O	0.0
1884	Tol-a	21	68	12	17	1	0	0		3		.250	.282	.265	79	-1	-2	5				1	1/O3P	0.0
1885	StL-N	2	6	2	3	1	0	0	1	2	1	.500	.625	.667	340	2	2	3				-2	/3	0.0
1886	StL-a	5	20	1	3	3	0	0		0		.150	.150	.300	39	-1	-2	1	0			-3	/S	-0.3
Total	3	28	94	15	23	5	0	0	1	5	1	.245	.283	.298	87	-1	-1	9	0			-3	/1SO3P	-0.3

■ PAUL McSWEENEY   McSweeney, Paul A. b: 4/3/1867, St.Louis, Mo.   d: 8/12/51, St.Louis, Mo.   Deb: 9/20/1891

| 1891 | StL-a | 3 | 12 | 2 | 3 | 1 | 0 | 0 | 2 | 0 | | .250 | .308 | .333 | 75 | -0 | -1 | 2 | 1 | | | -2 | /23 | -0.1 |

■ JIM McTAMANY   McTamany, James Edward b: 7/1/1863, Philadelphia, Pa.   d: 4/16/16, Lenni, Pa.   BR/TR, 5'8", 190 lbs.   Deb: 8/15/1885

1885	Bro-a	35	131	21	36	7	2	1		9		.275	.321	.382	123	4	3	16				-5	O	-0.3
1886	Bro-a	111	418	86	106	23	10	2		54		.254	.353	.371	128	16	15	63	18			14	*O	2.2
1887	Bro-a	134	520	123	134	22	10	1		76		.258	.365	.344	99	4	3	92	66			8	*O	0.4
1888	KC-a	130	516	94	127	12	10	4	41	67		.246	.345	.331	113	15	10	80	55			6	*O	1.0
1889	Col-a	139	529	113	146	21	7	4	52	116	66	.276	.407	.365	129	22	28	97	40			-5	*O	1.4
1890	Col-a	125	466	140	120	27	7	1		112		.258	.405	.352	136	22	28	86	43			2	*O	2.1
1891	Col-a	81	304	59	76	17	9	3	35	58	48	.250	.374	.395	130	10	14	54	20			-2	O	0.7
	Phi-a	58	218	57	49	6	3	3	21	43	44	.225	.365	.321	96	2	1	31	13			0	O	0.0

YEAR	TM/L	G	AB	R	H	2B	3B	HR	RBI	BB	SO	AVG	OBP	SLG	PRO+	BR	/A	RC	SB	CS	SBR	FR	POS	TPR
	Yr	139	522	116	125	23	12	6	56	101	92	.239	.370	.364	115	12	14	85	33			-2		0.7
Total	7	813	3102	693	794	135	58	19	149	535	158	.256	.373	.355	119	95	101	519	255			17	O	7.5

■ BILL McTIGUE
McTigue, William Patrick "Rebel" b: 1/3/1891, Nashville, Tenn. d: 5/8/20, Nashville, Tenn. BL/TL, 6'1.5", 175 lbs. Deb: 5/02/11

YEAR	TM/L	G	AB	R	H	2B	3B	HR	RBI	BB	SO	AVG	OBP	SLG	PRO+	BR	/A	RC	SB	CS	SBR	FR	POS	TPR
1911	Bos-N	14	12	1	1	1	0	0	0	0	5	.083	.083	.167	-28	-2	-2	0	0			-1	P	0.0
1912	Bos-N	10	13	2	1	0	0	0	1	1	5	.077	.143	.077	-38	-2	-3	0	0			0	P	0.0
1913	Bos-N	1	0	0	0	0	0	0	0	0	0	—	—	—	—	0	0	0	0			0	R	0.0
1916	Det-A	3	1	0	0	0	0	0	0	0	0	.000	.000	.000	-97	-0	-0	0	0			0	/P	0.0
Total	4	28	26	3	2	1	0	0	1	1	10	.077	.111	.115	-36	-5	-5	0	0			0	/P	0.0

■ CAL McVEY
McVey, Calvin Alexander b: 8/30/1850, Montrose, Iowa d: 8/20/26, San Francisco, Cal BR/TR, 5'9", 170 lbs. Deb: 5/05/1871 M

YEAR	TM/L	G	AB	R	H	2B	3B	HR	RBI	BB	SO	AVG	OBP	SLG	PRO+	BR	/A	RC	SB	CS	SBR	FR	POS	TPR
1871	Bos-n	29	153	43	66	9	5	0	43	1	2	.431	.435	.556	176	16	14	41	6				*C/O	0.9
1872	Bos-n	46	237	56	73	11	3	0		0		.308	.308	.380	105	3	-0	28					*C/O	0.0
1873	Bal-n	38	192	49	73	8	5	3			3	.380	.390	.521	166	15	15	40					C/OS123M	1.1
1874	Bos-n	70	341	91	124	22	4	4			0	.364	.364	.487	159	25	21	62					*OC	1.8
1875	Bos-n	82	389	88	137	33	9	3			1	.352	.354	.506	187	35	33	71					*1OC/P	2.6
1876	Chi-N	63	308	62	107	15	0	1	53	2	4	.347	.352	.406	136	16	10	45	3				*1P/CO3	1.3
1877	Chi-N	60	266	58	98	9	7	0	36	8	11	.368	.387	.455	147	19	14	48				-10	*C3P/21	0.8
1878	Cin-N	61	271	43	83	10	4	2	28	5	10	.306	.319	.395	147	9	13	35				-10	*3/CM	0.5
1879	Cin-N	81	354	64	105	18	6	0	55	8	13	.297	.312	.381	134	10	12	43				-7	*1/OP3CM	0.5
Total	5 n	265	1312	327	473	83	26	10	43	5	2	.361	.363	.486	160	93	84	242					C/O1SP23	6.4
Total	4	265	1199	227	393	52	17	3	172	23	38	.328	.340	.407	140	54	50	171				-24	1/3CPO2	2.6

■ GEORGE McVEY
McVey, George W. b: 1864, Port Jervis, N.Y. d: 5/3/1896, Quincy, Ill. 6'1", 185 lbs. Deb: 9/19/1885

YEAR	TM/L	G	AB	R	H	2B	3B	HR	RBI	BB	SO	AVG	OBP	SLG	PRO+	BR	/A	RC	SB	CS	SBR	FR	POS	TPR
1885	Bro-a	6	21	2	3	0	0	0		2		.143	.217	.143	17	-2	-2	1				-0	/1C	-0.1

■ BILL McWILLIAMS
McWilliams, William Henry b: 11/28/10, Dubuque, Iowa BR/TR, 6', 185 lbs. Deb: 7/08/31

YEAR	TM/L	G	AB	R	H	2B	3B	HR	RBI	BB	SO	AVG	OBP	SLG	PRO+	BR	/A	RC	SB	CS	SBR	FR	POS	TPR
1931	Bos-A	2	2	0	0	0	0	0	0	0	1	.000	.000	.000	-99	-1	-1	0	0	0	0	0	H	0.0

■ BOB MEACHAM
Meacham, Robert Andrew b: 8/25/60, Los Angeles, Cal. BB/TR, 6'1", 175 lbs. Deb: 6/30/83

YEAR	TM/L	G	AB	R	H	2B	3B	HR	RBI	BB	SO	AVG	OBP	SLG	PRO+	BR	/A	RC	SB	CS	SBR	FR	POS	TPR
1983	NY-A	22	51	5	12	2	0	0	4	4	10	.235	.304	.275	63	-3	-2	6	8	0	2	9	S/3	1.0
1984	NY-A	99	360	62	91	13	4	2	25	32	70	.253	.319	.328	83	-10	-8	41	9	5	-0	-12	S/2	-1.2
1985	NY-A	156	481	70	105	16	2	1	47	54	102	.218	.304	.266	59	-27	-25	45	25	7	3	-17	*S	-2.6
1986	NY-A	56	161	19	36	7	1	0	10	17	39	.224	.309	.280	62	-8	-8	13	3	6	-3	-5	S	-1.1
1987	NY-A	77	203	28	55	11	1	5	21	19	33	.271	.351	.409	102	1	1	30	6	5	-1	-1	S2/D	0.3
1988	NY-A	47	115	18	25	9	0	0	7	14	22	.217	.313	.296	72	-4	-4	13	7	1	2	-7	S2/3	-0.6
Total	6	457	1371	202	324	58	8	8	114	140	276	.236	.316	.308	73	-50	-46	147	58	24	3	-32	S/23D	-4.2

■ CHARLIE MEAD
Mead, Charles Richard b: 4/9/21, Vermilion, Alt., Canada BL/TR, 6'1.5", 185 lbs. Deb: 8/28/43

YEAR	TM/L	G	AB	R	H	2B	3B	HR	RBI	BB	SO	AVG	OBP	SLG	PRO+	BR	/A	RC	SB	CS	SBR	FR	POS	TPR
1943	NY-N	37	146	9	40	6	1	1	13	10	15	.274	.321	.349	93	-1	-2	16	3			-1	O	-0.4
1944	NY-N	39	78	5	14	1	0	1	8	5	7	.179	.229	.231	30	-7	-7	4	0			4	O	-0.4
1945	NY-N	11	37	4	10	1	0	1	6	5	2	.270	.357	.378	103	0	0	5	0			2	O	0.2
Total	3	87	261	18	64	8	1	3	27	20	24	.245	.299	.318	75	-8	-9	26	3			5	/O	-0.6

■ LOUIE MEADOWS
Meadows, Michael Ray b: 4/29/61, Maysville, N.C. BL/TL, 5'11", 190 lbs. Deb: 7/03/86

YEAR	TM/L	G	AB	R	H	2B	3B	HR	RBI	BB	SO	AVG	OBP	SLG	PRO+	BR	/A	RC	SB	CS	SBR	FR	POS	TPR
1986	Hou-N	6	6	1	2	0	0	0	0	0	0	.333	.333	.333	87	-0	-0	1	1	0	0	0	/O	0.0
1988	Hou-N	35	42	5	8	0	1	2	3	6	8	.190	.292	.381	95	-0	-0	5	4	2	0	2	O	0.1
1989	Hou-N	31	51	5	9	0	0	3	10	1	14	.176	.192	.353	55	-3	-3	3	1	2	-1	-2	O/1	-0.6
1990	Hou-N	15	14	3	2	0	0	0	2	4	4	.143	.250	.143	11	-2	-2	1	0	0	0	-0	/O	-0.1
	Phi-N	15	14	1	1	0	0	0	0	1	2	.071	.133	.071	-42	-3	-3	0	0	0	0	-0	/O	-0.2
	Yr	30	28	4	3	0	0	0	0	3	6	.107	.194	.107	-15	-4	-4	1	0	0	0	0		-0.3
Total	4	102	127	15	22	0	1	5	13	10	28	.173	.234	.307	54	-8	-8	9	6	4	-1	0	/O1	-0.8

■ PAT MEANEY
Meaney, Patrick J. b: 1870, Philadelphia, Pa. d: 10/20/22, Philadelphia, Pa. TL, Deb: 5/18/12

YEAR	TM/L	G	AB	R	H	2B	3B	HR	RBI	BB	SO	AVG	OBP	SLG	PRO+	BR	/A	RC	SB	CS	SBR	FR	POS	TPR
1912	Det-A	1	2	0	0	0	0	0	0	0	1	.000	.500	.000	48	0	0	0	0			0	/S	0.0

■ CHARLIE MEARA
Meara, Charles Edward "Goggy" b: 4/13/1891, New York, N.Y. d: 2/8/62, Bronx, N.Y. BL/TR, 5'10", 160 lbs. Deb: 6/01/14

YEAR	TM/L	G	AB	R	H	2B	3B	HR	RBI	BB	SO	AVG	OBP	SLG	PRO+	BR	/A	RC	SB	CS	SBR	FR	POS	TPR
1914	NY-A	4	7	2	2	0	0	0	1	2	2	.286	.444	.286	120	0	0	1	0	1	-1	-1	/O	-0.1

■ RAY MEDEIROS
Medeiros, Ray Antone "Pep" b: 5/9/26, Oakland, Cal. BR/TR, 5'10", 163 lbs. Deb: 4/25/45

YEAR	TM/L	G	AB	R	H	2B	3B	HR	RBI	BB	SO	AVG	OBP	SLG	PRO+	BR	/A	RC	SB	CS	SBR	FR	POS	TPR
1945	Cin-N	1	0	0	0	0	0	0	0	0	0	—	—	—	—	0	0	0	0	0	0	0	R	0.0

■ LUIS MEDINA
Medina, Luis Main b: 3/26/63, Santa Monica, Cal. BR/TL, 6'4", 200 lbs. Deb: 9/02/88

YEAR	TM/L	G	AB	R	H	2B	3B	HR	RBI	BB	SO	AVG	OBP	SLG	PRO+	BR	/A	RC	SB	CS	SBR	FR	POS	TPR
1988	Cle-A	16	51	10	13	0	0	6	8	2	18	.255	.309	.608	146	3	3	10	0	0	0	-0	1	0.2
1989	Cle-A	30	83	8	17	1	0	4	8	6	35	.205	.258	.361	72	-3	-3	7	0	1	-1	-1	D/O1	-0.4
Total	2	46	134	18	30	1	0	10	16	8	53	.224	.278	.455	101	-0	-1	17	0	1	-1	-1	/D1O	-0.2

■ JOE MEDWICK
Medwick, Joseph Michael "Ducky" or "Muscles" b: 11/24/11, Carteret, N.J. d: 3/21/75, St.Petersburg, Fla BR/TR, 5'10", 187 lbs. Deb: 9/02/32 H

YEAR	TM/L	G	AB	R	H	2B	3B	HR	RBI	BB	SO	AVG	OBP	SLG	PRO+	BR	/A	RC	SB	CS	SBR	FR	POS	TPR
1932	StL-N	26	106	13	37	12	1	2	12	2	10	.349	.367	.538	136	5	5	21	3			1	O	0.4
1933	StL-N	148	595	92	182	40	10	18	98	26	56	.306	.337	.497	129	25	21	97	5			6	*O	1.9
1934	*StL-N	149	620	110	198	40	18	18	106	21	83	.319	.343	.529	122	23	18	109	3			0	*O	1.0
1935	StL-N	154	634	132	224	46	13	23	126	30	59	.353	.386	.576	149	46	43	139	4			-0	*O	3.4
1936	StL-N	155	636	115	223	64	13	18	138	34	33	.351	.387	.577	157	47	47	141	13			0	*O	5.0
1937	StL-N	156	633	111	237	56	10	31	154	41	50	.374	.414	.641	179	69	67	170	4			0	*O	5.8
1938	StL-N	146	590	100	190	47	8	21	122	42	41	.322	.369	.536	138	34	30	113	0			9	*O	3.6
1939	StL-N	150	606	98	201	48	8	14	117	45	44	.332	.380	.507	128	29	25	114	6			1	*O	2.3
1940	StL-N	37	158	21	48	12	0	3	20	6	8	.304	.329	.437	104	1	0	20	2			-2	O	-0.2
	Bro-N	106	423	62	127	18	12	14	66	26	28	.300	.345	.499	123	16	12	70	2			5	*O	1.4
	Yr	143	581	83	175	30	12	17	86	32	36	.301	.341	.482	118	17	13	90	4			2		1.2
1941	*Bro-N	133	538	100	171	33	10	18	88	38	35	.318	.364	.517	140	30	27	95	2			-0	*O	2.2
1942	Bro-N	142	553	69	166	37	4	4	96	32	25	.300	.338	.403	115	10	9	72	2			-1	*O	0.4
1943	Bro-N	48	173	13	47	10	0	0	25	10	8	.272	.315	.329	86	-3	-3	18	1			-6	O	-1.1
	NY-N	78	324	41	91	20	3	5	45	9	14	.281	.300	.407	103	-1	-1	35	0			4	O/1	0.0
	Yr	126	497	54	138	30	3	5	70	19	22	.278	.306	.380	97	-4	-4	53	1			-3		-1.1
1944	NY-N	128	490	64	165	24	3	7	85	38	24	.337	.386	.441	133	21	21	82	2			5	*O	1.7
1945	NY-N	26	92	14	28	4	0	3	11	2	2	.304	.319	.446	110	1	1	12	2			-1	O	-0.1
	Bos-N	66	218	17	62	13	0	0	26	12	12	.284	.325	.344	85	-4	-4	23	3			-1	O1	-0.8
	Yr	92	310	31	90	17	0	3	37	14	14	.290	.323	.374	93	-4	-4	36	5			-2		-0.8
1946	Bro-N	41	77	7	24	4	0	2	18	6	5	.312	.369	.442	128	3	3	13	0			-2	O/1	0.1
1947	StL-N	75	150	19	46	12	0	4	28	16	12	.307	.373	.467	117	5	4	26	0			-2	/O	0.0
1948	StL-N	20	19	0	4	2	0	0	2	1	2	.211	.250	.211	24	-2	-2	1	0			0	/O	-0.1
Total	17	1984	7635	1198	2471	540	113	205	1383	437	551	.324	.362	.505	133	354	322	1372	42			29	*O/1	27.0

■ TOMMY MEE
Mee, Thomas William "Judge" b: 3/18/1890, Chicago, Ill. d: 5/16/81, Chicago, Ill. BR/TR, 5'8", 165 lbs. Deb: 6/14/10

YEAR	TM/L	G	AB	R	H	2B	3B	HR	RBI	BB	SO	AVG	OBP	SLG	PRO+	BR	/A	RC	SB	CS	SBR	FR	POS	TPR
1910	StL-A	8	19	1	3	2	0	0	1	0		.158	.158	.263	34	-2	-1	1	0			-1	/S23	-0.2

YEAR	TM/L	G	AB	R	H	2B	3B	HR	RBI	BB	SO	AVG	OBP	SLG	PRO+	BR	/A	RC	SB	CS	SBR	FR	POS	TPR

■ DAD MEEK   Meek, Frank J. b: St.Louis, Mo. d: 12/26/22, St.Louis, Mo.   Deb: 5/10/1889

1889	StL-a	2	2	2	1	0	0	0	1	0	0	.500	.500	.500	166	0	0	1	1			0	/C	0.0
1890	StL-a	4	16	3	5	0	0	0		0		.313	.313	.313	76	-0	-1	2	1			3	/C	0.2
Total	2	6	18	5	6	0	0	0	1	0	0	.333	.333	.333	86	-0	-0	3	2			3	/C	0.2

■ SAMMY MEEKS   Meeks, Samuel Mack b: 4/23/23, Anderson, S.C. BR/TR, 5'9", 160 lbs. Deb: 4/29/48

1948	Was-A	24	33	4	4	1	0	0	2	1	12	.121	.147	.152	-21	-6	-6	1	0	0	0	-0	S/2	-0.5
1949	Cin-N	16	36	10	11	2	0	2	6	2	6	.306	.342	.528	128	1	1	6	1			6	/2S	0.7
1950	Cin-N	39	95	7	27	5	0	1	8	6	14	.284	.327	.368	82	-2	-2	11	1			-4	S/3	-0.2
1951	Cin-N	23	35	4	8	0	0	0	2	0	4	.229	.229	.229	23	-4	-4	1	1	0	0	-1	/3S	-0.4
Total	4	102	199	25	50	8	0	3	18	9	36	.251	.284	.337	64	-11	-11	20	3	0		1	/S23	-0.4

■ DUTCH MEIER   Meier, Arthur Ernst b: 3/30/1879, St.Louis, Mo. d: 3/23/48, Chicago, Ill. BR/TR, 5'10", 175 lbs. Deb: 5/12/06

| 1906 | Pit-N | 82 | 273 | 32 | 70 | 11 | 4 | 0 | 16 | 13 | | .256 | .290 | .326 | 90 | -3 | -4 | 28 | 4 | | | -12 | OS | -1.7 |

■ DAVE MEIER   Meier, David Keith b: 8/8/59, Helena, Mont. BR/TR, 6', 185 lbs. Deb: 4/03/84

1984	Min-A	59	147	18	35	8	1	0	13	6	9	.238	.273	.306	57	-8	-9	11	0	1	-1	0	O/3D	-1.0
1985	Min-A	71	104	15	27	6	0	1	8	18	12	.260	.374	.346	93	1	-0	13	0	6	-4	3	O/D	-0.1
1987	Tex-A	13	21	4	6	1	0	0	0	0	4	.286	.286	.333	63	-1	-1	1	0	0	0	0	/O	0.0
1988	Chi-N	2	5	0	2	0	0	0	1	0	1	.400	.400	.400	125	0	0	1	0	0	0	-1	/3	0.0
Total	4	145	277	37	70	15	1	1	22	24	26	.253	.317	.325	73	-8	-10	27	0	7	-4	2	O/D3	-1.1

■ WALT MEINERT   Meinert, Walter Henry b: 12/11/1890, New York, N.Y. d: 11/9/58, Decatur, Ill. BL/TL, 5'7.5", 150 lbs. Deb: 9/06/13

| 1913 | StL-A | 4 | 8 | 1 | 3 | 0 | 0 | 0 | 0 | 1 | 3 | .375 | .444 | .375 | 144 | 0 | 1 | 2 | 1 | | | -0 | /O | 0.0 |

■ FRANK MEINKE   Meinke, Frank Louis b: 10/18/1863, Chicago, Ill. d: 11/8/31, Chicago, Ill. 5'10.5", 172 lbs. Deb: 5/01/1884

1884	Det-N	92	341	28	56	5	7	6	24	6	89	.164	.179	.273	42	-23	-20	17				-3	SP/O32	-1.1
1885	Det-N	1	3	0	0	0	0	0	0	0	1	.000	.000	.000	-99	-1	-1	0				0	/OP	0.0
Total	2	93	344	28	56	5	7	6	24	6	90	.163	.177	.270	41	-24	-21	17				-3	/SPO23	-1.1

■ BOB MEINKE   Meinke, Robert Bernard b: 6/25/1887, Chicago, Ill. d: 12/29/52, Chicago, Ill. BR/TR, 5'10", 135 lbs. Deb: 8/22/10

| 1910 | Cin-N | 2 | 1 | 0 | 0 | 0 | 0 | 0 | 0 | 0 | 1 | .000 | .500 | .000 | 51 | 0 | 0 | 0 | 0 | | | 1 | /S | 0.1 |

■ GEORGE MEISTER   Meister, George B. b: 6/5/1864, Germany d: 8/24/08, Pittsburgh, Pa. Deb: 8/15/1884

| 1884 | Tol-a | 34 | 119 | 9 | 23 | 6 | 0 | 0 | | 3 | | .193 | .244 | .244 | 60 | -5 | -5 | 7 | | | | -9 | 3 | -1.2 |

■ JOHN MEISTER   Meister, John F. b: 5/10/1863, Allentown, Pa. d: 1/17/23, Philadelphia, Pa. Deb: 8/24/1886

1886	NY-a	45	186	35	44	7	3	2		4		.237	.253	.339	90	-4	-2	17	1			-8	2	-0.9
1887	NY-a	39	157	24	35	6	2	1		16		.223	.303	.306	75	-6	-4	18	9			-9	O2/3S	-1.1
Total	2	84	343	59	79	13	5	3		20		.230	.277	.324	83	-9	-7	34	10			-17	/2O3S	-2.0

■ KARL MEISTER   Meister, Karl Daniel "Dutch" b: 5/15/1891, Marietta, Ohio d: 8/15/67, Marietta, Ohio BR/TR, 6', 178 lbs. Deb: 8/10/13

| 1913 | Cin-N | 4 | 7 | 1 | 2 | 1 | 0 | 0 | 2 | 0 | 4 | .286 | .286 | .429 | 103 | -0 | -0 | 1 | 0 | | | -1 | /O | 0.0 |

■ MOXIE MEIXELL   Meixell, Merton Merrill b: 10/18/1887, Lake Crystal, Minn d: 8/17/82, Los Angeles, Cal. BL/TR, 5'10", 168 lbs. Deb: 7/07/12

| 1912 | Cle-A | 3 | 2 | 0 | 1 | 0 | 0 | 0 | 0 | 0 | | .500 | .500 | .500 | 180 | 0 | 0 | 0 | 0 | | | 0 | /O | 0.0 |

■ ROMAN MEJIAS   Mejias, Roman (Gomez) b: 8/9/30, Abreus, Las Villas, Cuba BR/TR, 6', 175 lbs. Deb: 4/13/55

1955	Pit-N	71	167	14	36	8	1	3	21	9	13	.216	.256	.329	55	-11	-11	13	1	3	-2	2	O	-1.1
1957	Pit-N	58	142	12	39	7	4	2	15	6	13	.275	.309	.423	97	-2	-1	17	2	2	-1	1	O	-0.1
1958	Pit-N	76	157	17	42	3	2	5	19	2	27	.268	.281	.408	82	-5	-5	17	2	0	1	6	O	0.1
1959	Pit-N	96	276	28	65	6	1	7	28	21	48	.236	.301	.341	71	-12	-11	28	1	2	-1	2	O	-1.0
1960	Pit-N	3	1	1	0	0	0	0	0	0	1	.000	.000	.000	-99	-0	-0	0	0	0	0	0	H	0.0
1961	Pit-N	4	1	1	0	0	0	0	0	0	1	.000	.000	.000	-99	-0	-0	0	0	0	0	0	/O	0.0
1962	Hou-N	146	566	82	162	12	3	24	76	30	83	.286	.329	.445	114	3	8	81	12	4	1	-4	*O	-0.1
1963	Bos-A	111	357	43	81	18	0	11	39	14	36	.227	.262	.370	72	-13	-14	32	4	1	1	2	O	-1.5
1964	Bos-A	62	101	14	24	3	1	2	4	7	16	.238	.294	.347	74	-3	-4	9	0	0	0	3	O	-0.2
Total	9	627	1768	212	449	57	12	54	202	89	238	.254	.296	.391	86	-43	-38	197	22	12	-1	11	O	-4.0

■ SAM MEJIAS   Mejias, Samuel Elias b: 5/9/52, Santiago, D.R. BR/TR, 6', 170 lbs. Deb: 9/06/76

1976	StL-N	18	21	1	3	1	0	0	0	2	2	.143	.217	.190	16	-2	-2	1	2	0	1	2	O	0.0
1977	Mon-N	74	101	14	23	4	1	3	8	2	17	.228	.243	.376	65	-6	-5	9	1	0	0	3	O	-0.3
1978	Mon-N	67	56	9	13	1	0	0	6	2	5	.232	.259	.250	43	-4	-4	3	0	0	0	3	O/P	-0.3
1979	Chi-N	31	11	4	2	0	0	0	0	2	5	.182	.308	.182	34	-1	-1	1	0	0	0	1	O	0.0
	Cin-N	7	2	1	1	0	0	0	0	0	0	.500	.500	.500	173	0	0	1	0	0	0	0	/O	0.0
	Yr	38	13	5	3	0	0	0	0	2	5	.231	.333	.231	53	-1	-1	1	0	0	0	1		0.0
1980	Cin-N	71	108	16	30	5	1	1	10	6	13	.278	.322	.370	93	-1	-1	13	4	2	0	8	O	0.5
1981	Cin-N	66	49	6	14	2	0	0	7	2	9	.286	.314	.327	80	-1	-1	5	1	0	0	2	O	0.0
Total	6	334	348	51	86	13	2	4	31	16	51	.247	.282	.330	69	-15	-15	32	8	2	1	18	O/P	-0.1

■ DUTCH MELE   Mele, Albert Ernest b: 1/11/15, New York, N.Y. d: 2/12/75, Hollywood, Fla. BL/TL, 6'0.5", 195 lbs. Deb: 9/14/37

| 1937 | Cin-N | 6 | 14 | 1 | 2 | 1 | 0 | 0 | 1 | 1 | 1 | .143 | .200 | .214 | 13 | -2 | -2 | 1 | 0 | | | -1 | /O | -0.2 |

■ SAM MELE   Mele, Sabath Anthony b: 1/21/23, Astoria, N.Y. BR/TR, 6'1", 183 lbs. Deb: 4/15/47 MC

1947	Bos-A	123	453	71	137	14	8	12	73	37	35	.302	.356	.448	114	12	8	72	0	3	-2	0	*O/1	0.2
1948	Bos-A	66	180	25	42	12	1	2	25	13	21	.233	.292	.344	66	-9	-10	18	1	1	-0	-2	O	-1.3
1949	Bos-A	18	46	1	9	1	1	0	7	7	14	.196	.302	.261	46	-3	-4	4	2	0	1	-1	O	-0.3
	Was-A	78	264	21	64	12	2	3	25	17	34	.242	.288	.337	67	-14	-14	24	2	1	0	-3	O1	-1.7
	Yr	96	310	22	73	13	3	3	32	24	48	.235	.290	.326	63	-18	-18	28	4	1	1	-4		-2.0
1950	Was-A	126	435	57	119	21	6	12	86	51	40	.274	.351	.432	105	-1	-2	64	2	0	0	-3	O1	-0.2
1951	Was-A	143	558	58	153	**36**	7	5	94	32	31	.274	.315	.391	92	-10	-9	64	2	3	-1	-0	*O1	-1.4
1952	Was-A	9	28	2	12	3	0	2	10	1	2	.429	.448	.750	237	4	5	10	0	0	0	-1	/O	0.3
	Chi-A	123	423	46	105	18	2	14	59	48	40	.248	.328	.400	101	0	-0	53	1	2	-1	-11	*O/1	-1.5
	Yr	132	451	48	117	21	2	16	69	49	42	.259	.335	.421	109	5	4	62	1	2	-1	-12		-1.2
1953	Chi-A	140	481	64	132	26	8	12	82	58	47	.274	.353	.437	109	8	6	75	3	1	0	-7	*O/1	-0.4
1954	Bal-A	72	230	17	55	9	4	5	32	18	26	.239	.294	.378	90	-6	-4	23	1	0	0	-7	O	-1.1
	Bos-A	42	132	22	42	6	0	7	23	12	12	.318	.384	.523	132	8	6	25	0	1	-1	-3	1O	0.2
	Yr	114	362	39	97	15	4	12	55	30	38	.268	.327	.431	107	2	2	47	1	1	-0	-10		-0.9
1955	Bos-A	14	31	1	4	2	0	0	1	0	7	.129	.129	.194	-13	-5	-5	1	1	0	0	2	/O	-0.2
	Cin-N	35	62	4	13	1	0	2	7	5	13	.210	.279	.323	56	-4	-1	5	0	1	-1	0	O1/3	-0.2
1956	Cle-A	57	114	17	29	7	0	4	20	12	20	.254	.325	.421	94	-1	-1	15	0	1	-1	-0	O1/3	-0.2
Total	10	1046	3437	406	916	168	39	80	544	311	342	.267	.329	.408	97	-21	-25	451	15	14	-4	-36	O/1	-8.1

■ FRANCISCO MELENDEZ   Melendez, Francisco Javier (Villegas) b: 1/25/64, Rio Piedras, P.R. BL/TL, 6', 190 lbs. Deb: 8/26/84

| 1984 | Phi-N | 21 | 23 | 0 | 3 | 0 | 0 | 0 | 2 | 1 | 5 | .130 | .167 | .130 | -15 | -3 | -4 | 0 | 0 | 0 | 0 | 1 | 1 | -0.2 |
| 1986 | Phi-N | 9 | 8 | 0 | 2 | 0 | 0 | 0 | 0 | 0 | 2 | .250 | .250 | .250 | 37 | -1 | -1 | 1 | 0 | 0 | 0 | 0 | /1 | 0.0 |

YEAR	TM/L	G	AB	R	H	2B	3B	HR	RBI	BB	SO	AVG	OBP	SLG	PRO+	BR	/A	RC	SB	CS	SBR	FR	POS	TPR
1987	SF-N	12	16	2	5	0	0	1	1	0	3	.313	.313	.500	117	0	0	3	0	0	0	-1	/1	0.0
1988	SF-N	23	26	1	5	0	0	0	3	3	2	.192	.276	.192	38	-2	-2	1	0	0	0	-1	/1O	-0.2
1989	Bal-A	9	11	1	3	0	0	0	3	1	2	.273	.333	.273	75	-0	-0	1	0	0	0	0	/1	0.0
Total	5	74	84	4	18	0	0	1	9	5	14	.214	.258	.250	43	-6	-6	6	0	0	0	-0	/1O	-0.4

■ LUIS MELENDEZ
Melendez, Luis Antonio (Santana) b: 8/11/49, Aibonito, P.R. BR/TR, 6', 165 lbs. Deb: 9/07/70

YEAR	TM/L	G	AB	R	H	2B	3B	HR	RBI	BB	SO	AVG	OBP	SLG	PRO+	BR	/A	RC	SB	CS	SBR	FR	POS	TPR
1970	StL-N	21	70	11	21	1	0	0	8	2	12	.300	.319	.314	69	-3	-3	7	3	0	1	1	O	-0.1
1971	StL-N	88	173	25	39	3	1	0	11	24	29	.225	.320	.254	62	-7	-8	15	2	0	1	1	O	-0.9
1972	StL-N	118	332	32	79	11	3	5	28	25	34	.238	.293	.334	79	-10	-9	31	5	4	-1	1	*O	-1.5
1973	StL-N	121	341	35	91	18	1	2	35	27	50	.267	.321	.343	84	-7	-7	34	2	7	-4	5	O	-1.0
1974	StL-N	83	124	15	27	4	3	0	8	11	9	.218	.287	.298	64	-6	-6	11	2	2	-1	5	O/S	-0.3
1975	StL-N	110	291	33	77	8	5	2	27	16	25	.265	.303	.347	77	-8	-10	28	3	2	-0	3	O	-0.9
1976	StL-N	20	24	0	3	0	0	0	0	0	3	.125	.125	.125	-29	-4	-4	0	0	0	0	1	/O	-0.2
	SD-N	72	119	15	29	5	0	0	5	3	12	.244	.262	.286	60	-7	-6	8	1	1	-0	4	O	-0.4
	Yr	92	143	15	32	5	0	0	5	3	15	.224	.240	.259	44	-11	-10	7	1	1	-0	5		-0.6
1977	SD-N	8	3	1	0	0	0	0	0	1	1	.000	.250	.000	-29	-1	-0	0	0	0	0	0	/O	0.0
Total	8	641	1477	167	366	50	13	9	122	109	175	.248	.300	.318	73	-53	-54	135	18	16	-4	20	O/S	-5.3

■ SKI MELILLO
Melillo, Oscar Donald "Spinach" b: 8/4/1899, Chicago, Ill. d: 11/14/63, Chicago, Ill. BR/TR, 5'8", 150 lbs. Deb: 4/18/26 C

YEAR	TM/L	G	AB	R	H	2B	3B	HR	RBI	BB	SO	AVG	OBP	SLG	PRO+	BR	/A	RC	SB	CS	SBR	FR	POS	TPR
1926	StL-A	99	385	54	98	18	5	1	30	32	31	.255	.315	.335	66	-18	-20	41	6	7	-2	8	23	-0.9
1927	StL-A	107	356	45	80	18	2	0	26	25	28	.225	.276	.287	45	-29	-30	27	3	6	-3	-2	*2	-2.8
1928	StL-A	51	132	9	25	2	0	0	9	9	11	.189	.241	.205	18	-16	-16	7	2	1	0	4	23	-1.0
1929	StL-A	141	494	57	146	17	10	5	67	29	30	.296	.337	.401	86	-9	-11	67	11	6	-0	23	*2	1.3
1930	StL-A	149	574	62	147	30	10	5	59	23	44	.256	.287	.369	63	-32	-35	60	15	9	-1	27	*2	-0.6
1931	StL-A	151	617	88	189	34	11	2	75	37	29	.306	.346	.407	94	-3	-6	84	7	11	-5	33	*2	2.9
1932	StL-A	154	612	71	148	19	11	3	66	36	42	.242	.286	.324	54	-39	-44	57	6	6	-2	11	*2	-2.6
1933	StL-A	132	496	50	145	23	6	3	79	29	18	.292	.333	.381	83	-9	-13	61	12	10	-2	23	*2	0.5
1934	StL-A	144	552	54	133	19	3	2	55	28	27	.241	.279	.297	45	-43	-49	45	4	6	-2	18	*2	-2.4
1935	StL-A	19	62	8	13	3	0	0	5	8	4	.210	.300	.258	43	-5	-5	5	0	0	0	0	2	-0.3
	Bos-A	106	400	45	104	13	2	1	39	38	22	.260	.327	.310	61	-20	-24	42	3	2	-0	18	*2	0.0
	Yr	125	462	53	117	16	2	1	44	46	26	.253	.324	.303	59	-25	-29	48	3	2	-0	19		-0.3
1936	Bos-A	98	327	39	74	12	4	0	32	28	16	.226	.287	.287	40	-30	-33	29	0	0	0	-8	2	-3.0
1937	Bos-A	26	56	8	14	2	0	0	6	5	4	.250	.311	.286	50	-4	-4	5	0	1	-1	-3	2/S3	-0.5
Total	12	1377	5063	590	1316	210	64	22	548	327	306	.260	.306	.340	64	-256	-292	530	69	65	-18	152	*2/3S	-9.4

■ JOE MELLANA
Mellana, Joseph Peter b: 3/11/05, Oakland, Cal. d: 11/1/69, Larkspur, Cal. BR/TR, 5'10", 180 lbs. Deb: 9/21/27

YEAR	TM/L	G	AB	R	H	2B	3B	HR	RBI	BB	SO	AVG	OBP	SLG	PRO+	BR	/A	RC	SB	CS	SBR	FR	POS	TPR
1927	Phi-A	4	7	1	2	0	0	0	2	0	1	.286	.286	.286	46	-1	-1	1	0	0	0	2	/3	0.1

■ BILL MELLOR
Mellor, William Harpin b: 6/6/1874, Camden, N.J. d: 11/5/40, Bridgeton, R.I. BR/TR, 6', 190 lbs. Deb: 7/28/02

YEAR	TM/L	G	AB	R	H	2B	3B	HR	RBI	BB	SO	AVG	OBP	SLG	PRO+	BR	/A	RC	SB	CS	SBR	FR	POS	TPR
1902	Bal-A	10	36	4	13	3	0	0	5	3		.361	.410	.444	133	2	2	7	1			-1	1	0.1

■ PAUL MELOAN
Meloan, Paul B. "Molly" b: 8/23/1888, Paynesville, Mo. d: 2/11/50, Taft, Cal. BR/TL, 5'10.5", 175 lbs. Deb: 8/02/10

YEAR	TM/L	G	AB	R	H	2B	3B	HR	RBI	BB	SO	AVG	OBP	SLG	PRO+	BR	/A	RC	SB	CS	SBR	FR	POS	TPR
1910	Chi-A	65	222	23	54	6	6	0	23	17		.243	.314	.324	104	0	1	24	4			4	O	0.2
1911	Chi-A	1	3	0	1	0	0	0	0	1	0	.333	.333	.333	89	-0	-0	0	0			-1	/O	0.0
	StL-A	64	206	30	54	11	2	3	14	15		.262	.318	.379	98	-2	-1	27	7			-6	O	-1.0
	Yr	65	209	30	55	11	2	3	15	15		.263	.319	.378	98	-2	-1	27	7			-6		-1.0
Total	2	130	431	53	109	17	8	3	38	32		.253	.316	.350	101	-2	-0	51	11			-3	O	-0.8

■ DAVE MELTON
Melton, David Olin b: 10/3/28, Pampa, Tex. BR/TR, 6', 185 lbs. Deb: 4/17/56

YEAR	TM/L	G	AB	R	H	2B	3B	HR	RBI	BB	SO	AVG	OBP	SLG	PRO+	BR	/A	RC	SB	CS	SBR	FR	POS	TPR
1956	KC-A	3	3	0	1	0	0	0	0	0	0	.333	.333	.333	76	-0	-0	0	0	0	0	0	/O	0.0
1958	KC-A	9	6	0	0	0	0	0	0	0	5	.000	.000	.000	-98	-2	-2	0	0	0	0	1	/O	0.0
Total	2	12	9	0	1	0	0	0	0	0	5	.111	.111	.111	-39	-2	-2	0	0	0	0	1	/O	0.0

■ BILL MELTON
Melton, William Edwin b: 7/7/45, Gulfport, Miss. BR/TR, 6'2", 200 lbs. Deb: 5/04/68

YEAR	TM/L	G	AB	R	H	2B	3B	HR	RBI	BB	SO	AVG	OBP	SLG	PRO+	BR	/A	RC	SB	CS	SBR	FR	POS	TPR
1968	Chi-A	34	109	5	29	8	0	2	16	10	32	.266	.328	.394	117	2	2	14	1	1	-0	4	3	0.8
1969	Chi-A	157	556	67	142	26	2	23	87	56	106	.255	.329	.433	106	7	4	79	1	2	-1	7	*3O	1.3
1970	Chi-A	141	514	74	135	15	1	33	96	56	107	.263	.345	.488	123	18	16	88	2	4	-2	5	O3	1.6
1971	Chi-A	150	543	72	146	18	2	33	86	61	87	.269	.354	.492	133	26	24	96	3	3	-1	27	*3	4.7
1972	Chi-A	57	208	22	51	5	0	7	30	23	31	.245	.320	.370	103	1	1	26	1	1	-0	3	3	0.6
1973	Chi-A	152	560	83	155	29	1	20	87	75	66	.277	.364	.439	121	20	17	87	4	4	-1	14	*3/D	2.8
1974	Chi-A	136	495	63	120	17	0	21	63	59	60	.242	.329	.404	107	6	5	65	3	2	-0	-3	*3D	0.3
1975	Chi-A	149	512	62	123	16	0	15	70	78	106	.240	.349	.359	99	3	2	67	5	4	-1	1	*3D	0.4
1976	Cal-A	118	341	31	71	17	3	6	42	44	53	.208	.302	.328	90	-6	-3	36	2	0	1	-2	D13	-0.7
1977	Cle-A	50	133	17	32	11	0	0	14	17	21	.241	.336	.323	83	-3	-2	13	1	3	-2	1	1D3	-0.4
Total	10	1144	3971	496	1004	162	9	160	591	479	669	.253	.340	.419	112	74	64	571	23	24	-8	56	3/DO1	11.4

■ BOB MELVIN
Melvin, Robert Paul b: 10/28/61, Palo Alto, Cal. BR/TR, 6'4", 205 lbs. Deb: 5/25/85

YEAR	TM/L	G	AB	R	H	2B	3B	HR	RBI	BB	SO	AVG	OBP	SLG	PRO+	BR	/A	RC	SB	CS	SBR	FR	POS	TPR
1985	Det-A	41	82	10	18	4	1	0	4	3	21	.220	.247	.293	47	-6	-6	6	0	0	0	7	C	0.3
1986	SF-N	89	268	24	60	14	2	5	25	15	69	.224	.265	.347	71	-13	-11	23	3	2	-0	6	C/3	-0.2
1987	*SF-N	84	246	31	49	8	0	11	31	17	44	.199	.251	.366	64	-15	-13	20	0	4	-2	4	C/1	-0.4
1988	SF-N	92	273	23	64	13	1	8	27	13	46	.234	.269	.377	87	-7	-5	26	0	2	-1	-8	C/1	-1.0
1989	Bal-A	85	278	22	67	10	1	1	32	15	53	.241	.280	.295	64	-14	-13	20	1	4	-2	-13	C/D	-2.5
1990	Bal-A	93	301	30	73	14	1	5	37	11	53	.243	.269	.346	72	-13	-12	26	0	1	-1	0	CD/1	-0.9
Total	6	484	1448	140	331	63	6	30	156	74	286	.229	.266	.343	70	-66	-60	121	4	13	-7	-3	C/D13	-4.7

■ MINNIE MENDOZA
Mendoza, Cristobal Rigoberto (Carreras) b: 11/16/33, Ceiba Del Agua, Cuba BR/TR, 6', 180 lbs. Deb: 4/09/70

YEAR	TM/L	G	AB	R	H	2B	3B	HR	RBI	BB	SO	AVG	OBP	SLG	PRO+	BR	/A	RC	SB	CS	SBR	FR	POS	TPR
1970	Min-A	16	16	2	3	0	0	0	2	0	1	.188	.188	.188	4	-2	-2	1	0	0	0	0	/32	-0.1

■ MARIO MENDOZA
Mendoza, Mario (Aizpuru) b: 12/26/50, Chihuahua, Mex. BR/TR, 5'11", 170 lbs. Deb: 4/26/74 C

YEAR	TM/L	G	AB	R	H	2B	3B	HR	RBI	BB	SO	AVG	OBP	SLG	PRO+	BR	/A	RC	SB	CS	SBR	FR	POS	TPR
1974	*Pit-N	91	163	10	36	1	2	0	15	8	35	.221	.262	.252	46	-12	-11	10	1	1	-0	5	S	0.3
1975	Pit-N	56	50	8	9	1	0	0	2	3	11	.180	.226	.200	19	-5	-5	2	0	0	0	8	S/3	0.9
1976	Pit-N	50	92	6	17	5	0	0	12	4	15	.185	.219	.239	30	-9	-9	4	0	1	-1	12	S/32	0.7
1977	Pit-N	70	81	5	16	3	0	0	4	3	10	.198	.226	.235	23	-9	-9	4	0	0	0	12	S3/P	0.9
1978	Pit-N	57	55	5	12	1	0	1	3	2	9	.218	.283	.291	58	-3	-3	5	3	1	0	9	23S	0.9
1979	Sea-A	148	373	26	74	10	3	1	29	9	62	.198	.219	.249	26	-39	-40	19	3	0	1	28	*S	0.7
1980	Sea-A	114	277	27	68	6	3	2	14	16	42	.245	.287	.310	63	-14	-14	24	3	4	-2	7	*S	-0.8
1981	Tex-A	88	229	18	53	6	1	0	22	7	25	.231	.257	.266	54	-14	-13	15	2	1	0	-1	S	-0.8
1982	Tex-A	12	17	1	2	0	0	0	0	0	4	.118	.118	.118	-37	-3	-3	0	0	0	0	2	S/D	0.0
Total	9	686	1337	106	287	33	9	4	101	52	219	.215	.247	.262	41	-108	-107	84	12	8	-1	81	S/32DP	3.6

■ MIKE MENDOZA
Mendoza, Michael Joseph b: 11/26/55, Inglewood, Cal. BR/TR, 6'5", 215 lbs. Deb: 9/07/79

YEAR	TM/L	G	AB	R	H	2B	3B	HR	RBI	BB	SO	AVG	OBP	SLG	PRO+	BR	/A	RC	SB	CS	SBR	FR	POS	TPR
1979	Hou-N	2	0	0	0	0	0	0	0	0	0	—	—	—	—	0	0	0	0	0	0	0	/P	0.0

■ JOCK MENEFEE
Menefee, John b: 1/15/1868, West Virginia d: 3/11/53, Belle Vernon, Pa. BR/TR, 6', Deb: 8/17/1892

YEAR	TM/L	G	AB	R	H	2B	3B	HR	RBI	BB	SO	AVG	OBP	SLG	PRO+	BR	/A	RC	SB	CS	SBR	FR	POS	TPR
1892	Pit-N	2	3	0	0	0	0	0	0	0	0	.000	.000	.000	-99	-1	-1	0	0			0	/OP	0.0
1893	Lou-N	22	73	10	20	2	1	0	12	13	5	.274	.391	.329	102	0	1	10	2			2	P/O	0.0

YEAR	TM/L	G	AB	R	H	2B	3B	HR	RBI	BB	SO	AVG	OBP	SLG	PRO+	BR	/A	RC	SB	CS	SBR	FR	POS	TPR
1894	Lou-N	29	79	7	13	1	0	0	4	8	7	.165	.250	.177	6	-12	-11	4	2			3	P/2	0.0
	Pit-N	13	47	6	12	1	2	0	7	3	3	.255	.300	.362	61	-3	-3	6	2			2	P	0.0
	Yr	42	126	13	25	2	2	0	11	11	10	.198	.268	.246	27	-15	-14	10	4			5		0.0
1895	Pit-N	2	0	0	0	0	0	0	0	0	0	—	—	—	—	0	0	0	0			0	/P	0.0
1898	NY-N	1	5	0	0	0	0	0	0	0	0	.000	.000	.000	-99	-1	-1	0	0			0	/P	0.0
1900	Chi-N	17	46	5	5	0	0	0	4	2		.109	.180	.109	-19	-7	-7	1	0			-2	P	0.0
1901	Chi-N	48	152	19	39	5	3	0	13	8		.257	.311	.329	91	-2	-1	18	4			-1	OP/12	0.0
1902	Chi-N	65	216	24	50	4	1	0	15	15		.231	.303	.259	78	-5	-5	21	4			-3	OP1/32	-0.6
1903	Chi-N	22	64	3	13	3	0	0	2	3		.203	.239	.250	42	-5	-5	4	0			3	P/1	0.0
Total	9	221	685	74	152	16	7	0	57	52	15	.222	.291	.266	61	-37	-32	64	14			4	P/0123	-0.6

■ DENIS MENKE

Menke, Denis John b: 7/21/40, Algona, Iowa BR/TR, 6', 185 lbs. Deb: 4/14/62 C

YEAR	TM/L	G	AB	R	H	2B	3B	HR	RBI	BB	SO	AVG	OBP	SLG	PRO+	BR	/A	RC	SB	CS	SBR	FR	POS	TPR
1962	Mil-N	50	146	12	28	3	1	2	16	16	38	.192	.280	.267	49	-11	-10	11	0	1	-1	5	23/S10	-0.2
1963	Mil-N	146	518	58	121	16	4	11	50	37	106	.234	.292	.344	83	-12	-11	51	6	7	-2	13	S32/10	0.9
1964	Mil-N	151	505	79	143	29	5	20	65	68	77	.283	.373	.479	137	26	26	91	4	2	0	2	*S2/3	4.0
1965	Mil-N	71	181	16	44	13	1	4	18	18	28	.243	.315	.392	97	-1	-1	22	1	3	-2	-7	S/13	-0.3
1966	Atl-N	138	454	55	114	20	4	15	60	71	87	.251	.360	.412	112	10	10	68	0	7	-4	-22	*S3/1	-0.9
1967	Atl-N	129	418	37	95	14	3	7	39	65	62	.227	.335	.325	91	-3	-3	48	5	7	-3	-22	*S/3	-1.4
1968	Hou-N	150	542	56	135	23	6	6	56	64	81	.249	.335	.347	107	5	6	65	5	8	-3	-17	*2S/13	-0.3
1969	Hou-N	154	553	72	149	25	5	10	90	87	87	.269	.373	.387	115	12	14	81	2	7	-4	-9	*S2/13	1.8
1970	Hou-N	154	562	82	171	26	6	13	92	82	80	.304	.398	.441	130	22	25	103	6	5	-1	-15	*S2/130	2.7
1971	Hou-N	146	475	57	117	26	3	1	43	59	68	.246	.332	.320	88	-8	-6	51	4	5	-2	-3	*13S/2	-1.6
1972	*Cin-N	140	447	41	104	19	2	9	50	58	76	.233	.327	.345	97	-4	-1	53	0	1	-1	0	*31	-0.2
1973	*Cin-N	139	241	38	46	10	0	3	26	69	53	.191	.375	.270	86	-2	-1	29	1	1	-0	16	*3/S21	1.4
1974	Hou-N	30	29	2	3	1	0	0	4	10	9	.103	.212	.138	-1	-4	-4	1	0	0	0	3	1/32S	0.0
Total	13	1598	5071	605	1270	225	40	101	606	698	853	.250	.346	.370	104	32	45	675	34	54	-22	-56	S321/O	5.9

■ MIKE MENOSKY

Menosky, Michael William "Leaping Mike" b: 10/16/1894, Glen Campbell, Pa. d: 4/11/83, Detroit, Mich. BL/TR, 5'10", 163 lbs. Deb: 4/18/14

YEAR	TM/L	G	AB	R	H	2B	3B	HR	RBI	BB	SO	AVG	OBP	SLG	PRO+	BR	/A	RC	SB	CS	SBR	FR	POS	TPR
1914	Pit-F	68	140	26	37	4	1	2	9	16	30	.264	.352	.350	102	1	1	20	5			-3	O	-0.3
1915	Pit-F	17	21	3	2	0	0	0	1	2	0	.095	.208	.095	-9	-3	-3	1	2			-2	/O	-0.5
1916	Was-A	11	37	5	6	1	1	0	3	1	10	.162	.184	.243	29	-3	-3	2	1			1	/O	-0.2
1917	Was-A	114	322	46	83	12	10	1	34	45	55	.258	.359	.366	123	9	10	48	22			7	O	1.3
1919	Was-A	116	342	62	98	15	3	6	39	44	46	.287	.379	.401	120	10	10	54	13			0	*O	0.3
1920	Bos-A	141	532	80	158	24	9	3	64	65	52	.297	.383	.393	111	7	10	82	23	19	-5	-3	*O	-0.8
1921	Bos-A	133	477	77	143	18	5	3	45	60	45	.300	.388	.377	99	-0	2	75	12	6	0	-4	*O	-1.1
1922	Bos-A	126	406	61	115	16	5	0	32	40	33	.283	.355	.369	90	-6	-5	55	9	5	-0	6	*O	-0.6
1923	Bos-A	84	188	22	43	8	4	0	25	22	19	.229	.310	.314	64	-10	-10	18	3	6	-3	3	O	-1.3
Total	9	810	2465	382	685	98	38	18	252	295	290	.278	.364	.370	101	4	11	356	90	36		7	O	-3.2

■ ED MENSOR

Mensor, Edward "The Midget" b: 11/7/1886, Woodville, Ore. d: 4/20/70, Salem, Ore. BB, 5'6", 145 lbs. Deb: 7/15/12

YEAR	TM/L	G	AB	R	H	2B	3B	HR	RBI	BB	SO	AVG	OBP	SLG	PRO+	BR	/A	RC	SB	CS	SBR	FR	POS	TPR
1912	Pit-N	39	99	19	26	3	2	0	1	23	12	.263	.402	.333	104	2	2	17	10			0	O	0.1
1913	Pit-N	44	56	9	10	1	0	0	1	8	13	.179	.292	.196	43	-4	-4	4	2			3	O/2S	0.0
1914	Pit-N	44	89	15	18	2	1	1	6	22	13	.202	.372	.281	99	1	1	11	2			1	O	0.2
Total	3	127	244	43	54	6	3	1	8	53	38	.221	.367	.283	89	-2	-0	31	14			4	/OS2	0.3

■ TED MENZE

Menze, Theodore Charles b: 11/4/1897, St.Louis, Mo. d: 12/23/69, St.Louis, Mo. BR/TR, 5'9", 172 lbs. Deb: 4/23/18

YEAR	TM/L	G	AB	R	H	2B	3B	HR	RBI	BB	SO	AVG	OBP	SLG	PRO+	BR	/A	RC	SB	CS	SBR	FR	POS	TPR
1918	StL-N	1	3	0	0	0	0	0	0	0	2	.000	.000	.000	-99	-1	-1	0	0			-0	/O	0.0

■ RUDY MEOLI

Meoli, Rudolph Bartholomew b: 5/1/51, Troy, N.Y. BL/TR, 5'9", 165 lbs. Deb: 9/09/71

YEAR	TM/L	G	AB	R	H	2B	3B	HR	RBI	BB	SO	AVG	OBP	SLG	PRO+	BR	/A	RC	SB	CS	SBR	FR	POS	TPR
1971	Cal-A	7	3	0	0	0	0	0	0	0	1	.000	.000	.000	-99	-1	-1	0	0			0	H	0.0
1973	Cal-A	120	305	36	68	12	1	2	23	31	38	.223	.295	.289	70	-14	-11	26	2	4	-2	-2	S3/2	-0.1
1974	Cal-A	36	90	9	22	2	0	0	3	8	10	.244	.306	.267	70	-4	-3	6	2	4	-2	2	3/S12	-0.1
1975	Cal-A	70	126	12	27	2	1	0	6	15	20	.214	.298	.246	59	-7	-6	10	3	0	1	0	S32/D	0.0
1978	Chi-N	47	29	10	3	0	1	0	2	6	4	.103	.257	.172	20	-3	-3	2	1	0	0	6	/23	0.4
1979	Phi-N	30	73	2	13	4	1	0	6	9	15	.178	.268	.260	43	-6	-6	6	2	0	1	3	S2/3	0.1
Total	6	310	626	69	133	20	4	2	40	69	88	.212	.291	.267	61	-34	-30	51	10	8	-2	11	S/32D1	0.3

■ ORLANDO MERCADO

Mercado, Orlando (Rodriguez) b: 11/7/61, Arecibo, P.R. BR/TR, 6', 180 lbs. Deb: 9/13/82

YEAR	TM/L	G	AB	R	H	2B	3B	HR	RBI	BB	SO	AVG	OBP	SLG	PRO+	BR	/A	RC	SB	CS	SBR	FR	POS	TPR
1982	Sea-A	9	17	1	2	0	0	1	6	0	5	.118	.118	.294	8	-2	-2	1	0	0	0	1	/C	0.0
1983	Sea-A	66	178	10	35	11	2	1	16	14	27	.197	.259	.298	51	-12	-12	14	2	2	-1	4	C	-0.5
1984	Sea-A	30	78	5	17	3	1	0	5	4	12	.218	.265	.282	52	-5	-5	6	1	0	0	-5	C	-0.8
1986	Tex-A	46	102	7	24	1	1	1	7	6	13	.235	.284	.294	56	-6	-6	7	0	1	-1	16	C	1.2
1987	Det-A	10	22	2	3	0	0	0	1	2	0	.136	.208	.136	-6	-3	-3	1	0	0	0	3	C	0.1
	LA-N	7	5	1	3	1	0	0	1	1	1	.600	.667	.800	294	1	1	3	0	0	0	0	/C	0.2
1988	Oak-A	16	24	3	3	0	0	1	1	3	8	.125	.222	.250	33	-2	-2	2	0	0	0	0	C	0.0
1989	Min-A	19	38	1	4	0	0	0	1	4	4	.105	.190	.105	-14	-6	-6	1	1	0	0	4	C	0.0
1990	NY-N	42	90	10	19	1	0	3	7	8	11	.211	.290	.322	70	-4	-4	8	0	0	0	2	C	0.0
	Mon-N	8	8	0	2	0	0	0	0	0	1	.250	.250	.250	38	-1	-1	1	0	0	0	3	/C	0.2
	Yr	50	98	10	21	1	0	3	7	8	12	.214	.287	.316	67	-5	-4	8	0	0	0	5		0.2
Total	8	253	562	40	112	17	4	7	45	42	82	.199	.261	.281	48	-39	-40	42	4	3	-1	28	C	0.4

■ ORLANDO MERCED

Merced, Orlando Luis (Villanueva) b: 11/2/66, Hato Rey, P.R. BB/TR, 6', 180 lbs. Deb: 6/27/90

YEAR	TM/L	G	AB	R	H	2B	3B	HR	RBI	BB	SO	AVG	OBP	SLG	PRO+	BR	/A	RC	SB	CS	SBR	FR	POS	TPR
1990	Pit-N	25	24	3	5	1	0	0	0	1	9	.208	.240	.250	36	-2	-2	1	0	0	0	0	/CO	-0.1

■ WIN MERCER

Mercer, George Barclay b: 6/20/1874, Chester, W.Va. d: 1/12/03, San Francisco, Cal TR, 5'7", 140 lbs. Deb: 4/21/1894

YEAR	TM/L	G	AB	R	H	2B	3B	HR	RBI	BB	SO	AVG	OBP	SLG	PRO+	BR	/A	RC	SB	CS	SBR	FR	POS	TPR
1894	Was-N	52	162	27	46	5	2	2	29	9	20	.284	.322	.377	72	-8	-7	23	9			2	P/O	0.0
1895	Was-N	63	196	26	50	9	1	1	26	12	32	.255	.308	.327	66	-10	-10	22	7			-8	P/SO32	0.0
1896	Was-N	49	156	23	38	1	1	1	14	9	18	.244	.302	.282	56	-10	-10	16	9			1	P/O	0.0
1897	Was-N	48	135	22	43	2	5	0	19	6		.319	.357	.407	104	1	1	23	7			-1	P	0.0
1898	Was-N	80	249	38	80	3	5	2	25	18		.321	.369	.398	123	7	7	43	14			-8	PSO/32	0.5
1899	Was-N	108	375	73	112	6	7	1	35	32		.299	.360	.360	102	1	2	56	16			-14	3PO/S1	-0.6
1900	NY-N	76	248	32	73	4	0	0	27	26		.294	.366	.310	94	-2	-0	35	15			-1	P3O/S2	0.5
1901	Was-A	51	140	26	42	7	2	0	16	23		.300	.399	.379	121	5	5	26	10			-2	PO/1S3	0.7
1902	Det-A	35	100	8	18	2	0	0	6	6		.180	.226	.200	20	-11	-11	5	1			4	P	0.0
Total	9	562	1761	275	502	39	23	7	197	141	70	.285	.344	.345	89	-27	-23	249	88			-27	P/3OS12	1.1

■ JOHN MERCER

Mercer, John Locke b: 6/22/1892, Taylortown, La. d: 12/22/82, Shreveport, La. 5'10.5", 155 lbs. Deb: 6/25/12

YEAR	TM/L	G	AB	R	H	2B	3B	HR	RBI	BB	SO	AVG	OBP	SLG	PRO+	BR	/A	RC	SB	CS	SBR	FR	POS	TPR
1912	StL-N	1	1	0	0	0	0	0	0	0	0	.000	.000	.000	-99	-0	-0	0	0			-0	/1	0.0

■ ANDY MERCHANT

Merchant, James Anderson b: 8/30/50, Mobile, Ala. BL/TR, 5'11", 185 lbs. Deb: 9/28/75

YEAR	TM/L	G	AB	R	H	2B	3B	HR	RBI	BB	SO	AVG	OBP	SLG	PRO+	BR	/A	RC	SB	CS	SBR	FR	POS	TPR
1975	Bos-A	1	4	1	2	0	0	0	1	0	1	.500	.600	.500	197	1	1	1	0	0	0	-1	/C	0.0
1976	Bos-A	2	2	0	0	0	0	0	0	1	2	.000	.000	.000	-89	-0	-1	0	0	0	0	0	/C	0.0
Total	2	3	6	1	2	0	0	0	1	1	2	.333	.429	.333	109	0	0	1	0	0	0	-1	/C	0.0

YEAR	TM/L	G	AB	R	H	2B	3B	HR	RBI	BB	SO	AVG	OBP	SLG	PRO+	BR	/A	RC	SB	CS	SBR	FR	POS	TPR

■ ART MEREWETHER   Merewether, Arthur Francis "Merry" b: 7/1/02, E.Providence, R.I.   BR/TR, 5'9.5", 155 lbs.   Deb: 7/10/22

YEAR	TM/L	G	AB	R	H	2B	3B	HR	RBI	BB	SO	AVG	OBP	SLG	PRO+	BR	/A	RC	SB	CS	SBR	FR	POS	TPR
1922	Pit-N	1	1	0	0	0	0	0	0	0	0	.000	.000	.000	-99	-0	-0	0	0	0	0	0	H	0.0

■ FRED MERKLE   Merkle, Frederick Charles b: 12/20/1888, Watertown, Wis.   d: 3/2/56, Daytona Beach, Fla.   BR/TR, 6'1", 190 lbs.   Deb: 9/21/07   C

YEAR	TM/L	G	AB	R	H	2B	3B	HR	RBI	BB	SO	AVG	OBP	SLG	PRO+	BR	/A	RC	SB	CS	SBR	FR	POS	TPR
1907	NY-N	15	47	0	12	1	0	0	5	1		.255	.271	.277	71	-2	-2	4	0			-1	1	-0.3
1908	NY-N	38	41	6	11	2	1	1	7	4		.268	.333	.439	142	2	2	6	0			-2	1/O23	0.0
1909	NY-N	79	236	15	45	9	1	0	20	16		.191	.245	.237	49	-14	-14	15	8			-3	1/2	-2.0
1910	NY-N	144	506	75	148	35	14	4	70	44	59	.292	.353	.441	131	18	18	86	23			1	*1	1.8
1911	*NY-N	149	541	80	153	24	10	12	84	43	60	.283	.342	.431	112	9	7	95	49			15	*1	1.7
1912	*NY-N	129	479	82	148	22	6	11	84	42	70	.309	.374	.449	121	16	14	93	37			-1	*1	0.7
1913	*NY-N	153	563	78	147	30	13	2	69	41	60	.261	.315	.371	95	-5	-5	72	35			-4	*1	-1.6
1914	NY-N	146	512	71	132	25	7	7	63	52	80	.258	.327	.375	112	5	7	66	23			3	*1	0.8
1915	NY-N	140	505	52	151	25	3	4	62	36	39	.299	.348	.384	129	13	16	70	20	15	-3	0	*1O	0.7
1916	NY-N	112	401	45	95	19	3	7	44	33	46	.237	.308	.352	108	1	3	49	17			0	*1	0.0
	*Bro-N	23	69	6	16	1	0	0	2	7	4	.232	.312	.246	70	-2	-2	6	2			-0	1/O	-0.3
	Yr	135	470	51	111	20	3	7	46	40	50	.236	.308	.336	102	-1	1	55	19			-0		-0.3
1917	Bro-N	2	8	1	1	1	0	0	0	0	1	.125	.125	.250	13	-1	-1	0	0			0	/1	0.0
	Chi-N	146	549	65	146	30	9	3	57	42	60	.266	.323	.370	104	7	3	67	13			-3	*1/O	-0.2
	Yr	148	557	66	147	31	9	3	57	42	61	.264	.320	.368	103	7	2	67	13			-3		-0.2
1918	*Chi-N	129	482	55	143	25	5	3	65	35	36	.297	.349	.388	122	14	13	71	21			1	*1	1.2
1919	Chi-N	133	498	52	133	20	6	3	62	33	35	.267	.315	.349	99	-1	-1	58	20			-10	*1/2	-1.3
1920	Chi-N	92	330	33	94	20	4	3	38	24	32	.285	.335	.397	108	4	3	43	3	5	-2	0	1/O	0.0
1925	NY-A	7	13	4	5	1	0	0	1	1	1	.385	.429	.462	128	1	1	3	1	0	0	-0	/1	0.0
1926	NY-A	1	2	0	0	0	0	0	0	0	0	.000	.000	.000	-99	-1	-1	0	0	0	0	0	/1	0.0
Total	16	1638	5782	720	1580	290	82	60	733	454	583	.273	.331	.383	109	64	59	804	272	20		-3	*1/O23	1.2

■ ED MERRILL   Merrill, Edward Mason b: 1860, Chicago, Ill.   d: 8/18/24, Chicago, Ill.   5'11", 176 lbs.   Deb: 6/20/1882

YEAR	TM/L	G	AB	R	H	2B	3B	HR	RBI	BB	SO	AVG	OBP	SLG	PRO+	BR	/A	RC	SB	CS	SBR	FR	POS	TPR
1882	Wor-N	2	8	0	1	0	0	0	4	0	1	.125	.125	.125	-19	-1	-1	0				-1	/3	-0.1
1884	Ind-a	55	196	14	35	3	1	0		6		.179	.207	.204	38	-13	-12	8				-4	2	-1.3
Total	2	57	204	14	36	3	1	0	4	6	1	.176	.204	.201	35	-14	-13	9				-4	/23	-1.4

■ LLOYD MERRIMAN   Merriman, Lloyd Archer "Citation" b: 8/2/24, Clovis, Cal.   BL/TL, 6', 190 lbs.   Deb: 4/24/49

YEAR	TM/L	G	AB	R	H	2B	3B	HR	RBI	BB	SO	AVG	OBP	SLG	PRO+	BR	/A	RC	SB	CS	SBR	FR	POS	TPR
1949	Cin-N	103	287	35	66	12	5	4	26	21	36	.230	.285	.348	68	-13	-14	28	2			-4	O	-2.1
1950	Cin-N	92	298	44	77	15	3	2	31	30	23	.258	.330	.349	79	-9	-9	36	6			-7	O	-1.8
1951	Cin-N	114	359	34	87	23	2	5	36	31	34	.242	.303	.359	76	-12	-13	41	8	4	0	4	*O	-1.1
1954	Cin-N	73	112	12	30	8	1	0	16	23	10	.268	.406	.357	98	1	1	19	3	0	1	-1	O	-0.2
1955	Chi-A	1	1	0	0	0	0	0	0	0	0	.000	.000	.000	-97	-0	-0	0	0	0	0	0	H	0.0
	Chi-N	72	145	15	31	6	1	1	8	21	21	.214	.313	.290	62	-8	-8	15	1	0	0	1	O	-0.6
Total	5	455	1202	140	291	64	12	12	117	126	124	.242	.317	.345	75	-40	-42	140	20	4		-7	O	-5.6

■ GEORGE MERRITT   Merritt, George Washington b: 4/14/1880, Paterson, N.J.   d: 2/21/38, Memphis, Tenn.   TR, 6', 160 lbs.   Deb: 9/06/01

YEAR	TM/L	G	AB	R	H	2B	3B	HR	RBI	BB	SO	AVG	OBP	SLG	PRO+	BR	/A	RC	SB	CS	SBR	FR	POS	TPR
1901	Pit-N	4	11	2	3	0	1	0	0	0		.273	.385	.455	141	1	1	2	0			-0	/P	0.0
1902	Pit-N	2	9	2	3	1	0	0	2	0		.333	.333	.444	137	0	0	1	0			1	/O	0.1
1903	Pit-N	9	27	4	4	0	1	0	3	2		.148	.207	.222	23	-3	-3	2	1			-2	/OP	-0.4
Total	3	15	47	8	10	1	2	0	5	2		.213	.275	.319	72	-2	-2	5	1			-1	/OP	-0.3

■ HERM MERRITT   Merritt, Herman G. b: 11/12/1900, Independence, Kan.   d: 5/26/27, Kansas City, Mo.   BR/TR,   Deb: 8/25/21

YEAR	TM/L	G	AB	R	H	2B	3B	HR	RBI	BB	SO	AVG	OBP	SLG	PRO+	BR	/A	RC	SB	CS	SBR	FR	POS	TPR
1921	Det-A	20	46	3	17	1	2	0	6	1	5	.370	.396	.478	123	1	2	9	1	0	0	-6	S	-0.1

■ JOHN MERRITT   Merritt, John Howard b: 10/12/1894, Tupelo, Miss.   d: 11/3/55, Tupelo, Miss.   5'11", 170 lbs.   Deb: 9/27/13

YEAR	TM/L	G	AB	R	H	2B	3B	HR	RBI	BB	SO	AVG	OBP	SLG	PRO+	BR	/A	RC	SB	CS	SBR	FR	POS	TPR
1913	NY-N	1	0	0	0	0	0	0	0	0	0	—	—	—	—	0	0	0	0			0	/O	0.0

■ BILL MERRITT   Merritt, William Henry b: 7/30/1870, Lowell, Mass.   d: 11/17/37, Lowell, Mass.   5'7", 160 lbs.   Deb: 8/08/1891

YEAR	TM/L	G	AB	R	H	2B	3B	HR	RBI	BB	SO	AVG	OBP	SLG	PRO+	BR	/A	RC	SB	CS	SBR	FR	POS	TPR
1891	Chi-N	11	42	4	9	1	0	0	4	2	2	.214	.250	.238	44	-3	-3	3	0			-3	C/1	-0.4
1892	Lou-N	46	168	22	33	4	2	1	13	11	15	.196	.246	.262	60	-9	-7	12	3			-2	C	-0.5
1893	Bos-N	39	141	30	49	6	3	3	26	13	13	.348	.403	.496	130	8	6	30	3			-4	C/O	0.4
1894	Bos-N	10	26	3	6	1	0	0	6	8	0	.231	.412	.269	64	-1	-1	3	0			1	/CO	0.4
	Pit-N	36	109	18	30	1	2	1	18	15	7	.275	.363	.349	75	-4	-4	15	2			-2	C/1O	-0.2
	Cin-N	29	113	17	37	6	1	1	21	9	3	.327	.387	.425	94	-0	-1	21	4			-4	C/31O	-0.1
	Yr	75	248	38	73	8	3	2	45	32	10	.294	.379	.375	82	-5	-6	39	6			-4		-0.3
1895	Cin-N	22	79	9	14	2	0	0	12	6	5	.177	.235	.203	14	-10	-10	4	2			-0	C/2	-0.7
	Pit-N	67	239	32	68	5	1	0	27	18	16	.285	.340	.314	75	-10	-7	27	2			-2	C/1	-0.2
	Yr	89	318	41	82	7	1	0	39	24	21	.258	.314	.286	59	-19	-18	31	4			-2		-0.9
1896	Pit-N	77	282	26	82	8	2	1	42	18	10	.291	.336	.344	84	-7	-6	34	3			2	C/321S	-0.5
1897	Pit-N	62	209	21	55	6	1	1	26	9		.263	.297	.316	66	-11	-10	21	2			-5	C/1	-0.5
1899	Bos-N	1	2	0	0	0	0	0	0	0		.000	.333	.000	-3	-0	-0	0	0			0	/C	0.0
Total	8	400	1410	182	383	40	12	8	195	109	71	.272	.327	.334	77	-48	-44	169	21			-18	C/1302S	-2.0

■ JACK MERSON   Merson, John Warren b: 1/17/22, Elk Ridge, Md.   BR/TR, 5'11", 175 lbs.   Deb: 9/14/51

YEAR	TM/L	G	AB	R	H	2B	3B	HR	RBI	BB	SO	AVG	OBP	SLG	PRO+	BR	/A	RC	SB	CS	SBR	FR	POS	TPR
1951	Pit-N	13	50	6	18	2	2	1	14	1	7	.360	.373	.540	138	3	3	10	0	0	0	2	2	0.5
1952	Pit-N	111	398	41	98	20	2	5	38	22	38	.246	.287	.344	72	-15	-16	38	1	1	-0	-6	23	-1.7
1953	Bos-A	1	4	0	0	0	0	0	0	0	0	.000	.000	.000	-95	-1	-1	0	0	0	0	0	/2	0.0
Total	3	125	452	47	116	22	4	6	52	23	45	.257	.294	.363	78	-13	-14	49	1	1	-0	-3	/23	-1.2

■ SAM MERTES   Mertes, Samuel Blair "Sandow" b: 8/6/1872, San Francisco, Cal.   d: 3/11/45, San Francisco, Cal   BR/TR, 5'10", 185 lbs.   Deb: 6/30/1896

YEAR	TM/L	G	AB	R	H	2B	3B	HR	RBI	BB	SO	AVG	OBP	SLG	PRO+	BR	/A	RC	SB	CS	SBR	FR	POS	TPR
1896	Phi-N	37	143	20	34	4	4	0	14	8	10	.238	.288	.322	63	-8	-8	19	19			-1	O/S2	-0.8
1898	Chi-N	83	269	45	80	4	8	1	47	34		.297	.388	.383	124	10	10	52	27			2	OS/21	0.8
1899	Chi-N	117	426	83	127	13	16	9	81	33		.298	.349	.467	129	13	15	87	45			-1	*O/1S	0.6
1900	Chi-N	127	481	72	142	25	4	7	60	42		.295	.356	.407	117	8	11	85	38			-4	O1/S	0.0
1901	Chi-A	137	545	94	151	16	17	5	98	52		.277	.346	.396	110	6	8	95	46			-6	*2/O	-0.3
1902	Chi-A	129	497	60	140	23	7	1	79	37		.282	.334	.362	99	-3	-0	78	46			6	*O/SCP123	0.0
1903	NY-N	138	517	100	145	32	14	7	104	61		.280	.356	.437	123	18	15	100	45			8	*O/C1	1.5
1904	NY-N	148	532	83	147	28	11	4	78	54		.276	.343	.393	124	18	15	92	47			1	*O/S	0.9
1905	*NY-N	150	551	81	154	27	17	5	108	56		.279	.346	.417	127	19	18	101	52			-11	*O	-0.3
1906	NY-N	71	253	37	60	9	6	1	33	29		.237	.316	.332	102	1	1	35	21			1	O	0.1
	StL-N	53	191	20	47	7	4	0	19	16		.246	.304	.325	102	-1	0	23	10			-6	O	-0.7
	Yr	124	444	57	107	16	10	1	52	45		.241	.311	.329	102	1	1	58	31			-5		-0.6
Total	10	1190	4405	695	1227	188	108	40	721	422	10	.279	.344	.398	115	82	85	768	396			-13	O2/1SC3P	1.8

■ LENNIE MERULLO   Merullo, Leonard Richard b: 5/5/17, Boston, Mass.   BR/TR, 5'11.5", 166 lbs.   Deb: 9/12/41

YEAR	TM/L	G	AB	R	H	2B	3B	HR	RBI	BB	SO	AVG	OBP	SLG	PRO+	BR	/A	RC	SB	CS	SBR	FR	POS	TPR
1941	Chi-N	7	17	3	6	1	0	0	1	2	0	.353	.421	.412	140	1	1	3	1			2	/S	0.3
1942	Chi-N	143	515	53	132	23	3	2	37	35	45	.256	.310	.324	89	-10	-7	52	14			-1	*S	0.2
1943	Chi-N	129	453	37	115	18	3	1	25	26	42	.254	.297	.313	78	-14	-13	42	7			-12	*S	-1.4
1944	Chi-N	66	193	20	41	8	1	1	16	16	18	.212	.276	.280	57	-11	-11	16	3			2	S/1	-0.1
1945	*Chi-N	121	394	40	94	18	0	2	37	31	30	.239	.297	.299	68	-18	-17	34	7			-4	*S	-0.8

YEAR	TM/L	G	AB	R	H	2B	3B	HR	RBI	BB	SO	AVG	OBP	SLG	PRO+	BR	/A	RC	SB	CS	SBR	FR	POS	TPR
1946	Chi-N	65	126	14	19	8	0	0	7	11	13	.151	.219	.214	24	-13	-13	6	2			18	S	0.9
1947	Chi-N	108	373	24	90	16	1	0	29	15	26	.241	.274	.290	52	-27	-25	28	4			7	*S	-0.9
Total	7	639	2071	191	497	92	8	6	152	136	174	.240	.291	.301	69	-92	-86	180	38			11	S/1	-1.8

■ **MATT MERULLO**   Merullo, Matthew Bates b: 8/4/65, Winchester, Mass.   BL/TR, 6'2", 200 lbs.   Deb: 4/12/89

YEAR	TM/L	G	AB	R	H	2B	3B	HR	RBI	BB	SO	AVG	OBP	SLG	PRO+	BR	/A	RC	SB	CS	SBR	FR	POS	TPR
1989	Chi-A	31	81	5	18	1	0	1	8	6	14	.222	.276	.272	56	-5	-5	6	0	1	-1	-4	C	-0.7

■ **STEVE MESNER**   Mesner, Stephan Mathias b: 1/13/18, Los Angeles, Cal. d: 4/6/81, San Diego, Cal.   BR/TR, 5'9", 178 lbs.   Deb: 9/23/38

YEAR	TM/L	G	AB	R	H	2B	3B	HR	RBI	BB	SO	AVG	OBP	SLG	PRO+	BR	/A	RC	SB	CS	SBR	FR	POS	TPR
1938	Chi-N	2	4	2	1	0	0	0	0	1	1	.250	.400	.250	80	-0	-0	1	0			-1	/S	0.0
1939	Chi-N	17	43	7	12	4	0	0	6	3	4	.279	.340	.372	90	-0	-1	5	0			1	S/23	0.1
1941	StL-N	24	69	8	10	1	0	0	10	5	6	.145	.203	.159	3	-9	-9	2	0			5	3	-0.3
1943	Cin-N	137	504	53	137	26	1	0	52	26	20	.272	.309	.327	85	-11	-10	50	6			1	*3	-1.0
1944	Cin-N	121	414	31	100	17	4	1	47	34	20	.242	.301	.309	75	-15	-14	38	1			-7	*3	-1.4
1945	Cin-N	150	540	52	137	19	1	1	52	52	18	.254	.322	.298	74	-19	-17	52	4			12	*3/2	-0.7
Total	6	451	1574	153	397	67	6	2	167	121	69	.252	.308	.306	75	-55	-51	149	11			11	3/S2	-3.3

■ **BOBBY MESSENGER**   Messenger, Charles Walter b: 3/19/1884, Bangor, Me. d: 7/10/61, Bath, Maine   BB/TR, 5'10.5", 165 lbs.   Deb: 8/30/09

YEAR	TM/L	G	AB	R	H	2B	3B	HR	RBI	BB	SO	AVG	OBP	SLG	PRO+	BR	/A	RC	SB	CS	SBR	FR	POS	TPR
1909	Chi-A	31	112	18	19	1	1	0	0	13		.170	.268	.196	49	-6	-6	8	7			-1	O	-0.9
1910	Chi-A	9	26	7	6	0	1	0	4	4		.231	.375	.308	119	1	1	4	3			-0	/O	0.0
1911	Chi-A	13	17	4	2	0	1	0	0	3		.118	.250	.235	37	-1	-1	1	0			-1	/O	-0.1
1914	StL-A	1	2	0	0	0	0	0	0	0	0	.000	.000	.000	-99	-0	-0	0	0			-0	/O	0.0
Total	4	54	157	29	27	1	3	0	4	20	0	.172	.282	.217	57	-7	-7	13	10			-2	/O	-1.0

■ **TOM MESSITT**   Messitt, Thomas John b: 7/27/1874, Frankfort, Pa. d: 9/22/34, Chicago, Ill.   5'9", 177 lbs.   Deb: 9/14/1899

YEAR	TM/L	G	AB	R	H	2B	3B	HR	RBI	BB	SO	AVG	OBP	SLG	PRO+	BR	/A	RC	SB	CS	SBR	FR	POS	TPR
1899	Lou-N	3	11	0	1	0	0	0	0	0		.091	.091	.091	-49	-2	-2	0	0			1	/C	0.0

■ **AL METCALF**   Metcalf, Al b: Brooklyn, N.Y.   Deb: 5/27/1875

YEAR	TM/L	G	AB	R	H	2B	3B	HR	RBI	BB	SO	AVG	OBP	SLG	PRO+	BR	/A	RC	SB	CS	SBR	FR	POS	TPR
1875	Mut-n	8	31	2	7	0	0	0		1		.226	.250	.226	62	-1	-1	2					/3OS	0.0

■ **SCAT METHA**   Metha, Frank Joseph b: 12/13/13, Los Angeles, Cal. d: 3/2/75, Fountain Valley, Cal.   BR/TR, 5'11", 165 lbs.   Deb: 4/22/40

YEAR	TM/L	G	AB	R	H	2B	3B	HR	RBI	BB	SO	AVG	OBP	SLG	PRO+	BR	/A	RC	SB	CS	SBR	FR	POS	TPR
1940	Det-A	26	37	6	9	0	1	0	3	2	8	.243	.282	.297	46	-3	-3	3	0	1	-1	4	2/3	0.1

■ **BUD METHENY**   Metheny, Arthur Beauregard b: 6/1/15, St.Louis, Mo.   BL/TL, 5'11", 190 lbs.   Deb: 4/27/43

YEAR	TM/L	G	AB	R	H	2B	3B	HR	RBI	BB	SO	AVG	OBP	SLG	PRO+	BR	/A	RC	SB	CS	SBR	FR	POS	TPR
1943	*NY-A	103	360	51	94	18	2	9	36	39	34	.261	.333	.397	113	5	5	49	2	3	-1	-16	O	-1.5
1944	NY-A	137	518	72	124	16	1	14	67	56	57	.239	.316	.355	89	-6	-8	59	5	5	-2	-11	*O	-2.6
1945	NY-A	133	509	64	126	18	2	8	53	54	31	.248	.325	.338	88	-5	-8	60	5	2	0	-9	*O	-2.3
1946	NY-A	3	3	0	0	0	0	0	0	0	0	.000	.000	.000	-99	-1	-1	0	0	0	0	0	H	0.0
Total	4	376	1390	187	344	52	5	31	156	149	122	.247	.323	.359	94	-6	-11	169	12	10	-2	-37	O	-6.4

■ **CATFISH METKOVICH**   Metkovich, George Michael b: 10/8/21, Angel's Camp, Cal.   BL/TR, 6'1", 185 lbs.   Deb: 7/16/43

YEAR	TM/L	G	AB	R	H	2B	3B	HR	RBI	BB	SO	AVG	OBP	SLG	PRO+	BR	/A	RC	SB	CS	SBR	FR	POS	TPR
1943	Bos-A	78	321	34	79	14	4	5	27	19	38	.246	.294	.361	90	-5	-5	34	1	3	-2	-4	O/1	-1.4
1944	Bos-A	134	549	94	152	28	8	9	59	31	57	.277	.319	.406	108	2	3	73	13	4	2	4	O1	0.3
1945	Bos-A	138	539	65	140	26	3	5	62	51	70	.260	.331	.347	94	-2	-4	67	19	6	2	-3	1O	-0.9
1946	*Bos-A	86	281	42	69	15	2	4	25	36	39	.246	.333	.356	88	-2	-4	37	8	3	1	-12	O	-2.0
1947	Cle-A	126	473	68	120	22	7	5	40	32	51	.254	.302	.362	86	-12	-10	52	5	3	-0	-2	*O/1	-1.8
1949	Chi-A	93	338	50	80	9	4	5	45	41	24	.237	.321	.331	75	-14	-12	34	5	4	-1	-8	O1	-2.2
1951	Pit-N	120	423	51	124	21	3	3	40	28	23	.293	.338	.378	90	-5	-6	54	3	2	-0	-2	O1	-1.1
1952	Pit-N	125	373	41	101	18	3	7	41	32	29	.271	.335	.391	98	0	-1	50	5	2	0	-6	1O	-0.9
1953	Pit-N	26	41	5	6	0	1	1	7	6	3	.146	.255	.268	37	-4	-4	3	0	0	0	-0	/1O	-0.3
	Chi-N	61	124	19	29	9	0	2	12	16	10	.234	.326	.355	76	-4	-4	14	2	1	0	-0	O/1	-0.5
	Yr	87	165	24	35	9	1	3	19	22	13	.212	.309	.333	66	-8	-8	17	2	1	0	-0		-0.8
1954	Mil-N	68	123	7	34	5	1	1	15	15	15	.276	.360	.358	94	-2	-1	15	0	0	0	2	1O	0.0
Total	10	1055	3585	476	934	167	36	47	373	307	359	.261	.323	.367	91	-47	-49	434	61	28	2	-32	O1	-10.8

■ **CHARLIE METRO**   Metro, Charles (b: Charles Moreskonich) b: 4/28/19, Nanty-Glo, Pa.   BR/TR, 5'11.5", 178 lbs.   Deb: 5/04/43   MC

YEAR	TM/L	G	AB	R	H	2B	3B	HR	RBI	BB	SO	AVG	OBP	SLG	PRO+	BR	/A	RC	SB	CS	SBR	FR	POS	TPR
1943	Det-A	44	40	12	8	0	2	0	3	6	.200	.256	.200	32	-3	-4	2	1	1	-0	4	O	0.0
1944	Det-A	38	78	8	15	2	1	0	5	3	10	.192	.222	.218	25	-8	-8	4	1	0	0	2	O	-0.6
	Phi-A	24	40	4	4	0	0	0	1	7	6	.100	.234	.100	-3	-5	-5	1	0	0	0	1	O/32	-0.3
	Yr	62	118	12	19	2	1	0	6	10	16	.161	.227	.178	16	-13	-13	5	1	0	0	3		-0.9
1945	Phi-A	65	200	18	42	10	1	3	15	23	33	.210	.291	.315	76	-6	-6	20	1	1	-0	-3	O	-1.2
Total	3	171	358	42	69	10	2	3	23	36	55	.193	.266	.257	51	-22	-23	27	3	2	-0	4	O/32	-2.1

■ **LENNY METZ**   Metz, Leonard Raymond b: 7/6/1899, Louisville, Colo. d: 2/24/53, Denver, Colo.   BR/TR, 5'10.5", 170 lbs.   Deb: 9/11/23

YEAR	TM/L	G	AB	R	H	2B	3B	HR	RBI	BB	SO	AVG	OBP	SLG	PRO+	BR	/A	RC	SB	CS	SBR	FR	POS	TPR
1923	Phi-N	12	37	4	8	0	0	0	3	4	3	.216	.310	.216	37	-3	-4	3	0	0	0	1	/2S	-0.1
1924	Phi-N	7	7	1	2	0	0	0	1	1	0	.286	.375	.286	71	-0	0	1	0	0	0	0	/S	0.0
1925	Phi-N	11	14	1	0	0	0	0	0	0	2	.000	.000	.000	-92	-4	-4	0	0	0	0	2	/S2	-0.1
Total	3	30	58	6	10	0	0	0	4	5	5	.172	.250	.172	11	-7	-8	4	0	0	0	3	/S2	-0.2

■ **ROGER METZGER**   Metzger, Roger Henry b: 10/10/47, Fredericksburg, Tex   BB/TR, 6', 165 lbs.   Deb: 6/16/70

YEAR	TM/L	G	AB	R	H	2B	3B	HR	RBI	BB	SO	AVG	OBP	SLG	PRO+	BR	/A	RC	SB	CS	SBR	FR	POS	TPR
1970	Chi-N	1	2	0	0	0	0	0	0	0	0	.000	.000	.000	-89	-1	-1	0	0	0	0	1	/S	0.1
1971	Hou-N	150	562	64	132	14	11	0	26	44	50	.235	.295	.299	70	-23	-21	52	15	6	1	-5	*S	-0.5
1972	Hou-N	153	641	84	142	12	3	2	38	60	71	.222	.289	.259	58	-35	-34	52	23	9	2	5	*S	-0.9
1973	Hou-N	154	580	67	145	11	14	1	35	39	70	.250	.301	.322	73	-22	-21	57	10	4	1	-19	*S	-1.9
1974	Hou-N	143	572	66	145	18	10	0	30	37	73	.253	.299	.320	76	-21	-18	54	9	7	-2	-10	*S	-1.4
1975	Hou-N	127	450	54	102	7	9	2	26	41	39	.227	.291	.296	68	-22	-19	40	4	5	-2	11	*S	0.5
1976	Hou-N	152	481	37	101	13	8	0	29	52	63	.210	.287	.270	65	-25	-20	38	1	1	-0	-3	*S/2	-1.0
1977	Hou-N	97	269	24	50	9	6	0	16	32	24	.186	.272	.264	49	-21	-18	20	2	0	1	-4	S/2	-0.7
1978	Hou-N	45	123	11	27	4	1	0	6	12	9	.220	.289	.268	61	-7	-6	8	0	0	0	-4	S/2	-0.6
	SF-N	75	235	17	61	6	1	0	17	12	17	.260	.296	.294	68	-11	-10	21	8	1	2	-12	S	-1.4
	Yr	120	358	28	88	10	2	0	23	24	26	.246	.293	.285	66	-18	-16	30	8	1	2	-16		-2.0
1979	SF-N	94	259	24	65	7	8	0	31	33	31	.251	.312	.340	83	-8	-6	28	11	3	2	2	S2/3	0.6
1980	SF-N	28	27	5	2	0	0	0	0	3	2	.074	.167	.074	-31	-5	-5	0	0	0	0	3	S/2	0.3
Total	11	1219	4201	453	972	101	71	5	254	355	449	.231	.293	.293	67	-200	-178	372	83	36	3	-35	*S/23	-7.2

■ **WILLIAM METZIG**   Metzig, William Andrew b: 12/4/18, Ft.Dodge, Iowa   BR/TR, 6'1", 180 lbs.   Deb: 9/19/44

YEAR	TM/L	G	AB	R	H	2B	3B	HR	RBI	BB	SO	AVG	OBP	SLG	PRO+	BR	/A	RC	SB	CS	SBR	FR	POS	TPR
1944	Chi-A	5	16	1	2	0	0	0	1	1	4	.125	.176	.125	-13	-2	-2	0	0	0	0	2	/2	0.0

■ **ALEX METZLER**   Metzler, Alexander b: 1/4/03, Fresno, Cal. d: 11/30/73, Fresno, Cal.   BL/TR, 5'9", 167 lbs.   Deb: 9/16/25

YEAR	TM/L	G	AB	R	H	2B	3B	HR	RBI	BB	SO	AVG	OBP	SLG	PRO+	BR	/A	RC	SB	CS	SBR	FR	POS	TPR
1925	Chi-N	9	38	2	7	2	0	0	2	3	7	.184	.244	.237	23	-4	-4	2	0	0	0	2	/O	-0.1
1926	Phi-N	20	67	8	16	3	0	0	12	7	5	.239	.311	.284	53	-4	-5	6	1	0	0	2	O	-0.3
1927	Chi-A	134	543	87	173	29	11	3	61	61	39	.319	.396	.429	117	13	15	89	15	11	-2	16	*O	1.9
1928	Chi-A	139	464	71	141	18	14	3	55	77	30	.304	.410	.422	121	16	17	86	16	8	0	-4	*O	0.5
1929	Chi-A	146	568	80	156	23	13	2	49	80	45	.275	.367	.371	92	-6	-5	83	11	4	1	1	*O	-0.7
1930	Chi-A	56	79	12	14	4	0	0	5	11	6	.177	.278	.228	31	-8	-8	5	0	2	-1	-5	O	-1.3
	StL-A	56	209	30	54	6	3	1	23	21	12	.258	.326	.330	65	-10	-11	24	5	1	1	-5	O	-1.5
	Yr	112	288	42	68	10	3	1	28	32	18	.236	.313	.302	57	-19	-19	29	5	3	-0	-10		-2.8

YEAR	TM/L	G	AB	R	H	2B	3B	HR	RBI	BB	SO	AVG	OBP	SLG	PRO+	BR	/A	RC	SB	CS	SBR	FR	POS	TPR
Total	6	560	1968	290	561	85	41	9	207	260	144	.285	.374	.384	97	-4	-1	296	48	26	-1	7	O	-1.5

■ HENSLEY MEULENS
Meulens, Hensley Filemon Acasio "Bam-Bam" b: 6/23/67, Curaco, Neth.Antilles BR/TR, 6'4", 200 lbs. Deb: 8/23/89

YEAR	TM/L	G	AB	R	H	2B	3B	HR	RBI	BB	SO	AVG	OBP	SLG	PRO+	BR	/A	RC	SB	CS	SBR	FR	POS	TPR
1989	NY-A	8	28	2	5	0	0	0	1	2	8	.179	.233	.179	18	-3	-3	1	0	1	-1	2	/3	0.0
1990	NY-A	23	83	12	20	7	0	3	10	9	25	.241	.337	.434	113	2	1	12	1	0	0	0	O	0.2
Total	2	31	111	14	25	7	0	3	11	11	33	.225	.312	.369	90	-1	-1	13	1	1	-0	3	/O3	0.2

■ IRISH MEUSEL
Meusel, Emil Frederick b: 6/9/1893, Oakland, Cal. d: 3/1/63, Long Beach, Cal. BR/TR, 5'11.5", 178 lbs. Deb: 10/01/14 C

YEAR	TM/L	G	AB	R	H	2B	3B	HR	RBI	BB	SO	AVG	OBP	SLG	PRO+	BR	/A	RC	SB	CS	SBR	FR	POS	TPR
1914	Was-A	1	2	0	0	0	0	0	0	0	0	.000	.000	.000	-97	-0	-0	0	0			-0	/O	0.0
1918	Phi-N	124	473	48	132	25	6	4	62	30	21	.279	.323	.383	108	7	4	61	18			9	*O/2	0.7
1919	Phi-N	135	521	65	159	26	7	5	59	15	13	.305	.327	.411	113	11	7	74	24			-2	*O	0.1
1920	Phi-N	138	518	75	160	27	8	14	69	32	27	.309	.349	.473	129	21	18	83	17	11	-2	0	*O/1	1.0
1921	Phi-N	84	343	59	121	21	7	12	51	18	17	.353	.385	.560	136	22	18	72	8	4	0	1	O	1.4
	*NY-N	62	243	37	80	12	6	2	36	15	12	.329	.373	.465	117	6	6	38	5	9	-4	-0	O	0.0
	Yr	146	586	96	201	33	13	14	87	33	29	.343	.380	.515	129	28	24	110	13	13	-4	0		1.4
1922	*NY-N	154	617	100	204	28	17	16	132	35	33	.331	.369	.509	123	20	19	112	12	10	-2	-12	*O	0.0
1923	*NY-N	146	595	102	177	22	14	19	125	38	16	.297	.341	.477	115	9	10	94	8	8	-2	-12	*O	-0.7
1924	*NY-N	139	549	75	170	26	9	6	102	33	18	.310	.351	.423	109	4	6	81	11	7	-1	-7	*O	-0.4
1925	NY-N	135	516	82	169	35	8	21	111	26	19	.328	.363	.548	135	20	23	100	5	4	-1	-6	*O	1.1
1926	NY-N	129	449	51	131	25	10	6	65	16	18	.292	.322	.432	103	-1	-0	60	5			-11	*O	-1.5
1927	Bro-N	42	74	7	18	3	1	1	7	11	5	.243	.341	.351	85	-1	-1	9	0			-1	O	-0.2
Total	11	1289	4900	701	1521	250	93	106	819	269	199	.310	.348	.464	118	118	110	783	113	53		-41	*O/21	1.5

■ BOB MEUSEL
Meusel, Robert William "Long Bob" b: 7/19/1896, San Jose, Cal. d: 11/28/77, Downey, Cal. BR/TR, 6'3", 190 lbs. Deb: 4/14/20

YEAR	TM/L	G	AB	R	H	2B	3B	HR	RBI	BB	SO	AVG	OBP	SLG	PRO+	BR	/A	RC	SB	CS	SBR	FR	POS	TPR
1920	NY-A	119	460	75	151	40	7	11	83	20	72	.328	.359	.517	126	17	15	83	4	4	-1	-10	O3/1	0.1
1921	*NY-A	149	598	104	190	40	16	24	135	34	88	.318	.356	.559	128	22	21	117	17	6	2	5	*O	1.4
1922	*NY-A	121	473	61	151	26	11	16	84	40	58	.319	.376	.522	129	20	19	91	13	9	-2	0	*O	0.8
1923	*NY-A	132	460	59	144	29	10	9	91	31	52	.313	.359	.478	117	10	9	74	13	15	-5	-7	*O	-1.2
1924	NY-A	143	579	93	188	40	11	12	120	32	43	.325	.365	.494	120	14	14	102	26	14	-1	-7	*O/3	-0.3
1925	NY-A	156	624	101	181	34	12	33	138	54	55	.290	.348	.542	125	16	18	112	10	14	-5	-9	*O3	-0.5
1926	*NY-A	108	413	73	130	22	3	12	81	37	32	.315	.373	.470	120	10	11	68	16	17	-5	-5	*O	-0.7
1927	*NY-A	135	516	75	174	47	9	8	103	45	58	.337	.393	.510	137	24	26	96	24	10	1	-4	*O	1.4
1928	*NY-A	131	518	77	154	45	5	11	113	39	56	.297	.349	.467	116	8	10	82	6	9	-4	4	*O	0.3
1929	NY-A	100	391	46	102	15	3	10	57	17	42	.261	.292	.391	79	-16	-13	43	1	5	-3	3	O	-1.5
1930	Cin-N	113	443	62	128	30	8	10	62	26	63	.289	.330	.460	93	-10	-6	65	9			-13	*O	-2.3
Total	11	1407	5475	826	1693	368	95	156	1067	375	619	.309	.356	.497	119	116	123	932	139	103		-42	*O/31	-2.5

■ BENNY MEYER
Meyer, Bernhard "Earache" b: 1/1/1888, Hematite, Mo. d: 2/6/74, Festus, Mo. BR/TR, 5'9", 170 lbs. Deb: 4/09/13 C

YEAR	TM/L	G	AB	R	H	2B	3B	HR	RBI	BB	SO	AVG	OBP	SLG	PRO+	BR	/A	RC	SB	CS	SBR	FR	POS	TPR
1913	Bro-N	38	87	12	17	0	1	1	10	10	14	.195	.278	.253	51	-5	-6	8	8			-0	O/C	-0.5
1914	Bal-F	143	500	76	152	18	10	5	40	71	53	.304	.395	.410	127	23	20	95	23			-10	*O/S	0.4
1915	Bal-F	35	120	20	29	2	0	0	5	37	13	.242	.424	.258	101	4	3	17	6			-3	O	-0.1
	Buf-F	93	333	37	77	8	6	1	29	40	37	.231	.316	.300	81	-6	-7	36	9			-6	O	-1.8
	Yr	128	453	57	106	10	6	1	34	77	50	.234	.348	.289	87	-2	-4	53	15			-9		-1.9
1925	Phi-N	1	1	1	1	1	0	0	0	0	0	1.000	1.000	2.000	594	1	1	2	0	0	0	0	/2	0.1
Total	4	310	1041	146	276	29	17	7	84	158	117	.265	.365	.346	104	16	12	157	46	0		-20	O/S2C	-1.9

■ DAN MEYER
Meyer, Daniel Thomas b: 8/3/52, Hamilton, Ohio BL/TR, 5'11", 180 lbs. Deb: 9/14/74

YEAR	TM/L	G	AB	R	H	2B	3B	HR	RBI	BB	SO	AVG	OBP	SLG	PRO+	BR	/A	RC	SB	CS	SBR	FR	POS	TPR
1974	Det-A	13	50	5	10	1	1	3	7	1	1	.200	.231	.440	86	-1	-1	4	1	0	0	-1	O	-0.1
1975	Det-A	122	470	56	111	17	3	8	47	26	25	.236	.279	.336	70	-18	-20	41	8	3	1	-11	O1	-3.6
1976	Det-A	105	294	37	74	8	4	2	16	17	22	.252	.293	.327	78	-7	-9	28	10	0	3	-10	O1/D	-1.8
1977	Sea-A	159	582	75	159	24	4	22	90	43	51	.273	.324	.442	107	4	5	77	11	8	-2	1	*1	-0.4
1978	Sea-A	123	444	38	101	18	1	8	56	24	39	.227	.267	.327	66	-21	-20	38	7	3	0	-1	*1/OD	-2.7
1979	Sea-A	144	525	72	146	21	7	20	74	29	35	.278	.321	.459	106	4	3	72	11	7	-1	-13	*3O1	-1.0
1980	Sea-A	146	531	56	146	25	6	11	71	31	42	.275	.316	.407	96	-4	-4	66	8	4	0	-15	*O/31D	-2.1
1981	Sea-A	83	252	26	66	10	1	3	22	10	16	.262	.293	.345	80	-6	-7	24	4	3	-1	3	3O/1D	-0.4
1982	Oak-A	120	383	28	92	17	3	8	59	18	33	.240	.274	.363	77	-15	-13	37	1	1	-0	-0	1DO	-1.4
1983	Oak-A	69	169	15	32	9	0	1	13	19	11	.189	.271	.260	50	-12	-11	11	0	0	0	-2	1DO/3	-1.4
1984	Oak-A	20	22	1	7	3	1	0	4	0	2	.318	.318	.545	143	1	1	3	0	0	0	0	/1D	0.1
1985	Oak-A	14	12	2	0	0	0	0	0	1	0	.000	.077	.000	-83	-3	-3	0	0	0	0	0	/3OD	-0.2
Total	12	1118	3734	411	944	153	31	86	459	219	277	.253	.296	.379	86	-77	-80	402	61	29	1	-49	1O3/D	-15.0

■ GEORGE MEYER
Meyer, George Francis b: 8/3/09, Chicago, Ill. BR/TR, 5'9", 160 lbs. Deb: 9/03/38

YEAR	TM/L	G	AB	R	H	2B	3B	HR	RBI	BB	SO	AVG	OBP	SLG	PRO+	BR	/A	RC	SB	CS	SBR	FR	POS	TPR
1938	Chi-A	24	81	10	24	2	2	0	9	11	17	.296	.387	.370	89	-1	-1	13	3	1	0	6	2	0.5

■ DUTCH MEYER
Meyer, Lambert Dalton b: 10/6/15, Waco, Tex. BR/TR, 5'10.5", 181 lbs. Deb: 6/23/37

YEAR	TM/L	G	AB	R	H	2B	3B	HR	RBI	BB	SO	AVG	OBP	SLG	PRO+	BR	/A	RC	SB	CS	SBR	FR	POS	TPR
1937	Chi-N	1	0	0	0	0	0	0	0	0	0	—	—	—	—	0	0	0	0			0	R	0.0
1940	Det-A	23	58	12	15	3	0	0	6	4	10	.259	.317	.310	58	-3	-4	7	2	0	1	0	2	-0.1
1941	Det-A	46	153	12	29	9	1	1	14	8	13	.190	.230	.281	31	-15	-17	10	1	1	-0	6	2	-0.6
1942	Det-A	14	52	5	17	3	0	2	9	4	4	.327	.386	.500	137	3	3	9	0	1	-1	6	2	0.9
1945	Cle-A	130	524	71	153	29	8	7	48	40	32	.292	.342	.418	125	12	14	74	2	4	-2	-32	*2	-1.8
1946	Cle-A	72	207	13	48	5	3	0	16	26	16	.232	.321	.285	75	-8	-6	20	0	1	-1	-13	2	-1.5
Total	6	286	994	113	262	49	12	10	93	82	75	.264	.322	.367	94	-11	-10	119	5	7		-32	2	-3.1

■ LEE MEYER
Meyer, Lee TR , Deb: 9/27/09

YEAR	TM/L	G	AB	R	H	2B	3B	HR	RBI	BB	SO	AVG	OBP	SLG	PRO+	BR	/A	RC	SB	CS	SBR	FR	POS	TPR
1909	Bro-N	7	23	1	3	0	0	0	0	2		.130	.200	.130	3	-3	-2	1	0			2	/S	0.0

■ SCOTT MEYER
Meyer, Scott William b: 8/19/57, Evergreen Park, Ill BR/TR, 6'1", 195 lbs. Deb: 9/10/78

YEAR	TM/L	G	AB	R	H	2B	3B	HR	RBI	BB	SO	AVG	OBP	SLG	PRO+	BR	/A	RC	SB	CS	SBR	FR	POS	TPR
1978	Oak-A	8	9	1	1	1	0	0	0	0	4	.111	.111	.222	-9	-1	-1	0	0	0	0	-0	/C	-0.1

■ JOEY MEYER
Meyer, Tanner Joe b: 5/10/62, Honolulu, Hawaii BR/TR, 6'3", 260 lbs. Deb: 4/04/88

YEAR	TM/L	G	AB	R	H	2B	3B	HR	RBI	BB	SO	AVG	OBP	SLG	PRO+	BR	/A	RC	SB	CS	SBR	FR	POS	TPR
1988	Mil-A	103	327	22	86	18	0	11	45	23	88	.263	.313	.419	102	1	0	41	0	1	-1	0	D1	-0.1
1989	Mil-A	53	147	13	33	6	0	7	29	12	36	.224	.283	.408	93	-2	-2	17	1	0	0	-1	D1	-0.2
Total	2	156	474	35	119	24	0	18	74	35	124	.251	.304	.416	100	-1	-2	58	1	1	-0	-1	/D1	-0.3

■ BILLY MEYER
Meyer, William Adam b: 1/14/1892, Knoxville, Tenn. d: 3/31/57, Knoxville, Tenn. BR/TR, 5'9.5", 170 lbs. Deb: 9/06/13 M

YEAR	TM/L	G	AB	R	H	2B	3B	HR	RBI	BB	SO	AVG	OBP	SLG	PRO+	BR	/A	RC	SB	CS	SBR	FR	POS	TPR
1913	Chi-A	1	1	0	1	0	0	0	0	0	0	1.000	1.000	1.000	490	0	0	1	0			1	/C	0.1
1916	Phi-A	50	138	6	32	2	2	1	12	8	11	.232	.274	.297	75	-5	-5	13	3			7	C	0.5
1917	Phi-A	62	162	9	38	5	1	0	9	7	14	.235	.271	.278	68	-7	-6	12	0			10	C	0.8
Total	3	113	301	15	71	7	3	1	21	15	25	.236	.274	.289	73	-11	-11	25	3			18	C	1.4

■ LEVI MEYERLE
Meyerle, Levi Samuel "Long Levi" b: 7/1845, Philadelphia, Pa. d: 11/4/21, Philadelphia, Pa. BR/TR, 6'1", 177 lbs. Deb: 5/20/1871

YEAR	TM/L	G	AB	R	H	2B	3B	HR	RBI	BB	SO	AVG	OBP	SLG	PRO+	BR	/A	RC	SB	CS	SBR	FR	POS	TPR
1871	Ath-n	26	130	45	64	9	3	4	40	2	1	.492	.500	.700	243	23	23	49	4				*3/P	1.3
1872	Ath-n	27	146	31	48	7	6	1		0		.329	.329	.479	145	7	7	24					O/S3	0.6
1873	Phi-n	48	237	53	83	14	6	2		2		.350	.356	.485	140	13	11	42					*3	0.6
1874	Chi-n	53	253	66	102	20	0	1		3		.403	.410	.494	185	24	23	53					23/OS	1.7
1875	Phi-n	68	300	55	96	13	9	1		0		.320	.320	.433	152	17	15	43					231	1.2

YEAR	TM/L	G	AB	R	H	2B	3B	HR	RBI	BB	SO	AVG	OBP	SLG	PRO+	BR	/A	RC	SB	CS	SBR	FR	POS	TPR
1876	Phi-N	55	256	46	87	12	8	0	34	3	2	.340	.347	.449	165	16	17	41				-3	*3/O2P	1.1
1877	Cin-N	27	107	11	35	7	2	0	15	0	4	.327	.327	.430	154	4	6	15				1	S2/O	0.7
1884	Phi-U	3	11	0	1	1	0	0		0		.091	.091	.182	-11	-1	-1	0	0			-1	/1O	-0.1
Total	5 n	222	1066	250	393	63	24	9	40	7	1	.369	.373	.498	167	83	79	209	4				3/201SP	5.4
Total	3	85	374	57	123	20	10	0	49	3	6	.329	.334	.436	157	19	21	57	0			-3	/3S201P	1.7

■ HENRY MEYERS
Meyers, Henry L. b: 1860, Philadelphia, Pa. d: 6/28/1898, Harrisburg, Pa. Deb: 8/30/1890

YEAR	TM/L	G	AB	R	H	2B	3B	HR	RBI	BB	SO	AVG	OBP	SLG	PRO+	BR	/A	RC	SB	CS	SBR	FR	POS	TPR
1890	Phi-a	5	19	2	3	0	0	0			1	.158	.238	.158	19	-2	-2	1	2			-3	/3	-0.3

■ CHIEF MEYERS
Meyers, John Tortes b: 7/29/1880, Riverside, Cal. d: 7/25/71, San Bernardino, Cal. BR/TR, 5'11", 194 lbs. Deb: 4/16/09

YEAR	TM/L	G	AB	R	H	2B	3B	HR	RBI	BB	SO	AVG	OBP	SLG	PRO+	BR	/A	RC	SB	CS	SBR	FR	POS	TPR
1909	NY-N	90	220	15	61	10	5	1	30	22		.277	.359	.382	128	8	8	31	3			5	C	1.8
1910	NY-N	127	365	25	104	18	0	1	62	40	18	.285	.362	.342	106	4	4	48	5			6	*C	1.6
1911	*NY-N	133	391	48	130	18	9	1	61	25	33	.332	.392	.432	126	16	14	69	7			-3	*C	2.0
1912	*NY-N	126	371	60	133	16	5	6	54	47	20	.358	.441	.477	147	28	27	82	8			-10	*C	2.3
1913	*NY-N	120	378	37	118	18	5	3	47	37	20	.312	.387	.410	127	15	14	60	7			5	*C	2.7
1914	NY-N	134	381	33	109	13	5	1	55	34	25	.286	.357	.354	116	6	8	48	4			-14	*C	-0.1
1915	NY-N	110	289	24	67	10	5	1	26	26	18	.232	.311	.311	94	-4	-2	28	4	4	-1	-3	C	0.0
1916	*Bro-N	80	239	21	59	10	3	0	21	26	15	.247	.336	.314	97	1	0	26	2			7	C	1.3
1917	Bro-N	47	132	8	28	3	0	0	3	13	7	.212	.283	.235	58	-6	-6	10	4			-6	C	-1.1
	Bos-N	25	68	5	17	4	4	0	4	4	4	.250	.311	.426	133	2	2	9	0			7	C	1.2
	Yr	72	200	13	45	7	4	0	7	17	11	.225	.292	.300	82	-4	-4	18	4			1		0.1
Total	9	992	2834	276	826	120	41	14	363	274	162	.291	.367	.378	117	70	69	409	44	4		-6	C	11.7

■ LOU MEYERS
Meyers, Lewis Henry "Crazy Horse" b: 12/9/1859, Cincinnati, Ohio d: 11/30/20, Cincinnati, Ohio BR/TR, 5'11", 165 lbs. Deb: 5/10/1884

YEAR	TM/L	G	AB	R	H	2B	3B	HR	RBI	BB	SO	AVG	OBP	SLG	PRO+	BR	/A	RC	SB	CS	SBR	FR	POS	TPR
1884	Cin-U	2	3	1	0	0	0	0			1	.000	.250	.000	-8	-0	-0	0	0			-2	/CO	-0.1

■ MICKEY MICELOTTA
Micelotta, Robert Peter b: 10/20/28, Corona, N.Y. BR/TR, 5'11", 185 lbs. Deb: 4/20/54

YEAR	TM/L	G	AB	R	H	2B	3B	HR	RBI	BB	SO	AVG	OBP	SLG	PRO+	BR	/A	RC	SB	CS	SBR	FR	POS	TPR
1954	Phi-N	13	3	2	0	0	0	0	0	1	1	.000	.250	.000	-28	-1	-1	0	0	0	0	4	/S	0.3
1955	Phi-N	4	4	0	0	0	0	0	0	0	0	.000	.000	.000	-99	-1	-1	0	0	0	0	0	/S	0.0
Total	2	17	7	2	0	0	0	0	0	1	1	.000	.125	.000	-64	-2	-2	0	0	0	0	4	/S	0.3

■ GENE MICHAEL
Michael, Eugene Richard "Stick" b: 6/2/38, Kent, Ohio BB/TR, 6'2", 183 lbs. Deb: 7/15/66 MC

YEAR	TM/L	G	AB	R	H	2B	3B	HR	RBI	BB	SO	AVG	OBP	SLG	PRO+	BR	/A	RC	SB	CS	SBR	FR	POS	TPR
1966	Pit-N	30	33	9	5	2	1	0	2	0	7	.152	.152	.273	15	-4	-4	1	0	0	0	5	/S23	0.2
1967	LA-N	98	223	20	45	3	1	0	7	11	30	.202	.246	.224	39	-18	-16	12	1	3	-2	5	S	-0.3
1968	NY-A	61	116	8	23	3	0	1	8	2	23	.198	.218	.250	43	-8	-8	6	3	2	-0	-1	S/P	-0.6
1969	NY-A	119	412	41	112	24	4	2	31	43	56	.272	.342	.364	101	-1	1	52	7	4	-0	-1	*S	0.5
1970	NY-A	134	435	42	93	10	1	2	38	50	93	.214	.295	.255	56	-27	-24	35	3	1	0	2	*S/32	-1.1
1971	NY-A	139	456	36	102	15	0	3	35	48	64	.224	.302	.276	69	-20	-17	37	3	3	-1	17	*S	1.4
1972	NY-A	126	391	29	91	7	4	1	32	32	45	.233	.292	.279	73	-14	-12	31	4	2	0	24	*S	2.7
1973	NY-A	129	418	30	94	11	1	3	47	26	51	.225	.270	.278	56	-25	-24	29	1	3	-2	4	*S	-0.3
1974	NY-A	81	177	19	46	9	0	0	13	14	24	.260	.314	.311	83	-4	-4	17	0	0	0	5	2S/3	0.6
1975	Det-A	56	145	15	31	2	0	3	13	8	28	.214	.255	.290	51	-9	-10	11	0	0	0	-12	S/23	-1.7
Total	10	973	2806	249	642	86	12	15	226	234	421	.229	.290	.284	66	-131	-118	231	22	18	-4	47	S/23P	1.4

■ CASS MICHAELS
Michaels, Casimir Eugene (Played In 1943 Under Real Name Of Casimir Eugene Kwietniewski)
b: 3/4/26, Detroit, Mich. d: 11/12/82, Grosse Pointe, Mich. BR/TR, 5'11", 175 lbs. Deb: 8/19/43

YEAR	TM/L	G	AB	R	H	2B	3B	HR	RBI	BB	SO	AVG	OBP	SLG	PRO+	BR	/A	RC	SB	CS	SBR	FR	POS	TPR
1943	Chi-A	2	7	0	0	0	0	0	0	0	0	.000	.000	.000	-99	-2	-2	0	0	0	0	-1	/3	-0.3
1944	Chi-A	27	68	4	12	4	1	0	5	2	5	.176	.200	.265	33	-6	-6	4	0	0	0	6	S/3	0.1
1945	Chi-A	129	445	47	109	8	5	2	54	37	28	.245	.307	.299	78	-13	-12	41	8	7	-2	10	*S/2	0.1
1946	Chi-A	91	291	37	75	8	0	1	22	29	26	.258	.333	.296	80	-8	-7	32	9	3	1	3	23/S	0.3
1947	Chi-A	110	355	31	97	15	4	3	34	39	28	.273	.350	.363	102	-0	1	45	10	5	0	11	23/S	1.6
1948	Chi-A	145	484	47	120	12	6	5	56	69	42	.248	.344	.329	82	-13	-11	60	8	2	1	13	S2/O	0.5
1949	Chi-A	154	561	73	173	27	9	6	83	101	50	.308	.417	.421	126	21	24	102	5	7	-3	12	*2	3.3
1950	Chi-A	36	138	21	43	6	3	4	19	13	8	.312	.375	.486	122	3	4	25	0	0	0	-6	2	0.0
	Was-A	106	388	48	97	8	4	4	47	55	39	.250	.345	.322	75	-16	-13	45	2	3	-1	8	*2	0.1
	Yr	142	526	69	140	14	7	8	66	68	47	.266	.352	.365	88	-12	-9	70	2	3	-1	2		0.1
1951	Was-A	138	485	59	125	20	4	4	45	61	41	.258	.342	.340	86	-9	-8	58	1	1	-0	-23	*2	-2.6
1952	Was-A	22	86	10	20	4	1	1	7	7	15	.233	.290	.337	77	-3	-3	7	0	0	0	1	2	0.0
	StL-A	55	166	21	44	8	2	3	25	23	16	.265	.354	.392	104	2	1	25	1	0	0	0	3/2	0.2
	Phi-A	55	200	22	50	4	5	1	18	23	11	.250	.330	.335	80	-4	-5	24	3	0	1	-13	2	-1.5
	Yr	132	452	53	114	16	8	5	50	53	42	.252	.332	.356	89	-5	-7	56	4	0	1	-12		-1.3
1953	Phi-A	117	411	53	103	10	0	12	42	51	56	.251	.335	.363	85	-6	-9	55	7	0	2	-11	*2	-1.0
1954	Chi-A	101	380	35	74	13	2	7	44	56	31	.262	.392	.397	113	9	7	50	10	4	1	-4	3/2	0.0
Total	12	1288	4367	508	1142	147	46	53	501	566	406	.262	.349	.353	92	-46	-37	572	64	32	0	5	2S3/O	0.8

■ RALPH MICHAELS
Michaels, Ralph Joseph b: 5/3/02, Etna, Pa. d: 8/5/88, Monroeville, Pa. BR/TR, 5'10.5", 178 lbs. Deb: 4/16/24

YEAR	TM/L	G	AB	R	H	2B	3B	HR	RBI	BB	SO	AVG	OBP	SLG	PRO+	BR	/A	RC	SB	CS	SBR	FR	POS	TPR
1924	Chi-N	8	11	0	4	0	0	0	2	0	1	.364	.364	.364	95	-0	-0	1	0	0	0	1	/S	0.1
1925	Chi-N	22	50	10	14	1	0	0	6	6	9	.280	.357	.300	69	-2	-2	6	1	0	0	3	3/12S	0.2
1926	Chi-N	2	0	1	0	0	0	0	0	0	0	—	—	—	—		0	0	0	0		0	H	0.0
Total	3	32	61	11	18	1	0	0	8	6	10	.295	.358	.311	73	-2	-2	7	1	0		3	/3S21	0.3

■ ED MICKELSON
Mickelson, Edward Allen b: 9/9/26, Ottawa, Ill. BR/TR, 6'3", 205 lbs. Deb: 9/18/50

YEAR	TM/L	G	AB	R	H	2B	3B	HR	RBI	BB	SO	AVG	OBP	SLG	PRO+	BR	/A	RC	SB	CS	SBR	FR	POS	TPR
1950	StL-N	5	10	1	1	0	0	0	2		3	.100	.250	.100	-4	-1	-2	0	0			1	/1	0.0
1953	StL-A	7	15	1	2	1	0	0	2	2	6	.133	.235	.200	18	-2	-2	1	0	0	0	0	/1	-0.1
1957	Chi-N	6	12	0	0	0	0	0	1	0	4	.000	.000	.000	-99	-3	-3	0	0	0	0	1	/1	-0.2
Total	3	18	37	2	3	1	0	0	3	4	13	.081	.171	.108	-23	-7	-7	1	0	0		2	/1	-0.3

■ EZRA MIDKIFF
Midkiff, Ezra Millington "Salt Rock" b: 11/13/1882, Salt Rock, W.Va. d: 3/20/57, Huntington, W.Va. BL/TR, 5'10", 180 lbs. Deb: 10/05/09

YEAR	TM/L	G	AB	R	H	2B	3B	HR	RBI	BB	SO	AVG	OBP	SLG	PRO+	BR	/A	RC	SB	CS	SBR	FR	POS	TPR
1909	Cin-N	1	2	0	0	0	0	0	0	0		.000	.000	.000	-99	-0	-0	0	0			-1	/3	0.0
1912	NY-A	21	86	9	21	1	0	0	9	7		.244	.301	.256	56	-4	-5	8	4			3	3	-0.1
1913	NY-A	83	284	22	56	9	1	0	14	12	33	.197	.232	.236	37	-23	-23	17	9			18	3/S2	-0.3
Total	3	105	372	31	77	10	1	0	23	19	33	.207	.247	.239	41	-28	-29	25	13			20	/3S2	-0.4

■ ED MIERKOWICZ
Mierkowicz, Edward Frank "Butch" or "Mouse" b: 3/6/24, Wyandotte, Mich. BR/TR, 6'4", 205 lbs. Deb: 8/31/45

YEAR	TM/L	G	AB	R	H	2B	3B	HR	RBI	BB	SO	AVG	OBP	SLG	PRO+	BR	/A	RC	SB	CS	SBR	FR	POS	TPR
1945	*Det-A	10	15	0	2	0	0	0	2	1	3	.133	.188	.267	29	-1	-2	1	0	0	0	0	/O	-0.1
1947	Det-A	21	42	6	8	1	0	1	1	1	12	.190	.209	.286	36	-4	-4	2	1	0	0	-0	O	-0.4
1948	Det-A	3	5	0	1	0	0	0	1	2	2	.200	.429	.200	69	-0	-0	0	0	0	0	0	/O	0.0
1950	StL-N	1	1	0	0	0	0	0	0	0	0	.000	.000	.000	-95	-0	-0	0	0			0	H	0.0
Total	4	35	63	6	11	3	0	1	4	4	18	.175	.224	.270	36	-5	-6	3	1	0		-0	/O	-0.5

■ LARRY MIGGINS
Miggins, Lawrence Edward "Irish" b: 8/20/25, Bronx, N.Y. BR/TR, 6'4", 198 lbs. Deb: 10/03/48

YEAR	TM/L	G	AB	R	H	2B	3B	HR	RBI	BB	SO	AVG	OBP	SLG	PRO+	BR	/A	RC	SB	CS	SBR	FR	POS	TPR
1948	StL-N	1	1	1	0	0	0	0	0	0	0	.000	.000	.000	-95	-0	-0	0	0			0	H	0.0
1952	StL-N	42	96	7	22	5	1	2	10	3	19	.229	.253	.365	69	-4	-4	9	0	1	-1	-4	O/1	-0.9
Total	2	43	97	8	22	5	1	2	10	3	19	.227	.250	.361	67	-5	-5	9	0	1		-4	/O1	-0.9

YEAR	TM/L	G	AB	R	H	2B	3B	HR	RBI	BB	SO	AVG	OBP	SLG	PRO+	BR	/A	RC	SB	CS	SBR	FR	POS	TPR

■ JOHN MIHALIC Mihalic, John Michael b: 11/13/11, Cleveland, Ohio d: 4/24/87, Ft.Oglethorpe, Ga. BR/TR, 5'11", 172 lbs. Deb: 9/18/35

YEAR	TM/L	G	AB	R	H	2B	3B	HR	RBI	BB	SO	AVG	OBP	SLG	PRO+	BR	/A	RC	SB	CS	SBR	FR	POS	TPR
1935	Was-A	6	22	4	5	3	0	0	6	2	3	.227	.292	.364	71	-1	-1	3	1	0	0	-1	/S	0.0
1936	Was-A	25	88	15	21	2	1	0	8	14	14	.239	.343	.284	60	-6	-5	10	2	1	0	1	2	-0.1
1937	Was-A	38	107	13	27	5	2	0	8	17	9	.252	.355	.336	79	-4	-3	14	2	1	0	4	2/S	0.4
Total	3	69	217	32	53	10	3	0	22	33	26	.244	.344	.318	70	-10	-9	26	5	2	0	4	/2S	0.3

■ EDDIE MIKSIS Miksis, Edward Thomas b: 9/11/26, Burlington, N.J. BR/TR, 6'0.5", 185 lbs. Deb: 6/17/44

YEAR	TM/L	G	AB	R	H	2B	3B	HR	RBI	BB	SO	AVG	OBP	SLG	PRO+	BR	/A	RC	SB	CS	SBR	FR	POS	TPR
1944	Bro-N	26	91	12	20	2	0	0	11	6	11	.220	.268	.242	45	-7	-6	6	4			-4	3S	-0.8
1946	Bro-N	23	48	3	7	0	0	0	5	3	3	.146	.212	.146	2	-6	-6	1	0			0	3/2	-0.6
1947	*Bro-N	45	86	18	23	1	0	4	10	9	8	.267	.337	.419	96	-0	-1	12	0			4	2O/3S	0.4
1948	Bro-N	86	221	28	47	7	1	2	16	19	27	.213	.278	.281	50	-15	-16	19	5			4	23/S	-0.8
1949	*Bro-N	50	113	17	25	5	0	1	6	7	8	.221	.267	.292	48	-8	-9	8	3			6	3/S21	-0.1
1950	Bro-N	51	76	13	19	2	1	2	10	5	10	.250	.296	.382	75	-3	-3	8	3			5	2S/3	0.4
1951	Bro-N	19	10	6	2	1	0	0	0	1	2	.200	.333	.300	70	-0	-0	1	0	0	0	2	/32	0.2
	Chi-N	102	421	48	112	13	3	4	35	33	36	.266	.319	.340	76	-13	-14	46	11	5	0	3	*2	-0.7
	Yr	121	431	54	114	14	3	4	35	34	38	.265	.320	.339	76	-14	-15	48	11	5	0	5		-0.5
1952	Chi-N	93	383	44	89	20	1	2	19	20	32	.232	.272	.305	59	-21	-22	31	4	4	-1	-13	2S	-3.3
1953	Chi-N	142	577	61	145	17	6	8	39	33	59	.251	.293	.343	64	-30	-32	57	13	4	2	-13	2S	-3.3
1954	Chi-N	38	99	9	20	3	0	2	3	3	9	.202	.225	.293	33	-10	-10	6	1	0	0	4	2/3O	-0.3
1955	Chi-N	131	481	52	113	14	2	9	41	32	55	.235	.283	.328	62	-27	-27	42	3	6	-3	-0	*O3	-3.1
1956	Chi-N	114	356	54	85	10	3	9	27	32	40	.239	.303	.360	79	-11	-11	38	4	2	0	2	3O2/S	-0.8
1957	StL-N	49	38	3	8	0	0	1	2	7	7	.211	.333	.289	68	-1	-2	4	0	0	0	-0	H	-0.2
	Bal-A	1	1	0	0	0	0	0	0	0	0	.000	.000	.000	-99	-0	-0	0	0	0	0	0	H	0.0
1958	Bal-A	3	2	0	0	0	0	0	0	0	1	.000	.000	.000	-99	-1	-1	0	0	0	0	0	/S	0.0
	Cin-N	69	50	15	7	0	0	0	4	5	5	.140	.218	.140	-2	-7	-8	2	1	1	-0	8	03/2S1	0.0
Total	14	1042	3053	383	722	95	17	44	228	215	313	.236	.288	.322	62	-161	-166	283	52	22		6	203S/1	-13.0

■ HORACE MILAN Milan, Horace Robert b: 4/7/1894, Linden, Tenn. d: 6/29/55, Texarkana, Ark. BR/TR, 5'9", 175 lbs. Deb: 8/29/15

YEAR	TM/L	G	AB	R	H	2B	3B	HR	RBI	BB	SO	AVG	OBP	SLG	PRO+	BR	/A	RC	SB	CS	SBR	FR	POS	TPR
1915	Was-A	11	27	6	11	1	1	0	7	8	7	.407	.543	.519	216	5	5	9	2			-2	O	0.2
1917	Was-A	31	73	8	21	3	1	0	9	4	9	.288	.342	.356	114	1	1	10	4			-4	O	-0.3
Total	2	42	100	14	32	4	2	0	16	12	16	.320	.404	.400	145	6	6	18	6			-6	/O	-0.1

■ CLYDE MILAN Milan, Jesse Clyde "Deerfoot" b: 3/25/1887, Linden, Tenn. d: 3/3/53, Orlando, Fla. BL/TR, 5'9", 168 lbs. Deb: 8/19/07 MC

YEAR	TM/L	G	AB	R	H	2B	3B	HR	RBI	BB	SO	AVG	OBP	SLG	PRO+	BR	/A	RC	SB	CS	SBR	FR	POS	TPR
1907	Was-A	48	183	22	51	3	3	0	9	8		.279	.309	.328	114	1	2	22	8			4	O	0.4
1908	Was-A	130	485	55	116	10	12	1	32	38		.239	.294	.315	109	0	5	53	29			9	*O	0.9
1909	Was-A	130	400	36	80	12	4	1	15	31		.200	.268	.257	69	-15	-13	32	10			5	*O	-1.4
1910	Was-A	142	531	89	148	17	6	0	16	71		.279	.379	.333	129	18	21	83	44			11	*O	2.8
1911	Was-A	154	616	109	194	24	8	3	35	74		.315	.395	.394	123	19	21	117	58			11	*O	1.9
1912	Was-A	154	601	105	184	19	11	1	79	63		.306	.377	.379	116	14	14	117	88			8	*O	1.2
1913	Was-A	154	579	92	174	18	9	3	54	58	25	.301	.367	.378	116	14	12	102	75			-7	*O	-0.3
1914	Was-A	115	437	63	129	19	11	1	39	32	26	.295	.346	.396	120	11	9	63	38	21	-1	-4	*O	-0.2
1915	Was-A	153	583	83	165	13	7	2	66	53	32	.288	.353	.346	108	7	6	77	40	19	1	0	*O	0.0
1916	Was-A	150	565	58	154	14	3	1	45	56	31	.273	.343	.313	100	-1	1	66	34	21	-2	17	*O	0.7
1917	Was-A	155	579	60	170	15	4	1	48	58	26	.294	.364	.333	114	10	11	76	20			-5	*O	-0.2
1918	Was-A	128	503	56	146	18	5	0	56	36	14	.290	.344	.346	110	4	5	65	26			2	*O	0.2
1919	Was-A	88	321	43	92	12	6	0	37	40	16	.287	.371	.361	107	4	4	46	11			-3	O	-0.4
1920	Was-A	126	506	70	163	22	5	3	41	28	12	.322	.364	.403	106	2	9	72	10	12	-4	8	*O	-0.3
1921	Was-A	113	406	55	117	19	11	1	40	37	13	.288	.351	.397	95	-6	-3	57	4	5	-2	2	O	-0.9
1922	Was-A	42	74	8	17	5	0	0	5	2	2	.230	.250	.297	44	-6	-6	5	0	0	0	1	OM	-0.5
Total	16	1982	7359	1004	2100	240	105	17	617	685	197	.285	.352	.353	109	76	94	1052	495	78		58	*O	3.9

■ LARRY MILBOURNE Milbourne, Lawrence William b: 2/14/51, Port Norris, N.J. BB/TR, 6', 161 lbs. Deb: 4/06/74

YEAR	TM/L	G	AB	R	H	2B	3B	HR	RBI	BB	SO	AVG	OBP	SLG	PRO+	BR	/A	RC	SB	CS	SBR	FR	POS	TPR
1974	Hou-N	112	136	31	38	2	1	0	9	10	14	.279	.329	.309	83	-4	-3	15	6	2	1	18	2/SO	2.1
1975	Hou-N	73	151	17	32	1	2	1	9	6	14	.212	.247	.265	45	-12	-11	9	1	2	-1	10	2S	0.3
1976	Hou-N	59	145	22	36	4	0	0	7	14	10	.248	.319	.276	77	-5	-4	14	6	1	1	-1	2	-0.2
1977	Sea-A	86	242	24	53	10	2	0	21	6	20	.219	.244	.285	44	-19	-19	17	3	1	0	4	2S/3D	-0.6
1978	Sea-A	93	234	31	53	6	2	2	20	9	6	.226	.255	.295	55	-14	-14	15	5	7	-3	16	3S2D	0.1
1979	Sea-A	123	356	40	99	13	4	2	26	19	20	.278	.315	.354	79	-10	-11	38	5	3	-0	-17	S23	-1.7
1980	Sea-A	106	258	31	68	6	6	0	26	19	13	.264	.317	.333	78	-8	-8	26	7	6	-2	9	2S/3D	0.4
1981	*NY-A	61	163	24	51	7	2	1	12	9	14	.313	.353	.399	118	3	3	23	2	0	1	-6	S2/3D	0.1
1982	NY-A	14	27	2	4	1	0	0	0	1	4	.148	.179	.185	0	-4	-4	1	0	1	-1	1	/S23	-0.1
	Min-A	29	98	9	23	1	1	0	1	7	8	.235	.286	.265	51	-6	-7	7	1	1	-0	-10	2	-1.5
	Cle-A	82	291	29	80	11	4	2	25	12	20	.275	.308	.361	83	-7	-7	29	2	5		-6	2S/3D	-0.9
	Yr	125	416	40	107	13	5	2	26	20	32	.257	.295	.327	70	-17	-17	36	3	7	-3	-15		-2.5
1983	Phi-N	41	66	3	16	0	1	0	4	4	7	.242	.286	.273	56	-4	-4	5	2	1	0	1	2/S3	-0.1
	NY-A	31	70	5	14	4	0	0	2	5	10	.200	.263	.257	46	-5	-5	5	1	1	-0	3	2/SS3	0.0
1984	Sea-A	79	211	22	56	5	1	1	22	12	16	.265	.305	.313	72	-8	-8	19	0	2	-1	-9	32/SD	-1.6
Total	11	989	2448	290	623	71	24	11	184	133	176	.254	.295	.317	70	-103	-99	222	41	33	-8	12	2S3/DO	-3.6

■ DON MILES Miles, Donald Ray b: 3/13/36, Indianapolis, Ind. BL/TR, 6'1", 210 lbs. Deb: 9/09/58

YEAR	TM/L	G	AB	R	H	2B	3B	HR	RBI	BB	SO	AVG	OBP	SLG	PRO+	BR	/A	RC	SB	CS	SBR	FR	POS	TPR
1958	LA-N	8	22	2	4	0	0	0	0	0	6	.182	.217	.182	7	-3	-3	1	0	0	0	1	/O	-0.1

■ DEE MILES Miles, Wilson Daniel b: 2/15/09, Kellerman, Ala. d: 11/2/76, Birmingham, Ala. BL/TR, 6', 175 lbs. Deb: 7/07/35

YEAR	TM/L	G	AB	R	H	2B	3B	HR	RBI	BB	SO	AVG	OBP	SLG	PRO+	BR	/A	RC	SB	CS	SBR	FR	POS	TPR
1935	Was-A	60	215	28	57	5	2	0	29	7	13	.265	.291	.307	57	-14	-14	19	6	4	-1	-1	O	-1.4
1936	Was-A	25	59	8	14	1	2	0	7	1	5	.237	.250	.322	43	-6	-5	4	0	1	-1	-0	O	-0.5
1939	Phi-A	106	320	49	96	17	6	1	37	15	17	.300	.331	.400	88	-7	-6	42	3	4	-2	-6	O	-1.5
1940	Phi-A	88	236	26	71	9	6	1	23	8	18	.301	.327	.403	90	-5	-4	32	1	1	-0	0	O	-0.6
1941	Phi-A	80	170	14	53	7	1	0	15	4	8	.312	.331	.365	86	-4	-4	20	0	1	-1	0	O	-0.4
1942	Phi-A	99	346	41	94	12	5	0	22	12	10	.272	.300	.335	79	-11	-11	36	5	3	-0	-0	O	-1.6
1943	Bos-A	45	121	9	26	2	2	0	10	3	3	.215	.234	.264	45	-9	-9	7	0	2	-1	0	O	-1.1
Total	7	503	1467	175	411	53	24	2	143	50	74	.280	.306	.353	76	-56	-52	159	15	16	-5	-7	O	-7.1

■ MIKE MILEY Miley, Michael Wilfred b: 3/30/53, Yazoo City, Miss. d: 1/6/77, Baton Rouge, La. BB/TR, 6'1", 185 lbs. Deb: 7/06/75

YEAR	TM/L	G	AB	R	H	2B	3B	HR	RBI	BB	SO	AVG	OBP	SLG	PRO+	BR	/A	RC	SB	CS	SBR	FR	POS	TPR
1975	Cal-A	70	224	17	39	3	2	4	26	16	54	.174	.232	.259	42	-18	-16	13	0	1	-1	-9	S	-1.9
1976	Cal-A	14	38	4	7	2	0	0	4	4	8	.184	.262	.237	50	-2	-2	3	1	0	0	-1	S	-0.2
Total	2	84	262	21	46	5	2	4	30	20	62	.176	.237	.256	43	-21	-19	16	1	1	-0	-11	/S	-2.1

■ FELIX MILLAN Millan, Felix Bernardo (Martinez) b: 8/21/43, Yabucoa, P.R. BR/TR, 5'11", 172 lbs. Deb: 6/02/66

YEAR	TM/L	G	AB	R	H	2B	3B	HR	RBI	BB	SO	AVG	OBP	SLG	PRO+	BR	/A	RC	SB	CS	SBR	FR	POS	TPR
1966	Atl-N	37	91	20	25	6	2	0	5	2	6	.275	.290	.341	74	-3	-3	8	3	1	0	-2	2/S3	-0.3
1967	Atl-N	41	136	13	32	3	3	2	6	4	10	.235	.268	.346	75	-5	-5	11	0	3	-2	3	2	0.0
1968	Atl-N	149	570	49	165	22	2	1	33	22	26	.289	.323	.340	99	-1	-1	57	1	6	-2	3	*2	0.9
1969	*Atl-N	162	652	98	174	23	5	6	57	34	35	.267	.311	.345	83	-15	-15	69	14	3	2	-16	*2	-1.6
1970	Atl-N	142	590	100	183	25	5	2	37	35	23	.310	.354	.380	91	-2	-7	79	16	5	2	-19	*2	-0.7
1971	Atl-N	143	577	65	167	20	8	2	45	37	22	.289	.335	.362	92	-2	-6	69	11	7	-1	6	*2	0.6

YEAR	TM/L	G	AB	R	H	2B	3B	HR	RBI	BB	SO	AVG	OBP	SLG	PRO+	BR	/A	RC	SB	CS	SBR	FR	POS	TPR
1972	Atl-N	125	498	46	128	19	3	1	38	23	28	.257	.294	.313	66	-18	-23	46	6	4	-1	-16	*2	-3.4
1973	*NY-N	153	638	82	185	23	4	3	37	35	22	.290	.333	.353	91	-8	-7	72	2	2	-1	-4	*2	-0.5
1974	NY-N	136	518	50	139	15	2	1	33	31	14	.268	.320	.311	78	-16	-15	53	5	1	1	-20	*2	-2.7
1975	NY-N	162	676	81	191	37	2	1	56	36	28	.283	.330	.348	92	-11	-7	75	1	6	-3	-25	*2	-2.9
1976	NY-N	139	531	55	150	25	2	1	35	41	19	.282	.342	.343	101	-3	1	60	2	4	-2	-24	*2	-1.9
1977	NY-N	91	314	40	78	11	2	2	21	18	9	.248	.296	.315	67	-16	-14	28	1	1	-0	-16	2	-2.5
Total	12	1480	5791	699	1617	229	38	22	403	318	242	.279	.324	.343	87	-100	-103	628	67	43	-6	-128	*2/3S	-15.0

■ FRANK MILLARD
Millard, Frank E. b: 7/4/1865, E.St.Louis, Ill. d: 7/4/1892, Galveston, Tex. Deb: 5/04/1890

YEAR	TM/L	G	AB	R	H	2B	3B	HR	RBI	BB	SO	AVG	OBP	SLG	PRO+	BR	/A	RC	SB	CS	SBR	FR	POS	TPR
1890	StL-a	1	1	0	0	0	0	0			1	.000	.500	.000	45	0	0	0	0			1	/2	0.0

■ DUSTY MILLER
Miller, Charles Bradley b: 9/10/1868, Oil City, Pa. d: 9/3/45, Memphis, Tenn. BL/TR, 5'11.5", 170 lbs. Deb: 9/23/1889

YEAR	TM/L	G	AB	R	H	2B	3B	HR	RBI	BB	SO	AVG	OBP	SLG	PRO+	BR	/A	RC	SB	CS	SBR	FR	POS	TPR
1889	Bal-a	11	40	4	6	1	1	0	6	2	11	.150	.209	.225	25	-4	-4	3	3			-7	/SO	-0.9
1890	StL-a	26	96	17	21	5	3	1		8		.219	.279	.365	80	-1	-4	11	4			3	O/S	-0.1
1895	Cin-N	132	529	103	177	31	16	10	112	33	34	.335	.378	.510	125	21	17	121	43			11	*O	1.3
1896	Cin-N	125	504	91	162	38	12	4	93	33	30	.321	.368	.468	114	14	8	118	76			-2	*O	-0.1
1897	Cin-N	119	440	83	139	27	1	4	70	48		.316	.392	.409	107	10	5	84	29			2	*O	0.0
1898	Cin-N	152	586	99	175	24	12	3	90	38		.299	.350	.396	109	11	6	95	32			8	*O	0.4
1899	Cin-N	80	323	44	81	12	5	0	37	9		.251	.275	.319	64	-16	-17	34	18			7	O	-1.3
	StL-N	10	39	3	8	1	0	0	3	3		.205	.279	.231	41	-3	-3	3	1			-1	O	-0.3
	Yr	90	362	47	89	13	5	0	40	12		.246	.276	.309	61	-19	-20	37	19			6		-1.6
Total	7	655	2557	444	769	139	50	22	411	174	75	.301	.352	.420	104	32	9	468	206			21	O/S	-1.0

■ BRUCE MILLER
Miller, Charles Bruce b: 3/4/47, Fort Wayne, Ind. BR/TR, 6'1", 185 lbs. Deb: 8/04/73

YEAR	TM/L	G	AB	R	H	2B	3B	HR	RBI	BB	SO	AVG	OBP	SLG	PRO+	BR	/A	RC	SB	CS	SBR	FR	POS	TPR
1973	SF-N	12	21	1	3	0	0	0	2	2	3	.143	.217	.143	2	-3	-3	1	0	0	0	1	/32S	-0.1
1974	SF-N	73	198	19	55	7	1	0	16	11	15	.278	.319	.323	76	-5	-6	19	1	1	-0	13	3S/2	0.8
1975	SF-N	99	309	22	74	6	3	0	31	15	26	.239	.277	.288	55	-18	-20	21	0	1	-1	10	32/S	-0.9
1976	SF-N	12	25	1	4	1	0	0	2	2	5	.160	.222	.200	20	-3	-3	1	0	0	0	-1	/23	-0.3
Total	4	196	553	43	136	14	4	1	51	30	49	.246	.287	.291	59	-29	-32	42	1	2	-1	22	3/2S	-0.5

■ CHARLIE MILLER
Miller, Charles Elmer b: 1/4/1892, Warrensburg, Mo. d: 4/23/72, Warrensburg, Mo. TR , Deb: 9/18/12

YEAR	TM/L	G	AB	R	H	2B	3B	HR	RBI	BB	SO	AVG	OBP	SLG	PRO+	BR	/A	RC	SB	CS	SBR	FR	POS	TPR
1912	StL-A	1	2	0	0	0	0	0	0			.000	.000	.000	-99	-1	-1	0	0			0	/S	0.0

■ CHARLIE MILLER
Miller, Charles Hess b: 12/30/1877, Conestoga Center, Pa. d: 1/13/51, Millersville, Pa. BR/TR, 6', 190 lbs. Deb: 10/02/15

YEAR	TM/L	G	AB	R	H	2B	3B	HR	RBI	BB	SO	AVG	OBP	SLG	PRO+	BR	/A	RC	SB	CS	SBR	FR	POS	TPR
1915	Bal-F	1	1	0	0	0	0	0	0			.000	.000	.000	-97	-0	-0	0	0			0	H	0.0

■ CHUCK MILLER
Miller, Charles Marion b: 9/18/1889, Woodville, Ohio d: 6/16/61, Houston, Tex. BL/TL, 5'8.5", 155 lbs. Deb: 9/19/13

YEAR	TM/L	G	AB	R	H	2B	3B	HR	RBI	BB	SO	AVG	OBP	SLG	PRO+	BR	/A	RC	SB	CS	SBR	FR	POS	TPR
1913	StL-N	4	12	0	2	0	0	0	1	0	2	.167	.167	.167	-5	-2	-2	0	0			-1	/O	-0.1
1914	StL-N	36	36	4	7	1	0	0	2	3	9	.194	.256	.222	43	-3	-2	2	2			1	O	-0.1
Total	2	40	48	4	9	1	0	0	3	3	11	.188	.235	.208	31	-4	-4	2	2			0	/O	-0.2

■ DUSTY MILLER
Miller, Dakin Evans b: 9/2/1877, Malvern, Iowa d: 4/20/50, Stockton, Cal. 5'10", 175 lbs. Deb: 4/17/02

YEAR	TM/L	G	AB	R	H	2B	3B	HR	RBI	BB	SO	AVG	OBP	SLG	PRO+	BR	/A	RC	SB	CS	SBR	FR	POS	TPR
1902	Chi-N	51	187	17	46	4	1	0	13	7		.246	.299	.278	82	-4	-3	20	10			1	O	-0.5

■ DARRELL MILLER
Miller, Darrell Keith b: 2/26/58, Washington, D.C. BR/TR, 6'2", 200 lbs. Deb: 8/14/84

YEAR	TM/L	G	AB	R	H	2B	3B	HR	RBI	BB	SO	AVG	OBP	SLG	PRO+	BR	/A	RC	SB	CS	SBR	FR	POS	TPR
1984	Cal-A	17	41	5	7	0	0	0	1	4	9	.171	.244	.171	17	-5	-4	2	0	0	0	-0	1/O	-0.5
1985	Cal-A	51	48	8	18	2	1	2	7	1	10	.375	.400	.583	166	4	4	11	0	1	-1	4	O/C3D	0.7
1986	Cal-A	33	57	6	13	2	1	0	4	4	8	.228	.279	.298	58	-3	-3	4	0	0	0	-4	OC/D	-0.6
1987	Cal-A	53	108	14	26	5	0	4	16	9	13	.241	.311	.398	89	-2	-2	13	1	0	0	-3	CO/3D	-0.1
1988	Cal-A	70	140	21	31	4	1	2	7	9	29	.221	.292	.307	70	-6	-5	13	2	1	0	8	C/OD	0.4
Total	5	224	394	54	95	13	3	8	35	27	69	.241	.303	.350	80	-12	-11	43	3	2	-0	4	/CO1D3	-0.1

■ BING MILLER
Miller, Edmund John b: 8/30/1894, Vinton, Iowa d: 5/7/66, Philadelphia, Pa. BR/TR, 6', 185 lbs. Deb: 4/16/21 C

YEAR	TM/L	G	AB	R	H	2B	3B	HR	RBI	BB	SO	AVG	OBP	SLG	PRO+	BR	/A	RC	SB	CS	SBR	FR	POS	TPR
1921	Was-A	114	420	57	121	28	8	9	71	25	50	.288	.334	.457	105	-2	1	63	3	4	-2	2	*O	-0.6
1922	Phi-A	143	535	90	179	29	12	21	90	24	42	.335	.371	.551	134	26	24	104	10	10	-3	5	*O	1.5
1923	Phi-A	123	458	68	137	25	4	12	64	27	34	.299	.344	.450	106	3	2	71	9	3	1	-1	*O	-0.7
1924	Phi-A	113	398	62	136	22	4	6	62	12	24	.342	.376	.462	114	8	7	69	11	5	0	-2	O/1	0.0
1925	Phi-A	124	474	78	151	29	10	10	81	19	14	.319	.355	.485	105	6	1	80	11	6	-0	-10	*O1	-1.8
1926	Phi-A	38	110	13	32	6	2	2	13	11	6	.291	.355	.436	100	1	-0	18	4	1	1	-5	O/1	-0.6
	StL-A	94	353	60	117	27	5	4	50	22	12	.331	.382	.470	116	10	8	60	7	11	-5	4	O	0.1
	Yr	132	463	73	149	33	7	6	63	33	18	.322	.376	.462	112	11	8	78	11	12	-4	-1		-0.5
1927	StL-A	143	492	83	160	32	7	5	75	30	26	.325	.375	.449	109	9	6	88	9	7	-2	4	*O	0.1
1928	Phi-A	139	510	76	168	34	7	8	85	27	24	.329	.372	.471	117	14	12	88	10	6	-1	0	*O	0.4
1929	*Phi-A	147	556	84	186	32	16	8	93	40	25	.335	.383	.493	120	19	16	105	24	9	2	6	*O	1.7
1930	*Phi-A	154	585	89	177	38	7	9	100	47	22	.303	.357	.438	96	0	-4	90	13	13	-4	5	*O	-0.7
1931	*Phi-A	137	534	75	150	43	5	8	77	36	16	.281	.338	.425	94	-2	-6	77	5	3	-0	6	*O	-0.8
1932	Phi-A	95	305	40	90	17	4	7	58	20	11	.295	.343	.446	99	0	-1	47	7	3	0	3	O	-0.1
1933	Phi-A	67	120	22	33	7	1	2	17	12	7	.275	.346	.400	96	-1	-1	17	4	2	0	-2	O/1	-0.3
1934	Phi-A	81	177	22	43	10	2	1	22	16	14	.243	.309	.339	70	-9	-8	19	1	0	0	-2	O	-0.9
1935	Bos-A	78	138	18	42	8	1	3	26	10	8	.304	.356	.442	99	1	-1	22	0	1	-1	-1	O	-0.2
1936	Bos-A	30	47	9	14	2	1	1	6	5	5	.298	.377	.447	97	0	-0	8	0	0	0	-0	O	0.0
Total	16	1820	6212	946	1936	389	96	116	990	383	340	.312	.359	.461	108	83	57	1017	128	84	-12	11	*O/1	-2.9

■ EDDIE MILLER
Miller, Edward Lee b: 6/29/57, San Pablo, Cal. BB/TR, 5'9", 175 lbs. Deb: 9/05/77

YEAR	TM/L	G	AB	R	H	2B	3B	HR	RBI	BB	SO	AVG	OBP	SLG	PRO+	BR	/A	RC	SB	CS	SBR	FR	POS	TPR
1977	Tex-A	17	6	7	2	0	0	0	1	1	1	.333	.429	.333	110	0	0	1	3	1	0	-1	/OD	0.1
1978	Atl-N	6	21	5	3	1	0	0	2	2	4	.143	.250	.190	22	-2	-2	2	3	0	1	-1	/O	-0.2
1979	Atl-N	27	113	12	35	1	0	0	5	5	24	.310	.350	.319	78	-2	-3	15	15	2	3	3	O	0.2
1980	Atl-N	11	19	3	3	0	0	0	0	0	5	.158	.158	.158	-11	-3	-3	0	1	2	-1	-1	/O	-0.4
1981	Atl-N	50	134	29	31	3	1	0	7		29	.231	.285	.269	56	-7	-8	12	23	5	4	-1	O	-0.6
1982	Det-A	14	25	3	1	0	0	0	0	4	4	.040	.250	.040	-14	-4	-4	1	0	3	-2	0	/OD	-0.5
1984	SD-N	13	14	4	4	0	1	1	2	0	4	.286	.286	.643	155	1	1	3	4	0	1	2	/O	0.3
Total	7	138	332	63	79	5	2	2	17	19	71	.238	.297	.274	57	-17	-19	34	49	13	7	3	/OD	-1.1

■ EDDIE MILLER
Miller, Edward Robert "Eppie" b: 11/26/16, Pittsburgh, Pa. BR/TR, 5'9", 180 lbs. Deb: 9/09/36

YEAR	TM/L	G	AB	R	H	2B	3B	HR	RBI	BB	SO	AVG	OBP	SLG	PRO+	BR	/A	RC	SB	CS	SBR	FR	POS	TPR
1936	Cin-N	5	10	1	1	0	0	0	0	1	1	.100	.182	.100	-24	-2	-2	0	0			-0	/S2	-0.1
1937	Cin-N	36	60	3	9	3	1	0	5	3	8	.150	.190	.233	15	-7	-7	2	0			7	S/3	0.3
1939	Bos-N	77	296	32	79	12	2	4	31	16	21	.267	.315	.361	88	-8	-5	33	4			12	S	1.2
1940	Bos-N	151	569	78	157	33	3	14	79	41	43	.276	.330	.418	111	3	7	76	8			15	*S	3.6
1941	Bos-N	154	585	54	140	27	3	6	68	35	72	.239	.288	.326	76	-22	-19	54	8			12	*S	0.6
1942	Bos-N	142	534	47	130	28	2	6	47	22	42	.243	.279	.337	81	-15	-14	47	11			4	*S	0.0
1943	Cin-N	154	576	49	129	26	4	2	71	33	43	.224	.271	.293	64	-28	-27	47	8			**27**	*S	1.5
1944	Cin-N	155	548	48	112	21	5	4	55	41	44	.209	.269	.289	59	-31	-29	43	9			12	*S	0.4
1945	Cin-N	115	421	46	100	27	2	13	49	18	38	.238	.275	.404	89	-10	-9	44	4			5	*S	0.8
1946	Cin-N	91	299	30	58	10	0	6	36	25	34	.194	.258	.288	57	-18	-17	22	5			24	S	1.3
1947	Cin-N	151	545	69	146	**38**	4	19	87	49	40	.268	.333	.457	109	4	4	81	5			-5	*S	1.1

YEAR	TM/L	G	AB	R	H	2B	3B	HR	RBI	BB	SO	AVG	OBP	SLG	PRO+	BR	/A	RC	SB	CS	SBR	FR	POS	TPR
1948	Phi-N	130	468	45	115	20	1	14	61	19	40	.246	.281	.382	79	-16	-15	47	1			-14	*S	-1.5
1949	Phi-N	85	266	21	55	10	1	6	29	29	21	.207	.294	.320	66	-13	-13	26	1			-10	2/S	-1.9
1950	StL-N	64	172	17	39	8	0	3	22	19	21	.227	.307	.326	64	-8	-9	18	0			14	S/2	0.9
Total	14	1510	5337	539	1270	263	28	97	640	351	465	.238	.290	.352	80	-173	-155	540	64			103	*S/23	8.2

■ ED MILLER
Miller, Edwin J. "Big Ed" b: 11/24/1888, Annville, Pa. d: 4/17/80, S.Lebanon Twsp, Pa BR/TR, 6', 180 lbs. Deb: 6/29/12

YEAR	TM/L	G	AB	R	H	2B	3B	HR	RBI	BB	SO	AVG	OBP	SLG	PRO+	BR	/A	RC	SB	CS	SBR	FR	POS	TPR
1912	StL-A	13	46	4	9	1	0	0	5	2		.196	.245	.217	34	-4	-4	3	1			-4	/1S	-0.7
1914	StL-A	41	58	8	8	0	1	0	4	4	13	.138	.219	.172	18	-6	-6	2	1	3	-2	-1	/12O3	-0.9
1918	Cle-A	32	96	9	22	4	3	0	3	12	10	.229	.321	.333	89	-0	-1	11	2			1	1/O	-0.1
Total	3	86	200	21	39	5	4	0	12	18	23	.195	.275	.260	58	-10	-11	16	4	3		-5	/102S3	-1.7

■ ELMER MILLER
Miller, Elmer b: 7/28/1890, Sandusky, Ohio d: 11/28/44, Beloit, Wis. BR/TR, 6', 175 lbs. Deb: 4/27/12

YEAR	TM/L	G	AB	R	H	2B	3B	HR	RBI	BB	SO	AVG	OBP	SLG	PRO+	BR	/A	RC	SB	CS	SBR	FR	POS	TPR
1912	StL-N	12	37	5	7	1	0	0	3	4	9	.189	.268	.216	34	-3	-3	2	1			1	O	-0.2
1915	NY-A	26	83	4	12	1	0	0	3	4	14	.145	.193	.157	5	-10	-10	3	0			-4	O	-1.6
1916	NY-A	43	152	12	34	3	2	1	18	11	18	.224	.280	.289	70	-6	-6	15	8			5	O	-0.3
1917	NY-A	114	379	43	95	11	3	3	35	40	44	.251	.336	.319	99	1	1	45	11			-6	*O	-1.2
1918	NY-A	67	202	18	49	9	2	1	22	19	17	.243	.317	.322	91	-2	-2	22	2			4	O	-0.1
1921	*NY-A	56	242	41	72	9	8	4	36	19	16	.298	.356	.450	102	1	0	39	2	2	-1	3	O	-0.1
1922	NY-A	51	172	31	46	7	2	3	18	11	12	.267	.311	.384	79	-5	-6	20	2	3	-1	-2	O	-1.2
	Bos-A	44	147	16	28	2	3	4	16	5	10	.190	.222	.327	42	-13	-13	11	3	1	0	-0	O	-1.5
	Yr	95	319	47	74	9	5	7	34	16	22	.232	.271	.357	62	-19	-19	30	5	4	-1	-2		-2.7
Total	7	413	1414	170	343	43	20	16	151	113	140	.243	.307	.335	80	-37	-40	157	29	6		1	O	-6.2

■ ELMER MILLER
Miller, Elmer Joseph "Lefty" b: 4/17/03, Detroit, Mich. d: 1/8/87, Corona, Cal. BL/TL, 5'11", 189 lbs. Deb: 6/21/29

YEAR	TM/L	G	AB	R	H	2B	3B	HR	RBI	BB	SO	AVG	OBP	SLG	PRO+	BR	/A	RC	SB	CS	SBR	FR	POS	TPR
1929	Phi-N	31	38	3	9	1	0	1	4	1	5	.237	.256	.342	44	-3	-4	3	0			2	/PO	0.0

■ KOHLY MILLER
Miller, Frank A. b: Philadelphia, Pa. TR , Deb: 10/03/1892

YEAR	TM/L	G	AB	R	H	2B	3B	HR	RBI	BB	SO	AVG	OBP	SLG	PRO+	BR	/A	RC	SB	CS	SBR	FR	POS	TPR
1892	Was-N	1	3	0	0	0	0	0	0	0	1	.000	.000	.000	-99	-1	-1	0	0			-1	/S	-0.1
	StL-N	1	4	0	0	0	0	0	0	0	0	.000	.000	.000	-99	-1	-1	0	0			-1	/3	-0.1
	Yr	2	7	0	0	0	0	0	0	0	1	.000	.000	.000	-99	-2	-2	0	0			-2		-0.2
1897	Phi-N	3	11	2	2	0	0	0	1	2		.182	.308	.182	34	-1	-1	1	0			-2	/2	-0.2
Total	2	5	18	2	2	0	0	0	1	2	1	.111	.200	.111	-12	-3	-3	1	0			-4	/23S	-0.4

■ GEORGE MILLER
Miller, George C. b: 2/19/1853, Newport, Ky. d: 7/24/29, Norwood, Ohio BR/TR, 5'5", 160 lbs. Deb: 9/06/1877

YEAR	TM/L	G	AB	R	H	2B	3B	HR	RBI	BB	SO	AVG	OBP	SLG	PRO+	BR	/A	RC	SB	CS	SBR	FR	POS	TPR
1877	Cin-N	11	37	4	6	1	0	0	3	5	2	.162	.262	.189	50	-2	-1	2				0	C	0.0
1884	Cin-a	6	20	6	5	1	1	0		1		.250	.318	.400	130	1	1	3				2	/C	0.2
Total	2	17	57	10	11	2	1	0	3	6	2	.193	.281	.263	80	-1	-1	4				2	/C	0.2

■ DOGGIE MILLER
Miller, George Frederick "Foghorn" or "Calliope" b: 8/15/1864, Brooklyn, N.Y. d: 4/6/09, Brooklyn, N.Y. BR/TR, 5'6", Deb: 5/01/1884 M

YEAR	TM/L	G	AB	R	H	2B	3B	HR	RBI	BB	SO	AVG	OBP	SLG	PRO+	BR	/A	RC	SB	CS	SBR	FR	POS	TPR
1884	Pit-a	89	347	46	78	10	2	0		13		.225	.257	.265	72	-10	-11	24				-7	OC/32	-1.3
1885	Pit-a	42	166	19	27	3	1	0		4		.163	.182	.193	20	-14	-14	6				-5	C/OS3	-1.2
1886	Pit-a	83	317	70	80	15	1	2		43		.252	.343	.325	112	6	6	49	35			-26	CO/2	-1.4
1887	Pit-N	87	342	58	83	17	4	1	34	35	13	.243	.317	.325	85	-8	-5	47	33			-25	CO/3	-1.7
1888	Pit-N	103	404	50	112	17	5	0	36	18	16	.277	.319	.344	123	6	10	54	27			-15	CO/3	-0.1
1889	Pit-N	104	422	77	113	25	3	6	56	31	11	.268	.321	.384	108	-2	-4	59	16			-7	CO/3	-0.1
1890	Pit-N	138	549	85	150	24	3	4	66	68	11	.273	.357	.350	123	8	18	82	32			2	3OSC/2	2.1
1891	Pit-N	135	548	80	156	19	6	4	57	59	26	.285	.357	.363	115	9	12	86	35			-16	CS3O/1	0.0
1892	Pit-N	149	623	103	158	15	12	3	59	69	14	.254	.335	.326	101	3	3	79	28			-12	OCS/3	-0.6
1893	Pit-N	41	154	23	28	6	1	0	17	17	8	.182	.284	.234	40	-13	-12	11	3			-0	C	-0.7
1894	StL-N	127	481	93	163	9	11	8	86	58	9	.339	.414	.453	111	10	10	100	17			-15	3C21/OSM	0.0
1895	StL-N	121	490	81	143	15	4	5	74	25	12	.292	.334	.369	84	-13	-11	68	18			-24	3CO/S1	-2.5
1896	Lou-N	98	324	54	89	17	4	1	33	27	9	.275	.334	.361	89	-7	-5	46	16			-16	C2/O31S	-1.2
Total	13	1317	5167	839	1380	192	57	33	518	467	129	.267	.333	.345	99	-25	6	710	260			-165	CO3/S21	-8.7

■ HUGHIE MILLER
Miller, Hugh Stanley "Cotton" b: 12/28/1887, St.Louis, Mo. d: 12/24/45, Jefferson Barracks, Mo. BR/TR, 6'1.5", 175 lbs. Deb: 6/18/11

YEAR	TM/L	G	AB	R	H	2B	3B	HR	RBI	BB	SO	AVG	OBP	SLG	PRO+	BR	/A	RC	SB	CS	SBR	FR	POS	TPR
1911	Phi-N	1	0	0	0	0	0	0	0	0	0	—	—	—	—	0	0	0	0			0	R	0.0
1914	StL-F	132	490	51	109	20	5	0	46	27	57	.222	.264	.284	54	-28	-31	41	4			0	*1	-2.9
1915	StL-F	7	6	0	3	1	0	0	3	0	0	.500	.500	.667	232	1	1	2	0			0	/1	0.1
Total	3	140	496	51	112	21	5	0	49	27	57	.226	.267	.288	56	-27	-30	43	4			0	1	-2.8

■ JAKE MILLER
Miller, Jacob George (b: Jacob George Munzing) b: 12/1/1895, Baltimore, Md. d: 8/24/74, Towson, Md. BR/TR, 5'10", 170 lbs. Deb: 7/16/22

YEAR	TM/L	G	AB	R	H	2B	3B	HR	RBI	BB	SO	AVG	OBP	SLG	PRO+	BR	/A	RC	SB	CS	SBR	FR	POS	TPR
1922	Pit-N	3	11	0	1	0	0	0	0	2	0	.091	.231	.091	-14	-2	-2	0	1	0	0	-0	/O	-0.1

■ HACK MILLER
Miller, James Eldridge b: 2/13/13, Celeste, Tex. d: 11/21/66, Dallas, Tex. BR/TR, 5'11.5", 215 lbs. Deb: 4/18/44

YEAR	TM/L	G	AB	R	H	2B	3B	HR	RBI	BB	SO	AVG	OBP	SLG	PRO+	BR	/A	RC	SB	CS	SBR	FR	POS	TPR
1944	Det-A	5	5	1	1	0	0	1	3	1	1	.200	.333	.800	207	1	1	1	0	0	0	0	/C	0.1
1945	Det-A	2	4	0	3	0	0	0	1	0	0	.750	.750	.750	315	1	1	1	0	0	0	-0	/C	0.1
Total	2	7	9	1	4	0	0	1	4	1	1	.444	.500	.778	250	2	2	3	0	0	0	-0	/C	0.2

■ JIM MILLER
Miller, James McCurdy "Rabbit" b: 10/2/1880, Pittsburgh, Pa. d: 2/7/37, Pittsburgh, Pa. BR/TR, 5'8", 165 lbs. Deb: 9/09/01

YEAR	TM/L	G	AB	R	H	2B	3B	HR	RBI	BB	SO	AVG	OBP	SLG	PRO+	BR	/A	RC	SB	CS	SBR	FR	POS	TPR
1901	NY-N	18	58	3	8	0	0	0	3	6		.138	.219	.138	6	-7	-6	2	1			-2	2	-0.7

■ JOHN MILLER
Miller, John Allen b: 3/14/44, Alhambra, Cal. BR/TR, 5'11", 195 lbs. Deb: 9/11/66

YEAR	TM/L	G	AB	R	H	2B	3B	HR	RBI	BB	SO	AVG	OBP	SLG	PRO+	BR	/A	RC	SB	CS	SBR	FR	POS	TPR
1966	NY-A	6	23	1	2	0	0	2	0	9		.087	.087	.217	-16	-3	-3	0	0	0	0	-1	/1O	-0.4
1969	LA-N	26	38	3	8	1	0	1	1	2	9	.211	.250	.316	62	-2	-2	3	0	0	0	-0	/O132	-0.2
Total	2	32	61	4	10	1	0	2	3	2	18	.164	.190	.279	33	-6	-5	4	0	0	0	-1	/O132	-0.6

■ DOTS MILLER
Miller, John Barney b: 9/9/1886, Kearny, N.J. d: 9/5/23, Saranac Lake, N.Y. BR/TR, 5'11.5", 170 lbs. Deb: 4/16/09

YEAR	TM/L	G	AB	R	H	2B	3B	HR	RBI	BB	SO	AVG	OBP	SLG	PRO+	BR	/A	RC	SB	CS	SBR	FR	POS	TPR
1909	*Pit-N	151	560	71	156	31	13	3	87	39		.279	.329	.396	115	14	9	78	14			-11	*2	-0.2
1910	Pit-N	120	444	45	101	13	10	1	48	33	41	.227	.284	.309	69	-17	-20	43	11			-18	*2/1S	-3.7
1911	Pit-N	137	470	82	126	17	8	6	78	51	48	.268	.348	.377	99	2	-1	69	17			-6	*2	-0.9
1912	Pit-N	148	567	74	156	33	12	4	87	37	45	.275	.324	.397	98	-5	-4	78	18			1	*1	-0.8
1913	Pit-N	154	580	75	158	24	20	7	90	37	52	.272	.317	.419	114	4	8	81	20			-4	*1/S	-0.3
1914	StL-N	155	573	67	166	27	10	4	88	34	52	.290	.339	.393	119	11	12	79	16			0	1S/2	1.3
1915	StL-N	150	553	73	146	17	10	2	72	43	48	.264	.324	.342	101	1	1	65	27	19	-3	4	12/3S	-0.1
1916	StL-N	143	505	47	120	22	7	1	46	40	49	.238	.300	.315	89	-6	-6	54	18			2	12S/3	-0.5
1917	StL-N	148	544	61	135	15	9	2	45	33	52	.248	.295	.320	91	-8	-6	54	14			19	21S	1.9
1919	StL-N	101	346	38	80	10	4	1	24	13	23	.231	.265	.292	72	-14	-12	28	6			2	12	-1.1
1920	Phi-N	98	343	41	87	12	2	1	27	16	17	.254	.289	.309	68	-13	-14	31	13	6	0	-9	23S/10	-2.1
1921	Phi-N	84	320	37	95	11	3	0	23	15	27	.297	.330	.350	74	-9	-12	36	3	5	-2	1	31/2	-1.3
Total	12	1589	5805	711	1526	232	108	32	715	391	454	.263	.314	.357	95	-39	-46	696	177	30		-19	12S/30	-7.8

■ JOE MILLER
Miller, Joseph A. b: 2/17/1861, Baltimore, Md. d: 4/23/28, Wheeling, W.V.A 5'9.5", 165 lbs. Deb: 5/01/1884

YEAR	TM/L	G	AB	R	H	2B	3B	HR	RBI	BB	SO	AVG	OBP	SLG	PRO+	BR	/A	RC	SB	CS	SBR	FR	POS	TPR
1884	Tol-a	105	423	46	101	12	8	1		26		.239	.284	.312	94	-1	-3	38				1	*S	-0.3
1885	Lou-a	98	339	44	62	9	5	0		28		.183	.249	.239	57	-15	-15	21				3	*S3/2	-0.9
Total	2	203	762	90	163	21	13	1		54		.214	.269	.280	77	-16	-18	59				4	S/32	-1.2

YEAR	TM/L	G	AB	R	H	2B	3B	HR	RBI	BB	SO	AVG	OBP	SLG	PRO+	BR	/A	RC	SB	CS	SBR	FR	POS	TPR

■ JOE MILLER   Miller, Joseph Wick b: 7/24/1850, Germany   d: 8/30/1891, White Bear Lake, Minn.   5'10.5", 169 lbs.   Deb: 6/26/1872 M

1872	Nat-n	1	4	0	1	0	0	0		0		.250	.250	.250	47	-0	-0	0					/1M	0.0
1875	Wes-n	13	50	4	6	1	0	0		0		.120	.120	.140	-10	-5	-6	1					2	-0.4
	Chi-n	15	53	1	8	0	0	0		0		.151	.151	.151	5	-5	-5	1					2/O	-0.4
	Yr	28	103	5	14	1	0	0		0		.136	.136	.146	-3	-10	-11	2						-0.8
Total	2 n	29	107	5	15	1	0	0		0		.140	.140	.150	-0	-10	-11	2					/2O1	-0.8

■ KEITH MILLER   Miller, Keith Alan b: 6/12/63, Midland, Mich.   BR/TR, 5'11", 175 lbs.   Deb: 6/16/87

1987	NY-N	25	51	14	19	2	2	0	1	2	6	.373	.407	.490	144	3	3	11	8	1	2	2	2	0.7
1988	NY-N	40	70	9	15	1	1	1	5	6	10	.214	.276	.300	69	-3	-3	5	0	5	-3	-7	2/S3O	-1.2
1989	NY-N	57	143	15	33	7	0	1	7	5	27	.231	.262	.301	63	-8	-7	12	6	0	2	-3	2O/S3	-0.7
1990	NY-N	88	233	42	60	8	0	1	12	23	46	.258	.329	.305	77	-7	-6	27	16	3	3	9	O2/S	0.4
Total	4	210	497	80	127	18	3	3	25	36	89	.256	.311	.322	80	-15	-13	54	30	9	4	2	/O2S3	-0.8

■ ED MILLER   Miller, L. Edward b: Tecumseh, Mich.   Deb: 7/18/1884

| 1884 | Tol-a | 8 | 24 | 2 | 6 | 0 | 0 | 0 | | 1 | | .250 | .280 | .250 | 74 | -1 | -1 | 2 | | | | -1 | /O | 0.0 |

■ HACK MILLER   Miller, Lawrence H. b: 1/1/1894, New York, N.Y.   d: 9/17/71, Oakland, Cal.   BR/TR, 5'9", 195 lbs.   Deb: 9/22/16

1916	Bro-N	3	3	0	1	0	0	0	1	1	1	.333	.500	1.000	345	1	1	2	0			-0	/O	0.1
1918	*Bos-A	12	29	2	8	2	0	0	4	0	4	.276	.276	.345	89	-1	-1	3	0			-3	O	-0.4
1922	Chi-N	122	466	61	164	28	5	12	78	26	39	.352	.389	.511	128	20	18	91	3	3	-1	-5	*O	0.8
1923	Chi-N	135	485	74	146	24	2	20	88	27	39	.301	.343	.482	116	9	9	79	6	5	-1	2	*O	0.5
1924	Chi-N	53	131	17	44	8	1	4	25	8	11	.336	.379	.504	133	6	6	25	1	0		-5	O	0.1
1925	Chi-N	24	86	10	24	3	2	2	9	2	9	.279	.303	.430	84	-2	-2	11	0	1	-1	-4	O	-0.6
Total	6	349	1200	164	387	65	11	38	205	64	103	.322	.361	.490	120	33	31	209	10	9		-14	O	0.5

■ LEMMIE MILLER   Miller, Lemmie Earl b: 6/2/60, Dallas, Tex.   BR/TR, 6'1", 190 lbs.   Deb: 5/22/84

| 1984 | LA-N | 8 | 12 | 1 | 2 | 0 | 0 | 0 | 0 | 1 | 2 | .167 | .231 | .167 | 13 | -1 | -1 | 1 | 0 | 0 | 0 | -0 | /O | -0.1 |

■ OTTO MILLER   Miller, Lowell Otto "Moonie" b: 6/1/1889, Minden, Neb.   d: 3/29/62, Brooklyn, N.Y.   BR/TR, 6', 196 lbs.   Deb: 7/16/10 C

1910	Bro-N	31	66	5	11	3	0	0	2	2		.167	.203	.212	22	-7	-7	3	1			9	C	0.4
1911	Bro-N	25	62	7	13	2	2	0	8	0	4	.210	.210	.306	46	-5	-5	4	2			-3	C	-0.5
1912	Bro-N	98	316	35	88	18	1	1	31	18	50	.278	.325	.351	88	-7	-5	39	11			12	C	1.2
1913	Bro-N	104	320	26	87	11	7	0	26	10	31	.272	.294	.350	81	-8	-9	34	7			-37	*C/1	-4.1
1914	Bro-N	54	169	17	39	6	1	0	9	7	20	.231	.261	.278	59	-9	-9	12	0			0	C/1	-0.6
1915	Bro-N	84	254	20	57	4	6	0	25	6	28	.224	.245	.287	60	-13	-13	20	3			8	C	0.1
1916	*Bro-N	73	216	16	55	9	2	1	17	7	29	.255	.281	.329	85	-4	-4	22	6			4	C	0.4
1917	Bro-N	92	274	19	63	5	4	1	17	14	29	.230	.272	.288	70	-9	-10	23	5			1	C	-0.4
1918	Bro-N	75	228	9	44	6	1	0	8	9	20	.193	.230	.228	40	-16	-16	11	1			4	C/1	-0.7
1919	Bro-N	51	164	18	37	5	0	0	5	7	14	.226	.257	.256	53	-9	-9	11	2			2	C	-0.3
1920	*Bro-N	90	301	16	87	9	2	0	33	9	18	.289	.312	.332	82	-6	-7	30	0	5	-3	-1	C	-0.5
1921	Bro-N	91	286	22	67	8	6	1	27	9	26	.234	.260	.315	50	-20	-22	24	2	1	0	10	C	-0.5
1922	Bro-N	59	180	20	47	11	1	1	23	6	13	.261	.285	.350	63	-10	-10	18	0	0	0	4	C	-0.4
Total	13	927	2836	229	695	97	33	5	231	104	301	.245	.275	.308	67	-123	-126	250	40	6		14	C/1	-5.9

■ KEITH MILLER   Miller, Neal Keith b: 3/7/63, Dallas, Tex.   BB/TR, 5'11", 175 lbs.   Deb: 4/23/88

1988	Phi-N	47	48	4	8	3	0	0	6	5	13	.167	.245	.229	36	-4	-4	3	0	0	0	-2	/O3S	-0.6
1989	Phi-N	8	10	0	3	1	0	0	0	0	3	.300	.300	.400	98	-0	-0	1	0	0	0	0	/O	0.0
Total	2	55	58	4	11	4	0	0	6	5	16	.190	.254	.259	47	-4	-4	4	0	0	0	-2	/O3S	-0.6

■ NORM MILLER   Miller, Norman Calvin b: 2/5/46, Los Angeles, Cal.   BL/TR, 5'10", 185 lbs.   Deb: 9/11/65

1965	Hou-N	11	15	2	3	0	0	1	1	1	7	.200	.250	.333	67	-1	-1	1	0	0	0	-0	/O	0.0
1966	Hou-N	11	34	1	5	0	0	1	3	2	8	.147	.194	.235	20	-4	-3	2	0	0	0	0	/O3	-0.3
1967	Hou-N	64	190	15	39	9	3	4	14	19	42	.205	.278	.300	68	-8	-8	14	2	0	1	-1	O	-1.0
1968	Hou-N	79	257	35	61	18	2	6	28	22	48	.237	.310	.393	112	3	3	31	6	5	-1	-2	O	-0.4
1969	Hou-N	119	409	58	108	21	4	4	50	47	77	.264	.350	.364	102	1	2	54	4	4	-1	-0	*O	-0.5
1970	Hou-N	90	226	29	54	9	0	4	29	41	33	.239	.358	.332	90	-3	-2	29	3	1	0	-1	O/C	-0.5
1971	Hou-N	45	74	5	19	5	0	2	10	5	13	.257	.313	.405	105	0	0	9	0	0	0	-2	O/C	-0.2
1972	Hou-N	67	107	18	26	4	0	4	13	13	23	.243	.331	.393	107	1	1	14	0	0	0	-1	O	0.0
1973	Hou-N	3	3	0	0	0	0	0	0	0	2	.000	.000	.000	-99	-1	-1	0	0	0	0	0	/O	0.0
	Atl-N	9	8	2	3	1	0	1	6	3	3	.375	.545	.875	267	2	2	4	0	0	0	-0	/O	0.2
	Yr	12	11	2	3	1	0	1	6	3	5	.273	.429	.636	181	1	1	3	0	0	0	-0		0.2
1974	Atl-N	42	41	1	7	1	0	1	5	7	9	.171	.292	.268	55	-2	-2	4	0	0	0	0	/O	-0.1
Total	10	540	1364	166	325	68	10	24	159	160	265	.238	.325	.356	95	-12	-8	162	16	10	-1	-7	O/C3	-2.8

■ OTTO MILLER   Miller, Otis Louis b: 2/2/01, Belleville, Ill.   d: 7/26/59, Belleville, Ill.   BR/TR, 5'10.5", 168 lbs.   Deb: 4/17/27

1927	StL-A	51	76	8	17	5	0	0	8	8	5	.224	.306	.289	53	-5	-5	7	0	1	-1	-4	S3	-0.5
1930	Bos-A	112	370	49	106	22	5	0	40	26	21	.286	.333	.373	82	-12	-10	46	2	4	-2	-6	32	-1.2
1931	Bos-A	107	389	38	106	12	1	0	43	15	20	.272	.301	.308	64	-22	-19	36	1	1	-0	-1	32	-1.2
1932	Bos-A	2	2	0	0	0	0	0	0	0	0	.000	.000	.000	-99	-1	-1	0	0	0	0	0	H	0.0
Total	4	272	837	95	229	39	6	0	91	49	46	.274	.315	.335	71	-40	-35	89	3	6	-3	-10	3/2S	-2.9

■ RALPH MILLER   Miller, Ralph Joseph b: 2/29/1896, Ft. Wayne, Ind.   d: 3/18/39, Ft.Wayne, Ind.   BR/TR, 6', 190 lbs.   Deb: 4/14/20

1920	Phi-N	97	338	28	74	14	2	0	28	11	32	.219	.246	.266	45	-23	-25	22	3	4	-2	1	3/1SO	-2.2
1921	Phi-N	57	204	19	62	10	0	3	26	6	10	.304	.327	.397	84	-3	-5	25	3	5	-2	0	S3	-0.1
1924	*Was-A	9	15	1	2	0	0	0	0	1	1	.133	.188	.133	-17	-3	-3	0	0	0	0	0	/2	-0.1
Total	3	163	557	48	138	24	2	3	54	18	43	.248	.274	.311	59	-29	-33	47	6	9	-4	1	3/S210	-2.4

■ RAY MILLER   Miller, Raymond Peter b: 2/12/1888, Pittsburgh, Pa.   d: 4/7/27, Pittsburgh, Pa.   5'10", 168 lbs.   Deb: 4/14/17

| 1917 | Cle-A | 19 | 21 | 1 | 4 | 1 | 0 | 0 | 2 | 8 | 3 | .190 | .414 | .238 | 92 | 1 | 0 | 2 | 0 | | | 1 | /1 | 0.2 |
| | Pit-N | 6 | 27 | 1 | 4 | 1 | 0 | 0 | 2 | 0 | 3 | .148 | .207 | .185 | 20 | -3 | -3 | 1 | 0 | | | 0 | /1 | -0.2 |

■ RICK MILLER   Miller, Richard Alan b: 4/19/48, Grand Rapids, Mich.   BL/TL, 6', 175 lbs.   Deb: 9/04/71

1971	Bos-A	15	33	9	11	1	0	1	7	8	8	.333	.463	.576	180	4	4	9	0	2	-1	2	O	0.5
1972	Bos-A	89	98	13	21	4	1	3	15	11	27	.214	.294	.367	91	-1	-1	10	0	2	-1	10	O	0.7
1973	Bos-A	143	441	65	115	17	7	6	43	51	56	.261	.341	.372	95	-1	-2	58	12	7	-1	-11	*O	-1.7
1974	Bos-A	114	280	41	73	8	1	5	22	37	47	.261	.347	.350	94	1	-1	38	13	2	3	-4	*O	-0.4
1975	*Bos-A	77	108	21	21	2	1	0	15	21	20	.194	.326	.231	55	-5	-6	9	3	2	-0	7	O	0.0
1976	Bos-A	105	269	40	76	15	3	0	27	34	47	.283	.363	.361	100	5	1	36	11	10	-3	7	O/D	0.4
1977	Bos-A	86	189	34	48	9	3	0	24	22	30	.254	.341	.333	76	-3	-6	23	11	5	0	2	O/D	-0.6
1978	Cal-A	132	475	66	125	25	4	1	37	54	70	.263	.343	.339	96	-3	-1	53	3	13	-7	21	*O	1.0
1979	*Cal-A	120	427	60	125	15	5	2	28	50	69	.293	.368	.365	102	1	3	60	5	4	-1	6	*O	0.3
1980	Cal-A	129	412	52	113	14	3	2	33	48	71	.274	.351	.337	92	-4	-3	53	7	3	0	1	*O	-0.4
1981	Bos-A	97	316	38	92	17	2	2	33	28	36	.291	.351	.377	103	4	2	41	3	5	-2	-6	O	-0.8
1982	Bos-A	135	409	50	104	13	2	4	38	40	41	.254	.324	.325	75	-11	-14	43	5	6	-2	-12	*O	-3.2

YEAR	TM/L	G	AB	R	H	2B	3B	HR	RBI	BB	SO	AVG	OBP	SLG	PRO+	BR	/A	RC	SB	CS	SBR	FR	POS	TPR
1983	Bos-A	104	262	41	75	10	2	2	21	28	30	.286	.357	.363	92	0	-2	34	3	3	-1	1	O/1D	-0.2
1984	Bos-A	95	123	17	32	5	1	0	12	17	22	.260	.350	.317	82	-2	-2	14	1	1	-0	1	O/1	-0.3
1985	Bos-A	41	45	5	15	2	0	0	9	5	6	.333	.400	.378	110	1	1	7	1	0	0	0	/OD	0.1
Total	15	1482	3887	552	1046	161	35	28	369	454	583	.269	.348	.350	92	-11	-29	488	78	65	-16	24	*O/D1	-4.6

■ **ROD MILLER**   Miller, Rodney Carter   b: 1/16/40, Portland, Ore.   BL/TR, 5'10", 160 lbs.   Deb: 9/28/57

YEAR	TM/L	G	AB	R	H	2B	3B	HR	RBI	BB	SO	AVG	OBP	SLG	PRO+	BR	/A	RC	SB	CS	SBR	FR	POS	TPR
1957	Bro-N	1	1	0	0	0	0	0	0	0	1	.000	.000	.000	-91	-0	-0	0	0	0	0	0	H	0.0

■ **DOC MILLER**   Miller, Roy Oscar   b: 1883, Chatham, Ont., Canada   d: 7/31/38, Jersey City, N.J.   BL/TL, 5'10.5", 170 lbs.   Deb: 5/04/10

YEAR	TM/L	G	AB	R	H	2B	3B	HR	RBI	BB	SO	AVG	OBP	SLG	PRO+	BR	/A	RC	SB	CS	SBR	FR	POS	TPR
1910	Chi-N	1	1	0	0	0	0	0	0	0	0	.000	.000	.000	-99	-0	-0	0	0			0	H	0.0
	Bos-N	130	482	48	138	27	4	3	55	33	52	.286	.333	.378	103	3	-0	66	17			-14	*O	-1.9
	Yr	131	483	48	138	27	4	3	55	33	52	.286	.333	.377	102	3	-0	66	17			-14		-1.9
1911	Bos-N	146	577	69	192	36	3	7	91	43	43	.333	.379	.442	120	21	15	107	32			-2	*O	0.8
1912	Bos-N	51	201	26	47	8	1	2	24	14	17	.234	.287	.313	63	-10	-11	22	6			-2	O	-1.3
	Phi-N	67	177	24	51	12	5	0	21	9	13	.288	.323	.412	94	-1	-2	24	3			0	O	-0.2
	Yr	118	378	50	98	20	6	2	45	23	30	.259	.303	.360	78	-11	-13	44	9			-2		-1.5
1913	Phi-N	69	87	9	30	6	0	0	11	6	6	.345	.400	.414	127	4	3	14	2			-3	O	0.0
1914	Cin-N	93	192	8	49	7	2	0	33	16	18	.255	.313	.313	83	-3	-4	19	4			-3	O	-0.8
Total	5	557	1717	184	507	96	15	12	235	121	149	.295	.343	.390	102	13	1	251	64			-24	O	-3.4

■ **RUDY MILLER**   Miller, Rudel Charles   b: 7/12/1900, Kalamazoo, Mich.   BR/TR, 6'1", 180 lbs.   Deb: 9/19/29

YEAR	TM/L	G	AB	R	H	2B	3B	HR	RBI	BB	SO	AVG	OBP	SLG	PRO+	BR	/A	RC	SB	CS	SBR	FR	POS	TPR
1929	Phi-A	2	4	1	1	0	0	0	1	3	0	.250	.571	.250	115	1	0	1	0	0	0	-0	/3	0.0

■ **TOM MILLER**   Miller, Thomas P. "Reddy"   b: Philadelphia, Pa.   d: 5/29/1876, Philadelphia, Pa.   Deb: 10/24/1874

YEAR	TM/L	G	AB	R	H	2B	3B	HR	RBI	BB	SO	AVG	OBP	SLG	PRO+	BR	/A	RC	SB	CS	SBR	FR	POS	TPR
1874	Ath-n	4	16	1	8	0	0	0		0		.500	.500	.500	202	2	2	4					C	0.1
1875	StL-n	55	212	17	34	2	0	0		2		.160	.168	.170	19	-17	-14	6					*C/3	-1.0
Total	2 n	59	228	18	42	2	0	0		2		.184	.191	.193	35	-15	-12	10					/C3	-0.9

■ **TOM MILLER**   Miller, Thomas Royall   b: 7/5/1897, Powhatan Court House, Va.   d: 8/13/80, Richmond, Va.   BL/TR, 5'11", 180 lbs.   Deb: 7/29/18

YEAR	TM/L	G	AB	R	H	2B	3B	HR	RBI	BB	SO	AVG	OBP	SLG	PRO+	BR	/A	RC	SB	CS	SBR	FR	POS	TPR
1918	Bos-N	2	2	0	0	0	0	0	0	0	0	.000	.000	.000	-99	-0	-0	-0	1			0	H	0.0
1919	Bos-N	7	6	2	2	0	0	0	0	0	1	.333	.333	.333	105	-0	0	1	0			0	H	0.0
Total	2	9	8	2	2	0	0	0	0	0	1	.250	.250	.250	53	-0	-0	1	1			0		0.0

■ **WARD MILLER**   Miller, Ward Taylor "Windy" or "Grump"   b: 7/5/1884, Mt.Carroll, Ill.   d: 9/4/58, Dixon, Ill.   BL/TR, 5'11", 177 lbs.   Deb: 4/14/09

YEAR	TM/L	G	AB	R	H	2B	3B	HR	RBI	BB	SO	AVG	OBP	SLG	PRO+	BR	/A	RC	SB	CS	SBR	FR	POS	TPR
1909	Pit-N	15	56	2	8	0	1	0	4	4		.143	.213	.179	20	-5	-6	3	2			-1	O	-0.7
	Cin-N	43	113	17	35	3	1	0	4	6		.310	.345	.354	118	2	2	17	9			-6	O	-0.5
	Yr	58	169	19	43	3	2	0	8	10		.254	.300	.296	84	-3	-3	18	11			-7		-1.2
1910	Cin-N	81	126	21	30	6	0	0	10	22	13	.238	.356	.286	92	-1	-0	17	10			2	O	0.1
1912	Chi-N	86	241	45	74	11	4	0	22	26	18	.307	.377	.386	109	3	4	39	11			-5	O	-0.2
1913	Chi-N	80	203	23	48	5	7	1	16	34	33	.236	.349	.345	98	1	1	27	13			8	O	0.8
1914	StL-F	121	402	49	118	17	7	4	50	59	36	.294	.397	.400	122	18	15	74	18			10	*O	2.0
1915	StL-F	154	536	80	164	19	9	1	63	79	39	.306	.400	.381	125	25	21	101	33			3	*O	1.8
1916	StL-A	146	485	72	129	17	5	1	50	72	76	.266	.371	.328	116	9	12	65	25	21	-5	-5	*O	-0.6
1917	StL-A	43	82	13	17	1	1	1	2	16	15	.207	.350	.280	96	0	0	10	7			-4	O	-0.5
Total	8	769	2244	322	623	79	35	8	221	318	230	.278	.375	.355	113	52	49	353	128	21		1	O	2.2

■ **WARREN MILLER**   Miller, Warren Lemuel "Gitz"   b: 7/14/1885, Philadelphia, Pa.   d: 8/12/56, Philadelphia, Pa.   BL/TL, 5'10", 160 lbs.   Deb: 7/29/09

YEAR	TM/L	G	AB	R	H	2B	3B	HR	RBI	BB	SO	AVG	OBP	SLG	PRO+	BR	/A	RC	SB	CS	SBR	FR	POS	TPR
1909	Was-A	26	51	5	11	0	0	0	1	4		.216	.273	.216	57	-3	-2	3	0			-1	O	-0.4
1911	Was-A	21	34	3	5	0	0	0	0	0		.147	.147	.147	-18	-5	-5	1	0			-2	/O	-0.7
Total	2	47	85	8	16	0	0	0	1	4		.188	.225	.188	25	-8	-8	4	0			-3	/O	-1.1

■ **BILL MILLER**   Miller, William Alexander   b: 5/23/1879, Germany   d: 9/8/57, Ashtabula, Ohio   BL/TL, 6'2", 170 lbs.   Deb: 8/23/02

YEAR	TM/L	G	AB	R	H	2B	3B	HR	RBI	BB	SO	AVG	OBP	SLG	PRO+	BR	/A	RC	SB	CS	SBR	FR	POS	TPR
1902	Pit-N	1	5	0	1	0	0	0	2	0		.200	.200	.200	24	-0	-0	0				-0	/O	0.0

■ **WALLY MILLIES**   Millies, Walter Louis   b: 10/18/06, Chicago, Ill.   BR/TR, 5'10.5", 170 lbs.   Deb: 9/23/34

YEAR	TM/L	G	AB	R	H	2B	3B	HR	RBI	BB	SO	AVG	OBP	SLG	PRO+	BR	/A	RC	SB	CS	SBR	FR	POS	TPR
1934	Bro-N	2	7	0	0	0	0	0	0	0	0	.000	.000	.000	-99	-2	-2	0	0			1	/C	0.0
1936	Was-A	74	215	26	67	10	2	0	25	11	8	.312	.345	.377	83	-7	-6	28	1	0	0	-0	C	0.0
1937	Was-A	59	179	21	40	7	1	0	28	9	15	.223	.261	.274	36	-18	-17	13	1	0	0	2	C	-0.9
1939	Phi-N	84	205	12	48	3	0	0	12	9	5	.234	.270	.249	41	-17	-16	13	0			-8	C	-2.1
1940	Phi-N	26	43	1	3	0	0	0	0	4	4	.070	.149	.070	-39	-8	-8	0	0			2	C	-0.4
1941	Phi-N	1	2	0	0	0	0	0	0	0	0	.000	.000	.000	-99	-1	-1	0	0			0	/C	0.0
Total	6	246	651	60	158	20	3	0	65	33	32	.243	.280	.283	47	-53	-49	55	2	0		-3	C	-3.4

■ **JOCKO MILLIGAN**   Milligan, John   b: 8/8/1861, Philadelphia, Pa.   d: 8/29/23, Philadelphia, Pa.   BR/TR, 6', 192 lbs.   Deb: 5/01/1884

YEAR	TM/L	G	AB	R	H	2B	3B	HR	RBI	BB	SO	AVG	OBP	SLG	PRO+	BR	/A	RC	SB	CS	SBR	FR	POS	TPR
1884	Phi-a	66	268	39	77	20	3	3		8		.287	.308	.418	129	10	8	35				10	C/O	2.1
1885	Phi-a	67	265	35	71	15	4	2		7		.268	.289	.377	106	3	1	30				7	C/1O	1.4
1886	Phi-a	75	301	52	76	17	3	5		21		.252	.301	.379	113	4	4	41	18			2	C1/O3	0.5
1887	Phi-a	95	377	54	114	27	4	2		21		.302	.344	.411	112	5	5	57	8			5	1C/O	1.4
1888	*StL-a	63	219	19	55	6	2	5	37	17		.251	.311	.365	108	5	1	26	3			6	C/1	1.2
1889	StL-a	72	273	53	100	30	2	12	76	16	19	.366	.408	.623	172	31	25	72	2			16	C/1	3.9
1890	Phi-P	62	234	38	69	9	3	3	57	19	19	.295	.363	.397	102	2	1	35	2			5	C/1	0.6
1891	Phi-a	118	455	75	138	35	12	11	106	56	51	.303	.397	.505	157	35	33	94	2			-0	C1	2.9
1892	Was-N	88	323	40	89	20	9	4	43	26	24	.276	.335	.430	137	12	13	48	2			4	C1	1.7
1893	Bal-N	24	102	19	25	5	2	1	19	5	7	.245	.294	.363	74	-4	-4	12	2			2	1/C	-0.1
	NY-N	42	147	16	34	5	6	1	25	14	13	.231	.302	.367	79	-5	-5	17	2			15	C	1.1
	Yr	66	249	35	59	10	8	2	44	19	20	.237	.299	.365	77	-9	-9	29	4			17		1.0
Total	10	772	2964	440	848	189	50	49	363	210	133	.286	.341	.433	124	98	80	469	41			71	C1/O3	16.7

■ **RANDY MILLIGAN**   Milligan, Randy Andre   b: 11/27/61, San Diego, Cal.   BR/TR, 6'2", 200 lbs.   Deb: 9/12/87

YEAR	TM/L	G	AB	R	H	2B	3B	HR	RBI	BB	SO	AVG	OBP	SLG	PRO+	BR	/A	RC	SB	CS	SBR	FR	POS	TPR
1987	NY-N	3	1	0	0	0	0	0	0	1	1	.000	.500	.000	49	0	0	0	0	0	0	0	/H	0.0
1988	Pit-N	40	82	10	18	5	0	3	8	20	24	.220	.379	.390	123	3	3	13	1	2	-1	-1	1/O	0.0
1989	Bal-A	124	365	56	98	23	5	12	45	74	75	.268	.396	.458	144	22	24	68	9	5	-0	1	*1	1.7
1990	Bal-A	109	362	64	96	20	1	20	60	88	68	.265	.412	.492	155	29	30	78	6	3	0	5	1/D	2.8
Total	4	276	810	130	212	48	6	35	113	183	168	.262	.401	.465	147	54	57	159	16	10	-1	6	1/DO	4.5

■ **JACK MILLS**   Mills, Abbott Paige   b: 10/23/1889, S.Williamstown, Mass.   d: 6/3/73, Washington, D.C.   BL/TR, 6', 165 lbs.   Deb: 7/01/11

YEAR	TM/L	G	AB	R	H	2B	3B	HR	RBI	BB	SO	AVG	OBP	SLG	PRO+	BR	/A	RC	SB	CS	SBR	FR	POS	TPR
1911	Cle-A	13	17	5	5	0	0	0	1	1		.294	.368	.294	85	-0	-0	2	1			2	/3	0.1

■ **CHARLIE MILLS**   Mills, Charles   b: Brooklyn, N.Y.   d: 4/10/1874, Brooklyn, N.Y.   6',   Deb: 5/18/1871

YEAR	TM/L	G	AB	R	H	2B	3B	HR	RBI	BB	SO	AVG	OBP	SLG	PRO+	BR	/A	RC	SB	CS	SBR	FR	POS	TPR
1871	Mut-n	32	146	27	36	4	3	0	22	1	0	.247	.252	.315	68	-7	-4	12	2				*C/O2	-0.2
1872	Mut-n	6	31	6	4	0	0	0		0		.129	.129	.129	-22	-4	-4	1					/OC	-0.2
Total	2 n	38	177	33	40	4	3	0		1		.226	.230	.282	53	-11	-8	13					/CO2	-0.4

■ **BUSTER MILLS**   Mills, Colonel Buster "Bus"   b: 9/16/08, Ranger, Tex.   BR/TR, 5'11.5", 195 lbs.   Deb: 4/18/34   MC

YEAR	TM/L	G	AB	R	H	2B	3B	HR	RBI	BB	SO	AVG	OBP	SLG	PRO+	BR	/A	RC	SB	CS	SBR	FR	POS	TPR
1934	StL-N	29	72	7	17	4	1	1	8	4	11	.236	.295	.361	70	-3	-3	8	0			1	O	-0.2
1935	Bro-N	17	56	12	12	2	1	1	7	5	11	.214	.323	.339	80	-2	-1	6	0			-1	O	-0.3

YEAR	TM/L	G	AB	R	H	2B	3B	HR	RBI	BB	SO	AVG	OBP	SLG	PRO+	BR	/A	RC	SB	CS	SBR	FR	POS	TPR
1937	Bos-A	123	505	85	149	25	8	7	58	46	41	.295	.361	.418	92	-3	-6	77	11	8	-2	-4	*O	-1.4
1938	StL-A	123	466	66	133	24	4	3	46	43	46	.285	.350	.373	81	-13	-13	61	7	8	-3	3	*O	-1.1
1940	NY-A	34	63	10	25	3	3	1	15	7	5	.397	.457	.587	176	7	7	15	0	0	0	-1	O	0.4
1942	Cle-A	80	195	19	54	4	2	1	26	24	18	.277	.353	.333	99	-1	-0	23	5	4	-1	8	O	0.4
1946	Cle-A	9	22	1	6	0	0	0	3	3	5	.273	.360	.273	84	-0	-0	2	0	1	-1	-0	/O	-0.1
Total	7	415	1379	200	396	62	19	14	163	131	137	.287	.355	.390	91	-16	-17	191	23	21		6	O	-2.3

■ EVERETT MILLS Mills, Everett b: 1845, Newark, N.J. d: 6/22/08, Newark, N.J. 6'1", 174 lbs. Deb: 5/05/1871 M

YEAR	TM/L	G	AB	R	H	2B	3B	HR	RBI	BB	SO	AVG	OBP	SLG	PRO+	BR	/A	RC	SB	CS	SBR	FR	POS	TPR
1871	Oly-n	32	157	38	43	6	4	1	24	3	1	.274	.287	.382	95	-2	-0	18	2				*1	0.0
1872	Bal-n	55	267	55	76	13	3	0			3	.285	.293	.356	94	-1	-3	28					*1M	0.2
1873	Bal-n	54	264	64	86	16	6	0			2	.326	.331	.432	123	7	7	39					*1/O	0.6
1874	Har-n	53	241	40	70	6	2	0			6	.290	.308	.332	99	1	-1	25					*1	0.2
1875	Har-n	80	341	59	91	10	4	1			0	.267	.267	.328	100	1	-1	31					*1	-0.3
1876	Har-N	63	254	28	66	8	1	0	23	1	3	.260	.263	.299	80	-4	-7	20				-2	*1	-0.6
Total	5 n	274	1270	256	366	51	19	2	24	14	1	.288	.296	.363	103	7	2	141					1/O	0.5

■ FRANK MILLS Mills, Frank Le Moyne b: 5/13/1895, Knoxville, Ohio d: 8/31/83, Youngstown, Ohio BL/TR, 6', 180 lbs. Deb: 9/22/14

YEAR	TM/L	G	AB	R	H	2B	3B	HR	RBI	BB	SO	AVG	OBP	SLG	PRO+	BR	/A	RC	SB	CS	SBR	FR	POS	TPR
1914	Cle-A	4	8	0	1	0	0	0	0	1	2	.125	.222	.125	4	-1	-1	0	0			-1	/C	-0.1

■ BRAD MILLS Mills, James Bradley b: 1/19/57, Exter, Cal. BL/TR, 6', 195 lbs. Deb: 6/08/80

YEAR	TM/L	G	AB	R	H	2B	3B	HR	RBI	BB	SO	AVG	OBP	SLG	PRO+	BR	/A	RC	SB	CS	SBR	FR	POS	TPR
1980	Mon-N	21	60	1	18	1	0	0	8	5	6	.300	.354	.317	88	-1	-1	7	0	1	-1	-1	3	-0.2
1981	*Mon-N	17	21	3	5	1	0	0	1	2	1	.238	.304	.286	67	-1	-1	2	0	0	0	0	/32	0.0
1982	Mon-N	54	67	6	15	3	0	1	2	5	11	.224	.278	.313	64	-3	-3	5	0	0	0	-3	3	-0.6
1983	Mon-N	14	20	1	5	0	0	0	1	2	3	.250	.318	.250	60	-1	-1	2	0	0	0	-1	/31	-0.1
Total	4	106	168	11	43	5	0	1	12	14	21	.256	.313	.304	73	-6	-6	16	0	1	-1	-5	/321	-0.9

■ RUPERT MILLS Mills, Rupert Frank b: 10/12/1892, Newark, N.J. d: 7/20/29, Lake Hopatcong, N.J. BR/TR, 6'2", 185 lbs. Deb: 6/23/15

YEAR	TM/L	G	AB	R	H	2B	3B	HR	RBI	BB	SO	AVG	OBP	SLG	PRO+	BR	/A	RC	SB	CS	SBR	FR	POS	TPR
1915	New-F	41	134	12	27	5	1	0	16	6	21	.201	.241	.254	49	-9	-8	10	6			0	1	-0.7

■ BILL MILLS Mills, William Henry b: 11/2/20, Boston, Mass. BR/TR, 5'10", 175 lbs. Deb: 5/19/44

YEAR	TM/L	G	AB	R	H	2B	3B	HR	RBI	BB	SO	AVG	OBP	SLG	PRO+	BR	/A	RC	SB	CS	SBR	FR	POS	TPR
1944	Phi-A	5	4	0	1	0	0	0	0	1	1	.250	.400	.250	89	0	0	0	0	0	0	0	/C	0.0

■ PETE MILNE Milne, William James b: 4/10/25, Mobile, Ala. BL/TR, 6'1", 180 lbs. Deb: 9/15/48

YEAR	TM/L	G	AB	R	H	2B	3B	HR	RBI	BB	SO	AVG	OBP	SLG	PRO+	BR	/A	RC	SB	CS	SBR	FR	POS	TPR
1948	NY-N	12	27	0	6	0	1	0	2	1	6	.222	.250	.296	47	-2	-2	2	0			-1	/O	-0.3
1949	NY-N	31	29	5	7	1	0	1	6	3	6	.241	.313	.379	85	-1	-1	3	0			0	/O	0.0
1950	NY-N	4	4	1	1	0	1	0	1	0	1	.250	.250	.750	151	0	0	1	0			0	H	0.0
Total	3	47	60	6	14	1	2	1	9	4	13	.233	.281	.367	73	-2	-2	6	0			-1	/O	-0.3

■ BRIAN MILNER Milner, Brian Tate b: 11/17/59, Fort Worth, Tex. BR/TR, 6'2", 200 lbs. Deb: 6/23/78

YEAR	TM/L	G	AB	R	H	2B	3B	HR	RBI	BB	SO	AVG	OBP	SLG	PRO+	BR	/A	RC	SB	CS	SBR	FR	POS	TPR
1978	Tor-A	2	9	3	4	0	1	0	2	0	1	.444	.444	.667	204	1	1	3	0	0	0	-3	/C	0.0

■ EDDIE MILNER Milner, Eddie James b: 5/21/55, Columbus, Ohio BL/TL, 5'11", 173 lbs. Deb: 9/02/80

YEAR	TM/L	G	AB	R	H	2B	3B	HR	RBI	BB	SO	AVG	OBP	SLG	PRO+	BR	/A	RC	SB	CS	SBR	FR	POS	TPR
1980	Cin-N	6	3	1	0	0	0	0	0	0	0	.000	.000	.000	-99	-1	-1	0	0	0	0	0	/H	0.0
1981	Cin-N	8	5	0	1	0	0	0	1	1	1	.200	.333	.400	106	0	0	1	0	0	0	0	/O	0.0
1982	Cin-N	113	407	61	109	23	5	4	31	41	40	.268	.338	.378	98	0	-1	52	18	12	-2	6	*O	0.2
1983	Cin-N	146	502	77	131	23	6	9	33	68	60	.261	.350	.384	100	3	1	72	41	12	5	13	*O	1.7
1984	Cin-N	117	336	44	78	8	4	7	29	51	50	.232	.337	.342	87	-3	-5	42	21	13	-2	6	*O	-0.4
1985	Cin-N	145	453	82	115	19	7	3	33	61	31	.254	.344	.347	89	-2	-5	60	35	13	3	9	*O	0.3
1986	Cin-N	145	424	70	110	22	6	15	47	36	56	.259	.317	.446	104	3	1	59	18	11	-1	1	*O	0.0
1987	*SF-N	101	214	38	54	14	0	4	19	24	33	.252	.328	.374	90	-4	-3	26	10	9	-2	4	O	-0.4
1988	Cin-N	23	51	3	9	1	0	0	2	4	9	.176	.236	.196	24	-5	-5	2	2	2	-1	1	O	-0.4
Total	9	804	2395	376	607	111	28	42	195	286	280	.253	.335	.376	94	-8	-17	314	145	72		39	O	1.0

■ JOHN MILNER Milner, John David "The Hammer" b: 12/28/49, Atlanta, Ga. BL/TL, 6', 185 lbs. Deb: 9/15/71

YEAR	TM/L	G	AB	R	H	2B	3B	HR	RBI	BB	SO	AVG	OBP	SLG	PRO+	BR	/A	RC	SB	CS	SBR	FR	POS	TPR
1971	NY-N	9	18	1	3	1	0	1		0	3	.167	.167	.222	9	-2	-2	1	0	0	0	1	/O	0.0
1972	NY-N	117	362	52	86	12	2	17	38	51	74	.238	.340	.423	118	8	9	54	2	1	0	1	O1	0.5
1973	*NY-N	129	451	69	108	12	3	23	72	62	84	.239	.333	.432	112	6	7	64	1	1	-0	5	10	-0.4
1974	NY-N	137	507	70	128	19	0	20	63	66	77	.252	.339	.408	110	5	6	69	10	2	2	-1	*1	0.1
1975	NY-N	91	220	24	42	11	0	7	29	33	22	.191	.302	.336	81	-7	-6	23	1	1	-0	5	O1	-0.3
1976	NY-N	127	443	56	120	25	4	15	78	65	53	.271	.364	.447	137	17	21	70	0	7	-4	-2	*O1	1.0
1977	NY-N	131	388	43	99	20	3	12	57	61	55	.255	.356	.415	111	4	7	59	6	2	1	1	10	0.3
1978	Pit-N	108	295	39	80	17	0	6	38	34	25	.271	.347	.390	101	2	1	41	5	0	2	-2	O1	-0.3
1979	*Pit-N	128	326	52	90	9	4	16	60	53	37	.276	.379	.475	126	15	13	60	3	5	-2	-5	O1	0.2
1980	Pit-N	114	238	31	58	6	0	8	34	52	29	.244	.379	.370	108	5	5	36	2	2	-1	-2	10	-0.1
1981	Pit-N	34	59	6	14	1	0	2	9	5	3	.237	.297	.356	82	-1	-2	6	0	0	0	-2	/10	-0.3
	*Mon-N	31	76	6	18	5	0	3	9	12	6	.237	.341	.421	114	2	1	11	0	1	-1	1	1	0.1
	Yr	65	135	12	32	6	0	5	18	17	9	.237	.322	.393	100	0	-0	17	0	1	-1	-1		-0.2
1982	Mon-N	26	28	1	3	0	0	0	2	4	2	.107	.219	.107	-6	-4	-4	1	0	0	0	0	/1	-0.3
	Pit-N	33	25	5	6	2	0	2	8	6	3	.240	.406	.560	163	2	2	7	1	0	0	0	/1	0.3
	Yr	59	53	6	9	2	0	2	10	10	5	.170	.313	.321	76	-1	-2	6	1	0	0	0		0.0
Total	12	1215	3436	455	855	140	16	131	498	504	473	.249	.347	.413	112	53	59	501	31	22	-4	-11	10	0.8

■ MIKE MILOSEVICH Milosevich, Michael "Mollie" b: 1/13/15, Zeigler, Ill. d: 2/3/66, E.Chicago, Ind. BR/TR, 5'10.5", 172 lbs. Deb: 4/30/44

YEAR	TM/L	G	AB	R	H	2B	3B	HR	RBI	BB	SO	AVG	OBP	SLG	PRO+	BR	/A	RC	SB	CS	SBR	FR	POS	TPR
1944	NY-A	94	312	27	77	11	4	0	32	30	37	.247	.313	.308	75	-9	-10	29	1	2	-1	7	S	0.1
1945	NY-A	30	69	5	15	2	0	0	7	6	6	.217	.289	.246	54	-4	-4	5	0	0	1	1	S/2	-0.2
Total	2	124	381	32	92	13	4	0	39	36	43	.241	.309	.297	71	-13	-14	34	1	2	-1	8	S/2	-0.1

■ DON MINCHER Mincher, Donald Ray b: 6/24/38, Huntsville, Ala. BL/TR, 6'3", 205 lbs. Deb: 4/18/60

YEAR	TM/L	G	AB	R	H	2B	3B	HR	RBI	BB	SO	AVG	OBP	SLG	PRO+	BR	/A	RC	SB	CS	SBR	FR	POS	TPR
1960	Was-A	27	79	10	19	4	1	2	5	11	11	.241	.333	.392	96	-0	-0	9	0	1	-1	-4	1	-0.5
1961	Min-A	35	101	18	19	5	1	5	11	22	11	.188	.333	.406	91	-0	-1	13	0	1	-1	-1	1	-0.5
1962	Min-A	86	121	20	29	1	1	9	29	34	24	.240	.406	.488	134	8	7	26	0	0	0	-1	1	0.4
1963	Min-A	82	225	41	58	8	0	17	42	30	51	.258	.353	.520	138	12	12	44	0	0	0	-5	1	0.5
1964	Min-A	120	287	45	68	12	4	23	56	27	51	.237	.303	.547	130	10	10	45	0	0	0	0	1	0.8
1965	*Min-A	128	346	43	87	17	3	22	65	49	73	.251	.348	.509	134	18	16	62	1	3	-2	-3	1	0.7
1966	Min-A	139	431	53	108	30	0	14	62	58	68	.251	.342	.418	110	10	7	61	3	2	-0	5	*1	0.8
1967	Cal-A	147	487	81	133	23	3	25	76	69	69	.273	.368	.487	157	31	33	87	0	3	-2	-1	*1/O	2.1
1968	Cal-A	120	399	35	94	12	1	13	48	43	65	.236	.316	.368	111	3	5	47	0	2	-1	-3	*1	-0.4
1969	Sea-A	140	427	53	105	14	0	25	78	78	69	.246	.369	.454	131	18	19	72	10	11	-4	8	*1	1.5
1970	Oak-A	140	463	62	114	18	0	27	74	56	71	.246	.331	.460	120	9	11	70	5	4	-1	2	*1	0.6
1971	Oak-A	28	92	9	22	6	1	2	8	20	14	.239	.375	.391	120	3	3	14	1	1	0	3	1	0.5
	Was-A	100	323	35	94	15	1	10	45	53	52	.291	.394	.437	143	17	19	58	2	1	0	1	1	1.9
	Yr	128	415	44	116	21	2	12	53	73	66	.280	.390	.427	138	19	22	73	3	2	-0	6		2.4
1972	Tex-A	61	191	23	45	10	0	6	39	46	23	.236	.389	.382	136	9	10	33	2	1	0	6	1	1.2
	*Oak-A	47	54	2	8	1	0	0	5	10	16	.148	.281	.167	37	-4	-4	2	0	2	-1	-0	1	-0.6
	Yr	108	245	25	53	11	0	6	44	56	39	.216	.366	.335	115	6	7	33	2	3	-1	5		0.6

YEAR	TM/L	G	AB	R	H	2B	3B	HR	RBI	BB	SO	AVG	OBP	SLG	PRO+	BR	/A	RC	SB	CS	SBR	FR	POS	TPR
Total	13	1400	4026	530	1003	176	16	200	643	606	668	.249	.351	.450	127	144	147	644	24	32	-12	8	*1/O	9.0

■ ED MINCHER
Mincher, Edward John   b: Baltimore, Md.   Deb: 5/04/1871

YEAR	TM/L	G	AB	R	H	2B	3B	HR	RBI	BB	SO	AVG	OBP	SLG	PRO+	BR	/A	RC	SB	CS	SBR	FR	POS	TPR
1871	Kek-n	9	36	4	8	0	0	0	5	0	0	.222	.222	.222	28	-3	-3	2	1				/O	-0.1
1872	Nat-n	11	54	4	5	0	0	0		0		.093	.093	.093	-37	-9	-11	0					O	-0.6
Total	2 n	20	90	8	13	0	0	0		0		.144	.144	.144	-12	-12	-14	3					/O	-0.7

■ DAN MINNEHAN
Minnehan, Daniel Joseph   b: 11/28/1865, Troy, N.Y.   d: 8/8/29, Troy, N.Y.   BR/TR, 5'10", 145 lbs.   Deb: 9/20/1895

YEAR	TM/L	G	AB	R	H	2B	3B	HR	RBI	BB	SO	AVG	OBP	SLG	PRO+	BR	/A	RC	SB	CS	SBR	FR	POS	TPR
1895	Lou-N	8	34	6	13	0	0	0	6	1	1	.382	.400	.382	112	0	1	5	0			-0	/3O	0.0

■ MINNIE MINOSO
Minoso, Saturnino Orestes Armas (Arrieta)   b: 11/29/22, Havana, Cuba   BR/TR, 5'10", 175 lbs.   Deb: 4/19/49   C

YEAR	TM/L	G	AB	R	H	2B	3B	HR	RBI	BB	SO	AVG	OBP	SLG	PRO+	BR	/A	RC	SB	CS	SBR	FR	POS	TPR
1949	Cle-A	9	16	2	3	0	0	1	1	2	2	.188	.350	.375	94	-0	-0	1	0	1	-1	0	/O	0.0
1951	Cle-A	8	14	3	6	2	0	0	2	1	1	.429	.529	.571	209	2	2	5	0	0	0	0	/1	0.2
	Chi-A	138	516	109	167	32	14	10	74	71	41	.324	.419	.498	150	36	38	115	31	10	3	-11	O3/S	2.4
	Yr	146	530	112	173	34	14	10	76	72	42	.326	.422	.500	152	38	40	120	31	10	3	-11		2.6
1952	Chi-A	147	569	96	160	24	9	13	61	71	46	.281	.375	.424	121	18	17	92	22	16	-3	11	*O/3S	2.2
1953	Chi-A	151	556	104	174	24	8	15	104	74	43	.313	.410	.466	132	31	28	106	25	16	-2	0	*O3	2.2
1954	Chi-A	153	568	119	182	29	18	19	116	77	46	.320	.416	.535	154	47	45	125	18	11	-1	12	*O/3	5.2
1955	Chi-A	139	517	79	149	26	7	10	70	76	43	.288	.390	.424	136	16	14	87	19	8	1	11	*O/3	1.9
1956	Chi-A	151	545	106	172	29	11	21	88	86	40	.316	.430	.525	149	43	42	130	12	6	0	-5	*O/31	2.9
1957	Chi-A	153	568	96	176	36	5	12	103	79	54	.310	.413	.454	136	33	32	106	18	15	-4	-1	*O/3	1.9
1958	Cle-A	149	556	94	168	25	2	24	80	59	53	.302	.384	.484	141	29	31	101	14	14	-4	6	*O/3	2.4
1959	Cle-A	148	570	92	172	32	0	21	92	54	46	.302	.379	.468	136	25	28	100	8	10	-4	12	*O	2.9
1960	Chi-A	154	591	89	184	32	4	20	105	52	63	.311	.380	.481	132	26	26	104	17	13	-3	3	*O	2.0
1961	Chi-A	152	540	91	151	28	3	14	82	67	46	.280	.376	.420	114	11	13	89	9	4	0	-4	*O	0.4
1962	StL-N	39	97	14	19	5	0	1	10	7	17	.196	.271	.278	44	-7	-8	8	4	0	1	-2	O	-1.0
1963	Was-A	109	315	38	72	12	2	4	30	33	38	.229	.317	.317	79	-8	-8	30	8	6	-1	-8	O/3	-2.0
1964	Chi-A	30	31	4	7	0	0	1	5	5	3	.226	.351	.323	91	-0	-0	4	0	0	0	1	/O	0.0
1976	Chi-A	3	8	0	1	0	0	0	0	0	2	.125	.125	.125	-27	-1	-1	0	0	0	0	0	/D	0.0
1980	Chi-A	2	2	0	0	0	0	0	0	0	0	.000	.000	.000	-99	-1	-1	0	0	0	0	0	/H	0.0
Total	17	1835	6579	1136	1963	336	83	186	1023	814	584	.298	.391	.459	130	299	298	1204	205	130	-16	24	*O3/1DS	23.6

■ WILLIE MIRANDA
Miranda, Guillermo (Perez)   b: 5/24/26, Velasco, Cuba   BB/TR, 5'9.5", 150 lbs.   Deb: 5/06/51

YEAR	TM/L	G	AB	R	H	2B	3B	HR	RBI	BB	SO	AVG	OBP	SLG	PRO+	BR	/A	RC	SB	CS	SBR	FR	POS	TPR
1951	Was-A	7	9	2	4	0	0	0	0	0	0	.444	.444	.444	143	0	1	2	0	0	0	-0	/S1	0.0
1952	Chi-A	12	8	1	2	1	0	0	0	3	0	.250	.455	.375	131	1	1	2	0	0	0	5	/S32	0.6
	StL-A	7	11	2	1	0	1	0	1	3	1	.091	.286	.273	54	-1	-1	1	0	0	0	-1	/S	0.0
	Chi-A	58	142	13	31	3	1	0	7	10	14	.218	.275	.254	47	-10	-10	11	1	0	0	10	S/23	0.3
	Yr	77	161	16	34	4	2	0	8	16	15	.211	.287	.261	52	-10	-10	14	1	0	0	15		0.9
1953	StL-A	17	6	2	1	0	0	0	0	1	1	.167	.286	.167	24	-1	-1	0	1	1	-0	3	/S3	0.3
	NY-A	48	58	12	13	0	0	1	5	5	10	.224	.286	.276	54	-4	-4	4	1	1	-0	17	S	1.6
	Yr	65	64	14	14	0	0	1	5	6	11	.219	.286	.266	51	-4	-4	4	2	2	-1	20		1.9
1954	NY-A	92	116	12	29	4	2	1	12	10	14	.250	.310	.345	82	-4	-3	12	0	3	-2	16	S/23	1.9
1955	Bal-A	153	487	42	124	12	6	1	38	42	58	.255	.315	.310	74	-21	-17	48	4	3	-1	19	*S/2	1.8
1956	Bal-A	148	461	38	100	16	4	2	34	46	73	.217	.288	.282	55	-33	-28	38	3	6	-3	2	*S	-1.5
1957	Bal-A	115	314	29	61	3	0	0	20	24	42	.194	.251	.204	28	-32	-29	17	2	1	0	-3	*S	-2.3
1958	Bal-A	102	214	15	43	6	0	1	8	14	25	.201	.250	.243	38	-19	-17	13	1	1	-0	-2	*S	-0.4
1959	Bal-A	65	88	8	14	5	0	0	7	7	16	.159	.221	.216	21	-10	-9	4	0	0	0	22	S3/2	1.6
Total	9	824	1914	176	423	50	14	6	132	165	250	.221	.284	.271	54	-131	-118	152	13	16	-6	89	S/321	3.9

■ JOHN MISSE
Misse, John Beverly   b: 5/30/1885, Highland, Kan.   d: 3/18/70, St.Joseph, Mo.   BR/TR, 5'8", 150 lbs.   Deb: 5/26/14

YEAR	TM/L	G	AB	R	H	2B	3B	HR	RBI	BB	SO	AVG	OBP	SLG	PRO+	BR	/A	RC	SB	CS	SBR	FR	POS	TPR
1914	StL-F	99	306	28	60	8	1	0	22	36	52	.196	.281	.229	45	-20	-22	24	3			14	2S/3	-0.4

■ CLARENCE MITCHELL
Mitchell, Clarence Elmer   b: 2/22/1891, Franklin, Neb.   d: 11/6/63, Grand Island, Neb.   BL/TL, 5'11.5", 190 lbs.   Deb: 6/02/11   C

YEAR	TM/L	G	AB	R	H	2B	3B	HR	RBI	BB	SO	AVG	OBP	SLG	PRO+	BR	/A	RC	SB	CS	SBR	FR	POS	TPR
1911	Det-A	5	4	2	2	0	0	0	0		1	.500	.600	.500	198	1	1	1				-0	/P	0.0
1916	Cin-N	56	117	11	28	2	1	0	11	4	6	.239	.264	.274	67	-5	-5	9	1			0	P/1O	0.0
1917	Cin-N	47	90	13	25	3	0	0	5	5	5	.278	.316	.311	97	-1	-0	9	0			1	P/1O	0.0
1918	Bro-N	10	24	2	6	1	1	0	2	0	3	.250	.250	.375	90	-0	-0	2	0			-2	/O1P	-0.2
1919	Bro-N	34	49	7	18	1	0	1	2	4	4	.367	.415	.449	156	4	3	9	0			1	P	0.0
1920	*Bro-N	55	107	9	25	2	2	0	11	8	9	.234	.287	.290	64	-5	-5	9	1	0	0	1	P1/O	0.0
1921	Bro-N	46	91	11	24	5	0	0	12	5	7	.264	.316	.319	66	-4	-4	10	3	1	0	3	P/1	0.0
1922	Bro-N	56	155	21	45	6	3	3	28	19	6	.290	.371	.426	106	1	2	25	0	0	0	4	1/P	0.5
1923	Phi-N	53	78	10	21	3	2	1	9	4	11	.269	.305	.397	75	-2	-3	9	0	0	0	-3	P	0.0
1924	Phi-N	69	102	7	26	3	0	0	13	2	7	.255	.276	.284	45	-7	-9	8	1	0	0	3	P	0.0
1925	Phi-N	52	92	7	18	2	0	0	13	5	9	.196	.237	.217	16	-11	-13	5	2	0	1	4	P/1	0.0
1926	Phi-N	39	78	8	19	4	0	0	6	5	7	.244	.289	.295	55	-5	-5	7	0			4	P/1	0.0
1927	Phi-N	18	42	5	10	2	0	1	6	2	1	.238	.273	.357	67	-2	-2	4	0			1	P	0.0
1928	Phi-N	5	4	0	1	0	0	0	0	0	0	.250	.250	.250	30	-0	-0	0	0			-0	/P	0.0
	*StL-N	19	56	0	7	1	0	0	1	0	3	.125	.125	.143	-30	-11	-11	1	0			3	P	0.0
	Yr	24	60	0	8	1	0	0	1	0	3	.133	.133	.150	-26	-11	-11	1	0			3		0.0
1929	StL-N	26	66	9	18	3	1	0	9	4	6	.273	.314	.348	63	-4	-4	7	1			-1	P	0.0
1930	StL-N	1	2	0	1	0	0	0	0	0	0	.500	.500	.500	138	0	0	0	0			0	/P	0.0
	NY-N	24	47	9	12	1	0	0	1	1	5	.255	.271	.277	33	-5	-5	3	0			2	P	0.0
	Yr	25	49	9	13	1	0	0	1	1	5	.265	.280	.286	38	-5	-5	4	0			2		0.0
1931	NY-N	27	73	5	16	2	0	1	4	2	4	.219	.240	.288	42	-6	-6	5	0			-1	P	0.0
1932	NY-N	8	10	2	2	0	0	0	0	1	1	.200	.273	.200	30	-1	-1	1	0			-1	/P	0.0
Total	18	650	1287	138	324	41	10	7	133	72	92	.252	.293	.315	64	-63	-67	125	9	1		20	P/1O	0.3

■ FRED MITCHELL
Mitchell, Frederick Francis (b: Frederick Francis Yapp)   b: 6/5/1878, Cambridge, Mass.   d: 10/13/70, Newton, Mass.   BR/TR, 5'9.5", 185 lbs.   Deb: 4/27/01   M

YEAR	TM/L	G	AB	R	H	2B	3B	HR	RBI	BB	SO	AVG	OBP	SLG	PRO+	BR	/A	RC	SB	CS	SBR	FR	POS	TPR
1901	Bos-A	20	44	5	7	1	0	2	0	4	2	.159	.196	.250	25	-5	-4	2	0			-0	P/2S	0.0
1902	Bos-A	1	1	0	0	0	0	0	0	0	0	.000	.000	.000	-97	-0	-0	0	0			0	/P	0.0
	Phi-A	19	48	7	9	1	1	0		3	1	.188	.204	.250	25	-5	-5	3	1			2	P/O	0.0
	Yr	20	49	7	9	1	1	0		3	1	.184	.200	.245	23	-5	-5	3	1			3		0.0
1903	Phi-N	29	95	11	19	4	0	0	10	0		.200	.200	.242	28	-9	-9	5	0			-3	P	0.0
1904	Phi-N	25	82	9	17	3	1	0	3	5		.207	.253	.268	65	-4	-3	6	1			3	P/13O	0.0
	Bro-N	8	24	3	7	1	1	0	6	1		.292	.320	.417	132	1	1	3	0			1	/P	0.0
	Yr	33	106	12	24	4	2	0	9	6		.226	.268	.302	80	-3	-2	10	1			4		0.0
1905	Bro-N	27	79	4	15	0	0	0	8	4		.190	.229	.190	29	-7	-6	4	0			-2	P/13SO	-0.4
1910	NY-N	68	196	16	45	7	2	0	18	9		.230	.274	.286	71	-6	-7	16	6			-14	C	-1.6
1913	Bos-N	4	3	0	1	0	0	0	0	0	2	.333	.333	.333	89	-0	-0	0	0			0	H	0.0
Total	7	201	572	55	120	16	7	0	52	22	2	.210	.243	.262	52	-34	-34	40	8			-12	/PC130S2	-2.0

■ JOHNNY MITCHELL
Mitchell, John Franklin   b: 8/9/1894, Detroit, Mich.   d: 11/4/65, Birmingham, Mich.   BB/TR, 5'8", 155 lbs.   Deb: 5/21/21

YEAR	TM/L	G	AB	R	H	2B	3B	HR	RBI	BB	SO	AVG	OBP	SLG	PRO+	BR	/A	RC	SB	CS	SBR	FR	POS	TPR
1921	NY-A	13	42	4	11	1	0	0	2	4	4	.262	.326	.286	56	-3	-3	4	1	0	0	-6	/S2	-0.6
1922	NY-A	4	4	1	0	0	0	0	0	0	1	.000	.000	.000	-98	-1	-1	0	0	0	0	-1	/S	0.0

YEAR	TM/L	G	AB	R	H	2B	3B	HR	RBI	BB	SO	AVG	OBP	SLG	PRO+	BR	/A	RC	SB	CS	SBR	FR	POS	TPR
	Bos-A	59	203	20	51	4	1	1	8	16	17	.251	.318	.296	61	-11	-11	20	1	2	-1	-4	S	-0.8
	Yr	63	207	21	51	4	1	1	8	16	18	.246	.313	.290	58	-12	-12	20	1	2	-1	-5		-0.8
1923	Bos-A	92	347	40	78	15	4	0	19	34	18	.225	.296	.291	55	-23	-23	29	7	11	-5	0	S/2	-1.7
1924	Bro-N	64	243	42	64	10	0	1	16	37	22	.263	.361	.317	86	-4	-3	31	3	1	0	-1	S	0.2
1925	Bro-N	97	336	45	84	8	3	0	18	28	19	.250	.308	.292	55	-23	-21	32	2	0	1	-4	S	-1.5
Total	5	329	1175	152	288	38	8	2	63	119	81	.245	.317	.296	62	-65	-63	117	14	14	-4	-15	S/2	-4.4

■ KEVIN MITCHELL
Mitchell, Kevin Darnell b: 1/13/62, San Diego, Cal. BR/TR, 5'10", 186 lbs. Deb: 9/04/84

YEAR	TM/L	G	AB	R	H	2B	3B	HR	RBI	BB	SO	AVG	OBP	SLG	PRO+	BR	/A	RC	SB	CS	SBR	FR	POS	TPR
1984	NY-N	7	14	0	3	0	0	0	1	0	3	.214	.214	.214	21	-1	-1	0	0	1	-1	-1	/3	-0.2
1986	*NY-N	108	328	51	91	22	2	12	43	33	61	.277	.345	.466	125	9	10	52	3	3	-1	-7	OS/31	0.3
1987	SD-N	62	196	19	48	7	1	7	26	20	38	.245	.315	.398	91	-4	-3	24	0	0	0	4	3/O	0.0
	*SF-N	69	268	49	82	13	1	15	44	28	50	.306	.376	.530	144	14	16	52	9	6	-1	-4	3/OS	1.0
	Yr	131	464	68	130	20	2	22	70	48	88	.280	.350	.474	121	10	13	76	9	6	-1	0		1.0
1988	SF-N	148	505	60	127	25	7	19	80	48	85	.251	.323	.442	123	10	13	71	5	5	-2	-4	*3O	0.6
1989	SF-N	154	543	100	158	34	6	**47**	125	87	115	.291	.392	**.635**	**194**	62	64	136	3	4	-2	1	*O/3	6.4
1990	SF-N	140	524	90	152	24	2	35	93	58	87	.290	.363	.544	148	31	32	101	4	7	-3	2	*O	2.8
Total	6	688	2378	369	661	125	19	135	412	274	439	.278	.356	.517	144	122	130	437	24	26	-8	-9	O3/S1	10.9

■ DALE MITCHELL
Mitchell, Loren Dale b: 8/23/21, Colony, Okla. d: 1/5/87, Tulsa, Okla. BL/TL, 6'1", 195 lbs. Deb: 9/15/46

YEAR	TM/L	G	AB	R	H	2B	3B	HR	RBI	BB	SO	AVG	OBP	SLG	PRO+	BR	/A	RC	SB	CS	SBR	FR	POS	TPR
1946	Cle-A	11	44	7	19	3	0	0	5	1	2	.432	.444	.500	175	4	4	10	1	0	0	1	O	0.4
1947	Cle-A	123	493	69	156	16	10	1	34	23	14	.316	.347	.396	109	3	4	69	2	5	-2	2	*O	-0.1
1948	*Cle-A	141	608	82	204	30	8	4	56	45	17	.336	.383	.431	119	13	15	98	13	18	-7	3	*O	0.6
1949	Cle-A	149	640	81	**203**	16	**23**	3	56	43	11	.317	.360	.428	110	5	7	102	10	3	1	1	*O	0.5
1950	Cle-A	130	506	81	156	27	5	3	49	67	21	.308	.390	.399	106	4	6	83	3	7	-3	-12	*O	-1.0
1951	Cle-A	134	510	83	148	21	7	11	62	53	16	.290	.358	.424	117	7	11	79	7	7	-2	-3	*O	0.1
1952	Cle-A	134	511	61	165	26	3	5	58	52	9	.323	.387	.415	132	17	21	82	6	6	-2	-4	*O	1.1
1953	Cle-A	134	500	76	150	26	4	13	60	42	20	.300	.354	.446	118	9	11	80	3	1	0	-11	*O	-0.2
1954	*Cle-A	53	60	6	17	1	0	1	6	9	1	.283	.377	.350	98	0	0	8	0	0	0	-1	/O1	0.0
1955	Cle-A	61	58	4	15	2	1	0	10	4	3	.259	.306	.328	68	-2	-3	5	0	0	0	0	/1O	-0.2
1956	Cle-A	38	30	2	4	0	0	0	6	7	2	.133	.297	.133	17	-3	-3	2	0	0	0	-0	/O	-0.2
	*Bro-N	19	24	3	7	1	0	0	1	0	3	.292	.292	.333	63	-1	-1	2	0	0	0	-0	/O	-0.1
Total	11	1127	3984	555	1244	169	61	41	403	346	119	.312	.368	.416	114	54	71	622	45	47	-15	-25	O/1	0.9

■ MIKE MITCHELL
Mitchell, Michael Francis b: 12/12/1879, Springfield, Ohio d: 7/16/61, Phoenix, Ariz. BR/TR, 6'1", 185 lbs. Deb: 4/11/07

YEAR	TM/L	G	AB	R	H	2B	3B	HR	RBI	BB	SO	AVG	OBP	SLG	PRO+	BR	/A	RC	SB	CS	SBR	FR	POS	TPR
1907	Cin-N	148	558	64	163	17	12	3	47	37		.292	.336	.382	122	16	13	81	17			22	*O/1	3.3
1908	Cin-N	119	406	41	90	9	6	1	37	46		.222	.301	.281	90	-4	-3	40	18			1	*O/1	-0.3
1909	Cin-N	145	523	83	162	17	**17**	4	86	57		.310	.378	.430	152	30	31	98	37			6	*O/1	3.5
1910	Cin-N	156	583	79	167	16	**18**	5	88	59	56	.286	.356	.401	126	14	18	96	35			-6	*O/1	0.7
1911	Cin-N	142	529	74	154	22	22	2	84	44	34	.291	.348	.427	121	10	12	90	35			7	*O	1.5
1912	Cin-N	147	552	60	156	14	13	4	78	41	43	.283	.333	.377	97	-6	-3	76	23			-9	*O	-1.5
1913	Chi-N	82	279	37	73	11	6	4	35	32	33	.262	.340	.387	107	3	3	41	15			5	O	0.7
	Pit-N	54	199	25	54	8	2	1	16	14	15	.271	.319	.347	94	-3	-2	23	8			6	O	0.3
	Yr	136	478	62	127	19	8	5	51	46	48	.266	.331	.370	102	-0	-1	63	23			11		1.0
1914	Pit-N	76	273	31	64	11	5	2	23	16	16	.234	.279	.333	86	-7	-6	26	5			7	O	0.3
	Was-A	55	193	20	55	5	3	1	20	22	19	.285	.361	.358	113	4	4	27	9	7	-2	4	O	0.3
Total	8	1124	4095	514	1138	130	104	27	514	368	216	.278	.339	.380	114	57	66	597	202	7		43	*O/1	8.5

■ BOBBY MITCHELL
Mitchell, Robert McKasha b: 2/6/1856, Cincinnati, Ohio d: 5/1/33, Springfield, Ohio BL/TL, 5'5", 135 lbs. Deb: 9/06/1877

YEAR	TM/L	G	AB	R	H	2B	3B	HR	RBI	BB	SO	AVG	OBP	SLG	PRO+	BR	/A	RC	SB	CS	SBR	FR	POS	TPR
1877	Cin-N	13	49	5	10	3	0	0	5	1	2	.204	.220	.265	59	-3	-2	3				-0	P/O	0.0
1878	Cin-N	13	49	4	12	0	0	0	8	1	4	.245	.260	.245	74	-2	-1	3				0	/PSO	0.0
1879	Cle-N	30	109	11	16	2	2	0	6	0	14	.147	.147	.202	14	-10	-10	3				-6	P/O	0.0
1882	StL-a	1	4	0	0	0	0	0		0		.000	.000	.000	-96	-1	-1	0				-0	/OP	0.0
Total	4	57	211	20	38	5	2	0	19	2	20	.180	.188	.223	35	-15	-13	9				-6	/POS	0.0

■ BOBBY MITCHELL
Mitchell, Robert Van b: 4/7/55, Salt Lake City, Utah BL/TL, 5'10", 170 lbs. Deb: 9/01/80

YEAR	TM/L	G	AB	R	H	2B	3B	HR	RBI	BB	SO	AVG	OBP	SLG	PRO+	BR	/A	RC	SB	CS	SBR	FR	POS	TPR
1980	LA-N	9	3	1	1	0	0	0	0	1	0	.333	.500	.333	139	0	0	1	0	0	0	1	/O	0.1
1981	LA-N	10	8	0	1	0	0	0	0	1	4	.125	.222	.125	1	-1	-1	0	0	0	0	1	/O	0.0
1982	Min-A	124	454	48	113	11	6	2	28	54	53	.249	.331	.313	76	-12	-14	48	8	9	-3	10	*O	-1.0
1983	Min-A	59	152	26	35	4	2	1	15	28	21	.230	.354	.303	80	-2	-3	18	1	1	-0	-0	O	-0.4
Total	4	202	617	75	150	15	8	3	43	84	78	.243	.337	.308	76	-15	-18	67	9	10	-3	11	O	-1.3

■ BOBBY MITCHELL
Mitchell, Robert Vance b: 10/22/43, Norristown, Pa. BR/TR, 6'3", 185 lbs. Deb: 7/05/70

YEAR	TM/L	G	AB	R	H	2B	3B	HR	RBI	BB	SO	AVG	OBP	SLG	PRO+	BR	/A	RC	SB	CS	SBR	FR	POS	TPR
1970	NY-A	10	22	1	5	2	0	0	4	2	3	.227	.320	.318	81	-1	-1	2	0	2	-1	1	/O	0.0
1971	Mil-A	35	55	7	10	1	1	2	6	6	18	.182	.262	.345	72	-2	-2	5	0	2	-1	3	O	0.0
1973	Mil-A	47	130	12	29	6	0	5	20	5	32	.223	.252	.385	79	-5	-4	13	4	1	1	-2	OD	-0.5
1974	Mil-A	88	173	27	42	6	2	5	20	18	46	.243	.318	.387	103	0	0	20	7	6	-2	1	DO	0.0
1975	Mil-A	93	229	39	57	14	3	9	41	25	69	.249	.323	.454	117	5	4	32	3	4	-2	-2	OD	0.0
Total	5	273	609	86	143	29	6	21	91	56	168	.235	.301	.406	100	-3	-2	72	14	15	-5	3	O/D	-0.5

■ RALPH MITTERLING
Mitterling, Ralph "Sarge" b: 4/19/1890, Freeburg, Pa. d: 1/22/56, Pittsburg, Pa. 5'10", 165 lbs. Deb: 7/07/16

YEAR	TM/L	G	AB	R	H	2B	3B	HR	RBI	BB	SO	AVG	OBP	SLG	PRO+	BR	/A	RC	SB	CS	SBR	FR	POS	TPR
1916	Phi-A	13	39	1	6	0	0	0	2	3	6	.154	.214	.154	11	-4	-4	1	0			-2	O	-0.7

■ GEORGE MITTERWALD
Mitterwald, George Eugene b: 6/7/45, Berkeley, Cal. BR/TR, 6'2", 195 lbs. Deb: 9/15/66 C

YEAR	TM/L	G	AB	R	H	2B	3B	HR	RBI	BB	SO	AVG	OBP	SLG	PRO+	BR	/A	RC	SB	CS	SBR	FR	POS	TPR
1966	Min-A	3	5	1	1	0	0	0	0	0	0	.200	.200	.200	14	-1	-1	0	0	0	0	1	/C	0.0
1968	Min-A	11	34	1	7	1	0	0	1	3	8	.206	.270	.235	52	-2	-2	2	0	0	0	0	C	0.0
1969	*Min-A	69	187	18	48	8	0	5	13	17	47	.257	.329	.380	96	-1	-1	23	0	1	-1	11	C/O	1.3
1970	*Min-A	117	369	36	82	12	2	15	46	34	84	.222	.291	.388	84	-8	-9	39	3	5	-2	24	*C	1.5
1971	Min-A	125	388	38	97	13	1	13	44	39	104	.250	.319	.389	97	-1	-2	47	3	3	-1	-11	*C	-0.8
1972	Min-A	64	163	12	30	4	1	1	8	9	37	.184	.227	.239	37	-12	-13	8	0	1	-1	6	C	-0.8
1973	Min-A	125	432	50	112	15	0	16	64	39	111	.259	.328	.405	101	3	3	57	3	1	0	4	*C/D	0.8
1974	Chi-N	78	215	17	54	7	0	7	28	18	42	.251	.315	.381	90	-2	-3	25	1	3	-2	-2	C	-0.4
1975	Chi-N	84	200	19	44	4	3	5	26	19	44	.220	.288	.345	72	-7	-8	20	0	0	0	0	C1	-0.8
1976	Chi-N	101	303	19	65	7	0	5	28	16	63	.215	.254	.287	49	-19	-22	20	1	2	-1	0	C1	-2.2
1977	Chi-N	110	349	40	83	22	0	9	43	28	69	.238	.296	.378	72	-11	-16	34	3	1	0	12	*C/1	-0.4
Total	11	887	2645	251	623	93	7	76	301	222	607	.236	.298	.362	80	-61	-77	275	14	17	-6	43	C/1DO	-1.8

■ JOHNNY MIZE
Mize, John Robert "The Big Cat" b: 1/7/13, Demorest, Ga. BL/TR, 6'2", 215 lbs. Deb: 4/16/36 CH

YEAR	TM/L	G	AB	R	H	2B	3B	HR	RBI	BB	SO	AVG	OBP	SLG	PRO+	BR	/A	RC	SB	CS	SBR	FR	POS	TPR
1936	StL-N	126	414	76	136	30	8	19	93	50	32	.329	.402	.577	162	55	35	102	1			2	1/O	2.7
1937	StL-N	145	560	103	204	40	7	25	113	56	57	.364	.427	.595	171	57	56	150	2			-13	*1	3.4
1938	StL-N	149	531	85	179	34	**16**	27	102	74	47	.337	.422	**.614**	172	59	55	141	0			-2	*1	4.1
1939	StL-N	153	564	104	197	44	14	**28**	108	92	49	**.349**	.444	**.626**	**174**	69	64	162	0			-4	*1	**4.2**
1940	StL-N	155	579	111	182	31	13	**43**	**137**	82	49	.314	.404	**.636**	173	64	60	152	7			-7	*1	3.9
1941	StL-N	126	473	67	150	**39**	8	16	100	70	45	.317	.406	.535	153	40	36	106	4			3	*1	2.2
1942	NY-N	142	541	97	165	25	7	26	**110**	60	39	.305	.380	**.521**	161	41	40	110	3			-3	*1	2.8
1946	NY-N	101	377	70	127	18	3	22	70	62	26	.337	.437	.576	185	44	43	100	3			5	*1	4.1

YEAR	TM/L	G	AB	R	H	2B	3B	HR	RBI	BB	SO	AVG	OBP	SLG	PRO+	BR	/A	RC	SB	CS	SBR	FR	POS	TPR
1947	NY-N	154	586	**137**	177	26	2	51	**138**	74	42	.302	.384	.614	160	48	48	143	2			9	*1	4.5
1948	NY-N	152	560	110	162	26	4	40	125	94	37	.289	.395	.564	156	45	44	131	4			4	*1	4.6
1949	NY-N	106	388	59	102	15	0	18	62	50	19	.263	.351	.441	111	6	6	63	1			2	*1	0.8
	*NY-A	13	23	4	6	1	0	1	2	4	2	.261	.393	.435	119	1	1	5	0	0	0	-0	/1	0.0
1950	*NY-A	90	274	43	76	12	0	25	72	29	24	.277	.351	.595	143	13	14	59	0	1	-1	-3	1	0.6
1951	*NY-A	113	332	37	86	14	1	10	49	36	24	.259	.339	.398	102	-1	1	47	1	0	0	-4	1	-0.4
1952	*NY-A	78	137	9	36	9	0	4	29	11	15	.263	.327	.416	112	1	2	18	0	0	0	1	1	0.0
1953	*NY-A	81	104	6	26	3	0	4	27	12	17	.250	.339	.394	101	-0	0	15	0	0	0	-0	1	0.0
Total	15	1884	6443	1118	2011	367	83	359	1337	856	524	.312	.397	.562	157	520	505	1502	28	1		-12	*1/O	37.5

■ JOHN MIZEROCK

Mizerock, John Joseph b: 12/8/60, Punxsutawney, Pa. BL/TR, 5'11", 190 lbs. Deb: 4/12/83

YEAR	TM/L	G	AB	R	H	2B	3B	HR	RBI	BB	SO	AVG	OBP	SLG	PRO+	BR	/A	RC	SB	CS	SBR	FR	POS	TPR
1983	Hou-N	33	85	8	13	4	1	1	10	12	15	.153	.265	.259	49	-6	-6	6	0	0	0	2	C	-0.1
1985	Hou-N	15	38	6	9	4	0	0	6	2	8	.237	.293	.342	79	-1	-1	3	0	0	0	4	C	0.3
1986	Hou-N	44	81	9	15	1	1	1	6	24	16	.185	.377	.259	81	-1	-1	9	0	0	0	4	C	0.4
1989	Atl-N	11	27	1	6	0	0	0	2	0	3	.222	.222	.222	27	-3	-3	1	0	0	0	1	C	0.0
Total	4	103	231	24	43	9	2	2	24	38	42	.186	.309	.268	64	-11	-10	19	0	0	0	10	C	0.6

■ BILL MIZEUR

Mizeur, William Francis "Bad Bill" b: 6/22/1897, Nokomis, Ill. d: 8/27/76, Decatur, Ill. BL/TR, 6', 180 lbs. Deb: 9/30/23

YEAR	TM/L	G	AB	R	H	2B	3B	HR	RBI	BB	SO	AVG	OBP	SLG	PRO+	BR	/A	RC	SB	CS	SBR	FR	POS	TPR
1923	StL-A	1	1	0	0	0	0	0	0	0	0	.000	.000	.000	-95	-0	-0	0	0	0	0	0	H	0.0
1924	StL-A	1	1	0	0	0	0	0	0	0	0	.000	.000	.000	-94	-0	-0	0	0	0	0	0	H	0.0
Total	2	2	2	0	0	0	0	0	0	0	0	.000	.000	.000	-94	-1	-1	0	0	0	0	0		0.0

■ DAVE MOATES

Moates, David Allan b: 1/30/48, Great Lakes, Ill. BL/TL, 5'9", 163 lbs. Deb: 9/21/74

YEAR	TM/L	G	AB	R	H	2B	3B	HR	RBI	BB	SO	AVG	OBP	SLG	PRO+	BR	/A	RC	SB	CS	SBR	FR	POS	TPR
1974	Tex-A	1	0	0	0	0	0	0	0	0	0	—	—	—	—	0	0	0	0	0	0	0	R	0.0
1975	Tex-A	54	175	21	48	9	0	3	14	13	15	.274	.324	.377	99	-1	-1	20	9	2	2	6	O/D	0.5
1976	Tex-A	85	137	21	33	7	1	0	13	11	18	.241	.297	.307	75	-4	-4	13	6	3	0	9	O/D	0.3
Total	3	140	312	42	81	16	1	3	27	24	33	.260	.313	.346	88	-5	-5	33	15	5	2	14	O/D	0.8

■ DANNY MOELLER

Moeller, Daniel Edward b: 3/23/1885, DeWitt, Iowa d: 4/14/51, Florence, Ala. BB/TR, 5'11", 165 lbs. Deb: 9/24/07

YEAR	TM/L	G	AB	R	H	2B	3B	HR	RBI	BB	SO	AVG	OBP	SLG	PRO+	BR	/A	RC	SB	CS	SBR	FR	POS	TPR
1907	Pit-N	11	42	4	12	1	1	0	3	4		.286	.348	.357	121	1	1	6	2			-2	O	0.0
1908	Pit-N	36	109	14	21	3	1	0	9	9		.193	.254	.239	59	-5	-5	7	4			-4	O	-1.0
1912	Was-A	132	519	90	143	26	10	6	46	52		.276	.346	.399	112	8	7	81	30			10	*O	0.9
1913	Was-A	153	589	88	139	15	10	5	42	72	103	.236	.322	.331	86	-8	-10	75	62			6	*O	-1.2
1914	Was-A	151	571	83	143	19	10	1	45	71	89	.250	.341	.324	97	1	0	65	26	25	-7	-1	*O	-1.9
1915	Was-A	118	438	65	99	11	10	2	23	59	63	.226	.319	.311	88	-6	-6	51	32	10	4	-2	*O	-1.1
1916	Was-A	78	240	30	59	8	1	1	23	30	35	.246	.335	.300	93	-2	-1	29	13			2	O	-0.3
	Cle-A	25	30	5	2	0	0	0	1	5	6	.067	.200	.067	-19	-4	-4	1	2			-2	/O2	-0.7
	Yr	103	270	35	61	8	1	1	24	35	41	.226	.319	.274	79	-6	-6	29	15			-0		-1.0
Total	7	704	2538	379	618	83	43	15	192	302	296	.243	.328	.328	93	-15	-18	314	171	35		6	O/2	-5.3

■ JOE MOFFETT

Moffett, Joseph W. b: 6/1859, Wheeling, W.Va. 6', Deb: 5/06/1884

YEAR	TM/L	G	AB	R	H	2B	3B	HR	RBI	BB	SO	AVG	OBP	SLG	PRO+	BR	/A	RC	SB	CS	SBR	FR	POS	TPR
1884	Tol-a	56	204	17	41	5	3	0			2	.201	.209	.255	51	-10	-11	11				-5	13/2O	-1.6

■ SAM MOFFETT

Moffett, Samuel R. b: 3/14/1857, Wheeling, W.Va. d: 5/5/07, Butte, Mont. TR , 6', 175 lbs. Deb: 5/15/1884

YEAR	TM/L	G	AB	R	H	2B	3B	HR	RBI	BB	SO	AVG	OBP	SLG	PRO+	BR	/A	RC	SB	CS	SBR	FR	POS	TPR
1884	Cle-N	67	256	26	47	12	2	0	15	8	56	.184	.208	.246	41	-17	-18	13				8	OP/132	-0.5
1887	Ind-N	11	41	6	5	1	0	0	1	1	6	.122	.143	.146	-19	-6	-6	1	2			-1	/PO	0.0
1888	Ind-N	10	35	6	4	0	0	0	0	5	4	.114	.225	.114	12	-3	-3	1	0			-2	/PO	0.0
Total	3	88	332	38	56	13	2	0	16	14	66	.169	.202	.220	30	-26	-27	16	2			5	/OP123	-0.5

■ JOHN MOHARDT

Mohardt, John Henry b: 1/21/1898, Pittsburgh, Pa. d: 11/24/61, LaJolla, Cal. 5'10", 165 lbs. Deb: 4/15/22

YEAR	TM/L	G	AB	R	H	2B	3B	HR	RBI	BB	SO	AVG	OBP	SLG	PRO+	BR	/A	RC	SB	CS	SBR	FR	POS	TPR
1922	Det-A	5	1	2	1	0	0	0	0	1	0	1.000	1.000	1.000	436	1	1	1	0	1	-1	-1	/O	0.0

■ KID MOHLER

Mohler, Ernest Follette b: 12/13/1874, Oneida, Ill. d: 11/4/61, San Francisco, Cal. 5'4.5", 145 lbs. Deb: 9/29/1894

YEAR	TM/L	G	AB	R	H	2B	3B	HR	RBI	BB	SO	AVG	OBP	SLG	PRO+	BR	/A	RC	SB	CS	SBR	FR	POS	TPR
1894	Was-N	3	9	0	1	0	0	0	0	2	4	.111	.273	.111	-3	-1	-1	0	0			2	/2	0.0

■ JOHNNY MOKAN

Mokan, John Leo b: 9/23/1895, Buffalo, N.Y. d: 2/10/85, Buffalo, N.Y. BR/TR, 5'7", 165 lbs. Deb: 4/15/21

YEAR	TM/L	G	AB	R	H	2B	3B	HR	RBI	BB	SO	AVG	OBP	SLG	PRO+	BR	/A	RC	SB	CS	SBR	FR	POS	TPR
1921	Pit-N	19	52	7	14	3	2	0	9	5	3	.269	.333	.404	92	-0		7				-0	O	-0.1
1922	Pit-N	31	89	9	23	3	1	0	8	9	3	.258	.327	.315	65	-4	-4	9	0	1	-1	-4	O	-0.9
	Phi-N	47	151	20	38	7	1	3	27	16	25	.252	.327	.371	73	-5	-7	19	1	0	0	-5	O/3	-1.1
	Yr	78	240	29	61	10	2	3	35	25	28	.254	.327	.350	70	-9	-11	29	1	1	-0	-9		-2.0
1923	Phi-N	113	400	76	125	23	3	10	48	53	31	.313	.401	.460	113	17	10	73	6	11	-5	8	*O/3	-0.9
1924	Phi-N	96	366	50	95	15	1	7	44	30	27	.260	.321	.363	74	-9	-15	43	7	5	-1	0	O	-1.6
1925	Phi-N	75	209	30	69	11	2	6	42	27	9	.330	.417	.488	120	10	8	43	3	5	-2	-5	O	-0.1
1926	Phi-N	127	456	68	138	23	5	6	62	41	31	.303	.365	.414	104	6	3	69	4			-7	*O	-0.8
1927	Phi-N	74	213	22	61	13	2	0	33	25	21	.286	.361	.366	94	-1	-1	29	5			-6	O	-0.9
Total	7	582	1936	282	563	98	17	32	273	206	150	.291	.364	.409	97	15	-7	292	26	22		-20	O/3	-4.6

■ FENTON MOLE

Mole, Fenton Le Roy "Muscles" b: 6/14/25, San Leandro, Cal. BL/TL, 6'1.5", 200 lbs. Deb: 9/01/49

YEAR	TM/L	G	AB	R	H	2B	3B	HR	RBI	BB	SO	AVG	OBP	SLG	PRO+	BR	/A	RC	SB	CS	SBR	FR	POS	TPR
1949	NY-A	10	27	2	5	2	1	0	2	3	5	.185	.267	.333	58	-2	-2	2	0	0	0	1	/1	0.0

■ BOB MOLINARO

Molinaro, Robert Joseph b: 5/21/50, Newark, N.J. BL/TR, 6', 190 lbs. Deb: 9/18/75

YEAR	TM/L	G	AB	R	H	2B	3B	HR	RBI	BB	SO	AVG	OBP	SLG	PRO+	BR	/A	RC	SB	CS	SBR	FR	POS	TPR
1975	Det-A	6	19	2	5	0	0	0	1	1	0	.263	.300	.368	84	-0	-0	2	0	0	0	-1	/O	0.0
1977	Det-A	4	4	0	1	1	0	0	0	0	2	.250	.250	.500	94	-0	-0	1	0	0	0	0	H	0.0
	Chi-A	1	2	0	1	0	0	0	0	0	1	.500	.500	.500	174	0	0	1	1	0	0	0	/O	0.0
	Yr	5	6	0	2	1	0	0	0	0	3	.333	.333	.500	119	0	0	1	1	0	0	0		0.0
1978	Chi-A	105	286	39	75	5	5	6	27	19	12	.262	.315	.378	93	-3	-3	35	22	6	3	-3	OD	-0.3
1979	Bal-A	8	6	0	0	0	0	0	0	1	3	.000	.143	.000	-60	-1	-1	0	1	0	0	1	/O	0.0
1980	Chi-A	119	344	48	100	16	4	5	36	26	29	.291	.353	.404	107	4	4	50	18	7	1	-3	OD	0.1
1981	Chi-A	47	42	7	11	1	1	1	9	8	1	.262	.392	.405	133	2	2	7	1	0	0	1	/OD	0.3
1982	Chi-N	65	66	6	13	1	0	1	12	6	5	.197	.264	.258	45	-5	-5	5	1	1	-0	-1	/O	-0.6
	Phi-N	19	14	0	4	0	0	0	2	3	1	.286	.412	.286	96	0	0	2	1	0	0	0	H	0.0
	Yr	84	80	6	17	1	0	1	14	9	6	.213	.292	.262	55	-5	-5	7	2	1	0	-1		-0.6
1983	Phi-N	19	18	1	2	1	0	0	3	0	2	.111	.111	.333	19	-2	-2	1	0	0	0	0	H	-0.1
	Det-A	8	2	3	0	0	0	0	0	1	1	.000	.333	.000	1	-0	-0	0	1	0	0	0	/D	0.0
Total	8	401	803	106	212	25	11	14	90	65	57	.264	.328	.375	95	-5	-6	104	46	15	5	-6	O/D	-0.6

■ PAUL MOLITOR

Molitor, Paul Leo b: 8/22/56, St.Paul, Minn. BR/TR, 6', 185 lbs. Deb: 4/07/78

YEAR	TM/L	G	AB	R	H	2B	3B	HR	RBI	BB	SO	AVG	OBP	SLG	PRO+	BR	/A	RC	SB	CS	SBR	FR	POS	TPR
1978	Mil-A	125	521	73	142	26	4	6	45	19	54	.273	.303	.372	89	-9	-9	59	30	12	2	-5	2S/3D	
1979	Mil-A	140	584	88	188	27	16	9	62	48	48	.322	.375	.469	126	21	21	103	33	13	2	1	*	
1980	Mil-A	111	450	81	137	29	2	9	37	48	48	.304	.378	.438	126	14	16	78	34	7	6			
1981	*Mil-A	64	251	45	67	11	0	2	19	25	29	.267	.341	.335	100	-1	1	30	10	6				
1982	*Mil-A	160	666	**136**	201	26	8	19	71	69	93	.302	.368	.450	132	22	27	117	41	9				
1983	Mil-A	152	608	95	164	28	6	15	47	59	74	.270	.336	.410	113	3	10	88	41	8				
1984	Mil-A	13	46	3	10	1	0	0	6	2	8	.217	.250	.239	38	-4	-4	3	1	0				
1985	Mil-A	140	576	93	171	28	3	10	48	54	80	.297	.358	.408	110	8	8	85	21	7				
1986	Mil-A	105	437	62	123	24	6	9	55	40	81	.281	.342	.426	104	4	2	65	20	5				

YEAR	TM/L	G	AB	R	H	2B	3B	HR	RBI	BB	SO	AVG	OBP	SLG	PRO+	BR	/A	RC	SB	CS	SBR	FR	POS	TPR
1987	Mil-A	118	465	**114**	164	**41**	5	16	75	69	67	.353	.438	.566	159	45	43	125	45	10	8	1	D32	4.9
1988	Mil-A	154	609	115	190	34	6	13	60	71	54	.312	.386	.452	132	29	28	112	41	10	6	-8	*3D/2	2.6
1989	Mil-A	155	615	84	194	35	4	11	56	64	67	.315	.384	.439	133	27	27	106	27	11	2	4	*3D2	3.3
1990	Mil-A	103	418	64	119	27	6	12	45	37	51	.285	.344	.464	128	12	14	68	18	3	4	-1	21/3D	1.7
Total	13	1540	6246	1053	1870	337	66	131	626	605	754	.299	.364	.437	122	172	186	1039	362	101	48	-0	32D/SO1	23.9

■ FRED MOLLENKAMP
Mollenkamp, Frederick Henry b: 3/15/1890, Cincinnati, Ohio d: 11/1/48, Cincinnati, Ohio   Deb: 8/29/14

YEAR	TM/L	G	AB	R	H	2B	3B	HR	RBI	BB	SO	AVG	OBP	SLG	PRO+	BR	/A	RC	SB	CS	SBR	FR	POS	TPR
1914	Phi-N	3	8	0	1	0	0	0	0	2	0	.125	.300	.125	26	-1	-1	0	0			2	/1	0.1

■ FRITZ MOLLWITZ
Mollwitz, Frederick August b: 6/16/1890, Coburg, Germany d: 10/3/67, Bradenton, Fla.   BR/TR, 6'2", 170 lbs.   Deb: 9/26/13

YEAR	TM/L	G	AB	R	H	2B	3B	HR	RBI	BB	SO	AVG	OBP	SLG	PRO+	BR	/A	RC	SB	CS	SBR	FR	POS	TPR
1913	Chi-N	2	7	1	3	0	0	0	0	0	0	.429	.429	.429	145	0	0	1	0			-0	/1	0.0
1914	Chi-N	13	20	0	3	0	0	0	1	0	3	.150	.150	.150	-11	-3	-3	1	1			-0	/1O	-0.3
	Cin-N	32	111	12	18	2	0	0	5	3	9	.162	.198	.180	12	-12	-12	4	2			1	1	-1.2
	Yr	45	131	12	21	2	0	0	6	3	12	.160	.191	.176	9	-15	-15	5	3			0		-1.5
1915	Cin-N	153	525	36	136	21	3	1	51	15	49	.259	.281	.316	79	-14	-15	50	19	11	-1	0	*1	-2.5
1916	Cin-N	65	183	12	41	4	4	0	16	5	12	.224	.245	.290	65	-8	-8	15	6			-0	1	-1.1
	Chi-N	33	71	1	19	2	0	0	11	7	6	.268	.333	.296	85	-0	-1	8	4			-1	1/O	-0.2
	Yr	98	254	13	60	6	4	0	27	12	18	.236	.271	.291	71	-9	-9	24	10			-1		-1.3
1917	Pit-N	36	140	15	36	4	1	0	12	8	8	.257	.297	.300	81	-3	-3	14	4			-1	1/2	-0.4
1918	Pit-N	119	432	43	116	12	7	0	45	23	24	.269	.323	.329	90	-4	-6	50	23			-0	*1	-0.9
1919	Pit-N	56	168	11	29	2	4	0	12	15	12	.173	.249	.232	43	-11	-12	11	9			-3	1/O	-1.6
	StL-N	25	83	7	19	3	0	0	5	7	3	.229	.289	.265	71	-3	-3	7	2			1	1	-0.1
	Yr	81	251	18	48	5	4	0	17	22	21	.191	.262	.243	52	-14	-14	18	11			-2		-1.7
Total	7	534	1740	138	420	50	19	1	158	83	132	.241	.278	.294	72	-57	-61	162	70	11		-4	1/O2	-8.3

■ BLAS MONACO
Monaco, Blas b: 11/16/15, San Antonio, Tex.   BB/TR, 5'11", 170 lbs.   Deb: 8/18/37

YEAR	TM/L	G	AB	R	H	2B	3B	HR	RBI	BB	SO	AVG	OBP	SLG	PRO+	BR	/A	RC	SB	CS	SBR	FR	POS	TPR
1937	Cle-A	5	7	0	2	0	1	0	2	0	2	.286	.375	.571	134	0	0	2	0	0	0	0	/2	0.1
1946	Cle-A	12	6	2	0	0	0	0	0	1	1	.000	.143	.000	-62	-1	-1	0	0	0	0	0	H	0.0
Total	2	17	13	2	2	0	1	0	2	1	3	.154	.267	.308	53	-1	-1	2	0	0	0	0	/2	0.1

■ FREDDIE MONCEWICZ
Moncewicz, Frederick Alfred b: 9/1/03, Brockton, Mass. d: 4/23/69, Brockton, Mass.   BR/TR, 5'8.5", 175 lbs.   Deb: 6/19/28

YEAR	TM/L	G	AB	R	H	2B	3B	HR	RBI	BB	SO	AVG	OBP	SLG	PRO+	BR	/A	RC	SB	CS	SBR	FR	POS	TPR
1928	Bos-A	3	1	0	0	0	0	0	0	0	1	.000	.000	.000	-99	-0	-0	0	0	0	0	0	/S	0.0

■ ALEX MONCHAK
Monchak, Alex b: 12/22/19, Bayonne, N.J.   BR/TR, 6', 180 lbs.   Deb: 6/22/40   C

YEAR	TM/L	G	AB	R	H	2B	3B	HR	RBI	BB	SO	AVG	OBP	SLG	PRO+	BR	/A	RC	SB	CS	SBR	FR	POS	TPR
1940	Phi-N	19	14	1	2	0	0	0	0	0	6	.143	.143	.143	-22	-2	-2	0	1			0	/S2	0.0

■ RICK MONDAY
Monday, Robert James b: 11/20/45, Batesville, Ark.   BL/TL, 6'3", 193 lbs.   Deb: 9/03/66

YEAR	TM/L	G	AB	R	H	2B	3B	HR	RBI	BB	SO	AVG	OBP	SLG	PRO+	BR	/A	RC	SB	CS	SBR	FR	POS	TPR
1966	KC-A	17	41	4	4	1	1	0	2	6	16	.098	.213	.171	12	-5	-5	2	1	1	-0	1	O	-0.4
1967	KC-A	124	406	52	102	14	6	14	58	42	107	.251	.324	.419	122	9	10	55	3	6	-3	11	*O	1.7
1968	Oak-A	148	482	56	132	24	7	8	49	72	143	.274	.373	.402	142	22	25	78	14	6	1	-5	*O	1.7
1969	Oak-A	122	399	57	108	17	4	12	54	72	100	.271	.389	.424	133	17	19	71	12	3	2	-7	*O	1.1
1970	Oak-A	112	376	63	109	19	7	10	37	58	99	.290	.388	.457	137	18	20	68	17	11	-2	-1	*O	1.2
1971	*Oak-A	116	355	53	87	9	3	18	56	49	93	.245	.337	.439	121	8	9	52	6	9	-4	-2	*O	0.0
1972	Chi-N	138	434	68	108	22	5	11	42	78	102	.249	.365	.399	105	12	6	67	12	9	-2	-12	*O	-1.5
1973	Chi-N	149	554	93	148	24	5	26	56	92	124	.267	.372	.469	123	25	20	100	5	12	-6	-4	*O	0.3
1974	Chi-N	142	538	84	158	19	7	20	58	70	94	.294	.377	.467	130	25	23	97	7	9	-3	-2	*O	1.2
1975	Chi-N	136	491	89	131	29	4	17	60	83	95	.267	.374	.446	121	19	16	86	8	3	1	-2	*O	1.0
1976	Chi-N	137	534	107	145	20	5	32	77	60	125	.272	.347	.507	129	26	21	92	5	9	-4	2	*O1	1.5
1977	*LA-N	118	392	47	90	13	1	15	48	60	109	.230	.332	.383	91	-4	-4	52	1	4	-2	-17	*O/1	-2.7
1978	LA-N	119	342	54	87	14	1	19	57	49	100	.254	.349	.468	127	12	12	56	2	4	-2	-1	*O/1	0.6
1979	LA-N	12	33	2	10	0	0	0	2	5	6	.303	.395	.303	94	0	0	4	0	0	0	1	O	0.1
1980	LA-N	96	194	35	52	7	1	10	25	28	49	.268	.363	.469	133	8	9	35	2	2	-1	-2	O	0.5
1981	*LA-N	66	130	24	41	1	2	11	25	24	42	.315	.426	.608	198	16	16	35	1	2	-1	-5	O	1.0
1982	LA-N	104	210	37	54	6	4	11	42	39	51	.257	.376	.481	142	11	12	40	2	1	0	-6	O/1	0.5
1983	*LA-N	99	178	21	44	7	1	6	20	29	42	.247	.353	.399	108	2	3	26	0	0	0	-4	O/1	-0.1
1984	LA-N	31	44	4	9	2	0	1	7	8	16	.191	.309	.298	72	-2	-2	5	0	0	0	-1	1/O	-0.2
Total	19	1986	6136	950	1619	248	64	241	775	924	1513	.264	.362	.443	124	220	210	1020	98	91	-25	-56	*O/1	7.5

■ DON MONEY
Money, Donald Wayne "Brooks" b: 6/7/47, Washington, D.C.   BR/TR, 6'1", 170 lbs.   Deb: 4/10/68

YEAR	TM/L	G	AB	R	H	2B	3B	HR	RBI	BB	SO	AVG	OBP	SLG	PRO+	BR	/A	RC	SB	CS	SBR	FR	POS	TPR
1968	Phi-N	4	13	1	3	2	0	0	2	2	4	.231	.333	.385	115	0	0	1	0	1	-1	-1	/S	0.0
1969	Phi-N	127	450	41	103	22	2	6	42	43	83	.229	.298	.327	77	-15	-14	41	1	3	-2	17	*S	1.7
1970	Phi-N	120	447	66	132	25	4	14	66	43	68	.295	.366	.463	124	13	15	75	4	7	-3	11	*3/S	1.9
1971	Phi-N	121	439	40	98	22	8	7	38	31	80	.223	.279	.358	79	-13	-13	44	4	1	1	3	3O2	-1.0
1972	Phi-N	152	536	54	119	16	2	15	52	41	92	.222	.280	.343	74	-18	-19	50	5	7	-3	20	*3/S	-0.2
1973	Mil-A	145	556	75	158	28	2	11	61	53	53	.284	.350	.401	113	8	10	80	22	5	4	-23	*3S	-0.8
1974	Mil-A	159	629	85	178	32	3	15	65	62	80	.283	.349	.415	120	15	16	93	19	6	2	-9	*3/2D	1.1
1975	Mil-A	109	405	58	112	16	1	15	43	31	51	.277	.333	.432	114	7	7	58	7	9	-3	-21	3/S	-1.5
1976	Mil-A	117	439	51	117	18	4	12	62	47	50	.267	.337	.408	120	9	10	59	6	5	-1	-4	*3D/S	0.6
1977	Mil-A	152	570	86	159	28	3	25	83	57	70	.279	.352	.470	122	17	17	92	8	5	-1	-4	*2O3/2	2.0
1978	Mil-A	137	518	88	152	30	2	14	54	48	70	.293	.361	.440	124	17	17	84	3	0	1	-4	123D/S	1.5
1979	Mil-A	92	350	49	83	20	1	6	38	40	47	.237	.319	.351	81	-9	-9	40	1	0	0	-2	D312	-0.9
1980	Mil-A	86	289	39	74	17	1	17	46	40	36	.256	.348	.498	133	11	12	52	0	0	0	1	31D/2	1.2
1981	*Mil-A	60	185	17	40	7	0	2	14	19	27	.216	.293	.286	71	-7	-6	17	0	0	0	-6	3/1D	-1.1
1982	*Mil-A	96	275	40	78	14	3	16	55	32	38	.284	.360	.531	150	15	17	53	0	2	-1	5	D31/2	2.0
1983	Mil-A	43	114	5	17	5	0	1	8	11	17	.149	.224	.219	24	-12	-11	6	0	0	0	4	D3/1	-0.6
Total	16	1720	6215	798	1623	302	36	176	729	600	866	.261	.330	.406	106	38	48	847	80	51	-7	-9	*32DS1/O	5.9

■ FRANK MONROE
Monroe, Frank W. b: Hamilton, Ohio   Deb: 7/18/1884

YEAR	TM/L	G	AB	R	H	2B	3B	HR	RBI	BB	SO	AVG	OBP	SLG	PRO+	BR	/A	RC	SB	CS	SBR	FR	POS	TPR
1884	Ind-a	2	8	1	0	0	0	0	0	0	0	.000	.000	.000	-99	-2	-2	0				0	/OC	0.0

■ JOHN MONROE
Monroe, John Allen b: 8/24/1898, Farmersville, Tex. d: 6/19/56, Conroe, Tex.   BL/TR, 5'10", 160 lbs.   Deb: 4/16/21

YEAR	TM/L	G	AB	R	H	2B	3B	HR	RBI	BB	SO	AVG	OBP	SLG	PRO+	BR	/A	RC	SB	CS	SBR	FR	POS	TPR
1921	NY-N	19	21	4	3	0	0	1	3	3	6	.143	.280	.286	50	-2	-2	2	0	0	0	2	/2S	0.0
	Phi-N	41	133	13	38	4	2	1	8	11	9	.286	.345	.368	82	-2	-3	17	2	2	-1	5	2/3	0.2
	Yr	60	154	17	41	4	2	2	11	14	15	.266	.335	.357	79	-3	-5	19	2	2	-1	7		0.2

■ ED MONTAGUE
Montague, Edward Francis b: 7/24/05, San Francisco, Cal. d: 6/17/88, Daly City, Cal.   BR/TR, 5'10", 165 lbs.   Deb: 5/14/28

YEAR	TM/L	G	AB	R	H	2B	3B	HR	RBI	BB	SO	AVG	OBP	SLG	PRO+	BR	/A	RC	SB	CS	SBR	FR	POS	TPR
1928	Cle-A	32	51	12	12	0	1	0	3	6	7	.235	.339	.275	62	-2	-3	5	0	0	0	5	S/3	0.4
1930	Cle-A	58	179	37	47	5	2	1	16	37	38	.263	.392	.330	82	-2	-3	25	1	5	-3	-15	S3	-1.4
1931	Cle-A	64	193	27	55	8	3	1	26	21	22	.285	.358	.373	87	-2	-3	26	3	4	-2	16	S	1.6
1932	Cle-A	66	192	29	47	5	1	0	24	21	24	.245	.326	.281	55	-11	-13	19	3	3	-1	-13	S3	-2.0
Total	4	220	615	105	161	18	7	2	69	85	91	.262	.357	.324	74	-18	-22	76	7	12	-5	-6	S/3	-1.4

■ WILLIE MONTANEZ
Montanez, Guillermo (Naranjo) b: 4/1/48, Catano, P.R.   BL/TL, 6', 170 lbs.   Deb: 4/12/66

YEAR	TM/L	G	AB	R	H	2B	3B	HR	RBI	BB	SO	AVG	OBP	SLG	PRO+	BR	/A	RC	SB	CS	SBR	FR	POS	TPR
	Cal-A	8	2	2	0	0	0	0	0	0	2	.000	.000	.000	-99	-1	-0	0	1	0	0	0	/1	0.0
	Phi-N	18	25	3	6	0	0	0	3	1	4	.240	.269	.240	39	-2	-2	2	0	0	0	1	O/1	-0.1

YEAR	TM/L	G	AB	R	H	2B	3B	HR	RBI	BB	SO	AVG	OBP	SLG	PRO+	BR	/A	RC	SB	CS	SBR	FR	POS	TPR
1971	Phi-N	158	599	78	153	27	6	30	99	67	105	.255	.333	.471	126	19	19	89	4	7	-3	-2	*O/1	0.8
1972	Phi-N	147	531	60	131	**39**	3	13	64	58	108	.247	.322	.405	103	3	2	70	1	3	-2	8	*O1	0.2
1973	Phi-N	146	552	69	145	16	5	11	65	46	80	.263	.326	.370	90	-6	-7	65	2	6	-3	-2	1O	-2.0
1974	Phi-N	143	527	55	160	33	1	7	79	32	57	.304	.347	.410	107	7	4	72	3	6	-3	-1	*1/O	-0.5
1975	Phi-N	21	84	9	24	8	0	2	16	4	12	.286	.318	.452	108	1	0	11	1	0	0	2	1	0.1
	SF-N	135	518	52	158	26	2	8	85	45	50	.305	.365	.409	110	10	8	72	5	3	-0	-1	*1	0.0
	Yr	156	602	61	182	34	2	10	101	49	62	.302	.359	.415	110	11	8	84	6	3	0	1		0.1
1976	SF-N	60	230	22	71	15	2	2	20	15	15	.309	.354	.417	115	5	4	31	2	1	0	4	1	0.6
	Atl-N	103	420	52	135	14	0	9	64	21	32	.321	.354	.419	112	9	6	56	0	4	-2	-5	*1	-0.6
	Yr	163	650	74	206	29	2	11	84	36	47	.317	.354	.418	113	14	11	87	2	5	-2	-1		0.0
1977	Atl-N	136	544	70	156	31	1	20	68	35	60	.287	.330	.458	97	5	-3	77	1	1	-0	-4	*1	-1.3
1978	NY-N	159	609	66	156	32	0	17	96	60	92	.256	.324	.392	103	-1	1	76	9	4	0	3	*1	0.0
1979	NY-N	109	410	36	96	19	0	5	47	25	48	.234	.280	.317	65	-22	-20	33	0	1	-1	3	*1	-2.2
	Tex-A	38	144	19	46	6	0	8	24	8	14	.319	.359	.528	137	7	7	26	0	1	-1	1	1D	0.6
1980	SD-N	128	481	39	132	12	4	6	63	36	52	.274	.329	.353	96	-6	-3	55	3	4	-2	1	*1	-0.8
	Mon-N	14	19	1	4	0	0	0	1	3	3	.211	.318	.211	50	-1	-1	1	0	1	0	0	/1	-0.1
	Yr	142	500	40	136	12	4	6	64	39	55	.272	.328	.348	94	-7	-4	57	3	5	-2	1		-0.9
1981	Mon-N	26	62	6	11	0	1	0	5	4	9	.177	.227	.210	24	-6	-6	2	0	0	0	1	1	-0.5
	Pit-N	29	38	2	10	0	0	1	1	1	2	.263	.282	.342	74	-1	-1	3	0	0	0	-1	1	-0.2
	Yr	55	100	8	21	0	1	1	6	5	11	.210	.248	.260	43	-7	-8	5	0	0	0	0		-0.7
1982	Pit-N	36	32	4	9	1	0	0	3	3	3	.281	.343	.313	82	-1	-1	3	0	0	0	0	/1O	0.0
	Phi-N	18	16	0	1	0	0	0	1	1	3	.063	.118	.063	-47	-3	-3	0	0	0	0	1	/1	-0.2
	Yr	54	48	4	10	1	0	0	2	4	6	.208	.269	.229	40	-4	-4	3	0	0	0	1		-0.2
Total	14	1632	5843	645	1604	279	25	139	802	465	751	.275	.331	.402	101	16	4	744	32	42	-16	9	*1O/D	-6.2

■ RENE MONTEAGUDO
Monteagudo, Rene (Miranda)   b: 3/12/16, Havana, Cuba   d: 9/14/73, Hialeah, Fla.   BL/TL, 5'7", 165 lbs.   Deb: 9/06/38

YEAR	TM/L	G	AB	R	H	2B	3B	HR	RBI	BB	SO	AVG	OBP	SLG	PRO+	BR	/A	RC	SB	CS	SBR	FR	POS	TPR
1938	Was-A	5	6	0	3	0	0	0	1	0	0	.500	.500	.500	162	1	1	1	0	0	0	-1	/P	0.0
1940	Was-A	27	33	4	6	1	1	0	1	1	4	.182	.206	.273	24	-4	-4	2	0	0	0	-1	P	0.0
1944	Was-A	10	38	2	11	2	0	0	4	0	1	.289	.289	.342	84	-1	-1	4	0	0	0	-1	/O	-0.2
1945	Phi-N	114	193	26	58	6	0	0	15	28	7	.301	.389	.332	104	2	3	26	2			-3	OP	0.0
Total	4	156	270	32	78	9	1	0	21	29	12	.289	.358	.330	94	-3	-1	33	2	0		-6	/PO	-0.2

■ FELIPE MONTEMAYOR
Montemayor, Felipe Angel "Monty"   b: 2/7/30, Monterrey, Mexico   BL/TL, 6'2", 185 lbs.   Deb: 4/14/53

YEAR	TM/L	G	AB	R	H	2B	3B	HR	RBI	BB	SO	AVG	OBP	SLG	PRO+	BR	/A	RC	SB	CS	SBR	FR	POS	TPR
1953	Pit-N	28	55	5	6	4	0	0	2	4	13	.109	.210	.182	3	-8	-8	2	0	0	0	2	O	-0.5
1955	Pit-N	36	95	10	20	1	3	2	8	18	24	.211	.342	.347	85	-2	-2	12	1	0	0	-4	O	-0.5
Total	2	64	150	15	26	5	3	2	10	22	37	.173	.295	.287	55	-10	-10	15	1	0	0	-2	/O	-1.0

■ AL MONTGOMERY
Montgomery, Alvin Atlas   b: 7/3/20, Loving, N.Mex.   d: 4/26/42, Waverly, Va.   BR/TR, 5'10.5", 185 lbs.   Deb: 6/20/41

YEAR	TM/L	G	AB	R	H	2B	3B	HR	RBI	BB	SO	AVG	OBP	SLG	PRO+	BR	/A	RC	SB	CS	SBR	FR	POS	TPR
1941	Bos-N	42	52	4	10	1	0	0	4	9	8	.192	.323	.212	55	-3	-3	4	0			-6	C	-0.5

■ BOB MONTGOMERY
Montgomery, Robert Edward   b: 4/16/44, Nashville, Tenn.   BR/TR, 6'1", 195 lbs.   Deb: 9/06/70

YEAR	TM/L	G	AB	R	H	2B	3B	HR	RBI	BB	SO	AVG	OBP	SLG	PRO+	BR	/A	RC	SB	CS	SBR	FR	POS	TPR
1970	Bos-A	22	78	8	14	2	0	1	4	6	20	.179	.247	.244	33	-7	-8	4	0	0	0	1	C	-0.6
1971	Bos-A	67	205	19	49	11	2	2	24	16	43	.239	.304	.341	77	-5	-7	21	1	0	0	-2	C	-0.5
1972	Bos-A	24	77	7	22	1	0	2	7	3	17	.286	.313	.377	99	0	-0	9	0	0	0	-2	C	-0.1
1973	Bos-A	34	128	18	41	6	2	7	25	7	36	.320	.356	.563	146	8	8	23	0	0	0	-0	C	0.8
1974	Bos-A	88	254	26	64	10	0	4	38	13	50	.252	.291	.339	75	-7	-9	24	3	0	1	-6	C/D	-1.1
1975	*Bos-A	62	195	16	44	10	1	2	26	4	37	.226	.245	.318	53	-11	-13	15	1	1	-0	-5	C/1D	-1.7
1976	Bos-A	31	93	10	23	3	1	3	13	5	20	.247	.286	.398	88	-1	-2	10	0	1	-1	-1	C/D	-0.1
1977	Bos-A	17	40	6	12	2	0	2	7	4	9	.300	.378	.500	123	2	1	8	0	0	0	-0	C	0.1
1978	Bos-A	10	29	2	7	1	1	0	5	2	12	.241	.290	.345	70	-1	-1	3	0	0	0	1	C	0.0
1979	Bos-A	32	86	13	30	4	1	0	7	4	24	.349	.381	.419	109	2	1	13	1	0	0	-4	C	0.0
Total	10	387	1185	125	306	50	8	23	156	64	268	.258	.300	.372	83	-19	-30	129	6	2	1	-20	C/D1	-3.2

■ AL MONTREUIL
Montreuil, Allan Arthur   b: 8/23/43, New Orleans, La.   BR/TR, 5'5", 158 lbs.   Deb: 9/01/72

YEAR	TM/L	G	AB	R	H	2B	3B	HR	RBI	BB	SO	AVG	OBP	SLG	PRO+	BR	/A	RC	SB	CS	SBR	FR	POS	TPR
1972	Chi-N	5	11	0	1	0	0	0	0	1	4	.091	.167	.091	-23	-2	-2	0	0	0	0	0	/2	-0.1

■ DAN MONZON
Monzon, Daniel Francisco   b: 5/17/46, Bronx, N.Y.   BR/TR, 5'10", 182 lbs.   Deb: 4/25/72

YEAR	TM/L	G	AB	R	H	2B	3B	HR	RBI	BB	SO	AVG	OBP	SLG	PRO+	BR	/A	RC	SB	CS	SBR	FR	POS	TPR
1972	Min-A	55	55	13	15	1	0	0	5	8	12	.273	.365	.291	92	0	-0	7	1	0	0	9	2/3SO	1.2
1973	Min-A	39	76	10	17	1	1	0	4	11	9	.224	.330	.263	66	-3	-3	8	1	0	0	9	23/O	0.7
Total	2	94	131	23	32	2	1	0	9	19	21	.244	.344	.275	77	-3	-3	15	2	0	1	18	/23SO	1.9

■ JOE MOOCK
Moock, Joseph Geoffrey   b: 3/12/44, Plaquemine, La.   BL/TR, 6'1", 180 lbs.   Deb: 9/01/67

YEAR	TM/L	G	AB	R	H	2B	3B	HR	RBI	BB	SO	AVG	OBP	SLG	PRO+	BR	/A	RC	SB	CS	SBR	FR	POS	TPR
1967	NY-N	13	40	2	9	2	0	0	5	0	7	.225	.225	.275	43	-3	-3	2	0	0	0	2	3	-0.1

■ GEORGE MOOLIC
Moolic, George Henry "Prunes"   b: 3/12/1865, Lawrence, Mass.   d: 2/19/15, Lawrence, Mass.   5'7", 145 lbs.   Deb: 5/01/1886

YEAR	TM/L	G	AB	R	H	2B	3B	HR	RBI	BB	SO	AVG	OBP	SLG	PRO+	BR	/A	RC	SB	CS	SBR	FR	POS	TPR
1886	Chi-N	16	56	9	8	3	0	0	2	2	17	.143	.172	.196	10	-6	-7	2	0			6	C/O	0.0

■ WALLY MOON
Moon, Wallace Wade   b: 4/3/30, Bay, Ark.   BL/TR, 6', 169 lbs.   Deb: 4/13/54   C

YEAR	TM/L	G	AB	R	H	2B	3B	HR	RBI	BB	SO	AVG	OBP	SLG	PRO+	BR	/A	RC	SB	CS	SBR	FR	POS	TPR
1954	StL-N	151	635	106	193	29	9	12	76	71	73	.304	.375	.435	109	10	10	106	18	10	-1	-3	*O	0.1
1955	StL-N	152	593	86	175	24	8	19	76	47	65	.295	.350	.459	113	10	10	91	11	11	-3	-4	*O1	-0.2
1956	StL-N	149	540	86	161	22	11	16	68	80	50	.298	.390	.469	129	24	24	99	12	9	-2	-1	O1	1.6
1957	StL-N	142	516	86	152	28	5	24	73	62	57	.295	.371	.508	131	24	23	94	5	6	-2	-4	O	1.3
1958	StL-N	108	290	36	69	10	3	7	38	47	30	.238	.344	.366	85	-4	-6	37	2	3	-1	-9	O	-1.7
1959	*LA-N	145	543	93	164	26	**11**	19	74	81	64	.302	.396	.495	126	29	24	111	15	6	1	-0	*O/1	2.2
1960	LA-N	138	469	74	140	21	6	13	69	67	53	.299	.387	.452	121	20	16	77	6	10	-4	1	O	0.9
1961	LA-N	134	463	79	152	25	3	17	88	89	79	.328	**.438**	.505	137	37	31	107	7	5	-1	-9	O	1.3
1962	LA-N	95	244	36	59	9	1	4	31	30	33	.242	.327	.336	84	-7	-5	28	5	2	0	-2	O1	-0.8
1963	LA-N	122	343	41	90	13	2	8	48	45	43	.262	.350	.382	119	6	8	45	5	5	-2	-12	O	-1.0
1964	LA-N	68	118	8	26	2	1	2	9	12	22	.220	.292	.305	74	-5	-4	10	1	1	-0	-2	O	-0.6
1965	*LA-N	53	89	6	18	3	0	1	11	13	22	.202	.304	.270	67	-4	-3	8	2	0	1	-5	O	-0.8
Total	12	1457	4843	737	1399	212	60	142	661	644	591	.289	.374	.445	117	142	130	810	89	68	-14	-49	*O1	2.3

■ AL MOORE
Moore, Albert James   b: 8/4/02, Brooklyn, N.Y.   d: 11/29/74, AtSea N.Y.To PR   BR/TR, 5'10", 174 lbs.   Deb: 9/27/25

YEAR	TM/L	G	AB	R	H	2B	3B	HR	RBI	BB	SO	AVG	OBP	SLG	PRO+	BR	/A	RC	SB	CS	SBR	FR	POS	TPR
1925	NY-N	2	8	0	1	0	0	0	0	1	2	.125	.222	.125	-9	-1	-1	0	0	1	-1	-0	/O	-0.1
1926	NY-N	28	81	12	18	4	0	0	10	5	7	.222	.267	.272	46	-6	-6	6	2			3	O	-0.3
Total	2	30	89	12	19	4	0	0	10	6	9	.213	.263	.258	41	-8	-7	6	2	1		3	/O	-0.4

■ JUNIOR MOORE
Moore, Alvin Earl   b: 1/25/53, Waskom, Tex.   BR/TR, 5'11", 185 lbs.   Deb: 8/02/76

YEAR	TM/L	G	AB	R	H	2B	3B	HR	RBI	BB	SO	AVG	OBP	SLG	PRO+	BR	/A	RC	SB	CS	SBR	FR	POS	TPR
1976	Atl-N	20	26	1	7	1	0	0	2	4	4	.269	.387	.308	93	0	0	4	0	0	0	1	/32O	0.1
1977	Atl-N	112	361	41	94	9	3	5	34	33	29	.260	.324	.343	71	-10	-16	38	4	5	-2	-4	*3/2	-2.1
1978	Chi-A	24	65	8	19	0	1	0	4	6	7	.292	.352	.323	90	-1	-1	7	1	1	-0	0	D/3O	0.0
1979	Chi-A	88	201	24	53	6	2	1	23	12	20	.264	.305	.328	71	-8	-8	18	0	2	-1	-2	OD/2	-1.2
1980	Chi-A	45	121	9	31	4	1	1	10	7	11	.256	.297	.331	72	-5	-5	10	0	2	-1	-1	3/O1D	-0.6
Total	5	289	774	83	204	20	7	7	73	62	71	.264	.320	.335	73	-23	-29	77	5	10	-5	-6	3/OD21	-3.8

YEAR	TM/L	G	AB	R	H	2B	3B	HR	RBI	BB	SO	AVG	OBP	SLG	PRO+	BR	/A	RC	SB	CS	SBR	FR	POS	TPR

■ ANSE MOORE
Moore, Anselm Winn b: 9/22/17, Delhi, La. BL/TR, 6'1", 190 lbs. Deb: 4/17/46

| 1946 | Det-A | 51 | 134 | 16 | 28 | 4 | 0 | 1 | 8 | 12 | 9 | .209 | .279 | .261 | 48 | -9 | -10 | 11 | 1 | 1 | -0 | 0 | O | -1.1 |

■ ARCHIE MOORE
Moore, Archie Francis b: 8/30/41, Upper Darby, Pa. BL/TL, 6'2", 190 lbs. Deb: 4/20/64

1964	NY-A	31	23	4	4	2	0	0	1	2	9	.174	.240	.261	39	-2	-2	2	0	0	0	1	/O1	-0.1
1965	NY-A	9	17	1	7	2	0	1	4	4	4	.412	.524	.706	248	4	4	6	0	0	0	0	/O	0.4
Total	2	40	40	5	11	4	0	1	5	6	13	.275	.370	.450	128	2	2	8	0	0	0	1	/O1	0.3

■ CHARLEY MOORE
Moore, Charles Wesley b: 12/1/1884, Jackson Co., Ind. d: 7/29/70, Portland, Ore. 5'10", 160 lbs. Deb: 4/16/12

| 1912 | Chi-N | 5 | 9 | 2 | 2 | 0 | 1 | 0 | 2 | 0 | 1 | .222 | .222 | .444 | 80 | -0 | -0 | 1 | 0 | | | 1 | /S23 | 0.0 |

■ CHARLIE MOORE
Moore, Charles William b: 6/21/53, Birmingham, Ala. BR/TR, 5'11", 180 lbs. Deb: 9/08/73

1973	Mil-A	8	27	0	5	0	1	0	3	2	4	.185	.241	.259	42	-2	-2	2	0	0	0	3	/C	0.1
1974	Mil-A	72	204	17	50	10	4	0	19	21	34	.245	.316	.333	87	-3	-3	21	3	4	-2	3	C/D	0.0
1975	Mil-A	73	241	26	70	20	1	1	29	17	31	.290	.337	.394	106	2	1	30	1	5	-3	-6	CO/D	-0.5
1976	Mil-A	87	241	33	46	7	4	3	16	43	45	.191	.316	.290	80	-5	-5	24	1	2	-1	0	CO/3D	-0.4
1977	Mil-A	138	375	42	93	15	6	5	45	31	39	.248	.307	.360	81	-10	-10	38	1	7	-4	-5	*C	-1.5
1978	Mil-A	96	268	30	72	7	1	5	31	12	24	.269	.300	.358	84	-6	-6	28	4	2	0	-2	C	-0.5
1979	Mil-A	111	337	45	101	16	2	5	38	29	32	.300	.357	.404	105	3	3	46	8	5	-1	9	*C	1.5
1980	Mil-A	111	320	42	93	13	2	2	30	24	28	.291	.340	.363	96	-3	-2	39	10	5	0	-15	*C	-1.1
1981	*Mil-A	48	156	16	47	8	3	1	9	12	13	.301	.351	.410	125	4	5	21	1	4	-2	-0	C/OD	0.4
1982	*Mil-A	133	456	53	116	22	4	6	45	29	49	.254	.300	.360	86	-13	-9	45	2	10	-5	1	*OC/2	-1.5
1983	Mil-A	151	529	65	150	27	6	2	49	55	42	.284	.355	.369	108	1	7	71	11	4	1	-8	*O/CD	-0.1
1984	Mil-A	70	188	13	44	7	1	2	17	10	26	.234	.276	.314	66	-10	-9	14	0	4	-2	1	O/C	-1.1
1985	Mil-A	105	349	35	81	13	4	0	31	27	53	.232	.289	.292	60	-19	-19	29	4	0	1	5	*C/O	-0.7
1986	Mil-A	80	235	24	61	12	3	3	39	21	38	.260	.320	.374	86	-4	-5	27	5	5	-2	13	C/O2D	1.1
1987	Tor-A	51	107	15	23	10	1	1	7	13	12	.215	.300	.355	73	-4	-4	12	0	0	0	8	C/O	0.7
Total	15	1334	4033	456	1052	187	43	36	408	346	470	.261	.321	.355	89	-70	-58	447	51	57	-19	6	CO/D23	-3.6

■ DEE MOORE
Moore, D C b: 4/6/14, Hedley, Tex. BR/TR, 5'11", 190 lbs. Deb: 9/12/36

1936	Cin-N	6	10	4	4	2	1	0	1	0	3	.400	.400	.800	230	1	2	3	0			-0	/PC	0.1
1937	Cin-N	7	13	2	1	0	0	0	0	1	2	.077	.200	.077	-23	-2	-2	0	0			2	/C	0.0
1943	Bro-N	37	79	8	20	3	0	0	12	11	8	.253	.344	.291	84	-1	-1	9	1			-6	C/3	-0.6
	Phi-N	37	113	13	27	4	1	1	8	15	8	.239	.328	.319	91	-2	-1	12	0			-0	C/O31	0.0
	Yr	74	192	21	47	7	1	1	20	26	16	.245	.335	.307	88	-3	-2	21	1			-6		-0.6
1946	Phi-N	11	13	2	1	0	0	0	1	7	3	.077	.400	.077	41	-0	-0	1	0			1	/C1	0.0
Total	4	98	228	29	53	9	2	1	22	34	24	.232	.335	.303	85	-4	-3	25	1			-4	/C301P	-0.5

■ GENE MOORE
Moore, Eugene Jr. "Rowdy" b: 8/26/09, Lancaster, Tex. d: 3/12/78, Jackson, Miss. BL/TL, 5'11", 175 lbs. Deb: 9/20/31

1931	Cin-N	4	14	2	2	1	0	0	1	0	1	.143	.143	.214	-6	-2	-2	0	0			0	/O	-0.1
1933	StL-N	11	38	6	15	3	2	0	8	4	10	.395	.452	.579	183	5	4	10	1			1	O	0.5
1934	StL-N	9	18	2	5	1	0	0	1	2	2	.278	.350	.333	79	-0	-0	2	0			1	/O	0.0
1935	StL-N	3	3	0	0	0	0	0	0	0	1	.000	.000	.000	-96	-1	-1	0	0			0	H	0.0
1936	Bos-N	151	637	91	185	38	12	13	67	40	80	.290	.335	.449	117	6	12	100	6			13	*O	1.7
1937	Bos-N	148	561	88	159	29	10	16	70	61	73	.283	.358	.456	132	15	22	96	11			11	*O	2.6
1938	Bos-N	54	180	27	49	8	3	3	19	16	20	.272	.338	.400	114	1	3	25	1			-1	O	0.0
1939	Bro-N	107	306	45	69	13	6	3	39	40	50	.225	.315	.337	73	-11	-12	35	4			-7	O/1	-2.0
1940	Bro-N	10	26	3	7	2	0	0	2	1	3	.269	.296	.346	72	-1	-1	3	0			-1	/O	-0.1
	Bos-N	103	363	46	106	24	1	5	39	25	32	.292	.338	.405	110	2	4	48	2			3	O	0.3
	Yr	113	389	49	113	26	1	5	41	26	35	.290	.335	.401	107	1	3	51	2			2		0.2
1941	Bos-N	129	397	42	108	17	8	5	43	45	37	.272	.349	.393	114	5	7	57	5			1	*O	0.4
1942	Was-A	1	2	0	0	0	0	0	0	0	1	.000	.000	.000	-99	-1	-1	0	0	0	0	0	/O	0.0
1943	Was-A	92	254	41	68	14	3	2	39	19	29	.268	.321	.370	106	-0	-1	29	0	2	-1	-1	O/1	-0.2
1944	*StL-A	110	390	56	93	13	6	6	58	24	37	.238	.284	.349	76	-11	-14	37	0	5	-3	-1	*O	-2.2
1945	StL-A	110	354	48	92	16	2	5	50	40	26	.260	.337	.359	97	1	-1	46	1	3	-2	-6	*O	-1.2
Total	14	1042	3543	497	958	179	53	58	436	317	401	.270	.333	.400	105	7	21	489	31	10		13	O/1	-0.3

■ FERDIE MOORE
Moore, Ferdinand Depage b: 2/21/1896, Camden, N.J. d: 5/6/47, Atlantic City, N.J. Deb: 10/02/14

| 1914 | Phi-A | 2 | 4 | 1 | 2 | 0 | 0 | 0 | 1 | 0 | 2 | .500 | .500 | .500 | 208 | 0 | 0 | 1 | 0 | | | -1 | /1 | 0.0 |

■ GARY MOORE
Moore, Gary Douglas b: 2/24/45, Tulsa, Okla. BR/TL, 5'10", 175 lbs. Deb: 5/03/70

| 1970 | LA-N | 7 | 16 | 2 | 3 | 0 | 2 | 0 | 0 | 0 | 1 | .188 | .188 | .438 | 65 | -1 | -1 | 0 | 1 | 0 | 0 | -0 | /O1 | 0.0 |

■ EDDIE MOORE
Moore, Graham Edward b: 1/18/1899, Barlow, Ky. d: 2/10/76, Ft.Myers, Fla. BR/TR, 5'7", 165 lbs. Deb: 9/25/23

1923	Pit-N	6	26	6	7	1	0	0	1	2	3	.269	.321	.308	65	-1	-1	3	1	0	0	-5	/S	-0.5
1924	Pit-N	72	209	47	75	8	4	2	13	27	12	.359	.437	.464	139	6	7	42	6	7	-2	1	O3/2	1.1
1925	*Pit-N	142	547	106	163	29	8	6	77	73	26	.298	.383	.413	97	5	-1	92	19	7	2	-6	*2O/3	-0.6
1926	Pit-N	43	132	19	30	8	1	0	19	12	6	.227	.292	.303	57	-7	-8	12	3			-11	2/3S	-1.7
	Bos-N	54	184	17	49	3	2	0	15	16	12	.266	.325	.304	77	-7	-5	19	6			-3	2S/3	-0.4
	Yr	97	316	36	79	11	3	0	34	28	18	.250	.311	.304	68	-15	-14	31	9			-14		-2.1
1927	Bos-N	112	411	53	124	14	4	1	32	39	17	.302	.364	.363	103	-2	3	54	5			-2	32O/S	0.2
1928	Bos-N	68	215	27	51	9	0	2	18	19	12	.237	.299	.307	62	-13	-11	20	7			3	O/2	-1.0
1929	Bro-N	111	402	48	119	18	6	0	48	44	16	.296	.370	.371	86	-9	-7	56	3			-18	2S/O3	-1.6
1930	Bro-N	76	196	24	55	13	1	1	20	21	7	.281	.356	.372	77	-7	-7	26	1			4	2OS/3	0.0
1932	NY-N	37	87	9	23	3	0	1	6	9	6	.264	.340	.333	84	-2	-2	10	1			3	S/32	0.4
1934	Cle-A	27	65	4	10	2	0	0	4	8	4	.154	.267	.185	18	-8	-8	4	0	0	0	1	2/3S	-0.5
Total	10	748	2474	360	706	108	26	13	257	272	121	.285	.359	.366	89	-37	-35	338	52	14		-34	2O/S3	-4.6

■ HARRY MOORE
Moore, Henry S. Deb: 4/17/1884

| 1884 | Was-U | 111 | 461 | 77 | 155 | 23 | 5 | 1 | | 19 | | .336 | .363 | .414 | 168 | 29 | 31 | 71 | 0 | | | -9 | *O/S | 1.8 |

■ JACKIE MOORE
Moore, Jackie Spencer b: 2/19/39, Jay, Fla. BR/TR, 6', 180 lbs. Deb: 4/18/65 MC

| 1965 | Det-A | 21 | 53 | 2 | 5 | 0 | 0 | 0 | 2 | 6 | 12 | .094 | .186 | .094 | -17 | -8 | -8 | 1 | 0 | 0 | 0 | 3 | C | -0.3 |

■ JIMMY MOORE
Moore, James William b: 4/24/03, Paris, Tenn. d: 3/7/86, Memphis, Tenn. BR/TR, 6'0.5", 187 lbs. Deb: 8/31/30

1930	Chi-A	16	39	4	8	2	0	0	2	6	3	.205	.326	.256	52	-3	-3	4	0	0	0	0	O	-0.2
	*Phi-A	15	50	10	19	3	0	2	12	2	4	.380	.404	.560	136	3	3	11	1	1	-0	-0	O	0.1
	Yr	31	89	14	27	5	0	2	14	8	7	.303	.367	.427	100	0	0	14	1	1	-0	-0		-0.1
1931	*Phi-A	49	143	18	32	5	1	2	21	11	13	.224	.284	.315	54	-9	-10	13	0	1	-1	0	O	-1.1
Total	2	80	232	32	59	10	1	4	35	19	20	.254	.316	.358	71	-9	-10	27	1	2	-1	0	/O	-1.2

■ JERRIE MOORE
Moore, Jeremiah S. b: Detroit, Mich. d: 9/26/1890, Wayne, Mich. BL Deb: 4/17/1884

1884	Alt-U	20	80	10	25	3	1	1		0		.313	.313	.412	141	3	3	11	0			-11	C/O	-0.5
	Cle-N	9	30	1	6	0	0	0	10	0	5	.200	.200	.200	25	-2	-3	1				0	/C	0.0
1885	Det-N	6	23	2	4	1	0	0	0	1	3	.174	.208	.217	38	-2	-2	1				-2	/C	-0.2

YEAR	TM/L	G	AB	R	H	2B	3B	HR	RBI	BB	SO	AVG	OBP	SLG	PRO+	BR	/A	RC	SB	CS	SBR	FR	POS	TPR
Total	2	35	133	13	35	4	1	1	10	1	8	.263	.269	.331	95	-1	-1	13				-12	/CO	-0.7

■ JOHNNY MOORE
Moore, John Francis b: 3/23/02, Waterville, Conn.   BL/TR, 5'10.5", 175 lbs.   Deb: 9/15/28

YEAR	TM/L	G	AB	R	H	2B	3B	HR	RBI	BB	SO	AVG	OBP	SLG	PRO+	BR	/A	RC	SB	CS	SBR	FR	POS	TPR
1928	Chi-N	4	4	0	0	0	0	0	0	0	0	.000	.000	.000	-99	-1	-1	0	0			0	H	0.0
1929	Chi-N	37	63	13	18	1	0	2	8	4	6	.286	.338	.397	81	-2	-2	8	0			2	O	-0.1
1931	Chi-N	39	104	19	25	3	1	2	16	7	5	.240	.288	.346	69	-5	-5	11	1			0	O	-0.4
1932	*Chi-N	119	443	59	135	24	5	13	64	22	38	.305	.342	.470	117	9	9	71	4			-6	*O	-0.4
1933	Cin-N	135	514	60	135	19	5	1	44	29	16	.263	.306	.325	81	-13	-12	52	4			7	*O	-1.3
1934	Cin-N	16	42	5	8	1	1	0	5	3	2	.190	.244	.262	36	-4	-4	3	0			-0	O	-0.4
	Phi-N	116	458	68	157	34	6	11	93	40	18	.343	.397	.515	125	27	19	97	7			7	*O	1.9
	Yr	132	500	73	165	35	7	11	98	43	20	.330	.384	.494	120	23	16	98	7			6		1.5
1935	Phi-N	153	600	84	194	33	3	19	93	45	50	.323	.375	.483	117	24	16	114	4			-13	*O	-0.2
1936	Phi-N	124	472	85	155	24	3	16	68	26	22	.328	.365	.494	117	18	12	83	1			-9	*O	-0.1
1937	Phi-N	96	307	46	98	16	2	9	59	18	18	.319	.357	.472	114	9	6	52	2			-4	O	0.0
1945	Chi-N	7	6	0	1	0	0	0	2	1	1	.167	.286	.167	28	-1	-1	0	0			0	H	0.0
Total	10	846	3013	439	926	155	26	73	452	195	176	.307	.352	.449	109	62	38	492	23			-16	O	-1.0

■ JO-JO MOORE
Moore, Joseph Gregg "The Gause Ghost" b: 12/25/08, Gause, Tex.   BL/TR, 5'11", 155 lbs.   Deb: 9/17/30

YEAR	TM/L	G	AB	R	H	2B	3B	HR	RBI	BB	SO	AVG	OBP	SLG	PRO+	BR	/A	RC	SB	CS	SBR	FR	POS	TPR
1930	NY-N	3	5	1	1	0	0	0	0	0	1	.200	.200	.200	-3	-1	-1	0	0			0	/O	0.0
1931	NY-N	4	8	0	2	1	0	0	3	0	1	.250	.250	.375	67	-0	-0	1	1			-0	/O	0.0
1932	NY-N	86	361	53	110	15	2	2	27	20	18	.305	.341	.374	94	-4	-3	47	4			-7	O	-1.5
1933	*NY-N	132	524	56	153	16	5	0	42	21	27	.292	.323	.342	91	-7	-6	59	4			3	*O	-1.1
1934	NY-N	139	580	106	192	37	4	15	61	31	23	.331	.370	.486	130	21	23	109	5			-12	*O	0.5
1935	NY-N	155	681	108	201	28	9	15	71	53	24	.295	.353	.429	111	9	10	110	5			-1	*O	0.2
1936	*NY-N	152	649	110	205	29	9	7	63	37	27	.316	.358	.421	110	8	9	103	2			6	*O	0.8
1937	*NY-N	142	580	89	180	37	10	6	57	46	37	.310	.364	.440	116	14	13	96	7			-10	*O	-0.2
1938	NY-N	125	506	76	153	23	6	11	56	22	27	.302	.335	.437	110	6	5	77	2			-4	*O	0.0
1939	NY-N	138	562	80	151	23	2	10	47	45	17	.269	.324	.370	85	-11	-12	69	5			-0	*O	-1.4
1940	NY-N	138	543	83	150	33	4	6	46	43	30	.276	.337	.385	98	-1	-1	72	7			-2	*O	-0.7
1941	NY-N	121	428	47	117	16	2	7	40	30	15	.273	.322	.369	93	-4	-5	52	4			-5	*O	-1.4
Total	12	1335	5427	809	1615	258	53	79	513	348	247	.298	.344	.408	105	29	32	795	46			-30	*O	-4.8

■ KELVIN MOORE
Moore, Kelvin Orlando b: 9/26/57, LeRoy, Ala.   BR/TL, 6'1", 195 lbs.   Deb: 8/28/81

YEAR	TM/L	G	AB	R	H	2B	3B	HR	RBI	BB	SO	AVG	OBP	SLG	PRO+	BR	/A	RC	SB	CS	SBR	FR	POS	TPR
1981	*Oak-A	14	47	5	12	0	1	1	3	5	15	.255	.327	.362	103	-0	0	6	1	0	0	-1	1	0.0
1982	Oak-A	21	67	6	15	1	1	2	6	3	23	.224	.257	.358	70	-3	-3	5	0	1	-1	-2	1	-0.5
1983	Oak-A	41	124	12	26	4	0	5	16	10	39	.210	.274	.363	78	-5	-4	11	2	4	-2	-3	1	-1.0
Total	3	76	238	23	53	5	2	8	25	18	77	.223	.280	.361	81	-8	-6	22	3	5	-2	-5	/1	-1.5

■ MOLLY MOORE
Moore, Maurice d: 2/24/1881, New York, N.Y.   Deb: 6/30/1875

YEAR	TM/L	G	AB	R	H	2B	3B	HR	RBI	BB	SO	AVG	OBP	SLG	PRO+	BR	/A	RC	SB	CS	SBR	FR	POS	TPR
1875	Atl-n	22	88	5	20	5	0	0			0	.227	.227	.284	87	-2	-0	6					S/13	0.0

■ RANDY MOORE
Moore, Randolph Edward b: 6/21/05, Naples, Tex.   BL/TR, 6', 185 lbs.   Deb: 4/12/27

YEAR	TM/L	G	AB	R	H	2B	3B	HR	RBI	BB	SO	AVG	OBP	SLG	PRO+	BR	/A	RC	SB	CS	SBR	FR	POS	TPR
1927	Chi-A	6	15	0	0	0	0	0	0	0	2	.000	.000	.000	-99	-4	-4	0	0	0	0	1	/O	-0.3
1928	Chi-A	24	61	6	13	4	1	0	5	3	5	.213	.250	.311	47	-5	-5	5	0	1	-1	0	O	-0.5
1930	Bos-N	83	191	24	55	9	0	2	34	10	13	.288	.323	.366	69	-10	-9	22	3			1	O3	-0.8
1931	Bos-N	83	192	19	50	8	1	3	34	13	3	.260	.311	.359	83	-6	-5	22	1			1	O3/2	-0.3
1932	Bos-N	107	351	41	103	21	2	3	43	15	11	.293	.322	.390	94	-5	-3	44	1			-6	O31/C	-1.0
1933	Bos-N	135	497	64	150	23	7	8	70	40	16	.302	.356	.425	133	14	19	74	3			-1	*O1	1.1
1934	Bos-N	123	422	55	120	21	2	7	64	40	16	.284	.346	.393	105	-1	3	59	2			-3	O1	-0.5
1935	Bos-N	125	407	42	112	20	4	4	42	26	16	.275	.319	.373	93	-9	-4	48	1			-1	O1	-0.8
1936	Bro-N	42	88	4	21	3	0	0	14	8	1	.239	.302	.273	55	-5	-5	7	0			-3	O	-0.9
1937	Bro-N	13	22	3	3	1	0	0	2	3	2	.136	.240	.182	16	-3	-3	1	0			0	C	-0.1
	StL-N	8	7	0	0	0	0	0	0	0	0	.000	.000	.000	-98	-2	-2	0	0			0	/O	-0.1
	Yr	21	29	3	3	1	0	0	2	3	2	.103	.188	.138	-10	-4	-5	1	0			0		-0.2
Total	10	749	2253	258	627	110	17	27	308	158	85	.278	.326	.378	95	-35	-19	283	11	1		-11	O/13C2	-4.2

■ TERRY MOORE
Moore, Terry Bluford b: 5/27/12, Vernon, Ala.   BR/TR, 5'11", 195 lbs.   Deb: 4/16/35   MC

YEAR	TM/L	G	AB	R	H	2B	3B	HR	RBI	BB	SO	AVG	OBP	SLG	PRO+	BR	/A	RC	SB	CS	SBR	FR	POS	TPR
1935	StL-N	119	456	63	131	34	3	6	53	15	40	.287	.314	.414	90	-5	-7	60	13			12	*O	0.0
1936	StL-N	143	590	85	156	39	4	5	47	37	52	.264	.309	.369	82	-16	-16	70	9			17	*O	-0.4
1937	StL-N	115	461	76	123	17	3	5	43	32	41	.267	.317	.349	79	-12	-13	53	13			9	*O	-0.8
1938	StL-N	94	312	49	85	21	3	4	21	46	19	.272	.366	.397	104	5	3	49	9			7	O/3	0.8
1939	StL-N	130	417	65	123	25	2	17	77	43	38	.295	.362	.487	119	15	11	73	6			7	*O/P	1.6
1940	StL-N	136	537	92	163	33	4	17	64	42	44	.304	.356	.475	121	19	15	92	18			14	*O	2.4
1941	StL-N	122	493	86	145	26	4	6	68	52	31	.294	.364	.400	108	10	6	74	3			4	*O	0.5
1942	*StL-N	130	489	80	141	26	3	6	49	56	26	.288	.364	.391	112	13	9	72	10			-8	*O/3	-0.1
1946	*StL-N	91	278	32	73	14	1	3	28	18	26	.263	.312	.353	85	-5	-6	32	0			-1	O	-0.8
1947	StL-N	127	460	61	130	17	1	7	45	38	39	.283	.339	.370	84	-8	-11	58	1			-2	*O	-1.6
1948	StL-N	91	207	30	48	11	0	4	18	27	12	.232	.321	.343	75	-6	-7	24	0			-5	O	-1.7
Total	11	1298	4700	719	1318	263	28	80	513	406	368	.280	.340	.399	98	11	-16	656	82			53	*O/3P	-0.1

■ SCRAPPY MOORE
Moore, William Allen b: 12/16/1892, St.Louis, Mo.   d: 10/13/64, Little Rock, Ark.   BR/TR, 5'8", 153 lbs.   Deb: 6/21/17

YEAR	TM/L	G	AB	R	H	2B	3B	HR	RBI	BB	SO	AVG	OBP	SLG	PRO+	BR	/A	RC	SB	CS	SBR	FR	POS	TPR
1917	StL-A	4	8	1	1	0	0	0	0	1	0	.125	.222	.125	6	-1	-1	0	0			0	/3	0.0

■ BILL MOORE
Moore, William Henry "Willie" b: 12/12/01, Kansas City, Mo.   d: 5/24/72, Kansas City, Mo.   BL/TR, 5'11", 170 lbs.   Deb: 9/07/26

YEAR	TM/L	G	AB	R	H	2B	3B	HR	RBI	BB	SO	AVG	OBP	SLG	PRO+	BR	/A	RC	SB	CS	SBR	FR	POS	TPR
1926	Bos-A	5	18	0	3	0	0	0	0	0	0	.167	.167	.167	-13	-3	-3	0	0	0	0	0	/C	-0.1
1927	Bos-A	44	69	7	15	2	0	0	4	13	8	.217	.341	.246	56	-4	-4	7	0	0	0	2	C	0.0
Total	2	49	87	9	18	2	0	0	4	13	10	.207	.310	.230	43	-7	-7	7	0	0	0	2	/C	-0.1

■ BILL MOORE
Moore, William Ross b: 10/10/60, Los Angeles, Cal.   BR/TL, 6'1", 185 lbs.   Deb: 7/19/86

YEAR	TM/L	G	AB	R	H	2B	3B	HR	RBI	BB	SO	AVG	OBP	SLG	PRO+	BR	/A	RC	SB	CS	SBR	FR	POS	TPR
1986	Mon-N	6	12	0	2	0	0	0	0	0	4	.167	.167	.167	-8	-2	-2	0	0	0	0	-0	/10	-0.1

■ ANDRES MORA
Mora, Andres (Ibarra) b: 5/25/55, Rio Bravo, Mex.   BR/TR, 6', 180 lbs.   Deb: 4/13/76

YEAR	TM/L	G	AB	R	H	2B	3B	HR	RBI	BB	SO	AVG	OBP	SLG	PRO+	BR	/A	RC	SB	CS	SBR	FR	POS	TPR
1976	Bal-A	73	220	18	48	11	0	6	25	13	49	.218	.262	.350	83	-7	-5	20	1	0	0	-1	DO	-0.6
1977	Bal-A	77	233	32	57	8	2	13	44	5	53	.245	.264	.464	100	-3	-2	27	0	0	0	-9	O/3D	-1.1
1978	Bal-A	76	229	21	49	8	0	8	14	13	47	.214	.259	.354	75	-10	-8	20	0	0	1	-1	O/D	-1.0
1980	Cle-A	9	18	0	2	0	0	0	0	0	0	.111	.111	.111	-39	-3	-3	0	0	0	0	-0	/O	-0.3
Total	4	235	700	71	156	27	2	27	83	31	149	.223	.258	.383	83	-23	-18	67	1	1	-0	-10	O/D3	-3.0

■ JOSE MORALES
Morales, Jose Manuel (Hernandez) b: 12/30/44, Frederiksted, V.I.   BR/TR, 5'11", 187 lbs.   Deb: 8/13/73   C

YEAR	TM/L	G	AB	R	H	2B	3B	HR	RBI	BB	SO	AVG	OBP	SLG	PRO+	BR	/A	RC	SB	CS	SBR	FR	POS	TPR
1973	Oak-A	6	14	0	4	1	0	0	1	1	5	.286	.333	.357	100	-0	-0	1	0	1	-1	0	/D	0.0
	Mon-N	5	5	0	2	0	0	0	0	0	0	.400	.400	.400	118	0	0	1	0	0	0	0	H	0.0
1974	Mon-N	25	26	3	7	4	0	1	5	1	7	.269	.296	.538	123	1	1	3	0	0	0	-0	/C	0.0
1975	Mon-N	93	163	18	49	6	1	2	24	14	21	.301	.356	.387	102	1	1	20	0	2	-1	5	1/OC	0.3
1976	Mon-N	104	158	12	50	11	0	4	37	3	20	.316	.337	.462	120	4	4	23	0	0	0	1	1C	0.5
1977	Mon-N	65	74	3	15	4	1	1	9	5	12	.203	.253	.324	55	-5	-5	5	0	0	0	-2	/C1	-0.6

YEAR	TM/L	G	AB	R	H	2B	3B	HR	RBI	BB	SO	AVG	OBP	SLG	PRO+	BR	/A	RC	SB	CS	SBR	FR	POS	TPR
1978	Min-A	101	242	22	76	13	1	2	38	20	35	.314	.369	.401	114	6	5	34	0	1	-1	1	D/C1O	0.5
1979	Min-A	92	191	21	51	5	1	2	27	14	27	.267	.324	.335	75	-6	-7	19	0	0	0	0	D/1	-0.6
1980	Min-A	97	241	36	73	17	2	8	36	22	19	.303	.364	.490	123	10	8	40	0	0	0	-1	D/C1	0.7
1981	Bal-A	38	86	6	21	3	0	2	14	3	13	.244	.270	.349	77	-3	-3	6	0	0	0	-0	D/1	-0.2
1982	Bal-A	3	3	0	0	0	0	0	0	0	2	.000	.000	.000	-99	-1	-1	0	0	0	0	0	/H	0.0
	LA-N	35	30	1	9	1	0	1	8	4	8	.300	.382	.433	131	1	1	5	0	0	0	0	H	0.1
1983	*LA-N	47	53	4	15	3	0	3	8	1	11	.283	.296	.509	120	1	1	7	0	0	0	-0	/1	0.1
1984	LA-N	22	19	0	3	0	0	0	1	1	2	.158	.200	.158	2	-2	-2	1	0	0	0	0	H	-0.2
Total	12	733	1305	126	375	68	6	26	207	89	182	.287	.336	.408	102	8	3	164	0	4	-2	4	D/1CO	0.6

■ JERRY MORALES
Morales, Julio Ruben (Torres) b: 2/18/49, Yabucao, P.R. BR/TR, 5'10", 155 lbs. Deb: 9/05/69

YEAR	TM/L	G	AB	R	H	2B	3B	HR	RBI	BB	SO	AVG	OBP	SLG	PRO+	BR	/A	RC	SB	CS	SBR	FR	POS	TPR
1969	SD-N	19	41	5	8	2	0	1	6	5	7	.195	.283	.317	71	-2	-2	3	0	2	-1	2	O	-0.1
1970	SD-N	28	58	6	9	0	1	1	4	3	11	.155	.197	.241	17	-7	-7	2	0	0	0	-2	O	-0.9
1971	SD-N	12	17	1	2	0	0	0	1	2	2	.118	.211	.118	-5	-2	-2	0	1	0	0	0	/O	-0.1
1972	SD-N	115	347	38	83	15	7	4	18	35	54	.239	.309	.357	96	-5	-2	38	4	6	-2	9	O/3	0.0
1973	SD-N	122	388	47	109	23	2	9	34	27	55	.281	.328	.420	115	2	6	49	6	5	-1	4	*O	0.4
1974	Chi-N	151	534	70	146	21	7	15	82	46	63	.273	.333	.423	106	6	3	69	2	12	-7	-5	*O	-1.3
1975	Chi-N	153	578	62	156	21	0	12	91	50	65	.270	.333	.369	91	-4	-7	69	3	7	-3	-1	*O	-1.7
1976	Chi-N	140	537	66	147	17	0	16	67	41	49	.274	.325	.395	95	1	-4	62	3	8	-4	5	*O	-0.8
1977	Chi-N	136	490	56	142	34	5	11	69	43	75	.290	.350	.447	101	8	1	75	0	3	-2	-12	*O	-1.7
1978	StL-N	130	457	44	109	19	8	4	46	33	44	.239	.291	.341	77	-15	-14	43	4	4	-1	-1	*O	-2.2
1979	Det-A	129	440	50	93	23	1	14	56	30	56	.211	.265	.364	65	-21	-23	39	10	4	1	-7	*O/D	-3.3
1980	NY-N	94	193	19	49	7	1	3	30	13	31	.254	.304	.347	84	-5	-4	20	2	3	-1	3	O	-0.5
1981	Chi-N	84	245	27	70	6	2	1	25	22	29	.286	.347	.339	91	-1	-2	29	1	1	-0	-3	O	-0.7
1982	Chi-N	65	116	14	33	2	2	4	30	9	7	.284	.336	.440	112	2	2	15	1	2	-1	7	O	0.7
1983	Chi-N	63	87	11	17	9	0	0	11	7	19	.195	.255	.299	51	-6	-6	7	0	0	0	-0	O	-0.6
Total	15	1441	4528	516	1173	199	36	95	570	366	567	.259	.316	.382	91	-49	-63	520	37	57	-23	1	*O/D3	-12.8

■ RICH MORALES
Morales, Richard Angelo b: 9/20/43, San Francisco, Cal. BR/TR, 5'11", 170 lbs. Deb: 8/08/67 C

YEAR	TM/L	G	AB	R	H	2B	3B	HR	RBI	BB	SO	AVG	OBP	SLG	PRO+	BR	/A	RC	SB	CS	SBR	FR	POS	TPR
1967	Chi-A	8	10	0	0	0	0	0	0	0	2	.000	.000	.000	-99	-2	-2	0	0	0	0	2	/S	0.0
1968	Chi-A	10	29	2	5	0	0	0	0	2	5	.172	.226	.172	22	-3	-3	1	0	0	0	2	/S2	0.0
1969	Chi-A	55	121	12	26	0	1	0	6	7	18	.215	.269	.231	39	-9	-10	8	1	0	0	10	2S/3	0.2
1970	Chi-A	62	112	6	18	2	0	1	2	9	16	.161	.230	.205	20	-12	-13	6	1	0	0	6	S32	-0.2
1971	Chi-A	84	185	19	45	8	0	2	14	22	26	.243	.339	.319	84	-3	-3	20	2	3	-1	-1	S3/2O	-0.8
1972	Chi-A	110	287	24	59	7	1	2	20	19	49	.206	.262	.258	54	-16	-16	17	2	3	-1	-1	S23	-0.8
1973	Chi-A	7	4	1	0	0	0	0	1	1	1	.000	.200	.000	-38	-1	-1	0	0	0	0	1	/32	0.0
	SD-N	90	244	9	40	6	1	0	16	27	36	.164	.247	.197	27	-25	-22	13	0	1	-1	22	2S	0.4
1974	SD-N	54	61	8	12	3	0	1	5	8	6	.197	.290	.295	67	-3	-3	6	1	0	0	7	S2/31	0.9
Total	8	480	1053	81	205	26	3	6	64	95	159	.195	.268	.242	46	-73	-73	70	7	7	-2	48	S2/310	0.5

■ CHARLIE MORAN
Moran, Charles Barthell "Uncle Charlie" b: 2/22/1878, Nashville, Tenn. d: 6/14/49, Horse Cave, Ky. BR/TR, 5'8", 180 lbs. Deb: 9/09/03 U

YEAR	TM/L	G	AB	R	H	2B	3B	HR	RBI	BB	SO	AVG	OBP	SLG	PRO+	BR	/A	RC	SB	CS	SBR	FR	POS	TPR
1903	StL-N	4	14	2	6	0	0	0		1	0	.429	.429	.429	152	1	1	3	1			-1	/PS	0.0
1908	StL-N	21	63	2	11	1	2	0		2	0	.175	.175	.254	40	-5	-4	3	0			-2	C	-0.6
Total	2	25	77	4	17	1	2	0		3	0	.221	.221	.286	62	-4	-3	6	1			-3	/CPS	-0.6

■ CHARLES MORAN
Moran, Charles Vincent b: 3/26/1879, Washington, D.C. d: 4/11/34, Washington, D.C. TR , Deb: 4/29/03

YEAR	TM/L	G	AB	R	H	2B	3B	HR	RBI	BB	SO	AVG	OBP	SLG	PRO+	BR	/A	RC	SB	CS	SBR	FR	POS	TPR
1903	Was-A	98	373	41	84	14	5	1	24	33		.225	.288	.298	76	-9	-10	36	8			5	S/2	0.0
1904	Was-A	62	243	27	54	10	0	0	7	23		.222	.289	.263	79	-5	-5	22	7			-13	S/3	-1.9
	StL-A	82	272	15	47	3	1	0	14	25		.173	.242	.191	42	-17	-16	14	2			-3	3/O	-1.7
	Yr	144	515	42	101	13	1	0	21	48		.196	.265	.225	60	-23	-20	36	9			-16		-3.6
1905	StL-A	27	82	6	16	1	0	0	5	10		.195	.283	.207	61	-3	-3	7	3			-4	2/3	-0.7
Total	3	269	970	89	201	28	6	1	50	91		.207	.275	.252	67	-36	-34	79	20			-15	S/32O	-4.3

■ HERBIE MORAN
Moran, John Herbert b: 2/16/1884, Costello, Pa. d: 9/21/54, Clarkson, N.Y. BL/TR, 5'5", 150 lbs. Deb: 4/16/08

YEAR	TM/L	G	AB	R	H	2B	3B	HR	RBI	BB	SO	AVG	OBP	SLG	PRO+	BR	/A	RC	SB	CS	SBR	FR	POS	TPR
1908	Phi-A	19	59	4	9	0	0	0	4	6		.153	.231	.153	25	-4	-5	2	1			1	O	-0.5
	Bos-N	8	29	3	8	0	0	0	2	2		.276	.323	.276	95	-0	-0	3	1			2	/O	0.2
1909	Bos-N	8	31	8	7	1	0	0	0	5		.226	.333	.258	80	-0	-1	3	0			-0	/O	0.0
1910	Bos-N	20	67	11	8	0	0	0	3	13	14	.119	.280	.119	17	-6	-7	4	6			4	O	-0.3
1912	Bro-N	130	508	77	140	18	10	1	40	69	38	.276	.368	.356	102	1	4	76	28			1	*O	0.1
1913	Bro-N	132	515	71	137	15	5	0	26	45	29	.266	.333	.315	83	-8	-10	58	21			-5	*O	-1.7
1914	Cin-N	107	395	43	93	10	5	1	35	41	29	.235	.312	.294	78	-9	-10	42	26			-7	*O	-2.1
	*Bos-N	41	154	24	41	3	1	0	4	17	11	.266	.347	.299	93	-1	-1	17	4			-6	O	-0.8
	Yr	148	549	67	134	13	6	1	39	58	40	.244	.322	.295	82	-10	-11	59	30			-14		-2.9
1915	Bos-N	130	419	59	84	13	5	0	21	66	41	.200	.320	.255	79	-10	-7	38	10	10	-1	-7	*O	-2.0
Total	7	595	2177	300	527	60	26	2	135	264	162	.242	.331	.296	83	-38	-37	244	103	10		-18	O	-7.1

■ PAT MORAN
Moran, Patrick Joseph b: 2/7/1876, Fitchburg, Mass. d: 3/7/24, Orlando, Fla. TR , 5'10", 180 lbs. Deb: 5/15/01 M

YEAR	TM/L	G	AB	R	H	2B	3B	HR	RBI	BB	SO	AVG	OBP	SLG	PRO+	BR	/A	RC	SB	CS	SBR	FR	POS	TPR
1901	Bos-N	52	180	12	38	5	1	2	18	3		.211	.228	.283	45	-12	-14	13	3			-6	C1/3SO2	-1.5
1902	Bos-N	80	251	22	60	5	5	1	24	17		.239	.305	.311	91	-2	-2	27	6			1	C/1O	0.7
1903	Bos-N	109	389	40	102	25	5	7	54	29		.262	.313	.406	111	2	4	54	8			21	*C/1	3.2
1904	Bos-N	113	398	26	90	11	3	4	34	18		.226	.260	.299	77	-13	-11	35	10			4	C3/1	0.1
1905	Bos-N	85	267	22	64	11	5	2	22	8		.240	.262	.341	83	-7	-6	25	3			14	C	1.6
1906	*Chi-N	70	226	22	57	13	1	0	35	7		.252	.275	.319	82	-4	-6	23	6			2	C	0.2
1907	*Chi-N	65	198	8	45	5	1	1	19	10		.227	.264	.278	67	-7	-8	17	5			-0	C	-0.3
1908	Chi-N	50	150	12	39	5	1	0	12	13		.260	.319	.307	98	1	-0	17	6			2	C	0.4
1909	Chi-N	77	246	18	54	11	1	1	23	16		.220	.278	.285	73	-8	-8	20	2			0	C	-0.2
1910	Phi-N	68	199	13	47	7	1	0	11	17	16	.236	.306	.281	69	-7	-8	19	6			0	C	-0.4
1911	Phi-N	34	103	2	19	3	0	0	8	3	13	.184	.208	.214	18	-11	-12	5	0			-1	C	-0.9
1912	Phi-N	13	26	1	3	1	0	0	1	1	7	.115	.148	.154	-16	-4	-4	1	0			-1	C	-0.4
1913	Phi-N	1	1	0	0	0	0	0	0	0	0	.000	.000	.000	-96	-0	-0	0	0			0	H	0.0
1914	Phi-N	1	0	0	0	0	0	0	1	0	0	—	—	—		0	0	0	0			0	/C	0.0
Total	14	818	2634	198	618	102	24	18	262	142	36	.235	.278	.312	78	-73	-76	254	55			37	C/310S2	2.5

■ AL MORAN
Moran, Richard Alan b: 12/5/38, Detroit, Mich. BR/TR, 6'1.5", 190 lbs. Deb: 4/09/63

YEAR	TM/L	G	AB	R	H	2B	3B	HR	RBI	BB	SO	AVG	OBP	SLG	PRO+	BR	/A	RC	SB	CS	SBR	FR	POS	TPR
1963	NY-N	119	331	26	64	5	1	2	23	36	60	.193	.274	.230	46	-22	-22	21	3	7	-3	6	*S/3	-0.8
1964	NY-N	16	22	2	5	0	0	0	4	2	2	.227	.292	.227	50	-1	-1	1	0	0	0	4	S/3	0.4
Total	2	135	353	28	69	5	1	2	27	38	62	.195	.276	.229	46	-23	-24	22	3	7	-3	11	S/3	-0.4

■ ROY MORAN
Moran, Roy Ellis "Deedle" b: 9/17/1884, Vincennes, Ind. d: 7/18/66, Atlanta, Ga. BR/TR, 5'8", 155 lbs. Deb: 9/03/12

YEAR	TM/L	G	AB	R	H	2B	3B	HR	RBI	BB	SO	AVG	OBP	SLG	PRO+	BR	/A	RC	SB	CS	SBR	FR	POS	TPR
1912	Was-A	7	13	1	2	0	0	0	0	8		.154	.476	.154	82	1	1	3	3			-0	/O	0.0

■ BILL MORAN
Moran, William L. b: 10/10/1869, Joliet, Ill. d: 4/8/16, Joliet, Ill. Deb: 5/07/1892

YEAR	TM/L	G	AB	R	H	2B	3B	HR	RBI	BB	SO	AVG	OBP	SLG	PRO+	BR	/A	RC	SB	CS	SBR	FR	POS	TPR
1892	StL-N	24	81	2	11	1	0	0	5	2	12	.136	.157	.148	-7	-10	-10	2	0			-3	C/O	-1.0
1895	Chi-N	15	55	8	9	2	1	1	9	3	2	.164	.220	.291	30	-6	-6	4	2			-1	C	-0.4
Total	2	39	136	10	20	3	1	1	14	5	14	.147	.183	.206	11	-16	-16	6	2			-4	/CO	-1.4

YEAR	TM/L	G	AB	R	H	2B	3B	HR	RBI	BB	SO	AVG	OBP	SLG	PRO+	BR	/A	RC	SB	CS	SBR	FR	POS	TPR

■ BILLY MORAN   Moran, William Nelson   b: 11/27/33, Montgomery, Ala.   BR/TR, 5'11", 185 lbs.   Deb: 4/15/58

YEAR	TM/L	G	AB	R	H	2B	3B	HR	RBI	BB	SO	AVG	OBP	SLG	PRO+	BR	/A	RC	SB	CS	SBR	FR	POS	TPR
1958	Cle-A	115	257	26	58	11	0	1	18	13	23	.226	.263	.280	51	-18	-17	18	3	2	-0	13	2S	0.6
1959	Cle-A	11	17	1	5	1	0	0	2	0	1	.294	.294	.294	64	-1	-1	1	0	0	0	-1	/2S	0.0
1961	LA-A	54	173	17	45	7	1	2	22	17	16	.260	.330	.347	73	-4	-7	20	0	0	0	-5	2/S	-0.5
1962	LA-A	160	659	90	186	25	3	17	74	39	80	.282	.326	.407	99	-5	-2	89	5	1	1	19	*2	2.9
1963	LA-A	153	597	67	164	29	5	7	65	31	57	.275	.314	.375	98	-7	-3	68	1	1	-0	15	*2	2.4
1964	LA-A	50	198	26	53	10	1	0	11	13	20	.268	.316	.328	88	-5	-3	18	1	3	-2	-7	3/2S	-1.0
	Cle-A	69	151	14	31	6	0	1	10	18	16	.205	.294	.265	57	-8	-8	12	0	1	-1	3	32/1	-0.3
	Yr	119	349	40	84	16	1	1	21	31	36	.241	.306	.301	73	-14	-12	30	1	4	-2	-4		-1.3
1965	Cle-A	22	24	1	3	0	0	0	0	2	5	.125	.222	.125	1	-3	-3	1	0	0	0	1	/2S	-0.1
Total	7	634	2076	242	545	88	10	28	202	133	218	.263	.310	.355	85	-51	-44	227	10	8	-2	39	2/3S1	4.0

■ MICKEY MORANDINI   Morandini, Michael Robert   b: 4/22/66, Kittanning, Pa.   BL/TR, 5'11", 170 lbs.   Deb: 9/01/90

YEAR	TM/L	G	AB	R	H	2B	3B	HR	RBI	BB	SO	AVG	OBP	SLG	PRO+	BR	/A	RC	SB	CS	SBR	FR	POS	TPR
1990	Phi-N	25	79	9	19	4	0	1	3	6	19	.241	.294	.329	72	-3	-3	8	3	0	1	1	2	0.0

■ RAY MOREHART   Morehart, Raymond Anderson   b: 12/2/1899, Near Abner, Tex.   d: 1/13/89, Dallas, Tex.   BL/TR, 5'9", 157 lbs.   Deb: 8/09/24

YEAR	TM/L	G	AB	R	H	2B	3B	HR	RBI	BB	SO	AVG	OBP	SLG	PRO+	BR	/A	RC	SB	CS	SBR	FR	POS	TPR
1924	Chi-A	31	100	10	20	4	2	0	8	17	7	.200	.316	.280	56	-7	-6	10	3	1	0	-12	S/2	-1.3
1926	Chi-A	73	192	27	61	10	3	0	21	11	15	.318	.358	.401	101	-1	-0	24	3	11	-6	-5	2	-0.8
1927	NY-A	73	195	45	50	7	2	1	20	29	18	.256	.353	.328	80	-6	-5	23	4	4	-1	4	2	0.0
Total	3	177	487	82	131	21	7	1	49	57	40	.269	.347	.347	83	-13	-11	57	10	16	-7	-13	2/S	-2.1

■ DANNY MOREJON   Morejon, Daniel (Torres)   b: 7/21/30, Havana, Cuba   BR/TR, 6'1", 175 lbs.   Deb: 7/11/58

YEAR	TM/L	G	AB	R	H	2B	3B	HR	RBI	BB	SO	AVG	OBP	SLG	PRO+	BR	/A	RC	SB	CS	SBR	FR	POS	TPR
1958	Cin-N	12	26	4	5	0	0	0	1	9	2	.192	.400	.192	60	-1	-1	3	1	0	0	-1	O	-0.1

■ KEITH MORELAND   Moreland, Bobby Keith   b: 5/2/54, Dallas, Tex.   BR/TR, 6', 190 lbs.   Deb: 10/01/78

YEAR	TM/L	G	AB	R	H	2B	3B	HR	RBI	BB	SO	AVG	OBP	SLG	PRO+	BR	/A	RC	SB	CS	SBR	FR	POS	TPR
1978	Phi-N	1	2	0	0	0	0	0	0	0	0	.000	.000	.000	-99	-1	-1	0	0	0	0	0	/C	0.0
1979	Phi-N	14	48	3	18	3	2	0	8	3	5	.375	.412	.521	148	3	3	10	0	0	0	0	C	0.4
1980	*Phi-N	62	159	13	50	8	0	4	29	8	14	.314	.347	.440	112	4	3	22	3	1	0	-1	C/3O	0.2
1981	*Phi-N	61	196	16	50	7	0	6	37	15	13	.255	.311	.383	92	-1	-2	20	1	2	-1	-7	C/31O	-1.0
1982	Chi-N	138	476	50	124	17	2	15	68	46	71	.261	.330	.399	100	2	0	61	0	6	-4	-2	OC/3	-0.6
1983	Chi-N	154	533	76	161	30	3	16	70	68	73	.302	.384	.460	127	25	22	93	0	3	-2	-12	*O/C	0.5
1984	*Chi-N	140	495	59	138	17	3	16	80	34	71	.279	.329	.422	101	5	-0	64	1	4	-2	-11	*O1/3C	-1.7
1985	Chi-N	161	587	74	180	30	3	14	106	68	50	.307	.380	.440	116	23	16	100	12	3	2	-14	*O13/C	0.0
1986	Chi-N	156	586	72	159	30	0	12	79	53	48	.271	.332	.384	90	-3	-8	72	3	6	-3	-13	*O3C1	-2.7
1987	Chi-N	153	563	63	150	29	1	27	88	39	66	.266	.314	.465	99	0	-2	78	3	3	-1	4	*3/1	0.0
1988	SD-N	143	511	40	131	23	0	5	64	40	51	.256	.310	.331	86	-10	-9	50	2	3	-1	-3	1O/3	-2.0
1989	Det-A	90	318	34	95	16	0	5	35	27	33	.299	.357	.396	115	5	6	42	3	2	-0	-6	D13/C	-0.1
	Bal-A	33	107	11	23	4	0	1	10	4	12	.215	.243	.280	49	-8	-7	6	0	0	0	0	D	-0.6
	Yr	123	425	45	118	20	0	6	45	31	45	.278	.330	.367	99	-2	-1	46	3	2	-0	-6		-0.7
Total	12	1306	4581	511	1279	214	14	121	674	405	515	.279	.339	.411	103	45	19	616	28	33	-11	-65	O3C1/D	-7.6

■ HARRY MORELOCK   Morelock, A. Harry   b: Philadelphia, Pa.   Deb: 8/21/1891

YEAR	TM/L	G	AB	R	H	2B	3B	HR	RBI	BB	SO	AVG	OBP	SLG	PRO+	BR	/A	RC	SB	CS	SBR	FR	POS	TPR
1891	Phi-N	4	14	1	1	0	0	0	0	3	3	.071	.235	.071	-8	-2	-2	0	0			-3	/S	-0.4
1892	Phi-N	1	3	0	0	0	0	0	0	1	0	.000	.250	.000	-22	-0	-0	0	0			-1	/3	0.0
Total	2	5	17	1	1	0	0	0	0	4	3	.059	.238	.059	-10	-2	-2	0	0			-4	/S3	-0.4

■ JOSE MORENO   Moreno, Jose De Los Santos (b: Jose De Los Santos Mauricio (Moreno))   b: 11/1/57, Santo Domingo, D.R.   BB/TR, 6', 175 lbs.   Deb: 5/24/80

YEAR	TM/L	G	AB	R	H	2B	3B	HR	RBI	BB	SO	AVG	OBP	SLG	PRO+	BR	/A	RC	SB	CS	SBR	FR	POS	TPR
1980	NY-N	37	46	6	9	2	1	2	9	3	12	.196	.245	.413	83	-1	-1	4	1	0	0	0	/23	0.0
1981	SD-N	34	48	5	11	2	0	0	6	1	8	.229	.245	.271	50	-3	-3	3	4	1	1	1	/O2	-0.1
1982	Cal-A	11	3	3	0	0	0	0	0	2	0	.000	.400	.000	21	-0	-0	0	0	2	-1	1	/2D	0.0
Total	3	82	97	14	20	4	1	2	15	6	20	.206	.252	.330	66	-5	-5	7	5	3	-0	1	/O23D	-0.1

■ OMAR MORENO   Moreno, Omar Renan (Quintero)   b: 10/24/52, Puerto Armuelles, Panama   BL/TL, 6'2", 180 lbs.   Deb: 9/06/75

YEAR	TM/L	G	AB	R	H	2B	3B	HR	RBI	BB	SO	AVG	OBP	SLG	PRO+	BR	/A	RC	SB	CS	SBR	FR	POS	TPR
1975	Pit-N	6	6	1	1	0	0	0	0	1	1	.167	.286	.167	28	-1	-1	1	1	0	0	-0	/O	0.0
1976	Pit-N	48	122	24	33	4	1	2	12	16	24	.270	.360	.369	106	2	1	19	15	5	2	4	O	0.6
1977	Pit-N	150	492	69	118	19	9	7	34	38	102	.240	.296	.358	72	-18	-20	55	53	16	6	1	*O	-1.8
1978	Pit-N	155	515	95	121	15	7	2	33	81	104	.235	.342	.303	78	-10	-13	65	71	22	8	11	*O	0.0
1979	*Pit-N	162	695	110	196	21	12	8	69	51	104	.282	.334	.381	90	-5	-9	94	77	21	11	15	*O	1.2
1980	Pit-N	162	676	87	168	20	13	2	36	57	101	.249	.309	.325	76	-20	-21	71	96	33	9	18	*O	-2.2
1981	Pit-N	103	434	62	120	18	8	1	35	26	76	.276	.322	.362	91	-4	-6	53	39	14	3	5	*O	0.0
1982	Pit-N	158	645	82	158	18	9	3	44	44	121	.245	.294	.315	68	-26	-28	61	60	26	2	5	*O	-2.2
1983	Hou-N	97	405	48	98	12	11	0	25	22	72	.242	.283	.326	73	-18	-15	38	30	13	1	4	O	-1.1
	NY-A	48	152	17	38	9	1	1	17	8	31	.250	.287	.342	75	-6	-5	14	7	3	-0	4	O	-0.5
1984	NY-A	117	355	37	92	12	6	4	38	18	48	.259	.297	.361	84	-10	-8	37	20	11	-1	-3	*O/D	-1.4
1985	NY-A	34	66	12	13	4	1	1	4	1	16	.197	.209	.333	47	-5	-5	4	1	1	-0	6	O/D	0.0
	KC-A	24	70	9	17	1	3	2	12	3	8	.243	.284	.429	91	-1	-1	8	0	1	-1	-4	O	-0.5
	Yr	58	136	21	30	5	4	3	16	4	24	.221	.248	.382	70	-6	-6	12	1	2	-1	1		-0.5
1986	Atl-N	118	359	46	84	18	6	4	27	21	77	.234	.276	.351	68	-15	-17	32	17	16	-5	-4	O	-2.8
Total	12	1382	4992	699	1257	171	87	37	386	387	885	.252	.308	.343	79	-137	-147	553	487	182	37	61	*O/D	-8.0

■ CHET MORGAN   Morgan, Chester Collins "Chick"   b: 6/6/10, Cleveland, Miss.   BL/TR, 5'9", 160 lbs.   Deb: 4/19/35

YEAR	TM/L	G	AB	R	H	2B	3B	HR	RBI	BB	SO	AVG	OBP	SLG	PRO+	BR	/A	RC	SB	CS	SBR	FR	POS	TPR
1935	Det-A	14	23	2	4	1	0	0	1	5	0	.174	.321	.217	43	-2	-2	2	0	0	0	-0	/O	-0.1
1938	Det-A	74	306	50	87	6	1	0	27	20	12	.284	.330	.304	58	-18	-20	31	5	6	-2	-2	O	-2.2
Total	2	88	329	52	91	7	1	0	28	25	12	.277	.330	.304	57	-20	-22	33	5	6	-2	-3	/O	-2.3

■ ED MORGAN   Morgan, Edward Carre   b: 5/22/04, Cairo, Ill.   d: 4/9/80, New Orleans, La.   BR/TR, 6'0.5", 180 lbs.   Deb: 4/11/28

YEAR	TM/L	G	AB	R	H	2B	3B	HR	RBI	BB	SO	AVG	OBP	SLG	PRO+	BR	/A	RC	SB	CS	SBR	FR	POS	TPR
1928	Cle-A	76	265	42	83	24	6	4	54	21	17	.313	.366	.494	123	8	8	47	5	5	-2	1	1O3	0.4
1929	Cle-A	93	318	60	101	19	10	3	37	37	24	.318	.392	.469	116	10	9	59	4	3	-1	-11	O	-0.5
1930	Cle-A	150	584	122	204	47	11	26	136	62	66	.349	.413	.601	148	46	43	144	8	4	0	-3	*1O	2.2
1931	Cle-A	131	462	87	162	33	4	11	86	83	46	.351	.451	.511	144	39	35	110	4	5	-2	2	*1/3	2.3
1932	Cle-A	144	532	96	156	32	7	4	68	94	44	.293	.402	.402	102	11	6	92	7	6	-2	-8	*1/3	-1.6
1933	Cle-A	39	121	10	32	3	3	1	13	7	9	.264	.305	.364	73	-4	-5	13	1	1	-0	3	1/O	-0.4
1934	Bos-A	138	528	95	141	28	4	3	79	81	46	.267	.367	.352	80	-9	-14	74	7	1	2	-7	*1	-4.1
Total	7	771	2810	512	879	186	45	52	473	385	252	.313	.398	.467	117	102	81	540	36	25	-4	-23	1O/3	-1.7

■ EDDIE MORGAN   Morgan, Edwin Willis "Pepper"   b: 11/19/14, Brady Lake, Ohio   d: 6/27/82, Lakewood, Ohio   BL/TL, 5'10", 160 lbs.   Deb: 4/14/36

YEAR	TM/L	G	AB	R	H	2B	3B	HR	RBI	BB	SO	AVG	OBP	SLG	PRO+	BR	/A	RC	SB	CS	SBR	FR	POS	TPR
1936	StL-N	8	18	4	5	0	0	1	3	2	4	.278	.350	.444	113	0	0	3	0			-0	/O	0.0
1937	Bro-N	31	48	4	9	3	0	0	5	9	7	.188	.316	.250	55	-3	-3	5	0			-1	/1O	-0.4
Total	2	39	66	8	14	3	0	1	8	11	11	.212	.325	.303	70	-2	-3	8	0			-2	/O1	-0.4

■ BILL MORGAN   Morgan, Henry William   b: 10/1857, Washington, D.C.   Deb: 5/04/1875

YEAR	TM/L	G	AB	R	H	2B	3B	HR	RBI	BB	SO	AVG	OBP	SLG	PRO+	BR	/A	RC	SB	CS	SBR	FR	POS	TPR
1875	RS-n	19	69	11	18	4	0	0			5	.261	.311	.319	131	1	3	7					/OP3	0.3
1878	Mil-N	14	56	2	11	0	0	0	5	3	9	.196	.237	.196	41	-3	-4	3				-4	O/32	-0.7
1882	Pit-a	17	66	10	17	2	1	0		4		.258	.300	.318	114	1	1	6				-7	O/C	-0.5
1884	Ric-a	6	20	0	2	0	0	0		1		.100	.143	.100	-18	-2	-2	0				-2	/CO2	-0.3

YEAR	TM/L	G	AB	R	H	2B	3B	HR	RBI	BB	SO	AVG	OBP	SLG	PRO+	BR	/A	RC	SB	CS	SBR	FR	POS	TPR
	Bal-U	2	9	1	2	0	0	0		1		.222	.300	.222	72	-0	-0	1	0			-1	/C2O	0.0
Total	3	39	151	13	32	2	1	0	5	9	9	.212	.256	.238	65	-5	-5	10	0			-14	/OC23	-1.5

■ RED MORGAN
Morgan, James Edward b: 10/6/1883, Neola, Iowa Deceased TR , Deb: 6/20/06

YEAR	TM/L	G	AB	R	H	2B	3B	HR	RBI	BB	SO	AVG	OBP	SLG	PRO+	BR	/A	RC	SB	CS	SBR	FR	POS	TPR
1906	Bos-A	88	307	20	66	6	3	1	21	16		.215	.254	.264	64	-13	-13	24	7			-13	3	-2.0

■ JOE MORGAN
Morgan, Joe Leonard b: 9/19/43, Bonham, Tex. BL/TR, 5'7", 160 lbs. Deb: 9/21/63

YEAR	TM/L	G	AB	R	H	2B	3B	HR	RBI	BB	SO	AVG	OBP	SLG	PRO+	BR	/A	RC	SB	CS	SBR	FR	POS	TPR
1963	Hou-N	8	25	5	6	0	0	0	3	5	5	.240	.367	.320	106	0	0	4	1	0	0	-3	/2	-0.1
1964	Hou-N	10	37	4	7	0	0	0	0	6	7	.189	.302	.189	44	-3	-2	2	0	1	-1	-0	2	-0.1
1965	Hou-N	157	601	100	163	22	12	14	40	97	77	.271	.375	.418	132	21	27	103	20	9	1	-2	*2	3.5
1966	Hou-N	122	425	60	121	14	8	5	42	89	43	.285	.412	.391	134	19	23	77	11	8	-2	-16	*2	1.3
1967	Hou-N	133	494	73	136	27	11	6	42	81	51	.275	.380	.411	131	20	22	88	29	5	6	-5	*2/O	3.3
1968	Hou-N	10	20	6	5	0	1	0	0	7	4	.250	.444	.350	144	2	2	5	3	0	1	-4	/2O	-0.1
1969	Hou-N	147	535	94	126	18	5	15	43	110	74	.236	.367	.372	110	9	10	86	49	14	6	-2	*2O	2.5
1970	Hou-N	144	548	102	147	28	9	8	52	102	55	.268	.384	.396	114	11	14	92	42	13	5	11	*2	4.5
1971	Hou-N	160	583	87	149	27	11	13	56	88	52	.256	.354	.407	118	13	15	95	40	8	7	-3	*2	2.8
1972	*Cin-N	149	552	122	161	23	4	16	73	115	44	.292	.419	.435	152	37	41	117	58	17	7	-7	*2	5.4
1973	Cin-N	157	576	116	167	35	2	26	82	111	61	.290	.408	.493	157	42	46	128	67	15	11	-8	*2	5.6
1974	Cin-N	149	512	107	150	31	3	22	67	120	69	.293	.430	.494	160	45	46	125	58	12	10	-13	*2	5.1
1975	*Cin-N	146	498	107	163	27	6	17	94	132	52	.327	.471	.508	169	57	56	145	67	10	14	-7	*2	7.0
1976	*Cin-N	141	472	113	151	30	5	27	111	114	41	.320	.453	.576	186	61	60	144	60	9	13	-23	*2	5.8
1977	Cin-N	153	521	113	150	21	6	22	78	117	58	.288	.420	.478	138	35	34	121	49	10	9	-18	*2	3.4
1978	Cin-N	132	441	68	104	27	0	13	75	79	40	.236	.354	.385	107	6	6	67	19	5	3	-31	*2	-1.5
1979	*Cin-N	127	436	70	109	26	1	9	32	93	45	.250	.383	.376	107	9	8	72	28	6	5	-13	*2	0.8
1980	*Hou-N	141	461	66	112	17	5	11	49	93	47	.243	.370	.373	117	8	13	73	24	6	4	-12	*2	1.4
1981	SF-N	90	308	47	74	16	1	8	31	66	37	.240	.374	.377	116	8	9	49	14	5	1	-11	2	0.5
1982	SF-N	134	463	68	134	19	4	14	61	85	60	.289	.402	.438	135	25	25	92	24	4	5	-6	*2/3	3.0
1983	*Phi-N	123	404	72	93	20	1	16	59	89	54	.230	.374	.403	117	11	12	68	18	2	4	-2	*2	1.9
1984	Oak-A	116	365	50	89	21	0	6	43	66	39	.244	.361	.351	105	1	5	51	8	3	1	-31	*2/D	-2.0
Total	22	2649	9277	1650	2517	449	96	268	1133	1865	1015	.271	.395	.427	133	438	470	1804	689	162	110	-203	*2/OD3	54.0

■ JOE MORGAN
Morgan, Joseph Michael b: 11/19/30, Walpole, Mass. BL/TR, 5'10", 170 lbs. Deb: 4/14/59 MC

YEAR	TM/L	G	AB	R	H	2B	3B	HR	RBI	BB	SO	AVG	OBP	SLG	PRO+	BR	/A	RC	SB	CS	SBR	FR	POS	TPR
1959	Mil-N	13	23	2	5	1	0	0	1	2	4	.217	.280	.261	49	-2	-2	2	0	0	0	-2	/2	-0.2
	KC-A	20	21	2	4	0	1	0	3	3	7	.190	.292	.286	58	-1	-1	2	0	0	0	-1	/3	-0.1
1960	Phi-N	26	83	5	11	2	2	0	2	6	11	.133	.191	.205	8	-11	-11	3	0	0	0	1	3	-0.9
	Cle-A	22	47	6	14	2	0	2	4	6	4	.298	.377	.468	131	2	2	8	0	0	0	-1	3/O	0.1
1961	Cle-A	4	10	0	2	0	0	0	0	1	3	.200	.273	.200	29	-1	-1	1	0	0	0	0	/O	0.0
1964	StL-N	3	3	0	0	0	0	0	0	0	2	.000	.000	.000	-92	-1	-1	0	0	0	0	0	H	0.0
Total	4	88	187	15	36	5	3	2	10	18	31	.193	.263	.283	49	-13	-13	15	0	0	0	-2	/32O	-1.1

■ RAY MORGAN
Morgan, Raymond Caryll b: 6/14/1889, Baltimore, Md. d: 2/15/40, Baltimore, Md. BR/TR, 5'8.5", 155 lbs. Deb: 8/07/11

YEAR	TM/L	G	AB	R	H	2B	3B	HR	RBI	BB	SO	AVG	OBP	SLG	PRO+	BR	/A	RC	SB	CS	SBR	FR	POS	TPR
1911	Was-A	25	89	11	19	2	0	0	5	4		.213	.247	.236	36	-8	-8	6	2			-3	3	-1.0
1912	Was-A	81	273	40	65	10	7	1	30	29		.238	.318	.337	87	-5	-5	33	11			-7	2/S3	-1.1
1913	Was-A	138	481	58	131	19	8	0	57	68	63	.272	.369	.345	107	8	7	66	19			-5	*2/S	-0.1
1914	Was-A	147	491	50	126	22	8	1	49	62	34	.257	.352	.340	105	6	5	63	24	17	-3	-9	*2	-0.8
1915	Was-A	62	193	21	45	5	4	0	21	30	15	.233	.342	.301	92	-1	-1	22	6	5	-1	-4	2/S3	-0.6
1916	Was-A	99	315	41	84	12	4	1	29	59	29	.267	.398	.340	125	12	13	50	14			-17	2/S13	0.0
1917	Was-A	101	338	32	90	9	1	1	33	40	29	.266	.346	.308	101	1	1	38	7			-8	2/3	0.0
1918	Was-A	88	300	25	70	11	1	0	30	28	14	.233	.311	.277	79	-8	-7	27	4			-4	2/O	-0.8
Total	8	741	2480	278	630	90	33	4	254	320	184	.254	.348	.322	99	7	6	304	87	22		-57	2/3S10	-4.4

■ BOBBY MORGAN
Morgan, Robert Morris b: 6/29/26, Oklahoma City, Okla. BR/TR, 5'9", 175 lbs. Deb: 4/18/50

YEAR	TM/L	G	AB	R	H	2B	3B	HR	RBI	BB	SO	AVG	OBP	SLG	PRO+	BR	/A	RC	SB	CS	SBR	FR	POS	TPR
1950	Bro-N	67	199	38	45	10	3	7	21	32	43	.226	.342	.412	95	-1	-1	29	0			6	3S	0.6
1952	*Bro-N	67	191	36	45	7			16	46	35	.236	.392	.387	115	6	6	33	2	2	-1	3	3/2S	1.1
1953	*Bro-N	69	196	35	51	6	2	7	33	33	47	.260	.370	.418	103	2	2	31	2	2	-1	-2	3S	0.0
1954	Phi-N	135	455	58	119	25	2	14	50	70	68	.262	.360	.418	102	2	2	70	3	1	0	-22	*S/32	-1.0
1955	Phi-N	136	483	61	112	20	2	10	49	73	72	.232	.333	.344	81	-13	-11	57	6	4	-1	-13	2S/31	-1.6
1956	Phi-N	8	25	1	5	0	0	0	1	6	4	.200	.355	.200	56	-1	-1	2	0	0	0		/32	0.0
	StL-N	61	113	14	22	7	0	3	20	15	24	.195	.289	.336	67	-5	-5	10	0	2	-1	1	23/S	-0.3
	Yr	69	138	15	27	7	0	3	21	21	28	.196	.302	.312	65	-7	-7	13	0	2	-1	1		-0.3
1957	Phi-N	2	0	0	0	0	0	0	0	0	0	—	—	—		0	0	0	0	0	0	1	/2	0.1
	Chi-N	125	425	43	88	20	2	5	27	52	87	.207	.295	.299	61	-23	-23	41	5	0	2	8	*23	-0.2
	Yr	127	425	43	88	20	2	5	27	52	87	.207	.295	.299	61	-23	-23	41	5	0	2	9		-0.1
1958	Chi-N	1	1	0	0	0	0	0	0	0	1	.000	.000	.000	-99	-0	-0	0	0	0	0	0	H	0.0
Total	8	671	2088	286	487	96	11	53	217	327	381	.233	.339	.366	88	-33	-32	272	18	11		-17	2S3/1	-1.3

■ VERN MORGAN
Morgan, Vernon Thomas b: 8/8/28, Emporia, Va. d: 11/8/75, Minneapolis, Minn. BL/TR, 6'1", 190 lbs. Deb: 8/10/54 C

YEAR	TM/L	G	AB	R	H	2B	3B	HR	RBI	BB	SO	AVG	OBP	SLG	PRO+	BR	/A	RC	SB	CS	SBR	FR	POS	TPR
1954	Chi-N	24	64	3	15	2	0	0	2	1	10	.234	.246	.266	33	-6	-6	4	0	0	0	-4	3	-0.9
1955	Chi-N	7	7	1	1	0	0	0	1	3	4	.143	.400	.143	52	-0	-0	1	0	0	0	-0	/3	0.0
Total	2	31	71	4	16	2	0	0	3	4	14	.225	.267	.254	36	-7	-7	5	0	0	0	-4	/3	-0.9

■ BILL MORGAN
Morgan, William Deb: 8/06/1883

YEAR	TM/L	G	AB	R	H	2B	3B	HR	RBI	BB	SO	AVG	OBP	SLG	PRO+	BR	/A	RC	SB	CS	SBR	FR	POS	TPR
1883	Pit-a	32	114	12	18	2	1	0			7	.158	.207	.193	31	-9	-8	5				-1	S/OC2	-0.7
1884	Was-a	45	162	8	28	1	1	0			8	.173	.216	.191	41	-11	-8	7				-4	OC/2S	-0.9
Total	2	77	276	20	46	3	2	0			15	.167	.212	.192	36	-19	-16	12				-4	/OSC2	-1.6

■ MOE MORHARDT
Morhardt, Meredith Goodwin b: 1/16/37, Manchester, Conn. BL/TL, 6'1", 185 lbs. Deb: 9/07/61

YEAR	TM/L	G	AB	R	H	2B	3B	HR	RBI	BB	SO	AVG	OBP	SLG	PRO+	BR	/A	RC	SB	CS	SBR	FR	POS	TPR
1961	Chi-N	7	18	3	5	0	0	0	1	3	1	.278	.381	.278	78	-0	-0	2	0	0	0	-1	/1	-0.1
1962	Chi-N	18	16	1	2	0	0	0	2	2	8	.125	.222	.125	-4	-2	-2	1	0	0	0	0	H	-0.1
Total	2	25	34	4	7	0	0	0	3	5	13	.206	.308	.206	39	-3	-3	3	0	0	0	-1	/1	-0.2

■ ED MORIARTY
Moriarty, Edward Jerome b: 10/12/12, Holyoke, Mass. BR/TR, 5'10.5", 180 lbs. Deb: 6/21/35

YEAR	TM/L	G	AB	R	H	2B	3B	HR	RBI	BB	SO	AVG	OBP	SLG	PRO+	BR	/A	RC	SB	CS	SBR	FR	POS	TPR
1935	Bos-N	8	34	4	11	2	1	1	1	0	6	.324	.324	.529	136	1	1	6	0			-4	/2	-0.1
1936	Bos-N	6	6	1	1	0	0	0	0	0	1	.167	.167	.167	-11	-1	-1	0	0			0	H	0.0
Total	2	14	40	5	12	2	1	1	1	0	7	.300	.300	.475	114	0	0	6	0			-4	/2	-0.1

■ GENE MORIARITY
Moriarity, Eugene John b: Holyoke, Mass. BL/TL, 5'8", 130 lbs. Deb: 6/18/1884

YEAR	TM/L	G	AB	R	H	2B	3B	HR	RBI	BB	SO	AVG	OBP	SLG	PRO+	BR	/A	RC	SB	CS	SBR	FR	POS	TPR
1884	Bos-N	4	16	1	1	0	0	0		0		.063	.063	.063	-61	-3	-3	0				-0	/O	-0.2
	Ind-a	10	37	4	8	0	2	0		0		.216	.216	.324	79	-1	-1	3				-1	/OP3	-0.1
1885	Det-N	11	39	1	1	1	0	0		0	10	.026	.026	.051	-75	-7	-7	0				1	/O3SP	-0.5
1892	StL-N	47	177	20	31	4	1	3	19	4	37	.175	.207	.260	44	-13	-12	11	7			2	O	-1.0
Total	3	72	269	26	41	5	3	3	19	4	55	.152	.174	.227	25	-24	-23	14	7			2	/O3PS	-1.8

■ GEORGE MORIARTY
Moriarty, George Joseph b: 7/7/1884, Chicago, Ill. d: 4/8/64, Miami, Fla. TR , 6', 185 lbs. Deb: 9/27/03 MU

YEAR	TM/L	G	AB	R	H	2B	3B	HR	RBI	BB	SO	AVG	OBP	SLG	PRO+	BR	/A	RC	SB	CS	SBR	FR	POS	TPR
1903	Chi-N	1	5	1	0	0	0	0	0	0	0	.000	.000	.000	-99	-1	-1	0	0			-0	/3	-0.1

YEAR	TM/L	G	AB	R	H	2B	3B	HR	RBI	BB	SO	AVG	OBP	SLG	PRO+	BR	/A	RC	SB	CS	SBR	FR	POS	TPR
1904	Chi-N	4	13	0	0	0	0	0	0	0	1	.000	.071	.000	-77	-3	-3	0	0			-0	/3O	-0.2
1906	NY-A	65	197	22	46	7	7	0	23	17		.234	.294	.340	91	-0	-2	24	8			2	3O/12	0.1
1907	NY-A	126	437	51	121	16	5	0	43	25		.277	.316	.336	102	4	1	58	28			-9	31/02S	-0.3
1908	NY-A	101	348	25	82	12	1	0	27	11		.236	.259	.276	75	-10	-10	30	22			8	13O/2	-0.1
1909	*Det-A	133	473	43	129	20	4	1	39	24		.273	.309	.338	100	1	-1	59	34			2	*31	0.6
1910	Det-A	136	490	53	123	24	3	2	60	33		.251	.308	.324	92	-2	-6	58	33			-1	*3	0.0
1911	Det-A	130	478	51	116	20	4	1	60	27		.243	.287	.308	63	-23	-26	51	28			-4	*3/1	-2.8
1912	Det-A	105	375	38	93	23	1	0	54	26		.248	.316	.315	83	-10	-8	46	27			-8	13	-1.4
1913	Det-A	105	347	29	83	5	2	0	30	24	25	.239	.302	.265	67	-14	-14	36	33			-3	3/O	-1.5
1914	Det-A	132	465	56	118	19	5	1	40	39	27	.254	.318	.323	90	-4	-6	55	34	15	1	17	*3/1	1.6
1915	Det-A	31	38	2	8	1	0	0	0	5	7	.211	.318	.237	63	-1	-2	3	1	1	-0	-0	3/12O	-0.1
1916	Chi-A	7	5	1	1	0	0	0	0	2	0	.200	.429	.200	88	0	0	0	0			1	/13	0.1
Total	13	1076	3671	372	920	147	32	5	376	234	59	.251	.302	.312	84	-62	-78	422	248	16		6	31/02S	-4.1

■ **BILL MORIARTY** Moriarty, William Joseph b: 1883, Chicago, Ill. d: 12/25/16, Elgin, Ill. BR/TR, 6'2", 180 lbs. Deb: 4/29/09

YEAR	TM/L	G	AB	R	H	2B	3B	HR	RBI	BB	SO	AVG	OBP	SLG	PRO+	BR	/A	RC	SB	CS	SBR	FR	POS	TPR
1909	Cin-N	6	20	1	4	1	0	0	1	0		.200	.200	.250	40	-1	-1	1	2			0	/S	0.0

■ **BILL MORLEY** Morley, William M. (b: William Morley Jennings) b: 1/23/1890, Holland, Mich. d: 5/14/85, Lubbock, Tex. BR/TR, 5'11", 170 lbs. Deb: 9/08/13

YEAR	TM/L	G	AB	R	H	2B	3B	HR	RBI	BB	SO	AVG	OBP	SLG	PRO+	BR	/A	RC	SB	CS	SBR	FR	POS	TPR
1913	Was-A	2	3	0	0	0	0	0	0	0	0	.000	.000	.000	-98	-1	-1	0	0			0	/2	0.0

■ **RUSS MORMAN** Morman, Russell Lee b: 4/28/62, Independence, Mo. BR/TR, 6'4", 215 lbs. Deb: 8/03/86

YEAR	TM/L	G	AB	R	H	2B	3B	HR	RBI	BB	SO	AVG	OBP	SLG	PRO+	BR	/A	RC	SB	CS	SBR	FR	POS	TPR
1986	Chi-A	49	159	18	40	5	0	4	17	16	36	.252	.328	.358	84	-3	-3	19	1	0	0	-3	1	-0.8
1988	Chi-A	40	75	8	18	2	0	0	3	3	17	.240	.269	.267	51	-5	-5	4	0	0	0	-2	1O/D	-0.7
1989	Chi-A	37	58	5	13	2	0	0	8	6	16	.224	.297	.259	59	-3	-3	5	1	0	0	1	1	-0.4
1990	KC-A	12	37	5	10	4	2	1	3	3	3	.270	.325	.568	148	2	2	7	0	0	0	0	/O1D	0.2
Total	4	138	329	36	81	13	2	5	31	28	72	.246	.309	.343	80	-9	-9	35	2	0	1	-4	1/OD	-1.7

■ **JEFF MORONKO** Moronko, Jeffrey Robert b: 8/17/59, Houston, Tex. BR/TR, 6'2", 190 lbs. Deb: 9/01/84

YEAR	TM/L	G	AB	R	H	2B	3B	HR	RBI	BB	SO	AVG	OBP	SLG	PRO+	BR	/A	RC	SB	CS	SBR	FR	POS	TPR
1984	Cle-A	7	19	1	3	1	0	0	3	3	5	.158	.273	.211	35	-2	-2	1	0	0	0	0	/3D	-0.1
1987	NY-A	7	11	0	1	0	0	0	0	0	2	.091	.167	.091	-29	-2	-2	0	0	0	0	1	/3SO	0.0
Total	2	14	30	1	4	1	0	0	3	3	7	.133	.235	.167	12	-4	-4	2	0	0	0	1	/3OSD	-0.1

■ **JOHN MORRILL** Morrill, John Francis "Honest John" b: 2/19/1855, Boston, Mass. d: 4/2/32, Boston, Mass. BR/TR, 5'10.5", 155 lbs. Deb: 4/24/1876 M

YEAR	TM/L	G	AB	R	H	2B	3B	HR	RBI	BB	SO	AVG	OBP	SLG	PRO+	BR	/A	RC	SB	CS	SBR	FR	POS	TPR
1876	Bos-N	66	278	38	73	5	2	0	26	3	5	.263	.270	.295	87	-3	-4	23				8	2C/O1	0.4
1877	Bos-N	61	242	47	73	5	1	0	28	6	15	.302	.319	.331	101	1	0	26				-9	31O/2	-0.7
1878	Bos-N	60	233	26	56	5	1	0	23	5	16	.240	.256	.270	68	-7	-3	17				2	*1/O3	-0.3
1879	Bos-N	84	348	56	98	18	5	0	49	14	32	.282	.309	.362	118	8	7	40				2	31	0.7
1880	Bos-N	86	342	51	81	16	8	2	44	11	37	.237	.261	.348	108	1	3	32				0	13/P	0.1
1881	Bos-N	81	311	47	90	19	3	1	39	12	30	.289	.316	.379	123	6	8	38				9	*1/2P3	0.7
1882	Bos-N	83	349	73	101	19	11	2	54	18	29	.289	.324	.424	137	14	14	49				-3	*1/S2O3PM	0.0
1883	Bos-N	97	404	83	129	33	16	6	68	15	68	.319	.344	.525	155	28	26	75				-0	*1/O3S2PM	1.4
1884	Bos-N	111	438	80	114	19	7	3	61	30	87	.260	.308	.356	109	0	4	49				4	*12/P3OM	0.0
1885	Bos-N	111	394	74	89	20	7	4	44	64	78	.226	.334	.343	124	11	13	46				2	*12/3M	0.1
1886	Bos-N	117	430	86	106	25	6	7	69	56	81	.247	.333	.381	122	10	13	59	9			-2	S12/PM	0.3
1887	Bos-N	127	504	79	141	32	6	12	81	37	86	.280	.330	.438	113	8	8	81	19			4	*1M	-0.6
1888	Bos-N	135	486	60	96	18	7	4	39	55	68	.198	.282	.288	83	-7	-8	46	21			9	*1/2M	-1.1
1889	Was-N	44	146	20	27	5	0	2	16	30	23	.185	.328	.260	71	-5	-4	17	12			-1	1/32PM	-0.5
1890	Bos-P	2	7	1	1	0	0	0	2	2	1	.143	.333	.143	29	-1	-1	0	0			-0	/S1	0.0
Total	15	1265	4912	821	1275	239	80	43	643	358	656	.260	.310	.367	112	69	71	599	61			25	132/SOCP	0.5

■ **DOYT MORRIS** Morris, Doyt Theodore b: 7/15/16, Stanley, N.C. d: 7/4/84, Gastonia, N.C. BR/TR, 6'4", 195 lbs. Deb: 6/06/37

YEAR	TM/L	G	AB	R	H	2B	3B	HR	RBI	BB	SO	AVG	OBP	SLG	PRO+	BR	/A	RC	SB	CS	SBR	FR	POS	TPR
1937	Phi-A	6	13	0	2	0	0	0	0	0	3	.154	.154	.154	-23	-2	-2	0	0	0	0	0	/O	-0.1

■ **E. MORRIS** Morris, E. b: Trenton, N.J. Deb: 9/11/1884

YEAR	TM/L	G	AB	R	H	2B	3B	HR	RBI	BB	SO	AVG	OBP	SLG	PRO+	BR	/A	RC	SB	CS	SBR	FR	POS	TPR
1884	Bal-U	1	3	0	0	0	0	0		0		.000	.000	.000	-91	-1	-1	0				-1	/OP	0.0

■ **JOHN MORRIS** Morris, John Daniel b: 2/23/61, Freeport, N.Y. BL/TL, 6'1", 185 lbs. Deb: 8/05/86

YEAR	TM/L	G	AB	R	H	2B	3B	HR	RBI	BB	SO	AVG	OBP	SLG	PRO+	BR	/A	RC	SB	CS	SBR	FR	POS	TPR
1986	StL-N	39	100	8	24	0	1	1	14	7	15	.240	.290	.290	61	-5	-5	8	6	2	1	2	O	-0.2
1987	*StL-N	101	157	22	41	6	4	3	23	11	22	.261	.314	.408	88	-3	-3	20	5	2	0	1	O	-0.4
1988	StL-N	20	38	3	11	2	1	0	3	1	7	.289	.308	.395	99	-0	-0	5	0	0	0	-2	O	-0.2
1989	StL-N	96	117	8	28	4	1	2	14	4	22	.239	.264	.342	70	-5	-5	10	1	0	0	-0	O	-0.5
1990	StL-N	18	18	0	2	0	0	0	0	3	6	.111	.238	.111	-1	-2	-2	1	0	0	0	-0	/O	-0.2
Total	5	274	430	41	106	12	7	6	54	26	72	.247	.291	.349	74	-15	-16	44	12	4	1	1	O	-1.5

■ **WALTER MORRIS** Morris, John Walter b: 1/31/1880, Rockwall, Tex. d: 8/2/61, Dallas, Tex. BR/TR, 5'11", Deb: 8/31/08

YEAR	TM/L	G	AB	R	H	2B	3B	HR	RBI	BB	SO	AVG	OBP	SLG	PRO+	BR	/A	RC	SB	CS	SBR	FR	POS	TPR
1908	StL-N	23	73	1	13	1	1	0	2	0		.178	.178	.219	29	-6	-6	3	1			4	S	-0.1

■ **P. MORRIS** Morris, P. b: Rockford, Ill. Deb: 5/14/1884

YEAR	TM/L	G	AB	R	H	2B	3B	HR	RBI	BB	SO	AVG	OBP	SLG	PRO+	BR	/A	RC	SB	CS	SBR	FR	POS	TPR
1884	Was-U	1	3	0	0	0	0	0		0		.000	.000	.000	-99	-1	-1	0	0			0	/S	0.0

■ **HAL MORRIS** Morris, William Harold b: 4/9/65, Fort Rucker, Ala. BL/TL, 6'3", 200 lbs. Deb: 7/29/88

YEAR	TM/L	G	AB	R	H	2B	3B	HR	RBI	BB	SO	AVG	OBP	SLG	PRO+	BR	/A	RC	SB	CS	SBR	FR	POS	TPR
1988	NY-A	15	20	1	2	0	0	0	0	0	9	.100	.100	.100	-44	-4	-4	0	0	0	0	1	/OD	-0.2
1989	NY-A	15	18	2	5	0	0	0	4	1	4	.278	.316	.278	69	-1	-1	1	0	0	0	0	/O1D	0.0
1990	*Cin-N	107	309	50	105	22	3	7	36	21	32	.340	.384	.498	137	17	16	55	9	3	1	0	1/O	1.3
Total	3	137	347	53	112	22	3	7	40	22	45	.323	.365	.464	124	12	11	57	9	3	1	1	/1OD	1.1

■ **JIM MORRISON** Morrison, James Forrest b: 9/23/52, Pensacola, Fla. BR/TR, 5'11", 175 lbs. Deb: 9/18/77

YEAR	TM/L	G	AB	R	H	2B	3B	HR	RBI	BB	SO	AVG	OBP	SLG	PRO+	BR	/A	RC	SB	CS	SBR	FR	POS	TPR
1977	Phi-N	5	7	3	3	0	0	0	1	1	1	.429	.500	.429	145	1	1	2	0	0	0	1	/3	0.1
1978	*Phi-N	53	108	12	17	1	1	3	10	10	21	.157	.235	.269	40	-9	-9	7	1	1	-0	13	2/3O	0.6
1979	Chi-A	67	240	38	66	14	0	14	35	15	48	.275	.328	.508	122	6	6	41	11	3	2	0	23	1.0
1980	Chi-A	162	604	66	171	40	4	15	57	36	74	.283	.332	.424	106	4	4	80	9	6	-1	-3	*2/SD	0.9
1981	Chi-A	90	290	27	68	8	1	10	34	10	29	.234	.265	.372	84	-8	-7	26	3	2	-0	8	3/2D	0.1
1982	Chi-A	51	166	17	37	7	3	7	19	13	15	.223	.279	.428	91	-3	-3	18	0	1	-1	-6	3/D	-1.0
	Pit-N	44	86	10	24	4	1	4	15	5	14	.279	.319	.488	119	2	2	12	2	0	1	3	3/O2S	0.4
1983	Pit-N	66	158	16	48	7	2	6	25	9	25	.304	.349	.487	126	6	5	24	2	6	-3	3	23/S	0.6
1984	Pit-N	100	304	38	87	14	2	11	45	20	52	.286	.332	.454	119	7	7	43	0	1	-1	0	32/S1	0.7
1985	Pit-N	92	244	17	62	10	0	4	22	8	44	.254	.281	.344	75	-9	-9	23	3	0	1	1	32/O	-0.6
1986	Pit-N	154	537	58	147	35	4	23	88	47	88	.274	.337	.482	120	15	14	86	9	8	-2	-13	*3/2S	-0.4
1987	Pit-N	96	348	41	92	22	1	9	46	27	57	.264	.319	.411	91	-5	-5	44	8	5	-1	1	3S/2	-0.2
	*Det-A	34	117	15	24	1	1	4	19	2	26	.205	.225	.333	47	-9	-9	9	2	1	0	0	3/2SO1D	-0.5
1988	Det-A	24	74	7	16	5	0	0	6	0	14	.216	.216	.284	40	-6	-6	3	0	2	-1	-1	D/13OS	-0.7
	Atl-N	51	92	6	14	2	0	2	13	10	13	.152	.235	.239	35	-8	-8	5	0	1	-1	-0	3/OP	-0.9
Total	12	1089	3375	371	876	170	16	112	435	213	521	.260	.308	.419	98	-16	-17	424	50	37	-7	9	32/SDO1P	0.1

■ **JON MORRISON** Morrison, Jonathan W. b: 1859, Port Huron, Mich. Deb: 8/01/1884

YEAR	TM/L	G	AB	R	H	2B	3B	HR	RBI	BB	SO	AVG	OBP	SLG	PRO+	BR	/A	RC	SB	CS	SBR	FR	POS	TPR
1884	Ind-a	44	182	26	48	6	8	1		7		.264	.306	.401	136	6	7	23				3	O	0.8

YEAR	TM/L	G	AB	R	H	2B	3B	HR	RBI	BB	SO	AVG	OBP	SLG	PRO+	BR	/A	RC	SB	CS	SBR	FR	POS	TPR
1887	NY-a	9	34	7	4	0	0	0			6	.118	.268	.118	12	-4	-3	1	0			-4	/O	-0.5
Total	2	53	216	33	52	6	8	1			13	.241	.299	.356	114	2	4	24	0			-1	/O	0.3

■ TOM MORRISON
Morrison, Thomas J. b: 1875, St.Louis, Mo. 5'3", 145 lbs. Deb: 9/18/1895

YEAR	TM/L	G	AB	R	H	2B	3B	HR	RBI	BB	SO	AVG	OBP	SLG	PRO+	BR	/A	RC	SB	CS	SBR	FR	POS	TPR
1895	Lou-N	6	22	3	6	0	2	0	4	1	1	.273	.304	.455	102	-0	-0	3	0			-2	/S3	-0.1
1896	Lou-N	8	27	3	4	1	0	0	0	4	4	.148	.258	.185	20	-3	-3	1	0			-0	/3OS	-0.2
Total	2	14	49	6	10	1	2	0	4	5	5	.204	.278	.306	57	-3	-3	4	0			-3	/3SO	-0.3

■ JACK MORRISSEY
Morrissey, John Albert "King" b: 5/2/1876, Lansing, Mich. d: 10/30/36, Lansing, Mich. BB/TR, 5'10", 160 lbs. Deb: 9/18/02

YEAR	TM/L	G	AB	R	H	2B	3B	HR	RBI	BB	SO	AVG	OBP	SLG	PRO+	BR	/A	RC	SB	CS	SBR	FR	POS	TPR
1902	Cin-N	12	39	5	11	1	1	0	3	4		.282	.349	.359	110	1	1	5	0			-2	2/O	0.0
1903	Cin-N	29	89	14	22	1	0	0	9	14		.247	.350	.258	69	-2	-3	10	3			-10	2/OS	-1.2
Total	2	41	128	19	33	2	1	0	12	18		.258	.349	.289	80	-1	-3	15	3			-12	/2OS	-1.2

■ JOHN MORRISSEY
Morrissey, John J. b: 1856, Janesville, Wis. d: 4/29/1884, Janesville, Wis. Deb: 5/02/1881

YEAR	TM/L	G	AB	R	H	2B	3B	HR	RBI	BB	SO	AVG	OBP	SLG	PRO+	BR	/A	RC	SB	CS	SBR	FR	POS	TPR
1881	Buf-N	12	47	3	10	2	0	0	3	0	3	.213	.213	.255	47	-3	-3	3				-2	3	-0.2
1882	Det-N	2	7	1	2	0	0	0	0	0	2	.286	.286	.286	84	-0	-0	1				-1	/3	0.0
Total	2	14	54	4	12	2	0	0	3	0	5	.222	.222	.259	52	-3	-3	3				-3	/3	-0.2

■ JO-JO MORRISSEY
Morrissey, Joseph Anselm b: 1/16/04, Warren, R.I. d: 5/2/50, Worcester, Mass. BR/TR, 6'1.5", 178 lbs. Deb: 4/12/32

YEAR	TM/L	G	AB	R	H	2B	3B	HR	RBI	BB	SO	AVG	OBP	SLG	PRO+	BR	/A	RC	SB	CS	SBR	FR	POS	TPR
1932	Cin-N	89	269	15	65	10	1	3		14	15	.242	.282	.286	55	-17	-16	22	2			9	S23/O	0.0
1933	Cin-N	148	534	43	123	20	0	0	26	20	22	.230	.261	.268	52	-34	-33	35	5			-9	2S3	-3.2
1936	Chi-A	17	38	3	7	1	0	0	6	2	3	.184	.225	.211	8	-6	-6	2	0	0	0	0	/3S2	-0.4
Total	3	254	841	61	195	31	1	0	45	36	40	.232	.266	.271	51	-57	-55	59	7	0		0	2S/3O	-3.6

■ TOM MORRISSEY
Morrissey, Thomas J. b: 1861, Janesville, Wis. d: 9/23/41, Janesville, Wis. Deb: 9/27/1884

YEAR	TM/L	G	AB	R	H	2B	3B	HR	RBI	BB	SO	AVG	OBP	SLG	PRO+	BR	/A	RC	SB	CS	SBR	FR	POS	TPR
1884	Mil-U	12	47	3	8	2	0	0			0	.170	.170	.213	53	-3	-0	2	0			-1	3	0.0

■ BUD MORSE
Morse, Newell Obediah b: 9/4/04, Berkeley, Cal. d: 4/6/87, Sparks, Nev. BL/TR, 5'9", 150 lbs. Deb: 9/14/29

YEAR	TM/L	G	AB	R	H	2B	3B	HR	RBI	BB	SO	AVG	OBP	SLG	PRO+	BR	/A	RC	SB	CS	SBR	FR	POS	TPR
1929	Phi-A	8	27	1	2	0	0	0	0	0	0	.074	.074	.074	-60	-6	-7	0	0	0	0	2	/2	-0.3

■ HAP MORSE
Morse, Peter Raymond "Pete" b: 12/6/1886, St.Paul, Minn. d: 6/19/74, St.Paul, Minn. BR/TR, 5'8", 160 lbs. Deb: 4/18/11

YEAR	TM/L	G	AB	R	H	2B	3B	HR	RBI	BB	SO	AVG	OBP	SLG	PRO+	BR	/A	RC	SB	CS	SBR	FR	POS	TPR
1911	StL-N	4	8	0	0	0	0	0	0	1	2	.000	.111	.000	-70	-2	-2	0				0	/SO	-0.1

■ CHARLIE MORTON
Morton, Charles Hazen b: 10/12/1854, Kingsville, Ohio d: 12/9/21, Massillon, Ohio TR, Deb: 5/02/1882 MU

YEAR	TM/L	G	AB	R	H	2B	3B	HR	RBI	BB	SO	AVG	OBP	SLG	PRO+	BR	/A	RC	SB	CS	SBR	FR	POS	TPR
1882	Pit-a	25	103	12	29	0	3	0			5	.282	.315	.340	127	2	3	11				1	O/3S	0.3
	StL-a	9	32	2	2	0	1	0			2	.063	.118	.125	-17	-4	-4	0				-4	/2O	-0.7
	Yr	34	135	14	31	0	4	0			7	.230	.268	.289	90	-2	-1	11				-3		-0.4
1884	Tol-a	32	111	11	18	6	2	0			7	.162	.212	.252	51	-5	-6	6				-1	3O/P2M	-0.5
1885	Det-N	22	79	9	14	1	2	0	3	5	10	.177	.226	.241	51	-4	-4	4				2	3/SM	-0.1
Total	3	88	325	34	63	7	8	0	3	19	10	.194	.238	.265	66	-11	-11	22				-2	/O32SP	-1.0

■ MOOSE MORTON
Morton, Guy Jr. b: 11/4/30, Tuscaloosa, Ala. BR/TR, 6'2", 200 lbs. Deb: 9/17/54

YEAR	TM/L	G	AB	R	H	2B	3B	HR	RBI	BB	SO	AVG	OBP	SLG	PRO+	BR	/A	RC	SB	CS	SBR	FR	POS	TPR
1954	Bos-A	1	1	0	0	0	0	0	0	0	1	.000	.000	.000	-90	-0	-0	0	0	0	0	0	H	0.0

■ BUBBA MORTON
Morton, Wycliffe Nathaniel b: 12/13/31, Washington, D.C. BR/TR, 5'10", 175 lbs. Deb: 4/19/61

YEAR	TM/L	G	AB	R	H	2B	3B	HR	RBI	BB	SO	AVG	OBP	SLG	PRO+	BR	/A	RC	SB	CS	SBR	FR	POS	TPR
1961	Det-A	77	108	26	31	5	1	2	19	9	25	.287	.347	.407	98	0	-0	16	3	1	0	1	O	0.0
1962	Det-A	90	195	30	51	6	3	4	17	32	32	.262	.366	.385	99	1	1	28	1	1	-0	5	O/1	0.2
1963	Det-A	6	11	2	1	0	0	0	2	2	1	.091	.231	.091	-5	-2	-2	0	0	0	0	0	/O	-0.1
	Mil-N	15	28	1	5	0	0	0	4	2	3	.179	.258	.179	28	-2	-2	1	0	0	0	0	/O	-0.2
1966	Cal-A	15	50	4	11	1	0	0	4	2	6	.220	.250	.240	43	-4	-4	3	1	1	-0	0	/O	-0.4
1967	Cal-A	80	201	23	63	9	3	0	32	22	29	.313	.387	.388	135	8	9	29	0	3	-2	-5	O	0.1
1968	Cal-A	81	163	13	44	6	0	1	18	14	18	.270	.343	.325	107	1	2	18	2	1	0	-3	O/3	-0.3
1969	Cal-A	87	172	18	42	10	1	7	32	28	29	.244	.360	.436	128	5	6	28	0	0	0	0	O/1	0.5
Total	7	451	928	117	248	37	8	14	128	111	143	.267	.352	.370	106	8	10	124	7	7	-2	-2	O/13	-0.2

■ WALT MORYN
Moryn, Walter Joseph "Moose" b: 4/12/26, St.Paul, Minn. BL/TR, 6'2", 205 lbs. Deb: 6/29/54

YEAR	TM/L	G	AB	R	H	2B	3B	HR	RBI	BB	SO	AVG	OBP	SLG	PRO+	BR	/A	RC	SB	CS	SBR	FR	POS	TPR
1954	Bro-N	48	91	16	25	4	2	2	14	7	11	.275	.333	.429	94	-1	-1	13	0	0	0	-0	O	-0.1
1955	Bro-N	11	19	3	5	1	0	1	3	5	4	.263	.417	.474	132	1	1	4	0	0	0	-1	/O	0.0
1956	Chi-N	147	529	69	151	27	3	23	67	50	67	.285	.351	.478	122	14	16	89	4	2	0	8	*O	1.9
1957	Chi-N	149	568	76	164	33	0	19	88	50	90	.289	.349	.447	114	10	11	88	0	2	-1	3	*O	0.8
1958	Chi-N	143	512	77	135	26	7	26	77	62	83	.264	.352	.494	123	15	16	91	1	2	-1	-4	*O	0.7
1959	Chi-N	117	381	41	89	14	1	14	48	44	66	.234	.318	.386	87	-8	-7	46	0	0	0	-7	*O	-1.4
1960	Chi-N	38	109	12	32	4	0	2	11	13	19	.294	.369	.385	108	1	2	16	2	1	0	-1	O	0.0
	StL-N	75	200	24	49	4	3	11	35	17	38	.245	.304	.460	97	1	-1	26	0	0	0	-2	O	-0.5
	Yr	113	309	36	81	8	3	13	46	30	57	.262	.327	.434	101	2	0	43	2	1	0	-3		-0.5
1961	StL-N	17	32	0	4	2	0	0	2	1	5	.125	.152	.188	-10	-5	-5	1	0	0	0	-1	/O	-0.6
	Pit-N	40	65	6	13	1	0	3	9	2	10	.200	.235	.354	53	-5	-5	4	0	0	0	1	O	-0.3
	Yr	57	97	6	17	3	0	3	11	3	15	.175	.208	.299	31	-10	-10	4	0	0	0	-0		-0.9
Total	8	785	2506	324	667	116	16	101	354	251	393	.266	.338	.446	108	25	26	377	7	7	-2	-5	O	0.5

■ ROSS MOSCHITTO
Moschitto, Rosaire Allen b: 2/15/45, Fresno, Cal. BR/TR, 6'2", 175 lbs. Deb: 4/15/65

YEAR	TM/L	G	AB	R	H	2B	3B	HR	RBI	BB	SO	AVG	OBP	SLG	PRO+	BR	/A	RC	SB	CS	SBR	FR	POS	TPR
1965	NY-A	96	27	12	5	0	0	1	3	0	12	.185	.185	.296	35	-2	-2	2	0	0	0	7	O	0.1
1967	NY-A	14	9	1	1	0	0	0	0	1	2	.111	.200	.111	-6	-1	-1	0	0	0	0	1	/O	0.0
Total	2	110	36	13	6	0	0	1	3	1	14	.167	.189	.250	25	-4	-3	2	0	0	0	8	/O	0.1

■ LLOYD MOSEBY
Moseby, Lloyd Anthony b: 11/5/59, Portland, Ark. BL/TR, 6'3", 200 lbs. Deb: 5/24/80

YEAR	TM/L	G	AB	R	H	2B	3B	HR	RBI	BB	SO	AVG	OBP	SLG	PRO+	BR	/A	RC	SB	CS	SBR	FR	POS	TPR
1980	Tor-A	114	389	44	89	24	1	9	46	25	85	.229	.282	.365	73	-14	-16	37	4	6	-2	0	*O/D	-1.9
1981	Tor-A	100	378	36	88	16	2	9	43	24	86	.233	.280	.357	78	-9	-12	37	11	8	-2	-2	*O	-1.9
1982	Tor-A	147	487	51	115	20	9	9	52	33	106	.236	.288	.370	74	-13	-19	52	11	7	-1	-7	*O	-3.1
1983	Tor-A	151	539	104	170	31	7	18	81	51	85	.315	.380	.499	132	29	25	104	27	8	3	5	*O	3.1
1984	Tor-A	158	592	97	166	28	**15**	18	92	78	122	.280	.372	.470	126	26	23	110	39	9	6	8	*O	3.2
1985	*Tor-A	152	584	92	151	30	7	18	70	76	91	.259	.348	.426	108	9	7	89	37	15	2	-7	*O	0.0
1986	Tor-A	152	589	89	149	24	5	21	86	64	122	.253	.332	.418	100	2	0	86	32	11	3	-4	*O/D	-0.3
1987	Tor-A	155	592	106	167	27	4	26	96	70	124	.282	.360	.473	116	16	14	106	39	7	8	-13	*O/D	0.5
1988	Tor-A	128	472	77	113	17	7	10	42	70	93	.239	.345	.369	99	2	1	66	31	8	5	-8	*O/D	-0.4
1989	*Tor-A	135	502	72	111	25	3	11	43	56	101	.221	.299	.349	86	-10	-9	58	24	7	3	-7	*OD	-1.4
1990	Det-A	122	431	64	107	16	5	14	51	48	77	.248	.331	.406	105	3	3	57	17	5	2	3	*O/D	0.7
Total	11	1514	5555	832	1426	258	65	163	702	595	1092	.257	.335	.415	102	41	18	801	272	91	27	-33	*O/D	-1.5

■ ARNIE MOSER
Moser, Arnold Robert b: 8/9/15, Houston, Tex. BR/TR, 5'11", 165 lbs. Deb: 6/20/37

YEAR	TM/L	G	AB	R	H	2B	3B	HR	RBI	BB	SO	AVG	OBP	SLG	PRO+	BR	/A	RC	SB	CS	SBR	FR	POS	TPR
1937	Cin-N	5	5	0	0	0	0	0	0	0	2	.000	.000	.000	-99	-1	-1	0	0			0	H	0.0

■ JERRY MOSES
Moses, Gerald Braheen b: 8/9/46, Yazoo City, Miss. BR/TR, 6'3", 210 lbs. Deb: 5/09/65

YEAR	TM/L	G	AB	R	H	2B	3B	HR	RBI	BB	SO	AVG	OBP	SLG	PRO+	BR	/A	RC	SB	CS	SBR	FR	POS	TPR
1965	Bos-A	4	4	1	1	0	0	1	0	0	2	.250	.250	1.000	224	1	1	1	0	0	0	0	H	0.1
1968	Bos-A	6	18	2	6	0	0	2	4	1	4	.333	.368	.667	196	2	2	3	0	1	-1	-3	/C	0.0
1969	Bos-A	53	135	13	41	9	1	4	17	5	23	.304	.333	.474	117	4	3	21	0	1	-1	-5	C	0.0

YEAR	TM/L	G	AB	R	H	2B	3B	HR	RBI	BB	SO	AVG	OBP	SLG	PRO+	BR	/A	RC	SB	CS	SBR	FR	POS	TPR
1970	Bos-A	92	315	26	83	18	1	6	35	21	45	.263	.314	.384	85	-4	-7	37	1	1	-0	2	C/O	-0.3
1971	Cal-A	69	181	12	41	8	2	4	15	10	34	.227	.267	.359	82	-6	-5	15	0	0	0	6	C/O	0.4
1972	Cle-A	52	141	9	31	3	0	4	14	11	29	.220	.290	.326	81	-3	-3	14	0	0	0	1	C/1	-0.2
1973	NY-A	21	59	5	15	2	0	0	3	2	6	.254	.279	.288	62	-3	-3	4	0	0	0	4	C/D	0.2
1974	Det-A	74	198	19	47	6	3	4	19	11	38	.237	.284	.359	81	-5	-5	19	0	1	-1	-2	C	-0.5
1975	SD-N	13	19	1	3	2	0	0	1	2	3	.158	.238	.263	42	-2	-1	1	0	0	0	-1	/C	-0.1
	Chi-A	2	2	1	1	0	1	0	0	0	0	.500	.500	1.500	441	1	1	2	0	0	0	0	/1D	0.1
Total	9	386	1072	89	269	48	8	25	109	63	184	.251	.297	.381	89	-16	-19	116	1	4	-2	2	C/1DO	-0.3

■ JOHN MOSES
Moses, John William b: 8/9/57, Los Angeles, Cal. BB/TL, 5'10", 165 lbs. Deb: 8/23/82

YEAR	TM/L	G	AB	R	H	2B	3B	HR	RBI	BB	SO	AVG	OBP	SLG	PRO+	BR	/A	RC	SB	CS	SBR	FR	POS	TPR
1982	Sea-A	22	44	7	14	5	1	1	3	4	5	.318	.375	.545	145	3	3	10	5	1	1	-1	O	0.2
1983	Sea-A	93	130	19	27	4	1	0	6	12	20	.208	.280	.254	46	-9	-10	9	11	5	0	10	OD	0.0
1984	Sea-A	19	35	3	12	1	1	0	2	2	5	.343	.395	.429	129	1	1	6	1	0	0	2	O/D	0.3
1985	Sea-A	33	62	4	12	0	0	0	3	2	8	.194	.219	.194	14	-7	-7	2	5	2	0	-0	O	-0.7
1986	Sea-A	103	399	56	102	16	3	3	34	34	65	.256	.314	.333	76	-13	-13	40	25	18	-3	-3	O/1D	-2.1
1987	Sea-A	116	390	58	96	16	4	3	38	29	49	.246	.303	.331	65	-18	-21	38	23	15	-2	-4	*O/1D	-2.8
1988	Min-A	105	206	33	65	10	3	2	12	15	21	.316	.368	.422	117	6	5	31	11	6	-0	2	O/D	0.0
1989	Min-A	129	242	33	68	12	3	1	31	19	23	.281	.336	.368	92	-1	-3	30	14	7	0	4	*O/1PD	0.0
1990	Min-A	115	172	26	38	3	1	1	14	19	19	.221	.306	.267	58	-8	-10	14	2	3	-1	3	OD/1P	-0.8
Total	9	735	1680	239	434	67	17	11	143	136	215	.258	.318	.338	77	-45	-54	181	97	57	-5	13	O/D1P	-5.3

■ WALLY MOSES
Moses, Wallace b: 10/8/10, Uvalda, Ga. d: 10/10/90, Vidalia, Ga. BL/TL, 5'10", 160 lbs. Deb: 4/17/35 C

YEAR	TM/L	G	AB	R	H	2B	3B	HR	RBI	BB	SO	AVG	OBP	SLG	PRO+	BR	/A	RC	SB	CS	SBR	FR	POS	TPR
1935	Phi-A	85	345	60	112	21	3	5	35	25	18	.325	.375	.446	113	6	6	57	3	4	-2	-2	O	0.1
1936	Phi-A	146	585	98	202	35	11	7	66	62	32	.345	.410	.479	121	18	20	117	12	6	-0	-2	*O	1.2
1937	Phi-A	154	649	113	208	48	13	25	86	54	38	.320	.374	.550	132	27	28	132	9	7	-2	2	*O	2.1
1938	Phi-A	142	589	86	181	29	8	8	49	58	31	.307	.369	.424	101	-2	1	95	15	5	2	4	*O	0.6
1939	Phi-A	115	437	68	134	28	7	3	33	44	23	.307	.370	.423	105	2	3	71	7	4	-0	-2	*O	-0.2
1940	Phi-A	142	537	91	166	41	9	9	50	75	44	.309	.396	.469	126	20	22	108	6	4	-1	1	*O	1.2
1941	Phi-A	116	438	78	132	31	4	4	35	62	27	.301	.388	.418	116	10	11	76	3	3	-1	6	*O	0.9
1942	Chi-A	146	577	73	156	28	4	7	49	74	27	.270	.353	.369	106	4	5	81	16	10	-1	7	*O	0.0
1943	Chi-A	150	599	82	147	22	12	3	48	55	47	.245	.310	.337	89	-9	-9	69	56	14	8	6	*O	0.2
1944	Chi-A	136	535	82	150	26	9	3	34	52	22	.280	.345	.379	108	5	6	77	21	7	2	-6	*O	-0.2
1945	Chi-A	140	569	79	168	35	15	2	50	69	33	.295	.373	.420	134	22	24	97	11	5	0	5	*O	2.5
1946	Chi-A	56	168	20	46	9	1	4	16	17	20	.274	.344	.411	115	2	3	24	2	2	-1	-1	O	0.0
	*Bos-A	48	175	23	36	11	3	2	17	14	15	.206	.268	.337	65	-8	-9	16	2	4	-2	-0	O	-1.4
	Yr	104	343	43	82	20	4	6	33	31	35	.239	.306	.373	88	-6	-6	40	4	6	-2	-1		-1.4
1947	Bos-A	90	255	32	70	18	2	2	27	27	16	.275	.344	.384	95	1	-2	35	3	0	1	-7	O	-1.0
1948	Bos-A	78	189	26	49	12	1	2	29	21	19	.259	.340	.365	83	-4	-5	27	5	0	2	0	O	-0.4
1949	Phi-A	110	308	49	85	19	3	1	25	51	19	.276	.381	.367	102	1	2	48	1	3	-2	-7	O	-0.8
1950	Phi-A	88	265	47	70	16	5	2	21	40	17	.264	.365	.385	94	-3	-2	40	0	1	-1	1	O	-0.2
1951	Phi-A	70	136	17	26	6	0	0	9	21	9	.191	.304	.235	46	-10	-10	10	2	2	-1	-1	O	-1.1
Total	17	2012	7356	1124	2138	435	110	89	679	821	457	.291	.364	.416	109	81	94	1179	174	81	4	5	*O	3.5

■ DOC MOSKIMAN
Moskiman, William Bankhead b: 12/20/1879, Oakland, Cal. d: 1/11/53, San Leandro, Cal. BR/TR, 6', 170 lbs. Deb: 8/23/10

YEAR	TM/L	G	AB	R	H	2B	3B	HR	RBI	BB	SO	AVG	OBP	SLG	PRO+	BR	/A	RC	SB	CS	SBR	FR	POS	TPR
1910	Bos-A	5	9	1	1	0	0	0	1	2	.	.111	.273	.111	20	-1	-1	0	0			0	/1O	0.0

■ JIM MOSOLF
Mosolf, James Frederick b: 8/21/05, Puyallup, Wash. d: 12/28/79, Dallasyore. BL/TR, 5'10", 186 lbs. Deb: 9/09/29

YEAR	TM/L	G	AB	R	H	2B	3B	HR	RBI	BB	SO	AVG	OBP	SLG	PRO+	BR	/A	RC	SB	CS	SBR	FR	POS	TPR
1929	Pit-N	8	13	3	6	1	1	0	2	1	1	.462	.500	.692	188	2	2	4	0			0	/O	0.2
1930	Pit-N	40	51	16	17	2	1	0	9	8	7	.333	.424	.412	103	1	1	9	0			-1	O/P	0.0
1931	Pit-N	39	44	7	11	1	0	1	8	8	5	.250	.365	.341	92	-0	-0	6	0			-1	O	-0.1
1933	Chi-N	31	82	13	22	5	1	1	9	5	8	.268	.326	.390	104	0	0	11	0			1	O	0.0
Total	4	118	190	39	56	9	3	2	28	22	21	.295	.374	.405	107	3	3	31	0			-1	/OP	0.1

■ CHARLIE MOSS
Moss, Charles Crosby b: 3/20/11, Meridian, Miss. BR/TR, 5'10", 160 lbs. Deb: 5/19/34

YEAR	TM/L	G	AB	R	H	2B	3B	HR	RBI	BB	SO	AVG	OBP	SLG	PRO+	BR	/A	RC	SB	CS	SBR	FR	POS	TPR
1934	Phi-A	10	10	3	2	0	0	0	1	0	0	.200	.200	.200	4	-1	-1	0	0	0	0	-1	/C	0.0
1935	Phi-A	4	3	1	1	0	0	0	1	1	0	.333	.500	.333	120	0	0	1	0	0	0	0	/C	0.0
1936	Phi-A	33	44	2	11	1	1	0	10	6	5	.250	.340	.318	65	-2	-2	5	1	0	0	-1	C	-0.1
Total	3	47	57	6	14	1	1	0	12	7	5	.246	.328	.298	58	-4	-3	6	1	0	0	-2	/C	-0.1

■ HOWIE MOSS
Moss, Howard Glenn b: 10/17/19, Gastonia, N.C. d: 5/7/89, Baltimore, Md. BR/TR, 5'11.5", 185 lbs. Deb: 4/14/42

YEAR	TM/L	G	AB	R	H	2B	3B	HR	RBI	BB	SO	AVG	OBP	SLG	PRO+	BR	/A	RC	SB	CS	SBR	FR	POS	TPR
1942	NY-N	7	14	0	0	0	0	0	0	0	4	.000	.000	.000	-99	-3	-3	0	0			0	/O	-0.3
1946	Cin-N	7	26	1	5	0	0	0	1	0	4	.192	.222	.192	19	-3	-3	1	0			-0	/O	-0.3
	Cle-A	8	32	2	2	0	0	0	0	3	9	.063	.143	.063	-44	-6	-6	0	0	1	-1	0	/3	-0.5
Total	2	22	72	3	7	0	0	0	1	3	17	.097	.145	.097	-32	-12	-12	1	0	1		0	/O3	-1.1

■ LES MOSS
Moss, John Lester b: 5/14/25, Tulsa, Okla. BR/TR, 5'11", 205 lbs. Deb: 9/10/46 MC

YEAR	TM/L	G	AB	R	H	2B	3B	HR	RBI	BB	SO	AVG	OBP	SLG	PRO+	BR	/A	RC	SB	CS	SBR	FR	POS	TPR
1946	StL-A	12	35	4	13	3	0	0	5	3	5	.371	.436	.457	142	2	2	8	1	0	0	1	C	0.4
1947	StL-A	96	274	17	43	5	2	6	27	35	48	.157	.255	.255	41	-22	-23	20	0	0	0	-5	C	-2.0
1948	StL-A	107	335	35	86	12	1	14	46	39	50	.257	.334	.424	98	-1	-2	46	0	0	0	-9	*C	-0.3
1949	StL-A	97	278	28	81	11	0	10	39	49	32	.291	.399	.439	117	10	8	51	0	1	-1	-4	C	0.7
1950	StL-A	84	222	24	59	6	0	8	34	26	32	.266	.343	.401	87	-4	-5	30	0	1	-1	-0	C	-0.3
1951	StL-A	16	47	5	8	2	0	1	7	6	8	.170	.264	.277	45	-4	-4	3	0	0	0	-0	C	-0.2
	Bos-A	71	202	18	40	6	0	3	26	25	34	.198	.289	.272	48	-13	-16	16	0	0	0	-0	C	-1.0
	Yr	87	249	23	48	8	0	4	33	31	42	.193	.285	.273	47	-17	-20	19	0	0	0	-1		-1.2
1952	StL-A	52	118	11	29	3	0	3	12	15	13	.246	.331	.347	86	-2	-2	13	0	1	-1	-3	C	-0.3
1953	StL-A	78	239	21	66	14	1	2	28	18	31	.276	.329	.368	86	-4	-5	27	0	1	-1	-6	C	-0.8
1954	Bal-A	50	126	7	31	3	0	0	5	14	16	.246	.321	.270	68	-6	-5	11	0	0	0	-2	C	-0.4
1955	Bal-A	29	56	5	19	1	0	2	6	7	4	.339	.413	.464	146	3	3	10	0	1	-1	2	C	0.6
	Chi-A	32	59	5	15	2	0	2	7	6	10	.254	.333	.390	91	-1	-1	8	0	0	0	0	C	0.0
	Yr	61	115	10	34	3	0	4	13	13	14	.296	.372	.426	116	2	3	19	0	1	-1	2		0.6
1956	Chi-A	56	127	20	31	4	0	10	22	18	15	.244	.338	.512	120	3	3	20	0	0	0	-6	C	-0.1
1957	Chi-A	42	115	10	31	3	0	2	12	20	18	.270	.378	.348	99	1	1	16	0	0	0	-7	C	-0.4
1958	Chi-A	2	1	0	0	0	0	0	0	1	0	.000	.500	.000	51	0	0	0	0	0	0	0	H	0.0
Total	13	824	2234	210	552	75	4	63	276	282	316	.247	.333	.369	86	-37	-45	280	1	5	-3	-40	C	-4.1

■ JOHNNY MOSTIL
Mostil, John Anthony "Bananas" b: 6/1/1896, Chicago, Ill. d: 12/10/70, Midlothian, Ill. BR/TR, 5'8.5", 168 lbs. Deb: 6/20/18

YEAR	TM/L	G	AB	R	H	2B	3B	HR	RBI	BB	SO	AVG	OBP	SLG	PRO+	BR	/A	RC	SB	CS	SBR	FR	POS	TPR
1918	Chi-A	10	33	4	9	2	2	0	6	1	6	.273	.294	.455	125	1	1	4	1			-2	/2	0.0
1921	Chi-A	100	326	43	98	21	7	3	42	28	35	.301	.379	.436	109	4	5	53	10	12	-4	0	O/2	-0.5
1922	Chi-A	132	458	74	139	28	14	7	70	38	39	.303	.375	.472	108	12	13	81	14	10	-2	5	*O	0.7
1923	Chi-A	153	546	91	159	37	15	3	64	62	51	.291	.376	.430	113	10	11	92	41	17	2	22	*O/3S	2.2
1924	Chi-A	118	385	75	125	22	5	4	49	45	41	.325	.401	.439	120	10	12	67	7	11	-5	7	*O	0.7
1925	Chi-A	153	605	135	181	36	16	2	50	90	52	.299	.400	.421	120	11	11	108	43	21	0	7	*O	0.9
1926	Chi-A	148	600	120	197	41	15	4	42	79	55	.328	.415	.467	134	28	31	122	35	14	2	17	*O	3.8
1927	Chi-A	13	16	3	2	0	0	0	1	0	1	.125	.176	.125	-21	-3	-3	0	0	0	0	-2	/O	-0.3
1928	Chi-A	133	503	69	136	19	8	0	51	66	54	.270	.360	.340	86	-9	-8	63	23	21	-6	18	*O	-0.2

YEAR	TM/L	G	AB	R	H	2B	3B	HR	RBI	BB	SO	AVG	OBP	SLG	PRO+	BR	/A	RC	SB	CS	SBR	FR	POS	TPR
1929	Chi-A	12	35	4	8	3	0	0	3	6	2	.229	.341	.314	71	-1	-1	4	1	0	0	-1	O	-0.1
Total	10	972	3507	618	1054	209	82	23	376	415	336	.301	.386	.427	113	63	76	596	176	106		73	O/23S	7.2

■ MANNY MOTA
Mota, Manuel Rafael (Geronimo)   b: 2/18/38, Santo Domingo, D.R.   BR/TR, 5'10", 160 lbs.   Deb: 4/16/62   C

YEAR	TM/L	G	AB	R	H	2B	3B	HR	RBI	BB	SO	AVG	OBP	SLG	PRO+	BR	/A	RC	SB	CS	SBR	FR	POS	TPR
1962	SF-N	47	74	9	13	1	0	0	9	7	8	.176	.256	.189	22	-8	-8	4	3	2	-0	4	O/32	-0.5
1963	Pit-N	59	126	20	34	2	3	0	7	7	18	.270	.313	.333	86	-2	-2	12	0	2	-1	-4	O/2	-0.9
1964	Pit-N	115	271	43	75	8	3	5	32	10	31	.277	.310	.384	94	-2	-2	32	4	1	1	-8	O/C2	-1.3
1965	Pit-N	121	294	47	82	7	6	4	29	22	32	.279	.333	.384	101	1	0	37	2	2	-1	-1	O	-0.3
1966	Pit-N	116	322	54	107	16	7	5	46	25	28	.332	.387	.472	137	17	17	57	7	7	-2	-2	O/3	1.0
1967	Pit-N	120	349	53	112	14	8	4	56	14	46	.321	.351	.441	125	11	10	52	3	2	-0	-2	O/3	0.4
1968	Pit-N	111	331	35	93	10	2	1	33	20	19	.281	.324	.332	99	-1	-1	36	4	2	0	-5	O/23	-1.1
1969	Mon-N	31	89	6	28	1	1	0	0	6	11	.315	.358	.348	98	-0	-0	10	1	3	-2	-2	O	-0.4
	LA-N	85	294	35	95	6	4	3	30	26	25	.323	.380	.401	128	8	11	45	5	4	-1	-3	O	0.2
	Yr	116	383	41	123	7	5	3	30	32	36	.321	.375	.389	120	8	10	55	6	7	-2	-5		-0.2
1970	LA-N	124	417	63	127	12	6	3	37	47	37	.305	.379	.384	110	4	7	61	11	6	-0	-6	*O/3	-0.4
1971	LA-N	91	269	24	84	13	5	0	34	20	20	.312	.362	.398	122	5	7	37	4	3	-1	-9	O	-0.4
1972	LA-N	118	371	57	120	16	5	5	48	27	15	.323	.370	.434	133	15	16	58	4	4	-1	-10	O	0.0
1973	LA-N	89	293	33	92	11	2	0	23	25	12	.314	.370	.365	109	2	4	37	1	3	-2	-9	O	-1.0
1974	*LA-N	66	57	5	16	2	0	0	16	5	4	.281	.349	.316	91	-1	-0	7	0	0	0	-1	/O	0.0
1975	LA-N	52	49	3	13	1	0	0	10	5	1	.265	.357	.286	84	-1	-1	5	0	0	0	1	/O	0.0
1976	LA-N	50	52	1	15	3	0	0	13	7	5	.288	.373	.346	107	1	1	7	0	0	0	1	/O	0.2
1977	*LA-N	49	38	5	15	1	0	1	4	10	0	.395	.521	.500	176	5	5	10	1	1	-0	0	/O	0.5
1978	*LA-N	37	33	2	10	1	0	0	6	3	4	.303	.361	.333	95	-0	-0	4	0	0	0	0	H	0.0
1979	LA-N	47	42	1	15	0	0	0	3	3	4	.357	.400	.357	110	1	1	6	0	0	0	0	/O	0.1
1980	LA-N	7	7	0	3	0	0	0	2	0	0	.429	.429	.429	143	0	0	1	0	0	0	0	/H	0.0
1982	LA-N	1	1	0	0	0	0	0	0	0	0	.000	.000	.000	-99	-0	-0	0	0	0	0	0	/H	0.0
Total	20	1536	3779	496	1149	125	52	31	438	289	320	.304	.358	.389	112	53	64	517	50	42	-10	-56	*O/32C	-3.9

■ DARRYL MOTLEY
Motley, Darryl De Wayne   b: 1/21/60, Muskogee, Okla.   BR/TR, 5'9", 196 lbs.   Deb: 8/10/81

YEAR	TM/L	G	AB	R	H	2B	3B	HR	RBI	BB	SO	AVG	OBP	SLG	PRO+	BR	/A	RC	SB	CS	SBR	FR	POS	TPR
1981	KC-A	42	125	15	29	4	0	2	8	7	15	.232	.278	.312	70	-5	-5	10	1	3	-2	1	O	-0.6
1983	KC-A	19	68	9	16	1	2	3	11	2	8	.235	.268	.441	91	-1	-1	7	2	1	0	3	O/D	0.0
1984	*KC-A	146	522	64	148	25	6	15	70	28	73	.284	.321	.441	108	5	4	63	10	12	-4	0	*O	-0.3
1985	*KC-A	123	383	45	85	20	1	17	49	18	57	.222	.261	.413	81	-12	-12	35	6	4	-1	-11	*O/D	-2.4
1986	KC-A	72	217	22	44	9	1	7	20	11	31	.203	.241	.350	57	-13	-14	16	0	2	-1	-6	O/D	-2.1
	Atl-N	5	10	1	2	1	0	0	0	1	1	.200	.273	.300	55	-1	-1	1	0	0	0	0	/O	0.0
1987	Atl-N	6	8	0	0	0	0	0	1	0	1	.000	.000	.000	-95	-2	-2	0	0	0	0	0	/O	-0.1
Total	6	413	1333	156	324	60	10	44	159	67	186	.243	.282	.402	86	-29	-30	130	19	22	-8	-11	O/D	-5.3

■ BITSY MOTT
Mott, Elisha Matthew   b: 6/12/18, Arcadia, Fla.   BR/TR, 5'8", 155 lbs.   Deb: 4/17/45

YEAR	TM/L	G	AB	R	H	2B	3B	HR	RBI	BB	SO	AVG	OBP	SLG	PRO+	BR	/A	RC	SB	CS	SBR	FR	POS	TPR
1945	Phi-N	90	289	21	64	8	0	0	22	27	25	.221	.290	.249	52	-19	-18	22	2			13	S2/3	0.4

■ CURT MOTTON
Motton, Curtell Howard   b: 9/24/40, Darnell, La.   BR/TR, 5'8", 164 lbs.   Deb: 7/05/67

YEAR	TM/L	G	AB	R	H	2B	3B	HR	RBI	BB	SO	AVG	OBP	SLG	PRO+	BR	/A	RC	SB	CS	SBR	FR	POS	TPR
1967	Bal-A	27	65	5	13	2	0	2	9	5	14	.200	.278	.323	78	-2	-2	6	0	1	-1	0	O	-0.2
1968	Bal-A	83	217	27	43	7	0	8	25	31	43	.198	.301	.341	94	-1	-1	22	1	3	-2	-3	O	-0.8
1969	*Bal-A	56	89	15	27	6	0	6	21	13	10	.303	.398	.573	167	8	8	22	3	1	0	-2	O	0.6
1970	Bal-A	52	84	16	19	3	1	3	19	18	20	.226	.369	.393	109	2	2	14	1	2	-1	-0	O	0.0
1971	*Bal-A	38	53	13	10	1	0	4	8	10	12	.189	.317	.434	112	1	1	8	0	0	0	0	O	0.0
1972	Mil-A	6	6	1	1	0	0	1	2	1	2	.167	.286	.667	181	1	1	1	0	0	0	0	/O	0.0
	Cal-A	42	39	6	6	1	0	0	1	5	12	.154	.250	.179	31	-3	-3	2	0	0	0	2	/O	-0.1
	Yr	48	45	7	7	1	0	1	3	6	14	.156	.255	.244	52	-3	-3	3	0	0	0	2		-0.1
1973	Bal-A	5	6	2	2	0	0	1	4	1	1	.333	.429	.833	250	1	1	2	0	0	0	0	/OD	0.1
1974	*Bal-A	7	8	0	0	0	0	0	0	2	2	.000	.200	.000	-40	-1	-1	0	0	0	0	1	/OD	0.0
Total	8	316	567	85	121	20	1	25	89	86	116	.213	.322	.384	105	4	5	76	5	7	-3	-2	O/D	-0.4

■ FRANK MOTZ
Motz, Frank H.   b: 10/1/1868, Freeburg, Pa.   d: 3/18/44, Akron, Ohio   6', 160 lbs.   Deb: 8/27/1890

YEAR	TM/L	G	AB	R	H	2B	3B	HR	RBI	BB	SO	AVG	OBP	SLG	PRO+	BR	/A	RC	SB	CS	SBR	FR	POS	TPR
1890	Phi-N	1	2	1	0	0	0	0	3	1	1	.000	.333	.000	1	-0	-0	0	1			0	/1	0.0
1893	Cin-N	43	156	16	40	7	1	2	25	19	10	.256	.352	.353	87	-2	-3	21	3			6	1	0.2
1894	Cin-N	18	69	8	14	4	0	0	12	9	1	.203	.304	.261	37	-7	-7	6	2			4	1	-0.2
Total	3	62	227	25	54	11	1	2	40	29	12	.238	.337	.322	70	-9	-10	27	6			10	/1	0.0

■ ALLIE MOULTON
Moulton, Albert Theodore   b: 1/16/1886, Medway, Mass.   d: 7/10/68, Peabody, Mass.   BR/TR, 5'6", 155 lbs.   Deb: 9/25/11

YEAR	TM/L	G	AB	R	H	2B	3B	HR	RBI	BB	SO	AVG	OBP	SLG	PRO+	BR	/A	RC	SB	CS	SBR	FR	POS	TPR
1911	StL-A	4	15	4	1	0	0	0	1		4	.067	.263	.067	-6	-2	-2	0	0			-1	/2	-0.2

■ FRANK MOUNTAIN
Mountain, Frank Henry   b: 5/17/1860, Ft.Edward, N.Y.   d: 11/19/39, Schenectady, N.Y.   TR, 5'11", 185 lbs.   Deb: 7/19/1880

YEAR	TM/L	G	AB	R	H	2B	3B	HR	RBI	BB	SO	AVG	OBP	SLG	PRO+	BR	/A	RC	SB	CS	SBR	FR	POS	TPR
1880	Tro-N	2	9	1	2	0	0	0	0	0	4	.222	.222	.222	49	-0	-1	0				0	/P	0.0
1881	Det-N	7	25	0	4	1	1	0	4	2	8	.160	.222	.280	55	-1	-1	2				-1	/P	0.0
1882	Wor-N	5	16	1	1	0	0	0	1	0	5	.063	.063	.063	-58	-3	-3	0				-0	/P	0.0
	Phi-a	9	36	5	12	3	0	0			2	.333	.368	.417	147	2	2	6				1	/PO	0.0
	Wor-N	20	70	8	19	2	2	2	5	3	18	.271	.301	.443	132	3	2	10				-1	P/O1S	0.0
1883	Col-a	70	276	36	60	14	5	3			9	.217	.242	.337	92	-5	-1	23				1	PO	0.0
1884	Col-a	58	210	26	50	7	3	4			9	.238	.283	.357	120	2	5	22				3	PO	0.0
1885	Pit-a	5	20	1	2	0	1	0			1	.100	.143	.200	9	-2	-2	1				-0	/P	0.0
1886	Pit-a	18	55	6	8	1	1	0			13	.145	.319	.200	66	-1	-1	5	3			-0	1/P	-0.1
Total	7	194	717	84	158	28	13	9	10	39	35	.220	.265	.333	97	-5	-0	67	3			3	P/O1S	-0.1

■ RAY MOWE
Mowe, Raymond Benjamin   b: 7/12/1889, Rochester, Ind.   d: 8/14/68, Sarasota, Fla.   BL/TR, 5'7.5", 160 lbs.   Deb: 9/25/13

YEAR	TM/L	G	AB	R	H	2B	3B	HR	RBI	BB	SO	AVG	OBP	SLG	PRO+	BR	/A	RC	SB	CS	SBR	FR	POS	TPR
1913	Bro-N	5	9	0	1	0	0	0	0	0	1	.111	.200	.111	-10	-1	-1	0	0			1	/S	0.0

■ MIKE MOWREY
Mowrey, Harry Harlan   b: 4/20/1884, Browns Mill, Pa.   d: 3/20/47, Chambersburg, Pa.   BR/TR, 5'10", 180 lbs.   Deb: 9/24/05

YEAR	TM/L	G	AB	R	H	2B	3B	HR	RBI	BB	SO	AVG	OBP	SLG	PRO+	BR	/A	RC	SB	CS	SBR	FR	POS	TPR
1905	Cin-N	7	30	4	8	1	0	0	6	1		.267	.290	.300	70	-1	-1	3	0			-0	/3	0.0
1906	Cin-N	21	53	3	17	3	0	0	6	5		.321	.379	.377	133	2	2	9	2			4	3/2S	0.6
1907	Cin-N	138	448	43	113	16	6	1	44	35		.252	.306	.321	95	-1	-3	51	10			-19	*3S	-2.4
1908	Cin-N	77	227	17	50	9	1	0	23	12		.220	.259	.269	72	-8	-7	17	5			-7	3/SO2	-1.4
1909	Cin-N	38	115	10	22	5	0	0	5	20		.191	.311	.235	70	-3	-3	9	2			0	3S	-0.2
	StL-N	12	29	3	7	1	0	0	4	4		.241	.333	.276	95	-0	-0	3	1			-1	/23	0.0
	Yr	50	144	13	29	6	0	0	9	24		.201	.315	.243	75	-4	-3	13	3			-1		-0.2
1910	StL-N	143	489	69	138	24	6	2	70	67	38	.282	.375	.368	121	13	15	76	21			12	*3	2.8
1911	StL-N	137	471	59	126	29	7	0	61	59	46	.268	.359	.359	103	1	3	66	15			7	*3/S	1.5
1912	StL-N	114	408	59	104	13	8	2	50	46	29	.255	.335	.341	87	-8	-7	54	19			3	*3	-0.2
1913	StL-N	132	450	61	117	18	4	0	33	53	40	.260	.342	.318	90	-5	-4	55	21			14	*3	0.9
1914	Pit-N	79	284	24	72	7	5	1	25	22	20	.254	.316	.324	94	-3	-2	31	8			-2	3	0.0
1915	Pit-F	151	521	56	146	26	6	1	66	68	39	.280	.367	.359	116	12	13	88	40			-19	*3	-0.2
1916	*Bro-N	144	495	57	121	22	6	0	60	50	60	.244	.320	.313	92	-2	-3	59	16			0	*3	-0.1
1917	Bro-N	83	271	20	58	9	5	0	25	29	25	.214	.292	.284	75	-7	-8	24	7			-3	3/2	-1.2
Total	13	1276	4291	485	1099	183	54	7	461	469	297	.256	.334	.329	97	-10	-5	545	167			-12	*3/S2O	0.1

YEAR	TM/L	G	AB	R	H	2B	3B	HR	RBI	BB	SO	AVG	OBP	SLG	PRO+	BR	/A	RC	SB	CS	SBR	FR	POS	TPR

■ JOE MOWRY
Mowry, Joseph Aloysius b: 4/6/08, St.Louis, Mo. BB/TR, 6′, 198 lbs. Deb: 5/13/33

YEAR	TM/L	G	AB	R	H	2B	3B	HR	RBI	BB	SO	AVG	OBP	SLG	PRO+	BR	/A	RC	SB	CS	SBR	FR	POS	TPR
1933	Bos-N	86	249	25	55	8	5	0	20	15	22	.221	.273	.293	67	-12	-10	21	1			-0	O	-1.4
1934	Bos-N	25	79	9	17	3	0	1	4	3	13	.215	.244	.291	46	-6	-6	6	0			1	O/2	-0.4
1935	Bos-N	81	136	17	36	8	1	1	13	11	13	.265	.324	.360	91	-3	-2	17	0			0	O	-0.2
Total	3	192	464	51	108	19	6	2	37	29	48	.233	.284	.313	71	-22	-17	44	1			1	O/2	-2.0

■ MIKE MOYNAHAN
Moynahan, Michael b: 1856, Chicago, Ill. d: 4/9/1899, Chicago, Ill. BL/TR, Deb: 8/20/1880

YEAR	TM/L	G	AB	R	H	2B	3B	HR	RBI	BB	SO	AVG	OBP	SLG	PRO+	BR	/A	RC	SB	CS	SBR	FR	POS	TPR
1880	Buf-N	27	100	12	33	5	1	0	14	6	9	.330	.368	.400	157	6	6	15				-6	S	0.1
1881	Cle-N	33	135	12	31	5	1	0	8	3	14	.230	.246	.281	69	-5	-4	10				-3	O/3	-0.6
	Det-N	1	4	1	1	0	0	0	0	0	1	.250	.250	.250	55	-0	-0	0				1	/3	0.0
	Yr	34	139	13	32	5	1	0	8	3	15	.230	.246	.281	69	-5	-4	10				-2		-0.6
1883	Phi-a	95	400	90	123	18	10	1		30		.308	.356	.410	135	21	15	60				0	*S	1.1
1884	Phi-a	1	4	0	0	0	0	0		0		.000	.000	.000	-94	-1	-1	0				-0	/O	0.0
	Cle-N	12	45	9	13	2	1	0	6	7	11	.289	.385	.378	136	2	2	7				-0	/2SO	0.2
Total	4	169	688	124	201	30	13	1	28	46	35	.292	.337	.378	124	23	18	91				-9	S/O23	0.8

■ HEINIE MUELLER
Mueller, Clarence Francis b: 9/16/1899, Creve Coeur, Mo. d: 1/23/75, DeSoto, Mo. "Les" BL/TL, 5′8″, 158 lbs. Deb: 9/25/20

YEAR	TM/L	G	AB	R	H	2B	3B	HR	RBI	BB	SO	AVG	OBP	SLG	PRO+	BR	/A	RC	SB	CS	SBR	FR	POS	TPR
1920	StL-N	4	22	0	7	1	0	0	1	2	4	.318	.375	.364	117	0	1	3	1	0	0	0	/O	0.1
1921	StL-N	55	176	25	62	10	6	1	34	11	22	.352	.397	.494	137	9	9	33	2	4	-2	3	O	0.8
1922	StL-N	61	159	20	43	7	2	3	26	14	18	.270	.329	.396	91	-3	-2	21	2	1	0	1	O	-0.2
1923	StL-N	78	265	39	91	16	9	5	41	18	16	.343	.392	.528	144	15	16	54	4	3	-1	11	O	2.2
1924	StL-N	92	296	39	78	12	6	2	37	19	16	.264	.312	.365	82	-8	-8	33	8	7	-2	1	O1	-0.9
1925	StL-N	78	243	33	76	16	4	1	26	17	11	.313	.365	.424	99	0	-0	37	0	3	-2	-5	O	-0.8
1926	StL-N	52	191	36	51	7	5	3	28	11	6	.267	.330	.403	93	-1	-2	25	8			0	O	-0.3
	NY-N	85	305	36	76	6	2	4	29	21	17	.249	.300	.321	68	-14	-14	29	7			5	O	-1.0
	Yr	137	496	72	127	13	7	7	57	32	23	.256	.312	.353	78	-15	-16	54	15			5		-1.3
1927	NY-N	84	190	33	55	6	1	3	19	25	12	.289	.384	.379	105	2	2	29	2			-8	O/1	-0.7
1928	Bos-N	42	151	25	34	3	1	0	19	17	9	.225	.316	.258	54	-10	-9	14	1			7	O	-0.2
1929	Bos-N	46	93	10	19	2	1	0	11	12	12	.204	.302	.247	39	-9	-8	8	2			-1	O	-1.0
1935	StL-A	16	27	0	5	1	0	0	1	1	4	.185	.214	.222	12	-4	-4	1	0	0	0	0	/1O	-0.3
Total	11	693	2118	296	597	87	37	22	272	168	147	.282	.342	.389	94	-23	-19	287	37	18		15	O/1	-2.3

■ DON MUELLER
Mueller, Donald Frederick "Mandrake The Magician" b: 4/14/27, St.Louis, Mo. BL/TR, 6′, 185 lbs. Deb: 8/02/48

YEAR	TM/L	G	AB	R	H	2B	3B	HR	RBI	BB	SO	AVG	OBP	SLG	PRO+	BR	/A	RC	SB	CS	SBR	FR	POS	TPR
1948	NY-N	36	81	12	29	4	1	1	9	0	3	.358	.358	.469	121	2	2	12	0			0	O	0.1
1949	NY-N	51	56	5	13	4	0	0	1	5	6	.232	.295	.304	61	-3	-3	3	0			-0	/O	-0.3
1950	NY-N	132	525	60	153	15	6	7	84	10	26	.291	.309	.383	80	-16	-16	60	1			-9	*O	-2.9
1951	NY-N	122	469	58	130	10	7	16	69	19	13	.277	.307	.431	95	-4	-5	63	1	1	-0	-4	*O	-1.2
1952	NY-N	126	456	61	128	14	7	12	49	34	24	.281	.333	.421	107	4	4	65	2	1	0	-2	*O	-0.1
1953	NY-N	131	480	56	160	12	2	6	60	19	13	.333	.360	.404	97	-1	-2	71	2	0	1	-9	*O	-1.4
1954	*NY-N	153	619	90	212	35	8	4	71	22	17	.342	.367	.444	110	8	8	94	2	3	-1	-3	*O	0.0
1955	NY-N	147	605	67	185	21	4	8	83	19	12	.306	.330	.393	91	-8	-8	75	1	2	-1	-14	*O	-2.5
1956	NY-N	138	453	38	122	12	1	5	41	15	7	.269	.293	.333	68	-21	-20	39	0	1	-1	-10	*O	-3.6
1957	NY-N	135	450	45	116	7	1	6	37	13	16	.258	.280	.318	60	-25	-25	39	2	0	1	-5	*O	-3.3
1958	Chi-A	70	166	7	42	5	0	0	16	11	9	.253	.299	.283	62	-9	-8	14	0	0	0	-4	O	-1.5
1959	Chi-A	4	4	0	2	0	0	0	0	0	0	.500	.500	.500	178	0	0	1	0	0	0	0	H	0.0
Total	12	1245	4364	499	1292	139	37	65	520	167	146	.296	.324	.390	89	-72	-74	538	11	8		-59	*O	-16.7

■ HEINIE MUELLER
Mueller, Emmett Jerome b: 7/20/12, St.Louis, Mo. d: 10/3/86, Orlando, Fla. BB/TR, 5′6″, 167 lbs. Deb: 4/19/38

YEAR	TM/L	G	AB	R	H	2B	3B	HR	RBI	BB	SO	AVG	OBP	SLG	PRO+	BR	/A	RC	SB	CS	SBR	FR	POS	TPR
1938	Phi-N	136	444	53	111	12	4	4	34	64	43	.250	.346	.322	87	-7	-6	55	2			-27	*23	-2.5
1939	Phi-N	115	341	46	95	19	4	9	43	33	34	.279	.342	.437	111	3	5	49	4			-11	23O/S	-0.3
1940	Phi-N	97	263	24	65	13	2	3	28	37	23	.247	.344	.346	95	-2	-1	33	2			-8	2O3	-0.8
1941	Phi-N	93	233	21	53	11	1	1	22	22	24	.227	.302	.296	72	-9	-8	21	2			-2	2O3	-0.8
Total	4	441	1281	144	324	55	11	17	127	156	124	.253	.337	.353	93	-16	-10	159	10			-48	2/301S	-4.4

■ RAY MUELLER
Mueller, Ray Coleman "Iron Man" b: 3/8/12, Pittsburg, Kan. BR/TR, 5′9″, 175 lbs. Deb: 5/11/35 C

YEAR	TM/L	G	AB	R	H	2B	3B	HR	RBI	BB	SO	AVG	OBP	SLG	PRO+	BR	/A	RC	SB	CS	SBR	FR	POS	TPR
1935	Bos-N	42	97	10	22	5	0	3	11	3	11	.227	.250	.371	70	-5	-4	9	0			-2	C	-0.5
1936	Bos-N	24	71	5	14	4	0	0	5	5	17	.197	.250	.254	38	-6	-6	5	0			-3	C	-0.7
1937	Bos-N	64	187	21	47	9	2	2	26	18	36	.251	.317	.353	90	-5	-2	21	1			2	C	0.1
1938	Bos-N	83	274	23	65	8	6	4	35	16	28	.237	.282	.354	82	-10	-7	27	3			-3	C	-0.6
1939	Pit-N	86	180	14	42	8	1	2	18	14	22	.233	.289	.322	65	-9	-9	18	0			-4	C	-1.0
1940	Pit-N	3	3	1	1	0	0	0	1	2	0	.333	.600	.333	165	1	1	1	0			1	/C	0.2
1943	Cin-N	141	427	50	111	19	4	8	52	56	42	.260	.347	.379	111	6	7	59	1			20	*C	3.4
1944	Cin-N	155	555	54	159	24	4	10	73	53	47	.286	.353	.398	115	8	11	79	4			-6	*C	1.3
1946	Cin-N	114	378	35	96	18	4	8	48	27	37	.254	.309	.386	100	-3	-2	45	0			9	*C	1.0
1947	Cin-N	71	192	17	48	11	0	6	33	16	25	.250	.311	.401	88	-4	-4	22	1			-2	C	-0.3
1948	Cin-N	14	34	2	7	1	0	0	2	4	3	.206	.289	.235	45	-3	-2	2	0			1	C	0.0
1949	Cin-N	32	106	7	29	4	0	1	13	5	13	.274	.319	.340	76	-4	-4	12	1			-3	C	-0.4
	NY-N	56	170	17	38	2	2	5	23	13	14	.224	.279	.347	67	-8	-8	15	1			0	C	-0.5
	Yr	88	276	24	67	6	2	6	36	18	27	.243	.294	.344	70	-12	-12	27	2			-2		-0.9
1950	NY-N	4	11	0	1	1	0	0	0	0	2	.091	.091	.182	-30	-2	-2	0	0			2	/C	0.0
	Pit-N	67	156	17	42	7	0	6	24	11	14	.269	.321	.429	92	-1	-2	19	2			2	C	0.2
	Yr	71	167	17	43	8	0	6	24	11	16	.257	.307	.413	85	-4	-4	18	2			4		0.2
1951	Bos-N	28	70	8	11	2	0	1	9	7	11	.157	.234	.229	27	-7	-7	4	0	0	0	3	C	-0.3
Total	14	985	2911	281	733	123	23	56	373	250	322	.252	.314	.368	91	-54	-41	337	14	0		17	C	1.9

■ WALTER MUELLER
Mueller, Walter John b: 12/6/1894, Central, Mo. d: 8/16/71, St.Louis, Mo. BR/TR, 5′8″, 160 lbs. Deb: 5/08/22

YEAR	TM/L	G	AB	R	H	2B	3B	HR	RBI	BB	SO	AVG	OBP	SLG	PRO+	BR	/A	RC	SB	CS	SBR	FR	POS	TPR
1922	Pit-N	32	122	21	33	5	1	2	18	5	7	.270	.305	.377	74	-5	-5	14	1	0	0	5	O	0.0
1923	Pit-N	40	111	11	34	4	4	0	20	4	6	.306	.336	.414	95	-1	-1	15	2	2	-1	1	O	-0.1
1924	Pit-N	30	50	6	13	1	1	0	8	4	4	.260	.327	.320	73	-2	-2	6	1	0	0	2	O	0.1
1926	Pit-N	19	62	8	15	0	1	0	3	0	2	.242	.242	.274	37	-5	-6	4	0			0	O	-0.5
Total	4	121	345	46	95	10	7	2	49	13	19	.275	.307	.362	74	-13	-14	39	4	2		8	/O	-0.5

■ BILL MUELLER
Mueller, William Lawrence "Hawk" b: 11/9/20, Bay City, Mich. BR/TR, 6′1.5″, 180 lbs. Deb: 8/29/42

YEAR	TM/L	G	AB	R	H	2B	3B	HR	RBI	BB	SO	AVG	OBP	SLG	PRO+	BR	/A	RC	SB	CS	SBR	FR	POS	TPR
1942	Chi-A	26	85	5	14	1	0	0	5	12	9	.165	.276	.176	29	-8	-7	4	2	1	0	10	O	0.0
1945	Chi-A	13	9	3	0	0	0	0	0	2	1	.000	.182	.000	-47	-2	-2	0	1	0	0	0	/O	0.0
Total	2	39	94	8	14	1	0	0	5	14	10	.149	.266	.160	22	-9	-9	4	3	1	0	10	/O	0.0

■ MIKE MULDOON
Muldoon, Michael D. b: 1858, Ireland 5′8″, 165 lbs. Deb: 5/01/1882

YEAR	TM/L	G	AB	R	H	2B	3B	HR	RBI	BB	SO	AVG	OBP	SLG	PRO+	BR	/A	RC	SB	CS	SBR	FR	POS	TPR
1882	Cle-N	84	341	50	84	17	5	6	45	10	28	.246	.268	.378	108	1	3	35				3	*3O	0.6
1883	Cle-N	98	378	54	86	22	3	0	29	10	39	.228	.247	.320	67	-15	-14	29				-8	*3/O	-1.8
1884	Cle-N	110	422	46	101	16	6	2	38	18	67	.239	.270	.320	82	-7	-10	37				-7	*3/O2	-1.9
1885	Bal-a	102	410	47	103	20	6	2		20		.251	.293	.344	105	1	2	42				-3	*3/2	0.4
1886	Bal-a	101	381	57	76	13	8	0		34		.199	.269	.276	74	-12	-10	32	12			2	23	-0.5
Total	5	495	1932	254	450	88	28	10	112	92	134	.233	.270	.323	87	-31	-29	176	12			-13	3/2O	-3.2

YEAR	TM/L	G	AB	R	H	2B	3B	HR	RBI	BB	SO	AVG	OBP	SLG	PRO+	BR	/A	RC	SB	CS	SBR	FR	POS	TPR

■ TONY MULLANE Mullane, Anthony John "Count" or "The Apollo Of The Box" b: 1/20/1859, Cork, Ireland d: 4/25/44, Chicago, Ill. BB/TB, 5'10.5", 165 lbs. Deb: 8/27/1881

YEAR	TM/L	G	AB	R	H	2B	3B	HR	RBI	BB	SO	AVG	OBP	SLG	PRO+	BR	/A	RC	SB	CS	SBR	FR	POS	TPR
1881	Det-N	5	19	0	5	0	0	0	1	0	0	.263	.263	.263	63	-1	-1	1				0	/P	0.0
1882	Lou-a	77	303	46	78	13	1	0		13		.257	.288	.307	107	0	3	27				10	*P1O/2	0.0
1883	StL-a	83	307	38	69	11	6	0		13		.225	.256	.300	74	-7	-10	24				1	PO/21	0.0
1884	Tol-a	95	352	49	97	19	3	3		33		.276	.339	.372	131	14	12	46				6	PO/13S2	0.0
1886	Cin-a	91	324	59	73	12	5	0		25		.225	.283	.293	80	-6	-8	33	20			-1	PO/13S2	0.0
1887	Cin-a	56	199	35	44	6	3	3		16		.221	.292	.327	73	-7	-8	25	20			-2	P/O	0.0
1888	Cin-a	51	175	27	44	4	4	1	16	8		.251	.296	.337	101	1	-0	22	12			-2	P/1O2	0.0
1889	Cin-a	63	196	53	58	16	4	0	29	27	21	.296	.387	.418	128	9	8	42	24			-1	P3O/1	0.0
1890	Cin-N	81	286	41	79	9	8	0	34	39	30	.276	.375	.364	118	8	8	47	19			-2	OP3S/1	1.0
1891	Cin-N	64	209	16	31	1	2	0	10	18	33	.148	.229	.172	19	-21	-21	9	4			-2	PO/3	0.0
1892	Cin-N	39	118	14	20	3	1	0	9	9	8	.169	.246	.212	41	-8	-8	7	4			5	P/1	0.0
1893	Cin-N	16	52	11	15	0	0	1	6	5	3	.288	.383	.346	94	0	-0	7	1			0	P/3	0.0
	Bal-N	38	114	15	26	2	1	0	14	5	14	.228	.261	.263	40	-10	-10	9	5			2	P/O1	0.0
	Yr	54	166	26	41	2	1	1	20	10	17	.247	.302	.289	58	-10	-10	17	6			2		0.0
1894	Bal-N	21	53	3	21	3	0	0	9	6	3	.396	.475	.453	121	3	2	13	2			-1	P	0.0
	Cle-N	4	13	0	1	0	0	0	0	4	2	.077	.294	.077	-5	-2	-2	1	1			2	/P	0.0
	Yr	25	66	3	22	3	0	0	9	10	5	.333	.436	.379	96	1	0	13	3			1		0.0
Total	13	784	2720	407	661	99	38	8	128	221	114	.243	.307	.316	89	-27	-34	315	112			16	PO/31S2	1.0

■ GREG MULLEAVY Mulleavy, Gregory Thomas "Moe" b: 9/25/05, Detroit, Mich. d: 2/1/80, Arcadia, Cal. BR/TR, 5'9", 167 lbs. Deb: 7/04/30 C

YEAR	TM/L	G	AB	R	H	2B	3B	HR	RBI	BB	SO	AVG	OBP	SLG	PRO+	BR	/A	RC	SB	CS	SBR	FR	POS	TPR
1930	Chi-A	77	289	27	76	14	5	0	28	20	23	.263	.311	.346	69	-15	-13	32	5	2	0	-5	S	-0.9
1932	Chi-A	1	3	0	0	0	0	0	0	0	0	.000	.000	.000	-99	-1	-1	0	0	0	0	0	/2	0.0
1933	Bos-A	1	0	1	0	0	0	0	0	0	0	—	—	—	—	0	0	0	0	0	0	0	R	0.0
Total	3	79	292	28	76	14	5	0	28	20	23	.260	.308	.342	67	-16	-14	32	5	2	0	-5	/S2	-0.9

■ MULLEN Mullen Deb: 8/17/1872

YEAR	TM/L	G	AB	R	H	2B	3B	HR	RBI	BB	SO	AVG	OBP	SLG	PRO+	BR	/A	RC	SB	CS	SBR	FR	POS	TPR
1872	Cle-n	1	4	1	0	0	0	0		0		.000	.000	.000	-99	-1	-1	0					/O	0.0

■ CHARLIE MULLEN Mullen, Charles George b: 3/15/1889, Seattle, Wash. d: 6/6/63, Seattle, Wash. BR/TR, 5'10.5", 155 lbs. Deb: 5/18/10

YEAR	TM/L	G	AB	R	H	2B	3B	HR	RBI	BB	SO	AVG	OBP	SLG	PRO+	BR	/A	RC	SB	CS	SBR	FR	POS	TPR
1910	Chi-A	41	123	15	24	2	1	0	13	4		.195	.220	.228	42	-9	-8	8	4			1	1/O	-0.6
1911	Chi-A	20	59	7	12	2	1	0	5	5		.203	.266	.271	51	-4	-4	5	1			0	1	-0.2
1914	NY-A	93	323	33	84	8	0	0	44	33	55	.260	.332	.285	86	-5	-5	32	11	17	-7	3	1	-0.9
1915	NY-A	40	90	11	24	1	0	0	7	10	12	.267	.340	.278	85	-1	-1	10	5	2	0	1	1	-0.1
1916	NY-A	59	146	11	39	9	1	0	18	9	13	.267	.310	.342	94	-1	-2	18	7			-4	21/O	-0.5
Total	5	253	741	77	183	22	3	0	87	61	80	.247	.306	.285	78	-20	-19	72	28	19		0	1/2O	-2.3

■ MOON MULLEN Mullen, Ford Parker b: 2/9/17, Olympia, Wash. BL/TR, 5'9", 165 lbs. Deb: 4/18/44

YEAR	TM/L	G	AB	R	H	2B	3B	HR	RBI	BB	SO	AVG	OBP	SLG	PRO+	BR	/A	RC	SB	CS	SBR	FR	POS	TPR
1944	Phi-N	118	464	51	124	9	4	0	31	28	32	.267	.315	.304	77	-15	-13	46	4			-7	*2/3	-0.8

■ JOHN MULLEN Mullen, John b: Philadelphia, Pa. BL/TL, Deb: 9/09/1876

YEAR	TM/L	G	AB	R	H	2B	3B	HR	RBI	BB	SO	AVG	OBP	SLG	PRO+	BR	/A	RC	SB	CS	SBR	FR	POS	TPR
1876	Phi-N	1	3	0	0	0	0	0	0	0	0	.000	.000	.000	-99	-1	-1	0				1	/C	0.0

■ BILLY MULLEN Mullen, William John b: 1/23/1896, St.Louis, Mo. d: 5/4/71, St.Louis, Mo. BR/TR, 5'8", 160 lbs. Deb: 10/02/20

YEAR	TM/L	G	AB	R	H	2B	3B	HR	RBI	BB	SO	AVG	OBP	SLG	PRO+	BR	/A	RC	SB	CS	SBR	FR	POS	TPR
1920	StL-A	2	0	0	0	0	0	0	0	0	0	.000	.000	.000	-97	-1	-1	0	0	0	0	-1	/2	-0.1
1921	StL-A	4	4	0	0	0	0	0	0	2	1	.000	.333	.000	-8	-1	-1	0	0	0	0	0	/3	0.0
1923	Bro-N	4	11	1	3	0	0	0	0	0	0	.273	.273	.273	46	-1	-1	1	0	0	0	-0	/3	0.0
1926	Det-A	11	13	2	1	0	0	0	0	5	1	.077	.333	.077	11	-1	-2	1	1	0	0	-0	/3	0.0
1928	StL-A	15	18	2	7	1	0	0	2	3	4	.389	.476	.444	139	1	1	4	0	0	0	1	/3	0.2
Total	5	36	50	5	11	1	0	0	2	10	6	.220	.350	.240	56	-3	-3	6	1	0	0	-0	/32	0.1

■ FREDDIE MULLER Muller, Frederick William b: 12/21/07, Newark, Cal. d: 10/20/76, Davis, Cal. BR/TR, 5'10", 170 lbs. Deb: 7/08/33

YEAR	TM/L	G	AB	R	H	2B	3B	HR	RBI	BB	SO	AVG	OBP	SLG	PRO+	BR	/A	RC	SB	CS	SBR	FR	POS	TPR
1933	Bos-A	15	48	6	9	1	1	0	3	5	5	.188	.264	.250	37	-4	-4	4	1	0	0	-4	2	-0.7
1934	Bos-A	2	1	1	0	0	0	0	0	1	0	.000	.500	.000	36	0	-0	0	0	0	0	-0	/23	0.0
Total	2	17	49	7	9	1	1	0	3	6	5	.184	.273	.245	38	-4	-4	4	1	0	0	-5	/23	-0.7

■ MULLIGAN Mulligan Deb: 6/14/1884

YEAR	TM/L	G	AB	R	H	2B	3B	HR	RBI	BB	SO	AVG	OBP	SLG	PRO+	BR	/A	RC	SB	CS	SBR	FR	POS	TPR
1884	Was-U	1	4	2	1	0	0	0		0		.250	.250	.250	72	-0	-0	0	0			1	/3	0.1

■ JOE MULLIGAN Mulligan, Edward Joseph "Big Joe" b: 8/27/1894, St.Louis, Mo. d: 3/15/82, San Rafael, Cal. BR/TR, 5'9", 152 lbs. Deb: 9/23/15

YEAR	TM/L	G	AB	R	H	2B	3B	HR	RBI	BB	SO	AVG	OBP	SLG	PRO+	BR	/A	RC	SB	CS	SBR	FR	POS	TPR
1915	Chi-N	11	22	5	8	1	0	0	2	5	1	.364	.481	.409	170	2	2	5	2	2	-1	3	S/3	0.5
1916	Chi-N	58	189	13	29	3	4	0	9	8	30	.153	.200	.212	24	-16	-19	9	1			3	S	-1.3
1921	Chi-A	151	609	82	153	21	12	1	45	32	53	.251	.293	.330	59	-39	-38	57	13	18	-7	-13	*3/S	-4.3
1922	Chi-A	103	372	39	87	14	8	0	31	22	32	.234	.278	.315	55	-26	-25	33	7	7	-2	4	3/S	-1.3
1928	Pit-N	27	43	4	10	2	0	0	1	3	4	.233	.283	.279	45	-3	-4	4	0			0	/32	-0.2
Total	5	350	1235	143	287	41	24	1	88	70	120	.232	.278	.307	54	-82	-83	107	23	27		-3	3/S2	-6.6

■ GEORGE MULLIN Mullin, George Joseph "Wabash George" b: 7/4/1880, Toledo, Ohio d: 1/7/44, Wabash, Ind. BR/TR, 5'11", 188 lbs. Deb: 5/04/02

YEAR	TM/L	G	AB	R	H	2B	3B	HR	RBI	BB	SO	AVG	OBP	SLG	PRO+	BR	/A	RC	SB	CS	SBR	FR	POS	TPR
1902	Det-A	40	120	20	39	4	3	0	11	8		.325	.367	.408	114	3	2	19	1			1	P/O	0.0
1903	Det-A	46	126	11	35	9	1	1	12	2		.278	.289	.389	107	0	1	15	1			4	P/O	0.0
1904	Det-A	53	155	14	45	10	2	0	8	10		.290	.333	.381	132	5	5	21	1			7	P/O	0.0
1905	Det-A	47	135	15	35	4	0	0	12	12		.259	.320	.289	95	-0	-0	15	4			7	P/O	0.0
1906	Det-A	50	142	13	32	6	4	0	6	4		.225	.247	.324	78	-4	-4	12	2			2	P/2O	0.0
1907	*Det-A	70	157	16	34	5	3	0	13	12		.217	.272	.287	77	-3	-4	13	2			4	P/1	0.0
1908	*Det-A	55	125	13	32	2	2	1	8	7		.256	.295	.328	100	0	-0	13	2			3	P	0.0
1909	*Det-A	53	126	13	27	7	0	0	17	13		.214	.288	.270	73	-3	-4	10	2			0	P/O	0.0
1910	Det-A	50	129	15	33	6	2	1	11	8		.256	.290	.357	99	0	-1	14	1			0	P/O	0.0
1911	Det-A	40	98	4	28	7	2	0	5	10		.286	.352	.398	104	1	1	14	1			-2	P	0.0
1912	Det-A	38	90	13	25	5	1	0	12	17		.278	.393	.356	118	2	3	13	0			0	P	0.0
1913	Det-A	12	20	1	7	0	0	0	1	4	1	.350	.458	.350	139	1	1	3	0			1	/P	0.0
	Was-A	11	21	4	4	0	0	0	0	2	5	.190	.292	.190	41	-1	-1	1	1			1	P	0.0
	Yr	23	41	5	11	0	0	0	1	6	6	.268	.375	.268	89	-0	-0	4	1			2		0.0
1914	Ind-F	43	77	11	24	5	3	0	21	11	15	.312	.404	.455	132	5	4	15	0			-3	P	0.0
1915	New-F	6	10	0	1	0	0	0	0	1		.100	.250	.100	6	-1	-1	0	0			-1	/P	0.0
Total	14	614	1531	163	401	70	23	3	137	122	21	.262	.317	.344	100	5	1	177	18			23	P/O12	0.0

■ HENRY MULLIN Mullin, Henry b: Boston, Mass. BR, Deb: 6/04/1884

YEAR	TM/L	G	AB	R	H	2B	3B	HR	RBI	BB	SO	AVG	OBP	SLG	PRO+	BR	/A	RC	SB	CS	SBR	FR	POS	TPR
1884	Was-a	34	120	13	17	3	1	0		8		.142	.195	.183	29	-9	-7	4				-1	O/3	-0.6
	Bos-U	2	8	1	0	0	0	0		0		.000	.000	.000	-99	-2	-2	0	0			3	/O	0.1

■ JIM MULLIN Mullin, James Henry b: 10/16/1883, New York, N.Y. d: 1/24/25, Philadelphia, Pa. TR, 5'10", 173 lbs. Deb: 6/01/04

YEAR	TM/L	G	AB	R	H	2B	3B	HR	RBI	BB	SO	AVG	OBP	SLG	PRO+	BR	/A	RC	SB	CS	SBR	FR	POS	TPR
1904	Phi-A	22	52	5	14	1	0	1	5	3		.269	.309	.346	104	1	0	6	2			-5	/12SO	-0.5
	Was-A	27	102	10	19	2	2	0	4	4		.186	.217	.245	48	-6	-6	6	3			5	2	0.0
	Phi-A	19	58	4	10	1	0	0	4	2		.172	.200	.172	19	-5	-5	3	2			-0	1	-0.5

YEAR	TM/L	G	AB	R	H	2B	3B	HR	RBI	BB	SO	AVG	OBP	SLG	PRO+	BR	/A	RC	SB	CS	SBR	FR	POS	TPR
	Yr	68	212	19	43	3	2	1	13	9		.203	.235	.250	54	-11	-11	15	7			-0		-1.0
1905	Was-A	50	163	18	31	7	6	0	13	5		.190	.214	.307	69	-7	-6	13	5			-4	2/1	-1.0
Total	2	118	375	37	74	10	8	1	26	14		.197	.226	.275	60	-17	-17	28	12			-4	/21SO	-2.0

■ PAT MULLIN
Mullin, Patrick Joseph　b: 11/1/17, Trotter, Pa.　BL/TR, 6'2", 190 lbs.　Deb: 9/18/40　C

YEAR	TM/L	G	AB	R	H	2B	3B	HR	RBI	BB	SO	AVG	OBP	SLG	PRO+	BR	/A	RC	SB	CS	SBR	FR	POS	TPR
1940	Det-A	4	4	0	0	0	0	0	0	0	0	.000	.000	.000	-91	-1	-1	0	0	0	0	0	/O	0.0
1941	Det-A	54	220	42	76	11	5	5	23	18	18	.345	.400	.509	126	12	9	48	5	1	1	-2	O	0.5
1946	Det-A	93	276	34	68	13	4	3	35	25	36	.246	.311	.355	81	-6	-8	31	3	5	-2	-3	O	-1.7
1947	Det-A	116	398	62	102	28	6	15	62	63	66	.256	.359	.470	126	15	14	69	3	8	-4	5	*O	1.1
1948	Det-A	138	496	91	143	16	11	23	80	77	57	.288	.385	.504	132	24	22	103	1	2	-1	-3	*O	1.3
1949	Det-A	104	310	55	83	8	6	12	59	42	29	.268	.357	.448	112	4	4	52	1	2	-1	-3	O	0.0
1950	Det-A	69	142	16	31	5	0	6	23	20	23	.218	.315	.380	75	-5	-6	18	1	4	-2	0	O	-0.7
1951	Det-A	110	295	41	83	11	6	12	51	40	38	.281	.367	.481	128	11	11	55	2	2	-1	-6	O	0.1
1952	Det-A	97	255	29	64	13	5	7	35	31	30	.251	.332	.424	108	3	2	36	4	2	0	3	O	0.3
1953	Det-A	79	97	11	26	1	0	4	17	14	15	.268	.360	.402	107	1	1	14	0	1	-1	-2	O	-0.1
Total	10	864	2493	381	676	106	43	87	385	330	312	.271	.358	.453	115	58	48	426	20	27	-10	-11	O	0.8

■ RANCE MULLINIKS
Mulliniks, Steven Rance　b: 1/15/56, Tulare, Cal.　BL/TR, 5'11", 162 lbs.　Deb: 6/18/77

YEAR	TM/L	G	AB	R	H	2B	3B	HR	RBI	BB	SO	AVG	OBP	SLG	PRO+	BR	/A	RC	SB	CS	SBR	FR	POS	TPR
1977	Cal-A	78	271	36	73	13	2	3	21	23	36	.269	.329	.365	93	-4	-3	34	1	1	-0	0	S	0.6
1978	Cal-A	50	119	6	22	3	1	1	6	8	23	.185	.242	.252	41	-10	-9	7	2	0	1	2	S/D	-0.2
1979	Cal-A	22	68	7	10	0	0	1	8	4	14	.147	.205	.191	8	-9	-8	3	0	0	0	-7	S	-1.2
1980	KC-A	36	54	8	14	3	0	0	6	7	10	.259	.344	.315	81	-1	-1	6	0	0	0	2	S2	0.3
1981	KC-A	24	44	6	10	3	0	0	5	2	7	.227	.261	.295	61	-2	-2	3	0	1	-1	3	2/S3	0.1
1982	Tor-A	112	311	32	76	25	0	4	35	37	49	.244	.327	.363	82	-4	-8	36	3	2	-0	-16	*3S	-2.4
1983	Tor-A	129	364	54	100	34	3	10	49	57	43	.275	.374	.467	122	16	13	62	0	2	-1	-18	*3S/2	-0.4
1984	Tor-A	125	343	41	111	21	5	3	42	33	44	.324	.385	.440	123	13	12	58	2	3	-1	-13	*3/S2	0.0
1985	*Tor-A	129	366	55	108	26	1	10	57	55	54	.295	.387	.454	126	16	15	66	2	0	1	-16	*3	0.9
1986	Tor-A	117	348	50	90	22	0	11	45	43	60	.259	.342	.417	103	3	2	48	1	1	-0	-1	*3/2D	-0.1
1987	Tor-A	124	332	37	103	28	1	11	44	34	55	.310	.374	.500	127	14	13	60	1	1	-0	-6	3D/S	0.5
1988	Tor-A	119	337	49	101	21	1	12	48	56	57	.300	.399	.475	143	21	21	65	1	0	0	-0	*D/3	2.1
1989	*Tor-A	103	273	25	65	11	2	3	29	34	40	.238	.322	.326	85	-5	-5	27	0	0	0	2	D3	-0.2
1990	Tor-A	57	97	11	28	4	0	2	16	22	19	.289	.420	.392	131	5	5	18	2	1	0	-0	3D/1	0.5
Total	14	1225	3327	417	911	214	16	71	411	415	511	.274	.356	.412	108	53	44	495	15	12	-3	-68	3DS/21	-0.8

■ FRAN MULLINS
Mullins, Francis Joseph　b: 5/14/57, Oakland, Cal.　BR/TR, 6', 180 lbs.　Deb: 9/01/80

YEAR	TM/L	G	AB	R	H	2B	3B	HR	RBI	BB	SO	AVG	OBP	SLG	PRO+	BR	/A	RC	SB	CS	SBR	FR	POS	TPR
1980	Chi-A	21	62	9	12	4	0	0	3	9	8	.194	.296	.258	53	-4	-4	4	0	1	-1	-2	3	-0.6
1984	SF-N	57	110	8	24	8	0	2	10	9	29	.218	.277	.345	77	-4	-4	10	3	1	0	9	S3/2	0.9
1986	Cle-A	28	40	3	7	4	0	0	5	2	11	.175	.214	.275	33	-4	-3	3	0	0	0	9	2S/1D	0.6
Total	3	106	212	20	43	16	0	2	18	20	48	.203	.272	.307	61	-12	-11	17	3	2	-0	17	/3S2D1	0.9

■ JOE MULVEY
Mulvey, Joseph H.　b: 10/27/1858, Providence, R.I.　d: 8/21/28, Philadelphia, Pa.　BR/TR, 5'11.5", 178 lbs.　Deb: 5/31/1883

YEAR	TM/L	G	AB	R	H	2B	3B	HR	RBI	BB	SO	AVG	OBP	SLG	PRO+	BR	/A	RC	SB	CS	SBR	FR	POS	TPR
1883	Pro-N	4	16	1	2	1	0	0	2	0	1	.125	.125	.188	-6	-2	-2	0				-3	/S	-0.3
	Phi-N	3	12	2	6	1	0	0	3	0	1	.500	.500	.583	250	2	2	4				-1	/3	0.1
	Yr	7	28	3	8	2	0	0	5	0	2	.286	.286	.357	96	-0	-0	3				-3		-0.2
1884	Phi-N	100	401	47	92	11	2	2	32	4	49	.229	.237	.282	66	-17	-15	27				11	*3	-0.7
1885	Phi-N	107	443	74	119	25	6	6	64	3	18	.269	.274	.393	116	5	6	49				-7	*3	0.0
1886	Phi-N	107	430	71	115	16	10	2	53	15	31	.267	.292	.365	98	-1	-2	55	27			-18	*3/O	-1.3
1887	Phi-N	111	474	93	136	21	6	2	78	21	14	.287	.321	.369	88	-5	-9	72	43			-15	*3	-1.9
1888	Phi-N	100	398	37	86	12	3	0	39	9	33	.216	.235	.261	57	-18	-20	29	18			-14	*3	-3.0
1889	Phi-N	129	544	77	157	21	9	6	77	23	25	.289	.319	.393	92	-2	-9	77	23			0	*3	0.0
1890	Phi-P	120	519	96	149	26	15	6	87	27	36	.287	.326	.430	100	-1	-3	81	20			-16	*3	-0.7
1891	Phi-a	113	453	62	115	9	13	5	66	17	32	.254	.287	.364	86	-9	-11	52	11			2	*3	-0.4
1892	Phi-N	25	98	9	14	1	1	0	4	6	9	.143	.200	.173	14	-10	-10	4	2			3	3	-0.4
1893	Was-N	55	226	21	53	9	4	0	19	7	8	.235	.264	.310	55	-16	-15	19	2			5	3	-0.6
1895	Bro-N	13	49	8	15	4	1	0	8	2	0	.306	.333	.429	106	-0	0	8	1			2	3	0.2
Total	12	987	4063	598	1059	157	70	29	532	134	257	.261	.287	.355	86	-74	-88	478	147			-51	3/SO	-9.0

■ JERRY MUMPHREY
Mumphrey, Jerry Wayne　b: 9/9/52, Tyler, Tex.　BB/TR, 6'2", 185 lbs.　Deb: 9/10/74

YEAR	TM/L	G	AB	R	H	2B	3B	HR	RBI	BB	SO	AVG	OBP	SLG	PRO+	BR	/A	RC	SB	CS	SBR	FR	POS	TPR
1974	StL-N	5	2	2	0	0	0	0	0	0	0	.000	.000	.000	-99	-1	-1	0	0	0	0	0	/O	0.0
1975	StL-N	11	16	2	6	2	0	0	1	4	3	.375	.500	.500	172	2	2	5	0	0	0	0	/O	0.2
1976	StL-N	112	384	51	99	15	5	1	26	37	53	.258	.325	.331	86	-6	-7	46	22	6	3	4	O	-0.3
1977	StL-N	145	463	73	133	20	10	2	38	47	70	.287	.354	.387	100	-0	1	64	22	15	-2	-9	*O	-1.5
1978	StL-N	125	367	41	96	13	4	2	37	30	40	.262	.319	.335	84	-8	-8	37	14	10	-2	-6	*O	-2.1
1979	StL-N	124	339	53	100	10	3	3	32	26	39	.295	.345	.369	94	-2	-2	41	8	11	-4	-13	*O	-2.3
1980	SD-N	160	564	61	168	24	3	4	59	49	90	.298	.354	.372	109	3	7	79	52	5	13	-1	*O	1.2
1981	*NY-A	80	319	44	98	11	5	6	32	24	27	.307	.356	.429	127	10	10	47	14	9	-1	5	O	1.3
1982	NY-A	123	477	76	143	24	10	9	68	50	66	.300	.366	.449	124	15	16	76	11	3	2	4	*O	1.7
1983	NY-A	83	267	41	70	11	4	7	36	28	33	.262	.332	.412	107	1	3	34	2	3	-1	5	O	0.5
	Hou-N	44	143	17	48	10	2	1	17	22	23	.336	.428	.455	154	10	11	31	5	0	2	3	O	1.5
1984	Hou-N	151	524	66	152	20	3	9	83	56	79	.290	.359	.391	119	8	13	74	15	7	0	-5	*O	0.3
1985	Hou-N	130	444	52	123	25	2	6	61	37	57	.277	.333	.396	106	1	3	56	6	7	-2	-0	*O	-0.2
1986	Chi-N	111	309	37	94	11	2	5	32	26	45	.304	.358	.401	101	4	1	45	2	3	-1	-4	O	-0.5
1987	Chi-N	118	309	41	103	19	2	13	44	35	47	.333	.401	.534	140	20	19	66	1	1	-0	-6	O	0.9
1988	Chi-N	63	66	3	9	2	0	0	9	7	16	.136	.219	.167	12	-7	-8	2	0	0	0	-1	/O	-0.8
Total	15	1585	4993	660	1442	217	55	70	575	478	688	.289	.351	.396	109	50	60	702	174	80	4	-25	*O	-0.1

■ JOHN MUNCE
Munce, John Lewis "Big John"　b: 11/18/1857, Philadelphia, Pa.　d: 3/15/17, Philadelphia, Pa.　6',　Deb: 8/19/1884

YEAR	TM/L	G	AB	R	H	2B	3B	HR	RBI	BB	SO	AVG	OBP	SLG	PRO+	BR	/A	RC	SB	CS	SBR	FR	POS	TPR
1884	Wil-U	7	21	1	4	0	0	0		1		.190	.227	.190	41	-1	-1	1	0			-1	/O	-0.1

■ JAKE MUNCH
Munch, Jacob Ferdinand　b: 11/16/1890, Morton, Pa.　d: 6/8/66, Lansdowne, Pa.　BL/TL, 6'2.5", 170 lbs.　Deb: 5/27/18

YEAR	TM/L	G	AB	R	H	2B	3B	HR	RBI	BB	SO	AVG	OBP	SLG	PRO+	BR	/A	RC	SB	CS	SBR	FR	POS	TPR
1918	Phi-A	22	30	3	8	0	1	0	0	0	5	.267	.267	.333	80	-1	-1	2	0			-1	/O1	-0.2

■ GEORGE MUNDINGER
Mundinger, George　b: 11/20/1854, New Orleans, La.　d: 10/12/10, Covington, La.　BR/TR, 6'2", 200 lbs.　Deb: 5/09/1884

YEAR	TM/L	G	AB	R	H	2B	3B	HR	RBI	BB	SO	AVG	OBP	SLG	PRO+	BR	/A	RC	SB	CS	SBR	FR	POS	TPR
1884	Ind-a	3	8	1	2	0	0	0				.250	.250	.250	68	-0	-0	1				-2	/C	-0.1

■ BILL MUNDY
Mundy, William Edward　b: 6/28/1889, Salineville, Ohio　d: 9/23/58, Kalamazoo, Mich.　BL/TL, 5'10", 154 lbs.　Deb: 8/17/13

YEAR	TM/L	G	AB	R	H	2B	3B	HR	RBI	BB	SO	AVG	OBP	SLG	PRO+	BR	/A	RC	SB	CS	SBR	FR	POS	TPR
1913	Bos-A	16	47	4	12	0	0	0	4	4	12	.255	.314	.255	65	-2	-2	4	0			-2	1	-0.4

■ HORATIO MUNN
Munn, Horatio　Deb: 9/06/1875

YEAR	TM/L	G	AB	R	H	2B	3B	HR	RBI	BB	SO	AVG	OBP	SLG	PRO+	BR	/A	RC	SB	CS	SBR	FR	POS	TPR
1875	Atl-n	1	4	0	0	0	0	0		0		.000	.000	.000	-99	-1	-1	0					/2	0.0

■ PEDRO MUNOZ
Munoz, Pedro Javier　b: 9/19/68, Ponce, P.R.　BR/TR, 5'11", 170 lbs.　Deb: 9/01/90

YEAR	TM/L	G	AB	R	H	2B	3B	HR	RBI	BB	SO	AVG	OBP	SLG	PRO+	BR	/A	RC	SB	CS	SBR	FR	POS	TPR
1990	Min-A	22	85	13	23	4	1	0	5	2	16	.271	.287	.341	70	-3	-4	8	3	0	1	-3	O/D	-0.5

■ RED MUNSON
Munson, Clarence Hanford　b: 7/31/1883, Cincinnati, Ohio　d: 2/19/57, Mishawaka, Ind.　TR,　Deb: 8/28/05

YEAR	TM/L	G	AB	R	H	2B	3B	HR	RBI	BB	SO	AVG	OBP	SLG	PRO+	BR	/A	RC	SB	CS	SBR	FR	POS	TPR
1905	Phi-N	9	26	1	3	1	0	0	2	0		.115	.115	.154	-20	-4	-4	1	0			-1	/C	-0.3

YEAR	TM/L	G	AB	R	H	2B	3B	HR	RBI	BB	SO	AVG	OBP	SLG	PRO+	BR	/A	RC	SB	CS	SBR	FR	POS	TPR

■ JOE MUNSON
Munson, Joseph Martin Napoleon (b: Joseph Martin Napoleon Carlson) b: 11/6/1899, Renovo, Pa. BL/TR, 5'9", 184 lbs. Deb: 9/18/25

YEAR	TM/L	G	AB	R	H	2B	3B	HR	RBI	BB	SO	AVG	OBP	SLG	PRO+	BR	/A	RC	SB	CS	SBR	FR	POS	TPR
1925	Chi-N	9	35	5	13	3	1	0	3	3	1	.371	.436	.514	140	2	2	8	1	1	-0	-1	/O	0.1
1926	Chi-N	33	101	17	26	2	2	3	15	8	4	.257	.318	.406	93	-1	-1	13	0			-3	O	-0.4
Total	2	42	136	22	39	5	3	3	18	11	5	.287	.349	.434	105	1	1	21	1	1		-3	/O	-0.3

■ THURMAN MUNSON
Munson, Thurman Lee b: 6/7/47, Akron, Ohio d: 8/2/79, Canton, Ohio BR/TR, 5'11", 190 lbs. Deb: 8/08/69

YEAR	TM/L	G	AB	R	H	2B	3B	HR	RBI	BB	SO	AVG	OBP	SLG	PRO+	BR	/A	RC	SB	CS	SBR	FR	POS	TPR
1969	NY-A	26	86	6	22	1	2	1	9	10	10	.256	.333	.349	94	-1	-1	9	0	1	-1	-0	C	0.0
1970	NY-A	132	453	59	137	25	4	6	53	57	56	.302	.389	.415	128	15	18	72	5	7	-3	6	*C	2.4
1971	NY-A	125	451	71	113	15	4	10	42	52	65	.251	.337	.368	106	0	4	57	6	5	-1	-2	*C/O	0.7
1972	NY-A	140	511	54	143	16	3	7	46	47	58	.280	.344	.364	115	7	9	62	6	7	-2	-5	*C	0.2
1973	NY-A	147	519	80	156	29	4	20	74	48	64	.301	.364	.487	143	25	27	89	4	6	-2	6	*C/D	3.4
1974	NY-A	144	517	64	135	19	2	13	60	44	66	.261	.320	.381	104	0	2	61	2	0	1	1	*C/D	0.8
1975	NY-A	157	597	83	190	24	3	12	102	45	52	.318	.372	.429	129	20	22	90	3	2	-0	8	*CD/103	3.4
1976	*NY-A	152	616	79	186	27	1	17	105	29	38	.302	.343	.432	127	18	19	85	14	11	-2	-3	*CDO	1.8
1977	*NY-A	149	595	85	183	28	5	18	100	39	55	.308	.352	.462	121	15	16	90	5	6	-2	-5	*CD	1.3
1978	*NY-A	154	617	73	183	27	1	6	71	35	70	.297	.337	.373	102	-1	1	73	2	3	-1	-2	*CDO	0.2
1979	NY-A	97	382	42	110	18	3	3	39	32	37	.288	.343	.374	95	-3	-2	46	1	2	-1	-6	C/1D	-0.5
Total	11	1423	5344	696	1558	229	32	113	701	438	571	.292	.350	.410	117	97	116	735	48	50	-16	-2	*C/DO13	13.7

■ JOHN MUNYAN
Munyan, John B. b: 11/14/1860, Chester, Pa. d: 2/18/45, Endicott, N.Y. Deb: 7/12/1887

YEAR	TM/L	G	AB	R	H	2B	3B	HR	RBI	BB	SO	AVG	OBP	SLG	PRO+	BR	/A	RC	SB	CS	SBR	FR	POS	TPR
1887	Cle-a	16	58	9	14	1	1	0		3		.241	.279	.293	63	-3	-3	6	4			-1	O/C3	-0.2
1890	Col-a	2	7	1	1	0	0	0		0		.143	.250	.143	19	-1	-1	0	0			0	/O	0.0
	StL-a	96	342	61	91	15	7	4		32		.266	.341	.386	102	7	-1	50	11			-3	C/O23S	0.4
	Yr	98	349	62	92	15	7	4		32		.264	.339	.381	101	6	-2	50	11			-3		0.4
1891	StL-a	62	182	44	42	4	3	0	20	43	39	.231	.389	.286	84	2	-3	26	13			-4	CO/S3	-0.4
Total	3	176	589	115	148	20	11	4	20	78	39	.251	.351	.343	92	5	-8	82	28			-8	C/O3S2	-0.2

■ BOBBY MURCER
Murcer, Bobby Ray b: 5/20/46, Oklahoma City, Okla. BL/TR, 5'11", 160 lbs. Deb: 9/08/65

YEAR	TM/L	G	AB	R	H	2B	3B	HR	RBI	BB	SO	AVG	OBP	SLG	PRO+	BR	/A	RC	SB	CS	SBR	FR	POS	TPR
1965	NY-A	11	37	2	9	0	1	1	4	5	12	.243	.333	.378	102	0	0	5	0	0	0	7	S	0.8
1966	NY-A	21	69	3	12	1	1	0	5	4	5	.174	.219	.217	27	-7	-6	3	2	2	-1	-4	S	-1.0
1969	NY-A	152	564	82	146	24	4	26	82	50	103	.259	.323	.454	120	9	12	82	7	5	-1	-4	*O3	0.4
1970	NY-A	159	581	95	146	23	3	23	78	87	100	.251	.351	.420	118	10	14	89	15	10	-2	6	*O	1.2
1971	NY-A	146	529	94	175	25	6	25	94	91	60	.331	**.429**	.543	**185**	54	58	126	14	8	-1	-3	*O	**5.2**
1972	NY-A	153	585	**102**	171	30	7	33	96	63	67	.292	.363	.537	171	45	47	114	11	9	-2	4	*O	5.0
1973	NY-A	160	616	83	187	29	2	22	95	50	67	.304	.359	.464	135	23	26	100	6	7	-2	-0	*O	1.9
1974	NY-A	156	606	69	166	25	4	10	88	57	59	.274	.338	.378	109	5	7	79	14	5	1	4	*O	0.8
1975	SF-N	147	526	80	157	29	4	11	91	91	45	.298	.404	.432	127	26	23	97	9	5	-0	-12	*O	0.6
1976	SF-N	147	533	73	138	20	2	23	90	84	78	.259	.364	.433	122	19	17	86	12	7	-1	-2	*O	1.0
1977	Chi-N	154	554	90	147	18	3	27	89	80	77	.265	.361	.455	106	14	6	95	16	7	1	-8	*O/2S	-0.6
1978	Chi-N	146	499	66	140	22	6	9	64	60	57	.281	.380	.403	106	15	8	79	14	5	1	-12	*O	-0.8
1979	Chi-N	58	190	22	49	4	1	7	22	36	20	.258	.379	.400	103	5	2	31	2	3	-1	-1	O	0.0
	NY-A	74	264	42	72	12	0	8	33	25	32	.273	.340	.409	103	0	1	35	1	1	-0	-4	O	-0.5
1980	*NY-A	100	297	41	80	9	1	13	57	34	28	.269	.348	.438	116	6	6	45	2	0	1	-7	OD	0.0
1981	*NY-A	50	117	14	31	6	0	6	24	12	15	.265	.333	.470	131	4	4	18	0	0	0	0	D	0.4
1982	NY-A	65	141	12	32	6	0	7	30	12	15	.227	.292	.418	94	-2	-2	16	2	1	0	0	D	-0.1
1983	NY-A	9	22	2	4	2	0	1	1	1	1	.182	.217	.409	71	-1	-1	1	0	0	0	0	/D	0.0
Total	17	1908	6730	972	1862	285	45	252	1043	862	841	.277	.361	.445	124	226	222	1103	127	75	-7	-34	*OD/3S2	14.3

■ SIMMY MURCH
Murch, Simeon Augustus b: 11/21/1880, Castine, Me. d: 6/6/39, Exeter, N.H. TR, 6'4", 220 lbs. Deb: 9/20/04

YEAR	TM/L	G	AB	R	H	2B	3B	HR	RBI	BB	SO	AVG	OBP	SLG	PRO+	BR	/A	RC	SB	CS	SBR	FR	POS	TPR
1904	StL-N	13	51	3	7	1	0	0	1	1		.137	.154	.157	-3	-6	-6	1	0			-2	/23S	-0.8
1905	StL-N	4	9	0	1	0	0	0	0	0		.111	.111	.111	-34	-1	-1	0	0			-3	/2S	-0.4
1908	Bro-N	6	11	1	2	1	0	0	0	1		.182	.250	.273	71	-0	-0	1	0			-1	/1	0.0
Total	3	23	71	4	10	2	0	0	1	2		.141	.164	.169	4	-8	-7	2	0			-6	/231S	-1.2

■ WILBUR MURDOCH
Murdoch, Wilbur Edwin b: 3/14/1875, Avon, N.Y. d: 10/29/41, Los Angeles, Cal. Deb: 8/29/08

YEAR	TM/L	G	AB	R	H	2B	3B	HR	RBI	BB	SO	AVG	OBP	SLG	PRO+	BR	/A	RC	SB	CS	SBR	FR	POS	TPR
1908	StL-N	27	62	5	16	3	0	0	5	3		.258	.292	.306	98	-1	-0	7	4			-4	O	-0.5

■ TIM MURNANE
Murnane, Timothy Hayes b: 6/4/1852, Naugatuck, Conn. d: 2/7/17, Boston, Mass. BL/TR, 5'9.5", 172 lbs. Deb: 4/26/1872 M

YEAR	TM/L	G	AB	R	H	2B	3B	HR	RBI	BB	SO	AVG	OBP	SLG	PRO+	BR	/A	RC	SB	CS	SBR	FR	POS	TPR
1872	Man-n	24	115	29	39	3	0	0		1		.339	.345	.365	126	2	4	15				1		0.5
1873	Ath-n	42	182	53	40	3	1	1		8		.220	.253	.264	49	-10	-13	12					O/12	-0.8
1874	Ath-n	21	81	11	18	2	0	0		2		.222	.241	.247	51	-4	-5	5					O/21	-0.3
1875	Phi-n	69	311	70	85	4	0	0		8		.273	.292	.296	100	1	-1	27					1O2	-0.1
1876	Bos-N	69	308	60	87	4	3	2	34	4	12	.282	.301	.334	109	4	3	32				-3	*1/O2	0.0
1877	Bos-N	35	140	23	39	7	1	1	15	6	7	.279	.308	.364	107	2	1	16				-2	O/1	-0.1
1878	Pro-N	49	188	35	45	6	1	0	14	8	12	.239	.270	.282	82	-3	-3	15				1	*1/O	0.0
1884	Bos-U	76	311	55	73	5	2	0		22		.235	.285	.264	88	-4	-3	24	0			-5	1OM	-0.7
Total	4 n	156	689	163	182	12	1	2		19		.264	.284	.293	82	-10	-15	60	0				/O12	-0.7
Total	4	229	947	173	244	22	7	3	63	44	31	.258	.291	.305	97	-1	-2	87	0			-10	1/O2	-0.8

■ MURPHY
Murphy Deb: 8/16/1884

YEAR	TM/L	G	AB	R	H	2B	3B	HR	RBI	BB	SO	AVG	OBP	SLG	PRO+	BR	/A	RC	SB	CS	SBR	FR	POS	TPR
1884	Bos-U	1	3	0	0	0	0	0		1		.000	.250	.000	-9	-0	-0	0	0			-3	/CO	-0.2

■ CLARENCE MURPHY
Murphy, Clarence Deb: 6/17/1886

YEAR	TM/L	G	AB	R	H	2B	3B	HR	RBI	BB	SO	AVG	OBP	SLG	PRO+	BR	/A	RC	SB	CS	SBR	FR	POS	TPR
1886	Lou-a	1	3	0	0	0	0	0		0		.000	.000	.000	-95	-1	-1	0	0			0	/O	0.0

■ CONNIE MURPHY
Murphy, Cornelius David "Stone Face" b: 11/1/1870, Northfield, Mass. d: 12/14/45, New Bedford, Mass. BL/TR, 5'8", 155 lbs. Deb: 9/17/1893

YEAR	TM/L	G	AB	R	H	2B	3B	HR	RBI	BB	SO	AVG	OBP	SLG	PRO+	BR	/A	RC	SB	CS	SBR	FR	POS	TPR
1893	Cin-N	6	17	3	3	1	0	0	2	1	2	.176	.222	.235	22	-2	-2	1	0			-2	/C	-0.2
1894	Cin-N	1	4	0	0	0	0	0	0	1	1	.000	.200	.000	-46	-1	-1	0	0			-1	/C	-0.1
Total	2	7	21	3	3	1	0	0	2	2	3	.143	.217	.190	7	-3	-3	1	0			-2	/C	-0.3

■ DALE MURPHY
Murphy, Dale Bryan b: 3/12/56, Portland, Ore. BR/TR, 6'4", 210 lbs. Deb: 9/13/76

YEAR	TM/L	G	AB	R	H	2B	3B	HR	RBI	BB	SO	AVG	OBP	SLG	PRO+	BR	/A	RC	SB	CS	SBR	FR	POS	TPR
1976	Atl-N	19	65	3	17	6	0	0	9	7	9	.262	.333	.354	89	-0	-1	8	0	0	0	1	C	0.1
1977	Atl-N	18	76	5	24	8	1	2	14	0	9	.316	.316	.526	108	2	1	11	0	1	-1	-1	C	0.0
1978	Atl-N	151	530	66	120	14	3	23	79	42	145	.226	.287	.394	80	-10	-17	56	11	7	-1	5	*1C	-1.7
1979	Atl-N	104	384	53	106	7	2	21	57	38	67	.276	.344	.469	111	10	6	60	6	1	-1	-7	1C	-0.1
1980	Atl-N	156	569	98	160	27	2	33	89	59	133	.281	.350	.510	133	26	24	101	9	6	-1	-1	*O/1	1.7
1981	Atl-N	104	369	43	91	12	1	13	50	44	72	.247	.327	.390	100	1	0	47	14	5	1	-1	*O/1	-0.2
1982	*Atl-N	162	598	113	168	23	2	36	109	93	134	.281	.380	.507	140	38	35	118	23	11	0	-1	*O	3.3
1983	Atl-N	162	589	131	178	24	4	36	**121**	90	110	.302	.396	**.540**	146	46	41	131	30	4	7	-3	*O	4.3
1984	Atl-N	162	607	94	176	32	8	36	100	79	134	.290	.374	**.547**	145	44	38	123	19	7	2	-5	*O	3.0
1985	Atl-N	162	616	**118**	185	32	2	**37**	111	**90**	141	.300	.390	.539	148	48	43	**131**	10	3	1	-13	*O	2.9
1986	Atl-N	160	614	89	163	29	7	29	83	75	141	.265	.347	.477	118	20	16	102	7	7	-2	-10	*O	0.1
1987	Atl-N	159	566	115	167	27	1	44	105	115	136	.295	.420	.580	154	53	49	**143**	16	6	1	8	*O	5.0
1988	Atl-N	156	592	77	134	35	4	24	77	74	125	.226	.314	.421	104	6	3	72	3	5	-2	11	*O	0.8
1989	Atl-N	154	574	60	131	16	0	20	84	65	142	.228	.309	.361	88	-7	-9	64	3	2	-0	5	*O	-0.5

YEAR	TM/L	G	AB	R	H	2B	3B	HR	RBI	BB	SO	AVG	OBP	SLG	PRO+	BR	/A	RC	SB	CS	SBR	FR	POS	TPR
1990	Atl-N	97	349	38	81	14	0	17	55	41	84	.232	.315	.418	98	-1	-1	45	9	2	2	2	O	0.0
	Phi-N	57	214	22	57	9	1	7	28	20	46	.266	.329	.416	104	1	1	26	0	1	-1	-3	O	-0.4
	Yr	154	563	60	138	23	1	24	83	61	130	.245	.320	.417	100	0	-1	72	9	3	1	-1		-0.4
Total	15	1983	7312	1125	1958	315	38	378	1171	932	1627	.268	.353	.476	122	277	230	1237	160	68	7	-12	*O1/C	18.3

■ DANNY MURPHY
Murphy, Daniel Francis b: 8/11/1876, Philadelphia, Pa. d: 11/22/55, Jersey City, N.J. BR/TR, 5'9", 175 lbs. Deb: 9/17/00 C

YEAR	TM/L	G	AB	R	H	2B	3B	HR	RBI	BB	SO	AVG	OBP	SLG	PRO+	BR	/A	RC	SB	CS	SBR	FR	POS	TPR
1900	NY-N	22	74	11	20	1	0	0	6	8		.270	.341	.284	79	-2	-1	9	4			-6	2	-0.5
1901	NY-N	5	20	0	4	0	0	0	0	1		.200	.238	.200	30	-2	-2	1	0			-3	/2	-0.4
1902	Phi-A	76	291	48	91	11	8	1	48	13		.313	.351	.416	109	5	3	48	12			-12	2	-0.4
1903	Phi-A	133	513	66	140	31	11	1	60	13		.273	.291	.382	98	0	-3	65	17			-13	*2	-1.2
1904	Phi-A	150	557	78	160	30	17	7	77	22		.287	.314	.440	133	22	19	87	22			13	*2	3.6
1905	*Phi-A	151	537	71	149	34	4	6	71	42		.277	.330	.389	128	17	16	81	23			-9	*2	0.7
1906	Phi-A	119	448	48	135	24	7	2	60	21		.301	.333	.400	127	14	13	68	17			-11	*2	0.0
1907	Phi-A	124	469	51	127	23	3	2	57	30		.271	.315	.345	110	6	5	57	11			13	*2	1.9
1908	Phi-A	142	525	51	139	28	7	4	66	32		.265	.307	.368	114	11	7	64	16			10	O2/1	1.3
1909	Phi-A	149	541	61	152	28	14	5	69	35		.281	.332	.412	132	19	18	81	19			-2	*O	1.2
1910	*Phi-A	151	560	70	168	28	18	4	64	31		.300	.338	.436	143	24	24	88	18			-3	*O	1.5
1911	*Phi-A	141	508	104	167	27	11	6	66	50		.329	.398	.461	142	27	28	102	22			6	*O/2	2.2
1912	Phi-A	36	130	27	42	6	2	2	20	16		.323	.401	.446	148	7	8	26	8			-6	O	0.0
1913	Phi-A	40	59	3	19	5	1	0	6	4	8	.322	.365	.441	139	2	3	9	2			-2	/O	0.0
1914	Bro-F	52	161	16	49	9	0	4	32	17	16	.304	.374	.435	132	7	7	30	4			1	O	0.5
1915	Bro-F	5	6	0	1	0	0	0	0	0	0	.167	.167	.167	-1	-1	-1	0	0			-1	/2O	-0.1
Total	16	1496	5399	705	1563	285	103	44	702	335	24	.289	.333	.405	124	157	145	816	193			-24	2O/1	10.3

■ DANNY MURPHY
Murphy, Daniel Francis b: 8/23/42, Beverly, Mass. BL/TR, 5'11", 185 lbs. Deb: 6/18/60

YEAR	TM/L	G	AB	R	H	2B	3B	HR	RBI	BB	SO	AVG	OBP	SLG	PRO+	BR	/A	RC	SB	CS	SBR	FR	POS	TPR
1960	Chi-N	31	75	7	9	2	0	1	6	4	13	.120	.175	.187	-1	-10	-10	2	0	0	0	1	O	-1.0
1961	Chi-N	4	13	3	5	0	0	2	3	1	5	.385	.429	.846	225	2	2	5	0	0	0	0	/O	0.2
1962	Chi-N	14	35	5	7	3	1	0	3	2	9	.200	.243	.343	53	-2	-2	3	0	0	0	-1	/O	-0.3
1969	Chi-A	17	1	0	0	0	0	0	0	2	0	.000	.667	.000	95	0	0	0	0	0	0	-0	P	0.0
1970	Chi-A	51	6	3	2	0	0	1	1	2	2	.333	.500	.833	252	1	1	2	0	0	0	-0	P	0.0
Total	5	117	130	18	23	5	1	4	13	11	29	.177	.246	.323	53	-9	-9	13	0	0	0	-1	/PO	-1.1

■ DANNY MURPHY
Murphy, Daniel Joseph "Handsome Dan" b: 9/10/1864, Brooklyn, N.Y. d: 12/14/15, Brooklyn, N.Y. Deb: 4/26/1892

YEAR	TM/L	G	AB	R	H	2B	3B	HR	RBI	BB	SO	AVG	OBP	SLG	PRO+	BR	/A	RC	SB	CS	SBR	FR	POS	TPR
1892	NY-N	8	26	2	3	0	0	0	0	5	4	.115	.258	.115	15	-2	-2	1	0			-2	/C	-0.3

■ DAVE MURPHY
Murphy, David Francis "Dirty Dave" b: 5/4/1876, Adams, Mass. d: 4/8/40, Adams, Mass. TR, Deb: 8/28/05

YEAR	TM/L	G	AB	R	H	2B	3B	HR	RBI	BB	SO	AVG	OBP	SLG	PRO+	BR	/A	RC	SB	CS	SBR	FR	POS	TPR
1905	Bos-N	3	11	0	2	0	0	0				.182	.182	.182	10	-1	-1	0	0			-2	/S3	-0.2

■ DWAYNE MURPHY
Murphy, Dwayne Keith b: 3/18/55, Merced, Cal. BL/TR, 6'1", 185 lbs. Deb: 4/08/78

YEAR	TM/L	G	AB	R	H	2B	3B	HR	RBI	BB	SO	AVG	OBP	SLG	PRO+	BR	/A	RC	SB	CS	SBR	FR	POS	TPR
1978	Oak-A	60	52	15	10	2	0	0	5	7	14	.192	.288	.231	50	-3	-3	4	0	1	-1	5	O/D	0.0
1979	Oak-A	121	388	57	99	10	4	11	40	84	80	.255	.389	.387	116	9	12	62	15	11	-2	4	*O	0.9
1980	Oak-A	159	573	86	157	18	2	13	68	102	96	.274	.386	.380	119	13	18	90	26	15	-1	19	*O	3.3
1981	*Oak-A	107	390	58	98	10	3	15	60	73	91	.251	.372	.408	131	15	17	64	10	4	1	9	*O/D	2.5
1982	Oak-A	151	543	84	129	15	1	27	94	94	122	.238	.353	.418	116	10	13	88	26	8	3	15	*O/SD	2.6
1983	Oak-A	130	471	55	107	17	2	17	75	62	105	.227	.317	.380	97	-6	-2	55	7	5	-1	5	*O/D	0.1
1984	Oak-A	153	559	93	143	18	2	33	88	74	111	.256	.346	.472	133	18	23	90	4	5	-2	12	*O	2.8
1985	Oak-A	152	523	77	122	21	3	20	59	84	123	.233	.343	.400	111	3	9	73	4	5	-2	0	*O	0.5
1986	Oak-A	98	329	50	83	11	3	9	39	56	80	.252	.368	.386	114	4	8	51	3	1	0	7	O/D	1.2
1987	Oak-A	82	219	39	51	7	0	8	35	58	61	.233	.394	.374	113	4	7	36	4	4	-1	5	O/12	0.8
1988	Det-A	49	144	14	36	5	0	4	19	24	26	.250	.361	.368	109	2	2	21	1	1	-0	5	O/D	0.7
1989	Phi-N	98	156	20	34	5	0	9	27	29	44	.218	.341	.423	117	4	4	24	0	1	-1	-1	O	0.2
Total	12	1360	4347	648	1069	139	20	166	609	747	953	.246	.359	.402	116	72	109	659	100	61	-7	86	*O/D21S	15.6

■ ED MURPHY
Murphy, Edward Joseph b: 8/23/18, Joliet, Ill. BR/TR, 5'11", 190 lbs. Deb: 9/10/42

YEAR	TM/L	G	AB	R	H	2B	3B	HR	RBI	BB	SO	AVG	OBP	SLG	PRO+	BR	/A	RC	SB	CS	SBR	FR	POS	TPR
1942	Phi-N	13	28	2	7	2	0	0	4	2	4	.250	.300	.321	86	-1	-1	3	0			-0	/1	0.0

■ TONY MURPHY
Murphy, Frank J. b: Brooklyn, N.Y. Deb: 10/15/1884

YEAR	TM/L	G	AB	R	H	2B	3B	HR	RBI	BB	SO	AVG	OBP	SLG	PRO+	BR	/A	RC	SB	CS	SBR	FR	POS	TPR
1884	NY-a	1	3	1	1	0	0	0		0		.333	.333	.333	125	0	0	0				-1	/C	0.0

■ FRANK MURPHY
Murphy, Frank Morton b: 1880, Hackensack, N.J. d: 11/2/12, New York, N.Y. Deb: 7/02/01

YEAR	TM/L	G	AB	R	H	2B	3B	HR	RBI	BB	SO	AVG	OBP	SLG	PRO+	BR	/A	RC	SB	CS	SBR	FR	POS	TPR
1901	Bos-N	45	176	13	46	5	3	1	18	4		.261	.282	.341	75	-4	-6	19	6			4	O	-0.6
	NY-N	35	130	10	21	3	0	0	8	6		.162	.199	.185	13	-14	-13	6	2			-10	2O	-2.2
	Yr	80	306	23	67	8	3	1	26	10		.219	.246	.275	51	-18	-20	24	8			-5		-2.8

■ DUMMY MURPHY
Murphy, Herbert Courtland b: 12/18/1886, Olney, Ill. d: 8/10/62, Tallahassee, Fla. BR/TR, 5'10", 165 lbs. Deb: 4/14/14

YEAR	TM/L	G	AB	R	H	2B	3B	HR	RBI	BB	SO	AVG	OBP	SLG	PRO+	BR	/A	RC	SB	CS	SBR	FR	POS	TPR
1914	Phi-N	9	26	1	4	1	0	0	3	0	4	.154	.185	.192	12	-3	-3	1	0			3	/S	0.0

■ HOWARD MURPHY
Murphy, Howard b: 1/1/1882, Birmingham, Ala. d: 10/5/26, Fort Worth, Tex. 5'8.5", 150 lbs. Deb: 8/04/09

YEAR	TM/L	G	AB	R	H	2B	3B	HR	RBI	BB	SO	AVG	OBP	SLG	PRO+	BR	/A	RC	SB	CS	SBR	FR	POS	TPR
1909	StL-N	25	60	3	12	0	0	0	3	4		.200	.250	.200	42	-4	-4	3	1			-2	O	-0.6

■ JERRY MURPHY
Murphy, Jeremiah Francis b: 1871, Pawtucket, R.I. d: 6/1/14, Baker, Oregon Deb: 9/22/03

YEAR	TM/L	G	AB	R	H	2B	3B	HR	RBI	BB	SO	AVG	OBP	SLG	PRO+	BR	/A	RC	SB	CS	SBR	FR	POS	TPR
1903	Det-A	5	22	1	4	1	0	0	1	0		.182	.182	.227	24	-2	-2	1	0			-1	/S	-0.2

■ EDDIE MURPHY
Murphy, John Edward b: 10/2/1891, Hancock, N.Y. d: 2/21/69, Dunmore, Pa. BL/TR, 5'9", 155 lbs. Deb: 8/26/12

YEAR	TM/L	G	AB	R	H	2B	3B	HR	RBI	BB	SO	AVG	OBP	SLG	PRO+	BR	/A	RC	SB	CS	SBR	FR	POS	TPR
1912	Phi-A	33	142	24	45	4	1	0	6	11		.317	.370	.359	113	2	3	21	7			0	O	0.1
1913	*Phi-A	137	508	105	150	14	7	1	30	70	44	.295	.391	.356	122	16	17	76	21			-12	*O	-0.1
1914	*Phi-A	148	573	101	156	12	9	3	43	87	46	.272	.379	.340	121	16	18	77	36	32	-8	-5	*O	-0.4
1915	Phi-A	68	260	37	60	3	4	0	17	29	15	.231	.315	.273	78	-7	-6	25	13	3	2	-5	O/3	-1.2
	Chi-A	70	273	51	86	11	5	0	26	39	12	.315	.410	.392	136	15	14	47	20	12	-1	-1	O	0.9
	Yr	138	533	88	146	14	9	0	43	68	27	.274	.365	.334	109	8	8	71	33	15	1	-6		-0.3
1916	Chi-A	51	105	14	22	5	1	0	4	9	5	.210	.284	.276	68	-4	-4	9	3			-3	O/3	-0.9
1917	Chi-A	53	51	9	16	2	1	0	16	5	1	.314	.386	.392	135	2	2	9	4			-4	/O	-0.1
1918	Chi-A	91	286	36	85	9	3	0	23	22	18	.297	.350	.350	110	4	3	37	6			-10	O/2	-1.0
1919	*Chi-A	30	35	8	17	4	0	0	5	7	0	.486	.571	.600	228	7	7	12	0			0	/O	0.6
1920	Chi-A	58	118	22	40	2	1	0	19	12	4	.339	.405	.373	107	2	2	18	1	3	-2	1	O/3	0.0
1921	Chi-A	6	5	1	1	0	0	0	0	0	0	.200	.200	.200	2	-1	-1	0	0	0	0	0	H	0.0
1926	Pit-N	16	17	3	2	0	0	0	6	3	0	.118	.250	.118	2	-2	-2	1	0			0	/O	-0.2
Total	11	761	2373	411	680	66	32	4	195	294	145	.287	.374	.346	114	49	52	331	111	50		-38	O/32	-2.3

■ JOHN MURPHY
Murphy, John Patrick b: 1879, New Haven, Conn. d: 4/20/49, Andover, Mass. Deb: 9/10/02

YEAR	TM/L	G	AB	R	H	2B	3B	HR	RBI	BB	SO	AVG	OBP	SLG	PRO+	BR	/A	RC	SB	CS	SBR	FR	POS	TPR
1902	StL-N	1	3	1	2	1	0	0	1	1		.667	.750	1.000	463	1	1	2	0			-1	/3	0.1

■ LARRY MURPHY
Murphy, Lawrence Patrick BL, Deb: 5/30/1891

YEAR	TM/L	G	AB	R	H	2B	3B	HR	RBI	BB	SO	AVG	OBP	SLG	PRO+	BR	/A	RC	SB	CS	SBR	FR	POS	TPR
1891	Was-a	101	400	73	106	15	3	1	35	63	27	.265	.372	.325	108	4	7	61	29			-5	*O	-0.1

YEAR	TM/L	G	AB	R	H	2B	3B	HR	RBI	BB	SO	AVG	OBP	SLG	PRO+	BR	/A	RC	SB	CS	SBR	FR	POS	TPR

■ LEO MURPHY Murphy, Leo Joseph "Red" b: 1/7/1889, Terre Haute, Ind. d: 8/12/60, Racine, Wis. BR/TR, 6'1", 179 lbs. Deb: 5/02/15

1915	Pit-N	31	41	4	4	0	0	0	4	4	12	.098	.178	.098	-16	-6	-6	1	0			-3	C	-0.8

■ MIKE MURPHY Murphy, Michael Jerome b: 8/19/1888, Forestville, Pa. d: 10/26/52, Johnson City, N.Y. BR/TR, 5'9", 170 lbs. Deb: 5/17/12

1912	StL-N	1	1	0	0	0	0	0	1	0	0	.000	.000	.000	-99	-0	-0	0	0			0	/C	0.0
1916	Phi-A	14	27	0	3	0	0	0	1	1	3	.111	.143	.111	-25	-4	-4	1	0			-3	C	-0.7
Total	2	15	28	0	3	0	0	0	2	1	3	.107	.138	.107	-28	-4	-4	1	0			-3	/C	-0.7

■ MORGAN MURPHY Murphy, Morgan Edward b: 2/14/1867, E.Providence, R.I. d: 10/3/38, Providence, R.I. BR/TR, 5'8", 160 lbs. Deb: 4/22/1890

1890	Bos-P	68	246	38	56	10	2	2	32	24	31	.228	.301	.309	61	-12	-15	28	16			2	C/SO3	-0.7
1891	Bos-a	106	402	60	87	11	4	4	54	36	58	.216	.289	.294	70	-16	-15	40	17			7	*C/O	-0.3
1892	Cin-N	74	234	29	46	8	2	2	24	25	57	.197	.277	.274	69	-9	-8	19	4			-1	C	-0.4
1893	Cin-N	57	200	25	47	5	1	1	19	14	35	.235	.295	.285	55	-13	-13	18	1			-6	C/1	-1.1
1894	Cin-N	75	255	42	70	9	0	1	37	26	34	.275	.344	.322	60	-15	-17	31	6			-6	C/S3	-1.1
1895	Cin-N	25	82	15	22	2	0	0	16	11	8	.268	.355	.293	67	-3	-4	11	6			-4	C	-0.4
1896	StL-N	49	175	12	45	5	2	0	11	8	14	.257	.290	.309	62	-10	-9	16	1			-2	C	-0.5
1897	StL-N	62	207	13	35	2	0	0	12	6		.169	.196	.179	1	-29	-28	8	1			-4	C/1	-2.1
1898	Pit-N	5	16	0	2	0	0	0	2	1		.125	.176	.125	-12	-2	-2	0	0			1	/C	0.0
	Phi-N	25	86	6	17	3	0	0	11	6		.198	.258	.233	45	-6	-6	5	0			0	C	-0.3
	Yr	30	102	6	19	3	0	0	13	7		.186	.245	.216	36	-8	-8	6	0			1		-0.3
1900	Phi-N	11	36	2	10	0	1	0	3	0		.278	.278	.333	71	-2	-1	3	0			2	C	0.1
1901	Phi-A	9	28	5	6	1	0	0	6	0		.214	.214	.250	28	-3	-3	2	1			1	/C1	-0.1
Total	11	566	1967	247	443	56	12	10	227	157	237	.225	.287	.281	55	-120	-122	182	53			-11	C/10S3	-6.9

■ PAT MURPHY Murphy, Patrick J. b: 1/2/1857, Auburn, Mass. d: 5/16/27, Worcester, Mass. 5'10", 160 lbs. Deb: 9/02/1887

1887	NY-N	17	56	4	12	1	0	0	4	2	4	.214	.241	.250	40	-5	-4	4	1			1	C	0.0
1888	*NY-N	28	106	11	18	1	0	0	4	6	11	.170	.214	.179	28	-8	-8	5	3			4	C	-0.2
1889	NY-N	9	28	5	10	1	1	1	4	2	0	.357	.400	.571	171	2	2	7	0			-3	/C	0.2
1890	NY-N	32	119	14	28	5	1	0	9	14	13	.235	.321	.294	81	-2	-2	12	3			-3	C/OS	-0.3
Total	4	86	309	34	68	9	2	1	21	24	28	.220	.278	.272	66	-13	-12	28	7			-1	/COS	-0.5

■ DICK MURPHY Murphy, Richard Lee b: 10/25/31, Cincinnati, Ohio BL/TL, 5'11", 170 lbs. Deb: 6/13/54

1954	Cin-N	6	1	1	0	0	0	0	0	0	1	.000	.000	.000	-97	-0	-0	0	0	0	0	0	H	0.0

■ BUZZ MURPHY Murphy, Robert R. b: 4/26/1895, Denver, Colo. d: 5/11/38, Denver, Colo. BL/TL, 5'8.5", 155 lbs. Deb: 7/14/18

1918	Bos-N	9	32	6	12	2	3	1	9	3	5	.375	.429	.719	259	5	5	10	0			-2	/O	0.3
1919	Was-A	79	252	19	66	7	4	0	28	19	32	.262	.326	.321	83	-6	-5	28	5			5	O	-0.8
Total	2	88	284	25	78	9	7	1	37	22	37	.275	.338	.366	101	-0	-0	38	5			0	O	-0.5

■ BILLY MURPHY Murphy, William Eugene b: 5/7/44, Pineville, La. BR/TR, 6'1", 190 lbs. Deb: 4/15/66

1966	NY-N	84	135	15	31	4	1	3	13	7	34	.230	.273	.341	71	-6	-5	12	1	2	-1	3	O	-0.4

■ YALE MURPHY Murphy, William Henry "Tot" or "Midget" b: 11/11/1869, Southville, Mass. d: 2/14/06, Southville, Mass. BL/TR, 5'3", 125 lbs. Deb: 4/19/1894

1894	*NY-N	74	280	64	76	6	2	0	28	51	23	.271	.384	.307	70	-11	-11	45	28			-11	SO/321	-1.5
1895	NY-N	51	184	35	37	6	2	0	16	27	13	.201	.303	.255	48	-14	-13	17	7			-4	O/S32	-1.5
1897	NY-N	5	8	1	0	0	0	0	1	2		.000	.000	.000	-45	-2	-2	0	0			-2	/S2	-0.2
Total	3	130	472	100	113	12	4	0	45	80	36	.239	.350	.282	60	-27	-25	62	35			-17	/SO321	-3.2

■ WILLIE MURPHY Murphy, William N. "Gentle Willie" b: 1865, Boston, Mass. BL, 5'11", 198 lbs. Deb: 5/01/1884

1884	Cle-N	42	168	18	38	3	3	0	9	1	23	.226	.231	.298	63	-7	-8	12				-6	O	-1.2
	Was-a	5	21	3	10	0	0	0		0	1	.476	.542	.476	271	3	4	6				-0	/O2	0.3

■ TONY MURRAY Murray, Anthony Joseph b: 4/30/04, Chicago, Ill. d: 3/19/74, Chicago, Ill. BR/TR, 5'10.5", 154 lbs. Deb: 10/06/23

1923	Chi-N	2	4	0	1	0	0	0	0	0	0	.250	.400	.250	75	-0	-0	0	0	0	0	-0	/O	0.0

■ EDDIE MURRAY Murray, Eddie Clarence b: 2/24/56, Los Angeles, Cal. BB/TR, 6'2", 190 lbs. Deb: 4/07/77

1977	Bal-A	160	611	81	173	29	2	27	88	48	104	.283	.336	.470	125	13	18	90	0	1	-1	-5	*D1/O	1.0
1978	Bal-A	161	610	85	174	32	3	27	95	70	97	.285	.360	.480	143	27	32	104	6	5	-1	1	*1/3D	2.6
1979	*Bal-A	159	606	90	179	30	2	25	99	72	78	.295	.372	.475	132	23	26	107	10	2	2	-1	*1	1.8
1980	Bal-A	158	621	100	186	36	2	32	116	54	71	.300	.357	.519	138	30	30	111	7	2	1	-9	*1/D	1.2
1981	Bal-A	99	378	57	111	21	2	22	78	40	43	.294	.363	.534	156	26	26	70	2	3	-1	10	1	3.3
1982	Bal-A	151	550	87	174	30	1	32	110	70	82	.316	.395	.549	157	42	43	116	7	2	1	1	*1/D	4.0
1983	*Bal-A	156	582	115	178	30	3	33	111	86	90	.306	.398	.538	**158**	45	**46**	**133**	5	1	1	3	*1/D	4.3
1984	Bal-A	162	588	97	180	26	3	29	110	**107**	87	.306	**.415**	.509	157	**47**	**49**	130	10	2	2	8	*1/D	4.8
1985	Bal-A	156	583	111	173	37	1	31	124	84	68	.297	.387	.523	151	38	41	122	5	2	0	13	*1/D	4.2
1986	Bal-A	137	495	61	151	25	1	17	84	78	49	.305	.400	.463	136	26	27	92	3	0	1	-3	*1D	1.7
1987	Bal-A	160	618	89	171	28	3	30	91	73	80	.277	.353	.477	121	15	18	103	1	2	-1	12	*1/D	1.3
1988	Bal-A	161	603	75	171	27	2	28	84	75	78	.284	.363	.474	136	26	28	101	5	2	0	10	*1/D	3.3
1989	LA-N	160	594	66	147	29	1	20	88	87	85	.247	.346	.401	115	11	12	85	7	2	1	13	*1/3	1.5
1990	LA-N	155	558	96	184	22	3	26	95	82	64	.330	.417	.520	165	45	49	118	8	5	-1	4	*1	4.5
Total	14	2135	7997	1210	2352	402	29	379	1373	1026	1076	.294	.376	.494	141	414	445	1481	76	31	4	58	*1D/3O	39.5

■ ED MURRAY Murray, Edward Francis b: 5/8/1895, Mystic, Conn. d: 11/8/70, Cheyenne, Wyoming BR/TR, 5'6", 145 lbs. Deb: 6/24/17

1917	StL-A	1	1	0	0	0	0	0	0	0	1	.000	.000	.000	-99	-0	-0	0	0			0	/S	0.0

■ JIM MURRAY Murray, James Oscar b: 1/16/1878, Galveston, Tex. d: 4/25/45, Galveston, Tex. BR/TL, 5'10", 180 lbs. Deb: 9/02/02

1902	Chi-N	12	47	3	8	0	0	0	1	2		.170	.204	.170	17	-4	-4	2	0			-1	O	-0.5
1911	StL-A	31	102	8	19	5	0	3	11	5		.186	.224	.324	54	-7	-7	7	0			0	O	-0.8
1914	Bos-N	39	112	10	26	4	2	0	12	6	24	.232	.277	.304	73	-4	-4	10	2			-7	O	-1.2
Total	3	82	261	21	53	9	2	3	24	13	24	.203	.244	.287	56	-16	-15	18	2			-7	/O	-2.5

■ MIAH MURRAY Murray, Jeremiah J. b: 1/1/1865, Boston, Mass. d: 1/11/22, Boston, Mass. BR/TR, 5'11.5", 170 lbs. Deb: 5/17/1884 U

1884	Pro-N	8	27	1	5	0	0	0	1	1	8	.185	.214	.185	27	-2	-2	1				-3	/CO1	-0.3
1885	Lou-a	12	43	4	8	0	0	0		2		.186	.239	.186	38	-3	-3	2				1	C/1	0.1
1888	Was-N	12	42	1	4	1	0	0	3	1		.095	.116	.119	-25	-6	-5	1	0			-2	C/1	-0.6
1891	Was-a	2	8	0	0	0	0	0	0	1		.000	.000	.000	-99	-2	-2	0	0			3	/C	0.1
Total	4	34	120	6	17	1	0	0	4	4	16	.142	.176	.150	4	-13	-12	4	0			-1	/C10	-0.8

■ RED MURRAY Murray, John Joseph b: 3/4/1884, Arnot, Pa. d: 12/4/58, Sayre, Pa. BR/TR, 5'10.5", 190 lbs. Deb: 6/16/06

1906	StL-N	46	144	18	37	9	7	1	16	9		.257	.301	.438	138	4	5	21	5			-2	O/C	0.3
1907	StL-N	132	485	46	127	10	10	7	46	24		.262	.297	.367	114	3	5	62	23			5	*O	0.6
1908	StL-N	154	593	64	167	19	15	7	62	37		.282	.324	.400	140	20	23	89	48			-4	*O	2.0
1909	NY-N	149	570	74	150	15	12	7	91	45		.263	.319	.368	112	7	6	81	48			2	*O	0.4
1910	NY-N	149	553	99	153	27	8	4	87	52	51	.277	.345	.376	110	7	7	91	57			1	*O	1.0
1911	*NY-N	140	488	70	142	27	15	3	78	43	37	.291	.354	.426	114	10	8	89	48			-11	*O	-0.6
1912	*NY-N	143	549	83	152	26	20	3	92	27	45	.277	.320	.413	97	-3	-5	83	38			-3	*O	-1.1

YEAR	TM/L	G	AB	R	H	2B	3B	HR	RBI	BB	SO	AVG	OBP	SLG	PRO+	BR	/A	RC	SB	CS	SBR	FR	POS	TPR
1913	*NY-N	147	520	70	139	21	3	2	59	34	28	.267	.320	.331	85	-10	-10	63	35			2	*O	-1.0
1914	NY-N	86	139	19	31	6	3	0	23	9	7	.223	.270	.309	75	-5	-5	14	11			-2	O	-0.7
1915	NY-N	45	127	12	28	1	2	3	11	7	15	.220	.261	.331	83	-4	-3	10	2	3	-1	2	O	-0.3
	Chi-N	51	144	20	43	6	1	0	11	8	8	.299	.340	.354	110	2	2	18	6	5	-1	3	O/2	0.3
	Yr	96	271	32	71	7	3	3	22	15	23	.262	.303	.343	98	-2	-1	28	8	8	-2	5		0.0
1917	NY-N	22	22	1	1	1	0	0	3	4	3	.045	.192	.091	-12	-3	-3	0	0			0	O/C	-0.2
Total	11	1264	4334	555	1170	168	96	37	579	299	194	.270	.321	.379	108	29	30	623	321	8		-6	*O/C2	-0.1

■ LARRY MURRAY
Murray, Larry   b: 4/1/53, Chicago, Ill.   BB/TR, 5'11", 179 lbs.   Deb: 9/07/74

YEAR	TM/L	G	AB	R	H	2B	3B	HR	RBI	BB	SO	AVG	OBP	SLG	PRO+	BR	/A	RC	SB	CS	SBR	FR	POS	TPR
1974	NY-A	6	1	1	0	0	0	0	0	0	0	.000	.000	.000	-99	-0	-0	0	0	1	-1	0	/O	0.0
1975	NY-A	6	1	1	0	0	0	0	0	0	0	.000	.000	.000	-99	-0	-0	0	0	0	0	0	/O	0.0
1976	NY-A	8	10	2	1	0	0	0	2	1	2	.100	.182	.100	-16	-1	-1	0	2	0	1	1	/O	0.0
1977	Oak-A	90	162	19	29	5	2	1	9	17	36	.179	.257	.253	40	-13	-13	12	12	3	2	4	O/SD	-0.9
1978	Oak-A	11	12	1	1	0	0	0	0	3	2	.083	.267	.083	3	-1	-1	0	0	0	0	-0	/O	-0.1
1979	Oak-A	105	226	25	42	11	2	2	20	28	34	.186	.276	.279	53	-16	-14	18	6	6	-2	8	O/2	-1.1
Total	6	226	412	49	73	16	4	3	31	49	74	.177	.265	.257	44	-33	-31	31	20	10	0	13	O/2DS	-2.1

■ RAY MURRAY
Murray, Raymond Lee "Deacon"   b: 10/12/17, Spring Hope, N.C.   BR/TR, 6'3", 204 lbs.   Deb: 4/25/48

YEAR	TM/L	G	AB	R	H	2B	3B	HR	RBI	BB	SO	AVG	OBP	SLG	PRO+	BR	/A	RC	SB	CS	SBR	FR	POS	TPR
1948	Cle-A	4	4	0	0	0	0	0	0	0	3	.000	.000	.000	-99	-1	-1	0	0	0	0	0	H	0.0
1950	Cle-A	55	139	16	38	8	2	1	13	12	13	.273	.331	.381	85	-4	-3	16	1	0	0	-5	C	-0.5
1951	Cle-A	1	1	0	1	0	0	0	0	1	0	1.000	1.000	1.000	468	0	0	1	0	0	0	1	/C	0.1
	Phi-A	40	122	10	26	6	0	0	13	14	8	.213	.294	.262	50	-8	-9	10	0	0	0	-2	C	-0.7
	Yr	41	123	10	27	6	0	0	14	14	8	.220	.299	.268	53	-8	-8	10	0	0	0	-1		-0.6
1952	Phi-A	44	136	14	28	5	0	1	10	9	13	.206	.255	.265	42	-10	-11	9	0	0	0	8	C	0.0
1953	Phi-A	84	268	25	76	14	3	6	41	18	25	.284	.331	.425	99	0	-1	38	0	0	0	4	C	0.6
1954	Bal-A	22	61	4	15	4	1	0	2	2	5	.246	.270	.344	73	-3	-2	6	0	0	0	1	C	0.0
Total	6	250	731	69	184	37	6	8	80	55	67	.252	.305	.352	75	-26	-27	79	1	0	0	7	C	-0.5

■ RICH MURRAY
Murray, Richard Dale   b: 7/6/57, Los Angeles, Cal.   BR/TR, 6'4", 195 lbs.   Deb: 6/07/80

YEAR	TM/L	G	AB	R	H	2B	3B	HR	RBI	BB	SO	AVG	OBP	SLG	PRO+	BR	/A	RC	SB	CS	SBR	FR	POS	TPR
1980	SF-N	53	194	19	42	8	2	4	24	11	48	.216	.259	.340	67	-9	-9	15	2	1	0	0	1	-1.1
1983	SF-N	4	10	0	2	0	0	0	1	0	3	.200	.200	.200	11	-1	-1	0	0	0	0	-0	/1	-0.1
Total	2	57	204	19	44	8	2	4	25	11	51	.216	.256	.333	65	-11	-10	15	2	1	0	0	/1	-1.2

■ BOBBY MURRAY
Murray, Robert Hayes   b: 7/4/1894, St.Albans, Vt.   d: 1/4/79, Nashua, N.H.   TR, 5'7", 155 lbs.   Deb: 9/24/23

YEAR	TM/L	G	AB	R	H	2B	3B	HR	RBI	BB	SO	AVG	OBP	SLG	PRO+	BR	/A	RC	SB	CS	SBR	FR	POS	TPR
1923	Was-A	10	37	2	7	1	0	0	2	1	4	.189	.211	.216	13	-5	-4	2	1	0	0	2	3	0.0

■ TOM MURRAY
Murray, Thomas W.   b: 1866, Savannah, Ga.   Deb: 6/20/1894

YEAR	TM/L	G	AB	R	H	2B	3B	HR	RBI	BB	SO	AVG	OBP	SLG	PRO+	BR	/A	RC	SB	CS	SBR	FR	POS	TPR
1894	Phi-N	1	2	0	0	0	0	0	0	0	2	.000	.000	.000	-99	-1	-1	0	0			0	/S	0.0

■ BILL MURRAY
Murray, William Allenwood "Dasher"   b: 9/6/1893, Vinalhaven, Me.   d: 9/14/43, Boston, Mass.   BB/TR, 5'11", 165 lbs.   Deb: 6/27/17

YEAR	TM/L	G	AB	R	H	2B	3B	HR	RBI	BB	SO	AVG	OBP	SLG	PRO+	BR	/A	RC	SB	CS	SBR	FR	POS	TPR
1917	Was-A	8	21	2	3	0	1	0	4	2	2	.143	.217	.238	39	-2	-2	1	1			-2	/2S	-0.2

■ IVAN MURRELL
Murrell, Ivan Augustus (Peters)   b: 4/24/45, Almirante, Panama   BR/TR, 6'2", 195 lbs.   Deb: 9/28/63

YEAR	TM/L	G	AB	R	H	2B	3B	HR	RBI	BB	SO	AVG	OBP	SLG	PRO+	BR	/A	RC	SB	CS	SBR	FR	POS	TPR
1963	Hou-N	2	5	1	1	0	0	0	0	0	2	.200	.200	.200	17	-1	-1	0	0	0	0	0	/O	0.0
1964	Hou-N	10	14	1	2	1	0	0	1	0	6	.143	.143	.214	-1	-2	-2	0	0	0	0	-1	/O	-0.2
1967	Hou-N	10	29	2	9	0	0	0	1	1	9	.310	.333	.310	88	-1	-0	3	1	0	0	-1	/O	0.0
1968	Hou-N	32	59	3	6	1	1	0	3	1	17	.102	.117	.153	-20	-9	-8	1	0	0	0	3	O	-0.7
1969	SD-N	111	247	19	63	10	6	3	25	11	65	.255	.292	.381	91	-5	-4	26	3	4	-2	-0	O/1	-0.9
1970	SD-N	125	347	43	85	9	3	12	35	17	93	.245	.288	.392	84	-11	-9	36	9	7	-2	1	*O/1	-1.4
1971	SD-N	103	255	23	60	6	3	7	24	7	60	.235	.264	.365	82	-9	-7	22	5	2	0	1	O	-0.8
1972	SD-N	5	7	0	1	0	0	0	0	0	3	.143	.143	.143	-20	-1	-1	0	0	0	0	0	/O	0.0
1973	SD-N	93	210	23	48	13	1	9	21	2	52	.229	.236	.429	87	-7	-5	20	2	0	1	3	O1	-0.3
1974	Atl-N	73	133	11	33	1	1	2	12	5	35	.248	.275	.316	62	-7	-7	11	0	0	0	5	O1	-0.3
Total	10	564	1306	126	308	41	15	33	123	44	342	.236	.266	.366	77	-51	-44	120	20	13	-2	11	O/1	-4.6

■ DANNY MURTAUGH
Murtaugh, Daniel Edward   b: 10/8/17, Chester, Pa.   d: 12/2/76, Chester, Pa.   BR/TR, 5'9", 165 lbs.   Deb: 7/06/41   MC

YEAR	TM/L	G	AB	R	H	2B	3B	HR	RBI	BB	SO	AVG	OBP	SLG	PRO+	BR	/A	RC	SB	CS	SBR	FR	POS	TPR
1941	Phi-N	85	347	34	76	8	1	0	11	26	31	.219	.275	.248	50	-24	-22	25	**18**			2	2/S	-1.4
1942	Phi-N	144	506	48	122	16	4	0	27	49	39	.241	.311	.289	80	-15	-12	47	13			6	S32	0.1
1943	Phi-N	113	451	65	123	17	4	1	35	57	23	.273	.357	.335	104	2	4	57	4			0	*2	0.8
1946	Bos-N	6	19	1	4	1	0	1	3	2	2	.211	.286	.421	102	-0	-0	2	0			-3	/2	-0.3
1947	Bos-N	3	8	0	1	0	0	0	0	1	2	.125	.222	.125	-6	-1	-1	0	0			0	/23	0.0
1948	Pit-N	146	514	56	149	21	5	1	71	60	40	.290	.365	.356	94	-1	-2	70	10			1	*2	0.9
1949	Pit-N	75	236	16	48	7	2	2	24	29	17	.203	.291	.275	51	-16	-16	21	2			3	2	-1.0
1950	Pit-N	118	367	34	108	20	5	2	37	47	42	.294	.376	.392	99	3	1	56	2			3	*2	0.7
1951	Pit-N	77	151	9	30	7	0	1	11	16	19	.199	.284	.265	47	-11	-11	11	0	0	0	-2	2/3	-1.1
Total	9	767	2599	263	661	97	21	8	219	287	215	.254	.331	.317	81	-62	-60	290	49	0		10	2/S3	-1.3

■ TONY MUSER
Muser, Anthony Joseph   b: 8/1/47, Van Nuys, Cal.   BL/TL, 6'2", 180 lbs.   Deb: 9/14/69   C

YEAR	TM/L	G	AB	R	H	2B	3B	HR	RBI	BB	SO	AVG	OBP	SLG	PRO+	BR	/A	RC	SB	CS	SBR	FR	POS	TPR
1969	Bos-A	2	9	0	1	0	0	0	1	1	1	.111	.200	.111	-10	-1	-1	0	0	0	0	1	/1	0.0
1971	Chi-A	11	16	2	5	0	1	0	0	1	1	.313	.353	.438	119	0	0	2	0	0	0	0	/1	0.1
1972	Chi-A	44	61	6	17	2	2	1	9	2	6	.279	.302	.426	113	1	1	7	1	1	-0	0	1/O	-0.2
1973	Chi-A	109	309	38	88	14	3	4	30	33	36	.285	.354	.388	105	4	3	43	8	4	0	-2	1D/O	-0.4
1974	Chi-A	103	206	16	60	5	1	1	18	6	22	.291	.315	.340	86	-3	-4	20	1	4	-2	-4	1D	-1.3
1975	Chi-A	43	111	11	27	3	0	0	6	7	8	.243	.288	.270	58	-6	-6	12	8	1	0	2	1	-0.6
	Bal-A	80	82	11	26	3	0	0	11	8	9	.317	.378	.354	115	1	2	11	0	0	0	1	1	0.0
	Yr	123	193	22	53	6	0	0	17	15	17	.275	.327	.306	83	-5	-4	18	2	1	0	3		-0.6
1976	Bal-A	136	326	25	74	7	1	1	30	21	34	.227	.274	.264	62	-17	-15	23	1	1	-0	5	*1OD	-1.7
1977	Bal-A	120	118	14	27	6	0	0	7	13	16	.229	.305	.280	65	-6	-5	9	1	2	-1	4	1O/D	-0.6
1978	Mil-A	15	30	0	4	1	1	0	5	3	5	.133	.212	.233	25	-3	-3	1	0	0	0	0	1	-0.3
Total	9	663	1268	123	329	41	9	7	117	95	138	.259	.312	.323	82	-31	-29	124	14	13	-4	6	1/DO	-5.0

■ STAN MUSIAL
Musial, Stanley Frank "Stan The Man"   b: 11/21/20, Donora, Pa.   BL/TL, 6', 175 lbs.   Deb: 9/17/41   H

YEAR	TM/L	G	AB	R	H	2B	3B	HR	RBI	BB	SO	AVG	OBP	SLG	PRO+	BR	/A	RC	SB	CS	SBR	FR	POS	TPR
1941	StL-N	12	47	8	20	4	0	1	7	2	1	.426	.449	.574	175	5	5	12	1			-0	O	0.4
1942	*StL-N	140	467	87	147	32	10	10	72	62	25	.315	.397	.490	148	35	31	96	6			4	*O	3.3
1943	*StL-N	157	617	108	220	48	20	13	81	72	18	.357	.425	.562	176	66	62	147	9			12	*O	7.1
1944	*StL-N	146	568	112	197	51	14	12	94	90	28	.347	.440	.549	174	61	60	145	7			12	*O	6.0
1946	*StL-N	156	624	124	228	50	20	16	103	73	31	.365	.434	.587	180	71	68	164	7			-4	*1O	5.5
1947	StL-N	149	587	113	183	30	13	19	95	80	24	.312	.398	.504	132	33	29	118	4			-7	*1	1.3
1948	StL-N	155	611	135	230	46	18	39	131	79	34	.376	.450	.702	196	90	86	191	7			5	*O/1	7.7
1949	StL-N	157	612	128	207	41	13	36	123	107	38	.338	.438	.624	174	72	68	173	3			-4	*O/1	5.4
1950	StL-N	146	555	105	192	41	7	28	109	87	36	.346	.437	.596	161	57	54	149	5			-13	O1	3.4
1951	StL-N	152	578	124	205	30	12	32	108	98	40	.355	.449	.614	182	70	70	169	4	5	-2	6	O1	6.8
1952	StL-N	154	578	105	194	42	6	21	91	96	29	.336	.432	.538	167	56	56	141	7	7	-2	-9	O1/P	4.2
1953	StL-N	157	593	127	200	53	9	30	113	105	32	.337	.437	.609	169	63	63	166	3	4	-2	-3	*O	4.9
1954	StL-N	153	591	120	195	41	9	35	126	103	39	.330	.433	.607	166	61	60	153	1	7	-4	-3	*O1	4.6

YEAR	TM/L	G	AB	R	H	2B	3B	HR	RBI	BB	SO	AVG	OBP	SLG	PRO+	BR	/A	RC	SB	CS	SBR	FR	POS	TPR
1955	StL-N	154	562	97	179	30	5	33	108	80	39	.319	.411	.566	156	46	47	131	5	4	-1	5	*1O	4.1
1956	StL-N	156	594	87	184	33	6	27	109	75	39	.310	.390	.522	142	36	36	119	2	0	1	2	*1O	3.2
1957	StL-N	134	502	82	176	38	3	29	102	66	34	.351	.428	.612	172	54	53	129	1	1	-0	2	*1	4.3
1958	StL-N	135	472	64	159	35	2	17	62	72	26	.337	.426	.528	145	37	34	102	0	0	0	8	*1	3.4
1959	StL-N	115	341	37	87	13	2	14	44	60	25	.255	.367	.428	104	7	4	53	0	2	-1	3	1/O	-0.1
1960	StL-N	116	331	49	91	17	1	17	63	41	34	.275	.358	.486	118	13	9	59	1	1	-0	-6	O1	0.0
1961	StL-N	123	372	46	107	22	4	15	70	52	35	.288	.374	.489	116	15	10	69	0	0	0	-5	*O	0.0
1962	StL-N	135	433	57	143	18	1	19	82	64	46	.330	.420	.508	135	31	26	94	3	0	1	-10	*O	1.0
1963	StL-N	124	337	34	86	10	2	12	58	35	43	.255	.329	.404	100	4	1	47	2	0	1	-11	O	-1.6
Total	22	3026	10972	1949	3630	725	177	475	1951	1599	696	.331	.418	.559	157	983	930	2625	78	31		-15	*O1/P	74.9

■ DANNY MUSSER
Musser, William Daniel b: 9/5/05, Zion, Pa. BL/TR, 5'9.5", 160 lbs. Deb: 9/18/32

YEAR	TM/L	G	AB	R	H	2B	3B	HR	RBI	BB	SO	AVG	OBP	SLG	PRO+	BR	/A	RC	SB	CS	SBR	FR	POS	TPR
1932	Was-A	1	2	0	1	0	0	0	0	0	0	.500	.500	.500	162	0	0	0	0	0	0	0	/3	0.0

■ GEORGE MYATT
Myatt, George Edward "Mercury", "Stud" or "Foghorn" b: 6/14/14, Denver, Colo. BL/TR, 5'11", 167 lbs. Deb: 8/16/38 MC

YEAR	TM/L	G	AB	R	H	2B	3B	HR	RBI	BB	SO	AVG	OBP	SLG	PRO+	BR	/A	RC	SB	CS	SBR	FR	POS	TPR
1938	NY-N	43	170	27	52	2	1	3	10	14	13	.306	.362	.382	104	1	1	24	10			7	S3	1.0
1939	NY-N	22	53	7	10	2	0	0	3	6	6	.189	.271	.226	35	-5	-5	4	2			1	3	-0.3
1943	Was-A	42	53	11	13	3	0	0	3	13	7	.245	.394	.302	109	1	1	9	3	0	1	-1	2/S3	0.2
1944	Was-A	140	538	86	153	19	6	0	40	54	44	.284	.357	.342	105	2	5	72	26	10	2	-22	*2S/O	-1.0
1945	Was-A	133	490	81	145	17	7	1	39	63	43	.296	.378	.365	127	12	17	77	30	11	2	-19	2O/3S	0.0
1946	Was-A	15	34	7	8	1	0	0	4	2	3	.235	.297	.265	61	-2	-2	3	1	1	-0	-2	/32	-0.2
1947	Was-A	12	7	1	0	0	0	0	0	4	4	.000	.364	.000	6	-1	-1	0	0	0	0	0	/2	0.0
Total	7	407	1345	220	381	44	14	4	99	156	120	.283	.362	.346	108	9	17	188	72	22		-35	2/3SO	-0.3

■ GLENN MYATT
Myatt, Glenn Calvin b: 7/9/1897, Argenta, Ark. d: 8/9/69, Houston, Tex. BL/TR, 5'11", 165 lbs. Deb: 4/15/20

YEAR	TM/L	G	AB	R	H	2B	3B	HR	RBI	BB	SO	AVG	OBP	SLG	PRO+	BR	/A	RC	SB	CS	SBR	FR	POS	TPR
1920	Phi-A	70	196	14	49	8	3	0	18	12	22	.250	.293	.321	62	-11	-11	18	1	3	-2	-5	OC	-1.8
1921	Phi-A	44	69	6	14	2	0	0	5	6	7	.203	.267	.232	28	-7	-8	5	0	0		2	C	-0.3
1923	Cle-A	92	220	36	63	7	6	3	40	16	18	.286	.338	.414	97	-2	-2	30	0	2	-1	-8	C	-0.5
1924	Cle-A	105	342	55	117	22	7	8	73	33	12	.342	.402	.518	134	17	17	72	6	1	1	-15	C	0.8
1925	Cle-A	106	358	51	97	15	9	11	54	29	24	.271	.329	.455	97	-4	-4	54	2	1	0	-19	C/O	-1.5
1926	Cle-A	56	117	14	29	5	2	0	13	13	13	.248	.323	.325	69	-5	-5	13	1	0	0	-1	C	-0.3
1927	Cle-A	55	94	15	23	6	0	2	8	12	7	.245	.336	.372	83	-2	-2	12	1	1	-0	2	C	0.0
1928	Cle-A	58	125	9	36	7	2	1	15	13	9	.288	.355	.400	97	-0	-0	17	0	2	-1	-9	C	-0.7
1929	Cle-A	59	129	14	30	4	1	1	17	7	5	.233	.277	.302	47	-10	-11	11	0	1	-1	-1	C	-0.7
1930	Cle-A	86	265	30	78	23	2	2	37	18	17	.294	.342	.419	88	-4	-5	37	2	3	-1	-6	C	-0.5
1931	Cle-A	65	195	21	48	14	2	1	29	21	13	.246	.331	.354	73	-7	-8	23	2	1	0	-4	C	-0.7
1932	Cle-A	82	252	45	62	12	1	8	46	27	21	.246	.326	.397	81	-5	-8	34	2	2	-1	-8	C	-1.1
1933	Cle-A	40	77	10	18	4	0	0	7	15	8	.234	.372	.286	73	-2	-2	9	0	1	-1	-1	C	-0.1
1934	Cle-A	36	107	18	34	6	1	0	12	13	5	.318	.392	.393	101	1	1	17	1	0	0	-1	C	0.3
1935	Cle-A	10	36	1	3	1	0	0	2	4	3	.083	.175	.111	-24	-7	-7	1	0	0		-1	C	-0.6
	NY-N	13	18	2	4	0	1	1	6	0	3	.222	.222	.500	90	-0	-0	2	0			-1	/C	0.0
1936	Det-A	27	78	5	17	1	0	0	5	9	4	.218	.299	.231	32	-8	-8	6	0	0	0	-2	C	-0.6
Total	16	1004	2678	346	722	137	37	38	387	248	195	.270	.334	.391	85	-56	-65	362	18	18		-76	C/O	-8.3

■ BUDDY MYER
Myer, Charles Solomon b: 3/16/04, Ellisville, Miss. d: 10/31/74, Baton Rouge, La. BL/TR, 5'10.5", 163 lbs. Deb: 9/26/25

YEAR	TM/L	G	AB	R	H	2B	3B	HR	RBI	BB	SO	AVG	OBP	SLG	PRO+	BR	/A	RC	SB	CS	SBR	FR	POS	TPR
1925	*Was-A	4	8	1	2	0	0	0	0	0	1	.250	.250	.250	28	-1	-1	0	0	0	0	-2	/S	-0.1
1926	Was-A	132	434	66	132	18	6	1	62	45	19	.304	.370	.380	98	-1	-0	61	10	11	-4	-18	*S/3	-1.1
1927	Was-A	15	51	7	11	1	0	0	7	8	3	.216	.322	.235	47	-4	-4	4	3	1	0	-2	S	-0.3
	Bos-A	133	469	59	135	22	11	2	47	48	15	.288	.359	.394	97	-3	-1	65	9	5	-0	7	*S3O/2	1.3
	Yr	148	520	66	146	23	11	2	54	56	18	.281	.355	.379	92	-7	-5	69	12	6	0	4		1.0
1928	Bos-A	147	536	78	168	26	6	1	44	53	28	.313	.379	.390	104	4	5	82	30	16	-1	4	*3	1.0
1929	Was-A	141	563	80	169	29	10	3	82	63	33	.300	.373	.403	99	1	0	88	18	7	1	-15	23	-0.7
1930	Was-A	138	541	97	164	18	8	2	61	58	31	.303	.373	.377	90	-6	-6	78	14	11	-2	-19	*2/O	-2.2
1931	Was-A	139	591	114	173	33	11	4	56	58	42	.293	.360	.406	100	1	1	85	11	14	-5	-16	*2	-1.1
1932	Was-A	143	577	120	161	38	16	5	52	69	33	.279	.360	.426	104	3	4	91	12	7	-1	-18	*2	-0.7
1933	*Was-A	131	530	95	160	29	15	4	61	60	29	.302	.384	.436	115	11	12	87	6	8	-3	-1	*2	0.5
1934	Was-A	139	524	103	160	33	8	3	57	102	32	.305	.419	.416	121	17	21	98	6	6	-2	-12	*2	1.1
1935	Was-A	151	616	115	215	36	11	5	100	96	40	.349	.440	.468	139	37	40	132	7	6	-2	8	*2	4.8
1936	Was-A	51	156	31	42	5	2	0	15	42	11	.269	.427	.327	94	-0	1	27	7	2	1	3	2	0.8
1937	Was-A	125	430	54	126	16	10	1	65	78	41	.293	.407	.384	105	4	7	72	6	2	-3	-17	*2/O	0.0
1938	Was-A	127	437	79	147	22	8	6	71	93	32	.336	.454	.465	140	26	31	99	9	5	-0	2	*2	3.3
1939	Was-A	83	258	33	78	10	3	1	32	40	18	.302	.396	.376	106	1	4	42	4	1	1	-1	2	0.6
1940	Was-A	71	210	28	61	14	4	0	29	34	10	.290	.389	.395	111	2	4	34	6	3	0	4	2	1.0
1941	Was-A	53	107	14	27	3	1	0	9	18	10	.252	.360	.299	80	-3	-2	13	2	0	1	-8	2	-0.6
Total	17	1923	7038	1174	2131	353	130	38	850	965	428	.303	.389	.406	108	89	115	1158	156	109	-19	-102	*2S3/O	7.6

■ GEORGE MYERS
Myers, George D. b: 11/13/1860, Buffalo, N.Y. d: 12/14/26, Buffalo, N.Y. BR , Deb: 5/02/1884

YEAR	TM/L	G	AB	R	H	2B	3B	HR	RBI	BB	SO	AVG	OBP	SLG	PRO+	BR	/A	RC	SB	CS	SBR	FR	POS	TPR
1884	Buf-N	78	325	34	59	9	2	2	32	13	33	.182	.213	.240	41	-21	-23	17				-11	CO	-2.6
1885	Buf-N	89	326	40	67	7	2	0	19	23	40	.206	.258	.239	60	-13	-15	21				-5	CO	-1.3
1886	StL-N	79	295	26	56	7	3	0	27	18	42	.190	.236	.234	46	-20	-17	18	6			-12	C/O3	-1.3
1887	Ind-N	69	235	25	51	8	1	1	20	22	7	.217	.298	.272	63	-12	-10	27	26			-11	CO/13	-1.3
1888	Ind-N	66	248	36	59	9	0	2	16	16	14	.238	.292	.298	89	-2	-3	31	28			-9	C3O/1	-0.9
1889	Ind-N	43	149	22	29	3	0	0	12	17	13	.195	.294	.215	44	-10	-11	13	12			7	OC/1	-0.3
Total	6	424	1578	183	321	43	8	5	126	109	149	.203	.260	.250	57	-78	-77	127	72			-40	CO/31	-8.5

■ GREG MYERS
Myers, Gregory Richard b: 4/14/66, Riverside, Cal. BL/TR, 6'1", 200 lbs. Deb: 9/12/87

YEAR	TM/L	G	AB	R	H	2B	3B	HR	RBI	BB	SO	AVG	OBP	SLG	PRO+	BR	/A	RC	SB	CS	SBR	FR	POS	TPR
1987	Tor-A	7	9	1	1	0	0	0	0	0	3	.111	.111	.111	-40	-2	-2	-0	0	0	0	2	/C	0.1
1989	Tor-A	17	44	0	5	2	0	0	1	2	9	.114	.152	.159	-12	-7	-6	1	0	1	-1	2	C/D	-0.4
1990	Tor-A	87	250	33	59	7	1	5	22	22	33	.236	.298	.332	77	-8	-8	22	0	1	-1	-1	C	-0.6
Total	3	111	303	34	65	9	1	5	23	24	45	.215	.272	.300	61	-16	-16	23	0	2	-1	3	C/D	-0.9

■ HENRY MYERS
Myers, Henry C. b: 5/1858, Philadelphia, Pa. d: 4/18/1895, Philadelphia, Pa. BR/TR, 5'9", 159 lbs. Deb: 8/20/1881 M

YEAR	TM/L	G	AB	R	H	2B	3B	HR	RBI	BB	SO	AVG	OBP	SLG	PRO+	BR	/A	RC	SB	CS	SBR	FR	POS	TPR
1881	Pro-N	1	4	0	0	0	0	0	0	0	0	.000	.000	.000	-99	-1	-1	0				-0	/S	0.0
1882	Bal-a	69	294	43	53	3	0	0	12			.180	.212	.190	40	-19	-15	12				-7	*S/PM	-1.7
1884	Wil-U	6	24	3	3	0	0	0	0	0	0	.125	.125	.125	-15	-3	-3	0	0			4	/S2	0.1
Total	3	76	322	46	56	3	0	0	0	12	2	.174	.204	.183	34	-22	-19	13	0			-3	/SP2	-1.6

■ HI MYERS
Myers, Henry Harrison b: 4/27/1889, E.Liverpool, Ohio d: 5/1/65, Minerva, Ohio BR/TR, 5'9.5", 175 lbs. Deb: 8/30/09

YEAR	TM/L	G	AB	R	H	2B	3B	HR	RBI	BB	SO	AVG	OBP	SLG	PRO+	BR	/A	RC	SB	CS	SBR	FR	POS	TPR
1909	Bro-N	6	22	1	5	1	0	0		6	2	.227	.292	.273	78	-1	-1	2	1			-1	/O	-0.1
1911	Bro-N	13	43	2	7	1	0	0	0	2	3	.163	.200	.186	9	-5	-5	2	1			-0	O	-0.5
1914	Bro-N	70	227	35	65	3	9	0	17	7	24	.286	.316	.379	104	1	0	27	2			-5	O	-0.5
1915	Bro-N	153	605	69	150	21	7	2	36		19	.248	.275	.349	75	-17	-18	52	15	22	-8	-3	*O	-3.4
1916	*Bro-N	113	412	54	108	12	14	3	36	21	35	.262	.308	.381	108	4	3	55	17			-3	*O	-0.3
1917	Bro-N	120	471	37	126	15	10	3	41	18	25	.268	.294	.348	94	-3	-3	49	5			-1	O123	-0.7
1918	Bro-N	107	407	36	104	9	8	4	40	20	26	.256	.292	.346	95	-4	-4	44	17			9	*O	0.0

YEAR	TM/L	G	AB	R	H	2B	3B	HR	RBI	BB	SO	AVG	OBP	SLG	PRO+	BR	/A	RC	SB	CS	SBR	FR	POS	TPR
1919	Bro-N	133	512	62	157	23	**14**	5	**73**	23	34	.307	.339	**.436**	129	18	17	78	13			5	*O	1.8
1920	*Bro-N	154	582	83	177	36	**22**	4	80	35	54	.304	.345	.462	126	21	18	88	9	13	-5	0	*O/3	0.5
1921	Bro-N	144	549	51	158	14	4	4	68	22	51	.288	.318	.350	74	-18	-21	61	8	6	-1	2	*O2/3	-2.5
1922	Bro-N	153	618	82	196	20	9	6	89	13	26	.317	.331	.408	90	-11	-10	79	9	10	-3	2	*O/2	-1.6
1923	StL-N	96	330	29	99	18	2	2	48	12	19	.300	.330	.385	90	-6	-5	42	5	3	-0	4	O	-0.4
1924	StL-N	43	124	12	26	5	1	1	15	3	10	.210	.228	.290	39	-11	-11	8	1	2	-1	-1	O3/2	-1.1
1925	StL-N	1	1	0	0	0	0	0	0	0	0	.000	.000	.000	-98	-0	-0	0	0	0	0	0	H	0.0
	Cin-N	3	6	1	1	1	0	0	0	0	0	.167	.167	.333	25	-1	-1	0	0	0	0	0	/O	0.0
	StL-N	1	1	1	1	0	0	0	0	0	0	1.000	1.000	1.000	403	0	0	1	0	0	0	0	H	0.0
	Yr	5	8	2	2	1	0	0	0	0	0	.250	.250	.375	58	-1	-1	1	0	0	0	0		0.0
Total	14	1310	4910	555	1380	179	100	32	559	195	358	.281	.312	.378	95	-34	-41	587	107	56		11	*O/231	-8.8

■ BERT MYERS
Myers, James Albert b: 4/8/1874, Frederick, Md. d: 10/12/15, Washington, D.C. BR/TR, 5'10", Deb: 4/25/1896

YEAR	TM/L	G	AB	R	H	2B	3B	HR	RBI	BB	SO	AVG	OBP	SLG	PRO+	BR	/A	RC	SB	CS	SBR	FR	POS	TPR
1896	StL-N	122	454	47	116	12	8	0	37	40	32	.256	.320	.317	73	-19	-16	50	8			-9	*3/S	-1.5
1898	Was-N	31	110	14	29	1	4	0	13	13		.264	.341	.345	100	0	0	14	2			-3	3	-0.1
1900	Phi-N	7	28	5	5	1	0	0	2	3		.179	.258	.214	33	-2	-2	2	1			2	/3	0.0
Total	3	160	592	66	150	14	12	0	52	56	32	.253	.321	.318	76	-21	-18	66	11			-10	3/S	-1.6

■ AL MYERS
Myers, James Albert "Cod" b: 10/22/1863, Danville, Ill. d: 12/24/27, Marshall, Ill. 5'8.5", 165 lbs. Deb: 9/27/1884

YEAR	TM/L	G	AB	R	H	2B	3B	HR	RBI	BB	SO	AVG	OBP	SLG	PRO+	BR	/A	RC	SB	CS	SBR	FR	POS	TPR
1884	Mil-U	12	46	6	15	6	0	0		0		.326	.326	.457	299	3	6	7	0			2	2	0.7
1885	Phi-N	93	357	25	73	13	2	1	28	11	41	.204	.228	.261	59	-17	-16	22				-18	*2	-2.2
1886	KC-N	118	473	69	131	22	9	4	51	22	42	.277	.309	.387	104	5	1	59	3			1	*2	0.6
1887	Was-N	105	362	45	84	9	5	2	36	40	26	.232	.312	.301	77	-12	-9	41	18			-4	2S	-0.7
1888	Was-N	132	502	46	104	12	7	2	46	37	46	.207	.270	.271	79	-13	-9	43	20			-26	*2	-3.0
1889	Was-N	46	176	24	46	3	0	0	20	22	7	.261	.347	.278	82	-4	-2	21	10			3	2	0.4
	Phi-N	75	305	52	82	14	2	0	28	36	9	.269	.354	.328	85	-2	-6	39	8			-9	2	-0.7
	Yr	121	481	76	128	17	2	0	48	58	16	.266	.351	.310	84	-6	-8	60	18			-6		-0.3
1890	Phi-N	117	487	95	135	29	7	2	81	57	46	.277	.365	.378	116	13	11	85	44			14	*2	2.6
1891	Phi-N	135	514	67	118	27	2	2	69	69	46	.230	.331	.302	84	-6	-8	55	8			-10	*2	-1.2
Total	8	833	3222	429	788	135	34	13	359	294	263	.245	.314	.320	90	-33	-33	372	111			-46	2/S	-3.5

■ LYNN MYERS
Myers, Lynnwood Lincoln b: 2/23/14, Enola, Pa. BR/TR, 5'6.5", 145 lbs. Deb: 7/13/38

YEAR	TM/L	G	AB	R	H	2B	3B	HR	RBI	BB	SO	AVG	OBP	SLG	PRO+	BR	/A	RC	SB	CS	SBR	FR	POS	TPR
1938	StL-N	70	227	18	55	10	2	1	19	9	25	.242	.271	.317	58	-12	-14	20	9			-1	S	-0.9
1939	StL-N	74	117	24	28	6	1	0	10	12	23	.239	.310	.308	63	-5	-6	12	1			5	S3/2	0.2
Total	2	144	344	42	83	16	3	1	29	21	48	.241	.285	.314	60	-18	-20	32	10			4	S/32	-0.7

■ HAP MYERS
Myers, Ralph Edward b: 4/8/1888, San Francisco, Cal. d: 6/30/67, San Francisco, Cal BR/TR, 6'3", 175 lbs. Deb: 4/16/10

YEAR	TM/L	G	AB	R	H	2B	3B	HR	RBI	BB	SO	AVG	OBP	SLG	PRO+	BR	/A	RC	SB	CS	SBR	FR	POS	TPR
1910	Bos-A	3	6	0	2	0	0	0	0	0		.333	.333	.333	106	0	0	1	0			0	/O	0.0
1911	StL-A	11	37	4	11	1	0	0	1	1		.297	.316	.324	82	-1	-1	4	0			-2	1	-0.1
	Bos-A	13	38	3	14	2	0	0	0	4		.368	.429	.421	139	2	2	8	4			-1	1	0.1
	Yr	24	75	7	25	3	0	0	1	5		.333	.375	.373	111	1	1	12	4			-2		0.0
1913	Bos-N	140	524	74	143	20	1	2	50	38	48	.273	.333	.326	87	-7	-8	73	57			5	*1	-1.0
1914	Bro-F	92	305	61	67	10	5	1	29	44	43	.220	.322	.295	78	-8	-7	45	43			1	1	-0.4
1915	Bro-F	118	341	61	98	9	1	1	36	32	39	.287	.352	.328	103	2	2	54	28			1	*1	0.5
Total	5	377	1251	203	335	42	7	4	116	119	130	.268	.338	.322	90	-12	-12	184	132			5	1/O	-0.9

■ RICHIE MYERS
Myers, Richard b: 4/7/30, Sacramento, Cal. BR , 5'6", 150 lbs. Deb: 4/21/56

YEAR	TM/L	G	AB	R	H	2B	3B	HR	RBI	BB	SO	AVG	OBP	SLG	PRO+	BR	/A	RC	SB	CS	SBR	FR	POS	TPR
1956	Chi-N	4	1	1	0	0	0	0	0	0	0	.000	.000	.000	-99	-0	-0	0	0	0	0	0	H	0.0

■ BILLY MYERS
Myers, William Harrison b: 8/14/10, Enola, Pa. BR/TR, 5'8", 168 lbs. Deb: 4/16/35

YEAR	TM/L	G	AB	R	H	2B	3B	HR	RBI	BB	SO	AVG	OBP	SLG	PRO+	BR	/A	RC	SB	CS	SBR	FR	POS	TPR
1935	Cin-N	117	445	60	119	15	10	5	36	29	81	.267	.315	.380	89	-9	-7	55	10			3	*S	0.1
1936	Cin-N	98	323	45	87	9	6	6	27	28	56	.269	.328	.390	99	-4	-1	43	6			8	S	1.2
1937	Cin-N	124	335	35	84	13	3	7	43	44	57	.251	.339	.370	97	-3	-1	46	0			4	*S/2	1.3
1938	Cin-N	134	442	57	112	18	6	12	47	41	80	.253	.317	.403	99	-3	-1	58	2			2	*S2	1.0
1939	*Cin-N	151	509	79	143	18	6	9	56	71	90	.281	.369	.393	104	5	5	81	4			6	*S	2.0
1940	*Cin-N	90	282	33	57	14	2	5	30	30	56	.202	.283	.319	65	-13	-14	27	0			-5	S	-0.9
1941	Chi-N	24	63	10	14	1	0	1	4	7	25	.222	.310	.286	71	-2	-2	6	1			4	S/2	0.4
Total	7	738	2399	319	616	88	33	45	243	250	445	.257	.328	.377	93	-29	-21	316	23			23	S/2	5.1

■ TIM NAEHRING
Naehring, Timothy James b: 2/1/67, Cincinnati, Ohio BR/TR, 6'2", 190 lbs. Deb: 7/15/90

YEAR	TM/L	G	AB	R	H	2B	3B	HR	RBI	BB	SO	AVG	OBP	SLG	PRO+	BR	/A	RC	SB	CS	SBR	FR	POS	TPR
1990	Bos-A	24	85	10	23	6	0	2	12	8	15	.271	.333	.412	102	1	0	11	0	0	0	-2	S/32	0.0

■ BILL NAGEL
Nagel, William Taylor b: 8/19/15, Memphis, Tenn. d: 10/8/81, Freehold, N.J. BR/TR, 6'1", 190 lbs. Deb: 4/20/39

YEAR	TM/L	G	AB	R	H	2B	3B	HR	RBI	BB	SO	AVG	OBP	SLG	PRO+	BR	/A	RC	SB	CS	SBR	FR	POS	TPR
1939	Phi-A	105	341	39	86	19	4	12	39	25	86	.252	.307	.437	90	-8	-7	42	2	1	0	-15	23/P	-1.8
1941	Phi-N	17	56	2	8	1	1	0	6	3	14	.143	.186	.196	8	-7	-7	2	0			3	2/O3	-0.2
1945	Chi-A	67	220	21	46	10	3	3	27	15	41	.209	.263	.323	71	-9	-9	18	3	1	0	-3	1/3	-1.4
Total	3	189	617	62	140	30	8	15	72	43	141	.227	.281	.374	77	-24	-22	61	5	2		-15	/2130P	-3.4

■ LOU NAGELSEN
Nagelsen, Louis Marcellus (b: Louis Marcellus Nageleisen)
b: 6/29/1887, Piqua, Ohio d: 10/22/65, Fort Wayne, Ind. BR/TR, 6'2", 180 lbs. Deb: 9/10/12

YEAR	TM/L	G	AB	R	H	2B	3B	HR	RBI	BB	SO	AVG	OBP	SLG	PRO+	BR	/A	RC	SB	CS	SBR	FR	POS	TPR
1912	Cle-A	2	3	0	0	0	0	0	0	0		.000	.000	.000	-97	-1	-1	0	0			-1	/C	0.0

■ RUSS NAGELSON
Nagelson, Russell Charles b: 9/19/44, Cincinnati, Ohio BL/TR, 6', 205 lbs. Deb: 9/11/68

YEAR	TM/L	G	AB	R	H	2B	3B	HR	RBI	BB	SO	AVG	OBP	SLG	PRO+	BR	/A	RC	SB	CS	SBR	FR	POS	TPR
1968	Cle-A	5	3	0	1	0	0	0	0	2	2	.333	.600	.333	192	1	1	1	0	0	0	0	H	0.1
1969	Cle-A	12	17	1	6	0	0	0	0	3	3	.353	.450	.353	123	1	1	3	0	0	0	0	/O1	0.1
1970	Cle-A	17	24	3	3	1	0	1	2	3	9	.125	.222	.292	39	-2	-2	2	0	0	0	-0	/O	-0.2
	Det-A	28	32	5	6	0	0	0	2	5	6	.188	.297	.188	36	-3	-3	2	0	0	0	-1	/O1	-0.3
	Yr	45	56	8	9	1	0	1	4	8	15	.161	.266	.232	38	-5	-5	4	0	0	0	-1		-0.5
Total	3	62	76	9	16	1	0	1	4	13	20	.211	.326	.263	64	-3	-3	8	0	0	0	-1	/O1	-0.3

■ TOM NAGLE
Nagle, Thomas Edward b: 10/30/1865, Milwaukee, Wis. d: 3/9/46, Milwaukee, Wis. BR/TR, 5'10", 150 lbs. Deb: 4/22/1890

YEAR	TM/L	G	AB	R	H	2B	3B	HR	RBI	BB	SO	AVG	OBP	SLG	PRO+	BR	/A	RC	SB	CS	SBR	FR	POS	TPR
1890	Chi-N	38	144	21	39	5	1	1	11	7	24	.271	.318	.340	90	-1	-2	17	4			-6	C/O	-0.5
1891	Chi-N	8	25	3	3	0	0	0	1	1	3	.120	.154	.120	-19	-4	-4	0	0			-3	/CO	-0.5
Total	2	46	169	24	42	5	1	1	12	8	27	.249	.294	.308	75	-5	-6	18	4			-9	/CO	-1.0

■ BILL NAHORODNY
Nahorodny, William Gerard b: 8/31/53, Hamtramck, Mich. BR/TR, 6'2", 200 lbs. Deb: 9/27/76

YEAR	TM/L	G	AB	R	H	2B	3B	HR	RBI	BB	SO	AVG	OBP	SLG	PRO+	BR	/A	RC	SB	CS	SBR	FR	POS	TPR
1976	Phi-N	3	5	0	1	1	0	0	0	0	0	.200	.200	.400	65	-0	-0	0	0	0	0	0	/C	0.0
1977	Chi-A	7	23	3	6	1	0	1	4	2	3	.261	.320	.435	104	0	0	3	0	0	0	-1	/C	0.0
1978	Chi-A	107	347	29	82	11	2	8	35	23	52	.236	.288	.349	77	-11	-11	35	1	0	0	-3	*C/1D	-1.1
1979	Chi-A	65	179	20	46	10	0	6	29	18	23	.257	.325	.413	98	-1	-1	23	0	1	-1	0	C/D	0.1
1980	Atl-N	59	157	14	38	12	0	5	18	8	21	.242	.287	.414	91	-2	-3	19	0	2	-1	-7	C/1	-0.9
1981	Atl-N	14	13	0	3	1	0	0	2	1	3	.231	.286	.308	67	-1	-1	1	0	0	0	0	/C1	0.0
1982	Cle-A	39	94	6	21	5	1	4	18	2	9	.223	.240	.426	79	-3	-3	8	0	0	0	-4	C	-0.4
1983	Det-A	2	1	0	0	0	0	0	0	1	0	.000	.500	.000	89	0	0	0	0	0	0	0	/H	0.0
1984	Sea-A	12	25	2	6	0	0	1	3	1	7	.240	.321	.360	89	-0	-0	3	0	1	-1	-2	C/1	-0.2
Total	9	308	844	74	203	41	3	25	109	56	118	.241	.292	.385	85	-18	-19	91	1	4	-2	-17	C/1D	-2.5

YEAR	TM/L	G	AB	R	H	2B	3B	HR	RBI	BB	SO	AVG	OBP	SLG	PRO+	BR	/A	RC	SB	CS	SBR	FR	POS	TPR

■ FRANK NALEWAY
Naleway, Frank "Chick" b: 7/5/02, Chicago, Ill. d: 1/28/49, Chicago, Ill. BR/TR, 5'9.5", 165 lbs. Deb: 9/16/24

YEAR	TM/L	G	AB	R	H	2B	3B	HR	RBI	BB	SO	AVG	OBP	SLG	PRO+	BR	/A	RC	SB	CS	SBR	FR	POS	TPR
1924	Chi-A	1	2	0	0	0	0	0	0	1	0	.000	.333	.000	-10	-0	-0	0	0	0	0	-1	/S	0.0

■ DOC NANCE
Nance, William G. "Kid" (b: Willie G. Cooper) b: 8/2/1876, Ft.Worth, Tex. d: 5/28/58, Fort Worth, Tex. BR/TR, Deb: 8/19/1897

YEAR	TM/L	G	AB	R	H	2B	3B	HR	RBI	BB	SO	AVG	OBP	SLG	PRO+	BR	/A	RC	SB	CS	SBR	FR	POS	TPR
1897	Lou-N	35	120	25	29	5	3	3	17	20		.242	.355	.408	107	1	1	19	3			4	O	0.2
1898	Lou-N	22	76	13	24	5	0	1	16	12		.316	.416	.421	146	5	5	14	2			2	O	0.5
1901	Det-A	132	461	72	129	24	5	3	66	51		.280	.355	.373	100	4	1	69	9			1	*O	0.0
Total	3	189	657	110	182	34	8	7	99	83		.277	.362	.385	106	10	7	102	14			6	O	0.7

■ AL NAPLES
Naples, Aloysius Francis b: 8/29/27, St.George, S.I., N.Y. BR/TR, 5'9", 168 lbs. Deb: 6/25/49

YEAR	TM/L	G	AB	R	H	2B	3B	HR	RBI	BB	SO	AVG	OBP	SLG	PRO+	BR	/A	RC	SB	CS	SBR	FR	POS	TPR
1949	StL-A	2	7	0	1	1	0	0	0	0	1	.143	.143	.286	12	-1	-1	0	0	0	0	-1	/S	-0.1

■ DANNY NAPOLEON
Napoleon, Daniel b: 1/11/42, Claysburg, Pa. BR/TR, 5'11", 190 lbs. Deb: 4/14/65

YEAR	TM/L	G	AB	R	H	2B	3B	HR	RBI	BB	SO	AVG	OBP	SLG	PRO+	BR	/A	RC	SB	CS	SBR	FR	POS	TPR
1965	NY-N	68	97	5	14	1	1	0	7	8	23	.144	.224	.175	15	-11	-10	4	0	0	0	-0	O/3	-1.1
1966	NY-N	12	33	2	7	2	0	0	0	1	10	.212	.235	.273	42	-3	-3	2	0	1	-1	-0	/O3	-0.3
Total	2	80	130	7	21	3	1	0	7	9	33	.162	.227	.200	22	-14	-13	5	0	1	-1	-1	/O3	-1.4

■ HAL NARAGON
Naragon, Harold Richard b: 10/1/28, Zanesville, Ohio BL/TR, 6', 160 lbs. Deb: 9/23/51 C

YEAR	TM/L	G	AB	R	H	2B	3B	HR	RBI	BB	SO	AVG	OBP	SLG	PRO+	BR	/A	RC	SB	CS	SBR	FR	POS	TPR
1951	Cle-A	3	8	0	2	0	0	0	0	1	0	.250	.400	.250	83	-0	-0	1	0	0	0	0	/C	0.0
1954	*Cle-A	46	101	10	24	2	2	0	12	9	12	.238	.300	.297	63	-5	-5	10	0	0	0	-1	C	-0.4
1955	Cle-A	57	127	12	41	9	2	1	14	15	8	.323	.394	.449	122	5	4	23	1	0	0	-4	C	0.3
1956	Cle-A	53	122	11	35	3	1	3	18	13	9	.287	.360	.402	99	-0	-0	18	0	0	0	-11	C	-0.9
1957	Cle-A	57	121	12	31	1	1	0	8	12	9	.256	.328	.281	69	-5	-5	11	0	0	0	-2	C	-0.4
1958	Cle-A	9	9	2	3	0	1	0	0	0	0	.333	.333	.556	144	0	0	2	0	0	0	0	H	0.0
1959	Cle-A	14	36	6	10	4	1	0	5	3	2	.278	.350	.444	121	1	1	6	0	0	0	-1	C	0.0
	Was-A	71	195	12	47	3	2	0	11	8	9	.241	.275	.277	52	-13	-13	14	0	1	-1	-1	C	-1.1
	Yr	85	231	18	57	7	3	0	16	11	11	.247	.287	.303	63	-12	-12	20	0	1	-1	-2		-1.1
1960	Was-A	33	92	7	19	2	0	0	5	8	4	.207	.277	.228	39	-8	-8	6	0	0	0	-3	C	-0.8
1961	Min-A	57	139	10	42	2	1	2	11	4	8	.302	.326	.374	82	-3	-4	16	0	0	0	-5	C	-0.8
1962	Min-A	24	35	1	8	1	0	0	3	3	1	.229	.289	.257	47	-2	-3	3	0	0	0	0	/C	-0.1
Total	10	424	985	83	262	27	11	6	87	76	62	.266	.323	.334	77	-29	-31	109	1	1	-0	-27	C	-4.2

■ BILL NARLESKI
Narleski, William Edward "Cap" b: 6/9/1899, Perth Amboy, N.J. d: 7/22/64, Laurel Springs, N.J. BR/TR, 5'9", 160 lbs. Deb: 4/18/29

YEAR	TM/L	G	AB	R	H	2B	3B	HR	RBI	BB	SO	AVG	OBP	SLG	PRO+	BR	/A	RC	SB	CS	SBR	FR	POS	TPR
1929	Bos-A	96	260	30	72	16	1	0	25	21	22	.277	.333	.346	77	-9	-8	30	4	4	-1	-16	S2/3	-1.8
1930	Bos-A	39	98	11	23	9	0	0	7	7	5	.235	.306	.327	63	-6	-5	10	0	0	0	-8	S3/2	-0.9
Total	2	135	358	41	95	25	1	0	32	28	27	.265	.326	.341	73	-15	-14	41	4	4	-1	-25	/S23	-2.7

■ JERRY NARRON
Narron, Jerry Austin b: 1/15/56, Goldsboro, N.C. BL/TR, 6'3", 205 lbs. Deb: 4/13/79

YEAR	TM/L	G	AB	R	H	2B	3B	HR	RBI	BB	SO	AVG	OBP	SLG	PRO+	BR	/A	RC	SB	CS	SBR	FR	POS	TPR
1979	NY-A	61	123	17	21	3	1	4	18	9	26	.171	.227	.309	44	-10	-10	9	0	0	0	-4	C	-1.0
1980	Sea-A	48	107	7	21	3	0	4	18	13	18	.196	.283	.336	68	-5	-5	11	0	0	0	-8	C/D	-1.0
1981	Sea-A	76	203	13	45	5	0	3	17	16	35	.222	.285	.291	64	-9	-10	17	0	0	0	-14	C/D	-2.1
1983	Cal-A	10	22	1	3	0	0	1	4	1	3	.136	.174	.273	21	-2	-2	1	0	0	0	-1	/CD	-0.2
1984	Cal-A	69	150	9	37	5	0	3	17	8	12	.247	.289	.340	74	-6	-5	13	0	0	0	-8	C/1	-1.0
1985	Cal-A	67	132	12	29	4	0	5	14	11	11	.220	.280	.364	75	-5	-5	13	0	0	0	2	C/1D	0.0
1986	*Cal-A	57	95	5	21	3	1	1	8	9	14	.221	.295	.305	65	-5	-5	8	0	0	0	2	C/D	0.0
1987	Sea-A	4	8	0	0	0	0	0	0	0	2	.000	.000	.000	-95	-2	-2	0	0	0	0	-0	/C	-0.1
Total	8	392	840	64	177	23	2	21	96	67	127	.211	.272	.318	62	-43	-44	72	0	0	0	-31	C/D1	-5.4

■ SAM NARRON
Narron, Samuel b: 8/25/13, Middlesex, N.C. BR/TR, 5'10", 180 lbs. Deb: 9/15/35 C

YEAR	TM/L	G	AB	R	H	2B	3B	HR	RBI	BB	SO	AVG	OBP	SLG	PRO+	BR	/A	RC	SB	CS	SBR	FR	POS	TPR
1935	StL-N	4	7	0	3	0	0	0	0	0	0	.429	.429	.429	126	0	0	1	0			-0	/C	0.0
1942	StL-N	10	10	0	4	0	0	0	1	0	0	.400	.400	.400	125	0	0	2	0			-0	/C	0.0
1943	*StL-N	10	11	0	1	0	0	0	0	1	2	.091	.167	.091	-24	-2	-2	0	0			1	/C	0.0
Total	3	24	28	0	8	0	0	0	1	1	2	.286	.310	.286	67	-1	-1	3	0			0	/C	0.0

■ COTTON NASH
Nash, Charles Francis b: 7/24/42, Jersey City, N.J. BR/TR, 6'6", 220 lbs. Deb: 9/01/67

YEAR	TM/L	G	AB	R	H	2B	3B	HR	RBI	BB	SO	AVG	OBP	SLG	PRO+	BR	/A	RC	SB	CS	SBR	FR	POS	TPR
1967	Chi-A	3	4	1	0	0	0	0	0	1	0	.000	.250	.000	-21	-0	-0	0	0	0	0	-1	/1	0.0
1969	Min-A	6	9	0	2	0	0	0	0	1	2	.222	.300	.222	47	-1	-1	1	0	0	0	1	/1O	0.0
1970	Min-A	4	4	1	1	0	0	0	2	1	1	.250	.400	.250	82	-0	-0	0	0	1	-1	-0	/1	0.0
Total	3	13	16	2	3	0	0	0	2	3	3	.188	.316	.188	45	-1	-1	1	0	1	-1	1	/1O	0.0

■ KEN NASH
Nash, Kenneth Leland (Played One Game In 1912 Under Name Of Costello)
b: 7/14/1888, S.Weymouth, Mass. d: 2/16/77, Epsom, N.H. BB/TR, 5'8", 140 lbs. Deb: 7/04/12

YEAR	TM/L	G	AB	R	H	2B	3B	HR	RBI	BB	SO	AVG	OBP	SLG	PRO+	BR	/A	RC	SB	CS	SBR	FR	POS	TPR
1912	Cle-A	11	23	2	4	0	0	0	3			.174	.269	.174	27	-2	-2	1	0			-3	/S	-0.4
1914	StL-N	24	51	4	14	3	1	0	6	6	10	.275	.351	.373	116	1	1	6	0			-6	3/2S	-0.4
Total	2	35	74	6	18	3	1	0	6	9	10	.243	.325	.311	87	-1	-1	8	0			-10	/S32	-0.8

■ BILLY NASH
Nash, William Mitchell b: 6/24/1865, Richmond, Va. d: 11/15/29, E.Orange, N.J. BR/TR, 5'8.5", 167 lbs. Deb: 8/05/1884 MU

YEAR	TM/L	G	AB	R	H	2B	3B	HR	RBI	BB	SO	AVG	OBP	SLG	PRO+	BR	/A	RC	SB	CS	SBR	FR	POS	TPR
1884	Ric-a	45	166	31	33	8	8	1		12		.199	.281	.361	112	2	3	17				8	3	1.0
1885	Bos-N	26	94	9	24	4	0	0	11	2	9	.255	.271	.298	87	-2	-1	8				-4	3/2	-0.3
1886	Bos-N	109	417	61	117	11	8	1	45	24	28	.281	.320	.353	109	2	5	53	16			-3	*3S	0.4
1887	Bos-N	121	475	100	140	24	12	6	94	60	30	.295	.376	.434	126	18	18	96	43			9	*3/O	2.4
1888	Bos-N	135	526	71	149	18	15	4	75	50	46	.283	.350	.397	138	25	23	82	20			25	*32	5.2
1889	Bos-N	128	481	84	132	20	2	3	76	79	44	.274	.379	.343	98	6	1	74	26			12	*3/P	1.9
1890	Bos-P	129	488	103	130	28	6	6	90	88	43	.266	.383	.379	99	7	0	83	26			18	*3/P	2.2
1891	Bos-N	140	537	92	148	24	9	5	95	74	50	.276	.369	.382	108	16	6	88	28			-12	*3	0.0
1892	*Bos-N	135	526	94	137	25	5	4	95	59	41	.260	.338	.350	101	7	0	75	31			24	*3/O	3.0
1893	Bos-N	128	485	115	141	27	6	10	123	85	29	.291	.399	.433	114	18	11	98	30			3	*3	1.2
1894	Bos-N	132	512	132	148	23	6	8	87	91	23	.289	.399	.404	89	-0	-9	93	20			6	*3	-0.3
1895	Bos-N	132	508	97	147	23	6	10	108	74	19	.289	.383	.417	100	8	0	90	18			-8	*3	-0.4
1896	Phi-N	65	227	29	56	9	1	3	30	34	21	.247	.355	.335	85	-4	-4	29	3			7	3M	0.5
1897	Phi-N	104	337	45	87	20	2	0	39	60		.258	.373	.329	91	-3	-1	44	4			-7	3S/2	-0.5
1898	Phi-N	20	70	9	17	2	1	0	9	11		.243	.346	.300	92	-1	-0	7	0			-1	3	0.0
Total	15	1549	5849	1072	1606	266	87	60	977	803	383	.275	.366	.381	105	100	52	938	265			77	*3/2SOP	16.3

■ PETE NATON
Naton, Peter Alphonsus b: 9/9/31, Flushing, N.Y. BR/TR, 6'1", 200 lbs. Deb: 6/16/53

YEAR	TM/L	G	AB	R	H	2B	3B	HR	RBI	BB	SO	AVG	OBP	SLG	PRO+	BR	/A	RC	SB	CS	SBR	FR	POS	TPR
1953	Pit-N	6	12	2	2	0	0	0	1	2	1	.167	.286	.167	22	-1	-1	1	0	0	0	-1	/C	-0.1

■ SANDY NAVA
Nava, Vincent P. (b: Irwin Sandy) b: 4/12/1850, San Francisco, Cal d: 6/15/06, Baltimore, Md. 5'6", 155 lbs. Deb: 5/05/1882

YEAR	TM/L	G	AB	R	H	2B	3B	HR	RBI	BB	SO	AVG	OBP	SLG	PRO+	BR	/A	RC	SB	CS	SBR	FR	POS	TPR
1882	Pro-N	28	97	15	20	0	0	0	7	1	13	.206	.214	.227	42	-6	-6	5				-6	C/O	-0.9
1883	Pro-N	29	100	18	24	4	2	0	16	3	17	.240	.262	.320	74	-3	-3	9				-5	C/O	-0.5
1884	Pro-N	34	116	10	11	0	0	0	6	11	35	.095	.173	.095	-14	-15	-14	2				-1	C/S2	-1.0
1885	Bal-a	8	27	2	5	1	0	0		1		.185	.214	.222	41	-2	-2	1				-5	/C	-0.4
1886	Bal-a	2	5	0	1	0	0	0		0		.200	.200	.200	27	-0	-0	0	1			-1	/SC	0.0
Total	5	101	345	45	61	7	2	0	29	16	65	.177	.213	.209	33	-26	-26	17	1			-17	/CSO2	-2.8

YEAR	TM/L	G	AB	R	H	2B	3B	HR	RBI	BB	SO	AVG	OBP	SLG	PRO+	BR	/A	RC	SB	CS	SBR	FR	POS	TPR

■ EARL NAYLOR Naylor, Earl Eugene b: 5/19/19, Kansas City, Mo. d: 1/16/90, Winter Haven, Fla. BR/TR, 6', 190 lbs. Deb: 4/15/42

1942	Phi-N	76	168	9	33	4	1	0	14	11	18	.196	.246	.232	42	-13	-12	9	1			-5	OP	-1.5
1943	Phi-N	33	120	12	21	2	0	3	14	12	16	.175	.256	.267	53	-8	-7	7	1			8	O	0.0
1946	Bro-N	3	2	1	0	0	0	0	0	0	1	.000	.000	.000	-99	-1	-1	0	0			0	H	0.0
Total	3	112	290	22	54	6	1	3	28	23	35	.186	.248	.245	46	-21	-19	16	2			3	/OP	-1.5

■ JACK NEAGLE Neagle, John Henry b: 1/2/1858, Syracuse, N.Y. d: 9/20/04, Syracuse, N.Y. BR/TR, 5'6", 155 lbs. Deb: 7/08/1879

1879	Cin-N	3	12	1	2	0	0	0	2	0	0	.167	.167	.167	11	-1	-1	0				-0	/OP	0.0
1883	Phi-N	18	73	6	12	1	0	0	4	1	9	.164	.176	.178	9	-8	-7	2				-2	O/P	-0.5
	Bal-a	9	35	3	10	4	0	0		2		.286	.324	.400	128	1	1	5				-3	/PO	0.0
	Pit-a	27	101	14	19	0	1	0		5		.188	.226	.208	43	-6	-6	5				-3	PO	0.0
	Yr	36	136	17	29	4	1	0		7		.213	.252	.257	66	-5	-5	9				-5		0.0
1884	Pit-a	43	148	13	22	6	0	0		6		.149	.187	.189	24	-12	-12	5				-4	P/O	0.0
Total	3	100	369	37	65	11	1	0	6	14	9	.176	.208	.211	36	-26	-24	18				-12	/PO	-0.5

■ CHARLIE NEAL Neal, Charles Lenard b: 1/30/31, Longview, Tex. BR/TR, 5'10", 165 lbs. Deb: 4/17/56

1956	*Bro-N	62	136	22	39	5	1	2	14	14	19	.287	.353	.382	91	-0	-1	18	2	2	-1	2	2/S	0.4
1957	Bro-N	128	448	62	121	13	7	12	62	53	83	.270	.358	.411	96	5	-1	69	11	4	1	-3	*S3/2	0.2
1958	LA-N	140	473	87	120	9	6	22	65	61	91	.254	.345	.438	102	4	2	71	7	6	-2	12	*2/S	2.0
1959	*LA-N	151	616	103	177	30	11	19	83	43	86	.287	.338	.464	103	8	3	91	17	6	2	20	*2/S	3.6
1960	LA-N	139	477	60	122	23	2	8	40	48	75	.256	.325	.363	83	-8	-11	54	5	5	-2	-15	*2/S	-1.6
1961	LA-N	108	341	40	80	6	1	10	48	30	49	.235	.298	.346	65	-15	-18	35	3	2	-0	2	*2	-0.3
1962	NY-N	136	508	59	132	14	9	11	58	56	90	.260	.333	.388	91	-5	-6	62	2	8	-4	-8	2S3	-0.6
1963	NY-N	72	253	26	57	12	1	3	18	27	49	.225	.302	.316	77	-7	-7	25	1	2	-1	0	3/S	-0.7
	Cin-N	34	64	2	10	1	0	0	3	5	15	.156	.217	.172	13	-7	-7	3	0	1	-1	-2	3/2S	-1.0
	Yr	106	317	28	67	13	1	3	21	32	64	.211	.286	.287	64	-14	-14	28	1	3	-2	-2		-1.7
Total	8	970	3316	461	858	113	38	87	391	337	557	.259	.331	.394	90	-24	-48	429	48	36	-7	8	2S3	2.0

■ OFFA NEAL Neal, Theophilus Fountain b: 6/5/1876, Logan, Ill. d: 4/12/50, Mt.Vernon, Ill. BL/TR, 6', 185 lbs. Deb: 9/30/05

| 1905 | NY-N | 4 | 13 | 0 | 0 | 0 | 0 | 0 | 0 | 0 | | .000 | .000 | .000 | -98 | -3 | -3 | 0 | 0 | | | -0 | /32 | -0.3 |

■ GREASY NEALE Neale, Alfred Earle b: 11/5/1891, Parkersburg, W.Va. d: 11/2/73, Lake Worth, Fla. BL/TR, 6', 170 lbs. Deb: 4/12/16 C

1916	Cin-N	138	530	53	139	13	5	0	20	19	79	.262	.295	.306	87	-10	-9	54	17			16	*O	0.3
1917	Cin-N	121	385	40	113	14	9	3	33	24	36	.294	.343	.400	133	12	14	58	25			-3	*O	0.8
1918	Cin-N	107	371	57	100	11	11	1	32	24	38	.270	.324	.367	113	4	5	50	23			9	*O	0.9
1919	*Cin-N	139	500	57	121	10	12	1	54	47	51	.242	.316	.316	93	-5	-3	59	28			0	*O	-0.9
1920	Cin-N	150	530	55	135	10	7	3	46	45	48	.255	.322	.317	85	-10	-9	58	29	12	2	13	*O	-0.2
1921	Phi-N	22	57	7	12	1	0	0	1	14	9	.211	.366	.228	56	-2	-3	5	3	4	-2	-6	O	-1.1
	Cin-N	63	241	39	58	10	5	0	12	22	16	.241	.307	.324	70	-11	-10	24	9	6	-1	-2	O	-1.5
	Yr	85	298	46	70	11	5	0	13	36	25	.235	.319	.305	67	-14	-13	30	12	10	-2	-8		-2.6
1922	Cin-N	25	43	11	10	2	1	0	2	6	3	.233	.353	.326	77	-1	-1	6	5	2	0	-2	O	-0.2
1924	Cin-N	3	4	0	0	0	0	0	0	0	1	.000	.000	.000	-99	-1	-1	0	0	0	0	0	/O	0.0
Total	8	768	2661	319	688	71	50	8	200	201	281	.259	.319	.332	94	-25	-18	314	139	24		26	O	-1.9

■ JOE NEALE Neale, Joseph Hunt b: 5/7/1866, Wadsworth, Ohio d: 12/30/13, Akron, Ohio BR/TR, 5'8", 153 lbs. Deb: 6/21/1886

1886	Lou-a	2	5	0	0	0	0	0		0		.000	.000	.000	-95	-1	-1	0	0			0	/OP	0.0
1887	Lou-a	5	19	3	1	0	0	0		3		.053	.182	.053	-31	-3	-3	0	1			0	/P	0.0
1890	StL-a	11	30	4	2	0	0	0		3		.067	.152	.067	-30	-5	-6	0	0			-1	P/O	0.0
1891	StL-a	15	51	6	6	0	1	1	8	3	11	.118	.167	.216	9	-6	-7	2	1			2	P	0.0
Total	4	33	105	13	9	0	1	1	8	9	11	.086	.158	.133	-13	-15	-17	3	2			2	/PO	0.0

■ JIM NEALON Nealon, James Joseph b: 12/15/1884, Sacramento, Cal. d: 4/2/10, San Francisco, Cal. 6'1.5", Deb: 4/12/06

1906	Pit-N	154	556	82	142	21	12	3	83	53		.255	.320	.353	107	7	4	72	15			1	*1	0.0
1907	Pit-N	105	381	29	98	10	8	0	47	23		.257	.300	.325	96	-2	-2	43	11			0	*1	-0.4
Total	2	259	937	111	240	31	20	3	130	76		.256	.312	.342	103	5	2	114	26			1	1	-0.4

■ TOM NEEDHAM Needham, Thomas J. "Deerfoot" b: 4/7/1879, Ireland d: 12/13/26, Steubenville, Ohio BR/TR, 5'10", 180 lbs. Deb: 5/12/04

1904	Bos-N	84	269	18	70	12	3	4	19	11		.260	.289	.372	109	1	2	31	3			5	C/O	1.5
1905	Bos-N	83	271	21	59	6	1	2	17	24		.218	.281	.269	68	-11	-10	22	3			-8	C/O1	-1.0
1906	Bos-N	83	285	11	54	8	2	1	12	13		.189	.225	.242	48	-18	-17	17	3			-2	C/2130	-1.3
1907	Bos-N	86	260	19	51	6	2	1	19	18		.196	.248	.246	57	-13	-13	18	4			-10	C/1	-1.9
1908	NY-N	54	91	8	19	3	0	0	11	12		.209	.301	.242	72	-2	-2	7	0			8	C	0.9
1909	Chi-N	13	28	3	4	0	0	0	0	0		.143	.143	.143	-11	-4	-4	1	0			1	/C	-0.1
1910	*Chi-N	31	76	9	14	3	1	0	10	10	10	.184	.287	.250	57	-4	-4	6	1			3	C/1	0.1
1911	Chi-N	27	62	4	12	2	0	0	5	9	14	.194	.315	.226	52	-4	-4	5	2			6	C	0.4
1912	Chi-N	33	90	12	16	5	0	0	10	7	13	.178	.260	.233	36	-8	-8	6	3			-1	C	-0.6
1913	Chi-N	20	42	5	10	4	1	0	11	4	8	.238	.304	.381	95	-0	-0	5	0			5	C/1	0.5
1914	Chi-N	9	17	3	2	1	0	0	3	1	4	.118	.167	.176	2	-2	-2	1	1			2	/C	0.1
Total	11	523	1491	113	311	50	10	8	117	109	49	.209	.265	.272	65	-64	-62	118	20			8	C/1203	-1.5

■ CAL NEEMAN Neeman, Calvin Amandus b: 2/18/29, Valmeyer, Ill. BR/TR, 6'1", 192 lbs. Deb: 4/16/57

1957	Chi-N	122	415	37	107	17	1	10	39	22	87	.258	.300	.376	81	-12	-11	46	0	0	0	1	*C	-0.3
1958	Chi-N	76	201	30	52	7	0	12	29	21	41	.259	.338	.473	113	3	3	32	0	0	0	2	C	0.9
1959	Chi-N	44	105	7	17	2	0	3	9	11	23	.162	.241	.267	36	-10	-10	7	0	0	0	-1	C	-0.8
1960	Chi-N	9	13	0	2	1	0	0	0	0	5	.154	.154	.231	4	-2	-2	0	0	0	0	4	/C	0.2
	Phi-N	59	160	13	29	6	2	4	13	16	42	.181	.264	.319	59	-9	-9	13	0	0	0	5	C	-0.1
	Yr	68	173	13	31	7	2	4	13	16	47	.179	.257	.312	55	-11	-11	13	0	0	0	8		0.1
1961	Phi-N	19	31	0	7	1	0	0	2	4	8	.226	.314	.258	55	-2	-2	2	1	0	0	2	C	0.2
1962	Pit-N	24	50	5	9	1	1	1	5	3	10	.180	.226	.300	40	-4	-4	3	0	0	0	8	C	0.4
1963	Cle-A	9	9	0	0	0	0	0	0	1	5	.000	.100	.000	-70	-2	-2	0	0	0	0	3	/C	0.0
	Was-A	14	18	1	1	0	0	0	0	1	0	.056	.105	.056	-54	-4	-4	0	0	0	0	2	C	-0.1
	Yr	23	27	1	1	0	0	0	0	2	5	.037	.103	.037	-59	-6	-6	0	0	0	0	5		0.0
Total	7	376	1002	93	224	35	4	30	97	79	221	.224	.286	.356	72	-42	-41	104	1	0	0	25	C	0.5

■ DOUG NEFF Neff, Douglas Williams b: 10/8/1891, Harrisonburg, Va. d: 5/23/32, Cape Charles, Va. BR/TR, 5'9", 141 lbs. Deb: 6/26/14

1914	Was-A	3	2	0	0	0	0	0	0	0	0	.000	.000	.000	-97	-0	-0	0	0			2	/S	0.1
1915	Was-A	30	60	1	10	1	0	0	4	4	6	.167	.219	.183	20	-6	-6	3	1	2	-1	-3	32/S	-0.9
Total	2	33	62	1	10	1	0	0	4	4	6	.161	.212	.177	16	-6	-6	3	1	2		-2	/32S	-0.8

■ CY NEIGHBORS Neighbors, Flemon Cecil b: 9/23/1880, Fayetteville, Mo. d: 5/20/64, Tacoma, Wash. BR , Deb: 4/29/08

| 1908 | Pit-N | 1 | 0 | 0 | 0 | 0 | 0 | 0 | 0 | 0 | | — | — | — | — | 0 | 0 | 0 | 0 | | | -0 | /O | 0.0 |

■ BOB NEIGHBORS Neighbors, Robert Otis b: 11/9/17, Talahina, Okla. d: 8/8/52, North Korea (Mia) BR/TR, 5'11", 165 lbs. Deb: 9/16/39

| 1939 | StL-A | 7 | 11 | 3 | 2 | 0 | 0 | 1 | 1 | 0 | 1 | .182 | .182 | .455 | 56 | -1 | -1 | 1 | 0 | 0 | 0 | -0 | /S | 0.0 |

YEAR	TM/L	G	AB	R	H	2B	3B	HR	RBI	BB	SO	AVG	OBP	SLG	PRO+	BR	/A	RC	SB	CS	SBR	FR	POS	TPR
■ TOMMY NEILL			Neill, Thomas White		b: 11/7/19, Hartselle, Ala.			BL/TR, 6'2", 200 lbs.		Deb: 9/10/46													
1946	Bos-N	13	45	8	12	2	0	0	7	2	1	.267	.298	.311	72	-2	-2	4	0			-1	O	-0.2
1947	Bos-N	7	10	1	2	0	0	0	0	1	2	.200	.333	.400	96	-0	-0	1	0			-0	/O	0.0
Total	2	20	55	9	14	2	1	0	7	3	3	.255	.305	.327	77	-2	-2	5	0			-1	/O	-0.2
■ BERNIE NEIS			Neis, Bernard Edmund		b: 9/26/1895, Bloomington, Ill.		d: 11/29/72, Inverness, Fla.		BB/TR, 5'7", 160 lbs.		Deb: 4/14/20												
1920	*Bro-N	95	249	38	63	11	2	2	22	26	35	.253	.329	.337	89	-2	-3	28	9	9	-3	-2	O	-1.3
1921	Bro-N	102	230	34	59	5	4	4	34	25	41	.257	.332	.365	81	-5	-6	28	9	7	-2	4	O/2	-0.6
1922	Bro-N	61	70	15	16	4	1	1	9	13	8	.229	.349	.357	83	-2	-1	9	3	2	-0	2	O	0.0
1923	Bro-N	126	445	78	122	17	4	5	37	36	38	.274	.330	.364	85	-11	-9	53	8	8	-2	-0	*O	-1.4
1924	Bro-N	80	211	43	64	8	3	4	26	27	17	.303	.385	.427	121	6	7	36	4	2	-0	-1	O	0.4
1925	Bos-N	106	355	47	101	20	2	5	45	38	19	.285	.354	.394	100	-4	-0	49	8	10	-4	14	O	0.8
1926	Bos-N	30	93	16	20	5	2	0	8	8	10	.215	.277	.312	64	-6	-4	8	4			1	O	-0.3
1927	Cle-A	32	96	17	29	9	0	4	18	18	9	.302	.412	.521	140	6	6	20	0	1	-1	5	O	0.8
	Chi-A	45	76	9	22	5	0	0	11	10	9	.289	.372	.355	92	-1	-1	10	1	0	0	-3	O	-0.3
	Yr	77	172	26	51	14	0	4	29	28	18	.297	.395	.448	120	5	6	31	1	1	-0	2		0.5
Total	8	677	1825	297	496	84	18	25	210	201	186	.272	.346	.379	94	-19	-12	242	46	39		19	O/2	-1.9
■ ERNIE NEITZKE			Neitzke, Ernest Fredrich		b: 11/13/1894, Toledo, Ohio		d: 4/27/77, Sylvania, Ohio		BR/TR, 5'10", 180 lbs.		Deb: 6/02/21												
1921	Bos-A	11	25	3	6	0	0	0	2	4	4	.240	.345	.240	53	-2	-2	2	0	0	0	-1	/OP	-0.1
■ DAVE NELSON			Nelson, David Earl		b: 6/20/44, Fort Sill, Okla.		BR/TR, 5'10", 160 lbs.		Deb: 4/11/68 C													
1968	Cle-A	88	189	26	44	4	5	0	19	17	35	.233	.300	.307	85	-4	-3	20	23	7	3	-1	2S	0.1
1969	Cle-A	52	123	11	25	0	0	0	6	9	26	.203	.263	.203	31	-11	-11	7	4	3	-1	5	2/O	-0.5
1970	Was-A	47	107	5	17	1	0	0	4	7	24	.159	.211	.168	6	-14	-13	4	2	1	0	1	2	-0.8
1971	Was-A	85	329	47	92	11	3	5	33	23	29	.280	.329	.377	105	-1	1	39	17	8	0	-13	3/2	-1.5
1972	Tex-A	145	499	68	113	16	3	2	28	67	81	.226	.324	.283	85	-9	-7	54	51	17	5	-11	*3O	-1.0
1973	Tex-A	142	576	71	165	24	4	7	48	34	78	.286	.326	.378	102	-2	1	70	43	16	3	-12	*2	-0.1
1974	Tex-A	121	474	71	112	13	1	3	42	34	72	.236	.293	.287	69	-20	-18	38	25	13	-0	1	*2/D	-1.2
1975	Tex-A	28	80	9	17	1	0	2	10	8	10	.213	.292	.300	68	-3	-3	8	6	0	2	1	2/D	0.0
1976	*KC-A	78	153	24	36	4	2	1	17	14	26	.235	.299	.307	77	-4	-4	16	15	5	2	2	2D/1	0.2
1977	KC-A	27	48	8	9	3	1	0	4	7	11	.188	.291	.292	59	-3	-3	4	1	3	-2	-2	2/D	-0.4
Total	10	813	2578	340	630	77	19	20	211	220	392	.244	.307	.312	81	-70	-61	259	187	73	12	-29	23/DOS1	-5.2
■ ROCKY NELSON			Nelson, Glenn Richard		b: 11/18/24, Portsmouth, Ohio		BL/TL, 5'10.5", 175 lbs.		Deb: 4/27/49													
1949	StL-N	82	244	28	54	8	4	4	32	11	12	.221	.258	.336	55	-15	-17	20	1			-4	1	-2.0
1950	StL-N	76	235	27	58	10	4	1	20	26	9	.247	.324	.336	71	-9	-10	27	4			3	1	-0.9
1951	StL-N	9	18	3	4	1	0	0	1	1	0	.222	.263	.278	45	-1	-1	1	0	0	0	-1	/1O	-0.1
	Pit-N	71	195	29	52	7	4	1	14	10	7	.267	.302	.359	75	-7	-7	21	1	1	-0	1	1O	-0.7
	Yr	80	213	32	56	8	4	1	15	11	7	.263	.299	.352	73	-8	-9	22	1	1	-0	0		-0.8
	Chi-A	6	5	0	0	0	0	0	0	1	1	.000	.167	.000	-53	-1	-1	0	0	0	0	0	H	0.0
1952	*Bro-N	37	39	6	10	1	0	0	3	7	4	.256	.370	.282	82	-1	-1	5	0	0	0	-1	/1	-0.1
1954	Cle-A	4	4	0	0	0	0	0	0	0	1	.000	.000	.000	-98	-1	-1	0	0	0	0	0	/1	0.0
1956	Bro-N	31	96	7	20	2	0	4	15	4	10	.208	.240	.354	53	-6	-7	8	0	0	0	2	1	-0.6
	StL-N	38	56	6	13	5	0	3	8	6	6	.232	.306	.482	108	0	0	8	0	0	0	0	1/O	0.0
	Yr	69	152	13	33	7	0	7	23	10	16	.217	.265	.401	73	-6	-6	15	0	0	0	2		-0.6
1959	Pit-N	98	175	31	51	11	0	6	32	23	19	.291	.383	.457	124	6	6	32	0	0	0	-3	1/O	0.0
1960	*Pit-N	93	200	34	60	11	1	7	35	24	15	.300	.389	.470	133	10	10	38	1	2	-1	1	1	0.7
1961	Pit-N	75	127	15	25	5	1	5	13	17	11	.197	.301	.370	77	-4	-4	14	0	0	0	-1	1	-0.7
Total	9	620	1394	186	347	61	14	31	173	130	94	.249	.318	.379	84	-28	-33	174	7	3		-2	1/O	-4.4
■ JAMIE NELSON			Nelson, James Victor		b: 9/5/59, Clinton Okla.		BR/TR, 5'11", 180 lbs.		Deb: 7/21/83													
1983	Sea-A	40	96	9	21	3	0	1	5	13	12	.219	.312	.281	62	-4	-5	9	4	2	0	5	C	0.2
■ CANDY NELSON			Nelson, John W		b: 3/12/1854, Portland, Maine		d: 9/4/10, Brooklyn, N.Y.		BL/TR, 5'6", 145 lbs.		Deb: 6/11/1872											
1872	Tro-n	4	17	1	6	0	0	0		0		.353	.353	.353	116	0	0	2					/OS	0.0
	Eck-n	18	76	12	19	2	0	0		2		.250	.269	.276	80	-3	-0	6					/2O3	0.0
	Yr	22	93	13	25	2	0	0		2		.269	.284	.290	88	-2	-0	8						0.0
1873	Mut-n	36	168	28	56	6	1	0		1		.333	.337	.381	112	2	2	22					2/O3	0.0
1874	Mut-n	65	295	55	71	8	5	0		9		.241	.263	.302	77	-6	-8	24					*2S	-0.7
1875	Mut-n	70	276	29	56	8	0	0		10		.203	.231	.232	57	-10	-13	15					23/O	-1.1
1878	Ind-N	19	84	12	11	1	0	0	5	5	11	.131	.180	.143	8	-8	-6	2				-6	S	-1.0
1879	Tro-N	28	106	17	28	7	1	0	10	8	4	.264	.316	.349	127	2	3	12				4	S/O	0.8
1881	Wor-N	24	103	13	29	1	0	0	15	5	6	.282	.315	.320	95	0	-1	11				2	S	0.3
1883	NY-a	97	417	75	127	19	6	0		31		.305	.353	.379	131	17	14	57				-6	*S	0.5
1884	*NY-a	111	432	114	110	15	3	1		74		.255	.375	.310	133	19	21	51				-17	*S/2	0.1
1885	NY-a	107	420	98	107	12	4	1		61		.255	.353	.310	124	10	15	47				13	*S/3	2.6
1886	NY-a	109	413	89	93	7	2	0		64		.225	.332	.252	90	-3	-0	40	14			-8	SO	-0.4
1887	NY-a	68	257	61	63	5	1	0		48		.245	.380	.272	90	-1	1	39	29			10	OS/2	0.8
	NY-N	1	2	0	0	0	0	0	0	0		.000	.000	.000	-99	-1	-1	0	0			0	/3	0.0
1890	Bro-a	60	223	44	56	3	2	0		35		.251	.365	.283	97	0	2	28	12			-8	S/O	-0.2
Total	4 n	193	832	125	208	24	6	0		22		.250	.269	.293	79	-17	-19	69	0				2/3OS	-1.8
Total	9	624	2457	523	624	70	19	3	30	331	22	.254	.349	.302	110	35	49	287	55			-15	S/O32	3.5
■ LYNN NELSON			Nelson, Lynn Bernard "Line Drive"		b: 2/24/05, Sheldon, N.Dak.		d: 2/15/55, Kansas City, Mo.		BL/TR, 5'10.5", 170 lbs.		Deb: 4/18/30											
1930	Chi-N	37	18	0	4	1	1	0	2	0	1	.222	.222	.389	44	-2	-2	1	0			1	P	0.0
1933	Chi-N	29	21	5	5	1	1	0	1	1	3	.238	.273	.381	85	-0	-0	2	0			1	P	0.0
1934	Chi-N	2	0	0	0	0	0	0	0	0	0	—	—	—	—	0	0	0	0			0	/P	0.0
1937	Phi-A	74	113	18	40	6	2	4	29	6	13	.354	.387	.549	135	5	5	24	1	0	0	-1	P/O	1.0
1938	Phi-A	67	112	12	31	0	0	0	15	7	12	.277	.319	.277	52	-8	-8	10	0	0	0	-0	P	-0.1
1939	Phi-A	40	80	3	15	2	0	0	5	2	13	.188	.217	.213	10	-11	-11	3	0	1	-1	-1	P	-0.1
1940	Det-A	19	23	4	8	0	0	1	3	0	6	.348	.348	.478	102	0	0	4	0	0	0	0	/P	0.1
Total	7	268	367	42	103	10	4	5	55	16	48	.281	.313	.371	74	-16	-15	45	1	1		0	P/O	1.0
■ RAY NELSON			Nelson, Raymond "Kell" (b: Raymond Nelson Kellogg)		b: 8/4/1875, Holyoke, Mass.		d: 1/8/61, Mt.Vernon, N.Y.		BR/TR, 5'9", 150 lbs.		Deb: 5/06/01										
1901	NY-N	39	130	12	26	2	0	0	7	10		.200	.262	.215	43	-9	-9	9	3			-3	2	-0.8
■ RICKY NELSON			Nelson, Ricky Lee		b: 5/8/59, Eloy, Ariz.		BL/TR, 6', 200 lbs.		Deb: 5/17/83													
1983	Sea-A	98	291	32	74	13	3	5	36	17	50	.254	.295	.371	79	-8	-9	31	7	4	-0	-8	O/D	-1.7
1984	Sea-A	9	15	2	3	0	0	0	1	0	2	.200	.294	.400	91	-0	-0	2	0	0	0	0	/OD	0.0
1985	Sea-A	6	2	2	0	0	0	0	0	1	1	.000	.000	.000	-99	-1	-1	0	0	0	0	0	/O	0.0
1986	Sea-A	10	12	2	2	0	0	0	1	0	4	.167	.167	.167	-9	-2	-2	0	1	0	0	0	/OD	-0.1
Total	4	123	320	38	79	13	3	6	39	18	59	.247	.289	.363	75	-10	-11	34	8	4		-8	/OD	-1.8

YEAR	TM/L	G	AB	R	H	2B	3B	HR	RBI	BB	SO	AVG	OBP	SLG	PRO+	BR	/A	RC	SB	CS	SBR	FR	POS	TPR

■ ROB NELSON Nelson, Robert Augustus b: 5/17/64, Pasadena, Cal. BL/TL, 6'4", 215 lbs. Deb: 9/09/86

1986	Oak-A	5	9	1	2	1	0	0	0	1	4	.222	.300	.333	78	-0	-0	1	0	0	0	0	/1D	0.0
1987	Oak-A	7	24	1	4	1	0	0	0	0	12	.167	.167	.208	-2	-3	-3	1	0	0	0	3	/1	0.0
	SD-N	10	11	0	1	0	0	0	1	1	8	.091	.167	.091	-31	-2	-2	0	0	0	0	-0	/1	-0.1
1988	SD-N	7	21	4	4	0	0	1	3	2	9	.190	.261	.333	71	-1	-1	2	0	0	0	1	/1	0.0
1989	SD-N	42	82	6	16	0	1	3	7	20	29	.195	.353	.329	96	0	0	10	1	3	-2	3	1	0.0
1990	SD-N	5	5	0	0	0	0	0	0	0	4	.000	.000	.000	-99	-1	-1	0	0	0	0	0	/H	0.0
Total	5	76	152	12	27	2	1	4	11	24	66	.178	.290	.283	62	-8	-7	14	1	3	-2	6	/1D	-0.1

■ TEX NELSON Nelson, Robert Sidney "Babe" b: 8/7/36, Dallas, Tex. BL/TL, 6'3", 205 lbs. Deb: 6/22/55

1955	Bal-A	25	31	4	6	0	0	0	1	7	13	.194	.342	.194	50	-2	-2	3	0	0	0	1	/O1	-0.1
1956	Bal-A	39	68	5	14	2	0	0	5	7	22	.206	.280	.235	40	-6	-5	5	0	0	0	1	O	-0.5
1957	Bal-A	15	23	2	5	0	2	0	5	1	5	.217	.280	.391	87	-1	-1	3	0	0	0	-1	/O	-0.1
Total	3	79	122	11	25	2	2	0	11	15	40	.205	.297	.254	52	-9	-8	10	0	0	0	0	/O1	-0.7

■ TOMMY NELSON Nelson, Tom Cousineau b: 5/1/17, Chicago, Ill. d: 9/24/73, San Diego, Cal. BR/TR, 5'11.5", 180 lbs. Deb: 4/17/45

| 1945 | Bos-N | 40 | 121 | 6 | 20 | 2 | 0 | 0 | 6 | 4 | 13 | .165 | .192 | .182 | 4 | -16 | -16 | 3 | 1 | | | -3 | 32 | -1.7 |

■ DICK NEN Nen, Richard Le Roy b: 9/24/39, South Gate, Cal. BL/TL, 6'2", 200 lbs. Deb: 9/18/63

1963	LA-N	7	8	2	1	0	0	1	1	3	3	.125	.364	.500	157	1	1	1	0	0	0	-0	/1	0.0
1965	Was-A	69	246	18	64	7	1	6	31	19	47	.260	.316	.370	96	-2	-2	29	1	2	-1	9	1	0.4
1966	Was-A	94	235	20	50	8	0	6	30	28	46	.213	.297	.323	79	-6	-6	21	0	2	-1	-1	1	-1.1
1967	Was-A	110	238	21	52	7	1	6	29	21	39	.218	.282	.332	84	-6	-5	21	0	1	-1	2	1/O	-0.9
1968	Chi-N	81	94	8	17	1	1	2	16	6	17	.181	.230	.277	48	-6	-6	6	0	0	0	-0	1	-0.9
1970	Was-A	6	5	1	1	0	0	0	0	0	0	.200	.200	.200	11	-1	-1	0	0	0	0	0	/1	0.0
Total	6	367	826	70	185	23	3	21	107	77	152	.224	.291	.335	82	-20	-19	79	1	5	-3	9	1/O	-2.5

■ JACK NESS Ness, John Charles b: 11/11/1885, Chicago, Ill. d: 12/3/57, DeLand, Fla. BR/TR, 6'2", 165 lbs. Deb: 5/09/11

1911	Det-A	12	39	6	6	0	0	0	2	2		.154	.195	.154	-2	-5	-6	1	0			1	1	-0.4
1916	Chi-A	75	258	32	69	7	5	1	34	9	32	.267	.310	.345	96	-2	-2	30	4			-5	1	-0.9
Total	2	87	297	38	75	7	5	1	36	11	32	.253	.295	.320	82	-7	-8	31	4			-4	/1	-1.3

■ GRAIG NETTLES Nettles, Graig b: 8/20/44, San Diego, Cal. BL/TR, 6', 180 lbs. Deb: 9/06/67

1967	Min-A	3	3	0	1	0	0	0	0	0	0	.333	.333	.667	175	0	0	1	0	0	0	0	H	0.0
1968	Min-A	22	76	13	17	2	1	5	8	7	20	.224	.298	.474	125	2	2	10	0	0	0	0	O/31	0.2
1969	*Min-A	96	225	27	50	9	2	7	26	32	47	.222	.322	.373	92	-2	-2	27	1	2	-1	-0	O3	-0.4
1970	Cle-A	157	549	81	129	13	1	26	62	81	77	.235	.336	.404	99	3	-0	77	3	1	0	29	*3/O	2.9
1971	Cle-A	158	598	78	156	18	1	28	86	82	56	.261	.353	.435	112	18	11	93	7	4	-0	42	*3	5.0
1972	Cle-A	150	557	65	141	28	0	17	70	57	50	.253	.327	.395	110	9	7	73	2	3	-1	5	*3	1.8
1973	NY-A	160	552	65	129	18	0	22	81	78	76	.234	.336	.386	107	3	5	73	0	0	0	26	*3/D	3.0
1974	NY-A	155	566	74	139	21	1	22	75	59	75	.246	.320	.403	110	4	6	75	1	0	0	16	*3/S	2.6
1975	NY-A	157	581	71	155	24	4	21	91	51	88	.267	.328	.430	116	8	10	82	1	3	-2	11	*3	2.3
1976	*NY-A	158	583	88	148	29	2	32	93	62	94	.254	.330	.475	135	23	23	92	11	6	-0	17	*3/S	4.2
1977	*NY-A	158	589	99	150	23	4	37	107	68	79	.255	.333	.496	124	17	18	98	2	5	-2	-3	*3/D	0.9
1978	*NY-A	159	587	81	162	23	2	27	93	59	69	.276	.348	.460	128	19	21	91	1	1	-0	-6	*3/S	1.4
1979	NY-A	145	521	71	132	15	1	20	73	59	53	.253	.329	.401	98	-3	-2	68	1	2	-1	9	*3	0.9
1980	*NY-A	89	324	52	79	14	0	16	45	42	42	.244	.332	.435	110	4	4	47	0	0	0	-3	3/S	0.1
1981	*NY-A	103	349	46	85	7	1	15	46	47	49	.244	.335	.398	112	5	5	48	0	2	-1	8	3/D	1.3
1982	NY-A	122	405	47	94	11	2	18	55	51	49	.232	.319	.402	98	-2	-1	50	1	5	-3	8	*3/D	0.2
1983	NY-A	129	462	56	123	17	3	20	75	51	65	.266	.343	.446	120	10	12	71	0	1	-1	1	*3/D	1.2
1984	*SD-N	124	395	56	90	11	1	20	65	58	55	.228	.334	.413	109	5	5	55	0	0	0	-10	*3	-0.5
1985	SD-N	137	440	66	115	23	1	15	61	72	59	.261	.365	.420	121	13	14	70	0	0	0	-9	*3	0.6
1986	SD-N	126	354	36	77	9	0	16	55	41	62	.218	.302	.379	88	-7	-6	41	0	1	-1	-2	*3	-1.1
1987	Atl-N	112	177	16	37	8	1	5	33	22	25	.209	.296	.350	67	-8	-9	18	1	0	0	-0	3/1	-0.9
1988	Mon-N	80	93	5	16	4	0	1	14	9	19	.172	.245	.247	40	-7	-7	5	0	0	0	-1	3/1	-0.9
Total	22	2700	8986	1193	2225	328	28	390	1314	1088	1209	.248	.332	.421	110	115	118	1264	32	36	-12	138	*3/O1DS	24.8

■ JIM NETTLES Nettles, James William b: 3/2/47, San Diego, Cal. BL/TL, 6', 186 lbs. Deb: 9/07/70

1970	Min-A	13	20	3	5	0	0	0	0	1	5	.250	.286	.250	48	-1	-1	1	0	1	-1	-0	O	-0.2
1971	Min-A	70	168	17	42	5	1	6	24	19	24	.250	.326	.399	101	1	0	22	3	2	-0	10	O	0.8
1972	Min-A	102	235	28	48	5	2	4	15	32	52	.204	.302	.294	74	-6	-7	21	4	3	-1	6	O/1	-0.3
1974	Det-A	43	141	20	32	5	1	6	17	15	26	.227	.306	.404	99	0	-0	17	3	4	-2	-7	O	-0.9
1979	KC-A	11	23	0	2	0	0	0	1	3	2	.087	.192	.087	-21	-4	-4	1	0	0	0	1	/O1	-0.2
1981	Oak-A	1	0	0	0	0	0	0	0	0	0	—	—	—	—	0	0	0	0	0	0	0	/O	0.0
Total	6	240	587	68	129	15	4	16	57	70	109	.220	.305	.341	83	-10	-13	63	10	10	-3	10	O/1	-0.8

■ MORRIS NETTLES Nettles, Morris b: 1/26/52, Los Angeles, Cal. BL/TL, 6'1", 170 lbs. Deb: 4/26/74

1974	Cal-A	56	175	27	48	4	0	0	8	16	38	.274	.335	.297	88	-3	-2	18	20	11	-1	-3	O	-0.6
1975	Cal-A	112	294	50	68	11	0	0	23	26	57	.231	.296	.269	65	-15	-12	24	22	15	-2	-0	O/D	-1.7
Total	2	168	469	77	116	15	0	0	31	42	95	.247	.311	.279	74	-18	-14	41	42	26	-3	-3	O/D	-2.3

■ MILO NETZEL Netzel, Miles A. b: 5/12/1886, Eldred, Pa. d: 3/18/38, Oxnard, Cal. TL, Deb: 9/16/09

| 1909 | Cle-A | 10 | 37 | 2 | 7 | 1 | 0 | 0 | 3 | 3 | | .189 | .250 | .216 | 46 | -2 | -2 | 2 | 1 | | | -3 | /3O | -0.5 |

■ OTTO NEU Neu, Otto Adam b: 9/24/1894, Springfield, Ohio d: 9/19/32, Kenton, Ohio BR/TR, 5'11", 170 lbs. Deb: 7/10/17

| 1917 | StL-A | 1 | 0 | 0 | 0 | 0 | 0 | 0 | 0 | 0 | 0 | — | — | — | 0 | 0 | 0 | 0 | 0 | | | 0 | /S | 0.0 |

■ JOHNNY NEUN Neun, John Henry b: 10/28/1900, Baltimore, Md. d: 3/28/90, Baltimore, Md. BB/TL, 5'10.5", 175 lbs. Deb: 4/14/25 MC

1925	Det-A	60	75	15	20	3	3	0	4	9	12	.267	.345	.387	87	-2	-2	10	2	3	-1	-1	1	-0.2
1926	Det-A	97	242	47	72	14	4	0	15	27	26	.298	.370	.388	97	-0	-1	34	4	7	-3	-3	1	-0.7
1927	Det-A	79	204	38	66	9	4	0	27	35	13	.324	.427	.407	116	7	7	35	22	7	2	-3	1	0.4
1928	Det-A	36	108	15	23	3	1	0	5	7	10	.213	.261	.259	36	-10	-10	7	2	2	-1	0	1	-1.1
1930	Bos-N	81	212	39	69	12	2	0	23	21	18	.325	.389	.429	101	-0	1	35	9			0	1	0.0
1931	Bos-N	79	104	17	23	1	3	0	11	11	14	.221	.302	.288	62	-6	-5	10	2			-0	1	-0.7
Total	6	432	945	171	273	42	17	2	85	110	93	.289	.366	.376	91	-11	-10	131	41	19		-6	1	-2.3

■ NEVINS Nevins Deb: 6/17/1873

| 1873 | Res-n | 13 | 54 | 7 | 11 | 2 | 1 | 0 | | 0 | | .204 | .204 | .278 | 43 | -4 | -3 | 3 | | | | | 3/2O | -0.1 |

■ DON NEWCOMBE Newcombe, Donald "Newk" b: 6/14/26, Madison, N.J. BL/TR, 6'4", 220 lbs. Deb: 5/20/49

1949	*Bro-N	39	96	8	22	4	0	0	10	5	16	.229	.267	.271	43	-8	-8	6	0			0	P	0.0
1950	Bro-N	40	97	8	24	3	1	1	8	10	19	.247	.318	.330	69	-4	-4	10	0			0	P	0.0
1951	Bro-N	40	103	11	23	3	1	0	8	9	8	.223	.286	.272	50	-7	-7	9	0	0	0	0	P	0.0
1954	Bro-N	31	47	6	15	1	0	0	4	4	6	.319	.373	.340	85	-1	-1	7	0	0	0	-1	P	0.0
1955	*Bro-N	57	117	18	42	9	1	7	23	6	18	.359	.395	.632	163	11	10	30	1	0	0	-2	P	0.0

YEAR	TM/L	G	AB	R	H	2B	3B	HR	RBI	BB	SO	AVG	OBP	SLG	PRO+	BR	/A	RC	SB	CS	SBR	FR	POS	TPR
1956	*Bro-N	52	111	13	26	6	0	2	16	12	18	.234	.315	.342	71	-4	-5	12	1	0	0	0	P	0.0
1957	Bro-N	34	74	8	17	2	0	1	7	11	11	.230	.329	.297	64	-3	-4	7	0	1	-1	2	P	0.0
1958	LA-N	11	12	2	5	0	0	0	0	2	2	.417	.500	.417	141	1	1	3	0	0	0	0	P	0.0
	Cin-N	39	60	9	21	1	0	1	9	8	10	.350	.426	.417	118	3	2	12	0	0	0	-1	P	0.0
	Yr	50	72	11	26	1	0	1	9	10	12	.361	.439	.417	122	4	3	14	0	0	0	-1		0.0
1959	Cin-N	61	105	10	32	2	0	3	21	17	23	.305	.402	.410	113	3	3	19	0	0	0	-1	P	0.7
1960	Cin-N	24	36	0	5	1	0	0	1	3	8	.139	.205	.167	3	-5	-5	2	0	0	0	-1	P	0.0
	Cle-A	24	20	1	6	1	0	0	1	1	7	.300	.333	.350	88	-0	-0	2	0	0	0	-1	P	0.0
Total	10	452	878	94	238	33	3	15	108	87	147	.271	.339	.367	85	-13	-18	117	2	1		-4	P	0.7

■ JOHN NEWELL
Newell, John A.   b: 1/14/1868, Wilmington, Del.   d: 1/28/19, Wilmington, Del.   BR/TL, Deb: 7/22/1891

YEAR	TM/L	G	AB	R	H	2B	3B	HR	RBI	BB	SO	AVG	OBP	SLG	PRO+	BR	/A	RC	SB	CS	SBR	FR	POS	TPR
1891	Pit-N	5	18	1	2	0	0	0	2	0	0	.111	.158	.111	-21	-3	-3	0	0			-1	/3	-0.3

■ T. E. NEWELL
Newell, T. E.   b: St.Louis, Mo.   Deb: 8/08/1877

YEAR	TM/L	G	AB	R	H	2B	3B	HR	RBI	BB	SO	AVG	OBP	SLG	PRO+	BR	/A	RC	SB	CS	SBR	FR	POS	TPR
1877	StL-N	1	3	0	0	0	0	0	0	0	0	.000	.000	.000	-99	-1	-1	0				0	/S	0.0

■ AL NEWMAN
Newman, Albert Dwayne   b: 6/30/60, Kansas City, Mo.   BB/TR, 5'9", 175 lbs.   Deb: 6/14/85

YEAR	TM/L	G	AB	R	H	2B	3B	HR	RBI	BB	SO	AVG	OBP	SLG	PRO+	BR	/A	RC	SB	CS	SBR	FR	POS	TPR
1985	Mon-N	25	29	7	5	1	0	0	1	3	4	.172	.250	.207	31	-3	-3	2	2	1	0	10	2/S	0.8
1986	Mon-N	95	185	23	37	3	0	1	8	21	20	.200	.282	.232	44	-14	-14	12	11	11	-3	9	2S	-0.5
1987	*Min-A	110	307	44	68	15	5	0	29	34	27	.221	.299	.303	58	-17	-19	28	15	11	-2	-10	S23/OD	-2.2
1988	Min-A	105	260	35	58	7	0	0	19	29	34	.223	.301	.250	54	-14	-15	22	12	3	2	-4	3S2/D	-1.4
1989	Min-A	141	446	62	113	18	2	0	38	59	46	.253	.343	.303	78	-8	-12	52	25	12	0	-21	23S/OD	-2.8
1990	Min-A	144	388	43	94	14	0	0	30	33	34	.242	.305	.278	60	-18	-21	55	13	6	0	-1	2S3/O	-1.3
Total	6	620	1615	214	375	58	7	1	125	179	165	.232	.310	.279	62	-74	-83	150	78	44	-3	-17	2S3/DO	-7.4

■ CHARLIE NEWMAN
Newman, Charles "Decker"   b: 11/5/1868, Juda, Wis.   d: 11/23/47, San Diego, Cal.   BR/TR, Deb: N/A.

YEAR	TM/L	G	AB	R	H	2B	3B	HR	RBI	BB	SO	AVG	OBP	SLG	PRO+	BR	/A	RC	SB	CS	SBR	FR	POS	TPR
1892	NY-N	3	12	1	4	0	0	0	1	2	0	.333	.429	.333	136	1	1	3	3			-0	/O	0.0
	Chi-N	16	61	4	10	0	0	0	2	1	6	.164	.177	.164	4	-7	-7	2	2			-2	O	-0.9
	Yr	19	73	5	14	0	0	0	3	3	6	.192	.224	.192	27	-6	-6	4	5			-3		-0.9

■ JEFF NEWMAN
Newman, Jeffrey Lynn   b: 9/11/48, Fort Worth, Tex.   BR/TR, 6'2", 215 lbs.   Deb: 6/30/76   MC

YEAR	TM/L	G	AB	R	H	2B	3B	HR	RBI	BB	SO	AVG	OBP	SLG	PRO+	BR	/A	RC	SB	CS	SBR	FR	POS	TPR
1976	Oak-A	43	77	5	15	4	0	0	4	4	12	.195	.235	.247	43	-6	-5	5	0	0	0	6	C	0.2
1977	Oak-A	94	162	17	36	9	0	4	15	4	24	.222	.246	.352	61	-9	-9	14	2	0	1	10	C/P	0.4
1978	Oak-A	105	268	25	64	7	1	9	32	18	40	.239	.289	.373	90	-6	-4	28	0	3	-2	-5	C1/D	-1.0
1979	Oak-A	143	516	53	119	17	2	22	71	27	88	.231	.270	.399	82	-18	-14	51	2	1	0	-1	C1/3D	-1.3
1980	Oak-A	127	438	37	102	19	1	15	56	25	81	.233	.276	.384	85	-14	-10	43	3	4	-2	-15	1C/32D	-2.8
1981	*Oak-A	68	216	17	50	12	0	3	15	9	28	.231	.262	.329	73	-9	-8	16	0	2	-1	2	C1	-0.6
1982	Oak-A	72	251	19	50	11	0	6	30	14	49	.199	.242	.315	54	-17	-16	18	0	1	-1	-0	C/13D	-1.3
1983	Bos-A	59	132	11	25	4	0	3	7	10	31	.189	.257	.288	46	-9	-10	9	0	1	-1	1	C/D	-0.6
1984	Bos-A	24	63	5	14	2	0	1	3	5	16	.222	.279	.302	58	-3	-4	6	0	0	0	2	C	0.0
Total	9	735	2123	189	475	85	4	63	233	116	369	.224	.266	.357	73	-92	-81	190	7	12	-5	-0	C1/D32P	-7.0

■ PATRICK NEWNAM
Newnam, Patrick Henry   b: 12/10/1880, Hempstead, Tex.   d: 6/20/38, San Antonio, Tex.   BR/TR, 6', 180 lbs.   Deb: 5/29/10

YEAR	TM/L	G	AB	R	H	2B	3B	HR	RBI	BB	SO	AVG	OBP	SLG	PRO+	BR	/A	RC	SB	CS	SBR	FR	POS	TPR
1910	StL-A	103	384	45	83	3	8	2	26	29		.216	.275	.281	79	-12	-9	33	16			-4	*1	-0.9
1911	StL-A	20	62	11	12	4	0	0	5	12		.194	.351	.258	74	-2	-1	7	4			1	1	0.0
Total	2	123	446	56	95	7	8	2	31	41		.213	.287	.278	78	-14	-11	40	20			-3	1	-0.9

■ SKEETER NEWSOME
Newsome, Lamar Ashby   b: 10/18/10, Phenix City, Ala.   BR/TR, 5'9", 155 lbs.   Deb: 4/19/35

YEAR	TM/L	G	AB	R	H	2B	3B	HR	RBI	BB	SO	AVG	OBP	SLG	PRO+	BR	/A	RC	SB	CS	SBR	FR	POS	TPR
1935	Phi-A	59	145	18	30	7	1	1	10	5	9	.207	.233	.290	35	-15	-14	10	2	1		8	S2/3O	-0.4
1936	Phi-A	127	471	41	106	15	2	0	46	25	27	.225	.266	.265	32	-51	-50	35	13	4	2	7	*S/23O	-2.9
1937	Phi-A	122	438	53	111	22	1	1	30	37	22	.253	.312	.315	59	-28	-27	45	11	5	0	7	*S	-1.1
1938	Phi-A	17	48	7	13	4	0	0	7	1	4	.271	.286	.354	61	-3	-3	5	1	1	-0	1	S	0.0
1939	Phi-A	99	248	22	55	9	1	0	17	19	12	.222	.277	.266	40	-23	-22	17	5	7	-3	1	S/2	-1.2
1941	Bos-A	93	227	28	51	6	0	2	17	22	11	.225	.296	.278	51	-15	-16	20	10	4	1	15	S2	0.3
1942	Bos-A	29	95	7	26	6	0	0	9	9	5	.274	.337	.337	87	-1	-2	11	2	1	0	3	32/S	0.2
1943	Bos-A	114	449	48	119	21	2	1	22	21	21	.265	.301	.327	82	-10	-10	43	5	6	-2	14	S3	0.2
1944	Bos-A	136	472	41	114	26	3	0	41	33	21	.242	.291	.309	72	-18	-17	43	4	3	-1	11	*S/23	0.1
1945	Bos-A	125	438	45	127	30	1	1	48	20	15	.290	.322	.370	98	-1	-2	51	6	3	0	22	2S3	2.4
1946	Phi-N	112	375	35	87	10	2	1	23	30	23	.232	.289	.277	63	-19	-18	33	4			-12	*S/23	-2.3
1947	Phi-N	95	310	36	71	8	2	2	22	24	24	.229	.284	.287	54	-21	-20	26	4			2	S/23	-1.0
Total	12	1128	3716	381	910	164	15	9	292	246	194	.245	.293	.304	62	-206	-202	338	67	35		78	S2/3O	-5.7

■ GUS NIARHOS
Niarhos, Constantine Gregory   b: 12/6/20, Birmingham, Ala.   BR/TR, 6', 160 lbs.   Deb: 6/09/46   C

YEAR	TM/L	G	AB	R	H	2B	3B	HR	RBI	BB	SO	AVG	OBP	SLG	PRO+	BR	/A	RC	SB	CS	SBR	FR	POS	TPR
1946	NY-A	37	40	11	9	1	1	0	2	11	2	.225	.392	.300	94	0	0	6	1	0	0	7	C	0.9
1948	NY-A	83	228	41	61	12	2	0	19	52	15	.268	.404	.338	99	2	3	36	1	3	-2	11	C	1.7
1949	*NY-A	32	43	7	12	2	1	0	6	13	6	.279	.456	.372	120	2	2	9	0	0	0	8	C	0.8
1950	NY-A	1	0	0	0	0	0	0	0	0	0	—	—	—	—	0	0	0	0	0	0	0	R	0.0
	Chi-A	41	105	17	34	4	0	0	16	14	6	.324	.408	.362	101	1	1	16	0	0	0	8	C	1.0
	Yr	42	105	17	34	4	0	0	16	14	6	.324	.408	.362	101	1	1	16	0	0	0	8		1.0
1951	Chi-A	66	168	27	43	6	0	1	10	47	9	.256	.419	.310	101	3	3	26	4	3	-1	4	C	1.0
1952	Bos-A	29	58	4	6	1	0	0	4	12	6	.103	.268	.103	6	-7	-8	3	0	0	0	6	C	0.0
1953	Bos-A	16	35	6	7	1	1	0	2	4	4	.200	.300	.286	56	-2	-2	3	0	1	-1	4	C	0.1
1954	Phi-N	3	5	0	1	0	0	0	0	2	0	.200	.200	.200	5	-1	-1	0	0	0	0	1	/C	0.0
1955	Phi-N	7	9	1	1	0	0	0	0	0	2	.111	.111	.111	-42	-2	-2	0	0	0	0	1	/C	0.0
Total	9	315	691	114	174	26	5	1	59	153	56	.252	.390	.308	89	-3	-3	99	6	7	-2	45	C	5.5

■ SAM NICHOL
Nichol, Samuel Anderson   b: 4/20/1869, Ireland   d: 4/19/37, Steubenville, Ohio   BR/TR, 5'10", 178 lbs.   Deb: 10/05/1888

YEAR	TM/L	G	AB	R	H	2B	3B	HR	RBI	BB	SO	AVG	OBP	SLG	PRO+	BR	/A	RC	SB	CS	SBR	FR	POS	TPR
1888	Pit-N	8	22	3	1	0	0	0		2	2	.045	.125	.045	-47	-3	-3	0	0			2	/O	-0.1
1890	Col-a	14	56	7	9	0	0	0		2		.161	.190	.161	5	-7	-6	2	3			3	O	-0.3
Total	2	22	78	10	10	0	0	0		4	2	.128	.171	.128	-9	-10	-9	2	3			4	/O	-0.4

■ DON NICHOLAS
Nicholas, Donald Leigh   b: 10/30/30, Phoenix, Ariz.   BL/TR, 5'7", 150 lbs.   Deb: 4/16/52

YEAR	TM/L	G	AB	R	H	2B	3B	HR	RBI	BB	SO	AVG	OBP	SLG	PRO+	BR	/A	RC	SB	CS	SBR	FR	POS	TPR
1952	Chi-A	3	2	0	0	0	0	0	0	0	0	.000	.000	.000	-99	-1	-1	0	0	0	0	0	H	0.0
1954	Chi-A	7	0	3	0	0	0	0	0	0	0	—	1.000	—	185	0	0	0	0	1	-1	0	H	0.0
Total	2	10	2	3	0	0	0	0	0	0	0	.000	.333	.000	-2	-0	-0	0	0	1	-1	0		0.0

■ SIMON NICHOLLS
Nicholls, Simon Burdette   b: 7/18/1882, Germantown, Md.   d: 3/12/11, Baltimore, Md.   BL/TR,   Deb: 9/18/03

YEAR	TM/L	G	AB	R	H	2B	3B	HR	RBI	BB	SO	AVG	OBP	SLG	PRO+	BR	/A	RC	SB	CS	SBR	FR	POS	TPR
1903	Det-A	2	8		3	0	0	0	0	0		.375	.375	.375	132	0	0	1	0			-2	/S	-0.1
1906	Phi-A	12	44	1	8	1	0	0	1	3		.182	.234	.205	38	-3	-3	2	0			-2	S	-0.5
1907	Phi-A	124	460	75	139	12	2	0	23	24		.302	.337	.337	114	8	7	62	13			-20	S23	-1.0
1908	Phi-A	150	550	58	119	17	3	4	31	35		.216	.263	.280	73	-13	-17	45	14			-20	*S2/3	-3.9
1909	Phi-A	21	71	10	15	2	1	0	3	3		.211	.243	.268	60	-3	-3	4	0			0	S/31	0.0
1910	Cle-A	1	0	0	0	0	0	0	0	0		—	—	—		0	0	0				-1	/S	0.0
Total	6	312	1133	144	284	32	6	4	58	65		.251	.291	.300	88	-11	-16	115	27			-45	S/231	-5.7

YEAR	TM/L	G	AB	R	H	2B	3B	HR	RBI	BB	SO	AVG	OBP	SLG	PRO+	BR	/A	RC	SB	CS	SBR	FR	POS	TPR

■ AL NICHOLS
Nichols, Albert H.　b: Brooklyn, N.Y.　5'11", 180 lbs.　Deb: 4/24/1875

YEAR	TM/L	G	AB	R	H	2B	3B	HR	RBI	BB	SO	AVG	OBP	SLG	PRO+	BR	/A	RC	SB	CS	SBR	FR	POS	TPR
1875	Atl-n	32	129	4	20	3	0	0		0		.155	.155	.178	17	-11	-8	4					3	-0.5
1876	NY-N	57	212	20	38	4	0	0	9	2	3	.179	.187	.198	33	-15	-11	8				5	*3	-0.6
1877	Lou-N	6	19	1	4	0	1	0	0	0	2	.211	.211	.316	54	-1	-1	1				4	/2S31	0.2
Total	2	63	231	21	42	4	1	0	9	2	5	.182	.189	.208	35	-16	-13	9				9	/321S	-0.4

■ ART NICHOLS
Nichols, Arthur Francis (b: Arthur Francis Meikle)　b: 7/14/1871, Manchester, N.H.　d: 8/9/45, Willimantic, Conn.　5'10", 175 lbs.　Deb: 9/16/1898

YEAR	TM/L	G	AB	R	H	2B	3B	HR	RBI	BB	SO	AVG	OBP	SLG	PRO+	BR	/A	RC	SB	CS	SBR	FR	POS	TPR
1898	Chi-N	14	42	7	12	1	0	0	6	4		.286	.388	.310	104	1	1	8	6			1	C	0.2
1899	Chi-N	17	47	5	12	2	0	1	11	0		.255	.286	.362	81	-1	-1	6	3			-1	C	-0.1
1900	Chi-N	8	25	1	5	0	0	0	0	3		.200	.286	.200	39	-2	-2	2	1			-1	/C	-0.1
1901	StL-N	93	308	50	75	11	3	0	33	10		.244	.279	.308	76	-11	-9	32	14			-2	CO	-0.9
1902	StL-N	73	251	36	67	12	0	1	31	21		.267	.331	.327	109	2	3	35	18			-7	1C/O	-0.5
1903	StL-N	36	120	13	23	2	0	0	9	12		.192	.265	.208	38	-9	-9	9	9			-5	1/OC	-1.4
Total	6	241	793	112	194	28	3	3	90	50		.245	.300	.299	81	-21	-17	92	51			-16	/C1O	-2.8

■ CARL NICHOLS
Nichols, Carl Edward　b: 10/14/62, Los Angeles, Cal.　BR/TR, 6', 184 lbs.　Deb: 9/14/86

YEAR	TM/L	G	AB	R	H	2B	3B	HR	RBI	BB	SO	AVG	OBP	SLG	PRO+	BR	/A	RC	SB	CS	SBR	FR	POS	TPR
1986	Bal-A	5	5	0	0	0	0	0	0	1	4	.000	.167	.000	-51	-1	-1	0	0	0	0	-0	/C	0.0
1987	Bal-A	13	21	4	8	1	0	0	3	1	4	.381	.409	.429	126	1	1	4	0	0	0	1	C	0.3
1988	Bal-A	18	47	2	9	1	0	0	1	3	10	.191	.240	.213	29	-4	-4	2	0	0	0	6	C/O	0.3
1989	Hou-N	8	13	0	1	0	0	0	2	0	3	.077	.077	.077	-58	-3	-3	0	0	0	0	-0	/C	-0.2
1990	Hou-N	32	49	7	10	3	0	0	11	8	11	.204	.328	.265	66	-2	-2	5	0	0	0	3	C/1O	0.2
Total	5	76	135	13	28	5	0	0	17	13	32	.207	.282	.244	48	-9	-9	11	0	0	0	10	/CO1	0.6

■ ROY NICHOLS
Nichols, Roy　b: 3/3/21, Little Rock, Ark.　BR/TR, 5'11", 155 lbs.　Deb: 5/06/44

YEAR	TM/L	G	AB	R	H	2B	3B	HR	RBI	BB	SO	AVG	OBP	SLG	PRO+	BR	/A	RC	SB	CS	SBR	FR	POS	TPR
1944	NY-N	11	9	3	2	1	0	0	0	2	2	.222	.364	.333	97	0	0	1	0			2	/23	0.2

■ REID NICHOLS
Nichols, Thomas Reid　b: 8/5/58, Ocala, Fla.　BR/TR, 5'11", 165 lbs.　Deb: 9/16/80

YEAR	TM/L	G	AB	R	H	2B	3B	HR	RBI	BB	SO	AVG	OBP	SLG	PRO+	BR	/A	RC	SB	CS	SBR	FR	POS	TPR
1980	Bos-A	12	36	5	8	0	1	0	3	3	8	.222	.282	.278	51	-2	-2	3	0	1	-1	1	/OD	-0.1
1981	Bos-A	39	48	13	9	0	1	0	3	2	6	.188	.220	.229	28	-4	-5	3	0	1	-1	5	O/3D	0.0
1982	Bos-A	92	245	35	74	16	1	7	33	14	28	.302	.342	.461	112	6	4	38	5	3	-0	10	O/D	1.0
1983	Bos-A	100	274	35	78	22	1	6	22	26	36	.285	.353	.438	108	6	4	42	7	5	-1	7	OD/S	0.8
1984	Bos-A	74	124	14	28	5	1	1	14	12	18	.226	.309	.306	68	-5	-5	13	2	1	0	5	O/D	-0.1
1985	Bos-A	21	32	3	6	1	0	1	3	2	4	.188	.257	.313	53	-2	-2	3	1	0	0	1	O/2D	-0.1
	Chi-A	51	118	20	35	7	1	1	15	15	13	.297	.376	.398	108	2	2	18	5	5	-2	-2	O/D	-0.1
	Yr	72	150	23	41	8	1	2	18	17	17	.273	.351	.380	96	0	-0	20	6	5	-1	-1		-0.1
1986	Chi-A	74	136	9	31	4	0	2	18	11	23	.228	.286	.301	58	-8	-8	12	5	4	-1	5	O/2D	-0.4
1987	Mon-N	77	147	22	39	8	2	4	20	14	13	.265	.333	.429	97	-0	-1	21	2	1	0	7	O/3	0.4
Total	8	540	1160	156	308	63	8	22	131	99	149	.266	.328	.391	91	-7	-14	151	27	21	-5	38	O/D23S	1.5

■ DAVE NICHOLSON
Nicholson, David Lawrence　b: 8/29/39, St.Louis, Mo.　BR/TR, 6'2", 215 lbs.　Deb: 5/24/60

YEAR	TM/L	G	AB	R	H	2B	3B	HR	RBI	BB	SO	AVG	OBP	SLG	PRO+	BR	/A	RC	SB	CS	SBR	FR	POS	TPR
1960	Bal-A	54	113	17	21	1	1	5	11	20	55	.186	.308	.345	77	-4	-3	12	0	2	-1	-1	O	-0.6
1962	Bal-A	97	173	25	30	4	1	9	15	27	76	.173	.289	.364	78	-7	-5	19	3	4	-2	5	O	-0.4
1963	Chi-A	126	449	53	103	11	4	22	70	63	175	.229	.324	.419	108	4	5	65	2	1	0	-4	*O	-0.3
1964	Chi-A	97	294	40	60	6	1	13	39	52	126	.204	.330	.364	95	-2	-1	38	0	2	-1	-6	O	-1.2
1965	Chi-A	54	85	11	13	2	1	2	12	9	40	.153	.234	.271	46	-6	-6	6	0	0	0	-2	O	-0.9
1966	Hou-N	100	280	36	69	8	4	10	31	46	92	.246	.359	.411	122	6	9	45	1	1	-0	3	O	0.9
1967	Atl-N	10	25	2	5	0	0	0	1	2	9	.200	.259	.200	34	-2	-2	2	0	0	0	0	/O	-0.2
Total	7	538	1419	184	301	32	12	61	179	219	573	.212	.320	.381	97	-11	-4	186	6	10	-4	-5	O	-2.7

■ FRED NICHOLSON
Nicholson, Fred "Shoemaker"　b: 9/1/1894, Honey Grove, Tex.　d: 1/23/72, Kilgore, Tex.　BR/TR, 5'10.5", 173 lbs.　Deb: 4/11/17

YEAR	TM/L	G	AB	R	H	2B	3B	HR	RBI	BB	SO	AVG	OBP	SLG	PRO+	BR	/A	RC	SB	CS	SBR	FR	POS	TPR
1917	Det-A	13	14	4	4	1	1	0	1	1	2	.286	.333	.357	111	0	0	2	0			-1	/O	0.0
1919	Pit-N	30	66	8	18	2	2	1	6	6	11	.273	.333	.409	118	2	1	9	2			0	O/1	0.1
1920	Pit-N	99	247	33	89	16	7	4	30	18	31	.360	.404	.530	162	21	20	51	9	6	-1	3	O	1.9
1921	Bos-N	83	245	36	80	11	7	5	41	17	29	.327	.370	.490	133	9	10	43	5	4	-1	-4	O/12	0.2
1922	Bos-N	78	222	31	56	4	5	2	29	23	24	.252	.336	.342	79	-8	-6	26	5	7	-3	-4	O	-1.4
Total	5	303	794	112	247	34	21	12	107	65	97	.311	.367	.452	124	23	25	131	21	17		-5	O/12	0.8

■ OVID NICHOLSON
Nicholson, Ovid Edward　b: 12/30/1888, Salem, Ind.　d: 3/24/68, Salem, Ind.　BL/TR, 5'9.5", 155 lbs.　Deb: 9/17/12

YEAR	TM/L	G	AB	R	H	2B	3B	HR	RBI	BB	SO	AVG	OBP	SLG	PRO+	BR	/A	RC	SB	CS	SBR	FR	POS	TPR
1912	Pit-N	6	11	2	5	0	0	0	3	1	2	.455	.500	.455	165	1	1	3	1			0	/O	0.1

■ PARSON NICHOLSON
Nicholson, Thomas C. "Deacon"　b: 4/14/1863, Blaine, Ohio　d: 2/28/17, Bellaire, Ohio　6'6", 190 lbs.　Deb: 9/14/1888

YEAR	TM/L	G	AB	R	H	2B	3B	HR	RBI	BB	SO	AVG	OBP	SLG	PRO+	BR	/A	RC	SB	CS	SBR	FR	POS	TPR
1888	Det-N	24	85	11	22	2	3	1	9	2	7	.259	.284	.388	115	1	1	11	6			-2	2	0.0
1890	Tol-a	134	523	78	140	16	11	4		42		.268	.328	.363	103	3	1	79	46			-8	*2/C	-0.1
1895	Was-N	10	38	7	7	2	1	0	5	7	4	.184	.311	.289	58	-2	-2	5	6			-2	S	-0.2
Total	3	168	646	96	169	20	15	5	14	51	11	.262	.321	.362	102	2	-0	96	58			-11	2/SC	-0.3

■ BILL NICHOLSON
Nicholson, William Beck "Swish"　b: 12/11/14, Chestertown, Md.　BL/TR, 6', 205 lbs.　Deb: 6/13/36

YEAR	TM/L	G	AB	R	H	2B	3B	HR	RBI	BB	SO	AVG	OBP	SLG	PRO+	BR	/A	RC	SB	CS	SBR	FR	POS	TPR
1936	Phi-A	11	12	2	0	0	0	0	0	0	5	.000	.000	.000	-99	-4	-4	0	0	0	0	0	/O	-0.2
1939	Chi-N	58	220	37	65	12	5	5	38	20	29	.295	.354	.464	116	5	5	38	0			-0	O	0.3
1940	Chi-N	135	491	78	146	27	7	25	98	50	67	.297	.366	.534	148	29	30	97	2			-4	*O	2.2
1941	Chi-N	147	532	74	135	26	1	26	98	82	91	.254	.357	.453	132	19	22	90	1			-2	*O	1.4
1942	Chi-N	152	588	83	173	22	11	21	78	76	80	.294	.382	.476	156	38	40	112	8			10	*O	**4.9**
1943	Chi-N	154	608	95	188	30	9	**29**	**128**	71	86	.309	.386	.531	166	48	49	129	4			4	*O	4.9
1944	Chi-N	156	582	**116**	167	35	8	**33**	122	93	71	.287	.391	.545	162	47	48	132	3			-1	*O	3.5
1945	*Chi-N	151	559	82	136	28	4	13	88	92	73	.243	.356	.377	106	5	7	81	4			-2	*O	-0.1
1946	Chi-N	105	296	36	65	13	2	8	41	44	44	.220	.325	.358	95	-2	-2	37	1			-1	O	-0.3
1947	Chi-N	148	487	69	119	28	1	26	75	87	83	.244	.364	.466	124	14	16	90	1			-7	*O	0.5
1948	Chi-N	143	494	68	129	24	5	19	67	81	60	.261	.371	.445	125	15	18	88	2			-9	*O	0.0
1949	Phi-N	98	299	42	70	8	3	11	40	45	53	.234	.344	.391	99	-1	-0	44	1			-2	O	-0.6
1950	Phi-N	41	58	3	13	2	1	3	10	10	16	.224	.318	.448	101	-0	-0	8	0			-1	O	0.0
1951	Phi-N	85	170	23	41	9	2	8	30	25	24	.241	.342	.459	115	3	3	29	0	1	-1	-3	O	-0.1
1952	Phi-N	55	88	17	24	3	0	6	19	14	26	.273	.390	.511	150	6	6	20	0	0	0	-2	O	-0.3
1953	Phi-N	38	62	12	13	5	1	2	16	12	20	.210	.338	.419	97	-0	-0	9	0	0	0	-3	O	-0.3
Total	16	1677	5546	837	1484	272	60	235	948	800	828	.268	.365	.465	133	221	238	1005	27	1		-21	*O	16.5

■ GEORGE NICOL
Nicol, George Edward　b: 10/17/1870, Barry, Ill.　d: 8/10/24, Milwaukee, Wis.　TL, 5'7", 155 lbs.　Deb: 9/23/1890

YEAR	TM/L	G	AB	R	H	2B	3B	HR	RBI	BB	SO	AVG	OBP	SLG	PRO+	BR	/A	RC	SB	CS	SBR	FR	POS	TPR
1890	StL-a	3	7	4	2	1	0	0		4		.286	.545	.429	168	1	1	2	0			-0	/P	0.0
1891	Chi-N	3	6	0	2	0	1	0	3	0	1	.333	.333	.667	192	1	1	1	0			-1	/P	0.0
1894	Pit-N	8	20	8	9	1	0	0	3	0	1	.450	.450	.500	132	1	1	5	0			-1	/P	0.0
	Lou-N	27	108	12	38	6	4	0	19	2	3	.352	.375	.481	115	1	2	22	4			-5	O/P	-0.2
	Yr	35	128	20	47	7	4	0	22	2	4	.367	.386	.484	117	2	3	26	4			-6		-0.2
Total	3	41	141	24	51	8	5	0	25	6	5	.362	.396	.489	123	4	5	29	4			-7	/OP	-0.2

■ HUGH NICOL
Nicol, Hugh　b: 1/1/1858, Campsie, Scotland　d: 6/27/21, Lafayette, Ind.　BR/TR, 5'4", 145 lbs.　Deb: 5/03/1881　M

YEAR	TM/L	G	AB	R	H	2B	3B	HR	RBI	BB	SO	AVG	OBP	SLG	PRO+	BR	/A	RC	SB	CS	SBR	FR	POS	TPR
1881	Chi-N	26	108	13	22	2	0	0	7	4	12	.204	.232	.222	42	-7	-7	6				4	O/S	-0.2

YEAR	TM/L	G	AB	R	H	2B	3B	HR	RBI	BB	SO	AVG	OBP	SLG	PRO+	BR	/A	RC	SB	CS	SBR	FR	POS	TPR
1882	Chi-N	47	186	19	37	9	1	1	16	7	29	.199	.228	.274	58	-8	-9	12				9	O/S	0.0
1883	StL-a	94	368	73	106	13	3	0		18		.288	.321	.340	107	5	2	41				12	*O2	1.3
1884	StL-a	110	442	79	115	14	5	0		22		.260	.300	.314	100	2	-1	43				23	*O2/S3	2.0
1885	*StL-a	112	425	59	88	11	1	0		34		.207	.271	.238	61	-16	-19	28				13	*O/3	-1.0
1886	StL-a	67	253	44	52	6	3	0		26		.206	.280	.253	66	-8	-10	29	38			-4	O/S2	-1.3
1887	Cin-a	125	475	122	102	18	2	1		86		.215	.341	.267	72	-13	-15	93	**138**			-2	*O	-1.7
1888	Cin-a	135	548	112	131	10	2	1	35	67		.239	.330	.270	92	1	-3	85	103			-3	*O2/S	-0.9
1889	Cin-a	122	474	82	121	7	8	2	58	54	35	.255	.338	.316	86	-5	-8	80	80			1	*O/23	-0.8
1890	Cin-N	50	186	28	39	1	4	0	19	19	12	.210	.283	.258	60	-9	-9	21	24			-6	O/S2	-1.3
Total	10	888	3465	631	813	91	29	5	135	337	88	.235	.307	.282	80	-58	-79	437	383			49	O/2S3	-3.9

■ STEVE NICOSIA

Nicosia, Steven Richard   b: 8/6/55, Paterson, N.J.   BR/TR, 5'10", 185 lbs.   Deb: 7/08/78

YEAR	TM/L	G	AB	R	H	2B	3B	HR	RBI	BB	SO	AVG	OBP	SLG	PRO+	BR	/A	RC	SB	CS	SBR	FR	POS	TPR
1978	Pit-N	3	5	0	0	0	0	0	0	1	0	.000	.167	.000	-48	-1	-1	0	0	0	0	1	/C	0.0
1979	*Pit-N	70	191	22	55	16	0	4	13	23	17	.288	.364	.435	112	5	4	29	0	2	-1	4	C	0.8
1980	Pit-N	60	176	16	38	8	0	1	22	19	16	.216	.296	.278	60	-9	-9	14	0	1	-1	-1	C	-0.9
1981	Pit-N	54	169	21	39	10	1	2	18	13	10	.231	.286	.337	74	-6	-6	15	3	1	0	0	C	-0.4
1982	Pit-N	39	100	6	28	3	0	1	7	11	13	.280	.351	.340	91	-0	-1	12	0	1	-1	4	C/O	0.3
1983	Pit-N	21	46	4	6	2	0	1	1	1	7	.130	.149	.239	6	-6	-6	1	0	0	0	-1	C	-0.6
	SF-N	15	33	4	11	0	0	0	6	3	2	.333	.389	.333	105	0	0	4	0	0	0	2	/C	0.3
	Yr	36	79	8	17	2	0	1	7	4	9	.215	.253	.278	47	-6	-6	4	0	0	0	1		-0.3
1984	SF-N	48	132	9	40	11	2	2	19	8	14	.303	.343	.462	129	4	4	20	1	1	-0	-5	C	0.1
1985	Mon-N	42	71	4	12	2	0	0	1	7	11	.169	.244	.197	26	-7	-7	4	1	0	0	-6	C/1	-1.1
	Tor-A	6	15	0	4	0	0	0	1	0	0	.267	.267	.267	46	-1	-1	1	0	0	0	1	/C	0.0
Total	8	358	938	86	233	52	3	11	88	86	90	.248	.312	.345	82	-21	-23	99	5	6	-2	-1	C/O1	-1.5

■ CHARLIE NIEBERGALL

Niebergall, Charles Arthur "Nig"   b: 5/23/1899, New York, N.Y.   d: 8/29/82, Holiday, Fla.   BR/TR, 5'10", 160 lbs.   Deb: 6/17/21

YEAR	TM/L	G	AB	R	H	2B	3B	HR	RBI	BB	SO	AVG	OBP	SLG	PRO+	BR	/A	RC	SB	CS	SBR	FR	POS	TPR
1921	StL-N	5	6	1	1	0	0	0	0	0	0	.167	.167	.167	-12	-1	-1	0	0	0	0	-0	/C	0.0
1923	StL-N	9	28	2	3	1	0	0	1	2	2	.107	.167	.143	-18	-5	-5	1	0	0	0	-0	/C	-0.3
1924	StL-N	40	58	6	17	6	0	0	7	3	9	.293	.339	.397	98	-0	-0	8	0	0	0	1	C	0.2
Total	3	54	92	9	21	7	0	0	8	5	11	.228	.276	.304	55	-6	-6	9	0	0	0	1	/C	-0.1

■ AL NIEHAUS

Niehaus, Albert Bernard   b: 6/1/1899, Cincinnati, Ohio   d: 10/14/31, Cincinnati, Ohio   BR/TR, 5'11", 175 lbs.   Deb: 4/22/25

YEAR	TM/L	G	AB	R	H	2B	3B	HR	RBI	BB	SO	AVG	OBP	SLG	PRO+	BR	/A	RC	SB	CS	SBR	FR	POS	TPR
1925	Pit-N	17	64	7	14	8	0	0	7	1	5	.219	.242	.344	45	-5	-6	5	0	0	0	-1	1	-0.7
	Cin-N	51	147	16	44	10	2	0	14	13	10	.299	.360	.395	95	-1	-1	20	1	4	-2	2	1	-0.4
	Yr	68	211	23	58	18	2	0	21	14	15	.275	.326	.379	80	-7	-7	25	1	4	-2	1		-1.1

■ BERT NIEHOFF

Niehoff, John Albert   b: 5/13/1884, Louisville, Colo.   d: 12/8/74, Inglewood, Cal.   BR/TR, 5'10.5", 170 lbs.   Deb: 10/04/13   C

YEAR	TM/L	G	AB	R	H	2B	3B	HR	RBI	BB	SO	AVG	OBP	SLG	PRO+	BR	/A	RC	SB	CS	SBR	FR	POS	TPR
1913	Cin-N	2	8	0	0	0	0	0	0	0	2	.000	.000	.000	-99	-2	-2	0	0			2	/3	0.0
1914	Cin-N	142	484	46	117	16	9	4	49	38	77	.242	.298	.337	86	-8	-9	52	20			7	*3/2	0.3
1915	*Phi-N	148	529	61	126	27	2	2	49	30	63	.238	.280	.308	77	-15	-15	50	21	11	-0	-7	*2	-2.3
1916	Phi-N	146	548	65	133	**42**	4	4	61	37	57	.243	.292	.356	95	-2	-4	60	20	14	-2	-2	*2/3	-0.4
1917	Phi-N	114	361	30	92	17	4	2	42	23	29	.255	.303	.341	93	-2	-3	39	8			18	2/13	2.3
1918	StL-N	22	84	5	15	2	0	0	5	3	10	.179	.207	.202	26	-8	-7	4	2			2	2	-0.4
	NY-N	7	23	3	6	0	0	0	1	0	4	.261	.261	.261	60	-1	-1	1	0			-2	/2	-0.3
	Yr	29	107	8	21	2	0	0	6	3	14	.196	.218	.215	33	-9	-8	5	2			-1		-0.7
Total	6	581	2037	210	489	104	19	12	207	131	242	.240	.288	.327	84	-37	-43	206	71	25		18	23/1	-0.8

■ MILT NIELSEN

Nielsen, Milton Robert   b: 2/8/25, Tyler, Minn.   BL/TL, 5'11", 190 lbs.   Deb: 9/27/49

YEAR	TM/L	G	AB	R	H	2B	3B	HR	RBI	BB	SO	AVG	OBP	SLG	PRO+	BR	/A	RC	SB	CS	SBR	FR	POS	TPR
1949	Cle-A	3	9	1	1	0	0	0	0	2	4	.111	.273	.111	4	-1	-1	0	0	0	0	-0	/O	0.0
1951	Cle-A	16	6	1	0	0	0	0	0	1	1	.000	.143	.000	-63	-1	-1	0	0	0	0	0	H	0.0
Total	2	19	15	2	1	0	0	0	0	3	5	.067	.222	.067	-22	-3	-2	0	0	0	0	-0	/O	0.0

■ BUTCH NIEMAN

Nieman, Elmer Le Roy   b: 2/8/18, Herkimer, Kan.   BL/TL, 6'2", 195 lbs.   Deb: 5/02/43

YEAR	TM/L	G	AB	R	H	2B	3B	HR	RBI	BB	SO	AVG	OBP	SLG	PRO+	BR	/A	RC	SB	CS	SBR	FR	POS	TPR
1943	Bos-N	101	335	39	84	15	8	8	46	39	39	.251	.331	.406	114	5	5	47	4			-1	O	0.1
1944	Bos-N	134	468	65	124	16	6	16	65	47	47	.265	.332	.427	108	7	4	69	5			-2	*O	-0.6
1945	Bos-N	97	247	43	61	15	0	14	56	43	33	.247	.361	.478	131	10	10	44	11			-1	O	0.7
Total	3	332	1050	147	269	46	14	37	167	129	119	.256	.339	.432	116	22	20	161	20			-3	O	0.2

■ BOB NIEMAN

Nieman, Robert Charles   b: 1/26/27, Cincinnati, Ohio   d: 3/10/85, Corona, Cal.   BR/TR, 5'11", 195 lbs.   Deb: 9/14/51

YEAR	TM/L	G	AB	R	H	2B	3B	HR	RBI	BB	SO	AVG	OBP	SLG	PRO+	BR	/A	RC	SB	CS	SBR	FR	POS	TPR
1951	StL-A	12	43	6	16	3	1	2	8	3	5	.372	.413	.628	174	4	4	11	0	0	0	-0	O	0.3
1952	StL-A	131	478	66	138	22	2	18	74	46	73	.289	.352	.456	120	14	12	75	0	4	-2	-3	*O	0.3
1953	Det-A	142	508	72	143	32	5	15	69	57	57	.281	.354	.453	118	11	12	82	0	3	-2	1	*O	0.6
1954	Det-A	91	251	24	66	14	1	8	35	22	32	.263	.322	.422	105	-0	1	31	0	2	-1	-6	O	-0.7
1955	Chi-A	99	272	36	77	11	2	11	53	36	37	.283	.371	.460	119	8	7	46	1	0	0	-9	O	-0.4
1956	Chi-A	14	40	3	12	1	0	2	4	4	4	.300	.364	.475	118	1	1	5	0	1	-1	0	O	0.0
	Bal-A	114	388	60	125	20	6	12	64	86	59	.322	.445	.497	161	31	36	89	1	5	-3	1	*O	2.7
	Yr	128	428	63	137	21	6	14	68	90	63	.320	.438	.495	156	32	36	94	1	6	-3	1		2.7
1957	Bal-A	129	445	61	123	17	6	13	70	63	86	.276	.369	.429	125	12	15	70	4	4	-1	-0	*O	0.7
1958	Bal-A	105	366	56	119	20	2	16	60	44	57	.325	.398	.522	159	26	28	71	2	8	-4	-15	*O	0.2
1959	Bal-A	118	360	49	105	18	2	21	60	42	55	.292	.369	.528	146	21	22	67	1	2	-1	-3	O	1.3
1960	StL-N	81	188	19	54	13	5	4	31	24	31	.287	.374	.473	120	8	6	33	0	1	-1	-9	O	-0.5
1961	StL-N	6	17	0	8	1	0	0	2	0	2	.471	.471	.529	150	2	1	4	0	0	0	-1	O	0.0
	Cle-A	39	65	2	23	6	0	2	10	7	4	.354	.417	.538	157	5	5	16	1	0	0	0	O	0.5
1962	Cle-A	2	1	0	0	0	0	0	1	0	1	.000	.000	.000	-99	-0	-0	0	0	0	0	0	H	0.0
	*SF-N	30	30	1	9	2	0	1	3	1	9	.300	.323	.467	111	0	0	5	0	0	0	0	O	0.0
Total	12	1113	3452	455	1018	180	32	125	544	435	512	.295	.375	.474	132	142	150	605	10	30	-15	-45	O	5.0

■ AL NIEMIEC

Niemiec, Alfred Joseph   b: 5/18/11, Meriden, Conn.   BR/TR, 5'11", 158 lbs.   Deb: 9/19/34

YEAR	TM/L	G	AB	R	H	2B	3B	HR	RBI	BB	SO	AVG	OBP	SLG	PRO+	BR	/A	RC	SB	CS	SBR	FR	POS	TPR
1934	Bos-A	9	32	2	7	0	0	0	3	3	4	.219	.286	.219	30	-3	-4	2	0	0	0	4	/2	0.1
1936	Phi-A	69	203	22	40	3	2	1	20	26	16	.197	.291	.246	35	-21	-20	16	2	2	-1	10	2/S	-0.5
Total	2	78	235	24	47	3	2	1	23	29	20	.200	.291	.243	34	-24	-24	18	2	2	-1	15	/2S	-0.4

■ TOM NIETO

Nieto, Thomas Andrew   b: 10/27/60, Downey, Cal.   BR/TR, 6'1", 193 lbs.   Deb: 5/10/84

YEAR	TM/L	G	AB	R	H	2B	3B	HR	RBI	BB	SO	AVG	OBP	SLG	PRO+	BR	/A	RC	SB	CS	SBR	FR	POS	TPR
1984	StL-N	33	86	7	24	4	0	3	12	5	18	.279	.319	.430	112	1	1	11	0	0	0	4	C	0.6
1985	*StL-N	95	253	15	57	10	2	0	34	26	37	.225	.305	.281	65	-11	-11	21	0	2	-1	-3	C	-1.1
1986	Mon-N	30	65	5	13	3	1	1	7	6	21	.200	.278	.323	66	-3	-3	5	0	1	-1	-2	C	-0.4
1987	Min-A	41	105	7	21	7	1	1	12	8	24	.200	.276	.314	54	-7	-7	10	0	0	0	1	C/D	-0.2
1988	Min-A	24	60	1	4	0	0	1	10	1	17	.067	.097	.067	-52	-12	-12	0	0	0	0	3	C	-0.8
1989	Phi-N	11	20	1	3	0	0	0	6	1	9	.150	.370	.150	54	-1	-1	2	0	0	0	3	C	0.0
1990	Phi-N	17	30	1	5	1	0	0	4	3	11	.167	.265	.167	22	-3	-3	1	0	0	0	2	C	0.0
Total	7	251	619	37	127	24	4	5	69	55	135	.205	.281	.281	56	-37	-37	50	0	3	-2	8	C/D	-1.6

■ TOM NILAND

Niland, Thomas James "Honest Tom"   b: 4/14/1870, Brookfield, Mass.   d: 4/30/50, Lynn, Mass.   BR/TR, 5'11", 160 lbs.   Deb: 4/19/1896

YEAR	TM/L	G	AB	R	H	2B	3B	HR	RBI	BB	SO	AVG	OBP	SLG	PRO+	BR	/A	RC	SB	CS	SBR	FR	POS	TPR
1896	StL-N	18	68	3	12	0	1	0	3	5	4	.176	.243	.206	21	-8	-7	3	0			-4	O/S	-1.0

HARRY NILES
Niles, Herbert Clyde　b: 9/10/1880, Buchanan, Mich.　d: 4/18/53, Sturgis, Mich.　BR/TR, 5'8", 175 lbs.　Deb: 4/24/06

YEAR	TM/L	G	AB	R	H	2B	3B	HR	RBI	BB	SO	AVG	OBP	SLG	PRO+	BR	/A	RC	SB	CS	SBR	FR	POS	TPR
1906	StL-A	142	541	71	124	14	4	2	31	46		.229	.290	.281	84	-11	-8	56	30			6	*O3	-0.4
1907	StL-A	120	492	65	142	9	5	2	35	28		.289	.327	.339	115	8	8	63	19			-6	*2/O	0.2
1908	NY-A	96	362	43	90	14	6	4	24	25		.249	.297	.354	112	5	4	43	18			-24	2/O	-2.4
	Bos-A	17	32	4	8	0	0	1	3	6		.250	.368	.344	131	2	1	6	3			-1	/2S	0.1
	Yr	113	394	47	98	14	6	5	27	31		.249	.304	.353	114	6	6	48	21			-24		-2.3
1909	Bos-A	145	546	64	134	12	5	1	38	39		.245	.311	.291	88	-5	-7	58	27			0	*O3/S2	-1.1
1910	Bos-A	18	57	6	12	3	0	1	3	4		.211	.262	.316	79	-1	-2	5	1			-0	O	-0.2
	Cle-A	70	240	25	51	6	4	1	18	15		.213	.267	.283	72	-8	-8	20	9			-4	O/S3	-1.5
	Yr	88	297	31	63	9	4	2	21	19		.212	.266	.290	73	-9	-10	25	10			-4		-1.7
Total	5	608	2270	278	561	58	24	12	152	163		.247	.302	.310	95	-12	-12	250	107			-28	O2/3S	-5.3

BILL NILES
Niles, William A.　b: 1/1874, Vermont　d: 7/3/36, Springfield, Ohio　160 lbs.　Deb: 5/13/1895

YEAR	TM/L	G	AB	R	H	2B	3B	HR	RBI	BB	SO	AVG	OBP	SLG	PRO+	BR	/A	RC	SB	CS	SBR	FR	POS	TPR
1895	Pit-N	11	37	2	8	0	0	0	0	5	2	.216	.310	.216	41	-3	-3	3	2			1	3/2	-0.1

RABBIT NILL
Nill, George Charles　b: 7/14/1881, Ft.Wayne, Ind.　d: 5/24/62, Fort Wayne, Ind.　BR/TR, 5'7", 160 lbs.　Deb: 9/27/04

YEAR	TM/L	G	AB	R	H	2B	3B	HR	RBI	BB	SO	AVG	OBP	SLG	PRO+	BR	/A	RC	SB	CS	SBR	FR	POS	TPR
1904	Was-A	15	48	4	8	0	1	0	3	5		.167	.245	.208	47	-3	-3	3	0			-4	2	-0.6
1905	Was-A	103	319	46	58	7	3	3	31	33		.182	.259	.251	66	-12	-11	26	12			-3	32/S	-1.2
1906	Was-A	89	315	37	74	8	2	0	15	47		.235	.334	.273	97	-0	2	36	16			4	S23O	0.6
1907	Was-A	66	215	21	47	7	3	0	25	15		.219	.270	.279	83	-6	-4	19	6			-2	2O/3	-0.6
	Cle-A	12	43	5	12	1	0	0	2	3		.279	.326	.302	102	0	0	5	2			-4	/3S	-0.2
	Yr	78	258	26	59	8	3	0	27	18		.229	.279	.283	87	-5	-4	24	8			-5		-0.8
1908	Cle-A	11	23	3	5	0	0	0	1	0		.217	.217	.217	43	-1	-1	1	0			0	/SO2	0.0
Total	5	296	963	116	204	23	9	3	77	103		.212	.288	.264	80	-22	-17	91	36			-7	2/3SO	-2.0

AL NIXON
Nixon, Albert Richard "Humpty Dumpty"　b: 4/11/1886, Atlantic City, N.J　d: 11/9/60, Opelousas, La.　BR/TR, 5'7.5", 164 lbs.　Deb: 9/04/15

YEAR	TM/L	G	AB	R	H	2B	3B	HR	RBI	BB	SO	AVG	OBP	SLG	PRO+	BR	/A	RC	SB	CS	SBR	FR	POS	TPR
1915	Bro-N	14	26	3	6	1	0	0	2	2	4	.231	.286	.269	67	-1	-1	2	1	1	-0	-0	O	-0.1
1916	Bro-N	1	2	0	2	0	0	0	0	0	0	1.000	1.000	1.000	501	1	1	2	0			0	/O	0.1
1918	Bro-N	6	11	1	5	0	0	0	0	0	0	.455	.455	.455	178	1	1	2	0			0	/O	0.1
1921	Bos-N	55	138	25	33	6	3	1	9	7	11	.239	.281	.348	69	-7	-6	13	3	2	-0	4	O	-0.3
1922	Bos-N	86	318	35	84	14	4	2	22	9	19	.264	.284	.352	66	-18	-16	30	6	6	-2	2	O	-1.7
1923	Bos-N	88	321	53	88	12	4	0	19	24	14	.274	.334	.336	81	-10	-8	37	2	3	-1	12	O	0.0
1926	Phi-N	93	311	38	91	18	2	4	41	13	20	.293	.323	.402	90	-3	-5	39	5			1	O	-0.7
1927	Phi-N	54	154	18	48	7	0	0	18	5	5	.312	.333	.357	84	-3	-4	18	1			7	O	0.1
1928	Phi-N	25	64	7	15	2	0	0	7	6	4	.234	.300	.266	47	-5	-5	5	1			1	O	-0.4
Total	9	422	1345	180	372	60	13	7	118	66	77	.277	.314	.356	78	-46	-43	148	19	12		26	O	-2.9

OTIS NIXON
Nixon, Otis Junior　b: 1/9/59, Columbus Co., N.C.　BB/TR, 6'2", 180 lbs.　Deb: 9/09/83

YEAR	TM/L	G	AB	R	H	2B	3B	HR	RBI	BB	SO	AVG	OBP	SLG	PRO+	BR	/A	RC	SB	CS	SBR	FR	POS	TPR
1983	NY-A	13	14	2	2	0	0	0	0	1	5	.143	.200	.143	-4	-2	-2	1	2	0	1	2	/O	0.1
1984	Cle-A	49	91	16	14	0	0	0	1	8	11	.154	.222	.154	6	-11	-12	3	12	6	0	6	O	-0.6
1985	Cle-A	104	162	34	38	4	0	3	9	8	27	.235	.271	.315	60	-9	-9	12	20	11	-1	13	OD	0.3
1986	Cle-A	105	95	33	25	4	1	0	8	13	12	.263	.352	.326	88	-1	-1	13	23	6	3	8	O/D	0.8
1987	Cle-A	19	17	2	1	0	0	0	1	3	4	.059	.200	.059	-26	-3	-3	0	2	3	-1	2	O/D	-0.1
1988	Mon-N	90	271	47	66	8	2	0	15	28	42	.244	.314	.288	71	-8	-10	30	46	13	6	-6	O	-1.2
1989	Mon-N	126	258	41	56	7	2	0	21	33	36	.217	.306	.260	62	-11	-12	24	37	12	4	4	O	-0.4
1990	Mon-N	119	231	46	58	6	2	1	20	28	33	.251	.332	.307	78	-6	-6	29	50	13	7	6	O/S	0.5
Total	8	625	1139	221	260	29	7	4	75	122	170	.228	.303	.277	63	-53	-55	112	192	64	19	37	O/DS	-0.6

DONELL NIXON
Nixon, Robert Donell　b: 12/31/61, Evergreen, N.C.　BR/TR, 6'1", 185 lbs.　Deb: 4/07/87

YEAR	TM/L	G	AB	R	H	2B	3B	HR	RBI	BB	SO	AVG	OBP	SLG	PRO+	BR	/A	RC	SB	CS	SBR	FR	POS	TPR
1987	Sea-A	46	132	17	33	4	0	3	12	13	28	.250	.327	.348	75	-4	-5	16	21	7	2	2	O/D	-0.1
1988	SF-N	59	78	15	27	3	0	0	6	10	12	.346	.420	.385	138	4	4	12	11	8	-2	3	O	0.5
1989	*SF-N	95	166	23	44	2	0	1	15	11	30	.265	.311	.295	76	-5	-5	15	10	3	1	-0	O	-0.4
1990	Bal-A	8	20	1	5	2	0	0	2	1	7	.250	.286	.350	79	-1	-1	3	5	0	2	0	/OD	0.1
Total	4	208	396	56	109	11	0	4	35	35	77	.275	.337	.333	88	-6	-6	46	47	18	3	4	O/D	0.1

RUSS NIXON
Nixon, Russell Eugene　b: 2/19/35, Cleves, Ohio　BL/TR, 6'1", 195 lbs.　Deb: 4/20/57　MC

YEAR	TM/L	G	AB	R	H	2B	3B	HR	RBI	BB	SO	AVG	OBP	SLG	PRO+	BR	/A	RC	SB	CS	SBR	FR	POS	TPR
1957	Cle-A	62	185	15	52	7	1	2	18	12	12	.281	.325	.362	88	-3	-3	20	0	1	-1	-5	C	-0.5
1958	Cle-A	113	376	42	113	17	4	9	46	13	38	.301	.324	.439	111	3	4	47	0	3	-2	-10	*C	-0.6
1959	Cle-A	82	258	23	62	10	3	1	29	15	28	.240	.282	.314	66	-13	-12	21	0	0	0	-7	C	-1.5
1960	Cle-A	25	82	6	20	5	0	1	6	6	6	.244	.311	.341	79	-3	-2	8	0	1	-1	-0	C	-0.1
	Bos-A	80	272	24	81	17	3	5	33	13	23	.298	.330	.438	102	1	0	36	0	1	-1	-17	C	-1.2
	Yr	105	354	30	101	22	3	6	39	19	29	.285	.325	.415	97	-1	-2	44	0	2	-1	-17		-1.3
1961	Bos-A	87	242	24	70	12	2	1	19	13	19	.289	.331	.368	84	-5	-5	29	0	1	-1	-2	C	-0.7
1962	Bos-A	65	151	11	42	7	2	1	19	8	14	.278	.314	.371	81	-4	-4	17	0	0	0	-2	C	-0.4
1963	Bos-A	98	287	27	77	18	1	5	30	22	32	.268	.329	.390	98	0	-1	36	0	0	0	-10	C	-1.0
1964	Bos-A	81	163	10	38	7	0	1	20	14	29	.233	.302	.294	64	-7	-8	14	0	0	0	-4	C	-1.0
1965	Bos-A	59	137	11	37	5	1	0	11	6	23	.270	.301	.321	72	-4	-5	11	0	0	0	-6	C	-0.8
1966	Min-A	51	96	5	25	2	1	0	7	7	13	.260	.317	.302	74	-2	-3	9	0	0	0	-4	C	-0.5
1967	Min-A	74	170	16	40	6	1	1	22	18	29	.235	.309	.300	74	-4	-5	16	0	0	0	-11	C	-1.3
1968	Bos-A	29	85	1	13	2	0	0	12	6	13	.153	.217	.176	19	-8	-9	3	0	0	0	-5	C	-1.3
Total	12	906	2504	215	670	115	19	27	266	154	279	.268	.313	.361	84	-49	-54	266	0	7	-4	-83	C	-10.9

RAY NOBLE
Noble, Rafael Miguel (Magee)　b: 3/15/19, Central Hatillo, Cuba　BR/TR, 5'11", 210 lbs.　Deb: 4/18/51

YEAR	TM/L	G	AB	R	H	2B	3B	HR	RBI	BB	SO	AVG	OBP	SLG	PRO+	BR	/A	RC	SB	CS	SBR	FR	POS	TPR
1951	*NY-N	55	141	16	33	6	0	5	26	6	26	.234	.265	.383	72	-6	-6	13	0	0	0	-4	C	-1.0
1952	NY-N	6	5	0	0	0	0	0	0	0	1	.000	.000	.000	-99	-1	-1	0	0	0	0	0	/C	0.0
1953	NY-N	46	97	15	20	0	1	4	14	19	14	.206	.353	.351	83	-2	-2	14	1	0	0	0	/C	0.1
Total	3	107	243	31	53	6	1	9	40	25	41	.218	.299	.362	74	-9	-10	27	1	0	0	-4	/C	-0.9

JUNIOR NOBOA
Noboa, Miliciades Arturo (Diaz)　b: 11/10/64, Azua, D.R.　BR/TR, 5'10", 155 lbs.　Deb: 8/22/84

YEAR	TM/L	G	AB	R	H	2B	3B	HR	RBI	BB	SO	AVG	OBP	SLG	PRO+	BR	/A	RC	SB	CS	SBR	FR	POS	TPR
1984	Cle-A	23	11	3	4	0	0	0	0	0	2	.364	.364	.364	100	0	-0	1	1	0	0	4	2/D	0.5
1987	Cle-A	39	80	7	18	2	1	0	7	3	6	.225	.253	.275	40	-7	-7	6	1	0	0	4	2/S3D	0.0
1988	Cal-A	21	16	4	1	0	0	0	0	0	1	.063	.063	.063	-67	-3	-3	-0	0	0	0	9	/2S3	0.6
1989	Mon-N	21	44	3	10	0	0	0	1	1	3	.227	.244	.227	35	-4	-4	3	0	0	0	7	/2S3	0.4
1990	Mon-N	81	158	15	42	7	2	0	14	7	14	.266	.301	.335	75	-6	-5	16	4	1	1	-16	2/O3SP	-2.0
Total	5	185	309	32	75	9	3	0	22	11	26	.243	.271	.291	54	-19	-19	26	6	1	1	6	/2S3ODP	-0.5

PAUL NOCE
Noce, Paul David　b: 12/16/59, San Francisco, Cal.　BR/TR, 5'10", 175 lbs.　Deb: 6/01/87

YEAR	TM/L	G	AB	R	H	2B	3B	HR	RBI	BB	SO	AVG	OBP	SLG	PRO+	BR	/A	RC	SB	CS	SBR	FR	POS	TPR
1987	Chi-N	70	180	17	41	9	2	3	14	6	49	.228	.261	.350	58	-11	-12	16	5	3	-0	19	2S/3	1.1
1990	Cin-N	1	1	0	1	0	0	0	0	0	0	1.000	1.000	1.000	441	0	0	0	0	0	0	0	/H	0.0
Total	2	71	181	17	42	9	2	3	14	6	49	.232	.265	.354	60	-10	-11	17	5	3	-0	19	/2S3	1.1

GEORGE NOFTSKER
Noftsker, George Washington　b: 8/24/1859, Shippensburg, Pa.　d: 5/8/31, Shippensburg, Pa.　BR/TR, 5'8", 135 lbs.　Deb: 4/17/1884

YEAR	TM/L	G	AB	R	H	2B	3B	HR	RBI	BB	SO	AVG	OBP	SLG	PRO+	BR	/A	RC	SB	CS	SBR	FR	POS	TPR
1884	Alt-U	7	25	0	1					1		.040	.040	.040	-72	-4	-4	0	0			1	/OC	-0.2

YEAR	TM/L	G	AB	R	H	2B	3B	HR	RBI	BB	SO	AVG	OBP	SLG	PRO+	BR	/A	RC	SB	CS	SBR	FR	POS	TPR

■ MATT NOKES
Nokes, Matthew Dodge b: 10/31/63, San Diego, Cal. BL/TR, 6'1", 185 lbs. Deb: 9/03/85

YEAR	TM/L	G	AB	R	H	2B	3B	HR	RBI	BB	SO	AVG	OBP	SLG	PRO+	BR	/A	RC	SB	CS	SBR	FR	POS	TPR
1985	SF-N	19	53	3	11	2	0	2	5	1	9	.208	.236	.358	67	-3	-2	4	0	0	0	-1	C	-0.2
1986	Det-A	7	24	2	8	1	0	1	2	1	1	.333	.360	.500	132	1	1	4	0	0	0	1	/C	0.3
1987	*Det-A	135	461	69	133	14	2	32	87	35	70	.289	.347	.536	135	18	21	82	2	1	0	-10	*CD/O3	1.9
1988	Det-A	122	382	53	96	18	0	16	53	34	58	.251	.314	.424	109	2	3	49	0	1	-1	-3	*C/D	0.4
1989	Det-A	87	268	15	67	10	0	9	39	17	37	.250	.300	.388	95	-3	-3	30	1	0	0	-5	CD	-0.5
1990	Det-A	44	111	12	30	5	1	3	8	4	14	.270	.308	.414	101	-0	-0	12	0	0	0	-3	DC	-0.2
	NY-A	92	240	21	57	4	0	8	32	20	33	.237	.307	.354	84	-5	-5	25	2	2	-1	-5	CD/O	-0.9
	Yr	136	351	33	87	9	1	11	40	24	47	.248	.307	.373	89	-5	-6	38	2	2	-1	-8		-1.1
Total	6	506	1539	175	402	54	3	71	226	112	222	.261	.318	.439	109	9	15	207	5	4	-1	-25	CD/O3	0.8

■ JOE NOLAN
Nolan, Joseph William b: 5/12/51, St.Louis, Mo. BL/TR, 5'11", 175 lbs. Deb: 9/21/72

YEAR	TM/L	G	AB	R	H	2B	3B	HR	RBI	BB	SO	AVG	OBP	SLG	PRO+	BR	/A	RC	SB	CS	SBR	FR	POS	TPR
1972	NY-N	4	10	0	0	0	0	0	0	1	3	.000	.091	.000	-74	-2	-2	0	0	0	0	-0	/C	-0.2
1975	Atl-N	4	4	0	1	0	0	0	0	1	0	.250	.400	.250	80	-0	-0	1	0	0	0	-0	/C	0.0
1977	Atl-N	62	82	13	23	3	0	3	9	13	12	.280	.379	.427	103	2	1	14	1	0	0	0	C	0.1
1978	Atl-N	95	213	22	49	7	3	4	22	34	28	.230	.339	.347	83	-2	-4	27	3	2	-0	-4	C	-0.6
1979	Atl-N	89	230	28	57	9	3	4	21	27	28	.248	.335	.365	85	-3	-5	28	1	3	-2	-7	C	-1.1
1980	Atl-N	17	22	2	6	1	0	0	2	2	4	.273	.333	.318	80	-0	-1	2	0	0	0	1	/C	0.1
	Cin-N	53	154	14	48	7	0	3	24	13	8	.312	.365	.416	117	4	4	24	0	0	0	1	C	0.6
	Yr	70	176	16	54	8	0	3	26	15	12	.307	.361	.403	112	3	3	26	0	0	0	2		0.7
1981	Cin-N	81	236	25	73	18	1	1	26	24	19	.309	.375	.407	120	7	7	35	1	2	-1	-11	C	-0.4
1982	Bal-A	77	219	24	51	7	1	6	35	16	35	.233	.285	.356	75	-8	-8	22	1	1	-0	-4	C	-0.7
1983	*Bal-A	73	184	25	51	11	1	5	24	16	31	.277	.342	.429	113	3	3	26	0	0	0	-10	C	-0.3
1984	Bal-A	35	62	2	18	1	1	1	9	12	10	.290	.405	.387	123	2	3	11	0	0	0	2	D/C	0.5
1985	Bal-A	31	38	1	5	2	0	0	6	5	5	.132	.233	.184	16	-4	-4	2	0	0	0	1	/CD	-0.2
Total	11	621	1454	156	382	66	10	27	178	164	183	.263	.340	.378	95	-1	-7	190	7	8	-3	-31	C/D	-2.2

■ RED NONNENKAMP
Nonnenkamp, Leo William b: 7/7/11, St.Louis, Mo. BL/TL, 5'11", 165 lbs. Deb: 9/06/33

YEAR	TM/L	G	AB	R	H	2B	3B	HR	RBI	BB	SO	AVG	OBP	SLG	PRO+	BR	/A	RC	SB	CS	SBR	FR	POS	TPR
1933	Pit-N	1	1	0	0	0	0	0	0	0	1	.000	.000	.000	-99	-0	-0	0	0			0	H	0.0
1938	Bos-A	87	180	37	51	4	1	0	18	21	13	.283	.358	.317	67	-7	-9	22	6	1	1	3	O/1	-0.4
1939	Bos-A	58	75	12	18	2	1	0	5	12	6	.240	.345	.293	62	-4	-4	8	0	1	-1	-0	O	-0.4
1940	Bos-A	9	7	0	0	0	0	0	1	0	4	.000	.125	.000	-62	-2	-2	0	0	0	0	0	H	-0.1
Total	4	155	263	49	69	6	2	0	24	33	24	.262	.347	.300	62	-13	-15	30	6	2		3	/O1	-0.9

■ PETE NOONAN
Noonan, Peter John b: 11/24/1881, W.Stockbridge, Mass. d: 2/11/65, Great Barrington, Mass. BR/TR, 6', 180 lbs. Deb: 6/20/04

YEAR	TM/L	G	AB	R	H	2B	3B	HR	RBI	BB	SO	AVG	OBP	SLG	PRO+	BR	/A	RC	SB	CS	SBR	FR	POS	TPR
1904	Phi-N	39	114	13	23	3	1	2	13	1		.202	.209	.298	58	-5	-6	8	1			-3	C1	-0.6
1906	Chi-N	5	3	0	1	0	0	0	0	0		.333	.333	.333	104	0	0	0	0			0	/1	0.0
	StL-N	44	125	8	21	1	3	1	9	11	.168	.235	.248	54	-7	-6	8	1			4	C1	0.0
	Yr	49	128	8	22	1	3	1	9	11	.172	.237	.250	55	-7	-6	9	1			4		0.0
1907	StL-N	74	237	19	53	7	3	1	16	9	.224	.252	.291	74	-8	-7	19	3			3	C	0.2
Total	3	162	479	40	98	11	7	4	38	21	.205	.238	.282	65	-20	-20	36	5			4	C/1	-0.4

■ TIM NORDBROOK
Nordbrook, Timothy Charles b: 7/7/49, Baltimore, Md. BR/TR, 6'1", 180 lbs. Deb: 9/13/74

YEAR	TM/L	G	AB	R	H	2B	3B	HR	RBI	BB	SO	AVG	OBP	SLG	PRO+	BR	/A	RC	SB	CS	SBR	FR	POS	TPR
1974	Bal-A	6	15	4	4	0	0	0	1	2	2	.267	.353	.267	83	-0	-0	2	1	0	0	1	/S2	0.2
1975	Bal-A	40	34	6	4	1	0	0	0	7	7	.118	.268	.147	21	-3	-3	2	0	0	0	5	S/2	0.6
1976	Bal-A	27	22	4	5	0	0	0	0	3	5	.227	.320	.227	66	-1	-1	2	0	0	0	3	2S	0.4
	Cal-A	5	8	1	0	0	0	0	0	1	3	.000	.111	.000	-70	-2	-2	0	1	0	0	2	/S2D	0.1
	Yr	32	30	5	5	0	0	0	0	4	8	.167	.265	.167	30	-3	-2	2	1	0	0	5		0.5
1977	Chi-A	15	20	2	5	0	0	0	1	7	4	.250	.444	.250	95	0	0	3	1	0	0	-2	S/3D	0.0
	Tor-A	24	63	9	11	0	1	0	1	4	11	.175	.224	.206	18	-7	-7	3	1	0	0	1	S	-0.2
	Yr	39	83	11	16	0	1	0	2	11	15	.193	.287	.217	39	-7	-7	6	2	0	1	-1		-0.2
1978	Tor-A	7	0	1	0	0	0	0	0	0	0	—	1.000	—	200	0	0	0	0	0	0	2	/S	0.3
	Mil-A	2	5	0	0	0	0	0	0	1	1	.000	.167	.000	-49	-1	-1	0	0	0	0	0	/S	0.0
	Yr	9	5	1	0	0	0	0	0	1	1	.000	.286	.000	-13	-1	-1	0	0	0	0	2		0.3
1979	Mil-A	2	2	0	1	0	0	0	0	0	0	.500	.500	.500	171	0	0	1	0	0	0	-1	/S	0.0
Total	6	128	169	27	30	1	1	0	3	25	33	.178	.287	.195	38	-13	-13	12	4	0	1	12	S/2D3	1.4

■ WAYNE NORDHAGEN
Nordhagen, Wayne Oren b: 7/4/48, Thief River Falls, Minn. BR/TR, 6'2", 205 lbs. Deb: 7/16/76

YEAR	TM/L	G	AB	R	H	2B	3B	HR	RBI	BB	SO	AVG	OBP	SLG	PRO+	BR	/A	RC	SB	CS	SBR	FR	POS	TPR
1976	Chi-A	22	53	6	10	2	0	0	5	4	12	.189	.246	.226	39	-4	-4	3	0	0	0	1	O/CD	-0.3
1977	Chi-A	52	124	16	39	7	3	4	22	2	12	.315	.325	.516	125	4	4	20	1	0	0	-4	O/CD	0.0
1978	Chi-A	68	206	28	62	16	0	5	35	5	18	.301	.318	.451	113	3	3	27	0	1	-0	-4	ODC	-0.2
1979	Chi-A	78	193	20	54	15	0	7	25	13	22	.280	.325	.466	111	2	2	26	0	0	-1	2	DO/CP	0.3
1980	Chi-A	123	415	45	115	22	4	15	59	10	45	.277	.296	.458	104	-0	0	51	0	1	-1	-6	OD	-0.8
1981	Chi-A	65	208	19	64	8	1	6	33	10	25	.308	.342	.442	127	6	6	29	0	1	-1	-9	O	-0.4
1982	Tor-A	44	115	8	32	3	0	1	14	9	13	.278	.331	.330	75	-3	-4	11	0	2	-1	1	DO	-0.4
	Pit-N	1	4	0	2	0	0	0	2	0	1	.500	.500	.500	175	0	0	1	0	0	0	0	/O	0.0
	Yr	28	70	4	18	3	0	0	6	1	9	.257	.268	.300	51	-4	-5	5	0	0	0	0	D	-0.4
1983	Chi-N	21	35	1	5	1	0	1	4	0	5	.143	.167	.257	15	-4	-4	1	0	0	0	-1	/O	-0.5
Total	8	502	1423	147	401	77	8	39	205	54	162	.282	.309	.429	101	-0	-2	174	1	5	-3	-22	OD/CP	-2.7

■ LOU NORDYKE
Nordyke, Louis Ellis b: 8/7/1876, Brighton, Iowa d: 9/27/45, Los Angeles, Cal. TR, 6', 185 lbs. Deb: 4/18/06

YEAR	TM/L	G	AB	R	H	2B	3B	HR	RBI	BB	SO	AVG	OBP	SLG	PRO+	BR	/A	RC	SB	CS	SBR	FR	POS	TPR
1906	StL-A	25	53	4	13	1	0	0	7	10		.245	.365	.264	105	1	1	7	3			-3	1	-0.1

■ IRV NOREN
Noren, Irving Arnold b: 11/29/24, Jamestown, N.Y. BL/TL, 6', 190 lbs. Deb: 4/18/50 C

YEAR	TM/L	G	AB	R	H	2B	3B	HR	RBI	BB	SO	AVG	OBP	SLG	PRO+	BR	/A	RC	SB	CS	SBR	FR	POS	TPR
1950	Was-A	138	542	80	160	27	10	14	98	67	77	.295	.375	.459	118	10	13	98	5	2	0	13	*O1	2.2
1951	Was-A	129	509	82	142	33	5	8	86	51	35	.279	.345	.411	105	2	3	72	10	7	-1	16	*O	1.3
1952	Was-A	12	49	4	12	3	1	0	2	6	3	.245	.327	.347	91	-1	-1	6	1	0	0	4	O	0.3
	*NY-A	93	272	36	64	13	2	5	21	26	34	.235	.316	.353	91	-5	-3	33	4	2	0	-5	O1	-1.1
	Yr	105	321	40	76	16	3	5	23	32	37	.237	.318	.352	91	-6	-4	39	5	2	0	-1		-0.8
1953	*NY-A	109	345	55	92	12	6	6	46	42	39	.267	.350	.388	103	-0	1	50	3	3	-1	1	O	0.3
1954	NY-A	125	426	70	136	21	6	12	66	43	38	.319	.383	.481	140	20	22	79	4	6	-2	2	*O/1	2.0
1955	*NY-A	132	371	49	94	19	1	8	59	43	33	.253	.336	.375	92	-5	-4	48	5	2	0	-1	*O	-1.0
1956	NY-A	29	37	4	8	1	0	0	6	12	7	.216	.408	.243	78	-1	0	4	0	0	0	-1	O/1	-0.1
1957	KC-A	81	160	8	34	8	0	2	16	11	19	.213	.267	.300	54	-10	-10	12	0	0	0	-1	1/O	-1.2
	StL-N	17	30	3	11	4	1	1	10	4	6	.367	.441	.667	189	4	4	8	0	1	-1	-2	/O	0.1
1958	StL-N	117	178	24	47	9	1	4	22	13	21	.264	.328	.393	87	-3	-3	23	0	1	-1	-3	O	-0.8
1959	StL-N	8	8	0	1	1	0	0	0	0	2	.125	.125	.250	-3	-1	-1	0	0	0	0	-0	/O1	-0.1
	Chi-N	65	156	27	50	6	2	4	19	13	24	.321	.384	.462	125	6	6	29	2	0	1	2	O/1	0.8
	Yr	73	164	27	51	7	2	4	19	13	26	.311	.372	.451	118	4	4	29	2	0	1	2		0.7
1960	Chi-N	12	11	0	1	0	0	0	1	3	4	.091	.286	.091	9	-1	-1	0	0	0	0	-0	/1O	-0.1
	LA-N	26	25	1	5	0	0	1	1	1	8	.200	.231	.320	46	-2	-2	2	0	0	0	0	H	-0.1
	Yr	38	36	1	6	0	0	1	2	4	12	.167	.250	.250	36	-3	-3	2	0	0	0	-0		-0.2
Total	11	1093	3119	443	857	157	35	65	453	335	350	.275	.349	.410	106	12	22	464	34	24	-4	31	O/1	2.5

YEAR	TM/L	G	AB	R	H	2B	3B	HR	RBI	BB	SO	AVG	OBP	SLG	PRO+	BR	/A	RC	SB	CS	SBR	FR	POS	TPR

■ DAN NORMAN   Norman, Daniel Edmund b: 1/11/55, Los Angeles, Cal.   BR/TR, 6'2", 195 lbs.   Deb: 9/27/77

YEAR	TM/L	G	AB	R	H	2B	3B	HR	RBI	BB	SO	AVG	OBP	SLG	PRO+	BR	/A	RC	SB	CS	SBR	FR	POS	TPR
1977	NY-N	7	16	2	4	1	0	0	0	4	2	.250	.400	.313	99	0	0	2	0	0	0	-1	/O	0.0
1978	NY-N	19	64	7	17	0	1	4	10	2	14	.266	.288	.484	116	1	1	9	1	0	0	-0	O	0.0
1979	NY-N	44	110	9	27	3	1	3	11	10	26	.245	.314	.373	90	-2	-2	14	2	0	1	1	O	-0.1
1980	NY-N	69	92	5	17	1	1	2	9	6	14	.185	.235	.283	45	-7	-7	7	5	0	2	-1	O	-0.6
1982	Mon-N	53	66	6	14	3	0	2	7	7	20	.212	.288	.348	76	-2	-2	7	0	1	-1	1	O	-0.1
Total	5	192	348	29	79	8	3	11	37	29	76	.227	.288	.362	81	-11	-10	39	8	1	2	0	O	-0.8

■ BILL NORMAN   Norman, Henry Willis Patrick b: 7/16/10, St.Louis, Mo.   d: 4/21/62, Milwaukee, Wis.   BR/TR, 6'2", 190 lbs.   Deb: 8/08/31   MC

YEAR	TM/L	G	AB	R	H	2B	3B	HR	RBI	BB	SO	AVG	OBP	SLG	PRO+	BR	/A	RC	SB	CS	SBR	FR	POS	TPR
1931	Chi-A	24	55	7	10	2	0	0	6	4	10	.182	.237	.218	22	-6	-6	3	0	1	-1	-1	O	-0.7
1932	Chi-A	13	48	6	11	3	1	0	2	2	3	.229	.260	.333	56	-4	-3	4	0	0	0	-1	O	-0.3
Total	2	37	103	13	21	5	1	0	8	6	13	.204	.248	.272	38	-10	-9	7	0	1	-1	-2	/O	-1.0

■ NELSON NORMAN   Norman, Nelson Augusto b: 5/23/58, San Pedro De Macoris, D.R.   BB/TR, 6'2", 160 lbs.   Deb: 5/20/78

YEAR	TM/L	G	AB	R	H	2B	3B	HR	RBI	BB	SO	AVG	OBP	SLG	PRO+	BR	/A	RC	SB	CS	SBR	FR	POS	TPR
1978	Tex-A	23	34	1	9	2	0	0	1	0	5	.265	.265	.324	64	-2	-2	3	0	0	0	10	S/3	1.0
1979	Tex-A	147	343	36	76	9	3	0	21	19	41	.222	.262	.265	43	-27	-27	25	4	1	1	-15	*S/2	-2.3
1980	Tex-A	17	32	4	7	0	0	0	1	1	1	.219	.242	.219	28	-3	-3	1	0	1	-1	7	S	0.4
1981	Tex-A	7	13	1	3	1	0	0	2	1	2	.231	.286	.308	75	-0	-0	1	0	0	0	3	/S	0.3
1982	Pit-N	3	3	0	0	0	0	0	0	0	0	.000	.000	.000	-97	-1	-1	0	0	0	0	-1	/2S	0.0
1987	Mon-N	1	4	0	0	0	0	0	0	0	1	.000	.000	.000	-97	-1	-1	0	0	0	0	-1	/S	-0.1
Total	6	198	429	42	95	12	3	0	25	21	50	.221	.258	.263	42	-35	-34	30	4	2	0	3	S/32	-0.7

■ JIM NORRIS   Norris, James Francis b: 12/20/48, Brooklyn, N.Y.   BL/TL, 5'10", 175 lbs.   Deb: 4/07/77

YEAR	TM/L	G	AB	R	H	2B	3B	HR	RBI	BB	SO	AVG	OBP	SLG	PRO+	BR	/A	RC	SB	CS	SBR	FR	POS	TPR
1977	Cle-A	133	440	59	119	23	6	2	37	64	57	.270	.363	.364	102	1	3	59	26	17	-2	16	*O/1	1.2
1978	Cle-A	113	315	41	89	14	5	2	27	42	20	.283	.367	.378	111	5	6	45	12	7	-1	1	OD/1	0.4
1979	Cle-A	124	353	50	87	15	6	3	30	44	35	.246	.330	.348	83	-8	-8	39	15	10	-2	2	OD	-1.0
1980	Tex-A	119	174	23	43	5	0	0	16	23	16	.247	.335	.276	72	-6	-6	15	6	3	0	-3	O1/D	-1.0
Total	4	489	1282	173	338	57	17	7	110	173	128	.264	.351	.351	95	-7	-5	159	59	37	-5	17	O/D1	-0.4

■ LEO NORRIS   Norris, Leo John b: 5/17/08, Bay St.Louis, Miss   d: 2/13/87, Zachary, La.   BR/TR, 5'11", 165 lbs.   Deb: 4/14/36

YEAR	TM/L	G	AB	R	H	2B	3B	HR	RBI	BB	SO	AVG	OBP	SLG	PRO+	BR	/A	RC	SB	CS	SBR	FR	POS	TPR
1936	Phi-N	154	581	64	154	27	4	11	76	39	79	.265	.315	.382	79	-12	-19	69	4			-8	*S2	-1.7
1937	Phi-N	116	381	45	98	24	3	9	36	21	53	.257	.296	.407	82	-7	-11	48	3			-11	23S	-1.6
Total	2	270	962	109	252	51	7	20	112	60	132	.262	.307	.392	80	-19	-31	117	7			-19	S2/3	-3.3

■ BILL NORTH   North, William Alex b: 5/15/48, Seattle, Wash.   BB/TR, 5'11", 185 lbs.   Deb: 9/03/71

YEAR	TM/L	G	AB	R	H	2B	3B	HR	RBI	BB	SO	AVG	OBP	SLG	PRO+	BR	/A	RC	SB	CS	SBR	FR	POS	TPR
1971	Chi-N	8	16	3	6	0	0	0	4	4	6	.375	.524	.375	138	2	1	4	1	1	-0	-1	/O	0.0
1972	Chi-N	66	127	22	23	2	3	0	4	13	33	.181	.262	.244	40	-9	-11	9	6	0	2	0	O	-1.1
1973	Oak-A	146	554	98	158	10	5	5	34	78	89	.285	.376	.348	111	7	11	81	53	20	4	21	*O/D	3.3
1974	*Oak-A	149	543	79	141	20	5	4	33	69	86	.260	.348	.337	105	1	5	68	54	26	1	16	*O/D	1.9
1975	*Oak-A	140	524	74	143	17	5	1	43	81	80	.273	.374	.330	103	4	6	73	30	12	3	15	*O/D	1.9
1976	Oak-A	154	590	91	163	20	5	2	31	73	95	.276	.358	.337	109	6	9	78	75	29	5	-0	*O/D	1.1
1977	Oak-A	56	184	32	48	3	3	1	9	32	25	.261	.376	.326	95	-0	-0	24	17	13	-3	-4	O/D	-0.7
1978	Oak-A	24	52	5	11	4	0	0	5	9	13	.212	.348	.288	86	-1	-0	6	3	2	-0	-1	O	-0.1
	*LA-N	110	304	54	71	10	0	0	10	65	48	.234	.372	.266	81	-4	-4	38	27	8	3	-6	*O	-1.0
1979	SF-N	142	460	87	119	15	4	5	30	96	84	.259	.388	.341	108	5	9	71	58	24	3	-4	*O	0.5
1980	SF-N	128	415	73	104	12	1	1	19	81	78	.251	.374	.292	90	-2	-1	54	45	19	2	3	*O	0.0
1981	SF-N	46	131	22	29	7	0	1	12	26	28	.221	.354	.298	88	-1	-1	18	26	8	3	-1	O	0.1
Total	11	1169	3900	640	1016	120	31	20	230	627	665	.261	.366	.323	99	7	25	524	395	162	21	39	*O/D	5.9

■ HUB NORTHEN   Northen, Hubbard Elwin b: 8/16/1885, Atlanta, Tex.   d: 10/1/47, Shreveport, La.   BL/TL, 5'8", 175 lbs.   Deb: 9/10/10

YEAR	TM/L	G	AB	R	H	2B	3B	HR	RBI	BB	SO	AVG	OBP	SLG	PRO+	BR	/A	RC	SB	CS	SBR	FR	POS	TPR
1910	StL-A	26	96	6	19	1	0	0	16	5		.198	.238	.208	42	-7	-6	5	2			-2	O	-1.0
1911	Cin-N	1	0	0	0	0	0	0	0	0	0	—	—	—	—	0	0	0	0			0	H	0.0
	Bro-N	19	76	16	24	2	2	0	1	14	9	.316	.429	.395	137	4	4	14	4			2	O	0.6
	Yr	20	76	16	24	2	2	0	1	14	9	.316	.429	.395	137	4	4	14	4			2		0.6
1912	Bro-N	118	412	54	116	26	6	3	46	41	46	.282	.352	.396	109	2	4	60	8			-8	*O	-0.5
Total	3	164	584	76	159	29	8	3	63	60	55	.272	.345	.365	103	-0	3	79	14			-7	O	-0.9

■ RON NORTHEY   Northey, Ronald James b: 4/26/20, Mahanoy City, Pa.   d: 4/16/71, Pittsburgh, Pa.   BL/TR, 5'10", 195 lbs.   Deb: 4/14/42   C

YEAR	TM/L	G	AB	R	H	2B	3B	HR	RBI	BB	SO	AVG	OBP	SLG	PRO+	BR	/A	RC	SB	CS	SBR	FR	POS	TPR
1942	Phi-N	127	402	31	101	13	2	5	31	28	33	.251	.300	.331	89	-9	-6	41	2			-0	*O	-0.9
1943	Phi-N	147	586	72	163	31	5	16	68	51	52	.278	.339	.430	127	14	17	88	2			1	*O	1.4
1944	Phi-N	152	570	72	164	35	9	22	104	67	51	.288	.367	.496	146	30	32	107	1			1	*O	2.2
1946	Phi-N	128	438	55	109	24	6	16	62	39	59	.249	.313	.441	116	5	6	61	1			-9	*O	-0.5
1947	Phi-N	13	47	7	12	3	0	0	3	6	3	.255	.340	.319	79	-1	-1	6	1			-2	O	-0.2
	StL-N	110	311	52	91	19	3	15	63	48	29	.293	.391	.518	133	18	16	65	0			-9	O/3	0.4
	Yr	123	358	59	103	22	3	15	66	54	32	.288	.384	.492	127	16	14	70	1			-10		0.2
1948	StL-N	96	246	40	79	10	1	13	64	38	25	.321	.420	.528	147	20	18	55	0			-11	O	0.2
1949	StL-N	90	265	28	69	18	2	7	50	31	15	.260	.338	.423	98	1	-1	37	0			-12	O	-1.6
1950	Cin-N	27	77	11	20	5	0	5	9	15	6	.260	.380	.519	134	4	4	16	0			-6	O	-0.2
	Chi-N	53	114	11	32	9	0	4	20	10	9	.281	.339	.465	110	1	1	18	0			-2	O	0.0
	Yr	80	191	22	52	14	0	9	29	25	15	.272	.356	.487	120	5	5	33	0			-8		-0.2
1952	Chi-N	1	1	0	0	0	0	0	0	0	0	.000	.000	.000	-99	-0	-0	0	0	0	0	0	H	0.0
1955	Chi-A	14	14	1	5	2	0	1	4	3	3	.357	.471	.714	209	2	2	4	0	0	0	-0	/O	0.2
1956	Chi-A	53	48	4	17	2	0	3	23	8	1	.354	.446	.583	168	5	5	12	0	0	0	0	H	0.5
1957	Chi-A	40	27	0	5	1	0	0	7	11	5	.185	.421	.222	80	0	0	4	0	0	0	0	H	0.0
	Phi-N	33	26	1	7	0	0	1	5	6	6	.269	.406	.385	118	1	1	5	0	0	0	0	H	0.1
Total	12	1084	3172	385	874	172	28	108	513	361	297	.276	.352	.450	124	90	94	517	7	0		-48	O/3	1.6

■ SCOTT NORTHEY   Northey, Scott Richard b: 10/15/46, Philadelphia, Pa.   BR/TR, 6', 175 lbs.   Deb: 9/02/69

YEAR	TM/L	G	AB	R	H	2B	3B	HR	RBI	BB	SO	AVG	OBP	SLG	PRO+	BR	/A	RC	SB	CS	SBR	FR	POS	TPR
1969	KC-A	20	61	11	16	2	2	1	7	7	19	.262	.338	.410	108	1	1	9	6	3	0	0	O	0.1

■ JIM NORTHRUP   Northrup, James Thomas b: 11/24/39, Breckenridge, Mich.   BL/TR, 6'3", 190 lbs.   Deb: 9/30/64

YEAR	TM/L	G	AB	R	H	2B	3B	HR	RBI	BB	SO	AVG	OBP	SLG	PRO+	BR	/A	RC	SB	CS	SBR	FR	POS	TPR
1964	Det-A	5	12	1	1	1	0	0	0	0	3	.083	.083	.167	-32	-2	-2	0	1	0	0	0	/O	-0.1
1965	Det-A	80	219	20	45	12	3	2	16	12	50	.205	.253	.315	60	-12	-12	16	1	1	-0	-5	O	-2.0
1966	Det-A	123	419	53	111	24	6	16	58	33	52	.265	.325	.465	121	12	11	56	4	7	-3	10	*O	1.4
1967	Det-A	144	495	63	134	18	6	10	61	43	83	.271	.333	.392	110	8	7	63	7	1	2	-9	*O	-0.5
1968	*Det-A	154	580	76	153	29	7	21	90	50	87	.264	.326	.447	129	24	19	82	4	5	-2	13	*O	2.8
1969	Det-A	148	543	79	160	31	5	25	66	52	81	.295	.360	.508	135	27	25	100	4	2	0	3	*O	2.4
1970	Det-A	139	504	71	132	21	3	24	80	58	68	.262	.346	.458	119	13	13	78	3	6	-3	7	*O	1.2
1971	Det-A	136	459	72	124	27	2	16	71	60	43	.270	.355	.442	121	15	13	71	7	4	-0	-3	*O	0.5
1972	*Det-A	134	426	40	111	15	2	8	42	38	47	.261	.324	.362	101	2	0	45	4	7	-3	-2	*O/1	-0.8
1973	Det-A	119	404	55	124	14	7	12	44	38	41	.307	.368	.465	125	17	14	68	4	4	-3	-3	*O	0.7
1974	Det-A	97	376	41	89	12	1	11	42	36	46	.237	.303	.362	88	-5	-6	42	0	0	0	-3	O	-0.8
	Mon-N	21	54	3	13	1	0	2	8	5	9	.241	.305	.370	84	-1	-1	5	0	0	0	-3	O	-0.4
	Bal-A	8	7	2	4	0	0	1	3	2	1	.571	.667	1.000	386	3	3	5	0	0	0	1	/OD	0.4
1975	Bal-A	84	194	27	53	13	0	5	29	22	22	.273	.353	.418	125	4	6	27	0	1	-1	-4	O/D	0.0

YEAR	TM/L	G	AB	R	H	2B	3B	HR	RBI	BB	SO	AVG	OBP	SLG	PRO+	BR	/A	RC	SB	CS	SBR	FR	POS	TPR
Total	12	1392	4692	603	1254	218	42	153	610	449	635	.267	.335	.429	115	104	89	659	39	38	-11	6	*O/1D	4.8

■ FRANK NORTON Norton, Frank Prescott   Deb: 5/05/1871

YEAR	TM/L	G	AB	R	H	2B	3B	HR	RBI	BB	SO	AVG	OBP	SLG	PRO+	BR	/A	RC	SB	CS	SBR	FR	POS	TPR
1871	Oly-n	1	1	0	0	0	0	0	0	0	1	.000	.000	.000	-99	-0	-0	0	0				/O	0.0

■ WILLIE NORWOOD   Norwood, Willie   b: 11/7/50, Green County, Ala.   BR/TR, 6', 185 lbs.   Deb: 4/21/77

YEAR	TM/L	G	AB	R	H	2B	3B	HR	RBI	BB	SO	AVG	OBP	SLG	PRO+	BR	/A	RC	SB	CS	SBR	FR	POS	TPR
1977	Min-A	39	83	15	19	3	0	3	9	6	17	.229	.281	.373	78	-3	-3	9	6	1	1	2	O/D	0.0
1978	Min-A	125	428	56	109	22	3	8	46	28	64	.255	.305	.376	89	-6	-7	46	25	10	2	-6	*O/D	-1.4
1979	Min-A	96	270	32	67	13	3	6	30	20	51	.248	.300	.385	80	-7	-8	29	9	5	-0	1	OD	-0.9
1980	Min-A	34	73	6	12	2	0	1	8	3	13	.164	.197	.233	16	-8	-9	3	1	1	-0	2	O/D	-0.7
Total	4	294	854	109	207	40	6	18	93	57	145	.242	.292	.367	79	-24	-27	87	41	17	2	-1	O/D	-3.0

■ JOE NOSSEK   Nossek, Joseph Rudolph   b: 11/8/40, Cleveland, Ohio   BR/TR, 6', 178 lbs.   Deb: 4/18/64   C

YEAR	TM/L	G	AB	R	H	2B	3B	HR	RBI	BB	SO	AVG	OBP	SLG	PRO+	BR	/A	RC	SB	CS	SBR	FR	POS	TPR
1964	Min-A	7	1	1	0	0	0	0	0	0	0	.000	.000	.000	-99	-0	-0	0	0	0	0	0	/O	0.0
1965	*Min-A	87	170	19	37	9	0	2	16	7	22	.218	.253	.306	55	-10	-10	13	2	0	1	3	O/3	-0.8
1966	Min-A	4	0	0	0	0	0	0	0	0	0	—	—	—	—	0	0	0	0	0	0	0	O	0.0
	KC-A	87	230	13	60	10	3	1	27	8	21	.261	.286	.343	83	-6	-6	21	4	2	0	1	O/3	-0.8
	Yr	91	230	13	60	10	3	1	27	8	21	.261	.286	.343	82	-6	-6	21	4	2	0	1		-0.8
1967	KC-A	87	166	12	34	6	1	0	10	4	26	.205	.224	.253	42	-12	-12	9	2	0	1	7	O	-0.6
1969	Oak-A	13	6	0	0	0	0	0	0	0	0	.000	.000	.000	-99	-2	-2	0	0	0	0	1	O	0.0
	StL-N	9	5	2	1	0	0	0	0	0	3	.200	.200	.200	12	-1	-1	0	0	0	0	1	/O	0.0
1970	StL-N	1	1	0	0	0	0	0	0	0	0	.000	.000	.000	-98	-0	-0	0	0	0	0	0	H	0.0
Total	6	295	579	47	132	25	4	3	53	19	72	.228	.254	.301	60	-31	-30	43	8	2	1	12	O/3	-2.2

■ LOU NOVIKOFF   Novikoff, Louis Alexander "The Mad Russian"   b: 10/12/15, Glendale, Ariz.   d: 9/30/70, South Gate, Cal.   BR/TR, 5'10", 185 lbs.   Deb: 4/15/41

YEAR	TM/L	G	AB	R	H	2B	3B	HR	RBI	BB	SO	AVG	OBP	SLG	PRO+	BR	/A	RC	SB	CS	SBR	FR	POS	TPR
1941	Chi-N	62	203	22	49	8	0	5	24	11	15	.241	.284	.355	82	-6	-5	19	0			-3	O	-1.0
1942	Chi-N	128	483	48	145	25	5	7	64	24	28	.300	.337	.416	125	10	12	64	3			-1	*O	0.8
1943	Chi-N	78	233	22	65	7	3	0	28	18	15	.279	.333	.335	95	-2	-2	24	0			-8	O	-1.2
1944	Chi-N	71	139	15	39	4	2	3	19	10	11	.281	.329	.403	106	1	1	19	1			-5	O	-0.6
1946	Phi-N	17	23	0	7	1	0	0	3	1	2	.304	.333	.348	96	-0	-0	2	0			1	/O	0.0
Total	5	356	1081	107	305	45	10	15	138	64	71	.282	.325	.384	107	2	6	129	4			-17	O	-2.0

■ RUBE NOVOTNEY   Novotney, Ralph Joseph   b: 8/5/24, Streator, Ill.   BR/TR, 6', 187 lbs.   Deb: 4/29/49

YEAR	TM/L	G	AB	R	H	2B	3B	HR	RBI	BB	SO	AVG	OBP	SLG	PRO+	BR	/A	RC	SB	CS	SBR	FR	POS	TPR
1949	Chi-N	22	67	4	18	2	1	0	6	3	11	.269	.300	.328	70	-3	-3	6	0			1	C	-0.1

■ LES NUNAMAKER   Nunamaker, Leslie Grant   b: 1/25/1889, Malcolm, Neb.   d: 11/14/38, Hastings, Neb.   BR/TR, 6'2", 190 lbs.   Deb: 4/28/11

YEAR	TM/L	G	AB	R	H	2B	3B	HR	RBI	BB	SO	AVG	OBP	SLG	PRO+	BR	/A	RC	SB	CS	SBR	FR	POS	TPR
1911	Bos-A	62	183	18	47	4	3	0	19	12		.257	.303	.311	72	-7	-7	18	1			7	C	0.7
1912	Bos-A	35	103	15	26	5	2	0	6	6		.252	.313	.340	82	-2	-3	12	2			-3	C	-0.1
1913	Bos-A	29	65	9	14	5	2	0	9	8	8	.215	.311	.354	92	-1	-1	8	2			3	C	0.5
1914	Bos-A	5	5	0	1	0	0	0	0	1	0	.200	.333	.200	61	-0	-0	0	0			0	/C1	0.0
	NY-A	87	257	19	68	10	3	2	29	22	34	.265	.327	.350	104	1	1	30	11	9	-2	4	C/1	0.8
	Yr	92	262	19	69	10	3	2	29	23	34	.263	.328	.347	103	1	1	30	11	9	-2	4		0.8
1915	NY-A	87	249	24	56	6	3	0	17	23	24	.225	.293	.273	70	-9	-9	21	4			-4	C/1	-0.8
1916	NY-A	91	260	25	77	14	7	0	28	34	21	.296	.380	.404	133	12	11	41	4			-7	C	0.9
1917	NY-A	104	310	22	81	9	2	0	33	21	25	.261	.310	.303	86	-5	-5	30	5			-4	C	-0.2
1918	StL-N	85	274	22	71	9	2	0	22	28	16	.259	.339	.307	98	-1	-0	30	6			0	C/1O	0.8
1919	Cle-A	26	56	6	14	1	1	0	7	2	6	.250	.276	.304	59	-3	-3	5	0			-4	C	-0.6
1920	*Cle-A	34	54	10	18	3	3	0	14	4	5	.333	.379	.500	128	2	2	10	1	0	0	1	C/1	0.5
1921	Cle-A	46	131	16	47	7	2	0	25	11	8	.359	.408	.443	115	4	3	24	1	1	-0	4	C	0.8
1922	Cle-A	25	43	8	13	2	0	0	7	4	3	.302	.362	.349	85	-1	-1	6	0	0	0	-2	C	-0.2
Total	12	716	1990	194	533	75	30	2	216	176	150	.268	.332	.339	95	-11	-12	234	36	12		-5	C/1O	3.1

■ EMORY NUSZ   Nusz, Emory Moberly   b: 4/2/1866,   d: 8/3/1893, Point Of Rocks, Md.   Deb: 4/26/1884

YEAR	TM/L	G	AB	R	H	2B	3B	HR	RBI	BB	SO	AVG	OBP	SLG	PRO+	BR	/A	RC	SB	CS	SBR	FR	POS	TPR
1884	Was-U	1	4	1	0	0	0	0		0		.000	.000	.000	-99	-1	-1	0	0			-0	/O	0.0

■ DIZZY NUTTER   Nutter, Everett Clarence   b: 8/27/1893, Roseville, Ohio   d: 7/25/58, Battle Creek, Mich.   BL/TR, 5'9", 160 lbs.   Deb: 9/07/19

YEAR	TM/L	G	AB	R	H	2B	3B	HR	RBI	BB	SO	AVG	OBP	SLG	PRO+	BR	/A	RC	SB	CS	SBR	FR	POS	TPR
1919	Bos-N	18	52	4	11	0	0	0	3	4	5	.212	.268	.212	47	-3	-3	3	1			2	O	-0.1

■ CHARLIE NYCE   Nyce, Charles Reiff (b: Charles Reiff Nice)   b: 7/1/1870, Philadelphia, Pa.   d: 5/9/08, Philadelphia, Pa.   5'8", 160 lbs.   Deb: 5/28/1895

YEAR	TM/L	G	AB	R	H	2B	3B	HR	RBI	BB	SO	AVG	OBP	SLG	PRO+	BR	/A	RC	SB	CS	SBR	FR	POS	TPR
1895	Bos-N	9	35	7	8	5	0	2	9	4	2	.229	.325	.543	114	1	0	6	0			-0	/S	0.0

■ CHRIS NYMAN   Nyman, Christopher Curtis   b: 6/6/55, Pomona, Cal.   BR/TR, 6'4", 200 lbs.   Deb: 7/28/82

YEAR	TM/L	G	AB	R	H	2B	3B	HR	RBI	BB	SO	AVG	OBP	SLG	PRO+	BR	/A	RC	SB	CS	SBR	FR	POS	TPR
1982	Chi-A	28	65	6	16	1	0	0	2	3	9	.246	.279	.262	50	-4	-4	4	3	2	-0	1	1/O	-0.4
1983	Chi-A	21	28	12	8	0	0	2	4	4	7	.286	.394	.500	139	2	2	5	2	2	-1	1	1D	0.2
Total	2	49	93	18	24	1	0	2	6	7	16	.258	.317	.333	78	-3	-3	10	5	4	-1	2	/1DO	-0.2

■ NYLS NYMAN   Nyman, Nyls Wallace Rex   b: 3/7/54, Detroit, Mich.   BL/TR, 6', 170 lbs.   Deb: 9/06/74

YEAR	TM/L	G	AB	R	H	2B	3B	HR	RBI	BB	SO	AVG	OBP	SLG	PRO+	BR	/A	RC	SB	CS	SBR	FR	POS	TPR
1974	Chi-A	5	14	5	9	2	1	0	4	0	1	.643	.667	.929	347	5	4	8	1	0	0	1	/O	0.5
1975	Chi-A	106	327	36	74	6	3	2	28	11	34	.226	.256	.281	51	-21	-22	23	10	4	1	-13	O/D	-3.7
1976	Chi-A	8	15	2	2	1	0	0	1	0	3	.133	.133	.200	-3	-2	-2	0	1	0	0	1	O	0.0
1977	Chi-A	1	1	0	0	0	0	0	0	0	0	.000	.000	.000	-99	-0	-0	0	0	0	0	0	H	0.0
Total	4	120	357	43	85	9	4	2	33	11	38	.238	.267	.303	60	-19	-19	32	12	4	1	-11	O/D	-3.2

■ REBEL OAKES   Oakes, Ennis Telfair   b: 12/17/1886, Homer, La.   d: 2/29/48, Rocky Springs, Lisbon, La.   BL/TR, 5'8", 170 lbs.   Deb: 4/14/09   M

YEAR	TM/L	G	AB	R	H	2B	3B	HR	RBI	BB	SO	AVG	OBP	SLG	PRO+	BR	/A	RC	SB	CS	SBR	FR	POS	TPR
1909	Cin-N	120	415	55	112	10	5	3	31	40		.270	.341	.340	112	6	6	56	23			-2	*O	0.1
1910	StL-N	131	468	50	118	14	6	0	43	38	38	.252	.315	.308	85	-11	-9	51	18			-11	*O	-2.5
1911	StL-N	154	551	69	145	13	6	2	59	41	35	.263	.320	.319	81	-16	-14	64	25			6	*O	-1.2
1912	StL-N	136	495	57	139	19	5	3	58	31	24	.281	.328	.358	90	-9	-8	66	26			-3	*O	-1.4
1913	StL-N	147	539	60	139	14	5	0	49	43	32	.293	.350	.338	98	-1	-0	71	22			-6	*O	-0.8
1914	Pit-F	145	571	82	178	18	10	7	75	35	22	.312	.359	.415	122	15	16	100	28			6	*OM	1.5
1915	Pit-F	153	580	55	161	24	5	0	82	37	19	.278	.323	.336	96	-4	-3	75	21			-3	*OM	-1.4
Total	7	986	3619	428	1011	112	42	15	397	265	170	.279	.334	.346	98	-20	-11	483	163			-13	O	-5.7

■ PRINCE OANA   Oana, Henry Kauhane   b: 1/22/08, Waipahu, Hawaii   d: 6/19/76, Austin, Tex.   BR/TR, 6'2", 193 lbs.   Deb: 4/22/34

YEAR	TM/L	G	AB	R	H	2B	3B	HR	RBI	BB	SO	AVG	OBP	SLG	PRO+	BR	/A	RC	SB	CS	SBR	FR	POS	TPR
1934	Phi-N	6	21	3	5	1	0	0	3	0	1	.238	.238	.286	35	-2	-2	1	0			1	/O	-0.1
1943	Det-A	20	26	5	10	2	1	1	7	1	2	.385	.407	.654	193	3	3	6	0	0	0	-0	P	0.4
1945	Det-A	4	5	0	1	0	0	0	0	0	0	.200	.200	.200	15	-1	-1	0	0	0	0	-0	/P	0.0
Total	3	30	52	8	16	3	1	1	10	1	3	.308	.321	.462	108	1	0	7	0	0	0	0	/PO	0.3

■ JOHNNY OATES   Oates, Johnny Lane   b: 1/21/46, Sylva, N.C.   BL/TR, 5'11", 188 lbs.   Deb: 9/17/70   C

YEAR	TM/L	G	AB	R	H	2B	3B	HR	RBI	BB	SO	AVG	OBP	SLG	PRO+	BR	/A	RC	SB	CS	SBR	FR	POS	TPR
1970	Bal-A	5	18	2	5	0	1	0	2	0	2	.278	.350	.389	102	0	0	3	0	0	0	1	/C	0.1
1972	Bal-A	85	253	20	66	12	1	4	21	28	31	.261	.335	.364	105	3	2	29	5	7	-3	-3	C	-0.3
1973	Atl-N	93	322	27	80	6	0	4	27	22	31	.248	.299	.304	63	-14	-17	28	1	4	-2	3	C	-2.0
1974	Atl-N	100	291	22	65	10	0	1	21	23	24	.223	.280	.268	52	-18	-19	22	2	3	-1	13	C	-0.3
1975	Atl-N	8	18	0	4	0	0	0	1	4	4	.222	.263	.278	48	-1	-1	1	0	0	0	-0	/C	0.0
	Phi-N	90	269	28	77	14	0	1	25	33	29	.286	.364	.349	95	1	-1	35	1	0	0	1	C	0.3

YEAR	TM/L	G	AB	R	H	2B	3B	HR	RBI	BB	SO	AVG	OBP	SLG	PRO+	BR	/A	RC	SB	CS	SBR	FR	POS	TPR
	Yr	98	287	28	81	15	0	1	25	34	33	.282	.358	.345	92	-1	-2	36	1	0	0	0		0.3
1976	*Phi-N	37	99	10	25	2	0	0	8	8	12	.253	.308	.273	64	-4	-5	7	0	1	-1	1	C	-0.1
1977	*LA-N	60	156	18	42	4	0	3	11	11	11	.269	.317	.353	80	-5	-4	17	1	0	0	5	C	0.0
1978	*LA-N	40	75	5	23	1	0	0	6	5	3	.307	.350	.320	89	-1	-1	8	0	1	-1	-2	C	-0.2
1979	LA-N	26	46	4	6	2	0	0	2	4	1	.130	.200	.174	3	-6	-6	2	0	1	-1	3	C	-0.2
1980	NY-A	39	64	6	12	3	0	1	3	2	3	.188	.224	.281	38	-6	-5	3	1	2	-1	3	C	-0.1
1981	NY-A	10	26	4	5	1	0	0	0	2	0	.192	.250	.231	40	-2	-2	2	0	0	0	1	C	0.0
Total	11	593	1637	146	410	56	2	14	126	141	149	.250	.311	.313	73	-53	-60	158	11	19	-8	17	C	-2.8

■ HENRY OBERBECK
Oberbeck, Henry A.   b: 5/17/1858, Missouri   d: 8/26/21, St.Louis, Mo.   Deb: 5/07/1883

YEAR	TM/L	G	AB	R	H	2B	3B	HR	RBI	BB	SO	AVG	OBP	SLG	PRO+	BR	/A	RC	SB	CS	SBR	FR	POS	TPR
1883	Pit-a	2	9	1	2	1	0	0		0		.222	.222	.333	80	-0	-0	1				0	/1	0.0
	StL-a	4	14	0	0	0	0	0		0		.000	.000	.000	-94	-3	-3	0				1	/O	-0.1
	Yr	6	23	1	2	1	0	0		0		.087	.087	.130	-30	-3	-3	0				1		-0.1
1884	Bal-U	33	125	19	23	4	0	0		3		.184	.203	.216	38	-7	-9	6	0			2	O/3P	-0.6
	KC-U	27	90	7	17	3	0	0		7		.189	.247	.222	69	-3	-2	5	0			7	3/OP1	0.5
	Yr	60	215	26	40	7	0	0		10		.186	.222	.219	50	-11	-11	11	0			9		-0.1
Total	2	66	238	27	42	8	0	0		10		.176	.210	.210	41	-14	-14	11	0			10	/O3P1	-0.2

■ KEN OBERKFELL
Oberkfell, Kenneth Ray   b: 5/4/56, Highland, Ill.   BL/TR, 6', 175 lbs.   Deb: 8/22/77

YEAR	TM/L	G	AB	R	H	2B	3B	HR	RBI	BB	SO	AVG	OBP	SLG	PRO+	BR	/A	RC	SB	CS	SBR	FR	POS	TPR
1977	StL-N	9	9	0	1	0	0	0	1	0	3	.111	.111	.111	-41	-2	-2	0	0	0	0	-1	/2	-0.1
1978	StL-N	24	50	7	6	1	0	0	0	3	1	.120	.170	.140	-13	-8	-7	1	0	0	0	3	2/3	-0.2
1979	StL-N	135	369	53	111	19	5	1	35	57	35	.301	.400	.388	115	11	11	60	4	1	1	-4	*23/S	1.4
1980	StL-N	116	422	58	128	27	6	3	46	51	23	.303	.380	.417	118	14	12	66	4	4	-1	-8	*23	1.0
1981	StL-N	102	376	43	110	12	6	2	45	37	28	.293	.356	.372	104	4	3	49	13	5	1	11	*3/S	1.0
1982	*StL-N	137	470	55	136	22	5	2	34	40	31	.289	.346	.370	99	1	0	58	11	9	-2	11	*3/2	0.7
1983	StL-N	151	488	62	143	26	5	3	38	61	27	.293	.373	.385	110	9	9	71	12	6	0	4	*32/S	0.9
1984	StL-N	50	152	17	47	11	1	0	11	16	10	.309	.379	.395	121	4	4	22	1	2	-1	4	3/2S	0.8
	Atl-N	50	172	21	40	8	1	1	10	15	17	.233	.294	.308	65	-7	-8	15	1	3	-2	-5	3/2	-1.5
	Yr	100	324	38	87	19	2	1	21	31	27	.269	.334	.349	90	-3	-4	37	2	5	-2	-1		-0.7
1985	Atl-N	134	412	30	112	19	4	3	35	51	38	.272	.360	.359	96	3	-0	54	1	2	-1	-1	*32	-0.1
1986	Atl-N	151	503	62	136	24	3	5	48	83	40	.270	.376	.360	98	6	2	72	7	4	-0	9	*32	0.9
1987	Atl-N	135	508	59	142	29	2	3	48	48	29	.280	.344	.362	83	-8	-12	63	3	3	-1	-4	*32	-1.7
1988	Atl-N	120	422	42	117	20	4	3	40	32	28	.277	.331	.365	95	-3	-0	51	4	5	-2	-7	*3/2	-1.1
	Pit-N	20	54	7	12	2	0	0	2	5	6	.222	.288	.259	59	-3	-3	4	0	0	0	-3	2/S31	-0.5
	Yr	140	476	49	129	22	4	3	42	37	34	.271	.326	.353	91	-3	-5	55	4	5	-2	-10		-1.6
1989	Pit-N	14	40	2	5	1	0	0	2	2	2	.125	.167	.150	-9	-6	-5	1	0	0	0	-0	/12	-0.6
	SF-N	83	116	17	37	5	1	2	15	8	8	.319	.373	.431	133	4	5	18	0	1	-1	-4	3/12	0.0
	Yr	97	156	19	42	6	1	2	17	10	10	.269	.321	.359	97	-1	-1	17	0	1	-1	-4		-0.6
1990	Hou-N	77	150	10	31	6	1	1	12	15	17	.207	.283	.280	57	-9	-9	12	1	1	-0	-2	312	-1.1
Total	14	1508	4713	545	1314	232	44	29	422	524	343	.279	.354	.365	97	13	-3	620	62	46	-9	3	*32/1S	-0.2

■ MIKE O'BERRY
O'Berry, Preston Michael   b: 4/20/54, Birmingham, Ala.   BR/TR, 6'2", 190 lbs.   Deb: 4/08/79

YEAR	TM/L	G	AB	R	H	2B	3B	HR	RBI	BB	SO	AVG	OBP	SLG	PRO+	BR	/A	RC	SB	CS	SBR	FR	POS	TPR
1979	Bos-A	43	59	8	10	1	0	1	4	5	16	.169	.246	.237	29	-6	-6	3	0	0	0	0	C	-0.3
1980	Chi-N	19	48	7	10	1	0	0	5	5	13	.208	.283	.229	41	-3	-4	4	0	0	0	4	C	0.1
1981	Cin-N	55	111	6	20	3	1	1	5	14	19	.180	.272	.252	49	-7	-7	8	0	0	0	3	C	-0.3
1982	Cin-N	21	45	5	10	2	0	0	3	10	13	.222	.364	.267	77	-1	-1	5	0	0	0	-1	C	-0.1
1983	Cal-A	26	60	7	10	1	0	1	5	3	11	.167	.206	.233	21	-7	-6	3	0	0	0	-1	C	-0.5
1984	NY-A	13	32	3	8	2	0	0	5	2	2	.250	.294	.313	71	-1	-1	3	0	0	0	1	C/3	0.0
1985	Mon-N	20	21	2	4	0	0	0	0	4	3	.190	.320	.190	49	-1	-1	2	1	0	0	4	C	0.4
Total	7	197	376	38	72	10	1	3	27	43	77	.191	.276	.247	46	-26	-27	28	1	0	0	10	C/3	-0.7

■ JIM OBRADOVICH
Obradovich, James Thomas   b: 9/13/49, Fort Campbell, Ky.   BL/TL, 6'2", 200 lbs.   Deb: 9/12/78

YEAR	TM/L	G	AB	R	H	2B	3B	HR	RBI	BB	SO	AVG	OBP	SLG	PRO+	BR	/A	RC	SB	CS	SBR	FR	POS	TPR
1978	Hou-N	10	17	3	3	0	1	0	2	1	3	.176	.222	.294	47	-1	-1	1	0	0	0	-0	/1	-0.1

■ CHARLIE O'BRIEN
O'Brien, Charles Hugh   b: 5/1/60, Tulsa, Okla.   BR/TR, 6'2", 195 lbs.   Deb: 6/02/85

YEAR	TM/L	G	AB	R	H	2B	3B	HR	RBI	BB	SO	AVG	OBP	SLG	PRO+	BR	/A	RC	SB	CS	SBR	FR	POS	TPR
1985	Oak-A	16	11	3	3	1	0	0	1	3	3	.273	.429	.364	129	0	1	2	0	0	0	0	C	0.1
1987	Mil-A	10	35	2	7	3	1	0	0	4	4	.200	.282	.343	63	-2	-2	3	0	1	-1	5	C	0.3
1988	Mil-A	40	118	12	26	6	0	2	9	5	16	.220	.252	.322	59	-7	-7	9	0	1	-1	12	C	0.6
1989	Mil-A	62	188	22	44	10	0	6	35	21	11	.234	.339	.383	104	1	2	23	0	0	0	6	C	1.0
1990	Mil-A	46	145	11	27	7	2	0	11	11	26	.186	.253	.262	46	-11	-10	10	0	0	0	4	C	-0.4
	NY-N	28	68	6	11	3	0	0	9	10	8	.162	.278	.206	36	-6	-6	5	0	0	0	9	C	0.5
Total	5	202	565	56	118	30	3	8	65	54	68	.209	.292	.315	70	-23	-22	52	0	2	-1	36	C	2.1

■ EDDIE O'BRIEN
O'Brien, Edward Joseph   b: 12/11/30, S.Amboy, N.J.   BR/TR, 5'9", 165 lbs.   Deb: 4/25/53   C

YEAR	TM/L	G	AB	R	H	2B	3B	HR	RBI	BB	SO	AVG	OBP	SLG	PRO+	BR	/A	RC	SB	CS	SBR	FR	POS	TPR
1953	Pit-N	89	261	21	62	5	3	0	14	17	30	.238	.289	.280	50	-19	-19	23	6	1	1	-14	S	-2.4
1955	Pit-N	75	236	26	55	3	1	0	8	18	13	.233	.290	.254	47	-18	-17	18	4	5	-2	-1	O/3S	-2.0
1956	Pit-N	63	53	17	14	2	0	0	3	2	2	.264	.291	.302	61	-3	-3	5	1	1	-0	12	S/O32P	1.0
1957	Pit-N	3	4	0	0	0	0	0	0	0	0	.000	.000	.000	-99	-1	-1	0	0	0	0	0	/P	0.0
1958	Pit-N	1	0	0	0	0	0	0	0	0	0	—	—	—	—	0	0	0	0	0	0	0	/P	0.0
Total	5	231	554	64	131	10	4	0	25	37	45	.236	.288	.269	48	-41	-40	45	11	7	-1	-3	S/O3P2	-3.4

■ MICKEY O'BRIEN
O'Brien, Frank Aloysius   b: 9/13/1894, San Francisco, Cal.   d: 11/4/71, Monterey Park, Cal.   BR/TR, 5'8", 160 lbs.   Deb: 4/26/23

YEAR	TM/L	G	AB	R	H	2B	3B	HR	RBI	BB	SO	AVG	OBP	SLG	PRO+	BR	/A	RC	SB	CS	SBR	FR	POS	TPR
1923	Phi-N	15	21	3	7	2	0	0	2	1	.333		.391	.429	104	1	0	4	0	0	0	0	/C	0.1

■ GEORGE O'BRIEN
O'Brien, George Joseph   b: 11/4/1889, Cleveland, Ohio   d: 3/24/66, Columbus, Ohio   BR/TR, 6', 185 lbs.   Deb: 8/16/15

YEAR	TM/L	G	AB	R	H	2B	3B	HR	RBI	BB	SO	AVG	OBP	SLG	PRO+	BR	/A	RC	SB	CS	SBR	FR	POS	TPR
1915	StL-A	3	9	1	2	0	0	0	0	1	2	.222	.300	.222	59	-0	-0	1	0			-1	/C	0.0

■ JERRY O'BRIEN
O'Brien, Jeremiah   b: 2/2/1864, New York   d: 7/4/11, Binghamton, N.Y.   Deb: 7/30/1887

YEAR	TM/L	G	AB	R	H	2B	3B	HR	RBI	BB	SO	AVG	OBP	SLG	PRO+	BR	/A	RC	SB	CS	SBR	FR	POS	TPR
1887	Was-N	1	4	0	0	0	0	0	0	0	2	.000	.000	.000	-99	-1	-1	0	0			-0	/2	0.0

■ JOHN O'BRIEN
O'Brien, John E.   b: 10/22/1851, Columbus, Ohio   d: 12/31/14, Fall River, Mass.   TR , 5'11.5", 187 lbs.   Deb: 4/19/1884

YEAR	TM/L	G	AB	R	H	2B	3B	HR	RBI	BB	SO	AVG	OBP	SLG	PRO+	BR	/A	RC	SB	CS	SBR	FR	POS	TPR
1884	Bal-U	18	77	7	19	1	1	0		2		.247	.266	.286	78	-1	-2	6	0			1	O	-0.1

■ JOHN O'BRIEN
O'Brien, John J. "Chewing Gum"   b: 7/14/1870, St.John, N.B., Can   d: 5/13/13, Lewiston, Maine   BL/TR, 175 lbs.   Deb: 4/22/1891

YEAR	TM/L	G	AB	R	H	2B	3B	HR	RBI	BB	SO	AVG	OBP	SLG	PRO+	BR	/A	RC	SB	CS	SBR	FR	POS	TPR
1891	Bro-N	43	167	22	41	4	2	0	26	12	17	.246	.308	.293	78	-5	-4	17	4			-22	2	-2.2
1893	Chi-N	4	14	3	5	0	1	0	1	2	2	.357	.471	.500	164	1	1	3	0			-2	/2	0.0
1895	Lou-N	128	539	82	138	10	4	1	50	45	20	.256	.325	.295	66	-28	-22	58	15			3	*2/1	-0.9
1896	Lou-N	49	186	24	63	9	1	2	24	13	7	.339	.385	.430	121	4	6	33	4			-1	2	0.5
	Was-N	73	270	38	72	6	3	4	33	27	12	.267	.344	.356	87	-5	-5	35	4			2	2	0.0
	Yr	122	456	62	135	15	4	6	57	40	19	.296	.361	.386	100	-0	1	68	8			1		0.5
1897	Was-N	86	320	37	78	12	2	3	46	19		.244	.309	.322	69	-14	-14	34	6			3	2	-0.2
1899	Bal-N	39	135	14	26	4	0	1	17	15		.193	.283	.244	45	-9	-10	11	4			7	2	0.0
	Pit-N	79	279	26	63	2	4	1	33	21		.226	.285	.272	55	-17	-16	25	8			3	2	-0.7
	Yr	118	414	40	89	6	4	2	50	36		.215	.284	.263	52	-26	-27	35	12			10		-0.7
Total	6	501	1910	246	486	47	17	12	229	154	58	.254	.322	.316	73	-72	-65	216	45			-7	2/1	-3.5

YEAR	TM/L	G	AB	R	H	2B	3B	HR	RBI	BB	SO	AVG	OBP	SLG	PRO+	BR	/A	RC	SB	CS	SBR	FR	POS	TPR

■ JACK O'BRIEN
O'Brien, John Joseph b: 2/5/1873, Watervliet, N.Y. d: 6/10/33, Watervliet, N.Y. 6'1", 165 lbs. Deb: 4/14/1899

YEAR	TM/L	G	AB	R	H	2B	3B	HR	RBI	BB	SO	AVG	OBP	SLG	PRO+	BR	/A	RC	SB	CS	SBR	FR	POS	TPR
1899	Was-N	127	468	68	132	11	5	6	51	31		.282	.329	.365	94	-5	-4	63	17			4	*O/3	-0.6
1901	Was-A	11	45	5	8	0	0	0	5	3		.178	.245	.178	20	-5	-5	3	2			0	O	-0.3
	Cle-A	92	375	54	106	14	5	0	39	22		.283	.329	.347	93	-5	-3	49	13			-3	O/3	-0.5
	Yr	103	420	59	114	14	5	0	44	25		.271	.320	.329	85	-10	-7	51	15			-3		-0.8
1903	*Bos-A	96	338	44	71	14	4	3	38	21		.210	.256	.302	65	-13	-15	31	10			-6	O3/2S	-2.6
Total	3	326	1226	171	317	39	14	9	133	77		.259	.306	.335	83	-27	-26	146	42			-4	O/32S	-4.0

■ JACK O'BRIEN
O'Brien, John K. (b: John K. Bryne) b: 6/12/1860, Philadelphia, Pa. d: 11/20/10, Philadelphia, Pa. BR/TR, 5'10", 184 lbs. Deb: 5/02/1882

YEAR	TM/L	G	AB	R	H	2B	3B	HR	RBI	BB	SO	AVG	OBP	SLG	PRO+	BR	/A	RC	SB	CS	SBR	FR	POS	TPR
1882	Phi-a	62	241	44	73	13	3	3		13		.303	.339	.419	138	13	9	35				6	CO/31	1.4
1883	Phi-a	94	390	74	113	14	10	0		25		.290	.333	.377	118	12	7	50				-3	CO3/S	0.8
1884	Phi-a	36	138	25	39	6	1	1		9		.283	.340	.362	124	5	4	17				-1	C/O1	0.4
1885	Phi-a	62	225	35	60	9	1	2		20		.267	.340	.342	112	6	3	27				-7	C/S103	0.2
1886	Phi-a	105	423	65	107	25	7	0		38		.253	.325	.345	111	6	6	56	23			-13	C31S/20	-0.3
1887	Bro-a	30	123	18	28	4	1	1		6		.228	.264	.301	58	-7	-7	12	8			-6	C/O2	-0.7
1888	Bal-a	57	196	25	44	11	5	0	18	17		.224	.300	.332	108	1	2	24	14			-15	CO/1	-0.8
1890	Phi-a	109	433	80	113	24	14	4		52		.261	.354	.409	131	15	16	75	31			4	*1/OC	1.5
Total	8	555	2169	366	577	106	42	11	18	180		.266	.331	.369	116	52	41	297	76			-34	C1/O3S2	2.5

■ JOHNNY O'BRIEN
O'Brien, John Thomas b: 12/11/30, S.Amboy, N.J. BR/TR, 5'9", 170 lbs. Deb: 4/19/53

YEAR	TM/L	G	AB	R	H	2B	3B	HR	RBI	BB	SO	AVG	OBP	SLG	PRO+	BR	/A	RC	SB	CS	SBR	FR	POS	TPR
1953	Pit-N	89	279	28	69	13	2	2	22	21	36	.247	.309	.330	67	-13	-13	28	1	1	-0	-4	2/S	-1.3
1955	Pit-N	84	278	22	83	15	2	1	25	20	19	.299	.348	.378	94	-3	-2	36	1	1	-0	5	2	0.9
1956	Pit-N	73	104	13	18	1	0	0	3	5	7	.173	.211	.183	7	-13	-13	4	0	0	0	5	2/PS	-0.2
1957	Pit-N	34	35	7	11	2	1	0	1	1	4	.314	.368	.429	117	1	1	5	0	0	0	-2	P/S2	0.1
1958	Pit-N	3	1	1	0	0	0	0	0	0	1	.000	.000	.000	-99	-0	-0	0	0	0	0	0	H	0.0
	StL-N	12	2	3	0	0	0	0	0	1	0	.000	.333	.000	-2	-0	-0	0	0	0	0	0	/SP2	0.0
	Yr	15	3	4	0	0	0	0	0	1	1	.000	.250	.000	-26	-1	-1	0	0	0	0	0		0.0
1959	Mil-N	44	116	16	23	4	0	1	8	11	15	.198	.273	.259	47	-9	-8	9	0	0	0	-2	2	-0.7
Total	6	339	815	90	204	35	5	4	59	59	82	.250	.307	.320	68	-39	-36	82	2	2	-1	1	2/PS	-1.2

■ PETE O'BRIEN
O'Brien, Peter J. b: 6/17/1877, Binghamton, N.Y. d: 1/31/17, Jersey City, N.J. BL/TR, 5'7", 170 lbs. Deb: 9/21/01

YEAR	TM/L	G	AB	R	H	2B	3B	HR	RBI	BB	SO	AVG	OBP	SLG	PRO+	BR	/A	RC	SB	CS	SBR	FR	POS	TPR
1901	Cin-N	16	54	1	11	1	1	0	3	2		.204	.232	.278	52	-4	-3	4	0			-2	2	-0.3
1906	StL-A	151	524	44	122	9	4	2	57	42		.233	.290	.277	83	-11	-9	53	25			-41	*23S	-5.7
1907	Cle-A	43	145	13	33	5	2	0	6	7		.228	.263	.290	77	-4	-4	12	1			-11	23S	-1.5
	Was-A	39	134	6	25	3	1	0	12	12		.187	.253	.224	59	-7	-5	9	4			4	3S/2	0.0
	Yr	82	279	15	58	8	3	0	18	19		.208	.258	.258	69	-10	-9	21	5			-7		-1.5
Total	3	249	857	60	191	18	7	3	78	63		.223	.276	.271	76	-25	-21	78	30			-50	2/3S	-7.5

■ PETE O'BRIEN
O'Brien, Peter James b: 6/16/1867, Chicago, Ill. d: 6/30/37, York Township, Du Page County, Ill. BR/TR, 5'9.5", 165 lbs. Deb: 4/29/1890

YEAR	TM/L	G	AB	R	H	2B	3B	HR	RBI	BB	SO	AVG	OBP	SLG	PRO+	BR	/A	RC	SB	CS	SBR	FR	POS	TPR
1890	Chi-N	27	106	15	30	7	0	3	16	5	10	.283	.315	.434	115	2	1	16	4			-2	2	0.0

■ PETE O'BRIEN
O'Brien, Peter Michael b: 2/9/58, Santa Monica, Cal. BL/TL, 6'1", 185 lbs. Deb: 9/03/82

YEAR	TM/L	G	AB	R	H	2B	3B	HR	RBI	BB	SO	AVG	OBP	SLG	PRO+	BR	/A	RC	SB	CS	SBR	FR	POS	TPR
1982	Tex-A	20	67	13	16	4	1	4	13	6	8	.239	.301	.507	124	1	2	11	1	0	0	-0	O/1D	0.1
1983	Tex-A	154	524	53	124	24	5	8	53	58	62	.237	.314	.347	83	-13	-11	57	5	4	-1	14	*1O/D	-0.3
1984	Tex-A	142	520	57	149	26	2	18	80	53	50	.287	.353	.448	116	14	12	80	3	5	-2	1	*1/O	0.1
1985	Tex-A	159	573	69	153	34	3	22	92	69	53	.267	.347	.452	115	13	12	85	5	10	-5	-6	*1	-0.7
1986	Tex-A	156	551	86	160	23	3	23	90	87	66	.290	.387	.468	128	26	24	98	4	4	-1	2	*1	1.4
1987	Tex-A	159	569	84	163	26	1	23	88	59	61	.286	.354	.457	113	10	10	91	0	4	-2	17	*1/OD	0.9
1988	Tex-A	156	547	57	149	24	1	16	71	72	73	.272	.357	.408	111	11	9	80	1	4	-2	13	*1/D	1.1
1989	Cle-A	155	554	75	144	24	1	12	55	83	48	.260	.358	.372	104	7	6	77	3	1	0	3	*1/D	-0.1
1990	Sea-A	108	366	32	82	18	0	5	27	44	33	.224	.311	.314	74	-12	-12	36	0	0	0	6	1/OD	-1.3
Total	9	1209	4271	526	1140	203	17	131	569	531	454	.267	.349	.414	108	59	52	616	22	32	-13	48	*1/OD	1.2

■ RAY O'BRIEN
O'Brien, Raymond Joseph b: 10/31/1892, St.Louis, Mo. d: 3/31/42, St.Louis, Mo. BL/TL, 5'9", 175 lbs. Deb: 6/27/16

YEAR	TM/L	G	AB	R	H	2B	3B	HR	RBI	BB	SO	AVG	OBP	SLG	PRO+	BR	/A	RC	SB	CS	SBR	FR	POS	TPR
1916	Pit-N	16	57	5	12	3	2	0	3	1	14	.211	.224	.333	69	-2	-2	5	0			-2	O	-0.5

■ SYD O'BRIEN
O'Brien, Sydney Lloyd b: 12/18/44, Compton, Cal. BR/TR, 6'1", 185 lbs. Deb: 4/15/69

YEAR	TM/L	G	AB	R	H	2B	3B	HR	RBI	BB	SO	AVG	OBP	SLG	PRO+	BR	/A	RC	SB	CS	SBR	FR	POS	TPR
1969	Bos-A	100	263	47	64	10	5	9	29	15	37	.243	.287	.422	91	-3	-4	31	2	3	-1	-1	3S2	-0.4
1970	Chi-A	121	441	48	109	13	2	8	44	22	62	.247	.286	.340	69	-18	-20	41	3	3	-1	-6	32/S	-2.2
1971	Cal-A	90	251	25	50	8	1	5	21	15	33	.199	.247	.299	58	-16	-14	16	0	2	-1	-1	S/2310	-1.0
1972	Cal-A	36	39	10	7	2	0	1	1	6	10	.179	.289	.308	82	-1	-1	4	0	0	0	1	/3S21	0.1
	Mil-A	31	58	5	12	2	0	1	5	2	13	.207	.233	.293	57	-3	-3	3	0	1	-1	-1	/32	-0.3
	Yr	67	97	15	19	4	0	2	6	8	23	.196	.257	.299	68	-4	-4	7	0	1	-1	0		-0.2
Total	4	378	1052	135	242	35	8	24	100	60	155	.230	.274	.347	72	-40	-42	95	5	9	-4	-8	3/S210	-3.8

■ TOMMY O'BRIEN
O'Brien, Thomas Edward "Obie" b: 12/19/18, Anniston, Ala. d: 11/5/78, Anniston, Ala. BR/TR, 5'11", 195 lbs. Deb: 4/24/43

YEAR	TM/L	G	AB	R	H	2B	3B	HR	RBI	BB	SO	AVG	OBP	SLG	PRO+	BR	/A	RC	SB	CS	SBR	FR	POS	TPR
1943	Pit-N	89	232	35	72	12	7	2	26	15	24	.310	.352	.448	126	8	7	35	0			-3	O/3	0.2
1944	Pit-N	85	156	27	39	6	2	3	20	21	12	.250	.343	.372	97	1	-0	19	1			-4	O/3	-0.7
1945	Pit-N	58	161	23	54	6	5	0	18	9	13	.335	.374	.435	120	5	4	27	0			-4	O	-0.1
1949	Bos-A	49	125	24	28	5	0	3	10	21	12	.224	.336	.336	73	-4	-5	15	1	0	0	-2	O	-0.7
1950	Bos-A	9	31	0	4	1	0	0	3	3	5	.129	.206	.161	-5	-5	-5	1	0	0	0	-0	/O	-0.5
	Was-A	3	9	1	1	0	0	0	1	1	0	.111	.200	.111	-20	-2	-2	0	0	0	0	1	/O	0.0
	Yr	12	40	1	5	1	0	0	4	4	5	.125	.205	.150	-8	-7	-7	1	0	0	0	1		-0.5
Total	5	293	714	110	198	30	14	8	78	70	66	.277	.344	.392	100	3	-1	97	2	0		-12	O/3	-1.8

■ TOM O'BRIEN
O'Brien, Thomas H. b: 6/22/1860, Salem, Mass. d: 4/21/21, Worcester, Mass. Deb: 6/14/1882

YEAR	TM/L	G	AB	R	H	2B	3B	HR	RBI	BB	SO	AVG	OBP	SLG	PRO+	BR	/A	RC	SB	CS	SBR	FR	POS	TPR
1882	Wor-N	22	89	9	18	1	1	0	7	1	10	.202	.211	.236	42	-6	-6	5				-3	O/23	-0.7
1883	Bal-a	33	138	16	37	6	4	0		5		.268	.294	.370	109	2	1	15				-4	2/O	-0.1
1884	Bos-U	103	449	80	118	31	8	4		12		.263	.282	.394	128	12	13	51	0			2	*2/O1C	0.9
1885	Bal-a	8	33	4	7	3	0	0		2		.212	.257	.303	80	-1	-1	3				1	/12	0.0
1887	NY-a	31	129	13	25	3	2	0		2		.194	.212	.248	31	-12	-11	9	10			-2	1/O32P	-1.0
1890	Roc-a	73	273	36	52	6	5	0		30		.190	.273	.249	60	-15	-11	21	6			-4	1/2	-1.4
Total	6	270	1111	158	257	50	20	4	7	52	10	.231	.267	.323	88	-20	-15	104	16			-9	2/103PC	-2.3

■ TOM O'BRIEN
O'Brien, Thomas J. b: 2/20/1873, Verona, Pa. d: 2/4/01, Phoenix, Arizona Deb: 5/10/1897

YEAR	TM/L	G	AB	R	H	2B	3B	HR	RBI	BB	SO	AVG	OBP	SLG	PRO+	BR	/A	RC	SB	CS	SBR	FR	POS	TPR
1897	Bal-N	50	147	25	37	6	6	0	32	20		.252	.349	.293	72	-5	-5	18	7			0	1O	-0.5
1898	Bal-N	18	60	9	13	0	0	0	14	10		.217	.338	.217	61	-2	-2	5	0			0	O	-0.2
	Pit-N	107	413	53	107	10	8	1	45	25		.259	.318	.329	90	-6	-5	49	13			-3	O1/32S	-1.0
	Yr	125	473	62	120	10	8	1	59	35		.254	.321	.315	86	-8	-7	53	13			-3		-1.0
1899	NY-N	150	573	100	170	21	10	6	77	44		.297	.351	.400	112	6	6	91	23			-1	*O3/S21	0.0
1900	Pit-N	102	376	61	109	22	6	3	61	21		.290	.349	.404	109	5	4	59	12			-11	1O/2S	-0.6
Total	4	427	1569	248	436	59	24	10	229	120		.278	.341	.365	100	-2	1	220	55			-14	O1/32S	-2.3

■ DARBY O'BRIEN
O'Brien, William D. b: 9/1/1863, Peoria, Ill. d: 6/15/1893, Peoria, Ill. BR/TR, 6'1", 186 lbs. Deb: 4/16/1887

YEAR	TM/L	G	AB	R	H	2B	3B	HR	RBI	BB	SO	AVG	OBP	SLG	PRO+	BR	/A	RC	SB	CS	SBR	FR	POS	TPR
1887	NY-a	127	522	97	157	30	13	5		40		.301	.355	.437	128	15	19	101	49			6	*O1/S3P	1.7

YEAR	TM/L	G	AB	R	H	2B	3B	HR	RBI	BB	SO	AVG	OBP	SLG	PRO+	BR	/A	RC	SB	CS	SBR	FR	POS	TPR
1888	Bro-a	136	532	105	149	27	6	2	65	30		.280	.327	.365	125	14	14	83	55			2	*O	1.0
1889	*Bro-a	136	567	146	170	30	11	5	80	61	76	.300	.384	.418	130	24	24	129	91			-6	*O	1.0
1890	*Bro-N	85	350	78	110	28	6	2	63	32	43	.314	.378	.446	142	18	18	75	38			1	O	1.5
1891	Bro-N	103	395	79	100	18	6	5	57	39	53	.253	.331	.367	106	3	3	60	31			2	*O	0.0
1892	Bro-N	122	490	72	119	14	5	1	56	29	52	.243	.289	.298	82	-13	-10	60	57			4	*O	-0.9
Total	6	709	2856	577	805	147	47	20	321	231	224	.282	.344	.387	119	61	68	508	321			8	O/1SP3	4.3

■ BILLY O'BRIEN

O'Brien, William Smith   b: 3/14/1860, Albany, N.Y.   d: 5/26/11, Kansas City, Mo.   BR, 6', 185 lbs.   Deb: 9/27/1884

YEAR	TM/L	G	AB	R	H	2B	3B	HR	RBI	BB	SO	AVG	OBP	SLG	PRO+	BR	/A	RC	SB	CS	SBR	FR	POS	TPR
1884	StP-U	8	30	1	7	3	0	0		0		.233	.233	.333	165	-0	2	2	0			1	/3P	0.3
	KC-U	4	17	2	4	0	0	0		0		.235	.235	.235	68	-1	-0	1	0			1	/31	0.1
	Yr	12	47	3	11	3	0	0		0		.234	.234	.298	121	-1	1	3	0			2		0.4
1887	Was-N	113	453	71	126	16	12	**19**	73	21	17	.278	.317	.492	130	12	16	76	11			-3	*1/O32	-0.2
1888	Was-N	133	528	42	119	15	2	9	66	9	70	.225	.238	.313	81	-15	-11	43	10			-4	*1/3	-2.7
1889	Was-N	2	8	1	0	0	0	0	0	1	1	.000	.111	.000	-72	-2	-2	0	0			-0	/1	-0.1
1890	Bro-a	96	388	47	108	25	8	4		28		.278	.332	.415	127	9	11	56	5			-2	*1	0.4
Total	5	356	1424	164	364	59	22	32	139	59	88	.256	.289	.395	111	4	16	179	26			-7	1/3O2P	-2.2

■ WHITEY OCK

Ock, Harold David   b: 3/17/12, Brooklyn, N.Y.   d: 3/18/75, Mt.Kisco, N.Y.   BR/TR, 5'11", 180 lbs.   Deb: 9/29/35

YEAR	TM/L	G	AB	R	H	2B	3B	HR	RBI	BB	SO	AVG	OBP	SLG	PRO+	BR	/A	RC	SB	CS	SBR	FR	POS	TPR
1935	Bro-N	1	3	0	0	0	0	0	0	1	2	.000	.250	.000	-27	-1	-1	0	0			-0	/C	0.0

■ DANNY O'CONNELL

O'Connell, Daniel Francis   b: 1/21/27, Paterson, N.J.   d: 10/2/69, Clifton, N.J.   BR/TR, 5'11", 168 lbs.   Deb: 7/14/50   C

YEAR	TM/L	G	AB	R	H	2B	3B	HR	RBI	BB	SO	AVG	OBP	SLG	PRO+	BR	/A	RC	SB	CS	SBR	FR	POS	TPR
1950	Pit-N	79	315	39	92	16	1	8	32	24	33	.292	.342	.425	97	-0	-2	45	7			17	S3	2.1
1953	Pit-N	149	588	88	173	26	8	7	55	57	42	.294	.361	.401	99	-0	-0	87	3	4	-2	8	*32	0.5
1954	Mil-N	146	541	61	151	28	4	2	37	38	46	.279	.329	.357	84	-17	-12	64	2	2	-1	9	*23/1S	0.3
1955	Mil-N	124	453	47	102	15	4	6	40	28	43	.225	.278	.316	60	-28	-25	40	2	2	-1	16	*2/3S	0.0
1956	Mil-N	139	498	71	119	17	9	2	42	76	42	.239	.344	.321	86	-11	-7	61	3	3	-1	-6	*2/3S	-0.2
1957	Mil-N	48	183	29	43	9	1	1	8	19	20	.235	.314	.311	74	-8	-6	20	1	0	0	7	2	0.5
	NY-N	95	364	57	97	18	3	7	28	33	30	.266	.331	.390	93	-4	-3	47	8	3	1	6	23	0.9
	Yr	143	547	86	140	27	4	8	36	52	50	.256	.325	.364	87	-11	-9	66	9	3	1	12		1.4
1958	SF-N	107	306	44	71	12	2	3	23	51	35	.232	.342	.314	77	-10	-9	36	2	1	0	3	*2/3	0.0
1959	SF-N	34	58	6	11	3	0	0	0	5	15	.190	.254	.241	34	-6	-5	4	0	1	-1	7	3/2	0.1
1961	Was-A	138	493	61	128	30	1	1	37	77	62	.260	.363	.331	88	-6	-5	67	15	5	2	1	32	0.9
1962	Was-A	84	236	24	62	7	2	2	18	23	28	.263	.335	.335	80	-7	-6	27	5	1	1	-1	32	-0.4
Total	10	1143	4035	527	1049	181	35	39	320	431	396	.260	.335	.351	84	-96	-81	496	48	22		67	23/S1	4.7

■ JIMMY O'CONNELL

O'Connell, James Joseph   b: 2/11/01, Sacramento, Cal.   d: 11/11/76, Bakersfield, Cal.   BL/TR, 5'10.5", 175 lbs.   Deb: 4/17/23

YEAR	TM/L	G	AB	R	H	2B	3B	HR	RBI	BB	SO	AVG	OBP	SLG	PRO+	BR	/A	RC	SB	CS	SBR	FR	POS	TPR
1923	*NY-N	87	252	42	63	9	2	6	39	34	32	.250	.351	.373	92	-3	-2	35	7	3	0	-10	O/1	-1.3
1924	NY-N	52	104	24	33	4	2	2	18	11	16	.317	.388	.452	128	4	4	19	2	1	0	-2	O/2	0.1
Total	2	139	356	66	96	13	4	8	57	45	48	.270	.361	.396	102	1	2	54	9	4	0	-12	/O12	-1.2

■ JOHN O'CONNELL

O'Connell, John Charles   b: 6/13/04, Pittsburgh, Pa.   BR/TR, 6', 170 lbs.   Deb: 8/16/28

YEAR	TM/L	G	AB	R	H	2B	3B	HR	RBI	BB	SO	AVG	OBP	SLG	PRO+	BR	/A	RC	SB	CS	SBR	FR	POS	TPR
1928	Pit-N	1	1	0	0	0	0	0	0	0	0	.000	.000	.000	-96	-0	-0	0	0			1	/C	0.0
1929	Pit-N	2	7	1	1	1	0	0	0	1	1	.143	.250	.286	32	-1	-1	1	0			-0	/C	0.0
Total	2	3	8	1	1	1	0	0	0	1	1	.125	.222	.250	17	-1	-1	1	0			0	/C	0.0

■ JOHN O'CONNELL

O'Connell, John Joseph   b: 5/16/1872, Lawrence, Mass.   d: 5/14/08, Derry, N.H.   Deb: 8/22/1891

YEAR	TM/L	G	AB	R	H	2B	3B	HR	RBI	BB	SO	AVG	OBP	SLG	PRO+	BR	/A	RC	SB	CS	SBR	FR	POS	TPR
1891	Bal-a	8	29	2	5	1	0	0	7	3	6	.172	.250	.207	33	-2	-3	2	2			-3	/S2O	-0.4
1902	Det-A	8	22	1	4	0	0	0	0	3		.182	.280	.182	31	-2	-1	1	0			1	/21	0.0
Total	2	16	51	3	9	1	0	0	7	6	6	.176	.263	.196	32	-4	-4	3	2			-2	/2S1O	-0.4

■ PAT O'CONNELL

O'Connell, Patrick H.   b: 6/10/1861, Bangor, Me.   d: 1/24/43, Lewiston, Maine   BR/TR, 5'10", 175 lbs.   Deb: 7/22/1886

YEAR	TM/L	G	AB	R	H	2B	3B	HR	RBI	BB	SO	AVG	OBP	SLG	PRO+	BR	/A	RC	SB	CS	SBR	FR	POS	TPR
1886	Bal-a	42	166	20	30	3	2	0		11		.181	.236	.223	47	-10	-9	11	10			-4	O/1P	-1.2
1890	Bro-a	11	40	7	9	2	1	0		7		.225	.340	.325	102	0	0	6	3			-1	3/1	0.0
Total	2	53	206	27	39	5	3	0		18		.189	.258	.243	58	-10	-9	17	13			-5	/O31P	-1.2

■ DAN O'CONNOR

O'Connor, Daniel Cornelius   b: 8/1868, Guelph, Ont., Canada   d: 3/3/42, Guelph, Ont., Canada   6'2", 185 lbs.   Deb: 6/03/1890

YEAR	TM/L	G	AB	R	H	2B	3B	HR	RBI	BB	SO	AVG	OBP	SLG	PRO+	BR	/A	RC	SB	CS	SBR	FR	POS	TPR
1890	Lou-a	6	26	3	12	1	1	0		1		.462	.481	.577	220	3	4	10	5			-1	/1	0.2

■ JOHNNY O'CONNOR

O'Connor, John Charles "Bucky"   b: 12/1/1891, Cahersiveen, Ire.   d: 5/30/82, Bonner Springs, Kan.   BR/TR, 5'9",   Deb: 9/16/16

YEAR	TM/L	G	AB	R	H	2B	3B	HR	RBI	BB	SO	AVG	OBP	SLG	PRO+	BR	/A	RC	SB	CS	SBR	FR	POS	TPR
1916	Chi-N	1	0	0	0	0	0	0	0	0	0	—	—	—	—	0	0	0	0			0	/C	0.0

■ JACK O'CONNOR

O'Connor, John Joseph "Rowdy Jack" or "Peach Pie"
 b: 6/2/1869, St.Louis, Mo.   d: 11/14/37, St.Louis, Mo.   BR/TR, 5'10", 170 lbs.   Deb: 4/20/1887   M

YEAR	TM/L	G	AB	R	H	2B	3B	HR	RBI	BB	SO	AVG	OBP	SLG	PRO+	BR	/A	RC	SB	CS	SBR	FR	POS	TPR
1887	Cin-a	12	40	4	4	0	0	0		2		.100	.143	.100	-30	-7	-7	1	3			4	/OC	-0.1
1888	Cin-a	36	137	14	28	3	1	1	17	6		.204	.243	.263	62	-5	-6	12	12			1	O/C	-0.5
1889	Col-a	107	398	69	107	17	7	4	60	33	37	.269	.331	.377	109	1	5	60	26			-2	CO/21	0.9
1890	Col-a	121	457	89	148	14	10	2		38		.324	.377	.411	145	19	24	84	29			11	*C/OS23	4.1
1891	Col-a	56	229	28	61	12	3	0	37	11	14	.266	.300	.345	92	-5	-3	27	10			3	OC	0.0
1892	*Cle-N	140	572	71	142	22	5	1	58	25	48	.248	.282	.309	77	-15	-18	56	17			8	*OC	-1.0
1893	Cle-N	96	384	72	110	23	1	4	75	29	12	.287	.341	.383	89	-4	-8	62	29			-2	CO	-0.4
1894	Cle-N	86	330	67	104	23	7	2	51	15	7	.315	.345	.445	88	-6	-9	57	15			9	CO/1	0.2
1895	Cle-N	89	340	51	99	14	10	0	58	30	22	.291	.354	.391	89	-3	-7	52	11			-3	C1/3	-0.3
1896	*Cle-N	68	256	41	76	11	1	1	43	15	12	.297	.343	.359	82	-5	-7	38	15			-7	C1O	-0.8
1897	Cle-N	103	397	49	115	21	4	2	69	26		.290	.338	.378	86	-5	-9	59	20			-12	O1C	-1.9
1898	Cle-N	131	478	50	119	17	4	1	56	26		.249	.292	.308	75	-16	-15	46	8			2	1CO	-0.9
1899	StL-N	84	289	33	73	5	6	0	43	15		.253	.299	.311	68	-12	-13	30	7			2	C1	-0.6
1900	StL-N	10	32	4	7	0	0	0	6	2		.219	.306	.219	48	-2	-2	2	0			-0	C	0.0
	*Pit-N	43	147	15	35	4	1	0	19	3		.238	.258	.279	50	-10	-10	12	5			-10	C/1	-1.4
	Yr	53	179	19	42	4	1	0	25	5		.235	.267	.268	50	-12	-12	15	5			-10		-1.4
1901	Pit-N	61	202	16	39	7	3	0	22	10		.193	.238	.257	44	-14	-15	14	2			-1	C	-0.7
1902	Pit-N	49	170	13	50	1	2	1	28	3		.294	.306	.341	98	-0	-1	19	2			-3	C/1O	-0.8
1903	NY-A	64	212	13	43	4	1	0	12	8		.203	.232	.231	38	-15	-16	13	4			0	C/1	-0.8
1904	StL-A	14	47	4	10	1	0	0	2	2		.213	.245	.234	57	-2	-2	3	0			-4	C	-0.5
1906	StL-A	55	174	8	33	0	0	0	11	2		.190	.190	.190	24	-15	-14	8	4			10	C	0.0
1907	StL-A	25	89	2	14	2	0	0	4	0		.157	.157	.180	8	-9	-9	3	0			-2	C	-0.9
1910	StL-A	1	0	0	0	0	0	0	0	0		—	—	—	—	0	0	0	0			-0	/CM	0.0
Total	21	1451	5380	713	1417	201	66	19	671	301	152	.263	.306	.336	81	-129	-141	658	219			4	CO1/S23	-5.6

■ PADDY O'CONNOR

O'Connor, Patrick Francis   b: 8/4/1879, County Kerry, Ireland   d: 8/17/50, Springfield, Mass.   BR/TR, 5'8", 168 lbs.   Deb: 4/17/08

YEAR	TM/L	G	AB	R	H	2B	3B	HR	RBI	BB	SO	AVG	OBP	SLG	PRO+	BR	/A	RC	SB	CS	SBR	FR	POS	TPR
1908	Pit-N	12	16	1	3	0	0	0	2	0		.188	.188	.188	21	-1	-1	1	0			-1	/C	-0.2
1909	*Pit-N	9	16	1	5	1	0	0	3	0		.313	.313	.375	104	-1	-1	2	0			-2	/C3	-0.1
1910	Pit-N	6	4	0	1	0	0	0	0	1	1	.250	.400	.250	85	0	-0	0	0			-0	/C	0.0
1914	StL-N	10	9	0	0	0	0	0	0	2	2	.000	.250	.000	-24	-1	-1	0	0			-0	/C	-0.1
1915	Pit-F	70	219	15	50	10	1	0	16	14	30	.228	.278	.283	67	-9	-9	20	4			-14	C	-2.3
1918	NY-A	1	3	0	1	0	0	0	0	0	1	.333	.333	.333	99	-0	-0	0	0			-0	/C	0.0

YEAR	TM/L	G	AB	R	H	2B	3B	HR	RBI	BB	SO	AVG	OBP	SLG	PRO+	BR	/A	RC	SB	CS	SBR	FR	POS	TPR
Total	6	108	267	17	60	11	1	0	21	17	34	.225	.276	.273	64	-12	-12	23	4			-18	/C3	-2.7

■ KEN O'DEA
O'Dea, James Kenneth   b: 3/16/13, Lima, N.Y.   d: 12/17/85, Lima, N.Y.   BL/TR, 6', 180 lbs.   Deb: 4/21/35

YEAR	TM/L	G	AB	R	H	2B	3B	HR	RBI	BB	SO	AVG	OBP	SLG	PRO+	BR	/A	RC	SB	CS	SBR	FR	POS	TPR
1935	*Chi-N	76	202	30	52	13	2	6	38	26	18	.257	.345	.431	106	2	2	31	0			-1	C	0.0
1936	Chi-N	80	189	36	58	10	3	2	38	38	18	.307	.423	.423	126	10	9	37	0			-2	C	0.8
1937	Chi-N	83	219	31	66	7	5	4	32	24	26	.301	.370	.434	113	6	4	38	1			-7	C	0.0
1938	*Chi-N	86	247	22	65	12	1	3	33	12	18	.263	.297	.356	77	-8	-8	25	1			4	C	-0.1
1939	NY-N	52	97	7	17	1	0	3	11	10	16	.175	.252	.278	42	-8	-8	7	0			-2	C	-0.8
1940	NY-N	48	96	9	23	4	1	0	12	16	15	.240	.348	.302	80	-2	-2	11	0			2	C	0.2
1941	NY-N	59	89	13	19	5	1	3	17	8	20	.213	.278	.393	86	-2	-2	10	0			2	C	0.1
1942	*StL-N	58	192	22	45	7	1	5	32	17	23	.234	.297	.359	85	-3	-4	20	0			10	C	0.8
1943	*StL-N	71	203	15	57	11	2	3	25	19	25	.281	.345	.399	110	4	3	29	0			6	C	1.1
1944	*StL-N	85	265	35	66	11	2	6	37	37	29	.249	.343	.374	100	1	1	37	1			8	C	1.2
1945	StL-N	100	307	56	78	18	2	4	43	50	31	.254	.359	.365	99	2	1	43	0			3	C	0.5
1946	StL-N	22	57	2	7	2	0	1	3	8	8	.123	.231	.211	25	-6	-6	3	0			6	C	0.0
	Bos-N	12	32	4	7	0	0	0	2	8	4	.219	.375	.219	70	-1	-1	3	0			-1	C	-0.1
	Yr	34	89	6	14	2	0	1	5	16	12	.157	.286	.213	41	-6	-7	6	0			5		-0.1
Total	12	832	2195	262	560	101	20	40	323	273	251	.255	.338	.374	95	-5	-12	292	3			27	C	3.7

■ PAUL O'DEA
O'Dea, Paul "Lefty"   b: 7/3/20, Cleveland, Ohio   d: 12/11/78, Cleveland, Ohio   BL/TL, 6', 200 lbs.   Deb: 4/19/44

YEAR	TM/L	G	AB	R	H	2B	3B	HR	RBI	BB	SO	AVG	OBP	SLG	PRO+	BR	/A	RC	SB	CS	SBR	FR	POS	TPR
1944	Cle-A	76	173	25	55	9	0	0	13	23	21	.318	.401	.370	126	6	7	24	2	2	-1	-4	O/P1	0.1
1945	Cle-A	87	221	21	52	2	2	1	21	20	26	.235	.299	.276	70	-9	-8	18	3	0	1	0	O/P	-0.8
Total	2	163	394	46	107	11	2	1	34	43	47	.272	.345	.317	95	-3	-1	43	5	2	0	-4	/OP1	-0.7

■ HEINIE ODOM
Odom, Herman Boyd   b: 10/13/1900, Rusk, Tex.   d: 8/31/70, Rusk, Tex.   BB/TR, 6', 170 lbs.   Deb: 4/22/25

YEAR	TM/L	G	AB	R	H	2B	3B	HR	RBI	BB	SO	AVG	OBP	SLG	PRO+	BR	/A	RC	SB	CS	SBR	FR	POS	TPR
1925	NY-A	1	1	0	1	0	0	0	0	0	0	1.000	1.000	1.000	416	0	0	1	0	0	0	0	/3	0.1

■ BLUE MOON ODOM
Odom, Johnny Lee   b: 5/29/45, Macon, Ga.   BR/TR, 6', 178 lbs.   Deb: 9/05/64

YEAR	TM/L	G	AB	R	H	2B	3B	HR	RBI	BB	SO	AVG	OBP	SLG	PRO+	BR	/A	RC	SB	CS	SBR	FR	POS	TPR
1964	KC-A	5	5	1	0	0	0	0	0	1	4	.000	.167	.000	-47	-1	-1	0	0	0	0	0	/P	0.0
1965	KC-A	1	0	0	0	0	0	0	0	0	0	—	—	—	—	0	0	0	0	0	0	0	/P	0.0
1966	KC-A	17	31	1	3	0	0	0	2	3	16	.097	.176	.097	-20	-5	-5	1	0	0	0	2	P	0.0
1967	KC-A	33	28	4	8	1	0	0	1	1	14	.286	.310	.321	90	-0	-0	3	0	1	-1	0	P	0.0
1968	Oak-A	42	78	14	17	2	0	1	2	6	29	.218	.282	.282	75	-3	-2	7	0	0	0	1	P	0.0
1969	Oak-A	43	79	15	21	2	1	5	16	2	24	.266	.293	.506	125	1	2	12	0	0	0	1	P	0.0
1970	Oak-A	37	54	8	13	2	0	3	7	3	18	.241	.281	.444	100	-1	-0	7	1	0	0	3	P	0.0
1971	Oak-A	37	50	8	8	0	1	1	1	2	24	.160	.192	.260	28	-5	-5	2	0	0	0	-0	P	0.0
1972	*Oak-A	59	66	16	8	1	0	2	2	1	29	.121	.134	.227	7	-8	-7	2	4	2	0	1	P	0.0
1973	*Oak-A	51	1	5	0	0	0	0	0	0	0	.000	.000	.000	-99	-0	-0	-1	1	2	-1	-1	P	0.0
1974	*Oak-A	43	0	3	0	0	0	0	0	0	0	—	—	—	—	0	0	0	0	0	0	1	P	0.0
1975	Oak-A	8	0	1	0	0	0	0	0	0	0	—	—	—	—	0	0	0	0	0	0	0	/P	0.0
	Cle-A	3	0	0	0	0	0	0	0	0	0	—	—	—	—	0	0	0	0	0	0	-0	/P	0.0
	Yr	11	0	1	0	0	0	0	0	0	0	—	—	—	—	0	0	0	0	0	0	-0		0.0
	Atl-N	15	13	0	1	1	0	0	1	0	5	.077	.077	.154	-36	-2	-2	0	0	0	0	0	P	0.0
1976	Chi-A	8	0	0	0	0	0	0	0	0	0	—	—	—	—	0	0	0	0	0	0	-1	/P	0.0
Total	13	402	405	76	79	9	2	12	31	19	163	.195	.235	.316	60	-23	-22	32	6	5	-1	7	P	0.0

■ O'DONNELL
O'Donnell   b: Littlestown, Pa.   Deb: 7/16/1884

YEAR	TM/L	G	AB	R	H	2B	3B	HR	RBI	BB	SO	AVG	OBP	SLG	PRO+	BR	/A	RC	SB	CS	SBR	FR	POS	TPR
1884	Phi-U	1	4	0	1	0	0	0		0	0	.250	.250	.250	75	-0	-0	0	0			-0	/C	0.0

■ HARRY O'DONNELL
O'Donnell, Harry Herman "Butch"   b: 4/2/1894, Philadelphia, Pa.   d: 1/31/58, Philadelphia, Pa.   BR/TR, 5'8", 175 lbs.   Deb: 4/30/27

YEAR	TM/L	G	AB	R	H	2B	3B	HR	RBI	BB	SO	AVG	OBP	SLG	PRO+	BR	/A	RC	SB	CS	SBR	FR	POS	TPR
1927	Phi-N	16	16	1	1	0	0	0	2	2	2	.063	.167	.063	-36	-3	-3	0	0			1	C	0.0

■ LEFTY O'DOUL
O'Doul, Francis Joseph   b: 3/4/1897, San Francisco, Cal.   d: 12/7/69, San Francisco, Cal.   BL/TL, 6', 180 lbs.   Deb: 4/29/19

YEAR	TM/L	G	AB	R	H	2B	3B	HR	RBI	BB	SO	AVG	OBP	SLG	PRO+	BR	/A	RC	SB	CS	SBR	FR	POS	TPR
1919	NY-A	19	16	2	4	0	0	0	1	1	2	.250	.294	.250	53	-1	-1	1	1			-1	/PO	0.0
1920	NY-A	13	12	2	2	1	0	0	1	1	1	.167	.231	.250	26	-1	-1	1	0	0	0	-1	/PO	-0.1
1922	NY-A	8	9	0	3	1	0	0	4	0	2	.333	.333	.444	99	-0	-0	1	0	0	0	0	/P	0.0
1923	Bos-A	36	35	2	5	0	0	0	4	2	3	.143	.189	.143	-12	-6	-6	1	0	0	0	1	P/O	0.0
1928	NY-N	114	354	67	113	19	4	8	46	30	8	.319	.372	.463	117	8	8	60	9			-14	O	-0.8
1929	Phi-N	154	638	152	**254**	35	6	32	122	76	19	**.398**	**.465**	.622	157	69	62	180	2			-1	*O	4.2
1930	Phi-N	140	528	122	202	37	7	22	97	63	21	.383	.453	.604	142	47	41	141	3			-13	*O	1.6
1931	Bro-N	134	512	85	172	32	11	7	75	48	16	.336	.396	.482	136	26	26	100	5			-6	*O	1.3
1932	Bro-N	148	595	120	219	32	8	21	90	50	20	**.368**	.423	.555	164	51	53	142	11			-10	*O	3.2
1933	Bro-N	43	159	14	40	5	1	5	21	15	6	.252	.320	.390	106	0	1	21	2			-3	O	-0.4
	*NY-N	78	229	31	70	9	1	9	35	29	17	.306	.388	.472	147	14	14	43	1			-5	O	0.6
	Yr	121	388	45	110	14	2	14	56	44	23	.284	.361	.438	130	14	15	63	3			-8		0.2
1934	NY-N	83	177	27	56	4	3	9	46	18	7	.316	.383	.525	144	10	11	38	2			-6	O	0.3
Total	11	970	3264	624	1140	175	41	113	542	333	122	.349	.413	.532	142	217	208	730	36	0		-57	O/P	9.9

■ FRED ODWELL
Odwell, Frederick William "Fritz"   b: 9/25/1872, Downsville, N.Y.   d: 8/19/48, Downsville, N.Y.   BL/TR, 5'9.5", 160 lbs.   Deb: 4/16/04

YEAR	TM/L	G	AB	R	H	2B	3B	HR	RBI	BB	SO	AVG	OBP	SLG	PRO+	BR	/A	RC	SB	CS	SBR	FR	POS	TPR
1904	Cin-N	129	468	75	133	22	10	1	58	26		.284	.322	.380	109	9	4	70	30			14	*O/2	1.4
1905	Cin-N	130	468	79	113	10	9	9	65	26		.241	.281	.359	83	-6	-12	56	21			4	*O	-1.7
1906	Cin-N	58	202	20	45	5	4	0	21	15		.223	.276	.287	74	-5	-6	21	11			3	O	-0.4
1907	Cin-N	94	274	24	74	5	7	0	24	22		.270	.324	.339	106	3	2	36	10			5	O/2	0.4
Total	4	411	1412	198	365	42	30	10	168	89		.258	.302	.352	95	1	-13	183	72			26	O/2	-0.3

■ CHUCK OERTEL
Oertel, Charles Frank "Ducky" or "Snuffy"   b: 3/12/31, Coffeyville, Kan.   BL/TR, 5'8", 165 lbs.   Deb: 9/01/58

YEAR	TM/L	G	AB	R	H	2B	3B	HR	RBI	BB	SO	AVG	OBP	SLG	PRO+	BR	/A	RC	SB	CS	SBR	FR	POS	TPR
1958	Bal-A	14	12	4	2	0	0	1	1	1	1	.167	.231	.417	78	-1	-0	1	0	0	0	0	/O	0.0

■ RON OESTER
Oester, Ronald John   b: 5/5/56, Cincinnati, Ohio   BB/TR, 6'2", 185 lbs.   Deb: 9/10/78

YEAR	TM/L	G	AB	R	H	2B	3B	HR	RBI	BB	SO	AVG	OBP	SLG	PRO+	BR	/A	RC	SB	CS	SBR	FR	POS	TPR
1978	Cin-N	6	8	1	3	0	0	0	1	0	2	.375	.375	.375	110	0	0	1	0	0	0	1	/S	0.2
1979	Cin-N	6	3	0	0	0	0	0	0	0	1	.000	.000	.000	-99	-1	-1	0	0	0	0	-1	/S	0.1
1980	Cin-N	100	303	40	84	16	2	2	20	26	44	.277	.336	.363	95	-2	-2	37	6	2	1	-14	2S/3	-0.8
1981	Cin-N	105	354	45	96	16	7	5	42	42	49	.271	.348	.398	110	6	5	48	2	5	-2	5	*2/S	1.6
1982	Cin-N	151	549	63	143	19	4	9	47	35	82	.260	.305	.359	83	-12	-13	56	5	6	-2	4	*2S3	-0.3
1983	Cin-N	157	549	63	145	23	5	11	58	49	106	.264	.326	.384	93	-3	-6	66	2	2	-1	-25	*2/S	-2.6
1984	Cin-N	150	553	54	134	26	3	3	38	41	97	.242	.296	.316	69	-21	-23	50	7	2	1	-16	*2/S	-3.6
1985	Cin-N	152	526	59	155	26	3	1	34	51	65	.295	.357	.361	97	2	-1	68	5	0	2	5	*2	0.6
1986	Cin-N	153	523	52	135	23	2	8	44	52	84	.258	.326	.356	84	-8	-11	59	9	2	2	18	*2	1.1
1987	Cin-N	69	237	28	60	9	6	2	23	22	51	.253	.317	.367	77	-7	-7	26	2	3	-1	6	2	-0.1
1988	Cin-N	54	150	20	42	7	0	0	10	9	24	.280	.321	.327	83	-3	-3	15	0	2	-1	2	2/S	0.0
1989	Cin-N	109	305	23	75	15	0	1	14	32	47	.246	.318	.305	76	-8	-9	29	1	0	0	8	*2/S	0.0
1990	*Cin-N	64	154	10	46	10	1	0	13	10	29	.299	.341	.377	95	-1	-1	20	1	2	-1	-8	2/3	-0.9
Total	13	1276	4214	458	1118	190	33	42	344	369	681	.265	.325	.356	87	-56	-73	474	40	26	-4	-13	*2/S3	-4.7

BOB O'FARRELL
O'Farrell, Robert Arthur b: 10/19/1896, Waukegan, Ill. d: 2/20/88, Waukegan, Ill. BR/TR, 5'9.5", 180 lbs. Deb: 9/05/15 M

YEAR	TM/L	G	AB	R	H	2B	3B	HR	RBI	BB	SO	AVG	OBP	SLG	PRO+	BR	/A	RC	SB	CS	SBR	FR	POS	TPR
1915	Chi-N	2	3	0	1	0	0	0	0	0	0	.333	.333	.333	102	-0	-0	0	0			-1	/C	0.0
1916	Chi-N	1	0	0	0	0	0	0	0	0	0	—	—	—	—	0	0	0	0			0	/C	0.0
1917	Chi-N	3	8	1	3	2	0	0	1	1	0	.375	.444	.625	210	1	1	2	1			-1	/C	0.0
1918	*Chi-N	52	113	9	32	7	3	1	14	10	15	.283	.347	.425	132	5	4	16	0			-6	C	0.3
1919	Chi-N	49	125	11	27	4	2	0	9	7	10	.216	.258	.280	61	-6	-6	9	2			-4	C	-0.7
1920	Chi-N	94	270	29	67	11	4	3	19	34	23	.248	.332	.352	95	-1	-1	34	1	0	0	-6	C	-0.1
1921	Chi-N	96	260	32	65	12	7	4	32	18	14	.250	.299	.396	82	-7	-7	31	2	0	1	-5	C	-0.5
1922	Chi-N	128	392	68	127	18	8	4	60	79	34	.324	.439	.441	125	21	19	82	5	3	-0	15	*C	3.2
1923	Chi-N	131	452	73	144	25	4	12	84	67	38	.319	.408	.471	131	22	22	91	10	3	1	1	*C	2.9
1924	Chi-N	71	183	25	44	6	2	3	28	30	13	.240	.347	.344	85	-3	-3	24	2	0	1	-2	C	-0.3
1925	Chi-N	17	22	4	4	0	1	0	3	2	5	.182	.250	.273	33	-2	-2	2	0	0	0	-1	/C	-0.2
	StL-N	94	317	37	88	13	2	3	32	46	26	.278	.373	.360	86	-4	-5	45	0	1	-1	-5	C	-0.5
	Yr	111	339	39	92	13	3	3	35	48	31	.271	.365	.354	83	-6	-7	46	0	1	-1	-7		-0.7
1926	*StL-N	147	492	63	144	30	9	7	68	61	44	.293	.371	.433	111	11	9	79	1			8	*C	2.1
1927	StL-N	61	178	19	47	10	1	0	18	23	22	.264	.348	.331	80	-4	-4	21	3			-1	CM	-0.1
1928	StL-N	16	52	6	11	1	0	0	4	13	9	.212	.369	.231	59	-2	-2	5	2			-0	C	-0.1
	NY-N	75	133	23	26	6	0	2	20	34	16	.195	.359	.286	70	-4	-5	16	2			-1	C	-0.1
	Yr	91	185	29	37	7	0	2	24	47	25	.200	.362	.270	67	-7	-7	21	4			-1		-0.2
1929	NY-N	91	248	35	76	14	3	4	42	28	30	.306	.384	.435	103	2	2	41	3			-5	C	0.3
1930	NY-N	94	249	37	75	16	4	4	54	31	21	.301	.381	.446	101	0	1	42	1			0	C	0.4
1931	NY-N	85	174	11	39	8	3	1	19	21	23	.224	.311	.322	72	-7	-6	19	0			1	C	-0.1
1932	NY-N	50	67	7	16	3	0	0	8	11	10	.239	.354	.284	76	-2	-2	8	0			1	C	0.1
1933	StL-N	55	163	16	39	4	2	2	20	15	25	.239	.303	.325	76	-4	-5	16	0			-5	C	-0.8
1934	Cin-N	44	123	10	30	8	3	1	9	11	19	.244	.306	.382	85	-3	-3	14	0			0	CM	0.0
	Chi-N	22	67	3	15	3	0	0	5	3	11	.224	.257	.269	42	-6	-5	5	0			3	C	-0.1
	Yr	66	190	13	45	11	3	1	14	14	30	.237	.289	.342	70	-9	-8	19	0			3		-0.1
1935	StL-N	14	10	0	0	0	0	0	0	2	0	.000	.167	.000	-49	-2	-2	0	0			1	/C	-0.1
Total	21	1492	4101	517	1120	201	58	51	549	547	408	.273	.360	.388	97	4	-2	604	35	7		-14	*C	5.6

JOSE OFFERMAN
Offerman, Jose Antonio (Dono) b: 11/8/68, San Pedro De Macoris, D.R. BB/TR, 6', 150 lbs. Deb: 8/19/90

YEAR	TM/L	G	AB	R	H	2B	3B	HR	RBI	BB	SO	AVG	OBP	SLG	PRO+	BR	/A	RC	SB	CS	SBR	FR	POS	TPR
1990	LA-N	29	58	7	9	0	0	1	7	4	14	.155	.210	.207	16	-7	-6	3	1	0	0	-1	S	-0.4

ROWLAND OFFICE
Office, Rowland Johnie b: 10/25/52, Sacramento, Cal. BL/TL, 6', 170 lbs. Deb: 8/05/72

YEAR	TM/L	G	AB	R	H	2B	3B	HR	RBI	BB	SO	AVG	OBP	SLG	PRO+	BR	/A	RC	SB	CS	SBR	FR	POS	TPR
1972	Atl-N	2	5	1	2	0	0	0	0	1	2	.400	.500	.400	145	0	0	1	0	0	0	0	/O	0.0
1974	Atl-N	131	248	20	61	16	1	3	31	16	30	.246	.292	.355	77	-7	-9	23	5	3	-0	-29	*O	-4.4
1975	Atl-N	126	355	30	103	14	1	3	30	23	41	.290	.339	.361	91	-3	-4	42	2	2	-1	-9	*O	-1.8
1976	Atl-N	99	359	51	101	17	1	4	34	37	49	.281	.352	.368	98	3	-0	46	2	8	-4	-7	O	-1.5
1977	Atl-N	124	428	42	103	13	1	5	39	23	58	.241	.284	.311	53	-25	-31	36	2	4	-2	2	O/1	-3.4
1978	Atl-N	146	404	40	101	13	1	9	40	22	52	.250	.299	.354	73	-11	-16	41	8	6	-1	-8	*O	-3.1
1979	Atl-N	124	277	35	69	14	2	2	37	27	33	.249	.320	.336	74	-8	-10	30	5	4	-1	3	O	-1.1
1980	Mon-N	116	292	36	78	13	4	6	30	36	39	.267	.348	.401	108	4	4	42	3	3	-1	-5	O	-0.5
1981	Mon-N	26	40	4	7	0	0	0	0	4	6	.175	.250	.175	22	-4	-4	2	0	0	0	-1	O	-0.5
1982	Mon-N	3	3	0	1	1	0	0	0	1	1	.333	.333	.667	170	0	0	1	0	0	0	0	/O	0.1
1983	NY-A	2	2	0	0	0	0	0	0	1	0	.000	.000	.000	-99	-1	-1	0	0	0	0	0	/O	0.0
Total	11	899	2413	259	626	101	11	32	242	189	311	.259	.317	.350	79	-50	-70	264	27	30	-10	-53	O/1	-16.2

JIM OGLESBY
Oglesby, James Dorn b: 8/10/05, Schofield, Mo. d: 9/1/55, Tulsa, Okla. BL/TL, 6', 190 lbs. Deb: 4/14/36

YEAR	TM/L	G	AB	R	H	2B	3B	HR	RBI	BB	SO	AVG	OBP	SLG	PRO+	BR	/A	RC	SB	CS	SBR	FR	POS	TPR
1936	Phi-A	3	11	0	2	0	0	0	2	2	0	.182	.308	.182	24	-1	-1	1	0	0	0	0	/1	0.0

BEN OGLIVIE
Oglivie, Benjamin Ambrosio (Palmer) b: 2/11/49, Colon, Panama BL/TL, 6'2", 160 lbs. Deb: 9/04/71

YEAR	TM/L	G	AB	R	H	2B	3B	HR	RBI	BB	SO	AVG	OBP	SLG	PRO+	BR	/A	RC	SB	CS	SBR	FR	POS	TPR
1971	Bos-A	14	38	2	10	3	0	0	4	0	5	.263	.263	.342	66	-2	-2	3	0	0	0	1	O	0.0
1972	Bos-A	94	253	27	61	10	2	8	30	18	61	.241	.294	.391	97	0	-1	29	1	1	-0	-3	O	-0.6
1973	Bos-A	58	147	16	32	9	1	2	9	9	32	.218	.272	.333	66	-6	-7	13	1	1	-0	6	OD	-0.1
1974	Det-A	92	252	28	68	11	3	4	29	34	38	.270	.357	.385	109	5	4	36	12	3	2	6	O1/D	1.0
1975	Det-A	100	332	45	95	14	1	9	36	16	62	.286	.323	.416	103	2	0	40	11	8	-2	3	O/1D	0.0
1976	Det-A	115	305	36	87	12	3	15	47	11	44	.285	.317	.492	129	11	9	43	9	4	0	-6	O/1D	0.2
1977	Det-A	132	450	63	118	24	2	21	61	40	80	.262	.327	.464	107	7	4	64	9	9	-3	2	*O/D	0.0
1978	Mil-A	128	469	71	142	29	4	18	72	52	69	.303	.372	.497	142	26	26	85	11	7	-1	-3	OD1	1.9
1979	Mil-A	139	514	88	145	30	4	29	81	48	56	.282	.346	.525	131	21	21	91	12	5	1	-2	*OD/1	1.3
1980	Mil-A	156	592	94	180	26	2	41	118	54	71	.304	.367	.563	156	39	42	121	11	9	-2	15	*O/D	5.1
1981	*Mil-A	107	400	53	97	15	4	14	72	37	49	.243	.316	.395	109	2	4	49	2	2	-1	-5	*O/D	-0.3
1982	*Mil-A	159	602	92	147	22	1	34	102	70	81	.244	.327	.453	119	9	14	90	3	5	-2	7	*O	1.3
1983	Mil-A	125	411	49	115	19	3	13	66	60	64	.280	.377	.436	133	14	19	67	4	6	-2	2	*O/D	1.7
1984	Mil-A	131	461	49	121	16	2	12	60	44	56	.262	.328	.384	100	-2	0	55	0	6	-4	-3	*O/D	-0.9
1985	Mil-A	101	341	40	99	17	2	10	61	37	51	.290	.363	.440	119	9	9	54	0	2	-1	-2	O/D	0.5
1986	Mil-A	103	346	31	98	20	1	5	53	30	33	.283	.340	.390	95	-1	-2	45	1	2	-1	1	*OD/1	-0.1
Total	16	1754	5913	784	1615	277	33	235	901	560	852	.273	.340	.450	119	134	139	886	87	70	-16	17	*OD/1	10.8

BRUCE OGRODOWSKI
Ogrodowski, Ambrose Francis "Brusie" b: 2/17/12, Hoytville, Pa. d: 3/5/56, San Francisco, Cal. BR/TR, 5'11", 175 lbs. Deb: 4/14/36

YEAR	TM/L	G	AB	R	H	2B	3B	HR	RBI	BB	SO	AVG	OBP	SLG	PRO+	BR	/A	RC	SB	CS	SBR	FR	POS	TPR
1936	StL-N	94	237	28	54	15	1	1	20	10	20	.228	.259	.312	53	-16	-16	18	0			5	C	-0.7
1937	StL-N	90	279	37	65	10	3	3	31	11	17	.233	.267	.323	58	-16	-17	22	2			3	C	-1.0
Total	2	184	516	65	119	25	4	4	51	21	37	.231	.263	.318	56	-32	-33	39	2			8	C	-1.7

HAL O'HAGEN
O'Hagen, Harry P. b: 9/30/1873, Washington, D.C. d: 1/14/13, Newark, N.J. 6', 173 lbs. Deb: 9/24/1892

YEAR	TM/L	G	AB	R	H	2B	3B	HR	RBI	BB	SO	AVG	OBP	SLG	PRO+	BR	/A	RC	SB	CS	SBR	FR	POS	TPR
1892	Was-N	1	4	1	1	0	0	0	0	0	2	.250	.250	.250	54	-0	-0	0	0			1	/C	0.1
1902	Chi-N	31	108	10	21	1	3	0	10	11		.194	.269	.259	67	-4	-4	10	8			3	1	-0.2
	NY-N	4	11	0	1	0	0	0	0	0		.091	.091	.091	-44	-2	-2	0	0			-0	/O	-0.2
	Cle-A	3	13	2	5	2	0	0	1	0		.385	.385	.538	162	1	1	4	2			1	/1	0.2
	NY-N	22	73	5	11	2	1	0	8	2		.151	.195	.205	25	-6	-6	4	3			-0	1/O	-0.2
	Yr	57	192	15	33	2	4	0	18	13		.172	.232	.224	45	-12	-12	14	11			2		-1.1
Total	2	61	209	18	39	5	4	0	19	13	2	.187	.241	.249	53	-12	-11	18	13			4	/1OC	-0.8

KID O'HARA
O'Hara, James Francis b: 12/19/1875, Wilkes-Barre, Pa. d: 12/1/54, Canton, Ohio BB/TR, 5'7.5", 152 lbs. Deb: 9/15/04

YEAR	TM/L	G	AB	R	H	2B	3B	HR	RBI	BB	SO	AVG	OBP	SLG	PRO+	BR	/A	RC	SB	CS	SBR	FR	POS	TPR
1904	Bos-N	8	29	3	6	0	0	0	0	4		.207	.303	.207	62	-1	-1	2	0			0	/O	0.0

TOM O'HARA
O'Hara, Thomas F. b: 7/13/1885, Waverly, N.Y. d: 6/8/54, Denver, Colo. Deb: 9/19/06

YEAR	TM/L	G	AB	R	H	2B	3B	HR	RBI	BB	SO	AVG	OBP	SLG	PRO+	BR	/A	RC	SB	CS	SBR	FR	POS	TPR
1906	StL-N	14	53	8	16	1	0	0	0	3		.302	.339	.321	113	0	1	7	3			-2	O	0.0
1907	StL-N	48	173	11	41	2	1	0	5	12		.237	.286	.260	76	-5	-5	14	1			-1	O	-0.8
Total	2	62	226	19	57	3	1	0	5	15		.252	.299	.274	84	-5	-4	21	4			-3	/O	-0.8

BILL O'HARA
O'Hara, William Alexander b: 8/14/1883, Toronto, Ont., Can. d: 6/15/31, Jersey City, N.J. BL/TR, 5'10", Deb: 4/15/09

YEAR	TM/L	G	AB	R	H	2B	3B	HR	RBI	BB	SO	AVG	OBP	SLG	PRO+	BR	/A	RC	SB	CS	SBR	FR	POS	TPR
1909	NY-N	115	360	48	85	9	3	1	30	41		.236	.318	.286	86	-4	-5	42	31			1	*O	-0.7
1910	StL-N	9	20	1	3	0	0	0	2	1	3	.150	.190	.150	-0	-3	-2	1	0			0	/OP1	-0.2
Total	2	124	380	49	88	9	3	1	32	42	3	.232	.311	.279	82	-7	-7	43	31			1	O/1P	-0.9

YEAR	TM/L	G	AB	R	H	2B	3B	HR	RBI	BB	SO	AVG	OBP	SLG	PRO+	BR	/A	RC	SB	CS	SBR	FR	POS	TPR

■ LEN OKRIE   Okrie, Leonard Joseph   b: 7/16/23, Detroit, Mich.   BR/TR, 6', 185 lbs.   Deb: 6/16/48   C

YEAR	TM/L	G	AB	R	H	2B	3B	HR	RBI	BB	SO	AVG	OBP	SLG	PRO+	BR	/A	RC	SB	CS	SBR	FR	POS	TPR
1948	Was-A	19	42	1	10	0	1	0	1	1	7	.238	.256	.286	45	-3	-3	2	0	0	0	2	C	0.0
1950	Was-A	17	27	1	6	0	0	0	2	6	7	.222	.382	.222	61	-1	-1	3	0	0	0	1	C	0.1
1951	Was-A	5	8	1	1	1	0	0	0	2	1	.125	.300	.250	51	-1	-1	1	0	0	0	1	/C	0.0
1952	Bos-A	1	1	0	0	0	0	0	0	0	1	.000	.000	.000	-93	-0	-0	0	0	0	0	0	/C	0.0
Total	4	42	78	3	17	1	1	0	3	9	16	.218	.307	.256	51	-6	-5	6	0	0	0	4	/C	0.1

■ DAVE OLDFIELD   Oldfield, David   b: 12/18/1864, Philadelphia, Pa.   d: 8/28/39, Philadelphia, Pa.   BB/TL, 5'7", 175 lbs.   Deb: 6/28/1883

YEAR	TM/L	G	AB	R	H	2B	3B	HR	RBI	BB	SO	AVG	OBP	SLG	PRO+	BR	/A	RC	SB	CS	SBR	FR	POS	TPR
1883	Bal-a	1	4	0	0	0	0	0		0		.000	.000	.000	-97	-1	-1	0				-0	/C	0.0
1885	Bro-a	10	25	2	8	1	0	0		3		.320	.414	.360	149	2	2	4				1	/CO	0.3
1886	Bro-a	14	55	7	13	1	0	0		2		.236	.263	.255	63	-2	-2	4	1			-4	C/SO	-0.4
	Was-N	21	71	2	10	2	0	0	2	5	15	.141	.197	.169	13	-7	-7	2	0			-5	C/O	-0.9
Total	3	46	155	11	31	4	0	0	2	10	15	.200	.253	.226	51	-9	-8	10	1			-8	/COS	-1.0

■ JOHN OLDHAM   Oldham, John Hardin   b: 11/6/32, Salinas, Cal.   BL, 6'3", 198 lbs.   Deb: 9/02/56

YEAR	TM/L	G	AB	R	H	2B	3B	HR	RBI	BB	SO	AVG	OBP	SLG	PRO+	BR	/A	RC	SB	CS	SBR	FR	POS	TPR
1956	Cin-N	1	0	0	0	0	0	0	0	0	0	—	—	—	—	0	0	0	0	0	0	0	R	0.0

■ BOB OLDIS   Oldis, Robert Carl   b: 1/5/28, Preston, Iowa   BR/TR, 6'1", 185 lbs.   Deb: 4/28/53   C

YEAR	TM/L	G	AB	R	H	2B	3B	HR	RBI	BB	SO	AVG	OBP	SLG	PRO+	BR	/A	RC	SB	CS	SBR	FR	POS	TPR
1953	Was-A	7	16	0	4	0	0	0	3	1	2	.250	.294	.250	49	-1	-1	1	0	0	0	2	/C	0.1
1954	Was-A	11	24	1	8	1	0	0	0	1	3	.333	.360	.375	107	0	0	3	0	0	0	-1	/C3	0.0
1955	Was-A	6	6	0	0	0	0	0	0	0	0	.000	.143	.000	-62	-1	-1	0	0	0	0	0	/C	0.0
1960	*Pit-N	22	20	1	4	1	0	0	1	1	2	.200	.238	.250	34	-2	-2	1	0	0	0	3	C	0.2
1961	Pit-N	4	5	0	0	0	0	0	0	0	0	.000	.000	.000	-99	-1	-1	0	0	0	0	2	/C	0.1
1962	Phi-N	38	80	9	21	1	0	1	10	13	10	.262	.366	.313	87	-1	-1	10	0	1	-1	1	C	0.0
1963	Phi-N	47	85	8	19	3	0	0	8	3	5	.224	.250	.259	47	-6	-6	5	0	0	0	5	C	0.0
Total	7	135	236	20	56	6	0	1	22	20	22	.237	.297	.275	60	-13	-12	21	0	1	-1	12	C/3	0.4

■ RUBE OLDRING   Oldring, Reuben Henry   b: 5/30/1884, New York, N.Y.   d: 9/9/61, Bridgeton, N.J.   BR/TR, 5'10", 186 lbs.   Deb: 10/02/05

YEAR	TM/L	G	AB	R	H	2B	3B	HR	RBI	BB	SO	AVG	OBP	SLG	PRO+	BR	/A	RC	SB	CS	SBR	FR	POS	TPR
1905	NY-A	8	30	2	9	0	1	1	6	2		.300	.344	.467	142	2	1	6	4			5	/S	0.7
1906	Phi-A	59	174	15	42	10	1	0	19	2		.241	.250	.310	74	-5	-6	16	7			2	3/S21	0.0
1907	Phi-A	117	441	48	126	27	8	1	40	7		.286	.297	.390	118	8	6	62	29			-10	*O	-1.0
1908	Phi-A	116	434	38	96	14	2	1	39	18		.221	.252	.270	67	-14	-17	33	13			3	*O	-2.2
1909	Phi-A	90	326	39	75	13	8	1	28	20		.230	.287	.328	92	-3	-4	36	17			-1	O/1	-0.8
1910	Phi-A	134	546	79	168	27	14	4	57	23		.308	.340	.430	142	22	23	85	17			-2	*O	1.6
1911	*Phi-A	121	495	84	147	11	14	3	59	21		.297	.332	.394	104	-0	1	72	21			-9	*O	-1.6
1912	Phi-A	99	395	61	119	14	5	1	24	10		.301	.324	.370	102	-3	-1	53	17			-3	O	-0.9
1913	*Phi-A	137	538	101	152	27	9	5	71	34	37	.283	.328	.394	114	5	6	78	40			-7	*O/S	-0.7
1914	*Phi-A	119	466	68	129	21	7	3	49	18	35	.277	.308	.371	108	-0	1	53	14	16	-5	-6	*O	-1.8
1915	Phi-A	107	408	49	101	23	3	6	42	22	21	.248	.293	.363	99	-5	-3	45	11	6	-0	5	O/3	-0.2
1916	Phi-A	40	146	10	36	8	3	0	14	9	9	.247	.290	.342	94	-2	-2	15	1			-2	O	-0.6
	NY-A	43	158	17	37	8	0	1	12	12	13	.234	.288	.304	76	-5	-5	16	6			-3	O	-1.1
	Yr	83	304	27	73	16	3	1	26	21	22	.240	.289	.322	84	-7	-7	31	7			-5		-1.7
1918	Phi-A	49	133	5	31	2	1	0	11	8	10	.233	.282	.263	64	-6	-6	10	0			-8	O/23	-1.7
Total	13	1239	4690	616	1268	205	76	27	471	206	125	.270	.305	.364	103	-6	-3	578	197	22		-36	*O/3S21	-10.3

■ CHARLEY O'LEARY   O'Leary, Charles Timothy   b: 10/15/1882, Chicago, Ill.   d: 1/6/41, Chicago, Ill.   BR/TR, 5'7", 165 lbs.   Deb: 4/14/04   C

YEAR	TM/L	G	AB	R	H	2B	3B	HR	RBI	BB	SO	AVG	OBP	SLG	PRO+	BR	/A	RC	SB	CS	SBR	FR	POS	TPR
1904	Det-A	135	456	39	97	10	3	1	16	21		.213	.247	.254	62	-20	-18	34	9			6	*S	-1.2
1905	Det-A	148	512	47	109	13	1	0	33	29		.213	.255	.242	59	-23	-23	39	13			-8	*S	-2.8
1906	Det-A	128	443	34	97	13	2	2	34	17		.219	.248	.271	62	-19	-20	35	8			-8	*S	-2.8
1907	*Det-A	139	465	61	112	19	1	0	34	32		.241	.290	.286	82	-7	-9	45	11			-4	*S	-1.0
1908	*Det-A	65	211	21	53	9	3	0	17	9		.251	.282	.322	94	-1	-2	20	4			-12	S/2	-1.3
1909	*Det-A	76	261	29	53	10	0	0	13	6		.203	.224	.241	45	-16	-17	16	9			-3	32/SO	-2.1
1910	Det-A	65	211	23	51	7	1	0	9	9		.242	.276	.284	71	-6	-8	19	7			1	2S/3	-0.9
1911	Det-A	74	256	29	68	8	2	0	25	21		.266	.336	.313	77	-6	-8	32	10			4	2/3	-0.3
1912	Det-A	3	10	1	2	0	0	0	1	0		.200	.200	.200	15	-1	-1	0	0			2	/2	0.1
1913	StL-N	121	406	32	88	15	5	0	31	20	34	.217	.260	.278	55	-25	-24	30	3			-8	*S2	-2.6
1934	StL-A	1	1	1	1	0	0	0	0	0	0	1.000	1.000	1.000	385	0	0	1	0	0	0	0	H	0.0
Total	11	955	3232	317	731	104	18	3	213	164	34	.226	.266	.272	66	-123	-130	271	74	0		-30	S2/3O	-14.9

■ DAN O'LEARY   O'Leary, Daniel "Hustling Dan"   b: 10/22/1856, Detroit, Mich.   d: 6/24/22, Chicago, Ill.   BL,   Deb: 9/03/1879   M

YEAR	TM/L	G	AB	R	H	2B	3B	HR	RBI	BB	SO	AVG	OBP	SLG	PRO+	BR	/A	RC	SB	CS	SBR	FR	POS	TPR
1879	Pro-N	2	7	1	3	0	0	0	2	0	0	.429	.429	.429	187	1	1	1				0	/O	0.0
1880	Bos-N	3	12	1	3	2	0	0	1	0	3	.250	.250	.417	126	0	0	1				-1	/O	0.0
1881	Det-N	2	8	0	0	0	0	0	0	0	2	.000	.000	.000	-96	-2	-2	0				-0	/O	-0.1
1882	Wor-N	6	22	2	4	1	0	0	2	5	5	.182	.333	.227	82	-0	-0	2				-2	/O	-0.1
1884	Cin-U	32	132	14	34	0	2	1		5		.258	.285	.311	94	0	-1	12	0			2	OM	0.0
Total	5	45	181	18	44	3	2	1	5	10	10	.243	.283	.298	89	-1	-3	16	0			-1	/O	-0.2

■ JOHN OLERUD   Olerud, John Garrett   b: 8/5/68, Bellevue, Wash.   BL/TL, 6'5", 205 lbs.   Deb: 9/03/89

YEAR	TM/L	G	AB	R	H	2B	3B	HR	RBI	BB	SO	AVG	OBP	SLG	PRO+	BR	/A	RC	SB	CS	SBR	FR	POS	TPR
1989	Tor-A	6	8	2	3	0	0	0	0	1	3	.375	.375	.375	114	0	0	1	0	0	0	0	/1D	0.0
1990	Tor-A	111	358	43	95	15	1	14	48	57	75	.265	.368	.430	125	12	13	59	0	2	-1	-1	D1	1.0
Total	2	117	366	45	98	15	1	14	48	57	76	.268	.368	.429	125	12	13	60	0	2	-1	-0	/D1	1.0

■ FRANK OLIN   Olin, Franklin Walter   b: 1/9/1860, Woodford, Vt.   d: 5/21/51, St.Louis, Mo.   BL,   Deb: 7/04/1884

YEAR	TM/L	G	AB	R	H	2B	3B	HR	RBI	BB	SO	AVG	OBP	SLG	PRO+	BR	/A	RC	SB	CS	SBR	FR	POS	TPR
1884	Was-a	21	83	12	32	4	1	0		8		.386	.440	.458	223	9	10	17				-7	2O	0.3
	Was-U	1	4	0	0	0	0	0		0		.000	.000	.000	-99	-1	-1	0	0			-0	/O	0.0
	Tol-a	26	86	16	22	0	1	1		5		.256	.304	.314	101	1	0	8				0	O	0.0
1885	Det-N	1	4	1	2	0	0	0	0	0	0	.500	.500	.500	224	1	1	1				-0	/3	0.0
Total	2	49	177	29	56	4	2	1	0	13	0	.316	.366	.379	153	9	10	27				-6	/O23	0.3

■ TONY OLIVA   Oliva, Pedro (Lopez)   b: 7/20/40, Pinar Del Rio, Cuba   BL/TR, 6'1", 175 lbs.   Deb: 9/09/62   C

YEAR	TM/L	G	AB	R	H	2B	3B	HR	RBI	BB	SO	AVG	OBP	SLG	PRO+	BR	/A	RC	SB	CS	SBR	FR	POS	TPR
1962	Min-A	9	9	3	4	1	0	0	3	3	2	.444	.583	.556	201	2	2	3	0	0	0	0	/O	0.2
1963	Min-A	7	7	0	3	0	0	0	1	0	2	.429	.429	.429	138	0	0	1	0	0	0	0	H	0.0
1964	Min-A	161	672	109	217	43	9	32	94	34	68	.323	.361	.557	150	43	42	132	12	6	0	6	*O	4.4
1965	*Min-A	149	576	107	185	40	5	16	98	55	64	.321	.384	.491	141	35	32	109	19	9	0	7	*O	3.6
1966	Min-A	159	622	99	191	32	7	25	87	42	72	.307	.356	.502	135	33	29	106	13	7	-0	12	*O	3.6
1967	Min-A	146	557	76	161	34	6	17	83	44	61	.289	.350	.463	128	26	21	91	11	3	2	9	*O	3.0
1968	Min-A	128	470	54	136	24	5	18	68	45	61	.289	.360	.477	145	29	26	77	10	9	-2	4	*O	2.6
1969	*Min-A	153	637	97	197	39	4	24	101	45	66	.309	.358	.496	134	29	27	107	10	13	-5	9	*O	2.8
1970	*Min-A	157	628	96	204	36	7	23	107	38	67	.325	.366	.514	138	32	31	112	5	4	-1	15	*O	3.9
1971	Min-A	126	487	73	164	30	3	22	81	25	44	.337	.372	.546	152	34	32	90	4	1	-1	-4	*O	2.6
1972	Min-A	10	28	1	9	1	0	0	1	2	5	.321	.367	.357	111	1	0	4	0	0	0	-2	/O	-0.2
1973	Min-A	146	571	63	166	20	0	16	92	45	44	.291	.347	.410	123	16	9	79	2	1	0	0	*D	0.6
1974	Min-A	127	459	43	131	16	2	13	57	27	31	.285	.328	.414	108	6	4	58	0	1	-1	0	*D	0.4
1975	Min-A	131	455	46	123	10	0	13	58	41	45	.270	.088	.378	103	4	3	60	0	1	-1	0	*D	0.2
1976	Min-A	67	123	3	26	3	0	1	16	2	13	.211	.236	.260	44	-9	-9	7	0	0	0	0	D	-0.9

YEAR	TM/L	G	AB	R	H	2B	3B	HR	RBI	BB	SO	AVG	OBP	SLG	PRO+	BR	/A	RC	SB	CS	SBR	FR	POS	TPR
Total	15	1676	6301	870	1917	329	48	220	947	448	645	.304	.356	.476	130	272	246	1036	86	55	-7	56	*OD	26.8

■ ED OLIVARES
Olivares, Edward (Balzac) b: 11/5/38, Mayaguez, P.R. BR/TR, 5'11", 180 lbs. Deb: 9/16/60

YEAR	TM/L	G	AB	R	H	2B	3B	HR	RBI	BB	SO	AVG	OBP	SLG	PRO+	BR	/A	RC	SB	CS	SBR	FR	POS	TPR
1960	StL-N	3	5	0	0	0	0	0	0	0	3	.000	.000	.000	-92	-1	-1	0	0	0	0	-0	/3	-0.1
1961	StL-N	21	30	2	5	0	0	0	1	0	4	.167	.167	.167	-10	-5	-5	1	1	0	0	-1	O	-0.5
Total	2	24	35	2	5	0	0	0	1	0	7	.143	.143	.143	-21	-6	-6	1	1	0	0	-1	/O3	-0.6

■ AL OLIVER
Oliver, Albert b: 10/14/46, Portsmouth, Ohio BL/TL, 6', 195 lbs. Deb: 9/23/68

YEAR	TM/L	G	AB	R	H	2B	3B	HR	RBI	BB	SO	AVG	OBP	SLG	PRO+	BR	/A	RC	SB	CS	SBR	FR	POS	TPR
1968	Pit-N	4	8	1	1	0	0	0	0	0	4	.125	.125	.125	-25	-1	-1	0	0	0	0	0	/O	0.0
1969	Pit-N	129	463	55	132	19	2	17	70	21	38	.285	.334	.445	119	9	10	62	8	5	-1	-3	*1O	-0.3
1970	*Pit-N	151	551	63	149	33	5	12	83	35	35	.270	.330	.414	100	-2	-1	75	1	1	-0	-3	O1	-1.3
1971	Pit-N	143	529	69	149	31	7	14	64	27	72	.282	.323	.446	116	9	9	72	4	3	-1	3	*O1	0.6
1972	*Pit-N	140	565	88	176	27	4	12	89	34	44	.312	.356	.437	127	17	18	85	2	4	-2	-6	*O/1	0.4
1973	Pit-N	158	654	90	191	38	7	20	99	22	52	.292	.320	.463	118	10	12	92	6	0	-2	-6	*O1	0.0
1974	*Pit-N	147	617	96	198	38	12	11	85	33	58	.321	.360	.475	137	24	27	101	10	1	2	4	O1	2.7
1975	*Pit-N	155	628	90	176	39	8	18	84	25	73	.280	.313	.454	112	5	6	83	4	2	0	-2	*O/1	-0.1
1976	Pit-N	121	443	62	143	22	5	12	61	26	29	.323	.367	.476	137	21	20	74	6	2	1	2	*O/1	2.0
1977	Pit-N	154	568	75	175	29	6	19	82	40	38	.308	.358	.481	119	17	15	91	13	16	-6	0	*O	0.5
1978	Tex-A	133	525	65	170	35	5	14	89	31	41	.324	.364	.490	138	25	25	90	8	9	-3	1	*OD	2.0
1979	Tex-A	136	492	69	159	28	4	12	76	34	34	.323	.372	.470	127	17	18	81	4	5	-2	-9	*OD	0.2
1980	Tex-A	163	656	96	209	43	3	19	117	39	47	.319	.361	.480	132	24	27	108	5	7	-3	-2	*O/1D	1.9
1981	Tex-A	102	421	53	130	29	1	4	55	24	28	.309	.349	.411	125	9	12	56	3	0	1	0	*D/1	1.3
1982	Mon-N	160	617	90	**204**	**43**	2	22	**109**	61	59	**.331**	.394	.514	149	43	41	**125**	5	2	0	-9	*1	2.6
1983	Mon-N	157	614	70	184	**38**	3	8	84	44	44	.300	.348	.410	110	7	8	81	1	3	-2	3	*1/O	0.2
1984	SF-N	91	339	27	101	19	2	0	34	20	27	.298	.339	.366	101	-1	0	36	2	2	-1	-1	1	-0.3
	Phi-N	28	93	9	29	7	0	0	14	7	9	.312	.360	.387	108	1	1	11	1	2	-1	-3	1/O	-0.3
	Yr	119	432	36	130	26	2	0	48	27	36	.301	.343	.370	103	0	1	48	3	4	-2	-4		-0.6
1985	LA-N	35	79	1	20	5	0	0	8	5	11	.253	.298	.316	74	-3	-3	7	1	0	0	-3	O	-0.6
	*Tor-A	61	187	20	47	6	1	5	23	7	13	.251	.282	.374	76	-6	-7	17	0	0	0	0	D/1	-0.6
Total	18	2368	9049	1189	2743	529	77	219	1326	535	756	.303	.348	.451	122	224	237	1348	84	64	-13	-34	*O1D	10.9

■ DAVE OLIVER
Oliver, David Jacob b: 4/7/51, Stockton, Cal. BL/TR, 5'11", 175 lbs. Deb: 9/25/77 C

YEAR	TM/L	G	AB	R	H	2B	3B	HR	RBI	BB	SO	AVG	OBP	SLG	PRO+	BR	/A	RC	SB	CS	SBR	FR	POS	TPR
1977	Cle-A	7	22	2	7	0	1	0	3	4	0	.318	.444	.409	139	1	1	5	0	0	0	1	/2	0.2

■ GENE OLIVER
Oliver, Eugene George b: 3/22/35, Moline, Ill. BR/TR, 6'2", 225 lbs. Deb: 6/06/59

YEAR	TM/L	G	AB	R	H	2B	3B	HR	RBI	BB	SO	AVG	OBP	SLG	PRO+	BR	/A	RC	SB	CS	SBR	FR	POS	TPR
1959	StL-N	68	172	14	42	9	0	6	28	7	41	.244	.274	.401	72	-6	-8	17	3	2	-0	-3	O/C1	-1.1
1961	StL-N	22	52	8	14	2	0	4	9	6	10	.269	.367	.538	124	3	2	10	0	0	0	1	C/O	0.4
1962	StL-N	122	345	42	89	19	1	14	45	50	59	.258	.354	.441	102	6	2	54	5	2	0	-3	C/O1	0.0
1963	StL-N	39	102	10	23	4	0	6	18	13	19	.225	.313	.441	105	2	1	13	0	0	0	2	C	0.3
	Mil-N	95	296	34	74	12	2	11	47	27	59	.250	.323	.416	112	4	4	38	4	4	-1	-10	1O/C	-1.0
	Yr	134	398	44	97	16	2	17	65	40	78	.244	.321	.422	110	6	5	52	4	4	-1	-9		-0.7
1964	Mil-N	93	279	45	77	15	1	13	49	17	41	.276	.320	.477	120	7	7	37	3	7	-3	-5	1/C	-0.4
1965	Mil-N	122	392	56	106	20	0	21	58	36	61	.270	.336	.482	127	14	13	60	5	4	-1	4	C1/O	1.7
1966	Atl-N	76	191	19	37	9	1	8	24	16	43	.194	.256	.377	72	-7	-8	19	2	0	1	13	C/1O	0.7
1967	Atl-N	17	51	8	10	2	0	3	6	6	8	.196	.281	.412	97	-0	-0	5	0	0	0	2	C	0.2
	Phi-N	85	263	29	59	16	0	7	34	29	56	.224	.304	.365	90	-4	-4	35	2	2	-1	-12	C/1	-1.2
	Yr	102	314	37	69	18	0	10	40	35	64	.220	.300	.373	91	-4	-4	35	2	2	-1	-10		-1.0
1968	Bos-A	16	35	2	5	0	0	0	1	4	12	.143	.250	.143	20	-3	-3	2	0	0	0	-2	C/O	-0.4
	Chi-N	8	11	1	4	0	0	0	1	3	2	.364	.500	.364	152	1	1	2	0	0	0	0	/1CO	0.2
1969	Chi-N	23	27	0	6	3	0	0	0	1	9	.222	.276	.333	62	-1	-2	2	0	0	0	2	/C	0.1
Total	10	786	2216	268	546	111	5	93	320	215	420	.246	.317	.427	103	15	6	289	24	21	-5	-12	*C1/O	-0.5

■ JOE OLIVER
Oliver, Joseph Melton b: 7/24/65, Memphis, Tenn. BR/TR, 6'3", 215 lbs. Deb: 7/15/89

YEAR	TM/L	G	AB	R	H	2B	3B	HR	RBI	BB	SO	AVG	OBP	SLG	PRO+	BR	/A	RC	SB	CS	SBR	FR	POS	TPR
1989	Cin-N	49	151	13	41	8	0	3	23	6	28	.272	.304	.384	92	-1	-2	17	0	0	0	-1	C	0.0
1990	*Cin-N	121	364	34	84	23	0	8	52	37	75	.231	.305	.360	80	-9	-10	40	1	1	-0	2	*C	-0.2
Total	2	170	515	47	125	31	0	11	75	43	103	.243	.305	.367	84	-10	-12	57	1	1	-0	1	C	-0.2

■ NATE OLIVER
Oliver, Nathaniel "Peewee" b: 12/13/40, St.Petersburg, Fla. BR/TR, 5'10", 160 lbs. Deb: 4/09/63

YEAR	TM/L	G	AB	R	H	2B	3B	HR	RBI	BB	SO	AVG	OBP	SLG	PRO+	BR	/A	RC	SB	CS	SBR	FR	POS	TPR
1963	LA-N	65	163	23	39	2	3	1	9	13	25	.239	.299	.307	80	-5	-4	14	3	4	-2	5	2/S	0.4
1964	LA-N	99	321	28	78	9	0	0	21	31	57	.243	.310	.271	70	-14	-11	26	7	4	-0	-10	2/S	-1.3
1965	LA-N	8	1	3	1	0	0	0	0	0	0	1.000	1.000	1.000	498	0	0	1	1	0	0	3	/2	0.4
1966	*LA-N	80	119	17	23	2	0	0	3	13	17	.193	.278	.210	41	-10	-8	7	3	3	-1	11	2/S3	0.7
1967	LA-N	77	232	18	55	6	2	0	7	13	50	.237	.283	.280	67	-11	-9	18	3	2	-0	-8	2S/O	-1.2
1968	SF-N	36	73	3	13	2	0	0	1	1	13	.178	.189	.205	18	-7	-7	3	0	1	-1	1	2S/3	-0.5
1969	NY-A	1	1	0	0	0	0	0	0	0	0	.000	.000	.000	-99	-0	-0	0	0	0	0	0	H	0.0
	Chi-N	44	44	15	7	3	0	1	4	1	10	.159	.196	.295	32	-4	-5	2	1	1	-1	11	2	0.7
Total	7	410	954	107	216	24	5	2	45	72	172	.226	.284	.268	62	-51	-44	71	17	15	-4	12	2/S3O	-0.8

■ BOB OLIVER
Oliver, Robert Lee b: 2/8/43, Shreveport, La. BR/TR, 6'3", 205 lbs. Deb: 9/10/65

YEAR	TM/L	G	AB	R	H	2B	3B	HR	RBI	BB	SO	AVG	OBP	SLG	PRO+	BR	/A	RC	SB	CS	SBR	FR	POS	TPR
1965	Pit-N	3	2	1	0	0	0	0	0	0	0	.000	.000	.000	-99	-1	-1	0	0	0	0	0	/O	0.0
1969	KC-A	118	394	43	100	8	4	13	43	21	74	.254	.295	.393	91	-6	-7	39	5	5	-2	7	O1/3	-0.4
1970	KC-A	160	612	83	159	24	6	27	99	42	126	.260	.311	.451	108	4	4	82	3	3	-1	-8	*13	-1.0
1971	KC-A	128	373	35	91	12	2	8	52	14	88	.244	.281	.351	79	-12	-11	34	0	0	-0	-1	1O/3	-1.8
1972	KC-A	16	63	7	17	2	1	1	6	2	12	.270	.292	.381	100	-0	-0	7	1	0	0	2	O	0.2
	Cal-A	134	509	47	137	20	4	19	70	27	97	.269	.310	.436	127	10	13	64	4	3	-1	-6	*1/O	-0.6
	Yr	150	572	54	154	22	5	20	76	29	109	.269	.308	.430	124	10	13	70	5	3	-0	-4		-0.4
1973	Cal-A	151	544	51	144	24	1	18	89	33	100	.265	.313	.412	111	0	5	66	1	1	-0	-2	3O1D	0.0
1974	Cal-A	110	359	22	89	9	1	8	55	16	51	.248	.282	.345	84	-10	-8	29	2	1	0	-13	13/OD	-2.3
	Bal-A	9	20	1	3	2	0	0	4	0	5	.150	.150	.250	14	-2	-2	1	1	1	-0	2	/1D	0.0
	Yr	119	379	23	92	11	1	8	59	16	56	.243	.275	.340	81	-12	-10	30	3	2	-0	-11		-2.3
1975	NY-A	18	38	3	5	1	0	0	1	1	9	.132	.154	.158	-12	-6	-5	1	0	0	0	-0	/13D	-0.6
Total	8	847	2914	293	745	102	19	94	419	156	562	.256	.298	.400	100	-23	-12	322	17	14	-3	-19	1O3/D	-6.5

■ TOM OLIVER
Oliver, Thomas Noble "Rebel" b: 1/15/03, Montgomery, Ala. d: 2/26/88, Montgomery, Ala. BR/TR, 6', 168 lbs. Deb: 4/14/30 C

YEAR	TM/L	G	AB	R	H	2B	3B	HR	RBI	BB	SO	AVG	OBP	SLG	PRO+	BR	/A	RC	SB	CS	SBR	FR	POS	TPR
1930	Bos-A	154	646	86	189	34	2	0	46	42	25	.293	.339	.351	78	-23	-20	77	6	6	-2	15	*O	-1.0
1931	Bos-A	148	586	52	162	35	5	0	70	25	17	.276	.307	.353	77	-24	-19	62	4	6	-2	13	*O	-1.6
1932	Bos-A	122	455	39	120	23	3	0	37	25	12	.264	.305	.327	66	-24	-23	45	1	6	-3	4	*O	-2.4
1933	Bos-A	90	244	25	63	9	1	0	23	13	7	.258	.296	.303	60	-14	-14	22	1	1	-0	4	O	-1.2
Total	4	514	1931	202	534	101	11	0	176	105	61	.277	.316	.340	73	-86	-76	206	12	19	-7	36	O	-6.2

■ LUIS OLMO
Olmo, Luis Francisco (Rodriguez) (b: Luis Francisco Rodriguez (Olmo)) b: 8/11/19, Arecibo, P.R. BR/TR, 5'11.5", 185 lbs. Deb: 7/23/43

YEAR	TM/L	G	AB	R	H	2B	3B	HR	RBI	BB	SO	AVG	OBP	SLG	PRO+	BR	/A	RC	SB	CS	SBR	FR	POS	TPR
1943	Bro-N	57	238	29	72	6	4	4	37	8	20	.303	.325	.412	112	2	2	29	3			2	O	0.2
1944	Bro-N	136	520	65	134	20	5	9	85	17	37	.258	.284	.367	84	-14	-13	53	10			-6	O23	-1.8
1945	Bro-N	141	556	62	174	27	**13**	10	110	36	33	.313	.356	.462	127	17	18	90	15			-11	*O3/2	0.2
1949	*Bro-N	38	105	15	32	4	1	1	14	5	11	.305	.336	.390	91	-1	-2	12	2			0	O	-0.2

YEAR	TM/L	G	AB	R	H	2B	3B	HR	RBI	BB	SO	AVG	OBP	SLG	PRO+	BR	/A	RC	SB	CS	SBR	FR	POS	TPR
1950	Bos-N	69	154	23	35	7	1	5	22	18	23	.227	.308	.383	86	-5	-3	17	3			-3	O/3	-0.7
1951	Bos-N	21	56	4	11	1	1	0	4	4	4	.196	.250	.250	38	-5	-5	4	0	1	-1	-1	O	-0.6
Total	6	462	1629	208	458	65	25	29	272	88	128	.281	.319	.405	102	-5	-2	204	33	1		-18	O/32	-2.9

■ BARNEY OLSEN
Olsen, Bernard Charles b: 9/11/19, Everett, Mass. d: 3/30/77, Everett, Mass. BR/TR, 5'11", 179 lbs. Deb: 4/17/41

YEAR	TM/L	G	AB	R	H	2B	3B	HR	RBI	BB	SO	AVG	OBP	SLG	PRO+	BR	/A	RC	SB	CS	SBR	FR	POS	TPR
1941	Chi-N	24	73	13	21	6	1	1	4	4	11	.288	.325	.438	118	1	1	10	0			4	O	0.4

■ GREG OLSON
Olson, Gregory William b: 9/6/60, Marshall, Minn. BR/TR, 6', 200 lbs. Deb: 6/27/89

YEAR	TM/L	G	AB	R	H	2B	3B	HR	RBI	BB	SO	AVG	OBP	SLG	PRO+	BR	/A	RC	SB	CS	SBR	FR	POS	TPR
1989	Min-A	3	2	0	1	0	0	0	0	0	0	.500	.500	.500	171	0	0	1	0	0	0	0	/C	0.0
1990	Atl-N	100	298	36	78	12	1	7	36	30	51	.262	.333	.379	94	-1	-2	37	1	1	-0	-8	C/3	-0.6
Total	2	103	300	36	79	12	1	7	36	30	51	.263	.334	.380	94	-1	-2	38	1	1	-0	-8	C/3	-0.6

■ IVY OLSON
Olson, Ivan Massie b: 10/14/1885, Kansas City, Mo. d: 9/1/65, Inglewood, Cal. BR/TR, 5'10.5", 175 lbs. Deb: 4/12/11 C

YEAR	TM/L	G	AB	R	H	2B	3B	HR	RBI	BB	SO	AVG	OBP	SLG	PRO+	BR	/A	RC	SB	CS	SBR	FR	POS	TPR
1911	Cle-A	140	545	89	142	20	8	1	50	34		.261	.311	.332	78	-16	-17	63	20			-16	*S/3	-1.9
1912	Cle-A	125	467	68	118	13	1	0	33	21		.253	.291	.285	63	-22	-24	45	16			6	S32/O	-1.3
1913	Cle-A	104	370	47	92	13	3	0	32	22	28	.249	.296	.300	72	-12	-14	35	7			4	31/2	-0.8
1914	Cle-A	89	310	22	75	6	2	1	20	13	24	.242	.275	.284	65	-13	-14	26	15	9		12	S23/O1	-0.3
1915	Cin-N	63	207	18	48	5	4	0	14	12	13	.232	.274	.295	71	-7	-8	18	10	6	-1	13	23/1	0.5
	Bro-N	18	26	2	2	0	1	0	3	1	0	.077	.111	.154	-20	-4	-4	1	0			-1	/S23O	-0.4
	Yr	81	233	20	50	5	5	0	17	13	13	.215	.256	.279	61	-11	-11	18	10	6	-1	12		0.1
1916	*Bro-N	108	351	29	89	13	4	1	38	21	27	.254	.298	.322	88	-4	-5	40	14			-12	*S/21	-1.3
1917	Bro-N	139	580	64	156	18	5	2	38	14	34	.269	.291	.328	87	-9	-10	55	6			-6	*S/3	-1.6
1918	Bro-N	126	506	63	121	16	4	1	17	27	18	.239	.286	.292	77	-14	-14	46	21			-25	*S	-4.1
1919	Bro-N	140	590	73	**164**	14	9	1	38	30	12	.278	.316	.337	94	-3	-4	67	26			-2	*S	0.0
1920	*Bro-N	143	637	71	162	13	11	1	46	20	19	.254	.278	.314	68	-26	-28	54	4	7	-3	-7	*S2	-3.3
1921	Bro-N	151	652	86	174	22	10	3	35	28	26	.267	.301	.345	68	-28	-31	66	4	9	-4	5	*S2	-1.6
1922	Bro-N	136	551	63	150	26	6	1	47	25	10	.272	.306	.347	69	-27	-26	58	8	5	-1	-6	2S	-2.8
1923	Bro-N	82	292	33	76	11	1	1	35	14	10	.260	.296	.315	63	-16	-15	29	5	0	2	5	2/31S	-0.7
1924	Bro-N	10	27	0	6	1	0	0	0	3	1	.222	.300	.259	53	-2	-2	2	0	0	0	-2	/S2	-0.2
Total	14	1574	6111	730	1575	191	69	13	446	285	222	.258	.295	.318	74	-202	-216	605	156	36		-32	*S23/10	-19.5

■ KARL OLSON
Olson, Karl Arthur "Ole" b: 7/6/30, Ross, Cal. BR/TR, 6'3", 205 lbs. Deb: 6/30/51

YEAR	TM/L	G	AB	R	H	2B	3B	HR	RBI	BB	SO	AVG	OBP	SLG	PRO+	BR	/A	RC	SB	CS	SBR	FR	POS	TPR
1951	Bos-A	5	10	0	1	0	0	0	0	0	3	.100	.100	.100	-42	-2	-2	0	0	0	0	0	/O	-0.1
1953	Bos-A	25	57	5	7	2	0	1	6	1	9	.123	.138	.211	-7	-9	-9	1	0	0	0	-0	O	-0.9
1954	Bos-A	101	227	25	59	12	2	1	20	12	23	.260	.297	.344	68	-8	-11	21	2	1	0	6	O	-0.6
1955	Bos-A	26	48	7	12	1	2	0	1	1	10	.250	.265	.354	60	-3	-3	4	0	0	0	1	O	-0.2
1956	Was-A	106	313	34	77	10	2	4	22	28	41	.246	.310	.329	69	-14	-14	30	1	1	0	-15	*O	-3.3
1957	Was-A	8	12	2	2	0	0	0	0	1	2	.167	.231	.167	10	-1	-1	1	0	0	0	1	/O	0.0
	Det-A	8	14	1	2	0	0	0	1	0	6	.143	.143	.143	-21	-2	-2	0	0	0	0	-0	/O	-0.2
	Yr	16	26	3	4	0	0	0	1	1	8	.154	.185	.154	-6	-4	-4	1	0	0	0	1		-0.2
Total	6	279	681	74	160	25	6	6	50	43	94	.235	.281	.316	57	-40	-44	56	3	2	-0	-7	O	-5.3

■ MARV OLSON
Olson, Marvin Clement "Sparky" b: 5/28/07, Gayville, S.Dak. BR/TR, 5'7", 160 lbs. Deb: 9/13/31

YEAR	TM/L	G	AB	R	H	2B	3B	HR	RBI	BB	SO	AVG	OBP	SLG	PRO+	BR	/A	RC	SB	CS	SBR	FR	POS	TPR
1931	Bos-A	15	53	8	10	1	0	0	5	9	3	.189	.306	.208	40	-5	-4	4	0	0	0	3	2	0.0
1932	Bos-A	115	403	58	100	14	6	0	25	61	26	.248	.347	.313	74	-15	-13	47	1	5	-3	-15	*2/3	-2.4
1933	Bos-A	3	1	1	0	0	0	0	0	0	1	.000	.000	.000	-99	-0	-0	0	0	0	0	0	/2	0.0
Total	3	133	457	67	110	15	6	0	30	70	30	.241	.342	.300	70	-20	-17	51	1	5	-3	-12	2/3	-2.4

■ TOM O'MALLEY
O'Malley, Thomas Patrick b: 12/25/60, Orange, N.J. BL/TR, 6', 180 lbs. Deb: 5/08/82

YEAR	TM/L	G	AB	R	H	2B	3B	HR	RBI	BB	SO	AVG	OBP	SLG	PRO+	BR	/A	RC	SB	CS	SBR	FR	POS	TPR
1982	SF-N	92	291	26	80	12	4	2	27	33	39	.275	.351	.364	100	1	1	35	0	3	-2	0	3/2S	-0.1
1983	SF-N	135	410	40	106	16	1	5	45	52	47	.259	.348	.339	94	-3	-2	49	2	4	-2	1	*3	-0.7
1984	SF-N	13	25	2	3	0	0	0	0	2	2	.120	.185	.120	-13	-4	-4	1	0	0	0	-0	/3	-0.3
	Chi-A	12	16	0	2	0	0	0	3	0	5	.125	.125	.125	-29	-3	-3	0	0	0	0	-2	/3	-0.4
1985	Bal-A	8	14	1	1	0	0	1	2	0	2	.071	.071	.286	-8	-2	-2	0	0	0	0	-1	/3	-0.2
1986	Bal-A	56	181	19	46	9	0	1	18	17	21	.254	.318	.320	76	-6	-6	18	0	1	-1	-1	3	-0.8
1987	Tex-A	45	117	10	32	8	0	1	12	15	9	.274	.356	.368	92	-1	-1	14	0	0	0	-4	3/2	-0.4
1988	Mon-N	14	27	3	7	0	0	0	2	3	4	.259	.333	.259	69	-1	-1	3	0	0	0	1	/3	0.0
1989	NY-N	9	11	2	6	1	0	0	8	0	2	.545	.545	.727	274	2	2	4	0	0	0	0	/3	0.2
1990	NY-N	82	121	14	27	7	0	3	14	9	20	.223	.288	.355	78	-4	-4	13	0	0	0	2	3/1	0.0
Total	9	466	1213	117	310	54	5	13	131	133	151	.256	.332	.340	87	-21	-19	136	2	8	-4	-4	3/12S	-2.7

■ OLLIE O'MARA
O'Mara, Oliver Edward b: 3/8/1891, St.Louis, Mo. d: 10/24/89, Reno, Nev. TR, 5'9", 155 lbs. Deb: 9/08/12

YEAR	TM/L	G	AB	R	H	2B	3B	HR	RBI	BB	SO	AVG	OBP	SLG	PRO+	BR	/A	RC	SB	CS	SBR	FR	POS	TPR
1912	Det-A	1	4	0	0	0	0	0	0	0		.000	.000	.000	-99	-1	-1	0	0			0	/S	0.0
1914	Bro-N	67	247	41	65	10	2	1	7	16	26	.263	.316	.332	91	-2	-3	29	14			-12	S	-1.3
1915	Bro-N	149	577	77	141	26	3	0	31	51	40	.244	.308	.300	83	-10	-11	56	11	12	-4	-34	*S	-5.1
1916	*Bro-N	72	193	18	39	5	2	0	15	12	20	.202	.249	.249	52	-11	-11	15	10			-5	S	-1.5
1918	Bro-N	121	450	29	96	8	1	1	24	7	18	.213	.242	.242	48	-28	-28	29	11			-2	*3	-3.1
1919	Bro-N	2	7	1	0	0	0	0	0	0	0	.000	.000	.000	-98	-2	-2	-0	0			-0	/3	-0.1
Total	6	412	1478	166	341	49	8	2	77	86	104	.231	.280	.279	69	-54	-56	129	46	12		-52	S3	-11.1

■ TOM O'MEARA
O'Meara, Thomas Edward b: 12/12/1872, Chicago, Ill. d: 2/16/02, Fort Wayne, Ind. Deb: 9/29/1895

YEAR	TM/L	G	AB	R	H	2B	3B	HR	RBI	BB	SO	AVG	OBP	SLG	PRO+	BR	/A	RC	SB	CS	SBR	FR	POS	TPR
1895	Cle-N	1	1	1	1	0	0	0	0	1	0	.000	.500	.000	36	-0	-0	0	0			-0	/C	0.0
1896	Cle-N	12	33	5	5	0	0	0	0	5	7	.152	.263	.152	12	-4	-4	1	0			-2	/C1	-0.3
Total	2	13	34	6	5	0	0	0	0	6	7	.147	.275	.147	14	-4	-4	1	0			-2	/C1	-0.3

■ O'NEAL
O'Neal Deb: 10/23/1874

YEAR	TM/L	G	AB	R	H	2B	3B	HR	RBI	BB	SO	AVG	OBP	SLG	PRO+	BR	/A	RC	SB	CS	SBR	FR	POS	TPR
1874	Har-n	1	3	0	0	0	0	0		0		.000	.000	.000	-95	-1	-1	0					/O	0.0

■ DENNY O'NEIL
O'Neil, Dennis b: 11/22/1866, Holyoke, Mass. d: 11/15/22, Rushville, Ind. BL/TL, 6'2.5", 200 lbs. Deb: 6/18/1893

YEAR	TM/L	G	AB	R	H	2B	3B	HR	RBI	BB	SO	AVG	OBP	SLG	PRO+	BR	/A	RC	SB	CS	SBR	FR	POS	TPR
1893	StL-N	7	25	3	3	0	0	0	2	4	0	.120	.241	.120	-2	-4	-4	1	3			-1	/1	-0.3

■ MICKEY O'NEIL
O'Neil, George Michael b: 4/12/1900, St.Louis, Mo. d: 4/8/64, St.Louis, Mo. BR/TR, 5'10", 185 lbs. Deb: 9/12/19 C

YEAR	TM/L	G	AB	R	H	2B	3B	HR	RBI	BB	SO	AVG	OBP	SLG	PRO+	BR	/A	RC	SB	CS	SBR	FR	POS	TPR
1919	Bos-N	11	28	3	6	0	0	0	1	1	7	.214	.241	.214	39	-2	-2	2	0			3	C	0.2
1920	Bos-N	112	304	19	86	5	4	0	28	21	20	.283	.339	.326	96	-3	-1	35	4	4	-1	7	*C/2	1.2
1921	Bos-N	98	277	26	69	9	4	2	29	23	21	.249	.307	.332	73	-12	-10	29	2	2	-1	7	C	0.2
1922	Bos-N	83	251	18	56	5	2	0	26	14	11	.223	.267	.259	38	-24	-22	18	1	0	0	1	C	-1.9
1923	Bos-N	96	306	29	65	7	4	0	20	17	14	.212	.258	.261	39	-28	-26	21	3	2	-0	14	C	-0.6
1924	Bos-N	106	362	32	89	4	1	0	22	14	27	.246	.276	.262	47	-28	-28	26	4	3	-1	2	*C	-2.2
1925	Bos-N	70	222	29	57	6	5	2	30	21	16	.257	.327	.356	81	-8	-6	26	1	2	-1	-9	C	-1.0
1926	Bro-N	75	201	19	42	5	3	0	20	23	8	.209	.293	.264	52	-14	-13	17	3			-3	C	-1.3
1927	Was-A	5	6	0	0	0	0	0	0	0	0	.000	.000	.000	-99	-2	-2	0	0	0	0	0	C	-0.1
	NY-N	16	38	2	5	0	0	0	3	5	2	.132	.233	.132	-0	-5	-5	1	0			3	C	0.0
Total	9	672	1995	177	475	41	23	4	179	139	127	.238	.292	.288	58	-125	-113	175	18	13		25	C/2	-5.5

■ JOHN O'NEIL
O'Neil, John Francis b: 4/19/20, Shelbiana, Ky. BR/TR, 5'9", 155 lbs. Deb: 4/16/46

YEAR	TM/L	G	AB	R	H	2B	3B	HR	RBI	BB	SO	AVG	OBP	SLG	PRO+	BR	/A	RC	SB	CS	SBR	FR	POS	TPR
1946	Phi-N	46	94	12	25	3	0	0	9	5	12	.266	.303	.298	73	-4	-3	9	0			4	S	0.3

YEAR	TM/L	G	AB	R	H	2B	3B	HR	RBI	BB	SO	AVG	OBP	SLG	PRO+	BR	/A	RC	SB	CS	SBR	FR	POS	TPR

■ FRED O'NEILL   O'Neill, Frederick James "Tip" b: 1865, London, Ontario, Canada d: 3/7/1892, London, Ont., Can. 5'7", 142 lbs. Deb: 5/03/1887

YEAR	TM/L	G	AB	R	H	2B	3B	HR	RBI	BB	SO	AVG	OBP	SLG	PRO+	BR	/A	RC	SB	CS	SBR	FR	POS	TPR
1887	NY-a	6	26	4	8	1	1	0		1		.308	.357	.423	125	1	1	5	3			-1	/O	0.0

■ HARRY O'NEILL   O'Neill, Harry Mink b: 5/8/17, Philadelphia, Pa. d: 3/6/45, Iwo Jima, Marianas Islands BR/TR, 6'3", 205 lbs. Deb: 7/23/39

YEAR	TM/L	G	AB	R	H	2B	3B	HR	RBI	BB	SO	AVG	OBP	SLG	PRO+	BR	/A	RC	SB	CS	SBR	FR	POS	TPR
1939	Phi-A	1	0	0	0	0	0	0	0	0	0	—	—	—	—	0	0	0	0	0	0	0	/C	0.0

■ TIP O'NEILL   O'Neill, James Edward b: 5/25/1858, Woodstock, Ont., Canada d: 12/31/15, Montreal, Que., Can BR/TR, 6'1.5", 167 lbs. Deb: 5/05/1883

YEAR	TM/L	G	AB	R	H	2B	3B	HR	RBI	BB	SO	AVG	OBP	SLG	PRO+	BR	/A	RC	SB	CS	SBR	FR	POS	TPR
1883	NY-N	23	76	8	15	3	0	0	5	3	15	.197	.228	.237	42	-5	-5	4				-2	P/O	0.0
1884	StL-a	78	297	49	82	13	11	3		12		.276	.309	.424	135	12	11	40				-6	OP/1	0.6
1885	*StL-a	52	206	44	72	7	4	3		13		.350	.399	.466	168	18	16	39				-1	O	1.1
1886	*StL-a	138	579	106	190	28	14	3		47		.328	.385	.440	153	40	36	104	9			8	*O	3.4
1887	*StL-a	124	517	167	225	52	19	14		50		**.435**	**.490**	**.691**	208	88	78	194	30			-6	*O	**5.3**
1888	*StL-a	130	529	96	177	24	10	5	98	44		**.335**	.390	.446	155	42	33	105	26			-1	*O	2.5
1889	StL-a	134	534	123	179	33	8	9	110	72	37	.335	.419	.478	139	42	29	122	28			-2	*O	1.9
1890	Chi-P	137	577	112	174	20	16	3	75	65	36	.302	.377	.407	107	10	6	102	29			-12	*O	-0.9
1891	StL-a	129	521	112	167	28	4	10	95	62	33	.321	.402	.447	127	32	18	106	25			-13	*O	0.0
1892	Cin-N	109	419	63	105	14	6	2	52	53	25	.251	.339	.327	105	3	4	52	14			-3	*O	-0.2
Total	10	1054	4255	880	1386	222	92	52	435	421	146	.326	.392	.458	142	281	225	869	161			-37	*O/P1	13.7

■ JIM O'NEILL   O'Neill, James Leo b: 2/23/1893, Minooka, Pa. d: 9/5/76, Chambersburg, Pa. BR/TR, 5'10.5", 165 lbs. Deb: 4/15/20

YEAR	TM/L	G	AB	R	H	2B	3B	HR	RBI	BB	SO	AVG	OBP	SLG	PRO+	BR	/A	RC	SB	CS	SBR	FR	POS	TPR
1920	Was-A	86	294	27	85	17	7	1	40	13	30	.289	.324	.405	95	-4	-3	38	7	3	0	-5	S/2	0.0
1923	Was-A	23	33	6	9	1	0	0	3	1	3	.273	.294	.303	60	-2	-2	3	0	0	0	3	/23SO	0.1
Total	2	109	327	33	94	18	7	1	43	14	33	.287	.321	.394	91	-6	-5	41	7	3	0	-3	/S23O	0.1

■ JOHN O'NEILL   O'Neill, John J. b: New York, N.Y. TR, Deb: 9/06/1899

YEAR	TM/L	G	AB	R	H	2B	3B	HR	RBI	BB	SO	AVG	OBP	SLG	PRO+	BR	/A	RC	SB	CS	SBR	FR	POS	TPR
1899	NY-N	2	7	0	0	0	0	0	0			.000	.000	.000	-99	-2	-2	0	0			1	/C	0.0
1902	NY-N	2	8	0	0	0	0	0	0			.000	.000	.000	-99	-2	-2	0	0			0	/C	0.0
Total	2	4	15	0	0	0	0	0	0			.000	.000	.000	-99	-4	-4	0	0			1	/C	0.0

■ JACK O'NEILL   O'Neill, John Joseph b: 1/10/1873, Galway, Ireland d: 6/29/35, Scranton, Pa. TR, 5'10", 165 lbs. Deb: 4/21/02

YEAR	TM/L	G	AB	R	H	2B	3B	HR	RBI	BB	SO	AVG	OBP	SLG	PRO+	BR	/A	RC	SB	CS	SBR	FR	POS	TPR
1902	StL-N	63	192	13	27	1	1	0	12	13		.141	.211	.156	15	-18	-18	7	2			1	C	-1.0
1903	StL-N	75	246	23	58	9	1	0	27	13		.236	.274	.280	62	-13	-12	23	11			16	C	1.0
1904	Chi-N	51	168	8	36	5	0	1	19	6		.214	.241	.262	57	-9	-9	12	1			5	C	0.0
1905	Chi-N	53	172	16	34	4	2	0	12	8		.198	.233	.244	42	-12	-13	12	6			7	C	0.0
1906	Bos-N	61	167	14	30	5	1	0	4	12		.180	.235	.222	45	-11	-10	10	0			12	C/1O	0.6
Total	5	303	945	74	185	24	5	1	74	52		.196	.241	.235	45	-62	-61	63	20			40	C/1O	0.6

■ MIKE O'NEILL   O'Neill, Michael Joyce (a.k.a. Michael Joyce In 1901) b: 9/7/1877, Galway, Ireland d: 8/12/59, Scranton, Pa. BR/TR, 5'11", 185 lbs. Deb: 9/20/01

YEAR	TM/L	G	AB	R	H	2B	3B	HR	RBI	BB	SO	AVG	OBP	SLG	PRO+	BR	/A	RC	SB	CS	SBR	FR	POS	TPR
1901	StL-N	6	15	3	6	0	0	0	2	3		.400	.500	.400	174	2	2	3	0			-1	/P	0.0
1902	StL-N	51	135	21	43	5	3	2	15	2		.319	.333	.444	148	6	6	21	0			-0	P/O	0.0
1903	StL-N	41	110	12	25	2	2	0	6	8		.227	.280	.282	64	-5	-5	10	3			-0	PO	0.0
1904	StL-N	30	91	9	21	7	2	0	16	5		.231	.271	.352	98	-1	-0	9	0			2	P/O	0.0
1907	Cin-N	9	29	5	2	0	2	0	2	2		.069	.129	.207	6	-3	-3	1	1			-0	/O	-0.4
Total	5	137	380	50	97	14	9	2	41	20		.255	.294	.355	100	-2	-1	44	4			-0	/PO	-0.4

■ PAUL O'NEILL   O'Neill, Paul Andrew b: 2/25/63, Columbus, Ohio BL/TL, 6'4", 200 lbs. Deb: 9/03/85

YEAR	TM/L	G	AB	R	H	2B	3B	HR	RBI	BB	SO	AVG	OBP	SLG	PRO+	BR	/A	RC	SB	CS	SBR	FR	POS	TPR
1985	Cin-N	5	12	1	4	1	0	0	1	0	2	.333	.333	.417	103	0	0	2	0	0	0	0	/O	0.0
1986	Cin-N	3	2	0	0	0	0	0	0	1	1	.000	.333	.000	-0	-0	-0	0	0	0	0	0	/H	0.0
1987	Cin-N	84	160	24	41	14	1	7	28	18	29	.256	.331	.488	109	3	2	26	2	1	0	1	O/1P	0.1
1988	Cin-N	145	485	58	122	25	3	16	73	38	65	.252	.309	.414	102	2	0	61	8	6	-1	-2	*O1	-0.7
1989	Cin-N	117	428	49	118	24	2	15	74	46	64	.276	.349	.446	122	14	12	69	20	5	3	1	*O	1.5
1990	*Cin-N	145	503	59	136	28	0	16	78	53	103	.270	.342	.421	106	6	5	69	13	11	-3	3	*O	0.1
Total	6	499	1590	191	421	92	6	54	254	156	264	.265	.333	.432	109	25	19	227	43	23	-1	4	O/1P	1.0

■ PEACHES O'NEILL   O'Neill, Philip Bernard b: 8/30/1879, Anderson, Ind. d: 8/2/55, Anderson, Ind. TR, 5'11", 165 lbs. Deb: 4/16/04

YEAR	TM/L	G	AB	R	H	2B	3B	HR	RBI	BB	SO	AVG	OBP	SLG	PRO+	BR	/A	RC	SB	CS	SBR	FR	POS	TPR
1904	Cin-N	8	15	0	4	0	0	0	1	1		.267	.313	.267	75	-0	-0	1	0			-3	/C1	-0.3

■ STEVE O'NEILL   O'Neill, Stephen Francis b: 7/6/1891, Minooka, Pa. d: 1/26/62, Cleveland, Ohio BR/TR, 5'10", 165 lbs. Deb: 9/18/11 MC

YEAR	TM/L	G	AB	R	H	2B	3B	HR	RBI	BB	SO	AVG	OBP	SLG	PRO+	BR	/A	RC	SB	CS	SBR	FR	POS	TPR
1911	Cle-A	9	27	1	4	1	0	0	1	4		.148	.281	.185	31	-2	-2	2	2			4	/C	0.2
1912	Cle-A	69	215	17	49	4	0	0	14	12		.228	.272	.247	47	-14	-15	15	2			9	C	0.1
1913	Cle-A	80	234	19	69	13	3	0	29	10	24	.295	.329	.376	103	1	0	30	5			3	C	1.0
1914	Cle-A	87	269	28	68	12	2	0	20	15	35	.253	.292	.312	79	-7	-8	24	1	3	-2	1	C/1	-0.2
1915	Cle-A	121	386	32	91	14	2	2	34	26	41	.236	.293	.298	75	-12	-13	35	2	3	-1	5	*C	0.0
1916	Cle-A	130	378	30	89	23	0	0	29	24	33	.235	.288	.296	71	-12	-15	36	2			5	*C	-0.3
1917	Cle-A	129	370	21	68	10	2	0	29	41	55	.184	.272	.222	47	-21	-24	24	2			1	*C	-1.4
1918	Cle-A	114	359	34	87	8	7	1	35	48	22	.242	.343	.312	89	0	-3	39	5			1	*C	0.9
1919	Cle-A	125	398	46	115	35	7	2	47	48	21	.289	.373	.427	121	13	10	63	4			-7	*C	0.9
1920	*Cle-A	149	489	63	157	39	5	3	55	69	39	.321	.408	.440	121	20	17	91	3	5	-2	-8	*C	1.9
1921	Cle-A	106	335	39	108	22	1	1	50	57	22	.322	.424	.403	110	9	8	61	0	1	-1	3	*C	1.3
1922	Cle-A	133	392	33	122	27	4	2	65	73	25	.311	.423	.416	118	15	15	74	2	2	-1	-13	*C	0.5
1923	Cle-A	113	330	31	82	12	0	0	50	64	34	.248	.374	.285	75	-9	-9	39	0	4	-1	-11	*C	-1.2
1924	Bos-A	106	307	29	73	15	1	0	38	63	23	.238	.371	.293	73	-10	-10	38	0	2	-1	1	C	-0.3
1925	NY-A	35	91	7	26	5	0	1	13	10	3	.286	.363	.374	89	-2	-1	13	0	0	0	3	C	0.3
1927	StL-A	74	191	14	44	7	0	1	22	20	6	.230	.303	.283	51	-13	-14	17	0	3	-2	1	C	-1.1
1928	StL-A	10	24	4	7	1	0	0	6	8	0	.292	.485	.333	115	2	1	5	0	0	0	-4	C	-0.1
Total	17	1590	4795	448	1259	248	34	13	537	592	383	.263	.349	.337	88	-42	-62	604	30	23		-6	*C/1	2.5

■ BILL O'NEILL   O'Neill, William John b: 1/22/1880, St.John, N.B., Can. d: 7/27/20, St.John, N.B., Can BB, 5'11", 175 lbs. Deb: 5/07/04

YEAR	TM/L	G	AB	R	H	2B	3B	HR	RBI	BB	SO	AVG	OBP	SLG	PRO+	BR	/A	RC	SB	CS	SBR	FR	POS	TPR
1904	Bos-A	17	51	7	10	1	0	0	5	5		.196	.226	.216	39	-3	-4	3	0			-2	/OS	-0.6
	Was-A	95	365	33	89	10	1	1	16	22		.244	.287	.285	84	-7	-6	38	22			-10	O/2	-2.3
	Yr	112	416	40	99	11	1	1	21	24		.238	.280	.276	78	-10	-10	40	22			-12		-2.9
1906	*Chi-A	94	330	37	82	4	1	1	21	22		.248	.295	.276	83	-7	-7	35	19			-6	O	-1.6
Total	2	206	746	77	181	15	2	2	42	46		.243	.287	.276	81	-17	-15	75	41			-18	O/2S	-4.5

■ RALPH ONIS   Onis, Manuel Dominguez "Curly" b: 10/24/08, Tampa, Fla. BR/TR, 5'9", 180 lbs. Deb: 4/27/35

YEAR	TM/L	G	AB	R	H	2B	3B	HR	RBI	BB	SO	AVG	OBP	SLG	PRO+	BR	/A	RC	SB	CS	SBR	FR	POS	TPR
1935	Bro-N	1	1	0	1	0	0	0	0	0	0	1.000	1.000	1.000	449	0	0	1	0			-0	/C	0.0

■ EDDIE ONSLOW   Onslow, Edward Joseph b: 2/17/1893, Meadville, Pa. d: 5/8/81, Dennison, Ohio BL/TL, 6', 170 lbs. Deb: 8/07/12

YEAR	TM/L	G	AB	R	H	2B	3B	HR	RBI	BB	SO	AVG	OBP	SLG	PRO+	BR	/A	RC	SB	CS	SBR	FR	POS	TPR
1912	Det-A	36	128	11	29	1	2	1	13	3		.227	.250	.289	56	-8	-8	10	3			-3	1	-0.9
1913	Det-A	17	55	7	14	1	0	0	8	5	9	.255	.328	.273	77	-1	-1	5	1			-1	1	-0.2
1918	Cle-A	2	6	0	1	0	0	0	0	0	1	.167	.167	.167	1	-1	-1	0	0			-1	/O	-0.1
1927	Was-A	9	18	1	4	1	0	0	1	1	0	.222	.263	.278	41	-2	-2	1	0	0	0	0	/1	-0.1
Total	4	64	207	19	48	3	2	1	22	9	10	.232	.271	.280	59	-12	-11	16	4	0		-5	/1O	-1.3

YEAR	TM/L	G	AB	R	H	2B	3B	HR	RBI	BB	SO	AVG	OBP	SLG	PRO+	BR	/A	RC	SB	CS	SBR	FR	POS	TPR

■ JACK ONSLOW
Onslow, John James b: 10/13/1888, Scottdale, Pa. d: 12/22/60, Concord, Mass. BR/TR, 5'11", 180 lbs. Deb: 5/02/12 MC

YEAR	TM/L	G	AB	R	H	2B	3B	HR	RBI	BB	SO	AVG	OBP	SLG	PRO+	BR	/A	RC	SB	CS	SBR	FR	POS	TPR
1912	Det-A	36	69	7	11	1	0	0	4	10		.159	.284	.174	33	-6	-5	4	1			1	C/O	0.0
1917	NY-N	9	8	1	2	1	0	0	0	0	1	.250	.333	.375	121	0	0	1	0			-0	/C	0.0
Total	2	45	77	8	13	2	0	0	4	10	1	.169	.289	.195	41	-6	-5	5	1			1	/CO	0.0

■ STEVE ONTIVEROS
Ontiveros, Steven Robert b: 10/26/51, Bakersfield, Cal. BB/TR, 6', 185 lbs. Deb: 8/05/73

YEAR	TM/L	G	AB	R	H	2B	3B	HR	RBI	BB	SO	AVG	OBP	SLG	PRO+	BR	/A	RC	SB	CS	SBR	FR	POS	TPR
1973	SF-N	24	33	3	8	0	0	1	5	4	7	.242	.324	.333	79	-1	-1	4	0	0	0	1	/1O	0.0
1974	SF-N	120	343	45	91	15	1	4	30	57	41	.265	.375	.350	99	4	2	46	0	0	0	-5	31/O	-0.5
1975	SF-N	108	325	21	94	16	0	3	31	55	44	.289	.395	.366	108	8	6	50	2	0	1	0	3/O1	0.6
1976	SF-N	59	74	8	13	3	0	0	5	6	11	.176	.247	.216	31	-7	-7	4	0	0	0	-2	/3O1	-0.9
1977	Chi-N	156	546	54	163	32	3	10	68	81	69	.299	.392	.423	107	17	9	92	3	3	-1	-2	*3	0.5
1978	Chi-N	82	276	34	67	14	4	1	22	34	33	.243	.326	.333	75	-5	-9	31	0	2	-1	10	3/1	0.0
1979	Chi-N	152	519	58	148	28	2	4	57	58	68	.285	.365	.370	92	3	-4	69	0	1	-1	-4	*3/1	-1.4
1980	Chi-N	31	77	7	16	3	0	1	3	14	17	.208	.330	.286	68	-2	-3	8	0	0	0	-1	3	-0.3
Total	8	732	2193	230	600	111	10	24	224	309	290	.274	.367	.366	94	17	-6	305	5	6	-2	-3	3/1O	-2.0

■ JOSE OQUENDO
Oquendo, Jose Manuel (Contreras) b: 7/4/63, Rio Piedras, P.R. BB/TR, 5'10", 160 lbs. Deb: 5/02/83

YEAR	TM/L	G	AB	R	H	2B	3B	HR	RBI	BB	SO	AVG	OBP	SLG	PRO+	BR	/A	RC	SB	CS	SBR	FR	POS	TPR
1983	NY-N	120	328	29	70	7	0	1	17	19	60	.213	.261	.244	41	-26	-26	19	8	9	-3	6	*S	-1.2
1984	NY-N	81	189	23	42	5	0	0	10	15	26	.222	.286	.249	52	-12	-11	16	10	1	2	2	S	0.0
1986	StL-N	76	138	20	41	4	1	0	13	24	15	.297	.366	.341	97	-0	-0	17	2	3	-1	-5	S2/3O	-0.3
1987	*StL-N	116	248	43	71	9	0	1	24	54	29	.286	.414	.335	99	4	3	38	4	4	-1	8	O2S/31P	1.1
1988	StL-N	148	451	36	125	10	1	7	46	52	40	.277	.352	.350	101	3	2	57	4	6	-2	10	23S10/PC	1.3
1989	StL-N	163	556	59	162	28	7	1	48	79	59	.291	.380	.372	112	14	12	81	3	5	-2	20	*2/S1	3.4
1990	StL-N	156	469	38	118	17	5	1	37	74	46	.252	.354	.316	83	-7	-8	57	1	1	-0	-1	*2/S	-0.8
Total	7	860	2379	248	629	80	14	11	195	308	280	.264	.350	.324	88	-24	-28	283	32	29	-8	40	2S/O31PC	3.5

■ TOM ORAN
Oran, Thomas b: 1845, d: 9/22/1886, St.Louis, Mo. Deb: 5/04/1875

YEAR	TM/L	G	AB	R	H	2B	3B	HR	RBI	BB	SO	AVG	OBP	SLG	PRO+	BR	/A	RC	SB	CS	SBR	FR	POS	TPR
1875	RS-n	19	81	7	16	5	1	0	1			.198	.207	.284	75	-2	-1	5					O	0.0

■ ERNIE ORAVETZ
Oravetz, Ernest Eugene b: 1/24/32, Johnstown, Pa. BB/TL, 5'4", 145 lbs. Deb: 4/11/55

YEAR	TM/L	G	AB	R	H	2B	3B	HR	RBI	BB	SO	AVG	OBP	SLG	PRO+	BR	/A	RC	SB	CS	SBR	FR	POS	TPR
1955	Was-A	100	263	24	71	5	1	0	25	26	19	.270	.338	.297	76	-10	-8	27	1	2	-1	-6	O	-1.7
1956	Was-A	88	137	20	34	3	2	0	11	27	20	.248	.372	.299	79	-3	-3	18	1	0	0	-2	O	-0.5
Total	2	188	400	44	105	8	3	0	36	53	39	.262	.350	.298	77	-13	-11	45	2	2	-1	-8	/O	-2.2

■ TONY ORDENANA
Ordenana, Antonio (Rodriguez) "Mosquito" b: 10/30/18, Guanabacoa, Havana, Cuba d: 9/29/88, Miami, Fla. BR/TR, 5'9", 158 lbs. Deb: 10/03/43

YEAR	TM/L	G	AB	R	H	2B	3B	HR	RBI	BB	SO	AVG	OBP	SLG	PRO+	BR	/A	RC	SB	CS	SBR	FR	POS	TPR
1943	Pit-N	1	4	0	2	0	0	0	3	0		.500	.500	.500	183	0		1	0			1	/S	0.1

■ JOE ORENGO
Orengo, Joseph Charles b: 11/29/14, San Francisco, Cal. d: 7/24/88, San Francisco, Cal. BR/TR, 6', 185 lbs. Deb: 4/18/39

YEAR	TM/L	G	AB	R	H	2B	3B	HR	RBI	BB	SO	AVG	OBP	SLG	PRO+	BR	/A	RC	SB	CS	SBR	FR	POS	TPR
1939	StL-N	7	3	0	0	0	0	0	0	0	1	.000	.000	.000	-94	-1	-1	0	0			-0	/S	0.0
1940	StL-N	129	415	58	119	23	4	7	56	65	90	.287	.383	.412	113	13	10	72	9			5	23S	2.2
1941	NY-N	77	252	23	54	11	2	4	25	28	49	.214	.298	.321	73	-9	-9	24	1			18	3/S2	1.1
1943	NY-N	83	266	28	58	8	2	6	29	36	46	.218	.311	.331	85	-5	-5	28	1			4	1	-0.4
	Bro-N	7	15	1	3	2	0	0	1	4	2	.200	.368	.333	103	0	0	2	0			0	/3	-0.0
	Yr	90	281	29	61	10	2	6	30	40	48	.217	.315	.331	86	-5	-5	30	1			4		-0.4
1944	Det-A	46	154	14	31	10	0	0	10	20	29	.201	.297	.266	58	-7	-8	13	1	1	-0	6	S3/12	0.0
1945	Chi-A	17	15	5	1	0	0	0	1	3	2	.067	.222	.067	-15	-2	-2	0	0	0	0	1	/32	0.5
Total	6	366	1120	129	266	54	8	17	122	156	219	.237	.332	.346	88	-10	-16	139	12	1		35	3/12S	2.9

■ GEORGE ORME
Orme, George William b: 9/16/1891, Lebanon, Ind. d: 3/16/62, Indianapolis, Ind. BR/TR, 5'10", 160 lbs. Deb: 9/14/20

YEAR	TM/L	G	AB	R	H	2B	3B	HR	RBI	BB	SO	AVG	OBP	SLG	PRO+	BR	/A	RC	SB	CS	SBR	FR	POS	TPR
1920	Bos-A	4	6	4	2	0	0	0	1	3	0	.333	.556	.333	146	1	1	1	0				/O	0.1

■ JESS ORNDORFF
Orndorff, Jesse Walworth Thayer b: 1/15/1881, Chicago, Ill. d: 9/28/60, Cardiff-By-The-Sea, Cal. BB/TR, 6', 168 lbs. Deb: 4/18/07

YEAR	TM/L	G	AB	R	H	2B	3B	HR	RBI	BB	SO	AVG	OBP	SLG	PRO+	BR	/A	RC	SB	CS	SBR	FR	POS	TPR
1907	Bos-N	5	17	0	2	0	0	0	0	0		.118	.118	.118	-26	-2	-2	0				-2	/C	-0.4

■ FRANK O'ROURKE
O'Rourke, James Francis "Blackie" b: 11/28/1894, Hamilton, Ont., Can d: 5/14/86, Chatham, N.J. BR/TR, 5'10.5", 165 lbs. Deb: 6/12/12

YEAR	TM/L	G	AB	R	H	2B	3B	HR	RBI	BB	SO	AVG	OBP	SLG	PRO+	BR	/A	RC	SB	CS	SBR	FR	POS	TPR
1912	Bos-N	61	196	11	24	3	1	0	16	11	50	.122	.177	.148	-10	-30	-31	6	1			-7	S/3	-3.1
1917	Bro-N	64	198	18	47	7	1	0	15	14	25	.237	.294	.283	75	-5	-6	19	11			7	3	0.1
1918	Bro-N	4	12	0	2	0	0	0	2	1	3	.167	.231	.167	22	-1	-1	0	0			1	/2O	0.0
1920	Was-A	14	54	8	16	1	0	0	5	2	5	.296	.321	.315	71	-2	-2	6	2	1	0	4	S/3	0.3
1921	Was-A	123	444	51	104	17	8	3	54	26	56	.234	.287	.329	60	-30	-27	42	6	7	-2	-7	*S	-1.9
1922	Bos-A	67	216	28	57	14	3	1	17	20	28	.264	.335	.370	84	-5	-5	27	6	6	-2	-11	S3	-0.9
1924	Det-A	47	181	28	50	11	2	0	19	12	19	.276	.332	.359	79	-6	-6	22	7	4	0	11	2/S	0.6
1925	Det-A	124	482	88	141	40	7	5	57	32	37	.293	.350	.436	100	-3	-1	73	5	8	-3	15	*2/3	1.4
1926	Det-A	111	363	43	88	16	1	1	41	35	33	.242	.321	.300	62	-19	-20	37	8	6	-1	10	32S	-0.3
1927	StL-A	140	538	85	144	25	3	1	39	64	43	.268	.358	.331	77	-14	-16	64	19	8	1	11	*32/1	0.4
1928	StL-A	99	391	54	103	24	3	1	62	21	19	.263	.303	.348	68	-17	-19	43	10	2	2	-9	3/S	-2.4
1929	StL-A	154	585	81	147	23	9	2	62	41	28	.251	.306	.332	62	-32	-35	62	14	7	0	-17	*3/2S	-4.0
1930	StL-A	115	400	52	107	15	4	1	41	35	30	.268	.326	.333	65	-19	-21	44	11	9	-2	10	3S/1	-0.6
1931	StL-A	8	9	0	2	0	0	0	0	0	1	.222	.222	.222	17	-1	-1	0	1	1	-0	1	/S1	0.0
Total	14	1131	4069	547	1032	196	42	15	430	314	377	.254	.315	.333	68	-185	-191	444	101	59		17	3S2/1O	-10.4

■ JIM O'ROURKE
O'Rourke, James Henry "Orator Jim" b: 9/1/1850, Bridgeport, Conn. d: 1/8/19, Bridgeport, Conn. BR/TR, 5'8", 185 lbs. Deb: 4/26/1872 MUH

YEAR	TM/L	G	AB	R	H	2B	3B	HR	RBI	BB	SO	AVG	OBP	SLG	PRO+	BR	/A	RC	SB	CS	SBR	FR	POS	TPR
1872	Man-n	23	100	27	33	3	0	0			3	.330	.350	.360	126	2	4	13					S/DD	0.3
1873	Bos-n	57	275	80	100	22	3	1			15	.364	.397	.476	144	19	14	53					1O/C	1.1
1874	Bos-n	70	332	82	105	12	6	5			2	.316	.320	.434	130	13	10	47					*1	0.8
1875	Bos-n	75	364	98	106	16	8	6			10	.291	.310	.429	147	19	17	50					O3/1	1.6
1876	Bos-N	70	312	61	102	17	3	2	43	15	17	.327	.358	.420	156	19	18	48				-4	*O/1C	1.2
1877	Bos-N	61	265	68	96	14	4	0	23	20	9	.362	.407	.445	162	21	20	49				-2	*O/1	1.4
1878	Bos-N	60	255	44	71	17	7	1	29	5	21	.278	.292	.412	120	7	5	31				4	*O/1C	0.4
1879	Pro-N	81	362	69	126	19	9	1	46	13	10	.348	.371	.459	174	27	28	63				-10	*O1/C3	1.3
1880	Bos-N	86	363	71	100	20	11	6	45	21	8	.275	.315	.441	158	20	21	52				-3	O1S3/C	1.7
1881	Buf-N	83	348	71	105	21	7	0	30	27	18	.302	.352	.402	139	15	16	51				-20	*3O/CS1M	0.0
1882	Buf-N	84	370	62	104	15	6	2	37	13	13	.281	.305	.370	114	6	5	43				-2	*O/SC3M	0.2
1883	Buf-N	94	436	102	143	29	8	1	38	15	13	.328	.350	.438	135	19	18	69				-12	OC/3SPM	0.8
1884	Buf-N	108	467	119	162	33	7	5	63	35	17	.347	.392	.480	168	39	37	90				-10	*O1C/P3M	2.2
1885	NY-N	112	477	119	143	21	16	5	42	40	21	.300	.354	.442	158	30	30	77				-17	*O/C	1.0
1886	NY-N	105	440	106	136	26	6	1	34	39	21	.309	.365	.402	132	18	17	72	14			7	OC/1	2.5
1887	NY-N	103	397	73	113	15	3	3	38	36	11	.285	.352	.411	118	7	11	75	46			-10	C3O/2	1.5
1888	*NY-N	107	409	50	112	16	6	4	50	24	30	.274	.319	.372	123	10	10	58	25			2	OC/13	1.1
1889	*NY-N	128	502	89	161	36	7	3	81	40	34	.321	.372	.438	127	18	18	96	33			-10	*O/C	0.2
1890	NY-P	111	478	112	172	37	6	9	115	40	15	.360	.410	.515	136	31	24	113	5				*O	1.9
1891	NY-N	136	555	92	164	28	7	5	95	26	30	.295	.334	.398	120	8	12	82	19			1	*OC	0.7
1892	NY-N	115	448	62	136	21	5	0	56	30	30	.304	.354	.388	128	14	14	69	16			-10	*O/C1	0.1
1893	Was-N	129	547	75	157	22	5	2	95	49	26	.287	.354	.356	93	-6	-4	76	15			6	O1/CM	0.0

YEAR	TM/L	G	AB	R	H	2B	3B	HR	RBI	BB	SO	AVG	OBP	SLG	PRO+	BR	/A	RC	SB	CS	SBR	FR	POS	TPR
1904	NY-N	1	4	1	1	0	0	0	0	0		.250	.250	.250	54	-0	-0	0	0			-1	/C	0.0
Total	4 n	225	1071	287	344	53	17	12			30	.321	.340	.436	139	54	45	163	0				1/O3SDC	3.8
Total	19	1774	7435	1446	2304	414	132	50	1010	481	348	.310	.355	.421	134	303	300	1214	191			-86	*OC31/SP2	17.2

■ CHARLIE O'ROURKE

O'Rourke, James Patrick b: 6/22/37, Walla Walla, Wash BR/TR, 6'2", 195 lbs. Deb: 6/16/59

YEAR	TM/L	G	AB	R	H	2B	3B	HR	RBI	BB	SO	AVG	OBP	SLG	PRO+	BR	/A	RC	SB	CS	SBR	FR	POS	TPR
1959	StL-N	2	2	0	0	0	0	0	0	0	0	.000	.000	.000	-94	-1	-1	0	0	0	0	0	H	0.0

■ QUEENIE O'ROURKE

O'Rourke, James Stephen b: 12/26/1883, Bridgeport, Conn. d: 12/22/55, Sparrows Point, Md BR/TR, 5'7", 150 lbs. Deb: 8/15/08

YEAR	TM/L	G	AB	R	H	2B	3B	HR	RBI	BB	SO	AVG	OBP	SLG	PRO+	BR	/A	RC	SB	CS	SBR	FR	POS	TPR
1908	NY-A	34	108	5	25	1	0	0	3	4		.231	.259	.241	64	-4	-4	8	4			-6	OS/23	-1.2

■ JOHN O'ROURKE

O'Rourke, John b: 8/23/1849, Bridgeport, Conn. d: 6/23/11, Boston, Mass. BL, 6', 190 lbs. Deb: 5/01/1879

YEAR	TM/L	G	AB	R	H	2B	3B	HR	RBI	BB	SO	AVG	OBP	SLG	PRO+	BR	/A	RC	SB	CS	SBR	FR	POS	TPR
1879	Bos-N	72	317	69	108	17	11	6	**62**	8	32	.341	.357	**.521**	181	28	27	60				1	*O	2.3
1880	Bos-N	81	313	30	86	22	8	3	36	18	32	.275	.314	.425	153	16	17	43				3	*O	1.6
1883	NY-a	77	315	49	85	19	5	2		21		.270	.315	.381	119	8	6	39				-3	*O/1	0.3
Total	3	230	945	148	279	58	24	11	98	47	64	.295	.329	.442	150	52	50	142				0	O/1	4.2

■ JOE O'ROURKE

O'Rourke, Joseph Leo Jr. b: 10/28/04, Philadelphia, Pa. d: 6/27/90, Philadelphia, Pa. BL/TR, 5'7", 145 lbs. Deb: 4/19/29

YEAR	TM/L	G	AB	R	H	2B	3B	HR	RBI	BB	SO	AVG	OBP	SLG	PRO+	BR	/A	RC	SB	CS	SBR	FR	POS	TPR
1929	Phi-N	3	3	0	0	0	0	0	0	0	1	.000	.000	.000	-94	-1	-1	0	0			0	H	0.0

■ PATSY O'ROURKE

O'Rourke, Joseph Leo Sr. b: 4/13/1881, Philadelphia, Pa. d: 4/18/56, Philadelphia, Pa. TR, 5'7", 160 lbs. Deb: 4/16/08

YEAR	TM/L	G	AB	R	H	2B	3B	HR	RBI	BB	SO	AVG	OBP	SLG	PRO+	BR	/A	RC	SB	CS	SBR	FR	POS	TPR
1908	StL-N	53	164	8	32	4	2	0	16	14		.195	.258	.244	65	-7	-6	11	2			-7	S	-1.5

■ TOM O'ROURKE

O'Rourke, Thomas Joseph b: 1862, New York, N.Y. d: 7/19/29, New York, N.Y. TR, 5'9", 158 lbs. Deb: 5/11/1887

YEAR	TM/L	G	AB	R	H	2B	3B	HR	RBI	BB	SO	AVG	OBP	SLG	PRO+	BR	/A	RC	SB	CS	SBR	FR	POS	TPR
1887	Bos-N	22	78	12	12	3	0	0	10	7	6	.154	.233	.192	20	-8	-8	5	4			-5	C/O3	-0.8
1888	Bos-N	20	74	3	13	0	0	0	4	1	9	.176	.187	.176	17	-7	-7	3	2			1	C/O	-0.4
1890	NY-N	2	7	1	0	0	0	0	0	1	0	.000	.125	.000	-62	-1	-1	0	0			2	/C	0.1
	Syr-a	41	153	16	33	8	0	0		12		.216	.273	.268	68	-7	-5	12	2			-9	C/1	-0.8
Total	3	85	312	32	58	11	0	0	14	21	15	.186	.240	.221	40	-24	-21	19	8			-11	/CO13	-1.9

■ TIM O'ROURKE

O'Rourke, Timothy Patrick "Voiceless Tim" b: 5/18/1864, Chicago, Ill. d: 4/20/38, Seattle, Wash. BL/TR, 5'10", 170 lbs. Deb: 5/27/1890

YEAR	TM/L	G	AB	R	H	2B	3B	HR	RBI	BB	SO	AVG	OBP	SLG	PRO+	BR	/A	RC	SB	CS	SBR	FR	POS	TPR
1890	Syr-a	87	332	48	94	13	6	1		36		.283	.362	.367	130	8	13	53	22			-11	3	0.1
1891	Col-a	34	136	22	38	1	3	0	12	15	7	.279	.359	.331	107	1	2	20	9			0	3	0.3
1892	Bal-N	63	239	40	74	8	4	0	35	24	19	.310	.373	.377	125	9	7	39	12			-14	S/O3	-0.2
1893	Bal-N	31	135	22	49	4	1	0	19	12	4	.363	.423	.407	121	5	5	26	5			-4	O/3S	0.0
	Lou-N	92	352	80	99	8	4	0	53	77	15	.281	.421	.327	111	7	12	59	22			-21	SO/3	-0.5
	Yr	123	487	102	148	12	5	0	72	89	19	.304	.422	.349	114	12	17	85	27			-25		-0.5
1894	Lou-N	55	220	46	61	3	3	0	27	23	9	.277	.351	.318	68	-12	-9	28	9			-1	10/S32	-0.7
	StL-N	18	71	10	20	4	1	0	10	8	3	.282	.354	.366	76	-3	-3	10	2			-2	3	-0.3
	Was-N	7	25	4	5	2	1	0	2	2	1	.200	.259	.360	51	-2	-2	2	0			1	/2S	0.0
	Yr	80	316	60	86	9	5	0	39	33	13	.272	.345	.332	69	-17	-14	41	11			-2		-1.0
Total	5	387	1510	272	440	43	23	1	158	197	58	.291	.380	.352	107	12	25	238	81			-50	3S/O12	-1.3

■ DAVE ORR

Orr, David L. b: 9/29/1859, New York, N.Y. d: 6/3/15, Brooklyn, N.Y. BL/TR, 5'11", 250 lbs. Deb: 5/17/1883 M

YEAR	TM/L	G	AB	R	H	2B	3B	HR	RBI	BB	SO	AVG	OBP	SLG	PRO+	BR	/A	RC	SB	CS	SBR	FR	POS	TPR
1883	NY-a	1	4	1	1	1	0	0		0		.250	.250	.500	131	0	0	1				0	/1	0.0
	NY-N	1	3	0	0	0	0	0	0	0	1	.000	.000	.000	-99	-1	-1	0				0	/O	0.0
	NY-a	12	46	5	15	3	3	2		0		.326	.326	.652	200	5	5	10				-1	1	0.2
1884	*NY-a	110	458	82	**162**	32	13	9		5		**.354**	.362	.539	199	43	45	92				-5	*1/O	3.1
1885	NY-a	107	444	76	152	29	**21**	6		8		.342	.358	**.543**	201	39	45	88				-3	*1/P	2.9
1886	NY-a	136	571	93	**193**	25	**31**	7		17		.338	.363	**.527**	188	47	51	**118**	16			0	*1	3.8
1887	NY-a	84	345	63	127	25	10	2		22		.368	.408	.516	166	26	29	81	17			-1	1/OM	2.1
1888	Bro-a	99	394	57	120	20	5	1	59	7		.305	.330	.388	134	13	13	55	11			4	*1	1.0
1889	Col-a	134	560	70	183	31	12	4	87	9	38	.327	.340	.446	132	15	19	91	12			9	*1	1.4
1890	Bro-P	107	464	89	173	32	13	6	124	30	11	.373	.416	.537	147	34	29	110	10			-4	*1	1.1
Total	8	791	3289	536	1126	198	108	37	270	98	50	.342	.366	.502	165	223	236	647	66			-2	1/OP	15.6

■ BILLY ORR

Orr, William John b: 4/22/1891, San Francisco, Cal d: 3/10/67, Santarium, Cal. BR/TR, 5'11", 168 lbs. Deb: 5/03/13

YEAR	TM/L	G	AB	R	H	2B	3B	HR	RBI	BB	SO	AVG	OBP	SLG	PRO+	BR	/A	RC	SB	CS	SBR	FR	POS	TPR
1913	Phi-A	30	67	6	13	1	1	0	7	4	10	.194	.239	.239	41	-5	-5	4	1			-2	S/132	-0.5
1914	Phi-A	10	24	3	4	1	1	0	1	2	5	.167	.231	.292	59	-1	-1	2	1	1	-0	-4	/S3	-0.5
Total	2	40	91	9	17	2	2	0	8	6	15	.187	.237	.253	46	-7	-6	5	2	1		-6	/S312	-1.0

■ ERNIE ORSATTI

Orsatti, Ernest Ralph b: 9/8/02, Los Angeles, Cal. d: 9/4/68, Canoga Park, Cal. BL/TL, 5'7.5", 154 lbs. Deb: 9/04/27

YEAR	TM/L	G	AB	R	H	2B	3B	HR	RBI	BB	SO	AVG	OBP	SLG	PRO+	BR	/A	RC	SB	CS	SBR	FR	POS	TPR
1927	StL-N	27	92	15	29	7	3	0	12	11	12	.315	.388	.457	122	3	3	16	2			-0	O	0.2
1928	*StL-N	27	69	10	21	6	0	3	15	10	11	.304	.400	.522	137	4	4	14	0			-1	O/1	0.2
1929	StL-N	113	346	64	115	21	7	3	39	33	43	.332	.394	.460	110	6	6	62	7			6	O1	0.4
1930	*StL-N	48	131	24	42	8	4	1	15	12	18	.321	.382	.466	100	1	0	23	1			4	1O	0.2
1931	*StL-N	70	158	27	46	16	6	0	19	14	16	.291	.349	.468	113	4	3	26	1			-1	O/1	0.0
1932	StL-N	101	375	44	126	27	6	2	44	18	29	.336	.368	.456	117	10	9	63	5			-6	O/1	-0.3
1933	StL-N	120	436	55	130	21	6	0	38	33	33	.298	.348	.374	101	4	1	58	14			-1	*O/1	-0.6
1934	*StL-N	105	337	39	101	14	4	0	31	27	31	.300	.353	.365	87	-3	-6	45	6			-4	O	-1.3
1935	StL-N	90	221	28	53	9	3	1	24	18	25	.240	.297	.321	64	-10	-12	21	10			-1	O	-1.4
Total	9	701	2165	306	663	129	39	10	237	176	218	.306	.360	.416	102	19	9	328	46			-3	O/1	-2.6

■ JOHN ORSINO

Orsino, John Joseph "Horse" b: 4/22/38, Teaneck, N.J. BR/TR, 6'3", 215 lbs. Deb: 7/14/61

YEAR	TM/L	G	AB	R	H	2B	3B	HR	RBI	BB	SO	AVG	OBP	SLG	PRO+	BR	/A	RC	SB	CS	SBR	FR	POS	TPR
1961	SF-N	25	83	5	23	3	2	4	12	3	13	.277	.310	.506	116	1	1	13	0	0	0	-2	C	0.1
1962	*SF-N	18	48	4	13	2	0	0	4	5	11	.271	.340	.313	78	-1	-1	5	0	0	0	-2	C	-0.2
1963	Bal-A	116	379	53	103	18	1	19	56	38	53	.272	.352	.475	132	15	16	63	2	3	-1	-7	*C/1	1.0
1964	Bal-A	81	248	21	55	10	0	8	23	23	45	.222	.293	.359	81	-7	-7	26	0	0	0	1	C/1	-0.3
1965	Bal-A	77	232	30	54	10	2	9	28	23	51	.233	.315	.409	102	1	1	26	1	0	0	-8	C/1	-0.3
1966	Was-A	14	23	1	4	1	0	0	0	0	7	.174	.174	.217	12	-3	-3	1	0	0	0	0	/1C	-0.2
1967	Was-A	1	1	0	0	0	0	0	0	0	1	.000	.000	.000	-99	-0	-0	0	0	0	0	0	H	0.0
Total	7	332	1014	114	252	44	5	40	123	92	191	.249	.321	.420	106	6	7	135	3	3	-1	-18	C/1	0.1

■ JOE ORSULAK

Orsulak, Joseph Michael b: 5/31/62, Parispanny, N.J. BL/TL, 6'1", 185 lbs. Deb: 9/01/83

YEAR	TM/L	G	AB	R	H	2B	3B	HR	RBI	BB	SO	AVG	OBP	SLG	PRO+	BR	/A	RC	SB	CS	SBR	FR	POS	TPR
1983	Pit-N	7	11	0	2	0	0	0	1	0	2	.182	.182	.182	-1	-1	-1	0	0	1	-1	1	/O	0.0
1984	Pit-N	32	67	12	17	1	2	0	3	1	7	.254	.275	.328	69	-3	-3	6	3	1	0	2	O	-0.1
1985	Pit-N	121	397	54	119	14	6	0	21	26	27	.300	.344	.365	100	-1	-0	51	24	11	1	5	*O	0.3
1986	Pit-N	138	401	60	100	19	6	2	19	28	38	.249	.300	.342	75	-13	-14	42	24	11	1	-3	*O	-1.9
1988	Bal-A	125	379	48	109	21	3	8	27	23	30	.288	.333	.422	113	4	6	51	9	8	-2	-4	*O/D	-0.1
1989	Bal-A	123	390	59	111	22	5	7	55	41	35	.285	.356	.421	122	10	11	59	5	3	-0	5	*O/D	1.4
1990	Bal-A	124	413	49	111	14	3	11	57	46	48	.269	.343	.397	109	4	5	55	6	8	-3	7	*O/D	0.8
Total	7	670	2058	282	569	91	25	28	183	165	187	.277	.338	.386	101	-0	3	264	71	43	-5	12	O/D	0.4

■ JORGE ORTA

Orta, Jorge (Nunez) b: 11/26/50, Mazatlan, Mexico BL/TR, 5'10", 170 lbs. Deb: 4/15/72

YEAR	TM/L	G	AB	R	H	2B	3B	HR	RBI	BB	SO	AVG	OBP	SLG	PRO+	BR	/A	RC	SB	CS	SBR	FR	POS	TPR
1972	Chi-A	51	124	20	25	3	1	3	11	6	37	.202	.244	.315	64	-6	-6	9	3	3	-1	0	S2/3	-0.3
1973	Chi-A	128	425	46	113	9	10	4	40	37	87	.266	.326	.376	94	-2	-4	51	8	8	-2	-26	*2/S	-2.7
1974	Chi-A	139	525	73	166	31	2	10	67	40	88	.316	.368	.440	128	21	19	85	9	5	-0	-13	*2D/S	1.2

YEAR	TM/L	G	AB	R	H	2B	3B	HR	RBI	BB	SO	AVG	OBP	SLG	PRO+	BR	/A	RC	SB	CS	SBR	FR	POS	TPR
1975	Chi-A	140	542	64	165	26	10	11	83	48	67	.304	.365	.450	128	20	20	85	16	9	-1	-12	*2/D	1.1
1976	Chi-A	158	636	74	174	29	8	14	72	38	77	.274	.320	.410	112	8	8	81	24	8	2	-1	O3D	0.8
1977	Chi-A	144	564	71	159	27	8	11	84	46	49	.282	.338	.417	105	3	3	78	4	4	-1	-47	*2	-3.3
1978	Chi-A	117	420	45	115	19	2	13	53	42	39	.274	.345	.421	114	8	8	61	1	2	-1	-22	*2/D	-0.9
1979	Chi-A	113	325	49	85	18	3	11	46	44	33	.262	.351	.437	111	5	5	50	1	5	-3	-10	D2	-0.9
1980	Cle-A	129	481	78	140	18	3	10	64	71	44	.291	.384	.403	116	13	13	78	6	5	-1	6	*O/D	1.6
1981	Cle-A	88	338	50	92	14	3	5	34	21	43	.272	.317	.376	100	-1	-0	38	4	3	-1	-0	O	-0.3
1982	LA-N	86	115	13	25	5	0	2	8	12	13	.217	.297	.313	73	-4	-4	11	0	1	-1	1	O	-0.3
1983	Tor-A	103	245	30	58	6	3	10	38	19	29	.237	.292	.408	85	-4	-6	28	1	2	-1	1	DO	-0.5
1984	*KC-A	122	403	50	120	23	7	9	50	28	39	.298	.346	.457	119	10	10	63	0	1	-1	2	DO/2	1.0
1985	*KC-A	110	300	32	80	21	1	4	45	22	28	.267	.321	.383	92	-3	-4	36	2	1	0	0	D	-0.3
1986	KC-A	106	336	35	93	14	2	9	46	23	34	.277	.323	.411	96	-1	-2	42	0	3	-2	0	D	-0.3
1987	KC-A	21	50	3	9	4	0	2	4	3	8	.180	.226	.380	55	-3	-3	4	0	0	0	0	D	-0.2
Total	16	1755	5829	733	1619	267	63	130	745	500	715	.278	.338	.412	108	65	57	800	79	60	-12	-122	2DO/3S	-3.8

■ FRANK ORTENZIO
Ortenzio, Frank Joseph b: 2/24/51, Fresno, Cal. BR/TR, 6'2", 215 lbs. Deb: 9/09/73

YEAR	TM/L	G	AB	R	H	2B	3B	HR	RBI	BB	SO	AVG	OBP	SLG	PRO+	BR	/A	RC	SB	CS	SBR	FR	POS	TPR
1973	KC-A	9	25	1	7	2	0	1	6	2	6	.280	.333	.480	118	1	1	4	0	0	0	1	/1D	0.1

■ AL ORTH
Orth, Albert Lewis "Smiling Al" or "The Curveless Wonder" b: 9/5/1872, Tipton, Ind. d: 10/8/48, Lynchburg, Va. BL/TR, 6', 200 lbs. Deb: 8/15/1895 U

YEAR	TM/L	G	AB	R	H	2B	3B	HR	RBI	BB	SO	AVG	OBP	SLG	PRO+	BR	/A	RC	SB	CS	SBR	FR	POS	TPR
1895	Phi-N	11	45	8	16	4	0	1	13	1	6	.356	.370	.511	127	2	2	9	0			-1	P	0.0
1896	Phi-N	25	82	12	21	3	3	1	13	3	11	.256	.282	.402	82	-3	-3	10	2			1	P	0.0
1897	Phi-N	53	152	26	50	7	4	1	17	3		.329	.342	.447	112	1	2	26	5			0	P/O	0.0
1898	Phi-N	39	123	17	36	6	4	1	14	3		.293	.310	.431	119	1	2	17	1			1	P/O	0.0
1899	Phi-N	22	62	5	13	3	1	1	5	1		.210	.222	.339	56	-4	-4	5	2			-4	P/O	0.0
1900	Phi-N	39	129	6	40	4	1	1	21	2		.310	.326	.380	97	-1	-1	17	2			1	P/O	0.0
1901	Phi-N	41	128	14	36	6	0	1	15	3		.281	.303	.352	90	-2	-2	15	3			2	P/O	0.0
1902	Was-A	56	175	20	38	3	2	2	10	9		.217	.259	.291	53	-11	-11	14	2			0	PO/1S	0.0
1903	Was-A	55	162	19	49	9	7	0	11	4		.302	.319	.444	127	5	5	25	3			-2	P/SO1	0.0
1904	Was-A	31	102	7	22	3	1	0	11	1		.216	.223	.265	56	-5	-5	7	2			-2	OP	-0.6
	NY-A	24	64	6	19	1	1	0	7	0		.297	.297	.344	100	0	-0	7	2			1	P/O	0.0
	Yr	55	166	13	41	4	2	0	18	1		.247	.251	.295	73	-5	-5	14	4			-1		-0.6
1905	NY-A	55	131	13	24	3	1	1	8	4		.183	.207	.244	40	-8	-10	8	2			1	P/1O	0.0
1906	NY-A	47	135	12	37	2	2	1	17	6		.274	.305	.341	94	0	-1	15	2			1	P/O	0.0
1907	NY-A	44	105	11	34	6	0	1	13	4		.324	.349	.410	133	5	4	16	1			3	P/O	0.0
1908	NY-A	38	69	4	20	1	2	0	4	2		.290	.310	.362	119	1	1	8	0			0	P	0.0
1909	NY-A	22	34	3	9	0	1	0	5	5		.265	.359	.324	115	1	1	4	1			-2	/2P	0.0
Total	15	602	1698	183	464	61	30	12	184	51	17	.273	.296	.366	93	-17	-20	203	30			-0	P/OS21	-0.6

■ JUNIOR ORTIZ
Ortiz, Adalberto Colon b: 10/24/59, Humacao, P.R. BR/TR, 5'11", 174 lbs. Deb: 9/20/82

YEAR	TM/L	G	AB	R	H	2B	3B	HR	RBI	BB	SO	AVG	OBP	SLG	PRO+	BR	/A	RC	SB	CS	SBR	FR	POS	TPR
1982	Pit-N	7	15	1	3	1	0	0	0	1	3	.200	.250	.267	43	-1	-1	1	0	0	0	1	/C	0.0
1983	Pit-N	5	8	1	1	0	0	0	0	1	0	.125	.222	.125	-1	-1	-1	0	0	0	0	0	/C	0.0
	NY-N	68	185	10	47	5	0	0	12	3	34	.254	.270	.281	53	-12	-12	14	1	0	0	1	C	-0.8
	Yr	73	193	11	48	5	0	0	12	4	34	.249	.268	.275	51	-13	-13	15	1	0		1		-0.8
1984	NY-N	40	91	6	18	3	0	0	5	5	15	.198	.240	.231	33	-8	-8	5	1	0	0	-3	C	-1.0
1985	Pit-N	23	72	4	21	2	0	1	5	3	17	.292	.320	.361	91	-1	-1	8	1	0	0	1	C	0.1
1986	Pit-N	49	110	11	37	6	0	0	14	9	13	.336	.387	.391	112	2	2	16	0	1	-1	0	C	0.3
1987	Pit-N	75	192	16	52	8	1	1	22	15	23	.271	.324	.339	75	-6	-7	20	0	2	-1	0	C	-0.1
1988	Pit-N	49	118	8	33	6	0	2	18	9	9	.280	.341	.381	109	1	1	13	1	4	-2	-2	C	0.0
1989	Pit-N	91	230	16	50	6	1	1	22	20	20	.217	.286	.265	61	-12	-11	17	2	2	-1	-9	C	-1.5
1990	Min-A	71	170	18	57	7	1	0	18	12	16	.335	.386	.388	109	4	3	24	0	4	-2	2	C/D	0.4
Total	9	478	1191	91	319	44	3	5	122	78	150	.268	.317	.322	78	-34	-34	118	6	13	-6	-9	C/D	-2.6

■ JAVIER ORTIZ
Ortiz, Javier Victor b: 1/22/63, Boston, Mass. BR/TR, 6'4", 220 lbs. Deb: 6/15/90

YEAR	TM/L	G	AB	R	H	2B	3B	HR	RBI	BB	SO	AVG	OBP	SLG	PRO+	BR	/A	RC	SB	CS	SBR	FR	POS	TPR
1990	Hou-N	30	77	7	21	5	1	1	10	12	11	.273	.371	.403	115	2	2	12	1	1	-0	-1	O	0.0

■ JOSE ORTIZ
Ortiz, Jose Luis (Irizarry) b: 6/25/47, Ponce, P.R. BR/TR, 5'9.5", 155 lbs. Deb: 9/04/69

YEAR	TM/L	G	AB	R	H	2B	3B	HR	RBI	BB	SO	AVG	OBP	SLG	PRO+	BR	/A	RC	SB	CS	SBR	FR	POS	TPR
1969	Chi-A	16	11	0	3	1	0	0	2	1	0	.273	.333	.364	90	-0	-0	1	0	0	0	1	/O	0.1
1970	Chi-A	15	24	4	8	1	0	0	1	2	2	.333	.407	.375	113	1	1	4	1	0	0	2	O	0.3
1971	Chi-N	36	88	10	26	7	1	0	3	4	10	.295	.347	.398	96	1	-0	12	2	2	-1	1	O	0.0
Total	3	67	123	14	37	9	1	0	6	7	12	.301	.358	.390	99	2	0	18	3	2	-0	4	/O	0.4

■ ROBERTO ORTIZ
Ortiz, Roberto Gonzalo (Nunez) b: 6/30/15, Camaguey, Cuba d: 9/15/71, Miami, Fla. BR/TR, 6'4", 200 lbs. Deb: 9/06/41

YEAR	TM/L	G	AB	R	H	2B	3B	HR	RBI	BB	SO	AVG	OBP	SLG	PRO+	BR	/A	RC	SB	CS	SBR	FR	POS	TPR
1941	Was-A	22	79	10	26	1	2	1	17	3	10	.329	.354	.430	112	1	1	11	0	1	-1	-1	O	-0.1
1942	Was-A	20	42	4	7	1	3	1	4	5	11	.167	.271	.405	89	-1	-1	5	0	0	-1	-1	/O	-0.1
1943	Was-A	1	4	0	1	0	0	0	0	0	0	.250	.250	.250	48	-0	-0	0	0	1	-1	0	/O	0.0
1944	Was-A	85	316	36	80	11	4	5	35	19	47	.253	.312	.361	96	-4	-2	38	4	1	1	-8	O	-1.2
1949	Was-A	40	129	12	36	3	0	1	11	9	12	.279	.326	.326	74	-5	-5	13	0	0	0	-3	O	-0.7
1950	Was-A	39	75	4	17	2	1	0	8	7	12	.227	.301	.280	52	-6	-5	7	0	0	0	-2	O	-0.6
	Phi-A	6	14	1	1	0	0	0	3	0	3	.071	.071	.071	-65	-3	-3	0	0	0	0	-0	/O	-0.3
	Yr	45	89	5	18	2	1	0	11	7	15	.202	.268	.247	34	-9	-9	6	0	0	0	-2		-0.9
Total	6	213	659	67	168	18	10	8	78	43	95	.255	.310	.349	84	-19	-16	75	4	3	-1	-14	O	-3.0

■ JOHN ORTON
Orton, John Andrew b: 12/8/65, Santa Cruz, Cal. BR/TR, 6'1", 195 lbs. Deb: 8/20/89

YEAR	TM/L	G	AB	R	H	2B	3B	HR	RBI	BB	SO	AVG	OBP	SLG	PRO+	BR	/A	RC	SB	CS	SBR	FR	POS	TPR
1989	Cal-A	16	39	4	7	1	0	0	4	2	17	.179	.220	.205	21	-4	-4	2	0	0	0	4	C	0.0
1990	Cal-A	31	84	8	16	5	0	1	6	5	31	.190	.244	.286	48	-6	-6	5	0	1	-1	1	C	-0.4
Total	2	47	123	12	23	6	0	1	10	7	48	.187	.237	.260	39	-10	-10	7	0	1	-1	4	/C	-0.4

■ OSSIE ORWOLL
Orwoll, Oswald Christian b: 11/17/1900, Portland, Ore. d: 5/8/67, Decorah, Iowa BL/TL, 6', 174 lbs. Deb: 4/13/28

YEAR	TM/L	G	AB	R	H	2B	3B	HR	RBI	BB	SO	AVG	OBP	SLG	PRO+	BR	/A	RC	SB	CS	SBR	FR	POS	TPR
1928	Phi-A	64	170	28	52	13	2	0	22	16	24	.306	.366	.406	100	1	0	26	3	1	0	-1	1P	0.2
1929	Phi-A	30	51	6	13	2	1	0	6	2	11	.255	.283	.333	56	-3	-4	5	0	0	0	-1	P/O	-0.2
Total	2	94	221	34	65	15	3	0	28	18	35	.294	.347	.389	90	-3	-3	31	3	1	0	-3	/P1O	0.0

■ FRED OSBORN
Osborn, Wilfred Pearl "Ossie" b: 11/28/1883, Nevada, Ohio d: 9/2/54, Upper Sandusky, O. BL/TR, 5'9", 178 lbs. Deb: 6/08/07

YEAR	TM/L	G	AB	R	H	2B	3B	HR	RBI	BB	SO	AVG	OBP	SLG	PRO+	BR	/A	RC	SB	CS	SBR	FR	POS	TPR
1907	Phi-N	56	163	22	45	2	3	0	9	3		.276	.289	.325	96	-2	-1	17	4			-4	O/1	-0.7
1908	Phi-N	152	555	62	148	19	12	2	44	30		.267	.304	.355	109	6	4	64	16			2	*O	0.6
1909	Phi-N	58	189	14	35	4	1	0	19	12		.185	.238	.217	41	-13	-13	12	6			10	O	-0.5
Total	3	266	907	98	228	25	16	2	72	45		.251	.288	.321	92	-9	-10	93	26			8	O/1	-0.6

■ FRED OSBORNE
Osborne, Frederick W. b: Hampton, Iowa Deb: 7/14/1890

YEAR	TM/L	G	AB	R	H	2B	3B	HR	RBI	BB	SO	AVG	OBP	SLG	PRO+	BR	/A	RC	SB	CS	SBR	FR	POS	TPR
1890	Pit-N	41	168	24	40	8	3	1	14	6	18	.238	.269	.339	89	-5	-2	16	0			0	O/P	0.0

■ BOBO OSBORNE
Osborne, Lawrence Sidney b: 10/12/35, Chattahoochee, Ga. BL/TR, 6'1", 205 lbs. Deb: 6/27/57

YEAR	TM/L	G	AB	R	H	2B	3B	HR	RBI	BB	SO	AVG	OBP	SLG	PRO+	BR	/A	RC	SB	CS	SBR	FR	POS	TPR
1957	Det-A	11	27	4	4	1	0	0	3	3	7	.148	.233	.185	15	-3	-3	1	0	0	0	-0	/O1	-0.3
1958	Det-A	2	2	0	0	0	0	0	0	0	0	.000	.000	.000	-93	-1	-1	0	0	0	0	0	H	0.0
1959	Det-A	86	209	27	40	7	1	3	21	16	41	.191	.256	.278	44	-16	-17	15	1	0	0	-1	1/O	-1.7

YEAR	TM/L	G	AB	R	H	2B	3B	HR	RBI	BB	SO	AVG	OBP	SLG	PRO+	BR	/A	RC	SB	CS	SBR	FR	POS	TPR
1961	Det-A	71	93	8	20	7	0	2	13	20	15	.215	.354	.355	88	-1	-1	13	1	0	0	-2	/31	-0.3
1962	Det-A	64	74	12	17	1	0	0	7	16	25	.230	.374	.243	68	-2	-3	8	0	0	0	-1	3/1C	-0.3
1963	Was-A	125	358	42	76	14	1	12	44	49	83	.212	.312	.358	87	-6	-6	42	0	0	0	-3	13	-1.1
Total	6	359	763	93	157	30	2	17	86	104	171	.206	.306	.317	71	-28	-30	81	2	0	1	-8	1/3OC	-3.7

■ HARRY OSTDIEK

Ostdiek, Henry Girard b: 4/12/1881, Ottumwa, Iowa d: 5/6/56, Minneapolis, Minn. BR/TR, 5'11", 185 lbs. Deb: 9/10/04

YEAR	TM/L	G	AB	R	H	2B	3B	HR	RBI	BB	SO	AVG	OBP	SLG	PRO+	BR	/A	RC	SB	CS	SBR	FR	POS	TPR
1904	Cle-A	7	18	1	3	0	1	0	3	3		.167	.286	.278	81	-0	-0	2	1			-0	/C	0.0
1908	Bos-A	1	3	0	0	0	0	0	0	0		.000	.000	.000	-97	-1	-1	0	0			0	/C	0.0
Total	2	8	21	1	3	0	1	0	3	3		.143	.250	.238	57	-1	-1	2	1			-0	/C	0.0

■ CHAMP OSTEEN

Osteen, James Champlin b: 2/24/1877, Hendersonville, N.C. d: 12/14/62, Greenville, S.C. BL/TR, 5'8", 150 lbs. Deb: 9/18/03

YEAR	TM/L	G	AB	R	H	2B	3B	HR	RBI	BB	SO	AVG	OBP	SLG	PRO+	BR	/A	RC	SB	CS	SBR	FR	POS	TPR
1903	Was-A	10	40	4	8	0	2	0	4	2		.200	.238	.300	61	-2	-2	3	0			1	S	0.0
1904	NY-A	28	107	15	21	1	4	2	9	1		.196	.204	.336	67	-4	-4	8	0			-2	3/S1	-0.5
1908	StL-N	29	112	2	22	4	0	0	11	0		.196	.196	.232	40	-8	-7	5	0			-6	S3	-1.5
1909	StL-N	16	45	6	9	1	0	0	7	7		.200	.308	.222	69	-2	-1	4	1			-6	S	-0.7
Total	4	83	304	27	60	6	6	2	31	10		.197	.223	.276	58	-15	-15	19	1			-13	/S31	-2.7

■ RED OSTERGARD

Ostergard, Roy Lund b: 5/16/1896, Denmark, Wis. d: 1/13/77, Hemet, Cal. BR/TR, 5'10.5", 175 lbs. Deb: 6/14/21

YEAR	TM/L	G	AB	R	H	2B	3B	HR	RBI	BB	SO	AVG	OBP	SLG	PRO+	BR	/A	RC	SB	CS	SBR	FR	POS	TPR
1921	Chi-A	12	11	2	4	0	0	0	0	0	2	.364	.364	.364	87	-0	-0	1	0	0	0	0	H	0.0

■ CHARLIE OSTERHOUT

Osterhout, Charles H. b: 1856, Syracuse, N.Y. d: 5/21/33, Syracuse, N.Y. TR , Deb: 6/23/1879

YEAR	TM/L	G	AB	R	H	2B	3B	HR	RBI	BB	SO	AVG	OBP	SLG	PRO+	BR	/A	RC	SB	CS	SBR	FR	POS	TPR
1879	Syr-N	2	8	0	0	0	0	0	0	0		.000	.000	.000	-99	-2	-2	0				0	/OC	0.0

■ BRIAN OSTROSSER

Ostrosser, Brian Leonard b: 6/17/49, Hamilton, Ont., Can BL/TR, 6', 175 lbs. Deb: 8/05/73

YEAR	TM/L	G	AB	R	H	2B	3B	HR	RBI	BB	SO	AVG	OBP	SLG	PRO+	BR	/A	RC	SB	CS	SBR	FR	POS	TPR
1973	NY-N	4	5	0	0	0	0	0	0	0	2	.000	.000	.000	-99	-1	-1	0	0	0	0	-0	/S	0.0

■ JOHNNY OSTROWSKI

Ostrowski, John Thaddeus b: 10/17/17, Chicago, III. BR/TR, 5'10.5", 170 lbs. Deb: 9/24/43

YEAR	TM/L	G	AB	R	H	2B	3B	HR	RBI	BB	SO	AVG	OBP	SLG	PRO+	BR	/A	RC	SB	CS	SBR	FR	POS	TPR
1943	Chi-N	10	29	2	6	0	1	0	3	3	8	.207	.303	.276	69	-1	-1	2	0			-2	/O3	-0.2
1944	Chi-N	8	13	2	2	1	0	0	2	1	4	.154	.214	.231	25	-1	-1	1	0			-1	/O	-0.2
1945	Chi-N	7	10	4	3	2	0	0	1	0	0	.300	.300	.500	123	0	0	2	0			-1	/3	0.0
1946	Chi-N	64	160	20	34	4	2	3	12	20	31	.213	.300	.319	77	-5	-5	16	1			1	3/2	-0.3
1948	Bos-A	1	1	0	0	0	0	0	0	0	1	.000	.000	.000	-95	-0	-0	0	0	0	0	0	H	0.0
1949	Chi-A	49	158	19	42	9	4	5	31	15	41	.266	.333	.468	115	1	2	24	4	3	-1	-1	O/3	0.0
1950	Chi-A	21	45	9	10	1	1	2	2	9	8	.222	.364	.422	104	0	0	8	0	0	0	-0	O	0.0
	Was-A	55	141	16	32	2	1	4	23	20	31	.227	.327	.340	75	-6	-5	17	2	0	1	3	O	-0.1
	Chi-A	1	4	1	2	1	0	0	0	0	1	.500	.500	.750	223	1	1	2	0	0	0	-0	/O	0.0
	Yr	77	190	26	44	4	2	6	25	29	40	.232	.339	.368	85	-5	-4	26	2	0	1	3		-0.1
Total	7	216	561	73	131	20	9	14	74	68	125	.234	.321	.376	89	-12	-10	71	7	3		-1	O/32	-0.8

■ REGGIE OTERO

Otero, Regino Jose (Gomez) b: 9/7/15, Havana, Cuba d: 10/21/88, Hialeah, Fla. BL/TR, 6', 165 lbs. Deb: 9/02/45 C

YEAR	TM/L	G	AB	R	H	2B	3B	HR	RBI	BB	SO	AVG	OBP	SLG	PRO+	BR	/A	RC	SB	CS	SBR	FR	POS	TPR
1945	Chi-N	14	23	1	9	0	0	0	5	2	2	.391	.440	.391	135	1	1	4	0			0	/1	0.1

■ AMOS OTIS

Otis, Amos Joseph b: 4/26/47, Mobile, Ala. BR/TR, 5'11.5", 165 lbs. Deb: 9/06/67 C

YEAR	TM/L	G	AB	R	H	2B	3B	HR	RBI	BB	SO	AVG	OBP	SLG	PRO+	BR	/A	RC	SB	CS	SBR	FR	POS	TPR
1967	NY-N	19	59	6	13	2	0	0	1	5	13	.220	.292	.254	59	-3	-3	4	0	4	-2	-0	O/3	-0.6
1969	NY-N	48	93	6	14	3	1	0	4	6	27	.151	.202	.204	14	-11	-11	4	1	0	0	3	O/3	-0.9
1970	KC-A	159	620	91	176	36	9	11	58	68	67	.284	.356	.424	114	12	12	102	33	2	9	10	*O	2.5
1971	KC-A	147	555	80	167	26	4	15	79	40	74	.301	.350	.443	125	16	16	87	52	8	11	18	*O	4.2
1972	KC-A	143	540	75	158	28	2	11	54	50	59	.293	.356	.413	129	19	19	82	28	12	1	5	*O	2.4
1973	KC-A	148	583	89	175	21	4	26	93	63	47	.300	.369	.484	129	29	23	103	13	9	-2	1	*OD	1.9
1974	KC-A	146	552	87	157	31	9	12	73	58	67	.284	.355	.438	120	19	15	86	18	5	2	7	*O/D	2.2
1975	KC-A	132	470	87	116	26	6	9	46	66	48	.247	.344	.385	103	5	3	68	39	11	5	-1	*O	0.3
1976	*KC-A	153	592	93	165	40	2	18	86	55	100	.279	.345	.444	129	21	21	92	26	7	4	-11	*O	1.1
1977	*KC-A	142	478	85	120	20	8	17	78	71	88	.251	.348	.433	110	8	8	74	23	7	3	-7	*O	0.0
1978	*KC-A	141	486	74	145	30	7	22	96	66	54	.298	.387	.525	150	35	34	102	32	8	5	5	*O/D	4.0
1979	KC-A	151	577	100	170	28	2	18	90	68	92	.295	.372	.444	117	16	15	100	30	5	6	-1	*O/D	1.4
1980	*KC-A	107	394	56	99	16	3	10	53	39	70	.251	.323	.383	92	-4	-4	52	16	1	4	3	*O	0.1
1981	*KC-A	99	372	49	100	22	3	9	57	31	59	.269	.328	.417	114	6	6	74	16	7	1	8	O/D	1.3
1982	KC-A	125	475	73	136	25	3	11	88	37	65	.286	.340	.421	108	5	5	64	9	5	-0	-7	*O	-0.5
1983	KC-A	98	356	35	93	16	3	4	41	27	63	.261	.313	.357	84	-8	-8	39	5	2	0	4	O/D	-0.4
1984	Pit-N	40	97	6	16	4	0	0	10	7	15	.165	.221	.206	21	-10	-10	4	0	0	0	2	O	-0.9
Total	17	1998	7299	1092	2020	374	66	193	1007	757	1008	.277	.347	.425	114	155	140	1114	341	93	47	39	*O/D3	18.1

■ BILL OTIS

Otis, Paul Franklin b: 12/24/1889, Scituate, Mass. 5'10.5", 150 lbs. Deb: 7/04/12

YEAR	TM/L	G	AB	R	H	2B	3B	HR	RBI	BB	SO	AVG	OBP	SLG	PRO+	BR	/A	RC	SB	CS	SBR	FR	POS	TPR
1912	NY-A	4	17	1	1	0	0	0	2	3		.059	.200	.059	-24	-3	-3	0	0			1	/O	-0.2

■ MEL OTT

Ott, Melvin Thomas "Master Melvin" b: 3/2/09, Gretna, La. d: 11/21/58, New Orleans, La. BL/TR, 5'9", 170 lbs. Deb: 4/27/26 MH

YEAR	TM/L	G	AB	R	H	2B	3B	HR	RBI	BB	SO	AVG	OBP	SLG	PRO+	BR	/A	RC	SB	CS	SBR	FR	POS	TPR
1926	NY-N	35	60	7	23	2	0	0	4	1	9	.383	.393	.417	120	1	2	9	1			1	O	0.2
1927	NY-N	82	163	23	46	7	3	1	19	13	9	.282	.335	.380	91	-2	-2	20	2			-4	O	-0.7
1928	NY-N	124	435	69	140	26	4	18	77	52	36	.322	.397	.524	138	24	24	89	3			-3	*O/23	1.6
1929	NY-N	150	545	138	179	37	2	42	151	113	38	.328	.449	.635	166	58	59	157	6			13	*O/2	5.2
1930	NY-N	148	521	122	182	34	5	25	119	103	35	.349	.458	.578	152	45	47	139	9			11	*O	4.1
1931	NY-N	138	497	104	145	23	8	29	115	80	44	.292	.392	.545	153	35	37	111	10			-2	*O	2.8
1932	NY-N	154	566	119	180	30	8	38	123	100	39	.318	.424	.601	175	60	62	151	6			1	*O	5.0
1933	*NY-N	152	580	98	164	36	1	23	103	75	48	.283	.367	.467	140	28	29	105	1			-9	*O	1.2
1934	NY-N	153	582	119	190	29	10	35	135	85	43	.326	.415	.591	170	55	57	150	0			-10	*O	3.8
1935	NY-N	152	593	113	191	33	6	31	114	82	58	.322	.407	.555	159	48	49	144	7			3	*O3	4.5
1936	*NY-N	150	534	120	175	28	6	33	135	111	41	.328	.448	.588	179	62	63	153	6			-5	*O	4.9
1937	*NY-N	151	545	99	160	28	2	31	95	102	69	.294	.408	.523	149	41	40	128	7			-2	3O	3.6
1938	NY-N	150	527	116	164	23	6	36	116	118	47	.311	.442	.583	178	62	61	149	2			0	*3O	5.7
1939	NY-N	125	396	85	122	23	2	27	80	100	50	.308	.449	.581	173	46	45	112	6			-6	O3	3.8
1940	NY-N	151	536	89	155	27	3	19	79	100	50	.289	.407	.457	137	32	31	107	6			-1	*O3	2.5
1941	NY-N	148	525	89	150	29	0	27	90	100	68	.286	.403	.495	149	39	37	115	5			-3	*O	2.8
1942	NY-N	152	549	118	162	21	0	30	93	109	61	.295	.415	.497	165	49	49	122	6			-3	*OM	4.5
1943	NY-N	125	380	65	89	12	2	18	47	95	44	.234	.391	.418	133	20	20	71	7			-1	*O/3M	1.6
1944	NY-N	120	399	91	115	16	4	26	82	90	47	.288	.423	.544	171	40	41	101	2			-6	*O/3M	2.7
1945	NY-N	135	451	73	139	23	0	21	79	71	41	.308	.411	.499	150	33	33	98	1			-5	*OM	2.2
1946	NY-N	31	68	2	5	1	0	1	4	8	15	.074	.171	.132	-13	-10	-10	2	0			-1	OM	-1.2
1947	NY-N	4	4	0	0	0	0	0	0	0	0	.000	.000	.000	-99	-1	-1	0	0			0	HM	0.0
Total	22	2730	9456	1859	2876	488	72	511	1860	1708	896	.304	.414	.533	155	767	773	2235	89			-32	*O3/2	60.8

■ ED OTT

Ott, Nathan Edward b: 7/11/51, Muncy, Pa. BL/TR, 5'10", 190 lbs. Deb: 6/10/74 C

YEAR	TM/L	G	AB	R	H	2B	3B	HR	RBI	BB	SO	AVG	OBP	SLG	PRO+	BR	/A	RC	SB	CS	SBR	FR	POS	TPR
1974	Pit-N	7	5	1	0	0	0	0	0	0	1	.000	.000	.000	-99	-1	-1	0	0	0	0	0	/O	0.0
1975	Pit-N	5	5	0	1	0	0	0	0	0	0	.200	.200	.200	11	-1	-1	0	0	0	0	0	/C	0.0
1976	Pit-N	27	39	2	12	2	0	0	5	3	5	.308	.357	.359	103	0	0	5	0	0	0	-1	/C	0.0
1977	Pit-N	104	311	40	82	14	3	7	38	32	41	.264	.336	.395	93	-2	-3	41	7	7	-2	-5	C	-1.1

YEAR	TM/L	G	AB	R	H	2B	3B	HR	RBI	BB	SO	AVG	OBP	SLG	PRO+	BR	/A	RC	SB	CS	SBR	FR	POS	TPR
1978	Pit-N	112	379	49	102	18	4	9	38	27	56	.269	.318	.409	97	-0	-2	49	4	1	1	-9	C/O	-0.8
1979	*Pit-N	117	403	49	110	20	2	7	51	26	62	.273	.317	.385	86	-6	-8	48	0	1	-1	-3	*C	-0.8
1980	Pit-N	120	392	35	102	14	0	8	41	33	47	.260	.318	.357	87	-6	-7	42	1	6	-3	-3	*C/O	-1.1
1981	Cal-A	75	258	20	56	8	1	2	22	17	42	.217	.268	.279	58	-14	-14	19	2	1	0	0	C	-1.0
Total	8	567	1792	196	465	76	10	33	195	138	254	.259	.314	.368	86	-30	-36	203	14	16	-5	-20	C/O	-4.8

■ BILLY OTT
Ott, William Joseph   b: 11/23/40, New York, N.Y.   BB/TR, 6'1", 180 lbs.   Deb: 9/04/62

YEAR	TM/L	G	AB	R	H	2B	3B	HR	RBI	BB	SO	AVG	OBP	SLG	PRO+	BR	/A	RC	SB	CS	SBR	FR	POS	TPR
1962	Chi-N	12	28	3	4	0	0	1	2	2	10	.143	.200	.250	19	-3	-3	1	0	0	0	0	/O	-0.3
1964	Chi-N	20	39	4	7	3	0	0	1	3	10	.179	.238	.256	38	-3	-3	2	0	1	-1	-1	O	-0.5
Total	2	32	67	7	11	3	0	1	3	5	20	.164	.222	.254	30	-6	-7	4	0	1	-1	-1	/O	-0.8

■ JOE OTTEN
Otten, Joseph G.   b: Murphysboro, Ill.   TR ,   Deb: 7/05/1895

YEAR	TM/L	G	AB	R	H	2B	3B	HR	RBI	BB	SO	AVG	OBP	SLG	PRO+	BR	/A	RC	SB	CS	SBR	FR	POS	TPR
1895	StL-N	26	87	8	21	0	0	0	8	5	8	.241	.283	.241	38	-8	-8	7	2			-4	C/O	-0.7

■ BILLY OTTERSON
Otterson, William John   b: 5/4/1862, Pittsburgh, Pa.   d: 9/21/40, Pittsburgh, Pa.   BR/TR, 5'7", 124 lbs.   Deb: 9/04/1887

YEAR	TM/L	G	AB	R	H	2B	3B	HR	RBI	BB	SO	AVG	OBP	SLG	PRO+	BR	/A	RC	SB	CS	SBR	FR	POS	TPR
1887	Bro-a	30	100	16	20	4	1	2	8			.200	.259	.320	62	-5	-5	11	8			1	S	-0.3

■ PHIL OUELLETTE
Ouellette, Philip Roland   b: 11/10/61, Salem, Ore.   BB/TR, 6', 190 lbs.   Deb: 9/10/86

YEAR	TM/L	G	AB	R	H	2B	3B	HR	RBI	BB	SO	AVG	OBP	SLG	PRO+	BR	/A	RC	SB	CS	SBR	FR	POS	TPR
1986	SF-N	10	23	1	4	0	0	0	3	1	4	.174	.269	.174	26	-2	-2	1	0	0	0	0	/C	-0.1

■ JOHNNY OULLIBER
Oulliber, John Andrew   b: 2/24/11, New Orleans, La.   d: 12/26/80, New Orleans, La.   BR/TR, 5'11", 165 lbs.   Deb: 7/25/33

YEAR	TM/L	G	AB	R	H	2B	3B	HR	RBI	BB	SO	AVG	OBP	SLG	PRO+	BR	/A	RC	SB	CS	SBR	FR	POS	TPR
1933	Cle-A	22	75	9	20	1	0	0	4	5		.267	.313	.280	55	-4	-5	7	0	0	0	-4	O	-0.8

■ CHINK OUTEN
Outen, William Austin   b: 6/17/05, Mt.Holly, N.C.   d: 9/11/61, Durham, N.C.   BL/TR, 6', 200 lbs.   Deb: 4/16/33

YEAR	TM/L	G	AB	R	H	2B	3B	HR	RBI	BB	SO	AVG	OBP	SLG	PRO+	BR	/A	RC	SB	CS	SBR	FR	POS	TPR
1933	Bro-N	93	153	20	38	10	4	4	17	20	15	.248	.335	.392	112	2	2	22	1			-13	C	-0.8

■ JIMMY OUTLAW
Outlaw, James Paulus   b: 1/20/13, Orme, Tenn.   BR/TR, 5'8", 165 lbs.   Deb: 4/20/37

YEAR	TM/L	G	AB	R	H	2B	3B	HR	RBI	BB	SO	AVG	OBP	SLG	PRO+	BR	/A	RC	SB	CS	SBR	FR	POS	TPR
1937	Cin-N	49	165	18	45	7	3	0	11	3	31	.273	.290	.352	77	-6	-5	17	2			4	3	0.0
1938	Cin-N	4	0	1	0	0	0	0	0	0	0	—	—	—	—	0	0	0	0			0	R	0.0
1939	Bos-N	65	133	15	35	2	0	0	5	10	14	.263	.315	.278	65	-7	-6	13	1			2	O/3	-0.3
1943	Det-A	20	67	8	18	1	0	1	6	8	4	.269	.347	.328	91	-0	-1	8	0	0	0	-1	O	-0.1
1944	Det-A	139	535	69	146	20	6	3	57	41	40	.273	.327	.350	88	-5	-8	60	7	8	-3	-3	*O	-1.9
1945	*Det-A	132	446	56	121	16	5	0	34	45	33	.271	.338	.330	88	-3	-6	52	6	7	-2	-3	*O3	-1.6
1946	Det-A	92	299	36	78	14	2	2	31	29	24	.261	.328	.341	82	-5	-7	33	5	4	-1	-6	O3	-1.3
1947	Det-A	70	127	20	29	7	1	0	15	21	14	.228	.338	.299	76	-3	-4	15	3	1	0	-2	O/3	-0.6
1948	Det-A	74	198	33	56	12	0	0	25	31	15	.283	.383	.343	91	-0	-1	27	0	1	-1	3	3O	0.0
1949	Det-A	5	4	1	1	0	0	0	0	0	1	.250	.250	.250	32	-0	0	0	0	0	0	0	H	0.0
Total	10	650	1974	257	529	79	17	6	184	188	176	.268	.333	.334	85	-30	-39	225	24	21		-6	O3	-5.8

■ MICKEY OWEN
Owen, Arnold Malcolm   b: 4/4/16, Nixa, Mo.   BR/TR, 5'10", 190 lbs.   Deb: 5/02/37   C

YEAR	TM/L	G	AB	R	H	2B	3B	HR	RBI	BB	SO	AVG	OBP	SLG	PRO+	BR	/A	RC	SB	CS	SBR	FR	POS	TPR
1937	StL-N	80	234	17	54	4	2	0	20	15	13	.231	.277	.265	47	-17	-17	17	1			-3	C	-1.7
1938	StL-N	122	397	45	106	25	2	4	36	32	14	.267	.325	.370	86	-5	-8	46	2			1	*C	-0.2
1939	StL-N	131	344	32	89	18	2	3	35	43	28	.259	.344	.349	82	-6	-8	42	6			5	*C	0.0
1940	StL-N	117	307	27	81	16	2	0	27	34	13	.264	.341	.329	81	-5	-7	35	4			3	*C	0.0
1941	*Bro-N	128	386	32	89	15	2	1	44	34	14	.231	.296	.288	62	-18	-20	33	1			6	*C	-0.1
1942	Bro-N	133	421	53	109	16	3	0	44	44	17	.259	.330	.311	87	-5	-6	43	10			4	*C	0.1
1943	Bro-N	106	365	31	95	11	2	0	54	25	15	.260	.309	.301	77	-11	-11	34	4			-5	*C/3S	-1.1
1944	Bro-N	130	461	43	126	20	3	1	42	36	17	.273	.326	.336	88	-8	-7	48	4			-10	*C/2	-1.0
1945	Bro-N	24	84	5	24	9	0	0	11	10	2	.286	.368	.393	113	2	2	11	0			-3	C	0.0
1949	Chi-N	62	198	15	54	9	3	2	18	12	13	.273	.318	.379	88	-4	-4	24	1			-1	C	-0.1
1950	Chi-N	86	259	22	63	11	0	2	21	13	16	.243	.282	.309	56	-17	-17	21	2			3	C	-1.0
1951	Chi-N	58	125	10	23	6	0	0	15	19	13	.184	.292	.232	42	-10	-10	9	1	0	0	8	C	0.0
1954	Bos-A	32	68	6	16	3	0	1	11	9	6	.235	.325	.324	70	-2	-3	7	0	1	-1	-2	C	-0.4
Total	13	1209	3649	338	929	163	21	14	378	326	181	.255	.318	.322	76	-106	-116	371	36	1		5	*C/32S	-5.5

■ DAVE OWEN
Owen, Dave   b: 4/25/58, Cleburne, Tex.   BB/TR, 6'2", 170 lbs.   Deb: 9/06/83

YEAR	TM/L	G	AB	R	H	2B	3B	HR	RBI	BB	SO	AVG	OBP	SLG	PRO+	BR	/A	RC	SB	CS	SBR	FR	POS	TPR
1983	Chi-N	16	22	1	2	0	1	0	2	2	7	.091	.167	.182	-3	-3	-3	1	1	0	0	4	S/3	0.2
1984	Chi-N	47	93	8	18	2	2	1	10	8	15	.194	.272	.290	53	-5	-6	8	1	2	-1	1	S/32	-0.2
1985	Chi-N	22	19	6	7	0	0	0	4	1	5	.368	.400	.368	105	0	0	3	1	1	-0	2	/S32	0.2
1988	KC-A	7	5	0	0	0	0	0	0	0	3	.000	.000	.000	-99	-1	-1	0	0	0	0	4	/S	0.3
Total	4	92	139	15	27	2	3	1	16	11	30	.194	.263	.273	47	-9	-11	11	3	3	-1	10	/S32	0.5

■ LARRY OWEN
Owen, Lawrence Thomas   b: 5/31/55, Cleveland, Ohio   BR/TR, 5'11", 185 lbs.   Deb: 8/14/81

YEAR	TM/L	G	AB	R	H	2B	3B	HR	RBI	BB	SO	AVG	OBP	SLG	PRO+	BR	/A	RC	SB	CS	SBR	FR	POS	TPR
1981	Atl-N	13	16	0	0	0	0	0	1	1	4	.000	.059	.000	-80	-4	-4	0	0	0	0	2	C	-0.1
1982	Atl-N	2	3	1	1	1	0	0	0	0	1	.333	.333	.667	167	0	0	1	0	0	0	-0	/C	0.0
1983	Atl-N	17	17	0	2	0	0	0	1	0	2	.118	.118	.118	-32	-3	-3	0	0	1	-1	1	C	-0.1
1985	Atl-N	26	71	7	17	3	0	2	12	8	17	.239	.316	.366	85	-1	-1	8	0	0	0	2	C	0.2
1987	KC-A	76	164	17	31	6	0	5	14	16	51	.189	.261	.317	51	-11	-12	13	0	0	0	19	C	1.2
1988	KC-A	37	81	5	17	1	0	1	3	9	23	.210	.304	.259	59	-4	-4	7	0	0	0	5	C	0.2
Total	6	171	352	30	68	11	0	8	30	34	98	.193	.268	.293	51	-23	-25	30	0	1	-1	29	C	1.4

■ MARV OWEN
Owen, Marvin James "Freck"   b: 3/22/06, Agnew, Cal.   BR/TR, 6'1", 175 lbs.   Deb: 4/16/31

YEAR	TM/L	G	AB	R	H	2B	3B	HR	RBI	BB	SO	AVG	OBP	SLG	PRO+	BR	/A	RC	SB	CS	SBR	FR	POS	TPR
1931	Det-A	105	377	35	84	11	6	3	39	29	38	.223	.282	.308	53	-25	-27	34	2	2	-1	1	S31/2	-2.1
1933	Det-A	138	550	77	144	24	9	2	65	44	29	.262	.321	.349	76	-18	-19	63	2	2	-1	-11	*3	-1.8
1934	*Det-A	154	565	79	179	34	9	8	96	59	37	.317	.385	.451	115	13	13	100	3	3	-1	-7	*3	0.4
1935	*Det-A	134	483	52	127	24	5	2	71	43	37	.263	.326	.346	76	-19	-16	56	1	4	-2	-10	*3	-2.5
1936	Det-A	154	583	72	172	20	4	9	105	53	41	.295	.361	.389	85	-13	-13	84	9	6	-1	-4	*3/1	-1.4
1937	Det-A	107	396	48	114	22	5	1	45	41	24	.288	.358	.376	83	-8	-10	54	3	4	-2	0	*3	-0.8
1938	Chi-A	141	577	84	162	23	6	6	55	45	31	.281	.337	.373	76	-20	-22	74	6	4	-1	0	*3	-1.6
1939	Chi-A	58	194	22	46	9	0	0	15	16	15	.237	.302	.284	49	-14	-15	17	4	5	-2	-2	3	-1.8
1940	Bos-A	20	57	4	12	0	0	0	6	8	4	.211	.308	.211	36	-5	-5	4	0	0	0	-2	/31	-0.2
Total	9	1011	3782	473	1040	167	44	31	497	338	283	.275	.339	.367	80	-110	-116	485	30	30	-9	-30	3/1S2	-11.8

■ SPIKE OWEN
Owen, Spike Dee   b: 4/19/61, Cleburne, Tex.   BB/TR, 5'9", 165 lbs.   Deb: 6/25/83

YEAR	TM/L	G	AB	R	H	2B	3B	HR	RBI	BB	SO	AVG	OBP	SLG	PRO+	BR	/A	RC	SB	CS	SBR	FR	POS	TPR
1983	Sea-A	80	306	36	60	11	3	2	21	24	44	.196	.259	.271	44	-22	-24	23	10	6	-1	0	S	-1.9
1984	Sea-A	152	530	67	130	18	8	3	43	46	63	.245	.309	.326	77	-17	-16	56	16	8	0	16	*S	1.2
1985	Sea-A	118	352	41	91	10	6	6	37	34	27	.259	.324	.372	89	-5	-5	44	11	5	0	27	*S	3.0
1986	Sea-A	112	402	46	99	22	6	0	35	34	42	.246	.307	.331	73	-15	-15	40	1	3	-2	34	*S	2.3
	*Bos-A	42	126	21	23	2	1	1	10	17	9	.183	.285	.238	44	-9	-10	10	3	1	-0	-2	S	-0.7
	Yr	154	528	67	122	24	7	1	45	51	51	.231	.301	.309	66	-24	-24	49	4	4	-1	32		1.6
1987	Bos-A	132	437	50	113	17	7	2	48	53	43	.259	.340	.343	80	-10	-12	52	11	8	-0	-14	*S	-1.9
1988	*Bos-A	89	257	40	64	14	1	5	18	27	27	.249	.325	.370	90	-2	-3	31	0	1	-1	-0	S/D	0.0
1989	Mon-N	142	437	52	102	17	4	6	41	39	34	.234	.295	.332	95	1	-0	53	3	2	-0	11	*S	2.0
1990	Mon-N	149	453	55	106	24	5	5	35	70	60	.234	.337	.342	88	-6	-6	55	8	6	-1	-13	*S	-0.6
Total	8	1016	3300	408	788	135	41	30	288	381	359	.239	.320	.332	79	-86	-90	363	63	40	-5	59	S/D	3.4

YEAR	TM/L	G	AB	R	H	2B	3B	HR	RBI	BB	SO	AVG	OBP	SLG	PRO+	BR	/A	RC	SB	CS	SBR	FR	POS	TPR

■ FRANK OWENS   Owens, Frank Walter "Yip"   b: 1/26/1886, Toronto, Ont., Can.   d: 7/2/58, Minneapolis, Minn.   BR/TR, 6', 170 lbs.   Deb: 9/11/05

1905	Bos-A	1	2	0	0	0	0	0	0	0		.000	.000	.000	-99	-0	-0	0	0			0	/C	0.0
1909	Chi-A	64	174	12	35	4	1	0	17	8		.201	.245	.236	54	-10	-9	11	3			-5	C	-1.0
1914	Bro-F	58	184	15	51	7	3	2	20	9	16	.277	.314	.380	99	-1	-1	23	2			-31	C	-3.1
1915	Bal-F	99	334	32	84	14	7	3	28	17	34	.251	.290	.362	90	-4	-6	38	4			-28	C	-3.3
Total	4	222	694	59	170	25	11	5	65	34	50	.245	.284	.334	84	-15	-16	73	9			-64	C	-7.4

■ JACK OWENS   Owens, Furman Lee   b: 5/6/08, Converse, S.C.   d: 11/14/58, Greenville, S.C.   BR/TR, 6'1", 186 lbs.   Deb: 9/21/35

| 1935 | Phi-A | 2 | 8 | 0 | 2 | 0 | 0 | 0 | 1 | 0 | 1 | .250 | .250 | .250 | 30 | -1 | -1 | 0 | 0 | 0 | 0 | -0 | /C | 0.0 |

■ RED OWENS   Owens, Thomas Llewellyn   b: 11/1/1874, Pottsville, Pa.   d: 8/20/52, Harrisburg, Pa.   BR/TR,   Deb: 7/28/1899

1899	Phi-N	8	21	0	1	0	0	0	1	2		.048	.130	.048	-51	-4	-4	0	0			-0	/2	-0.3
1905	Bro-N	43	168	14	36	6	2	1	20	6		.214	.241	.292	65	-8	-7	13	1			4	2	0.0
Total	2	51	189	14	37	6	2	1	21	8		.196	.228	.265	50	-13	-11	13	1			3	/2	-0.3

■ HENRY OXLEY   Oxley, Henry Havelock   b: 1/4/1858, Covehead, P.E.I., Canada.   d: 10/12/45, Somerville, Mass.   Deb: 7/30/1884

| 1884 | NY-N | 3 | 4 | 0 | 0 | 0 | 0 | 0 | 0 | 1 | 2 | .000 | .200 | .000 | -31 | -1 | -1 | 0 | | | | 2 | /C | 0.1 |
| | NY-a | 1 | 3 | 0 | 0 | 0 | 0 | 0 | 0 | 0 | | .000 | .000 | .000 | -99 | -1 | -1 | 0 | | | | 0 | /C | 0.0 |

■ ANDY OYLER   Oyler, Andrew Paul "Pepper"   b: 5/5/1880, Newville, Pa.   d: 10/24/70, E.Pennsboro Twp., Cumberland County, Pa.   BR/TR, 5'6.5", 138 lbs.   Deb: 5/08/02

| 1902 | Bal-A | 27 | 77 | 9 | 17 | 1 | 0 | 1 | 6 | 8 | | .221 | .310 | .273 | 61 | -3 | -4 | 8 | 3 | | | -8 | 3/OS2 | -1.1 |

■ RAY OYLER   Oyler, Raymond Francis   b: 8/4/38, Indianapolis, Ind.   d: 1/26/81, Seattle, Wash.   BR/TR, 5'11", 165 lbs.   Deb: 4/18/65

1965	Det-A	82	194	22	36	6	0	5	13	21	61	.186	.265	.294	58	-11	-11	14	1	0	0	6	S2/13	-0.1
1966	Det-A	71	210	16	36	8	3	1	9	23	62	.171	.263	.252	48	-14	-14	14	0	0	0	15	S	0.4
1967	Det-A	148	367	33	76	14	2	1	29	37	91	.207	.283	.264	61	-16	-18	28	0	2	-1	15	*S	0.6
1968	*Det-A	111	215	13	29	6	1	1	12	20	59	.135	.215	.186	22	-20	-21	9	1	2	-1	9	*S	-0.4
1969	Sea-A	106	255	24	42	5	0	7	22	31	80	.165	.260	.267	48	-18	-18	17	1	2	-1	9	*S	-0.4
1970	Cal-A	24	24	2	2	0	0	0	1	3	6	.083	.185	.083	-24	-4	-4	1	0	0	0	-1	S/3	-0.3
Total	6	542	1265	110	221	39	6	15	86	135	359	.175	.259	.251	48	-83	-85	83	2	6	-3	52	S/231	-0.2

■ CHARLIE PABOR   Pabor, Charles Henry   b: 9/24/1846, New York, N.Y.   d: 4/22/13, New Haven, Conn.   TL, 5'8", 155 lbs.   Deb: 5/04/1871   M

1871	Cle-n	29	142	24	42	2	4	0	18	1	3	.296	.301	.366	96	-2	0	16	1				*O/PM	0.1
1872	Cle-n	21	90	12	19	0	0	0		0	0	.211	.211	.211	32	-7	-6	4					O/P	-0.2
1873	Atl-n	55	226	36	80	7	4	0			6	.354	.371	.420	148	9	14	36					*O	1.1
1874	Phi-n	17	77	11	18	0	0	1			0	.234	.234	.273	59	-3	-4	5					/O	-0.2
1875	Atl-n	42	153	15	36	1	3	0			1	.235	.240	.281	91	-3	0	11					O/PM	0.1
	NH-n	6	23	4	8	0	2	0			0	.348	.348	.522	230	2	3	4					OM	0.2
	Yr	48	176	19	44	1	5	0			1	.250	.254	.313	109	-1	3	14						0.3
Total	5 n	170	711	102	203	10	13	1			8	.286	.293	.340	103	-4	7	76					O/P	1.1

■ ED PABST   Pabst, Edward D. A.   b: 1868, St.Louis, Mo.   d: 6/19/40, St.Louis, Mo.   5'11", 170 lbs.   Deb: 9/26/1890

1890	Phi-a	8	25	7	10	2	0	0		5		.400	.500	.480	198	3	3	8	3			4	/O	0.6
	StL-a	4	14	1	2	0	1	0		0		.143	.143	.286	24	-1	-2	1	0			1	/O	0.0
	Yr	12	39	8	12	2	1	0		5		.308	.386	.410	134	2	2	8	3			5		0.6

■ JIM PACIOREK   Paciorek, James Joseph   b: 6/7/60, Detroit, Mich.   BB/TR, 6'3", 203 lbs.   Deb: 4/09/87

| 1987 | Mil-A | 48 | 101 | 16 | 23 | 5 | 0 | 2 | 10 | 12 | 20 | .228 | .310 | .337 | 69 | -4 | -4 | 11 | 1 | 0 | 0 | -3 | 13/OD | -0.8 |

■ JOHN PACIOREK   Paciorek, John Francis   b: 2/11/45, Detroit, Mich.   BR/TR, 6'2", 200 lbs.   Deb: 9/29/63

| 1963 | Hou-N | 1 | 3 | 4 | 3 | 0 | 0 | 0 | 3 | 2 | 0 | 1.000 | 1.000 | 1.000 | 509 | 2 | 2 | 4 | 0 | 0 | 0 | 0 | /O | 0.2 |

■ TOM PACIOREK   Paciorek, Thomas Marian   b: 11/2/46, Detroit, Mich.   BR/TR, 6'4", 215 lbs.   Deb: 9/12/70

1970	LA-N	8	9	2	2	1	0	0	0	0	3	.222	.300	.333	73	-0	-0	1	0	0	0	-0	/O	0.0
1971	LA-N	2	2	0	1	0	0	0	1	0	0	.500	.500	.500	196	0	0	1	0	0	0	0	/O	0.0
1972	LA-N	11	47	4	12	4	0	1	6	1	7	.255	.271	.404	92	-1	-1	5	1	0	0	1	/1O	0.0
1973	LA-N	96	195	26	51	8	0	5	18	11	35	.262	.304	.379	92	-3	-2	20	3	3	-1	-1	O/1	-0.8
1974	*LA-N	85	175	23	42	8	6	1	24	10	32	.240	.285	.371	86	-5	-4	17	1	3	-2	-3	O/1	-1.1
1975	LA-N	62	145	14	28	8	0	1	5	11	29	.193	.250	.269	46	-11	-10	9	4	3	-1	-3	O	-1.6
1976	Atl-N	111	324	39	94	10	4	4	36	19	57	.290	.335	.383	97	1	-1	40	2	3	-1	-8	O1/3	-1.4
1977	Atl-N	72	155	20	37	8	0	3	15	6	46	.239	.267	.348	57	-8	-11	15	1	0	0	-1	1/O3	-1.2
1978	Atl-N	5	9	2	3	0	0	0	0	0	1	.333	.333	.333	78	-0	-0	1	0	0	0	-0	/1	0.0
	Sea-A	70	251	32	75	20	3	4	30	15	39	.299	.338	.450	121	6	6	36	2	2	-1	-5	OD/1	-0.1
1979	Sea-A	103	310	38	89	23	4	6	42	28	62	.287	.356	.445	113	6	6	49	6	4	-1	-7	O1	-0.4
1980	Sea-A	126	418	44	114	19	1	15	59	17	67	.273	.303	.431	98	-2	-3	50	3	2	-0	2	O1D	-0.4
1981	Sea-A	104	405	50	132	28	2	14	66	35	50	.326	.385	.509	150	28	26	76	13	10	-2	7	*O	3.0
1982	Chi-A	104	382	49	119	27	4	11	55	24	53	.312	.366	.490	133	17	17	68	3	3	-1	1	*1/O	1.4
1983	*Chi-A	115	420	65	129	32	3	9	63	25	58	.307	.350	.462	117	10	10	67	6	1	1	-7	1O/D	0.7
1984	Chi-A	111	363	35	93	21	2	4	29	25	69	.256	.311	.358	81	-8	-10	42	6	0	2	-15	1O	-2.8
1985	Chi-A	46	122	14	30	2	0	0	9	8	22	.246	.298	.262	53	-7	-8	10	2	0	1	0	OD/1	-0.7
	NY-A	46	116	14	33	3	1	1	11	6	14	.284	.325	.353	92	-2	-1	13	1	0	0	-3	O/1	-0.4
1986	Tex-A	88	213	17	61	7	0	4	22	3	41	.286	.306	.376	82	-5	-6	22	1	3	-2	2	O13/SD	-0.6
1987	Tex-A	27	60	6	17	3	0	3	12	1	19	.283	.306	.483	105	0	0	7	0	1	-1	1	1O/D	0.0
Total	18	1392	4121	494	1162	232	30	86	503	245	704	.282	.328	.415	102	17	7	548	55	38	-6	-38	O1/D3S	-7.1

■ FRANKIE PACK   Pack, Frank   b: 4/10/28, Morristown, Tenn.   BL/TR, 6', 190 lbs.   Deb: 6/05/49

| 1949 | StL-A | 1 | 1 | 0 | 0 | 0 | 0 | 0 | 0 | 0 | 1 | .000 | .000 | .000 | -96 | -0 | -0 | 0 | 0 | 0 | 0 | 0 | H | 0.0 |

■ DICK PADDEN   Padden, Richard Joseph "Brains"   b: 9/17/1870, Martins Ferry, O.   d: 10/31/22, Martins Ferry, O.   BR/TR, 5'10", 165 lbs.   Deb: 7/15/1896

1896	Pit-N	61	219	33	53	4	8	2	24	14	9	.242	.294	.361	77	-9	-7	26	8			-12	2	-1.4
1897	Pit-N	134	517	84	146	16	10	2	58	38		.282	.349	.364	94	-6	-3	74	18			2	*2	0.8
1898	Pit-N	128	463	61	119	7	6	2	43	35		.257	.328	.311	88	-7	-6	52	11			-3	/2	-0.2
1899	Was-N	134	451	66	125	20	7	2	61	24		.277	.335	.366	96	-3	-3	66	27			9	S2	1.3
1901	StL-N	123	489	77	125	17	7	2	62	31		.256	.307	.331	91	-3	-5	60	26			-0	*2/S	0.4
1902	StL-A	117	413	54	109	26	3	1	40	30		.264	.333	.349	92	-4	-3	54	11			18	*2	1.8
1903	StL-A	29	94	7	19	3	0	0	6	9		.202	.272	.234	56	-5	-5	8	5			6	2	0.2
1904	StL-A	132	453	42	108	19	4	0	36	40		.238	.300	.298	98	-3	-0	50	23			-9	*2	-0.9
1905	StL-A	16	58	5	10	1	1	0	4	3		.172	.213	.224	42	-4	-4	3	3			0	2	0.2
Total	9	874	3157	423	814	113	46	11	334	224	9	.258	.320	.333	90	-50	-35	393	132			11	2/S	1.7

■ TOM PADDEN   Padden, Thomas Francis   b: 10/6/08, Manchester, N.H.   d: 6/10/73, Manchester, N.H.   BR/TR, 5'11.5", 170 lbs.   Deb: 5/29/32

1932	Pit-N	47	118	13	31	6	1	0	10	9	7	.263	.315	.331	75	-4	-4	13	0			-1	C	-0.2
1933	Pit-N	30	90	5	19	2	0	0	8	2	6	.211	.237	.233	35	-8	-8	5	0			6	C	0.0
1934	Pit-N	82	237	27	76	12	2	0	22	30	23	.321	.399	.388	109	5	5	37	3			-5	C	0.2
1935	Pit-N	97	302	35	82	9	1	1	30	48	26	.272	.371	.318	84	-3	-5	39	1			14	C	0.9

YEAR	TM/L	G	AB	R	H	2B	3B	HR	RBI	BB	SO	AVG	OBP	SLG	PRO+	BR	/A	RC	SB	CS	SBR	FR	POS	TPR
1936	Pit-N	88	281	22	70	9	2	1	31	22	41	.249	.304	.306	63	-14	-15	27	0			2	C	-0.9
1937	Pit-N	35	98	14	28	2	0	0	8	13	11	.286	.369	.306	85	-1	-1	12	1			7	C	0.7
1943	Phi-N	17	41	5	12	0	0	0	1	2	6	.293	.341	.293	87	-1	-1	4	0			4	C	0.4
	Was-A	3	3	1	0	0	0	0	0	0	1	.000	.250	.000	-25	-0	-0	0	0	0	0	0	/C	0.0
Total	7	399	1170	122	318	40	6	2	110	127	121	.272	.345	.321	80	-26	-28	136	5	0		26	C	1.1

■ DEL PADDOCK

Paddock, Delmar Harold   b: 6/8/1887, Volga, S.Dak.   d: 2/6/52, Remer, Minn   BL/TR, 5'9", 165 lbs.   Deb: 4/14/12

YEAR	TM/L	G	AB	R	H	2B	3B	HR	RBI	BB	SO	AVG	OBP	SLG	PRO+	BR	/A	RC	SB	CS	SBR	FR	POS	TPR
1912	Chi-A	1	1	0	0	0	0	0	0	0	0	.000	.000	.000	-99	-0	-0	0	0			0	H	0.0
	NY-A	46	156	26	45	5	3	1	14	23		.288	.393	.378	114	5	4	27	9			-7	3/2O	-0.3
	Yr	47	157	26	45	5	3	1	14	23		.287	.391	.376	113	5	4	26	9			-7		-0.3

■ DON PADGETT

Padgett, Don Wilson   b: 12/5/11, Caroleen, N.C.   d: 12/9/80, High Point, N.C.   BL/TR, 6', 190 lbs.   Deb: 4/23/37

YEAR	TM/L	G	AB	R	H	2B	3B	HR	RBI	BB	SO	AVG	OBP	SLG	PRO+	BR	/A	RC	SB	CS	SBR	FR	POS	TPR
1937	StL-N	123	446	62	140	22	6	10	74	30	43	.314	.357	.457	117	11	10	75	4			1	*O	0.6
1938	StL-N	110	388	59	105	26	5	8	65	18	28	.271	.303	.425	93	-3	-5	48	0			3	O1/C	-0.4
1939	StL-N	92	233	38	93	15	3	5	53	18	11	.399	.444	.554	157	22	20	54	1			-3	C/1	1.8
1940	StL-N	93	240	24	58	15	1	6	41	26	14	.242	.321	.387	89	-2	-4	30	1			-8	C/1	-0.8
1941	StL-N	107	324	39	80	18	0	5	44	21	16	.247	.293	.349	75	-9	-12	32	0			-8	OC/1	-2.1
1946	Bro-N	19	30	2	5	1	0	1	9	4	4	.167	.265	.300	59	-2	-2	2	0			-1	C	-0.2
	Bos-N	44	98	6	25	3	0	2	21	5	7	.255	.291	.347	80	-3	-3	10	0			-6	C	-0.7
	Yr	63	128	8	30	4	0	3	30	9	11	.234	.285	.336	75	-4	-5	13	0			-7		-0.9
1947	Phi-N	75	158	14	50	8	1	0	24	16	5	.316	.383	.380	107	1	2	22	0			-7	C	-0.3
1948	Phi-N	36	74	3	17	3	0	0	7	3	2	.230	.260	.270	44	-6	-6	5	0			-4	C	-0.7
Total	8	699	1991	247	573	111	16	37	338	141	130	.288	.336	.415	101	10	1	279	6			-32	CO/1	-2.8

■ ERNIE PADGETT

Padgett, Ernest Kitchen "Red"   b: 3/1/1899, Philadelphia, Pa.   d: 4/15/57, E.Orange, N.J.   BR/TR, 5'8", 155 lbs.   Deb: 10/03/23

YEAR	TM/L	G	AB	R	H	2B	3B	HR	RBI	BB	SO	AVG	OBP	SLG	PRO+	BR	/A	RC	SB	CS	SBR	FR	POS	TPR
1923	Bos-N	4	11	3	2	0	0	0	0	2	0	.182	.308	.182	33	-1	-1	1	0	0	0	2	/S2	0.1
1924	Bos-N	138	502	42	128	25	9	1	46	37	56	.255	.310	.347	79	-17	-15	53	4	9	-4	-10	*32	-2.1
1925	Bos-N	86	256	31	78	9	7	0	29	14	14	.305	.341	.395	96	-5	-2	33	3	5	-2	-20	2S/3	-2.0
1926	Cle-A	36	62	7	13	0	1	0	6	8	3	.210	.300	.242	42	-5	-5	5	1	0	0	2	3/S	0.0
1927	Cle-A	7	7	1	2	0	0	0	0	0	2	.286	.286	.286	48	-1	-1	1	0	0	0	0	/2	0.0
Total	5	271	838	84	223	34	17	1	81	61	75	.266	.318	.351	80	-29	-23	92	8	14	-6	-26	3/2S	-4.0

■ DENNIS PAEPKE

Paepke, Dennis Ray   b: 4/17/45, Long Beach, Cal.   BR/TR, 6', 202 lbs.   Deb: 6/02/69

YEAR	TM/L	G	AB	R	H	2B	3B	HR	RBI	BB	SO	AVG	OBP	SLG	PRO+	BR	/A	RC	SB	CS	SBR	FR	POS	TPR
1969	KC-A	12	27	2	3	1	0	0	2	3		.111	.172	.148	-10	-4	-4	1	0	0	0	3	/C	0.0
1971	KC-A	60	152	11	31	6	0	2	14	8	29	.204	.244	.283	49	-10	-10	9	0	0	0	-2	CO	-1.1
1972	KC-A	2	6	0	0	0	0	0	0	1	2	.000	.143	.000	-55	-1	-1	0	0	0	0	1	/C	0.0
1974	KC-A	6	12	0	2	0	0	0	0	1	2	.167	.231	.167	15	-1	-1	0	0	1	-1	-0	/CO	-0.1
Total	4	80	197	13	36	7	0	2	14	12	36	.183	.230	.249	36	-17	-17	10	0	1	-1	2	/CO	-1.2

■ ANDY PAFKO

Pafko, Andrew "Handy Andy" or "Pruschka"   b: 2/25/21, Boyceville, Wis.   BR/TR, 6', 190 lbs.   Deb: 9/24/43   C

YEAR	TM/L	G	AB	R	H	2B	3B	HR	RBI	BB	SO	AVG	OBP	SLG	PRO+	BR	/A	RC	SB	CS	SBR	FR	POS	TPR
1943	Chi-N	13	58	7	22	3	0	0	10	2	5	.379	.400	.431	142	3	3	9	1			-2	O	0.0
1944	Chi-N	128	469	47	126	16	2	6	62	28	23	.269	.315	.350	87	-9	-8	50	2			13	*O	-0.4
1945	*Chi-N	144	534	64	159	24	12	12	110	45	36	.298	.361	.455	129	17	19	92	5			-1	*O	1.1
1946	Chi-N	65	234	18	66	6	4	3	39	27	15	.282	.366	.380	114	4	5	33	4			10	O	1.5
1947	Chi-N	129	513	68	155	25	7	13	66	31	39	.302	.346	.454	115	6	9	75	4			4	*O	0.8
1948	Chi-N	142	548	82	171	30	2	26	101	50	50	.312	.375	.516	145	28	31	105	3			13	*3	4.0
1949	Chi-N	144	519	79	146	29	2	18	69	63	33	.281	.369	.449	121	14	16	86	4			-11	O3	0.0
1950	Chi-N	146	514	95	156	24	8	36	92	69	32	.304	.397	.591	158	41	42	124	4			-6	*O	3.0
1951	Chi-N	49	178	26	47	5	3	12	35	17	10	.264	.342	.528	128	7	6	31	1	1	-0	4	O	0.9
	Bro-N	84	277	42	69	11	0	18	58	35	27	.249	.350	.484	120	8	7	47	1	4	-2	-0	O	0.3
	Yr	133	455	68	116	16	3	30	93	52	37	.255	.347	.501	123	15	14	78	2	5	-2	4		1.2
1952	*Bro-N	150	551	76	158	17	5	19	85	64	48	.287	.366	.439	121	17	16	91	4	3	-1	-3	*O3	1.0
1953	Mil-N	140	516	70	153	23	4	17	72	37	33	.297	.347	.455	114	5	7	81	2	1	0	-9	*O	-0.4
1954	Mil-N	138	510	61	146	22	4	14	69	37	36	.286	.339	.427	105	-2	2	72	1	2	-1	-5	*O	-0.7
1955	Mil-N	86	252	29	67	3	5	5	34	7	23	.266	.297	.377	81	-9	-7	26	1	2	-1	-5	O3	-1.3
1956	Mil-N	45	93	15	24	5	0	2	9	10	13	.258	.330	.376	95	-1	-1	12	0	0	0	-2	O	-0.3
1957	*Mil-N	83	220	31	61	6	1	8	27	10	22	.277	.312	.423	102	-2	-0	28	1	0	0	-4	O	-0.5
1958	*Mil-N	95	164	17	39	7	1	3	23	15	17	.238	.309	.348	80	-6	-4	18	0	0	0	2	O	-0.4
1959	Mil-N	71	142	17	31	8	2	1	15	14	15	.218	.293	.324	70	-7	-6	13	0	0	0	1	O	-0.5
Total	17	1852	6292	844	1796	264	62	213	976	561	477	.285	.351	.449	118	115	140	992	38	13		-0	*O3	8.1

■ JOSE PAGAN

Pagan, Jose Antonio (Rodriguez)   b: 5/5/35, Barceloneta, P.R.   BR/TR, 5'9", 160 lbs.   Deb: 8/04/59   C

YEAR	TM/L	G	AB	R	H	2B	3B	HR	RBI	BB	SO	AVG	OBP	SLG	PRO+	BR	/A	RC	SB	CS	SBR	FR	POS	TPR
1959	SF-N	31	46	7	8	1	0	0	1	2	8	.174	.196	.196	9	-6	-6	2	1	0	0	3	3/S2	-0.1
1960	SF-N	18	49	8	14	2	2	0	2	1	6	.286	.300	.408	97	-1	-1	5	2	2	-1	-8	S/3	-0.8
1961	SF-N	134	434	38	110	15	2	5	46	31	45	.253	.306	.332	72	-19	-17	42	8	5	-1	-17	*S/O	-2.1
1962	*SF-N	164	580	73	150	25	6	7	57	47	77	.259	.315	.359	82	-16	-15	63	13	9	-2	-25	*S	-2.5
1963	SF-N	148	483	46	113	12	1	6	39	26	70	.234	.279	.300	67	-21	-20	40	10	7	-1	-18	*S/2O	-2.7
1964	SF-N	134	367	33	82	10	1	1	28	35	66	.223	.293	.264	57	-19	-20	29	5	4	-1	-17	*S/O	-3.0
1965	SF-N	26	83	10	17	4	0	0	5	8		.205	.275	.253	48	-5	-6	6	1	0	0	-5	S	-0.7
	Pit-N	42	38	6	9	1	0	0	1	1	7	.237	.275	.263	52	-2	-2	3	1	0	0	8	3/S	0.6
	Yr	68	121	16	26	5	0	0	6	9	16	.215	.275	.256	50	-8	-8	8	2	0	1	3		-0.1
1966	Pit-N	109	368	44	97	15	6	6	54	13	38	.264	.296	.370	84	-8	-9	38	0	2	-1	3	3S/2O	-0.6
1967	Pit-N	81	211	17	61	6	2	1	19	10	28	.289	.330	.351	95	-1	-1	24	1	1	-0	10	30S/2C	0.8
1968	Pit-N	80	163	24	36	7	1	4	21	11	32	.221	.282	.350	90	-2	-2	15	2	3	-1	-2	30/S21	-0.5
1969	Pit-N	108	274	29	78	11	4	9	42	17	46	.285	.329	.453	119	5	6	41	1	0	0	-3	30/2	0.2
1970	*Pit-N	95	230	21	61	14	1	7	29	20	24	.265	.324	.426	101	-1	-0	31	1	1	-0	-1	3/012	-0.3
1971	*Pit-N	57	158	16	38	1	0	5	15	16	25	.241	.314	.342	86	-3	-3	17	0	0	0	-2	3/O1	-0.4
1972	Pit-N	53	127	11	32	9	0	3	8	5	17	.252	.286	.394	93	-2	-2	14	0	0	0	-8	3/O	-1.0
1973	Phi-N	46	78	4	16	5	0	0	5	1	15	.205	.215	.269	33	-7	-7	3	0	1	-1	-1	3/1O2	-0.9
Total	15	1326	3689	387	922	138	26	52	372	244	510	.250	.300	.344	79	-109	-105	373	46	35	-7	-83	S3/O21C	-14.0

■ MIKE PAGE

Page, Michael Randy   b: 7/12/40, Woodruff, S.C.   BL/TR, 6'2.5", 210 lbs.   Deb: 6/30/68

YEAR	TM/L	G	AB	R	H	2B	3B	HR	RBI	BB	SO	AVG	OBP	SLG	PRO+	BR	/A	RC	SB	CS	SBR	FR	POS	TPR
1968	Atl-N	20	28	1	5	0	0	0	1	1	9	.179	.207	.179	16	-3	-3	1	0	0	0	-1	/O	-0.3

■ MITCHELL PAGE

Page, Mitchell Otis   b: 10/15/51, Los Angeles, Cal.   BL/TR, 6'2", 205 lbs.   Deb: 4/09/77

YEAR	TM/L	G	AB	R	H	2B	3B	HR	RBI	BB	SO	AVG	OBP	SLG	PRO+	BR	/A	RC	SB	CS	SBR	FR	POS	TPR
1977	Oak-A	145	501	85	154	28	8	21	75	78	95	.307	.407	.521	153	37	38	117	42	5	10	3	*O/D	4.5
1978	Oak-A	147	516	62	147	25	7	17	70	53	95	.285	.356	.459	135	19	22	82	23	19	-5	-5	*OD	1.0
1979	Oak-A	133	478	51	118	11	2	9	42	52	93	.247	.325	.335	83	-14	-10	51	17	16	-5	0	*D/O	-1.4
1980	Oak-A	110	348	58	85	10	4	17	51	35	87	.244	.315	.443	113	2	5	47	14	7	0	0	*D	0.5
1981	Oak-A	34	92	9	13	1	0	4	13	7	29	.141	.202	.283	40	-8	-7	5	2	1	0	0	D	-0.6
1982	Oak-A	31	78	14	20	5	0	4	7	7	24	.256	.333	.474	124	2	2	10	3	4	-2	0	D	0.1
1983	Oak-A	57	79	16	19	3	0	0	8	12	26	.241	.341	.278	77	-2	-2	8	3	3	-1	2	DO	0.1
1984	Pit-N	16	12	2	4	1	0	0	0	1	5	.333	.467	.417	150	1	1	2	0	0	0	0	H	0.1
Total	8	673	2104	297	560	84	21	72	259	245	449	.266	.348	.429	118	37	49	322	104	55	-2	0	DO	4.2

YEAR	TM/L	G	AB	R	H	2B	3B	HR	RBI	BB	SO	AVG	OBP	SLG	PRO+	BR	/A	RC	SB	CS	SBR	FR	POS	TPR

■ KARL PAGEL   Pagel, Karl Douglas   b: 3/29/55, Madison, Wis.   BL/TL, 6'2", 188 lbs.   Deb: 9/21/78

YEAR	TM/L	G	AB	R	H	2B	3B	HR	RBI	BB	SO	AVG	OBP	SLG	PRO+	BR	/A	RC	SB	CS	SBR	FR	POS	TPR
1978	Chi-N	2	2	0	0	0	0	0	0	0	2	.000	.000	.000	-89	-1	-1	0	0	0	0	0	H	0.0
1979	Chi-N	1	1	0	0	0	0	0	0	0	1	.000	.000	.000	-91	-0	-0	0	0	0	0	0	/H	0.0
1981	Cle-A	14	15	3	4	0	2	1	4	4	1	.267	.421	.733	230	3	3	5	0	0	0	2	/1D	0.4
1982	Cle-A	23	18	3	3	0	0	0	2	7	11	.167	.400	.167	63	-0	-0	2	0	0	0	0	1/D	0.0
1983	Cle-A	8	20	1	6	0	0	0	1	0	5	.300	.300	.300	63	-1	-1	2	0	0	0	-0	/OD	0.0
Total	5	48	56	7	13	0	2	1	7	11	20	.232	.358	.357	99	0	0	9	0	0	0	2	/1DO	0.4

■ JIM PAGLIARONI   Pagliaroni, James Vincent "Pag"   b: 12/8/37, Dearborn, Mich.   BR/TR, 6'4", 210 lbs.   Deb: 8/13/55

YEAR	TM/L	G	AB	R	H	2B	3B	HR	RBI	BB	SO	AVG	OBP	SLG	PRO+	BR	/A	RC	SB	CS	SBR	FR	POS	TPR
1955	Bos-A	1	0	0	0	0	0	0	1	0	0	—	—	—	—	0	-0	0	0	0	0	0	/C	0.0
1960	Bos-A	28	62	7	19	5	2	2	9	13	11	.306	.434	.548	158	6	6	16	0	0	0	-3	C	0.4
1961	Bos-A	120	376	50	91	17	0	16	58	55	74	.242	.345	.415	100	1	0	56	1	1	-0	-4	*C	-0.4
1962	Bos-A	90	260	39	67	14	0	11	37	36	55	.258	.359	.438	110	5	4	43	2	1	0	-3	C	0.5
1963	Pit-N	92	252	27	58	5	0	11	26	36	57	.230	.331	.381	104	2	2	31	0	0	0	4	C	0.9
1964	Pit-N	97	302	33	89	12	3	10	36	41	56	.295	.383	.454	135	15	15	52	1	0	0	0	C	1.9
1965	Pit-N	134	403	42	108	15	0	17	65	41	84	.268	.340	.432	115	8	8	57	0	0	0	-6	*C	0.8
1966	Pit-N	123	374	37	88	20	0	11	49	50	71	.235	.332	.377	96	-1	-1	47	0	5	-3	-16	*C	-1.7
1967	Pit-N	44	100	4	20	1	1	0	9	16	26	.200	.316	.230	59	-5	-5	7	0	0	0	-0	C	-0.2
1968	Oak-A	66	199	19	49	4	0	6	20	24	42	.246	.333	.357	115	3	4	25	0	0	0	-8	C	-0.1
1969	Oak-A	14	27	1	4	1	0	1	2	5	2	.148	.303	.296	71	-1	-1	3	0	0	0	2	/C	0.1
	Sea-A	40	110	10	29	4	1	5	14	13	16	.264	.341	.455	123	3	3	18	0	0	0	-5	C/1O	0.0
	Yr	54	137	11	33	5	1	6	16	18	18	.241	.333	.423	113	2	2	21	0	0	0	-4		0.1
Total	11	849	2465	269	622	98	7	90	326	330	494	.252	.346	.407	109	37	35	355	4	7	-3	-39	C/1O	2.2

■ MIKE PAGLIARULO   Pagliarulo, Michael Timothy   b: 3/15/60, Medford, Mass.   BL/TR, 6'1", 205 lbs.   Deb: 7/07/84

YEAR	TM/L	G	AB	R	H	2B	3B	HR	RBI	BB	SO	AVG	OBP	SLG	PRO+	BR	/A	RC	SB	CS	SBR	FR	POS	TPR
1984	NY-A	67	201	24	48	15	3	7	34	15	46	.239	.292	.448	105	-0	1	25	0	0	0	6	3	0.7
1985	NY-A	138	380	55	91	16	2	19	62	45	86	.239	.326	.442	111	4	5	56	0	0	0	-17	*3	-1.6
1986	NY-A	149	504	71	120	24	3	28	71	54	120	.238	.317	.464	111	5	6	74	4	1	1	6	*3/S	1.0
1987	NY-A	150	522	76	122	26	3	32	87	53	111	.234	.307	.479	105	1	2	75	1	3	-2	4	*3/1	0.3
1988	NY-A	125	444	46	96	20	1	15	67	37	104	.216	.280	.367	80	-13	-13	46	1	0	0	-0	*3	-1.2
1989	NY-A	74	223	19	44	10	0	4	16	19	43	.197	.266	.296	59	-12	-12	18	1	1	-0	-4	3/D	-1.6
	SD-N	50	148	12	29	7	0	3	14	18	39	.196	.287	.304	69	-6	-6	14	2	0	1	0	3	-0.5
1990	SD-N	128	398	29	101	23	2	7	38	39	66	.254	.325	.374	90	-4	-5	47	1	3	-2	1	*3	-0.1
Total	7	881	2820	332	651	141	14	115	389	280	615	.231	.304	.413	96	-26	-22	356	10	8	-2	-4	3/SD1	-3.0

■ TOM PAGNOZZI   Pagnozzi, Thomas Alan   b: 7/30/62, Tucson, Ariz.   BR/TR, 6', 190 lbs.   Deb: 4/12/87

YEAR	TM/L	G	AB	R	H	2B	3B	HR	RBI	BB	SO	AVG	OBP	SLG	PRO+	BR	/A	RC	SB	CS	SBR	FR	POS	TPR
1987	*StL-N	27	48	8	9	1	0	2	9	4	13	.188	.250	.333	52	-3	-4	4	1	0	0	-4	C/1	-0.4
1988	StL-N	81	195	17	55	9	0	0	15	11	32	.282	.320	.328	86	-3	-4	20	0	0	0	-2	C1/3	-0.5
1989	StL-N	52	80	3	12	2	0	0	3	6	19	.150	.218	.175	13	-9	-9	2	0	0	0	-3	C/13	-1.0
1990	StL-N	69	220	20	61	15	0	2	23	14	37	.277	.323	.373	88	-3	-4	28	1	1	-0	9	C/1	0.8
Total	4	229	543	48	137	27	0	4	50	35	101	.252	.300	.324	73	-18	-20	54	2	1	0	1	C/13	-1.1

■ REY PALACIOS   Palacios, Robert Rey   b: 11/8/62, Brooklyn, N.Y.   BR/TR, 5'10", 190 lbs.   Deb: 9/08/88

YEAR	TM/L	G	AB	R	H	2B	3B	HR	RBI	BB	SO	AVG	OBP	SLG	PRO+	BR	/A	RC	SB	CS	SBR	FR	POS	TPR
1988	KC-A	5	11	2	1	0	0	0	0	0	4	.091	.091	.091	-48	-2	-2	0	0	0	0	1	/C3D	0.0
1989	KC-A	55	47	12	8	2	0	1	8	2	14	.170	.220	.277	39	-4	-4	3	0	1	-1	4	31C/O	-0.1
1990	KC-A	41	56	8	13	3	0	2	9	5	24	.232	.295	.393	93	-1	-1	6	2	2	-1	4	C/13O	0.3
Total	3	101	114	22	22	5	0	3	17	7	42	.193	.246	.316	57	-7	-7	9	2	3	-1	8	/C130D	0.2

■ ERV PALICA   Palica, Ervin Martin (b: Ervin Martin Pavliecivich)   b: 2/9/28, Lomita, Cal.   d: 5/29/82, Huntington Beach, Cal.   BR/TR, 6'1.5", 180 lbs.   Deb: 4/21/45

YEAR	TM/L	G	AB	R	H	2B	3B	HR	RBI	BB	SO	AVG	OBP	SLG	PRO+	BR	/A	RC	SB	CS	SBR	FR	POS	TPR
1945	Bro-N	2	0	0	0	0	0	0	0	0	0	—	—	—	—	0	0	0	0			0	R	0.0
1947	Bro-N	3	0	0	0	0	0	0	0	0	0	—	—	—	—	0	0	0	0			0	/P	0.0
1948	Bro-N	45	39	6	5	1	1	0	3	4	12	.128	.209	.205	12	-5	-5	2	0			-1	P	0.0
1949	*Bro-N	49	19	2	3	1	0	0	2	2	6	.158	.238	.211	20	-2	-2	1	0			0	P	0.0
1950	Bro-N	48	68	4	15	4	0	1	8	0	8	.221	.221	.324	40	-6	-6	5	2			-4	P	0.0
1951	Bro-N	20	13	1	2	0	0	0	0	2	5	.154	.267	.154	16	-1	-2	1	0			1	P	0.0
1953	Bro-N	4	1	0	1	0	0	0	0	0	0	1.000	1.000	1.000	414	0	0	1	0			0	/P	0.0
1954	Bro-N	28	16	2	4	1	0	0	1	1	4	.250	.294	.313	56	-1	-1	2	0			-1	P	0.0
1955	Bal-A	33	55	3	13	1	0	0	3	4	18	.236	.288	.255	50	-4	-4	4	0			-1	P	0.0
1956	Bal-A	30	32	4	5	0	0	0	0	0	10	.156	.156	.156	-19	-5	-5	1	0			0	P	0.0
Total	10	262	243	22	48	8	1	1	17	13	63	.198	.238	.251	31	-24	-24	16	2	0		-7	P	0.0

■ RAFAEL PALMEIRO   Palmeiro, Rafael (Corrales)   b: 9/24/64, Havana, Cuba   BL/TL, 6', 175 lbs.   Deb: 9/08/86

YEAR	TM/L	G	AB	R	H	2B	3B	HR	RBI	BB	SO	AVG	OBP	SLG	PRO+	BR	/A	RC	SB	CS	SBR	FR	POS	TPR
1986	Chi-N	22	73	9	18	4	0	3	12	4	6	.247	.295	.425	89	-1	-1	8	1	1	-0	-0	O	-0.1
1987	Chi-N	84	221	32	61	15	1	14	30	20	26	.276	.339	.543	124	8	7	40	2	2	-1	-4	O1	0.0
1988	Chi-N	152	580	75	178	41	5	8	53	38	34	.307	.353	.436	120	18	15	89	12	2	2	0	*O/1	1.4
1989	Tex-A	156	559	76	154	23	4	8	64	63	48	.275	.355	.374	104	6	5	74	4	3	-1	10	*1/D	0.4
1990	Tex-A	154	598	72	**191**	35	6	14	89	40	59	.319	.365	.468	129	24	23	94	3	3	-1	11	*1/D	1.0
Total	5	568	2031	264	602	118	16	47	248	165	173	.296	.353	.440	118	55	48	304	22	11	0	5	1O/D	2.7

■ DEAN PALMER   Palmer, Dean William   b: 12/27/68, Tallahassee, Fla.   BR/TR, 6'1", 175 lbs.   Deb: 9/01/89

YEAR	TM/L	G	AB	R	H	2B	3B	HR	RBI	BB	SO	AVG	OBP	SLG	PRO+	BR	/A	RC	SB	CS	SBR	FR	POS	TPR
1989	Tex-A	16	19	0	2	2	0	0	1	0	12	.105	.105	.211	-13	-3	-3	0	0	0	0	0	/3SOD	-0.2

■ EDDIE PALMER   Palmer, Edwin Henry "Baldy"   b: 6/1/1893, Petty, Tex.   d: 1/9/83, Marlow, Okla.   BR/TR, 5'9.5", 175 lbs.   Deb: 9/06/17

YEAR	TM/L	G	AB	R	H	2B	3B	HR	RBI	BB	SO	AVG	OBP	SLG	PRO+	BR	/A	RC	SB	CS	SBR	FR	POS	TPR
1917	Phi-A	16	52	7	11	1	0	0	5	7	7	.212	.305	.231	65	-2	-2	4	1			0	3/S	0.0

■ JOE PALMISANO   Palmisano, Joseph   b: 11/19/02, West Point, Ga.   d: 11/5/71, Albuquerque, N.Mex.   BR/TR, 5'8", 160 lbs.   Deb: 5/31/31

YEAR	TM/L	G	AB	R	H	2B	3B	HR	RBI	BB	SO	AVG	OBP	SLG	PRO+	BR	/A	RC	SB	CS	SBR	FR	POS	TPR
1931	Phi-A	19	44	5	10	2	0	0	4	6	3	.227	.320	.273	54	-3	-3	4	0	0	0	-1	C/2	-0.2

■ STAN PALYS   Palys, Stanley Francis   b: 5/1/30, Blakely, Pa.   BR/TR, 6'2", 190 lbs.   Deb: 9/20/53

YEAR	TM/L	G	AB	R	H	2B	3B	HR	RBI	BB	SO	AVG	OBP	SLG	PRO+	BR	/A	RC	SB	CS	SBR	FR	POS	TPR
1953	Phi-N	2	2	0	0	0	0	0	0	1	0	.000	.333	.000	-4	-0	-0	0	0	0	0	0	/O	0.0
1954	Phi-N	2	4	0	1	0	0	0	0	1	1	.250	.400	.250	74	-0	-0	1	0	0	0	0	/O	0.0
1955	Phi-N	15	52	8	15	3	0	1	8	6	5	.288	.362	.404	105	0	0	8	1	0	0	0	O	0.0
	Cin-N	79	222	29	51	14	0	7	30	12	35	.230	.272	.387	69	-9	-11	23	1	1	-0	1	O/1	-1.1
	Yr	94	274	37	66	17	0	8	38	18	40	.241	.290	.391	75	-9	-11	31	2	1		1		-1.1
1956	Cin-N	40	53	5	12	0	0	2	5	6	13	.226	.305	.340	69	-2	-2	6	0	0	0	-1	O	-0.3
Total	4	138	333	42	79	17	0	10	43	26	54	.237	.294	.378	74	-11	-13	37	2	1	0	-0	/O1	-1.4

■ JIM PANKOVITS   Pankovits, James Franklin   b: 8/6/55, Pennington Gap, Va.   BR/TR, 5'10", 195 lbs.   Deb: 5/27/84

YEAR	TM/L	G	AB	R	H	2B	3B	HR	RBI	BB	SO	AVG	OBP	SLG	PRO+	BR	/A	RC	SB	CS	SBR	FR	POS	TPR
1984	Hou-N	53	81	6	23	7	0	1	14	2	20	.284	.301	.407	105	-1	0	10	2	1	0	-5	2/S/O	-0.3
1985	Hou-N	75	172	24	42	3	0	4	14	17	29	.244	.316	.331	84	-4	-4	19	1	4	0	0	O2/3	-0.3
1986	*Hou-N	70	113	12	32	6	1	1	7	11	25	.283	.347	.381	103	0	1	14	1	1	-0	4	2/OC	0.4
1987	Hou-N	50	61	7	14	2	0	1	8	6	13	.230	.299	.311	64	-3	-3	6	2	0	1	5	/2O3	0.2
1988	Hou-N	68	140	13	31	7	1	2	12	8	28	.221	.273	.329	75	-5	-5	13	2	1	0	-2	23/1	-0.6
1990	Bos-A	2	0	0	0	0	0	0	0	0	0	—	—	—	—	0	0	0	0	0	0	0	/2	0.0

YEAR	TM/L	G	AB	R	H	2B	3B	HR	RBI	BB	SO	AVG	OBP	SLG	PRO+	BR	/A	RC	SB	CS	SBR	FR	POS	TPR
Total	6	318	567	62	142	25	2	9	55	44	115	.250	.308	.349	86	-13	-11	61	8	3	1	2	2/03S1C	-0.6

■ **KEN PAPE**   Pape, Kenneth Wayne   b: 10/1/51, San Antonio, Tex.   BR/TR, 5'11", 195 lbs.   Deb: 5/17/76

YEAR	TM/L	G	AB	R	H	2B	3B	HR	RBI	BB	SO	AVG	OBP	SLG	PRO+	BR	/A	RC	SB	CS	SBR	FR	POS	TPR
1976	Tex-A	21	23	7	5	1	0	1	4	3	2	.217	.357	.391	117	1	1	3	0	1	-1	4	/S32D	0.5

■ **STAN PAPI**   Papi, Stanley Gerard   b: 2/4/51, Fresno, Cal.   BR/TR, 6', 170 lbs.   Deb: 4/11/74

YEAR	TM/L	G	AB	R	H	2B	3B	HR	RBI	BB	SO	AVG	OBP	SLG	PRO+	BR	/A	RC	SB	CS	SBR	FR	POS	TPR
1974	StL-N	8	4	0	1	0	0	0	1	0	0	.250	.250	.250	40	-0	-0	0	0	0	0	1	/S2	0.1
1977	Mon-N	13	43	5	10	2	1	0	4	1	9	.233	.250	.326	55	-3	-3	3	1	0	0	-4	3/S2	-0.6
1978	Mon-N	67	152	15	35	11	0	0	11	10	28	.230	.287	.303	65	-7	-7	12	0	0	0	-3	S3/2	-0.7
1979	Bos-A	50	117	9	22	8	0	1	6	5	20	.188	.221	.282	33	-11	-12	8	0	0	0	12	2S	0.4
1980	Bos-A	1	0	0	0	0	0	0	0	0	0	—	—	—	—	0	0	0	0	0	0	0	/3	0.0
	Det-A	46	114	12	27	3	4	3	17	5	24	.237	.269	.412	82	-3	-3	12	0	0	0	-2	23/S/1	-0.2
	Yr	47	114	12	27	3	4	3	17	5	24	.237	.269	.412	82	-3	-3	12	0	0	0	-2		-0.2
1981	Det-A	40	93	8	19	2	1	3	12	3	18	.204	.229	.344	61	-5	-5	7	1	0	0	-1	3/120D	-0.5
Total	6	225	523	49	114	26	6	7	51	24	99	.218	.255	.331	60	-29	-30	42	2	0	1	3	/32SD10	-1.5

■ **AL PARDO**   Pardo, Alberto Judas   b: 9/8/62, Oviedo, Spain   BB/TR, 6'2", 187 lbs.   Deb: 7/03/85

YEAR	TM/L	G	AB	R	H	2B	3B	HR	RBI	BB	SO	AVG	OBP	SLG	PRO+	BR	/A	RC	SB	CS	SBR	FR	POS	TPR
1985	Bal-A	34	75	3	10	1	0	0	1	3	15	.133	.167	.147	-14	-12	-11	2	0	0	0	3	C	-0.6
1986	Bal-A	16	51	3	7	1	0	1	3	0	14	.137	.137	.216	-6	-7	-7	1	0	0	0	-2	C/D	-0.8
1988	Phi-N	2	2	0	0	0	0	0	0	0	2	.000	.000	.000	-98	-1	-1	0	0	0	0	0	/C	0.0
1989	Phi-N	1	1	0	0	0	0	0	0	0	0	.000	.000	.000	-99	-0	-0	0	0	0	0	0	/C	0.0
Total	4	53	129	6	17	2	0	1	4	3	31	.132	.152	.171	-12	-20	-19	3	0	0	0	0	/CD	-1.4

■ **JOHNNY PAREDES**   Paredes, Johnny Alfonso (Isambert)   b: 9/2/62, Maracaibo, Venez.   BR/TR, 5'11", 165 lbs.   Deb: 4/29/88

YEAR	TM/L	G	AB	R	H	2B	3B	HR	RBI	BB	SO	AVG	OBP	SLG	PRO+	BR	/A	RC	SB	CS	SBR	FR	POS	TPR
1988	Mon-N	35	91	6	17	2	0	1	10	9	17	.187	.282	.242	49	-5	-6	7	5	2	0	1	2/O	-0.4
1990	Det-A	6	8	2	1	0	0	0	0	1	0	.125	.222	.125	-0	-1	-1	0	0	0	0	1	/2	0.0
	Mon-N	3	6	0	2	1	0	0	1	1	0	.333	.429	.500	155	0	0	1	0	0	0	1	/2	0.1
Total	2	44	105	8	20	3	0	1	11	11	17	.190	.286	.248	52	-6	-6	9	5	2	0	2	/2O	-0.3

■ **FREDDY PARENT**   Parent, Frederick Alfred   b: 11/25/1875, Biddeford, Me.   d: 11/2/72, Sanford, Maine   BR/TR, 5'7", 154 lbs.   Deb: 7/14/1899

YEAR	TM/L	G	AB	R	H	2B	3B	HR	RBI	BB	SO	AVG	OBP	SLG	PRO+	BR	/A	RC	SB	CS	SBR	FR	POS	TPR
1899	StL-N	2	8	0	1	0	0	0	1	0		.125	.125	.125	-30	-1	-1	0	0			-1	/2	-0.1
1901	Bos-A	138	517	87	158	23	9	4	59	41		.306	.367	.408	119	12	14	88	16			-0	*S	2.0
1902	Bos-A	138	567	91	156	31	8	3	62	24		.275	.310	.374	88	-8	-10	74	16			4	*S	0.5
1903	*Bos-A	139	560	83	170	31	17	4	80	13		.304	.319	.441	122	17	13	90	24			9	*S	3.0
1904	Bos-A	155	591	85	172	22	9	6	77	28		.291	.323	.389	120	17	13	86	20			-8	*S	0.7
1905	Bos-A	153	602	55	141	16	5	0	33	47		.234	.290	.277	81	-11	-12	61	25			-7	*S	-1.5
1906	Bos-A	149	600	67	141	14	10	1	49	31		.235	.273	.297	80	-14	-14	56	16			-7	*S/2	-2.0
1907	Bos-A	114	409	51	113	19	5	1	26	22		.276	.313	.355	116	6	6	52	12			-0	OS/32	0.5
1908	Chi-A	119	391	28	81	7	5	0	35	50		.207	.297	.251	82	-6	-6	33	9			5	*S	0.3
1909	Chi-A	136	472	61	123	10	5	0	30	46		.261	.335	.303	106	2	5	60	32			17	SO/2	2.5
1910	Chi-A	81	258	23	46	6	1	1	16	29		.178	.266	.221	55	-13	-12	19	14			-2	O2/S3	-1.9
1911	Chi-A	3	9	3	4	1	0	0	3	2		.444	.545	.556	214	1	2	3	0			1	/2	0.2
Total	12	1327	4984	633	1306	180	74	20	471	333		.262	.311	.340	100	-1	-2	623	184			10	*SO/23	4.2

■ **MARK PARENT**   Parent, Mark Allen   b: 9/16/61, Ashland, Ore.   BR/TR, 6'5", 215 lbs.   Deb: 9/20/86

YEAR	TM/L	G	AB	R	H	2B	3B	HR	RBI	BB	SO	AVG	OBP	SLG	PRO+	BR	/A	RC	SB	CS	SBR	FR	POS	TPR
1986	SD-N	8	14	1	2	0	0	0	1	1	3	.143	.200	.143	-4	-2	-2	0	0	0	0	-1	/C	-0.2
1987	SD-N	12	25	0	2	0	0	0	2	0	9	.080	.080	.080	-60	-6	-5	0	0	0	0	0	C	-0.3
1988	SD-N	41	118	9	23	3	0	6	15	6	23	.195	.234	.373	73	-5	-5	10	0	0	0	5	C	0.3
1989	SD-N	52	141	12	27	4	0	7	21	8	34	.191	.235	.369	70	-6	-6	11	1	0	0	5	C/1	0.2
1990	SD-N	65	189	13	42	11	0	3	16	16	29	.222	.283	.328	67	-9	-9	18	1	0	0	7	C	0.1
Total	5	178	487	35	96	18	0	16	54	31	98	.197	.245	.333	61	-27	-27	40	2	0	1	17	C/1	0.1

■ **KELLY PARIS**   Paris, Kelly Jay   b: 10/17/57, Encino, Cal.   BR/TR, 6', 175 lbs.   Deb: 9/01/82

YEAR	TM/L	G	AB	R	H	2B	3B	HR	RBI	BB	SO	AVG	OBP	SLG	PRO+	BR	/A	RC	SB	CS	SBR	FR	POS	TPR
1982	StL-N	12	29	1	3	0	0	0	1	0	7	.103	.103	.103	-42	-5	-4	0	0	0	0	2	/3S	-0.2
1983	Cin-N	56	120	13	30	6	0	0	7	15	22	.250	.338	.300	75	-3	-4	13	8	2	-1	-2	32/S1	-0.3
1985	Bal-A	5	9	0	0	0	0	0	0	0	1	.000	.000	.000	-99	-2	-2	0	0	0	0	-0	/2D	-0.2
1986	Bal-A	5	10	0	2	0	0	0	0	0	3	.200	.200	.200	9	-1	-1	0	0	1	-1	1	/3D	0.0
1988	Chi-A	14	44	6	11	0	0	3	6	0	6	.250	.250	.455	93	-1	-1	5	0	0	0	0	/13D	0.0
Total	5	92	212	20	46	6	0	3	14	15	39	.217	.272	.288	54	-13	-13	18	8	3	1	1	/312SD	-0.7

■ **TONY PARISSE**   Parisse, Louis Peter   b: 6/25/11, Philadelphia, Pa.   d: 6/2/56, Philadelphia, Pa.   BR/TR, 5'10", 165 lbs.   Deb: 9/22/43

YEAR	TM/L	G	AB	R	H	2B	3B	HR	RBI	BB	SO	AVG	OBP	SLG	PRO+	BR	/A	RC	SB	CS	SBR	FR	POS	TPR
1943	Phi-A	6	17	0	3	0	0	0	1	2	2	.176	.263	.176	30	-1	-1	1	0	0	0	1	/C	0.0
1944	Phi-A	4	4	0	0	0	0	0	0	0	1	.000	.000	.000	-99	-1	-1	0	0	0	0	-1	/C	-0.1
Total	2	10	21	0	3	0	0	0	1	2	3	.143	.217	.143	6	-2	-2	1	0	0	0	0	/C	-0.1

■ **ACE PARKER**   Parker, Clarence McKay   b: 5/17/12, Portsmouth, Va.   BR/TR, 6', 180 lbs.   Deb: 4/24/37

YEAR	TM/L	G	AB	R	H	2B	3B	HR	RBI	BB	SO	AVG	OBP	SLG	PRO+	BR	/A	RC	SB	CS	SBR	FR	POS	TPR
1937	Phi-A	38	94	8	11	0	1	2	13	4	17	.117	.153	.202	-11	-16	-16	3	0	0	0	-4	S/2O	-1.7
1938	Phi-A	56	113	12	26	5	0	0	12	10	16	.230	.293	.274	44	-10	-10	9	1	2	-1	-5	S/23	-1.1
Total	2	94	207	20	37	5	1	2	25	14	33	.179	.231	.242	19	-26	-26	12	1	2	-1	-9	/S23O	-2.8

■ **PAT PARKER**   Parker, Clarence Perkins   b: 5/22/1893, Somerville, Mass.   d: 3/21/67, Claremont, N.H.   5'7", 160 lbs.   Deb: 8/10/15

YEAR	TM/L	G	AB	R	H	2B	3B	HR	RBI	BB	SO	AVG	OBP	SLG	PRO+	BR	/A	RC	SB	CS	SBR	FR	POS	TPR
1915	StL-A	3	6	0	1	0	0	0	1	0	3	.167	.167	.167	-0	-1	-1	0	0	1	-1	-0	/O	-0.1

■ **DAVE PARKER**   Parker, David Gene   b: 6/9/51, Calhoun, Miss.   BL/TR, 6'5", 230 lbs.   Deb: 7/12/73

YEAR	TM/L	G	AB	R	H	2B	3B	HR	RBI	BB	SO	AVG	OBP	SLG	PRO+	BR	/A	RC	SB	CS	SBR	FR	POS	TPR
1973	Pit-N	54	139	17	40	9	1	4	14	2	27	.288	.308	.453	111	1	1	18	1	1	-0	3	O	0.2
1974	*Pit-N	73	220	27	62	10	3	4	29	10	53	.282	.322	.409	107	0	1	28	3	3	-1	2	O/1	0.0
1975	Pit-N	148	558	75	172	35	10	25	101	38	89	.308	.358	.541	148	32	32	101	8	6	-1	6	*O	3.3
1976	Pit-N	138	537	82	168	28	10	13	90	30	80	.313	.351	.475	132	21	20	85	19	7	2	6	*O	2.4
1977	Pit-N	159	637	107	215	44	8	21	88	58	107	.338	.399	.531	143	42	40	130	17	19	-6	28	*O/2	5.6
1978	Pit-N	148	581	102	194	32	12	30	117	57	92	.334	.395	.585	163	53	50	134	20	7	2	4	*O	5.2
1979	*Pit-N	158	622	109	193	45	7	25	94	67	101	.310	.385	.526	140	39	36	131	20	4	4	9	*O	4.5
1980	Pit-N	139	518	71	153	31	1	17	79	25	69	.295	.330	.458	116	10	9	75	10	7	-1	-1	*O	0.2
1981	Pit-N	67	240	29	62	14	3	9	48	9	25	.258	.291	.454	106	1	0	30	6	2	1	-8	O	-0.9
1982	Pit-N	73	244	41	66	19	3	6	29	22	45	.270	.333	.447	113	5	4	34	7	5	-1	-6	O	-0.3
1983	Pit-N	144	552	68	154	29	4	12	69	28	89	.279	.314	.411	97	-2	-4	67	12	9	-2	1	*O	-0.7
1984	Cin-N	156	607	73	173	28	0	16	94	41	89	.285	.331	.410	103	5	2	80	11	10	-3	0	*O	-0.6
1985	Cin-N	160	635	88	198	42	4	34	125	52	80	.312	.365	.551	146	43	39	112	5	13	-6	7	*O	3.7
1986	Cin-N	162	637	89	174	31	3	31	116	56	126	.273	.333	.477	116	16	12	94	1	6	-3	-6	*O	0.0
1987	Cin-N	153	589	77	149	28	0	26	97	44	104	.253	.314	.433	91	-5	-9	77	7	3	0	4	*O/1	-1.0
1988	*Oak-A	101	377	43	97	18	1	12	55	32	70	.257	.314	.406	104	-0	-1	49	0	1	-1	0	DO/1	0.4
1989	*Oak-A	144	553	56	146	27	0	22	97	38	91	.264	.313	.432	112	4	6	68	0	0	0	0	*D/O	0.6
1990	Mil-A	157	610	71	176	30	3	21	92	41	102	.289	.337	.451	122	13	16	86	4	7	-3	-1	*D/1	1.2
Total	18	2334	8856	1225	2592	500	73	328	1434	650	1439	.293	.345	.477	123	276	258	1400	151	110	-21	50	*OD/12	23.8

■ **DIXIE PARKER**   Parker, Douglas Woolley   b: 4/24/1895, Forest Home, Ala.   d: 5/15/72, Tuscaloosa, Ala.   BL/TR, 5'11", 160 lbs.   Deb: 7/28/23

YEAR	TM/L	G	AB	R	H	2B	3B	HR	RBI	BB	SO	AVG	OBP	SLG	PRO+	BR	/A	RC	SB	CS	SBR	FR	POS	TPR
1923	Phi-N	4	5	0	1	0	0	0	1	0	1	.200	.200	.200	5	-1	-1	0	0	0	0	-1	/C	-0.1

YEAR	TM/L	G	AB	R	H	2B	3B	HR	RBI	BB	SO	AVG	OBP	SLG	PRO+	BR	/A	RC	SB	CS	SBR	FR	POS	TPR

■ SALTY PARKER
Parker, Francis James b: 7/8/13, E.St.Louis, Ill. BR/TR, 6′, 173 lbs. Deb: 8/13/36 MC

YEAR	TM/L	G	AB	R	H	2B	3B	HR	RBI	BB	SO	AVG	OBP	SLG	PRO+	BR	/A	RC	SB	CS	SBR	FR	POS	TPR
1936	Det-A	11	25	6	7	2	0	0	4	2	3	.280	.333	.360	71	-1	-1	2	0	2	-1	3	/S1	0.1

■ WES PARKER
Parker, Maurice Wesley b: 11/13/39, Evanston, Ill. BB/TL, 6′1″, 180 lbs. Deb: 4/19/64

YEAR	TM/L	G	AB	R	H	2B	3B	HR	RBI	BB	SO	AVG	OBP	SLG	PRO+	BR	/A	RC	SB	CS	SBR	FR	POS	TPR
1964	LA-N	124	214	29	55	7	1	3	10	14	45	.257	.306	.341	88	-5	-3	23	5	4	-1	6	O1	0.0
1965	*LA-N	154	542	80	129	24	7	8	51	75	95	.238	.336	.352	101	-2	2	70	13	7	-0	0	*1/O	-0.5
1966	*LA-N	156	475	67	120	17	5	12	51	69	83	.253	.353	.385	114	5	10	67	7	3	0	0	*1O	0.3
1967	LA-N	139	413	56	102	16	5	5	31	65	83	.247	.359	.346	112	4	8	55	10	5	0	5	*1O	0.8
1968	LA-N	135	468	42	112	22	2	3	27	49	87	.239	.314	.314	96	-5	-2	49	4	6	-2	2	*1O	-0.9
1969	LA-N	132	471	76	131	23	4	13	68	56	46	.278	.357	.427	128	12	16	73	4	1	1	1	*1/O	0.8
1970	LA-N	161	614	84	196	**47**	4	10	111	79	70	.319	.397	.458	134	26	30	113	8	2	1	4	*1	2.1
1971	LA-N	157	533	69	146	24	1	6	62	63	63	.274	.352	.356	107	2	6	69	6	1	1	5	*1O	0.0
1972	LA-N	130	427	45	119	14	3	4	59	62	43	.279	.371	.354	110	6	7	57	3	5	-2	1	*1/O	-0.1
Total	9	1288	4157	548	1110	194	32	64	470	532	615	.267	.353	.375	112	44	75	575	60	34	-2	24	*1O	2.5

■ RICK PARKER
Parker, Richard Allen b: 3/20/63, Kansas City, Mo. BR/TR, 6′, 185 lbs. Deb: 5/04/90

YEAR	TM/L	G	AB	R	H	2B	3B	HR	RBI	BB	SO	AVG	OBP	SLG	PRO+	BR	/A	RC	SB	CS	SBR	FR	POS	TPR
1990	SF-N	54	107	19	26	5	0	2	14	10	15	.243	.314	.346	82	-3	-3	13	6	1	1	-4	O/23S	-0.5

■ BILLY PARKER
Parker, William David b: 1/14/47, Hayneville, Ala. BR/TR, 5′8″, 168 lbs. Deb: 9/09/71

YEAR	TM/L	G	AB	R	H	2B	3B	HR	RBI	BB	SO	AVG	OBP	SLG	PRO+	BR	/A	RC	SB	CS	SBR	FR	POS	TPR
1971	Cal-A	20	70	4	16	0	1	1	6	2	20	.229	.250	.300	59	-4	-4	5	1	1	-0	-1	2	-0.4
1972	Cal-A	36	80	11	17	2	0	2	8	9	17	.213	.292	.313	85	-2	-1	7	0	2	-1	0	3/2OS	0.0
1973	Cal-A	38	102	14	23	2	1	0	7	8	23	.225	.288	.265	61	-6	-5	8	0	1	-1	-3	2/SD	-0.6
Total	3	94	252	29	56	4	2	3	21	19	60	.222	.279	.290	68	-12	-10	19	1	4	-2	-4	/23OSD	-1.0

■ FRANK PARKINSON
Parkinson, Frank Joseph "Parky" b: 3/23/1895, Dickson City, Pa. d: 7/4/60, Trenton, N.J. BR/TR, 5′11″, 175 lbs. Deb: 4/13/21

YEAR	TM/L	G	AB	R	H	2B	3B	HR	RBI	BB	SO	AVG	OBP	SLG	PRO+	BR	/A	RC	SB	CS	SBR	FR	POS	TPR
1921	Phi-N	108	391	36	99	20	2	5	32	13	81	.253	.277	.353	61	-20	-24	37	3	4	-2	9	*S/3	-0.5
1922	Phi-N	141	545	86	150	18	6	15	70	55	93	.275	.344	.413	86	-5	-13	79	3	4	-2	**31**	*2	1.4
1923	Phi-N	67	219	21	53	12	0	3	28	13	31	.242	.288	.338	58	-12	-15	20	0	4	-2	3	2S3	-1.1
1924	Phi-N	62	156	14	33	7	0	1	19	14	28	.212	.281	.276	44	-11	-14	13	3	1	0	7	3S2	-0.2
Total	4	378	1311	157	335	57	8	24	149	95	233	.256	.308	.366	69	-48	-65	149	9	13	-5	50	2S/3	-0.4

■ ART PARKS
Parks, Artie William b: 11/1/11, Paris, Ark. d: 12/6/89, Little Rock, Ark. BL/TR, 5′9″, 170 lbs. Deb: 9/25/37

YEAR	TM/L	G	AB	R	H	2B	3B	HR	RBI	BB	SO	AVG	OBP	SLG	PRO+	BR	/A	RC	SB	CS	SBR	FR	POS	TPR
1937	Bro-N	7	16	2	5	2	0	0	2	2	2	.313	.389	.438	122	1	1	3				0	/O	0.0
1939	Bro-N	71	239	27	65	13	2	1	19	28	14	.272	.348	.356	86	-3	-4	30	2			-5	/O	-1.0
Total	2	78	255	29	70	15	2	1	19	30	16	.275	.351	.361	89	-2	-4	33	2			-5	/O	-1.0

■ BILL PARKS
Parks, William Robert b: 6/4/1849, Easton, Pa. d: 10/10/11, Easton, Pa. 5′8″, 150 lbs. Deb: 4/26/1875

YEAR	TM/L	G	AB	R	H	2B	3B	HR	RBI	BB	SO	AVG	OBP	SLG	PRO+	BR	/A	RC	SB	CS	SBR	FR	POS	TPR
1875	Was-n	26	112	13	20	1	0	0				.179	.179	.188	28	-8	-7	4					OPM	0.0
	Phi-n	2	6	0	1	0	0	0				.167	.167	.167	15	-0	-1	0					/PO	0.0
	Yr	28	118	13	21	1	0	0				.178	.178	.186	27	-8	-8	4						0.0
1876	Bos-N	1	4	0	0	0	0	0	0	0	0	.000	.000	.000	-98	-1	-1	0				0	/O	0.0

■ SAM PARRILLA
Parrilla, Samuel b: 6/12/43, Santurce, P.R. BR/TR, 5′11″, 185 lbs. Deb: 4/11/70

YEAR	TM/L	G	AB	R	H	2B	3B	HR	RBI	BB	SO	AVG	OBP	SLG	PRO+	BR	/A	RC	SB	CS	SBR	FR	POS	TPR
1970	Phi-N	11	16	0	2	1	0	0	0	1	4	.125	.176	.188	-3	-2	-2	1	0	0	0	0	/O	-0.1

■ LANCE PARRISH
Parrish, Lance Michael b: 6/15/56, Clairton, Pa. BR/TR, 6′3″, 210 lbs. Deb: 9/05/77

YEAR	TM/L	G	AB	R	H	2B	3B	HR	RBI	BB	SO	AVG	OBP	SLG	PRO+	BR	/A	RC	SB	CS	SBR	FR	POS	TPR
1977	Det-A	12	46	10	9	2	0	3	7	5	12	.196	.275	.435	85	-1	-1	5	0	0	0	2	C	0.1
1978	Det-A	85	288	37	63	11	3	14	41	11	71	.219	.255	.424	85	-6	-7	29	0	0	0	5	C	0.0
1979	Det-A	143	493	65	136	26	3	19	65	49	105	.276	.344	.456	110	9	7	73	6	7	-2	3	*C	1.3
1980	Det-A	144	553	79	158	34	6	24	82	31	109	.286	.327	.499	120	15	13	80	6	4	-1	-2	*CD/1O	1.5
1981	Det-A	96	348	39	85	18	2	10	46	34	52	.244	.312	.394	98	0	-1	38	2	3	-1	-2	C/D	0.0
1982	Det-A	133	486	75	138	19	2	32	87	40	99	.284	.340	.529	134	21	21	86	3	4	-2	7	*C/O	3.3
1983	Det-A	155	605	80	163	42	3	27	114	44	106	.269	.320	.483	120	12	14	86	1	3	-1	1	*CD	1.9
1984	*Det-A	147	578	75	137	16	2	33	98	41	120	.237	.290	.443	100	-3	-2	71	2	3	-1	2	*CD	0.6
1985	Det-A	140	549	64	150	27	1	28	98	41	90	.273	.326	.479	118	11	12	82	2	6	-3	-6	*CD	0.8
1986	Det-A	91	327	53	84	6	1	22	62	38	83	.257	.343	.483	122	10	10	57	0	0	0	2	C/D	1.7
1987	Phi-N	130	466	42	114	21	0	17	67	47	104	.245	.315	.399	85	-9	-11	53	0	1	-1	-2	*C	-0.3
1988	Phi-N	123	424	44	91	17	2	15	60	42	93	.215	.296	.370	88	-6	-7	46	0	0	0	-3	*C/1	-0.3
1989	Cal-A	124	433	48	103	12	1	17	50	42	104	.238	.308	.388	97	-3	-2	51	1	1	-0	2	*C/D	0.4
1990	Cal-A	133	470	54	126	14	0	24	70	46	107	.268	.340	.451	119	11	11	71	2	2	-1	12	*C/1D	2.6
Total	14	1656	6066	765	1557	265	26	285	947	516	1255	.257	.318	.450	109	62	56	828	25	34	-13	21	*CD/1O	13.6

■ LARRY PARRISH
Parrish, Larry Alton b: 11/10/53, Winter Haven, Fla. BR/TR, 6′3″, 190 lbs. Deb: 9/06/74

YEAR	TM/L	G	AB	R	H	2B	3B	HR	RBI	BB	SO	AVG	OBP	SLG	PRO+	BR	/A	RC	SB	CS	SBR	FR	POS	TPR
1974	Mon-N	25	69	9	14	5	0	4	4	6	19	.203	.286	.275	54	-4	-4	6	0	0	0	8	3	0.3
1975	Mon-N	145	532	50	146	32	5	10	65	28	74	.274	.316	.410	96	-2	-5	64	4	5	-2	-3	*3/2S	-1.0
1976	Mon-N	154	543	65	126	28	5	11	61	41	91	.232	.288	.363	81	-13	-16	54	2	6	-3	5	*3	-1.6
1977	Mon-N	123	402	50	99	19	2	11	46	37	71	.246	.316	.386	90	-8	-6	47	2	4	-2	-9	*3	-1.7
1978	Mon-N	144	520	68	144	39	4	15	70	32	103	.277	.321	.454	116	8	9	69	2	3	-1	-5	*3	0.1
1979	Mon-N	153	544	83	167	39	2	30	82	41	101	.307	.358	.551	146	31	31	106	5	1	1	-9	*3	1.7
1980	Mon-N	126	452	55	115	27	3	15	72	36	80	.254	.315	.427	105	2	2	57	2	6	-3	-8	*3	-0.9
1981	*Mon-N	97	349	41	85	19	3	8	44	28	73	.244	.300	.384	92	-4	-5	39	0	0	0	-17	3	-2.8
1982	Tex-A	128	440	59	116	15	0	17	62	30	84	.264	.316	.414	104	-2	1	56	5	2	0	-12	*O/3D	-1.3
1983	Tex-A	145	555	76	151	26	4	26	88	46	91	.272	.331	.474	121	13	14	82	0	0	0	-12	*OD	0.0
1984	Tex-A	156	613	72	175	42	1	22	101	42	116	.285	.337	.465	116	15	12	89	2	4	-2	-3	OD3	0.6
1985	Tex-A	94	346	44	86	11	1	17	51	33	77	.249	.316	.434	101	1	0	44	0	2	-1	-7	OD/3	-0.8
1986	Tex-A	129	464	67	128	22	1	28	94	52	114	.276	.351	.509	127	19	17	80	3	1	0	-5	D3	1.1
1987	Tex-A	152	557	79	149	22	1	32	100	49	154	.268	.330	.483	112	8	8	88	3	1	0	-8	*D3/O	0.0
1988	Tex-A	68	248	22	47	9	1	7	26	20	79	.190	.256	.319	58	-14	-15	20	0	0	0	0	D	-1.4
	*Bos-A	52	158	10	41	5	0	7	26	8	32	.259	.299	.424	96	-0	-1	19	0	1	-1	3	1D	0.0
	Yr	120	406	32	88	14	1	14	52	28	111	.217	.272	.360	73	-14	-16	39	0	1	-1	3		-1.4
Total	15	1891	6792	850	1789	360	33	256	992	529	1359	.263	.321	.439	106	49	44	919	30	36	-13	-82	*3OD/1S2	-7.7

■ TOM PARROTT
Parrott, Thomas William "Tacky Tom" b: 4/10/1868, Portland, Ore. d: 1/1/32, Dundee, Ore. BR/TR, 5′10.5″, 170 lbs. Deb: 6/18/1893

YEAR	TM/L	G	AB	R	H	2B	3B	HR	RBI	BB	SO	AVG	OBP	SLG	PRO+	BR	/A	RC	SB	CS	SBR	FR	POS	TPR
1893	Chi-N	7	27	4	7	1	0	0	3	1	2	.259	.286	.296	57	-2	-2	2	0			-1	/P32	0.0
	Cin-N	24	68	5	13	1	1	1	9	1	9	.191	.203	.279	28	-7	-7	4	0			1	P/O	0.0
	Yr	31	95	9	20	2	1	1	12	2	11	.211	.227	.284	36	-9	-9	6	0					0.0
1894	Cin-N	68	229	51	74	12	6	4	40	17	10	.323	.372	.480	102	2	-0	44	4			5	PO1/S32	0.0
1895	Cin-N	64	201	35	69	13	7	3	41	11	8	.343	.377	.522	127	9	7	44	10			1	P1/O	0.0
1896	StL-N	118	474	62	138	13	12	7	70	11	24	.291	.307	.414	94	-9	-6	65	12			13	*O/P1	0.1
Total	4	281	999	157	301	40	26	15	163	41	53	.301	.329	.438	98	-8	-8	160	26			19	OP/132S	0.1

■ JIGGS PARROTT
Parrott, Walter Edward b: 7/14/1871, Portland, Ore. d: 4/16/1898, Phoenix, Ariz. 5′11″, 160 lbs. Deb: 7/11/1892

YEAR	TM/L	G	AB	R	H	2B	3B	HR	RBI	BB	SO	AVG	OBP	SLG	PRO+	BR	/A	RC	SB	CS	SBR	FR	POS	TPR
1892	Chi-N	78	333	38	67	8	5	2	22	8	30	.201	.222	.273	51	-21	-21	22	7			-2	3	-1.6
1893	Chi-N	110	455	54	111	10	9	1	65	13	25	.244	.267	.312	56	-31	-29	46	25			9	*3/2O	-1.5
1894	Chi-N	124	517	82	128	17	9	3	64	16	35	.248	.274	.333	45	-46	-51	57	30			-6	*2/3	-3.7

YEAR	TM/L	G	AB	R	H	2B	3B	HR	RBI	BB	SO	AVG	OBP	SLG	PRO+	BR	/A	RC	SB	CS	SBR	FR	POS	TPR
1895	Chi-N	3	4	0	1	0	0	0	0	0	0	.250	.250	.250	29	-0	-0	0	0			-1	/OS1	0.0
Total	4	315	1309	174	307	35	23	6	151	37	90	.235	.258	.310	50	-97	-101	125	62			0	32/01S	-6.8

■ CASEY PARSONS
Parsons, Casey Robert b: 4/14/54, Wenatchee, Wash.   BL/TR, 6'1", 180 lbs.   Deb: 5/31/81

YEAR	TM/L	G	AB	R	H	2B	3B	HR	RBI	BB	SO	AVG	OBP	SLG	PRO+	BR	/A	RC	SB	CS	SBR	FR	POS	TPR
1981	Sea-A	36	22	6	5	1	0	1	5	1	4	.227	.320	.409	105	0	0	3	0	0	0	3	O/1	0.3
1983	Chi-A	8	5	1	1	0	0	0	0	2	1	.200	.429	.200	77	0	-0	1	0	0	0	0	/OD	0.0
1984	Chi-A	1	1	0	0	0	0	0	0	0	1	.000	.000	.000	-96	-0	-0	0	0	0	0	0	/H	0.0
1987	Cle-A	18	25	2	4	0	0	1	5	0	5	.160	.160	.280	13	-3	-3	1	0	0	0	0	/O1D	-0.2
Total	4	63	53	9	10	1	0	2	10	3	11	.189	.259	.321	57	-3	-3	4	0	0	0	4	/OD1	0.1

■ DIXIE PARSONS
Parsons, Edward Dixon b: 5/12/16, Talladega, Ala.   BR/TR, 6'2", 180 lbs.   Deb: 8/16/39

YEAR	TM/L	G	AB	R	H	2B	3B	HR	RBI	BB	SO	AVG	OBP	SLG	PRO+	BR	/A	RC	SB	CS	SBR	FR	POS	TPR
1939	Det-A	5	1	0	0	0	0	0	0	1	1	.000	.500	.000	36	-0	-0	0	0	0	0	0	/C	0.0
1942	Det-A	63	188	8	37	4	0	2	11	13	22	.197	.249	.250	37	-15	-17	12	1	0	0	9	C	0.0
1943	Det-A	40	106	2	15	3	0	0	4	6	16	.142	.188	.170	4	-13	-14	3	0	0	0	6	C	-0.6
Total	3	108	295	10	52	7	0	2	15	20	39	.176	.229	.220	26	-28	-31	15	1	0	0	15	C	-0.6

■ JOHN PARSONS
Parsons, John S. b: Napoleon, Ohio   Deb: 10/15/1884

YEAR	TM/L	G	AB	R	H	2B	3B	HR	RBI	BB	SO	AVG	OBP	SLG	PRO+	BR	/A	RC	SB	CS	SBR	FR	POS	TPR
1884	Cin-a	1	3	0	0	0	0	0		0		.000	.000	.000	-95	-1	-1	0				-1	/O	0.0

■ ROY PARTEE
Partee, Roy Robert b: 9/7/17, Los Angeles, Cal.   BR/TR, 5'10", 180 lbs.   Deb: 4/23/43

YEAR	TM/L	G	AB	R	H	2B	3B	HR	RBI	BB	SO	AVG	OBP	SLG	PRO+	BR	/A	RC	SB	CS	SBR	FR	POS	TPR
1943	Bos-A	96	299	30	84	14	2	0	31	39	33	.281	.368	.341	106	4	4	40	0	0	0	-6	C	0.3
1944	Bos-A	89	280	18	68	12	0	2	41	37	29	.243	.333	.307	85	-5	-5	30	0	1	-1	-6	C	-0.5
1946	*Bos-A	40	111	13	35	5	2	0	9	13	14	.315	.387	.396	113	3	2	17	0	0	0	-6	C	-0.1
1947	Bos-A	60	169	14	39	2	0	0	16	18	23	.231	.305	.243	50	-10	-12	14	0	0	0	-1	C	-0.8
1948	StL-A	82	231	14	47	8	1	0	17	25	21	.203	.284	.247	41	-19	-20	16	2	2	-1	1	C	-1.3
Total	5	367	1090	89	273	41	5	2	114	132	120	.250	.334	.303	78	-27	-30	116	2	3	-1	-17	C	-2.4

■ STEVE PARTENHEIMER
Partenheimer, Harold Philip b: 8/30/1891, Greenfield, Mass. d: 6/16/71, Mansfield, Ohio   TR, 5'8.5", 145 lbs.   Deb: 6/18/13

YEAR	TM/L	G	AB	R	H	2B	3B	HR	RBI	BB	SO	AVG	OBP	SLG	PRO+	BR	/A	RC	SB	CS	SBR	FR	POS	TPR
1913	Det-A	1	2	0	0	0	0	0	0	0	0	.000	.333	.000	-1	-0	-0	0	0			0	/3	0.0

■ JAY PARTRIDGE
Partridge, James Bugg b: 11/15/02, Mountville, Ga. d: 1/14/74, Nashville, Tenn.   BL/TR, 5'11", 160 lbs.   Deb: 4/12/27

YEAR	TM/L	G	AB	R	H	2B	3B	HR	RBI	BB	SO	AVG	OBP	SLG	PRO+	BR	/A	RC	SB	CS	SBR	FR	POS	TPR
1927	Bro-N	146	572	72	149	17	6	7	40	20	36	.260	.289	.348	70	-25	-26	56	9			-15	*2	-4.2
1928	Bro-N	37	73	18	18	0	1	0	12	13	6	.247	.368	.274	71	-2	-2	8	2			-5	2/3	-0.6
Total	2	183	645	90	167	17	7	7	52	33	42	.259	.299	.340	70	-28	-28	64	11			-20	2/3	-4.8

■ BEN PASCHAL
Paschal, Benjamin Edwin b: 10/13/1895, Enterprise, Ala. d: 11/10/74, Charlotte, N.C.   BR/TR, 5'11", 185 lbs.   Deb: 8/16/15

YEAR	TM/L	G	AB	R	H	2B	3B	HR	RBI	BB	SO	AVG	OBP	SLG	PRO+	BR	/A	RC	SB	CS	SBR	FR	POS	TPR
1915	Cle-A	9	9	0	1	0	0	0	0	0	3	.111	.111	.111	-33	-1	-1	0	0			0	H	-0.1
1920	Bos-A	9	28	5	10	0	0	0	5	5	2	.357	.455	.357	122	1	1	5	1	0	0	-0	/O	0.1
1924	NY-A	4	12	2	3	1	0	0	3	1	0	.250	.308	.333	65	-1	-1	1	0	0	0	-0	/O	0.0
1925	NY-A	89	247	49	89	16	5	12	56	22	29	.360	.417	.611	161	21	21	60	14	9	-1	-4	O	0.9
1926	*NY-A	96	258	46	74	12	3	7	33	26	35	.287	.354	.438	107	2	2	40	7	6	-2	-3	O	-0.7
1927	NY-A	50	82	16	26	9	2	2	16	4	10	.317	.349	.549	134	3	3	14	0	2	-1	-5	O	-0.3
1928	*NY-A	65	79	12	25	6	1	1	15	8	11	.316	.379	.456	122	2	2	14	1	0	0	-6	O	-0.3
1929	NY-A	42	72	13	15	3	0	2	11	6	3	.208	.269	.333	58	-5	-4	7	1	1	-0	-1	O	-0.5
Total	8	364	787	143	243	47	11	24	139	72	93	.309	.369	.488	123	21	24	141	24	18		-19	O	-0.9

■ JOHNNY PASEK
Pasek, John Paul b: 6/25/05, Niagara Falls, N.Y. d: 3/13/76, Niagara Falls, N.Y   BR/TR, 5'10", 175 lbs.   Deb: 7/28/33

YEAR	TM/L	G	AB	R	H	2B	3B	HR	RBI	BB	SO	AVG	OBP	SLG	PRO+	BR	/A	RC	SB	CS	SBR	FR	POS	TPR
1933	Det-A	28	61	6	15	4	0	0	4	7	7	.246	.324	.311	68	-3	-3	7	2	0	1	-0	C	0.0
1934	Chi-A	4	9	1	3	0	0	0	0	1	1	.333	.400	.333	88	-0	-0	1	0	0	0	-0	/C	0.0
Total	2	32	70	7	18	4	0	0	4	8	8	.257	.333	.314	70	-3	-3	8	2	0	1	-0	/C	0.0

■ DODE PASKERT
Paskert, George Henry b: 8/28/1881, Cleveland, Ohio d: 2/12/59, Cleveland, Ohio   BR/TR, 5'11", 165 lbs.   Deb: 9/21/07

YEAR	TM/L	G	AB	R	H	2B	3B	HR	RBI	BB	SO	AVG	OBP	SLG	PRO+	BR	/A	RC	SB	CS	SBR	FR	POS	TPR
1907	Cin-N	16	50	10	14	4	0	1	8	2		.280	.308	.420	125	1	1	7	2			1	O	0.1
1908	Cin-N	118	395	40	96	14	4	1	36	27		.243	.291	.306	96	-3	-2	42	25			5	*O	0.2
1909	Cin-N	104	322	49	81	7	4	0	33	34		.252	.327	.298	95	-2	-1	39	23			0	O/1	-0.3
1910	Cin-N	144	506	63	152	21	5	4	46	70	60	.300	.389	.374	128	17	20	93	51			10	*O/1	2.5
1911	Phi-N	153	560	96	153	18	5	4	47	70	70	.273	.358	.345	96	-1	-2	81	28			3	*O	-0.3
1912	Phi-N	145	540	102	170	37	5	2	43	91	67	.315	.420	.413	120	26	21	108	36			4	*O/23	1.9
1913	Phi-N	124	454	83	119	21	9	4	29	65	69	.262	.358	.374	105	7	5	65	12			15	*O	1.8
1914	Phi-N	132	451	59	119	25	6	3	44	56	68	.264	.349	.366	106	8	4	64	23			6	*O/S	0.7
1915	*Phi-N	109	328	51	80	17	4	3	39	35	38	.244	.319	.348	100	1	0	41	9	6	-1	4	O/1	0.1
1916	Phi-N	149	555	82	155	30	7	8	46	54	76	.279	.346	.402	125	19	17	77	22	21	-6	4	*O/S	0.3
1917	Phi-N	141	546	78	137	27	11	4	43	62	63	.251	.331	.363	108	9	6	68	19			-6	*O	-0.4
1918	*Chi-N	127	461	69	132	24	4	2	59	53	49	.286	.362	.369	120	14	13	68	20			-8	*O/3	-0.1
1919	Chi-N	88	270	21	53	11	3	2	29	28	33	.196	.274	.281	67	-10	-11	22	7			-8	*O	-2.4
1920	Chi-N	139	487	57	136	22	10	5	71	64	58	.279	.366	.396	117	14	12	72	16	14	-4	-3	*O	-0.1
1921	Cin-N	27	92	8	16	1	1	0	4	4	8	.174	.208	.207	11	-12	-11	4	0	2	-1	1	O	-1.2
Total	15	1716	6017	868	1613	279	78	41	577	715	659	.268	.349	.361	108	88	73	853	293	43		19	*O/13S2	2.8

■ KEVIN PASLEY
Pasley, Kevin Patrick b: 7/22/53, Bronx, N.Y.   BR/TR, 6', 185 lbs.   Deb: 10/02/74

YEAR	TM/L	G	AB	R	H	2B	3B	HR	RBI	BB	SO	AVG	OBP	SLG	PRO+	BR	/A	RC	SB	CS	SBR	FR	POS	TPR
1974	LA-N	1	0	0	0	0	0	0	0	0	0	—	—	—	—	0	0	0	0	0	0	0	/C	0.0
1976	LA-N	23	52	4	12	2	0	0	2	3	7	.231	.273	.269	55	-3	-3	4	0	0	0	5	C	0.3
1977	LA-N	2	3	0	1	0	0	0	0	0	0	.333	.333	.333	80	-0	-0	0	0	0	0	1	/C	0.1
	Sea-A	4	13	1	5	0	0	0	2	1	2	.385	.429	.385	125	0	1	2	0	0	0	-2	/C	0.0
1978	Sea-A	25	54	3	13	5	0	1	5	2	4	.241	.268	.389	83	-1	-1	5	0	0	0	-0	C	0.0
Total	4	55	122	8	31	7	0	1	9	6	13	.254	.289	.336	76	-4	-4	12	0	0	0	3	/C	0.4

■ DAN PASQUA
Pasqua, Daniel Anthony b: 10/17/61, Yonkers, N.Y.   BL/TL, 6', 203 lbs.   Deb: 5/30/85

YEAR	TM/L	G	AB	R	H	2B	3B	HR	RBI	BB	SO	AVG	OBP	SLG	PRO+	BR	/A	RC	SB	CS	SBR	FR	POS	TPR
1985	NY-A	60	148	17	31	3	1	9	25	16	38	.209	.291	.426	96	-2	-1	19	0	0	0	9	OD	0.7
1986	NY-A	102	280	44	82	17	0	16	45	47	78	.293	.400	.525	151	20	21	62	2	0	1	-5	O/1D	1.4
1987	NY-A	113	318	42	74	7	1	17	42	40	99	.233	.320	.421	96	-3	-0	43	0	2	-1	0	OD1	-0.5
1988	Chi-A	129	422	48	96	16	2	20	50	46	100	.227	.308	.417	101	-0	0	54	1	0	0	6	*O/1D	0.4
1989	Chi-A	73	246	26	61	9	1	11	47	25	58	.248	.320	.427	111	2	3	35	1	2	-1	2	O/D	0.3
1990	Chi-A	112	325	43	89	27	3	13	58	37	66	.274	.352	.495	137	14	15	57	1	1	-0	1	DO	1.5
Total	6	589	1739	220	433	79	8	86	267	211	439	.249	.334	.452	116	32	36	270	5	5	-2	13	OD/1	3.8

■ MIKE PASQUARIELLO
Pasquariello, Michael John "Toney" b: 11/7/1898, Philadelphia, Pa. d: 4/5/65, Bridgeport, Conn.   BR/TR, 5'11", 167 lbs.   Deb: 7/09/19

YEAR	TM/L	G	AB	R	H	2B	3B	HR	RBI	BB	SO	AVG	OBP	SLG	PRO+	BR	/A	RC	SB	CS	SBR	FR	POS	TPR
1919	Phi-N	1	1	1	1	0	0	0	0	0	0	1.000	1.000	1.000	469	0	0	1	0			0	/1	0.0
	StL-N	1	1	0	0	0	0	0	0	0	1	.000	.000	.000	-99	-0	-0	0	0			0	H	0.0
	Yr	2	2	1	1	0	0	0	0	0	1	.500	.500	.500	200	0	0	0	0			0		0.0

■ CLIFF PASTORNICKY
Pastornicky, Clifford Scott b: 11/18/58, Seattle, Was.   BR/TR, 5'10", 170 lbs.   Deb: 6/14/83

YEAR	TM/L	G	AB	R	H	2B	3B	HR	RBI	BB	SO	AVG	OBP	SLG	PRO+	BR	/A	RC	SB	CS	SBR	FR	POS	TPR
1983	KC-A	10	32	4	4	0	0	2	5	0	3	.125	.125	.313	16	-4	-4	0	0	0	0	-1	3	-0.3

■ BOB PATE
Pate, Robert Wayne b: 12/3/53, Los Angeles, Cal.   BR/TR, 6'3.5", 200 lbs.   Deb: 6/02/80

YEAR	TM/L	G	AB	R	H	2B	3B	HR	RBI	BB	SO	AVG	OBP	SLG	PRO+	BR	/A	RC	SB	CS	SBR	FR	POS	TPR
1980	Mon-N	23	39	3	10	2	0	0	5	3	6	.256	.310	.308	73	-1	-1	4	0	1	-1	-1	O	-0.3

YEAR	TM/L	G	AB	R	H	2B	3B	HR	RBI	BB	SO	AVG	OBP	SLG	PRO+	BR	/A	RC	SB	CS	SBR	FR	POS	TPR
1981	Mon-N	8	6	0	2	0	0	0	0	1	0	.333	.429	.333	117	0	0	1	0	0	0	0	/O	0.0
Total	2	31	45	3	12	2	0	0	5	4	6	.267	.327	.311	79	-1	-1	5	0	1	-1	-1	/O	-0.3

■ FREDDIE PATEK   Patek, Frederick Joseph "The Flea" b: 10/9/44, Seguin, Tex.   BR/TR, 5'5", 148 lbs.   Deb: 6/03/68

YEAR	TM/L	G	AB	R	H	2B	3B	HR	RBI	BB	SO	AVG	OBP	SLG	PRO+	BR	/A	RC	SB	CS	SBR	FR	POS	TPR
1968	Pit-N	61	208	31	53	4	2	2	18	12	37	.255	.302	.322	89	-3	-3	22	18	7	1	-1	S/O3	0.3
1969	Pit-N	147	460	48	110	9	1	5	32	53	86	.239	.319	.296	75	-15	-14	43	15	8	-0	-2	*S	0.1
1970	*Pit-N	84	237	42	58	10	5	1	19	29	46	.245	.327	.342	81	-7	-6	29	8	2	1	11	S	1.4
1971	KC-A	147	591	86	158	21	11	6	36	44	80	.267	.323	.371	97	-4	-3	75	49	14	6	10	*S	3.0
1972	KC-A	136	518	59	110	25	4	0	32	47	64	.212	.282	.276	67	-21	-21	44	33	7	6	30	*S	3.2
1973	KC-A	135	501	82	117	19	5	5	45	54	63	.234	.312	.321	73	-14	-19	53	36	14	2	35	*S	3.7
1974	KC-A	149	537	72	121	18	6	3	38	77	69	.225	.326	.298	76	-11	-15	58	33	15	1	4	*S	0.1
1975	KC-A	136	483	58	110	14	5	5	45	42	65	.228	.292	.308	68	-19	-21	47	32	7	5	-6	*S/D	-0.8
1976	*KC-A	144	432	58	104	19	3	1	43	50	63	.241	.322	.306	84	-7	-8	48	51	15	6	-5	*S/D	0.2
1977	*KC-A	154	497	72	130	26	6	5	60	41	84	.262	.324	.368	88	-8	-8	65	53	13	8	-19	*S	0.0
1978	*KC-A	138	440	54	109	23	1	2	46	42	56	.248	.315	.318	76	-12	-13	48	38	11	5	-25	*S	-2.2
1979	KC-A	106	306	30	77	17	0	1	37	16	42	.252	.295	.317	64	-15	-16	26	11	12	-4	-28	*S	-3.4
1980	Cal-A	86	273	41	72	10	5	5	34	15	26	.264	.304	.392	92	-5	-4	28	7	6	-2	-18	S	-1.6
1981	Cal-A	27	47	3	11	1	0	0	5	1	6	.234	.250	.298	57	-3	-3	3	1	0	0	2	2/3S	0.0
Total	14	1650	5530	736	1340	216	55	41	490	523	787	.242	.311	.324	79	-143	-153	592	385	131	37	-15	*S/230D	4.0

■ BOB PATRICK   Patrick, Robert Lee b: 10/27/17, Ft.Smith, Ark.   BR/TR, 6'2", 190 lbs.   Deb: 9/20/41

YEAR	TM/L	G	AB	R	H	2B	3B	HR	RBI	BB	SO	AVG	OBP	SLG	PRO+	BR	/A	RC	SB	CS	SBR	FR	POS	TPR
1941	Det-A	5	7	2	2	0	0	0	0	0	1	.286	.286	.286	47	-0	-1	1	0	0	0	-0	/O	0.0
1942	Det-A	4	8	1	2	1	0	1	3	1	0	.250	.333	.750	185	1	1	2	0	0	0	0	/O	0.1
Total	2	9	15	3	4	1	0	1	3	1	1	.267	.313	.533	118	0	0	3	0	0	0	0	/O	0.1

■ HARRY PATTEE   Pattee, Harry Ernest b: 1/17/1882, Charlestown, Mass.   d: 7/17/71, Lynchburg, Va.   BL/TR, 5'8", 149 lbs.   Deb: 4/14/08

YEAR	TM/L	G	AB	R	H	2B	3B	HR	RBI	BB	SO	AVG	OBP	SLG	PRO+	BR	/A	RC	SB	CS	SBR	FR	POS	TPR
1908	Bro-N	80	264	19	57	5	2	0	9	25		.216	.284	.250	76	-7	-6	26	24			12	2	0.6

■ DAN PATTERSON   Patterson, Daniel Thomas b: 1846, New York, N.Y.   5'9", 143 lbs.   Deb: 5/18/1871

YEAR	TM/L	G	AB	R	H	2B	3B	HR	RBI	BB	SO	AVG	OBP	SLG	PRO+	BR	/A	RC	SB	CS	SBR	FR	POS	TPR
1871	Mut-n	32	151	31	31	2	0	0	13	1	0	.205	.211	.219	26	-14	-11	8	2				*O/2	-0.5
1872	Eck-n	12	47	6	8	1	0	0		0		.170	.170	.191	13	-5	-3	2					O/1	-0.1
1874	Mut-n	1	5	1	2	0	0	0		0		.400	.400	.400	150	0	0	1					/1O	0.0
1875	Atl-n	11	41	3	8	0	0	0		0		.195	.195	.195	41	-3	-2	2					/2O	-0.1
Total	4 n	56	244	41	49	3	0	0		1		.201	.204	.213	28	-21	-16	12					/O21	-0.7

■ HAM PATTERSON   Patterson, Hamilton b: 10/13/1877, Belleville, Ill.   d: 11/25/45, E.St.Louis, Ill.   TR , 6'2", 185 lbs.   Deb: 5/18/09

YEAR	TM/L	G	AB	R	H	2B	3B	HR	RBI	BB	SO	AVG	OBP	SLG	PRO+	BR	/A	RC	SB	CS	SBR	FR	POS	TPR
1909	StL-A	17	49	2	10	1	0	0	5	0		.204	.204	.224	38	-4	-3	2	1			-1	/1O	-0.4
	Chi-A	1	3	2	0	0	0	0	0	1		.000	.250	.000	-21	-0	-0	0	0			1	/1	0.0
	Yr	18	52	4	10	1	0	0	5	1		.192	.208	.212	35	-4	-4	2	1			-0		-0.4

■ HANK PATTERSON   Patterson, Henry Joseph Colquit b: 7/17/07, San Francisco, Cal.   d: 9/30/70, Panorama City, Cal.   BR/TR, 5'11.5", 170 lbs.   Deb: 9/05/32

YEAR	TM/L	G	AB	R	H	2B	3B	HR	RBI	BB	SO	AVG	OBP	SLG	PRO+	BR	/A	RC	SB	CS	SBR	FR	POS	TPR
1932	Bos-A	1	1	0	0	0	0	0	0	0	0	.000	.000	.000	-99	-0	-0	0	0	0	0	0	/C	0.0

■ CLAIRE PATTERSON   Patterson, Lorenzo Claire b: 10/5/1887, Arkansas City, Kan.   d: 3/28/13, Mojave, Cal.   BL/TR, 6' ", 180 lbs.   Deb: 9/05/09

YEAR	TM/L	G	AB	R	H	2B	3B	HR	RBI	BB	SO	AVG	OBP	SLG	PRO+	BR	/A	RC	SB	CS	SBR	FR	POS	TPR
1909	Cin-N	4	8	0	1	0	0	0	1	0		.125	.125	.125	-23	-1	-1	0	0			-0	/O	-0.1

■ MIKE PATTERSON   Patterson, Michael Lee b: 1/26/58, Santa Monica, Cal.   BL/TR, 5'10", 170 lbs.   Deb: 4/15/81

YEAR	TM/L	G	AB	R	H	2B	3B	HR	RBI	BB	SO	AVG	OBP	SLG	PRO+	BR	/A	RC	SB	CS	SBR	FR	POS	TPR
1981	Oak-A	12	23	4	8	1	1	0	1	2	5	.348	.400	.478	160	2	2	4	0	1	-1	0	/OD	0.1
	NY-A	4	9	2	2	0	2	0	0	0		.222	.222	.667	150	0	0	1	0	0	0	0	/O	0.0
	Yr	16	32	6	10	1	3	0	1	2	5	.313	.353	.531	158	2	2	6	0	1	-1	0		0.1
1982	NY-A	11	16	3	3	1	0	1	1	2	6	.188	.278	.438	94	-0	-0	2	1	0	0	-0	/OD	0.0
Total	2	27	48	9	13	2	3	1	2	4	11	.271	.327	.500	135	2	2	8	1	1	-0	-0	/OD	0.1

■ PAT PATTERSON   Patterson, William Jennings Bryan b: 1/29/01, Belleville, Ill.   d: 10/1/77, St.Louis, Mo.   BR/TR, 6', 175 lbs.   Deb: 4/14/21

YEAR	TM/L	G	AB	R	H	2B	3B	HR	RBI	BB	SO	AVG	OBP	SLG	PRO+	BR	/A	RC	SB	CS	SBR	FR	POS	TPR
1921	NY-N	23	35	5	14	0	0	1	5	2	5	.400	.432	.486	142	2	2	7	0	1	-1	4	3/S	0.6

■ GEORGE PATTISON   Pattison, George   Deb: 4/24/1884

YEAR	TM/L	G	AB	R	H	2B	3B	HR	RBI	BB	SO	AVG	OBP	SLG	PRO+	BR	/A	RC	SB	CS	SBR	FR	POS	TPR
1884	Phi-U	2	7	0	1	0	0	0	0			.143	.143	.143	-3	-1	-1	0				-0	/O	0.0

■ GENE PATTON   Patton, Gene Tunney b: 7/8/26, Coatesville, Pa.   BL/TR, 5'10", 165 lbs.   Deb: 6/17/44

YEAR	TM/L	G	AB	R	H	2B	3B	HR	RBI	BB	SO	AVG	OBP	SLG	PRO+	BR	/A	RC	SB	CS	SBR	FR	POS	TPR
1944	Bos-N	1	0	0	0	0	0	0	0	0	0					0	0	0	0			0	R	0.0

■ BILL PATTON   Patton, George William b: 10/7/12, Cornwall, Pa.   d: 3/15/86, Philadelphia, Pa.   BR/TR, 6'2", 180 lbs.   Deb: 6/29/35

YEAR	TM/L	G	AB	R	H	2B	3B	HR	RBI	BB	SO	AVG	OBP	SLG	PRO+	BR	/A	RC	SB	CS	SBR	FR	POS	TPR
1935	Phi-A	9	10	1	3	1	0	0	2	2	3	.300	.417	.400	113	0	0	2	0	0	0	1	/C	0.1

■ TOM PATTON   Patton, Thomas Allen b: 9/5/35, Honey Brook, Pa.   BR/TR, 5'9.5", 185 lbs.   Deb: 4/30/57

YEAR	TM/L	G	AB	R	H	2B	3B	HR	RBI	BB	SO	AVG	OBP	SLG	PRO+	BR	/A	RC	SB	CS	SBR	FR	POS	TPR
1957	Bal-A	1	2	0	0	0	0	0	0	0	2	.000	.000	.000	-99	-1	-1	0	0	0	0	1	/C	0.1

■ LOU PAUL   Paul, Louis BR/TR   Deb: 9/05/1876

YEAR	TM/L	G	AB	R	H	2B	3B	HR	RBI	BB	SO	AVG	OBP	SLG	PRO+	BR	/A	RC	SB	CS	SBR	FR	POS	TPR
1876	Phi-N	3	12	2	2	1	0	0	0	0	0	.167	.167	.250	37	-1	-1	1				-1	/C	0.0

■ CARLOS PAULA   Paula, Carlos (Conill) b: 11/28/27, Havana, Cuba   d: 4/25/83, Miami, Fla.   BR/TR, 6'3", 195 lbs.   Deb: 9/06/54

YEAR	TM/L	G	AB	R	H	2B	3B	HR	RBI	BB	SO	AVG	OBP	SLG	PRO+	BR	/A	RC	SB	CS	SBR	FR	POS	TPR
1954	Was-A	9	24	2	4	1	0	0	2	2	4	.167	.231	.208	22	-3	-2	1	0	0	0	1	/O	-0.1
1955	Was-A	115	351	34	105	20	7	6	45	17	43	.299	.335	.447	115	3	5	49	2	3	-1	-4	O	-0.4
1956	Was-A	33	82	8	15	2	1	3	13	8	15	.183	.256	.341	56	-6	-6	5	0	2	-1	-2	O	-0.9
Total	3	157	457	44	124	23	8	9	60	27	62	.271	.315	.416	99	-6	-3	56	2	5	-2	-5	O	-1.4

■ GENE PAULETTE   Paulette, Eugene Edward b: 5/26/1891, Centralia, Ill.   d: 2/8/66, Little Rock, Ark.   BR/TR, 6', 150 lbs.   Deb: 6/16/11

YEAR	TM/L	G	AB	R	H	2B	3B	HR	RBI	BB	SO	AVG	OBP	SLG	PRO+	BR	/A	RC	SB	CS	SBR	FR	POS	TPR
1911	NY-N	10	12	1	2	0	0	0	0	0	0	.167	.167	.167	-6	-2	-2	0				-1	/1S3	-0.2
1916	StL-A	5	4	1	2	0	0	0	0	1	1	.500	.600	.500	242	1	1	1	0			0	H	0.1
1917	StL-A	12	22	3	4	0	0	0	0	3	3	.182	.280	.182	43	-1	-1	1	0			0	/123	0.0
	StL-N	95	332	32	88	21	7	0	34	16	16	.265	.303	.370	109	1	2	38	9			-1	1	0.1
1918	StL-N	125	461	33	126	15	3	0	52	27	16	.273	.316	.319	97	-3	-2	49	11			4	1S/203P	0.1
1919	StL-N	43	144	11	31	6	0	0	11	9	6	.215	.261	.257	60	-8	-7	10	4			2	1/S	-0.5
	Phi-N	67	243	20	63	8	3	1	31	19	10	.259	.316	.329	88	-2	-3	27	10			1	2O/1	0.0
	Yr	110	387	31	94	14	3	1	42	28	16	.243	.296	.302	78	-9	-10	36	14			3		-0.5
1920	Phi-N	143	562	59	162	16	6	1	36	33	16	.288	.332	.343	90	-4	-7	64	9	8	-2	6	*1/S	-0.3
Total	6	500	1780	160	478	66	19	2	165	108	69	.269	.314	.330	92	-18	-19	191	43	8		11	1/2SO3P	-0.8

■ SI PAUXTIS   Pauxtis, Simon Francis b: 7/20/1885, Pittston, Pa.   d: 3/13/61, Philadelphia, Pa.   BR/TR, 6' ", 175 lbs.   Deb: 9/18/09

YEAR	TM/L	G	AB	R	H	2B	3B	HR	RBI	BB	SO	AVG	OBP	SLG	PRO+	BR	/A	RC	SB	CS	SBR	FR	POS	TPR
1909	Cin-N	4	8	2	1	0	0	0	0	0		.125	.222	.125	8	-1	-1	0	0			-1	/C	0.0

■ DON PAVLETICH   Pavletich, Donald Stephen b: 7/13/38, Milwaukee, Wis.   BR/TR, 5'11", 190 lbs.   Deb: 4/20/57

YEAR	TM/L	G	AB	R	H	2B	3B	HR	RBI	BB	SO	AVG	OBP	SLG	PRO+	BR	/A	RC	SB	CS	SBR	FR	POS	TPR
1957	Cin-N	1	1	0	0	0	0	0	0	0	0	.000	.000	.000	-93	-0	-0	0	0	0	0	0	H	0.0
1959	Cin-N	1	0	1	0	0	0	0	0	0	0	—				0	0	0	0	0	0	0	R	0.0
1962	Cin-N	34	63	7	14	3	0	1	7	8	18	.222	.310	.317	67	-3	-3	7	0	0	0	-2	1/C	-0.5
1963	Cin-N	71	183	18	38	11	0	5	18	17	12	.208	.275	.350	76	-5	-6	18	0	0	0	-3	1C	-0.9

YEAR	TM/L	G	AB	R	H	2B	3B	HR	RBI	BB	SO	AVG	OBP	SLG	PRO+	BR	/A	RC	SB	CS	SBR	FR	POS	TPR
1964	Cin-N	34	91	12	22	4	0	5	11	10	17	.242	.317	.451	109	1	1	13	0	0	0	-3	C/1	0.0
1965	Cin-N	68	191	25	61	11	1	8	32	23	27	.319	.395	.513	144	14	12	38	1	1	-0	-2	C/1	1.2
1966	Cin-N	83	235	29	69	13	2	12	38	18	37	.294	.346	.519	126	11	9	41	1	0	0	-11	C1	0.0
1967	Cin-N	74	231	25	55	14	3	6	34	21	38	.238	.313	.403	93	1	2	26	2	1	0	-5	C/13	-0.3
1968	Cin-N	46	98	11	28	3	1	2	11	8	23	.286	.352	.398	117	3	2	12	0	0	0	-0	1/C	0.2
1969	Chi-A	78	188	26	46	12	0	6	33	28	45	.245	.343	.404	103	2	1	28	0	0	0	-6	C1	-0.2
1970	Bos-A	32	65	4	9	1	1	0	6	10	15	.138	.253	.185	21	-7	-7	3	1	0	0	1	1C	-0.6
1971	Bos-A	14	27	5	7	1	0	1	3	5	5	.259	.375	.407	113	1	1	5	0	0	0	-1	/C	0.0
Total	12	536	1373	163	349	73	8	46	193	148	237	.254	.330	.420	103	18	7	190	5	2	0	-31	C1/3	-1.1

■ TED PAWELEK
Pawelek, Theodore John "Porky" b: 8/15/19, Chicago Heights, Ill. d: 2/12/64, Chicago Heights, Ill. BL/TR, 5'10.5", 202 lbs. Deb: 9/13/46

YEAR	TM/L	G	AB	R	H	2B	3B	HR	RBI	BB	SO	AVG	OBP	SLG	PRO+	BR	/A	RC	SB	CS	SBR	FR	POS	TPR
1946	Chi-N	4	4	0	1	1	0	0	0	0	0	.250	.250	.500	112	0	0	1				0	/C	0.0

■ STAN PAWLOSKI
Pawloski, Stanley Walter b: 9/6/31, Wanamie, Pa. BR/TR, 6'1", 175 lbs. Deb: 9/24/55

YEAR	TM/L	G	AB	R	H	2B	3B	HR	RBI	BB	SO	AVG	OBP	SLG	PRO+	BR	/A	RC	SB	CS	SBR	FR	POS	TPR
1955	Cle-A	2	8	0	1	0	0	0	0	0	2	.125	.125	.125	-31	-1	-2	0	0	0	0	1	/2	0.0

■ FRED PAYNE
Payne, Frederick Thomas b: 9/2/1880, Camden, N.Y. d: 1/16/54, Camden, N.Y. BR/TR, 5'10", 162 lbs. Deb: 4/21/06

YEAR	TM/L	G	AB	R	H	2B	3B	HR	RBI	BB	SO	AVG	OBP	SLG	PRO+	BR	/A	RC	SB	CS	SBR	FR	POS	TPR
1906	Det-A	72	222	23	60	5	5	0	20	13		.270	.311	.338	102	1	0	26	4			-1	CO	0.3
1907	*Det-A	53	169	17	28	2	2	0	14	7		.166	.199	.201	28	-13	-14	8	4			3	C/O	-0.7
1908	Det-A	20	45	3	3	0	0	0	2	3		.067	.125	.067	-35	-6	-7	1	1			-3	C/O	-0.9
1909	Chi-A	32	82	8	20	2	0	0	12	5		.244	.295	.268	82	-2	-2	7	0			-1	C/O	0.0
1910	Chi-A	91	252	17	56	5	4	0	19	11		.222	.260	.274	70	-10	-9	20	6			-4	C/O	-0.4
1911	Chi-A	66	133	14	27	2	1	1	19	8		.203	.259	.256	45	-10	-10	10	6			-4	C	-0.6
Total	6	334	903	82	194	16	12	1	86	47		.215	.258	.262	62	-41	-40	72	21			-10	C/O	-2.3

■ GEORGE PAYNTER
Paynter, George Washington (b: George Washington Paner)
b: 7/6/1871, Cincinnati, Ohio d: 10/1/50, Cincinnati, Ohio 5'9", 125 lbs. Deb: 8/12/1894

YEAR	TM/L	G	AB	R	H	2B	3B	HR	RBI	BB	SO	AVG	OBP	SLG	PRO+	BR	/A	RC	SB	CS	SBR	FR	POS	TPR
1894	StL-N	1	4	0	0	0	0	0	0	1		.000	.200	.000	-47	-1	-1	0	1			1	/O	0.0

■ JOHNNY PEACOCK
Peacock, John Gaston b: 1/10/10, Fremont, N.C. d: 10/17/81, Wilson, N.C. BL/TR, 5'11", 165 lbs. Deb: 9/23/37

YEAR	TM/L	G	AB	R	H	2B	3B	HR	RBI	BB	SO	AVG	OBP	SLG	PRO+	BR	/A	RC	SB	CS	SBR	FR	POS	TPR
1937	Bos-A	9	32	3	10	2	1	0	6	1	0	.313	.333	.438	89	-0	-1	5	0	0	0	1	/C	0.1
1938	Bos-A	72	195	29	59	7	1	1	39	17	4	.303	.358	.364	78	-5	-7	26	4	1	1	-9	C/1O	-1.2
1939	Bos-A	92	274	33	76	11	4	0	36	29	11	.277	.347	.347	75	-9	-10	35	1	1	-0	-8	C	-1.1
1940	Bos-A	63	131	20	37	4	1	0	13	23	10	.282	.390	.328	85	-1	-2	17	1	1	-0	-7	C	-0.4
1941	Bos-A	79	261	28	74	20	1	0	27	21	3	.284	.339	.368	85	-5	-6	34	2	1	0	-4	C	-0.5
1942	Bos-A	88	286	17	76	7	3	0	25	21	11	.266	.316	.311	74	-9	-10	29	1	1	-0	-6	C	-0.6
1943	Bos-A	48	114	7	23	3	1	0	7	10	9	.202	.266	.246	49	-7	-7	8	1	1	-0	-1	C	-0.7
1944	Bos-A	4	4	0	0	0	0	0	0	0	0	.000	.000	.000	-99	-1	-1	0	0	0	0	0	/C	0.0
	Phi-N	83	253	21	57	9	3	0	21	31	15	.225	.310	.285	70	-10	-9	23	1			2	C/2	-0.3
1945	Phi-N	33	74	6	15	6	0	0	6	6	0	.203	.262	.284	53	-5	-5	5	1			-5	C	-0.9
	Bro-N	48	110	11	28	5	1	0	14	24	10	.255	.388	.318	98	1	1	16	2			0	C	0.2
	Yr	81	184	17	43	11	1	0	20	30	10	.234	.341	.304	82	-4	-4	21	3			-5		-0.7
Total	9	619	1734	175	455	74	16	1	194	183	73	.262	.333	.325	76	-51	-56	197	14	6		-37	C/2O1	-5.4

■ ELIAS PEAK
Peak, Elias b: 5/23/1859, Philadelphia, Pa. d: 12/17/16, Philadelphia, Pa. Deb: 4/19/1884

YEAR	TM/L	G	AB	R	H	2B	3B	HR	RBI	BB	SO	AVG	OBP	SLG	PRO+	BR	/A	RC	SB	CS	SBR	FR	POS	TPR
1884	Bos-U	1	3	2	2	0	0	0			1	.667	.750	.667	389	1	1	2	0			0	/O	0.1
	Phi-U	54	215	35	42	6	4	0			7	.195	.221	.260	67	-8	-6	13	0			-6	2/OS	-1.1
	Yr	55	218	37	44	6	4	0			8	.202	.230	.266	73	-7	-5	14	0			-6		-1.0

■ HARRY PEARCE
Pearce, Harry James b: 7/12/1889, Philadelphia, Pa. d: 1/8/42, Philadelphia, Pa. BR/TR, 5'9", 158 lbs. Deb: 10/02/17

YEAR	TM/L	G	AB	R	H	2B	3B	HR	RBI	BB	SO	AVG	OBP	SLG	PRO+	BR	/A	RC	SB	CS	SBR	FR	POS	TPR
1917	Phi-N	7	16	2	4	3	0	0	2	0	4	.250	.294	.438	118	0	0	2	0			5	/S	0.5
1918	Phi-N	60	164	16	40	3	2	0	18	9	31	.244	.295	.287	73	-4	-5	15	5			5	2/S13	0.2
1919	Phi-N	68	244	24	44	3	3	0	9	8	27	.180	.209	.217	26	-21	-23	12	6			-1	2S/3	-2.4
Total	3	135	424	42	88	9	5	0	29	17	62	.208	.247	.252	48	-25	-28	29	11			9	/2S31	-1.7

■ DICKEY PEARCE
Pearce, Richard J. b: 2/29/1836, Brooklyn, N.Y. d: 10/12/08, Onset, Mass. BR/TR, 5'3.5", 161 lbs. Deb: 5/18/1871 MU

YEAR	TM/L	G	AB	R	H	2B	3B	HR	RBI	BB	SO	AVG	OBP	SLG	PRO+	BR	/A	RC	SB	CS	SBR	FR	POS	TPR
1871	Mut-n	33	163	31	44	5	0	0	20	4	1	.270	.287	.301	76	-6	-3	14	0				*S	0.0
1872	Mut-n	44	206	32	40	1	1	1		4		.194	.210	.223	36	-16	-13	10					*S/OM	-0.8
1873	Atl-n	55	259	42	71	6	0	1		10		.274	.301	.309	89	-6	-0	25					*S	0.1
1874	Atl-n	56	254	48	75	4	0	0		7		.295	.314	.311	113	0	6	25					*S/3	0.1
1875	StL-n	70	312	51	77	5	3	0		7		.247	.263	.282	98	-3	1	24					*S/PM	0.0
1876	StL-N	25	102	12	21	1	0	0	10	3	5	.206	.229	.216	51	-5	-4	5	5				S/O2	0.0
1877	StL-N	8	29	1	5	0	0	0	4	1	4	.172	.200	.172	19	-3	-2	1	3				/S	0.0
Total	5 n	258	1194	204	307	21	4	2	20	32	1	.257	.277	.286	84	-31	-8	98					S/P3O	-0.7
Total	2	33	131	13	26	1	0	0	14	4	9	.198	.222	.206	44	-8	-7	6	8				/S2O	0.0

■ DUCKY PEARCE
Pearce, William C. b: 3/17/1885, Corning, Ohio d: 5/22/33, Brownstown, Ind. BR/TR, 6'1", 185 lbs. Deb: 7/01/08

YEAR	TM/L	G	AB	R	H	2B	3B	HR	RBI	BB	SO	AVG	OBP	SLG	PRO+	BR	/A	RC	SB	CS	SBR	FR	POS	TPR
1908	Cin-N	2	2	0	0	0	0	0	0	0		.000	.000	.000	-99	-0	-0	-0	0			1	/C	0.1
1909	Cin-N	2	2	0	0	0	0	0	0	0		.000	.000	.000	-99	-0	-0	0	0			-0	/C	0.0
Total	2	4	4	0	0	0	0	0	0	0		.000	.000	.000	-99	-1	-1	-0	0			1	/C	0.1

■ ALBIE PEARSON
Pearson, Albert Gregory b: 9/12/34, Alhambra, Cal. BL/TL, 5'5", 140 lbs. Deb: 4/14/58

YEAR	TM/L	G	AB	R	H	2B	3B	HR	RBI	BB	SO	AVG	OBP	SLG	PRO+	BR	/A	RC	SB	CS	SBR	FR	POS	TPR
1958	Was-A	146	530	63	146	25	5	3	33	64	31	.275	.356	.358	99	-0	1	69	7	8	-3	2	*O	-0.8
1959	Was-A	25	80	9	15	1	0	0	2	14	3	.188	.309	.200	43	-6	-6	6	1	1	-0	-3	O	-0.9
	Bal-A	80	138	22	32	4	2	0	6	13	5	.232	.298	.290	64	-7	-7	12	4	0	1	3	O	-0.4
	Yr	105	218	31	47	5	2	0	8	27	8	.216	.302	.257	56	-13	-12	19	5	1	1	0		-1.3
1960	Bal-A	48	82	17	20	2	0	1	6	17	3	.244	.374	.305	87	-1	-1	11	4	0	1	-1	O	-0.1
1961	LA-A	144	427	92	123	21	3	7	41	96	40	.288	.422	.400	109	18	11	84	11	3	2	0	*O	1.2
1962	LA-A	160	614	**115**	160	29	6	5	42	95	36	.261	.361	.352	96	-3	-1	85	15	6	1	0	*O	-0.5
1963	LA-A	154	578	92	176	26	5	6	47	92	37	.304	.403	.398	133	24	28	100	17	10	-1	-0	*O	2.3
1964	LA-A	107	265	34	59	5	1	2	16	35	22	.223	.316	.272	72	-11	-8	25	6	4	-1	-7	O	-1.8
1965	Cal-A	122	360	41	100	17	2	4	21	51	17	.278	.370	.369	114	7	8	55	12	1	3	-2	*O	0.5
1966	Cal-A	2	3	0	0	0	0	0	0	0	1	.000	.000	.000	-99	-1	-1	0	0	0	0	0	/O	0.0
Total	9	988	3077	485	831	130	24	28	214	477	195	.270	.370	.355	102	20	26	447	77	33	3	-4	O	-0.5

■ CHARLIE PECHOUS
Pechous, Charles Edward b: 10/5/1896, Chicago, Ill. d: 9/13/80, Kenosha, Wis. BR/TR, 6', 170 lbs. Deb: 9/14/15

YEAR	TM/L	G	AB	R	H	2B	3B	HR	RBI	BB	SO	AVG	OBP	SLG	PRO+	BR	/A	RC	SB	CS	SBR	FR	POS	TPR
1915	Chi-F	18	51	4	9	3	0	0	4	4	15	.176	.235	.235	42	-4	-3	4	1			-1	3	-0.3
1916	Chi-N	22	69	5	10	1	1	0	4	3	21	.145	.181	.188	12	-7	-8	3	1			8	3	0.1
1917	Chi-N	13	41	2	10	0	0	0	1	2	9	.244	.295	.244	61	-2	-2	3	1			-2	/3S	-0.3
Total	3	53	161	11	29	4	1	0	9	9	45	.180	.228	.217	34	-12	-13	9	3			6	/3S	-0.5

■ HAL PECK
Peck, Harold Arthur b: 4/20/17, Big Bend, Wis. BL/TL, 5'11", 175 lbs. Deb: 5/13/43

YEAR	TM/L	G	AB	R	H	2B	3B	HR	RBI	BB	SO	AVG	OBP	SLG	PRO+	BR	/A	RC	SB	CS	SBR	FR	POS	TPR
1943	Bro-N	1	1	0	0	0	0	0	0	0	0	.000	.000	.000	-99	-0	-0	0	0			0	H	-0.2
1944	Phi-A	2	8	0	2	0	0	0	1	0	2	.250	.250	.250	44	-1	-1	0	0	2	-1	0	/O	-0.2
1945	Phi-A	112	449	51	124	22	9	5	39	37	28	.276	.331	.399	112	5	5	61	5	3	-0	-12	*O	-1.1
1946	Phi-A	48	150	14	37	8	2	2	11	16	14	.247	.319	.367	92	-2	-2	18	1	2	-1	-5	O	-0.9

YEAR	TM/L	G	AB	R	H	2B	3B	HR	RBI	BB	SO	AVG	OBP	SLG	PRO+	BR	/A	RC	SB	CS	SBR	FR	POS	TPR
1947	Cle-A	114	392	58	115	18	2	8	44	27	31	.293	.342	.411	112	3	5	56	3	3	-1	-11	O	-1.1
1948	*Cle-A	45	63	12	18	3	0	0	8	4	8	.286	.328	.333	78	-2	-2	8	1	0	0	-1	/O	-0.2
1949	Cle-A	33	29	1	9	1	0	0	9	3	3	.310	.375	.345	93	-0	-0	4	0	0	0	0	/O	0.0
Total	7	355	1092	136	305	52	13	15	112	87	86	.279	.334	.392	106	5		147	10	10		-29	O	-3.5

■ **ROGER PECKINPAUGH** Peckinpaugh, Roger Thorpe b: 2/5/1891, Wooster, Ohio d: 11/17/77, Cleveland, Ohio BR/TR, 5'10.5", 165 lbs. Deb: 9/15/10 M

YEAR	TM/L	G	AB	R	H	2B	3B	HR	RBI	BB	SO	AVG	OBP	SLG	PRO+	BR	/A	RC	SB	CS	SBR	FR	POS	TPR
1910	Cle-A	15	45	1	9	0	0	0	6	1		.200	.234	.200	36	-3	-3	3	3			-6	S	-1.0
1912	Cle-A	70	236	18	50	4	1	1	22	16		.212	.262	.250	45	-17	-18	18	11			-2	S	-1.2
1913	Cle-A	1	0	1	0	0	0	0	0	0	0	—	—	—	—	0	0	0	0			0	H	0.0
	NY-A	95	340	35	91	10	7	1	32	24	47	.268	.316	.347	94	-3	-4	41	19			-6	S	0.0
	Yr	96	340	36	91	10	7	1	32	24	47	.268	.316	.347	94	-3	-4	41	19			-6		0.0
1914	NY-A	157	570	55	127	14	6	3	51	51	73	.223	.288	.284	72	-20	-20	52	38	17	1	3	*SM	0.0
1915	NY-A	142	540	67	119	18	7	5	44	49	72	.220	.289	.307	79	-16	-16	53	19	12	-2	11	*S	0.6
1916	NY-A	145	552	65	141	22	8	4	58	62	50	.255	.332	.346	101	2	1	72	18			1	*S	1.5
1917	NY-A	148	543	63	141	24	7	0	41	64	46	.260	.340	.330	103	4	3	66	17			10	*S	2.0
1918	NY-A	122	446	59	103	15	3	0	43	43	41	.231	.303	.278	74	-13	-14	42	12			25	*S	2.1
1919	NY-A	122	453	89	138	20	2	7	33	59	37	.305	.390	.404	122	16	15	75	10			28	*S	5.4
1920	NY-A	139	534	109	144	26	6	8	54	72	47	.270	.356	.386	93	-2	-5	75	8	12	-5	3	*S	0.6
1921	*NY-A	149	577	128	166	25	7	8	71	84	44	.288	.380	.397	96	1	-1	93	2	2	-1	-4	*S	1.2
1922	Was-A	147	520	62	132	14	4	2	48	55	36	.254	.329	.308	70	-24	-21	57	11	6	-0	22	*S	1.7
1923	Was-A	154	568	73	150	18	4	2	62	64	30	.264	.340	.320	78	-20	-16	66	10	8	-2	23	*S	2.0
1924	*Was-A	155	523	72	142	20	5	2	73	72	45	.272	.360	.340	84	-13	-11	69	11	7	-1	9	*S	1.3
1925	*Was-A	126	422	67	124	16	4	4	64	49	23	.294	.367	.379	91	-6	-5	63	13	4	2	-15	*S/1	0.0
1926	Was-A	57	147	19	35	4	1	1	14	28	12	.238	.360	.299	75	-5	-4	18	3	0	1	-1	S/1	0.0
1927	Chi-A	68	217	23	64	6	3	0	23	21	6	.295	.360	.350	87	-4	-3	27	2	3	-1	-1	S/1	0.0
Total	17	2012	7233	1006	1876	256	75	48	739	814	609	.259	.336	.335	87	-124	-120	889	207	71		100	*S/1	16.2

■ **BILL PECOTA** Pecota, William Joseph b: 2/16/60, Redwood City, Cal. BR/TR, 6'2", 195 lbs. Deb: 9/19/86

YEAR	TM/L	G	AB	R	H	2B	3B	HR	RBI	BB	SO	AVG	OBP	SLG	PRO+	BR	/A	RC	SB	CS	SBR	FR	POS	TPR
1986	KC-A	12	29	3	6	2	0	0	2	3	3	.207	.303	.276	58	-2	-2	2	0	2	-1	10	3/SD	0.6
1987	KC-A	66	156	22	43	5	1	3	14	15	25	.276	.343	.378	89	-2	-2	21	5	0	2	8	S32/D	0.9
1988	KC-A	90	178	25	37	3	3	1	15	18	34	.208	.288	.275	58	-10	-10	16	7	2	1	13	S31/OD2C	0.5
1989	KC-A	65	83	21	17	4	2	3	5	7	9	.205	.275	.410	91	-1	-1	9	5	0	2	8	SO2/31	1.1
1990	KC-A	87	240	43	58	15	2	5	20	33	39	.242	.336	.383	103	1	1	32	8	5	-1	8	2S3/O1D	1.2
Total	5	320	686	114	161	29	8	12	56	76	110	.235	.316	.353	85	-14	-14	80	25	9	2	46	S/2301DC	4.3

■ **LES PEDEN** Peden, Leslie Earl "Gooch" b: 9/17/23, Azle, Tex. BR/TR, 6'1.5", 212 lbs. Deb: 4/17/53

YEAR	TM/L	G	AB	R	H	2B	3B	HR	RBI	BB	SO	AVG	OBP	SLG	PRO+	BR	/A	RC	SB	CS	SBR	FR	POS	TPR
1953	Was-A	9	28	4	7	1	0	1	4	3		.250	.323	.393	101	-0	0	4	0	0	0	-1	/C	0.0

■ **STU PEDERSON** Pederson, Stuart Russell b: 1/28/60, Palo Alto, Cal. BL/TL, 6', 185 lbs. Deb: 9/08/85

YEAR	TM/L	G	AB	R	H	2B	3B	HR	RBI	BB	SO	AVG	OBP	SLG	PRO+	BR	/A	RC	SB	CS	SBR	FR	POS	TPR
1985	LA-N	8	4	1	0	0	0	0	0	0	2	.000	.000	.000	-99	-1	-1	0	0	0	0	0	/O	0.0

■ **AL PEDRIQUE** Pedrique, Alfredo Jose (Garcia) b: 8/11/60, Aragua, Venez. BR/TR, 6' ", 155 lbs. Deb: 4/14/87

YEAR	TM/L	G	AB	R	H	2B	3B	HR	RBI	BB	SO	AVG	OBP	SLG	PRO+	BR	/A	RC	SB	CS	SBR	FR	POS	TPR
1987	NY-N	5	6	1	0	0	0	0	0	1	2	.000	.143	.000	-61	-1	-1	0	0	0	0	1	/S2	0.0
	Pit-N	88	246	23	74	10	1	1	27	18	27	.301	.356	.362	90	-3	-3	31	5	4	-1	-11	S/32	-0.6
	Yr	93	252	24	74	10	1	1	27	19	29	.294	.350	.353	87	-4	-4	30	5	4	-1	-10		-0.6
1988	Pit-N	50	128	7	23	5	0	0	4	8	17	.180	.234	.219	31	-11	-11	6	0	0	0	8	S/3	-0.6
1989	Det-A	31	69	1	14	3	0	0	5	2	15	.203	.225	.246	34	-6	-6	3	0	0	0	8	3S/2	0.3
Total	3	174	449	32	111	18	1	1	36	29	61	.247	.299	.298	64	-22	-21	39	5	4	-1	-1	S/32	-0.9

■ **CHICK PEDROES** Pedroes, Charles P. b: 10/27/1869, Chicago, Ill. d: 8/6/27, Chicago, Ill. Deb: 8/21/02

YEAR	TM/L	G	AB	R	H	2B	3B	HR	RBI	BB	SO	AVG	OBP	SLG	PRO+	BR	/A	RC	SB	CS	SBR	FR	POS	TPR
1902	Chi-N	2	6	0	0	0	0	0	0	0		.000	.000	.000	-99	-1	-1	0	0			-0	/O	-0.1

■ **HOMER PEEL** Peel, Homer Hefner b: 10/10/02, Port Sullivan, Tex BR/TR, 5'9.5", 170 lbs. Deb: 9/13/27

YEAR	TM/L	G	AB	R	H	2B	3B	HR	RBI	BB	SO	AVG	OBP	SLG	PRO+	BR	/A	RC	SB	CS	SBR	FR	POS	TPR
1927	StL-N	2	2	0	0	0	0	0	0	0	1	.000	.000	.000	-97	-1	-1	0	0			0	/O	0.0
1929	Phi-N	53	156	16	42	12	1	0	19	12	7	.269	.329	.359	66	-7	-9	18	1			2	O/1	-0.8
1930	StL-N	26	73	9	12	2	0	0	10	3	4	.164	.197	.192	-5	-13	-13	3	0			-2	O	-1.4
1933	*NY-N	84	148	16	38	1	1	1	12	14	10	.257	.325	.297	80	-4	-3	15	0			-5	O/1	-1.0
1934	NY-N	21	41	7	8	0	0	1	3	1	2	.195	.214	.268	29	-4	-4	2	0			-1	O	-0.5
Total	5	186	420	48	100	15	2	2	44	30	24	.238	.294	.298	53	-28	-30	38	1			-6	O/1	-3.7

■ **JACK PEERSON** Peerson, Jack Chiles b: 8/28/10, Brunswick, Ga. d: 10/23/66, Ft.Walton Beach, Fla. BR/TR, 5'11", 175 lbs. Deb: 9/07/35

YEAR	TM/L	G	AB	R	H	2B	3B	HR	RBI	BB	SO	AVG	OBP	SLG	PRO+	BR	/A	RC	SB	CS	SBR	FR	POS	TPR
1935	Phi-A	10	19	3	6	1	0	0	1	1	1	.316	.350	.368	87	-0	-0	2	0	0	0	0	/S	0.0
1936	Phi-A	8	34	7	11	1	1	0	5	0	3	.324	.324	.412	82	-1	-1	4	0	1	-1	4	/S2	0.2
Total	2	18	53	10	17	2	1	0	6	1	4	.321	.333	.396	84	-2	-1	6	0	1	-1	4	/S2	0.2

■ **CHARLIE PEETE** Peete, Charles "Mule" b: 2/22/29, Franklin, Va. d: 11/27/56, Caracas, Venez. BL/TR, 5'9.5", 190 lbs. Deb: 7/17/56

YEAR	TM/L	G	AB	R	H	2B	3B	HR	RBI	BB	SO	AVG	OBP	SLG	PRO+	BR	/A	RC	SB	CS	SBR	FR	POS	TPR
1956	StL-N	23	52	3	10	2	2	0	6	6	10	.192	.288	.308	60	-3	-3	3	0	2	-1	3	O	-0.1

■ **MONTE PEFFER** Peffer, Monte (b: Montague Pfeiffer) b: 10/8/1891, New York, N.Y. d: 9/27/41, New York, N.Y. BR/TR, 5'4.5", 147 lbs. Deb: 9/29/13

YEAR	TM/L	G	AB	R	H	2B	3B	HR	RBI	BB	SO	AVG	OBP	SLG	PRO+	BR	/A	RC	SB	CS	SBR	FR	POS	TPR
1913	Phi-A	1	3	0	0	0	0	0	0	0	1	.000	.250	.000	-26	-0	-0	0	0			-0	/S	0.0

■ **HEINIE PEITZ** Peitz, Henry Clement b: 11/28/1870, St.Louis, Mo. d: 10/23/43, Cincinnati, Ohio BR/TR, 5'11", 165 lbs. Deb: 10/15/1892 C

YEAR	TM/L	G	AB	R	H	2B	3B	HR	RBI	BB	SO	AVG	OBP	SLG	PRO+	BR	/A	RC	SB	CS	SBR	FR	POS	TPR
1892	StL-N	1	3	0	0	0	0	0	0	0	0	.000	.000	.000	-99	-1	-1	0	0			-0	/C	0.0
1893	StL-N	96	362	53	92	12	9	1	45	54	20	.254	.353	.345	87	-5	-5	50	12			9	CSO/1	0.8
1894	StL-N	99	338	52	89	19	9	3	49	43	21	.263	.348	.399	81	-11	-11	53	14			4	3C1/P	-0.2
1895	StL-N	90	334	44	95	14	12	2	65	29	20	.284	.345	.416	99	-2	-1	52	9			-1	C13	0.4
1896	Cin-N	68	211	33	63	12	5	2	34	30	15	.299	.386	.431	110	6	3	39	7			0	C	0.8
1897	Cin-N	77	266	35	78	11	7	1	44	18		.293	.340	.398	91	-2	-5	38	3			6	C/P	0.9
1898	Cin-N	105	330	49	90	15	5	1	43	35		.273	.344	.358	97	2	-1	45	9			-5	*C	0.1
1899	Cin-N	93	290	45	79	13	2	1	43	45		.272	.374	.341	98	2	1	42	11			-1	C/P	0.5
1900	Cin-N	91	294	34	75	14	1	2	34	20		.255	.309	.330	80	-8	-7	32	5			5	C/1	0.5
1901	Cin-N	82	269	24	82	13	5	1	24	23		.305	.360	.401	131	8	10	41	3			1	C2/31	1.8
1902	Cin-N	112	387	54	122	22	5	1	60	24		.315	.371	.406	129	19	14	63	7			0	2C/13	2.3
1903	Cin-N	105	358	45	93	15	3	0	42	37		.260	.329	.318	78	-5	-11	42	7			-1	C1/32	-0.4
1904	Cin-N	84	272	32	66	13	2	1	30	14		.243	.280	.316	79	-5	-8	25	1			4	C1/3	0.2
1905	Pit-N	88	278	18	62	10	0	0	27	24		.223	.285	.259	63	-12	-12	24	2			-11	C/2	-1.5
1906	Pit-N	40	125	13	30	8	0	0	20	13		.240	.312	.304	90	-1	-1	13	1			0	C	0.2
1913	StL-N	3	4	1	1	0	1	0	0	0		.250	.250	.750	182	0	0	1	0			-1	/CO	0.0
Total	16	1234	4121	532	1117	191	66	16	560	409	76	.271	.340	.361	94	-14	-34	560	91			10	C/3120SP	6.4

■ **JOE PEITZ** Peitz, Joseph b: 11/8/1869, St.Louis, Mo. d: 12/4/19, St.Louis, Mo. Deb: 7/05/1894

YEAR	TM/L	G	AB	R	H	2B	3B	HR	RBI	BB	SO	AVG	OBP	SLG	PRO+	BR	/A	RC	SB	CS	SBR	FR	POS	TPR
1894	StL-N	7	26	10	11	2	3	0	3	6	1	.423	.531	.731	204	5	5	11	2			1	/O	0.4

■ **EDDIE PELLAGRINI** Pellagrini, Edward Charles b: 3/13/18, Boston, Mass. BR/TR, 5'9", 160 lbs. Deb: 4/22/46

YEAR	TM/L	G	AB	R	H	2B	3B	HR	RBI	BB	SO	AVG	OBP	SLG	PRO+	BR	/A	RC	SB	CS	SBR	FR	POS	TPR
1946	Bos-A	22	71	7	15	3	1	2	4	3	18	.211	.253	.366	68	-3	-4	6	1	0	0	-0	3/S	-0.1
1947	Bos-A	74	231	29	47	8	1	4	19	23	35	.203	.281	.299	57	-12	-15	21	2	2	-1	-6	3S	-2.1

YEAR	TM/L	G	AB	R	H	2B	3B	HR	RBI	BB	SO	AVG	OBP	SLG	PRO+	BR	/A	RC	SB	CS	SBR	FR	POS	TPR
1948	StL-A	105	290	31	69	8	3	2	27	34	40	.238	.320	.307	65	-13	-14	30	1	2	-1	**24**	S	0.9
1949	StL-A	79	235	26	56	8	1	2	15	14	24	.238	.284	.306	54	-16	-17	21	2	1	0	7	S	-0.8
1951	Phi-N	86	197	31	46	4	5	5	30	23	25	.234	.326	.381	91	-3	-3	26	5	1	1	-17	2/S3	-1.5
1952	Cin-N	46	100	15	17	2	0	1	3	8	18	.170	.231	.220	26	-10	-10	5	1	0	0	10	2/1S3	0.1
1953	Pit-N	78	174	16	44	3	2	4	19	14	20	.253	.309	.362	75	-7	-7	21	1	1	-0	-4	23/S	-0.9
1954	Pit-N	73	125	12	27	6	0	0	16	9	21	.216	.290	.264	46	-10	-10	11	0	0	0	2	3/2S	-0.6
Total	8	563	1423	167	321	42	13	20	133	128	201	.226	.295	.316	62	-74	-78	140	13	7	-0	15	S23/1	-5.0

■ BILL PELOUZE
Pelouze, William Nelson b: 9/12/1865, Washington, D.C. d: 6/20/43, Lake Geneva, Wis. BR/TR, 5'8", 170 lbs. Deb: 7/22/1886

YEAR	TM/L	G	AB	R	H	2B	3B	HR	RBI	BB	SO	AVG	OBP	SLG	PRO+	BR	/A	RC	SB	CS	SBR	FR	POS	TPR
1886	StL-N	1	3	0	0	0	0	0	0	0	2	.000	.000	.000	-99	-1	-1	0	0			0	/O	0.0

■ JOHN PELTZ
Peltz, John b: 4/23/1861, New Orleans, La. d: 2/27/06, New Orleans, La. BR/TR, Deb: 5/01/1884

YEAR	TM/L	G	AB	R	H	2B	3B	HR	RBI	BB	SO	AVG	OBP	SLG	PRO+	BR	/A	RC	SB	CS	SBR	FR	POS	TPR
1884	Ind-a	106	393	40	86	13	17	3			7	.219	.236	.361	98	-3	-1	34				4	*O	0.2
1888	Bal-a	1	4	1	1	0	0	0			0	.250	.250	.250	65	-0	-0	1	1			-0	/O	0.0
1890	Bro-a	98	384	55	87	9	6	1			32	.227	.289	.289	75	-13	-11	36	10			3	*O	-1.1
	Syr-a	5	17	2	3	1	1	0			3	.176	.300	.353	105	-0	0	2	0			0	O	0.0
	Tol-a	20	73	8	18	2	2	0			3	.247	.276	.329	78	-2	-2	9	7			-2	O	-0.4
	Yr	123	474	65	108	12	9	1			38	.228	.288	.297	77	-15	-13	47	17			1		-1.5
Total	3	230	871	106	195	25	26	4	0		45	.224	.265	.326	86	-18	-14	81	18			5	O	-1.3

■ BROCK PEMBERTON
Pemberton, Brock b: 11/5/53, Tulsa, Okla. BB/TL, 6'3", 190 lbs. Deb: 9/10/74

YEAR	TM/L	G	AB	R	H	2B	3B	HR	RBI	BB	SO	AVG	OBP	SLG	PRO+	BR	/A	RC	SB	CS	SBR	FR	POS	TPR
1974	NY-N	11	22	0	4	0	0	0	1	0	3	.182	.182	.182	2	-3	-3	1	0	1	-1	1	/1	-0.2
1975	NY-N	2	2	0	0	0	0	0	0	0	1	.000	.000	.000	-99	-1	-1	0	0	0	0	0	H	0.5
Total	2	13	24	0	4	0	0	0	1	0	4	.167	.167	.167	-7	-3	-3	1	0	1	-1	1	/1	-0.2

■ BERT PENA
Pena, Adalberto (Rivera) b: 7/11/59, Santurce, P.R. BR/TR, 5'11", 165 lbs. Deb: 9/14/81

YEAR	TM/L	G	AB	R	H	2B	3B	HR	RBI	BB	SO	AVG	OBP	SLG	PRO+	BR	/A	RC	SB	CS	SBR	FR	POS	TPR
1981	Hou-N	4	2	0	1	0	0	0	0	0	0	.500	.500	.500	194	0	0	1	0	0	0	0	/S	0.1
1983	Hou-N	4	8	0	1	0	0	0	0	2	2	.125	.300	.125	23	-1	-1	0	0	0	0	-1	/S	-0.1
1984	Hou-N	24	39	3	8	1	0	1	4	3	8	.205	.262	.308	64	-2	-2	2	0	0	0	6	S	0.6
1985	Hou-N	20	29	7	8	2	0	0	4	1	6	.276	.300	.345	82	-1	-1	3	0	0	0	1	/3S2	0.0
1986	Hou-N	15	29	3	6	1	0	0	2	5	5	.207	.324	.241	60	-1	-1	2	1	0	0	1	S/32	0.1
1987	Hou-N	21	46	5	7	0	0	0	0	2	7	.152	.204	.152	-4	-7	-7	1	0	0	0	-1	S/3	-0.5
Total	6	88	153	18	31	4	0	1	10	13	28	.203	.269	.248	45	-12	-11	9	1	0	0	4	/S32	0.2

■ TONY PENA
Pena, Antonio Francisco (Padilla) b: 6/4/57, Monte Cristi, D.R. BR/TR, 6', 175 lbs. Deb: 9/01/80

YEAR	TM/L	G	AB	R	H	2B	3B	HR	RBI	BB	SO	AVG	OBP	SLG	PRO+	BR	/A	RC	SB	CS	SBR	FR	POS	TPR
1980	Pit-N	8	21	1	9	1	1	0	1	0	4	.429	.429	.571	174	2	2	4	0	1	-1	1	/C	0.3
1981	Pit-N	66	210	16	63	9	1	2	17	8	23	.300	.329	.381	98	-0	-1	25	1	2	-1	2	C	0.1
1982	Pit-N	138	497	53	147	28	4	11	63	17	57	.296	.324	.435	107	5	4	63	2	5	-2	-7	*C	-0.4
1983	Pit-N	151	542	51	163	22	3	15	70	31	73	.301	.339	.435	110	8	6	75	6	7	-2	-1	*C	0.8
1984	Pit-N	147	546	77	156	27	2	15	78	36	79	.286	.334	.425	112	8	8	74	12	8	-1	12	*C	2.4
1985	Pit-N	147	546	53	136	27	2	10	59	29	67	.249	.287	.361	81	-16	-15	51	12	8	-1	8	*C/1	-0.2
1986	Pit-N	144	510	56	147	26	2	10	52	53	69	.288	.356	.406	107	7	6	68	9	10	-3	3	*C/1	0.9
1987	*StL-N	116	384	40	82	13	4	5	44	36	54	.214	.283	.307	55	-24	-25	30	6	1	1	1	*C/1O	-1.3
1988	StL-N	149	505	55	133	23	1	10	51	33	60	.263	.310	.372	94	-4	-5	56	6	2	1	6	*C/1	0.9
1989	StL-N	141	424	36	110	17	2	4	37	35	33	.259	.319	.337	85	-7	-8	41	5	3	-0	10	*C/O	1.2
1990	*Bos-A	143	491	62	129	19	1	7	56	43	71	.263	.323	.348	84	-8	-11	50	8	6	-1	10	*C/1	0.2
Total	11	1350	4676	500	1275	212	23	89	528	321	590	.273	.321	.385	95	-28	-39	536	67	53	-12	45	*C/1O	4.9

■ GERONIMO PENA
Pena, Geronimo b: 3/29/67, Distrito Nacional, D.R. BB/TR, 6'1", 170 lbs. Deb: 9/05/90

YEAR	TM/L	G	AB	R	H	2B	3B	HR	RBI	BB	SO	AVG	OBP	SLG	PRO+	BR	/A	RC	SB	CS	SBR	FR	POS	TPR
1990	StL-N	18	45	5	11	2	0	0	2	4	14	.244	.320	.289	67	-2	-2	5	1	1	-0	-1	2	-0.2

■ ROBERTO PENA
Pena, Roberto Cesar "Baby" (b: Roberto Cesar Zapata (Pena))
b: 4/17/37, Santo Domingo, D.R. d: 7/23/82, Santiago, D.R. BR/TR, 5'8", 170 lbs. Deb: 4/12/65

YEAR	TM/L	G	AB	R	H	2B	3B	HR	RBI	BB	SO	AVG	OBP	SLG	PRO+	BR	/A	RC	SB	CS	SBR	FR	POS	TPR
1965	Chi-N	51	170	17	37	5	1	2	12	16	19	.218	.293	.294	64	-7	-8	14	1	2	-1	-10	S	-1.3
1966	Chi-N	6	17	0	3	2	0	0	1	0	4	.176	.176	.294	28	-2	-2	1	0	0	0	0	/S	0.0
1968	Phi-N	138	500	56	130	13	2	1	38	34	63	.260	.310	.300	84	-9	-9	45	3	5	-2	6	*S	1.2
1969	SD-N	139	472	44	118	16	3	4	30	21	63	.250	.286	.322	73	-19	-17	41	0	3	-2	-23	S231	-3.4
1970	Oak-A	19	58	4	15	1	0	0	3	3	4	.259	.295	.276	61	-3	-3	4	1	1	-0	-1	S/3	-0.2
	Mil-A	121	416	36	99	19	1	3	42	25	45	.238	.284	.310	63	-21	-21	34	3	5	-2	-16	S2/1	-3.0
	Yr	140	474	40	114	20	1	3	45	28	49	.241	.286	.306	63	-24	-24	38	4	6	-2	-17		-3.2
1971	Mil-A	113	274	17	65	9	3	3	28	15	37	.237	.279	.325	71	-11	-11	24	2	1	0	-5	13S/2	-1.7
Total	6	587	1907	174	467	65	10	13	154	114	235	.245	.291	.310	72	-73	-71	164	10	17	-7	-48	S/132	-8.4

■ ELMER PENCE
Pence, Elmer Clair b: 8/17/1900, Valley Springs, Cal. d: 9/17/68, San Francisco, Cal. BR/TR, 6', 185 lbs. Deb: 8/23/22

YEAR	TM/L	G	AB	R	H	2B	3B	HR	RBI	BB	SO	AVG	OBP	SLG	PRO+	BR	/A	RC	SB	CS	SBR	FR	POS	TPR
1922	Chi-A	1	0	0	0	0	0	0	0	0	0	—	—	—	0	0	0	0	0	0	0	-0	/O	0.0

■ JIM PENDLETON
Pendleton, James Edward b: 1/7/24, St.Charles, Mo. BR/TR, 6', 185 lbs. Deb: 4/17/53

YEAR	TM/L	G	AB	R	H	2B	3B	HR	RBI	BB	SO	AVG	OBP	SLG	PRO+	BR	/A	RC	SB	CS	SBR	FR	POS	TPR
1953	Mil-N	120	251	48	75	12	4	7	27	7	36	.299	.323	.462	108	-0	2	35	6	5	-1	9	*O/S	0.6
1954	Mil-N	71	173	20	38	3	1	1	16	4	21	.220	.237	.266	33	-18	-16	11	2	1	0	3	O	-1.4
1955	Mil-N	8	10	0	0	0	0	0	0	1	0	.000	.000	.000	-99	-3	-3	0	0	0	0	0	/S3O	-0.2
1956	Mil-N	14	11	0	0	0	0	0	0	1	3	.000	.083	.000	-80	-3	-3	0	0	0	0	-0	/S312	-0.2
1957	Pit-N	46	59	9	18	1	1	0	9	9	14	.305	.406	.356	110	1	1	9	0	0	0	-2	/O3S	0.0
1958	Pit-N	3	3	0	1	0	0	0	0	0	0	.333	.333	.333	79	-0	-0	0	0	0	0	0	H	0.0
1959	Cin-N	65	113	13	29	2	0	3	9	8	18	.257	.311	.354	75	-4	-4	12	3	0	1	4	O3/S	0.0
1962	Hou-N	117	321	30	79	12	2	8	36	14	57	.246	.282	.371	79	-13	-10	33	0	0	0	-4	O/13S	-1.8
Total	8	444	941	120	240	30	8	19	97	43	151	.255	.292	.365	76	-39	-32	100	11	6	-0	9	O/3S12	-3.0

■ TERRY PENDLETON
Pendleton, Terry Lee b: 7/16/60, Los Angeles, Cal. BB/TR, 5'9", 178 lbs. Deb: 7/18/84

YEAR	TM/L	G	AB	R	H	2B	3B	HR	RBI	BB	SO	AVG	OBP	SLG	PRO+	BR	/A	RC	SB	CS	SBR	FR	POS	TPR
1984	StL-N	67	262	37	85	16	3	1	33	16	32	.324	.363	.420	123	6	7	40	20	5	3	9	3	1.9
1985	*StL-N	149	559	56	134	16	3	5	69	37	75	.240	.287	.306	66	-26	-25	45	17	12	-2	23	*3	-0.3
1986	StL-N	159	578	56	138	26	5	1	59	34	59	.239	.282	.306	63	-30	-29	50	24	6	4	25	*3/O	-0.4
1987	*StL-N	159	583	82	167	29	4	12	96	70	74	.286	.365	.412	103	6	4	86	19	12	-2	16	*3	1.7
1988	StL-N	110	391	44	99	20	2	6	53	21	51	.253	.295	.361	86	-7	-8	39	3	3	-1	11	*3	0.2
1989	StL-N	162	613	83	162	28	5	13	74	44	81	.264	.314	.390	97	-1	-3	72	9	5	-0	30	*3	2.7
1990	StL-N	121	447	46	103	20	2	6	58	30	58	.230	.280	.324	64	-21	-23	38	7	5	-1	7	*3	-1.2
Total	7	927	3433	404	888	155	24	44	442	252	430	.259	.310	.356	84	-73	-77	370	99	48	1	120	3/O	4.6

■ JIMMY PEOPLES
Peoples, James Elsworth b: 10/8/1863, Big Beaver, Mich. d: 8/29/20, Detroit, Mich. TR, 5'8", 200 lbs. Deb: 5/29/1884 U

YEAR	TM/L	G	AB	R	H	2B	3B	HR	RBI	BB	SO	AVG	OBP	SLG	PRO+	BR	/A	RC	SB	CS	SBR	FR	POS	TPR
1884	Cin-a	69	267	28	45	2	2	1			6	.169	.187	.202	27	-20	-22	10				-1	SCO/31	-2.0
1885	Cin-a	7	22	1	4	0	0	0			0	.182	.217	.182	28	-2	-2	1				-1	/CPO	0.0
	Bro-a	41	151	21	30	4	1	1			5	.199	.229	.258	55	-7	-7	9				-6	C/S130	-0.7
	Yr	48	173	22	34	4	1	1			6	.197	.228	.249	52	-9	-9	10				-7		-0.7
1886	Bro-a	93	340	43	74	7	3	3			20	.218	.261	.282	71	-11	-12	31	20			14	CS/O3	0.6
1887	Bro-a	73	268	36	68	14	2	1			16	.254	.306	.332	79	-7	-8	35	22			-9	C/OS12	-0.5
1888	Bro-a	32	103	15	20	5	3	0			8	.194	.259	.301	82	-2	-2	11	10			8	C/SO	0.8

YEAR	TM/L	G	AB	R	H	2B	3B	HR	RBI	BB	SO	AVG	OBP	SLG	PRO+	BR	/A	RC	SB	CS	SBR	FR	POS	TPR
1889	Col-a	29	100	13	23	6	2	1	16	6	8	.230	.274	.360	86	-3	-2	11	3			-3	C/O2S	-0.2
Total	6	344	1251	157	264	38	13	7	33	62	8	.211	.252	.279	63	-52	-54	108	55			2	C/SO123P	-2.0

■ JOE PEPITONE
Pepitone, Joseph Anthony "Pepi" b: 10/9/40, Brooklyn, N.Y. BL/TL, 6'2", 185 lbs. Deb: 4/10/62 C

YEAR	TM/L	G	AB	R	H	2B	3B	HR	RBI	BB	SO	AVG	OBP	SLG	PRO+	BR	/A	RC	SB	CS	SBR	FR	POS	TPR
1962	NY-A	63	138	14	33	3	2	7	17	3	21	.239	.255	.442	86	-4	-3	13	1	1	-0	-2	O1	-0.7
1963	*NY-A	157	580	79	157	16	3	27	89	23	63	.271	.307	.448	109	5	5	76	3	5	-2	4	*1O	0.3
1964	*NY-A	160	613	71	154	12	3	28	100	24	63	.251	.283	.418	90	-9	-10	67	2	1	0	6	*1O	-0.9
1965	NY-A	143	531	51	131	18	3	18	62	43	59	.247	.306	.394	98	-3	-2	62	4	2	0	-6	*1O	-1.6
1966	NY-A	152	585	85	149	21	4	31	83	29	58	.255	.292	.463	118	8	10	74	4	3	-1	9	*1O	1.3
1967	NY-A	133	501	45	126	18	3	13	64	34	62	.251	.303	.377	104	-1	1	53	1	3	-2	-1	*O/1	-0.6
1968	NY-A	108	380	41	93	9	3	15	56	37	45	.245	.313	.403	119	7	8	48	8	2	1	-9	O1	-1.6
1969	NY-A	135	513	49	124	16	3	27	70	30	42	.242	.285	.442	105	-3	-0	59	8	6	-1	-6	*1	-1.6
1970	Hou-N	75	279	44	70	9	5	14	35	18	28	.251	.299	.470	107	-1	1	37	5	2	0	-1	1O	-0.4
	Chi-N	56	213	38	57	9	2	12	44	15	15	.268	.316	.498	102	3	-0	33	0	2	-1	2	O1	-0.2
	Yr	131	492	82	127	18	7	26	79	33	43	.258	.306	.482	105	2	1	70	5	4	-1	1		-0.6
1971	Chi-N	115	427	50	131	19	4	16	61	24	41	.307	.349	.482	117	17	10	67	1	2	-1	-1	1O	0.0
1972	Chi-N	66	214	23	56	5	0	8	21	13	22	.262	.313	.397	91	-0	-3	26	1	2	-1	-0	1	-0.8
1973	Chi-N	31	112	16	30	3	0	3	18	8	6	.268	.322	.375	86	-1	-2	14	3	1	0	0	1	-0.2
	Atl-N	3	11	0	4	0	0	0	1	1	1	.364	.417	.364	110	0	0	1	0	0	0	-1	/1	0.0
	Yr	34	123	16	34	3	0	3	19	9	7	.276	.331	.374	88	-1	-2	15	3	1	0	-1		-0.2
Total	12	1397	5097	606	1315	158	35	219	721	302	526	.258	.303	.432	105	18	14	629	41	32	-7	-4	1O	-5.8

■ HENRY PEPLOSKI
Peploski, Henry Stephen "Pep" b: 9/15/05, Garlin, Poland d: 1/28/82, Dover, N.J. BL/TR, 5'9", 155 lbs. Deb: 9/19/29

YEAR	TM/L	G	AB	R	H	2B	3B	HR	RBI	BB	SO	AVG	OBP	SLG	PRO+	BR	/A	RC	SB	CS	SBR	FR	POS	TPR
1929	Bos-N	6	10	1	2	0	0	0	1	1	3	.200	.273	.200	20	-1	-1	1	0			-0	/3	0.0

■ PEPPER PEPLOSKI
Peploski, Joseph Aloysius b: 9/12/1891, Brooklyn, N.Y. Deceased BR/TR, 5'8", 155 lbs. Deb: 6/24/13

YEAR	TM/L	G	AB	R	H	2B	3B	HR	RBI	BB	SO	AVG	OBP	SLG	PRO+	BR	/A	RC	SB	CS	SBR	FR	POS	TPR
1913	Det-A	2	4	1	2	0	0	0	0	0	0	.500	.500	.500	196	0	0	1	0			-1	/3	0.0

■ DON PEPPER
Pepper, Donald Hoyte b: 10/8/43, Saratoga Sprgs., N.Y BL/TR, 6'4.5", 215 lbs. Deb: 9/10/66

YEAR	TM/L	G	AB	R	H	2B	3B	HR	RBI	BB	SO	AVG	OBP	SLG	PRO+	BR	/A	RC	SB	CS	SBR	FR	POS	TPR
1966	Det-A	4	3	0	0	0	0	0	0	0	1	.000	.000	.000	-98	-1	-1	0	0	0	0	0	/1	0.0

■ ROY PEPPER
Pepper, Raymond Watson b: 8/5/05, Decatur, Ala. BR/TR, 6'2", 195 lbs. Deb: 4/15/32

YEAR	TM/L	G	AB	R	H	2B	3B	HR	RBI	BB	SO	AVG	OBP	SLG	PRO+	BR	/A	RC	SB	CS	SBR	FR	POS	TPR
1932	StL-N	21	57	3	14	2	1	0	7	5	13	.246	.306	.316	66	-3	-3	6	1			0	O	-0.3
1933	StL-N	3	9	2	2	0	0	1	2	0	1	.222	.222	.556	110	0	0	1	0			-0	/O	0.0
1934	StL-A	148	564	71	168	24	6	7	101	29	67	.298	.333	.399	81	-11	-18	73	1	4	-2	9	*O	-1.1
1935	StL-A	92	261	20	66	15	3	4	37	20	32	.253	.306	.379	73	-10	-12	30	0	2	-1	-5	O	-1.7
1936	StL-A	75	124	13	35	5	0	2	23	5	23	.282	.310	.371	66	-7	-7	13	0	2	-1	-2	O	-0.9
Total	5	339	1015	109	285	46	10	14	170	59	136	.281	.321	.387	77	-30	-39	123	2	8		2	O	-4.0

■ JACK PERCONTE
Perconte, John Patrick b: 8/31/54, Joliet, Ill. BL/TR, 5'10", 160 lbs. Deb: 9/13/80

YEAR	TM/L	G	AB	R	H	2B	3B	HR	RBI	BB	SO	AVG	OBP	SLG	PRO+	BR	/A	RC	SB	CS	SBR	FR	POS	TPR
1980	LA-N	14	17	2	4	0	0	0	2	2	1	.235	.316	.235	57	-1	-1	2	3	0	1	3	/2	0.4
1981	LA-N	8	9	2	2	0	1	0	1	2	2	.222	.364	.444	133	0	0	1	1	1	-0	5	/2	0.5
1982	Cle-A	93	219	27	52	4	4	0	15	22	25	.237	.307	.292	66	-10	-10	22	9	3	1	8	2/D	0.4
1983	Cle-A	14	26	1	7	1	0	0	0	5	2	.269	.387	.308	91	0	-0	4	3	1	0	8	2	0.8
1984	Sea-A	155	612	93	180	24	4	0	31	57	47	.294	.359	.346	97	-1	-0	84	29	6	5	0	*2	1.3
1985	Sea-A	125	485	60	128	17	7	2	23	50	36	.264	.336	.340	85	-8	-9	62	31	2	8	0	*2	0.4
1986	Chi-A	24	73	6	16	1	0	0	4	11	10	.219	.321	.233	52	-4	-5	6	2	0	1	-7	2	-0.8
Total	7	433	1441	191	389	47	16	2	76	149	123	.270	.342	.329	86	-24	-23	181	78	13	16	18	2/D	3.0

■ TONY PEREZ
Perez, Atanacio (Rigal) b: 5/14/42, Camaguey, Cuba BR/TR, 6'2", 175 lbs. Deb: 7/26/64 C

YEAR	TM/L	G	AB	R	H	2B	3B	HR	RBI	BB	SO	AVG	OBP	SLG	PRO+	BR	/A	RC	SB	CS	SBR	FR	POS	TPR
1964	Cin-N	12	25	1	2	1	0	0	1	3	9	.080	.179	.120	-14	-4	-4	1	0	0	0	-1	/1	-0.5
1965	Cin-N	104	281	40	73	14	4	12	47	21	67	.260	.316	.466	110	6	3	38	0	2	-1	-1	1	-0.2
1966	Cin-N	99	257	25	68	10	4	4	39	14	44	.265	.308	.381	83	-4	-6	27	1	0	0	-5	1	-1.5
1967	Cin-N	156	600	78	174	28	7	26	102	33	102	.290	.331	.490	119	22	15	91	0	3	-2	-24	*31/2	-1.9
1968	Cin-N	160	625	93	176	25	7	18	92	51	92	.282	.342	.430	124	23	19	88	3	2	-0	5	*3	2.6
1969	Cin-N	160	629	103	185	31	2	37	122	63	131	.294	.360	.526	138	36	32	114	4	2	0	1	*3	3.5
1970	*Cin-N	158	587	107	186	28	6	40	129	83	134	.317	.405	.589	162	52	52	140	8	3	1	-7	*3/1	4.0
1971	Cin-N	158	609	72	164	22	3	25	91	51	120	.269	.327	.438	117	10	12	86	4	1	1	7	*31	1.7
1972	*Cin-N	136	515	64	146	33	7	21	90	55	121	.283	.353	.497	148	25	28	90	4	2	0	-5	*1	1.5
1973	*Cin-N	151	564	73	177	33	3	27	101	74	117	.314	.396	.527	162	41	45	118	3	1	0	-4	*1	3.5
1974	Cin-N	158	596	81	158	28	2	28	101	61	112	.265	.335	.460	123	14	15	88	1	3	-2	-5	*1	0.1
1975	*Cin-N	137	511	74	144	28	3	20	109	54	101	.282	.354	.466	124	17	16	83	1	2	-1	-5	*1	0.2
1976	*Cin-N	139	527	77	137	32	6	19	91	50	88	.260	.330	.452	117	12	11	78	10	5	0	-4	*1	0.1
1977	Mon-N	154	559	71	158	32	6	19	91	63	111	.283	.357	.463	122	14	16	91	4	3	-1	9	*1	1.7
1978	Mon-N	148	544	63	158	38	3	14	78	38	104	.290	.339	.449	120	12	13	82	2	0	1	-1	*1	0.7
1979	Mon-N	132	489	58	132	29	4	13	73	38	82	.270	.326	.425	104	1	2	65	2	1	0	-6	*1	-1.0
1980	Bos-A	151	585	73	161	31	3	25	105	41	93	.275	.324	.467	108	9	5	80	1	0	0	-1	*1D	-0.3
1981	Bos-A	84	306	35	77	11	3	9	39	27	66	.252	.312	.395	97	1	-2	37	0	0	0	0	1D	-0.2
1982	Bos-A	69	196	18	51	14	2	6	31	19	48	.260	.326	.444	103	2	1	27	0	1	-1	0	D/1	0.0
1983	*Phi-N	91	253	18	61	11	2	6	43	28	57	.241	.319	.372	92	-3	-3	29	1	1	0	1	1	-0.4
1984	Cin-N	71	137	9	33	6	1	2	15	11	21	.241	.297	.343	76	-4	-5	12	0	0	0	-2	1	-0.7
1985	Cin-N	72	183	25	60	8	0	6	33	22	22	.328	.400	.470	136	11	10	35	0	2	-1	-2	1	0.5
1986	Cin-N	77	200	14	51	12	1	2	29	25	25	.255	.338	.355	87	-2	-3	24	0	0	0	-3	1	-0.8
Total	23	2777	9778	1272	2732	505	79	379	1652	925	1867	.279	.344	.463	122	292	272	1523	49	33	-5	-52	*13/D2	12.6

■ MARTY PEREZ
Perez, Martin Roman b: 2/28/47, Visalia, Cal. BR/TR, 5'11", 160 lbs. Deb: 9/09/69

YEAR	TM/L	G	AB	R	H	2B	3B	HR	RBI	BB	SO	AVG	OBP	SLG	PRO+	BR	/A	RC	SB	CS	SBR	FR	POS	TPR
1969	Cal-A	13	13	3	3	0	0	0	0	2	1	.231	.333	.231	63	-1	-1	1	0	0	0	6	/S23	0.6
1970	Cal-A	3	3	0	0	0	0	0	1	0	0	.000	.000	.000	-99	-1	-1	0	0	0	0	1	/S	0.0
1971	Atl-N	130	410	28	93	15	3	4	32	25	44	.227	.273	.307	60	-20	-23	32	1	2	-1	-14	*S/2	-2.2
1972	Atl-N	141	479	33	109	13	1	1	28	30	55	.228	.277	.265	50	-28	-33	32	0	3	-2	-33	*S	-5.6
1973	Atl-N	141	501	66	125	15	5	8	57	49	66	.250	.319	.347	79	-10	-15	54	2	3	-1	-9	*S	-0.6
1974	Atl-N	127	447	51	116	20	5	2	34	35	51	.260	.315	.340	80	-10	-13	47	2	0	1	-9	*2S/3	-1.4
1975	Atl-N	120	461	50	127	14	2	2	34	37	44	.275	.329	.328	80	-10	-12	48	2	2	-1	-8	*2/S	-1.5
1976	Atl-N	31	96	12	24	4	0	1	6	8	9	.250	.308	.323	74	-3	-3	9	0	0	0	-2	2S/3	-0.2
	SF-N	93	332	37	86	13	1	2	26	30	28	.259	.320	.322	80	-7	-8	36	3	4	-2	7	2/S	0.2
	Yr	124	428	49	110	17	1	3	32	38	37	.257	.318	.322	79	-10	-12	45	3	4	-2	5		0.0
1977	NY-A	1	4	0	2	0	0	0	0	0	1	.500	.500	.500	175	0	0	1	0	0	0	1	/3	0.1
	Oak-A	115	373	32	86	14	5	2	23	29	65	.231	.291	.311	65	-18	-18	33	1	3	-2	0	*23/S	-0.9
	Yr	116	377	32	88	14	5	2	23	29	66	.233	.293	.313	65	-18	-17	34	1	3	-2	1		-0.8
1978	Oak-A	16	12	1	0	0	0	0	0	0	5	.000	.000	.000	-99	-3	-3	0	0	0	0	2	3/S2	0.0
Total	10	931	3131	313	771	108	22	22	241	245	369	.246	.303	.316	70	-111	-129	291	11	17	-7	-59	S2/3	-11.5

■ TONY PEREZCHICA
Perezchica, Antonio Llamas (Gonzales) b: 4/20/66, Mexicali, Mex. BR/TR, 5'11", 165 lbs. Deb: 9/07/88

YEAR	TM/L	G	AB	R	H	2B	3B	HR	RBI	BB	SO	AVG	OBP	SLG	PRO+	BR	/A	RC	SB	CS	SBR	FR	POS	TPR
1988	SF-N	7	8	1	1	0	0	0	1	2	1	.125	.300	.125	27	-1	-1	1	0	0	0	-1	/2	-0.1
1990	SF-N	4	3	1	1	0	0	0	0	1	2	.333	.500	.333	136	0	0	1	0	0	0	-1	/2S	0.0

YEAR	TM/L	G	AB	R	H	2B	3B	HR	RBI	BB	SO	AVG	OBP	SLG	PRO+	BR	/A	RC	SB	CS	SBR	FR	POS	TPR
Total	2	11	11	2	2	0	0	0	1	3	3	.182	.357	.182	59	-0	-0	1	0	0	0	-3	/2S	-0.1

■ BRODERICK PERKINS
Perkins, Broderick Phillip b: 11/23/54, Pittsburg, Cal. BL/TL, 5'10", 180 lbs. Deb: 7/07/78

YEAR	TM/L	G	AB	R	H	2B	3B	HR	RBI	BB	SO	AVG	OBP	SLG	PRO+	BR	/A	RC	SB	CS	SBR	FR	POS	TPR
1978	SD-N	62	217	14	52	14	1	2	33	5	29	.240	.257	.341	71	-11	-9	18	4	0	1	3	1	-0.6
1979	SD-N	57	87	8	23	0	0	0	8	8	12	.264	.326	.264	67	-4	-3	7	0	0	0	-0	1	-0.4
1980	SD-N	43	100	18	37	9	0	2	14	11	10	.370	.432	.520	175	9	10	24	2	1	0	-2	1O	0.6
1981	SD-N	92	254	27	71	18	3	2	40	14	16	.280	.317	.398	110	-0	2	29	0	4	-2	-2	1/O	-0.5
1982	SD-N	125	347	32	94	10	4	2	34	26	20	.271	.327	.340	92	-6	-4	39	2	1	0	1	1O	-0.7
1983	Cle-A	79	184	23	50	10	0	0	24	9	19	.272	.306	.326	71	-6	-7	17	1	5	-3	-0	1OD	-1.0
1984	Cle-A	58	66	5	13	1	0	0	4	7	10	.197	.284	.212	39	-5	-5	4	0	0	0	-0	D/1	-0.5
Total	7	516	1255	127	340	62	8	8	157	80	116	.271	.317	.352	90	-23	-17	138	9	11	-4	-1	1/OD	-3.1

■ CY PERKINS
Perkins, Ralph Foster b: 2/27/1896, Gloucester, Mass. d: 10/2/63, Philadelphia, Pa. BR/TR, 5'10.5", 158 lbs. Deb: 9/25/15 MC

YEAR	TM/L	G	AB	R	H	2B	3B	HR	RBI	BB	SO	AVG	OBP	SLG	PRO+	BR	/A	RC	SB	CS	SBR	FR	POS	TPR
1915	Phi-A	7	20	2	4	1	0	0	3	3	3	.200	.304	.250	68	-1	-1	2	0			1	/C	0.0
1917	Phi-A	6	18	1	3	0	0	0	2	2	1	.167	.250	.167	28	-2	-1	1	0			4	/C	0.3
1918	Phi-A	68	218	9	41	4	1	0	14	8	15	.188	.217	.229	34	-18	-18	11	1			12	C	0.0
1919	Phi-A	101	305	22	77	12	7	2	29	27	22	.252	.313	.357	87	-5	-6	33	2			7	C/S	0.7
1920	Phi-A	148	492	40	128	24	6	5	52	28	35	.260	.303	.364	75	-18	-19	53	5	6	-2	24	*C/2	1.4
1921	Phi-A	141	538	58	155	31	4	12	73	32	32	.288	.329	.428	91	-9	-9	73	5	9	-4	5	*C	-0.2
1922	Phi-A	148	505	58	135	20	6	6	69	40	30	.267	.322	.366	77	-16	-18	59	1	7	-4	-3	*C	-1.9
1923	Phi-A	143	500	53	135	34	5	2	65	65	30	.270	.356	.370	90	-5	-6	69	1	3	-2	-6	*C	-0.3
1924	Phi-A	128	392	31	95	19	4	0	32	31	20	.242	.304	.311	58	-24	-25	38	3	4	-2	-1	*C	-1.7
1925	Phi-A	65	140	21	43	10	0	1	18	26	6	.307	.426	.400	104	4	2	26	0	0	0	11	C/3	1.5
1926	Phi-A	63	148	14	43	6	0	0	19	18	7	.291	.371	.331	80	-3	-4	19	0	2	-1	9	C	0.7
1927	Phi-A	59	137	11	35	7	2	1	15	12	8	.255	.315	.358	70	-5	-7	15	0	2	-1	1	C/1	-0.3
1928	Phi-A	19	29	1	5	0	0	0	1	1	1	.172	.200	.172	-1	-4	-4	1	0	1	-1	4	C	0.0
1929	Phi-A	38	76	4	16	4	0	0	9	5	4	.211	.259	.263	34	-7	-8	5	0	0	0	2	C	-0.2
1930	Phi-A	20	38	1	6	2	0	0	4	2	3	.158	.200	.211	4	-6	-6	2	0	0	0	0	C/1	-0.3
1931	NY-A	16	47	3	12	1	0	0	7	1	4	.255	.286	.277	51	-3	-3	4	0	0	0	-5	C	-0.6
1934	Det-A	1	1	0	0	0	0	0	0	0	0	.000	.000	.000	-99	-0	-0	0	0	0	0	0	H	0.0
Total	17	1171	3604	329	933	175	35	30	409	301	221	.259	.319	.352	75	-124	-133	411	18	34		64	*C/S132	-0.9

■ SAM PERLOZZO
Perlozzo, Samuel Benedict b: 3/4/51, Cumberland, Md. BR/TR, 5'9", 170 lbs. Deb: 9/13/77 C

YEAR	TM/L	G	AB	R	H	2B	3B	HR	RBI	BB	SO	AVG	OBP	SLG	PRO+	BR	/A	RC	SB	CS	SBR	FR	POS	TPR
1977	Min-A	10	24	6	7	0	2	0	0	2	3	.292	.346	.458	119	1	1	4	0	0	0	-3	2/3	-0.1
1979	SD-N	2	2	0	0	0	0	0	0	1	0	.000	.333	.000	-1	-0	-0	0	0	0	0	-1	/2	-0.1
Total	2	12	26	6	7	0	2	0	0	3	3	.269	.345	.423	110	0	0	4	0	0	0	-4	/23	-0.2

■ JOHN PERRIN
Perrin, John Stephenson b: 2/4/1898, Escanaba, Mich. d: 6/24/69, Detroit, Mich. BL/TR, 5'9", 160 lbs. Deb: 7/11/21

YEAR	TM/L	G	AB	R	H	2B	3B	HR	RBI	BB	SO	AVG	OBP	SLG	PRO+	BR	/A	RC	SB	CS	SBR	FR	POS	TPR
1921	Bos-A	4	13	3	3	0	0	0	1	0	3	.231	.231	.231	19	-2	-2	1	0	0	0	-2	/O	-0.2

■ NIG PERRINE
Perrine, John Grover b: 1/14/1885, Clinton, Wis. d: 8/13/48, Kansas City, Mo. TR, 5'9", 160 lbs. Deb: 4/11/07

YEAR	TM/L	G	AB	R	H	2B	3B	HR	RBI	BB	SO	AVG	OBP	SLG	PRO+	BR	/A	RC	SB	CS	SBR	FR	POS	TPR
1907	Was-A	44	146	13	25	4	1	0	15	13		.171	.239	.212	49	-9	-7	10	10			-3	2S/3	-1.0

■ GEORGE PERRING
Perring, George Wilson b: 8/13/1884, Sharon, Wis. d: 8/20/60, Beloit, Wis. BR/TR, 6', 190 lbs. Deb: 4/30/08

YEAR	TM/L	G	AB	R	H	2B	3B	HR	RBI	BB	SO	AVG	OBP	SLG	PRO+	BR	/A	RC	SB	CS	SBR	FR	POS	TPR
1908	Cle-A	89	310	23	67	8	5	0	19	16		.216	.255	.274	73	-9	-9	23	8			-6	S3	-1.2
1909	Cle-A	88	283	26	63	10	9	0	20	19		.223	.283	.322	87	-3	-5	27	6			7	3S/2	0.5
1910	Cle-A	39	122	14	27	6	3	0	8	3		.221	.240	.320	74	-4	-4	10	3			2	3/1	0.0
1914	KC-F	144	496	68	138	28	10	2	69	59	39	.278	.355	.387	117	9	12	74	7			9	*31/PS	2.4
1915	KC-F	153	553	67	143	23	7	7	67	57	30	.259	.329	.363	109	3	6	77	10			15	*312/S	2.6
Total	5	513	1764	198	438	75	34	9	183	154	69	.248	.311	.345	100	-4	-0	208	34			26	3/1S2P	4.3

■ BOYD PERRY
Perry, Boyd Glenn b: 3/21/14, Snow Camp, N.C. d: 6/29/90, Burlington, N.C. BR/TR, 5'10", 158 lbs. Deb: 5/23/41

YEAR	TM/L	G	AB	R	H	2B	3B	HR	RBI	BB	SO	AVG	OBP	SLG	PRO+	BR	/A	RC	SB	CS	SBR	FR	POS	TPR
1941	Det-A	36	83	9	15	5	0	0	11	10	9	.181	.269	.241	32	-8	-9	6	1	0	0	-0	S2	-0.6

■ CLAY PERRY
Perry, Clayton Shields b: 12/18/1881, Rice Lake, Wis. d: 1/16/54, Rice Lake, Wis. TR, 5'10.5", 175 lbs. Deb: 9/02/08

YEAR	TM/L	G	AB	R	H	2B	3B	HR	RBI	BB	SO	AVG	OBP	SLG	PRO+	BR	/A	RC	SB	CS	SBR	FR	POS	TPR
1908	Det-A	7	17	0	2	0	0	0	0	0		.118	.118	.118	-22	-2	-2	0				-1	/3	-0.2

■ GERALD PERRY
Perry, Gerald June b: 10/30/60, Savannah, Ga. BL/TR, 5'11", 180 lbs. Deb: 8/11/83

YEAR	TM/L	G	AB	R	H	2B	3B	HR	RBI	BB	SO	AVG	OBP	SLG	PRO+	BR	/A	RC	SB	CS	SBR	FR	POS	TPR
1983	Atl-N	27	39	5	14	2	0	1	6	5	4	.359	.432	.487	144	3	3	8	0	1	-1	-2	/1O	0.0
1984	Atl-N	122	347	52	92	12	2	7	47	61	38	.265	.378	.372	104	8	5	50	15	12	-3	-10	1O	-1.2
1985	Atl-N	110	238	22	51	5	0	3	13	23	28	.214	.284	.273	53	-14	-15	18	9	5	-0	-10	1/O	-1.7
1986	Atl-N	29	70	6	19	2	0	2	11	8	4	.271	.346	.386	96	-0	-0	8	0	1	-1	-4	O/1	-0.5
1987	Atl-N	142	533	77	144	35	2	12	74	48	63	.270	.332	.411	91	-4	-7	69	42	16	3	-10	*1/O	-2.1
1988	Atl-N	141	547	61	164	29	1	8	74	36	49	.300	.344	.400	108	9	6	70	29	14	0	1	*1	0.0
1989	Atl-N	72	266	24	67	11	0	4	21	32	28	.252	.339	.338	92	-1	-2	31	10	6	-1	1	1	-0.7
1990	KC-A	133	465	57	118	22	2	8	57	39	56	.254	.316	.361	91	-7	-6	53	17	4	3	2	D1	-0.4
Total	8	776	2505	304	669	118	7	45	303	252	270	.267	.336	.374	94	-6	-18	307	122	59	1	-22	1/OD	-6.6

■ BOB PERRY
Perry, Melvin Gray b: 9/14/34, New Bern, N.C. BR/TR, 6'2", 180 lbs. Deb: 5/17/63

YEAR	TM/L	G	AB	R	H	2B	3B	HR	RBI	BB	SO	AVG	OBP	SLG	PRO+	BR	/A	RC	SB	CS	SBR	FR	POS	TPR
1963	LA-A	61	166	16	42	9	0	3	14	9	31	.253	.303	.361	91	-3	-2	18	1	1	-0	-6	O	-1.0
1964	LA-A	70	221	19	61	8	1	3	16	14	52	.276	.319	.362	99	-4	-1	25	1	1	-0	0	O	-0.3
Total	2	131	387	35	103	17	1	6	30	23	83	.266	.312	.362	95	-7	-3	43	2	2	-1	-6	O	-1.3

■ HANK PERRY
Perry, William Henry "Socks" b: 7/28/1886, Howell, Mich. d: 7/18/56, Pontiac, Mich. BL/TR, 5'11", 190 lbs. Deb: 4/12/12

YEAR	TM/L	G	AB	R	H	2B	3B	HR	RBI	BB	SO	AVG	OBP	SLG	PRO+	BR	/A	RC	SB	CS	SBR	FR	POS	TPR
1912	Det-A	13	36	3	6	1	0	0	3			.167	.231	.194	23	-4	-3	2				2	/O	-0.1

■ JOHNNY PESKY
Pesky, John Michael (b: John Michael Paveskovich) b: 9/27/19, Portland, Ore. BL/TR, 5'9", 168 lbs. Deb: 4/14/42 MC

YEAR	TM/L	G	AB	R	H	2B	3B	HR	RBI	BB	SO	AVG	OBP	SLG	PRO+	BR	/A	RC	SB	CS	SBR	FR	POS	TPR
1942	Bos-A	147	620	105	205	29	9	2	51	42	36	.331	.375	.416	118	18	15	100	12	7	-1	18	*S	4.0
1946	*Bos-A	153	621	115	208	43	4	2	55	65	29	.335	.401	.427	124	27	23	111	9	8	-2	12	*S	3.6
1947	Bos-A	155	638	106	207	27	8	0	39	72	22	.324	.393	.392	110	18	12	103	12	9	-2	-11	*S3	0.0
1948	Bos-A	143	565	124	159	26	6	3	55	99	32	.281	.394	.365	98	6	2	90	3	5	-2	6	*3	0.0
1949	Bos-A	148	604	111	185	27	7	2	69	100	19	.306	.408	.384	103	13	7	104	8	4	0	21	*3	2.7
1950	Bos-A	127	490	112	153	22	6	1	49	104	31	.312	.437	.388	103	16	9	93	2	1	0	22	*3/S	2.4
1951	Bos-A	131	480	93	153	20	6	3	41	84	15	.313	.417	.398	110	18	12	87	2	2	-1	9	*S3/2	2.6
1952	Bos-A	25	67	10	10	2	0	0	2	15	5	.149	.313	.179	36	-5	-6	4	0	3	-2	-6	3/S	-1.3
	Det-A	69	177	26	45	4	0	0	9	41	11	.254	.394	.294	93	1	1	25	1	2	-1	-5	S2/3	-0.2
	Yr	94	244	36	55	6	0	0	11	56	16	.225	.372	.262	77	-4	-5	28	1	5	-3	-11		-1.5
1953	Det-A	103	308	43	90	22	1	2	24	27	10	.292	.353	.390	102	0	1	43	3	7	-3	-13	2	-1.1
1954	Det-A	20	17	5	3	0	0	0	1	3	1	.176	.300	.353	80	-1	-0	1	0	0	0	0	H	0.0
	Was-A	49	158	17	40	4	3	0	9	10	7	.253	.298	.316	72	-7	-6	15	1	1	-0	-8	2/S	-1.3
	Yr	69	175	22	43	4	3	0	10	13	8	.246	.298	.320	72	-8	-7	16	1	1	-0	-8		-1.3
Total	10	1270	4745	867	1455	226	50	17	404	662	218	.307	.394	.386	106	105	69	777	53	49	-14	44	S32	11.4

■ BILL PETERMAN
Peterman, William David b: 3/20/21, Philadelphia, Pa. BR/TR, 6'2", 185 lbs. Deb: 4/26/42

YEAR	TM/L	G	AB	R	H	2B	3B	HR	RBI	BB	SO	AVG	OBP	SLG	PRO+	BR	/A	RC	SB	CS	SBR	FR	POS	TPR
1942	Phi-N	1	1	0	1	0	0	0	0	0	0	1.000	1.000	1.000	512	0	0	1	0			0	/C	0.1

YEAR	TM/L	G	AB	R	H	2B	3B	HR	RBI	BB	SO	AVG	OBP	SLG	PRO+	BR	/A	RC	SB	CS	SBR	FR	POS	TPR

■ JOHN PETERS   Peters, John Paul b: 4/8/1850, Louisiana, Mo. d: 1/4/24, St.Louis, Mo.   BR/TR, 5'7", 180 lbs.   Deb: 5/23/1874

YEAR	TM/L	G	AB	R	H	2B	3B	HR	RBI	BB	SO	AVG	OBP	SLG	PRO+	BR	/A	RC	SB	CS	SBR	FR	POS	TPR
1874	Chi-n	55	240	39	69	10	0	1		2		.287	.293	.342	101	0	-0	25					S2/3	-0.1
1875	Chi-n	69	298	40	86	18	0	0		0		.289	.289	.349	118	5	5	31					*S/2	0.3
1876	Chi-N	66	316	70	111	14	2	1	47	3	2	.351	.357	.418	141	18	13	48				-1	*S/P	0.9
1877	Chi-N	60	265	45	84	10	3	0	41	1	7	.317	.320	.377	106	5	1	33				19	*S	1.8
1878	Mil-N	55	246	33	76	6	1	0	22	5	8	.309	.323	.341	111	5	2	28				5	2S	1.0
1879	Chi-N	83	379	45	93	13	2	1	31	1	19	.245	.247	.298	74	-9	-12	29				-9	*S	-1.3
1880	Pro-N	86	359	30	82	5	0	0	24	5	15	.228	.239	.242	66	-13	-12	21				-2	*S	-0.8
1881	Buf-N	54	229	21	49	8	1	0	25	3	12	.214	.224	.258	52	-13	-12	14				7	S/O	0.0
1882	Pit-a	78	333	46	96	10	1	0		4		.288	.297	.324	115	3	5	33				6	*S/2	1.1
1883	Pit-a	8	28	3	3	0	0	0		0		.107	.107	.107	-32	-4	-4	0				3	/S	0.0
1884	Pit-a	1	4	0	0	0	0	0		0		.000	.000	.000	-98	-1	-1	0				-1	/S	-0.1
Total	2 n	124	538	79	155	28	0	1		2		.288	.291	.346	110	6	5	55					/S23	0.2
Total	9	491	2159	293	594	66	10	2	190	22	63	.275	.282	.318	94	-8	-20	206				27	S/2OP	2.6

■ JOHN PETERS   Peters, John William "Big Pete" or "Shotgun" b: 7/14/1893, Kansas City, Kan. d: 2/21/32, Kansas City, Mo.   BR/TR, 6', 192 lbs.   Deb: 5/01/15

YEAR	TM/L	G	AB	R	H	2B	3B	HR	RBI	BB	SO	AVG	OBP	SLG	PRO+	BR	/A	RC	SB	CS	SBR	FR	POS	TPR
1915	Det-A	1	3	0	0	0	0	0	0	0	1	.000	.000	.000	-95	-1	-1	0	0			1	/C	0.1
1918	Cle-A	1	1	0	0	0	0	0	0	1	1	.000	.500	.000	46	0	0	0	0			-1	/C	0.0
1921	Phi-N	55	155	7	45	4	0	3	23	6	13	.290	.329	.374	79	-3	-5	19	1	0	0	-13	C	-1.4
1922	Phi-N	55	143	15	35	9	1	4	24	9	18	.245	.308	.406	75	-4	-6	18	0	1	-1	-5	C	-1.0
Total	4	112	302	22	80	13	1	7	47	16	33	.265	.317	.384	76	-8	-12	37	1	1		-17	/C	-2.3

■ RICK PETERS   Peters, Richard Devin b: 11/21/55, Lynwood, Cal.   BB/TR, 5'9", 170 lbs.   Deb: 9/08/79

YEAR	TM/L	G	AB	R	H	2B	3B	HR	RBI	BB	SO	AVG	OBP	SLG	PRO+	BR	/A	RC	SB	CS	SBR	FR	POS	TPR
1979	Det-A	12	19	3	5	0	0	0	2	5	3	.263	.417	.263	85	0	-0	3	0	0	0	-1	/32OD	0.0
1980	Det-A	133	477	79	139	19	7	2	42	54	48	.291	.371	.373	102	5	3	66	13	7	-0	-4	*OD	-0.3
1981	Det-A	63	207	26	53	7	3	0	15	29	28	.256	.353	.319	91	-0	-1	22	1	6	-3	3	OD	-0.2
1983	Oak-A	55	178	20	51	7	0	0	20	12	21	.287	.335	.326	88	-4	-2	18	4	9	-4	9	O/D	0.2
1986	Oak-A	44	38	7	7	1	0	0	1	7	7	.184	.311	.211	49	-3	-2	2	2	2	-1	3	O/2	0.0
Total	5	307	919	135	255	34	10	2	80	107	107	.277	.358	.343	95	-2	-3	111	20	24	-8	9	O/D23	-0.3

■ RUSTY PETERS   Peters, Russell Dixon b: 12/14/14, Roanoke, Va.   BR/TR, 5'11", 170 lbs.   Deb: 4/14/36

YEAR	TM/L	G	AB	R	H	2B	3B	HR	RBI	BB	SO	AVG	OBP	SLG	PRO+	BR	/A	RC	SB	CS	SBR	FR	POS	TPR
1936	Phi-A	45	119	12	26	3	2	3	16	4	28	.218	.244	.353	47	-11	-11	10	1	1	-0	1	S3/O2	-0.6
1937	Phi-A	116	339	39	88	17	6	3	43	41	59	.260	.339	.372	80	-11	-10	44	4	4	-1	-13	23S	-1.5
1938	Phi-A	2	7	0	0	0	0	0	0	0	1	.000	.000	.000	-99	-2	-2	0	0	0	0	-2	/S	-0.3
1940	Cle-A	30	71	5	17	3	2	0	7	4	14	.239	.280	.338	61	-4	-4	7	1	0	0	-0	/2S31	-0.2
1941	Cle-A	29	63	6	13	2	0	0	2	7	10	.206	.286	.238	42	-5	-5	4	0	1	-1	2	S/32	-0.2
1942	Cle-A	34	58	6	13	5	1	0	2	2	14	.224	.250	.345	70	-3	-3	4	0	0	0	2	S/23	0.1
1943	Cle-A	79	215	22	47	6	2	1	19	18	29	.219	.282	.279	69	-10	-8	18	1	1	-0	-6	3S/2O	-1.4
1944	Cle-A	88	282	23	63	13	3	1	24	15	35	.223	.268	.301	65	-14	-13	23	2	1	0	-3	2S/3	-1.3
1946	Cle-A	9	21	0	6	0	0	0	2	1	1	.286	.318	.286	74	-1	-1	2	0	1	-1	0	/S	0.0
1947	StL-A	39	47	10	16	4	0	0	2	6	8	.340	.415	.426	131	2	2	9	0	0	0	7	2/S	1.0
Total	10	471	1222	123	289	53	16	8	117	98	199	.236	.295	.326	69	-59	-54	120	9	9	-3	-12	2S3/O1	-4.4

■ BUDDY PETERSON   Peterson, Carl Francis b: 4/23/25, Portland, Ore.   BR/TR, 5'9.5", 170 lbs.   Deb: 9/14/55

YEAR	TM/L	G	AB	R	H	2B	3B	HR	RBI	BB	SO	AVG	OBP	SLG	PRO+	BR	/A	RC	SB	CS	SBR	FR	POS	TPR
1955	Chi-A	6	21	7	6	1	0	0	2	3	1	.286	.400	.333	96	0	0	3	0	0	0	-1	/S	0.0
1957	Bal-A	7	17	1	3	2	0	0	0	2	2	.176	.263	.294	55	-1	-1	1	0	0	0	-1	/S	-0.1
Total	2	13	38	8	9	3	0	0	2	5	3	.237	.341	.316	80	-1	-1	4	0	0	0	-2	/S	-0.1

■ CAP PETERSON   Peterson, Charles Andrew b: 8/15/42, Tacoma, Wash. d: 5/16/80, Tacoma, Wash.   BR/TR, 6'2", 195 lbs.   Deb: 9/12/62

YEAR	TM/L	G	AB	R	H	2B	3B	HR	RBI	BB	SO	AVG	OBP	SLG	PRO+	BR	/A	RC	SB	CS	SBR	FR	POS	TPR
1962	SF-N	4	6	1	1	0	0	0	0	1	4	.167	.286	.167	25	-1	-1	0	0	0	0	-1	/S	0.0
1963	SF-N	22	54	7	14	2	0	1	2	2	13	.259	.286	.352	83	-1	-1	6	0	0	0	-6	/23OS	-0.6
1964	SF-N	66	74	8	15	1	1	1	8	3	20	.203	.234	.284	44	-5	-6	5	0	0	0	-1	O/123	-0.6
1965	SF-N	63	105	14	26	7	0	3	15	10	16	.248	.313	.400	97	-0	-1	12	0	0	0	-3	O	-0.3
1966	SF-N	89	190	13	45	6	1	2	19	11	32	.237	.282	.311	63	-9	-10	15	2	0	1	-3	O/1	-1.3
1967	Was-A	122	405	35	97	17	2	8	46	32	61	.240	.300	.351	95	-5	-3	41	0	3	-2	0	*O	-0.7
1968	Was-A	94	226	20	46	8	1	3	18	18	31	.204	.265	.288	70	-9	-8	18	2	1	0	-5	O	-1.6
1969	Cle-A	76	110	8	25	3	0	1	14	24	18	.227	.370	.282	82	-1	-2	12	0	0	0	-0	O/3	-0.2
Total	8	536	1170	106	269	44	5	19	122	101	195	.230	.294	.325	80	-31	-30	109	4	4	-1	-17	O/321S	-5.3

■ HARDY PETERSON   Peterson, Harding William b: 10/17/29, Perth Amboy, N.J.   BR/TR, 6', 205 lbs.   Deb: 5/05/55

YEAR	TM/L	G	AB	R	H	2B	3B	HR	RBI	BB	SO	AVG	OBP	SLG	PRO+	BR	/A	RC	SB	CS	SBR	FR	POS	TPR
1955	Pit-N	32	81	7	20	6	0	1	10	7	7	.247	.315	.358	79	-3	-2	9	0	0	0	6	C	0.4
1957	Pit-N	30	73	10	22	2	1	2	11	9	10	.301	.378	.438	122	2	2	10	0	1	-1	2	C	0.5
1958	Pit-N	2	6	0	2	0	0	0	0	1	0	.333	.429	.333	108	0	0	1	0	0	0	-0	/C	0.0
1959	Pit-N	2	1	0	0	0	0	0	0	0	0	.000	.000	.000	-99	-0	-0	0	0	0	0	1	/C	0.0
Total	4	66	161	17	44	8	1	3	21	17	17	.273	.346	.391	99	-1	-0	20	0	1	-1	7	/C	0.9

■ BOB PETERSON   Peterson, Robert A. b: 7/16/1884, Philadelphia, Pa. d: 11/27/62, Eveshan Township, N.J.   BR/TR, 6'1", 160 lbs.   Deb: 4/18/06

YEAR	TM/L	G	AB	R	H	2B	3B	HR	RBI	BB	SO	AVG	OBP	SLG	PRO+	BR	/A	RC	SB	CS	SBR	FR	POS	TPR
1906	Bos-A	39	118	10	24	1	1	1	9	11		.203	.271	.254	67	-4	-4	9	1			-6	C/21O	-0.8
1907	Bos-A	4	13	1	1	0	0	0	0	0		.077	.077	.077	-51	-2	-2	0	0			0	/C	0.0
Total	2	43	131	11	25	1	1	1	9	11		.191	.254	.237	56	-6	-6	9	1			-6	/C21O	-0.8

■ TED PETOSKEY   Petoskey, Frederick Lee b: 1/5/11, St.Charles, Mich.   BR/TR, 5'11.5", 183 lbs.   Deb: 9/09/34

YEAR	TM/L	G	AB	R	H	2B	3B	HR	RBI	BB	SO	AVG	OBP	SLG	PRO+	BR	/A	RC	SB	CS	SBR	FR	POS	TPR
1934	Cin-N	6	7	0	0	0	0	0	1	0	5	.000	.000	.000	-99	-2	-2	0	1			2	/O	0.0
1935	Cin-N	4	5	0	2	0	0	0	0	0	1	.400	.400	.400	119	0	0	1	1			-0	/O	0.0
Total	2	10	12	0	2	0	0	0	1	0	6	.167	.167	.167	-11	-2	-2	1	1			2	/O	0.0

■ GENO PETRALLI   Petralli, Eugene James b: 9/25/59, Sacramento, Cal.   BL/TR, 6'2", 185 lbs.   Deb: 9/04/82

YEAR	TM/L	G	AB	R	H	2B	3B	HR	RBI	BB	SO	AVG	OBP	SLG	PRO+	BR	/A	RC	SB	CS	SBR	FR	POS	TPR
1982	Tor-A	16	44	3	16	2	0	0	1	4	6	.364	.417	.409	117	2	1	8	0	0	0	-2	C/3	0.0
1983	Tor-A	6	4	0	0	0	0	0	0	1	1	.000	.200	.000	-37	-1	-1	0	0	0	0	0	/CD	0.0
1984	Tor-A	3	3	0	0	0	0	0	0	0	0	.000	.000	.000	-97	-1	-1	0	0	0	0	0	/CD	0.0
1985	Tex-A	42	100	7	27	2	0	0	11	8	12	.270	.330	.290	71	-4	-4	10	1	0	0	1	C	0.0
1986	Tex-A	69	137	17	35	9	3	2	18	5	14	.255	.282	.409	83	-3	-4	14	3	0	1	-8	C3/2D	-0.7
1987	Tex-A	101	202	28	61	11	2	7	31	27	29	.302	.390	.480	129	9	9	38	0	2	-1	6	C3/120D	1.8
1988	Tex-A	129	351	35	99	14	2	7	36	41	52	.282	.360	.393	108	6	5	49	0	1	-1	5	CD/312	1.3
1989	Tex-A	70	184	18	56	7	0	4	23	17	24	.304	.369	.408	117	5	5	28	0	0	0	-11	CD	-0.4
1990	Tex-A	133	325	28	83	13	1	0	21	50	49	.255	.360	.302	85	-3	-4	36	0	2	-1	-1	*C/32	-0.2
Total	9	569	1350	136	377	58	8	20	141	153	187	.279	.357	.379	101	10	7	181	4	5	-2	-8	C/3D210	1.8

■ RICO PETROCELLI   Petrocelli, Americo Peter b: 6/27/43, Brooklyn, N.Y.   BR/TR, 6', 175 lbs.   Deb: 9/21/63

YEAR	TM/L	G	AB	R	H	2B	3B	HR	RBI	BB	SO	AVG	OBP	SLG	PRO+	BR	/A	RC	SB	CS	SBR	FR	POS	TPR
1963	Bos-A	1	4	0	1	1	0	0	1	0	1	.250	.250	.500	101	-0	-0	1	0	0	0	-0	/S	0.0
1965	Bos-A	103	323	38	75	15	2	13	33	36	71	.232	.311	.412	98	1	-1	41	0	2	-1	10	S	1.3
1966	Bos-A	139	522	58	124	20	1	18	59	41	99	.238	.297	.383	85	-5	-11	60	1	1	-0	1	*S/3	-0.3
1967	*Bos-A	142	491	53	127	24	2	17	66	49	93	.259	.332	.420	112	8	8	70	2	4	-2	3	*S	2.0
1968	Bos-A	123	406	41	95	17	2	12	46	31	73	.234	.295	.374	95	0	-3	45	0	1	-1	11	*S/1	1.8
1969	Bos-A	154	535	92	159	32	2	40	97	98	68	.297	.407	.589	167	55	51	129	3	5	-2	5	*S/3	6.2

YEAR	TM/L	G	AB	R	H	2B	3B	HR	RBI	BB	SO	AVG	OBP	SLG	PRO+	BR	/A	RC	SB	CS	SBR	FR	POS	TPR
1970	Bos-A	157	583	82	152	31	3	29	103	67	82	.261	.339	.473	114	16	11	92	1	1	-0	-10	*S3	1.3
1971	Bos-A	158	553	82	139	24	4	28	89	91	108	.251	.359	.461	122	23	18	92	2	0	1	-1	*3	1.4
1972	Bos-A	147	521	62	125	15	2	15	75	78	91	.240	.341	.363	104	8	5	68	0	1	-1	-1	*3	0.9
1973	Bos-A	100	356	44	87	13	1	13	45	47	64	.244	.334	.396	99	3	-0	47	0	0	0	6	3	0.4
1974	Bos-A	129	454	53	121	23	1	15	76	48	74	.267	.339	.421	110	10	6	65	1	0	0	-18	*3/D	-1.0
1975	*Bos-A	115	402	31	96	15	1	7	59	41	66	.239	.314	.333	76	-9	-13	40	0	2	-1	-18	*3/D	-3.1
1976	Bos-A	85	240	17	51	7	1	3	24	34	36	.213	.310	.287	67	-7	-11	20	0	5	-3	-4	3/21SD	-1.7
Total	13	1553	5390	653	1352	237	22	210	773	661	926	.251	.336	.420	108	107	60	769	10	22	-10	-16	S3/D21	9.2

■ PAT PETTEE
Pettee, Patrick E.   b: 1/10/1863, Natick, Mass.   d: 10/9/34, Natick, Mass.   BR/TR, 5'10", 170 lbs.   Deb: 4/08/1891

YEAR	TM/L	G	AB	R	H	2B	3B	HR	RBI	BB	SO	AVG	OBP	SLG	PRO+	BR	/A	RC	SB	CS	SBR	FR	POS	TPR
1891	Lou-a	2	5	1	0	0	0	0	0	3	1	.000	.375	.000	12	-0	-0	0	1			-0	/2	0.0

■ NED PETTIGREW
Pettigrew, Jim Ned   b: 8/25/1881, Honey Grove, Tex.   d: 8/20/52, Duncan, Okla.   5'11", 175 lbs.   Deb: 4/23/14

YEAR	TM/L	G	AB	R	H	2B	3B	HR	RBI	BB	SO	AVG	OBP	SLG	PRO+	BR	/A	RC	SB	CS	SBR	FR	POS	TPR
1914	Buf-F	2	2	0	0	0	0	0	0	0	0	.000	.000	.000	-98	-1	-1	0	0			0	H	0.0

■ JOE PETTINI
Pettini, Joseph Paul   b: 1/26/55, Wheeling, W.Va.   BR/TR, 5'9", 165 lbs.   Deb: 7/10/80

YEAR	TM/L	G	AB	R	H	2B	3B	HR	RBI	BB	SO	AVG	OBP	SLG	PRO+	BR	/A	RC	SB	CS	SBR	FR	POS	TPR
1980	SF-N	63	190	19	44	3	1	1	9	17	33	.232	.295	.274	61	-10	-9	17	5	2	0	-13	S3/2	-1.7
1981	SF-N	35	29	3	2	1	0	0	2	4	5	.069	.182	.103	-18	-4	-4	1	1	0	0	4	2S/3	0.2
1982	SF-N	29	39	5	8	1	0	0	2	3	4	.205	.262	.231	39	-3	-3	2	0	1	-1	-0	S/3	-0.1
1983	SF-N	61	86	11	16	0	1	0	7	9	11	.186	.273	.209	33	-8	-7	5	4	1	1	11	S23	0.7
Total	4	188	344	38	70	5	2	1	20	33	53	.203	.273	.238	45	-25	-24	25	10	4	1	2	S/32	-0.9

■ GARY PETTIS
Pettis, Gary George   b: 4/3/58, Oakland, Cal.   BB/TR, 6'1", 165 lbs.   Deb: 9/13/82

YEAR	TM/L	G	AB	R	H	2B	3B	HR	RBI	BB	SO	AVG	OBP	SLG	PRO+	BR	/A	RC	SB	CS	SBR	FR	POS	TPR
1982	Cal-A	10	5	5	1	0	0	1	1	0	2	.200	.200	.800	159	0	0	1	0	0	0	1	/O	0.1
1983	Cal-A	22	85	19	25	2	3	3	6	7	15	.294	.348	.494	130	3	3	15	8	3	1	2	O	0.5
1984	Cal-A	140	397	63	90	11	6	2	29	60	115	.227	.333	.300	77	-11	-10	46	48	17	4	-7	*O	-1.6
1985	Cal-A	125	443	67	114	10	8	1	32	62	125	.257	.344	.323	86	-7	-7	61	56	9	11	10	*O	1.3
1986	*Cal-A	154	539	93	139	23	4	5	58	69	132	.258	.342	.343	88	-8	-7	71	50	13	7	13	*O/D	1.0
1987	Cal-A	133	394	49	82	13	2	1	17	52	124	.208	.302	.259	53	-27	-25	35	24	5	4	2	*O	-2.0
1988	Det-A	129	458	65	96	14	4	3	36	47	85	.210	.285	.277	60	-25	-23	42	44	10	7	5	*O	-1.2
1989	Det-A	119	444	77	114	8	6	1	18	84	106	.257	.375	.309	97	1	2	58	43	15	4	1	*O	0.6
1990	Tex-A	136	423	66	101	16	8	3	31	57	118	.239	.335	.336	86	-5	-6	52	38	15	2	-1	*O/D	-0.6
Total	9	968	3188	504	762	97	41	20	228	438	822	.239	.333	.314	80	-78	-72	382	311	87	41	26	O/D	-1.9

■ BOB PETTIT
Pettit, Robert Henry   b: 7/19/1861, Williamstown, Mass.   d: 11/1/10, Derby, Conn.   BL/TR, 5'9", 160 lbs.   Deb: 9/03/1887

YEAR	TM/L	G	AB	R	H	2B	3B	HR	RBI	BB	SO	AVG	OBP	SLG	PRO+	BR	/A	RC	SB	CS	SBR	FR	POS	TPR
1887	Chi-N	32	138	29	36	3	3	2	12	8	15	.261	.301	.370	77	-3	-6	21	16			-2	O/CP	-0.5
1888	Chi-N	43	169	23	43	1	4	4	23	7	9	.254	.288	.379	106	2	1	21	7			-3	O	-0.6
1891	Mil-a	21	80	10	14	4	0	1	5	7	7	.175	.267	.262	45	-5	-8	6	2			-6	/2O3	-1.1
Total	3	96	387	62	93	8	7	7	40	22	31	.240	.288	.351	81	-5	-12	48	25			-11	/O23PC	-1.8

■ MARTY PEVEY
Pevey, Marty Ashley   b: 12/25/62, Savannah, Ga.   BL/TR, 6'1", 185 lbs.   Deb: 5/16/89

YEAR	TM/L	G	AB	R	H	2B	3B	HR	RBI	BB	SO	AVG	OBP	SLG	PRO+	BR	/A	RC	SB	CS	SBR	FR	POS	TPR
1989	Mon-N	13	41	2	9	1	1	0	3	0	8	.220	.220	.293	45	-3	-3	2	0	0	0	-1	C/O	-0.3

■ LARRY PEZOLD
Pezold, Lorenz Johannes   b: 6/22/1893, New Orleans, La.   d: 10/22/57, Baton Rouge, La.   BR/TR, 5'9.5", 175 lbs.   Deb: 7/28/14

YEAR	TM/L	G	AB	R	H	2B	3B	HR	RBI	BB	SO	AVG	OBP	SLG	PRO+	BR	/A	RC	SB	CS	SBR	FR	POS	TPR
1914	Cle-A	23	71	4	16	0	1	0	5	9	6	.225	.313	.254	68	-2	-3	6	2	3	-1	-1	3/O	-0.4

■ FRED PFEFFER
Pfeffer, Nathaniel Frederick "Fritz" or "Dandelion"
b: 3/17/1860, Louisville, Ky.   d: 4/10/32, Chicago, Ill.   BR/TR, 5'10.5", 184 lbs.   Deb: 5/01/1882   M

YEAR	TM/L	G	AB	R	H	2B	3B	HR	RBI	BB	SO	AVG	OBP	SLG	PRO+	BR	/A	RC	SB	CS	SBR	FR	POS	TPR
1882	Tro-N	85	330	26	72	7	4	1	43	1	24	.218	.221	.273	60	-16	-13	20				11	*S/2	0.6
1883	Chi-N	96	371	41	87	22	7	1	45	8	50	.235	.251	.340	73	-10	-14	32				16	*2S/31	0.0
1884	Chi-N	112	467	105	135	10	10	25	101	25	47	.289	.325	.514	147	30	24	80				46	*2/P	6.3
1885	*Chi-N	112	469	90	113	12	7	5	73	26	47	.241	.281	.328	84	-2	-12	44				25	*2/PO	2.3
1886	*Chi-N	118	474	88	125	17	8	7	95	36	46	.264	.316	.378	96	6	-6	68	30			8	*2/1	0.6
1887	Chi-N	123	479	95	133	21	6	16	89	34	20	.278	.327	.447	101	8	-2	91	57			25	*2/O	2.5
1888	Chi-N	135	517	90	129	22	10	8	57	32	38	.250	.297	.377	108	9	4	79	64			39	*2	4.6
1889	Chi-N	134	531	85	121	15	7	7	77	53	51	.228	.302	.322	72	-17	-22	67	45			21	*2	0.8
1890	Chi-P	124	499	86	128	21	8	5	80	44	23	.257	.319	.361	80	-13	-17	68	27			24	*2	1.1
1891	Chi-N	137	498	93	123	12	9	7	77	79	60	.247	.353	.349	108	7	7	78	40			25	*2	3.2
1892	Lou-N	124	470	78	121	14	9	2	76	67	36	.257	.353	.338	121	8	14	67	27			12	*21/PM	2.4
1893	Lou-N	125	508	85	129	29	12	3	75	51	18	.254	.322	.376	94	-11	-4	74	32			6	*2	0.1
1894	Lou-N	104	409	68	126	12	14	5	59	30	14	.308	.357	.443	100	-5	0	78	31			12	*2S/P	1.4
1895	Lou-N	11	45	8	13	1	0	0	5	5	3	.289	.360	.311	81	-1	-1	6	2			-3	/S21	-0.1
1896	NY-N	4	14	1	2	0	0	0	4	1	1	.143	.250	.143	7	-2	-2	1	0			-2	/S2	-0.2
	Chi-N	94	360	45	88	16	7	2	52	23	20	.244	.294	.344	67	-17	-19	44	22			10	*2	-0.5
	Yr	98	374	46	90	16	7	2	56	24	21	.241	.292	.337	65	-18	-21	44	22			8		-0.7
1897	Chi-N	32	114	10	26	0	1	0	11		12	.228	.318	.246	50	-7	-8	11	5			-6	2	-0.9
Total	16	1670	6555	1094	1671	231	119	94	1019	527	498	.255	.312	.369	93	-33	-68	906	382			268	*2S/1PO3	24.2

■ BOBBY PFEIL
Pfeil, Robert Raymond   b: 11/13/43, Passaic, N.J.   BR/TR, 6'1", 180 lbs.   Deb: 6/26/69

YEAR	TM/L	G	AB	R	H	2B	3B	HR	RBI	BB	SO	AVG	OBP	SLG	PRO+	BR	/A	RC	SB	CS	SBR	FR	POS	TPR
1969	NY-N	62	211	20	49	9	0	0	10	7	27	.232	.260	.275	49	-14	-15	14	0	1	-1	-3	32/O	-1.8
1971	Phi-N	44	70	5	19	3	0	2	9	6	9	.271	.329	.400	106	0	0	8	1	1	-0	-0	3/CO12S	0.0
Total	2	106	281	25	68	12	0	2	19	13	36	.242	.278	.306	63	-14	-14	22	1	2	-1	-4	/32OCS1	-1.8

■ GEORGE PFISTER
Pfister, George Edward   b: 9/4/18, Bound Brook, N.J.   BR/TR, 6', 200 lbs.   Deb: 9/27/41

YEAR	TM/L	G	AB	R	H	2B	3B	HR	RBI	BB	SO	AVG	OBP	SLG	PRO+	BR	/A	RC	SB	CS	SBR	FR	POS	TPR
1941	Bro-N	1	2	0	0	0	0	0	0	0	0	.000	.000	.000	-96	-1	-1	0	0			0	/C	0.0

■ MONTE PFYL
Pfyl, Meinhard Charles   b: 5/11/1884, St.Louis, Mo.   d: 10/18/45, San Francisco, Cal   BL/TL, 6'3", 190 lbs.   Deb: 7/30/07

YEAR	TM/L	G	AB	R	H	2B	3B	HR	RBI	BB	SO	AVG	OBP	SLG	PRO+	BR	/A	RC	SB	CS	SBR	FR	POS	TPR
1907	NY-N	1	0	0	0	0	0	0	0	0	0	-	-	-	-0	-0		0	0			0	/1	0.0

■ ART PHELAN
Phelan, Arthur Thomas "Dugan"   b: 8/14/1887, Niantic, Ill.   d: 12/27/64, Ft.Worth, Tex.   BR/TR, 5'8", 160 lbs.   Deb: 6/25/10

YEAR	TM/L	G	AB	R	H	2B	3B	HR	RBI	BB	SO	AVG	OBP	SLG	PRO+	BR	/A	RC	SB	CS	SBR	FR	POS	TPR
1910	Cin-N	23	42	7	9	0	0	0	4	7	6	.214	.327	.214	61	-2	-2	5	5			-1	/32OS	-0.2
1912	Cin-N	130	461	56	112	9	11	3	54	46	37	.243	.314	.330	79	-15	-13	56	25			-1	*3/2	-1.3
1913	Chi-N	91	261	41	65	11	6	2	35	29	26	.249	.331	.360	97	-1	-1	33	8			-9	23/S	-1.0
1914	Chi-N	25	46	5	13	2	1	0	3	4	3	.283	.340	.370	111	1	1	6	0			-0	/32S	0.1
1915	Chi-N	133	448	41	98	16	7	3	35	55	42	.219	.307	.306	86	-7	-7	45	12	9	-2	-2	*32	-0.5
Total	5	402	1258	150	297	38	25	8	131	141	114	.236	.317	.325	85	-24	-22	144	50	9		-13	3/2SO	-2.9

■ DAN PHELAN
Phelan, Daniel T.   b: 7/1865, Thomaston, Conn.   d: 12/7/45, West Haven, Conn.   Deb: 4/18/1890

YEAR	TM/L	G	AB	R	H	2B	3B	HR	RBI	BB	SO	AVG	OBP	SLG	PRO+	BR	/A	RC	SB	CS	SBR	FR	POS	TPR
1890	Lou-a	8	32	4	8	1	1	0			0	.250	.250	.344	79	-1	-1	3	1			0	/1	0.0

■ DICK PHELAN
Phelan, James Dickson   b: 12/10/1854, Towanda, Pa.   d: 2/13/31, San Antonio, Tex.   Deb: 4/17/1884

YEAR	TM/L	G	AB	R	H	2B	3B	HR	RBI	BB	SO	AVG	OBP	SLG	PRO+	BR	/A	RC	SB	CS	SBR	FR	POS	TPR
1884	Bal-U	101	402	63	99	13	3	3			12	.246	.268	.316	88	-1	-8	35	0			-8	*2/3O	-1.7
1885	Buf-N	4	16	2	2	0	0	1	3	0	3	.125	.125	.313	37	-1	-1	1				-1	/2	-0.1
	StL-N	2	4	1	1	1	0	0	1	0	2	.250	.250	.500	147	0	0	1				-1	/3	0.0
	Yr	6	20	3	3	1	0	1	4	0	5	.150	.150	.350	58	-1	-1	1				-2		-0.1
Total	2	107	422	66	102	14	3	4	4	12	5	.242	.263	.318	86	-2	-9	36				-9	2/3O	-1.8

YEAR	TM/L	G	AB	R	H	2B	3B	HR	RBI	BB	SO	AVG	OBP	SLG	PRO+	BR	/A	RC	SB	CS	SBR	FR	POS	TPR

■ NEALY PHELPS Phelps, Cornelius Carman b: 11/19/1840, New York, N.Y. d: 2/12/1885, New York, N.Y. Deb: 7/01/1871

YEAR	TM/L	G	AB	R	H	2B	3B	HR	RBI	BB	SO	AVG	OBP	SLG	PRO+	BR	/A	RC	SB	CS	SBR	FR	POS	TPR
1871	Kek-n	1	3	0	0	0	0	0	0	1	0	.000	.250	.000	-20	-0	-0	0	0				/1	0.0
1873	Mut-n	1	6	0	0	0	0	0		0		.000	.000	.000	-99	-1	-1	0					/O	0.0
1874	Mut-n	6	24	5	3	0	0	0		0		.125	.125	.125	-19	-3	-3	0					/O	-0.1
1875	Mut-n	2	6	1	2	0	0	0		0		.333	.333	.333	124	0	0	1					/O	0.0
1876	NY-N	1	3	0	0	0	0	0	0	0	1	.000	.000	.000	-99	-1	-1	0				-0	/O	0.0
	Phi-N	1	4	0	0	0	0	0	0	0	0	.000	.000	.000	-99	-1	-1	0				0	/C	0.0
	Yr	2	7	0	0	0	0	0	0	0	1	.000	.000	.000	-99	-1	-1	0				-0		0.0
Total	4 n	10	39	6	5	0	0	0		1		.128	.150	.128	-11	-5	-5	1					/O1	-0.1

■ ED PHELPS Phelps, Edward Jaykill "Yaller" b: 3/3/1879, Albany, N.Y. d: 1/31/42, E.Greenbush, N.Y. BR/TR, 5'11", 185 lbs. Deb: 9/03/02

YEAR	TM/L	G	AB	R	H	2B	3B	HR	RBI	BB	SO	AVG	OBP	SLG	PRO+	BR	/A	RC	SB	CS	SBR	FR	POS	TPR
1902	Pit-N	18	61	5	13	1	0	0	6	4		.213	.284	.230	58	-3	-3	5	2			-5	C/1	-0.6
1903	*Pit-N	81	273	32	77	7	3	2	31	17		.282	.324	.352	92	-2	-3	34	2			-7	C/1	-0.3
1904	Pit-N	94	302	29	73	5	3	0	28	15		.242	.278	.278	72	-9	-10	26	2			-10	C/1	-1.2
1905	Cin-N	44	156	18	36	5	3	0	18	12		.231	.286	.301	69	-4	-6	15	4			-6	C	-0.7
1906	Cin-N	12	40	3	11	0	2	1	5	3		.275	.326	.450	138	2	2	7	2			-1	C	0.2
	Pit-N	43	118	9	28	3	1	0	12	9		.237	.291	.280	77	-3	-3	10	1			-3	C	-0.3
	Yr	55	158	12	39	3	3	1	17	12		.247	.300	.323	92	-1	-2	17	3			-4		-0.1
1907	Pit-N	43	113	11	24	1	0	0	12	9		.212	.270	.221	55	-5	-6	8	1			-3	C/1	-0.6
1908	Pit-N	34	64	3	15	2	2	0	11	2		.234	.258	.328	89	-1	-1	5	0			0	C	-0.3
1909	StL-N	104	306	43	76	13	1	0	22	39		.248	.350	.297	108	2	5	35	7			-10	C	0.1
1910	StL-N	93	270	25	71	4	2	0	37	36	29	.263	.356	.293	93	-2	-1	32	9			-15	C	-1.1
1912	Bro-N	52	111	8	32	4	3	0	23	16	15	.288	.388	.378	114	2	3	17	1			-5	C	0.0
1913	Bro-N	15	18	0	4	0	0	0	0	1	2	.222	.263	.222	38	-1	-1	1	0			-2	/C	-0.2
Total	11	633	1832	186	460	45	20	3	205	163	46	.251	.318	.302	87	-25	-26	195	31			-66	C/1	-4.7

■ BABE PHELPS Phelps, Ernest Gordon "Blimp" b: 4/19/08, Odenton, Md. BL/TR, 6'2", 225 lbs. Deb: 9/17/31

YEAR	TM/L	G	AB	R	H	2B	3B	HR	RBI	BB	SO	AVG	OBP	SLG	PRO+	BR	/A	RC	SB	CS	SBR	FR	POS	TPR
1931	Was-A	3	3	0	1	0	0	0	0	0	0	.333	.333	.333	75	-0	-0	0	0	0	0	0	H	0.0
1933	Chi-N	3	7	0	2	0	0	0	2	0	1	.286	.286	.286	64	-0	-0	1	0			1	/C	0.1
1934	Chi-N	44	70	7	20	5	2	2	12	1	8	.286	.296	.500	111	0	1	10	0			-2	C	0.0
1935	Bro-N	47	121	17	44	7	2	5	22	9	10	.364	.408	.579	165	10	11	28	0			-2	C	0.8
1936	Bro-N	115	319	36	117	23	2	5	57	27	18	.367	.421	.498	145	21	21	69	1			-15	C/O	0.8
1937	Bro-N	121	409	42	128	37	3	7	58	25	28	.313	.357	.469	121	12	11	67	2			-5	*C	0.9
1938	Bro-N	66	208	33	64	12	2	5	46	23	15	.308	.379	.457	126	8	8	35	2			-3	C	0.6
1939	Bro-N	98	323	33	92	21	2	6	42	24	24	.285	.336	.418	98	0	-1	43	0			1	C	0.2
1940	Bro-N	118	370	47	109	24	5	13	61	30	27	.295	.349	.492	122	14	11	59	2			-9	C/1	0.6
1941	Bro-N	16	30	3	7	3	0	2	4	1	2	.233	.258	.533	114	0	0	4	0			-1	C	0.1
1942	Pit-N	95	257	21	73	11	1	9	41	20	24	.284	.345	.440	126	9	8	39	2			-3	C	0.7
Total	11	726	2117	239	657	143	19	54	345	160	157	.310	.362	.472	124	75	68	356	9	0		-38	C/1O	4.8

■ KEN PHELPS Phelps, Kenneth Allen b: 8/6/54, Seattle, Wash. BL/TL, 6'1", 209 lbs. Deb: 9/20/80

YEAR	TM/L	G	AB	R	H	2B	3B	HR	RBI	BB	SO	AVG	OBP	SLG	PRO+	BR	/A	RC	SB	CS	SBR	FR	POS	TPR
1980	KC-A	3	4	0	0	0	0	0	0	0	2	.000	.000	.000	-99	-1	-1	0	0	0	0	-0	/1	0.0
1981	KC-A	21	22	1	3	0	1	0	1	1	13	.136	.174	.227	15	-2	-2	1	0	0	0	0	/1D	-0.1
1982	Mon-N	10	8	0	2	0	0	0	0	0	3	.250	.333	.250	64	-0	-0	1	0	0	0	0	H	0.0
1983	Sea-A	50	127	10	30	4	1	7	16	13	25	.236	.307	.449	101	1	-0	19	0	0	0	3	1D	0.1
1984	Sea-A	101	290	52	70	9	0	24	51	61	73	.241	.382	.521	149	20	21	63	3	3	-1	-1	D/1	1.8
1985	Sea-A	61	116	18	24	3	0	9	24	24	33	.207	.343	.466	118	3	3	20	2	0	1	1	D/1	0.4
1986	Sea-A	125	344	69	85	16	4	24	64	88	96	.247	.409	.526	151	28	28	81	2	3	-1	-3	1D	2.0
1987	Sea-A	120	332	68	86	13	1	27	68	80	75	.259	.414	.548	145	28	25	81	1	1	-0	-0	*D/1	2.3
1988	Sea-A	72	190	37	54	8	0	14	32	51	35	.284	.438	.547	167	21	20	50	1	0	0	0	D/1	2.0
	NY-A	45	107	17	24	5	0	10	22	19	26	.224	.341	.551	147	6	6	20	0	0	0	0	D/1	0.6
	Yr	117	297	54	78	13	0	24	54	70	61	.263	.405	.549	160	28	27	70	1	0	0	0		2.6
1989	NY-A	86	185	26	46	3	0	7	29	27	47	.249	.344	.378	105	1	2	26	0	0	0	-1	D/1	0.0
	*Oak-A	11	9	0	1	1	0	0	0	4	0	.111	.385	.222	78	-0	-0	1	0	0	0	0	/1D	0.0
	Yr	97	194	26	47	4	0	7	29	31	47	.242	.347	.371	104	1	2	27	0	0	0	-1		-0.1
1990	Oak-A	32	59	6	11	2	0	1	6	12	10	.186	.324	.271	70	-2	-2	6	0	0	0	0	D/1	-0.1
	Cle-A	24	61	4	7	0	0	0	0	10	11	.115	.239	.115	2	-8	-8	2	1	0	0	0	1/D	-0.8
	Yr	56	120	10	18	2	0	1	6	22	21	.150	.282	.192	35	-10	-10	7	1	0	0	0		-0.9
Total	11	761	1854	308	443	64	7	123	313	390	449	.239	.377	.480	132	95	91	369	10	7	-1	-1	D1	8.2

■ DAVE PHILLEY Philley, David Earl b: 5/16/20, Paris, Tex. BB/TR, 6', 188 lbs. Deb: 9/06/41

YEAR	TM/L	G	AB	R	H	2B	3B	HR	RBI	BB	SO	AVG	OBP	SLG	PRO+	BR	/A	RC	SB	CS	SBR	FR	POS	TPR
1941	Chi-A	7	9	4	2	1	0	0	0	3	3	.222	.417	.333	102	0	0	2	0	0	0	0	/O	0.0
1946	Chi-A	17	68	10	24	2	3	0	17	4	4	.353	.389	.471	145	3	4	14	5	0	2	4	O	0.9
1947	Chi-A	143	551	55	142	25	11	2	45	35	39	.258	.303	.354	85	-15	-12	56	21	16	-3	-6	*O/3	-2.7
1948	Chi-A	137	488	51	140	28	3	5	42	50	33	.287	.353	.387	100	-3	-0	67	8	10	-4	10	*O	0.1
1949	Chi-A	146	598	84	171	20	8	0	44	54	51	.286	.347	.346	86	-14	-12	76	13	4	2	-4	*O	-1.7
1950	Chi-A	156	619	69	150	21	5	14	80	52	57	.242	.302	.360	71	-31	-29	67	6	3	0	-4	*O	-3.2
1951	Chi-A	7	25	0	6	2	0	0	2	2	3	.240	.296	.320	68	-1	-1	2	0	0	0	-0	/O	-0.1
	Phi-A	125	468	71	123	18	7	7	59	63	38	.263	.354	.376	95	-1	-2	68	9	6	-1	-4	*O/3	-1.0
	Yr	132	493	71	129	20	7	7	61	65	41	.262	.351	.373	94	-2	-3	70	9	6	-1	-4		-1.1
1952	Phi-A	151	586	80	154	25	4	7	71	59	35	.263	.334	.355	86	-6	-11	67	11	4	1	5	*O/3	-0.8
1953	Phi-A	157	620	80	188	30	9	9	59	51	35	.303	.358	.424	106	8	5	92	13	5	1	0	*O/3	0.2
1954	*Cle-A	133	452	48	102	13	3	12	60	57	48	.226	.312	.347	79	-12	-13	48	2	4	-2	-9	*O	-2.7
1955	Cle-A	43	104	15	31	4	2	2	9	12	10	.298	.371	.433	111	2	2	15	0	2	-1	-1	O	-0.1
	Bal-A	83	311	50	93	13	3	6	41	34	38	.299	.368	.418	119	5	8	47	1	2	-1	-2	O/3	0.0
	Yr	126	415	65	124	17	5	8	50	46	48	.299	.369	.422	116	7	9	62	1	4	-2	-3		-0.1
1956	Bal-A	32	117	13	24	4	2	1	17	18	13	.205	.311	.299	67	-6	-5	10	3	1	0	-3	O/3	-0.8
	Chi-A	86	279	44	74	14	2	4	47	28	27	.265	.334	.373	85	-6	-6	33	1	3	-2	-7	1O	-1.7
	Yr	118	396	57	98	18	4	5	64	46	40	.247	.327	.351	80	-12	-11	44	4	4	-1	-9		-2.5
1957	Chi-A	22	71	9	23	4	0	0	9	4	10	.324	.360	.380	102	0	0	10	1	1	-0	-0	O/1	-0.1
	Det-A	65	173	15	49	8	1	2	16	7	16	.283	.311	.376	85	-4	-4	19	3	1	0	2	1O/3	-0.2
	Yr	87	244	24	72	12	1	2	25	11	26	.295	.325	.377	90	-3	-4	29	4	2	0	2		-0.2
1958	Phi-N	91	207	30	64	11	4	3	31	15	20	.309	.359	.444	113	4	3	31	1	1	-0	-2	O1	0.0
1959	Phi-N	99	254	32	74	18	3	2	37	18	27	.291	.341	.461	109	3	3	40	0	1	0	0	O1	0.0
1960	Phi-N	14	15	2	5	2	0	0	4	3	2	.333	.444	.467	149	1	1	3	0	0	0	-1	/O1	0.0
	SF-N	39	61	5	10	0	0	1	7	6	14	.164	.239	.213	26	-6	-6	3	0	0	0	-2	O/3	-0.7
	Yr	53	76	7	15	2	0	1	11	9	16	.197	.282	.263	53	-5	-5	6	0	0	0	-2		-0.7
	Bal-A	14	34	6	9	2	1	1	5	4	5	.265	.342	.471	119	1	1	6	1	0	0	-1	/O3	0.0
1961	Bal-A	99	144	13	36	9	2	1	23	10	20	.250	.299	.361	77	-5	-5	13	2	0	1	-5	O/1	-0.9
1962	Bos-A	38	42	3	6	2	0	0	5	4	5	.143	.250	.190	20	-5	-5	1	0	0	0	-0	/O	-0.4
Total	18	1904	6296	789	1700	276	72	84	729	594	551	.270	.335	.377	91	-87	-84	790	101	63	-8	-30	*O1/3	-15.8

■ ADOLFO PHILLIPS Phillips, Adolfo Emilio (Lopez) b: 12/16/41, Bethania, Panama BR/TR, 6'1", 175 lbs. Deb: 9/02/64

YEAR	TM/L	G	AB	R	H	2B	3B	HR	RBI	BB	SO	AVG	OBP	SLG	PRO+	BR	/A	RC	SB	CS	SBR	FR	POS	TPR
1964	Phi-N	13	13	4	3	0	0	0	3	3	3	.231	.375	.231	76	-0	-0	2	0	0	0	1	/O	0.1

YEAR	TM/L	G	AB	R	H	2B	3B	HR	RBI	BB	SO	AVG	OBP	SLG	PRO+	BR	/A	RC	SB	CS	SBR	FR	POS	TPR
1965	Phi-N	41	87	14	20	4	0	3	5	5	34	.230	.272	.379	83	-2	-2	9	3	3	-1	1	O	-0.2
1966	Phi-N	2	3	1	0	0	0	0	0	0	0	.000	.000	.000	-99	-1	-1	0	0	0	0	0	/O	0.0
	Chi-N	116	416	68	109	29	1	16	36	43	135	.262	.348	.452	119	12	11	66	32	15	1	7	*O	1.6
	Yr	118	419	69	109	29	1	16	36	43	135	.260	.346	.449	118	11	10	66	32	15	1	7		1.6
1967	Chi-N	144	448	66	120	20	7	17	70	80	93	.268	.386	.458	134	26	24	82	24	10	1	12	*O	3.2
1968	Chi-N	143	439	49	106	20	5	13	33	47	90	.241	.322	.399	108	8	5	55	9	7	-2	3	*O	0.0
1969	Chi-N	28	49	5	11	3	1	0	1	16	15	.224	.424	.327	100	2	1	7	1	3	-2	1	O	0.0
	Mon-N	58	199	25	43	4	4	4	7	19	62	.216	.288	.337	74	-7	-7	19	6	5	-1	-3	O	-1.4
	Yr	86	248	30	54	7	5	4	8	35	77	.218	.319	.335	80	-5	-6	27	7	8	-3	-2		-1.4
1970	Mon-N	92	214	36	51	6	3	6	21	36	51	.238	.353	.379	96	-0	-0	31	7	1	2	-8	O	-0.9
1972	Cle-A	12	7	2	0	0	0	0	0	2	2	.000	.222	.000	-29	-1	-1	0	0	0	0	1	O	0.0
Total	8	649	1875	270	463	86	21	59	173	251	485	.247	.344	.410	110	36	29	270	82	44	-2	16	O	2.4

■ DAMON PHILLIPS
Phillips, Damon Roswell "Dee"   b: 6/8/19, Corsicana, Tex.   BR/TR, 6', 176 lbs.   Deb: 7/19/42

YEAR	TM/L	G	AB	R	H	2B	3B	HR	RBI	BB	SO	AVG	OBP	SLG	PRO+	BR	/A	RC	SB	CS	SBR	FR	POS	TPR
1942	Cin-N	28	84	4	17	2	0	0	6	7	5	.202	.264	.226	44	-6	-6	5	0			7	S	0.3
1944	Bos-N	140	489	35	126	30	1	1	53	28	34	.258	.301	.329	74	-15	-18	49	1			-4	3S	-0.9
1946	Bos-N	2	2	0	1	0	0	0	0	0	0	.500	.500	.500	182	0	0	1	0			0	H	0.0
Total	3	170	575	39	144	32	1	1	59	35	39	.250	.296	.315	70	-21	-23	55	1			3	/3S	-0.6

■ EDDIE PHILLIPS
Phillips, Edward David   b: 2/17/01, Worcester, Mass.   d: 1/26/68, Buffalo, N.Y.   BR/TR, 6', 178 lbs.   Deb: 5/04/24

YEAR	TM/L	G	AB	R	H	2B	3B	HR	RBI	BB	SO	AVG	OBP	SLG	PRO+	BR	/A	RC	SB	CS	SBR	FR	POS	TPR
1924	Bos-N	3	3	0	0	0	0	0	0	0	2	.000	.000	.000	-99	-1	-1	0	0	0	0	0	/C	0.0
1929	Det-A	68	221	24	52	13	1	2	21	20	16	.235	.302	.330	62	-13	-13	23	0	1	-1	-5	C	-1.1
1931	Pit-N	106	353	30	82	18	3	7	44	41	49	.232	.317	.360	82	-9	-9	43	1			-7	*C	-1.0
1932	NY-A	9	31	4	9	1	0	2	4	2	3	.290	.333	.516	123	1	1	5	1	0	0	1	/C	0.2
1934	Was-A	56	169	6	33	6	1	2	16	26	24	.195	.306	.278	54	-12	-11	16	1	0	0	-7	C	-1.1
1935	Cle-A	70	220	18	60	16	1	1	41	15	21	.273	.319	.368	76	-8	-8	26	0	0	0	-9	C	-1.3
Total	6	312	997	82	236	54	6	14	126	104	115	.237	.312	.345	72	-42	-41	113	3	1		-27	C	-4.3

■ EDDIE PHILLIPS
Phillips, Howard Edward   b: 7/8/31, St.Louis, Mo.   BB/TR, 6'1", 180 lbs.   Deb: 9/10/53

YEAR	TM/L	G	AB	R	H	2B	3B	HR	RBI	BB	SO	AVG	OBP	SLG	PRO+	BR	/A	RC	SB	CS	SBR	FR	POS	TPR
1953	StL-N	9	0	4	0	0	0	0	0	0	0	.000	—	—	—	0	0	0	0	0	0	0	R	0.0

■ JACK PHILLIPS
Phillips, Jack Dorn "Stretch"   b: 9/6/21, Clarence, N.Y.   BR/TR, 6'4", 193 lbs.   Deb: 8/22/47

YEAR	TM/L	G	AB	R	H	2B	3B	HR	RBI	BB	SO	AVG	OBP	SLG	PRO+	BR	/A	RC	SB	CS	SBR	FR	POS	TPR
1947	*NY-A	16	36	5	10	1	1	1	2	3	5	.278	.333	.417	109	0	0	5	0	0	0	-2	1	-0.1
1948	NY-A	1	2	0	0	0	0	0	0	0	1	.000	.000	.000	-99	-1	-1	0	0	0	0	-0	/1	0.0
1949	NY-A	45	91	16	28	4	1	1	10	12	9	.308	.388	.407	110	2	2	15	1	0	0	-2	1	0.0
	Pit-N	18	56	6	13	3	1	0	3	4	6	.232	.283	.321	60	-3	-3	5	1			0	1/3	-0.2
1950	Pit-N	69	208	25	61	7	6	5	34	20	17	.293	.355	.457	108	3	2	35	1			2	1/3P	0.2
1951	Pit-N	70	156	12	37	7	3	0	12	15	17	.237	.304	.321	66	-7	-8	15	1	2	-1	-1	1/3	-1.0
1952	Pit-N	1	1	0	0	0	0	0	0	0	0	.000	.000	.000	-97	-0	-0	0	0	0	0	0	/1	0.0
1955	Det-A	55	117	15	37	8	2	1	20	10	12	.316	.370	.444	121	3	3	19	0	0	0	-1	1/3	0.0
1956	Det-A	67	224	31	66	13	2	1	20	21	19	.295	.355	.384	95	-1	-2	28	1	1	-0	-1	1/2O	-0.4
1957	Det-A	1	1	0	0	0	0	0	0	0	0	.000	.000	.000	-97	-0	-0	0	0	0	0	0	H	0.0
Total	9	343	892	111	252	42	16	9	101	85	86	.283	.345	.396	95	-5	-6	122	5	3		-5	1/302P	-1.5

■ BUBBA PHILLIPS
Phillips, John Melvin   b: 2/24/30, West Point, Miss.   BR/TR, 5'9", 180 lbs.   Deb: 4/30/55

YEAR	TM/L	G	AB	R	H	2B	3B	HR	RBI	BB	SO	AVG	OBP	SLG	PRO+	BR	/A	RC	SB	CS	SBR	FR	POS	TPR
1955	Det-A	95	184	18	43	4	0	0	23	14	20	.234	.295	.304	63	-10	-10	17	2	1	0	8	O/3	-0.4
1956	Chi-A	67	99	16	27	6	0	2	11	6	12	.273	.321	.394	87	-2	-2	13	1	2	-1	6	O/3	0.1
1957	Chi-A	121	393	38	106	13	3	7	42	28	32	.270	.323	.372	89	-6	-6	48	5	3	-0	16	3O	1.0
1958	Chi-A	84	260	26	71	10	0	5	30	15	14	.273	.315	.369	89	-5	-4	29	3	0	1	7	3O	0.4
1959	*Chi-A	117	379	43	100	27	1	5	40	27	28	.264	.320	.380	92	-5	-4	45	1	1	-0	6	*3O	0.0
1960	Cle-A	113	304	34	63	14	1	4	33	14	37	.207	.252	.372	50	-23	-21	23	1	0	0	-2	3O/S	-2.3
1961	Cle-A	143	546	64	144	23	1	18	72	29	61	.264	.307	.408	92	-10	-8	66	1	0	0	-18	*3	-1.6
1962	Cle-A	148	562	53	145	26	0	10	54	20	55	.258	.292	.358	76	-22	-19	56	4	0	1	-15	*3/O2	-3.1
1963	Det-A	128	464	42	114	11	2	5	45	19	42	.246	.281	.310	63	-21	-23	38	6	2	1	1	*3/O	-2.1
1964	Det-A	46	87	14	22	1	0	3	6	10	13	.253	.330	.368	92	-1	-1	10	1	2	-1	2	3/O	0.0
Total	10	1062	3278	348	835	135	8	62	356	182	314	.255	.300	.358	79	-104	-99	343	25	11	1	10	3O/2S	-8.0

■ JACK PHILLIPS
Phillips, John Stephen   b: 5/24/19, St.Louis, Mo.   d: 6/16/58, St.Louis, Mo.   BR/TR, 6'1", 185 lbs.   Deb: 7/13/45

YEAR	TM/L	G	AB	R	H	2B	3B	HR	RBI	BB	SO	AVG	OBP	SLG	PRO+	BR	/A	RC	SB	CS	SBR	FR	POS	TPR
1945	NY-N	2	2	1	1	0	0	0	0	0	0	.500	.500	.500	176	0	0	1	0			0	/P	0.0

■ TONY PHILLIPS
Phillips, Keith Anthony   b: 4/25/59, Atlanta, Ga.   BB/TR, 5'9", 155 lbs.   Deb: 5/10/82

YEAR	TM/L	G	AB	R	H	2B	3B	HR	RBI	BB	SO	AVG	OBP	SLG	PRO+	BR	/A	RC	SB	CS	SBR	FR	POS	TPR
1982	Oak-A	40	81	11	17	2	0	0	8	12	26	.210	.326	.284	73	-3	-2	8	2	3	-1	-5	S	-0.4
1983	Oak-A	148	412	54	102	12	3	4	35	48	70	.248	.329	.320	85	-10	-7	48	16	5	2	-3	*S2/3D	0.0
1984	Oak-A	154	451	62	120	24	3	4	37	42	86	.266	.329	.359	97	-6	-2	55	10	6	-1	-11	S2/O	-0.1
1985	Oak-A	42	161	23	45	12	2	4	17	13	34	.280	.333	.453	122	3	4	25	3	2	-0	-0	32	0.3
1986	Oak-A	118	441	76	113	14	5	5	52	76	82	.256	.369	.345	103	0	5	63	15	10	-2	1	23/OSD	0.8
1987	Oak-A	111	379	48	91	20	0	10	46	57	76	.240	.339	.372	95	-5	-2	49	7	6	-2	-2	23/SOD	0.0
1988	*Oak-A	79	212	32	43	8	4	2	17	36	50	.203	.321	.307	80	-6	-5	22	0	2	-1	-12	3O2S/1D	-1.6
1989	*Oak-A	143	451	48	118	15	6	4	47	58	66	.262	.350	.348	101	0	2	53	3	8	-4	-20	23SO/1	-1.9
1990	Det-A	152	573	97	144	23	5	8	55	99	85	.251	.365	.351	102	5	5	81	19	9	0	8	*32S/OD	1.7
Total	9	987	3161	451	793	130	30	41	314	441	575	.251	.345	.350	97	-22	-1	403	75	51	-8	-45	2S3/OD1	-1.0

■ MARR PHILLIPS
Phillips, Marr B.   b: 6/16/1857, Pittsburgh, Pa.   d: 4/1/28, Pittsburgh, Pa.   Deb: 5/01/1884

YEAR	TM/L	G	AB	R	H	2B	3B	HR	RBI	BB	SO	AVG	OBP	SLG	PRO+	BR	/A	RC	SB	CS	SBR	FR	POS	TPR
1884	Ind-a	97	413	41	111	18	8	0			5	.269	.279	.351	111	2	4	42				14	*S	1.5
1885	Det-N	33	139	13	29	5	0	0	17	0	13	.209	.209	.245	46	-8	-8	7				3	S	-0.3
	Pit-a	4	15	1	4	0	0	0			2	.267	.353	.267	102	0	0	1				-1	/S	0.0
1890	Roc-a	64	257	18	53	8	0	0			16	.206	.261	.237	53	-16	-13	19	10			6	S	-0.3
Total	3	198	824	73	197	31	8	0	17		13	.239	.263	.296	81	-22	-17	69	10			21	S	0.9

■ MIKE PHILLIPS
Phillips, Michael Dwaine   b: 8/19/50, Beaumont, Tex.   BL/TR, 6', 170 lbs.   Deb: 4/15/73

YEAR	TM/L	G	AB	R	H	2B	3B	HR	RBI	BB	SO	AVG	OBP	SLG	PRO+	BR	/A	RC	SB	CS	SBR	FR	POS	TPR
1973	SF-N	63	104	18	25	3	4	1	9	6	17	.240	.288	.375	79	-3	-3	10	0	3	-2	-0	3S/2	-0.2
1974	SF-N	100	283	19	62	6	1	2	20	14	37	.219	.258	.269	45	-20	-22	19	4	5	-2	4	32S	-1.6
1975	SF-N	10	31	3	6	0	0	0	1	6	4	.194	.324	.194	44	-2	-2	2	1	0	0	4	/23	0.2
	NY-N	116	383	31	98	10	7	1	28	25	47	.256	.303	.326	78	-13	-11	38	3	0	1	1	*S/2	0.4
	Yr	126	414	34	104	10	7	1	29	31	51	.251	.305	.316	76	-15	-14	40	4	0	1	4		0.6
1976	NY-N	87	262	30	67	4	6	4	29	25	29	.256	.321	.363	99	-2	-1	31	2	5	-1	-9	S23	-0.4
1977	NY-N	38	86	5	18	2	1	1	3	2	15	.209	.244	.291	45	-7	-7	6	0	1	-1	-5	S2/3	-0.7
	StL-N	48	87	17	21	3	2	0	9	9	13	.241	.320	.322	74	-3	-3	10	1	0	0	5	2/S3	0.5
	Yr	86	173	22	39	5	3	1	12	11	28	.225	.283	.306	60	-10	-10	15	1	1	-0	1		-0.2
1978	StL-N	76	164	14	44	8	1	1	28	13	25	.268	.330	.348	91	-2	-2	19	0	0	0	-1	2S/3	0.1
1979	StL-N	44	97	10	22	3	1	1	6	10	9	.227	.306	.309	68	-4	-4	9	0	0	0	13	S2/3	1.2
1980	StL-N	63	128	13	30	5	0	0	7	9	17	.234	.285	.273	55	-7	-8	9	0	0	0	13	S/23	1.0
1981	SD-N	14	29	1	6	0	1	0	0	0	3	.207	.207	.276	39	-2	-2	1	1	0	0	4	/2S	0.3
	*Mon-N	34	55	5	12	2	0	0	4	5	15	.218	.283	.255	53	-3	-3	4	0	1	-1	0	S/2	0.0
	Yr	48	84	6	18	2	1	0	4	5	18	.214	.258	.262	49	-6	-6	5	1	1	-0	4		0.3

YEAR	TM/L	G	AB	R	H	2B	3B	HR	RBI	BB	SO	AVG	OBP	SLG	PRO+	BR	/A	RC	SB	CS	SBR	FR	POS	TPR
1982	Mon-N	14	8	0	1	0	0	0	1	0	3	.125	.125	.125	-29	-1	-1	0	0	0	0	3	2/S	0.2
1983	Mon-N	5	2	0	0	0	0	0	0	0	0	.000	.000	.000	-99	-1	-1	0	0	0	0	-1	/S3	-0.1
Total	11	712	1719	166	412	46	24	11	145	124	234	.240	.294	.314	70	-72	-70	156	12	12	-4	30	S23	0.9

■ DICK PHILLIPS
Phillips, Richard Eugene b: 11/24/31, Racine, Wis. BL/TR, 6′, 180 lbs. Deb: 4/15/62 C

YEAR	TM/L	G	AB	R	H	2B	3B	HR	RBI	BB	SO	AVG	OBP	SLG	PRO+	BR	/A	RC	SB	CS	SBR	FR	POS	TPR
1962	SF-N	5	3	1	0	0	0	0	1	1	1	.000	.250	.000	-27	-1	-1	0	0	0	0	0	/1	0.0
1963	Was-A	124	321	33	76	8	0	10	32	29	35	.237	.304	.355	84	-7	-7	36	1	0	0	4	1/23	-0.3
1964	Was-A	109	234	17	54	6	1	2	23	27	22	.231	.313	.291	70	-9	-9	23	1	2	-1	2	1/3	-0.9
1966	Was-A	25	37	3	6	0	0	0	4	2	5	.162	.225	.162	13	-4	-4	1	0	0	0	-0	/1	-0.4
Total	4	263	595	54	136	14	1	12	60	59	63	.229	.302	.316	74	-21	-20	60	2	2	-1	6	1/32	-1.6

■ BILL PHILLIPS
Phillips, William B. b: 1857, St.John, N.B., Canada d: 10/7/1900, Chicago, Ill. BR/TR, 202 lbs. Deb: 5/01/1879

YEAR	TM/L	G	AB	R	H	2B	3B	HR	RBI	BB	SO	AVG	OBP	SLG	PRO+	BR	/A	RC	SB	CS	SBR	FR	POS	TPR
1879	Cle-N	81	365	58	99	15	4	0	29	2	20	.271	.275	.334	101	-0	0	34				-1	*1C/O	-0.6
1880	Cle-N	85	334	41	85	14	10	1	36	6	29	.254	.268	.365	115	4	5	33				2	*1	0.3
1881	Cle-N	85	357	51	97	18	10	1	44	5	19	.272	.282	.387	114	3	5	40				-1	*1	-0.6
1882	Cle-N	78	335	40	87	17	7	4	47	7	18	.260	.275	.388	114	3	5	37				3	*1/C	-0.4
1883	Cle-N	97	382	42	94	29	8	2	40	8	49	.246	.262	.380	93	-4	-3	39				-2	*1	-1.5
1884	Cle-N	111	464	58	128	25	12	3	46	18	80	.276	.303	.401	115	9	7	58				-1	*1	-0.5
1885	Bro-a	99	391	65	118	16	11	3		27		.302	.364	.422	150	23	23	62				0	*1	1.3
1886	Bro-a	141	585	68	160	26	15	0		33		.274	.313	.369	114	9	8	74	13			-2	*1	0.0
1887	Bro-a	132	533	82	142	34	11	2		45		.266	.330	.383	99	0	-1	75	16			4	*1	0.0
1888	KC-a	129	509	57	120	20	10	1	56	27		.236	.284	.320	90	-2	-7	50	10			3	*1	-1.1
Total	10	1038	4255	562	1130	214	98	17	298	178	215	.266	.299	.374	110	45	41	501	39			5	*1/CO	-3.1

■ BILL PHYLE
Phyle, William Joseph b: 6/25/1875, Duluth, Minn. d: 8/6/53, Los Angeles, Cal. TR , Deb: 9/17/1898

YEAR	TM/L	G	AB	R	H	2B	3B	HR	RBI	BB	SO	AVG	OBP	SLG	PRO+	BR	/A	RC	SB	CS	SBR	FR	POS	TPR
1898	Chi-N	4	9	1	1	0	0	0	0	2		.111	.273	.111	13	-1	-1	0	0			-0	/P	0.0
1899	Chi-N	10	34	2	6	0	0	0	1	0		.176	.176	.176	-2	-5	-4	1	0			1	P	0.0
1901	NY-N	25	66	8	12	2	0	0	3	2		.182	.206	.212	24	-6	-6	3	0			1	P/S	0.0
1906	StL-N	22	73	6	13	3	1	0	4	5		.178	.231	.247	52	-4	-4	5	2			2	3	-0.2
Total	4	61	182	17	32	5	1	0	8	9		.176	.215	.214	29	-16	-15	9	2			4	/P3S	-0.2

■ ROB PICCIOLO
Picciolo, Robert Michael b: 2/4/53, Santa Monica, Cal. BR/TR, 6′2″, 185 lbs. Deb: 4/09/77 C

YEAR	TM/L	G	AB	R	H	2B	3B	HR	RBI	BB	SO	AVG	OBP	SLG	PRO+	BR	/A	RC	SB	CS	SBR	FR	POS	TPR
1977	Oak-A	148	419	35	84	12	3	2	22	9	55	.200	.219	.258	30	-41	-40	22	1	4	-2	7	*S	-1.7
1978	Oak-A	78	93	16	21	1	0	2	7	2	13	.226	.242	.301	55	-6	-6	6	1	1	-0	4	S23	0.2
1979	Oak-A	115	348	37	88	16	2	2	27	3	45	.253	.261	.328	61	-21	-19	27	2	1	0	-2	*S/23O	-0.7
1980	Oak-A	95	271	32	65	9	2	5	18	2	63	.240	.245	.343	64	-16	-13	21	1	1	-0	-24	S2/O	-3.1
1981	*Oak-A	82	179	23	48	5	3	4	13	5	22	.268	.292	.397	102	-1	-0	19	0	1	-1	-15	S	-0.9
1982	Oak-A	18	49	3	11	1	0	0	3	1	10	.224	.240	.245	35	-4	-4	3	1	0	0	3	S	0.1
	Mil-A	22	21	7	6	1	0	0	1	1	4	.286	.318	.333	84	-1	-0	2	0	0	0	2	2/SD	0.3
	Yr	40	70	10	17	2	0	0	4	2	14	.243	.264	.271	50	-5	-5	6	1	0	0	5		0.4
1983	Mil-A	14	27	2	6	3	0	0	1	0	4	.222	.222	.333	55	-2	-2	2	0	0	0	2	/S231	0.1
1984	Cal-A	87	119	18	24	6	0	1	9	0	21	.202	.202	.277	31	-11	-11	6	0	1	-1	13	S3/2O	0.7
1985	Oak-A	71	102	19	28	2	0	1	8	2	17	.275	.288	.324	73	-5	-4	9	3	2	-0	6	321D/SO	0.2
Total	9	730	1628	192	381	56	10	17	109	25	254	.234	.247	.312	55	-108	-99	118	9	11	-4	-3	S2/31DO	-4.8

■ NICK PICCIUTO
Picciuto, Nicholas Thomas b: 8/27/21, Newark, N.J. BR/TR, 5′8.5″, 165 lbs. Deb: 5/11/45

YEAR	TM/L	G	AB	R	H	2B	3B	HR	RBI	BB	SO	AVG	OBP	SLG	PRO+	BR	/A	RC	SB	CS	SBR	FR	POS	TPR
1945	Phi-N	36	89	7	12	6	0	0	6	6	17	.135	.189	.202	9	-11	-11	4	0			-6	3/2	-1.6

■ VAL PICINICH
Picinich, Valentine John b: 9/8/1896, New York, N.Y. d: 12/5/42, Nobleboro, Maine BR/TR, 5′9″, 165 lbs. Deb: 7/25/16 C

YEAR	TM/L	G	AB	R	H	2B	3B	HR	RBI	BB	SO	AVG	OBP	SLG	PRO+	BR	/A	RC	SB	CS	SBR	FR	POS	TPR
1916	Phi-A	40	118	8	23	3	1	0	5	6	33	.195	.234	.237	43	-9	-8	7	1			0	C	-0.6
1917	Phi-A	2	6	0	2	0	0	0	0	1	2	.333	.429	.333	135	0	0	1	0			-1	/C	0.0
1918	Was-A	47	148	13	34	3	3	0	12	9	25	.230	.274	.291	72	-6	-5	12	0			-2	C	-0.2
1919	Was-A	80	212	18	58	12	3	3	22	17	43	.274	.330	.401	106	1	1	30	6			15	C	2.0
1920	Was-A	48	133	14	27	6	2	3	14	9	33	.203	.259	.346	61	-8	-8	12	0	0	0	9	C	0.5
1921	Was-A	45	141	10	39	9	0	0	12	16	21	.277	.354	.340	82	-4	-3	17	0	3	-2	3	C	0.3
1922	Was-A	76	210	16	48	12	2	0	19	23	33	.229	.311	.305	64	-12	-10	22	1	0	0	7	C	0.0
1923	Bos-A	87	268	33	74	21	1	2	31	46	32	.276	.386	.384	103	3	3	42	3	5	-2	-2	C	0.4
1924	Bos-A	69	161	25	44	6	3	1	24	29	19	.273	.394	.366	97	1	0	26	5	1	1	-3	C	0.1
1925	Bos-A	90	251	31	64	21	0	1	25	33	21	.255	.344	.351	77	-9	-9	33	2	0	1	-7	C/1	-0.9
1926	Cin-N	89	240	33	63	16	1	2	31	29	22	.262	.342	.363	92	-3	-2	30	4			0	C	0.1
1927	Cin-N	65	173	16	44	8	3	0	12	24	15	.254	.345	.335	85	-4	-3	21	3			5	C	0.6
1928	Cin-N	96	324	29	98	15	1	7	35	20	25	.302	.343	.420	100	-1	-1	45	1			-3	C	0.2
1929	Bro-N	93	273	28	71	16	6	4	31	34	24	.260	.342	.407	86	-7	-6	38	3			-3	C	-0.1
1930	Bro-N	23	46	4	10	3	0	0	3	5	6	.217	.294	.283	41	-4	-4	4	1			-1	C	-0.3
1931	Bro-N	24	45	5	12	4	0	1	4	4	9	.267	.327	.422	101	-0	-0	6	1			1	C	0.2
1932	Bro-N	41	70	8	18	6	0	1	11	4	8	.257	.297	.386	84	-2	-2	8	0			-2	C	-0.2
1933	Bro-N	6	6	1	1	1	0	0	0	0	1	.167	.167	.333	42	-0	-0	0	0			0	/C	0.0
	Pit-N	16	52	6	13	4	1	0	7	5	10	.250	.316	.385	99	-0	-0	7	0			-3	C	-0.1
	Yr	22	58	7	14	5	1	0	7	5	11	.241	.302	.379	95	-1	-0	7	0			-2		-0.1
Total	18	1037	2877	298	743	166	26	26	298	314	382	.258	.334	.361	86	-65	-58	362	31	9		16	C/1	1.7

■ CHARLIE PICK
Pick, Charles Thomas b: 4/10/1888, Brookneal, Va. d: 6/26/54, Lynchburg, Va. BL/TR, 5′10″, 160 lbs. Deb: 9/20/14

YEAR	TM/L	G	AB	R	H	2B	3B	HR	RBI	BB	SO	AVG	OBP	SLG	PRO+	BR	/A	RC	SB	CS	SBR	FR	POS	TPR
1914	Was-A	10	23	0	9	0	0	0	1	4	4	.391	.481	.391	159	2	2	4	1	2	-1	-0	/O	0.0
1915	Was-A	3	2	0	0	0	0	0	0	0	0	.000	.000	.000	-99	-0	-0	0	0			0	H	0.0
1916	Phi-A	121	398	29	96	10	3	0	20	40	24	.241	.315	.281	83	-9	-8	39	25	16	-2	4	*3/O	0.0
1918	*Chi-N	29	89	13	29	4	1	0	12	14	4	.326	.417	.393	144	6	6	17	7			0	2/3	0.7
1919	Chi-N	75	269	27	65	8	6	0	18	14	12	.242	.292	.316	82	-6	-6	29	17			12	2/3	0.8
	Bos-N	34	114	12	29	1	1	1	7	7	5	.254	.325	.307	94	-1	-0	12	4			-2	2/3O1	-0.1
	Yr	109	383	39	94	9	7	1	25	21	17	.245	.302	.313	86	-7	-6	41	21			10		0.7
1920	Bos-N	95	383	34	105	16	6	2	28	23	11	.274	.320	.363	100	-2	-0	41	10	16	-7	0	2	-0.4
Total	6	367	1278	115	333	39	17	3	86	102	60	.261	.323	.325	95	-11	-7	143	64	34		14	23/O1	1.0

■ EDDIE PICK
Pick, Edgar Everett b: 5/7/1899, Attleboro, Mass. d: 5/13/67, Santa Monica, Cal. BB/TR, 6′, 185 lbs. Deb: 9/13/23

YEAR	TM/L	G	AB	R	H	2B	3B	HR	RBI	BB	SO	AVG	OBP	SLG	PRO+	BR	/A	RC	SB	CS	SBR	FR	POS	TPR
1923	Cin-N	9	8	2	3	0	0	0	2	3	3	.375	.545	.375	150	1	1	2	0	0	0	-0	/O	0.0
1924	Cin-N	3	2	0	0	0	0	0	0	0	1	.000	.000	.000	-99	-1	-0	0	0	0	0	0	/O	0.0
1927	Chi-N	54	181	23	31	5	2	2	15	20	26	.171	.254	.254	36	-16	-17	12	0			-5	3/2O	-1.8
Total	3	66	191	25	34	5	2	2	17	23	30	.178	.266	.257	40	-16	-16	15	0	0		-6	/3O2	-1.8

■ OLLIE PICKERING
Pickering, Oliver Daniel b: 4/9/1870, Olney, Ill. d: 1/20/52, Vincennes, Ind. BL/TR, 5′11″, 170 lbs. Deb: 8/09/1896

YEAR	TM/L	G	AB	R	H	2B	3B	HR	RBI	BB	SO	AVG	OBP	SLG	PRO+	BR	/A	RC	SB	CS	SBR	FR	POS	TPR
1896	Lou-N	45	165	28	50	6	4	1	22	12	11	.303	.350	.406	105	0	1	29	13			3	O	0.1
1897	Lou-N	63	246	34	62	5	2	1	20	25		.252	.326	.301	70	-10	-9	31	20			5	O	-0.7
	Cle-N	46	182	33	64	5	2	1	22	11		.352	.392	.412	110	4	3	38	18			0	O/2	0.0
	Yr	109	428	67	126	10	4	2	42	36		.294	.353	.350	88	-6	-6	68	38			5		-0.7
1901	Cle-A	137	547	102	169	25	3	0	40	58		.309	.382	.377	118	12	16	95	36			15	*O	2.6
1902	Cle-A	69	293	46	75	5	2	3	26	19		.256	.306	.317	78	-10	-8	36	22			-2	O/1	-1.3

YEAR	TM/L	G	AB	R	H	2B	3B	HR	RBI	BB	SO	AVG	OBP	SLG	PRO+	BR	/A	RC	SB	CS	SBR	FR	POS	TPR
1903	Phi-A	137	512	93	144	18	6	1	36	53		.281	.349	.346	106	9	6	81	40			4	*O	0.1
1904	Phi-A	124	455	56	103	10	3	0	30	45		.226	.296	.262	75	-9	-12	43	17			-0	*O	-2.1
1907	StL-A	151	576	63	159	15	10	0	60	35		.276	.318	.337	111	6	7	70	15			-11	*O	-1.3
1908	Was-A	113	373	45	84	7	4	2	30	28		.225	.279	.282	92	-6	-3	32	13			-7	O	-1.7
Total	8	885	3349	500	910	96	39	9	286	286	11	.272	.331	.332	98	-4	0	456	194			5	O/12	-4.3

■ URBANE PICKERING   Pickering, Urbane Henry "Pick"   b: 6/3/1899, Hoxie, Kan.   d: 5/13/70, Modesto, Cal.   BR/TR, 5'10", 180 lbs.   Deb: 4/18/31

YEAR	TM/L	G	AB	R	H	2B	3B	HR	RBI	BB	SO	AVG	OBP	SLG	PRO+	BR	/A	RC	SB	CS	SBR	FR	POS	TPR
1931	Bos-A	103	341	48	86	13	4	9	52	33	53	.252	.318	.393	91	-8	-5	43	3	4	-2	-2	32	-0.2
1932	Bos-A	132	457	47	119	28	5	2	40	39	71	.260	.320	.357	77	-17	-15	53	3	4	-2	-7	*3/C	-1.3
Total	2	235	798	95	205	41	9	11	92	72	124	.257	.319	.372	83	-25	-20	95	6	8	-3	-8	3/2C	-1.5

■ DAVE PICKETT   Pickett, David T.   b: 5/26/1874, Brookline, Mass.   d: 4/22/50, Easton, Mass.   5'7.5", 170 lbs.   Deb: 6/21/1898

YEAR	TM/L	G	AB	R	H	2B	3B	HR	RBI	BB	SO	AVG	OBP	SLG	PRO+	BR	/A	RC	SB	CS	SBR	FR	POS	TPR
1898	Bos-N	14	43	3	12	1	0	0	3	6		.279	.380	.302	94	0	0	6	2			-2	O	-0.2

■ JOHN PICKETT   Pickett, John Thomas   b: 2/20/1866, Chicago, Ill.   d: 7/4/22, Chicago, Ill.   BR/TR,   Deb: 6/06/1889

YEAR	TM/L	G	AB	R	H	2B	3B	HR	RBI	BB	SO	AVG	OBP	SLG	PRO+	BR	/A	RC	SB	CS	SBR	FR	POS	TPR
1889	KC-a	53	201	20	45	7	0	0	12	11	21	.224	.271	.259	50	-12	-14	16	7			-16	O32	-2.6
1890	Phi-P	100	407	82	114	7	9	4	64	40	17	.280	.347	.371	92	-4	-5	58	12			-21	*2	-1.6
1892	Bal-N	36	141	13	30	2	3	1	12	7	10	.213	.260	.291	66	-6	-6	11	2			-5	2	-0.9
Total	3	189	749	115	189	16	12	5	88	58	48	.252	.311	.326	76	-21	-26	86	21			-42	2/O3	-5.1

■ TY PICKUP   Pickup, Clarence William   b: 10/29/1897, Philadelphia, Pa.   d: 8/2/74, Philadelphia, Pa.   6', 180 lbs.   Deb: 4/30/18

YEAR	TM/L	G	AB	R	H	2B	3B	HR	RBI	BB	SO	AVG	OBP	SLG	PRO+	BR	/A	RC	SB	CS	SBR	FR	POS	TPR
1918	Phi-N	1	1	0	1	0	0	0	0	0	0	1.000	1.000	1.000	478	0	0	1	0			0	/O	0.1

■ GRACIE PIERCE   Pierce, Grayson S.   b: New York, N.Y.   d: 8/28/1894, New York, N.Y.   BR/TR,   Deb: 5/02/1882   U

YEAR	TM/L	G	AB	R	H	2B	3B	HR	RBI	BB	SO	AVG	OBP	SLG	PRO+	BR	/A	RC	SB	CS	SBR	FR	POS	TPR
1882	Lou-a	9	33	3	10	1	0	0		1		.303	.324	.333	130	1	1	4				1	/2	0.2
	Bal-a	41	151	8	30	2	1	0		3		.199	.214	.225	52	-8	-6	7				-10	2/OS	-1.1
	Yr	50	184	11	40	3	1	0		4		.217	.234	.245	67	-7	-5	11				-9		-0.9
1883	Col-a	11	41	5	7	0	0	0		0		.171	.171	.171	11	-4	-3	1				-1	/2O	-0.3
	NY-N	18	62	3	5	0	1	0		1	9	.081	.095	.113	-37	-10	-10	1				-1	O/2	-0.9
1884	NY-a	5	20	2	5	1	0	0		0		.250	.250	.300	83	-0	-0	2				-5	O/2	-0.4
Total	3	84	307	21	57	4	2	0	2	5	9	.186	.199	.212	37	-21	-19	15				-15	/2OS	-2.5

■ JACK PIERCE   Pierce, Lavern Jack   b: 6/2/48, Laurel, Miss.   BL/TR, 6', 210 lbs.   Deb: 4/27/73

YEAR	TM/L	G	AB	R	H	2B	3B	HR	RBI	BB	SO	AVG	OBP	SLG	PRO+	BR	/A	RC	SB	CS	SBR	FR	POS	TPR
1973	Atl-N	11	20	4	1	0	0	0	0	1	8	.050	.095	.050	-55	-4	-4	0	0	0	0	1	/1	-0.3
1974	Atl-N	6	9	1	1	0	0	0	0	1	0	.111	.200	.111	-11	-1	-1	0	0	0	0	0	/1	0.0
1975	Det-A	53	170	19	40	6	1	8	22	20	40	.235	.323	.424	105	2	1	24	0	0	0	-5	1	-0.6
Total	3	70	199	20	42	6	1	8	22	22	48	.211	.296	.372	83	-4	-5	25	0	0	0	-4	/1	-0.9

■ MAURY PIERCE   Pierce, Maurice   b: Baltimore, Md.   Deb: 4/23/1884

YEAR	TM/L	G	AB	R	H	2B	3B	HR	RBI	BB	SO	AVG	OBP	SLG	PRO+	BR	/A	RC	SB	CS	SBR	FR	POS	TPR
1884	Was-U	2	7	0	1	0	0	0		0		.143	.143	.143	-3	-1	-1	0	0			0	/3	0.0

■ ANDY PIERCY   Piercy, Andrew J.   b: 8/1856, San Jose, Cal.   d: 12/27/32, San Jose, Cal.   TR,   Deb: 5/12/1881

YEAR	TM/L	G	AB	R	H	2B	3B	HR	RBI	BB	SO	AVG	OBP	SLG	PRO+	BR	/A	RC	SB	CS	SBR	FR	POS	TPR
1881	Chi-N	2	8	1	2	0	0	0	0	1		.250	.250	.250	55	-0	-0	1				-1	/32	-0.1

■ DICK PIERRE   Pierre, Richard J.   b: Grand Haven, Mich.   Deb: 9/25/1883

YEAR	TM/L	G	AB	R	H	2B	3B	HR	RBI	BB	SO	AVG	OBP	SLG	PRO+	BR	/A	RC	SB	CS	SBR	FR	POS	TPR
1883	Phi-N	5	19	1	3	0	0	0	0	0		.158	.158	.158	-4	-2	-2	0				-4	/S	-0.4

■ JIM PIERSALL   Piersall, James Anthony   b: 11/14/29, Waterbury, Conn.   BR/TR, 6', 175 lbs.   Deb: 9/07/50   C

YEAR	TM/L	G	AB	R	H	2B	3B	HR	RBI	BB	SO	AVG	OBP	SLG	PRO+	BR	/A	RC	SB	CS	SBR	FR	POS	TPR
1950	Bos-A	6	7	4	2	0	0	0	0	4	0	.286	.545	.286	107	1	1	2	0	0	0	1	/O	0.1
1952	Bos-A	56	161	28	43	8	0	1	16	28	26	.267	.379	.335	93	1	-0	23	3	3	-1	-6	SO/3	-0.6
1953	Bos-A	151	585	76	159	21	9	3	52	41	52	.272	.329	.354	80	-13	-17	69	11	10	-3	15	*O	-0.8
1954	Bos-A	133	474	77	135	24	2	8	38	36	42	.285	.339	.395	90	-0	-7	63	5	1	1	-0	*O	-0.9
1955	Bos-A	149	515	68	146	25	5	13	62	67	52	.283	.368	.427	104	10	4	82	6	1	1	7	*O	0.5
1956	Bos-A	155	601	91	176	40	6	14	87	58	48	.293	.356	.449	99	9	-1	92	7	7	-2	11	*O	-0.5
1957	Bos-A	151	609	103	159	27	5	19	63	62	54	.261	.333	.415	98	2	-2	83	14	6	1	5	*O	-0.5
1958	Bos-A	130	417	55	99	13	5	8	48	42	43	.237	.307	.350	75	-11	-15	46	12	2	2	5	*O	-1.5
1959	Cle-A	100	317	42	78	13	2	4	30	25	31	.246	.305	.338	79	-10	-9	34	6	3	0	-4	O/3	-1.7
1960	Cle-A	138	486	70	137	12	4	18	66	24	38	.282	.316	.434	104	-1	0	62	18	5	2	5	*O	0.2
1961	Cle-A	121	484	81	156	26	7	6	40	43	46	.322	.380	.442	122	13	15	79	8	5	2	10	*O	2.1
1962	Was-A	135	471	38	115	20	4	4	31	39	53	.244	.302	.329	70	-20	-20	45	12	7	-1	0	*O	-2.4
1963	Was-A	29	94	9	23	1	0	1	5	6	11	.245	.290	.287	63	-5	-5	8	4	0	1	2	O	-0.2
	NY-N	40	124	13	24	4	1	1	10	10	14	.194	.254	.266	49	-8	-8	8	1	2	-1	1	O	-1.0
	LA-A	20	52	4	16	1	0	0	4	5	5	.308	.368	.327	103	-0	0	6	0	1	-1	-1	O	-0.1
1964	LA-A	87	255	28	80	11	0	2	13	16	32	.314	.354	.380	116	2	5	34	5	3	-0	-2	O	0.0
1965	Cal-A	53	112	10	30	5	2	2	12	5	15	.268	.305	.402	101	-0	0	13	2	2	-1	1	O	-0.8
1966	Cal-A	75	123	14	26	5	0	0	14	13	19	.211	.287	.252	58	-7	-6	8	1	2	-1	1	O	-0.8
1967	Cal-A	5	3	0	0	0	0	0	0	0	0	.000	.000	.000	-99	-1	-1	0	0	0	0	0	O	0.0
Total	17	1734	5890	811	1604	256	52	104	591	524	583	.272	.334	.386	92	-39	-66	756	115	57		52	*O/S3	-7.6

■ DAVE PIERSON   Pierson, David P.   b: 8/20/1855, Wilkes-Barre, Pa.   d: 11/11/22, Trenton, N.J.   BR/TR, 5'7", 142 lbs.   Deb: 4/25/1876

YEAR	TM/L	G	AB	R	H	2B	3B	HR	RBI	BB	SO	AVG	OBP	SLG	PRO+	BR	/A	RC	SB	CS	SBR	FR	POS	TPR
1876	Cin-N	57	233	33	55	4	1	0	13	1	9	.236	.239	.262	78	-8	-3	15				-1	CO/S32P	-0.1

■ DICK PIERSON   Pierson, Edmund Dana   b: 10/24/1857, Wilkes-Barre, Pa.   d: 7/20/22, Newark, N.J.   TR,   Deb: 6/23/1885

YEAR	TM/L	G	AB	R	H	2B	3B	HR	RBI	BB	SO	AVG	OBP	SLG	PRO+	BR	/A	RC	SB	CS	SBR	FR	POS	TPR
1885	NY-a	3	9	1	1	0	0	0		2		.111	.273	.111	29	-1	-1	0				-2	/2	-0.1

■ TONY PIET   Piet, Anthony Francis (b: Anthony Francis Pietruszka)   b: 12/7/06, Berwick, Pa.   d: 12/1/81, Hinsdale, Ill.   BR/TR, 6', 175 lbs.   Deb: 8/15/31

YEAR	TM/L	G	AB	R	H	2B	3B	HR	RBI	BB	SO	AVG	OBP	SLG	PRO+	BR	/A	RC	SB	CS	SBR	FR	POS	TPR
1931	Pit-N	44	167	22	50	12	4	0	24	13	24	.299	.354	.419	108	2	2	25	10			-4	2/S	0.0
1932	Pit-N	154	574	66	162	25	8	7	85	46	56	.282	.343	.390	98	-2	-1	80	19			-28	*2	-1.6
1933	Pit-N	107	362	45	117	21	5	1	42	19	28	.323	.367	.417	124	11	11	57	12			-5	2	1.3
1934	Cin-N	106	421	58	109	20	5	1	38	23	44	.259	.307	.337	74	-16	-15	43	6			-10	32	-1.5
1935	Cin-N	6	5	2	1	1	0	0	2	0	0	.200	.200	.400	59	-0	-0	0	0			0	/O	0.0
	Chi-A	77	292	47	87	17	5	3	27	33	27	.298	.375	.421	103	3	2	48	2	1	0	4	23	0.7
1936	Chi-A	109	352	69	96	15	2	7	42	66	48	.273	.400	.386	92	-0	-2	61	15	5	2	6	23	0.9
1937	Chi-A	100	332	34	78	15	1	4	38	32	36	.235	.314	.322	61	-20	-20	36	14	6	1	2	32	-1.3
1938	Det-A	41	80	9	17	6	0	0	14	15	11	.213	.351	.287	58	-4	-5	8	2	4	-2	0	3/2	-0.5
Total	8	744	2585	352	717	132	30	23	312	247	274	.277	.350	.378	91	-28	-29	359	80	16		-36	23/OS	-2.0

■ SANDY PIEZ   Piez, Charles William   b: 10/13/1892, New York, N.Y.   d: 12/29/30, Atlantic City, N.J   BR/TR, 5'10", 170 lbs.   Deb: 4/17/14

YEAR	TM/L	G	AB	R	H	2B	3B	HR	RBI	BB	SO	AVG	OBP	SLG	PRO+	BR	/A	RC	SB	CS	SBR	FR	POS	TPR
1914	NY-N	37	8	9	3	0	1	0	3	0	1	.375	.375	.625	202	1	1	3	4			5	/O	0.6

■ JOE PIGNATANO   Pignatano, Joseph Benjamin   b: 8/4/29, Brooklyn, N.Y.   BR/TR, 5'10", 180 lbs.   Deb: 4/28/57   C

YEAR	TM/L	G	AB	R	H	2B	3B	HR	RBI	BB	SO	AVG	OBP	SLG	PRO+	BR	/A	RC	SB	CS	SBR	FR	POS	TPR
1957	Bro-N	8	14	0	3	1	0	1	1	0	5	.214	.214	.286	30	-1	-1	1	0	0	0	3	/C	0.2
1958	LA-N	63	142	18	31	4	0	9	17	16	26	.218	.306	.437	91	-2	-2	19	4	1	1	9	C	1.0
1959	*LA-N	52	139	17	33	4	1	1	11	21	15	.237	.346	.302	69	-4	-6	16	1	0	0	7	C	0.5
1960	LA-N	58	90	11	21	4	0	2	9	15	17	.233	.343	.344	83	-1	-2	12	1	1	-0	15	C	1.5
1961	KC-A	92	243	31	59	10	3	4	22	36	42	.243	.350	.358	89	-3	-3	34	2	2	-1	1	C/3	-0.3

YEAR	TM/L	G	AB	R	H	2B	3B	HR	RBI	BB	SO	AVG	OBP	SLG	PRO+	BR	/A	RC	SB	CS	SBR	FR	POS	TPR
1962	SF-N	7	5	2	1	0	0	0	0	4	0	.200	.556	.200	114	1	1	0	0	0	0	-1	/C	0.0
	NY-N	27	56	2	13	2	0	0	2	2	11	.232	.259	.268	41	-5	-5	3	0	0	0	4	C	0.0
	Yr	34	61	4	14	2	0	0	2	6	11	.230	.299	.262	51	-4	-4	4	0	0	0	4		0.0
Total	6	307	689	81	161	25	4	16	62	94	116	.234	.332	.351	80	-15	-18	86	8	4	0	39	C/3	2.9

■ JAY PIKE
Pike, Jacob Emanuel b: Brooklyn, N.Y. BL/TL, Deb: 8/27/1877

YEAR	TM/L	G	AB	R	H	2B	3B	HR	RBI	BB	SO	AVG	OBP	SLG	PRO+	BR	/A	RC	SB	CS	SBR	FR	POS	TPR
1877	Har-N	1	4	0	1	0	0	0	0	0	0	.250	.250	.250	65	-0	-0	0				-1	/O	0.0

■ JESS PIKE
Pike, Jess Willard b: 7/31/15, Dustin, Okla. d: 3/28/84, San Diego, Cal. BL/TR, 6'3", 175 lbs. Deb: 4/18/46

YEAR	TM/L	G	AB	R	H	2B	3B	HR	RBI	BB	SO	AVG	OBP	SLG	PRO+	BR	/A	RC	SB	CS	SBR	FR	POS	TPR
1946	NY-N	16	41	4	7	1	1	1	6	6	9	.171	.277	.317	68	-2	-2	4	0			-3	O	-0.4

■ LIP PIKE
Pike, Lipman Emanuel b: 5/25/1845, New York, N.Y. d: 10/10/1893, Brooklyn, N.Y. BL/TL, 5'8", 158 lbs. Deb: 5/09/1871 M

YEAR	TM/L	G	AB	R	H	2B	3B	HR	RBI	BB	SO	AVG	OBP	SLG	PRO+	BR	/A	RC	SB	CS	SBR	FR	POS	TPR
1871	Tro-n	28	130	43	49	10	7	4	39	5	7	.377	.400	.654	194	16	15	36	3				O/21M	1.0
1872	Bal-n	56	285	68	84	10	4	6		5	3	.295	.302	.421	115	6	3	37					O2/3	0.1
1873	Bal-n	56	288	71	89	18	8	4		6		.309	.323	.469	130	10	10	45					*O/2	0.9
1874	Har-n	52	238	58	81	24	5	1		0		.340	.340	.496	155	16	14	41					OS/2M	1.0
1875	StL-n	70	312	61	107	21	10	0		3		.343	.349	.474	200	25	29	53					*O/2	2.5
1876	StL-N	63	282	55	91	19	10	1	50	8	9	.323	.341	.472	178	20	22	47				-6	*O/2	1.4
1877	Cin-N	58	262	45	78	12	4	4	23	9	7	.298	.321	.420	148	9	14	36				-4	O2/SM	0.8
1878	Cin-N	31	145	28	47	5	1	0	11	4	9	.324	.342	.372	149	5	7	19				-4	O	0.0
	Pro-N	5	22	4	5	0	1	0	4	1	1	.227	.261	.318	90	-0	-0	2				-3	/2	-0.2
	Yr	36	167	32	52	5	2	0	15	5	10	.311	.331	.365	140	5	7	21				-7		-0.2
1881	Wor-N	5	18	1	2	0	0	0	0	4	3	.111	.273	.111	24	-1	-2	1				-1	O	-0.2
1887	NY-a	1	4	0	0	0	0	0		0		.000	.000	.000	-99	-1	-1	0	0			0	/O	0.0
Total	5 n	262	1253	301	410	83	34	15	39	17	7	.327	.336	.484	153	72	72	212	3				O/2S31	5.5
Total	5	163	733	133	223	36	16	5	88	26	29	.304	.328	.417	152	31	40	104	0			-18	O/2S	1.8

■ AL PILARCIK
Pilarcik, Alfred James b: 7/3/30, Whiting, Ind. BL/TL, 5'10", 180 lbs. Deb: 7/13/56

YEAR	TM/L	G	AB	R	H	2B	3B	HR	RBI	BB	SO	AVG	OBP	SLG	PRO+	BR	/A	RC	SB	CS	SBR	FR	POS	TPR
1956	KC-A	69	239	28	60	10	1	4	22	30	32	.251	.335	.351	81	-6	-6	31	9	2	2	-0	O	-0.7
1957	Bal-A	142	407	52	113	16	3	9	49	53	28	.278	.366	.398	116	6	9	62	14	7	0	5	*O	0.7
1958	Bal-A	141	379	40	92	21	0	1	24	42	37	.243	.322	.306	78	-13	-10	39	7	3	0	-4	*O	-2.1
1959	Bal-A	130	273	37	77	12	1	3	16	30	25	.282	.355	.366	101	0	1	37	9	3	1	-4	*O	-0.6
1960	Bal-A	104	194	30	48	5	1	4	17	15	16	.247	.315	.345	79	-6	-6	21	0	2	-1	-2	O	-1.1
1961	KC-A	35	60	9	12	1	1	0	9	6	7	.200	.273	.250	41	-5	-5	4	1	0	0	2	O	-0.3
	Chi-A	47	62	9	11	1	0	1	6	9	5	.177	.282	.242	42	-5	-5	4	1	1	-0	3	O	-0.2
	Yr	82	122	18	23	2	1	1	15	15	12	.189	.277	.246	41	-10	-10	8	2	1	0	4		-0.5
Total	6	668	1614	205	413	66	7	22	143	185	150	.256	.336	.346	89	-29	-22	198	41	18	2	-1	O	-4.3

■ ANDY PILNEY
Pilney, Antone James b: 1/19/13, Frontenac, Kan. BR/TR, 5'11", 174 lbs. Deb: 6/12/36

YEAR	TM/L	G	AB	R	H	2B	3B	HR	RBI	BB	SO	AVG	OBP	SLG	PRO+	BR	/A	RC	SB	CS	SBR	FR	POS	TPR
1936	Bos-N	3	2	0	0	0	0	0	0	0	1	.000	.000	.000	-99	-1	-1	0	0			0	H	0.0

■ BABE PINELLI
Pinelli, Ralph Arthur (b: Rinaldo Angelo Paolinelli)
b: 10/18/1895, San Francisco, Cal d: 10/2/ 22, 84 Daly City, Cal. BR/TR, 5'9", 165 lbs. Deb: 8/03/18 U

YEAR	TM/L	G	AB	R	H	2B	3B	HR	RBI	BB	SO	AVG	OBP	SLG	PRO+	BR	/A	RC	SB	CS	SBR	FR	POS	TPR
1918	Chi-A	24	78	7	18	1	1	1	7	7	8	.231	.302	.308	83	-2	-2	8	3			-7	3	-0.9
1920	Det-A	102	284	33	65	9	3	0	21	25	16	.229	.296	.282	55	-19	-18	24	6	8	-3	20	3S/2	0.6
1922	Cin-N	156	547	77	167	19	7	1	72	48	37	.305	.368	.371	93	-6	-4	73	17	22	-8	21	*3	2.0
1923	Cin-N	117	423	44	117	14	5	0	51	27	29	.277	.320	.333	74	-17	-15	43	10	14	-5	9	*3	-0.8
1924	Cin-N	144	510	61	156	16	7	0	70	32	32	.306	.353	.365	94	-4	-3	65	23	17	-3	27	*3	3.0
1925	Cin-N	130	492	68	139	33	6	2	49	22	28	.283	.316	.386	80	-17	-15	55	8	19	-9	21	*3S	0.5
1926	Cin-N	71	207	26	46	7	4	0	24	15	5	.222	.284	.295	58	-13	-12	18	2			1	3S/2	-0.7
1927	Cin-N	30	76	11	15	2	0	1	4	6	7	.197	.265	.263	43	-6	-6	5	2			-1	3/S2	-0.4
Total	8	774	2617	327	723	101	33	5	298	182	162	.276	.328	.346	79	-83	-75	292	71	80		91	3/S2	3.3

■ LOU PINIELLA
Piniella, Louis Victor b: 8/28/43, Tampa, Fla. BR/TR, 6', 182 lbs. Deb: 9/04/64 MC

YEAR	TM/L	G	AB	R	H	2B	3B	HR	RBI	BB	SO	AVG	OBP	SLG	PRO+	BR	/A	RC	SB	CS	SBR	FR	POS	TPR
1964	Bal-A	4	1	0	0	0	0	0	0	0	0	.000	.000	.000	-99	-0	-0	0	0	0	0	0	H	0.0
1968	Cle-A	6	5	1	0	0	0	0	1	0	0	.000	.000	.000	-99	-1	-1	0	0	0	0	0	/O	0.0
1969	KC-A	135	493	43	139	21	6	11	68	33	56	.282	.331	.416	107	4	3	65	2	4	-2	12	*O	1.1
1970	KC-A	144	542	54	163	24	5	11	88	35	42	.301	.345	.424	111	7	7	74	3	6	-3	-3	*O/1	-0.4
1971	KC-A	126	448	43	125	21	5	3	51	21	43	.279	.314	.368	94	-5	-5	49	5	3	-0	-5	*O	-1.5
1972	KC-A	151	574	65	179	33	4	11	72	34	59	.312	.359	.441	138	25	25	84	7	2	1	-3	*O	2.2
1973	KC-A	144	513	53	128	28	1	9	69	30	65	.250	.294	.361	77	-12	-17	47	5	7	-3	-9	*O/D	-3.3
1974	NY-A	140	518	71	158	26	0	9	70	32	58	.305	.348	.407	112	10	10	66	1	8	-5	6	*O/1D	1.0
1975	NY-A	74	199	7	39	4	1	0	22	16	22	.196	.266	.226	41	-15	-15	10	0	0	0	-1	OD	-1.7
1976	*NY-A	100	327	36	92	16	6	3	38	18	34	.281	.323	.394	110	3	3	41	0	1	-1	-0	OD	0.2
1977	*NY-A	103	339	47	112	19	3	12	45	20	31	.330	.369	.510	138	16	17	59	2	2	-1	-3	OD/1	1.2
1978	*NY-A	130	472	67	148	34	5	6	69	34	36	.314	.362	.445	129	16	17	74	3	1	0	-2	*OD	1.3
1979	NY-A	130	461	49	137	22	2	11	69	17	31	.297	.325	.425	103	-1	1	58	3	2	-0	-0	*OD	-0.3
1980	*NY-A	116	321	39	92	18	0	2	27	29	20	.287	.346	.361	96	-2	-1	36	0	2	-1	-3	*O/D	-0.7
1981	*NY-A	60	159	16	44	9	0	5	18	13	9	.277	.331	.428	119	3	3	20	0	1	-1	2	OD	0.4
1982	NY-A	102	261	33	80	17	1	6	37	19	18	.307	.354	.448	120	6	7	37	0	1	-1	4	DO	0.8
1983	NY-A	53	148	19	43	9	1	2	16	11	12	.291	.344	.405	109	1	2	20	1	1	-0	-2	O/D	0.1
1984	NY-A	29	86	8	26	4	1	1	6	7	5	.302	.355	.407	115	1	2	10	0	0	0	0	OD	0.1
Total	18	1747	5867	651	1705	305	41	102	766	368	541	.291	.336	.409	109	56	60	750	32	41	-15	-9	*OD/1	0.4

■ ED PINKHAM
Pinkham, Edward b: 1849, Brooklyn, N.Y. TL , 5'7", 142 lbs. Deb: 5/08/1871

YEAR	TM/L	G	AB	R	H	2B	3B	HR	RBI	BB	SO	AVG	OBP	SLG	PRO+	BR	/A	RC	SB	CS	SBR	FR	POS	TPR
1871	Chi-n	24	95	27	25	5	5	1	17	18	3	.263	.381	.453	125	5	3	19	5				3/OP	0.1

■ GEORGE PINKNEY
Pinkney, George Burton b: 1/11/1862, Orange Prairie, Ill. d: 11/10/26, Peoria, Ill. BR/TR, 5'7", 160 lbs. Deb: 8/16/1884

YEAR	TM/L	G	AB	R	H	2B	3B	HR	RBI	BB	SO	AVG	OBP	SLG	PRO+	BR	/A	RC	SB	CS	SBR	FR	POS	TPR
1884	Cle-N	36	144	18	45	9	0	0	16	10	7	.313	.357	.375	126	5	4	20				-8	2S	-0.1
1885	Bro-a	110	447	77	124	16	5	0	27			.277	.328	.336	112	7	7	51				-11	23/S	0.1
1886	Bro-a	141	597	119	156	22	7	0	70			.261	.339	.322	108	8	8	78	32			-16	*3/P	-0.1
1887	Bro-a	138	580	133	155	26	6	3	61			.267	.343	.348	94	-2	-3	92	59			13	*3/S	0.4
1888	Bro-a	143	575	134	156	18	8	4	52	66		.271	.358	.351	132	23	23	93	51			-25	*3	-0.1
1889	*Bro-a	138	545	103	134	25	7	4	82	59	43	.246	.327	.339	92	-5	-5	78	47			-8	*3	-0.9
1890	*Bro-N	126	485	115	150	20	9	7	83	80	19	.309	.411	.431	148	32	32	108	47			-14	*3	2.0
1891	Bro-N	135	501	80	137	19	6	2	71	66	32	.273	.366	.347	111	9	10	82	44			-20	*3/S	-0.4
1892	StL-N	78	290	31	50	3	2	0	25	36	26	.172	.268	.197	45	-19	-17	17	4			-8	3	-1.8
1893	Lou-N	118	446	64	105	12	6	1	62	50	8	.235	.323	.296	72	-20	-14	48	12			-1	*3	-1.1
Total	10	1163	4610	874	1212	170	56	21	391	525	135	.263	.345	.338	105	39	45	665	296			-98	*3/2SP	-2.0

■ VADA PINSON
Pinson, Vada Edward b: 8/11/36, Memphis, Tenn. BL/TL, 5'11", 170 lbs. Deb: 4/15/58 C

YEAR	TM/L	G	AB	R	H	2B	3B	HR	RBI	BB	SO	AVG	OBP	SLG	PRO+	BR	/A	RC	SB	CS	SBR	FR	POS	TPR
1958	Cin-N	27	96	20	26	7	0	1	8	11	18	.271	.352	.375	88	-1	-1	13	2	1	0	1	O	0.0
1959	Cin-N	154	648	131	205	47	9	20	84	55	98	.316	.371	.509	128	28	26	124	21	6	3	12	*O	3.8
1960	Cin-N	154	652	107	187	37	12	20	61	47	96	.287	.339	.472	117	16	15	104	32	12	2	3	*O	1.6
1961	*Cin-N	154	607	101	208	34	8	16	87	39	63	.343	.383	.504	131	28	27	116	23	10	1	13	*O	3.1

YEAR	TM/L	G	AB	R	H	2B	3B	HR	RBI	BB	SO	AVG	OBP	SLG	PRO+	BR	/A	RC	SB	CS	SBR	FR	POS	TPR
1962	Cin-N	155	619	107	181	31	7	23	100	45	68	.292	.344	.477	114	14	11	101	26	8	3	0	*O	0.6
1963	Cin-N	162	652	96	**204**	37	**14**	22	106	36	80	.313	.350	.514	141	35	33	113	27	8	3	3	*O	3.4
1964	Cin-N	156	625	99	166	23	11	23	84	42	99	.266	.317	.448	109	9	7	89	8	2	1	-2	*O	0.2
1965	Cin-N	159	669	97	204	34	10	22	94	43	81	.305	.353	.484	125	28	23	112	21	8	2	8	*O	2.9
1966	Cin-N	156	618	70	178	35	6	16	76	33	83	.288	.329	.442	103	9	3	87	18	10	-1	1	*O	-0.1
1967	Cin-N	158	650	90	187	28	**13**	18	66	26	86	.288	.318	.454	106	13	5	94	26	8	3	1	*O	0.2
1968	Cin-N	130	499	60	135	29	6	5	48	32	59	.271	.315	.383	102	4	1	59	17	11	-2	-3	*O	-1.0
1969	StL-N	132	495	58	126	22	6	10	70	35	63	.255	.308	.384	92	-6	-6	56	4	4	-1	1	*O	-1.3
1970	Cle-A	148	574	74	164	28	6	24	82	28	69	.286	.322	.481	113	12	8	84	7	6	-2	5	*O/1	0.5
1971	Cle-A	146	566	60	149	23	4	11	35	21	58	.263	.297	.376	82	-10	-15	63	25	6	4	9	*O/1	-0.6
1972	Cal-A	136	484	56	133	24	2	7	49	30	54	.275	.324	.376	114	4	7	59	17	6	2	-2	*O	-0.1
1973	Cal-A	124	466	56	121	14	6	8	57	20	55	.260	.290	.367	91	-11	-7	46	5	5	-2	0	*O	-1.1
1974	KC-A	115	406	46	112	18	2	6	41	21	45	.276	.315	.374	92	-2	-5	49	21	5	3	-8	*O/1D	-1.2
1975	KC-A	103	319	38	71	14	5	4	22	10	21	.223	.251	.335	63	-16	-17	24	5	6	-2	-2	O/1D	-2.4
Total	18	2469	9645	1366	2757	485	127	256	1170	574	1196	.286	.330	.442	110	155	114	1394	305	122	18	39	*O/1D	8.8

■ WALLY PIPP

Pipp, Walter Clement b: 2/17/1893, Chicago, Ill. d: 1/11/65, Grand Rapids, Mich BL/TL, 6'1", 180 lbs. Deb: 6/29/13

YEAR	TM/L	G	AB	R	H	2B	3B	HR	RBI	BB	SO	AVG	OBP	SLG	PRO+	BR	/A	RC	SB	CS	SBR	FR	POS	TPR
1913	Det-A	12	31	3	5	0	3	0	5	2	6	.161	.235	.355	73	-1	-1	2	0			-1	1	-0.1
1915	NY-A	136	479	59	118	20	13	4	60	66	81	.246	.339	.367	112	6	7	65	18	7	1	3	*1	0.5
1916	NY-A	151	545	70	143	20	14	**12**	93	54	82	.262	.331	.417	122	14	12	82	16			6	*1	1.7
1917	NY-A	155	587	82	143	29	12	**9**	70	60	66	.244	.320	.380	112	8	7	72	11			4	*1	0.6
1918	NY-A	91	349	48	106	15	9	2	44	22	34	.304	.345	.415	127	10	10	52	11			0	1	0.5
1919	NY-A	138	523	74	144	23	10	7	50	39	42	.275	.330	.398	103	1	1	71	9			1	*1	-0.9
1920	NY-A	153	610	109	171	30	14	11	76	48	54	.280	.339	.430	99	0	-3	87	4	10	-5	0	*1	-0.6
1921	*NY-A	153	588	96	174	35	9	8	97	45	28	.296	.347	.427	94	-4	-6	87	17	10	-1	-4	*1	-1.1
1922	*NY-A	152	577	96	190	32	10	9	90	56	32	.329	.392	.466	120	20	18	104	7	12	-5	-5	*1	-0.4
1923	*NY-A	144	569	79	173	19	8	6	108	36	28	.304	.352	.397	95	-3	-5	77	6	13	-6	-3	*1	-1.9
1924	NY-A	153	589	88	174	30	**19**	9	113	51	36	.295	.352	.457	108	4	4	95	12	6	0	2	*1	-0.1
1925	NY-A	62	178	19	41	6	3	3	24	13	12	.230	.286	.348	61	-11	-11	18	3	3	-1	4	1	-0.8
1926	Cin-N	155	574	72	167	22	15	6	99	49	26	.291	.352	.413	108	4	6	83	8			2	*1	0.2
1927	Cin-N	122	443	49	115	19	6	2	41	32	11	.260	.309	.343	77	-16	-14	47	2			0	1	-2.1
1928	Cin-N	95	272	30	77	11	3	2	26	23	13	.283	.341	.368	87	-6	-5	34	1			1	1	-1.1
Total	15	1872	6914	974	1941	311	148	90	996	596	551	.281	.341	.408	104	25	19	976	125	61		10	*1	-5.6

■ JIM PISONI

Pisoni, James Pete b: 8/14/29, St.Louis, Mo. BR/TR, 5'10", 169 lbs. Deb: 9/25/53

YEAR	TM/L	G	AB	R	H	2B	3B	HR	RBI	BB	SO	AVG	OBP	SLG	PRO+	BR	/A	RC	SB	CS	SBR	FR	POS	TPR
1953	StL-A	3	12	1	1	0	0	1	1	0	5	.083	.083	.333	8	-2	-2	0	0	0	0	0	/O	-0.1
1956	KC-A	10	30	4	8	0	0	2	5	2	8	.267	.313	.467	103	-0	-0	4	0	0	0	4	/O	0.4
1957	KC-A	44	97	14	23	2	2	3	12	10	17	.237	.321	.392	92	-1	-1	13	0	0	0	7	O	0.3
1959	Mil-N	9	24	4	4	1	0	0	0	2	6	.167	.231	.208	20	-3	-3	1	0	0	0	1	/O	-0.1
	NY-A	17	17	2	3	0	1	0	1	1	9	.176	.222	.294	42	-1	-1	1	0	0	0	1	O	0.0
1960	NY-A	20	9	1	1	0	0	0	1	1	2	.111	.200	.111	-14	-1	-1	0	0	0	0	2	O	0.0
Total	5	103	189	26	40	3	3	6	20	16	47	.212	.280	.354	71	-8	-8	20	0	0	0	15	/O	0.5

■ ALEX PITKO

Pitko, Alexander "Spunk" b: 11/22/14, Burlington, N.J. BR/TR, 5'10", 180 lbs. Deb: 9/11/38

YEAR	TM/L	G	AB	R	H	2B	3B	HR	RBI	BB	SO	AVG	OBP	SLG	PRO+	BR	/A	RC	SB	CS	SBR	FR	POS	TPR
1938	Phi-N	7	19	2	6	1	0	0	2	3	3	.316	.409	.368	118	1	1	3	1			-1	/O	0.0
1939	Was-A	4	8	0	1	0	0	0	1	1	3	.125	.222	.125	-10	-1	-1	0	0	0	0	-0	/O	-0.1
Total	2	11	27	2	7	1	0	0	3	4	6	.259	.355	.296	80	-1	-1	3	1	0		-2	/O	-0.1

■ JAKE PITLER

Pitler, Jacob Albert b: 4/22/1894, New York, N.Y. d: 2/3/68, Binghamton, N.Y. BR/TR, 5'8", 150 lbs. Deb: 5/30/17 C

YEAR	TM/L	G	AB	R	H	2B	3B	HR	RBI	BB	SO	AVG	OBP	SLG	PRO+	BR	/A	RC	SB	CS	SBR	FR	POS	TPR
1917	Pit-N	109	382	39	89	8	5	0	23	30	24	.233	.297	.280	75	-9	-11	34	6			-11	*2/O	-1.7
1918	Pit-N	2	1	1	0	0	0	0	0	1	0	.000	.500	.000	55	0	0	1	2			0	/2	0.1
Total	2	111	383	40	89	8	5	0	23	31	24	.232	.298	.279	75	-9	-11	35	8			-11	2/O	-1.6

■ CHRIS PITTARO

Pittaro, Christopher Francis b: 9/16/61, Trenton, N.J. BB/TR, 5'11", 170 lbs. Deb: 4/08/85

YEAR	TM/L	G	AB	R	H	2B	3B	HR	RBI	BB	SO	AVG	OBP	SLG	PRO+	BR	/A	RC	SB	CS	SBR	FR	POS	TPR
1985	Det-A	28	62	10	15	3	1	0	7	5	13	.242	.299	.323	71	-3	-2	6	1	1	-0	-1	3/2D	-0.3
1986	Min-A	11	21	0	2	0	0	0	0	0	8	.095	.095	.095	-47	-4	-4	0	0	0	0	2	/2S	0.0
1987	Min-A	14	12	6	4	0	0	0	0	1	0	.333	.385	.333	90	-0	-0	2	1	0	0	3	/2D	0.3
Total	3	53	95	16	21	3	1	0	7	6	21	.221	.267	.274	48	-7	-7	8	2	1	0	4	/32SD	0.0

■ PINKY PITTINGER

Pittinger, Clarke Alonzo b: 2/24/1899, Hudson, Mich. d: 11/4/77, Ft.Lauderdale, Fla. BR/TR, 5'10", 160 lbs. Deb: 4/15/21

YEAR	TM/L	G	AB	R	H	2B	3B	HR	RBI	BB	SO	AVG	OBP	SLG	PRO+	BR	/A	RC	SB	CS	SBR	FR	POS	TPR
1921	Bos-A	40	91	6	18	1	0	0	5	4	13	.198	.232	.209	13	-12	-12	5	3	2	-0	3	O/3S2	-0.9
1922	Bos-A	66	186	16	48	3	0	0	7	9	10	.258	.299	.274	51	-13	-13	15	2	5	-2	5	3S	-0.3
1923	Bos-A	60	177	15	38	5	0	0	15	5	10	.215	.236	.243	26	-19	-19	10	3	1	0	-11	2S/3	-2.6
1925	Chi-N	59	173	21	54	7	2	0	15	12	7	.312	.364	.376	88	-2	-3	24	5	4	-1	4	S3	0.4
1927	Cin-N	31	84	17	23	5	0	1	10	2	5	.274	.291	.369	78	-3	-3	9	4			3	2/S3	0.1
1928	Cin-N	40	38	12	9	0	1	0	4	0	1	.237	.237	.289	37	-4	-3	2	2			8	S/23	0.6
1929	Cin-N	77	210	31	62	11	0	0	27	5	10	.295	.318	.348	68	-12	-10	22	8			2	S/32	0.6
Total	7	373	959	118	252	32	3	1	83	37	50	.263	.294	.306	55	-65	-63	87	27	12		13	S/32O	-2.7

■ JOE PITTMAN

Pittman, Joseph Wayne b: 1/1/54, Houston, Tex. BR/TR, 6'1", 180 lbs. Deb: 4/25/81

YEAR	TM/L	G	AB	R	H	2B	3B	HR	RBI	BB	SO	AVG	OBP	SLG	PRO+	BR	/A	RC	SB	CS	SBR	FR	POS	TPR
1981	*Hou-N	52	135	11	38	4	2	0	7	11	16	.281	.336	.341	97	-1	-0	15	4	4	-1	-9	2/3	-0.9
1982	Hou-N	15	10	0	2	1	0	0	0	0	2	.200	.200	.300	41	-1	-1	1	0	0	0	1	/3O	0.0
	SD-N	55	118	16	30	2	0	0	7	9	13	.254	.307	.271	66	-6	-5	10	8	3	1	-2	2S	-0.4
	Yr	70	128	16	32	3	0	0	7	9	15	.250	.299	.273	65	-6	-6	11	8	3	1	-2		-0.4
1984	SF-N	17	22	2	5	0	0	0	2	0	6	.227	.227	.227	29	-2	-2	1	1	1	-0	-2	/S23	-0.3
Total	3	139	285	29	75	7	2	0	16	20	37	.263	.311	.302	77	-10	-8	26	13	8	-1	-13	/2S3O	-1.6

■ GAYLEN PITTS

Pitts, Gaylen Richard b: 6/6/46, Wichita, Kan. BR/TR, 6'1", 175 lbs. Deb: 5/12/74

YEAR	TM/L	G	AB	R	H	2B	3B	HR	RBI	BB	SO	AVG	OBP	SLG	PRO+	BR	/A	RC	SB	CS	SBR	FR	POS	TPR
1974	Oak-A	18	41	4	10	3	0	0	3	5	4	.244	.326	.317	92	-1	-0	4	0	0	0	0	3/21	0.0
1975	Oak-A	10	3	1	1	1	0	0	0	1	0	.333	.333	.667	181	0	0	0	0	0	0	2	/3S2	0.2
Total	2	28	44	5	11	4	0	0	4	5	4	.250	.327	.341	98	-0	-0	4	0	0	0	2	/32S1	0.2

■ HERMAN PITZ

Pitz, Herman b: 7/18/1865, Brooklyn, N.Y. d: 9/3/24, Far Rockaway, N.Y. 5'6", 140 lbs. Deb: 4/18/1890

YEAR	TM/L	G	AB	R	H	2B	3B	HR	RBI	BB	SO	AVG	OBP	SLG	PRO+	BR	/A	RC	SB	CS	SBR	FR	POS	TPR
1890	Bro-a	61	189	26	26	0	0	0		45		.138	.312	.138	36	-12	-11	16	25			-7	C3/OS2	-1.3
	Syr-a	29	95	17	21	0	0	0		13		.221	.321	.221	69	-4	-2	12	14			-5	C/SO	-0.3
	Yr	90	284	43	47	0	0	0		58		.165	.315	.165	47	-16	-13	28	39			-13		-1.6

■ PHIL PLANTIER

Plantier, Phillip Alan b: 1/27/69, Manchester, N.H. BL/TR, 6', 175 lbs. Deb: 8/21/90

YEAR	TM/L	G	AB	R	H	2B	3B	HR	RBI	BB	SO	AVG	OBP	SLG	PRO+	BR	/A	RC	SB	CS	SBR	FR	POS	TPR
1990	Bos-A	14	15	1	2	1	0	0	3	4	6	.133	.350	.200	55	-1	-1	1	0	0	0	0	/OD	0.0

■ DON PLARSKI

Plarski, Donald Joseph b: 11/9/29, Chicago, Ill. d: 12/29/81, St.Louis, Mo. BR/TR, 5'6", 160 lbs. Deb: 7/20/55

YEAR	TM/L	G	AB	R	H	2B	3B	HR	RBI	BB	SO	AVG	OBP	SLG	PRO+	BR	/A	RC	SB	CS	SBR	FR	POS	TPR
1955	KC-A	8	11	0	1	0	0	0	0	0	2	.091	.091	.091	-50	-2	-2	0	1	0	0	0	/O	-0.1

■ ELMO PLASKETT

Plaskett, Elmo Alexander b: 6/27/38, Frederiksted, V.I. BR/TR, 5'10", 195 lbs. Deb: 9/08/62

YEAR	TM/L	G	AB	R	H	2B	3B	HR	RBI	BB	SO	AVG	OBP	SLG	PRO+	BR	/A	RC	SB	CS	SBR	FR	POS	TPR
1962	Pit-N	7	14	2	4	0	0	1	3	1	3	.286	.333	.500	120	0	0	2	0	0	0	-1	/C	0.0
1963	Pit-N	10	21	1	3	0	0	0	2	0	5	.143	.143	.143	-17	-3	-3	0	0	0	0	-2	/C3	-0.4

YEAR	TM/L	G	AB	R	H	2B	3B	HR	RBI	BB	SO	AVG	OBP	SLG	PRO+	BR	/A	RC	SB	CS	SBR	FR	POS	TPR
Total	2	17	35	3	7	0	0	1	5	1	8	.200	.222	.286	41	-3	-3	3	0	0	0	-3	/C3	-0.4

■ WHITEY PLATT Platt, Mizell George b: 8/21/20, W.Palm Beach, Fla. d: 7/27/70, W.Palm Beach, Fla BR/TR, 6'1.5", 190 lbs. Deb: 9/16/42

1942	Chi-N	4	16	1	1	0	0	0	2	0	3	.063	.063	.063	-66	-3	-3	-0	0			0	/O	-0.2
1943	Chi-N	20	41	2	7	3	0	0	2	1	7	.171	.190	.244	25	-4	-4	2	0			-1	O	-0.5
1946	Chi-A	84	247	28	62	8	5	3	32	17	34	.251	.307	.360	89	-5	-4	24	1	7	-4	-1	O	-1.2
1948	StL-A	123	454	57	123	22	10	7	82	39	51	.271	.331	.410	94	-4	-6	60	1	4	-2	-8	*O	-1.8
1949	StL-A	102	244	29	63	8	2	3	29	24	27	.258	.325	.344	74	-9	-10	27	0	1	-1	2	O/1	-0.9
Total	5	333	1002	117	256	41	17	13	147	81	122	.255	.314	.369	83	-25	-27	112	2	12		-7	O/1	-4.6

■ AL PLATTE Platte, Alfred Frederick Joseph b: 4/13/1890, Grand Rapids, Mich d: 8/29/76, Grand Rapids, Mich BL/TL, 5'7", 160 lbs. Deb: 9/01/13

| 1913 | Det-A | 9 | 18 | 1 | 2 | 1 | 0 | 0 | 0 | 1 | 1 | .111 | .158 | .167 | -5 | -2 | -2 | 1 | 0 | | | -1 | /O | -0.3 |

■ RANCE PLESS Pless, Rance b: 12/6/25, Greeneville, Tenn. BR/TR, 6', 145 lbs. Deb: 4/21/56

| 1956 | KC-A | 48 | 85 | 4 | 23 | 3 | 1 | 0 | 9 | 10 | 13 | .271 | .354 | .329 | 81 | -2 | -2 | 9 | 0 | 1 | -1 | 2 | 1/3 | 0.0 |

■ HERB PLEWS Plews, Herbert Eugene b: 6/14/28, Helena, Mont. BL/TR, 5'11", 160 lbs. Deb: 4/18/56

1956	Was-A	91	256	24	69	10	7	1	25	26	40	.270	.339	.375	88	-4	-4	32	1	2	-1	-3	2/S3	-0.2
1957	Was-A	104	329	51	89	19	4	1	26	28	39	.271	.331	.362	90	-5	-4	38	0	3	-2	-14	23/S	-1.5
1958	Was-A	111	380	46	98	12	6	2	29	17	45	.258	.291	.337	74	-15	-14	36	2	3	-1	-21	23	-3.0
1959	Was-A	27	40	4	9	0	0	0	2	3	5	.225	.279	.225	40	-3	-3	2	0	1	-1	1	/2	-0.1
	Bos-A	13	12	0	1	1	0	0	0	0	4	.083	.083	.167	-32	-2	-2	0	0	0	0	1	/2	0.0
	Yr	40	52	4	10	1	0	0	2	3	9	.192	.236	.212	24	-5	-5	2	0	1	-1	2		-0.1
Total	4	346	1017	125	266	42	17	4	82	74	133	.262	.314	.348	80	-29	-28	107	3	9	-5	-36	2/3S	-4.8

■ WALTER PLOCK Plock, Walter S. b: 7/2/1869, Philadelphia, Pa. d: 4/28/1900, Richmond, Va. 6'3", Deb: 8/21/1891

| 1891 | Phi-N | 2 | 5 | 2 | 2 | 0 | 0 | 0 | 0 | 0 | 1 | .400 | .500 | .400 | 162 | 1 | 0 | 1 | 0 | | | -1 | /O | 0.0 |

■ BILL PLUMMER Plummer, William Francis b: 3/21/47, Oakland, Cal. BR/TR, 6'1", 190 lbs. Deb: 4/19/68 C

1968	Chi-N	2	2	0	0	0	0	0	0	0	1	.000	.000	.000	-94	-0	-0	0	0	0	0	0	/C	0.0
1970	Cin-N	4	8	0	1	0	0	0	0	0	2	.125	.222	.125	-4	-1	-1	0	0	0	0	-2	/C	-0.2
1971	Cin-N	10	19	0	0	0	0	0	0	0	4	.000	.000	.000	-99	-5	-5	0	0	0	0	0	/C3	-0.4
1972	Cin-N	38	102	8	19	4	0	2	9	4	20	.186	.217	.284	44	-8	-7	6	0	0	0	1	C/13	-0.4
1973	Cin-N	50	119	8	18	3	0	2	11	18	26	.151	.268	.227	41	-10	-9	8	1	0	0	-0	C/3	-0.6
1974	Cin-N	50	120	7	27	7	0	2	10	6	21	.225	.262	.333	67	-6	-6	10	1	0	0	6	C/3	0.2
1975	Cin-N	65	159	17	29	7	0	1	19	24	28	.182	.297	.245	51	-10	-10	14	1	0	0	-3	C	-1.1
1976	Cin-N	56	153	16	38	6	1	4	19	14	36	.248	.311	.379	93	-1	-2	16	0	2	-1	6	C	0.6
1977	Cin-N	51	117	10	16	5	0	1	7	17	34	.137	.246	.205	22	-13	-13	7	1	1	-0	-1	C	-1.4
1978	Sea-A	41	93	6	20	5	0	2	7	12	19	.215	.305	.333	80	-2	-2	9	0	0	0	-5	C	-0.6
Total	10	367	892	72	168	37	1	14	82	95	191	.188	.269	.279	53	-57	-56	70	4	3	-1	1	C/31	-3.9

■ BIFF POCOROBA Pocoroba, Biff b: 7/25/53, Burbank, Cal. BB/TR, 5'10", 175 lbs. Deb: 4/25/75

1975	Atl-N	67	188	15	48	7	1	2	22	20	11	.255	.327	.319	77	-5	-6	20	0	0	0	-3	C	-0.6
1976	Atl-N	54	174	16	42	7	0	0	14	19	12	.241	.316	.282	66	-6	-8	15	1	0	0	5	C	0.0
1977	Atl-N	113	321	46	93	24	1	8	44	57	27	.290	.398	.445	113	14	9	57	3	4	-2	4	*C	0.9
1978	Atl-N	92	289	21	70	8	0	6	34	29	14	.242	.316	.332	73	-7	-11	27	0	3	-2	2	C	-0.8
1979	Atl-N	28	38	6	12	4	0	0	4	7	0	.316	.422	.421	122	2	2	6	1	1	-0	0	/C	0.2
1980	Atl-N	70	83	7	22	4	0	2	8	11	11	.265	.351	.386	102	1	0	12	1	0	0	-1	C	0.0
1981	Atl-N	57	122	4	22	4	0	0	8	12	15	.180	.265	.213	36	-10	-10	7	0	0	0	-5	3/C	-1.6
1982	*Atl-N	56	120	5	33	7	0	2	22	13	12	.275	.351	.383	101	1	1	16	0	0	0	-4	C/3	-0.3
1983	Atl-N	55	120	11	32	6	0	2	16	12	7	.267	.333	.367	87	-1	-2	14	0	0	0	-3	C	-0.3
1984	Atl-N	4	2	1	0	0	0	0	0	0	2	.000	.500	.000	48	0	0	0	0	0	0	0	/H	0.0
Total	10	596	1457	132	374	71	2	21	172	182	109	.257	.342	.351	86	-11	-25	175	6	8	-3	-4	C/3	-2.5

■ MIKE POEPPING Poepping, Michael Harold b: 8/7/50, Little Falls, Minn. BR/TR, 6'6", 230 lbs. Deb: 9/06/75

| 1975 | Min-A | 14 | 37 | 0 | 5 | 1 | 0 | 1 | 5 | 1 | 7 | .135 | .238 | .162 | 15 | -4 | -4 | 1 | 0 | 0 | 0 | -1 | O | -0.5 |

■ JIMMY POFAHL Pofahl, James Willard b: 6/18/17, Faribault, Minn. d: 9/14/84, Owatonna, Minn. BR/TR, 5'11", 185 lbs. Deb: 4/16/40

1940	Was-A	119	406	34	95	23	5	2	36	37	55	.234	.298	.330	67	-23	-19	41	2	0	1	-5	*S/2	-1.2
1941	Was-A	22	75	9	14	3	2	0	6	10	11	.187	.282	.280	52	-6	-5	7	1	0	0	-4	S	-0.7
1942	Was-A	84	283	22	59	7	2	0	28	29	30	.208	.282	.247	50	-19	-18	20	4	3	-1	1	S23	-1.4
Total	3	225	764	65	168	33	9	2	70	76	96	.220	.290	.295	59	-47	-42	67	7	3	0	-8	S/23	-3.3

■ JOHN POFF Poff, John William b: 10/23/52, Chillicothe, Ohio BL/TL, 6'2", 190 lbs. Deb: 9/08/79

1979	Phi-N	12	19	2	2	1	0	0	1	4	4	.105	.150	.158	-15	-3	-3	0	0	0	0	-0	/O1	-0.3
1980	Mil-A	19	68	7	17	1	2	1	7	3	7	.250	.282	.368	79	-2	-2	7	0	0	0	-1	/O1D	-0.3
Total	2	31	87	9	19	2	2	1	8	4	11	.218	.253	.322	57	-5	-5	7	0	0	0	-2	/OD1	-0.6

■ AARON POINTER Pointer, Aaron Elton "Hawk" b: 4/19/42, Little Rock, Ark. BR/TR, 6'2", 185 lbs. Deb: 9/22/63

1963	Hou-N	2	5	0	1	0	0	0	0	0	1	.200	.200	.200	17	-1	-1	0	0	0	0	-0	O	0.0
1966	Hou-N	11	26	5	9	1	0	1	5	5	6	.346	.469	.500	182	3	3	7	1	1	-0	2	O	0.5
1967	Hou-N	27	70	6	11	4	0	0	10	13	26	.157	.298	.257	62	-3	-3	6	1	0	0	1	O	-0.2
Total	3	40	101	11	21	5	0	2	15	18	33	.208	.339	.317	91	-1	-0	13	2	1	0	2	/O	0.3

■ HUGH POLAND Poland, Hugh Reid b: 1/19/13, Tompkinsville, Ky. d: 3/30/84, Guthrie, Ky. BL/TR, 5'11.5", 185 lbs. Deb: 4/22/43

1943	NY-N	4	12	1	1	0	1	0	2	1	0	.083	.154	.250	16	-1	-1	1	0			-2	/C	-0.2
	Bos-N	44	141	5	27	7	0	0	13	4	11	.191	.214	.241	32	-13	-12	7	0			-2	C	-1.3
	Yr	48	153	6	28	7	1	0	15	5	11	.183	.209	.242	30	-14	-14	7	0			-4		-1.5
1944	Bos-N	8	23	1	3	1	0	0	2	0	1	.130	.130	.174	-14	-3	-4	0	0			1	/C	-0.2
1946	Bos-N	4	6	0	1	1	0	0	0	0	0	.167	.167	.333	40	-1	-1	0	0			0	/C	0.0
1947	Phi-N	4	8	0	0	0	0	0	0	0	1	.000	.000	.000	-99	-2	-2	0	0			1	/C	-0.1
	Cin-N	16	18	1	6	0	0	0	2	1	4	.333	.368	.389	102	0	0	3	0			-1	/C	0.0
	Yr	20	26	1	6	0	0	0	2	1	4	.231	.259	.269	41	-2	-2	2	0			-1		-0.1
1948	Cin-N	3	3	0	1	0	0	0	0	0	0	.333	.333	.333	84	-0	-0	0	0			0	H	0.0
Total	5	83	211	8	39	10	1	0	19	6	16	.185	.207	.242	28	-20	-20	11	0			-4	/C	-1.8

■ MARK POLHEMUS Polhemus, Mark S. "Humpty Dumpty" b: 10/4/1862, Brooklyn, N.Y. d: 11/12/23, Lynn, Mass. 5'6.5", 185 lbs. Deb: 7/13/1887

| 1887 | Ind-N | 20 | 75 | 6 | 18 | 1 | 0 | 0 | 8 | 2 | 9 | .240 | .260 | .253 | 46 | -5 | -5 | 6 | 4 | | | -0 | O | -0.3 |

■ GUS POLIDOR Polidor, Gustavo Adolfo (Gonzalez) b: 10/26/61, Caracas, Venezuela BR/TR, 6', 170 lbs. Deb: 9/07/85

1985	Cal-A	2	1	1	1	0	0	0	0	0	0	1.000	1.000	1.000	452	0	0	1	0	0	0	0	/SO	0.1
1986	Cal-A	6	19	1	5	1	0	0	1	1	0	.263	.300	.316	69	-1	-1	1	0	0	0	0	/2S3	0.0
1987	Cal-A	63	137	12	36	3	0	2	15	2	15	.263	.279	.328	62	-8	-7	12	0	0	0	-5	S3/2	-0.4
1988	Cal-A	54	81	4	12	3	0	0	4	3	11	.148	.179	.185	2	-11	-10	2	0	0	0	4	S3/2D	-0.4
1989	Mil-A	79	175	15	34	7	0	0	14	6	18	.194	.230	.234	31	-16	-16	9	3	0	1	3	32S/D	-0.9
1990	Mil-A	18	15	0	1	0	0	0	1	0	1	.067	.067	.067	-65	-3	-3	0	0	0	0	2	3/2S	0.0

YEAR	TM/L	G	AB	R	H	2B	3B	HR	RBI	BB	SO	AVG	OBP	SLG	PRO+	BR	/A	RC	SB	CS	SBR	FR	POS	TPR
Total	6	222	428	33	89	14	0	2	35	12	45	.208	.235	.255	35	-38	-37	26	3	0	1	3	/S32DO	-2.1

■ **NICK POLLY** Polly, Nicholas (b: Nicholas Joseph Polachanin) b: 4/18/17, Chicago, Ill. BR/TR, 5'11", 190 lbs. Deb: 9/11/37

YEAR	TM/L	G	AB	R	H	2B	3B	HR	RBI	BB	SO	AVG	OBP	SLG	PRO+	BR	/A	RC	SB	CS	SBR	FR	POS	TPR
1937	Bro-N	10	18	2	4	0	0	0	2	0	1	.222	.222	.222	21	-2	-2	1	0			2	/3	0.1
1945	Bos-A	4	7	0	1	0	0	0	1	0	0	.143	.143	.143	-17	-1	-1	0	0	0	0	-0	/3	0.0
Total	2	14	25	2	5	0	0	0	3	0	1	.200	.200	.200	11	-3	-3	1	0	0		2	/3	0.1

■ **LUIS POLONIA** Polonia, Luis Andrew (Almonte) b: 12/10/64, Santiago, D.R. BL/TL, 5'8", 155 lbs. Deb: 4/24/87

YEAR	TM/L	G	AB	R	H	2B	3B	HR	RBI	BB	SO	AVG	OBP	SLG	PRO+	BR	/A	RC	SB	CS	SBR	FR	POS	TPR
1987	Oak-A	125	435	78	125	16	10	4	49	32	64	.287	.336	.398	100	-4	0	61	29	7	5	-4	*OD	-0.1
1988	*Oak-A	84	288	51	84	11	4	2	27	21	40	.292	.340	.378	104	0	2	38	24	9	2	-2	O/D	0.0
1989	Oak-A	59	206	31	59	6	4	1	17	9	15	.286	.316	.369	96	-2	-1	23	13	4	2	1	O	0.0
	NY-A	66	227	39	71	11	2	2	29	16	29	.313	.363	.405	118	5	5	32	9	4	0	-2	O/D	0.3
	Yr	125	433	70	130	17	6	3	46	25	44	.300	.341	.388	108	3	4	55	22	8	2	-0		0.3
1990	NY-A	11	22	2	7	0	0	0	3	0	1	.318	.318	.318	78	-1	-1	2	1	0	0	0	/D	0.0
	Cal-A	109	381	50	128	7	9	2	32	25	42	.336	.378	.417	122	11	11	57	20	14	-2	-7	OD	0.1
	Yr	120	403	52	135	7	9	2	35	25	43	.335	.375	.412	120	11	11	59	21	14	-2	-7		0.1
Total	4	454	1559	251	474	51	29	11	157	103	191	.304	.348	.395	108	10	16	214	96	38	6	-13	O/D	0.3

■ **CARLOS PONCE** Ponce, Carlos Antonio (Diaz) b: 2/7/59, Rio Piedras, P.R. BR/TR, 5'10", 170 lbs. Deb: 8/14/85

YEAR	TM/L	G	AB	R	H	2B	3B	HR	RBI	BB	SO	AVG	OBP	SLG	PRO+	BR	/A	RC	SB	CS	SBR	FR	POS	TPR
1985	Mil-A	21	62	4	10	2	0	1	5	1	9	.161	.175	.242	13	-7	-7	2	0	0	0	-1	1/OD	-0.8

■ **RALPH POND** Pond, Ralph Benjamin b: 5/4/1888, Eau Claire, Wis. d: 9/8/47, Cleveland, Ohio Deb: 6/08/10

YEAR	TM/L	G	AB	R	H	2B	3B	HR	RBI	BB	SO	AVG	OBP	SLG	PRO+	BR	/A	RC	SB	CS	SBR	FR	POS	TPR
1910	Bos-A	1	4	0	1	0	0	0	0	0	0	.250	.250	.250	55	-0	-0	0	1			-1	/O	0.0

■ **HARLIN POOL** Pool, Harold G "Samson" b: 3/12/08, Lakeport, Cal. d: 2/15/63, Rodeo, Cal. BL/TR, 5'10", 195 lbs. Deb: 5/30/34

YEAR	TM/L	G	AB	R	H	2B	3B	HR	RBI	BB	SO	AVG	OBP	SLG	PRO+	BR	/A	RC	SB	CS	SBR	FR	POS	TPR
1934	Cin-N	99	358	38	117	22	5	2	50	17	18	.327	.369	.433	117	7	8	58	3			-3	O	0.1
1935	Cin-N	28	68	8	12	6	2	0	11	2	2	.176	.200	.324	39	-6	-6	4	0			-2	O	-0.8
Total	2	127	426	46	129	28	7	2	61	19	20	.303	.343	.415	105	1	2	62	3			-5	O	-0.7

■ **ED POOLE** Poole, Edward I. b: 9/7/1874, Canton, Ohio d: 3/11/19, Malvern, Ohio TR , 5'10", 175 lbs. Deb: 10/06/00

YEAR	TM/L	G	AB	R	H	2B	3B	HR	RBI	BB	SO	AVG	OBP	SLG	PRO+	BR	/A	RC	SB	CS	SBR	FR	POS	TPR
1900	Pit-N	2	4	1	2	0	1	1	3	0		.500	.500	1.750	507	2	2	4	0			-0	/OP	0.2
1901	Pit-N	26	78	6	16	4	0	1	4	4		.205	.244	.295	56	-4	-5	6	1			-2	PO/23	-0.4
1902	Pit-N	1	4	0	1	0	0	0	0	0		.250	.250	.250	54	-0	-0	0	0			0	/P	0.0
	Cin-N	17	61	7	7	2	0	0	1	0		.115	.115	.148	-17	-8	-9	1	0			-1	P/O	0.0
	Yr	18	65	7	8	2	0	0	1	0		.123	.123	.154	-13	-9	-9	1	0			-1		0.0
1903	Cin-N	25	70	7	17	1	0	0	7	2		.243	.264	.257	45	-4	-6	5	0			2	P	0.0
1904	Bro-N	25	62	3	8	1	0	0	0	0		.129	.129	.145	-15	-8	-8	1	0			3	P	0.0
Total	5	96	279	24	51	8	1	2	15	6		.183	.200	.240	30	-23	-25	18	1			3	/PO32	-0.2

■ **JIM POOLE** Poole, James Robert "Easy" b: 5/12/1895, Taylorsville, N.C. d: 1/2/75, Hickory, N.C. BL/TR, 6', 175 lbs. Deb: 4/14/25

YEAR	TM/L	G	AB	R	H	2B	3B	HR	RBI	BB	SO	AVG	OBP	SLG	PRO+	BR	/A	RC	SB	CS	SBR	FR	POS	TPR
1925	Phi-A	133	480	65	143	29	8	5	67	27	37	.298	.338	.423	86	-8	-12	68	5	4	-1	-7	*1	-2.1
1926	Phi-A	112	361	49	106	23	5	8	63	23	25	.294	.339	.452	99	1	2	55	4	3	-1	0	*1/O	-0.6
1927	Phi-A	38	99	4	22	2	0	0	10	9	6	.222	.287	.242	36	-9	-10	7	0	0	0	1	*1	-0.9
Total	3	283	940	118	271	54	13	13	140	59	68	.288	.333	.415	86	-16	-24	130	9	7	-2	-7	1/O	-3.6

■ **RAY POOLE** Poole, Raymond Herman b: 1/16/20, Salisbury, N.C. BL/TR, 6', 180 lbs. Deb: 9/09/41

YEAR	TM/L	G	AB	R	H	2B	3B	HR	RBI	BB	SO	AVG	OBP	SLG	PRO+	BR	/A	RC	SB	CS	SBR	FR	POS	TPR
1941	Phi-A	2	2	0	0	0	0	0	0	0	1	.000	.000	.000	-99	-1	-1	0	0	0	0	0	H	0.0
1947	Phi-A	13	13	1	3	0	0	0	1	1	4	.231	.286	.231	44	-1	-1	1	0	0	0	0	H	0.0
Total	2	15	15	1	3	0	0	0	1	1	5	.200	.250	.200	25	-2	-2	1	0	0	0	0		0.0

■ **TOM POORMAN** Poorman, Thomas Iverson b: 10/14/1857, Lock Haven, Pa. d: 2/18/05, Lock Haven, Pa. BL/TR, 5'10.5", 170 lbs. Deb: 5/05/1880

YEAR	TM/L	G	AB	R	H	2B	3B	HR	RBI	BB	SO	AVG	OBP	SLG	PRO+	BR	/A	RC	SB	CS	SBR	FR	POS	TPR
1880	Buf-N	19	70	5	11	1	0	0		1	13	.157	.157	.171	11	-6	-6	2				-0	PO	0.0
	Chi-N	7	25	3	5	1	2	0	0	0	2	.200	.200	.400	92	-0	-0	2				-1	/OP	0.0
	Yr	26	95	8	16	2	2	0	1	0	15	.168	.168	.232	33	-6	-7	4				-1		0.0
1884	Tol-a	94	382	56	89	8	7	0			10	.233	.254	.291	77	-8	-10	29				4	*O/P	-0.6
1885	Bos-N	56	227	44	54	5	3	3	25	7	32	.238	.261	.326	92	-3	-2	20				-3	O	-0.5
1886	Bos-N	88	371	72	97	16	6	3	41	19	52	.261	.297	.361	104	-1	1	50	31			5	*O	0.7
1887	Phi-a	135	585	140	155	18	**19**	4		35		.265	.317	.381	96	-4	-4	101	88			3	*O/2P	-0.4
1888	Phi-a	97	383	76	87	16	6	2	44	31		.227	.294	.316	99	-0	-0	50	46			-10	*O	-1.2
Total	6	496	2043	396	498	65	43	12	111	102	99	.244	.285	.335	91	-22	-21	254	165			-2	O/P2	-2.0

■ **DAVE POPE** Pope, David b: 6/17/25, Talladega, Ala. BL/TR, 5'10.5", 170 lbs. Deb: 7/01/52

YEAR	TM/L	G	AB	R	H	2B	3B	HR	RBI	BB	SO	AVG	OBP	SLG	PRO+	BR	/A	RC	SB	CS	SBR	FR	POS	TPR
1952	Cle-A	12	34	9	10	1	1	1	4	1	7	.294	.314	.471	124	0	1	5	0	0	0	-1	O	0.0
1954	*Cle-A	60	102	21	30	2	1	4	13	10	22	.294	.357	.451	118	3	2	16	2	1	0	0	O	0.2
1955	Cle-A	35	104	17	31	5	0	6	22	12	31	.298	.376	.519	134	5	5	21	0	0	0	-0	O	0.3
	Bal-A	86	222	21	55	8	4	1	30	16	34	.248	.304	.333	77	-9	-7	22	5	2	0	5	O	-0.5
	Yr	121	326	38	86	13	4	7	52	28	65	.264	.328	.393	97	-4	-2	42	5	2	0	4		-0.2
1956	Bal-A	12	19	1	3	0	0	1	0	7		.158	.200	.158	-5	-3	-3	1	0	0	0	-1	/O	-0.3
	Cle-A	25	70	6	17	3	1	0	3	1	12	.243	.254	.314	48	-5	-6	6	0	0	0	1	O	-0.5
	Yr	37	89	7	20	3	1	0	4	1	19	.225	.242	.281	38	-8	-8	6	0	0	0	-0		-0.8
Total	4	230	551	75	146	19	7	12	73	40	113	.265	.319	.390	92	-9	-7	71	7	3	0	3	O	-0.8

■ **PAUL POPOVICH** Popovich, Paul Edward b: 8/18/40, Flemington, W.Va. BB/TR, 6', 175 lbs. Deb: 4/19/64

YEAR	TM/L	G	AB	R	H	2B	3B	HR	RBI	BB	SO	AVG	OBP	SLG	PRO+	BR	/A	RC	SB	CS	SBR	FR	POS	TPR
1964	Chi-N	1	1	0	1	0	0	0	0	0	0	1.000	1.000	1.000	447	0	0	1	0	0	0	0	H	0.0
1966	Chi-N	2	6	0	0	0	0	0	0	0	2	.000	.000	.000	-99	-2	-2	0	0	0	0	-1	/2	-0.2
1967	Chi-N	49	159	18	34	4	0	0	2	9	12	.214	.265	.239	43	-11	-12	9	0	1	-1	-4	S2/3	-1.2
1968	LA-N	134	418	35	97	8	1	2	25	29	37	.232	.283	.270	72	-16	-13	32	1	3	-2	3	2S/3	0.0
1969	LA-N	28	50	5	10	0	0	0	4	1	4	.200	.216	.200	18	-5	-5	2	0	0	0	0	2/S	-0.2
	Chi-N	60	154	26	48	6	0	1	14	18	14	.312	.387	.370	100	3	1	24	0	1	-1	-6	2/S3O	-0.2
	Yr	88	204	31	58	6	0	1	18	19	18	.284	.348	.328	85	-2	-4	25	0	1	-1	-6		-0.4
1970	Chi-N	78	186	22	47	5	1	4	20	18	18	.253	.319	.355	73	-5	-8	22	0	1	-1	-5	2S3	-0.9
1971	Chi-N	89	226	24	49	7	1	4	28	14	17	.217	.262	.310	54	-12	-15	17	0	1	-1	4	23/S	-1.0
1972	Chi-N	58	129	8	25	3	2	1	11	12	8	.194	.262	.271	47	-8	-10	9	0	1	-1	19	2/S3	1.2
1973	Chi-N	99	280	24	66	3	2	2	24	18	22	.236	.284	.300	58	-14	-17	23	3	2	-0	**26**	2/S3	1.3
1974	*Pit-N	59	83	9	18	2	1	0	6	5	10	.217	.261	.265	49	-6	-6	6	0	0	0	-1	2S	-0.4
1975	Pit-N	25	40	5	8	1	0	0	1	3	2	.200	.273	.225	40	-3	-3	3	0	0	0	-3	/2S	-0.4
Total	11	682	1732	176	403	42	9	14	134	127	151	.233	.288	.292	62	-79	-89	147	4	10	-5	32	2S/3O	-2.0

■ **GEORGE POPPLEIN** Popplein, George J. b: Baltimore, Md. Deb: 7/11/1873

YEAR	TM/L	G	AB	R	H	2B	3B	HR	RBI	BB	SO	AVG	OBP	SLG	PRO+	BR	/A	RC	SB	CS	SBR	FR	POS	TPR
1873	Mar-n	1	4	0	0	0	0	0		0	0	.000	.000	.000	-99	-1	-1	0					/O	0.0

■ **TOM POQUETTE** Poquette, Thomas Arthur b: 10/30/51, Eau Claire, Wis. BL/TR, 5'10", 175 lbs. Deb: 9/01/73

YEAR	TM/L	G	AB	R	H	2B	3B	HR	RBI	BB	SO	AVG	OBP	SLG	PRO+	BR	/A	RC	SB	CS	SBR	FR	POS	TPR
1973	KC-A	21	28	4	6	1	0	0	3	1	4	.214	.267	.250	43	-2	-2	2	1	1	-0	1	O	-0.2
1976	*KC-A	104	344	43	104	18	10	2	34	29	31	.302	.363	.430	131	14	13	52	6	5	-1	-8	O/D	0.2
1977	*KC-A	106	342	43	100	23	6	2	33	19	21	.292	.339	.412	103	1	1	47	1	4	-2	-3	O	-0.7
1978	*KC-A	80	204	16	44	9	2	4	30	14	9	.216	.266	.338	67	-9	-10	18	2	0	1	4	O/D	-0.5

YEAR	TM/L	G	AB	R	H	2B	3B	HR	RBI	BB	SO	AVG	OBP	SLG	PRO+	BR	/A	RC	SB	CS	SBR	FR	POS	TPR
1979	KC-A	21	26	1	5	0	0	0	3	1	4	.192	.222	.192	13	-3	-3	1	0	0	0	0	O	-0.2
	Bos-A	63	154	14	51	9	0	2	23	8	7	.331	.376	.429	110	4	2	25	2	2	-1	-2	O/D	-0.1
	Yr	84	180	15	56	9	0	2	26	9	11	.311	.354	.394	97	0	-1	25	2	2	-1	-2		-0.3
1981	Bos-A	3	2	0	0	0	0	0	0	0	0	.000	.000	.000	-94	-1	-1	0	0	0	0	0	/O	0.0
	Tex-A	30	64	2	10	1	0	0	7	5	1	.156	.229	.172	18	-7	-6	2	0	1	-1	-2	O	-1.0
	Yr	33	66	2	10	1	0	0	7	5	1	.152	.222	.167	14	-7	-7	2	0	1	-1	-2		-1.0
1982	KC-A	24	62	4	9	1	0	0	3	4	5	.145	.209	.161	3	-8	-8	3	1	0	0	0	O	-0.7
Total	7	452	1226	127	329	62	18	10	136	81	82	.268	.321	.373	92	-11	-13	149	13	13	-4	-11	O/D	-3.2

■ DAN PORTER
Porter, Daniel Edward b: 10/17/31, Decatur, Ill. BL/TL, 6', 164 lbs. Deb: 8/16/51

YEAR	TM/L	G	AB	R	H	2B	3B	HR	RBI	BB	SO	AVG	OBP	SLG	PRO+	BR	/A	RC	SB	CS	SBR	FR	POS	TPR
1951	Was-A	13	19	2	4	0	0	0	0	2	4	.211	.286	.211	36	-2	-2	1	0	0	0	-1	/O	-0.1

■ DARRELL PORTER
Porter, Darrell Ray b: 1/17/52, Joplin, Mo. BL/TR, 6', 193 lbs. Deb: 9/02/71

YEAR	TM/L	G	AB	R	H	2B	3B	HR	RBI	BB	SO	AVG	OBP	SLG	PRO+	BR	/A	RC	SB	CS	SBR	FR	POS	TPR
1971	Mil-A	22	70	4	15	2	0	2	9	9	20	.214	.304	.329	80	-2	-2	7	2	2	-1	2	C	0.1
1972	Mil-A	18	56	2	7	1	0	1	2	5	21	.125	.210	.196	22	-5	-5	2	0	0	0	5	C	0.0
1973	Mil-A	117	350	50	89	19	2	16	67	57	85	.254	.365	.457	133	15	16	61	5	2	0	-4	CD	1.4
1974	Mil-A	131	432	59	104	15	4	12	56	50	88	.241	.326	.377	103	1	2	54	8	7	-2	-3	*C/D	0.1
1975	Mil-A	130	409	66	95	12	5	18	60	89	77	.232	.376	.418	123	16	16	68	2	5	-2	-0	*C/D	1.7
1976	Mil-A	119	389	43	81	14	1	5	32	51	61	.208	.302	.288	75	-12	-11	37	2	0	1	-4	*C/D	-1.1
1977	*KC-A	130	425	61	117	21	3	16	60	53	70	.275	.357	.452	118	11	11	71	1	0	0	1	*C/D	1.5
1978	*KC-A	150	520	77	138	27	6	18	78	75	75	.265	.360	.444	122	18	16	82	0	5	-3	-5	*C/D	1.3
1979	KC-A	157	533	101	155	23	10	20	112	**121**	65	.291	**.429**	.484	143	41	39	119	3	4	-2	-1	*CD	4.1
1980	*KC-A	118	418	51	104	14	2	7	51	69	50	.249	.358	.342	92	-2	-2	54	1	1	-0	3	CD	0.4
1981	StL-N	61	174	22	39	10	2	6	31	39	32	.224	.369	.408	117	6	5	28	1	2	-1	-3	C	0.2
1982	*StL-N	120	373	46	86	18	5	12	48	66	66	.231	.349	.402	109	6	6	55	1	1	-0	-6	*C	0.0
1983	StL-N	145	443	57	116	24	3	15	66	68	94	.262	.365	.431	120	13	13	71	1	3	-2	-7	*C	0.9
1984	StL-N	127	422	56	98	16	3	11	68	60	79	.232	.335	.363	98	-1	0	52	5	3	-0	-12	*C	-0.8
1985	*StL-N	84	240	30	53	12	2	10	36	41	48	.221	.337	.412	109	3	3	36	6	1	1	-2	C	0.6
1986	Tex-A	68	155	21	41	6	0	12	29	22	51	.265	.360	.535	136	8	8	30	1	1	0	3	CD	1.1
1987	Tex-A	85	130	19	31	3	0	7	21	30	43	.238	.389	.423	115	4	4	24	0	0	0	0	D/C1	0.4
Total	17	1782	5539	765	1369	237	48	188	826	905	1025	.247	.357	.409	113	120	118	853	39	37	-11	-33	*CD/1	11.9

■ IRV PORTER
Porter, Irving Marble b: 5/17/1888, Lynn, Mass. d: 2/20/71, Lynn, Mass. BB/TR, 5'9", 155 lbs. Deb: 8/20/14

YEAR	TM/L	G	AB	R	H	2B	3B	HR	RBI	BB	SO	AVG	OBP	SLG	PRO+	BR	/A	RC	SB	CS	SBR	FR	POS	TPR
1914	Chi-A	1	4	1	1	0	0	0	0	0	1	.250	.250	.250	51	-0	-0	0	0			-0	/O	0.0

■ JAY PORTER
Porter, J W "J W" b: 1/17/33, Shawnee, Okla. BR/TR, 6'2", 180 lbs. Deb: 7/30/52

YEAR	TM/L	G	AB	R	H	2B	3B	HR	RBI	BB	SO	AVG	OBP	SLG	PRO+	BR	/A	RC	SB	CS	SBR	FR	POS	TPR
1952	StL-A	33	104	12	26	4	1	0	7	10	10	.250	.316	.308	72	-4	-4	11	4	0	1	3	O/3	0.0
1955	Det-A	24	55	6	13	2	0	0	3	8	15	.236	.333	.273	66	-3	-2	5	0	0	0	-3	/1CO	-0.4
1956	Det-A	14	21	0	2	0	0	0	3	0	8	.095	.095	.095	-49	-4	-5	0	0	0	0	-1	/CO	-0.4
1957	Det-A	58	140	14	35	8	0	2	18	14	20	.250	.323	.350	82	-3	-4	17	0	0	0	-2	OC/1	-0.6
1958	Cle-A	40	85	13	17	1	0	4	19	9	23	.200	.284	.353	76	-3	-3	8	0	0	0	-1	C/13	-0.3
1959	Was-A	37	106	8	24	4	0	1	10	11	16	.226	.305	.292	65	-5	-5	10	0	0	0	-0	C/1	-0.3
	StL-N	23	33	5	7	3	0	1	2	1	4	.212	.257	.394	66	-2	-2	3	0	0	0	1	C/1	0.0
Total	6	229	544	58	124	22	1	8	62	53	96	.228	.301	.316	68	-23	-24	54	4	0	1	-3	/CO13	-2.0

■ MATTHEW PORTER
Porter, Matthew Sheldon b: Kansas City, Mo. Deb: 6/27/1884 M

YEAR	TM/L	G	AB	R	H	2B	3B	HR	RBI	BB	SO	AVG	OBP	SLG	PRO+	BR	/A	RC	SB	CS	SBR	FR	POS	TPR
1884	KC-U	3	12	1	1	1	0	0			0	.083	.083	.167	-20	-1	-1	0	0			1	/OM	0.0

■ DICK PORTER
Porter, Richard Twilley "Wiggles" or "Twitches" b: 12/30/01, Princess Anne, Md. d: 9/24/74, Philadelphia, Pa. BL/TR, 5'10", 170 lbs. Deb: 4/16/29

YEAR	TM/L	G	AB	R	H	2B	3B	HR	RBI	BB	SO	AVG	OBP	SLG	PRO+	BR	/A	RC	SB	CS	SBR	FR	POS	TPR
1929	Cle-A	71	192	26	63	16	5	1	24	17	14	.328	.386	.479	117	6	5	34	3	5	-2	-5	O2	-0.2
1930	Cle-A	119	480	100	168	43	8	4	57	55	31	.350	.420	.498	127	25	22	102	3	3	-1	-4	*O	1.1
1931	Cle-A	114	414	82	129	24	3	1	38	56	36	.312	.395	.391	102	7	3	65	6	9	-4	-6	*O/2	-1.1
1932	Cle-A	146	621	106	191	42	8	4	60	64	43	.308	.373	.420	99	6	0	99	2	4	-2	-16	*O	-2.2
1933	Cle-A	132	499	73	133	19	6	0	41	51	42	.267	.335	.329	73	-16	-19	57	4	4	-1	-5	*O	-2.8
1934	Cle-A	13	44	9	10	2	1	1	6	4	5	.227	.292	.386	73	-2	-2	5	0	0	0	-2	O	-0.3
	Bos-A	80	265	30	80	13	6	0	56	21	15	.302	.355	.396	87	-3	-5	38	5	2	0	-10	O	-1.4
	Yr	93	309	39	90	15	7	1	62	25	20	.291	.346	.395	85	-5	-7	43	5	2	0	-12		-1.7
Total	6	675	2515	426	774	159	37	11	282	268	186	.308	.376	.414	99	22	3	400	23	27	-9	-47	O/2	-6.9

■ BOB PORTER
Porter, Robert Lee b: 7/22/59, Yuma, Ariz. BL/TL, 5'10", 180 lbs. Deb: 5/13/81

YEAR	TM/L	G	AB	R	H	2B	3B	HR	RBI	BB	SO	AVG	OBP	SLG	PRO+	BR	/A	RC	SB	CS	SBR	FR	POS	TPR
1981	Atl-N	17	14	2	4	1	0	0	4	2	1	.286	.375	.357	106	0	0	2	0	0	0	0	/H	0.0
1982	Atl-N	24	27	1	3	0	0	0	0	1	9	.111	.143	.111	-27	-5	-5	1	0	0	0	-0	/O1	-0.4
Total	2	41	41	3	7	1	0	0	4	3	10	.171	.227	.195	19	-4	-5	3	0	0	0	-0	/O1	-0.4

■ LEO POSADA
Posada, Leopoldo Jesus (Hernandez) b: 4/15/36, Havana, Cuba BR/TR, 5'11", 175 lbs. Deb: 9/21/60

YEAR	TM/L	G	AB	R	H	2B	3B	HR	RBI	BB	SO	AVG	OBP	SLG	PRO+	BR	/A	RC	SB	CS	SBR	FR	POS	TPR
1960	KC-A	10	36	8	13	0	2	1	2	3	7	.361	.410	.556	158	3	3	8	1	0	0	-1	/O	0.1
1961	KC-A	116	344	37	87	10	4	7	53	36	84	.253	.331	.366	86	-7	-7	43	0	0	0	1	*O	-0.8
1962	KC-A	29	46	6	9	1	1	0	3	7	14	.196	.302	.261	51	-3	-3	4	0	0	0	0	O	-0.2
Total	3	155	426	51	109	11	7	8	58	46	105	.256	.334	.371	88	-7	-7	55	1	0	0	0	O	-0.9

■ LEW POST
Post, Lewis G. b: 4/12/1875, Hastings, Mich. d: 8/21/44, Chicago, Ill. Deb: 9/21/02

YEAR	TM/L	G	AB	R	H	2B	3B	HR	RBI	BB	SO	AVG	OBP	SLG	PRO+	BR	/A	RC	SB	CS	SBR	FR	POS	TPR
1902	Det-A	3	12	2	1	0	0	0	2	0		.083	.083	.083	-52	-2	-2	0	0			-1	/O	-0.2

■ SAM POST
Post, Samuel Gilbert b: 11/17/1896, Richmond, Va. d: 3/31/71, Portsmouth, Va. BL/TL, 6'1.5", 170 lbs. Deb: 4/22/22

YEAR	TM/L	G	AB	R	H	2B	3B	HR	RBI	BB	SO	AVG	OBP	SLG	PRO+	BR	/A	RC	SB	CS	SBR	FR	POS	TPR
1922	Bro-N	9	25	3	7	0	0	0	4	1	4	.280	.308	.280	53	-2	-2	2	1	0	0	-1	/1	-0.1

■ WALLY POST
Post, Walter Charles b: 7/9/29, St.Wendelin, Ohio d: 1/6/82, St.Henry, Ohio BR/TR, 6'1", 190 lbs. Deb: 9/18/49

YEAR	TM/L	G	AB	R	H	2B	3B	HR	RBI	BB	SO	AVG	OBP	SLG	PRO+	BR	/A	RC	SB	CS	SBR	FR	POS	TPR
1949	Cin-N	6	8	1	2	0	0	0	1	0	3	.250	.250	.250	34	-1	-1	0				-0	/O	0.0
1951	Cin-N	15	41	6	9	3	0	1	7	3	4	.220	.273	.366	69	-2	-2	4	0	0	0	1	/O	0.0
1952	Cin-N	19	58	5	9	1	0	2	7	4	20	.155	.222	.276	37	-5	-5	4	0	0	0	1	O	-0.3
1953	Cin-N	11	33	3	8	1	0	1	4	4	6	.242	.324	.364	78	-1	-1	4	1	0	0	1	O	0.0
1954	Cin-N	130	451	46	115	21	3	18	83	26	70	.255	.300	.435	86	-9	-11	56	2	2	-1	3	*O	-1.2
1955	Cin-N	154	601	116	186	33	3	40	109	60	102	.309	.374	.574	139	39	34	125	7	4	-0	-0	*O	3.0
1956	Cin-N	143	539	94	134	25	3	36	83	37	124	.249	.302	.506	105	7	3	81	6	2	0	10	*O	0.9
1957	Cin-N	134	467	68	114	26	2	20	74	33	84	.244	.294	.437	87	-6	-10	57	2	2	-1	6	*O	-0.8
1958	Phi-N	110	379	51	107	21	3	12	62	32	74	.282	.343	.449	109	4	4	59	0	2	-1	5	O	0.6
1959	Phi-N	132	468	62	119	17	6	22	94	36	101	.254	.312	.457	100	-0	-1	67	0	0	0	6	*O	0.3
1960	Phi-N	34	84	11	24	6	1	2	12	9	24	.286	.355	.452	119	2	2	14	0	1	0	-0	O	0.1
	Cin-N	77	249	36	70	14	0	17	38	28	51	.281	.354	.542	139	13	13	43	0	2	-1	2	O	1.1
	Yr	111	333	47	94	20	1	19	50	37	75	.282	.354	.520	134	16	15	58	0	2	-1			1.2
1961	*Cin-N	99	282	44	83	16	3	20	57	22	61	.294	.348	.585	140	15	15	55	0	1	-1	-1	O	0.9
1962	Cin-N	109	285	43	75	10	3	17	62	32	67	.263	.342	.498	118	8	7	48	1	0	0	-10	O	-0.7
1963	Cin-N	5	7	1	0	0	0	0	0	0	1	.000	.125	.000	-59	-1	-1	-0	0	0	0	0	/O	0.0
	Min-A	21	47	6	9	0	1	2	6	2	17	.191	.224	.362	60	-3	-3	4	0	0	0	-1	O	-0.4

YEAR	TM/L	G	AB	R	H	2B	3B	HR	RBI	BB	SO	AVG	OBP	SLG	PRO+	BR	/A	RC	SB	CS	SBR	FR	POS	TPR
1964	Cle-A	5	8	1	0	0	0	0	0	3	4	.000	.273	.000	-16	-1	-1	0	0	0	0	-1	/O	-0.1
Total	15	1204	4007	594	1064	194	28	210	699	331	813	.266	.325	.485	109	59	42	620	19	13		21	*O	3.4

■ MIKE POTTER
Potter, Michael Gary b: 5/16/51, Montebello, Cal. BR/TR, 6'1", 195 lbs. Deb: 9/06/76

YEAR	TM/L	G	AB	R	H	2B	3B	HR	RBI	BB	SO	AVG	OBP	SLG	PRO+	BR	/A	RC	SB	CS	SBR	FR	POS	TPR
1976	StL-N	9	16	0	0	0	0	0	0	1	6	.000	.059	.000	-82	-4	-4	0	0	0	0	0	/O	-0.3
1977	StL-N	5	7	0	0	0	0	0	0	0	2	.000	.000	.000	-99	-2	-2	0	0	0	0	0	/O	-0.1
Total	2	14	23	0	0	0	0	0	0	1	8	.000	.042	.000	-87	-6	-6	0	0	0	0	0	/O	-0.4

■ DAN POTTS
Potts, Daniel b: Kent, Ohio Deb: 10/03/1892

YEAR	TM/L	G	AB	R	H	2B	3B	HR	RBI	BB	SO	AVG	OBP	SLG	PRO+	BR	/A	RC	SB	CS	SBR	FR	POS	TPR
1892	Was-N	1	4	0	1	0	0	0	0	0	1	.250	.250	.250	54	-0	-0	0	0			1	/C	0.1

■ JOHN POTTS
Potts, John Frederick "Fred" b: 2/6/1887, Tipp City, Ohio d: 9/5/62, Cleveland, Ohio BL/TR, 5'7", 165 lbs. Deb: 4/18/14

YEAR	TM/L	G	AB	R	H	2B	3B	HR	RBI	BB	SO	AVG	OBP	SLG	PRO+	BR	/A	RC	SB	CS	SBR	FR	POS	TPR
1914	KC-F	41	102	14	27	4	0	1	9	25	13	.265	.414	.333	121	4	4	18	7			-4	O	0.0

■ KEN POULSEN
Poulsen, Ken Sterling b: 8/4/47, Van Nuys, Cal. BL/TR, 6'1", 190 lbs. Deb: 7/03/67

YEAR	TM/L	G	AB	R	H	2B	3B	HR	RBI	BB	SO	AVG	OBP	SLG	PRO+	BR	/A	RC	SB	CS	SBR	FR	POS	TPR
1967	Bos-A	5	5	0	1	1	0	0	0	0	2	.200	.200	.400	68	-0	-0	0	0	0	0	-0	/3S	0.0

■ ALONZO POWELL
Powell, Alonzo Sidney b: 12/12/64, San Francisco, Cal. BR/TR, 6'2", 190 lbs. Deb: 4/06/87

YEAR	TM/L	G	AB	R	H	2B	3B	HR	RBI	BB	SO	AVG	OBP	SLG	PRO+	BR	/A	RC	SB	CS	SBR	FR	POS	TPR
1987	Mon-N	14	41	3	8	3	0	0	4	5	17	.195	.283	.268	46	-3	-3	3	0	0	0	-2	O	-0.5

■ JAKE POWELL
Powell, Alvin Jacob b: 7/15/08, Silver Spring, Md d: 11/4/48, Washington, D.C. BR/TR, 5'11.5", 180 lbs. Deb: 8/03/30

YEAR	TM/L	G	AB	R	H	2B	3B	HR	RBI	BB	SO	AVG	OBP	SLG	PRO+	BR	/A	RC	SB	CS	SBR	FR	POS	TPR
1930	Was-A	3	4	1	0	0	0	0	0	0	1	.000	.000	.000	-99	-1	-1	0	0	0	0	-0	/O	0.0
1934	Was-A	9	35	6	10	2	0	0	1	4	2	.286	.359	.343	85	-1	-1	4	1	1	-0	1	/O	0.0
1935	Was-A	139	551	88	172	26	10	6	98	37	37	.312	.360	.428	107	2	4	85	15	7	0	-3	*O/2	0.0
1936	Was-A	53	210	40	62	11	5	1	30	19	21	.295	.357	.410	94	-4	-2	31	10	4	1	-3	O	-0.4
	*NY-A	87	328	62	99	13	3	7	48	33	30	.302	.366	.424	98	-3	-1	52	16	7	1	4	O	0.0
	Yr	140	538	102	161	24	8	8	78	52	51	.299	.362	.418	96	-7	-3	83	26	11	1	0		-0.4
1937	*NY-A	97	365	54	96	22	3	3	45	25	36	.263	.314	.364	70	-17	-18	42	7	5	-1	0	O	-1.9
1938	*NY-A	45	164	27	42	12	1	2	20	15	20	.256	.326	.378	76	-6	-6	21	3	1	0	-3	O	-0.8
1939	NY-A	31	86	12	21	4	1	1	9	3	8	.244	.270	.349	58	-6	-6	7	1	2	-1	2	O	-0.4
1940	NY-A	12	27	3	5	0	0	0	2	1	4	.185	.214	.185	5	-4	-4	1	0	0	0	1	/O	-0.2
1943	Was-A	37	132	14	35	10	2	0	20	5	13	.265	.297	.371	99	-1	-1	13	3	5	-2	3	O	0.0
1944	Was-A	96	367	29	88	9	1	1	37	16	26	.240	.272	.278	60	-21	-19	29	7	2	1	-1	O/3	-2.3
1945	Was-A	31	98	4	19	2	0	0	3	8	8	.194	.255	.214	40	-8	-7	6	1	1	-0	-1	O	-1.0
	Phi-N	48	173	13	40	5	0	1	14	8	13	.231	.265	.277	52	-12	-11	11	1			-5	O	-1.7
Total	11	688	2540	353	689	116	26	22	327	174	219	.271	.320	.363	81	-82	-72	303	65	35		-6	O/23	-8.7

■ ABNER POWELL
Powell, Charles Abner "Ab" b: 12/15/1860, Shenandoah, Pa. d: 8/7/53, New Orleans, La. BR/TR, 5'7", 160 lbs. Deb: 8/04/1884

YEAR	TM/L	G	AB	R	H	2B	3B	HR	RBI	BB	SO	AVG	OBP	SLG	PRO+	BR	/A	RC	SB	CS	SBR	FR	POS	TPR
1884	Was-U	48	191	36	54	10	5	0			3	.283	.294	.387	133	5	6	22	0			-1	OP/3S2	0.5
1886	Bal-a	11	39	4	7	2	1	0			1	.179	.200	.282	53	-2	-2	3	4			1	/PO	0.0
	Cin-a	19	74	13	17	1	1	0			4	.230	.269	.270	69	-2	-3	6	0			1	O/SP	-0.1
	Yr	30	113	17	24	3	2	0			5	.212	.246	.274	64	-5	-5	9	4			2		-0.1
Total	2	78	304	53	78	13	7	0			8	.257	.276	.345	105	0	1	31	4			0	/OPS32	0.4

■ HOSKEN POWELL
Powell, Hosken b: 5/14/55, Selma, Ala. BL/TL, 6'1", 175 lbs. Deb: 4/05/78

YEAR	TM/L	G	AB	R	H	2B	3B	HR	RBI	BB	SO	AVG	OBP	SLG	PRO+	BR	/A	RC	SB	CS	SBR	FR	POS	TPR
1978	Min-A	121	381	55	94	20	2	3	31	45	31	.247	.326	.333	84	-6	-7	44	11	5	0	-17	*O	-2.7
1979	Min-A	104	338	49	99	17	3	2	36	33	25	.293	.361	.379	96	1	-1	47	5	1	1	-7	O/D	-1.0
1980	Min-A	137	485	58	127	17	5	6	35	32	46	.262	.312	.355	76	-12	-17	53	14	3	2	-1	*O	-1.7
1981	Min-A	80	264	30	63	11	3	2	25	17	31	.239	.287	.326	71	-8	-10	24	7	4	-0	-1	O/D	-1.3
1982	Tor-A	112	265	43	73	13	4	3	26	12	23	.275	.307	.389	82	-4	-7	30	4	4	-1	-3	OD	-1.3
1983	Tor-A	40	83	6	14	0	0	1	7	5	8	.169	.216	.205	16	-9	-10	4	2	0	1	1	O/1D	-0.8
Total	6	594	1816	241	470	78	17	17	160	144	164	.259	.316	.349	79	-40	-52	202	43	17	3	-29	O/D1	-8.8

■ JIM POWELL
Powell, James E. b: 8/1859, Richmond, Va. 5'10", 170 lbs. Deb: 8/05/1884

YEAR	TM/L	G	AB	R	H	2B	3B	HR	RBI	BB	SO	AVG	OBP	SLG	PRO+	BR	/A	RC	SB	CS	SBR	FR	POS	TPR
1884	Ric-a	41	151	23	37	8	4	0			7	.245	.296	.351	115	2	3	16				1	1	0.1

■ BOOG POWELL
Powell, John Wesley b: 8/17/41, Lakeland, Fla. BL/TR, 6'4.5", 230 lbs. Deb: 9/26/61

YEAR	TM/L	G	AB	R	H	2B	3B	HR	RBI	BB	SO	AVG	OBP	SLG	PRO+	BR	/A	RC	SB	CS	SBR	FR	POS	TPR
1961	Bal-A	4	13	0	1	0	0	0	1	0	2	.077	.077	.077	-60	-3	-3	0	0	0	0	-1	/O	-0.3
1962	Bal-A	124	400	44	97	13	2	15	53	38	79	.243	.311	.398	94	-7	-4	47	1	1	-0	-9	*O/1	-1.7
1963	Bal-A	140	491	67	130	22	2	25	82	49	87	.265	.331	.470	124	13	15	74	1	2	-1	-11	*O1	-0.2
1964	Bal-A	134	424	74	123	17	0	39	99	76	91	.290	.400	.606	176	44	44	105	2	0	0	-1	*O/1	3.9
1965	Bal-A	144	472	54	117	20	2	17	72	71	93	.248	.351	.407	112	10	9	71	1	1	-0	2	1O	0.5
1966	*Bal-A	140	491	78	141	18	0	34	109	67	125	.287	.374	.532	159	36	37	97	0	4	-2	-5	*1	2.6
1967	Bal-A	125	415	53	97	14	1	13	55	55	94	.234	.326	.366	105	3	3	51	1	3	-2	-4	*1	-1.1
1968	Bal-A	154	550	60	137	21	1	22	85	73	97	.249	.340	.411	127	18	18	79	7	1	2	-4	*1	1.0
1969	*Bal-A	152	533	83	162	25	0	37	121	72	76	.304	.388	.559	161	43	43	112	1	1	-0	-2	*1	3.1
1970	*Bal-A	154	526	82	156	28	0	35	114	104	80	.297	.417	.549	163	49	48	123	1	1	-0	-2	*1	4.0
1971	*Bal-A	128	418	59	107	19	0	22	92	82	64	.256	.383	.459	139	23	23	77	1	0	0	-3	*1	1.6
1972	*Bal-A	140	465	53	117	20	1	21	81	65	92	.252	.348	.434	129	19	17	71	4	0	1	-3	*1	0.3
1973	*Bal-A	114	370	52	98	13	1	11	54	85	64	.265	.402	.395	126	17	17	62	0	2	-1	2	*1	1.1
1974	*Bal-A	110	344	37	91	13	1	12	45	52	58	.265	.361	.413	126	11	12	49	0	1	-1	1	*1/D	0.8
1975	Cle-A	134	435	64	129	18	0	27	86	59	72	.297	.382	.524	154	31	31	89	1	3	-2	-2	*1/D	2.0
1976	Cle-A	95	293	29	63	9	0	9	33	41	43	.215	.311	.338	91	-3	-3	31	1	1	-0	1	1	-0.6
1977	LA-N	50	41	0	10	0	0	0	5	12	9	.244	.415	.244	82	-0	-0	5	0	0	0	-1	/1	0.0
Total	17	2042	6681	889	1776	270	11	339	1187	1001	1226	.266	.364	.462	134	305	309	1145	20	21	-7	-41	*1O/D	17.0

■ MARTIN POWELL
Powell, Martin J. b: 3/25/1856, Fitchburg, Mass. d: 2/5/1888, Fitchburg, Mass. BL/TL, 6'4.5", Deb: 6/18/1881

YEAR	TM/L	G	AB	R	H	2B	3B	HR	RBI	BB	SO	AVG	OBP	SLG	PRO+	BR	/A	RC	SB	CS	SBR	FR	POS	TPR
1881	Det-N	55	219	47	74	9	4	1	38	15	9	.338	.380	.429	148	14	12	37				-3	1/C	0.2
1882	Det-N	80	338	44	81	13	0	0	29	19	27	.240	.280	.278	80	-7	-7	27				-5	*1	-2.2
1883	Det-N	101	421	76	115	17	5	1	48	28	23	.273	.318	.344	106	1	4	47				-3	*1	-0.9
1884	Cin-U	43	185	46	59	4	2	1		13		.319	.364	.378	140	10	8	26	0			-2	1	0.4
1885	Phi-a	19	75	5	12	0	3	0		1		.160	.192	.240	35	-5	-6	4				-0	1	-0.6
Total	5	298	1238	218	341	43	14	3	115	76	59	.275	.318	.340	108	13	12	141				-12	1/C	-3.1

■ PAUL POWELL
Powell, Paul Ray b: 3/19/48, San Angelo, Tex. BR/TR, 5'11", 185 lbs. Deb: 4/07/71

YEAR	TM/L	G	AB	R	H	2B	3B	HR	RBI	BB	SO	AVG	OBP	SLG	PRO+	BR	/A	RC	SB	CS	SBR	FR	POS	TPR
1971	Min-A	20	31	7	5	0	0	1	2	3	12	.161	.235	.258	38	-3	-3	2	0	0	0	2	O	-0.1
1973	LA-N	2	1	0	0	0	0	0	0	0	1	.000	.000	.000	-99	-0	-0	0	0	0	0	0		0.0
1975	LA-N	8	10	2	2	1	0	0	0	1	2	.200	.273	.300	61	-1	-1	1	0	0	0	1	/CO	0.1
Total	3	30	42	9	7	1	0	1	2	4	15	.167	.239	.262	41	-3	-3	2	0	0	0	3	/OC	0.0

■ RAY POWELL
Powell, Raymond Reath "Rabbit" b: 11/20/1888, Siloam Springs, Ark. d: 10/16/62, Chillicothe, Mo. BL/TR, 5'9", 160 lbs. Deb: 4/16/13

YEAR	TM/L	G	AB	R	H	2B	3B	HR	RBI	BB	SO	AVG	OBP	SLG	PRO+	BR	/A	RC	SB	CS	SBR	FR	POS	TPR
1913	Det-A	2	0	0	0	0	0	0	0	0	0	—	—	—		0	0	0	0	0	0	0	/O	0.0
1917	Bos-N	88	357	42	97	10	4	4	30	24	54	.272	.318	.356	113	2	4	42	12			6	O	0.9
1918	Bos-N	53	188	31	40	7	5	0	20	29	30	.213	.321	.303	95	-1	-0	19	2			-3	O	-0.6
1919	Bos-N	123	470	51	111	12	12	3	33	41	79	.236	.303	.326	93	-6	-4	49	16			-2	*O	-1.1
1920	Bos-N	147	609	69	137	12	12	6	29	44	83	.225	.282	.314	74	-23	-20	51	10	18	-8	2	*O	-3.7

YEAR	TM/L	G	AB	R	H	2B	3B	HR	RBI	BB	SO	AVG	OBP	SLG	PRO+	BR	/A	RC	SB	CS	SBR	FR	POS	TPR
1921	Bos-N	149	624	114	191	25	**18**	12	74	58	85	.306	.369	.462	125	16	21	102	6	17	-8	-3	*O	0.2
1922	Bos-N	142	550	82	163	22	11	6	37	59	66	.296	.369	.409	105	1	5	82	3	12	-6	8	*O	0.1
1923	Bos-N	97	338	57	102	20	4	4	38	45	36	.302	.385	.420	117	7	9	55	1	6	-3	-6	O	-0.2
1924	Bos-N	74	188	21	49	9	1	1	15	21	28	.261	.338	.335	85	-5	-3	22	1	3	-2	7	O	0.1
Total	9	875	3324	467	890	117	67	35	276	321	461	.268	.336	.375	102	-8	12	421	51	<u>56</u>		7	O	-4.3

■ **LEROY POWELL**   Powell, Robert Leroy b: 10/17/33, Flint, Mich. BR/TR, 6'1", 190 lbs. Deb: 9/16/55

YEAR	TM/L	G	AB	R	H	2B	3B	HR	RBI	BB	SO	AVG	OBP	SLG	PRO+	BR	/A	RC	SB	CS	SBR	FR	POS	TPR
1955	Chi-A	1	0	0	0	0	0	0	0	0	0	—	—	—	—	0	0	0	0	0	0	0	R	0.0
1957	Chi-A	1	0	1	0	0	0	0	0	0	0	—	—	—	—	0	0	0	0	0	0	0	R	0.0
Total	2	2	0	1	0	0	0	0	0	0	0	—	—	—	—	0	0	0	0	0	0	0		0.0

■ **TOM POWER**   Power, Thomas E. b: San Francisco, Cal. d: 2/25/1898, San Francisco, Cal 5'11", 164 lbs. Deb: 8/27/1890

YEAR	TM/L	G	AB	R	H	2B	3B	HR	RBI	BB	SO	AVG	OBP	SLG	PRO+	BR	/A	RC	SB	CS	SBR	FR	POS	TPR
1890	Bal-a	38	125	11	26	3	1	0		13		.208	.288	.248	58	-6	-7	11	6			-3	12	-0.9

■ **VIC POWER**   Power, Victor Pellot (b: b: 11/1/31, Arecibo, P.R. BR/TR, 6', 186 lbs. Deb: 4/13/54

YEAR	TM/L	G	AB	R	H	2B	3B	HR	RBI	BB	SO	AVG	OBP	SLG	PRO+	BR	/A	RC	SB	CS	SBR	FR	POS	TPR
1954	Phi-A	127	462	36	118	17	5	8	38	19	19	.255	.288	.366	78	-16	-16	44	2	1	0	15	*O1/S3	-0.3
1955	KC-A	147	596	91	190	34	10	19	76	35	27	.319	.357	.505	128	21	20	103	0	2	-1	14	*1	2.6
1956	KC-A	127	530	77	164	21	5	14	63	24	16	.309	.341	.447	106	3	3	80	2	2	-1	7	12/O	0.9
1957	KC-A	129	467	48	121	15	1	14	42	19	21	.259	.292	.385	82	-12	-13	50	3	2	-0	11	*1/O2	-0.2
1958	KC-A	52	205	35	62	13	4	4	27	7	3	.302	.325	.463	112	3	3	28	1	1	-0	6	1/2	0.7
	Cle-A	93	385	63	122	24	6	12	53	13	11	.317	.341	.504	133	13	15	65	2	1	0	6	312/SO	2.3
	Yr	145	590	98	184	37	**10**	16	80	20	14	.312	.336	.490	125	17	17	92	3	2	0	12		3.0
1959	Cle-A	147	595	102	172	31	6	10	60	40	22	.289	.336	.412	108	3	5	75	9	13	-5	10	*12/3	1.1
1960	Cle-A	147	580	69	167	26	3	10	84	24	20	.288	.316	.395	94	-9	-6	69	9	5	-3	21	*1/S3	0.5
1961	Cle-A	147	563	64	151	34	4	5	63	38	16	.268	.316	.369	85	-15	-13	62	4	3	-1	19	*1/2	-0.6
1962	Min-A	144	611	80	177	28	2	16	63	22	35	.290	.318	.421	93	-4	-7	79	7	1	2	9	*1/2	-0.5
1963	Min-A	138	541	65	146	28	2	10	52	22	24	.270	.298	.384	88	-8	-10	59	3	1	0	-1	*12/3	-1.2
1964	Min-A	19	45	6	10	2	0	0	1	1	3	.222	.239	.267	40	-4	-4	3	0	0	0	1	1/2	-0.2
	LA-A	68	221	17	55	6	0	3	13	8	14	.249	.278	.317	72	-11	-8	18	1	1	-0	3	13/2	-0.6
	Yr	87	266	23	65	8	0	3	14	9	17	.244	.272	.308	66	-14	-12	21	1	1	-0	4		-0.8
	Phi-N	18	48	1	10	4	0	0	3	2	3	.208	.240	.292	50	-3	-3	3	0	0	0	1	1	-0.2
1965	Cal-A	124	197	11	51	7	1	1	20	5	13	.259	.281	.320	72	-8	-7	17	2	2	-1	6	*1/23	-0.6
Total	12	1627	6046	765	1716	290	49	126	658	279	247	.284	.317	.411	97	-46	-41	755	45	35	-7	128	*120/3S	3.7

■ **MIKE POWERS**   Powers, Ellis Foree b: 3/2/06, Crestwood, Ky. d: 12/2/83, Louisville, Ky. BL/TL, 6'1", 185 lbs. Deb: 8/19/32

YEAR	TM/L	G	AB	R	H	2B	3B	HR	RBI	BB	SO	AVG	OBP	SLG	PRO+	BR	/A	RC	SB	CS	SBR	FR	POS	TPR
1932	Cle-A	14	33	4	6	4	0	0	5	2	2	.182	.229	.303	34	-3	-4	3	0	0	0	-1	/O	-0.4
1933	Cle-A	24	47	6	13	2	1	0	2	6	6	.277	.358	.362	87	-0	-1	6	2	1	0	-1	O	-0.1
Total	2	38	80	10	19	6	1	0	7	8	8	.237	.307	.338	65	-4	-4	9	2	1	0	-2	/O	-0.5

■ **JOHN POWERS**   Powers, John Calvin b: 7/8/29, Birmingham, Ala. BL/TR, 6'1", 185 lbs. Deb: 9/24/55

YEAR	TM/L	G	AB	R	H	2B	3B	HR	RBI	BB	SO	AVG	OBP	SLG	PRO+	BR	/A	RC	SB	CS	SBR	FR	POS	TPR
1955	Pit-N	2	4	0	1	0	0	0	0	0	0	.250	.250	.250	34	-0	-0	0	0	0	0	0	/O	0.0
1956	Pit-N	11	21	0	1	0	0	0	0	1	4	.048	.091	.048	-63	-5	-5	0	0	0	0	-0	/O	-0.4
1957	Pit-N	20	35	7	10	3	0	2	8	5	9	.286	.419	.543	161	3	3	9	0	0	0	-0	/O	0.3
1958	Pit-N	57	82	6	15	1	0	2	2	8	19	.183	.256	.268	40	-7	-7	5	0	0	0	1	O	-0.6
1959	Cin-N	43	43	8	11	2	1	2	4	3	13	.256	.319	.488	108	1	0	7	0	0	0	-0	/O	0.0
1960	Bal-A	10	18	3	2	0	0	0	0	3	1	.111	.238	.111	-2	-3	-3	1	0	0	0	-1	/O	-0.3
	Cle-A	8	12	2	2	1	1	0	0	2	2	.167	.286	.417	90	-0	-0	1	0	0	0	0	/O	0.0
	Yr	18	30	5	4	1	1	0	0	5	3	.133	.257	.233	34	-3	-3	2	0	0	0	-0		-0.3
Total	6	151	215	26	42	7	2	6	14	22	48	.195	.282	.330	64	-12	-11	23	0	0	0	0	/O	-1.0

■ **LES POWERS**   Powers, Leslie Edwin b: 11/5/09, Ballard, Wash. d: 11/13/78, Santa Monica, Cal. BL/TL, 6', 175 lbs. Deb: 9/17/38

YEAR	TM/L	G	AB	R	H	2B	3B	HR	RBI	BB	SO	AVG	OBP	SLG	PRO+	BR	/A	RC	SB	CS	SBR	FR	POS	TPR
1938	NY-N	2	3	0	0	0	0	0	0	0	1	.000	.000	.000	-99	-1	-1	0	0			0	H	0.0
1939	Phi-N	19	52	7	18	1	1	0	2	4	6	.346	.393	.404	118	1	1	9	0			-2	1	-0.1
Total	2	21	55	7	18	1	1	0	2	4	7	.327	.373	.382	106	0	1	9	0			-2	/1	-0.1

■ **MIKE POWERS**   Powers, Michael Riley "Doc" b: 9/22/1870, Pittsfield, Mass. d: 4/26/09, Philadelphia, Pa. BR/TR, Deb: 6/12/1898

YEAR	TM/L	G	AB	R	H	2B	3B	HR	RBI	BB	SO	AVG	OBP	SLG	PRO+	BR	/A	RC	SB	CS	SBR	FR	POS	TPR
1898	Lou-N	34	99	13	27	4	3	1	19	5		.273	.308	.404	108	0	1	13	1			-3	C/1O	0.0
1899	Lou-N	49	169	15	35	8	2	0	22	6		.207	.239	.278	43	-13	-13	12	1			-8	C/1	-1.7
	Was-N	14	38	3	10	2	0	0	3	1		.263	.282	.316	67	-2	-2	3	0			1	C/1	0.0
	Yr	63	207	18	45	10	2	0	25	7		.217	.247	.285	48	-15	-15	15	1			-8		-1.7
1901	Phi-A	116	431	53	108	26	5	1	47	18		.251	.292	.341	73	-14	-17	47	10			-5	*C/1	-1.0
1902	Phi-A	71	246	35	65	7	1	2	39	14		.264	.312	.325	75	-7	-8	27	3			3	C/1	0.0
1903	Phi-A	75	247	19	56	11	1	0	23	5		.227	.242	.279	55	-13	-14	18	1			-2	C/1	-0.7
1904	Phi-A	57	184	11	35	3	0	0	11	6		.190	.216	.207	34	-13	-14	10	3			-4	C/O	-1.3
1905	*Phi-A	21	60	6	10	0	0	0	5	0		.167	.167	.167	7	-6	-6	2	2			4	C	0.0
	NY-A	11	33	3	6	1	0	0	2	1		.182	.206	.212	31	-2	-3	1	0			0	/1C	-0.2
	*Phi-A	19	61	2	8	0	0	0	5	3		.131	.172	.131	-2	-7	-7	2	2			-5	C	-1.0
	Yr	51	154	11	24	1	0	0	12	4		.156	.177	.162	9	-15	-16	6	4			-1		-1.2
1906	Phi-A	58	185	5	29	1	0	0	7	1		.157	.161	.162	2	-20	-21	6	2			10	C/1	-0.6
1907	Phi-A	59	159	9	29	3	0	0	9	7		.182	.217	.201	34	-11	-12	9	1			14	C	0.8
1908	Phi-A	62	172	8	31	6	1	0	7	5		.180	.203	.227	39	-11	-12	8	1			7	C/1	0.1
1909	Phi-A	1	4	1	1	0	0	0	0	0		.250	.250	.250	57	-0	-0	0	0			0	/C	0.0
Total	11	647	2088	183	450	72	13	4	199	72		.216	.246	.268	51	-119	-128	159	27			11	C/1O	-5.6

■ **PHIL POWERS**   Powers, Phillip B. "Grandmother" b: 7/26/1854, New York, N.Y. d: 12/22/14, New York, N.Y. BR/TR, 5'7", 166 lbs. Deb: 8/31/1878 U

YEAR	TM/L	G	AB	R	H	2B	3B	HR	RBI	BB	SO	AVG	OBP	SLG	PRO+	BR	/A	RC	SB	CS	SBR	FR	POS	TPR
1878	Chi-N	8	31	2	5	1	1	0	2	1	5	.161	.188	.258	42	-2	-2	2				6	/C	0.4
1880	Bos-N	37	126	11	18	5	0	0	10	5	15	.143	.176	.183	22	-10	-9	4				-2	C/O	-0.8
1881	Cle-N	5	15	1	1	0	0	0	0	1	2	.067	.125	.067	-40	-2	-2	0				0	/C3	-0.1
1882	Cin-a	16	60	4	13	1	1	0		3		.217	.254	.267	71	-1	-2	4				2	C/1O	0.0
1883	Cin-a	30	114	16	28	1	4	0		3		.246	.265	.325	84	-1	-3	10				-4	CO	-0.3
1884	Cin-a	34	130	10	18	1	0	0		5		.138	.170	.146	6	-13	-14	3				1	C/O1	-0.8
1885	Cin-a	15	60	6	16	2	0	0		0		.267	.267	.300	80	-1	-2	5				-4	C	-0.2
	Bal-a	9	34	6	4	1	0	0		1		.118	.143	.147	-7	-4	-4	1				-4	/CO	-0.5
	Yr	24	94	12	20	3	0	0		1		.213	.221	.245	49	-5	-5	5				-7		-0.7
Total	7	154	570	56	103	12	6	0	<u>12</u>	19	<u>22</u>	.181	.207	.223	40	-35	-37	29				-4	C/O13	-2.3

■ **CARL POWIS**   Powis, Carl Edgar "Jug" b: 1/11/28, Philadelphia, Pa. BR/TR, 6', 185 lbs. Deb: 4/15/57

YEAR	TM/L	G	AB	R	H	2B	3B	HR	RBI	BB	SO	AVG	OBP	SLG	PRO+	BR	/A	RC	SB	CS	SBR	FR	POS	TPR
1957	Bal-A	15	41	4	8	1	0	0	2	7	9	.195	.327	.317	82	-1	-1	5	2	0	1	-1	O	-0.1

■ **JOHNNY PRAMESA**   Pramesa, John Steven b: 8/28/25, Barton, Ohio BR/TR, 6'2", 210 lbs. Deb: 4/24/49

YEAR	TM/L	G	AB	R	H	2B	3B	HR	RBI	BB	SO	AVG	OBP	SLG	PRO+	BR	/A	RC	SB	CS	SBR	FR	POS	TPR
1949	Cin-N	17	25	2	6	1	0	1	2	3	5	.240	.321	.400	91	-0	-0	3	0			-1	C	0.0
1950	Cin-N	74	228	14	70	10	1	5	30	19	15	.307	.363	.425	106	2	2	34	0			2	C	0.6
1951	Cin-N	72	227	12	52	5	2	6	22	5	17	.229	.246	.348	57	-14	-15	18	0			-6	C	-2.0
1952	Chi-N	22	46	1	13	1	0	1	5	4	4	.283	.340	.370	96	-0	-0	6	0	0	0	2	C	0.2
Total	4	185	526	29	141	17	3	13	59	31	41	.268	.310	.386	84	-12	-13	61	0	<u>0</u>		-3	C	-1.2

YEAR	TM/L	G	AB	R	H	2B	3B	HR	RBI	BB	SO	AVG	OBP	SLG	PRO+	BR	/A	RC	SB	CS	SBR	FR	POS	TPR

■ DEL PRATT Pratt, Derrill Burnham b: 1/10/1888, Walhalla, S.C. d: 9/30/77, Texas City, Tex. BR/TR, 5'11", 175 lbs. Deb: 4/11/12

YEAR	TM/L	G	AB	R	H	2B	3B	HR	RBI	BB	SO	AVG	OBP	SLG	PRO+	BR	/A	RC	SB	CS	SBR	FR	POS	TPR
1912	StL-A	152	570	76	172	26	15	5	69	36		.302	.348	.426	125	13	16	91	24			14	*2S/O3	2.9
1913	StL-A	155	592	60	175	31	13	2	87	40	57	.296	.341	.402	121	11	12	89	37			5	*2/1	1.4
1914	StL-A	158	584	85	165	34	13	5	65	50	45	.283	.341	.411	131	16	19	83	37	28	-6	-2	*2	1.2
1915	StL-A	159	602	61	175	31	11	3	78	26	43	.291	.323	.394	119	7	9	80	32	23	-4	12	*2	1.6
1916	StL-A	158	596	64	159	35	12	5	**103**	54	56	.267	.331	.391	123	10	13	80	26	17	-2	22	*2	4.1
1917	StL-A	123	450	40	111	22	8	1	53	33	36	.247	.301	.338	98	-4	-2	49	18			15	*2/1	2.2
1918	NY-A	126	477	65	131	19	7	2	55	35	26	.275	.327	.356	104	2	1	59	12			12	*2	2.1
1919	NY-A	140	527	69	154	27	7	4	56	36	24	.292	.342	.393	105	3	3	75	22			**28**	*2	4.4
1920	NY-A	154	574	84	180	37	8	4	97	50	24	.314	.372	.427	107	9	6	91	12	10	-2	12	*2	1.8
1921	Bos-A	135	521	80	169	36	10	5	102	44	10	.324	.378	.461	116	10	12	89	8	10	-4	-1	*2	1.0
1922	Bos-A	154	607	73	183	44	7	6	86	53	20	.301	.361	.427	106	4	4	93	7	10	-4	-13	*2	-0.1
1923	Det-A	101	297	43	92	18	3	0	40	25	9	.310	.375	.391	104	1	2	46	5	1	1	-10	213	-0.3
1924	Det-A	121	429	56	130	32	3	1	77	31	10	.303	.353	.399	95	-5	-4	59	6	9	-2	-2	21/3O	-0.8
Total	13	1836	6826	856	1996	392	117	43	968	513	360	.292	.345	.403	112	76	91	984	246	108		92	*2/1S3O	21.5

■ FRANK PRATT Pratt, Francis Bruce "Truckhorse" b: 8/24/1897, Blocton, Ala. d: 3/8/74, Centreville, Ala. TR, 5'9.5", 155 lbs. Deb: 5/13/21

YEAR	TM/L	G	AB	R	H	2B	3B	HR	RBI	BB	SO	AVG	OBP	SLG	PRO+	BR	/A	RC	SB	CS	SBR	FR	POS	TPR
1921	Chi-A	1	1	0	0	0	0	0	0	0	0	.000	.000	.000	-99	-0	-0	0	0	0	0	0	H	0.0

■ LARRY PRATT Pratt, Lester John b: 10/8/1886, Gibson City, Ill. d: 1/8/69, Peoria, Ill. BR/TR, 6', 183 lbs. Deb: 9/19/14

YEAR	TM/L	G	AB	R	H	2B	3B	HR	RBI	BB	SO	AVG	OBP	SLG	PRO+	BR	/A	RC	SB	CS	SBR	FR	POS	TPR
1914	Bos-A	5	4	0	0	0	0	0	0	0	4	.000	.000	.000	-99	-1	-1	0	0			2	/C	0.1
1915	Bro-F	20	49	5	9	1	0	1	2	2	18	.184	.216	.265	42	-4	-4	3	2			-5	C	-0.8
	New-F	5	4	2	2	2	0	0	0	3	1	.500	.714	1.000	429	2	2	4	2			-1	/C	0.1
	Yr	25	53	7	11	3	0	1	2	5	19	.208	.276	.321	78	-2	-2	6	4			-6		-0.7
Total	2	30	57	7	11	3	0	1	2	5	23	.193	.258	.298	65	-3	-3	8	4			-4	/C	-0.6

■ TOM PRATT Pratt, Thomas J. b: 1844, Chelsea, Mass. d: 9/28/08, Philadelphia, Pa. TL, 5'7.5", 150 lbs. Deb: 10/18/1871 U

YEAR	TM/L	G	AB	R	H	2B	3B	HR	RBI	BB	SO	AVG	OBP	SLG	PRO+	BR	/A	RC	SB	CS	SBR	FR	POS	TPR
1871	Ath-n	1	6	2	2	0	0	0	1	0	0	.333	.333	.333	93	-0	-0	1	0				/1	0.0

■ MEL PREIBISCH Preibisch, Melvin Adolphus "Primo" b: 11/23/14, Sealy, Tex. d: 4/12/80, Sealy, Tex. BR/TR, 5'11", 185 lbs. Deb: 9/17/40

YEAR	TM/L	G	AB	R	H	2B	3B	HR	RBI	BB	SO	AVG	OBP	SLG	PRO+	BR	/A	RC	SB	CS	SBR	FR	POS	TPR
1940	Bos-N	11	40	3	9	2	0	0	5	2	4	.225	.262	.275	51	-3	-3	3	0			2	O	-0.1
1941	Bos-N	5	4	0	0	0	0	0	0	1	2	.000	.200	.000	-42	-1	-1	0	0			0	/O	0.0
Total	2	16	44	3	9	2	0	0	5	3	6	.205	.255	.250	42	-4	-3	3	0			2	/O	-0.1

■ BOBBY PRESCOTT Prescott, George Bertrand b: 3/27/31, Colon, Panama BR/TR, 5'11", 180 lbs. Deb: 6/17/61

YEAR	TM/L	G	AB	R	H	2B	3B	HR	RBI	BB	SO	AVG	OBP	SLG	PRO+	BR	/A	RC	SB	CS	SBR	FR	POS	TPR
1961	KC-A	10	12	0	1	0	0	0	0	2	5	.083	.214	.083	-17	-2	-2	0	0	0	0	0	/O	-0.1

■ JIM PRESLEY Presley, James Arthur b: 10/23/61, Pensacola, Fla. BR/TR, 6'1", 200 lbs. Deb: 6/24/84

YEAR	TM/L	G	AB	R	H	2B	3B	HR	RBI	BB	SO	AVG	OBP	SLG	PRO+	BR	/A	RC	SB	CS	SBR	FR	POS	TPR
1984	Sea-A	70	251	27	57	12	1	10	36	6	63	.227	.248	.402	78	-9	-9	24	1	1	-0	-3	3/D	-1.0
1985	Sea-A	155	570	71	157	33	1	28	84	44	100	.275	.328	.484	118	13	13	80	2	2	-1	6	*3	1.3
1986	Sea-A	155	616	83	163	33	4	27	107	32	172	.265	.305	.463	105	2	2	80	4	4	-2	6	*3	0.2
1987	Sea-A	152	575	78	142	23	6	24	88	38	157	.247	.298	.433	86	-9	-13	72	2	0	1	11	*3/SD	-0.3
1988	Sea-A	150	544	50	125	26	0	14	62	36	114	.230	.283	.355	74	-17	-20	52	3	5	-2	-13	*3/D	-3.5
1989	Sea-A	117	390	42	92	20	1	12	41	21	107	.236	.277	.385	82	-9	-11	39	0	0	0	-4	31/D	-1.6
1990	Atl-N	140	541	59	131	34	1	19	72	29	130	.242	.284	.414	88	-10	-11	62	1	1	0	-2	*31	-1.0
Total	7	939	3487	410	867	181	14	134	490	206	843	.249	.294	.424	92	-39	-49	407	9	13	-5	1	3/1DS	-5.9

■ WALT PRESTON Preston, Walter B. b: 1870, Richmond, Va. BL/TR, 6', 175 lbs. Deb: 4/18/1895

YEAR	TM/L	G	AB	R	H	2B	3B	HR	RBI	BB	SO	AVG	OBP	SLG	PRO+	BR	/A	RC	SB	CS	SBR	FR	POS	TPR
1895	Lou-N	50	197	42	55	6	4	1	24	17	17	.279	.366	.365	97	-2	0	31	11			-7	O3	-0.6

■ JIM PRICE Price, Jimmie William b: 10/13/41, Harrisburg, Pa. BR/TR, 6', 192 lbs. Deb: 4/11/67

YEAR	TM/L	G	AB	R	H	2B	3B	HR	RBI	BB	SO	AVG	OBP	SLG	PRO+	BR	/A	RC	SB	CS	SBR	FR	POS	TPR
1967	Det-A	44	92	9	24	4	0	0	8	4	10	.261	.292	.304	74	-3	-3	7	0	0	0	0	C	0.0
1968	*Det-A	64	132	12	23	4	0	3	13	13	14	.174	.253	.273	58	-6	-7	8	0	0	0	2	C	-0.3
1969	Det-A	72	192	21	45	8	0	9	28	18	20	.234	.300	.417	95	-1	-2	24	0	0	0	3	C	0.4
1970	Det-A	52	132	12	24	4	0	2	15	21	23	.182	.294	.326	70	-5	-5	13	0	0	0	-1	C	-0.5
1971	Det-A	29	54	4	13	2	0	1	7	6	3	.241	.328	.333	84	-1	-1	6	0	0	0	1	C	0.2
Total	5	261	602	58	129	22	0	18	71	62	70	.214	.290	.341	78	-16	-18	58	0	0	0	5	C	-0.2

■ JACKIE PRICE Price, John Thomas Reid "Johnny" b: 11/13/12, Windborn, Miss. d: 10/2/67, San Francisco, Cal. BL/TR, 5'10.5", 150 lbs. Deb: 8/18/46

YEAR	TM/L	G	AB	R	H	2B	3B	HR	RBI	BB	SO	AVG	OBP	SLG	PRO+	BR	/A	RC	SB	CS	SBR	FR	POS	TPR
1946	Cle-A	7	13	1	3	0	0	0	0	0	0	.231	.231	.231	31	-1	-1	0	0			2	/S	0.0

■ JOE PRICE Price, Joseph Preston "Lumber" b: 4/10/1897, Milligan College, Tenn. d: 1/15/61, Washington, D.C. BR/TR, 6'1.5", 187 lbs. Deb: 9/05/28

YEAR	TM/L	G	AB	R	H	2B	3B	HR	RBI	BB	SO	AVG	OBP	SLG	PRO+	BR	/A	RC	SB	CS	SBR	FR	POS	TPR
1928	NY-N	1	1	0	0	0	0	0	0	0	1	.000	.000	.000	-99	-0	-0	0	0			0	/O	0.0

■ BOB PRICHARD Prichard, Robert Alexander b: 10/21/17, Paris, Tex. BL/TL, 6'1", 195 lbs. Deb: 6/14/39

YEAR	TM/L	G	AB	R	H	2B	3B	HR	RBI	BB	SO	AVG	OBP	SLG	PRO+	BR	/A	RC	SB	CS	SBR	FR	POS	TPR
1939	Was-A	26	85	8	20	5	0	0	8	19	16	.235	.375	.294	79	-3	-2	11	0	2	-1	-1	1	-0.5

■ JERRY PRIDDY Priddy, Gerald Edward b: 11/9/19, Los Angeles, Cal. d: 3/3/80, N.Hollywood, Cal. BR/TR, 5'11.5", 180 lbs. Deb: 4/17/41

YEAR	TM/L	G	AB	R	H	2B	3B	HR	RBI	BB	SO	AVG	OBP	SLG	PRO+	BR	/A	RC	SB	CS	SBR	FR	POS	TPR
1941	NY-A	56	174	18	37	7	0	1	26	18	16	.213	.290	.270	50	-13	-12	14	4	2	0	9	231	0.0
1942	*NY-A	59	189	23	53	9	2	2	28	31	27	.280	.385	.381	118	5	6	31	0	1	-1	5	31/2S	1.1
1943	Was-A	149	560	68	152	31	3	4	62	67	76	.271	.350	.359	112	6	9	72	5	5	-2	4	*2S/3	1.8
1946	Was-A	138	511	54	130	22	8	6	58	57	79	.254	.332	.364	100	-4	-0	64	9	3	1	2	*2	1.4
1947	Was-A	147	505	42	108	20	3	3	49	62	79	.214	.301	.283	65	-25	-23	44	7	6	-2	-2	*2	-2.0
1948	StL-A	151	560	96	166	40	9	8	79	86	71	.296	.391	.443	118	18	16	101	6	5	-1	24	*2	4.0
1949	StL-A	145	544	83	158	26	4	11	63	80	81	.290	.382	.414	106	9	6	89	5	3	-0	-3	*2	0.4
1950	Det-A	157	618	104	171	26	6	13	75	95	95	.277	.376	.401	96	0	-3	95	2	7	-4	**31**	*2	3.3
1951	Det-A	154	584	73	152	22	6	8	57	69	73	.260	.338	.360	88	-9	-9	73	4	3	-1	10	*2/S	0.6
1952	Det-A	75	279	37	79	23	3	4	20	42	29	.283	.379	.430	124	10	10	46	1	8	-1	-2	*2	-0.3
1953	Det-A	65	196	14	46	6	2	1	24	17	19	.235	.299	.301	63	-10	-10	18	1	1	-0	4	21/3	-0.3
Total	11	1296	4720	612	1252	232	46	61	541	624	639	.265	.353	.373	97	-12	-11	646	44	44	-13	82	*2/31S	11.1

■ JOHNNY PRIEST Priest, John Gooding b: 6/23/1886, St.Joseph, Mo. d: 11/4/79, Washington, D.C. BR/TR, 5'11", 170 lbs. Deb: 5/30/11

YEAR	TM/L	G	AB	R	H	2B	3B	HR	RBI	BB	SO	AVG	OBP	SLG	PRO+	BR	/A	RC	SB	CS	SBR	FR	POS	TPR
1911	NY-A	8	21	2	3	0	0	0		2	2	.143	.250	.143	10	-2	-3	1	3			-3	/23	-0.5
1912	NY-A	2	2	1	1	0	0	0		1	0	.500	.500	.500	176	0	0	0	0			0	H	0.0
Total	2	10	23	3	4	0	0	0		3	2	.174	.269	.174	23	-2	-2	2	3			-3	/23	-0.5

■ TOM PRINCE Prince, Thomas Albert b: 8/13/64, Kankakee, Ill. BR/TR, 5'11", 185 lbs. Deb: 9/22/87

YEAR	TM/L	G	AB	R	H	2B	3B	HR	RBI	BB	SO	AVG	OBP	SLG	PRO+	BR	/A	RC	SB	CS	SBR	FR	POS	TPR
1987	Pit-N	4	9	1	2	1	0	1	2	0	2	.222	.222	.667	123	0	0	1	0	0	0	1	/C	0.1
1988	Pit-N	29	74	3	13	2	0	0	6	4	15	.176	.218	.203	22	-7	-7	3	0	0	0	-2	C	-0.8
1989	Pit-N	21	52	1	7	4	0	0	5	6	12	.135	.224	.212	26	-5	-5	2	1	1	-0	-0	C	-0.3
1990	Pit-N	4	10	1	1	0	0	0	0	3	2	.100	.182	.100	-21	-2	-2	0	0	1	-1	0	/C	-0.1
Total	4	58	145	6	23	7	0	1	13	11	31	.159	.218	.228	27	-14	-14	6	1	2	-1	-1	/C	-1.1

■ WALTER PRINCE Prince, Walter Farr b: 5/9/1861, Amherst, N.H. d: 3/2/38, Bristol, N.H. BL/TR, 5'9", 150 lbs. Deb: 8/07/1883

YEAR	TM/L	G	AB	R	H	2B	3B	HR	RBI	BB	SO	AVG	OBP	SLG	PRO+	BR	/A	RC	SB	CS	SBR	FR	POS	TPR
1883	Lou-a	4	11	1	2	0	0	0		0		.182	.182	.182	19	-1	-1	0				-2	/O1S	-0.2
1884	Det-N	7	21	0	3	0	0	0	1	3	4	.143	.250	.143	29	-2	-1	1				-3	/O	-0.3

YEAR	TM/L	G	AB	R	H	2B	3B	HR	RBI	BB	SO	AVG	OBP	SLG	PRO+	BR	/A	RC	SB	CS	SBR	FR	POS	TPR
	Was-a	43	166	22	36	3	2	1		13		.217	.286	.277	98	-2	1	13				-5	1	-0.5
	Was-U	1	4	0	1	0	0	0		0		.250	.250	.250	72	-0	-0	0	0			-0	/1	0.0
Total	2	55	202	23	42	3	2	1	1	16	4	.208	.276	.257	86	-5	-1	15	0			-11	/1OS	-1.0

■ BUDDY PRITCHARD

Pritchard, Harold William b: 1/25/36, South Gate, Cal. BR/TR, 6'1", 195 lbs. Deb: 4/21/57

YEAR	TM/L	G	AB	R	H	2B	3B	HR	RBI	BB	SO	AVG	OBP	SLG	PRO+	BR	/A	RC	SB	CS	SBR	FR	POS	TPR
1957	Pit-N	23	11	1	1	0	0	0	0	0	4	.091	.091	.091	-53	-2	-2	0	0	0	0	5	S/O	0.3

■ GEORGE PROESER

Proeser, George "Yatz" b: 5/30/1864, Cincinnati, Ohio d: 10/13/41, New Burlington, O. BL/TL, 5'10", 190 lbs. Deb: 9/15/1888

YEAR	TM/L	G	AB	R	H	2B	3B	HR	RBI	BB	SO	AVG	OBP	SLG	PRO+	BR	/A	RC	SB	CS	SBR	FR	POS	TPR
1888	Cle-a	7	23	5	7	2	0	0	1	1		.304	.333	.391	139	1	1	3	0			-1	/P	0.0
1890	Syr-a	13	53	11	13	1	1	1		10		.245	.365	.358	128	1	2	7	1			-2	O	0.0
Total	2	20	76	16	20	3	1	1	1	11		.263	.356	.368	131	2	3	11	1			-2	/OP	0.0

■ JAKE PROPST

Propst, William Jacob b: 3/10/1895, Kennedy, Ala. d: 2/24/67, Columbus, Miss. 5'10", 165 lbs. Deb: 8/07/23

YEAR	TM/L	G	AB	R	H	2B	3B	HR	RBI	BB	SO	AVG	OBP	SLG	PRO+	BR	/A	RC	SB	CS	SBR	FR	POS	TPR
1923	Was-A	1	1	0	0	0	0	0	0	0	0	.000	.000	.000	-99	-0	-0	0	0	0	0	0	H	0.0

■ DOC PROTHRO

Prothro, James Thompson b: 7/16/1893, Memphis, Tenn. d: 10/14/71, Memphis, Tenn. BR/TR, 5'10.5", 170 lbs. Deb: 9/26/20 M

YEAR	TM/L	G	AB	R	H	2B	3B	HR	RBI	BB	SO	AVG	OBP	SLG	PRO+	BR	/A	RC	SB	CS	SBR	FR	POS	TPR
1920	Was-A	6	13	2	5	0	0	0	2	0	4	.385	.385	.385	107	0	0	2	0	0	0	-1	/S3	0.20
1923	Was-A	6	8	2	2	0	1	0	3	1	3	.250	.333	.500	124	0	0	1	0	0	0	3	/3	0.4
1924	Was-A	46	159	17	53	11	5	0	24	15	11	.333	.394	.465	125	5	6	29	4	4	-1	-11	3	-0.2
1925	Bos-A	119	415	44	130	23	3	0	51	52	21	.313	.390	.383	97	-0	-0	62	9	11	-4	-6	*3/S	-0.2
1926	Cin-N	3	5	1	1	0	1	0	1	1	1	.200	.333	.600	151	0	0	1	0			-0	/3	0.0
Total	5	180	600	66	191	34	10	0	81	69	40	.318	.390	.408	105	5	6	95	13	15		-14	3/S	0.0

■ EARL PRUESS

Pruess, Earl Henry "Gibby" b: 4/2/1895, Chicago, Ill. d: 8/28/79, Branson, Mo. BR/TR, 5'10.5", 170 lbs. Deb: 9/15/20

YEAR	TM/L	G	AB	R	H	2B	3B	HR	RBI	BB	SO	AVG	OBP	SLG	PRO+	BR	/A	RC	SB	CS	SBR	FR	POS	TPR
1920	StL-A	1	0	1	0	0	0	0	0	1	0	—	1.000	—	176	0	0	1	0	0	0	0	/O	0.0

■ JIM PRUETT

Pruett, James Calvin b: 12/16/17, Nashville, Tenn. BR/TR, 5'10", 178 lbs. Deb: 9/26/44

YEAR	TM/L	G	AB	R	H	2B	3B	HR	RBI	BB	SO	AVG	OBP	SLG	PRO+	BR	/A	RC	SB	CS	SBR	FR	POS	TPR
1944	Phi-A	3	4	1	1	0	0	0	0	1	0	.250	.500	.250	119	0	0	1	0	0	0	1	/C	0.1
1945	Phi-A	6	9	1	2	0	0	0	0	1	2	.222	.300	.222	53	-1	-1	0	0	1	-1	1	/C	0.0
Total	2	9	13	2	3	0	0	0	0	2	2	.231	.375	.231	77	-0	-0	1	0	1	-1	1	/C	0.1

■ RON PRUITT

Pruitt, Ronald Ralph b: 10/21/51, Flint, Mich. BR/TR, 6', 185 lbs. Deb: 6/25/75

YEAR	TM/L	G	AB	R	H	2B	3B	HR	RBI	BB	SO	AVG	OBP	SLG	PRO+	BR	/A	RC	SB	CS	SBR	FR	POS	TPR
1975	Tex-A	14	17	2	3	0	0	0	0	1	3	.176	.222	.176	14	-2	-2	1	0	0	0	-0	C/O	-0.1
1976	Cle-A	47	86	7	23	1	1	0	5	16	8	.267	.382	.302	103	1	1	11	2	3	-1	6	O/C31D	0.6
1977	Cle-A	78	219	29	63	10	2	2	32	28	22	.288	.373	.379	109	3	4	30	2	3	-1	-6	O/C3D	-0.4
1978	Cle-A	71	187	17	44	6	1	6	17	16	20	.235	.296	.374	88	-4	-3	21	2	1	0	-5	CO/3D	-0.7
1979	Cle-A	64	166	23	47	7	0	2	21	19	21	.283	.357	.361	94	-1	-1	22	2	0	1	-3	ODC/3	-0.3
1980	Cle-A	23	36	1	11	1	0	0	4	4	6	.306	.375	.333	95	-0	-0	5	0	0	0	0	/O3D	0.0
	Chi-A	33	70	8	21	2	0	2	11	8	7	.300	.372	.414	116	2	2	10	0	0	0	-1	O/C31D	0.0
	Yr	56	106	9	32	3	0	2	15	12	13	.302	.373	.387	109	2	2	15	0	0	0	-1		0.0
1981	Cle-A	5	9	0	0	0	0	0	0	1	2	.000	.100	.000	-70	-2	-2	0	0	0	0	-0	/OCD	-0.2
1982	SF-N	5	4	1	2	1	0	0	2	1	1	.500	.600	.750	276	1	1	2	0	0	0	0	/CO	0.1
1983	SF-N	1	1	0	0	0	0	0	0	0	0	.000	.000	.000	-99	-0	-0	0	0	0	0	/H	0.0
Total	9	341	795	88	214	28	4	12	92	94	90	.269	.348	.360	97	-2	-1	100	8	7	-2	-10	O/CD31	-1.0

■ GREG PRYOR

Pryor, Gregory Russell b: 10/2/49, Marietta, Ohio BR/TR, 6', 180 lbs. Deb: 6/04/76

YEAR	TM/L	G	AB	R	H	2B	3B	HR	RBI	BB	SO	AVG	OBP	SLG	PRO+	BR	/A	RC	SB	CS	SBR	FR	POS	TPR
1976	Tex-A	5	8	2	3	0	0	0	1	0	1	.375	.375	.375	118	0	0	1	0	0	0	0	/2S3	0.1
1978	Chi-A	82	222	27	58	11	0	2	15	11	18	.261	.299	.338	78	-6	-7	22	3	1	0	6	2S3	0.4
1979	Chi-A	143	476	60	131	23	3	3	34	35	41	.275	.327	.355	84	-10	-10	52	3	4	-2	-5	*S23	-0.1
1980	Chi-A	122	338	32	81	18	4	1	29	12	35	.240	.270	.325	63	-18	-18	28	2	2	-1	22	S3/2D	1.0
1981	Chi-A	47	76	4	17	1	0	0	6	6	8	.224	.298	.237	57	-4	-4	6	0	0	0	2	3S/2	0.0
1982	KC-A	73	152	23	41	10	1	2	12	10	20	.270	.315	.388	92	-2	-2	18	2	0	1	8	321/S	0.7
1983	KC-A	68	115	9	25	4	0	1	14	7	8	.217	.262	.278	49	-8	-8	8	0	0	0	8	3/12	0.0
1984	*KC-A	123	270	32	71	11	1	4	25	12	28	.263	.302	.356	80	-7	-7	26	0	3	-2	17	*32S/1D	1.1
1985	*KC-A	63	114	8	25	3	0	1	3	8	12	.219	.270	.272	49	-8	-8	7	0	1	-1	8	32S/1D	0.1
1986	KC-A	63	112	7	19	4	0	0	7	3	14	.170	.191	.205	8	-14	-14	3	1	1	-0	4	3S2/1	-0.9
Total	10	789	1883	204	471	85	9	14	146	104	185	.250	.293	.327	70	-78	-78	172	11	12	-4	71	3S2/1D	2.4

■ GEORGE PUCCINELLI

Puccinelli, George Lawrence "Pooch" or "Count"
b: 6/22/07, San Francisco, Cal. d: 4/16/56, San Francisco, Cal BR/TR, 6'0.5", 190 lbs. Deb: 7/17/30

YEAR	TM/L	G	AB	R	H	2B	3B	HR	RBI	BB	SO	AVG	OBP	SLG	PRO+	BR	/A	RC	SB	CS	SBR	FR	POS	TPR
1930	*StL-N	11	16	5	9	1	0	3	8	0	1	.563	.563	1.188	298	5	5	10	0			-0	/O	0.4
1932	StL-N	31	108	17	30	8	0	3	11	12	13	.278	.350	.435	107	2	1	17	1			1	O	0.0
1934	StL-A	10	26	4	6	1	0	2	5	1	8	.231	.286	.500	92	-0	-1	4	0	0	0	1	/O	0.0
1936	Phi-A	135	457	83	127	30	3	11	78	65	70	.278	.369	.429	98	-3	-1	75	2	3	-1	-2	*O	-0.6
Total	4	187	607	109	172	40	3	19	102	78	92	.283	.367	.453	105	4	4	105	3	3		0	O	-0.2

■ KIRBY PUCKETT

Puckett, Kirby b: 3/14/61, Chicago, Ill. BR/TR, 5'8", 178 lbs. Deb: 5/08/84

YEAR	TM/L	G	AB	R	H	2B	3B	HR	RBI	BB	SO	AVG	OBP	SLG	PRO+	BR	/A	RC	SB	CS	SBR	FR	POS	TPR
1984	Min-A	128	557	63	165	12	5	0	31	16	69	.296	.321	.336	78	-14	-17	58	14	7	0	22	*O	0.2
1985	Min-A	161	691	80	199	29	13	4	74	41	87	.288	.332	.385	90	-4	-9	88	21	12	-1	13	*O	0.0
1986	Min-A	161	680	119	223	37	6	31	96	34	99	.328	.366	.537	138	37	35	127	20	12	-1	3	*O	3.3
1987	*Min-A	157	624	96	207	32	5	28	99	32	91	.332	.370	.534	131	30	27	116	12	7	-1	1	*O/D	2.3
1988	Min-A	158	657	109	234	42	5	24	121	23	83	.356	.380	.545	151	46	43	126	6	7	-2	13	*O	5.0
1989	Min-A	159	635	75	215	45	4	9	85	41	59	.339	.381	.465	129	30	25	107	11	4	1	14	*O/D	3.8
1990	Min-A	146	551	82	164	40	3	12	80	57	73	.298	.367	.446	118	20	15	88	5	4	-1	1	*O/23SD	1.4
Total	7	1070	4395	624	1407	237	41	108	586	244	561	.320	.360	.466	120	145	119	710	89	53	-5	67	*O/DS32	16.0

■ JOHN PUHL

Puhl, John G. b: 1875, New York, N.Y. d: 8/24/1900, Bayonne, N.J. Deb: 10/13/1898

YEAR	TM/L	G	AB	R	H	2B	3B	HR	RBI	BB	SO	AVG	OBP	SLG	PRO+	BR	/A	RC	SB	CS	SBR	FR	POS	TPR
1898	NY-N	2	9	1	2	0	0	0	1	0		.222	.222	.222	30	-1	-1	0	0			-0	/3	0.0
1899	NY-N	1	2	0	0	0	0	0	0	0		.000	.333	.000	-3	-0	-0	0	0			-0	/3	0.0
Total	2	3	11	1	2	0	0	0	1	0		.182	.250	.182	26	-1	-1	0	0			-1	/3	0.0

■ TERRY PUHL

Puhl, Terry Stephen b: 7/8/56, Melville, Sask., Can BL/TR, 6'2", 195 lbs. Deb: 7/12/77

YEAR	TM/L	G	AB	R	H	2B	3B	HR	RBI	BB	SO	AVG	OBP	SLG	PRO+	BR	/A	RC	SB	CS	SBR	FR	POS	TPR
1977	Hou-N	60	229	40	69	13	5	0	10	30	31	.301	.385	.402	122	5	7	39	10	1	2	1	O	0.8
1978	Hou-N	149	585	87	169	25	6	3	35	48	46	.289	.347	.368	108	0	5	75	32	14	1	19	*O	2.1
1979	Hou-N	157	600	87	172	22	4	8	49	58	46	.287	.353	.377	105	1	5	80	30	22	-4	-6	*O	-0.9
1980	*Hou-N	141	535	75	151	24	5	13	55	60	52	.282	.359	.419	126	12	18	85	27	11	2	14	*O	2.9
1981	*Hou-N	96	350	43	88	19	4	3	28	31	49	.251	.319	.354	96	-4	-2	44	22	4	3	0	O	0.2
1982	Hou-N	145	507	64	133	17	9	8	50	51	49	.262	.332	.379	106	-1	4	66	17	9	-0	-2	*O	0.1
1983	Hou-N	137	465	66	136	25	7	8	44	36	48	.292	.346	.428	121	8	11	70	24	11	1	-5	*O	0.4
1984	Hou-N	132	449	66	135	19	7	9	55	59	45	.301	.383	.434	139	19	23	77	13	8	-1	-4	*O	1.4
1985	Hou-N	57	194	34	55	14	3	2	23	18	23	.284	.347	.418	116	3	4	30	6	2	1	-2	O	0.1
1986	*Hou-N	81	172	17	42	10	0	3	14	15	24	.244	.305	.355	84	-5	-4	18	3	2	-0	-4	O	-0.8
1987	Hou-N	90	122	9	28	5	0	2	15	11	11	.230	.293	.320	65	-7	-6	11	1	1	-0	1	O	-0.6
1988	Hou-N	113	234	42	71	7	2	3	19	35	30	.303	.396	.389	131	10	11	42	22	4	4	-1	O	1.2
1989	Hou-N	121	354	41	96	25	0	0	27	45	39	.271	.355	.364	110	4	5	46	9	8	-2	-1	*O/1	0.0
1990	Hou-N	37	41	5	12	1	0	0	8	5	7	.293	.383	.317	97	0	0	5	1	2	-1	-1	/O1	-0.1

YEAR	TM/L	G	AB	R	H	2B	3B	HR	RBI	BB	SO	AVG	OBP	SLG	PRO+	BR	/A	RC	SB	CS	SBR	FR	POS	TPR
Total	14	1516	4837	676	1357	226	56	62	432	502	505	.281	.351	.389	113	45	81	689	217	99	6	11	*O/1	6.7

■ **RICH PUIG**   Puig, Richard Gerald   b: 3/16/53, Tampa, Fla.   BL/TR, 5'10", 165 lbs.   Deb: 9/13/74

YEAR	TM/L	G	AB	R	H	2B	3B	HR	RBI	BB	SO	AVG	OBP	SLG	PRO+	BR	/A	RC	SB	CS	SBR	FR	POS	TPR
1974	NY-N	4	10	0	0	0	0	0	0	1	2	.000	.091	.000	-74	-2	-2	0	0	0	0	-0	/23	-0.2

■ **LUIS PUJOLS**   Pujols, Luis Bienvenido (Toribio)   b: 11/18/55, Santiago, D.R.   BR/TR, 6'2", 175 lbs.   Deb: 9/22/77

YEAR	TM/L	G	AB	R	H	2B	3B	HR	RBI	BB	SO	AVG	OBP	SLG	PRO+	BR	/A	RC	SB	CS	SBR	FR	POS	TPR
1977	Hou-N	6	15	0	1	0	0	0	0	0	5	.067	.067	.067	-70	-3	-3	0	0	0	0	0	/C	-0.2
1978	Hou-N	56	153	11	20	8	1	1	11	12	45	.131	.199	.216	17	-18	-16	6	0	0	0	2	C/1	-1.3
1979	Hou-N	26	75	7	17	2	1	0	8	2	14	.227	.247	.280	46	-6	-5	5	0	0	0	1	C	-0.3
1980	*Hou-N	78	221	15	44	6	1	0	20	13	29	.199	.247	.235	38	-19	-17	13	0	0	0	-2	C/3	-1.7
1981	*Hou-N	40	117	5	28	3	1	1	14	10	17	.239	.299	.308	76	-4	-4	10	1	0	0	0	C	-0.2
1982	Hou-N	65	176	8	35	6	2	4	15	10	40	.199	.242	.324	62	-11	-9	12	0	3	-2	8	C	-0.1
1983	Hou-N	40	87	4	17	2	0	0	12	5	14	.195	.239	.218	29	-8	-8	4	0	0	0	6	C	0.0
1984	KC-A	4	5	0	1	0	0	0	1	0	0	.200	.200	.200	11	-1	-1	0	0	0	0	0	/C	0.0
1985	Tex-A	1	1	0	1	0	0	0	0	0	0	1.000	1.000	1.000	444	0	0	1	0	0	0	0	/C	0.0
Total	9	316	850	50	164	27	6	6	81	52	164	.193	.241	.260	43	-69	-62	51	1	3	-2	17	C/31	-3.8

■ **BLONDIE PURCELL**   Purcell, William Aloysius   b: Paterson, N.J.   5'9.5", 159 lbs.   Deb: 5/01/1879   M

YEAR	TM/L	G	AB	R	H	2B	3B	HR	RBI	BB	SO	AVG	OBP	SLG	PRO+	BR	/A	RC	SB	CS	SBR	FR	POS	TPR
1879	Syr-N	63	277	32	72	6	3	0	25	3	13	.260	.268	.303	99	-4	1	23				-14	OP/C	-1.0
	Cin-N	12	50	10	11	0	0	0	4	0	3	.220	.220	.220	48	-3	-2	2				0	O/P	-0.1
	Yr	75	327	42	83	6	3	0	29	3	16	.254	.261	.291	91	-6	-2	25				-13		-1.1
1880	Cin-N	77	325	48	95	13	6	1	24	5	13	.292	.303	.378	131	9	10	38				-3	OP/S	0.6
1881	Cle-N	20	80	3	14	2	1	0	4	5	8	.175	.224	.225	44	-5	-5	4				-2	O	-0.6
	Buf-N	30	113	15	33	7	2	0	17	8	8	.292	.339	.389	130	4	4	15				-6	O/P	0.0
	Yr	50	193	18	47	9	3	0	21	13	16	.244	.291	.321	95	-1	-1	19				-8		-0.6
1882	Buf-N	84	380	79	105	18	6	2	40	14	27	.276	.302	.371	113	6	5	44				-6	*O/P	-0.1
1883	Phi-N	97	425	70	114	20	5	1	32	13	26	.268	.290	.346	101	-4	2	44				5	3OPM	0.9
1884	Phi-N	103	428	67	108	11	7	1	31	29	30	.252	.300	.318	99	-2	1	44				-1	O/P	-0.6
1885	Phi-a	66	304	71	90	15	5	0		16		.296	.337	.378	121	10	7	40				-1	O/P	0.2
	Bos-N	21	87	9	19	1	1	0	3	3	15	.218	.244	.253	63	-4	-3	6				-3	O	-0.6
1886	Bal-a	26	85	17	19	0	1	0		17		.224	.365	.247	98	1	1	13	13			-1	O/SP	0.2
1887	Bal-a	140	567	101	142	25	8	4		46		.250	.318	.344	92	-10	-4	92	88			-4	*O/P	-0.9
1888	Bal-a	101	406	53	96	9	4	2	39	27		.236	.289	.293	92	-4	-3	40	16			-6	*O/S1	-1.1
	Phi-a	18	66	10	11	3	1	0	6	5		.167	.236	.242	56	-3	-3	6	10			0	O/3	-0.2
	Yr	119	472	63	107	12	5	2	45	32		.227	.281	.286	87	-7	-6	46	26			-6		-1.3
1889	Phi-a	129	507	72	160	19	7	0	85	50	27	.316	.383	.381	122	15	16	84	22			-10	*O	0.1
1890	Phi-a	110	463	110	128	28	3	2		43		.276	.343	.363	114	6	8	76	48			-1	*O	0.1
Total	12	1097	4563	767	1217	177	60	13	310	284	170	.267	.314	.340	105	11	35	569	197			-52	O/P3S1C	-2.7

■ **PID PURDY**   Purdy, Everett Virgil   b: 6/15/04, Beatrice, Neb.   d: 1/16/51, Beatrice, Neb.   BL/TR, 5'6", 150 lbs.   Deb: 9/07/26

YEAR	TM/L	G	AB	R	H	2B	3B	HR	RBI	BB	SO	AVG	OBP	SLG	PRO+	BR	/A	RC	SB	CS	SBR	FR	POS	TPR
1926	Chi-A	11	33	5	6	2	1	0	6	2	1	.182	.229	.303	39	-3	-3	2	0	1	-1	0	/O	-0.3
1927	Cin-N	18	62	15	22	2	4	1	12	4	3	.355	.412	.565	164	5	5	14	0			-2	O	0.2
1928	Cin-N	70	223	32	69	11	1	0	25	23	13	.309	.377	.368	97	-1	-0	31	1			-3	O	-0.4
1929	Cin-N	82	181	22	49	7	5	1	16	19	8	.271	.350	.381	85	-5	-4	24	2			-2	O	-0.8
Total	4	181	499	74	146	22	11	2	59	48	25	.293	.362	.393	97	-4	-2	72	3	1		-7	O	-1.3

■ **JESSE PURNELL**   Purnell, Jesse Rhoades   b: 5/11/1881, Glenside, Pa.   d: 7/4/66, Philadelphia, Pa.   5'5.5", 140 lbs.   Deb: 10/01/04

YEAR	TM/L	G	AB	R	H	2B	3B	HR	RBI	BB	SO	AVG	OBP	SLG	PRO+	BR	/A	RC	SB	CS	SBR	FR	POS	TPR
1904	Phi-N	7	19	2	2	0	0	0	1	4		.105	.261	.105	17	-2	-2	1	1			-1	/3	-0.1

■ **BILLY PURTELL**   Purtell, William Patrick   b: 1/6/1886, Columbus, Ohio   d: 3/17/62, Bradenton, Fla.   BR/TR, 5'9", 170 lbs.   Deb: 4/16/08

YEAR	TM/L	G	AB	R	H	2B	3B	HR	RBI	BB	SO	AVG	OBP	SLG	PRO+	BR	/A	RC	SB	CS	SBR	FR	POS	TPR
1908	Chi-A	26	69	3	9	2	0	0	3	2		.130	.155	.159	3	-7	-7	2	2			6	3	0.1
1909	Chi-A	103	361	34	93	9	3	0	40	19		.258	.302	.299	94	-4	-3	39	14			5	32	0.5
1910	Chi-A	102	368	21	82	5	3	1	36	21		.223	.272	.261	70	-14	-12	28	5			4	*3	-0.3
	Bos-A	49	168	15	35	1	2	1	15	18		.208	.289	.256	69	-5	-6	14	2			-5	3/S	-0.9
	Yr	151	536	36	117	6	5	2	51	39		.218	.278	.259	70	-19	-18	43	7			-0		-1.2
1911	Bos-A	27	82	5	23	5	3	0	7	1		.280	.298	.415	99	-1	-1	10	1			0	3/2SO	-0.9
1914	Det-A	28	76	4	13	4	0	0	3	2	7	.171	.203	.224	27	-7	-7	3	0	2	-1	-1	3/S2	-0.9
Total	5	335	1124	82	255	26	11	2	104	63	7	.227	.275	.275	73	-39	-36	97	24	2		10	3/2SO	-1.5

■ **ED PUTMAN**   Putman, Eddy William   b: 9/25/53, Los Angeles, Cal.   BR/TR, 6'1", 190 lbs.   Deb: 9/07/76

YEAR	TM/L	G	AB	R	H	2B	3B	HR	RBI	BB	SO	AVG	OBP	SLG	PRO+	BR	/A	RC	SB	CS	SBR	FR	POS	TPR
1976	Chi-N	5	7	0	3	0	0	0	0	0	0	.429	.429	.429	132	0	0	0	0	0	0	0	/C1	0.0
1978	Chi-N	17	25	2	5	0	0	0	3	4	6	.200	.310	.200	40	-2	-2	2	0	0	0	1	/31C	-0.1
1979	Det-A	21	39	4	9	3	0	2	4	4	12	.231	.302	.462	99	-0	-0	5	0	1	-1	1	C/1	0.0
Total	3	43	71	6	17	3	0	2	7	8	18	.239	.316	.366	81	-1	-2	7	0	1	-1	1	/C13	-0.1

■ **PAT PUTNAM**   Putnam, Patrick Edward   b: 12/3/53, Bethel, Vt.   BL/TR, 6', 205 lbs.   Deb: 9/02/77

YEAR	TM/L	G	AB	R	H	2B	3B	HR	RBI	BB	SO	AVG	OBP	SLG	PRO+	BR	/A	RC	SB	CS	SBR	FR	POS	TPR
1977	Tex-A	11	26	3	8	4	0	0	3	1	4	.308	.333	.462	113	0	0	3	0	1	-1	-1	/1D	0.0
1978	Tex-A	20	46	4	7	1	0	1	2	2	5	.152	.188	.239	19	-5	-5	2	0	0	0	0	D/1	-0.4
1979	Tex-A	139	426	57	118	19	2	18	64	23	50	.277	.323	.458	109	3	4	57	1	6	-3	0	1D	-0.3
1980	Tex-A	147	410	42	108	16	2	13	55	36	49	.263	.323	.407	102	-1	0	51	0	2	-1	5	*1/3D	-0.4
1981	Tex-A	95	297	33	79	17	2	8	35	17	38	.266	.306	.418	113	1	3	37	4	2	0	4	1/O	0.5
1982	Tex-A	43	122	14	28	8	0	2	9	10	18	.230	.293	.344	78	-4	-4	11	0	2	-1	1	1/3O	-0.4
1983	Sea-A	144	469	58	126	23	2	19	67	39	57	.269	.329	.448	107	6	4	67	2	1	0	3	*1D	0.2
1984	Sea-A	64	155	11	31	6	0	2	16	12	27	.200	.257	.277	49	-11	-11	11	3	0	1	0	DO/1	-0.9
	Min-A	14	38	1	3	1	0	0	4	4	12	.079	.167	.105	-22	-6	-7	1	0	0	0	0	D	-0.6
	Yr	78	193	12	34	7	0	2	20	16	39	.176	.239	.244	34	-17	-17	12	3	0	1	0		-1.5
Total	8	677	1989	223	508	95	8	63	255	144	260	.255	.309	.406	96	-16	-14	241	10	14	-5	12	1D/O3	-2.3

■ **JIM PYBURN**   Pyburn, James Edward   b: 11/1/32, Fairfield, Ala.   BR/TR, 6', 190 lbs.   Deb: 4/17/55

YEAR	TM/L	G	AB	R	H	2B	3B	HR	RBI	BB	SO	AVG	OBP	SLG	PRO+	BR	/A	RC	SB	CS	SBR	FR	POS	TPR
1955	Bal-A	39	98	5	20	2	2	0	7	8	24	.204	.271	.265	48	-8	-7	7	1	1	-0	-4	3/O	-1.0
1956	Bal-A	84	156	23	27	3	3	2	11	17	26	.173	.254	.269	41	-14	-13	11	4	1	1	7	O	-0.7
1957	Bal-A	35	40	8	9	0	0	1	2	9	6	.225	.367	.300	90	-0	-0	5	1	0	0	6	O/C	0.4
Total	3	158	294	36	56	5	5	3	20	34	56	.190	.277	.272	51	-22	-20	23	6	2	1	9	O/3C	-1.3

■ **FRANKIE PYTLAK**   Pytlak, Frank Anthony   b: 7/30/08, Buffalo, N.Y.   d: 5/8/77, Buffalo, N.Y.   BR/TR, 5'7.5", 160 lbs.   Deb: 4/22/32

YEAR	TM/L	G	AB	R	H	2B	3B	HR	RBI	BB	SO	AVG	OBP	SLG	PRO+	BR	/A	RC	SB	CS	SBR	FR	POS	TPR
1932	Cle-A	12	29	5	7	1	1	0	4	3	2	.241	.333	.345	71	-1	-1	4	0	0	0	3	C	0.2
1933	Cle-A	80	248	36	77	10	6	2	33	17	10	.310	.355	.423	101	2	0	36	3	4	-2	10	C	1.1
1934	Cle-A	91	289	46	75	12	4	0	35	36	11	.260	.352	.329	75	-9	-10	37	11	2	2	-11	C	-0.9
1935	Cle-A	55	149	14	44	6	1	1	12	11	4	.295	.348	.369	84	-3	-4	19	3	2	-0	-1	C	0.0
1936	Cle-A	75	224	35	72	15	4	0	31	24	11	.321	.394	.424	101	1	1	39	5	2	0	-6	C	0.0
1937	Cle-A	125	397	60	125	15	6	1	44	52	15	.315	.404	.390	100	3	3	68	16	5	2	8	*C	1.9
1938	Cle-A	113	364	46	112	14	7	1	43	36	15	.308	.374	.393	95	-3	-2	50	5	5	-0	-2	C	-0.7
1939	Cle-A	63	183	20	49	2	5	0	14	20	5	.268	.343	.333	76	-7	-6	22	4	1	1	2	C	0.0
1940	Cle-A	62	149	16	21	2	1	0	16	17	5	.141	.234	.168	6	-21	-20	7	0	1	-1	7	C/O	-0.8
1941	Bos-A	106	336	36	91	23	1	2	39	28	19	.271	.329	.363	81	-9	-10	40	5	7	-3	0	C	-0.5

YEAR	TM/L	G	AB	R	H	2B	3B	HR	RBI	BB	SO	AVG	OBP	SLG	PRO+	BR	/A	RC	SB	CS	SBR	FR	POS	TPR
1945	Bos-A	9	17	1	2	0	0	0	0	3	0	.118	.250	.118	8	-2	-2	1	0	0	0	1	/C	0.0
1946	Bos-A	4	14	1	2	0	0	0	1	0	0	.143	.143	.143	-19	-2	-2	0	0	0	0	2	/C	0.0
Total	12	795	2399	316	677	100	36	7	272	247	97	.282	.355	.363	84	-51	-53	328	56	29	-1	8	C/O	0.1

■ TIM PYZNARSKI   Pyznarski, Timothy Matthew   b: 2/4/60, Chicago, Ill.   BR/TR, 6'2", 195 lbs.   Deb: 9/14/86

YEAR	TM/L	G	AB	R	H	2B	3B	HR	RBI	BB	SO	AVG	OBP	SLG	PRO+	BR	/A	RC	SB	CS	SBR	FR	POS	TPR
1986	SD-N	15	42	3	10	1	0	0	0	4	11	.238	.319	.262	63	-2	-2	4	2	0	1	-0	1	-0.1

■ JIM QUALLS   Qualls, James Robert   b: 10/9/46, Exeter, Cal.   BB/TR, 5'10", 158 lbs.   Deb: 4/10/69

YEAR	TM/L	G	AB	R	H	2B	3B	HR	RBI	BB	SO	AVG	OBP	SLG	PRO+	BR	/A	RC	SB	CS	SBR	FR	POS	TPR
1969	Chi-N	43	120	12	30	5	3	0	9	2	14	.250	.268	.342	62	-5	-7	11	2	1	0	-0	O/2	-0.9
1970	Mon-N	9	9	1	1	0	0	0	1	0	0	.111	.111	.111	-40	-2	-2	0	0	0	0	-0	/2O	-0.1
1972	Chi-A	11	10	0	0	0	0	0	0	0	2	.000	.000	.000	-98	-2	-2	0	0	0	0	1	/O	-0.1
Total	3	63	139	13	31	5	3	0	10	2	16	.223	.239	.302	46	-9	-11	11	2	1	0	-0	/O2	-1.1

■ MEL QUEEN   Queen, Melvin Douglas   b: 3/26/42, Johnson City, N.Y.   BL/TR, 6'1", 189 lbs.   Deb: 4/13/64   C

YEAR	TM/L	G	AB	R	H	2B	3B	HR	RBI	BB	SO	AVG	OBP	SLG	PRO+	BR	/A	RC	SB	CS	SBR	FR	POS	TPR
1964	Cin-N	48	95	7	19	2	0	2	12	4	19	.200	.232	.284	43	-7	-7	5	0	1	-1	2	O	-0.7
1965	Cin-N	5	3	0	0	0	0	0	0	0	1	.000	.000	.000	-94	-1	-1	0	0	0	0	0	/O	0.0
1966	Cin-N	56	55	4	7	1	0	0	5	10	12	.127	.262	.145	16	-6	-7	3	0	0	0	3	O/P	-0.3
1967	Cin-N	49	81	6	17	4	0	0	5	4	10	.210	.247	.259	40	-6	-7	5	2	0	1	-2	P	0.0
1968	Cin-N	10	8	2	1	0	0	0	0	1	3	.125	.222	.125	6	-1	-1	0	0	0	0	0	/P	0.0
1969	Cin-N	2	6	0	1	0	0	0	1	0	2	.167	.167	.167	-6	-1	-1	0	0	0	0	-0	/P	0.0
1970	Cal-A	37	16	1	4	0	0	0	1	0	2	.250	.250	.250	40	-1	-1	1	0	0	0	-1	P	0.0
1971	Cal-A	45	8	0	0	0	0	0	1	1	0	.000	.111	.000	-71	-2	-2	0	0	0	0	-1	P	0.0
1972	Cal-A	17	2	0	0	0	0	0	0	1	1	.000	.333	.000	5	-0	-0	0	0	0	0	-0	P	0.0
Total	9	269	274	20	49	7	0	2	25	21	50	.179	.237	.226	30	-25	-27	15	2	1	0	0	P/O	-1.0

■ BILLY QUEEN   Queen, William Eddleman "Doc"   b: 11/28/28, Gastonia, N.C.   BR/TR, 6'1", 185 lbs.   Deb: 4/13/54

YEAR	TM/L	G	AB	R	H	2B	3B	HR	RBI	BB	SO	AVG	OBP	SLG	PRO+	BR	/A	RC	SB	CS	SBR	FR	POS	TPR
1954	Mil-N	3	2	0	0	0	0	0	0	0	2	.000	.000	.000	-99	-1	-1	0	0	0	0	0	/O	0.0

■ GEORGE QUELLICH   Quellich, George William   b: 2/10/06, Johnsville, Cal.   d: 8/31/58, Johnsville, Cal.   BR/TR, 6'1", 180 lbs.   Deb: 8/01/31

YEAR	TM/L	G	AB	R	H	2B	3B	HR	RBI	BB	SO	AVG	OBP	SLG	PRO+	BR	/A	RC	SB	CS	SBR	FR	POS	TPR
1931	Det-A	13	54	6	12	5	0	1	11	3	4	.222	.263	.370	63	-3	-3	5	1	0	0	1	O	-0.1

■ JOE QUEST   Quest, Joseph L.   b: 11/3/1851, New Castle, Pa.   d: 4/7/23, Cleveland, Ohio   BR/TR, 5'6", 150 lbs.   Deb: 8/30/1871   U

YEAR	TM/L	G	AB	R	H	2B	3B	HR	RBI	BB	SO	AVG	OBP	SLG	PRO+	BR	/A	RC	SB	CS	SBR	FR	POS	TPR
1871	Cle-n	3	13	1	3	1	0	0	2	1	0	.231	.286	.308	75	-0	-0	1	0				/2S	0.0
1878	Ind-n	62	278	45	57	3	2	0	13	12	24	.205	.238	.230	63	-13	-8	16	1				*2	-0.1
1879	Chi-N	83	334	38	69	16	1	0	22	9	33	.207	.227	.260	57	-14	-17	20	14				*2	0.5
1880	Chi-N	82	300	37	71	12	1	0	27	8	16	.237	.256	.283	78	-5	-8	22	4				*2/S3	0.0
1881	Chi-N	78	293	35	72	6	0	1	26	2	29	.246	.251	.276	63	-11	-13	21	6				*2/S	-0.4
1882	Chi-N	42	159	24	32	5	2	0	15	8	16	.201	.240	.258	57	-7	-8	10	-5				2/S	-1.0
1883	Det-N	37	137	22	32	8	2	0	25	10	18	.234	.286	.321	88	-2	-1	13	0				2	-0.2
	StL-a	19	78	12	20	3	1	0			1	.256	.266	.321	83	-1	-2	7	-6				2	-0.6
1884	StL-a	81	310	46	64	9	5	0			19	.206	.257	.268	71	-8	-10	22	-9				*2	-1.5
	Pit-a	12	43	2	9	3	0	0			0	.209	.227	.279	65	-2	-2	3	0				/2S	0.0
	Yr	93	353	48	73	12	5	0			19	.207	.253	.269	70	-10	-12	25	-9					-1.5
1885	Det-N	55	200	24	39	8	2	0	21	14	25	.195	.248	.255	63	-8	-8	13	-1				2S/O	-0.3
1886	Phi-a	42	150	14	31	4	1	0			20	.207	.300	.247	73	-4	-4	13	5				2 S/2	0.0
Total	9	593	2282	299	496	77	17	1	149	103	161	.217	.252	.267	68	-75	-80	159	5				5	2/SO3	-3.6

■ HAL QUICK   Quick, James Harold "Blondie"   b: 10/4/17, Rome, Ga.   d: 3/9/74, Swansea, Ill.   BR/TR, 5'10.5", 163 lbs.   Deb: 9/07/39

YEAR	TM/L	G	AB	R	H	2B	3B	HR	RBI	BB	SO	AVG	OBP	SLG	PRO+	BR	/A	RC	SB	CS	SBR	FR	POS	TPR
1939	Was-A	12	41	3	10	1	0	0	2	1	1	.244	.279	.268	44	-4	-3	3	1	0	0	1	S	0.0

■ FRANK QUILICI   Quilici, Francis Ralph "Guido"   b: 5/11/39, Chicago, Ill.   BR/TR, 6'1", 170 lbs.   Deb: 7/18/65   MC

YEAR	TM/L	G	AB	R	H	2B	3B	HR	RBI	BB	SO	AVG	OBP	SLG	PRO+	BR	/A	RC	SB	CS	SBR	FR	POS	TPR
1965	*Min-A	56	149	16	31	5	1	0	7	15	33	.208	.280	.255	51	-9	-10	11	1	1	-0	3	2/S	-0.3
1967	Min-A	23	19	2	2	1	0	0	0	3	4	.105	.227	.158	14	-2	-2	1	0	0	0	1	2/3S	0.0
1968	Min-A	97	229	22	56	11	4	1	22	21	45	.245	.311	.341	93	-1	-2	25	0	0	0	17	23/S1	2.1
1969	Min-A	118	144	19	25	3	1	2	12	12	22	.174	.237	.250	36	-12	-13	9	2	0	1	24	32/S	1.5
1970	*Min-A	111	141	19	32	3	0	2	12	15	16	.227	.301	.291	63	-7	-7	11	0	2	-1	15	23/S	1.4
Total	5	405	682	78	146	23	6	5	53	66	120	.214	.284	.287	63	-31	-33	57	3	3	-1	60	23/S1	4.7

■ LEE QUILLEN   Quillen, Leon Abner   b: 5/5/1882, North Branch, Minn.   d: 5/14/65, St.Paul, Minn.   TR, 5'10", 165 lbs.   Deb: 9/30/06

YEAR	TM/L	G	AB	R	H	2B	3B	HR	RBI	BB	SO	AVG	OBP	SLG	PRO+	BR	/A	RC	SB	CS	SBR	FR	POS	TPR
1906	Chi-A	4	9	1	3	0	0	0	0	0	0	.333	.333	.333	114	0	0	1	1			-2	/S	-0.1
1907	Chi-A	49	151	17	29	5	0	0	14	10		.192	.242	.225	52	-8	-8	11	8			0	3	-0.4
Total	2	53	160	18	32	5	0	0	14	10		.200	.247	.231	56	-8	-7	12	9			-2	/3S	-0.5

■ QUINLAN   Quinlan   Deb: 9/07/1874

YEAR	TM/L	G	AB	R	H	2B	3B	HR	RBI	BB	SO	AVG	OBP	SLG	PRO+	BR	/A	RC	SB	CS	SBR	FR	POS	TPR
1874	Phi-n	1	4	0	1	0	0	0			0	.250	.250	.250	58	-0	-0	0					S	0.0

■ FRANK QUINLAN   Quinlan, Francis Patrick   b: 3/9/1869, Marlboro, Mass.   d: 5/4/04, Brockton, Mass.   Deb: 10/05/1891

YEAR	TM/L	G	AB	R	H	2B	3B	HR	RBI	BB	SO	AVG	OBP	SLG	PRO+	BR	/A	RC	SB	CS	SBR	FR	POS	TPR
1891	Bos-a	2	5	0	0	0	0	0	0	0	2	.000	.000	.000	-99	-1	-1	0	0			-0	/CO	-0.1

■ FINNERS QUINLAN   Quinlan, Thomas Finners   b: 10/21/1887, Scranton, Pa.   d: 2/17/66, Scranton, Pa.   BL/TL, 5'8", 154 lbs.   Deb: 9/06/13

YEAR	TM/L	G	AB	R	H	2B	3B	HR	RBI	BB	SO	AVG	OBP	SLG	PRO+	BR	/A	RC	SB	CS	SBR	FR	POS	TPR
1913	StL-N	13	50	1	8	0	0	0	1	1	9	.160	.176	.160	-4	-7	-7	1	0			1	O	-0.6
1915	Chi-A	42	114	11	22	3	0	0	7	4	11	.193	.270	.219	45	-7	-8	7	3	4	-2	-1	O	-1.3
Total	2	55	164	12	30	3	0	0	8	5	20	.183	.243	.201	31	-14	-14	9	3	4		-1	/O	-1.9

■ TOM QUINLAN   Quinlan, Thomas Raymond   b: 3/27/68, St.Paul, Minn.   BR/TR, 6'3", 200 lbs.   Deb: 9/04/90

YEAR	TM/L	G	AB	R	H	2B	3B	HR	RBI	BB	SO	AVG	OBP	SLG	PRO+	BR	/A	RC	SB	CS	SBR	FR	POS	TPR
1990	Tor-A	1	2	0	1	0	0	0	0	0	1	.500	.667	.500	235	1	1	1	0	0	0	-0	/3	0.0

■ QUINN   Quinn   Deb: 9/09/1875

YEAR	TM/L	G	AB	R	H	2B	3B	HR	RBI	BB	SO	AVG	OBP	SLG	PRO+	BR	/A	RC	SB	CS	SBR	FR	POS	TPR
1875	Atl-n	2	7	2	1	0	0	0			0	.143	.143	.143	-1	-1	-1	0					/O	0.0

■ QUINN   Quinn   Deb: 6/21/1877

YEAR	TM/L	G	AB	R	H	2B	3B	HR	RBI	BB	SO	AVG	OBP	SLG	PRO+	BR	/A	RC	SB	CS	SBR	FR	POS	TPR
1877	Chi-N	4	14	1	1	0	0	0	0	1	0	.071	.133	.071	-30	-2	-2	0				-0	/O	-0.1

■ QUINN   Quinn   Deb: 9/07/1881

YEAR	TM/L	G	AB	R	H	2B	3B	HR	RBI	BB	SO	AVG	OBP	SLG	PRO+	BR	/A	RC	SB	CS	SBR	FR	POS	TPR
1881	Bos-N	1	4	0	0	0	0	0	0	0	0	.000	.000	.000	-99	-1	-1	0				0	/1	0.0
	Wor-N	2	7	0	1	0	0	0	1	0	2	.143	.250	.143	25	-1	-1	0				-1	/C	-0.1
	Yr	3	11	0	1	0	0	0	1	0	2	.091	.167	.091	-16	-1	-1	0				-1		-0.1

■ FRANK QUINN   Quinn, Frank J.   b: 1876, Grand Rapids, Mich.   d: 2/17/20, Camden, Ind.   5'8",   Deb: 8/09/1899

YEAR	TM/L	G	AB	R	H	2B	3B	HR	RBI	BB	SO	AVG	OBP	SLG	PRO+	BR	/A	RC	SB	CS	SBR	FR	POS	TPR
1899	Chi-N	12	34	6	6	0	1	0	1		6	.176	.300	.235	51	-2	-2	3	1			-3	O/2	-0.5

■ JOHN QUINN   Quinn, John Edward "Pick"   b: 9/12/1885, Framingham, Mass.   d: 4/9/56, Marlboro, Mass.   BR/TR, 5'11", 150 lbs.   Deb: 10/09/11

YEAR	TM/L	G	AB	R	H	2B	3B	HR	RBI	BB	SO	AVG	OBP	SLG	PRO+	BR	/A	RC	SB	CS	SBR	FR	POS	TPR
1911	Phi-N	1	2	0	0	0	0	0	0	0	0	.000	.000	.000	-99	-1	-1	0	0			0	/C	0.0

■ JOE QUINN   Quinn, Joseph C.   b: 1851, Chicago, Ill.   d: 1/2/09, Chicago, Ill.   5'8.5", 148 lbs.   Deb: 7/26/1871

YEAR	TM/L	G	AB	R	H	2B	3B	HR	RBI	BB	SO	AVG	OBP	SLG	PRO+	BR	/A	RC	SB	CS	SBR	FR	POS	TPR
1871	Kek-n	5	17	8	4	0	0	0	2	4	0	.235	.381	.235	81	-0	-0	3	3				/C	0.0
1875	Wes-n	11	43	4	14	2	0	0			0	.326	.326	.372	133	2	1	5					/CO	0.1

YEAR	TM/L	G	AB	R	H	2B	3B	HR	RBI	BB	SO	AVG	OBP	SLG	PRO+	BR	/A	RC	SB	CS	SBR	FR	POS	TPR
	Har-n	5	13	1	3	0	0	0		1		.231	.286	.231	77	-0	-0	1					/CO	0.0
	Chi-n	17	59	12	14	0	0	0		0		.237	.237	.237	64	-2	-2	3					C/O	-0.1
	Yr	33	115	17	31	2	0	0		1		.270	.276	.287	92	-1	-1	9						0.0
Total	2 n	38	132	25	35	2	0	0		5		.265	.292	.280	91	-1	-1	12					/CO	0.0

■ JOE QUINN

Quinn, Joseph J. b: 12/25/1864, Sydney, Australia d: 11/12/40, St.Louis, Mo. BR/TR, 5'7", 158 lbs. Deb: 4/26/1884 M

YEAR	TM/L	G	AB	R	H	2B	3B	HR	RBI	BB	SO	AVG	OBP	SLG	PRO+	BR	/A	RC	SB	CS	SBR	FR	POS	TPR
1884	StL-U	103	429	74	116	21	1	0			9	.270	.285	.324	102	2	-0	41	0			-1	*1/OS	-0.1
1885	StL-N	97	343	27	73	8	2	0	15	9	38	.213	.233	.248	59	-17	-14	20				-10	O31	-2.5
1886	StL-N	75	271	33	63	11	3	1	21	8	31	.232	.254	.306	75	-10	-8	25	12			1	O2/13S	-0.5
1888	Bos-N	38	156	19	47	8	3	4	29	2	5	.301	.310	.468	145	7	7	27	12			-7	2	0.1
1889	Bos-N	112	444	57	116	13	5	2	69	25	21	.261	.308	.327	74	-13	-17	53	24			-29	S2/3	-3.4
1890	Bos-P	130	509	87	153	19	8	7	82	44	24	.301	.359	.411	100	4	-2	87	29			15	*2	1.6
1891	Bos-N	124	508	70	122	8	10	3	63	28	28	.240	.288	.313	69	-16	-25	54	24			-23	*2	-3.9
1892	*Bos-N	143	532	63	116	14	1	1	59	35	40	.218	.275	.254	57	-24	-31	43	17			2	*2	-2.6
1893	StL-N	135	547	68	126	18	6	0	71	33	7	.230	.279	.285	51	-38	-39	51	24			-30	*2	-5.7
1894	StL-N	106	405	59	116	18	1	4	61	24	8	.286	.328	.365	68	-21	-21	58	25			22	*2	0.5
1895	StL-N	134	543	84	169	19	9	2	74	36	6	.311	.356	.390	96	-4	-3	85	22			-2	*2M	0.2
1896	StL-N	48	191	19	40	6	1	1	17	9	5	.209	.252	.267	40	-17	-16	15	8			3	2	-0.9
	*Bal-N	24	82	22	27	1	1	0	5	6	1	.329	.375	.366	96	-0	-0	14	6			-3	/2O3S	-0.2
	Yr	72	273	41	67	7	2	1	22	15	6	.245	.290	.297	58	-17	-16	28	14			-1		-1.1
1897	Bal-N	75	285	33	74	11	4	1	45	13		.260	.299	.337	70	-13	-13	33	12			9	3S2/O1	-0.1
1898	Bal-N	12	32	5	8	1	0	0	5	1		.250	.273	.281	60	-2	-2	3	0			1	/32O	0.0
	StL-N	103	375	35	94	10	5	0	36	24		.251	.301	.304	74	-12	-13	39	13			-1	2S/O	-0.8
	Yr	115	407	40	102	11	5	0	41	25		.251	.299	.302	73	-13	-14	42	13			-1		-0.8
1899	Cle-N	147	615	73	176	24	6	0	72	21		.286	.312	.345	89	-16	-9	75	22			3	*2M	0.2
1900	StL-N	22	80	12	21	2	0	1	11	10		.262	.344	.325	88	-1	-1	11	4			-9	2/S3	-0.7
	Cin-N	74	266	18	73	5	2	0	25	16		.274	.316	.308	77	-9	-8	29	7			-18	2	-1.9
	Yr	96	346	30	94	7	2	1	36	26		.272	.323	.312	79	-10	-9	39	11			-27		-2.6
1901	Was-A	66	266	33	67	11	2	2	34	11		.252	.287	.331	74	-10	-9	28	7			-14	2	-2.3
Total	17	1768	6879	891	1797	228	70	29	794	364	214	.261	.302	.327	77	-207	-222	792	268			-93	*2SO1/3	-23.0

■ TOM QUINN

Quinn, Thomas Oscar b: 4/25/1864, Annapolis, Md. d: 7/24/32, Pittsburgh, Pa. BR/TR, 5'8", 180 lbs. Deb: 9/02/1886

YEAR	TM/L	G	AB	R	H	2B	3B	HR	RBI	BB	SO	AVG	OBP	SLG	PRO+	BR	/A	RC	SB	CS	SBR	FR	POS	TPR
1886	Pit-a	3	11	1	0	0	0	0		0		.000	.000	.000	-99	-2	-2	0	1			-1	/C	-0.2
1889	Bal-a	55	194	18	34	2	1	1	15	19	22	.175	.252	.211	34	-16	-17	12	6			7	C	-0.3
1890	Pit-P	55	207	23	44	4	3	1	15	17	8	.213	.282	.275	55	-14	-11	17	1			-25	C	-2.7
Total	3	113	412	42	78	6	4	2	30	36	30	.189	.261	.238	41	-33	-30	29	8			-19	C	-3.2

■ LUIS QUINONES

Quinones, Luis Raul b: 4/28/62, Ponce, P.R. BB/TR, 5'11", 165 lbs. Deb: 5/27/83

YEAR	TM/L	G	AB	R	H	2B	3B	HR	RBI	BB	SO	AVG	OBP	SLG	PRO+	BR	/A	RC	SB	CS	SBR	FR	POS	TPR
1983	Oak-A	19	42	5	8	2	1	0	4	1	4	.190	.209	.286	37	-4	-3	2	1	1	-0	3	/23OSD	0.0
1986	SF-N	71	106	13	19	1	3	0	11	3	17	.179	.209	.245	26	-11	-10	6	3	1	-0	-7	S3/2	-1.4
1987	Chi-N	49	101	12	22	6	0	0	8	10	16	.218	.288	.277	49	-7	-8	9	0	0	0	-6	S/23	-1.0
1988	Cin-N	23	52	4	12	3	0	1	11	2	11	.231	.259	.346	70	-2	-2	5	1	1	0	1	S/23	0.0
1989	Cin-N	97	340	43	83	13	4	12	34	25	46	.244	.302	.412	99	-0	-1	42	2	4	-2	-5	23/S	-0.7
1990	*Cin-N	83	145	10	35	7	0	2	17	13	29	.241	.308	.331	74	-5	-5	15	1	0	0	9	32/S1	0.6
Total	6	342	786	87	179	32	8	15	85	54	123	.228	.282	.346	73	-29	-30	79	8	7	-2	-5	3/S2DO1	-2.5

■ REY QUINONES

Quinones, Rey Francisco (Santiago) b: 11/11/63, Rio Pedras, P.R. BR/TR, 5'11", 160 lbs. Deb: 5/17/86

YEAR	TM/L	G	AB	R	H	2B	3B	HR	RBI	BB	SO	AVG	OBP	SLG	PRO+	BR	/A	RC	SB	CS	SBR	FR	POS	TPR
1986	Bos-A	62	190	26	45	12	1	2	15	19	26	.237	.316	.342	79	-5	-5	20	3	2	-0	-8	S	-0.9
	Sea-A	36	122	6	23	4	0	0	7	5	31	.189	.220	.221	21	-13	-13	6	1	1	-0	1	S	-1.0
	Yr	98	312	32	68	16	1	2	22	24	57	.218	.280	.295	56	-19	-19	26	4	3	-1	-7		-1.9
1987	Sea-A	135	478	55	132	18	2	12	56	26	71	.276	.319	.397	84	-8	-12	57	1	3	-2	-10	*S	-1.5
1988	Sea-A	140	499	63	124	30	3	12	52	23	71	.248	.286	.393	84	-9	-12	52	0	3	-2	3	*S/D	-0.4
1989	Sea-A	7	19	2	2	0	0	0	0	1	1	.105	.150	.105	-26	-3	-3	0	0	0	0	-2	/S	-0.4
	Pit-N	71	225	21	47	11	0	3	29	15	40	.209	.261	.298	62	-12	-11	17	0	2	-1	-11	S	-2.0
Total	4	451	1533	173	373	75	6	29	159	89	240	.243	.290	.357	74	-52	-57	153	5	11	-5	-27	S/D	-6.2

■ CARLOS QUINTANA

Quintana, Carlos Narcis (Hernandez) b: 8/26/65, Estado Miranda, Ven BR/TR, 6', 175 lbs. Deb: 9/16/88

YEAR	TM/L	G	AB	R	H	2B	3B	HR	RBI	BB	SO	AVG	OBP	SLG	PRO+	BR	/A	RC	SB	CS	SBR	FR	POS	TPR
1988	Bos-A	5	6	1	2	0	0	0	2	3		.333	.500	.333	133	1	0	1	0	0	0	0	/OD	0.1
1989	Bos-A	34	77	6	16	5	0	0	6	7	12	.208	.274	.273	51	-5	-5	5	0	0	0	-1	O/1D	-0.6
1990	*Bos-A	149	512	56	147	28	0	7	67	52	74	.287	.355	.383	102	5	2	67	1	2	-1	14	*1/O	0.4
Total	3	188	595	63	165	33	0	7	75	61	89	.277	.347	.368	95	1	-3	73	1	2	-1	13	1/OD	-0.1

■ MARSHALL QUINTON

Quinton, Marshall J. b: Philadelphia, Pa. 5'11", 190 lbs. Deb: 8/07/1884

YEAR	TM/L	G	AB	R	H	2B	3B	HR	RBI	BB	SO	AVG	OBP	SLG	PRO+	BR	/A	RC	SB	CS	SBR	FR	POS	TPR
1884	Ric-a	26	94	12	22	5	0	0		0		.234	.242	.287	75	-3	-2	7				-8	CO/S	-0.8
1885	Phi-a	7	29	6	6	1	0	0		1		.207	.258	.241	57	-1	-1	2				2	/C	0.1
Total	2	33	123	18	28	6	0	0		1		.228	.246	.276	71	-4	-4	9				-6	/COS	-0.7

■ JAMIE QUIRK

Quirk, James Patrick b: 10/22/54, Whittier, Cal. BL/TR, 6'4", 190 lbs. Deb: 9/04/75 C

YEAR	TM/L	G	AB	R	H	2B	3B	HR	RBI	BB	SO	AVG	OBP	SLG	PRO+	BR	/A	RC	SB	CS	SBR	FR	POS	TPR
1975	KC-A	14	39	2	10	0	0	1	5	2	7	.256	.293	.333	75	-1	-1	4	0	0	0	0	O/3D	0.0
1976	*KC-A	64	114	11	28	6	0	1	15	2	22	.246	.259	.325	70	-5	-5	8	0	0	0	-1	DS3/1	-0.4
1977	Mil-A	93	221	16	48	14	1	3	13	8	47	.217	.251	.330	57	-14	-14	17	0	1	-1	0	DO/3	-1.3
1978	KC-A	17	29	3	6	2	0	0	2	5	4	.207	.324	.276	68	-1	-1	3	0	0	0	2	3/SD	0.1
1979	KC-A	51	79	8	24	6	1	1	11	5	13	.304	.353	.443	111	1	1	13	0	0	0	2	/CS3D	0.4
1980	KC-A	62	163	13	45	5	0	5	21	7	24	.276	.310	.399	92	-2	-2	18	3	2	-0	1	3C/O1D	0.0
1981	KC-A	46	100	8	25	7	0	0	10	6	17	.250	.299	.320	79	-3	-3	8	0	2	-1	-1	C/32O	-0.4
1982	KC-A	36	78	8	18	3	0	1	11	5	15	.231	.259	.308	55	-5	-5	6	0	0	0	2	C/13O	0.1
1983	StL-N	48	86	3	18	2	1	2	11	6	27	.209	.269	.326	64	-4	-4	7	0	0	0	-5	C/3S	-0.8
1984	Chi-A	3	2	0	0	0	0	0	1	0	2	.000	.000	.000	-96	-1	-1	0	0	0	0	0	/3	0.1
	Cle-A	1	1	1	1	0	0	0	1	0	0	1.000	1.000	4.000	1189	1	1	4	0	0	0	0	/C	0.1
	Yr	4	3	1	1	0	0	0	2	0	2	.333	.333	1.333	324	1	1	1	0	0	0	0		0.1
1985	*KC-A	19	57	3	16	3	1	0	4	2	9	.281	.305	.368	83	-1	-1	6	0	0	0	-4	C/1	-0.4
1986	KC-A	80	219	24	47	10	0	8	26	17	41	.215	.274	.370	72	-9	-9	22	0	1	-1	9	C3/1O	0.1
1987	KC-A	109	296	24	70	17	0	5	33	28	56	.236	.311	.345	72	-11	-12	32	1	0	0	-4	*C/S	-0.6
1988	KC-A	84	196	22	47	7	1	8	25	28	41	.240	.338	.408	107	2	2	27	1	5	-3	13	C/13	1.6
1989	NY-A	13	24	0	2	0	0	0	0	0	3	.083	.185	.083	-22	-4	-4	0	0	1	-1	1	/CSD	-0.2
	Oak-A	9	10	1	2	0	0	0	1	0	4	.200	.200	.500	95	-0	-0	1	0	0	0	-0	/3C1O	0.1
	Bal-A	25	51	5	11	2	0	0	9	9	11	.216	.333	.255	70	-2	-2	4	0	1	-1	3	C	0.1
	Yr	47	85	6	15	2	0	1	10	12	20	.176	.278	.235	47	-6	-6	5	0	2	-1	3		-0.1
1990	*Oak-A	56	121	12	34	5	1	3	26	14	34	.281	.360	.413	119	3	3	19	0	0	0	-2	C/13OD	0.1
Total	16	830	1886	164	452	89	6	40	219	145	379	.240	.298	.357	79	-54	-56	199	5	13	-6	17	C3/DO1S2	-1.6

■ JOHN RABB

Rabb, John Andrew b: 6/23/60, Los Angeles, Cal. BR/TR, 6'1", 180 lbs. Deb: 9/04/82

YEAR	TM/L	G	AB	R	H	2B	3B	HR	RBI	BB	SO	AVG	OBP	SLG	PRO+	BR	/A	RC	SB	CS	SBR	FR	POS	TPR
1982	SF-N	2	2	0	1	0	0	0	0	0	1	.500	.500	1.500	441	1	1	2	0	0	0	0	/O	0.1
1983	SF-N	40	104	10	24	9	0	1	14	9	17	.231	.292	.346	79	-3	-3	10	0	1	0	4	C/O	0.2
1984	SF-N	54	82	10	16	1	0	3	9	10	33	.195	.283	.317	71	-3	-3	8	1	1	-0	-0	1/OC	-0.4

YEAR	TM/L	G	AB	R	H	2B	3B	HR	RBI	BB	SO	AVG	OBP	SLG	PRO+	BR	/A	RC	SB	CS	SBR	FR	POS	TPR
1985	Atl-N	3	2	0	0	0	0	0	0	0	1	.000	.000	.000	-94	-1	-1	0	0	0	0	0	/O	0.0
1988	Sea-A	9	14	2	5	2	0	0	4	0	1	.357	.357	.500	131	1	1	3	0	0	0	0	/O1D	0.1
Total	5	108	204	22	46	12	1	4	27	19	53	.225	.291	.353	81	-6	-5	22	2	1	0	4	/C1OD	0.0

■ **JOE RABBITT**   Rabbitt, Joseph Patrick   b: 1/16/1900, Frontenac, Kan.   d: 12/5/69, Norwalk, Conn.   BL/TR, 5'10", 165 lbs.   Deb: 9/15/22

YEAR	TM/L	G	AB	R	H	2B	3B	HR	RBI	BB	SO	AVG	OBP	SLG	PRO+	BR	/A	RC	SB	CS	SBR	FR	POS	TPR
1922	Cle-A	2	3	1	1	0	0	0	0	0	0	.333	.333	.333	74	-0	-0	0	0	0	0	-0	/O	0.0

■ **MARV RACKLEY**   Rackley, Marvin Eugene   b: 7/25/21, Seneca, S.C.   BL/TL, 5'10", 170 lbs.   Deb: 4/15/47

YEAR	TM/L	G	AB	R	H	2B	3B	HR	RBI	BB	SO	AVG	OBP	SLG	PRO+	BR	/A	RC	SB	CS	SBR	FR	POS	TPR
1947	Bro-N	18	9	2	2	0	0	0	2	1	0	.222	.300	.222	39	-1	-1	1	0			2	/O	0.1
1948	Bro-N	88	281	55	92	13	5	0	15	19	25	.327	.370	.409	107	4	3	44	8			-2	O	-0.3
1949	*Bro-N	9	9	2	4	1	0	0	1	1	0	.444	.500	.556	175	1	1	3	0			-0	/O	0.1
	Pit-N	11	35	5	11	2	0	0	2	2	3	.314	.351	.371	92	-0	-0	5	1			0	/O	0.0
	*Bro-N	54	141	23	41	4	1	1	14	13	8	.291	.351	.355	86	-2	-3	18	1			-3	O	-0.7
	Yr	74	185	30	56	7	1	1	17	16	11	.303	.358	.368	91	-1	-2	25	2			-3		-0.6
1950	Cin-N	5	2	0	1	0	0	0	1	0	0	.500	.500	.500	163	0	0	1	0			0	H	0.0
Total	4	185	477	87	151	20	6	1	35	36	36	.317	.365	.390	100	3	1	71	10			-2	O	-0.8

■ **CHARLEY RADBOURN**   Radbourn, Charles Gardner "Old Hoss"   b: 12/11/1854, Rochester, N.Y.   d: 2/5/1897, Bloomington, Ill.   BR/TL, 5'9", 168 lbs.   Deb: 5/05/1880   H

YEAR	TM/L	G	AB	R	H	2B	3B	HR	RBI	BB	SO	AVG	OBP	SLG	PRO+	BR	/A	RC	SB	CS	SBR	FR	POS	TPR
1880	Buf-N	6	21	1	3	0	0	0	1	0	1	.143	.143	.143	-3	-2	-2	0				4	/O2	0.2
1881	Pro-N	72	270	27	59	9	0	0	28	10	15	.219	.246	.252	58	-13	-12	17				-2	POS	0.0
1882	Pro-N	83	326	30	78	11	0	1	32	12	22	.239	.266	.282	76	-8	-8	25				1	PO/S	0.0
1883	Pro-N	89	381	59	108	11	3	3	48	14	16	.283	.309	.352	98	0	-1	42				3	*PO/1	0.0
1884	*Pro-N	87	361	48	83	7	1	1	37	26	42	.230	.282	.263	74	-11	-9	27				-5	*P/O1S2	0.0
1885	Pro-N	66	249	34	58	9	2	0	22	36	27	.233	.330	.285	104	2	3	24				1	PO/2	0.0
1886	Bos-N	66	253	30	60	5	1	2	22	17	36	.237	.285	.289	78	-7	-6	23	5			3	P	0.0
1887	Bos-N	51	175	25	40	2	1	1	24	18	21	.229	.308	.280	66	-7	-7	17	6			-3	P/O	0.0
1888	Bos-N	24	79	6	17	1	0	0	6	3	14	.215	.262	.228	58	-3	-4	6	4			-1	P	0.0
1889	Bos-N	35	122	17	23	1	0	1	13	9	19	.189	.256	.221	33	-10	-12	8	3			4	P/O3	0.0
1890	Bos-P	45	154	20	39	6	0	0	16	9	20	.253	.299	.292	56	-9	-11	16	7			1	P/O1	0.0
1891	Cin-N	29	96	11	17	2	2	0	10	4	11	.177	.225	.240	36	-8	-8	6	1			-3	P/O3	0.0
Total	12	653	2487	308	585	64	11	9	259	158	244	.235	.283	.281	73	-77	-77	212	26			2	PO/S123	0.2

■ **JOHN RADCLIFF**   Radcliff, John Y.   b: 6/1848, Pennsylvania   d: 7/26/11, Ocean City, N.J.   5'6", 140 lbs.   Deb: 5/20/1871

YEAR	TM/L	G	AB	R	H	2B	3B	HR	RBI	BB	SO	AVG	OBP	SLG	PRO+	BR	/A	RC	SB	CS	SBR	FR	POS	TPR
1871	Ath-n	28	145	47	44	7	5	0	22	6	1	.303	.331	.421	115	3	3	22	5				*S	0.2
1872	Bal-n	56	298	70	87	10	4	1			1	.292	.294	.362	97	0	-3	33					*S/32	-0.1
1873	Bal-n	45	247	60	71	10	1	0			3	.287	.296	.336	86	-4	-4	25					S3	-0.2
1874	Phi-n	23	102	20	26	6	0	1			2	.255	.269	.343	90	-1	-1	10					O/2S13	0.0
1875	Cen-n	5	24	2	4	0	0	0			0	.167	.167	.167	17	-2	-2	1					/S	-0.1
Total	5 n	157	816	199	232	33	10	2			12	.284	.295	.357	94	-4	-7	91					S/3021	-0.2

■ **RIP RADCLIFF**   Radcliff, Raymond Allen   b: 1/19/06, Kiowa, Okla.   d: 5/23/62, Enid, Okla.   BL/TL, 5'10", 170 lbs.   Deb: 9/17/34

YEAR	TM/L	G	AB	R	H	2B	3B	HR	RBI	BB	SO	AVG	OBP	SLG	PRO+	BR	/A	RC	SB	CS	SBR	FR	POS	TPR
1934	Chi-A	14	56	7	15	2	1	0	5	0	2	.268	.268	.339	54	-4	-4	5	1	0	0	0	O	-0.2
1935	Chi-A	146	623	95	178	28	8	10	68	53	21	.286	.346	.404	91	-7	-9	88	4	4	-1	-16	*O	-2.5
1936	Chi-A	138	618	120	207	31	7	8	82	44	12	.335	.381	.447	100	3	-0	105	6	3	0	-21	*O	-2.1
1937	Chi-A	144	584	105	190	38	10	4	79	53	25	.325	.383	.445	108	8	8	102	6	1	1	-5	*O	0.0
1938	Chi-A	129	503	64	166	23	6	5	81	36	17	.330	.376	.429	99	1	-1	80	5	7	-3	-1	O1	-0.6
1939	Chi-A	113	397	49	105	25	2	2	53	26	21	.264	.313	.353	68	-18	-20	44	6	4	-1	-12	O1	-3.4
1940	StL-A	150	584	105	**200**	33	9	7	81	47	20	.342	.392	.466	119	19	17	109	6	4	1	-7	*O/1	0.0
1941	StL-A	19	71	12	20	2	2	2	14	10	1	.282	.370	.451	112	2	1	12	1	1	-0	-3	O/1	-0.2
	Det-A	96	379	47	120	14	5	3	40	19	13	.317	.351	.404	90	-1	-6	53	4	4	-1	-6	O	-1.7
	Yr	115	450	59	140	16	7	5	54	29	14	.311	.354	.411	94	1	-5	66	5	5	-2	-9		-1.9
1942	Det-A	62	144	13	36	5	0	1	20	9	6	.250	.294	.306	64	-6	-8	13	0	1	-1	-1	O/1	-1.0
1943	Det-A	70	115	3	30	4	0	0	10	13	3	.261	.341	.296	81	-1	-2	12	1	1	-0	-1	O/1	-0.4
Total	10	1081	4074	598	1267	205	50	42	533	310	141	.311	.362	.417	96	-5	-24	623	40	30	-6	-72	O/1	-12.1

■ **DAVE RADER**   Rader, David Martin   b: 12/26/48, Claremore, Okla.   BL/TR, 5'11", 165 lbs.   Deb: 9/05/71

YEAR	TM/L	G	AB	R	H	2B	3B	HR	RBI	BB	SO	AVG	OBP	SLG	PRO+	BR	/A	RC	SB	CS	SBR	FR	POS	TPR
1971	SF-N	3	4	0	0	0	0	0	0	0	0	.000	.000	.000	-99	-1	-1	0	0	0	0	-0	/C	0.0
1972	SF-N	133	459	44	119	14	1	6	41	29	31	.259	.308	.333	81	-11	-12	45	1	2	-1	-14	*C	-2.0
1973	SF-N	148	462	59	106	15	4	9	41	63	22	.229	.330	.338	82	-8	-10	51	0	0	0	-14	*C	-1.5
1974	SF-N	113	323	26	94	16	2	1	26	31	21	.291	.353	.362	96	1	-1	41	1	0	0	-9	*C	-0.5
1975	SF-N	98	292	39	85	15	0	5	31	32	30	.291	.363	.394	106	4	3	41	1	0	0	-3	C	0.4
1976	SF-N	88	255	20	67	15	0	1	22	27	21	.263	.333	.333	87	-3	-4	27	2	0	1	-8	C	-0.7
1977	StL-N	66	114	15	30	7	1	1	16	9	10	.263	.317	.368	85	-3	-2	15	1	0	0	4	C	0.1
1978	Chi-N	116	305	29	62	13	3	3	36	34	26	.203	.285	.295	56	-15	-20	24	0	1	-0	-13	*C	-3.1
1979	Phi-N	31	54	3	11	1	1	1	5	6	7	.204	.283	.315	61	-3	-3	4	0	0	0	-4	C	-0.5
1980	Bos-A	50	137	14	45	11	0	3	17	14	12	.328	.391	.474	129	7	6	25	1	1	-0	3	C/D	1.0
Total	10	846	2405	254	619	107	12	30	235	245	180	.257	.329	.349	86	-32	-45	272	8	4	0	-58	C/D	-6.8

■ **DON RADER**   Rader, Donald Russell   b: 9/5/1893, Wolcott, Ind.   d: 6/26/83, Walla Walla, Wash   BL/TR, 5'10", 164 lbs.   Deb: 7/25/13

YEAR	TM/L	G	AB	R	H	2B	3B	HR	RBI	BB	SO	AVG	OBP	SLG	PRO+	BR	/A	RC	SB	CS	SBR	FR	POS	TPR
1913	Chi-A	4	3	1	1	0	0	0	0	0	0	.333	.333	.667	193	0	0	1	0			-0	/3O	0.0
1921	Phi-N	9	32	4	9	2	0	0	3	3	5	.281	.343	.344	76	-1	-1	4	0	0	0	-6	/S	-0.5
Total	2	13	35	5	10	3	0	0	3	3	5	.286	.342	.371	84	-0	-1	5	0	0		-6	/SO3	-0.5

■ **DOUG RADER**   Rader, Douglas Lee "Rojo" or "The Red Rooster"   b: 7/30/44, Chicago, Ill.   BR/TR, 6'2", 208 lbs.   Deb: 7/31/67   MC

YEAR	TM/L	G	AB	R	H	2B	3B	HR	RBI	BB	SO	AVG	OBP	SLG	PRO+	BR	/A	RC	SB	CS	SBR	FR	POS	TPR
1967	Hou-N	47	162	24	54	10	4	2	26	7	31	.333	.368	.481	146	8	9	27	0	3	-2	-1	1/3	0.5
1968	Hou-N	98	333	42	89	16	4	6	43	31	51	.267	.332	.393	119	7	8	43	2	2	-1	1	3/1	0.9
1969	Hou-N	155	569	62	140	25	3	11	83	62	103	.246	.327	.359	94	-6	-4	65	1	5	-3	14	*3/1	0.8
1970	Hou-N	156	576	90	145	25	3	25	87	57	102	.252	.323	.436	106	0	3	76	3	2	-0	24	*3/1	2.1
1971	Hou-N	135	484	51	118	21	4	12	56	40	112	.244	.306	.378	95	-5	-4	56	5	1	1	2	*3	-0.1
1972	Hou-N	152	553	70	131	24	7	22	90	57	120	.237	.314	.425	110	5	6	70	5	5	-2	18	*3	2.3
1973	Hou-N	154	574	79	146	26	0	21	89	46	97	.254	.313	.409	99	-2	-2	73	4	3	-1	-5	*3	-1.1
1974	Hou-N	152	533	61	137	27	3	17	78	60	131	.257	.337	.415	114	6	9	74	7	2	1	5	*3	1.2
1975	Hou-N	129	448	41	100	23	2	12	48	42	101	.223	.297	.364	89	-12	-8	60	3	4	-2	14	*3/S	1.8
1976	SD-N	139	471	45	121	22	4	9	55	55	150	.257	.338	.378	112	2	7	60	3	4	-2	14	*3	1.8
1977	SD-N	52	170	19	46	8	3	5	27	33	40	.271	.392	.441	137	7	9	30	0	1	-1	1	3	0.9
	Tor-A	96	313	47	75	18	2	13	40	38	65	.240	.328	.435	104	2	2	44	2	1	0	0	3D/1O	0.1
Total	11	1465	5186	631	1302	245	39	155	722	528	1055	.251	.325	.403	106	11	33	665	37	33	-9	82	*3/1DSO	9.4

■ **PAUL RADFORD**   Radford, Paul Revere "Shorty"   b: 10/14/1861, Roxbury, Mass.   d: 2/21/45, Boston, Mass.   BR/TR, 5'6", 148 lbs.   Deb: 5/01/1883

YEAR	TM/L	G	AB	R	H	2B	3B	HR	RBI	BB	SO	AVG	OBP	SLG	PRO+	BR	/A	RC	SB	CS	SBR	FR	POS	TPR
1883	Bos-N	79	258	46	53	6	3	0	14	9	26	.205	.232	.252	46	-16	-17	15				-3	*O	-1.5
1884	*Pro-N	97	355	56	70	11	2	1	29	25	43	.197	.250	.248	58	-17	-16	23				4	*O/P	-1.0
1885	Pro-N	105	371	55	90	12	5	0	32	33	43	.243	.304	.302	100	-1	1	35				1	*OS/P2	0.1
1886	KC-N	122	493	78	113	17	5	0	20	58	48	.229	.310	.284	77	-9	-14	57	39			9	*OS/2	-0.3
1887	NY-a	128	486	127	129	15	5	4	**106**			.265	.403	.342	116	14	19	99	73			-2	SO2/P	1.2

YEAR	TM/L	G	AB	R	H	2B	3B	HR	RBI	BB	SO	AVG	OBP	SLG	PRO+	BR	/A	RC	SB	CS	SBR	FR	POS	TPR
1888	Bro-a	90	308	48	67	9	3	2	29	35		.218	.305	.286	93	-1	-1	38	33			9	O/2	0.4
1889	Cle-N	136	487	94	116	21	5	1	46	91	37	.238	.365	.308	92	-2	-0	67	30			0	*O/3	-0.4
1890	Cle-P	122	466	98	136	24	12	2	62	82	28	.292	.406	.408	131	17	24	90	25			8	OS/32P	2.6
1891	Bos-a	133	456	102	118	11	5	0	65	96	36	.259	.393	.305	105	8	9	78	55			20	*S/OP	3.0
1892	Was-N	137	510	93	130	19	4	1	37	86	47	.255	.366	.314	111	9	11	73	35			-7	O3S/2	0.6
1893	Was-N	124	464	87	106	18	3	2	34	105	42	.228	.380	.293	84	-6	-4	65	32			7	*O/2P	0.0
1894	Was-N	95	325	61	78	13	5	0	49	65	23	.240	.378	.311	71	-14	-11	48	24			-1	S2O	-0.7
Total	12	1361	4979	945	1206	176	57	13	417	791	373	.242	.351	.308	94	-17	3	688	346			45	OS/32P	4.0

■ JACK RADTKE
Radtke, Jack William b: 4/14/13, Denver, Colo. BB/TR, 5'7", 160 lbs. Deb: 8/01/36

YEAR	TM/L	G	AB	R	H	2B	3B	HR	RBI	BB	SO	AVG	OBP	SLG	PRO+	BR	/A	RC	SB	CS	SBR	FR	POS	TPR
1936	Bro-N	33	31	8	3	0	0	0	2	4	9	.097	.200	.097	-18	-5	-5	1	3			5	2/3S	0.1

■ JACK RAFTER
Rafter, John Cornelius b: 2/20/1875, Troy, N.Y. d: 1/5/43, Troy, N.Y. TR , 5'8", 165 lbs. Deb: 9/24/04

YEAR	TM/L	G	AB	R	H	2B	3B	HR	RBI	BB	SO	AVG	OBP	SLG	PRO+	BR	/A	RC	SB	CS	SBR	FR	POS	TPR
1904	Pit-N	1	3	0	0	0	0	0	0	0	0	.000	.000	.000	-97	-1	-1	0	0			0	/C	0.0

■ TOM RAFTERY
Raftery, Thomas Francis b: 10/5/1881, Boston, Mass. d: 12/31/54, Boston, Mass. 5'10.5", 175 lbs. Deb: 4/18/09

YEAR	TM/L	G	AB	R	H	2B	3B	HR	RBI	BB	SO	AVG	OBP	SLG	PRO+	BR	/A	RC	SB	CS	SBR	FR	POS	TPR
1909	Cle-A	8	32	6	7	2	1	0	0	4		.219	.306	.344	101	0	0	4	1			-1	/O	0.0

■ TOM RAGLAND
Ragland, Thomas b: 6/16/46, Talladega, Ala. BR/TR, 5'10", 155 lbs. Deb: 4/05/71

YEAR	TM/L	G	AB	R	H	2B	3B	HR	RBI	BB	SO	AVG	OBP	SLG	PRO+	BR	/A	RC	SB	CS	SBR	FR	POS	TPR
1971	Was-A	10	23	1	4	0	0	0	0	0	5	.174	.208	.174	10	-3	-3	0	0	0	0	-1	2	-0.2
1972	Tex-A	25	58	3	10	2	0	0	2	5	11	.172	.238	.207	35	-5	-4	3	0	1	-1	-3	2/3S	-0.7
1973	Cle-A	67	183	16	47	7	1	0	12	8	31	.257	.292	.306	67	-8	-8	16	2	3	-1	13	2/S	0.7
Total	3	102	264	20	61	9	1	0	14	13	47	.231	.272	.273	56	-15	-15	19	2	4	-2	10	/2S3	-0.2

■ LARRY RAINES
Raines, Lawrence Glenn Hope b: 3/9/30, St.Albans, W.Va. d: 1/28/78, Lansing, Mich. BR/TR, 5'10", 165 lbs. Deb: 4/16/57

YEAR	TM/L	G	AB	R	H	2B	3B	HR	RBI	BB	SO	AVG	OBP	SLG	PRO+	BR	/A	RC	SB	CS	SBR	FR	POS	TPR
1957	Cle-A	96	244	39	64	14	0	2	16	19	40	.262	.318	.344	82	-6	-6	27	5	2	0	-5	3S2/O	-0.7
1958	Cle-A	7	9	1	0	0	0	0	0	0	5	.000	.000	.000	-99	-2	-2	0	0	1	-1	4	/2	0.1
Total	2	103	253	40	64	14	0	2	16	19	45	.253	.308	.332	76	-9	-8	27	5	3	-0	-1	/3S2O	-0.6

■ TIM RAINES
Raines, Timothy b: 9/16/59, Sanford, Fla. BB/TR, 5'8", 160 lbs. Deb: 9/11/79

YEAR	TM/L	G	AB	R	H	2B	3B	HR	RBI	BB	SO	AVG	OBP	SLG	PRO+	BR	/A	RC	SB	CS	SBR	FR	POS	TPR
1979	Mon-N	6	0	3	0	0	0	0	0	0	0	—	—	—		0	0	0	2	1	0	0	/R	0.1
1980	Mon-N	15	20	5	1	0	0	0	0	0	6	.050	.269	.050	-6	-3	-3	1	5	0	2	2	/2O	0.2
1981	*Mon-N	88	313	61	95	13	7	5	37	45	31	.304	.394	.438	134	16	16	64	71	11	15	-1	O/2	2.8
1982	Mon-N	156	647	90	179	32	8	4	43	75	83	.277	.354	.369	101	4	2	96	78	16	14	-1	*O2	1.6
1983	Mon-N	156	615	133	183	32	8	11	71	97	70	.298	.395	.429	129	27	27	120	90	14	19	1	*O/2	5.6
1984	Mon-N	160	622	106	192	38	9	8	60	87	69	.309	.395	.437	140	30	34	124	75	10	17	3	*O/2	5.0
1985	Mon-N	150	575	115	184	30	13	11	41	81	60	.320	.407	.475	155	38	42	124	70	9	16	1	*O	5.6
1986	Mon-N	151	580	91	194	35	10	9	62	78	60	.334	.415	.476	146	38	39	130	70	9	16	3	*O	5.5
1987	Mon-N	139	530	123	175	34	8	18	68	90	52	.330	.431	.526	148	43	41	132	50	5	12	9	*O	5.5
1988	Mon-N	109	429	66	116	19	7	12	48	53	44	.270	.353	.431	119	14	12	69	33	7	6	4	*O	1.9
1989	Mon-N	145	517	76	148	29	6	9	60	93	48	.286	.398	.418	132	26	26	96	41	9	7	-2	*O	3.0
1990	Mon-N	130	457	65	131	11	5	9	62	70	43	.287	.385	.392	115	12	12	75	49	16	5	-5	*O	0.9
Total	12	1405	5305	934	1598	273	81	96	552	775	563	.301	.393	.438	131	245	247	1030	634	106	127	25	*O/2	37.7

■ JOHN RAINEY
Rainey, John Paul b: 7/26/1864, Birmingham, Mich. d: 11/11/12, Detroit, Mich. BL/TR, 6'1.5", 164 lbs. Deb: 8/25/1887

YEAR	TM/L	G	AB	R	H	2B	3B	HR	RBI	BB	SO	AVG	OBP	SLG	PRO+	BR	/A	RC	SB	CS	SBR	FR	POS	TPR
1887	NY-N	17	58	6	17	3	0	0	12	5	6	.293	.349	.345	100	-0	0	7				-3	3	-0.1
1890	Buf-P	42	166	29	39	5	1	1	20	24	15	.235	.349	.295	81	-5	-2	22	12			0	O/S32	-0.1
Total	2	59	224	35	56	8	1	1	32	29	21	.250	.349	.308	86	-5	-2	29	12			-2	/O3S2	-0.2

■ GARY RAJSICH
Rajsich, Gary Louis b: 10/28/54, Youngstown, Ohio BL/TL, 6'2", 210 lbs. Deb: 4/09/82

YEAR	TM/L	G	AB	R	H	2B	3B	HR	RBI	BB	SO	AVG	OBP	SLG	PRO+	BR	/A	RC	SB	CS	SBR	FR	POS	TPR
1982	NY-N	80	162	17	42	8	3	2	12	17	40	.259	.333	.383	100	0	0	20	1	3	-2	-3	O/1	-0.4
1983	NY-N	11	36	5	12	3	0	1	3	3	1	.333	.400	.500	149	2	2	7	0	0	0	-0	1	0.2
1984	StL-N	7	7	1	1	0	0	0	2	2	1	.143	.333	.143	39	-0	-0	1	0	0	0	-0	/1	0.0
1985	SF-N	51	91	5	15	6	0	0	10	17	22	.165	.296	.231	52	-6	-5	7	0	1	-1	-1	1	-0.7
Total	4	149	296	28	70	17	3	3	27	39	64	.236	.329	.345	90	-4	-3	35	1	4	-2	-5	/1O	-0.9

■ DOC RALSTON
Ralston, Samuel Beryl b: 8/3/1885, Pierpont, Ohio d: 8/29/50, Lancaster, Pa. BR/TR, 6', 185 lbs. Deb: 9/08/10

YEAR	TM/L	G	AB	R	H	2B	3B	HR	RBI	BB	SO	AVG	OBP	SLG	PRO+	BR	/A	RC	SB	CS	SBR	FR	POS	TPR
1910	Was-A	21	73	4	15	1	0	0	3	3		.205	.256	.219	51	-4	-4	5	2			2	O	-0.3

■ BOB RAMAZZOTTI
Ramazzotti, Robert Louis b: 1/16/17, Elanora, Pa. BR/TR, 5'8.5", 175 lbs. Deb: 4/20/46

YEAR	TM/L	G	AB	R	H	2B	3B	HR	RBI	BB	SO	AVG	OBP	SLG	PRO+	BR	/A	RC	SB	CS	SBR	FR	POS	TPR
1946	Bro-N	62	120	10	25	4	0	0	7	9	13	.208	.264	.242	43	-9	-9	8	0			5	32	-0.3
1948	Bro-N	4	3	0	0	0	0	0	0	0	1	.000	.000	.000	-97	-1	-1	0	0			0	/32	0.0
1949	Bro-N	5	13	1	2	0	0	1	3	0	3	.154	.154	.385	38	-1	-1	1	0			-1	/3	-0.1
	Chi-N	65	190	14	34	3	1	0	6	5	33	.179	.200	.205	9	-24	-24	6	9			6	3S/2	-1.5
	Yr	70	203	15	36	3	1	1	9	5	36	.177	.197	.217	11	-26	-25	7	9			5		-1.6
1950	Chi-N	61	145	19	38	3	3	1	6	4	16	.262	.287	.345	66	-8	-7	14	3			-2	23/S	-0.7
1951	Chi-N	73	158	13	39	5	2	1	15	10	23	.247	.292	.323	64	-8	-8	15	0	0	0	13	S/23	0.9
1952	Chi-N	50	183	26	52	5	3	1	12	14	14	.284	.338	.361	93	-1	-2	22	3	1	0	-2	2	-0.1
1953	Chi-N	26	39	3	6	2	0	0	4	3	4	.154	.214	.205	10	-5	-5	2	0	0	0	0	2	-0.4
Total	7	346	851	86	196	22	9	4	53	53	107	.230	.271	.291	52	-57	-57	68	15	1		19	2/3S	-2.2

■ MARIO RAMIREZ
Ramirez, Mario (Torres) b: 9/12/57, Yauco, P.R. BR/TR, 5'9", 155 lbs. Deb: 4/25/80

YEAR	TM/L	G	AB	R	H	2B	3B	HR	RBI	BB	SO	AVG	OBP	SLG	PRO+	BR	/A	RC	SB	CS	SBR	FR	POS	TPR
1980	NY-N	18	24	2	5	0	0	0	1	7		.208	.240	.208	27	-2	-2	1	0	0	0	3	/S/23	0.2
1981	SD-N	13	13	1	1	0	0	0	1	2	5	.077	.200	.077	-21	-2	-2	0	0	0	0	4	/S3	0.2
1982	SD-N	13	23	1	4	1	0	0	1	2	4	.174	.240	.217	30	-2	-2	1	0	0	0	2	/S23	0.0
1983	SD-N	55	107	11	21	6	3	0	12	20	23	.196	.328	.308	80	-3	-2	12	0	0	0	-2	S/3	0.0
1984	*SD-N	48	59	12	7	1	0	2	9	13	14	.119	.278	.237	46	-4	-4	4	0	0	0	-0	S/32	0.0
1985	SD-N	37	60	6	17	0	0	2	5	3	11	.283	.317	.383	97	-1	-0	8	0	0	0	-5	S/2	-0.2
Total	6	184	286	33	55	8	3	4	28	41	64	.192	.296	.283	64	-14	-13	27	0	0	0	2	S/23	0.2

■ MILT RAMIREZ
Ramirez, Milton (Barboza) b: 4/2/50, Mayaguez, P.R. BR/TR, 5'9", 150 lbs. Deb: 4/11/70

YEAR	TM/L	G	AB	R	H	2B	3B	HR	RBI	BB	SO	AVG	OBP	SLG	PRO+	BR	/A	RC	SB	CS	SBR	FR	POS	TPR
1970	StL-N	62	79	8	15	2	1	0	3	8	9	.190	.264	.241	36	-7	-7	4	0	1	-1	10	S/3	1.0
1971	StL-N	4	11	2	3	0	0	0	0	2	1	.273	.385	.273	86	-0	-0	1	0	0	0	-1	/S	0.0
1979	Oak-A	28	62	4	10	1	1	0	3	3	8	.161	.200	.210	11	-8	-7	3	0	0	0	-5	32/S	-1.0
Total	3	94	152	14	28	3	2	0	6	13	18	.184	.248	.230	30	-15	-15	8	0	1	-1	4	/S32	0.0

■ ORLANDO RAMIREZ
Ramirez, Orlando (Leal) b: 12/18/51, Cartagena, Colombia BR/TR, 5'10", 175 lbs. Deb: 7/06/74

YEAR	TM/L	G	AB	R	H	2B	3B	HR	RBI	BB	SO	AVG	OBP	SLG	PRO+	BR	/A	RC	SB	CS	SBR	FR	POS	TPR
1974	Cal-A	31	86	4	14	0	0	0	7	6	23	.163	.217	.163	11	-10	-9	4	2	1	0	5	S	-0.1
1975	Cal-A	44	100	10	24	4	1	0	4	11	22	.240	.315	.300	80	-3	-2	9	9	6	-1	0	S	0.1
1976	Cal-A	30	70	3	14	1	0	0	5	6	11	.200	.263	.214	44	-5	-4	4	3	2	-0	4	S	0.1
1977	Cal-A	25	13	6	1	0	0	0	0	0	3	.077	.077	.077	-60	-3	-3	0	1	0	0	9	/2SD	0.7
1979	Cal-A	13	12	1	0	0	0	0	0	1	6	.000	.143	.000	-60	-3	-3	0	1	0	0	4	S	0.2
Total	5	143	281	24	53	5	1	0	16	24	65	.189	.255	.214	37	-23	-21	17	16	9	-1	22	S/2D	1.0

■ RAFAEL RAMIREZ
Ramirez, Rafael Emilio (Peguero) b: 2/18/58, San Pedro De Macoris, D.R. BR/TR, 6', 170 lbs. Deb: 8/04/80

YEAR	TM/L	G	AB	R	H	2B	3B	HR	RBI	BB	SO	AVG	OBP	SLG	PRO+	BR	/A	RC	SB	CS	SBR	FR	POS	TPR
1980	Atl-N	50	165	17	44	6	1	2	11	2	33	.267	.292	.352	76	-5	-6	17	2	1	0	-10	S	-1.1

YEAR	TM/L	G	AB	R	H	2B	3B	HR	RBI	BB	SO	AVG	OBP	SLG	PRO+	BR	/A	RC	SB	CS	SBR	FR	POS	TPR
1981	Atl-N	95	307	30	67	16	2	2	20	24	47	.218	.277	.303	63	-15	-15	27	7	3	0	-2	S	-0.7
1982	*Atl-N	157	609	74	169	24	4	10	52	36	49	.278	.321	.379	91	-5	-8	73	27	14	-0	17	*S	2.1
1983	Atl-N	152	622	82	185	13	5	7	58	36	48	.297	.338	.368	89	-4	-9	76	16	12	-2	7	*S	0.9
1984	Atl-N	145	591	51	157	22	4	2	48	26	70	.266	.298	.327	70	-20	-25	53	14	17	-6	-3	*S	-1.8
1985	Atl-N	138	568	54	141	25	4	5	58	20	63	.248	.274	.333	65	-25	-29	45	2	6	-3	9	*S	-1.2
1986	Atl-N	134	496	57	119	21	1	8	33	21	60	.240	.275	.335	64	-23	-26	42	19	8	1	14	S3/O	-0.4
1987	Atl-N	56	179	22	47	12	0	1	21	8	16	.263	.302	.346	68	-8	-9	18	6	3	0	-6	S3	-0.9
1988	Hou-N	155	566	51	156	30	5	6	59	18	61	.276	.302	.378	98	-6	-3	60	3	2	-0	-10	*S	-0.2
1989	Hou-N	151	537	46	132	20	2	6	54	29	64	.246	.284	.324	76	-19	-17	49	3	1	0	-41	*S	-5.2
1990	Hou-N	132	445	44	116	19	3	2	37	24	46	.261	.300	.330	75	-16	-15	43	10	5	0	-18	*S	-2.2
Total	11	1365	5085	528	1333	208	31	51	451	244	557	.262	.299	.345	77	-144	-162	503	109	72	-11	-43	*S/3O	-10.7

■ DOMINGO RAMOS

Ramos, Domingo Antonio (De Ramos) b: 3/29/58, Santiago, D.R. BR/TR, 5'10", 154 lbs. Deb: 9/08/78

YEAR	TM/L	G	AB	R	H	2B	3B	HR	RBI	BB	SO	AVG	OBP	SLG	PRO+	BR	/A	RC	SB	CS	SBR	FR	POS	TPR
1978	NY-A	1	0	0	0	0	0	0	0	0	0	—	—	—	—	0	0	0	0	0	0	0	/S	0.0
1980	Tor-A	5	16	0	2	0	0	0	0	2	5	.125	.222	.125	-2	-2	-2	1	0	0	0	-0	/2SD	-0.1
1982	Sea-A	8	26	3	4	2	0	0	1	3	2	.154	.241	.231	30	-2	-3	2	0	0	0	-5	/S	-0.7
1983	Sea-A	53	127	14	36	4	0	2	10	7	12	.283	.326	.362	86	-2	-2	14	3	1	0	9	S/23D	0.8
1984	Sea-A	59	81	6	15	2	0	0	2	5	12	.185	.233	.210	24	-8	-8	3	2	2	-1	4	3S/12	-0.2
1985	Sea-A	75	168	19	33	6	0	1	15	17	23	.196	.270	.250	43	-13	-13	12	0	1	-1	-9	S21/3	-1.9
1986	Sea-A	49	99	8	18	2	0	0	5	8	13	.182	.250	.202	25	-10	-10	4	0	1	-1	14	S2/3D	0.4
1987	Sea-A	42	103	9	32	6	0	2	11	3	12	.311	.336	.427	96	-0	-1	14	0	1	-1	7	S/32D	0.7
1988	Cle-A	22	46	7	12	1	0	0	5	3	7	.261	.320	.283	68	-2	-2	5	0	0	0	2	2/1S3	0.0
	Cal-A	10	15	3	2	0	0	0	0	0	0	.133	.133	.133	-26	-2	-2	0	0	0	0	0	/3O	-0.2
	Yr	32	61	10	14	1	0	0	5	3	7	.230	.277	.246	47	-4	-4	4	0	0	0	2		-0.2
1989	*Chi-N	85	179	18	47	6	2	1	19	17	23	.263	.333	.335	85	-2	-3	18	1	1	-0	3	S3	0.2
1990	Chi-N	98	226	22	60	5	0	2	17	27	29	.265	.346	.314	76	-4	-7	25	0	2	-1	-15	3S/2	-1.9
Total	11	507	1086	109	261	34	2	8	85	92	138	.240	.304	.297	64	-48	-54	97	6	9	-4	8	S3/21DO	-2.9

■ CHUCHO RAMOS

Ramos, Jesus Manuel (Garcia) b: 4/12/18, Maturin, Venez. BR/TL, 5'10.5", 167 lbs. Deb: 5/07/44

YEAR	TM/L	G	AB	R	H	2B	3B	HR	RBI	BB	SO	AVG	OBP	SLG	PRO+	BR	/A	RC	SB	CS	SBR	FR	POS	TPR
1944	Cin-N	4	10	1	5	1	0	0	0	0	0	.500	.500	.600	217	1	1	3	0			-0	/O	0.1

■ PEDRO RAMOS

Ramos, Pedro (Guerra) "Pete" b: 4/28/35, Pinar Del Rio, Cuba BB/TR, 6', 175 lbs. Deb: 4/11/55

YEAR	TM/L	G	AB	R	H	2B	3B	HR	RBI	BB	SO	AVG	OBP	SLG	PRO+	BR	/A	RC	SB	CS	SBR	FR	POS	TPR
1955	Was-A	59	38	6	3	0	0	0	0	2	18	.079	.125	.079	-47	-8	-7	0	0	1	-1	-0	P	0.0
1956	Was-A	56	44	9	9	0	2	0	2	2	16	.205	.239	.295	40	-4	-4	3	0	1	-1	0	P	0.0
1957	Was-A	56	76	6	13	0	0	1	10	2	27	.171	.192	.211	10	-9	-9	3	0	0	0	0	P	0.0
1958	Was-A	53	88	9	21	1	0	0	10	0	33	.239	.239	.250	35	-8	-8	6	0	0	0	-0	P	0.0
1959	Was-A	45	75	7	11	1	1	1	2	4	38	.147	.190	.227	14	-9	-9	4	1	0	0	0	P	0.0
1960	Was-A	53	86	6	10	3	0	2	4	1	36	.116	.126	.221	-8	-13	-13	3	0	0	0	0	P	0.0
1961	Min-A	53	93	8	16	1	0	3	11	3	42	.172	.206	.280	27	-10	-10	5	0	0	0	-3	P	0.0
1962	Cle-A	39	68	6	10	3	0	3	8	1	29	.147	.171	.324	31	-7	-7	3	0	0	0	0	P	0.0
1963	Cle-A	54	55	13	6	0	0	0	3	7	32	.109	.155	.273	17	-6	-6	3	0	0	0	-2	P	0.0
1964	Cle-A	44	39	6	7	0	0	2	2	2	22	.179	.220	.333	52	-3	-3	3	0	0	0	-1	P	0.0
	NY-A	13	5	0	0	0	0	0	0	0	2	.000	.000	.000	-98	-1	-1	0	0	0	0	-1	P	0.0
	Yr	57	44	6	7	0	0	2	2	2	24	.159	.196	.295	34	-4	-4	3	0	0	0	-1		0.0
1965	NY-A	65	12	0	1	0	0	0	0	0	8	.083	.083	.083	-53	-2	-2	0	1	0	0	-1	P	0.0
1966	NY-A	52	13	0	2	0	0	0	0	0	8	.154	.154	.154	-12	-2	-2	0	0	0	0	-0	P	0.0
1967	Phi-N	6	1	0	0	0	0	0	0	0	0	.000	.000	.000	-99	-0	-0	0	0	0	0	1	/P	0.0
1969	Pit-N	5	1	0	0	0	0	0	0	0	0	.000	.000	.000	-99	-0	-0	0	0	0	0	0	/P	0.0
	Cin-N	38	8	0	0	0	0	0	0	1	4	.000	.111	.000	-63	-2	-2	0	0	0	0	0	P	0.0
	Yr	43	9	0	0	0	0	0	0	1	5	.000	.100	.000	-67	-2	-2	0	0	0	0	0		0.0
1970	Was-A	5	1	0	0	0	0	0	0	1	0	.000	.500	.000	52	0	0	0	0	0	0	0	/P	0.0
Total	15	696	703	76	109	9	3	15	56	22	316	.155	.183	.240	14	-84	-84	34	2	2	-1	-6	P	0.0

■ BOBBY RAMOS

Ramos, Roberto b: 11/5/55, Havana, Cuba BR/TR, 5'11", 190 lbs. Deb: 9/26/78

YEAR	TM/L	G	AB	R	H	2B	3B	HR	RBI	BB	SO	AVG	OBP	SLG	PRO+	BR	/A	RC	SB	CS	SBR	FR	POS	TPR
1978	Mon-N	2	4	0	0	0	0	0	0	0	1	.000	.000	.000	-99	-1	-1	0	0	0	0	0	/C	0.0
1980	Mon-N	13	32	5	5	2	0	0	2	5	5	.156	.270	.219	38	-3	-3	2	0	0	0	1	C	-0.1
1981	Mon-N	26	41	4	8	1	0	1	3	3	5	.195	.250	.293	53	-3	-3	3	0	0	0	4	C	0.1
1982	NY-A	4	11	1	1	0	0	1	2	0	3	.091	.091	.364	18	-1	-1	0	0	0	0	1	/C	0.0
1983	Mon-N	27	61	2	14	3	1	0	5	8	11	.230	.329	.311	79	-2	-2	7	0	0	0	4	C	0.4
1984	Mon-N	31	83	8	16	1	0	2	5	6	13	.193	.247	.277	49	-6	-5	5	0	0	0	6	C	0.2
Total	6	103	232	20	44	7	1	4	17	22	38	.190	.263	.280	53	-15	-15	17	0	0	0	16	/C	0.6

■ MIKE RAMSEY

Ramsey, Michael James b: 7/8/60, Thomson, Ga. BB/TL, 6'", 170 lbs. Deb: 4/06/87

YEAR	TM/L	G	AB	R	H	2B	3B	HR	RBI	BB	SO	AVG	OBP	SLG	PRO+	BR	/A	RC	SB	CS	SBR	FR	POS	TPR
1987	LA-N	48	125	18	29	4	2	0	12	10	32	.232	.289	.296	57	-8	-8	10	2	4	-2	-0	O	-1.0

■ MIKE RAMSEY

Ramsey, Michael Jeffrey b: 3/29/54, Roanoke, Va. BB/TR, 6'1", 170 lbs. Deb: 9/04/78

YEAR	TM/L	G	AB	R	H	2B	3B	HR	RBI	BB	SO	AVG	OBP	SLG	PRO+	BR	/A	RC	SB	CS	SBR	FR	POS	TPR
1978	StL-N	12	5	4	1	0	0	0	0	0	1	.200	.200	.200	12	-1	-1	0	0	0	0	5	/S	0.5
1980	StL-N	59	126	11	33	8	1	0	8	3	17	.262	.279	.341	70	-5	-5	11	0	0	0	0	2S/3	0.0
1981	StL-N	47	124	19	32	3	0	0	9	8	16	.258	.303	.282	65	-5	-6	10	4	0	1	13	S/32O	1.3
1982	*StL-N	112	256	18	59	8	2	1	21	22	34	.230	.294	.289	63	-12	-12	21	6	5	-4	9	23S/O	-0.1
1983	StL-N	97	175	25	46	4	3	1	16	12	23	.263	.314	.337	80	-5	-5	18	4	2	0	3	2S/3O	0.2
1984	StL-N	21	15	1	1	1	0	0	0	1	3	.067	.125	.133	-28	-3	-3	0	0	0	0	4	/2S3	0.3
	Mon-N	37	70	2	15	1	0	0	3	0	13	.214	.214	.229	26	-7	-7	3	0	0	0	1	S2	-0.1
	Yr	58	85	3	16	2	0	0	3	1	16	.188	.198	.212	16	-10	-9	3	0	0	0	5		0.2
1985	LA-N	9	15	1	2	1	0	0	0	2	4	.133	.235	.200	24	-2	-1	1	0	0	0	0	/S2	0.0
Total	7	394	786	81	189	26	6	2	57	48	111	.240	.286	.296	63	-39	-39	65	14	7	0	36	2S/3O	2.1

■ BILL RAMSEY

Ramsey, William Thrace "Square Jaw" b: 2/20/21, Osceola, Ark. BR/TR, 6'1", 190 lbs. Deb: 4/19/45

YEAR	TM/L	G	AB	R	H	2B	3B	HR	RBI	BB	SO	AVG	OBP	SLG	PRO+	BR	/A	RC	SB	CS	SBR	FR	POS	TPR
1945	Bos-N	78	137	16	40	8	0	1	12	4	22	.292	.326	.372	93	-1	-2	16	1			2	O	-0.1

■ DICK RAND

Rand, Richard Hilton b: 3/7/31, South Gate, Cal. BR/TR, 6'2", 185 lbs. Deb: 9/16/53

YEAR	TM/L	G	AB	R	H	2B	3B	HR	RBI	BB	SO	AVG	OBP	SLG	PRO+	BR	/A	RC	SB	CS	SBR	FR	POS	TPR
1953	StL-N	9	31	3	9	1	0	0	1	2	6	.290	.333	.323	72	-1	-1	4	0	0	0	3	/C	0.2
1955	StL-N	3	10	1	3	0	0	0	3	1	1	.300	.364	.600	150	1	1	2	0	1	-1	-1	/C	0.0
1957	Pit-N	60	105	7	23	2	1	1	9	11	24	.219	.293	.286	58	-6	-6	10	0	0	0	0	C	-0.2
Total	3	72	146	11	35	3	1	1	13	14	31	.240	.306	.315	68	-7	-6	15	0	1	-1	2	/C	0.0

■ SAP RANDALL

Randall, James Odell b: 8/19/60, Mobile, Ala. BB/TR, 5'11", 195 lbs. Deb: 8/02/88

YEAR	TM/L	G	AB	R	H	2B	3B	HR	RBI	BB	SO	AVG	OBP	SLG	PRO+	BR	/A	RC	SB	CS	SBR	FR	POS	TPR
1988	Chi-A	4	12	1	0	0	0	0	1	2	3	.000	.143	.000	-57	-3	-3	0	0	0	0	0	/1OD	-0.2

■ NEWT RANDALL

Randall, Newton J. b: 2/3/1880, New Lowell, Ont., Canada d: 5/3/55, Duluth, Minn. 5'10", Deb: 4/18/07

YEAR	TM/L	G	AB	R	H	2B	3B	HR	RBI	BB	SO	AVG	OBP	SLG	PRO+	BR	/A	RC	SB	CS	SBR	FR	POS	TPR
1907	Chi-N	22	78	6	16	4	2	0	4	8		.205	.279	.308	81	-1	-2	8	2			1	O	-0.1
	Bos-N	75	258	16	55	6	3	0	15	19		.213	.267	.260	67	-10	-10	19	4			-7	O	-2.2
	Yr	97	336	22	71	10	5	0	19	27		.211	.270	.271	70	-11	-11	27	6			-7		-2.3

■ BOB RANDALL
Randall, Robert Lee b: 6/10/48, Norton, Kan. BR/TR, 6'2", 175 lbs. Deb: 4/13/76 C

YEAR	TM/L	G	AB	R	H	2B	3B	HR	RBI	BB	SO	AVG	OBP	SLG	PRO+	BR	/A	RC	SB	CS	SBR	FR	POS	TPR
1976	Min-A	153	475	55	127	18	4	1	34	28	38	.267	.319	.328	87	-6	-8	51	3	5	-2	-6	*2	-0.6
1977	Min-A	103	306	36	73	13	2	0	22	15	25	.239	.290	.294	60	-17	-16	27	1	4	-2	10	*2/13D	0.0
1978	Min-A	119	330	36	89	11	3	0	21	24	22	.270	.331	.321	82	-6	-7	36	5	3	-0	10	*2/3D	0.9
1979	Min-A	80	199	25	49	7	0	0	14	15	17	.246	.299	.281	55	-12	-13	18	2	2	-1	7	2/3SO	-0.2
1980	Min-A	5	15	2	3	1	0	0	0	1	0	.200	.250	.267	39	-1	-1	1	0	0	0	0	/32	0.2
Total	5	460	1325	154	341	50	9	1	91	83	102	.257	.311	.311	74	-42	-45	132	11	14	-5	21	2/3DOS1	0.1

■ LEN RANDLE
Randle, Leonard Shenoff b: 2/12/49, Long Beach, Cal. BB/TR, 5'10", 169 lbs. Deb: 6/16/71

YEAR	TM/L	G	AB	R	H	2B	3B	HR	RBI	BB	SO	AVG	OBP	SLG	PRO+	BR	/A	RC	SB	CS	SBR	FR	POS	TPR
1971	Was-A	75	215	27	47	11	0	2	13	24	56	.219	.300	.298	74	-8	-7	21	1	1	-0	5	2	0.1
1972	Tex-A	74	249	23	48	13	0	2	21	13	51	.193	.236	.269	52	-16	-15	14	4	5	-2	1	2/SO	-1.2
1973	Tex-A	10	29	3	6	1	1	1	1	0	2	.207	.207	.414	74	-1	-1	2	0	2	-1	-2	/2O	-0.3
1974	Tex-A	151	520	65	157	17	4	1	49	29	43	.302	.341	.356	103	0	2	61	26	17	-2	4	32O/SD	0.6
1975	Tex-A	156	601	85	166	24	7	4	57	57	80	.276	.343	.359	99	-0	-0	73	16	19	-7	13	2O3/CSD	0.2
1976	Tex-A	142	539	53	121	11	6	1	51	46	63	.224	.288	.273	63	-23	-25	45	30	15	-0	-4	*2O/3D	-2.4
1977	NY-N	136	513	78	156	22	7	5	27	65	70	.304	.384	.404	117	11	14	78	33	21	-3	-6	*32/OS	0.5
1978	NY-N	132	437	53	102	16	8	2	35	64	57	.233	.333	.320	86	-8	-6	49	14	11	-2	-7	*3/2	-1.6
1979	NY-A	20	39	2	7	0	0	0	3	3	2	.179	.238	.179	15	-5	-4	2	0	0	0	1	0	-0.3
1980	Chi-N	130	489	67	135	19	6	3	39	50	55	.276	.344	.370	93	-0	4	61	19	13	-2	-5	*32/O	-1.0
1981	Sea-A	82	273	22	63	9	1	4	25	17	22	.231	.278	.315	68	-11	-12	24	11	6	-0	4	32/OS	-0.6
1982	Sea-A	30	46	10	8	2	0	0	4	3	4	.174	.240	.217	26	-5	-5	2	2	2	-1	9	D/32	0.4
Total	12	1138	3950	488	1016	145	40	27	322	372	505	.257	.323	.335	87	-65	-63	430	156	112	-20	15	32O/DSC	-5.0

■ WILLIE RANDOLPH
Randolph, Willie Larry b: 7/6/54, Holly Hill, S.C. BR/TR, 5'11", 165 lbs. Deb: 7/29/75

YEAR	TM/L	G	AB	R	H	2B	3B	HR	RBI	BB	SO	AVG	OBP	SLG	PRO+	BR	/A	RC	SB	CS	SBR	FR	POS	TPR
1975	*Pit-N	30	61	9	10	1	0	0	3	7	6	.164	.250	.180	21	-6	-6	3	1	0	0	4	2/3	-0.1
1976	*NY-A	125	430	59	115	15	4	1	40	58	39	.267	.358	.328	103	3	4	55	37	12	4	15	*2	3.2
1977	*NY-A	147	551	91	151	28	11	4	40	64	53	.274	.351	.387	102	2	3	77	13	6	0	6	*2	2.0
1978	NY-A	134	499	87	139	18	6	3	42	82	51	.279	.385	.357	112	10	12	78	36	7	7	-8	*2	1.8
1979	NY-A	153	574	98	155	15	13	5	61	95	39	.270	.376	.368	104	5	7	82	33	12	3	9	*2	2.5
1980	NY-A	138	513	99	151	23	7	7	46	**119**	45	.294	.429	.407	133	29	30	105	30	5	6	-7	*2	3.6
1981	*NY-A	93	357	59	83	14	3	2	24	57	24	.232	.338	.305	88	-4	-4	40	14	5	1	-3	2	-0.2
1982	NY-A	144	553	85	155	21	4	3	36	75	35	.280	.369	.349	100	2	3	75	16	9	-1	-3	*2/D	0.8
1983	NY-A	104	420	73	117	21	1	2	38	53	32	.279	.361	.348	100	-0	2	55	12	4	1	3	*2	0.9
1984	NY-A	142	564	86	162	24	2	2	31	86	42	.287	.382	.348	108	6	9	79	10	6	-1	11	*2	2.7
1985	NY-A	143	497	75	137	21	2	5	40	85	39	.276	.386	.356	107	7	9	69	16	9	-1	-3	*2	1.1
1986	NY-A	141	492	76	136	15	2	5	50	94	49	.276	.396	.346	105	8	8	77	15	2	3	-12	*2/D	0.7
1987	NY-A	120	449	96	137	24	2	7	67	82	25	.305	.415	.414	122	18	18	82	11	1	3	-2	*2/D	2.7
1988	NY-A	110	404	43	93	20	1	2	34	55	39	.230	.325	.300	77	-11	-11	42	8	4	0	8	*2	0.4
1989	LA-N	145	549	62	155	18	0	2	36	71	51	.282	.369	.326	102	3	4	69	7	6	-2	-1	*2	0.4
1990	LA-N	26	96	15	26	4	0	1	9	13	9	.271	.364	.344	101	-0	1	13	1	0	0	-2	2	0.0
	*Oak-A	93	292	37	75	9	3	1	21	32	25	.257	.332	.318	85	-6	-5	31	6	1	1	-11	2/D	-1.0
Total	16	1988	7301	1150	1997	291	61	52	618	1128	603	.274	.373	.351	104	65	85	1032	266	89	26	4	*2/D3	21.5

■ MERRITT RANEW
Ranew, Merritt Thomas b: 5/10/38, Albany, Ga. BL/TR, 5'11", 170 lbs. Deb: 4/13/62

YEAR	TM/L	G	AB	R	H	2B	3B	HR	RBI	BB	SO	AVG	OBP	SLG	PRO+	BR	/A	RC	SB	CS	SBR	FR	POS	TPR
1962	Hou-N	71	218	26	51	6	8	4	24	14	43	.234	.289	.390	87	-7	-5	24	2	2	-1	-4	C	-0.8
1963	Chi-N	78	154	18	52	8	1	3	15	9	32	.338	.382	.461	134	8	7	27	1	0	0	-4	C/1	0.5
1964	Chi-N	16	33	0	3	0	0	0	1	2	6	.091	.167	.091	-24	-5	-6	1	0	0	0	2	/C	-0.3
	Mil-N	9	17	1	2	0	0	0	0	0	3	.118	.118	.118	-33	-3	-3	0	0	1	-1	-1	/C	-0.4
	Yr	25	50	1	5	0	0	0	1	2	9	.100	.151	.100	-27	-8	-9	1	0	1	-1	1		-0.7
1965	Cal-A	41	91	12	19	4	0	1	10	7	22	.209	.265	.286	58	-5	-5	7	0	0	0	-10	C	-1.3
1969	Sea-A	54	81	11	20	2	0	0	4	10	14	.247	.330	.272	71	-3	-3	7	0	0	0	-5	C/O3	-0.6
Total	5	269	594	68	147	20	9	8	54	42	120	.247	.304	.352	83	-15	-14	66	3	3	-1	-21	C/1O3	-2.9

■ JEFF RANSOM
Ransom, Jeffrey Dean b: 11/11/60, Fresno, Cal. BR/TR, 5'11", 185 lbs. Deb: 9/05/81

YEAR	TM/L	G	AB	R	H	2B	3B	HR	RBI	BB	SO	AVG	OBP	SLG	PRO+	BR	/A	RC	SB	CS	SBR	FR	POS	TPR
1981	SF-N	5	15	2	4	1	0	0	1	1	1	.267	.313	.333	85	-0	-0	1	0	0	0	2	/C	0.2
1982	SF-N	15	44	5	7	0	0	0	3	6	7	.159	.260	.159	20	-5	-5	2	0	0	0	1	C	-0.2
1983	SF-N	6	20	3	4	0	0	1	3	4	7	.200	.333	.350	92	-0	-0	2	0	0	0	-2	/C	-0.1
Total	3	26	79	10	15	1	0	1	6	11	15	.190	.289	.241	50	-5	-5	5	0	0	0	1	/C	-0.1

■ EARL RAPP
Rapp, Earl Wellington b: 5/20/21, Corunna, Mich. BL/TR, 6'2", 185 lbs. Deb: 4/28/49

YEAR	TM/L	G	AB	R	H	2B	3B	HR	RBI	BB	SO	AVG	OBP	SLG	PRO+	BR	/A	RC	SB	CS	SBR	FR	POS	TPR
1949	Det-A	1	0	0	0	0	0	0	0	1	0	—	1.000	—	175	0	0	0	0	0	0	0	H	0.0
	Chi-A	19	54	3	14	1	1	0	11	5	6	.259	.322	.315	71	-2	-2	6	1	1	-0	2	O	0.0
	Yr	20	54	3	14	1	1	0	11	6	6	.259	.333	.315	74	-2	-2	6	1	1	-0	2		0.0
1951	NY-N	13	11	0	1	0	0	0	1	2	3	.091	.231	.091	-10	-2	-2	0	0	0	0	0	H	-0.1
	StL-A	26	98	14	32	5	3	2	14	11	11	.327	.394	.500	137	5	5	21	1	0	0	-3	O	0.1
1952	StL-A	30	49	3	7	4	0	0	4	0	8	.143	.143	.224	1	-7	-7	1	0	0	0	-1	/O	-0.7
	Was-A	46	67	7	19	6	0	0	9	6	13	.284	.351	.373	105	0	0	10	0	0	0	-3	O	-0.2
	Yr	76	116	10	26	10	0	0	13	6	21	.224	.268	.310	61	-6	-6	10	0	0	0	-3		-0.9
Total	3	135	279	27	73	16	4	2	39	25	41	.262	.325	.369	89	-5	-5	38	2	1	0	-4	/O	-0.9

■ GOLDIE RAPP
Rapp, Joseph Aloysius b: 2/6/1892, Cincinnati, Ohio d: 7/1/66, LaMesa, Cal. BB/TR, 5'10", 165 lbs. Deb: 4/13/21

YEAR	TM/L	G	AB	R	H	2B	3B	HR	RBI	BB	SO	AVG	OBP	SLG	PRO+	BR	/A	RC	SB	CS	SBR	FR	POS	TPR
1921	NY-N	58	181	21	39	9	1	0	15	15	13	.215	.276	.276	46	-14	-14	12	3	11	-6	13	3	-0.6
	Phi-N	52	202	28	56	7	1	1	10	14	8	.277	.324	.337	70	-7	-9	21	6	7	-2	-2	3/2	-1.3
	Yr	110	383	49	95	16	2	1	25	29	21	.248	.301	.308	59	-21	-23	33	9	18	-8	10		-1.9
1922	Phi-N	119	502	58	127	26	3	0	38	32	29	.253	.299	.317	54	-31	-37	46	6	12	-5	5	*3/S	-2.7
1923	Phi-N	47	179	27	47	5	0	1	10	14	14	.263	.320	.307	59	-8	-11	18	1	1	-0	-0	3	-1.0
Total	3	276	1064	134	269	47	5	2	73	75	64	.253	.303	.312	57	-60	-72	97	16	31	-14	15	3/S2	-5.6

■ BILL RARIDEN
Rariden, William Angel "Bedford Bill" b: 2/4/1888, Bedford, Ind. d: 8/28/42, Bedford, Ind. BR/TR, 5'10", 168 lbs. Deb: 8/12/09

YEAR	TM/L	G	AB	R	H	2B	3B	HR	RBI	BB	SO	AVG	OBP	SLG	PRO+	BR	/A	RC	SB	CS	SBR	FR	POS	TPR
1909	Bos-N	13	42	1	6	1	0	0	1	4		.143	.217	.167	18	-4	-4	2	1			-3	C	-0.6
1910	Bos-N	49	137	15	31	5	1	1	14	12	22	.226	.293	.299	70	-5	-6	13	1			3	C	0.0
1911	Bos-N	70	246	22	56	9	0	0	21	21	18	.228	.288	.264	51	-15	-17	19	3			1	C/32	-1.0
1912	Bos-N	79	247	27	55	3	1	1	14	18	35	.223	.281	.255	46	-18	-18	19	3			-5	C	-1.8
1913	Bos-N	95	246	31	58	9	2	3	30	30	21	.236	.324	.325	84	-4	-5	27	5			3	C	0.3
1914	Ind-F	131	396	44	93	15	5	0	47	61	43	.235	.337	.298	75	-7	-13	47	12			-24	*C	-3.1
1915	New-F	142	444	49	120	30	7	0	40	60	29	.270	.361	.369	123	11	14	65	8			-18	*C	0.0
1916	NY-N	120	351	23	78	9	3	1	29	55	32	.222	.333	.274	92	-3	-1	34	4			-9	*C	-0.3
1917	*NY-N	101	266	20	72	10	1	0	25	42	17	.271	.372	.316	116	6	7	32	3			-17	*C	-0.5
1918	NY-N	69	183	15	41	5	1	0	17	15	15	.224	.283	.262	68	-7	-7	14	1			-9	C	-1.1
1919	*Cin-N	74	218	16	47	6	3	0	24	17	19	.216	.275	.284	70	-8	-8	18	4			3	C	0.0
1920	Cin-N	39	101	9	25	3	0	0	10	5	0	.248	.283	.277	62	-5	-5	8	2	0	1	-0	C	-0.1
Total	12	982	2877	272	682	105	24	7	272	340	251	.237	.320	.298	81	-59	-62	297	47	0		-76	C/32	-8.2

YEAR	TM/L	G	AB	R	H	2B	3B	HR	RBI	BB	SO	AVG	OBP	SLG	PRO+	BR	/A	RC	SB	CS	SBR	FR	POS	TPR

■ MORRIE RATH
Rath, Morris Charles b: 12/25/1886, Mobeetie, Tex. d: 11/18/45, Upper Darby, Pa. BL/TR, 5'8.5", 160 lbs. Deb: 9/28/09

YEAR	TM/L	G	AB	R	H	2B	3B	HR	RBI	BB	SO	AVG	OBP	SLG	PRO+	BR	/A	RC	SB	CS	SBR	FR	POS	TPR
1909	Phi-A	7	26	4	7	1	0	0	3	2		.269	.387	.308	117	1	1	3	1			2	/S3	0.3
1910	Phi-A	18	26	3	4	0	0	0	1	5		.154	.290	.154	40	-2	-2	2	0			-2	3/2	-0.3
	Cle-A	24	67	5	13	3	0	0	0	10		.194	.299	.239	68	-2	-2	5	2			2	3/S	0.1
	Yr	42	93	8	17	3	0	0	1	15		.183	.296	.215	60	-4	-4	7	2			0		-0.2
1912	Chi-A	157	591	104	161	10	2	1	19	95		.272	.380	.301	98	2	5	80	30			18	*2	2.0
1913	Chi-A	92	295	37	59	2	0	0	12	46	22	.200	.310	.207	52	-16	-16	26	22			-1	2	-2.0
1919	*Cin-N	138	537	77	142	13	1	1	29	64	24	.264	.343	.298	96	-2	0	61	17			13	*2	1.9
1920	Cin-N	129	506	61	135	7	4	2	28	36	24	.267	.319	.308	82	-12	-11	51	10	11	-4	-7	*2/3O	-1.9
Total	6	565	2048	291	521	36	7	4	92	258	70	.254	.342	.285	86	-30	-24	227	82	11		26	2/3SO	0.1

■ GENE RATLIFF
Ratliff, Kelly Eugene b: 9/28/45, Macon, Ga. BR/TR, 6'5", 185 lbs. Deb: 5/15/65

YEAR	TM/L	G	AB	R	H	2B	3B	HR	RBI	BB	SO	AVG	OBP	SLG	PRO+	BR	/A	RC	SB	CS	SBR	FR	POS	TPR
1965	Hou-N	4	4	0	0	0	0	0	0	0	4	.000	.000	.000	-99	-1	-1	0	0	0	0	0	H	0.0

■ PAUL RATLIFF
Ratliff, Paul Hawthorne b: 1/23/44, San Diego, Cal. BL/TR, 6'2", 190 lbs. Deb: 4/14/63

YEAR	TM/L	G	AB	R	H	2B	3B	HR	RBI	BB	SO	AVG	OBP	SLG	PRO+	BR	/A	RC	SB	CS	SBR	FR	POS	TPR
1963	Min-A	10	21	2	4	1	0	1	3	2	7	.190	.292	.381	85	-0	-0	3	0	0	0	2	/C	0.2
1970	*Min-A	69	149	19	40	7	2	5	22	15	51	.268	.363	.443	119	4	4	25	0	0	0	-16	C	-1.0
1971	Min-A	21	44	3	7	1	0	2	6	4	17	.159	.229	.318	52	-3	-3	5	0	0	0	1	C	-0.1
	Mil-A	23	41	3	7	1	0	3	7	5	21	.171	.277	.415	95	-1	-0	5	0	0	0	-1	C	0.0
	Yr	44	85	6	14	2	0	5	13	9	38	.165	.253	.365	72	-3	-3	8	0	0	0	-0		-0.1
1972	Mil-A	22	42	1	3	0	0	1	4	2	23	.071	.114	.143	-25	-6	-6	1	0	0	0	-2	C	-0.9
Total	4	145	297	28	61	10	2	12	42	28	119	.205	.293	.374	86	-6	-6	37	0	0	0	-16	C	-1.8

■ TOMMY RAUB
Raub, Thomas Jefferson b: 12/1/1870, Raubsville, Pa. d: 2/16/49, Phillipsburg, N.J. BR/TR, 5'10", 155 lbs. Deb: 5/03/03

YEAR	TM/L	G	AB	R	H	2B	3B	HR	RBI	BB	SO	AVG	OBP	SLG	PRO+	BR	/A	RC	SB	CS	SBR	FR	POS	TPR
1903	Chi-N	36	84	6	19	3	2	0	7	5		.226	.270	.310	68	-4	-3	8	3			-4	C/1O3	-0.6
1906	StL-N	24	78	9	22	2	4	0	2	4		.282	.317	.410	134	2	2	11	2			-4	C	0.0
Total	2	60	162	15	41	5	6	0	9	9		.253	.292	.358	98	-2	-1	19	5			-8	/C1O3	-0.6

■ BOB RAUDMAN
Raudman, Robert Joyce "Shorty" b: 3/14/42, Erie, Pa. BL/TL, 5'9.5", 185 lbs. Deb: 9/13/66

YEAR	TM/L	G	AB	R	H	2B	3B	HR	RBI	BB	SO	AVG	OBP	SLG	PRO+	BR	/A	RC	SB	CS	SBR	FR	POS	TPR
1966	Chi-N	8	29	1	7	2	0	0	2	1	4	.241	.267	.310	59	-2	-2	2	0	0	0	0	/O	-0.1
1967	Chi-N	8	26	0	4	0	0	0	1	1	4	.154	.185	.154	-2	-3	-4	0	0	0	0	0	/O	-0.3
Total	2	16	55	1	11	2	0	0	3	2	8	.200	.228	.236	30	-5	-5	3	0	0	0	0	/O	-0.4

■ JOHNNY RAWLINGS
Rawlings, John William "Red" b: 8/17/1892, Bloomfield, Iowa d: 10/16/72, Inglewood, Cal. BR/TR, 5'8", 158 lbs. Deb: 4/14/14

YEAR	TM/L	G	AB	R	H	2B	3B	HR	RBI	BB	SO	AVG	OBP	SLG	PRO+	BR	/A	RC	SB	CS	SBR	FR	POS	TPR
1914	Cin-N	33	60	9	13	1	0	0	8	6	8	.217	.288	.233	54	-3	-3	5	1			0	3/2S	-0.2
	KC-F	61	193	19	41	3	0	0	15	22	25	.212	.296	.228	54	-11	-10	16	6			17	S	1.1
1915	KC-F	120	399	40	86	9	2	2	24	27	40	.216	.269	.263	60	-21	-19	37	17			-4	*S	-1.4
1917	Bos-N	122	371	37	95	9	4	2	31	38	32	.256	.337	.318	107	2	4	43	12			11	2S/3O	2.4
1918	Bos-N	111	410	32	85	7	3	0	21	30	31	.207	.265	.239	56	-22	-20	29	10			1	S2O	-1.9
1919	Bos-N	77	275	30	70	8	2	1	16	16	20	.255	.298	.309	86	-6	-5	28	10			-9	2O/S	-1.3
1920	Bos-N	5	3	0	0	0	0	0	2	0	1	.000	.000	.000	-99	-1	-1	0	0	0	0	-0	/2	0.0
	Phi-N	98	384	39	90	19	2	3	30	22	25	.234	.278	.318	67	-15	-17	34	9	6	-1	-2	2	-1.8
	Yr	103	387	39	90	19	2	3	32	22	26	.233	.276	.315	67	-16	-18	34	9	6	-1	-2		-1.8
1921	Phi-N	60	254	20	74	14	2	1	16	8	12	.291	.318	.374	76	-7	-9	29	4	5	-2	5	2	-0.5
	*NY-N	86	307	40	82	8	1	1	30	18	19	.267	.316	.309	66	-14	-14	31	4	4	-1	-1	2/S	-1.5
	Yr	146	561	60	156	22	3	2	46	26	31	.278	.317	.339	71	-21	-23	60	8	9	-3	3		-2.0
1922	NY-N	88	308	46	87	13	8	1	30	23	15	.282	.342	.386	87	-6	-6	41	7	6	-2	-4	2/3	-1.1
1923	Pit-N	119	461	53	131	18	4	1	45	25	29	.284	.322	.347	75	-16	-17	54	9	0	3	-8	*2	-2.0
1924	Pit-N	3	3	0	1	0	0	0	2	0	0	.333	.333	.333	78	-0	-0	0	0	0	0	0	H	0.0
1925	Pit-N	36	110	17	31	7	0	2	13	8	8	.282	.336	.400	82	-2	-3	15	0	1	-1	3	2	0.0
1926	Pit-N	61	181	27	42	6	0	0	20	14	10	.232	.287	.265	47	-13	-14	15	3			-3	2	-1.3
Total	12	1080	3719	409	928	122	28	14	303	257	275	.250	.303	.309	72	-134	-134	375	92	22		5	2S/O3	-9.5

■ IRV RAY
Ray, Irving Burton "Stubby" b: 1/22/1864, Harrington, Me. d: 2/21/48, Harrington, Me. TL, 5'6", 165 lbs. Deb: 7/07/1888

YEAR	TM/L	G	AB	R	H	2B	3B	HR	RBI	BB	SO	AVG	OBP	SLG	PRO+	BR	/A	RC	SB	CS	SBR	FR	POS	TPR
1888	Bos-N	50	206	26	51	2	3	2	26	6	11	.248	.272	.316	87	-3	-3	20	7			-11	S/2	-1.2
1889	Bos-N	9	33	8	10	1	0	0	2	4	0	.303	.378	.333	96	-0	-0	5	1			-4	/S3	-0.2
	Bal-a	26	106	20	36	4	1	0	17	7	6	.340	.397	.396	126	4	4	22	12			-7	S/O	-0.1
1890	Bal-a	38	139	28	50	6	2	1		15		.360	.433	.453	157	12	10	33	11			-10	S	0.2
1891	Bal-a	103	418	72	116	17	5	0	58	54	18	.278	.366	.342	104	5	4	64	28			-14	OS	-0.8
Total	4	226	902	154	263	30	11	3	103	86	35	.292	.360	.359	112	18	15	144	59			-46	S/O32	-2.1

■ JOHNNY RAY
Ray, John Cornelius b: 3/1/57, Chouteau, Okla. BB/TR, 5'11", 170 lbs. Deb: 9/02/81

YEAR	TM/L	G	AB	R	H	2B	3B	HR	RBI	BB	SO	AVG	OBP	SLG	PRO+	BR	/A	RC	SB	CS	SBR	FR	POS	TPR
1981	Pit-N	31	102	10	25	11	0	0	6	6	9	.245	.287	.353	78	-3	-3	10	0	0	0	2	2	0.1
1982	Pit-N	162	647	79	182	30	7	7	63	36	34	.281	.320	.382	93	-5	-7	80	16	7	1	8	*2	0.9
1983	Pit-N	151	576	68	163	38	7	5	53	35	26	.283	.324	.399	97	-2	-3	73	18	9	0	17	*2	2.0
1984	Pit-N	155	555	75	173	38	6	6	67	37	31	.312	.358	.434	122	15	15	83	11	6	-0	-9	*2	1.0
1985	Pit-N	154	594	67	163	33	3	7	70	46	24	.274	.328	.375	97	-3	-3	71	13	9	-2	-15	*2	-1.8
1986	Pit-N	155	579	67	174	33	0	7	78	58	47	.301	.367	.394	107	9	7	79	6	9	-4	5	*2	1.1
1987	Pit-N	123	472	48	129	19	3	5	54	41	36	.273	.331	.358	82	-11	-12	53	4	2	0	4	*2	-0.5
	Cal-A	30	127	16	44	11	0	0	15	3	10	.346	.362	.433	113	2	2	19	0	0	0	-1	2/D	0.3
1988	Cal-A	153	602	75	184	42	7	6	83	36	38	.306	.349	.429	120	12	15	90	4	1	1	-5	*2O/D	1.6
1989	Cal-A	134	530	52	153	16	3	5	62	36	30	.289	.334	.358	97	-3	-2	62	6	3	0	4	*2	0.4
1990	Cal-A	105	404	47	112	23	0	5	43	19	44	.277	.310	.371	89	-6	-6	44	2	3	-1	12	*2/D	1.0
Total	10	1353	5188	604	1502	294	36	53	594	353	329	.290	.336	.391	101	5	3	662	80	49	-5	23	*2/OD	6.1

■ LARRY RAY
Ray, Larry Dale b: 3/11/58, Madison, Ind. BL/TR, 6'1", 195 lbs. Deb: 9/10/82

YEAR	TM/L	G	AB	R	H	2B	3B	HR	RBI	BB	SO	AVG	OBP	SLG	PRO+	BR	/A	RC	SB	CS	SBR	FR	POS	TPR
1982	Hou-N	5	6	0	1	0	0	0	1	0	4	.167	.167	.167	-7	-1	-1	0	0	0	0	-0	/O	0.0

■ FLOYD RAYFORD
Rayford, Floyd Kinnard b: 7/27/57, Memphis, Tenn. BR/TR, 5'10", 190 lbs. Deb: 4/17/80

YEAR	TM/L	G	AB	R	H	2B	3B	HR	RBI	BB	SO	AVG	OBP	SLG	PRO+	BR	/A	RC	SB	CS	SBR	FR	POS	TPR
1980	Bal-A	8	18	1	4	0	0	0	1	0	5	.222	.222	.222	22	-2	-2	1	0	0	0	0	/32D	-0.1
1982	Bal-A	34	53	7	7	0	0	3	5	6	14	.132	.220	.302	42	-4	-4	4	0	1	-1	5	3/CD	0.0
1983	StL-N	56	104	5	22	4	0	3	14	10	27	.212	.281	.337	70	-4	-4	10	1	0	0	-4	3	-0.8
1984	Bal-A	86	250	24	64	14	0	4	27	12	51	.256	.298	.360	83	-7	-6	25	0	3	-2	10	C3/1	0.6
1985	Bal-A	105	359	55	110	21	1	18	48	10	69	.306	.325	.521	131	12	13	56	3	1	0	-2	3C/D	0.9
1986	Bal-A	81	210	15	37	4	0	8	19	15	50	.176	.231	.310	46	-16	-16	14	0	0	0	4	3C/D	-1.2
1987	Bal-A	20	50	5	11	0	0	2	3	2	9	.220	.250	.340	56	-3	-3	4	0	0	0	6	C/3D	0.4
Total	7	390	1044	112	255	43	1	38	117	55	225	.244	.284	.397	86	-25	-23	113	4	5	-2	20	3C/D12	-0.2

■ FRED RAYMER
Raymer, Frederick Charles b: 11/12/1875, Leavenworth, Kan. d: 6/11/57, Los Angeles, Cal. TR, 5'11", 185 lbs. Deb: 4/24/01

YEAR	TM/L	G	AB	R	H	2B	3B	HR	RBI	BB	SO	AVG	OBP	SLG	PRO+	BR	/A	RC	SB	CS	SBR	FR	POS	TPR
1901	Chi-N	120	463	41	108	14	2	0	43	11		.233	.254	.272	56	-27	-24	39	18			-18	3S/12	-3.4
1904	Bos-N	114	419	28	88	12	3	1	27	13		.210	.234	.260	56	-23	-21	32	17			7	*2	-1.1
1905	Bos-N	137	498	26	105	14	2	0	31	8		.211	.223	.247	42	-36	-34	32	15			-18	*2/1O	-4.7
Total	3	371	1380	95	301	40	7	1	101	32		.218	.237	.259	51	-85	-80	103	50			-29	2/3S1O	-9.2

YEAR	TM/L	G	AB	R	H	2B	3B	HR	RBI	BB	SO	AVG	OBP	SLG	PRO+	BR	/A	RC	SB	CS	SBR	FR	POS	TPR

■ HARRY RAYMOND   Raymond, Harry H. "Jack" b: 2/20/1862, Utica, N.Y. d: 3/21/25, San Diego, Cal. 5'9", 179 lbs. Deb: 9/09/1888

1888	Lou-a	32	123	8	26	2	0	0	13	1		.211	.218	.228	46	-7	-7	8	7			-1	3/O	-0.6
1889	Lou-a	130	515	58	123	12	9	0	47	19	45	.239	.270	.297	64	-25	-24	48	19			-1	*3/OP	-1.9
1890	*Lou-a	123	521	91	135	7	4	2		22		.259	.293	.299	79	-16	-14	52	18			-2	*3/S	-1.5
1891	Lou-a	14	59	4	12	2	0	0	2	5	6	.203	.288	.237	53	-3	-3	5	3			5	S	0.2
1892	Pit-N	12	49	4	4	0	1	0	2	4	8	.082	.151	.122	-16	-7	-7	1	1			-1	3	-0.6
	Was-N	4	15	2	1	0	0	0	0	3	2	.067	.222	.067	-11	-2	-2	0	1			1	/3	0.0
	Yr	16	64	6	5	0	1	0	2	7	10	.078	.169	.109	-15	-9	-9	2	2			-1		-0.6
Total	5	315	1282	167	301	23	14	2	64	54	61	.235	.270	.279	64	-61	-57	114	49			1	3/SOP	-4.4

■ LOU RAYMOND   Raymond, Louis Anthony (b: Louis Anthony Raymondjack) b: 12/11/1894, Buffalo, N.Y. d: 5/2/79, Rochester, N.Y. 5'10.5", 187 lbs. Deb: 5/02/19

| 1919 | Phi-N | 1 | 2 | 0 | 1 | 0 | 0 | 0 | 0 | 0 | | .500 | .500 | .500 | 188 | 0 | 0 | 0 | 0 | | | 0 | /2 | 0.0 |

■ AL REACH   Reach, Alfred James b: 5/25/1840, London, England d: 1/14/28, Atlantic City, N.J TL , 5'6", 155 lbs. Deb: 5/20/1871 M

1871	Ath-n	26	133	43	47	7	6	0	34	5	6	.353	.377	.496	150	8	8	26	2				*2	0.5
1872	Ath-n	24	118	21	23	0	0	0		4		.195	.221	.195	29	-9	-9	5					O/1	-0.5
1873	Ath-n	16	73	13	16	5	1	0		0		.219	.219	.315	51	-4	-5	5					/O2	-0.3
1874	Ath-n	14	55	8	7	2	0	0		0		.127	.127	.164	-7	-6	-7	1					O	-0.4
1875	Ath-n	3	14	4	4	1	0	0		0		.286	.286	.357	109	0	0	1					/O2	0.0
Total	5 n	83	393	89	97	15	7	0		9		.247	.264	.321	73	-11	-13	39					/O21	-0.7

■ BOB REACH   Reach, Robert b: 8/28/1843, Williamsburg, N.Y. d: 5/19/22, Springfield, Mass. 5'5", 155 lbs. Deb: 4/23/1872

1872	Oly-n	2	8	1	2	0	0	0		0		.250	.250	.250	57	-0	-0	1					/S	0.0
1873	Was-n	1	5	1	1	0	0	0		0		.200	.200	.200	19	-0	-0	0					/S	0.0
Total	2 n	3	13	2	3	0	0	0		0		.231	.231	.231	42	-1	-1	1					/S	0.0

■ RANDY READY   Ready, Randy Max b: 1/8/60, Fremont, Cal. BR/TR, 5'11", 180 lbs. Deb: 9/04/83

1983	Mil-A	12	37	8	15	3	2	1	6	6	3	.405	.488	.676	234	6	7	12	0	1	-1	0	/3D	0.6
1984	Mil-A	37	123	13	23	6	1	3	13	14	18	.187	.270	.325	66	-6	-6	11	0	0	0	3	3	-0.1
1985	Mil-A	48	181	29	48	9	5	1	21	14	23	.265	.321	.387	93	-2	-2	22	0	0	0	0	O/32D	-0.1
1986	Mil-A	23	79	8	15	4	0	1	4	9	9	.190	.273	.278	49	-5	-6	6	2	0	1	-4	O/23D	-0.8
	SD-N	1	3	0	0	0	0	0	0	0	1	.000	.000	.000	-99	-1	-1	0	0	0	0	0	/3	0.0
1987	SD-N	124	350	69	108	26	6	12	54	67	44	.309	.424	.520	154	27	29	81	7	3	0	1	32O	3.0
1988	SD-N	114	331	43	88	16	2	7	39	39	38	.266	.349	.390	114	6	6	48	6	2	1	-8	32O	0.2
1989	SD-N	28	67	4	17	2	1	0	5	11	6	.254	.359	.313	94	-0	-0	8	0	0	0	2	3/2O	0.2
	Phi-N	72	187	33	50	11	1	8	21	31	31	.267	.377	.465	140	10	10	35	4	3	-1	-6	O3/2	0.3
	Yr	100	254	37	67	13	2	8	26	42	37	.264	.372	.425	127	10	10	43	4	3	-1	-4		0.5
1990	Phi-N	101	217	26	53	9	1	1	26	29	35	.244	.336	.309	79	-5	-5	25	3	2	-0	-3	O2	-0.9
Total	8	560	1575	233	417	86	19	34	189	220	208	.265	.358	.408	113	29	33	248	22	11	0	-14	3O2/D	2.2

■ LEROY REAMS   Reams, Leroy b: 8/11/43, Pine Bluff, Ark. BL/TR, 6'2", 175 lbs. Deb: 5/07/69

| 1969 | Phi-N | 1 | 1 | 0 | 0 | 0 | 0 | 0 | 0 | 0 | 1 | .000 | .000 | .000 | -99 | -0 | -0 | 0 | 0 | 0 | 0 | 0 | H | 0.0 |

■ PHIL REARDON   Reardon, Philip Michael b: 10/3/1883, Brooklyn, N.Y. d: 9/28/20, Brooklyn, N.Y. BR/TR, Deb: 9/19/06

| 1906 | Bro-N | 5 | 14 | 0 | 1 | 0 | 0 | 0 | 0 | 0 | | .071 | .071 | .071 | -60 | -2 | -2 | 0 | 0 | | | 1 | /O | -0.1 |

■ ART REBEL   Rebel, Arthur Anthony b: 3/4/15, Cincinnati, Ohio BL/TL, 5'8", 180 lbs. Deb: 4/19/38

1938	Phi-N	7	9	2	2	0	0	0	1	1	1	.222	.300	.222	47	-1	-1	0	0			0	/O	0.0
1945	StL-N	26	72	12	25	4	0	0	5	6	4	.347	.397	.403	120	2	2	11	1			2	O	0.3
Total	2	33	81	14	27	4	0	0	6	7	5	.333	.386	.383	112	2	2	11	1			2	/O	0.3

■ JOHN RECCIUS   Reccius, John b: 6/7/1862, Louisville, Ky. d: 9/1/30, Louisville, Ky. 5'6.5", Deb: 5/02/1882

1882	Lou-a	74	266	46	63	12	3	1		23		.237	.298	.316	114	3	5	26				-3	*OP	0.3
1883	Lou-a	18	63	10	9	2	0	0		7		.143	.229	.175	34	-4	-4	3				-1	O/P	-0.3
Total	2	92	329	56	72	14	3	1		30		.219	.284	.289	98	-2	1	28				-4	/OP	0.0

■ PHIL RECCIUS   Reccius, Phillip b: 6/7/1862, Louisville, Ky. d: 2/15/03, Louisville, Ky. 5'9", 163 lbs. Deb: 9/25/1882

1882	Lou-a	4	15	2	2	0	0	0		0		.133	.133	.133	-10	-2	-2	0				0	/O	-0.1
1883	Lou-a	1	3	1	1	1	0	0		0		.333	.333	.667	232	0	0	1				-0	/O	0.0
1884	Lou-a	73	263	23	63	9	2	3		5		.240	.267	.323	99	-2	0	23				-2	3PS	0.1
1885	Lou-a	102	402	57	97	8	10	1		13		.241	.267	.318	87	-6	-6	35				-1	*3/P	0.1
1886	Lou-a	5	13	4	4	1	1	0		3		.308	.471	.538	206	2	2	3	0			1	/OP	0.2
1887	Lou-a	11	37	9	9	2	0	0		8		.243	.391	.297	94	0	0	6	3			2	O/S	0.1
	Cle-a	62	229	23	47	6	3	0		24		.205	.295	.258	58	-12	-11	21	9			8	3/P	-0.3
	Yr	73	266	32	56	8	3	0		32		.211	.309	.263	64	-12	-11	26	12			10		-0.2
1888	Lou-a	2	9	0	2	1	0	0	4	1		.222	.300	.333	108	0	0	1	0			-1	/3	0.0
1890	Roc-a	1	4	0	0	0	0	0		0		.000	.000	.000	-99	-1	-1	0	0			-0	/O	0.0
Total	8	261	975	117	225	28	16	4	4	54		.231	.280	.305	83	-20	-17	90	12			6	3/POS	0.0

■ JOHNNY REDER   Reder, John Anthony b: 9/24/09, Lublin, Poland BR/TR, 6', 184 lbs. Deb: 4/16/32

| 1932 | Bos-A | 17 | 37 | 4 | 5 | 1 | 0 | 0 | 3 | 6 | 6 | .135 | .256 | .162 | 11 | -5 | -5 | 2 | 0 | 0 | 0 | 0 | 1/3 | -0.4 |

■ BUCK REDFERN   Redfern, George Howard b: 4/7/02, Asheville, N.C. d: 9/8/64, Asheville, N.C. BR/TR, 5'11", 165 lbs. Deb: 4/11/28

1928	Chi-A	86	261	22	61	6	3	0	35	12	19	.234	.267	.280	44	-21	-21	21	8	2	1	6	2S/3	-0.7
1929	Chi-A	21	46	0	6	0	0	0	3	3	3	.130	.184	.130	-18	-8	-8	1	1	1	-0	-5	2/3S	-1.1
Total	2	107	307	22	67	6	3	0	38	15	22	.218	.255	.257	35	-29	-29	22	9	3	1	1	/2S3	-1.8

■ JOE REDFIELD   Redfield, Joseph Randall b: 1/14/61, Doylestown, Pa. BR/TR, 6'2", 190 lbs. Deb: 6/04/88

| 1988 | Cal-A | 1 | 2 | 0 | 0 | 0 | 0 | 0 | 0 | 0 | 0 | .000 | .000 | .000 | -99 | -1 | -1 | 0 | 0 | 0 | 0 | 0 | /3 | 0.0 |

■ GLENN REDMON   Redmon, Glenn Vincent b: 1/11/48, Detroit, Mich. BR/TR, 5'11", 180 lbs. Deb: 9/08/74

| 1974 | SF-N | 7 | 17 | 0 | 4 | 3 | 0 | 0 | 4 | 1 | 3 | .235 | .278 | .412 | 87 | -0 | -0 | 2 | 0 | 0 | 0 | -1 | /2 | 0.0 |

■ HARRY REDMOND   Redmond, Harry John b: 9/13/1887, Cleveland, Ohio d: 7/10/60, Cleveland, Ohio TR , Deb: 9/07/09

| 1909 | Bro-N | 6 | 19 | 3 | 0 | 0 | 0 | 0 | 1 | 0 | | .000 | .000 | .000 | -99 | -4 | -4 | -0 | 0 | | | 4 | /2 | 0.0 |

■ WAYNE REDMOND   Redmond, Howard Wayne b: 11/25/45, Athens, Ala. BR/TR, 5'10", 165 lbs. Deb: 9/07/65

1965	Det-A	4	4	1	0	0	0	0	0	1	1	.000	.200	.000	-38	-1	-1	0	0	0	0	0	/O	0.0
1969	Det-A	5	3	0	0	0	0	0	0	0	2	.000	.000	.000	-96	-1	-1	0	0	0	0	0	H	0.0
Total	2	9	7	1	0	0	0	0	0	1	3	.000	.125	.000	-60	-2	-2	0	0	0	0	0	/O	0.0

■ JACK REDMOND   Redmond, John McKittrick "Red" b: 9/3/10, Florence, Ariz. d: 7/27/68, Garland, Tex. BL/TR, 5'11", 185 lbs. Deb: 4/22/35

| 1935 | Was-A | 22 | 34 | 8 | 6 | 1 | 0 | 1 | 7 | 3 | 1 | .176 | .243 | .294 | 40 | -3 | -3 | 3 | 0 | 0 | 0 | 2 | C | 0.0 |

■ BILLY REDMON   Redmon, William T. b: Brooklyn, N.Y. BL/TL, Deb: 5/04/1875

| 1875 | RS-n | 19 | 82 | 12 | 16 | 2 | 0 | 0 | | 2 | | .195 | .214 | .220 | 56 | -4 | -3 | 4 | | | | | S/3 | -0.2 |

YEAR	TM/L	G	AB	R	H	2B	3B	HR	RBI	BB	SO	AVG	OBP	SLG	PRO+	BR	/A	RC	SB	CS	SBR	FR	POS	TPR
1877	Cin-N	3	12	1	3	1	0	0	3	1	1	.250	.308	.333	115	0	0	1				2	/S	0.2
1878	Mil-N	48	187	16	43	8	0	0	21	8	13	.230	.262	.273	71	-5	-6	14				-17	S/O3C	-1.9
Total	2	51	199	17	46	9	0	0	24	9	14	.231	.264	.276	73	-5	-6	15				-15	/SO3C	-1.7

■ GARY REDUS   Redus, Gary Eugene   b: 11/1/56, Athens, Ala.   BR/TR, 6'1", 180 lbs.   Deb: 9/07/82

YEAR	TM/L	G	AB	R	H	2B	3B	HR	RBI	BB	SO	AVG	OBP	SLG	PRO+	BR	/A	RC	SB	CS	SBR	FR	POS	TPR
1982	Cin-N	20	83	12	18	3	2	1	7	5	21	.217	.261	.337	65	-4	-4	8	11	2	2	-1	O	-0.3
1983	Cin-N	125	453	90	112	20	9	17	51	71	111	.247	.353	.444	115	12	10	76	39	14	3	5	*O	1.7
1984	Cin-N	123	394	69	100	21	3	7	22	52	71	.254	.342	.376	97	2	-1	58	48	11	8	-3	*O	0.0
1985	Cin-N	101	246	51	62	14	4	6	28	44	52	.252	.368	.415	113	7	6	45	48	12	7	-6	O	0.5
1986	Phi-N	90	340	62	84	22	4	11	33	47	78	.247	.344	.432	109	6	4	55	25	7	3	5	O	1.1
1987	Chi-A	130	475	78	112	26	6	12	48	69	90	.236	.333	.392	89	-5	-7	69	52	11	9	6	*O/D	0.5
1988	Chi-A	77	262	42	69	10	4	6	34	33	52	.263	.350	.401	110	4	4	42	26	2	7	-3	O/D	0.7
	Pit-N	30	71	12	14	2	0	2	4	15	19	.197	.345	.310	90	-0	-0	9	5	2	0	1	O	0.1
1989	Pit-N	98	279	42	79	18	7	6	33	40	51	.283	.375	.462	143	14	16	52	25	6	4	2	1O	1.7
1990	*Pit-N	96	227	32	56	15	3	6	23	33	38	.247	.347	.419	114	3	5	36	11	5	0	-3	1/O	-0.1
Total	9	890	2830	490	706	151	42	74	283	409	583	.249	.347	.411	107	39	33	450	290	72	44	4	O1/D	5.9

■ BOB REECE   Reece, Robert Scott   b: 1/5/51, Sacramento, Cal.   BR/TR, 6'1", 190 lbs.   Deb: 4/22/78

YEAR	TM/L	G	AB	R	H	2B	3B	HR	RBI	BB	SO	AVG	OBP	SLG	PRO+	BR	/A	RC	SB	CS	SBR	FR	POS	TPR
1978	Mon-N	9	11	2	2	1	0	0	3	0	4	.182	.182	.273	26	-1	-1	1	0	0	0	1	/C	0.0

■ DARREN REED   Reed, Darren Douglas   b: 10/16/65, Ventura, Cal.   BR/TR, 6'1", 190 lbs.   Deb: 5/01/90

YEAR	TM/L	G	AB	R	H	2B	3B	HR	RBI	BB	SO	AVG	OBP	SLG	PRO+	BR	/A	RC	SB	CS	SBR	FR	POS	TPR
1990	NY-N	26	39	5	8	4	1	1	2	3	11	.205	.262	.436	90	-1	-1	5	1	0	0	1	O	0.0

■ HUGH REED   Reed, Hugh   b: 1837, Chicago, Ill.   d: 11/3/1883, Chicago, Ill.   Deb: 8/26/1874

YEAR	TM/L	G	AB	R	H	2B	3B	HR	RBI	BB	SO	AVG	OBP	SLG	PRO+	BR	/A	RC	SB	CS	SBR	FR	POS	TPR
1874	Bal-n	1	4	0	0	0	0	0		0		.000	.000	.000	-99	-1	-1	0					/O	0.0

■ JEFF REED   Reed, Jeffrey Scott   b: 11/12/62, Joliet, Ill.   BL/TR, 6'2", 190 lbs.   Deb: 4/05/84

YEAR	TM/L	G	AB	R	H	2B	3B	HR	RBI	BB	SO	AVG	OBP	SLG	PRO+	BR	/A	RC	SB	CS	SBR	FR	POS	TPR
1984	Min-A	18	21	3	3	3	0	0	1	2	6	.143	.217	.286	36	-2	-2	1	0	0	0	2	C	0.1
1985	Min-A	7	10	2	2	0	0	0	0	0	3	.200	.200	.200	9	-1	-1	0	0	0	0	-0	/C	0.0
1986	Min-A	68	165	13	39	6	1	2	9	16	19	.236	.308	.321	70	-6	-7	17	1	0	0	8	C	0.5
1987	Mon-N	75	207	15	44	11	0	1	21	12	20	.213	.259	.280	42	-17	-18	14	0	1	-1	-4	C	-1.6
1988	Mon-N	43	123	10	27	3	2	0	9	13	22	.220	.294	.276	62	-5	-6	10	1	0	0	2	C	-0.1
	Cin-N	49	142	10	33	6	0	1	7	15	19	.232	.306	.296	71	-5	-5	13	0	0	0	6	C	0.3
	Yr	92	265	20	60	9	2	1	16	28	41	.226	.300	.287	66	-10	-11	24	1	0	0	8		0.2
1989	Cin-N	102	287	16	64	11	0	3	23	34	46	.223	.310	.293	71	-9	-10	27	0	0	0	-5	C	-0.8
1990	*Cin-N	72	175	12	44	8	1	3	16	24	26	.251	.342	.360	91	-1	-2	22	0	0	0	1	C	0.3
Total	7	434	1130	81	256	48	4	10	86	116	161	.227	.301	.303	66	-47	-51	106	2	1	0	10	C	-1.3

■ JODY REED   Reed, Jody Eric   b: 7/26/62, Tampa, Fla.   BR/TR, 5'9", 170 lbs.   Deb: 9/12/87

YEAR	TM/L	G	AB	R	H	2B	3B	HR	RBI	BB	SO	AVG	OBP	SLG	PRO+	BR	/A	RC	SB	CS	SBR	FR	POS	TPR
1987	Bos-A	9	30	4	9	1	1	0	8	4	0	.300	.382	.400	105	0	0	5	1	1	-0	5	/S23	0.5
1988	*Bos-A	109	338	60	99	23	1	1	28	45	21	.293	.382	.376	109	8	6	51	1	3	-2	3	S2/3D	1.2
1989	Bos-A	146	524	76	151	42	2	3	40	73	44	.288	.379	.393	111	15	11	81	4	5	-2	1	S2/3OD	1.7
1990	*Bos-A	155	598	70	173	**45**	0	5	51	75	65	.289	.372	.390	108	13	9	87	4	4	-1	-7	*2S/D	1.0
Total	4	419	1490	210	432	111	4	9	127	197	130	.290	.377	.388	109	36	26	224	10	13	-5	1	S2/3DO	4.4

■ JACK REED   Reed, John Burwell   b: 2/2/33, Silver City, Miss.   BR/TR, 6', 185 lbs.   Deb: 4/23/61

YEAR	TM/L	G	AB	R	H	2B	3B	HR	RBI	BB	SO	AVG	OBP	SLG	PRO+	BR	/A	RC	SB	CS	SBR	FR	POS	TPR
1961	*NY-A	28	13	4	2	0	0	0	1	1	1	.154	.214	.154	0	-2	-2	0	0	0	0	1	O	-0.1
1962	NY-A	88	43	17	13	2	1	1	4	4	7	.302	.362	.465	125	1	1	7	2	1	0	5	O	0.4
1963	NY-A	106	73	18	15	3	1	0	1	9	14	.205	.293	.274	60	-4	-4	7	5	1	1	9	O	0.3
Total	3	222	129	39	30	5	2	1	6	14	22	.233	.308	.326	76	-4	-4	14	7	2	1	16	O	0.6

■ MILT REED   Reed, Milton D.   b: 7/4/1890, Atlanta, Ga.   d: 7/27/38, Atlanta, Ga.   BL/TR, 5'9.5", 150 lbs.   Deb: 9/09/11

YEAR	TM/L	G	AB	R	H	2B	3B	HR	RBI	BB	SO	AVG	OBP	SLG	PRO+	BR	/A	RC	SB	CS	SBR	FR	POS	TPR
1911	StL-N	1	1	0	0	0	0	0	0	0	0	.000	.000	.000	-99	-0	-0	0	0			0	H	0.0
1913	Phi-N	13	24	4	6	1	0	0	0	1	5	.250	.280	.292	61	-1	-1	2	1			-4	/S2	-0.4
1914	Phi-N	44	107	10	22	2	1	0	2	10	13	.206	.280	.243	52	-6	-6	8	4			-17	S2/3	-2.5
1915	Bro-F	10	31	2	9	1	1	0	8	2	0	.290	.353	.387	120	1	1	5	2			-4	S	-0.2
Total	4	68	163	16	37	4	2	0	10	13	18	.227	.292	.276	65	-6	-7	16	7			-25	/S23	-3.1

■ TED REED   Reed, Ralph Edwin   b: 10/18/1890, Beaver, Pa.   d: 2/16/59, Beaver, Pa.   BR/TR, 5'11", 190 lbs.   Deb: 9/10/15

YEAR	TM/L	G	AB	R	H	2B	3B	HR	RBI	BB	SO	AVG	OBP	SLG	PRO+	BR	/A	RC	SB	CS	SBR	FR	POS	TPR
1915	New-F	20	77	5	20	1	2	0	4	2	7	.260	.287	.325	86	-2	-1	9	1			-3	3	-0.3

■ BILLY REED   Reed, William Joseph   b: 11/12/22, Shawano, Wis.   BL/TR, 5'10.5", 175 lbs.   Deb: 4/15/52

YEAR	TM/L	G	AB	R	H	2B	3B	HR	RBI	BB	SO	AVG	OBP	SLG	PRO+	BR	/A	RC	SB	CS	SBR	FR	POS	TPR
1952	Bos-N	15	52	4	13	0	0	0	0	0	5	.250	.264	.250	45	-4	-4	3	0	0	0	-6	2	-0.9

■ ICICLE REEDER   Reeder, James Edward   b: 1865, Cincinnati, Ohio   Deb: 6/24/1884

YEAR	TM/L	G	AB	R	H	2B	3B	HR	RBI	BB	SO	AVG	OBP	SLG	PRO+	BR	/A	RC	SB	CS	SBR	FR	POS	TPR
1884	Cin-a	3	14	0	2	0	0	0		0		.143	.143	.143	-5	-2	-2	0				-0	/O	-0.1
	Was-U	3	12	0	2	0	0	0		0		.167	.167	.167	13	-1	-1	0	0			-1	/O	-0.1

■ NICK REEDER   Reeder, Nicholas (b: Nicholas Herchenroeder)   b: 3/22/1867, Louisville, Ky.   d: 9/26/1894, Louisville, Ky.   BR/TR, 5'9", 189 lbs.   Deb: 4/11/1891

YEAR	TM/L	G	AB	R	H	2B	3B	HR	RBI	BB	SO	AVG	OBP	SLG	PRO+	BR	/A	RC	SB	CS	SBR	FR	POS	TPR
1891	Lou-a	1	2	0	0	0	0	0	0	0	1	.000	.000	.000	-99	-1	-1	0				0	/3	0.0

■ RANDY REESE   Reese, Andrew Jackson   b: 2/7/04, Tupelo, Miss.   d: 1/10/66, Tupelo, Miss.   BR/TR, 5'11", 180 lbs.   Deb: 4/15/27

YEAR	TM/L	G	AB	R	H	2B	3B	HR	RBI	BB	SO	AVG	OBP	SLG	PRO+	BR	/A	RC	SB	CS	SBR	FR	POS	TPR
1927	NY-N	97	355	43	94	14	2	4	21	13	52	.265	.298	.349	73	-14	-14	36	5			-2	3O/1	-1.2
1928	NY-N	109	406	61	125	18	4	6	44	13	24	.308	.331	.416	94	-5	-5	53	7			-8	02/1S3	-1.3
1929	NY-N	58	209	36	55	11	3	0	21	15	19	.263	.316	.344	64	-12	-12	23	8			2	2/O3	-0.8
1930	NY-N	67	172	26	47	4	2	4	25	10	12	.273	.313	.390	70	-9	-8	20	1			-3	O3/1	-1.1
Total	4	331	1142	166	321	47	11	14	111	51	107	.281	.315	.378	78	-40	-39	132	21			-11	O/321S	-4.4

■ PEE WEE REESE   Reese, Harold Henry   b: 7/23/18, Ekron, Ky.   BR/TR, 5'10", 160 lbs.   Deb: 4/23/40   CH

YEAR	TM/L	G	AB	R	H	2B	3B	HR	RBI	BB	SO	AVG	OBP	SLG	PRO+	BR	/A	RC	SB	CS	SBR	FR	POS	TPR
1940	Bro-N	84	312	58	85	8	4	5	28	45	42	.272	.366	.372	98	3	1	47	15			-14	S	-0.5
1941	*Bro-N	152	595	76	136	23	5	2	46	68	56	.229	.311	.294	68	-22	-25	59	10			8	*S	-0.3
1942	Bro-N	151	564	87	144	24	5	3	53	82	55	.255	.350	.332	98	2	1	71	15			17	*S	3.1
1946	Bro-N	152	542	79	154	16	10	5	60	87	71	.284	.384	.378	116	15	14	85	10			-3	*S	2.3
1947	*Bro-N	142	476	81	135	24	4	12	73	**104**	67	.284	.414	.426	119	21	18	93	7			-2	*S	2.6
1948	Bro-N	151	566	96	155	31	4	9	75	79	63	.274	.363	.390	100	5	2	82	25			10	*S	2.8
1949	*Bro-N	155	617	**132**	172	27	3	16	73	116	59	.279	.396	.410	112	19	15	111	26			2	*S	3.3
1950	Bro-N	141	531	97	138	21	5	11	52	91	62	.260	.369	.380	96	1	-1	81	17			2	*S/3	1.4
1951	*Bro-N	154	616	94	176	20	8	10	84	81	57	.286	.371	.393	103	7	5	91	20	14	-2	-8	*S	0.7
1952	*Bro-N	149	559	94	152	18	8	6	58	86	59	.272	.369	.365	103	6	5	84	**30**	5	**6**	-11	*S	0.4
1953	*Bro-N	140	524	108	142	25	7	13	61	82	61	.271	.374	.420	104	7	6	88	22	6	**3**	-1	*S	1.8
1954	Bro-N	141	554	98	171	35	8	10	69	90	62	.309	.408	.455	121	23	21	104	8	5	-1	2	*S	2.5
1955	*Bro-N	145	553	99	156	29	4	10	61	78	60	.282	.374	.403	103	7	5	82	8	7	-2	-13	*S	-1.9
1956	*Bro-N	147	572	85	147	19	2	9	46	56	69	.257	.324	.344	74	-15	-21	66	13	4	2	-9	*S3	-1.2
1957	Bro-N	103	330	33	74	3	1	1	29	29	32	.224	.308	.248	47	-21	-25	27	5	2	0	10	3S	-1.2
1958	LA-N	59	147	21	33	7	2	4	17	26	15	.224	.341	.381	88	-2	-2	20	1	2	-1	-8	S3	-0.9
Total	16	2166	8058	1338	2170	330	80	126	885	1210	890	.269	.366	.377	98	56	19	1191	232	_45_		-24	*S3	15.6

YEAR	TM/L	G	AB	R	H	2B	3B	HR	RBI	BB	SO	AVG	OBP	SLG	PRO+	BR	/A	RC	SB	CS	SBR	FR	POS	TPR

■ JIMMIE REESE
Reese, James Herman (b: James Herman Soloman) b: 10/1/05, Los Angeles, Cal.   BL/TR, 5'11.5", 165 lbs.   Deb: 4/19/30 C

YEAR	TM/L	G	AB	R	H	2B	3B	HR	RBI	BB	SO	AVG	OBP	SLG	PRO+	BR	/A	RC	SB	CS	SBR	FR	POS	TPR
1930	NY-A	77	188	44	65	14	2	3	18	11	8	.346	.382	.489	125	5	6	35	1	1	-0	-9	2/3	-0.1
1931	NY-A	65	245	41	59	10	2	3	26	17	10	.241	.293	.335	68	-13	-11	24	2	3	-1	5	2	-0.2
1932	StL-N	90	309	38	82	15	0	2	26	20	19	.265	.314	.333	72	-11	-12	33	4			9	2	0.2
Total	3	232	742	123	206	39	4	8	70	48	37	.278	.324	.373	84	-19	-17	92	7	4		4	2/3	-0.1

■ RICH REESE
Reese, Richard Benjamin b: 9/29/41, Leipsic, Ohio BL/TL, 6'3", 185 lbs.   Deb: 9/04/64

YEAR	TM/L	G	AB	R	H	2B	3B	HR	RBI	BB	SO	AVG	OBP	SLG	PRO+	BR	/A	RC	SB	CS	SBR	FR	POS	TPR
1964	Min-A	10	7	0	0	0	0	0	0	0	1	.000	.000	.000	-99	-2	-2	0	0	0	0	0	/1	-0.1
1965	Min-A	14	7	0	2	1	0	0	0	2	2	.286	.444	.429	143	1	1	1	0	0	0	0	/1O	0.0
1966	Min-A	3	2	0	0	0	0	0	0	1	2	.000	.333	.000	5	-0	-0	0	0	0	0	0	H	0.0
1967	Min-A	95	101	13	25	5	0	4	20	8	17	.248	.303	.416	102	1	0	13	0	0	0	0	1O	-0.2
1968	Min-A	126	332	40	86	15	2	4	28	18	36	.259	.303	.352	93	-1	-3	35	3	1	0	-1	1O	-0.8
1969	*Min-A	132	419	52	135	24	4	16	69	23	57	.322	.365	.513	140	22	21	76	1	5	-3	-3	*1/O	0.7
1970	*Min-A	153	501	63	131	15	5	10	56	48	70	.261	.335	.371	93	-3	-4	64	5	4	-1	-2	*1	-1.4
1971	Min-A	120	329	40	72	8	3	10	39	20	35	.219	.274	.353	74	-11	-12	30	7	4	-0	-1	1/O	-1.9
1972	Min-A	132	197	23	43	3	2	5	26	25	27	.218	.306	.330	85	-2	-3	20	0	1	-1	3	1O	-1.2
1973	Det-A	59	102	10	14	1	0	2	4	7	17	.137	.193	.206	11	-12	-13	4	0	0	0	-1	1O	-1.6
	Min-A	22	23	7	4	1	1	1	3	6	6	.174	.345	.435	114	1	1	4	0	0	0	1	1	0.0
	Yr	81	125	17	18	2	1	3	7	13	23	.144	.225	.248	31	-11	-12	7	0	0	0	-0		-1.6
Total	10	866	2020	248	512	73	17	52	245	158	270	.253	.314	.384	95	-8	-16	247	16	15	-4	-3	1/O	-6.5

■ BOBBY REEVES
Reeves, Robert Edwin "Gunner" b: 6/24/04, Hill City, Tenn. BR/TR, 5'11", 170 lbs.   Deb: 6/09/26

YEAR	TM/L	G	AB	R	H	2B	3B	HR	RBI	BB	SO	AVG	OBP	SLG	PRO+	BR	/A	RC	SB	CS	SBR	FR	POS	TPR
1926	Was-A	20	49	4	11	0	1	0	7	6	9	.224	.321	.265	56	-3	-3	4	1	1	-0	1	3/2S	0.0
1927	Was-A	112	380	37	97	11	5	1	39	21	53	.255	.296	.318	60	-23	-23	35	3	1	0	-7	S3/2	-1.8
1928	Was-A	102	353	44	107	16	8	3	42	24	47	.303	.351	.419	102	0	1	50	4	8	-4	-4	S2/3O	0.1
1929	Bos-A	140	460	66	114	19	2	2	28	60	57	.248	.343	.311	71	-19	-17	52	7	8	-3	1	*3/2S1	-1.0
1930	Bos-A	92	272	41	59	7	4	2	18	50	36	.217	.345	.294	66	-14	-12	32	6	2	1	5	3S2	-0.1
1931	Bos-A	36	84	11	14	2	2	0	1	14	16	.167	.293	.238	43	-7	-6	7	0	1	-1	-8	2/P	-1.1
Total	6	502	1598	203	402	55	22	8	135	175	218	.252	.331	.329	73	-66	-60	180	21	21	-6	-11	3S/2P10	-3.9

■ RUDY REGALADO
Regalado, Rudolph Valentino b: 5/21/30, Los Angeles, Cal. BR/TR, 6'1", 185 lbs.   Deb: 4/13/54

YEAR	TM/L	G	AB	R	H	2B	3B	HR	RBI	BB	SO	AVG	OBP	SLG	PRO+	BR	/A	RC	SB	CS	SBR	FR	POS	TPR
1954	*Cle-A	65	180	21	45	5	0	2	24	19	16	.250	.335	.311	76	-5	-5	19	0	2	-1	-5	3/2	-1.4
1955	Cle-A	10	26	2	7	2	0	0	5	2	4	.269	.321	.346	77	-1	-1	3	0	0	0	2	/32	0.1
1956	Cle-A	16	47	4	11	1	0	0	2	4	1	.234	.308	.255	49	-3	-3	4	0	0	0	-6	3/1	-0.9
Total	3	91	253	27	63	8	0	2	31	25	21	.249	.329	.304	71	-9	-10	26	0	2	-1	-10	/321	-2.2

■ JOE REGAN
Regan, Joseph Charles b: 7/12/1872, Seymour, Conn. d: 11/18/48, Hartford, Conn. BR/TR, 6'1", Deb: 9/21/1898

YEAR	TM/L	G	AB	R	H	2B	3B	HR	RBI	BB	SO	AVG	OBP	SLG	PRO+	BR	/A	RC	SB	CS	SBR	FR	POS	TPR
1898	NY-N	2	5	1	1	0	0	0	2	0		.200	.200	.200	17	-1	-1	0	0			-1	/O	0.0

■ BILL REGAN
Regan, William Wright b: 1/23/1899, Pittsburgh, Pa. d: 6/11/68, Pittsburgh, Pa. BR/TR, 5'10", 155 lbs.   Deb: 6/02/26

YEAR	TM/L	G	AB	R	H	2B	3B	HR	RBI	BB	SO	AVG	OBP	SLG	PRO+	BR	/A	RC	SB	CS	SBR	FR	POS	TPR
1926	Bos-A	108	403	40	106	21	3	4	34	23	37	.263	.309	.360	76	-16	-15	45	6	3	0	17	*2	0.7
1927	Bos-A	129	468	43	128	37	10	2	66	26	51	.274	.315	.408	88	-11	-10	55	10	10	-3	3	*2	-0.4
1928	Bos-A	138	511	53	135	30	6	7	75	21	44	.264	.296	.387	80	-18	-17	58	9	6	-1	15	*2/O	0.0
1929	Bos-A	104	371	38	107	27	7	1	54	22	38	.288	.328	.407	90	-7	-6	49	7	5	-1	-16	23/1	-1.9
1930	Bos-A	134	507	54	135	35	10	3	53	25	60	.266	.303	.393	78	-21	-18	60	4	2	0	-10	*2/3	-2.3
1931	Pit-N	28	104	8	21	8	0	1	10	5	19	.202	.239	.308	46	-8	-8	8	2			-0	2	-0.6
Total	6	641	2364	236	632	158	36	18	292	122	245	.267	.306	.387	81	-82	-73	275	38	26		9	2/31O	-4.1

■ TONY REGO
Rego, Antone (b: Antone Do Rego) b: 10/31/1897, Wailuku, Hawaii d: 1/6/78, Tulsa, Okla. BR/TR, 5'4", 165 lbs.   Deb: 6/21/24

YEAR	TM/L	G	AB	R	H	2B	3B	HR	RBI	BB	SO	AVG	OBP	SLG	PRO+	BR	/A	RC	SB	CS	SBR	FR	POS	TPR
1924	StL-A	24	59	5	13	1	0	0	5	1	3	.220	.233	.237	20	-7	-7	3	0	0	0	-0	C	-0.5
1925	StL-A	20	32	5	13	2	1	0	3	3	2	.406	.472	.531	147	3	3	8	0	0	0	2	C	0.5
Total	2	44	91	10	26	3	1	0	8	4	5	.286	.323	.341	66	-4	-5	11	0	0	0	2	/C	0.0

■ WALLY REHG
Rehg, Walter Phillip b: 8/31/1888, Summerfield, Ill. d: 4/5/46, Burbank, Cal. BR/TR, 5'8", 160 lbs.   Deb: 4/14/12

YEAR	TM/L	G	AB	R	H	2B	3B	HR	RBI	BB	SO	AVG	OBP	SLG	PRO+	BR	/A	RC	SB	CS	SBR	FR	POS	TPR
1912	Pit-N	8	9	1	0	0	0	0	0	0	1	.000	.000	.000	-99	-2	-2	0	0			0	/O	-0.1
1913	Bos-A	30	101	13	28	3	2	0	9	2	7	.277	.291	.347	84	-2	-3	11	4			-3	O	-0.7
1914	Bos-A	88	151	14	33	4	2	0	11	18	11	.219	.306	.272	74	-5	-5	12	5	8	-3	-5	O	-1.7
1915	Bos-A	5	5	2	1	0	0	0	0	0	1	.200	.200	.200	20	-1	-0	0	1			-0	/OS	0.0
1917	Bos-N	87	341	48	92	12	6	1	31	24	32	.270	.320	.349	111	2	4	41	13			-13	O	-1.2
1918	Bos-N	40	133	6	32	5	1	1	12	5	14	.241	.268	.316	81	-4	-3	11	3			3	O	-0.2
1919	Cin-N	5	12	1	2	0	0	0	3	1	0	.167	.231	.167	21	-1	-1	1	0			1	/O	0.0
Total	7	263	752	85	188	24	11	2	66	50	66	.250	.299	.319	90	-13	-10	76	26	8		-18	O	-3.9

■ FRANK REIBER
Reiber, Frank Bernard "Tubby" b: 9/19/09, Huntington, W.Va. BR/TR, 5'8.5", 169 lbs.   Deb: 4/13/33

YEAR	TM/L	G	AB	R	H	2B	3B	HR	RBI	BB	SO	AVG	OBP	SLG	PRO+	BR	/A	RC	SB	CS	SBR	FR	POS	TPR
1933	Det-A	13	18	3	5	0	1	1	3	2	3	.278	.350	.556	134	1	1	4	0	0	0	-2	/C	0.0
1934	Det-A	3	1	0	0	0	0	0	0	2	0	.000	.667	.000	84	0	0	0	0	0	0	0	H	0.0
1935	Det-A	8	11	3	3	0	0	0	1	3	3	.273	.429	.273	88	-0	0	2	0	0	0	-0	/C	0.0
1936	Det-A	20	55	7	15	2	0	1	5	5	7	.273	.333	.364	72	-2	-2	7	0	1	-1	-3	C/O	-0.3
Total	4	44	85	13	23	2	1	2	9	12	13	.271	.361	.388	89	-1	-1	12	0	1	-1	-5	/CO	-0.3

■ HERMAN REICH
Reich, Herman Charles b: 11/23/17, Bell, Cal. BR/TL, 6'2", 200 lbs.   Deb: 5/03/49

YEAR	TM/L	G	AB	R	H	2B	3B	HR	RBI	BB	SO	AVG	OBP	SLG	PRO+	BR	/A	RC	SB	CS	SBR	FR	POS	TPR
1949	Was-A	2	2	0	0	0	0	0	0	0	1	.000	.000	.000	-99	-1	-1	0	0	0	0	0	H	0.0
	Cle-A	1	2	0	1	0	0	0	0	1	0	.500	.667	.500	215	0	0	1	0	0	0	0	/O	0.0
	Yr	3	4	0	1	0	0	0	0	1	1	.250	.400	.250	75	-0	-0	1	0	0	0	0		0.0
	Chi-N	108	386	43	108	18	2	3	34	13	32	.280	.305	.360	80	-13	-12	41	4			14	1O	0.1

■ RICK REICHARDT
Reichardt, Frederic Carl b: 3/16/43, Madison, Wis. BR/TR, 6'3", 210 lbs.   Deb: 9/01/64

YEAR	TM/L	G	AB	R	H	2B	3B	HR	RBI	BB	SO	AVG	OBP	SLG	PRO+	BR	/A	RC	SB	CS	SBR	FR	POS	TPR
1964	LA-A	11	37	0	6	0	0	0	1	1	12	.162	.184	.162	-3	-5	-5	1	1	0	0	1	O	-0.3
1965	Cal-A	20	75	8	20	4	0	1	6	5	12	.267	.321	.360	95	-1	-0	9	4	1	1	0	O	0.0
1966	Cal-A	89	319	48	92	5	4	16	44	27	61	.288	.368	.480	145	17	18	57	8	4	0	1	O	1.6
1967	Cal-A	146	498	56	132	14	2	17	69	35	90	.265	.322	.404	118	7	9	61	5	3	-0	5	*O	1.1
1968	Cal-A	151	534	62	136	20	3	21	73	42	118	.255	.330	.421	131	17	19	72	8	7	-2	4	*O	1.7
1969	Cal-A	137	493	60	125	11	4	13	68	43	100	.254	.324	.371	99	-4	-1	56	3	6	-3	5	*O/1	-0.2
1970	Cal-A	9	6	1	1	0	0	0	1	3	0	.167	.444	.167	78	0	0	1	0	0	0	0	/O	0.0
	Was-A	107	277	42	70	14	2	15	46	23	69	.253	.330	.480	127	7	9	39	2	4	-2	-4	O/3	0.0
	Yr	116	283	43	71	14	2	15	47	26	69	.251	.333	.473	126	7	9	40	2	4	-2	-4		0.0
1971	Chi-A	138	496	53	138	14	2	19	62	37	90	.278	.336	.429	112	9	7	68	5	10	-5	-11	*O/1	-1.3
1972	Chi-A	101	291	31	73	14	4	8	43	28	63	.251	.323	.409	114	6	5	39	2	2	-1	-12	O	-1.0
1973	Chi-A	46	153	15	42	8	1	3	16	8	29	.275	.315	.399	96	-0	-1	18	2	3	-1	0	O/D	-0.5
	KC-A	41	127	15	28	5	2	3	17	11	28	.220	.283	.362	75	-4	-5	12	0	1	-1	0	D/O	-0.5
	Yr	87	280	30	70	13	3	6	33	19	57	.250	.300	.382	86	-4	-6	30	2	4	-2	0		-1.0
1974	KC-A	1	1	0	1	0	0	0	0	0	0	1.000	1.000	1.000	451	0	0	1	0	0	0	-0	H	0.0
Total	11	997	3307	391	864	109	24	116	445	263	672	.261	.328	.414	115	49	55	434	40	41	-13	-14	O/D13	0.6

YEAR	TM/L	G	AB	R	H	2B	3B	HR	RBI	BB	SO	AVG	OBP	SLG	PRO+	BR	/A	RC	SB	CS	SBR	FR	POS	TPR
■ **DICK REICHLE** Reichle, Richard Wendell b: 11/23/1896, Lincoln, Ill. d: 6/13/67, St.Louis, Mo. BL/TR, 6', 185 lbs. Deb: 9/19/22																								
1922	Bos-A	6	24	3	6	1	0	0	0	0	2	.250	.280	.292	50	-2	-2	2	0	0	0	-0	/O	-0.2
1923	Bos-A	122	361	40	93	17	3	1	39	22	34	.258	.315	.330	69	-16	-16	37	3	6	-3	-6	O/1	-3.3
Total	2	128	385	43	99	18	3	1	39	22	36	.257	.313	.327	68	-18	-18	39	3	6	-3	-7	/O1	-3.5
■ **JESSIE REID** Reid, Jessie Thomas b: 6/1/62, Honolulu, Hawaii BL/TL, 6'1", 200 lbs. Deb: 9/09/87																								
1987	SF-N	6	8	1	1	0	0	1	1	1	5	.125	.222	.500	89	-0	-0	1	0	0	0	0	/O	0.0
1988	SF-N	2	2	0	0	0	0	0	0	0	1	.000	.000	.000	-99	-1	-0	0	0	0	0	0	H	0.0
Total	2	8	10	1	1	0	0	1	1	1	6	.100	.182	.400	54	-1	-1	1	0	0	0	0	/O	0.0
■ **SCOTT REID** Reid, Scott Donald b: 1/7/47, Chicago, Ill. BL/TR, 6'1", 195 lbs. Deb: 9/10/69																								
1969	Phi-N	13	19	5	4	0	0	0	0	7	5	.211	.423	.211	85	0	0	2	0	1	-1	-0	/O	0.0
1970	Phi-N	25	49	5	6	1	0	0	1	11	22	.122	.283	.143	18	-5	-5	3	0	0	0	5	O	0.0
Total	2	38	68	10	10	1	0	0	1	18	27	.147	.326	.162	37	-5	-5	5	0	1	-1	5	/O	0.0
■ **BILLY REID** Reid, William Alexander b: 5/17/1857, London, Ont., Can. d: 6/26/40, London, Ont., Can. BR/TR, 6', 170 lbs. Deb: 5/01/1883																								
1883	Bal-a	24	97	14	27	3	0	0			4	.278	.307	.309	96	-0	-1	9				-8	2/S	-0.6
1884	Pit-a	19	70	11	17	2	0	0			4	.243	.293	.271	87	-1	-1	6				-4	O/32	-0.4
Total	2	43	167	25	44	5	0	0			8	.263	.301	.293	92	-1	-1	15				-12	/2O3S	-1.0
■ **DUKE REILLEY** Reilley, Alexander Aloysius "Midget" b: 8/25/1884, Chicago, Ill. d: 3/4/68, Indianapolis, Ind. BB/TR, 5'4.5", 148 lbs. Deb: 8/28/09																								
1909	Cle-A	20	62	10	13	0	0	0	0	4		.210	.258	.210	46	-4	-4	5	5			1	O	-0.3
■ **CHARLIE REILLEY** Reilley, Charles E. b: 1856, Hartford, Conn. d: 1888, BR/TR, 5'10", 165 lbs. Deb: 5/01/1879																								
1879	Tro-N	62	236	17	54	5	1	0	19	1	20	.229	.232	.258	66	-10	-7	15				-10	C1/O	-1.7
1880	Cin-N	30	103	8	21	1	0	0	9	0	5	.204	.204	.214	42	-6	-6	5				-3	OC/3	-0.8
1881	Det-N	19	70	8	12	2	0	0	3	0	10	.171	.171	.200	16	-7	-7	2				-3	C/OS31	-0.8
	Wor-N	2	8	2	3	0	0	0	1	0	1	.375	.375	.375	129	0	0	1				-2	/C	-0.1
	Yr	21	78	10	15	2	0	0	4	0	11	.192	.192	.218	28	-6	-7	3				-5		-0.9
1882	Pro-N	3	11	0	2	0	0	0	2	1	2	.182	.250	.182	41	-1	-1	1				-3	/C	-0.2
Total	4	116	428	35	92	8	1	0	34	2	38	.215	.219	.238	52	-23	-21	23				-21	/CO13S	-3.6
■ **ARCH REILLY** Reilly, Archer Edwin b: 8/17/1891, Alton, Ill. d: 11/29/63, Columbus, Ohio BR/TR, 5'10", 163 lbs. Deb: 6/01/17																								
1917	Pit-N	1	0	0	0	0	0	0	0	0	0	—	—	—	—	0	0	0	0			0	/3	0.0
■ **BARNEY REILLY** Reilly, Bernard Eugene b: 2/7/1885, Brockton, Mass. d: 11/15/34, St.Joseph, Mo. BR/TR, 6' ", 175 lbs. Deb: 7/02/09																								
1909	Chi-A	12	25	3	5	0	0	0	3	3		.200	.286	.200	56	-1	-1	2	2			4	2/O	0.2
■ **JOSH REILLY** Reilly, Charles b: 1868, San Francisco, Cal. d: 6/13/38, San Francisco, Cal. Deb: 5/02/1896																								
1896	Chi-N	9	42	6	9	1	0	0	2	1	1	.214	.233	.238	24	-4	-5	3	2			-1	/2S	-0.4
■ **CHARLIE REILLY** Reilly, Charles Thomas "Princeton Charlie" b: 6/24/1855, Princeton, N.J. d: 12/16/37, Los Angeles, Cal. BB/TR, 5'11", 190 lbs. Deb: 10/09/1889																								
1889	Col-a	6	23	5	11	1	0	3	6	2	2	.478	.538	.913	330	6	6	17	9			2	/3	0.7
1890	Col-a	137	530	75	141	23	3	4		35		.266	.319	.343	105	-3	3	74	43			28	*3	2.6
1891	Pit-N	114	415	43	91	8	5	3	44	29	58	.219	.277	.284	67	-18	-17	39	20			2	*3S/O	-0.9
1892	Phi-N	91	331	42	65	7	3	1	24	18	43	.196	.242	.245	49	-21	-20	23	13			10	3O/2	-0.5
1893	Phi-N	104	416	64	102	16	7	4	56	33	36	.245	.314	.346	77	-14	-14	51	13			-0	*3	-1.0
1894	Phi-N	39	135	21	40	1	2	0	19	16	10	.296	.383	.333	78	-4	-4	21	9			2	3/O2S1	-0.1
1895	Phi-N	49	179	28	48	6	1	0	25	13	12	.268	.335	.313	69	-8	-8	22	7			-1	S3/2O	-0.2
1897	Was-N	101	351	64	97	18	3	2	60	34		.276	.359	.362	93	-3	-2	53	18			18	*3	1.3
Total	8	641	2380	342	595	80	24	17	234	180	161	.250	.314	.325	82	-64	-55	299	132			60	3/SO21	1.7
■ **HAL REILLY** Reilly, Harold J. Deb: 6/19/19																								
1919	Chi-N	1	3	0	0	0	0	0	0	0	1	.000	.000	.000	-99	-1	-1	0	0			0	/O	0.0
■ **JOHN REILLY** Reilly, John Good "Long Jong" b: 10/5/1858, Cincinnati, Ohio d: 5/31/37, Cincinnati, Ohio BR/TR, 6'3", 178 lbs. Deb: 5/18/1880																								
1880	Cin-N	73	272	21	56	8	4	0	16	3	36	.206	.215	.265	62	-11	-10	16				-3	*1/O	-1.6
1883	Cin-a	98	437	103	136	21	14	9		9		.311	.325	.485	148	26	22	71				-1	*1/O	1.0
1884	Cin-a	105	448	114	152	24	19	**11**		5		.339	.366	**.551**	190	46	43	**93**				-2	*1/OS	3.2
1885	Cin-a	111	482	92	143	18	11	5		11		.297	.322	.411	131	17	15	65				-5	*1/O	0.1
1886	Cin-a	115	441	92	117	12	11	6		31		.265	.321	.383	119	10	9	62	19			-1	*1/O	0.1
1887	Cin-a	134	551	106	170	35	14	10		22		.309	.352	.477	130	21	19	113	50			-0	*1/O	1.3
1888	Cin-a	127	527	112	169	28	14	**13**	103	17		.321	.363	**.501**	171	44	40	**129**	82			-0	*1O	2.9
1889	Cin-a	111	427	84	111	24	13	5	66	34	37	.260	.340	.412	113	8	6	76	43			-1	*1/O	-0.3
1890	Cin-a	133	553	114	166	25	**26**	4	86	16	41	.300	.328	.472	135	19	20	98	29			-3	*1/O	0.7
1891	Cin-N	135	546	60	132	20	13	4	64	9	42	.242	.267	.348	80	-16	-16	58	22			-7	*1O	-2.5
Total	10	1142	4684	898	1352	215	139	69	335	157	156	.289	.325	.438	130	166	148	780	245			-23	*1/OS	4.9
■ **JOE REILLY** Reilly, Joseph J. b: 1861, New York, N.Y. 5'10", 140 lbs. Deb: 4/23/1884																								
1884	Bos-U	3	11	1	0	0	0	0		1		.000	.083	.000	-71	-2	-2	0	0			-1	/O3	-0.2
1885	NY-a	10	40	6	7	3	0	0		2		.175	.214	.250	52	-2	-2	2				1	/23	0.0
Total	2	13	51	7	7	3	0	0		3		.137	.185	.196	25	-4	-4	2				0	/23O	-0.2
■ **TOM REILLY** Reilly, Thomas Henry b: 8/3/1884, St.Louis, Mo. d: 10/18/18, New Orleans, La. BR/TR, 5'10", Deb: 7/27/08																								
1908	StL-N	29	81	5	14	1	0	1	3	2		.173	.193	.222	35	-6	-6	4	4			-6	S	-1.3
1909	StL-N	5	7	0	2	0	1	0	2	0		.286	.286	.571	176	0	0	1	0			0	/S	0.1
1914	Cle-A	1	1	0	0	0	0	0	0	0	0	.000	.000	.000	-96	-0	-0	0	0			0	H	0.0
Total	3	35	89	5	16	1	1	1	5	2	0	.180	.198	.247	45	-6	-6	4	4			-6	/S	-1.2
■ **KEVIN REIMER** Reimer, Kevin Michael b: 6/28/64, Macon, Ga. BL/TR, 6'2", 215 lbs. Deb: 9/13/88																								
1988	Tex-A	12	25	2	3	0	0	1	2	0	6	.120	.120	.240	-2	-3	-3	1	0	0	0	0	/OD	-0.3
1989	Tex-A	3	5	0	0	0	0	0	0	0	1	.000	.000	.000	-98	-1	-1	0	0	0	0	0	/D	0.0
1990	Tex-A	64	100	5	26	9	1	2	15	10	22	.260	.333	.430	110	1	1	14	0	1	-1	-0	D/O	0.0
Total	3	79	130	7	29	9	1	3	17	10	29	.223	.284	.377	82	-3	-3	14	0	1	-1	-0	/DO	-0.3
■ **MIKE REINBACH** Reinbach, Michael Wayne b: 8/6/49, San Diego, Cal. BL/TR, 6'2", 195 lbs. Deb: 4/07/74																								
1974	Bal-A	12	20	2	5	1	0	0	2	2	5	.250	.318	.300	81	-1	-0	2	0	0	0	1	/OD	-0.3
■ **ART REINHOLZ** Reinholz, Arthur August b: 1/27/03, Detroit, Mich. d: 12/29/80, Newport Richey, Fla. BR/TR, 5'10.5", 175 lbs. Deb: 9/25/28																								
1928	Cle-A	2	3	0	1	0	0	0	0	0	0	.333	.500	.333	122	0	0	1	0	0	0	1	/3	0.1
■ **WALLY REINECKER** Reinecker, Walter (b: Walter Joseph Smith) b: 4/21/1890, Pittsburgh, Pa. d: 4/18/57, Pittsburgh, Pa. BR/TR, 5'6", 150 lbs. Deb: 9/17/15																								
1915	Bal-F	3	8	0	1	0	0	0	0	0	0	.125	.222	.125	4	-1	-1	0				-2	/3	-0.2
■ **CHARLIE REIPSCHLAGER** Reipschlager, Charles W. BR/TR, 5'6.5", 160 lbs. Deb: 5/02/1883																								
1883	NY-a	37	145	8	27	4	2	0		4		.186	.208	.241	43	-9	-10	7				6	C/O	0.0

YEAR	TM/L	G	AB	R	H	2B	3B	HR	RBI	BB	SO	AVG	OBP	SLG	PRO+	BR	/A	RC	SB	CS	SBR	FR	POS	TPR
1884	*NY-a	59	233	21	56	13	2	0			1	.240	.250	.313	87	-4	-3	19				17	C/O	1.6
1885	NY-a	72	268	29	65	11	1	0		9		.243	.270	.291	86	-6	-3	22	2			-12	C/O3S2	-0.5
1886	NY-a	65	232	21	49	4	6	0		9		.211	.244	.280	68	-9	-8	17	2			-7	C/O	-1.0
1887	Cle-a	63	231	20	49	8	3	0			11	.212	.251	.273	49	-16	-15	18	7			2	C1	-0.3
Total	5	296	1109	99	246	40	14	0		34		.222	.248	.283	68	-44	-39	82	9			6	C/O132S	-0.2

■ BOBBY REIS
Reis, Robert Joseph Thomas b: 1/2/09, Woodside, N.Y. d: 5/1/73, St.Paul, Minn. BR/TR, 6'1", 175 lbs. Deb: 9/19/31

YEAR	TM/L	G	AB	R	H	2B	3B	HR	RBI	BB	SO	AVG	OBP	SLG	PRO+	BR	/A	RC	SB	CS	SBR	FR	POS	TPR
1931	Bro-N	6	17	3	5	0	0	0	2	2	0	.294	.368	.294	81	-0	-0	2	0			-1	/3	0.0
1932	Bro-N	1	4	0	1	0	0	0	0	0	1	.250	.250	.250	36	-0	-0	0	0			-1	/3	0.0
1935	Bro-N	52	85	10	21	3	2	0	4	6	13	.247	.297	.329	70	-4	-4	8	2			5	OP/213	0.3
1936	Bos-N	37	60	3	13	2	0	0	5	3	6	.217	.254	.250	39	-5	-5	4	0			4	P/O	0.0
1937	Bos-N	45	86	10	21	5	0	0	6	13	12	.244	.343	.302	84	-2	-1	10	2			-2	O/P1	-0.2
1938	Bos-N	34	49	6	9	0	0	0	4	1	3	.184	.200	.184	7	-6	-6	2	1			-1	PO/SC2	-0.3
Total	6	175	301	32	70	10	2	0	21	25	35	.233	.291	.279	59	-18	-16	26	5			6	/PO312SC	-0.2

■ PETE REISER
Reiser, Harold Patrick b: 3/17/19, St.Louis, Mo. d: 10/25/81, Palm Springs, Cal. BL/TR, 5'11", 185 lbs. Deb: 7/23/40 C

YEAR	TM/L	G	AB	R	H	2B	3B	HR	RBI	BB	SO	AVG	OBP	SLG	PRO+	BR	/A	RC	SB	CS	SBR	FR	POS	TPR
1940	Bro-N	58	225	34	66	11	4	3	20	15	33	.293	.338	.418	101	2	0	31	2			-2	3O/S	-0.1
1941	*Bro-N	137	536	117	184	39	17	14	76	46	71	.343	.406	.558	163	48	45	124	4			9	*O	4.9
1942	Bro-N	125	480	89	149	33	5	10	64	48	45	.310	.375	.463	142	26	25	88	20			-7	*O	1.7
1946	Bro-N	122	423	75	117	21	5	11	73	55	58	.277	.361	.428	122	13	12	70	34			7	O3	1.8
1947	*Bro-N	110	388	68	120	23	2	5	46	68	41	.309	.415	.418	117	15	13	74	14			-3	*O	0.6
1948	Bro-N	64	127	17	30	8	2	1	19	29	21	.236	.382	.354	97	1	1	20	4			-2	O/3	-0.3
1949	Bos-N	84	221	32	60	8	3	8	40	33	42	.271	.369	.443	123	6	7	38	3			3	O/3	0.7
1950	Bos-N	53	78	12	16	2	0	1	10	18	22	.205	.367	.269	75	-2	-2	9	1			1	O/3	-0.1
1951	Pit-N	74	140	22	38	9	3	2	13	27	20	.271	.389	.421	115	4	4	25	4	2	0	-2	O/3	0.1
1952	Cle-A	34	44	7	6	1	0	3	7	4	16	.136	.208	.364	61	-3	-3	3	1	1	-0	1	O	-0.1
Total	10	861	2662	473	786	155	41	58	368	343	369	.295	.380	.450	127	110	103	483	87	3		6	O/3S	9.2

■ CHARLIE REISING
Reising, Charles "Pop" b: 8/28/1861, Indiana d: 7/26/15, Louisville, Ky. Deb: 7/19/1884

YEAR	TM/L	G	AB	R	H	2B	3B	HR	RBI	BB	SO	AVG	OBP	SLG	PRO+	BR	/A	RC	SB	CS	SBR	FR	POS	TPR
1884	Ind-a	2	8	0	0	0	0	0	1			.000	.111	.000	-62	-1	-1	0				-1	/O	-0.2

■ AL REISS
Reiss, Albert Allen b: 1/8/09, Elizabeth, N.J. d: 5/13/89, Red Bank, N.J. BB/TR, 5'10.5", 165 lbs. Deb: 6/22/32

YEAR	TM/L	G	AB	R	H	2B	3B	HR	RBI	BB	SO	AVG	OBP	SLG	PRO+	BR	/A	RC	SB	CS	SBR	FR	POS	TPR
1932	Phi-A	9	5	0	1	0	0	0	1	1	1	.200	.333	.200	40	-0	-0	0	0	0	0	0	/S	0.0

■ HEINIE REITZ
Reitz, Henry P. b: 6/29/1867, Chicago, Ill. d: 11/10/14, Sacramento, Cal BL/TR, 5'7", 158 lbs. Deb: 4/27/1893

YEAR	TM/L	G	AB	R	H	2B	3B	HR	RBI	BB	SO	AVG	OBP	SLG	PRO+	BR	/A	RC	SB	CS	SBR	FR	POS	TPR
1893	Bal-N	130	490	90	140	17	13	1	76	65	32	.286	.377	.380	101	4	2	81	24			-1	*2	0.1
1894	*Bal-N	108	446	86	135	22	31	2	105	42	24	.303	.372	.504	106	6	2	93	18			26	*23	2.6
1895	Bal-N	71	245	45	72	15	5	0	29	18	11	.294	.350	.396	91	-2	-4	40	15			-3	23/S	-0.2
1896	*Bal-N	120	464	76	133	15	6	4	106	49	32	.287	.357	.371	93	-3	-4	73	28			-17	*2/S	-1.4
1897	*Bal-N	128	477	76	138	15	6	2	84	50		.289	.370	.358	95	-1	-1	74	23			21	*2	2.6
1898	Was-N	132	489	62	148	20	2	2	47	32		.303	.357	.364	110	6	7	69	11			6	*2	1.7
1899	Pit-N	34	130	11	34	4	2	0	15	10		.262	.314	.323	77	-4	-4	14	3			1	2	0.0
Total	7	723	2741	446	800	108	65	11	462	266	99	.292	.363	.391	99	6	-2	444	122			35	2/3S	5.4

■ KEN REITZ
Reitz, Kenneth John b: 6/24/51, San Francisco, Cal BR/TR, 6', 180 lbs. Deb: 9/05/72

YEAR	TM/L	G	AB	R	H	2B	3B	HR	RBI	BB	SO	AVG	OBP	SLG	PRO+	BR	/A	RC	SB	CS	SBR	FR	POS	TPR
1972	StL-N	21	78	5	28	6	4	0	10	2	4	.359	.375	.410	125	2	2	10	0	1	-1	-4	3	-0.1
1973	StL-N	147	426	40	100	20	2	6	42	9	25	.235	.257	.333	63	-23	-23	31	0	1	-1	-6	*3/S	-3.3
1974	StL-N	154	579	48	157	28	2	7	54	23	63	.271	.301	.363	86	-13	-13	56	0	0	0	-17	*3/S2	-3.3
1975	StL-N	161	592	43	159	25	1	5	63	22	54	.269	.300	.340	75	-19	-22	56	1	1	-0	-21	*3	-4.5
1976	SF-N	155	577	40	154	21	1	5	66	24	48	.267	.297	.333	76	-17	-19	51	5	4	-1	2	*3/S	-2.1
1977	StL-N	157	587	58	153	36	1	17	79	19	74	.261	.292	.412	88	-13	-12	64	2	6	-3	-2	*3	-1.7
1978	StL-N	150	540	41	133	26	2	10	75	23	61	.246	.283	.357	79	-17	-16	52	1	0	0	1	*3	-1.6
1979	StL-N	159	605	42	162	41	2	8	73	25	85	.268	.301	.382	84	-14	-14	67	1	0	0	-13	*3	-3.4
1980	StL-N	151	523	39	141	33	0	8	58	22	44	.270	.303	.379	86	-9	-11	56	0	1	-1	-4	*3	-1.6
1981	Chi-N	82	260	10	56	9	1	2	28	15	56	.215	.260	.281	53	-15	-17	18	0	0	0	5	3	-1.6
1982	Pit-N	7	10	0	0	0	0	0	0	0	2	.000	.091	.000	-70	-2	-2	0	0	0	0	1	/3	-0.1
Total	11	1344	4777	366	1243	243	12	68	548	184	518	.260	.293	.359	79	-141	-146	461	10	14	-5	-57	*3/S2	-23.3

■ BUTCH REMENTER
Rementer, Willis J. H. b: 3/14/1878, Philadelphia, Pa. d: 9/23/22, Philadelphia, Pa. TR Deb: 10/08/04

YEAR	TM/L	G	AB	R	H	2B	3B	HR	RBI	BB	SO	AVG	OBP	SLG	PRO+	BR	/A	RC	SB	CS	SBR	FR	POS	TPR
1904	Phi-N	1	2	0	0	0	0	0				.000	.000	.000	-99	-0	-0	0				-0	/C	0.0

■ JACK REMSEN
Remsen, John J. b: 4/1850, Brooklyn, N.Y. BR, 5'11", 189 lbs. Deb: 5/02/1872

YEAR	TM/L	G	AB	R	H	2B	3B	HR	RBI	BB	SO	AVG	OBP	SLG	PRO+	BR	/A	RC	SB	CS	SBR	FR	POS	TPR
1872	Atl-n	37	164	26	40	6	5	0			2	.244	.253	.341	69	-4	-10	15					*O	-0.5
1873	Atl-n	50	207	39	60	7	6	1			2	.290	.297	.396	114	0	5	25					*O	0.5
1874	Mut-n	64	285	52	65	11	4	2			0	.228	.228	.316	69	-9	-11	21					*O/1	-0.6
1875	Har-n	86	354	69	96	10	4	0			5	.271	.281	.322	103	3	0	33					*O	0.1
1876	Har-N	69	324	62	89	12	5	1	30	1	15	.275	.277	.352	100	2	-2	32				7	*O	0.4
1877	StL-N	33	123	14	32	3	4	0	13	4	3	.260	.283	.350	104	-0	1	12				1	O	0.1
1878	Chi-N	56	224	32	52	11	1	1	19	17	33	.232	.286	.304	88	-1	-3	20				6	*O	-0.1
1879	Chi-N	42	152	14	33	4	2	0	8	2	23	.217	.227	.270	59	-6	-7	10				-3	O1	-1.0
1881	Cle-N	48	172	14	30	4	3	0	13	9	31	.174	.215	.233	43	-11	-10	9				-1	O	-1.0
1884	Phi-N	12	43	9	9	2	0	0	3	6	9	.209	.306	.256	83	-1	-0	3				-0	O	0.0
	Bro-a	81	301	45	67	6	6	3		23		.223	.278	.312	94	-1	-1	27				4	*O	0.1
Total	4 n	237	1010	176	261	34	19	3			9	.258	.265	.339	89	-9	-16	93					O/1	-0.5
Total	6	341	1339	190	312	42	21	5	86	62	114	.233	.267	.307	85	-18	-23	113				13	O/1	-1.5

■ JERRY REMY
Remy, Gerald Peter b: 11/8/52, Fall River, Mass. BL/TR, 5'9", 165 lbs. Deb: 4/07/75

YEAR	TM/L	G	AB	R	H	2B	3B	HR	RBI	BB	SO	AVG	OBP	SLG	PRO+	BR	/A	RC	SB	CS	SBR	FR	POS	TPR
1975	Cal-A	147	569	82	147	17	5	1	46	45	55	.258	.313	.311	82	-17	-12	53	34	21	-2	10	*2	0.0
1976	Cal-A	143	502	64	132	14	3	0	28	38	43	.263	.315	.303	87	-11	-7	50	35	16	1	15	*2/D	1.7
1977	Cal-A	154	575	74	145	19	10	4	44	59	59	.252	.324	.341	85	-14	-11	67	41	17	2	-13	*2/3	-0.8
1978	Bos-A	148	583	87	162	24	6	2	44	40	55	.278	.324	.350	81	-8	-16	66	30	13	1	2	*2/SD	-0.4
1979	Bos-A	80	306	49	91	11	2	0	29	26	25	.297	.352	.346	85	-4	-6	39	14	9	1	-21	2/O	-2.4
1980	Bos-A	63	230	24	72	7	2	0	9	10	14	.313	.342	.361	88	-2	-4	27	14	6	1	-3	2/O	-0.2
1981	Bos-A	88	358	55	110	9	1	0	31	36	30	.307	.371	.338	99	4	1	48	9	2	2	-8	2	-0.2
1982	Bos-A	155	636	89	178	22	3	0	47	55	77	.280	.339	.324	79	-13	-18	71	16	9	1	-16	*2	-2.5
1983	Bos-A	146	592	73	163	16	5	0	43	40	35	.275	.321	.319	72	-18	-23	62	11	3	2	-31	*2	-4.8
1984	Bos-A	30	104	8	26	1	1	0	8	7	11	.250	.297	.279	58	-5	-6	9	4	3	1	-3	2	-0.7
Total	10	1154	4455	605	1226	140	38	7	329	356	404	.275	.329	.328	82	-89	-101	492	208	99	3	-67	*2/DOS3	-10.3

■ RICK RENICK
Renick, Warren Richard b: 3/16/44, London, Ohio BR/TR, 6', 188 lbs. Deb: 7/11/68 C

YEAR	TM/L	G	AB	R	H	2B	3B	HR	RBI	BB	SO	AVG	OBP	SLG	PRO+	BR	/A	RC	SB	CS	SBR	FR	POS	TPR
1968	Min-A	42	97	16	21	5	2	3	13	9	42	.216	.283	.402	101	-0	-0	11	0	0	0	0	S	0.3
1969	*Min-A	71	139	21	34	3	0	5	17	12	32	.245	.309	.374	88	-2	-2	15	0	1	-1	-5	3O/S	-0.7
1970	*Min-A	81	179	20	41	0	0	7	25	22	29	.229	.317	.391	93	-2	-2	21	0	2	-1	-1	3O/S	-0.4
1971	Min-A	27	45	4	10	2	0	1	8	5	14	.222	.314	.333	81	-1	-1	5	0	0	0	-2	/3O	-0.3
1972	Min-A	55	93	10	16	2	0	4	8	15	25	.172	.287	.323	77	-2	-3	8	0	1	-1	-3	O/13S	-0.7

YEAR	TM/L	G	AB	R	H	2B	3B	HR	RBI	BB	SO	AVG	OBP	SLG	PRO+	BR	/A	RC	SB	CS	SBR	FR	POS	TPR
Total	5	276	553	71	122	20	2	20	71	63	142	.221	.304	.373	89	-6	-8	60	0	4	-2	-10	/3OS1	-1.8

■ BILL RENNA
Renna, William Beneditto "Big Bill" b: 10/14/24, Hanford, Cal. BR/TR, 6'3", 218 lbs. Deb: 4/14/53

YEAR	TM/L	G	AB	R	H	2B	3B	HR	RBI	BB	SO	AVG	OBP	SLG	PRO+	BR	/A	RC	SB	CS	SBR	FR	POS	TPR
1953	NY-A	61	121	19	38	6	3	2	13	13	31	.314	.385	.463	133	5	5	22	0	1	-1	-3	O	0.1
1954	Phi-A	123	422	52	98	15	4	13	53	41	60	.232	.305	.379	86	-9	-9	49	1	3	-2	2	*O	-1.1
1955	KC-A	100	249	33	53	7	3	7	28	31	42	.213	.305	.349	75	-9	-9	27	0	3	-2	-4	O	-1.8
1956	KC-A	33	48	12	13	3	0	2	5	3	10	.271	.314	.458	101	-0	-0	7	1	0	0	-1	O	-0.1
1958	Bos-A	39	56	5	15	5	0	4	18	6	14	.268	.339	.571	136	3	3	11	0	0	0	-1	O	0.1
1959	Bos-A	14	22	2	2	0	0	0	2	5	9	.091	.259	.091	0	-3	-3	1	0	0	0	-1	/O	-0.4
Total	6	370	918	123	219	36	10	28	119	99	166	.239	.317	.391	91	-13	-14	117	2	7	-4	-7	O	-3.2

■ TONY RENSA
Rensa, George Anthony "Pug" b: 9/29/01, Parsons, Pa. d: 1/4/87, Wilkes-Barre, Pa. BR/TR, 5'10", 180 lbs. Deb: 5/05/30

YEAR	TM/L	G	AB	R	H	2B	3B	HR	RBI	BB	SO	AVG	OBP	SLG	PRO+	BR	/A	RC	SB	CS	SBR	FR	POS	TPR
1930	Det-A	20	37	6	10	2	1	1	3	6	7	.270	.386	.459	111	1	1	7	1	0	0	-1	C	0.1
	Phi-N	54	172	31	49	11	2	3	31	10	18	.285	.328	.424	75	-6	-8	23	0			-11	C	-1.3
1931	Phi-N	19	29	2	3	1	0	0	2	6	2	.103	.257	.138	8	-4	-4	1	0			3	C	0.0
1933	NY-A	8	29	4	9	2	1	0	3	1	3	.310	.333	.448	112	0	0	4	0	1	-1	-1	/C	0.0
1937	Chi-A	26	57	10	17	5	1	0	5	8	6	.298	.385	.421	103	0	0	10	3	0	1	1	C	0.4
1938	Chi-A	59	165	15	41	5	0	3	19	25	16	.248	.351	.333	71	-7	-7	21	1	1	-0	6	C	0.0
1939	Chi-A	14	25	3	5	0	0	0	2	1	2	.200	.231	.200	11	-3	-3	1	0	0	0	1	C	0.0
Total	6	200	514	71	134	26	5	7	65	57	54	.261	.338	.372	74	-18	-21	67	5	2		-2	C	-0.8

■ RICH RENTERIA
Renteria, Richard Avina b: 12/25/61, Harbor City, Cal. BR/TR, 5'9", 172 lbs. Deb: 9/14/86

YEAR	TM/L	G	AB	R	H	2B	3B	HR	RBI	BB	SO	AVG	OBP	SLG	PRO+	BR	/A	RC	SB	CS	SBR	FR	POS	TPR
1986	Pit-N	10	12	2	3	1	0	0	1	0	4	.250	.250	.333	58	-1	-1	1	0	0	0	0	/3	0.0
1987	Sea-A	12	10	2	1	1	0	0	0	1	2	.100	.182	.200	1	-1	-2	0	1	0	0	1	/2SD	0.0
1988	Sea-A	31	88	6	18	9	0	0	6	2	8	.205	.222	.307	45	-6	-7	4	1	3	-2	4	DS/32	-0.2
Total	3	53	110	10	22	11	0	0	7	3	14	.200	.221	.300	42	-9	-9	6	2	3	-1	5	/DS23	-0.2

■ BOB REPASS
Repass, Robert Willis b: 11/6/17, W.Pittston, Pa. BR/TR, 6'1", 185 lbs. Deb: 9/18/39

YEAR	TM/L	G	AB	R	H	2B	3B	HR	RBI	BB	SO	AVG	OBP	SLG	PRO+	BR	/A	RC	SB	CS	SBR	FR	POS	TPR
1939	StL-N	3	6	0	2	1	0	0	1	0	2	.333	.333	.500	114	0	0	1	0			0	/2	0.1
1942	Was-A	81	259	30	62	11	1	2	23	33	30	.239	.328	.313	81	-6	-6	29	6	1	1	-2	23S	-0.4
Total	2	84	265	30	64	12	1	2	24	33	32	.242	.328	.317	82	-6	-6	29	6	1		-2	/23S	-0.3

■ ROGER REPOZ
Repoz, Roger Allen b: 8/3/40, Bellingham, Wash. BL/TL, 6'3", 190 lbs. Deb: 9/11/64

YEAR	TM/L	G	AB	R	H	2B	3B	HR	RBI	BB	SO	AVG	OBP	SLG	PRO+	BR	/A	RC	SB	CS	SBR	FR	POS	TPR
1964	NY-A	11	1	1	0	0	0	0	0	1	1	.000	.500	.000	52	0	0	0	0	0	0	0	/O	0.0
1965	NY-A	79	218	34	48	7	4	12	28	25	57	.220	.300	.454	112	3	3	30	1	1	-0	-4	O	-0.3
1966	NY-A	37	43	4	15	4	1	0	9	4	8	.349	.404	.488	161	3	3	9	0	0	0	0	O	0.2
	KC-A	101	319	40	69	10	3	11	34	44	80	.216	.315	.370	99	-1	0	38	3	3	-1	-2	O1	-0.6
	Yr	138	362	44	84	14	4	11	43	48	88	.232	.325	.384	106	2	3	47	3	3	-1	-3		-0.4
1967	KC-A	40	87	9	21	6	1	2	8	12	20	.241	.340	.402	122	2	3	12	4	2	0	3	O	0.5
	Cal-A	74	176	25	44	9	1	5	20	19	37	.250	.323	.398	116	3	3	24	2	2	-1	5	O	0.6
	Yr	114	263	34	65	15	2	7	28	31	57	.247	.329	.399	118	5	6	36	6	4	-1	8		1.1
1968	Cal-A	133	375	30	90	8	1	13	54	38	83	.240	.315	.371	111	3	5	46	8	7	-2	4	*O	0.3
1969	Cal-A	103	219	25	36	1	1	8	19	32	52	.164	.271	.288	59	-13	-12	19	1	3	-2	2	O1	-1.4
1970	Cal-A	137	407	50	97	17	6	18	47	45	90	.238	.319	.442	112	3	5	60	4	2	0	-2	*O1	-0.1
1971	Cal-A	113	297	39	59	11	1	13	41	60	69	.199	.335	.374	108	1	4	40	3	5	-2	-3	O1	-0.5
1972	Cal-A	3	3	0	1	0	0	0	0	0	2	.333	.333	.333	105	-0	-0	0	0	0	0	0	H	0.0
Total	9	831	2145	257	480	73	19	82	260	280	499	.224	.316	.390	106	4	14	279	26	25	-7	3	O1	-1.3

■ RIP REPULSKI
Repulski, Eldon John b: 10/4/27, Sauk Rapids, Minn. BR/TR, 6', 195 lbs. Deb: 4/14/53

YEAR	TM/L	G	AB	R	H	2B	3B	HR	RBI	BB	SO	AVG	OBP	SLG	PRO+	BR	/A	RC	SB	CS	SBR	FR	POS	TPR
1953	StL-N	153	567	75	156	25	4	15	66	33	71	.275	.325	.413	91	-8	-8	74	3	6	-3	-11	*O	-2.7
1954	StL-N	152	619	99	175	39	5	19	79	43	75	.283	.333	.454	102	1	0	88	8	10	-4	-5	*O	-1.2
1955	StL-N	147	512	64	138	28	2	23	73	49	66	.270	.338	.467	111	7	7	75	5	7	-3	-7	*O	-0.4
1956	StL-N	112	376	44	104	18	3	11	55	24	46	.277	.332	.428	102	1	1	50	2	2	-1	-4	*O	-0.7
1957	Phi-N	134	516	65	134	23	4	20	68	19	74	.260	.293	.436	95	-7	-5	64	7	1	2	2	*O	-0.4
1958	Phi-N	85	238	33	58	9	4	13	40	15	47	.244	.300	.479	103	-0	-0	31	0	0	0	-8	O	-0.9
1959	*LA-N	53	94	11	24	4	0	2	14	13	23	.255	.346	.362	83	-1	-2	11	0	1	-1	-3	O	-0.5
1960	LA-N	4	5	0	1	0	0	0	0	0	1	.200	.200	.200	9	-1	-1	0	0	0	0	0	/O	0.0
	Bos-A	73	136	14	33	6	1	3	20	10	25	.243	.295	.368	75	-4	-4	13	0	0	0	-1	O	-0.6
1961	Bos-A	15	25	2	7	1	0	0	1	1	5	.280	.308	.320	66	-1	-1	2	0	2	-1	-1	/O	-0.2
Total	9	928	3088	407	830	153	23	106	416	207	433	.269	.322	.436	98	-15	-14	409	25	29	-10	-36	O	-7.6

■ LARRY RESSLER
Ressler, Lawrence P. b: 8/10/1848, France d: 6/12/18, Reading, Pa. Deb: 4/26/1875

YEAR	TM/L	G	AB	R	H	2B	3B	HR	RBI	BB	SO	AVG	OBP	SLG	PRO+	BR	/A	RC	SB	CS	SBR	FR	POS	TPR
1875	Was-n	27	106	17	21	1	0	0		1		.198	.206	.208	45	-6	-5	5					O/2	-0.3

■ DINO RESTELLI
Restelli, Dino Paul "Dingo" b: 9/23/24, St.Louis, Mo. BR/TR, 6'1.5", 191 lbs. Deb: 6/14/49

YEAR	TM/L	G	AB	R	H	2B	3B	HR	RBI	BB	SO	AVG	OBP	SLG	PRO+	BR	/A	RC	SB	CS	SBR	FR	POS	TPR
1949	Pit-N	72	232	41	58	11	0	12	40	35	26	.250	.358	.453	113	5	5	38	3			1	O/1	0.2
1951	Pit-N	21	38	1	7	1	0	1	3	2	4	.184	.225	.289	36	-3	-4	3	0	0	0	2	O	-0.1
Total	2	93	270	42	65	12	0	13	43	37	30	.241	.341	.430	103	2	1	41	3	0		2	/O1	0.1

■ MERV RETTENMUND
Rettenmund, Mervin Weldon b: 6/6/43, Flint, Mich. BR/TR, 5'10", 190 lbs. Deb: 4/14/68 C

YEAR	TM/L	G	AB	R	H	2B	3B	HR	RBI	BB	SO	AVG	OBP	SLG	PRO+	BR	/A	RC	SB	CS	SBR	FR	POS	TPR
1968	Bal-A	31	64	10	19	5	0	2	7	18	20	.297	.458	.469	181	8	8	16	1	1	-0	-1	O	0.6
1969	*Bal-A	95	190	27	47	10	3	4	25	28	28	.247	.344	.395	105	2	2	27	6	1	1	2	O	0.3
1970	*Bal-A	106	338	60	109	17	2	18	58	38	59	.322	.396	.544	155	26	25	72	13	7	-0	7	O	2.8
1971	*Bal-A	141	491	81	156	23	4	11	75	87	60	.318	.424	.448	149	35	35	99	15	6	1	4	*O	3.8
1972	Bal-A	102	301	40	70	10	2	6	21	41	37	.233	.325	.339	95	-0	-1	33	6	4	-1	-0	O	-0.5
1973	*Bal-A	95	321	59	84	17	2	9	44	57	39	.262	.380	.411	124	12	12	56	11	2	2	-2	O	1.0
1974	Cin-N	80	208	30	45	6	0	6	28	37	39	.216	.340	.332	90	-2	-2	25	5	1	1	-4	O	-0.7
1975	*Cin-N	93	188	24	45	6	1	3	19	35	22	.239	.359	.314	86	-2	-2	23	5	2	2	-5	O/3	-0.5
1976	SD-N	86	140	16	32	7	0	2	11	29	23	.229	.361	.321	103	0	2	19	4	1	1	5	O	0.6
1977	SD-N	107	126	23	36	6	1	4	17	33	28	.286	.438	.444	153	9	11	27	1	2	-1	-4	O/3	0.5
1978	Cal-A	50	108	16	29	5	1	1	14	30	13	.269	.436	.361	131	6	7	19	0	3	-2	-1	OD	0.4
1979	*Cal-A	35	76	7	20	2	0	1	10	11	14	.263	.364	.329	91	-1	-0	9	1	0	0	0	D/O	0.0
1980	Cal-A	2	4	0	1	0	0	0	0	1	1	.250	.400	.250	84	-0	-0	1	0	0	0	0	/D	0.0
Total	13	1023	2555	393	693	114	16	66	329	445	382	.271	.383	.406	124	92	95	425	68	28	4	2	O/D3	8.3

■ KEN RETZER
Retzer, Kenneth Leo b: 4/30/34, Wood River, Ill. BL/TR, 6', 185 lbs. Deb: 9/09/61

YEAR	TM/L	G	AB	R	H	2B	3B	HR	RBI	BB	SO	AVG	OBP	SLG	PRO+	BR	/A	RC	SB	CS	SBR	FR	POS	TPR
1961	Was-A	16	53	7	18	4	0	1	3	4	5	.340	.386	.472	130	2	2	10	1	0	0	1	C	0.3
1962	Was-A	109	340	36	97	11	2	8	37	26	21	.285	.336	.400	98	-2	-1	45	2	0	1	-0	C	0.4
1963	Was-A	95	265	21	64	10	0	5	31	17	20	.242	.292	.336	76	-9	-9	26	2	0	1	-11	C	-1.8
1964	Was-A	17	32	1	3	0	0	0	1	5	4	.094	.237	.094	-4	-4	-4	1	0	0	0	4	C	0.0
Total	4	237	690	65	182	25	2	14	72	52	50	.264	.318	.367	87	-13	-12	82	5	0	2	-6	C	-1.1

■ DAVE REVERING
Revering, David Alvin b: 2/12/53, Roseville, Cal. BL/TR, 6'4", 210 lbs. Deb: 4/08/78

YEAR	TM/L	G	AB	R	H	2B	3B	HR	RBI	BB	SO	AVG	OBP	SLG	PRO+	BR	/A	RC	SB	CS	SBR	FR	POS	TPR
1978	Oak-A	152	521	49	141	21	3	16	46	26	55	.271	.305	.415	106	-1	2	63	0	1	-1	9	*1/D	0.5
1979	Oak-A	125	472	63	136	25	5	19	77	34	65	.288	.337	.483	125	11	14	75	1	4	-2	2	*1D	0.8

YEAR	TM/L	G	AB	R	H	2B	3B	HR	RBI	BB	SO	AVG	OBP	SLG	PRO+	BR	/A	RC	SB	CS	SBR	FR	POS	TPR
1980	Oak-A	106	376	48	109	21	5	15	62	32	37	.290	.346	.492	136	13	16	64	1	0	0	2	1/D	1.2
1981	Oak-A	31	87	12	20	1	1	2	10	11	12	.230	.323	.333	94	-1	-0	9	0	1	-1	-1	1/D	-0.2
	*NY-A	45	119	8	28	4	1	2	7	11	20	.235	.300	.336	84	-3	-2	12	0	1	-1	3	1	0.0
	Yr	76	206	20	48	5	2	4	17	22	32	.233	.310	.335	88	-4	-3	21	0	2	-1	2		-0.2
1982	NY-A	14	40	2	6	2	0	0	2	3	4	.150	.209	.200	13	-5	-5	1	0	0	0	-2	1/D	-0.6
	Tor-A	55	135	15	29	6	0	5	18	22	30	.215	.325	.370	83	-2	-3	16	0	3	-2	0	D/1	-0.4
	Sea-A	29	82	8	17	3	1	3	12	9	17	.207	.286	.378	78	-2	-3	8	0	0	0	-2	1	-0.5
	Yr	98	257	25	52	11	1	8	32	34	51	.202	.296	.346	71	-9	-11	25	0	3	-2	-4		-1.5
Total	5	557	1832	205	486	83	16	62	234	148	240	.265	.321	.430	110	10	18	248	2	10	-5	12	1/D	0.8

■ HENRY REVILLE
Reville, Henry   b: Baltimore, Md.   Deb: 10/14/1874

YEAR	TM/L	G	AB	R	H	2B	3B	HR	RBI	BB	SO	AVG	OBP	SLG	PRO+	BR	/A	RC	SB	CS	SBR	FR	POS	TPR
1874	Bal-n	1	4	0	0	0	0	0		0	0	.000	.000	.000	-99	-1	-1	0					/O	0.0

■ WILLIAM REXTER
Rexter, William H.   b: Brooklyn, N.Y.   Deb: 9/25/1875

YEAR	TM/L	G	AB	R	H	2B	3B	HR	RBI	BB	SO	AVG	OBP	SLG	PRO+	BR	/A	RC	SB	CS	SBR	FR	POS	TPR
1875	Atl-n	1	4	0	0	0	0	0		0	0	.000	.000	.000	-99	-1	-1	0					/O	0.0

■ GIL REYES
Reyes, Gilberto R. (Polanco)   b: 12/10/63, Santo Domingo, D.R.   BR/TR, 6'2", 200 lbs.   Deb: 6/11/83

YEAR	TM/L	G	AB	R	H	2B	3B	HR	RBI	BB	SO	AVG	OBP	SLG	PRO+	BR	/A	RC	SB	CS	SBR	FR	POS	TPR
1983	LA-N	19	31	1	5	2	0	0	0	0	5	.161	.188	.226	14	-4	-4	1	0	0	0	3	C	0.0
1984	LA-N	4	5	0	0	0	0	0	0	0	0	.000	.000	.000	-99	-1	-1	0	0	0	0	0	/C	0.0
1985	LA-N	6	1	0	0	0	0	0	0	1	1	.000	.667	.000	105	0	0	0	0	0	0	2	/C	0.2
1987	LA-N	1	0	0	0	0	0	0	0	0	0	—	—	—	—	0	0	0	0	0	0	0	/C	0.0
1988	LA-N	5	9	1	1	0	0	0	0	0	3	.111	.111	.111	-37	-2	-2	0	0	0	0	0	/C	0.0
1989	Mon-N	4	5	0	1	0	0	0	0	1	0	.200	.200	.200	14	-1	-1	0	0	0	0	1	/C	0.0
Total	6	39	51	2	7	2	0	0	1	1	13	.137	.185	.176	2	-7	-7	1	0	0	0	5	/C	0.2

■ NAP REYES
Reyes, Napoleon Aguilera   b: 11/24/19, Santiago De Cuba, Cuba   BR/TR, 6'1", 205 lbs.   Deb: 5/19/43

YEAR	TM/L	G	AB	R	H	2B	3B	HR	RBI	BB	SO	AVG	OBP	SLG	PRO+	BR	/A	RC	SB	CS	SBR	FR	POS	TPR
1943	NY-N	40	125	13	32	4	2	0	13	4	12	.256	.290	.320	76	-4	-4	12	2			-5	1/3	-1.1
1944	NY-N	116	374	38	108	16	5	8	53	15	24	.289	.325	.422	109	3	3	49	2			3	13/O	0.2
1945	NY-N	122	431	39	124	15	4	5	44	25	26	.288	.338	.376	97	-1	-2	53	1			-3	*3/1	-0.7
1950	NY-N	1	1	0	0	0	0	0	0	0	0	.000	.000	.000	-99	-0	-0	0	0			-0	/1	0.0
Total	4	279	931	90	264	35	11	13	110	44	62	.284	.326	.387	99	-3	-4	113	5			-6	31/O	-1.6

■ CARL REYNOLDS
Reynolds, Carl Nettles   b: 2/1/03, LaRue, Tex.   d: 5/29/78, Houston, Tex.   BR/TR, 6', 194 lbs.   Deb: 9/01/27

YEAR	TM/L	G	AB	R	H	2B	3B	HR	RBI	BB	SO	AVG	OBP	SLG	PRO+	BR	/A	RC	SB	CS	SBR	FR	POS	TPR
1927	Chi-A	14	42	5	9	3	0	1	7	5	7	.214	.313	.357	75	-2	-2	4	1	2	-1	2	O	-0.1
1928	Chi-A	84	291	51	94	21	11	2	36	17	13	.323	.371	.491	126	10	10	54	15	3	3	-2	O	0.7
1929	Chi-A	131	517	81	164	24	12	11	67	20	37	.317	.348	.474	111	5	8	83	19	9	0	-1	*O	0.0
1930	Chi-A	138	563	103	202	25	18	22	104	20	39	.359	.388	.584	148	34	37	126	16	4	2	10	*O	3.9
1931	Chi-A	118	462	71	134	24	14	6	77	20	26	.290	.333	.442	108	-0	4	68	17	6	2	-4	*O	-0.4
1932	Was-A	102	406	53	124	28	7	9	63	14	19	.305	.332	.475	108	2	3	62	8	4	0	1	O	0.0
1933	StL-A	135	475	81	136	26	14	8	71	50	25	.286	.357	.451	106	8	4	77	5	4	-1	-1	*O	-0.2
1934	Bos-A	113	413	61	125	26	9	4	86	27	28	.303	.350	.438	95	0	4	63	5	3	-0	-2	*O	-0.6
1935	Bos-A	78	244	33	66	13	4	6	35	24	20	.270	.336	.430	91	-2	-4	36	4	1	1	4	O	0.0
1936	Was-A	89	293	41	81	18	2	4	41	21	22	.276	.329	.392	82	-11	-9	38	8	4	0	-1	O	-0.9
1937	Chi-N	7	11	0	3	1	0	0	1	2	2	.273	.385	.364	100	0	0	1				-0	/O	0.0
1938	*Chi-N	125	497	59	150	28	10	3	67	22	32	.302	.335	.416	103	3	1	69	9			2	*O	0.0
1939	Chi-N	88	281	33	69	10	6	4	44	16	32	.246	.298	.367	76	-9	-10	30	5			3	O	-0.8
Total	13	1222	4495	672	1357	247	107	80	699	262	308	.302	.346	.458	107	37	35	713	112	40		11	*O	1.6

■ CHARLIE REYNOLDS
Reynolds, Charles Lawrence   b: 5/1/1865, Williamsburg, Ind.   d: 7/3/44, Denver, Colo.   5'9", 175 lbs.   Deb: 5/08/1889

YEAR	TM/L	G	AB	R	H	2B	3B	HR	RBI	BB	SO	AVG	OBP	SLG	PRO+	BR	/A	RC	SB	CS	SBR	FR	POS	TPR
1889	KC-a	1	4	1	1	0	0	0	1	0	1	.250	.250	.250	42	-0	-0	0	0			-1	/C	0.0
	Bro-a	12	42	5	9	1	1	0	3	1	6	.214	.233	.286	49	-3	-3	3	2			-0	C	-0.1
	Yr	13	46	6	10	1	1	0	4	1	7	.217	.234	.283	48	-3	-3	4	2			-1		-0.1

■ DANNY REYNOLDS
Reynolds, Daniel Vance "Squirrel"   b: 11/27/19, Stony Point, N.C.   BR/TR, 5'11", 158 lbs.   Deb: 5/26/45

YEAR	TM/L	G	AB	R	H	2B	3B	HR	RBI	BB	SO	AVG	OBP	SLG	PRO+	BR	/A	RC	SB	CS	SBR	FR	POS	TPR
1945	Chi-A	29	72	6	12	2	1	0	4	3	8	.167	.200	.222	23	-7	-7	2	1	2	-1	2	S2	-0.5

■ DON REYNOLDS
Reynolds, Donald Edward   b: 4/16/53, Arkadelphia, Ark.   BR/TR, 5'8", 178 lbs.   Deb: 4/07/78

YEAR	TM/L	G	AB	R	H	2B	3B	HR	RBI	BB	SO	AVG	OBP	SLG	PRO+	BR	/A	RC	SB	CS	SBR	FR	POS	TPR
1978	SD-N	57	87	8	22	2	0	0	10	15	14	.253	.363	.276	87	-1	-1	10	1	0	0	-2	O	-0.3
1979	SD-N	30	45	6	10	1	2	0	6	7	6	.222	.327	.333	86	-1	-1	4	0	1	-1	1	O	0.0
Total	2	87	132	14	32	3	2	0	16	22	20	.242	.351	.295	87	-3	-1	14	1	1	-0	-2	/O	-0.3

■ CRAIG REYNOLDS
Reynolds, Gordon Craig   b: 12/27/52, Houston, Tex.   BL/TR, 6'1", 175 lbs.   Deb: 8/01/75

YEAR	TM/L	G	AB	R	H	2B	3B	HR	RBI	BB	SO	AVG	OBP	SLG	PRO+	BR	/A	RC	SB	CS	SBR	FR	POS	TPR
1975	*Pit-N	31	76	8	17	3	0	0	4	3	5	.224	.253	.263	44	-6	-6	5	0	1	-1	4	S	0.1
1976	Pit-N	7	4	1	1	0	0	1	1	0	0	.250	.250	1.000	241	1	1	1	0	0	0	2	/S2	0.3
1977	Sea-A	135	420	41	104	12	3	4	28	15	23	.248	.279	.319	63	-22	-21	36	6	6	-2	8	*S	0.1
1978	Sea-A	148	548	57	160	16	7	6	44	36	41	.292	.339	.374	101	0	1	71	9	6	-1	4	*S	1.6
1979	Hou-N	146	555	63	147	20	9	0	39	21	49	.265	.294	.333	75	-23	-19	57	12	6	0	-16	*S	-2.0
1980	*Hou-N	137	381	64	86	9	6	3	28	20	39	.226	.264	.304	63	-22	-18	32	2	1	0	12	*S	1.0
1981	*Hou-N	87	323	43	84	10	12	1	31	12	31	.260	.287	.402	99	-4	-2	35	3	3	-1	-5	S	0.1
1982	Hou-N	54	118	16	30	2	3	1	7	11	9	.254	.323	.347	95	-2	-1	14	3	1	0	2	S/3	0.5
1983	Hou-N	65	98	10	21	3	0	1	6	6	10	.214	.260	.276	52	-7	-6	7	0	1	-1	-4	23/SO	-0.9
1984	Hou-N	146	527	61	137	15	11	6	60	22	53	.260	.290	.364	89	-13	-9	57	7	1	2	18	*S/3	2.7
1985	Hou-N	107	379	43	103	18	8	4	32	12	30	.272	.294	.393	93	-6	-5	42	4	4	-1	10	*S/2	1.3
1986	*Hou-N	114	313	32	78	7	3	6	41	12	31	.249	.277	.348	73	-13	-12	28	3	1	0	-11	S/13OP	-1.4
1987	Hou-N	135	374	35	95	17	3	4	28	30	44	.254	.309	.348	77	-14	-12	42	5	1	1	-12	*S/3	-0.7
1988	Hou-N	78	161	20	41	7	0	1	14	8	23	.255	.290	.317	77	-5	-5	15	3	0	1	-4	S321	-0.7
1989	Hou-N	101	189	16	38	4	0	2	14	19	18	.201	.274	.254	54	-12	-11	14	1	0	0	8	2S3/1PO	0.0
Total	15	1491	4466	480	1142	143	65	42	377	227	406	.256	.293	.345	80	-148	-126	457	58	32	-2	17	*S/2310P	2.0

■ HAROLD REYNOLDS
Reynolds, Harold Craig   b: 11/26/60, Eugene, Ore.   BB/TR, 5'11", 165 lbs.   Deb: 9/02/83

YEAR	TM/L	G	AB	R	H	2B	3B	HR	RBI	BB	SO	AVG	OBP	SLG	PRO+	BR	/A	RC	SB	CS	SBR	FR	POS	TPR
1983	Sea-A	20	59	8	12	4	1	0	1	2	9	.203	.230	.305	44	-4	-5	3	0	2	-1	-1	2	-0.6
1984	Sea-A	10	10	3	3	0	0	0	0	0	1	.300	.364	.300	87	-0	-0	1	1	1	-0	4	/2	0.4
1985	Sea-A	67	104	15	15	3	1	0	6	17	14	.144	.264	.192	27	-10	-10	7	3	2	-0	19	2	1.1
1986	Sea-A	126	445	46	99	19	4	1	24	29	42	.222	.275	.290	53	-28	-29	37	30	12	2	29	*2	0.9
1987	Sea-A	160	530	73	146	31	8	1	35	39	34	.275	.327	.370	80	-15	-15	67	60	20	6	19	*2	2.1
1988	Sea-A	158	598	61	169	26	11	4	41	51	51	.283	.341	.383	98	2	-1	74	35	29	-7	6	*2	0.8
1989	Sea-A	153	613	87	184	24	9	0	43	55	45	.300	.361	.369	103	6	4	83	25	18	-3	27	*2/D	3.0
1990	Sea-A	160	642	100	162	36	5	5	55	81	52	.252	.339	.347	91	-5	-6	80	31	16	-0	16	*2	1.8
Total	8	854	3001	393	790	143	39	11	205	274	248	.263	.328	.348	84	-51	-62	352	185	100	-5	118	2/D	9.5

■ R.J. REYNOLDS
Reynolds, Robert James   b: 4/19/59, Sacramento, Cal.   BB/TR, 6', 190 lbs.   Deb: 9/01/83

YEAR	TM/L	G	AB	R	H	2B	3B	HR	RBI	BB	SO	AVG	OBP	SLG	PRO+	BR	/A	RC	SB	CS	SBR	FR	POS	TPR
1983	LA-N	24	55	5	13	0	0	2	11	3	11	.236	.276	.345	72	-2	-2	6	5	0	2	0	O	0.0
1984	LA-N	73	240	24	62	12	2	2	24	14	38	.258	.302	.350	84	-6	-6	24	7	5	-1	-4	O	-1.3
1985	LA-N	73	207	22	55	10	4	0	25	13	31	.266	.312	.353	88	-4	-3	23	6	3	0	-2	O	-0.6
	Pit-N	31	130	22	40	5	3	3	17	9	18	.308	.357	.462	129	4	5	22	12	2	2	0	O	0.7

YEAR	TM/L	G	AB	R	H	2B	3B	HR	RBI	BB	SO	AVG	OBP	SLG	PRO+	BR	/A	RC	SB	CS	SBR	FR	POS	TPR
	Yr	104	337	44	95	15	7	3	42	22	49	.282	.330	.395	104	0	1	45	18	5	2	-2		0.1
1986	Pit-N	118	402	63	108	30	2	9	48	40	78	.269	.336	.420	105	4	3	55	16	9	-1	-9	*O	-0.9
1987	Pit-N	117	335	47	87	24	1	7	51	34	80	.260	.328	.400	91	-4	-4	46	14	1	4	-9	O	-1.3
1988	Pit-N	130	323	35	80	14	2	6	51	20	62	.248	.292	.359	87	-6	-6	35	15	2	3	-8	O	-1.4
1989	Pit-N	125	363	45	98	16	2	6	48	34	66	.270	.334	.375	106	1	3	45	22	5	4	1	O	0.7
1990	*Pit-N	95	215	25	62	10	1	0	19	23	35	.288	.357	.344	98	-1	0	26	12	2	2	-2	O	-0.1
Total	8	786	2270	288	605	121	17	35	294	190	419	.267	.325	.381	97	-15	-12	282	109	29	15	-32	O	-4.2

■ RONN REYNOLDS
Reynolds, Ronn Dwayne b: 8/28/58, Wichita, Kan. BR/TR, 6', 200 lbs. Deb: 9/29/82

YEAR	TM/L	G	AB	R	H	2B	3B	HR	RBI	BB	SO	AVG	OBP	SLG	PRO+	BR	/A	RC	SB	CS	SBR	FR	POS	TPR
1982	NY-N	2	4	0	0	0	0	0	1	1	1	.000	.200	.000	-40	-1	-1	0	0	0	0	-1	/C	-0.1
1983	NY-N	24	66	4	13	1	0	0	2	8	12	.197	.284	.212	40	-5	-5	4	0	0	0	-1	C	-0.5
1985	NY-N	28	43	4	9	2	0	0	1	0	18	.209	.227	.256	36	-4	-4	2	0	0	0	6	C	0.3
1986	Phi-N	43	126	8	27	4	0	3	10	5	30	.214	.244	.317	52	-8	-9	9	0	0	0	1	C	-0.6
1987	Hou-N	38	102	5	17	4	0	1	7	3	29	.167	.190	.235	12	-13	-12	4	0	1	-1	4	C	-0.5
1990	SD-N	8	15	1	1	1	0	0	1	1	6	.067	.125	.133	-28	-3	-3	0	0	0	0	1	/C	-0.1
Total	6	143	356	22	67	12	0	4	21	18	96	.188	.229	.256	32	-34	-33	20	0	1	-1	9	C	-1.5

■ TOMMIE REYNOLDS
Reynolds, Tommie D b: 8/15/41, Arizona, La. BR/TR, 6'2", 190 lbs. Deb: 9/05/63 M

YEAR	TM/L	G	AB	R	H	2B	3B	HR	RBI	BB	SO	AVG	OBP	SLG	PRO+	BR	/A	RC	SB	CS	SBR	FR	POS	TPR
1963	KC-A	8	19	1	1	1	0	0	0	1	7	.053	.143	.105	-28	-3	-3	0	0	0	0	-1	/O	-0.4
1964	KC-A	31	94	11	19	1	0	2	9	10	22	.202	.292	.277	58	-5	-5	7	0	0	0	-2	O/3	-0.8
1965	KC-A	90	270	34	64	11	3	1	22	36	41	.237	.327	.311	83	-5	-5	28	9	2	2	5	O/3	-0.1
1967	NY-N	101	136	16	28	1	0	2	9	11	26	.206	.280	.257	56	-8	-7	10	1	1	-0	3	O/3C	-0.8
1969	Oak-A	107	315	51	81	10	0	2	20	34	29	.257	.345	.308	87	-6	-4	34	1	3	-2	3	O	-0.4
1970	Cal-A	59	120	11	30	3	1	1	6	6	10	.250	.291	.317	70	-5	-5	10	1	1	-0	2	O/3	-0.4
1971	Cal-A	45	86	4	16	3	0	2	8	9	6	.186	.286	.291	68	-4	-3	6	0	1	-1	1	O/3	-0.3
1972	Mil-A	72	130	13	26	5	1	2	13	10	25	.200	.262	.300	68	-5	-5	10	0	0	0	2	O/13	-0.4
Total	8	513	1170	141	265	35	5	12	87	117	166	.226	.307	.296	73	-42	-38	106	12	8	-1	13	O/31C	-3.6

■ BILL REYNOLDS
Reynolds, William Dee b: 8/14/1884, Eastland, Tex. d: 6/5/24, Carnegie, Okla. BR/TR, 6', 185 lbs. Deb: 9/15/13

YEAR	TM/L	G	AB	R	H	2B	3B	HR	RBI	BB	SO	AVG	OBP	SLG	PRO+	BR	/A	RC	SB	CS	SBR	FR	POS	TPR
1913	NY-A	5	5	0	0	0	0	0	0	0	1	.000	.000	.000	-99	-1	-1	0	0			0	/C	0.0
1914	NY-A	4	5	0	2	0	0	0	0	0	3	.400	.400	.400	141	0	0	1	0			0	/C	0.1
Total	2	9	10	0	2	0	0	0	0	0	4	.200	.200	.200	19	-1	-1	1	0			0	/C	0.1

■ ROCKY RHAWN
Rhawn, Robert John b: 2/13/19, Catawissa, Pa. d: 6/9/84, Danville, Pa. BR/TR, 5'8", 180 lbs. Deb: 9/17/47

YEAR	TM/L	G	AB	R	H	2B	3B	HR	RBI	BB	SO	AVG	OBP	SLG	PRO+	BR	/A	RC	SB	CS	SBR	FR	POS	TPR
1947	NY-N	13	45	7	14	3	0	1	3	8	1	.311	.415	.444	128	2	2	9	0			0	/23	0.3
1948	NY-N	36	44	11	12	2	1	1	8	6	6	.273	.385	.432	120	1	1	7	3			1	S/3	0.3
1949	NY-N	14	29	8	5	0	0	0	2	7	2	.172	.333	.172	40	-2	-2	2	1			4	/2	0.2
	Pit-N	3	7	0	1	0	0	0	0	0	0	.143	.143	.143	-23	-1	-1	0	0			1	/3	0.0
	Yr	17	36	8	6	0	0	0	2	7	2	.167	.302	.167	29	-3	-3	2	1			4		0.2
	Chi-A	24	73	12	15	4	1	0	5	12	8	.205	.318	.288	63	-4	-4	7	0	1	-1	3	3/S	-0.1
Total	3	90	198	38	47	9	2	2	18	35	17	.237	.352	.333	84	-4	-4	26	4	1		8	/3S2	0.7

■ CY RHEAM
Rheam, Kenneth Johnston b: 9/28/1893, Pittsburgh, Pa. d: 10/23/47, Pittsburgh, Pa. BR/TR, 6' ", 175 lbs. Deb: 5/20/14

YEAR	TM/L	G	AB	R	H	2B	3B	HR	RBI	BB	SO	AVG	OBP	SLG	PRO+	BR	/A	RC	SB	CS	SBR	FR	POS	TPR
1914	Pit-F	73	214	15	45	5	3	0	20	9	33	.210	.242	.262	45	-16	-15	16	6			-4	132/O	-1.9
1915	Pit-F	34	69	10	12	0	0	1	5	1	7	.174	.186	.217	19	-7	-7	4	4			0	O/1	-0.8
Total	2	107	283	25	57	5	3	1	25	10	40	.201	.229	.251	39	-23	-22	20	10			-4	/1O32	-2.7

■ BILLY RHIEL
Rhiel, William Joseph b: 8/16/1900, Youngstown, Ohio d: 8/16/46, Youngstown, Ohio BR/TR, 5'11", 175 lbs. Deb: 4/20/29

YEAR	TM/L	G	AB	R	H	2B	3B	HR	RBI	BB	SO	AVG	OBP	SLG	PRO+	BR	/A	RC	SB	CS	SBR	FR	POS	TPR
1929	Bro-N	76	205	27	57	9	4	4	25	19	25	.278	.339	.420	89	-5	-4	29	0			1	2/3S	0.0
1930	Bos-N	20	47	3	8	4	0	0	4	2	5	.170	.204	.255	11	-7	-7	2	0			-4	3/2	-0.8
1932	Det-A	85	250	30	70	13	3	3	38	17	23	.280	.328	.392	82	-6	-7	33	2	0	1	-6	31/O2	-1.0
1933	Det-A	19	17	1	3	0	1	0	1	5	4	.176	.364	.294	75	-0	-0	2	0	0	0	0	/O	0.0
Total	4	200	519	61	138	26	8	7	68	43	57	.266	.323	.387	78	-18	-18	66	2	0		-8	/3210S	-1.8

■ DUSTY RHODES
Rhodes, James Lamar b: 5/13/27, Mathews, Ala. BL/TR, 6', 178 lbs. Deb: 7/15/52

YEAR	TM/L	G	AB	R	H	2B	3B	HR	RBI	BB	SO	AVG	OBP	SLG	PRO+	BR	/A	RC	SB	CS	SBR	FR	POS	TPR
1952	NY-N	67	176	34	44	8	1	10	36	23	33	.250	.340	.477	123	5	5	29	1	0	0	-3	O	0.1
1953	NY-N	76	163	18	38	7	0	11	30	10	28	.233	.277	.479	91	-3	-3	21	0	1	-1	3	O	-0.2
1954	*NY-N	82	164	31	56	7	3	15	50	18	25	.341	.410	.695	181	19	19	47	1	0	0	-4	O	1.4
1955	NY-N	94	187	22	57	5	2	6	32	27	26	.305	.393	.449	122	7	7	35	1	1	-0	-4	O	0.2
1956	NY-N	111	244	20	53	10	3	8	33	30	41	.217	.303	.381	83	-6	-6	27	0	0	0	-5	O	-1.3
1957	NY-N	92	190	20	39	5	1	4	19	18	34	.205	.278	.305	72	-12	-12	15	0	0	0	-6	O	-1.8
1959	SF-N	54	48	1	9	2	0	0	7	5	9	.188	.264	.229	34	-5	-4	3	0	0	0	0	H	-0.3
Total	7	576	1172	146	296	44	10	54	207	131	196	.253	.329	.445	104	6	6	178	3	2	-0	-18	O	-1.9

■ KARL RHODES
Rhodes, Karl Derrick b: 8/21/68, Cincinnati, Ohio BL/TL, 6', 175 lbs. Deb: 8/07/90

YEAR	TM/L	G	AB	R	H	2B	3B	HR	RBI	BB	SO	AVG	OBP	SLG	PRO+	BR	/A	RC	SB	CS	SBR	FR	POS	TPR
1990	Hou-N	39	86	12	21	6	1	1	3	13	12	.244	.343	.372	99	-0	0	12	4	1	1	2	O/2	0.1

■ KEVIN RHOMBERG
Rhomberg, Kevin Jay b: 11/22/55, Dubuque, Iowa BR/TR, 6', 175 lbs. Deb: 9/01/82

YEAR	TM/L	G	AB	R	H	2B	3B	HR	RBI	BB	SO	AVG	OBP	SLG	PRO+	BR	/A	RC	SB	CS	SBR	FR	POS	TPR
1982	Cle-A	16	18	3	6	0	0	1	1	2	4	.333	.400	.500	146	1	1	3	0	2	-1	2	/O3D	0.1
1983	Cle-A	12	21	2	10	0	0	0	2	2	4	.476	.522	.476	170	2	2	5	1	1	-0	-0	/OD	0.2
1984	Cle-A	13	8	0	2	0	0	0	0	0	3	.250	.250	.250	38	-1	-1	1	0	0	0	1	/O12D	0.0
Total	3	41	47	5	18	0	0	1	3	4	11	.383	.431	.447	140	3	3	9	1	3	-2	3	/OD213	0.3

■ HAL RHYNE
Rhyne, Harold J. b: 3/30/1899, Paso Robles, Cal. d: 1/7/71, Orangeville, Cal. BR/TR, 5'8.5", 163 lbs. Deb: 4/18/26

YEAR	TM/L	G	AB	R	H	2B	3B	HR	RBI	BB	SO	AVG	OBP	SLG	PRO+	BR	/A	RC	SB	CS	SBR	FR	POS	TPR
1926	Pit-N	109	366	46	92	14	3	2	39	35	21	.251	.327	.322	71	-12	-15	40	1			8	2S/3	0.0
1927	*Pit-N	62	168	21	46	5	0	0	17	14	9	.274	.330	.304	66	-7	-8	17	0			-6	23/S	-1.3
1929	Bos-A	120	346	41	87	24	5	0	38	25	14	.251	.309	.350	71	-16	-15	39	4	1	1	-3	*S/3O	-0.6
1930	Bos-A	107	296	34	60	8	5	0	23	25	19	.203	.269	.264	37	-29	-27	22	1	4	-2	4	*S	-1.2
1931	Bos-A	147	565	75	154	34	3	0	51	57	41	.273	.341	.343	85	-15	-11	68	3	3	-1	17	*S	1.8
1932	Bos-A	71	207	26	47	12	5	0	14	24	14	.227	.310	.333	69	-10	-9	22	3	2	-0	-2	S/32	-0.5
1933	Chi-A	39	83	9	22	1	1	0	10	5	9	.265	.315	.301	67	-4	-4	8	1	1	-0	5	23/S	0.2
Total	7	655	2031	252	508	98	22	2	192	184	127	.250	.318	.323	69	-93	-89	217	13	11		23	S2/3O	-1.6

■ DEL RICE
Rice, Delbert b: 10/27/22, Portsmouth, Ohio d: 1/26/83, Buena Park, Cal. BR/TR, 6'2", 190 lbs. Deb: 5/02/45 MC

YEAR	TM/L	G	AB	R	H	2B	3B	HR	RBI	BB	SO	AVG	OBP	SLG	PRO+	BR	/A	RC	SB	CS	SBR	FR	POS	TPR
1945	StL-N	83	253	27	66	17	3	1	28	16	33	.261	.313	.364	86	-5	-6	28	0			9	C	0.5
1946	*StL-N	55	139	10	38	8	1	1	12	8	16	.273	.313	.367	89	-2	-2	15	0			-0	C	-0.1
1947	StL-N	97	261	28	57	7	3	12	44	36	40	.218	.315	.406	87	-4	-6	35	1			4	C	0.0
1948	StL-N	100	290	24	57	10	1	4	34	37	46	.197	.298	.279	54	-17	-19	26	1			7	C	-0.4
1949	StL-N	92	284	25	67	16	1	4	29	30	40	.236	.320	.342	74	-9	-11	32	0			-3	C	-1.0
1950	StL-N	130	414	39	101	20	3	9	54	43	65	.244	.323	.372	78	-11	-14	50	0			6	*C	-0.2
1951	StL-N	122	374	34	94	13	1	9	47	34	26	.251	.319	.364	83	-9	-9	44	0	0	0	2	*C	-0.6
1952	StL-N	147	495	43	128	27	2	11	65	33	38	.259	.313	.388	93	-6	-6	60	0	1	-1	-5	*C	-0.8
1953	StL-N	135	419	32	99	22	1	6	37	48	49	.236	.323	.344	72	-16	-16	47	0	0	0	-5	*C	-1.2
1954	StL-N	56	147	13	37	10	1	2	16	16	21	.252	.325	.374	81	-4	-4	18	0	1	-1	6	C	0.3
1955	StL-N	20	59	6	12	3	0	1	7	7	6	.203	.288	.305	58	-4	-4	5	0	0	0	-5	C	-0.7

YEAR	TM/L	G	AB	R	H	2B	3B	HR	RBI	BB	SO	AVG	OBP	SLG	PRO+	BR	/A	RC	SB	CS	SBR	FR	POS	TPR
	Mil-N	27	71	5	14	0	1	2	7	6	12	.197	.260	.310	53	-5	-5	6	0	0	0	0	C	-0.3
	Yr	47	130	11	26	3	1	3	14	13	18	.200	.273	.308	55	-9	-8	11	0	0	0	-5		-1.0
1956	Mil-N	71	188	15	40	9	1	3	17	18	34	.213	.282	.319	65	-10	-9	16	0	0	0	1	C	-0.5
1957	*Mil-N	54	144	15	33	1	1	9	20	17	37	.229	.311	.438	106	-1	1	18	0	0	0	6	C	0.9
1958	Mil-N	43	121	10	27	7	0	1	8	8	30	.223	.271	.306	57	-8	-7	10	0	0	0	-0	C	-0.5
1959	Mil-N	13	29	3	6	0	0	0	1	2	3	.207	.258	.207	28	-3	-3	1	0	0	0	0	/C	-0.1
1960	Chi-N	18	52	2	12	3	0	0	4	2	7	.231	.259	.288	50	-4	-4	3	0	0	0	-2	C	-0.4
	StL-N	1	2	0	0	0	0	0	0	1	0	.000	.333	.000	1	-0	-0	0	0	0	0	-0	/C	0.0
	Yr	19	54	2	12	3	0	0	4	3	7	.222	.263	.278	49	-4	-4	3	0	0	0	-2		-0.4
	Bal-A	1	1	0	0	0	0	0	0	0	0	.000	.000	.000	-99	-0	-0	0	0	0	0	0	/C	0.0
1961	LA-A	44	83	11	20	4	0	4	11	20	19	.241	.388	.434	107	3	1	15	0	1	-1	2	C	0.2
Total	17	1309	3826	342	908	177	20	79	441	382	522	.237	.312	.356	78	-115	-122	430	2	3		23	*C	-4.9

■ SAM RICE
Rice, Edgar Charles b: 2/20/1890, Morocco, Ind. d: 10/13/74, Rossmor, Md. BL/TR, 5'9", 150 lbs. Deb: 8/07/15 H

YEAR	TM/L	G	AB	R	H	2B	3B	HR	RBI	BB	SO	AVG	OBP	SLG	PRO+	BR	/A	RC	SB	CS	SBR	FR	POS	TPR
1915	Was-A	4	8	0	3	0	0	0	0	0	1	.375	.375	.375	124	0	0	1	0			0	/P	0.0
1916	Was-A	58	197	26	59	8	3	1	17	15	13	.299	.352	.386	124	5	5	28	4			2	O/P	0.6
1917	Was-A	155	586	77	177	25	7	0	69	50	41	.302	.360	.369	124	15	16	86	35			8	*O	1.7
1918	Was-A	7	23	3	8	1	0	0	3	2	0	.348	.400	.391	141	1	1	4	1			3	/O	0.4
1919	Was-A	141	557	80	179	23	9	3	71	42	26	.321	.376	.411	122	16	16	91	26			8	*O	1.5
1920	Was-A	153	624	83	211	29	9	3	80	39	23	.338	.381	.428	117	12	15	100	63	30	1	21	*O	2.3
1921	Was-A	143	561	83	185	39	13	4	79	38	10	.330	.382	.467	121	12	16	100	25	12	0	11	*O	1.5
1922	Was-A	154	633	91	187	37	13	6	69	48	13	.295	.347	.423	105	-3	3	93	20	9	1	9	*O	0.1
1923	Was-A	148	595	117	188	35	18	3	75	57	12	.316	.381	.450	125	15	20	105	20	8	1	8	*O	1.4
1924	*Was-A	154	646	106	216	39	14	1	76	46	24	.334	.382	.443	116	11	14	109	24	13	-1	4	*O	0.5
1925	*Was-A	152	649	111	227	31	13	1	87	37	10	.350	.388	.442	113	10	12	112	26	11	1	9	*O	0.8
1926	Was-A	152	641	98	216	32	14	3	76	42	20	.337	.380	.445	117	13	15	103	25	23	-6	7	*O	0.4
1927	Was-A	142	603	98	179	33	14	2	65	36	11	.297	.336	.408	93	-8	-7	78	19	6	2	-0	*O	-1.3
1928	Was-A	148	616	95	202	32	15	2	55	49	15	.328	.379	.438	115	13	13	105	16	3	3	-8	*O	0.0
1929	Was-A	150	616	119	199	39	10	1	62	55	9	.323	.382	.424	106	8	7	102	16	8	0	7	*O	0.7
1930	Was-A	147	593	121	207	35	13	1	73	55	14	.349	.407	.457	118	19	18	111	13	8	-1	4	*O	1.4
1931	Was-A	120	413	81	128	21	8	0	42	35	11	.310	.365	.400	100	1	1	61	6	5	-1	1	*O	-0.5
1932	Was-A	106	288	58	93	16	7	1	34	32	6	.323	.391	.438	116	7	7	50	7	4	-0	-2	O	0.2
1933	*Was-A	73	85	19	25	4	3	1	12	3	7	.294	.326	.447	104	-0	0	11	0	2	-1	6	O	0.3
1934	Cle-A	97	335	48	98	19	1	1	33	28	9	.293	.351	.364	83	-7	-8	44	5	1	1	-8	O	-1.5
Total	20	2404	9269	1514	2987	498	184	34	1078	709	275	.322	.374	.427	113	140	164	1495	351	143		89	*O/P	10.5

■ HAL RICE
Rice, Harold Housten "Hoot" b: 2/11/24, Morganette, W.Va. BL/TR, 6'1", 195 lbs. Deb: 4/29/48

YEAR	TM/L	G	AB	R	H	2B	3B	HR	RBI	BB	SO	AVG	OBP	SLG	PRO+	BR	/A	RC	SB	CS	SBR	FR	POS	TPR
1948	StL-N	8	31	3	10	1	2	0	3	2	4	.323	.364	.484	121	1	1	6	0			-0	/O	0.0
1949	StL-N	40	46	3	9	2	1	1	9	3	7	.196	.245	.348	55	-3	-3	4	0			0	O	-0.3
1950	StL-N	44	128	12	27	3	1	2	11	10	10	.211	.268	.297	46	-10	-11	11	0			-0	O	-1.1
1951	StL-N	69	236	20	60	12	1	4	38	24	22	.254	.323	.364	84	-5	-5	27	0	1	-1	-4	O	-1.1
1952	StL-N	98	295	37	85	14	5	7	45	16	26	.288	.325	.441	110	3	3	39	1	3	-2	-5	O	-0.5
1953	StL-N	8	8	0	2	0	0	0	0	0	3	.250	.250	.250	31	-1	-1	1	0	0	0	0	H	0.0
	Pit-N	78	286	39	89	16	1	4	42	17	22	.311	.350	.416	99	-1	-0	42	0	1	-1	9	O	0.5
	Yr	86	294	39	91	16	1	4	42	17	25	.310	.347	.412	97	-1	-1	42	0	1	-1	9		0.5
1954	Pit-N	28	81	10	14	4	1	1	9	14	24	.173	.295	.284	52	-6	-6	7	0	2	-1	2	O	-0.4
	Chi-N	51	72	5	11	0	0	0	5	8	15	.153	.237	.153	4	-10	-10	3	0	0	0	-0	O	-1.0
	Yr	79	153	15	25	4	1	1	14	22	39	.163	.269	.222	29	-16	-16	10	0	2	-1	2		-1.4
Total	7	424	1183	129	307	52	12	19	162	94	133	.260	.314	.372	82	-31	-32	139	1	7		1	O	-3.9

■ HARRY RICE
Rice, Harry Francis b: 11/22/01, Ware Station, Ill. d: 1/1/71, Portland, Ore. BL/TR, 5'9", 185 lbs. Deb: 4/18/23

YEAR	TM/L	G	AB	R	H	2B	3B	HR	RBI	BB	SO	AVG	OBP	SLG	PRO+	BR	/A	RC	SB	CS	SBR	FR	POS	TPR
1923	StL-A	4	3	0	0	0	0	0	0	0	0	.000	.000	.000	-95	-1	-1	0	0	0	0	0	H	0.0
1924	StL-A	54	93	19	26	7	0	0	15	7	5	.280	.350	.355	77	-2	-3	11	1	3	-2	-0	3/21SO	-0.3
1925	StL-A	103	354	87	127	25	8	11	47	54	15	.359	.450	.568	149	32	29	92	8	7	-2	6	O/1C23	2.4
1926	StL-A	148	578	86	181	27	10	9	58	69	63	.313	.384	.441	110	13	9	98	10	11	-4	7	*O/32S	0.3
1927	StL-A	137	520	90	149	26	9	7	68	50	21	.287	.351	.412	94	-3	-5	73	6	4	-1	12	*O/3	-0.1
1928	Det-A	131	510	87	154	21	12	6	81	44	27	.302	.360	.425	104	4	3	78	20	13	-2	1	*O/3	-0.4
1929	Det-A	130	536	97	163	33	7	6	69	61	23	.304	.379	.425	106	7	6	87	6	10	-4	6	*O/3	0.2
1930	Det-A	37	128	16	39	6	0	2	24	19	8	.305	.403	.398	102	2	1	21	0	3	-2	-0	O	-0.1
	NY-A	100	346	62	103	17	5	7	74	31	21	.298	.361	.436	106	0	3	55	3	3	-1	8	O/13	0.5
	Yr	137	474	78	142	23	5	9	98	50	29	.300	.372	.426	105	2	4	76	3	6	-3	8		0.4
1931	Was-A	47	162	32	43	5	6	0	15	12	10	.265	.320	.370	81	-5	-5	20	2	1	0	-1	O	-0.7
1933	Cin-N	143	510	44	133	19	6	0	54	35	24	.261	.316	.322	84	-11	-10	53	4			2	*O/3	-1.7
Total	10	1034	3740	620	1118	186	63	48	506	376	194	.299	.368	.421	104	36	28	587	60	55		39	O/312SC	0.1

■ JIM RICE
Rice, James Edward b: 3/8/53, Anderson, S.C. BR/TR, 6'2", 200 lbs. Deb: 8/19/74

YEAR	TM/L	G	AB	R	H	2B	3B	HR	RBI	BB	SO	AVG	OBP	SLG	PRO+	BR	/A	RC	SB	CS	SBR	FR	POS	TPR
1974	Bos-A	24	67	6	18	2	1	1	13	4	12	.269	.319	.373	92	-0	-1	8	0	0	0	-0	D/O	0.0
1975	Bos-A	144	564	92	174	29	4	22	102	36	122	.309	.354	.491	126	25	19	92	10	5	0	-5	OD	1.2
1976	Bos-A	153	581	75	164	25	8	25	85	28	123	.282	.320	.482	118	20	11	83	8	5	-1	-8	OD	0.2
1977	Bos-A	160	644	104	206	29	15	39	114	53	120	.320	.379	.593	143	51	42	136	5	4	-1	-2	*DO	3.6
1978	Bos-A	163	677	121	213	25	15	46	139	58	126	.315	.373	.600	153	59	50	147	7	5	-1	5	*OD	5.2
1979	Bos-A	158	619	117	201	39	6	39	130	57	97	.325	.385	.596	152	50	46	138	9	4	0	-3	*OD	3.7
1980	Bos-A	124	504	81	148	22	6	24	86	30	87	.294	.338	.504	121	17	14	81	8	3	1	2	*OD	1.4
1981	Bos-A	108	451	51	128	18	1	17	62	34	76	.284	.338	.441	116	12	9	64	2	2	-1	3	*O	0.9
1982	Bos-A	145	573	86	177	24	5	24	97	55	98	.309	.376	.494	129	24	25	98	0	1	-1	-6	*O	1.3
1983	Bos-A	155	626	90	191	34	1	39	126	52	102	.305	.364	.550	137	39	33	113	0	2	-1	13	*O/D	4.2
1984	Bos-A	159	657	98	184	25	7	28	122	44	102	.280	.326	.467	111	13	9	88	4	0	-1	7	*O/D	1.2
1985	Bos-A	140	546	85	159	20	3	27	103	51	75	.291	.354	.487	122	20	17	83	2	0	1	-6	*O/D	0.9
1986	*Bos-A	157	618	98	200	39	2	20	110	62	78	.324	.389	.490	137	33	32	115	0	1	-1	10	*O/D	3.7
1987	Bos-A	108	404	66	112	14	0	13	62	45	77	.277	.360	.408	100	3	1	55	1	1	-0	1	OD	0.0
1988	*Bos-A	135	485	57	128	18	3	15	72	48	89	.264	.334	.406	102	4	1	63	1	1	-0	-1	*DO	0.0
1989	Bos-A	56	209	22	49	3	0	2	28	13	39	.234	.283	.344	71	-7	-9	20	1	1	0	0	D	-0.8
Total	16	2089	8225	1249	2452	373	79	382	1451	670	1423	.298	.356	.502	127	367	299	1382	58	34	-3	9	*OD	26.7

■ LEN RICE
Rice, Leonard Oliver b: 9/2/18, Lead, S.Dak. BR/TR, 6', 175 lbs. Deb: 4/26/44

YEAR	TM/L	G	AB	R	H	2B	3B	HR	RBI	BB	SO	AVG	OBP	SLG	PRO+	BR	/A	RC	SB	CS	SBR	FR	POS	TPR
1944	Cin-N	10	4	1	0	0	0	0	0	0	0	.000	.000	.000	-99	-1	-1	0	0			1	/C	0.0
1945	Chi-N	32	99	10	23	3	0	0	7	5	8	.232	.269	.263	49	-7	-7	6	2			-1	C	-0.6
Total	2	42	103	11	23	3	0	0	7	5	8	.223	.259	.252	44	-8	-8	6	2			1	/C	-0.6

■ BOB RICE
Rice, Robert Turnbull b: 5/28/1899, Philadelphia, Pa. d: 2/20/86, Elizabethtown, Pa BR/TR, 5'10", 170 lbs. Deb: 9/01/26

YEAR	TM/L	G	AB	R	H	2B	3B	HR	RBI	BB	SO	AVG	OBP	SLG	PRO+	BR	/A	RC	SB	CS	SBR	FR	POS	TPR
1926	Phi-N	19	54	3	8	0	1	0	10	3	4	.148	.193	.185	2	-7	-8	2	0			1	3/2S	-0.6

■ LEE RICHARD
Richard, Lee Edward "Bee Bee" b: 9/18/48, Lafayette, La. BR/TR, 5'11", 165 lbs. Deb: 4/07/71

YEAR	TM/L	G	AB	R	H	2B	3B	HR	RBI	BB	SO	AVG	OBP	SLG	PRO+	BR	/A	RC	SB	CS	SBR	FR	POS	TPR
1971	Chi-A	87	260	38	60	7	3	2	17	20	46	.231	.288	.304	66	-11	-12	21	8	9	-3	2	SO	-0.5

YEAR	TM/L	G	AB	R	H	2B	3B	HR	RBI	BB	SO	AVG	OBP	SLG	PRO+	BR	/A	RC	SB	CS	SBR	FR	POS	TPR
1972	Chi-A	11	29	5	7	0	0	0	1	0	7	.241	.241	.241	43	-2	-2	2	1	0	0	0	/OS	-0.1
1974	Chi-A	32	67	5	11	1	0	0	1	5	8	.164	.222	.179	16	-7	-7	3	0	0	0	3	3/S2OD	-0.2
1975	Chi-A	43	45	11	9	0	1	0	5	4	7	.200	.265	.244	44	-3	-3	3	2	3	-1	6	3/S2D	0.3
1976	StL-N	66	91	12	16	4	2	0	5	4	9	.176	.211	.264	34	-8	-8	4	1	0	0	12	2S/3	0.6
Total	5	239	492	71	103	12	6	2	29	33	77	.209	.260	.270	50	-32	-33	33	12	12	-4	23	/S230D	0.1

■ GENE RICHARDS

Richards, Eugene b: 9/29/53, Monticello, S.C. BL/TL, 6', 175 lbs. Deb: 4/06/77

YEAR	TM/L	G	AB	R	H	2B	3B	HR	RBI	BB	SO	AVG	OBP	SLG	PRO+	BR	/A	RC	SB	CS	SBR	FR	POS	TPR
1977	SD-N	146	525	79	152	16	11	5	32	60	80	.290	.365	.390	114	3	10	81	56	12	10	1	*O1	1.5
1978	SD-N	154	555	90	171	26	12	4	45	64	80	.308	.384	.420	135	20	25	92	37	17	1	-21	*O1	0.0
1979	SD-N	150	545	77	152	17	9	4	41	47	62	.279	.345	.365	100	-4	0	72	24	8	2	-6	*O	-0.6
1980	SD-N	158	642	91	193	26	8	4	41	61	73	.301	.363	.385	116	9	13	96	61	16	9	6	*O	2.3
1981	SD-N	104	393	47	113	14	12	3	42	53	44	.288	.374	.407	131	12	16	63	20	8	1	-2	*O	1.3
1982	SD-N	132	521	63	149	13	8	3	28	36	52	.286	.335	.359	99	-4	-1	62	30	20	-3	-3	*O/1	-0.9
1983	SD-N	95	233	37	64	11	3	3	22	17	17	.275	.327	.386	100	-1	-0	28	14	5	1	-4	O	-0.3
1984	SF-N	87	135	18	34	4	0	0	4	18	26	.252	.340	.281	79	-4	-3	13	5	3	-0	-1	O	-0.4
Total	8	1026	3549	502	1028	127	63	26	255	356	436	.290	.358	.383	113	32	60	508	247	89	21	-29	O/1	2.9

■ FRED RICHARDS

Richards, Fred Charles "Fuzzy" b: 11/3/27, Warren, Ohio BL/TL, 6'1.5", 185 lbs. Deb: 9/15/51

YEAR	TM/L	G	AB	R	H	2B	3B	HR	RBI	BB	SO	AVG	OBP	SLG	PRO+	BR	/A	RC	SB	CS	SBR	FR	POS	TPR
1951	Chi-N	10	27	1	8	2	0	0	4	2	3	.296	.345	.370	91	-0	-0	4	0	0	0	1	/1	0.1

■ PAUL RICHARDS

Richards, Paul Rapier b: 11/21/08, Waxahachie, Tex. d: 5/4/86, Waxahachie, Tex. BR/TR, 6'1.5", 180 lbs. Deb: 4/17/32 M

YEAR	TM/L	G	AB	R	H	2B	3B	HR	RBI	BB	SO	AVG	OBP	SLG	PRO+	BR	/A	RC	SB	CS	SBR	FR	POS	TPR
1932	Bro-N	3	8	0	0	0	0	0	0	0	2	.000	.000	.000	-99	-2	-2	0	0			4	/C	0.1
1933	NY-N	51	87	4	17	3	0	0	10	3	12	.195	.222	.230	30	-8	-8	4	0			1	C	-0.5
1934	NY-N	42	75	10	12	1	0	0	3	13	8	.160	.284	.173	26	-8	-7	4	0			2	C	-0.3
1935	NY-N	7	4	0	1	0	0	0	0	2	1	.250	.500	.250	110	0	0	1	0			1	/C	0.1
	Phi-A	85	257	31	63	10	1	4	29	24	12	.245	.310	.339	68	-13	-12	28	0	0	0	-3	C	-1.1
1943	Det-A	100	313	32	69	7	1	5	33	38	35	.220	.307	.297	71	-9	-11	31	1	0	0	21	*C	1.6
1944	Det-A	95	300	24	71	13	0	3	37	35	30	.237	.318	.310	76	-7	-9	30	8	3	1	16	C	1.4
1945	*Det-A	83	234	26	60	12	1	3	32	19	31	.256	.315	.355	88	-2	-4	29	4	0	1	11	C	1.6
1946	Det-A	57	139	13	28	5	2	0	11	23	18	.201	.315	.266	60	-6	-7	13	2	0	1	15	C	1.1
Total	8	523	1417	140	321	51	5	15	157	149	.227	.305	.301	68	-55	-61	139	15	3		67	C	4.0

■ HARDY RICHARDSON

Richardson, Abram Harding "Old True Blue"
b: 4/21/1855, Clarksboro, N.J. d: 1/14/31, Utica, N.Y. BR/TR, 5'9.5", 170 lbs. Deb: 5/01/1879

YEAR	TM/L	G	AB	R	H	2B	3B	HR	RBI	BB	SO	AVG	OBP	SLG	PRO+	BR	/A	RC	SB	CS	SBR	FR	POS	TPR
1879	Buf-N	79	336	54	95	18	10	0	37	16	30	.283	.315	.396	130	12	11	43				-6	*3/C	0.6
1880	Buf-N	83	343	48	89	18	8	0	17	14	37	.259	.289	.359	116	6	5	36				-5	*3/C	0.0
1881	Buf-N	83	344	62	100	18	9	2	53	12	27	.291	.315	.413	129	10	11	46				25	*O/2S3	3.2
1882	Buf-N	83	354	61	96	20	8	2	57	11	33	.271	.293	.390	115	6	5	41				15	*2	1.9
1883	Buf-N	92	399	73	124	34	7	1	56	22	20	.311	.347	.439	134	17	16	62				22	*2	2.9
1884	Buf-N	102	439	85	132	27	9	6	60	22	41	.301	.334	.444	139	21	19	67				8	2O/31	2.3
1885	Buf-N	96	426	90	136	19	11	6	44	20	22	.319	.350	.458	155	27	25	70				12	2O/SP	3.8
1886	Det-N	125	538	125	189	27	11	11	61	46	27	.351	.402	.504	169	47	45	129	42			10	O2/PS3	5.2
1887	*Det-N	120	543	131	178	25	18	8	94	31	40	.328	.366	.484	132	25	22	110	29			14	2O	3.3
1888	Det-N	58	266	60	77	18	2	6	32	17	23	.289	.335	.440	148	14	14	45	13			4	2	1.9
1889	Bos-N	132	536	122	163	33	10	6	79	48	44	.304	.367	.437	119	18	12	106	47			13	2O	2.6
1890	Bos-P	130	555	126	181	26	14	13	146	52	46	.326	.384	.494	127	26	19	124	42			2	*O/S1	1.3
1891	Bos-a	74	278	45	71	9	4	7	52	40	26	.255	.351	.392	117	6	6	45	16			-0	O/3S1	0.3
1892	Was-N	10	37	2	4	0	0	0	0	5	3	.108	.214	.108	-1	-4	-4	1	2			0	/O32	-0.3
	NY-N	64	248	36	53	11	5	2	34	21	26	.214	.278	.323	84	-6	-5	27	14			-1	2O/1S	-0.5
	Yr	74	285	38	57	11	5	2	34	26	29	.200	.269	.295	73	-10	-9	28	16			-1		-0.8
Total	14	1331	5642	1120	1688	303	126	70	822	377	445	.299	.344	.435	131	225	201	952	205			111	203/S1CP	28.5

■ ART RICHARDSON

Richardson, Arthur L. b: 1862, Hamilton, Ont., Can. d: 25, Deb: 7/10/1884

YEAR	TM/L	G	AB	R	H	2B	3B	HR	RBI	BB	SO	AVG	OBP	SLG	PRO+	BR	/A	RC	SB	CS	SBR	FR	POS	TPR
1884	CP-U	1	4	0	0	0	0	0	0	0		.000	.000	.000	-99	-1	-1	0	0			-1	/2	-0.1

■ NOLEN RICHARDSON

Richardson, Clifford Nolen b: 1/18/03, Chattanooga, Tenn. d: 9/25/51, Athens, Ga. BR/TR, 6'1.5", 170 lbs. Deb: 4/16/29

YEAR	TM/L	G	AB	R	H	2B	3B	HR	RBI	BB	SO	AVG	OBP	SLG	PRO+	BR	/A	RC	SB	CS	SBR	FR	POS	TPR
1929	Det-A	13	21	2	4	0	0	0	2	2	1	.190	.261	.190	18	-3	-3	1	1	1	-0	-4	S	-0.4
1931	Det-A	38	148	13	40	9	2	0	16	6	3	.270	.299	.358	70	-6	-7	16	2	1	0	-2	3	-0.5
1932	Det-A	69	155	13	34	5	2	0	12	9	13	.219	.262	.277	38	-14	-15	12	5	2	0	11	3/S	0.1
1935	NY-A	12	46	3	10	1	1	0	5	3	1	.217	.265	.283	44	-4	-4	4	0	0	0	-6	S	-0.8
1938	Cin-N	35	100	8	29	4	0	0	10	3	4	.290	.311	.330	78	-3	-3	10	0			-1	S	0.0
1939	Cin-N	1	3	0	0	0	0	0	0	0	0	.000	.000	.000	-99	-1	-1	0	0			1	/S	0.0
Total	6	168	473	39	117	19	5	0	45	23	22	.247	.282	.309	55	-31	-32	42	8	4		-1	3/S	-1.6

■ DANNY RICHARDSON

Richardson, Daniel b: 1/25/1863, Elmira, N.Y. d: 9/12/26, New York, N.Y. BR/TR, 5'8", 165 lbs. Deb: 5/22/1884 M

YEAR	TM/L	G	AB	R	H	2B	3B	HR	RBI	BB	SO	AVG	OBP	SLG	PRO+	BR	/A	RC	SB	CS	SBR	FR	POS	TPR
1884	NY-N	74	277	36	70	8	1	1	27	16	17	.253	.294	.300	85	-4	-5	25				0	OS	-0.2
1885	NY-N	49	198	26	52	9	3	0	25	10	14	.263	.298	.338	107	1	1	20				0	O3/P	0.3
1886	NY-N	68	237	43	55	9	1	1	27	17	21	.232	.283	.291	74	-7	-7	24	12			-4	O/PS32	-0.7
1887	*NY-N	122	450	79	125	19	10	3	62	36	25	.278	.337	.384	107	1	5	74	41			14	*23/P	2.1
1888	*NY-N	135	561	82	127	16	7	8	61	15	35	.226	.248	.323	83	-11	-11	55	35			12	*2	0.5
1889	*NY-N	125	497	88	139	22	8	7	100	46	37	.280	.342	.398	108	5	5	81	32			9	*2	2.0
1890	NY-P	123	528	102	135	12	9	4	80	37	19	.256	.307	.335	67	-21	-29	67	37			25	S2	0.2
1891	NY-N	123	516	85	139	18	5	4	51	33	27	.269	.313	.347	98	-5	-2	66	28			49	*2/S	4.5
1892	Was-N	142	551	48	132	13	4	3	58	25	45	.240	.274	.294	75	-19	-16	52	25			58	S2/3M	4.2
1893	Bro-N	54	206	36	46	6	2	0	27	13	18	.223	.279	.272	50	-15	-14	18	7			-17	2/3S	-2.5
1894	Lou-N	116	430	51	109	17	2	1	40	35	31	.253	.317	.309	57	-32	-27	46	8			2	*S2	-1.3
Total	11	1131	4451	676	1129	149	52	32	558	283	289	.254	.301	.332	83	-107	-99	528	225			148	2SO/3P	9.1

■ JEFF RICHARDSON

Richardson, Jeffrey Scott b: 8/26/65, Grand Island, Neb. BR/TR, 6'2", 175 lbs. Deb: 7/14/89

YEAR	TM/L	G	AB	R	H	2B	3B	HR	RBI	BB	SO	AVG	OBP	SLG	PRO+	BR	/A	RC	SB	CS	SBR	FR	POS	TPR
1989	Cin-N	53	125	10	21	4	0	2	11	10	23	.168	.235	.248	37	-10	-11	8	1	0	0	-2	S/3	-0.9

■ KEN RICHARDSON

Richardson, Kenneth Franklin b: 5/2/15, Orleans, Ind. d: 12/7/87, Woodland Hills, Cal BR/TR, 5'10.5", 187 lbs. Deb: 4/14/42

YEAR	TM/L	G	AB	R	H	2B	3B	HR	RBI	BB	SO	AVG	OBP	SLG	PRO+	BR	/A	RC	SB	CS	SBR	FR	POS	TPR
1942	Phi-A	6	15	1	1	0	0	0	0	2	2	.067	.176	.067	-30	-3	-3	0	0	0	0	0	/O13	-0.2
1946	Phi-N	6	20	1	3	1	0	0	2	0	2	.150	.150	.200	-1	-3	-3	0	0			-0	/2	-0.2
Total	2	12	35	2	4	1	0	0	2	2	2	.114	.162	.143	-14	-5	-5	1	0	0		0	/2O31	-0.4

■ BOBBY RICHARDSON

Richardson, Robert Clinton b: 8/19/35, Sumter, S.C. BR/TR, 5'9", 170 lbs. Deb: 8/05/55

YEAR	TM/L	G	AB	R	H	2B	3B	HR	RBI	BB	SO	AVG	OBP	SLG	PRO+	BR	/A	RC	SB	CS	SBR	FR	POS	TPR
1955	NY-A	11	26	2	4	0	0	0	3	2	0	.154	.214	.154	0	-4	-4	1	1	1	-0	-5	/2S	-0.8
1956	NY-A	5	7	1	1	0	0	0	0	1	1	.143	.143	.143	-25	-1	-1	0	0	0	0	2	S	0.1
1957	*NY-A	97	305	36	78	11	1	0	19	9	26	.256	.277	.298	58	-18	-18	23	1	3	-2	5	2	-0.9
1958	*NY-A	73	182	18	45	6	2	0	14	8	5	.247	.279	.302	62	-10	-9	15	1	3	-2	8	23/S	0.1
1959	*NY-A	134	469	53	141	18	6	2	33	26	20	.301	.337	.377	99	-3	-4	60	5	5	-2	2	*2S3	2.3
1960	*NY-A	150	460	45	116	12	3	1	26	35	19	.252	.305	.298	68	-23	-20	42	6	6	-2	-4	*23	-1.5
1961	*NY-A	162	662	80	173	17	5	3	49	30	23	.261	.295	.316	67	-35	-30	59	9	7	-2	-9	*2	-2.1
1962	*NY-A	161	692	99	209	38	5	8	59	37	24	.302	.338	.406	103	-1	1	92	11	9	-2	-3	*2	0.8

YEAR	TM/L	G	AB	R	H	2B	3B	HR	RBI	BB	SO	AVG	OBP	SLG	PRO+	BR	/A	RC	SB	CS	SBR	FR	POS	TPR
1963	*NY-A	151	630	72	167	20	6	3	48	25	22	.265	.295	.330	76	-21	-21	63	15	1	4	7	*2	0.1
1964	*NY-A	159	679	90	181	25	4	4	50	28	36	.267	.296	.333	73	-24	-25	66	11	2	2	-14	*2/S	-2.1
1965	NY-A	160	664	76	164	28	2	6	47	37	39	.247	.288	.322	74	-24	-23	61	7	5	-1	-3	*2	-1.9
1966	NY-A	149	610	71	153	21	3	7	42	25	28	.251	.281	.330	78	-20	-18	52	6	6	-2	3	*2/3	-0.4
Total	12	1412	5386	643	1432	196	37	34	390	262	243	.266	.301	.335	77	-184	-168	534	73	48	-7	-10	*2/3S	-8.2

■ **TOM RICHARDSON**   Richardson, Thomas Mitchell b: 8/7/1883, Louisville, Ill. d: 11/15/39, Onawa, Iowa BR/TR, 6', 190 lbs. Deb: 8/02/17

YEAR	TM/L	G	AB	R	H	2B	3B	HR	RBI	BB	SO	AVG	OBP	SLG	PRO+	BR	/A	RC	SB	CS	SBR	FR	POS	TPR
1917	StL-A	1	1	0	0	0	0	0	0	0	0	.000	.000	.000	-99	-0	-0	0				0	H	0.0

■ **BILL RICHARDSON**   Richardson, William Henry b: 9/24/1878, Salem, Ind. d: 11/6/49, Sullivan, Ind. BR/TR, 5'11", 200 lbs. Deb: 9/20/01

YEAR	TM/L	G	AB	R	H	2B	3B	HR	RBI	BB	SO	AVG	OBP	SLG	PRO+	BR	/A	RC	SB	CS	SBR	FR	POS	TPR
1901	StL-N	15	52	7	11	2	0	2	7	6		.212	.293	.365	97	-1	-1	6	1			-1	1	0.0

■ **MIKE RICHARDT**   Richardt, Michael Anthony b: 5/24/58, Los Angeles, Cal. BR/TR, 6', 170 lbs. Deb: 8/30/80

YEAR	TM/L	G	AB	R	H	2B	3B	HR	RBI	BB	SO	AVG	OBP	SLG	PRO+	BR	/A	RC	SB	CS	SBR	FR	POS	TPR
1980	Tex-A	22	71	2	16	2	0	0	8	1	7	.225	.236	.254	35	-6	-6	4	0	0	0	-1	2/D	-0.5
1982	Tex-A	119	402	34	97	10	0	3	43	23	42	.241	.284	.289	61	-23	-20	32	9	1	2	5	2D/O	-0.8
1983	Tex-A	22	83	9	13	2	1	1	7	2	11	.157	.176	.241	14	-10	-10	3	2	1	0	2	2	-0.6
1984	Tex-A	6	9	0	1	0	0	0	0	1	1	.111	.200	.111	-11	-1	-1	0	0	0	-1	1	/2	0.0
	Hou-N	16	15	1	4	1	0	0	2	0	1	.267	.267	.333	73	-1	-1	1	0	0	0	0	H	0.0
Total	4	185	580	46	131	15	1	4	60	27	62	.226	.262	.276	50	-41	-38	41	11	3	2	7	2/DO	-1.9

■ **LANCE RICHBOURG**   Richbourg, Lance Clayton b: 12/18/1897, DeFuniak Springs Fla. d: 9/10/75, Crestview, Fla. BL/TR, 5'10.5", 160 lbs. Deb: 7/04/21

YEAR	TM/L	G	AB	R	H	2B	3B	HR	RBI	BB	SO	AVG	OBP	SLG	PRO+	BR	/A	RC	SB	CS	SBR	FR	POS	TPR
1921	Phi-N	10	5	2	1	1	0	0	0	0	3	.200	.200	.400	51	-0	-0	0	1	1	-0	3	/2	0.2
1924	Was-A	15	32	3	9	2	1	0	1	2	0	.281	.324	.406	90	-1	-1	4	0	0	0	1	/O	0.0
1927	Bos-N	115	450	57	139	12	9	2	34	22	30	.309	.342	.389	104	-3	1	58	24			-4	*O	-0.6
1928	Bos-N	148	612	105	206	26	12	2	52	62	39	.337	.399	.428	123	17	21	104	11			6	*O	2.1
1929	Bos-N	139	557	76	170	24	13	3	56	42	26	.305	.355	.411	93	-9	-6	80	7			8	*O	-0.8
1930	Bos-N	130	529	81	161	23	8	3	54	19	31	.304	.331	.395	77	-22	-19	66	13			1	*O	-2.3
1931	Bos-N	97	286	32	82	11	6	2	29	19	14	.287	.331	.388	96	-3	-2	38	9			-4	O	-0.8
1932	Chi-N	44	148	22	38	2	2	1	21	8	4	.257	.295	.318	65	-7	-7	14	0			-3	O	-1.1
Total	8	698	2619	378	806	101	51	13	247	174	147	.308	.352	.400	97	-30	-13	364	65	1		9	O/2	-3.3

■ **ROB RICHIE**   Richie, Robert Eugene b: 9/5/65, Reno, Nev. BL/TR, 6'2", 190 lbs. Deb: 8/19/89

YEAR	TM/L	G	AB	R	H	2B	3B	HR	RBI	BB	SO	AVG	OBP	SLG	PRO+	BR	/A	RC	SB	CS	SBR	FR	POS	TPR
1989	Det-A	19	49	6	13	4	2	1	10	5	10	.265	.333	.490	132	2	2	7	0	1	-1	-0	O/D	0.1

■ **DON RICHMOND**   Richmond, Donald Lester b: 10/27/19, Gillett, Pa. d: 5/24/81, Elmira, N.Y. BL/TR, 6'1", 175 lbs. Deb: 9/16/41

YEAR	TM/L	G	AB	R	H	2B	3B	HR	RBI	BB	SO	AVG	OBP	SLG	PRO+	BR	/A	RC	SB	CS	SBR	FR	POS	TPR
1941	Phi-A	9	35	3	7	1	1	0	5	0	1	.200	.200	.286	28	-4	-4	1	0	2	-1	-2	/3	-0.6
1946	Phi-A	16	62	3	18	3	0	1	9	0	10	.290	.290	.387	89	-1	-1	7	1	0	0	-3	3	-0.2
1947	Phi-A	19	21	2	4	1	1	0	4	3	3	.190	.292	.333	72	-1	-1	2	0	0	0	-3	/32	-0.3
1951	StL-N	12	34	3	3	1	0	1	4	3	3	.088	.162	.206	-2	-5	-5	1	0	1	-1	5	3	0.0
Total	4	56	152	11	32	6	2	2	22	6	17	.211	.241	.316	51	-11	-11	11	1	3	-2	-3	/32	-1.1

■ **JOHN RICHMOND**   Richmond, John H. b: 1854, Pennsylvania TR, Deb: 4/22/1875

YEAR	TM/L	G	AB	R	H	2B	3B	HR	RBI	BB	SO	AVG	OBP	SLG	PRO+	BR	/A	RC	SB	CS	SBR	FR	POS	TPR
1875	Ath-n	29	126	29	25	1	0	0		0		.198	.198	.206	36	-7	-9	5					2O/C	-0.8
1879	Syr-N	62	254	31	54	8	4	1	23	4	24	.213	.225	.287	76	-9	-5	17				-8	OS/C	-1.0
1880	Bos-N	32	129	12	32	3	1	0	9	2	18	.248	.260	.287	88	-2	-2	10				-12	S/O	-1.1
1881	Bos-N	27	98	13	27	2	2	1	12	6	7	.276	.317	.367	120	2	2	12				-0	S/O	0.2
1882	Cle-N	41	140	12	24	6	2	0	11	11	27	.171	.232	.243	54	-7	-6	8				1	O	-0.4
	Phi-a	18	65	8	12	2	2	0		11		.185	.303	.277	87	-0	-1	6				0	0	0.0
1883	Col-a	92	385	63	109	7	8	0		25		.283	.327	.343	126	7	12	44				26	*S/O	3.0
1884	Col-a	105	398	57	100	13	7	3		35		.251	.317	.342	128	9	14	44				-9	*S	0.2
1885	Pit-a	34	131	14	27	2	2	0		8		.206	.262	.252	66	-5	-4	9				-10	SO	-1.2
Total	7	411	1600	210	385	43	28	5	55	102	76	.241	.288	.312	102	-5	10	149				-11	SO/C	-0.3

■ **LEE RICHMOND**   Richmond, J. Lee b: 5/5/1857, Sheffield, Ohio d: 10/1/29, Toledo, Ohio TL, 5'10", 142 lbs. Deb: 9/27/1879

YEAR	TM/L	G	AB	R	H	2B	3B	HR	RBI	BB	SO	AVG	OBP	SLG	PRO+	BR	/A	RC	SB	CS	SBR	FR	POS	TPR
1879	Bos-N	1	6	0	2	0	0	0	1	0	1	.333	.333	.333	118	-0	0	1				0	/P	0.0
1880	Wor-N	77	309	44	70	8	4	0	34	9	32	.227	.248	.278	72	-7	-10	22				-7	*PO	0.0
1881	Wor-N	61	252	31	63	5	1	0	28	10	10	.250	.279	.278	71	-7	-9	20				0	PO	0.0
1882	Wor-N	55	228	50	64	8	9	2	28	9	11	.281	.308	.421	128	8	7	30				2	PO	0.0
1883	Pro-N	49	194	41	55	8	6	1	19	15	19	.284	.335	.402	120	6	5	27				-10	OP	-0.1
1886	Cin-a	8	29	3	8	0	0	0		3		.276	.344	.276	94	0	-0	3	0			-3	/OP	-0.2
Total	6	251	1018	169	262	29	20	3	110	46	73	.257	.289	.334	95	-0	-7	102	0			-18	P/O	-0.3

■ **AL RICHTER**   Richter, Allen Gordon b: 2/7/27, Norfolk, Va. BR/TR, 6', 175 lbs. Deb: 9/23/51

YEAR	TM/L	G	AB	R	H	2B	3B	HR	RBI	BB	SO	AVG	OBP	SLG	PRO+	BR	/A	RC	SB	CS	SBR	FR	POS	TPR
1951	Bos-A	5	11	1	1	0	0	0	0	3	0	.091	.286	.091	5	-1	-2	0	0	0	0	2	/S	0.1
1953	Bos-A	1	0	0	0	0	0	0	0	0	0	—	—	—	—	0	0	0	0	0	0	0	/S	0.0
Total	2	6	11	1	1	0	0	0	0	3	0	.091	.286	.091	5	-1	-2	0	0	0	0	3	/S	0.1

■ **JOHN RICHTER**   Richter, John M. b: 2/8/1873, Louisville, Ky. d: 10/4/27, Louisville, Ky. Deb: 10/06/1898

YEAR	TM/L	G	AB	R	H	2B	3B	HR	RBI	BB	SO	AVG	OBP	SLG	PRO+	BR	/A	RC	SB	CS	SBR	FR	POS	TPR
1898	Lou-N	3	13	1	2	0	0	0	0	0		.154	.154	.154	-11	-2	-2	0	0			1	/3	0.0

■ **JOE RICKERT**   Rickert, Joseph Francis "Diamond Joe" b: 12/12/1876, London, Ohio d: 10/15/43, Springfield, Ohio 5'10.5", 165 lbs. Deb: 10/12/1898

YEAR	TM/L	G	AB	R	H	2B	3B	HR	RBI	BB	SO	AVG	OBP	SLG	PRO+	BR	/A	RC	SB	CS	SBR	FR	POS	TPR
1898	Pit-N	2	6	0	1	0	0	0	0	0		.167	.167	.167	-3	-1	-1	0	0			1	/O	0.0
1901	Bos-N	13	60	6	10	1	2	0	1	3		.167	.206	.250	31	-5	-6	3	1			2	O	-0.4
Total	2	15	66	6	11	1	2	0	1	3		.167	.203	.242	28	-6	-7	4	1			3	/O	-0.4

■ **MARV RICKERT**   Rickert, Marvin August "Twitch" b: 1/8/21, Long Branch, Wash. d: 6/3/78, Oakville, Wash. BL/TR, 6'2", 195 lbs. Deb: 9/10/42

YEAR	TM/L	G	AB	R	H	2B	3B	HR	RBI	BB	SO	AVG	OBP	SLG	PRO+	BR	/A	RC	SB	CS	SBR	FR	POS	TPR
1942	Chi-N	8	26	5	7	0	0	0	1	1	5	.269	.296	.269	69	-1	-1	2	0			2	/O	0.0
1946	Chi-N	111	392	44	103	18	3	7	47	28	54	.263	.314	.378	98	-4	-3	46	3			-7	*O	-1.1
1947	Chi-N	71	137	7	20	0	0	2	15	15	17	.146	.230	.190	13	-17	-16	6	0			1	O/1	-1.6
1948	Cin-N	8	6	0	1	0	0	0	0	0	0	.167	.167	.167	-10	-1	-1	0	0			0	H	0.0
	*Bos-N	3	13	1	3	0	1	0	2	0	1	.231	.286	.385	81	-0	-0	2	0			1	/O	0.0
	Yr	11	19	1	4	0	1	0	2	0	1	.211	.250	.316	54	-1	-1	2	0			1		0.0
1949	Bos-N	100	277	44	81	18	3	6	49	23	38	.292	.347	.444	117	4	5	42	1			-1	O1	0.0
1950	Pit-N	17	20	0	3	0	0	0	4	0	4	.150	.150	.150	-20	-3	-4	0	0			0	O	-0.3
	Chi-A	84	278	38	66	9	2	4	27	21	42	.237	.291	.327	60	-18	-17	25	0	1	-1	-6	O/1	-2.3
Total	6	402	1149	139	284	45	9	19	145	88	161	.247	.302	.352	79	-41	-37	122	4	1		-9	O/1	-5.3

■ **DAVE RICKETTS**   Ricketts, David William b: 7/12/35, Pottstown, Pa. BB/TR, 6', 190 lbs. Deb: 9/25/63 C

YEAR	TM/L	G	AB	R	H	2B	3B	HR	RBI	BB	SO	AVG	OBP	SLG	PRO+	BR	/A	RC	SB	CS	SBR	FR	POS	TPR
1963	StL-N	3	8	0	2	0	0	0	0	0	2	.250	.250	.250	41	-1	-1	1	0	0	0	-0	/C	0.0
1965	StL-N	11	29	1	7	0	0	0	0	1	3	.241	.267	.241	40	-2	-2	2	0	0	0	-2	C	-0.4
1967	*StL-N	52	99	11	27	8	0	1	14	4	7	.273	.301	.384	96	-1	-1	11	0	0	0	0	C	0.0
1968	*StL-N	20	22	1	3	0	0	0	1	0	3	.136	.136	.136	-18	-3	-3	0	0	0	0	0	/C	-0.2
1969	StL-N	30	44	2	12	1	0	0	5	4	5	.273	.333	.295	77	-1	-1	5	0	0	0	1	/C	0.0
1970	Pit-N	14	11	0	2	0	0	0	1	0	3	.182	.250	.182	18	-1	-1	1	0	0	0	0	/C	0.0
Total	6	130	213	15	53	9	0	1	20	10	23	.249	.283	.305	67	-9	-9	19	0	0	0	-1	/C	-0.6

YEAR	TM/L	G	AB	R	H	2B	3B	HR	RBI	BB	SO	AVG	OBP	SLG	PRO+	BR	/A	RC	SB	CS	SBR	FR	POS	TPR

■ BRANCH RICKEY   Rickey, Wesley Branch "The Mahatma" b: 12/20/1881, Lucasville, Ohio d: 12/9/65, Columbia, Mo. BL/TR, 5'9", 175 lbs. Deb: 6/16/05 MH

YEAR	TM/L	G	AB	R	H	2B	3B	HR	RBI	BB	SO	AVG	OBP	SLG	PRO+	BR	/A	RC	SB	CS	SBR	FR	POS	TPR
1905	StL-A	1	3	0	0	0	0	0	0	0		.000	.000	.000	-99	-1	-1	0	0			-0	/C	0.0
1906	StL-A	65	201	22	57	7	3	3	24	16		.284	.336	.393	136	7	8	29	4			-8	C/O	0.4
1907	NY-A	52	137	16	25	1	3	0	15	11		.182	.243	.234	50	-7	-8	9	4			-5	OC/1	-1.4
1914	StL-A	2	2	0	0	0	0	0	0	0	1	.000	.000	.000	-99	-0	-0	0	0			0	HM	0.0
Total	4	120	343	38	82	8	6	3	39	27	1	.239	.295	.324	96	-1	-2	38	8			-13	/CO1	-1.0

■ CHRIS RICKLEY   Rickley, Christian b: 10/7/1859, Philadelphia, Pa. d: 10/25/11, Philadelphia, Pa. 5'8", 160 lbs. Deb: 6/09/1884

YEAR	TM/L	G	AB	R	H	2B	3B	HR	RBI	BB	SO	AVG	OBP	SLG	PRO+	BR	/A	RC	SB	CS	SBR	FR	POS	TPR
1884	Phi-U	6	25	5	5	2	0	0		2		.200	.259	.280	89	-0	-0	2	0			0	/S	0.0

■ JOHN RICKS   Ricks, John   Deb: 9/21/1891

YEAR	TM/L	G	AB	R	H	2B	3B	HR	RBI	BB	SO	AVG	OBP	SLG	PRO+	BR	/A	RC	SB	CS	SBR	FR	POS	TPR
1891	StL-a	5	18	3	3	0	0	0	0	0	2	.167	.167	.167	-3	-2	-3	1	0			-1	/3	-0.2
1894	StL-N	1	1	0	0	0	0	0	0	0	0	.000	.000	.000	-99	-0	-0	0	0			-1	/3	0.0
Total	2	6	19	3	3	0	0	0	0	0	2	.158	.158	.158	-8	-3	-3	1	0			-1	/3	-0.2

■ FRED RICO   Rico, Alfredo (Cruz) b: 7/4/44, Jerome, Ariz. BR/TR, 5'10", 180 lbs. Deb: 9/01/69

YEAR	TM/L	G	AB	R	H	2B	3B	HR	RBI	BB	SO	AVG	OBP	SLG	PRO+	BR	/A	RC	SB	CS	SBR	FR	POS	TPR
1969	KC-A	12	26	2	6	2	0	0	2	9	10	.231	.429	.308	108	1	1	4	0	1	-1	4	/O3	0.4

■ ART RICO   Rico, Arthur Raymond b: 7/23/1896, Roxbury, Mass. d: 1/3/19, Boston, Mass. BR/TR, 5'9.5", 185 lbs. Deb: 7/31/16

YEAR	TM/L	G	AB	R	H	2B	3B	HR	RBI	BB	SO	AVG	OBP	SLG	PRO+	BR	/A	RC	SB	CS	SBR	FR	POS	TPR
1916	Bos-N	4	4	0	0	0	0	0	0	0	0	.000	.000	.000	-99	-1	-1	0	0			-0	/C	0.0
1917	Bos-N	13	14	1	4	1	0	0	2	0	2	.286	.286	.357	102	-1	-0	1	0			-1	C/O	0.0
Total	2	17	18	1	4	1	0	0	2	0	2	.222	.222	.278	56	-1	-1	1	0			-1	/CO	0.0

■ HARRY RICONDA   Riconda, Henry Paul b: 3/17/1897, New York, N.Y. d: 11/15/58, Mahopac, N.Y. BR/TR, 5'10", 175 lbs. Deb: 4/19/23

YEAR	TM/L	G	AB	R	H	2B	3B	HR	RBI	BB	SO	AVG	OBP	SLG	PRO+	BR	/A	RC	SB	CS	SBR	FR	POS	TPR
1923	Phi-A	55	175	23	46	11	4	0	12	12	18	.263	.317	.371	80	-5	-6	21	4	2	0	4	3/S	0.4
1924	Phi-A	83	281	34	71	16	3	1	21	27	43	.253	.323	.342	71	-12	-13	32	3	4	-2	1	3/S	-0.5
1926	Bos-N	4	12	1	2	0	0	0	0	2	2	.167	.286	.167	27	-1	-1	1	0			-1	/3	-0.1
1928	Bro-N	92	281	22	63	15	4	3	35	20	28	.224	.285	.338	63	-16	-16	27	6			3	23S	-0.8
1929	Pit-N	8	15	3	7	2	0	0	2	0	0	.467	.467	.600	158	1	1	4	0			-0	/S	0.1
1930	Cin-N	1	1	0	0	0	0	0	0	0	0	.000	.000	.000	-99	-0	-0	0	0			0	H	0.0
Total	6	243	765	83	189	44	11	4	70	61	91	.247	.309	.349	71	-34	-34	84	13	6		7	3/2S	-0.9

■ JOHN RIDDLE   Riddle, John H. b: 2/1864, Pennsylvania BR , Deb: 9/18/1889

YEAR	TM/L	G	AB	R	H	2B	3B	HR	RBI	BB	SO	AVG	OBP	SLG	PRO+	BR	/A	RC	SB	CS	SBR	FR	POS	TPR
1889	Was-N	11	37	3	8	3	0	0	3	2	8	.216	.256	.297	59	-2	-2	3	0			-0	/CO	-0.1
1890	Phi-a	27	85	7	7	0	1	0		17		.082	.243	.106	5	-9	-9	3	4			-1	CO/23	-0.7
Total	2	38	122	10	15	3	1	0	3	19	8	.123	.246	.164	22	-12	-11	6	4			-1	/CO23	-0.8

■ JOHNNY RIDDLE   Riddle, John Ludy "Mutt" b: 10/3/05, Clinton, S.C. BR/TR, 5'11", 190 lbs. Deb: 4/17/30 C

YEAR	TM/L	G	AB	R	H	2B	3B	HR	RBI	BB	SO	AVG	OBP	SLG	PRO+	BR	/A	RC	SB	CS	SBR	FR	POS	TPR
1930	Chi-A	25	58	7	14	3	1	0	4	3	6	.241	.290	.328	58	-4	-4	6	0	0	0	-2	C	-0.2
1937	Was-A	8	26	2	7	0	0	0	3	0	2	.269	.296	.269	46	-2	-2	2	0	0	0	0	/C	0.0
	Bos-N	2	3	0	0	0	0	0	0	1	0	.000	.250	.000	-29	-1	-0	0	0			1	/C	0.0
1938	Bos-N	19	57	6	16	1	0	0	2	4	2	.281	.328	.298	81	-2	-1	6	0			4	C	0.3
1941	Cin-N	10	10	2	3	0	0	0	0	0	1	.300	.300	.300	69	-0	-0	1	0			1	C	0.2
1944	Cin-N	1	0	0	0	0	0	0	0	0	0	—	—	—	—	0	0	0	0			0	/C	0.0
1945	Cin-N	23	45	0	8	0	0	0	2	4	6	.178	.245	.178	19	-5	-5	2	0			3	C	0.0
1948	Pit-N	10	15	1	3	0	0	0	0	1	2	.200	.250	.200	23	-2	-2	1	0			0	C	0.0
Total	7	98	214	18	51	4	1	0	11	13	19	.238	.288	.266	51	-15	-14	18	0	0		8	/C	0.3

■ HANK RIEBE   Riebe, Harvey Donald b: 10/10/21, Cleveland, Ohio BR/TR, 5'9.5", 175 lbs. Deb: 8/26/42

YEAR	TM/L	G	AB	R	H	2B	3B	HR	RBI	BB	SO	AVG	OBP	SLG	PRO+	BR	/A	RC	SB	CS	SBR	FR	POS	TPR
1942	Det-A	11	35	1	11	2	0	0	2	0	6	.314	.314	.371	85	-1	-1	4	0	0	0	-0	C	0.0
1947	Det-A	8	7	0	0	0	0	0	2	0	2	.000	.000	.000	-97	-2	-2	0	0	0	0	-0	/C	-0.1
1948	Det-A	25	62	0	12	0	0	0	5	3	5	.194	.231	.194	13	-8	-8	2	0	1	-1	0	C	-0.5
1949	Det-A	17	33	1	6	2	0	0	2	0	5	.182	.182	.242	12	-4	-4	1	1	0	0	-2	C	-0.4
Total	4	61	137	2	29	4	0	0	11	3	18	.212	.229	.241	26	-14	-15	7	1	1	-0	-2	/C	-1.0

■ JOE RIGGERT   Riggert, Joseph Aloysius b: 12/11/1886, Janesville, Wis. d: 12/10/73, Kansas City, Mo. BR/TR, 5'9.5", 170 lbs. Deb: 5/12/11

YEAR	TM/L	G	AB	R	H	2B	3B	HR	RBI	BB	SO	AVG	OBP	SLG	PRO+	BR	/A	RC	SB	CS	SBR	FR	POS	TPR
1911	Bos-A	50	146	19	31	4	4	2	13	12		.212	.290	.336	75	-5	-5	16	5			-4	O	-1.1
1914	Bro-N	27	83	6	16	1	3	2	6	4	20	.193	.230	.349	70	-3	-4	7	2			-1	O	-0.4
	StL-N	34	89	9	19	5	2	0	8	5	14	.213	.255	.315	70	-4	-4	8	4			-1	O	-0.5
	Yr	61	172	15	35	6	5	2	14	9	34	.203	.243	.331	70	-7	-7	15	6			-1		-0.9
1919	Bos-N	63	240	34	68	8	5	4	17	25	30	.283	.356	.408	135	9	10	36	9			-0	O	0.8
Total	3	174	558	68	134	18	14	8	44	46	64	.240	.305	.366	98	-4	-3	66	20			-5	O	-1.2

■ LEW RIGGS   Riggs, Lewis Sidney b: 4/22/10, Mebane, N.C. d: 8/12/75, Durham, N.C. BL/TR, 6', 175 lbs. Deb: 4/28/34

YEAR	TM/L	G	AB	R	H	2B	3B	HR	RBI	BB	SO	AVG	OBP	SLG	PRO+	BR	/A	RC	SB	CS	SBR	FR	POS	TPR
1934	StL-N	2	1	0	0	0	0	0	0	0	1	.000	.000	.000	-94	-0	-0	0	0			0	H	0.0
1935	Cin-N	142	532	73	148	26	8	5	46	43	32	.278	.334	.385	96	-5	-3	72	8			8	*3	0.9
1936	Cin-N	141	538	69	138	20	12	6	57	38	33	.257	.314	.372	90	-13	-8	63	5			12	*3	1.4
1937	Cin-N	122	384	43	93	17	5	6	45	24	17	.242	.289	.359	79	-14	-12	40	4			20	*3/2S	1.2
1938	Cin-N	142	531	53	134	21	13	2	55	40	28	.252	.311	.352	84	-13	-12	60	3			-1	*3	-1.5
1939	Cin-N	22	38	5	6	1	0	0	1	5	4	.158	.256	.184	20	-4	-4	2	1			-1	3	-0.4
1940	*Cin-N	41	72	8	21	7	1	1	9	2	4	.292	.311	.458	109	1	0	10	0			2	3	0.2
1941	*Bro-N	77	197	27	60	13	4	5	36	16	12	.305	.357	.487	131	9	8	35	1			-7	3/12	0.1
1942	Bro-N	70	180	20	50	5	0	3	22	13	9	.278	.333	.356	100	0	0	22	0			-6	3/1	-0.5
1946	Bro-N	1	4	0	0	0	0	0	0	0	0	.000	.000	.000	-99	-1	-1	0	0			0	/3	0.0
Total	10	760	2477	298	650	110	43	28	271	181	140	.262	.317	.375	91	-42	-32	304	22			27	3/21S	1.4

■ TOPPER RIGNEY   Rigney, Emory Elmo b: 1/7/1897, Groveton, Tex. d: 6/6/72, San Antonio, Tex. BR/TR, 5'9", 150 lbs. Deb: 4/12/22

YEAR	TM/L	G	AB	R	H	2B	3B	HR	RBI	BB	SO	AVG	OBP	SLG	PRO+	BR	/A	RC	SB	CS	SBR	FR	POS	TPR
1922	Det-A	155	536	68	161	17	7	2	63	68	44	.300	.380	.369	99	-1	2	81	17	8	0	-11	*S	0.8
1923	Det-A	129	470	63	148	24	11	3	74	55	35	.315	.389	.419	115	10	11	80	7	5	-1	-16	*S	0.6
1924	Det-A	147	499	81	144	29	9	4	94	102	39	.289	.410	.407	113	12	14	90	11	11	-3	10	*S	3.3
1925	Det-A	62	146	21	36	5	2	2	18	21	15	.247	.341	.349	77	-5	-5	18	2	2	-1	-14	S/3	-1.0
1926	Bos-A	148	525	71	142	32	6	4	53	108	31	.270	.395	.377	105	6	8	85	6	8	-3	20	*S	3.5
1927	Bos-A	8	18	0	2	1	0	0	0	1	2	.111	.158	.167	-16	-3	-3	1	0	0	0	-1	/3S	-0.3
	Was-A	45	132	20	36	5	4	0	13	22	10	.273	.381	.371	97	-0	-0	19	1	2	-1	-3	S/3	0.0
	Yr	53	150	20	38	6	4	0	13	23	12	.253	.356	.347	84	-3	-3	19	1	2	-1	-4		-0.3
Total	6	694	2326	324	669	113	39	13	315	377	176	.288	.388	.387	104	19	27	374	44	36	-8	-15	S/3	6.9

■ BILL RIGNEY   Rigney, William Joseph "Specs" or "The Cricket" b: 1/29/18, Alameda, Cal. BR/TR, 6'1", 178 lbs. Deb: 4/16/46 MC

YEAR	TM/L	G	AB	R	H	2B	3B	HR	RBI	BB	SO	AVG	OBP	SLG	PRO+	BR	/A	RC	SB	CS	SBR	FR	POS	TPR
1946	NY-N	110	360	38	85	9	1	3	31	36	29	.236	.307	.292	70	-14	-14	34	9			3	3S	-0.8
1947	NY-N	130	531	84	142	24	3	17	59	51	54	.267	.337	.420	99	-1	-1	76	7			1	23S	0.8
1948	NY-N	113	424	72	112	17	3	10	43	47	54	.264	.342	.389	97	-1	-2	58	4			-11	*2/S	-0.4
1949	NY-N	122	389	53	108	19	6	6	47	47	38	.278	.356	.404	103	2	2	58	5			-17	S23	-0.7
1950	NY-N	56	83	9	15	2	0	0	8	9	13	.181	.253	.205	22	-9	-9	4	0			6	23	-0.2
1951	*NY-N	44	69	9	16	2	0	4	9	8	7	.232	.321	.435	100	-0	-0	10	0	1	-1	5	3/2	0.5
1952	NY-N	60	90	15	27	5	1	1	14	11	6	.300	.388	.411	121	3	3	14	2	3	-1	-1	3/2S1	0.2

YEAR	TM/L	G	AB	R	H	2B	3B	HR	RBI	BB	SO	AVG	OBP	SLG	PRO+	BR	/A	RC	SB	CS	SBR	FR	POS	TPR
1953	NY-N	19	20	2	5	0	0	0	1	0	5	.250	.250	.250	30	-2	-2	1	0	0	0	0	/32	-0.1
Total	8	654	1966	281	510	78	14	41	212	208	206	.259	.334	.376	91	-22	-23	254	25	4		-13	23S/1	-0.3

■ **CULLEY RIKARD** Rikard, Culley b: 5/9/14, Oxford, Miss. BL/TR, 5'11", 183 lbs. Deb: 9/20/41

YEAR	TM/L	G	AB	R	H	2B	3B	HR	RBI	BB	SO	AVG	OBP	SLG	PRO+	BR	/A	RC	SB	CS	SBR	FR	POS	TPR
1941	Pit-N	6	20	1	4	1	0	0	1	1	5	.200	.238	.250	38	-2	-2	1	0			1	/O	0.0
1942	Pit-N	38	52	6	10	2	1	0	5	7	8	.192	.288	.269	62	-2	-2	4	0			-0	O	-0.2
1947	Pit-N	109	324	57	93	16	4	4	32	50	39	.287	.384	.398	105	5	4	51	1			-5	O	-0.3
Total	3	153	396	64	107	19	5	4	37	58	48	.270	.365	.374	97	1	-0	57	1			-4	O	-0.5

■ **ERNIE RILES** Riles, Ernest b: 10/2/60, Cairo, Ga. BL/TR, 6'1", 180 lbs. Deb: 5/14/85

YEAR	TM/L	G	AB	R	H	2B	3B	HR	RBI	BB	SO	AVG	OBP	SLG	PRO+	BR	/A	RC	SB	CS	SBR	FR	POS	TPR
1985	Mil-A	116	448	54	128	12	7	5	45	36	54	.286	.342	.377	97	-2	-1	55	2	2	-1	-19	*S/D	-1.1
1986	Mil-A	145	524	69	132	24	2	9	47	54	80	.252	.323	.357	82	-11	-13	59	7	7	-2	-30	*S	-3.6
1987	Mil-A	83	276	38	72	11	1	4	38	30	47	.261	.336	.351	80	-6	-7	33	3	4	-2	-9	3S	-1.6
1988	Mil-A	41	127	7	32	6	1	1	9	7	26	.252	.291	.339	75	-4	-4	12	2	2	-1	1	3/SD	-0.2
	SF-N	79	187	26	55	7	2	3	28	10	33	.294	.330	.401	114	2	3	23	1	2	-1	8	32S	1.2
1989	*SF-N	122	302	43	84	13	2	7	40	28	50	.278	.343	.404	116	5	6	39	0	6	-4	-9	32/SO	-0.6
1990	SF-N	92	155	22	31	2	1	8	21	26	26	.200	.315	.381	91	-2	-2	20	0	0	0	-4	S23	-0.2
Total	6	678	2019	259	534	75	16	37	228	191	316	.264	.330	.372	93	-18	-19	241	15	23	-9	-61	S3/2DO	-6.1

■ **JIM RILEY** Riley, James Joseph b: 11/10/1886, Buffalo, N.Y. d: 3/25/49, Buffalo, N.Y. BR/TR, 6', 165 lbs. Deb: 8/02/10

YEAR	TM/L	G	AB	R	H	2B	3B	HR	RBI	BB	SO	AVG	OBP	SLG	PRO+	BR	/A	RC	SB	CS	SBR	FR	POS	TPR
1910	Bos-N	1	1	0	0	0	0	0	0	1	1	.000	.500	.000	46	0	0	0	0			0	/O	0.0

■ **JIM RILEY** Riley, James Norman b: 5/25/1895, Bayfield, N.B., Can d: 5/25/69, Seguin, Tex. BL/TR, 5'10.5", 185 lbs. Deb: 7/03/21

YEAR	TM/L	G	AB	R	H	2B	3B	HR	RBI	BB	SO	AVG	OBP	SLG	PRO+	BR	/A	RC	SB	CS	SBR	FR	POS	TPR
1921	StL-A	4	11	0	0	0	0	0	0	1	3	.000	.083	.000	-73	-3	-3	0	0	0	0	-3	/2	-0.5
1923	Was-A	2	3	1	0	0	0	0	0	2	0	.000	.400	.000	12	-0	-0	0	0	0	0	-1	/1	0.0
Total	2	6	14	1	0	0	0	0	0	3	3	.000	.176	.000	-50	-3	-3	0	0	0	0	-3	/21	-0.5

■ **LEE RILEY** Riley, Leon Francis b: 8/20/06, Princeton, Neb. d: 9/13/70, Schenectady, N.Y. BL/TR, 6'1", 185 lbs. Deb: 4/19/44

YEAR	TM/L	G	AB	R	H	2B	3B	HR	RBI	BB	SO	AVG	OBP	SLG	PRO+	BR	/A	RC	SB	CS	SBR	FR	POS	TPR
1944	Phi-N	4	12	1	1	1	0	0	1	0	0	.083	.083	.167	-32	-2	-2	0	0			-1	/O	-0.3

■ **BILLY RILEY** Riley, William James "Pigtail Billy" b: 1857, Cincinnati, Ohio d: 11/9/1887, Cincinnati, Ohio 5'10", 160 lbs. Deb: 5/05/1875

YEAR	TM/L	G	AB	R	H	2B	3B	HR	RBI	BB	SO	AVG	OBP	SLG	PRO+	BR	/A	RC	SB	CS	SBR	FR	POS	TPR
1875	Wes-n	8	33	4	5	0	0	0		1		.152	.176	.182	23	-2	-3	1					/O	-0.1
1879	Cle-N	44	165	14	24	2	0	0	9	2	26	.145	.156	.158	4	-16	-16	4				5	O/1C	-1.1

■ **FRANK RINGO** Ringo, Frank C. b: 10/12/1860, Parkville, Mo. d: 4/12/1889, Kansas City, Mo. 5'11", 175 lbs. Deb: 5/01/1883

YEAR	TM/L	G	AB	R	H	2B	3B	HR	RBI	BB	SO	AVG	OBP	SLG	PRO+	BR	/A	RC	SB	CS	SBR	FR	POS	TPR
1883	Phi-N	60	221	24	42	10	1	0	12	6	34	.190	.211	.244	42	-16	-13	12				-6	CO/S32	-1.4
1884	Phi-N	26	91	4	12	2	0	0	6	3	19	.132	.160	.154	-1	-10	-10	2				-15	C	-2.0
	Phi-a	2	6	0	0	0	0	0		0	0	.000	.000	.000	-94	-1	-1	0				2	/C	0.1
1885	Det-N	17	65	12	16	3	0	0	2	0	7	.246	.246	.292	73	-2	-2	5				6	/C3O	0.4
	Pit-a	3	11	0	2	0	0	0		0	0	.182	.182	.182	17	-1	-1	0				3	/C	0.2
1886	Pit-a	15	56	3	12	2	2	0		0	1	.214	.228	.321	73	-2	-2	4	0			-0	/1C	-0.1
	KC-N	16	56	6	13	7	0	0	7	5	10	.232	.295	.357	92	-0	-1	6	0			-4	C/O3	-0.2
Total	4	139	506	49	97	24	3	0	27	15	70	.192	.215	.251	46	-33	-29	29	0			-13	/C3O1S2	-3.0

■ **BOB RINKER** Rinker, Robert John b: 4/21/21, Audenried, Pa. BR/TR, 6', 190 lbs. Deb: 9/06/50

YEAR	TM/L	G	AB	R	H	2B	3B	HR	RBI	BB	SO	AVG	OBP	SLG	PRO+	BR	/A	RC	SB	CS	SBR	FR	POS	TPR
1950	Phi-A	3	3	0	1	0	0	0	0	0	0	.333	.333	.333	72	-0	-0	0	0	0	0	0	/C	0.0

■ **JUAN RIOS** Rios, Juan Onofre Velez (b: Juan Onofre Velez (Rios)) b: 6/14/42, Mayaguez, P.R. BR/TR, 6'3", 185 lbs. Deb: 4/09/69

YEAR	TM/L	G	AB	R	H	2B	3B	HR	RBI	BB	SO	AVG	OBP	SLG	PRO+	BR	/A	RC	SB	CS	SBR	FR	POS	TPR
1969	KC-A	87	196	20	44	5	1	1	5	7	19	.224	.262	.276	50	-13	-13	12	1	3	-2	-16	2S/3	-2.8

■ **CAL RIPKEN** Ripken, Calvin Edwin Jr. b: 8/24/60, Havre De Grace, Md. BR/TR, 6'4", 200 lbs. Deb: 8/10/81

YEAR	TM/L	G	AB	R	H	2B	3B	HR	RBI	BB	SO	AVG	OBP	SLG	PRO+	BR	/A	RC	SB	CS	SBR	FR	POS	TPR
1981	Bal-A	23	39	1	5	0	0	0	0	1	8	.128	.150	.128	-19	-6	-6	0	0	0	0	0	S/3	-0.4
1982	Bal-A	160	598	90	158	32	5	28	93	46	95	.264	.320	.475	115	10	11	87	3	3	-1	-7	S3	0.9
1983	*Bal-A	162	663	121	211	47	2	27	102	58	97	.318	.373	.517	145	37	39	120	0	4	-2	16	*S	6.0
1984	Bal-A	162	641	103	195	37	7	27	86	71	89	.304	.375	.510	146	37	38	122	2	1	-0	39	*S	8.7
1985	Bal-A	161	642	116	181	32	5	26	110	67	68	.282	.351	.469	125	19	21	96	2	3	-1	7	*S	3.8
1986	Bal-A	162	627	98	177	35	1	25	81	70	60	.282	.358	.461	123	18	20	102	4	2	0	10	*S	3.8
1987	Bal-A	162	624	97	157	28	3	27	98	81	77	.252	.339	.436	106	3	6	90	3	5	-2	-4	*S	0.7
1988	Bal-A	161	575	87	152	25	1	23	81	102	69	.264	.377	.431	129	23	25	99	2	2	-1	-2	*S	3.0
1989	Bal-A	162	646	80	166	30	0	21	93	57	72	.257	.320	.401	105	1	3	79	3	2	-0	4	*S	2.0
1990	Bal-A	161	600	78	150	28	4	21	84	82	66	.250	.345	.415	114	10	12	88	3	1	0	-30	*S	-0.7
Total	10	1476	5655	871	1552	294	28	225	828	635	701	.274	.350	.456	123	152	169	882	22	23	-7	32	*S/3	27.8

■ **BILLY RIPKEN** Ripken, William Oliver b: 12/16/64, Havre De Grace, Md. BR/TR, 6'1", 180 lbs. Deb: 7/11/87

YEAR	TM/L	G	AB	R	H	2B	3B	HR	RBI	BB	SO	AVG	OBP	SLG	PRO+	BR	/A	RC	SB	CS	SBR	FR	POS	TPR
1987	Bal-A	58	234	27	72	9	0	2	20	21	23	.308	.365	.372	99	-1	0	33	4	1	1	-3	2	0.2
1988	Bal-A	150	512	52	106	18	1	2	34	33	63	.207	.262	.258	47	-37	-35	35	8	2	1	2	*2/3D	-2.1
1989	Bal-A	115	318	31	76	11	2	2	26	22	53	.239	.288	.305	69	-14	-12	27	1	2	-1	12	*2	0.1
1990	Bal-A	129	406	48	118	28	1	3	38	28	43	.291	.342	.387	106	2	3	55	5	2	0	-8	*2	0.1
Total	4	452	1470	158	372	66	4	9	118	104	182	.253	.306	.322	77	-49	-44	149	18	7	1	3	2/3D	-1.7

■ **JIMMY RIPPLE** Ripple, James Albert b: 10/14/09, Export, Pa. d: 7/16/59, Greensburg, Pa. BL/TR, 5'10", 170 lbs. Deb: 4/20/36

YEAR	TM/L	G	AB	R	H	2B	3B	HR	RBI	BB	SO	AVG	OBP	SLG	PRO+	BR	/A	RC	SB	CS	SBR	FR	POS	TPR
1936	*NY-N	96	311	42	95	17	2	7	47	28	15	.305	.365	.441	117	7	7	51	1			-3	O	0.0
1937	*NY-N	121	426	70	135	23	3	5	66	29	20	.317	.362	.420	110	7	6	65	3			-17	*O	-1.6
1938	NY-N	134	501	68	131	21	3	10	60	49	21	.261	.333	.375	94	-4	-4	62	2			-3	*O	-0.9
1939	NY-N	66	123	10	28	4	0	1	12	8	7	.228	.286	.285	53	-8	-8	10	0			-2	O	-0.9
	Bro-N	28	106	18	35	8	4	0	22	11	8	.330	.398	.481	131	5	5	19	0			-3	O	0.1
	Yr	94	229	28	63	12	4	1	34	19	15	.275	.339	.376	90	-3	-3	28	0			-5		-0.8
1940	Bro-N	7	13	0	3	0	0	0	0	2	2	.231	.333	.231	55	-1	-1	0	0			1	/O	0.0
	*Cin-N	32	101	15	31	10	0	4	20	13	2	.307	.397	.525	151	7	7	22	1			-5	O	0.1
	Yr	39	114	15	34	10	0	4	20	15	7	.298	.389	.491	139	7	6	23	1			-4		0.1
1941	Cin-N	38	102	10	22	6	1	1	9	9	4	.216	.279	.324	69	-4	-4	9	0			-4	O	-0.8
1943	Phi-A	32	126	8	30	3	1	0	15	7	7	.238	.284	.278	65	-6	-6	11	0	0	0	-6	O	-1.3
Total	7	554	1809	241	510	92	14	28	251	156	89	.282	.343	.395	101	4	3	252	7	0		-43	O	-5.3

■ **SWEDE RISBERG** Risberg, Charles August b: 10/13/1894, San Francisco, Cal d: 10/13/75, Red Bluff, Cal. BR/TR, 6', 175 lbs. Deb: 4/11/17

YEAR	TM/L	G	AB	R	H	2B	3B	HR	RBI	BB	SO	AVG	OBP	SLG	PRO+	BR	/A	RC	SB	CS	SBR	FR	POS	TPR
1917	*Chi-A	149	474	59	96	20	8	1	45	59	65	.203	.297	.285	76	-12	-13	45	16			-39	*S	-5.2
1918	Chi-A	82	273	36	70	12	3	1	27	23	32	.256	.321	.333	97	-1	-2	30	5			-8	S32/10	-0.7
1919	*Chi-A	119	414	48	106	19	6	2	38	35	38	.256	.317	.345	86	-8	-8	49	19			-13	S1	-1.5
1920	Chi-A	126	458	53	122	21	10	2	65	31	45	.266	.316	.369	81	-14	-14	53	12	10	-2	-4	*S	-0.8
Total	4	476	1619	196	394	72	27	6	175	148	180	.243	.311	.332	83	-35	-37	177	52	10		-64	S/1320	-8.2

■ **POP RISING** Rising, Percival Sumner b: 1/2/1872, Industry, Pa. d: 1/28/38, Rochester, Pa. Deb: 8/10/05

YEAR	TM/L	G	AB	R	H	2B	3B	HR	RBI	BB	SO	AVG	OBP	SLG	PRO+	BR	/A	RC	SB	CS	SBR	FR	POS	TPR
1905	Bos-A	11	29	2	3	1	0	0	2	2		.103	.161	.207	17	-3	-3	1	0			0	/O3	-0.2

■ **CLAUDE RITCHEY** Ritchey, Claude Cassius "Little All Right" b: 10/5/1873, Emlenton, Pa. d: 11/8/51, Emlenton, Pa. BB/TR, 5'6.5", 167 lbs. Deb: 4/22/1897

YEAR	TM/L	G	AB	R	H	2B	3B	HR	RBI	BB	SO	AVG	OBP	SLG	PRO+	BR	/A	RC	SB	CS	SBR	FR	POS	TPR
1897	Cin-N	101	337	58	95	12	4	0	41	42		.282	.368	.341	85	-3	-7	48	11			-16	SO/2	-1.8

YEAR	TM/L	G	AB	R	H	2B	3B	HR	RBI	BB	SO	AVG	OBP	SLG	PRO+	BR	/A	RC	SB	CS	SBR	FR	POS	TPR
1898	Lou-N	151	551	65	140	10	4	5	51	46		.254	.321	.314	86	-10	-9	63	19			-15	S2	-1.5
1899	Lou-N	147	536	65	161	15	7	4	71	49		.300	.370	.377	108	7	7	85	21			-6	*2S	0.9
1900	*Pit-N	123	476	62	139	17	8	1	67	29		.292	.339	.368	97	-2	-2	67	18			7	*2	1.0
1901	Pit-N	140	540	66	160	20	4	1	74	47		.296	.356	.354	105	7	5	78	15			3	*2/S	1.7
1902	Pit-N	115	405	54	112	13	1	2	55	53		.277	.370	.328	114	12	10	57	10			6	*2/O	2.4
1903	*Pit-N	138	506	66	145	28	10	0	59	55		.287	.357	.381	109	9	7	78	15			19	*2	3.2
1904	Pit-N	156	544	79	143	22	12	0	51	59		.263	.335	.347	110	9	8	71	12			-2	*2/S	1.0
1905	Pit-N	153	533	54	136	29	6	0	52	51		.255	.320	.332	94	-2	-3	63	12			-5	*2/S	0.1
1906	Pit-N	152	484	46	130	21	5	1	62	68		.269	.359	.339	115	13	11	66	6			1	*2	1.3
1907	Bos-N	144	499	45	127	17	4	2	51	50		.255	.322	.317	103	2	2	57	8			14	*2	2.1
1908	Bos-N	121	421	44	115	10	3	2	36	50		.273	.350	.325	120	10	11	52	7			16	*2	2.9
1909	Bos-N	30	87	4	15	1	0	0	3	8		.172	.242	.184	31	-7	-7	4	1			0	2	-0.7
Total	13	1671	5919	708	1618	215	68	18	673	607		.273	.345	.342	102	47	32	789	155			22	*2S/O	12.6

■ CHARLIE RITTER
Ritter, Charles J.   Deb: 9/21/1885

YEAR	TM/L	G	AB	R	H	2B	3B	HR	RBI	BB	SO	AVG	OBP	SLG	PRO+	BR	/A	RC	SB	CS	SBR	FR	POS	TPR
1885	Buf-N	2	6	0	1	0	0	0	0	0	2	.167	.167	.167	8	-1	-1	0				0	/2	0.0

■ FLOYD RITTER
Ritter, Floyd Alexander   b: 6/1/1870, Dorset, Ohio   d: 2/7/43, Stevenson, Wash.   BR/TR, 5'8", 155 lbs.   Deb: 6/04/1890

YEAR	TM/L	G	AB	R	H	2B	3B	HR	RBI	BB	SO	AVG	OBP	SLG	PRO+	BR	/A	RC	SB	CS	SBR	FR	POS	TPR
1890	Tol-a	1	3	0	0	0	0	0	0		0	.000	.000	.000	-97	-1	-1	0	0			1	/C	0.0

■ LEW RITTER
Ritter, Lewis Elmer "Old Dog"   b: 9/7/1875, Liverpool, Pa.   d: 5/27/52, Harrisburg, Pa.   BR/TR, 5'9", 150 lbs.   Deb: 9/10/02

YEAR	TM/L	G	AB	R	H	2B	3B	HR	RBI	BB	SO	AVG	OBP	SLG	PRO+	BR	/A	RC	SB	CS	SBR	FR	POS	TPR
1902	Bro-N	16	57	5	12	1	0	0	2	1		.211	.224	.228	41	-4	-4	4	2			3	C	0.0
1903	Bro-N	78	259	26	61	9	6	0	37	19		.236	.288	.317	76	-9	-8	28	9			-19	C/O	-1.9
1904	Bro-N	72	214	23	53	4	1	0	19	20		.248	.312	.276	86	-3	-3	25	17			5	C/23	0.8
1905	Bro-N	92	311	32	68	10	5	1	28	15		.219	.255	.293	70	-14	-11	29	16			-15	C/O3	-1.7
1906	Bro-N	73	226	22	47	1	3	0	15	16		.208	.260	.239	62	-11	-9	17	6			-9	C/O13	-1.5
1907	Bro-N	93	271	15	55	6	1	0	17	18		.203	.253	.232	58	-14	-12	19	5			-1	C	-0.6
1908	Bro-N	38	99	6	19	2	1	0	2	7		.192	.245	.232	57	-5	-5	6	0			-3	C	-0.6
Total	7	462	1437	129	315	33	17	1	120	96		.219	.268	.268	68	-60	-51	126	55			-40	C/O321	-5.5

■ WHITEY RITTERSON
Ritterson, Edward West   b: 4/26/1855, Philadelphia, Pa.   d: 7/28/17, Sellersville, Pa.   BR/TR, 5'8",   Deb: 5/03/1876

YEAR	TM/L	G	AB	R	H	2B	3B	HR	RBI	BB	SO	AVG	OBP	SLG	PRO+	BR	/A	RC	SB	CS	SBR	FR	POS	TPR
1876	Phi-N	16	52	8	13	3	0	0	4	0	2	.250	.250	.308	86	-1	-1	4				-4	C/O3	-0.3

■ JIM RITZ
Ritz, James L.   b: 1874, Pittsburgh, Pa.   d: 11/10/1896, Pittsburgh, Pa.   Deb: 7/20/1894

YEAR	TM/L	G	AB	R	H	2B	3B	HR	RBI	BB	SO	AVG	OBP	SLG	PRO+	BR	/A	RC	SB	CS	SBR	FR	POS	TPR
1894	Pit-N	1	4	1	0	0	0	0	0	0	0	.000	.200	.000	-48	-1	-1	0	1			-0	/3	0.0

■ GERMAN RIVERA
Rivera, German (Diaz)   b: 7/6/60, Santurce, P.R.   BR/TR, 6'2", 195 lbs.   Deb: 9/02/83

YEAR	TM/L	G	AB	R	H	2B	3B	HR	RBI	BB	SO	AVG	OBP	SLG	PRO+	BR	/A	RC	SB	CS	SBR	FR	POS	TPR
1983	LA-N	13	17	1	6	1	0	0	0	2	2	.353	.421	.412	132	1	1	3	0	1	-1	2	/3	0.2
1984	LA-N	94	227	20	59	12	2	2	17	21	30	.260	.325	.357	92	-2	-2	23	1	0	0	16	3	1.4
1985	Hou-N	13	36	3	7	2	1	0	2	4	8	.194	.275	.306	64	-2	-2	3	0	0	0	3	3	0.1
Total	3	120	280	24	72	15	3	2	19	27	40	.257	.325	.354	91	-3	-3	28	1	1	-0	20	3	1.7

■ BOMBO RIVERA
Rivera, Jesus Manuel (Torres)   b: 8/2/52, Ponce, Pr.   BR/TR, 5'10", 187 lbs.   Deb: 4/17/75

YEAR	TM/L	G	AB	R	H	2B	3B	HR	RBI	BB	SO	AVG	OBP	SLG	PRO+	BR	/A	RC	SB	CS	SBR	FR	POS	TPR
1975	Mon-N	5	9	1	1	0	0	0	0	2	3	.111	.273	.111	9	-1	-1	0	0	0	0	0	/O	0.0
1976	Mon-N	68	185	22	51	11	4	2	19	13	32	.276	.323	.411	103	1	0	24	1	0	0	0	O	0.0
1978	Min-A	101	251	35	68	8	2	3	23	35	47	.271	.365	.355	101	2	2	35	5	3	-0	0	O/D	0.0
1979	Min-A	112	263	37	74	13	5	2	31	17	40	.281	.325	.392	89	-3	-4	32	5	5	-2	-5	*O	-1.4
1980	Min-A	44	113	13	25	7	0	3	10	4	20	.221	.248	.363	61	-6	-7	9	0	0	0	-2	O/D	-0.9
1982	KC-A	5	10	1	1	0	0	0	0	0	2	.100	.100	.100	-45	-2	-2	0	0	0	0	-0	/O	-0.1
Total	6	335	831	109	220	39	11	10	83	71	144	.265	.324	.374	90	-8	-12	100	11	8	-2	-7	O/D	-2.4

■ LUIS RIVERA
Rivera, Luis Antonio (Pedraza)   b: 1/3/64, Cidra, P.R.   BR/TR, 5'11", 165 lbs.   Deb: 8/03/86

YEAR	TM/L	G	AB	R	H	2B	3B	HR	RBI	BB	SO	AVG	OBP	SLG	PRO+	BR	/A	RC	SB	CS	SBR	FR	POS	TPR
1986	Mon-N	55	166	20	34	11	1	0	13	17	33	.205	.286	.283	58	-9	-9	15	1	1	-0	-9	S	-1.3
1987	Mon-N	18	32	0	5	2	0	0	1	1	8	.156	.182	.219	5	-4	-4	1	0	0	0	2	S	0.0
1988	Mon-N	123	371	35	83	17	3	4	30	24	69	.224	.273	.318	66	-15	-17	30	3	4	-2	-6	*S	-1.7
1989	Bos-A	93	323	35	83	17	1	5	29	20	60	.257	.302	.362	81	-6	-9	34	2	3	-1	-3	S/2D	-0.5
1990	*Bos-A	118	346	38	78	20	0	7	45	25	58	.225	.280	.344	70	-13	-15	32	4	3	-1	10	*S/23	0.2
Total	5	407	1238	128	283	67	5	16	118	87	228	.229	.282	.330	69	-48	-54	112	10	11	-4	-6	S/23D	-3.3

■ JIM RIVERA
Rivera, Manuel Joseph "Jungle Jim"   b: 7/22/22, New York, N.Y.   BL/TL, 6', 196 lbs.   Deb: 4/15/52

YEAR	TM/L	G	AB	R	H	2B	3B	HR	RBI	BB	SO	AVG	OBP	SLG	PRO+	BR	/A	RC	SB	CS	SBR	FR	POS	TPR
1952	StL-A	97	336	45	86	13	6	4	30	29	59	.256	.319	.366	88	-5	-6	40	8	7	-2	3	O	-0.6
	Chi-A	53	201	27	50	7	3	3	18	21	27	.249	.320	.358	88	-3	-4	26	13	2	3	1	O	-0.1
	Yr	150	537	72	136	20	9	7	48	50	86	.253	.319	.363	88	-8	-10	67	21	9	1	4		-0.7
1953	Chi-A	156	567	79	147	26	**16**	11	78	53	70	.259	.329	.420	98	-1	-3	76	22	15	-2	-7	*O	-1.6
1954	Chi-A	145	490	62	140	16	8	13	61	49	68	.286	.358	.431	111	10	8	77	18	10	-1	-12	*O	-0.8
1955	Chi-A	147	454	71	120	24	4	10	52	62	59	.264	.354	.401	100	2	0	66	**25**	16	-2	13	*O	0.5
1956	Chi-A	139	491	76	125	23	5	12	66	49	75	.255	.326	.395	88	-8	-9	66	20	9	1	1	*O	-1.4
1957	Chi-A	125	402	51	103	21	6	14	52	40	80	.256	.328	.443	108	4	4	59	18	2	**4**	-9	O1	-0.6
1958	Chi-A	116	276	37	62	8	4	4	35	24	49	.225	.289	.380	84	-7	-7	31	21	3	5	-6	O	-1.4
1959	*Chi-A	80	177	18	39	9	4	4	19	11	19	.220	.270	.384	78	-6	-6	18	5	3	-0	-2	O	-1.1
1960	Chi-A	48	17	17	5	0	0	1	1	3	3	.294	.400	.471	136	1	1	4	4	0	1	0	O	0.5
1961	Chi-A	1	0	0	0	0	0	0	0	0	0	—	—	—	—	0	0	0	0	1	-1	0	H	0.0
	KC-A	64	141	20	34	8	0	2	10	24	14	.241	.352	.340	86	-2	-2	18	6	2	1	-7	O	-0.9
	Yr	65	141	20	34	8	0	2	10	24	14	.241	.352	.340	86	-2	-2	18	6	3	0	-7		-0.9
Total	10	1171	3552	503	911	155	56	83	422	365	523	.256	.330	.402	96	-17	-24	484	160	70	6	-20	*O/1	-7.5

■ MICKEY RIVERS
Rivers, John Milton   b: 10/31/48, Miami, Fla.   BL/TL, 5'10", 165 lbs.   Deb: 8/04/70

YEAR	TM/L	G	AB	R	H	2B	3B	HR	RBI	BB	SO	AVG	OBP	SLG	PRO+	BR	/A	RC	SB	CS	SBR	FR	POS	TPR
1970	Cal-A	17	25	6	8	2	0	0	3	3	5	.320	.414	.400	130	1	1	5	1	0	0	0	/O	0.1
1971	Cal-A	78	268	31	71	12	2	1	12	19	38	.265	.316	.336	91	-5	-3	32	13	1	3	2	O	0.0
1972	Cal-A	58	159	18	34	6	2	0	7	8	26	.214	.256	.277	62	-8	-7	11	4	3	-1	2	O	-0.7
1973	Cal-A	30	129	26	45	6	4	0	16	8	11	.349	.391	.457	150	6	8	24	8	3	-3	0	O	0.5
1974	Cal-A	118	466	69	133	19	**11**	2	31	39	47	.285	.342	.393	118	6	10	64	30	13	1	8	*O	1.7
1975	Cal-A	155	616	70	175	17	**13**	1	53	43	42	.284	.333	.359	103	-4	1	81	**70**	14	**13**	5	*O/D	1.5
1976	*NY-A	137	590	95	184	31	8	8	67	13	51	.312	.330	.432	123	14	14	88	43	7	9	4	*O	2.5
1977	*NY-A	138	565	79	184	18	5	12	69	18	45	.326	.351	.439	115	10	10	86	22	14	-2	5	*O/D	0.9
1978	*NY-A	141	559	78	148	25	8	11	48	29	51	.265	.305	.397	98	-5	-3	69	25	5	5	5	*O	0.3
1979	NY-A	74	286	37	82	18	5	3	25	13	21	.287	.320	.416	99	-2	-1	36	3	7	-3	-4	O	-1.0
	Tex-A	58	247	35	74	9	3	6	25	9	18	.300	.327	.433	104	0	1	35	7	2	1	4	O	0.3
	Yr	132	533	72	156	27	8	9	50	22	39	.293	.323	.424	101	-2	-0	71	10	9	-2	-1		-0.7
1980	Tex-A	147	630	96	210	32	6	7	60	20	34	.333	.355	.437	119	12	14	98	18	7	1	6	*O/D	1.8
1981	Tex-A	99	399	62	114	21	2	3	26	24	31	.286	.328	.371	107	0	3	49	9	5	-0	1	O	0.1
1982	Tex-A	19	68	6	16	1	1	0	4	0	7	.235	.235	.324	54	-5	-4	5	0	0	0	0	D	-0.3
1983	Tex-A	96	309	37	88	17	0	1	20	11	21	.285	.312	.350	83	-8	-7	35	9	4	0	-2	DO	-0.8
1984	Tex-A	102	313	40	94	13	1	4	33	9	23	.300	.320	.387	91	-3	-4	38	5	5	-2	0	DO	-0.5
Total	15	1467	5629	785	1660	247	71	61	499	266	471	.295	.329	.397	106	10	32	756	267	90	26	33	*OD	6.4

YEAR	TM/L	G	AB	R	H	2B	3B	HR	RBI	BB	SO	AVG	OBP	SLG	PRO+	BR	/A	RC	SB	CS	SBR	FR	POS	TPR

■ JOHNNY RIZZO   Rizzo, John Costa b: 7/30/12, Houston, Tex. d: 12/4/77, Houston, Tex. BR/TR, 6', 190 lbs. Deb: 4/19/38

YEAR	TM/L	G	AB	R	H	2B	3B	HR	RBI	BB	SO	AVG	OBP	SLG	PRO+	BR	/A	RC	SB	CS	SBR	FR	POS	TPR
1938	Pit-N	143	555	97	167	31	9	23	111	54	61	.301	.368	.514	139	29	29	105	1			-7	*O	1.9
1939	Pit-N	94	330	49	86	23	3	6	55	42	27	.261	.349	.403	103	1	2	46	0			-3	O	-0.1
1940	Pit-N	9	28	1	5	1	0	0	2	5	5	.179	.324	.214	51	-2	-2	2	0			-2	O	-0.3
	Cin-N	31	110	17	31	6	0	4	17	14	14	.282	.363	.445	121	3	3	19	1			4	O	0.6
	Phi-N	103	367	53	107	12	2	20	53	37	31	.292	.358	.499	139	16	18	67	2			8	O/3	2.3
	Yr	143	505	71	143	19	2	24	72	56	50	.283	.357	.471	130	18	18	88	3			10		2.6
1941	Phi-N	99	235	20	51	9	2	4	24	24	34	.217	.295	.323	77	-8	-7	22	1			2	O/3	-0.7
1942	Bro-N	78	217	31	50	8	0	4	27	24	25	.230	.307	.323	83	-4	-5	21	2			2	O	-0.4
Total	5	557	1842	268	497	90	16	61	289	200	197	.270	.345	.435	116	35	38	282	7			4	O/3	3.3

■ PHIL RIZZUTO   Rizzuto, Philip Francis "Scooter" b: 9/25/17, Brooklyn, N.Y. BR/TR, 5'6", 150 lbs. Deb: 4/15/41

YEAR	TM/L	G	AB	R	H	2B	3B	HR	RBI	BB	SO	AVG	OBP	SLG	PRO+	BR	/A	RC	SB	CS	SBR	FR	POS	TPR
1941	*NY-A	133	515	65	158	20	9	3	46	27	36	.307	.343	.398	97	-4	-3	70	14	5	1	16	*S	1.6
1942	*NY-A	144	553	79	157	24	7	4	68	44	40	.284	.343	.374	104	1	2	74	22	6	3	25	*S	3.8
1946	*NY-A	126	471	53	121	17	1	2	38	34	39	.257	.315	.310	74	-15	-16	48	14	7	0	13	*S	0.0
1947	*NY-A	153	549	78	150	26	9	2	60	57	31	.273	.350	.364	100	-0	0	76	11	6	-0	16	*S	1.7
1948	NY-A	128	464	65	117	13	2	6	50	60	24	.252	.340	.328	79	-14	-13	57	6	5	-1	-11	*S	-2.3
1949	*NY-A	153	614	110	169	22	7	5	65	72	34	.275	.352	.358	88	-10	-10	82	18	6	2	3	*S	1.3
1950	*NY-A	155	617	125	200	36	7	7	66	92	39	.324	.418	.439	123	22	24	124	12	8	-1	9	*S	3.6
1951	*NY-A	144	540	87	148	21	6	2	43	58	27	.274	.350	.346	92	-7	-5	73	18	3	4	6	*S	1.4
1952	*NY-A	152	578	89	147	24	10	2	43	67	42	.254	.337	.341	95	-8	-3	73	17	6	2	19	*S	2.6
1953	*NY-A	134	413	54	112	21	3	2	54	71	39	.271	.383	.351	103	3	5	63	4	3	-1	-3	*S	1.1
1954	NY-A	127	307	47	60	11	0	2	15	41	23	.195	.292	.251	51	-21	-19	25	3	2	-0	-1	*S/2	-0.9
1955	*NY-A	81	143	19	37	4	1	1	9	22	18	.259	.369	.322	88	-2	-1	20	7	1	2	-9	*S	0.0
1956	NY-A	31	52	6	12	0	0	0	6	6	6	.231	.310	.231	46	-4	-4	5	3	0	1	3	S	0.3
Total	13	1661	5816	877	1588	239	62	38	563	651	398	.273	.351	.355	93	-60	-43	789	149	58	10	86	*S/2	12.6

■ MIKE ROACH   Roach, James Michael b: 1876, New York, N.Y. d: 11/12/16, Binghamton, N.Y. Deb: 8/10/1899

YEAR	TM/L	G	AB	R	H	2B	3B	HR	RBI	BB	SO	AVG	OBP	SLG	PRO+	BR	/A	RC	SB	CS	SBR	FR	POS	TPR
1899	Was-N	24	78	7	17	1	0	0	7	3		.218	.265	.231	39	-6	-6	6	3			-4	C/1	-0.8

■ MEL ROACH   Roach, Melvin Earl b: 1/25/33, Richmond, Va. BR/TR, 6'1", 190 lbs. Deb: 7/31/53

YEAR	TM/L	G	AB	R	H	2B	3B	HR	RBI	BB	SO	AVG	OBP	SLG	PRO+	BR	/A	RC	SB	CS	SBR	FR	POS	TPR
1953	Mil-N	5	2	1	0	0	0	0	0	0	1	.000	.000	.000	-99	-1	-1	0	0	0	0	0	/2	0.0
1954	Mil-N	3	4	0	0	0	0	0	0	0	0	.000	.000	.000	-99	-1	-1	0	0	0	0	0	/1	0.0
1957	Mil-N	7	6	1	1	0	0	0	0	0	3	.167	.167	.167	-11	-1	-1	0	0	0	0	0	/2	0.0
1958	Mil-N	44	136	14	42	7	0	3	10	6	15	.309	.338	.426	110	-0	1	20	0	0	0	-1	2/O1	0.2
1959	Mil-N	19	31	1	3	0	0	0	2	4		.097	.152	.097	-35	-6	-6	1	0	0	0	1	/2O3	-0.3
1960	Mil-N	48	140	12	42	12	0	3	18	6	19	.300	.333	.450	121	2	3	17	0	0	0	-10	O2/13	-0.5
1961	Mil-N	13	36	3	6	0	0	1	6	2	4	.167	.250	.250	35	-3	-3	3	0	0	0	-2	/O1	-0.5
	Chi-N	23	39	1	5	2	0	0	1	3	9	.128	.190	.179	-1	-6	-6	1	1	0	0	-1	/12	-0.5
	Yr	36	75	4	11	2	0	1	7	5	13	.147	.220	.213	16	-9	-9	3	1	0	0	-3		-1.0
1962	Phi-N	65	105	9	20	4	0	0	8	5	19	.190	.227	.229	23	-11	-11	5	0	0	0	-1	3/21O	-1.0
Total	8	227	499	42	119	25	0	7	43	24	75	.238	.278	.331	66	-27	-23	47	1	0	0	-13	/2O31	-2.6

■ ROXEY ROACH   Roach, Wilbur Charles b: 11/28/1882, Anita, Pa. d: 12/26/47, Bay City, Mich. BR/TR, 5'11", 160 lbs. Deb: 5/02/10

YEAR	TM/L	G	AB	R	H	2B	3B	HR	RBI	BB	SO	AVG	OBP	SLG	PRO+	BR	/A	RC	SB	CS	SBR	FR	POS	TPR
1910	NY-A	70	220	27	47	9	2	0	20	29		.214	.313	.273	79	-3	-5	24	15			-7	S/O	-1.1
1911	NY-A	13	40	4	10	2	1	0	2	6		.250	.348	.350	89	-0	-1	5	0			-1	/S2	0.0
1912	Was-A	2	2	1	1	0	0	1	1	0		.500	.500	2.000	601	1	1	2	0			-1	/S	0.1
1915	Buf-F	92	346	35	93	20	3	2	31	17	34	.269	.303	.361	94	-3	-4	43	11			16	S	2.1
Total	4	177	608	67	151	31	6	3	54	52	34	.248	.311	.334	90	-5	-8	74	26			8	S/O2	1.1

■ MIKE ROARKE   Roarke, Michael Thomas b: 11/8/30, West Warwick, R.I. BR/TR, 6'2", 195 lbs. Deb: 4/19/61 C

YEAR	TM/L	G	AB	R	H	2B	3B	HR	RBI	BB	SO	AVG	OBP	SLG	PRO+	BR	/A	RC	SB	CS	SBR	FR	POS	TPR
1961	Det-A	86	229	21	51	6	1	2	22	20	31	.223	.285	.284	51	-15	-16	18	0	0	0	4	C	-1.2
1962	Det-A	56	136	11	29	4	1	4	14	13	17	.213	.287	.346	67	-6	-7	13	0	0	0	6	C	0.2
1963	Det-A	23	44	5	14	0	0	1	2	3		.318	.362	.318	89	-0	-0	5	0	0	0	1	C	0.1
1964	Det-A	29	82	4	19	1	0	0	7	10	10	.232	.315	.244	57	-4	-4	7	0	0	0	3	C	0.0
Total	4	194	491	41	113	11	2	6	44	45	61	.230	.297	.297	60	-26	-28	43	0	0	0	14	C	-0.9

■ FRED ROAT   Roat, Frederick R. b: 11/10/1867, Oregon, Ill. d: 9/24/13, Oregon, Ill. TR , Deb: 5/10/1890

YEAR	TM/L	G	AB	R	H	2B	3B	HR	RBI	BB	SO	AVG	OBP	SLG	PRO+	BR	/A	RC	SB	CS	SBR	FR	POS	TPR
1890	Pit-N	57	215	18	48	2	0	2	17	16	22	.223	.286	.260	70	-10	-6	18	7			3	3/1O	-0.1
1892	Chi-N	8	31	4	6	0	1	0	2	2	3	.194	.242	.258	52	-2	-2	2	2			-3	/2	-0.4
Total	2	65	246	22	54	2	1	2	19	18	25	.220	.281	.260	67	-12	-8	21	9			-0	/312O	-0.5

■ TOMMY ROBELLO   Robello, Thomas Vardasco "Tony" b: 2/9/13, San Leandro, Cal. BR/TR, 5'10.5", 175 lbs. Deb: 8/13/33

YEAR	TM/L	G	AB	R	H	2B	3B	HR	RBI	BB	SO	AVG	OBP	SLG	PRO+	BR	/A	RC	SB	CS	SBR	FR	POS	TPR
1933	Cin-N	14	30	1	7	3	0	0	3	1	5	.233	.258	.333	69	-1	-1	3	0			2	2/3	0.1
1934	Cin-N	2	2	0	0	0	0	0	0	0	1	.000	.000	.000	-99	-1	-1	0	0			0	H	0.0
Total	2	16	32	1	7	3	0	0	3	1	6	.219	.242	.313	58	-2	-2	3	0			2	/23	0.1

■ SKIPPY ROBERGE   Roberge, Joseph Albert Armand b: 5/19/17, Lowell, Mass. BR/TR, 5'11", 185 lbs. Deb: 7/18/41

YEAR	TM/L	G	AB	R	H	2B	3B	HR	RBI	BB	SO	AVG	OBP	SLG	PRO+	BR	/A	RC	SB	CS	SBR	FR	POS	TPR
1941	Bos-N	55	167	12	36	6	0	0	15	18		.216	.256	.251	45	-13	-12	12	0			5	2/3S	-0.3
1942	Bos-N	74	172	10	37	7	0	1	12	9	19	.215	.258	.273	57	-10	-9	13	1			8	23/S	0.1
1946	Bos-N	48	169	13	39	6	2	2	20	7	12	.231	.270	.325	68	-8	-8	15	1			2	3	-0.5
Total	3	177	508	35	112	19	2	3	47	25	49	.220	.261	.283	57	-30	-29	39	2			15	/32S	-0.7

■ RED ROBERTS   Roberts, Charles Emory b: 8/8/18, Carrollton, Ga. BR/TR, 6', 170 lbs. Deb: 9/03/43

YEAR	TM/L	G	AB	R	H	2B	3B	HR	RBI	BB	SO	AVG	OBP	SLG	PRO+	BR	/A	RC	SB	CS	SBR	FR	POS	TPR
1943	Was-A	9	23	1	6	1	0	1	3	4	2	.261	.370	.435	140	1	1	4	0	0	0	-4	/S3	-0.3

■ SKIPPER ROBERTS   Roberts, Clarence Ashley b: 1/11/1888, Wardner, Idaho d: 12/24/63, Long Beach, Cal. BL/TR, 5'10.5", 175 lbs. Deb: 6/12/13

YEAR	TM/L	G	AB	R	H	2B	3B	HR	RBI	BB	SO	AVG	OBP	SLG	PRO+	BR	/A	RC	SB	CS	SBR	FR	POS	TPR
1913	StL-N	26	41	4	6	2	0	0	3	3	13	.146	.205	.195	15	-5	-5	2	1			-1	C	-0.4
1914	Pit-F	33	55	7	12	2	1	0	4	1	11	.218	.246	.291	54	-3	-3	5	2			-4	C	-0.6
	Chi-F	4	3	0	1	0	0	0	1	1	1	.333	.500	.333	150	0	0	1	0			0	H	0.0
	Pit-F	19	39	5	10	2	1	1	4	1	8	.256	.293	.436	108	0	0	5	1			-6	/CO	-0.5
	Yr	56	97	12	23	4	2	1	9	3	20	.237	.275	.351	79	-3	-3	11	3			-10		-1.1
Total	2	82	138	16	29	6	2	1	12	6	33	.210	.253	.304	60	-8	-7	12	4			-11	/CO	-1.5

■ CURT ROBERTS   Roberts, Curtis Benjamin b: 8/16/29, Pineland, Tex. d: 11/14/69, Oakland, Cal. BR/TR, 5'8", 165 lbs. Deb: 4/13/54

YEAR	TM/L	G	AB	R	H	2B	3B	HR	RBI	BB	SO	AVG	OBP	SLG	PRO+	BR	/A	RC	SB	CS	SBR	FR	POS	TPR
1954	Pit-N	134	496	47	115	18	7	1	36	55	49	.232	.311	.302	62	-28	-27	50	6	3	0	2	*2	-1.6
1955	Pit-N	6	17	1	2	1	0	0	0	2	1	.118	.211	.176	4	-2	-2	1	0	0	0	-1	/2	-0.2
1956	Pit-N	31	62	6	11	5	2	0	4	5	12	.177	.239	.323	50	-5	-4	5	1	0	0	-1	2	-0.3
Total	3	171	575	54	128	24	9	1	40	62	62	.223	.300	.301	59	-35	-34	56	7	3	0	0	2	-2.1

■ DAVE ROBERTS   Roberts, David Leonard b: 6/30/33, Panama City, Pan. BL/TL, 6', 172 lbs. Deb: 9/05/62

YEAR	TM/L	G	AB	R	H	2B	3B	HR	RBI	BB	SO	AVG	OBP	SLG	PRO+	BR	/A	RC	SB	CS	SBR	FR	POS	TPR
1962	Hou-N	16	53	3	13	3	0	1	10	8	8	.245	.355	.358	99	-0	0	8	0	0	0	-1	O/1	-0.1
1964	Hou-N	61	125	9	23	4	1	1	7	14	28	.184	.271	.256	52	-8	-7	9	0	1	-1	4	1/O	-0.5
1966	Pit-N	14	16	3	2	1	0	0	0	0	7	.125	.125	.188	-15	-2	-2	0	0	0	0	0	/1	-0.1
Total	3	91	194	15	38	8	1	2	17	22	43	.196	.284	.278	60	-11	-10	17	0	1	-1	3	/1O	-0.7

YEAR	TM/L	G	AB	R	H	2B	3B	HR	RBI	BB	SO	AVG	OBP	SLG	PRO+	BR	/A	RC	SB	CS	SBR	FR	POS	TPR

■ DAVE ROBERTS
Roberts, David Wayne b: 2/17/51, Lebanon, Ore. BR/TR, 6'3", 215 lbs. Deb: 6/07/72 C

YEAR	TM/L	G	AB	R	H	2B	3B	HR	RBI	BB	SO	AVG	OBP	SLG	PRO+	BR	/A	RC	SB	CS	SBR	FR	POS	TPR
1972	SD-N	100	418	38	102	17	0	5	33	18	64	.244	.275	.321	74	-18	-15	37	7	2	1	-6	32/SC	-1.9
1973	SD-N	127	479	56	137	20	3	21	64	17	83	.286	.312	.472	124	7	11	70	11	2	2	3	*32	1.4
1974	SD-N	113	318	26	53	10	1	5	18	32	69	.167	.247	.252	41	-26	-24	20	2	0	1	-4	*3/SO	-3.0
1975	SD-N	33	113	7	32	2	0	2	12	13	19	.283	.367	.354	107	1	1	16	3	1	0	-4	3/2	-0.1
1977	SD-N	82	186	15	41	14	1	1	23	11	32	.220	.268	.323	64	-11	-9	16	2	1	0	-4	C/23S	-1.3
1978	SD-N	54	97	7	21	4	1	1	7	12	25	.216	.309	.309	79	-3	-2	9	0	0	0	-0	C/1O	-0.1
1979	Tex-A	44	84	12	22	2	1	3	14	7	17	.262	.319	.417	98	-1	-0	11	1	0	0	3	CO/213	0.3
1980	Tex-A	101	235	27	56	4	0	10	30	13	38	.238	.281	.383	83	-7	-6	24	0	1	-1	-19	3SC/O12	-2.2
1981	*Hou-N	27	54	4	13	3	0	1	5	3	6	.241	.281	.352	83	-2	-1	5	1	0	0	0	1/32C	-0.1
1982	Phi-N	28	33	2	6	1	0	0	2	2	8	.182	.229	.212	23	-3	-3	2	0	1	-1	1	3C/2	-0.1
Total	10	709	2017	194	483	77	7	49	208	128	361	.239	.288	.357	83	-64	-49	210	27	8	3	-30	3C/2S10	-7.2

■ BIP ROBERTS
Roberts, Leon Joseph b: 10/27/63, Berkeley, Cal. BB/TR, 5'7", 150 lbs. Deb: 4/07/86

YEAR	TM/L	G	AB	R	H	2B	3B	HR	RBI	BB	SO	AVG	OBP	SLG	PRO+	BR	/A	RC	SB	CS	SBR	FR	POS	TPR
1986	SD-N	101	241	34	61	5	2	1	12	14	29	.253	.294	.303	66	-11	-11	20	14	12	-3	4	2	-0.8
1988	SD-N	5	9	1	3	0	0	0	0	1	2	.333	.400	.333	115	0	0	1	0	2	-1	-1	/32	-0.1
1989	SD-N	117	329	81	99	15	8	3	25	49	45	.301	.393	.422	133	16	16	58	21	11	-0	-6	O3S/2	1.0
1990	SD-N	149	556	104	172	36	3	9	44	55	65	.309	.378	.433	121	18	17	97	46	12	7	-3	O3S/2	2.2
Total	4	372	1135	220	335	56	13	13	81	119	141	.295	.366	.402	113	23	22	176	81	37	2	-6	O2/3S	2.3

■ LEON ROBERTS
Roberts, Leon Kauffman b: 1/22/51, Vicksburg, Mich. BR/TR, 6'3", 200 lbs. Deb: 9/03/74

YEAR	TM/L	G	AB	R	H	2B	3B	HR	RBI	BB	SO	AVG	OBP	SLG	PRO+	BR	/A	RC	SB	CS	SBR	FR	POS	TPR
1974	Det-A	17	63	5	17	3	2	0	7	3	10	.270	.303	.381	92	-1	-1	6	0	2	-1	-5	O	-0.7
1975	Det-A	129	447	51	115	17	5	10	38	36	94	.257	.318	.385	94	-2	-4	53	3	7	-3	4	*O/D	-0.6
1976	Hou-N	87	235	31	68	11	2	7	33	19	43	.289	.350	.443	136	7	9	38	1	0	0	-7	O	0.1
1977	Hou-N	19	27	1	2	0	0	0	2	1	8	.074	.107	.074	-55	-6	-5	0	0	0	0	0	/O	-0.5
1978	Sea-A	134	472	78	142	21	7	22	92	41	52	.301	.367	.515	146	27	28	90	6	3	0	6	*O/D	3.1
1979	Sea-A	140	450	61	122	24	6	15	54	56	64	.271	.354	.451	114	10	9	73	3	3	-1	0	*O	0.3
1980	Sea-A	119	374	48	94	18	3	10	33	43	59	.251	.330	.396	97	-1	-1	48	8	4	0	2	*O/D	0.0
1981	Tex-A	72	233	26	65	17	2	4	31	25	38	.279	.351	.421	128	7	8	33	3	4	-2	-6	O	0.0
1982	Tex-A	31	73	7	17	3	0	1	6	4	14	.233	.282	.315	67	-4	-3	6	0	0	0	-1	O/D	-0.4
	Tor-A	40	105	6	24	4	0	1	5	7	16	.229	.277	.295	52	-6	-7	8	1	1	-0	-1	DO	-0.8
	Yr	71	178	13	41	7	0	2	11	11	30	.230	.279	.303	58	-10	-10	14	1	1	-0	-2		-1.2
1983	KC-A	84	213	24	55	7	0	8	24	17	27	.258	.316	.404	96	-1	-1	26	1	1	0	1	O/D	0.0
1984	KC-A	29	45	4	10	1	1	0	3	4	3	.222	.300	.289	63	-2	-2	4	0	0	0	1	O/PD	-0.1
Total	11	901	2737	342	731	126	28	78	328	256	428	.267	.335	.419	108	28	28	383	26	25	-7	-4	O/DP	0.4

■ JIM ROBERTSON
Robertson, Alfred James b: 1/29/28, Chicago, Ill. BR/TR, 5'9", 183 lbs. Deb: 4/15/54

YEAR	TM/L	G	AB	R	H	2B	3B	HR	RBI	BB	SO	AVG	OBP	SLG	PRO+	BR	/A	RC	SB	CS	SBR	FR	POS	TPR
1954	Phi-A	63	147	9	27	8	0	0	8	23	25	.184	.298	.238	48	-10	-10	12	0	0	0	-2	C	-0.9
1955	KC-A	6	8	1	2	0	0	0	0	1	2	.250	.333	.250	58	-0	-0	1	0	0	0	0	/C	-0.0
Total	2	69	155	10	29	8	0	0	8	24	27	.187	.300	.239	49	-10	-10	13	0	0	0	-2	/C	-0.9

■ ANDRE ROBERTSON
Robertson, Andre Levett b: 10/2/57, Orange, Tex. BR/TR, 5'10", 155 lbs. Deb: 9/03/81

YEAR	TM/L	G	AB	R	H	2B	3B	HR	RBI	BB	SO	AVG	OBP	SLG	PRO+	BR	/A	RC	SB	CS	SBR	FR	POS	TPR
1981	*NY-A	10	19	1	5	1	0	0	0	0	3	.263	.263	.316	67	-1	-1	1	1	1	-0	4	/S2	0.3
1982	NY-A	44	118	16	26	5	0	2	9	8	19	.220	.270	.314	61	-7	-6	9	0	0	0	8	S2/3	0.5
1983	NY-A	98	322	37	80	16	3	1	22	8	54	.248	.273	.326	67	-16	-15	28	2	4	-2	22	S2	1.1
1984	NY-A	52	140	10	30	5	1	0	6	4	20	.214	.236	.264	40	-12	-11	6	0	1	-1	11	S/2	0.3
1985	NY-A	50	125	16	41	5	0	2	17	6	24	.328	.364	.416	116	2	3	18	1	2	-1	-6	3S/2	-0.4
Total	5	254	724	80	182	32	4	5	54	26	120	.251	.281	.327	69	-33	-30	62	4	8	-4	38	S/23	1.8

■ DARYL ROBERTSON
Robertson, Daryl Berdene b: 1/5/36, Cripple Creek, Colo BR/TR, 6', 184 lbs. Deb: 5/04/62

YEAR	TM/L	G	AB	R	H	2B	3B	HR	RBI	BB	SO	AVG	OBP	SLG	PRO+	BR	/A	RC	SB	CS	SBR	FR	POS	TPR
1962	Chi-N	9	19	0	2	0	0	0	2	2	10	.105	.190	.105	-18	-3	-3	1	0	0	0	-1	/S3	-0.3

■ DAVE ROBERTSON
Robertson, Davis Aydelotte b: 9/25/1889, Portsmouth, Va. d: 11/5/70, Virginia Beach, Va. BL/TL, 6', 186 lbs. Deb: 6/05/12

YEAR	TM/L	G	AB	R	H	2B	3B	HR	RBI	BB	SO	AVG	OBP	SLG	PRO+	BR	/A	RC	SB	CS	SBR	FR	POS	TPR
1912	NY-N	3	2	0	1	0	0	0	1	0	1	.500	.500	.500	169	0	0	1	1			0	/1O	0.0
1914	NY-N	82	256	25	68	12	3	2	32	10	26	.266	.299	.359	99	-3	-2	29	9			-2	O	-0.5
1915	NY-N	141	544	72	160	17	10	3	58	22	52	.294	.326	.379	120	7	10	71	22	10	1	-5	*O	0.1
1916	NY-N	150	587	88	180	18	8	12	69	14	56	.307	.326	.426	137	18	21	82	21	17	-4	-2	*O	1.1
1917	*NY-N	142	532	64	138	16	9	12	54	10	47	.259	.276	.391	107	-1	-1	59	17			-6	*O	-1.0
1919	NY-N	1	0	0	0	0	0	0	0	0	0	—	—	—	—	0	0	0	0			0	R	0.0
	Chi-N	27	96	8	20	2	0	1	10	1	10	.208	.224	.260	45	-6	-7	6	3			-1	O	-0.8
	Yr	28	96	8	20	2	0	1	10	1	10	.208	.224	.260	45	-6	-6	6	3			-1		-0.8
1920	Chi-N	134	500	68	150	29	11	10	75	40	44	.300	.353	.462	130	20	19	75	17	23	-9	-10	*O	-0.8
1921	Chi-N	22	36	7	8	3	0	0	14	1	3	.222	.243	.306	44	-3	-3	2	0	2	-1	-1	/O	-0.5
	Pit-N	60	230	29	74	18	3	6	48	12	16	.322	.361	.504	123	8	7	40	4	5	-2	-7	O	-0.3
	Yr	82	266	36	82	21	3	6	62	13	19	.308	.345	.477	113	5	4	41	4	7	-3	-8		-0.8
1922	NY-N	42	47	5	13	2	0	1	3	3	7	.277	.320	.383	80	-1	-1	6	0	0	0	1	/O	0.0
Total	9	804	2830	366	812	117	44	47	364	113	262	.287	.318	.409	117	38	45	370	94	57		-34	O/1	-2.7

■ DON ROBERTSON
Robertson, Donald Alexander b: 10/15/30, Harvey, Ill. BL/TL, 5'10", 180 lbs. Deb: 4/13/54

YEAR	TM/L	G	AB	R	H	2B	3B	HR	RBI	BB	SO	AVG	OBP	SLG	PRO+	BR	/A	RC	SB	CS	SBR	FR	POS	TPR
1954	Chi-N	14	6	2	0	0	0	0	0	0	2	.000	.000	.000	-99	-2	-2	0	0	0	0	0	/O	-0.1

■ GENE ROBERTSON
Robertson, Eugene Edward b: 12/25/1899, St.Louis, Mo. d: 10/21/81, Fallon, Nev. BL/TR, 5'7", 152 lbs. Deb: 7/04/19

YEAR	TM/L	G	AB	R	H	2B	3B	HR	RBI	BB	SO	AVG	OBP	SLG	PRO+	BR	/A	RC	SB	CS	SBR	FR	POS	TPR
1919	StL-A	5	7	1	1	0	0	0	0	1	1	.143	.250	.143	11	-1	-1	0	0			-1	/S	-0.1
1922	StL-A	18	27	2	8	2	1	0	1	1	1	.296	.321	.444	95	-0	-0	4	1	0	0	1	/3S2	0.2
1923	StL-A	78	251	36	62	10	1	0	17	21	7	.247	.310	.295	57	-14	-16	25	4	2	0	-14	3/2	-2.0
1924	StL-A	121	439	40	140	25	4	4	52	36	14	.319	.373	.421	99	3	-1	69	3	5	-2	-11	*3/2	-0.4
1925	StL-A	154	582	97	158	26	5	14	76	81	30	.271	.364	.405	90	-4	-6	90	10	7	-1	-2	*3/S	-0.2
1926	StL-A	78	247	23	62	12	6	0	19	17	10	.251	.302	.360	69	-11	-12	28	5	1	1	-5	3S/2	-0.9
1928	*NY-A	83	251	29	73	9	0	1	36	14	6	.291	.328	.339	78	-9	-8	28	2	4	-2	-8	3/2	-1.5
1929	NY-A	90	309	45	92	15	6	0	35	28	6	.298	.358	.385	98	-4	-1	43	3	3	-1	-11	3	-0.7
	Bos-N	8	28	1	8	0	0	0	6	1	0	.286	.310	.286	51	-2	-2	2	1			-1	/3S	-0.2
1930	Bos-N	21	59	7	11	1	0	0	7	5	3	.186	.250	.203	12	-8	-8	3	0			-2	3	-0.8
Total	9	656	2200	311	615	100	23	20	249	205	79	.280	.344	.373	83	-51	-58	292	29	22		-55	3/S2	-6.6

■ BOB ROBERTSON
Robertson, Robert Eugene b: 10/2/46, Frostburg, Md. BR/TR, 6'1", 195 lbs. Deb: 9/18/67

YEAR	TM/L	G	AB	R	H	2B	3B	HR	RBI	BB	SO	AVG	OBP	SLG	PRO+	BR	/A	RC	SB	CS	SBR	FR	POS	TPR
1967	Pit-N	9	35	4	6	0	0	2	4	3	12	.171	.237	.343	64	-2	-2	3	0	0	0	-0	/1	-0.2
1969	Pit-N	32	96	7	20	4	1	1	9	8	30	.208	.269	.302	61	-5	-5	7	1	0	0	1	1	-0.5
1970	*Pit-N	117	390	69	112	19	4	27	82	51	98	.287	.372	.564	150	25	26	83	4	1	1	3	1/3O	2.1
1971	*Pit-N	131	469	65	127	18	2	26	72	60	101	.271	.358	.484	137	22	23	83	1	2	-1	15	*1	2.9
1972	*Pit-N	115	306	25	59	11	0	12	41	41	84	.193	.294	.346	83	-8	-7	33	1	1	-0	10	1O3	-0.3
1973	Pit-N	119	397	43	95	16	0	14	40	55	77	.239	.333	.385	101	-0	-0	50	0	4	-2	5	*1	-0.1
1974	*Pit-N	91	236	25	54	11	0	16	48	33	48	.229	.323	.479	127	6	7	36	0	0	0	-1	1	0.4
1975	*Pit-N	75	124	17	34	4	0	6	18	23	25	.274	.396	.452	136	7	7	25	0	0	0	1	1	0.7
1976	Pit-N	61	129	10	28	5	1	2	25	16	23	.217	.303	.318	76	-4	-4	13	0	1	-1	-0	1	-0.6
1978	Sea-A	64	174	17	40	5	2	8	28	24	39	.230	.327	.420	109	2	2	24	0	0	0	-1	D1	-0.1

YEAR	TM/L	G	AB	R	H	2B	3B	HR	RBI	BB	SO	AVG	OBP	SLG	PRO+	BR	/A	RC	SB	CS	SBR	FR	POS	TPR
1979	Tor-A	15	29	1	3	0	0	1	1	3	9	.103	.188	.207	6	-4	-4	1	0	0	0	1	/1	-0.3
Total	11	829	2385	283	578	93	10	115	368	317	546	.242	.334	.434	115	39	44	357	7	9	-3	35	1/DO3	4.1

■ SHERRY ROBERTSON
Robertson, Sherrard Alexander b: 1/1/19, Montreal, Que., Can. d: 10/23/70, Houghton, S.Dak. BL/TR, 6', 180 lbs. Deb: 9/08/40 C

YEAR	TM/L	G	AB	R	H	2B	3B	HR	RBI	BB	SO	AVG	OBP	SLG	PRO+	BR	/A	RC	SB	CS	SBR	FR	POS	TPR
1940	Was-A	10	33	4	7	0	1	0	0	5	6	.212	.316	.273	58	-2	-2	3	0	0	0	1	S	0.0
1941	Was-A	1	3	0	0	0	0	0	0	0	3	.000	.000	.000	-99	-1	-1	0	0	0	0	0	/3	0.0
1943	Was-A	59	120	22	26	4	1	3	14	17	19	.217	.319	.342	97	-1	-0	14	0	2	-1	-4	3/S	-0.5
1946	Was-A	74	230	30	46	6	3	6	19	30	42	.200	.292	.330	78	-8	-7	25	6	2	1	-6	32S/O	-0.8
1947	Was-A	95	266	25	62	9	3	1	23	32	52	.233	.318	.301	74	-9	-9	27	4	5	-2	-2	O3/2	-1.4
1948	Was-A	71	187	19	46	11	3	2	22	24	26	.246	.335	.369	90	-4	-3	27	8	0	2	-3	O	-0.4
1949	Was-A	110	374	59	94	17	3	11	42	42	35	.251	.329	.401	95	-6	-5	52	10	3	1	-6	23O	-0.8
1950	Was-A	71	123	19	32	3	3	2	16	22	18	.260	.372	.382	98	-1	0	19	1	1	-0	-8	O2/3	-0.6
1951	Was-A	62	111	14	21	2	1	1	10	9	22	.189	.256	.252	38	-10	-10	8	2	1	0	2	O	-0.7
1952	Was-A	1	0	0	0	0	0	0	0	0	0	—	—	—	—	0	0	0	0	0	0	0	R	0.0
	Phi-A	43	60	8	12	3	0	0	5	21	15	.200	.407	.250	81	0	-0	8	1	2	-1	-4	/2O3	-0.5
	Yr	44	60	8	12	3	0	0	5	21	15	.200	.407	.250	81	0	-0	8	1	2.	-1	-4		-0.5
Total	10	597	1507	200	346	55	18	26	151	202	238	.230	.323	.342	83	-41	-36	184	32	16	0	-30	O2/3S	-5.7

■ BILLY JOE ROBIDOUX
Robidoux, William Joseph b: 1/13/64, Ware, Mass. BL/TR, 6'1", 200 lbs. Deb: 9/11/85

YEAR	TM/L	G	AB	R	H	2B	3B	HR	RBI	BB	SO	AVG	OBP	SLG	PRO+	BR	/A	RC	SB	CS	SBR	FR	POS	TPR
1985	Mil-A	18	51	5	9	2	0	3	8	12	16	.176	.333	.392	98	0	0	7	0	0	0	0	O/1D	0.0
1986	Mil-A	56	181	15	41	8	0	1	21	33	36	.227	.346	.287	72	-5	-6	19	0	0	0	-2	1D	-0.9
1987	Mil-A	23	62	9	12	0	0	0	4	8	17	.194	.286	.194	30	-6	-6	4	0	1	-1	0	1D	-0.7
1988	Mil-A	33	91	9	23	5	0	0	5	8	14	.253	.313	.308	74	-3	-3	8	1	1	-0	2	1/D	-0.2
1989	Chi-A	16	39	2	5	2	0	0	1	4	9	.128	.209	.179	11	-5	-4	2	0	0	-0	-0	1/O	-0.5
1990	Bos-A	27	44	3	8	4	0	1	4	6	14	.182	.294	.341	74	-1	-2	4	0	0	0	1	1/D	-0.1
Total	6	173	468	43	98	21	0	5	43	71	106	.209	.315	.286	65	-20	-21	44	1	2	-1	1	1/DO	-2.4

■ AARON ROBINSON
Robinson, Aaron Andrew b: 6/23/15, Lancaster, S.C. d: 3/9/66, Lancaster, S.C. BL/TR, 6'2", 205 lbs. Deb: 5/06/43

YEAR	TM/L	G	AB	R	H	2B	3B	HR	RBI	BB	SO	AVG	OBP	SLG	PRO+	BR	/A	RC	SB	CS	SBR	FR	POS	TPR
1943	NY-A	1	1	0	0	0	0	0	0	0	1	.000	.000	.000	-99	-0	-0	0	0	0	0	0	H	0.0
1945	NY-A	50	160	19	45	6	1	8	24	21	23	.281	.368	.481	139	9	8	30	0	0	0	-4	C	0.8
1946	NY-A	100	330	32	98	17	2	16	64	48	39	.297	.388	.506	146	21	21	69	0	1	-1	-12	C	1.3
1947	*NY-A	82	252	23	68	11	5	5	36	40	26	.270	.370	.413	119	6	7	41	0	1	-1	0	C	1.2
1948	Chi-A	98	326	47	82	14	2	8	39	46	30	.252	.344	.380	96	-4	-2	45	0	1	-1	-4	C	0.0
1949	Det-A	110	331	38	89	12	0	13	56	73	21	.269	.402	.423	118	11	11	60	0	2	-1	-1	*C	1.4
1950	Det-A	107	283	37	64	7	0	9	37	75	35	.226	.388	.346	86	-2	-3	45	0	1	-1	-3	*C	-0.1
1951	Det-A	36	82	3	17	6	0	0	9	17	9	.207	.343	.280	70	-3	-3	8	0	0	0	-1	C	-0.1
	Bos-A	26	74	9	15	1	1	2	7	17	10	.203	.352	.324	76	-1	-2	10	0	0	0	-1	C	0.0
	Yr	62	156	12	32	7	1	2	16	34	19	.205	.347	.301	73	-4	-5	18	0	0	0	-2		-0.1
Total	8	610	1839	208	478	74	11	61	272	337	194	.260	.375	.412	112	38	36	307	0	6	-4	-26	C	4.5

■ VAL ROBINSON
Robinson, Alfred Valentine Deb: 5/01/1872

YEAR	TM/L	G	AB	R	H	2B	3B	HR	RBI	BB	SO	AVG	OBP	SLG	PRO+	BR	/A	RC	SB	CS	SBR	FR	POS	TPR
1872	Oly-n	7	32	6	6	0	0	0	0			.188	.188	.188	17	-3	-3	1					/O	-0.1

■ BROOKS ROBINSON
Robinson, Brooks Calbert b: 5/18/37, Little Rock, Ark. BR/TR, 6'1", 180 lbs. Deb: 9/17/55 CH

YEAR	TM/L	G	AB	R	H	2B	3B	HR	RBI	BB	SO	AVG	OBP	SLG	PRO+	BR	/A	RC	SB	CS	SBR	FR	POS	TPR
1955	Bal-A	6	22	0	2	0	0	0	1	0	10	.091	.091	.091	-55	-5	-4	0	0	0	0	-2	/3	-0.6
1956	Bal-A	15	44	5	10	4	0	1	1	1	5	.227	.244	.386	70	-3	-2	4	0	0	0	0	3/2	0.0
1957	Bal-A	50	117	13	28	6	1	2	14	7	10	.239	.288	.359	81	-4	-3	11	1	0	0	4	3	0.1
1958	Bal-A	145	463	31	110	16	3	3	32	31	51	.238	.293	.305	68	-22	-19	38	1	2	-1	10	*32	-0.3
1959	Bal-A	88	313	29	89	15	2	4	24	17	37	.284	.325	.383	96	-3	-2	38	2	2	-1	7	3/2	0.4
1960	Bal-A	152	595	74	175	27	9	14	88	35	49	.294	.333	.440	109	4	5	78	2	2	-1	12	*3/2	2.0
1961	Bal-A	163	668	89	192	38	7	7	61	47	57	.287	.338	.397	98	-5	-3	85	1	3	-2	-6	*3/2S	0.0
1962	Bal-A	162	634	77	192	29	9	23	86	42	70	.303	.347	.486	127	17	21	102	3	1	0	7	*3/S2	3.0
1963	Bal-A	161	589	67	148	26	4	11	67	46	84	.251	.307	.365	89	-10	-9	66	2	3	-1	9	*3/S	-0.9
1964	Bal-A	163	612	82	194	35	3	28	**118**	51	64	.317	.373	.521	146	37	37	115	1	0	-0	-2	*3	3.9
1965	Bal-A	144	559	81	166	25	2	18	80	47	47	.297	.354	.445	123	18	17	86	3	0	1	-6	*3	1.4
1966	*Bal-A	157	620	91	167	35	2	23	100	56	36	.269	.333	.444	123	17	18	88	2	3	-1	4	*3	1.8
1967	Bal-A	158	610	88	164	25	5	22	77	54	54	.269	.332	.434	126	18	18	83	1	3	-2	**31**	*3	5.5
1968	Bal-A	162	608	65	154	36	6	17	75	44	55	.253	.308	.416	118	11	11	76	1	1	-1	17	*3	3.6
1969	*Bal-A	156	598	73	140	21	3	23	84	56	55	.234	.303	.395	93	-7	-7	69	2	1	0	19	*3	1.4
1970	*Bal-A	158	608	84	168	31	4	18	94	53	53	.276	.338	.429	109	8	7	85	1	1	-0	-1	*3	0.6
1971	*Bal-A	156	589	67	160	21	1	20	92	63	50	.272	.345	.413	115	11	11	83	0	0	0	7	*3	1.4
1972	Bal-A	153	556	48	139	23	2	8	64	43	45	.250	.306	.342	90	-6	-7	58	1	0	0	6	*3	0.4
1973	Bal-A	155	549	53	141	17	2	9	72	55	50	.257	.328	.344	90	-7	-6	61	2	0	1	9	*3	0.1
1974	*Bal-A	153	553	46	159	27	0	7	59	56	41	.288	.356	.374	114	8	10	74	0	0	1	19	*3	3.3
1975	Bal-A	144	482	50	97	15	1	6	53	44	33	.201	.269	.274	57	-29	-25	37	0	0	0	4	*3	-1.9
1976	Bal-A	71	218	16	46	8	2	3	11	8	24	.211	.242	.307	64	-12	-10	16	0	0	0	0	3	-0.9
1977	Bal-A	24	47	3	7	2	0	1	4	4	4	.149	.216	.255	30	-5	-4	2	0	0	0	2	3	-0.2
Total	23	2896	10654	1232	2848	482	68	268	1357	860	990	.267	.325	.401	105	32	52	1358	28	22	-5	151	*3/2S	25.0

■ BRUCE ROBINSON
Robinson, Bruce Philip b: 4/16/54, LaJolla, Cal. BL/TR, 6'1", 185 lbs. Deb: 8/19/78

YEAR	TM/L	G	AB	R	H	2B	3B	HR	RBI	BB	SO	AVG	OBP	SLG	PRO+	BR	/A	RC	SB	CS	SBR	FR	POS	TPR
1978	Oak-A	28	84	5	21	3	1	0	8	3	8	.250	.276	.310	68	-4	-4	7	0	0	0	7	C	0.5
1979	NY-A	6	12	0	2	0	0	0	2	1	0	.167	.231	.167	9	-2	-1	1	0	0	0	2	/C	0.1
1980	NY-A	4	5	0	0	0	0	0	0	0	4	.000	.000	.000	-99	-1	-1	0	0	0	0	-0	/C	0.0
Total	3	38	101	5	23	3	1	0	10	4	12	.228	.257	.277	52	-7	-6	7	0	0	0	9	/C	0.6

■ CHARLIE ROBINSON
Robinson, Charles Henry b: 7/27/1856, Westerly, R.I. d: 5/18/13, Deb: 8/02/1884

YEAR	TM/L	G	AB	R	H	2B	3B	HR	RBI	BB	SO	AVG	OBP	SLG	PRO+	BR	/A	RC	SB	CS	SBR	FR	POS	TPR
1884	Ind-a	20	80	11	23	2	0	0			3	.287	.313	.313	111	1	1	8				-2	C/SO	0.0
1885	Bro-a	11	40	5	6	2	1	0			3	.150	.209	.250	46	-2	-2	2				-5	C	-0.4
Total	2	31	120	16	29	4	1	0			6	.242	.278	.292	88	-2	-1	10				-7	/CSO	-0.4

■ RABBIT ROBINSON
Robinson, Clyde b: 3/5/1882, Wellsburg, W.Va. d: 4/9/15, Waterbury, Conn. BR/TR, 5'6", 148 lbs. Deb: 4/22/03

YEAR	TM/L	G	AB	R	H	2B	3B	HR	RBI	BB	SO	AVG	OBP	SLG	PRO+	BR	/A	RC	SB	CS	SBR	FR	POS	TPR
1903	Was-A	103	373	41	79	10	8	1	20	33		.212	.276	.290	70	-12	-13	35	16			2	2OS/3	-1.0
1904	Det-A	101	320	30	77	13	6	0	37	29		.241	.304	.319	102	0	1	38	14			1	S3O2	0.3
1910	Cin-N	2	7	0	0	0	0	0	1	1	0	.000	.125	.000	-66	-1	-1	0	0			-1	/3	-0.2
Total	3	206	700	71	156	23	14	1	58	63	0	.223	.287	.300	83	-13	-13	73	30			3	/2SO3	-0.9

■ CRAIG ROBINSON
Robinson, Craig George b: 8/21/48, Abington, Pa. BR/TR, 5'10", 165 lbs. Deb: 9/09/72

YEAR	TM/L	G	AB	R	H	2B	3B	HR	RBI	BB	SO	AVG	OBP	SLG	PRO+	BR	/A	RC	SB	CS	SBR	FR	POS	TPR
1972	Phi-N	5	15	0	3	1	0	0	0	1	2	.200	.200	.267	46	-1	-1	1	0	0	0	2	/S	0.2
1973	Phi-N	46	146	11	33	7	0	0	7	0	25	.226	.226	.274	37	-12	-13	8	1	1	-0	1	S/2	-0.6
1974	Atl-N	145	452	52	104	4	6	0	29	30	57	.230	.282	.265	52	-28	-30	34	11	2	2	-17	*S	-3.0
1975	Atl-N	10	17	1	1	0	0	0	0	0	5	.059	.059	.059	-65	-4	-4	0	0	0	0	1	/S	-0.1
	SF-N	29	29	4	2	1	0	0	0	2	6	.069	.104	.103	-34	-5	-5	0	0	0	0	5	S/2	0.1
	Yr	39	46	5	3	1	0	0	0	2	11	.065	.104	.087	-45	-9	-9	0	0	0	0	6		0.0
1976	SF-N	15	13	4	4	1	0	0	2	3	4	.308	.438	.385	131	1	1	2	0	0	0	4	/23S	0.5
	Atl-N	15	17	4	4	0	0	0	3	5	2	.235	.409	.235	81	0	-0	2	0	0	0	2	/2S3	0.2

YEAR	TM/L	G	AB	R	H	2B	3B	HR	RBI	BB	SO	AVG	OBP	SLG	PRO+	BR	/A	RC	SB	CS	SBR	FR	POS	TPR
	Yr	30	30	8	8	1	0	0	5	8	6	.267	.421	.300	102	1	1	5	0	1	-1	6		0.7
1977	Atl-N	27	29	4	6	1	0	0	1	1	6	.207	.233	.241	25	-3	-3	2	0	0	0	6	S	0.6
Total	6	292	718	80	157	15	6	0	42	42	107	.219	.265	.256	44	-52	-56	50	12	4	1	3	S/23	-2.1

■ DAVE ROBINSON
Robinson, David Tanner b: 5/22/46, Minneapolis, Minn. BB/TL, 6'1", 186 lbs. Deb: 9/10/70

YEAR	TM/L	G	AB	R	H	2B	3B	HR	RBI	BB	SO	AVG	OBP	SLG	PRO+	BR	/A	RC	SB	CS	SBR	FR	POS	TPR
1970	SD-N	15	38	5	12	2	0	2	6	5	4	.316	.395	.526	151	2	3	8	2	0	1	1	O	0.4
1971	SD-N	7	6	0	0	0	0	0	0	1	3	.000	.143	.000	-61	-1	-1	0	0	0	0	0	H	0.0
Total	2	22	44	5	12	2	0	2	6	6	7	.273	.360	.455	124	1	1	8	2	0	1	1	/O	0.4

■ EARL ROBINSON
Robinson, Earl John b: 11/3/36, New Orleans, La. BR/TR, 6'1", 190 lbs. Deb: 9/10/58

YEAR	TM/L	G	AB	R	H	2B	3B	HR	RBI	BB	SO	AVG	OBP	SLG	PRO+	BR	/A	RC	SB	CS	SBR	FR	POS	TPR
1958	LA-N	8	15	3	3	0	0	0	1	4	.200	.250	.200	20	-2	-2	0	0	0	0	1	/3	0.0
1961	Bal-A	96	222	37	59	12	3	8	30	31	54	.266	.356	.455	117	5	5	36	4	3	-1	5	O	0.6
1962	Bal-A	29	63	12	18	3	1	1	4	8	10	.286	.366	.413	115	1	1	10	2	0	1	1	O	0.2
1964	Bal-A	37	121	11	33	5	1	3	10	7	24	.273	.313	.405	98	-1	-1	15	1	2	-1	2	O	0.0
Total	4	170	421	63	113	20	5	12	44	47	92	.268	.342	.425	108	3	4	61	7	5	-1	9	O/3	0.8

■ FLOYD ROBINSON
Robinson, Floyd Andrew b: 5/9/36, Prescott, Ark. BL/TR, 5'9", 175 lbs. Deb: 8/10/60

YEAR	TM/L	G	AB	R	H	2B	3B	HR	RBI	BB	SO	AVG	OBP	SLG	PRO+	BR	/A	RC	SB	CS	SBR	FR	POS	TPR
1960	Chi-A	22	46	7	13	0	0	1	11	8	.283	.431	.283	98	1	1	7	2	3	-1	-2	O	-0.2
1961	Chi-A	132	432	69	134	20	7	11	59	52	32	.310	.389	.465	129	18	19	82	7	4	-0	3	*O	1.7
1962	Chi-A	156	600	89	187	45	10	11	109	72	47	.312	.387	.475	131	27	27	113	4	2	0	1	*O	2.2
1963	Chi-A	146	527	71	149	21	6	13	71	62	43	.283	.363	.419	120	14	15	81	4	3	-1	-3	*O	0.8
1964	Chi-A	141	525	83	158	17	3	11	59	70	41	.301	.388	.408	125	18	20	87	9	5	-0	-5	*O	0.9
1965	Chi-A	156	577	70	153	15	6	14	66	76	51	.265	.356	.385	117	10	14	83	4	1	1	-5	*O	0.4
1966	Chi-A	127	342	44	81	11	2	5	35	44	32	.237	.332	.325	96	-3	-1	41	8	2	1	-16	*O	-2.1
1967	Cin-N	55	130	19	31	6	2	1	10	14	14	.238	.313	.338	77	-2	-4	14	3	1	0	-3	O	-0.8
1968	Oak-A	53	81	5	20	5	0	1	14	4	10	.247	.282	.346	94	-1	-1	8	0	0	0	-1	O	-0.2
	Bos-A	24	24	1	3	0	0	0	2	3	4	.125	.250	.125	15	-2	-2	1	1	0	0	-1	O	-0.3
	Yr	77	105	6	23	5	0	1	16	7	14	.219	.274	.295	73	-4	-3	9	1	0	0	-2		-0.5
Total	9	1012	3284	458	929	140	36	67	426	408	282	.283	.367	.409	118	78	88	517	42	21	0	-31	O	2.4

■ FRANK ROBINSON
Robinson, Frank b: 8/31/35, Beaumont, Tex. BR/TR, 6'1", 183 lbs. Deb: 4/17/56 MCH

YEAR	TM/L	G	AB	R	H	2B	3B	HR	RBI	BB	SO	AVG	OBP	SLG	PRO+	BR	/A	RC	SB	CS	SBR	FR	POS	TPR
1956	Cin-N	152	572	122	166	27	6	38	83	64	95	.290	.381	.558	139	39	34	121	8	4	0	1	*O	3.0
1957	Cin-N	150	611	97	197	29	5	29	75	44	92	.322	.379	.529	131	34	29	122	10	2	2	21	*O1	4.5
1958	Cin-N	148	554	90	149	25	6	31	83	62	80	.269	.350	.504	116	17	13	99	10	1	2	9	*O3	2.0
1959	Cin-N	146	540	106	168	31	4	36	125	69	93	.311	.397	.583	152	44	42	122	18	8	1	-5	*1O	2.7
1960	Cin-N	139	464	86	138	33	6	31	83	82	67	.297	.413	.595	169	48	47	113	13	6	0	1	1O/3	4.3
1961	*Cin-N	153	545	117	176	32	7	37	124	71	64	.323	.411	.611	164	52	51	137	22	3	5	8	*O/3	5.4
1962	Cin-N	162	609	134	208	51	2	39	136	76	62	.342	.424	.624	172	67	64	160	18	9	0	9	*O	6.2
1963	Cin-N	140	482	79	125	19	3	21	91	81	69	.259	.381	.442	132	26	24	87	26	10	2	5	*O/1	2.5
1964	Cin-N	156	568	103	174	38	6	29	96	79	67	.306	.399	.548	158	50	47	127	23	5	4	4	*O	5.3
1965	Cin-N	156	582	109	172	33	5	33	113	70	100	.296	.388	.540	148	46	41	120	13	9	-2	3	*O	3.9
1966	*Bal-A	155	576	122	182	34	2	49	122	87	90	.316	.415	.637	200	74	75	146	8	5	-1	-6	*O/1	6.5
1967	Bal-A	129	479	83	149	23	7	30	94	71	84	.311	.408	.576	189	53	54	113	2	3	-1	-4	*O/1	4.8
1968	Bal-A	130	421	69	113	27	1	15	52	73	84	.268	.391	.444	153	30	30	77	11	2	2	-6	*O/1	2.4
1969	*Bal-A	148	539	111	166	19	5	32	100	88	62	.308	.417	.540	164	50	49	126	9	3	1	-5	*O1	4.2
1970	*Bal-A	132	471	88	144	24	1	25	78	69	70	.306	.402	.520	151	35	34	99	2	1	0	1	*O/1	3.1
1971	*Bal-A	133	455	82	128	16	2	28	99	72	62	.281	.390	.510	154	33	34	88	3	0	1	-8	O1	2.3
1972	LA-N	103	342	41	86	6	1	19	59	55	76	.251	.358	.442	129	12	13	55	2	3	-1	-2	O	0.6
1973	Cal-A	147	534	85	142	29	0	30	97	82	93	.266	.374	.489	153	30	36	99	1	1	0	2	*DO	3.7
1974	Cal-A	129	427	75	107	26	2	20	63	75	85	.251	.375	.461	148	24	27	77	5	1	1	0	*D/O	2.9
	Cle-A	15	50	6	10	1	1	2	5	10	10	.200	.333	.380	106	0	1	7	0	1	-1	-1	D/1	0.0
	Yr	144	477	81	117	27	3	22	68	85	95	.245	.371	.453	143	24	27	85	5	2	0	-1		2.9
1975	Cle-A	49	118	19	28	5	0	9	24	29	15	.237	.388	.508	152	9	9	25	0	0	0	0	DM	0.9
1976	Cle-A	36	67	5	15	0	0	3	10	11	12	.224	.333	.358	104	0	1	8	0	0	0	-0	D/1OM	0.0
Total	21	2808	10006	1829	2943	528	72	586	1812	1420	1532	.294	.392	.537	154	773	754	2126	204	77	15	25	*OD13/1	71.2

■ FRED ROBINSON
Robinson, Frederic Henry b: 7/6/1856, South Acton, Mass. d: 12/18/33, Hudson, Mass. BR/TR, Deb: 4/17/1884

YEAR	TM/L	G	AB	R	H	2B	3B	HR	RBI	BB	SO	AVG	OBP	SLG	PRO+	BR	/A	RC	SB	CS	SBR	FR	POS	TPR
1884	Cin-U	3	13	1	3	0	0	0	0	.231	.231	.231	52	-1	-1	1				-3	/2	-0.3

■ JACKIE ROBINSON
Robinson, Jack Roosevelt b: 1/31/19, Cairo, Ga. d: 10/24/72, Stamford, Conn. BR/TR, 5'11.5", 195 lbs. Deb: 4/15/47 H

YEAR	TM/L	G	AB	R	H	2B	3B	HR	RBI	BB	SO	AVG	OBP	SLG	PRO+	BR	/A	RC	SB	CS	SBR	FR	POS	TPR
1947	*Bro-N	151	590	125	175	31	5	12	48	74	36	.297	.383	.427	111	14	11	104	29			-3	*1	0.0
1948	Bro-N	147	574	108	170	38	8	12	85	57	37	.296	.367	.453	117	16	14	99	22			1	*21/3	2.2
1949	*Bro-N	156	593	122	203	38	12	16	124	86	27	.342	.432	.528	150	50	46	135	37			-1	*2	5.0
1950	Bro-N	144	518	99	170	39	4	14	81	80	24	.328	.423	.500	139	34	33	114	12			11	*2	4.5
1951	Bro-N	153	548	106	185	33	7	19	88	79	27	.338	.429	.527	153	46	44	133	25	8	3	17	*2	6.7
1952	*Bro-N	149	510	104	157	17	3	19	75	106	40	.308	.440	.465	149	42	41	116	24	7	3	4	*2	5.5
1953	Bro-N	136	484	109	159	34	7	12	95	74	30	.329	.425	.502	137	32	30	111	17	4	3	7	O3/21S	3.4
1954	Bro-N	124	386	62	120	22	4	15	59	63	20	.311	.417	.505	135	24	22	83	7	3	0	-6	O3/2	1.5
1955	*Bro-N	105	317	51	81	6	2	8	36	61	18	.256	.381	.363	96	2	1	49	12	3	1	8	3O/12	1.0
1956	*Bro-N	117	357	61	98	15	2	10	43	60	32	.275	.383	.412	106	9	5	60	12	5	1	15	32/1O	2.2
Total	10	1382	4877	947	1518	273	54	137	734	740	291	.311	.410	.474	131	269	248	1002	197	30		53	2310/S	32.0

■ JACK ROBINSON
Robinson, John W. "Bridgeport" b: 7/15/1880, Portland, Maine d: 7/22/21, Macon, Ga. TR, Deb: 9/06/02

YEAR	TM/L	G	AB	R	H	2B	3B	HR	RBI	BB	SO	AVG	OBP	SLG	PRO+	BR	/A	RC	SB	CS	SBR	FR	POS	TPR
1902	NY-N	4	9	0	0	0	0	0	0	0	.000	.000	.000	-99	-2	-2	0				1	/C	0.0

■ WILBERT ROBINSON
Robinson, Wilbert "Uncle Robby" b: 6/29/1863, Bolton, Mass. d: 8/8/34, Atlanta, Ga. BR/TR, 5'8.5", 215 lbs. Deb: 4/19/1886 MCH

YEAR	TM/L	G	AB	R	H	2B	3B	HR	RBI	BB	SO	AVG	OBP	SLG	PRO+	BR	/A	RC	SB	CS	SBR	FR	POS	TPR
1886	Phi-a	87	342	57	69	11	3	1		21		.202	.254	.260	62	-14	-15	32	33			-7	C1/O	-1.6
1887	Phi-a	68	264	28	60	6	2	1		14		.227	.269	.277	54	-16	-16	24	15			6	C1/O	0.1
1888	Phi-a	66	254	32	62	7	2	1	31	9		.244	.270	.299	86	-4	-4	24	11			25	C/1	2.5
1889	Phi-a	69	264	31	61	13	2	0	28	6	34	.231	.251	.295	58	-15	-15	22	9			0	C	-0.5
1890	Phi-a	82	329	32	78	13	4	0		16		.237	.279	.337	86	-8	-7	37	20			-14	C	-0.9
	Bal-a	14	48	7	13	1	0	0		3		.271	.314	.292	77	-1	-1	5	1			6	C/1	0.5
	Yr	96	377	39	91	14	4	0		19		.241	.283	.332	85	-9	-8	42	21			-8		-0.4
1891	Bal-a	93	334	25	72	8	5	2	46	16	37	.216	.251	.287	56	-20	-20	29	18			2	C/O	-1.2
1892	Bal-N	90	330	36	88	14	4	2	57	15	35	.267	.303	.352	96	-1	-3	38	5			-19	C/1O	-1.5
1893	Bal-N	95	359	49	120	21	3	2	57	26	22	.334	.382	.435	116	9	8	68	17			-8	*C/1	0.6
1894	*Bal-N	109	414	69	146	21	4	1	98	46	18	.353	.421	.430	103	7	4	82	12			-6	*C	0.6
1895	*Bal-N	77	282	38	74	19	1	0	48	12	19	.262	.295	.337	62	-15	-17	32	11			13	C	0.2
1896	*Bal-N	67	245	43	85	9	6	2	38	14	13	.347	.385	.457	122	8	7	48	9			2	C	1.3
1897	Bal-N	48	181	25	57	9	0	0	23	8		.315	.347	.365	90	-2	-2	23	0			-2	C	0.2
1898	Bal-N	79	289	29	80	12	2	0	38	16		.277	.317	.332	87	-4	-5	32	3			-5	C	-0.4
1899	Bal-N	108	356	40	101	15	2	0	47	31		.284	.344	.337	85	-4	-7	44	5			-19	*C	-1.7
1900	StL-N	60	210	26	52	5	1	0	28	11		.248	.291	.281	61	-11	-11	20	7			-1	C	-0.5
1901	Bal-A	68	239	32	72	12	3	0	26	10		.301	.335	.377	95	-0	-2	34	9			-3	C	0.1
1902	Bal-A	91	335	38	98	16	7	1	57	12		.293	.323	.391	95	-1	-3	47	11			-14	CM	-0.9

YEAR	TM/L	G	AB	R	H	2B	3B	HR	RBI	BB	SO	AVG	OBP	SLG	PRO+	BR	/A	RC	SB	CS	SBR	FR	POS	TPR
Total	17	1371	5075	637	1388	212	51	18	622	286	178	.273	.316	.346	85	-95	-110	642	196			-43	*C/1O	-3.1

■ EDDIE ROBINSON　Robinson, William Edward　b: 12/15/20, Paris, Tex.　BL/TR, 6′2.5″, 210 lbs.　Deb: 9/09/42　C

YEAR	TM/L	G	AB	R	H	2B	3B	HR	RBI	BB	SO	AVG	OBP	SLG	PRO+	BR	/A	RC	SB	CS	SBR	FR	POS	TPR
1942	Cle-A	8	8	1	1	0	0	0	2	1	0	.125	.222	.125	-1	-1	-1	0	0	0	0	0	/1	0.0
1946	Cle-A	8	30	6	12	1	0	3	4	2	4	.400	.438	.733	238	5	5	10	0	0	0	-2	/1	0.3
1947	Cle-A	95	318	52	78	10	1	14	52	30	18	.245	.314	.415	105	-1	0	41	1	0	0	-1	1	-0.2
1948	*Cle-A	134	493	53	125	18	5	16	83	36	42	.254	.307	.408	91	-11	-9	61	1	0	0	-0	*1	-0.2
1949	Was-A	143	527	66	155	27	3	18	78	67	30	.294	.381	.459	125	16	17	93	3	4	-2	-2	*1	1.5
1950	Was-A	36	129	21	30	4	2	1	13	25	4	.233	.365	.318	80	4	-3	17	0	0	0	0	1	-0.3
	Chi-A	119	424	62	133	11	2	20	73	60	28	.314	.405	.491	132	19	20	90	0	0	0	-7	*1	0.7
	Yr	155	553	83	163	15	4	21	86	85	32	.295	.395	.450	120	15	17	106	0	0	0	-7		0.4
1951	Chi-A	151	564	85	159	23	5	29	117	77	54	.282	.371	.495	135	25	26	107	2	5	-2	-6	*1	1.5
1952	Chi-A	155	594	79	176	33	1	22	104	70	49	.296	.382	.466	134	28	28	113	2	0	1	-8	*1	1.1
1953	Phi-A	156	615	64	152	28	4	22	102	63	56	.247	.322	.413	94	-4	-7	84	1	2	-1	-14	*1	-2.4
1954	NY-A	85	142	11	37	9	0	3	27	19	21	.261	.348	.387	105	0	1	21	0	0	0	1	1	0.1
1955	*NY-A	88	173	25	36	1	0	16	42	36	26	.208	.360	.491	129	7	7	31	0	0	0	-2	1	0.3
1956	NY-A	26	54	7	12	1	0	5	11	5	3	.222	.323	.519	123	1	1	9	0	1	-1	-0	1	0.0
	KC-A	75	172	13	34	5	1	2	12	26	20	.198	.310	.273	55	-11	-11	15	0	0	0	-4	1	-1.5
	Yr	101	226	20	46	6	1	7	23	31	23	.204	.313	.332	71	-10	-10	24	0	1	-1	-4		-1.5
1957	Det-A	13	9	0	0	0	0	0	0	3	0	.000	.308	.000	-9	-1	-1	0	0	0	0	0	/1	0.0
	Cle-A	19	27	1	6	1	0	1	3	0	3	.222	.250	.370	68	-1	-1	2	0	0	0	0	/1	0.0
	Bal-A	4	3	0	0	0	0	0	0	1	1	.000	.250	.000	-28	-1	-0	0	0	0	0	0	H	0.0
	Yr	36	39	1	6	1	0	1	3	4	4	.154	.267	.256	44	-3	-3	2	0	0	0	1		0.0
Total	13	1315	4282	546	1146	172	24	172	723	521	359	.268	.354	.440	113	65	72	694	10	12	-4	-43	*1	0.9

■ YANK ROBINSON　Robinson, William H.　b: 9/19/1859, Philadelphia, Pa.　d: 8/25/1894, St.Louis, Mo.　BR/TR, 5′6.5″, 170 lbs.　Deb: 8/24/1882

YEAR	TM/L	G	AB	R	H	2B	3B	HR	RBI	BB	SO	AVG	OBP	SLG	PRO+	BR	/A	RC	SB	CS	SBR	FR	POS	TPR
1882	Det-N	11	39	1	7	1	0	0	2	1	13	.179	.200	.205	30	-3	-3	2				-4	S/OP	-0.5
1884	Bal-U	102	415	101	111	24	4	2		37		.267	.327	.359	120	15	8	50	0			15	3SCP/2	2.2
1885	*StL-a	78	287	63	75	8	8	0		29		.261	.344	.345	115	8	6	35				-5	O2/C31	0.0
1886	*StL-a	133	481	89	132	26	9	3		64		.274	.377	.385	135	26	22	91	51			-3	*2/3OSP	1.6
1887	*StL-a	125	430	102	131	32	4	1		92		.305	.445	.405	127	31	21	114	75			-13	*2/3OSCP	0.7
1888	*StL-a	134	455	111	105	17	6	3	53	116		.231	.400	.314	121	27	18	82	56			-44	*2S	-1.9
1889	StL-a	132	452	97	94	17	3	5	70	118	55	.208	.378	.292	83	4	-8	66	39			-35	*2	-3.4
1890	Pit-P	98	306	59	70	10	3	0	38	101	33	.229	.434	.281	104	7	12	46	17			-19	*2	0.0
1891	Cin-a	97	342	48	61	9	4	1	37	68	51	.178	.328	.237	59	-12	-18	35	23			-11	*2	-1.9
	StL-a	1	3	0	0	0	0	0	0	0	0	.000	.000	.000	-87	-1	-1	0	0			-1	/2	0.0
	Yr	98	345	48	61	9	4	1	37	68	51	.177	.325	.235	58	-13	-19	35	23			-12		-1.9
1892	Was-N	67	218	26	39	4	3	0	19	38	28	.179	.301	.225	63	-9	-8	18	11			-4	3/S2	-0.6
Total	10	978	3428	697	825	148	44	15	219	664	180	.241	.375	.323	105	92	49	538	272			-123	23/SOCP1	-3.8

■ BILL ROBINSON　Robinson, William Henry　b: 6/26/43, McKeesport, Pa.　BR/TR, 6′2″, 189 lbs.　Deb: 9/20/66　C

YEAR	TM/L	G	AB	R	H	2B	3B	HR	RBI	BB	SO	AVG	OBP	SLG	PRO+	BR	/A	RC	SB	CS	SBR	FR	POS	TPR
1966	Atl-N	6	11	1	3	0	1	0	3	0	1	.273	.273	.455	96	-0	-0	1	0	0	0	-0	/O	0.0
1967	NY-A	116	342	31	67	6	1	7	29	28	56	.196	.261	.281	62	-17	-16	24	2	2	-1	1	*O	-2.0
1968	NY-A	107	342	34	82	16	7	6	40	26	54	.240	.297	.380	107	1	2	36	7	6	-2	3	O	0.0
1969	NY-A	87	222	23	38	11	2	3	21	16	39	.171	.227	.279	42	-18	-17	13	3	1	0	-2	O/1	-2.1
1972	Phi-N	82	188	19	45	9	1	8	21	5	30	.239	.259	.426	89	-3	-4	16	2	3	-1	-6	O	-1.4
1973	Phi-N	124	452	62	130	32	1	25	65	27	91	.288	.329	.529	131	18	17	74	5	4	-1	2	*O3	1.2
1974	Phi-N	100	280	32	66	14	1	5	29	17	61	.236	.282	.346	72	-10	-12	24	5	3	-0	1	O	-1.4
1975	*Pit-N	92	200	26	56	12	2	6	33	11	36	.280	.318	.450	112	2	2	27	3	1	0	2	O	0.5
1976	Pit-N	122	393	55	119	23	3	21	64	16	73	.303	.332	.534	142	19	18	62	2	4	-2	-8	O3/1	0.5
1977	Pit-N	137	507	74	154	32	1	26	104	25	92	.304	.340	.525	125	18	16	88	12	6	0	-11	1O3	-0.1
1978	Pit-N	136	499	70	123	36	2	14	80	35	105	.246	.302	.411	93	-3	-6	60	14	11	-2	-4	*O3/1	-1.8
1979	*Pit-N	148	421	59	111	17	6	24	75	24	81	.264	.305	.504	111	7	5	60	13	2	3	-19	*O1/3	-1.6
1980	Pit-N	100	272	28	78	10	1	12	36	15	45	.287	.324	.463	116	5	5	36	1	4	-2	-5	1O	-0.5
1981	Pit-N	39	88	8	19	3	0	2	8	5	18	.216	.258	.318	61	-5	-5	7	1	0	0	-0	1/O3	-0.6
1982	Pit-N	31	71	8	17	3	0	4	12	5	19	.239	.289	.451	101	0	0	8	0	1	-1	0	O/1	0.1
	Phi-N	35	69	6	18	6	0	3	19	7	15	.261	.329	.478	121	2	2	10	1	1	-0	0	O/1	0.1
	Yr	66	140	14	35	9	0	7	31	12	34	.250	.309	.464	111	2	2	18	1	2	-1	0		0.1
1983	Phi-N	10	7	0	1	0	0	0	2	1	4	.143	.250	.143	12	-1	-1	0	0	0	0	-1	/13O	-0.1
Total	16	1472	4364	536	1127	229	29	166	641	263	820	.258	.303	.438	104	14	6	545	71	49	-8	-48	*O13	-9.5

■ RAFAEL ROBLES　Robles, Rafael Orlando (Natera)　b: 10/20/47, San Pedro De Macoris, D.R.　BR/TR, 6′, 170 lbs.　Deb: 4/08/69

YEAR	TM/L	G	AB	R	H	2B	3B	HR	RBI	BB	SO	AVG	OBP	SLG	PRO+	BR	/A	RC	SB	CS	SBR	FR	POS	TPR
1969	SD-N	6	20	1	2	0	0	0	0	1	3	.100	.143	.100	-32	-3	-3	0	1	1	-0	-4	/S	-0.7
1970	SD-N	23	89	5	19	1	0	0	3	5	11	.213	.263	.225	33	-8	-8	6	3	0	1	2	S	-0.2
1972	SD-N	18	24	1	4	0	0	0	0	0	3	.167	.167	.167	-5	-3	-3	1	0	0	0	-2	S/3	-0.3
Total	3	47	133	7	25	1	0	0	3	6	17	.188	.229	.195	17	-15	-14	7	4	1	1	-4	/S3	-1.2

■ SERGIO ROBLES　Robles, Sergio (Valenzuela)　b: 4/16/46, Magdalena, Mexico　BR/TR, 6′2″, 190 lbs.　Deb: 8/27/72

YEAR	TM/L	G	AB	R	H	2B	3B	HR	RBI	BB	SO	AVG	OBP	SLG	PRO+	BR	/A	RC	SB	CS	SBR	FR	POS	TPR
1972	Bal-A	2	5	0	1	0	0	0	0	0	0	.200	.200	.200	19	-0	-1	0	0	0	0	-1	/C	-0.1
1973	Bal-A	8	13	0	1	0	0	0	0	3	1	.077	.250	.077	-4	-2	-2	0	0	0	0	3	/C	0.1
1976	LA-N	6	3	0	0	0	0	0	0	0	2	.000	.000	.000	-99	-1	-1	0	0	0	0	1	/C	0.1
Total	3	16	21	0	2	0	0	0	0	3	3	.095	.208	.095	-11	-3	-3	1	0	0	0	3	/C	0.1

■ TOM ROBSON　Robson, Thomas James　b: 1/15/46, Rochester, N.Y.　BR/TR, 6′3″, 215 lbs.　Deb: 9/14/74　C

YEAR	TM/L	G	AB	R	H	2B	3B	HR	RBI	BB	SO	AVG	OBP	SLG	PRO+	BR	/A	RC	SB	CS	SBR	FR	POS	TPR
1974	Tex-A	6	13	2	3	1	0	0	2	4	3	.231	.412	.308	112	0	0	2	0	0	0	0	/1D	0.0
1975	Tex-A	17	35	3	7	0	0	0	2	1	3	.200	.222	.200	20	-4	-4	1	0	0	0	0	/1D	-0.3
Total	2	23	48	5	10	1	0	0	4	5	6	.208	.283	.229	48	-3	-3	3	0	0	0	0	/D1	-0.3

■ ADAM ROCAP　Rocap, Adam　b: 1854, Philadelphia, Pa.　d: 3/29/1892, Philadelphia, Pa.　5′9″, 170 lbs.　Deb: 5/05/1875

YEAR	TM/L	G	AB	R	H	2B	3B	HR	RBI	BB	SO	AVG	OBP	SLG	PRO+	BR	/A	RC	SB	CS	SBR	FR	POS	TPR
1875	Ath-n	16	70	13	12	0	0	0		0		.171	.171	.171	17	-5	-7	2					O/2	-0.5

■ MIKE ROCCO　Rocco, Michael Dominick　b: 3/2/16, St.Paul, Minn.　BL/TL, 5′11″, 188 lbs.　Deb: 6/05/43

YEAR	TM/L	G	AB	R	H	2B	3B	HR	RBI	BB	SO	AVG	OBP	SLG	PRO+	BR	/A	RC	SB	CS	SBR	FR	POS	TPR
1943	Cle-A	108	405	43	97	14	4	5	46	51	40	.240	.328	.331	99	-3	-0	47	1	2	-1	-5	*1	-0.9
1944	Cle-A	155	653	87	174	29	7	13	70	56	51	.266	.325	.392	108	2	5	84	4	8	-4	17	*1	1.0
1945	Cle-A	143	565	81	149	28	6	10	56	52	40	.264	.326	.388	111	3	6	72	0	4	-2	4	*1	0.3
1946	Cle-A	34	98	8	24	2	0	2	14	15	15	.245	.345	.327	94	-1	-0	12	1	1	-0	5	1	0.3
Total	4	440	1721	219	444	73	17	30	186	174	146	.258	.327	.372	106	1	11	215	6	15	-7	21	1	0.7

■ JACK ROCHE　Roche, John Joseph "Red"　b: 11/22/1890, Los Angeles, Cal.　d: 3/30/83, Peoria, Ariz.　BR/TR, 6′1″, 178 lbs.　Deb: 5/24/14

YEAR	TM/L	G	AB	R	H	2B	3B	HR	RBI	BB	SO	AVG	OBP	SLG	PRO+	BR	/A	RC	SB	CS	SBR	FR	POS	TPR
1914	StL-N	12	9	1	6	2	0	0	3	0	1	.667	.700	1.111	441	4	4	7	1			-2	/C	0.2
1915	StL-N	46	39	2	8	0	1	0	6	4	8	.205	.295	.256	68	-1	-1	3	1			0	/C	0.0
1917	StL-N	1	1	0	0	0	0	0	0	0	0	.000	.000	.000	-99	-0	-0	0	0			-1	/C	0.0
Total	3	59	49	3	14	2	2	0	9	4	9	.286	.364	.408	133	2	2	11	2			-2	/C	0.2

YEAR	TM/L	G	AB	R	H	2B	3B	HR	RBI	BB	SO	AVG	OBP	SLG	PRO+	BR	/A	RC	SB	CS	SBR	FR	POS	TPR

■ BEN ROCHEFORT Rochefort, Bennett Harold (b: Bennett Harold Rochefort Gilbert)
b: 8/15/1896, Camden, N.J. d: 4/2/81, Red Bank, N.J. BL/TR, 6'2", 185 lbs. Deb: 10/03/14

| 1914 | Phi-A | 1 | 2 | 0 | 1 | 0 | 0 | 0 | 0 | 0 | 1 | .500 | .500 | .500 | 208 | 0 | 0 | 1 | 0 | | | 0 | /1 | 0.1 |

■ LOU ROCHELLI Rochelli, Louis Joseph b: 1/11/19, Williamson, Ill. BR/TR, 6'1", 175 lbs. Deb: 8/25/44

| 1944 | Bro-N | 5 | 17 | 0 | 3 | 0 | 1 | 0 | 2 | 2 | 6 | .176 | .263 | .294 | 58 | -1 | -1 | 1 | 0 | | | -0 | /2 | 0.0 |

■ LES ROCK Rock, Lester Henry (b: Lester Henry Schwarzrock) b: 8/19/12, Springfield, Minn. BL/TR, 6'2", 184 lbs. Deb: 9/11/36

| 1936 | Chi-A | 2 | 1 | 0 | 0 | 0 | 0 | 0 | 1 | 0 | 0 | .000 | .000 | .000 | -97 | -0 | -0 | 0 | 0 | 0 | 0 | 0 | /1 | 0.0 |

■ IKE ROCKENFIELD Rockenfield, Isaac Broc b: 11/3/1876, Omaha, Neb. d: 2/21/27, San Diego, Cal. BR/TR, 5'7", 150 lbs. Deb: 5/05/05

1905	StL-A	95	322	40	70	12	6	0	16	46		.217	.315	.255	88	-4	-2	33	11			-9	2	-1.1
1906	StL-A	27	89	3	21	4	0	0	8	1		.236	.244	.281	69	-4	-3	7	0			-5	2	-0.9
Total	2	122	411	43	91	16	6	0	24	47		.221	.301	.260	84	-7	-5	40	11			-14	2	-2.0

■ PAT ROCKETT Rockett, Patrick Edward b: 1/9/55, San Antonio, Tex. BR/TR, 5'11", 170 lbs. Deb: 9/17/76

1976	Atl-N	4	5	0	1	0	0	0	0	0	1	.200	.200	.200	13	-1	-1	0	0	0	0	-1	/S	0.0
1977	Atl-N	93	264	27	67	10	0	1	24	27	32	.254	.330	.303	64	-10	-14	26	1	2	-1	-11	S	-1.3
1978	Atl-N	55	142	6	20	2	0	0	4	13	12	.141	.213	.155	4	-18	-20	4	1	2	-1	-10	S	-2.8
Total	3	152	411	33	88	12	0	1	28	40	45	.214	.289	.251	43	-29	-34	31	2	4	-2	-21	S	-4.1

■ ANDRE RODGERS Rodgers, Kenneth Andre Ian "Andy" b: 12/2/34, Nassau, Bahamas BR/TR, 6'3", 200 lbs. Deb: 4/16/57

1957	NY-N	32	86	8	21	2	1	3	9	9	21	.244	.323	.395	92	-1	-1	12	0	0	0	5	S/3	0.5
1958	SF-N	22	63	7	13	3	1	2	11	4	14	.206	.254	.381	67	-3	-3	6	0	0	0	-3	S	-0.4
1959	SF-N	71	228	32	57	12	1	6	24	32	50	.250	.345	.390	98	-1	-0	32	2	1	0	-9	S	-0.6
1960	SF-N	81	217	22	53	8	5	2	22	24	44	.244	.328	.355	92	-4	-2	25	1	1	-0	-3	S3/1O	-0.4
1961	Chi-N	73	214	27	57	17	0	6	23	25	54	.266	.346	.430	103	1	1	31	1	1	-0	1	1S/O2	0.1
1962	Chi-N	138	461	40	128	20	8	5	44	44	93	.278	.344	.388	93	-2	-4	60	5	6	-2	7	*S/1	1.3
1963	Chi-N	150	516	51	118	17	4	5	33	65	90	.229	.325	.306	79	-9	-13	52	5	7	-3	-3	*S	-0.3
1964	Chi-N	129	448	50	107	17	3	12	46	53	88	.239	.319	.371	90	-3	-5	55	5	1	1	19	*S	2.5
1965	Pit-N	75	178	17	51	12	0	2	25	18	28	.287	.352	.388	108	2	2	24	2	1	0	-6	S3/12	0.0
1966	Pit-N	36	49	6	9	1	0	0	4	8	7	.184	.298	.204	43	-4	-4	3	0	1	-1	-1	/S3O1	-0.4
1967	Pit-N	47	61	8	14	3	0	2	4	8	18	.230	.319	.377	98	-0	-0	7	1	1	-0	2	/13S2	0.2
Total	11	854	2521	268	628	112	23	45	245	290	507	.249	.331	.365	90	-23	-29	305	22	20	-5	10	S/1302	2.5

■ BOB RODGERS Rodgers, Robert Leroy b: 8/16/38, Delaware, Ohio BB/TR, 6'2", 190 lbs. Deb: 9/08/61 MC

1961	LA-A	16	56	8	18	2	0	2	13	1	6	.321	.333	.464	99	1	-0	7	0	0	0	-1	C	0.0
1962	LA-A	155	565	65	146	34	6	6	61	45	68	.258	.313	.372	86	-14	-11	61	1	8	-5	0	*C	-0.7
1963	LA-A	100	300	24	70	6	0	4	23	29	35	.233	.305	.293	73	-12	-10	28	2	2	-1	-13	C	-2.3
1964	LA-A	148	514	38	125	18	3	4	54	40	71	.243	.303	.313	80	-19	-13	47	4	3	-1	12	*C	0.4
1965	Cal-A	132	411	33	86	14	3	1	32	35	61	.209	.276	.265	56	-24	-23	28	4	5	-2	4	*C	-1.1
1966	Cal-A	133	454	45	107	20	3	7	48	29	57	.236	.285	.339	81	-13	-12	41	3	4	-2	-4	*C	-1.1
1967	Cal-A	139	429	29	94	13	3	6	41	34	55	.219	.280	.305	76	-15	-13	35	1	4	-2	2	*C/O	-0.4
1968	Cal-A	91	258	13	49	6	0	1	14	16	48	.190	.245	.225	45	-17	-16	15	2	1	0	0	C	-1.4
1969	Cal-A	18	46	4	9	1	0	0	2	5	8	.196	.288	.217	46	-3	-3	3	0	0	0	0	C	-0.1
Total	9	932	3033	259	704	114	18	31	288	234	409	.232	.291	.312	74	-117	-101	265	17	27	-11	-1	C/O	-6.7

■ BILL RODGERS Rodgers, Wilbur Kincaid "Rawmeat Bill" b: 4/18/1887, Pleasant Ridge, O. d: 12/24/78, Goliad, Tex. BL/TR, 5'9.5", 170 lbs. Deb: 4/15/15

1915	Cle-A	16	45	8	14	2	0	0	7	8	7	.311	.415	.356	128	2	2	7	3	3	-1	-4	2	-0.2
	Bos-A	11	6	2	0	0	0	0	0	3	2	.000	.333	.000	-0	-1	-0	0	0			1	/2	0.1
	Yr	27	51	10	14	2	0	0	7	11	9	.275	.403	.314	115	2	2	7	3	3	-1	-3		-0.1
	Cin-N	72	213	20	51	13	4	0	12	11	29	.239	.299	.338	91	-2	-3	22	8	5	-1	5	2/S3O	0.3
1916	Cin-N	3	4	0	0	0	0	0	0	0	2	.000	.000	.000	-99	-1	-1	0	0			-0	/S	0.0
Total	2	102	268	30	65	15	4	0	19	22	40	.243	.316	.328	91	-1	-2	29	11	8		3	/2SO3	0.2

■ BILL RODGERS Rodgers, William Sherman b: 12/5/22, Harrisburg, Pa. BL/TL, 6', 162 lbs. Deb: 9/27/44

1944	Pit-N	2	4	1	1	0	0	0	0	0	1	.250	.250	.250	39	-0	-0	0	0			0	/O	0.0
1945	Pit-N	1	1	0	1	0	0	0	0	0	0	1.000	1.000	1.000	440	0	0	1	0			0	H	0.0
Total	2	3	5	1	2	0	0	0	0	0	1	.400	.400	.400	120	0	0	1	0			0	/OS	0.0

■ ERIC RODIN Rodin, Eric Chapman b: 2/5/30, Orange, N.J. BR/TR, 6'2", 215 lbs. Deb: 9/07/54

| 1954 | NY-N | 5 | 6 | 0 | 0 | 0 | 0 | 0 | 0 | 0 | 2 | .000 | .000 | .000 | -99 | -2 | -2 | 0 | 0 | 0 | 0 | 0 | /O | -0.1 |

■ AURELIO RODRIGUEZ Rodriguez, Aurelio (Ituarte) b: 12/28/47, Cananea, Sonora, Mex BR/TR, 5'10", 180 lbs. Deb: 9/01/67

1967	Cal-A	29	130	14	31	3	1	1	8	2	21	.238	.250	.300	64	-6	-6	10	1	0	0	5	3	0.0
1968	Cal-A	76	223	14	54	10	1	1	16	17	36	.242	.299	.309	88	-4	-3	19	0	2	-1	-6	3/2	-0.9
1969	Cal-A	159	561	47	130	17	2	7	49	32	88	.232	.276	.307	66	-29	-26	45	5	3	-0	8	*3	-1.5
1970	Cal-A	17	63	6	17	2	2	0	7	3	6	.270	.313	.365	90	-1	-1	6	0	1	-1	4	3	0.2
	Was-A	142	547	64	135	31	5	19	76	37	81	.247	.303	.426	104	-3	-1	67	15	5	2	13	*3/S	1.6
	Yr	159	610	70	152	33	7	19	83	40	87	.249	.304	.420	102	-4	-1	73	15	6	1	17		1.8
1971	Det-A	154	604	68	153	30	7	15	39	27	93	.253	.289	.401	90	-8	-10	65	4	6	-2	15	*3/S	-0.3
1972	*Det-A	153	601	65	142	23	5	13	56	28	104	.236	.273	.356	83	-12	-14	55	2	3	-1	24	*3/S	1.6
1973	Det-A	160	555	46	123	27	3	9	58	31	85	.222	.267	.330	63	-25	-30	48	3	1	0	10	*3/S	-2.2
1974	Det-A	159	571	54	127	23	5	5	49	26	70	.222	.258	.306	60	-29	-31	43	2	0	1	22	*3	-0.6
1975	Det-A	151	507	47	124	20	6	13	60	30	63	.245	.287	.385	85	-10	-12	55	1	1	-0	18	*3	0.8
1976	Det-A	128	480	40	115	13	2	8	50	19	61	.240	.270	.325	71	-17	-19	37	0	4	-2	13	*3	-0.7
1977	Det-A	96	306	30	67	14	1	10	32	16	36	.219	.258	.369	65	-14	-16	27	1	1	-0	16	3/S	-0.2
1978	Det-A	134	385	40	102	25	2	7	43	19	37	.265	.305	.395	82	-9	-5	44	0	1	-1	-7	*3	-1.3
1979	Det-A	106	343	27	87	18	0	5	36	11	40	.254	.279	.350	66	-16	-17	31	0	2	-1	6	*3/1	-0.7
1980	SD-N	89	175	7	35	7	2	2	13	6	26	.200	.227	.297	48	-13	-12	11	1	1	-0	10	3/S	-0.1
	*NY-A	52	164	14	36	6	1	3	14	7	35	.220	.251	.323	57	-10	-10	12	0	0	0	-5	3/2	-1.4
1981	*NY-A	27	52	4	18	2	0	2	8	2	10	.346	.370	.500	151	3	3	9	0	0	0	4	3/21D	0.8
1982	Chi-A	118	257	24	62	15	1	3	31	11	35	.241	.275	.342	68	-11	-11	23	0	1	-0	14	*3/2S	0.0
1983	Bal-A	45	67	0	8	0	0	0	2	0	13	.119	.132	.119	-31	-12	-12	1	0	0	0	-0	*3	-0.9
	*Chi-A	22	20	1	4	1	0	1	1	0	3	.200	.200	.400	58	-1	-1	1	0	0	0	4	3	0.3
	Yr	67	87	1	12	1	0	1	3	0	16	.138	.148	.184	-9	-13	-13	2	0	0	0	6		-0.6
Total	17	2017	6611	612	1570	287	46	124	648	324	943	.237	.276	.351	75	-223	-235	610	35	31	-8	168	*3/S2D1	-5.8

■ EDWIN RODRIGUEZ Rodriguez, Edwin (Morales) b: 8/14/60, Ponce, P.R. BR/TR, 5'11", 175 lbs. Deb: 9/28/82

1982	NY-A	3	9	2	3	0	0	0	1	1	1	.333	.400	.333	106	0	0	1	0	0	0	1	/2	0.1
1983	SD-N	7	12	1	2	1	0	0	0	1	3	.167	.231	.250	34	-1	-1	1	0	0	0	-1	/2S3	-0.1
1985	SD-N	1	1	0	0	0	0	0	0	0	0	.000	.000	.000	-99	-0	-0	0	0	0	0	0	/H	0.0
Total	3	11	22	3	5	1	0	0	1	2	4	.227	.292	.273	58	-1	-1	2	0	0	0	0	/2S3	0.0

YEAR	TM/L	G	AB	R	H	2B	3B	HR	RBI	BB	SO	AVG	OBP	SLG	PRO+	BR	/A	RC	SB	CS	SBR	FR	POS	TPR

■ ELLIE RODRIGUEZ
Rodriguez, Eliseo (Delgado) b: 5/24/46, Fajardo, P.R. BR/TR, 5'11", 185 lbs. Deb: 5/26/68

YEAR	TM/L	G	AB	R	H	2B	3B	HR	RBI	BB	SO	AVG	OBP	SLG	PRO+	BR	/A	RC	SB	CS	SBR	FR	POS	TPR
1968	NY-A	9	24	1	5	0	0	0	1	3	3	.208	.296	.208	57	-1	-1	2	0	0	0	0	/C	0.0
1969	KC-A	95	267	27	63	10	0	2	20	31	26	.236	.333	.296	77	-7	-7	27	3	2	-0	-9	C	-1.0
1970	KC-A	80	231	25	52	8	2	1	15	27	35	.225	.317	.290	68	-9	-9	21	2	1	0	12	C	0.4
1971	Mil-A	115	319	28	67	10	1	1	30	41	51	.210	.315	.257	64	-14	-13	27	1	1	-0	6	*C	-0.2
1972	Mil-A	116	355	31	101	14	2	2	35	52	43	.285	.386	.352	123	12	13	51	1	4	-2	-12	*C	0.0
1973	Mil-A	94	290	30	78	8	1	0	30	41	28	.269	.378	.303	96	0	1	36	4	3	-1	4	CD	0.6
1974	Cal-A	140	395	48	100	20	0	7	36	69	56	.253	.376	.357	119	9	12	56	4	5	-2	-8	*C/D	0.7
1975	Cal-A	90	226	20	53	6	0	3	27	49	37	.235	.384	.301	103	2	4	30	2	2	-1	-8	C	-0.1
1976	LA-N	36	66	10	14	0	0	0	9	19	12	.212	.409	.212	82	-0	-0	8	0	0	0	5	C	0.7
Total	9	775	2173	220	533	76	6	16	203	332	291	.245	.359	.308	94	-8	-0	258	17	18	-6	-9	C/D	1.1

■ HECTOR RODRIGUEZ
Rodriguez, Hector Antonio (Ordenana) b: 6/13/20, Alquizar, Cuba BR/TR, 5'8", 165 lbs. Deb: 4/15/52

YEAR	TM/L	G	AB	R	H	2B	3B	HR	RBI	BB	SO	AVG	OBP	SLG	PRO+	BR	/A	RC	SB	CS	SBR	FR	POS	TPR
1952	Chi-A	124	407	55	108	14	0	1	40	47	22	.265	.346	.307	82	-8	-8	45	7	6	-2	3	*3	-0.7

■ JOSE RODRIGUEZ
Rodriguez, Jose "El Hombre Goma" b: 2/23/1894, Havana, Cuba d: 1/21/53, Havana, Cuba BR/TR, 5'8", 150 lbs. Deb: 10/05/16

YEAR	TM/L	G	AB	R	H	2B	3B	HR	RBI	BB	SO	AVG	OBP	SLG	PRO+	BR	/A	RC	SB	CS	SBR	FR	POS	TPR
1916	NY-N	1	0	0	0	0	0	0	0	0	0	—	—	—	—	0	0	0	0			0	R	0.0
1917	NY-N	7	20	2	4	0	1	0	2	2	1	.200	.273	.300	78	-1	-1	2	2			-1	/1	-0.1
1918	NY-N	50	125	15	20	0	2	0	15	12	3	.160	.239	.192	33	-10	-10	7	6			4	2/13	-0.3
Total	3	58	145	17	24	0	3	0	17	14	4	.166	.244	.207	39	-10	-10	9	8			3	/213	-0.4

■ RUBEN RODRIGUEZ
Rodriguez, Ruben Dario (Martinez) b: 8/4/64, Cabrera, D.R. BR/TR, 6'3", 190 lbs. Deb: 9/17/86

YEAR	TM/L	G	AB	R	H	2B	3B	HR	RBI	BB	SO	AVG	OBP	SLG	PRO+	BR	/A	RC	SB	CS	SBR	FR	POS	TPR
1986	Pit-N	2	3	0	0	0	0	0	0	0	1	.000	.000	.000	-98	-1	-1	0	0	0	0	1	/C	0.0
1988	Pit-N	2	5	1	1	0	1	0	1	0	2	.200	.200	.600	123	0	0	1	0	0	0	0	/C	0.0
Total	2	4	8	1	1	0	1	0	1	0	3	.125	.125	.375	36	-1	-1	1	0	0	0	1	/C	0.0

■ VIC RODRIGUEZ
Rodriguez, Victor Manuel (Rivera) b: 7/14/61, New York, N.Y. BR/TR, 5'11", 173 lbs. Deb: 9/05/84

YEAR	TM/L	G	AB	R	H	2B	3B	HR	RBI	BB	SO	AVG	OBP	SLG	PRO+	BR	/A	RC	SB	CS	SBR	FR	POS	TPR
1984	Bal-A	11	17	4	7	3	0	0	2	0	2	.412	.412	.588	177	2	2	4	0	0	0	3	/2D	0.4
1989	Min-A	6	11	2	5	2	0	0	0	0	1	.455	.455	.636	191	1	1	3	0	0	0	1	/3	0.2
Total	2	17	28	6	12	5	0	0	2	0	3	.429	.429	.607	183	3	3	7	0	0	0	3	/23D	0.6

■ GARY ROENICKE
Roenicke, Gary Steven b: 12/5/54, Covina, Cal. BR/TR, 6'3", 205 lbs. Deb: 6/08/76

YEAR	TM/L	G	AB	R	H	2B	3B	HR	RBI	BB	SO	AVG	OBP	SLG	PRO+	BR	/A	RC	SB	CS	SBR	FR	POS	TPR
1976	Mon-N	29	90	9	20	3	1	2	5	4	18	.222	.263	.344	69	-4	-4	8	0	0	0	-1	O	-0.6
1978	Bal-A	27	58	5	15	3	0	3	15	8	3	.259	.358	.466	138	2	3	9	0	1	-1	-3	O	-0.0
1979	*Bal-A	133	376	60	98	16	1	25	64	61	74	.261	.381	.508	143	21	23	73	1	3	-2	-2	*O	1.4
1980	Bal-A	118	297	40	71	13	0	10	28	41	49	.239	.343	.384	100	0	1	40	2	0	1	-7	*O	-0.7
1981	Bal-A	85	219	31	59	16	0	3	20	23	29	.269	.344	.384	110	3	3	26	1	2	-1	-3	O	-0.2
1982	Bal-A	137	393	58	106	25	1	21	74	70	73	.270	.392	.499	143	25	25	79	6	7	-2	3	*O1	2.2
1983	*Bal-A	115	323	45	84	13	0	19	64	30	35	.260	.331	.477	121	8	9	49	2	2	-1	-8	*O/13D	0.0
1984	Bal-A	121	326	36	73	19	1	10	44	58	43	.224	.348	.380	104	2	3	45	1	2	-1	-9	*O	-1.0
1985	Bal-A	114	225	36	49	9	0	15	43	44	36	.218	.346	.458	121	6	7	37	2	2	-1	5	OD	1.0
1986	NY-A	69	136	11	36	5	0	3	18	27	30	.265	.390	.368	109	3	3	22	1	1	-0	-3	OD/31	0.2
1987	Atl-N	67	151	25	33	8	0	9	28	32	23	.219	.359	.450	107	3	3	26	0	0	0	-3	O/1	-0.2
1988	Atl-N	49	114	11	26	5	0	1	7	8	15	.228	.279	.298	63	-5	-6	9	0	0	0	-2	O/1	-0.9
Total	12	1064	2708	367	670	135	4	121	410	406	428	.247	.354	.434	117	65	69	424	16	20	-7	-29	O/D13	1.2

■ RON ROENICKE
Roenicke, Ronald Jon b: 8/19/56, Covina, Cal. BB/TL, 6', 180 lbs. Deb: 9/02/81

YEAR	TM/L	G	AB	R	H	2B	3B	HR	RBI	BB	SO	AVG	OBP	SLG	PRO+	BR	/A	RC	SB	CS	SBR	FR	POS	TPR
1981	LA-N	22	47	6	11	1	0	0	6	8	12	.234	.321	.234	62	-2	-2	4	1	1	-0	3	O	0.0
1982	LA-N	109	143	18	37	8	0	1	12	21	32	.259	.361	.336	99	0	1	20	5	0	2	-2	O	0.0
1983	LA-N	81	145	12	32	4	0	2	12	14	26	.221	.289	.290	61	-8	-7	12	3	2	-0	-0	O	-0.9
	Sea-A	59	198	23	50	12	0	4	23	33	22	.253	.365	.374	100	2	1	30	6	2	1	10	O/1D	1.1
1984	*SD-N	12	20	4	6	1	0	1	2	2	5	.300	.364	.500	141	1	1	4	0	0	0	-0	O	0.0
1985	SF-N	65	133	23	34	9	1	3	13	35	27	.256	.411	.406	136	7	8	26	6	2	1	-2	O	0.6
1986	Phi-N	102	275	42	68	13	1	5	42	61	52	.247	.384	.356	102	5	3	42	2	2	-1	3	O	0.4
1987	Phi-N	63	78	9	13	3	1	1	4	14	15	.167	.293	.269	49	-5	-6	7	1	0	0	-0	O	-0.6
1988	Cin-N	14	37	4	5	1	0	0	5	4	8	.135	.238	.162	16	-4	-4	2	0	0	0	-1	O	-0.5
Total	8	527	1076	141	256	51	3	17	113	190	195	.238	.355	.338	92	-4	-5	146	24	9	2	10	O/1D	1.1

■ OSCAR ROETTGER
Roettger, Oscar Frederick Louis "Okkie" b: 2/19/1900, St.Louis, Mo. d: 7/4/86, St.Louis, Mo. BR/TR, 6', 170 lbs. Deb: 7/07/23

YEAR	TM/L	G	AB	R	H	2B	3B	HR	RBI	BB	SO	AVG	OBP	SLG	PRO+	BR	/A	RC	SB	CS	SBR	FR	POS	TPR
1923	NY-A	5	2	0	0	0	0	0	0	0	0	.000	.000	.000	-98	-1	-1	0	0	0	0	0	/P	0.0
1924	NY-A	1	0	0	0	0	0	0	0	0	0	—	—	—	—	0	0	0	0	0	0	0	/P	0.0
1927	Bro-N	5	4	0	0	0	0	0	0	1	1	.000	.333	.000	-4	-0	-0	0	0	0	0	0	/O	0.0
1932	Phi-A	26	60	7	14	1	0	0	6	5	4	.233	.292	.250	40	-5	-5	5	0	0	0	-1	1	-0.7
Total	4	37	66	7	14	1	0	0	6	6	5	.212	.288	.227	34	-6	-6	5	0	0	0	-1	/1PO	-0.7

■ WALLY ROETTGER
Roettger, Walter Henry b: 8/28/02, St.Louis, Mo. d: 9/14/51, Champaign, Ill. BR/TR, 6'1.5", 190 lbs. Deb: 5/01/27

YEAR	TM/L	G	AB	R	H	2B	3B	HR	RBI	BB	SO	AVG	OBP	SLG	PRO+	BR	/A	RC	SB	CS	SBR	FR	POS	TPR
1927	StL-N	5	1	0	0	0	0	0	0	1	0	.000	.500	.000	42	0	0	0	0			0	/O	0.0
1928	StL-N	68	261	27	89	17	4	6	44	10	22	.341	.372	.506	125	9	9	47	2			-5	O	0.2
1929	StL-N	79	269	27	68	11	3	3	42	13	27	.253	.287	.349	56	-19	-19	26	0			-4	O	-2.6
1930	NY-N	121	420	51	119	15	5	5	51	25	29	.283	.330	.379	72	-20	-19	51	1			-9	*O	-3.1
1931	Cin-N	44	185	25	65	11	4	1	20	7	9	.351	.378	.470	135	7	8	33	1			-3	O	0.3
	*StL-N	45	151	16	43	12	2	0	17	9	14	.285	.337	.391	92	-1	-2	21	0			-5	O	-0.8
	Yr	89	336	41	108	23	6	1	37	16	23	.321	.360	.435	114	6	6	53	1			-8		-0.5
1932	Cin-N	106	347	26	96	18	3	3	43	23	24	.277	.323	.372	89	-7	-5	43	0			-2	O	-1.2
1933	Cin-N	84	209	13	50	7	1	1	17	8	10	.239	.267	.297	62	-11	-10	15	0			3	O	-1.1
1934	Pit-N	47	106	7	26	5	1	0	11	3	8	.245	.266	.311	53	-7	-7	8	0			2	O	-0.6
Total	8	599	1949	192	556	96	23	19	245	99	143	.285	.324	.387	85	-48	-45	244	4			-22	O	-8.9

■ ED ROETZ
Roetz, Edward Bernard b: 8/6/05, Philadelphia, Pa. d: 3/16/65, Philadelphia, Pa. BR/TR, 5'10", 160 lbs. Deb: 5/26/29

YEAR	TM/L	G	AB	R	H	2B	3B	HR	RBI	BB	SO	AVG	OBP	SLG	PRO+	BR	/A	RC	SB	CS	SBR	FR	POS	TPR
1929	StL-A	16	45	7	11	4	1	0	5	4	6	.244	.306	.378	72	-2	-2	5	0	0	0	-1	/S123	-0.2

■ BILLY ROGELL
Rogell, William George b: 11/24/04, Springfield, Ill. BB/TR, 5'10.5", 163 lbs. Deb: 4/14/25

YEAR	TM/L	G	AB	R	H	2B	3B	HR	RBI	BB	SO	AVG	OBP	SLG	PRO+	BR	/A	RC	SB	CS	SBR	FR	POS	TPR
1925	Bos-A	58	169	12	33	5	1	0	17	11	17	.195	.244	.237	22	-20	-20	10	0	3	-2	6	2/S	-1.1
1927	Bos-A	82	207	35	55	14	6	2	28	24	28	.266	.342	.420	99	-1	-1	29	3	1	0	6	3/2O	0.8
1928	Bos-A	102	296	33	69	10	4	0	29	22	47	.233	.295	.294	56	-19	-18	26	2	6	-3	-13	S2/O3	-2.6
1930	Det-A	54	144	20	24	4	2	0	9	15	23	.167	.250	.222	20	-17	-18	9	1	2	-1	4	S3/O	-0.9
1931	Det-A	48	185	21	56	12	3	2	24	24	17	.303	.383	.432	110	4	3	30	8	8	-2	11	S	1.5
1932	Det-A	144	554	88	150	29	6	9	61	50	38	.271	.332	.394	84	-11	-14	74	14	6	1	8	*S/3	0.5
1933	Det-A	155	587	67	173	42	11	0	57	79	33	.295	.384	.404	106	9	7	93	6	9	-4	20	*S	3.3
1934	*Det-A	154	592	114	175	32	8	3	100	74	36	.296	.374	.392	97	-1	-1	92	13	3	2	19	*S	2.0
1935	*Det-A	150	560	88	154	23	11	6	71	80	29	.275	.367	.387	99	-3	0	83	3	6	-3	12	*S	1.6
1936	Det-A	146	585	85	160	27	5	6	68	73	44	.274	.357	.368	79	-18	-19	80	14	10	-2	-1	*S/3	-0.9
1937	Det-A	146	536	85	148	30	7	8	64	83	46	.276	.376	.403	94	-1	-3	86	5	5	-2	2	*S	0.1
1938	Det-A	136	501	76	130	22	3	3	55	86	37	.259	.373	.353	78	-11	-15	73	9	5	2	8	*S	0.1
1939	Det-A	74	174	24	40	6	3	2	23	26	14	.230	.330	.333	65	-8	-10	21	3	1	0	2	S3/2	-0.2

YEAR	TM/L	G	AB	R	H	2B	3B	HR	RBI	BB	SO	AVG	OBP	SLG	PRO+	BR	/A	RC	SB	CS	SBR	FR	POS	TPR
1940	Chi-N	33	59	7	8	0	0	1	3	2	8	.136	.164	.186	-4	-8	-8	2	1			-5	S/32	-1.1
Total	14	1482	5149	755	1375	256	75	42	609	649	416	.267	.351	.370	84	-106	-116	707	82	62		68	*S3/2O	3.5

■ EMMETT ROGERS   Rogers, Emmett b: 1865, Rome, N.Y. BB , 5'10", 165 lbs. Deb: 4/19/1890

YEAR	TM/L	G	AB	R	H	2B	3B	HR	RBI	BB	SO	AVG	OBP	SLG	PRO+	BR	/A	RC	SB	CS	SBR	FR	POS	TPR
1890	Tol-a	35	110	18	19	3	3	0		14		.173	.266	.255	54	-6	-6	8	2			9	C/O	0.6

■ FRALEY ROGERS   Rogers, Fraley W. b: 1850, Brooklyn, N.Y. d: 5/10/1881, New York, N.Y. 5'8", 184 lbs. Deb: 4/30/1872

YEAR	TM/L	G	AB	R	H	2B	3B	HR	RBI	BB	SO	AVG	OBP	SLG	PRO+	BR	/A	RC	SB	CS	SBR	FR	POS	TPR
1872	Bos-n	45	204	39	58	10	1	1		1		.284	.288	.358	93	-1	-3	22					O/1	0.0
1873	Bos-n	1	6	1	2	2	0	0		0		.333	.333	.667	172	1	0	1					/O	0.0
Total	2 n	46	210	40	60	12	1	1		1		.286	.289	.367	95	-0	-3	23					/O1	0.0

■ JIM ROGERS   Rogers, James F. b: 4/9/1872, Hartford, Conn. 5'7.5", 180 lbs. Deb: 4/17/1896 M

YEAR	TM/L	G	AB	R	H	2B	3B	HR	RBI	BB	SO	AVG	OBP	SLG	PRO+	BR	/A	RC	SB	CS	SBR	FR	POS	TPR
1896	Was-N	38	154	21	43	6	4	1	30	10	9	.279	.323	.390	89	-3	-3	21	3			-6	3/2O	-0.5
	Lou-N	72	290	39	75	8	6	0	38	15	14	.259	.297	.328	69	-14	-12	33	13			-2	1S	-1.0
	Yr	110	444	60	118	14	10	1	68	25	23	.266	.306	.349	76	-17	-15	54	16			-8		-1.5
1897	Lou-N	41	150	22	22	3	2	2	22	22		.147	.260	.233	34	-14	-14	10	4			-5	2/1M	-1.3
Total	2	151	594	82	140	17	12	3	90	47	23	.236	.294	.320	65	-32	-29	64	20			-13	/123SO	-2.8

■ JAY ROGERS   Rogers, Jay Lewis b: 8/3/1888, Sandusky, N.Y. d: 7/1/64, Carlisle, N.Y. BR/TR, 5'11.5", 178 lbs. Deb: 5/22/14

YEAR	TM/L	G	AB	R	H	2B	3B	HR	RBI	BB	SO	AVG	OBP	SLG	PRO+	BR	/A	RC	SB	CS	SBR	FR	POS	TPR
1914	NY-A	5	8	0	0	0	0	0	0	0	4	.000	.000	.000	-99	-2	-2	0	0			0	/C	-0.1

■ PACKY ROGERS   Rogers, Stanley Frank (b: Stanley Frank Hazinski) b: 4/26/13, Swoyersville, Pa. BR/TR, 5'8", 175 lbs. Deb: 7/12/38

YEAR	TM/L	G	AB	R	H	2B	3B	HR	RBI	BB	SO	AVG	OBP	SLG	PRO+	BR	/A	RC	SB	CS	SBR	FR	POS	TPR
1938	Bro-N	23	37	3	7	1	1	0	5	6		.189	.302	.270	57	-2	-2	3	0			-0	/S32O	-0.1

■ MIKE ROGODZINSKI   Rogodzinski, Michael George b: 2/22/48, Evanston, Ill. BL/TR, 6', 185 lbs. Deb: 5/04/73

YEAR	TM/L	G	AB	R	H	2B	3B	HR	RBI	BB	SO	AVG	OBP	SLG	PRO+	BR	/A	RC	SB	CS	SBR	FR	POS	TPR
1973	Phi-N	66	80	13	19	3	0	2	7	12	19	.237	.337	.350	88	-1	-1	10	0	0	0	0	O	-0.1
1974	Phi-N	17	15	1	1	0	0	0	1	2	3	.067	.176	.067	-29	-3	-3	0	0	0	0	0	/O	-0.2
1975	Phi-N	16	19	3	5	1	0	0	4	3	2	.263	.364	.316	86	-0	-0	2	0	1	-1	-1	/O	-0.1
Total	3	99	114	17	25	4	0	2	12	17	24	.219	.321	.307	73	-4	-4	12	0	1	-1	-1	/O	-0.4

■ DAVE ROHDE   Rohde, David Grant b: 5/8/64, Los Altos, Cal. BR/TR, 6'2", 180 lbs. Deb: 4/09/90

YEAR	TM/L	G	AB	R	H	2B	3B	HR	RBI	BB	SO	AVG	OBP	SLG	PRO+	BR	/A	RC	SB	CS	SBR	FR	POS	TPR
1990	Hou-N	58	98	8	18	4	0	0	5	9	20	.184	.286	.224	43	-7	-7	7	0	0	0	0	2/3S	-0.6

■ GEORGE ROHE   Rohe, George Anthony "Whitey" b: 9/15/1875, Cincinnati, Ohio d: 6/10/57, Cincinnati, Ohio BR/TR, 5'9", 165 lbs. Deb: 5/07/01

YEAR	TM/L	G	AB	R	H	2B	3B	HR	RBI	BB	SO	AVG	OBP	SLG	PRO+	BR	/A	RC	SB	CS	SBR	FR	POS	TPR
1901	Bal-A	14	36	7	10	2	0	0	4	5		.278	.381	.333	97	0	0	5	1			-2	/13	-0.2
1905	Chi-A	34	113	14	24	1	0	1	12	12		.212	.288	.248	75	-3	-3	9	2			-4	23	-0.6
1906	*Chi-A	77	225	14	58	5	1	0	25	16		.258	.307	.289	91	-3	-2	24	8			2	3/2O	0.4
1907	Chi-A	144	494	46	105	11	2	2	51	39		.213	.270	.255	72	-16	-14	42	16			-5	32S	-1.5
Total	4	269	868	81	197	19	3	3	92	72		.227	.287	.266	79	-21	-19	80	27			-9	3/2S10	-1.9

■ DAN ROHN   Rohn, Daniel Jay b: 1/10/56, Alpena, Mich. BL/TR, 5'7", 165 lbs. Deb: 9/02/83

YEAR	TM/L	G	AB	R	H	2B	3B	HR	RBI	BB	SO	AVG	OBP	SLG	PRO+	BR	/A	RC	SB	CS	SBR	FR	POS	TPR
1983	Chi-N	23	31	3	12	3	2	0	6	2	2	.387	.424	.613	176	3	3	8	1	0	0	-0	/2S	0.4
1984	Chi-N	25	31	1	4	0	0	1	3	1	6	.129	.156	.226	6	-4	-4	1	0	0	0	0	/32S	-0.3
1986	Cle-A	6	10	1	2	0	0	0	2	1	1	.200	.273	.200	32	-1	-1	1	0	0	0	1	/23S	0.0
Total	3	54	72	5	18	3	2	1	11	4	9	.250	.289	.389	82	-1	-2	10	1	0	0	1	/23S	0.1

■ RAY ROHWER   Rohwer, Ray b: 6/5/1895, Dixon, Cal. d: 1/24/88, Davis, Cal. BL/TL, 5'10", 155 lbs. Deb: 4/13/21

YEAR	TM/L	G	AB	R	H	2B	3B	HR	RBI	BB	SO	AVG	OBP	SLG	PRO+	BR	/A	RC	SB	CS	SBR	FR	POS	TPR
1921	Pit-N	30	40	6	10	3	2	0	6	4	8	.250	.318	.425	93	-0	-1	5	0	1	-1	1	O	0.0
1922	Pit-N	53	129	19	38	6	3	3	22	10	17	.295	.350	.457	105	1	1	21	1	0	0	-0	O	0.0
Total	2	83	169	25	48	9	5	3	28	14	25	.284	.342	.450	102	1	0	26	1	1	-0	1	/O	0.0

■ TONY ROIG   Roig, Anton Ambrose b: 12/23/27, New Orleans, La. BR/TR, 6'1", 180 lbs. Deb: 9/13/53

YEAR	TM/L	G	AB	R	H	2B	3B	HR	RBI	BB	SO	AVG	OBP	SLG	PRO+	BR	/A	RC	SB	CS	SBR	FR	POS	TPR
1953	Was-A	3	8	0	1	1	0	0	0	0	1	.125	.125	.250	-1	-1	-1	0	0	0	0	2	/2	0.0
1955	Was-A	29	57	3	13	1	1	0	4	2	15	.228	.254	.281	46	-5	-4	4	0	0	0	1	S/32	0.0
1956	Was-A	44	119	11	25	5	2	0	7	20	29	.210	.324	.286	62	-6	-6	11	2	0	1	7	2S	0.5
Total	3	76	184	14	39	7	3	0	11	22	45	.212	.296	.283	55	-12	-12	15	2	0	1	9	/S23	0.5

■ COOKIE ROJAS   Rojas, Octavio Victor (Rivas) b: 3/6/39, Havana, Cuba BR/TR, 5'10", 160 lbs. Deb: 4/10/62 MC

YEAR	TM/L	G	AB	R	H	2B	3B	HR	RBI	BB	SO	AVG	OBP	SLG	PRO+	BR	/A	RC	SB	CS	SBR	FR	POS	TPR
1962	Cin-N	39	86	9	19	2	0	0	6	9	4	.221	.302	.244	47	-6	-6	6	1	1	-0	-2	2/3	-0.5
1963	Phi-N	64	77	18	17	0	1	1	2	3	8	.221	.259	.286	57	-4	-4	5	4	1	1	17	2/O	1.6
1964	Phi-N	109	340	58	99	19	5	2	31	22	17	.291	.338	.394	107	2	3	42	1	3	-2	-6	O2S/C3	-0.3
1965	Phi-N	142	521	78	158	25	3	3	42	42	33	.303	.359	.380	110	7	8	71	5	5	-2	1	2OS/C1	1.2
1966	Phi-N	156	626	77	168	18	1	6	55	35	46	.268	.311	.329	79	-18	-18	63	4	6	-0	-9	*2O/S	-0.9
1967	Phi-N	147	528	60	137	21	2	4	45	30	58	.259	.299	.330	79	-14	-15	50	8	4	0	-3	*2/OCSP3	-0.9
1968	Phi-N	152	621	53	144	19	0	9	48	16	55	.232	.251	.306	67	-26	-26	43	4	8	-4	11	*2/C	-1.2
1969	Phi-N	110	391	35	89	11	1	4	30	23	28	.228	.272	.292	60	-22	-21	28	1	6	-3	-3	2/O	-2.0
1970	StL-N	23	47	2	5	0	0	0	2	3	4	.106	.176	.106	-22	-8	-8	1	0	0		1	2/OS	-0.5
	KC-A	98	384	36	100	13	3	2	28	20	29	.260	.297	.326	72	-15	-15	34	3	7	-3	-1	2	-0.9
1971	KC-A	115	414	56	124	22	2	6	59	39	35	.300	.363	.406	118	10	10	60	8	3	1	-12	*2/SO	0.4
1972	KC-A	137	487	49	127	25	0	3	53	41	35	.261	.319	.331	94	-4	-3	47	2	8	-2	-2	*2/3S	0.0
1973	KC-A	139	551	78	152	29	3	6	69	37	38	.276	.323	.372	88	-4	-9	65	18	4	3	9	*2	0.8
1974	KC-A	144	542	52	147	17	1	6	60	30	43	.271	.313	.339	83	-9	-13	52	8	4	0	-24	*2	-3.2
1975	KC-A	120	406	34	103	18	2	2	37	30	24	.254	.305	.323	75	-12	-13	37	4	5	-2	-15	*2/D	-2.7
1976	*KC-A	63	132	11	32	6	0	0	16	8	15	.242	.286	.288	68	-5	-5	11	2	0	1	-12	2/31D	-1.5
1977	*KC-A	64	156	8	39	9	1	0	10	8	17	.250	.287	.321	65	-8	-8	12	1	3	-2	3	32/D	-0.4
Total	16	1822	6309	714	1660	254	25	54	593	396	489	.263	.309	.337	83	-137	-145	630	74	68	-19	-46	*2O/3SDC1	-12.5

■ STAN ROJEK   Rojek, Stanley Andrew b: 4/21/19, N.Tonawanda, N.Y. BR/TR, 5'10", 170 lbs. Deb: 9/22/42

YEAR	TM/L	G	AB	R	H	2B	3B	HR	RBI	BB	SO	AVG	OBP	SLG	PRO+	BR	/A	RC	SB	CS	SBR	FR	POS	TPR
1942	Bro-N	1	0	1	0	0	0	0	0	0	0	—	—	—	—	0	0	0	0			0	R	0.0
1946	Bro-N	45	47	11	13	2	1	0	2	4	1	.277	.333	.362	96	-0	-0	5	1			5	S/23	0.7
1947	Bro-N	32	80	7	21	0	1	0	7	7	3	.262	.322	.287	61	-4	-4	7	1			8	S/32	0.5
1948	Pit-N	156	641	85	186	27	5	4	51	61	41	.290	.355	.367	94	-3	-5	87	24			-8	*S	0.4
1949	Pit-N	144	557	72	136	19	2	0	31	50	31	.244	.309	.285	59	-30	-32	52	4			1	*S	-1.5
1950	Pit-N	76	230	28	59	12	1	0	17	18	13	.257	.313	.317	64	-11	-12	23	2			-15	S/2	-1.9
1951	Pit-N	8	16	0	3	0	0	0	0	0	1	.188	.188	.188	1	-2	-2	1	0	0	0	-1	/S	-0.2
	StL-N	51	186	21	51	7	3	0	14	10	10	.274	.318	.344	78	-6	-6	19	0	3	-2	1	S	-0.2
	Yr	59	202	21	54	7	3	0	14	10	11	.267	.308	.332	72	-8	-8	19	0	3	-2	-1		-0.4
1952	StL-A	9	7	0	1	0	0	0	0	2	0	.143	.333	.143	35	-1	-1	0	0	0	0	2	/S2	0.1
Total	8	522	1764	225	470	67	13	4	122	152	100	.266	.327	.326	74	-57	-62	193	32	3		-8	S/23	-2.1

■ RED ROLFE   Rolfe, Robert Abial b: 10/17/08, Penacook, N.H. d: 7/8/69, Guilford, N.H. BL/TR, 5'11.5", 170 lbs. Deb: 6/29/31 MC

YEAR	TM/L	G	AB	R	H	2B	3B	HR	RBI	BB	SO	AVG	OBP	SLG	PRO+	BR	/A	RC	SB	CS	SBR	FR	POS	TPR
1931	NY-A	1	0	0	0	0	0	0	0	0	0	—	—	—	—	0	0	0	0	0	0	-0	/S	0.0
1934	NY-A	89	279	54	80	13	2	0	18	26	16	.287	.348	.348	86	-8	-5	34	4	3	1	-6	*S	-0.1
1935	NY-A	149	639	108	192	33	9	5	67	57	39	.300	.361	.404	103	-2	3	95	7	3	-1	-6	*3S	-0.1
1936	*NY-A	135	568	116	181	39	**15**	10	70	68	38	.319	.392	.493	121	15	18	113	3	0	1	3	*3	2.0
1937	*NY-A	154	648	143	179	34	10	4	62	90	53	.276	.365	.378	87	-11	-11	94	4	2	0	5	*3	-0.2

YEAR	TM/L	G	AB	R	H	2B	3B	HR	RBI	BB	SO	AVG	OBP	SLG	PRO+	BR	/A	RC	SB	CS	SBR	FR	POS	TPR
1938	*NY-A	151	631	132	196	36	8	10	80	74	44	.311	.386	.441	107	7	8	113	13	1	3	-7	*3	0.8
1939	*NY-A	152	648	**139**	**213**	**46**	10	14	80	81	41	.329	.404	.495	131	29	30	134	7	6	-2	-15	*3	1.0
1940	NY-A	139	588	102	147	26	6	10	53	50	48	.250	.311	.366	78	-23	-19	71	4	2	0	-1	*3	-1.0
1941	*NY-A	136	561	106	148	22	5	8	42	57	38	.264	.332	.364	85	-13	-12	73	3	2	-0	-9	*3	-1.4
1942	*NY-A	69	265	42	58	8	2	8	25	23	18	.219	.281	.355	80	-9	-8	28	1	1	-0	5	3	-0.2
Total	10	1175	4827	942	1394	257	67	69	497	526	335	.289	.360	.413	100	-15	3	756	44	20	1	-21	*3/S	1.0

■ **RAY ROLLING**   Rolling, Raymond Copeland b: 9/8/1886, Martinsburg, Mo. d: 8/25/66, St.Paul, Minn. BR/TR, 5'10.5", 160 lbs. Deb: 9/06/12

YEAR	TM/L	G	AB	R	H	2B	3B	HR	RBI	BB	SO	AVG	OBP	SLG	PRO+	BR	/A	RC	SB	CS	SBR	FR	POS	TPR
1912	StL-N	5	15	0	3	0	0	0	0	0	5	.200	.200	.200	10	-2	-2	1	0			-0	/2	-0.1

■ **RED ROLLINGS**   Rollings, William Russell b: 3/21/04, Mobile, Ala. d: 12/31/64, Mobile, Ala. BL/TR, 5'11", 167 lbs. Deb: 4/17/27

YEAR	TM/L	G	AB	R	H	2B	3B	HR	RBI	BB	SO	AVG	OBP	SLG	PRO+	BR	/A	RC	SB	CS	SBR	FR	POS	TPR
1927	Bos-A	82	184	19	49	4	1	0	9	12	10	.266	.325	.299	64	-10	-9	18	3	1	0	-5	31/2	-1.0
1928	Bos-A	50	48	7	11	3	1	0	9	6	8	.229	.315	.333	72	-2	-2	5	0	0	0	-2	/1203	-0.4
1930	Bos-N	52	123	10	29	6	0	0	10	9	5	.236	.288	.285	40	-12	-11	10	2			3	32	-0.5
Total	3	184	355	36	89	13	2	0	28	27	23	.251	.311	.299	57	-24	-23	34	5	1		-4	/3210	-1.9

■ **RICH ROLLINS**   Rollins, Richard John "Red" b: 4/16/38, Mount Pleasant, Pa. BR/TR, 5'10", 185 lbs. Deb: 6/16/61

YEAR	TM/L	G	AB	R	H	2B	3B	HR	RBI	BB	SO	AVG	OBP	SLG	PRO+	BR	/A	RC	SB	CS	SBR	FR	POS	TPR
1961	Min-A	13	17	3	5	1	0	0	3	2	2	.294	.400	.353	98	0	0	3	0	0	0	1	/23	0.1
1962	Min-A	159	624	96	186	23	5	16	96	75	61	.298	.379	.428	112	16	13	104	3	1	0	-5	*3/S	1.0
1963	Min-A	136	531	75	163	23	1	16	61	36	59	.307	.360	.444	122	17	16	84	2	0	1	-7	*3/2	1.1
1964	Min-A	148	596	87	161	25	**10**	12	68	53	80	.270	.335	.406	104	4	3	80	2	5	-2	-2	*3	0.2
1965	*Min-A	140	469	59	117	22	1	5	32	37	54	.249	.310	.333	79	-10	-13	48	4	0	1	-4	*32	-1.4
1966	Min-A	90	269	30	66	7	1	10	40	13	34	.245	.290	.390	88	-3	-5	28	0	2	-4	3/20	-1.1
1967	Min-A	109	339	31	83	11	2	6	39	27	58	.245	.306	.342	84	-4	-7	34	1	1	-0	-10	3	-1.6
1968	Min-A	93	203	14	49	5	0	6	30	10	34	.241	.287	.355	89	-2	-3	20	3	1	0	-1	3	-0.2
1969	Sea-A	58	187	15	42	7	0	4	21	7	19	.225	.271	.326	68	-9	-8	16	2	0	1	3	3/S	-0.4
1970	Mil-A	14	25	3	5	1	0	0	5	3	4	.200	.286	.240	46	-2	-2	2	0	0	0	1	/3	0.0
	Cle-A	42	43	6	10	0	0	2	4	3	5	.233	.283	.372	75	-1	-2	5	0	0	0	-1	/3	-0.2
	Yr	56	68	9	15	1	0	2	9	6	9	.221	.284	.324	65	-3	-3	7	0	0	0	-0		-0.2
Total	10	1002	3303	419	887	125	20	77	399	266	410	.269	.330	.388	98	6	-7	424	17	10	-1	-30	3/2SO	-2.5

■ **ROLLINSON**   Rollinson Deb: 6/17/1884

YEAR	TM/L	G	AB	R	H	2B	3B	HR	RBI	BB	SO	AVG	OBP	SLG	PRO+	BR	/A	RC	SB	CS	SBR	FR	POS	TPR
1884	Was-U	1	3	0	0	0	0	0	0	0	0	.000	.000	.000	-99	-1	-1	0	0			0	/C	0.0

■ **BILL ROMAN**   Roman, William Anthony b: 10/11/38, Detroit, Mich. BL/TL, 6'4", 190 lbs. Deb: 9/30/64

YEAR	TM/L	G	AB	R	H	2B	3B	HR	RBI	BB	SO	AVG	OBP	SLG	PRO+	BR	/A	RC	SB	CS	SBR	FR	POS	TPR
1964	Det-A	3	8	2	3	0	0	1	1	0	2	.375	.375	.750	201	1	1	2	0	0	0	0	/1	0.1
1965	Det-A	21	27	0	2	0	0	0	0	2	7	.074	.138	.074	-38	-5	-5	0	0	0	0	-0	/1	-0.5
Total	2	24	35	2	5	0	0	1	1	2	9	.143	.189	.229	17	-4	-4	3	0	0	0	-0	/1	-0.4

■ **JOHN ROMANO**   Romano, John Anthony "Honey" b: 8/23/34, Hoboken, N.J. BR/TR, 5'11", 205 lbs. Deb: 9/12/58

YEAR	TM/L	G	AB	R	H	2B	3B	HR	RBI	BB	SO	AVG	OBP	SLG	PRO+	BR	/A	RC	SB	CS	SBR	FR	POS	TPR
1958	Chi-A	4	7	1	2	0	0	0	1	1	0	.286	.375	.286	86	-0	-0	1	0	0	0	1	/C	0.1
1959	*Chi-A	53	126	20	37	5	1	5	25	23	18	.294	.407	.468	141	8	8	25	0	1	-1	1	C	1.1
1960	Cle-A	108	316	40	86	12	2	16	52	37	50	.272	.354	.475	126	9	11	53	0	0	0	-11	C	0.5
1961	Cle-A	142	509	76	152	29	1	21	80	61	60	.299	.379	.483	132	21	23	95	0	0	0	-10	*C	1.2
1962	Cle-A	135	459	71	120	19	3	25	81	73	64	.261	.369	.460	130	18	20	82	0	1	-1	-8	*C	1.7
1963	Cle-A	89	255	28	55	5	2	10	34	38	49	.216	.322	.369	94	-2	-2	32	4	3	-1	-11	C/O	-1.2
1964	Cle-A	106	352	46	85	18	1	19	47	51	83	.241	.349	.460	124	11	12	54	2	2	-1	-5	C/1	1.1
1965	Chi-A	122	356	39	86	11	0	18	48	59	74	.242	.357	.424	129	11	14	54	0	2	-1	4	*C/O1	2.5
1966	Chi-A	122	329	33	76	12	0	15	47	58	72	.231	.348	.404	124	8	11	50	0	0	0	3	*C	2.0
1967	StL-N	24	58	1	7	1	0	0	2	13	15	.121	.282	.138	24	-5	-5	3	1	0	0	-0	C	-0.4
Total	10	905	2767	355	706	112	10	129	417	414	485	.255	.358	.443	123	79	90	450	7	9	-3	-35	C/O1	8.6

■ **TOM ROMANO**   Romano, Thomas Michael b: 10/25/58, Syracuse, N.Y. BR/TR, 5'10", 170 lbs. Deb: 9/01/87

YEAR	TM/L	G	AB	R	H	2B	3B	HR	RBI	BB	SO	AVG	OBP	SLG	PRO+	BR	/A	RC	SB	CS	SBR	FR	POS	TPR
1987	Mon-N	7	3	1	0	0	0	0	0	0	1	.000	.000	.000	-97	-1	-1	0	0	0	0	0	/O	0.0

■ **ED ROMERO**   Romero, Edgardo Ralph (Rivera) b: 12/9/57, Santurce, P.R. BR/TR, 5'11", 160 lbs. Deb: 7/16/77

YEAR	TM/L	G	AB	R	H	2B	3B	HR	RBI	BB	SO	AVG	OBP	SLG	PRO+	BR	/A	RC	SB	CS	SBR	FR	POS	TPR
1977	Mil-A	10	25	4	7	1	0	0	2	4	3	.280	.379	.320	93	-0	-0	3	0	0	0	0	S	0.1
1980	Mil-A	42	104	20	27	7	0	1	10	9	11	.260	.319	.356	87	-2	-2	12	2	0	1	4	S2/3	0.6
1981	*Mil-A	44	91	6	18	3	0	1	10	4	9	.198	.232	.264	45	-7	-6	4	0	2	-1	10	S2/3	0.5
1982	Mil-A	52	144	18	36	8	0	1	7	8	16	.250	.289	.326	73	-6	-5	13	0	0	0	-1	2S/3O	-0.2
1983	Mil-A	59	145	17	46	7	0	1	18	8	8	.317	.353	.386	112	1	2	20	1	0	0	-8	SO/32D	-0.4
1984	Mil-A	116	357	36	90	12	0	1	31	29	25	.252	.310	.294	71	-15	-13	31	3	3	-1	2	3S2/10D	-0.7
1985	Mil-A	88	251	24	63	11	1	0	21	26	20	.251	.321	.303	72	-9	-9	26	1	1	-0	11	S2O/3	0.6
1986	*Bos-A	100	233	41	49	11	0	2	23	18	16	.210	.273	.283	51	-16	-16	19	2	0	1	-8	S3/2O	-1.7
1987	Bos-A	88	235	23	64	5	0	0	14	18	22	.272	.324	.294	64	-11	-12	21	0	2	-1	2	2S3/1	-0.7
1988	*Bos-A	31	75	3	18	3	0	0	5	3	8	.240	.278	.280	55	-4	-5	5	0	0	0	0	3/S/21D	-0.4
1989	Bos-A	46	113	14	24	4	0	0	6	7	7	.212	.264	.248	42	-8	-9	7	0	2	-1	13	23S	0.4
	Atl-N	7	19	1	5	1	0	1	1	0	0	.263	.263	.474	104	0	-0	2	0	0	0	5	/2S3	0.5
	Mil-A	15	50	3	10	3	0	0	3	0	10	.200	.200	.260	29	-5	-5	2	0	0	0	2	2/3SD	-0.3
1990	Det-A	32	70	8	16	3	0	0	4	6	4	.229	.289	.271	58	-4	-4	6	0	0	0	0	3/D	0.2
Total	12	730	1912	218	473	79	1	8	155	140	159	.247	.300	.302	67	-86	-83	172	9	10	-3	36	S23/O1D	-1.5

■ **KEVIN ROMINE**   Romine, Kevin Andrew b: 5/23/61, Exeter, N.H. BR/TR, 5'11", 185 lbs. Deb: 9/05/85

YEAR	TM/L	G	AB	R	H	2B	3B	HR	RBI	BB	SO	AVG	OBP	SLG	PRO+	BR	/A	RC	SB	CS	SBR	FR	POS	TPR
1985	Bos-A	24	28	3	6	2	0	0	1	1	4	.214	.241	.286	42	-2	-2	2	1	0	0	2	O/D	0.0
1986	Bos-A	35	35	6	9	2	0	0	2	3	9	.257	.316	.314	72	-1	-1	4	2	0	1	6	O/D	0.4
1987	Bos-A	9	24	5	7	2	0	0	2	2	6	.292	.346	.375	89	-0	-0	3	0	0	0	2	/OD	0.1
1988	*Bos-A	57	78	17	15	2	1	1	6	7	15	.192	.259	.282	49	-5	-5	6	2	0	1	1	O/D	-0.4
1989	Bos-A	92	274	30	75	13	0	1	23	21	53	.274	.330	.332	82	-4	-6	28	1	1	-0	0	O/D	-0.8
1990	Bos-A	70	136	21	37	8	0	2	14	12	27	.272	.336	.368	92	-1	-1	16	4	0	1	-2	O/D	-0.2
Total	6	287	575	82	149	28	1	4	48	46	114	.259	.317	.332	78	-14	-17	59	10	1	2	8	O/D	-0.9

■ **HENRI RONDEAU**   Rondeau, Henri Joseph b: 5/5/1887, Danielson, Conn. d: 5/28/43, Woonsocket, R.I. BR/TR, 5'10.5", 175 lbs. Deb: 4/11/13

YEAR	TM/L	G	AB	R	H	2B	3B	HR	RBI	BB	SO	AVG	OBP	SLG	PRO+	BR	/A	RC	SB	CS	SBR	FR	POS	TPR
1913	Det-A	35	70	5	13	2	0	0	5	14	16	.186	.321	.214	58	-3	-3	5	1			-2	C/1	-0.3
1915	Was-A	14	40	3	7	0	0	0	4	4	3	.175	.250	.175	27	-3	-4	2	1	2	-1	3	O	-0.2
1916	Was-A	50	162	20	36	5	3	1	28	18	18	.222	.301	.309	88	-3	-2	18	7			3	O	-0.1
Total	3	99	272	28	56	7	3	1	37	36	37	.206	.305	.265	71	-9	-9	25	9	2		4	/OC1	-0.6

■ **GENE ROOF**   Roof, Eugene Lawrence b: 1/13/58, Paducah, Ky. BB/TR, 6'2", 180 lbs. Deb: 9/03/81

YEAR	TM/L	G	AB	R	H	2B	3B	HR	RBI	BB	SO	AVG	OBP	SLG	PRO+	BR	/A	RC	SB	CS	SBR	FR	POS	TPR
1981	StL-N	23	60	11	18	6	0	0	3	12	16	.300	.417	.400	129	3	3	11	5	1	1	-2	O	0.2
1982	StL-N	11	15	3	4	0	0	0	2	1	4	.267	.313	.267	63	-1	-1	1	2	0	1	-0	/O	0.0
1983	StL-N	6	3	1	0	0	0	0	0	0	0	.000	.000	.000	-99	-1	-1	0	0	0	0	-0	/O	0.0
	Mon-N	8	12	2	2	2	0	0	1	1	3	.167	.231	.333	55	-1	-1	1	0	0	0	-0	/O	0.0
	Yr	14	15	3	2	2	0	0	1	1	3	.133	.188	.267	25	-2	-2	1	0	0	0	-0		0.0
Total	3	48	90	17	24	8	0	0	6	14	23	.267	.365	.356	102	1	1	14	7	1	2	-2	/O	0.2

YEAR	TM/L	G	AB	R	H	2B	3B	HR	RBI	BB	SO	AVG	OBP	SLG	PRO+	BR	/A	RC	SB	CS	SBR	FR	POS	TPR

■ PHIL ROOF
Roof, Phillip Anthony　b: 3/5/41, Paducah, Ky.　BR/TR, 6'2", 190 lbs.　Deb: 4/29/61　C

YEAR	TM/L	G	AB	R	H	2B	3B	HR	RBI	BB	SO	AVG	OBP	SLG	PRO+	BR	/A	RC	SB	CS	SBR	FR	POS	TPR
1961	Mil-N	1	0	0	0	0	0	0	0	0	0	—	—	—	—	0	0	0	0	0	0	0	/C	0.0
1964	Mil-N	1	2	0	0	0	0	0	0	0	1	.000	.000	.000	-99	-1	-1	0	0	0	0	1	/C	0.1
1965	Cal-A	9	22	1	3	0	0	0	0	0	6	.136	.136	.136	-23	-3	-3	0	0	0	0	5	/C	0.3
	Cle-A	43	52	3	9	1	0	0	3	5	13	.173	.259	.192	30	-5	-5	3	0	0	0	13	C	1.2
	Yr	52	74	4	12	1	0	0	3	5	19	.162	.225	.176	15	-8	-8	3	0	0	0	19		1.5
1966	KC-A	127	369	33	77	14	3	7	44	37	95	.209	.286	.320	76	-12	-11	31	2	5	-2	0	*C/1	-0.7
1967	KC-A	114	327	23	67	14	5	6	24	23	85	.205	.268	.333	79	-10	-9	30	4	1	1	-1	*C	-0.2
1968	Oak-A	34	64	5	12	0	0	1	2	2	15	.188	.212	.234	37	-5	-5	3	1	0	0	-1	*C	-0.4
1969	Oak-A	106	247	19	58	6	1	2	19	33	55	.235	.337	.291	81	-6	-5	25	1	0	0	-1	*C	0.1
1970	Mil-A	110	321	39	73	7	1	13	37	32	72	.227	.307	.377	87	-6	-6	36	3	2	-0	7	*C/1	0.2
1971	Mil-A	41	114	6	22	2	1	1	10	8	28	.193	.252	.254	44	-8	-8	7	0	0	0	3	C	-0.3
	Min-A	31	87	6	21	4	0	0	6	8	18	.241	.305	.287	67	-3	-4	6	0	1	-1	8	C	0.6
	Yr	72	201	12	43	6	1	1	16	16	46	.214	.275	.269	54	-12	-12	13	0	1	-1	11		0.3
1972	Min-A	61	146	16	30	11	1	3	12	6	27	.205	.237	.356	71	-5	-6	12	0	1	-1	-3	C	-0.9
1973	Min-A	47	117	10	23	4	1	1	15	13	27	.197	.277	.274	53	-7	-7	9	0	0	0	3	C	-0.3
1974	Min-A	44	97	10	19	1	0	2	13	6	24	.196	.257	.268	49	-6	-7	6	0	0	0	7	C	0.2
1975	Min-A	63	126	18	38	2	0	7	21	9	28	.302	.353	.484	132	5	5	22	0	0	0	7	C	1.3
1976	Min-A	18	46	1	10	3	0	0	4	2	6	.217	.250	.283	54	-3	-3	3	0	0	0	5	C/D	0.3
	Chi-A	4	9	0	1	0	0	0	0	0	3	.111	.111	.111	-35	-2	-2	0	0	0	0	-0	/C	-0.1
	Yr	22	55	1	11	3	0	0	4	2	9	.200	.228	.255	40	-4	-4	3	0	0	0	5		0.2
1977	Tor-A	3	5	0	0	0	0	0	0	0	0	.000	.000	.000	-99	-1	-1	0	0	0	0	1	/C	0.0
Total	15	857	2151	190	463	69	13	43	210	184	504	.215	.284	.319	73	-79	-77	193	11	10	-3	54	C/1D	1.4

■ GEORGE ROOKS
Rooks, George Brinton McClellan (b: George Brinton Mc Clellan Ruckser)
b: 10/21/1863, Chicago, Ill.　d: 3/11/35, Chicago, Ill.　BR/TR, 5'11", 170 lbs.　Deb: 5/12/1891

YEAR	TM/L	G	AB	R	H	2B	3B	HR	RBI	BB	SO	AVG	OBP	SLG	PRO+	BR	/A	RC	SB	CS	SBR	FR	POS	TPR
1891	Bos-N	5	16	1	2	0	0	0	0	4	1	.125	.300	.125	24	-1	-2	1	0			1	/O	0.0

■ ROLANDO ROOMES
Roomes, Rolando Audley　b: 2/15/62, Kingston, Jamaica　BR/TR, 6'3", 180 lbs.　Deb: 4/12/88

YEAR	TM/L	G	AB	R	H	2B	3B	HR	RBI	BB	SO	AVG	OBP	SLG	PRO+	BR	/A	RC	SB	CS	SBR	FR	POS	TPR
1988	Chi-N	17	16	3	3	0	0	0	0	0	4	.188	.188	.188	8	-2	-2	0	0	1	-1	0	/O	-0.2
1989	Cin-N	107	315	36	83	18	5	7	34	13	100	.263	.299	.419	100	0	-1	38	12	8	-1	0	*O	-0.3
1990	Cin-N	30	61	5	13	0	0	2	7	0	20	.213	.213	.311	41	-5	-5	3	0	0	0	2	O	-0.3
	Mon-N	16	14	1	4	0	1	0	1	1	6	.286	.333	.429	109	0	0	1	0	2	-1	1	/O	0.0
	Yr	46	75	6	17	0	1	2	8	1	26	.227	.237	.333	54	-5	-5	5	0	2	-1	2		-0.3
Total	3	170	406	45	103	18	6	9	42	14	130	.254	.284	.394	88	-7	-8	43	12	11	-3	3	O	-0.8

■ FRANK ROONEY
Rooney, Frank (b: Frank Rovny)　b: 10/12/1884, Podebrady, Bohemia (Austria-Hungary)　d: 4/6/77, Bessemer, Mich.　Deb: 4/18/14

YEAR	TM/L	G	AB	R	H	2B	3B	HR	RBI	BB	SO	AVG	OBP	SLG	PRO+	BR	/A	RC	SB	CS	SBR	FR	POS	TPR
1914	Ind-F	12	35	1	7	0	1	1	8	2	.	.200	.222	.343	54	-2	-2	3	2			-1	/1	-0.2

■ PAT ROONEY
Rooney, Patrick Eugene　b: 11/28/57, Chicago, Ill.　BR/TR, 6'1", 190 lbs.　Deb: 9/09/81

YEAR	TM/L	G	AB	R	H	2B	3B	HR	RBI	BB	SO	AVG	OBP	SLG	PRO+	BR	/A	RC	SB	CS	SBR	FR	POS	TPR
1981	Mon-N	4	5	0	0	0	0	0	0	0	3	.000	.000	.000	-99	-1	-1	0	0	0	0	0	/O	-0.1

■ JORGE ROQUE
Roque, Jorge (Vargas)　b: 4/28/50, Ponce, P.R.　BR/TR, 5'10", 158 lbs.　Deb: 9/04/70

YEAR	TM/L	G	AB	R	H	2B	3B	HR	RBI	BB	SO	AVG	OBP	SLG	PRO+	BR	/A	RC	SB	CS	SBR	FR	POS	TPR
1970	StL-N	5	1	2	0	0	0	0	0	0	1	.000	.500	.000	45	0	0	0	0	0	0	0	/O	0.0
1971	StL-N	3	10	2	3	0	0	0	1	0	3	.300	.300	.300	68	-0	-0	1	1	0	0	0	/O	0.0
1972	StL-N	32	67	3	7	2	1	1	5	6	19	.104	.178	.209	10	-8	-8	2	1	1	-0	2	O	-0.7
1973	Mon-N	25	61	7	9	2	0	1	6	4	17	.148	.212	.230	22	-7	-7	2	2	2	-1	2	O	-0.6
Total	4	65	139	14	19	4	1	2	12	10	40	.137	.205	.223	20	-15	-15	6	4	3	-1	4	/O	-1.3

■ LUIS ROSADO
Rosado, Luis (Robles)　b: 12/6/55, Santurce, P.R.　BR/TR, 6', 180 lbs.　Deb: 9/08/77

YEAR	TM/L	G	AB	R	H	2B	3B	HR	RBI	BB	SO	AVG	OBP	SLG	PRO+	BR	/A	RC	SB	CS	SBR	FR	POS	TPR
1977	NY-N	9	24	1	5	1	0	0	3	1	3	.208	.269	.250	42	-2	-2	2	0	0	0	-0	/1C	-0.1
1980	NY-N	2	4	0	0	0	0	0	0	0	1	.000	.000	.000	-99	-1	-1	0	0	0	0	-0	/1	0.0
Total	2	11	28	1	5	1	0	0	3	1	4	.179	.233	.214	23	-3	-3	2	0	0	0	-0	/1C	-0.1

■ BUDDY ROSAR
Rosar, Warren Vincent　b: 7/3/14, Buffalo, N.Y.　BR/TR, 5'9", 190 lbs.　Deb: 4/29/39

YEAR	TM/L	G	AB	R	H	2B	3B	HR	RBI	BB	SO	AVG	OBP	SLG	PRO+	BR	/A	RC	SB	CS	SBR	FR	POS	TPR
1939	NY-A	43	105	18	29	5	1	0	12	13	10	.276	.356	.343	81	-3	-3	14	4	0	1	4	C	0.4
1940	NY-A	73	228	34	68	11	3	4	37	19	11	.298	.357	.425	106	1	2	36	7	1	2	0	C	0.8
1941	*NY-A	67	209	25	60	17	2	1	36	22	10	.287	.355	.402	101	-0	0	29	0	0	0	3	C	0.4
1942	*NY-A	69	209	18	48	10	0	2	34	17	20	.230	.288	.306	68	-9	-9	17	1	2	-1	3	C	0.0
1943	Cle-A	115	382	53	108	17	1	1	41	33	12	.283	.340	.340	106	-0	2	44	0	4	-2	5	*C	1.2
1944	Cle-A	99	331	29	87	9	3	0	30	34	17	.263	.339	.308	89	-5	-4	37	1	2	-1	2	C	0.5
1945	Phi-A	92	300	23	63	12	1	1	25	20	16	.210	.262	.267	54	-18	-18	20	2	1	0	-1	C	-1.2
1946	Phi-A	121	424	34	120	22	2	2	47	36	17	.283	.339	.358	96	-3	-3	48	1	3	-2	5	*C	0.7
1947	Phi-A	102	359	40	93	20	2	1	33	40	13	.259	.335	.334	85	-6	-7	41	1	3	-2	12	*C	1.2
1948	Phi-A	90	302	30	77	13	0	4	41	39	12	.255	.344	.338	82	-7	-8	38	0	2	-1	-4	C	-0.5
1949	Phi-A	32	95	7	19	2	0	0	6	16	5	.200	.315	.221	45	-7	-7	8	0	0	0	-2	C	-0.7
1950	Bos-A	27	84	13	25	2	0	1	12	7	4	.298	.352	.357	75	-2	-3	10	0	0	0	-0	C	-0.2
1951	Bos-A	58	170	11	39	7	0	1	13	19	14	.229	.307	.288	56	-9	-11	16	0	0	0	-0	C	-0.7
Total	13	988	3198	335	836	147	15	18	367	315	161	.261	.330	.334	84	-70	-67	358	17	18	-6	25	C	1.9

■ JIMMY ROSARIO
Rosario, Angel Ramon (Ferrer)　b: 5/5/45, Bayamon, P.R.　BB/TR, 5'10", 155 lbs.　Deb: 4/08/71

YEAR	TM/L	G	AB	R	H	2B	3B	HR	RBI	BB	SO	AVG	OBP	SLG	PRO+	BR	/A	RC	SB	CS	SBR	FR	POS	TPR
1971	*SF-N	92	192	26	43	6	1	0	13	33	35	.224	.341	.266	75	-5	-5	20	7	4	-0	8	O	0.1
1972	SF-N	7	2	1	0	0	0	0	0	0	0	.000	.000	.000	-99	-1	-1	0	0	1	-1	0	/O	0.0
1976	Mil-A	15	37	4	7	0	0	1	5	3	8	.189	.250	.270	53	-2	-2	2	1	3	-2	-0	O/D	-0.4
Total	3	114	231	31	50	6	1	1	18	36	43	.216	.325	.264	70	-8	-8	22	8	8	-2	8	/OD	-0.3

■ SANTIAGO ROSARIO
Rosario, Santiago　b: 7/25/39, Guayanilla, P.R.　BL/TL, 5'11", 165 lbs.　Deb: 6/23/65

YEAR	TM/L	G	AB	R	H	2B	3B	HR	RBI	BB	SO	AVG	OBP	SLG	PRO+	BR	/A	RC	SB	CS	SBR	FR	POS	TPR
1965	KC-A	81	85	8	20	3	0	2	8	6	16	.235	.293	.341	81	-2	-2	8	0	0	0	0	1/O	-0.3

■ VICTOR ROSARIO
Rosario, Victor Manuel　b: 8/28/66, Hato Mayor Del Rey, D.R.　BR/TR, 5'11", 155 lbs.　Deb: 9/06/90

YEAR	TM/L	G	AB	R	H	2B	3B	HR	RBI	BB	SO	AVG	OBP	SLG	PRO+	BR	/A	RC	SB	CS	SBR	FR	POS	TPR
1990	Atl-N	9	7	3	1	0	0	0	0	1	1	.143	.250	.143	11	-1	-1	0	0	0	0	1	/S2	0.0

■ PETE ROSE
Rose, Peter Edward "Charlie Hustle"　b: 4/14/41, Cincinnati, Ohio　BB/TR, 5'11", 192 lbs.　Deb: 4/08/63　M

YEAR	TM/L	G	AB	R	H	2B	3B	HR	RBI	BB	SO	AVG	OBP	SLG	PRO+	BR	/A	RC	SB	CS	SBR	FR	POS	TPR
1963	Cin-N	157	623	101	170	25	9	6	41	55	72	.273	.337	.371	101	4	1	77	13	15	-5	-22	*2/O	-1.7
1964	Cin-N	136	516	64	139	13	2	4	34	36	51	.269	.319	.326	79	-12	-14	53	4	10	-5	-14	*2	-2.3
1965	Cin-N	162	670	117	**209**	35	11	11	81	69	76	.312	.383	.446	124	31	25	118	8	3	1	-18	*2	1.7
1966	Cin-N	156	654	97	205	38	5	16	70	37	61	.313	.351	.460	113	20	13	100	4	9	-4	-8	*23	1.0
1967	Cin-N	148	585	86	176	32	8	12	76	56	66	.301	.365	.444	117	23	16	95	11	6	0	-9	*O2	0.3
1968	Cin-N	149	626	94	210	42	6	10	49	56	76	**.335**	**.394**	.470	149	45	40	**113**	3	7	-3	9	*O/21	4.3
1969	Cin-N	156	627	**120**	218	33	11	16	82	88	65	**.348**	.432	.512	155	56	52	138	7	10	-4	7	*O/2	4.8
1970	*Cin-N	159	649	120	205	37	9	15	52	73	64	.316	.387	.470	128	27	26	121	12	7	-1	2	*O	2.1
1971	Cin-N	160	632	86	192	27	4	13	44	68	50	.304	.374	.421	127	22	23	100	13	9	-2	2	*O	1.9
1972	*Cin-N	154	645	107	**198**	31	11	6	57	73	46	.307	.383	.417	135	25	29	109	10	5	1	12	*O	3.7
1973	*Cin-N	160	680	115	**230**	36	8	5	64	65	42	**.338**	.401	.437	139	31	35	119	10	7	-1	9	*O	3.7
1974	Cin-N	163	652	**110**	185	**45**	7	3	51	106	54	.284	.388	.388	119	19	21	104	2	4	-2	9	*O	2.2

YEAR	TM/L	G	AB	R	H	2B	3B	HR	RBI	BB	SO	AVG	OBP	SLG	PRO+	BR	/A	RC	SB	CS	SBR	FR	POS	TPR
1975	*Cin-N	162	662	112	210	47	4	7	74	89	50	.317	.407	.432	130	33	31	120	0	1	-1	-35	*3O	-0.6
1976	*Cin-N	162	665	130	215	42	6	10	63	86	54	.323	.406	.450	139	40	38	123	9	5	-0	-12	*3/O	2.5
1977	Cin-N	162	655	95	204	38	7	9	64	66	42	.311	.379	.432	115	17	15	111	16	4	2	-24	*3	-0.6
1978	Cin-N	159	655	103	198	51	3	7	52	62	30	.302	.365	.421	119	17	17	102	13	9	-2	-24	*3/O1	-1.0
1979	Phi-N	163	628	90	208	40	5	4	59	95	32	.331	.421	.430	128	33	30	116	20	11	-1	-5	*1/32	1.8
1980	*Phi-N	162	655	95	185	42	1	1	64	66	33	.282	.354	.354	93	0	-4	83	12	8	-1	9	*1	-0.3
1981	*Phi-N	107	431	73	140	18	5	0	33	46	26	.325	.394	.390	118	15	12	67	4	4	-1	9	*1	1.7
1982	Phi-N	162	634	80	172	25	4	3	54	66	32	.271	.347	.338	90	-5	-6	75	8	8	-2	6	*1	-1.2
1983	*Phi-N	151	493	52	121	14	3	0	45	52	28	.245	.320	.286	70	-19	-18	46	7	7	-2	0	*1O	-2.7
1984	Mon-N	95	278	34	72	6	2	0	23	31	20	.259	.335	.295	82	-7	-5	27	1	1	-0	5	1O	-0.2
	Cin-N	26	96	9	35	9	0	0	11	9	7	.365	.430	.458	143	7	6	20	0	0		-3	1/M	0.3
	Yr	121	374	43	107	15	2	0	34	40	27	.286	.360	.337	99	-0	1	46	1	1	-0	2		0.1
1985	Cin-N	119	405	60	107	12	2	2	46	86	35	.264	.398	.319	98	7	4	59	8	1	2	0	*1/M	0.3
1986	Cin-N	72	237	15	52	8	2	0	29	30	31	.219	.317	.270	61	-11	-12	23	3	0	1	-1	1/M	-1.4
Total	24	3562	14053	2165	4256	746	135	160	1314	1566	1143	.303	.377	.409	117	416	378	2220	198	149	-30	-94	*O132	20.3

■ BOBBY ROSE   Rose, Robert Richard b: 3/15/67, Covina, Cal. BR/TR, 5'11", 170 lbs. Deb: 8/12/89

YEAR	TM/L	G	AB	R	H	2B	3B	HR	RBI	BB	SO	AVG	OBP	SLG	PRO+	BR	/A	RC	SB	CS	SBR	FR	POS	TPR
1989	Cal-A	14	38	4	8	1	2	1	3	2	10	.211	.268	.421	93	-1	-1	4	0	0	0	-1	3/2	-0.1
1990	Cal-A	7	13	5	5	0	0	1	2	2	1	.385	.467	.615	200	2	2	4	0	0	0	-1	/23	0.1
Total	2	21	51	9	13	1	2	2	5	4	11	.255	.321	.471	122	1	1	8	0	0	0	-2	/32	0.0

■ JOHN ROSEBORO   Roseboro, John Junior b: 5/13/33, Ashland, Ohio BL/TR, 5'11.5", 190 lbs. Deb: 6/14/57 C

YEAR	TM/L	G	AB	R	H	2B	3B	HR	RBI	BB	SO	AVG	OBP	SLG	PRO+	BR	/A	RC	SB	CS	SBR	FR	POS	TPR
1957	Bro-N	35	69	6	10	2	0	2	6	10	20	.145	.253	.261	35	-6	-7	5	0	0	0	3	C/1	-0.3
1958	LA-N	114	384	52	104	11	9	14	43	36	56	.271	.336	.456	104	3	2	58	11	8	-2	-16	*C/O	-0.9
1959	*LA-N	118	397	39	92	14	7	10	38	52	69	.232	.325	.378	81	-7	-11	50	7	5	-1	8	*C	0.2
1960	LA-N	103	287	22	61	15	3	8	42	44	53	.213	.325	.369	84	-4	-6	37	7	6	-2	4	C/13	0.0
1961	LA-N	128	394	59	99	16	6	18	59	56	62	.251	.345	.459	104	7	3	67	6	4	-1	6	*C	1.8
1962	LA-N	128	389	45	97	16	7	7	55	50	60	.249	.345	.380	101	-2	1	54	12	3	2	-3	*C	0.2
1963	*LA-N	135	470	50	111	13	7	9	49	36	50	.236	.295	.351	91	-9	-6	48	7	6	-2	-10	*C	-1.4
1964	LA-N	134	414	42	119	24	1	3	45	44	61	.287	.361	.372	115	5	9	57	3	3	-1	0	*C	1.3
1965	*LA-N	136	437	42	102	10	0	8	57	34	51	.233	.292	.311	75	-17	-14	39	1	6	-3	-3	*C/3	-1.6
1966	*LA-N	142	445	47	123	23	2	9	53	44	51	.276	.346	.398	115	4	9	60	3	2	-0	5	*C	1.7
1967	LA-N	116	334	37	91	18	2	4	24	38	33	.272	.350	.374	117	4	7	43	2	4	-2	-12	*C	0.0
1968	Min-A	135	380	31	82	12	0	8	39	46	57	.216	.304	.311	82	-6	-8	37	2	3	-1	-6	*C	-1.0
1969	*Min-A	115	361	33	95	12	0	3	32	39	44	.263	.335	.321	83	-7	-8	39	5	5	-2	-0	*C	-0.1
1970	Was-A	46	86	7	20	4	0	1	6	18	10	.233	.365	.314	94	-1	0	11	1	1	-0	-2	C	-0.1
Total	14	1585	4847	512	1206	190	44	104	548	547	677	.249	.329	.371	95	-34	-28	604	67	56	-14	-26	*C/1O3	-0.2

■ BOB ROSELLI   Roselli, Robert Edward b: 12/10/31, San Francisco, Cal BR/TR, 5'11", 185 lbs. Deb: 8/16/55

YEAR	TM/L	G	AB	R	H	2B	3B	HR	RBI	BB	SO	AVG	OBP	SLG	PRO+	BR	/A	RC	SB	CS	SBR	FR	POS	TPR
1955	Mil-N	6	9	1	2	1	0	0	0	1	4	.222	.364	.333	91	-0	-0	1	0	0	0	0	/C	0.0
1956	Mil-N	4	2	1	1	1	0	0	1	0	1	.500	.500	2.000	564	1	1	2	0	0	0	0	/C	0.3
1958	Mil-N	1	1	0	0	0	0	0	0	0	0	.000	.000	.000	-99	-0	-0	0	0	0	0	0	H	0.0
1961	Chi-A	22	38	2	10	3	0	0	4	0	11	.263	.263	.342	61	-2	-2	3	0	0	0	-1	C	-0.3
1962	Chi-A	35	64	4	12	3	1	1	5	11	15	.188	.316	.313	70	-3	-3	7	1	0	0	-1	C	-0.2
Total	5	68	114	8	25	7	1	2	10	12	31	.219	.305	.351	76	-4	-4	13	1	0	0	-0	/C	-0.2

■ DAVE ROSELLO   Rosello, David (Rodriguez) b: 6/26/50, Mayaguez, P.R. BR/TR, 5'11", 160 lbs. Deb: 9/10/72

YEAR	TM/L	G	AB	R	H	2B	3B	HR	RBI	BB	SO	AVG	OBP	SLG	PRO+	BR	/A	RC	SB	CS	SBR	FR	POS	TPR
1972	Chi-N	5	12	2	3	1	0	0	3	3	2	.250	.400	.500	139	1	1	3	0	0	0	1	/S	0.2
1973	Chi-N	16	38	4	10	2	0	0	2	2	4	.263	.300	.316	66	-2	-2	2	2	2	-1	3	2/S	0.1
1974	Chi-N	62	148	9	30	7	0	0	10	10	28	.203	.253	.250	39	-12	-12	10	1	1	-0	3	2S	-0.5
1975	Chi-N	19	58	7	15	2	0	1	8	9	8	.259	.358	.345	92	-0	-0	7	0	1	-1	1	S	0.2
1976	Chi-N	91	227	27	55	5	1	1	11	41	33	.242	.361	.286	78	-2	-5	25	1	2	-1	-7	S/2	-0.4
1977	Chi-N	56	82	18	18	2	1	1	9	12	12	.220	.319	.305	62	-3	-5	9	0	0	0	-2	3S/2	-0.5
1979	Cle-A	59	107	20	26	6	1	3	14	15	27	.243	.336	.402	98	-0	-0	16	1	0	0	-4	23S	-0.1
1980	Cle-A	71	117	16	29	3	0	2	12	9	19	.248	.302	.325	71	-5	-5	12	0	0	0	4	23/SD	0.2
1981	Cle-A	43	84	11	20	4	0	1	7	7	12	.238	.297	.321	79	-2	-2	8	0	1	-1	3	2/3SD	0.1
Total	9	422	873	114	206	31	3	10	76	108	145	.236	.321	.313	73	-25	-30	92	5	7	-3	1	2S/3D	-0.7

■ CHIEF ROSEMAN   Roseman, James John b: 1856, New York, N.Y. d: 7/4/38, Brooklyn, N.Y. BR/TR, 5'7", 167 lbs. Deb: 5/01/1882 M

YEAR	TM/L	G	AB	R	H	2B	3B	HR	RBI	BB	SO	AVG	OBP	SLG	PRO+	BR	/A	RC	SB	CS	SBR	FR	POS	TPR
1882	Tro-N	82	331	41	78	21	6	1	29	3	41	.236	.243	.344	90	-5	-3	28				-5	*O	-0.7
1883	NY-a	93	398	48	100	13	6	0	11			.251	.271	.314	85	-5	-8	35				-3	*O/1	-0.8
1884	*NY-a	107	436	97	130	16	11	4	21			.298	.339	.413	152	22	24	63				-2	*O	1.9
1885	NY-a	101	410	72	114	13	14	4	25			.278	.345	.407	148	17	22	57				-7	*O/P	0.9
1886	NY-a	134	559	90	127	19	10	5	24			.227	.269	.324	91	-9	-6	52	6			-3	*O/P	-1.0
1887	Phi-a	21	73	16	16	2	1	0	10			.219	.352	.274	78	-1	-1	8	3			-0	O	-0.1
	NY-a	60	241	30	55	10	1	1	9			.228	.265	.290	59	-14	-12	20	3			-7	O/1P	-1.7
	Bro-a	1	3	2	1	0	0	0	0			.333	.333	.333	136	0	0	1				-3	/O	-0.2
	Yr	82	317	48	72	12	2	1	19			.227	.290	.287	65	-15	-13	29	6			-11		-2.0
1890	StL-a	80	302	47	103	26	0	2	30			.341	.447	.447	146	28	21	65	7			-8	O1M	0.7
	Lou-a	2	8	0	2	0	0	0	0			.250	.250	.250	50	-1	0	1				-1	/1	0.0
	Yr	82	310	47	105	26	0	2	30			.339	.443	.442	144	28	20	65	7			-9		0.7
Total	7	681	2761	443	726	120	49	17	29	133	41	.263	.311	.360	111	31	36	329	19			-38	O/1P	-1.0

■ AL ROSEN   Rosen, Albert Leonard "Flip" b: 2/29/24, Spartanburg, S.C. BR/TR, 5'10.5", 180 lbs. Deb: 9/10/47

YEAR	TM/L	G	AB	R	H	2B	3B	HR	RBI	BB	SO	AVG	OBP	SLG	PRO+	BR	/A	RC	SB	CS	SBR	FR	POS	TPR
1947	Cle-A	7	9	1	1	0	0	0	0	0	3	.111	.111	.111	-39	-2	-2	0	0	0	0	0	/3O	0.0
1948	*Cle-A	5	5	0	1	0	0	0	0	0	2	.200	.200	.200	7	-1	-1	0	0	0	0	0	/3	0.0
1949	Cle-A	23	44	3	7	2	0	0	5	7	4	.159	.275	.205	28	-5	-4	3	0	1	-1	-1	3	-0.5
1950	Cle-A	155	554	100	159	23	4	37	116	100	72	.287	.405	.543	146	34	37	120	5	7	-3	1	*3	2.7
1951	Cle-A	154	573	82	152	30	1	24	102	85	71	.265	.362	.447	125	14	18	96	7	5	-1	-15	*3	-0.2
1952	Cle-A	148	567	101	171	32	5	28	105	75	54	.302	.387	.524	162	39	43	115	8	6	-1	-20	*3/1S	2.3
1953	Cle-A	155	599	115	201	27	5	43	145	85	48	.336	.422	.613	181	63	65	155	8	7	-2	1	*3/1S	5.6
1954	*Cle-A	137	466	76	140	20	2	24	102	85	43	.300	.412	.506	148	34	33	100	6	2	1	-14	31/2S	1.4
1955	Cle-A	139	492	61	120	13	1	21	81	92	44	.244	.357	.402	103	7	4	76	4	2	0	3	*31	0.7
1956	Cle-A	121	416	64	111	18	2	15	61	58	44	.267	.357	.428	104	4	2	62	1	3	-2	-7	*3	-0.3
Total	10	1044	3725	603	1063	165	20	192	717	587	385	.285	.386	.495	138	188	197	729	39	33	-8	-52	3/1S2O	11.7

■ GOODY ROSEN   Rosen, Goodwin George b: 8/28/12, Toronto, Ont., Can. BL/TL, 5'10", 155 lbs. Deb: 9/14/37

YEAR	TM/L	G	AB	R	H	2B	3B	HR	RBI	BB	SO	AVG	OBP	SLG	PRO+	BR	/A	RC	SB	CS	SBR	FR	POS	TPR
1937	Bro-N	22	77	10	24	5	1	0	6	6	6	.312	.361	.403	106	1	1	12	2			2	O	0.1
1938	Bro-N	148	473	75	133	17	11	4	51	65	43	.281	.368	.389	106	7	6	74	0			16	*O	1.9
1939	Bro-N	54	183	22	46	6	4	1	12	23	21	.251	.335	.344	80	-4	-5	23	4			-2	O	-0.7
1944	Bro-N	89	264	38	69	8	3	0	23	26	27	.261	.330	.314	83	-6	-5	29	0			11	O	0.0
1945	Bro-N	145	606	126	197	24	11	12	75	50	48	.325	.379	.460	134	26	26	110	4			-2	*O	1.8
1946	Bro-N	3	3	0	1	0	0	0	0	0	1	.333	.333	.333	89	-0	-0	0	0			0	/O	0.0
	NY-N	100	310	39	87	11	4	5	30	48	32	.281	.377	.390	117	9	8	47	2			2	O	0.9

YEAR	TM/L	G	AB	R	H	2B	3B	HR	RBI	BB	SO	AVG	OBP	SLG	PRO+	BR	/A	RC	SB	CS	SBR	FR	POS	TPR
Yr		103	313	39	88	11	4	5	30	48	33	.281	.377	.390	117	8	8	47	2			2		0.9
Total	6	551	1916	310	557	71	34	22	197	218	166	.291	.364	.398	111	32	31	295	12			26	O	4.0

■ HARRY ROSENBERG
Rosenberg, Harry b: 6/22/09, San Francisco, Cal. BR/TR, 5'9.5", 160 lbs. Deb: 7/15/30

YEAR	TM/L	G	AB	R	H	2B	3B	HR	RBI	BB	SO	AVG	OBP	SLG	PRO+	BR	/A	RC	SB	CS	SBR	FR	POS	TPR
1930	NY-N	9	5	1	0	0	0	0	0	1	4	.000	.167	.000	-56	-1	-1	0	0			0	/O	0.0

■ LOU ROSENBERG
Rosenberg, Louis C. b: 3/5/03, San Francisco, Cal. BR/TR, 5'7", 155 lbs. Deb: 5/22/23

YEAR	TM/L	G	AB	R	H	2B	3B	HR	RBI	BB	SO	AVG	OBP	SLG	PRO+	BR	/A	RC	SB	CS	SBR	FR	POS	TPR
1923	Chi-A	3	4	0	1	0	0	0	0	0	1	.250	.250	.250	32	-0	-0	0	0	1	-1	-1	/2	-0.1

■ MAX ROSENFELD
Rosenfeld, Max b: 12/23/02, New York, N.Y. d: 3/10/69, Miami, Fla. BR/TR, 5'8", 175 lbs. Deb: 4/21/31

YEAR	TM/L	G	AB	R	H	2B	3B	HR	RBI	BB	SO	AVG	OBP	SLG	PRO+	BR	/A	RC	SB	CS	SBR	FR	POS	TPR
1931	Bro-N	3	9	0	2	1	0	0	0	1	1	.222	.300	.333	71	-0	-0	1	0			0	/O	0.0
1932	Bro-N	34	39	8	14	3	0	2	7	0	10	.359	.359	.590	153	2	3	8	2			3	O	0.3
1933	Bro-N	5	9	0	1	0	0	0	0	1	1	.111	.200	.111	-10	-1	-1	0	0			1	/O	0.0
Total	3	42	57	8	17	4	0	2	7	2	12	.298	.322	.474	115	1	1	9	2			3	/O	0.3

■ LARRY ROSENTHAL
Rosenthal, Lawrence John b: 5/21/12, St.Paul, Minn. BL/TL, 6'0.5", 190 lbs. Deb: 6/20/36

YEAR	TM/L	G	AB	R	H	2B	3B	HR	RBI	BB	SO	AVG	OBP	SLG	PRO+	BR	/A	RC	SB	CS	SBR	FR	POS	TPR
1936	Chi-A	85	317	71	89	15	8	3	46	59	37	.281	.394	.407	95	1	-1	55	2	0	1	3	O	0.0
1937	Chi-A	58	97	20	28	5	3	0	9	9	20	.289	.355	.402	90	-1	-1	14	1	0	0	3	O	0.1
1938	Chi-A	61	105	14	30	5	1	1	12	12	13	.286	.359	.381	83	-2	-3	15	0	1	-1	2	O	-0.1
1939	Chi-A	107	324	50	86	21	5	10	51	53	46	.265	.369	.454	106	5	3	58	6	4	-1	-2	O	-0.2
1940	Chi-A	107	276	46	83	14	5	6	42	64	32	.301	.432	.453	128	15	15	61	2	3	-1	4	O	1.1
1941	Chi-A	20	59	9	14	4	0	0	1	12	5	.237	.366	.305	80	-1	-1	7	0	0	0	-1	O	-0.3
	Cle-A	45	75	10	14	3	1	1	8	9	10	.187	.274	.293	53	-6	-5	7	1	0	0	1	O/1	-0.3
	Yr	65	134	19	28	7	1	1	9	21	15	.209	.316	.299	66	-7	-6	14	1	0	0	-0		-0.6
1944	NY-A	36	101	9	20	3	0	0	9	19	15	.198	.325	.228	57	-5	-5	9	1	0	0	2	O	-0.3
	Phi-A	32	54	5	11	2	0	1	6	5	9	.204	.271	.296	63	-3	-3	5	0	0	0	-1	O	-0.4
	Yr	68	155	14	31	5	0	1	15	24	24	.200	.307	.252	60	-7	-7	14	1	0	0	1		-0.7
1945	Phi-A	28	75	6	15	3	2	0	5	9	8	.200	.286	.293	68	-3	-3	7	0	1	-1	-2	O	-0.6
Total	8	579	1483	240	390	75	25	22	189	251	195	.263	.370	.392	96	-0	-4	237	13	9	-2	8	O/1	-1.0

■ SI ROSENTHAL
Rosenthal, Simon b: 11/13/03, Boston, Mass. d: 4/7/69, Boston, Mass. BL/TL, 5'9", 165 lbs. Deb: 9/08/25

YEAR	TM/L	G	AB	R	H	2B	3B	HR	RBI	BB	SO	AVG	OBP	SLG	PRO+	BR	/A	RC	SB	CS	SBR	FR	POS	TPR
1925	Bos-A	19	72	6	19	5	2	0	8	7	3	.264	.329	.389	82	-2	-2	10	1	0	0	0	O	-0.2
1926	Bos-A	104	285	34	76	12	3	4	34	19	18	.267	.317	.372	82	-9	-8	34	4	1	1	-13	O	-2.4
Total	2	123	357	40	95	17	5	4	42	26	21	.266	.319	.375	82	-12	-10	44	5	1	1	-13	/O	-2.6

■ BUNNY ROSER
Roser, John William Joseph "Jack" b: 11/15/01, St.Louis, Mo. d: 5/6/79, Rocky Hill, Conn. BL/TL, 5'11", 175 lbs. Deb: 8/24/22

YEAR	TM/L	G	AB	R	H	2B	3B	HR	RBI	BB	SO	AVG	OBP	SLG	PRO+	BR	/A	RC	SB	CS	SBR	FR	POS	TPR
1922	Bos-N	32	113	13	27	3	4	0	16	10	19	.239	.306	.336	69	-6	-5	12	2	1	0	-4	O	-0.9

■ CHET ROSS
Ross, Chester James b: 4/1/17, Buffalo, N.Y. d: 2/21/89, Buffalo, N.Y. BR/TR, 6'1", 195 lbs. Deb: 9/15/39

YEAR	TM/L	G	AB	R	H	2B	3B	HR	RBI	BB	SO	AVG	OBP	SLG	PRO+	BR	/A	RC	SB	CS	SBR	FR	POS	TPR
1939	Bos-N	11	31	4	10	1	1	0	0	2	10	.323	.364	.419	118	0	1	5	0			1	/O	0.2
1940	Bos-N	149	569	84	160	23	14	17	89	59	127	.281	.352	.460	130	17	21	96	4			6	*O	2.2
1941	Bos-N	29	50	1	6	1	0	0	4	9	17	.120	.254	.140	14	-6	-5	2	0			-0	O	-0.5
1942	Bos-N	76	220	20	43	7	2	5	19	16	37	.195	.250	.314	66	-11	-10	17	0			-0	O	-1.2
1943	Bos-N	94	285	27	62	12	2	7	32	26	67	.218	.285	.347	84	-7	-7	28	1			1	O	-0.8
1944	Bos-N	54	154	20	35	9	2	5	26	12	23	.227	.287	.409	91	-2	-3	18	1			2	O	-0.3
Total	6	413	1309	156	316	53	21	34	170	124	281	.241	.309	.392	100	-8	-4	166	6			11	O	-0.4

■ DON ROSS
Ross, Donald Raymond b: 7/16/14, Pasadena, Cal. BR/TR, 6'1", 185 lbs. Deb: 4/19/38

YEAR	TM/L	G	AB	R	H	2B	3B	HR	RBI	BB	SO	AVG	OBP	SLG	PRO+	BR	/A	RC	SB	CS	SBR	FR	POS	TPR
1938	Det-A	77	265	22	69	7	1	1	30	29	11	.260	.333	.306	58	-15	-18	29	1	0	0	4	3	-0.9
1940	Bro-N	10	38	4	11	2	0	1	8	3	3	.289	.341	.421	103	0	0	6	1			-0	3	0.0
1942	Det-A	87	226	29	62	10	2	3	30	36	16	.274	.379	.376	104	5	3	34	2	1	0	-6	O3	-0.5
1943	Det-A	89	247	19	66	13	0	0	18	20	3	.267	.325	.320	82	-3	-6	27	2	0	1	-7	OS/23	-1.3
1944	Det-A	66	167	14	35	5	0	2	15	14	9	.210	.275	.275	54	-9	-10	13	2	1	0	-3	O/S1	-1.5
1945	Det-A	8	29	3	11	4	0	0	4	5	1	.379	.471	.517	175	3	3	8	2	0	1	-0	/3	0.4
	Cle-A	106	363	26	95	15	1	2	43	42	15	.262	.340	.325	97	-2	-0	41	0	4	-2	-13	*3	-1.4
	Yr	114	392	29	106	19	1	2	47	47	16	.270	.350	.339	104	1	3	48	2	4	-2	-13		-1.0
1946	Cle-A	55	153	12	41	7	0	3	14	17	12	.268	.341	.373	106	-0	1	20	0	0	0	-11	3/O	-0.6
Total	7	498	1488	129	390	63	4	12	162	166	70	.262	.338	.334	86	-22	-27	177	10	6		-36	30/S21	-5.8

■ JOE ROSSI
Rossi, Joseph Anthony b: 3/13/23, Oakland, Cal. BR/TR, 6'1", 205 lbs. Deb: 4/20/52

YEAR	TM/L	G	AB	R	H	2B	3B	HR	RBI	BB	SO	AVG	OBP	SLG	PRO+	BR	/A	RC	SB	CS	SBR	FR	POS	TPR
1952	Cin-N	55	145	14	32	0	1	1	6	20	20	.221	.319	.255	61	-7	-7	13	1	0	0	1	C	-0.4

■ CLAUDE ROSSMAN
Rossman, Claude R. b: 6/17/1881, Philmont, N.Y. d: 1/16/28, Poughkeepsie, N.Y. BL/TL, 6', Deb: 9/16/04

YEAR	TM/L	G	AB	R	H	2B	3B	HR	RBI	BB	SO	AVG	OBP	SLG	PRO+	BR	/A	RC	SB	CS	SBR	FR	POS	TPR
1904	Cle-A	18	62	5	13	5	0	0	6	0		.210	.210	.290	59	-3	-3	4	0			-4	O	-0.8
1906	Cle-A	118	396	49	122	13	2	1	53	17		.308	.337	.359	121	8	9	55	11			-8	*1/O	-0.2
1907	*Det-A	153	571	60	158	21	8	0	69	33		.277	.316	.342	108	7	4	73	20			-14	*1	-1.1
1908	*Det-A	138	524	45	154	33	13	2	71	27		.294	.328	.418	139	23	21	74	8			6	*1	2.6
1909	Det-A	82	287	16	75	8	3	0	39	13		.261	.293	.310	87	-4	-5	29	10			-6	1	-1.2
	StL-A	2	8	0	1	0	0	0	0	0		.125	.125	.125	-23	-1	-1	0	0			-0	/O	-0.1
	Yr	84	295	16	76	8	3	0	39	13		.258	.289	.305	84	-5	-6	29	10			-6		-1.3
Total	5	511	1848	175	523	80	26	3	238	90		.283	.316	.359	114	30	25	235	49			-25	1/O	-0.8

■ FRANK ROTH
Roth, Francis Charles b: 10/11/1878, Chicago, Ill. d: 3/27/55, Burlington, Wis. BR/TR, 5'10", 160 lbs. Deb: 4/18/03 C

YEAR	TM/L	G	AB	R	H	2B	3B	HR	RBI	BB	SO	AVG	OBP	SLG	PRO+	BR	/A	RC	SB	CS	SBR	FR	POS	TPR
1903	Phi-N	68	220	27	60	11	4	0	22	9		.273	.301	.359	93	-4	-3	25	3			-7	C/3	-0.3
1904	Phi-N	81	229	28	59	8	1	1	20	12		.258	.295	.314	93	-3	-2	25	8			-11	C/12	-0.6
1905	StL-A	35	107	9	25	3	0	0	7	6		.234	.274	.262	76	-3	-3	8	1			-6	C	-0.6
1906	Chi-A	16	51	4	10	1	1	0	7	3		.196	.241	.255	58	-3	-2	4	1			3	C	0.2
1909	Cin-N	56	147	12	35	7	2	0	16	6		.238	.287	.313	87	-3	-3	14	5			-2	C	0.0
1910	Cin-N	26	29	3	7	2	0	0	3	0	2	.241	.267	.310	71	-1	-1	3	1			0	/CO	0.0
Total	6	282	783	83	196	32	8	1	75	36	2	.250	.288	.315	87	-16	-13	79	19			-22	C/0213	-1.3

■ BRAGGO ROTH
Roth, Robert Frank b: 8/28/1892, Burlington, Wis. d: 9/11/36, Chicago, Ill. BR/TR, 5'7.5", 170 lbs. Deb: 9/01/14

YEAR	TM/L	G	AB	R	H	2B	3B	HR	RBI	BB	SO	AVG	OBP	SLG	PRO+	BR	/A	RC	SB	CS	SBR	FR	POS	TPR
1914	Chi-A	34	126	14	37	4	6	1	10	8	25	.294	.355	.444	142	6	6	20	3	3	-1	2	O	0.5
1915	Chi-A	70	240	44	60	6	10	3	35	29	50	.250	.338	.396	116	5	4	34	12	6	0	-15	3O	-1.1
	Cle-A	39	144	23	43	4	7	4	20	22	22	.299	.399	.507	168	12	12	32	14	4	2	-6	O	0.6
	Yr	109	384	67	103	10	17	7	55	51	72	.268	.361	.438	135	18	16	66	26	10	2	-21		-0.5
1916	Cle-A	125	409	50	117	19	7	4	72	38	48	.286	.350	.396	117	11	8	62	29	14	0	3	*O	0.5
1917	Cle-A	145	495	69	141	30	9	1	72	52	73	.285	.355	.388	118	15	11	82	51			0	*O	0.3
1918	Cle-A	106	375	53	106	21	12	1	59	53	41	.283	.383	.411	127	19	15	69	35			-3	O	0.7
1919	Phi-A	48	195	33	63	13	8	5	29	15	21	.323	.377	.549	156	14	14	42	11			-5	O	0.6
	Bos-A	63	227	32	58	9	4	0	23	24	32	.256	.337	.330	93	-3	-1	27	9			-4	O	-0.9
	Yr	111	422	65	121	22	12	5	52	39	53	.287	.355	.431	124	11	12	68	20			-8		-0.3
1920	Was-A	138	468	80	136	23	8	9	92	75	57	.291	.395	.432	122	15	17	85	24	12		-10	*O	-0.3
1921	NY-A	43	152	29	43	9	2	0	10	19	20	.283	.370	.408	96	-0	-1	24	1	2		-3	O	-0.6
Total	8	811	2831	427	804	138	73	30	422	335	389	.284	.367	.416	122	94	85	477	189	41		-41	O/3	0.3

YEAR	TM/L	G	AB	R	H	2B	3B	HR	RBI	BB	SO	AVG	OBP	SLG	PRO+	BR	/A	RC	SB	CS	SBR	FR	POS	TPR

■ BOB ROTHEL Rothel, Robert Burton b: 9/17/23, Columbia Station Ohio d: 3/21/84, Huron, Ohio BR/TR, 5'10.5", 170 lbs. Deb: 4/22/45

| 1945 | Cle-A | 4 | 10 | 0 | 2 | 0 | 0 | 0 | 3 | 1 | | .200 | .385 | .200 | 75 | -0 | -0 | 1 | 0 | 0 | 0 | -1 | /3 | 0.0 |

■ BOBBY ROTHERMEL Rothermel, Edward Hill b: 12/18/1870, Fleetwood, Pa. d: 2/11/27, Detroit, Mich. Deb: 6/18/1899

| 1899 | Bal-N | 10 | 21 | 1 | 2 | 0 | 0 | 0 | 3 | 1 | | .095 | .136 | .095 | -33 | -4 | -4 | 0 | 0 | | | -2 | /23S | -0.4 |

■ JACK ROTHFUSS Rothfuss, John Albert b: 4/18/1872, Newark, N.J. d: 4/20/47, Basking Ridge, N.J 5'11.5", 195 lbs. Deb: 8/02/1897

| 1897 | Pit-N | 35 | 115 | 20 | 36 | 3 | 1 | 2 | 18 | 5 | | .313 | .352 | .409 | 107 | 0 | 1 | 18 | 3 | | | -1 | 1 | 0.0 |

■ CLAUDE ROTHGEB Rothgeb, Claude James b: 1/1/1880, Milford, Ill. d: 7/6/44, Manitowoc, Wis. BB , 6'0.5", 200 lbs. Deb: 6/17/05

| 1905 | Was-A | 7 | 16 | 2 | 2 | 0 | 0 | 0 | 0 | 0 | | .125 | .125 | .125 | -21 | -2 | -2 | 0 | 1 | | | 0 | /O | -0.1 |

■ JACK ROTHROCK Rothrock, John Houston b: 3/14/05, Long Beach, Cal. d: 2/2/80, San Bernardino, Cal BB/TR, 5'11.5", 165 lbs. Deb: 7/28/25

1925	Bos-A	22	55	6	19	3	3	0	7	3	7	.345	.379	.509	124	2	2	10	0	0	0	-4	S	0.1
1926	Bos-A	15	17	3	5	1	0	0	2	3	1	.294	.400	.353	101	0	0	3	0	0	0	-1	/S	0.0
1927	Bos-A	117	428	61	111	24	8	1	36	24	46	.259	.302	.360	73	-19	-18	44	5	5	-2	4	S231	-0.9
1928	Bos-A	117	344	52	92	9	4	3	22	33	40	.267	.333	.343	79	-11	-10	41	12	6	0	-17	O31S/2PC	-2.8
1929	Bos-A	143	473	70	142	19	7	6	59	43	47	.300	.361	.408	100	-1	0	70	23	13	-1	2	*O	-0.3
1930	Bos-A	45	65	4	18	3	1	0	4	2	9	.277	.299	.354	67	-4	-3	6	0	2	-1	1	/O3	-0.3
1931	Bos-A	133	475	81	132	32	3	4	42	47	48	.278	.343	.383	96	-6	-3	64	13	7	-0	-1	O2/13S	-0.6
1932	Bos-A	12	48	3	10	1	0	0	0	5	5	.208	.283	.229	35	-5	-4	4	3	0	1	0	O	-0.2
	Chi-A	39	64	8	12	2	1	0	6	5	9	.188	.246	.250	31	-7	-6	4	1	0	0	-2	O/31	-0.7
	Yr	51	112	11	22	3	1	0	6	10	14	.196	.262	.241	33	-11	-10	8	4	0	1	-1		-0.9
1934	*StL-N	154	647	106	184	35	3	11	72	49	56	.284	.336	.399	90	-4	-10	91	10			3	*O/2	-1.2
1935	StL-N	129	502	76	137	18	5	3	56	57	29	.273	.347	.347	84	-8	-10	66	7			-2	*O	-1.6
1937	Phi-A	88	232	29	62	15	0	0	21	28	15	.267	.346	.332	73	-9	-9	28	1	0	0	0	O/2	-0.9
Total	11	1014	3350	498	924	162	35	28	327	299	312	.276	.336	.370	85	-72	-71	431	75	33		-16	O/S231CP	-9.4

■ EDD ROUSH Roush, Edd J b: 5/8/1893, Oakland City, Ind. d: 3/21/88, Bradenton, Fla. BL/TL, 5'11", 170 lbs. Deb: 8/20/13 CH

1913	Chi-A	9	10	2	1	0	0	0	0	0	2	.100	.100	.100	-42	-2	-2	0	0			-0	/O	-0.2
1914	Ind-F	74	166	26	54	8	4	1	30	6	20	.325	.353	.440	114	5	3	32	12			2	O/1	0.2
1915	New-F	145	551	73	164	20	11	3	60	38	25	.298	.350	.390	126	12	16	89	28			4	*O	1.4
1916	NY-N	39	69	4	13	0	1	0	5	1	4	.188	.200	.217	30	-6	-6	4	4			-0	O	-0.6
	Cin-N	69	272	34	78	7	14	0	15	13	19	.287	.336	.415	133	9	10	43	15			4	O	1.2
	Yr	108	341	38	91	7	15	0	20	14	23	.267	.309	.375	114	3	4	46	19			4		0.6
1917	Cin-N	136	522	82	178	19	14	4	67	27	24	.341	.379	.454	162	32	35	94	21			-2	*O	3.2
1918	Cin-N	113	435	61	145	18	10	5	62	22	10	.333	.368	.455	153	24	25	80	24			4	*O	2.5
1919	*Cin-N	133	504	73	162	19	13	3	71	42	19	.321	.380	.429	147	27	28	87	20			6	*O	3.1
1920	Cin-N	149	579	81	196	22	16	4	90	42	19	.339	.386	.453	142	30	31	98	36	24	-4	12	*O1/2	3.2
1921	Cin-N	112	418	68	147	27	12	4	71	31	8	.352	.403	.502	145	23	26	80	19	17	-5	-2	*O	1.4
1922	Cin-N	49	165	29	58	7	4	1	24	19	5	.352	.428	.461	132	8	9	33	5	3	-0	2	O	0.8
1923	Cin-N	138	527	88	185	41	18	6	88	46	16	.351	.406	.531	149	34	35	109	10	15	-6	-8	*O	1.6
1924	Cin-N	121	483	67	168	23	21	3	72	22	11	.348	.376	.501	135	21	22	86	17	13	-5	-7	*O	0.9
1925	Cin-N	134	540	91	183	28	16	8	83	35	14	.339	.381	.494	125	18	19	97	22	20	-5	-1	*O	0.8
1926	Cin-N	144	563	95	182	37	10	7	79	38	17	.323	.366	.462	125	16	18	92	8			-14	*O/1	-0.1
1927	NY-N	140	570	83	173	27	4	7	58	26	15	.304	.335	.402	97	-4	-4	74	18			-8	*O	-1.7
1928	NY-N	46	163	20	41	5	3	2	13	14	8	.252	.311	.356	75	-6	-6	18	1			4	O	-0.3
1929	NY-N	115	450	76	146	19	7	8	52	45	16	.324	.390	.451	108	6	6	78	6			-5	*O	-0.6
1931	Cin-N	101	376	46	102	12	5	1	41	17	5	.271	.308	.338	78	-14	-11	40	2			-2	O	-1.6
Total	18	1967	7363	1099	2376	339	183	67	981	484	260	.323	.369	.446	127	233	254	1235	268	92		-13	*O/12	15.2

■ PHIL ROUTCLIFFE Routcliffe, Philip John "Chicken" b: 10/24/1870, Oswego, N.Y. d: 10/4/18, Oswego, N.Y. 6', 175 lbs. Deb: 4/21/1890

| 1890 | Pit-N | 1 | 4 | 1 | 1 | 0 | 0 | 0 | 1 | 0 | 0 | .250 | .400 | .250 | 105 | 0 | 0 | 1 | 1 | | | 0 | /O | 0.0 |

■ DAVE ROWAN Rowan, David (b: David Drohan) b: 12/6/1882, Elora, Ont., Canada d: 7/30/55, Toronto, Ont., Can BL/TL, 5'11", 175 lbs. Deb: 5/27/11

| 1911 | StL-A | 18 | 65 | 7 | 25 | 1 | 1 | 0 | 11 | 4 | | .385 | .420 | .431 | 143 | 3 | 4 | 12 | 0 | | | -2 | 1 | 0.2 |

■ WADE ROWDON Rowdon, Wade Lee b: 9/7/60, Riverhead, N.Y. BR/TR, 6'2", 170 lbs. Deb: 9/08/84

1984	Cin-N	4	7	0	2	0	0	0	0	1		.286	.286	.286	58	-0	-0	1	0	0	0	1	/S3	0.1
1985	Cin-N	5	9	2	2	0	0	0	2	2	1	.222	.364	.222	64	-0	-0	1	0	0	0	-1	/3	-0.1
1986	Cin-N	38	80	9	20	5	1	0	10	9	17	.250	.333	.338	82	-1	-2	10	2	0	1	-5	/3SO2	-0.5
1987	Chi-N	11	31	2	7	1	1	1	4	3	10	.226	.294	.419	83	-1	-1	3	0	2	-1	-1	/3	-0.3
1988	Bal-A	20	30	1	3	0	0	0	0	0	6	.100	.100	.100	-45	-6	-6	-0	1	1	-0	3	/3OD	-0.2
Total	5	78	157	14	34	6	2	1	16	14	35	.217	.285	.299	59	-8	-9	15	3	3	-1	-3	/3OSD2	-1.0

■ DAVE ROWE Rowe, David E. b: 2/1856, Jacksonville, Ill. BR , 5'9", 180 lbs. Deb: 5/30/1877 M

1877	Chi-N	2	7	0	2	0	0	0		0	3	.286	.286	.286	72	-0	-0	1				-0	/OP	0.0
1882	Cle-N	24	97	13	25	4	3	1	17	4	9	.258	.287	.392	119	2	2	11				-3	O/P	-0.1
1883	Bal-a	59	256	40	80	11	6	0		2		.313	.318	.402	127	8	7	34				-9	O/S1P	-0.1
1884	StL-U	109	485	95	142	32	11	4		10		.293	.307	.429	141	22	19	65	0			-1	*OS/21P	1.5
1885	StL-N	16	62	8	10	3	0	0	3	5	8	.161	.224	.210	44	-4	-3	3				-2	O	-0.5
1886	KC-N	105	429	53	103	24	8	3	57	15	43	.240	.266	.354	82	-8	-12	42	2			-6	*OS/2M	-1.4
1888	KC-a	32	122	14	21	3	4	0	13	6		.172	.217	.262	52	-6	-7	8	2			2	OM	-0.5
Total	7	347	1458	223	383	77	32	8	90	42	63	.263	.284	.376	107	14	6	163	4			-21	O/S21P	-1.1

■ HARLAND ROWE Rowe, Harland Stimson "Hypie" b: 4/20/1896, Springvale, Me. d: 5/26/69, Springvale, Maine BL/TR, 6'1", 170 lbs. Deb: 6/23/16

| 1916 | Phi-A | 17 | 36 | 2 | 5 | 1 | 0 | 0 | 3 | 2 | 8 | .139 | .184 | .167 | 6 | -4 | -4 | 1 | 0 | | | -2 | /3O | -0.6 |

■ JACK ROWE Rowe, John Charles b: 12/8/1856, Harrisburg, Pa. d: 4/25/11, St.Louis, Mo. BL/TR, 5'8", 170 lbs. Deb: 9/06/1879 M

1879	Buf-N	8	34	8	12	1	0	0	8	0	1	.353	.353	.382	139	1	1	5				2	/CO	0.3
1880	Buf-N	79	326	43	82	6	1	0	36	6	17	.252	.265	.328	98	-0	-1	29				-19	*CO/3	-1.5
1881	Buf-N	64	246	30	82	11	11	0	43	1	12	.333	.336	.480	156	14	14	41				-8	C/S3O	0.6
1882	Buf-N	75	308	43	82	14	5	1	42	12	0	.266	.294	.354	105	2	1	33				-15	CS/3O	-0.6
1883	Buf-N	87	374	65	104	18	7	1	38	15	14	.278	.306	.372	102	2	1	44				-19	COS/3	-1.2
1884	Buf-N	93	400	85	126	14	14	4	61	23	14	.315	.352	.450	146	23	21	65				-13	CO/S	1.2
1885	Buf-N	98	421	62	122	28	8	2	51	13	19	.290	.311	.409	128	13	11	55				-16	SCO	0.1
1886	Det-N	111	468	97	142	21	9	6	87	26	27	.303	.340	.425	128	17	15	74	12			-20	*S/C	-0.5
1887	*Det-N	124	537	135	171	30	10	6	96	39	11	.318	.364	.445	123	19	16	98	22			-31	*S	-1.5
1888	Det-N	105	451	62	125	19	8	2	74	19	28	.277	.311	.368	118	9	9	56	10			-9	*S	0.2
1889	Pit-N	75	317	57	82	14	3	2	32	22	16	.259	.313	.341	93	-7	-2	36	5			-5	S	-0.3
1890	Buf-P	125	504	77	126	8	2	4	76	48		.250	.324	.333	84	-16	-8	59	10			-1	*SM	0.0
Total	12	1044	4386	764	1256	202	88	28	644	224	177	.286	.323	.402	116	77	78	594	59			-154	SCO/3	-3.2

■ SCHOOLBOY ROWE Rowe, Lynwood Thomas b: 1/11/10, Waco, Tex. d: 1/8/61, ElDorado, Ark. BR/TR, 6'4.5", 210 lbs. Deb: 4/15/33 C

| 1933 | Det-A | 21 | 50 | 6 | 11 | 1 | 0 | 0 | 6 | 1 | 4 | .220 | .235 | .240 | 26 | -5 | -5 | 3 | 0 | 0 | 0 | 1 | P | 0.0 |

YEAR	TM/L	G	AB	R	H	2B	3B	HR	RBI	BB	SO	AVG	OBP	SLG	PRO+	BR	/A	RC	SB	CS	SBR	FR	POS	TPR
1934	*Det-A	51	109	15	33	8	1	2	22	6	20	.303	.339	.450	102	-0	-0	17	0	0	0	-1	P	0.0
1935	*Det-A	45	109	19	34	3	2	3	28	12	12	.312	.380	.459	120	3	3	19	0	0	0	-2	P	0.0
1936	Det-A	45	90	16	23	2	1	1	12	13	15	.256	.356	.333	71	-4	-4	12	0	0	0	2	P	0.0
1937	Det-A	10	10	2	2	0	0	0	1	1	4	.200	.273	.200	21	-1	-1	1	0	0	0	1	P	0.0
1938	Det-A	4	6	1	1	1	0	0	0	0	1	.167	.167	.333	21	-1	-1	0	0	0	0	1	/P	0.0
1939	Det-A	31	61	7	15	0	1	1	12	5	7	.246	.303	.328	57	-4	-4	5	1	1	-0	1	P	0.0
1940	*Det-A	27	67	7	18	6	1	1	18	5	13	.269	.319	.433	85	-1	-2	9	1	1	-0	0	P	0.0
1941	Det-A	32	55	10	15	0	3	1	12	5	8	.273	.333	.436	93	-0	-1	8	0	0	0	1	P	0.0
1942	Det-A	2	4	0	0	0	0	0	0	0	0	.000	.000	.000	-93	-1	-1	0	0	0	0	0	/P	0.0
	Bro-N	14	19	2	4	0	0	0	2	1	4	.211	.250	.211	35	-2	-2	1	0			0	/P	0.0
1943	Phi-N	82	120	14	36	7	0	4	18	15	21	.300	.382	.458	148	7	7	20	0			0	P	1.2
1946	Phi-N	30	61	4	11	5	0	1	6	3	16	.180	.219	.311	51	-4	-4	4	0			-2	P	0.0
1947	Phi-N	43	79	9	22	2	0	2	11	13	18	.278	.380	.380	106	1	1	12	0			-1	P	0.0
1948	Phi-N	31	52	3	10	0	0	1	4	4	10	.192	.250	.250	36	-5	-5	4	1			1	P	0.0
1949	Phi-N	23	17	1	4	1	0	1	1	2	4	.235	.316	.471	111	0	0	3	0			1	P	0.0
Total	15	491	909	116	239	36	9	18	153	86	157	.263	.328	.382	87	-17	-18	119	3	2		3	P	1.2

■ BAMA ROWELL
Rowell, Carvel William b: 1/13/16, Citronelle, Ala. BL/TR, 5'11", 185 lbs. Deb: 9/04/39

YEAR	TM/L	G	AB	R	H	2B	3B	HR	RBI	BB	SO	AVG	OBP	SLG	PRO+	BR	/A	RC	SB	CS	SBR	FR	POS	TPR
1939	Bos-N	21	59	5	11	2	2	0	6	1	4	.186	.200	.288	32	-6	-5	3	0			-1	O	-0.5
1940	Bos-N	130	486	46	148	19	8	3	58	18	22	.305	.331	.395	105	-1	2	64	12			-2	*2/O	0.8
1941	Bos-N	138	483	49	129	23	6	7	60	39	36	.267	.322	.383	102	-2	0	61	11			-9	2O3	-0.2
1946	Bos-N	95	293	37	82	12	6	3	31	29	15	.280	.345	.392	108	3	3	41	5			-1	O	0.0
1947	Bos-N	113	384	48	106	23	2	5	40	18	14	.276	.310	.385	86	-10	-9	47	7			-11	*O/23	-2.1
1948	Phi-N	77	196	15	47	16	2	1	22	8	14	.240	.270	.357	70	-9	-9	18	2			-12	3O2	-2.1
Total	6	574	1901	200	523	95	26	19	217	113	105	.275	.316	.382	95	-26	-19	233	37			-34	2O/3	-4.1

■ ED ROWEN
Rowen, W. Edward b: 10/22/1857, Bridgeport, Conn. d: 2/22/1892, Bridgeport, Conn. 6'1", 170 lbs. Deb: 5/01/1882

YEAR	TM/L	G	AB	R	H	2B	3B	HR	RBI	BB	SO	AVG	OBP	SLG	PRO+	BR	/A	RC	SB	CS	SBR	FR	POS	TPR
1882	Bos-N	83	327	36	81	7	4	1	43	19	18	.248	.289	.303	90	-3	-3	29				-12	OC/S3	-1.1
1883	Phi-a	49	196	28	43	10	1	0		10		.219	.257	.281	67	-6	-8	15				-1	C/O32	-0.4
1884	Phi-a	4	15	4	6	1	0	0		1		.400	.471	.467	198	2	2	3				-3	/C	0.0
Total	3	136	538	68	130	18	5	1	43	30	18	.242	.283	.299	85	-7	-10	47				-16	/COS32	-1.5

■ CHUCK ROWLAND
Rowland, Charles Leland b: 7/23/1899, Warrenton, N.C. BR/TR, 6'1", 185 lbs. Deb: 5/11/23

YEAR	TM/L	G	AB	R	H	2B	3B	HR	RBI	BB	SO	AVG	OBP	SLG	PRO+	BR	/A	RC	SB	CS	SBR	FR	POS	TPR
1923	Phi-A	5	6	0	0	0	0	0	0	0	2	.000	.000	.000	-99	-2	-2	0	0	0	0	0	/C	0.0

■ RICH ROWLAND
Rowland, Richard Garnet b: 2/25/67, Cloverdale, Cal. BR/TR, 6'1", 210 lbs. Deb: 9/07/90

YEAR	TM/L	G	AB	R	H	2B	3B	HR	RBI	BB	SO	AVG	OBP	SLG	PRO+	BR	/A	RC	SB	CS	SBR	FR	POS	TPR
1990	Det-A	7	19	3	3	1	0	0	2	4	4	.158	.238	.211	27	-2	-2	1	0	0	0	-0	/CD	-0.1

■ JIM ROXBURGH
Roxburgh, James A. b: 1/17/1858, San Francisco, Cal d: 2/21/34, San Francisco, Csl BR/TR, Deb: 5/30/1884

YEAR	TM/L	G	AB	R	H	2B	3B	HR	RBI	BB	SO	AVG	OBP	SLG	PRO+	BR	/A	RC	SB	CS	SBR	FR	POS	TPR
1884	Bal-a	2	4	1	2	0	0	0		1		.500	.667	.500	281	1	1	1				0	/C	0.1
1887	Phi-a	2	8	0	1	0	0	0		0	1	.125	.125	.125	-29	-1	-1	0	0			-0	/C2	0.0
Total	2	4	12	1	3	0	0	0		1		.250	.357	.250	83	-0	-0	1	0			-0	/C2	0.1

■ JERRY ROYSTER
Royster, Jeron Kennis b: 10/18/52, Sacramento, Cal. BR/TR, 6', 165 lbs. Deb: 8/14/73

YEAR	TM/L	G	AB	R	H	2B	3B	HR	RBI	BB	SO	AVG	OBP	SLG	PRO+	BR	/A	RC	SB	CS	SBR	FR	POS	TPR
1973	LA-N	10	19	1	4	0	0	0	2	0	5	.211	.211	.211	18	-2	-2	1	1	0	0	2	/32	0.0
1974	LA-N	6	0	2	0	0	0	0	0	0	0	—	—	—		0	0	0	0	0	0	2	/23O	0.2
1975	LA-N	13	36	2	9	2	1	0	1	1	3	.250	.270	.361	77	-1	-1	3	1	0	0	-1	/O23S	-0.1
1976	Atl-N	149	533	65	132	13	1	5	45	52	53	.248	.316	.304	72	-16	-20	52	24	13	-1	17	*3/S	-0.5
1977	Atl-N	140	445	64	96	10	2	6	28	38	67	.216	.279	.288	47	-30	-37	36	28	10	2	-28	3S2/O	-5.5
1978	Atl-N	140	529	67	137	17	8	2	35	56	49	.259	.333	.333	78	-8	-15	60	27	17	-2	-12	2S/3	-2.1
1979	Atl-N	154	601	103	164	25	6	3	51	62	59	.273	.341	.349	83	-8	-14	78	35	8	6	13	32	0.7
1980	Atl-N	123	392	42	95	17	5	1	20	37	48	.242	.309	.319	73	-12	-14	39	22	13	-1	-15	23O	-3.0
1981	Atl-N	64	93	13	19	4	1	0	9	7	14	.204	.260	.269	49	-6	-6	7	5	5	-3	3	32	-0.3
1982	*Atl-N	108	261	43	77	13	2	2	25	22	36	.295	.354	.383	102	2	1	37	14	6	1	-2	3O2S	0.0
1983	Atl-N	91	268	32	63	10	3	3	30	28	35	.235	.307	.328	71	-9	-11	25	11	7	-1	8	32OS	-0.3
1984	Atl-N	81	227	22	47	13	2	1	21	15	41	.207	.259	.295	52	-14	-16	16	6	4	-1	3	23SO	-0.9
1985	SD-N	90	249	31	70	13	2	5	31	32	31	.281	.365	.410	118	6	7	37	6	5	-1	2	23/SO	0.9
1986	SD-N	118	257	31	66	12	0	5	26	32	45	.257	.339	.362	95	-2	-1	31	3	5	-2	-2	3S2/O	-0.4
1987	Chi-A	55	154	25	37	11	0	7	23	19	28	.240	.328	.448	101	-0	-0	23	2	1	0	-7	3O/2D	-0.7
	NY-A	18	42	1	15	2	0	0	4	4	4	.357	.413	.405	120	1	1	6	2	1	0	3	3/2SO	0.4
	Yr	73	196	26	52	13	0	7	27	23	32	.265	.345	.439	104	2	1	30	4	2	0	-5		-0.3
1988	Atl-N	68	102	8	18	3	0	0	1	6	16	.176	.222	.206	22	-10	-11	5	0	0	0	3	O3/2S	-0.8
Total	16	1428	4208	552	1049	165	33	40	352	411	534	.249	.318	.333	76	-108	-138	456	189	95	-0	-10	32SO/D	-12.4

■ WILLIE ROYSTER
Royster, Willie Arthur b: 4/11/54, Clarksville, Va. BR/TR, 5'11", 180 lbs. Deb: 9/03/81

YEAR	TM/L	G	AB	R	H	2B	3B	HR	RBI	BB	SO	AVG	OBP	SLG	PRO+	BR	/A	RC	SB	CS	SBR	FR	POS	TPR
1981	Bal-A	4	4	0	0	0	0	0	0	0	2	.000	.000	.000	-99	-1	-1	0	0	0	0	-0	/C	0.0

■ VIC ROZNOVSKY
Roznovsky, Victor Joseph b: 10/19/38, Shiner, Tex. BL/TR, 6', 170 lbs. Deb: 6/28/64

YEAR	TM/L	G	AB	R	H	2B	3B	HR	RBI	BB	SO	AVG	OBP	SLG	PRO+	BR	/A	RC	SB	CS	SBR	FR	POS	TPR
1964	Chi-N	35	76	2	15	1	0	0	2	5	18	.197	.247	.211	29	-7	-7	4	0	1	-1	-6	C	-1.3
1965	Chi-N	71	172	9	38	4	1	3	15	16	30	.221	.298	.308	70	-6	-7	17	1	0	0	1	C	-0.2
1966	Bal-A	41	97	4	23	5	0	1	10	9	21	.237	.308	.320	82	-2	-2	10	0	0	0	-2	C	-0.2
1967	Bal-A	45	97	7	20	5	0	0	10	1	20	.206	.214	.258	39	-7	-7	4	0	0	0	-2	C	-0.7
1969	Phi-N	13	13	0	3	0	0	0	1	1	4	.231	.286	.231	47	-1	-1	1	0	0	0	0	/C	0.0
Total	5	205	455	22	99	15	1	4	38	32	83	.218	.275	.281	59	-24	-24	36	1	1	-0	-8	C	-2.4

■ AL RUBELING
Rubeling, Albert William b: 5/10/13, Baltimore, Md. d: 1/28/88, Baltimore, Md. BR/TR, 6', 185 lbs. Deb: 4/16/40

YEAR	TM/L	G	AB	R	H	2B	3B	HR	RBI	BB	SO	AVG	OBP	SLG	PRO+	BR	/A	RC	SB	CS	SBR	FR	POS	TPR
1940	Phi-A	108	376	49	92	16	6	4	38	48	58	.245	.330	.351	78	-13	-11	45	4	5	-2	-7	32	-1.3
1941	Phi-A	6	19	0	5	0	0	0	2	2	1	.263	.333	.263	61	-1	-1	2	0	0	0	-2	/3	-0.1
1943	Pit-N	47	168	23	44	8	4	0	9	8	17	.262	.295	.357	85	-3	-4	17	0			0	2/3	-0.2
1944	Pit-N	92	184	22	45	7	2	4	30	19	19	.245	.322	.370	90	-1	-2	23	4			0	O23	0.0
Total	4	253	747	94	186	31	12	8	79	77	95	.249	.321	.355	82	-18	-19	87	8	5		-9	3/2O	-1.6

■ SONNY RUBERTO
Ruberto, John Edward b: 1/2/46, Staten Island, N.Y. BR/TR, 5'11", 175 lbs. Deb: 5/25/69 C

YEAR	TM/L	G	AB	R	H	2B	3B	HR	RBI	BB	SO	AVG	OBP	SLG	PRO+	BR	/A	RC	SB	CS	SBR	FR	POS	TPR
1969	SD-N	19	21	3	3	0	0	0	0	1	7	.143	.182	.143	-8	-3	-3	1	0	0	0	4	C	0.2
1972	Cin-N	2	3	0	0	0	0	0	0	0	1	.000	.250	.000	-25	-0	-0	0	0	0	0	-0	/C	0.0
Total	2	21	24	3	3	0	0	0	0	1	8	.125	.192	.125	-10	-3	-3	1	0	0	0	4	/C	0.2

■ ART RUBLE
Ruble, William Arthur "Speedy" b: 3/11/03, Knoxville, Tenn. d: 11/1/83, Maryville, Tenn. BL/TR, 5'10.5", 168 lbs. Deb: 4/18/27

YEAR	TM/L	G	AB	R	H	2B	3B	HR	RBI	BB	SO	AVG	OBP	SLG	PRO+	BR	/A	RC	SB	CS	SBR	FR	POS	TPR
1927	Det-A	56	91	16	15	4	2	0	11	14	15	.165	.283	.253	39	-8	-8	7	2	2	-1	-7	O	-1.7
1934	Phi-N	19	54	7	15	4	0	0	8	7	3	.278	.361	.352	81	-0	-1	7	0			-1	O	-0.2
Total	2	75	145	23	30	8	2	0	19	21	18	.207	.311	.290	55	-9	-10	14	2	2		-8	/O	-1.9

■ JOHNNY RUCKER
Rucker, John Joel b: 1/15/17, Crabapple, Ga. d: 8/7/85, Moultrie, Ga. BL/TR, 6'2", 175 lbs. Deb: 4/16/40

YEAR	TM/L	G	AB	R	H	2B	3B	HR	RBI	BB	SO	AVG	OBP	SLG	PRO+	BR	/A	RC	SB	CS	SBR	FR	POS	TPR
1940	NY-N	86	277	38	82	7	5	4	23	7	32	.296	.313	.401	95	-2	-3	34	4			-3	O	-0.7
1941	NY-N	143	622	95	179	38	9	1	42	29	61	.288	.320	.383	95	-4	-6	76	8			1	*O	-0.9
1943	NY-N	132	505	56	138	19	4	2	46	22	44	.273	.304	.339	85	-11	-11	53	4			-2	*O	-1.7

YEAR	TM/L	G	AB	R	H	2B	3B	HR	RBI	BB	SO	AVG	OBP	SLG	PRO+	BR	/A	RC	SB	CS	SBR	FR	POS	TPR
1944	NY-N	144	587	79	143	14	8	6	39	24	48	.244	.275	.325	69	-26	-26	54	8			-9	*O	-4.6
1945	NY-N	105	429	58	117	19	11	7	51	20	36	.273	.305	.417	98	-3	-3	55	7			-4	O	-1.1
1946	NY-N	95	197	28	52	8	2	1	13	7	27	.264	.300	.340	81	-5	-6	20	4			-3	O	-1.0
Total	6	705	2617	354	711	105	39	21	214	109	248	.272	.302	.366	87	-51	-54	293	35			-19	O	-10.0

■ JOHN RUDDERHAM
Rudderham, John Edmund b: 8/30/1863, Quincy, Mass. d: 4/3/42, Randolph, Mass. BR/TR, 5'8", 170 lbs. Deb: 9/18/1884

YEAR	TM/L	G	AB	R	H	2B	3B	HR	RBI	BB	SO	AVG	OBP	SLG	PRO+	BR	/A	RC	SB	CS	SBR	FR	POS	TPR
1884	Bos-U	1	4	0	1	0	0	0		0	0	.250	.250	.250	71	-0	-0	0	0			-1	/O	0.0

■ JOE RUDI
Rudi, Joseph Oden b: 9/7/46, Modesto, Cal. BR/TR, 6'2", 200 lbs. Deb: 4/11/67 C

YEAR	TM/L	G	AB	R	H	2B	3B	HR	RBI	BB	SO	AVG	OBP	SLG	PRO+	BR	/A	RC	SB	CS	SBR	FR	POS	TPR
1967	KC-A	19	43	4	8	2	0	0	1	3	7	.186	.239	.233	41	-3	-3	2	0	0	0	-1	/1O	-0.5
1968	Oak-A	68	181	10	32	5	1	1	12	12	32	.177	.236	.232	44	-13	-12	10	1	1	-0	-4	O	-2.1
1969	Oak-A	35	122	10	23	3	1	2	6	5	16	.189	.220	.279	41	-10	-10	7	1	1	-0	1	O1	-1.0
1970	Oak-A	106	350	40	108	23	2	11	42	16	61	.309	.342	.480	129	10	12	54	3	1	0	0	O1	0.4
1971	*Oak-A	127	513	62	137	23	4	10	52	28	62	.267	.306	.386	97	-5	-4	57	3	2	-0	2	*O/1	-0.6
1972	*Oak-A	147	593	94	181	32	9	19	75	37	62	.305	.348	.486	154	31	34	95	3	4	-2	-6	*O/3	2.6
1973	*Oak-A	120	437	53	118	25	1	12	66	30	72	.270	.320	.414	111	2	5	55	0	0	0	-0	*O/1D	0.1
1974	*Oak-A	158	593	73	174	39	4	22	99	34	92	.293	.337	.484	143	23	28	94	2	3	-1	-15	*O1/D	0.7
1975	*Oak-A	126	468	66	130	26	6	21	75	40	56	.278	.339	.494	136	18	19	76	2	1	0	-10	1O/D	0.3
1976	Oak-A	130	500	54	135	32	3	13	94	41	71	.270	.329	.424	124	11	14	68	6	1	1	-5	*O1/D	0.7
1977	Cal-A	64	242	48	64	13	2	13	53	22	48	.264	.336	.496	128	7	8	42	1	0	0	-0	O/D	0.6
1978	Cal-A	133	497	58	127	27	1	17	79	28	82	.256	.298	.416	103	-3	-0	60	2	1	0	0	*OD1	-0.3
1979	Cal-A	90	330	35	80	11	3	11	61	24	61	.242	.296	.394	87	-8	-7	38	0	0	0	-0	O/1D	-0.9
1980	Cal-A	104	372	42	88	17	1	16	53	17	84	.237	.279	.417	90	-8	-6	41	1	0	0	5	O/1D	-0.3
1981	Bos-A	49	122	14	22	3	0	6	24	8	29	.180	.242	.352	66	-5	-6	10	0	0	0	-1	D/1O	-0.7
1982	Oak-A	71	193	21	41	6	1	5	18	24	35	.212	.303	.332	77	-7	-6	21	0	0	0	-4	1O/D	-1.0
Total	16	1547	5556	684	1468	287	39	179	810	369	870	.264	.314	.427	112	41	66	730	25	15	-1	-43	*O1/D3	-2.0

■ DUTCH RUDOLPH
Rudolph, John Herman b: 7/10/1882, Natrona, Pa. d: 4/17/67, Natrona, Pa. 5'10", 160 lbs. Deb: 7/03/03

YEAR	TM/L	G	AB	R	H	2B	3B	HR	RBI	BB	SO	AVG	OBP	SLG	PRO+	BR	/A	RC	SB	CS	SBR	FR	POS	TPR
1903	Phi-N	1	1	0	0	0	0	0	0	0		.000	.000	.000	-99	-0	-0	0	0			0	H	0.0
1904	Chi-N	2	3	0	1	0	0	0	0	0		.333	.333	.333	108	0	0	0	0			-1	/O	0.0
Total	2	3	4	0	1	0	0	0	0	0		.250	.250	.250	53	-0	-0	0	0			-1	/O	0.0

■ KEN RUDOLPH
Rudolph, Kenneth Victor b: 12/29/46, Rockford, Ill. BR/TR, 6'1", 180 lbs. Deb: 4/20/69

YEAR	TM/L	G	AB	R	H	2B	3B	HR	RBI	BB	SO	AVG	OBP	SLG	PRO+	BR	/A	RC	SB	CS	SBR	FR	POS	TPR
1969	Chi-N	27	34	7	7	1	0	1	6	6	11	.206	.325	.324	73	-1	-1	4	0	0	0	0	C/O	0.0
1970	Chi-N	20	40	1	4	1	0	0	2	1	12	.100	.122	.125	-30	-8	-8	1	0	0	0	1	C	-0.5
1971	Chi-N	25	76	5	15	3	0	0	7	6	20	.197	.265	.237	38	-6	-7	5	0	0	0	7	C	0.0
1972	Chi-N	42	106	10	25	1	1	2	9	6	14	.236	.283	.321	64	-4	-5	8	1	2	-1	6	C	0.2
1973	Chi-N	64	170	12	35	8	1	2	17	7	25	.206	.242	.300	46	-12	-13	10	1	4	-2	-3	C	-1.5
1974	SF-N	57	158	11	41	3	0	0	10	21	15	.259	.350	.278	74	-4	-5	15	0	0	0	3	C	0.0
1975	StL-N	44	80	5	16	2	0	1	6	3	10	.200	.229	.262	35	-7	-7	4	0	0	0	2	C	-0.4
1976	StL-N	27	50	1	8	3	0	0	5	1	7	.160	.176	.220	12	-6	-6	2	0	0	0	2	C	-0.3
1977	SF-N	11	15	1	3	0	0	0	1	3	.200	.250	.200	22	-2	-2	1	0	0	0	2	C	0.1
	Bal-A	11	14	2	4	1	0	0	2	0	4	.286	.286	.357	79	-1	-0	1	0	0	0	5	C	0.4
Total	9	328	743	55	158	23	2	6	64	52	121	.213	.268	.273	48	-49	-55	51	2	6	-3	25	C/O	-2.0

■ MUDDY RUEL
Ruel, Herold Dominic b: 2/20/1896, St.Louis, Mo. d: 11/13/63, Palo Alto, Cal. BR/TR, 5'9", 150 lbs. Deb: 5/29/15 MC

YEAR	TM/L	G	AB	R	H	2B	3B	HR	RBI	BB	SO	AVG	OBP	SLG	PRO+	BR	/A	RC	SB	CS	SBR	FR	POS	TPR
1915	StL-A	10	14	0	0	0	0	0	1	5	5	.000	.263	.000	-22	-2	-2	0	0			-1	/C	-0.2
1917	NY-A	6	17	1	2	0	0	0	1	2	2	.118	.211	.118	0	-2	-2	1	1			-1	/C	-0.2
1918	NY-A	3	6	0	2	0	0	0	0	0	1	.333	.500	.333	148	1	1	1	1			0	/C	0.1
1919	NY-A	79	233	18	56	6	0	0	31	34	26	.240	.340	.266	71	-7	-8	22	4			2	C	-0.1
1920	NY-A	82	261	30	70	14	1	1	15	15	18	.268	.310	.341	70	-11	-12	28	4	2	0	0	C	-0.4
1921	Bos-A	113	358	41	99	21	1	1	45	41	15	.277	.352	.349	82	-10	-9	45	2	7	-4	-10	*C	-1.7
1922	Bos-A	116	361	34	92	15	1	0	28	41	26	.255	.333	.302	67	-17	-16	39	4	2	0	-2	*C	-1.4
1923	Was-A	136	449	63	142	24	3	0	54	55	21	.316	.394	.383	111	6	9	70	4	6	-2	18	*C	3.2
1924	*Was-A	149	501	50	142	20	2	0	57	62	20	.283	.370	.331	84	-11	-9	65	7	11	-5	12	*C	0.7
1925	*Was-A	127	393	55	122	9	2	0	54	63	14	.310	.411	.344	95	-0	1	60	4	5	-2	10	*C/1	1.5
1926	Was-A	117	368	42	110	22	4	1	53	61	14	.299	.401	.389	109	6	8	61	7	6	-2	0	*C	1.3
1927	Was-A	131	428	61	132	16	5	1	52	63	18	.308	.403	.376	104	5	6	65	9	6	-1	-4	*C	0.6
1928	Was-A	108	350	31	90	18	2	0	55	44	14	.257	.342	.320	75	-12	-11	40	12	10	-2	7	*C/1	0.0
1929	Was-A	69	188	16	46	4	2	0	20	31	7	.245	.352	.287	66	-8	-9	20	0	4	-2	9	C	0.4
1930	Was-A	66	198	18	50	3	4	0	26	24	13	.253	.342	.308	66	-9	-10	23	1	0	0	3	C	0.4
1931	Bos-A	33	83	6	25	5	0	0	6	9	6	.301	.370	.361	98	-1	0	12	0	0	0	1	C	0.3
	Det-A	14	50	1	6	1	0	0	3	5	1	.120	.200	.140	-9	-8	-8	2	0	0	0	3	C	-0.3
	Yr	47	133	7	31	6	0	0	9	14	7	.233	.306	.278	56	-9	-8	12	0	0	0	4		0.0
1932	Det-A	51	136	10	32	4	2	0	18	17	6	.235	.320	.294	58	-8	-9	14	1	0	0	-2	C	-0.6
1933	StL-A	36	63	13	12	2	0	0	8	24	4	.190	.414	.222	68	-1	-1	8	0	0	0	2	C	0.2
1934	Chi-A	22	57	4	12	3	0	0	7	8	5	.211	.308	.263	47	-4	-5	5	0	0	0	-2	C	-0.3
Total	19	1468	4514	494	1242	187	29	4	534	606	238	.275	.365	.332	83	-93	-85	581	61	59		47	*C/1	3.1

■ DUTCH RUETHER
Ruether, Walter Henry b: 9/13/1893, Alameda, Cal. d: 5/16/70, Phoenix, Ariz. BL/TL, 6'1.5", 180 lbs. Deb: 4/13/17

YEAR	TM/L	G	AB	R	H	2B	3B	HR	RBI	BB	SO	AVG	OBP	SLG	PRO+	BR	/A	RC	SB	CS	SBR	FR	POS	TPR
1917	Chi-N	31	44	3	12	1	3	0	11	8	11	.273	.385	.432	139	3	2	7	0			0	P/1	0.5
	Cin-N	19	24	1	5	2	0	0	1	3	6	.208	.296	.292	84	-0	-0	2	1			-0	/P	0.0
	Yr	50	68	4	17	3	3	0	12	11	17	.250	.354	.382	122	2	2	9	1			0		0.5
1918	Cin-N	2	3	0	0	0	0	0	0	0	2	.000	.000	.000	-99	-1	-1	0	0			-0	/P	0.0
1919	*Cin-N	42	92	8	24	2	3	0	6	4	18	.261	.292	.348	94	-1	-1	9	1			-3	P	0.0
1920	Cin-N	45	104	3	20	4	0	0	10	5	24	.192	.229	.231	33	-9	-9	6	0	0	0	-0	P/1	0.0
1921	Bro-N	49	97	12	34	5	2	2	13	4	9	.351	.376	.505	127	4	4	18	1	0	0	-1	P	0.0
1922	Bro-N	67	125	12	26	6	1	2	20	12	11	.208	.283	.320	56	-9	-8	12	0	0	0	-0	P	0.0
1923	Bro-N	49	117	6	32	1	0	0	10	12	12	.274	.341	.282	68	-5	-5	12	0	0	0	-2	P/1	0.0
1924	Bro-N	34	62	5	15	1	4	0	4	5	2	.242	.299	.290	60	-4	-3	6	0	0	0	2	P	0.0
1925	*Was-A	55	108	18	36	3	2	1	15	10	8	.333	.390	.426	109	1	2	18	0	1	-1	-2	P/1	0.0
1926	Was-A	47	92	6	23	2	0	1	11	6	10	.250	.296	.304	58	-6	-6	9	0	0	0	-2	P	-0.2
	*NY-A	13	21	2	2	0	0	0	0	0	1	.095	.136	.095	-39	-4	-4	0	0	0	0	-1	/P	-0.3
	Yr	60	113	8	25	2	0	1	11	6	11	.221	.267	.265	40	-10	-10	8	0	0	0	-3	P	-0.5
1927	NY-A	35	80	7	21	3	0	1	10	8	15	.262	.330	.338	76	-3	-3	9	0	0	0	1	P	0.0
Total	11	488	969	83	250	30	12	7	111	77	129	.258	.314	.335	76	-34	-32	108	3	1		-7	P/1	0.0

■ RUDY RUFER
Rufer, Rudolph Joseph b: 10/28/26, Ridgewood, N.Y. BR/TR, 6'0.5", 165 lbs. Deb: 9/22/49

YEAR	TM/L	G	AB	R	H	2B	3B	HR	RBI	BB	SO	AVG	OBP	SLG	PRO+	BR	/A	RC	SB	CS	SBR	FR	POS	TPR
1949	NY-N	7	15	1	1	0	0	0	2	2	0	.067	.176	.067	-32	-3	-3	0	0			-0	/S	-0.2
1950	NY-N	15	11	1	1	0	0	0	0	0	1	.091	.091	.091	-52	-2	-2	0	1			1	/S	0.0
Total	2	22	26	2	2	0	0	0	2	2	1	.077	.143	.077	-40	-5	-5	0	1			1	/S	-0.2

■ RED RUFFING
Ruffing, Charles Herbert b: 5/3/04, Granville, Ill. d: 2/17/86, Mayfield Hts., O. BR/TR, 6'1.5", 205 lbs. Deb: 5/31/24 CH

YEAR	TM/L	G	AB	R	H	2B	3B	HR	RBI	BB	SO	AVG	OBP	SLG	PRO+	BR	/A	RC	SB	CS	SBR	FR	POS	TPR
1924	Bos-A	8	7	0	1	0	0	0		0	1	.143	.143	.429	44	-1	-1	0	0	0	0	-1	/P	0.0
1925	Bos-A	37	79	6	17	4	2	0	11	1	22	.215	.235	.316	39	-8	-8	6	0	0	0	-1	P	0.0

YEAR	TM/L	G	AB	R	H	2B	3B	HR	RBI	BB	SO	AVG	OBP	SLG	PRO+	BR	/A	RC	SB	CS	SBR	FR	POS	TPR
1926	Bos-A	37	51	8	10	1	0	1	5	2	12	.196	.226	.275	31	-5	-5	3	0	1	-1	-1	P	0.0
1927	Bos-A	29	55	5	14	3	1	0	4	0	6	.255	.268	.345	59	-4	-3	5	0	0	0	-0	P	0.0
1928	Bos-A	60	121	12	38	13	1	2	19	3	12	.314	.331	.488	115	1	2	19	0	0	0	-3	P	0.0
1929	Bos-A	60	114	9	35	9	0	2	17	2	13	.307	.325	.439	97	-1	-1	16	0	0	0	-2	P/O	0.0
1930	Bos-A	6	11	2	3	2	0	0	1	0	1	.273	.273	.455	84	-0	-0	1	0	0	0	-1	/P	0.0
	NY-A	52	99	15	37	6	2	4	21	7	7	.374	.415	.596	160	8	8	24	0	0	0	-3	P	0.0
	Yr	58	110	17	40	8	2	4	22	7	8	.364	.402	.582	153	7	8	25	0	0	0	-4		0.0
1931	NY-A	48	109	14	36	8	1	3	12	1	13	.330	.336	.505	125	2	3	18	0	0	0	-4	P/O	0.0
1932	*NY-A	55	124	20	38	6	1	3	19	6	10	.306	.338	.444	106	-0	1	18	0	0	0	-3	P	0.0
1933	NY-A	55	115	10	29	3	1	2	13	7	15	.252	.295	.348	74	-5	-4	12	0	0	0	0	P	0.0
1934	NY-A	45	113	11	28	3	0	2	13	3	17	.248	.274	.327	58	-8	-7	10	0	0	0	-3	P	0.0
1935	NY-A	50	109	13	37	10	0	2	18	3	9	.339	.363	.486	125	2	3	19	0	0	0	-2	P	0.0
1936	*NY-A	53	127	14	37	5	0	5	22	11	12	.291	.348	.449	99	-1	-1	20	0	0	0	2	P	0.0
1937	*NY-A	54	129	11	26	3	0	1	10	13	24	.202	.275	.248	32	-13	-13	9	0	0	0	-4	P	0.0
1938	*NY-A	45	107	12	24	4	1	3	17	17	21	.224	.331	.364	74	-4	-4	14	0	0	0	-2	P	0.0
1939	*NY-A	44	114	12	35	1	0	1	20	7	18	.307	.347	.342	78	-4	-4	14	1	0	0	-1	P	0.0
1940	NY-A	33	89	8	11	4	0	1	7	3	9	.124	.152	.202	-9	-15	-14	2	0	0	0	-3	P	0.0
1941	*NY-A	38	89	10	27	8	1	2	22	4	12	.303	.333	.483	115	1	1	14	0	0	0	-3	P	0.0
1942	*NY-A	30	80	8	20	4	0	1	13	5	13	.250	.302	.338	81	-2	-2	8	0	0	0	-2	P	0.0
1945	NY-A	21	46	4	10	0	1	1	5	0	8	.217	.217	.326	54	-3	-3	3	0	0	0	-1	P	0.0
1946	NY-A	8	25	1	3	1	0	0	1	1	8	.120	.154	.160	-12	-4	-4	1	0	0	0	-1	/P	0.0
1947	Chi-A	14	24	2	5	0	0	0	3	1	3	.208	.240	.208	26	-2	-2	1	0	0	0	-0	/P	0.0
Total	22	882	1937	207	521	98	13	36	273	97	266	.269	.306	.389	81	-67	-59	238	1	1	-0	-37	P/O	0.0

■ CHICO RUIZ Ruiz, Hiraldo (Sablon) b: 12/5/38, Santo Domingo, Cuba d: 2/9/72, San Diego, Cal. BB/TR, 6', 169 lbs. Deb: 4/13/64

YEAR	TM/L	G	AB	R	H	2B	3B	HR	RBI	BB	SO	AVG	OBP	SLG	PRO+	BR	/A	RC	SB	CS	SBR	FR	POS	TPR
1964	Cin-N	77	311	33	76	13	2	2	16	7	41	.244	.270	.318	63	-15	-16	28	11	3	2	-10	32	-2.6
1965	Cin-N	29	18	7	2	1	0	0	1	0	5	.111	.111	.167	-21	-3	-3	-0	1	2	-1	4	/3S	-0.6
1966	Cin-N	82	110	13	28	2	1	0	5	5	14	.255	.287	.291	56	-6	-7	9	1	2	-1	1	3/OS	-0.6
1967	Cin-N	105	250	32	55	12	4	0	13	11	35	.220	.259	.300	53	-13	-16	18	9	4	0	2	23S/O	-1.0
1968	Cin-N	85	139	15	36	2	1	0	9	12	18	.259	.318	.288	78	-3	-3	13	4	3	-1	8	21/3S	0.6
1969	Cin-N	88	196	19	48	4	1	0	13	14	28	.245	.295	.276	58	-10	-11	17	4	2	0	-6	2S/310	-1.1
1970	Cal-A	68	107	10	26	3	1	0	12	7	16	.243	.296	.290	64	-5	-5	9	3	0	1	0	3/2S1C	-0.3
1971	Cal-A	31	19	4	5	0	0	0	0	2	7	.263	.333	.263	76	-1	-0	2	1	0	0	3	/32	0.3
Total	8	565	1150	133	276	37	10	2	69	58	164	.240	.281	.295	60	-55	-62	96	34	16	1	1	23/S10C	-4.7

■ CHICO RUIZ Ruiz, Manuel (Cruz) b: 11/1/51, Santurce, P.R. BR/TR, 5'11.5", 170 lbs. Deb: 7/29/78

YEAR	TM/L	G	AB	R	H	2B	3B	HR	RBI	BB	SO	AVG	OBP	SLG	PRO+	BR	/A	RC	SB	CS	SBR	FR	POS	TPR
1978	Atl-N	18	46	3	13	3	0	0	2	2	4	.283	.313	.348	76	-1	-2	5	0	0	0	1	2/3	0.1
1980	Atl-N	25	26	3	8	2	1	0	2	3	7	.308	.379	.462	129	1	1	4	0	1	-1	2	3/S2	0.3
Total	2	43	72	6	21	5	1	0	4	5	11	.292	.338	.389	95	0	-0	9	0	1	-1	3	/32S	0.4

■ JOE RULLO Rullo, Joseph Vincent b: 6/16/16, New York, N.Y. d: 10/28/69, Philadelphia, Pa. BR/TR, 5'11", 168 lbs. Deb: 9/22/43

YEAR	TM/L	G	AB	R	H	2B	3B	HR	RBI	BB	SO	AVG	OBP	SLG	PRO+	BR	/A	RC	SB	CS	SBR	FR	POS	TPR
1943	Phi-A	16	55	2	16	3	0	0	6	8	7	.291	.381	.345	114	1	1	8	0	0	0	-1	2	0.1
1944	Phi-A	35	96	5	16	0	0	0	5	6	19	.167	.223	.167	12	-11	-11	4	1	0	0	4	2/1	-0.5
Total	2	51	151	7	32	3	0	0	11	14	26	.212	.283	.232	50	-10	-9	12	1	0	0	3	/21	-0.4

■ WILLIAM RUMLER Rumler, William George b: 3/27/1891, Milford, Neb. d: 5/26/66, Lincoln, Neb. BR/TR, 6'1", 190 lbs. Deb: 5/04/14

YEAR	TM/L	G	AB	R	H	2B	3B	HR	RBI	BB	SO	AVG	OBP	SLG	PRO+	BR	/A	RC	SB	CS	SBR	FR	POS	TPR
1914	StL-A	34	46	2	8	1	0	0	6	3	12	.174	.240	.196	32	-4	-4	3	2	2	-1	-3	C/O	-0.7
1916	StL-A	27	37	6	12	3	0	0	10	3	7	.324	.375	.405	141	1	2	6	0			0	/C	0.3
1917	StL-A	78	88	7	23	3	4	1	16	8	9	.261	.323	.420	132	2	3	12	2			0	/O	0.2
Total	3	139	171	15	43	7	4	1	32	14	28	.251	.312	.357	107	-0	1	20	4	2		-3	/CO	-0.2

■ PAUL RUNGE Runge, Paul William b: 5/21/58, Kingston, N.Y. BR/TR, 6', 165 lbs. Deb: 9/25/81

YEAR	TM/L	G	AB	R	H	2B	3B	HR	RBI	BB	SO	AVG	OBP	SLG	PRO+	BR	/A	RC	SB	CS	SBR	FR	POS	TPR
1981	Atl-N	10	27	2	7	1	0	0	2	4	4	.259	.355	.296	84	-0	-0	3	0	0	0	-1	S	0.0
1982	Atl-N	4	2	0	0	0	0	0	0	0	0	.000	.000	.000	-96	-1	-1	0	0	0	0	0	/H	0.0
1983	Atl-N	5	8	0	2	0	0	0	1	1	4	.250	.333	.250	59	-0	-0	1	0	0	0	-1	/2	0.0
1984	Atl-N	28	90	5	24	3	1	0	3	10	14	.267	.340	.322	81	-1	-2	10	5	3	-0	10	2/S3	0.9
1985	Atl-N	50	87	15	19	3	0	1	5	18	18	.218	.352	.287	76	-1	-2	10	0	1	-1	4	3/S2	0.1
1986	Atl-N	7	8	1	2	0	0	0	0	2	4	.250	.400	.250	79	-0	-0	1	0	0	0	2	/2	0.2
1987	Atl-N	27	47	9	10	1	0	3	8	5	10	.213	.288	.426	82	-1	-1	5	0	1	-1	1	3/S2	0.0
1988	Atl-N	52	76	11	16	5	0	0	7	14	21	.211	.333	.276	73	-2	-2	7	0	0	0	-1	3/2S	-0.2
Total	8	183	345	43	80	13	1	4	26	54	75	.232	.336	.310	77	-7	-9	37	5	5	-2	13	/32S	1.0

■ TOMMY RUNNELLS Runnells, Thomas William b: 4/17/55, Greeley, Colo. BB/TR, 6', 175 lbs. Deb: 8/09/85 C

YEAR	TM/L	G	AB	R	H	2B	3B	HR	RBI	BB	SO	AVG	OBP	SLG	PRO+	BR	/A	RC	SB	CS	SBR	FR	POS	TPR
1985	Cin-N	28	35	3	7	1	0	0	3	0	4	.200	.263	.229	37	-3	-3	2	0	0	0	1	S/2	0.0
1986	Cin-N	12	11	1	1	1	0	0	0	0	2	.091	.091	.182	-26	-2	-2	0	0	0	0	1	/23	0.0
Total	2	40	46	4	8	2	0	0	3	6	.174	.224	.217	23	-5	-5	2	0	0	0	2	/S23	0.0

■ PETE RUNNELS Runnels, James Edward (b: James Edward Runnells) b: 1/28/28, Lufkin, Tex. BL/TR, 6', 170 lbs. Deb: 7/01/51 MC

YEAR	TM/L	G	AB	R	H	2B	3B	HR	RBI	BB	SO	AVG	OBP	SLG	PRO+	BR	/A	RC	SB	CS	SBR	FR	POS	TPR
1951	Was-A	78	273	31	76	12	2	0	25	31	24	.278	.354	.337	89	-4	-3	34	0	3	-2	-21	S	-2.0
1952	Was-A	152	555	70	158	18	3	1	64	72	55	.285	.368	.333	99	-0	-3	69	0	10	-6	-15	*S/2	-1.0
1953	Was-A	137	486	64	125	15	5	2	50	64	36	.257	.347	.321	83	-11	-9	55	3	4	-2	-33	*S2	-3.4
1954	Was-A	139	488	75	131	17	15	3	56	78	60	.268	.369	.383	112	6	9	72	2	3	-1	-19	*S2/O	0.0
1955	Was-A	134	503	66	143	16	4	2	49	55	51	.284	.356	.344	94	-7	-7	60	3	9	-5	-3	*2/S	-0.1
1956	Was-A	147	578	72	179	29	9	8	76	58	64	.310	.375	.433	113	11	11	91	5	5	-2	0	12/S	1.1
1957	Was-A	134	473	53	109	18	4	2	35	55	51	.230	.313	.298	69	-20	-19	46	2	3	-1	2	132	-1.7
1958	Bos-A	147	568	103	183	32	5	8	59	87	49	.322	.418	.438	127	32	27	107	1	2	-1	8	*21	4.0
1959	Bos-A	147	560	95	176	33	6	6	57	95	48	.314	.415	.427	126	29	25	102	6	5	-1	6	*21/S	3.4
1960	Bos-A	143	528	80	169	29	2	2	35	71	51	.320	.403	.394	112	15	13	86	5	2	0	9	*21/3	2.7
1961	Bos-A	143	360	44	114	20	3	3	38	46	32	.317	.399	.414	115	11	10	60	5	1	1	1	*13/2S	0.9
1962	Bos-A	152	562	80	183	33	5	10	60	79	57	.326	.411	.456	129	29	29	110	3	4	-2	-1	*1	1.4
1963	Hou-N	124	388	35	98	9	1	2	23	45	42	.253	.335	.296	89	-7	-4	38	2	0	1	-10	12/3	-1.2
1964	Hou-N	22	51	3	10	1	0	0	3	8	7	.196	.305	.216	53	-3	-3	3	0	0	0	-2	1	-0.4
Total	14	1799	6373	876	1854	282	64	49	630	844	627	.291	.376	.378	106	81	82	934	37	51	-20	-76	12S/30	3.0

■ REB RUSSELL Russell, Ewell Albert b: 4/12/1889, Jackson, Miss. d: 9/30/73, Indianapolis, Ind BL/TL, 5'11", 185 lbs. Deb: 4/18/13

YEAR	TM/L	G	AB	R	H	2B	3B	HR	RBI	BB	SO	AVG	OBP	SLG	PRO+	BR	/A	RC	SB	CS	SBR	FR	POS	TPR
1913	Chi-A	52	106	9	20	5	3	1	7	1	29	.189	.204	.321	54	-7	-7	7	0			-5	P	0.0
1914	Chi-A	46	64	6	17	1	1	0	7	1	14	.266	.277	.313	78	-2	-2	6	0			0	P	0.0
1915	Chi-A	45	86	11	21	2	3	0	7	4	14	.244	.293	.337	86	-2	-2	9	1			-2	P	0.0
1916	Chi-A	56	91	9	13	2	0	0	6	0	18	.143	.152	.165	-5	-12	-12	3	1			-1	P	0.0
1917	*Chi-A	39	68	5	19	3	3	0	9	2	10	.279	.300	.412	115	1	1	8	0			-0	P/O	0.0
1918	Chi-A	27	50	2	7	3	0	0	3	0	6	.140	.157	.200	8	-6	-6	2	0			-1	P/O	0.0
1919	Chi-A	1	0	0	0	0	0	0	0	0	0	—	—	—				0	0			0	/P	0.0
1922	Pit-N	60	220	51	81	14	8	12	75	14	18	.368	.423	.668	175	24	24	61	4	2	0	-3	O	1.7
1923	Pit-N	94	291	49	84	18	7	9	58	20	21	.289	.341	.491	115	6	5	49	3	1	0	-3	O	0.0
Total	9	420	976	142	262	48	25	22	172	42	130	.268	.309	.436	104	2	1	144	9	3		-15	PO	1.7

RIP RUSSELL
Russell, Glen David b: 1/26/15, Los Angeles, Cal. d: 9/26/76, Los Alamitos, Cal   BR/TR, 6'1", 180 lbs.   Deb: 5/05/39

YEAR	TM/L	G	AB	R	H	2B	3B	HR	RBI	BB	SO	AVG	OBP	SLG	PRO+	BR	/A	RC	SB	CS	SBR	FR	POS	TPR
1939	Chi-N	143	542	55	148	24	5	9	79	36	56	.273	.318	.386	87	-10	-11	66	2			-5	*1	-3.2
1940	Chi-N	68	215	15	53	7	2	5	33	8	23	.247	.277	.367	78	-8	-7	20	1			-6	1/3	-1.7
1941	Chi-N	6	17	1	5	1	0	0	1	1	5	.294	.333	.353	97	-0	-0	2	0			0	/1	0.0
1942	Chi-N	102	302	32	73	9	0	8	41	17	21	.242	.282	.351	88	-7	-6	29	0			-12	123/O	-1.9
1946	*Bos-A	80	274	22	57	10	1	6	35	13	30	.208	.247	.318	54	-17	-19	19	1	1	-0	-1	3/2	-1.4
1947	Bos-A	26	52	8	8	1	0	1	3	8	7	.154	.267	.231	36	-4	-5	3	0	0	0	1	3	-0.2
Total	6	425	1402	133	344	52	8	29	192	83	142	.245	.289	.356	77	-46	-47	140	4	1		-22	1/32O	-8.4

HARVEY RUSSELL
Russell, Harvey Holmes b: 1/10/1887, Marshall, Va. d: 1/8/80, Alexnadria, Va.   BL/TR, 5'9.5", 163 lbs.   Deb: 4/17/14

YEAR	TM/L	G	AB	R	H	2B	3B	HR	RBI	BB	SO	AVG	OBP	SLG	PRO+	BR	/A	RC	SB	CS	SBR	FR	POS	TPR
1914	Bal-F	81	168	18	39	3	2	0	13	18	17	.232	.310	.274	66	-6	-7	16	2			-31	C/SO	-3.7
1915	Bal-F	53	73	5	19	1	2	0	11	14	5	.260	.407	.329	115	3	3	11	1			-9	C	-0.6
Total	2	134	241	23	58	4	4	0	24	32	22	.241	.342	.290	81	-4	-5	27	3			-40	/COS	-4.3

JIM RUSSELL
Russell, James William b: 10/1/18, Fayette City, Pa. d: 11/24/87, Pittsburgh, Pa.   BB/TR, 6'1", 181 lbs.   Deb: 9/12/42

YEAR	TM/L	G	AB	R	H	2B	3B	HR	RBI	BB	SO	AVG	OBP	SLG	PRO+	BR	/A	RC	SB	CS	SBR	FR	POS	TPR
1942	Pit-N	5	14	2	1	0	0	0	0	1	4	.071	.133	.071	-38	-2	-2	0	0			1	/O	-0.1
1943	Pit-N	146	533	79	138	19	11	4	44	77	67	.259	.354	.358	102	6	4	70	12			1	*O/1	1.4
1944	Pit-N	152	580	109	181	34	14	8	66	79	63	.312	.399	.460	136	34	31	112	6			10	*O	3.0
1945	Pit-N	146	510	88	145	24	8	12	77	71	40	.284	.377	.433	120	18	15	88	15			0	*O	0.9
1946	Pit-N	146	516	68	143	29	6	8	50	67	54	.277	.362	.403	114	12	11	78	11			-11	*O/1	-0.3
1947	Pit-N	128	478	68	121	21	8	8	51	63	58	.253	.343	.381	89	-5	-7	64	7			14	*O	0.3
1948	Bos-N	89	322	44	85	18	1	9	54	46	31	.264	.361	.410	110	4	5	49	4			2	O	0.1
1949	Bos-N	130	415	57	96	22	1	8	54	64	68	.231	.337	.347	88	-9	-5	52	3			-14	*O	-2.5
1950	Bro-N	77	214	37	49	8	2	10	32	31	36	.229	.329	.425	95	-1	-2	30	1			4	O	0.1
1951	Bro-N	16	13	2	0	0	0	0	0	4	6	.000	.278	.000	-18	-2	-2	0	0	0	0	0	/O	-0.1
Total	10	1035	3595	554	959	175	51	67	428	503	427	.267	.360	.400	108	55	46	544	59	0		8	O/1	1.4

JOHN RUSSELL
Russell, John William b: 1/5/61, Oklahoma City, Okla.   BR/TR, 6', 200 lbs.   Deb: 6/22/84

YEAR	TM/L	G	AB	R	H	2B	3B	HR	RBI	BB	SO	AVG	OBP	SLG	PRO+	BR	/A	RC	SB	CS	SBR	FR	POS	TPR
1984	Phi-N	39	99	11	28	8	1	2	11	12	33	.283	.360	.444	123	3	3	16	0	1	-1	-1	O/C	0.1
1985	Phi-N	81	216	22	47	12	0	9	23	18	72	.218	.278	.398	85	-5	-5	24	2	0	1	-5	O1	-1.1
1986	Phi-N	93	315	35	76	21	2	13	60	25	103	.241	.303	.444	100	0	-1	42	0	1	-1	-3	C	-0.2
1987	Phi-N	24	62	5	9	1	0	3	8	3	17	.145	.185	.306	26	-7	-7	2	0	1	-1	-0	O/C	-0.7
1988	Phi-N	22	49	5	12	1	0	2	4	3	15	.245	.302	.388	95	-0	-0	5	0	0	0	3	C	0.4
1989	Atl-N	74	159	14	29	2	0	2	9	8	53	.182	.226	.233	31	-14	-15	8	0	0	0	-4	CO/13P	-1.6
1990	Tex-A	68	128	16	35	4	0	2	8	11	41	.273	.331	.352	89	-1	-2	15	1	0	0	4	CD/O13	0.3
Total	7	401	1028	108	236	49	3	33	123	80	334	.230	.288	.379	82	-24	-27	111	3	3	-1	-6	CO/1D3P	-2.8

LLOYD RUSSELL
Russell, Lloyd Opal b: 4/10/13, Atoka, Okla. d: 5/24/68, Waco, Tex.   BR/TR, 5'11", 166 lbs.   Deb: 4/26/38

YEAR	TM/L	G	AB	R	H	2B	3B	HR	RBI	BB	SO	AVG	OBP	SLG	PRO+	BR	/A	RC	SB	CS	SBR	FR	POS	TPR
1938	Cle-A	2	0	0	0	0	0	0	0	0	0	—	—	—	—	0	0	0	0	0	0	0	R	0.0

PAUL RUSSELL
Russell, Paul A. b: 1870, Reading, Pa. d: Pottstown, Pa.   Deb: 7/29/1894

YEAR	TM/L	G	AB	R	H	2B	3B	HR	RBI	BB	SO	AVG	OBP	SLG	PRO+	BR	/A	RC	SB	CS	SBR	FR	POS	TPR
1894	StL-N	3	10	1	1	0	0	0	0	0	2	.100	.100	.100	-51	-2	-2	0	0			0	/O32	-0.1

BILL RUSSELL
Russell, William Ellis b: 10/21/48, Pittsburg, Kan.   BR/TR, 6', 175 lbs.   Deb: 4/07/69 C

YEAR	TM/L	G	AB	R	H	2B	3B	HR	RBI	BB	SO	AVG	OBP	SLG	PRO+	BR	/A	RC	SB	CS	SBR	FR	POS	TPR
1969	LA-N	98	212	35	48	6	2	5	15	22	45	.226	.302	.344	87	-6	-4	23	4	1	1	7	O	0.0
1970	LA-N	81	278	30	72	11	9	0	28	16	28	.259	.306	.363	82	-9	-7	32	9	1	2	6	O/S	-0.1
1971	LA-N	91	211	29	48	7	4	2	15	11	39	.227	.266	.327	71	-10	-8	18	6	3	0	4	2O/S	-0.2
1972	LA-N	129	434	47	118	19	5	4	34	34	64	.272	.328	.366	99	-2	-1	53	14	7	0	17	*S/O	3.1
1973	LA-N	162	615	55	163	26	3	4	56	34	63	.265	.305	.337	81	-19	-16	62	15	7	0	9	*S	1.6
1974	*LA-N	160	553	61	149	18	6	5	65	53	51	.269	.338	.351	97	-5	-2	64	14	5	1	-19	*S/O	-0.1
1975	LA-N	84	252	24	52	9	2	0	14	23	28	.206	.278	.258	52	-17	-16	19	5	0	2	-21	S	-2.7
1976	LA-N	149	554	53	152	17	3	5	65	21	46	.274	.304	.343	85	-13	-12	55	15	5	2	-14	*S	-1.0
1977	LA-N	153	634	84	176	28	6	4	51	24	43	.278	.306	.360	78	-20	-20	64	16	7	1	10	*S	1.2
1978	*LA-N	155	625	72	179	32	4	3	46	30	34	.286	.321	.365	92	-8	-8	69	10	6	-1	12	*S	1.7
1979	LA-N	153	627	72	170	26	4	7	56	24	43	.271	.299	.359	80	-19	-18	60	6	9	-4	-27	*S	-3.4
1980	LA-N	130	466	38	123	23	2	3	34	18	44	.264	.296	.341	79	-15	-14	48	13	2	0	-22	*S	-1.9
1981	*LA-N	82	262	20	61	9	2	0	22	19	20	.233	.287	.282	64	-13	-12	17	2	1	0	10	S	0.7
1982	*LA-N	153	497	64	136	20	2	3	46	63	30	.274	.360	.340	99	0	2	63	10	2	2	-4	*S	1.1
1983	*LA-N	131	451	47	111	13	1	1	30	33	31	.246	.303	.286	64	-21	-21	40	13	9	-2	1	*S	-1.0
1984	LA-N	89	262	25	70	12	1	0	19	25	24	.267	.331	.321	85	-5	-5	28	4	4	-1	-3	SO/2	-0.2
1985	LA-N	76	169	19	44	6	1	0	13	18	9	.260	.335	.308	83	-4	-3	19	4	0	1	-5	SO/23	-0.5
1986	LA-N	105	216	21	54	11	0	0	18	15	23	.250	.305	.301	73	-9	-7	21	7	0	2	-1	OS/23	-0.3
Total	18	2181	7318	796	1926	293	57	46	627	483	667	.263	.312	.338	83	-195	-172	759	167	69	9	-39	*SO/23	-2.0

RUST
Rust b: Louisville, Ky.   Deb: 7/04/1882

YEAR	TM/L	G	AB	R	H	2B	3B	HR	RBI	BB	SO	AVG	OBP	SLG	PRO+	BR	/A	RC	SB	CS	SBR	FR	POS	TPR
1882	Bal-a	1	3	0	1	0	0	0			0	.333	.333	.333	136	0	0					-1	/OP	0.0

HANK RUSZKOWSKI
Ruszkowski, Henry Alexander b: 11/10/25, Cleveland, Ohio   BR/TR, 6', 190 lbs.   Deb: 9/26/44

YEAR	TM/L	G	AB	R	H	2B	3B	HR	RBI	BB	SO	AVG	OBP	SLG	PRO+	BR	/A	RC	SB	CS	SBR	FR	POS	TPR
1944	Cle-A	3	8	1	3	0	0	0	1	0	1	.375	.375	.375	119	0	0	1	0	0	0	-0	/C	0.0
1945	Cle-A	14	49	2	10	0	0	0	5	4	9	.204	.264	.204	38	-4	-4	3	0	0	0	3	C	0.1
1947	Cle-A	23	27	5	7	2	0	3	4	2	6	.259	.310	.667	172	2	2	6	0	0	0	-2	C	0.2
Total	3	40	84	8	20	2	0	3	10	6	16	.238	.289	.369	91	-2	-1	9	0	0	0	2	/C	0.3

BABE RUTH
Ruth, George Herman "The Bambino" or "The Sultan Of Swat"
b: 2/6/1895, Baltimore, Md. d: 8/16/48, New York, N.Y.   BL/TL, 6'2", 215 lbs.   Deb: 7/11/14 CH

YEAR	TM/L	G	AB	R	H	2B	3B	HR	RBI	BB	SO	AVG	OBP	SLG	PRO+	BR	/A	RC	SB	CS	SBR	FR	POS	TPR
1914	Bos-A	5	10	1	2	1	0	0	2	0	4	.200	.200	.300	50	-1	-1	1	0			0	/P	0.0
1915	*Bos-A	42	92	16	29	10	1	4	21	9	23	.315	.376	.576	191	9	9	20	0			1	P	0.0
1916	*Bos-A	67	136	18	37	5	3	3	15	10	23	.272	.322	.419	122	3	3	19	0			-0	P	0.0
1917	Bos-A	52	123	14	40	6	3	2	12	12	18	.325	.385	.472	163	9	9	22	0			2	P	0.0
1918	*Bos-A	95	317	50	95	26	11	**11**	66	57	58	.300	.410	.555	194	35	35	72	6			3	OP1	4.1
1919	Bos-A	130	432	**103**	139	34	12	**29**	114	101	58	.322	**.456**	**.657**	**224**	67	70	128	7			5	*OP/1	7.0
1920	NY-A	142	458	**158**	172	36	9	**54**	137	**148**	80	.376	**.530**	**.847**	**252**	**113**	**110**	**211**	14	14	-4	0	*O/1	8.8
1921	*NY-A	152	540	**177**	204	44	16	**59**	**171**	**144**	81	.378	**.512**	**.846**	**236**	**119**	**117**	**238**	17	13	-3	4	*O/1	9.6
1922	*NY-A	110	406	94	128	24	8	35	96	84	80	.315	.434	**.672**	**181**	51	49	120	2	6	-3	1	*O/1	3.7
1923	*NY-A	152	522	151	205	45	13	41	130	**170**	93	**.393**	**.545**	**.764**	**238**	**119**	**118**	**238**	17	21	-8	16	*O/1	10.5
1924	*NY-A	153	529	**143**	200	39	7	**46**	121	**142**	81	**.378**	**.513**	**.739**	**221**	**101**	**101**	**205**	9	13	-5	7	*O	8.4
1925	NY-A	98	359	61	104	12	2	25	66	59	68	.290	.393	.543	138	19	20	78	2	4	-2	9	O	1.6
1926	*NY-A	152	495	**139**	184	30	5	**47**	**146**	**144**	76	.372	**.516**	**.737**	**228**	97	99	**196**	11	9	-2	1	*O/1	8.1
1927	*NY-A	151	540	**158**	192	29	8	**60**	**164**	138	89	.356	**.487**	**.772**	**229**	**101**	103	202	7	6	-2	5	*O	8.9
1928	*NY-A	154	536	**163**	173	29	8	**54**	142	135	87	.323	.461	**.709**	**210**	84	87	182	4	5	-3	-0	*O	6.9
1929	NY-A	135	499	121	172	26	6	46	154	72	60	.345	.430	.697	199	62	67	150	5	3	-0	-9	*O	4.8
1930	NY-A	145	518	150	186	28	9	49	153	**136**	61	.359	**.493**	**.732**	**216**	90	94	**191**	10	10	-3	-0	*O	7.5
1931	NY-A	145	534	149	199	31	3	**46**	163	**128**	51	.373	**.495**	**.700**	**223**	92	96	192	5	4	-1	-11	*O/1	6.8
1932	*NY-A	133	457	120	156	13	5	41	137	**130**	62	.341	**.489**	.661	**206**	71	75	157	2	2	-1	-9	*O/1	5.5
1933	NY-A	137	459	97	138	21	3	34	103	**114**	90	.301	.442	.582	180	50	54	124	4	5	-2	-10	*O/P1	3.5

YEAR	TM/L	G	AB	R	H	2B	3B	HR	RBI	BB	SO	AVG	OBP	SLG	PRO+	BR	/A	RC	SB	CS	SBR	FR	POS	TPR
1934	NY-A	125	365	78	105	17	4	22	84	103	63	.288	.447	.537	164	33	37	95	1	3	-2	-9	*O	2.3
1935	Bos-N	28	72	13	13	0	0	6	12	20	24	.181	.359	.431	121	2	2	12	0			-3	O	-0.1
Total	22	2503	8399	2174	2873	506	136	714	2209	2056	1330	.342	.474	.690	209	1322	1355	2838	123	118		0	*OP/1	107.9

■ JIM RUTHERFORD Rutherford, James Hollis b: 9/26/1886, Stillwater, Minn. d: 9/18/56, Cleveland, Ohio 6'1", 180 lbs. Deb: 7/12/10

YEAR	TM/L	G	AB	R	H	2B	3B	HR	RBI	BB	SO	AVG	OBP	SLG	PRO+	BR	/A	RC	SB	CS	SBR	FR	POS	TPR
1910	Cle-A	1	2	0	1	0	0	0	0	0		.500	.500	.500	210	0	0	0	0			0	/O	0.0

■ MICKEY RUTNER Rutner, Milton b: 3/18/20, Hempstead, N.Y. BR/TR, 5'11", 190 lbs. Deb: 9/11/47

YEAR	TM/L	G	AB	R	H	2B	3B	HR	RBI	BB	SO	AVG	OBP	SLG	PRO+	BR	/A	RC	SB	CS	SBR	FR	POS	TPR
1947	Phi-A	12	48	4	12	1	0	1	4	3	2	.250	.294	.333	73	-2	-2	4	0	0	0	-3	3	-0.4

■ MARK RYAL Ryal, Mark Dwayne b: 4/28/60, Henryetta, Okla. BL/TL, 6'1", 185 lbs. Deb: 9/07/82

YEAR	TM/L	G	AB	R	H	2B	3B	HR	RBI	BB	SO	AVG	OBP	SLG	PRO+	BR	/A	RC	SB	CS	SBR	FR	POS	TPR
1982	KC-A	6	13	0	1	0	0	0	0	1	3	.077	.143	.077	-38	-2	-2	0	0	0	0	0	/O	-0.2
1985	Chi-A	12	33	4	5	3	0	0	3	3	3	.152	.222	.242	26	-3	-4	2	0	0	0	-0	O	-0.3
1986	Cal-A	13	32	6	12	0	0	2	5	2	4	.375	.412	.563	164	3	3	7	1	0	0	-0	/O1D	0.2
1987	Cal-A	58	100	7	20	6	0	5	18	3	15	.200	.223	.410	65	-6	-5	8	0	0	0	-2	O/1D	-0.7
1989	Phi-N	29	33	2	8	2	0	0	5	1	6	.242	.265	.303	62	-2	-2	3	0	0	0	-0	/1O	-0.2
1990	Pit-N	9	12	0	1	0	0	0	0	0	3	.083	.083	.083	-56	-2	-2	0	0	0	0	0	/O	-0.2
Total	6	127	223	19	47	11	0	7	31	10	34	.211	.245	.354	61	-13	-13	19	1	0	0	-3	/O1D	-1.4

■ CONNIE RYAN Ryan, Cornelius Joseph b: 2/27/20, New Orleans, La. BR/TR, 5'11", 175 lbs. Deb: 4/14/42 MC

YEAR	TM/L	G	AB	R	H	2B	3B	HR	RBI	BB	SO	AVG	OBP	SLG	PRO+	BR	/A	RC	SB	CS	SBR	FR	POS	TPR
1942	NY-N	11	27	4	5	0	0	0	2	4	3	.185	.290	.185	40	-2	-2	2	1			7	2	0.6
1943	Bos-N	132	457	52	97	10	2	1	24	58	56	.212	.301	.249	61	-22	-21	38	7			-19	*23	-4.1
1944	Bos-N	88	332	59	98	18	5	4	25	36	40	.295	.364	.416	114	9	7	50	13			13	23	2.8
1946	Bos-N	143	502	55	121	28	8	1	48	55	63	.241	.317	.335	84	-10	-11	56	7			-2	*23	-0.8
1947	Bos-N	150	544	60	144	33	5	5	69	71	60	.265	.351	.371	94	-5	-4	74	5			-7	*2/S	0.6
1948	*Bos-N	51	122	14	26	3	0	0	10	21	16	.213	.333	.238	58	-6	-6	11	0			4	2/3	0.1
1949	Bos-N	85	208	28	52	13	1	6	20	21	30	.250	.319	.409	99	-2	-1	27	1			6	3S2/1	0.8
1950	Bos-N	20	72	12	14	2	0	3	6	12	9	.194	.326	.347	82	-2	-2	8	0			1	2	0.0
	Cin-N	106	367	45	95	18	5	3	43	52	46	.259	.352	.360	87	-5	-6	48	4			11	*2	0.8
	Yr	126	439	57	109	20	5	6	49	64	55	.248	.348	.358	87	-8	-7	57	4			12		0.8
1951	Cin-N	136	473	75	112	17	4	16	53	79	72	.237	.350	.391	97	1	-0	69	11	6	-0	-3	*2/31O	0.1
1952	Phi-N	154	577	81	139	24	6	12	49	69	72	.241	.327	.366	93	-6	-5	73	13	5	1	-5	*2	-0.2
1953	Phi-N	90	247	47	73	14	6	5	26	30	35	.296	.372	.462	116	6	6	45	5	1	1	-5	2/1	0.5
	Chi-A	17	54	6	12	1	0	0	6	9	12	.222	.333	.241	55	-3	-3	5	2	0	1	-1	3	-0.3
1954	Cin-N	1	0	0	0	0	0	0	0	1	0	—	1.000	—	182	0	0	0	0	0	0	0	H	0.0
Total	12	1184	3982	535	988	181	42	56	381	518	514	.248	.337	.357	90	-49	-47	506	69	12		0	23/S1O	0.9

■ CYCLONE RYAN Ryan, Daniel R. b: 1866, Capperwhite, Ireland d: 1/30/17, Medfield, Mass. TR , 6', Deb: 8/08/1887

YEAR	TM/L	G	AB	R	H	2B	3B	HR	RBI	BB	SO	AVG	OBP	SLG	PRO+	BR	/A	RC	SB	CS	SBR	FR	POS	TPR
1887	NY-a	8	32	4	7	1	0	0			3	.219	.286	.250	54	-2	-2	3	1			0	/1P	0.0
1891	Bos-N	1	1	0	0	0	0	0	0	0	0	.000	.000	.000	-89	-0	-0	0	0			0	/P	0.0
Total	2	9	33	4	7	1	0	0	0	3	0	.212	.278	.242	50	-2	-2	3	1			0	/1P	0.0

■ MIKE RYAN Ryan, J. b: St.Louis, Mo. Deb: 7/25/1895

YEAR	TM/L	G	AB	R	H	2B	3B	HR	RBI	BB	SO	AVG	OBP	SLG	PRO+	BR	/A	RC	SB	CS	SBR	FR	POS	TPR
1895	StL-N	2	2	0	0	0	0	0	0	0	0	.000	.000	.000	-99	-1	-1	0	0			-1	/3	0.0

■ JIMMY RYAN Ryan, James Edward "Pony" b: 2/11/1863, Clinton, Mass. d: 10/26/23, Chicago, Ill. BR/TL, 5'9", 162 lbs. Deb: 10/08/1885

YEAR	TM/L	G	AB	R	H	2B	3B	HR	RBI	BB	SO	AVG	OBP	SLG	PRO+	BR	/A	RC	SB	CS	SBR	FR	POS	TPR
1885	Chi-N	3	13	2	6	1	0	0	2	1	1	.462	.500	.538	205	2	2	4				1	/SO	0.2
1886	*Chi-N	84	327	58	100	17	6	4	53	12	28	.306	.330	.431	113	11	3	51	10			-1	O/S32P	0.5
1887	Chi-N	126	508	117	145	23	10	11	74	53	19	.285	.360	.435	108	15	4	100	50			-8	*O/P2	0.5
1888	Chi-N	129	549	115	182	33	10	16	64	35	50	.332	.377	.515	172	51	45	133	60			3	*O/P	4.7
1889	Chi-N	135	576	140	177	31	14	17	72	70	62	.307	.388	.498	141	37	32	132	45			6	*OS	3.0
1890	Chi-P	118	486	99	165	32	5	6	89	60	36	.340	.416	.463	131	27	23	109	30			2	*O	1.6
1891	Chi-N	118	505	110	140	22	15	9	66	53	38	.277	.355	.434	132	19	20	90	27			5	*O/SP	1.7
1892	Chi-N	128	505	105	148	21	11	10	65	61	41	.293	.375	.438	147	29	29	95	27			5	*O/S	2.8
1893	Chi-N	83	341	82	102	21	7	3	30	59	25	.299	.407	.428	117	14	15	64	8			-1	OS/P	0.9
1894	Chi-N	108	474	132	171	37	7	6	62	50	23	.361	.425	.487	115	18	12	105	11			9	*O	1.1
1895	Chi-N	108	438	83	139	22	8	6	49	48	22	.317	.392	.445	111	12	7	86	18			2	*O	0.6
1896	Chi-N	128	489	83	149	24	0	6	86	46	16	.305	.369	.413	104	6	3	87	29			-0	*O	-0.5
1897	Chi-N	136	520	103	156	33	17	5	85	50		.300	.369	.458	116	14	11	100	27			7	*O	0.6
1898	Chi-N	144	572	122	185	32	13	4	79	73		.323	.405	.446	147	36	36	118	29			-7	*O	1.9
1899	Chi-N	125	525	91	158	20	10	3	68	43		.301	.356	.394	111	6	8	79	9			-1	*O	0.0
1900	Chi-N	105	415	66	115	25	4	5	59	29		.277	.329	.393	105	-0	2	61	19			-11	*O	-1.6
1902	Was-A	120	484	92	155	32	6	4	44	43		.320	.385	.448	131	22	21	90	10			3	*O	1.6
1903	Was-A	114	437	42	109	25	4	7	46	17		.249	.278	.373	94	-3	-4	50	9			3	*O	-0.8
Total	18	2012	8164	1642	2502	451	157	118	1093	803	361	.306	.374	.444	125	315	269	1554	418			18	*O/SP23	17.7

■ JOHN RYAN Ryan, John A. (Played 1 Game Under Real Name Of Daniel Sheehan) b: Birmingham, Mich. Deb: 5/27/1884

YEAR	TM/L	G	AB	R	H	2B	3B	HR	RBI	BB	SO	AVG	OBP	SLG	PRO+	BR	/A	RC	SB	CS	SBR	FR	POS	TPR
1884	Was-U	7	28	2	4	0	1	0		1		.143	.172	.214	31	-2	-2	1	0			-1	/O3	-0.2
	Wil-U	2	6	0	1	0	0	0		0		.167	.286	.167	55	-0	-0	0	0			0	/O	0.0
	Yr	9	34	2	5	0	1	0		2		.147	.194	.206	36	-2	-2	1	0			-1		-0.2

■ JACK RYAN Ryan, John Bernard b: 11/12/1868, Haverhill, Mass. d: 8/21/52, Boston, Mass. BR/TR, 5'10.5", 165 lbs. Deb: 9/02/1889 C

YEAR	TM/L	G	AB	R	H	2B	3B	HR	RBI	BB	SO	AVG	OBP	SLG	PRO+	BR	/A	RC	SB	CS	SBR	FR	POS	TPR
1889	Lou-a	21	79	8	14	1	0	0	2	3	17	.177	.207	.190	15	-9	-8	4	2			-7	C/O3	-1.1
1890	*Lou-a	93	337	43	73	16	4	0		12		.217	.244	.288	60	-19	-17	26	6			6	C/OS1	0.0
1891	Lou-a	75	253	24	57	5	4	2	25	15	40	.225	.271	.300	67	-12	-11	22	3			2	C1/302	-0.5
1894	Bos-N	53	201	39	54	12	7	1	29	13	16	.269	.316	.413	70	-9	-12	28	3			0	C/1	-0.4
1895	Bos-N	49	189	22	55	7	0	0	18	6	6	.291	.313	.328	62	-9	-12	21	3			6	C/2O	-0.1
1896	Bos-N	8	32	2	3	1	0	0	0	0	1	.094	.094	.125	-40	-6	-7	0	0			2	/C	-0.3
1898	Bro-N	87	301	39	57	11	4	0	24	15		.189	.233	.252	41	-23	-23	19	5			2	C/31	-1.3
1899	Bal-N	2	4	0	2	1	0	0	1	0		.500	.500	.750	232	1	1	2	1			2	/C	0.2
1901	StL-N	83	300	27	59	6	5	0	31	7		.197	.215	.250	38	-24	-22	19	5			3	C/21O	-1.0
1902	StL-N	76	267	23	48	4	4	0	14	4		.180	.195	.225	32	-22	-20	14	2			-8	C/132S	-2.2
1903	StL-N	67	227	18	54	5	1	1	10	10		.238	.270	.282	61	-12	-11	19	2			-9	C1/S	-1.6
1912	Was-A	1	1	0	0	0	0	0	0	0		.000	.000	.000	-99	-0	-0	0	0			0	/3	0.0
1913	Was-A	1	1	0	0	0	0	0	0	0		.000	.000	.000	-99	-0	-0	0	0			0	/C	0.0
Total	13	616	2192	245	476	69	29	4	154	85	80	.217	.248	.281	51	-144	-144	173	32			-0	C/1230S	-8.3

■ BUDDY RYAN Ryan, John Budd b: 10/6/1885, Denver, Colo. d: 7/9/56, Sacramento, Cal. BL/TR, 5'9.5", 172 lbs. Deb: 4/11/12

YEAR	TM/L	G	AB	R	H	2B	3B	HR	RBI	BB	SO	AVG	OBP	SLG	PRO+	BR	/A	RC	SB	CS	SBR	FR	POS	TPR
1912	Cle-A	93	328	53	89	12	9	1	31	30		.271	.343	.372	101	2	0	46	12			4	O	0.0
1913	Cle-A	73	243	26	72	6	1	0	32	11	13	.296	.332	.329	91	-2	-3	29	9			-1	O/1	-0.8
Total	2	166	571	79	161	18	10	1	63	41	13	.282	.339	.354	97	-0	-3	75	21			3	O/1	-0.8

■ BLONDY RYAN Ryan, John Collins b: 1/4/06, Lynn, Mass d: 11/28/59, Swampscott, Mass. BR/TR, 6'1", 178 lbs. Deb: 7/13/30

YEAR	TM/L	G	AB	R	H	2B	3B	HR	RBI	BB	SO	AVG	OBP	SLG	PRO+	BR	/A	RC	SB	CS	SBR	FR	POS	TPR
1930	Chi-A	28	87	9	18	0	4	1	10	6	13	.207	.258	.333	50	-7	-7	8	2	0	1	-1	3/S2	-0.5
1933	*NY-N	146	525	47	125	10	5	3	48	15	62	.238	.259	.293	58	-29	-28	38	0			17	*S	-0.1

YEAR	TM/L	G	AB	R	H	2B	3B	HR	RBI	BB	SO	AVG	OBP	SLG	PRO+	BR	/A	RC	SB	CS	SBR	FR	POS	TPR
1934	NY-N	110	385	35	93	19	0	2	41	19	68	.242	.277	.306	57	-24	-23	31	3			12	3S2	-0.2
1935	Phi-N	39	129	13	34	3	0	1	10	7	20	.264	.312	.310	61	-6	-7	12	1			2	S/23	-0.3
	NY-A	30	105	12	25	1	3	0	11	3	10	.238	.259	.305	48	-9	-8	8	0	0	0	-4	S	-0.9
1937	*NY-N	21	75	10	18	3	1	1	13	6	8	.240	.296	.347	73	-3	-3	7	0			1	S/23	-0.2
1938	NY-N	12	24	1	5	0	0	0	0	1	3	.208	.240	.208	24	-2	-2	4	0			-1	/23S	-0.2
Total	6	386	1330	127	318	36	13	8	133	57	184	.239	.271	.304	57	-80	-78	105	6	0		26	S/32	-2.2

■ JACK RYAN Ryan, John Francis b: 5/5/05, Mineral, Minn. d: 9/2/67, Rochester, Minn. BR/TR, 6', 185 lbs. Deb: 6/18/29

YEAR	TM/L	G	AB	R	H	2B	3B	HR	RBI	BB	SO	AVG	OBP	SLG	PRO+	BR	/A	RC	SB	CS	SBR	FR	POS	TPR
1929	Bos-A	2	3	0	0	0	0	0	0	0	0	.000	.000	.000	-99	-1	-1	0	0	0	0	-1	/O	-0.1

■ JOHNNY RYAN Ryan, John Joseph b: 10/1853, Philadelphia, Pa. d: 3/22/02, Philadelphia, Pa. 5'7.5", 150 lbs. Deb: 8/19/1873

YEAR	TM/L	G	AB	R	H	2B	3B	HR	RBI	BB	SO	AVG	OBP	SLG	PRO+	BR	/A	RC	SB	CS	SBR	FR	POS	TPR
1873	Phi-n	2	8	1	2	0	0	0			0	.250	.250	.250	46	-1	-1	1					/1O	0.0
1874	Bal-n	47	184	29	33	7	1	0			5	.179	.201	.228	37	-13	-12	9					*O/P	-0.8
1875	NH-n	37	146	17	23	2	1	0			3	.158	.174	.185	29	-11	-7	5					O/PS3	-0.4
1876	Lou-N	64	241	32	61	5	1	1	18	6	23	.253	.271	.295	75	-3	-9	20				-8	*O/P	-1.5
1877	Cin-N	6	26	2	4	0	1	0	2	1	5	.154	.185	.231	34	-2	-2	1				-1	/O	-0.2
Total	3 n	86	338	47	58	9	2	0			8	.172	.191	.210	34	-24	-20	14					/OP3S1	-1.2
Total	2	70	267	34	65	5	2	1	20	7	28	.243	.263	.288	72	-5	-11	21				-9	/OP	-1.7

■ MIKE RYAN Ryan, Michael James b: 11/25/41, Haverhill, Mass. BR/TR, 6'2", 205 lbs. Deb: 10/03/64 C

YEAR	TM/L	G	AB	R	H	2B	3B	HR	RBI	BB	SO	AVG	OBP	SLG	PRO+	BR	/A	RC	SB	CS	SBR	FR	POS	TPR
1964	Bos-A	1	3	0	1	0	0	0	2	1	0	.333	.500	.333	131	0	0	1	0	0	0	-1	/C	0.0
1965	Bos-A	33	107	7	17	0	1	3	9	5	19	.159	.196	.262	27	-10	-11	4	0	0	0	1	C	-0.8
1966	Bos-A	116	369	27	79	15	3	2	32	29	66	.214	.271	.287	55	-19	-23	28	1	0	0	1	*C	-1.6
1967	*Bos-A	79	226	21	45	4	2	2	27	26	42	.199	.285	.261	58	-10	-12	17	2	0	1	0	C	-0.6
1968	Phi-N	96	296	12	53	6	1	1	15	15	59	.179	.219	.216	31	-25	-25	12	0	3	-2	-4	C	-3.1
1969	Phi-N	133	446	41	91	17	2	12	44	30	66	.204	.257	.332	66	-23	-21	36	1	1	-0	1	*C	-1.2
1970	Phi-N	46	134	14	24	8	0	2	11	16	24	.179	.267	.284	49	-10	-10	9	0	0	0	-13	C	-2.0
1971	Phi-N	43	134	9	22	5	1	3	6	10	32	.164	.222	.284	42	-10	-10	8	0	0	0	12	C	0.2
1972	Phi-N	46	106	6	19	4	0	2	10	10	25	.179	.256	.274	49	-7	-7	7	0	0	0	6	C	0.1
1973	Phi-N	28	69	7	16	1	2	1	5	6	19	.232	.293	.348	75	-2	-2	6	0	0	0	0	C	0.0
1974	Pit-N	15	30	2	3	0	0	0	0	4	16	.100	.206	.100	-13	-4	-4	1	0	0	0	3	C	0.0
Total	11	636	1920	146	370	60	12	28	161	152	370	.193	.253	.280	51	-120	-126	128	4	4	-1	7	C	-9.0

■ TOM RYDER Ryder, Thomas BL , Deb: 7/22/1884

YEAR	TM/L	G	AB	R	H	2B	3B	HR	RBI	BB	SO	AVG	OBP	SLG	PRO+	BR	/A	RC	SB	CS	SBR	FR	POS	TPR
1884	StL-U	8	28	4	7	1	0	0			2	.250	.300	.286	96	0	-0	2	0			0	/O	0.0

■ GENE RYE Rye, Eugene Rudolph "Half-Pint" (b: Eugene Rudolph Mercantelli) b: 11/15/06, Chicago, Ill. d: 1/21/80, Park Ridge, Ill. BL/TR, 5'6", 165 lbs. Deb: 4/22/31

YEAR	TM/L	G	AB	R	H	2B	3B	HR	RBI	BB	SO	AVG	OBP	SLG	PRO+	BR	/A	RC	SB	CS	SBR	FR	POS	TPR
1931	Bos-A	17	39	3	7	1	0	0		2	5	.179	.220	.179	6	-5	-5	2	0	0	0	-1	O	-0.6

■ ALEX SABO Sabo, Alexander "Giz" (b: Alexander Szabo) b: 2/14/10, New Brunswick, N.J BR/TR, 6', 192 lbs. Deb: 8/01/36

YEAR	TM/L	G	AB	R	H	2B	3B	HR	RBI	BB	SO	AVG	OBP	SLG	PRO+	BR	/A	RC	SB	CS	SBR	FR	POS	TPR
1936	Was-A	4	8	1	3	0	0	0	1	0	2	.375	.375	.375	91	-0	-0	1	0	0	0	1	/C	0.1
1937	Was-A	1	0	0	0	0	0	0	0	0	0	—	—	—	—	-0	-0	0	0	0	0	0	/C	0.0
Total	2	5	8	1	3	0	0	0	1	0	2	.375	.375	.375	91	-0	-0	1	0	0	0	1	/C	0.1

■ CHRIS SABO Sabo, Christopher Andrew b: 1/19/62, Detroit, Mich. BR/TR, 5'11", 185 lbs. Deb: 4/04/88

YEAR	TM/L	G	AB	R	H	2B	3B	HR	RBI	BB	SO	AVG	OBP	SLG	PRO+	BR	/A	RC	SB	CS	SBR	FR	POS	TPR
1988	Cin-N	137	538	74	146	40	2	11	44	29	52	.271	.316	.414	104	4	2	69	46	14	5	19	*3/S	2.7
1989	Cin-N	82	304	40	79	21	1	6	29	25	33	.260	.318	.395	99	-1	-3	34	14	9	-1	-3	3	-0.5
1990	*Cin-N	148	567	95	153	38	2	25	71	61	58	.270	.345	.476	121	17	16	94	25	10	2	-6	*3	1.6
Total	3	367	1409	209	378	99	5	42	144	115	143	.268	.328	.435	110	22	17	202	85	33	6	10	3/S	3.8

■ FRANK SACKA Sacka, Frank b: 8/30/24, Romulus, Mich. BR/TR, 6', 195 lbs. Deb: 4/29/51

YEAR	TM/L	G	AB	R	H	2B	3B	HR	RBI	BB	SO	AVG	OBP	SLG	PRO+	BR	/A	RC	SB	CS	SBR	FR	POS	TPR
1951	Was-A	7	16	1	4	0	0	0	3	0	5	.250	.250	.250	36	-1	-1	1	0	0	0	2	/C	0.1
1953	Was-A	7	18	2	5	0	0	0	3	3	1	.278	.381	.278	82	-0	-0	2	0	0	0	2	/C	0.2
Total	2	14	34	3	9	0	0	0	6	3	6	.265	.324	.265	62	-2	-2	3	0	0	0	3	/C	0.3

■ MIKE SADEK Sadek, Michael George b: 5/30/46, Minneapolis, Minn. BR/TR, 5'9", 165 lbs. Deb: 4/13/73

YEAR	TM/L	G	AB	R	H	2B	3B	HR	RBI	BB	SO	AVG	OBP	SLG	PRO+	BR	/A	RC	SB	CS	SBR	FR	POS	TPR
1973	SF-N	39	66	6	11	1	1	0	4	11	9	.167	.286	.212	38	-5	-5	5	1	0	0	8	C	0.5
1975	SF-N	42	106	14	25	5	2	0	9	14	14	.236	.325	.321	76	-3	-3	10	1	0	0	6	C	0.5
1976	SF-N	55	93	8	19	2	0	0	7	11	10	.204	.295	.226	48	-6	-6	7	0	0	0	8	C	0.4
1977	SF-N	61	126	12	29	7	0	1	15	12	5	.230	.297	.310	63	-7	-6	12	2	1	0	10	C	0.3
1978	SF-N	40	109	15	26	3	0	2	9	10	11	.239	.303	.321	77	-4	-3	11	1	0	0	2	C	0.3
1979	SF-N	63	126	14	30	5	0	1	11	15	24	.238	.324	.302	77	-5	-3	12	1	0	0	3	C/O	0.1
1980	SF-N	64	151	14	38	4	1	1	16	27	18	.252	.365	.311	93	-1	-0	19	0	0	0	4	C	0.5
1981	SF-N	19	36	5	6	3	0	0	3	8	7	.167	.318	.250	64	-2	-1	4	0	0	0	7	C	0.6
Total	8	383	813	88	184	30	4	5	74	108	97	.226	.319	.292	70	-31	-30	80	6	1	1	47	C/O	2.9

■ ED SADOWSKI Sadowski, Edward Roman b: 1/19/32, Pittsburgh, Pa. BR/TR, 5'11", 175 lbs. Deb: 4/20/60

YEAR	TM/L	G	AB	R	H	2B	3B	HR	RBI	BB	SO	AVG	OBP	SLG	PRO+	BR	/A	RC	SB	CS	SBR	FR	POS	TPR
1960	Bos-A	38	93	10	20	2	0	3	8	8	13	.215	.284	.333	64	-5	-5	8	0	0	0	5	C	0.3
1961	LA-A	69	164	16	38	13	0	4	12	11	33	.232	.280	.384	68	-6	-9	16	2	3	-1	8	C	-0.2
1962	LA-A	27	55	4	11	4	0	1	3	2	14	.200	.228	.327	49	-4	-4	4	1	0	0	4	C	0.0
1963	LA-A	80	174	24	30	1	1	4	15	17	33	.172	.246	.259	44	-14	-12	11	2	1	0	20	C	0.9
1966	Atl-N	3	9	1	1	0	0	0	1	1	1	.111	.200	.111	-10	-1	-1	0	0	0	0	1	/C	0.0
Total	5	217	495	55	100	20	1	12	39	39	94	.202	.262	.319	56	-30	-31	39	5	4	-1	37	C	1.0

■ BOB SADOWSKI Sadowski, Robert Frank "Sid" b: 1/15/37, St.Louis, Mo. BL/TR, 6', 175 lbs. Deb: 9/16/60

YEAR	TM/L	G	AB	R	H	2B	3B	HR	RBI	BB	SO	AVG	OBP	SLG	PRO+	BR	/A	RC	SB	CS	SBR	FR	POS	TPR
1960	StL-N	1	1	0	0	0	0	0	0	1	0	.000	.500	.000	47	0	0	0	0	0	0	-1	/2	0.0
1961	Phi-N	16	54	4	7	0	0	0	0	4	7	.130	.203	.130	-9	-8	-8	1	1	0	0	-1	3	-0.9
1962	Chi-A	79	130	22	30	3	3	6	24	13	22	.231	.301	.438	97	-1	-1	17	0	0	0	5	32	0.5
1963	LA-A	88	144	12	36	6	0	1	22	15	34	.250	.321	.313	83	-4	-3	15	2	1	0	-2	O/32	-0.5
Total	4	184	329	38	73	9	3	7	46	33	63	.222	.295	.331	73	-13	-12	34	3	1	0	1	/3O2	-0.9

■ TOM SAFFELL Saffell, Thomas Judson b: 7/26/21, Etowah, Tenn. BL/TR, 5'11", 170 lbs. Deb: 7/02/49

YEAR	TM/L	G	AB	R	H	2B	3B	HR	RBI	BB	SO	AVG	OBP	SLG	PRO+	BR	/A	RC	SB	CS	SBR	FR	POS	TPR
1949	Pit-N	73	205	36	66	7	1	2	25	21	27	.322	.385	.395	107	3	3	32	5			0	O	0.0
1950	Pit-N	67	182	18	37	7	0	2	6	14	34	.203	.264	.275	41	-15	-16	14	1			9	O	-0.8
1951	Pit-N	49	65	11	13	0	0	1	5	5	18	.200	.257	.246	35	-6	-6	4	1	0	0	4	O	-0.5
1955	Pit-N	73	113	21	19	1	0	1	3	15	22	.168	.266	.204	27	-12	-11	7	1	0	0	0	O	-0.7
	KC-A	9	37	5	8	0	0	0	1	4	7	.216	.293	.216	38	-3	-3	3	1	0	0	-0	/O	-0.3
Total	4	271	602	91	143	15	1	6	40	59	108	.238	.307	.296	60	-33	-34	61	9	1		14	O	-2.3

■ HARRY SAGE Sage, Harry "Doc" b: 3/16/1864, Rock Island, Ill. d: 5/27/47, Rock Island, Ill. BR/TR, 5'10", 185 lbs. Deb: 4/17/1890

YEAR	TM/L	G	AB	R	H	2B	3B	HR	RBI	BB	SO	AVG	OBP	SLG	PRO+	BR	/A	RC	SB	CS	SBR	FR	POS	TPR
1890	Tol-a	81	275	40	41	8	4	2	29			.149	.235	.229	38	-21	-22	18	10			6	C/O	-0.6

■ PONY SAGER Sager, Samuel B. b: 1847, Marshalltown, Iowa 140 lbs. Deb: 5/06/1871

YEAR	TM/L	G	AB	R	H	2B	3B	HR	RBI	BB	SO	AVG	OBP	SLG	PRO+	BR	/A	RC	SB	CS	SBR	FR	POS	TPR
1871	Rok-n	8	39	9	11	0	0	0	5	2	2	.282	.317	.282	77	-1	-1	5	5				/SO	0.0

YEAR	TM/L	G	AB	R	H	2B	3B	HR	RBI	BB	SO	AVG	OBP	SLG	PRO+	BR	/A	RC	SB	CS	SBR	FR	POS	TPR

■ VIC SAIER Saier, Victor Sylvester b: 5/4/1891, Lansing, Mich. d: 5/14/67, E.Lansing, Mich. BL/TR, 5'11", 185 lbs. Deb: 5/03/11

1911	Chi-N	86	259	42	67	15	1	1	37	25	37	.259	.340	.336	89	-3	-3	34	11			-4	1	-0.9
1912	Chi-N	122	451	74	130	25	14	2	61	34	65	.288	.340	.419	107	3	3	67	11			-5	*1	-0.6
1913	Chi-N	149	519	94	150	15	21	14	92	62	62	.289	.370	.480	141	28	27	97	26			-5	*1	1.6
1914	Chi-N	153	537	87	129	24	8	18	72	94	61	.240	.357	.415	130	21	21	85	19			-11	*1	0.9
1915	Chi-N	144	497	74	131	35	11	11	64	64	62	.264	.350	.445	140	24	23	83	29	9	3	-5	*1	1.6
1916	Chi-N	147	498	60	126	25	3	7	50	79	68	.253	.356	.357	108	14	8	66	20	17	-4	-0	*1	-0.2
1917	Chi-N	6	21	5	5	1	0	0	2	2	1	.238	.304	.286	75	-0	-1	2	0			2	/1	0.1
1919	Pit-N	58	166	19	37	3	3	2	17	18	13	.223	.306	.313	83	-2	-3	17	5			-5	1	-0.8
Total	8	865	2948	455	775	143	61	55	395	378	369	.263	.351	.409	119	83	76	450	121	26		-33	1	1.7

■ EBBA ST.CLAIRE St.Claire, Edward Joseph b: 8/5/21, Whitehall, N.Y. d: 8/22/82, Whitehill, N.Y. BB/TR, 6'1", 219 lbs. Deb: 4/17/51

1951	Bos-N	72	220	22	62	17	2	1	25	12	24	.282	.322	.391	98	-3	-1	29	2	0	1	3	C	0.3
1952	Bos-N	39	108	5	23	2	0	2	4	8	12	.213	.267	.287	56	-7	-6	8	0	1	-1	5	C	0.0
1953	Mil-N	33	80	7	16	3	0	2	5	3	9	.200	.229	.313	42	-7	-7	6	0	0	0	3	C	-0.1
1954	NY-N	20	42	5	11	1	0	2	6	12	7	.262	.436	.429	126	2	2	9	0	0	0	2	C	0.5
Total	4	164	450	39	112	23	2	7	40	35	52	.249	.306	.356	81	-15	-12	52	2	1	0	13	C	0.7

■ LENN SAKATA Sakata, Lenn Haruki b: 6/8/54, Honolulu, Hawaii BR/TR, 5'9", 160 lbs. Deb: 7/21/77

1977	Mil-A	53	154	13	25	2	0	2	12	9	22	.162	.209	.214	16	-18	-18	7	1	3	-2	17	2	0.2
1978	Mil-A	30	78	8	15	4	0	0	3	8	11	.192	.267	.244	44	-6	-6	5	1	0	0	2	2	-0.3
1979	Mil-A	4	14	1	7	2	0	0	1	0	1	.500	.500	.643	206	2	2	5	0	0	0	2	/2	0.4
1980	Bal-A	43	83	12	16	3	2	1	9	6	10	.193	.247	.313	53	-6	-5	6	2	1	0	6	2/SD	0.3
1981	Bal-A	61	150	19	34	4	0	5	15	11	18	.227	.284	.353	83	-4	-4	15	4	0	1	2	S2	0.3
1982	Bal-A	136	343	40	89	18	1	6	31	30	39	.259	.326	.370	91	-4	-4	42	7	4	-0	-5	2S	0.3
1983	*Bal-A	66	134	23	34	7	0	3	12	16	17	.254	.338	.373	97	-1	-0	17	8	4	0	8	2/CD	1.0
1984	Bal-A	81	157	23	30	1	0	3	11	6	15	.191	.221	.255	32	-15	-14	8	4	1	1	5	2/O	-0.4
1985	Bal-A	55	97	15	22	3	0	3	6	6	15	.227	.279	.351	73	-4	-4	9	3	2	-0	-1	2/D	-0.2
1986	Oak-A	17	34	4	12	2	0	0	5	3	6	.353	.405	.412	133	1	2	5	0	1	-1	5	2/D	0.6
1987	NY-A	19	45	5	12	0	1	2	4	2	4	.267	.313	.444	99	-0	-0	5	0	1	-1	1	3/2	0.0
Total	11	565	1289	163	296	46	4	25	109	97	158	.230	.288	.330	71	-53	-51	123	30	17	-1	40	2S/3DOC	1.9

■ MARK SALAS Salas, Mark Bruce b: 3/8/61, Montebello, Cal. BL/TR, 6', 180 lbs. Deb: 6/19/84

1984	StL-N	14	20	1	2	1	0	0	1	0	3	.100	.100	.150	-31	-3	-3	0	0	0	0	-0	/CO	-0.3
1985	Min-A	120	360	51	108	20	5	9	41	18	37	.300	.335	.458	108	6	4	53	0	1	-1	3	*C/D	1.0
1986	Min-A	91	258	28	60	7	4	8	33	18	32	.233	.285	.384	78	-8	-9	27	3	1	0	-6	C/D	-0.9
1987	Min-A	22	45	8	17	2	0	3	9	5	6	.378	.440	.622	171	5	5	12	0	1	-1	1	C	0.6
	NY-A	50	115	13	23	4	0	3	12	10	17	.200	.281	.313	58	-7	-7	11	0	0	0	-1	C/OD	-0.4
	Yr	72	160	21	40	6	0	6	21	15	23	.250	.326	.400	91	-2	-2	21	0	1	-1	-1		0.2
1988	Chi-A	75	196	17	49	7	0	3	9	12	17	.250	.303	.332	78	-6	-6	20	0	0	0	0	C/D	-0.2
1989	Cle-A	30	77	4	17	4	1	2	7	5	13	.221	.277	.377	81	-2	-2	8	0	0	0	-0	D/C	-0.1
1990	Det-A	74	164	18	38	3	0	9	24	21	28	.232	.323	.415	105	1	1	22	0	0	0	-4	C/3D	-0.1
Total	7	476	1235	140	314	48	10	37	136	89	153	.254	.310	.399	91	-14	-17	153	3	3	-1	-8	C/DO3	-0.4

■ ANGEL SALAZAR Salazar, Argenis Antonio (Yepez) b: 11/4/61, ElTigre, Venez. BR/TR, 6', 170 lbs. Deb: 8/10/83

1983	Mon-N	36	37	5	8	1	1	0	1	1	8	.216	.237	.297	47	-3	-3	2	0	0	0	2	S	0.3
1984	Mon-N	80	174	12	27	4	2	0	12	4	38	.155	.179	.201	7	-22	-21	6	1	1	-0	-3	S	-1.5
1986	KC-A	117	298	24	73	20	2	0	24	7	47	.245	.267	.326	59	-17	-17	26	1	1	-0	-5	*S/2	-1.5
1987	KC-A	116	317	24	65	7	0	2	21	6	46	.205	.220	.246	23	-35	-36	16	4	4	-1	22	*S	-0.8
1988	Chi-N	34	60	4	15	1	1	0	1	1	11	.250	.262	.300	58	-3	-3	5	0	0	0	7	S/23	0.5
Total	5	383	886	69	188	33	6	2	59	19	150	.212	.231	.270	36	-79	-80	55	6	6	-2	23	S/23	-3.0

■ LUIS SALAZAR Salazar, Luis Ernesto (Garcia) b: 5/19/56, Barcelona, Venez. BR/TR, 6', 185 lbs. Deb: 8/15/80

1980	SD-N	44	169	28	57	4	7	1	25	9	25	.337	.374	.462	140	7	8	29	11	2	2	-2	3/O	0.8
1981	SD-N	109	400	37	121	19	6	3	38	16	72	.303	.331	.403	116	3	6	51	11	8	-2	1	3O	0.0
1982	SD-N	145	524	55	127	15	5	8	62	23	80	.242	.277	.336	75	-22	-18	48	32	9	4	16	*3S/O	0.1
1983	SD-N	134	481	52	124	16	2	14	45	17	80	.258	.286	.387	88	-12	-10	53	24	9	2	10	*3S	0.2
1984	*SD-N	93	228	20	55	7	2	3	17	6	38	.241	.261	.329	65	-11	-11	17	11	7	-1	9	3O/S	-0.3
1985	Chi-A	122	327	39	80	18	2	10	45	12	60	.245	.271	.404	79	-9	-11	35	14	4	2	0	O3/1D	-1.1
1986	Chi-A	4	7	1	1	0	0	0	0	1	3	.143	.250	.143	10	-1	-1	0	0	0	0	0	/D	0.0
1987	SD-N	84	189	13	48	5	0	3	17	14	30	.254	.305	.328	70	-9	-8	19	3	3	-1	-6	3SO/P1	-1.2
1988	Det-A	130	452	61	122	14	1	12	62	21	70	.270	.307	.385	96	-5	-3	52	6	0	2	-8	OS3/1	-0.8
1989	SD-N	95	246	27	66	7	2	8	22	11	44	.268	.302	.411	102	-0	-0	29	1	3	-2	8	3O/S1	0.7
	*Chi-N	26	80	7	26	5	0	1	12	4	13	.325	.357	.425	114	2	2	11	0	1	-1	-6	3/O	-0.4
	Yr	121	326	34	92	12	2	9	34	15	57	.282	.316	.414	105	2	1	40	1	4	-2	3		0.3
1990	Chi-N	115	410	44	104	13	3	12	47	19	59	.254	.293	.388	79	-9	-13	47	3	1	0	-17	3O	-2.9
Total	11	1101	3513	384	931	123	30	75	392	153	574	.265	.298	.381	89	-66	-60	391	116	47	7	6	3OS/1D2P	-5.1

■ ED SALES Sales, Edward A. b: 1861, Harrisburg, Pa. d: 8/10/12, New Haven, Conn. TR, Deb: 7/15/1890

| 1890 | Pit-N | 51 | 189 | 19 | 43 | 7 | 3 | 1 | 23 | 16 | 15 | .228 | .298 | .312 | 90 | -5 | -1 | 19 | 3 | | | -13 | S | -1.3 |

■ BILL SALKELD Salkeld, William Franklin b: 3/8/17, Pocatello, Idaho d: 4/22/67, Los Angeles, Cal. BL/TR, 5'10", 190 lbs. Deb: 4/18/45

1945	Pit-N	95	267	45	83	16	1	15	52	50	16	.311	.420	.547	161	25	24	63	2			-9	C	1.6
1946	Pit-N	69	160	18	47	8	0	3	19	39	16	.294	.432	.400	133	10	10	32	2			-0	C	1.1
1947	Pit-N	47	61	5	13	2	0	0	8	6	8	.213	.284	.246	41	-5	-5	4	0			-3	C	-0.6
1948	*Bos-N	78	198	26	48	8	1	8	28	42	37	.242	.378	.414	116	5	6	34	1			5	C	1.5
1949	Bos-N	66	161	17	41	5	0	5	25	44	24	.255	.417	.379	121	6	7	29	1			-4	C	0.5
1950	Chi-A	1	3	0	0	0	0	0	0	1	0	.000	.250	.000	-33	-1	-1	0	0	0	0	-0	/C	0.0
Total	6	356	850	111	232	39	2	31	132	182	101	.273	.402	.433	129	41	40	162	6	0		-10	C	4.1

■ CHICO SALMON Salmon, Ruthford Eduardo b: 12/3/40, Colon, Panama BR/TR, 5'10", 160 lbs. Deb: 6/28/64

1964	Cle-A	86	283	43	87	17	2	4	25	13	37	.307	.342	.424	113	4	4	41	10	6	-1	-8	O21	-0.3
1965	Cle-A	79	120	20	29	8	0	3	12	5	19	.242	.283	.383	87	-2	-2	12	7	4	-0	-2	1O/23	-0.6
1966	Cle-A	126	422	46	108	13	2	7	40	21	41	.256	.291	.346	82	-10	-10	44	10	1	2	-16	S210/3	-2.0
1967	Cle-A	90	203	19	46	13	1	2	19	17	29	.227	.290	.330	82	-4	-5	20	10	4	1	6	O12S/3	0.1
1968	Cle-A	103	276	24	59	8	1	3	12	12	30	.214	.254	.283	63	-13	-12	19	7	7	-2	-13	23SO1	-2.9
1969	*Bal-A	52	91	18	27	5	0	3	12	10	22	.297	.379	.451	130	4	4	16	0	0	0	-4	1/2S3O	0.0
1970	Bal-A	63	172	19	43	4	0	7	22	8	30	.250	.287	.395	85	-4	-4	19	2	2	-1	-20	S23/1	-2.1
1971	Bal-A	42	84	11	15	1	0	2	7	3	21	.179	.207	.262	32	-8	-8	4	0	0	0	-3	/123S	-1.0
1972	Bal-A	17	16	2	1	0	0	0	1	0	4	.063	.063	.125	-44	-3	-3	0	0	0	0	0	/13	-0.2
Total	9	658	1667	202	415	70	6	31	149	89	233	.249	.291	.354	84	-36	-36	174	46	24	-1	-61	2S10/3	-9.0

■ JACK SALTZGAVER Saltzgaver, Otto Hamlin b: 1/23/03, Croton, Iowa d: 2/1/78, Keokuk, Iowa BL/TR, 5'11", 165 lbs. Deb: 4/12/32

| 1932 | NY-A | 20 | 47 | 10 | 6 | 2 | 1 | 0 | 5 | 10 | 10 | .128 | .281 | .213 | 31 | -5 | -4 | 4 | 1 | 1 | -0 | -3 | 2 | -0.6 |
| 1934 | NY-A | 94 | 350 | 64 | 95 | 8 | 1 | 6 | 36 | 48 | 28 | .271 | .359 | .351 | 90 | -7 | -4 | 48 | 8 | 1 | 2 | -16 | 3/1 | -1.6 |

YEAR	TM/L	G	AB	R	H	2B	3B	HR	RBI	BB	SO	AVG	OBP	SLG	PRO+	BR	/A	RC	SB	CS	SBR	FR	POS	TPR
1935	NY-A	61	149	17	39	6	0	3	18	23	12	.262	.368	.362	95	-2	-0	21	0	2	-1	-13	23/1	-1.3
1936	NY-A	34	90	14	19	5	0	1	13	13	18	.211	.311	.300	53	-7	-6	9	0	0	0	-5	3/21	-0.9
1937	NY-A	17	11	6	2	0	0	0	0	3	4	.182	.357	.182	40	-1	-1	1	0	0	0	0	/1	0.0
1945	Pit-N	52	117	20	38	5	3	0	10	8	8	.325	.368	.419	114	3	2	18	0			-4	2/3	0.1
Total	6	278	764	131	199	26	5	10	82	105	80	.260	.351	.347	85	-19	-14	101	9	4		-39	3/21	-4.3

■ ED SAMCOFF
Samcoff, Edward William   b: 9/1/24, Sacramento, Cal.   BR/TR, 5'10", 165 lbs.   Deb: 4/21/51

YEAR	TM/L	G	AB	R	H	2B	3B	HR	RBI	BB	SO	AVG	OBP	SLG	PRO+	BR	/A	RC	SB	CS	SBR	FR	POS	TPR
1951	Phi-A	4	11	0	0	0	0	0	0	1	2	.000	.083	.000	-75	-3	-3	0	0	0	0	-1	/2	-0.3

■ RON SAMFORD
Samford, Ronald Edward   b: 2/28/30, Dallas, Tex.   BR/TR, 5'11", 156 lbs.   Deb: 4/15/54

YEAR	TM/L	G	AB	R	H	2B	3B	HR	RBI	BB	SO	AVG	OBP	SLG	PRO+	BR	/A	RC	SB	CS	SBR	FR	POS	TPR
1954	NY-N	12	5	2	0	0	0	0	0	0	1	.000	.000	.000	-99	-1	-1	0	0	1	-1	3	/2	0.1
1955	Det-A	1	1	0	0	0	0	0	0	0	1	.000	.000	.000	-99	-0	-0	0	0	0	0	0	/S	0.0
1957	Det-A	54	91	6	20	1	2	0	5	6	15	.220	.276	.275	49	-6	-6	7	1	0	0	13	S2/3	1.1
1959	Was-A	91	237	23	53	13	0	5	22	11	29	.224	.264	.342	65	-12	-12	19	1	0	0	0	S2	-0.5
Total	4	158	334	31	73	14	2	5	27	17	46	.219	.263	.317	58	-20	-20	27	2	1	0	17	S/23	0.7

■ BILL SAMPLE
Sample, William Amos   b: 4/2/55, Roanoke, Va.   BR/TR, 5'9", 175 lbs.   Deb: 9/02/78

YEAR	TM/L	G	AB	R	H	2B	3B	HR	RBI	BB	SO	AVG	OBP	SLG	PRO+	BR	/A	RC	SB	CS	SBR	FR	POS	TPR
1978	Tex-A	8	15	2	7	2	0	0	3	0	3	.467	.467	.600	197	2	2	4	0	0	0	0	/OD	0.2
1979	Tex-A	128	325	60	95	21	2	5	35	37	28	.292	.368	.415	112	6	6	50	8	6	-1	-5	*O/D	-0.3
1980	Tex-A	99	204	29	53	10	0	4	19	18	15	.260	.338	.368	96	-2	-1	26	8	5	-1	-2	O/D	-0.4
1981	Tex-A	66	230	36	65	16	0	3	25	17	21	.283	.350	.391	120	4	6	33	4	1	1	-1	O	0.4
1982	Tex-A	97	360	56	94	14	2	10	29	27	35	.261	.318	.394	99	-3	-1	47	10	2	2	0	O/D	-0.1
1983	Tex-A	147	554	80	152	28	3	12	57	44	46	.274	.333	.401	103	1	2	79	44	8	8	2	*O	1.1
1984	Tex-A	130	489	67	121	20	2	5	33	29	46	.247	.290	.327	68	-20	-22	46	18	6	2	4	*O/D	-1.9
1985	NY-A	59	139	18	40	5	0	1	15	9	10	.288	.340	.345	90	-2	-2	17	2	1	0	-3	O	-0.4
1986	Atl-N	92	200	23	57	11	0	6	14	14	26	.285	.341	.430	105	3	1	31	4	2	0	-6	O/2	-0.5
Total	9	826	2516	371	684	127	9	46	230	195	230	.272	.331	.384	98	-11	-8	334	98	31	11	-9	O/D2	-1.9

■ AMADO SAMUEL
Samuel, Amado Ruperto   b: 12/6/38, San Pedro De Macoris, D.R.   BR/TR, 6'1", 170 lbs.   Deb: 4/10/62

YEAR	TM/L	G	AB	R	H	2B	3B	HR	RBI	BB	SO	AVG	OBP	SLG	PRO+	BR	/A	RC	SB	CS	SBR	FR	POS	TPR
1962	Mil-N	76	209	16	43	10	0	3	20	12	54	.206	.249	.297	47	-16	-16	15	0	2	-1	-4	S2/3	-1.4
1963	Mil-N	15	17	0	3	1	0	0	0	0	4	.176	.176	.235	18	-2	-2	1	0	1	-1	2	/S2	0.1
1964	NY-N	53	142	7	33	7	0	0	5	4	24	.232	.264	.282	55	-9	-8	10	0	1	-1	7	S3/2	0.0
Total	3	144	368	23	79	18	0	3	25	16	82	.215	.251	.288	49	-27	-26	26	0	4	-2	5	/S23	-1.3

■ JUAN SAMUEL
Samuel, Juan Milton   b: 12/9/60, San Pedro De Macoris, , D.R.   BR/TR, 5'11", 170 lbs.   Deb: 8/24/83

YEAR	TM/L	G	AB	R	H	2B	3B	HR	RBI	BB	SO	AVG	OBP	SLG	PRO+	BR	/A	RC	SB	CS	SBR	FR	POS	TPR
1983	*Phi-N	18	65	14	18	1	2	2	5	4	16	.277	.329	.446	114	1	1	9	3	2	-0	3	2	0.5
1984	Phi-N	160	701	105	191	36	**19**	15	69	28	168	.272	.307	.442	107	5	3	99	72	15	13	-22	*2	-0.1
1985	Phi-N	161	663	101	175	31	13	19	74	33	141	.264	.305	.436	102	2	-0	87	53	19	5	-2	*2	0.3
1986	Phi-N	145	591	90	157	36	12	16	78	26	142	.266	.306	.448	102	2	-1	80	42	14	4	-9	*2	-0.3
1987	Phi-N	160	655	113	178	37	**15**	28	100	60	162	.272	.338	.502	115	16	13	109	35	15	2	-19	*2	-0.1
1988	Phi-N	157	629	68	153	32	9	12	67	39	151	.243	.300	.380	92	-6	-7	73	33	10	4	-26	*2/O3	-2.6
1989	Phi-N	51	199	32	49	3	1	8	20	18	45	.246	.312	.392	100	-0	-0	26	11	3	2	7	O	0.8
	NY-N	86	333	37	76	13	1	3	28	24	75	.228	.300	.300	76	-12	-10	33	31	9	4	2	O	-0.4
	Yr	137	532	69	125	16	2	11	48	42	120	.235	.304	.335	85	-12	-10	58	42	12	5	9		0.4
1990	LA-N	143	492	62	119	24	3	13	52	51	126	.242	.319	.382	98	-5	-2	60	38	20	-1	-6	*2O	-0.8
Total	8	1081	4328	622	1116	213	75	116	493	283	1026	.258	.312	.422	101	1	-4	575	318	107	31	-71	2O/3	-2.7

■ IKE SAMULS
Samuls, Samuel Earl   b: 2/20/1876, Chicago, Ill.   d: 1/1/42, Los Angeles, Cal.   BR/TR,   Deb: 8/03/1895

YEAR	TM/L	G	AB	R	H	2B	3B	HR	RBI	BB	SO	AVG	OBP	SLG	PRO+	BR	/A	RC	SB	CS	SBR	FR	POS	TPR
1895	StL-N	24	74	5	17	2	0	0	5	5	7	.230	.278	.257	41	-6	-6	7	5			-2	3/S	-0.6

■ GUS SANBERG
Sanberg, Gustave E.   b: 2/23/1896, Long Island City, N.Y.   d: 2/3/30, Los Angeles, Cal.   BR/TR, 6'1", 189 lbs.   Deb: 5/11/23

YEAR	TM/L	G	AB	R	H	2B	3B	HR	RBI	BB	SO	AVG	OBP	SLG	PRO+	BR	/A	RC	SB	CS	SBR	FR	POS	TPR
1923	Cin-N	7	17	1	3	1	0	0	1	1	1	.176	.222	.235	21	-2	-2	1	0	0	0	-1	/C	-0.1
1924	Cin-N	24	52	1	9	0	0	0	3	2	7	.173	.204	.173	2	-7	-7	2	0	0	0	0	C	-0.5
Total	2	31	69	2	12	1	0	0	4	3	8	.174	.208	.188	7	-9	-9	3	0	0	0	-0	/C	-0.6

■ ALEJANDRO SANCHEZ
Sanchez, Alejandro (Pimentel)   b: 2/14/59, San Pedro, D.R.   BR/TR, 6', 185 lbs.   Deb: 9/06/82

YEAR	TM/L	G	AB	R	H	2B	3B	HR	RBI	BB	SO	AVG	OBP	SLG	PRO+	BR	/A	RC	SB	CS	SBR	FR	POS	TPR
1982	Phi-N	7	14	3	4	1	0	2	4	0	4	.286	.286	.786	186	1	1	3	0	0	0	0	/O	0.2
1983	Phi-N	8	7	2	2	0	0	0	2	0	2	.286	.286	.286	59	-0	-0	0	0	0	0	0	/O	0.0
1984	SF-N	13	41	3	8	0	1	0	2	0	12	.195	.195	.244	23	-4	-4	1	2	3	-1	1	O	-0.4
1985	Det-A	71	133	19	33	6	2	6	12	0	39	.248	.248	.459	89	-3	-3	13	2	2	-1	1	OD	-0.2
1986	Min-A	8	16	1	2	0	0	0	1	1	8	.125	.176	.125	-16	-3	-3	0	0	0	0	0	/OD	-0.2
1987	Oak-A	2	3	0	0	0	0	0	0	0	1	.000	.000	.000	-99	-1	-1	0	0	0	0	0	/OD	0.0
Total	6	109	214	28	49	7	3	8	21	1	66	.229	.233	.402	71	-9	-9	18	4	5	-2	2	/OD	-0.6

■ CELERINO SANCHEZ
Sanchez, Celerino (Perez)   b: 2/3/44, Veracruz, Mexico   BR/TR, 5'11", 160 lbs.   Deb: 6/13/72

YEAR	TM/L	G	AB	R	H	2B	3B	HR	RBI	BB	SO	AVG	OBP	SLG	PRO+	BR	/A	RC	SB	CS	SBR	FR	POS	TPR
1972	NY-A	71	250	18	62	8	3	0	22	12	30	.248	.293	.304	81	-7	-6	21	0	0	0	4	3	0.0
1973	NY-A	34	64	12	14	3	0	1	9	2	12	.219	.242	.313	57	-4	-4	5	1	1	-0	2	3D/SO	-0.1
Total	2	105	314	30	76	11	3	1	31	14	42	.242	.283	.306	76	-11	-10	26	1	1	-0	6	/3DOS	-0.1

■ ORLANDO SANCHEZ
Sanchez, Orlando (Marquez)   b: 9/7/56, Canovanas, P.R.   BL/TR, 6'1", 195 lbs.   Deb: 5/06/81

YEAR	TM/L	G	AB	R	H	2B	3B	HR	RBI	BB	SO	AVG	OBP	SLG	PRO+	BR	/A	RC	SB	CS	SBR	FR	POS	TPR
1981	StL-N	27	49	5	14	2	1	0	6	2	6	.286	.314	.367	90	-1	-1	5	1	0	0	-2	C	-0.1
1982	StL-N	26	37	6	7	0	1	0	3	5	5	.189	.286	.243	49	-2	-2	3	0	0	0	-1	/C	-0.2
1983	StL-N	6	6	0	0	0	0	0	0	0	4	.000	.000	.000	-99	-2	-2	0	0	0	0	0	/C	-0.1
1984	KC-A	10	10	0	1	1	0	0	2	0	2	.100	.100	.200	-19	-2	-2	0	0	0	0	0	/C	-0.1
	Bal-A	4	8	0	2	0	0	0	1	0	2	.250	.250	.250	40	-1	-1	1	0	0	0	0	/C	0.0
	Yr	14	18	0	3	1	0	0	3	0	4	.167	.167	.222	7	-2	-2	0	0	0	0	0		-0.1
Total	4	73	110	11	24	3	2	0	12	7	19	.218	.265	.282	53	-7	-7	9	1	0	0	-3	/C	-0.5

■ HEINIE SAND
Sand, John Henry   b: 7/3/1897, San Francisco, Cal   d: 11/3/58, San Francisco, Cal.   BR/TR, 5'8", 160 lbs.   Deb: 4/17/23

YEAR	TM/L	G	AB	R	H	2B	3B	HR	RBI	BB	SO	AVG	OBP	SLG	PRO+	BR	/A	RC	SB	CS	SBR	FR	POS	TPR
1923	Phi-N	132	470	85	107	16	5	4	32	82	56	.228	.347	.309	67	-15	-23	57	7	3	0	-2	*S3	-1.3
1924	Phi-N	137	539	79	132	21	6	6	40	52	57	.245	.316	.340	67	-18	-27	60	5	4	-1	2	*S	-1.4
1925	Phi-N	148	496	69	138	30	7	3	55	64	65	.278	.364	.385	84	-5	-11	73	1	1	-0	-5	*S	-0.4
1926	Phi-N	149	567	99	154	30	5	4	37	66	56	.272	.350	.363	88	-5	-9	73	2			-3	*S	-0.1
1927	Phi-N	141	535	87	160	22	8	1	49	58	59	.299	.369	.376	98	1	1	75	5			-15	S3	-0.3
1928	Phi-N	141	426	38	90	26	1	0	38	60	47	.211	.310	.277	53	-27	-29	40	1			-1	*S	-1.0
Total	6	848	3033	457	781	145	32	18	251	382	340	.258	.343	.344	77	-69	-99	378	21	8		-25	S/3	-4.5

■ RYNE SANDBERG
Sandberg, Ryne Dee   b: 9/18/59, Spokane, Wash.   BR/TR, 6'1", 175 lbs.   Deb: 9/02/81

YEAR	TM/L	G	AB	R	H	2B	3B	HR	RBI	BB	SO	AVG	OBP	SLG	PRO+	BR	/A	RC	SB	CS	SBR	FR	POS	TPR
1981	Phi-N	13	6	2	1	0	0	0	0	0	1	.167	.167	.167	-5	-1	-1	0	0	0	0	4	/S2	0.4
1982	Chi-N	156	635	103	172	33	5	7	54	36	90	.271	.314	.372	89	-8	-10	75	32	12	2	5	*32	-0.4
1983	Chi-N	158	633	94	165	25	4	8	48	51	79	.261	.319	.351	81	-13	-16	75	37	11	5	**41**	*2/S	3.6
1984	*Chi-N	156	636	**114**	200	36	**19**	19	84	52	101	.314	.369	.520	135	38	31	**126**	32	7	5	23	*2	**6.6**
1985	Chi-N	153	609	113	186	31	6	26	83	57	97	.305	.364	.504	127	32	24	117	54	11	10	8	*2/S	4.4
1986	Chi-N	154	627	68	178	28	5	14	76	46	79	.284	.333	.411	97	2	-3	86	34	11	4	5	*2	0.8
1987	Chi-N	132	523	81	154	25	2	16	59	59	79	.294	.368	.442	109	11	8	89	21	2	5	1	*2	1.6
1988	Chi-N	155	618	77	163	23	8	19	69	54	91	.264	.324	.419	107	8	5	82	25	10	2	11	*2	2.4

YEAR	TM/L	G	AB	R	H	2B	3B	HR	RBI	BB	SO	AVG	OBP	SLG	PRO+	BR	/A	RC	SB	CS	SBR	FR	POS	TPR
1989	*Chi-N	157	606	**104**	176	25	5	30	76	59	85	.290	.357	.497	132	32	26	109	15	5	2	1	*2	3.2
1990	Chi-N	155	615	**116**	188	30	3	**40**	100	50	84	.306	.359	.559	136	38	31	124	25	7	3	7	*2	4.3
Total	10	1389	5508	872	1583	256	57	179	649	464	786	.287	.345	.452	113	139	95	883	275	76	37	106	*23/S	26.9

■ BEN SANDERS
Sanders, Alexander Bennett b: 2/16/1865, Catharpen, Va. d: 8/29/30, Memphis, Tenn. BR/TR, 6′, 210 lbs. Deb: 6/06/1888

YEAR	TM/L	G	AB	R	H	2B	3B	HR	RBI	BB	SO	AVG	OBP	SLG	PRO+	BR	/A	RC	SB	CS	SBR	FR	POS	TPR
1888	Phi-N	57	236	26	58	11	2	1	25	8	12	.246	.276	.322	88	-2	-4	25	13			3	PO/3	0.0
1889	Phi-N	44	169	21	47	8	2	0	21	6	11	.278	.307	.349	78	-4	-6	20	4			-2	P/O	0.0
1890	Phi-P	52	189	31	59	6	6	0	30	10	10	.312	.347	.407	101	0	-1	28	2			1	PO	0.0
1891	Phi-a	40	156	24	39	6	4	1	19	7	12	.250	.291	.359	86	-3	-4	17	2			-5	OP	-0.5
1892	Lou-N	54	198	30	54	12	2	3	18	16	17	.273	.330	.399	133	5	7	29	6			-2	P1/O	0.0
Total	5	247	948	132	257	43	16	5	113	47	62	.271	.310	.366	96	-4	-7	119	27			-6	P/O13	-0.5

■ DEION SANDERS
Sanders, Deion Luwynn b: 8/9/67, Ft.Myers, Fla. BL/TL, 6′1″, 195 lbs. Deb: 6/01/89

YEAR	TM/L	G	AB	R	H	2B	3B	HR	RBI	BB	SO	AVG	OBP	SLG	PRO+	BR	/A	RC	SB	CS	SBR	FR	POS	TPR
1989	NY-A	14	47	7	11	2	0	2	7	3	8	.234	.280	.404	92	-1	-1	6	1	0	0	0	O	0.0
1990	NY-A	57	133	24	21	2	2	3	9	13	27	.158	.238	.271	42	-11	-11	9	8	2	1	-1	O/D	-1.0
Total	2	71	180	31	32	4	2	5	16	16	35	.178	.249	.306	54	-11	-11	15	9	2	2	-0	/OD	-1.0

■ JOHN SANDERS
Sanders, John Frank b: 11/20/45, Grand Island, Neb. BR/TR, 6′2″, 200 lbs. Deb: 4/13/65

YEAR	TM/L	G	AB	R	H	2B	3B	HR	RBI	BB	SO	AVG	OBP	SLG	PRO+	BR	/A	RC	SB	CS	SBR	FR	POS	TPR
1965	KC-A	1	0	0	0	0	0	0	0	0	0	—	—	—	—	0	0	0	0	0	0	0	R	0.0

■ RAY SANDERS
Sanders, Raymond Floyd b: 12/4/16, Bonne Terre, Mo. d: 10/28/83, Washington, Mo. BL/TR, 6′2″, 185 lbs. Deb: 4/14/42

YEAR	TM/L	G	AB	R	H	2B	3B	HR	RBI	BB	SO	AVG	OBP	SLG	PRO+	BR	/A	RC	SB	CS	SBR	FR	POS	TPR
1942	*StL-N	95	282	37	71	17	2	5	39	42	31	.252	.351	.379	106	6	3	39	2			-3	1	-0.6
1943	*StL-N	144	478	69	134	21	5	11	73	77	33	.280	.381	.414	124	20	18	80	1			-7	*1	0.5
1944	*StL-N	154	601	87	177	34	9	12	102	71	50	.295	.371	.441	126	23	21	101	2			-13	*1	-0.3
1945	StL-N	143	537	85	148	29	3	8	78	83	55	.276	.375	.385	109	11	9	84	3			-4	*1	-0.1
1946	Bos-N	80	259	43	63	12	0	6	35	50	38	.243	.368	.359	105	4	4	38	0			4	1	0.1
1948	*Bos-N	5	4	0	1	0	0	0	2	1	0	.250	.400	.250	81	-0	-0	0	0			0	H	0.0
1949	Bos-N	9	21	0	3	1	0	0	0	4	9	.143	.280	.190	30	-2	-2	1	0			2	/1	0.0
Total	7	630	2182	321	597	114	19	42	329	328	216	.274	.370	.401	115	61	52	344	8			-21	1	-0.4

■ REGGIE SANDERS
Sanders, Reginald Jerome b: 9/9/49, Birmingham, Ala. BR/TR, 6′2″, 205 lbs. Deb: 9/01/74

YEAR	TM/L	G	AB	R	H	2B	3B	HR	RBI	BB	SO	AVG	OBP	SLG	PRO+	BR	/A	RC	SB	CS	SBR	FR	POS	TPR
1974	Det-A	26	99	12	27	7	0	3	10	5	20	.273	.308	.434	108	1	1	13	1	0	0	2	1/D	0.2

■ MIKE SANDLOCK
Sandlock, Michael Joseph b: 10/17/15, Old Greenwich, Conn. BB/TR, 6′1″, 180 lbs. Deb: 9/19/42

YEAR	TM/L	G	AB	R	H	2B	3B	HR	RBI	BB	SO	AVG	OBP	SLG	PRO+	BR	/A	RC	SB	CS	SBR	FR	POS	TPR
1942	Bos-N	2	1	1	1	0	0	0	0	0	0	1.000	1.000	1.000	496	0	0	1	0			0	/S	0.1
1944	Bos-N	30	30	1	3	0	0	0	2	5	3	.100	.250	.100	1	-4	-4	1	0			7	3/S	0.5
1945	Bro-N	80	195	21	55	14	2	2	17	18	19	.282	.346	.405	109	2	2	28	2			1	CS/23	0.7
1946	Bro-N	19	34	1	5	0	0	0	0	3	4	.147	.216	.147	4	-4	-4	1	0			6	C/3	0.6
1953	Pit-N	64	186	10	43	5	0	0	12	12	19	.231	.281	.258	42	-16	-15	14	0	0	0	19	C	0.6
Total	5	195	446	34	107	19	2	2	31	38	45	.240	.304	.305	66	-21	-21	46	2	0		33	C/S32	2.1

■ CHARLIE SANDS
Sands, Charles Duane b: 12/17/47, Newport News, Va. BL/TR, 6′2″, 200 lbs. Deb: 6/21/67

YEAR	TM/L	G	AB	R	H	2B	3B	HR	RBI	BB	SO	AVG	OBP	SLG	PRO+	BR	/A	RC	SB	CS	SBR	FR	POS	TPR
1967	NY-A	1	1	0	0	0	0	0	0	0	1	.000	.000	.000	-99	-0	-0	0	0	0	0	0	H	0.0
1971	*Pit-N	28	25	4	5	2	0	1	5	7	6	.200	.375	.400	120	1	1	4	0	0	0	0	/C	0.1
1972	Pit-N	1	1	0	0	0	0	0	0	0	0	.000	.000	.000	-99	-0	-0	0	0	0	0	0	H	0.0
1973	Cal-A	17	33	5	9	2	1	1	5	5	10	.273	.368	.485	150	2	2	6	0	0	0	-7	C	-0.4
1974	Cal-A	43	83	6	16	2	0	4	13	23	17	.193	.374	.361	119	2	3	12	0	0	0	-1	D/C	0.3
1975	Oak-A	3	2	0	1	0	0	0	0	1	1	.500	.667	.500	239	1	1	1	0	0	0	0	/D	0.1
Total	6	93	145	15	31	6	1	6	23	36	35	.214	.374	.393	125	5	6	24	0	0	0	-7	/DC	0.1

■ TOMMY SANDT
Sandt, Thomas James b: 12/22/50, Brooklyn, N.Y. BR/TR, 5′11″, 175 lbs. Deb: 6/29/75 C

YEAR	TM/L	G	AB	R	H	2B	3B	HR	RBI	BB	SO	AVG	OBP	SLG	PRO+	BR	/A	RC	SB	CS	SBR	FR	POS	TPR
1975	Oak-A	1	0	0	0	0	0	0	0	0	0	—	—	—	—	0	0	0	0	0	0	0	/2	0.0
1976	Oak-A	41	67	6	14	1	0	0	3	7	9	.209	.284	.224	52	-4	-4	5	0	0	0	3	S/23	0.2
Total	2	42	67	6	14	1	0	0	3	7	9	.209	.284	.224	52	-4	-4	5	0	0	0	3	/S23	0.2

■ JACK SANFORD
Sanford, John Doward b: 6/23/17, Chatham, Va. BR/TR, 6′3″, 195 lbs. Deb: 8/24/40

YEAR	TM/L	G	AB	R	H	2B	3B	HR	RBI	BB	SO	AVG	OBP	SLG	PRO+	BR	/A	RC	SB	CS	SBR	FR	POS	TPR
1940	Was-A	34	122	5	24	4	2	0	10	6	17	.197	.234	.262	30	-13	-12	8	0	0	0	-2	1	-1.4
1941	Was-A	3	5	1	2	0	1	0	0	1	1	.400	.500	.800	251	1	1	2	0	0	0	-0	/1	0.1
1946	Was-A	10	26	7	6	0	1	0	1	2	6	.231	.286	.308	70	-1	-1	2	0	0	0	-1	/1	-0.2
Total	3	47	153	13	32	4	4	0	11	9	24	.209	.253	.288	44	-13	-12	12	0	0	0	-3	/1	-1.5

■ MANNY SANGUILLEN
Sanguillen, Manuel De Jesus (Magan) b: 3/21/44, Colon, Panama BR/TR, 6′, 193 lbs. Deb: 7/23/67

YEAR	TM/L	G	AB	R	H	2B	3B	HR	RBI	BB	SO	AVG	OBP	SLG	PRO+	BR	/A	RC	SB	CS	SBR	FR	POS	TPR
1967	Pit-N	30	96	6	26	4	0	0	8	4	12	.271	.300	.313	75	-3	-3	8	0	1	-1	-5	C	-0.6
1969	Pit-N	129	459	62	139	21	6	5	57	12	48	.303	.325	.407	106	1	2	56	8	4	0	4	*C	1.3
1970	*Pit-N	128	486	63	158	19	9	7	61	17	45	.325	.348	.444	113	6	7	69	2	3	-1	1	*C	1.2
1971	*Pit-N	138	533	60	170	26	5	7	81	19	32	.319	.346	.426	118	11	11	70	6	4	-1	4	*C	1.9
1972	*Pit-N	136	520	55	155	18	8	7	71	21	38	.298	.325	.404	108	3	4	65	1	2	-1	-4	*C/O	0.6
1973	Pit-N	149	589	64	166	26	7	12	65	17	29	.282	.305	.411	99	-5	-3	67	2	5	-2	-1	CO	-0.3
1974	*Pit-N	151	596	77	171	21	4	7	68	21	27	.287	.317	.371	95	-8	-6	65	2	2	-1	-7	*C	-0.7
1975	*Pit-N	133	481	60	158	24	4	9	58	48	31	.328	.393	.451	135	22	23	83	5	4	-1	-5	*C	2.2
1976	Pit-N	114	389	52	113	16	6	2	36	28	18	.290	.341	.378	103	2	1	46	2	4	-2	-7	*C	-0.1
1977	Oak-A	152	571	42	157	17	5	6	58	22	35	.275	.304	.354	80	-17	-16	57	2	5	-2	-8	CD/O1	-2.5
1978	Pit-N	85	220	15	58	5	1	3	16	9	10	.264	.299	.336	74	-7	-8	21	2	2	-1	-2	1C	-1.2
1979	*Pit-N	56	74	8	17	5	2	0	4	2	5	.230	.250	.351	59	-4	-4	6	0	0	0	0	/C1	-0.3
1980	Pit-N	47	48	2	12	3	0	0	2	3	1	.250	.294	.313	68	-2	-2	4	3	2	-0	0	/1	-0.2
Total	13	1448	5062	566	1500	205	57	65	585	223	331	.296	.329	.398	103	-2	6	616	35	38	-12	-29	*C/OD1	1.3

■ ED SANICKI
Sanicki, Edward Robert "Butch" b: 7/7/23, Wallington, N.J. BR/TR, 5′9″, 175 lbs. Deb: 9/14/49

YEAR	TM/L	G	AB	R	H	2B	3B	HR	RBI	BB	SO	AVG	OBP	SLG	PRO+	BR	/A	RC	SB	CS	SBR	FR	POS	TPR
1949	Phi-N	7	13	4	3	0	0	3	7	1	4	.231	.286	.923	217	2	2	3	0			1	/O	0.2
1951	Phi-N	13	4	1	2	1	0	0	1	1	1	.500	.600	.750	265	1	1	2	1	0	0	0	O	0.1
Total	2	20	17	5	5	1	0	3	8	2	5	.294	.368	.882	231	3	3	6	1	0		1	/O	0.3

■ BEN SANKEY
Sankey, Benjamin Turner b: 9/2/07, Nauvoo, Ala. BR/TR, 5′10″, 155 lbs. Deb: 10/05/29

YEAR	TM/L	G	AB	R	H	2B	3B	HR	RBI	BB	SO	AVG	OBP	SLG	PRO+	BR	/A	RC	SB	CS	SBR	FR	POS	TPR
1929	Pit-N	2	7	1	1	0	0	0	0	0	1	.143	.143	.143	-28	-1	-1	0	0			-0	/S	0.0
1930	Pit-N	13	30	6	5	0	0	0	3	2	3	.167	.219	.167	-5	-5	-5	1	0			-0	/S2	-0.3
1931	Pit-N	57	132	14	30	2	5	0	14	14	10	.227	.301	.318	67	-6	-6	14	0			-9	S/23	-1.0
Total	3	72	169	21	36	2	5	0	14	16	14	.213	.281	.284	49	-13	-13	15	0			-9	/S23	-1.3

■ ANDRES SANTANA
Santana, Andres Confesor (Belonis) b: 3/19/68, San Pedro De Macoris, D.R. BB/TR, 5′11″, 160 lbs. Deb: 9/16/90

YEAR	TM/L	G	AB	R	H	2B	3B	HR	RBI	BB	SO	AVG	OBP	SLG	PRO+	BR	/A	RC	SB	CS	SBR	FR	POS	TPR
1990	SF-N	6	2	0	0	0	0	0	0	1	0	.000	.000	.000	-99	-1	-1	0	0	0	0	1	/S	0.1

■ RAFAEL SANTANA
Santana, Rafael Francisco (De La Cruz) b: 1/31/58, LaRomana, D.R. BR/TR, 6′1″, 165 lbs. Deb: 4/05/83

YEAR	TM/L	G	AB	R	H	2B	3B	HR	RBI	BB	SO	AVG	OBP	SLG	PRO+	BR	/A	RC	SB	CS	SBR	FR	POS	TPR
1983	StL-N	30	14	1	3	0	0	0	2	2	2	.214	.353	.214	61	-1	-1	1	0	1	-1	2	/2S3	0.2
1984	NY-N	51	152	14	42	11	1	1	12	9	17	.276	.317	.382	97	-1	-1	17	0	3	-2	-3	S	0.0
1985	NY-N	154	529	41	136	19	1	1	29	29	54	.257	.296	.302	69	-23	-21	45	1	0	0	-11	*S	-2.0
1986	*NY-N	139	394	38	86	11	0	1	28	36	43	.218	.287	.254	52	-26	-25	27	0	0	0	17	*S/2	0.6

YEAR	TM/L	G	AB	R	H	2B	3B	HR	RBI	BB	SO	AVG	OBP	SLG	PRO+	BR	/A	RC	SB	CS	SBR	FR	POS	TPR
1987	NY-N	139	439	41	112	21	2	5	44	29	57	.255	.303	.346	75	-18	-15	44	1	1	-0	15	*S	1.5
1988	NY-A	148	480	50	115	12	1	4	38	33	61	.240	.290	.294	64	-23	-22	38	1	2	-1	-9	*S	-2.5
1990	Cle-A	7	13	3	3	0	0	1	3	0	0	.231	.231	.462	88	-0	-0	1	0	0	0	-2	/S	-0.1
Total	7	668	2021	188	497	74	5	13	156	138	234	.246	.296	.307	68	-92	-85	173	3	7	-3	10	S/23	-2.3

■ BENITO SANTIAGO
Santiago, Benito (Rivera) b: 3/9/65, Ponce, P.R.   BR/TR, 6'1", 180 lbs.   Deb: 9/14/86

YEAR	TM/L	G	AB	R	H	2B	3B	HR	RBI	BB	SO	AVG	OBP	SLG	PRO+	BR	/A	RC	SB	CS	SBR	FR	POS	TPR
1986	SD-N	17	62	10	18	2	0	3	6	2	12	.290	.313	.468	115	1	1	9	0	1	-1	-5	C	-0.4
1987	SD-N	146	546	64	164	33	2	18	79	16	112	.300	.326	.467	111	4	6	77	21	12	-1	-5	*C	1.2
1988	SD-N	139	492	49	122	22	2	10	46	24	82	.248	.284	.362	86	-11	-10	46	15	7	-0	-5	*C	-0.8
1989	SD-N	129	462	50	109	16	3	16	62	26	89	.236	.278	.387	88	-9	-9	47	11	6	-0	-5	*C	-0.4
1990	SD-N	100	344	42	93	8	5	11	53	27	55	.270	.329	.419	103	1	1	47	5	5	-2	-5	C	0.0
Total	5	531	1906	215	506	81	12	58	246	95	350	.265	.304	.412	98	-14	-11	226	52	31	-3	-24	C	-0.4

■ RON SANTO
Santo, Ronald Edward b: 2/25/40, Seattle, Wash.   BR/TR, 6', 190 lbs.   Deb: 6/26/60

YEAR	TM/L	G	AB	R	H	2B	3B	HR	RBI	BB	SO	AVG	OBP	SLG	PRO+	BR	/A	RC	SB	CS	SBR	FR	POS	TPR
1960	Chi-N	95	347	44	87	24	2	9	44	31	44	.251	.312	.409	97	-3	-2	42	0	3	-2	-19	3	-2.4
1961	Chi-N	154	578	84	164	32	6	23	83	73	77	.284	.364	.479	120	18	17	95	2	3	-1	5	*3	1.4
1962	Chi-N	162	604	44	137	20	4	17	83	65	94	.227	.304	.358	74	-20	-23	65	4	1	1	11	*3/S	-0.6
1963	Chi-N	162	630	79	187	29	6	25	99	42	92	.297	.345	.481	128	27	23	99	6	4	-1	13	*3	3.8
1964	Chi-N	161	592	94	185	33	13	30	114	86	96	.313	.401	.564	162	55	52	135	3	4	-2	17	*3	6.0
1965	Chi-N	164	608	88	173	30	4	33	101	88	109	.285	.379	.510	144	40	38	121	3	1	0	19	*3	5.2
1966	Chi-N	155	561	93	175	21	8	30	94	95	78	.312	.417	.538	161	51	50	127	4	5	-2	28	*3/S	7.7
1967	Chi-N	161	586	107	176	23	4	31	98	96	103	.300	.401	.512	153	48	45	120	1	5	-3	31	*3	6.7
1968	Chi-N	162	577	86	142	17	3	26	98	96	106	.246	.357	.421	124	25	21	87	3	4	-2	17	*3	4.1
1969	Chi-N	160	575	97	166	18	4	29	123	96	97	.289	.392	.485	128	36	27	108	1	3	-2	6	*3	3.3
1970	Chi-N	154	555	83	148	30	4	26	114	92	108	.267	.372	.476	112	21	11	100	2	0	1	13	*3/O	2.0
1971	Chi-N	154	555	77	148	22	1	21	88	79	95	.267	.358	.423	105	16	6	84	4	0	1	-3	*3/O	0.5
1972	Chi-N	133	464	68	140	25	5	17	74	69	75	.302	.397	.487	135	32	26	89	1	4	-2	6	*3/2SO	3.1
1973	Chi-N	149	536	65	143	29	2	20	77	63	97	.267	.348	.440	109	12	7	76	1	2	-1	-12	*3	-0.8
1974	Chi-A	117	375	29	83	12	1	5	41	37	72	.221	.295	.299	69	-14	-15	31	0	2	-1	6	D23/1S	-0.7
Total	15	2243	8143	1138	2254	365	67	342	1331	1108	1343	.277	.366	.464	123	345	284	1379	35	41	-14	138	*3/D2SO1	39.3

■ RAFAEL SANTO DOMINGO
Santo Domingo, Rafael (Molina) b: 11/24/55, Orocovis, P.R.   BB/TR, 6', 160 lbs.   Deb: 9/07/79

YEAR	TM/L	G	AB	R	H	2B	3B	HR	RBI	BB	SO	AVG	OBP	SLG	PRO+	BR	/A	RC	SB	CS	SBR	FR	POS	TPR
1979	Cin-N	7	6	0	1	0	0	0	0	1	3	.167	.286	.167	26	-1	-1	0	0	0	0	0	/H	0.0

■ NELSON SANTOVENIA
Santovenia, Nelson Gil (Mayol) b: 7/27/61, Pinar Del Rio, Cuba   BR/TR, 6'3", 195 lbs.   Deb: 9/16/87

YEAR	TM/L	G	AB	R	H	2B	3B	HR	RBI	BB	SO	AVG	OBP	SLG	PRO+	BR	/A	RC	SB	CS	SBR	FR	POS	TPR
1987	Mon-N	2	1	0	0	0	0	0	0	0	0	.000	.000	.000	-97	-0	-0	0	0	0	0	0	/C	0.0
1988	Mon-N	92	309	26	73	20	2	8	41	24	77	.236	.298	.392	92	-2	-4	36	2	3	-1	3	C/1	0.2
1989	Mon-N	97	304	30	76	14	1	5	31	24	37	.250	.311	.352	88	-4	-5	31	2	1	0	12	C/1	1.4
1990	Mon-N	59	163	13	31	3	1	6	28	8	31	.190	.228	.331	52	-11	-11	10	0	3	-2	3	C	-0.7
Total	4	250	777	69	180	37	4	19	100	56	145	.232	.288	.363	82	-18	-20	78	4	7	-3	17	C/1	0.9

■ EDWARD SANTRY
Santry, Edward b: Chicago, Ill. d: 3/6/1899, Chicago, Ill.   Deb: 8/07/1884

YEAR	TM/L	G	AB	R	H	2B	3B	HR	RBI	BB	SO	AVG	OBP	SLG	PRO+	BR	/A	RC	SB	CS	SBR	FR	POS	TPR
1884	Det-N	6	22	1	4	0	0	0	0	1	2	.182	.217	.182	29	-2	-2	1				-0	/S2	0.0

■ JOE SARGENT
Sargent, Joseph Alexander "Horse Belly" b: 9/24/1893, Rochester, N.Y. d: 7/5/50, Rochester, N.Y.   BR/TR, 5'10", 165 lbs.   Deb: 4/27/21

YEAR	TM/L	G	AB	R	H	2B	3B	HR	RBI	BB	SO	AVG	OBP	SLG	PRO+	BR	/A	RC	SB	CS	SBR	FR	POS	TPR
1921	Det-A	66	178	21	45	8	5	2	22	24	26	.253	.342	.388	87	-4	-4	24	2	3	-1	3	23S	0.3

■ BILL SARNI
Sarni, William Florine b: 9/19/27, Los Angeles, Cal. d: 4/15/83, Creve Coeur, Mo.   BR/TR, 5'11", 180 lbs.   Deb: 5/09/51

YEAR	TM/L	G	AB	R	H	2B	3B	HR	RBI	BB	SO	AVG	OBP	SLG	PRO+	BR	/A	RC	SB	CS	SBR	FR	POS	TPR
1951	StL-N	36	86	7	15	1	0	0	2	9	13	.174	.253	.186	20	-10	-10	4	1	0	0	0	C	-0.8
1952	StL-N	3	5	0	1	0	0	0	0	0	1	.200	.200	.200	11	-1	-1	0	0	0	0	2	/C	0.2
1954	StL-N	123	380	40	114	18	4	9	70	25	42	.300	.343	.439	101	1	0	55	3	3	-1	-13	*C	-1.0
1955	StL-N	107	325	32	83	15	2	3	34	27	33	.255	.314	.342	74	-12	-12	33	1	1	-0	-7	C	-1.5
1956	StL-N	43	148	12	43	7	2	5	22	8	15	.291	.331	.466	111	2	2	22	1	0	0	3	C	0.6
	NY-N	78	238	16	55	9	3	5	23	20	31	.231	.293	.357	74	-9	-9	25	0	1	-1	-5	C	-1.2
	Yr	121	386	28	98	16	5	10	45	28	46	.254	.308	.399	88	-7	-7	47	1	1	-0	-3		-0.6
Total	5	390	1182	107	311	50	11	22	151	89	135	.263	.316	.380	84	-28	-29	139	6	5	-1	-20	C	-3.7

■ MACKEY SASSER
Sasser, Mack Daniel b: 8/3/62, Fort Gaines, Ga.   BL/TR, 6'1", 190 lbs.   Deb: 7/17/87

YEAR	TM/L	G	AB	R	H	2B	3B	HR	RBI	BB	SO	AVG	OBP	SLG	PRO+	BR	/A	RC	SB	CS	SBR	FR	POS	TPR
1987	SF-N	2	4	0	0	0	0	0	0	0	0	.000	.000	.000	-99	-1	-1	0	0	0	0	0	/C	0.0
	Pit-N	12	23	2	5	0	0	0	2	0	0	.217	.217	.217	16	-3	-3	1	0	0	0	-1	/C	-0.3
	Yr	14	27	2	5	0	0	0	2	0	2	.185	.185	.185	-2	-4	-4	1	0	0	0	-1		-0.3
1988	*NY-N	60	123	9	35	10	1	1	17	6	9	.285	.318	.407	112	1	1	15	0	0	0	9	C/3O	1.3
1989	NY-N	72	182	17	53	14	2	1	22	7	15	.291	.317	.407	111	1	2	22	0	1	-1	0	C/3	0.6
1990	NY-N	100	270	31	83	14	0	6	41	15	19	.307	.346	.426	114	4	4	38	0	0	0	-10	C/1	0.0
Total	4	246	602	59	176	38	3	8	82	28	45	.292	.325	.405	107	1	4	75	0	1	-1	-2	C/31O	1.6

■ TOM SATRIANO
Satriano, Thomas Victor Nicholas b: 8/28/40, Pittsburgh, Pa.   BL/TR, 6'1", 185 lbs.   Deb: 7/23/61

YEAR	TM/L	G	AB	R	H	2B	3B	HR	RBI	BB	SO	AVG	OBP	SLG	PRO+	BR	/A	RC	SB	CS	SBR	FR	POS	TPR
1961	LA-A	35	96	15	19	5	1	1	8	12	16	.198	.294	.302	53	-5	-7	10	2	0	1	0	32/S	-0.3
1962	LA-A	10	19	4	8	2	0	2	6	0	1	.421	.421	.842	238	3	3	6	0	0	0	-0	/3	0.3
1963	LA-A	23	50	1	9	1	0	0	2	9	10	.180	.305	.200	48	-3	-3	4	0	0	0	3	3/C1	0.0
1964	LA-A	108	255	18	51	9	0	1	17	30	37	.200	.284	.247	55	-17	-14	17	0	2	-1	-1	31C/S2	-1.6
1965	Cal-A	47	79	8	13	2	0	1	4	10	10	.165	.258	.228	40	-6	-6	5	1	1	-0	0	3C2/1	-0.4
1966	Cal-A	103	226	16	54	5	3	0	24	27	32	.239	.320	.288	78	-6	-6	21	3	3	-1	-9	C13/2	-1.5
1967	Cal-A	90	201	13	45	7	0	4	21	28	25	.224	.319	.318	92	-2	-1	21	1	0	0	-7	3C2/1	-0.6
1968	Cal-A	111	297	20	75	9	0	8	35	37	44	.253	.337	.364	117	5	6	37	0	0	0	-9	C23/1	0.2
1969	Cal-A	41	108	5	28	2	0	1	16	18	15	.259	.370	.306	95	-0	-0	13	0	2	-1	0	C/12	0.1
	Bos-A	47	127	9	24	2	0	0	11	22	12	.189	.318	.205	46	-8	-9	9	0	0	0	-2	C	-0.8
	Yr	88	235	14	52	4	0	1	27	40	27	.221	.342	.251	68	-8	-8	21	0	2	-1	-2		-0.7
1970	Bos-A	59	165	21	39	9	1	3	13	21	23	.236	.326	.358	83	-2	-4	19	0	0	0	-0	C	-0.2
Total	10	674	1623	130	365	53	5	21	157	214	225	.225	.317	.303	79	-43	-39	160	7	8	-3	-25	C3/12S	-4.8

■ FRANK SAUCIER
Saucier, Francis Field b: 5/28/26, Leslie, Mo.   BL/TR, 6'1", 180 lbs.   Deb: 7/21/51

YEAR	TM/L	G	AB	R	H	2B	3B	HR	RBI	BB	SO	AVG	OBP	SLG	PRO+	BR	/A	RC	SB	CS	SBR	FR	POS	TPR
1951	StL-A	18	14	4	1	1	0	0	1	3	4	.071	.278	.143	16	-2	-2	1	0	0	0	0	/O	0.0

■ EDDIE SAUER
Sauer, Edward "Horn" b: 1/3/20, Pittsburgh, Pa. d: 7/1/88, Thousand Oaks, Cal   BR/TR, 6'1", 188 lbs.   Deb: 9/17/43

YEAR	TM/L	G	AB	R	H	2B	3B	HR	RBI	BB	SO	AVG	OBP	SLG	PRO+	BR	/A	RC	SB	CS	SBR	FR	POS	TPR
1943	Chi-N	14	55	3	15	3	0	0	9	3	6	.273	.322	.327	89	-1	-1	6	1			1	O	0.0
1944	Chi-N	23	50	3	11	4	0	0	5	2	6	.220	.250	.300	55	-3	-3	4	0			0	O	-0.3
1945	*Chi-N	49	93	8	24	1	2	1	11	8	23	.258	.317	.387	97	-1	-1	12	2			0	O	-0.1
1949	StL-N	24	45	5	10	2	1	0	1	3	8	.222	.271	.311	53	-3	-3	4	0			-1	O	-0.4
	Bos-N	79	214	26	57	12	0	3	31	17	34	.266	.323	.364	89	-5	-3	25	0			1	O	-0.6
	Yr	103	259	31	67	14	1	3	32	20	42	.259	.314	.355	82	-8	-7	29	0			-0		-1.0
Total	4	189	457	45	117	25	5	2	57	33	77	.256	.309	.352	83	-13	-11	50	3			1	O	-1.4

■ HANK SAUER
Sauer, Henry John b: 3/17/17, Pittsburgh, Pa.   BR/TR, 6'3", 198 lbs.   Deb: 9/09/41   C

YEAR	TM/L	G	AB	R	H	2B	3B	HR	RBI	BB	SO	AVG	OBP	SLG	PRO+	BR	/A	RC	SB	CS	SBR	FR	POS	TPR
1941	Cin-N	9	33	4	10	4	0	0	5	1	4	.303	.324	.424	109	0	0	4	0			1	/O	0.1
1942	Cin-N	7	20	4	5	0	0	2	4	2	2	.250	.318	.550	152	1	1	4	0			0	/1	0.1

YEAR	TM/L	G	AB	R	H	2B	3B	HR	RBI	BB	SO	AVG	OBP	SLG	PRO+	BR	/A	RC	SB	CS	SBR	FR	POS	TPR
1945	Cin-N	31	116	18	34	1	0	5	20	6	16	.293	.328	.431	112	1	1	17	2			1	O/1	0.1
1948	Cin-N	145	530	78	138	22	1	35	97	60	85	.260	.340	.504	130	17	19	92	2			4	*O1	1.3
1949	Cin-N	42	152	22	36	6	0	4	16	18	19	.237	.318	.355	79	-4	-4	16	0			3	O/1	-0.3
	Chi-N	96	357	59	104	17	1	27	83	37	47	.291	.363	.571	151	22	23	75	0			0	O	1.7
	Yr	138	509	81	140	23	1	31	99	55	66	.275	.349	.507	129	17	18	89	0			3		1.4
1950	Chi-N	145	540	85	148	32	2	32	103	60	67	.274	.350	.519	127	18	19	96	1			1	*O1	1.4
1951	Chi-N	141	525	77	138	19	4	30	89	45	77	.263	.325	.486	113	9	7	84	2	1	0	9	*O	1.2
1952	Chi-N	151	567	89	153	31	3	37	121	77	92	.270	.361	.531	143	33	32	111	1	2	-1	12	*O	4.0
1953	Chi-N	108	395	61	104	16	5	19	60	50	56	.263	.349	.473	109	7	5	66	0			1	*O	0.1
1954	Chi-N	142	520	98	150	18	1	41	103	70	68	.288	.379	.563	140	31	30	114	2	1	0	-1	*O	2.4
1955	Chi-N	79	261	29	55	8	1	12	28	26	47	.211	.287	.387	77	-9	-9	28	0	0	0	-6	O	-1.6
1956	StL-N	75	151	11	45	4	0	5	24	25	31	.298	.408	.424	124	6	6	27	0	0	0	-5	O	0.0
1957	NY-N	127	378	46	98	14	1	26	76	49	59	.259	.344	.508	126	13	13	67	1	0	0	-15	O	-0.4
1958	SF-N	88	236	27	59	8	0	12	46	35	37	.250	.356	.436	111	3	4	39	0	0	0	-9	O	-0.6
1959	SF-N	13	15	1	1	0	0	0	1	0	7	.067	.067	.267	-17	-3	-2	0	0	0	0	0	/O	-0.2
Total	15	1399	4796	709	1278	200	19	288	876	561	714	.266	.347	.496	123	144	145	840	11	4		-4	*O/1	9.3

■ RUSTY SAUNDERS
Saunders, Russell Collier b: 3/12/06, Trenton, N.J. d: 11/24/67, Trenton, N.J. BR/TR, 6'2", 205 lbs. Deb: 9/24/27

YEAR	TM/L	G	AB	R	H	2B	3B	HR	RBI	BB	SO	AVG	OBP	SLG	PRO+	BR	/A	RC	SB	CS	SBR	FR	POS	TPR
1927	Phi-A	5	15	2	2	1	0	0	2	3	2	.133	.278	.200	24	-2	-2	1	0	0	0	0	/O	-0.1

■ AL SAUTERS
Sauters, Al b: Philadelphia, Pa.   Deb: 9/08/1890

| 1890 | Phi-a | 14 | 41 | 1 | 4 | 0 | 0 | 0 | | | 11 | .098 | .288 | .098 | 17 | -4 | -3 | 1 | 0 | | | -4 | 3/O2 | -0.6 |

■ DON SAVAGE
Savage, Donald Anthony b: 3/5/19, Bloomfield, N.J. d: 12/25/61, Montclair, N.J. BR/TR, 6', 180 lbs. Deb: 4/18/44

1944	NY-A	71	239	31	63	7	5	4	24	20	41	.264	.323	.385	98	0	-1	29	1	1	-0	-10	3	-1.2
1945	NY-A	34	58	5	13	1	0	0	3	3	14	.224	.262	.241	44	-4	-4	4	1	0	0	1	3/O	-0.2
Total	2	105	297	36	76	8	5	4	27	23	55	.256	.312	.357	88	-4	-5	33	2	1	0	-9	/3O	-1.4

■ JIMMIE SAVAGE
Savage, James Harold b: 8/29/1883, Southington, Conn. d: 6/26/40, New Castle, Pa. BB/TR, 5'5", 150 lbs. Deb: 9/03/12

1912	Phi-N	2	3	1	0	0	0	0	0	1	0	.000	.250	.000	-27	-1	-1	0	0			-0	/2	0.0
1914	Pit-F	132	479	81	136	9	9	1	26	67	32	.284	.372	.347	107	7	7	71	17			-9	O3S/2	-0.4
1915	Pit-F	14	21	0	3	0	0	0	0	1	0	.143	.182	.143	-3	-3	-3	1	0			-1	/O3	-0.3
Total	3	148	503	82	139	9	9	1	26	69	32	.276	.364	.336	102	4	4	72	17			-10	/O3S2	-0.7

■ TED SAVAGE
Savage, Theodore Edmund (b: Ephesian Savage) b: 2/21/36, Venice, Ill. BR/TR, 6'1", 185 lbs. Deb: 4/09/62

1962	Phi-N	127	335	54	89	11	2	7	39	40	66	.266	.347	.373	96	-2	-1	46	16	5	2	-3	*O	-0.7
1963	Pit-N	85	149	22	29	2	1	5	14	14	31	.195	.268	.322	69	-6	-6	11	4	3	-1	-2	O	-1.1
1965	StL-N	30	63	7	10	3	0	1	4	6	9	.159	.232	.254	34	-5	-6	3	1	1	-0	0	O	-0.6
1966	StL-N	16	29	4	5	2	1	0	3	4	7	.172	.273	.310	61	-1	-2	3	4	0	1	-1	/O	0.0
1967	StL-N	9	8	1	1	0	0	0	0	1	3	.125	.222	.125	2	-1	-1	0	0	0	0	0	H	0.0
	Chi-N	96	225	40	49	10	1	5	33	40	54	.218	.348	.338	93	1	-1	27	7	6	-2	-4	O/3	-0.9
	Yr	105	233	41	50	10	1	5	33	41	57	.215	.344	.330	90	-0	-1	27	7	6	-2	-4		-0.9
1968	Chi-N	3	8	0	2	0	0	0	0	0	1	.250	.250	.250	47	-0	-1	0	0	0	-1	-0	/O	-0.1
	LA-N	61	126	7	26	6	1	2	7	10	20	.206	.270	.317	82	-4	-3	9	1	2	-1	4	O	-0.1
	Yr	64	134	7	28	6	1	2	7	10	21	.209	.269	.313	80	-4	-4	9	1	3	-2	3		-0.2
1969	Cin-N	68	110	20	25	7	0	2	11	20	27	.227	.346	.345	90	-0	-1	15	3	0	1	3	O/2	0.2
1970	Mil-A	114	276	43	77	10	5	12	50	57	44	.279	.406	.482	143	19	18	57	10	6	-1	-7	O/1	0.7
1971	Mil-A	14	17	2	3	0	0	0	1	5	4	.176	.364	.176	58	-1	-1	2	1	0	0	-1	/O	0.0
	KC-A	19	29	2	5	0	0	0	1	3	6	.172	.250	.172	22	-3	-3	1	2	0	1	-0	/O	-0.2
	Yr	33	46	4	8	0	0	0	2	8	10	.174	.296	.174	36	-4	-4	3	3	0	1	-1		-0.2
Total	9	642	1375	202	321	51	11	34	163	200	272	.233	.335	.361	94	-5	-6	175	49	24	0	-10	O/123	-2.8

■ BOB SAVERINE
Saverine, Robert Paul "Rabbit" b: 6/2/41, Norwalk, Conn. BB/TR, 5'10", 160 lbs. Deb: 9/12/59

1959	Bal-A	1	0	1	0	0	0	0	0	0	0	—	—	—	—	0	0	0	0	0	0	0	R	0.0
1962	Bal-A	8	21	2	5	2	0	0	3	1	3	.238	.273	.333	65	-1	-1	1	0	2	-1	2	/2	0.0
1963	Bal-A	115	167	21	39	1	2	1	12	25	44	.234	.333	.281	76	-5	-4	17	8	3	1	11	O2S	0.7
1964	Bal-A	46	34	14	5	1	0	0	0	3	6	.147	.216	.176	11	-4	-4	1	3	1	0	6	S/O	0.2
1966	Was-A	120	406	54	102	10	4	5	24	27	62	.251	.301	.333	83	-10	-9	41	4	3	-1	-18	23S/O	-2.3
1967	Was-A	89	233	22	55	13	0	0	8	17	34	.236	.288	.292	75	-8	-7	20	8	0	2	-19	2S/3O	-2.3
Total	6	379	861	114	206	27	6	6	47	73	149	.239	.300	.305	76	-28	-26	81	23	9	2	-19	2/OS3	-3.7

■ CARL SAWATSKI
Sawatski, Carl Ernest "Swats" b: 11/4/27, Shickshinny, Pa. BL/TR, 5'10", 210 lbs. Deb: 9/29/48

1948	Chi-N	2	2	0	0	0	0	0	0	0	0	.000	.000	.000	-99	-1	-1	0	0			0	H	0.0
1950	Chi-N	38	103	4	18	1	0	1	7	11	19	.175	.254	.214	25	-11	-11	6	0			-1	C	-1.0
1953	Chi-N	43	59	5	13	3	0	1	5	7	7	.220	.303	.322	62	-3	-3	6	0	0	0	-1	C	-0.2
1954	Chi-A	43	109	6	20	3	3	1	12	15	20	.183	.282	.294	56	-6	-7	9	0	0	0	6	C	-0.5
1957	*Mil-N	58	105	13	25	4	0	6	17	10	15	.238	.316	.448	110	0	1	15	0	0	0	6	C	0.9
1958	Mil-N	10	10	1	1	0	0	0	1	2	5	.100	.250	.100	-3	-1	-1	0	0	0	0	1	/C	0.0
	Phi-N	60	183	12	42	4	1	5	12	16	42	.230	.302	.344	72	-8	-7	19	0	0	0	-3	C	-0.7
	Yr	70	193	13	43	4	1	5	13	18	47	.223	.299	.332	68	-9	-9	19	0	0	0	-2		-0.7
1959	Phi-N	74	198	15	58	10	0	6	43	32	36	.293	.394	.480	129	10	9	38	0	0	0	-14	C	-1.0
1960	StL-N	78	179	16	41	4	0	6	27	22	24	.229	.313	.352	75	-4	-6	19	0	0	0	-7	C	-1.0
1961	StL-N	86	174	23	52	8	0	10	33	25	17	.299	.387	.517	125	10	7	35	0	0	0	-6	C/O	0.5
1962	StL-N	85	222	26	56	9	1	13	42	36	38	.252	.357	.477	111	7	4	39	0	0	0	0	C	0.5
1963	StL-N	56	105	12	25	0	0	6	14	15	28	.238	.333	.410	103	2	1	15	2	0	1	-6	C	-0.3
Total	11	633	1449	133	351	46	5	58	213	191	251	.242	.333	.401	92	-7	-15	202	2	0		-31	C/O	-1.8

■ CARL SAWYER
Sawyer, Carl Everett "Huck" b: 10/19/1890, Seattle, Wash. d: 1/17/57, Los Angeles, Cal. BR/TR, 5'11", 160 lbs. Deb: 9/11/15

1915	Was-A	10	32	8	8	1	0	0	3	4	5	.250	.351	.281	89	-0	-0	4	2			-2	/2S	-0.1
1916	Was-A	16	31	3	6	1	0	0	2	4	4	.194	.306	.226	61	-1	-1	3	3			2	/2S3	0.1
Total	2	26	63	11	14	2	0	0	5	8	9	.222	.329	.254	75	-2	-1	7	5			-0	/2S3	0.0

■ DAVE SAX
Sax, David John b: 9/22/58, Sacramento, Cal. BR/TR, 6', 185 lbs. Deb: 9/01/82

1982	LA-N	2	2	0	0	0	0	0	0	0	0	.000	.000	.000	-99	-1	-1	0	0	0	0	0	/O	0.0
1983	LA-N	7	8	0	0	0	0	0	1	0	0	.000	.000	.000	-99	-2	-2	0	0	0	0	-1	/C	-0.1
1985	Bos-A	22	36	2	11	3	0	0	6	3	6	.306	.359	.389	101	0	0	5	0	1	-1	-1	C/O	0.1
1986	Bos-A	4	11	1	5	1	0	1	1	0	1	.455	.455	.818	237	2	2	4	0	0	0	-1	/C1	0.1
1987	Bos-A	2	3	0	0	0	0	0	0	0	1	.000	.000	.000	-97	-1	-1	0	0	0	0	1	/C	0.0
Total	5	37	60	3	16	4	0	1	8	3	5	.267	.302	.383	84	-1	-1	9	0	1	-1	-0	/CO1	0.0

■ OLLIE SAX
Sax, Erik Oliver b: 11/5/04, Branford, Conn. d: 3/21/82, Newark, N.J. BR/TR, 5'8", 164 lbs. Deb: 4/13/28

| 1928 | StL-A | 16 | 17 | 4 | 3 | 0 | 0 | 0 | 0 | 5 | 3 | .176 | .364 | .176 | 45 | -1 | -1 | 2 | 0 | 0 | 0 | 3 | /3 | 0.2 |

■ STEVE SAX
Sax, Stephen Louis b: 1/29/60, Sacramento, Cal. BR/TR, 5'11", 185 lbs. Deb: 8/18/81

| 1981 | *LA-N | 31 | 119 | 15 | 33 | 2 | 0 | 2 | 9 | 7 | 14 | .277 | .317 | .345 | 91 | -2 | -2 | 12 | 5 | 7 | -3 | 2 | 2 | 0.0 |

YEAR	TM/L	G	AB	R	H	2B	3B	HR	RBI	BB	SO	AVG	OBP	SLG	PRO+	BR	/A	RC	SB	CS	SBR	FR	POS	TPR
1982	LA-N	150	638	88	180	23	7	4	47	49	53	.282	.335	.359	97	-5	-3	79	49	19	3	-9	*2	-0.1
1983	*LA-N	155	623	94	175	18	5	5	41	58	73	.281	.343	.350	93	-5	-5	76	56	30	-1	-29	*2	-3.1
1984	LA-N	145	569	70	138	24	4	1	35	47	53	.243	.301	.304	71	-22	-21	51	34	19	-1	12	*2	-0.6
1985	*LA-N	136	488	62	136	8	4	1	42	54	43	.279	.354	.318	92	-5	-3	56	27	11	2	-9	*2/3	-0.9
1986	LA-N	157	633	91	210	43	4	6	56	59	58	.332	.391	.441	139	26	31	110	40	17	2	5	*2	3.1
1987	LA-N	157	610	84	171	22	7	6	46	44	61	.280	.332	.369	88	-13	-10	76	37	11	5	2	*2/3O	-0.1
1988	*LA-N	160	632	70	175	19	4	5	57	45	51	.277	.326	.343	95	-6	-4	73	42	12	5	-19	*2	-1.3
1989	NY-A	158	651	88	205	26	3	5	63	52	44	.315	.366	.387	114	12	13	91	43	17	3	-10	*2	0.8
1990	NY-A	155	615	70	160	24	2	4	42	49	46	.260	.319	.325	80	-15	-16	68	43	9	8	-13	*2	-1.3
Total	10	1404	5578	732	1583	209	40	39	438	464	496	.284	.341	.357	97	-35	-19	691	376	152	22	-78	*2/3O	-3.5

■ JIMMY SAY
Say, James I.   b: 1862, Baltimore, Md.   d: 6/23/1894, Baltimore, Md.   Deb: 7/22/1882

YEAR	TM/L	G	AB	R	H	2B	3B	HR	RBI	BB	SO	AVG	OBP	SLG	PRO+	BR	/A	RC	SB	CS	SBR	FR	POS	TPR
1882	Lou-a	1	4	1	1	0	0	0			0	.250	.250	.250	74	-0	-0	0				-1	/3	0.0
	Phi-a	22	82	12	17	2	0	1			1	.207	.217	.268	56	-3	-4	5				1	S	-0.1
	Yr	23	86	13	18	2	0	1			1	.209	.218	.267	57	-3	-5	5				0		-0.1
1884	Wil-U	16	59	3	13	1	2	0			1	.220	.233	.305	79	-1	-1	4	0			-3	3	-0.3
	KC-U	2	8	0	2	0	0	0			0	.250	.250	.250	80	-0	-0	1	0			-2	/3	-0.1
	Yr	18	67	3	15	1	2	0			1	.224	.235	.299	79	-1	-2	5	0			-5		-0.4
1887	Cle-a	16	64	9	24	5	3	0			1	.375	.385	.547	165	5	5	14	0			-4	3	0.0
Total	3	57	217	25	57	8	5	1			3	.263	.273	.359	97	-0	-1	24	0			-9	/3S	-0.5

■ LOU SAY
Say, Louis I.   b: 2/4/1854, Baltimore, Md.   d: 6/5/30, Fallston, Md.   BR/TR, 5'7", 145 lbs.   Deb: 4/14/1873

YEAR	TM/L	G	AB	R	H	2B	3B	HR	RBI	BB	SO	AVG	OBP	SLG	PRO+	BR	/A	RC	SB	CS	SBR	FR	POS	TPR
1873	Mar-n	3	11	1	2	0	0	0			0	.182	.182	.182	10	-1	-1	0					/SO	0.0
1874	Bal-n	18	67	4	14	3	0	0			0	.209	.209	.254	47	-4	-4	4					S	-0.3
1875	Was-n	11	39	4	10	0	0	0			0	.256	.256	.256	81	-1	-1	3					/S2O	-0.3
1880	Cin-N	48	191	14	38	8	1	0	15	4	31	.199	.215	.251	58	-8	-8	11				1	S	-0.3
1882	Phi-a	49	199	35	45	4	3	1			8	.226	.256	.291	75	-3	-6	15				6	S	0.1
1883	Bal-a	74	324	52	83	13	2	1			10	.256	.278	.318	89	-3	-5	29				7	*S	-0.3
1884	Bal-U	78	339	65	81	14	2	2			11	.239	.263	.310	84	-2	-8	28	0			2	*S	-0.3
	KC-U	17	70	6	14	2	0	1			2	.200	.222	.271	76	-2	-1	4	0			9	S/2	0.7
	Yr	95	409	71	95	16	2	3			13	.232	.256	.303	83	-5	-9	33	0			10		0.4
Total	3 n	32	117	9	26	3	0	0			0	.222	.222	.248	54	-6	-5	7	0				/SO2	-0.3
Total	4	266	1123	172	261	41	8	5	15	35	31	.232	.256	.297	79	-19	-28	88	0			25	S/2	0.2

■ JERRY SCALA
Scala, Gerard Daniel   b: 9/27/26, Bayonne, N.J.   BL/TR, 5'11", 178 lbs.   Deb: 4/22/48

YEAR	TM/L	G	AB	R	H	2B	3B	HR	RBI	BB	SO	AVG	OBP	SLG	PRO+	BR	/A	RC	SB	CS	SBR	FR	POS	TPR
1948	Chi-A	3	6	1	0	0	0	0	0	0	3	.000	.000	.000	-99	-2	-2	0	0	0	0	0	/O	0.0
1949	Chi-A	37	120	17	30	7	1	1	13	17	19	.250	.348	.350	88	-3	-2	16	3	3	-1	1	O	-0.2
1950	Chi-A	40	67	8	13	2	1	0	6	10	10	.194	.299	.254	44	-6	-5	5	0	0	0	2	O	-0.3
Total	3	80	193	26	43	9	2	1	19	27	32	.223	.321	.306	67	-10	-9	22	3	3	-1	3	/O	-0.5

■ SKEETER SCALZI
Scalzi, Frank John   b: 6/16/13, Lafferty, Ohio   d: 8/25/84, Pittsburgh, Pa.   BR/TR, 5'6", 160 lbs.   Deb: 7/21/39

YEAR	TM/L	G	AB	R	H	2B	3B	HR	RBI	BB	SO	AVG	OBP	SLG	PRO+	BR	/A	RC	SB	CS	SBR	FR	POS	TPR
1939	NY-N	11	18	3	6	0	0	0	0	3	2	.333	.429	.333	106	0	0	2	1			2	/S3	0.3

■ JOHNNY SCALZI
Scalzi, John Anthony   b: 3/22/07, Stamford, Conn.   d: 9/27/62, Port Chester, N.Y   BR/TR, 5'7", 170 lbs.   Deb: 6/19/31

YEAR	TM/L	G	AB	R	H	2B	3B	HR	RBI	BB	SO	AVG	OBP	SLG	PRO+	BR	/A	RC	SB	CS	SBR	FR	POS	TPR
1931	Bos-N	2	1	0	0	0	0	0	0	0	1	.000	.000	.000	-99	-0	-0	0	0			0	H	0.0

■ MORT SCANLAN
Scanlan, Mortimer J.   b: 3/18/1861, Chicago, Ill.   d: 12/29/28, Chicago, Ill.   6'1", 186 lbs.   Deb: 4/21/1890

YEAR	TM/L	G	AB	R	H	2B	3B	HR	RBI	BB	SO	AVG	OBP	SLG	PRO+	BR	/A	RC	SB	CS	SBR	FR	POS	TPR
1890	NY-N	3	10	0	0	0	0	0	0	2	5	.000	.167	.000	-49	-2	-2	0	1			-0	/1	-0.1

■ PAT SCANLON
Scanlon, James Patrick   b: 9/23/52, Minneapolis, Minn.   BL/TR, 6', 180 lbs.   Deb: 9/27/74

YEAR	TM/L	G	AB	R	H	2B	3B	HR	RBI	BB	SO	AVG	OBP	SLG	PRO+	BR	/A	RC	SB	CS	SBR	FR	POS	TPR
1974	Mon-N	2	4	1	1	0	0	0	0	0	1	.250	.250	.250	38	-0	-0	0	0	0	0	1	/3	0.0
1975	Mon-N	60	109	5	20	3	1	2	15	17	25	.183	.294	.284	58	-6	-6	9	0	1	-1	2	3/1	-0.4
1976	Mon-N	11	27	2	5	1	0	1	2	2	5	.185	.241	.333	59	-1	-2	2	0	0	0	-1	/31	-0.2
1977	SD-N	47	79	9	15	3	0	1	11	12	20	.190	.297	.266	58	-5	-4	6	0	0	0	-5	23/O	-0.7
Total	4	120	219	17	41	7	1	4	28	31	51	.187	.288	.283	58	-13	-12	17	0	1	-1	-3	/321O	-1.3

■ JOHN SCANNELL
Scannell, John J. (b: P. Scanlan)   Deb: 7/04/1884

YEAR	TM/L	G	AB	R	H	2B	3B	HR	RBI	BB	SO	AVG	OBP	SLG	PRO+	BR	/A	RC	SB	CS	SBR	FR	POS	TPR
1884	Bos-U	6	24	2	7	1	0	0			0	.292	.292	.333	113	0	0	2				0	/O	0.0

■ RUSS SCARRITT
Scarritt, Russell Mallory   b: 1/14/03, Pensacola, Fla.   BL/TR, 5'10.5", 165 lbs.   Deb: 4/18/29

YEAR	TM/L	G	AB	R	H	2B	3B	HR	RBI	BB	SO	AVG	OBP	SLG	PRO+	BR	/A	RC	SB	CS	SBR	FR	POS	TPR
1929	Bos-A	151	540	69	159	26	17	1	71	34	38	.294	.337	.411	94	-8	-6	73	13	11	-3	1	*O	-1.2
1930	Bos-A	113	447	48	129	17	8	2	48	12	49	.289	.312	.376	76	-19	-16	50	4	7	-3	4	*O	-1.7
1931	Bos-A	10	39	2	6	1	0	0	1	2	2	.154	.195	.179	-1	-6	-5	1	0	0	0	1	/O	-0.4
1932	Phi-N	11	11	0	2	0	0	0	0	1	2	.182	.250	.182	16	-1	-1	1	0			0	/O	0.0
Total	4	285	1037	119	296	44	25	3	120	49	91	.285	.320	.385	82	-33	-29	125	17	_18_		6	O	-3.3

■ LES SCARSELLA
Scarsella, Leslie George   b: 11/23/13, Santa Cruz, Cal.   d: 12/17/58, San Francisco, Cal   BL/TL, 5'11", 185 lbs.   Deb: 9/15/35

YEAR	TM/L	G	AB	R	H	2B	3B	HR	RBI	BB	SO	AVG	OBP	SLG	PRO+	BR	/A	RC	SB	CS	SBR	FR	POS	TPR
1935	Cin-N	6	10	4	2	1	0	0	0	3	1	.200	.385	.300	89	-0	0	1	0			1	/1	0.1
1936	Cin-N	115	485	63	152	21	9	3	65	14	36	.313	.335	.412	107	-1	3	66	6			2	*1	-0.4
1937	Cin-N	110	329	35	81	11	4	3	34	17	26	.246	.285	.331	70	-15	-13	30	5			-4	1O	-2.0
1939	Cin-N	16	14	0	2	0	0	0	2	0	2	.143	.143	.143	-23	-2	-2	0	0			0	H	-0.1
1940	Bos-N	18	60	7	18	1	3	0	8	3	5	.300	.344	.417	115	1	1	9	2			-1	1	0.0
Total	5	265	898	109	255	34	16	6	109	37	70	.284	.315	.378	92	-18	-12	107	13			-2	1/O	-2.4

■ PAUL SCHAAL
Schaal, Paul   b: 3/3/43, Pittsburgh, Pa.   BR/TR, 5'11", 165 lbs.   Deb: 9/03/64

YEAR	TM/L	G	AB	R	H	2B	3B	HR	RBI	BB	SO	AVG	OBP	SLG	PRO+	BR	/A	RC	SB	CS	SBR	FR	POS	TPR
1964	LA-A	17	32	3	4	0	0	0	0	2	5	.125	.176	.125	-16	-5	-5	1	0	1	-1	-1	/23	-0.4
1965	Cal-A	155	483	48	108	12	2	9	45	61	88	.224	.312	.313	80	-13	-12	50	6	3	0	-10	*3/2	-2.1
1966	Cal-A	138	386	59	94	15	7	6	24	68	56	.244	.364	.365	113	8	9	55	6	4	-1	-2	*3	-0.8
1967	Cal-A	99	272	31	51	9	1	6	20	38	39	.188	.289	.294	76	-9	-7	25	2	2	-1	2	3/S2	-0.3
1968	Cal-A	60	219	22	46	7	1	2	16	29	25	.210	.308	.279	82	-5	-4	19	5	7	-3	9	3	0.5
1969	KC-A	61	205	22	54	6	0	1	13	25	27	.263	.349	.307	84	-3	-3	24	2	1	0	-19	3/2S	-1.1
1970	KC-A	124	380	50	102	12	3	6	35	43	39	.268	.344	.355	93	-3	-3	47	7	4	-0	-16	3S/2	-1.8
1971	KC-A	161	548	80	150	31	6	11	63	103	51	.274	.391	.412	129	24	24	95	7	5	-1	-12	*3	0.6
1972	KC-A	127	435	47	99	19	3	6	41	61	59	.228	.326	.326	95	-2	-1	46	1	3	-2	-16	*3/S	-1.6
1973	KC-A	121	396	61	114	14	3	8	42	63	45	.288	.392	.399	114	15	11	63	5	6	-2	-12	*3	-0.5
1974	KC-A	12	34	2	6	2	0	1	4	5	5	.176	.300	.324	75	-1	-1	3	0	0	0	1	*3	0.0
	Cal-A	53	165	10	41	5	0	2	20	18	27	.248	.322	.315	89	-3	-2	16	2	2	-1	-10	3	-1.1
	Yr	65	199	13	47	7	0	3	24	23	32	.236	.319	.317	86	-4	-3	19	2	2	-1	-9		-1.1
Total	11	1128	3555	436	869	132	26	57	323	516	466	.244	.344	.344	98	4	6	444	43	38	-10	-90	*3/2S	-9.0

■ GERMANY SCHAEFER
Schaefer, Herman A.   b: 2/4/1877, Chicago, Ill.   d: 5/16/19, Saranac Lake, N.Y.   BR/TR, 5'9", 175 lbs.   Deb: 10/05/01

YEAR	TM/L	G	AB	R	H	2B	3B	HR	RBI	BB	SO	AVG	OBP	SLG	PRO+	BR	/A	RC	SB	CS	SBR	FR	POS	TPR
1901	Chi-N	2	5	0	3	1	0	0	0	2		.600	.714	.800	357	2	2	3	0			1	/23	0.3
1902	Chi-N	81	291	32	57	2	3	0	14	19		.196	.250	.223	49	-17	-16	21	12			-8	3/1OS	-2.2
1905	Det-A	153	554	64	135	17	9	2	47	45		.244	.301	.318	97	-1	-1	64	19			7	*2/S	0.5
1906	Det-A	124	446	48	106	14	3	0	42	32		.238	.289	.296	83	-7	-9	50	31			9	*2/S	-0.2
1907	*Det-A	109	372	45	96	12	3	1	32	30		.258	.313	.315	99	1	-0	46	21			-5	2S3/O	-0.4

YEAR	TM/L	G	AB	R	H	2B	3B	HR	RBI	BB	SO	AVG	OBP	SLG	PRO+	BR	/A	RC	SB	CS	SBR	FR	POS	TPR
1908	*Det-A	153	584	96	151	20	10	3	52	37		.259	.303	.342	107	7	4	74	40			3	S23	1.0
1909	Det-A	87	280	26	70	12	0	0	22	14		.250	.286	.293	79	-6	-7	27	12			14	2/O	0.5
	Was-A	37	128	13	31	5	1	1	4	6		.242	.281	.320	94	-2	-1	12	2			0	2/3	-0.1
	Yr	124	408	39	101	17	1	1	26	20		.248	.284	.301	84	-8	-9	39	14			14		0.4
1910	Was-A	74	229	27	63	6	5	0	14	25		.275	.352	.345	124	5	7	34	17			-0	2O/3	0.3
1911	Was-A	125	440	74	147	14	7	0	45	57		.334	.412	.398	129	18	19	82	22			0	*1/O	2.1
1912	Was-A	60	166	21	41	7	3	0	19	23		.247	.342	.325	91	-1	-2	22	11			-11	O12/P	-1.3
1913	Was-A	54	100	17	32	1	1	0	7	15	12	.320	.419	.350	123	4	4	17	6			-2	2/13PO	0.2
1914	Was-A	30	29	6	7	1	0	0	2	3	5	.241	.313	.276	75	-1	-1	3	4	1	1	0	/2O	0.0
1915	New-F	59	154	26	33	5	3	0	8	25	11	.214	.328	.286	87	-2	-1	16	3			-1	O1/32	-0.2
1916	NY-A	1	1	0	0	0	0	0	0	0	0	.000	.000	.000	-98	-0	-0	0	0			0	/O	0.0
1918	Cle-A	1	5	2	0	0	0	0	0	0	0	.000	.000	.000	-91	-1	-1	-0	1			-0	/2	-0.1
Total	15	1150	3784	497	972	117	48	9	308	333	28	.257	.319	.320	98	-2	-5	471	201	1		4	213/SOP	0.4

■ JEFF SCHAEFER
Schaefer, Jeffrey Scott b: 5/31/60, Patchogue, N.Y. BR/TR, 5'10", 170 lbs. Deb: 4/07/89

YEAR	TM/L	G	AB	R	H	2B	3B	HR	RBI	BB	SO	AVG	OBP	SLG	PRO+	BR	/A	RC	SB	CS	SBR	FR	POS	TPR
1989	Chi-A	15	10	2	1	0	0	0	0	0	2	.100	.100	.100	-45	-2	-2	0	1	1	-0	1	/S23D	0.0
1990	Sea-A	55	107	11	22	3	0	0	6	3	11	.206	.241	.234	33	-9	-10	7	4	1	1	12	3S/2	0.5
Total	2	70	117	13	23	3	0	0	6	3	13	.197	.230	.222	27	-11	-11	7	5	2	0	13	/3S2D	0.5

■ HARRY SCHAFER
Schafer, Harry C. "Silk Stocking" b: 8/14/1846, Philadelphia, Pa. d: 2/28/35, Philadelphia, Pa. BR/TR, 5'9.5", 143 lbs. Deb: 5/05/1871

YEAR	TM/L	G	AB	R	H	2B	3B	HR	RBI	BB	SO	AVG	OBP	SLG	PRO+	BR	/A	RC	SB	CS	SBR	FR	POS	TPR
1871	Bos-n	31	149	38	42	7	5	0	28	3	1	.282	.296	.396	94	-1	-2	22	13				*3/2	-0.2
1872	Bos-n	48	226	50	66	12	5	1		1	0	.292	.292	.403	106	3	0	27					*3/O	-0.1
1873	Bos-n	60	290	65	80	7	4	2			4	.276	.286	.348	79	-5	-10	30					*3O	-0.7
1874	Bos-n	71	325	69	84	13	3	1			0	.258	.258	.326	80	-5	-9	28					*3	-0.7
1875	Bos-n	51	216	47	62	9	0	0			0	.287	.287	.329	108	2	1	21					*3/O	0.3
1876	Bos-N	70	286	47	72	11	0	0	35	4	11	.252	.262	.290	82	-5	-5	22				3	*3	-0.3
1877	Bos-N	33	141	20	39	5	2	0	13	0	7	.277	.277	.340	90	-1	-2	14				-12	O/3S	-1.2
1878	Bos-n	2	8	0	1	0	0	0	0	0	1	.125	.125	.125	-16	-1	-1	0				-0	/O	-0.1
Total	5 n	261	1206	269	334	48	17	4	28	7	1	.277	.281	.355	91	-6	-20	128					3/O2	-1.4
Total	3	105	435	67	112	16	2	0	48	4	19	.257	.264	.303	83	-7	-8	36				-9	/3OS	-1.6

■ JIMMIE SCHAFFER
Schaffer, Jimmie Ronald b: 4/5/36, Limeport, Pa. BR/TR, 5'9", 170 lbs. Deb: 5/20/61 C

YEAR	TM/L	G	AB	R	H	2B	3B	HR	RBI	BB	SO	AVG	OBP	SLG	PRO+	BR	/A	RC	SB	CS	SBR	FR	POS	TPR
1961	StL-N	68	153	15	39	7	0	1	16	9	29	.255	.301	.320	59	-8	-10	14	0	0	0	4	C	0.0
1962	StL-N	70	66	7	16	2	1	0	6	6	16	.242	.306	.303	58	-3	-4	6	1	0	0	7	C	0.4
1963	Chi-N	57	142	17	34	7	0	7	19	11	35	.239	.294	.437	102	1	0	16	0	0	0	0	C	0.2
1964	Chi-N	54	122	9	25	6	1	2	9	17	17	.205	.307	.320	74	-3	-4	10	2	4	-2	-7	C	-1.2
1965	Chi-A	17	31	2	6	3	1	0	1	3	4	.194	.265	.355	79	-1	-1	2	0	0	0	3	C	0.3
	NY-N	24	37	0	5	2	0	0	0	1	15	.135	.158	.189	-3	-5	-5	1	0	0	0	-1	C	-0.4
1966	Phi-N	8	15	2	2	1	0	1	4	1	7	.133	.188	.400	58	-1	-1	1	0	0	0	-0	/C	0.0
1967	Phi-N	2	2	1	0	0	0	0	0	1	1	.000	.333	.000	3	-0	-0	0	0	0	0	0	/C	0.0
1968	Cin-N	4	6	0	1	0	0	0	1	0	3	.167	.167	.167	0	-1	-1	0	0	0	0	-1	/C	-0.1
Total	8	304	574	53	128	28	3	11	56	49	127	.223	.286	.340	69	-21	-25	51	3	4	-2	5	C	-0.8

■ JOHNNY SCHAIVE
Schaive, John Edward b: 2/25/34, Springfield, Ill. BR/TR, 5'8", 175 lbs. Deb: 9/19/58

YEAR	TM/L	G	AB	R	H	2B	3B	HR	RBI	BB	SO	AVG	OBP	SLG	PRO+	BR	/A	RC	SB	CS	SBR	FR	POS	TPR
1958	Was-A	7	24	1	6	0	0	0	1	1	4	.250	.280	.250	48	-2	-2	1	0	0	0	-1	/2	-0.1
1959	Was-A	16	59	3	9	2	0	0	2	0	7	.153	.167	.186	-3	-8	-8	2	0	0	0	4	2	-0.2
1960	Was-A	6	12	1	3	1	0	0	0	0	3	.250	.250	.333	57	-1	-1	1	0	0	0	-0	/2	0.0
1962	Was-A	82	225	20	57	15	1	6	29	6	25	.253	.273	.409	81	-7	-7	21	0	1	-1	4	3/2	-0.2
1963	Was-A	3	3	0	0	0	0	0	0	0	1	.000	.000	.000	-99	-1	-1	0	0	0	0	0	H	0.0
Total	5	114	323	25	75	18	1	6	32	7	40	.232	.251	.350	61	-19	-18	24	0	1	-1	7	/32	-0.5

■ ROY SCHALK
Schalk, Le Roy John b: 11/9/08, Chicago, Ill. BR/TR, 5'10", 168 lbs. Deb: 9/17/32

YEAR	TM/L	G	AB	R	H	2B	3B	HR	RBI	BB	SO	AVG	OBP	SLG	PRO+	BR	/A	RC	SB	CS	SBR	FR	POS	TPR
1932	NY-A	3	12	3	3	1	0	0	0	2	2	.250	.357	.333	84	-0	-0	2	0	0	0	-1	/2	0.0
1944	Chi-A	146	587	47	129	14	4	1	44	45	52	.220	.276	.262	55	-35	-34	43	5	4		-14	*2/S	-4.6
1945	Chi-A	133	513	50	127	23	1	1	65	32	41	.248	.293	.302	75	-18	-17	45	3	6	-3	6	*2	-1.1
Total	3	282	1112	100	259	38	5	2	109	79	95	.233	.285	.281	64	-53	-51	90	8	10	-4	-9	2/S	-5.7

■ RAY SCHALK
Schalk, Raymond William "Cracker" b: 8/12/1892, Harvey, Ill. d: 5/19/70, Chicago, Ill. BR/TR, 5'9", 165 lbs. Deb: 8/11/12 MCH

YEAR	TM/L	G	AB	R	H	2B	3B	HR	RBI	BB	SO	AVG	OBP	SLG	PRO+	BR	/A	RC	SB	CS	SBR	FR	POS	TPR
1912	Chi-A	23	63	7	18	2	0	0	8	3		.286	.357	.317	96	-0	-0	8	2			4	C	0.6
1913	Chi-A	129	401	38	98	15	5	1	38	27	36	.244	.297	.314	80	-11	-11	40	14			-0	*C	-0.1
1914	Chi-A	136	392	30	106	13	2	0	36	38	24	.270	.347	.314	100	1	1	50	24	11	1	6	*C	1.8
1915	Chi-A	135	413	46	110	14	4	1	54	62	21	.266	.366	.327	104	6	4	51	15	18	-6	-3	*C	0.5
1916	Chi-A	129	410	36	95	12	9	0	41	41	31	.232	.311	.305	84	-7	-8	45	30	13	1	8	*C	0.7
1917	*Chi-A	140	424	48	96	12	5	2	51	59	27	.226	.331	.292	88	-3	-4	47	19			4	*C	1.2
1918	Chi-A	108	333	35	73	6	3	0	22	36	22	.219	.301	.255	67	-12	-13	29	12			-4	*C	-0.7
1919	*Chi-A	131	394	57	111	9	3	0	34	51	25	.282	.367	.320	93	-1	-1	50	11			0	*C	0.6
1920	Chi-A	151	485	64	131	25	5	1	61	68	19	.270	.362	.348	89	-6	-6	67	10	4	1	-1	*C	0.6
1921	Chi-A	128	416	32	105	24	4	0	47	40	36	.252	.328	.329	69	-20	-19	47	3	4	-2	8	*C	-0.7
1922	Chi-A	142	442	57	124	22	3	4	60	67	36	.281	.379	.371	97	-0	0	68	12	4	1	19	*C	2.3
1923	Chi-A	123	382	42	87	12	2	1	44	39	28	.228	.306	.277	55	-25	-24	38	6	4	-1	4	*C	-1.1
1924	Chi-A	57	153	15	30	4	2	1	11	21	10	.196	.301	.268	49	-12	-11	13	1	5	-3	7	C	-0.3
1925	Chi-A	125	343	44	94	18	1	0	52	57	27	.274	.382	.332	87	-7	-4	49	11	5		2	C	0.6
1926	Chi-A	82	226	26	60	9	0	0	32	27	11	.265	.349	.314	77	-8	-7	27	5	1	1	-7	C	-0.6
1927	Chi-A	16	26	2	6	2	0	0	2	2	1	.231	.286	.308	55	-2	-2	1	2	0	0	1	CM	0.0
1928	Chi-A	2	1	0	1	0	0	0	1	0	0	1.000	1.000	1.000	433	0	0	1	1	0	0	1	/CM	0.1
1929	NY-N	5	2	0	0	0	0	0	0	0	1	.000	.000	.000	-99	-1	-1	0	0			1	/C	0.1
Total	18	1762	5306	579	1345	199	49	11	594	638	355	.253	.340	.316	83	-108	-103	630	176	69		48	*C	5.6

■ BIFF SCHALLER
Schaller, Walter b: 9/23/1889, Chicago, Ill. d: 10/9/39, Emeryville, Cal. BL/TR, 5'11", 168 lbs. Deb: 4/30/11

YEAR	TM/L	G	AB	R	H	2B	3B	HR	RBI	BB	SO	AVG	OBP	SLG	PRO+	BR	/A	RC	SB	CS	SBR	FR	POS	TPR
1911	Det-A	40	60	8	8	0	1	1	7	4		.133	.200	.217	15	-7	-7	3	1			-1	O/1	-0.8
1913	Chi-A	36	96	12	21	3	0	0	4	20	16	.219	.353	.250	78	-2	-2	10	5			-6	O	-0.9
Total	2	76	156	20	29	3	1	1	11	24	16	.186	.298	.237	54	-9	-9	13	6			-7	/O1	-1.7

■ BOBBY SCHANG
Schang, Robert Martin b: 12/7/1886, Wales Center, N.Y. d: 8/29/66, Sacramento, Cal. BR/TR, 5'7", 165 lbs. Deb: 9/23/14

YEAR	TM/L	G	AB	R	H	2B	3B	HR	RBI	BB	SO	AVG	OBP	SLG	PRO+	BR	/A	RC	SB	CS	SBR	FR	POS	TPR
1914	Pit-N	11	35	0	8	1	1	0	1	0	10	.229	.229	.314	64	-2	-2	2	0			-1	C	-0.2
1915	Pit-N	56	125	13	23	6	3	0	4	14	32	.184	.271	.280	68	-5	-5	10	2	2	-1	-6	C	-0.9
	NY-N	12	21	1	3	0	0	0	1	4	5	.143	.280	.143	31	-2	-1	1	1			-2	/C	0.0
	Yr	68	146	14	26	6	3	0	5	18	37	.178	.273	.260	63	-6	-6	12	3	2	-0	-8		-1.2
1927	StL-N	3	5	0	1	0	0	0	0	0	0	.200	.200	.200	7	-1	-1	0	0			-0	/C	0.0
Total	3	82	186	14	35	7	4	0	6	18	47	.188	.263	.269	62	-9	-9	14	3	2		-10	/C	-1.4

■ WALLY SCHANG
Schang, Walter Henry b: 8/22/1889, S.Wales, N.Y. d: 3/6/65, St.Louis, Mo. BB/TR, 5'10", 180 lbs. Deb: 5/01/13 C

YEAR	TM/L	G	AB	R	H	2B	3B	HR	RBI	BB	SO	AVG	OBP	SLG	PRO+	BR	/A	RC	SB	CS	SBR	FR	POS	TPR
1913	*Phi-A	79	207	32	55	16	3	3	30	34	44	.266	.392	.415	140	11	12	34	4			-5	C	1.3
1914	*Phi-A	107	307	44	88	11	8	3	45	32	33	.287	.371	.404	137	13	14	47	7	7	-2	2	*C	2.2
1915	Phi-A	116	359	64	89	9	11	1	44	66	47	.248	.385	.343	121	12	13	55	18	3	4	-1	3OC	1.8

YEAR	TM/L	G	AB	R	H	2B	3B	HR	RBI	BB	SO	AVG	OBP	SLG	PRO+	BR	/A	RC	SB	CS	SBR	FR	POS	TPR
1916	Phi-A	110	338	41	90	15	8	7	38	38	44	.266	.358	.420	139	14	15	57	14			5	OC	2.0
1917	Phi-A	118	316	41	90	14	9	3	36	29	24	.285	.362	.415	139	14	14	49	6			-9	C3/O	1.2
1918	*Bos-A	88	225	36	55	7	1	0	20	46	35	.244	.377	.284	101	3	3	26	4			-13	CO/3S	-0.5
1919	Bos-A	113	330	43	101	16	3	0	55	71	42	.306	.436	.373	136	18	20	58	15			-3	*C	2.3
1920	Bos-A	122	387	58	118	30	7	4	51	64	37	.305	.413	.450	134	18	21	75	7	7	-2	-3	CO	1.7
1921	*NY-A	134	424	77	134	30	5	6	55	78	35	.316	.428	.453	122	20	18	88	7	4	-0	-6	*C	1.5
1922	*NY-A	124	408	46	130	21	7	1	53	53	36	.319	.405	.412	111	10	9	72	12	6	0	1	*C	1.3
1923	*NY-A	84	272	39	75	8	2	2	29	27	17	.276	.360	.342	84	-5	-5	36	5	2	0	-8	*C	-0.6
1924	NY-A	114	356	46	104	19	7	5	52	48	43	.292	.382	.427	109	5	5	59	2	6	-3	-2	*C	0.6
1925	NY-A	73	167	17	40	8	1	2	24	17	9	.240	.310	.335	65	-10	-9	18	3	1	0	3	C	-0.1
1926	StL-A	103	285	36	94	19	5	8	50	32	20	.330	.405	.516	133	16	14	59	5	5	-2	-0	C/O	1.7
1927	StL-A	97	264	40	84	15	2	5	42	41	33	.318	.414	.447	119	11	9	49	3	2	-0	-8	C	0.3
1928	StL-A	91	245	41	70	10	5	3	39	68	26	.286	.448	.404	121	14	13	52	8	2	1	-13	C	0.6
1929	StL-A	94	249	43	59	10	5	5	36	74	22	.237	.424	.378	104	7	6	46	1	4	-2	-6	C	0.5
1930	Phi-A	45	92	16	16	4	1	1	9	17	15	.174	.309	.272	47	-7	-8	9	0			3	C	-0.1
1931	Det-A	30	76	9	14	2	0	0	2	14	11	.184	.311	.211	38	-6	-7	6	1	0	0	0	C	-0.3
Total	19	1842	5307	769	1506	264	90	59	710	849	573	.284	.393	.401	117	156	157	896	122	49		-63	*CO/3S	17.4

■ ART SCHAREIN
Scharein, Arthur Otto "Scoop" b: 6/30/05, Decatur, Ill. d: 7/2/69, San Antonio, Tex. BR/TR, 5'11", 155 lbs. Deb: 7/06/32

YEAR	TM/L	G	AB	R	H	2B	3B	HR	RBI	BB	SO	AVG	OBP	SLG	PRO+	BR	/A	RC	SB	CS	SBR	FR	POS	TPR
1932	StL-A	81	303	43	92	19	2	0	42	25	10	.304	.363	.380	87	-3	-5	41	4	8	-4	18	3/S2	1.4
1933	StL-A	123	471	49	96	13	3	0	26	41	21	.204	.269	.244	35	-43	-47	32	7	9	-3	14	3S/2	-2.5
1934	StL-A	1	2	0	1	0	0	0	0	2	0	.500	.500	.500	146	0	0	0	0	0	0	0	H	0.0
Total	3	205	776	92	189	32	5	0	70	66	31	.244	.306	.298	56	-45	-52	73	11	17	-7	32	3/S2	-1.1

■ GEORGE SCHAREIN
Scharein, George Albert "Tom" b: 11/21/14, Decatur, Ill. d: 12/23/81, Decatur, Ill. BR/TR, 6'1", 174 lbs. Deb: 4/19/37

YEAR	TM/L	G	AB	R	H	2B	3B	HR	RBI	BB	SO	AVG	OBP	SLG	PRO+	BR	/A	RC	SB	CS	SBR	FR	POS	TPR
1937	Phi-N	146	511	44	123	20	1	0	57	36	47	.241	.293	.284	53	-30	-35	44	13			10	*S	-1.2
1938	Phi-N	117	390	47	93	16	4	1	29	16	33	.238	.268	.308	60	-23	-21	32	11			-2	S2/3	-1.5
1939	Phi-N	118	399	35	95	17	1	1	33	13	40	.238	.262	.293	50	-29	-28	31	4			-9	*S	-2.9
1940	Phi-N	7	17	0	5	0	0	0	0	0	3	.294	.294	.294	65	-1	-1	1	0			-1	/S	0.0
Total	4	388	1317	126	316	53	6	2	119	65	123	.240	.277	.294	54	-82	-85	108	28			-2	S/23	-5.6

■ NICK SCHARF
Scharf, Edward T. b: 7/1858, Baltimore, Md. d: 5/12/37, Baltimore, Md. TR , Deb: 5/18/1882

YEAR	TM/L	G	AB	R	H	2B	3B	HR	RBI	BB	SO	AVG	OBP	SLG	PRO+	BR	/A	RC	SB	CS	SBR	FR	POS	TPR
1882	Bal-a	10	39	4	8	1	1	1		0		.205	.205	.359	94	-1	-0	3				-1	/O3	-0.1
1883	Bal-a	3	13	1	2	1	0	0		1		.154	.214	.231	42	-1	-1	1				-3	/S	-0.3
Total	2	13	52	5	10	2	1	1		1		.192	.208	.327	79	-1	-1	4				-4	/OS3	-0.4

■ AL SCHEER
Scheer, Allan G. b: 10/21/1888, Dayton, Ohio d: 5/6/59, Logansport, Ind. BL/TR, 5'9", 165 lbs. Deb: 8/02/13

YEAR	TM/L	G	AB	R	H	2B	3B	HR	RBI	BB	SO	AVG	OBP	SLG	PRO+	BR	/A	RC	SB	CS	SBR	FR	POS	TPR
1913	Bro-N	6	22	3	5	0	0	0	0	2	4	.227	.292	.227	48	-1	-1	2	1			-2	/O	-0.3
1914	Ind-F	120	363	63	111	23	6	3	45	49	39	.306	.396	.427	122	18	13	68	9			-5	*O/2S	0.3
1915	New-F	155	546	75	146	25	14	2	60	65	38	.267	.353	.375	123	12	16	87	31			-2	*O	0.6
Total	3	281	931	141	262	48	20	5	105	116	81	.281	.368	.392	121	29	27	156	41			-9	O/2S	0.6

■ HEINIE SCHEER
Scheer, Henry b: 7/31/1900, New York, N.Y. d: 3/21/76, New Haven, Conn. BR/TR, 5'8", 146 lbs. Deb: 4/20/22

YEAR	TM/L	G	AB	R	H	2B	3B	HR	RBI	BB	SO	AVG	OBP	SLG	PRO+	BR	/A	RC	SB	CS	SBR	FR	POS	TPR
1922	Phi-A	51	135	10	23	3	0	4	12	3	25	.170	.188	.281	21	-16	-17	7	1	0	0	9	23	-0.4
1923	Phi-A	69	210	26	50	8	1	2	21	17	41	.238	.301	.314	61	-12	-12	21	3	4	-2	-8	2	-1.9
Total	2	120	345	36	73	11	1	6	33	20	66	.212	.259	.301	46	-28	-29	28	4	4	-1	0	/23	-2.3

■ FRITZ SCHEEREN
Scheeren, Frederick "Dutch" b: 9/8/1891, Kokomo, Ind. d: 6/17/73, Oil City, Pa. BR/TR, 6', 180 lbs. Deb: 9/14/14

YEAR	TM/L	G	AB	R	H	2B	3B	HR	RBI	BB	SO	AVG	OBP	SLG	PRO+	BR	/A	RC	SB	CS	SBR	FR	POS	TPR
1914	Pit-N	11	31	4	9	0	1	1	2	1	6	.290	.313	.452	132	1	1	4	1			-2	O	0.0
1915	Pit-N	4	3	0	0	0	0	0	0	0	0	.000	.000	.000	-99	-1	-1	0	0			0	/O	0.0
Total	2	15	34	4	9	0	1	1	2	1	6	.265	.286	.412	111	0	0	4	1			-2	/O	0.0

■ BOB SCHEFFING
Scheffing, Robert Boden b: 8/11/13, Overland, Mo. d: 10/26/85, Phoenix, Ariz. BR/TR, 6'2", 180 lbs. Deb: 4/27/41 MC

YEAR	TM/L	G	AB	R	H	2B	3B	HR	RBI	BB	SO	AVG	OBP	SLG	PRO+	BR	/A	RC	SB	CS	SBR	FR	POS	TPR
1941	Chi-N	51	132	9	32	8	0	1	20	5	19	.242	.270	.326	70	-6	-6	10	2			-3	C	-0.4
1942	Chi-N	44	102	7	20	3	0	2	12	7	11	.196	.248	.284	58	-6	-6	7	2			4	C	0.0
1946	Chi-N	63	115	8	32	4	1	0	18	12	18	.278	.346	.330	94	-1	-1	13	0			-6	C	-0.5
1947	Chi-N	110	363	33	96	11	5	5	50	25	25	.264	.312	.364	82	-12	-10	39	2			-5	C	-1.2
1948	Chi-N	102	293	23	88	18	2	5	45	22	27	.300	.351	.427	114	3	5	44	0			-5	C	0.5
1949	Chi-N	55	149	12	40	6	1	3	19	9	9	.268	.314	.383	88	-3	-3	16	0			-3	C	-0.3
1950	Chi-N	12	16	0	3	1	0	0	1	0	2	.188	.188	.250	14	-2	-2	1	0			0	/C	0.0
	Cin-N	21	47	4	13	0	0	2	6	4	2	.277	.333	.404	93	-1	-1	5	0			-3	C	-0.3
	Yr	33	63	4	16	1	0	2	7	4	4	.254	.299	.365	74	-3	-3	6	0			-3		-0.3
1951	Cin-N	47	122	9	31	2	0	2	14	16	9	.254	.345	.320	79	-3	-3	15	0	0	0	-3	C	-0.5
	StL-N	12	18	0	2	0	0	0	2	3	5	.111	.238	.111	-3	-3	-3	1	0	0	0	1	C	0.0
	Yr	59	140	9	33	2	0	2	16	19	14	.236	.331	.293	68	-5	-6	15	0	0	0	-2		-0.5
Total	8	517	1357	105	357	53	9	20	187	103	127	.263	.316	.360	86	-32	-27	150	6	0		-23	C	-2.7

■ TED SCHEFFLER
Scheffler, Theodore J. b: 4/5/1864, New York, N.Y. d: 2/24/49, Jamaica, N.Y. BR/TR, 5'10", 160 lbs. Deb: 8/07/1888

YEAR	TM/L	G	AB	R	H	2B	3B	HR	RBI	BB	SO	AVG	OBP	SLG	PRO+	BR	/A	RC	SB	CS	SBR	FR	POS	TPR
1888	Det-N	27	94	17	19	3	1	0	4	9	9	.202	.286	.255	76	-2	-2	8	4			-5	O	-0.6
1890	Roc-a	119	445	111	109	12	6	3		78		.245	.373	.319	116	8	14	84	77			9	*O/C	1.5
Total	2	146	539	128	128	15	7	3	4	87	9	.237	.359	.308	109	6	12	92	81			4	O/C	0.9

■ FRANK SCHEIBECK
Scheibeck, Frank S. b: 6/28/1865, Detroit, Mich. d: 10/22/56, Detroit, Mich. BR/TR, 5'7", 145 lbs. Deb: 5/09/1887

YEAR	TM/L	G	AB	R	H	2B	3B	HR	RBI	BB	SO	AVG	OBP	SLG	PRO+	BR	/A	RC	SB	CS	SBR	FR	POS	TPR
1887	Cle-a	3	9	2	2	0	0	0		2		.222	.364	.222	69	-0	-0	1	0			-2	/S3P	-0.1
1888	Det-N	1	4	0	0	0	0	0	0	0	0	.000	.000	.000	-99	-1	-1	0	0			-1	/S	-0.2
1890	Tol-a	134	485	72	117	13	5	1		76		.241	.348	.295	90	-2	-4	71	57			1	*S	0.4
1894	Pit-N	28	102	20	36	2	3	1	10	11	9	.353	.416	.461	114	2	3	23	7			-8	S/O32	-0.3
	Was-N	52	196	49	45	2	4	0	17	45	24	.230	.384	.281	66	-9	-8	26	11			5	S	0.0
	Yr	80	298	69	81	4	7	1	27	56	33	.272	.394	.342	83	-7	-5	48	18			-3		-0.3
1895	Was-N	48	167	17	31	5	2	0	25	17	21	.186	.265	.240	32	-17	-16	12	5			-1	S/32	-1.1
1899	Was-N	27	94	19	27	4	1	0	9	11		.287	.368	.351	101	0	1	14	5			-10	S	-0.6
1901	Cle-A	93	329	33	70	11	3	0	38	18		.213	.256	.264	48	-24	-22	25	3			-14	S	-2.6
1906	Det-A	3	10	1	1	0	0	0	0	2		.100	.250	.100	12	-1	-1	0	0			-1	/2	-0.1
Total	8	389	1396	213	329	37	18	2	99	182	54	.236	.328	.292	72	-50	-48	173	88			-31	S/O23P	-4.6

■ RICHIE SCHEINBLUM
Scheinblum, Richard Alan b: 11/5/42, New York, N.Y. BB/TR, 6'1", 180 lbs. Deb: 9/01/65

YEAR	TM/L	G	AB	R	H	2B	3B	HR	RBI	BB	SO	AVG	OBP	SLG	PRO+	BR	/A	RC	SB	CS	SBR	FR	POS	TPR
1965	Cle-A	4	1	1	0	0	0	0	0	0	0	.000	.000	.000	-99	-0	-0	0	0	0	0	0	H	0.0
1967	Cle-A	18	66	8	21	4	2	0	6	5	10	.318	.366	.439	136	3	3	10	0	2	-1	-1	O	0.0
1968	Cle-A	19	55	3	12	5	0	0	5	5	8	.218	.295	.309	84	-1	-1	5	0	0	0	1	O	0.0
1969	Cle-A	102	199	13	37	5	1	1	13	19	30	.186	.257	.236	37	-16	-17	11	0	2	-1	0	O	-2.0
1971	Was-A	27	49	5	7	3	0	0	4	8	5	.143	.263	.204	36	-4	-4	3	0	0	0	3	O	0.0
1972	KC-A	134	450	60	135	21	4	8	66	58	46	.300	.383	.418	139	23	23	71	0	1	-1	-0	*O	1.8
1973	Cin-N	29	54	5	12	2	0	1	8	10	4	.222	.344	.315	88	-1	-1	6	0	0	0	-1	O	-0.1
	Cal-A	77	229	28	75	10	2	3	21	35	27	.328	.419	.428	150	13	16	42	0	0	0	-4	O/D	1.0
1974	Cal-A	10	26	1	4	0	0	0	2	1	2	.154	.185	.154	-2	-3	-3	0	0	0	0	-0	/OD	-0.3

YEAR	TM/L	G	AB	R	H	2B	3B	HR	RBI	BB	SO	AVG	OBP	SLG	PRO+	BR	/A	RC	SB	CS	SBR	FR	POS	TPR
	KC-A	36	83	7	15	2	0	0	2	8	8	.181	.253	.205	31	-7	-8	4	0	1	-1	0	D/O	-0.8
	Yr	46	109	8	19	2	0	0	4	9	10	.174	.237	.193	24	-10	-11	4	0	1	-1	-0		-1.1
	StL-N	6	6	0	2	0	0	0	0	0	1	.333	.333	.333	88	-0	-0	1	0	0	0	0	H	0.0
Total	8	462	1218	131	320	52	9	13	127	149	135	.263	.346	.352	104	6	8	153	0	6	-4	-6	O/D	-0.4

■ DANNY SCHELL
Schell, Clyde Daniel b: 12/26/27, Fostoria, Mich. d: 5/11/72, Mayville, Mich. BR/TR, 6'1", 195 lbs. Deb: 4/13/54

YEAR	TM/L	G	AB	R	H	2B	3B	HR	RBI	BB	SO	AVG	OBP	SLG	PRO+	BR	/A	RC	SB	CS	SBR	FR	POS	TPR
1954	Phi-N	92	272	25	77	14	3	7	33	17	31	.283	.330	.434	97	-2	-2	34	0	3	-2	0	O	-0.5
1955	Phi-N	2	2	0	0	0	0	0	0	0	1	.000	.000	.000	-99	-1	-1	0	0	0	0	0	H	0.0
Total	2	94	274	25	77	14	3	7	33	17	32	.281	.328	.431	96	-2	-2	34	0	3	-2	0	/O	-0.5

■ AL SCHELLHASE
Schellhase, Albert Herman "Schelley" b: 9/13/1864, Evansville, Ind. d: 1/3/19, Evansville, Ind. TR, 5'8", 148 lbs. Deb: 5/07/1890

YEAR	TM/L	G	AB	R	H	2B	3B	HR	RBI	BB	SO	AVG	OBP	SLG	PRO+	BR	/A	RC	SB	CS	SBR	FR	POS	TPR
1890	Bos-N	9	29	1	4	0	0	0	1	1	10	.138	.167	.138	-9	-4	-4	1	0			-1	/OCS3	-0.3
1891	Lou-a	7	20	4	3	0	0	0	1	1	2	.150	.190	.150	-1	-3	-3	1	3			1	/C	0.0
Total	2	16	49	5	7	0	0	0	2	2	12	.143	.176	.143	-6	-7	-7	2	3			0	/CO3S	-0.3

■ FRED SCHEMANSKE
Schemanske, Frederick George "Buck" b: 4/28/03, Detroit, Mich. d: 2/18/60, Detroit, Mich. BR/TR, 6'2", 190 lbs. Deb: 9/15/23

YEAR	TM/L	G	AB	R	H	2B	3B	HR	RBI	BB	SO	AVG	OBP	SLG	PRO+	BR	/A	RC	SB	CS	SBR	FR	POS	TPR
1923	Was-A	2	2	0	2	0	0	0	0	0	0	1.000	1.000	1.000	450	1	1	2	0	0	0	0	/P	0.1

■ MIKE SCHEMER
Schemer, Michael "Lefty" b: 11/20/17, Baltimore, Md. d: 4/22/83, Miami, Fla. BL/TL, 6', 180 lbs. Deb: 8/08/45

YEAR	TM/L	G	AB	R	H	2B	3B	HR	RBI	BB	SO	AVG	OBP	SLG	PRO+	BR	/A	RC	SB	CS	SBR	FR	POS	TPR
1945	NY-N	31	108	10	36	3	1	1	10	6	1	.333	.368	.407	114	2	2	14	2			4	1	0.5
1946	NY-N	1	1	0	0	0	0	0	0	0	0	.000	.000	.000	-99	-0	-0	0	0			0	H	0.0
Total	2	32	109	10	36	3	1	1	10	6	1	.330	.365	.404	112	2	2	14	2			4	/1	0.5

■ BILL SCHENCK
Schenck, William G. b: Brooklyn, N.Y. 5'7", 171 lbs. Deb: 5/29/1882

YEAR	TM/L	G	AB	R	H	2B	3B	HR	RBI	BB	SO	AVG	OBP	SLG	PRO+	BR	/A	RC	SB	CS	SBR	FR	POS	TPR
1882	Lou-a	60	231	37	60	11	3	0		8		.260	.285	.333	115	2	4	22				-7	*3/SP	-0.4
1884	Ric-a	42	151	14	31	4	0	3		1		.205	.216	.291	67	-5	-5	10				-5	S/2	-0.9
1885	Bro-a	1	4	0	0	0	0	0		0		.000	.000	.000	-99	-1	-1	0				0	/3	0.0
Total	3	103	386	51	91	15	3	3		9		.236	.255	.313	93	-5	-2	32				-12	/3S2P	-1.3

■ HANK SCHENZ
Schenz, Henry Leonard b: 4/11/19, New Richmond, Ohio d: 5/12/88, Cincinnati, Ohio BR/TR, 5'9.5", 175 lbs. Deb: 9/18/46

YEAR	TM/L	G	AB	R	H	2B	3B	HR	RBI	BB	SO	AVG	OBP	SLG	PRO+	BR	/A	RC	SB	CS	SBR	FR	POS	TPR
1946	Chi-N	6	11	0	2	0	0	0	1	0	0	.182	.182	.182	3	-1	-1	0	1			0	/3	0.0
1947	Chi-N	7	14	2	1	0	0	0	0	2	1	.071	.235	.071	-16	-2	-2	1	0			0	/3	-0.1
1948	Chi-N	96	337	43	88	17	1	1	14	18	15	.261	.306	.326	74	-14	-12	34	3			-5	2/3	-1.1
1949	Chi-N	7	14	2	6	0	0	0	1	1	0	.429	.467	.429	146	1	1	3	2			1	/3	0.2
1950	Pit-N	58	101	17	23	4	2	1	5	6	7	.228	.271	.337	57	-6	-7	8	0			3	23/S	-0.2
1951	Pit-N	25	61	5	13	1	0	0	3	0	2	.213	.226	.230	22	-7	-7	3	0	2	-1	-3	2/3	-0.9
	*NY-N	8	0	1	0	0	0	0	0	0	0	—	—	—	—	0	0	0	0	0	0	0	R	
	Yr	33	61	6	13	1	0	0	3	0	2	.213	.226	.230	22	-7	-7	3	0	2	-1	-3		-0.9
Total	6	207	538	70	133	22	3	2	24	27	25	.247	.291	.310	63	-29	-28	49	6	2		-4	2/3S	-2.1

■ JOE SCHEPNER
Schepner, Joseph Maurice "Gentleman Joe" b: 8/10/1895, Aliquippa, Pa. d: 7/25/59, Mobile, Ala. BR/TR, 5'10", 160 lbs. Deb: 9/11/19

YEAR	TM/L	G	AB	R	H	2B	3B	HR	RBI	BB	SO	AVG	OBP	SLG	PRO+	BR	/A	RC	SB	CS	SBR	FR	POS	TPR
1919	StL-A	14	48	2	10	4	0	0	6	1	5	.208	.224	.292	43	-4	-4	3	0			-1	3	-0.3

■ BOB SCHERBARTH
Scherbarth, Robert Elmer b: 1/18/26, Milwaukee, Wis. BR/TR, 6', 180 lbs. Deb: 4/23/50

YEAR	TM/L	G	AB	R	H	2B	3B	HR	RBI	BB	SO	AVG	OBP	SLG	PRO+	BR	/A	RC	SB	CS	SBR	FR	POS	TPR
1950	Bos-A	1	0	0	0	0	0	0	0	0	0	—	—	—	—	0	0	0	0	0	0	0	/C	0.0

■ HARRY SCHERER
Scherer, Harry Deb: 7/24/1889

YEAR	TM/L	G	AB	R	H	2B	3B	HR	RBI	BB	SO	AVG	OBP	SLG	PRO+	BR	/A	RC	SB	CS	SBR	FR	POS	TPR
1889	Lou-a	1	3	0	1	0	0	0	0	0	0	.333	.333	.333	94	-0	-0	0	0			-1	/O	0.0

■ LOU SCHIAPPACASSE
Schiappacasse, Louis Joseph b: 3/29/1881, Ann Arbor, Mich. d: 9/20/10, Ann Arbor, Mich. BR/TR, Deb: 9/07/02

YEAR	TM/L	G	AB	R	H	2B	3B	HR	RBI	BB	SO	AVG	OBP	SLG	PRO+	BR	/A	RC	SB	CS	SBR	FR	POS	TPR
1902	Det-A	2	5	0	0	0	0	0	1	1		.000	.167	.000	-49	-1	-1	0	0			-1	/O	-0.1

■ MORRIE SCHICK
Schick, Maurice Francis b: 4/17/1892, Chicago, Ill. d: 10/25/79, Hazel Crest, Ill. BR/TR, 5'11", 170 lbs. Deb: 4/15/17

YEAR	TM/L	G	AB	R	H	2B	3B	HR	RBI	BB	SO	AVG	OBP	SLG	PRO+	BR	/A	RC	SB	CS	SBR	FR	POS	TPR
1917	Chi-N	14	34	3	5	0	0	0	3	3	10	.147	.216	.147	11	-3	-4	1	0			2	O	-0.1

■ CHUCK SCHILLING
Schilling, Charles Thomas b: 10/25/37, Brooklyn, N.Y. BR/TR, 5'10", 160 lbs. Deb: 4/11/61

YEAR	TM/L	G	AB	R	H	2B	3B	HR	RBI	BB	SO	AVG	OBP	SLG	PRO+	BR	/A	RC	SB	CS	SBR	FR	POS	TPR
1961	Bos-A	158	646	87	167	25	2	5	62	78	77	.259	.340	.327	77	-17	-19	76	7	6	-2	15	*2	1.3
1962	Bos-A	119	413	48	95	17	1	7	35	29	48	.230	.287	.327	63	-21	-22	38	1	0	0	13	*2	0.0
1963	Bos-A	146	576	63	135	25	0	8	33	41	72	.234	.291	.319	69	-22	-24	54	3	2	-0	-14	*2	-2.9
1964	Bos-A	47	163	18	32	6	0	0	7	15	22	.196	.264	.233	38	-13	-14	11	0	1	-1	-0	2	-1.0
1965	Bos-A	71	171	14	41	3	2	3	9	13	17	.240	.293	.333	73	-5	-6	15	0	1	-1	10	2	0.6
Total	5	541	1969	230	470	76	5	23	146	176	236	.239	.305	.317	68	-78	-86	193	11	10	-3	25	2	-2.0

■ BILL SCHINDLER
Schindler, William Gibbons b: 7/10/1896, Perryville, Mo. d: 2/6/79, Perryville, Mo. BR/TR, 5'11", 160 lbs. Deb: 9/03/20

YEAR	TM/L	G	AB	R	H	2B	3B	HR	RBI	BB	SO	AVG	OBP	SLG	PRO+	BR	/A	RC	SB	CS	SBR	FR	POS	TPR
1920	StL-N	1	2	0	0	0	0	0	0	0	1	.000	.000	.000	-99	-1	-0	0	0	0	0	0	/C	0.0

■ DUTCH SCHIRICK
Schirick, Harry Ernest b: 6/15/1890, Ruby, N.Y. d: 11/12/68, Kingston, N.Y. BR/TR, 5'8", 160 lbs. Deb: 9/17/14

YEAR	TM/L	G	AB	R	H	2B	3B	HR	RBI	BB	SO	AVG	OBP	SLG	PRO+	BR	/A	RC	SB	CS	SBR	FR	POS	TPR
1914	StL-A	1	0	0	0	0	0	0	0	1	0	—	1.000	—	211	0	0	2	2			0	H	0.1

■ LARRY SCHLAFLY
Schlafly, Harry Linton b: 9/20/1878, Port Washington, Ohio d: 6/27/19, Canton, Ohio BR/TR, 5'11", 182 lbs. Deb: 9/18/02 M

YEAR	TM/L	G	AB	R	H	2B	3B	HR	RBI	BB	SO	AVG	OBP	SLG	PRO+	BR	/A	RC	SB	CS	SBR	FR	POS	TPR
1902	Chi-N	10	31	5	10	0	3	0	5	6		.323	.432	.516	201	4	4	8	2			-3	/O23	0.0
1906	Was-A	123	426	60	105	13	8	2	30	50		.246	.326	.329	112	5	7	59	29			14	*2	1.9
1907	Was-A	24	74	10	10	0	0	1	4	22		.135	.333	.176	71	-1	-1	8	7			-9	2	-1.0
1914	Buf-F	51	127	16	33	7	1	2	19	12	22	.260	.338	.378	103	1	1	18	3			2	2/1C3OM	0.3
Total	4	208	658	91	158	20	12	5	58	90	22	.240	.334	.330	110	8	11	92	41			3	2/103C	1.2

■ ADMIRAL SCHLEI
Schlei, George Henry b: 1/12/1878, Cincinnati, Ohio d: 1/24/58, Huntington, W.Va. BR/TR, 5'8.5", 179 lbs. Deb: 4/24/04

YEAR	TM/L	G	AB	R	H	2B	3B	HR	RBI	BB	SO	AVG	OBP	SLG	PRO+	BR	/A	RC	SB	CS	SBR	FR	POS	TPR
1904	Cin-N	97	291	25	69	8	3	0	32	17		.237	.279	.285	70	-8	-11	26	7			11	C	0.8
1905	Cin-N	99	314	32	71	8	3	1	36	22		.226	.277	.280	61	-12	-16	29	9			16	C/1	0.9
1906	Cin-N	116	388	44	95	13	8	4	54	29		.245	.297	.351	99	1	-1	45	7			8	C1	1.5
1907	Cin-N	84	246	28	67	3	2	0	27	28		.272	.347	.301	101	3	1	29	5			6	C/1O	1.4
1908	Cin-N	92	300	31	66	6	4	1	22	22		.220	.273	.277	80	-7	-7	24	2			-7	C	-1.0
1909	NY-N	92	279	25	68	12	0	0	30	40		.244	.343	.287	94	0	-0	30	4			5	C	1.3
1910	NY-N	55	99	10	19	2	1	0	8	14	10	.192	.304	.232	57	-5	-5	9	4			0	C	-0.2
1911	NY-N	1	1	0	0	0	0	0	0	0	1	.000	.000	.000	-97	-0	-0	0	0			0	H	0.0
Total	8	636	1918	195	455	52	21	6	209	172	11	.237	.301	.296	82	-29	-39	191	38			40	C/1O	4.7

■ RUDY SCHLESINGER
Schlesinger, William Cordes b: 11/5/41, Cincinnati, Ohio BR/TR, 6'2", 175 lbs. Deb: 5/04/65

YEAR	TM/L	G	AB	R	H	2B	3B	HR	RBI	BB	SO	AVG	OBP	SLG	PRO+	BR	/A	RC	SB	CS	SBR	FR	POS	TPR
1965	Bos-A	1	1	0	0	0	0	0	0	0	0	.000	.000	.000	-94	-0	-0	0	0	0	0	0	H	0.0

■ DUTCH SCHLIEBNER
Schliebner, Frederick Paul b: 5/19/1891, Charlottenburg, Germany d: 4/15/75, Toledo, Ohio BR/TR, 5'10", 180 lbs. Deb: 4/17/23

YEAR	TM/L	G	AB	R	H	2B	3B	HR	RBI	BB	SO	AVG	OBP	SLG	PRO+	BR	/A	RC	SB	CS	SBR	FR	POS	TPR
1923	Bro-N	19	76	11	19	4	0	0	4	5	7	.250	.296	.303	60	-5	-4	7	1	0	0	3	1	-0.2
	StL-A	127	444	50	122	19	6	4	52	39	60	.275	.339	.372	82	-9	-12	58	3	2	-0	-0	*1	-1.7

■ JAY SCHLUETER
Schlueter, Jay D b: 7/31/49, Phoenix, Ariz. BR/TR, 6', 182 lbs. Deb: 6/18/71

YEAR	TM/L	G	AB	R	H	2B	3B	HR	RBI	BB	SO	AVG	OBP	SLG	PRO+	BR	/A	RC	SB	CS	SBR	FR	POS	TPR
1971	Hou-N	7	3	1	1	0	0	0	0	0	1	.333	.333	.333	92	-0	-0	0	0	0	0	1	/O	0.1

YEAR	TM/L	G	AB	R	H	2B	3B	HR	RBI	BB	SO	AVG	OBP	SLG	PRO+	BR	/A	RC	SB	CS	SBR	FR	POS	TPR
■ **NORM SCHLUETER**				Schlueter, Norman John "Duke" b: 9/25/16, Belleville, Ill. BR/TR, 5'10", 175 lbs. Deb: 5/28/38																				
1938	Chi-A	35	118	11	27	5	1	0	7	4	15	.229	.254	.288	35	-12	-12	9	1	0	0	-3	C	-1.3
1939	Chi-A	34	56	5	13	2	1	0	8	1	11	.232	.246	.304	39	-5	-5	3	2	0	1	1	C	-0.1
1944	Cle-A	49	122	2	15	4	0	0	11	12	22	.123	.201	.156	3	-15	-15	4	0	2	-1	-7	C	-2.1
Total	3	118	296	18	55	11	2	0	26	17	48	.186	.230	.236	24	-33	-33	16	3	2	-0	-10	C	-3.5
■ **RAY SCHMANDT**				Schmandt, Raymond Henry b: 1/25/1896, St.Louis, Mo. d: 2/2/69, St.Louis, Mo. BR/TR, 6'1", 175 lbs. Deb: 6/24/15																				
1915	StL-A	3	4	0	0	0	0	0	0	0	1	.000	.000	.000	-99	-1	-1	0	0			0	/1	0.0
1918	Bro-N	34	114	11	35	5	4	0	18	7	7	.307	.347	.421	134	4	4	16	1			-4	2	0.3
1919	Bro-N	47	127	8	21	4	0	0	10	4	13	.165	.191	.197	16	-13	-13	4	0			0	21/3	-1.3
1920	*Bro-N	28	63	7	15	2	1	0	7	3	4	.238	.273	.302	63	-3	-3	5	1	1	-0	3	1	0.0
1921	Bro-N	95	350	42	107	8	5	1	43	11	22	.306	.329	.366	81	-8	-10	41	3	4	-2	0	1	-1.2
1922	Bro-N	110	396	54	106	17	3	2	44	21	28	.268	.306	.341	67	-20	-19	41	6	6	-2	5	*1	-1.6
Total	6	317	1054	122	284	36	13	3	122	46	75	.269	.301	.337	72	-41	-42	108	11	11		5	1/23	-3.8
■ **GEORGE SCHMEES**				Schmees, George Edward "Rocky" b: 9/6/24, Cincinnati, Ohio BL/TL, 6', 190 lbs. Deb: 4/15/52																				
1952	StL-A	34	61	9	8	1	0	3	2	18	.131	.159	.180	-6	-9	-9	2	0	0	0	2	O/1	-0.7
	Bos-A	42	64	8	13	3	0	0	3	10	11	.203	.311	.250	53	-3	-4	5	0	1	-1	0	O/P1	-0.4
	Yr	76	125	17	21	4	1	0	6	12	29	.168	.241	.216	26	-12	-13	7	0	1	-1	3		-1.1
■ **BOSS SCHMIDT**				Schmidt, Charles b: 9/12/1880, Coal Hill, Ark. d: 11/14/32, Clarksville, Ark. BB/TR, 5'11", 200 lbs. Deb: 4/30/06																				
1906	Det-A	68	216	13	47	4	3	0	10	6		.218	.239	.264	57	-10	-11	15	1			7	C	0.1
1907	*Det-A	104	349	32	85	6	6	0	23	5		.244	.254	.295	74	-10	-11	30	8			4	*C	0.1
1908	Det-A	122	419	45	111	14	3	1	38	16		.265	.292	.320	97	-0	-2	41	5			7	*C	1.9
1909	*Det-A	84	253	21	53	8	2	1	28	7		.209	.240	.269	58	-12	-13	19	7			-7	C/O	-1.6
1910	Det-A	71	197	22	51	7	7	1	23	2		.259	.277	.381	99	-0	-2	21	2			-6	C	0.0
1911	Det-A	28	46	4	13	2	1	0	2	0		.283	.298	.370	82	-1	-1	5	0			-2	C/O	-0.1
Total	6	477	1480	137	360	41	22	3	124	36		.243	.265	.307	79	-34	-41	130	23			2	C/O	0.4
■ **BUTCH SCHMIDT**				Schmidt, Charles John "Butcher Boy" b: 7/19/1886, Baltimore, Md. d: 9/4/52, Baltimore, Md. BL/TL, 6'1.5", 200 lbs. Deb: 5/11/09																				
1909	NY-A	1	2	0	0	0	0	0	0	0	0	.000	.000	.000	-99	-0	-0	0	0			-0	/P	0.0
1913	Bos-N	22	78	6	24	2	2	1	14	2	5	.308	.333	.423	113	1	1	11	1			1	1	0.1
1914	*Bos-N	147	537	67	153	17	9	1	71	43	55	.285	.350	.356	111	7	8	71	14			3	*1	0.8
1915	Bos-N	127	458	46	115	26	7	2	60	36	59	.251	.318	.352	107	1	4	52	3	10	-5	-4	*1	-1.3
Total	4	297	1075	119	292	45	18	4	145	81	119	.272	.335	.358	109	9	12	134	18	10		-1	1/P	-0.4
■ **DAVE SCHMIDT**				Schmidt, David Frederick b: 12/22/56, Mesa, Ariz. BR/TR, 6'1", 190 lbs. Deb: 4/28/81																				
1981	Bos-A	15	42	6	10	1	0	2	5	3	7	17	.238	.347	.405	109	1	1	6	0	0	0	-3	C	-0.1
■ **MIKE SCHMIDT**				Schmidt, Michael Jack b: 9/27/49, Dayton, Ohio BR/TR, 6'2", 195 lbs. Deb: 9/12/72																				
1972	Phi-N	13	34	2	7	0	0	1	3	5	15	.206	.325	.294	75	-1	-1	4	0	0	0	2	3/2	0.1
1973	Phi-N	132	367	43	72	11	0	18	52	62	136	.196	.326	.373	91	-2	-4	48	8	2	1	21	*3/21S	1.7
1974	Phi-N	162	568	108	160	28	7	**36**	116	106	138	.282	.398	.546	156	48	45	130	23	12	-0	26	*3	6.9
1975	Phi-N	158	562	93	140	34	3	**38**	95	101	180	.249	.367	.523	139	34	31	113	29	12	-0	**24**	*3S	5.8
1976	*Phi-N	160	584	112	153	31	4	**38**	107	100	149	.262	.380	.524	150	43	40	121	14	9	-1	**25**	*3	6.4
1977	*Phi-N	154	544	114	149	27	11	38	101	104	122	.274	.399	.574	151	46	42	129	15	8	-0	29	*3/S2	6.9
1978	*Phi-N	145	513	93	129	27	2	21	78	91	103	.251	.368	.435	122	18	18	90	19	6	2	10	*3/S	3.0
1979	Phi-N	160	541	109	137	25	4	45	114	**120**	115	.253	.392	.564	153	45	42	123	9	5	-0	18	*3/S	5.5
1980	*Phi-N	150	548	104	157	25	8	**48**	121	89	119	.286	.388	**.624**	169	56	53	137	12	5	1	23	*3	7.8
1981	*Phi-N	102	354	**78**	112	19	2	**31**	91	**73**	71	.316	**.439**	**.644**	195	50	48	102	12	4	1	23	*3	6.9
1982	Phi-N	148	514	108	144	26	3	35	87	**107**	131	.280	**.407**	.547	161	47	46	118	14	7	0	19	*3	6.3
1983	Phi-N	154	534	104	136	16	4	**40**	109	**128**	148	.255	**.402**	.524	156	43	44	117	7	8	-3	23	*3/S	6.1
1984	Phi-N	151	528	93	146	23	3	**36**	106	92	116	.277	.388	.536	155	41	40	108	5	7	-3	12	*3/1S	5.0
1985	Phi-N	158	549	89	152	31	5	33	93	87	117	.277	.379	.532	148	39	37	113	1	3	-2	5	*13/S	3.8
1986	Phi-N	160	552	97	160	29	1	**37**	**119**	89	84	.290	.395	**.547**	152	44	41	122	1	2	-1	-7	*31	3.1
1987	Phi-N	147	522	88	153	28	0	35	113	83	80	.293	.392	.548	141	35	33	111	2	1	0	13	*3/1S	4.3
1988	Phi-N	108	390	52	97	21	2	12	62	49	42	.249	.342	.405	111	7	7	55	3	0	1	3	*3/1	1.1
1989	Phi-N	42	148	19	30	7	0	6	28	21	17	.203	.302	.372	91	-2	-2	16	0	1	-1	-5	3	-0.7
Total	18	2404	8352	1506	2234	408	59	548	1595	1507	1883	.267	.384	.527	147	592	561	1757	174	92	-3	265	*31/S2	80.0
■ **BOB SCHMIDT**				Schmidt, Robert Benjamin b: 4/22/33, St.Louis, Mo. BR/TR, 6'2", 205 lbs. Deb: 4/16/58																				
1958	SF-N	127	393	46	96	20	2	14	54	33	59	.244	.308	.412	90	-7	-6	44	0	1	-1	-4	*C	-0.3
1959	SF-N	71	181	17	44	7	1	5	20	13	24	.243	.297	.376	80	-6	-5	19	0	2	-1	-4	*C	-0.2
1960	SF-N	110	344	31	92	12	1	8	37	26	51	.267	.319	.378	96	-5	-2	39	0	3	-2	-4	*C	-0.3
1961	SF-N	2	6	0	1	0	0	0	1	0	1	.167	.167	.167	-12	-1	-1	0	0	0	0	1	/C	0.0
	Cin-N	27	70	4	9	0	0	1	4	8	14	.129	.218	.171	5	-10	-10	2	0	0	0	1	C	-0.6
	Yr	29	76	4	10	0	0	1	5	8	15	.132	.214	.171	4	-11	-11	2	0	0	0	2		-0.6
1962	Was-A	88	256	28	62	14	0	10	31	14	37	.242	.284	.414	86	-6	-6	30	0	0	0	-2	C	-0.2
1963	Was-A	9	15	3	3	1	0	0	3	3	5	.200	.333	.267	71	-0	-0	1	0	0	0	-1	/C	-0.1
1965	NY-A	20	40	4	10	1	0	2	3	3	8	.250	.302	.350	85	-1	-1	4	0	0	0	0	C	0.3
Total	7	454	1305	133	317	55	4	39	150	100	199	.243	.299	.381	84	-36	-32	141	0	6	-4	-6	C	-1.4
■ **WALTER SCHMIDT**				Schmidt, Walter Joseph b: 3/20/1887, Coal Hill, Ark. d: 7/4/73, Modesto, Cal. BR/TR, 5'9", 159 lbs. Deb: 4/13/16																				
1916	Pit-N	64	184	16	35	1	2	1	15	10	13	.190	.236	.250	49	-11	-11	12	3			-1	C	-1.0
1917	Pit-N	72	183	9	45	7	0	0	17	11	11	.246	.296	.284	76	-5	-5	16	4			9	C	0.7
1918	Pit-N	105	323	31	77	6	3	0	27	17	19	.238	.281	.276	67	-12	-13	27	7			15	*C	1.2
1919	Pit-N	85	267	23	67	9	2	0	29	23	9	.251	.310	.300	81	-5	-6	26	5			-0	C	0.0
1920	Pit-N	94	310	22	86	8	4	0	20	24	15	.277	.337	.329	89	-3	-4	36	9	3	1	-5	C	-0.1
1921	Pit-N	114	393	30	111	9	3	0	38	12	13	.282	.307	.321	65	-19	-20	38	10	6	-1	5	*C	-0.7
1922	Pit-N	40	152	21	50	11	1	0	22	1	5	.329	.333	.414	91	-2	-2	20	2	1	0	-5	C	-0.6
1923	Pit-N	97	335	39	83	7	2	0	37	22	12	.248	.300	.281	53	-22	-23	29	10	5	0	-10	C	-2.6
1924	Pit-N	58	177	16	43	3	2	1	20	13	5	.243	.295	.299	59	-10	-10	17	6	1	1	1	C	-0.6
1925	StL-N	37	87	9	22	2	1	0	9	4	3	.253	.290	.299	51	-6	-7	8	1	0	0	6	C	0.1
Total	10	766	2411	216	619	63	20	3	234	137	105	.257	.301	.303	68	-94	-101	231	57	16		15	C	-3.6
■ **HANK SCHMULBACH**				Schmulbach, Henry Alrives b: 1/17/25, E.St.Louis, Ill. BL/TL, 5'11", 165 lbs. Deb: 9/27/43																				
1943	StL-A	1	0	1	0	0	0	0	0	0	0	—	—	—	—	0	0	0	0	0	0	0	R	0.0
■ **DAVE SCHNECK**				Schneck, David Lee b: 6/18/49, Allentown, Pa. BL/TL, 5'10", 200 lbs. Deb: 7/14/72																				
1972	NY-N	37	123	7	23	3	2	3	10	10	26	.187	.254	.317	63	-7	-6	10	0	1	-1	-0	O	-0.8
1973	NY-N	13	36	2	7	0	1	0	0	1	4	.194	.216	.250	29	-3	-3	1	0	0	0	2	O	-0.2
1974	NY-N	93	254	23	52	11	1	5	25	16	43	.205	.255	.315	60	-15	-14	21	4	1	1	11	O	-0.6
Total	3	143	413	32	82	14	4	8	35	27	73	.199	.251	.310	58	-25	-24	32	4	2	0	12	O	-1.6

YEAR	TM/L	G	AB	R	H	2B	3B	HR	RBI	BB	SO	AVG	OBP	SLG	PRO+	BR	/A	RC	SB	CS	SBR	FR	POS	TPR

■ RED SCHOENDIENST Schoendienst, Albert Fred b: 2/2/23, Germantown, Ill. BB/TR, 6', 170 lbs. Deb: 4/17/45 MCH

YEAR	TM/L	G	AB	R	H	2B	3B	HR	RBI	BB	SO	AVG	OBP	SLG	PRO+	BR	/A	RC	SB	CS	SBR	FR	POS	TPR
1945	StL-N	137	565	89	157	22	6	1	47	21	17	.278	.305	.343	78	-17	-18	59	26			0	*OS/2	-2.1
1946	*StL-N	142	606	94	170	28	5	0	34	37	27	.281	.322	.343	85	-10	-13	67	12			-0	*23/S	-0.8
1947	StL-N	151	659	91	167	25	9	3	48	48	27	.253	.304	.332	66	-30	-34	65	6			-2	*2/3O	-1.9
1948	StL-N	119	408	64	111	21	4	4	36	28	16	.272	.319	.373	82	-8	-11	49	1			1	2	-0.3
1949	StL-N	151	640	102	190	25	2	3	54	51	18	.297	.351	.356	86	-8	-12	82	8			24	*2S/3O	1.8
1950	StL-N	153	642	81	177	43	9	7	63	33	32	.276	.313	.403	83	-14	-18	79	3			8	*2S/3	-0.4
1951	StL-N	135	553	88	160	32	7	6	54	35	23	.289	.335	.405	98	-2	-3	75	0	1	-1	16	*2/S	1.7
1952	StL-N	152	620	91	188	40	7	7	67	42	30	.303	.347	.424	113	10	10	89	9	6	-1	33	*23/S	4.9
1953	StL-N	146	564	107	193	35	5	15	79	60	23	.342	.405	.502	135	30	30	114	3	3	-1	25	*2	5.7
1954	StL-N	148	610	98	192	38	8	5	79	54	22	.315	.371	.428	107	7	7	96	4	2	0	33	*2	4.7
1955	StL-N	145	553	68	148	21	3	11	51	54	28	.268	.337	.376	89	-8	-8	70	7	7	-2	-15	*2	-1.2
1956	StL-N	40	153	22	48	9	0	0	15	13	5	.314	.367	.373	100	0	0	21	0	1	-1	-1	2	0.1
	NY-N	92	334	39	99	12	3	2	14	28	10	.296	.354	.368	95	-2	-1	42	1	2	-1	-10	2	-0.5
	Yr	132	487	61	147	21	3	2	29	41	15	.302	.358	.370	97	-1	-1	63	1	3	-2	-12		-0.4
1957	NY-N	57	254	35	78	8	4	9	33	10	8	.307	.338	.476	116	5	5	40	2	1	-0	-1	2	0.8
	*Mil-N	93	394	56	122	23	4	6	32	23	7	.310	.349	.434	117	5	8	59	2	3	-1	5	2/O	2.0
	Yr	150	648	91	200	31	8	15	65	33	15	.309	.345	.451	117	10	13	99	4	4	-1	4		2.8
1958	*Mil-N	106	427	47	112	23	1	1	24	31	21	.262	.314	.328	77	-18	-13	44	3	1	0	1	*2	-0.6
1959	Mil-N	5	3	0	0	0	0	0	0	0	0	.000	.000	.000	-99	-1	-1	0	0	0	0	-0	/2	0.0
1960	Mil-N	68	226	21	58	9	1	1	19	17	13	.257	.311	.319	79	-8	-6	23	1	0	0	-17	2	-1.8
1961	StL-N	72	120	9	36	9	0	1	12	12	6	.300	.364	.400	93	1	-1	18	1	0	0	-10	2	-0.6
1962	StL-N	98	143	21	43	4	0	2	12	9	12	.301	.346	.371	84	-1	-3	17	0	0	0	-0	2/3	-0.1
1963	StL-N	6	5	0	0	0	0	0	0	0	1	.000	.000	.000	-91	-1	-1	0	0	0	0	0	H	0.0
Total	19	2216	8479	1223	2449	427	78	84	773	606	346	.289	.338	.387	93	-70	-83	1109	89	27		87	*2O/S3	11.4

■ JUMBO SCHOENECK Schoeneck, Louis N. b: 3/3/1862, Chicago, Ill. d: 1/20/30, Chicago, Ill. BR/TR, 6'3", 223 lbs. Deb: 4/20/1884

YEAR	TM/L	G	AB	R	H	2B	3B	HR	RBI	BB	SO	AVG	OBP	SLG	PRO+	BR	/A	RC	SB	CS	SBR	FR	POS	TPR
1884	CP-U	90	366	56	116	22	2	2		8		.317	.332	.404	149	17	17	50	0			0	*1	1.4
	Bal-U	16	60	5	15	2	0	0		0		.250	.250	.283	72	-1	-2	4	0			2	1	0.0
	Yr	106	426	61	131	24	2	2		8		.308	.320	.387	137	16	15	54	0			2		1.4
1888	Ind-N	48	169	15	40	4	0	0	20	9	24	.237	.283	.260	75	-4	-5	16	11			-1	1/P	-0.9
1889	Ind-N	16	62	3	15	2	2	0	8	3	3	.242	.299	.339	78	-2	-2	7	1			2	1	0.0
Total	3	170	657	79	186	30	4	2	28	20	27	.283	.308	.350	114	10	9	77	12			3	1/P	0.5

■ DICK SCHOFIELD Schofield, John Richard "Ducky" b: 1/7/35, Springfield, Ill. BB/TR, 5'9", 163 lbs. Deb: 7/03/53

YEAR	TM/L	G	AB	R	H	2B	3B	HR	RBI	BB	SO	AVG	OBP	SLG	PRO+	BR	/A	RC	SB	CS	SBR	FR	POS	TPR
1953	StL-N	33	39	9	7	0	0	0	4	2	11	.179	.220	.333	42	-3	-3	3	0	0	0	10	S	0.7
1954	StL-N	43	7	17	1	0	1	0	1	0	3	.143	.143	.429	42	-1	-1	-1	1	1	-0	14	S	1.3
1955	StL-N	12	4	3	0	0	0	0	0	0	1	.000	.000	.000	-99	-1	-1	0	0	0	0	3	/S	0.2
1956	StL-N	16	30	3	3	2	0	0	1	0	6	.100	.100	.167	-30	-5	-5	0	0	0	0	-1	/S	-0.5
1957	StL-N	65	56	10	9	0	0	0	1	7	13	.161	.254	.161	14	-7	-7	2	1	3	-2	10	S	0.2
1958	StL-N	39	108	16	23	4	0	1	8	23	15	.213	.351	.278	67	-4	-5	12	0	2	-1	-5	S	-0.8
	Pit-N	26	27	4	4	0	1	0	2	3	6	.148	.233	.222	22	-3	-3	1	0	1	-1	0	/S3	-0.2
	Yr	65	135	20	27	4	1	1	10	26	21	.200	.329	.267	59	-7	-7	13	0	3	-2	-4		-1.0
1959	Pit-N	81	145	21	34	10	1	1	9	16	22	.234	.311	.338	73	-6	-5	16	1	1	-0	11	2/SO	0.8
1960	*Pit-N	65	102	9	34	4	1	0	10	16	20	.333	.429	.392	126	5	5	18	0	1	-1	8	S2/3	1.4
1961	Pit-N	60	78	16	15	2	1	0	2	10	19	.192	.284	.244	42	-6	-6	6	0	1	-1	3	3/S2O	0.4
1962	Pit-N	54	104	19	30	3	0	2	10	17	22	.288	.388	.375	106	2	2	17	0	1	-1	-6	3/2S	-0.3
1963	Pit-N	138	541	54	133	18	2	3	32	69	83	.246	.334	.303	84	-8	-8	58	2	4	-2	10	*S2/3	1.4
1964	Pit-N	121	398	50	98	22	5	3	36	54	60	.246	.346	.349	97	0	0	52	1	2	-1	2	*S	0.9
1965	Pit-N	31	109	13	25	5	0	0	6	15	19	.229	.323	.275	70	-4	-4	11	1	0	0	4	S	0.4
	SF-N	101	379	39	77	10	1	2	19	33	50	.203	.272	.251	47	-25	-27	26	2	4	-2	-6	S	-2.5
	Yr	132	488	52	102	15	1	2	25	48	69	.209	.284	.256	52	-29	-30	37	3	4	-2	-2		-2.1
1966	SF-N	11	16	4	1	0	0	0	0	2	2	.063	.167	.063	-32	-3	-3	0	0	0	0	2	/S	0.0
	NY-A	25	58	5	9	2	0	0	2	9	8	.155	.269	.190	36	-5	-4	4	0	0	0	5	S	0.1
	LA-N	20	70	10	18	0	0	0	4	8	8	.257	.350	.257	78	-2	-1	7	1	1	-0	-2	3/S	-0.4
1967	LA-N	84	232	23	50	10	1	2	15	31	40	.216	.308	.293	79	-7	-5	20	1	2	-1	-0	S/23	0.2
1968	*StL-N	69	127	14	28	7	1	1	8	13	31	.220	.303	.315	87	-2	-2	12	1	2	-1	9	S2	1.4
1969	Bos-A	94	226	30	58	9	3	2	20	29	44	.257	.351	.350	92	-0	-2	29	0	2	-1	4	2S/3O	0.3
1970	Bos-A	76	139	16	26	1	2	1	14	21	26	.187	.298	.245	48	-9	-10	10	0	1	-1	4	23/S	-1.3
1971	Mil-A	23	28	2	3	2	0	0	1	2	8	.107	.194	.179	6	-4	-3	1	0	0	0	-1	3/S2	-0.4
	StL-N	34	60	7	13	2	0	1	6	10	9	.217	.347	.300	82	-1	-1	7	0	0	0	2	S2/3	0.4
Total	19	1321	3083	394	699	113	20	21	211	390	526	.227	.319	.297	73	-100	-101	311	12	29	-14	77	S2/3O	3.7

■ DICK SCHOFIELD Schofield, Richard Craig b: 11/21/62, Springfield, Ill. BR/TR, 5'10", 175 lbs. Deb: 9/08/83

YEAR	TM/L	G	AB	R	H	2B	3B	HR	RBI	BB	SO	AVG	OBP	SLG	PRO+	BR	/A	RC	SB	CS	SBR	FR	POS	TPR
1983	Cal-A	21	54	4	11	2	0	3	4	6	8	.204	.295	.407	92	-1	-1	6	0	0	0	5	S	0.5
1984	Cal-A	140	400	39	77	10	3	4	21	33	79	.192	.264	.262	47	-29	-29	29	5	2	0	3	*S	-1.3
1985	Cal-A	147	438	50	96	19	3	8	41	35	70	.219	.289	.331	70	-19	-18	43	11	4	1	1	*S	-0.5
1986	*Cal-A	139	458	67	114	17	6	13	57	48	55	.249	.327	.397	97	-3	-2	63	23	5	4	15	*S	2.5
1987	Cal-A	134	479	52	120	17	3	9	46	37	63	.251	.307	.355	78	-17	-15	56	19	3	4	-18	*S/2D	-2.1
1988	Cal-A	155	527	61	126	11	6	6	34	40	57	.239	.304	.317	76	-18	-16	55	20	5	3	21	*S	1.5
1989	Cal-A	91	302	42	69	11	2	4	26	28	47	.228	.300	.318	76	-10	-9	31	9	3	1	-8	S	-0.8
1990	Cal-A	99	310	41	79	8	1	1	18	52	61	.255	.365	.297	87	-3	-3	38	3	4	0	12	S	1.4
Total	8	926	2968	356	692	95	24	48	247	279	440	.233	.307	.330	76	-99	-92	323	90	26	11	31	S/2D	1.2

■ OTTO SCHOMBERG Schomberg, Otto H. (b: Otto H. Shambrick) b: 11/14/1864, Milwaukee, Wis. d: 5/3/27, Ottawa, Kan. TL , Deb: 7/07/1886

YEAR	TM/L	G	AB	R	H	2B	3B	HR	RBI	BB	SO	AVG	OBP	SLG	PRO+	BR	/A	RC	SB	CS	SBR	FR	POS	TPR
1886	Pit-a	72	246	53	67	6	6	1		57		.272	.417	.358	147	17	17	41	7			-7	1	0.6
1887	Ind-N	112	419	91	129	18	16	5	83	56	32	.308	.397	.463	145	24	27	88	21			-10	*1/O	0.0
1888	Ind-N	30	112	11	24	5	1	1	10	10	12	.214	.290	.304	90	-1	-1	12	6			-4	O1	-0.5
Total	3	214	777	155	220	29	23	7	93	123	44	.283	.389	.407	139	41	44	140	34			-21	1/O	0.1

■ JERRY SCHOONMAKER Schoonmaker, Jerald Lee b: 12/14/33, Seymour, Mo. BR/TR, 5'11", 190 lbs. Deb: 6/11/55

YEAR	TM/L	G	AB	R	H	2B	3B	HR	RBI	BB	SO	AVG	OBP	SLG	PRO+	BR	/A	RC	SB	CS	SBR	FR	POS	TPR
1955	Was-A	20	46	5	7	0	1	1	4	5	11	.152	.235	.261	35	-4	-4	3	1	0	0	0	O	-0.4
1957	Was-A	30	23	5	2	1	0	0	0	2	11	.087	.160	.130	-20	-4	-4	1	0	0	0	2	O	-0.2
Total	2	50	69	10	9	1	1	1	4	7	22	.130	.211	.217	16	-8	-8	4	1	0	0	2	/O	-0.6

■ GENE SCHOTT Schott, Eugene Arthur b: 7/14/13, Batavia, Ohio BR/TR, 6'2", 185 lbs. Deb: 4/16/35

YEAR	TM/L	G	AB	R	H	2B	3B	HR	RBI	BB	SO	AVG	OBP	SLG	PRO+	BR	/A	RC	SB	CS	SBR	FR	POS	TPR
1935	Cin-N	36	60	6	12	2	0	0	2	3	13	.200	.238	.233	28	-6	-6	3	0					
1936	Cin-N	39	60	10	18	3	1	1	8	5	18	.300	.354	.433	118	1	1	10	0					
1937	Cin-N	50	49	5	7	0	0	0	4	1	14	.143	.160	.184	-7	-7	-7	1	0					
1938	Cin-N	31	24	3	3	0	0	0	0	1	4	.125	.160	.125	-21	-4	-4	0	0					
1939	Phi-N	8	6	3	2	1	0	0	0	0	0	.333	.333	.667	168	1	1	1	0					
	Bro-N	1	0	0	0	0	0	0	0	0	0	—	—	—		0	0	0	0					
	Yr	9	6	3	2	1	0	0	0	0	0	.333	.333	.667	166	1	1	1	0					
Total	5	165	199	27	42	7	2	1	14	10	49	.211	.249	.281	45	-16	-15	16	0					

YEAR	TM/L	G	AB	R	H	2B	3B	HR	RBI	BB	SO	AVG	OBP	SLG	PRO+	BR	/A	RC	SB	CS	SBR	FR	POS	TPR

■ PAUL SCHRAMKA
Schramka, Paul Edward b: 3/22/28, Milwaukee, Wis. BL/TL, 6', 185 lbs. Deb: 4/14/53

1953	Chi-N	2	0	0	0	0	0	0	0	0	0	—	—	—	—	0	0	0	0	0	0	0	/O	0.0

■ OSSEE SCHRECKENGOST
Schreckengost, Ossee Freeman (a.k.a. Of Ossee Schreck)
b: 4/11/1875, New Bethlehem, Pa. d: 7/9/14, Philadelphia, Pa. BR/TR, 5'10", 180 lbs. Deb: 9/08/1897

1897	Lou-N	1	3	0	0	0	0	0	0	0	0	.000	.000	.000	-99	-1	-1	0	0			0	/C	0.0
1898	Cle-N	10	35	5	11	2	3	0	10	0	0	.314	.314	.543	149	2	2	6	1			0	/C	0.2
1899	StL-N	6	8	0	0	0	0	0	0	0	1	.000	.111	.000	-66	-2	-2	0	0			-1	/1O	-0.1
	Cle-N	43	150	15	47	8	3	0	10	6		.313	.344	.407	117	1	3	23	4			-6	C/1SO	0.0
	StL-N	66	269	42	77	12	2	2	37	14		.286	.324	.368	90	-3	-4	38	14			-3	1C/2	-0.4
	Yr	115	427	57	124	20	5	2	47	21		.290	.327	.375	96	-4	-3	60	18			-10		-0.5
1901	Bos-A	86	280	37	85	13	5	0	38	19		.304	.356	.386	110	3	4	42	6			2	C/1	1.1
1902	Cle-A	18	74	5	25	0	0	0	9	0		.338	.338	.338	93	-1	-1	10	2			-1	1	-0.1
	Phi-A	79	284	45	92	17	2	2	43	9		.324	.347	.419	109	4	3	44	3			22	C/1O	2.8
	Yr	97	358	50	117	17	2	2	52	9		.327	.345	.402	106	3	2	54	5			20		2.7
1903	Phi-A	92	306	26	78	13	4	3	30	11		.255	.281	.353	87	-4	-5	31	0			18	C1	2.3
1904	Phi-A	95	311	23	58	9	1	1	21	5		.186	.199	.232	36	-22	-23	16	3			5	C/1	-0.9
1905	*Phi-A	123	420	30	114	19	6	0	45	3		.271	.277	.345	97	-2	-3	44	9			11	*C/1	2.1
1906	Phi-A	98	338	29	96	20	1	1	41	10		.284	.305	.358	106	2	1	40	5			8	C/1	1.7
1907	Phi-A	101	356	30	97	16	3	0	38	17		.272	.306	.334	103	2	1	39	4			16	C/1	2.8
1908	Phi-A	71	207	16	46	7	1	0	16	6		.222	.244	.266	63	-8	-9	14	1			9	C/1	0.7
	Chi-A	6	16	1	3	0	0	0	0	1		.188	.235	.188	40	-1	-1	1	0			4	/C	0.4
	Yr	77	223	17	49	7	1	0	16	7		.220	.243	.260	62	-9	-10	14	1			13		1.1
Total	11	895	3057	304	829	136	31	9	338	102		.271	.296	.345	92	-29	-36	347	52			84	C/102S	12.6

■ HANK SCHREIBER
Schreiber, Henry Walter b: 7/12/1891, Cleveland, Ohio d: 2/23/68, Indianapolis, Ind. BR/TR, 5'11", 165 lbs. Deb: 4/14/14

1914	Chi-A	1	2	0	0	0	0	0	0	0	1	.000	.000	.000	-99	-0	-0	0	0			-0	/O	0.0
1917	Bos-N	2	7	1	2	0	0	0	0	0	1	.286	.286	.286	80	-0	-0	1	0			-1	/S3	0.0
1919	Cin-N	19	58	5	13	4	0	0	4	0	12	.224	.224	.293	56	-3	-3	4	0			7	3/S	0.4
1921	NY-N	4	6	2	2	0	0	0	2	1	1	.333	.429	.333	104	0	0	1	0	0	0	-0	/2S3	0.0
1926	Chi-N	10	18	2	1	1	0	0	0	0	1	.056	.056	.111	-55	-4	-4	0	0			1	/S32	-0.2
Total	5	36	91	10	18	5	0	0	6	1	16	.198	.207	.253	34	-8	-8	5	0	0		6	/3S2O	0.2

■ TED SCHREIBER
Schreiber, Theodore Henry b: 7/11/38, Brooklyn, N.Y. BR/TR, 5'11", 175 lbs. Deb: 4/14/63

1963	NY-N	39	50	1	8	0	0	0	2	4	14	.160	.236	.160	16	-5	-5	2	0	1	-1	8	3/S2	0.3

■ POP SCHRIVER
Schriver, William Frederick b: 7/11/1865, Brooklyn, N.Y. d: 12/27/32, Brooklyn, N.Y. BR/TR, 5'9.5", 172 lbs. Deb: 4/29/1886

1886	Bro-a	8	21	2	1	0	0	0			2	.048	.130	.048	-42	-3	-3	0	0			1	/OC	-0.1
1888	Phi-N	40	134	15	26	5	2	1	23	7	21	.194	.250	.284	68	-4	-5	10	2			-4	C/S3O	-0.7
1889	Phi-N	55	211	24	56	10	0	1	19	16	8	.265	.323	.327	77	-5	-8	25	5			3	C/23	-0.2
1890	Phi-N	57	223	37	61	9	6	0	35	22	15	.274	.339	.368	105	2	1	32	9			-1	C1/32O	0.2
1891	Chi-N	27	90	15	30	1	4	1	21	10	9	.333	.412	.467	159	7	7	18	1			3	C/1	1.0
1892	Chi-N	92	326	40	73	10	6	1	34	27	25	.224	.297	.301	82	-7	-7	31	4			-11	CO	-1.2
1893	Chi-N	64	229	49	65	8	3	4	34	14	9	.284	.336	.397	98	-2	-1	33	4			2	C/O	0.5
1894	Chi-N	96	349	55	96	12	3	3	47	29	21	.275	.341	.352	65	-17	-21	46	9			-2	*C/S31	-1.1
1895	NY-N	24	92	16	29	2	1	1	16	9	10	.315	.382	.391	104	1	1	15	3			-4	C/1	0.0
1897	Cin-N	61	178	29	54	12	4	1	30	19		.303	.374	.433	108	4	2	31	3			-4	C	0.4
1898	Pit-N	95	315	25	72	15	3	0	32	23		.229	.285	.295	70	-13	-12	27	0			-5	C/1	-0.9
1899	Pit-N	91	301	31	85	19	5	1	49	23		.282	.339	.389	102	1	1	42	4			6	C/1	1.0
1900	*Pit-N	37	92	12	27	7	0	1	12	10		.293	.381	.402	118	3	3	14	0			-4	C/1	0.0
1901	StL-N	53	166	17	45	7	3	1	23	12		.271	.324	.367	108	0	2	22	2			4	C1	0.8
Total	14	800	2727	367	720	117	40	16	375	223	118	.264	.328	.354	89	-33	-41	346	46			-18	C/1032S	-0.3

■ BOB SCHRODER
Schroder, Robert James b: 12/30/44, Ridgefield, N.J. BL/TR, 6', 175 lbs. Deb: 4/20/65

1965	SF-N	31	9	4	2	0	0	0	1	1	1	.222	.300	.222	48	-1	-1	1	0	0	0	10	/23	1.0
1966	SF-N	10	33	0	8	0	0	0	2	0	2	.242	.242	.242	34	-3	-3	2	0	0	0	-5	/S	-0.7
1967	SF-N	62	135	20	31	4	0	0	7	15	15	.230	.307	.259	64	-6	-6	12	1	0	0	-10	2/3	-1.3
1968	SF-N	35	44	5	7	1	1	0	2	7	3	.159	.288	.227	56	-2	-2	3	0	0	0	-3	2/S3	-0.4
Total	4	138	221	29	48	5	1	0	12	23	21	.217	.294	.249	58	-11	-11	18	1	0	0	-8	/2S3	-1.4

■ BILL SCHROEDER
Schroeder, Alfred William b: 9/7/58, Baltimore, Md. BR/TR, 6'2", 200 lbs. Deb: 7/13/83

1983	Mil-A	23	73	7	13	2	1	3	7	3	23	.178	.221	.356	60	-5	-4	6	0	1	-1	-3	C	-0.5
1984	Mil-A	61	210	29	54	6	0	14	25	8	54	.257	.291	.486	115	2	3	27	0	1	-1	-5	C/1D	0.1
1985	Mil-A	53	194	18	47	8	0	8	25	12	61	.242	.293	.407	90	-3	-3	22	0	1	-1	-8	C/1D	-0.9
1986	Mil-A	64	217	32	46	14	0	7	19	9	59	.212	.263	.373	69	-9	-10	22	1	0	0	-4	C1D	-1.2
1987	Mil-A	75	250	35	83	12	0	14	42	16	56	.332	.379	.548	138	15	14	52	5	2	0	-8	C/1D	1.1
1988	Mil-A	41	122	9	19	2	0	5	10	6	36	.156	.208	.295	39	-10	-10	6	0	0	0	5	C1/D	-0.4
1989	Cal-A	41	138	16	28	2	0	6	15	3	44	.203	.220	.348	59	-8	-8	10	0	0	0	7	C/1	0.0
1990	Cal-A	18	58	7	13	3	0	4	9	1	10	.224	.237	.483	96	-1	-1	5	0	0	0	2	C/1	0.1
Total	8	376	1262	153	303	49	1	61	152	58	343	.240	.282	.426	91	-20	-20	149	6	5	-1	-13	C/1D	-1.7

■ RICH SCHU
Schu, Rick Spencer b: 1/26/62, Philadelphia, Pa. BR/TR, 6', 170 lbs. Deb: 9/01/84

1984	Phi-N	17	29	12	8	2	1	2	5	6	6	.276	.400	.621	180	3	3	8	0	0	0	-0	3	0.3
1985	Phi-N	112	416	54	105	21	4	7	24	38	78	.252	.318	.373	90	-4	-6	49	8	6	-1	-10	*3	-1.7
1986	Phi-N	92	208	32	57	10	1	8	25	18	44	.274	.338	.447	111	4	3	32	2	2	-1	1	3	0.2
1987	Phi-N	92	196	24	46	6	3	7	23	20	36	.235	.312	.403	85	-4	-5	25	0	2	-1	-1	31	-0.8
1988	Bal-A	89	270	22	69	9	4	4	20	21	49	.256	.316	.363	92	-4	-3	30	6	4	-1	-12	3/1D	-1.5
1989	Bal-A	1	0	0	0	0	0	0	0	0	0	—	—	—	—	0	0	0	0	0	0	-0	/2	0.0
	Det-A	98	266	25	57	11	0	7	21	24	37	.214	.279	.335	74	-10	-9	24	1	2	-1	-2	3/21SD	-1.1
	Yr	99	266	25	57	11	0	7	21	24	37	.214	.279	.335	74	-10	-9	24	1	2	-1	-2		-1.1
1990	Cal-A	61	157	19	42	8	0	6	14	11	25	.268	.315	.433	107	1	1	21	0	0	0	2	31/O2	0.2
Total	7	562	1542	188	384	67	13	41	132	138	275	.249	.314	.389	93	-14	-15	189	17	16	-5	-22	3/1D2OS	-4.4

■ HEINIE SCHUBLE
Schuble, Henry George b: 11/1/06, Houston, Tex. BR/TR, 5'9", 152 lbs. Deb: 7/08/27

1927	StL-N	65	218	29	56	6	2	4	28	7	27	.257	.283	.358	69	-10	-10	21	0			-6	S	-1.0
1929	Det-A	92	258	35	60	11	7	2	28	19	23	.233	.288	.353	64	-15	-15	27	3	2	-0	-10	S/3	-1.5
1932	Det-A	102	340	58	92	20	6	5	52	24	37	.271	.319	.409	84	-7	-9	45	14	5	1	8	3S	0.5
1933	Det-A	49	96	12	21	4	1	0	6	5	17	.219	.257	.281	42	-8	-8	7	2	0	1	1	3/S2	-0.3
1934	Det-A	11	15	2	4	2	0	0	4	2	1	.267	.313	.400	83	-0	-0	2	0	0	0	0	/S32	0.0
͗35	Det-A	11	8	3	2	0	0	0	0	1	0	.250	.333	.250	55	-1	-1	1	0	0	0	1	/32	0.1
	StL-N	2	0	0	0	0	0	0	0	0	0	—	—	—	—	0	0	0	0	0	0	0	/3	0.0
	7	332	935	139	235	43	16	11	116	57	108	.251	.296	.367	70	-41	-44	103	19	7		-6	S3/2	-2.2

CHULMERICH
Schulmerich, Edward Wesley b: 8/21/01, Hillsboro, Ore. d: 6/26/85, Corvallis, Ore. BR/TR, 5'11", 210 lbs. Deb: 5/01/31

		95	327	36	101	17	7	2	43	28	30	.309	.363	.422	115	5	6	51	0			-2	O	0.0

YEAR	TM/L	G	AB	R	H	2B	3B	HR	RBI	BB	SO	AVG	OBP	SLG	PRO+	BR	/A	RC	SB	CS	SBR	FR	POS	TPR
1932	Bos-N	119	404	47	105	22	5	11	57	27	61	.260	.314	.421	99	-3	-1	55	5			2	*O	-0.5
1933	Bos-N	29	85	10	21	6	1	1	13	5	10	.247	.289	.376	97	-1	-1	10	0			1	O	0.0
	Phi-N	97	365	53	122	19	4	8	59	32	45	.334	.394	.474	130	23	17	69	1			-3	O	0.9
	Yr	126	450	63	143	25	5	9	72	37	55	.318	.375	.456	126	21	17	78	1			-2		0.9
1934	Phi-N	15	52	2	13	1	0	0	1	4	8	.250	.316	.269	51	-3	-4	4	0			-1	O	-0.4
	Cin-N	74	209	21	55	8	3	5	19	22	43	.263	.333	.402	98	-1	-1	28	1			-3	O	-0.5
	Yr	89	261	23	68	9	3	5	20	26	51	.261	.330	.375	88	-4	-4	33	1			-4		-0.9
Total	4	429	1442	169	417	73	20	27	192	118	197	.289	.347	.424	109	19	17	217	7			-6	O	-0.5

■ ART SCHULT
Schult, Arthur William "Dutch" b: 6/20/28, Brooklyn, N.Y.   BR/TR, 6'3", 210 lbs.   Deb: 5/17/53

YEAR	TM/L	G	AB	R	H	2B	3B	HR	RBI	BB	SO	AVG	OBP	SLG	PRO+	BR	/A	RC	SB	CS	SBR	FR	POS	TPR
1953	NY-A	7	0	3	0	0	0	0	0	0	0	—	—	—		0	0	0	0	0	0	0	R	0.0
1956	Cin-N	5	7	3	3	0	0	0	2	1	1	.429	.500	.429	144	1	1	2	0	0	0	0	/O	0.1
1957	Cin-N	21	34	4	9	2	0	0	4	0	2	.265	.286	.324	59	-2	-2	3	0	0	0	1	/O	-0.1
	Was-A	77	247	30	65	14	0	4	35	14	30	.263	.305	.368	84	-6	-6	26	0	1	-1	-3	1O	-1.1
1959	Chi-N	42	118	17	32	7	0	2	14	7	14	.271	.323	.381	88	-2	-2	13	0	0	0	-4	1O	-0.7
1960	Chi-N	12	15	1	2	1	0	0	1	1	3	.133	.188	.200	6	-2	-2	1	0	0	0	-0	/O	-0.2
Total	5	164	421	58	111	24	0	6	56	23	50	.264	.308	.363	81	-12	-11	44	0	1	-1	-6	/1O	-2.0

■ FRANK SCHULTE
Schulte, Frank M. "Wildfire" b: 9/17/1882, Cohocton, N.Y.   d: 10/2/49, Oakland, Cal.   BL/TR, 5'11", 170 lbs.   Deb: 9/21/04

YEAR	TM/L	G	AB	R	H	2B	3B	HR	RBI	BB	SO	AVG	OBP	SLG	PRO+	BR	/A	RC	SB	CS	SBR	FR	POS	TPR
1904	Chi-N	20	84	16	24	4	3	2	13	2		.286	.302	.476	141	3	3	13	1			0	O	0.3
1905	Chi-N	123	493	67	135	15	14	1	47	32		.274	.318	.367	102	3	0	66	16			-6	*O	-1.4
1906	*Chi-N	146	563	77	158	18	**13**	7	60	31		.281	.318	.396	118	13	10	84	25			0	O	0.8
1907	*Chi-N	97	342	44	98	14	7	2	32	22		.287	.330	.386	119	9	7	49	7			-3	O	0.0
1908	*Chi-N	102	386	42	91	20	2	1	43	29		.236	.289	.306	88	-4	-5	40	15			-6	*O	-1.3
1909	Chi-N	140	538	57	142	16	11	4	60	24		.264	.298	.357	101	-1	-2	64	23			-13	*O	-2.1
1910	*Chi-N	151	559	93	168	29	15	**10**	68	39	57	.301	.349	.460	137	22	22	97	22			-11	*O	0.6
1911	Chi-N	154	577	105	173	30	21	**21**	**107**	76	71	.300	.384	**.534**	155	41	40	127	23			-9	*O	2.6
1912	Chi-N	139	553	90	146	27	11	12	64	53	70	.264	.336	.418	106	2	3	83	17			-12	*O	-1.2
1913	Chi-N	132	497	85	138	28	6	9	68	39	68	.278	.336	.412	113	7	7	73	21			-16	*O	-1.1
1914	Chi-N	137	465	54	112	22	7	5	61	39	55	.241	.306	.351	95	-4	-3	53	16			-14	*O	-2.1
1915	Chi-N	151	550	66	137	20	6	12	62	49	68	.249	.313	.373	107	4	4	66	19	17	-5	10	*O	0.5
1916	Chi-N	72	230	31	68	11	1	5	27	20	35	.296	.352	.417	123	9	7	37	9			-2	O	0.3
	Pit-N	55	177	12	45	5	3	0	14	17	19	.254	.323	.316	96	-0	-0	29	5			-4	O	-0.6
	Yr	127	407	43	113	16	4	5	41	37	54	.278	.339	.373	111	9	6	56	14			-6		-0.3
1917	Pit-N	30	103	11	22	5	1	0	7	10	14	.214	.283	.282	71	-3	-3	9	5			-2	O	-0.6
	Phi-N	64	149	21	32	10	0	1	15	16	22	.215	.299	.302	81	-2	-3	14	4			-8	O	-1.4
	Yr	94	252	32	54	15	1	1	22	26	36	.214	.293	.294	77	-6	-7	23	9			-10		-2.0
1918	Was-A	93	267	35	77	14	3	0	44	47	36	.288	.406	.363	135	13	14	41	5			1	O	1.2
Total	15	1806	6533	906	1766	288	124	92	792	545	515	.270	.330	.395	114	113	99	937	233	17		-95	*O	-5.5

■ FRED SCHULTE
Schulte, Fred William "Fritz" (b: Fred William Schult) b: 1/13/01, Belvidere, Ill.   d: 5/20/83, Belvidere, Ill.   BR/TR, 6'1", 183 lbs.   Deb: 4/15/27

YEAR	TM/L	G	AB	R	H	2B	3B	HR	RBI	BB	SO	AVG	OBP	SLG	PRO+	BR	/A	RC	SB	CS	SBR	FR	POS	TPR
1927	StL-A	60	189	32	60	16	5	3	34	20	14	.317	.383	.503	124	7	6	34	5	3	-0	-2	O	0.1
1928	StL-A	146	556	90	159	44	6	7	85	51	60	.286	.347	.424	99	1	-2	83	6	5	-1	17	*O	0.6
1929	StL-A	121	446	63	137	24	5	3	71	59	44	.307	.389	.404	101	5	2	74	8	3	1	13	*O	1.0
1930	StL-A	113	392	59	109	23	5	5	62	41	44	.278	.348	.401	86	-6	-8	55	12	8	-1	-1	O/1	-1.3
1931	StL-A	134	553	100	168	32	7	9	65	56	49	.304	.369	.436	107	9	6	89	6	8	-3	6	*O	0.0
1932	StL-A	146	565	106	166	35	6	9	73	71	44	.294	.373	.425	100	6	1	90	5	9	-4	-5	*O/1	-1.2
1933	*Was-A	144	550	98	162	30	7	5	87	61	27	.295	.366	.402	104	3	4	81	10	12	-4	14	*O	0.8
1934	Was-A	136	524	72	156	32	6	3	73	53	34	.298	.363	.399	100	-2	1	76	3	7	-3	-3	O	-0.7
1935	Was-A	76	226	33	60	6	4	2	0	0	0	.265	.265	.354	61	-15	-14	19	0	3	-2	-3	O	-1.7
1936	Pit-N	74	238	28	62	7	3	1	17	20	20	.261	.320	.328	73	-8	-9	26	1			-0	O	-1.0
1937	Pit-N	29	20	5	2	0	0	0	3	4	3	.100	.280	.100	7	-2	-2	1	0			1	/O	-0.1
Total	11	1179	4259	686	1241	249	54	47	570	436	339	.291	.358	.408	97	-3	-14	629	56	58		35	*O/1	-3.5

■ HAM SCHULTE
Schulte, Herman Joseph (b: Herman Joseph Schultenhenrich) b: 9/1/12, St.Charles, Mo.   BR/TR, 5'8.5", 158 lbs.   Deb: 4/16/40

YEAR	TM/L	G	AB	R	H	2B	3B	HR	RBI	BB	SO	AVG	OBP	SLG	PRO+	BR	/A	RC	SB	CS	SBR	FR	POS	TPR
1940	Phi-N	120	436	44	103	18	2	1	21	32	30	.236	.288	.294	63	-23	-21	40	3			-10	*2/S	-2.2

■ JOHNNY SCHULTE
Schulte, John Clement b: 9/8/1896, Fredericktown, Mo.   d: 6/28/78, St.Louis, Mo.   BL/TR, 5'11", 190 lbs.   Deb: 4/18/23   C

YEAR	TM/L	G	AB	R	H	2B	3B	HR	RBI	BB	SO	AVG	OBP	SLG	PRO+	BR	/A	RC	SB	CS	SBR	FR	POS	TPR
1923	StL-A	7	3	1	0	0	0	0	1	4	0	.000	.571	.000	56	0	0	1	0	0	0	1	/C1	0.1
1927	StL-N	64	156	35	45	8	2	9	32	47	19	.288	.456	.538	160	17	16	41	1			3	C	2.3
1928	Phi-N	65	113	14	28	2	2	4	17	15	12	.248	.336	.407	90	-1	-2	16	0			-5	C	-0.4
1929	Chi-N	31	69	6	18	3	0	0	9	7	11	.261	.329	.304	58	-4	-4	7	0			1	C	0.0
1932	StL-A	15	24	2	5	2	0	0	3	1	6	.208	.240	.292	35	-2	-2	2	0	0	0	-1	/C	-0.2
	Bos-N	10	9	1	2	0	0	1	2	2	1	.222	.364	.556	149	1	1	2	0			1	C	0.2
Total	5	192	374	59	98	15	4	14	64	76	49	.262	.388	.436	112	10	9	68	1	0		-0	C/1	2.0

■ JACK SCHULTE
Schulte, John Herman Frank b: 11/15/1881, Cincinnati, Ohio   d: 8/17/75, Roseville, Mich.   BR/TR, 5'9", 180 lbs.   Deb: 8/19/06

YEAR	TM/L	G	AB	R	H	2B	3B	HR	RBI	BB	SO	AVG	OBP	SLG	PRO+	BR	/A	RC	SB	CS	SBR	FR	POS	TPR
1906	Bos-N	2	7	0	0	0	0	0	0	0	0	.000	.000	.000	-99	-2	-2	0	0			-1	/S	-0.2

■ LEN SCHULTE
Schulte, Leonard Bernard (b: Leonard Bernard Schultehenrich) b: 12/5/16, St.Charles, Mo.   d: 5/6/86, Orlando, Fla.   BR/TR, 5'10", 160 lbs.   Deb: 9/27/44

YEAR	TM/L	G	AB	R	H	2B	3B	HR	RBI	BB	SO	AVG	OBP	SLG	PRO+	BR	/A	RC	SB	CS	SBR	FR	POS	TPR
1944	StL-A	1	0	0	0	0	0	0	0	1	0	—	1.000	—	188	0	0	0	0	0	0	0	H	0.0
1945	StL-A	119	430	37	106	16	1	0	36	24	35	.247	.286	.288	64	-19	-21	36	0	3	-2	-8	32S	-3.0
1946	StL-A	4	5	1	2	0	0	0	2	0	0	.400	.400	.400	118	0	0	0	0	0	0	1	/23	0.1
Total	3	124	435	38	108	16	1	0	38	25	35	.248	.289	.290	65	-18	-21	37	0	3	-2	-7	/32S	-2.9

■ HOWIE SCHULTZ
Schultz, Howard Henry "Stretch" or "Steeple" b: 7/3/22, St.Paul, Minn.   BR/TR, 6'6", 200 lbs.   Deb: 8/16/43

YEAR	TM/L	G	AB	R	H	2B	3B	HR	RBI	BB	SO	AVG	OBP	SLG	PRO+	BR	/A	RC	SB	CS	SBR	FR	POS	TPR
1943	Bro-N	45	182	20	49	12	0	1	34	6	24	.269	.300	.352	88	-3	-3	18	3			2	1	-0.3
1944	Bro-N	138	526	59	134	32	3	11	83	24	67	.255	.290	.390	92	-9	-8	55	6			0	*1	-1.9
1945	Bro-N	39	142	18	34	8	2	1	19	10	14	.239	.294	.345	78	-5	-5	14	2			3	1	-0.2
1946	Bro-N	90	249	27	63	14	1	3	27	16	34	.253	.298	.353	84	-6	-6	26	2			5	1	-0.8
1947	Bro-N	2	1	0	0	0	0	0	0	0	0	.000	.000	.000	-96	-0	-0	0	0			0	/1	0.0
	Phi-N	114	403	30	90	19	1	6	35	21	70	.223	.264	.320	56	-27	-26	33	0			-1	*1	-3.2
	Yr	116	404	30	90	19	1	6	35	21	70	.223	.263	.319	56	-28	-26	32	0			-1		-3.2
1948	Phi-N	6	13	0	1	0	0	0	1	1	2	.077	.143	.077	-40	-3	-2	0	0			0	/1	-0.1
	Cin-N	36	72	9	12	0	0	2	9	4	7	.167	.211	.250	25	-8	-7	4	2			-3	1	1.0
	Yr	42	85	9	13	0	0	2	10	5	9	.153	.200	.224	15	-10	-10	4	2					
Total	6	470	1588	163	383	85	7	24	208	82	218	.241	.281	.349	75	-61	-58	150	15					

■ JOHN SCHULTZ
Schultz, John b: St.Louis, Mo.   Deb: 8/07/1891

YEAR	TM/L	G	AB	R	H	2B	3B	HR	RBI	BB	SO	AVG	OBP	SLG	PRO+	BR	/A	RC	SB
1891	StL-a	1	2	0	0	0	0	0	0	0	0	.000	.000	.000	-87	-1	-1	0	0

■ JOE SCHULTZ
Schultz, Joseph Charles Jr. "Dode" b: 8/29/18, Chicago, Ill.   BL/TR, 5'11", 180 lbs.   Deb: 9/27/39   MC

YEAR	TM/L	G	AB	R	H	2B	3B	HR	RBI	BB	SO	AVG	OBP	SLG	PRO+	BR	/A	RC	SB
1939	Pit-N	4	14	3	4	2	0	0	2	2	0	.286	.375	.429	117	0	0	2	0

YEAR	TM/L	G	AB	R	H	2B	3B	HR	RBI	BB	SO	AVG	OBP	SLG	PRO+	BR	/A	RC	SB	CS	SBR	FR	POS	TPR
1940	Pit-N	16	36	2	7	0	1	0	4	2	1	.194	.237	.250	35	-3	-3	2	0			-3	C	-0.5
1941	Pit-N	2	2	1	1	0	0	0	0	0	0	.500	.500	.500	183	0	0	1	0			0	/C	0.0
1943	StL-A	46	92	6	22	5	0	0	8	9	8	.239	.307	.293	74	-3	-3	8	0	1	-1	-5	C	-0.7
1944	StL-A	3	8	1	2	0	0	0	0	0	1	.250	.250	.250	41	-1	-1	1	0	0	0	-1	/C	0.0
1945	StL-A	41	44	1	13	2	0	0	8	3	1	.295	.340	.341	93	-3	-0	5	0	0	0	0	/C	0.0
1946	StL-A	42	57	1	22	4	0	0	14	11	2	.386	.485	.456	156	6	5	14	0	0	0	-5	C	0.2
1947	StL-A	43	38	3	7	0	0	1	1	4	5	.184	.262	.263	45	-3	-3	3	0	0	0	0	H	-0.2
1948	StL-A	43	37	0	7	0	0	0	9	6	3	.189	.302	.189	32	-3	-4	2	0	0	0	0	H	-0.2
Total	9	240	328	18	85	13	1	1	46	37	21	.259	.334	.314	81	-7	-8	38	0	1		-12	/C	-1.3

■ JOE SCHULTZ
Schultz, Joseph Charles Sr. "Germany" b: 7/24/1893, Pittsburgh, Pa. d: 4/13/41, Columbia, S.C. BR/TR, 5'11.5", 172 lbs. Deb: 9/28/12

YEAR	TM/L	G	AB	R	H	2B	3B	HR	RBI	BB	SO	AVG	OBP	SLG	PRO+	BR	/A	RC	SB	CS	SBR	FR	POS	TPR
1912	Bos-N	4	12	1	3	1	0	0	4	0	2	.250	.250	.333	58	-1	-1	1	0			-0	/2	0.0
1913	Bos-N	9	18	2	4	0	0	0	1	2	7	.222	.333	.222	59	-1	-1	2	0			0	/O2	0.0
1915	Bro-N	56	120	13	35	3	2	0	4	10	18	.292	.346	.350	109	2	1	14	3	4	-2	-4	3/S	-0.2
	Chi-N	7	8	1	2	0	0	0	3	0	2	.250	.250	.250	51	-0	-0	1	0			0	/2	0.0
	Yr	63	128	14	37	3	2	0	7	10	20	.289	.341	.344	106	1	1	15	3	4	-2	-3		-0.2
1916	Pit-N	77	204	18	53	8	2	0	22	7	14	.260	.298	.319	88	-3	-3	22	6			-14	23/OS	-1.8
1919	StL-N	88	229	24	58	9	1	2	21	11	7	.253	.287	.328	90	-5	-3	22	4			-7	O/23	-1.2
1920	StL-N	99	320	38	84	5	5	0	32	21	11	.262	.308	.309	81	-9	-8	31	5	4	-1	-4	O	-1.8
1921	StL-N	92	275	37	85	20	3	6	45	15	11	.309	.348	.469	116	5	6	44	4	3	-1	-3	O/31	0.0
1922	StL-N	112	344	50	108	13	4	2	64	19	10	.314	.350	.392	96	-5	-2	48	3	1	0	0	O	-0.4
1923	StL-N	2	7	0	2	0	0	0	1	1	0	.286	.375	.286	78	-0	-0	1	0	0	0	0	/O	0.0
1924	StL-N	12	12	0	2	0	0	0	2	3	0	.167	.333	.167	39	-1	-1	1	0	0	0	-0	/O	0.0
	Phi-N	88	284	35	80	15	1	5	29	20	18	.282	.329	.394	83	-3	-8	37	6	2	1	-4	O	-1.2
	Yr	100	296	35	82	15	1	5	31	23	18	.277	.329	.385	82	-4	-8	38	6	2	1	-5		-1.2
1925	Phi-N	24	64	10	22	6	0	0	8	4	1	.344	.382	.438	100	1	0	10	1	1	-0	0	O	0.0
	Cin-N	33	62	6	20	3	1	0	13	3	1	.323	.354	.403	95	-1	-0	9	3	1	0	-2	O/2	-0.1
	Yr	57	126	16	42	9	1	0	21	7	2	.333	.368	.421	99	0	0	19	4	2	0	-2		-0.1
Total	11	703	1959	235	558	83	19	15	249	116	102	.285	.327	.370	93	-20	-20	242	35	16		-38	O/321S	-6.7

■ JEFF SCHULZ
Schulz, Jeffrey Alan b: 6/2/61, Evansville, Ind. BL/TR, 6'1", 190 lbs. Deb: 9/02/89

YEAR	TM/L	G	AB	R	H	2B	3B	HR	RBI	BB	SO	AVG	OBP	SLG	PRO+	BR	/A	RC	SB	CS	SBR	FR	POS	TPR
1989	KC-A	7	9	0	2	0	0	0	1	0	2	.222	.222	.222	26	-1	-1	0	0	0	0	0	/O	0.0
1990	KC-A	30	66	5	17	5	1	0	6	6	13	.258	.319	.364	93	-1	-1	7	0	0	0	-1	O/D	-0.1
Total	2	37	75	5	19	5	1	0	7	6	15	.253	.309	.347	85	-2	-2	8	0	0	0	-1	/OD	-0.1

■ BILL SCHUSTER
Schuster, William Charles "Broadway Bill" b: 8/4/12, Buffalo, N.Y. d: 6/28/87, ElMonte, Cal. BR/TR, 5'9", 164 lbs. Deb: 9/29/37

YEAR	TM/L	G	AB	R	H	2B	3B	HR	RBI	BB	SO	AVG	OBP	SLG	PRO+	BR	/A	RC	SB	CS	SBR	FR	POS	TPR
1937	Pit-N	3	6	2	3	0	0	0	1	1	0	.500	.571	.500	193	1	1	2	0			1	/S	0.2
1939	Bos-N	2	3	0	0	0	0	0	0	0	1	.000	.000	.000	-99	-1	-1	0	0			-0	/S3	0.0
1943	Chi-N	13	51	3	15	2	1	0	0	3	2	.294	.333	.373	105	0	0	6	0			7	S	0.8
1944	Chi-N	60	154	14	34	7	1	1	14	12	16	.221	.277	.299	62	-8	-8	12	4			-4	S/2	-0.6
1945	*Chi-N	45	47	8	9	2	1	0	2	7	4	.191	.296	.277	61	-2	-2	4	2			8	S/23	0.8
Total	5	123	261	27	61	11	3	1	17	23	23	.234	.296	.310	72	-10	-10	23	6			12	/S23	1.2

■ RANDY SCHWARTZ
Schwartz, Douglas Randall b: 2/9/44, Los Angeles, Cal. BL/TL, 6'3", 230 lbs. Deb: 9/08/65

YEAR	TM/L	G	AB	R	H	2B	3B	HR	RBI	BB	SO	AVG	OBP	SLG	PRO+	BR	/A	RC	SB	CS	SBR	FR	POS	TPR
1965	KC-A	6	7	0	2	0	0	0	1	0	4	.286	.286	.286	64	-0	-0	1	0	0	0	1	/1	0.0
1966	KC-A	10	11	0	1	0	0	0	1	1	3	.091	.167	.091	-24	-2	-2	0	0	0	0	-0	/1	-0.1
Total	2	16	18	0	3	0	0	0	2	1	7	.167	.211	.167	10	-2	-2	1	0	0	0	0	/1	-0.1

■ BILL SCHWARTZ
Schwartz, William August "Pop" or "Scooper Bill" b: 4/3/1864, Jamestown, Ky. d: 12/22/40, Newport, Ky. BR/TR, 6'1", 195 lbs. Deb: 5/03/1883

YEAR	TM/L	G	AB	R	H	2B	3B	HR	RBI	BB	SO	AVG	OBP	SLG	PRO+	BR	/A	RC	SB	CS	SBR	FR	POS	TPR
1883	Col-a	2	4	0	1	0	0	0			0	.250	.250	.250	67	-0	0	0				-2	/1C	-0.1
1884	Cin-U	29	106	14	25	4	0	1			3	.236	.257	.302	82	-1	-3	8	0			-5	C/O3	-0.5
Total	2	31	110	14	26	4	0	1			3	.236	.257	.300	81	-1	-3	9	0			-7	/CO31	-0.6

■ BILL SCHWARTZ
Schwartz, William Charles "Blab" b: 4/22/1884, Cleveland, Ohio d: 8/29/61, Nashville, Tenn. TR , 6'2", 185 lbs. Deb: 5/02/04

YEAR	TM/L	G	AB	R	H	2B	3B	HR	RBI	BB	SO	AVG	OBP	SLG	PRO+	BR	/A	RC	SB	CS	SBR	FR	POS	TPR
1904	Cle-A	24	86	5	13	2	0	0	0	0		.151	.151	.174	4	-9	-9	3	4			-4	1/3	-1.3

■ BILL SCHWARZ
Schwarz, William De Witt b: 1/30/1891, Birmingham, Ala. d: 6/24/49, Jacksonville, Fla TR , Deb: 8/20/14

YEAR	TM/L	G	AB	R	H	2B	3B	HR	RBI	BB	SO	AVG	OBP	SLG	PRO+	BR	/A	RC	SB	CS	SBR	FR	POS	TPR
1914	NY-A	1	1	0	0	0	0	0	0	0	1	.000	.000	.000	-99	-0	-0	0	0			0	/C	0.0

■ AL SCHWEITZER
Schweitzer, Albert Caspar "Cheese" b: 12/23/1882, Cleveland, Ohio d: 1/27/69, Newark, Ohio BR/TR, 5'6", 170 lbs. Deb: 4/30/08

YEAR	TM/L	G	AB	R	H	2B	3B	HR	RBI	BB	SO	AVG	OBP	SLG	PRO+	BR	/A	RC	SB	CS	SBR	FR	POS	TPR
1908	StL-A	64	182	22	53	4	2	1	14	20		.291	.361	.352	134	7	7	26	6			5	O	1.1
1909	StL-A	27	76	7	17	2	0	0	2	5		.224	.298	.250	79	-2	-2	6	3			-3	O	-0.5
1910	StL-A	113	379	37	87	11	2	2	37	36		.230	.303	.285	90	-6	-4	40	26			-4	*O	-1.4
1911	StL-A	76	237	31	51	11	4	0	34	43		.215	.338	.295	80	-6	-5	28	12			-1	O	-1.0
Total	4	280	874	97	208	28	8	3	87	104		.238	.325	.299	95	-7	-2	100	47			-2	O	-1.8

■ PI SCHWERT
Schwert, Pius Louis b: 11/22/1892, Angola, N.Y. d: 3/11/41, Washington, D.C. BR/TR, 5'10.5", 160 lbs. Deb: 10/06/14

YEAR	TM/L	G	AB	R	H	2B	3B	HR	RBI	BB	SO	AVG	OBP	SLG	PRO+	BR	/A	RC	SB	CS	SBR	FR	POS	TPR
1914	NY-A	2	5	0	0	0	0	0	2	2	2	.000	.286	.000	-13	-1	-1	0	0			1	/C	0.0
1915	NY-A	9	18	6	5	3	0	0	6	1	6	.278	.316	.444	128	0	-0	3	0			1	/C	0.2
Total	2	11	23	6	5	3	0	0	6	3	8	.217	.308	.348	97	-0	-0	3	0			1	/C	0.2

■ ART SCHWIND
Schwind, Arthur Edwin b: 11/4/1889, Ft.Wayne, Ind. d: 1/13/68, Sullivan, Ill. BB/TR, 5'8", 150 lbs. Deb: 10/03/12

YEAR	TM/L	G	AB	R	H	2B	3B	HR	RBI	BB	SO	AVG	OBP	SLG	PRO+	BR	/A	RC	SB	CS	SBR	FR	POS	TPR
1912	Bos-N	1	2	0	1	0	0	0	0	0	0	.500	.500	.500	171	0	0	0	0			0	/3	0.0

■ JERRY SCHYPINSKI
Schypinski, Gerald Albert b: 9/16/31, Detroit, Mich. BL/TR, 5'10", 170 lbs. Deb: 8/31/55

YEAR	TM/L	G	AB	R	H	2B	3B	HR	RBI	BB	SO	AVG	OBP	SLG	PRO+	BR	/A	RC	SB	CS	SBR	FR	POS	TPR
1955	KC-A	22	69	7	15	2	0	0	5	1	6	.217	.229	.246	27	-7	-7	4	0	0	0	-2	S/2	-0.6

■ MIKE SCIOSCIA
Scioscia, Michael Lorri b: 11/27/58, Upper Darby, Pa. BL/TR, 6'2", 200 lbs. Deb: 4/20/80

YEAR	TM/L	G	AB	R	H	2B	3B	HR	RBI	BB	SO	AVG	OBP	SLG	PRO+	BR	/A	RC	SB	CS	SBR	FR	POS	TPR
1980	LA-N	54	134	8	34	5	1	1	8	12	9	.254	.315	.328	81	-4	-3	15	1	0	0	3	C	0.1
1981	*LA-N	93	290	27	80	10	0	2	29	36	18	.276	.358	.331	100	-0	1	34	0	2	-1	-2	C	0.0
1982	LA-N	129	365	31	80	11	1	5	38	44	31	.219	.305	.296	70	-15	-13	34	2	0	1	-6	*C	-1.7
1983	LA-N	12	35	3	11	3	0	1	7	5	2	.314	.400	.486	145	2	2	7	0	0	0	-3	C	0.0
1984	LA-N	114	341	29	93	18	0	5	38	52	26	.273	.371	.370	110	6	6	48	2	1	0	13	*C	2.3
1985	*LA-N	141	429	47	127	26	3	7	53	77	21	.296	.409	.420	136	22	24	78	3	3	-1	1	*C	3.0
1986	LA-N	122	374	36	94	18	1	5	26	62	23	.251	.362	.345	103	0	4	49	3	3	-1	-1	*C	0.4
1987	LA-N	142	461	44	122	26	1	6	38	55	23	.265	.342	.364	90	-7	-5	58	7	4	-0	10	*C	1.5
1988	*LA-N	130	408	29	105	18	0	3	35	38	31	.257	.321	.324	88	-7	-6	40	0	3	-2	8	*C	0.7
1989	LA-N	133	408	40	102	16	0	10	44	52	29	.250	.339	.363	102	1	2	52	0	2	-1	18	*C	2.9
1990	LA-N	135	435	46	115	25	0	12	66	55	31	.264	.351	.405	114	5	8	62	4	1	1	3	*C	1.8
Total	11	1205	3680	340	963	176	7	57	382	488	244	.262	.351	.360	102	5	20	476	22	19	-5	44	*C	11.0

■ LOU SCOFFIC
Scoffic, Louis "Weaser" b: 5/20/13, Herrin, Ill. BR/TR, 5'10", 182 lbs. Deb: 4/16/36

YEAR	TM/L	G	AB	R	H	2B	3B	HR	RBI	BB	SO	AVG	OBP	SLG	PRO+	BR	/A	RC	SB	CS	SBR	FR	POS	TPR
	StL-N	4	7	2	3	0	0	0	2	1	2	.429	.500	.429	153	1	1	2	0			0	/O	0.1

■ DARYL SCONIERS
Sconiers, Daryl Anthony b: 10/3/58, San Bernardino, Cal. BL/TL, 6'2", 185 lbs. Deb: 9/13/81

YEAR	TM/L	G	AB	R	H	2B	3B	HR	RBI	BB	SO	AVG	OBP	SLG	PRO+	BR	/A	RC	SB	CS	SBR	FR	POS	TPR
		15	52	6	14	1	1	1	7	1	10	.269	.283	.385	91	-1	-1	6	0	0	0	1	1/D	0.0

YEAR	TM/L	G	AB	R	H	2B	3B	HR	RBI	BB	SO	AVG	OBP	SLG	PRO+	BR	/A	RC	SB	CS	SBR	FR	POS	TPR
1982	Cal-A	12	13	0	2	0	0	0	2	2	1	.154	.267	.154	19	-1	-1	0	0	0	0	0	/1D	0.0
1983	Cal-A	106	314	49	86	19	3	8	46	17	41	.274	.311	.430	102	-0	0	39	4	2	0	-5	1D/O	-0.6
1984	Cal-A	57	160	14	39	4	0	4	17	13	17	.244	.301	.344	78	-5	-5	15	1	2	-1	-1	1/D	-0.8
1985	Cal-A	44	98	14	28	6	1	2	12	15	18	.286	.381	.429	122	3	3	17	2	1	0	-1	D/1	0.2
Total	5	234	637	83	169	30	5	15	84	48	87	.265	.317	.399	97	-4	-3	77	7	5	-1	-5	1/DO	-1.2

■ SCOTT
Scott Deb: 7/16/1884

YEAR	TM/L	G	AB	R	H	2B	3B	HR	RBI	BB	SO	AVG	OBP	SLG	PRO+	BR	/A	RC	SB	CS	SBR	FR	POS	TPR
1884	Bal-U	13	53	10	12	1	1	1		2		.226	.255	.340	90	-0	-1	5	0			-2	O/3	-0.2

■ TONY SCOTT
Scott, Anthony b: 9/18/51, Cincinnati, Ohio BB/TR, 6', 164 lbs. Deb: 9/01/73

YEAR	TM/L	G	AB	R	H	2B	3B	HR	RBI	BB	SO	AVG	OBP	SLG	PRO+	BR	/A	RC	SB	CS	SBR	FR	POS	TPR
1973	Mon-N	11	1	2	0	0	0	0	0	0	1	.000	.000	.000	-97	-0	-0	0	0	0	0	1	/O	0.0
1974	Mon-N	19	7	2	2	0	0	0	1	1	3	.286	.375	.286	82	-0	-0	1	1	1	-0	1	O	0.0
1975	Mon-N	92	143	19	26	4	2	0	11	12	38	.182	.259	.238	37	-12	-13	8	5	6	-2	7	O	-1.0
1977	StL-N	95	292	38	85	16	3	3	41	33	48	.291	.369	.397	107	3	4	42	13	10	-2	9	O	0.8
1978	StL-N	96	219	28	50	5	2	1	14	14	41	.228	.281	.283	59	-12	-12	16	5	6	-2	-2	O	-1.9
1979	StL-N	153	587	69	152	22	10	6	68	34	92	.259	.305	.361	80	-16	-17	62	37	17	1	10	*O	-0.9
1980	StL-N	143	415	51	104	19	3	0	28	35	68	.251	.310	.311	72	-14	-16	40	22	10	1	-8	*O	-2.9
1981	StL-N	45	176	21	40	5	2	2	17	5	22	.227	.253	.313	58	-10	-10	12	10	7	-1	4	O	-0.8
	*Hou-N	55	225	28	66	13	2	2	22	15	32	.293	.338	.396	113	2	3	31	8	3	1	-1	O	0.1
	Yr	100	401	49	106	18	4	4	39	20	54	.264	.301	.359	88	-8	-7	43	18	10	-1	3		-0.7
1982	Hou-N	132	460	43	110	16	3	1	29	15	56	.239	.265	.293	61	-27	-23	35	18	4	3	-9	*O	-3.2
1983	Hou-N	80	186	20	42	6	1	2	17	11	39	.226	.269	.301	62	-11	-9	16	5	4	-1	-1	O	-1.2
1984	Hou-N	25	21	2	4	1	0	0	0	4	3	.190	.320	.238	63	-1	-1	2	0	0	0	1	/O	0.0
	Mon-N	45	71	8	18	4	0	0	5	7	21	.254	.321	.310	81	-2	-2	7	1	1	-0	-1	O	-0.2
	Yr	70	92	10	22	5	0	0	5	11	24	.239	.320	.293	78	-3	-2	9	1	1	-0	0		-0.2
Total	11	991	2803	331	699	111	28	17	253	186	464	.249	.300	.327	75	-100	-96	272	125	69	-4	12	O	-11.2

■ DONNIE SCOTT
Scott, Donald Malcolm b: 8/16/61, Dunedin, Fla. BB/TR, 5'11", 185 lbs. Deb: 9/30/83

YEAR	TM/L	G	AB	R	H	2B	3B	HR	RBI	BB	SO	AVG	OBP	SLG	PRO+	BR	/A	RC	SB	CS	SBR	FR	POS	TPR
1983	Tex-A	2	4	0	0	0	0	0	0	0	0	.000	.000	.000	-99	-1	-1	0	0	0	0	1	/C	0.0
1984	Tex-A	81	235	16	52	9	0	3	20	20	44	.221	.282	.298	59	-12	-13	20	0	1	-1	7	C	-0.1
1985	Sea-A	80	185	18	41	13	0	4	23	15	41	.222	.280	.357	72	-7	-7	19	1	1	-0	-6	C	-0.9
Total	3	163	424	34	93	22	0	7	43	35	85	.219	.279	.321	63	-21	-22	38	1	2	-1	2	C	-1.0

■ PETE SCOTT
Scott, Floyd John b: 12/21/1898, Woodland, Cal. d: 5/3/53, Daly City, Cal. BR/TR, 5'11.5", 175 lbs. Deb: 4/13/26

YEAR	TM/L	G	AB	R	H	2B	3B	HR	RBI	BB	SO	AVG	OBP	SLG	PRO+	BR	/A	RC	SB	CS	SBR	FR	POS	TPR
1926	Chi-N	77	189	34	54	13	1	3	34	22	31	.286	.363	.413	107	3	2	29	3			4	O/3	0.4
1927	Chi-N	71	156	28	49	18	1	0	21	19	18	.314	.392	.442	123	6	6	27	1			-2	O	0.2
1928	Pit-N	60	177	33	55	10	4	5	33	18	14	.311	.378	.497	122	7	6	33	1			3	O/1	0.6
Total	3	208	522	95	158	41	6	8	88	59	63	.303	.377	.450	117	15	13	88	5			5	O/13	1.2

■ GEORGE SCOTT
Scott, George Charles "Boomer" b: 3/23/44, Greenville, Miss. BR/TR, 6'2", 200 lbs. Deb: 4/12/66

YEAR	TM/L	G	AB	R	H	2B	3B	HR	RBI	BB	SO	AVG	OBP	SLG	PRO+	BR	/A	RC	SB	CS	SBR	FR	POS	TPR
1966	Bos-A	162	601	73	147	18	7	27	90	65	152	.245	.326	.433	105	12	5	81	4	0	1	5	*1/3	0.6
1967	*Bos-A	159	565	74	171	21	7	19	82	63	119	.303	.377	.465	136	34	29	97	10	8	-2	-4	*1/3	1.2
1968	Bos-A	124	350	23	60	14	0	3	25	26	88	.171	.239	.237	42	-23	-26	18	3	5	-2	2	*1/3	-3.5
1969	Bos-A	152	549	63	139	14	5	16	52	61	74	.253	.332	.384	95	-0	-4	69	4	3	-1	-5	*31	-1.2
1970	Bos-A	127	480	50	142	24	5	16	63	44	95	.296	.357	.467	117	16	12	74	4	11	-5	-8	31	-0.4
1971	Bos-A	146	537	72	141	16	4	24	78	41	102	.263	.321	.441	106	8	4	69	0	3	-2	-7	*1	-1.2
1972	Mil-A	152	578	71	154	24	4	20	88	43	130	.266	.322	.426	123	13	14	76	16	4	2	-5	*13	-0.1
1973	Mil-A	158	604	98	185	30	4	24	107	61	94	.306	.372	.488	144	32	33	106	9	5	-0	7	*1/D	3.0
1974	Mil-A	158	604	74	170	36	2	17	82	59	90	.281	.348	.432	124	18	18	84	9	9	-3	8	*1/D	1.7
1975	Mil-A	158	617	86	176	26	4	**36**	**109**	51	97	.285	.343	.515	139	29	29	99	6	5	-1	3	*1D/3	2.2
1976	Mil-A	156	606	73	166	21	5	18	77	53	118	.274	.337	.414	122	14	15	82	0	1	-1	-2	*1	0.5
1977	Bos-A	157	584	103	157	26	5	33	95	57	112	.269	.340	.500	112	19	10	93	1	1	-0	0	*1	0.1
1978	Bos-A	120	412	51	96	16	4	12	54	44	86	.233	.307	.379	83	-5	-10	44	1	1	-0	-8	*1/D	-2.4
1979	Bos-A	45	156	18	35	9	1	4	23	17	22	.224	.301	.372	76	-5	-6	14	0	0	0	-2	1	-0.9
	KC-A	44	146	19	39	8	2	1	20	12	32	.267	.331	.370	87	-2	-3	15	1	1	-0	-4	1/3D	-0.8
	NY-A	16	44	9	14	3	1	1	6	2	7	.318	.348	.500	128	1	2	8	1	0	0	0	D/1	0.2
	Yr	105	346	46	88	20	4	6	49	31	61	.254	.319	.387	87	-5	-7	37	2	1	0	-6		-1.5
Total	14	2034	7433	957	1992	306	60	271	1051	699	1418	.268	.335	.435	113	161	123	1027	69	57	-14	-21	*13/D	-1.0

■ JIM SCOTT
Scott, James Walter b: 9/22/1888, Shenandoah, Pa. d: 5/12/72, S.Pasadena, Fla. BR/TR, 5'9.5", 165 lbs. Deb: 4/22/14

YEAR	TM/L	G	AB	R	H	2B	3B	HR	RBI	BB	SO	AVG	OBP	SLG	PRO+	BR	/A	RC	SB	CS	SBR	FR	POS	TPR
1914	Pit-F	8	24	2	6	1	0	0	1	5	0	.250	.379	.292	95	0	0	3	1			-3	/S	-0.1

■ JOHN SCOTT
Scott, John Henry b: 1/24/52, Jackson, Miss. BR/TR, 6'2", 165 lbs. Deb: 9/07/74

YEAR	TM/L	G	AB	R	H	2B	3B	HR	RBI	BB	SO	AVG	OBP	SLG	PRO+	BR	/A	RC	SB	CS	SBR	FR	POS	TPR
1974	SD-N	14	15	3	1	0	0	0	0	0	4	.067	.067	.067	-65	-3	-3	0	1	0	0	1	/O	-0.1
1975	SD-N	25	9	6	0	0	0	0	0	0	2	.000	.000	.000	-99	-2	-2	0	2	0	1	0	/O	-0.1
1977	Tor-A	79	233	26	56	9	0	2	15	8	39	.240	.266	.305	54	-15	-15	17	10	8	-2	-1	O/D	-1.9
Total	3	118	257	35	57	9	0	2	15	8	45	.222	.245	.280	43	-20	-21	17	13	8	-1	1	/OD	-2.1

■ LE GRANT SCOTT
Scott, Le Grant Edward b: 7/25/10, Cleveland, Ohio BL/TL, 5'8.5", 170 lbs. Deb: 4/19/39

YEAR	TM/L	G	AB	R	H	2B	3B	HR	RBI	BB	SO	AVG	OBP	SLG	PRO+	BR	/A	RC	SB	CS	SBR	FR	POS	TPR
1939	Phi-N	76	232	31	65	15	1	1	26	22	14	.280	.343	.366	93	-3	-2	29	5			-1	O	-0.3

■ EVERETT SCOTT
Scott, Lewis Everett "Deacon" b: 11/19/1892, Bluffton, Ind. d: 11/2/60, Fort Wayne, Ind. BR/TR, 5'8", 148 lbs. Deb: 4/14/14

YEAR	TM/L	G	AB	R	H	2B	3B	HR	RBI	BB	SO	AVG	OBP	SLG	PRO+	BR	/A	RC	SB	CS	SBR	FR	POS	TPR
1914	Bos-A	144	539	66	129	15	6	2	37	32	43	.239	.286	.301	76	-17	-17	48	9	14	-6	-10	*S	-2.1
1915	*Bos-A	100	359	25	72	11	0	0	28	17	21	.201	.237	.231	41	-27	-26	22	4	7	-3	4	*S	-1.6
1916	*Bos-A	123	366	37	85	19	2	0	27	23	24	.232	.283	.295	73	-13	-13	37	8			7	*S/23	0.4
1917	Bos-A	157	528	40	127	24	7	0	50	20	46	.241	.268	.313	78	-17	-16	49	12			8	*S	-0.2
1918	*Bos-A	126	443	40	98	11	5	0	43	12	16	.221	.242	.269	55	-26	-26	32	11			18	*S	0.0
1919	Bos-A	138	507	41	141	19	0	0	38	19	26	.278	.306	.316	79	-18	-14	50	8			7	*S	0.4
1920	Bos-A	154	569	41	153	21	12	4	61	21	15	.269	.300	.369	80	-21	-18	60	4	11	-5	17	*S	0.7
1921	Bos-A	154	576	65	151	21	9	1	62	27	21	.262	.295	.335	62	-35	-33	55	5	9	-4	**38**	*S	1.9
1922	*NY-A	154	557	64	150	23	5	3	45	23	22	.269	.304	.345	67	-26	-28	59	2	3	-1	19	*S	0.7
1923	*NY-A	152	533	48	131	16	4	6	60	13	19	.246	.266	.325	54	-37	-38	45	1	3	-2	-10	*S	-3.3
1924	NY-A	153	548	56	137	12	6	4	64	21	15	.250	.278	.316	53	-40	-40	47	3	7	-3	10	*S	-1.6
1925	NY-A	22	60	3	13	0	0	0	4	2	7	.217	.242	.217	17	-8	-7	3	0	1	-1	3	S	-0.1
	Was-A	33	103	10	28	6	1	0	18	4	4	.272	.299	.350	65	-6	-6	10	1	2	-1	3	S/3	0.1
	Yr	55	163	13	41	6	1	0	22	6	6	.252	.278	.301	48	-13	-13	13	1	3	-2	6		0.0
1926	Chi-A	40	143	15	36	10	1	0	13	9	8	.252	.296	.350	67	-8	-7	14	1	3	-2	5	S	0.0
	Cin-N	1	4	0	1	0	0	0	1	0	0	.667	.667	.667	267	1	1	2	0					0.0
Total	13	1654	5837	552	1455	208	58	20	551	243	282	.249	.281	.315	65	-297	-287	532	69	60				

■ MILT SCOTT
Scott, Milton Parker "Mikado Milt" b: 1/17/1866, Chicago, Ill. d: 11/3/38, Baltimore, Md. 5'9", 160 lbs. Deb: 9/30/1882

YEAR	TM/L	G	AB	R	H	2B	3B	HR	RBI	BB	SO	AVG	OBP	SLG	PRO+	BR	/A	RC
1882	Chi-N	1	5	1	2	0	0	0	0	0	0	.400	.400	.400	151	0	0	1
1884	Det-N	110	438	29	108	17	5	3	50	9	62	.247	.262	.329	90	-8	-4	39
1885	Det-N	38	148	14	39	7	0	0	12	4	16	.264	.283	.311	92	-1	-2	13
	Pit-a	55	210	15	52	7	1	0		5		.248	.272	.290	81	-5	-4	17

YEAR	TM/L	G	AB	R	H	2B	3B	HR	RBI	BB	SO	AVG	OBP	SLG	PRO+	BR	/A	RC	SB	CS	SBR	FR	POS	TPR
1886	Bal-a	137	484	48	92	11	4	2		22		.190	.239	.242	53	-26	-24	31	11			8	*1/P	-1.9
Total	4	341	1285	107	293	42	10	5	62	40	78	.228	.257	.288	75	-40	-34	101	11			12	1/P	-4.2

■ **DICK SCOTT**   Scott, Richard Edward b: 7/19/62, Ellsworth, Maine BR/TR, 6'1", 170 lbs. Deb: 5/19/89

YEAR	TM/L	G	AB	R	H	2B	3B	HR	RBI	BB	SO	AVG	OBP	SLG	PRO+	BR	/A	RC	SB	CS	SBR	FR	POS	TPR
1989	Oak-A	3	2	0	0	0	0	0	1	0	0	.000	.000	.000	-99	-1	-1	0	0	0	0	0	/S	0.0

■ **ROD SCOTT**   Scott, Rodney Darrell b: 10/16/53, Indianapolis, Ind. BB/TR, 6', 160 lbs. Deb: 4/11/75

YEAR	TM/L	G	AB	R	H	2B	3B	HR	RBI	BB	SO	AVG	OBP	SLG	PRO+	BR	/A	RC	SB	CS	SBR	FR	POS	TPR
1975	KC-A	48	15	13	1	0	0	0	0	1	3	.067	.125	.067	-43	-3	-3	0	4	2	0	6	D/2SR	0.4
1976	Mon-N	7	10	3	4	0	0	0	0	1	1	.400	.455	.400	138	1	1	2	2	0	1	0	/2S	0.2
1977	Oak-A	133	364	56	95	4	4	0	20	43	50	.261	.344	.294	77	-10	-10	41	33	18	-1	-30	2S/3OD	-2.6
1978	Chi-N	78	227	41	64	5	1	0	15	43	41	.282	.403	.313	91	4	0	35	27	10	2	-8	3O/2S	-0.5
1979	Mon-N	151	562	69	134	12	5	3	42	66	82	.238	.321	.294	69	-23	-22	61	39	12	5	-15	*2S	-2.1
1980	Mon-N	154	567	84	127	13	13	0	46	70	75	.224	.310	.293	69	-22	-22	60	63	13	11	-16	*2S	-1.7
1981	*Mon-N	95	336	43	69	9	3	0	26	50	35	.205	.310	.250	60	-16	-16	32	30	7	5	-15	2	-2.1
1982	Mon-N	14	25	2	5	0	0	0	1	3	2	.200	.286	.200	37	-2	-2	2	5	0	2	-1	2	0.0
	NY-A	10	26	5	5	0	0	0	0	4	2	.192	.300	.192	39	-2	-2	2	2	0	1	1	/S2	0.0
Total	8	690	2132	316	504	43	26	3	150	281	291	.236	.328	.285	71	-73	-76	235	205	62	24	-79	2S/3DO	-8.4

■ **JIM SCRANTON**   Scranton, James Dean b: 4/5/60, Torrance, Cal. BR/TR, 6', 175 lbs. Deb: 9/05/84

YEAR	TM/L	G	AB	R	H	2B	3B	HR	RBI	BB	SO	AVG	OBP	SLG	PRO+	BR	/A	RC	SB	CS	SBR	FR	POS	TPR
1984	KC-A	2	2	0	0	0	0	0	0	0	0	.000	.000	.000	-99	-1	-1	0	0	0	0	-0	/S3	0.0
1985	KC-A	6	4	1	0	0	0	0	0	0	0	.000	.000	.000	-99	-1	-1	0	0	0	0	2	/S	0.1
Total	2	8	6	1	0	0	0	0	0	0	0	.000	.000	.000	-99	-2	-2	0	0	0	0	2	/S3	0.1

■ **CHUCK SCRIVENER**   Scrivener, Wayne Allison b: 10/3/47, Alexandria, Va. BR/TR, 5'9", 170 lbs. Deb: 9/18/75

YEAR	TM/L	G	AB	R	H	2B	3B	HR	RBI	BB	SO	AVG	OBP	SLG	PRO+	BR	/A	RC	SB	CS	SBR	FR	POS	TPR
1975	Det-A	4	16	0	4	1	0	0	0	0	1	.250	.250	.313	56	-1	-1	1	1	0	0	-2	/3S	-0.2
1976	Det-A	80	222	28	49	7	1	2	16	19	34	.221	.282	.288	65	-9	-10	19	1	0	0	6	2S/3	0.1
1977	Det-A	61	72	10	6	0	0	0	2	5	9	.083	.143	.083	-35	-14	-14	1	0	0	0	9	S/23	0.2
Total	3	145	310	38	59	8	1	2	18	24	44	.190	.249	.242	40	-24	-25	22	2	0	1	13	/S23	0.1

■ **KEN SEARS**   Sears, Kenneth Eugene "Ziggy" b: 7/6/17, Streator, Ill. d: 7/17/68, Bridgeport, Tex. BL/TR, 6'1", 200 lbs. Deb: 5/02/43

YEAR	TM/L	G	AB	R	H	2B	3B	HR	RBI	BB	SO	AVG	OBP	SLG	PRO+	BR	/A	RC	SB	CS	SBR	FR	POS	TPR
1943	NY-A	60	187	22	52	7	0	2	22	11	18	.278	.328	.348	97	-1	-1	21	1	3	-2	1	C	0.1
1946	StL-A	7	15	1	5	0	0	0	1	3	0	.333	.444	.333	114	1	1	2	0	0	0	-3	/C	-0.1
Total	2	67	202	23	57	7	0	2	23	14	18	.282	.338	.347	99	-0	-0	23	1	3	-2	-1	/C	0.0

■ **JIMMY SEBRING**   Sebring, James Dennison b: 3/22/1882, Liberty, Pa. d: 12/22/09, Williamsport, Pa. BL/TR, 6', 180 lbs. Deb: 9/08/02

YEAR	TM/L	G	AB	R	H	2B	3B	HR	RBI	BB	SO	AVG	OBP	SLG	PRO+	BR	/A	RC	SB	CS	SBR	FR	POS	TPR
1902	Pit-N	19	80	15	26	4	4	0	15	5		.325	.365	.475	156	5	5	15	2			4	O	0.7
1903	*Pit-N	124	506	71	140	16	13	4	64	32		.277	.320	.383	99	-0	-2	71	20			7	*O	-0.1
1904	Pit-N	80	305	28	82	11	7	0	32	17		.269	.307	.351	102	1	0	36	8			9	O	0.6
	Cin-N	56	222	22	50	9	2	0	24	14		.225	.271	.284	67	-7	-7	20	8			4	O	-0.7
	Yr	136	527	50	132	20	9	0	56	31		.250	.292	.323	87	-6	-9	56	16			12		-0.1
1905	Cin-N	58	217	31	62	10	5	2	28	14		.286	.329	.406	109	5	2	34	11			-6	O	-0.8
1909	Bro-N	25	81	11	8	1	1	0	5	11		.099	.207	.136	7	-9	-8	3	3			-2	O	-1.2
	Was-A	1	0	0	0	0	0	0	0	0		—	—	—	—	0	0	0	0			-0	/O	0.0
Total	5	363	1411	178	368	51	32	6	168	93		.261	.307	.355	94	-4	-13	179	52			14	O	-1.5

■ **FRANK SECORY**   Secory, Frank Edward b: 8/24/12, Mason City, Iowa BR/TR, 6'1", 200 lbs. Deb: 4/28/40 U

YEAR	TM/L	G	AB	R	H	2B	3B	HR	RBI	BB	SO	AVG	OBP	SLG	PRO+	BR	/A	RC	SB	CS	SBR	FR	POS	TPR
1940	Det-A	1	1	0	0	0	0	0	0	0	1	.000	.000	.000	-91	-0	-0	0	0	0	0	0	H	0.0
1942	Cin-N	2	5	1	0	0	0	0	1	3	2	.000	.375	.000	14	-0	-0	0	0			0	/O	0.0
1944	Chi-N	22	56	10	18	1	0	4	17	6	8	.321	.387	.554	163	4	4	13	1			1	O	0.4
1945	*Chi-N	35	57	4	9	1	0	0	6	2	7	.158	.186	.175	1	-8	-7	2	0			-1	O	-0.8
1946	Chi-N	33	43	6	10	3	0	3	12	6	6	.233	.327	.512	139	2	2	7	0			-1	/O	0.0
Total	5	93	162	21	37	5	0	3	36	17	24	.228	.302	.389	95	-2	-2	22	1	0		-1	/O	-0.4

■ **CHARLIE SEE**   See, Charles Henry "Chad" b: 10/13/1896, Pleasantville, N.Y. d: 7/19/48, Bridgeport, Conn. BL/TR, 5'10.5", 175 lbs. Deb: 8/06/19

YEAR	TM/L	G	AB	R	H	2B	3B	HR	RBI	BB	SO	AVG	OBP	SLG	PRO+	BR	/A	RC	SB	CS	SBR	FR	POS	TPR
1919	Cin-N	8	14	1	4	0	0	0	1	1	0	.286	.333	.286	89	-0	-0	1	0			-1	/O	0.0
1920	Cin-N	47	82	9	25	4	0	0	15	1	7	.305	.329	.354	97	-0	-0	9	2	4	-2	4	O/P	0.1
1921	Cin-N	37	106	11	26	5	1	1	7	7	5	.245	.298	.340	72	-5	-4	11	3	2	-0	0	O	-0.5
Total	3	92	202	21	55	9	1	1	23	9	12	.272	.313	.342	83	-6	-5	21	5	6		3	/OP	-0.4

■ **LARRY SEE**   See, Ralph Laurence b: 6/20/60, Norwalk, Cal. BR/TR, 6'1", 195 lbs. Deb: 9/03/86

YEAR	TM/L	G	AB	R	H	2B	3B	HR	RBI	BB	SO	AVG	OBP	SLG	PRO+	BR	/A	RC	SB	CS	SBR	FR	POS	TPR
1986	LA-N	13	20	1	5	2	0	0	2	0	7	.250	.318	.350	90	-0	-0	2	0	0	0	1	/1	0.0
1988	Tex-A	13	23	0	3	0	0	0	0	1	8	.130	.167	.130	-15	-4	-4	1	0	0	0	0	/C1/3D	-0.3
Total	2	26	43	1	8	2	0	0	2	3	15	.186	.239	.233	32	-4	-4	3	0	0	0	1	/1DC3	-0.3

■ **BOB SEEDS**   Seeds, Robert Ira "Suitcase Bob" b: 2/24/07, Ringgold, Tex. BR/TR, 6', 180 lbs. Deb: 4/19/30

YEAR	TM/L	G	AB	R	H	2B	3B	HR	RBI	BB	SO	AVG	OBP	SLG	PRO+	BR	/A	RC	SB	CS	SBR	FR	POS	TPR
1930	Cle-A	85	277	37	79	11	3	3	32	12	22	.285	.315	.379	72	-11	-12	32	1	3	-2	2	O	-1.3
1931	Cle-A	48	134	26	41	4	1	1	10	11	11	.306	.359	.373	88	-1	-2	18	1	0	0	-2	O/1	-0.5
1932	Cle-A	2	4	0	0	0	0	0	0	0	0	.000	.000	.000	-94	-1	-1	0	0	0	0	0	/O	0.0
	Chi-A	116	434	53	126	18	6	2	45	31	37	.290	.342	.373	91	-9	-5	55	5	7	-3	-3	*O	-1.4
	Yr	118	438	53	126	18	6	2	45	31	37	.288	.339	.370	89	-11	-7	54	5	7	-3	-3		-1.4
1933	Bos-A	82	230	26	56	13	4	0	23	21	20	.243	.310	.335	71	-10	-9	24	1	3	-2	0	1O	-1.3
1934	Bos-A	8	6	0	1	0	0	0	1	0	1	.167	.167	.167	-13	-1	-1	0	0	0	0	0	/O	0.0
	Cle-A	61	186	28	46	8	1	0	18	21	13	.247	.327	.301	62	-10	-10	20	2	1	0	-4	O	-1.3
	Yr	69	192	28	47	8	1	0	19	21	14	.245	.322	.297	59	-11	-12	20	2	1	0	-4		-1.3
1936	*NY-A	13	42	12	11	1	0	4	10	5	3	.262	.340	.571	126	1	1	8	3	1	0	1	/O3	0.2
1938	NY-N	81	296	35	86	12	3	9	52	20	33	.291	.338	.443	112	4	4	44	0			-3	O	0.0
1939	NY-N	63	173	33	46	5	1	5	26	22	31	.266	.352	.426	99	0	0	25	1			-5	O	-0.4
1940	NY-N	56	155	18	45	5	2	4	16	17	19	.290	.371	.426	118	4	4	25	0			-3	O	0.0
Total	9	615	1937	268	537	77	21	28	233	160	190	.277	.336	.382	89	-33	-32	251	14	15		-16	O/13	-6.0

■ **PAT SEEREY**   Seerey, James Patrick b: 3/17/23, Wilburton, Okla. d: 4/28/86, Jennings, Mo. BR/TR, 5'10", 200 lbs. Deb: 6/09/43

YEAR	TM/L	G	AB	R	H	2B	3B	HR	RBI	BB	SO	AVG	OBP	SLG	PRO+	BR	/A	RC	SB	CS	SBR	FR	POS	TPR
1943	Cle-A	26	72	8	16	3	0	1	5	4	19	.222	.263	.306	70	-3	-3	5	0	0	0	1	O	-0.1
1944	Cle-A	101	342	39	80	16	0	15	39	19	99	.234	.276	.412	99	-4	-3	36	0	2	-1	4	O	-0.2
1945	Cle-A	126	414	56	98	22	2	14	56	66	97	.237	.342	.401	120	8	10	60	1	2	-1	-7	*O	-0.2
1946	Cle-A	117	404	57	91	17	2	26	62	65	101	.225	.334	.470	131	11	15	64	2	3	-1	-11	*O	-0.3
1947	Cle-A	82	216	24	37	4	1	11	29	34	66	.171	.284	.352	78	-8	-7	22	0	1	-1	-2	O	-1.2
1948	Cle-A	10	23	7	6	0	0	1	6	7	8	.261	.433	.391	123	1	1	4	0	0	0	-2	/O	0.0
	Chi-A	95	340	44	78	11	0	18	64	61	94	.229	.347	.421	107	1	3	53	0	0	0	1	O	0.0
	Yr	105	363	51	84	11	0	19	70	68	102	.231	.353	.419	108	2	4	57	0	0	0	-1		0.0
1949	Chi-A	4	4	1	0	0	0	0	0	1	4	.000	.429	.000	19	-0	-0	0	0	0	0	-0	/O	0.0
Total	7	561	1815	236	406	73	5	86	261	259	485	.224	.321	.412	109	6	16	246	3	8	-4	-16	O	-2.0

■ **EMMETT SEERY**   Seery, John Emmett b: 2/13/1861, Princeville, Ill. BL/TR, Deb: 4/17/1884

YEAR	TM/L	G	AB	R	H	2B	3B	HR	RBI	BB	SO	AVG	OBP	SLG	PRO+	BR	/A	RC	SB	CS	SBR	FR	POS	TPR
	Bal-U	105	463	113	144	25	7	2		20		.311	.340	.408	137	24	17	66	0			7	*O/C3	1.9
	?-U	1	4	2	2	1	0	0		1		.500	.600	.750	407	1	1	2	0			-0	/O	0.1
		106	467	115	146	26	7	2		21		.313	.342	.411	139	25	18	67	0			7		2.0

YEAR	TM/L	G	AB	R	H	2B	3B	HR	RBI	BB	SO	AVG	OBP	SLG	PRO+	BR	/A	RC	SB	CS	SBR	FR	POS	TPR
1885	StL-N	59	216	20	35	7	0	1	14	16	37	.162	.220	.208	42	-14	-12	10				5	O/3	-0.7
1886	StL-N	126	453	73	108	22	6	2	48	57	82	.238	.324	.327	105	1	5	57	24			-3	*O/P	0.4
1887	Ind-N	122	465	104	104	18	15	4	28	71	68	.224	.331	.353	95	-3	-0	72	48			6	*O/S	0.6
1888	Ind-N	133	500	87	110	20	10	5	50	64	73	.220	.316	.330	106	7	6	79	80			9	*O/S	1.3
1889	Ind-N	127	526	123	165	26	12	8	59	67	59	.314	.401	.454	138	30	28	106	19			0	*O	2.0
1890	Bro-P	104	394	78	88	12	7	1	50	70	36	.223	.348	.297	70	-12	-16	57	44			7	*O	-1.0
1891	Cin-a	97	372	77	106	15	10	4	36	81	52	.285	.423	.411	131	25	19	75	19			3	*O	1.5
1892	Lou-N	42	154	18	31	6	1	0	15	24	19	.201	.309	.253	78	-4	-2	14	6			3	O	0.0
Total	9	916	3547	695	893	152	68	27	300	471	426	.252	.345	.356	108	55	45	538	240			37	O/3CSP	6.1

■ KAL SEGRIST
Segrist, Kal Hill   b: 4/14/31, Greenville, Tex.   BR/TR, 6', 180 lbs.   Deb: 7/16/52

YEAR	TM/L	G	AB	R	H	2B	3B	HR	RBI	BB	SO	AVG	OBP	SLG	PRO+	BR	/A	RC	SB	CS	SBR	FR	POS	TPR
1952	NY-A	13	23	3	1	0	0	0	1	3	1	.043	.154	.043	-46	-4	-4	0	0	0	0	0	2/3	-0.3
1955	Bal-A	7	9	1	3	0	0	0	0	2	0	.333	.455	.333	123	0	0	1	0	0	0	0	/312	0.1
Total	2	20	32	4	4	0	0	0	1	5	1	.125	.243	.125	4	-4	-4	2	0	0	0	1	/231	-0.2

■ DAVID SEGUI
Segui, David Vincent   b: 7/19/66, Kansas City, Kan.   BB/TL, 6'1", 170 lbs.   Deb: 5/08/90

YEAR	TM/L	G	AB	R	H	2B	3B	HR	RBI	BB	SO	AVG	OBP	SLG	PRO+	BR	/A	RC	SB	CS	SBR	FR	POS	TPR
1990	Bal-A	40	123	14	30	7	0	2	15	11	15	.244	.311	.350	86	-3	-2	10	0	0	0	1	1/D	-0.3

■ KURT SEIBERT
Seibert, Kurt Elliott   b: 10/16/55, Cheverly, Md.   BB/TR, 6', 165 lbs.   Deb: 9/03/79

YEAR	TM/L	G	AB	R	H	2B	3B	HR	RBI	BB	SO	AVG	OBP	SLG	PRO+	BR	/A	RC	SB	CS	SBR	FR	POS	TPR
1979	Chi-N	7	2	2	0	0	0	0	0	0	1	.000	.000	.000	-91	-1	-1	0	0	0	0	2	/2	0.2

■ SOCKS SEIBOLD
Seibold, Harry   b: 4/3/1896, Philadelphia, Pa.   d: 9/21/65, Philadelphia, Pa.   BR/TR, 5'8.5", 162 lbs.   Deb: 9/18/15

YEAR	TM/L	G	AB	R	H	2B	3B	HR	RBI	BB	SO	AVG	OBP	SLG	PRO+	BR	/A	RC	SB	CS	SBR	FR	POS	TPR
1915	Phi-A	10	26	3	3	1	0	0	2	4	4	.115	.233	.154	16	-3	-3	1	0			-4	/S	-0.5
1916	Phi-A	5	12	0	2	1	0	0	1	0	4	.167	.167	.250	26	-1	-1	1	0			2	/PO	0.0
1917	Phi-A	36	59	6	13	1	1	0	5	4	8	.220	.281	.271	70	-2	-2	5	1			-1	P/O	0.0
1919	Phi-A	15	13	1	2	0	0	0	1	0	4	.154	.154	.154	-13	-2	-2	0	0			0	P	0.0
1929	Bos-N	33	70	6	20	2	0	0	9	6	6	.286	.342	.314	66	-4	-3	8	0			-1	P	0.0
1930	Bos-N	36	90	6	19	2	0	1	5	6	6	.211	.260	.267	29	-11	-10	6	0			-3	P	0.0
1931	Bos-N	33	70	3	9	0	0	0	2	1	9	.129	.141	.129	-28	-12	-12	2	0			0	P	0.0
1932	Bos-N	28	46	2	7	0	0	0	2	2	0	.152	.188	.152	-8	-7	-7	1	0			2	P	0.0
1933	Bos-N	11	9	0	1	0	0	0	0	2	2	.111	.273	.111	14	-1	-1	0	0			0	P	0.0
Total	9	207	395	27	76	7	1	1	27	25	43	.192	.242	.223	25	-43	-41	24	1			-4	P/SO	-0.5

■ RICKY SEILHEIMER
Seilheimer, Ricky Allen   b: 8/30/60, Brenham, Tex.   BL/TR, 5'11", 185 lbs.   Deb: 7/05/80

YEAR	TM/L	G	AB	R	H	2B	3B	HR	RBI	BB	SO	AVG	OBP	SLG	PRO+	BR	/A	RC	SB	CS	SBR	FR	POS	TPR
1980	Chi-A	21	52	4	11	3	1	1	3	4	15	.212	.268	.365	72	-2	-2	5	1	0	0	-3	C	-0.3

■ KEVIN SEITZER
Seitzer, Kevin Lee   b: 3/26/62, Springfield, Ill.   BR/TR, 5'11", 180 lbs.   Deb: 9/03/86

YEAR	TM/L	G	AB	R	H	2B	3B	HR	RBI	BB	SO	AVG	OBP	SLG	PRO+	BR	/A	RC	SB	CS	SBR	FR	POS	TPR
1986	KC-A	28	96	16	31	4	1	2	11	19	14	.323	.440	.448	140	7	7	21	0	0	0	1	1/O3	0.5
1987	KC-A	161	641	105	207	33	8	15	83	80	85	.323	.400	.470	126	29	27	120	12	7	-1	8	*31/OD	2.9
1988	KC-A	149	559	90	170	32	5	5	60	72	64	.304	.389	.406	122	20	19	89	10	8	-2	3	*3/OD	2.1
1989	KC-A	160	597	78	168	17	2	4	48	102	76	.281	.391	.337	107	11	11	85	17	8	0	-9	*3/SO1	0.3
1990	KC-A	158	622	91	171	31	5	6	38	67	66	.275	.347	.370	103	2	3	82	7	5	-1	-9	*32	-0.3
Total	5	656	2515	380	747	117	21	32	240	340	305	.297	.384	.398	116	69	68	397	46	28	-3	-6	3/102SD	5.5

■ KIP SELBACH
Selbach, Albert Karl   b: 3/24/1872, Columbus, Ohio   d: 2/17/56, Columbus, Ohio   BR/TR, 5'7", 190 lbs.   Deb: 4/24/1894

YEAR	TM/L	G	AB	R	H	2B	3B	HR	RBI	BB	SO	AVG	OBP	SLG	PRO+	BR	/A	RC	SB	CS	SBR	FR	POS	TPR
1894	Was-N	97	372	69	114	21	17	7	71	51	20	.306	.390	.511	121	10	12	84	21			-9	OS	0.0
1895	Was-N	129	516	115	166	21	22	6	55	69	28	.322	.403	.483	132	23	25	116	31			16	*O/S2	2.5
1896	Was-N	127	487	100	148	17	13	5	100	76	28	.304	.405	.423	121	18	18	106	49			7	*O	1.3
1897	Was-N	124	486	113	152	25	16	5	59	80		.313	.414	.461	134	26	26	115	46			13	*O	2.5
1898	Was-N	132	515	88	156	28	11	3	60	64		.303	.383	.417	133	23	23	94	25			20	*O/S	3.2
1899	Cin-N	140	521	104	154	27	11	3	87	70		.296	.384	.407	118	16	15	98	38			17	*O	2.0
1900	NY-N	141	523	98	176	29	12	4	68	72		.337	.420	.461	153	35	39	119	36			10	*O	3.3
1901	NY-N	125	502	89	145	29	6	1	56	45		.289	.347	.376	116	8	11	71	8			-9	*O	-1.1
1902	Bal-A	128	503	86	161	27	9	3	60	58		.320	.394	.427	124	22	18	97	22			9	*O	1.9
1903	Was-A	140	533	68	134	23	12	3	49	41		.251	.305	.356	98	-0	-1	67	20			-3	*O/3	-1.3
1904	Was-A	48	178	15	49	8	4	0	14	24		.275	.361	.365	135	7	8	28	9			3	O	0.9
	Bos-A	98	376	50	97	19	8	0	30	48		.258	.342	.351	115	11	8	51	10			1	O	0.4
	Yr	146	554	65	146	27	12	0	44	72		.264	.348	.356	121	18	16	78	19			4		1.3
1905	Bos-A	121	418	54	103	16	6	4	47	67		.246	.351	.342	121	13	13	57	12			-1	*O	0.7
1906	Bos-A	60	228	15	48	9	2	0	23	18		.211	.268	.268	70	-8	-8	19	7			1	O	-0.9
Total	13	1610	6158	1064	1803	299	149	44	779	783	76	.293	.375	.411	123	204	206	1122	334			75	*O/S23	15.4

■ GEORGE SELKIRK
Selkirk, George Alexander "Twinkletoes"
b: 1/4/08, Huntsville, Ont., Canada   d: 1/19/87, Ft.Lauderdale, Fla   BL/TR, 6'1", 182 lbs.   Deb: 8/12/34

YEAR	TM/L	G	AB	R	H	2B	3B	HR	RBI	BB	SO	AVG	OBP	SLG	PRO+	BR	/A	RC	SB	CS	SBR	FR	POS	TPR
1934	NY-A	46	176	23	55	7	1	5	38	15	17	.313	.370	.449	118	2	4	29	1	1	-0	-0	O	0.3
1935	NY-A	128	491	64	153	29	12	11	94	44	36	.312	.372	.487	128	14	17	87	2	7	-4	2	*O	1.4
1936	*NY-A	137	493	93	152	28	9	18	107	94	60	.308	.420	.511	133	24	27	111	13	7	-0	1	*O	2.1
1937	*NY-A	78	256	49	84	13	5	18	68	34	24	.328	.411	.629	157	22	22	68	8	2	1	0	O	2.0
1938	*NY-A	99	335	58	85	12	5	10	62	68	52	.254	.384	.409	99	1	1	58	9	4	0	-3	O	-0.1
1939	*NY-A	128	418	103	128	17	4	21	101	103	49	.306	.452	.517	149	35	36	110	12	5	1	-5	*O	2.5
1940	NY-A	118	379	68	102	17	5	19	71	84	43	.269	.406	.491	137	20	22	83	3	6	-3	-3	*O	0.8
1941	*NY-A	70	164	30	36	5	0	6	25	28	30	.220	.340	.360	86	-3	-3	22	1	0	-0	-0	O	-0.5
1942	*NY-A	42	78	15	15	3	0	0	10	16	8	.192	.330	.231	60	-4	-3	7	0	0	0	-1	O	-0.5
Total	9	846	2790	503	810	131	41	108	576	486	319	.290	.400	.483	128	111	124	575	49	32	-5	-9	O	8.0

■ RUBE SELLERS
Sellers, Oliver   b: 3/7/1881, Duquesne, Pa.   d: 1/14/52, Pittsburgh, Pa.   BR/TR, 5'10", 180 lbs.   Deb: 8/12/10

YEAR	TM/L	G	AB	R	H	2B	3B	HR	RBI	BB	SO	AVG	OBP	SLG	PRO+	BR	/A	RC	SB	CS	SBR	FR	POS	TPR
1910	Bos-N	12	32	3	5	0	0	0	2	6	5	.156	.289	.156	29	-3	-3	2	1			-2	/O	-0.5

■ FRANK SELMAN
Selman, Frank C. (a.k.a. Frank C. Williams 1871-75)   b: Baltimore, Md.   Deb: 5/04/1871

YEAR	TM/L	G	AB	R	H	2B	3B	HR	RBI	BB	SO	AVG	OBP	SLG	PRO+	BR	/A	RC	SB	CS	SBR	FR	POS	TPR
1871	Kek-n	14	65	14	15	3	0	1	10	4	0	.231	.275	.323	70	-2	-3	6	1				3/CS	-0.2
1872	Oly-n	9	41	3	10	3	0	0		1		.244	.262	.317	81	-1	-1	3					/C3	0.0
1873	Mar-n	1	4	1	1	0	0	0		0		.250	.250	.250	62	-0	-0	0					/P	0.0
1874	Bal-n	12	54	9	16	4	1	0		0		.296	.296	.407	122	1	1	7					/SCO	0.1
1875	Was-n	1	3	0	1	0	0	0		0		.333	.333	.333	136	0	0	0					/1	0.0
Total	5 n	37	167	27	43	10	1	1		5		.257	.279	.347	89	-2	-2	17					/3CS10P	-0.1

■ CAREY SELPH
Selph, Carey Isom   b: 12/5/01, Donaldson, Ark.   d: 2/24/76, Houston, Tex.   BR/TR, 5'9.5", 175 lbs.   Deb: 5/25/29

YEAR	TM/L	G	AB	R	H	2B	3B	HR	RBI	BB	SO	AVG	OBP	SLG	PRO+	BR	/A	RC	SB	CS	SBR	FR	POS	TPR
1929	StL-N	25	51	8	12	1	1	0	7	6	4	.235	.316	.294	52	-4	-4	5	1			-5	2	-0.7
1932	Chi-A	116	396	50	112	19	8	0	51	31	9	.283	.341	.371	90	-9	-5	50	7	6	-2	-6	32	-0.5
Total	2	141	447	58	124	20	9	0	58	37	13	.277	.338	.362	85	-13	-9	55	8	6		-11	/32	-1.2

■ MIKE SEMBER
Sember, Michael David   b: 2/24/53, Hammond, Ind.   BR/TR, 6', 185 lbs.   Deb: 8/18/77

YEAR	TM/L	G	AB	R	H	2B	3B	HR	RBI	BB	SO	AVG	OBP	SLG	PRO+	BR	/A	RC	SB	CS	SBR	FR	POS	TPR
1977	Chi-N	3	4	0	1	0	0	0	0	0	2	.250	.250	.250	31	-0	-0	0	0	0	0	1	/2	0.0
1978	Chi-N	9	3	2	1	0	0	0	0	1	1	.333	.500	.333	122	0	0	1	0	0	0	1	/3S	0.1
Total	2	12	7	2	2	0	0	0	0	1	3	.286	.375	.286	74	-0	-0	1	0	0	0	1	/3S2	0.1

YEAR	TM/L	G	AB	R	H	2B	3B	HR	RBI	BB	SO	AVG	OBP	SLG	PRO+	BR	/A	RC	SB	CS	SBR	FR	POS	TPR

■ ANDY SEMINICK Seminick, Andrew Wasil b: 9/12/20, Pierce, W.Va. BR/TR, 5'11", 187 lbs. Deb: 9/14/43 C

1943	Phi-N	22	72	9	13	2	0	2	5	7	22	.181	.253	.292	60	-4	-4	5	0			1	C/O	-0.2
1944	Phi-N	22	63	9	14	2	1	0	4	6	17	.222	.300	.286	68	-3	-3	5	2			1	C/O	-0.1
1945	Phi-N	80	188	18	45	7	2	6	26	18	38	.239	.313	.394	98	-2	-1	23	3			0	C/3O	0.1
1946	Phi-N	124	406	55	107	15	5	12	52	39	86	.264	.334	.414	115	5	6	52	2			-6	*C	0.4
1947	Phi-N	111	337	48	85	16	2	13	50	58	69	.252	.370	.427	115	6	8	56	4			9	*C	1.9
1948	Phi-N	125	391	49	88	11	3	13	44	58	68	.225	.328	.368	90	-6	-5	49	4			7	*C	1.0
1949	Phi-N	109	334	52	81	11	2	24	68	69	74	.243	.380	.503	138	17	19	67	0			7	C	2.8
1950	*Phi-N	130	393	55	113	15	3	24	68	68	50	.288	.400	.524	143	25	26	84	0			4	*C	3.2
1951	Phi-N	101	291	42	66	8	1	11	37	63	67	.227	.370	.375	102	2	3	46	1	0	0	-3	C	0.1
1952	Cin-N	108	336	38	86	16	1	14	50	35	65	.256	.330	.435	111	4	4	48	1	3	-2	-4	*C	0.5
1953	Cin-N	119	387	46	91	12	0	19	64	49	82	.235	.323	.413	90	-6	-6	53	2	2	-1	-6	*C	-0.5
1954	Cin-N	86	247	25	58	9	4	7	30	48	39	.235	.364	.389	93	-0	-1	37	0	0	-1	3	C	0.4
1955	Cin-N	6	15	1	2	0	0	1	1	0	3	.133	.133	.333	18	-2	-2	1	0	0	0	2	/C	0.0
	Phi-N	93	289	32	71	12	1	11	34	32	59	.246	.333	.408	97	-2	-1	39	1	2	-1	10	C	1.1
	Yr	99	304	33	73	12	1	12	35	32	62	.240	.325	.405	93	-4	-3	39	1	2	-1	12		1.1
1956	Phi-N	60	161	16	32	3	1	7	23	31	38	.199	.332	.360	88	-3	-2	19	3	0	1	-8	C	-0.8
1957	Phi-N	8	11	0	1	0	0	0	0	0	2	.091	.167	.091	-29	-2	-2	0	0	0	0	1	/C	0.0
Total	15	1304	3921	495	953	139	26	164	556	582	780	.243	.347	.417	107	31	39	584	23	7		16	*C/O3	9.4

■ SONNY SENERCHIA Senerchia, Emanuel Robert b: 4/6/31, Newark, N.J. BR/TR, 6'1", 195 lbs. Deb: 8/22/52

| 1952 | Pit-N | 29 | 100 | 5 | 22 | 5 | 0 | 3 | 11 | 4 | 21 | .220 | .250 | .360 | 66 | -5 | -5 | 8 | 0 | 3 | -2 | -8 | 3 | -1.4 |

■ COUNT SENSENDERFER Sensenderfer, John Phillips Jenkins b: 12/28/1847, Philadelphia, Pa. d: 5/3/03, Philadelphia, Pa. 5'9", 170 lbs. Deb: 5/20/1871

1871	Ath-n	25	127	38	41	5	2	0	23	0	1	.323	.323	.394	106	1	1	18	5				*O	0.1
1872	Ath-n	1	5	2	2	0	0	0		0		.400	.400	.400	146	0	0	1					/O	0.0
1873	Ath-n	19	85	12	23	1	0	0		0		.271	.271	.282	59	-4	-5	7					O	-0.2
1874	Ath-n	5	16	3	3	0	0	0		0		.188	.188	.188	18	-1	-2	1					/O	0.0
Total	4 n	50	233	55	69	6	2	0	n	0		.296	.296	.339	83	-4	-6	26					/O	-0.1

■ PAUL SENTELL Sentell, Leopold Theodore b: 8/27/1879, New Orleans, La. d: 4/27/23, Cincinnati, Ohio TR, 5'9", 176 lbs. Deb: 4/12/06 U

1906	Phi-N	63	192	19	44	5	1	1	14	14		.229	.282	.281	77	-5	-5	21	15			-9	32/OS	-1.6
1907	Phi-N	3	3	0	0	0	0	0	0	0	1	.000	.250	.000	-20	-0	-0	0	0			-2	/SO	-0.2
Total	2	66	195	19	44	5	1	1	14	15		.226	.281	.277	76	-5	-5	21	15			-10	/32SO	-1.8

■ TED SEPKOWSKI Sepkowski, Theodore Walter (b: Theodore Walter Sczepkowski) b: 11/9/23, Baltimore, Md. BL/TR, 5'11", 190 lbs. Deb: 9/09/42

1942	Cle-A	5	10	1	1	0	0	0	0	0	3	.100	.100	.100	-46	-2	-2	0	0	0	0	0	/2	0.0
1946	Cle-A	2	8	2	4	1	0	0	1	0	0	.500	.500	.625	228	1	1	3	0	0	0	-0	/3	0.1
1947	Cle-A	10	8	0	1	1	0	0	0	1	1	.125	.222	.250	32	-1	-1	1	0	0	0	0	/O	0.0
	NY-A	2	0	1	0	0	0	0	0	0	0	—	—	—	—	0	0	0	0	1	-1	0	R	0.0
	Yr	12	8	1	1	1	0	0	0	1	1	.125	.222	.250	32	-1	-1	1	0	1	-1	0	/O	0.0
Total	3	19	26	3	6	2	0	0	1	1	4	.231	.259	.308	61	-2	-2	3	0	1	-1	0	/32O	0.1

■ BILL SERENA Serena, William Robert b: 10/2/24, Alameda, Cal. BR/TR, 5'9.5", 175 lbs. Deb: 9/16/49

1949	Chi-N	12	37	3	8	3	0	1	7	7	9	.216	.341	.378	95	-0	-0	5	0			-4	3	-0.3
1950	Chi-N	127	435	56	104	20	4	17	61	65	75	.239	.339	.421	100	-1	-0	64	1			-2	*3	-0.1
1951	Chi-N	13	39	8	13	3	1	1	4	11	4	.333	.490	.538	173	5	5	11	0	2	-1	-4	3	0.0
1952	Chi-N	122	390	49	107	21	5	15	61	39	83	.274	.345	.469	122	12	11	62	1	0	0	-1	32	1.4
1953	Chi-N	93	275	30	69	10	5	10	52	41	46	.251	.350	.433	100	1	0	43	0	0	0	-15	23	-1.2
1954	Chi-N	41	63	8	10	0	1	4	13	14	18	.159	.321	.381	81	-2	-2	8	0	0	0	-3	3/2	-0.4
Total	6	408	1239	154	311	57	16	48	198	177	235	.251	.348	.439	108	15	14	193	2	2		-29	32	-0.6

■ PAUL SERNA Serna, Paul David b: 11/16/58, ElCentro, Cal. BR/TR, 5'8", 170 lbs. Deb: 9/01/81

1981	Sea-A	30	94	11	24	2	0	4	9	3	11	.255	.293	.404	95	-0	-1	11	2	3	-1	-3	S/2	-0.2
1982	Sea-A	65	169	15	38	3	0	3	8	4	13	.225	.247	.296	47	-12	-13	10	0	5	-3	6	S23/D	-0.5
Total	2	95	263	26	62	5	0	7	17	7	24	.236	.264	.335	64	-13	-14	21	2	8	-4	3	/S23D	-0.7

■ WALTER SESSI Sessi, Walter Anthony "Watsie" b: 7/23/18, Finleyville, Pa. BL/TL, 6'3", 225 lbs. Deb: 9/18/41

1941	StL-N	5	13	2	0	0	0	0	0	1	2	.000	.071	.000	-74	-3	-3	0	0			-1	/O	-0.4
1946	StL-N	15	14	2	2	0	0	1	2	1	4	.143	.200	.357	54	-1	-1	1	0			0	H	0.0
Total	2	20	27	4	2	0	0	1	2	2	6	.074	.138	.185	-9	-4	-4	1	0			-1	/O	-0.4

■ JOHN SEVCIK Sevcik, John Joseph b: 7/11/42, Oak Park, Ill. BR/TR, 6'2", 205 lbs. Deb: 4/24/65

| 1965 | Min-A | 12 | 16 | 1 | 1 | 1 | 0 | 0 | 0 | 1 | 5 | .063 | .118 | .125 | -30 | -3 | -3 | 0 | 0 | 0 | 0 | 3 | C | 0.1 |

■ HANK SEVEREID Severeid, Henry Levai b: 6/1/1891, Story City, Iowa d: 12/17/68, San Antonio, Tex. BR/TR, 6', 175 lbs. Deb: 5/15/11

1911	Cin-N	37	56	5	17	6	1	0	10	3	6	.304	.350	.446	127	1	2	8	0			-3	C	0.1
1912	Cin-N	50	114	10	27	0	3	0	13	8	11	.237	.287	.289	60	-7	-6	10	0			-8	C/1O	-1.2
1913	Cin-N	8	6	0	0	0	0	0	0	1	1	.000	.143	.000	-58	-1	-1	0	0			-0	/CO	-0.1
1915	StL-A	80	203	12	45	6	1	1	22	16	25	.222	.279	.276	68	-9	-8	16	2	1	0	-10	C	-1.3
1916	StL-A	100	293	23	80	8	2	0	34	26	17	.273	.341	.314	102	-1	1	33	3			-16	C/13	-1.2
1917	StL-A	143	501	45	133	23	4	1	57	28	20	.265	.306	.333	99	-5	-3	51	6			-19	*C/1	-1.1
1918	StL-A	51	133	8	34	4	0	0	11	18	4	.256	.357	.286	97	-0	0	14	4			-5	C	0.0
1919	StL-A	112	351	16	87	12	2	0	36	21	13	.248	.298	.293	65	-16	-17	30	2			-5	*C	-1.6
1920	StL-A	123	422	46	117	14	5	2	49	33	11	.277	.336	.348	79	-11	-13	51	5	3	-0	2	*C	0.0
1921	StL-A	143	472	66	153	23	7	2	78	42	9	.324	.379	.415	97	2	-2	76	7	2	1	-4	*C	0.0
1922	StL-A	137	517	49	166	32	7	3	78	28	12	.321	.356	.427	100	2	-1	77	1	4	-2	6	*C	0.7
1923	StL-A	122	432	50	133	27	6	3	51	31	11	.308	.350	.419	98	-1	-2	66	0	3	0	8	*C	1.5
1924	StL-A	137	432	37	133	23	2	4	48	36	15	.308	.362	.398	90	-3	-7	62	1	6	-3	-3	*C	-0.4
1925	StL-A	34	109	15	40	9	0	1	21	11	2	.367	.425	.477	122	5	4	22	0	2	-1	-0	*C	0.4
	*Was-A	50	110	11	39	8	1	0	14	13	6	.355	.423	.445	123	4	4	21	0	0	0	3	C	0.8
	Yr	84	219	26	79	17	1	1	35	24	8	.361	.424	.461	123	9	9	43	0	2	-1	2		1.2
1926	Was-A	22	34	2	7	1	0	0	4	3	2	.206	.270	.235	33	-3	-3	2	0	0	0	2	C	0.0
	*NY-A	41	127	13	34	8	1	0	13	13	4	.268	.336	.346	79	-4	-4	15	1	1	-0	-3	C	-0.4
	Yr	63	161	15	41	9	1	0	17	16	6	.255	.322	.323	70	-7	-7	17	1	1	-0	-2		-0.4
Total	15	1390	4312	408	1245	204	42	17	539	331	169	.289	.342	.367	91	-44	-55	556	35	19		-54	*C/1O3	-3.8

■ RICH SEVERSON Severson, Richard Allen b: 1/18/45, Artesia, Cal. BR/TR, 6', 174 lbs. Deb: 4/10/70

1970	KC-A	77	240	22	60	11	1	1	22	16	33	.250	.300	.317	70	-10	-10	23	0	0	0	1	S2	-0.1
1971	KC-A	16	30	4	9	0	2	0	1	3	5	.300	.364	.433	126	1	1	5	0	0	0	6	/2S3	0.8
Total	2	93	270	26	69	11	3	1	23	19	38	.256	.307	.330	76	-9	-9	28	0	0	0	7	/S23	0.7

■ ED SEWARD Seward, Edward William (b: Edward William Sourhardt) b: 6/29/1867, Cleveland, Ohio d: 7/30/47, Cleveland, Ohio TR, 5'7", 175 lbs. Deb: 9/30/1885 U

| 1885 | Pro-N | 1 | 3 | 0 | 0 | 0 | 0 | 0 | 0 | 0 | 2 | .000 | .000 | .000 | -99 | -1 | -1 | 0 | | | | 1 | /P | 0.0 |

YEAR	TM/L	G	AB	R	H	2B	3B	HR	RBI	BB	SO	AVG	OBP	SLG	PRO+	BR	/A	RC	SB	CS	SBR	FR	POS	TPR
1887	Phi-a	74	266	31	50	10	0	5		16		.188	.239	.282	47	-19	-19	22	14			-2	PO	0.0
1888	Phi-a	64	225	27	32	3	3	2	14	18		.142	.215	.209	39	-15	-15	13	12			3	P/O	0.0
1889	Phi-a	46	143	22	31	5	3	2	17	22	19	.217	.333	.336	94	-1	-1	18	6			-3	P/O2	0.0
1890	Phi-a	26	72	7	10	4	0	0		8		.139	.244	.194	32	-6	-6	4	3			-2	P/O	0.0
1891	Cle-N	7	19	2	4	2	0	0	1	3	4	.211	.318	.316	83	-0	-0	2	0			-2	/OP1	-0.1
Total	6	218	728	89	127	24	6	9	32	67	25	.174	.253	.261	53	-42	-41	60	35			-6	P/O12	-0.1

■ GEORGE SEWARD
Seward, George E.   b: St.Louis, Mo.   5'7.5", 145 lbs.   Deb: 5/19/1875

YEAR	TM/L	G	AB	R	H	2B	3B	HR	RBI	BB	SO	AVG	OBP	SLG	PRO+	BR	/A	RC	SB	CS	SBR	FR	POS	TPR
1875	StL-n	25	97	13	24	2	0	0		1		.247	.255	.268	89	-2	-0	7					C/O2	0.0
1876	NY-N	1	3	0	0	0	0	0	0	0	0	.000	.000	.000	-99	-1	-1	0				1	/2	0.0
1882	StL-a	38	144	23	31	1	1	0		12		.215	.276	.236	71	-3	-4	10				-1	O/C	-0.4
Total	2	39	147	23	31	1	1	0	0	12	0	.211	.270	.231	68	-4	-5	10				0	/OC2	-0.4

■ LUKE SEWELL
Sewell, James Luther   b: 1/5/01, Titus, Ala.   d: 5/14/87, Akron, Ohio   BR/TR, 5'9", 160 lbs.   Deb: 6/30/21   MC

YEAR	TM/L	G	AB	R	H	2B	3B	HR	RBI	BB	SO	AVG	OBP	SLG	PRO+	BR	/A	RC	SB	CS	SBR	FR	POS	TPR
1921	Cle-A	3	6	0	0	0	0	0	1	0	3	.000	.000	.000	-99	-2	-2	0	0	0	0	1	/C	0.0
1922	Cle-A	41	87	14	23	5	0	0	10	5	8	.264	.312	.322	65	-4	-4	9	1	1	-0	0	C	-0.2
1923	Cle-A	10	10	2	2	0	1	0	1	1	0	.200	.273	.400	76	-0	-0	1	0	0	0	1	/C	0.1
1924	Cle-A	63	165	27	48	9	1	0	17	22	13	.291	.387	.358	92	-1	-1	25	1	0	0	5	C	0.7
1925	Cle-A	74	220	30	51	10	2	0	18	33	18	.232	.337	.295	61	-12	-12	25	6	1	1	7	C/O	0.0
1926	Cle-A	126	433	41	103	16	4	0	46	36	27	.238	.302	.293	55	-28	-29	42	9	3	1	1	*C	-1.7
1927	Cle-A	128	470	52	138	27	6	0	53	20	23	.294	.328	.377	82	-13	-13	54	4	8	-4	-2	*C	-1.2
1928	Cle-A	122	411	52	111	16	9	3	52	26	27	.270	.318	.375	81	-12	-12	49	3	4	-2	14	*C	0.7
1929	Cle-A	124	406	41	96	16	3	1	39	29	26	.236	.287	.298	49	-30	-32	36	6	6	-2	5	*C	-1.6
1930	Cle-A	76	292	40	75	21	2	1	43	14	9	.257	.293	.353	61	-17	-19	30	5	2	0	-2	C	-1.2
1931	Cle-A	108	375	45	103	30	4	1	53	36	17	.275	.341	.384	86	-5	-8	51	1	1	-0	-8	*C	-0.7
1932	Cle-A	87	300	36	76	20	2	2	52	38	24	.253	.337	.353	74	-9	-12	37	4	5	-2	3	C	-0.5
1933	*Was-A	141	474	65	125	30	4	2	61	48	24	.264	.335	.357	84	-11	-10	60	7	2	1	-7	*C	-0.8
1934	Was-A	72	207	21	49	7	3	2	21	22	10	.237	.313	.329	68	-11	-10	22	0	1	-1	-1	C/O123	-0.6
1935	Chi-A	118	421	52	120	19	3	2	67	32	18	.285	.336	.359	78	-13	-14	51	3	2	-0	6	*C	-0.4
1936	Chi-A	128	451	59	113	20	5	5	73	54	16	.251	.332	.350	66	-23	-25	56	11	2	2	12	*C	0.0
1937	Chi-A	122	412	51	111	21	6	1	61	46	18	.269	.343	.357	77	-14	-14	51	4	5	-2	6	*C	-0.1
1938	Chi-A	65	211	23	45	4	1	0	27	20	20	.213	.284	.242	32	-22	-22	16	0	0	0	7	C	-1.2
1939	Cle-A	16	20	1	3	1	0	0	1	3	1	.150	.261	.200	20	-2	-2	1	0	0	0	-1	C/1	-0.1
1942	StL-A	6	12	1	1	0	0	0	0	1	5	.083	.154	.083	-32	-2	-2	0	0	0	0	1	/CM	-0.1
Total	20	1630	5383	653	1393	272	56	20	696	486	307	.259	.323	.341	70	-231	-246	616	65	43	-6	48	*C/0132	-8.8

■ JOE SEWELL
Sewell, Joseph Wheeler   b: 10/9/1898, Titus, Ala.   d: 3/6/90, Mobile, Ala.   BL/TR, 5'6.5", 155 lbs.   Deb: 9/10/20   CH

YEAR	TM/L	G	AB	R	H	2B	3B	HR	RBI	BB	SO	AVG	OBP	SLG	PRO+	BR	/A	RC	SB	CS	SBR	FR	POS	TPR
1920	*Cle-A	22	70	14	23	4	1	0	12	9	4	.329	.412	.414	116	2	2	13	1	0	0	3	S	0.7
1921	Cle-A	154	572	101	182	36	12	4	93	80	17	.318	.412	.444	117	19	18	109	7	6	-2	-3	*S	3.0
1922	Cle-A	153	558	80	167	28	7	2	83	73	20	.299	.386	.385	101	4	3	86	10	12	-4	15	*S2	2.9
1923	Cle-A	153	553	98	195	41	10	3	109	98	12	.353	.456	.479	147	43	43	128	9	6	-1	5	*S	5.9
1924	Cle-A	153	594	99	188	45	5	4	106	67	13	.316	.388	.429	109	10	9	102	3	2	-0	21	*S	4.2
1925	Cle-A	155	608	78	204	37	7	1	98	64	4	.336	.402	.424	109	11	10	106	7	6	-2	16	*S/2	4.4
1926	Cle-A	154	578	91	187	41	5	4	85	65	6	.324	.399	.433	116	16	15	104	17	7	1	3	*S	2.9
1927	Cle-A	153	569	83	180	48	5	1	92	51	7	.316	.382	.424	108	8	7	85	3	16	-9	6	*S	1.6
1928	Cle-A	155	588	79	190	40	2	4	70	58	9	.323	.391	.418	111	12	12	100	7	1	2	27	*S3	5.1
1929	Cle-A	152	578	90	182	38	3	7	73	48	4	.315	.372	.427	102	5	2	93	6	6	-2	15	*3	2.2
1930	Cle-A	109	353	44	102	17	6	0	48	42	3	.289	.374	.371	86	-4	-6	51	1	4	-2	0	3	-0.3
1931	NY-A	130	484	102	146	22	1	6	64	61	8	.302	.390	.388	111	6	10	78	1	1	-0	-2	*3/2	1.4
1932	*NY-A	125	503	95	137	21	3	11	68	56	3	.272	.349	.392	96	-6	-2	71	0	2	-1	2	*3	0.6
1933	NY-A	135	524	87	143	18	1	2	54	71	4	.273	.361	.323	87	-11	-6	65	2	2	-1	3	*3	0.6
Total	14	1903	7132	1141	2226	436	68	49	1055	843	114	.312	.391	.413	109	116	117	1193	74	71	-20	110	*S3/2	35.2

■ TOMMY SEWELL
Sewell, Thomas Wesley   b: 4/16/06, Titus, Ala.   d: 7/30/56, Montgomery, Ala.   BL/TR, 5'7.5", 155 lbs.   Deb: 6/21/27

YEAR	TM/L	G	AB	R	H	2B	3B	HR	RBI	BB	SO	AVG	OBP	SLG	PRO+	BR	/A	RC	SB	CS	SBR	FR	POS	TPR
1927	Chi-N	1	1	0	0	0	0	0	0	0	0	.000	.000	.000	-99	-0	-0	0	0			0	H	0.0

■ JIMMY SEXTON
Sexton, Jimmy Dale   b: 12/15/51, Mobile, Ala.   BR/TR, 5'10", 175 lbs.   Deb: 9/02/77

YEAR	TM/L	G	AB	R	H	2B	3B	HR	RBI	BB	SO	AVG	OBP	SLG	PRO+	BR	/A	RC	SB	CS	SBR	FR	POS	TPR
1977	Sea-A	14	37	5	8	1	1	1	3	2	6	.216	.256	.378	71	-2	-2	3	1	1	-0	3	S	0.2
1978	Hou-N	88	141	17	29	3	2	2	6	13	28	.206	.273	.298	64	-8	-7	14	16	2	4	-3	S/32	0.0
1979	Hou-N	52	43	8	9	0	0	0	1	7	7	.209	.320	.209	50	-3	-3	3	1	3	-2	7	S/32	0.4
1981	Oak-A	7	3	3	0	0	0	0	0	0	2	.000	.000	.000	-99	-1	-1	0	2	0	1	1	/3D	0.1
1982	Oak-A	69	139	19	34	4	0	2	14	9	24	.245	.295	.317	71	-6	-6	16	16	0	5	-2	S/3D	0.2
1983	StL-N	6	9	1	1	1	0	0	0	1	4	.111	.200	.222	17	-1	-1	0	0	0	0	1	/S3	0.1
Total	6	236	372	53	81	9	3	5	24	32	71	.218	.281	.298	64	-20	-18	37	36	6	7	7	S/3D2	0.9

■ TOM SEXTON
Sexton, Thomas William   b: 3/14/1865, Rock Island, Ill.   d: 2/8/34, Rock Island, Ill.   Deb: 9/27/1884

YEAR	TM/L	G	AB	R	H	2B	3B	HR	RBI	BB	SO	AVG	OBP	SLG	PRO+	BR	/A	RC	SB	CS	SBR	FR	POS	TPR
1884	Mil-U	12	47	9	11	2	0	0		4		.234	.294	.277	173	-0	3	4	0			-1	S	0.2

■ SOCKS SEYBOLD
Seybold, Ralph Orlando   b: 11/23/1870, Washingtonville, O   d: 12/22/21, Greensburg, Pa.   BR/TR, 5'11", 175 lbs.   Deb: 8/20/1899

YEAR	TM/L	G	AB	R	H	2B	3B	HR	RBI	BB	SO	AVG	OBP	SLG	PRO+	BR	/A	RC	SB	CS	SBR	FR	POS	TPR
1899	Cin-N	22	85	13	19	5	1	0	8	6		.224	.275	.306	60	-5	-5	8	2			1	O	-0.4
1901	Phi-A	114	449	74	150	24	14	8	90	40		.334	.396	.503	144	30	27	99	15			-6	*O1	1.7
1902	Phi-A	137	522	91	165	27	12	16	97	43		.316	.375	.506	139	30	27	105	6			2	*O	1.9
1903	Phi-A	137	522	76	156	45	8	8	84	38		.299	.346	.462	137	26	23	88	5			-2	*O1	1.4
1904	Phi-A	143	510	56	149	26	9	3	64	42		.292	.346	.396	130	21	18	78	12			1	*O	1.3
1905	*Phi-A	133	492	64	135	37	4	6	59	42		.274	.331	.402	133	18	18	71	5			9	*O	2.1
1906	Phi-A	116	411	41	130	23	2	5	59	30		.316	.363	.418	142	21	20	69	9			-5	*O	1.1
1907	Phi-A	147	564	58	153	29	4	5	92	40		.271	.320	.363	117	12	10	73	10			1	*O	0.3
1908	Phi-A	48	130	5	28	2	0	0	3	12		.215	.282	.231	65	-4	-5	9	2			-3	O	-1.1
Total	6	997	3685	478	1085	218	54	51	556	293		.294	.348	.424	130	150	133	599	66			-4	O/1	8.3

■ CY SEYMOUR
Seymour, James Bentley   b: 12/9/1872, Albany, N.Y.   d: 9/20/19, New York, N.Y.   BL/TL, 6', 200 lbs.   Deb: 4/22/1896

YEAR	TM/L	G	AB	R	H	2B	3B	HR	RBI	BB	SO	AVG	OBP	SLG	PRO+	BR	/A	RC	SB	CS	SBR	FR	POS	TPR
1896	NY-N	12	32	2	7	0	0	0	0	0	7	.219	.219	.219	17	-4	-4	2	0			0	P/O	0.0
1897	NY-N	44	137	13	33	5	1	2	14	4		.241	.262	.336	61	-8	-8	13	3			6	P/O	0.0
1898	NY-N	80	297	41	82	5	2	4	23	9		.276	.300	.347	90	-6	-4	34	8			5	PO/2	0.0
1899	NY-N	50	159	25	52	3	2	2	27	4		.327	.364	.409	112	1	2	24	2			2	P/O13	0.0
1900	NY-N	23	40	9	12	0	0	0	2	3		.300	.349	.300	86	-1	-1	4	0			-0	P/O1	0.0
1901	Bal-A	134	547	84	166	19	8	1	77	28		.303	.337	.373	95	-1	-5	85	38			14	*O/1	0.6
1902	Bal-A	72	280	38	75	8	8	3	41	18		.268	.314	.386	91	-2	-4	40	12			1	O	-0.6
	Cin-N	62	244	27	83	8	2	2	37	12		.340	.376	.414	133	13	10	42				4	O/P3	0.6
1903	Cin-N	135	558	85	191	25	15	7	72	33		.342	.379	.478	131	31	22	115	25			5	*O	1.8
1904	Cin-N	131	531	71	166	26	13	5	58	29		.313	.348	.439	133	25	20	88	11			13	*O	2.9
1905	Cin-N	149	581	95	219	40	21	8	121	51		.377	.427	.559	177	66	58	152	21			12	*O	6.1
1906	Cin-N	79	307	35	79	7	2	4	38	24		.257	.311	.332	98	1	-1	36	10			10	O	0.8
	NY-N	72	269	35	86	12	3	4	42	18		.320	.362	.431	147	14	14	51	20			-2	O	1.1
	Yr	151	576	70	165	19	5	8	80	42		.286	.335	.378	121	15	13	86	29			8		1.9

YEAR	TM/L	G	AB	R	H	2B	3B	HR	RBI	BB	SO	AVG	OBP	SLG	PRO+	BR	/A	RC	SB	CS	SBR	FR	POS	TPR
1907	NY-N	131	473	46	139	25	8	3	75	36		.294	.344	.400	131	18	16	75	21			4	*O	1.7
1908	NY-N	156	587	60	157	23	2	5	92	30		.267	.303	.339	102	3	0	67	18			11	*O	1.2
1909	NY-N	80	280	37	87	12	5	1	30	25		.311	.369	.400	137	12	12	46	14			-0	O	1.0
1910	NY-N	79	287	32	76	9	4	1	40	23	18	.265	.324	.334	92	-3	-3	34	10			-2	O	-0.8
1913	Bos-N	39	73	2	13	2	0	0	10	7	7	.178	.259	.205	33	-6	-6	4	2			2	O	-0.4
Total	16	1528	5682	737	1723	229	96	52	799	354	32	.303	.345	.405	118	153	119	912	222			83	*OP/132	16.4

■ TILLIE SHAFER
Shafer, Arthur Joseph b: 3/22/1889, Los Angeles, Cal. d: 1/10/62, Los Angeles, Cal. BB/TR, 5'10", 165 lbs. Deb: 4/24/09

YEAR	TM/L	G	AB	R	H	2B	3B	HR	RBI	BB	SO	AVG	OBP	SLG	PRO+	BR	/A	RC	SB	CS	SBR	FR	POS	TPR
1909	NY-N	38	84	11	15	2	1	0	7	14		.179	.296	.226	61	-3	-3	8	6			-1	32/O	-0.3
1910	NY-N	29	21	5	4	1	0	0	1	0	6	.190	.190	.238	25	-2	-2	1	0			5	/32S	0.3
1912	*NY-N	78	163	48	47	4	1	0	23	30	19	.288	.408	.325	99	3	2	31	22			-7	S32	-0.2
1913	*NY-N	138	508	74	146	17	12	5	52	61	55	.287	.369	.398	118	14	13	82	32			-10	32SO	0.2
Total	4	283	776	138	212	24	14	5	83	105	80	.273	.366	.360	106	11	10	122	60			-14	3/2SO	0.0

■ RALPH SHAFER
Shafer, Ralph Newton b: 3/17/1894, Cincinnati, Ohio d: 2/5/50, Akron, Ohio 5'11". Deb: 7/25/14

YEAR	TM/L	G	AB	R	H	2B	3B	HR	RBI	BB	SO	AVG	OBP	SLG	PRO+	BR	/A	RC	SB	CS	SBR	FR	POS	TPR
1914	Pit-N	1	0	0	0	0	0	0	0	0	0	—	—	—	—	0	0	0	0			0	H	0.0

■ SHAFFER
Shaffer Deb: 9/15/1875

YEAR	TM/L	G	AB	R	H	2B	3B	HR	RBI	BB	SO	AVG	OBP	SLG	PRO+	BR	/A	RC	SB	CS	SBR	FR	POS	TPR
1875	Atl-n	1	4	0	0	0	0	0	0			.000	.000	.000	-99	-1	-1	0					/O	0.0

■ FRANK SHAFFER
Shaffer, Frank Deb: 4/24/1884

YEAR	TM/L	G	AB	R	H	2B	3B	HR	RBI	BB	SO	AVG	OBP	SLG	PRO+	BR	/A	RC	SB	CS	SBR	FR	POS	TPR
1884	Alt-U	19	74	11	21	2	0	0		3		.284	.312	.311	110	1	1	7	0			-3	O/C3	-0.1
	KC-U	44	164	18	28	3	2	0		15		.171	.240	.213	63	-7	-4	9	0			-2	O/C2S3	-0.5
	Bal-U	3	13	1	1	0	0	0		0		.077	.077	.077	-43	-2	-2	0	0			-0	/O	-0.1
	Yr	66	251	30	50	5	2	0		18		.199	.253	.235	71	-8	-5	15	0			-5		-0.7

■ ORATOR SHAFFER
Shaffer, George b: 1852, Philadelphia, Pa. BL/TR, 5'9", 165 lbs. Deb: 5/23/1874

YEAR	TM/L	G	AB	R	H	2B	3B	HR	RBI	BB	SO	AVG	OBP	SLG	PRO+	BR	/A	RC	SB	CS	SBR	FR	POS	TPR
1874	Har-n	9	34	6	8	0	0	1		0		.235	.235	.324	72	-1	-1	3					/O	0.0
	Mut-n	1	5	1	1	0	0	0		0		.200	.200	.200	27	-0	-0	0					/O	0.0
	Yr	10	39	7	9	0	0	1		0		.231	.231	.308	67	-1	-2	3						0.0
1875	Phi-n	19	70	10	17	2	1	0		0		.243	.243	.300	83	-1	-1	5					O/31	0.0
1877	Lou-N	61	260	38	74	9	5	3	34	9	17	.285	.309	.392	101	6	-1	32				13	*O/1	0.9
1878	Ind-N	63	266	40	90	19	6	0	30	13	20	.338	.369	.455	**196**	20	**25**	46				6	*O	2.3
1879	Chi-N	73	316	53	96	13	0	0	35	6	28	.304	.317	.345	111	6	3	35				19	*O/3	1.8
1880	Cle-N	83	338	62	90	14	9	0	21	17	36	.266	.301	.361	126	8	9	38				15	*O	2.0
1881	Cle-N	85	343	48	88	13	6	1	34	23	20	.257	.303	.338	107	1	4	36				0	*O	0.3
1882	Cle-N	84	313	37	67	14	2	3	28	27	27	.214	.276	.300	88	-4	-3	27				-10	*O	-1.2
1883	Buf-N	95	401	67	117	11	3	0	41	27	39	.292	.336	.334	103	3	2	46				20	*O	2.1
1884	StL-U	106	467	130	168	40	10	2		30		.360	.398	.501	195	49	46	96	0			-3	*O/21	3.6
1885	StL-N	69	257	30	50	11	2	0	18	19	31	.195	.250	.253	67	-10	-8	17				10	*O	0.1
	Phi-a	2	9	1	2	0	1	0		1		.222	.300	.444	128	0	0	1				-1	/O	0.0
1886	Phi-a	21	82	15	22	3	3	0		8		.268	.333	.378	123	2	2	12	3			0	O	0.2
1890	Phi-a	100	390	55	110	15	5	1		47		.282	.367	.354	118	9	10	63	29			2	*O/1	0.6
Total	2 n	29	109	17	26	2	1	1		0		.239	.239	.303	77	-2	-3	8	0				/O31	0.0
Total	11	842	3442	584	974	162	52	10	241	227	218	.283	.328	.369	123	89	90	448	32			72	O/213	12.7

■ TAYLOR SHAFFER
Shaffer, Taylor b: 7/1870, Philadelphia, Pa. Deb: 4/17/1890

YEAR	TM/L	G	AB	R	H	2B	3B	HR	RBI	BB	SO	AVG	OBP	SLG	PRO+	BR	/A	RC	SB	CS	SBR	FR	POS	TPR
1890	Phi-a	69	261	28	45	3	4	0		28		.172	.258	.215	42	-19	-17	20	19			4	2	-0.9

■ ART SHAMSKY
Shamsky, Arthur Louis b: 10/14/41, St.Louis, Mo. BL/TL, 6'1", 168 lbs. Deb: 4/17/65

YEAR	TM/L	G	AB	R	H	2B	3B	HR	RBI	BB	SO	AVG	OBP	SLG	PRO+	BR	/A	RC	SB	CS	SBR	FR	POS	TPR
1965	Cin-N	64	96	13	25	4	3	2	10	10	29	.260	.330	.427	104	1	1	15	1	0	0	1	O/1	0.2
1966	Cin-N	96	234	41	54	5	0	21	47	32	45	.231	.323	.521	120	9	6	39	0	2	-1	-2	O	0.1
1967	Cin-N	76	147	6	29	3	1	3	13	15	34	.197	.276	.293	56	-7	-9	12	0	1	-1	0	O	-1.1
1968	NY-N	116	345	30	82	14	4	12	48	21	58	.238	.295	.406	108	3	3	41	1	0	0	-3	O1	-0.5
1969	*NY-N	100	303	42	91	9	3	14	47	36	32	.300	.380	.488	139	17	16	57	1	2	-1	-6	O/1	0.4
1970	NY-N	122	403	48	118	19	2	11	49	49	33	.293	.374	.432	115	9	9	64	1	1	-0	1	O1	0.2
1971	NY-N	68	135	13	25	6	2	5	18	21	18	.185	.299	.370	90	-2	-2	14	1	1	-0	3	O/1	0.0
1972	Chi-N	15	16	1	2	0	0	0	1	3	3	.125	.263	.125	12	-2	-2	1	0	0	0	0	/1	-0.1
	Oak-A	8	7	0	0	0	0	0	0	1	2	.000	.125	.000	-64	-1	-1	0	0	0	0	0	H	-0.1
Total	8	665	1686	194	426	60	15	68	233	188	254	.253	.333	.427	109	27	21	243	5	7	-3	-6	O/1	-0.9

■ JIM SHANDLEY
Shandley, James J. b: New York d: 11/4/04, Brooklyn, N.Y. Deb: 5/03/1876

YEAR	TM/L	G	AB	R	H	2B	3B	HR	RBI	BB	SO	AVG	OBP	SLG	PRO+	BR	/A	RC	SB	CS	SBR	FR	POS	TPR
1876	NY-N	2	8	0	1	0	0	0	0	0	0	.125	.125	.125	-19	-1	-1	0				-1	/O	0.0

■ WALLY SHANER
Shaner, Walter Dedaker "Skinny" b: 5/24/1900, Lynchburg, Va. BR/TR, 6'2", 195 lbs. Deb: 5/04/23

YEAR	TM/L	G	AB	R	H	2B	3B	HR	RBI	BB	SO	AVG	OBP	SLG	PRO+	BR	/A	RC	SB	CS	SBR	FR	POS	TPR
1923	Cle-A	3	4	1	1	0	0	0	1	1	1	.250	.400	.250	74	-0	-0	0	0	0	0	-1	/O3	0.0
1926	Bos-A	69	191	20	54	12	2	0	21	17	13	.283	.348	.366	89	-4	-3	25	1	0	0	0	O	-0.5
1927	Bos-A	122	406	54	111	33	6	3	49	21	35	.273	.311	.406	87	-11	-10	48	11	4	1	-8	*O/1	-2.2
1929	Cin-N	13	28	5	9	0	0	1	4	4	5	.321	.406	.429	112	0	1	5	1			-1	/1O	0.0
Total	4	207	629	80	175	45	8	4	74	43	54	.278	.327	.394	89	-14	-12	79	13	4		-9	O/13	-2.7

■ HOWIE SHANKS
Shanks, Howard Samuel "Hank" b: 7/21/1890, Chicago, Ill. d: 7/30/41, Monaca, Pa. BR/TR, 5'11", 170 lbs. Deb: 5/09/12 C

YEAR	TM/L	G	AB	R	H	2B	3B	HR	RBI	BB	SO	AVG	OBP	SLG	PRO+	BR	/A	RC	SB	CS	SBR	FR	POS	TPR
1912	Was-A	116	399	52	92	14	7	1	48	40		.231	.305	.308	75	-13	-13	45	21			-2	*O	-2.1
1913	Was-A	109	390	38	99	11	5	1	37	15	40	.254	.287	.315	75	-13	-14	39	24			3	*O	-1.7
1914	Was-A	143	500	44	112	22	10	4	64	29	51	.224	.269	.332	79	-14	-16	47	18	16	-4	-0	*O	-3.1
1915	Was-A	141	492	52	123	19	8	0	47	30	42	.250	.297	.321	84	-11	-11	48	12	14	-5	7	O32	-1.1
1916	Was-A	140	471	51	119	15	7	1	48	41	34	.253	.317	.321	94	-5	-4	54	23	12	-0	10	O3/S1	0.3
1917	Was-A	126	430	45	87	15	5	0	28	33	37	.202	.269	.260	62	-20	-20	35	15			13	SO/1	-0.5
1918	Was-A	120	436	42	112	19	4	1	56	31	21	.257	.312	.326	94	-5	-4	50	23			1	O2/3	-0.3
1919	Was-A	135	491	33	122	8	7	1	54	25	48	.248	.289	.299	66	-23	-23	47	13			-11	S2/O	-2.4
1920	Was-A	128	444	56	119	16	7	4	37	29	43	.268	.316	.363	82	-14	-12	51	11	6	-0	-6	301/2S	-1.6
1921	Was-A	154	562	81	170	24	**18**	7	69	57	38	.302	.370	.447	113	6	10	93	11	10	-3	5	*3/2	2.3
1922	Was-A	84	272	35	77	10	9	1	32	25	25	.283	.352	.397	100	-2	-0	41	6	0	2	7	3O	1.2
1923	Bos-A	131	464	38	118	19	5	3	57	19	37	.254	.285	.336	63	-26	-27	44	6	6	-2	-19	O2/OS	-3.5
1924	Bos-A	72	193	22	50	16	3	0	25	21	12	.259	.332	.373	81	-6	-6	25	1	0	0	7	S3/O12	0.7
1925	NY-A	66	155	15	40	3	1	1	18	20	15	.258	.343	.310	68	-7	-7	18	1	0	0	-6	32/O	-0.9
Total	14	1665	5699	604	1440	211	96	25	620	415	443	.253	.308	.337	82	-154	-146	637	185	64		10	O3S2/1	-12.7

■ DOC SHANLEY
Shanley, Harry Root b: 1890, Granbury, Tex. d: 12/13/34, St.Petersburg, Fla BR/TR, 6', 174 lbs. Deb: 9/15/12

YEAR	TM/L	G	AB	R	H	2B	3B	HR	RBI	BB	SO	AVG	OBP	SLG	PRO+	BR	/A	RC	SB	CS	SBR	FR	POS	TPR
1912	StL-A	5	8	1	0	0	0	0	1	2		.000	.200	.000	-43	-1	-1	0	0			-1	/S	-0.2

■ WARREN SHANNABROOK
Shannabrook, Warren H. b: 11/30/1880, Massillon, Ohio d: 3/10/64, N.Canton, Ohio BR/TR, 6', 170 lbs. Deb: 8/13/06

YEAR	TM/L	G	AB	R	H	2B	3B	HR	RBI	BB	SO	AVG	OBP	SLG	PRO+	BR	/A	RC	SB	CS	SBR	FR	POS	TPR
1906	Was-A	1	2	0	0	0	0	0	0	0		.000	.000	.000	-99	-0	-0	0	0			-0	/3	0.0

■ DAN SHANNON
Shannon, Daniel W. b: 3/23/1865, Bridgeport, Conn. d: 10/25/13, Bridgeport, Conn. 175 lbs. Deb: 4/17/1889 M

YEAR	TM/L	G	AB	R	H	2B	3B	HR	RBI	BB	SO	AVG	OBP	SLG	PRO+	BR	/A	RC	SB	CS	SBR	FR	POS	TPR
1889	Lou-a	121	498	90	128	22	12	4	48	42	52	.257	.315	.373	100	-3	-1	68	26			7	*2M	0.7

YEAR	TM/L	G	AB	R	H	2B	3B	HR	RBI	BB	SO	AVG	OBP	SLG	PRO+	BR	/A	RC	SB	CS	SBR	FR	POS	TPR
1890	Phi-P	19	75	15	18	5	1	1	16	4	12	.240	.278	.373	73	-3	-3	9	4			-4	2	-0.4
	NY-P	83	324	59	70	7	8	3	44	25	34	.216	.274	.315	54	-20	-25	35	21			1	2/S	-1.5
	Yr	102	399	74	88	12	9	4	60	29	46	.221	.275	.326	57	-23	-28	44	25			-3		-1.9
1891	Was-a	19	67	7	9	2	0	0	3	6	9	.134	.205	.164	8	-8	-7	3	6			1	S/2M	-0.4
Total	3	242	964	171	225	36	21	8	111	77	107	.233	.291	.339	75	-33	-37	115	54			5	2/S	-1.6

■ FRANK SHANNON Shannon, John Francis b: 12/3/1873, San Francisco, Cal. d: 2/27/34, Boston, Mass. 5'3", 155 lbs. Deb: 10/01/1892

YEAR	TM/L	G	AB	R	H	2B	3B	HR	RBI	BB	SO	AVG	OBP	SLG	PRO+	BR	/A	RC	SB	CS	SBR	FR	POS	TPR
1892	Was-N	1	4	0	1	0	0	0	2	0	2	.250	.250	.250	54	-0	-0	0	0			-1	/S	0.0
1896	Lou-N	31	115	14	18	1	1	1	15	13	15	.157	.248	.209	23	-13	-12	7	3			-12	S/3	-2.0
Total	2	32	119	14	19	1	1	1	17	13	17	.160	.248	.210	24	-13	-12	7	3			-13	/S3	-2.0

■ JOE SHANNON Shannon, Joseph Aloysius b: 2/11/1897, Jersey City, N.J. d: 7/28/55, Jersey City, N.J. BR/TR, 5'11", 170 lbs. Deb: 7/07/15

YEAR	TM/L	G	AB	R	H	2B	3B	HR	RBI	BB	SO	AVG	OBP	SLG	PRO+	BR	/A	RC	SB	CS	SBR	FR	POS	TPR
1915	Bos-N	5	10	3	2	0	0	0	1	0	3	.200	.200	.200	22	-1	-1	1	0			1	/O2	0.0

■ RED SHANNON Shannon, Maurice Joseph b: 2/11/1897, Jersey City, N.J. d: 4/12/70, Jersey City, N.J. BB/TR, 5'11", 170 lbs. Deb: 10/07/15

YEAR	TM/L	G	AB	R	H	2B	3B	HR	RBI	BB	SO	AVG	OBP	SLG	PRO+	BR	/A	RC	SB	CS	SBR	FR	POS	TPR
1915	Bos-N	1	3	0	0	0	0	0	0	0	0	.000	.000	.000	-99	-1	-1	0	0			0	/2	0.0
1917	Phi-A	11	35	8	10	0	0	0	7	6	9	.286	.390	.286	108	1	1	4	2			-0	S	0.1
1918	Phi-A	72	225	23	54	6	5	0	16	42	52	.240	.367	.311	103	3	3	28	5			-4	S2	0.4
1919	Phi-A	39	155	14	42	7	2	0	14	12	28	.271	.331	.342	88	-2	-2	18	4			-5	2	-0.3
	Bos-N	80	290	36	75	11	7	0	17	17	42	.259	.313	.345	90	-6	-4	32	7			-4	2	-0.1
	Yr	119	445	50	117	18	9	0	31	29	70	.263	.320	.344	89	-9	-7	50	11			-9		-0.4
1920	Was-A	63	222	30	64	8	7	0	30	22	32	.288	.352	.387	99	-1	-0	30	2	5	-2	-19	S23	-1.7
	Phi-A	24	88	4	15	1	1	0	3	4	12	.170	.207	.205	9	-12	-12	4	1	1	-0	-1	S	-1.0
	Yr	87	310	34	79	9	8	0	33	26	44	.255	.313	.335	73	-13	-12	32	3	6	-3	-20		-2.7
1921	Phi-A	1	1	0	0	0	0	0	0	0	0	.000	.000	.000	-99	-0	-0	0	0	0	0	0	H	0.0
1926	Chi-N	19	51	9	17	5	0	0	4	6	3	.333	.414	.431	126	2	2	9	0			-2	S	0.1
Total	7	310	1070	124	277	38	22	0	91	109	178	.259	.334	.336	89	-16	-14	125	21	6		-35	2S/3	-2.5

■ MIKE SHANNON Shannon, Thomas Michael "Moonman" b: 7/5/39, St.Louis, Mo. BR/TR, 6'3", 195 lbs. Deb: 9/11/62

YEAR	TM/L	G	AB	R	H	2B	3B	HR	RBI	BB	SO	AVG	OBP	SLG	PRO+	BR	/A	RC	SB	CS	SBR	FR	POS	TPR
1962	StL-N	10	15	3	2	0	0	0	0	1	3	.133	.188	.133	-11	-2	-3	0	0	0	0	1	/O	-0.1
1963	StL-N	32	26	3	8	0	0	1	2	0	6	.308	.333	.423	106	0	0	3	0	1	-1	2	O	0.0
1964	*StL-N	88	253	30	66	8	2	9	43	19	54	.261	.313	.415	95	1	-2	32	4	0	1	-6	O	-0.9
1965	StL-N	124	244	32	54	17	3	3	25	28	46	.221	.307	.352	78	-5	-7	26	2	1	0	-1	*O/C	-1.1
1966	StL-N	137	459	61	132	20	6	16	64	37	106	.288	.341	.462	120	12	12	70	8	4	0	7	*O/C	1.6
1967	*StL-N	130	482	53	118	18	3	12	77	37	89	.245	.304	.369	93	-6	-5	52	2	4	-2	-10	*3/O	-2.5
1968	*StL-N	156	576	62	153	29	2	15	79	37	114	.266	.312	.401	114	8	8	70	1	2	-1	-7	*3	0.0
1969	StL-N	150	551	51	140	15	5	12	55	49	87	.254	.316	.365	90	-8	-8	63	1	4	-2	-19	*3	-2.9
1970	StL-N	55	174	18	37	9	2	0	22	16	20	.213	.279	.287	51	-12	-12	14	1	1	-0	-13	3	-2.7
Total	9	882	2780	313	710	116	23	68	367	224	525	.255	.313	.387	96	-11	-16	331	19	17	-5	-46	3O/C	-8.6

■ OWEN SHANNON Shannon, Owen Dennis Ignatius b: 12/22/1885, Omaha, Neb. d: 4/10/18, Omaha, Neb. BR/TR, Deb: 9/06/03

YEAR	TM/L	G	AB	R	H	2B	3B	HR	RBI	BB	SO	AVG	OBP	SLG	PRO+	BR	/A	RC	SB	CS	SBR	FR	POS	TPR
1903	StL-A	9	28	1	6	2	0	0	3	1		.214	.241	.286	61	-1	-1	2	0			-0	/C1	0.0
1907	Was-A	4	7	0	1	0	0	0	0	0		.143	.143	.143	-9	-1	-1	0	0			3	/C	0.2
Total	2	13	35	1	7	2	0	0	3	1		.200	.222	.257	48	-2	-2	2	0			2	/C1	0.2

■ WALLY SHANNON Shannon, Walter Charles b: 1/23/34, Cleveland, Ohio BL/TR, 6', 178 lbs. Deb: 7/09/59

YEAR	TM/L	G	AB	R	H	2B	3B	HR	RBI	BB	SO	AVG	OBP	SLG	PRO+	BR	/A	RC	SB	CS	SBR	FR	POS	TPR
1959	StL-N	47	95	5	27	5	0	0	5	0	12	.284	.292	.337	63	-5	-5	9	0	0	0	-10	S2	-1.4
1960	StL-N	18	23	2	4	0	0	0	1	3	6	.174	.296	.174	30	-2	-2	1	0	0	0	2	2/S	0.1
Total	2	65	118	7	31	5	0	0	6	3	18	.263	.293	.305	56	-7	-8	11	0	0	0	-8	/2S	-1.3

■ SPIKE SHANNON Shannon, William Porter b: 2/7/1878, Pittsburgh, Pa. d: 5/16/40, Minneapolis, Minn. BB/TR, 5'11", 180 lbs. Deb: 4/15/04 U

YEAR	TM/L	G	AB	R	H	2B	3B	HR	RBI	BB	SO	AVG	OBP	SLG	PRO+	BR	/A	RC	SB	CS	SBR	FR	POS	TPR
1904	StL-N	134	500	84	140	10	3	1	26	50		.280	.345	.318	112	6	9	72	34			9	*O	1.3
1905	StL-N	140	544	73	146	16	3	0	41	47		.268	.327	.309	95	-4	-2	68	27			1	*O	-1.1
1906	StL-N	80	302	36	78	4	0	0	25	36		.258	.337	.272	96	-1	0	35	15			6	O	0.5
	NY-N	76	287	42	73	5	1	0	25	34		.254	.333	.279	91	-1	-2	35	18			-7	O	-1.0
	Yr	156	589	78	151	9	1	0	50	70		.256	.335	.275	94	-2	-1	70	33			-1		-0.5
1907	NY-N	155	585	**104**	155	12	5	1	33	82		.265	.355	.308	107	10	8	79	33			2	*O	0.5
1908	NY-N	77	268	34	60	2	1	1	21	28		.224	.297	.250	74	-6	-7	24	13			-3	O	-1.2
	Pit-N	32	127	10	25	0	2	0	12	9		.197	.250	.228	55	-6	-6	8	5			1	O	-0.6
	Yr	109	395	44	85	2	3	1	33	37		.215	.282	.243	68	-12	-13	32	18			-2		-1.8
Total	5	694	2613	383	677	49	15	3	183	286		.259	.332	.293	96	-2	0	322	145			8	O	-1.6

■ BILLY SHANTZ Shantz, Wilmer Ebert b: 7/31/27, Pottstown, Pa. BR/TR, 6'1", 160 lbs. Deb: 4/13/54

YEAR	TM/L	G	AB	R	H	2B	3B	HR	RBI	BB	SO	AVG	OBP	SLG	PRO+	BR	/A	RC	SB	CS	SBR	FR	POS	TPR
1954	Phi-A	51	164	13	42	9	3	1	17	17	23	.256	.326	.366	89	-3	-3	19	0	0	0	-12	C	-1.2
1955	KC-A	79	217	18	56	4	1	1	12	11	14	.258	.294	.300	59	-12	-13	18	0	0	0	-11	C	-2.0
1960	NY-A	1	0	0	0	0	0	0	0	0	0	—	—	—	—	0	0	0	0	0	0	0	/C	0.0
Total	3	131	381	31	98	13	4	2	29	28	37	.257	.308	.328	72	-15	-15	38	0	0	0	-23	C	-3.2

■ RALPH SHARMAN Sharman, Ralph Edward "Bally" b: 4/11/1895, Cleveland, Ohio d: 5/24/18, Camp Sheridan, Ala BR/TR, 5'11", 176 lbs. Deb: 9/10/17

YEAR	TM/L	G	AB	R	H	2B	3B	HR	RBI	BB	SO	AVG	OBP	SLG	PRO+	BR	/A	RC	SB	CS	SBR	FR	POS	TPR
1917	Phi-A	13	37	2	11	2	1	0	2	3	2	.297	.366	.405	137	2	2	6	1			-1	O	0.0

■ DICK SHARON Sharon, Richard Louis b: 4/15/50, San Mateo, Cal. BR/TR, 6'2", 195 lbs. Deb: 5/13/73

YEAR	TM/L	G	AB	R	H	2B	3B	HR	RBI	BB	SO	AVG	OBP	SLG	PRO+	BR	/A	RC	SB	CS	SBR	FR	POS	TPR
1973	Det-A	91	178	20	43	9	0	7	16	10	31	.242	.282	.410	87	-3	-4	20	2	0	1	7	O	0.1
1974	Det-A	60	129	12	28	4	0	2	10	14	29	.217	.294	.295	67	-5	-5	11	4	4	-1	-2	O	-0.9
1975	SD-N	91	160	14	31	7	0	4	20	26	35	.194	.306	.313	77	-6	-5	15	0	2	-1	-0	O	-0.7
Total	3	242	467	46	102	20	0	13	46	50	95	.218	.294	.345	79	-13	-14	46	6	6	-2	5	O	-1.5

■ BILL SHARP Sharp, William Howard b: 1/18/50, Lima, Ohio BL/TL, 5'10", 178 lbs. Deb: 5/26/73

YEAR	TM/L	G	AB	R	H	2B	3B	HR	RBI	BB	SO	AVG	OBP	SLG	PRO+	BR	/A	RC	SB	CS	SBR	FR	POS	TPR
1973	Chi-A	77	196	23	54	8	3	4	22	19	28	.276	.349	.408	109	3	2	28	2	3	-1	7	O/D	0.6
1974	Chi-A	100	320	45	81	13	2	4	24	25	37	.253	.311	.344	86	-5	-6	33	0	3	-2	-2	O	-1.2
1975	Chi-A	18	35	1	7	0	0	0	4	2	3	.200	.243	.200	26	-3	-3	2	0	3	-2	-1	O	-0.4
	Mil-A	125	373	37	95	27	3	1	34	19	26	.255	.293	.351	81	-10	-10	36	0	3	-2	10	*O	-0.4
	Yr	143	408	38	102	27	3	1	38	21	29	.250	.288	.338	76	-13	-14	38	0	3	-2	9		-0.8
1976	Mil-A	78	180	16	44	4	0	0	11	10	15	.244	.288	.267	64	-8	-8	13	1	3	-2	5	O/D	-0.4
Total	4	398	1104	122	281	52	8	9	95	75	109	.255	.306	.341	83	-23	-25	113	3	12	-6	20	O/D	-1.8

■ BUD SHARPE Sharpe, Bayard Heston b: 8/6/1881, West Chester, Pa. d: 5/31/16, Haddock, Ga. BL/TR, Deb: 4/14/05

YEAR	TM/L	G	AB	R	H	2B	3B	HR	RBI	BB	SO	AVG	OBP	SLG	PRO+	BR	/A	RC	SB	CS	SBR	FR	POS	TPR
1905	Bos-N	46	170	8	31	3	2	0	11	7		.182	.215	.224	33	-14	-14	9	0			3	O/C1	-1.3
1910	Bos-N	115	439	30	105	14	3	0	29	14	31	.239	.264	.285	58	-24	-26	34	4			7	*1	-2.0
	Pit-N	4	16	2	3	0	1	0	1	0	2	.188	.188	.313	43	-1	-1	1	0			0	/1	0.0
	Yr	119	455	32	108	14	4	0	30	14	33	.237	.262	.286	57	-25	-27	35	4			8		-2.0
Total	2	165	625	40	139	17	6	0	41	21	33	.222	.249	.269	51	-39	-41	44	4			11	1/OC	-3.3

■ MIKE SHARPERSON Sharperson, Michael Tyrone b: 10/4/61, Orangeburg, S.C. BR/TR, 6'1", 175 lbs. Deb: 4/06/87

YEAR	TM/L	G	AB	R	H	2B	3B	HR	RBI	BB	SO	AVG	OBP	SLG	PRO+	BR	/A	RC	SB	CS	SBR	FR	POS	TPR
1987	Tor-A	32	96	4	20	4	1	0	9	7	15	.208	.269	.271	43	-8	-8	7	2	1	0	-5	2	-0.9
	LA-N	10	33	7	9	2	0	0	1	4	5	.273	.351	.333	85	-1	-1	4	0	0	0	2	/32	0.1

YEAR	TM/L	G	AB	R	H	2B	3B	HR	RBI	BB	SO	AVG	OBP	SLG	PRO+	BR	/A	RC	SB	CS	SBR	FR	POS	TPR
1988	*LA-N	46	59	8	16	1	0	0	4	1	12	.271	.295	.288	70	-2	-2	5	0	1	-1	-0	2/3S	-0.1
1989	LA-N	27	28	2	7	3	0	0	5	4	7	.250	.344	.357	102	0	0	3	0	1	-1	0	/213S	0.0
1990	LA-N	129	357	42	106	14	2	3	36	46	39	.297	.379	.373	114	5	8	54	15	6	1	6	*3S/21	1.9
Total	4	244	573	63	158	24	3	3	55	62	78	.276	.350	.344	95	-5	-3	73	17	9	-0	2	3/2S1	1.0

■ JACK SHARROTT
Sharrott, John Henry b: 8/13/1869, Bangor, Me. d: 12/31/27, Los Angeles, Cal. BR/TR, 5'9", 165 lbs. Deb: 4/22/1890

YEAR	TM/L	G	AB	R	H	2B	3B	HR	RBI	BB	SO	AVG	OBP	SLG	PRO+	BR	/A	RC	SB	CS	SBR	FR	POS	TPR
1890	NY-N	32	109	16	22	3	2	0	14	0	14	.202	.202	.266	37	-9	-9	7	6			-0	P/O	0.0
1891	NY-N	10	30	5	10	2	0	1	7	1	2	.333	.355	.500	156	2	2	7	3			1	P	0.0
1892	NY-N	4	8	1	1	0	0	0	0	0	1	.125	.125	.125	-24	-1	-1	0	0			-1	/OP	-0.1
1893	Phi-N	50	152	25	38	4	3	1	22	8	14	.250	.287	.336	67	-8	-8	17	6			-7	OP	-1.1
Total	4	96	299	47	71	9	5	2	43	9	31	.237	.260	.321	63	-16	-16	31	15			-8	/PO	-1.2

■ SHAG SHAUGHNESSY
Shaughnessy, Francis Joseph b: 4/8/1883, Amboy, Ill. d: 5/15/69, Montreal, Que., Can BR/TR, 6'1.5", 185 lbs. Deb: 4/17/05 C

YEAR	TM/L	G	AB	R	H	2B	3B	HR	RBI	BB	SO	AVG	OBP	SLG	PRO+	BR	/A	RC	SB	CS	SBR	FR	POS	TPR
1905	Was-A	1	3	0	0	0	0	0	0	0	0	.000	.000	.000	-99	-1	-1	0	0			-0	/O	0.0
1908	Phi-A	8	29	2	9	0	0	0	1		2	.310	.355	.310	112	1	0	4	3			-1	/O	0.0
Total	2	9	32	2	9	0	0	0	1		2	.281	.324	.281	93	-0	-0	4	3			-1	/O	0.0

■ AL SHAW
Shaw, Albert Simpson b: 3/1/1881, Toledo, Ill. d: 12/30/74, Danville, Ill. BL/TR, 5'8.5", 165 lbs. Deb: 9/28/07

YEAR	TM/L	G	AB	R	H	2B	3B	HR	RBI	BB	SO	AVG	OBP	SLG	PRO+	BR	/A	RC	SB	CS	SBR	FR	POS	TPR
1907	StL-N	9	25	2	7	0	0	0	1		3	.280	.357	.280	106	0	0	3	1			-0	/O	0.0
1908	StL-N	107	367	40	97	13	4	1	19		25	.264	.311	.330	112	3	4	40	9			7	O/S3	1.2
1909	StL-N	114	331	45	82	12	7	2	34		55	.248	.355	.344	125	8	11	45	15			-1	O	0.8
1914	Bro-F	112	376	81	122	27	7	5	49	44	59	.324	.395	.473	149	24	24	83	24			1	*O	2.0
1915	KC-F	132	448	67	126	22	10	6	67	46	45	.281	.348	.415	131	14	16	73	15			-14	*O	-0.3
Total	5	474	1547	235	434	74	28	14	170	173	104	.281	.353	.392	130	48	55	244	64			-7	O/S3	3.7

■ AL SHAW
Shaw, Alfred "Shoddy" b: 10/3/1874, Burslem, England d: 3/25/58, Uhrichsville, Ohio BR/TR, 5'8", 170 lbs. Deb: 6/08/01

YEAR	TM/L	G	AB	R	H	2B	3B	HR	RBI	BB	SO	AVG	OBP	SLG	PRO+	BR	/A	RC	SB	CS	SBR	FR	POS	TPR
1901	Det-A	55	171	20	46	7	0	1	23		10	.269	.321	.327	78	-4	-5	20	2			-1	C/13S	-0.1
1907	Bos-A	76	198	10	38	1	3	0	7		18	.192	.259	.227	57	-9	-9	13	4			15	C/1	1.4
1908	Chi-A	32	49	0	4	1	0	0	2		2	.082	.118	.102	-28	-7	-7	1	0			3	C	0.0
1909	Bos-N	18	41	1	4	0	0	0	0		5	.098	.213	.098	-3	-5	-5	1	0			4	C	0.0
Total	4	181	459	31	92	9	3	1	32		35	.200	.263	.240	53	-24	-25	35	6			21	C/13S	1.3

■ BEN SHAW
Shaw, Benjamin Nathaniel b: 6/18/1893, LaCenter, Ky. d: 3/16/59, Aurora, Ohio BR/TR, 5'11.5", 190 lbs. Deb: 4/11/17

YEAR	TM/L	G	AB	R	H	2B	3B	HR	RBI	BB	SO	AVG	OBP	SLG	PRO+	BR	/A	RC	SB	CS	SBR	FR	POS	TPR
1917	Pit-N	2	2	0	0	0	0	0	0	0	0	.000	.000	.000	-97	-0	-0	0	0			0	H	0.0
1918	Pit-N	21	36	5	7	1	0	0	2	2	2	.194	.275	.222	50	-2	-2	2	0			-2	/1C	-0.3
Total	2	23	38	5	7	1	0	0	2	2	2	.184	.262	.211	43	-2	-3	2	0			-2	/1C	-0.3

■ HUNKY SHAW
Shaw, Royal N b: 9/29/1884, Yakima, Wash. d: 7/3/69, Yakima, Wash. BB/TR, 5'8", 165 lbs. Deb: 5/16/08

YEAR	TM/L	G	AB	R	H	2B	3B	HR	RBI	BB	SO	AVG	OBP	SLG	PRO+	BR	/A	RC	SB	CS	SBR	FR	POS	TPR
1908	Pit-N	1	1	0	0	0	0	0	0		0	.000	.000	.000	-99	-0	-0	0	0			0	H	0.0

■ MARTY SHAY
Shay, Arthur Joseph b: 4/25/1896, Boston, Mass. d: 2/20/51, Worcester, Mass. BR/TR, 5'7.5", 148 lbs. Deb: 9/16/16

YEAR	TM/L	G	AB	R	H	2B	3B	HR	RBI	BB	SO	AVG	OBP	SLG	PRO+	BR	/A	RC	SB	CS	SBR	FR	POS	TPR
1916	Chi-N	2	7	0	2	0	0	0	0	0	1	.286	.286	.286	68	-0	-0	1	0			0	/S	0.0
1924	Bos-N	19	68	4	16	3	1	0	2	5	5	.235	.297	.309	65	-4	-3	6	2	1	0	-12	2/S	-1.6
Total	2	21	75	4	18	3	1	0	2	5	6	.240	.296	.307	66	-4	-3	7	2	1		-12	/2S	-1.6

■ DANNY SHAY
Shay, Daniel C. b: 11/8/1876, Springfield, Ohio d: 12/1/27, Kansas City, Mo. TR, 5'10", Deb: 4/30/01

YEAR	TM/L	G	AB	R	H	2B	3B	HR	RBI	BB	SO	AVG	OBP	SLG	PRO+	BR	/A	RC	SB	CS	SBR	FR	POS	TPR
1901	Cle-A	19	75	4	17	2	2	0	10		2	.227	.266	.307	62	-4	-4	6	0			-3	S	-0.5
1904	StL-N	99	340	45	87	11	1	1	18		39	.256	.332	.303	103	1	3	48	36			-7	S/2	-0.3
1905	StL-N	78	281	30	67	12	1	0	28		35	.238	.323	.288	87	-4	-3	31	11			-13	2S	-1.3
1907	NY-N	35	79	10	15	1	1	1	6		12	.190	.297	.266	76	-2	-2	8	5			-7	2/SO	-0.9
Total	4	231	775	89	186	26	5	2	62		88	.240	.317	.294	90	-9	-6	92	52			-31	S/2O	-3.0

■ GERRY SHEA
Shea, Gerald J. b: 7/26/1881, St.Louis, Mo. d: 5/3/64, Berkeley, Mo. TR, 5'7", 160 lbs. Deb: 10/01/05

YEAR	TM/L	G	AB	R	H	2B	3B	HR	RBI	BB	SO	AVG	OBP	SLG	PRO+	BR	/A	RC	SB	CS	SBR	FR	POS	TPR
1905	StL-N	2	6	0	2	0	0	0	0		0	.333	.333	.333	104	-0	-0	1	0			1	/C	0.1

■ NAP SHEA
Shea, John Edward "Napoleon" b: 5/23/1874, Ware, Mass. d: 7/8/68, Bloomfield Hills, Mich. BR/TR, 5'5", 155 lbs. Deb: 9/11/02

YEAR	TM/L	G	AB	R	H	2B	3B	HR	RBI	BB	SO	AVG	OBP	SLG	PRO+	BR	/A	RC	SB	CS	SBR	FR	POS	TPR
1902	Phi-N	3	8	1	1	0	0	0	0		1	.125	.300	.125	34	-0	-0	0	0			0	/C	0.0

■ MERV SHEA
Shea, Mervyn David John b: 9/5/1900, San Francisco, Cal d: 1/27/53, Sacramento, Cal. BR/TR, 5'11", 175 lbs. Deb: 4/23/27 C

YEAR	TM/L	G	AB	R	H	2B	3B	HR	RBI	BB	SO	AVG	OBP	SLG	PRO+	BR	/A	RC	SB	CS	SBR	FR	POS	TPR
1927	Det-A	34	85	5	15	6	3	0	9	7	15	.176	.239	.318	43	-8	-8	6	0	0	0	0	C	-0.5
1928	Det-A	39	85	8	20	2	3	0	9	9	11	.235	.316	.329	69	-4	-4	9	2	2	-1	4	C	0.1
1929	Det-A	50	162	23	47	6	0	3	24	19	18	.290	.365	.383	92	-1	-1	23	2	1	0	-6	C	-0.2
1933	Bos-A	16	56	1	8	3	0	0	8	4	7	.143	.200	.196	5	-8	-8	2	0	0	0	-2	C	-0.7
	StL-A	94	279	26	73	11	1	1	27	43	26	.262	.360	.319	76	-6	-9	35	2	0	1	8	C	0.4
	Yr	110	335	27	81	14	1	1	35	47	33	.242	.335	.299	65	-14	-16	37	2	0	1	7		-0.3
1934	Chi-A	62	176	8	28	3	0	0	5	24	19	.159	.260	.176	14	-22	-23	9	0	1	-1	2	C	-1.4
1935	Chi-A	46	122	8	28	2	0	0	13	30	9	.230	.382	.246	64	-5	-5	14	0	0	0	8	C	0.0
1936	Chi-A	14	24	3	3	0	0	0	2	6	5	.125	.300	.125	8	-3	-4	1	0	0	0	1	C	-0.1
1937	Chi-A	25	71	7	15	1	0	0	5	15	10	.211	.349	.225	48	-5	-5	7	1	0	0	3	C	0.0
1938	Bro-N	48	120	14	22	5	0	0	12	28	20	.183	.338	.225	56	-6	-6	11	1			-1	C	-0.5
1939	Det-A	4	2	0	0	0	0	0	0	0	1	.000	.000	.000	-93	-1	-1	0	0	0	0	-1	/C	0.0
1944	Phi-N	7	15	2	4	0	0	1	1	4	4	.267	.421	.467	155	1	1	3	0			-0	/C	0.1
Total	11	439	1197	105	263	39	7	5	115	189	145	.220	.327	.277	58	-67	-72	122	8	4		16	C	-2.4

■ DANNY SHEAFFER
Sheaffer, Danny Todd b: 8/2/61, Jacksonville, Fla. BR/TR, 6' ", 185 lbs. Deb: 4/09/87

YEAR	TM/L	G	AB	R	H	2B	3B	HR	RBI	BB	SO	AVG	OBP	SLG	PRO+	BR	/A	RC	SB	CS	SBR	FR	POS	TPR
1987	Bos-A	25	66	5	8	1	0	1	5	0	14	.121	.121	.182	-21	-11	-12	1	0	0	0	-3	C	-1.1
1989	Cle-A	7	16	1	1	0	0	0	0	2	2	.063	.167	.063	-32	-3	-3	0	0	0	0	0	/3OD	-0.2
Total	2	32	82	6	9	1	0	1	5	2	16	.110	.131	.159	-22	-14	-14	1	0	0	0	-2	/CD3O	-1.3

■ DAVE SHEAN
Shean, David William b: 7/9/1883, Arlington, Mass. d: 5/22/63, Boston, Mass. BR/TR, 5'11", 175 lbs. Deb: 9/10/06

YEAR	TM/L	G	AB	R	H	2B	3B	HR	RBI	BB	SO	AVG	OBP	SLG	PRO+	BR	/A	RC	SB	CS	SBR	FR	POS	TPR
1906	Phi-A	22	75	7	16	3	2	0	3	5		.213	.262	.307	77	-2	-2	8	6			-2	2	-0.4
1908	Phi-N	14	48	4	7	2	0	0	2	1		.146	.163	.188	13	-5	-5	2	1			-6	S	-1.3
1909	Phi-N	36	112	14	26	2	2	0	4	14		.232	.323	.286	88	-1	-1	11	3			-2	21/OS	-0.3
	Bos-N	75	267	32	66	11	4	1	29	17		.247	.297	.330	90	-2	-4	31	14			8	2	0.4
	Yr	111	379	46	92	13	6	1	33	31		.243	.305	.317	90	-4	-5	42	17			6		0.1
1910	Bos-N	150	543	52	130	12	7	3	36	42	45	.239	.294	.304	71	-19	-22	53	16			**43**	*2	2.5
1911	Chi-N	54	145	17	28	4	0	0	15	8	15	.193	.240	.221	29	-14	-14	9	4			1	2S/3	-1.2
1912	Bos-N	4	10	1	3	0	0	0	0	1	2	.300	.417	.300	96	0	0	1	0			-1	/S	0.0
1917	Cin-N	131	442	36	93	9	5	2	35	22	39	.210	.249	.267	61	-22	-20	31	10			19	*2	0.7
1918	*Bos-N	115	425	58	112	16	3	0	34	40	25	.264	.331	.315	97	-2	-1	51	11			-8	*2	-0.4
1919	Bos-A	29	100	4	14	0	0	0	8	5	7	.140	.189	.140	-7	-14	-13	3	1			4	2	-0.6
Total	9	630	2167	225	495	59	23	6	166	155	133	.228	.283	.285	70	-81	-82	200	66			56	2/S103	-0.6

■ RAY SHEARER
Shearer, Ray Solomon b: 9/19/29, Jacobus, Pa. d: 2/21/82, York, Pa. BR/TR, 6', 200 lbs. Deb: 9/18/57

YEAR	TM/L	G	AB	R	H	2B	3B	HR	RBI	BB	SO	AVG	OBP	SLG	PRO+	BR	/A	RC	SB	CS	SBR	FR	POS	TPR
1957	Mil-N	2	2	1	1	0	0	0	0	1	1	.500	.667	.500	237	1	1	1	0	0	0	0	/O	0.0

■ JOHN SHEARON
Shearon, John M. b: 1870, Pittsburgh, Pa. d: 2/1/23, Bradford, Pa. Deb: 7/28/1891

YEAR	TM/L	G	AB	R	H	2B	3B	HR	RBI	BB	SO	AVG	OBP	SLG	PRO+	BR	/A	RC	SB	CS	SBR	FR	POS	TPR
1891	Cle-N	30	124	10	30	1	1	0	13	1	15	.242	.248	.266	49	-8	-9	10	6			-4	O/P	-1.1

YEAR	TM/L	G	AB	R	H	2B	3B	HR	RBI	BB	SO	AVG	OBP	SLG	PRO+	BR	/A	RC	SB	CS	SBR	FR	POS	TPR
1896	Cle-N	16	64	6	11	0	1	0	3	4	6	.172	.221	.203	13	-8	-9	4	3			-4	O	-1.1
Total	2	46	188	16	41	1	2	0	16	5	21	.218	.238	.245	36	-16	-17	14	9			-8	/OP	-2.2

■ JIMMY SHECKARD

Sheckard, Samuel James Tilden   b: 11/23/1878, Upper Chanceford, Pa.   d: 1/15/47, Lancaster, Pa.   BL/TR, 5'9", 175 lbs.   Deb: 9/14/1897

YEAR	TM/L	G	AB	R	H	2B	3B	HR	RBI	BB	SO	AVG	OBP	SLG	PRO+	BR	/A	RC	SB	CS	SBR	FR	POS	TPR
1897	Bro-N	13	49	12	14	3	2	3	14	6		.286	.364	.612	166	4	4	13	5			-3	S/O	0.1
1898	Bro-N	105	408	51	113	17	9	4	64	37		.277	.349	.392	115	8	8	60	8			-3	*O/3	-0.1
1899	Bal-N	147	536	104	158	18	10	3	75	56		.295	.380	.382	106	11	7	110	77			21	*O/1	1.6
1900	Bro-N	85	273	74	82	19	10	1	39	42		.300	.401	.454	131	16	13	63	30			2	O	0.7
1901	Bro-N	133	554	116	196	29	19	11	104	47		.354	.407	**.534**	170	51	49	138	35			7	*O3	4.2
1902	Bal-A	4	15	3	4	1	0	0	0	1		.267	.313	.333	77	-0	-0	2	2			-1	/O	-0.1
	Bro-N	123	486	86	129	20	10	4	37	57		.265	.351	.372	124	16	15	74	23			8	*O	1.5
1903	Bro-N	139	515	99	171	29	9	9	75	75		.332	.417	.476	161	40	**42**	135	67			23	*O	5.4
1904	Bro-N	143	507	70	121	23	6	1	46	56		.239	.314	.314	98	-1	1	60	21			7	*O/2	0.3
1905	Bro-N	130	480	58	140	20	11	3	41	61		.292	.372	.398	142	20	25	83	23			15	*O	3.2
1906	*Chi-N	149	549	90	144	27	10	1	45	67		.262	.343	.353	113	13	9	83	30			0	*O	0.7
1907	*Chi-N	143	484	76	129	23	1	1	36	76		.267	.366	.324	112	14	10	75	31			-10	*O	-0.5
1908	*Chi-N	115	403	54	93	18	3	2	22	62		.231	.333	.305	102	5	3	48	18			-2	*O	0.0
1909	Chi-N	148	525	81	134	29	5	1	43	72		.255	.346	.335	109	9	7	70	15			-3	*O	0.0
1910	*Chi-N	144	507	82	130	27	6	5	51	83	53	.256	.366	.363	114	11	11	78	22			12	*O	1.8
1911	Chi-N	156	539	**121**	149	26	11	4	50	**147**	58	.276	**.434**	.388	130	32	32	106	32			17	*O	**4.3**
1912	Chi-N	146	523	85	128	22	10	3	47	**122**	81	.245	.392	.342	102	8	8	76	15			12	*O	1.5
1913	StL-N	52	136	18	27	2	1	0	17	41	25	.199	.388	.228	79	-1	-1	15	5			-2	O	-0.3
	Cin-N	47	116	16	22	1	3	0	7	27	16	.190	.343	.250	71	-3	-3	12	6			-2	O	-0.5
	Yr	99	252	34	49	3	4	0	24	68	41	.194	.368	.238	76	-4	-4	26	11			-4		-0.8
Total	17	2122	7605	1296	2084	354	136	56	813	1135	233	.274	.372	.378	121	250	240	1304	465			96	*O/3S21	23.8

■ DAN SHEEHAN

Sheehan, Daniel   b: 12/18/1872, Cleveland, Ohio   5'6", 142 lbs.   Deb: 8/02/00

YEAR	TM/L	G	AB	R	H	2B	3B	HR	RBI	BB	SO	AVG	OBP	SLG	PRO+	BR	/A	RC	SB	CS	SBR	FR	POS	TPR
1900	NY-N	1	2	0	0	0	0	0	0	0	0	.000	.000	.000	-99	-1	-1	0	0			0	/S	0.0

■ JIM SHEEHAN

Sheehan, James Thomas "Big Jim"   b: 6/3/13, New Haven, Conn.   BR/TR, 6'2", 196 lbs.   Deb: 9/26/36

YEAR	TM/L	G	AB	R	H	2B	3B	HR	RBI	BB	SO	AVG	OBP	SLG	PRO+	BR	/A	RC	SB	CS	SBR	FR	POS	TPR
1936	NY-N	1	4	0	0	0	0	0	0	0	2	.000	.000	.000	-99	-1	-1	0	0			-0	/C	0.0

■ JACK SHEEHAN

Sheehan, John Thomas   b: 4/15/1893, Chicago, Ill.   d: 5/29/87, W.Palm Beach, Fla.   BB/TR, 5'8.5", 165 lbs.   Deb: 9/11/20

YEAR	TM/L	G	AB	R	H	2B	3B	HR	RBI	BB	SO	AVG	OBP	SLG	PRO+	BR	/A	RC	SB	CS	SBR	FR	POS	TPR
1920	*Bro-N	3	5	0	2	1	0	0	0	1	0	.400	.500	.600	208	1	1	2	0	0	0	0	/S3	0.1
1921	Bro-N	5	12	2	0	0	0	0	0	0	1	.000	.000	.000	-97	-3	-3	0	0	0	0	0	/2S3	-0.3
Total	2	8	17	2	2	1	0	0	0	1	1	.118	.167	.176	-7	-3	-3	2	0	0	0	0	/S23	-0.2

■ TOMMY SHEEHAN

Sheehan, Thomas H.   b: 11/6/1877, Sacramento, Cal.   d: 5/22/59, Panama City, Pan.   TR, 5'8", 160 lbs.   Deb: 4/12/06

YEAR	TM/L	G	AB	R	H	2B	3B	HR	RBI	BB	SO	AVG	OBP	SLG	PRO+	BR	/A	RC	SB	CS	SBR	FR	POS	TPR
1906	Pit-N	95	315	28	76	6	3	1	34	18		.241	.282	.289	77	-8	-9	32	13			-5	3	-1.9
1907	Pit-N	75	226	23	62	2	3	0	25	23		.274	.341	.310	105	2	2	30	10			-1	3S	0.2
1908	Bro-N	146	468	45	100	18	2	0	29	53		.214	.294	.261	82	-9	-7	40	9			-6	*3	-1.0
Total	3	316	1009	96	238	26	8	1	88	94		.236	.301	.280	86	-15	-14	102	32			-11	3/S	-2.7

■ BIFF SHEEHAN

Sheehan, Timothy James   b: 2/13/1868, Hartford, Conn.   d: 10/21/23, Hartford, Conn.   5'9", 165 lbs.   Deb: 7/22/1895

YEAR	TM/L	G	AB	R	H	2B	3B	HR	RBI	BB	SO	AVG	OBP	SLG	PRO+	BR	/A	RC	SB	CS	SBR	FR	POS	TPR
1895	StL-N	52	180	24	57	3	6	1	18	20	6	.317	.394	.417	113	4	4	33	7			-2	O1	0.0
1896	StL-N	6	19	0	3	0	0	0	1	4	0	.158	.304	.158	27	-2	-2	1	0			-1	/O	-0.1
Total	2	58	199	24	60	3	6	1	19	24	6	.302	.385	.392	105	2	2	34	7			-3	/O1	-0.1

■ EARL SHEELY

Sheely, Earl Homer "Whitey"   b: 2/12/1893, Bushnell, Ill.   d: 9/16/52, Seattle, Wash.   BR/TR, 6'3.5", 195 lbs.   Deb: 4/14/21

YEAR	TM/L	G	AB	R	H	2B	3B	HR	RBI	BB	SO	AVG	OBP	SLG	PRO+	BR	/A	RC	SB	CS	SBR	FR	POS	TPR
1921	Chi-A	154	563	68	171	25	6	11	95	57	34	.304	.375	.428	106	4	5	90	4	9	-4	5	*1	0.5
1922	Chi-A	149	526	72	167	37	4	6	80	60	27	.317	.393	.437	117	14	14	92	4	6	-2	2	*1	0.2
1923	Chi-A	156	570	74	169	25	3	4	88	79	30	.296	.387	.372	102	3	4	87	5	5	-2	-1	*1	-0.4
1924	Chi-A	146	535	84	171	34	3	3	103	95	28	.320	.426	.411	120	18	21	102	7	4	-0	-10	*1	0.4
1925	Chi-A	153	600	93	189	43	3	9	111	68	23	.315	.389	.442	117	10	15	106	3	3	-1	-5	*1	0.5
1926	Chi-A	145	525	77	157	40	2	6	89	75	13	.299	.394	.417	116	11	14	92	3	1	0	-5	*1	0.8
1927	Chi-A	45	129	11	27	3	0	2	16	20	5	.209	.320	.279	58	-8	-7	12	1	3	-2	-4	1	-1.3
1929	Pit-N	139	485	63	142	22	4	6	88	75	24	.293	.392	.392	93	-1	-3	77	6			-0	*1	-0.8
1931	Bos-N	147	538	30	147	15	2	1	77	34	21	.273	.319	.314	73	-21	-19	56	0			-3	*1	-3.2
Total	9	1234	4471	572	1340	244	27	48	747	563	205	.300	.383	.399	104	30	44	715	33	31		-14	*1	-3.3

■ BUD SHEELY

Sheely, Hollis Kimball   b: 11/26/20, Spokane, Wash.   d: 10/17/85, Sacramento, Cal.   BL/TR, 6'1", 200 lbs.   Deb: 7/26/51

YEAR	TM/L	G	AB	R	H	2B	3B	HR	RBI	BB	SO	AVG	OBP	SLG	PRO+	BR	/A	RC	SB	CS	SBR	FR	POS	TPR
1951	Chi-A	34	89	2	16	2	0	0	7	6	7	.180	.240	.202	21	-10	-10	5	0	0	0	3	C	-0.3
1952	Chi-A	36	75	1	18	2	0	0	3	12	7	.240	.352	.267	73	-2	-2	8	0	1	-1	-1	C	-0.1
1953	Chi-A	31	46	4	10	1	0	0	2	9	8	.217	.345	.239	58	-2	-2	5	0	0	0	0	C	0.0
Total	3	101	210	7	44	5	0	0	12	27	22	.210	.305	.233	49	-14	-14	17	0	1	-1	2	/C	-0.4

■ CHUCK SHEERIN

Sheerin, Charles Joseph   b: 4/17/09, Brooklyn, N.Y.   d: 9/27/86, Valley Stream, N.Y.   BR/TR, 5'11.5", 198 lbs.   Deb: 4/21/36

YEAR	TM/L	G	AB	R	H	2B	3B	HR	RBI	BB	SO	AVG	OBP	SLG	PRO+	BR	/A	RC	SB	CS	SBR	FR	POS	TPR
1936	Phi-N	39	72	4	19	4	0	0	4	7	18	.264	.329	.319	68	-2	-3	8	0			-3	23/S	-0.3

■ LARRY SHEETS

Sheets, Larry Kent   b: 12/6/59, Staunton, Va.   BL/TR, 6'3", 217 lbs.   Deb: 9/18/84

YEAR	TM/L	G	AB	R	H	2B	3B	HR	RBI	BB	SO	AVG	OBP	SLG	PRO+	BR	/A	RC	SB	CS	SBR	FR	POS	TPR
1984	Bal-A	8	16	3	7	1	0	1	2	1	3	.438	.471	.688	221	2	2	5	0	0	0	1	/O	0.3
1985	Bal-A	113	328	43	86	8	0	17	50	28	52	.262	.324	.442	110	3	4	43	0	1	-1	-0	D/O1	0.3
1986	Bal-A	112	338	42	92	17	1	18	60	21	56	.272	.319	.488	117	6	7	47	2	0	1	-1	DO/C13	0.6
1987	Bal-A	135	469	74	148	23	0	31	94	31	67	.316	.362	.563	144	25	27	90	1	1	-0	-7	*O/1D	1.6
1988	Bal-A	136	452	38	104	19	1	10	47	42	72	.230	.304	.343	83	-11	-10	45	1	6	-3	-1	OD/1	-1.5
1989	Bal-A	102	304	33	74	12	1	7	33	26	58	.243	.309	.359	90	-5	-4	34	1	1	-0	0	D	-0.3
1990	Det-A	131	360	40	94	17	2	10	52	24	42	.261	.311	.403	99	-2	-2	41	1	3	-2	-5	OD	-0.8
Total	7	737	2267	273	605	97	5	94	338	173	350	.267	.322	.438	110	18	25	305	6	12	-5	-12	DO/1C3	0.2

■ GARY SHEFFIELD

Sheffield, Gary Antonian   b: 11/18/68, Tampa, Fla.   BR/TR, 5'11", 190 lbs.   Deb: 9/03/88

YEAR	TM/L	G	AB	R	H	2B	3B	HR	RBI	BB	SO	AVG	OBP	SLG	PRO+	BR	/A	RC	SB	CS	SBR	FR	POS	TPR
1988	Mil-A	24	80	12	19	1	0	4	12	7	7	.237	.299	.400	93	-1	-1	8	3	1	0	-10	S	-0.9
1989	Mil-A	95	368	34	91	18	0	5	32	27	33	.247	.306	.337	82	-9	-9	39	10	6	-1	-17	S3/D	-2.1
1990	Mil-A	125	487	67	143	30	1	10	67	44	41	.294	.356	.421	120	11	13	73	25	10	2	-4	*3	1.2
Total	3	244	935	113	253	49	1	19	111	78	81	.271	.331	.386	103	1	3	120	38	17	1	-31	3/SD	-1.8

■ JOHN SHELBY

Shelby, John T.   b: 2/23/58, Lexington, Ky.   BB/TR, 6'1", 175 lbs.   Deb: 9/15/81

YEAR	TM/L	G	AB	R	H	2B	3B	HR	RBI	BB	SO	AVG	OBP	SLG	PRO+	BR	/A	RC	SB	CS	SBR	FR	POS	TPR
1981	Bal-A	7	2	2	0	0	0	0	0	0	1	.000	.000	.000	-99	-1	-1	0	2	0	1	0	/O	0.0
1982	Bal-A	26	35	8	11	3	0	1	2	0	5	.314	.314	.486	116	1	1	5	0	1	-1	1	O	0.0
1983	*Bal-A	126	325	52	84	15	2	5	27	18	64	.258	.297	.363	82	-9	-8	37	15	2	3	-8	*O/D	-1.3
1984	Bal-A	128	383	44	80	12	5	6	30	20	71	.209	.248	.313	55	-24	-23	31	12	4	1	-1	*O	-2.2
1985	Bal-A	69	205	28	58	6	2	7	27	7	44	.283	.307	.434	103	-1	0	26	5	1	1	6	O/2D	0.7
1986	Bal-A	135	404	54	92	14	4	11	49	18	75	.228	.264	.364	70	-18	-18	39	18	6	2	-5	*O/D	-2.3
1987	Bal-A	21	32	4	6	0	0	1	3	1	13	.188	.212	.281	30	-3	-3	2	1	0	1	1	O/D	-0.2
	LA-N	120	476	61	132	26	0	21	69	31	97	.277	.323	.464	108	2	4	70	16	6	1	6	*O	0.3
1988	*LA-N	140	494	65	130	23	6	10	64	44	128	.263	.323	.395	109	3	5	62	16	5	2	0	*O	0.3
1989	LA-N	108	345	28	63	11	1	1	12	25	92	.183	.238	.229	35	-29	-29	18	10	7	-1	-5	O	-3.9
1990	LA-N	25	24	2	6	1	0	0	2	0	7	.250	.250	.292	51	-2	-2	2	1	0	0	0	O	0.0

YEAR	TM/L	G	AB	R	H	2B	3B	HR	RBI	BB	SO	AVG	OBP	SLG	PRO+	BR	/A	RC	SB	CS	SBR	FR	POS	TPR
	Det-A	78	222	22	55	9	3	4	20	10	51	.248	.280	.369	81	-7	-6	20	3	5	-2	3	O/D	-0.6
Total	10	983	2947	370	717	120	23	67	305	174	648	.243	.286	.368	81	-88	-80	312	98	38	7	1	O/D2	-9.1

■ BOB SHELDON   Sheldon, Bob Mitchell b: 11/27/50, Montebello, Cal. BL/TR, 6', 170 lbs. Deb: 4/10/74

YEAR	TM/L	G	AB	R	H	2B	3B	HR	RBI	BB	SO	AVG	OBP	SLG	PRO+	BR	/A	RC	SB	CS	SBR	FR	POS	TPR
1974	Mil-A	10	17	4	2	1	1	0	0	4	2	.118	.286	.294	67	-1	-1	2	0	1	-1	-1	/2D	-0.1
1975	Mil-A	53	181	17	52	3	3	0	14	13	14	.287	.342	.337	92	-2	-2	20	0	3	-2	-8	2/D	-1.0
1977	Mil-A	31	64	9	13	4	1	0	3	6	9	.203	.271	.297	55	-4	-4	6	0	0	0	1	D/2	-0.2
Total	3	94	262	30	67	8	5	0	17	23	25	.256	.321	.324	81	-6	-6	27	0	4	-2	-8	/2D	-1.3

■ HUGH SHELLEY   Shelley, Hubert Leneirre b: 10/26/10, Rogers, Tex. d: 6/16/78, Beaumont, Tex. BR/TR, 6', 170 lbs. Deb: 6/25/35

YEAR	TM/L	G	AB	R	H	2B	3B	HR	RBI	BB	SO	AVG	OBP	SLG	PRO+	BR	/A	RC	SB	CS	SBR	FR	POS	TPR
1935	Det-A	7	8	1	2	0	0	0	1	2	1	.250	.400	.250	74	-0	-0	1	0	0	0	0	/O	0.0

■ SKEETER SHELTON   Shelton, Andrew Kemper b: 6/29/1888, Huntington, W.Va. d: 1/9/54, Huntington, W.Va. BR/TR, 5'11", 175 lbs. Deb: 8/25/15

YEAR	TM/L	G	AB	R	H	2B	3B	HR	RBI	BB	SO	AVG	OBP	SLG	PRO+	BR	/A	RC	SB	CS	SBR	FR	POS	TPR
1915	NY-A	10	40	1	1	0	0	0	2	10		.025	.071	.025	-71	-8	-8	0	0		0		O	-0.9

■ STEVE SHEMO   Shemo, Stephen Michael b: 4/9/15, Swoyersville, Pa. BR/TR, 5'11", 175 lbs. Deb: 4/18/44

YEAR	TM/L	G	AB	R	H	2B	3B	HR	RBI	BB	SO	AVG	OBP	SLG	PRO+	BR	/A	RC	SB	CS	SBR	FR	POS	TPR
1944	Bos-N	18	31	3	9	2	0	0	1	1	3	.290	.313	.355	84	-1	-1	4	0			3	2/3	0.4
1945	Bos-N	17	46	4	11	1	0	0	7	1	3	.239	.255	.261	43	-4	-4	3	0			-6	2/3S	-0.8
Total	2	35	77	7	20	3	0	0	8	2	6	.260	.278	.299	60	-4	-4	7	0			-2	/23S	-0.4

■ JACK SHEPARD   Shepard, Jack Leroy b: 5/13/32, Clovis, Cal. BR/TR, 6'2", 195 lbs. Deb: 6/19/53

YEAR	TM/L	G	AB	R	H	2B	3B	HR	RBI	BB	SO	AVG	OBP	SLG	PRO+	BR	/A	RC	SB	CS	SBR	FR	POS	TPR
1953	Pit-N	2	4	0	1	0	0	0	0	0	2	.250	.250	.250	31	-0	-0	0	0	0	0	-0	/C	0.0
1954	Pit-N	82	227	24	69	8	2	3	22	26	33	.304	.375	.396	103	1	2	33	0	0	0	2	C	0.5
1955	Pit-N	94	264	24	63	10	2	2	23	33	25	.239	.323	.314	71	-11	-10	27	1	0	0	-9	C	-1.6
1956	Pit-N	100	256	24	62	11	2	7	30	25	37	.242	.310	.383	87	-6	-5	29	1	1	-0	1	C/1	-0.1
Total	4	278	751	72	195	29	6	12	75	84	97	.260	.334	.362	86	-16	-14	90	2	1	0	-7	C/1	-1.2

■ RAY SHEPARDSON   Shepardson, Raymond Francis b: 5/3/1897, Little Falls, N.Y. d: 11/8/75, Little Falls, N.Y. BR/TR, 5'11.5", 170 lbs. Deb: 9/19/24

YEAR	TM/L	G	AB	R	H	2B	3B	HR	RBI	BB	SO	AVG	OBP	SLG	PRO+	BR	/A	RC	SB	CS	SBR	FR	POS	TPR
1924	StL-N	3	6	1	0	0	0	0	0		3	.000	.000	.000	-99	-2	-2	0	0	0	0	0	/C	-0.1

■ RON SHEPHERD   Shepherd, Ronald Wayne b: 10/27/60, Longview, Tex. BR/TR, 6'4", 175 lbs. Deb: 9/05/84

YEAR	TM/L	G	AB	R	H	2B	3B	HR	RBI	BB	SO	AVG	OBP	SLG	PRO+	BR	/A	RC	SB	CS	SBR	FR	POS	TPR
1984	Tor-A	12	4	0	0	0	0	0	0	0	3	.000	.000	.000	-97	-1	-1	0	0	1	-1	1	/OD	0.0
1985	Tor-A	38	35	7	4	2	0	0	1	2	12	.114	.162	.171	-8	-5	-5	1	3	0	1	3	OD	0.0
1986	Tor-A	65	69	16	14	4	0	2	4	3	22	.203	.236	.348	55	-4	-5	6	0	0	0	3	OD	-0.2
Total	3	115	108	23	18	6	0	2	5	5	37	.167	.204	.278	29	-11	-11	7	3	1	0	7	/OD	-0.2

■ JOHN SHEPPARD   Sheppard, John b: Baltimore, Md. Deb: 6/27/1873

YEAR	TM/L	G	AB	R	H	2B	3B	HR	RBI	BB	SO	AVG	OBP	SLG	PRO+	BR	/A	RC	SB	CS	SBR	FR	POS	TPR
1873	Mar-n	3	11	1	0	0	0	0	0			.000	.000	.000	-99	-3	-3						/CO	

■ SHERIDAN   Sheridan Deb: 10/09/1875

YEAR	TM/L	G	AB	R	H	2B	3B	HR	RBI	BB	SO	AVG	OBP	SLG	PRO+	BR	/A	RC	SB	CS	SBR	FR	POS	TPR
1875	Atl-n	1	4	0	0	0	0	0	0			.000	.000	.000	-99	-1	-1	0					/O	0.0

■ RED SHERIDAN   Sheridan, Eugene Anthony b: 11/14/1896, Brooklyn, N.Y. d: 11/25/75, Queens Village, N.Y. BR/TR, 5'10.5", 160 lbs. Deb: 7/03/18

YEAR	TM/L	G	AB	R	H	2B	3B	HR	RBI	BB	SO	AVG	OBP	SLG	PRO+	BR	/A	RC	SB	CS	SBR	FR	POS	TPR
1918	Bro-N	2	4	0	1	0	0	0	0	1	0	.250	.400	.250	100	0	0	1	1			-1	/2	0.0
1920	Bro-N	3	2	0	0	0	0	0	0	0	1	.000	.000	.000	-97	-1	-1	0	0	0	0	1	/S	0.1
Total	2	5	6	0	1	0	0	0	0	1	1	.167	.286	.167	37	-0	-0	1	1	0		1	/S2	0.1

■ NEILL SHERIDAN   Sheridan, Neill Rawlins "Wild Horse" b: 11/20/21, Sacramento, Cal. BR/TR, 6'1.5", 195 lbs. Deb: 9/19/48

YEAR	TM/L	G	AB	R	H	2B	3B	HR	RBI	BB	SO	AVG	OBP	SLG	PRO+	BR	/A	RC	SB	CS	SBR	FR	POS	TPR
1948	Bos-A	2	1	0	0	0	0	0	0	0	1	.000	.000	.000	-95	-0	-0	0	0	0	0	0	H	0.0

■ PAT SHERIDAN   Sheridan, Patrick Arthur b: 12/4/57, Ann Arbor, Mich. BL/TR, 6'3", 175 lbs. Deb: 9/16/81

YEAR	TM/L	G	AB	R	H	2B	3B	HR	RBI	BB	SO	AVG	OBP	SLG	PRO+	BR	/A	RC	SB	CS	SBR	FR	POS	TPR
1981	KC-A	3	1	0	0	0	0	0	0	0	1	.000	.000	.000	-99	-0	-0	0	0	0	0	0	/O	0.0
1983	KC-A	109	333	43	90	12	2	7	36	20	64	.270	.312	.381	89	-5	-5	41	12	3	2	3	*O	-0.1
1984	*KC-A	138	481	64	136	24	4	8	53	41	91	.283	.340	.399	103	3	2	68	19	6	2	-3	*O	-0.2
1985	*KC-A	78	206	18	47	9	2	3	17	23	38	.228	.309	.335	76	-7	-7	23	11	3	2	-6	O/D	-1.1
1986	Det-A	98	236	41	56	9	1	6	19	21	57	.237	.302	.360	80	-7	-7	27	9	2	2	3	O/D	-0.4
1987	*Det-A	141	421	57	109	19	3	6	49	44	90	.259	.330	.361	87	-10	-7	50	18	13	-2	-9	*O	-2.0
1988	Det-A	127	347	47	88	9	5	11	47	44	64	.254	.341	.403	112	4	6	48	8	6	-1	-8	*O/D	-0.5
1989	Det-A	50	120	16	29	3	0	3	15	17	21	.242	.336	.342	93	-1	-1	15	4	0	1	-1	O/D	0.0
	*SF-N	70	161	20	33	3	4	3	14	13	45	.205	.264	.329	71	-7	-6	15	4	1	1	3	O	-0.2
Total	8	814	2306	306	588	88	21	47	250	223	471	.255	.322	.373	92	-30	-25	286	85	34	5	-17	O/D	-4.5

■ ED SHERLING   Sherling, Edward Creech "Shine" b: 7/17/1897, Coalsburg, Pa. d: 11/16/65, Enterprise, Cal. BR/TR, 6'1", 185 lbs. Deb: 8/13/24

YEAR	TM/L	G	AB	R	H	2B	3B	HR	RBI	BB	SO	AVG	OBP	SLG	PRO+	BR	/A	RC	SB	CS	SBR	FR	POS	TPR
1924	Phi-A	4	2	2	1	1	0	0	0	0		.500	.500	1.000	278	0	0	1	0	0	0	0	H	0.0

■ MONK SHERLOCK   Sherlock, John Clinton b: 10/26/04, Buffalo, N.Y. d: 11/26/85, Buffalo, N.Y. BR/TR, 5'10", 175 lbs. Deb: 4/20/30

YEAR	TM/L	G	AB	R	H	2B	3B	HR	RBI	BB	SO	AVG	OBP	SLG	PRO+	BR	/A	RC	SB	CS	SBR	FR	POS	TPR
1930	Phi-N	92	299	51	97	18	2	0	38	27	28	.324	.380	.398	83	-5	-8	45	0			4	1/2O	-0.5

■ VINCE SHERLOCK   Sherlock, Vincent Thomas "Baldy" b: 3/27/09, Buffalo, N.Y. BR/TR, 6', 180 lbs. Deb: 9/18/35

YEAR	TM/L	G	AB	R	H	2B	3B	HR	RBI	BB	SO	AVG	OBP	SLG	PRO+	BR	/A	RC	SB	CS	SBR	FR	POS	TPR
1935	Bro-N	9	26	4	12	1	0	0	6	1	2	.462	.481	.500	168	2	2	7	1			-1	/2	0.2

■ DENNIS SHERRILL   Sherrill, Dennis Lee b: 3/3/56, Miami, Fla. BR/TR, 6', 165 lbs. Deb: 9/04/78

YEAR	TM/L	G	AB	R	H	2B	3B	HR	RBI	BB	SO	AVG	OBP	SLG	PRO+	BR	/A	RC	SB	CS	SBR	FR	POS	TPR
1978	NY-A	2	1	1	0	0	0	0	0	0	1	.000	.000	.000	-99	-0	-0	0	0	0	0	-0	/3D	0.0
1980	NY-A	3	4	0	1	0	0	0	0	0	1	.250	.250	.250	38	-0	-0	0	0	0	0	-0	/S2	0.0
Total	2	5	5	1	1	0	0	0	0	0	2	.200	.200	.200	11	-1	-1	0	0	0	0	-0	/S2D3	0.0

■ NORM SHERRY   Sherry, Norman Burt b: 7/16/31, New York, N.Y. BR/TR, 5'11", 180 lbs. Deb: 4/12/59 MC

YEAR	TM/L	G	AB	R	H	2B	3B	HR	RBI	BB	SO	AVG	OBP	SLG	PRO+	BR	/A	RC	SB	CS	SBR	FR	POS	TPR
1959	LA-N	2	3	0	1	0	0	0	2	0	0	.333	.500	.333	119	0	0	0	0	0	0	-1	/C	0.0
1960	LA-N	47	138	22	39	4	1	8	19	12	29	.283	.353	.500	122	6	4	25	0	0	0	-4	C	0.2
1961	LA-N	47	121	10	31	2	0	5	21	9	30	.256	.308	.397	78	-3	-4	13	0	0	0	4	C	0.3
1962	LA-N	35	88	7	16	2	0	3	16	6	17	.182	.242	.307	49	-7	-6	6	0	0	0	9	C	0.3
1963	NY-N	63	147	6	20	1	0	2	11	10	26	.136	.206	.184	13	-16	-17	5	1	0	0	3	C	-1.2
Total	5	194	497	45	107	9	1	18	69	37	102	.215	.280	.346	69	-20	-22	49	1	0	0	10	C	-0.4

■ BARRY SHETRONE   Shetrone, Barry Stevan b: 7/6/38, Baltimore, Md. BL/TR, 6'2", 190 lbs. Deb: 7/27/59

YEAR	TM/L	G	AB	R	H	2B	3B	HR	RBI	BB	SO	AVG	OBP	SLG	PRO+	BR	/A	RC	SB	CS	SBR	FR	POS	TPR
1959	Bal-A	33	79	8	16	1	1	0	5	5	9	.203	.250	.241	36	-7	-7	6	3	0	1	-2	O	-0.8
1960	Bal-A	1	0	1	0	0	0	0	0	0	0	—	—	—	—	0	0	0	0	0	0	0	R	0.0
1961	Bal-A	3	7	0	1	0	0	0	1	0	2	.143	.143	.143	-24	-1	-1	0	0	0	0	0	/O	0.0
1962	Bal-A	21	24	3	6	1	0	1	1	0	5	.250	.250	.417	80	-1	-1	3	0	0	0	1	/O	0.0
1963	Was-A	2	2	0	0	0	0	0	0	0	0	.000	.000	.000	-99	-1	-1	0	0	0	0	0	H	0.0
Total	5	60	112	12	23	2	1	1	7	5	16	.205	.239	.268	39	-10	-9	8	3	0	1	-1	/O	-0.8

■ JOHN SHETZLINE   Shetzline, John Henry b: 1850, Philadelphia, Pa. d: 12/15/1892, Philadelphia, Pa. 5'11.5", 190 lbs. Deb: 5/02/1882

YEAR	TM/L	G	AB	R	H	2B	3B	HR	RBI	BB	SO	AVG	OBP	SLG	PRO+	BR	/A	RC	SB	CS	SBR	FR	POS	TPR
1882	Bal-a	73	282	23	62	8	3	0		5		.220	.233	.270	75	-9	-6	18				3	32/OS	-0.2

■ JIMMY SHEVLIN   Shevlin, James Cornelius b: 7/9/09, Cincinnati, Ohio d: 10/30/74, Ft.Lauderdale, Fla BL/TL, 5'10.5", 155 lbs. Deb: 6/29/30

YEAR	TM/L	G	AB	R	H	2B	3B	HR	RBI	BB	SO	AVG	OBP	SLG	PRO+	BR	/A	RC	SB	CS	SBR	FR	POS	TPR
1930	Det-A	28	14	4	2	0	0	0	2	2	3	.143	.250	.143	2	-2	-2	1	0	0	0	1	1	-0.3

YEAR	TM/L	G	AB	R	H	2B	3B	HR	RBI	BB	SO	AVG	OBP	SLG	PRO+	BR	/A	RC	SB	CS	SBR	FR	POS	TPR
1932	Cin-N	7	24	3	5	2	0	0	4	4	0	.208	.345	.292	76	-1	-1	3	4			-0	/1	0.0
1934	Cin-N	18	39	6	12	2	0	0	6	6	5	.308	.400	.359	107	1	1	6	0			0	1	0.0
Total	3	53	77	13	19	4	0	0	12	12	8	.247	.356	.299	77	-2	-2	9	4	0		1	/1	-0.3

■ PETE SHIELDS
Shields, Francis Leroy b: 9/21/1891, Swiftwater, Miss. d: 2/11/61, Jackson, Miss. BR/TR, 6', 175 lbs. Deb: 4/14/15

YEAR	TM/L	G	AB	R	H	2B	3B	HR	RBI	BB	SO	AVG	OBP	SLG	PRO+	BR	/A	RC	SB	CS	SBR	FR	POS	TPR
1915	Cle-A	23	72	4	15	6	0	0	6	4	14	.208	.250	.292	61	-4	-4	5	3	3	-1	0	1	-0.5

■ JIM SHILLING
Shilling, James Robert b: 5/14/14, Tulsa, Okla. d: 9/12/86, Tulsa, Okla. BR/TR, 5'11", 175 lbs. Deb: 4/21/39

YEAR	TM/L	G	AB	R	H	2B	3B	HR	RBI	BB	SO	AVG	OBP	SLG	PRO+	BR	/A	RC	SB	CS	SBR	FR	POS	TPR
1939	Cle-A	31	98	8	27	7	2	0	12	7	9	.276	.324	.388	84	-3	-2	12	1	0	0	4	2/S	0.2
	Phi-N	11	33	3	10	1	3	0	4	1	4	.303	.324	.515	126	1	1	5	0			-1	/2S3O	0.0

■ GINGER SHINAULT
Shinault, Enoch Erskine b: 9/7/1892, Benton, Ark. d: 12/29/30, Denver, Colo. BR/TR, 5'11", 170 lbs. Deb: 7/04/21

YEAR	TM/L	G	AB	R	H	2B	3B	HR	RBI	BB	SO	AVG	OBP	SLG	PRO+	BR	/A	RC	SB	CS	SBR	FR	POS	TPR
1921	Cle-A	22	29	5	11	1	0	0	4	6	5	.379	.486	.414	129	2	2	7	1	0	0	3	C	0.5
1922	Cle-A	13	15	1	2	1	0	0	0	0	2	.133	.133	.200	-14	-3	-3	0	0	0	0	-4	C	-0.5
Total	2	35	44	6	13	2	0	0	4	6	7	.295	.380	.341	85	-1	-1	7	1	0	0	-1	/C	0.0

■ BILLY SHINDLE
Shindle, William b: 12/5/1860, Gloucester, N.J. d: 6/3/36, Lakeland, N.J. TR, 5'8.5", 155 lbs. Deb: 10/04/1886

YEAR	TM/L	G	AB	R	H	2B	3B	HR	RBI	BB	SO	AVG	OBP	SLG	PRO+	BR	/A	RC	SB	CS	SBR	FR	POS	TPR
1886	Det-N	7	26	4	7	1	0	0	4	0	5	.269	.269	.269	62	-1	-1	2	2			1	/S	0.0
1887	Det-N	22	84	17	24	3	2	0	12	7	10	.286	.341	.369	96	-0	-0	15	13			-5	3/O	-0.4
1888	Bal-a	135	514	61	107	14	8	1	53	20		.208	.249	.272	71	-17	-15	49	52			37	*3	2.0
1889	Bal-a	138	567	122	178	24	7	3	64	42	37	.314	.369	.397	118	15	13	106	56			20	*3	2.9
1890	Phi-P	132	584	127	188	21	21	10	90	40	30	.322	.369	.481	125	21	18	126	51			8	*S/3	2.7
1891	Phi-N	103	415	68	87	13	1	0	38	33	39	.210	.278	.246	53	-23	-25	34	17			6	*3/S	-1.3
1892	Bal-N	143	619	100	156	20	18	3	50	35	34	.252	.301	.357	97	-2	-4	75	24			36	*3/S	3.7
1893	Bal-N	125	521	100	136	22	11	1	75	66	17	.261	.353	.351	87	-7	-9	72	17			8	*3	0.0
1894	Bro-N	116	476	94	141	22	9	4	96	29	20	.296	.344	.405	88	-15	-8	75	19			1	*3	-0.6
1895	Bro-N	116	477	91	133	21	2	3	69	47	28	.279	.357	.350	92	-9	-2	67	17			0	*3	0.0
1896	Bro-N	131	516	75	144	24	9	1	61	24	20	.279	.316	.366	86	-15	-10	69	24			-12	*3	-1.2
1897	Bro-N	134	542	83	154	32	6	4	105	35		.284	.336	.387	98	-6	-1	80	23			-12	*3	-1.0
1898	Bro-N	120	540	50	105	10	3	1	41	10		.225	.249	.266	50	-30	-30	32	3			7	*3	-1.8
Total	13	1422	5807	992	1560	226	97	31	758	388	240	.269	.323	.357	90	-90	-75	804	318			95	*3S/O	5.0

■ RAY SHINES
Shines, Anthony Raymond b: 7/18/56, Durham, N.C. BB/TR, 6'1", 210 lbs. Deb: 9/09/83

YEAR	TM/L	G	AB	R	H	2B	3B	HR	RBI	BB	SO	AVG	OBP	SLG	PRO+	BR	/A	RC	SB	CS	SBR	FR	POS	TPR
1983	Mon-N	3	2	0	1	0	0	0	0	0	0	.500	.500	.500	179	0	0	1	0	0	0	0	/O	0.0
1984	Mon-N	12	20	0	6	1	0	0	2	0	3	.300	.300	.350	86	-1	-0	2	0	0	0	-1	/13	-0.1
1985	Mon-N	47	50	0	6	0	0	0	3	4	9	.120	.185	.120	-14	-7	-7	1	0	1	-1	0	/1P	-0.7
1987	Mon-N	6	9	0	2	0	0	0	0	1	0	.222	.364	.222	58	-0	-0	1	1	0	0	0	/1	0.0
Total	4	68	81	0	15	1	0	0	5	5	12	.185	.241	.198	24	-8	-8	4	1	1	-0	-1	/1P3O	-0.8

■ RALPH SHINNERS
Shinners, Ralph Peter b: 10/4/1895, Monches, Wis. d: 7/23/62, Milwaukee, Wis. BR/TR, 6', 180 lbs. Deb: 4/12/22

YEAR	TM/L	G	AB	R	H	2B	3B	HR	RBI	BB	SO	AVG	OBP	SLG	PRO+	BR	/A	RC	SB	CS	SBR	FR	POS	TPR
1922	NY-N	56	135	16	34	4	2	0	15	5	22	.252	.308	.311	60	-8	-8	12	3	5	-2	-0	O	-1.0
1923	NY-N	33	13	5	2	1	0	0	0	2	1	.154	.267	.231	33	-1	-1	1	0	0	0	3	/O	0.2
1925	StL-N	74	251	39	74	9	2	7	36	12	19	.295	.330	.430	90	-3	-4	35	8	5	-1	1	O	-0.4
Total	3	163	399	60	110	14	4	7	51	19	42	.276	.320	.383	78	-13	-14	48	11	10	-3	4	O	-1.2

■ TIM SHINNICK
Shinnick, Timothy James "Dandy" or "Good Eye" b: 11/6/1867, Exeter, N.H. d: 5/18/44, Exeter, N.H. BB/TR, 6', 150 lbs. Deb: 4/19/1890

YEAR	TM/L	G	AB	R	H	2B	3B	HR	RBI	BB	SO	AVG	OBP	SLG	PRO+	BR	/A	RC	SB	CS	SBR	FR	POS	TPR
1890	*Lou-a	133	493	87	126	16	11	1		62		.256	.348	.339	107	5	7	82	62			-25	*2/3	-1.1
1891	Lou-a	128	443	79	98	10	11	1	54	54	47	.221	.314	.300	79	-11	-11	54	36			-21	*2/3S	-1.9
Total	2	261	936	166	224	26	22	2	54	116	47	.239	.332	.321	94	-7	-4	136	98			-45	2/3S	-3.0

■ BILL SHIPKE
Shipke, William Martin "Skipper Bill" or "Muskrat Bill" (b: William Martin Shipkrethaver) b: 11/18/1882, St.Louis, Mo. d: 9/10/40, Omaha, Neb. TR, 5'7", 145 lbs. Deb: 4/23/06

YEAR	TM/L	G	AB	R	H	2B	3B	HR	RBI	BB	SO	AVG	OBP	SLG	PRO+	BR	/A	RC	SB	CS	SBR	FR	POS	TPR
1906	Cle-A	2	6	0	0	0	0	0	0	0		.000	.000	.000	-99	-1	-1	0	0			2	/2	0.0
1907	Was-A	64	189	17	37	3	2	1	9	15		.196	.255	.249	67	-8	-6	14	6			7	3	0.5
1908	Was-A	111	341	40	71	7	8	0	20	38		.208	.288	.276	93	-4	-1	33	15			-6	*3/2	0.0
1909	Was-A	9	16	2	2	1	0	0	0	2		.125	.222	.188	31	-1	-1	1	0			2	/3S	0.1
Total	4	186	552	59	110	11	10	1	29	55		.199	.272	.261	80	-15	-10	48	21			5	3/2S	0.6

■ CRAIG SHIPLEY
Shipley, Craig Barry b: 1/7/63, Parramatta, Australia BR/TR, 6'1", 175 lbs. Deb: 6/22/86

YEAR	TM/L	G	AB	R	H	2B	3B	HR	RBI	BB	SO	AVG	OBP	SLG	PRO+	BR	/A	RC	SB	CS	SBR	FR	POS	TPR
1986	LA-N	12	27	3	3	1	0	0	4	2	5	.111	.200	.148	-3	-4	-4	1	0	0	0	-1	S/23	-0.3
1987	LA-N	26	35	3	9	1	0	0	2	0	6	.257	.257	.286	45	-3	-3	2	0	0	0	3	S/3	0.2
1989	NY-N	4	7	3	1	0	0	0	0	0	1	.143	.143	.143	-19	-1	-1	0	0	0	0	0	/S3	0.0
Total	3	42	69	9	13	2	0	0	6	2	12	.188	.222	.217	21	-8	-7	3	0	0	0	2	/S32	-0.1

■ ART SHIRES
Shires, Charles Arthur "Art The Great" b: 8/13/07, Italy, Tex. d: 7/13/67, Italy, Tex. BL/TR, 6'1", 195 lbs. Deb: 8/20/28

YEAR	TM/L	G	AB	R	H	2B	3B	HR	RBI	BB	SO	AVG	OBP	SLG	PRO+	BR	/A	RC	SB	CS	SBR	FR	POS	TPR
1928	Chi-A	33	123	20	42	6	1	1	11	13	10	.341	.409	.431	122	4	4	21	0	3	-2	3	1	0.4
1929	Chi-A	100	353	41	110	20	7	3	41	32	20	.312	.370	.433	108	3	4	56	4	5	-2	0	1/2	-0.9
1930	Chi-A	37	128	14	33	5	1	1	18	6	6	.258	.291	.336	61	-8	-8	13	2	0	1	-2	1	-1.1
	Was-A	38	84	11	31	5	0	1	19	5	5	.369	.404	.464	119	3	3	15	1	3	0	-2	1	
	Yr	75	212	25	64	10	1	2	37	11	11	.302	.336	.387	84	-6	-5	27	3	3	-1	-2		-1.1
1932	Bos-N	82	298	32	71	9	3	5	30	25	21	.238	.299	.339	74	-12	-10	32	1			-2	1	-1.6
Total	4	290	986	118	287	45	12	11	119	81	62	.291	.347	.395	95	-10	-7	137	8	11		-1	1/2	-3.2

■ BART SHIRLEY
Shirley, Barton Arvin b: 1/4/40, Corpus Christi, Tex. BR/TR, 5'10", 183 lbs. Deb: 9/14/64

YEAR	TM/L	G	AB	R	H	2B	3B	HR	RBI	BB	SO	AVG	OBP	SLG	PRO+	BR	/A	RC	SB	CS	SBR	FR	POS	TPR
1964	LA-N	18	62	6	17	1	1	0	7	4	8	.274	.318	.323	87	-1	-1	5	0	0	0	1	3/S	0.0
1966	LA-N	12	5	2	1	0	0	0	0	0	2	.200	.200	.200	13	-1	-1	0	0	0	0	3	/S	0.2
1967	NY-N	6	12	1	0	0	0	0	0	0	0	.000	.000	.000	-99	-3	-3	0	0	0	0	0	/2	-0.2
1968	LA-N	39	83	6	15	3	0	0	4	10	13	.181	.269	.217	51	-5	-4	4	0	1	-1	3	S2	0.1
Total	4	75	162	15	33	4	1	0	11	14	28	.204	.267	.241	53	-10	-9	10	0	1	-1	6	/S23	0.1

■ MULE SHIRLEY
Shirley, Ernest Raeford b: 5/24/01, Snow Hill, N.C. d: 8/4/55, Goldsboro, N.C. BL/TL, 5'11", 180 lbs. Deb: 5/06/24

YEAR	TM/L	G	AB	R	H	2B	3B	HR	RBI	BB	SO	AVG	OBP	SLG	PRO+	BR	/A	RC	SB	CS	SBR	FR	POS	TPR
1924	*Was-A	30	77	12	18	2	2	0	16	3	7	.234	.262	.312	49	-6	-6	7	0	0	0	0	1	-0.6
1925	Was-A	14	23	2	3	1	0	0	2	1	7	.130	.167	.174	-14	-4	-4	1	0	0	0	0	/1	-0.3
Total	2	44	100	14	21	3	2	0	18	4	14	.210	.240	.280	34	-10	-10	7	0	0	0	0	/1	-0.9

■ IVEY SHIVER
Shiver, Ivey Merwin "Chick" b: 1/22/07, Sylvester, Ga. d: 8/31/72, Savannah, Ga. BR/TR, 6'1.5", 190 lbs. Deb: 4/14/31

YEAR	TM/L	G	AB	R	H	2B	3B	HR	RBI	BB	SO	AVG	OBP	SLG	PRO+	BR	/A	RC	SB	CS	SBR	FR	POS	TPR
1931	Det-A	2	9	2	1	0	0	0	0	0	3	.111	.111	.111	-40	-2	-2	0	0	0	0	-0	/O	-0.1
1934	Cin-N	19	59	6	12	1	0	2	6	3	15	.203	.242	.322	51	-4	-4	5	1			-2	O	-0.6
Total	2	21	68	8	13	1	0	2	6	3	18	.191	.225	.294	38	-6	-6	5	1	0		-3	/O	-0.7

■ GEORGE SHOCH
Shoch, George Quintus b: 1/6/1859, Philadelphia, Pa. d: 9/30/37, Philadelphia, Pa. BR/TR, Deb: 9/10/1886

YEAR	TM/L	G	AB	R	H	2B	3B	HR	RBI	BB	SO	AVG	OBP	SLG	PRO+	BR	/A	RC	SB	CS	SBR	FR	POS	TPR
1886	Was-N	26	95	11	28	2	1	1	18	2	13	.295	.309	.368	112	0	1	12	2			-5	O/S	-0.2
1887	Was-N	70	264	47	63	9	1	1	18	21	16	.239	.304	.292	73	-11	-8	33	29			6	O/S2	0.0
1888	Was-N	90	317	46	58	6	3	2	24	25	22	.183	.262	.240	66	-12	-10	27	23			3	SO/2P	-0.5
1889	Was-N	30	109	12	26	2	0	0	11	20	5	.239	.385	.257	88	-1	0	15	9			3	O/S	0.2
1891	Mil-a	34	127	29	40	7	1	1	16	18	5	.315	.435	.409	121	9	4	29	12			3	S/3	0.7

YEAR	TM/L	G	AB	R	H	2B	3B	HR	RBI	BB	SO	AVG	OBP	SLG	PRO+	BR	/A	RC	SB	CS	SBR	FR	POS	TPR
1892	Bal-N	76	308	42	85	15	3	1	50	24	19	.276	.340	.354	108	4	3	43	14			0	SO/3	0.6
1893	Bro-N	94	327	53	86	17	1	2	54	48	13	.263	.366	.339	94	-3	-0	45	9			-3	O3S/2	-0.3
1894	Bro-N	64	239	47	77	6	5	1	37	26	6	.322	.400	.402	103	-1	3	46	16			-1	O3/2S	0.0
1895	Bro-N	61	216	49	56	9	7	0	29	36	6	.259	.368	.366	99	-2	2	32	7			-6	O2/S3	-0.5
1896	Bro-N	76	250	36	73	7	4	1	28	33	10	.292	.381	.364	105	1	4	40	11			-11	2O/3S	-0.5
1897	Bro-N	85	284	42	79	9	2	0	38	49		.278	.393	.324	98	0	3	40	6			4	2S/O	1.1
Total	11	706	2536	414	671	89	28	10	323	298	115	.265	.355	.334	95	-14	2	360	138			-9	OS2/3P	0.5

■ COSTEN SHOCKLEY

Shockley, John Costen b: 2/8/42, Georgetown, Del. BL/TL, 6'2", 200 lbs. Deb: 7/17/64

YEAR	TM/L	G	AB	R	H	2B	3B	HR	RBI	BB	SO	AVG	OBP	SLG	PRO+	BR	/A	RC	SB	CS	SBR	FR	POS	TPR
1964	Phi-N	11	35	4	8	0	0	1	2	2	8	.229	.270	.314	65	-2	-2	3	0	0	0	-1	/1	-0.2
1965	Cal-A	40	107	5	20	2	0	2	17	9	16	.187	.256	.262	49	-7	-7	7	0	0	0	1	1/O	-0.8
Total	2	51	142	9	28	2	0	3	19	11	24	.197	.260	.275	53	-9	-9	10	0	0	0	-0	/1O	-1.0

■ CHARLIE SHOEMAKER

Shoemaker, Charles Landis b: 8/10/39, Los Angeles, Cal. d: 5/31/90, Mount Penn, Pa. BL/TR, 5'10", 155 lbs. Deb: 9/09/61

YEAR	TM/L	G	AB	R	H	2B	3B	HR	RBI	BB	SO	AVG	OBP	SLG	PRO+	BR	/A	RC	SB	CS	SBR	FR	POS	TPR
1961	KC-A	7	26	5	10	2	0	0	1	2	2	.385	.429	.462	138	1	1	5	0	0	0	0	/2	0.2
1962	KC-A	5	11	1	2	0	0	0	0	0	2	.182	.182	.182	-2	-2	-2	0	0	0	0	1	/2	0.0
1964	KC-A	16	52	6	11	2	2	0	3	0	9	.212	.212	.327	46	-4	-4	4	0	0	0	-5	2	-0.7
Total	3	28	89	12	23	4	2	0	4	2	13	.258	.275	.348	68	-4	-4	9	0	0	0	-3	/2	-0.5

■ STRICK SHOFNER

Shofner, Frank Strickland b: 7/23/19, Crawford, Tex. BL/TR, 5'10.5", 187 lbs. Deb: 4/19/47

YEAR	TM/L	G	AB	R	H	2B	3B	HR	RBI	BB	SO	AVG	OBP	SLG	PRO+	BR	/A	RC	SB	CS	SBR	FR	POS	TPR
1947	Bos-A	5	13	1	2	0	1	0	0	1	3	.154	.154	.308	25	-1	-1	1	0	0	0	1	/3	0.0

■ EDDIE SHOKES

Shokes, Edward Christopher b: 1/27/20, Charleston, S.C. BL/TL, 6', 170 lbs. Deb: 6/09/41

YEAR	TM/L	G	AB	R	H	2B	3B	HR	RBI	BB	SO	AVG	OBP	SLG	PRO+	BR	/A	RC	SB	CS	SBR	FR	POS	TPR
1941	Cin-N	1	1	0	0	0	0	0	0	0	1	.000	.000	.000	-99	-0	-0	0	0			0	H	0.0
1946	Cin-N	31	83	3	10	1	0	0	5	18	21	.120	.277	.133	19	-8	-8	4	1			-1	1	-1.2
Total	2	32	84	3	10	1	0	0	5	18	22	.119	.275	.131	18	-9	-8	4	1			-1	/1	-1.2

■ RAY SHOOK

Shook, Raymond Curtis b: 11/18/1889, Perry, Ohio d: 9/16/70, South Bend, Ind. BR/TR, 5'7.5", 155 lbs. Deb: 4/16/16

YEAR	TM/L	G	AB	R	H	2B	3B	HR	RBI	BB	SO	AVG	OBP	SLG	PRO+	BR	/A	RC	SB	CS	SBR	FR	POS	TPR
1916	Chi-A	1	0	0	0	0	0	0	0	0	0	—	—	—	—	0	0	0	0			0	R	0.0

■ RON SHOOP

Shoop, Ronald Lee b: 9/19/31, Rural Valley, Pa. BR/TR, 5'11", 180 lbs. Deb: 8/22/59

YEAR	TM/L	G	AB	R	H	2B	3B	HR	RBI	BB	SO	AVG	OBP	SLG	PRO+	BR	/A	RC	SB	CS	SBR	FR	POS	TPR
1959	Det-A	3	7	1	1	0	0	0	1	0	1	.143	.143	.143	-20	-1	-1	0	0	0	0	-1	/C	-0.1

■ TOM SHOPAY

Shopay, Thomas Michael b: 2/21/45, Bristol, Conn. BL/TR, 5'9.5", 160 lbs. Deb: 9/17/67

YEAR	TM/L	G	AB	R	H	2B	3B	HR	RBI	BB	SO	AVG	OBP	SLG	PRO+	BR	/A	RC	SB	CS	SBR	FR	POS	TPR
1967	NY-A	8	27	2	8	1	0	2	6	1	5	.296	.321	.556	161	2	2	5	2	0	1	0	/O	0.2
1969	NY-A	28	48	2	4	1	0	0	2	10	10	.083	.120	.125	-33	-8	-8	1	0	1	-1	1	O	-0.7
1971	*Bal-A	47	74	10	19	2	0	0	5	3	7	.257	.286	.284	62	-4	-4	6	2	1	0	-0	O	-0.4
1972	Bal-A	49	40	3	9	0	0	0	2	5	12	.225	.311	.225	60	-2	-2	3	0	0	0	1	/O	0.0
1975	Bal-A	40	31	4	5	1	0	0	2	4	7	.161	.257	.194	31	-3	-3	2	3	0	1	4	O/CD	0.2
1976	Bal-A	14	20	4	4	0	0	0	1	3	3	.200	.304	.200	53	-1	-1	2	1	0	0	0	O/C	0.0
1977	Bal-A	67	69	15	13	3	0	1	4	8	7	.188	.273	.275	53	-5	-4	5	3	3	-1	5	O/D	-0.1
Total	7	253	309	40	62	7	1	3	20	26	51	.201	.263	.259	50	-21	-20	23	11	5	0	11	O/DC	-0.8

■ DAVE SHORT

Short, David Orvis b: 5/11/17, Magnolia, Ark. d: 11/22/83, Shreveport, La. BL/TR, 5'11.5", 162 lbs. Deb: 9/16/40

YEAR	TM/L	G	AB	R	H	2B	3B	HR	RBI	BB	SO	AVG	OBP	SLG	PRO+	BR	/A	RC	SB	CS	SBR	FR	POS	TPR
1940	Chi-A	4	3	1	1	0	0	0	0	1	2	.333	.500	.333	119	0	0	1	0	0	0	0	H	0.0
1941	Chi-A	3	8	0	0	0	0	0	0	2	1	.000	.200	.000	-44	-2	-2	0	0	0	0	-0	/O	-0.1
Total	2	7	11	1	1	0	0	0	0	3	3	.091	.286	.091	3	-1	-1	1	0	0	0	-0	/O	-0.1

■ CHICK SHORTEN

Shorten, Charles Henry b: 4/19/1892, Scranton, Pa. d: 10/23/65, Scranton, Pa. BL/TL, 6', 175 lbs. Deb: 9/22/15

YEAR	TM/L	G	AB	R	H	2B	3B	HR	RBI	BB	SO	AVG	OBP	SLG	PRO+	BR	/A	RC	SB	CS	SBR	FR	POS	TPR
1915	Bos-A	6	14	1	3	1	0	0	0	0	2	.214	.214	.286	51	-1	-1	1	0			-0	/O	-0.1
1916	*Bos-A	53	112	14	33	2	1	0	11	10	8	.295	.352	.330	105	1	1	14	1			-8	O	-0.9
1917	Bos-A	69	168	12	30	4	2	0	16	10	10	.179	.229	.226	39	-13	-12	9	2			-5	O	-2.2
1919	Det-A	95	270	37	85	9	3	0	22	22	13	.315	.366	.370	110	3	4	40	5			-6	O	-0.7
1920	Det-A	116	364	35	105	9	6	1	40	28	14	.288	.339	.354	86	-8	-7	44	2	4	-2	-1	O	-1.8
1921	Det-A	92	217	33	59	11	3	0	23	20	11	.272	.333	.350	75	-8	-8	26	2	3	-1	-4	O	-1.6
1922	StL-A	55	131	22	36	12	5	2	16	16	8	.275	.354	.489	114	3	2	23	0	1	-1	-2	O	-0.2
1924	Cin-N	41	69	7	19	3	0	0	6	4	2	.275	.315	.319	71	-3	-3	7	0	0	0	-2	O	-0.5
Total	8	527	1345	161	370	51	20	3	134	110	68	.275	.330	.349	87	-26	-24	163	12	8		-29	O	-8.0

■ BURT SHOTTON

Shotton, Burton Edwin "Barney" b: 10/18/1884, Brownhelm, Ohio d: 7/29/62, Lake Wales, Fla. BL/TR, 5'11", 175 lbs. Deb: 9/13/09 MC

YEAR	TM/L	G	AB	R	H	2B	3B	HR	RBI	BB	SO	AVG	OBP	SLG	PRO+	BR	/A	RC	SB	CS	SBR	FR	POS	TPR
1909	StL-A	17	61	5	16	0	1	0	0	5		.262	.328	.295	104	-0	0	7	3			1	O	0.1
1911	StL-A	139	572	84	146	11	8	0	36	51		.255	.317	.302	76	-20	-17	62	26			7	*O	-2.0
1912	StL-A	154	580	87	168	15	8	2	40	86		.290	.390	.353	117	14	17	92	35			6	*O	1.4
1913	StL-A	147	549	105	163	23	8	1	28	99	63	.297	.405	.373	132	24	26	95	43			13	*O	3.3
1914	StL-A	154	579	82	156	19	9	0	38	64	66	.269	.344	.333	108	3	6	69	40	29	-5	-3	*O	-0.7
1915	StL-A	156	559	93	158	18	11	1	30	118	62	.283	.409	.360	135	27	30	87	43	32	-6	-3	*O	1.4
1916	StL-A	157	618	97	174	23	6	1	36	111	67	.282	.391	.343	127	21	24	88	41	28	-5	10	*O	2.3
1917	StL-A	118	398	47	89	9	1	1	20	62	47	.224	.330	.259	83	-7	-5	38	16			-12	*O	-2.6
1918	Was-A	126	505	68	132	16	7	0	21	67	28	.261	.349	.321	104	3	4	61	25			6	*O	0.4
1919	StL-N	85	270	35	77	13	5	1	20	22	25	.285	.341	.381	125	6	7	39	16			-7	O	-0.1
1920	StL-N	62	180	28	41	5	0	1	12	18	14	.228	.305	.272	69	-7	-6	17	5	1	1	2	O	-0.7
1921	StL-N	38	48	9	12	1	1	1	7	7	4	.250	.357	.375	96	-0	-0	6	0	2	-1	0	O	-0.2
1922	StL-N	34	30	5	6	1	0	0	2	4	6	.200	.294	.233	39	-3	-3	2	0	1	-1	-0	/O	-0.2
1923	StL-N	1	0	0	0	0	0	0	0	0		—	—	—	—	0	0	0	0	0	0	0	R	0.0
Total	14	1388	4949	746	1338	154	65	9	290	714	382	.270	.365	.333	110	61	84	663	293	93		26	*O	2.6

■ JOHN SHOUPE

Shoupe, John F. b: 9/30/1851, Cincinnati, Ohio d: 2/13/20, Cincinnati, Ohio BL/TL, 5'7", 140 lbs. Deb: 5/03/1879

YEAR	TM/L	G	AB	R	H	2B	3B	HR	RBI	BB	SO	AVG	OBP	SLG	PRO+	BR	/A	RC	SB	CS	SBR	FR	POS	TPR
1879	Tro-N	11	44	5	4	0	0	0	1	0	3	.091	.091	.091	-43	-6	-6	0				-3	S/2	-0.7
1882	StL-a	2	7	1	0	0	0	0	0	0		.000	.000	.000	-96	-1	-1	0				1	/2	0.0
1884	Was-U	1	4	1	3	0	0	0	0	0	0	.750	.750	.750	423	1	1	2	0			2	/O	0.3
Total	3	14	55	7	7	0	0	0	1	0	3	.127	.127	.127	-16	-7	-6	3	0			0	/S2O	-0.4

■ JOHN SHOVLIN

Shovlin, John Joseph "Brode" b: 1/14/1891, Drifton, Pa. d: 2/16/76, Bethesda, Md. BR/TR, 5'7", 163 lbs. Deb: 6/21/11

YEAR	TM/L	G	AB	R	H	2B	3B	HR	RBI	BB	SO	AVG	OBP	SLG	PRO+	BR	/A	RC	SB	CS	SBR	FR	POS	TPR
1911	Pit-N	2	1	0	0	0	0	0	0	0	1	.000	.000	.000	-96	-0	-0	0				0	H	0.0
1919	StL-A	9	35	4	7	0	0	0	1	5		.200	.300	.200	41	-3	-3	2	0			-2	/2	-0.3
1920	StL-A	7	7	2	2	0	0	0	2	0		.286	.286	.286	50	-0	-0	1	0	0	0	1	/S	0.1
Total	3	18	43	7	9	0	0	0	3	5	3	.209	.292	.209	39	-3	-3	3	0	0		-1	/2S	-0.2

■ GEORGE SHUBA

Shuba, George Thomas "Shotgun" b: 12/13/24, Youngstown, Ohio BL/TR, 5'11", 180 lbs. Deb: 7/02/48

YEAR	TM/L	G	AB	R	H	2B	3B	HR	RBI	BB	SO	AVG	OBP	SLG	PRO+	BR	/A	RC	SB	CS	SBR	FR	POS	TPR
1948	Bro-N	63	161	21	43	6	0	4	32	34	31	.267	.395	.379	107	4	3	27	1			-5	O	-0.5
1949	Bro-N	1	1	0	0	0	0	0	0	0	0	.000	.000	.000	-96	-0	-0	0	0			0	H	0.0
1950	Bro-N	34	111	15	23	8	2	3	12	13	22	.207	.302	.396	80	-3	-4	14	2			2	O	-0.2
1952	*Bro-N	94	256	40	78	12	1	9	40	38	29	.305	.395	.465	136	14	13	47	1			-6	O	0.4
1953	*Bro-N	74	169	19	43	12	1	5	23	17	20	.254	.326	.426	92	-2	-2	23	1	3	-2	-6	O	-1.0
1954	Bro-N	45	65	3	10	3	0	2	10	7	10	.154	.247	.323	46	-5	-6	5	0	0	0	-1	O	-0.6
1955	*Bro-N	44	51	8	14	2	0	1	8	11	10	.275	.422	.373	110	2	2	9	0	0	0	-1	/O	0.0

YEAR	TM/L	G	AB	R	H	2B	3B	HR	RBI	BB	SO	AVG	OBP	SLG	PRO+	BR	/A	RC	SB	CS	SBR	FR	POS	TPR
Total	7	355	814	106	211	45	4	24	125	120	122	.259	.359	.413	104	9	6	125	5	5		-18	O	-1.9

■ FRANK SHUGART
Shugart, Frank Harry (b: Frank Harry Shugarts) b: 12/10/1866, Luthersburg, Pa. d: 9/9/44, Clearfield, Pa.   BR/TR, 5'8", 170 lbs. Deb: 8/23/1890

YEAR	TM/L	G	AB	R	H	2B	3B	HR	RBI	BB	SO	AVG	OBP	SLG	PRO+	BR	/A	RC	SB	CS	SBR	FR	POS	TPR
1890	Chi-P	29	106	8	20	5	5	0	15	5	13	.189	.232	.330	49	-8	-9	10	5			-5	S/O	-0.9
1891	Pit-N	75	320	57	88	19	8	3	33	20	26	.275	.324	.412	119	5	6	51	21			4	S	1.2
1892	Pit-N	137	554	94	148	19	14	0	62	47	48	.267	.329	.352	107	5	5	75	28			9	*S/CO	1.9
1893	Pit-N	52	210	37	55	7	3	1	32	19	15	.262	.332	.338	81	-6	-5	28	12			-3	S	-0.4
	StL-N	59	246	41	69	10	4	0	28	22	10	.280	.354	.354	90	-3	-3	36	13			-3	OS/3	-0.4
	Yr	111	456	78	124	17	7	1	60	41	25	.272	.344	.346	86	-9	-8	65	25			-5		-0.8
1894	StL-N	133	527	103	154	19	18	7	72	38	37	.292	.348	.436	90	-10	-10	90	21			-3	*O/S3	-1.6
1895	Lou-N	113	473	61	125	14	13	4	70	31	25	.264	.315	.374	84	-16	-10	62	14			-17	*SO	-1.8
1897	Phi-N	40	163	20	41	8	2	5	25	8		.252	.287	.417	89	-4	-3	21	5			-5	S	-0.6
1901	Chi-A	107	415	62	104	9	12	2	47	28		.251	.301	.345	83	-11	-9	49	12			-8	*S	-0.9
Total	8	745	3014	483	804	110	79	22	384	218	174	.267	.323	.378	92	-48	-40	422	131			-31	SO/3C	-3.5

■ TERRY SHUMPERT
Shumpert, Terrance Darnell b: 8/16/66, Paducah, Ky. BR/TR, 6'1", 190 lbs. Deb: 5/01/90

YEAR	TM/L	G	AB	R	H	2B	3B	HR	RBI	BB	SO	AVG	OBP	SLG	PRO+	BR	/A	RC	SB	CS	SBR	FR	POS	TPR
1990	KC-A	32	91	7	25	6	1	0	8	2	17	.275	.298	.363	86	-2	-2	8	3	3	-1	0	2	-0.1

■ VINCE SHUPE
Shupe, Vincent William b: 9/5/21, E.Canton, Ohio d: 4/5/62, Canton, Ohio BL/TL, 5'11", 180 lbs. Deb: 7/07/45

YEAR	TM/L	G	AB	R	H	2B	3B	HR	RBI	BB	SO	AVG	OBP	SLG	PRO+	BR	/A	RC	SB	CS	SBR	FR	POS	TPR
1945	Bos-N	78	283	22	76	8	0	0	15	17	16	.269	.312	.297	69	-11	-11	26	3			1	1	-1.3

■ ED SICKING
Sicking, Edward Joseph b: 3/30/1897, St.Bernard, Ohio d: 8/30/78, Cincinnati, Ohio BR/TR, 5'9.5", 165 lbs. Deb: 8/26/16

YEAR	TM/L	G	AB	R	H	2B	3B	HR	RBI	BB	SO	AVG	OBP	SLG	PRO+	BR	/A	RC	SB	CS	SBR	FR	POS	TPR
1916	Chi-N	1	1	0	0	0	0	0	0	0	0	.000	.000	.000	-90	-0	-0	0	0			0	H	0.0
1918	NY-N	46	132	9	33	4	0	0	12	6	11	.250	.283	.280	73	-4	-4	10	2			-8	32/S	-1.2
1919	NY-N	6	15	2	5	0	0	0	3	1	0	.333	.412	.333	127	1	1	2	0			3	/S	0.4
	Phi-N	61	185	16	40	2	1	0	15	8	17	.216	.253	.238	45	-12	-13	12	4			5	S2	-0.6
	Yr	67	200	18	45	2	1	0	18	9	17	.225	.265	.245	51	-11	-12	14	4			8		-0.2
1920	NY-N	46	134	11	23	3	1	0	9	10	10	.172	.234	.209	28	-12	-12	7	6	2	1	4	32/S	-0.6
	Cin-N	37	123	12	33	3	0	0	17	13	5	.268	.338	.293	83	-2	-2	12	2	3	-1	1	2/S3	-0.1
	Yr	83	257	23	56	6	1	0	26	23	15	.218	.285	.249	55	-15	-14	19	8	5	-1	4		-0.7
1927	Pit-N	6	7	1	1	1	0	0	3	1	0	.143	.250	.286	40	-1	-1	1	0			2	/2	0.1
Total	5	203	597	51	135	13	2	0	59	39	43	.226	.277	.255	57	-31	-32	45	14	5		5	/2S3	-2.0

■ NORM SIEBERN
Siebern, Norman Leroy b: 7/26/33, St.Louis, Mo. BL/TR, 6'2", 200 lbs. Deb: 6/15/56

YEAR	TM/L	G	AB	R	H	2B	3B	HR	RBI	BB	SO	AVG	OBP	SLG	PRO+	BR	/A	RC	SB	CS	SBR	FR	POS	TPR
1956	*NY-A	54	162	27	33	1	4	4	21	19	38	.204	.287	.333	66	-9	-8	16	1	1	-0	-2	O	-1.2
1958	*NY-A	134	460	79	138	19	5	14	55	66	87	.300	.389	.454	136	21	23	82	5	8	-3	2	*O	1.4
1959	NY-A	120	380	52	103	17	0	11	53	41	71	.271	.345	.403	108	3	4	56	3	1	0	-3	O/1	-0.2
1960	KC-A	144	520	69	145	31	6	19	69	72	68	.279	.369	.471	125	19	18	93	0	0	0	-2	O1	0.9
1961	KC-A	153	560	68	166	36	5	18	98	82	91	.296	.387	.475	129	24	24	108	2	4	-2	-2	*1O	0.8
1962	KC-A	162	600	114	185	25	6	25	117	110	88	.308	.416	.495	140	41	39	**129**	3	1	0	5	*1	3.3
1963	KC-A	152	556	80	151	25	2	16	83	79	82	.272	.362	.410	111	14	11	85	1	4	-2	4	*1O	0.8
1964	Bal-A	150	478	92	117	24	2	12	56	**106**	87	.245	.384	.379	114	13	13	78	2	3	-1	4	*1	1.2
1965	Bal-A	106	297	44	76	13	4	8	32	50	49	.256	.365	.407	117	9	8	47	1	2	-1	2	1	0.5
1966	Cal-A	125	336	29	83	14	1	5	41	63	61	.247	.366	.339	107	4	5	45	0	1	-1	3	1	0.4
1967	SF-N	46	58	6	9	1	1	0	4	14	13	.155	.319	.207	54	-3	-3	5	0	0	0	0	1/O	-0.3
	*Bos-A	33	44	2	9	0	2	0	7	6	8	.205	.300	.295	71	-1	-2	4	0	0	0	1	1/O	-0.1
1968	Bos-A	27	30	0	2	0	0	0	0	0	5	.067	.067	.067	-56	-6	-6	0	0	0	0	0	/1O	-0.6
Total	12	1406	4481	662	1217	206	38	132	636	708	748	.272	.372	.423	118	129	128	749	18	25	-10	11	1O	6.9

■ DICK SIEBERT
Siebert, Richard Walther b: 2/19/12, Fall River, Mass. d: 12/9/78, Minneapolis, Minn. BL/TL, 6', 170 lbs. Deb: 9/07/32

YEAR	TM/L	G	AB	R	H	2B	3B	HR	RBI	BB	SO	AVG	OBP	SLG	PRO+	BR	/A	RC	SB	CS	SBR	FR	POS	TPR
1932	Bro-N	6	7	1	2	0	0	0	0	2	2	.286	.444	.286	104	0	0	1	0			-0	/1	0.0
1936	Bro-N	2	2	0	0	0	0	0	0	0	0	.000	.000	.000	-99	-1	-1	0	0			1	/O	0.0
1937	StL-N	22	38	3	7	2	0	0	2	4	8	.184	.279	.237	41	-3	-3	3	1			-1	/1	-0.3
1938	StL-N	1	1	0	1	0	0	0	0	0	0	1.000	1.000	1.000	427	0	0	1	0			0	H	0.0
	Phi-A	48	194	24	55	8	3	0	28	10	9	.284	.329	.356	73	-9	-8	22	2	3	-1	5	1	-0.8
1939	Phi-A	101	402	58	118	28	3	6	47	21	22	.294	.329	.423	93	-7	-6	56	4	1	1	5	1	-0.8
1940	Phi-A	154	595	69	170	31	6	5	77	33	34	.286	.325	.383	85	-16	-14	74	8	6	-1	8	*1	-1.3
1941	Phi-A	123	467	63	156	28	8	5	79	37	22	.334	.385	.460	126	15	17	82	1	3	-2	6	*1	1.7
1942	Phi-A	153	612	57	159	25	7	2	74	24	17	.260	.291	.333	76	-22	-21	59	4	5	-2	-1	*1	-2.7
1943	Phi-A	146	558	50	140	26	7	1	72	33	21	.251	.295	.328	83	-14	-14	50	6	7	-2	4	*1	-1.7
1944	Phi-A	132	468	52	143	27	5	6	52	62	17	.306	.387	.423	133	20	21	83	2	0	1	-0	1O	1.6
1945	Phi-A	147	573	62	153	29	1	7	51	50	33	.267	.327	.358	92	-2	-1	68	2	7	-4	10	*1	0.0
Total	11	1035	3917	439	1104	204	40	32	482	276	185	.282	.331	.379	96	-36	-29	500	30	32		36	1/O	-4.3

■ FRED SIEFKE
Siefke, Frederick Edwin b: 3/27/1870, New York, N.Y. d: 4/18/1893, New York, N.Y. Deb: 5/02/1890

YEAR	TM/L	G	AB	R	H	2B	3B	HR	RBI	BB	SO	AVG	OBP	SLG	PRO+	BR	/A	RC	SB	CS	SBR	FR	POS	TPR
1890	Bro-a	16	58	1	8	2	0	0		5		.138	.206	.172	14	-6	-6	3	2			0	3	-0.4

■ JOHN SIEGEL
Siegel, John b: York, Pa. Deb: 6/09/1884

YEAR	TM/L	G	AB	R	H	2B	3B	HR	RBI	BB	SO	AVG	OBP	SLG	PRO+	BR	/A	RC	SB	CS	SBR	FR	POS	TPR
1884	Phi-U	8	31	4	7	2	0	0		1		.226	.250	.290	89	-1	-0	2	0			-5	/3	-0.3

■ JOHNNY SIEGLE
Siegle, John Herbert b: 7/8/1874, Urbana, Ohio d: 2/12/68, Urbana, Ohio BR/TR, 5'10", 165 lbs. Deb: 9/15/05

YEAR	TM/L	G	AB	R	H	2B	3B	HR	RBI	BB	SO	AVG	OBP	SLG	PRO+	BR	/A	RC	SB	CS	SBR	FR	POS	TPR
1905	Cin-N	17	56	9	17	1	2	1	8	7		.304	.381	.446	134	3	3	10	0			-1	O	0.0
1906	Cin-N	22	68	4	8	2	2	0	7	3		.118	.155	.206	13	-7	-7	3	0			0	O	-0.8
Total	2	39	124	13	25	3	4	1	15	10		.202	.261	.315	72	-4	-5	13	0			-1	/O	-0.8

■ OSCAR SIEMER
Siemer, Oscar Sylvester "Cotton" b: 8/14/01, St.Louis, Mo. d: 12/5/59, St.Louis, Mo. BR/TR, 5'9", 162 lbs. Deb: 5/20/25

YEAR	TM/L	G	AB	R	H	2B	3B	HR	RBI	BB	SO	AVG	OBP	SLG	PRO+	BR	/A	RC	SB	CS	SBR	FR	POS	TPR
1925	Bos-N	16	46	5	14	0	1	1	6	1	0	.304	.319	.413	94	-1	-1	6	0	0	0	-2	C	0.0
1926	Bos-N	31	73	3	15	1	0	0	5	2	7	.205	.227	.219	22	-8	-7	4	0	0	0	-1	C	-0.6
Total	2	47	119	8	29	1	1	1	11	3	7	.244	.262	.294	51	-9	-8	10	0	0		-3	/C	-0.6

■ RUBEN SIERRA
Sierra, Ruben Angel (Garcia) b: 10/6/65, Rio Piedras, P.R. BB/TR, 6'1", 175 lbs. Deb: 6/01/86

YEAR	TM/L	G	AB	R	H	2B	3B	HR	RBI	BB	SO	AVG	OBP	SLG	PRO+	BR	/A	RC	SB	CS	SBR	FR	POS	TPR
1986	Tex-A	113	382	50	101	13	10	16	55	22	65	.264	.306	.476	106	3	2	51	7	8	-3	-2	*O/D	-0.4
1987	Tex-A	158	643	97	169	35	4	30	109	39	114	.263	.307	.470	102	-0	-0	85	16	11	-2	1	*O	-0.3
1988	Tex-A	156	615	77	156	32	2	23	91	44	91	.254	.305	.424	99	-0	-2	77	18	4	3	2	*O/D	0.0
1989	Tex-A	162	634	101	194	35	**14**	29	**119**	43	82	.306	.352	**.543**	146	37	36	122	8	2	1	4	*O	3.9
1990	Tex-A	159	608	70	170	37	2	16	96	49	86	.280	.334	.426	109	8	7	85	9	0	3	-5	*O/D	0.2
Total	5	748	2882	395	790	152	32	114	470	197	438	.274	.322	.468	113	48	42	420	58	25	2	-0	O/D	3.4

■ ROY SIEVERS
Sievers, Roy Edward "Squirrel" b: 11/18/26, St.Louis, Mo. BR/TR, 6'1", 195 lbs. Deb: 4/21/49 C

YEAR	TM/L	G	AB	R	H	2B	3B	HR	RBI	BB	SO	AVG	OBP	SLG	PRO+	BR	/A	RC	SB	CS	SBR	FR	POS	TPR
1949	StL-A	140	471	84	144	28	1	16	91	70	75	.306	.398	.471	124	20	17	89	1	5	-3	10	*O/3	2.1
1950	StL-A	113	370	46	88	20	4	10	57	34	42	.238	.305	.395	75	-14	-16	43	1	3	-2	3	O3	-1.5
1951	StL-A	31	89	10	20	2	1	1	11	9	21	.225	.303	.303	62	-4	-5	8	0	0		2	O	-0.3
1952	StL-A	11	30	3	6	3	0	0	5	1	4	.200	.226	.300	44	-2	-2	2	0	0		-1	/1	-0.3
1953	StL-A	92	285	37	77	15	3	8	35	32	47	.270	.344	.407	100	1	-0	40	0	1	-1	-6	1	-0.7
1954	Was-A	145	514	75	119	26	6	24	102	80	77	.232	.337	.446	120	8	12	78	2	1	0	4	*O/1	1.2

YEAR	TM/L	G	AB	R	H	2B	3B	HR	RBI	BB	SO	AVG	OBP	SLG	PRO+	BR	/A	RC	SB	CS	SBR	FR	POS	TPR
1955	Was-A	144	509	74	138	20	8	25	106	73	66	.271	.367	.489	136	20	23	90	1	2	-1	-4	*O1/3	1.1
1956	Was-A	152	550	92	139	27	2	29	95	100	88	.253	.373	.467	121	17	17	100	0	2	0	-4	O1	0.6
1957	Was-A	152	572	99	172	23	5	**42**	**114**	76	55	.301	.389	.579	163	47	48	131	1	1	-0	-2	*O1	3.9
1958	Was-A	148	550	85	162	18	1	39	108	53	63	.295	.361	.544	148	32	33	106	3	1	0	-1	*O1	2.5
1959	Was-A	115	385	55	93	19	0	21	49	53	62	.242	.336	.455	116	8	8	59	1	1	-0	4	1O	1.1
1960	Chi-A	127	444	87	131	22	0	28	93	74	69	.295	.399	.534	152	32	33	95	1	1	-0	-6	*1/O	1.9
1961	Chi-A	141	492	76	145	26	6	27	92	61	62	.295	.379	.537	144	29	30	101	1	0	0	1	*1	1.8
1962	Phi-N	144	477	61	125	19	5	21	80	56	80	.262	.348	.455	117	9	11	78	2	1	0	4	*1/O	1.0
1963	Phi-N	138	450	46	108	19	2	19	82	43	72	.240	.313	.418	110	4	5	60	0	2	-1	-0	*1	0.1
1964	Phi-N	49	120	7	22	3	1	4	16	13	20	.183	.269	.325	67	-5	-5	10	0	0	0	-2	1	-0.8
	Was-A	33	58	5	10	1	0	4	11	9	14	.172	.284	.397	87	-1	-1	7	0	0	0	1	1	0.0
1965	Was-A	12	21	3	4	1	0	0	0	4	3	.190	.320	.238	62	-1	-1	2	0	0	0	-1	/1	-0.1
Total	17	1887	6387	945	1703	292	42	318	1147	841	920	.267	.357	.475	124	198	206	1097	14	19	-7	4	1O/3	13.6

■ FRANK SIFFELL   Siffell, Frank   b: 1860, Germany   d: 10/26/09, Philadelphia, Pa.   Deb: 6/14/1884

YEAR	TM/L	G	AB	R	H	2B	3B	HR	RBI	BB	SO	AVG	OBP	SLG	PRO+	BR	/A	RC	SB	CS	SBR	FR	POS	TPR
1884	Phi-a	7	17	3	3	1	0	0	0			.176	.222	.235	48	-1	-1	1				-2	/C	-0.1
1885	Phi-a	3	10	0	1	0	0	0	0			.100	.100	.100	-34	-1	-2	0				-3	/CO	-0.3
Total	2	10	27	3	4	1	0	0	0			.148	.179	.185	18	-2	-3	1				-5	/CO	-0.4

■ FRANK SIGAFOOS   Sigafoos, Francis Leonard   b: 3/21/04, Easton, Pa.   d: 4/12/68, Indianapolis, Ind.   BR/TR, 5'9", 170 lbs.   Deb: 9/03/26

YEAR	TM/L	G	AB	R	H	2B	3B	HR	RBI	BB	SO	AVG	OBP	SLG	PRO+	BR	/A	RC	SB	CS	SBR	FR	POS	TPR
1926	Phi-A	13	43	4	11	0	0	0	2	0	3	.256	.256	.256	32	-4	-4	3	0	0	0	-3	S	-0.6
1929	Det-A	14	23	3	4	1	0	0	2	5	2	.174	.321	.217	41	-2	-2	2	0	2	-1	-2	/3S	-0.3
	Chi-A	7	3	1	1	0	0	0	1	2	1	.333	.600	.333	148	0	1	1	0	0	0	1	/2	0.2
	Yr	21	26	4	5	1	0	0	3	7	5	.192	.364	.231	56	-1	-1	2	0	2	-1	-1		-0.1
1931	Cin-N	21	65	6	11	2	0	0	8	0	6	.169	.182	.200	3	-9	-8	3	0			-3	3/S	-1.0
Total	3	55	134	14	27	3	0	0	13	7	14	.201	.246	.224	25	-14	-14	8	0	2		-7	/3S2	-1.7

■ PADDY SIGLIN   Siglin, Wesley Peter   b: 9/24/1891, Aurelia, Iowa   d: 8/5/56, Oakland, Cal.   BR/TR, 5'10", 160 lbs.   Deb: 9/12/14

YEAR	TM/L	G	AB	R	H	2B	3B	HR	RBI	BB	SO	AVG	OBP	SLG	PRO+	BR	/A	RC	SB	CS	SBR	FR	POS	TPR
1914	Pit-N	14	39	4	6	0	0	0	2	4	6	.154	.233	.154	16	-4	-4	2	1			-6	2	-1.0
1915	Pit-N	6	7	1	2	0	0	0	0	1	2	.286	.375	.286	103	0	0	1	0			-0	/2	0.0
1916	Pit-N	3	4	0	1	0	0	0	0	0	0	.250	.250	.250	53	-0	-0	0	0			0	/2	0.0
Total	3	23	50	5	9	0	0	0	2	5	10	.180	.255	.180	32	-4	-4	3	2			-5	/2	-1.0

■ TRIPP SIGMAN   Sigman, Wesley Triplett   b: 1/17/1899, Mooresville, N.C.   d: 3/8/71, Augusta, Ga.   BL/TR, 6', 180 lbs.   Deb: 9/18/29

YEAR	TM/L	G	AB	R	H	2B	3B	HR	RBI	BB	SO	AVG	OBP	SLG	PRO+	BR	/A	RC	SB	CS	SBR	FR	POS	TPR
1929	Phi-N	10	29	8	15	1	0	2	9	3	1	.517	.563	.759	210	6	5	12	0			-0	O	0.4
1930	Phi-N	52	100	15	27	4	1	4	6	6	9	.270	.324	.450	79	-3	-4	14	1			0	O	-0.4
Total	2	62	129	23	42	5	1	6	15	9	10	.326	.379	.519	108	3	2	26	1			-0	/O	0.0

■ EDDIE SILBER   Silber, Edward James   b: 6/6/14, Philadelphia, Pa.   d: 10/26/76, Dunedin, Fla.   BR/TR, 5'11", 170 lbs.   Deb: 9/03/37

YEAR	TM/L	G	AB	R	H	2B	3B	HR	RBI	BB	SO	AVG	OBP	SLG	PRO+	BR	/A	RC	SB	CS	SBR	FR	POS	TPR
1937	StL-A	22	83	10	26	2	0	0	4	5	13	.313	.352	.337	74	-3	-3	9	0	2	-1	-6	/O	-0.9
1939	StL-A	1	1	0	0	0	0	0	0	0	1	.000	.000	.000	-98	-0	-0	0	0	0	0	0	H	0.0
Total	2	23	84	10	26	2	0	0	4	5	14	.310	.348	.333	72	-3	-3	9	0	2	-1	-6	/O	-0.9

■ ED SILCH   Silch, Edward "Baldy"   b: 2/22/1865, St.Louis, Mo.   d: 1/15/1895, St.Louis, Mo.   TR,   Deb: 4/29/1888

YEAR	TM/L	G	AB	R	H	2B	3B	HR	RBI	BB	SO	AVG	OBP	SLG	PRO+	BR	/A	RC	SB	CS	SBR	FR	POS	TPR
1888	Bro-a	14	48	5	13	4	0	0	3	4		.271	.327	.354	122	1	1	7	4			-2	O	0.0

■ DANNY SILVA   Silva, Daniel James   b: 10/5/1896, Everett, Mass.   d: 4/4/74, Hyannis, Mass.   BR/TR, 6', 170 lbs.   Deb: 8/11/19

YEAR	TM/L	G	AB	R	H	2B	3B	HR	RBI	BB	SO	AVG	OBP	SLG	PRO+	BR	/A	RC	SB	CS	SBR	FR	POS	TPR
1919	Was-A	1	4	0	1	0	0	0	0	0	0	.250	.250	.250	41	-0	-0	0	0			1	/3	0.1

■ AL SILVERA   Silvera, Aaron Albert   b: 8/26/35, San Diego, Cal.   BR/TR, 6', 180 lbs.   Deb: 6/12/55

YEAR	TM/L	G	AB	R	H	2B	3B	HR	RBI	BB	SO	AVG	OBP	SLG	PRO+	BR	/A	RC	SB	CS	SBR	FR	POS	TPR
1955	Cin-N	13	7	3	1	0	0	0	2	0	1	.143	.143	.143	-23	-1	-1	0	0	0	0	0	/O	0.0
1956	Cin-N	1	0	0	0	0	0	0	0	0	0	—	—	—	—	0	0	0	0	0	0	0	R	0.0
Total	2	14	7	3	1	0	0	0	2	0	1	.143	.143	.143	-23	-1	-1	0	0	0	0	0	/O	0.0

■ CHARLIE SILVERA   Silvera, Charles Anthony Ryan "Swede"   b: 10/13/24, San Francisco, Cal   BR/TR, 5'10", 175 lbs.   Deb: 9/29/48   C

YEAR	TM/L	G	AB	R	H	2B	3B	HR	RBI	BB	SO	AVG	OBP	SLG	PRO+	BR	/A	RC	SB	CS	SBR	FR	POS	TPR
1948	NY-A	4	14	1	8	0	0	0	0	1	0	.571	.571	.714	243	3	3	6	0	0	0	0	/C	0.3
1949	*NY-A	58	130	8	41	2	0	0	13	18	5	.315	.403	.331	95	0	0	18	2	1	0	4	C	0.6
1950	NY-A	18	25	2	4	0	0	0	1	1	2	.160	.192	.160	-9	-4	-4	1	0	0	0	3	C	0.0
1951	NY-A	18	51	5	14	3	0	1	7	5	3	.275	.339	.392	101	-0	-0	5	0	0	0	0	C	0.1
1952	NY-A	20	55	4	18	3	0	0	11	5	2	.327	.383	.382	121	1	1	7	0	3	-2	-3	C	-0.1
1953	NY-A	42	82	11	23	3	1	0	12	9	5	.280	.352	.341	91	-1	-1	11	0	1	-1	6	C/3	0.6
1954	NY-A	20	37	1	10	1	0	0	4	3	2	.270	.341	.297	79	-1	-1	3	0	1	-1	6	C	0.5
1955	NY-A	14	26	1	5	0	0	0	1	6	4	.192	.344	.192	48	-2	-2	2	0	0	0	3	C	0.2
1956	NY-A	7	9	0	2	0	0	0	0	2	3	.222	.222	.222	60	-0	-0	1	0	0	0	-1	/C	0.0
1957	Chi-N	26	53	1	11	3	0	0	2	4	5	.208	.263	.264	43	-4	-4	3	0	0	0	3	C	0.0
Total	10	227	482	34	136	15	2	1	52	53	32	.282	.356	.328	86	-9	-8	58	2	6	-3	21	C/3	2.2

■ LUIS SILVERIO   Silverio, Luis Pascual (Delmonte)   b: 10/23/56, Villa Gonzalez, D.R   BR/TR, 5'11", 165 lbs.   Deb: 9/09/78

YEAR	TM/L	G	AB	R	H	2B	3B	HR	RBI	BB	SO	AVG	OBP	SLG	PRO+	BR	/A	RC	SB	CS	SBR	FR	POS	TPR
1978	KC-A	8	11	7	6	2	1	0	3	2	3	.545	.615	.909	315	3	3	6	1	1	-0	-0	/OD	0.3

■ TOM SILVERIO   Silverio, Tomas Roberto (Veloz)   b: 10/14/45, Santiago, D.R.   BL/TL, 5'10", 170 lbs.   Deb: 4/30/70

YEAR	TM/L	G	AB	R	H	2B	3B	HR	RBI	BB	SO	AVG	OBP	SLG	PRO+	BR	/A	RC	SB	CS	SBR	FR	POS	TPR
1970	Cal-A	15	15	1	0	0	0	0	0	0	4	.000	.118	.000	-67	-3	-3	0	0	1	-1	-0	/O1	-0.4
1971	Cal-A	3	3	0	1	0	0	0	0	0	0	.333	.333	.333	96	-0	-0	0	0	0	0	0	/O	0.0
1972	Cal-A	13	12	1	2	0	0	0	0	2	5	.167	.167	.167	-1	-1	-1	0	0	0	0	-0	/O	-0.1
Total	3	31	30	2	3	0	0	0	0	2	9	.100	.156	.100	-27	-5	-5	1	0	1	-1	-0	/O1	-0.5

■ KEN SILVESTRI   Silvestri, Kenneth Joseph "Hawk"   b: 5/3/16, Chicago, Ill.   BB/TR, 6'1", 200 lbs.   Deb: 4/18/39   MC

YEAR	TM/L	G	AB	R	H	2B	3B	HR	RBI	BB	SO	AVG	OBP	SLG	PRO+	BR	/A	RC	SB	CS	SBR	FR	POS	TPR
1939	Chi-A	22	75	6	13	3	0	2	5	6	13	.173	.244	.293	36	-7	-8	6	0	1	-1	-1	C	-0.6
1940	Chi-A	28	24	5	6	2	0	2	10	4	7	.250	.357	.583	138	1	1	4	0	0	0	0	/C	0.1
1941	NY-A	17	40	6	10	5	0	1	4	7	6	.250	.362	.450	115	1	1	7	0	0	0	0	C	0.2
1946	NY-A	13	21	4	6	1	0	0	1	3	7	.286	.375	.333	98	0	0	3	0	0	0	3	/C	0.3
1947	NY-A	3	10	0	2	0	0	0	0	2	2	.200	.333	.200	51	-1	-1	1	0	0	0	-2	/C	-0.1
1949	Phi-N	4	4	1	0	0	0	0	0	2	1	.000	.333	.000	-3	-0	-0	0	0			0	/C2S	0.0
1950	*Phi-N	11	20	2	5	0	1	0	4	4	3	.250	.400	.350	101	0	0	3	0			-1	/C	0.0
1951	Phi-N	4	9	2	2	0	0	0	1	3	2	.222	.417	.222	78	-0	-0	1	0	0	0	-3	/C2	-0.2
Total	8	102	203	26	44	11	1	5	25	31	41	.217	.326	.355	78	-6	-6	25	0	1		-3	/C2S	-0.3

■ AL SIMMONS   Simmons, Aloysius Harry "Bucketfoot Al" (b: Aloys Szymanski)
b: 5/22/02, Milwaukee, Wis.   d: 5/26/56, Milwaukee, Wis.   BR/TR, 5'11", 190 lbs.   Deb: 4/15/24   CH

YEAR	TM/L	G	AB	R	H	2B	3B	HR	RBI	BB	SO	AVG	OBP	SLG	PRO+	BR	/A	RC	SB	CS	SBR	FR	POS	TPR
1924	Phi-A	152	594	69	183	31	9	8	102	30	60	.308	.343	.431	98	-4	-4	84	16	15	-4	6	*O	-1.2
1925	Phi-A	153	654	122	**253**	43	12	24	129	35	41	.387	.419	**.599**	146	51	45	**155**	7	14	-6	5	*O	2.8
1926	Phi-A	147	583	90	199	53	10	19	109	48	49	.341	.392	.564	139	37	33	127	10	6	-1	-4	*O	1.6
1927	Phi-A	106	406	86	159	36	11	15	108	31	30	.392	.436	.645	168	44	41	107	10	2		3	*O	3.6
1928	Phi-A	119	464	78	163	33	9	15	107	31	30	.351	.396	.558	144	30	29	100	4	4	-2	2	*O	2.1
1929	*Phi-A	143	581	114	212	41	9	34	**157**	31	38	.365	.398	.642	158	50	47	145	4	2	0	17	*O	**5.4**
1930	*Phi-A	138	554	**152**	211	41	16	36	165	39	34	**.381**	.423	.708	173	64	60	163	9	2	2	6	*O	5.5

YEAR	TM/L	G	AB	R	H	2B	3B	HR	RBI	BB	SO	AVG	OBP	SLG	PRO+	BR	/A	RC	SB	CS	SBR	FR	POS	TPR
1931	*Phi-A	128	513	105	200	37	13	22	128	47	45	**.390**	.444	.641	172	60	55	145	3	3	-1	9	*O	5.0
1932	Phi-A	154	670	144	**216**	28	9	35	151	47	76	.322	.368	.548	129	30	27	134	4	2	0	-7	*O	1.2
1933	Chi-A	146	605	85	200	29	10	14	119	39	49	.331	.373	.481	130	20	23	109	5	1	1	14	*O	3.1
1934	Chi-A	138	558	102	192	36	7	18	104	53	58	.344	.403	.530	135	31	29	120	3	2	-0	6	*O	3.0
1935	Chi-A	128	525	68	140	22	7	16	79	33	43	.267	.313	.427	87	-11	-13	68	4	6	-2	-4	*O	-1.8
1936	Det-A	143	568	96	186	38	6	13	112	49	35	.327	.383	.484	112	10	10	105	6	4	-1	-8	*O/1	-0.1
1937	Was-A	103	419	60	117	21	10	8	84	27	35	.279	.329	.434	95	-8	-5	60	3	2	-0	5	*O	-0.3
1938	Was-A	125	470	79	142	23	6	21	95	38	40	.302	.357	.511	123	8	13	86	2	1	0	-6	*O	0.6
1939	Bos-N	93	330	39	93	17	5	7	43	22	40	.282	.331	.427	110	0	3	43	0			-4	O	-0.1
	*Cin-N	9	21	0	3	0	0	0	1	2	3	.143	.217	.143	-1	-3	-3	1	0			1	/O	-0.1
	Yr	102	351	39	96	17	5	7	44	24	43	.274	.324	.410	103	-3	0	44	0			-3		-0.2
1940	Phi-A	37	81	7	25	4	0	1	19	4	8	.309	.341	.395	92	-1	-1	10	0	0	0	3	O	0.1
1941	Phi-A	9	24	1	3	1	0	0	1	1	2	.125	.160	.167	-14	-4	-4	0	0	0	0	1	/O	-0.3
1943	Bos-N	40	133	9	27	5	0	1	12	8	21	.203	.248	.263	49	-9	-9	8	0	1	-1	-1	/O	-1.2
1944	Phi-A	4	6	1	3	0	0	0	2	0	0	.500	.500	.500	189	1	1	1	0	0	0	0	/O	0.1
Total	20	2215	8759	1507	2927	539	149	307	1827	615	737	.334	.380	.535	132	399	378	1770	87	67		42	*O/1	29.0

■ HACK SIMMONS
Simmons, George Washington b: 1/29/1885, Brooklyn, N.Y. d: 4/26/42, Arverne, N.Y. BR/TR, 5'8", 179 lbs. Deb: 4/15/10

YEAR	TM/L	G	AB	R	H	2B	3B	HR	RBI	BB	SO	AVG	OBP	SLG	PRO+	BR	/A	RC	SB	CS	SBR	FR	POS	TPR
1910	Det-A	42	110	12	25	3	1	0	9	10		.227	.303	.273	75	-2	-3	10	1			-0	1/3O	-0.2
1912	NY-A	110	401	45	96	17	2	0	41	33		.239	.308	.292	68	-14	-18	41	19			-19	21/S	-3.7
1914	Bal-F	114	352	50	95	16	5	1	38	32	26	.270	.341	.352	96	0	-1	47	7			-8	O2/1S3	-1.2
1915	Bal-F	39	88	8	18	7	1	1	14	10	9	.205	.293	.341	85	-1	-2	10	1			-3	2O	-0.5
Total	4	305	951	115	234	43	9	2	102	85	35	.246	.318	.317	80	-18	-24	108	28			-30	2/013S	-5.6

■ JOHN SIMMONS
Simmons, John Earl b: 7/7/24, Birmingham, Ala. BR/TR, 6'1.5", 192 lbs. Deb: 4/22/49

YEAR	TM/L	G	AB	R	H	2B	3B	HR	RBI	BB	SO	AVG	OBP	SLG	PRO+	BR	/A	RC	SB	CS	SBR	FR	POS	TPR
1949	Was-A	62	93	12	20	0	0	0	5	11	6	.215	.298	.215	38	-8	-8	6	0	0	0	-1	O	-0.8

■ JOE SIMMONS
Simmons, Joseph S. b: 6/13/1845, New York, N.Y. 5'9", 166 lbs. Deb: 5/08/1871 M

YEAR	TM/L	G	AB	R	H	2B	3B	HR	RBI	BB	SO	AVG	OBP	SLG	PRO+	BR	/A	RC	SB	CS	SBR	FR	POS	TPR
1871	Chi-n	27	129	29	28	6	1	0	17	1	0	.217	.223	.279	39	-9	-13	9	4				*O/1	-0.6
1872	Cle-n	18	89	11	23	5	1	0		1		.258	.267	.337	90	-2	-1	8					1/O	0.1
1875	Wes-n	13	53	5	9	1	0	0		0		.170	.170	.189	23	-4	-4	2					O/1M	-0.3
Total	3 n	58	271	45	60	12	2	0		2		.221	.227	.280	51	-15	-17	19					/O1	-0.8

■ NELSON SIMMONS
Simmons, Nelson Bernard b: 6/27/63, Washington, D.C. BB/TR, 6'1", 185 lbs. Deb: 9/04/84

YEAR	TM/L	G	AB	R	H	2B	3B	HR	RBI	BB	SO	AVG	OBP	SLG	PRO+	BR	/A	RC	SB	CS	SBR	FR	POS	TPR
1984	Det-A	9	30	4	13	2	0	0	3	2	5	.433	.469	.500	169	3	3	6	1	0	0	-0	/OD	0.3
1985	Det-A	75	251	31	60	11	0	10	33	26	41	.239	.310	.402	94	-3	-2	32	1	0	0	-4	OD	-0.6
1987	Bal-A	16	49	3	13	1	1	1	4	3	8	.265	.308	.388	85	-1	-1	5	0	1	-1	1	O/D	-0.0
Total	3	100	330	38	86	14	1	11	40	31	54	.261	.324	.409	99	-1	-1	43	2	1	0	-4	/OD	-0.3

■ TED SIMMONS
Simmons, Ted Lyle b: 8/9/49, Highland Park, Mich. BB/TR, 5'11", 193 lbs. Deb: 9/21/68

YEAR	TM/L	G	AB	R	H	2B	3B	HR	RBI	BB	SO	AVG	OBP	SLG	PRO+	BR	/A	RC	SB	CS	SBR	FR	POS	TPR
1968	StL-N	2	3	0	1	0	0	0	0	1	1	.333	.500	.333	156	0	0	1	0	0	0	-0	/C	0.0
1969	StL-N	5	14	0	3	0	1	0	3	1	1	.214	.267	.357	73	-1	-1	1	0	0	0	-0	/C	-0.1
1970	StL-N	82	284	29	69	8	2	3	24	37	37	.243	.334	.317	74	-9	-10	31	2	2	-1	-1	C	-0.7
1971	StL-N	133	510	64	155	32	4	7	77	36	50	.304	.353	.424	115	12	10	71	1	3	-2	-13	*C	-0.1
1972	StL-N	152	594	70	180	36	6	16	96	29	57	.303	.338	.465	127	18	18	86	1	3	-2	7	*C1	3.2
1973	StL-N	161	619	62	192	36	2	13	91	61	47	.310	.374	.438	124	21	21	94	2	2	-1	12	*C/1O	4.2
1974	StL-N	152	599	66	163	33	6	20	103	47	35	.272	.331	.447	117	11	11	83	0	0	-0	-4	*C1	1.3
1975	StL-N	157	581	80	193	32	3	18	100	63	35	.332	.398	.491	141	36	33	108	1	3	-2	-3	*C/1O	3.4
1976	StL-N	150	546	60	159	35	3	5	75	73	35	.291	.375	.394	117	15	14	80	0	7	-4	-9	*C1/O3	0.5
1977	StL-N	150	516	82	164	25	3	21	95	79	37	.318	.410	.500	145	33	35	100	2	6	-3	-15	*C/O	1.5
1978	StL-N	152	516	71	148	40	5	22	80	77	39	.287	.383	.512	150	33	34	98	1	1	-0	-6	*CO	3.2
1979	StL-N	123	448	68	127	22	0	26	87	61	34	.283	.374	.507	137	24	23	84	0	1	-1	-5	*C	2.1
1980	StL-N	145	495	84	150	33	2	21	98	59	45	.303	.379	.505	140	30	28	94	1	0	-0	-9	*C/O	2.3
1981	*Mil-A	100	380	45	82	13	3	14	61	23	32	.216	.266	.376	88	-9	-7	36	0	1	-1	-8	CD/1	-1.3
1982	*Mil-A	137	539	73	145	29	0	23	97	32	40	.269	.312	.451	114	3	7	70	0	0	0	-1	*CD	1.3
1983	Mil-A	153	600	76	185	39	3	13	108	41	51	.308	.355	.448	129	15	21	89	4	2	0	-4	CD	2.0
1984	Mil-A	132	497	44	110	23	2	4	52	30	40	.221	.270	.300	60	-29	-26	36	3	0	-1	-1	D13	-2.9
1985	Mil-A	143	528	60	144	28	2	12	76	57	32	.273	.345	.402	104	3	4	71	1	1	-0	-3	D1C/3	0.0
1986	Atl-N	76	127	14	32	5	0	4	25	12	14	.252	.321	.386	89	-1	-2	16	1	0	0	-3	1C/3	-0.4
1987	Atl-N	73	177	20	49	8	0	4	30	21	23	.277	.354	.390	92	-0	-2	24	1	1	-0	-1	1C/3	-0.3
1988	Atl-N	78	107	6	21	6	0	2	11	15	9	.196	.295	.308	70	-4	-4	10	0	0	0	-1	1C	-0.5
Total	21	2456	8680	1074	2472	483	47	248	1389	855	694	.285	.352	.437	118	201	209	1284	21	33	-14	-69	*CD1/O3	18.7

■ MIKE SIMMS
Simms, Michael Howard b: 1/12/67, Orange, Cal. BR/TR, 6'4", 185 lbs. Deb: 9/05/90

YEAR	TM/L	G	AB	R	H	2B	3B	HR	RBI	BB	SO	AVG	OBP	SLG	PRO+	BR	/A	RC	SB	CS	SBR	FR	POS	TPR
1990	Hou-N	12	13	3	4	1	0	1	2	0	4	.308	.308	.615	150	1	1	2	0	0	0	0	/1	0.0

■ HANK SIMON
Simon, Henry Joseph b: 8/25/1862, Hawkinsville, N.Y. d: 1/1/25, Albany, N.Y. BR/TR, Deb: 10/07/1887

YEAR	TM/L	G	AB	R	H	2B	3B	HR	RBI	BB	SO	AVG	OBP	SLG	PRO+	BR	/A	RC	SB	CS	SBR	FR	POS	TPR
1887	Cle-a	3	10	1	1	0	0	0	0			.100	.100	.100	-45	-2	-2	0	0			-1	/O	-0.1
1890	Bro-a	89	373	66	96	17	11	0	34			.257	.321	.362	107	1	3	52	23			6	O	0.4
	Syr-a	38	156	33	47	5	3	2	17			.301	.370	.410	147	6	9	29	12			-3	O	0.3
	Yr	127	529	99	143	22	14	2	51			.270	.336	.376	119	7	12	81	35			4		0.7
Total	2	130	539	100	144	22	14	2	51			.267	.332	.371	115	5	10	81	35			3	O	0.6

■ MIKE SIMON
Simon, Michael Edward b: 4/13/1883, Hayden, Ind. d: 6/10/63, Los Angeles, Cal. BR/TR, 5'11", 188 lbs. Deb: 6/27/09

YEAR	TM/L	G	AB	R	H	2B	3B	HR	RBI	BB	SO	AVG	OBP	SLG	PRO+	BR	/A	RC	SB	CS	SBR	FR	POS	TPR
1909	Pit-N	12	18	2	3	0	0	0	2	1		.167	.211	.167	16	-2	-2	1	0			0	/C	0.0
1910	Pit-N	22	50	3	10	0	1	0	5	1	2	.200	.216	.240	31	-4	-5	3	1			-4	C	-0.8
1911	Pit-N	71	215	19	49	4	3	0	22	10	14	.228	.275	.274	52	-14	-15	16	1			-0	C	-0.9
1912	Pit-N	42	113	10	34	2	1	0	11	5	9	.301	.331	.336	84	-3	-3	12	1			4	C	0.3
1913	Pit-N	92	255	23	63	6	2	1	17	10	15	.247	.281	.298	68	-12	-10	21	3			23	C	1.8
1914	StL-F	93	276	21	57	11	2	0	21	18	21	.207	.263	.261	48	-18	-20	21	2			11	C	-0.5
1915	Bro-F	47	142	7	25	5	1	0	12	9	12	.176	.225	.225	34	-12	-12	8	1			-12	C	-2.4
Total	7	379	1069	85	241	28	10	1	90	54	73	.225	.269	.273	54	-64	-65	82	9			21	C	-2.5

■ SYL SIMON
Simon, Sylvester Adam "Sammy" b: 12/14/1897, Evansville, Ind. d: 2/28/73, Chandler, Ind. BR/TR, 5'10.5", 170 lbs. Deb: 10/01/23

YEAR	TM/L	G	AB	R	H	2B	3B	HR	RBI	BB	SO	AVG	OBP	SLG	PRO+	BR	/A	RC	SB	CS	SBR	FR	POS	TPR
1923	StL-A	1	1	0	0	0	0	0	0	0	0	.000	.000	.000	-95	-0	-0	0	0	0	0	0	H	0.0
1924	StL-A	23	32	5	8	1	1	0	6	3	5	.250	.314	.344	66	-2	-2	4	0	0	0	-0	/3S	0.0
Total	2	24	33	5	8	1	1	0	6	3	5	.242	.306	.333	61	-2	-2	4	0	0	0	-0	/3S	0.0

■ MEL SIMONS
Simons, Melbern Ellis "Butch" b: 7/1/1900, Carlyle, Ill. d: 11/10/74, Paducah, Ky. BL/TR, 5'10", 175 lbs. Deb: 4/14/31

YEAR	TM/L	G	AB	R	H	2B	3B	HR	RBI	BB	SO	AVG	OBP	SLG	PRO+	BR	/A	RC	SB	CS	SBR	FR	POS	TPR
1931	Chi-A	68	189	24	52	9	0	0	12	12	17	.275	.318	.323	73	-8	-7	20	1	1	-0	-9	O	-1.8
1932	Chi-A	7	5	0	0	0	0	0	0	0	1	.000	.000	.000	-99	-1	-1	0	0	0	0	0	/O	-0.1
Total	2	75	194	24	52	9	0	0	12	12	18	.268	.311	.314	69	-10	-8	20	1	1	-0	-9	/O	-1.9

■ HARRY SIMPSON
Simpson, Harry Leon "Suitcase" or "Goody" b: 12/3/25, Atlanta, Ga. d: 4/3/79, Akron, Ohio BL/TR, 6'1", 180 lbs. Deb: 4/21/51

YEAR	TM/L	G	AB	R	H	2B	3B	HR	RBI	BB	SO	AVG	OBP	SLG	PRO+	BR	/A	RC	SB	CS	SBR	FR	POS	TPR
1951	Cle-A	122	332	51	76	7	0	7	24	45	48	.229	.325	.313	77	-12	-9	36	6	4	-1	-3	O1	-1.5

YEAR	TM/L	G	AB	R	H	2B	3B	HR	RBI	BB	SO	AVG	OBP	SLG	PRO+	BR	/A	RC	SB	CS	SBR	FR	POS	TPR
1952	Cle-A	146	545	66	145	21	10	10	65	56	82	.266	.337	.396	111	2	6	75	5	3	-0	-8	*O1	-0.6
1953	Cle-A	82	242	25	55	3	1	7	22	18	27	.227	.284	.335	68	-12	-11	23	0	0	0	-4	O/1	-1.7
1955	Cle-A	3	1	1	0	0	0	0	0	2	0	.000	.667	.000	88	0	0	0	0	0	0	0	H	0.0
	KC-A	112	396	42	119	16	7	5	52	34	61	.301	.359	.414	106	4	3	57	3	5	-2	-2	*O/1	-0.5
	Yr	115	397	43	119	16	7	5	52	36	61	.300	.361	.413	106	4	4	57	3	5	-2	-2		-0.5
1956	KC-A	141	543	76	159	22	11	21	105	47	82	.293	.350	.490	119	13	13	87	2	3	-1	-14	*O1	-0.8
1957	KC-A	50	179	24	53	9	6	6	24	12	28	.296	.340	.514	128	7	6	28	0	1	-1	1	1O	0.5
	*NY-A	75	224	27	56	7	3	7	39	19	36	.250	.309	.402	94	-3	-2	27	1	0	0	-4	O1	-0.8
	Yr	125	403	51	109	16	9	13	63	31	64	.270	.323	.452	110	4	4	55	1	1	-0	-3		-0.3
1958	NY-A	24	51	1	11	2	1	0	6	6	12	.216	.310	.294	70	-2	-2	5	0	0	0	-1	O	-0.3
	KC-A	78	212	21	56	7	1	7	27	26	33	.264	.345	.406	104	2	1	31	0	2	-1	-3	1O	-0.4
	Yr	102	263	22	67	9	2	7	33	32	45	.255	.338	.384	98	-0	-0	35	0	2	-1	-4		-0.7
1959	KC-A	8	14	1	4	0	0	1	2	2	4	.286	.412	.500	146	1	1	3	0	0	0	0	/1	0.1
	Chi-A	38	75	5	14	5	1	2	13	4	14	.187	.228	.360	59	-5	-4	6	0	0	0	-3	O/1	-0.7
	Yr	46	89	6	18	5	1	3	15	6	18	.202	.260	.382	75	-4	-3	9	0	0	0	-3		-0.6
	Pit-N	9	15	3	4	2	0	0	2	0	2	.267	.267	.400	75	-1	-1	2	0	0	0	0	/O	0.0
Total	8	888	2829	343	752	101	41	73	381	271	429	.266	.332	.408	102	-6	1	380	17	18	-6	-39	O1	-6.7

■ JOE SIMPSON
Simpson, Joe Allen b: 12/31/51, Purcell, Okla. BL/TL, 6'3", 175 lbs. Deb: 9/02/75

YEAR	TM/L	G	AB	R	H	2B	3B	HR	RBI	BB	SO	AVG	OBP	SLG	PRO+	BR	/A	RC	SB	CS	SBR	FR	POS	TPR
1975	LA-N	9	6	3	2	0	0	0	0	0	2	.333	.333	.333	89	-0	-0	1	0	0	0	1	/O	0.0
1976	LA-N	23	30	2	4	1	0	0	0	1	6	.133	.161	.167	-7	-4	-4	1	0	1	-1	1	O	-0.3
1977	LA-N	29	23	2	4	0	0	0	1	2	6	.174	.240	.174	13	-3	-3	1	1	1	-0	3	O/1	-0.1
1978	LA-N	10	5	1	2	0	0	0	1	0	2	.400	.400	.400	125	0	0	1	0	0	0	1	O	0.1
1979	Sea-A	120	265	29	75	11	0	2	27	11	21	.283	.314	.347	77	-8	-9	28	6	3	0	-7	*O	-1.9
1980	Sea-A	129	365	42	91	15	3	3	34	28	43	.249	.305	.332	74	-13	-13	39	17	4	3	-21	*O/1	-3.4
1981	Sea-A	91	288	32	64	11	3	2	30	15	41	.222	.263	.302	60	-14	-16	24	12	3	2	-3	O	-1.9
1982	Sea-A	105	296	39	76	14	4	2	23	22	48	.257	.313	.351	80	-7	-8	30	8	14	-6	-3	O	-2.0
1983	KC-A	91	119	16	20	2	2	0	8	11	21	.168	.250	.218	30	-11	-11	7	1	1	-0	10	1O/PD	-0.3
Total	9	607	1397	166	338	54	12	9	124	90	190	.242	.291	.317	67	-61	-64	132	45	27	-3	-19	O/1PD	-9.8

■ MARTY SIMPSON
Simpson, Martin b: Baltimore, Md. Deb: 5/14/1873

YEAR	TM/L	G	AB	R	H	2B	3B	HR	RBI	BB	SO	AVG	OBP	SLG	PRO+	BR	/A	RC	SB	CS	SBR	FR	POS	TPR
1873	Mar-n	4	14	4	2	0	0	0	0			.143	.143	.143	-20	-2	-1	0					/2C	0.0

■ DICK SIMPSON
Simpson, Richard Charles b: 7/28/43, Washington, D.C. BR/TR, 6'4", 176 lbs. Deb: 9/21/62

YEAR	TM/L	G	AB	R	H	2B	3B	HR	RBI	BB	SO	AVG	OBP	SLG	PRO+	BR	/A	RC	SB	CS	SBR	FR	POS	TPR
1962	LA-A	6	8	1	2	0	0	0	1	2	3	.250	.400	.375	114	0	0	1	0	0	0	1	/O	0.1
1964	LA-A	21	50	11	7	1	0	2	4	8	15	.140	.259	.280	55	-3	-3	4	2	2	-1	0	O	-0.3
1965	Cal-A	8	27	2	6	1	0	0	3	2	8	.222	.276	.259	54	-2	-2	2	1	0	0	-1	O	-0.1
1966	Cin-N	92	84	26	20	2	0	4	14	10	32	.238	.333	.405	96	1	0	12	0	1	-1	-1	O	-0.3
1967	Cin-N	44	54	8	14	3	0	1	6	7	11	.259	.344	.370	94	0	-0	7	0	1	-1	4	O	0.2
1968	StL-N	26	56	11	13	0	0	3	8	8	21	.232	.328	.393	117	1	1	7	0	1	-1	-0	O	0.0
	Hou-N	59	177	25	33	7	2	3	11	20	61	.186	.284	.299	77	-5	-5	15	4	4	-1	-6	O	-1.6
	Yr	85	233	36	46	7	2	6	19	28	82	.197	.294	.322	86	-4	-3	23	4	5	-2	-6		-1.6
1969	NY-A	6	11	2	3	2	0	0	4	3	6	.273	.429	.455	153	1	1	2	0	0	0	0	/O	0.1
	Sea-A	26	51	8	9	2	0	2	5	4	17	.176	.236	.333	59	-3	-3	4	3	1	0	-0	O	-0.3
	Yr	32	62	10	12	4	0	2	9	7	23	.194	.275	.355	77	-2	-2	6	3	1	0	-0		-0.2
Total	7	288	518	94	107	19	2	15	56	64	174	.207	.301	.338	84	-10	-10	54	10	10	-3	-3	O	-2.2

■ DUKE SIMS
Sims, Duane B b: 6/5/41, Salt Lake City, Ut. BL/TR, 6'2", 197 lbs. Deb: 9/22/64

YEAR	TM/L	G	AB	R	H	2B	3B	HR	RBI	BB	SO	AVG	OBP	SLG	PRO+	BR	/A	RC	SB	CS	SBR	FR	POS	TPR
1964	Cle-A	2	6	0	0	0	0	0	0	0	2	.000	.000	.000	-99	-2	-2	0	0	0	0	0	/C	0.0
1965	Cle-A	48	118	9	21	0	0	6	15	15	33	.178	.271	.331	69	-5	-5	11	0	0	0	-2	C	-0.4
1966	Cle-A	52	133	12	35	2	2	6	19	11	31	.263	.338	.444	122	4	4	19	0	1	-1	-5	C	0.1
1967	Cle-A	88	272	25	55	8	2	12	37	30	64	.202	.295	.379	97	-1	-1	30	3	3	-1	-2	C	0.1
1968	Cle-A	122	361	48	90	21	0	11	44	62	68	.249	.367	.399	134	16	17	54	1	3	-2	-0	C1/O	2.0
1969	Cle-A	114	326	40	77	8	0	18	45	66	80	.236	.374	.426	120	12	11	57	1	2	-1	-4	*C/O1	1.3
1970	Cle-A	110	345	46	91	12	0	23	56	46	59	.264	.360	.499	128	16	14	63	0	4	-2	-2	CO1	0.8
1971	LA-N	90	230	23	63	7	2	6	25	30	39	.274	.360	.400	122	5	7	34	0	1	-1	-0	C	0.8
1972	LA-N	51	151	7	29	7	0	2	11	17	23	.192	.278	.278	60	-8	-8	11	0	0	0	-1	C	-0.6
	*Det-A	38	98	11	31	4	0	4	19	19	18	.316	.432	.480	166	10	9	22	0	0	0	-3	C/O	-0.3
1973	Det-A	80	252	31	61	10	0	8	30	30	36	.242	.327	.377	92	-1	-1	32	1	2	-1	3	C/O	0.0
	NY-A	4	9	3	3	0	0	1	1	3	1	.333	.500	.667	234	2	2	3	0	0	0	1	/CD	0.3
	Yr	84	261	34	64	10	0	9	31	33	37	.245	.334	.387	97	1	-1	35	1	2	-1	4		0.3
1974	NY-A	5	15	1	2	1	0	0	2	1	5	.133	.188	.200	12	-2	-2	1	0	0	0	0	/CD	-0.1
	Tex-A	39	106	7	22	0	0	3	6	8	24	.208	.282	.292	67	-5	-4	9	0	0	0	-3	C/OD	-0.6
	Yr	44	121	8	24	1	0	3	8	9	29	.198	.271	.281	60	-6	-6	9	0	0	0	-3		-0.7
Total	11	843	2422	263	580	80	6	100	310	338	483	.239	.341	.401	111	42	39	346	6	16	-8	-17	C/1OD	4.4

■ GREG SIMS
Sims, Gregory Emmett b: 6/28/46, San Francisco, Cal BB/TR, 6', 190 lbs. Deb: 4/15/66

YEAR	TM/L	G	AB	R	H	2B	3B	HR	RBI	BB	SO	AVG	OBP	SLG	PRO+	BR	/A	RC	SB	CS	SBR	FR	POS	TPR
1966	Hou-N	7	6	1	1	0	0	0	0	0	3	.167	.286	.167	32	-1	-0	0	0	0	0	0	/O	0.0

■ MATT SINATRO
Sinatro, Matthew Stephen b: 3/22/60, Hartford, Conn. BR/TR, 5'9", 174 lbs. Deb: 9/22/81

YEAR	TM/L	G	AB	R	H	2B	3B	HR	RBI	BB	SO	AVG	OBP	SLG	PRO+	BR	/A	RC	SB	CS	SBR	FR	POS	TPR
1981	Atl-N	12	32	4	9	1	1	0	4	5	4	.281	.378	.375	111	1	1	5	1	0	0	4	C	0.5
1982	Atl-N	37	81	10	11	2	0	1	4	4	9	.136	.176	.198	4	-10	-11	2	0	1	-1	4	C	-0.7
1983	Atl-N	7	12	0	2	0	0	0	2	2	1	.167	.286	.167	26	-1	-1	1	0	0	0	2	/C	0.1
1984	Atl-N	2	4	0	0	0	0	0	0	0	0	.000	.000	.000	-93	-1	-1	0	0	0	0	-0	/C	-0.1
1987	Oak-A	6	3	0	0	0	0	0	0	0	1	.000	.000	.000	-99	-1	-1	0	0	0	0	-0	/C	0.0
1988	Oak-A	10	9	1	3	2	0	0	5	0	1	.333	.333	.556	149	0	1	1	0	0	0	2	/C	0.3
1989	Det-A	13	25	2	3	0	0	0	1	1	3	.120	.185	.120	-13	-4	-4	1	0	0	0	0	C	-0.2
1990	Sea-A	30	50	2	15	1	0	0	4	4	10	.300	.352	.320	88	-1	-1	5	1	0	0	7	C	0.7
Total	8	117	216	19	43	6	1	1	20	16	29	.199	.258	.250	42	-16	-17	15	2	1	0	18	C	0.6

■ HOSEA SINER
Siner, Hosea John b: 3/20/1885, Shelburn, Ind. d: 6/10/48, Sullivan, Ind. BR/TR, 5'10.5", 185 lbs. Deb: 7/28/09

YEAR	TM/L	G	AB	R	H	2B	3B	HR	RBI	BB	SO	AVG	OBP	SLG	PRO+	BR	/A	RC	SB	CS	SBR	FR	POS	TPR
1909	Bos-N	10	23	1	3	0	0	0	1		2	.130	.200	.130	3	-3	-3	1	0			-1	/32S	-0.4

■ KEN SINGLETON
Singleton, Kenneth Wayne b: 6/10/47, New York, N.Y. BB/TR, 6'4", 210 lbs. Deb: 6/24/70

YEAR	TM/L	G	AB	R	H	2B	3B	HR	RBI	BB	SO	AVG	OBP	SLG	PRO+	BR	/A	RC	SB	CS	SBR	FR	POS	TPR
1970	NY-N	69	198	22	52	8	0	5	26	30	48	.263	.362	.379	99	0	0	28	1	1	-0	-3	O	-0.4
1971	NY-N	115	298	34	73	5	0	13	46	61	64	.245	.377	.393	120	9	10	45	0	1	-1	-6	O	0.0
1972	Mon-N	142	507	77	139	23	2	14	50	70	99	.274	.364	.410	118	15	13	75	5	10	-5	-2	*O	0.0
1973	Mon-N	162	560	100	169	26	2	23	103	123	91	.302	**.429**	.479	146	45	42	113	2	8	-4	2	*O	3.4
1974	Mon-N	148	511	68	141	20	2	9	74	93	84	.276	.387	.376	108	13	10	77	5	2	0	-12	*O	-0.7
1975	Bal-A	155	586	88	176	37	4	15	55	118	82	.300	.418	.454	156	41	46	118	3	5	-2	-11	*O	3.0
1976	Bal-A	154	544	62	151	25	2	13	70	79	76	.278	.369	.403	134	20	24	82	2	2	-1	-3	*OD	1.8
1977	Bal-A	152	536	90	176	24	0	24	99	107	101	.328	.442	.507	168	49	53	124	0	1	-1	-6	*O/D	4.0
1978	Bal-A	149	502	67	147	21	2	20	81	99	94	.293	.411	.462	**154**	34	38	100	0	2	-1	-15	*O/D	2.0
1979	*Bal-A	159	570	93	168	29	1	35	111	109	118	.295	.409	.533	158	44	47	127	3	1	-0	-9	*OD	3.2
1980	Bal-A	156	583	85	177	28	3	24	104	92	94	.304	.399	.485	143	35	36	113	0	2	-1	-19	*O/D	1.2

YEAR	TM/L	G	AB	R	H	2B	3B	HR	RBI	BB	SO	AVG	OBP	SLG	PRO+	BR	/A	RC	SB	CS	SBR	FR	POS	TPR
1981	Bal-A	103	363	48	101	16	1	13	49	61	59	.278	.382	.435	135	18	18	57	0	0	0	-7	OD	1.0
1982	Bal-A	156	561	71	141	27	2	14	77	86	93	.251	.353	.381	102	3	4	75	0	1	-1	-0	*D/O	0.3
1983	*Bal-A	151	507	52	140	21	3	18	84	99	83	.276	.395	.436	131	24	25	86	0	2	-1	0	*D	2.4
1984	Bal-A	111	363	28	78	7	1	6	36	37	60	.215	.287	.289	61	-19	-18	27	0	0	0	0	*D	-1.7
Total	15	2082	7189	985	2029	317	25	246	1065	1263	1246	.282	.391	.436	132	332	350	1247	21	36	-15	-92	*OD	19.5

■ FRED SINGTON
Sington, Frederic William b: 2/24/10, Brimingham, Ala. BR/TR, 6'2", 215 lbs. Deb: 9/23/34

YEAR	TM/L	G	AB	R	H	2B	3B	HR	RBI	BB	SO	AVG	OBP	SLG	PRO+	BR	/A	RC	SB	CS	SBR	FR	POS	TPR
1934	Was-A	9	35	2	10	2	0	0	6	4	3	.286	.359	.343	85	-1	-1	4	0	1	-1	-1	/O	-0.2
1935	Was-A	20	22	1	4	0	0	0	3	5	1	.182	.333	.182	38	-2	-2	2	0	0	0	1	/O	0.0
1936	Was-A	25	94	13	30	8	0	1	28	15	9	.319	.413	.436	116	2	3	18	0	0	0	-2	O	0.0
1937	Was-A	78	228	27	54	15	4	3	36	37	33	.237	.348	.377	87	-6	-4	32	1	1	-0	-3	O	-0.9
1938	Bro-N	17	53	10	19	6	1	2	5	13	5	.358	.493	.623	200	8	8	18	1			-2	O	0.6
1939	Bro-N	32	84	13	23	5	0	1	7	15	15	.274	.384	.369	100	1	1	11	0			-1	O	0.0
Total	6	181	516	66	140	36	5	7	85	89	66	.271	.382	.401	104	3	5	85	2	2		-9	O	-0.5

■ DICK SIPEK
Sipek, Richard Francis b: 1/16/23, Chicago, Ill. BL/TR, 5'9", 170 lbs. Deb: 4/28/45

YEAR	TM/L	G	AB	R	H	2B	3B	HR	RBI	BB	SO	AVG	OBP	SLG	PRO+	BR	/A	RC	SB	CS	SBR	FR	POS	TPR
1945	Cin-N	82	156	14	38	6	2	0	13	9	15	.244	.302	.308	71	-6	-6	14	0			-0	O	-0.7

■ JOHN SIPIN
Sipin, John White b: 8/29/46, Watsonville, Cal. BR/TR, 6'1.5", 175 lbs. Deb: 5/24/69

YEAR	TM/L	G	AB	R	H	2B	3B	HR	RBI	BB	SO	AVG	OBP	SLG	PRO+	BR	/A	RC	SB	CS	SBR	FR	POS	TPR
1969	SD-N	68	229	24	51	12	2	9	8	44	.223	.252	.319	61	-13	-12	18	2	0	1	-2	2	-0.8

■ GEORGE SISLER
Sisler, George Harold "Georgeous George"
b: 3/24/1893, Manchester, Ohio d: 3/26/73, Richmond Heights, Mo. BL/TL, 5'11", 170 lbs. Deb: 6/28/15 MCH

YEAR	TM/L	G	AB	R	H	2B	3B	HR	RBI	BB	SO	AVG	OBP	SLG	PRO+	BR	/A	RC	SB	CS	SBR	FR	POS	TPR
1915	StL-A	81	274	28	78	10	2	3	29	7	27	.285	.307	.369	106	-1	0	32	10	9	-2	-3	1OP	-0.6
1916	StL-A	151	580	83	177	21	11	4	76	40	37	.305	.355	.400	133	17	20	84	34	26	-5	-2	*1/PO3	1.1
1917	StL-A	135	539	60	190	30	9	2	52	30	19	.353	.390	.453	163	34	36	104	37			4	*1/2	3.8
1918	StL-A	114	452	69	154	21	9	2	41	40	17	.341	.400	.440	159	29	30	92	45			9	*1/P	3.5
1919	StL-A	132	511	96	180	31	15	10	83	27	20	.352	.390	.530	153	36	34	112	28			13	*1	3.8
1920	StL-A	154	631	137	257	49	18	19	122	46	19	.407	.449	.632	179	73	71	176	42	17	2	15	*1/P	8.3
1921	StL-A	138	582	125	216	38	18	12	104	34	27	.371	.411	.560	137	38	33	133	35	11	4	8	*1	4.0
1922	StL-A	142	586	134	246	42	18	8	105	49	14	.420	.467	.594	169	64	62	162	51	19	4	12	*1	6.3
1924	StL-A	151	636	94	194	27	10	9	74	31	29	.305	.340	.421	90	-7	-12	87	19	17	-5	1	*1M	-2.1
1925	StL-A	150	649	100	224	21	15	12	105	27	24	.345	.371	.479	109	12	7	110	11	12	-4	11	*1/PM	0.9
1926	StL-A	150	613	78	178	21	12	7	71	30	30	.290	.327	.398	84	-13	-16	79	12	8	-1	-4	*1/PM	-2.6
1927	StL-A	149	614	87	201	32	8	5	97	24	15	.327	.357	.430	100	2	-1	87	27	7	4	11	*1	0.7
1928	Was-A	20	49	1	12	1	0	0	2	1	2	.245	.260	.265	39	-4	-4	3	0	1	-1	-2	/1O	-0.6
	Bos-N	118	491	71	167	26	4	4	68	30	15	.340	.380	.434	119	9	12	78	11			7	*1/P	0.7
1929	Bos-N	154	629	67	205	40	8	2	79	33	17	.326	.363	.424	98	-5	-2	94	6			3	*1	-0.5
1930	Bos-N	116	431	54	133	15	7	3	67	23	15	.309	.346	.397	82	-14	-12	58	7			5	*1	-0.9
Total	15	2055	8267	1284	2812	425	164	102	1175	472	327	.340	.379	.468	124	269	258	1490	375	127		88	*1/OP23	25.8

■ DICK SISLER
Sisler, Richard Allan b: 11/2/20, St.Louis, Mo. BL/TR, 6'2", 205 lbs. Deb: 4/16/46 MC

YEAR	TM/L	G	AB	R	H	2B	3B	HR	RBI	BB	SO	AVG	OBP	SLG	PRO+	BR	/A	RC	SB	CS	SBR	FR	POS	TPR
1946	*StL-N	83	235	17	61	11	2	3	42	14	28	.260	.307	.362	86	-4	-5	26	0			0	1O	-0.8
1947	StL-N	46	74	4	15	2	1	0	9	3	8	.203	.234	.257	29	-7	-8	5	0			0	1/O	-0.7
1948	Phi-N	121	446	60	122	21	3	11	56	47	46	.274	.344	.408	105	2	3	66	1			-3	*1	-0.1
1949	Phi-N	121	412	42	119	19	6	7	50	25	38	.289	.333	.415	102	-1	0	57	0			-9	1	-0.8
1950	*Phi-N	141	523	79	155	29	4	13	83	64	50	.296	.373	.442	115	11	12	88	1			4	*O	1.1
1951	Phi-N	125	428	46	123	20	5	8	52	40	39	.287	.351	.414	107	3	4	63	1	0	0	-1	*O	0.0
1952	Cin-N	11	27	3	5	1	1	0	4	3	5	.185	.267	.296	56	-2	-2	2	0	0	0	-0	/O	-0.2
	StL-N	119	418	48	109	14	5	13	60	29	35	.261	.312	.411	99	-2	-2	53	3	3	-1	2	*1	-0.4
	Yr	130	445	51	114	15	6	13	64	32	40	.256	.309	.404	96	-3	-4	56	3	3	-1	1		-0.6
1953	StL-N	32	43	3	11	1	1	0	4	1	4	.256	.273	.326	55	-3	-3	4	0	0	0	1	1	-0.1
Total	8	799	2606	302	720	118	28	55	360	226	253	.276	.336	.406	101	-4	-1	365	6	3		-6	1O	-2.0

■ SIBBY SISTI
Sisti, Sebastian Daniel b: 7/26/20, Buffalo, N.Y. BR/TR, 5'11", 175 lbs. Deb: 7/21/39 C

YEAR	TM/L	G	AB	R	H	2B	3B	HR	RBI	BB	SO	AVG	OBP	SLG	PRO+	BR	/A	RC	SB	CS	SBR	FR	POS	TPR
1939	Bos-N	63	215	19	49	7	1	1	11	12	38	.228	.269	.284	52	-16	-14	16	4			0	23S	-1.0
1940	Bos-N	123	459	73	115	19	5	6	34	36	64	.251	.311	.353	87	-11	-8	53	4			-2	*32	-0.9
1941	Bos-N	140	541	72	140	24	3	1	45	38	76	.259	.309	.320	81	-17	-14	54	7			-8	*3/2S	-2.0
1942	Bos-N	129	407	50	86	11	4	4	35	45	55	.211	.296	.287	73	-14	-13	36	5			-4	*2/O	-0.8
1946	Bos-N	1	0	0	0	0	0	0	0	0	0	—	—	—	—	0	0	0	0			0	/3	0.0
1947	Bos-N	56	153	22	43	8	0	2	15	20	17	.281	.371	.373	100	0	1	22	2			-9	S/2	-0.3
1948	*Bos-N	83	221	30	54	6	2	0	21	31	34	.244	.340	.290	73	-8	-7	24	0			-5	2S	-0.9
1949	Bos-N	101	268	39	69	12	0	5	22	34	42	.257	.343	.358	93	-4	-2	33	1			-8	O2S/3	-0.5
1950	Bos-N	69	105	21	18	3	1	2	11	16	19	.171	.287	.276	52	-8	-7	9	1			0	S23/10	-0.3
1951	Bos-N	114	362	46	101	20	2	2	38	32	50	.279	.341	.362	96	-5	-2	46	4	5	-2	-23	S2/310	-2.0
1952	Bos-N	90	245	19	52	10	1	4	24	14	43	.212	.255	.310	58	-15	-14	19	2	0	1	-9	2OS/3	-2.1
1953	Mil-N	38	23	8	5	1	0	0	4	5	2	.217	.357	.261	69	-1	-1	2	0	0	0	4	2/S3	0.4
1954	Mil-N	9	0	2	0	0	0	0	0	0	0	—	—	—	—	0	0	0	0	0	0	0	R	0.0
Total	13	1016	2999	401	732	121	19	27	260	283	440	.244	.313	.324	79	-98	-81	315	30	5		-63	23S/O1	-10.4

■ ED SIXSMITH
Sixsmith, Edward b: 2/26/1863, Philadelphia, Pa. d: 12/12/26, Philadelphia, Pa. BR/TR, Deb: 9/11/1884

YEAR	TM/L	G	AB	R	H	2B	3B	HR	RBI	BB	SO	AVG	OBP	SLG	PRO+	BR	/A	RC	SB	CS	SBR	FR	POS	TPR
1884	Phi-N	1	2	0	0	0	0	0	0	0	0	.000	.000	.000	-99	-0	-0	0				-0	/C	0.0

■ TED SIZEMORE
Sizemore, Theodore Crawford b: 4/15/45, Gadsden, Ala. BR/TR, 5'10", 165 lbs. Deb: 4/07/69

YEAR	TM/L	G	AB	R	H	2B	3B	HR	RBI	BB	SO	AVG	OBP	SLG	PRO+	BR	/A	RC	SB	CS	SBR	FR	POS	TPR
1969	LA-N	159	590	69	160	20	5	4	46	45	40	.271	.328	.342	95	-9	-4	66	5	5	-2	-6	*2S/O	0.3
1970	LA-N	96	340	40	104	10	1	1	34	34	19	.306	.369	.350	98	-2	-0	42	5	1	1	-6	2/OS	0.4
1971	StL-N	135	478	53	126	14	5	3	42	42	26	.264	.324	.333	83	-8	-10	50	4	6	-2	-1	2SO/3	-0.4
1972	StL-N	120	439	53	116	17	4	2	38	37	36	.264	.327	.335	90	-6	-5	49	8	3	1	0	*2	0.3
1973	StL-N	142	521	69	147	22	1	1	54	68	34	.282	.367	.334	96	-0	-0	69	6	4	1	9	*2/3	1.4
1974	StL-N	129	504	68	126	21	0	2	47	70	37	.250	.341	.296	80	-12	-11	55	8	4	0	13	*2/SO	0.9
1975	StL-N	153	562	56	135	23	1	3	49	45	37	.240	.299	.301	64	-25	-28	51	1	5	-3	-25	*2	-5.0
1976	LA-N	84	266	18	64	8	1	0	18	15	22	.241	.281	.278	60	-14	-14	21	2	3	-1	2	2/3C	-0.9
1977	*Phi-N	152	519	64	146	20	3	4	47	52	40	.281	.348	.355	85	-7	-10	56	8	11	-4	9	*2	0.4
1978	*Phi-N	108	351	38	77	12	0	0	25	29	29	.219	.273	.254	48	-24	-24	23	8	1	2	4	*2	-1.1
1979	Chi-N	98	330	36	82	17	0	2	30	24	25	.248	.321	.318	68	-11	-15	34	3	3	-1	15	2	0.6
	Bos-A	26	88	12	23	7	0	1	6	4	5	.261	.301	.375	77	-2	-3	16	1	0	0	9	2/C	0.7
1980	Bos-A	9	23	1	5	1	0	0	0	0	0	.217	.217	.261	29	-2	-2	1	0	0	0	3	/2	0.2
Total	12	1411	5011	577	1311	188	21	23	430	469	350	.262	.327	.321	80	-123	-126	526	59	46	-10	28	*2/SO3C	-2.2

■ FRANK SKAFF
Skaff, Francis Michael b: 9/30/13, LaCrosse, Wis. d: 4/12/88, Towson, Md. BR/TR, 5'10", 185 lbs. Deb: 9/11/35 MC

YEAR	TM/L	G	AB	R	H	2B	3B	HR	RBI	BB	SO	AVG	OBP	SLG	PRO+	BR	/A	RC	SB	CS	SBR	FR	POS	TPR
1935	Bro-N	6	11	4	6	1	1	0	3	0	2	.545	.545	.818	267	2	2	4	0			-0	/3	0.2
1943	Phi-A	32	64	8	18	2	1	1	8	6	11	.281	.343	.391	115	1	1	9	0	0	0	1	1/3S	0.2
Total	2	38	75	12	24	3	2	1	11	6	13	.320	.370	.453	138	3	3	14	0	0		1	/13S	0.4

YEAR	TM/L	G	AB	R	H	2B	3B	HR	RBI	BB	SO	AVG	OBP	SLG	PRO+	BR	/A	RC	SB	CS	SBR	FR	POS	TPR

■ DAVE SKAGGS Skaggs, David Lindsey b: 6/12/51, Santa Monica, Cal. BR/TR, 6'2", 200 lbs. Deb: 4/17/77

1977	Bal-A	80	216	22	62	9	1	1	24	20	34	.287	.347	.352	97	-2	-0	28	0	0	0	-1	C	0.1
1978	Bal-A	36	86	6	13	1	1	0	2	9	14	.151	.232	.186	20	-9	-9	4	0	1	-1	4	C	-0.3
1979	*Bal-A	63	137	9	34	8	0	1	14	13	14	.248	.313	.328	76	-5	-4	13	0	0	0	3	C	0.1
1980	Bal-A	2	5	0	1	0	0	0	0	0	1	.200	.200	.200	10	-1	-1	0	0	0	0	1	C	0.0
	Cal-A	24	66	7	13	0	0	1	9	9	13	.197	.293	.242	50	-4	-4	5	0	0	0	-10	C	-1.3
	Yr	26	71	7	14	0	0	1	9	9	14	.197	.287	.239	47	-5	-5	5	0	0	0	-10		-1.3
Total	4	205	510	44	123	18	2	3	49	51	76	.241	.310	.302	72	-21	-18	50	0	1	-1	-3	C	-1.4

■ BUD SKETCHLEY Sketchley, Harry Clement b: 3/30/19, Virden, Man., Can. d: 12/19/79, Los Angeles, Cal. BL/TL, 5'10", 180 lbs. Deb: 4/14/42

| 1942 | Chi-A | 13 | 36 | 1 | 7 | 1 | 0 | 0 | 3 | 7 | 4 | .194 | .326 | .222 | 57 | -2 | -2 | 3 | 0 | 1 | -1 | -1 | O | -0.3 |

■ ROE SKIDMORE Skidmore, Robert Roe b: 10/30/45, Decatur, Ill. BR/TR, 6'3", 188 lbs. Deb: 9/17/70

| 1970 | Chi-N | 1 | 1 | 0 | 1 | 0 | 0 | 0 | 0 | 0 | 0 | 1.000 | 1.000 | 1.000 | 390 | 0 | 0 | 1 | 0 | 0 | 0 | 0 | H | 0.0 |

■ BILL SKIFF Skiff, William Franklin b: 10/16/1895, New Rochelle, N.Y. d: 12/25/76, Bronxville, N.Y. BR/TR, 5'10", 170 lbs. Deb: 5/17/21

1921	Pit-N	16	45	7	13	2	0	0	11	0	4	.289	.289	.333	63	-2	-2	4	1	1	-0	-1	C	-0.2
1926	NY-A	6	11	0	1	0	0	0	0	0	1	.091	.091	.091	-53	-2	-2	0	0	0	0	-1	/C	-0.2
Total	2	22	56	7	14	2	0	0	11	0	5	.250	.250	.286	40	-5	-5	4	1	1	-0	-2	/C	-0.4

■ CHARLES SKINNER Skinner, Charles Louis b: 8/14/1856, Chicago, Ill. d: 3/5/01, Washington, Mass. Deb: 7/12/1884

1884	Bal-U	1	3	0	1	0	0	0		0		.333	.333	.333	114	0	0	0	0			0	/O	0.0
	CP-U	1	3	1	1	0	0	0		0		.333	.333	.333	127	0	0	0	0			-0	/O	0.0
	Yr	2	6	1	2	0	0	0		0		.333	.333	.333	120	0	0	1	0			-0		0.0

■ CAMP SKINNER Skinner, Elisha Harrison b: 6/25/1897, Douglasville, Ga. d: 8/4/44, Douglasville, Ga. BL/TR, 5'11", 165 lbs. Deb: 5/02/22

1922	NY-A	27	33	1	6	0	0	0	2	0	4	.182	.206	.182	2	-5	-5	1	1	0	0	-0	/O	-0.4
1923	Bos-A	7	13	1	3	2	0	0	1	0	0	.231	.231	.385	60	-1	-1	1	0	0	0	-1	/O	-0.1
Total	2	34	46	2	9	2	0	0	3	0	4	.196	.213	.239	18	-6	-6	2	1	0	0	-1	/O	-0.5

■ JOEL SKINNER Skinner, Joel Patrick b: 2/21/61, LaJolla, Cal. BR/TR, 6'4", 198 lbs. Deb: 6/12/83

1983	Chi-A	6	11	2	3	0	0	0	1	0	1	.273	.273	.273	49	-1	-1	0	0	0	0	2	/C	0.2
1984	Chi-A	43	80	4	17	2	0	0	3	7	19	.213	.276	.237	42	-6	-6	5	1	0	0	9	C	0.5
1985	Chi-A	22	44	9	15	4	1	1	5	5	13	.341	.408	.545	153	4	3	9	0	0	0	3	C	0.7
1986	NY-A	54	166	6	43	4	0	1	17	7	40	.259	.289	.301	62	-9	-9	13	0	4	-2	5	C	-0.1
	Chi-A	60	149	17	30	5	1	4	20	9	43	.201	.252	.329	55	-9	-10	13	1	0	0	-7	C	-1.2
	Yr	114	315	23	73	9	1	5	37	16	83	.232	.271	.314	58	-18	-19	25	1	4	-2	-2		-1.3
1987	NY-A	64	139	9	19	4	0	3	14	8	46	.137	.189	.230	11	-18	-18	5	0	0	0	-3	C	-1.5
1988	NY-A	88	251	23	57	15	0	4	23	14	72	.227	.268	.335	68	-11	-11	22	0	0	0	-7	C/O1	-1.4
1989	Cle-A	79	178	10	41	10	0	1	13	9	42	.230	.271	.303	61	-9	-10	14	1	1	-0	-4	C	-1.0
1990	Cle-A	49	139	16	35	4	1	2	16	7	44	.252	.288	.338	73	-5	-5	13	0	0	0	0	C	-0.3
Total	8	465	1157	96	260	48	3	16	112	66	320	.225	.268	.313	59	-65	-66	94	3	5	-2	-2	C/O1	-4.1

■ BOB SKINNER Skinner, Robert Ralph b: 10/3/31, LaJolla, Cal. BL/TR, 6'4", 190 lbs. Deb: 4/13/54 MC

1954	Pit-N	132	470	67	117	15	9	8	46	47	59	.249	.317	.370	80	-15	-14	56	4	0	1	-2	*1/O	-1.9
1956	Pit-N	113	233	29	47	8	3	5	29	26	59	.202	.285	.326	65	-12	-11	22	1	1	-0	-7	O1/3	-2.1
1957	Pit-N	126	387	58	118	12	6	13	45	38	50	.305	.370	.468	127	13	14	70	10	4	1	0	O/13	1.1
1958	Pit-N	144	529	93	170	33	9	13	70	58	55	.321	.390	.491	135	25	27	102	12	4	1	-1	*O	2.3
1959	Pit-N	143	547	78	153	18	4	13	61	67	65	.280	.358	.399	102	2	3	81	10	7	-1	-2	*O/1	0.2
1960	*Pit-N	145	571	83	156	33	6	15	86	59	86	.273	.342	.431	109	8	7	82	11	8	-2	-1	*O	0.0
1961	Pit-N	119	381	61	102	20	3	3	42	51	49	.268	.360	.360	91	-3	-3	51	3	5	-2	-1	O	-1.1
1962	Pit-N	144	510	87	154	29	7	20	75	76	89	.302	.397	.504	140	30	30	106	10	4	1	-9	*O	1.4
1963	Pit-N	34	122	18	33	5	5	0	8	13	22	.270	.341	.393	110	2	2	16	4	1	1	-2	O	0.0
	Cin-N	72	194	25	49	10	2	3	17	21	42	.253	.332	.371	99	1	0	23	1	2	-1	-2	O	-0.5
	Yr	106	316	43	82	15	7	3	25	34	64	.259	.335	.380	103	3	2	39	5	3	-0	-4		-0.5
1964	Cin-N	25	59	6	13	3	0	3	5	4	12	.220	.270	.424	89	-1	-1	7	0	0	0	-0	O	-0.1
	*StL-N	55	118	10	32	5	0	1	16	11	20	.271	.333	.339	83	-1	-3	14	0	0	0	-0	O	-0.3
	Yr	80	177	16	45	8	0	4	21	15	32	.254	.313	.367	85	-2	-4	21	0	0	0	-1		-0.4
1965	StL-N	80	152	25	47	5	4	5	26	12	30	.309	.360	.493	126	7	6	26	1	0	0	-4	O	0.1
1966	StL-N	49	45	2	7	1	0	1	5	2	17	.156	.208	.244	25	-5	-5	2	0	0	0	0	H	-0.4
Total	12	1381	4318	642	1198	197	58	103	531	485	646	.277	.353	.421	108	51	52	656	67	36	-2	-27	O1/3	-1.3

■ LOU SKIZAS Skizas, Louis Peter "The Nervous Greek" b: 6/2/32, Chicago, Ill. BR/TR, 5'11", 175 lbs. Deb: 4/19/56

1956	NY-A	6	6	0	1	0	0	0	1	0	2	.167	.167	.167	-12	-1	-1	0	0	0	0	0	H	0.0
	KC-A	83	297	39	94	11	3	11	39	15	17	.316	.349	.485	118	6	6	45	3	1	0	2	O	0.5
	Yr	89	303	39	95	11	3	11	40	15	19	.314	.346	.479	116	5	5	45	3	1	0	2		0.5
1957	KC-A	119	376	34	92	14	1	18	44	27	15	.245	.299	.431	95	-3	-4	47	5	2	0	-9	O3	-1.7
1958	Det-A	23	33	4	8	2	0	1	2	5	1	.242	.342	.394	95	0	-0	4	0	0	0	-2	/O3	-0.1
1959	Chi-A	8	13	3	1	0	0	0	0	3	2	.077	.250	.077	-6	-2	-2	0	0	0	0	-0	/O	-0.1
Total	4	239	725	80	196	27	4	30	86	50	37	.270	.319	.443	102	0	-1	97	8	3	1	-9	O/3	-1.4

■ BILL SKOWRON Skowron, William Joseph "Moose" b: 12/18/30, Chicago, Ill. BR/TR, 5'11", 195 lbs. Deb: 4/13/54

1954	NY-A	87	215	37	73	12	9	7	41	19	18	.340	.396	.577	170	18	19	47	2	1	0	-1	1/32	1.6
1955	*NY-A	108	288	46	92	17	3	12	61	21	32	.319	.372	.524	141	14	15	52	1	1	-0	-2	1/3	0.8
1956	*NY-A	134	464	78	143	21	6	23	90	50	60	.308	.383	.528	143	24	26	90	4	4	-1	3	*1/3	2.3
1957	*NY-A	122	457	54	139	15	5	17	88	31	60	.304	.352	.470	125	13	14	70	3	2	-0	6	*1	1.9
1958	*NY-A	126	465	61	127	22	3	14	73	28	69	.273	.320	.424	107	1	3	59	1	1	-0	-2	*1/3	-0.3
1959	NY-A	74	282	39	84	13	5	15	59	20	47	.298	.351	.539	145	14	16	50	1	0	0	0	1	1.6
1960	*NY-A	146	538	63	166	34	3	26	91	38	95	.309	.356	.528	144	25	28	95	2	3	-1	9	*1	2.6
1961	*NY-A	150	561	76	150	23	4	28	89	35	108	.267	.320	.472	115	4	8	78	0	0	0	-0	*1	-0.6
1962	*NY-A	140	478	63	129	16	6	23	80	36	99	.270	.328	.473	116	7	9	71	0	1	-1	-5	*1	-0.5
1963	*LA-N	89	237	19	48	8	0	4	19	13	49	.203	.253	.287	59	-14	-12	15	0	1	-1	-1	1/3	-1.5
1964	Was-A	73	262	28	71	10	0	13	41	11	56	.271	.308	.458	110	2	3	35	0	0	0	-1	1	0.0
	Chi-A	73	273	19	80	11	3	4	38	19	36	.293	.341	.399	108	2	2	36	0	0	0	-1	1	0.0
	Yr	146	535	47	151	21	3	17	79	30	92	.282	.325	.428	109	4	5	71	0	0	0	-2		0.0
1965	Chi-A	146	559	63	153	24	3	18	78	32	77	.274	.319	.424	116	5	9	68	1	3	-2	-3	*1	-0.2
1966	Chi-A	120	337	27	84	15	2	6	29	26	45	.249	.309	.359	98	-4	-1	35	1	1	-0	-1	1	-0.4
1967	Chi-A	8	8	0	0	0	0	0	1	0	1	.000	.000	.000	-99	-2	-2	0	0	0	0	0	H	-0.1
	Cal-A	62	123	8	27	2	1	1	10	4	18	.220	.267	.276	63	-6	-6	8	0	0	0	-0	1	-0.9
	Yr	70	131	8	27	2	1	1	11	4	19	.206	.252	.260	53	-8	-7	7	0	0	0	-0		-1.0
Total	14	1658	5547	681	1566	243	53	211	888	383	870	.282	.335	.459	121	104	131	810	16	18	-6	1	*1/32	6.3

■ BOB SKUBE Skube, Robert Jacob b: 10/8/57, Northridge, Cal. BL/TL, 6', 180 lbs. Deb: 9/17/82

| 1982 | Mil-A | 4 | 3 | 0 | 2 | 0 | 0 | 0 | 0 | 0 | 0 | .667 | .667 | .667 | 285 | 1 | 1 | 1 | 0 | 0 | 0 | 0 | /OD | 0.1 |
| 1983 | Mil-A | 12 | 25 | 2 | 5 | 1 | 1 | 0 | 9 | 4 | 7 | .200 | .310 | .320 | 80 | -1 | -1 | 2 | 0 | 0 | 0 | 0 | /O1D | 0.0 |

YEAR	TM/L	G	AB	R	H	2B	3B	HR	RBI	BB	SO	AVG	OBP	SLG	PRO+	BR	/A	RC	SB	CS	SBR	FR	POS	
Total	2	16	28	2	7	1	1	0	9	4	7	.250	.344	.357	101	-0	0	4	0	0	0	0	/OD1	

■ GORDON SLADE Slade, Gordon Leigh "Oskie" b: 10/9/04, Salt Lake City, Utah d: 1/2/74, Long Beach, Cal. BR/TR, 5'10.5", 160 lbs. Deb: 4/21/30

YEAR	TM/L	G	AB	R	H	2B	3B	HR	RBI	BB	SO	AVG	OBP	SLG	PRO+	BR	/A	RC	SB	CS	SBR	FR	POS	
1930	Bro-N	25	37	8	8	2	0	1	2	3	5	.216	.275	.351	51	-3	-3	4	0			10	S	0.
1931	Bro-N	85	272	27	65	13	2	1	29	23	28	.239	.310	.313	68	-12	-12	28	2			11	S/3	0.6
1932	Bro-N	79	250	23	60	15	1	1	23	11	26	.240	.280	.320	62	-14	-13	23	3			11	S3	0.4
1933	StL-N	39	62	6	7	1	0	0	3	6	7	.113	.191	.129	-7	-9	-9	2	1			3	S/2	-0.4
1934	Cin-N	138	555	61	158	19	8	4	52	25	34	.285	.320	.369	86	-13	-11	66	6			2	S2	-0.2
1935	Cin-N	71	196	22	55	10	0	1	14	16	16	.281	.341	.347	88	-4	-3	24	0			-11	S2/O3	-1.0
Total	6	437	1372	147	353	60	11	8	123	84	116	.257	.307	.335	73	-54	-50	146	12			25	S/23O	0.2

■ ART SLADEN Sladen, Arthur b: 10/28/1860, Dracut, Mass. d: 2/28/14, Dracut, Mass. Deb: 4/17/1884

YEAR	TM/L	G	AB	R	H	2B	3B	HR	RBI	BB	SO	AVG	OBP	SLG	PRO+	BR	/A	RC	SB	CS	SBR	FR	POS	
1884	Bos-U	2	7	0	0	0	0	0		0		.000	.000	.000	-99	-1	-1	0	0			-0	/O	-0.1

■ JIMMY SLAGLE Slagle, James Franklin "Rabbit" or "Shorty" b: 7/11/1873, Worthville, Pa. d: 5/10/56, Chicago, Ill. BL/TR, 5'7", 144 lbs. Deb: 4/17/1899

YEAR	TM/L	G	AB	R	H	2B	3B	HR	RBI	BB	SO	AVG	OBP	SLG	PRO+	BR	/A	RC	SB	CS	SBR	FR	POS	
1899	Was-N	147	599	92	163	15	8	0	41	55		.272	.338	.324	85	-11	-10	75	22			20	*O	0.1
1900	Phi-N	141	574	115	165	16	9	0	45	60		.287	.357	.347	98	-0	-0	85	34			1	*O	-0.9
1901	Phi-N	48	183	20	37	6	2	1	20	16		.202	.277	.273	60	-8	-9	16	5			6	O	-0.7
	Bos-N	66	255	35	69	7	0	0	7	34		.271	.359	.298	86	-0	-3	34	14			-2	O	-1.1
	Yr	114	438	55	106	13	2	1	27	50		.242	.325	.288	76	-9	-12	50	19			4		-1.8
1902	Chi-N	115	454	64	143	11	4	0	28	53		.315	.387	.357	136	19	21	81	40			7	*O	2.1
1903	Chi-N	139	543	104	162	20	6	0	44	81		.298	.389	.357	119	15	17	93	33			2	*O	1.0
1904	Chi-N	120	481	73	125	12	10	1	31	41		.260	.318	.333	103	2	2	62	28			-2	*O	-0.4
1905	Chi-N	155	568	96	153	19	4	0	37	97		.269	.376	.317	105	12	9	82	27			5	*O	0.3
1906	Chi-N	127	498	71	119	8	6	0	33	63		.239	.324	.279	85	-3	-7	56	25			2	*O	-0.7
1907	*Chi-N	136	489	71	126	6	6	0	32	76		.258	.358	.294	100	8	4	64	28			-10	*O	-1.2
1908	Chi-N	104	352	38	78	4	1	0	26	43		.222	.306	.239	73	-7	-9	33	17			-6	*O	-1.7
Total	10	1298	4996	779	1340	124	56	2	344	619		.268	.350	.317	98	25	16	682	273			23	*O	-3.2

■ JACK SLATTERY Slattery, John Terrence b: 1/6/1878, S.Boston, Mass. d: 7/17/49, Boston, Mass. TR , 6'2", 191 lbs. Deb: 9/28/01 MC

YEAR	TM/L	G	AB	R	H	2B	3B	HR	RBI	BB	SO	AVG	OBP	SLG	PRO+	BR	/A	RC	SB	CS	SBR	FR	POS	
1901	Bos-A	1	3	1	1	0	0	0	1	1	1	.333	.500	.333	140	0	0	1	0			0	/C	0.0
1903	Cle-A	4	11	1	0	0	0	0	0	0		.000	.000	.000	-99	-3	-3	0	0			-1	/1	-0.2
	Chi-A	63	211	8	46	3	2	0	20	2		.218	.225	.251	46	-14	-13	13	2			-7	C/1	-1.2
	Yr	67	222	9	46	3	2	0	20	2		.207	.214	.239	39	-17	-16	12	2			-7		-1.4
1906	StL-N	3	7	0	2	0	0	0	0	1		.286	.375	.286	113	0	0	1	0			-1	/C	0.0
1909	Was-A	32	56	4	12	2	0	0	6	2		.214	.254	.250	62	-3	-2	4	1			-1	1/C	-0.2
Total	4	103	288	14	61	5	2	0	27	6		.212	.231	.243	47	-19	-17	18	3			-8	/C1	-1.6

■ MIKE SLATTERY Slattery, Michael J. b: 11/26/1866, Boston, Mass. d: 10/16/04, Boston, Mass. BL/TL, 6'2", 210 lbs. Deb: 4/19/1884

YEAR	TM/L	G	AB	R	H	2B	3B	HR	RBI	BB	SO	AVG	OBP	SLG	PRO+	BR	/A	RC	SB	CS	SBR	FR	POS	
1884	Bos-U	106	413	60	86	6	2	0		4		.208	.216	.232	52	-20	-19	21	0			6	*O1	-1.2
1888	*NY-N	103	391	50	96	12	6	1	35	13	28	.246	.272	.315	89	-5	-5	41	26			-1	*O	-0.6
1889	*NY-N	12	48	7	14	2	0	1	12	4	3	.292	.346	.396	108	0	0	7	2			0	O	0.0
1890	NY-P	97	411	80	126	20	11	5	67	27	25	.307	.352	.445	105	7	-0	73	18			-14	*O	-1.3
1891	Cin-N	41	158	24	33	3	2	1	16	10	10	.209	.256	.272	55	-9	-9	12	1			-0	O	-1.0
	Was-a	15	60	8	17	1	0	0	5	4	5	.283	.358	.300	96	-0	-0	9	6			-2	O	-0.1
Total	5	374	1481	229	372	44	21	8	135	62	71	.251	.284	.325	83	-28	-33	163	53			-11	O/1	-4.2

■ DON SLAUGHT Slaught, Donald Martin b: 9/11/58, Long Beach, Cal. BR/TR, 6'1", 190 lbs. Deb: 7/06/82

YEAR	TM/L	G	AB	R	H	2B	3B	HR	RBI	BB	SO	AVG	OBP	SLG	PRO+	BR	/A	RC	SB	CS	SBR	FR	POS	
1982	KC-A	43	115	14	32	6	0	3	8	9	12	.278	.331	.409	102	0	0	15	0	0	0	2	C	0.5
1983	KC-A	83	276	21	86	13	4	0	28	11	27	.312	.338	.388	99	-1	-1	34	3	1	0	-5	C/D	-0.1
1984	*KC-A	124	409	48	108	27	4	4	42	20	55	.264	.302	.379	86	-8	-8	46	0	0	0	-13	*C/D	-1.3
1985	Tex-A	102	343	34	96	17	4	8	35	20	41	.280	.331	.423	103	2	1	46	5	4	-1	-10	*C	-0.5
1986	Tex-A	95	314	39	83	17	1	13	46	16	59	.264	.310	.449	101	1	-0	42	3	2	-0	-5	C/D	0.0
1987	Tex-A	95	237	25	53	15	2	8	16	24	51	.224	.298	.405	84	-6	-6	27	0	3	-2	2	C/D	0.1
1988	NY-A	97	322	33	91	25	1	9	43	24	54	.283	.338	.450	120	7	8	47	1	0	0	-13	*C/D	0.0
1989	NY-A	117	350	34	88	21	3	5	38	30	57	.251	.319	.371	95	-3	-2	41	1	1	-0	-6	*C/D	-0.3
1990	*Pit-N	84	230	27	69	18	3	4	29	27	27	.300	.381	.457	135	10	11	42	0	1	-1	-4	C	1.0
Total	9	840	2596	275	706	159	22	54	285	181	383	.272	.325	.413	102	3	3	339	13	12	-3	-51	C/D	-0.6

■ ENOS SLAUGHTER Slaughter, Enos Bradsher "Country" b: 4/27/16, Roxboro, N.C. BL/TR, 5'9.5", 180 lbs. Deb: 4/19/38 H

YEAR	TM/L	G	AB	R	H	2B	3B	HR	RBI	BB	SO	AVG	OBP	SLG	PRO+	BR	/A	RC	SB	CS	SBR	FR	POS	
1938	StL-N	112	395	59	109	20	10	8	58	32	38	.276	.330	.438	104	4	1	57	1			0	O	0.0
1939	StL-N	149	604	95	193	52	5	12	86	44	53	.320	.371	.482	120	22	17	108	2			14	*O	2.9
1940	StL-N	140	516	96	158	25	13	17	73	50	35	.306	.370	.504	131	26	23	99	8			-0	*O	1.7
1941	StL-N	113	425	71	132	22	9	13	76	53	28	.311	.390	.496	139	27	24	86	4			-14	*O	0.5
1942	*StL-N	152	591	100	188	31	17	13	98	88	30	.318	.412	.494	153	50	45	128	9			2	*O	4.6
1946	*StL-N	156	609	100	183	30	8	18	130	69	41	.300	.374	.465	131	29	26	110	9			1	*O	2.5
1947	StL-N	147	551	100	162	31	13	10	86	59	27	.294	.366	.452	111	12	9	93	4			4	*O	0.8
1948	StL-N	146	549	91	176	27	11	11	90	81	29	.321	.409	.470	130	31	27	110	4			-11	*O	0.5
1949	StL-N	151	568	92	191	34	13	13	96	79	37	.336	.418	.511	141	40	37	127	3			-2	*O	2.6
1950	StL-N	148	556	82	161	26	7	10	101	66	33	.290	.367	.415	100	5	2	87	3			-6	*O	-0.8
1951	StL-N	123	409	48	115	17	8	4	64	67	25	.281	.386	.391	109	8	8	67	7	2	1	-3	*O	0.3
1952	StL-N	140	510	73	153	17	12	11	101	70	25	.300	.386	.445	130	22	22	93	6	1	1	0	*O	2.0
1953	StL-N	143	492	64	143	34	9	6	89	80	28	.291	.395	.433	116	14	14	90	4	4	-1	-11	*O	-0.2
1954	NY-A	69	125	19	31	4	2	1	19	28	8	.248	.386	.336	102	1	2	18	0	2	-1	-6	O	-0.5
1955	NY-A	10	9	1	1	0	0	0	1	1	1	.111	.200	.111	-15	-1	-1	0	0	0	0	0	H	0.0
	KC-A	108	267	49	86	12	4	5	34	40	17	.322	.414	.453	132	14	13	50	2	3	-1	-5	O	0.3
	Yr	118	276	50	87	12	4	5	35	41	18	.315	.408	.442	127	12	12	50	2	3	-1	-5		0.3
1956	KC-A	91	223	37	62	14	3	2	23	29	20	.278	.364	.395	100	0	0	33	1	0	0	-5	O	-0.6
	*NY-A	24	83	15	24	4	2	0	4	5	6	.289	.330	.386	91	-2	-1	11	1	1	-0	-3	O	-0.5
	Yr	115	306	52	86	18	5	2	27	34	26	.281	.355	.392	97	-1	-1	44	2	1	-0	-8		-1.1
1957	*NY-A	96	209	24	53	7	1	5	34	40	19	.254	.373	.368	105	2	3	30	0	2	-1	-6	O	-0.7
1958	*NY-A	77	138	21	42	4	1	4	19	21	16	.304	.396	.435	133	6	7	25	2	0	1	-4	O	0.1
1959	NY-A	74	99	10	17	2	0	6	21	13	19	.172	.268	.374	77	-4	-3	10	1	0	0	-6	O	-0.6
	Mil-N	11	18	0	3	0	0	1	3	1	3	.167	.286	.167	27	-2	-2	1	0	0	0	-1	/O	-0.1
Total	19	2380	7946	1247	2383	413	148	169	1304	1018	538	.300	.382	.453	122	306	270	1432	71	15		-54	*O	14.8

■ SCOTTIE SLAYBACK Slayback, Elbert b: 10/5/01, Paducah, Ky. d: 11/30/79, Cincinnati, Ohio BR/TR, 5'8", 165 lbs. Deb: 9/26/26

YEAR	TM/L	G	AB	R	H	2B	3B	HR	RBI	BB	SO	AVG	OBP	SLG	PRO+	BR	/A	RC	SB	CS	SBR	FR	POS	
1926	NY-N	2	8	0	0	0	0	0	0	0	0	.000	.000	.000	-99	-2	-2	0	0			-1	/2	-0.3

■ BRUCE SLOAN Sloan, Bruce Adams "Fatso" b: 10/4/14, McAlester, Okla. d: 9/24/73, Oklahoma City, Okla. BL/TL, 5'9", 195 lbs. Deb: 4/29/44

YEAR	TM/L	G	AB	R	H	2B	3B	HR	RBI	BB	SO	AVG	OBP	SLG	PRO+	BR	/A	RC	SB	CS	SBR	FR	POS	
1944	NY-N	59	104	7	28	4	1	1	9	13	8	.269	.350	.356	99	0	0	13	0			-4	O	-0.5

■ TOD SLOAN Sloan, Yale Yeastman b: 12/24/1890, Madisonville, Tenn d: 9/12/56, Akron, Ohio BL/TR, 6', 175 lbs. Deb: 9/22/13

YEAR	TM/L	G	AB	R	H	2B	3B	HR	RBI	BB	SO	AVG	OBP	SLG	PRO+	BR	/A	RC	SB	CS	SBR	FR	POS	
1913	StL-A	7	26	2	7	1	0	0	2	1	9	.269	.321	.308	87	-1	-0	3	1			2	/O	0.1
1917	StL-A	109	313	32	72	6	2	2	25	28	34	.230	.307	.281	83	-7	-6	28	8			-3	O	-1.4

		AB	R	H	2B	3B	HR	RBI	BB	SO	AVG	OBP	SLG	PRO+	BR	/A	RC	SB	CS	SBR	FR	POS	TPR
		63	9	15	1	3	0	6	12	3	.238	.368	.349	99	1	0	8	0			-1	O	-0.1
		43	402	43	94	8	5	2	33	41	46	.234	.319	.294	86	-7	-6	39	9			-1	O	-1.4

□ OCUM   Slocum, Ronald Reece   b: 7/2/45, Modesto, Cal.   BR/TR, 6'2", 185 lbs.   Deb: 9/08/69

		AB	R	H	2B	3B	HR	RBI	BB	SO	AVG	OBP	SLG	PRO+	BR	/A	RC	SB	CS	SBR	FR	POS	TPR
	N	13	24	6	7	1	0	1	5	0	5	.292	.292	.458	112	0	0	3	0	0	0	-1	/23S	0.0
	SD-N	60	71	8	10	2	2	1	11	8	24	.141	.237	.268	37	-7	-6	4	0	1	-1	13	CS3/2	0.9
	SD-N	7	18	1	0	0	0	0	0	0	8	.000	.053	.000	-90	-4	-4	0	0	0	0	1	/3	-0.2
	3	80	113	15	17	3	2	2	16	8	37	.150	.220	.265	33	-11	-10	8	0	1	-1	13	/3CS2	0.7

■ CRAIG SMAJSTRLA   Smajstrla, Craig Lee   b: 6/19/62, Houston, Tex.   BB/TR, 5'9", 165 lbs.   Deb: 9/06/88

1988	Hou-N	8	3	2	0	0	0	0	0	1	.000	.000	.000	-99	-1	-1	0	0	0	0	1	/2	0.1

■ CHARLIE SMALL   Small, Charles Albert   b: 10/24/05, Auburn, Me.   d: 1/14/53, Auburn, Me.   BL/TR, 5'11", 180 lbs.   Deb: 7/07/30

1930	Bos-A	25	18	1	3	1	0	0	2	5	.167	.250	.222	22	-2	-2	1	1	0	0	-0	/O	-0.1

■ HANK SMALL   Small, George Henry   b: 7/31/53, Atlanta, Ga.   BR/TR, 6'3", 205 lbs.   Deb: 9/27/78

1978	Atl-N	1	4	0	0	0	0	0	0	0	0	.000	.000	.000	-90	-1	-1	0	0	0	0	0	/1	0.0

■ JIM SMALL   Small, James Arthur   b: 3/8/37, Portland, Ore.   BL/TL, 6'1.5", 180 lbs.   Deb: 6/22/55

1955	Det-A	12	4	2	0	0	0	0	1	1	.000	.200	.000	-44	-1	-1	0	0	0	0	2	/O	0.1
1956	Det-A	58	91	13	29	4	2	0	10	6	10	.319	.361	.407	102	0	0	14	0	0	0	1	O	0.0
1957	Det-A	36	42	7	9	2	0	0	0	2	11	.214	.250	.262	39	-3	-4	2	0	2	-1	1	O	-0.4
1958	KC-A	2	4	0	0	0	0	0	0	1	0	.000	.200	.000	-39	-1	-1	0	0	0	0	0	/O	0.0
Total	4	108	141	22	38	6	2	0	10	10	22	.270	.318	.340	75	-5	-5	16	0	2	-1	3	/O	-0.3

■ ROY SMALLEY   Smalley, Roy Frederick Jr.   b: 10/25/52, Los Angeles, Cal.   BB/TR, 6'1", 185 lbs.   Deb: 4/30/75

1975	Tex-A	78	250	22	57	8	0	3	33	30	42	.228	.311	.296	73	-9	-8	25	4	0	1	4	S2/C	0.3
1976	Tex-A	41	129	15	29	2	0	1	8	29	27	.225	.367	.264	85	-1	-1	15	2	0	1	-6	2/S	-0.3
	Min-A	103	384	46	104	16	3	2	36	47	79	.271	.353	.344	102	4	2	49	0	4	-2	5	*S	1.1
	Yr	144	513	61	133	18	3	3	44	76	106	.259	.357	.324	98	3	1	64	2	4	-2	-1		0.8
1977	Min-A	150	584	93	135	21	5	6	56	74	89	.231	.319	.315	75	-20	-19	62	5	5	-2	19	*S	1.6
1978	Min-A	158	586	80	160	31	3	19	77	85	70	.273	.366	.433	122	20	19	92	2	8	-4	18	*S	4.6
1979	Min-A	162	621	94	168	28	3	24	95	80	80	.271	.357	.441	110	13	10	101	2	3	-1	33	*S/1	5.8
1980	Min-A	133	486	64	135	24	1	12	63	65	65	.278	.365	.405	103	9	4	72	3	3	-1	21	*S/1D	3.3
1981	Min-A	56	167	24	44	7	1	7	22	31	24	.263	.374	.443	128	9	7	27	0	0	0	-12	SD/1	-0.1
1982	Min-A	4	13	2	2	1	0	0	0	3	4	.154	.313	.231	51	-1	-1	1	0	0	0	1	/S	0.0
	NY-A	142	486	55	125	14	2	20	67	68	100	.257	.348	.418	111	7	8	75	0	1	-1	-18	S3/2D	-0.3
	Yr	146	499	57	127	15	2	20	67	71	104	.255	.347	.413	109	6	7	76	0	1	-1	-17		-0.3
1983	NY-A	130	451	70	124	24	1	18	62	58	68	.275	.360	.452	127	14	16	75	3	3	-1	-16	S31	0.4
1984	NY-A	67	209	17	50	8	1	7	26	15	35	.239	.290	.388	89	-5	-3	23	2	1	0	0	3S/1D	-0.1
	Chi-A	47	135	15	23	4	0	4	13	22	30	.170	.287	.289	57	-7	-8	12	1	1	-0	-5	3/S1D	-1.2
	Yr	114	344	32	73	12	1	11	39	37	65	.212	.289	.349	76	-12	-11	35	3	2	-0	-4		-1.3
1985	Min-A	129	388	57	100	20	0	12	45	60	65	.258	.359	.402	102	6	3	58	0	2	-1	-15	DS3/1	-1.0
1986	Min-A	143	459	59	113	20	4	20	57	68	80	.246	.343	.438	108	7	6	70	1	3	-2	-3	*DS/3	0.2
1987	*Min-A	110	309	32	85	16	1	8	34	36	52	.275	.353	.411	98	1	-0	46	2	0	1	-3	D3/S	-0.1
Total	13	1653	5657	745	1454	244	25	163	694	771	908	.257	.348	.395	103	48	33	801	27	34	-12	25	*SD3/21C	14.2

■ ROY SMALLEY   Smalley, Roy Frederick Sr.   b: 6/9/26, Springfield, Mo.   BR/TR, 6'3", 190 lbs.   Deb: 4/20/48

1948	Chi-N	124	361	25	78	11	4	4	36	23	76	.216	.265	.302	55	-24	-22	27	0			9	*S	0.0
1949	Chi-N	135	477	57	117	21	10	8	35	36	77	.245	.304	.382	85	-13	-11	54	2			14	*S	1.7
1950	Chi-N	154	557	58	128	21	9	21	85	49	114	.230	.297	.413	85	-15	-14	68	2			21	*S	2.2
1951	Chi-N	79	238	24	55	7	4	8	31	25	53	.231	.304	.395	85	-5	-6	29	0	0	0	-13	S	-1.1
1952	Chi-N	87	261	36	58	14	1	5	30	29	58	.222	.305	.341	78	-8	-8	29	0	0	0	-11	S	-1.6
1953	Chi-N	82	253	20	63	9	0	6	25	28	57	.249	.329	.356	77	-8	-8	32	0	0	0	-6	S	-0.7
1954	Mil-N	25	36	5	8	0	0	1	7	4	9	.222	.317	.306	67	-2	-2	3	0	0	0	4	/S21	0.3
1955	Phi-N	92	260	33	51	11	1	7	39	39	58	.196	.306	.327	69	-12	-11	26	0	0	0	-16	S/23	-2.3
1956	Phi-N	65	168	14	38	9	3	0	16	23	29	.226	.323	.315	74	-6	-6	18	0	0	0	-1	S	-0.1
1957	Phi-N	28	31	5	5	0	1	1	1	1	7	.161	.212	.323	42	-3	-3	2	0	0	0	1	S	0.0
1958	Phi-N	1	2	0	0	0	0	0	0	0	1	.000	.000	.000	-99	-1	-1	0	0	0	0	0	/S	0.0
Total	11	872	2644	277	601	103	33	61	305	257	541	.227	.300	.360	77	-95	-91	288	4	0		4	S/213	-1.6

■ WILL SMALLEY   Smalley, William Darwin "Deacon"   b: 6/27/1871, Oakland, Cal.   d: 10/11/1891, Bay City, Mich.   BR/TR,   Deb: 4/19/1890

1890	Cle-N	136	502	62	107	11	1	0	42	60	44	.213	.303	.239	62	-23	-21	40	10			18	*3	0.2
1891	Was-a	11	38	5	6	0	1	0	3	5	2	.158	.256	.211	37	-3	-3	2	0			-2	/32	-0.3
Total	2	147	540	67	113	11	2	0	45	65	46	.209	.300	.237	60	-26	-24	43	10			16	3/2	-0.1

■ JOE SMAZA   Smaza, Joseph Paul   b: 7/7/23, Detroit, Mich.   d: 5/30/79, Royal Oak, Mich.   BL/TL, 5'11", 175 lbs.   Deb: 9/18/46

1946	Chi-A	2	5	2	1	0	0	0	0	0	0	.200	.200	.200	12	-1	-1	0	0	0	0	0	/O	0.0

■ BILL SMILEY   Smiley, William B.   b: 1856, Baltimore, Md.   d: 7/11/1884, Baltimore, Md.   Deb: 10/13/1874

1874	Bal-n	2	7	0	0	0	0	0		0	0	.000	.000	.000	-99	-2	-1	0					/3	0.0
1882	StL-a	59	240	30	51	4	2	0		6		.213	.232	.246	59	-9	-11	14				-7	*2/O	-1.1
	Bal-a	16	61	3	9	0	0	0		0		.148	.148	.148	-0	-6	-6	1				2	2/S	-0.2
	Yr	75	301	33	60	4	2	0		6		.199	.215	.226	48	-16	-16	15				-5		-1.3

■ EDGAR SMITH   Smith, Albert Edgar   b: 10/15/1860, North Haven, Conn.   TR, 6', 200 lbs.   Deb: 7/06/1883

1883	Bos-N	30	115	10	25	5	3	0	16	5	11	.217	.250	.313	68	-4	-4	9				-1	O/C	-0.3

■ ALECK SMITH   Smith, Alexander Benjamin "Broadway Aleck"   b: 1871, New York, N.Y.   d: 7/9/19, New York, N.Y.   TR,   Deb: 4/23/1897

1897	Bro-N	66	237	36	71	13	1	1	39	4		.300	.317	.376	89	-6	-4	33	12			-5	CO/1	-0.3
1898	Bro-N	52	199	25	52	6	5	0	23	3		.261	.276	.342	79	-6	-6	21	7			-10	OC/321	-1.4
1899	Bro-N	17	61	6	11	0	1	0	6	2		.180	.206	.213	16	-7	-7	3	0			-3	C	-0.7
	Bal-N	41	120	17	46	6	4	0	25	4		.383	.417	.500	146	8	8	29	7			-3	C/O1	0.6
	Yr	58	181	23	57	6	5	0	31	6		.315	.347	.403	104	2	0	28	7			-5		-0.1
1900	Bro-N	7	25	2	6	0	0	0	3	1		.240	.269	.240	40	-2	-2	2	2			-1	/3C	-0.2
1901	NY-N	26	78	5	11	0	0	0	6	0		.141	.141	.141	-18	-11	-11	2	2			-0	C	-0.7
1902	Bal-A	41	145	10	34	3	0	0	21	8		.234	.275	.255	47	-10	-11	12	5			-6	C/1023	-1.3
1903	Bos-A	11	33	4	10	1	0	0	4	0		.303	.303	.333	88	-0	-1	3	0			1	C	0.1
1904	Chi-N	10	29	2	6	1	0	0	1	3		.207	.281	.241	64	-1	-1	2	1			-2	/OC3	-0.2
1906	NY-N	16	28	0	5	0	0	0	1	2		.179	.207	.179	21	-2	-3	1	1			-0	/C1O	-0.2
Total	9	287	955	107	252	30	11	1	130	26		.264	.288	.321	71	-37	-37	109	37			-29	C/O132	-4.3

■ AL SMITH   Smith, Alphonse Eugene "Fuzzy"   b: 2/7/28, Kirkwood, Mo.   BR/TR, 6'0.5", 189 lbs.   Deb: 7/10/53

1953	Cle-A	47	150	28	36	9	0	3	14	20	25	.240	.341	.360	92	-2	-1	21	2	0	1	-7	O/3	-0.8
1954	*Cle-A	131	481	101	135	29	6	11	50	88	65	.281	.399	.435	126	22	21	90	2	9	-5	-4	*O3/S	0.8
1955	Cle-A	154	607	123	186	27	4	22	77	93	77	.306	.411	.473	132	35	32	128	11	6	-0	-16	*O3/S2	1.0

YEAR	TM/L	G	AB	R	H	2B	3B	HR	RBI	BB	SO	AVG	OBP	SLG	PRO+	BR	/A	RC	SB	CS	SBR	FR	POS	TM
1956	Cle-A	141	526	87	144	26	5	16	71	84	72	.274	.382	.433	112	13	11	90	6	3	0	-5	*O3/2	0
1957	Cle-A	135	507	78	125	23	5	11	49	79	70	.247	.353	.377	100	1	2	73	12	6	0	-10	3O	-9
1958	Chi-A	139	480	61	121	23	5	12	58	48	77	.252	.326	.396	100	-2	-0	59	3	3	-1	-3	*O/3	-13
1959	*Chi-A	129	472	65	112	16	4	17	55	46	74	.237	.312	.396	94	-5	-5	58	7	5	-1	7	*O/3	-24
1960	Chi-A	142	536	80	169	31	3	12	72	50	65	.315	.377	.451	124	17	18	89	8	3	1	-6	*O	17
1961	Chi-A	147	532	88	148	29	4	28	93	56	67	.278	.352	.506	128	18	20	91	4	4	-1	-10	3O	19
1962	Chi-A	142	511	62	149	23	8	16	82	57	60	.292	.366	.462	122	15	16	83	3	3	-1	-20	*3O	-24
1963	Bal-A	120	368	45	100	17	1	10	39	32	74	.272	.335	.405	109	3	4	49	9	0	3	-6	O	-22
1964	Cle-A	61	136	15	22	1	1	4	9	8	32	.162	.214	.272	34	-12	-12	7	0	1	-1	1	O/3	-14
	Bos-A	29	51	10	11	4	0	2	7	13	10	.216	.385	.412	116	2	2	9	0	0	0	-1	3/O	03
	Yr	90	187	25	33	5	1	6	16	21	42	.176	.267	.310	59	-10	-10	15	0	1	-1	0		-13
Total	12	1517	5357	843	1458	258	46	164	676	674	768	.272	.360	.429	113	106	106	846	67	43	-6	-79	*O3/S2	-16

■ TONY SMITH

Smith, Anthony   b: 5/14/1884, Chicago, Ill.   d: 2/27/64, Galveston, Tex.   BR/TR, 5'9", 150 lbs.   Deb: 8/12/07

YEAR	TM/L	G	AB	R	H	2B	3B	HR	RBI	BB	SO	AVG	OBP	SLG	PRO+	BR	/A	RC	SB	CS	SBR	FR	POS	TM
1907	Was-A	51	139	12	26	1	1	0	8	18		.187	.280	.209	63	-6	-4	11	3			-9	S	-13
1910	Bro-N	106	321	31	58	10	1	1	16	69	53	.181	.329	.227	65	-12	-11	30	9			12	*S/3	06
1911	Bro-N	13	40	3	6	1	0	0	2	8	7	.150	.292	.175	33	-3	-3	2	1			0	S/2	-02
Total	3	170	500	46	90	12	2	1	26	95	60	.180	.313	.218	62	-21	-18	43	13			4	S/32	-09

■ KLONDIKE SMITH

Smith, Armstrong Frederick   b: 1/4/1887, London, England   d: 11/15/59, Springfield, Mass.   BL/TL, 5'9", 160 lbs.   Deb: 9/28/12

YEAR	TM/L	G	AB	R	H	2B	3B	HR	RBI	BB	SO	AVG	OBP	SLG	PRO+	BR	/A	RC	SB	CS	SBR	FR	POS	TM
1912	NY-A	7	27	0	5	1	0	0	0	0		.185	.185	.222	15	-3	-3	1	1			-1	/O	-04

■ BILLY SMITH

Smith, Billy Edward   b: 7/14/53, Jonesboro, La.   BB/TR, 6'2.5", 185 lbs.   Deb: 4/13/75

YEAR	TM/L	G	AB	R	H	2B	3B	HR	RBI	BB	SO	AVG	OBP	SLG	PRO+	BR	/A	RC	SB	CS	SBR	FR	POS	TM
1975	Cal-A	59	143	10	29	5	1	0	14	12	27	.203	.265	.252	50	-10	-9	10	1	3	-2	-9	S/13D	-1.4
1976	Cal-A	13	8	0	3	0	0	0	0	0	2	.375	.375	.375	128	0	0	1	0	0	0	-1	S/D	0.0
1977	Bal-A	109	367	44	79	12	2	5	29	33	71	.215	.282	.300	62	-21	-18	33	3	2	-0	4	*2/S13	-0.4
1978	Bal-A	85	250	29	65	12	2	5	30	27	40	.260	.335	.384	108	1	3	34	3	0	1	-1	2/S	0.7
1979	*Bal-A	68	189	18	47	9	4	6	33	15	33	.249	.311	.434	102	-1	0	27	1	0	0	-8	2/S	-0.3
1981	SF-N	36	61	6	11	0	0	1	5	9	16	.180	.286	.230	48	-4	-4	5	0	0	0	-0	S/23	-0.1
Total	6	370	1018	107	234	38	9	17	111	96	189	.230	.299	.335	79	-35	-28	110	8	5	-1	-14	2/S13D	-1.5

■ BOBBY GENE SMITH

Smith, Bobby Gene   b: 5/28/34, Hood River, Ore.   BR/TR, 5'11", 180 lbs.   Deb: 4/16/57

YEAR	TM/L	G	AB	R	H	2B	3B	HR	RBI	BB	SO	AVG	OBP	SLG	PRO+	BR	/A	RC	SB	CS	SBR	FR	POS	TM
1957	StL-N	93	185	24	39	7	1	3	18	13	35	.211	.263	.308	52	-12	-13	14	1	1	-0	11	O	-0.4
1958	StL-N	28	88	8	25	3	0	2	5	2	18	.284	.308	.386	79	-2	-3	11	1	0	0	2	O	0.0
1959	StL-N	43	60	11	13	1	1	1	7	1	9	.217	.230	.317	41	-5	-5	4	0	0	0	3	O	-0.2
1960	Phi-N	98	217	24	62	5	2	4	27	10	28	.286	.317	.382	90	-3	-3	24	2	3	-1	5	O/3	-0.1
1961	Phi-N	79	174	16	44	7	0	2	18	15	32	.253	.316	.328	72	-7	-7	17	0	1	-1	7	O	-0.2
1962	NY-N	8	22	1	3	0	1	0	2	3	2	.136	.240	.227	26	-2	-2	1	0	1	-1	0	/O	-0.2
	Chi-N	13	29	3	5	0	0	1	2	2	6	.172	.226	.276	33	-3	-3	2	0	1	-1	-0	/O	-0.3
	StL-N	91	130	13	30	9	0	0	12	7	14	.231	.270	.300	48	-9	-10	9	1	1	-0	3	O	-1.1
	Yr	112	181	17	38	9	1	1	16	12	22	.210	.259	.287	43	-14	-16	12	1	3	-2	3		-1.6
1965	Cal-A	23	57	1	13	3	0	0	5	2	10	.228	.267	.281	57	-3	-3	4	0	1	-1	-0	O	-0.4
Total	7	476	962	101	234	35	5	13	96	55	154	.243	.286	.331	64	-47	-50	86	5	9	-4	30	O/3	-2.9

■ BRICK SMITH

Smith, Brick Dudley   b: 5/2/59, Charlotte, N.C.   BR/TR, 6'4", 225 lbs.   Deb: 9/13/87

YEAR	TM/L	G	AB	R	H	2B	3B	HR	RBI	BB	SO	AVG	OBP	SLG	PRO+	BR	/A	RC	SB	CS	SBR	FR	POS	TM
1987	Sea-A	5	8	1	1	0	0	0	0	2	4	.125	.300	.125	18	-1	-1	0	0	0	0	0	/1D	0.0
1988	Sea-A	4	10	1	1	0	0	0	1	0	1	.100	.100	.100	-42	-2	-2	0	0	0	0	1	/1	0.0
Total	2	9	18	2	2	0	0	0	1	2	5	.111	.200	.111	-12	-3	-3	1	0	0	0	1	/1D	0.0

■ BERNIE SMITH

Smith, Calvin Bernard   b: 9/4/41, Ponchatoula, La.   BR/TR, 5'9", 164 lbs.   Deb: 7/31/70

YEAR	TM/L	G	AB	R	H	2B	3B	HR	RBI	BB	SO	AVG	OBP	SLG	PRO+	BR	/A	RC	SB	CS	SBR	FR	POS	TM
1970	Mil-A	44	76	8	21	3	1	1	6	11	12	.276	.382	.382	110	2	2	11	1	3	-2	0	O	-0.1
1971	Mil-A	15	36	1	5	1	0	1	3	0	5	.139	.162	.250	15	-4	-4	1	0	0	0	-1	O	-0.5
Total	2	59	112	9	26	4	1	2	9	11	17	.232	.317	.339	83	-2	-2	12	1	3	-2	-1	/O	-0.6

■ REGGIE SMITH

Smith, Carl Reginald   b: 4/2/45, Shreveport, La.   BB/TR, 6', 180 lbs.   Deb: 9/18/66

YEAR	TM/L	G	AB	R	H	2B	3B	HR	RBI	BB	SO	AVG	OBP	SLG	PRO+	BR	/A	RC	SB	CS	SBR	FR	POS	TM
1966	Bos-A	6	26	1	4	1	0	0	0	0	5	.154	.154	.192	-1	-3	-4	1	0	0	0	0	/O	-0.3
1967	*Bos-A	158	565	78	139	24	6	15	61	57	95	.246	.316	.389	99	5	-0	71	16	6	1	11	*O/2	0.9
1968	Bos-A	155	558	78	148	37	5	15	69	64	77	.265	.345	.430	125	23	19	80	22	18	-4	5	*O	1.5
1969	Bos-A	143	543	87	168	29	7	25	93	54	67	.309	.373	.527	142	34	30	99	7	13	-6	-1	*O	2.1
1970	Bos-A	147	580	109	176	32	7	22	74	51	60	.303	.364	.497	126	26	21	102	10	7	-1	13	*O	2.7
1971	Bos-A	159	618	85	175	33	2	30	96	63	82	.283	.354	.489	128	28	23	106	11	3	2	18	*O	4.0
1972	Bos-A	131	467	75	126	25	4	21	74	68	63	.270	.367	.475	142	29	26	85	15	4	2	3	*O	3.2
1973	Bos-A	115	423	79	128	23	2	21	69	68	49	.303	.400	.515	148	33	29	88	3	2	-0	16	*O/1D	4.2
1974	StL-N	143	517	79	160	26	9	23	100	71	70	.309	.394	.528	158	38	39	105	4	3	-1	3	*O/1	3.7
1975	StL-N	135	477	67	144	26	3	19	76	63	59	.302	.387	.488	137	27	25	87	9	7	-2	-7	O1/3	1.1
1976	StL-N	47	170	20	37	7	1	8	23	14	28	.218	.281	.412	94	-2	-2	18	1	2	-1	6	1O3	0.2
	LA-N	65	225	35	63	8	4	10	26	18	42	.280	.336	.484	133	8	8	36	2	0	1	2	O/3	1.0
	Yr	112	395	55	100	15	5	18	49	32	70	.253	.312	.453	116	6	6	54	3	2	-0	9		1.2
1977	*LA-N	148	488	104	150	27	4	32	87	104	76	.307	.432	.576	168	50	51	129	7	5	-1	-7	*O	3.7
1978	*LA-N	128	447	82	132	27	2	29	93	70	90	.295	.392	.559	164	38	38	102	12	5	1	-7	*O	2.8
1979	LA-N	68	234	41	64	13	1	10	32	31	50	.274	.363	.466	126	8	9	39	6	5	-1	4	O	1.0
1980	LA-N	92	311	47	100	13	0	15	55	41	63	.322	.402	.508	155	22	23	64	5	6	-2	6	O	2.5
1981	*LA-N	41	35	5	7	1	0	1	8	7	8	.200	.333	.314	88	-1	-0	3	0	0	0	0	/1	0.0
1982	SF-N	106	349	51	99	11	0	18	56	46	46	.284	.367	.470	133	15	15	61	7	0	2	2	1	1.5
Total	17	1987	7033	1123	2020	363	57	314	1092	890	1030	.287	.370	.489	136	379	351	1277	137	86	-11	68	*O1/3D2	35.8

■ CHARLIE SMITH

Smith, Charles J.   b: 12/11/1840, Brooklyn, N.Y.   d: 11/15/1897, Great Neck, N.Y.   5'10.5", 150 lbs.   Deb: 5/18/1871

YEAR	TM/L	G	AB	R	H	2B	3B	HR	RBI	BB	SO	AVG	OBP	SLG	PRO+	BR	/A	RC	SB	CS	SBR	FR	POS	TM
1871	Mut-n	14	72	15	19	2	1	0	5	1	1	.264	.274	.319	77	-3	-1	8	6				3/2	-0.1

■ POP SMITH

Smith, Charles Marvin   b: 10/12/1856, Digby, N.S., Canada   d: 4/18/27, Boston, Mass.   BR/TR, 5'11", 170 lbs.   Deb: 5/01/1880

YEAR	TM/L	G	AB	R	H	2B	3B	HR	RBI	BB	SO	AVG	OBP	SLG	PRO+	BR	/A	RC	SB	CS	SBR	FR	POS	TM
1880	Cin-N	83	334	35	69	10	9	0	27	6	36	.207	.221	.290	72	-10	-9	22				-10	*2	-1.5
1881	Cle-N	10	34	1	4	0	0	0	3	0	8	.118	.118	.118	-27	-5	-4	0				-2	3	-0.3
	Wor-N	11	41	1	3	0	0	0	2	3	5	.073	.136	.073	-31	-6	-6	0				2	/O2	-0.3
	Buf-N	3	11	3	0	0	0	0	1	3	5	.000	.214	.000	-27	-1	-1	0				-1	/2	-0.1
	Yr	24	86	5	7	0	0	0	6	6	18	.081	.141	.081	-28	-12	-12	1				-1		-0.8
1882	Bal-a	1	3	0	0	0	0	0		0		.000	.000	.000	-99	-1	-1	0				-0	/O	0.0
	Lou-a	3	11	1	2	0	0	0		0		.182	.182	.182	24	-1	-1	0				0	/S	0.0
	Yr	4	14	1	2	0	0	0		0		.143	.143	.143	-4	-1	-1	0				-0		0.0
1883	Col-a	97	405	82	106	18	17	6		22		.262	.300	.410	137	12	17	51				18	*23/P	3.2
1884	Col-a	108	445	78	106	18	10	6		20		.238	.289	.364	124	7	13	48				29	*2	4.0
1885	Pit-a	106	453	85	113	11	13	0		25		.249	.293	.331	101	-0	1	45				33	*2	3.4
1886	Pit-a	126	483	75	105	20	9	2		26		.217	.288	.308	89	-6	-6	55	38			21	*S2/C	1.8
1887	Pit-N	122	456	69	98	12	7	2	54	30	48	.215	.283	.285	63	-24	-19	46	30			-4	*2S	-1.6
1888	Pit-N	131	481	61	99	15	2	4	52	22	78	.206	.248	.270	72	-17	-12	42	37			-1	S2	-0.8
1889	Pit-N	72	258	26	54	10	2	5	27	24	38	.209	.292	.322	80	-10	-5	28	12			6	S/23O	0.3

YEAR	TM/L	G	AB	R	H	2B	3B	HR	RBI	BB	SO	AVG	OBP	SLG	PRO+	BR	/A	RC	SB	CS	SBR	FR	POS	TPR
	Bos-N	59	208	21	54	13	4	0	32	23	30	.260	.345	.361	93	0	-2	30	11			-0	S	0.0
	Yr	131	466	47	108	23	6	5	59	47	68	.232	.315	.339	87	-10	-7	59	23			6		0.3
1890	Bos-N	134	463	82	106	16	12	1	53	80	81	.229	.353	.322	92	3	-3	68	39			-21	*2/S	-1.7
1891	Was-a	27	90	13	16	2	2	0	13	13	16	.178	.295	.244	60	-5	-4	7	2			7	2/S3	0.4
Total	12	1093	4176	633	935	141	87	24	264	313	345	.224	.288	.317	89	-63	-44	445	169			77	2S/3OPC	6.7

■ CHARLEY SMITH
Smith, Charles William b: 9/15/37, Charleston, S.C. BR/TR, 6'1", 170 lbs. Deb: 9/08/60

YEAR	TM/L	G	AB	R	H	2B	3B	HR	RBI	BB	SO	AVG	OBP	SLG	PRO+	BR	/A	RC	SB	CS	SBR	FR	POS	TPR
1960	LA-N	19	60	2	10	1	1	0	5	1	15	.167		.217	8	-8	-8	3	0	0	0	0	3	-0.8
1961	LA-N	9	24	4	6	1	0	2	3	1	6	.250	.280	.542	103	0	-0	4	0	0	0	-0	/3S	0.0
	Phi-N	112	411	43	102	13	4	9	47	23	76	.248	.296	.365	75	-16	-15	43	3	4	-2	-2	3S	-2.1
	Yr	121	435	47	108	14	4	11	50	24	82	.248	.295	.375	77	-15	-15	47	3	4	-2	-3		-2.1
1962	Chi-A	65	145	11	30	4	0	2	17	9	32	.207	.258	.276	44	-12	-11	9	0	1	-1	2	3	-0.9
1963	Chi-A	4	7	0	2	0	1	0	1	0	2	.286	.286	.571	136	0	0	1	0	0	0	2	/S	0.2
1964	Chi-A	2	7	1	1	0	0	0	0	1	1	.143	.250	.429	87	-0	-0	0	0	0	0	3	/3	0.3
	NY-N	127	443	44	106	12	0	20	58	19	101	.239	.275	.402	90	-8	-7	47	2	2	-1	-11	3SO	-2.2
1965	NY-N	135	499	49	122	20	3	16	62	17	123	.244	.275	.393	89	-11	-9	50	2	1	0	10	*3/S2	-0.2
1966	StL-N	116	391	34	104	13	4	10	43	22	81	.266	.305	.396	93	-4	-4	45	0	2	-1	-1	*3/S	-0.7
1967	NY-A	135	425	38	95	15	3	9	38	32	110	.224	.279	.336	84	-10	-9	37	0	2	-1	11	*3	0.3
1968	NY-A	46	70	2	16	4	1	1	7	5	18	.229	.280	.357	95	-1	-1	7	0	0	0	4	3	0.4
1969	Chi-N	2	2	0	0	0	0	0	0	0	0	.000	.000	.000	-89	-1	-1	0	0	0	0	0	H	0.0
Total	10	771	2484	228	594	83	18	69	281	130	565	.239	.281	.370	82	-70	-65	246	7	12	-5	17	3/SO2	-5.7

■ CHRIS SMITH
Smith, Christopher William b: 7/18/57, Torrance, Cal. BB/TR, 6', 185 lbs. Deb: 5/14/81

YEAR	TM/L	G	AB	R	H	2B	3B	HR	RBI	BB	SO	AVG	OBP	SLG	PRO+	BR	/A	RC	SB	CS	SBR	FR	POS	TPR
1981	Mon-N	7	7	0	0	0	0	0	0	0	2	.000	.000	.000	-99	-2	-2	0	0	0	0	0	/2	-0.1
1982	Mon-N	2	2	0	0	0	0	0	0	0	1	.000	.000	.000	-98	-1	-1	0	0	0	0	0	/H	0.0
1983	SF-N	22	67	13	22	6	1	1	11	7	12	.328	.408	.493	153	5	5	14	0	0	0	-2	1/O3	0.2
Total	3	31	76	13	22	6	1	1	11	7	15	.289	.365	.434	124	2	2	14	0	0	0	-2	/1O32	0.1

■ EARL SMITH
Smith, Earl Calvin b: 3/14/28, Sunnyside, Wash. BR/TR, 6', 185 lbs. Deb: 4/14/55

YEAR	TM/L	G	AB	R	H	2B	3B	HR	RBI	BB	SO	AVG	OBP	SLG	PRO+	BR	/A	RC	SB	CS	SBR	FR	POS	TPR
1955	Pit-N	5	16	1	1	0	0	0	0	4	2	.063	.286	.063	-1	-2	-2	1	0	0	0	-0	/O	-0.2

■ EARL SMITH
Smith, Earl Leonard "Sheriff" b: 1/20/1891, Oak Hill, Ohio d: 3/14/43, Portsmouth, Ohio BB/TR, 5'11", 170 lbs. Deb: 9/12/16

YEAR	TM/L	G	AB	R	H	2B	3B	HR	RBI	BB	SO	AVG	OBP	SLG	PRO+	BR	/A	RC	SB	CS	SBR	FR	POS	TPR
1916	Chi-N	14	27	2	7	1	1	0	4	2	5	.259	.310	.370	98	-0	-0	4	1			-2	/O	-0.2
1917	StL-A	52	199	31	56	7	7	0	10	15	21	.281	.332	.387	124	4	5	27	5			6	O	0.8
1918	StL-A	89	286	28	77	10	5	0	32	13	16	.269	.303	.339	97	-3	-2	33	13			1	O	-0.5
1919	StL-A	88	252	21	63	12	5	1	36	18	27	.250	.300	.349	80	-7	-7	27	1			10	O	-0.1
1920	StL-A	103	353	45	108	21	8	3	55	13	18	.306	.336	.436	100	0	-1	51	11	4	1	-5	3O	-0.1
1921	StL-A	25	78	7	26	4	2	2	14	3	4	.333	.366	.513	115	2	2	14	0	0	0	-3	3/O	0.0
	Was-A	59	180	20	39	5	2	2	12	10	19	.217	.266	.300	46	-16	-14	15	1	0	0	4	O/3	-1.2
	Yr	84	258	27	65	9	4	4	26	13	23	.252	.296	.364	69	-13	-13	28	1	0	0	1		-1.2
1922	Was-A	65	205	22	53	12	2	1	23	8	17	.259	.293	.351	71	-10	-9	20	4	4	-1	1	O/3	-1.1
Total	7	495	1580	176	429	72	32	9	186	82	127	.272	.311	.375	90	-30	-29	191	36	8		12	O/3	-2.4

■ EARL SMITH
Smith, Earl Sutton "Oil" b: 2/14/1897, Hot Springs, Ark. d: 6/8/63, Little Rock, Ark. BL/TR, 5'10.5", 180 lbs. Deb: 4/24/19

YEAR	TM/L	G	AB	R	H	2B	3B	HR	RBI	BB	SO	AVG	OBP	SLG	PRO+	BR	/A	RC	SB	CS	SBR	FR	POS	TPR
1919	NY-N	21	36	5	9	1	1	0	8	3	3	.250	.308	.361	102	-0	0	4	1			-3	C/2	-0.1
1920	NY-N	91	262	20	77	7	1	1	30	18	16	.294	.344	.340	98	-1	-0	31	5	2	0	-5	C	0.1
1921	*NY-N	89	229	35	77	8	4	10	51	27	8	.336	.409	.537	148	16	16	50	4	3	-1	-10	C	1.0
1922	*NY-N	90	234	29	65	11	4	9	39	37	12	.278	.383	.474	119	7	7	44	1	1	-0	-1	C	0.6
1923	NY-N	24	34	2	7	1	1	1	4	4	1	.206	.289	.382	77	-1	-1	4	0	0	0	2	C	0.1
	Bos-N	72	191	22	55	15	1	3	19	22	10	.288	.364	.424	112	2	3	30	0	1	-1	-3	C	0.3
	Yr	96	225	24	62	16	2	4	23	26	11	.276	.353	.418	106	1	2	34	0	1	-1	-1		0.4
1924	Bos-N	33	59	1	16	3	0	0	8	6	3	.271	.338	.322	81	-2	-1	6	0	1	-1	-1	C	-0.1
	Pit-N	39	111	12	41	10	1	4	21	13	4	.369	.435	.586	169	11	11	29	2	0	1	1	C	1.2
	Yr	72	170	13	57	13	1	4	29	19	7	.335	.402	.494	140	10	10	34	2	1	0	0		1.1
1925	*Pit-N	109	329	34	103	22	3	8	64	31	13	.313	.374	.471	107	7	4	59	4	1	1	12	C	1.9
1926	Pit-N	105	292	29	101	17	2	2	46	28	7	.346	.407	.438	121	12	10	52	1			4	C	1.7
1927	*Pit-N	66	189	16	51	3	1	5	25	21	11	.270	.346	.376	87	-2	-3	25	0			-4	C	-0.2
1928	Pit-N	32	85	8	21	6	0	2	11	11	7	.247	.333	.388	85	-2	-2	11	0			-4	C	-0.3
	*StL-N	24	58	3	13	2	0	0	7	5	4	.224	.286	.259	42	-5	-5	4	0			-1	C	-0.3
	Yr	56	143	11	34	8	0	2	18	16	11	.238	.314	.336	66	-6	-7	15	0			-4		-0.6
1929	StL-N	57	145	9	50	8	0	1	22	18	6	.345	.417	.421	107	3	3	26	0			-5	C	0.2
1930	StL-N	8	10	0	0	0	0	0	0	3	1	.000	.231	.000	-36	-2	-2	0	0			1	/C	0.0
Total	12	860	2264	225	686	115	19	46	355	247	106	.303	.374	.432	111	45	38	377	18	9		-14	C/2	6.1

■ EDGAR SMITH
Smith, Edgar Eugene b: 6/12/1862, Providence, R.I. d: 11/3/1892, Providence, R.I. BR/TR, 5'10", 160 lbs. Deb: 5/25/1883

YEAR	TM/L	G	AB	R	H	2B	3B	HR	RBI	BB	SO	AVG	OBP	SLG	PRO+	BR	/A	RC	SB	CS	SBR	FR	POS	TPR
1883	Pro-N	2	9	2	2	1	0	0	1	0	2	.222	.222	.333	64	-0	-0	1				-0	/1O	0.0
	Phi-N	1	4	1	3	0	0	0	1	0	0	.750	.750	.750	393	1	1	2				-1	/PO	0.0
	Yr	3	13	3	5	1	0	0	2	0	2	.385	.385	.462	158	1	1	2				-1		0.0
1884	Was-a	14	57	5	5	0	1	0		1		.088	.103	.123	-29	-7	-6	1				5	O/P	0.0
1885	Pro-N	1	4	0	1	0	0	0		0		.250	.250	.250	64	-0	-0	0				0	P	0.0
1890	Cle-N	8	24	2	7	0	1	0	4	4	1	.292	.393	.375	129	1	1	4	0			2	/PO	0.0
Total	4	26	98	10	18	1	2	0	6	5	3	.184	.223	.235	49	-6	-5	8	0			5	/OP1	0.0

■ MAYO SMITH
Smith, Edward Mayo b: 1/17/15, New London, Mo. d: 11/24/77, Boynton Beach, Fla BL/TR, 6', 183 lbs. Deb: 6/24/45 M

YEAR	TM/L	G	AB	R	H	2B	3B	HR	RBI	BB	SO	AVG	OBP	SLG	PRO+	BR	/A	RC	SB	CS	SBR	FR	POS	TPR
1945	Phi-A	73	203	18	43	5	0	0	11	36	13	.212	.333	.236	67	-7	-7	19	0	1	-1	-6	O	-1.6

■ ELMER SMITH
Smith, Elmer Ellsworth b: 3/23/1868, Pittsburgh, Pa. d: 11/3/45, Pittsburgh, Pa. BL/TL, 5'11", 178 lbs. Deb: 5/31/1886

YEAR	TM/L	G	AB	R	H	2B	3B	HR	RBI	BB	SO	AVG	OBP	SLG	PRO+	BR	/A	RC	SB	CS	SBR	FR	POS	TPR
1886	Cin-a	10	32	7	9	1	1	0		9		.281	.439	.375	154	3	3	5	0			-3	P/O	0.0
1887	Cin-a	52	186	26	47	10	6	0		11		.253	.298	.375	86	-3	-4	23	5			-7	P/O	0.0
1888	Cin-a	40	129	15	29	4	1	0	9	20		.225	.329	.271	92	0	0	12	2			-6	P/O	0.0
1889	Cin-a	29	83	12	23	3	1	2	17	7	18	.277	.348	.410	114	2	1	12	1			-4	P	0.0
1892	Pit-N	138	511	86	140	16	14	4	63	82	43	.274	.375	.384	131	22	22	84	22			-5	*OP	1.4
1893	Pit-N	128	518	121	179	26	23	7	103	78	27	.346	.435	.525	160	43	45	133	26			3	*O	3.4
1894	Pit-N	125	489	128	174	33	19	6	72	65	12	.356	.436	.538	137	29	30	132	33			4	*O/P	2.0
1895	Pit-N	124	480	88	145	14	12	1	81	55	25	.302	.381	.387	106	2	7	86	34			-3	*O	-0.5
1896	Pit-N	123	467	121	175	20	14	7	94	74	18	.362	.454	.504	161	42	45	129	33			9	*O	3.8
1897	Pit-N	123	467	99	145	19	17	6	54	70		.310	.408	.463	137	24	27	101	25			3	*O	1.7
1898	Cin-N	123	486	79	166	21	10	0	66	69		.342	.424	.432	139	33	28	100	20			4	*O/P	2.3
1899	Cin-N	87	339	65	101	13	6	1	24	47		.298	.385	.381	111	8	7	55	10			-1	O	0.0
1900	Cin-N	29	111	14	31	4	4	1	18	18		.279	.385	.414	126	4	5	20	5			0	O	0.2
	NY-N	85	312	47	81	9	7	2	34	24		.260	.313	.353	90	-6	-4	40	14			-8	O	-1.7
	Yr	114	423	61	112	13	11	3	52	42		.265	.333	.369	100	-2	0	60	19			-8		-1.5
1901	Pit-N	4	4	0	0	0	0	0	0		2	.000	.333	.000	3	-0	0	0	0			-0	/O	0.0
	Bos-N	16	57	5	10	2	1	0	3		6	.175	.254	.246	43	-4	-4	4	2			-3	O	-0.8
	Yr	20	61	5	10	2	1	0	3		8	.164	.261	.230	41	-4	-5	4	2			-3		-0.8

YEAR	TM/L	G	AB	R	H	2B	3B	HR	RBI	BB	SO	AVG	OBP	SLG	PRO+	BR	/A	RC	SB	CS	SBR	FR	POS	TPR
Total	14	1235	4688	913	1455	195	136	38	638	636	139	.310	.397	.434	129	199	206	937	232			-18	*OP	11.8

■ ELMER SMITH   Smith, Elmer John   b: 9/21/1892, Sandusky, Ohio   d: 8/3/84, Columbia, Ky.   BL/TR, 5'10", 165 lbs.   Deb: 9/20/14

YEAR	TM/L	G	AB	R	H	2B	3B	HR	RBI	BB	SO	AVG	OBP	SLG	PRO+	BR	/A	RC	SB	CS	SBR	FR	POS	TPR
1914	Cle-A	13	53	5	17	3	0	0	8	2	11	.321	.345	.377	113	1	1	7	1	1	-0	1	O	0.1
1915	Cle-A	144	476	37	118	23	12	3	67	36	75	.248	.301	.366	97	-3	-4	53	10	11	-4	0	*O	-1.4
1916	Cle-A	79	213	25	59	15	3	3	40	18	35	.277	.336	.418	119	6	4	32	3			-2	O	0.0
	Was-A	45	168	12	36	10	3	2	27	18	28	.214	.298	.345	95	-2	-1	19	4			1	O	-0.2
	Yr	124	381	37	95	25	6	5	67	36	63	.249	.319	.386	108	4	3	51	7			-1		-0.2
1917	Was-A	35	117	8	26	4	3	0	17	5	14	.222	.260	.308	74	-4	-4	10	1			-0	O	-0.6
	Cle-A	64	161	21	42	5	1	3	22	13	18	.261	.316	.360	99	1	-1	20	6			-1	O	-0.4
	Yr	99	278	29	68	9	4	3	39	18	32	.245	.293	.338	89	-4	-5	29	7			-1		-1.0
1919	Cle-A	114	395	60	110	24	6	9	54	41	30	.278	.354	.438	115	11	8	64	15			-6	*O	-0.6
1920	*Cle-A	129	456	82	144	37	10	12	103	53	35	.316	.391	.520	135	25	23	93	5	4	-1	-8	*O	0.3
1921	Cle-A	129	431	98	125	28	9	16	85	56	46	.290	.374	.508	121	14	13	83	0	2	-1	-8	*O	-0.5
1922	Bos-A	73	231	43	66	13	6	6	32	25	21	.286	.358	.472	116	4	5	39	2	0	3	-2	O	0.1
	*NY-A	21	27	1	5	0	0	1	5	3	5	.185	.267	.296	46	-2	-2	2	0	0	0	-2	O	-0.4
	Yr	94	258	44	71	13	6	7	37	28	26	.275	.348	.453	108	2	2	41	0	3	-2	-1		-0.3
1923	NY-A	70	183	30	56	6	2	7	35	21	21	.306	.377	.475	121	6	5	34	3	1	0	-2	O	0.0
1925	Cin-N	96	284	47	77	13	7	8	46	28	20	.271	.339	.451	102	-1	0	43	6	5	-1	-8	O	-1.0
Total	10	1012	3195	469	881	181	62	70	541	319	359	.276	.344	.437	112	55	46	499	54	27		-31	O	-4.6

■ MIKE SMITH   Smith, Elwood Hope   b: 11/16/04, Norfolk, Va.   d: 5/31/81, Chesapeake, Va.   BL/TR, 5'11.5", 170 lbs.   Deb: 9/04/26

YEAR	TM/L	G	AB	R	H	2B	3B	HR	RBI	BB	SO	AVG	OBP	SLG	PRO+	BR	/A	RC	SB	CS	SBR	FR	POS	TPR
1926	NY-N	4	7	0	1	0	0	0	0	0	2	.143	.143	.143	-23	-1	-1	0	0			0	/OP	0.0

■ CARR SMITH   Smith, Emamuel Carr   b: 4/8/01, Kernersville, N.C.   d: 4/14/89, Miami, Fla.   BR/TR, 6'1", 175 lbs.   Deb: 9/23/23

YEAR	TM/L	G	AB	R	H	2B	3B	HR	RBI	BB	SO	AVG	OBP	SLG	PRO+	BR	/A	RC	SB	CS	SBR	FR	POS	TPR
1923	Was-A	5	9	0	1	1	0	0	1	0	0	.111	.111	.222	-14	-2	-1	0	0	0	0	-1	/O	-0.2
1924	Was-A	5	10	1	2	0	0	0	0	0	3	.200	.200	.200	3	-1	-1	0	0	0	0	-1	/O	-0.2
Total	2	10	19	1	3	1	0	0	1	0	3	.158	.158	.211	-5	-3	-3	1	0	0	0	-2	/O	-0.4

■ ERNIE SMITH   Smith, Ernest Henry "Kansas City Kid"   b: 10/11/1899, Totowa, N.J.   d: 4/6/73, Brooklyn, N.Y.   BR/TR, 5'8", 155 lbs.   Deb: 4/17/30

YEAR	TM/L	G	AB	R	H	2B	3B	HR	RBI	BB	SO	AVG	OBP	SLG	PRO+	BR	/A	RC	SB	CS	SBR	FR	POS	TPR
1930	Chi-A	24	79	5	19	3	0	0	3	5	6	.241	.286	.278	45	-7	-6	7	2	0	1	0	S	-0.2

■ FRANK SMITH   Smith, Frank L.   b: 11/24/1857, Canada   d: 10/11/28, Canandaigua, N.Y.   Deb: 8/06/1884

YEAR	TM/L	G	AB	R	H	2B	3B	HR	RBI	BB	SO	AVG	OBP	SLG	PRO+	BR	/A	RC	SB	CS	SBR	FR	POS	TPR
1884	Pit-a	10	36	3	9	0	1	0			0	.250	.250	.306	81	-1	-1	3				-1	/CO	-0.1

■ FRED SMITH   Smith, Fred Vincent   b: 7/29/1886, Cleveland, Ohio   d: 5/28/61, Cleveland, Ohio   BR/TR, 5'11.5", 185 lbs.   Deb: 4/17/13

YEAR	TM/L	G	AB	R	H	2B	3B	HR	RBI	BB	SO	AVG	OBP	SLG	PRO+	BR	/A	RC	SB	CS	SBR	FR	POS	TPR
1913	Bos-N	92	285	35	65	9	3	0	27	29	55	.228	.302	.281	65	-12	-13	26	7			-14	32S/O	-2.8
1914	Buf-F	145	473	48	104	12	10	2	45	49	78	.220	.297	.300	70	-17	-18	52	24			0	*3S/1	-1.5
1915	Buf-F	35	114	8	27	2	4	0	11	13	15	.237	.320	.325	89	-1	-1	13	2			3	S/3	0.4
	Bro-F	110	385	41	95	16	6	5	58	25	49	.247	.298	.358	94	-4	-4	50	21			1	S3	0.5
	Yr	145	499	49	122	18	10	5	69	38	64	.244	.303	.351	93	-5	-5	63	23			4		0.9
1917	StL-N	56	165	11	30	0	2	1	17	17	22	.182	.262	.224	51	-9	-9	10	4			7	3/2S	-0.9
Total	4	438	1422	143	321	39	25	8	158	133	219	.226	.296	.305	75	-43	-45	152	58			-3	3S/2OI	-3.6

■ GEORGE SMITH   Smith, George Cornelius   b: 7/7/37, St.Petersburg, Fla.   d: 6/15/87, St.Petersburg, Fla.   BR/TR, 5'10", 170 lbs.   Deb: 8/04/63

YEAR	TM/L	G	AB	R	H	2B	3B	HR	RBI	BB	SO	AVG	OBP	SLG	PRO+	BR	/A	RC	SB	CS	SBR	FR	POS	TPR
1963	Det-A	52	171	16	37	8	2	0	17	18	34	.216	.298	.287	63	-8	-8	16	4	0	1	11	2	0.8
1964	Det-A	5	7	1	2	0	0	0	2	1	4	.286	.375	.286	86	-0	-0	1	1	0	0	1	/2	0.1
1965	Det-A	32	53	6	5	0	0	1	1	3	18	.094	.143	.151	-16	-8	-8	1	0	0	0	3	2/S3	-0.3
1966	Bos-A	128	403	41	86	19	4	8	37	37	86	.213	.284	.340	71	-11	-16	39	4	0	1	16	*2S	1.2
Total	4	217	634	64	130	27	6	9	57	59	142	.205	.278	.309	62	-27	-33	57	9	0	3	30	2/S3	1.8

■ HEINIE SMITH   Smith, George Henry   b: 10/24/1871, Pittsburgh, Pa.   d: 6/25/39, Buffalo, N.Y.   BR/TR, 5'9.5", 160 lbs.   Deb: 9/08/1897 M

YEAR	TM/L	G	AB	R	H	2B	3B	HR	RBI	BB	SO	AVG	OBP	SLG	PRO+	BR	/A	RC	SB	CS	SBR	FR	POS	TPR
1897	Lou-N	21	76	7	20	3	0	1	7	3		.263	.300	.342	74	-3	-3	8	1			-2	2	-0.2
1898	Lou-N	35	121	14	23	4	0	0	13	6		.190	.240	.223	35	-10	-10	8	6			-6	2	-1.3
1899	Pit-N	15	53	9	15	3	1	0	12	5		.283	.345	.377	101	0	0	8	2			-4	2/S	-0.2
1901	NY-N	9	29	5	6	2	1	1	4	1		.207	.233	.448	101	-0	-0	3	1			-1	/2P	0.0
1902	NY-N	138	511	46	129	19	2	0	33	17		.252	.279	.297	80	-13	-12	53	32			4	*2M	0.1
1903	Det-A	93	336	36	75	11	3	1	22	19		.223	.265	.283	68	-13	-12	36	12			-2	2	-1.2
Total	6	311	1126	117	268	42	7	3	91	51		.238	.274	.296	73	-40	-37	112	54			-11	2/PS	-2.8

■ GERMANY SMITH   Smith, George J.   b: 4/21/1863, Pittsburgh, Pa.   d: 12/1/27, Altoona, Pa.   BR/TR, 6', 175 lbs.   Deb: 4/17/1884

YEAR	TM/L	G	AB	R	H	2B	3B	HR	RBI	BB	SO	AVG	OBP	SLG	PRO+	BR	/A	RC	SB	CS	SBR	FR	POS	TPR
1884	Alt-U	25	108	9	34	8	1	0		1		.315	.321	.407	143	5	4	14	0			6	S/P	1.0
	Cle-N	72	291	31	74	14	4	4	26	2	45	.254	.259	.371	93	-2	-3	29				10	2S	0.8
1885	Bro-a	108	419	63	108	17	11	4		10		.258	.275	.379	107	3	2	45				40	*S	3.8
1886	Bro-a	105	426	66	105	17	6	2		19		.246	.279	.329	91	-5	-6	46	22			12	*S/OC	1.1
1887	Bro-a	103	435	79	128	19	16	4		13		.294	.316	.439	110	4	3	70	26			**32**	*S/3	2.7
1888	Bro-a	103	402	47	86	10	7	3	61	22		.214	.255	.296	79	-10	-9	38	27			6	*S/2	0.1
1889	*Bro-a	121	446	89	103	22	3	3	53	40	42	.231	.296	.314	75	-14	-14	53	35			-4	*S/O	-0.7
1890	*Bro-N	129	481	76	92	6	5	1	47	42	23	.191	.260	.231	45	-33	-33	36	24			4	*S	-2.7
1891	Cin-N	138	512	50	103	11	5	3	53	38	32	.201	.258	.260	52	-31	-31	39	16			11	*S	-1.1
1892	Cin-N	139	506	58	121	13	6	8	63	42	52	.239	.297	.336	94	-5	-4	58	19			25	*S	2.5
1893	Cin-N	130	500	63	118	18	6	0	56	38	20	.236	.293	.320	63	-26	-29	52	14			20	*S	-0.3
1894	Cin-N	127	482	73	127	33	5	3	76	41	28	.263	.324	.371	66	-25	-29	64	15			20	*S	-0.1
1895	Cin-N	127	503	75	151	23	6	4	74	34	24	.300	.345	.394	88	-7	-10	75	13			2	*S	0.2
1896	Cin-N	120	456	65	131	22	9	2	71	28	22	.287	.330	.388	85	-7	-12	67	22			-10	*S	-1.8
1897	Bro-N	112	428	47	86	17	3	0	29	14		.201	.233	.255	32	-43	-39	26	1			-11	*S	-4.0
1898	StL-N	51	157	16	25	2	1	1	9	24		.159	.275	.204	39	-11	-12	9	1			-7	S	-1.4
Total	15	1710	6552	907	1592	252	94	46	618	408	288	.243	.289	.331	76	-207	-222	723	235			156	*S/23OCP	0.1

■ GREG SMITH   Smith, Gregory Allen   b: 4/5/67, Baltimore, Md.   BB/TR, 5'11", 170 lbs.   Deb: 9/02/89

YEAR	TM/L	G	AB	R	H	2B	3B	HR	RBI	BB	SO	AVG	OBP	SLG	PRO+	BR	/A	RC	SB	CS	SBR	FR	POS	TPR
1989	Chi-N	4	5	1	2	0	0	0	2	0	0	.400	.500	.400	149	0	0	1	0	0	0	0	/2	0.1
1990	Chi-N	18	44	4	9	2	1	0	5	2	5	.205	.239	.295	42	-3	-4	3	1	0	0	4	/2S	0.1
Total	2	22	49	5	11	2	1	0	7	2	5	.224	.269	.306	54	-3	-3	4	1	0	0	4	/2S	0.2

■ HAL SMITH   Smith, Harold Raymond "Cura"   b: 6/1/31, Barling, Ark.   BR/TR, 5'10.5", 186 lbs.   Deb: 5/02/56 C

YEAR	TM/L	G	AB	R	H	2B	3B	HR	RBI	BB	SO	AVG	OBP	SLG	PRO+	BR	/A	RC	SB	CS	SBR	FR	POS	TPR
1956	StL-N	75	227	27	64	12	0	5	23	15	22	.282	.326	.401	94	-2	-2	28	1	0	0	-3	C	-0.2
1957	StL-N	100	333	25	93	12	3	2	37	18	18	.279	.316	.351	78	-10	-11	35	2	2	-1	1	C	-0.4
1958	StL-N	77	220	13	50	4	1	1	24	14	14	.227	.274	.268	42	-17	-19	16	0	0	0	-1	C	-1.6
1959	StL-N	142	452	35	122	15	3	13	50	15	28	.270	.295	.403	78	-12	-15	47	2	6	-3	4	*C	-0.5
1960	StL-N	127	337	20	77	16	0	2	28	29	33	.228	.292	.294	56	-18	-21	27	1	0	0	17	*C	0.2
1961	StL-N	45	125	6	31	4	1	0	10	11	12	.248	.314	.296	57	-6	-8	12	0	0	0	17	C	1.2
1965	Pit-N	4	3	0	0	0	0	0	0	0	1	.000	.000	.000	-99	-1	-1	0	0	0	0	2	/C	0.1
Total	7	570	1697	126	437	63	8	23	172	102	128	.258	.301	.345	69	-66	-77	165	6	8	-3	37	C	-1.2

■ HAL SMITH   Smith, Harold Wayne   b: 12/7/30, W.Frankfort, Ill.   BR/TR, 6', 195 lbs.   Deb: 4/11/55

YEAR	TM/L	G	AB	R	H	2B	3B	HR	RBI	BB	SO	AVG	OBP	SLG	PRO+	BR	/A	RC	SB	CS	SBR	FR	POS	TPR
1955	Bal-A	135	424	41	115	23	4	4	52	30	21	.271	.322	.373	93	-9	-5	47	1	3	-2	-1	*C	-0.3

YEAR	TM/L	G	AB	R	H	2B	3B	HR	RBI	BB	SO	AVG	OBP	SLG	PRO+	BR	/A	RC	SB	CS	SBR	FR	POS	TPR
1956	Bal-A	77	229	16	60	14	0	3	18	17	22	.262	.316	.362	85	-7	-5	22	1	0	0	3	C	0.0
	KC-A	37	142	15	39	9	2	2	24	3	12	.275	.290	.408	82	-4	-4	16	1	1	-0	2	C	-0.1
	Yr	114	371	31	99	23	2	5	42	20	34	.267	.306	.380	85	-12	-9	38	2	1	0	5		-0.1
1957	KC-A	107	360	41	109	26	0	13	41	14	44	.303	.331	.483	118	8	7	52	2	2	-1	0	*C	1.1
1958	KC-A	99	315	32	86	19	2	5	46	25	47	.273	.330	.394	97	-1	-2	41	0	0	0	1	3C1	0.1
1959	KC-A	108	292	36	84	12	0	5	31	34	39	.288	.368	.380	104	3	3	42	0	3	-2	7	3C	0.9
1960	*Pit-N	77	258	37	76	18	2	11	45	22	48	.295	.355	.508	132	11	11	45	1	1	-0	-5	C	0.9
1961	Pit-N	67	193	12	43	10	0	3	26	11	38	.223	.268	.321	55	-12	-13	16	0	0	0	-0	C	-0.6
1962	Hou-N	109	345	32	81	14	0	12	35	24	55	.235	.288	.380	84	-12	-8	35	0	0	0	1	C/31	-0.5
1963	Hou-N	31	58	1	14	2	0	0	2	4	15	.241	.290	.276	68	-3	-2	4	0	0	0	-3	C	-0.4
1964	Cin-N	32	66	6	8	1	0	0	3	12	20	.121	.256	.136	14	-7	-8	2	1	0	0	-3	C	-1.0
Total	10	879	2682	269	715	148	10	58	323	196	361	.267	.320	.394	94	-33	-26	323	7	10	-4	1	C3/1	0.1

■ **HARRY SMITH**   Smith, Harry Thomas b: 10/31/1874, Yorkshire, England d: 2/17/33, Salem, N.J. BR/TR, Deb: 7/11/01 M

YEAR	TM/L	G	AB	R	H	2B	3B	HR	RBI	BB	SO	AVG	OBP	SLG	PRO+	BR	/A	RC	SB	CS	SBR	FR	POS	TPR
1901	Phi-A	11	34	3	11	1	0	0	3	2		.324	.378	.353	101	0	0	5	1			-2	/CO	0.0
1902	Pit-N	50	185	14	35	4	1	0	12	4		.189	.211	.222	33	-14	-15	10	4			-3	C	-1.2
1903	*Pit-N	61	212	15	37	3	2	0	19	12		.175	.219	.208	22	-21	-22	11	2			-4	C/O	-2.0
1904	Pit-N	47	141	17	35	3	1	0	18	16		.248	.325	.284	88	-1	-1	15	5			-4	C/O	-0.1
1905	Pit-N	1	3	0	0	0	0	0	1	0		.000	.000	.000	-98	-1	-1	0	1			0	/C	0.0
1906	Pit-N	1	1	0	0	0	0	0	0	0		.000	.000	.000	-96	-0	-0	0	0			0	/C	0.0
1907	Pit-N	18	38	4	10	1	0	0	1	4		.263	.333	.289	96	0	-0	4	0			-2	C	0.0
1908	Bos-N	41	130	13	32	2	2	1	16	7		.246	.285	.315	95	-1	-1	12	2			0	C	0.1
1909	Bos-N	43	113	9	19	4	1	0	4	5		.168	.203	.221	30	-9	-10	5	3			2	CM	-0.6
1910	Bos-N	70	147	8	35	4	0	1	15	5	14	.238	.263	.286	57	-8	-9	12	5			3	C	-0.3
Total	10	343	1004	83	214	22	7	2	89	55	14	.213	.255	.255	53	-55	-58	76	23			-10	C/O	-4.1

■ **HARRY SMITH**   Smith, Harry W. b: 2/5/1856, N.Vernon, Ind. d: 6/4/1898, N.Vernon, Ind. BR/TR, 6', 175 lbs. Deb: 5/08/1877

YEAR	TM/L	G	AB	R	H	2B	3B	HR	RBI	BB	SO	AVG	OBP	SLG	PRO+	BR	/A	RC	SB	CS	SBR	FR	POS	TPR
1877	Chi-N	24	94	7	19	1	0	0	3	4	6	.202	.235	.213	37	-6	-8	5				-8	2O	-1.3
	Cin-N	10	36	4	9	2	1	0	3	1	5	.250	.270	.361	109	-0	0	4				4	/C2O	0.4
	Yr	34	130	11	28	3	1	0	6	5	11	.215	.254	.254	54	-6	-7	8				-4		-0.9
1889	Lou-a	1	2	0	1	0	0	0	1	0	1	.500	.500	.500	192	0	0	1	0			-1	/OC	0.0
Total	2	35	132	11	29	3	1	0	7	5	12	.220	.248	.258	56	-6	-7	9	0			-5	/2OC	-0.9

■ **HARVEY SMITH**   Smith, Harvey Fetterhoff b: 7/24/1871, Union Deposit, Pa d: 11/12/62, Harrisburg, Pa. BL/TR, 5'8", 160 lbs. Deb: 8/19/1896

YEAR	TM/L	G	AB	R	H	2B	3B	HR	RBI	BB	SO	AVG	OBP	SLG	PRO+	BR	/A	RC	SB	CS	SBR	FR	POS	TPR
1896	Was-N	36	131	21	36	7	2	0	17	12	7	.275	.345	.359	88	-2	-2	20	9			3	3	0.2

■ **HAPPY SMITH**   Smith, Henry Joseph b: 7/14/1883, Coquille, Ore. d: 2/26/61, San Jose, Cal. BL/TR, 6', 185 lbs. Deb: 4/15/10

YEAR	TM/L	G	AB	R	H	2B	3B	HR	RBI	BB	SO	AVG	OBP	SLG	PRO+	BR	/A	RC	SB	CS	SBR	FR	POS	TPR
1910	Bro-N	35	76	6	18	2	0	0	5	4	14	.237	.275	.263	59	-4	-4	6	4			3	O	-0.1

■ **JACK SMITH**   Smith, Jack b: 6/23/1895, Chicago, Ill. d: 5/2/72, Westchester, Ill. BL/TL, 5'8", 165 lbs. Deb: 9/30/15

YEAR	TM/L	G	AB	R	H	2B	3B	HR	RBI	BB	SO	AVG	OBP	SLG	PRO+	BR	/A	RC	SB	CS	SBR	FR	POS	TPR
1915	StL-N	4	16	2	3	0	1	0	0	1	5	.188	.235	.313	65	-1	-1	1	0			-1	/O	-0.1
1916	StL-N	130	357	43	87	6	5	6	34	20	50	.244	.291	.350	94	-3	-3	37	24	16	-2	-16	*O	-2.9
1917	StL-N	137	462	64	137	16	11	3	34	38	65	.297	.351	.398	133	16	17	70	25			-20	*O	-0.6
1918	StL-N	42	166	24	35	2	1	0	4	7	21	.211	.260	.235	53	-9	-9	11	5			2	O	-0.9
1919	StL-N	119	408	47	91	16	3	0	15	26	29	.223	.271	.277	69	-17	-15	37	30			1	*O	-1.9
1920	StL-N	91	313	53	104	22	5	1	28	25	23	.332	.385	.444	143	15	17	53	14	9	-1	-3	O	0.8
1921	StL-N	116	411	86	135	22	9	7	33	21	24	.328	.361	.477	122	11	12	69	11	6	-0	-8	*O	0.0
1922	StL-N	143	510	117	158	23	12	8	46	50	30	.310	.375	.449	117	9	12	88	18	7	1	-17	*O	-0.7
1923	StL-N	124	407	98	126	16	6	5	41	27	20	.310	.356	.415	105	1	3	61	32	11	3	3	*O	0.5
1924	StL-N	124	459	91	130	18	6	2	33	33	27	.283	.333	.362	88	-9	-8	54	24	16	-2	10	*O	-0.1
1925	StL-N	80	243	53	61	11	4	4	31	19	13	.251	.308	.379	73	-10	-11	31	20	2	5	4	O	-0.3
1926	StL-N	1	1	0	0	0	0	0	0	0	1	.000	.000	.000	-96	-0	-0	0	0				H	0.0
	Bos-N	96	322	46	100	15	2	2	25	28	12	.311	.369	.388	114	2	6	46	11			-1	O	0.2
	Yr	97	323	46	100	15	2	2	25	28	13	.310	.368	.387	113	2	6	46	11			-1		0.2
1927	Bos-N	84	183	27	58	6	4	1	24	16	12	.317	.375	.410	119	3	5	28	8			3	O	0.6
1928	Bos-N	96	254	30	71	9	2	1	32	21	14	.280	.345	.343	82	-8	-6	29	6			-4	O	-1.1
1929	Bos-N	19	20	2	5	0	0	0	2	2	2	.250	.318	.250	45	-2	-2	2	0			-0	/O	-0.1
Total	15	1406	4532	783	1301	182	71	40	382	334	348	.287	.339	.385	103	-2	18	618	228	67		-46	*O	-6.6

■ **STUB SMITH**   Smith, James A. b: 11/26/1876, Elmwood, Ill. BL/TR, 145 lbs. Deb: 9/10/1898

YEAR	TM/L	G	AB	R	H	2B	3B	HR	RBI	BB	SO	AVG	OBP	SLG	PRO+	BR	/A	RC	SB	CS	SBR	FR	POS	TPR
1898	Bos-N	3	10	1	1	0	0	0	0			.100	.100	.100	-40	-2	-2	0	0			0	/S	0.0

■ **RED SMITH**   Smith, James Carlisle b: 4/6/1890, Greenville, S.C. d: 10/11/66, Atlanta, Ga. BR/TR, 5'11", 165 lbs. Deb: 9/05/11

YEAR	TM/L	G	AB	R	H	2B	3B	HR	RBI	BB	SO	AVG	OBP	SLG	PRO+	BR	/A	RC	SB	CS	SBR	FR	POS	TPR
1911	Bro-N	28	111	10	29	6	1	0	19	5	13	.261	.299	.333	80	-4	-3	12	5			-2	3	-0.3
1912	Bro-N	128	486	75	139	28	6	4	57	54	51	.286	.362	.393	111	5	7	77	22			5	*3	1.3
1913	Bro-N	151	540	70	160	40	10	6	76	45	67	.296	.358	.441	124	18	16	90	22			-3	*3	1.2
1914	Bro-N	90	330	39	81	10	8	4	48	30	26	.245	.310	.361	97	-1	-2	39	11			12	3	1.5
	Bos-N	60	207	30	65	17	1	3	37	28	24	.314	.401	.449	153	14	14	39	4			10	3	2.8
	Yr	150	537	69	146	27	9	7	85	58	50	.272	.346	.395	119	13	12	78	15			23		4.3
1915	Bos-N	157	549	66	145	34	4	2	65	67	49	.264	.345	.352	116	9	12	71	10	5	0	-6	*3	1.4
1916	Bos-N	150	509	48	132	16	10	3	60	53	55	.259	.333	.348	114	6	9	66	13			-4	*3	0.7
1917	Bos-N	147	505	60	149	31	6	2	62	53	61	.295	.369	.392	142	21	24	78	16			-21	*3	0.2
1918	Bos-N	119	429	55	128	20	3	2	65	45	47	.298	.373	.373	133	16	18	63	8			4	*3	2.6
1919	Bos-N	87	241	24	59	6	0	1	25	40	22	.245	.359	.282	98	1	2	27	6			5	O3	0.5
Total	9	1117	3907	477	1087	208	49	27	514	420	415	.278	.353	.377	120	85	97	562	117	5		1	*3/O	11.9

■ **HARRY SMITH**   Smith, James Harry b: 5/15/1890, Baltimore, Md. d: 4/1/22, Charlotte, N.C. BR/TR, 5'10", 180 lbs. Deb: 9/21/14

YEAR	TM/L	G	AB	R	H	2B	3B	HR	RBI	BB	SO	AVG	OBP	SLG	PRO+	BR	/A	RC	SB	CS	SBR	FR	POS	TPR
1914	NY-N	5	7	0	3	0	0	0	2	3	1	.429	.600	.429	215	1	1	2	1			2	/C	0.3
1915	NY-N	21	32	1	4	0	1	0	3	6	12	.125	.263	.188	40	-2	-2	1	0	1	-1	-2	C	-0.3
	Bro-F	28	65	5	13	0	0	1	4	7	16	.200	.278	.246	56	-3	-3	5	2			-9	C/O	-1.3
1917	Cin-N	8	17	0	2	0	0	0	1	2	7	.118	.211	.118	2	-2	-2	1	0			4	/C	0.3
1918	Cin-N	13	24	4	5	1	2	0	4	3	6	.185	.267	.250	95	-0	-0	3	1			-2	/CO	-0.1
Total	4	75	148	10	27	1	3	1	14	21	42	.182	.284	.250	63	-7	-6	12	4	1		-7	/CO	-1.1

■ **JIMMY SMITH**   Smith, James Lawrence "Greenfield Jimmy" b: 5/15/1895, Pittsburgh, Pa. d: 1/1/74, Pittsburgh, Pa. BB/TR, 5'9", 152 lbs. Deb: 9/26/14

YEAR	TM/L	G	AB	R	H	2B	3B	HR	RBI	BB	SO	AVG	OBP	SLG	PRO+	BR	/A	RC	SB	CS	SBR	FR	POS	TPR
1914	Chi-F	3	6	1	3	1	0	0	1	0	0	.500	.500	.667	247	1	1	2	0			1	/S	0.2
1915	Chi-F	95	318	32	69	11	4	4	30	14	65	.217	.250	.314	71	-14	-12	27	4			-13	S/2	-1.9
	Bal-F	33	108	9	19	1	1	1	11	11	23	.176	.258	.231	44	-7	-8	8	3			-4	S	-0.9
	Yr	128	426	41	88	12	5	5	41	25	88	.207	.252	.293	63	-21	-20	35	7			-16		-2.8
1916	Pit-N	36	96	4	18	1	1	0	5	6	22	.188	.257	.219	46	-6	-6	6	0			1	S/3	-0.3
1917	NY-N	36	96	12	22	5	1	0	9	9	18	.229	.295	.302	86	-2	-1	10	6			-2	2/S	-0.9
1918	Bos-N	34	102	8	23	3	4	1	14	3	13	.225	.255	.363	91	-2	-2	10	1			-1	2/SO3	-0.1
1919	*Cin-N	28	40	9	11	1	0	1	10	4	8	.275	.341	.525	163	3	3	7	1			0	/3S2O	0.3
1921	Phi-N	67	247	31	57	6	1	4	22	11	28	.231	.266	.320	50	-16	-19	19	2	8	-4	8	2	-1.4
1922	Phi-N	38	114	13	25	1	0	1	6	5	9	.219	.258	.254	30	-11	-13	7	1	3	-2	-3	S2/3	-1.4

YEAR	TM/L	G	AB	R	H	2B	3B	HR	RBI	BB	SO	AVG	OBP	SLG	PRO+	BR	/A	RC	SB	CS	SBR	FR	POS	TPR
Total	8	370	1127	119	247	32	15	12	108	63	186	.219	.265	.306	63	-55	-57	96	18	11		-13	S2/3O	-5.6

■ JIM SMITH
Smith, James Lorne b: 9/8/54, Santa Monica, Cal. BR/TR, 6'3", 185 lbs. Deb: 4/12/82

YEAR	TM/L	G	AB	R	H	2B	3B	HR	RBI	BB	SO	AVG	OBP	SLG	PRO+	BR	/A	RC	SB	CS	SBR	FR	POS	TPR
1982	Pit-N	42	42	5	10	2	1	0	4	5	7	.238	.319	.333	80	-1	-1	5	0	1	-1	8	S/23	0.9

■ JOHN SMITH
Smith, John b: Baltimore, Md.   Deb: 4/14/1873

YEAR	TM/L	G	AB	R	H	2B	3B	HR	RBI	BB	SO	AVG	OBP	SLG	PRO+	BR	/A	RC	SB	CS	SBR	FR	POS	TPR
1873	Mar-n	6	24	2	5	0	0	0		0		.208	.208	.208	30	-2	-1	1					/SO2M	0.0
1874	Bal-n	6	20	1	3	1	0	0		0		.150	.150	.200	10	-2	-2	1					/SO	-0.1
1875	NH-n	1	3	0	0	0	0	0		1		.000	.250	.000	-6	-0	-0	0					/S	0.0
Total	3 n	13	47	3	8	1	0	0		1		.170	.188	.191	19	-4	-3	2					/SO2	-0.1

■ DWIGHT SMITH
Smith, John Dwight b: 11/8/63, Tallahassee, Fla. BL/TR, 5'11", 175 lbs. Deb: 5/01/89

YEAR	TM/L	G	AB	R	H	2B	3B	HR	RBI	BB	SO	AVG	OBP	SLG	PRO+	BR	/A	RC	SB	CS	SBR	FR	POS	TPR
1989	*Chi-N	109	343	52	111	19	6	9	52	31	51	.324	.383	.493	138	21	18	66	9	4	0	-1	*O	1.7
1990	Chi-N	117	290	34	76	15	0	6	27	28	46	.262	.331	.376	86	-2	-5	36	11	6	-0	-3	O	-1.1
Total	2	226	633	86	187	34	6	15	79	59	97	.295	.359	.439	114	19	13	102	20	10	0	-4	O	0.6

■ JOHN SMITH
Smith, John J. b: San Francisco, Cal. 5'11", 210 lbs. Deb: 5/01/1882

YEAR	TM/L	G	AB	R	H	2B	3B	HR	RBI	BB	SO	AVG	OBP	SLG	PRO+	BR	/A	RC	SB	CS	SBR	FR	POS	TPR
1882	Tro-N	35	149	27	36	4	3	0	14	3	24	.242	.257	.309	84	-3	-2	12				0	1	-0.7
	Wor-N	19	70	10	17	3	2	0	5	5	10	.243	.293	.343	101	0	0	7				1	1	-0.1
	Yr	54	219	37	53	7	5	0	19	8	34	.242	.269	.320	90	-3	-2	19				1		-0.8

■ JACK SMITH
Smith, John Joseph (b: John Joseph Coffey) b: 8/8/1893, Oswayo, Pa. d: 12/4/62, New York, N.Y. TR, 5'9", Deb: 5/18/12

YEAR	TM/L	G	AB	R	H	2B	3B	HR	RBI	BB	SO	AVG	OBP	SLG	PRO+	BR	/A	RC	SB	CS	SBR	FR	POS	TPR
1912	Det-A	1	0	0	0	0	0	0	0	0		—	—	—		0	0	0				1	/3	0.1

■ JOHN SMITH
Smith, John Marshall b: 9/27/06, Washington, D.C. d: 5/9/82, Silver Spring, Md. BB/TR, 6'1", 180 lbs. Deb: 9/17/31

YEAR	TM/L	G	AB	R	H	2B	3B	HR	RBI	BB	SO	AVG	OBP	SLG	PRO+	BR	/A	RC	SB	CS	SBR	FR	POS	TPR
1931	Bos-A	4	15	2	2	0	0	0	1	2	1	.133	.235	.133	-1	-2	-2	1	1	0	0	-1	/1	-0.2

■ JUD SMITH
Smith, Judson Grant b: 1/13/1869, Green Oak, Mich. d: 12/7/47, Los Angeles, Cal. BR/TR, Deb: 5/21/1893

YEAR	TM/L	G	AB	R	H	2B	3B	HR	RBI	BB	SO	AVG	OBP	SLG	PRO+	BR	/A	RC	SB	CS	SBR	FR	POS	TPR
1893	Cin-N	17	43	7	10	1	0	1	5	9	5	.233	.365	.326	84	-1	-1	6	1			-2	/O3S	-0.1
	StL-N	4	13	1	1	0	0	0	0	1	2	.077	.200	.077	-24	-2	-2	0	0			1	/3	0.0
	Yr	21	56	8	11	1	0	1	5	10	7	.196	.328	.268	60	-3	-3	5	1			-1		-0.1
1896	Pit-N	10	35	6	12	2	1	0	4	2	2	.343	.395	.457	132	1	2	8	3			2	3	0.3
1898	Was-N	66	234	33	71	7	5	3	28	22		.303	.378	.415	130	9	9	42	11			-9	3S/12	0.2
1901	Pit-N	6	21	1	3	1	0	0	3			.143	.250	.190	29	-2	-2	1	0			0	/3	0.0
Total	4	103	346	48	97	11	6	4	37	37	9	.280	.363	.382	112	6	6	56	15			-9	/3SO12	0.4

■ KEITH SMITH
Smith, Keith Lavarne b: 5/3/53, Palmetto, Fla. BR/TR, 5'9", 178 lbs. Deb: 8/02/77

YEAR	TM/L	G	AB	R	H	2B	3B	HR	RBI	BB	SO	AVG	OBP	SLG	PRO+	BR	/A	RC	SB	CS	SBR	FR	POS	TPR
1977	Tex-A	23	67	13	16	4	0	2	6	4	7	.239	.301	.388	85	-1	-1	9	2	0	1	-1	O	-0.2
1979	StL-N	6	13	1	3	0	0	0	0	0	1	.231	.231	.231	26	-1	-1	0	0	1	-1	2	/O	0.0
1980	StL-N	24	31	3	4	1	0	0	2	2	2	.129	.182	.161	-3	-4	-4	1	0	0	0	0	/O	-0.4
Total	3	53	111	17	23	5	0	2	8	6	10	.207	.261	.306	54	-7	-7	10	2	1	0	1	/O	-0.6

■ KEN SMITH
Smith, Kenneth Earl b: 2/12/58, Youngstown, Ohio BL/TR, 6'1", 195 lbs. Deb: 9/22/81

YEAR	TM/L	G	AB	R	H	2B	3B	HR	RBI	BB	SO	AVG	OBP	SLG	PRO+	BR	/A	RC	SB	CS	SBR	FR	POS	TPR
1981	Atl-N	5	3	0	1	1	0	0	0	0	1	.333	.333	.667	174	0	0	1	0	0	0	0	/1	0.0
1982	Atl-N	48	41	6	12	1	0	1	3	6	13	.293	.383	.317	94	0	-0	6	0	0	0	-0	/1O	0.0
1983	Atl-N	30	12	2	2	0	0	1	2	1	5	.167	.231	.417	71	-0	-1	1	1	0	0	3	1	0.2
Total	3	83	56	8	15	2	0	2	5	7	19	.268	.349	.357	93	-0	-0	8	1	0	0	3	/1O	0.2

■ PADDY SMITH
Smith, Lawrence Patrick b: 5/16/1894, Pelham, N.Y. BL/TR, 6', 195 lbs. Deb: 7/06/20

YEAR	TM/L	G	AB	R	H	2B	3B	HR	RBI	BB	SO	AVG	OBP	SLG	PRO+	BR	/A	RC	SB	CS	SBR	FR	POS	TPR
1920	Bos-A	2	2	0	0	0	0	0	0	0	1	.000	.000	.000	-99	-1	-1	0	0	0	0	0	/C	0.0

■ BULL SMITH
Smith, Lewis Oscar b: 8/20/1880, Plum, W.Va. d: 5/1/28, Charleston, W.Va. BR/TR, 6', 180 lbs. Deb: 8/30/04

YEAR	TM/L	G	AB	R	H	2B	3B	HR	RBI	BB	SO	AVG	OBP	SLG	PRO+	BR	/A	RC	SB	CS	SBR	FR	POS	TPR
1904	Pit-N	13	42	2	6	0	1	0	0	1		.143	.163	.190	10	-4	-4	1	0			-0	O	-0.5
1906	Chi-N	1	1	0	0	0	0	0	0	0		.000	.000	.000	-95	-0	-0	0	0			0	H	0.0
1911	Was-A	1	0	0	0	0	0	0	0	0		—	—	—	—	0	0	0	0			0	R	0.0
Total	3	15	43	2	6	0	1	0	0	1		.140	.159	.186	7	-5	-5	1	0			-0	/O	-0.5

■ LEO SMITH
Smith, Lionel H. b: 5/13/1859, Brooklyn, N.Y. d: 8/30/35, Brooklyn, N.Y. 5'6", 142 lbs. Deb: 8/28/1890

YEAR	TM/L	G	AB	R	H	2B	3B	HR	RBI	BB	SO	AVG	OBP	SLG	PRO+	BR	/A	RC	SB	CS	SBR	FR	POS	TPR
1890	Roc-a	35	112	11	21	1	3	0		14		.188	.283	.250	64	-5	-4	8	1			8	S	0.5

■ LONNIE SMITH
Smith, Lonnie b: 12/22/55, Chicago, Ill. BR/TR, 5'9", 170 lbs. Deb: 9/02/78

YEAR	TM/L	G	AB	R	H	2B	3B	HR	RBI	BB	SO	AVG	OBP	SLG	PRO+	BR	/A	RC	SB	CS	SBR	FR	POS	TPR
1978	Phi-N	17	4	6	0	0	0	0	0	4	3	.000	.500	.000	50	0	0	2	4	0	1	2	O	0.3
1979	Phi-N	17	30	4	5	2	0	0	3	1	7	.167	.194	.233	15	-4	-4	1	2	1	0	2	O	-0.1
1980	*Phi-N	100	298	69	101	14	4	3	20	26	48	.339	.399	.443	128	15	13	54	33	13	2	-10	O	0.1
1981	Phi-N	62	176	40	57	14	3	2	11	18	14	.324	.402	.472	141	11	10	35	21	10	0	3	O	1.3
1982	*StL-N	156	592	120	182	35	8	8	69	64	74	.307	.383	.434	127	24	23	102	68	26	5	6	O	3.3
1983	StL-N	130	492	83	158	31	5	8	45	41	55	.321	.384	.453	131	21	21	85	43	18	2	-2	*O	2.0
1984	StL-N	145	504	77	126	20	4	6	49	70	90	.250	.352	.341	98	-1	1	70	50	13	7	-11	*O	-0.7
1985	StL-N	28	96	15	25	2	2	0	7	15	20	.260	.377	.323	98	1	1	16	12	6	0	-3	O	-0.2
	*KC-A	120	448	77	115	23	4	6	41	41	69	.257	.325	.366	88	-7	-7	60	40	7	8	-9	*O	-0.8
1986	KC-A	134	508	80	146	25	7	8	44	46	78	.287	.358	.411	107	7	6	77	26	9	2	-2	*OD	0.3
1987	KC-A	48	167	26	42	7	1	3	8	24	31	.251	.359	.359	89	-1	-2	24	9	4	0	-3	OD	-0.4
1988	Atl-N	43	114	14	27	3	0	3	9	10	25	.237	.298	.342	79	-2	-3	12	4	2	0	-1	O	-0.4
1989	Atl-N	134	482	89	152	34	4	21	79	76	95	.315	.420	.533	166	47	45	113	25	12	0	4	*O	5.0
1990	Atl-N	135	466	72	142	27	9	9	42	58	69	.305	.389	.459	130	22	21	86	10	10	-3	1	*O	1.6
Total	13	1269	4377	772	1278	237	51	77	427	494	678	.292	.373	.422	119	133	126	734	347	131	26	-22	O/D	11.3

■ RED SMITH
Smith, Marvin Harold b: 7/17/1900, Ashley, Ill. d: 2/19/61, Los Angeles, Cal. BL/TR, 5'7", 165 lbs. Deb: 4/14/25

YEAR	TM/L	G	AB	R	H	2B	3B	HR	RBI	BB	SO	AVG	OBP	SLG	PRO+	BR	/A	RC	SB	CS	SBR	FR	POS	TPR
1925	Phi-A	20	14	1	4	0	0	0	1	2	5	.286	.375	.286	65	-1	-1	2	0	0	0	1	S/3	0.3

■ MILT SMITH
Smith, Milton b: 3/27/29, Columbus, Ga. BR/TR, 5'10", 165 lbs. Deb: 7/21/55

YEAR	TM/L	G	AB	R	H	2B	3B	HR	RBI	BB	SO	AVG	OBP	SLG	PRO+	BR	/A	RC	SB	CS	SBR	FR	POS	TPR
1955	Cin-N	36	102	15	20	3	1	3	8	13	24	.196	.293	.333	62	-5	-6	10	2	2	-1	-2	3/2	-0.7

■ NATE SMITH
Smith, Nathaniel Beverly b: 4/26/35, Chicago, Ill. BR/TR, 5'11", 170 lbs. Deb: 9/19/62

YEAR	TM/L	G	AB	R	H	2B	3B	HR	RBI	BB	SO	AVG	OBP	SLG	PRO+	BR	/A	RC	SB	CS	SBR	FR	POS	TPR
1962	Bal-A	5	9	3	2	1	0	0	1	2		.222	.364	.333	94	-0	-0	1	0	0	0	1	/C	0.1

■ OLLIE SMITH
Smith, Oliver H. b: 1868, Mt.Vernon, Ohio BL/TL, Deb: 7/11/1894

YEAR	TM/L	G	AB	R	H	2B	3B	HR	RBI	BB	SO	AVG	OBP	SLG	PRO+	BR	/A	RC	SB	CS	SBR	FR	POS	TPR
1894	Lou-N	38	134	26	40	6	1	3	20	27	15	.299	.427	.425	116	3	5	31	13			-2	O	0.0

■ OZZIE SMITH
Smith, Osborne Earl b: 12/26/54, Mobile, Ala. BB/TR, 5'11", 150 lbs. Deb: 4/07/78

YEAR	TM/L	G	AB	R	H	2B	3B	HR	RBI	BB	SO	AVG	OBP	SLG	PRO+	BR	/A	RC	SB	CS	SBR	FR	POS	TPR
1978	SD-N	159	590	69	152	17	6	1	46	47	43	.258	.312	.312	81	-19	-14	61	40	12	5	26	*S	3.1
1979	SD-N	156	587	77	124	18	6	0	27	37	37	.211	.260	.262	46	-46	-42	42	28	7	4	20	*S	-0.1
1980	SD-N	158	609	67	140	18	5	0	35	71	49	.230	.315	.276	70	-25	-21	62	57	15	8	41	*S	4.7
1981	SD-N	110	450	53	100	11	2	0	21	41	37	.222	.294	.256	62	-24	-20	36	22	12	-1	26	*S	1.8
1982	*StL-N	140	488	58	121	24	1	2	43	68	32	.248	.342	.314	84	-8	-8	58	25	5	5	33	*S	4.1
1983	StL-N	159	552	69	134	30	6	3	50	64	36	.243	.323	.335	82	-12	-12	65	34	7	6	19	*S	2.7
1984	StL-N	124	412	53	106	20	5	1	44	56	17	.257	.349	.337	96	-2	-0	55	35	7	6	26	*S	4.7

YEAR	TM/L	G	AB	R	H	2B	3B	HR	RBI	BB	SO	AVG	OBP	SLG	PRO+	BR	/A	RC	SB	CS	SBR	FR	POS	TPR
1985	*StL-N	158	537	70	148	22	3	6	54	65	27	.276	.356	.361	102	3	3	73	31	8	5	16	*S	3.7
1986	StL-N	153	514	67	144	19	4	0	54	79	27	.280	.378	.333	99	2	3	73	31	7	5	-8	*S	1.3
1987	*StL-N	158	600	104	182	40	4	0	75	89	36	.303	.394	.383	105	10	8	102	43	9	8	19	*S	5.2
1988	StL-N	153	575	80	155	27	1	3	51	74	43	.270	.354	.336	98	2	1	80	57	9	12	23	*S	4.9
1989	StL-N	155	593	82	162	30	8	2	50	55	37	.273	.337	.361	96	0	-2	76	29	7	5	6	*S	1.9
1990	StL-N	143	512	61	130	21	1	1	50	61	33	.254	.336	.305	75	-14	-16	60	32	6	6	-13	*S	-1.0
Total	13	1926	7019	910	1798	297	52	19	600	807	454	.256	.335	.321	85	-134	-120	842	464	111	73	233	*S	37.0

■ KEITH SMITH
Smith, Patrick Keith b: 10/20/61, Los Angeles, Cal. BB/TR, 6'1", 175 lbs. Deb: 4/12/84

YEAR	TM/L	G	AB	R	H	2B	3B	HR	RBI	BB	SO	AVG	OBP	SLG	PRO+	BR	/A	RC	SB	CS	SBR	FR	POS	TPR
1984	NY-A	2	4	0	0	0	0	0	0	0	2	.000	.200	.000	-41	-1	-1	0	0	0	0	2	/S	0.2
1985	NY-A	4	0	1	0	0	0	0	0	0	0	—	—	—	—	0	0	0	0	0	0	1	/S	0.1
Total	2	6	4	1	0	0	0	0	0	0	2	.000	.200	.000	-41	-1	-1	0	0	0	0	3	/S	0.3

■ PAUL SMITH
Smith, Paul Leslie b: 3/19/31, New Castle, Pa. BL/TL, 5'8", 165 lbs. Deb: 4/14/53

YEAR	TM/L	G	AB	R	H	2B	3B	HR	RBI	BB	SO	AVG	OBP	SLG	PRO+	BR	/A	RC	SB	CS	SBR	FR	POS	TPR
1953	Pit-N	118	389	41	110	12	7	4	44	24	23	.283	.329	.380	85	-9	-9	50	3	0	1	-1	1O	-1.0
1957	Pit-N	81	150	12	38	4	0	3	11	12	17	.253	.313	.340	78	-5	-5	15	0	2	-1	-2	O/1	-0.8
1958	Pit-N	6	3	0	1	0	0	0	0	3	0	.333	.667	.333	180	1	1	1	0	0	0	0	H	0.1
	Chi-N	18	20	1	3	0	0	0	0	3	4	.150	.261	.150	13	-2	-2	1	0	0	0	0	/1	-0.2
	Yr	24	23	1	4	0	0	0	1	6	4	.174	.345	.174	44	-2	-2	2	0	0	0	0		-0.1
Total	3	223	562	54	152	16	7	7	56	42	44	.270	.326	.361	81	-16	-15	67	3	2	-0	-3	/1O	-1.9

■ PAUL SMITH
Smith, Paul Stoner b: 5/7/1888, Mt.Zion, Ill. d: 7/3/58, Decatur, Ill. BL/TR, 6'1", 190 lbs. Deb: 9/19/16

YEAR	TM/L	G	AB	R	H	2B	3B	HR	RBI	BB	SO	AVG	OBP	SLG	PRO+	BR	/A	RC	SB	CS	SBR	FR	POS	TPR
1916	Cin-N	10	44	5	10	0	1	0	1	1	8	.227	.244	.273	60	-2	-2	4	3			-1	O	-0.4

■ RAY SMITH
Smith, Raymond Edward b: 9/18/55, Glendale, Cal. BR/TR, 6'1", 185 lbs. Deb: 4/09/81

YEAR	TM/L	G	AB	R	H	2B	3B	HR	RBI	BB	SO	AVG	OBP	SLG	PRO+	BR	/A	RC	SB	CS	SBR	FR	POS	TPR
1981	Min-A	15	40	4	8	1	0	1	1	0	3	.200	.200	.300	40	-3	-3	2	0	0	0	1	C	-0.1
1982	Min-A	9	23	1	5	0	1	0	1	1	3	.217	.250	.304	50	-2	-2	2	0	0	0	1	/C	0.0
1983	Min-A	59	152	11	34	5	0	0	8	10	12	.224	.276	.257	46	-11	-11	11	1	0	0	11	C	0.2
Total	3	83	215	16	47	6	1	1	10	11	18	.219	.260	.270	45	-15	-16	15	1	0	0	13	/C	0.1

■ DICK SMITH
Smith, Richard Arthur b: 5/17/39, Lebanon, Ore. BR/TR, 6'2", 205 lbs. Deb: 7/20/63

YEAR	TM/L	G	AB	R	H	2B	3B	HR	RBI	BB	SO	AVG	OBP	SLG	PRO+	BR	/A	RC	SB	CS	SBR	FR	POS	TPR
1963	NY-N	20	42	4	10	0	1	0	3	5	10	.238	.319	.286	74	-1	-1	4	3	2	-0	-1	O/1	-0.2
1964	NY-N	46	94	14	21	6	1	0	3	1	29	.223	.247	.309	57	-6	-5	7	6	2	1	-0	1O	-0.5
1965	LA-N	10	6	0	0	0	0	0	1	0	3	.000	.000	.000	-99	-2	-2	0	0	0	0	-1	/O	-0.2
Total	3	76	142	18	31	6	2	0	7	6	42	.218	.260	.289	56	-8	-8	11	9	4	0	-2	/O1	-0.9

■ DICK SMITH
Smith, Richard Harrison b: 7/21/27, Blandburg, Pa. BR/TR, 5'8", 160 lbs. Deb: 9/14/51

YEAR	TM/L	G	AB	R	H	2B	3B	HR	RBI	BB	SO	AVG	OBP	SLG	PRO+	BR	/A	RC	SB	CS	SBR	FR	POS	TPR
1951	Pit-N	12	46	2	8	0	0	0	4	8	8	.174	.296	.174	29	-4	-4	3	0	2	-1	2	3	-0.2
1952	Pit-N	29	66	8	7	1	0	0	5	9	3	.106	.213	.121	-5	-9	-10	2	0	0	0	5	3/2S	-0.3
1953	Pit-N	13	43	4	7	0	1	0	2	6	6	.163	.265	.209	26	-5	-5	2	0	1	-1	5	S	0.1
1954	Pit-N	12	31	2	3	1	1	0	0	6	5	.097	.243	.194	16	-4	-4	2	0	0	0	2	/3	-0.1
1955	Pit-N	4	0	1	0	0	0	0	0	1	0	—	1.000	—	198	0	0	0	0	0	0	0	/S	0.0
Total	5	70	186	17	25	2	2	0	11	30	22	.134	.255	.167	15	-22	-22	9	0	3	-2	14	/3S2	-0.5

■ DICK SMITH
Smith, Richard Kelly b: 8/25/44, Lincolnton, N.C. BR/TR, 6'5", 200 lbs. Deb: 8/20/69

YEAR	TM/L	G	AB	R	H	2B	3B	HR	RBI	BB	SO	AVG	OBP	SLG	PRO+	BR	/A	RC	SB	CS	SBR	FR	POS	TPR
1969	Was-A	21	28	2	3	0	0	0		4	7	.107	.242	.107	1	-4	-3	1	0	0	0	-0	/O	-0.3

■ RED SMITH
Smith, Richard Paul b: 5/18/04, Brokaw, Wis. d: 3/8/78, Toledo, Ohio BR/TR, 5'10", 185 lbs. Deb: 5/31/27 C

YEAR	TM/L	G	AB	R	H	2B	3B	HR	RBI	BB	SO	AVG	OBP	SLG	PRO+	BR	/A	RC	SB	CS	SBR	FR	POS	TPR
1927	NY-N	1	0	0	0	0	0	0	0	0	0	—	—	—	—	0	0	0	0			0	/C	0.0

■ BOB SMITH
Smith, Robert Eldridge b: 4/22/1895, Rogersville, Tenn. d: 7/19/87, Waycross, Ga. BR/TR, 5'10", 175 lbs. Deb: 4/19/23

YEAR	TM/L	G	AB	R	H	2B	3B	HR	RBI	BB	SO	AVG	OBP	SLG	PRO+	BR	/A	RC	SB	CS	SBR	FR	POS	TPR
1923	Bos-N	115	375	30	94	16	3	0	40	17	35	.251	.285	.309	59	-24	-22	32	4	9	-4	14	*S/2	-0.2
1924	Bos-N	106	347	32	79	12	3	2	38	15	26	.228	.260	.297	51	-25	-24	27	5	2	0	8	S3	-0.6
1925	Bos-N	58	174	17	49	9	4	0	23	5	6	.282	.302	.339	80	-7	-5	19	2	2	-1	3	S2P/O	0.1
1926	Bos-N	40	84	10	25	6	2	0	13	2	4	.298	.314	.417	105	-1	0	10	0			3	P	0.0
1927	Bos-N	54	109	10	27	3	1	1	10	2	4	.248	.261	.321	60	-7	-6	9	0			2	P	0.0
1928	Bos-N	39	92	11	23	2	0	1	8	1	6	.250	.258	.304	49	-7	-7	7	2			3	P	0.0
1929	Bos-N	39	99	12	17	4	2	1	8	2	8	.172	.188	.283	16	-14	-13	5	1			4	P/S	0.0
1930	Bos-N	39	81	7	19	2	0	0	4	0	5	.235	.235	.259	20	-10	-10	5	0			1	P	0.0
1931	Chi-N	36	87	7	19	2	0	0	4	5	2	.218	.261	.241	35	-8	-8	6	0			1	P	0.0
1932	*Chi-N	36	42	5	10	4	1	0	4	0	2	.238	.238	.381	64	-2	-2	4	1			3	P/2	0.0
1933	Cin-N	23	25	2	5	1	0	0	1	1	0	.200	.231	.240	35	-2	-2	1	1			-1	P/S	0.0
	Bos-N	14	20	1	4	0	1	0	2	0	1	.200	.200	.300	45	-2	-1	1	0			1	P	0.0
	Yr	37	45	3	9	1	1	0	3	1	1	.200	.217	.267	39	-4	-3	3	1			0		0.0
1934	Bos-N	42	36	5	9	1	0	0	3	0	1	.250	.250	.278	44	-3	-3	3	0			1	P	0.0
1935	Bos-N	47	63	3	17	0	0	0	4	1	5	.270	.281	.270	53	-4	-4	4	0			-1	P	0.0
1936	Bos-N	35	45	1	10	2	0	0	4	0	4	.222	.222	.267	33	-4	-4	3	0			1	P	0.0
1937	Bos-N	19	10	1	2	0	0	0	0	1	1	.200	.273	.200	33	-1	-1	1	0			-1	P	0.0
Total	15	742	1689	154	409	64	17	5	166	52	110	.242	.265	.309	53	-122	-111	136	16	13		44	PS/230	-0.7

■ JOE SMITH
Smith, Salvatore (b: Salvatore Persico) b: 12/29/1893, New York, N.Y. d: 1/12/74, Yonkers, N.Y. BR/TR, 5'7", 170 lbs. Deb: 7/07/13

YEAR	TM/L	G	AB	R	H	2B	3B	HR	RBI	BB	SO	AVG	OBP	SLG	PRO+	BR	/A	RC	SB	CS	SBR	FR	POS	TPR
1913	NY-A	14	32	1	5	0	0	0	2	1	14	.156	.182	.156	-1	-4	-4	1	1			1	C	-0.2

■ SKYROCKET SMITH
Smith, Samuel J. b: 3/19/1868, St.Louis, Mo. d: 4/26/16, St.Louis, Mo. BR, Deb: 4/18/1888

YEAR	TM/L	G	AB	R	H	2B	3B	HR	RBI	BB	SO	AVG	OBP	SLG	PRO+	BR	/A	RC	SB	CS	SBR	FR	POS	TPR
1888	Lou-a	58	206	27	49	9	4	1	31	24		.238	.349	.335	126	7	7	26	5			0	1	0.3

■ SYD SMITH
Smith, Sydney E. b: 8/31/1883, Smithville, S.C. d: 6/5/61, Orangeburg, S.C. BR/TR, 5'10", 190 lbs. Deb: 4/14/08

YEAR	TM/L	G	AB	R	H	2B	3B	HR	RBI	BB	SO	AVG	OBP	SLG	PRO+	BR	/A	RC	SB	CS	SBR	FR	POS	TPR
1908	Phi-A	46	128	8	26	8	0	1	10	4		.203	.227	.289	65	-5	-5	8	0			-1	C/1O	-0.3
	StL-A	27	76	6	14	4	0	0	5	4		.184	.225	.237	51	-4	-4	4	2			9	C	0.8
	Yr	73	204	14	40	12	0	1	15	8		.196	.226	.270	60	-9	-9	12	2			8		0.5
1910	Cle-A	9	27	1	9	1	0	0	3	3		.333	.400	.370	140	1	1	4	0			0	/C	0.3
1911	Cle-A	58	154	8	46	8	1	1	21	11		.299	.353	.383	104	1	1	21	0			9	C/13	1.5
1914	Pit-N	5	11	1	3	0	0	0	1	0	1	.273	.273	.273	65	-1	-0	1	0			0	/C	0.0
1915	Pit-N	1	1	0	0	0	0	0	0	0	0	.000	.000	.000	-99	-0	-0	0	0			0	H	0.0
Total	5	146	397	24	98	21	1	2	40	22	1	.247	.290	.320	84	-7	-8	38	2			17	C/13O	2.3

■ TOM SMITH
Smith, Thomas N. b: 1851, Guelph, Ontario, Canada d: 3/28/1889, Detroit, Mich. Deb: 9/15/1875

YEAR	TM/L	G	AB	R	H	2B	3B	HR	RBI	BB	SO	AVG	OBP	SLG	PRO+	BR	/A	RC	SB	CS	SBR	FR	POS	TPR
1875	Atl-n	3	12	0	1	0	0	0		0		.083	.083	.083	-48	-2	-1	0					/2	0.0
1882	Phi-a	20	65	10	6	0	0	0			12	.092	.234	.092	12	-5	-7	1				2	3/SO2	-0.3

■ TOMMY SMITH
Smith, Tommy Alexander b: 8/1/48, Albemarle, N.C. BL/TR, 6'4", 210 lbs. Deb: 9/06/73

YEAR	TM/L	G	AB	R	H	2B	3B	HR	RBI	BB	SO	AVG	OBP	SLG	PRO+	BR	/A	RC	SB	CS	SBR	FR	POS	TPR
1973	Cle-A	14	41	6	10	2	0	2	3	1	2	.244	.262	.439	93	-1	-1	4	1	0	0	1	O	0.0
1974	Cle-A	23	31	4	3	1	0	0	1	0	7	.097	.176	.129	-11	-4	-4	1	0	0	0	3	O/D	-0.1
1975	Cle-A	8	8	0	1	0	0	0	2	0	1	.125	.125	.125	-29	-1	-1	0	0	0	0	1	/OD	0.0
1976	Cle-A	55	164	17	42	3	1	2	12	8	8	.256	.291	.323	80	-4	-4	16	5	8	0	2	O/D	-0.2
1977	Sea-A	21	27	1	7	1	1	0	4	0	6	.259	.259	.370	70	-1	-1	2	0	1	-1	2	O	0.0

YEAR	TM/L	G	AB	R	H	2B	3B	HR	RBI	BB	SO	AVG	OBP	SLG	PRO+	BR	/A	RC	SB	CS	SBR	FR	POS	TPR
Total	5	121	271	28	63	7	2	4	21	11	24	.232	.265	.317	68	-12	-12	23	9	1	2	6	/OD	-0.3

■ VINNIE SMITH   Smith, Vincent Ambrose   b: 12/7/15, Richmond, Va.   d: 12/14/79, Virginia Beach, Va   BR/TR, 6'1", 176 lbs.   Deb: 9/10/41   U

YEAR	TM/L	G	AB	R	H	2B	3B	HR	RBI	BB	SO	AVG	OBP	SLG	PRO+	BR	/A	RC	SB	CS	SBR	FR	POS	TPR
1941	Pit-N	9	33	3	10	1	0	0	5	1	5	.303	.324	.333	86	-1	-1	3	0			-2	/C	0.0
1946	Pit-N	7	21	2	4	0	0	0	0	1	5	.190	.227	.190	19	-2	-2	1	0			1	/C	-0.1
Total	2	16	54	5	14	1	0	0	5	2	10	.259	.286	.278	59	-3	-3	3	0			-1	/C	-0.1

■ WALLY SMITH   Smith, Wallace H.   b: 3/13/1889, Philadelphia, Pa.   d: 6/10/30, Florence, Ariz.   BR/TR, 5'11.5", 180 lbs.   Deb: 4/17/11

YEAR	TM/L	G	AB	R	H	2B	3B	HR	RBI	BB	SO	AVG	OBP	SLG	PRO+	BR	/A	RC	SB	CS	SBR	FR	POS	TPR
1911	StL-N	81	194	23	42	6	5	2	19	21	33	.216	.303	.330	79	-6	-6	21	5			2	3S/2O	-0.1
1912	StL-N	75	219	22	56	5	5	0	26	29	27	.256	.351	.324	87	-4	-3	26	4			-1	3S/1	-0.1
1914	Was-A	45	97	11	19	4	1	0	8	3	12	.196	.235	.258	47	-6	-7	6	3	4	-2	-3	2/1S30	-1.1
Total	3	201	510	56	117	15	11	2	53	53	72	.229	.312	.314	77	-16	-15	53	12	4		-3	/3S210	-1.3

■ WIB SMITH   Smith, Wilbur Floyd   b: 8/30/1886, Evart, Mich.   d: 11/18/59, Fargo, N.D.   BL/TR, 5'10.5", 165 lbs.   Deb: 5/31/09

YEAR	TM/L	G	AB	R	H	2B	3B	HR	RBI	BB	SO	AVG	OBP	SLG	PRO+	BR	/A	RC	SB	CS	SBR	FR	POS	TPR
1909	StL-A	17	42	3	8	0	0	0	2		0	.190	.190	.190	22	-4	-4	2	0			-8	C/1	-1.2

■ RED SMITH   Smith, Willard Jehu   b: 4/11/1892, Logansport, Ind.   d: 7/17/72, Noblesville, Ind.   BR/TR, 5'8", 165 lbs.   Deb: 9/17/17

YEAR	TM/L	G	AB	R	H	2B	3B	HR	RBI	BB	SO	AVG	OBP	SLG	PRO+	BR	/A	RC	SB	CS	SBR	FR	POS	TPR
1917	Pit-N	11	21	1	3	1	0	0	2	3	4	.143	.250	.190	35	-2	-2	1	1			2	/C	0.0
1918	Pit-N	15	24	1	4	1	0	0	3	3	0	.167	.259	.208	42	-2	-2	1	0			-1	C	-0.1
Total	2	26	45	2	7	2	0	0	5	6	4	.156	.255	.200	38	-3	-3	2	1			1	/C	-0.1

■ BILL SMITH   Smith, William E.   b: E.Liverpool, Ohio   151 lbs.   Deb: 9/17/1884

YEAR	TM/L	G	AB	R	H	2B	3B	HR	RBI	BB	SO	AVG	OBP	SLG	PRO+	BR	/A	RC	SB	CS	SBR	FR	POS	TPR
1884	Cle-N	1	3	0	0	0	0	0	0	0	2	.000	.000	.000	-97	-1	-1	0				-0	/O	0.0

■ BILL SMITH   Smith, William J.   b: Baltimore, Md.   d: 8/9/1886,   Deb: 4/14/1873   M

YEAR	TM/L	G	AB	R	H	2B	3B	HR	RBI	BB	SO	AVG	OBP	SLG	PRO+	BR	/A	RC	SB	CS	SBR	FR	POS	TPR
1873	Mar-n	5	19	2	2	0	0	0	0			.105	.105	.105	-49	-3	-2	0					/OC	-0.1

■ WILLIE SMITH   Smith, Willie   b: 2/11/39, Anniston, Ala.   BL/TL, 6', 182 lbs.   Deb: 6/18/63

YEAR	TM/L	G	AB	R	H	2B	3B	HR	RBI	BB	SO	AVG	OBP	SLG	PRO+	BR	/A	RC	SB	CS	SBR	FR	POS	TPR
1963	Det-A	17	8	2	1	0	0	0	0	0	1	.125	.125	.125	-29	-1	-1	0	0	0	0	0	P	0.0
1964	LA-A	118	359	46	108	14	6	11	51	8	39	.301	.320	.465	128	6	10	49	7	5	-1	-6	OP	0.1
1965	Cal-A	136	459	52	120	14	9	14	57	32	60	.261	.311	.423	109	3	4	58	9	8	-2	-3	*O/1	-0.5
1966	Cal-A	90	195	18	36	3	2	1	20	12	37	.185	.243	.236	39	-15	-15	12	1	0	0	-2	O	-2.0
1967	Cle-A	21	32	0	7	2	0	0	2	1	10	.219	.242	.281	54	-2	-2	1	0	2	-1	-1	/O1	-0.4
1968	Cle-A	33	42	1	6	0	0	0	3	1	14	.143	.217	.190	25	-4	-4	2	0	0	0	-0	/1PO	-0.4
	Chi-N	55	142	13	39	8	2	5	25	12	33	.275	.335	.465	129	6	5	23	0	0	0	-6	O/1P	-0.4
1969	Chi-N	103	195	21	48	9	1	9	25	25	49	.246	.332	.441	102	4	0	29	1	0	0	-6	O1	-0.8
1970	Chi-N	87	167	15	36	9	1	5	24	11	32	.216	.268	.371	62	-8	-10	17	2	1	0	-5	1/O	-1.8
1971	Cin-N	31	55	3	9	2	0	1	9	3	9	.164	.207	.255	31	-5	-5	2	0	0	0	1	1	-0.4
Total	9	691	1654	171	410	63	21	46	211	107	284	.248	.297	.395	94	-17	-18	194	20	16	-4	-27	O/1P	-6.4

■ HOMER SMOOT   Smoot, Homer Vernon "Doc"   b: 3/26/1878, Galestown, Md.   d: 3/25/28, Salisbury, Md.   BL/TR, 5'10", 180 lbs.   Deb: 4/17/02

YEAR	TM/L	G	AB	R	H	2B	3B	HR	RBI	BB	SO	AVG	OBP	SLG	PRO+	BR	/A	RC	SB	CS	SBR	FR	POS	TPR
1902	StL-N	129	518	58	161	19	4	3	48		23	.311	.351	.380	133	16	18	80	20			-0	*O	0.9
1903	StL-N	129	500	67	148	22	8	4	49		32	.296	.338	.396	115	6	8	77	17			-6	*O	-0.4
1904	StL-N	137	520	58	146	23	6	3	66		37	.281	.329	.365	122	9	12	73	23			2	*O	1.0
1905	StL-N	139	534	73	166	21	16	4	58		33	.311	.351	.433	140	21	23	92	21			1	*O	1.5
1906	StL-N	86	343	41	85	9	10	0	31		11	.248	.271	.332	94	-5	-4	34	3			2	O	-0.4
	Cin-N	60	220	11	57	8	1	1	17		13	.259	.300	.318	91	-2	-3	22	0			1	O	-0.3
	Yr	146	563	52	142	17	11	1	48		24	.252	.283	.327	92	-7	-7	55	3			2		-0.7
Total	5	680	2635	308	763	102	45	15	269		149	.290	.330	.380	120	45	55	377	84			-2	O	2.3

■ HENRY SMOYER   Smoyer, Henry Neitz "Hennie" (b: Henry Neitz Smowery)   b: 4/24/1890, Fredricksburg, Pa.   d: 2/28/58, Dubois, Pa.   BR/TR, 5'6",   Deb: 8/14/12

YEAR	TM/L	G	AB	R	H	2B	3B	HR	RBI	BB	SO	AVG	OBP	SLG	PRO+	BR	/A	RC	SB	CS	SBR	FR	POS	TPR
1912	StL-A	6	14	1	3	0	0	0	0		2	.214	.313	.214	53	-1	-1	1	0			-0	/S3	0.0

■ FRANK SMYKAL   Smykal, Frank John (b: Frank John Smejkal)   b: 10/13/1889, Chicago, Ill.   d: 8/11/50, Chicago, Ill.   BR/TR, 5'7", 150 lbs.   Deb: 8/30/16

YEAR	TM/L	G	AB	R	H	2B	3B	HR	RBI	BB	SO	AVG	OBP	SLG	PRO+	BR	/A	RC	SB	CS	SBR	FR	POS	TPR
1916	Pit-N	6	10	1	3	0	0	0	0	2	3	.300	.500	.300	147	1	1	2	1			-1	/S3	0.1

■ CLANCY SMYRES   Smyres, Clarence Melvin   b: 5/24/22, Culver City, Cal.   BB/TR, 5'11.5", 175 lbs.   Deb: 4/18/44

YEAR	TM/L	G	AB	R	H	2B	3B	HR	RBI	BB	SO	AVG	OBP	SLG	PRO+	BR	/A	RC	SB	CS	SBR	FR	POS	TPR
1944	Bro-N	5	2	1	0	0	0	0	0	0	0	.000	.000	.000	-99	-1	-1	0	0			0	H	0.0

■ RED SMYTH   Smyth, James Daniel   b: 1/30/1893, Holly Springs, Miss.   d: 4/14/58, Inglewood, Cal.   BL/TR, 5'9", 152 lbs.   Deb: 8/11/15

YEAR	TM/L	G	AB	R	H	2B	3B	HR	RBI	BB	SO	AVG	OBP	SLG	PRO+	BR	/A	RC	SB	CS	SBR	FR	POS	TPR
1915	Bro-N	19	22	3	3	0	0	0	3	4	2	.136	.269	.182	37	-2	-2	1	1	2	-1	1	/O	-0.1
1916	Bro-N	2	5	0	0	0	0	0	0	0	3	.000	.000	.000	-97	-1	-1	0	0			-0	/2	-0.1
1917	Bro-N	29	24	5	3	0	0	0	1	4	6	.125	.250	.125	16	-2	-2	1	0			0	/3O	-0.2
	StL-N	38	72	5	15	0	2	0	4	4	9	.208	.269	.264	66	-3	-3	5	3			-3	O	-0.6
	Yr	67	96	10	18	0	2	0	5	8	15	.188	.264	.229	52	-5	-5	6	3			-3		-0.8
1918	StL-N	40	113	19	24	1	2	0	4	16	11	.212	.315	.257	78	-3	-2	10	3			-2	O2	-0.4
Total	4	128	236	32	45	2	4	0	12	28	31	.191	.285	.233	60	-11	-10	17	7	2		-3	/O23	-1.4

■ JOHN SNEED   Sneed, Jonathon L.   b: Columbus, Ohio   d: 1/4/1899, Memphis, Tenn.   Deb: 5/01/1884

YEAR	TM/L	G	AB	R	H	2B	3B	HR	RBI	BB	SO	AVG	OBP	SLG	PRO+	BR	/A	RC	SB	CS	SBR	FR	POS	TPR
1884	Ind-a	27	102	14	22	4	0	1	6			.216	.259	.284	82	-2	-2	8				-0	O	-0.1
1890	Tol-a	9	30	3	6	0	0	0	8			.200	.368	.200	69	-1	-1	4	5			2	/O	0.1
	Col-a	128	484	114	141	13	15	2	63			.291	.383	.393	141	21	26	90	39			-8	*O/S	1.1
	Yr	137	514	117	147	13	15	2	71			.286	.382	.381	136	20	26	94	44			-5		1.2
1891	Col-a	99	366	66	94	9	6	1	61	55	29	.257	.366	.322	106	3	6	53	24			-4	*O	-0.1
Total	3	263	982	197	263	26	21	4	61	132	29	.268	.364	.349	120	21	30	155	68			-10	O/S	1.0

■ CHARLIE SNELL   Snell, Charles Anthony (b: Charles Anthony Schnell)   b: 11/29/1893, Hampstead, Md.   d: 4/4/88, Reading, Pa.   BR/TR, 5'11", 160 lbs.   Deb: 7/19/12

YEAR	TM/L	G	AB	R	H	2B	3B	HR	RBI	BB	SO	AVG	OBP	SLG	PRO+	BR	/A	RC	SB	CS	SBR	FR	POS	TPR
1912	StL-A	8	19	0	4	1	0	0		3		.211	.348	.263	78	-0	-0	2	0			2	/C	0.2

■ WALLY SNELL   Snell, Walter Henry "Doc"   b: 5/19/1889, W.Bridgewater, Mass.   d: 7/23/80, Providence, R.I.   BR/TR, 5'10", 170 lbs.   Deb: 8/01/13

YEAR	TM/L	G	AB	R	H	2B	3B	HR	RBI	BB	SO	AVG	OBP	SLG	PRO+	BR	/A	RC	SB	CS	SBR	FR	POS	TPR
1913	Bos-A	5	8	0	3	0	0	0	0	0		.375	.375	.375	117	0	1	1	1			0	/C	0.1

■ DUKE SNIDER   Snider, Edwin Donald "The Silver Fox"   b: 9/19/26, Los Angeles, Cal.   BL/TR, 6', 179 lbs.   Deb: 4/17/47   H

YEAR	TM/L	G	AB	R	H	2B	3B	HR	RBI	BB	SO	AVG	OBP	SLG	PRO+	BR	/A	RC	SB	CS	SBR	FR	POS	TPR
1947	Bro-N	40	83	6	20	3	1	0	5	3	24	.241	.276	.301	51	-6	-6	7	2			1	O	-0.5
1948	Bro-N	53	160	22	39	6	6	5	21	12	27	.244	.297	.450	96	-1	-2	21	4			2	O	-0.2
1949	*Bro-N	146	552	100	161	28	7	23	92	56	92	.292	.361	.493	122	20	17	100	12			-2	*O	0.7
1950	Bro-N	152	620	109	199	31	10	31	107	58	79	.321	.379	.553	139	36	34	131	16			4	*O	3.2
1951	Bro-N	150	606	96	168	26	6	29	101	62	97	.277	.344	.483	118	15	14	96	14	10	-2	-4	*O	0.3
1952	*Bro-N	144	534	80	162	25	7	21	92	55	77	.303	.368	.494	136	26	25	96	7	4	-0	-0	*O	2.1
1953	Bro-N	153	590	132	198	38	4	42	126	82	90	.336	.419	.627	165	59	57	161	16	7	1	-6	*O	4.3
1954	Bro-N	149	584	120	199	39	10	40	130	84	96	.341	.427	.647	170	65	62	161	6	6	-3	-9	*O	4.5
1955	*Bro-N	148	538	126	166	34	6	42	136	104	87	.309	.421	.628	169	59	57	145	9	7	-2	-4	*O	4.7
1956	*Bro-N	151	542	112	158	33	2	43	101	99	101	.292	.402	.598	152	50	45	128	3	3	-1	-4	*O	3.4
1957	Bro-N	139	508	91	139	25	7	40	92	77	104	.274	.368	.587	139	37	30	106	3	4	-2	-12	*O	1.3
1958	LA-N	106	327	45	102	12	3	15	58	32	49	.312	.375	.505	126	14	13	59	2	2	-1	-18	O	-0.8
1959	*LA-N	126	370	59	114	11	2	23	88	58	71	.308	.402	.535	137	26	22	78	1	5	-3	-9	*O	0.9

YEAR	TM/L	G	AB	R	H	2B	3B	HR	RBI	BB	SO	AVG	OBP	SLG	PRO+	BR	/A	RC	SB	CS	SBR	FR	POS	TPR
1960	LA-N	101	235	38	57	13	5	14	36	46	54	.243	.369	.519	131	13	11	46	1	0	0	-3	O	0.6
1961	LA-N	85	233	35	69	8	3	16	56	29	43	.296	.376	.562	133	15	12	48	1	1	-0	3	O	1.1
1962	LA-N	80	158	28	44	11	3	5	30	36	32	.278	.418	.481	150	11	12	34	2	0	1	-2	O	0.8
1963	NY-N	129	354	44	86	8	3	14	45	56	74	.243	.348	.401	113	8	7	53	0	1	-1	-11	*O	-1.0
1964	SF-N	91	167	16	35	7	0	4	17	22	40	.210	.302	.323	74	-5	-5	17	0	0	0	-3	O	-1.0
Total	18	2143	7161	1259	2116	358	85	407	1333	971	1237	.295	.381	.540	138	441	405	1487	99	50		-78	*O	24.4

■ VAN SNIDER Snider, Van Voorhees b: 8/11/63, Birmingham, Ala. BL/TR, 6'3", 185 lbs. Deb: 9/02/88

YEAR	TM/L	G	AB	R	H	2B	3B	HR	RBI	BB	SO	AVG	OBP	SLG	PRO+	BR	/A	RC	SB	CS	SBR	FR	POS	TPR
1988	Cin-N	11	28	4	6	1	0	1	6	0	13	.214	.214	.357	59	-2	-2	2	0	1	-1	0	/O	-0.2
1989	Cin-N	8	7	1	1	0	0	0	0	0	5	.143	.143	.143	-17	-1	-1	0	0	0	0	1	/O	0.0
Total	2	19	35	5	7	1	0	1	6	0	18	.200	.200	.314	44	-3	-3	2	0	1	-1	1	/O	-0.2

■ ROXY SNIPES Snipes, Wyatt Eure "Rock" b: 10/28/1896, Marion, S.C. d: 5/1/41, Fayetteville, N.C. BL/TR, 6', 185 lbs. Deb: 7/15/23

YEAR	TM/L	G	AB	R	H	2B	3B	HR	RBI	BB	SO	AVG	OBP	SLG	PRO+	BR	/A	RC	SB	CS	SBR	FR	POS	TPR
1923	Chi-A	1	1	0	0	0	0	0	0	0	0	.000	.000	.000	-99	-0	-0	0	0	0	0	0	H	0.0

■ CHAPPIE SNODGRASS Snodgrass, Amzie Beal b: 3/18/1870, Springfield, Ohio d: 9/9/51, New York, N.Y. BR/TR, 5'10", 165 lbs. Deb: 5/15/01

YEAR	TM/L	G	AB	R	H	2B	3B	HR	RBI	BB	SO	AVG	OBP	SLG	PRO+	BR	/A	RC	SB	CS	SBR	FR	POS	TPR
1901	Bal-A	3	10	0	1	0	0	0				.100	.100	.100	-42	-2	-2	0				-1	/O	-0.2

■ FRED SNODGRASS Snodgrass, Frederick Carlisle "Snow" b: 10/19/1887, Ventura, Cal. d: 4/5/74, Ventura, Cal. BR/TR, 5'11.5", 175 lbs. Deb: 6/04/08

YEAR	TM/L	G	AB	R	H	2B	3B	HR	RBI	BB	SO	AVG	OBP	SLG	PRO+	BR	/A	RC	SB	CS	SBR	FR	POS	TPR
1908	NY-N	6	4	2	1	0	0	0				.250	.250	.250	59	-0	-0	1				1	/C	0.1
1909	NY-N	28	70	10	21	5	0	1	6	7		.300	.387	.414	146	4	4	15	10			-0	O/C1	0.3
1910	NY-N	123	396	69	127	22	8	2	44	71	52	.321	.440	.432	154	32	32	90	33			-2	*O/1C3	2.7
1911	*NY-N	151	534	83	157	27	10	1	77	72	59	.294	.393	.388	115	16	14	102	51			5	O/13	1.4
1912	*NY-N	146	535	91	144	24	9	3	69	70	65	.269	.362	.364	96	1	-1	87	43			-2	*O/1/2	-0.6
1913	*NY-N	141	457	65	133	21	6	3	49	53	44	.291	.373	.383	115	11	11	72	27			1	O/12	1.0
1914	NY-N	113	392	54	103	20	4	0	44	37	43	.263	.336	.334	103	0	2	50	25			3	O1/23	0.2
1915	NY-N	80	252	36	49	9	0	0	20	35	33	.194	.307	.230	68	-9	-8	19	11	12	-4	-0	O	-1.6
	Bos-N	23	79	10	22	2	0	0	9	7	9	.278	.352	.304	104	0	1	8	0	4	-2	-0	O/1	-0.2
	Yr	103	331	46	71	11	0	0	29	42	42	.215	.318	.248	76	-9	-7	27	11	16	-6	-1		-1.8
1916	Bos-N	112	382	33	95	13	5	1	32	34	54	.249	.318	.317	100	-1	0	45	14			9	*O	0.7
Total	9	923	3101	453	852	143	42	11	351	386	359	.275	.367	.359	110	54	54	488	215	16		14	O/1C23	4.1

■ CHARLIE SNOW Snow, Charles M. b: 8/3/1849, Lowell, Mass. Deb: 10/01/1874

YEAR	TM/L	G	AB	R	H	2B	3B	HR	RBI	BB	SO	AVG	OBP	SLG	PRO+	BR	/A	RC	SB	CS	SBR	FR	POS	TPR
1874	Atl-n	1	2	0	1	0	0	0		0		.500	.500	.500	248	0	0	1					/O	0.0

■ BERNIE SNYDER Snyder, Bernard Austin b: 8/25/13, Philadelphia, Pa. BR/TR, 6', 165 lbs. Deb: 9/15/35

YEAR	TM/L	G	AB	R	H	2B	3B	HR	RBI	BB	SO	AVG	OBP	SLG	PRO+	BR	/A	RC	SB	CS	SBR	FR	POS	TPR
1935	Phi-A	10	32	5	11	1	0	0	3	1	2	.344	.364	.375	92	-0	-0	4	0	0	0	-2	/2S	-0.1

■ CHARLES SNYDER Snyder, Charles b: Camden, N.J. d: 3/3/01, Philadelphia, Pa. TR, Deb: 9/19/1890 M

YEAR	TM/L	G	AB	R	H	2B	3B	HR	RBI	BB	SO	AVG	OBP	SLG	PRO+	BR	/A	RC	SB	CS	SBR	FR	POS	TPR
1890	Phi-a	9	33	5	9	1	0	0			2	.273	.314	.303	87	-1	-1	3	0			-3	/OC	-0.2

■ POP SNYDER Snyder, Charles N. b: 10/6/1854, Washington, D.C. d: 10/29/24, Washington, D.C. BR/TR, 5'11.5", 184 lbs. Deb: 6/16/1873 MU

YEAR	TM/L	G	AB	R	H	2B	3B	HR	RBI	BB	SO	AVG	OBP	SLG	PRO+	BR	/A	RC	SB	CS	SBR	FR	POS	TPR
1873	Was-n	28	108	16	22	2	0	0			2	.204	.218	.222	31	-9	-8	5					C/O	-0.5
1874	Bal-n	39	152	24	33	4	2	1			2	.217	.227	.289	64	-6	-6	10					C	-0.2
1875	Phi-n	66	263	37	64	7	2	1			4	.243	.255	.297	87	-2	-4	20					*C/O	-0.1
1876	Lou-N	56	224	21	44	4	1	1	9	2	7	.196	.204	.237	39	-12	-18	11	7				*C/O	-0.6
1877	Lou-N	61	248	23	64	7	2	2	28	3	14	.258	.267	.327	73	-4	-11	22	15				*C/OS	0.5
1878	Bos-N	60	226	21	48	5	0	0	14	1	19	.212	.216	.235	44	-12	-15	12	0				*C/O	-1.1
1879	Bos-N	81	329	42	78	16	3	2	35	5	31	.237	.249	.322	85	-5	-6	27	20				*C/O	1.2
1881	Bos-N	62	219	14	50	8	0	0	16	3	23	.228	.239	.265	61	-10	-9	14	12				*C/OS2	0.2
1882	Cin-a	72	309	49	90	12	2	1			9	.291	.311	.353	116	7	4	35	13				*C/1OM	1.6
1883	Cin-a	58	250	38	64	14	6	0			8	.256	.279	.360	98	1	-1	26	7				C/SM	0.9
1884	Cin-a	67	268	32	69	9	9	0			7	.257	.276	.358	103	2	0	27	20				C/1OM	2.2
1885	Cin-a	39	152	13	36	4	3	1			6	.237	.276	.322	87	-2	-2	14	-1				C/1	0.2
1886	Cin-a	60	220	33	41	8	3	0			13	.186	.242	.250	54	-11	-12	16	11			-8	C1/O	-1.6
1887	Cle-a	74	282	33	72	12	6	0			9	.255	.281	.340	76	-10	-9	29	5			18	C1	1.6
1888	Cle-a	64	237	22	51	7	3	0	14	6		.215	.238	.270	67	-9	-8	18	9			10	C/1O	0.6
1889	Cle-N	22	83	5	16	3	0	0	12	2	12	.193	.221	.229	27	-8	-8	5	4			2	C	-0.4
1890	Cle-P	13	48	5	9	1	0	0	12	1	9	.188	.220	.208	17	-6	-5	2	1			-0	C	-0.3
1891	Was-a	8	27	4	5	0	1	0	2	0	3	.185	.241	.259	47	-2	-2	2	0			0	/1COM	0.0
Total	3 n	133	523	77	119	13	4	2			8	.228	.239	.279	68	-18	-18	36	0				C/OD	-0.8
Total	15	797	3122	355	737	110	39	7	142	75	118	.236	.256	.303	74	-82	-101	260	30			115	C/1OS2	5.0

■ REDLEG SNYDER Snyder, Emanuel Sebastian (b: Emanuel Sebastian Schneider) b: 12/12/1854, Camden, N.J. d: 11/24/32, Camden, N.J. BR/TR, 5'10", 175 lbs. Deb: 4/25/1876

YEAR	TM/L	G	AB	R	H	2B	3B	HR	RBI	BB	SO	AVG	OBP	SLG	PRO+	BR	/A	RC	SB	CS	SBR	FR	POS	TPR
1876	Cin-N	55	205	10	31	3	1	0	12	1	19	.151	.155	.176	12	-19	-14	6				4	*O	-0.8
1884	Wil-U	17	52	4	10	0	0	0		1		.192	.208	.192	35	-3	-4	2	0			1	1/O	-0.2
Total	2	72	257	14	41	3	1	0	12	2	19	.160	.166	.179	17	-22	-18	8	0			5	/O1	-1.0

■ COONEY SNYDER Snyder, Frank C. b: Toronto, Ontario, Canada d: 3/9/17, Toronto, Ont., Can. Deb: 5/19/1898

YEAR	TM/L	G	AB	R	H	2B	3B	HR	RBI	BB	SO	AVG	OBP	SLG	PRO+	BR	/A	RC	SB	CS	SBR	FR	POS	TPR
1898	Lou-N	17	61	4	10	0	0	0	6	3		.164	.215	.164	11	-7	-7	2	0			-6	C	-1.0

■ FRANK SNYDER Snyder, Frank Elton "Pancho" b: 5/27/1893, San Antonio, Tex. d: 1/5/62, San Antonio, Tex. BR/TR, 6'2", 185 lbs. Deb: 8/25/12 C

YEAR	TM/L	G	AB	R	H	2B	3B	HR	RBI	BB	SO	AVG	OBP	SLG	PRO+	BR	/A	RC	SB	CS	SBR	FR	POS	TPR
1912	StL-N	11	18	2	2	0	0	0	2	0	7	.111	.200	.111	-14	-3	-3	1	1			0	C	-0.1
1913	StL-N	7	21	1	4	0	1	0	2	0	4	.190	.190	.286	35	-2	-2	1	0			2	/C	0.1
1914	StL-N	100	326	19	75	15	4	1	25	13	28	.230	.262	.310	71	-13	-13	27	1			4	C	-0.5
1915	StL-N	144	473	41	141	22	7	2	55	39	49	.298	.353	.387	124	13	13	65	3	6	-3	7	*C	2.8
1916	StL-N	132	406	23	105	12	4	0	39	18	31	.259	.290	.308	84	-8	-8	39	7			9	C1/S	0.3
1917	StL-N	115	313	18	74	9	2	1	33	27	43	.236	.301	.288	83	-7	-6	27	4			-0	C/2	0.0
1918	StL-N	39	112	10	28	7	1	0	10	6	13	.250	.288	.330	92	-2	-1	11	4			4	C/1	0.3
1919	StL-N	50	154	7	28	4	2	0	14	5	13	.182	.213	.234	36	-12	-11	8	2			4	C/1	-0.4
	NY-N	32	92	7	21	6	0	0	11	8	9	.228	.297	.293	79	-2	-2	8	1			-4	C	-0.4
	Yr	82	246	14	49	10	2	0	25	13	22	.199	.245	.256	53	-15	-14	16	3			0		-0.8
1920	NY-N	87	264	26	66	13	4	3	27	17	18	.250	.295	.364	89	-4	-4	29	2	2	-1	1	C	0.2
1921	*NY-N	108	309	36	99	13	2	8	45	27	24	.320	.382	.453	120	9	9	53	3	4	-2	4	*C	1.8
1922	*NY-N	104	318	36	109	21	5	5	51	23	25	.343	.387	.487	123	11	11	58	1	5	-3	-3	C	0.5
1923	*NY-N	120	402	37	103	13	6	5	63	24	29	.256	.298	.396	73	-17	-16	43	5	3	-0	2	*C	-0.8
1924	*NY-N	118	354	37	107	18	3	5	53	30	43	.302	.357	.412	109	3	4	53	3	0	1	-17	*C	-0.9
1925	NY-N	107	325	21	78	9	1	11	51	20	49	.240	.286	.375	70	-17	-15	35	0			2	C	-0.7
1926	NY-N	55	148	10	32	5	0	3	16	13	13	.216	.280	.365	73	-6	-6	15	0			-1	C	-0.8
1927	StL-N	63	194	7	50	5	0	1	30	9	18	.258	.291	.299	56	-11	-12	17	0			-1	C	-0.8
Total	16	1392	4229	331	1122	170	44	47	525	281	416	.265	.313	.360	90	-69	-63	489	37	20		11	*C/12S	1.0

■ JERRY SNYDER Snyder, Gerald George b: 7/21/29, Jenks, Okla. BR/TR, 6', 170 lbs. Deb: 5/08/52

YEAR	TM/L	G	AB	R	H	2B	3B	HR	RBI	BB	SO	AVG	OBP	SLG	PRO+	BR	/A	RC	SB	CS	SBR	FR	POS	TPR
1952	Was-A	36	57	5	9	2	0	0	2	5	8	.158	.226	.193	18	-6	-6	3	1	0	0	7	2/S	0.2
1953	Was-A	29	62	10	21	4	0	0	4	5	8	.339	.388	.403	117	1	1	9	1	1	-0	7	S/2	0.9

YEAR	TM/L	G	AB	R	H	2B	3B	HR	RBI	BB	SO	AVG	OBP	SLG	PRO+	BR	/A	RC	SB	CS	SBR	FR	POS	TPR
1954	Was-A	64	154	17	36	3	1	0	17	15	18	.234	.302	.266	60	-9	-8	13	3	0	1	9	S/2	0.6
1955	Was-A	46	107	7	24	5	0	0	5	6	6	.224	.265	.271	47	-8	-8	7	1	1	-0	1	2S	-0.2
1956	Was-A	43	148	14	40	3	1	2	14	10	9	.270	.321	.345	76	-5	-5	15	1	0	0	-4	S/2	-0.5
1957	Was-A	42	93	6	14	1	0	1	4	4	9	.151	.186	.194	4	-12	-12	3	0	1	-1	1	S2/3	-1.0
1958	Was-A	6	9	1	1	0	0	0	1	1	1	.111	.200	.111	-12	-1	-1	0	0	0	0	-1	/2S	-0.1
Total	7	266	630	60	145	18	2	3	47	46	59	.230	.284	.279	54	-42	-39	51	7	3	0	20	S/23	-0.1

■ JIM SNYDER
Snyder, James C. A. b: 9/15/1847, Brooklyn, N.Y. d: 12/1/22, Rockaway Beach, N.Y 5'7", 130 lbs. Deb: 5/07/1872

YEAR	TM/L	G	AB	R	H	2B	3B	HR	RBI	BB	SO	AVG	OBP	SLG	PRO+	BR	/A	RC	SB	CS	SBR	FR	POS	TPR
1872	Eck-n	26	106	16	27	2	3	0		0		.255	.255	.330	93	-3	1	9					S/OC	0.1

■ CORY SNYDER
Snyder, James Cory b: 11/11/62, Inglewood, Cal. BR/TR, 6'4", 175 lbs. Deb: 6/13/86

YEAR	TM/L	G	AB	R	H	2B	3B	HR	RBI	BB	SO	AVG	OBP	SLG	PRO+	BR	/A	RC	SB	CS	SBR	FR	POS	TPR
1986	Cle-A	103	416	58	113	21	1	24	69	16	123	.272	.299	.500	115	5	6	58	2	3	-1	-12	OS3/D	-0.6
1987	Cle-A	157	577	74	136	24	2	33	82	31	166	.236	.276	.456	89	-11	-12	74	5	1	1	0	*OS	-1.1
1988	Cle-A	142	511	71	139	24	3	26	75	42	101	.272	.329	.483	121	15	13	79	5	1	1	11	*O/D	2.3
1989	Cle-A	132	489	49	105	17	0	18	59	23	134	.215	.253	.360	70	-21	-22	41	6	5	-1	16	*O/SD	-0.7
1990	Cle-A	123	438	46	102	27	3	14	55	21	118	.233	.271	.404	85	-10	-11	44	1	4	-2	-3	*O/S	-1.6
Total	5	657	2431	298	595	113	9	115	340	133	642	.245	.286	.441	96	-22	-25	296	19	14	-3	13	O/S3D	-1.7

■ JIM SNYDER
Snyder, James Robert b: 8/15/32, Dearbon, Mich. BR/TR, 6'1", 185 lbs. Deb: 9/15/61 MC

YEAR	TM/L	G	AB	R	H	2B	3B	HR	RBI	BB	SO	AVG	OBP	SLG	PRO+	BR	/A	RC	SB	CS	SBR	FR	POS	TPR
1961	Min-A	3	5	0	0	0	0	0	0	0	1	.000	.000	.000	-95	-1	-1	0	0	0	0	0	/2	0.0
1962	Min-A	12	10	1	1	0	0	0	1	0	0	.100	.100	.100	-44	-2	-2	0	0	1	-1	-6	/21	-0.8
1964	Min-A	26	71	3	11	2	0	1	9	4	11	.155	.211	.225	21	-8	-8	3	0	0	0	-4	2	-0.9
Total	3	41	86	4	12	2	0	1	10	4	12	.140	.187	.198	6	-11	-11	3	0	1	-1	-10	/21	-1.7

■ JACK SNYDER
Snyder, John William b: 10/6/1886, Lincoln Township, P d: 12/13/81, Brownsville, Pa. BR/TR, 5'9", 168 lbs. Deb: 6/13/14

YEAR	TM/L	G	AB	R	H	2B	3B	HR	RBI	BB	SO	AVG	OBP	SLG	PRO+	BR	/A	RC	SB	CS	SBR	FR	POS	TPR
1914	Buf-F	1	0	0	0	0	0	0	0	1	0	—	1.000	—	197	0	0	0	0				0	/C	0.0
1917	Bro-N	7	11	1	3	0	0	0	1	0	2	.273	.273	.273	66	-0	-0	1	0				0	/C	0.0
Total	2	8	11	1	3	0	0	0	1	1	2	.273	.333	.273	84	-0	-0	1	0			0	/C	0.0

■ JOSH SNYDER
Snyder, Joshua M. b: 3/1844, Brooklyn, N.Y. d: 4/21/1881, Brooklyn, N.Y. Deb: 5/18/1872

YEAR	TM/L	G	AB	R	H	2B	3B	HR	RBI	BB	SO	AVG	OBP	SLG	PRO+	BR	/A	RC	SB	CS	SBR	FR	POS	TPR
1872	Eck-n	9	42	3	6	2	0	0		1		.143	.163	.190	10	-4	-3	1					/O	-0.1

■ RUSS SNYDER
Snyder, Russell Henry b: 6/22/34, Oak, Neb. BL/TR, 6'1", 190 lbs. Deb: 4/18/59

YEAR	TM/L	G	AB	R	H	2B	3B	HR	RBI	BB	SO	AVG	OBP	SLG	PRO+	BR	/A	RC	SB	CS	SBR	FR	POS	TPR
1959	KC-A	73	243	41	76	13	2	3	21	19	29	.313	.367	.420	113	5	5	38	6	2	1	5	O	0.7
1960	KC-A	125	304	45	79	10	5	4	26	20	28	.260	.308	.365	81	-8	-9	34	7	3	0	-8	O	-1.9
1961	Bal-A	115	312	46	91	13	5	1	13	20	32	.292	.334	.375	91	-5	-4	39	5	3	-0	-12	*O	-1.9
1962	Bal-A	139	416	47	127	19	4	9	40	17	46	.305	.336	.435	111	2	5	58	7	4	-0	0	*O	0.0
1963	Bal-A	148	429	51	110	21	2	7	36	40	48	.256	.323	.364	94	-4	-3	53	18	5	2	-3	*O	-0.8
1964	Bal-A	56	93	11	27	3	0	1	7	11	22	.290	.365	.355	102	1	1	12	0	2	-1	-3	O	-0.5
1965	Bal-A	132	345	49	93	11	2	1	29	27	38	.270	.324	.322	83	-7	-7	36	3	4	-2	-0	*O	-1.4
1966	*Bal-A	117	373	66	114	21	5	3	41	38	37	.306	.370	.413	127	12	13	57	2	1	0	6	*O	1.6
1967	Bal-A	108	275	40	65	8	2	4	23	32	48	.236	.318	.324	91	-3	-3	31	5	2	0	-1	O	-0.5
1968	Chi-A	38	82	2	11	2	0	1	5	4	16	.134	.174	.195	12	-9	-9	3	0	0	0	-4	O	-1.5
	Cle-A	68	217	30	61	8	2	2	23	25	21	.281	.355	.364	120	5	6	29	1	1	-0	1	O/1	0.5
	Yr	106	299	32	72	10	2	3	28	29	37	.241	.308	.318	90	-3	-3	30	1	1	-0	-2		-1.0
1969	Cle-A	122	266	26	66	10	0	2	24	25	33	.248	.313	.308	72	-9	-10	26	3	2	-0	-3	O	-1.6
1970	Mil-A	124	276	34	64	11	0	4	31	16	40	.232	.274	.315	62	-15	-15	23	1	3	-2	-25	*O	-4.7
Total	12	1365	3631	488	984	150	29	42	319	294	438	.271	.327	.363	94	-33	-31	441	58	32	-2	-46	*O/1	-12.0

■ CHIEF SOCKALEXIS
Sockalexis, Louis M. b: 10/24/1871, Old Town, Maine d: 12/24/13, Burlington, Maine BL/TR, 5'11", 185 lbs. Deb: 4/22/1897

YEAR	TM/L	G	AB	R	H	2B	3B	HR	RBI	BB	SO	AVG	OBP	SLG	PRO+	BR	/A	RC	SB	CS	SBR	FR	POS	TPR
1897	Cle-N	66	278	43	94	9	8	3	42	18		.338	.385	.460	119	10	7	57	16			1	O	0.2
1898	Cle-N	21	67	11	15	2	0	0	10	1		.224	.246	.254	46	-5	-5	4	0			2	O	-0.2
1899	Cle-N	7	22	0	6	1	0	0	3	1		.273	.304	.318	79	-1	-1	2	0			1	/O	0.0
Total	3	94	367	54	115	12	8	3	55	20		.313	.355	.414	105	4	2	63	16			4	/O	0.0

■ BILL SODD
Sodd, William b: 9/18/14, Ft.Worth, Tex. BR/TR, 6'2", 210 lbs. Deb: 9/27/37

YEAR	TM/L	G	AB	R	H	2B	3B	HR	RBI	BB	SO	AVG	OBP	SLG	PRO+	BR	/A	RC	SB	CS	SBR	FR	POS	TPR
1937	Cle-A	1	1	0	0	0	0	0	0	0	1	.000	.000	.000	-99	-0	-0	0	0	0	0	0	H	0.0

■ ERIC SODERHOLM
Soderholm, Eric Thane b: 9/24/48, Cortland, N.Y. BR/TR, 5'11", 187 lbs. Deb: 9/03/71

YEAR	TM/L	G	AB	R	H	2B	3B	HR	RBI	BB	SO	AVG	OBP	SLG	PRO+	BR	/A	RC	SB	CS	SBR	FR	POS	TPR
1971	Min-A	21	64	9	10	4	0	1	4	10	17	.156	.299	.266	59	-3	-3	6	0	1	-1	3	3	0.0
1972	Min-A	93	287	28	54	10	0	13	39	19	48	.188	.246	.359	75	-9	-10	24	3	3	-1	2	3	-0.7
1973	Min-A	35	111	22	33	7	2	1	9	21	16	.297	.414	.423	131	6	6	20	1	2	-0	3/S	0.4
1974	Min-A	141	464	63	128	18	3	10	51	48	68	.276	.350	.392	109	8	6	63	7	3	0	-6	*3/S	0.3
1975	Min-A	117	419	62	120	17	2	11	58	53	66	.286	.367	.415	118	12	11	62	3	5	-2	13	*3/D	2.3
1977	Chi-A	130	460	77	129	20	3	25	67	47	47	.280	.352	.500	129	18	18	77	2	4	-2	0	*3/D	1.3
1978	Chi-A	143	457	57	118	17	1	20	67	39	44	.258	.322	.431	109	5	4	61	2	2	-1	0	*3D/2	0.3
1979	Chi-A	56	210	31	53	8	2	6	34	19	19	.252	.314	.395	90	-3	-3	24	0	1	-1	15	3	1.2
	Tex-A	63	147	15	40	6	0	4	19	12	9	.272	.331	.395	96	-1	-1	19	0	0	0	1	3D/1	0.1
	Yr	119	357	46	93	14	2	10	53	31	28	.261	.321	.395	93	-4	-4	42	0	1	-1	16		1.3
1980	*NY-A	95	275	38	79	13	1	11	35	27	25	.287	.353	.462	123	8	8	43	0	0	0	-1	D3	0.7
Total	9	894	2894	402	764	120	14	102	383	295	359	.264	.337	.421	109	41	36	398	18	21	-7	27	3/D1S2	5.9

■ RICK SOFIELD
Sofield, Richard Michael b: 12/16/56, Cheyenne, Wyo. BL/TR, 6'1", 195 lbs. Deb: 4/06/79

YEAR	TM/L	G	AB	R	H	2B	3B	HR	RBI	BB	SO	AVG	OBP	SLG	PRO+	BR	/A	RC	SB	CS	SBR	FR	POS	TPR
1979	Min-A	35	93	8	28	5	0	0	12	12	27	.301	.381	.355	96	1	0	12	2	3	-1	-1	O	-0.2
1980	Min-A	131	417	52	103	18	4	9	49	24	92	.247	.291	.374	75	-12	-16	46	4	5	-2	-2	*O/D	-2.1
1981	Min-A	41	102	9	18	2	0	0	5	8	22	.176	.236	.196	24	-10	-10	4	3	2	-0	1	O/D	-1.0
Total	3	207	612	69	149	25	4	9	66	44	141	.243	.296	.342	71	-21	-26	62	9	10	-3	-2	O/D	-3.3

■ LUIS SOJO
Sojo, Luis Beltran (Sojo) b: 1/3/66, Caracas, Venez. BR/TR, 5'11", 170 lbs. Deb: 7/14/90

YEAR	TM/L	G	AB	R	H	2B	3B	HR	RBI	BB	SO	AVG	OBP	SLG	PRO+	BR	/A	RC	SB	CS	SBR	FR	POS	TPR
1990	Tor-A	33	80	14	18	3	0	1	9	5	5	.225	.271	.300	61	-4	-4	6	1	1	-0	-3	2/SO3D	-0.6

■ TONY SOLAITA
Solaita, Tolia b: 1/15/47, Nuuyli, Amer.Samoa d: 2/10/90, Tafuna, Amer.Samoa BL/TL, 6', 210 lbs. Deb: 9/16/68

YEAR	TM/L	G	AB	R	H	2B	3B	HR	RBI	BB	SO	AVG	OBP	SLG	PRO+	BR	/A	RC	SB	CS	SBR	FR	POS	TPR
1968	NY-A	1	1	0	0	0	0	0	0	0	1	.000	.000	.000	-99	-0	-0	0	0	0	0	0	/1	0.0
1974	KC-A	96	239	31	64	12	0	7	30	35	70	.268	.364	.406	115	7	6	36	0	3	-2	3	1D/O	0.4
1975	KC-A	93	231	35	60	11	0	16	44	39	79	.260	.371	.515	145	15	14	45	0	1	-1	3	D1	1.5
1976	KC-A	31	68	4	16	4	0	0	9	6	17	.235	.297	.294	73	-2	-2	7	0	0	0	0	D/1	-0.2
	Cal-A	63	215	25	58	9	0	9	33	34	44	.270	.369	.437	145	10	12	36	1	1	-0	8	1/D	1.8
	Yr	94	283	29	74	13	0	9	42	40	61	.261	.353	.403	126	8	10	42	1	1	-0	8		1.6
1977	Cal-A	116	324	40	78	15	0	14	53	56	77	.241	.353	.417	113	5	7	49	1	3	-2	1	1/D	0.1
1978	Cal-A	60	94	10	21	3	0	4	16	15	16	.223	.336	.287	80	-2	-2	10	0	0	0	0	D1	0.3
1979	Mon-N	29	42	5	12	4	0	1	7	11	16	.286	.434	.452	143	3	3	9	0	0	0	0	1	0.3
	Tor-A	36	102	14	27	8	1	2	13	17	16	.265	.370	.422	112	2	2	17	0	0	0	1	D/1	0.3
Total	7	525	1316	164	336	66	1	50	203	214	345	.255	.361	.421	120	38	39	209	2	8	-4	18	1D/O	4.2

■ MOSE SOLOMON
Solomon, Morris Hirsch "The Rabbi Of Swat" b: 12/8/1900, New York, N.Y. d: 6/25/66, Miami, Fla. BL/TL, 5'9.5", 180 lbs. Deb: 9/30/23

YEAR	TM/L	G	AB	R	H	2B	3B	HR	RBI	BB	SO	AVG	OBP	SLG	PRO+	BR	/A	RC	SB	CS	SBR	FR	POS	TPR
1923	NY-N	2	8	0	3	1	0	0	1	0	1	.375	.375	.500	131	0	0	1	0	0	0	-0	/O	0.0

YEAR	TM/L	G	AB	R	H	2B	3B	HR	RBI	BB	SO	AVG	OBP	SLG	PRO+	BR	/A	RC	SB	CS	SBR	FR	POS	TPR

■ MOOSE SOLTERS
Solters, Julius Joseph (b: Julius Joseph Soltesz) b: 3/22/06, Pittsburgh, Pa.   d: 9/28/75, Pittsburgh, Pa.   BR/TR, 6', 190 lbs.   Deb: 4/17/34

YEAR	TM/L	G	AB	R	H	2B	3B	HR	RBI	BB	SO	AVG	OBP	SLG	PRO+	BR	/A	RC	SB	CS	SBR	FR	POS	TPR
1934	Bos-A	101	365	61	109	25	4	7	58	18	50	.299	.333	.447	93	-2	-5	54	9	4	0	5	O	0.0
1935	Bos-A	24	79	15	19	6	1	0	8	2	7	.241	.268	.342	53	-5	-6	7	1	1	-0	3	O	-0.3
	StL-A	127	552	79	182	39	6	18	104	34	35	.330	.369	.520	122	20	16	106	10	1	2	19	*O	3.3
	Yr	151	631	94	201	45	7	18	112	36	42	.319	.356	.498	113	14	10	112	11	2	2	22		3.0
1936	StL-A	152	628	100	183	45	7	17	134	41	76	.291	.336	.467	93	-7	-10	99	3	0	1	10	*O	-0.1
1937	Cle-A	152	589	90	190	42	11	20	109	42	56	.323	.372	.533	125	20	20	113	6	9	-4	1	*O	1.0
1938	Cle-A	67	199	30	40	6	3	2	22	13	28	.201	.250	.291	36	-21	-20	15	4	1	1	0	O	-1.7
1939	Cle-A	41	102	19	28	7	2	2	19	9	15	.275	.333	.441	100	-1	-0	15	2	1	0	-2	O	-0.2
	StL-A	40	131	14	27	6	1	0	14	10	20	.206	.262	.267	35	-13	-13	9	1	0	0	-1	O	-1.3
	Yr	81	233	33	55	13	3	2	33	19	35	.236	.294	.343	63	-14	-14	24	3	1	0	-3		-1.5
1940	Chi-A	116	428	65	132	28	3	12	80	27	54	.308	.351	.472	110	6	5	70	3	3	-1	5	*O	0.1
1941	Chi-A	76	251	24	65	9	4	4	43	18	31	.259	.311	.375	82	-8	-7	28	3	2	-0	-1	O	-1.1
1943	Chi-A	42	97	6	15	0	0	1	8	7	5	.155	.212	.186	17	-10	-10	3	0	1	-1	-3	O	-1.5
Total	9	938	3421	503	990	213	42	83	599	221	377	.289	.334	.449	96	-21	-32	519	42	23	-1	37	O	-1.8

■ JOCK SOMERLOTT
Somerlott, John Wesley b: 10/26/1882, Flint, Ind.   d: 4/21/65, Butler, Ind.   TR, 6', 160 lbs.   Deb: 9/19/10

YEAR	TM/L	G	AB	R	H	2B	3B	HR	RBI	BB	SO	AVG	OBP	SLG	PRO+	BR	/A	RC	SB	CS	SBR	FR	POS	TPR
1910	Was-A	16	63	6	14	0	0	0	2	3		.222	.258	.222	53	-4	-3	4	2			0	1	-0.2
1911	Was-A	13	40	2	7	0	0	0	2	0		.175	.195	.175	4	-5	-5	2	2			2	1	-0.2
Total	2	29	103	8	21	0	0	0	4	3		.204	.234	.204	32	-9	-8	6	4			2	/1	-0.4

■ ED SOMERVILLE
Somerville, Edward b: 3/1/1853, Philadelphia, Pa.   d: 10/1/1877, London, Ont., Canada   BR/TR,   Deb: 4/30/1875

YEAR	TM/L	G	AB	R	H	2B	3B	HR	RBI	BB	SO	AVG	OBP	SLG	PRO+	BR	/A	RC	SB	CS	SBR	FR	POS	TPR
1875	Cen-n	14	55	6	13	3	0	0			2	.236	.263	.291	100	-0	-0	4					2	0.0
	NH-n	33	134	14	29	4	0	0			1	.216	.222	.246	72	-5	-5	8					2/1S3	-0.1
	Yr	47	189	20	42	7	0	0			3	.222	.234	.259	81	-5	-2	12						-0.1
1876	Lou-N	64	256	29	48	5	1	0	14	1	6	.188	.191	.215	30	-17	-24	11				30	*2	0.5

■ JOE SOMMER
Sommer, Joseph John b: 11/20/1858, Covington, Ky.   d: 1/16/38, Cincinnati, Ohio   BR/TR,   Deb: 7/08/1880

YEAR	TM/L	G	AB	R	H	2B	3B	HR	RBI	BB	SO	AVG	OBP	SLG	PRO+	BR	/A	RC	SB	CS	SBR	FR	POS	TPR
1880	Cin-N	24	88	10	16	1	0	0	6	0	2	.182	.182	.193	28	-6	-6	3				-1	O/S3C	-0.7
1882	Cin-a	80	354	82	102	12	6	1	24			.288	.333	.364	127	13	10	44				4	*O	1.2
1883	Cin-a	97	413	79	115	5	7	3	20			.278	.312	.346	105	5	1	46				-1	*O/3P	0.1
1884	Bal-a	107	479	96	129	11	10	4	8			.269	.293	.359	110	7	4	52				6	*3/O2	1.0
1885	Bal-a	110	471	84	118	23	6	1	24			.251	.291	.331	100	-0	1	47				12	*O/S3P1	0.6
1886	Bal-a	139	560	79	118	18	4	1	24			.209	.266	.261	61	-26	-24	41	31			13	*023/SP	-1.1
1887	Bal-a	131	463	88	123	11	5	0	63			.266	.358	.311	95	-3	2	64	29			0	*023/SP	-0.1
1888	Bal-a	79	297	31	65	10	0	0	35	18		.219	.266	.253	71	-10	-9	24	13			-4	OS/21	-1.1
1889	Bal-a	106	386	51	85	13	2	1	36	42	49	.220	.298	.272	64	-17	-18	38	18			9	*O/S	-1.0
1890	Cle-N	9	35	4	8	1	0	0	0	2	2	.229	.270	.257	57	-2	-2	2	0			-2	/OP	-0.2
	Bal-a	38	129	13	33	4	2	0		13		.256	.324	.318	88	-1	-2	17	10			1	O	-0.2
Total	10	920	3675	617	911	109	42	11	77	238	53	.248	.297	.309	89	-40	-42	380	101			39	03/2SP1C	-1.5

■ PETE SOMMERS
Sommers, Joseph Andrews b: 10/26/1866, Cleveland, Ohio   d: 7/22/08, Cleveland, Ohio   BR/TL, 5'11.5", 181 lbs.   Deb: 4/27/1887

YEAR	TM/L	G	AB	R	H	2B	3B	HR	RBI	BB	SO	AVG	OBP	SLG	PRO+	BR	/A	RC	SB	CS	SBR	FR	POS	TPR
1887	NY-a	33	116	9	21	3	0	1		7		.181	.234	.233	33	-10	-10	8	6			-10	C/O1	-1.1
1888	Bos-N	4	13	1	3	1	0	0	0	0	3	.231	.231	.308	71	-0	-0	1	0			-1	/C	0.0
1889	Chi-N	12	45	5	10	5	0	0	8	2	8	.222	.271	.333	66	-2	-2	4	0			-4	C/O	-0.4
	Ind-N	23	84	12	21	2	2	2	14	1	16	.250	.267	.393	83	-2	-2	10	2			1	C/O	-0.1
	Yr	35	129	17	31	7	2	2	22	3	24	.240	.269	.372	77	-4	-5	14	2			-3		-0.5
1890	NY-N	17	47	4	5	1	1	0	1	4	13	.106	.192	.170	7	-5	-6	2	0			3	C/1O	-0.1
	Cle-N	9	34	4	7	1	1	0	1	2	3	.206	.250	.294	61	-2	-2	3	0			1	/CO	0.0
	Yr	26	81	8	12	2	2	0	2	6	16	.148	.216	.222	29	-7	-7	4	0			4		-0.1
Total	4	98	339	35	67	13	4	3	24	16	43	.198	.242	.286	51	-22	-22	27	8			-11	/CO1	-1.7

■ BILL SOMMERS
Sommers, William Dunn b: 2/17/23, Brooklyn, N.Y.   BR/TR, 6', 180 lbs.   Deb: 4/25/50

YEAR	TM/L	G	AB	R	H	2B	3B	HR	RBI	BB	SO	AVG	OBP	SLG	PRO+	BR	/A	RC	SB	CS	SBR	FR	POS	TPR
1950	StL-A	65	137	24	35	5	1	0	14	25	14	.255	.370	.307	72	-4	-5	17	0	1	-1	-9	32	-1.3

■ BILL SORRELL
Sorrell, William b: 10/14/40, Morehead, Ky.   BL/TR, 6', 190 lbs.   Deb: 9/02/65

YEAR	TM/L	G	AB	R	H	2B	3B	HR	RBI	BB	SO	AVG	OBP	SLG	PRO+	BR	/A	RC	SB	CS	SBR	FR	POS	TPR
1965	Phi-N	10	13	2	5	0	0	1	2	2	1	.385	.467	.615	206	2	2	4	0	0	0	0	/3	0.2
1967	SF-N	18	17	1	3	1	0	0	1	3	2	.176	.300	.235	56	-1	-1	2	0	0	0	-1	/O	-0.1
1970	KC-A	57	135	12	36	2	0	4	14	10	13	.267	.317	.370	89	-2	-2	15	1	0	0	-6	3/O1	-0.8
Total	3	85	165	15	44	3	0	5	17	15	16	.267	.328	.376	95	-1	-1	20	1	0	0	-6	/3O1	-0.7

■ CHICK SORRELLS
Sorrells, Raymond Edwin b: 7/31/1896, Stringtown, Okla.   d: 7/20/83, Terrell, Tex.   BR/TR, 5'9", 155 lbs.   Deb: 9/18/22

YEAR	TM/L	G	AB	R	H	2B	3B	HR	RBI	BB	SO	AVG	OBP	SLG	PRO+	BR	/A	RC	SB	CS	SBR	FR	POS	TPR
1922	Cle-A	2	1	0	0	0	0	0	0	0	0	.000	.000	.000	-99	-0	-0	0	0	0	0	0	/S	0.0

■ PAUL SORRENTO
Sorrento, Paul Anthony b: 11/17/65, Somerville, Mass.   BL/TR, 6'2", 195 lbs.   Deb: 9/08/89

YEAR	TM/L	G	AB	R	H	2B	3B	HR	RBI	BB	SO	AVG	OBP	SLG	PRO+	BR	/A	RC	SB	CS	SBR	FR	POS	TPR
1989	Min-A	14	21	2	5	0	0	1	5	4	4	.238	.385	.238	74	-0	-0	2	0	0	0	-0	/1D	0.0
1990	Min-A	41	121	11	25	4	1	5	13	12	31	.207	.284	.380	78	-3	-4	13	1	1	-0	-1	D1	-0.6
Total	2	55	142	13	30	4	1	5	14	17	35	.211	.300	.359	78	-3	-4	15	1	1	-0	-1	/D1	-0.6

■ SAMMY SOSA
Sosa, Samuel Peralta b: 11/10/68, San Pedro De Macoris, D.R.   BR/TR, 6', 165 lbs.   Deb: 6/16/89

YEAR	TM/L	G	AB	R	H	2B	3B	HR	RBI	BB	SO	AVG	OBP	SLG	PRO+	BR	/A	RC	SB	CS	SBR	FR	POS	TPR
1989	Tex-A	25	84	8	20	3	0	1	3	0	20	.238	.238	.310	52	-5	-6	5	0	2	-1	-2	O	-0.9
	Chi-A	33	99	19	27	5	0	3	10	11	27	.273	.357	.414	120	2	3	15	7	3	0	1	O/D	0.3
	Yr	58	183	27	47	8	0	4	13	11	47	.257	.306	.366	89	-3	-3	19	7	5	-1	-1	O	-0.6
1990	Chi-A	153	532	72	124	26	10	15	70	33	150	.233	.285	.404	93	-9	-7	58	32	16	0	4	*O	-0.4
Total	2	211	715	99	171	34	10	19	83	44	197	.239	.291	.394	92	-12	-10	77	39	21	-1	2	O/D	-1.0

■ DENNY SOTHERN
Sothern, Dennis Elwood b: 1/20/04, Washington, D.C.   d: 12/7/77, Durham, N.C.   BR/TR, 5'11", 175 lbs.   Deb: 9/10/26

YEAR	TM/L	G	AB	R	H	2B	3B	HR	RBI	BB	SO	AVG	OBP	SLG	PRO+	BR	/A	RC	SB	CS	SBR	FR	POS	TPR
1926	Phi-N	14	53	5	13	1	0	3	10	4	10	.245	.310	.434	94	-0	-1	7	0			1	O	0.0
1928	Phi-N	141	579	82	165	27	5	5	38	34	53	.285	.327	.375	80	-15	-18	69	17			5	*O	-1.7
1929	Phi-N	76	294	52	90	21	3	5	27	16	24	.306	.346	.449	89	-3	-6	44	13			0	O	-1.0
1930	Phi-N	90	347	66	97	26	1	5	36	22	37	.280	.326	.403	70	-14	-18	45	6			7	O	-1.5
	Pit-N	17	51	4	9	4	0	1	4	3	4	.176	.222	.314	28	-6	-6	3	2			1	O	-0.5
	Yr	107	398	70	106	30	1	6	40	25	41	.266	.313	.392	65	-21	-24	48	8			8		-2.0
1931	Bro-N	19	31	10	5	1	0	0	4	8	8	.161	.257	.194	23	-3	-3	2	0			1	O	-0.2
Total	5	357	1355	219	379	80	9	19	115	83	136	.280	.325	.394	77	-42	-52	170	38			14	O	-4.9

■ BUD SOUCHOCK
Souchock, Stephen b: 3/3/19, Yatesboro, Pa.   BR/TR, 6'2.5", 203 lbs.   Deb: 5/25/46

YEAR	TM/L	G	AB	R	H	2B	3B	HR	RBI	BB	SO	AVG	OBP	SLG	PRO+	BR	/A	RC	SB	CS	SBR	FR	POS	TPR
1946	NY-A	47	86	15	26	3	2	2	10	7	13	.302	.362	.477	131	4	3	15	0	3	-2	-2	1	-0.1
1948	NY-A	44	118	11	24	3	1	3	11	7	13	.203	.248	.322	51	-9	-9	9	3	0	1	-2	1	-0.7
1949	Chi-A	84	252	29	59	13	5	7	37	25	38	.234	.303	.409	90	-6	-5	32	5	2	0	1	O1	-0.3
1951	Det-A	91	188	33	46	10	3	11	28	18	27	.245	.314	.505	118	3	3	27	0	2	-1	-1	O/312	-0.1
1952	Det-A	92	269	40	66	16	4	13	45	21	44	.245	.314	.517	120	4	4	34	1	4	-1	1	O/1	0.3
1953	Det-A	89	278	29	84	13	3	11	46	8	35	.302	.326	.489	119	5	5	42	5	1	1	-1	O/1	0.3
1954	Det-A	25	39	6	7	0	1	3	8	2	10	.179	.220	.462	84	-1	-1	3	1	1	-0	0	/O3	-0.1
1955	Det-A	1	1	0	1	0	0	0	0	0	0	1.000	1.000	1.000	449	0	0	1	0	0	0	0	H	0.0

YEAR	TM/L	G	AB	R	H	2B	3B	HR	RBI	BB	SO	AVG	OBP	SLG	PRO+	BR	/A	RC	SB	CS	SBR	FR	POS	TPR
Total	8	473	1227	163	313	58	20	50	186	88	164	.255	.307	.457	106	-0	1	163	15	9	-1	-3	O/132	-0.7

■ CLYDE SOUTHWICK   Southwick, Clyde Aubra   b: 11/3/1886, Maxwell, Iowa   d: 10/14/61, Freeport, Ill.   BL/TR, 6', 180 lbs.   Deb: 8/22/11

YEAR	TM/L	G	AB	R	H	2B	3B	HR	RBI	BB	SO	AVG	OBP	SLG	PRO+	BR	/A	RC	SB	CS	SBR	FR	POS	TPR
1911	StL-A	4	12	3	3	0	0	0	0	0	1	.250	.308	.250	58	-1	-1	1	0			-1	/C	0.0

■ BILL SOUTHWORTH   Southworth, William Frederick   b: 11/10/45, Madison, Wis.   BR/TR, 6'2", 205 lbs.   Deb: 10/02/64

YEAR	TM/L	G	AB	R	H	2B	3B	HR	RBI	BB	SO	AVG	OBP	SLG	PRO+	BR	/A	RC	SB	CS	SBR	FR	POS	TPR
1964	Mil-N	3	7	2	2	0	0	1	2	0	3	.286	.444	.714	219	1	1	2	0	0	0	-1	/3	0.0

■ BILLY SOUTHWORTH   Southworth, William Harrison   b: 3/9/1893, Harvard, Neb.   d: 11/15/69, Columbus, Ohio   BL/TR, 5'9", 170 lbs.   Deb: 8/04/13   MC

YEAR	TM/L	G	AB	R	H	2B	3B	HR	RBI	BB	SO	AVG	OBP	SLG	PRO+	BR	/A	RC	SB	CS	SBR	FR	POS	TPR
1913	Cle-A	1	0	0	0	0	0	0	0	0	0	—	—	—	—	0	0	0	0			0	/O	0.0
1915	Cle-A	60	177	25	39	2	5	0	8	36	12	.220	.352	.288	90	-0	-1	18	2	4	-2	1	O	-0.3
1918	Pit-N	64	246	37	84	5	7	2	43	26	9	.341	.409	.443	154	18	17	49	19			6	O	2.2
1919	Pit-N	121	453	56	127	14	**14**	4	61	32	22	.280	.329	.400	114	9	7	64	23			4	*O	0.7
1920	Pit-N	146	546	64	155	17	13	2	53	52	20	.284	.348	.374	104	6	4	68	23	25	-8	4	*O	-0.3
1921	Bos-N	141	569	86	175	25	15	3	79	36	13	.308	.351	.441	115	6	10	84	22	20	-5	4	*O	0.2
1922	Bos-N	43	158	27	51	4	4	4	18	18	1	.323	.392	.475	128	5	6	30	4	1	1	2	O	0.7
1923	Bos-N	153	611	95	195	29	16	6	78	61	23	.319	.383	.448	124	17	21	103	14	16	-5	3	*O/2	1.3
1924	NY-N	94	281	40	72	13	0	3	36	32	16	.256	.332	.335	81	-8	-7	32	1	6	-3	-1	O	-1.1
1925	NY-N	123	473	79	138	19	5	6	44	51	11	.292	.363	.391	97	-4	-1	66	6	13	-6	-9	*O	-1.8
1926	NY-N	36	116	23	38	6	1	5	30	7	1	.328	.366	.526	139	6	6	21	1			-1	O	0.3
	StL-N	99	391	76	124	22	6	11	69	26	9	.317	.364	.488	123	14	12	67	13			-4	O	0.4
	Yr	135	507	99	162	28	7	16	99	33	10	.320	.365	.497	127	19	18	88	14			-5		0.7
1927	StL-N	92	306	52	92	15	5	2	39	23	7	.301	.350	.402	98	0	-1	42	10			-8	O	-1.1
1929	StL-N	19	32	1	6	2	0	0	3	2	4	.188	.235	.250	20	-4	-2	2	0			0	/OM	-0.3
Total	13	1192	4359	661	1296	173	91	52	561	402	148	.297	.359	.415	111	65	70	647	138	85		6	*O/2	0.9

■ JOHN SOWDERS   Sowders, John   b: 12/10/1866, Louisville, Ky.   d: 7/29/08, Indianapolis, Ind   BR/TL, 6',   Deb: 6/28/1887

YEAR	TM/L	G	AB	R	H	2B	3B	HR	RBI	BB	SO	AVG	OBP	SLG	PRO+	BR	/A	RC	SB	CS	SBR	FR	POS	TPR
1887	Ind-N	1	2	0	0	0	0	0	0	0	1	.000	.000	.000	-99	-1	-1	0	0			-0	/OP	0.0
1889	KC-a	28	87	11	19	3	0	0	6	4	20	.218	.269	.253	48	-5	-6	6	1			-3	P/O	0.0
1890	Bro-P	40	132	14	25	3	0	1	20	10	12	.189	.246	.235	28	-13	-15	8	0			-2	P/O	0.0
Total	3	69	221	25	44	6	0	1	26	14	33	.199	.253	.240	35	-19	-21	14	1			-6	/PO	0.0

■ LEN SOWDERS   Sowders, Leonard   b: 6/29/1861, Louisville, Ky.   d: 11/19/1888, Indianapolis, Ind.   Deb: 9/10/1886

YEAR	TM/L	G	AB	R	H	2B	3B	HR	RBI	BB	SO	AVG	OBP	SLG	PRO+	BR	/A	RC	SB	CS	SBR	FR	POS	TPR
1886	Bal-a	23	76	10	20	3	1	0		12	3	.263	.364	.329	123	2	3	12	6			-1	O/1	0.1

■ AL SPALDING   Spalding, Albert Goodwill   b: 9/2/1850, Byron, Ill.   d: 9/9/15, San Diego, Cal.   BR/TR, 6'1", 170 lbs.   Deb: 5/05/1871   MH

YEAR	TM/L	G	AB	R	H	2B	3B	HR	RBI	BB	SO	AVG	OBP	SLG	PRO+	BR	/A	RC	SB	CS	SBR	FR	POS	TPR
1871	Bos-n	31	144	43	39	10	1	1	31	8	1	.271	.309	.375	92	-1	-2	18	2				*P/D	0.0
1872	Bos-n	48	244	60	87	13	5	0			3	.357	.364	.451	142	14	11	41					*P/O	0.0
1873	Bos-n	60	323	84	107	13	2	1			3	.331	.337	.393	105	5	-0	44					*P/O	0.0
1874	Bos-n	71	359	80	119	15	1	0			3	.331	.337	.379	121	11	7	47					*P	0.0
1875	Bos-n	74	343	68	107	12	3	0			4	.312	.320	.364	131	12	10	41					*PO/1	0.0
1876	Chi-N	66	292	54	91	14	2	0	44	3	6	.312	.326	.373	118	10	4	36				4	*PO/1M	0.0
1877	Chi-N	60	254	29	65	7	6	0	35	3	16	.256	.265	.331	77	-4	-8	23				6	*12/P3M	-0.2
1878	Chi-N	1	4	0	2	0	0	0	0	0	0	.500	.500	.500	215	1	0	1				-2	/2	0.0
Total	5 n	284	1413	335	459	63	12	2	31	21	1	.325	.335	.391	120	41	26	191					P/O1D	0.0
Total	3	127	550	83	158	21	8	0	79	9	19	.287	.299	.355	99	6	-4	60				8	/P1203	-0.2

■ DICK SPALDING   Spalding, Charles Harry   b: 10/13/1893, Philadelphia, Pa.   d: 2/3/50, Philadelphia, Pa.   BL/TR, 5'11", 185 lbs.   Deb: 4/18/27   C

YEAR	TM/L	G	AB	R	H	2B	3B	HR	RBI	BB	SO	AVG	OBP	SLG	PRO+	BR	/A	RC	SB	CS	SBR	FR	POS	TPR
1927	Phi-N	115	442	68	131	16	3	0	25	38	40	.296	.352	.346	86	-7	-7	54	5			-1	*O	-1.2
1928	Was-A	16	23	1	8	0	0	0	0	0	4	.348	.348	.348	84	-1	-1	2	0	2	-1	-3	O	-0.5
Total	2	131	465	69	139	16	3	0	25	38	44	.299	.352	.346	86	-7	-8	56	5	2		-4	O	-1.7

■ AL SPANGLER   Spangler, Albert Donald   b: 7/8/33, Philadelphia, Pa.   BL/TL, 6', 175 lbs.   Deb: 9/16/59   C

YEAR	TM/L	G	AB	R	H	2B	3B	HR	RBI	BB	SO	AVG	OBP	SLG	PRO+	BR	/A	RC	SB	CS	SBR	FR	POS	TPR
1959	Mil-N	6	12	3	5	0	1	0	1	1	1	.417	.462	.583	192	1	1	4	1	0	0	0	/O	0.2
1960	Mil-N	101	105	26	28	5	2	0	6	14	17	.267	.358	.352	103	-0	1	15	6	2	1	8	O	0.7
1961	Mil-N	68	97	23	26	2	0	0	6	28	9	.268	.432	.289	102	1	2	15	4	2	0	1	O	0.1
1962	Hou-N	129	418	51	119	10	9	5	35	70	46	.285	.391	.388	119	9	13	69	7	6	-2	-4	*O	0.1
1963	Hou-N	120	430	52	121	25	4	4	27	50	38	.281	.358	.386	122	9	12	60	5	8	-3	2	*O	0.6
1964	Hou-N	135	449	51	110	18	5	4	38	41	43	.245	.314	.334	88	-10	-7	48	7	8	-3	-11	*O	-2.4
1965	Hou-N	38	112	18	24	1	1	1	7	14	18	.214	.302	.268	66	-5	-4	10	1	1	-0	-2	O	-0.8
	Cal-A	51	96	17	25	1	0	0	1	8	9	.260	.317	.271	70	-4	-3	10	4	0	1	-1	O	-0.3
1966	Cal-A	6	9	2	6	0	0	0	0	2	2	.667	.727	.667	312	3	3	5	0	0	0	-0	/O	0.2
1967	Chi-N	62	130	18	33	7	0	0	13	23	17	.254	.366	.308	91	0	-1	16	2	2	-1	-1	O	-0.3
1968	Chi-N	88	177	21	48	9	3	2	18	20	24	.271	.348	.390	114	5	4	24	0	1	-1	-3	O	-0.2
1969	Chi-N	82	213	23	45	8	1	4	23	21	16	.211	.285	.315	60	-9	-13	20	0	2	-1	-8	O	-2.6
1970	Chi-N	21	14	2	2	1	0	1	1	3	3	.143	.294	.429	81	-0	-2	2	0	0	0	1	O	0.0
1971	Chi-N	5	5	0	2	0	0	0	0	0	1	.400	.400	.400	111	0	0	1	0	0	0	0	H	0.0
Total	13	912	2267	307	594	87	26	21	175	295	234	.262	.350	.351	100	0	8	298	37	32	-8	-18	O	-4.7

■ BOB SPEAKE   Speake, Robert Charles "Spook"   b: 8/22/30, Springfield, Mo.   BL/TL, 6'1", 178 lbs.   Deb: 4/16/55

YEAR	TM/L	G	AB	R	H	2B	3B	HR	RBI	BB	SO	AVG	OBP	SLG	PRO+	BR	/A	RC	SB	CS	SBR	FR	POS	TPR
1955	Chi-N	95	261	36	57	9	5	12	43	28	71	.218	.301	.429	91	-4	-4	34	3	4	-2	-6	O/1	-1.2
1957	Chi-N	129	418	65	97	14	5	16	50	38	68	.232	.301	.404	89	-8	-7	51	5	6	-2	6	O1	-0.8
1958	SF-N	66	71	9	15	3	0	3	10	13	15	.211	.333	.380	90	-1	-1	9	0	1	-1	1	O	0.0
1959	SF-N	15	11	0	1	0	0	0	1	1	4	.091	.167	.091	-30	-2	-2	0	0	0	0	0	H	-0.1
Total	4	305	761	110	170	26	10	31	104	80	158	.223	.302	.406	88	-15	-14	95	8	11	-4	1	O/1	-2.1

■ TRIS SPEAKER   Speaker, Tristram E "The Grey Eagle"   b: 4/4/1888, Hubbard, Tex.   d: 12/8/58, Lake Whitney, Tex.   BL/TL, 5'11.5", 193 lbs.   Deb: 9/14/07   MH

YEAR	TM/L	G	AB	R	H	2B	3B	HR	RBI	BB	SO	AVG	OBP	SLG	PRO+	BR	/A	RC	SB	CS	SBR	FR	POS	TPR
1907	Bos-A	7	19	0	3	0	0	0	1	1		.158	.200	.158	16	-2	-2	1	0			1	/O	0.0
1908	Bos-A	31	116	12	26	2	2	0	9	4		.224	.250	.276	71	-4	-4	9	3			4	O	-0.1
1909	Bos-A	143	544	73	168	26	13	7	77	38		.309	.362	.443	151	32	30	99	35			**22**	*O	5.2
1910	Bos-A	141	538	92	183	20	14	7	65	52		.340	.404	.468	169	45	43	115	35			15	*O	5.6
1911	Bos-A	141	500	88	167	34	13	8	70	59		.334	.418	.502	158	38	39	115	25			6	O	3.3
1912	*Bos-A	153	580	136	222	**53**	12	**10**	90	82		.383	**.464**	.567	185	73	69	**175**	52			21	*O	7.8
1913	Bos-A	141	520	94	189	35	22	3	71	65	22	.363	.441	.533	180	56	54	136	46			24	*O	7.3
1914	Bos-A	158	571	101	**193**	46	18	4	90	77	25	.338	.423	**.503**	178	55	55	124	42	29	-5	28	*O/P1	7.4
1915	*Bos-A	150	547	108	176	25	12	0	69	81	14	.322	.416	.411	152	35	37	97	29	25	-6	13	*O	3.8
1916	Cle-A	151	546	102	**211**	41	8	2	79	82	20	**.386**	**.470**	.502	181	65	61	132	35	27	-6	9	*O	**6.0**
1917	Cle-A	142	523	90	184	42	11	2	60	67	14	.352	.432	.486	168	51	47	118	30			8	*O	5.0
1918	Cle-A	127	471	73	150	33	11	0	61	64	9	.318	.403	.435	140	31	26	90	27			11	*O	3.4
1919	Cle-A	134	494	83	146	38	12	2	63	73	12	.296	.395	.433	125	23	19	89	15			19	*OM	3.0
1920	*Cle-A	150	552	137	214	**50**	11	8	107	97	13	.388	.483	.562	171	66	63	152	10	13	-5	10	*OM	5.2
1921	Cle-A	132	506	107	183	**52**	14	3	75	68	12	.362	.439	.538	146	38	37	121	2	4	-2	10	*OM	3.2
1922	Cle-A	131	426	85	161	48	8	11	71	77	11	.378	**.474**	.606	182	49	52	127	8	3	-1	8	*OM	5.0
1923	Cle-A	150	574	133	218	**59**	11	17	**130**	93	15	.380	.469	.610	183	71	71	166	8	9	-2	10	*OM	6.1
1924	Cle-A	135	486	94	167	36	9	9	65	72	13	.344	.432	.510	141	32	31	109	5	7	-3	5	*OM	2.2

YEAR	TM/L	G	AB	R	H	2B	3B	HR	RBI	BB	SO	AVG	OBP	SLG	PRO+	BR	/A	RC	SB	CS	SBR	FR	POS	TPR
1925	Cle-A	117	429	79	167	35	5	12	87	70	12	.389	**.479**	.578	166	47	46	123	5	2	0	10	*OM	4.3
1926	Cle-A	150	539	96	164	52	8	7	86	94	15	.304	.408	.469	127	24	24	110	6	1	1	10	*OM	2.3
1927	Was-A	141	523	71	171	43	6	2	73	55	8	.327	.395	.444	119	14	15	88	9	8	-2	1	*O1	0.6
1928	Phi-A	64	191	28	51	22	2	3	30	10	5	.267	.310	.450	95	-2	-2	27	5	1	1	1	O	-0.2
Total	22	2789	10195	1882	3514	792	222	117	1529	1381	220	.345	.428	.500	156	843	813	2320	434	129		246	*O/1P	86.4

■ HORACE SPEED
Speed, Horace Arthur b: 10/4/51, Los Angeles, Cal. BR/TR, 6'1", 180 lbs. Deb: 4/10/75

YEAR	TM/L	G	AB	R	H	2B	3B	HR	RBI	BB	SO	AVG	OBP	SLG	PRO+	BR	/A	RC	SB	CS	SBR	FR	POS	TPR
1975	SF-N	17	15	2	2	1	0	0	1	1	8	.133	.235	.200	21	-2	-2	1	0	0	0	1	/O	0.0
1978	Cle-A	70	106	13	24	4	1	0	4	14	31	.226	.322	.283	72	-4	-3	9	2	4	-2	4	O/D	-0.2
1979	Cle-A	26	14	6	2	0	0	0	1	5	7	.143	.368	.143	44	-1	-1	1	2	1	0	1	O	0.0
Total	3	113	135	21	28	5	1	0	6	20	46	.207	.318	.259	63	-6	-6	11	4	5	-2	6	/OD	-0.2

■ CHRIS SPEIER
Speier, Chris Edward b: 6/28/50, Alameda, Cal. BR/TR, 6'1", 175 lbs. Deb: 4/07/71

YEAR	TM/L	G	AB	R	H	2B	3B	HR	RBI	BB	SO	AVG	OBP	SLG	PRO+	BR	/A	RC	SB	CS	SBR	FR	POS	TPR
1971	*SF-N	157	601	74	141	17	6	8	46	56	90	.235	.307	.323	80	-16	-15	58	4	7	-3	-12	*S	-0.9
1972	SF-N	150	562	74	151	25	2	15	71	82	92	.269	.365	.400	116	15	14	87	9	4	0	-5	*S	2.9
1973	SF-N	153	542	58	135	17	4	11	71	66	69	.249	.333	.356	87	-6	-9	63	4	5	-2	-10	*S/2	0.1
1974	SF-N	141	501	55	125	19	5	9	53	62	64	.250	.337	.361	91	-3	-5	64	3	2	-0	3	*S/2	1.3
1975	SF-N	141	487	60	132	30	5	10	69	70	50	.271	.364	.415	111	11	9	73	4	5	-2	1	*S/3	2.4
1976	SF-N	145	495	51	112	18	4	3	40	60	52	.226	.315	.297	72	-15	-17	47	2	2	-1	-1	*S/231	-0.5
1977	SF-N	6	17	1	3	1	0	0	0	0	3	.176	.176	.235	9	-2	-2	1	0	0	0	2	/S	0.0
	Mon-N	139	531	58	125	30	6	5	38	67	78	.235	.322	.343	81	-15	-13	59	1	2	-1	-15	*S	-0.6
	Yr	145	548	59	128	31	6	5	38	67	81	.234	.318	.339	79	-18	-16	60	1	2	-1	-10		-0.6
1978	Mon-N	150	501	47	126	18	3	5	51	60	75	.251	.333	.329	87	-8	-8	56	1	0	0	1	*S	0.6
1979	Mon-N	113	344	31	78	13	1	7	26	43	45	.227	.318	.331	78	-10	-10	35	0	0	0	4	*S	0.5
1980	Mon-N	128	388	35	103	14	4	1	32	52	38	.265	.352	.330	91	-3	-3	45	0	3	-2	-0	*S/3	1.0
1981	*Mon-N	96	307	33	69	10	2	2	25	38	29	.225	.310	.290	70	-11	-11	27	1	2	-1	-10	S	-1.3
1982	Mon-N	156	530	41	136	26	4	7	60	47	67	.257	.318	.360	88	-7	-9	58	1	6	-3	-21	*S	-2.1
1983	Mon-N	88	261	31	67	12	2	2	22	29	37	.257	.336	.341	88	-4	-4	31	2	1	0	-11	S3/2	-0.8
1984	Mon-N	25	40	1	6	0	0	0	1	1	8	.150	.171	.150	-10	-6	-6	1	0	0	0	-1	S/3	-0.5
	StL-N	38	118	9	21	7	1	3	8	9	19	.178	.242	.331	61	-7	-6	9	0	0	0	10	S/3	0.7
	Yr	63	158	10	27	7	1	3	9	10	27	.171	.225	.285	44	-12	-12	9	0	0	0	8		0.2
	Min-A	12	33	2	7	0	0	0	1	3	7	.212	.278	.212	36	-3	-3	2	0	0	0	-3	S	-0.4
1985	Chi-N	106	218	16	53	11	0	4	24	17	34	.243	.298	.349	72	-6	-9	21	1	3	-2	2	S32	-0.3
1986	Chi-N	95	155	21	44	8	0	6	23	15	32	.284	.351	.452	111	4	2	24	2	2	-1	9	3S/2	1.2
1987	*SF-N	111	317	39	79	13	0	11	39	42	51	.249	.343	.394	99	-2	-0	43	4	7	-3	2	23S	0.2
1988	SF-N	82	171	26	37	9	1	3	18	23	39	.216	.313	.333	89	-3	-2	17	3	3	-1	2	23S	0.2
1989	SF-N	28	37	7	9	4	0	0	2	5	9	.243	.333	.351	99	-0	0	4	0	0	0	-2	/3S21	-0.1
Total	19	2260	7156	770	1759	302	50	112	720	847	988	.246	.329	.349	88	-97	-106	826	42	54	-20	-51	*S32/1	3.6

■ BOB SPENCE
Spence, John Robert b: 2/10/46, San Diego, Cal. BL/TR, 6'4", 215 lbs. Deb: 9/05/69

YEAR	TM/L	G	AB	R	H	2B	3B	HR	RBI	BB	SO	AVG	OBP	SLG	PRO+	BR	/A	RC	SB	CS	SBR	FR	POS	TPR
1969	Chi-A	12	26	0	4	1	0	0	3	0	9	.154	.154	.192	-4	-4	-4	1	0	0	0	-0	/1	-0.4
1970	Chi-A	46	130	11	29	4	1	4	15	11	32	.223	.289	.362	75	-4	-5	14	0	0	0	3	1	-0.3
1971	Chi-A	14	27	2	4	0	0	0	1	5	6	.148	.281	.148	24	-3	-3	1	0	0	0	-1	/1	-0.3
Total	3	72	183	13	37	5	1	4	19	16	47	.202	.270	.306	57	-10	-11	16	0	0	0	2	/1	-1.0

■ STAN SPENCE
Spence, Stanley Orville b: 3/20/15, S.Portsmouth, Ky. d: 1/9/83, Kinston, N.C. BL/TL, 5'10.5", 180 lbs. Deb: 6/08/40

YEAR	TM/L	G	AB	R	H	2B	3B	HR	RBI	BB	SO	AVG	OBP	SLG	PRO+	BR	/A	RC	SB	CS	SBR	FR	POS	TPR
1940	Bos-A	51	68	5	19	2	1	2	13	4	9	.279	.319	.426	88	-1	-1	9	0	1	-1	-1	O	-0.3
1941	Bos-A	86	203	22	47	10	3	2	28	18	14	.232	.304	.340	68	-9	-10	22	1	0	0	3	O/1	-0.9
1942	Was-A	149	629	94	203	27	**15**	4	79	62	16	.323	.384	.432	131	25	25	111	5	2	-0	-5	*O	1.0
1943	Was-A	149	570	72	152	23	10	12	88	84	39	.267	.366	.405	130	20	22	93	8	1	2	1	*O	2.2
1944	Was-A	153	592	83	187	31	8	18	100	64	28	.316	.391	.486	157	38	41	118	3	7	-3	17	*O/1	5.1
1946	Was-A	152	578	83	169	50	10	16	87	62	31	.292	.365	.497	148	28	33	104	1	7	-4	4	*O	2.6
1947	Was-A	147	506	62	141	22	6	16	73	81	41	.279	.378	.441	131	19	21	89	2	2	-1	3	*O	1.8
1948	Bos-A	114	391	71	92	17	4	12	61	82	33	.235	.368	.391	97	2	-0	62	0	2	-1	-3	O1	-0.6
1949	Bos-A	7	20	3	3	1	0	0	1	6	1	.150	.346	.200	43	-1	-2	2	0	0	0	1	/O	0.0
	StL-A	104	314	46	77	13	3	13	45	52	36	.245	.356	.430	103	3	1	50	1	1	-0	1		0.0
	Yr	111	334	49	80	14	3	13	46	58	37	.240	.355	.416	99	1	-1	52	1	1	-0	1		0.0
Total	9	1112	3871	541	1090	196	60	95	575	520	248	.282	.369	.437	126	124	130	660	21	23	-8	20	O/1	10.9

■ SPENCER
Spencer Deb: 6/03/1872

YEAR	TM/L	G	AB	R	H	2B	3B	HR	RBI	BB	SO	AVG	OBP	SLG	PRO+	BR	/A	RC	SB	CS	SBR	FR	POS	TPR
1872	Nat-n	1	4	1	0	0	0	0		0		.000	.000	.000	-86	-1	-1	0					/S	0.0

■ CHET SPENCER
Spencer, Chester Arthur b: 3/4/1883, S.Webster, Ohio d: 11/10/38, Portsmouth, Ohio BL/TR, 6', 180 lbs. Deb: 8/22/06

YEAR	TM/L	G	AB	R	H	2B	3B	HR	RBI	BB	SO	AVG	OBP	SLG	PRO+	BR	/A	RC	SB	CS	SBR	FR	POS	TPR
1906	Bos-N	8	27	1	4	1	0	0	0	0		.148	.148	.185	5	-3	-3	1	0			-1	/O	-0.4

■ DARYL SPENCER
Spencer, Daryl Dean "Big Dee" b: 7/13/29, Wichita, Kan. BR/TR, 6'2.5", 185 lbs. Deb: 9/17/52

YEAR	TM/L	G	AB	R	H	2B	3B	HR	RBI	BB	SO	AVG	OBP	SLG	PRO+	BR	/A	RC	SB	CS	SBR	FR	POS	TPR
1952	NY-N	7	17	0	5	0	1	0	3	1	4	.294	.333	.412	105	0	0	2	0	0	0	1	/S3	0.2
1953	NY-N	118	408	55	85	18	5	20	56	42	74	.208	.287	.424	81	-12	-13	49	0	1	-1	-9	S32	-1.7
1956	NY-N	146	489	46	108	13	2	14	42	35	65	.221	.277	.342	66	-25	-24	45	1	3	-2	-2	2S3	-1.7
1957	NY-N	148	534	65	133	31	2	11	50	50	65	.249	.315	.376	85	-12	-11	62	3	1	0	14	*S2/3	1.0
1958	SF-N	148	539	71	138	20	5	17	74	73	60	.256	.348	.406	101	0	2	77	0	0	0	-1	*S2	1.1
1959	SF-N	152	555	59	147	20	1	12	62	58	67	.265	.334	.369	89	-9	-8	69	5	0	2	-4	*2/S	0.1
1960	StL-N	148	507	70	131	20	3	16	58	81	74	.258	.366	.404	102	10	4	77	1	1	-0	-24	*S2	-1.3
1961	StL-N	37	130	19	33	4	0	4	21	23	17	.254	.366	.377	89	-0	-2	17	1	0	0	-1	S	0.1
	LA-N	60	189	27	46	7	0	8	27	20	35	.243	.329	.407	86	-2	-4	25	0	1	-1	5	3/S	-0.1
	Yr	97	319	46	79	11	0	12	48	43	52	.248	.344	.395	88	-1	-5	43	1	1	-0	4		0.0
1962	LA-N	77	157	24	37	5	1	2	12	32	31	.236	.353	.318	91	-1	-1	19	0	0	0	7	3S	0.8
1963	LA-N	7	9	0	1	0	0	0	0	3	2	.111	.333	.111	37	-1	-1	1	0	0	0	-0	/3	0.0
	Cin-N	50	155	21	37	7	0	1	23	31	37	.239	.369	.303	93	1	0	21	1	0	0	3	3	0.4
	Yr	57	164	21	38	7	0	1	23	34	39	.232	.367	.293	91	-0	-0	21	1	0	0	2		0.4
Total	10	1098	3689	457	901	145	20	105	428	449	516	.244	.329	.380	88	-51	-57	465	13	7	-0	-12	S23	-1.1

■ TUBBY SPENCER
Spencer, Edward Russell b: 1/26/1884, Oil City, Pa. d: 2/1/45, San Francisco, Cal. BR/TR, 5'10", 215 lbs. Deb: 7/23/05

YEAR	TM/L	G	AB	R	H	2B	3B	HR	RBI	BB	SO	AVG	OBP	SLG	PRO+	BR	/A	RC	SB	CS	SBR	FR	POS	TPR
1905	StL-A	35	115	6	27	1	2	0	11	7		.235	.279	.278	83	-3	-2	10	2			-6	C	-0.4
1906	StL-A	58	188	15	33	6	1	0	17	7		.176	.205	.218	35	-14	-13	10	4			-5	C	-1.4
1907	StL-A	71	230	27	61	11	1	1	25	7		.265	.287	.335	100	-1	-1	23	1			-2	C	0.3
1908	StL-A	91	286	19	60	6	1	0	28	17		.210	.254	.238	62	-12	-12	17	1			-0	C	-0.3
1909	Bos-A	28	74	6	12	1	0	0	9	6		.162	.225	.176	26	-6	-6	3	2			-4	C	-0.9
1911	Phi-N	11	32	2	5	1	0	0	3	3	7	.156	.229	.281	42	-3	-3	2	0			-1	C	-0.1
1916	Det-A	19	54	7	20	1	1	1	10	6	6	.370	.443	.481	172	5	5	13	2			-7	C	0.0
1917	Det-A	70	192	13	46	8	3	0	22	15	15	.240	.324	.313	95	-1	-1	19	0			-2	C	0.2
1918	Det-A	66	155	11	34	8	1	0	8	19	18	.219	.313	.284	83	-3	-3	14	1			-12	C/1	-1.1
Total	9	449	1326	106	298	43	10	3	133	87	46	.225	.279	.279	77	-37	-35	111	13			-39	C/1	-3.7

YEAR	TM/L	G	AB	R	H	2B	3B	HR	RBI	BB	SO	AVG	OBP	SLG	PRO+	BR	/A	RC	SB	CS	SBR	FR	POS	TPR

■ TOM SPENCER
Spencer, Hubert Thomas   b: 2/28/51, Gallipolis, Ohio   BR/TR, 6′, 170 lbs.   Deb: 7/17/78   C

YEAR	TM/L	G	AB	R	H	2B	3B	HR	RBI	BB	SO	AVG	OBP	SLG	PRO+	BR	/A	RC	SB	CS	SBR	FR	POS	TPR
1978	Chi-A	29	65	3	12	1	0	0	4	2	9	.185	.209	.200	15	-7	-7	2	0	1	-1	4	O/D	-0.4

■ JIM SPENCER
Spencer, James Lloyd   b: 7/30/47, Hanover, Pa.   BL/TL, 6′2″, 195 lbs.   Deb: 9/07/68

YEAR	TM/L	G	AB	R	H	2B	3B	HR	RBI	BB	SO	AVG	OBP	SLG	PRO+	BR	/A	RC	SB	CS	SBR	FR	POS	TPR
1968	Cal-A	19	68	2	13	1	0	0	5	3	10	.191	.236	.206	36	-5	-5	3	0	0	0	3	1	-0.2
1969	Cal-A	113	386	39	98	14	3	10	31	26	53	.254	.304	.383	96	-6	-3	45	1	0	0	-1	*1	-1.1
1970	Cal-A	146	511	61	140	20	4	12	68	28	61	.274	.312	.399	98	-5	-3	61	0	2	-1	-1	*1	-1.2
1971	Cal-A	148	510	50	121	21	2	18	59	48	63	.237	.307	.392	104	-3	1	59	0	1	-1	2	*1	-0.4
1972	Cal-A	82	212	13	47	5	0	1	14	12	25	.222	.263	.259	59	-12	-10	13	0	1	-1	0	1O	-1.6
1973	Cal-A	29	87	10	21	4	2	2	11	9	9	.241	.320	.402	111	0	1	11	0	0	0	-2	1/D	-0.2
	Tex-A	102	352	35	94	12	3	4	43	34	41	.267	.333	.352	97	-3	-1	40	0	3	-2	5	1/D	-0.3
	Yr	131	439	45	115	16	5	6	54	43	50	.262	.331	.362	100	-3	0	51	0	3	-2	3		-0.5
1974	Tex-A	118	352	36	98	11	4	7	44	22	27	.278	.326	.392	109	2	3	44	1	2	-1	1	1D	0.1
1975	Tex-A	132	403	50	107	18	1	11	47	35	43	.266	.327	.397	105	1	2	51	0	1	-1	5	1D	0.1
1976	Chi-A	150	518	53	131	13	2	14	70	49	52	.253	.319	.367	100	-0	-1	60	6	4	-1	8	*1/D	0.0
1977	Chi-A	128	470	56	116	16	1	18	69	36	50	.247	.303	.400	90	-7	-7	55	1	2	-1	2	*1	-1.2
1978	*NY-A	71	150	12	34	9	1	7	24	15	32	.227	.297	.440	107	0	1	18	0	1	-1	1	D1	0.0
1979	NY-A	106	295	60	85	15	3	23	53	38	25	.288	.369	.593	158	22	23	60	0	2	-1	0	D1	1.9
1980	*NY-A	97	259	38	61	9	0	13	43	30	44	.236	.317	.421	102	-0	0	34	1	0	0	2	1D	-0.2
1981	NY-A	25	63	6	9	2	0	2	4	9	7	.143	.250	.270	50	-4	-4	5	0	0	0	2	1	-0.2
	*Oak-A	54	171	14	35	6	0	2	9	10	20	.205	.249	.275	53	-11	-10	11	1	0	0	2	1	-0.8
	Yr	79	234	20	44	8	0	4	13	19	27	.188	.249	.274	52	-15	-14	15	1	0	0	4		-1.0
1982	Oak-A	33	101	6	17	3	1	2	5	3	20	.168	.192	.277	28	-10	-10	5	0	0	0	2	1	-0.8
Total	15	1553	4908	541	1227	179	27	146	599	407	582	.250	.310	.387	98	-41	-24	574	11	19	-8	32	*1D/O	-6.1

■ BEN SPENCER
Spencer, Lloyd Benjamin   b: 5/15/1890, Patapsco, Md.   d: 9/1/70, Finksburg, Md.   BL/TL, 5′8″, 160 lbs.   Deb: 9/08/13

YEAR	TM/L	G	AB	R	H	2B	3B	HR	RBI	BB	SO	AVG	OBP	SLG	PRO+	BR	/A	RC	SB	CS	SBR	FR	POS	TPR
1913	Was-A	8	21	2	6	1	1	0	2	2	4	.286	.348	.429	124	1	1	3	0			-1	/O	0.0

■ ROY SPENCER
Spencer, Roy Hampton   b: 2/22/1900, Scranton, N.C.   d: 2/8/73, Port Charlotte, Fla   BR/TR, 5′10″, 168 lbs.   Deb: 4/19/25

YEAR	TM/L	G	AB	R	H	2B	3B	HR	RBI	BB	SO	AVG	OBP	SLG	PRO+	BR	/A	RC	SB	CS	SBR	FR	POS	TPR
1925	Pit-N	14	28	1	6	1	0	0	2	1	3	.214	.241	.250	24	-3	-3	2	1	0	0	-2	C	-0.3
1926	Pit-N	28	43	5	17	3	0	0	4	1	0	.395	.409	.465	128	2	2	8	0			-1	C	0.1
1927	*Pit-N	38	92	9	26	3	1	0	13	3	3	.283	.305	.337	67	-4	-5	9	0			3	C	0.0
1929	Was-A	50	116	18	18	4	0	1	9	8	15	.155	.222	.216	13	-15	-15	6	0	0	0	-1	C	-1.2
1930	Was-A	93	321	32	82	11	4	0	36	18	27	.255	.303	.315	57	-21	-21	32	3	0	1	4	C	-0.6
1931	Was-A	145	483	48	133	16	3	1	60	35	21	.275	.327	.327	72	-19	-19	53	0	0	0	7	*C	-0.1
1932	Was-A	102	317	28	78	9	0	1	41	24	17	.246	.301	.284	53	-22	-21	28	0	1	-1	-10	C	-2.4
1933	Cle-A	75	227	26	46	5	2	0	23	23	17	.203	.282	.242	38	-19	-21	17	0	0	0	5	C	-1.1
1934	Cle-A	5	7	0	1	1	0	0	2	0	1	.143	.143	.286	8	-1	-1	0	0	0	0	1	/C	0.0
1936	NY-N	19	18	3	5	1	0	0	3	2	3	.278	.350	.333	86	-0	-0	2	0			1	C	0.1
1937	Bro-N	51	117	5	24	2	2	0	4	8	17	.205	.256	.256	39	-10	-10	8	0			9	C	0.1
1938	Bro-N	16	45	2	12	1	1	0	6	5	6	.267	.340	.333	84	-1	-1	5	0			-0	C	0.0
Total	12	636	1814	177	448	57	13	3	203	128	130	.247	.301	.298	56	-113	-116	171	4	1		16	C	-5.4

■ VERN SPENCER
Spencer, Vernon Murray   b: 2/23/1896, Wixom, Mich.   d: 6/3/71, Wixon, Mich.   BL/TR, 5′7″, 165 lbs.   Deb: 7/04/20

YEAR	TM/L	G	AB	R	H	2B	3B	HR	RBI	BB	SO	AVG	OBP	SLG	PRO+	BR	/A	RC	SB	CS	SBR	FR	POS	TPR
1920	NY-N	45	140	15	28	2	3	0	19	11	17	.200	.258	.257	49	-9	-9	9	4	3	-1	0	O	-1.2

■ PAUL SPERAW
Speraw, Paul Bachman "Polly" or "Birdie"   b: 10/5/1893, Annville, Pa.   d: 2/22/62, Cedar Rapids, Iowa   BR/TR, 5′8.5″, 145 lbs.   Deb: 9/15/20

YEAR	TM/L	G	AB	R	H	2B	3B	HR	RBI	BB	SO	AVG	OBP	SLG	PRO+	BR	/A	RC	SB	CS	SBR	FR	POS	TPR
1920	StL-A	1	2	0	0	0	0	0	0	0	0	.000	.000	.000	-97	-1	-1	0	0	0	0	0	/3	0.0

■ ED SPERBER
Sperber, Edwin George   b: 1/21/1895, Cincinnati, Ohio   d: 1/5/76, Cincinnati, Ohio   BL/TL, 5′11″, 175 lbs.   Deb: 4/16/24

YEAR	TM/L	G	AB	R	H	2B	3B	HR	RBI	BB	SO	AVG	OBP	SLG	PRO+	BR	/A	RC	SB	CS	SBR	FR	POS	TPR
1924	Bos-N	24	59	8	17	2	0	1	12	10	9	.288	.400	.373	113	1	2	10	3	1	0	-3	O	-0.1
1925	Bos-N	2	2	0	0	0	0	0	0	0	0	.000	.000	.000	-99	-1	-1	0	0	0	0	0	H	0.0
Total	2	26	61	8	17	2	0	1	12	10	9	.279	.389	.361	106	1	1	10	3	1	0	-3	/O	-0.1

■ ROB SPERRING
Sperring, Robert Walter   b: 10/10/49, San Francisco, Cal.   BR/TR, 6′1″, 185 lbs.   Deb: 8/11/74

YEAR	TM/L	G	AB	R	H	2B	3B	HR	RBI	BB	SO	AVG	OBP	SLG	PRO+	BR	/A	RC	SB	CS	SBR	FR	POS	TPR
1974	Chi-N	42	107	9	22	3	0	1	5	9	28	.206	.267	.262	46	-7	-8	8	1	2	-1	5	2/S	-0.1
1975	Chi-N	65	144	25	30	4	1	1	9	16	31	.208	.292	.271	54	-8	-9	11	0	2	-1	13	32S/O	0.5
1976	Chi-N	43	93	8	24	3	0	0	7	9	25	.258	.324	.290	69	-3	-4	9	0	2	-1	-9	3S/2O	-1.3
1977	Hou-N	58	129	6	24	3	0	1	9	12	23	.186	.255	.233	35	-12	-11	8	0	0	0	-2	S23	-0.8
Total	4	208	473	48	100	13	1	3	30	46	107	.211	.283	.262	51	-31	-32	35	1	6	-3	7	/2S3O	-1.7

■ STAN SPERRY
Sperry, Stanley Kenneth   b: 2/19/14, Evansville, Wis.   d: 9/27/62, Evansville, Wis.   BL/TR, 5′10.5″, 164 lbs.   Deb: 7/28/36

YEAR	TM/L	G	AB	R	H	2B	3B	HR	RBI	BB	SO	AVG	OBP	SLG	PRO+	BR	/A	RC	SB	CS	SBR	FR	POS	TPR
1936	Phi-A	20	37	2	5	3	0	0	4	3	5	.135	.200	.216	11	-5	-5	2	0			-4	2	-0.7
1938	Phi-A	60	253	28	69	6	3	0	27	15	9	.273	.313	.320	61	-16	-15	25	1	2	-1	-8	2	-1.9
Total	2	80	290	30	74	9	3	0	31	18	14	.255	.299	.307	54	-21	-20	27	1	2		-12	/2	-2.6

■ BILL SPIERS
Spiers, William James   b: 6/5/66, Orangeburg, S.C.   BL/TR, 6′2″, 190 lbs.   Deb: 4/07/89

YEAR	TM/L	G	AB	R	H	2B	3B	HR	RBI	BB	SO	AVG	OBP	SLG	PRO+	BR	/A	RC	SB	CS	SBR	FR	POS	TPR
1989	Mil-A	114	345	44	88	9	3	4	33	21	63	.255	.300	.333	79	-10	-10	37	10	2	2	14	S3/21D	1.3
1990	Mil-A	112	363	44	88	15	3	2	36	16	46	.242	.276	.317	68	-17	-16	29	11	6	-0	-5	*S	-1.4
Total	2	226	708	88	176	24	6	6	69	37	109	.249	.288	.325	73	-27	-26	66	21	8	2	9	S/3D21	-0.1

■ HARRY SPIES
Spies, Henry   b: 6/12/1866, New Orleans, La.   d: 7/8/42, Los Angeles, Cal.   5′11.5″, 170 lbs.   Deb: 4/20/1895

YEAR	TM/L	G	AB	R	H	2B	3B	HR	RBI	BB	SO	AVG	OBP	SLG	PRO+	BR	/A	RC	SB	CS	SBR	FR	POS	TPR
1895	Cin-N	14	50	2	11	0	1	0	5	3	2	.220	.264	.260	35	-5	-5	4	0			2	C/1	-0.1
	Lou-N	72	276	42	74	14	7	2	35	11	19	.268	.313	.391	88	-8	-5	36	4			-4	1C/S	-0.3
	Yr	86	326	44	85	14	8	2	40	14	21	.261	.305	.371	79	-13	-10	39	4			-2		-0.4

■ ED SPIEZIO
Spiezio, Edward Wayne   b: 10/31/41, Joliet, Ill.   BR/TR, 5′11″, 180 lbs.   Deb: 7/23/64

YEAR	TM/L	G	AB	R	H	2B	3B	HR	RBI	BB	SO	AVG	OBP	SLG	PRO+	BR	/A	RC	SB	CS	SBR	FR	POS	TPR
1964	StL-N	12	12	0	4	0	0	0	0	0	1	.333	.333	.333	81	-0	-0	1	0	0	0	0	H	0.0
1965	StL-N	10	18	0	3	0	0	0	5	1	4	.167	.250	.167	18	-2	-2	1	0	0	0	0	/3	-0.1
1966	StL-N	26	73	4	16	5	1	2	10	5	11	.219	.269	.397	82	-2	-2	6	1	0	0	-4	3	-0.5
1967	*StL-N	55	105	9	22	2	0	3	10	7	18	.210	.265	.314	66	-5	-5	8	2	1	0	1	3/O	-0.4
1968	*StL-N	29	51	1	8	0	0	0	2	5	6	.157	.232	.157	19	-5	-5	2	1	1	-0	1	O/3	-0.4
1969	SD-N	121	355	29	83	9	0	13	43	38	64	.234	.315	.369	95	-4	-3	41	1	2	-1	1	3/O	-0.1
1970	SD-N	110	316	45	90	18	1	12	42	43	42	.285	.377	.462	129	11	13	57	4	0	1	2	3	1.3
1971	SD-N	97	308	16	71	10	1	7	36	22	50	.231	.290	.338	83	-9	-7	29	6	5	-1	1	3/O	-0.7
1972	SD-N	20	29	2	4	2	0	0	4	1	6	.138	.167	.207	6	-4	-3	1	1	0	0	-2	/3	-0.4
	Chi-A	74	277	20	66	10	1	2	22	13	43	.238	.277	.303	71	-10	-10	22	0	1	-1	7	3	-0.1
Total	9	554	1544	126	367	56	4	39	174	135	245	.238	.306	.355	88	-30	-24	168	16	10	-1	8	3/O	-1.4

■ CHARLIE SPIKES
Spikes, Leslie Charles   b: 1/23/51, Bogalusa, La.   BR/TR, 6′3″, 215 lbs.   Deb: 9/01/72

YEAR	TM/L	G	AB	R	H	2B	3B	HR	RBI	BB	SO	AVG	OBP	SLG	PRO+	BR	/A	RC	SB	CS	SBR	FR	POS	TPR
1972	NY-A	14	34	2	5	1	0	0	3	1	13	.147	.171	.176	4	-4	-4	1	0	1	-1	0	/O	-0.4
1973	Cle-A	140	506	68	120	12	3	23	73	45	103	.237	.306	.409	98	-2	-3	62	5	3	-0	1	*OD	-0.4
1974	Cle-A	155	568	63	154	23	1	22	80	34	100	.271	.320	.431	116	9	9	74	10	7	-1	-5	*O	0.0
1975	Cle-A	111	345	41	79	13	3	11	33	30	51	.229	.291	.380	88	-6	-6	35	7	6	-2	-2	*O/D	-1.2
1976	Cle-A	101	334	34	79	11	5	3	31	23	50	.237	.296	.326	83	-8	-7	32	5	6	-2	-2	O/D	-1.4

YEAR	TM/L	G	AB	R	H	2B	3B	HR	RBI	BB	SO	AVG	OBP	SLG	PRO+	BR	/A	RC	SB	CS	SBR	FR	POS	TPR
1977	Cle-A	32	95	13	22	2	0	3	11	11	17	.232	.324	.347	86	-2	-2	10	0	2	-1	-4	O/D	-0.6
1978	Det-A	10	28	1	7	1	0	0	2	2	6	.250	.344	.286	77	-1	-1	3	0	0	0	-2	I/O	-0.2
1979	Atl-N	66	93	12	26	8	0	3	21	5	30	.280	.316	.462	102	1	0	13	0	0	0	-3	O	-0.3
1980	Atl-N	41	36	6	10	1	0	0	2	3	18	.278	.350	.306	82	-1	-1	4	0	0	0	0	I/O	0.0
Total	9	670	2039	240	502	72	12	65	256	154	388	.246	.306	.389	96	-13	-14	233	27	25	-7	-16	O/D	-4.5

■ HARRY SPILMAN
Spilman, William Harry   b: 7/18/54, Albany, Ga.   BL/TR, 6'1", 180 lbs.   Deb: 9/11/78

YEAR	TM/L	G	AB	R	H	2B	3B	HR	RBI	BB	SO	AVG	OBP	SLG	PRO+	BR	/A	RC	SB	CS	SBR	FR	POS	TPR
1978	Cin-N	4	4	1	1	0	0	0	0	0	1	.250	.250	.250	40	-0	-0	0	0	0	0	0	H	0.0
1979	*Cin-N	43	56	7	12	3	0	0	5	7	5	.214	.323	.268	63	-3	-3	5	0	0	0	-0	1/3	-0.3
1980	Cin-N	65	101	14	27	4	0	4	19	9	19	.267	.333	.426	110	1	1	14	0	0	0	1	1/OC3	0.1
1981	Cin-N	23	24	4	4	1	0	0	3	3	7	.167	.259	.208	33	-2	-2	1	0	0	0	-0	/31	-0.1
	*Hou-N	28	34	5	10	0	0	0	1	2	3	.294	.333	.294	83	-1	-1	3	0	1	0	-0	1	-0.1
	Yr	51	58	9	14	1	0	0	4	5	10	.241	.302	.259	61	-3	-3	4	0	1	-1	-0		-0.2
1982	Hou-N	38	61	7	17	2	0	3	11	5	10	.279	.333	.459	129	1	2	9	0	0	0	-1	1	0.1
1983	Hou-N	42	78	7	13	3	0	1	9	5	12	.167	.217	.244	29	-8	-7	4	0	0	0	-2	1/C	-0.9
1984	Hou-N	32	72	14	19	2	0	2	15	12	10	.264	.369	.375	118	1	2	11	0	0	0	-3	1/C	0.0
1985	Hou-N	44	66	3	9	1	0	1	4	3	7	.136	.174	.197	4	-9	-8	2	0	0	0	-1	1/C	-0.9
1986	Det-A	24	49	6	12	2	0	3	8	3	8	.245	.288	.469	102	-0	-0	6	0	0	0	0	D/3C1	0.0
	SF-N	58	94	12	27	7	0	2	22	12	13	.287	.368	.426	124	2	3	16	0	0	0	0	1/3C20	0.3
1987	*SF-N	83	90	5	24	5	0	1	14	9	20	.267	.333	.356	87	-2	-2	10	1	1	-0	-2	3/1C	-0.4
1988	SF-N	40	40	4	7	1	1	1	3	4	6	.175	.250	.325	67	-2	-2	3	0	0	0	0	/1CO	-0.1
	Hou-N	7	5	0	0	0	0	0	0	0	3	.000	.000	.000	-99	-1	-1	0	0	0	0	0	/1	0.0
	Yr	47	45	4	7	1	1	1	3	4	9	.156	.224	.289	48	-3	-3	3	0	0	0	1		-0.1
1989	Hou-N	32	36	7	10	3	0	0	3	7	2	.278	.395	.361	122	1	1	5	0	0	0	0	1/C	0.1
Total	12	563	810	96	192	34	1	18	117	81	126	.237	.309	.348	85	-20	-16	92	1	2	-1	-7	1/3CDO2	-2.2

■ HAL SPINDEL
Spindel, Harold Stewart   b: 5/27/13, Chandler, Okla.   BR/TR, 6', 185 lbs.   Deb: 4/23/39

YEAR	TM/L	G	AB	R	H	2B	3B	HR	RBI	BB	SO	AVG	OBP	SLG	PRO+	BR	/A	RC	SB	CS	SBR	FR	POS	TPR
1939	StL-A	48	119	13	32	3	1	0	11	8	7	.269	.315	.311	59	-7	-7	11	0	2	-1	1	C	-0.4
1945	Phi-N	36	87	7	20	3	0	0	8	6	7	.230	.280	.264	53	-6	-5	7	0			0	C	-0.4
1946	Phi-N	1	3	0	1	0	0	0	1	0	0	.333	.333	.333	92	-0	-0	0	0			-0	/C	0.0
Total	3	85	209	20	53	6	1	0	20	14	14	.254	.300	.292	57	-13	-13	17	0	2		1	/C	-0.8

■ ANDY SPOGNARDI
Spognardi, Andrea Ettore   b: 10/18/08, Boston, Mass.   BR/TR, 5'9.5", 160 lbs.   Deb: 9/02/32

YEAR	TM/L	G	AB	R	H	2B	3B	HR	RBI	BB	SO	AVG	OBP	SLG	PRO+	BR	/A	RC	SB	CS	SBR	FR	POS	TPR
1932	Bos-A	17	34	9	10	1	0	0	1	6	6	.294	.400	.324	92	-0	-0	5	0	0	0	3	/2S3	0.3

■ AL SPOHRER
Spohrer, Alfred Ray   b: 12/3/02, Philadelphia, Pa.   d: 7/17/72, Plymouth, N.H.   BR/TR, 5'10.5", 175 lbs.   Deb: 4/13/28

YEAR	TM/L	G	AB	R	H	2B	3B	HR	RBI	BB	SO	AVG	OBP	SLG	PRO+	BR	/A	RC	SB	CS	SBR	FR	POS	TPR
1928	NY-N	2	2	0	0	0	0	0	0	0	0	.000	.000	.000	-99	-1	-1	0	0			0	/C	0.0
	Bos-N	51	124	15	27	3	0	0	9	5	11	.218	.254	.242	32	-13	-12	7	1			-5	C	-1.3
	Yr	53	126	15	27	3	0	0	9	5	11	.214	.250	.238	30	-13	-12	7	1			-5		-1.3
1929	Bos-N	114	342	42	93	21	8	2	48	26	35	.272	.327	.398	82	-12	-10	44	1			-9	*C	-0.9
1930	Bos-N	112	356	44	113	22	8	0	37	22	24	.317	.361	.441	96	-4	-2	55	3			-17	*C	-1.2
1931	Bos-N	114	350	23	84	17	5	0	27	22	27	.240	.285	.317	64	-19	-18	32	2			-1	*C	-1.2
1932	Bos-N	104	335	31	90	12	2	0	33	15	26	.269	.300	.316	69	-16	-14	32	2			10	*C	0.0
1933	Bos-N	67	184	11	46	6	1	1	12	11	13	.250	.292	.310	78	-7	-5	17	3			-6	C	-0.8
1934	Bos-N	100	265	25	59	15	0	0	17	14	18	.223	.262	.279	49	-21	-18	19	1			0	C	-1.4
1935	Bos-N	92	260	22	63	7	1	0	16	9	12	.242	.273	.288	55	-18	-15	20	0			-11	C	-2.5
Total	8	756	2218	213	575	103	25	6	199	124	166	.259	.301	.336	70	-110	-95	226	13			-39	C	-9.3

■ JIM SPOTTS
Spotts, James Russell   b: 4/10/09, Honey Brook, Pa.   d: 6/15/64, Medford, N.J.   BR/TR, 5'10.5", 175 lbs.   Deb: 4/23/30

YEAR	TM/L	G	AB	R	H	2B	3B	HR	RBI	BB	SO	AVG	OBP	SLG	PRO+	BR	/A	RC	SB	CS	SBR	FR	POS	TPR
1930	Phi-N	3	2	1	0	0	0	0	0	0	1	.000	.000	.000	-93	-1	-1	0	0			0	/C	0.0

■ CHARLIE SPRAGUE
Sprague, Charles Wellington   b: 10/10/1864, Cleveland, Ohio   d: 12/31/12, Des Moines, Iowa   5'11", 150 lbs.   Deb: 9/17/1887

YEAR	TM/L	G	AB	R	H	2B	3B	HR	RBI	BB	SO	AVG	OBP	SLG	PRO+	BR	/A	RC	SB	CS	SBR	FR	POS	TPR
1887	Chi-N	3	13	0	2	0	0	0	0	0	2	.154	.154	.154	-12	-2	-2	0	0			-1	/PO	0.0
1889	Cle-N	2	7	2	1	0	0	0	1	1	0	.143	.250	.143	12	-1	-1	1	1			1	/P	0.0
1890	Tol-a	55	199	25	47	5	6	1	16			.236	.303	.337	88	-3	-4	24	10			-6	OP	-0.6
Total	3	60	219	27	50	5	6	1	17		2	.228	.293	.320	79	-5	-7	25	11			-6	/OP	-0.6

■ HARRY SPRATT
Spratt, Henry Lee   b: 7/10/1887, Broadford, Va.   d: 7/3/69, Washington, D.C.   BL/TR, 5'8.5", 175 lbs.   Deb: 4/13/11

YEAR	TM/L	G	AB	R	H	2B	3B	HR	RBI	BB	SO	AVG	OBP	SLG	PRO+	BR	/A	RC	SB	CS	SBR	FR	POS	TPR
1911	Bos-N	62	154	22	37	4	4	2	13	13	25	.240	.299	.357	77	-4	-6	17	1			-8	S/23O	-1.2
1912	Bos-N	27	89	6	23	3	2	3	15	7	11	.258	.313	.438	102	-0	-0	12	2			-13	S	-1.0
Total	2	89	243	28	60	7	6	5	28	20	36	.247	.304	.387	86	-4	-6	29	3			-21	/S2O3	-2.2

■ GEORGE SPRIGGS
Spriggs, George Herman   b: 5/22/41, Newell, Md.   BL/TR, 5'11", 175 lbs.   Deb: 9/15/65

YEAR	TM/L	G	AB	R	H	2B	3B	HR	RBI	BB	SO	AVG	OBP	SLG	PRO+	BR	/A	RC	SB	CS	SBR	FR	POS	TPR
1965	Pit-N	9	2	5	1	0	0	0	0	0	0	.500	.500	.500	182	0	0	1	2	0	1	0	/O	0.1
1966	Pit-N	9	7	0	1	0	0	0	0	0	0	.143	.143	.143	-20	-1	-1	0	0	0	0	0	H	0.0
1967	Pit-N	38	57	14	10	1	1	0	5	6	20	.175	.254	.228	39	-4	-4	4	3	0	1	-1	/O	-0.5
1969	KC-A	23	29	4	4	2	1	0	0	3	8	.138	.242	.276	44	-2	-2	2	0	0	0	-0	/O	-0.2
1970	KC-A	51	130	12	27	2	3	1	7	14	32	.208	.285	.292	59	-7	-7	12	4	3	-1	0	O	-0.9
Total	5	130	225	35	43	5	5	1	12	23	63	.191	.269	.271	51	-15	-15	19	9	3	1	-1	/O	-1.5

■ STEVE SPRINGER
Springer, Steven Michael   b: 2/11/61, Long Beach, Cal.   BR/TR, 6', 190 lbs.   Deb: 5/22/90

YEAR	TM/L	G	AB	R	H	2B	3B	HR	RBI	BB	SO	AVG	OBP	SLG	PRO+	BR	/A	RC	SB	CS	SBR	FR	POS	TPR
1990	Cle-A	4	12	1	2	0	0	0	0	0	0	.167	.167	.167	-6	-2	-2	0	0	0	0	-0	/3D	-0.1

■ JOE SPRINZ
Sprinz, Joseph Conrad "Mule"   b: 8/3/02, St.Louis, Mo.   BR/TR, 5'11", 185 lbs.   Deb: 7/16/30

YEAR	TM/L	G	AB	R	H	2B	3B	HR	RBI	BB	SO	AVG	OBP	SLG	PRO+	BR	/A	RC	SB	CS	SBR	FR	POS	TPR
1930	Cle-A	17	45	5	8	1	0	0	2	4	4	.178	.245	.200	14	-6	-6	2	0	0	0	6	C	0.1
1931	Cle-A	1	3	0	0	0	0	0	0	0	0	.000	.000	.000	-95	-1	-1	0	0	0	0	0	/C	0.0
1933	StL-N	3	5	1	1	0	0	0	0	1	1	.200	.333	.200	53	-0	-0	0	0			2	/C	0.2
Total	3	21	53	6	9	1	0	0	2	5	5	.170	.241	.189	12	-7	-7	3	0			8	/C	0.3

■ FREDDY SPURGEON
Spurgeon, Fred   b: 10/9/1900, Wabash, Ind.   d: 11/5/70, Kalamazoo, Mich.   BR/TR, 5'11.5", 160 lbs.   Deb: 9/19/24

YEAR	TM/L	G	AB	R	H	2B	3B	HR	RBI	BB	SO	AVG	OBP	SLG	PRO+	BR	/A	RC	SB	CS	SBR	FR	POS	TPR
1924	Cle-A	3	7	0	1	1	0	0	0	0	0	.143	.250	.286	37	-1	-1	1	0	0	0	1	/2	0.0
1925	Cle-A	107	376	50	108	9	3	0	32	15	21	.287	.315	.327	62	-21	-22	39	8	4	0	-4	32/S	-1.8
1926	Cle-A	149	614	101	181	31	3	0	49	27	36	.295	.327	.355	77	-21	-22	73	7	2	1	-7	*2	-2.0
1927	Cle-A	57	179	30	45	6	1	1	19	18	14	.251	.323	.313	65	-9	-9	19	8	1	2	-8	2	-1.1
Total	4	316	1176	181	335	47	7	1	100	60	71	.285	.322	.339	70	-52	-53	131	23	7	3	-18	2/3S	-4.9

■ ED SPURNEY
Spurney, Edward Frederick   b: 1/19/1872, Cleveland, Ohio   d: 10/12/32, Cleveland, Ohio   Deb: 6/26/1891

YEAR	TM/L	G	AB	R	H	2B	3B	HR	RBI	BB	SO	AVG	OBP	SLG	PRO+	BR	/A	RC	SB	CS	SBR	FR	POS	TPR
1891	Pit-N	3	7	2	2	1	0	0	0	2	1	.286	.444	.429	161	1	1	1	1			-1	/S	0.0

■ MIKE SQUIRES
Squires, Michael Lynn   b: 3/5/52, Kalamazoo, Mich.   BL/TL, 5'11", 185 lbs.   Deb: 9/01/75   C

YEAR	TM/L	G	AB	R	H	2B	3B	HR	RBI	BB	SO	AVG	OBP	SLG	PRO+	BR	/A	RC	SB	CS	SBR	FR	POS	TPR
1975	Chi-A	20	65	5	15	0	0	0	4	8	5	.231	.315	.231	55	-3	-4	5	3	0	1	0	1	-0.3
1977	Chi-A	3	3	0	0	0	0	0	0	0	1	.000	.000	.000	-99	-1	-1	0	0	0	0	0	/1	0.0
1978	Chi-A	46	150	25	42	9	2	0	19	16	21	.280	.351	.367	101	1	0	20	4	4	-1	-2	1	-0.4
1979	Chi-A	122	295	44	78	10	1	2	22	22	19	.264	.320	.325	74	-10	-10	30	15	5	2	4	*1/O	-1.0
1980	Chi-A	131	343	38	97	11	3	2	33	33	24	.283	.347	.350	92	-3	-3	41	8	9	-3	4	*1/C	-0.8
1981	Chi-A	92	294	35	78	9	0	0	25	22	17	.265	.316	.296	79	-8	-7	29	7	2	1	1	1/O	-0.8

YEAR	TM/L	G	AB	R	H	2B	3B	HR	RBI	BB	SO	AVG	OBP	SLG	PRO+	BR	/A	RC	SB	CS	SBR	FR	POS	TPR
1982	Chi-A	116	195	33	52	9	3	1	21	14	13	.267	.316	.359	85	-4	-4	21	3	3	-1	7	*1	0.0
1983	*Chi-A	143	153	21	34	4	1	1	11	22	11	.222	.328	.281	67	-6	-6	15	3	3	-1	6	*1/3D	-0.6
1984	Chi-A	104	82	9	15	1	0	0	6	6	7	.183	.239	.195	21	-9	-9	4	2	2	-1	3	13/OP	-1.0
1985	Chi-A	2	0	1	0	0	0	0	0	0	0	—	—	—	—	0	0	0	0	0	0	0	/R	0.0
Total	10	779	1580	211	411	53	10	6	141	143	108	.260	.323	.318	78	-43	-44	166	45	28	-3	23	1/3DOCP	-4.9

■ MARV STAEHLE
Staehle, Marvin Gustave b: 3/13/42, Oak Park, Ill. BL/TR, 5'10", 165 lbs. Deb: 9/15/64

YEAR	TM/L	G	AB	R	H	2B	3B	HR	RBI	BB	SO	AVG	OBP	SLG	PRO+	BR	/A	RC	SB	CS	SBR	FR	POS	TPR
1964	Chi-A	6	5	0	2	0	0	0	2	0	0	.400	.400	.400	127	0	0	1	1	0	0	0	H	0.0
1965	Chi-A	7	7	0	3	0	0	0	2	0	0	.429	.429	.429	154	0	0	1	0	0	0	0	H	0.0
1966	Chi-A	8	15	2	2	0	0	0	0	4	2	.133	.316	.133	37	-1	-1	1	1	0	0	1	/2	0.1
1967	Chi-A	32	54	1	6	1	0	0	1	4	8	.111	.172	.130	-10	-7	-7	1	1	1	-0	1	2/S	-0.6
1969	Mon-N	6	17	4	7	2	0	1	1	2	0	.412	.474	.706	226	3	3	6	0	0	0	-1	/2	0.3
1970	Mon-N	104	321	41	70	9	1	0	26	39	21	.218	.309	.252	52	-21	-21	27	1	3	-2	-13	2/S	-2.4
1971	Atl-N	22	36	5	4	0	0	0	1	5	4	.111	.238	.111	2	-5	-5	1	0	0	0	4	/23	0.0
Total	7	185	455	53	94	12	1	1	33	54	35	.207	.296	.244	50	-30	-30	38	4	4	-1	-8	2/S3	-2.6

■ HEINIE STAFFORD
Stafford, Henry Alexander b: 11/1/1891, Orleans, Vt. d: 1/29/72, Lake Worth, Fla. TR, 5'7", 160 lbs. Deb: 10/05/16

YEAR	TM/L	G	AB	R	H	2B	3B	HR	RBI	BB	SO	AVG	OBP	SLG	PRO+	BR	/A	RC	SB	CS	SBR	FR	POS	TPR
1916	NY-N	1	1	0	0	0	0	0	0	0	0	.000	.000	.000	-99	-0	-0	0	0			0	H	0.0

■ GENERAL STAFFORD
Stafford, James Joseph "Jamsey" b: 7/9/1868, Webster, Mass. d: 9/11/23, Worcester, Mass. BR/TR, 5'8", 165 lbs. Deb: 8/27/1890

YEAR	TM/L	G	AB	R	H	2B	3B	HR	RBI	BB	SO	AVG	OBP	SLG	PRO+	BR	/A	RC	SB	CS	SBR	FR	POS	TPR
1890	Buf-P	15	49	11	7	1	0	0	3	7	8	.143	.250	.163	14	-6	-5	3	2			-2	P/O	0.0
1893	NY-N	67	281	58	79	7	4	5	27	25	31	.281	.344	.388	96	-2	-2	45	19			-7	O	-0.9
1894	NY-N	14	46	10	10	1	1	0	4	10	7	.217	.368	.283	61	-3	-2	6	2			-3	/3O21	-0.4
1895	NY-N	123	463	79	129	12	5	3	73	40	32	.279	.344	.346	82	-13	-11	71	42			-8	*2O/3	-1.0
1896	NY-N	59	230	28	66	9	1	0	40	13	18	.287	.333	.335	80	-7	-6	31	15			-5	O/S	-1.1
1897	NY-N	7	23	0	2	0	0	0	3	3		.087	.192	.087	-24	-4	-4	0	0			-3	/OS	-0.6
	Lou-N	111	432	68	120	16	5	7	53	31		.278	.330	.387	94	-6	-4	61	14			-12	*S/O3	-1.1
	Yr	118	455	68	122	16	5	7	56	34		.268	.323	.371	88	-10	-8	61	14			-15		-1.7
1898	Lou-N	49	181	26	54	3	0	1	25	19		.298	.365	.331	104	1	2	25	7			-8	2O/3	-0.5
	Bos-N	37	123	21	32	2	0	1	8	4		.260	.289	.301	68	-5	-6	12	3			-3	O/1	-1.0
	Yr	86	304	47	86	5	0	2	33	23		.283	.335	.319	89	-3	-4	37	10			-12		-1.5
1899	Bos-N	55	182	29	55	4	2	3	40	7		.302	.328	.396	92	-0	-3	27	9			-8	O/2S	-1.1
	Was-N	31	118	11	29	5	1	1	14	5		.246	.276	.331	69	-5	-5	12	4			-5	2S/3	-0.7
	Yr	86	300	40	84	9	3	4	54	12		.280	.308	.370	83	-6	-8	39	13			-13		-1.8
Total	8	568	2128	341	583	60	19	21	290	164	96	.274	.331	.350	84	-50	-46	294	117			-64	O2S/3P1	-8.4

■ BOB STAFFORD
Stafford, Robert M. b: Oak Ridge, N.C. Deb: 10/12/1890

YEAR	TM/L	G	AB	R	H	2B	3B	HR	RBI	BB	SO	AVG	OBP	SLG	PRO+	BR	/A	RC	SB	CS	SBR	FR	POS	TPR
1890	Phi-a	1	2	0	0	0	0	0		0		.000	.000	.000	-99	-0	-0	0	0			-0	/O	0.0

■ STEVE STAGGS
Staggs, Stephen Robert b: 5/6/51, Anchorage, Alaska BR/TR, 5'9", 150 lbs. Deb: 7/01/77

YEAR	TM/L	G	AB	R	H	2B	3B	HR	RBI	BB	SO	AVG	OBP	SLG	PRO+	BR	/A	RC	SB	CS	SBR	FR	POS	TPR
1977	Tor-A	72	290	37	75	11	6	2	28	36	38	.259	.340	.359	90	-3	-4	36	5	9	-4	-14	2	-1.5
1978	Oak-A	47	78	10	19	2	2	0	0	19	17	.244	.392	.321	108	1	2	11	2	3	-1	-3	2/S3D	0.0
Total	2	119	368	47	94	13	8	2	28	55	55	.255	.352	.351	94	-2	-2	47	7	12	-5	-17	2/D3S	-1.5

■ CHICK STAHL
Stahl, Charles Sylvester b: 1/10/1873, Avila, Ind. d: 3/28/07, W.Baden, Ind. BL/TL, 5'10", 160 lbs. Deb: 4/19/1897 M

YEAR	TM/L	G	AB	R	H	2B	3B	HR	RBI	BB	SO	AVG	OBP	SLG	PRO+	BR	/A	RC	SB	CS	SBR	FR	POS	TPR
1897	*Bos-N	114	469	112	166	30	13	4	97	38		.354	.406	.499	132	27	22	105	18			-3	*O	0.9
1898	Bos-N	125	467	72	144	21	8	5	52	46		.308	.375	.407	121	17	13	75	6			-1	*O	0.4
1899	Bos-N	148	576	122	202	23	19	7	52	72		.351	.426	.493	141	45	36	139	33			6	*O/P	2.9
1900	Bos-N	136	553	88	163	23	16	5	82	34		.295	.336	.421	98	6	-4	89	27			9	*O	-0.5
1901	Bos-N	131	515	105	156	20	16	6	72	54		.303	.376	.439	130	20	21	100	29			-1	*O	1.7
1902	Bos-A	127	508	92	164	22	11	2	58	37		.323	.373	.421	118	15	13	93	24			-4	*O	0.1
1903	*Bos-A	77	299	60	82	12	6	2	44	28		.274	.336	.375	109	6	4	43	10			-2	O	-0.2
1904	Bos-A	157	587	83	170	27	19	3	67	64		.290	.359	.416	139	32	28	97	11			-14	*O	0.5
1905	Bos-A	134	500	61	129	17	4	0	47	50		.258	.325	.308	102	3	3	59	18			-5	*O	-0.9
1906	Bos-A	155	595	62	170	24	6	4	51	47		.286	.338	.366	123	15	15	82	13			10	*OM	2.1
Total	10	1304	5069	857	1546	219	118	36	622	470		.305	.366	.416	123	186	152	882	189			-6	*O/P	7.0

■ JAKE STAHL
Stahl, Garland b: 4/13/1879, Elkhart, Ill. d: 9/18/22, Monrovia, Cal. BR/TR, 6'2", 195 lbs. Deb: 4/20/03 M

YEAR	TM/L	G	AB	R	H	2B	3B	HR	RBI	BB	SO	AVG	OBP	SLG	PRO+	BR	/A	RC	SB	CS	SBR	FR	POS	TPR
1903	Bos-A	40	92	14	22	3	5	2	8	4		.239	.271	.446	108	1	1	12	1			-1	C/O	0.3
1904	Was-A	142	520	54	136	29	12	3	50	21		.262	.290	.381	115	6	7	67	25			6	*1O	1.6
1905	Was-A	141	501	66	125	22	12	5	66	28		.250	.289	.371	116	5	7	69	41			2	*1M	0.6
1906	Was-A	137	482	38	107	9	8	0	51	21		.222	.254	.274	70	-18	-16	44	30			-2	*1M	-2.3
1908	NY-A	75	274	34	70	18	5	2	42	11		.255	.284	.380	116	4	4	34	17			4	O/1	0.5
	Bos-A	78	262	29	64	9	11	0	23	20		.244	.298	.363	113	4	3	32	13			-2	1	0.1
	Yr	153	536	63	134	27	16	2	65	31		.250	.291	.371	115	8	7	66	30			2		0.5
1909	Bos-A	127	435	62	128	19	12	6	60	43		.294	.377	.434	153	28	27	77	16			-11	*1	1.8
1910	Bos-A	144	531	68	144	19	16	10	77	42		.271	.334	.424	134	21	19	82	22			-7	*1	1.9
1912	*Bos-A	95	326	40	98	21	6	3	60	31		.301	.372	.429	123	12	10	57	13			-2	1M	0.9
1913	Bos-A	2	2	0	0	0	0	0	0	0	1	.000	.000	.000	-98	-0	-1	0	0			0	HM	0.0
Total	9	981	3425	405	894	149	87	31	437	221	1	.261	.311	.382	118	63	62	473	178			-13	1/OC	5.3

■ LARRY STAHL
Stahl, Larry Floyd b: 6/29/41, Belleville, Ill. BL/TL, 6', 175 lbs. Deb: 9/11/64

YEAR	TM/L	G	AB	R	H	2B	3B	HR	RBI	BB	SO	AVG	OBP	SLG	PRO+	BR	/A	RC	SB	CS	SBR	FR	POS	TPR
1964	KC-A	15	46	7	12	1	0	3	6	1	10	.261	.277	.478	102	0	-0	6	0	0	0	0	O	0.0
1965	KC-A	28	81	9	16	2	1	4	14	5	16	.198	.253	.395	82	-2	-2	8	1	0	0	2	O	0.0
1966	KC-A	119	312	37	78	11	5	5	34	17	63	.250	.291	.365	90	-6	-5	34	5	3	-0	-1	O	-1.0
1967	NY-N	71	155	9	37	5	0	1	18	8	25	.239	.285	.290	66	-7	-7	12	2	2	-1	6	O	-0.2
1968	NY-N	53	183	15	43	7	2	3	10	21	38	.235	.314	.344	97	-0	-0	22	3	0	1	6	O/1	0.5
1969	SD-N	95	162	10	32	6	2	3	10	17	31	.198	.278	.315	68	-8	-7	13	3	3	-1	4	O1	-0.6
1970	SD-N	52	66	5	12	2	0	3	9	2	14	.182	.206	.212	13	-8	-8	3	2	2	-1	0	O	-0.8
1971	SD-N	114	308	27	78	13	4	8	36	26	59	.253	.311	.399	107	-1	-2	37	4	3	-1	5	O/1	0.3
1972	SD-N	107	297	31	67	9	3	7	20	31	67	.226	.299	.347	89	-7	-4	31	1	3	-2	-2	O/1	-1.2
1973	*Cin-N	76	111	17	25	2	2	2	12	14	34	.225	.317	.333	85	-3	-2	13	1	0	0	-1	O/1	-0.3
Total	10	730	1721	167	400	58	19	36	163	142	357	.232	.293	.351	86	-41	-33	180	22	16	-3	19	O/1	-3.3

■ ROY STAIGER
Staiger, Roy Joseph b: 1/6/50, Tulsa, Okla. BR/TR, 6', 195 lbs. Deb: 9/12/75

YEAR	TM/L	G	AB	R	H	2B	3B	HR	RBI	BB	SO	AVG	OBP	SLG	PRO+	BR	/A	RC	SB	CS	SBR	FR	POS	TPR
1975	NY-N	13	19	2	3	1	0	0	0	0	4	.158	.158	.211	2	-3	-2	0	0	0	0	1	3	0.0
1976	NY-N	95	304	23	67	8	1	2	26	25	35	.220	.282	.273	62	-17	-15	23	3	3	-1	19	3/S	0.3
1977	NY-N	40	123	16	31	9	0	2	11	4	20	.252	.276	.374	76	-5	-4	12	1	0	0	6	3/S	0.1
1979	NY-A	4	11	1	3	1	0	0	1	1	0	.273	.333	.364	90	-0	-0	1	0	0	0	0	/3	0.0
Total	4	152	457	42	104	19	1	4	38	30	59	.228	.277	.300	64	-24	-22	36	4	3	-1	26	3/S	0.4

■ TUCK STAINBACK
Stainback, George Tucker b: 8/4/10, Los Angeles, Cal. BR/TR, 5'11.5", 175 lbs. Deb: 4/17/34

YEAR	TM/L	G	AB	R	H	2B	3B	HR	RBI	BB	SO	AVG	OBP	SLG	PRO+	BR	/A	RC	SB	CS	SBR	FR	POS	TPR
1934	Chi-N	104	359	47	110	14	3	2	46	8	42	.306	.327	.379	90	-6	-8	45	7			-3	O/3	-1.2
1935	Chi-N	47	94	16	24	4	0	3	11	0	13	.255	.271	.394	76	-3	-4	9	1			-1	O	-0.5
1936	Chi-N	44	75	13	13	3	0	1	5	6	14	.173	.235	.253	31	-7	-8	5	1			1	O	-0.7

YEAR	TM/L	G	AB	R	H	2B	3B	HR	RBI	BB	SO	AVG	OBP	SLG	PRO+	BR	/A	RC	SB	CS	SBR	FR	POS	TPR
1937	Chi-N	72	160	18	37	7	1	0	14	7	16	.231	.268	.287	49	-11	-12	12	3			5	O	-0.8
1938	StL-N	6	10	2	0	0	0	0	0	0	3	.000	.000	.000	-95	-3	-3	0	0			1	/O	-0.1
	Phi-N	30	81	9	21	3	0	1	11	3	3	.259	.294	.333	74	-3	-3	8	1			1	O	-0.2
	Bro-N	35	104	15	34	6	3	0	20	2	4	.327	.346	.442	113	2	2	16	1			-0	O	0.1
	Yr	71	195	26	55	9	3	1	31	5	10	.282	.307	.374	86	-4	-4	23	2			1		-0.2
1939	Bro-N	68	201	22	54	7	0	3	19	4	23	.269	.290	.348	68	-9	-10	21	0			-1	O	-1.0
1940	Det-A	15	40	4	9	2	0	0	1	1	9	.225	.262	.275	36	-4	-4	3	0	0	0	4	/O	0.0
1941	Det-A	94	200	19	49	8	1	2	10	3	21	.245	.260	.325	49	-14	-16	18	6	3	0	1	O	-2.0
1942	*NY-A	15	10	0	2	0	0	0	0	0	2	.200	.200	.200	13	-1	-1	0	0	0	0	1	/O	0.0
1943	*NY-A	71	231	31	60	11	2	0	10	7	16	.260	.285	.325	77	-7	-7	21	3	3	-1	3	O	-0.7
1944	NY-A	30	78	13	17	3	0	0	5	3	7	.218	.247	.256	42	-6	-6	6	1	0	0	-0	O	-0.6
1945	NY-A	95	327	40	84	12	2	5	32	13	20	.257	.289	.352	82	-7	-9	33	0	4	-2	6	O	-0.8
1946	Phi-A	91	291	35	71	10	2	0	20	7	20	.244	.264	.292	56	-18	-18	23	3	2	-0	1	O	-2.0
Total	13	817	2261	284	585	90	14	17	204	64	213	.259	.284	.333	68	-97	-104	219	27	12		20	O/3	-10.5

■ GALE STALEY
Staley, George Gaylord b: 5/2/1899, DePere, Wis. d: 4/19/89, Walnut Creek, Cal. BL/TR, 5'8.5", 167 lbs. Deb: 9/16/25

YEAR	TM/L	G	AB	R	H	2B	3B	HR	RBI	BB	SO	AVG	OBP	SLG	PRO+	BR	/A	RC	SB	CS	SBR	FR	POS	TPR
1925	Chi-N	7	26	2	11	2	0	0	3	2	1	.423	.464	.500	144	2	2	6	0	1	-1	4	/2	0.5

■ VIRGIL STALLCUP
Stallcup, Thomas Virgil "Red" b: 1/3/22, Ravensford, N.C. d: 5/2/89, Greenville, S.C. BR/TR, 6'3", 185 lbs. Deb: 4/18/47

YEAR	TM/L	G	AB	R	H	2B	3B	HR	RBI	BB	SO	AVG	OBP	SLG	PRO+	BR	/A	RC	SB	CS	SBR	FR	POS	TPR
1947	Cin-N	8	1	1	0	0	0	0	0	0	1	.000	.000	.000	-99	-0	-0	0	0			0	/S	0.0
1948	Cin-N	149	539	40	123	30	4	3	65	18	52	.228	.253	.315	55	-37	-34	40	2			-0	*S	-1.8
1949	Cin-N	141	575	49	146	28	5	3	45	9	44	.254	.268	.336	60	-33	-34	49	1			-10	*S	-2.7
1950	Cin-N	136	483	44	121	23	2	8	54	17	39	.251	.276	.356	65	-26	-26	44	4			-5	*S	-1.6
1951	Cin-N	121	428	33	103	17	2	5	49	6	40	.241	.251	.346	58	-26	-27	34	2	4	-2	-8	*S	-2.6
1952	Cin-N	2	1	0	0	0	0	0	0	0	0	.000	.000	.000	-99	-0	-0	0	0	0	0	0	/S	0.0
	StL-N	29	31	4	4	1	0	0	1	1	5	.129	.156	.161	-12	-5	-5	1	0	0	0	2	S	-0.1
	Yr	31	32	4	4	1	0	0	1	1	5	.125	.152	.156	-15	-5	-5	1	0	0	0	2		-0.1
1953	StL-N	1	1	0	0	0	0	0	0	0	0	.000	.000	.000	-99	-0	-0	0	0	0	0	0	H	0.0
Total	7	587	2059	171	497	99	13	22	214	51	181	.241	.260	.334	58	-127	-126	168	9	4		-21	S	-8.8

■ GEORGE STALLER
Staller, George Walborn "Stopper" b: 4/1/16, Rutherford Heights, Pa. BL/TL, 5'11", 190 lbs. Deb: 9/14/43 C

YEAR	TM/L	G	AB	R	H	2B	3B	HR	RBI	BB	SO	AVG	OBP	SLG	PRO+	BR	/A	RC	SB	CS	SBR	FR	POS	TPR
1943	Phi-A	21	85	14	23	1	3	3	12	5	6	.271	.326	.459	129	3	3	13	1	0	0	-2	O	0.1

■ GEORGE STALLINGS
Stallings, George Tweedy "Gentleman George"
b: 11/17/1867, Augusta, Ga. d: 5/13/29, Haddock, Ga. BR/TR, 6'1", 187 lbs. Deb: 5/22/1890 M

YEAR	TM/L	G	AB	R	H	2B	3B	HR	RBI	BB	SO	AVG	OBP	SLG	PRO+	BR	/A	RC	SB	CS	SBR	FR	POS	TPR
1890	Bro-N	4	11	1	0	0	0	0	0	1	3	.000	.154	.000	-53	-2	-2	0	0			-2	/C	-0.2
1897	Phi-N	2	9	1	2	1	0	0	0	0		.222	.222	.333	48	-1	-1	1	0			1	/O1M	0.0
1898	Phi-N	1	0	1	0	0	0	0	0	0		—	—	—	—	0	0	0	0			0	/HM	0.0
Total	3	7	20	3	2	1	0	0	0	1	3	.100	.182	.150	-6	-3	-3	1	0			-1	/C1O	-0.2

■ OSCAR STANAGE
Stanage, Oscar Harland b: 3/17/1883, Tulare, Cal. d: 11/11/64, Detroit, Mich. BR/TR, 5'11", 190 lbs. Deb: 5/19/06 C

YEAR	TM/L	G	AB	R	H	2B	3B	HR	RBI	BB	SO	AVG	OBP	SLG	PRO+	BR	/A	RC	SB	CS	SBR	FR	POS	TPR
1906	Cin-N	1	1	0	0	0	0	0	0	0		.000	.000	.000	-96	-0	-0	0	0			-0	/C	0.0
1909	*Det-A	77	252	17	66	8	6	0	21	11		.262	.298	.341	98	-0	-1	26	2			-9	C	-0.4
1910	Det-A	88	275	24	57	7	4	2	25	20		.207	.266	.284	68	-9	-11	21	1			-3	C	-0.5
1911	Det-A	141	503	45	133	13	7	3	51	20		.264	.297	.336	73	-18	-21	51	3			-15	*C	-1.8
1912	Det-A	121	394	35	103	9	4	0	41	34		.261	.326	.305	83	-9	-8	40	3			-27	*C	-2.2
1913	Det-A	80	241	19	54	13	2	0	21	21	35	.224	.292	.295	73	-9	-8	22	5			-9	C	-1.1
1914	Det-A	122	400	16	77	8	4	0	25	24	58	.192	.242	.233	41	-29	-30	25	2	1	0	-6	*C	-3.0
1915	Det-A	100	300	27	67	9	2	1	31	20	41	.223	.274	.277	62	-14	-15	25	5	1	1	-9	*C	-1.6
1916	Det-A	94	291	16	69	17	3	0	30	17	48	.237	.286	.316	78	-8	-9	28	3			-9	C	-1.4
1917	Det-A	99	297	19	61	14	1	0	30	20	35	.205	.262	.259	59	-15	-15	21	3			-4	C	-1.2
1918	Det-A	54	186	9	47	4	0	1	14	11	18	.253	.294	.290	80	-6	-5	16	2			-8	C/1S	-0.9
1919	Det-A	38	120	9	29	4	1	1	15	7	12	.242	.295	.317	73	-5	-4	11	1			1	C	-0.1
1920	Det-A	78	238	12	55	17	0	0	17	14	21	.231	.277	.303	55	-16	-16	21	0	0	0	-9	C	-1.7
1925	Det-A	3	5	0	1	0	0	0	0	0	0	.200	.200	.200	2	-1	-1	0	0	0	0	-1	/C	0.0
Total	14	1096	3503	248	819	123	34	8	321	219	268	.234	.284	.295	69	-138	-144	305	30	2		-108	*C/1S	-15.9

■ JERRY STANDAERT
Standaert, Jerome John b: 11/2/01, Chicago, Ill. d: 8/4/64, Chicago, Ill. BR/TR, 5'10", 168 lbs. Deb: 4/16/25

YEAR	TM/L	G	AB	R	H	2B	3B	HR	RBI	BB	SO	AVG	OBP	SLG	PRO+	BR	/A	RC	SB	CS	SBR	FR	POS	TPR
1925	Bro-N	1	1	0	0	0	0	0	0	0	1	.000	.000	.000	-99	-0	-0	0	0	0	0	0	H	0.0
1926	Bro-N	66	113	13	39	8	2	0	14	5	7	.345	.378	.451	124	3	4	19	0			-11	23/S	-0.5
1929	Bos-A	19	18	1	3	2	0	0	4	3	2	.167	.286	.278	47	-1	-1	2	0	0	0	0	1	-0.2
Total	3	86	132	14	42	10	2	0	18	8	10	.318	.362	.424	111	2	2	20	0	0		-11	/231S	-0.7

■ PETE STANICEK
Stanicek, Peter Louis b: 4/18/63, Harvey, Ill. BB/TR, 5'11", 175 lbs. Deb: 9/01/87

YEAR	TM/L	G	AB	R	H	2B	3B	HR	RBI	BB	SO	AVG	OBP	SLG	PRO+	BR	/A	RC	SB	CS	SBR	FR	POS	TPR
1987	Bal-A	30	113	9	31	3	0	6	9	8	19	.274	.333	.301	72	-5	-4	13	8	1	2	-6	2D/3	-0.5
1988	Bal-A	83	261	29	60	7	1	4	17	28	45	.230	.314	.310	78	-8	-7	25	12	6	0	-9	O2/D	-1.6
Total	2	113	374	38	91	10	1	4	26	36	64	.243	.320	.307	76	-12	-11	38	20	7	2	-15	/O2D3	-2.1

■ STEVE STANICEK
Stanicek, Stephen Blair b: 6/19/61, Lake Forest, Ill. BR/TR, 6', 190 lbs. Deb: 9/16/87

YEAR	TM/L	G	AB	R	H	2B	3B	HR	RBI	BB	SO	AVG	OBP	SLG	PRO+	BR	/A	RC	SB	CS	SBR	FR	POS	TPR
1987	Mil-A	4	7	2	2	0	0	0	0	0	2	.286	.286	.286	51	-0	-0	1	0	0	0	0	/D	0.0
1989	Phi-N	9	9	0	1	0	0	0	1	0	3	.111	.111	.111	-36	-2	-2	0	0	0	0	0	H	-0.1
Total	2	13	16	2	3	0	0	0	1	0	5	.188	.188	.188	4	-2	-2	1	0	0	0	0	/D	-0.1

■ TOM STANKARD
Stankard, Thomas Francis b: 3/20/1882, Waltham, Mass. d: 6/13/58, Waltham, Mass. BR/TR, 6', 190 lbs. Deb: 7/02/04

YEAR	TM/L	G	AB	R	H	2B	3B	HR	RBI	BB	SO	AVG	OBP	SLG	PRO+	BR	/A	RC	SB	CS	SBR	FR	POS	TPR
1904	Pit-N	2	2	0	0	0	0	0	0	0		.000	.000	.000	-97	-0	-0	0	0			-0	/S3	0.0

■ EDDIE STANKY
Stanky, Edward Raymond "The Brat" or "Muggsy" b: 9/3/16, Philadelphia, Pa. BR/TR, 5'8", 170 lbs. Deb: 4/21/43 MC

YEAR	TM/L	G	AB	R	H	2B	3B	HR	RBI	BB	SO	AVG	OBP	SLG	PRO+	BR	/A	RC	SB	CS	SBR	FR	POS	TPR
1943	Chi-N	142	510	92	125	15	1	0	47	92	42	.245	.363	.278	88	-4	-3	58	4			12	*2S/3	1.4
1944	Chi-N	13	25	4	6	0	1	0	0	2	2	.240	.296	.320	74	-1	-1	2	1			2	/2S3	0.2
	Bro-N	89	261	32	72	9	2	0	16	44	13	.276	.382	.326	102	3	3	37	3			-18	2S/3	-0.4
	Yr	102	286	36	78	9	3	0	16	46	15	.273	.375	.325	100	2	2	39	4			-16		-0.2
1945	Bro-N	153	555	128	143	29	5	1	39	148	42	.258	.417	.333	111	18	18	93	6			9	*2/S	3.9
1946	Bro-N	144	483	98	132	24	7	0	36	137	56	.273	.436	.352	124	26	25	90	8			-5	*2	2.6
1947	*Bro-N	146	559	97	141	24	5	3	53	103	39	.252	.373	.329	85	-5	-8	78	3			7	*2	1.4
1948	*Bos-N	67	247	49	79	14	2	2	29	61	13	.320	.455	.417	140	17	18	52	3			5	2	2.7
1949	Bos-N	138	506	90	144	24	5	1	42	113	41	.285	.417	.358	116	14	18	86	3			-8	*2	1.4
1950	NY-N	152	527	115	158	25	5	8	51	144	50	.300	.460	.412	131	35	35	116	9			2	*2	3.9
1951	*NY-N	145	515	88	127	17	2	14	43	127	63	.247	.401	.369	108	13	12	90	8	5	-1	-1	*2	1.6
1952	StL-N	53	83	13	19	4	0	0	7	19	9	.229	.373	.277	83	-1	-1	11	0	0	0	-1	2M	0.0
1953	StL-N	17	30	5	8	0	0	0	1	6	4	.267	.405	.267	80	-0	-0	4	0	0	0	1	/2M	0.1
Total	11	1259	4301	811	1154	185	35	29	364	996	374	.268	.410	.348	109	114	116	717	48	5		4	*2/S3	18.8

■ FRED STANLEY
Stanley, Frederick Blair b: 8/13/47, Farnhamville, Iowa BR/TR, 5'10", 165 lbs. Deb: 9/11/69

YEAR	TM/L	G	AB	R	H	2B	3B	HR	RBI	BB	SO	AVG	OBP	SLG	PRO+	BR	/A	RC	SB	CS	SBR	FR	POS	TPR
1969	Sea-A	17	43	2	12	2	1	0	4	3	8	.279	.326	.372	96	-0	-0	6	1	0	0	-4	S/2	-0.3
1970	Mil-A	6	0	1	0	0	0	0	0	0	0	—	—	—		0	0	0	0	0	0	2	/2	0.3

YEAR	TM/L	G	AB	R	H	2B	3B	HR	RBI	BB	SO	AVG	OBP	SLG	PRO+	BR	/A	RC	SB	CS	SBR	FR	POS	TPR
1971	Cle-A	60	129	14	29	4	0	2	12	27	25	.225	.363	.302	83	-0	-2	16	1	0	0	7	S/2	1.2
1972	Cle-A	6	12	1	2	1	0	0	0	2	3	.167	.286	.250	58	-1	-1	1	0	0	0	-3	/S2	-0.3
	SD-N	39	85	15	17	2	0	0	2	12	19	.200	.306	.224	57	-5	-4	7	1	0	0	3	2S/3	0.3
1973	NY-A	26	66	6	14	0	1	1	5	7	16	.212	.288	.288	65	-3	-3	6	0	0	0	3	S/2	0.3
1974	NY-A	33	38	2	7	0	0	0	3	3	2	.184	.244	.184	25	-4	-3	1	1	2	-1	12	S2	1.0
1975	NY-A	117	252	34	56	5	1	0	15	21	27	.222	.285	.250	54	-15	-15	18	3	1	0	4	S2/3	-0.1
1976	*NY-A	110	260	32	62	2	2	1	20	34	29	.238	.329	.273	78	-6	-6	26	1	0	0	-23	*S/2	-2.3
1977	*NY-A	48	46	6	12	0	0	1	7	8	6	.261	.370	.326	93	-0	-0	6	1	1	-0	3	S/32	0.8
1978	*NY-A	81	160	14	35	7	0	1	9	25	31	.219	.324	.281	73	-5	-5	16	0	0	0	-4	S2/3	-0.2
1979	NY-A	57	100	9	20	1	0	2	14	5	17	.200	.238	.270	38	-9	-9	6	0	1	-1	13	S3/210	0.8
1980	NY-A	49	86	13	18	3	0	0	5	5	5	.209	.269	.244	42	-7	-7	6	0	0	0	7	S23	0.3
1981	*Oak-A	66	145	15	28	4	0	0	7	15	23	.193	.269	.221	44	-10	-10	11	2	0	1	-17	S/2	-2.1
1982	Oak-A	101	228	33	44	7	0	2	17	29	32	.193	.287	.250	51	-15	-14	17	0	1	-1	-20	S/2	-2.6
Total	14	816	1650	197	356	38	5	10	120	196	243	.216	.302	.263	62	-81	-77	144	11	6	-0	-18	S2/301	-2.9

■ JIM STANLEY
Stanley, James F. b: 1889, BB/TR, 5'6", 148 lbs. Deb: 4/19/14

YEAR	TM/L	G	AB	R	H	2B	3B	HR	RBI	BB	SO	AVG	OBP	SLG	PRO+	BR	/A	RC	SB	CS	SBR	FR	POS	TPR
1914	Chi-F	54	98	13	19	3	0	0	4	19	14	.194	.347	.224	70	-3	-2	9	2			-10	S/32O	-0.9

■ JOE STANLEY
Stanley, Joseph b: New Jersey Deb: 4/24/1884

YEAR	TM/L	G	AB	R	H	2B	3B	HR	RBI	BB	SO	AVG	OBP	SLG	PRO+	BR	/A	RC	SB	CS	SBR	FR	POS	TPR
1884	Bal-U	6	21	3	5	1	0	0		0		.238	.238	.286	69	-1	-1	1	0			-2	/O	-0.2

■ JOE STANLEY
Stanley, Joseph Bernard b: 4/2/1881, Washington, D.C. d: 9/13/67, Detroit, Mich. BB/TR, 5'9.5", 150 lbs. Deb: 9/11/1897

YEAR	TM/L	G	AB	R	H	2B	3B	HR	RBI	BB	SO	AVG	OBP	SLG	PRO+	BR	/A	RC	SB	CS	SBR	FR	POS	TPR
1897	Was-N	1	1	0	0	0	0	0	0	0		.000	.000	.000	-99	-0	-0	0	0			0	/P	0.0
1902	Was-A	3	12	2	4	0	0	0	1	0		.333	.333	.333	86	-0	-0	1	0			-1	/O	0.0
1903	Bos-N	86	308	40	77	12	5	1	47	18		.250	.291	.331	82	-9	-7	34	10			3	O/PS	-0.7
1904	Bos-N	3	8	0	0	0	0	0	0	0		.000	.000	.000	-99	-2	-2	0	0			1	/O	0.0
1905	Was-A	28	92	13	24	2	1	1	17	7		.261	.313	.337	113	1	1	12	4			0	O	0.0
1906	Was-A	73	221	18	36	0	4	0	9	20		.163	.232	.199	39	-15	-14	14	6			-5	O/P	-2.3
1909	Chi-N	22	52	4	7	1	0	0	2	6		.135	.224	.154	17	-5	-5	2	0			-4	O	-1.0
Total	7	216	694	77	148	15	10	2	76	51		.213	.267	.272	66	-31	-27	63	20			-6	O/PS	-4.0

■ MICKEY STANLEY
Stanley, Mitchell Jack b: 7/20/42, Grand Rapids, Mich BR/TR, 6'1", 185 lbs. Deb: 9/13/64

YEAR	TM/L	G	AB	R	H	2B	3B	HR	RBI	BB	SO	AVG	OBP	SLG	PRO+	BR	/A	RC	SB	CS	SBR	FR	POS	TPR
1964	Det-A	4	11	3	3	0	0	0	1	0	1	.273	.273	.273	52	-1	-1	1	0	0	0	0	/O	0.0
1965	Det-A	30	117	14	28	6	0	3	13	3	12	.239	.258	.368	75	-4	-4	11	1	0	0	2	O	-0.2
1966	Det-A	92	235	28	68	15	4	3	19	17	20	.289	.337	.426	115	5	4	33	2	1	0	12	O	1.4
1967	Det-A	145	333	38	70	7	3	7	24	29	46	.210	.273	.312	71	-12	-13	30	9	2	2	-2	*O/1	-1.8
1968	*Det-A	153	583	88	151	16	6	11	60	42	57	.259	.313	.364	102	3	1	62	4	3	-1	-1	*O1/S2	-0.6
1969	Det-A	149	592	73	139	28	1	16	70	52	56	.235	.299	.367	82	-13	-16	64	8	4	0	-15	*OS/1	-3.3
1970	Det-A	142	568	83	143	21	11	13	47	45	56	.252	.307	.396	92	-7	-8	67	10	1	2	3	*O/1	-0.8
1971	Det-A	139	401	43	117	14	5	7	41	24	44	.292	.332	.404	103	3	1	52	1	3	-2	4	*O	0.0
1972	*Det-A	142	435	45	102	16	6	14	55	29	49	.234	.282	.395	97	-2	-3	45	1	0	0	1	*O	-0.5
1973	Det-A	157	602	81	147	23	5	17	57	48	65	.244	.300	.384	86	-8	-13	68	0	4	-2	10	*O	-0.9
1974	Det-A	99	394	40	87	13	2	8	34	26	63	.221	.271	.325	68	-16	-17	32	5	3	-0	4	O1/2	-1.7
1975	Det-A	52	164	26	42	7	3	3	19	15	27	.256	.322	.390	96	-0	-1	21	1	1	-0	3	O1/3D	0.0
1976	Det-A	84	214	34	55	17	1	4	29	14	19	.257	.303	.402	101	1	-0	25	2	0	1	1	O13/S2D	0.0
1977	Det-A	75	222	30	51	9	1	8	23	18	30	.230	.287	.387	78	-6	-8	24	0	0	0	-1	O/1SD	-1.0
1978	Det-A	53	151	15	40	9	0	3	8	9	19	.265	.306	.384	90	-2	-2	17	0	1	-1	-4	O1	-0.7
Total	15	1516	5022	641	1243	201	48	117	500	371	564	.248	.300	.377	89	-59	-80	549	44	23	-1	17	*O/1S3D2	-10.1

■ MIKE STANLEY
Stanley, Robert Michael b: 6/25/63, Ft.Lauderdale, Fla BR/TR, 6'1", 185 lbs. Deb: 6/24/86

YEAR	TM/L	G	AB	R	H	2B	3B	HR	RBI	BB	SO	AVG	OBP	SLG	PRO+	BR	/A	RC	SB	CS	SBR	FR	POS	TPR
1986	Tex-A	15	30	4	10	3	0	1	1	3	7	.333	.394	.533	146	2	2	7	1	0	0	-0	/3COD	0.2
1987	Tex-A	78	216	34	59	8	1	6	37	31	48	.273	.367	.403	104	2	2	33	3	0	1	-8	C1/OD	-0.1
1988	Tex-A	94	249	21	57	8	0	3	27	37	62	.229	.329	.297	75	-7	-7	26	0	0	0	-1	CD/13	-0.5
1989	Tex-A	67	122	9	30	3	1	1	11	12	29	.246	.324	.311	78	-3	-3	12	1	0	0	-1	CD/13	-0.5
1990	Tex-A	103	189	21	47	8	1	2	19	30	25	.249	.352	.333	91	-1	-1	24	1	0	0	-1	CD/31	0.0
Total	5	357	806	89	203	30	3	13	95	113	171	.252	.346	.345	90	-7	-8	102	6	0	2	-14	C/D130	-0.9

■ JACK STANSBURY
Stansbury, John James b: 12/6/1885, Phillipsburg, N.J. d: 12/26/70, Easton, Pa. BR/TR, 5'9", 165 lbs. Deb: 6/30/18

YEAR	TM/L	G	AB	R	H	2B	3B	HR	RBI	BB	SO	AVG	OBP	SLG	PRO+	BR	/A	RC	SB	CS	SBR	FR	POS	TPR
1918	Bos-A	20	47	3	6	1	0	0	2	6	3	.128	.241	.149	18	-5	-4	2	0			2	3/O	-0.1

■ BUCK STANTON
Stanton, George Washington b: 6/19/06, Stantonsburg, N.C BL/TL, 5'10", 150 lbs. Deb: 9/05/31

YEAR	TM/L	G	AB	R	H	2B	3B	HR	RBI	BB	SO	AVG	OBP	SLG	PRO+	BR	/A	RC	SB	CS	SBR	FR	POS	TPR
1931	StL-A	13	15	3	3	2	0	0	0	0	6	.200	.200	.333	37	-1	-1	1	0	0	0	0	/O	-0.1

■ HARRY STANTON
Stanton, Harry Andrew b: St.Louis, Mo. TR , Deb: 10/14/00

YEAR	TM/L	G	AB	R	H	2B	3B	HR	RBI	BB	SO	AVG	OBP	SLG	PRO+	BR	/A	RC	SB	CS	SBR	FR	POS	TPR
1900	StL-N	1	0	0	0	0	0	0	0	0		—	—	—	—	0	0	0	0			0	/C	0.0

■ LEROY STANTON
Stanton, Leroy Bobby b: 4/10/46, Latta, S.C. BR/TR, 6'1", 195 lbs. Deb: 9/10/70

YEAR	TM/L	G	AB	R	H	2B	3B	HR	RBI	BB	SO	AVG	OBP	SLG	PRO+	BR	/A	RC	SB	CS	SBR	FR	POS	TPR
1970	NY-N	4	4	0	1	0	1	0	0	0	0	.250	.250	.750	157	0	0	0	0	0	0	0	/O	0.0
1971	NY-N	5	21	2	4	1	0	0	2	2	4	.190	.261	.238	43	-2	-2	1	0	0	0	-1	/O	-0.2
1972	Cal-A	127	402	44	101	15	3	12	39	22	100	.251	.297	.393	110	1	3	42	2	3	-1	1	*O	0.0
1973	Cal-A	119	306	41	72	9	2	8	34	27	88	.235	.301	.356	92	-7	-4	31	3	3	-1	-9	*O	-1.6
1974	Cal-A	118	415	48	111	21	2	11	62	33	107	.267	.329	.407	117	5	8	54	10	8	-2	4	*O	0.8
1975	Cal-A	137	440	67	115	20	3	14	82	52	85	.261	.347	.416	124	9	13	66	18	6	2	-0	*O/D	1.1
1976	Cal-A	93	231	12	44	13	1	2	25	24	57	.190	.270	.281	66	-11	-9	16	2	6	-3	-4	O/D	-1.9
1977	Sea-A	133	454	56	125	24	1	27	90	42	115	.275	.343	.511	131	17	18	79	0	1	-1	1	OD	1.5
1978	Sea-A	93	302	24	55	11	0	3	24	34	80	.182	.267	.248	46	-21	-21	21	1	0	-1	-1	DO	-2.3
Total	9	829	2575	294	628	114	13	77	358	236	636	.244	.313	.388	103	-9	6	310	36	27	-5	-9	O/D	-2.6

■ TOM STANTON
Stanton, Thomas Patrick b: 10/25/1874, St.Louis, Mo. d: 1/17/57, St.Louis, Mo. BB/TR, 5'10", 175 lbs. Deb: 4/19/04

YEAR	TM/L	G	AB	R	H	2B	3B	HR	RBI	BB	SO	AVG	OBP	SLG	PRO+	BR	/A	RC	SB	CS	SBR	FR	POS	TPR
1904	Chi-N	1	3	0	0	0	0	0	0	0		.000	.000	.000	-99	-1	-1	0	0			0	/C	0.0

■ JOE STAPLES
Staples, Joseph F. b: Buffalo, N.Y. Deb: 9/19/1885

YEAR	TM/L	G	AB	R	H	2B	3B	HR	RBI	BB	SO	AVG	OBP	SLG	PRO+	BR	/A	RC	SB	CS	SBR	FR	POS	TPR
1885	Buf-N	7	22	0	1	0	0	0	0	0	9	.045	.045	.045	-69	-4	-4	0				-2	/O2	-0.5

■ DAVE STAPLETON
Stapleton, David Leslie b: 1/16/54, Fairhope, Ala. BR/TR, 6'1", 178 lbs. Deb: 5/30/80

YEAR	TM/L	G	AB	R	H	2B	3B	HR	RBI	BB	SO	AVG	OBP	SLG	PRO+	BR	/A	RC	SB	CS	SBR	FR	POS	TPR
1980	Bos-A	106	449	61	144	33	5	7	45	13	32	.321	.341	.463	112	10	7	67	3	2	-0	11	2/103D	2.2
1981	Bos-A	93	355	45	101	17	1	10	42	21	22	.285	.326	.423	108	6	3	45	0	4	-2	-8	S321/D	-0.3
1982	Bos-A	150	538	66	142	28	1	14	65	31	40	.264	.308	.398	87	-7	-11	58	2	4	-2	2	*1S/230D	-0.9
1983	Bos-A	151	542	54	134	31	1	10	66	40	44	.247	.301	.363	76	-14	-19	56	1	1	-0	-2	*1/2	-2.7
1984	Bos-A	13	39	4	9	2	0	0	1	3	3	.231	.286	.282	55	-2	-2	3	0	0	0	1	1/D	-0.1
1985	Bos-A	30	66	4	15	6	0	0	2	4	11	.227	.271	.318	58	-4	-4	6	0	0	0	1	2/1D	-0.3
1986	*Bos-A	39	39	4	5	1	0	0	3	2	10	.128	.171	.154	-11	-6	-6	1	0	0	0	3	1/23	-0.4
Total	7	582	2028	238	550	118	8	41	224	114	162	.271	.312	.398	90	-17	-32	236	6	11	-5	9	12/S3DO	-2.4

■ WILLIE STARGELL
Stargell, Wilver Dornel b: 3/6/40, Earlsboro, Okla. BL/TL, 6'2", 188 lbs. Deb: 9/16/62 CH

YEAR	TM/L	G	AB	R	H	2B	3B	HR	RBI	BB	SO	AVG	OBP	SLG	PRO+	BR	/A	RC	SB	CS	SBR	FR	POS	TPR
1962	Pit-N	10	31	1	9	3	1	0	4	3	10	.290	.353	.452	114	1	1	5	0	1	-1	-0	/O	0.0

YEAR	TM/L	G	AB	R	H	2B	3B	HR	RBI	BB	SO	AVG	OBP	SLG	PRO+	BR	/A	RC	SB	CS	SBR	FR	POS	TPR
1963	Pit-N	108	304	34	74	11	6	11	47	19	85	.243	.292	.428	104	1	1	36	0	2	-1	-10	O1	-1.5
1964	Pit-N	117	421	53	115	19	7	21	78	17	92	.273	.305	.501	123	10	11	62	1	1	-0	-10	O1	-0.2
1965	Pit-N	144	533	68	145	25	8	27	107	39	127	.272	.330	.501	130	20	19	87	1	1	-0	-6	*O/1	0.9
1966	Pit-N	140	485	84	153	30	0	33	102	48	109	.315	.384	.581	164	41	41	107	2	3	-1	-10	*O1	2.6
1967	Pit-N	134	462	54	125	18	6	20	73	67	103	.271	.367	.465	136	23	23	78	1	0	-0	-6	O1	1.2
1968	Pit-N	128	435	57	103	15	1	24	67	47	105	.237	.320	.441	129	14	14	61	5	0	2	-10	*O1	0.0
1969	Pit-N	145	522	89	160	31	6	29	92	61	120	.307	.385	.556	164	41	43	112	1	0	0	-10	*O1	2.6
1970	*Pit-N	136	474	70	125	18	3	31	85	44	119	.264	.333	.511	125	13	14	77	0	1	-1	-1	*O/1	0.7
1971	*Pit-N	141	511	104	151	26	0	**48**	125	83	154	.295	.401	.628	188	59	59	131	0	0	-0	-5	*O	**5.1**
1972	*Pit-N	138	495	75	145	28	2	33	112	65	129	.293	.377	.558	166	40	41	105	1	1	-0	-12	*1O	2.1
1973	Pit-N	148	522	106	156	**43**	3	**44**	**119**	80	129	.299	.395	**.646**	**189**	58	59	136	0	0	0	1	*O	5.5
1974	*Pit-N	140	508	90	153	37	4	25	96	87	106	.301	.409	.537	**169**	44	47	115	0	2	-1	-5	*O/1	3.6
1975	*Pit-N	124	461	71	136	32	2	22	90	58	109	.295	.377	.516	147	28	28	91	0	0	0	-10	*1	1.2
1976	Pit-N	117	428	54	110	20	3	20	65	50	101	.257	.342	.458	124	13	13	70	2	0	1	-10	*1	-0.1
1977	Pit-N	63	186	29	51	12	0	13	35	31	55	.274	.386	.548	144	13	12	39	0	1	-1	-1	1	0.7
1978	Pit-N	122	390	60	115	18	2	28	97	50	93	.295	.385	.567	156	32	30	85	3	2	-1	-1	*1	2.5
1979	*Pit-N	126	424	60	119	19	0	32	82	47	105	.281	.357	.552	138	24	22	81	0	1	-1	-6	*1	1.0
1980	Pit-N	67	202	28	53	10	1	11	38	26	52	.262	.352	.485	129	8	8	35	0	0	0	0	1	0.6
1981	Pit-N	38	60	2	17	4	0	0	9	5	9	.283	.338	.350	93	-0	-1	8	0	0	0	-2	/1	-0.3
1982	Pit-N	74	73	6	17	4	0	3	17	10	24	.233	.325	.411	102	0	0	10	0	0	0	0	/1	0.0
Total	21	2360	7927	1195	2232	423	55	475	1540	937	1936	.282	.363	.529	147	483	485	1531	17	16	-5	-115	*O1	28.2

■ MATT STARK

Stark, Matthew Scott b: 1/21/65, Whittier, Cal. BR/TR, 6'4", 225 lbs. Deb: 4/08/87

YEAR	TM/L	G	AB	R	H	2B	3B	HR	RBI	BB	SO	AVG	OBP	SLG	PRO+	BR	/A	RC	SB	CS	SBR	FR	POS	TPR
1987	Tor-A	5	12	0	1	0	0	0	0	0	0	.083	.083	.083	-55	-3	-3	-0	0	0	0	1	/C	0.0
1990	Chi-A	8	16	0	4	1	0	0	3	1	6	.250	.294	.313	71	-1	-1	1	0	0	0	0	/D	0.0
Total	2	13	28	0	5	1	0	0	3	1	6	.179	.207	.214	15	-3	-3	1	0	0	0	1	/DC	0.0

■ DOLLY STARK

Stark, Monroe Randolph b: 1/19/1885, Ripley, Miss. d: 12/1/24, Memphis, Tenn. BR/TR, 5'9", 160 lbs. Deb: 9/12/09

YEAR	TM/L	G	AB	R	H	2B	3B	HR	RBI	BB	SO	AVG	OBP	SLG	PRO+	BR	/A	RC	SB	CS	SBR	FR	POS	TPR
1909	Cle-A	19	60	4	12	0	0	0	1	6		.200	.273	.200	48	-3	-3	4	4			-9	S	-1.4
1910	Bro-N	30	103	7	17	3	0	0	8	7	19	.165	.225	.194	23	-10	-10	5	2			-1	S	-1.0
1911	Bro-N	70	193	25	57	4	1	0	19	20	24	.295	.370	.326	100	-0	1	26	6			-3	S2/3	-0.6
1912	Bro-N	8	22	2	4	0	0	0	2	1	3	.182	.217	.182	10	-3	-3	1	2			0	/S	-0.1
Total	4	127	378	38	90	7	1	0	30	34	46	.238	.308	.262	66	-16	-15	37	14			-13	/S23	-2.5

■ GEORGE STARNAGLE

Starnagle, George Henry (b: George Henry Steuernagel) b: 10/6/1873, Belleville, Ill. d: 2/15/46, Belleville, Ill. BR/TR, 5'11", 175 lbs. Deb: 9/14/02

YEAR	TM/L	G	AB	R	H	2B	3B	HR	RBI	BB	SO	AVG	OBP	SLG	PRO+	BR	/A	RC	SB	CS	SBR	FR	POS	TPR
1902	Cle-A	1	3	0	0	0	0	0	0	0	0	.000	.000	.000	-99	-1	-1	0	0			-1	/C	0.0

■ CHARLIE STARR

Starr, Charles Watkin b: 8/30/1878, Pike Co., Ohio d: 10/18/37, Pasadena, Cal. TR , Deb: 4/29/05

YEAR	TM/L	G	AB	R	H	2B	3B	HR	RBI	BB	SO	AVG	OBP	SLG	PRO+	BR	/A	RC	SB	CS	SBR	FR	POS	TPR
1905	StL-A	26	97	9	20	0	0	0	6	7		.206	.260	.206	53	-5	-5	6	0			-4	2/3	-0.8
1908	Pit-N	20	59	8	11	2	0	0	8	13		.186	.333	.220	80	-1	-1	7	6			-5	2/S3	-0.6
1909	Bos-N	61	216	16	48	2	3	0	6	31		.222	.333	.259	80	-2	-4	22	7			-9	2/S3	-1.3
	Phi-N	3	3	0	0	0	0	0	0	0		.000	.000	.000	-99	-1	-1	0	0			0	H	0.0
	Yr	64	219	16	48	2	3	0	6	31		.219	.329	.256	78	-3	-4	21	7			-9		-1.3
Total	3	110	375	33	79	4	3	0	20	51		.211	.313	.237	73	-9	-9	34	13			-18	/2S3	-2.7

■ CHICK STARR

Starr, William b: 2/26/11, Brooklyn, N.Y. BR/TR, 6'1", 175 lbs. Deb: 8/23/35

YEAR	TM/L	G	AB	R	H	2B	3B	HR	RBI	BB	SO	AVG	OBP	SLG	PRO+	BR	/A	RC	SB	CS	SBR	FR	POS	TPR
1935	Was-A	12	24	1	5	0	0	0	1	0	1	.208	.208	.208	8	-3	-3	1	0	0	0	2	C	0.0
1936	Was-A	1	0	0	0	0	0	0	0	0	0	—	—	—	—	0	0	0	0	0	0	0	/C	0.0
Total	2	13	24	1	5	0	0	0	1	0	1	.208	.208	.208	8	-3	-3	1	0	0	0	2	/C	0.0

■ JOE START

Start, Joseph "Old Reliable" or "Rocks" b: 10/14/1842, New York, N.Y. d: 3/27/27, Providence, R.I. BL/TL, 5'9", 165 lbs. Deb: 5/18/1871 M

YEAR	TM/L	G	AB	R	H	2B	3B	HR	RBI	BB	SO	AVG	OBP	SLG	PRO+	BR	/A	RC	SB	CS	SBR	FR	POS	TPR
1871	Mut-n	33	161	35	58	5	1	1	34	3	0	.360	.372	.422	140	6	9	27	4				*1	0.6
1872	Mut-n	55	280	62	74	6	0	0		1		.264	.267	.286	75	-10	-6	22					*1	0.0
1873	Mut-n	53	251	42	67	11	3	1		5		.267	.281	.347	84	-5	-5	25					*1M	-0.2
1874	Mut-n	63	306	67	94	14	4	2		4		.307	.316	.399	122	9	7	40					*1	0.5
1875	Mut-n	68	309	56	87	9	5	4		3		.282	.288	.382	122	9	6	35					*1	0.3
1876	NY-N	56	264	40	73	6	0	0	21	1	2	.277	.279	.299	107	-2	3	23				3	*1	0.6
1877	Har-N	60	271	55	90	3	6	1	21	6	2	.332	.347	.399	150	10	14	38				-2	*1	0.8
1878	Chi-N	61	285	58	**100**	12	5	1	27	2	3	.351	.355	.439	150	17	15	46				-2	*1	1.4
1879	Pro-N	66	317	70	101	11	5	2	37	7	4	.319	.333	.404	144	14	14	44				0	*1/O	0.9
1880	Pro-N	82	345	53	96	14	6	0	27	13	20	.278	.304	.354	126	8	9	38				-3	*1	0.2
1881	Pro-N	79	348	56	114	12	6	0	29	9	7	.328	.345	.397	135	12	13	49				-4	*1	-0.1
1882	Pro-N	82	356	58	117	8	10	0	48	11	7	.329	.349	.407	142	16	16	52				2	*1	0.4
1883	Pro-N	87	370	63	105	16	7	1	57	22	16	.284	.324	.373	108	5	4	46				-1	*1	-0.7
1884	*Pro-N	93	381	80	105	10	5	2	32	35	25	.276	.337	.344	117	7	9	45				1	*1	0.0
1885	Pro-N	101	374	47	103	11	4	0	41	39	10	.275	.344	.326	122	9	11	43				1	*1	-0.5
1886	Was-N	31	122	10	27	4	1	0	17	5	13	.221	.252	.270	62	-6	-5	10	4			-2	1	-1.0
Total	5 n	272	1307	262	380	45	13	8	34	16		.291	.299	.363	107	9	11	149	4				1	1.2
Total	11	798	3433	590	1031	107	55	7	357	150	109	.300	.330	.370	127	90	103	432	4			-6	1/O	2.0

■ JOE STATON

Staton, Joseph b: 3/8/48, Seattle, Wash. BL/TL, 6'3", 175 lbs. Deb: 9/05/72

YEAR	TM/L	G	AB	R	H	2B	3B	HR	RBI	BB	SO	AVG	OBP	SLG	PRO+	BR	/A	RC	SB	CS	SBR	FR	POS	TPR
1972	Det-A	6	2	1	0	0	0	0	0	0	1	.000	.000	.000	-97	-0	-0	0	0	1	-1	0	/1	0.0
1973	Det-A	9	17	2	4	0	0	0	3	0	3	.235	.235	.235	31	-2	-2	1	1	0	0	2	/1	0.0
Total	2	15	19	3	4	0	0	0	3	0	4	.211	.211	.211	18	-2	-2	1	1	1	-0	2	/1	0.0

■ JIGGER STATZ

Statz, Arnold John b: 10/20/1897, Waukegan, Ill. d: 3/16/88, Corona Del Mar, Cal. BR/TR, 5'7.5", 150 lbs. Deb: 7/30/19

YEAR	TM/L	G	AB	R	H	2B	3B	HR	RBI	BB	SO	AVG	OBP	SLG	PRO+	BR	/A	RC	SB	CS	SBR	FR	POS	TPR
1919	NY-N	21	60	7	18	2	1	0	6	3	8	.300	.333	.367	112	1	1	7	2			1	O/2	0.1
1920	NY-N	16	30	0	4	0	1	0	5	2	9	.133	.188	.200	11	-3	-3	1	0	1	-1	0	O	-0.4
	Bos-A	2	3	0	0	0	0	0	0	0	0	.000	.000	.000	-99	-1	-1	0	0	0	0	-1	/O	-0.1
1922	Chi-N	110	462	77	137	19	5	1	34	41	31	.297	.355	.366	85	-9	-10	60	16	13	-3	6	*O	-0.9
1923	Chi-N	154	655	110	209	33	8	10	70	56	42	.319	.375	.440	114	14	14	105	29	23	-5	13	*O	1.6
1924	Chi-N	135	549	69	152	22	5	3	49	37	50	.277	.325	.352	80	-14	-15	63	13	9	-2	12	*O/2	-0.7
1925	Chi-N	38	148	21	38	6	3	2	14	11	16	.257	.317	.378	76	-5	-6	19	4	0	1	3	O	-0.1
1927	Bro-N	130	507	64	139	24	7	1	21	26	43	.274	.310	.355	77	-17	-17	54	10			11	*O/2	-1.0
1928	Bro-N	77	171	28	40	8	1	0	16	18	12	.234	.311	.292	59	-10	-10	16	3			3	O/2	-0.8
Total	8	683	2585	376	737	114	31	17	215	194	211	.285	.337	.373	87	-45	-47	325	77	46		47	O/2	-2.3

■ RUSTY STAUB

Staub, Daniel Joseph b: 4/1/44, New Orleans, La. BL/TR, 6'2", 190 lbs. Deb: 4/09/63 C

YEAR	TM/L	G	AB	R	H	2B	3B	HR	RBI	BB	SO	AVG	OBP	SLG	PRO+	BR	/A	RC	SB	CS	SBR	FR	POS	TPR
1963	Hou-N	150	513	43	115	17	4	6	45	59	58	.224	.310	.308	84	-13	-9	51	0	0	0	0	*1O	-1.4
1964	Hou-N	89	292	26	63	10	2	8	35	21	31	.216	.275	.346	78	-10	-9	27	1	1	-0	-1	1O	-1.2
1965	Hou-N	131	410	43	105	20	1	14	63	52	57	.256	.343	.412	120	7	10	56	3	0	1	4	O/1	1.2
1966	Hou-N	153	554	60	155	28	3	13	81	58	61	.280	.349	.412	119	9	10	79	2	1	0	11	*O/1	2.1
1967	Hou-N	149	546	71	182	**44**	1	10	74	60	47	.333	.402	.473	155	36	38	100	0	4	-2	6	*O	3.8
1968	Hou-N	161	591	54	172	37	1	6	72	73	57	.291	.376	.387	132	24	25	88	2	0	1	-0	*1O	2.1

YEAR	TM/L	G	AB	R	H	2B	3B	HR	RBI	BB	SO	AVG	OBP	SLG	PRO+	BR	/A	RC	SB	CS	SBR	FR	POS	TPR
1969	Mon-N	158	549	89	166	26	5	29	79	110	61	.302	.427	.526	165	53	52	128	3	4	-2	5	*O	4.9
1970	Mon-N	160	569	98	156	23	7	30	94	112	93	.274	.396	.497	138	33	33	117	12	11	-3	8	*O	3.0
1971	Mon-N	162	599	94	186	34	6	19	97	74	42	.311	.394	.482	147	39	38	111	9	5	-0	2	*O	3.6
1972	NY-N	66	239	32	70	11	0	9	38	31	13	.293	.379	.452	139	11	12	41	0	1	-1	-4	O	0.5
1973	*NY-N	152	585	77	163	36	1	15	76	74	52	.279	.363	.421	118	14	15	89	1	1	-0	9	*O	1.8
1974	NY-N	151	561	65	145	22	2	19	78	77	39	.258	.351	.406	113	9	10	78	2	1	0	5	*O	1.0
1975	NY-N	155	574	93	162	30	4	19	105	77	55	.282	.376	.448	134	22	26	97	2	0	1	2	*O	2.4
1976	Det-A	161	589	73	176	28	3	15	96	83	49	.299	.392	.433	136	33	30	99	3	1	0	-10	*OD	1.9
1977	Det-A	158	623	84	173	34	3	22	101	59	47	.278	.341	.448	107	11	6	89	1	1	-0	0	*D	0.6
1978	Det-A	162	642	75	175	30	1	24	121	76	35	.273	.352	.435	117	17	15	96	3	1	0	0	*D	1.6
1979	Det-A	68	246	32	58	12	1	9	40	32	18	.236	.336	.402	95	-0	-2	33	1	0	0	0	D	0.0
	Mon-N	38	86	9	23	3	0	3	14	14	10	.267	.370	.407	113	2	2	13	0	0	0	-2	1/O	0.0
1980	Tex-A	109	340	42	102	23	2	9	55	39	18	.300	.375	.459	131	13	15	55	1	1	-0	-2	D1O	1.0
1981	NY-N	70	161	9	51	9	0	5	21	22	12	.317	.402	.466	148	10	10	30	1	0	0	-2	1	0.8
1982	NY-N	112	219	11	53	9	0	3	27	24	10	.242	.317	.324	80	-6	-5	22	0	0	0	0	O1	-0.6
1983	NY-N	104	115	5	34	6	0	3	28	14	10	.296	.377	.426	123	4	4	18	0	0	0	-1	1/O	0.3
1984	NY-N	78	72	2	19	4	0	1	18	4	9	.264	.303	.361	87	-1	-1	8	0	0	0	-0	/1	-0.1
1985	NY-N	54	45	2	12	3	0	1	8	10	4	.267	.400	.400	128	2	2	8	0	0	0	0	/O	0.2
Total	23	2951	9720	1189	2716	499	47	292	1466	1255	888	.279	.366	.431	125	318	333	1534	47	33	-6	31	*OD1	29.5

■ ECKY STEARNS

Stearns, Daniel Eckford b: 10/17/1861, Buffalo, N.Y. d: 6/28/44, Glendale, Cal. BL/TR, 6'1", 185 lbs. Deb: 8/17/1880

YEAR	TM/L	G	AB	R	H	2B	3B	HR	RBI	BB	SO	AVG	OBP	SLG	PRO+	BR	/A	RC	SB	CS	SBR	FR	POS	TPR
1880	Buf-N	28	104	8	19	6	1	0	13	3	23	.183	.206	.260	55	-5	-5	6				-7	O/C3S	-1.1
1881	Det-N	3	11	1	1	1	0	0	0	0	2	.091	.091	.182	-16	-1	-1	0				-1	/S	-0.1
1882	Cin-a	49	214	28	55	10	2	0		6		.257	.277	.322	96	0	-2	20				-2	1O/2S	-0.3
1883	Bal-a	93	382	54	94	10	9	1		34		.246	.308	.327	102	3	1	39				3	*1/O	-0.3
1884	Bal-a	100	396	61	94	12	3	3		28		.237	.298	.306	96	1	-1	37				4	*1/2	-0.1
1885	Bal-a	67	253	40	47	3	8	1		38		.186	.306	.273	88	-2	-1	22				1	1/OC	-0.4
	Buf-N	30	105	7	21	6	1	0	9	8	23	.200	.257	.276	70	-3	-4	8				-6	S1/C	-0.6
1889	KC-a	139	560	96	160	24	12	3	87	56	69	.286	.351	.387	106	9	3	102	67			0	*1/3	-0.6
Total	7	509	2025	295	491	72	36	6	109	173	117	.242	.306	.325	96	2	-10	233	67			-8	1/OSC32	-3.8

■ JOHN STEARNS

Stearns, John Hardin b: 8/21/51, Denver, Col. BR/TR, 6', 185 lbs. Deb: 9/22/74 C

YEAR	TM/L	G	AB	R	H	2B	3B	HR	RBI	BB	SO	AVG	OBP	SLG	PRO+	BR	/A	RC	SB	CS	SBR	FR	POS	TPR
1974	Phi-N	1	2	0	1	0	0	0	0	0	0	.500	.500	.500	173	0	0	1	0	0	0	-1	/C	0.0
1975	NY-N	59	169	25	32	5	1	3	10	17	15	.189	.271	.284	57	-11	-10	13	4	1	1	6	C	0.0
1976	NY-N	32	103	13	27	6	0	2	10	16	11	.262	.367	.379	119	2	3	14	1	2	-1	3	C	0.7
1977	NY-N	139	431	52	108	25	1	12	55	77	76	.251	.373	.397	112	7	9	64	9	8	-2	4	*C/1	0.9
1978	NY-N	143	477	65	126	24	1	15	73	70	57	.264	.368	.413	122	13	15	75	25	13	-0	-3	*C/3	1.6
1979	NY-N	155	538	58	131	29	2	9	66	52	57	.243	.315	.355	86	-13	-11	54	15	15	-5	5	*C13/O	-0.8
1980	NY-N	91	319	42	91	25	1	0	45	33	24	.285	.354	.370	105	2	3	44	7	3	0	4	C1/3	0.8
1981	NY-N	80	273	25	74	12	1	1	24	24	17	.271	.330	.333	90	-4	-3	30	12	2	2	-3	C/13	-0.3
1982	NY-N	98	352	46	103	25	3	4	28	30	35	.293	.352	.415	114	6	7	51	17	7	1	-8	C3	0.0
1983	NY-N	4	0	2	0	0	0	0	0	0	0	—	—	—	—	0	0	0	0			0	/R	0.0
1984	NY-N	8	17	6	3	1	0	0	1	4	2	.176	.333	.235	63	-1	-1	2	1	0	0	-1	/C1	0.0
Total	11	810	2681	334	696	152	10	46	312	323	294	.260	.345	.375	102	2	13	347	91	51	-3	7	C/13O	2.9

■ JOHN STEDRONSKY

Stedronsky, John b: Troy, N.Y. Deb: 9/25/1879

YEAR	TM/L	G	AB	R	H	2B	3B	HR	RBI	BB	SO	AVG	OBP	SLG	PRO+	BR	/A	RC	SB	CS	SBR	FR	POS	TPR
1879	Chi-N	4	12	0	1	0	0	0	0	0	3	.083	.083	.083	-42	-2	-2	0				1	/3	0.0

■ FARMER STEELMAN

Steelman, Morris James b: 6/29/1875, Millville, N.J. d: 9/16/44, Merchantville, N.J. TR, Deb: 9/15/1899

YEAR	TM/L	G	AB	R	H	2B	3B	HR	RBI	BB	SO	AVG	OBP	SLG	PRO+	BR	/A	RC	SB	CS	SBR	FR	POS	TPR
1899	Lou-N	4	15	2	1	0	1	0	2	2		.067	.176	.200	4	-2	-2	1	0			-2	/C	-0.2
1900	Bro-N	1	4	0	0	0	0	0	0	0		.000	.000	.000	-94	-1	-1	0	0			1	/C	0.0
1901	Bro-N	1	3	0	1	0	0	0	0	0		.333	.333	.333	93	-0	-0	0	0			1	/C	0.1
	Phi-A	27	88	5	23	2	0	0	7	10		.261	.343	.284	74	-2	-3	11	4			1	CO	0.0
1902	Sea-A	10	32	1	6	1	0	0	6	2		.188	.235	.219	26	-3	-3	2	2			1	/CO	-0.1
Total	4	43	142	8	31	3	1	0	15	14		.218	.293	.254	52	-8	-9	14	6			2	/CO	-0.2

■ JIM STEELS

Steels, James Earl b: 5/30/61, Jackson, Miss. BL/TL, 5'10", 185 lbs. Deb: 4/06/87

YEAR	TM/L	G	AB	R	H	2B	3B	HR	RBI	BB	SO	AVG	OBP	SLG	PRO+	BR	/A	RC	SB	CS	SBR	FR	POS	TPR
1987	SD-N	62	68	9	13	1	1	0	6	11	14	.191	.304	.235	47	-5	-5	5	3	2	-0	0	O	-0.5
1988	Tex-A	36	53	4	10	1	0	0	5	0	15	.189	.189	.208	11	-6	-6	2	2	0	1	1	O/1D	-0.5
1989	SF-N	13	12	0	1	0	0	0	0	2	4	.083	.214	.083	-12	-2	-2	0	0	0	1	1	/1O	0.0
Total	3	111	133	13	24	2	1	0	11	13	33	.180	.253	.211	28	-13	-13	8	5	2	0	2	/O1D	-1.0

■ GENE STEERE

Steere, Frederick Eugene b: 8/16/1872, S.Scituate, R.I. d: 3/13/42, San Francisco, Cal Deb: 8/29/1894

YEAR	TM/L	G	AB	R	H	2B	3B	HR	RBI	BB	SO	AVG	OBP	SLG	PRO+	BR	/A	RC	SB	CS	SBR	FR	POS	TPR
1894	Pit-N	10	39	3	8	0	0	0	4	2	1	.205	.244	.205	10	-6	-6	3	2			-3	S	-0.5

■ JOHN STEFERO

Stefero, John Robert b: 9/22/59, Sumter, S.C. BL/TR, 5'8", 185 lbs. Deb: 6/24/83

YEAR	TM/L	G	AB	R	H	2B	3B	HR	RBI	BB	SO	AVG	OBP	SLG	PRO+	BR	/A	RC	SB	CS	SBR	FR	POS	TPR
1983	Bal-A	9	11	2	5	1	0	0	4	3	2	.455	.571	.545	213	2	2	4	0	0	0	1	/C	0.3
1986	Bal-A	52	120	14	28	2	0	2	13	16	25	.233	.324	.300	72	-4	-4	12	0	1	-1	-2	C/2	-0.3
1987	Mon-N	18	56	4	11	0	0	1	3	3	17	.196	.237	.250	28	-6	-6	3	0	0	0	-0	C	-0.4
Total	3	79	187	20	44	3	0	3	20	22	44	.235	.316	.299	67	-8	-8	19	0	1	-1	-2	/C2	-0.4

■ DAVE STEGMAN

Stegman, David William b: 1/30/54, Inglewood, Cal. BR/TR, 5'11", 190 lbs. Deb: 9/04/78

YEAR	TM/L	G	AB	R	H	2B	3B	HR	RBI	BB	SO	AVG	OBP	SLG	PRO+	BR	/A	RC	SB	CS	SBR	FR	POS	TPR
1978	Det-A	8	14	3	4	2	0	1	3	1	2	.286	.333	.643	164	1	1	2	0	0	0	0	/O	0.1
1979	Det-A	12	31	6	6	0	0	3	5	2	3	.194	.242	.484	88	-1	-1	3	1	1	-0	3	O	0.1
1980	Det-A	65	130	12	23	5	0	2	9	14	23	.177	.257	.262	41	-10	-11	10	1	1	-0	0	O/D	-1.1
1982	NY-A	2	0	0	0	0	0	0	0	0	0	—	—	—	—	0	0	0	0			0	/O	0.0
1983	Chi-A	30	53	5	9	2	0	0	4	10	9	.170	.302	.208	42	-4	-4	4	0	1	-1	-1	O	-0.5
1984	Chi-A	55	92	13	24	1	2	2	11	4	18	.261	.306	.380	85	-2	-2	11	3	0	1	4	O/D	0.1
Total	6	172	320	39	66	10	2	8	32	31	55	.206	.280	.325	64	-15	-17	31	5	3	-0	6	O/D	-1.3

■ JUSTIN STEIN

Stein, Justin Marion "Ott" b: 8/9/11, St.Louis, Mo. BR/TR, 5'11", 180 lbs. Deb: 5/28/38

YEAR	TM/L	G	AB	R	H	2B	3B	HR	RBI	BB	SO	AVG	OBP	SLG	PRO+	BR	/A	RC	SB	CS	SBR	FR	POS	TPR
1938	Phi-N	11	39	6	10	0	1	0	2	2	4	.256	.293	.308	67	-2	-2	4	0			0	/32	-0.1
	Cin-N	11	18	3	6	1	0	0	1	0	1	.333	.333	.389	101	-0	-0	2	0			1	/S2	0.1
	Yr	22	57	9	16	1	1	0	3	2	5	.281	.305	.333	78	-2	-2	6	0			1		0.0

■ BILL STEIN

Stein, William Allen b: 1/21/47, Battle Creek, Mich. BR/TR, 5'10", 170 lbs. Deb: 9/06/72

YEAR	TM/L	G	AB	R	H	2B	3B	HR	RBI	BB	SO	AVG	OBP	SLG	PRO+	BR	/A	RC	SB	CS	SBR	FR	POS	TPR
1972	StL-N	14	35	2	11	1	0	0	3	0	7	.314	.314	.543	141	1	2	6	1	0	0	-3	/3O	0.0
1973	StL-N	32	55	4	12	2	0	0	2	7	18	.218	.306	.255	57	-3	-3	5	0	0	0	-1	O/13	-0.4
1974	Chi-A	13	43	5	12	1	0	0	5	7	8	.279	.380	.302	96	0	0	5	0	0	0	-2	3/D	-0.1
1975	Chi-A	76	226	23	61	7	1	3	21	18	32	.270	.327	.350	90	-3	-3	25	2	2	-1	4	23D/O	0.1
1976	Chi-A	117	392	32	105	15	2	4	36	22	67	.268	.310	.347	92	-4	-5	41	4	2	0	-11	23/1SOD	-1.2
1977	Sea-A	151	556	53	144	26	5	13	67	29	79	.259	.302	.394	89	-10	-10	62	4	2	-1	-11	*3/SD	-2.5
1978	Sea-A	114	403	41	105	24	4	4	37	37	56	.261	.323	.370	95	-3	-3	48	1	0	0	-6	*3/D	-0.9
1979	Sea-A	88	250	28	62	9	2	7	27	17	28	.248	.301	.384	82	-6	-7	26	1	2	-1	11	32/S	0.5
1980	Sea-A	67	198	16	53	5	1	5	27	16	25	.268	.326	.379	92	-2	-2	24	1	1	-0	8	32/1D	0.6

YEAR	TM/L	G	AB	R	H	2B	3B	HR	RBI	BB	SO	AVG	OBP	SLG	PRO+	BR	/A	RC	SB	CS	SBR	FR	POS	TPR
1981	Tex-A	53	115	21	38	6	0	2	22	7	15	.330	.369	.435	138	4	5	16	1	2	-1	1	1/O32S	0.5
1982	Tex-A	85	184	14	44	8	0	1	16	12	23	.239	.293	.299	66	-9	-8	16	0	0	0	3	23/S10D	-0.2
1983	Tex-A	78	232	21	72	15	1	2	33	8	31	.310	.333	.409	105	1	1	30	2	3	-1	0	213/D	0.0
1984	Tex-A	27	43	3	12	1	0	0	3	5	9	.279	.354	.302	81	-1	-1	5	0	0	0	-2	2/13D	-0.2
1985	Tex-A	44	79	5	20	3	1	1	12	1	15	.253	.272	.354	69	-3	-4	7	0	0	0	3	3/120D	-0.1
Total	14	959	2811	268	751	122	18	44	311	186	413	.267	.316	.370	91	-38	-37	315	16	16	-5	-7	32/1DOS	-3.9

■ TERRY STEINBACH
Steinbach, Terry Lee   b: 3/2/62, New Ulm, Minn.   BR/TR, 6'1", 195 lbs.   Deb: 9/12/86

YEAR	TM/L	G	AB	R	H	2B	3B	HR	RBI	BB	SO	AVG	OBP	SLG	PRO+	BR	/A	RC	SB	CS	SBR	FR	POS	TPR
1986	Oak-A	6	15	3	5	0	0	2	4	1	0	.333	.375	.733	208	2	2	4	0	0	0	-0	/C	0.2
1987	Oak-A	122	391	66	111	16	3	16	56	32	66	.284	.352	.463	122	8	11	62	1	2	-1	-12	*C3/1D	0.7
1988	*Oak-A	104	351	42	93	19	1	9	51	33	47	.265	.338	.402	110	3	5	47	3	0	1	4	C/310D	1.3
1989	*Oak-A	130	454	37	124	13	1	7	42	30	66	.273	.321	.352	93	-6	-4	49	1	2	-1	-6	*CO1/3D	-0.7
1990	*Oak-A	114	379	32	95	15	2	9	57	19	66	.251	.294	.372	87	-9	-7	39	0	1	-1	-3	CD/1	-0.8
Total	5	476	1590	180	428	63	7	43	210	115	245	.269	.327	.399	104	-2	7	201	5	5	-2	-17	C/D130	0.7

■ HANK STEINBACHER
Steinbacher, Henry John   b: 3/22/13, Sacramento, Cal.   d: 4/3/77, Sacramento, Cal.   BL/TR, 5'11", 180 lbs.   Deb: 4/21/37

YEAR	TM/L	G	AB	R	H	2B	3B	HR	RBI	BB	SO	AVG	OBP	SLG	PRO+	BR	/A	RC	SB	CS	SBR	FR	POS	TPR
1937	Chi-A	26	73	13	19	4	1	1	9	4	7	.260	.299	.384	71	-4	-4	9	2	0	1	-3	O	-0.5
1938	Chi-A	106	399	59	132	23	8	4	61	41	19	.331	.393	.459	110	8	7	72	1	3	-2	-3	*O	0.2
1939	Chi-A	71	111	16	19	2	1	1	15	21	8	.171	.303	.234	38	-10	-10	9	0	0	0	-2	O	-1.1
Total	3	203	583	88	170	29	10	6	85	66	34	.292	.364	.407	92	-5	-7	90	3	3	-1	-8	O	-1.4

■ GENE STEINBRENNER
Steinbrenner, Eugene Gass   b: 11/17/1892, Pittsburgh, Pa.   d: 4/25/70, Pittsburgh, Pa.   TR , 5'8.5", 155 lbs.   Deb: 4/25/12

YEAR	TM/L	G	AB	R	H	2B	3B	HR	RBI	BB	SO	AVG	OBP	SLG	PRO+	BR	/A	RC	SB	CS	SBR	FR	POS	TPR
1912	Phi-N	3	9	0	2	1	0	0	1	0	3	.222	.222	.333	48	-1	-1	1	0			-1	/2	-0.1

■ BILL STEINECKE
Steinecke, William Robert   b: 2/7/07, Cincinnati, Ohio   d: 7/20/86, St.Augustine, Fla   BR/TR, 5'8.5", 175 lbs.   Deb: 9/16/31

YEAR	TM/L	G	AB	R	H	2B	3B	HR	RBI	BB	SO	AVG	OBP	SLG	PRO+	BR	/A	RC	SB	CS	SBR	FR	POS	TPR
1931	Pit-N	4	4	0	0	0	0	0	0	0	1	.000	.000	.000	-99	-1	-1	0	0			0	/C	0.0

■ BEN STEINER
Steiner, Benjamin Saunders   b: 7/28/21, Alexandria, Va.   d: 10/27/88, Venice, Fla.   BL/TR, 5'11", 165 lbs.   Deb: 4/17/45

YEAR	TM/L	G	AB	R	H	2B	3B	HR	RBI	BB	SO	AVG	OBP	SLG	PRO+	BR	/A	RC	SB	CS	SBR	FR	POS	TPR
1945	Bos-A	78	304	39	78	8	3	3	20	31	29	.257	.327	.332	89	-3	-4	35	10	6	-1	-4	2	-0.7
1946	Bos-A	3	4	1	1	0	0	0	0	0	0	.250	.250	.250	38	-0	-0	0	0	0	0	0	/3	0.0
1947	Det-A	1	0	1	0	0	0	0	0	0	0	—	—	—	—	0	0	0	0	0	0	0	R	0.0
Total	3	82	308	41	79	8	3	3	20	31	29	.256	.326	.331	89	-3	-4	35	10	6	-1	-4	/23	-0.7

■ RED STEINER
Steiner, James Harry   b: 1/7/15, Los Angeles, Cal.   BL/TR, 6', 185 lbs.   Deb: 5/11/45

YEAR	TM/L	G	AB	R	H	2B	3B	HR	RBI	BB	SO	AVG	OBP	SLG	PRO+	BR	/A	RC	SB	CS	SBR	FR	POS	TPR
1945	Cle-A	12	20	0	3	0	0	0	2	1	4	.150	.190	.150	-1	-3	-2	0	0	0	0	1	/C	0.0
	Bos-A	26	59	6	12	1	0	0	4	14	2	.203	.356	.220	67	-2	-2	6	0	0	0	-4	C	-0.4
	Yr	38	79	6	15	1	0	0	6	15	6	.190	.319	.203	52	-4	-4	6	0	0	0	-4		-0.4

■ HARRY STEINFELDT
Steinfeldt, Harry M.   b: 9/29/1877, St.Louis, Mo.   d: 8/17/14, Bellevue, Ky.   BR/TR, 5'9.5", 180 lbs.   Deb: 4/22/1898

YEAR	TM/L	G	AB	R	H	2B	3B	HR	RBI	BB	SO	AVG	OBP	SLG	PRO+	BR	/A	RC	SB	CS	SBR	FR	POS	TPR
1898	Cin-N	88	308	47	91	18	6	0	43	27		.295	.354	.393	109	7	3	47	9			0	203/S1	0.3
1899	Cin-N	107	386	62	94	16	8	0	43	40		.244	.323	.326	79	-10	-11	48	19			-6	32/SO	-1.2
1900	Cin-N	134	510	57	125	29	7	2	66	27		.245	.288	.341	77	-18	-16	56	14			36	32/OS	2.2
1901	Cin-N	105	382	40	95	18	7	6	47	28		.249	.300	.380	105	-2	2	49	10			10	32	1.8
1902	Cin-N	129	479	53	133	20	7	1	49	24		.278	.320	.355	101	5	-0	61	12			21	*3/O	2.8
1903	Cin-N	118	439	71	137	32	12	6	83	47		.312	.379	.481	132	26	18	86	6			7	*3S	2.5
1904	Cin-N	99	349	35	85	11	6	1	52	29		.244	.302	.318	86	-3	-6	41	16			-7	3	-0.9
1905	Cin-N	114	384	49	104	16	9	1	39	30		.271	.324	.367	97	3	-2	53	15			14	*3/120	2.0
1906	*Chi-N	151	539	81	176	27	10	3	83	47		.327	.381	.430	147	33	30	104	29			-17	*3/2	0.8
1907	*Chi-N	152	542	52	144	25	5	1	70	37		.266	.313	.336	99	2	-1	67	19			-6	3	-0.7
1908	*Chi-N	150	539	63	130	20	6	1	62	36		.241	.289	.306	88	-5	-8	53	12			-11	*3	-1.7
1909	Chi-N	151	528	73	133	27	6	2	59	57		.252	.331	.337	105	5	3	68	22			10	*3	1.9
1910	*Chi-N	129	448	70	113	21	1	2	58	36	29	.252	.323	.317	88	-7	-7	51	10			0	*3	-0.6
1911	Bos-N	19	63	5	16	4	0	1	8	6	3	.254	.338	.365	89	-0	-1	8	1			-5	3	-0.4
Total	14	1646	5896	758	1576	284	90	27	762	471	32	.267	.325	.360	101	37	5	791	194			47	*32/OS1	8.8

■ BILL STELLBAUER
Stellbauer, William Jennings   b: 3/20/1894, Bremond, Tex.   d: 2/16/74, New Braunfels, Tex   BR/TR, 5'10", 175 lbs.   Deb: 4/12/16

YEAR	TM/L	G	AB	R	H	2B	3B	HR	RBI	BB	SO	AVG	OBP	SLG	PRO+	BR	/A	RC	SB	CS	SBR	FR	POS	TPR
1916	Phi-A	25	48	2	13	2	1	0	5	6	7	.271	.352	.354	117	1	1	7	2			-3	O	-0.3

■ RICK STELMASZEK
Stelmaszek, Richard Francis   b: 10/8/48, Chicago, Ill.   BL/TR, 6'1", 195 lbs.   Deb: 6/25/71   C

YEAR	TM/L	G	AB	R	H	2B	3B	HR	RBI	BB	SO	AVG	OBP	SLG	PRO+	BR	/A	RC	SB	CS	SBR	FR	POS	TPR
1971	Was-A	6	9	0	0	0	0	0	0	0	3	.000	.000	.000	-99	-2	-2	0	0	0	0	-1	/C	-0.2
1973	Tex-A	7	9	0	1	0	0	0	0	1	2	.111	.200	.111	-11	-1	-1	0	0	0	0	-0	/C	0.0
	Cal-A	22	26	2	4	1	0	0	3	6	7	.154	.313	.192	49	-2	-1	2	0	0	0	-2	C	-0.2
	Yr	29	35	2	5	1	0	0	3	7	9	.143	.286	.171	34	-3	-3	2	0	0	0	-2		-0.2
1974	Chi-N	25	44	2	10	2	0	1	7	10	6	.227	.370	.341	96	0	0	6	0	0	0	-5	C	-0.4
Total	3	60	88	4	15	3	0	1	10	17	18	.170	.305	.239	55	-5	-5	8	0	0	0	-8	/C	-0.8

■ FRED STEM
Stem, Frederick Boothe   b: 9/22/1885, Oxford, N.C.   d: 9/5/64, Darlington, S.C.   BL/TR, 6'2", 160 lbs.   Deb: 9/15/08

YEAR	TM/L	G	AB	R	H	2B	3B	HR	RBI	BB	SO	AVG	OBP	SLG	PRO+	BR	/A	RC	SB	CS	SBR	FR	POS	TPR
1908	Bos-N	20	72	9	20	0	1	0	3	2		.278	.297	.306	96	-1	-0	7	1			-1	1	-0.1
1909	Bos-N	73	245	13	51	2	3	0	11	12		.208	.254	.241	51	-14	-15	17	5			10	1	-0.5
Total	2	93	317	22	71	2	4	0	14	14		.224	.263	.256	60	-14	-15	24	6			10	/1	-0.6

■ CASEY STENGEL
Stengel, Charles Dillon "The Old Professor"   b: 7/30/1890, Kansas City, Mo.   d: 9/29/75, Glendale, Cal.   BL/TL, 5'11", 175 lbs.   Deb: 9/17/12   MCH

YEAR	TM/L	G	AB	R	H	2B	3B	HR	RBI	BB	SO	AVG	OBP	SLG	PRO+	BR	/A	RC	SB	CS	SBR	FR	POS	TPR
1912	Bro-N	17	57	9	18	1	0	1	13	15	9	.316	.466	.386	140	4	4	13	5			-2	O	0.2
1913	Bro-N	124	438	60	119	16	8	7	43	56	58	.272	.356	.393	110	8	7	65	19			-1	*O	0.3
1914	Bro-N	126	412	55	130	13	10	4	60	56	55	.316	.404	.425	143	26	24	76	19			-11	*O	1.0
1915	Bro-N	132	459	52	109	20	12	3	50	34	46	.237	.294	.353	94	-3	-4	48	5	10	-5	-6	*O	-2.0
1916	*Bro-N	127	462	66	129	27	8	8	53	33	51	.279	.329	.424	127	15	14	70	11			-5	*O	0.5
1917	Bro-N	150	549	69	141	23	12	6	73	60	62	.257	.336	.375	115	12	11	72	18			5	*O	1.3
1918	Pit-N	39	122	18	30	4	1	1	12	16	14	.246	.343	.320	99	1	1	16	11			2	O	0.0
1919	Pit-N	89	321	38	94	10	10	4	43	35	35	.293	.364	.424	131	15	13	53	12			1	O	1.1
1920	Phi-N	129	445	53	130	25	6	9	50	38	35	.292	.356	.436	121	15	13	66	7	13	-6	-3	*O	-0.3
1921	Phi-N	24	59	7	18	3	1	0	4	6	7	.305	.369	.390	94	0	-0	9	1	1	-0	2	O	-0.2
	NY-N	18	22	4	5	1	0	0	2	1	5	.227	.261	.273	41	-2	-2	1	0	1	-1	-1	/O	-0.2
	Yr	42	81	11	23	4	1	0	6	7	12	.284	.341	.358	81	-2	-2	10	1	2	-1	1		-0.2
1922	*NY-N	84	250	48	92	8	10	7	48	21	17	.368	.436	.564	155	21	21	62	4	2	0	-6	O	1.1
1923	*NY-N	75	218	39	74	11	5	5	43	20	18	.339	.400	.505	139	12	12	45	6	2	1	-3	O	0.8
1924	Bos-N	131	461	57	129	20	6	5	39	45	39	.280	.348	.382	100	-2	-2	61	13	13	-4	-9	*O	-1.4
1925	Bos-N	12	13	0	1	0	0	0	2	1	2	.077	.143	.077	-46	-3	-3	0	0	1	-1	-0	/O	-0.2
Total	14	1277	4288	575	1219	182	89	60	535	437	453	.284	.356	.410	119	118	110	654	131	43		-38	*O	2.2

■ MIKE STENHOUSE
Stenhouse, Michael Steven   b: 5/29/58, Pueblo, Colo.   BL/TR, 6'1", 195 lbs.   Deb: 10/03/82

YEAR	TM/L	G	AB	R	H	2B	3B	HR	RBI	BB	SO	AVG	OBP	SLG	PRO+	BR	/A	RC	SB	CS	SBR	FR	POS	TPR
1982	Mon-N	1	1	0	0	0	0	0	0	0	0	.000	.000	-0	-98	-0	-0	0	0	0	0	0	/H	0.0
1983	Mon-N	24	40	2	5	1	0	0	2	10	10	.125	.205	.150	-0	-5	-5	1	0	0	0	-1	/O1	-0.6
1984	Mon-N	80	175	14	32	8	0	4	16	26	32	.183	.292	.297	69	-8	-7	16	0	0	0	-2	O1	-1.1
1985	Min-A	81	179	23	40	5	0	5	21	29	18	.223	.332	.335	79	-3	-5	22	1	0	0	1	DO/1	-0.3

YEAR	TM/L	G	AB	R	H	2B	3B	HR	RBI	BB	SO	AVG	OBP	SLG	PRO+	BR	/A	RC	SB	CS	SBR	FR	POS	TPR
1986	Bos-A	21	21	1	2	1	0	0	1	12	5	.095	.424	.143	63	-0	-0	3	0	0	0	0	/O1	0.0
Total	5	207	416	40	79	15	0	9	40	71	66	.190	.309	.291	67	-17	-17	41	1	0	0	-1	/O1D	-2.0

■ RENNIE STENNETT
Stennett, Renaldo Antonio (Porte) b: 4/5/51, Colon, Panama BR/TR, 5'11", 160 lbs. Deb: 7/10/71

YEAR	TM/L	G	AB	R	H	2B	3B	HR	RBI	BB	SO	AVG	OBP	SLG	PRO+	BR	/A	RC	SB	CS	SBR	FR	POS	TPR
1971	Pit-N	50	153	24	54	5	4	1	15	7	9	.353	.381	.458	137	7	7	26	1	1	-0	2	2	1.1
1972	*Pit-N	109	370	43	106	14	5	3	30	9	43	.286	.307	.376	95	-4	-4	37	4	3	-1	10	2O/S	0.8
1973	Pit-N	128	466	45	113	18	3	10	55	16	63	.242	.268	.358	74	-19	-18	42	2	3	-1	1	2S/O	-0.9
1974	*Pit-N	157	673	84	196	29	3	7	56	32	51	.291	.325	.374	99	-6	-3	77	8	9	-3	13	*2/O	1.5
1975	*Pit-N	148	616	89	176	25	7	7	62	33	42	.286	.326	.383	97	-4	-4	74	5	4	-1	13	*2	1.5
1976	Pit-N	157	654	59	168	31	9	2	60	19	32	.257	.279	.341	75	-23	-24	59	18	6	2	17	*2/S	0.4
1977	Pit-N	116	453	53	152	20	4	5	51	29	24	.336	.378	.430	113	11	9	71	28	18	-2	-7	*2	0.6
1978	Pit-N	106	333	30	81	9	2	3	35	13	22	.243	.276	.309	60	-17	-18	26	2	1	0	-12	2/3	-2.6
1979	*Pit-N	108	319	31	76	13	2	0	24	24	25	.238	.292	.292	57	-18	-19	25	1	4	-2	6	*2	-0.8
1980	SF-N	120	397	34	97	13	2	2	37	22	31	.244	.287	.302	66	-19	-18	32	4	4	-1	-13	*2	-2.6
1981	SF-N	38	87	8	20	0	0	1	7	3	6	.230	.264	.264	51	-6	-6	6	2	1	0	-2	2	-0.5
Total	11	1237	4521	500	1239	177	41	41	432	207	348	.274	.308	.359	85	-98	-96	475	75	54	-10	29	*2/SO3	-1.5

■ JAKE STENZEL
Stenzel, Jacob Charles (b: Jacob Charles Stelzle) b: 6/24/1867, Cincinnati, Ohio d: 1/6/19, Cincinnati, Ohio BR/TR, 5'10", 168 lbs. Deb: 6/16/1890

YEAR	TM/L	G	AB	R	H	2B	3B	HR	RBI	BB	SO	AVG	OBP	SLG	PRO+	BR	/A	RC	SB	CS	SBR	FR	POS	TPR
1890	Chi-N	11	41	3	11	1	0	0	3	1	0	.268	.286	.293	68	-2	-2	4	0			-3	/OC	-0.3
1892	Pit-N	3	9	0	0	0	0	0	0	1	3	.000	.100	.000	-68	-2	-2	0	1			1	/OC	0.0
1893	Pit-N	60	224	57	81	13	4	4	37	24	17	.362	.423	.509	152	16	16	56	16			-8	OC/S2	0.6
1894	Pit-N	131	522	148	185	39	20	13	121	75	13	.354	.441	.580	148	40	41	165	61			-1	*O	2.3
1895	Pit-N	129	514	114	192	38	13	7	97	57	25	.374	.447	.539	165	44	49	151	53			-5	*O	2.7
1896	Pit-N	114	479	104	173	26	14	2	82	32	13	.361	.409	.486	143	26	29	122	57			-3	*O/1	1.5
1897	*Bal-N	131	536	113	189	**43**	7	4	116	36		.353	.404	.481	136	27	27	135	69			-11	*O	0.5
1898	Bal-N	35	138	33	35	5	2	0	22	12		.254	.340	.319	90	-1	-1	17	4			-2	O	-0.4
	StL-N	108	404	64	114	15	11	1	33	41		.282	.365	.381	114	10	9	66	21			0	*O	0.2
	Yr	143	542	97	149	20	13	1	55	53		.275	.359	.365	108	9	7	82	25			-2		-0.2
1899	StL-N	35	128	21	35	9	0	1	19	16		.273	.367	.367	102	1	1	21	8			-1	O	-0.1
	Cin-N	9	29	5	9	1	0	0	3	4		.310	.412	.345	109	1	1	5	2			-1	/O	0.0
	Yr	44	157	26	44	10	0	1	22	20		.280	.376	.363	103	2	2	26	10			-2		-0.1
Total	9	766	3024	662	1024	190	71	32	533	299	71	.339	.408	.480	137	160	167	741	292			-34	O/C12S	7.0

■ RAY STEPHENS
Stephens, Carl Ray b: 9/22/62, Houston, Tex. BR/TR, 6', 190 lbs. Deb: 9/20/90

YEAR	TM/L	G	AB	R	H	2B	3B	HR	RBI	BB	SO	AVG	OBP	SLG	PRO+	BR	/A	RC	SB	CS	SBR	FR	POS	TPR
1990	StL-N	5	15	2	2	1	0	1	1	0	3	.133	.133	.400	40	-1	-1	0	0	0	0	2	/C	0.1

■ GENE STEPHENS
Stephens, Glen Eugene b: 1/20/33, Gravette, Ark. BL/TR, 6'3.5", 175 lbs. Deb: 4/16/52

YEAR	TM/L	G	AB	R	H	2B	3B	HR	RBI	BB	SO	AVG	OBP	SLG	PRO+	BR	/A	RC	SB	CS	SBR	FR	POS	TPR
1952	Bos-A	21	53	10	12	5	0	0	5	3	8	.226	.268	.321	59	-3	-3	4	4	2	0	-0	O	-0.3
1953	Bos-A	78	221	30	45	6	2	3	18	29	56	.204	.302	.290	57	-12	-14	22	3	3	-1	-7	O	-2.3
1955	Bos-A	109	157	25	46	9	4	3	18	20	34	.293	.380	.459	114	6	4	29	0	0	0	3	O	0.3
1956	Bos-A	104	63	22	17	2	0	1	7	12	12	.270	.387	.349	85	-0	-1	9	0	1	-1	8	O	0.3
1957	Bos-A	120	173	25	46	6	4	3	26	26	20	.266	.362	.399	102	2	1	26	0	2	-1	-1	O	-0.6
1958	Bos-A	134	270	38	59	10	1	9	25	22	46	.219	.280	.363	71	-10	-12	27	1	2	-1	2	*O	-1.8
1959	Bos-A	92	270	34	75	13	1	3	39	29	33	.278	.356	.367	95	0	-1	38	5	2	0	4	O	0.0
1960	Bos-A	35	109	9	25	4	0	2	11	14	22	.229	.317	.321	71	-4	-4	13	5	1	1	-1	O	-0.5
	Bal-A	84	193	38	46	11	0	5	11	25	25	.238	.329	.373	91	-3	-2	26	4	2	0	5	O	0.0
	Yr	119	302	47	71	15	0	7	22	39	47	.235	.325	.354	83	-7	-7	39	9	3	1	4		-0.5
1961	Bal-A	32	58	4	11	2	0	0	2	14	7	.190	.347	.224	57	-3	-3	6	1	1	-0	4	O	-0.3
	KC-A	62	183	22	38	6	1	4	26	16	27	.208	.279	.317	59	-11	-11	17	3	2	-0	0	O	-0.8
	Yr	94	241	26	49	8	1	4	28	30	34	.203	.297	.295	59	-14	-14	23	4	3	-1	5		-1.1
1962	KC-A	5	4	0	0	0	0	0	0	1	1	.000	.200	.000	-40	-1	-1	0	0	0	0	0	H	0.0
1963	Chi-A	6	18	5	7	0	0	1	2	1	3	.389	.421	.556	174	2	2	4	0	0	0	1	/O	0.3
1964	Chi-A	82	141	21	33	4	2	3	17	21	28	.234	.341	.355	97	-1	-0	18	1	2	-1	4	O	0.1
Total	12	964	1913	283	460	78	15	37	207	233	322	.240	.327	.355	82	-37	-46	239	27	20	-4	23	O	-5.6

■ JIM STEPHENS
Stephens, James Walter "Little Nemo" b: 12/10/1883, Salineville, Ohio d: 1/2/65, Oxford, Ala. BR/TR, 5'6.5", 157 lbs. Deb: 4/11/07

YEAR	TM/L	G	AB	R	H	2B	3B	HR	RBI	BB	SO	AVG	OBP	SLG	PRO+	BR	/A	RC	SB	CS	SBR	FR	POS	TPR
1907	StL-A	58	173	15	35	6	3	0	11	15		.202	.266	.272	73	-5	-5	14	3			-3	C	-0.3
1908	StL-A	47	150	14	30	4	1	0	6	9		.200	.245	.240	59	-6	-7	9	0			-0	C	-0.2
1909	StL-A	79	223	18	49	5	0	3	18	13		.220	.278	.283	83	-6	-4	18	5			3	C	0.5
1910	StL-A	99	289	24	62	3	7	0	23	16		.215	.261	.273	72	-11	-9	22	2			3	C	0.4
1911	StL-A	70	212	11	49	5	5	0	17	17		.231	.300	.302	71	-9	-8	19	1			-3	C	-0.2
1912	StL-A	75	205	13	51	7	5	0	22	7		.249	.274	.332	75	-8	-7	19	3			3	C	0.2
Total	6	428	1252	95	276	30	21	3	97	77		.220	.272	.285	73	-46	-40	101	14			2	C	0.4

■ VERN STEPHENS
Stephens, Vernon Decatur "Junior" or "Buster" b: 10/23/20, McAlister, N.Mex. d: 11/3/68, Long Beach, Cal. BR/TR, 5'10", 185 lbs. Deb: 9/13/41

YEAR	TM/L	G	AB	R	H	2B	3B	HR	RBI	BB	SO	AVG	OBP	SLG	PRO+	BR	/A	RC	SB	CS	SBR	FR	POS	TPR
1941	StL-A	3	2	0	1	0	0	0	0	0	0	.500	.500	.500	160	0	0	1	0	0	0	-0	/S	0.0
1942	StL-A	145	575	84	169	26	6	14	92	41	53	.294	.341	.433	115	10	9	83	1	3	-2	-10	*S	0.6
1943	StL-A	137	512	75	148	27	3	22	91	54	73	.289	.357	.482	142	26	25	90	3	2	-0	-24	*SO	0.2
1944	*StL-A	145	559	91	164	32	1	20	**109**	62	54	.293	.365	.462	128	25	21	101	2	2	-1	-4	*S	2.5
1945	StL-A	149	571	90	165	27	3	**24**	89	55	70	.289	.352	.473	132	25	22	98	2	1	0	-17	*S/3	1.2
1946	StL-A	115	450	67	138	19	4	14	64	35	49	.307	.357	.460	121	15	12	73	0	1	-1	0	*S	1.4
1947	StL-A	150	562	74	157	18	4	15	83	70	61	.279	.359	.406	110	9	8	88	8	4	0	12	*S	2.0
1948	Bos-A	155	635	114	171	25	8	29	137	77	56	.269	.350	.471	112	12	8	103	1	0	0	10	*S	1.9
1949	Bos-A	155	610	113	177	31	2	39	**159**	101	73	.290	.391	.539	135	37	31	132	2	2	-1	4	*S	3.4
1950	Bos-A	149	628	125	185	34	6	30	**144**	65	43	.295	.361	.511	110	16	8	114	1	0	0	-0	*S	1.3
1951	Bos-A	109	377	62	113	21	2	17	78	38	33	.300	.364	.501	120	15	11	62	1	2	-1	14	3/S	2.0
1952	Bos-A	92	295	35	75	13	2	7	44	39	31	.254	.343	.383	95	1	-2	40	2	2	-1	4	S3	0.4
1953	Chi-A	44	129	14	24	6	0	1	14	13	18	.186	.261	.256	39	-11	-11	9	2	0	-1	-3	3/S	-1.4
	StL-A	46	165	16	53	8	0	4	17	18	24	.321	.388	.442	121	6	5	28	0	0	0	-2	3	0.1
	Yr	90	294	30	77	14	0	5	31	31	42	.262	.332	.361	85	-5	-6	36	2	0	1	-5		-1.3
1954	Bal-A	101	365	31	104	17	1	8	46	17	36	.285	.317	.403	104	-3	-0	46	0	3	-2	-6	3	-1.3
1955	Bal-A	3	6	0	1	0	0	0	0	0	0	.167	.286	.167	26	-1	-1	0	0	0	0	-1	/3	0.0
	Chi-A	22	56	10	14	3	0	3	7	7	11	.250	.333	.464	110	1	1	9	0	0	0	4	3	0.5
	Yr	25	62	10	15	3	0	3	7	7	11	.242	.329	.435	102	0	0	9	0	0	0	4		0.5
Total	15	1720	6497	1001	1859	307	42	247	1174	692	685	.286	.355	.460	118	185	147	1076	25	22	-6	-18	*S3/O	14.8

■ RIGGS STEPHENSON
Stephenson, Jackson Riggs "Old Hoss" b: 1/5/1898, Akron, Ala. d: 11/15/85, Tuscaloosa, Ala. BR/TR, 5'10", 185 lbs. Deb: 4/13/21

YEAR	TM/L	G	AB	R	H	2B	3B	HR	RBI	BB	SO	AVG	OBP	SLG	PRO+	BR	/A	RC	SB	CS	SBR	FR	POS	TPR
1921	Cle-A	65	206	45	68	17	2	2	34	23	15	.330	.408	.461	119	7	7	40	4	1	1	-1	2/3	0.8
1922	Cle-A	86	233	47	79	24	5	2	32	27	18	.339	.421	.511	141	15	15	52	3	0	1	-5	32/O	1.5
1923	Cle-A	91	301	48	96	20	6	5	65	15	25	.319	.357	.475	118	6	6	50	6	5	-1	9	2O/3	1.6
1924	Cle-A	71	240	33	89	20	4	0	44	27	10	.371	.439	.504	141	16	15	53	1	2	-1	-13	2/O	0.2
1925	Cle-A	19	54	8	16	3	1	1	9	7	3	.296	.387	.444	110	1	1	10	1	1	-0	1	O	0.0
1926	Chi-N	82	281	40	95	18	3	3	44	31	16	.338	.404	.456	129	13	12	51	2			-8	O	0.2

YEAR	TM/L	G	AB	R	H	2B	3B	HR	RBI	BB	SO	AVG	OBP	SLG	PRO+	BR	/A	RC	SB	CS	SBR	FR	POS	TPR
1927	Chi-N	152	579	101	199	**46**	9	7	82	65	28	.344	.415	.491	142	36	36	117	8			-1	*O/3	2.8
1928	Chi-N	137	512	75	166	36	9	8	90	68	29	.324	.407	.477	132	24	25	99	8			-2	*O	1.8
1929	*Chi-N	136	495	91	179	36	6	17	110	67	21	.362	.445	.562	147	39	39	123	10			-6	*O	1.9
1930	Chi-N	109	341	56	125	21	1	5	68	32	20	.367	.421	.478	116	11	10	67	2			-9	O	-0.3
1931	Chi-N	80	263	34	84	14	4	1	52	37	14	.319	.405	.414	119	9	9	47	1			-7	O	-0.1
1932	*Chi-N	147	583	86	189	49	4	4	85	54	27	.324	.383	.443	123	19	20	102	3			-10	*O	0.0
1933	Chi-N	97	346	45	114	17	4	4	51	34	16	.329	.397	.436	138	18	18	60	5			-3	O	1.0
1934	Chi-N	38	74	5	16	0	0	0	7	7	5	.216	.293	.216	39	-6	-6	5	0			1	O	-0.5
Total	14	1310	4508	714	1515	321	54	63	773	494	247	.336	.407	.473	130	208	207	876	54	9		-55	O2/3	10.9

■ JOHN STEPHENSON
Stephenson, John Herman b: 4/13/41, S.Portsmouth, Ky. BL/TR, 5'11", 180 lbs. Deb: 4/14/64

YEAR	TM/L	G	AB	R	H	2B	3B	HR	RBI	BB	SO	AVG	OBP	SLG	PRO+	BR	/A	RC	SB	CS	SBR	FR	POS	TPR
1964	NY-N	37	57	2	9	0	0	1	2	4	18	.158	.226	.211	24	-6	-6	3	0	0	0	-2	3/O	-0.8
1965	NY-N	62	121	9	26	5	0	4	15	8	19	.215	.264	.355	75	-5	-4	9	0	1	-1	-1	C/O	-1.1
1966	NY-N	63	143	17	28	1	1	1	11	8	28	.196	.248	.238	37	-12	-12	7	0	0	0	-1	C/O	-1.1
1967	Chi-N	18	49	3	11	3	1	0	5	1	6	.224	.255	.327	62	-2	-3	4	0	0	0	0	C	-0.1
1968	Chi-N	2	2	0	0	0	0	0	0	0	0	.000	.000	.000	-94	-0	-0	0	0	0	0	0	H	0.0
1969	SF-N	22	27	2	6	2	0	0	3	0	4	.222	.222	.296	45	-2	-2	1	0	0	0	-3	/C3	-0.3
1970	SF-N	23	43	3	3	1	0	0	6	2	7	.070	.111	.093	-45	-9	-9	0	0	0	0	3	/CO	-0.5
1971	Cal-A	98	279	24	61	17	0	3	25	22	21	.219	.283	.312	74	-12	-10	24	0	0	0	-8	C	-1.4
1972	Cal-A	66	146	14	40	3	1	2	17	11	8	.274	.342	.349	112	1	2	16	0	0	0	-7	C	-0.4
1973	Cal-A	60	122	9	30	5	0	1	9	7	7	.246	.292	.311	76	-5	-4	11	0	0	0	-8	C	-0.9
Total	10	451	989	83	214	37	3	12	93	63	118	.216	.272	.296	64	-52	-46	75	0	1	-1	-32	C/3O	-6.6

■ JOE STEPHENSON
Stephenson, Joseph Chester b: 6/30/21, Detroit, Mich. BR/TR, 6'2", 185 lbs. Deb: 9/19/43

YEAR	TM/L	G	AB	R	H	2B	3B	HR	RBI	BB	SO	AVG	OBP	SLG	PRO+	BR	/A	RC	SB	CS	SBR	FR	POS	TPR
1943	NY-N	9	24	4	6	1	0	0	1	0	5	.250	.250	.292	56	-1	-1	2	0			2	/C	0.1
1944	Chi-A	4	8	1	1	0	0	0	0	1	3	.125	.222	.125	-1	-1	-1	0	1			1	/C	0.0
1947	Chi-A	16	35	3	5	0	0	0	3	1	7	.143	.211	.143	-1	-5	-5	1	0	0	0	0	C	-0.2
Total	3	29	67	8	12	1	0	0	4	2	15	.179	.225	.194	19	-7	-7	3	1	0		3	/C	-0.1

■ PHIL STEPHENSON
Stephenson, Phillip Raymond b: 9/19/60, Guthrie, Okla. BL/TL, 6'1", 195 lbs. Deb: 4/05/89

YEAR	TM/L	G	AB	R	H	2B	3B	HR	RBI	BB	SO	AVG	OBP	SLG	PRO+	BR	/A	RC	SB	CS	SBR	FR	POS	TPR
1989	Chi-N	17	21	0	3	0	0	0	0	2	3	.143	.217	.143	5	-3	-3	1	1	0	0	-0	/O	-0.2
	SD-N	10	17	4	6	0	0	2	2	3	2	.353	.450	.706	225	3	3	6	0	0	0	0	/1	0.3
	Yr	27	38	4	9	0	0	2	2	5	5	.237	.326	.395	100	0	0	6	1	0	0	-0		0.1
1990	SD-N	103	182	26	38	9	1	4	19	30	43	.209	.321	.335	79	-4	-5	21	2	1	0	3	1	-0.4
Total	2	130	220	30	47	9	1	6	21	35	48	.214	.322	.345	83	-4	-5	28	3	1	0	3	/1O	-0.3

■ DUMMY STEPHENSON
Stephenson, Reuben Crandol b: 9/22/1869, Petersburg, N.J. d: 12/1/24, Trenton, N.J. 5'11.5", 180 lbs. Deb: 9/09/1892

YEAR	TM/L	G	AB	R	H	2B	3B	HR	RBI	BB	SO	AVG	OBP	SLG	PRO+	BR	/A	RC	SB	CS	SBR	FR	POS	TPR
1892	Phi-N	8	37	4	10	3	0	0	5	0	2	.270	.289	.351	95	-0	-0	4	0			-2	/O	-0.1

■ BOB STEPHENSON
Stephenson, Robert Lloyd b: 8/11/28, Blair, Okla. BR/TR, 6', 165 lbs. Deb: 4/14/55

YEAR	TM/L	G	AB	R	H	2B	3B	HR	RBI	BB	SO	AVG	OBP	SLG	PRO+	BR	/A	RC	SB	CS	SBR	FR	POS	TPR
1955	StL-N	67	111	19	27	3	0	0	6	5	18	.243	.276	.270	46	-9	-9	8	2	1	0	-1	S/23	-0.7

■ WALTER STEPHENSON
Stephenson, Walter McQueen "Tarzan" b: 3/27/11, Saluda, N.C. BR/TR, 6', 180 lbs. Deb: 4/29/35

YEAR	TM/L	G	AB	R	H	2B	3B	HR	RBI	BB	SO	AVG	OBP	SLG	PRO+	BR	/A	RC	SB	CS	SBR	FR	POS	TPR
1935	*Chi-N	16	26	2	10	1	1	0	2	1	5	.385	.407	.500	142	2	1	6	0			2	/C	0.3
1936	Chi-N	6	12	0	1	0	0	0	1	0	5	.083	.083	.083	-54	-3	-3	0	0			0	/C	-0.2
1937	Phi-N	10	23	1	6	0	0	0	2	2	3	.261	.320	.261	55	-1	-1	2	0			0	/C	0.0
Total	3	32	61	3	17	1	1	0	5	3	13	.279	.313	.328	70	-2	-3	7	0			2	/C	0.1

■ DUTCH STERRETT
Sterrett, Charles Hurlbut b: 10/1/1889, Milroy, Pa. d: 12/9/65, Baltimore, Md. BR/TR, 5'11.5", 165 lbs. Deb: 6/20/12

YEAR	TM/L	G	AB	R	H	2B	3B	HR	RBI	BB	SO	AVG	OBP	SLG	PRO+	BR	/A	RC	SB	CS	SBR	FR	POS	TPR
1912	NY-A	66	230	30	61	4	7	1	32	11		.265	.310	.357	85	-4	-5	28	8			-7	O1C/2	-1.3
1913	NY-A	21	35	0	6	0	0	0	3	1	5	.171	.216	.171	14	-4	-4	1	1			-1	/1C	-0.4
Total	2	87	265	30	67	4	7	1	35	12	5	.253	.298	.332	77	-7	-9	29	9			-8	/O1C2	-1.7

■ CHUCK STEVENS
Stevens, Charles Augustus b: 7/10/18, Van Houten, N.Mex BB/TL, 6'1", 180 lbs. Deb: 9/16/41

YEAR	TM/L	G	AB	R	H	2B	3B	HR	RBI	BB	SO	AVG	OBP	SLG	PRO+	BR	/A	RC	SB	CS	SBR	FR	POS	TPR
1941	StL-A	4	13	2	2	0	0	0	2	0	1	.154	.154	.154	-18	-2	-2	0	0	0	0	-1	/1	-0.2
1946	StL-A	122	432	53	107	17	4	3	27	47	62	.248	.324	.326	78	-10	-12	46	4	6	-2	3	*1	-1.8
1948	StL-A	85	287	34	75	12	4	1	26	41	26	.261	.354	.341	83	-5	-6	39	2	2	-1	1	1	-0.1
Total	3	211	732	89	184	29	8	4	55	88	89	.251	.333	.329	79	-17	-21	86	6	8	-3	3	1	-2.1

■ STEVENS
Stevens *' ", Deb: 5/04/1875

YEAR	TM/L	G	AB	R	H	2B	3B	HR	RBI	BB	SO	AVG	OBP	SLG	PRO+	BR	/A	RC	SB	CS	SBR	FR	POS	TPR
1875	Was-n	1	4	0	1	0	0	0		0		.250	.250	.250	76	-0	-0	0					/O	0.0

■ LEE STEVENS
Stevens, De Wain Lee b: 7/10/67, Kansas City, Mo. BL/TL, 6'4", 205 lbs. Deb: 7/16/90

YEAR	TM/L	G	AB	R	H	2B	3B	HR	RBI	BB	SO	AVG	OBP	SLG	PRO+	BR	/A	RC	SB	CS	SBR	FR	POS	TPR
1990	Cal-A	67	248	28	53	10	0	7	32	22	75	.214	.278	.339	71	-10	-10	22	1	1	-0	-3	1	-1.8

■ ED STEVENS
Stevens, Edward Lee "Big Ed" b: 1/12/25, Galveston, Tex. BL/TL, 6'1", 190 lbs. Deb: 8/09/45 C

YEAR	TM/L	G	AB	R	H	2B	3B	HR	RBI	BB	SO	AVG	OBP	SLG	PRO+	BR	/A	RC	SB	CS	SBR	FR	POS	TPR
1945	Bro-N	55	201	29	55	14	3	4	29	32	20	.274	.376	.433	125	7	7	35	0			0	1	0.5
1946	Bro-N	103	310	34	75	13	7	10	60	27	44	.242	.303	.426	104	0	0	40	2			-4	1	-1.2
1947	Bro-N	5	13	0	2	1	0	0	0	1	5	.154	.214	.231	18	-2	-2	1	0			1	/1	0.0
1948	Pit-N	128	429	47	109	19	6	10	69	35	53	.254	.313	.396	89	-7	-8	54	4			5	*1	-0.2
1949	Pit-N	67	221	22	58	10	1	4	32	22	24	.262	.332	.371	86	-4	-4	29	1			10	1	0.6
1950	Pit-N	17	46	2	9	2	0	0	3	4	5	.196	.260	.239	31	-5	-5	3	0			1	1	-0.4
Total	6	375	1220	134	308	59	17	28	193	121	151	.252	.322	.398	95	-9	-11	162	7			13	1	-0.7

■ R C STEVENS
Stevens, R C b: 7/22/34, Moultrie, Ga. BL/TR, 6'5", 219 lbs. Deb: 4/15/58

YEAR	TM/L	G	AB	R	H	2B	3B	HR	RBI	BB	SO	AVG	OBP	SLG	PRO+	BR	/A	RC	SB	CS	SBR	FR	POS	TPR
1958	Pit-N	59	90	16	24	3	1	7	18	5	25	.267	.320	.556	129	3	3	17	0	0	0	3	1	0.2
1959	Pit-N	3	7	2	2	0	0	1	1	0	0	.286	.286	.714	157	0	0	1	0	0	0	0	/1	0.0
1960	Pit-N	9	3	1	0	0	0	0	0	0	1	.000	.000	.000	-99	-1	-1	0	0	0	0	1	/1	0.0
1961	Was-A	33	62	2	8	1	0	0	2	7	15	.129	.217	.145	-1	-9	-9	2	1	0	0	0	1	-1.0
Total	4	104	162	21	34	4	1	8	21	12	41	.210	.273	.395	77	-6	-6	20	1	0	0	3	/1	-0.8

■ BOBBY STEVENS
Stevens, Robert Jordan b: 4/17/07, Chevy Chase, Md. BL/TR, 5'8", 149 lbs. Deb: 7/03/31

YEAR	TM/L	G	AB	R	H	2B	3B	HR	RBI	BB	SO	AVG	OBP	SLG	PRO+	BR	/A	RC	SB	CS	SBR	FR	POS	TPR
1931	Phi-N	12	35	3	12	0	0	0	4	2	2	.343	.410	.343	97	1	0	5	0			-5	S	-0.3

■ ACE STEWART
Stewart, Asa b: 2/14/1869, Terre Haute, Ind. d: 4/17/12, Terre Haute, Ind. BR/TR, 5'10", 176 lbs. Deb: 4/18/1895

YEAR	TM/L	G	AB	R	H	2B	3B	HR	RBI	BB	SO	AVG	OBP	SLG	PRO+	BR	/A	RC	SB	CS	SBR	FR	POS	TPR
1895	Chi-N	97	365	52	88	8	10	8	76	39	40	.241	.314	.384	76	-11	-15	50	14			-8	*2	-1.4

■ TUFFY STEWART
Stewart, Charles Eugene b: 7/31/1883, Chicago, Ill. d: 11/18/34, Chicago, Ill. BL/TL, 5'10", 167 lbs. Deb: 8/08/13

YEAR	TM/L	G	AB	R	H	2B	3B	HR	RBI	BB	SO	AVG	OBP	SLG	PRO+	BR	/A	RC	SB	CS	SBR	FR	POS	TPR
1913	Chi-N	9	8	1	1	0	0	0	2	2	5	.125	.300	.250	58	-0	-0	1	1			0	/O	0.0
1914	Chi-N	2	1	0	0	0	0	0	0	0	0	.000	.000	.000	-99	-0	-0	0	0			0	H	0.0
Total	2	11	9	1	1	0	0	0	2	2	5	.111	.273	.222	43	-1	-1	1	1			0	/O	0.0

■ BUD STEWART
Stewart, Edward Perry b: 6/15/16, Sacramento, Cal. BL/TR, 5'11", 160 lbs. Deb: 4/19/41

YEAR	TM/L	G	AB	R	H	2B	3B	HR	RBI	BB	SO	AVG	OBP	SLG	PRO+	BR	/A	RC	SB	CS	SBR	FR	POS	TPR
1941	Pit-N	73	172	22	46	7	0	0	10	12	17	.267	.315	.308	76	-5	-5	18	3			-1	O	-0.7
1942	Pit-N	82	183	21	40	8	4	0	20	22	16	.219	.302	.306	76	-5	-5	18	2			-3	O3/2	-0.9
1948	NY-A	6	5	1	1	0	0	0	0	0	0	.200	.200	.400	58	-0	-0	0	0	0	0	0	H	0.0

YEAR	TM/L	G	AB	R	H	2B	3B	HR	RBI	BB	SO	AVG	OBP	SLG	PRO+	BR	/A	RC	SB	CS	SBR	FR	POS	TPR
	Was-A	118	401	56	112	17	13	7	69	49	27	.279	.361	.439	115	6	8	66	8	9	-3	-0	*O	0.0
	Yr	124	406	57	113	18	13	7	69	49	27	.278	.359	.438	115	6	7	66	8	9	-3	-0		0.0
1949	Was-A	118	388	58	110	23	4	8	43	49	33	.284	.368	.425	112	5	6	65	6	4	-1	-5	*O	-0.1
1950	Was-A	118	378	46	101	15	6	4	35	46	33	.267	.348	.370	88	-9	-6	53	5	4	-1	-1	*O	-0.9
1951	Chi-A	95	217	40	60	13	5	6	40	29	9	.276	.367	.465	127	7	8	36	1	6	-3	-3	O	0.0
1952	Chi-A	92	225	23	60	10	0	5	30	28	17	.267	.350	.378	102	1	1	34	3	0	1	-4	O	-0.4
1953	Chi-A	53	59	16	16	2	0	2	13	14	3	.271	.411	.407	118	2	2	11	1	0	0	-2	O	0.0
1954	Chi-A	18	13	0	1	0	0	0	0	3	2	.077	.250	.077	-7	-2	-2	0	0	0	0	1	/O	-0.1
Total	9	773	2041	288	547	96	32	32	260	252	157	.268	.351	.393	102	-0	5	301	29	23		-18	O/32	-3.1

■ GLEN STEWART Stewart, Glen Weldon "Gabby" b: 9/29/12, Tullahoma, Tenn. BR/TR, 6', 175 lbs. Deb: 6/26/40

YEAR	TM/L	G	AB	R	H	2B	3B	HR	RBI	BB	SO	AVG	OBP	SLG	PRO+	BR	/A	RC	SB	CS	SBR	FR	POS	TPR
1940	NY-N	15	29	1	4	1	0	0	0	1	2	.138	.167	.172	-6	-4	-4	1	0			1	/3S	-0.2
1943	Phi-N	110	336	23	71	10	1	2	24	32	41	.211	.284	.265	61	-17	-16	26	1			-9	S2/1C	-1.8
1944	Phi-N	118	377	32	83	11	5	0	29	28	40	.220	.274	.276	57	-22	-21	27	0			5	3S/2	-0.7
Total	3	243	742	56	158	22	6	2	53	61	83	.213	.275	.267	56	-44	-41	54	1			-4	S/321C	-2.7

■ JIMMY STEWART Stewart, James Franklin b: 6/11/39, Opelika, Ala. BB/TR, 6', 165 lbs. Deb: 9/03/63

YEAR	TM/L	G	AB	R	H	2B	3B	HR	RBI	BB	SO	AVG	OBP	SLG	PRO+	BR	/A	RC	SB	CS	SBR	FR	POS	TPR
1963	Chi-N	13	37	1	11	2	0	0	1	1	7	.297	.316	.351	87	-0	-1	4	1	1	-0	1	/S2	0.0
1964	Chi-N	132	415	59	105	17	0	3	33	49	61	.253	.335	.316	81	-7	-9	47	10	8	-2	-6	2S/O3	-0.9
1965	Chi-N	116	282	26	63	9	4	0	19	30	53	.223	.303	.284	65	-12	-13	27	13	3	2	-13	OS	-2.1
1966	Chi-N	57	90	4	16	4	1	0	4	7	12	.178	.253	.244	38	-7	-7	6	1	1	-0	-1	O/2S3	-0.8
1967	Chi-N	6	6	1	1	0	0	0	1	0	0	.167	.167	.167	-4	-1	-1	0	0	0	0	0	H	0.0
	Chi-A	24	18	5	3	0	0	0	1	1	6	.167	.211	.167	13	-2	-2	1	1	0	0	2	/O2S	0.1
1969	Cin-N	119	221	26	56	3	4	4	24	19	33	.253	.313	.357	83	-4	-5	25	4	2	0	-1	O2/3S	-0.8
1970	*Cin-N	101	105	15	28	3	1	1	8	8	13	.267	.325	.343	79	-3	-3	12	5	3	0	3	O2/3C1	-0.4
1971	Cin-N	80	82	7	19	2	2	0	9	9	12	.232	.308	.305	76	-3	-2	8	3	1	0	-2	O/32	-0.4
1972	Hou-N	68	96	14	21	5	2	0	9	6	9	.219	.265	.313	65	-5	-5	8	0	1	-1	-2	O/123	-0.7
1973	Hou-N	61	68	6	13	0	0	0	3	9	12	.191	.295	.191	37	-5	-5	5	0	0	0	1	/3O2	0.0
Total	10	777	1420	164	336	45	14	8	112	139	218	.237	.308	.305	71	-49	-53	142	38	20	-1	-19	O2S/31C	-6.0

■ STUFFY STEWART Stewart, John Franklin b: 1/31/1894, Jasper, Fla. d: 12/30/80, Lake City, Fla. BR/TR, 5'9.5", 160 lbs. Deb: 9/03/16

YEAR	TM/L	G	AB	R	H	2B	3B	HR	RBI	BB	SO	AVG	OBP	SLG	PRO+	BR	/A	RC	SB	CS	SBR	FR	POS	TPR
1916	StL-N	9	17	0	3	0	0	0	1	0	3	.176	.176	.176	9	-2	-2	1	0			-1	/2	-0.3
1917	StL-N	13	9	4	0	0	0	0	0	0	0	.000	.000	.000	-99	-2	-2	0	0			0	/O2	-0.1
1922	Pit-N	3	13	3	2	0	0	0	0	0	1	.154	.154	.154	-20	-2	-2	0	0	0	0	-1	/2	-0.2
1923	Bro-N	4	11	3	4	1	0	1	1	1	1	.364	.417	.727	202	1	1	3	0	0	0	-1	/2	0.0
1925	Was-A	7	17	3	6	1	0	0	3	1	2	.353	.389	.412	105	0	0	3	1	0	0	1	/32	0.1
1926	Was-A	62	63	27	17	6	1	0	9	6	6	.270	.333	.397	92	-1	-1	8	8	4	0	7	2/3	0.7
1927	Was-A	56	129	24	31	6	2	0	4	8	15	.240	.285	.318	57	-9	-8	11	12	2	2	1	2/3	-0.2
1929	Was-A	22	6	10	0	0	0	0	0	1	0	.000	.143	.000	-60	-1	-1	0	0	1	-1	8	/2	0.6
Total	8	176	265	74	63	14	3	1	18	17	32	.238	.284	.325	61	-16	-15	26	21	7		13	/23O	0.6

■ MARK STEWART Stewart, Mark "Big Slick" b: 10/11/1889, Whitlock, Tenn. d: 1/17/32, Memphis, Tenn. BL/TR, 6'1", 180 lbs. Deb: 10/04/13

YEAR	TM/L	G	AB	R	H	2B	3B	HR	RBI	BB	SO	AVG	OBP	SLG	PRO+	BR	/A	RC	SB	CS	SBR	FR	POS	TPR
1913	Cin-N	1	1	0	0	0	0	0	0	0	0	.000	.000	.000	-99	-0	-0	0	0			0	/C	0.0

■ NEB STEWART Stewart, Walter Nesbitt b: 5/21/18, S.Charleston, Ohio BR/TR, 6'1", 195 lbs. Deb: 9/08/40

YEAR	TM/L	G	AB	R	H	2B	3B	HR	RBI	BB	SO	AVG	OBP	SLG	PRO+	BR	/A	RC	SB	CS	SBR	FR	POS	TPR
1940	Phi-N	10	31	3	4	0	0	0	0	1	5	.129	.156	.129	-21	-5	-5	1	0			1	/O	-0.3

■ BILL STEWART Stewart, William Wayne b: 4/15/28, Bay City, Mich. BR/TR, 5'11", 200 lbs. Deb: 4/17/55

YEAR	TM/L	G	AB	R	H	2B	3B	HR	RBI	BB	SO	AVG	OBP	SLG	PRO+	BR	/A	RC	SB	CS	SBR	FR	POS	TPR
1955	KC-A	11	18	2	2	1	0	0	1	1	6	.111	.158	.167	-13	-3	-3	1	0	0	0	1	/O	-0.2

■ ROYLE STILLMAN Stillman, Royle Eldon b: 1/2/51, Santa Monica, Cal. BL/TL, 5'11", 180 lbs. Deb: 6/22/75

YEAR	TM/L	G	AB	R	H	2B	3B	HR	RBI	BB	SO	AVG	OBP	SLG	PRO+	BR	/A	RC	SB	CS	SBR	FR	POS	TPR
1975	Bal-A	13	14	1	6	0	0	0	1	1	3	.429	.467	.429	165	1	1	3	0	0	0	0	/O	0.1
1976	Bal-A	20	22	0	2	0	0	0	1	3	4	.091	.200	.091	-14	-3	-3	1	0	0	0	0	/1D	-0.2
1977	Chi-A	56	119	18	25	7	1	3	13	17	21	.210	.309	.361	82	-3	-3	14	2	1	0	-0	OD/1	-0.3
Total	3	89	155	19	33	7	1	3	15	21	28	.213	.307	.329	77	-5	-5	18	2	1	0	-0	/OD1	-0.4

■ KURT STILLWELL Stillwell, Kurt Andrew b: 6/4/65, Glendale, Cal. BB/TR, 5'11", 165 lbs. Deb: 4/13/86

YEAR	TM/L	G	AB	R	H	2B	3B	HR	RBI	BB	SO	AVG	OBP	SLG	PRO+	BR	/A	RC	SB	CS	SBR	FR	POS	TPR
1986	Cin-N	104	279	31	64	6	1	0	26	30	47	.229	.309	.258	56	-15	-17	24	6	2	1	-2	S	-1.0
1987	Cin-N	131	395	54	102	20	7	4	33	32	50	.258	.317	.375	79	-10	-12	46	4	6	-2	-21	S23	-2.9
1988	KC-A	128	459	63	115	28	5	10	53	47	76	.251	.324	.399	100	1	1	60	6	5	-1	-18	*S	-1.2
1989	KC-A	130	463	52	121	20	7	7	54	42	64	.261	.327	.380	99	-1	-1	60	9	6	-1	-31	*S	-2.2
1990	KC-A	144	506	60	126	35	4	3	51	39	60	.249	.308	.352	86	-11	-10	54	0	2	-1	-20	*S	-2.2
Total	5	637	2102	260	528	109	24	24	217	190	297	.251	.317	.360	86	-37	-39	244	25	21	-5	-93	S/23	-9.5

■ RON STILLWELL Stillwell, Ronald Roy b: 12/3/39, Los Angeles, Cal. BR/TR, 5'11", 165 lbs. Deb: 7/03/61

YEAR	TM/L	G	AB	R	H	2B	3B	HR	RBI	BB	SO	AVG	OBP	SLG	PRO+	BR	/A	RC	SB	CS	SBR	FR	POS	TPR
1961	Was-A	8	16	3	2	1	0	0	1	1	4	.125	.176	.188	-3	-2	-2	1	0	0	0	-1	/S	-0.2
1962	Was-A	6	22	5	6	0	0	0	2	2	2	.273	.333	.273	66	-1	-1	2	0	0	0	-2	/2S	-0.2
Total	2	14	38	8	8	1	0	0	3	3	6	.211	.268	.237	37	-3	-3	3	0	0	0	-3	/2S	-0.4

■ CRAIG STIMAC Stimac, Craig Steven b: 11/18/54, Oak Park, Ill. BR/TR, 6'2", 185 lbs. Deb: 8/12/80

YEAR	TM/L	G	AB	R	H	2B	3B	HR	RBI	BB	SO	AVG	OBP	SLG	PRO+	BR	/A	RC	SB	CS	SBR	FR	POS	TPR
1980	SD-N	20	50	5	11	2	0	0	7	1	6	.220	.235	.260	40	-4	-4	3	0	0	0	4	C/3	0.0
1981	SD-N	9	9	0	1	0	0	0	0	0	3	.111	.111	.111	-40	-2	-2	0	0	0	0	0	/H	-0.1
Total	2	29	59	5	12	2	0	0	7	1	9	.203	.217	.237	29	-6	-5	4	0	0	0	4	/C3	-0.1

■ BOB STINSON Stinson, Gorrell Robert b: 10/11/45, Elkin, N.C. BB/TR, 5'11", 180 lbs. Deb: 9/23/69

YEAR	TM/L	G	AB	R	H	2B	3B	HR	RBI	BB	SO	AVG	OBP	SLG	PRO+	BR	/A	RC	SB	CS	SBR	FR	POS	TPR
1969	LA-N	4	8	1	3	0	0	0	2	0	2	.375	.375	.375	119	0	0	0	0	1	-1	1	/C	0.0
1970	LA-N	4	3	1	0	0	0	0	0	0	1	.000	.000	.000	-99	-1	-0	0	0	0	0	-0	/C	0.0
1971	StL-N	17	19	3	4	1	0	0	1	1	7	.211	.250	.263	44	-1	-1	1	0	0	0	3	/CO	0.2
1972	Hou-N	27	35	3	6	1	0	0	2	1	6	.171	.216	.200	19	-4	-4	2	0	0	0	-4	C/O	-0.6
1973	Mon-N	48	111	12	29	6	1	3	12	17	15	.261	.374	.414	114	3	3	18	0	1	-1	-2	C/3	0.2
1974	Mon-N	38	87	4	15	2	0	1	6	15	16	.172	.294	.230	45	-6	-6	6	1	1	-0	0	C	-0.4
1975	KC-A	63	147	18	39	9	1	1	9	18	29	.265	.349	.361	98	1	0	20	1	0	0	8	C/120D	1.0
1976	*KC-A	79	209	26	55	7	1	2	25	25	29	.263	.345	.335	99	1	0	25	3	1	0	-6	C	-0.2
1977	Sea-A	105	297	20	80	11	1	8	32	37	50	.269	.362	.394	107	3	4	41	0	3	-3	-7	C/D	-0.1
1978	Sea-A	124	364	46	94	14	3	11	55	45	42	.258	.349	.404	112	6	6	52	2	1	-1	-18	*C/D	-0.8
1979	Sea-A	95	247	19	60	8	0	4	28	33	38	.243	.342	.348	85	-4	-4	30	1	2	-1	-7	C/D	-0.8
1980	Sea-A	48	107	6	23	2	0	1	8	9	19	.215	.282	.262	50	-7	-7	8	0	0	0	-9	C	-1.4
Total	12	652	1634	166	408	61	7	33	180	201	254	.250	.340	.356	93	-9	-10	205	8	10	-4	-42	C/OD213	-2.9

■ GAT STIRES Stires, Garrett b: 10/13/1849, Hunterdon Co., N.J. d: 6/13/33, Byron, Ill. 5'8", 180 lbs. Deb: 5/06/1871

YEAR	TM/L	G	AB	R	H	2B	3B	HR	RBI	BB	SO	AVG	OBP	SLG	PRO+	BR	/A	RC	SB	CS	SBR	FR	POS	TPR
1871	Rok-n	25	110	23	30	4	6	2	24	7	5	.273	.316	.473	129	3	4	18	3				*O	0.4

■ SNUFFY STIRNWEISS Stirnweiss, George Henry b: 10/26/18, New York, N.Y. d: 9/15/58, Newark Bay, N.J. BR/TR, 5'8.5", 175 lbs. Deb: 4/22/43

YEAR	TM/L	G	AB	R	H	2B	3B	HR	RBI	BB	SO	AVG	OBP	SLG	PRO+	BR	/A	RC	SB	CS	SBR	FR	POS	TPR
1943	*NY-A	83	274	34	60	8	4	1	25	47	37	.219	.333	.288	82	-5	-5	28	11	9	-2	-6	S/2	-1.3
1944	NY-A	154	643	125	205	35	16	8	43	73	87	.319	.389	.460	137	35	33	128	55	11	10	19	*2	6.8
1945	NY-A	152	632	107	195	32	22	10	64	78	62	.309	.385	.476	143	39	36	121	33	17	-0	26	*2	6.6

YEAR	TM/L	G	AB	R	H	2B	3B	HR	RBI	BB	SO	AVG	OBP	SLG	PRO+	BR	/A	RC	SB	CS	SBR	FR	POS	TPR
1946	NY-A	129	487	75	122	19	7	0	37	66	58	.251	.340	.318	83	-8	-9	57	18	6	**2**	-6	32/S	-0.2
1947	*NY-A	148	571	102	146	18	8	5	41	89	47	.256	.358	.342	96	-1	-1	76	5	3	-0	-10	*2	-0.4
1948	NY-A	141	515	90	130	20	7	3	32	86	62	.252	.360	.336	87	-8	-8	68	5	4	-1	-11	*2	-1.5
1949	*NY-A	70	157	29	41	8	2	0	11	29	20	.261	.380	.338	91	-1	-1	23	3	2	-0	4	2/3	0.3
1950	NY-A	7	2	0	0	0	0	0	0	0	0	.000	.000	.000	-99	-1	-1	0	0	0	0	1	/2	0.1
	StL-A	93	326	32	71	16	2	1	24	51	49	.218	.324	.288	56	-20	-22	33	3	3	-1	-24	23/S	-4.1
	Yr	100	328	32	71	16	2	1	24	51	49	.216	.322	.287	55	-21	-22	33	3	3	-1	-23		-4.0
1951	Cle-A	50	88	10	19	1	0	1	4	22	25	.216	.373	.261	78	-2	-1	11	1	0	0	7	2/3	0.7
1952	Cle-A	1	0	0	0	0	0	0	0	0	0	—	—	—	—	0	0	0	0	0	0	0	/3	0.0
Total	10	1028	3695	604	989	157	68	29	281	541	447	.268	.362	.371	102	28	21	545	134	55	7	0	23/S	7.0

■ JACK STIVETTS
Stivetts, John Elmer "Happy Jack" b: 3/31/1868, Ashland, Pa. d: 4/18/30, Ashland, Pa. BR/TR, 6'2", 185 lbs. Deb: 6/26/1889

YEAR	TM/L	G	AB	R	H	2B	3B	HR	RBI	BB	SO	AVG	OBP	SLG	PRO+	BR	/A	RC	SB	CS	SBR	FR	POS	TPR
1889	StL-a	27	79	12	18	2	2	0	7	3	13	.228	.265	.304	56	-4	-6	7	0			-1	P/O	0.0
1890	StL-a	67	226	36	65	15	6	7		16		.288	.337	.500	131	12	7	40	2			3	PO/1	0.0
1891	StL-a	85	302	45	92	10	2	7	54	10	32	.305	.331	.421	102	5	-2	44	4			2	PO	0.0
1892	*Bos-N	71	240	40	71	14	2	3	36	27	28	.296	.369	.408	126	11	8	40	8			-0	PO/1	0.0
1893	Bos-N	50	172	32	51	5	6	3	25	12	14	.297	.342	.448	103	2	-1	29	6			-4	P/O3	0.0
1894	Bos-N	68	244	55	80	12	7	8	64	16	21	.328	.369	.533	108	5	1	50	3			-4	PO/1	0.0
1895	Bos-N	46	158	20	30	6	4	0	24	6	18	.190	.220	.278	27	-17	-19	10	1			-2	P/1O	0.0
1896	Bos-N	67	221	42	76	9	6	3	49	12	10	.344	.380	.480	121	8	6	43	4			-6	PO/13	0.0
1897	*Bos-N	61	199	41	73	9	9	2	37	15		.367	.417	.533	143	14	12	46	2			-3	OP/21	0.9
1898	Bos-N	41	111	16	28	1	1	2	16	10		.252	.314	.333	83	-2	-3	12	1			-5	O1/S2P	-0.6
1899	Cle-N	18	39	8	8	1	1	0	2	6		.205	.326	.282	75	-1	-1	4	0			1	/OPS3	0.1
Total	11	601	1991	347	592	84	46	35	<u>314</u>	133	<u>136</u>	.297	.344	.438	106	33	3	325	31			-19	PO/1S32	0.4

■ MILT STOCK
Stock, Milton Joseph b: 7/11/1893, Chicago, Ill. d: 7/16/77, Montrose, Ala. BR/TR, 5'8", 154 lbs. Deb: 9/29/13 C

YEAR	TM/L	G	AB	R	H	2B	3B	HR	RBI	BB	SO	AVG	OBP	SLG	PRO+	BR	/A	RC	SB	CS	SBR	FR	POS	TPR
1913	NY-N	7	17	2	3	1	0	0	1	2	1	.176	.263	.235	43	-1	-1	1	2			2	/S	0.2
1914	NY-N	115	365	52	96	17	1	3	41	34	21	.263	.333	.340	103	0	2	44	11			15	*3/S	2.3
1915	*Phi-N	69	227	37	59	7	3	1	15	22	26	.260	.325	.330	98	-0	-0	26	6	2	1	2	3/S	0.5
1916	Phi-N	132	509	61	143	25	6	1	43	27	33	.281	.320	.360	105	4	2	56	21	26	-9	-6	*3S	-1.2
1917	Phi-N	150	564	76	149	27	6	3	53	51	34	.264	.326	.349	103	5	2	71	25			-9	*3S	-0.8
1918	Phi-N	123	481	62	132	14	1	1	42	35	22	.274	.325	.314	89	-2	-6	54	20			-5	*3	-0.9
1919	StL-N	135	492	56	151	16	4	0	52	49	21	.307	.371	.356	127	13	16	70	17			17	23	3.9
1920	StL-N	155	639	85	204	28	6	0	76	40	27	.319	.360	.382	117	11	14	86	15	17	-6	-8	*3	0.8
1921	StL-N	149	587	96	180	27	6	3	84	48	26	.307	.360	.388	100	-1	1	85	11	3	2	-22	*3	-1.8
1922	StL-N	151	581	85	177	33	9	5	79	42	29	.305	.352	.418	103	-2	1	83	7	12	-5	-9	*3/S	0.0
1923	StL-N	151	603	63	174	33	3	2	96	40	21	.289	.334	.363	86	-14	-12	74	9	6	-1	-14	*3/2	-2.2
1924	Bro-N	142	561	66	136	14	4	2	52	26	32	.242	.277	.292	54	-37	-35	45	3	8	-4	-23	*3	-5.1
1925	Bro-N	146	615	98	202	28	9	1	62	38	28	.328	.368	.408	101	-1	1	93	8	1	2	1	*2/3	0.1
1926	Bro-N	3	8	0	0	0	0	0	0	1	0	.000	.111	.000	-69	-2	-2	0	0			-0	/2	-0.1
Total	14	1628	6249	839	1806	270	58	22	696	455	321	.289	.339	.361	98	-28	-16	789	155	<u>75</u>		-58	*32/S	-4.3

■ LEN STOCKWELL
Stockwell, Leonard Clark b: 8/25/1859, Cordova, Ill. d: 1/28/05, Niles, Cal. TR, 5'11", 165 lbs. Deb: 5/17/1879

YEAR	TM/L	G	AB	R	H	2B	3B	HR	RBI	BB	SO	AVG	OBP	SLG	PRO+	BR	/A	RC	SB	CS	SBR	FR	POS	TPR
1879	Cle-N	2	6	0	0	0	0	0	0	0	2	.000	.000	.000	-99	-1	-1	0				2	/O	0.0
1884	Lou-a	2	9	0	1	0	0	0	0	0		.111	.111	.111	-28	-1	-1	0				-1	/OC	-0.1
1890	Cle-N	2	7	2	2	1	0	0	0	0	3	.286	.286	.429	111	0	0	1	0			0	/O1	0.0
Total	3	6	22	2	3	1	0	0	0	0	5	.136	.136	.182	0	-2	-2	1				1	/O1C	-0.1

■ STODDARD
Stoddard Deb: 9/25/1875

YEAR	TM/L	G	AB	R	H	2B	3B	HR	RBI	BB	SO	AVG	OBP	SLG	PRO+	BR	/A	RC	SB	CS	SBR	FR	POS	TPR
1875	Atl-n	2	9	1	1	1	0	0				.111	.111	.222	14	-1	-1	0					/O	0.0

■ AL STOKES
Stokes, Albert John (b: Albert John Stocek) b: 1/1/1900, Chicago, Ill. BR/TR, 5'9", 175 lbs. Deb: 5/10/25

YEAR	TM/L	G	AB	R	H	2B	3B	HR	RBI	BB	SO	AVG	OBP	SLG	PRO+	BR	/A	RC	SB	CS	SBR	FR	POS	TPR
1925	Bos-A	17	52	7	11	0	1	0	4	8		.212	.268	.250	32	-5	-5	4	0	0	0	3	C	0.0
1926	Bos-A	30	86	7	14	3	3	0	6	8	28	.163	.234	.267	32	-9	-9	6	0	0	0	-3	C	-0.9
Total	2	47	138	14	25	3	4	0	7	12	36	.181	.247	.261	32	-15	-14	9	0	0	0	-0	/C	-0.9

■ GENE STONE
Stone, Eugene Daniel b: 1/16/44, Burbank, Cal. BL/TL, 5'11", 190 lbs. Deb: 5/13/69

YEAR	TM/L	G	AB	R	H	2B	3B	HR	RBI	BB	SO	AVG	OBP	SLG	PRO+	BR	/A	RC	SB	CS	SBR	FR	POS	TPR
1969	Phi-N	18	28	4	6	0	1	0	0	4	9	.214	.313	.286	70	-1	-1	3	0	0	0	-1	/1	-0.1

■ GEORGE STONE
Stone, George Robert b: 9/3/1877, Lost Nation, Iowa d: 1/3/45, Clinton, Iowa BL/TL, 5'9", 175 lbs. Deb: 4/20/03

YEAR	TM/L	G	AB	R	H	2B	3B	HR	RBI	BB	SO	AVG	OBP	SLG	PRO+	BR	/A	RC	SB	CS	SBR	FR	POS	TPR
1903	Bos-A	2	2	0	0	0	0	0	0	0	0	.000	.000	.000	-95	-0	-0	0				0	H	0.0
1905	StL-A	154	632	76	187	25	13	7	52	44		.296	.342	.410	148	27	31	101	26			1	*O	2.7
1906	StL-A	154	581	91	208	25	20	6	71	52		**.358**	**.411**	**.501**	**196**	**57**	**60**	**139**	35			-1	*O	5.6
1907	StL-A	155	596	77	191	13	11	4	59	59		.320	.382	.399	152	35	35	104	23			-3	*O	2.6
1908	StL-A	148	588	89	165	21	8	5	31	55		.281	.342	.369	133	22	21	80	20			0	*O	1.6
1909	StL-A	83	310	53	89	5	4	1	15	24		.287	.340	.339	123	5	8	39	8			2	O	0.7
1910	StL-A	152	562	60	144	17	12	0	40	48		.256	.315	.329	108	1	5	65	20			-3	*O	-0.5
Total	7	848	3271	426	984	106	68	23	268	282		.301	.356	.396	145	147	159	528	132			-4	O	12.7

■ RON STONE
Stone, Harry Ronald b: 9/9/42, Corning, Cal. BL/TL, 6'2", 185 lbs. Deb: 4/13/66

YEAR	TM/L	G	AB	R	H	2B	3B	HR	RBI	BB	SO	AVG	OBP	SLG	PRO+	BR	/A	RC	SB	CS	SBR	FR	POS	TPR
1966	KC-A	26	22	2	6	1	0	0	0	0	2	.273	.273	.318	71	-1	-1	2	1	1	-0	1	/O1	0.0
1969	Phi-N	103	222	22	53	7	1	1	24	29	28	.239	.335	.293	79	-6	-5	21	3	1	0	-3	O	-1.1
1970	Phi-N	123	321	30	84	12	5	3	39	38	45	.262	.342	.358	90	-5	-4	40	5	6	-2	-4	O/1	-1.4
1971	Phi-N	95	185	16	42	8	1	2	23	25	36	.227	.319	.314	80	-4	-4	19	2	2	-1	-1	O/1	-0.7
1972	Phi-N	41	54	3	9	0	1	0	3	9	11	.167	.286	.204	40	-4	-4	3	0	0	0	3	O	-0.1
Total	5	388	804	73	194	28	8	6	89	101	122	.241	.329	.318	81	-20	-18	85	11	10	-3	-3	O/1	-3.3

■ JEFF STONE
Stone, Jeffrey Glen b: 12/26/60, Kennett, Mo. BL/TR, 6', 175 lbs. Deb: 9/09/83

YEAR	TM/L	G	AB	R	H	2B	3B	HR	RBI	BB	SO	AVG	OBP	SLG	PRO+	BR	/A	RC	SB	CS	SBR	FR	POS	TPR
1983	Phi-N	9	4	2	3	0	0	0	3	0	1	.750	.750	1.750	580	2	2	7	4	0	1	0	/O	0.4
1984	Phi-N	51	185	27	67	4	6	1	15	9	26	.362	.398	.465	139	10	10	37	27	5	5	-7	O	0.6
1985	Phi-N	88	264	36	70	4	3	3	11	15	50	.265	.307	.337	78	-7	-8	28	15	5	2	-10	O	-1.8
1986	Phi-N	82	249	32	69	6	4	6	19	20	52	.277	.341	.406	101	2	1	36	19	6	2	-0	O	0.1
1987	Phi-N	66	125	19	32	7	1	1	16	8	38	.256	.316	.352	74	-4	-5	14	3	1	0	-1	O	-0.6
1988	Bal-A	26	61	4	10	1	0	0	1	0	11	.164	.215	.180	12	-7	-7	2	4	1	1	-0	O/D	-0.6
1989	Tex-A	22	36	5	6	1	2	0	5	3	5	.167	.250	.306	55	-2	-2	2	2	1	0	0	D/O	-0.1
	Bos-A	18	15	3	3	0	0	0	1	1	2	.200	.250	.200	27	-1	-2	1	1	0	0	1	O	-0.1
	Yr	40	51	8	9	1	2	0	6	4	7	.176	.250	.275	46	-4	-4	3	3	1	0	1		-0.1
1990	Bos-A	10	2	1	1	0	0	0	0	1	0	.500	.500	.500	172	0	0	0	1	-1	0	0	/D	0.0
Total	8	372	941	129	261	23	18	11	72	60	186	.277	.328	.375	92	-8	-10	128	75	20	11	-18	O/D	-2.0

■ JOHN STONE
Stone, John Thomas "Rocky" b: 10/10/05, Lynchburg, Tenn. d: 11/30/55, Shelbyville, Tenn. BL/TR, 6'1", 178 lbs. Deb: 8/31/28

YEAR	TM/L	G	AB	R	H	2B	3B	HR	RBI	BB	SO	AVG	OBP	SLG	PRO+	BR	/A	RC	SB	CS	SBR	FR	POS	TPR
1928	Det-A	26	113	20	40	10	3	2	21	5	8	.354	.387	.549	141	6	7	21				-0	-1 O	0.4
1929	Det-A	51	150	23	39	11	1	2	15	11	13	.260	.311	.400	81	-5	-5	19	1	1	-0	-1	O	-0.6
1930	Det-A	126	422	60	132	29	11	3	56	32	49	.313	.363	.455	104	3	2	67	6	9	-4	1	*O	-0.4
1931	Det-A	147	584	86	191	28	11	10	76	56	48	.327	.388	.464	119	20	17	103	13	13	-4	4	*O	0.7

YEAR	TM/L	G	AB	R	H	2B	3B	HR	RBI	BB	SO	AVG	OBP	SLG	PRO+	BR	/A	RC	SB	CS	SBR	FR	POS	TPR
1932	Det-A	145	582	106	173	35	12	17	108	58	64	.297	.361	.486	113	13	10	103	2	1	0	7	*O	1.0
1933	Det-A	148	574	86	161	33	11	11	80	54	37	.280	.344	.434	103	3	1	86	1	4	-2	-3	*O	-0.7
1934	Was-A	113	419	77	132	28	7	7	67	52	26	.315	.395	.465	126	14	16	79	1	2	-1	6	*O	1.8
1935	Was-A	125	455	78	143	27	18	1	78	39	29	.314	.372	.459	118	9	11	77	4	5	-2	-1	*O	0.6
1936	Was-A	123	437	95	149	22	11	15	90	60	26	.341	.421	.545	145	25	29	104	8	0	2	4	*O	2.8
1937	Was-A	139	542	84	179	33	15	6	88	66	36	.330	.403	.480	127	19	22	107	6	4	-1	6	*O	2.0
1938	Was-A	56	213	24	52	12	4	3	28	30	16	.244	.337	.380	85	-7	-5	29	2	1	0	-3	O	-0.6
Total	11	1199	4491	739	1391	268	105	77	707	463	352	.310	.376	.468	116	101	106	798	45	40	-10	17	*O	7.0

■ TIGE STONE
Stone, William Arthur b: 9/18/01, Macon, Ga. d: 1/1/60, Jacksonville, Fla. 5'8", 145 lbs. Deb: 8/23/23

YEAR	TM/L	G	AB	R	H	2B	3B	HR	RBI	BB	SO	AVG	OBP	SLG	PRO+	BR	/A	RC	SB	CS	SBR	FR	POS	TPR
1923	StL-N	5	1	0	1	0	0	0	0	0	0	1.000	1.000	1.000	438	1	1	1	0	0	0	0	/OP	0.1

■ JOHN STONEHAM
Stoneham, John Andrew b: 11/8/08, Wood River, Ill. BL/TR, 5'9.5", 168 lbs. Deb: 9/18/33

YEAR	TM/L	G	AB	R	H	2B	3B	HR	RBI	BB	SO	AVG	OBP	SLG	PRO+	BR	/A	RC	SB	CS	SBR	FR	POS	TPR
1933	Chi-A	10	25	4	3	0	0	0	3	2	2	.120	.185	.240	12	-3	-3	1	0	0	0	-1	/O	-0.3

■ HOWIE STORIE
Storie, Howard Edward "Sponge" b: 5/15/11, Pittsfield, Mass. d: 7/27/68, Pittsfield, Mass. BR/TR, 5'10", 175 lbs. Deb: 9/07/31

YEAR	TM/L	G	AB	R	H	2B	3B	HR	RBI	BB	SO	AVG	OBP	SLG	PRO+	BR	/A	RC	SB	CS	SBR	FR	POS	TPR
1931	Bos-A	6	17	2	2	0	0	0	0	3	2	.118	.250	.118	-1	-2	-2	1	0	0	0	0	/C	-0.1
1932	Bos-A	6	8	0	3	0	0	0	0	0	0	.375	.375	.375	98	-0	-0	1	0	0	0	1	/C	0.1
Total	2	12	25	2	5	0	0	0	0	3	2	.200	.286	.200	31	-2	-2	2	0	0	0	1	/C	0.0

■ ALAN STORKE
Storke, Alan Marshall b: 9/27/1884, Auburn, N.Y. d: 3/18/10, Newton, Mass. TR , Deb: 9/24/06

YEAR	TM/L	G	AB	R	H	2B	3B	HR	RBI	BB	SO	AVG	OBP	SLG	PRO+	BR	/A	RC	SB	CS	SBR	FR	POS	TPR
1906	Pit-N	5	12	1	3	1	0	0	1	1		.250	.308	.333	98	0	-0	2	1			0	/3S	0.0
1907	Pit-N	112	357	24	92	6	6	1	39	16		.258	.290	.317	90	-4	-5	37	6			-13	31/2S	-1.9
1908	Pit-N	64	202	20	51	5	3	1	12	9		.252	.284	.322	95	-1	-1	20	4			-5	1/32	-0.8
1909	Pit-N	37	118	12	30	5	2	0	12	7		.254	.302	.331	89	-1	-2	12	1			-0	13	-0.2
	StL-N	48	174	11	49	5	0	0	10	12		.282	.328	.310	105	-0	1	19	5			-1	S/21	0.0
	Yr	85	292	23	79	10	2	0	22	19		.271	.317	.318	97	-1	-1	32	6			-2		-0.2
Total	4	266	863	68	225	22	11	2	74	45		.261	.298	.319	94	-7	-8	89	17			-19	/13S2	-2.9

■ LIN STORTI
Storti, Lindo Ivan b: 12/5/06, Santa Monica, Cal. d: 7/24/82, Ontario, Cal. BB/TR, 5'11", 165 lbs. Deb: 9/18/30

YEAR	TM/L	G	AB	R	H	2B	3B	HR	RBI	BB	SO	AVG	OBP	SLG	PRO+	BR	/A	RC	SB	CS	SBR	FR	POS	TPR
1930	StL-A	7	28	6	9	1	1	0	2	2	6	.321	.367	.429	98	0	-0	4	0	0	0	1	/2	0.1
1931	StL-A	86	273	32	60	15	4	3	26	15	50	.220	.263	.337	55	-18	-19	24	0	2	-1	9	3/2	-0.6
1932	StL-A	53	193	19	50	11	2	3	26	5	20	.259	.278	.383	66	-9	-11	20	1	0		-4	3	-1.0
1933	StL-A	70	210	26	41	7	4	3	21	25	31	.195	.281	.310	53	-14	-15	19	2	2	-1	-2	32	-1.5
Total	4	216	704	83	160	34	11	9	75	47	107	.227	.277	.345	59	-41	-46	68	3	4	-2	4	3/2	-3.0

■ TOM STOUCH
Stouch, Thomas Carl b: 12/2/1870, Perryville, Ohio d: 10/7/56, Lancaster, Pa. BR/TR, 6'2", 165 lbs. Deb: 7/07/1898

YEAR	TM/L	G	AB	R	H	2B	3B	HR	RBI	BB	SO	AVG	OBP	SLG	PRO+	BR	/A	RC	SB	CS	SBR	FR	POS	TPR
1898	Lou-N	4	16	4	5	1	0	0	6	1		.313	.353	.375	113	0	0	2	0			-2	/2	-0.1

■ GEORGE STOVALL
Stovall, George Thomas "Firebrand" b: 11/23/1878, Independence, Mo. d: 11/5/51, Burlington, Iowa BR/TR, 6'2", 180 lbs. Deb: 7/04/04 M

YEAR	TM/L	G	AB	R	H	2B	3B	HR	RBI	BB	SO	AVG	OBP	SLG	PRO+	BR	/A	RC	SB	CS	SBR	FR	POS	TPR
1904	Cle-A	52	181	18	54	10	1	1	31	2		.298	.306	.381	120	3	3	23	3			-2	1/2O3	0.2
1905	Cle-A	112	423	41	115	31	1	1	47	13		.272	.294	.357	107	2	2	50	13			-5	12/O	-0.4
1906	Cle-A	116	443	54	121	19	5	0	37	8		.273	.286	.339	98	-3	-2	50	15			-4	132	-0.7
1907	Cle-A	124	466	38	110	17	6	1	36	18		.236	.264	.305	82	-10	-10	44	13			-3	*1/3	-1.6
1908	Cle-A	138	534	71	156	29	6	2	45	17		.292	.314	.380	127	14	14	69	14			3	*1/OS	1.5
1909	Cle-A	145	565	60	139	17	10	2	49	6		.246	.259	.322	80	-13	-16	53	25			10	*1	-0.7
1910	Cle-A	142	521	49	136	19	4	0	52	14		.261	.284	.313	86	-10	-10	52	16			7	*1/2	0.1
1911	Cle-A	126	458	48	124	17	7	0	79	21		.271	.306	.338	79	-14	-14	50	11			7	*1/2M	-0.4
1912	StL-A	116	398	35	101	17	5	0	45	14		.254	.286	.322	76	-15	-13	39	11			5	1M	-0.6
1913	StL-A	89	303	34	87	14	3	1	24	7	23	.287	.305	.363	98	-3	-2	34	7			8	1M	0.5
1914	KC-F	124	450	51	128	20	5	7	75	23	35	.284	.325	.398	111	2	5	63	6			4	*1/3M	1.2
1915	KC-F	130	480	48	111	21	3	0	44	29	36	.231	.283	.287	72	-18	-16	44	8			5	*1M	-0.9
Total	12	1414	5222	547	1382	231	56	15	564	172	94	.265	.291	.339	93	-65	-61	569	142			34	*1/230S	-1.8

■ HARRY STOVEY
Stovey, Harry Duffield (b: Harry Duffield Stowe)
b: 12/20/1856, Philadelphia, Pa. d: 9/20/37, New Bedford, Mass BR/TR, 5'11.5", 175 lbs. Deb: 5/01/1880 M

YEAR	TM/L	G	AB	R	H	2B	3B	HR	RBI	BB	SO	AVG	OBP	SLG	PRO+	BR	/A	RC	SB	CS	SBR	FR	POS	TPR
1880	Wor-N	83	355	76	94	21	**14**	**6**	28	12	46	.265	.289	.454	136	17	13	48				-6	O1/P	0.4
1881	Wor-N	75	341	57	92	25	7	2	30	12	23	.270	.295	.402	111	6	3	41				-5	*1OM	-0.8
1882	Wor-N	84	360	90	104	13	10	5	26	22	34	.289	.330	.422	136	16	14	51				3	1O	0.9
1883	Phi-a	94	421	**110**	127	**31**	6	**14**		26		.302	.342	**.504**	156	31	26	74				0	*1/OP	1.5
1884	Phi-a	104	448	**124**	146	22	**23**	10		26		.326	.368	.545	185	46	42	92				-1	*1	3.2
1885	Phi-a	112	486	**130**	153	27	9	**13**		39		.315	.371	.488	163	39	35	90				4	*1OM	2.7
1886	Phi-a	123	489	115	144	28	11	7		64		.294	.377	.440	156	33	33	109	**68**			3	O1/P	2.6
1887	Phi-a	124	497	125	142	31	12	4		56		.286	.366	.421	121	15	15	74	74			12	O1	1.9
1888	Phi-a	130	530	127	152	25	**20**	9	65	62		.287	.365	.460	168	40	40	124	87			4	*O1	3.5
1889	Phi-a	137	556	**152**	171	38	13	**19**	**119**	77	68	.308	.393	**.525**	165	45	46	143	63			18	*O/1	**4.9**
1890	Bos-P	118	481	142	143	25	11	12	85	81	38	.297	.404	.470	127	26	19	134	**97**			2	*O/1	1.3
1891	Bos-N	134	544	118	152	31	**20**	**16**	95	78	69	.279	.372	**.498**	138	37	20	119	57			9	*O/1	2.4
1892	Bos-N	38	146	21	24	8	1	0	12	14	19	.164	.252	.233	44	-9	-11	14	20			0	O	-1.0
	Bal-N	74	283	58	77	14	11	4	55	40	32	.272	.364	.442	141	16	14	54	20			-3	O1	0.7
	Yr	112	429	79	101	22	12	4	67	54	51	.235	.326	.371	107	7	3	67	40			-3		-0.3
1893	Bal-N	8	26	4	4	2	0	0	5	8	3	.154	.353	.231	57	-1	-1	3	1			0	/O	0.0
	Bro-N	48	175	43	44	6	6	1	29	44	11	.251	.402	.371	113	4	6	36	22			-3	O	0.1
	Yr	56	201	47	48	8	6	1	34	52	14	.239	.395	.353	105	3	4	38	23			-2		0.1
Total	14	1486	6138	1492	1769	347	174	122	549	661	343	.288	.360	.461	143	360	320	1244	509			38	O1/P	24.3

■ RAY STOVIAK
Stoviak, Raymond Thomas b: 6/6/15, Scottdale, Pa. BL/TL, 6'1", 195 lbs. Deb: 6/05/38

YEAR	TM/L	G	AB	R	H	2B	3B	HR	RBI	BB	SO	AVG	OBP	SLG	PRO+	BR	/A	RC	SB	CS	SBR	FR	POS	TPR
1938	Phi-N	10	10	1	0	0	0	0	0	0	3	.000	.000	.000	-99	-3	-3	0	0			1	/O	-0.1

■ JOE STRAIN
Strain, Joseph Allan b: 4/30/54, Denver, Colo. BR/TR, 5'10", 169 lbs. Deb: 6/28/79

YEAR	TM/L	G	AB	R	H	2B	3B	HR	RBI	BB	SO	AVG	OBP	SLG	PRO+	BR	/A	RC	SB	CS	SBR	FR	POS	TPR
1979	SF-N	67	257	27	62	8	1	1	12	13	21	.241	.286	.292	62	-15	-13	22	8	4	0	-1	2/3	-0.9
1980	SF-N	77	189	26	54	6	0	0	16	10	10	.286	.322	.317	81	-5	-5	18	1	2	-1	-11	2/3S	-1.4
1981	Chi-N	25	74	7	14	1	0	0	1	5	7	.189	.250	.203	28	-7	-7	4	0	0	0	7	2	0.2
Total	3	169	520	60	130	15	1	1	29	28	38	.250	.293	.288	64	-27	-24	43	9	6	-1	-4	2/3S	-2.1

■ PAUL STRAND
Strand, Paul Edward b: 12/19/1893, Carbonado, Wash. d: 7/2/74, Salt Lake City, Utah BR/TL, 6'0.5", 190 lbs. Deb: 5/15/13

YEAR	TM/L	G	AB	R	H	2B	3B	HR	RBI	BB	SO	AVG	OBP	SLG	PRO+	BR	/A	RC	SB	CS	SBR	FR	POS	TPR
1913	Bos-N	7	6	1	1	0	0	0	0	0	0	.167	.167	.167	-5	-1	-1	0	0			0	/P	0.0
1914	Bos-N	18	24	2	8	2	0	0	3	0	2	.333	.333	.417	123	0	1	3	0			-1	P	0.0
1915	Bos-N	24	22	3	2	0	0	0	2	0	4	.091	.091	.091	-47	-4	-4	0	0			-0	/PO	-0.3
1924	Phi-A	47	167	15	38	9	4	0	13	4	9	.228	.254	.329	49	-13	-14	13	3	3	-1	-6	O	-2.2
Total	4	96	219	20	49	11	4	0	18	4	15	.224	.244	.311	47	-17	-18	17	3	3		-7	/OP	-2.5

■ LARRY STRANDS
Strands, John Lawrence b: 12/5/1885, Chicago, Ill. d: 1/19/57, Forest Park, Ill. BR/TR, 5'10.5", 165 lbs. Deb: 4/25/15

YEAR	TM/L	G	AB	R	H	2B	3B	HR	RBI	BB	SO	AVG	OBP	SLG	PRO+	BR	/A	RC	SB	CS	SBR	FR	POS	TPR
1915	New-F	35	75	7	14	3	1	1	11	6	11	.187	.247	.293	63	-4	-3	6	1			-7	3/2O	-1.0

YEAR	TM/L	G	AB	R	H	2B	3B	HR	RBI	BB	SO	AVG	OBP	SLG	PRO+	BR	/A	RC	SB	CS	SBR	FR	POS	TPR

■ SAMMY STRANG
Strang, Samuel Nicklin "The Dixie Thrush" (b: Samuel Strang Nicklin)
b: 12/16/1876, Chattanooga, Tenn.   d: 3/13/32, Chattanooga, Tenn.   BB/TR, 5'8", 160 lbs.   Deb: 7/10/1896

YEAR	TM/L	G	AB	R	H	2B	3B	HR	RBI	BB	SO	AVG	OBP	SLG	PRO+	BR	/A	RC	SB	CS	SBR	FR	POS	TPR
1896	Lou-N	14	46	6	12	0	0	0	7	6	6	.261	.346	.261	66	-2	-2	6	4			-8	S	-0.7
1900	Chi-N	27	102	15	29	3	0	0	9	8		.284	.348	.314	89	-2	-1	12	1			-11	3/S2	-0.9
1901	NY-N	135	493	55	139	14	6	1	34	59		.282	.361	.341	111	6	9	80	40			2	32/OS	1.8
1902	Chi-A	137	536	108	158	18	5	3	46	76		.295	.387	.364	116	12	15	94	38			5	*3	1.5
	Chi-N	3	11	1	4	0	0	0	0	0		.364	.364	.364	131	0	0	2	1			-1	/23	0.0
1903	Bro-N	135	508	101	138	21	5	0	38	75		.272	.365	.333	105	4	6	82	46			-7	*3/O2	0.7
1904	Bro-N	77	271	28	52	11	0	1	9	45		.192	.307	.244	74	-7	-6	26	16			-32	23/S	-3.8
1905	*NY-N	111	294	51	76	9	4	3	29	58		.259	.381	.347	117	10	9	50	23			-16	20/S13	-0.5
1906	NY-N	113	313	50	100	16	4	4	49	54		.319	.420	.435	165	27	26	68	21			3	20/S31	3.1
1907	NY-N	123	306	56	77	20	4	4	30	60		.252	.374	.382	135	16	15	53	21			-1	02/31S	1.3
1908	NY-N	28	53	8	5	0	0	0	2	23		.094	.368	.094	49	-1	-1	4	5			-3	2/OS	-0.4
Total	10	903	2933	479	790	112	28	16	253	464	6	.269	.371	.343	114	65	72	477	216			-68	320/S1	1.4

■ ALAN STRANGE
Strange, Alan Cochrane "Inky"   b: 11/7/09, Philadelphia, Pa.   BR/TR, 5'9", 162 lbs.   Deb: 4/17/34

YEAR	TM/L	G	AB	R	H	2B	3B	HR	RBI	BB	SO	AVG	OBP	SLG	PRO+	BR	/A	RC	SB	CS	SBR	FR	POS	TPR
1934	StL-A	127	430	39	100	17	2	1	45	48	28	.233	.310	.288	51	-28	-34	41	3	1	0	4	*S	-1.8
1935	StL-A	49	147	8	34	6	1	0	17	17	7	.231	.311	.286	53	-10	-11	14	0	0	0	2	S	-0.5
	Was-A	20	54	3	10	2	1	0	5	4	1	.185	.241	.259	30	-6	-6	4	0	0	0	3	S	-0.1
	Yr	69	201	11	44	8	2	0	22	21	8	.219	.293	.279	47	-15	-16	18	0	0	0	5		-0.6
1940	StL-A	54	167	26	31	8	3	0	6	22	12	.186	.284	.269	43	-14	-14	14	2	1	0	3	S/2	-0.7
1941	StL-A	45	112	14	26	4	0	0	11	15	5	.232	.323	.268	56	-6	-7	10	1	0	0	2	S/13	-0.3
1942	StL-A	19	37	3	10	2	0	0	5	3	1	.270	.325	.324	82	-1	-1	4	0	1	-1	5	3/S2	0.3
Total	5	314	947	93	211	39	7	1	89	109	54	.223	.304	.282	50	-65	-72	86	6	3	0	18	S/321	-3.1

■ DOUG STRANGE
Strange, Joseph Douglas   b: 4/13/64, Greenville, S.C.   BB/TR, 6'2", 170 lbs.   Deb: 7/13/89

YEAR	TM/L	G	AB	R	H	2B	3B	HR	RBI	BB	SO	AVG	OBP	SLG	PRO+	BR	/A	RC	SB	CS	SBR	FR	POS	TPR
1989	Det-A	64	196	16	42	4	1	1	14	17	36	.214	.280	.260	54	-12	-11	14	3	3	-1	1	3/2SD	-1.0

■ ASA STRATTON
Stratton, Asa Evans   b: 2/10/1853, Grafton, Mass.   d: 8/14/25, Fitchburg, Mass.   Deb: 6/17/1881

YEAR	TM/L	G	AB	R	H	2B	3B	HR	RBI	BB	SO	AVG	OBP	SLG	PRO+	BR	/A	RC	SB	CS	SBR	FR	POS	TPR
1881	Wor-N	1	4	0	1	0	0	0	0	0	2	.250	.250	.250	55	-0	-0	0				-1	/S	-0.1

■ SCOTT STRATTON
Stratton, C. Scott   b: 10/2/1869, Campbellsburg, Ky.   d: 3/8/39, Louisville, Ky.   BL/TR, 6', 180 lbs.   Deb: 4/21/1888

YEAR	TM/L	G	AB	R	H	2B	3B	HR	RBI	BB	SO	AVG	OBP	SLG	PRO+	BR	/A	RC	SB	CS	SBR	FR	POS	TPR
1888	Lou-a	67	249	35	64	8	1	1	29	12		.257	.310	.309	104	1	2	28	10			-4	OP	0.1
1889	Lou-a	62	229	30	66	7	5	4	34	13	36	.288	.332	.415	117	3	4	36	10			5	OP1	0.9
1890	*Lou-a	55	189	29	61	3	5	0	16			.323	.385	.392	135	8	8	32	8			5	P/O	0.0
1891	Pit-N	2	8	1	1	0	0	0	0	0		.125	.125	.125	-27	-1	-1	0				1	/P	0.0
	Lou-a	34	115	9	27	2	0	0	8	11	13	.235	.307	.252	64	-5	-5	12	8			3	P/1O	0.0
1892	Lou-N	63	219	22	56	2	9	0	23	17	21	.256	.318	.347	112	1	3	28	9			1	PO/1	0.0
1893	Lou-N	61	221	34	50	8	5	0	16	25	15	.226	.308	.308	71	-11	-8	23	6			5	PO/1	0.0
1894	Lou-N	13	37	9	12	1	2	0	4	4	2	.324	.390	.459	114	0	1	7	1			2	/PO	0.0
	Chi-N	23	96	29	36	5	4	3	23	6	1	.375	.417	.604	138	7	6	26	3			-1	P/O1	0.0
	Yr	36	133	38	48	6	6	3	27	10	3	.361	.410	.564	133	7	7	33	4			1		0.0
1895	Chi-N	10	24	3	7	1	1	0	2	4	2	.292	.393	.417	104	1	0	4	1			-1	/PO	0.0
Total	8	390	1387	201	380	37	32	8	139	108	93	.274	.334	.364	105	2	10	196	56			16	PO/1	1.0

■ JOE STRAUB
Straub, Joseph   b: 1/19/1858, Germany   d: 2/13/29, Pueblo, Colo.   BR/TR, 5'10", 160 lbs.   Deb: 6/24/1880

YEAR	TM/L	G	AB	R	H	2B	3B	HR	RBI	BB	SO	AVG	OBP	SLG	PRO+	BR	/A	RC	SB	CS	SBR	FR	POS	TPR
1880	Tro-N	3	12	1	3	0	0	0	3	1	3	.250	.308	.250	87	-0	-0	1				1	/C	0.1
1882	Phi-a	8	32	2	6	2	0	0		0	1	.188	.212	.250	50	-1	-2	2				-1	/CO	-0.2
1883	Col-a	27	100	4	13	0	0	0		4		.130	.163	.130	-5	-11	-10	2				-5	C1/O	-1.2
Total	3	38	144	7	22	2	0	0	3	6	3	.153	.187	.167	17	-13	-12	5				-5	/C1O	-1.3

■ JOE STRAUSS
Strauss, Joseph "Dutch" or "The Socker" (b: Joseph Strasser)   b: 11/1858, Ohio   d: 6/25/06, Cincinnati, Ohio   BR/TR,   Deb: 7/27/1884

YEAR	TM/L	G	AB	R	H	2B	3B	HR	RBI	BB	SO	AVG	OBP	SLG	PRO+	BR	/A	RC	SB	CS	SBR	FR	POS	TPR
1884	KC-U	16	60	4	12	3	0	0		1		.200	.213	.250	64	-3	-1	3	0			1	O/C23	0.0
1885	Lou-a	2	6	0	1	0	0	0		0		.167	.167	.167	7	-1	-1	0				-2	/OC	-0.1
1886	Lou-a	74	297	36	64	5	6	1		8		.215	.239	.283	61	-13	-15	27	25			5	O/PC	-1.0
	Bro-a	9	36	6	9	1	1	0		1		.250	.270	.333	89	-1	-1	4	4			1	/OC	0.0
	Yr	83	333	42	73	6	7	1		9		.219	.242	.288	64	-13	-16	31	29			6		-1.0
Total	3	101	399	46	86	9	7	1		10		.216	.237	.281	63	-16	-18	35	29			5	/OCP23	-1.1

■ DARRYL STRAWBERRY
Strawberry, Darryl Eugene   b: 3/12/62, Los Angeles, Cal.   BL/TL, 6'6", 190 lbs.   Deb: 5/06/83

YEAR	TM/L	G	AB	R	H	2B	3B	HR	RBI	BB	SO	AVG	OBP	SLG	PRO+	BR	/A	RC	SB	CS	SBR	FR	POS	TPR
1983	NY-N	122	420	63	108	15	7	26	74	47	128	.257	.338	.512	134	17	17	74	19	6	2	1	*O	1.8
1984	NY-N	147	522	75	131	27	4	26	97	75	131	.251	.345	.467	128	18	19	87	27	8	3	5	*O	2.3
1985	NY-N	111	393	78	109	15	4	29	79	73	96	.277	.392	.557	167	34	35	87	26	11	1	0	*O	3.5
1986	*NY-N	136	475	76	123	27	5	27	93	72	141	.259	.363	.507	142	24	26	92	28	12	1	-2	*O	2.4
1987	NY-N	154	532	108	151	32	5	39	104	97	122	.284	.401	.583	165	45	49	132	36	12	4	-3	*O	4.2
1988	*NY-N	153	543	101	146	27	3	39	101	85	127	.269	.371	.545	168	42	45	111	29	14	0	1	*O	4.5
1989	NY-N	134	476	69	107	26	1	29	77	61	105	.225	.314	.466	126	11	14	72	11	4	1	3	*O	1.7
1990	NY-N	152	542	92	150	18	1	37	108	70	110	.277	.364	.518	143	29	30	104	15	8	-0	3	*O	2.9
Total	8	1109	3903	662	1025	187	30	252	733	580	960	.263	.362	.520	147	219	235	760	191	75	12	9	*O	23.3

■ GABBY STREET
Street, Charles Evard "Old Sarge"   b: 9/30/1882, Huntsville, Ala.   d: 2/6/51, Joplin, Mo.   BR/TR, 5'11", 180 lbs.   Deb: 9/13/04   MC

YEAR	TM/L	G	AB	R	H	2B	3B	HR	RBI	BB	SO	AVG	OBP	SLG	PRO+	BR	/A	RC	SB	CS	SBR	FR	POS	TPR
1904	Cin-N	11	33	1	4	1	0	0	0	1		.121	.147	.152	-6	-4	-4	1	2			5	C	0.2
1905	Cin-N	2	2	0	0	0	0	0	0	2		.000	.500	.000	51	-0	-0	0	0			1	/C	0.1
	Bos-N	3	12	0	2	0	0	0	0	0		.167	.167	.167	0	-1	-1	1	1			-1	/C	-0.2
	Cin-N	29	91	8	23	5	1	0	8	6		.253	.299	.330	80	-3	-2	9	1			4	C	0.4
	Yr	34	105	8	25	5	1	0	8	8		.238	.292	.305	73	-3	-4	10	2			3		0.3
1908	Was-A	131	394	31	81	12	7	1	32	40		.206	.279	.279	91	-6	-3	32	5			-1	*C	1.0
1909	Was-A	137	407	25	86	12	1	0	29	26		.211	.262	.246	63	-18	-16	27	2			11	*C	0.6
1910	Was-A	89	257	18	52	6	0	1	16	23		.202	.273	.237	63	-11	-10	17	1			10	C	1.0
1911	Was-A	72	216	16	48	7	1	0	14	14		.222	.279	.264	53	-14	-13	17	4			6	C	0.1
1912	NY-A	29	88	4	16	1	1	0	6	7		.182	.258	.216	34	-7	-8	5	1			0	C	-0.4
1931	StL-N	1	1	0	0	0	0	0	0	0		.000	.000	.000	-96	-0	-0	0	0			0	/CM	0.0
Total	8	504	1501	98	312	44	11	2	105	119	0	.208	.270	.256	65	-64	-59	110	17			34	C	2.8

■ WALT STREULI
Streuli, Walter Herbert   b: 9/26/35, Memphis, Tenn.   BR/TR, 6'2", 195 lbs.   Deb: 9/25/54

YEAR	TM/L	G	AB	R	H	2B	3B	HR	RBI	BB	SO	AVG	OBP	SLG	PRO+	BR	/A	RC	SB	CS	SBR	FR	POS	TPR
1954	Det-A	1	0	0	0	0	0	0	0	0	0	—	1.000	—	195	0	0	0	0	0	0	0	/C	0.0
1955	Det-A	2	4	1	1	1	0	0	1	0	0	.250	.250	.500	100	-0	-0	1	0	0	0	0	/C	0.0
1956	Det-A	3	8	0	2	1	0	0	1	1	2	.250	.333	.375	87	-0	-0	1	0	0	0	0	/C	0.0
Total	3	6	12	1	3	2	0	0	2	1	2	.250	.357	.417	106	0	0	0	0	0	0	0	/C	0.0

■ CUB STRICKER
Stricker, John A. (b: John A. Streaker)   b: 2/15/1860, Philadelphia, Pa.   d: 11/19/37, Philadelphia, Pa.   BR/TR, 5'3", 138 lbs.   Deb: 5/02/1882   M

YEAR	TM/L	G	AB	R	H	2B	3B	HR	RBI	BB	SO	AVG	OBP	SLG	PRO+	BR	/A	RC	SB	CS	SBR	FR	POS	TPR
1882	Phi-a	72	272	34	59	6	1	0		15		.217	.258	.246	63	-8	-12	18				23	*2/PO	1.4
1883	Phi-a	89	330	67	90	8	0	1		19		.273	.312	.306	92	-0	-4	32				-20	*2/C	-1.9
1884	Phi-a	107	399	59	92	16	11	1		19		.231	.267	.333	91	-1	-5	36				-34	*2/OCP	-3.3
1885	Phi-a	106	398	71	93	9	3	1		21		.234	.284	.279	76	-8	-12	32				-13	*2	-1.7

YEAR	TM/L	G	AB	R	H	2B	3B	HR	RBI	BB	SO	AVG	OBP	SLG	PRO+	BR	/A	RC	SB	CS	SBR	FR	POS	TPR
1887	Cle-a	131	534	122	141	19	4	2			53	.264	.334	.326	89	-8	-6	89	86			10	*2/SP	0.5
1888	Cle-a	127	493	80	115	13	6	1	33	50		.233	.311	.290	99	-0	2	65	60			23	*2/OP	2.6
1889	Cle-N	136	566	83	142	10	4	1	47	58	18	.251	.323	.288	74	-19	-17	64	32			6	*2/S	0.0
1890	Cle-P	127	544	93	133	19	8	2	65	54	16	.244	.318	.320	79	-21	-13	65	24			5	*2S	0.0
1891	Bos-a	139	514	96	111	15	4	0	46	63	34	.216	.309	.261	67	-21	-20	59	54			**24**	*2	1.2
1892	StL-N	28	98	12	20	1	0	0	11	10	7	.204	.297	.214	60	-5	-4	8	5			-4	2/SM	-0.6
	Bal-N	75	269	45	71	5	5	3	37	32	18	.264	.344	.353	109	5	3	38	13			3	2	0.6
	Yr	103	367	57	91	6	5	3	48	42	25	.248	.332	.316	97	0	-0	46	18			-2		0.0
1893	Was-N	59	218	28	40	7	1	0	20	20	12	.183	.252	.225	29	-22	-21	14	4			7	2O/S3	-1.2
Total	11	1196	4635	790	1107	128	47	12	259	414	105	.239	.306	.294	80	-107	-108	521	278			29	*2/SOP3C	-2.4

■ GEORGE STRICKLAND

Strickland, George Bevan "Bo"   b: 1/10/26, New Orleans, La.   BR/TR, 6'1", 175 lbs.   Deb: 5/07/50   MC

YEAR	TM/L	G	AB	R	H	2B	3B	HR	RBI	BB	SO	AVG	OBP	SLG	PRO+	BR	/A	RC	SB	CS	SBR	FR	POS	TPR
1950	Pit-N	23	27	0	3	0	0	0	2	3	8	.111	.226	.111	-8	-4	-4	1	0			3	S/3	0.0
1951	Pit-N	138	454	59	98	12	7	9	47	65	83	.216	.318	.333	73	-15	-17	52	4	2	0	12	*S2	0.6
1952	Pit-N	76	232	17	41	6	2	5	22	21	45	.177	.248	.284	46	-17	-18	17	4	2	0	15	2S/13	0.0
	Cle-A	31	88	8	19	4	0	1	8	14	15	.216	.324	.295	78	-3	-2	10	0	0	0	10	S/2	0.9
1953	Cle-A	123	419	43	119	17	4	5	47	51	52	.284	.362	.379	103	1	3	63	0	0	0	16	*S/1	2.7
1954	*Cle-A	112	361	42	77	12	3	6	37	55	62	.213	.319	.313	72	-12	-13	39	2	1	0	-12	*S	-1.6
1955	Cle-A	130	388	34	81	9	5	2	34	49	60	.209	.302	.273	54	-24	-26	35	1	0	0	8	*S	-0.3
1956	Cle-A	85	171	22	36	1	2	3	17	22	27	.211	.301	.292	56	-11	-11	15	0	1	-1	16	2S3	0.9
1957	Cle-A	89	201	21	47	8	2	1	19	26	29	.234	.325	.308	75	-7	-6	20	0	3	-2	15	2S3	1.1
1959	Cle-A	132	441	55	105	15	2	3	48	51	64	.238	.317	.302	74	-17	-15	45	1	1	-0	-9	3S/2	-2.0
1960	Cle-A	32	42	4	7	0	0	1	3	4	8	.167	.255	.238	35	-4	-4	3	0	0	0	1	S3/2	-0.1
Total	10	971	2824	305	633	84	27	36	284	361	453	.224	.314	.311	70	-112	-113	299	12	10		74	S23/1	2.2

■ GEORGE STRIEF

Strief, George Andrew   b: 10/16/1856, Cincinnati, Ohio   d: 4/1/46, Cleveland, Ohio   5'7", 172 lbs.   Deb: 5/01/1879   U

YEAR	TM/L	G	AB	R	H	2B	3B	HR	RBI	BB	SO	AVG	OBP	SLG	PRO+	BR	/A	RC	SB	CS	SBR	FR	POS	TPR
1879	Cle-N	71	264	24	46	7	1	0	15	10	23	.174	.204	.208	37	-17	-17	12				-10	O2	-2.4
1882	Pit-a	79	297	45	58	9	6	2			13	.195	.229	.286	76	-8	-6	20				0	*2/S	0.0
1883	StL-a	82	302	22	68	9	0	1			12	.225	.255	.265	64	-10	-13	21				6	*2O	-0.4
1884	StL-a	48	184	22	37	5	2	2			13	.201	.254	.283	74	-4	-5	14				-3	O/21	-0.7
	KC-U	15	56	5	6	5	0	0			4	.107	.167	.196	26	-4	-3	2	0			8	2	0.4
	CP-U	15	53	6	11	5	0	0			3	.208	.250	.302	86	-1	-1	4	0			-2	2	-0.2
	Yr	30	109	11	17	10	0	0			7	.156	.207	.248	57	-5	-4	6	0			7		0.2
	Cle-N	8	29	2	7	2	0	0	0	0	5	.241	.241	.310	70	-1	-1	2				0	/O3	0.0
1885	Phi-a	44	175	19	48	8	5	0			9	.274	.310	.377	112	4	2	21				-2	3S/O2	0.1
Total	5	362	1360	145	281	50	14	5	15	64	28	.207	.242	.275	69	-43	-45	95				-1	2O/3S1	-3.2

■ JOHN STRIKE

Strike, John   b: 1865, Pennsylvania   Deb: 5/18/1882

YEAR	TM/L	G	AB	R	H	2B	3B	HR	RBI	BB	SO	AVG	OBP	SLG	PRO+	BR	/A	RC	SB	CS	SBR	FR	POS	TPR
1882	Lou-a	32	110	17	18	6	1	0			9	.164	.227	.236	60	-5	-4	6	0			0	C/O2S1	-0.2
1886	Phi-N	2	7	0	0	0	0	0	0	0	4	.000	.000	.000	-99	-2	-2	0	0			-1	/PO	0.0
Total	2	34	117	17	18	6	1	0	0	9	4	.154	.214	.222	49	-6	-5	6	0			-1	/CO2P1S	-0.2

■ LOU STRINGER

Stringer, Louis Bernard   b: 5/13/17, Grand Rapids, Mich   BR/TR, 5'11", 173 lbs.   Deb: 4/15/41

YEAR	TM/L	G	AB	R	H	2B	3B	HR	RBI	BB	SO	AVG	OBP	SLG	PRO+	BR	/A	RC	SB	CS	SBR	FR	POS	TPR
1941	Chi-N	145	512	59	126	31	4	5	53	59	86	.246	.324	.352	94	-6	-4	62	3			20	*2/S	2.6
1942	Chi-N	121	406	45	96	10	5	9	41	31	55	.236	.292	.352	92	-7	-5	42	3			2	*2/3	0.5
1946	Chi-N	80	209	26	51	3	1	3	19	26	34	.244	.328	.311	83	-5	-4	22	0			-4	2/S3	-0.6
1948	Bos-A	4	11	1	1	0	0	1	0	0	3	.091	.091	.364	17	-1	-2	0	0	0	0	2	/2	0.1
1949	Bos-A	35	41	10	11	4	0	1	6	5	10	.268	.348	.439	100	0	-0	6	0	0	0	3	/2	0.3
1950	Bos-A	24	17	7	5	1	0	0	2	0	4	.294	.294	.353	59	-1	-1	2	1	0	0	3	/32S	0.2
Total	6	409	1196	148	290	49	10	19	122	121	192	.242	.313	.348	90	-20	-17	135	7	0		26	2/S3	3.1

■ JOE STRIPP

Stripp, Joseph Valentine "Jersey Joe"   b: 2/3/03, Harrison, N.J.   d: 6/10/89, Orlando, Fla.   BR/TR, 5'11.5", 175 lbs.   Deb: 7/02/28

YEAR	TM/L	G	AB	R	H	2B	3B	HR	RBI	BB	SO	AVG	OBP	SLG	PRO+	BR	/A	RC	SB	CS	SBR	FR	POS	TPR
1928	Cin-N	42	139	18	40	7	3	1	17	8	8	.288	.340	.403	95	-1	-1	19	0			-5	O3/S	-0.6
1929	Cin-N	64	187	24	40	3	2	3	20	24	15	.214	.313	.299	55	-14	-12	19	2			8	3/2	0.0
1930	Cin-N	130	464	74	142	37	6	3	64	51	37	.306	.377	.431	100	-3	1	75	15			0	13	-0.1
1931	Cin-N	105	426	71	138	26	2	3	42	21	31	.324	.359	.415	114	4	7	64	5			4	3/1	1.6
1932	Bro-N	138	534	94	162	36	9	6	64	36	30	.303	.350	.438	113	7	9	84	14			16	31	3.0
1933	Bro-N	141	537	69	149	20	7	1	51	26	23	.277	.312	.346	92	-9	-6	59	5			5	*3	0.2
1934	Bro-N	104	384	50	121	19	6	1	40	22	20	.315	.354	.404	108	1	4	55	2			-6	3/1S	0.4
1935	Bro-N	109	373	44	114	13	5	3	43	22	15	.306	.344	.391	99	-1	-0	49	2			7	31/O	1.0
1936	Bro-N	110	439	51	139	31	1	1	60	22	12	.317	.351	.399	100	1	0	62	2			8	*3	1.5
1937	Bro-N	90	300	37	73	10	2	1	26	20	18	.243	.291	.300	60	-16	-17	25	1			-6	31/S	-2.0
1938	StL-N	54	199	24	57	7	0	0	18	18	10	.286	.349	.322	81	-3	-5	23	0			-8	3	-1.4
	Bos-N	59	229	19	63	10	0	1	19	10	7	.275	.305	.332	84	-8	-5	24	2			1	3	-0.5
	Yr	113	428	43	120	17	0	1	37	28	17	.280	.326	.327	82	-11	-10	46	2			-7		-1.9
Total	11	1146	4211	575	1238	219	43	24	464	280	226	.294	.340	.384	96	-42	-26	555	50			24	31/OS2	3.1

■ ALLIE STROBEL

Strobel, Albert Irving   b: 6/11/1884, Boston, Mass.   d: 2/10/55, Hollywood, Fla.   TR, 6', 160 lbs.   Deb: 8/29/05

YEAR	TM/L	G	AB	R	H	2B	3B	HR	RBI	BB	SO	AVG	OBP	SLG	PRO+	BR	/A	RC	SB	CS	SBR	FR	POS	TPR
1905	Bos-N	5	19	1	2	0	0	0	2	0		.105	.105	.105	-37	-3	-3	0	0			-0	/3O	-0.3
1906	Bos-N	100	317	28	64	10	3	1	24	29		.202	.269	.262	69	-12	-11	25	2			-6	2/SO	-1.7
Total	2	105	336	29	66	10	3	1	26	29		.196	.260	.253	63	-15	-14	25	2			-6	/2S3O	-2.0

■ JIM STRONER

Stroner, James M.   b: 9/26/1892, Chicago, Ill.   d: 11/16/71, Chicago, Ill.   BR/TR, 5'10", 175 lbs.   Deb: 5/01/29

YEAR	TM/L	G	AB	R	H	2B	3B	HR	RBI	BB	SO	AVG	OBP	SLG	PRO+	BR	/A	RC	SB	CS	SBR	FR	POS	TPR
1929	Pit-N	6	8	0	3	1	0	0	1	0		.375	.444	.500	130	0	0	2	0			-0	/3	0.0

■ ED STROUD

Stroud, Edwin Marvin   b: 10/31/39, Lapine, Ala.   BL/TR, 5'11", 180 lbs.   Deb: 9/11/66

YEAR	TM/L	G	AB	R	H	2B	3B	HR	RBI	BB	SO	AVG	OBP	SLG	PRO+	BR	/A	RC	SB	CS	SBR	FR	POS	TPR
1966	Chi-A	12	36	3	6	2	0	0	1	0	8	.167	.231	.222	33	-3	-3	2	3	0	1	-0	O	-0.2
1967	Chi-A	20	27	6	8	0	1	0	3	1	5	.296	.345	.370	116	0	0	3	7	2	1	2	O	0.4
	Was-A	87	204	36	41	5	3	1	10	25	29	.201	.291	.270	69	-8	-7	17	8	6	-1	-0	O	-1.1
	Yr	107	231	42	49	5	4	1	13	26	34	.212	.297	.281	75	-8	-7	20	15	8	-0	2		-0.7
1968	Was-A	105	306	41	73	10	10	4	23	20	50	.239	.285	.376	102	-1	-0	30	9	3	1	-4	O	-0.7
1969	Was-A	123	206	35	52	5	6	4	29	30	33	.252	.353	.393	114	3	4	31	12	8	2	1	O	0.5
1970	Was-A	129	433	69	115	11	5	5	32	40	79	.266	.332	.349	92	-7	-4	51	29	8	4	12	*O	0.6
1971	Chi-A	53	141	19	25	4	3	0	2	11	20	.177	.237	.248	36	-12	-12	7	4	5	-2	-5	O	-2.1
Total	6	529	1353	209	320	37	28	14	100	129	224	.237	.307	.336	87	-28	-22	141	72	26	6	5	O	-2.6

■ STEVE STROUGHTER

Stroughter, Stephen Lewis   b: 3/15/52, Visalia, Cal.   BL/TR, 6'2", 190 lbs.   Deb: 4/07/82

YEAR	TM/L	G	AB	R	H	2B	3B	HR	RBI	BB	SO	AVG	OBP	SLG	PRO+	BR	/A	RC	SB	CS	SBR	FR	POS	TPR
1982	Sea-A	26	47	4	8	1	0	1	3	3	9	.170	.235	.255	34	-4	-4	3	0	0	0	2	/OD	-0.2

■ AMOS STRUNK

Strunk, Amos Aaron   b: 1/22/1889, Philadelphia, Pa.   d: 7/22/79, Llanerch, Pa.   BL/TL, 5'11.5", 175 lbs.   Deb: 9/24/08

YEAR	TM/L	G	AB	R	H	2B	3B	HR	RBI	BB	SO	AVG	OBP	SLG	PRO+	BR	/A	RC	SB	CS	SBR	FR	POS	TPR
1908	Phi-A	12	34	4	8	1	0	0	0	4		.235	.316	.265	86	-0	-0	3	0			1	O	0.0
1909	Phi-A	11	35	1	4	0	0	0	2	1		.114	.139	.114	-20	-5	-5	1	2			-1	/O	-0.6
1910	*Phi-A	16	48	9	16	0	1	0	2	5		.333	.373	.375	135	2	2	8	4			1	O	0.2
1911	*Phi-A	74	215	42	55	7	2	1	21	35		.256	.363	.321	93	-1	-1	31	13			1	O/1	-0.3
1912	Phi-A	122	412	58	119	13	12	3	63	47		.289	.366	.400	124	10	13	72	29			11	*O	1.6

YEAR	TM/L	G	AB	R	H	2B	3B	HR	RBI	BB	SO	AVG	OBP	SLG	PRO+	BR	/A	RC	SB	CS	SBR	FR	POS	TPR
1913	*Phi-A	94	292	30	89	11	12	0	46	29	23	.305	.368	.425	135	11	12	49	14			-1	O	0.6
1914	*Phi-A	122	404	58	111	15	3	2	45	57	38	.275	.364	.342	116	8	9	53	25	22	-6	8	*O	0.5
1915	Phi-A	132	485	76	144	28	16	1	45	56	45	.297	.371	.427	143	22	24	78	17	19	-6	12	*O1	2.4
1916	Phi-A	150	544	71	172	30	9	3	49	66	59	.316	.393	.421	151	30	33	91	21	23	-8	2	*O/1	2.1
1917	Phi-A	148	540	83	152	26	7	1	45	68	37	.281	.363	.361	123	15	16	76	16			-2	*O	0.5
1918	*Bos-A	114	413	50	106	18	9	0	35	36	13	.257	.316	.344	101	-1	-1	50	20			-5	*O	-1.2
1919	Bos-A	48	184	27	50	11	3	0	17	13	13	.272	.323	.364	98	-2	-1	22	3			-1	O	-0.5
	Phi-A	60	194	15	41	6	4	0	13	23	15	.211	.298	.284	63	-9	-9	17	3			1	O	-1.2
	Yr	108	378	42	91	17	7	0	30	36	28	.241	.310	.323	79	-11	-10	39	6			-1		-1.7
1920	Phi-A	58	202	23	60	9	3	0	20	21	9	.297	.363	.371	94	-1	-1	26	0	6	-4	-4	O	-1.3
	Chi-A	53	188	33	45	8	1	1	16	28	15	.239	.338	.309	72	-7	-7	21	1	0	0	-1	O	-1.0
	Yr	111	390	56	105	17	4	1	36	49	24	.269	.351	.341	83	-8	-8	48	1	6	-3	-5		-2.3
1921	Chi-A	121	401	68	133	19	10	3	69	38	27	.332	.391	.451	116	9	10	69	7	10	-4	-8	*O	-0.9
1922	Chi-A	92	311	36	90	11	4	0	33	33	28	.289	.358	.350	85	-6	-6	40	9	6	-1	2	O/1	-1.0
1923	Chi-A	54	54	7	17	0	0	0	8	8	5	.315	.403	.315	92	-0	-0	8	1	0	0	-0	/O1	0.0
1924	Chi-A	1	1	0	0	0	0	0	0	0	0	.000	.000	.000	-99	-0	-0	0	0	0	0	0	H	0.0
	Phi-A	30	42	5	6	0	0	0	1	7	4	.143	.265	.143	7	-6	-6	2	0	0	0	-3	/O	-0.8
	Yr	31	43	5	6	0	0	0	1	7	4	.140	.260	.140	5	-6	-6	2	0	0	0	-3		-0.8
Total	17	1512	4999	696	1418	213	96	15	530	573	331	.284	.359	.374	112	68	81	720	185	86		14	*O/1	-0.9

■ AL STRUVE
Struve, Al   b: St.Louis, Mo.   Deb: 6/22/1884

YEAR	TM/L	G	AB	R	H	2B	3B	HR	RBI	BB	SO	AVG	OBP	SLG	PRO+	BR	/A	RC	SB	CS	SBR	FR	POS	TPR
1884	StL-a	2	7	2	2	0	0	0		0		.286	.286	.286	86	-0	-0	1				2	/OC	0.2

■ LUKE STUART
Stuart, Luther Lane   b: 5/23/1892, Alamance Co., N.C.   d: 6/15/47, Winston-Salem, N.C.   BR/TR, 5'8", 165 lbs.   Deb: 7/28/21

YEAR	TM/L	G	AB	R	H	2B	3B	HR	RBI	BB	SO	AVG	OBP	SLG	PRO+	BR	/A	RC	SB	CS	SBR	FR	POS	TPR
1921	StL-A	3	3	2	1	0	0	0	2	0	1	.333	.333	1.333	291	1	1	1	0	0	0	-1	/2	0.0

■ DICK STUART
Stuart, Richard Lee "Dr. Strangeglove"   b: 11/7/32, San Francisco, Cal.   BR/TR, 6'4", 212 lbs.   Deb: 7/10/58

YEAR	TM/L	G	AB	R	H	2B	3B	HR	RBI	BB	SO	AVG	OBP	SLG	PRO+	BR	/A	RC	SB	CS	SBR	FR	POS	TPR
1958	Pit-N	67	254	38	68	12	5	16	48	11	75	.268	.311	.543	124	6	7	41	0	0	0	0	1	0.3
1959	Pit-N	118	397	64	118	15	2	27	78	42	86	.297	.367	.549	141	22	22	78	1	1	-0	1	*1/O	1.5
1960	*Pit-N	122	438	48	114	17	5	23	83	39	107	.260	.321	.479	115	8	8	63	0	0	0	-1	*1/O	0.1
1961	Pit-N	138	532	83	160	28	8	35	117	34	121	.301	.347	.581	140	28	28	97	0	3	-2	-1	*1/O	1.6
1962	Pit-N	114	394	52	90	11	4	16	64	32	94	.228	.290	.398	83	-11	-11	44	0	1	-1	2	*1	-1.2
1963	Bos-A	157	612	81	160	25	4	42	118	44	144	.261	.312	.521	125	20	18	91	0	0	0	9	*1	2.3
1964	Bos-A	156	603	73	168	27	1	33	114	37	130	.279	.323	.491	117	16	13	93	0	0	0	2	*1	1.0
1965	Phi-N	149	538	53	126	19	1	28	95	39	136	.234	.290	.429	101	-2	-1	66	1	0	0	6	*1/3	-0.1
1966	NY-N	31	87	7	19	0	0	4	13	9	26	.218	.292	.356	81	-2	-2	8	0	-1	-1	-1	1	-0.5
	*LA-N	38	91	4	24	1	0	3	9	11	17	.264	.356	.374	112	1	2	12	0	1	-1	3	1	0.3
	Yr	69	178	11	43	1	0	7	22	20	43	.242	.325	.365	97	-2	-1	19	0	2	-1	2		-0.2
1969	Cal-A	22	51	3	8	2	0	1	4	3	21	.157	.204	.255	29	-5	-5	2	0	0	0	-1	1	-0.7
Total	10	1112	3997	506	1055	157	30	228	743	301	957	.264	.319	.489	117	81	79	595	2	7	-4	18	*1/O3	4.6

■ BILL STUART
Stuart, William Alexander "Chauncey"   b: 8/28/1873, Boalsburg, Pa.   d: 10/14/28, Fort Worth, Tex.   5'11", 170 lbs.   Deb: 8/15/1895

YEAR	TM/L	G	AB	R	H	2B	3B	HR	RBI	BB	SO	AVG	OBP	SLG	PRO+	BR	/A	RC	SB	CS	SBR	FR	POS	TPR
1895	Pit-N	19	77	5	19	3	0	0	10	2	6	.247	.275	.286	49	-6	-5	7	2			-1	S/2	-0.3
1899	NY-N	1	3	0	0	0	0	0	0	0	0	.000	.000	.000	-99	-1	-1	0	0			-0	/2	0.0
Total	2	20	80	5	19	3	0	0	10	2	6	.237	.265	.275	43	-7	-6	7	2			-1	/S2	-0.3

■ FRANKLIN STUBBS
Stubbs, Franklin Lee   b: 10/21/60, Richland, N.C.   BL/TL, 6'2", 215 lbs.   Deb: 4/28/84

YEAR	TM/L	G	AB	R	H	2B	3B	HR	RBI	BB	SO	AVG	OBP	SLG	PRO+	BR	/A	RC	SB	CS	SBR	FR	POS	TPR
1984	LA-N	87	217	22	42	2	3	8	17	24	63	.194	.274	.341	73	-9	-8	22	2	2	-1	3	1O	-0.8
1985	LA-N	10	9	0	2	0	0	0	2	0	3	.222	.222	.222	25	-1	-1	0	0	0	0	-0	/1	0.0
1986	LA-N	132	420	55	95	11	1	23	58	37	107	.226	.292	.421	101	-5	-1	51	7	1	2	-2	*O1	-0.4
1987	LA-N	129	386	48	90	16	3	16	52	31	85	.233	.292	.415	87	-10	-9	47	8	1	2	7	*1O	-0.6
1988	*LA-N	115	242	30	54	13	0	8	34	23	61	.223	.293	.376	94	-3	-2	28	11	3	2	6	1O	0.0
1989	LA-N	69	103	11	30	6	0	4	15	16	27	.291	.387	.466	145	6	6	18	3	2	-0	4	O/1	1.0
1990	Hou-N	146	448	59	117	23	2	23	71	48	114	.261	.335	.475	123	11	12	74	19	6	2	-6	1O	0.3
Total	7	688	1825	225	430	71	9	82	249	179	460	.236	.306	.419	101	-10	-3	240	50	15	6	12	1O	-0.5

■ MOOSE STUBING
Stubing, Lawrence George   b: 3/31/38, Bronx, N.Y.   BL/TL, 6'3", 220 lbs.   Deb: 4/14/67   MC

YEAR	TM/L	G	AB	R	H	2B	3B	HR	RBI	BB	SO	AVG	OBP	SLG	PRO+	BR	/A	RC	SB	CS	SBR	FR	POS	TPR
1967	Cal-A	5	5	0	0	0	0	0	0	0	4	.000	.000	.000	-99	-1	-1	0	0	0	0	0	H	0.0

■ SEEM STUDLEY
Studley, Seymour L. "Warhorse"   b: Washington, D.C.   d: 1874, Washington, D.C.   Deb: 4/20/1872

YEAR	TM/L	G	AB	R	H	2B	3B	HR	RBI	BB	SO	AVG	OBP	SLG	PRO+	BR	/A	RC	SB	CS	SBR	FR	POS	TPR
1872	Nat-n	5	21	3	2	0	0	0		0		.095	.095	.095	-35	-3	-4	0					/O	-0.2

■ GEORGE STUMPF
Stumpf, George Frederick   b: 12/15/10, New Orleans, La.   BL/TL, 5'8", 155 lbs.   Deb: 9/19/31

YEAR	TM/L	G	AB	R	H	2B	3B	HR	RBI	BB	SO	AVG	OBP	SLG	PRO+	BR	/A	RC	SB	CS	SBR	FR	POS	TPR
1931	Bos-A	7	28	2	7	1	1	0	4	1	2	.250	.276	.357	69	-2	-1	3	0	0	0	-1	/O	-0.2
1932	Bos-A	79	169	18	34	2	2	1	18	18	24	.201	.278	.254	40	-15	-15	13	1	1	-0	-3	O	-1.8
1933	Bos-A	22	41	8	14	3	0	0	5	4	2	.341	.400	.415	117	1	1	8	4	0	1	0	O	0.2
1936	Chi-A	10	22	3	6	1	0	0	5	2	1	.273	.333	.318	59	-1	-1	2	0	0	0	1	/O	0.0
Total	4	118	260	31	61	7	3	1	32	25	26	.235	.302	.296	57	-17	-16	26	5	1	1	-4	/O	-1.8

■ BILL STUMPF
Stumpf, William Frederick   b: 3/21/1892, Baltimore, Md.   d: 2/14/66, Crownsville, Md.   BR/TR, 6'0.5", 175 lbs.   Deb: 5/11/12

YEAR	TM/L	G	AB	R	H	2B	3B	HR	RBI	BB	SO	AVG	OBP	SLG	PRO+	BR	/A	RC	SB	CS	SBR	FR	POS	TPR
1912	NY-A	42	129	8	31	0	0	0	10	6		.240	.279	.240	46	-8	-9	10	5			-10	S/2310	-1.7
1913	NY-A	12	29	5	6	1	0	0	1	3	3	.207	.281	.241	53	-2	-2	2	0			-3	/S2O	-0.4
Total	2	54	158	13	37	1	0	0	11	9	3	.234	.280	.241	47	-10	-11	12	5			-13	/S2301	-2.1

■ GUY STURDY
Sturdy, Guy R.   b: 8/7/1899, Sherman, Tex.   d: 5/4/65, Marshall, Tex.   BL/TL, 6'0.5", 180 lbs.   Deb: 9/30/27

YEAR	TM/L	G	AB	R	H	2B	3B	HR	RBI	BB	SO	AVG	OBP	SLG	PRO+	BR	/A	RC	SB	CS	SBR	FR	POS	TPR
1927	StL-A	5	21	5	9	1	0	0	5	1	0	.429	.455	.476	137	1	1	4	2	0	1	-1	/1	0.1
1928	StL-A	54	45	3	10	1	0	1	8	8	4	.222	.340	.311	70	-2	-2	5	1	0	0	0	/1	-0.1
Total	2	59	66	8	19	2	0	1	13	9	4	.288	.373	.364	91	-0	-1	10	3	0	1	-1	/1	0.0

■ BOBBY STURGEON
Sturgeon, Robert Howard   b: 8/6/19, Clinton, Ind.   BR/TR, 6', 175 lbs.   Deb: 4/16/40

YEAR	TM/L	G	AB	R	H	2B	3B	HR	RBI	BB	SO	AVG	OBP	SLG	PRO+	BR	/A	RC	SB	CS	SBR	FR	POS	TPR
1940	Chi-N	7	21	1	4	1	0	0		0		.190	.190	.238	18	-2	-2	1	0			2	/S	0.0
1941	Chi-N	129	433	45	106	15	3	0	25	9	30	.245	.260	.293	58	-26	-24	31	5			-4	*S/23	-1.8
1942	Chi-N	63	162	8	40	7	1	0	7	4	13	.247	.269	.302	70	-7	-6	13	2			21	2S/3	1.9
1946	Chi-N	100	294	26	87	12	2	1	21	10	18	.296	.319	.361	94	-4	-3	33	0			-13	S2	-1.1
1947	Chi-N	87	232	16	59	10	5	0	21	7	12	.254	.276	.341	66	-13	-12	19	0			13	S2/3	0.8
1948	Bos-N	34	78	10	17	3	0	0	4	4	5	.218	.256	.282	46	-6	-6	5	0			-3	2/S3	-0.7
Total	6	420	1220	106	313	48	12	1	80	34	79	.257	.277	.318	68	-58	-54	103	7			14	S2/3	-0.9

■ DEAN STURGIS
Sturgis, Dean Donnell   b: 12/1/1892, Beloit, Kan.   d: 6/4/50, Uniontown, Pa.   BR/TR, 6'1", 180 lbs.   Deb: 5/01/14

YEAR	TM/L	G	AB	R	H	2B	3B	HR	RBI	BB	SO	AVG	OBP	SLG	PRO+	BR	/A	RC	SB	CS	SBR	FR	POS	TPR
1914	Phi-A	4	4	1	1	0	0	0	0	1	2	.250	.400	.250	99	0	0	0	0			0	/C	0.0

■ JOHNNY STURM
Sturm, John Peter Joseph   b: 1/23/16, St.Louis, Mo.   BL/TL, 6'1", 185 lbs.   Deb: 4/15/41

YEAR	TM/L	G	AB	R	H	2B	3B	HR	RBI	BB	SO	AVG	OBP	SLG	PRO+	BR	/A	RC	SB	CS	SBR	FR	POS	TPR
1941	*NY-A	124	524	58	125	17	3	3	36	37	50	.239	.293	.300	58	-33	-32	46	3	5	-2	-2	*1	-3.8

■ GEORGE STUTZ
Stutz, George "Kid" or "Satan"   b: 2/12/1893, Philadelphia, Pa.   d: 12/29/30, Philadelphia, Pa.   BL/TR, 5'5", 150 lbs.   Deb: 8/17/26

YEAR	TM/L	G	AB	R	H	2B	3B	HR	RBI	BB	SO	AVG	OBP	SLG	PRO+	BR	/A	RC	SB	CS	SBR	FR	POS	TPR
1926	Phi-N	6	9	0	0	0	0	0	0	0	2	.000	.000	.000	-95	-2	-3	0	0			1	/S	0.0

YEAR	TM/L	G	AB	R	H	2B	3B	HR	RBI	BB	SO	AVG	OBP	SLG	PRO+	BR	/A	RC	SB	CS	SBR	FR	POS	TPR

■ LENA STYLES   Styles, William Graves   b: 11/27/1899, Gurley, Ala.   d: 3/14/56, Gurley, Ala.   BR/TR, 6'1", 185 lbs.   Deb: 9/10/19

1919	Phi-A	8	22	0	6	1	0	0	5	1	6	.273	.304	.318	74	-1	-1	2	0			0	/C	0.0
1920	Phi-A	24	50	5	13	3	1	0	5	6	7	.260	.339	.360	84	-1	-1	7	1	0	0	2	/C1	0.1
1921	Phi-A	4	5	0	1	0	0	0	0	0	2	.200	.200	.200	2	-1	-1	0	0	0	0	-1	/C	-0.1
1930	Cin-N	7	12	2	3	0	1	0	1	1	2	.250	.357	.417	91	-0	-0	2	0			0	/C	0.0
1931	Cin-N	34	87	7	21	3	0	0	5	8	7	.241	.313	.276	63	-5	-4	8	0			-7	C	-0.8
Total	5	77	176	14	44	7	2	0	16	16	24	.250	.320	.313	71	-7	-7	19	1	0		-6	/C1	-0.8

■ NEIL STYNES   Stynes, Cornelius William   b: 12/10/1868, Arlington, Mass.   d: 3/26/44, Somerville, Mass.   6', 165 lbs.   Deb: 9/08/1890

1890	Cle-P	2	8	0	0	0	0	0	0	0	0	.000	.000	.000	-99	-2	-2	0	0			-1	/C	-0.1

■ KEN SUAREZ   Suarez, Kenneth Raymond   b: 4/12/43, Tampa, Fla.   BR/TR, 5'9", 175 lbs.   Deb: 4/14/66

1966	KC-A	35	69	5	10	0	1	0	2	15	26	.145	.298	.174	41	-5	-5	5	2	0	1	5	C	0.3
1967	KC-A	39	63	7	15	5	0	2	9	16	21	.238	.392	.413	143	4	4	12	1	0	0	7	C	1.4
1968	Cle-A	17	10	1	1	0	0	0	0	1	3	.100	.182	.100	-13	-1	-1	0	0	0	0	1	C/23O	0.1
1969	Cle-A	36	85	7	25	5	0	1	9	15	12	.294	.400	.388	117	3	3	13	1	0	0	6	C	1.1
1971	Cle-A	50	123	10	25	7	0	1	9	18	15	.203	.315	.285	65	-4	-6	12	0	1	-1	8	C	0.4
1972	Tex-A	25	33	2	5	1	0	0	4	1	4	.152	.176	.182	7	-4	-4	1	0	0	0	1	C	-0.2
1973	Tex-A	93	278	25	69	11	0	1	27	33	16	.248	.339	.299	84	-6	-4	29	1	2	-1	2	C	0.0
Total	7	295	661	57	150	29	1	5	60	99	97	.227	.334	.297	81	-13	-13	71	5	3	-0	31	C/O32	3.1

■ LUIS SUAREZ   Suarez, Luis Abelardo   b: 8/24/16, Alto Songo, Cuba   BR/TR, 5'11", 170 lbs.   Deb: 5/28/44

1944	Was-A	1	2	0	0	0	0	0	0	0	0	.000	.000	.000	-99	-1	-1	0	0	0	0	0	/3	0.0

■ TONY SUCK   Suck, Anthony (b: Charles Anthony Zuck)   b: 6/11/1858, Chicago.Ill.   d: 1/29/1895, Chicago, Ill.   5'9", 164 lbs.   Deb: 8/09/1883

1883	Buf-N	2	7	1	0	0	0	0	0	1	4	.000	.125	.000	-56	-1	-1	0				-1	/OC	-0.2
1884	CP-U	53	188	18	28	2	0	0		13		.149	.204	.160	25	-14	-14	6	0			-6	CSO/3	-1.5
	Bal-U	3	10	2	3	0	0	0		0		.300	.300	.300	94	-0	-0	1	0			2	/C	0.1
	Yr	56	198	20	31	2	0	0		13		.157	.209	.167	28	-14	-14	7	0			-5		-1.4
Total	2	58	205	21	31	2	0	0	0	14	4	.151	.205	.161	25	-15	-15	7	0			-6	/CSO3	-1.6

■ BILL SUDAKIS   Sudakis, William Paul "Suds"   b: 3/27/46, Joliet, Ill.   BB/TR, 6'1", 190 lbs.   Deb: 9/03/68

1968	LA-N	24	87	11	24	4	2	3	12	15	14	.276	.382	.471	168	6	7	15	1	0	0	4	3	1.2
1969	LA-N	132	462	50	108	17	5	14	53	40	94	.234	.296	.383	96	-8	-4	52	3	2	-0	11	*3	0.8
1970	LA-N	94	269	37	71	11	0	14	44	35	46	.264	.355	.461	122	6	8	45	4	0	1	-4	C3/O1	0.5
1971	LA-N	41	83	10	16	3	0	3	7	12	22	.193	.302	.337	86	-2	-1	8	0	1	-1	1	C/31O	0.1
1972	NY-N	18	49	3	7	0	0	1	7	6	14	.143	.236	.204	27	-5	-5	3	0	0	0	0	/1C	-0.4
1973	Tex-A	82	235	32	60	11	0	15	43	23	53	.255	.322	.494	132	7	8	36	0	1	-1	-4	31/COD	0.2
1974	NY-A	89	259	26	60	8	0	7	39	25	48	.232	.302	.344	88	-5	-4	29	0	0	0	2	D1/3C	-0.3
1975	Cal-A	30	58	4	7	2	0	1	6	12	15	.121	.282	.207	43	-4	-4	4	1	1	-0	-1	D/C1	-0.4
	Cle-A	20	46	4	9	0	0	1	3	4	7	.196	.260	.261	48	-3	-3	3	0	1	-1	-1	1/C	-0.5
	Yr	50	104	8	16	2	0	2	9	16	22	.154	.273	.231	45	-8	-7	7	1	2	-1	-2		-0.9
Total	8	530	1548	177	362	56	7	59	214	172	313	.234	.313	.393	103	-8	2	194	9	6	-1	8	3/C1DO	1.1

■ PETE SUDER   Suder, Peter "Pecky"   b: 4/16/16, Aliquippa, Pa.   BR/TR, 6', 175 lbs.   Deb: 4/15/41

1941	Phi-A	139	531	45	130	20	9	4	52	19	47	.245	.271	.339	62	-32	-30	43	1	3	-2	-7	*3/S	-3.0
1942	Phi-A	128	476	46	122	20	4	4	54	24	39	.256	.293	.340	78	-15	-15	43	4	4	-1	3	S32	-0.8
1943	Phi-A	131	475	30	105	14	5	3	41	14	40	.221	.243	.291	56	-28	-28	31	1	1	-0	-8	23/S	-3.3
1946	Phi-A	128	455	38	128	20	3	2	50	18	37	.281	.309	.352	85	-11	-10	48	1	1	-0	1	S32/10	-0.5
1947	Phi-A	145	528	45	127	28	4	5	60	35	44	.241	.290	.337	73	-20	-21	51	0	3	-2	-17	*2/S3	-3.4
1948	Phi-A	148	519	64	125	23	5	7	60	60	60	.241	.321	.345	77	-18	-18	60	1	3	-2	-1	*2	-1.6
1949	Phi-A	118	445	44	119	24	6	10	75	23	35	.267	.306	.416	93	-10	-8	52	0	1	-1	7	23/S	0.0
1950	Phi-A	77	248	34	61	10	0	8	35	23	31	.246	.310	.383	78	-10	-9	29	2	2	-1	1	23S/1	-0.5
1951	Phi-A	123	440	46	108	18	1	1	42	30	24	.245	.295	.298	59	-24	-26	37	5	5	-2	10	*2S/3	-1.1
1952	Phi-A	74	228	22	55	7	2	1	20	16	17	.241	.291	.303	61	-11	-13	21	1	1	-0	3	2S3	-0.6
1953	Phi-A	115	454	44	130	11	3	4	35	7	35	.286	.312	.350	76	-14	-16	48	3	3	-1	1	32/S	-1.3
1954	Phi-A	69	205	8	41	11	1	0	16	7	16	.200	.226	.263	34	-19	-19	11	0	0	-0	9	23/S	-0.9
1955	KC-A	26	81	3	17	4	1	0	1	2	13	.210	.229	.284	37	-7	-7	5	0	1	-1	-3	2	-0.9
Total	13	1421	5085	469	1268	210	44	49	541	288	456	.249	.291	.337	71	-219	-221	478	19	28	-11	2	23S/10	-17.9

■ JOE SUGDEN   Sugden, Joseph   b: 7/31/1870, Philadelphia, Pa.   d: 6/28/59, Philadelphia, Pa.   BB/TR, 5'10", 180 lbs.   Deb: 7/20/1893   C

1893	Pit-N	27	92	20	24	4	3	0	12	10	11	.261	.340	.370	92	-1	-1	12	1			0	C	0.1
1894	Pit-N	39	139	23	46	13	2	2	23	14	2	.331	.404	.496	119	4	4	30	3			-5	C/3SO	0.5
1895	Pit-N	49	155	28	48	4	1	1	17	16	12	.310	.385	.368	102	0	2	24	4			3	C	0.7
1896	Pit-N	80	301	42	89	5	7	0	36	19	9	.296	.348	.359	92	-5	-3	40	5			1	C/1O	0.4
1897	Pit-N	84	288	31	64	6	4	0	38	18		.222	.275	.271	48	-22	-20	25	9			-5	C/1	-1.0
1898	StL-N	89	289	29	73	7	1	0	34	23		.253	.314	.284	72	-9	-10	28	5			-1	CO/1	-0.6
1899	Cle-N	76	250	19	69	5	1	0	14	11		.276	.307	.304	76	-10	-7	25	2			0	C/O13	-0.2
1901	Chi-A	48	153	21	42	7	1	0	19	13		.275	.335	.333	90	-2	-1	19	4			5	C/1	0.6
1902	StL-A	68	200	25	50	7	2	0	15	20		.250	.327	.305	79	-5	-5	22	2			-3	C/1P	-0.1
1903	StL-A	79	241	18	51	4	0	0	22	25		.212	.286	.228	59	-11	-10	19	4			5	C/1	0.3
1904	StL-A	105	348	25	93	6	3	0	30	28		.267	.322	.302	107	1	3	38	6			-1	C1	1.2
1905	StL-A	90	266	21	46	4	0	0	23	23		.173	.239	.188	40	-18	-16	14	3			22	C/1	1.4
1912	Det-A	1	4	1	1	0	0	0	0	0		.250	.250	.250	44	-0	-0	0	0			1	/1	0.1
Total	13	835	2726	303	696	72	25	3	283	220	34	.255	.316	.303	79	-79	-65	297	48			22	C/103SP	2.9

■ GUS SUHR   Suhr, August Richard   b: 1/3/06, San Francisco, Cal.   BL/TR, 6', 180 lbs.   Deb: 4/15/30

1930	Pit-N	151	542	93	155	26	14	17	107	80	56	.286	.380	.480	106	6	5	99	11			-7	*1	-0.6
1931	Pit-N	87	270	26	57	13	4	4	32	38	25	.211	.308	.333	73	-10	-10	30	4			0	1	-1.5
1932	Pit-N	154	581	78	153	31	16	5	81	63	39	.263	.337	.398	99	-2	-1	82	7			-10	*1	-1.8
1933	Pit-N	154	566	72	151	31	11	10	75	72	52	.267	.350	.413	117	14	14	87	2			-4	*1	0.7
1934	Pit-N	151	573	67	162	36	13	13	103	66	52	.283	.360	.459	115	14	13	98	4			-5	*1	-0.4
1935	Pit-N	153	529	68	144	33	12	10	81	70	54	.272	.357	.437	109	10	7	89	6			-6	*1/O	-0.1
1936	Pit-N	156	583	111	182	33	12	11	118	95	34	.312	.410	.467	133	33	31	119	8			-4	*1	1.3
1937	Pit-N	151	575	69	160	28	14	5	97	83	42	.278	.369	.402	109	9	9	92	2			-4	*1	-0.2
1938	Pit-N	145	530	82	156	35	14	3	64	87	37	.294	.394	.430	126	22	22	97	4			-8	*1	0.1
1939	Pit-N	63	204	23	59	10	2	1	31	25	23	.289	.367	.373	101	0	1	31	4			-4	1	-0.9
	Phi-N	60	198	21	63	12	2	3	24	34	14	.318	.421	.444	137	11	11	40	1			1	1	0.5
	Yr	123	402	44	122	22	4	4	55	59	37	.303	.394	.408	118	11	12	71	5			-3		-0.4
1940	Phi-N	10	25	4	4	0	0	0	2	5	5	.160	.300	.400	95	-0	-0	3	0			1	/1	-0.1
Total	11	1435	5176	714	1446	288	114	84	818	718	433	.279	.368	.428	112	106	102	867	53			-51	*1/O	-3.0

■ CLYDE SUKEFORTH   Sukeforth, Clyde Leroy "Sukey"   b: 11/30/01, Washington, Me.   BL/TR, 5'10", 155 lbs.   Deb: 5/23/26   MC

1926	Cin-N	1	1	0	0	0	0	0	0	0	1	.000	.000	.000	-99	-0	-0	0				0	H	0.0
1927	Cin-N	38	58	12	11	2	0	0	2	7	2	.190	.277	.224	37	-5	-5	4	2			1	C	-0.1

YEAR	TM/L	G	AB	R	H	2B	3B	HR	RBI	BB	SO	AVG	OBP	SLG	PRO+	BR	/A	RC	SB	CS	SBR	FR	POS	TPR
1928	Cin-N	33	53	5	7	2	1	0	3	3	5	.132	.179	.208	1	-8	-8	2	0			1	C	-0.4
1929	Cin-N	84	237	31	84	16	2	1	33	17	6	.354	.398	.451	115	4	6	41	8			-8	C	0.4
1930	Cin-N	94	296	30	84	9	3	1	19	17	12	.284	.325	.345	65	-18	-16	33	1			-3	C	-1.2
1931	Cin-N	112	351	22	90	15	4	0	25	38	13	.256	.334	.322	82	-10	-7	40	0			-8	*C	-0.9
1932	Bro-N	59	111	14	26	4	4	0	12	6	10	.234	.280	.342	68	-5	-5	11	1			-3	C	-0.6
1933	Bro-N	20	36	1	2	0	0	0	0	2	1	.056	.105	.056	-55	-7	-7	0	0			3	C	-0.3
1934	Bro-N	27	43	5	7	1	0	0	1	1	6	.163	.182	.186	-1	-6	-6	1	0			-0	C	-0.4
1945	Bro-N	18	51	2	15	1	0	0	1	4	1	.294	.345	.314	85	-1	-1	6	0			-3	C	-0.3
Total	10	486	1237	122	326	50	14	2	96	95	57	.264	.319	.331	71	-57	-49	138	12			-19	C	-3.8

■ GUY SULARZ

Sularz, Guy Patrick b: 11/7/55, Minneapolis, Minn. BR/TR, 5'11", 165 lbs. Deb: 9/02/80

YEAR	TM/L	G	AB	R	H	2B	3B	HR	RBI	BB	SO	AVG	OBP	SLG	PRO+	BR	/A	RC	SB	CS	SBR	FR	POS	TPR
1980	SF-N	25	65	3	16	1	1	0	3	9	6	.246	.338	.292	79	-2	-1	7	1	0	0	12	2/3	1.2
1981	SF-N	10	20	0	4	0	0	0	2	2	4	.200	.304	.200	46	-1	-1	1	0	1	-1	4	/23	0.3
1982	SF-N	63	101	15	23	3	0	1	7	9	11	.228	.291	.287	62	-5	-5	9	3	0	1	10	S3/2	1.0
1983	SF-N	10	20	3	2	0	0	0	0	3	2	.100	.217	.100	-10	-3	-3	0	0	0	0	3	S3	0.0
Total	4	108	206	21	45	4	1	1	12	23	23	.218	.300	.262	59	-11	-11	18	4	1	1	29	/S23	2.5

■ ERNIE SULIK

Sulik, Ernest Richard "Dave" b: 7/7/10, San Francisco, Cal. d: 5/31/63, Oakland, Cal. BL/TL, 5'10", 178 lbs. Deb: 4/15/36

YEAR	TM/L	G	AB	R	H	2B	3B	HR	RBI	BB	SO	AVG	OBP	SLG	PRO+	BR	/A	RC	SB	CS	SBR	FR	POS	TPR
1936	Phi-N	122	404	69	116	14	4	6	36	40	22	.287	.353	.386	90	-0	-6	57	4			-1	*O	-1.0

■ SULLIVAN

Sullivan b: Bristol, R.I. Deb: 5/14/1875

YEAR	TM/L	G	AB	R	H	2B	3B	HR	RBI	BB	SO	AVG	OBP	SLG	PRO+	BR	/A	RC	SB	CS	SBR	FR	POS	TPR
1875	NH-n	2	8	3	3	0	0	0		0		.375	.375	.375	187	0	1	1					/O	0.1

■ ANDY SULLIVAN

Sullivan, Andrew R. b: 8/30/1884, Southborough, Mass d: 2/14/20, Framingham, Mass. TR , Deb: 9/13/04

YEAR	TM/L	G	AB	R	H	2B	3B	HR	RBI	BB	SO	AVG	OBP	SLG	PRO+	BR	/A	RC	SB	CS	SBR	FR	POS	TPR
1904	Bos-N	1	1	0	0	0	0	0	0	0	1	.000	.500	.000	64	0	0	0	0			-0	/S	0.0

■ JACKIE SULLIVAN

Sullivan, Carl Mancel b: 2/22/18, Princeton, Tex. BR/TR, 5'11", 172 lbs. Deb: 7/06/44

YEAR	TM/L	G	AB	R	H	2B	3B	HR	RBI	BB	SO	AVG	OBP	SLG	PRO+	BR	/A	RC	SB	CS	SBR	FR	POS	TPR
1944	Det-A	1	1	0	0	0	0	0	0	0	0	.000	.000	.000	-95	-0	-0	0	0	0	0	-0	/2	0.0

■ DAN SULLIVAN

Sullivan, Daniel C. "Link" b: 5/9/1857, Providence, R.I. d: 10/26/1893, Providence, R.I. TR , 5'11", 194 lbs. Deb: 5/02/1882

YEAR	TM/L	G	AB	R	H	2B	3B	HR	RBI	BB	SO	AVG	OBP	SLG	PRO+	BR	/A	RC	SB	CS	SBR	FR	POS	TPR
1882	Lou-a	67	286	44	78	8	2	0		9		.273	.295	.315	113	2	4	27				10	*C3/OS	1.2
1883	Lou-a	37	147	8	31	5	2	0		3		.211	.227	.272	65	-6	-5	9				-10	C/O3S	-1.0
1884	Lou-a	63	247	27	59	8	6	0		9		.239	.268	.320	98	-2	0	22				-17	C/O	-1.0
1885	Lou-a	13	44	3	8	1	0	0		2		.182	.234	.205	42	-3	-3	2				-0	C	0.0
	StL-a	17	60	4	7	2	0	0		6		.117	.197	.150	12	-6	-6	2				1	C/1	-0.2
	Yr	30	104	7	15	3	0	0		8		.144	.212	.173	24	-8	-9	4				1		-0.2
1886	Pit-a	1	4	0	0	0	0	0		0		.000	.000	.000	-99	-1	-1	0	0			-1	/C	-0.1
Total	5	198	788	86	183	24	10	0		29		.232	.261	.288	85	-16	-10	62	0			-17	C/301S	-1.1

■ DENNY SULLIVAN

Sullivan, Dennis J. b: 6/26/1858, Boston, Mass. d: 12/31/25, Boston, Mass. TR , Deb: 8/25/1879

YEAR	TM/L	G	AB	R	H	2B	3B	HR	RBI	BB	SO	AVG	OBP	SLG	PRO+	BR	/A	RC	SB	CS	SBR	FR	POS	TPR
1879	Pro-N	5	19	5	5	2	0	0	2	1	1	.263	.300	.368	121	0	0	2				-3	/3O	-0.2
1880	Bos-N	1	4	1	1	0	0	0	1	0	1	.250	.250	.250	72	-0	-0	0				-1	/C	0.0
Total	2	6	23	6	6	2	0	0	3	1	2	.261	.292	.348	113	0	0	2				-4	/3CO	-0.2

■ DENNY SULLIVAN

Sullivan, Dennis William b: 9/28/1882, Hillsboro, Wis. d: 6/2/56, W.Los Angeles, Cal BL/TR , Deb: 4/22/05

YEAR	TM/L	G	AB	R	H	2B	3B	HR	RBI	BB	SO	AVG	OBP	SLG	PRO+	BR	/A	RC	SB	CS	SBR	FR	POS	TPR
1905	Was-A	3	11	0	0	0	0	0	0	0	1	.000	.083	.000	-75	-2	-2	0	0			-0	/O	-0.2
1907	Bos-A	144	551	73	135	18	0	1	26	44		.245	.301	.283	89	-6	-6	56	16			1	*O	-1.3
1908	Bos-A	101	355	33	85	7	8	0	25	14		.239	.268	.304	86	-5	-6	33	14			8	O	-0.3
	Cle-A	4	6	0	0	0	0	0	0	0		.000	.000	.000	-99	-1	-1	0	0			-0	O	-0.1
	Yr	105	361	33	85	7	8	0	25	14		.235	.264	.299	83	-7	-8	32	14			8		-0.4
1909	Cle-A	3	2	0	1	0	0	0	0	0		.500	.500	.500	207	0	0	0	0			-1	/O	0.0
Total	4	255	925	106	221	25	8	1	51	59		.239	.285	.286	85	-15	-15	90	30			7	O	-1.9

■ HAYWOOD SULLIVAN

Sullivan, Haywood Cooper b: 12/15/30, Donalsonville, Ga. BR/TR, 6'4", 210 lbs. Deb: 9/20/55 M

YEAR	TM/L	G	AB	R	H	2B	3B	HR	RBI	BB	SO	AVG	OBP	SLG	PRO+	BR	/A	RC	SB	CS	SBR	FR	POS	TPR
1955	Bos-A	2	6	1	0	0	0	0	0	0	1	.000	.000	.000	-92	-2	-2	0	0	0	0	1	/C	0.0
1957	Bos-A	2	1	0	0	0	0	0	0	0	0	.000	.000	.000	-95	-0	-0	0	0	0	0	0	/C	0.0
1959	Bos-A	4	2	0	0	0	0	0	0	1	1	.000	.333	.000	-0	-0	-0	0	0	0	0	1	/C	0.0
1960	Bos-A	52	124	9	20	1	0	3	10	16	24	.161	.257	.242	35	-11	-12	8	0	0	0	5	C	-0.3
1961	KC-A	117	331	42	80	16	2	6	40	46	45	.242	.334	.356	84	-7	-7	41	1	0	0	-5	C1/O	-1.3
1962	KC-A	95	274	33	68	7	2	4	29	31	54	.248	.327	.332	75	-8	-9	31	1	0	0	-9	C/1	-1.2
1963	KC-A	40	113	9	24	6	1	0	8	15	15	.212	.305	.292	63	-5	-5	9	0	0	0	7	C	0.2
Total	7	312	851	94	192	30	5	13	87	109	140	.226	.314	.318	70	-33	-35	89	2	0	1	-1	C/1O	-2.6

■ JOHN SULLIVAN

Sullivan, John Eugene b: 2/16/1873, Illinois d: 6/5/24, St.Paul, Minn. TR , Deb: 4/19/05

YEAR	TM/L	G	AB	R	H	2B	3B	HR	RBI	BB	SO	AVG	OBP	SLG	PRO+	BR	/A	RC	SB	CS	SBR	FR	POS	TPR
1905	Det-A	13	32	4	5	0	0	0	4	4		.156	.250	.156	31	-2	-2	2	0			4	C	0.3
1908	Pit-N	1	1	0	0	0	0	0	0	0		.000	.000	.000	-99	-0	-0	0	0			0	/C	0.0
Total	2	14	33	4	5	0	0	0	4	4		.152	.243	.152	28	-2	-3	2	0			4	/C	0.3

■ CHUB SULLIVAN

Sullivan, John Frank b: 1/12/1856, Boston, Mass. d: 9/12/1881, Boston, Mass. BR/TR, 6', 164 lbs. Deb: 9/24/1877

YEAR	TM/L	G	AB	R	H	2B	3B	HR	RBI	BB	SO	AVG	OBP	SLG	PRO+	BR	/A	RC	SB	CS	SBR	FR	POS	TPR
1877	Cin-N	8	32	4	8	0	0	0	4	1	0	.250	.273	.250	74	-1	-1	2				-0	/1	0.0
1878	Cin-N	61	244	29	63	4	2	0	20	2	9	.258	.264	.291	91	-5	-1	19				5	*1	0.5
1880	Wor-N	43	166	22	43	6	3	0	0	4	6	.259	.276	.331	97	1	-1	16				3	1	0.0
Total	3	112	442	55	114	10	5	0	24	7	15	.258	.269	.303	92	-5	-3	37				7	1	0.5

■ JOHN SULLIVAN

Sullivan, John Lawrence b: 3/21/1890, Williamsport, Pa. d: 4/1/66, Milton, Pa. BR/TR, 5'11", 180 lbs. Deb: 4/18/20

YEAR	TM/L	G	AB	R	H	2B	3B	HR	RBI	BB	SO	AVG	OBP	SLG	PRO+	BR	/A	RC	SB	CS	SBR	FR	POS	TPR
1920	Bos-N	81	250	36	74	14	4	1	28	29	29	.296	.374	.396	126	8	9	39	3	2	-0	-2	O/1	0.3
1921	Bos-N	5	5	0	0	0	0	0	0	0	0	.000	.000	.000	-99	-1	-1	0	0	0	0	0	H	0.0
	Chi-N	76	240	28	79	14	4	4	41	19	26	.329	.381	.471	124	8	8	42	3	5	-2	-7	O	-0.3
	Yr	81	245	28	79	14	4	4	41	19	26	.322	.374	.461	120	7	7	41	3	5	-2	-7		-0.3
Total	2	162	495	64	153	28	8	5	69	48	55	.309	.374	.428	123	15	16	80	6	7	-2	-9	O/1	0.0

■ JOHN SULLIVAN

Sullivan, John Paul b: 11/2/20, Chicago, Ill. BR/TR, 5'10", 170 lbs. Deb: 6/07/42 C

YEAR	TM/L	G	AB	R	H	2B	3B	HR	RBI	BB	SO	AVG	OBP	SLG	PRO+	BR	/A	RC	SB	CS	SBR	FR	POS	TPR
1942	Was-A	94	357	38	84	16	1	0	42	26	30	.235	.285	.286	61	-19	-18	31	2	0	1	-11	S	-2.4
1943	Was-A	134	456	49	95	12	2	1	55	57	59	.208	.298	.250	63	-21	-19	39	6	2	1	11	*S	-0.6
1944	Was-A	138	471	49	118	12	1	0	30	52	43	.251	.325	.280	77	-14	-12	46	3	3	-1	-14	*S	-1.9
1947	Was-A	49	133	13	34	0	1	0	5	22	14	.256	.361	.271	79	-3	-3	15	0	2	-1	8	S/2	0.4
1948	Was-A	85	173	25	36	4	1	0	12	22	25	.208	.297	.243	46	-13	-13	14	2	2	-1	2	S/2	-0.9
1949	StL-A	105	243	29	55	8	3	0	18	38	35	.226	.331	.284	61	-12	-14	25	5	2	0	-9	S3/2	-2.1
Total	6	605	1833	203	422	52	9	1	162	216	206	.230	.312	.270	66	-83	-78	169	18	11	-1	-13	S/32	-7.5

■ JOHN SULLIVAN

Sullivan, John Peter b: 1/3/41, Somerville, N.J. BL/TR, 6', 195 lbs. Deb: 9/20/63

YEAR	TM/L	G	AB	R	H	2B	3B	HR	RBI	BB	SO	AVG	OBP	SLG	PRO+	BR	/A	RC	SB	CS	SBR	FR	POS	TPR
1963	Det-A	3	5	0	0	0	0	0	0	0	2	.000	.286	.000	-11	-1	-1	0	0	0	0	0	/C	0.0
1964	Det-A	2	3	0	0	0	0	0	0	0	1	.000	.000	.000	-99	-1	-1	0	0	0	0	0	/C	0.0
1965	Det-A	34	86	5	23	0	0	2	11	9	13	.267	.344	.337	93	-0	-1	11	0	0	0	1	C	0.2
1967	NY-N	65	147	4	32	5	0	0	6	6	26	.218	.248	.252	44	-11	-10	9	0	2	-1	-11	C	-2.1
1968	Phi-N	12	18	0	4	0	0	0	1	2	4	.222	.300	.222	59	-1	-1	1	0	0	0	-0	/C	0.0

YEAR	TM/L	G	AB	R	H	2B	3B	HR	RBI	BB	SO	AVG	OBP	SLG	PRO+	BR	/A	RC	SB	CS	SBR	FR	POS	TPR
Total	5	116	259	9	59	5	0	2	18	19	45	.228	.283	.270	59	-13	-13	21	0	2	-1	-11	/C	-1.9

■ JOE SULLIVAN
Sullivan, Joseph Daniel b: 1/6/1870, Charlestown, Mass. d: 11/2/1897, Charlestown, Mass. Deb: 4/27/1893

YEAR	TM/L	G	AB	R	H	2B	3B	HR	RBI	BB	SO	AVG	OBP	SLG	PRO+	BR	/A	RC	SB	CS	SBR	FR	POS	TPR
1893	Was-N	128	508	72	135	16	13	2	64	36	24	.266	.324	.360	86	-13	-10	63	7			-29	*S	-2.8
1894	Was-N	17	60	7	15	3	0	0	5	6	2	.250	.357	.300	63	-3	-3	8	3			-3	/2S3O	-0.3
	Phi-N	75	304	63	107	10	8	3	63	23	10	.352	.407	.467	115	6	8	63	10			-16	S	-0.2
	Yr	92	364	70	122	13	8	3	68	29	12	.335	.398	.440	106	3	5	71	13			-19		-0.5
1895	Phi-N	94	373	75	126	7	3	2	50	24	20	.338	.395	.389	104	4	4	65	15			-18	*S/O	-0.6
1896	Phi-N	48	191	45	48	5	3	2	24	18	12	.251	.347	.340	84	-4	-3	26	9			-4	O/S3	-0.8
	StL-N	51	212	25	62	4	2	2	21	9	12	.292	.351	.358	93	-3	-2	29	5			-6	O/2	-0.8
	Yr	99	403	70	110	9	5	4	45	27	24	.273	.349	.350	89	-7	-5	55	14			-9		-1.6
Total	4	413	1648	287	493	45	29	11	227	116	80	.299	.363	.382	96	-13	-7	254	49			-75	S/O23	-5.5

■ MARC SULLIVAN
Sullivan, Marc Cooper b: 7/25/58, Quincy, Mass. BR/TR, 6'4", 205 lbs. Deb: 10/01/82

YEAR	TM/L	G	AB	R	H	2B	3B	HR	RBI	BB	SO	AVG	OBP	SLG	PRO+	BR	/A	RC	SB	CS	SBR	FR	POS	TPR
1982	Bos-A	2	6	0	2	0	0	0	0	0	2	.333	.333	.333	79	-0	-0	1	0	0	0	1	/C	0.1
1984	Bos-A	2	6	1	3	0	0	0	1	1	0	.500	.571	.500	191	1	1	2	0	0	0	1	/C	0.2
1985	Bos-A	32	69	10	12	2	0	2	3	6	15	.174	.240	.290	43	-5	-6	5	0	0	0	4	C	0.0
1986	Bos-A	41	119	15	23	4	0	1	14	7	32	.193	.262	.252	40	-10	-10	9	0	0	0	-5	C	-1.1
1987	Bos-A	60	160	11	27	5	0	2	10	4	43	.169	.199	.237	15	-20	-20	7	0	0	0	1	C	-1.3
Total	5	137	360	37	67	11	0	5	28	18	92	.186	.237	.258	33	-34	-35	23	0	0	0	2	C	-2.1

■ MARTY SULLIVAN
Sullivan, Martin C. b: 10/20/1862, Lowell, Mass. d: 1/6/1894, Lowell, Mass. BR/TR, Deb: 4/30/1887

YEAR	TM/L	G	AB	R	H	2B	3B	HR	RBI	BB	SO	AVG	OBP	SLG	PRO+	BR	/A	RC	SB	CS	SBR	FR	POS	TPR
1887	Chi-N	115	472	98	134	13	16	7	77	36	53	.284	.340	.424	100	8	-3	82	35			-8	*O/P	-0.7
1888	Chi-N	75	314	40	74	12	6	7	39	15	32	.236	.273	.379	101	2	-1	36	9			3	O	0.2
1889	Ind-N	69	256	45	73	11	3	4	35	50	31	.285	.404	.398	124	11	10	48	15			-6	O/1	0.1
1890	Bos-N	121	505	82	144	19	7	6	61	56	48	.285	.357	.386	110	12	6	83	33			2	*O/3	0.5
1891	Bos-N	17	67	15	15	1	0	2	7	5	3	.224	.288	.328	72	-2	-3	9	7			-2	O	-0.4
	Cle-N	1	4	0	1	0	0	0	1	0	1	.250	.250	.250	45	-0	-0	0	0			-0	/O	0.0
	Yr	18	71	15	16	1	0	2	8	5	4	.225	.286	.324	71	-2	-3	9	7			-2		-0.4
Total	5	398	1618	280	441	56	32	26	220	162	168	.273	.341	.395	106	32	10	258	99			-10	O/13P	-0.3

■ MIKE SULLIVAN
Sullivan, Michael Joseph b: 6/10/1860, Webster, Mass. d: 3/21/29, Webster, Mass. BR/TR, 5'8.5", 165 lbs. Deb: 4/26/1888

YEAR	TM/L	G	AB	R	H	2B	3B	HR	RBI	BB	SO	AVG	OBP	SLG	PRO+	BR	/A	RC	SB	CS	SBR	FR	POS	TPR
1888	Phi-a	28	112	20	31	5	6	1	19	3		.277	.296	.455	143	5	5	18	10			-6	O3	-0.1

■ PAT SULLIVAN
Sullivan, Patrick J. b: 12/22/1862, Milwaukee, Wis. TR , 5'11", 165 lbs. Deb: 8/30/1884

YEAR	TM/L	G	AB	R	H	2B	3B	HR	RBI	BB	SO	AVG	OBP	SLG	PRO+	BR	/A	RC	SB	CS	SBR	FR	POS	TPR
1884	KC-U	31	114	15	22	3	1	0		4		.193	.220	.237	63	-5	-3	6	0			1	3/OCP	-0.1

■ RUSS SULLIVAN
Sullivan, Russell Guy b: 2/19/23, Fredericksburg, Va BL/TR, 6', 196 lbs. Deb: 9/08/51

YEAR	TM/L	G	AB	R	H	2B	3B	HR	RBI	BB	SO	AVG	OBP	SLG	PRO+	BR	/A	RC	SB	CS	SBR	FR	POS	TPR
1951	Det-A	7	26	2	5	1	0	1	1	2	1	.192	.250	.346	60	-2	-2	2	0	0	0	0	/O	-0.1
1952	Det-A	15	52	7	17	2	1	3	5	3	5	.327	.375	.577	161	4	4	12	1	0	0	-2	O	0.2
1953	Det-A	23	72	7	18	5	1	1	6	13	5	.250	.379	.389	109	1	1	11	0	0	0	1	O	0.2
Total	3	45	150	16	40	8	2	5	12	18	11	.267	.357	.447	118	4	4	25	1	0	0	-1	/O	0.3

■ SUTER SULLIVAN
Sullivan, Suter G. b: 10/14/1872, Baltimore, Md. d: 4/19/25, Baltimore, Md. Deb: 7/24/1898

YEAR	TM/L	G	AB	R	H	2B	3B	HR	RBI	BB	SO	AVG	OBP	SLG	PRO+	BR	/A	RC	SB	CS	SBR	FR	POS	TPR
1898	StL-N	42	144	10	32	3	0	0	12	13		.222	.300	.243	57	-7	-8	11	1			-13	SO/21P	-1.8
1899	Cle-N	127	473	37	116	16	3	0	55	25		.245	.296	.292	69	-23	-18	47	16			5	*30/S12	-1.1
Total	2	169	617	47	148	19	3	0	67	38		.240	.297	.280	66	-30	-25	58	17			-8	3/OS21P	-2.9

■ TOM SULLIVAN
Sullivan, Thomas Brandon b: 12/19/06, Nome, Alaska d: 8/16/44, Seattle, Wash. BR/TR, 6', 190 lbs. Deb: 6/14/25

YEAR	TM/L	G	AB	R	H	2B	3B	HR	RBI	BB	SO	AVG	OBP	SLG	PRO+	BR	/A	RC	SB	CS	SBR	FR	POS	TPR
1925	Cin-N	1	1	0	0	0	0	0	0	0	0	.000	.000	.000	-99	-0	-0	0	0	0	0	0	/C	0.0

■ SLEEPER SULLIVAN
Sullivan, Thomas Jefferson "Old Iron Hands" b: St.Louis, Mo. d: 9/25/1899, Camden, N.J. TR , 175 lbs. Deb: 5/03/1881

YEAR	TM/L	G	AB	R	H	2B	3B	HR	RBI	BB	SO	AVG	OBP	SLG	PRO+	BR	/A	RC	SB	CS	SBR	FR	POS	TPR
1881	Buf-N	35	121	13	23	4	0	0	15	1	21	.190	.197	.223	32	-9	-9	5				-7	C/O	-1.5
1882	StL-a	51	188	24	34	3	3	0		3		.181	.194	.229	40	-11	-12	9				-10	C/P	-1.9
1883	StL-a	8	27	2	6	0	1	0		0		.222	.222	.296	62	-1	-1	2				5	/CO	0.3
1884	StL-U	2	9	0	1	0	0	0		0		.111	.111	.111	-24	-1	-1	0	0			-1	/OCP	-0.1
Total	4	96	345	39	64	7	4	0	15	4	21	.186	.195	.229	38	-22	-24	16	0			-14	/COP	-3.2

■ TED SULLIVAN
Sullivan, Timothy Paul b: 1851, County Clare, Ireland d: 7/5/29, Washington, D.C. Deb: 9/09/1884 MU

YEAR	TM/L	G	AB	R	H	2B	3B	HR	RBI	BB	SO	AVG	OBP	SLG	PRO+	BR	/A	RC	SB	CS	SBR	FR	POS	TPR
1884	KC-U	3	9	0	3	0	0	0		1		.333	.400	.333	173	1	1	1	0			-2	/OSM	1.0

■ BILL SULLIVAN
Sullivan, William b: 7/4/1853, Holyoke, Mass. d: 11/13/1884, Holyoke, Mass. Deb: 8/09/1878 M

YEAR	TM/L	G	AB	R	H	2B	3B	HR	RBI	BB	SO	AVG	OBP	SLG	PRO+	BR	/A	RC	SB	CS	SBR	FR	POS	TPR
1878	Chi-N	2	6	1	1	0	0	0	0	0	0	.167	.167	.167	9	-1	-1	0				-0	/O	0.0

■ BILLY SULLIVAN
Sullivan, William Joseph Jr. b: 10/23/10, Chicago, Ill. BL/TR, 6', 170 lbs. Deb: 6/09/31

YEAR	TM/L	G	AB	R	H	2B	3B	HR	RBI	BB	SO	AVG	OBP	SLG	PRO+	BR	/A	RC	SB	CS	SBR	FR	POS	TPR
1931	Chi-A	92	363	48	100	16	5	2	33	20	14	.275	.315	.364	83	-12	-9	41	4	4	-1	-9	3/O1	-1.3
1932	Chi-A	93	307	31	97	16	1	1	45	20	9	.316	.358	.384	99	-3	-0	41	1	3	-2	-3	13/CO	-0.7
1933	Chi-A	54	125	9	24	0	1	0	13	10	5	.192	.252	.208	24	-14	-13	7	0	0	0	-3	1/C	-1.6
1935	Cin-N	85	241	29	64	9	4	2	36	19	16	.266	.324	.361	87	-5	-4	29	4			2	13/2	-0.1
1936	Cle-A	93	319	39	112	32	6	2	48	16	9	.351	.382	.508	117	8	7	61	5	2	0	-1	C/31O	1.1
1937	Cle-A	72	168	26	48	12	3	3	22	17	7	.286	.355	.446	100	-0	-0	26	1	4	-2	-5	C/13	-0.4
1938	StL-A	111	375	35	104	16	1	7	49	20	10	.277	.316	.381	74	-16	-16	45	8	5	-1	-2	C/1	-1.5
1939	StL-A	118	332	53	96	17	5	5	50	34	18	.289	.362	.416	96	-1	-2	49	3	3	-1	2	OC/1	-0.1
1940	*Det-A	78	220	36	68	14	4	3	41	31	11	.309	.399	.450	109	7	4	44	2	0	1	1	C/3	0.9
1941	Det-A	85	234	29	66	15	1	3	29	35	11	.282	.375	.393	94	2	-1	36	0	3	-2	5	C	0.6
1942	Bro-N	43	101	11	27	2	1	1	14	12	6	.267	.345	.337	98	0	0	13	1			-1	C	0.0
1947	Pit-N	38	55	1	14	3	0	0	8	6	3	.255	.328	.309	68	-2	-2	6	1			1	C	-0.1
Total	12	962	2840	347	820	152	32	29	388	240	119	.289	.346	.395	91	-36	-37	397	30	24		-12	C13/02	-3.2

■ BILLY SULLIVAN
Sullivan, William Joseph Sr. b: 2/1/1875, Oakland, Wis. d: 1/28/65, Newberg.Ore. BR/TR, 5'9", 155 lbs. Deb: 9/13/1899

YEAR	TM/L	G	AB	R	H	2B	3B	HR	RBI	BB	SO	AVG	OBP	SLG	PRO+	BR	/A	RC	SB	CS	SBR	FR	POS	TPR
1899	Bos-N	22	74	10	20	2	0	2	12	1		.270	.308	.378	82	-1	-2	9	2			6	C	0.4
1900	Bos-N	72	238	36	65	6	0	8	41	9		.273	.302	.399	84	-3	-7	31	4			0	C/S2	0.4
1901	Chi-A	98	367	54	90	15	6	4	56	10		.245	.271	.351	75	-14	-12	40	12			-1	C/3	-0.4
1902	Chi-A	76	263	36	64	12	3	1	26	6		.243	.266	.323	67	-13	-11	27	11			-3	C/1O	-0.8
1903	Chi-A	32	111	10	21	4	0	1	7	5		.189	.224	.252	46	-7	-7	7	3			-2	C	-0.4
1904	Chi-A	108	371	29	85	18	4	1	44	12		.229	.253	.307	82	-9	-8	34	11			2	*C	-0.3
1905	Chi-A	98	323	25	65	10	3	2	26	13		.201	.232	.269	63	-15	-13	25	14			-4	C/13	-0.8
1906	*Chi-A	118	387	37	83	18	4	0	33	22		.214	.257	.297	77	-12	-10	35	10			-5	*C	-0.6
1907	Chi-A	112	329	30	59	8	4	0	36	21		.179	.229	.228	49	-19	-18	20	6			-1	*C/2	-1.0
1908	Chi-A	137	430	40	82	8	4	0	29	22		.191	.230	.228	51	-23	-22	27	15			-21	*C	-3.3
1909	Chi-A	97	265	11	43	3	0	0	16	17		.162	.226	.174	28	-22	-20	13	9			5	CM	-0.8
1910	Chi-A	45	142	10	26	4	1	0	6	7		.183	.227	.225	43	-10	-17	6	1			13	C	1.0
1911	Chi-A	89	256	26	55	9	3	0	16	19		.215	.266	.270	52	-17	-16	19	1			2	C	-0.3
1912	Chi-A	41	91	9	19	2	1	0	15	9		.209	.287	.253	56	-5	-5	7	0			1	C	-0.3
1914	Chi-A	1	0	0	0	0	0	0	0	0	0	—	—	—		0	0	0				-0	/C	0.0
1916	Det-A	1	0	0	0	0	0	0	0	0	0	—	—	—		0	0	0				0	/C	0.0

YEAR	TM/L	G	AB	R	H	2B	3B	HR	RBI	BB	SO	AVG	OBP	SLG	PRO+	BR	/A	RC	SB	CS	SBR	FR	POS	TPR
Total	16	1147	3647	363	777	119	33	21	378	170	0	.213	.252	.281	63	-170	-162	302	98			-9	*C/1O32S	-6.4

■ **HOMER SUMMA**   Summa, Homer Wayne b: 11/3/1898, Gentry, Mo. d: 1/29/66, Los Angeles, Cal. BL/TR, 5'10.5", 170 lbs. Deb: 9/13/20

YEAR	TM/L	G	AB	R	H	2B	3B	HR	RBI	BB	SO	AVG	OBP	SLG	PRO+	BR	/A	RC	SB	CS	SBR	FR	POS	TPR
1920	Pit-N	10	22	1	7	1	1	0	3	1	5	.318	.400	.455	141	1	1	4	1	0	0	1	/O	0.2
1922	Cle-A	12	46	9	16	3	3	1	6	1	1	.348	.400	.609	159	4	4	11	1	1	-0	0	O	0.2
1923	Cle-A	137	525	92	172	27	6	3	69	33	20	.328	.374	.419	109	6	6	80	9	13	-5	-13	*O	-2.2
1924	Cle-A	111	390	55	113	21	6	2	38	11	16	.290	.311	.390	79	-13	-14	46	4	2	0	-6	O	-2.4
1925	Cle-A	75	224	28	74	10	1	0	25	13	6	.330	.375	.384	92	-2	-2	33	3	2	0	-9	O/3	-1.4
1926	Cle-A	154	581	74	179	31	6	4	76	47	9	.308	.368	.403	100	1	0	88	15	8	-0	7	*O	-0.3
1927	Cle-A	145	574	73	164	41	7	4	74	32	18	.286	.331	.402	89	-10	-11	73	6	5	-1	-8	*O	-2.8
1928	Cle-A	134	504	60	143	26	3	3	57	20	15	.284	.319	.365	78	-16	-16	59	4	2	-0	-4	*O	-2.7
1929	*Phi-A	37	81	12	22	4	0	0	10	2	1	.272	.298	.321	57	-5	-5	8	1	1	-0	-5	O	-1.0
1930	Phi-A	25	54	10	15	2	1	1	5	4	1	.278	.339	.407	85	-1	-1	8	0	0	0	0	O	-0.1
Total	10	840	3001	414	905	166	34	18	361	166	88	.302	.346	.398	92	-35	-39	410	44	34	-7	-36	O/3	-12.5

■ **CHAMP SUMMERS**   Summers, John Junior b: 6/15/46, Bremerton, Wash. BL/TR, 6'2", 205 lbs. Deb: 5/04/74 C

YEAR	TM/L	G	AB	R	H	2B	3B	HR	RBI	BB	SO	AVG	OBP	SLG	PRO+	BR	/A	RC	SB	CS	SBR	FR	POS	TPR
1974	Oak-A	20	24	2	3	1	0	0	3	1	5	.125	.160	.167	-6	-3	-3	1	0	0	0	0	O/D	-0.3
1975	Chi-N	76	91	14	21	5	1	1	16	10	13	.231	.314	.341	78	-2	-3	10	0	0	0	-2	O	-0.5
1976	Chi-N	83	126	11	26	2	0	3	13	13	31	.206	.286	.294	59	-6	-7	11	1	0	0	-2	O1/C	-1.0
1977	Cin-N	59	76	11	13	4	0	3	6	6	16	.171	.241	.342	53	-5	-5	6	0	0	0	1	O/3	-0.4
1978	Cin-N	13	35	4	9	2	0	1	3	7	4	.257	.381	.400	118	1	1	5	2	1	0	-2	O	-0.1
1979	Cin-N	27	60	10	12	2	1	1	11	13	15	.200	.351	.317	83	-1	-1	7	0	1	-1	-1	O/1	-0.2
	Det-A	90	246	47	77	12	1	20	51	40	33	.313	.415	.614	168	26	25	63	7	6	-2	-6	OD/1	1.4
1980	Det-A	120	347	61	103	19	1	17	60	52	52	.297	.396	.504	142	23	21	69	4	3	-1	-5	DO/1	1.5
1981	Det-A	64	165	16	42	8	0	3	21	19	35	.255	.342	.358	98	1	0	22	1	1	-0	-1	DO	-0.1
1982	SF-N	70	125	15	31	5	0	4	19	16	17	.248	.347	.384	105	1	1	17	0	1	-1	-3	O/1	-0.2
1983	SF-N	29	22	3	3	0	0	0	3	7	8	.136	.345	.136	39	-1	-1	1	0	0	0	0	O	0.0
1984	*SD-A	47	54	5	10	3	0	1	12	4	15	.185	.254	.296	54	-3	-3	4	0	0	0	-1	/1	-0.4
Total	11	698	1371	199	350	63	4	54	218	188	244	.255	.353	.425	111	29	25	215	15	13	-3	-21	OD/13C	-0.3

■ **KID SUMMERS**   Summers, William b: Toronto, Ont., Canada d: 10/16/1895, Toronto, Ont., Can. TR , Deb: 8/05/1893

YEAR	TM/L	G	AB	R	H	2B	3B	HR	RBI	BB	SO	AVG	OBP	SLG	PRO+	BR	/A	RC	SB	CS	SBR	FR	POS	TPR
1893	StL-N	2	1	1	0	0	0	0	0	0	0	.000	.500	.000	40	0	0	0	0			-0	/OC	0.0

■ **CARL SUMNER**   Sumner, Carl Ringdahl "Lefty" b: 9/28/08, Cambridge, Mass. BL/TL, 5'8", 170 lbs. Deb: 7/28/28

YEAR	TM/L	G	AB	R	H	2B	3B	HR	RBI	BB	SO	AVG	OBP	SLG	PRO+	BR	/A	RC	SB	CS	SBR	FR	POS	TPR
1928	Bos-A	16	29	6	8	1	1	0	3	5	6	.276	.382	.379	103	0	0	5	0	0	0	-3	O	-0.2

■ **ART SUNDAY**   Sunday, Arthur (b: August Wacher) b: 1/21/1862, Springfield, Ohio BL/TL, 5'9", 193 lbs. Deb: 5/05/1890

YEAR	TM/L	G	AB	R	H	2B	3B	HR	RBI	BB	SO	AVG	OBP	SLG	PRO+	BR	/A	RC	SB	CS	SBR	FR	POS	TPR
1890	Bro-P	24	83	26	22	5	1	0	13	15	9	.265	.419	.349	102	2	1	12	0			-5	O	-0.3

■ **BILLY SUNDAY**   Sunday, William Ashley "Parson" or "The Evangelist" b: 11/19/1862, Ames, Iowa d: 11/6/35, Chicago, Ill. BL , 5'10", 160 lbs. Deb: 5/22/1883

YEAR	TM/L	G	AB	R	H	2B	3B	HR	RBI	BB	SO	AVG	OBP	SLG	PRO+	BR	/A	RC	SB	CS	SBR	FR	POS	TPR
1883	Chi-N	14	54	6	13	4	0	0	5	1	18	.241	.255	.315	68	-2	-2	4				-5	O	-0.5
1884	Chi-N	43	176	25	39	4	1	4	28	4	36	.222	.239	.324	69	-5	-7	14				-9	O	-1.5
1885	*Chi-N	46	172	36	44	3	3	2	20	12	33	.256	.304	.343	95	2	-2	18				-8	O	-1.0
1886	Chi-N	28	103	16	25	2	2	0	6	7	26	.243	.291	.301	70	-2	-5	12	10			-0	O	-0.3
1887	Chi-N	50	199	41	58	6	6	3	32	21	20	.291	.362	.427	106	6	1	44	34			-7	O	-0.4
1888	Pit-N	120	505	69	119	14	3	0	15	12	36	.236	.256	.275	77	-16	-11	55	71			16	*O	0.3
1889	Pit-N	81	321	62	77	10	6	2	25	27	33	.240	.307	.327	87	-9	-4	48	47			9	O	0.2
1890	Pit-N	86	358	58	92	9	2	1	33	32	20	.257	.327	.302	97	-6	1	55	56			7	O/P	0.6
	Phi-N	31	119	26	31	3	1	0	6	18	7	.261	.367	.303	96	1	0	24	28			5	O	0.4
	Yr	117	477	84	123	12	3	1	39	50	27	.258	.337	.302	96	-5	1	79	84			12		1.0
Total	8	499	2007	339	498	55	24	12	170	134	229	.248	.300	.317	87	-32	-29	275	246			8	O/P	-2.2

■ **JIM SUNDBERG**   Sundberg, James Howard b: 5/18/51, Galesburg, Ill. BR/TR, 6', 190 lbs. Deb: 4/04/74

YEAR	TM/L	G	AB	R	H	2B	3B	HR	RBI	BB	SO	AVG	OBP	SLG	PRO+	BR	/A	RC	SB	CS	SBR	FR	POS	TPR
1974	Tex-A	132	368	45	91	13	3	3	36	62	61	.247	.356	.323	99	1	2	43	2	4	-2	5	*C	1.0
1975	Tex-A	155	472	45	94	9	0	6	36	51	77	.199	.283	.256	54	-28	-28	35	3	1	0	5	*C	-1.7
1976	Tex-A	140	448	33	102	24	2	3	34	37	61	.228	.287	.310	73	-14	-16	39	0	0	0	16	*C	0.6
1977	Tex-A	149	453	61	132	20	3	6	65	53	77	.291	.368	.389	105	6	5	67	2	3	-1	22	*C	2.9
1978	Tex-A	149	518	54	144	23	6	6	58	64	70	.278	.361	.380	108	7	7	69	2	5	-2	16	*C/D	2.6
1979	Tex-A	150	495	50	136	23	4	5	64	51	51	.275	.348	.368	94	-3	-3	62	3	3	-1	9	*C	1.1
1980	Tex-A	151	505	59	138	24	1	10	63	64	67	.273	.356	.384	106	3	5	69	2	2	-1	7	*C	1.9
1981	Tex-A	102	339	42	94	17	2	3	28	50	48	.277	.372	.366	120	8	10	48	2	5	-2	-3	C/O	0.9
1982	Tex-A	139	470	37	118	22	5	10	47	49	57	.251	.323	.383	98	-4	-1	57	2	6	-3	-1	*C/O	0.2
1983	Tex-A	131	378	30	76	14	0	2	28	35	64	.201	.272	.254	47	-27	-26	26	0	4	-2	5	*C	-1.7
1984	Mil-A	110	348	43	91	19	4	7	43	38	63	.261	.334	.399	106	1	3	48	1	1	-0	6	*C	1.5
1985	*KC-A	115	367	38	90	12	4	10	35	33	67	.245	.309	.381	88	-6	-6	42	0	2	-1	-6	*C	-0.8
1986	KC-A	140	429	41	91	9	1	12	42	57	91	.212	.305	.322	69	-17	-18	44	1	1	-0	-1	*C	-1.0
1987	Chi-N	61	139	9	28	2	0	4	15	19	40	.201	.306	.302	60	-7	-8	13	0	0	0	8	C	0.4
1988	Chi-N	24	54	8	13	1	0	2	9	8	15	.241	.339	.370	99	0	0	7	0	0	0	-1	C	0.0
	Tex-A	38	91	13	26	4	0	4	13	5	17	.286	.323	.462	114	2	1	13	0	0	0	-2	C	0.1
1989	Tex-A	76	147	13	29	7	1	2	8	23	37	.197	.306	.299	70	-5	-6	15	0	0	0	2	C/D	0.0
Total	16	1962	6021	621	1493	243	36	95	624	699	963	.248	.328	.348	89	-86	-78	698	20	37	-16	88	*C/OD	8.0

■ **B.J. SURHOFF**   Surhoff, William James b: 8/4/64, Bronx, N.Y. BL/TR, 6'1", 185 lbs. Deb: 4/08/87

YEAR	TM/L	G	AB	R	H	2B	3B	HR	RBI	BB	SO	AVG	OBP	SLG	PRO+	BR	/A	RC	SB	CS	SBR	FR	POS	TPR
1987	Mil-A	115	395	50	118	22	3	7	68	36	30	.299	.357	.423	103	4	2	56	11	10	-3	7	C3/1D	1.3
1988	Mil-A	139	493	47	121	21	0	5	38	31	49	.245	.294	.318	71	-19	-19	46	21	6	3	-8	*C3/1SO	-2.0
1989	Mil-A	126	436	42	108	17	4	5	55	25	29	.248	.293	.339	79	-13	-13	41	14	12	-3	-5	*CD/3	-1.6
1990	Mil-A	135	474	55	131	21	4	6	59	41	37	.276	.335	.376	102	-1	1	61	18	7	1	-8	*C3	-0.1
Total	4	515	1798	194	478	81	11	23	220	133	145	.266	.319	.362	88	-29	-29	204	64	35	-2	-14	C/3D1OS	-2.4

■ **GEORGE SUSCE**   Susce, George Cyril Methodius "Good Kid" b: 8/13/08, Pittsburgh, Pa. d: 2/25/86, Sarasota, Fla. BR/TR, 5'11.5", 200 lbs. Deb: 4/23/29 C

YEAR	TM/L	G	AB	R	H	2B	3B	HR	RBI	BB	SO	AVG	OBP	SLG	PRO+	BR	/A	RC	SB	CS	SBR	FR	POS	TPR
1929	Phi-N	17	17	5	5	3	0	1	1	1	2	.294	.368	.647	137	1	1	4	0			-1	C	0.0
1932	Det-A	2	0	0	0	0	0	0	0	0	0	—	—	—		0	0	0	0	0	0	0	/C	0.0
1939	Pit-N	31	75	8	17	3	1	1	4	12	5	.227	.333	.333	81	-2	-2	8	0			3	C	0.2
1940	StL-A	61	113	6	24	4	0	0	13	9	9	.212	.282	.248	38	-10	-10	7	1	0	0	7	C	0.1
1941	Cle-A	1	0	0	0	0	0	0	0	0	0	—	—	—		0	0	0	0	0	0	0	/C	0.0
1942	Cle-A	2	1	1	1	0	0	0	0	0	0	1.000	1.000	1.000	492	1	1	1	0			-0	/C	0.1
1943	Cle-A	3	1	0	0	0	0	0	0	0	0	.000	.000	.000	-99	-0	-0	0	0			1	/C	0.0
1944	Cle-A	29	61	3	14	1	0	0	4	2	5	.230	.254	.246	45	-5	-4	4	0	0	0	2	C	0.0
Total	8	146	268	23	61	11	1	2	22	25	21	.228	.301	.299	60	-15	-15	24	1	0		11	C	0.4

■ **PETE SUSKO**   Susko, Peter Jonathan b: 7/2/04, Laura, Ohio d: 5/22/78, Jacksonville, Fla. BL/TL, 5'11", 172 lbs. Deb: 8/01/34

YEAR	TM/L	G	AB	R	H	2B	3B	HR	RBI	BB	SO	AVG	OBP	SLG	PRO+	BR	/A	RC	SB	CS	SBR	FR	POS	TPR
1934	Was-A	58	224	25	64	5	3	2	25	18	10	.286	.342	.362	89	-6	-5	28	3	4	-2	3	1	-1.2

■ **BUTCH SUTCLIFFE**   Sutcliffe, Charles Inigo b: 7/22/15, Fall River, Mass. BR/TR, 5'8.5", 165 lbs. Deb: 8/28/38

YEAR	TM/L	G	AB	R	H	2B	3B	HR	RBI	BB	SO	AVG	OBP	SLG	PRO+	BR	/A	RC	SB	CS	SBR	FR	POS	TPR
1938	Bos-N	4	4	1	1	0	0	0	2	2	1	.250	.500	.250	124	0	0	1	0			0	/C	0.1

YEAR	TM/L	G	AB	R	H	2B	3B	HR	RBI	BB	SO	AVG	OBP	SLG	PRO+	BR	/A	RC	SB	CS	SBR	FR	POS	TPR

■ SY SUTCLIFFE   Sutcliffe, Elmer Ellsworth b: 4/15/1862, Wheaton, Ill. d: 2/13/1893, Wheaton, Ill.   BL, 6'2", 170 lbs. Deb: 10/02/1884

YEAR	TM/L	G	AB	R	H	2B	3B	HR	RBI	BB	SO	AVG	OBP	SLG	PRO+	BR	/A	RC	SB	CS	SBR	FR	POS	TPR
1884	Chi-N	4	15	4	3	1	0	0	2	2	4	.200	.294	.267	72	-0	-1	1				4	/C	0.3
1885	Chi-N	11	43	5	8	1	1	0	4	2	5	.186	.222	.256	47	-2	-3	1				-3	C/O	-0.4
	StL-N	16	49	2	6	1	0	0	4	5	10	.122	.204	.143	15	-4	-4	1				-0	C/O	-0.2
	Yr	27	92	7	14	2	1	0	8	7	15	.152	.212	.196	32	-7	-7	4				-4		-0.6
1888	Det-N	49	191	17	49	5	3	0	23	5	14	.257	.276	.314	90	-2	-2	19	6			6	SC/102	0.4
1889	Cle-N	46	161	17	40	3	2	1	21	14	6	.248	.309	.311	76	-5	-5	17	5			10	C/1O	0.4
1890	Cle-P	99	386	62	127	14	8	2	60	33	16	.329	.382	.422	127	9	15	68	10			-32	CO/S3	-1.0
1891	Was-a	53	201	29	71	8	3	2	33	17	17	.353	.409	.453	157	13	14	42	8			-2	OC/S3	1.0
1892	Bal-N	66	276	41	77	10	7	1	27	14	15	.279	.316	.377	108	3	1	38	12			-7	1	-0.9
Total	7	344	1322	177	381	43	24	6	174	92	87	.288	.336	.371	109	10	16	188	41			-24	C/1OS32	-0.4

■ GARY SUTHERLAND   Sutherland, Gary Lynn b: 9/27/44, Glendale, Cal. BR/TR, 6', 185 lbs. Deb: 9/17/66

YEAR	TM/L	G	AB	R	H	2B	3B	HR	RBI	BB	SO	AVG	OBP	SLG	PRO+	BR	/A	RC	SB	CS	SBR	FR	POS	TPR
1966	Phi-N	3	3	0	0	0	0	0	0	0	0	.000	.000	.000	-99	-1	-1	0	0	0	0	1	/S	0.0
1967	Phi-N	103	231	23	57	12	1	1	19	17	22	.247	.298	.320	76	-7	-7	20	0	3	-2	-14	SO	-1.7
1968	Phi-N	67	138	16	38	7	0	0	15	8	15	.275	.315	.326	93	-1	-1	14	0	0	0	-2	2S3/O	0.0
1969	Mon-N	141	544	63	130	26	1	3	35	37	31	.239	.290	.307	67	-24	-24	46	5	7	-3	10	*2S/O	-0.4
1970	Mon-N	116	359	37	74	10	0	3	26	31	22	.206	.273	.259	43	-29	-29	26	2	2	-1	3	2S/3	-1.2
1971	Mon-N	111	304	25	78	7	2	4	26	18	12	.257	.302	.332	79	-8	-8	28	3	4	-2	0	2S/O3	-0.4
1972	Hou-N	5	8	0	1	0	0	0	1	0	0	.125	.125	.125	-29	-1	-1	0	0	0	0	-0	/23	-0.1
1973	Hou-N	16	54	8	14	5	0	0	3	3	5	.259	.298	.352	80	-2	-2	5	0	0	0	-4	2/S	-0.4
1974	Det-A	149	619	60	157	20	1	5	49	26	37	.254	.284	.313	69	-23	-26	51	1	3	-2	-25	*2S/3	-4.7
1975	Det-A	129	503	51	130	12	3	6	39	45	41	.258	.323	.330	81	-10	-12	53	0	2	-1	-7	*2	-1.6
1976	Det-A	42	117	10	24	5	2	0	6	7	12	.205	.250	.282	53	-7	-7	7	0	1	-1	1	2	-0.3
	Mil-A	59	115	9	25	2	0	1	9	8	7	.217	.274	.261	58	-6	-6	7	0	2	-1	-0	2/1D	-0.4
	Yr	101	232	19	49	7	2	1	15	15	19	.211	.262	.272	56	-13	-13	14	0	3	-2	1		-0.7
1977	SD-N	80	103	5	25	3	0	1	11	7	15	.243	.291	.301	66	-6	-5	9	0	0	0	-4	23/1	-0.6
1978	StL-N	10	6	1	1	0	0	0	0	0	0	.167	.167	.167	-7	-1	-1	0	0	0	0	2	/2	0.1
Total	13	1031	3104	308	754	109	10	24	239	207	219	.243	.292	.308	69	-125	-130	267	11	24	-11	-39	2S/3OD1	-11.3

■ LEO SUTHERLAND   Sutherland, Leonardo (Cantin) b: 4/6/58, Santiago, Cuba BL/TL, 5'10", 165 lbs. Deb: 8/11/80

YEAR	TM/L	G	AB	R	H	2B	3B	HR	RBI	BB	SO	AVG	OBP	SLG	PRO+	BR	/A	RC	SB	CS	SBR	FR	POS	TPR
1980	Chi-A	34	89	9	23	3	0	0	5	1	11	.258	.267	.292	53	-6	-6	7	4	1	1	-1	O	-0.6
1981	Chi-A	11	12	6	2	0	0	0	0	3	1	.167	.333	.167	49	-1	-1	1	2	1	0	-0	/O	0.0
Total	2	45	101	15	25	3	0	0	5	4	12	.248	.276	.277	53	-6	-6	8	6	2	1	-1	/O	-0.6

■ GLENN SUTKO   Sutko, Glenn Edward b: 5/9/68, Atlanta, Ga. BR/TR, 6'3", 225 lbs. Deb: 10/03/90

YEAR	TM/L	G	AB	R	H	2B	3B	HR	RBI	BB	SO	AVG	OBP	SLG	PRO+	BR	/A	RC	SB	CS	SBR	FR	POS	TPR
1990	Cin-N	1	1	0	0	0	0	0	0	0	1	.000	.000	.000	-98	-0	-0	0	0	0	0	0	/C	0.0

■ EZRA SUTTON   Sutton, Ezra Ballou b: 9/17/1850, Palmyra, N.Y. d: 6/20/07, Braintree, Mass. BR/TR, 5'8.5", 153 lbs. Deb: 5/04/1871

YEAR	TM/L	G	AB	R	H	2B	3B	HR	RBI	BB	SO	AVG	OBP	SLG	PRO+	BR	/A	RC	SB	CS	SBR	FR	POS	TPR
1871	Cle-n	29	128	35	45	3	7	3	23	1	0	.352	.357	.555	166	9	10	27	3				*3	0.5
1872	Cle-n	22	108	30	30	8	1	0		0		.278	.278	.370	103	-0	1	11					3	0.0
1873	Ath-n	51	242	51	81	7	7	0		0	2	.335	.340	.421	114	6	3	36					*3/S2	0.1
1874	Ath-n	55	244	54	72	10	2	0		0	0	.295	.295	.352	97	1	-3	26					3S	-0.2
1875	Ath-n	75	358	83	116	11	7	2		1		.324	.326	.411	138	18	12	49					*3/P1O	1.3
1876	Phi-N	54	236	45	70	12	7	1	31	3	2	.297	.305	.419	141	9	10	31				-4	12/3O	0.5
1877	Bos-N	58	253	43	74	10	6	0	39	4	10	.292	.304	.379	110	4	2	30				-8	S3	-0.2
1878	Bos-N	60	239	31	54	9	3	1	29	2	14	.226	.232	.301	69	-7	-9	17				-1	*3/S	-0.6
1879	Bos-N	84	339	54	84	13	4	0	34	2	18	.248	.252	.310	82	-6	-7	27				-12	S3	-1.3
1880	Bos-N	76	288	41	72	9	2	0	25	7	7	.250	.268	.295	94	-3	-2	23				4	S3	0.4
1881	Bos-N	83	333	43	97	12	4	0	31	13	9	.291	.318	.351	116	4	4	38				-3	*3/S	0.9
1882	Bos-N	81	319	44	80	8	1	2	38	24	25	.251	.303	.301	94	-1	-1	30				-4	*3/S	-0.3
1883	Bos-N	94	414	101	134	28	15	3	73	17	12	.324	.350	.486	147	24	23	72				-1	*3/OS	2.0
1884	Bos-N	110	468	102	**162**	28	7	3	61	29	22	.346	.384	.455	164	33	34	84				-3	*3	2.2
1885	Bos-N	110	457	78	143	23	8	4	47	17	25	.313	.338	.425	151	21	24	67				-0	*3S/21	2.4
1886	Bos-N	116	499	83	138	21	6	3	48	26	21	.277	.312	.361	108	2	5	63	18			-4	OS32	0.2
1887	Bos-N	77	326	58	99	14	9	3	46	13	6	.304	.342	.429	115	6	6	55	17			17	SO23	1.9
1888	Bos-N	28	110	16	24	3	1	1	16	7	3	.218	.277	.291	82	-2	-2	12	10			-5	3/S	-0.6
Total	5 n	232	1080	253	344	39	24	5	23	4		.319	.321	.413	122	34	23	149	3				3/SPO12	1.7
Total	13	1031	4281	739	1231	190	73	21	518	164	174	.288	.315	.381	119	86	88	550	45			-25	3S/O21	7.5

■ DALE SVEUM   Sveum, Dale Curtis b: 11/23/63, Richmond, Cal. BB/TR, 6'2", 185 lbs. Deb: 5/12/86

YEAR	TM/L	G	AB	R	H	2B	3B	HR	RBI	BB	SO	AVG	OBP	SLG	PRO+	BR	/A	RC	SB	CS	SBR	FR	POS	TPR
1986	Mil-A	91	317	35	78	13	2	7	35	32	63	.246	.317	.366	83	-6	-8	37	4	3	-1	-8	32S	-1.5
1987	Mil-A	153	535	86	135	27	3	25	95	40	133	.252	.306	.454	95	-3	-5	70	2	6	-3	-13	*S2	-1.2
1988	Mil-A	129	467	41	113	14	4	9	51	21	122	.242	.276	.347	73	-17	-18	45	1	0	0	-6	*S/2D	-2.0
1990	Mil-A	48	117	15	23	7	0	1	12	12	30	.197	.282	.282	60	-6	-6	10	0	1	-1	-5	32/1S	-1.0
Total	4	421	1436	177	349	61	9	42	193	105	348	.243	.297	.386	83	-34	-37	161	7	10	-4	-32	S/321D	-5.4

■ HARRY SWACINA   Swacina, Harry Joseph "Swats" b: 8/22/1881, St.Louis, Mo. d: 6/21/44, Birmingham, Ala. BR/TR, 6'2", 190 lbs. Deb: 9/13/07

YEAR	TM/L	G	AB	R	H	2B	3B	HR	RBI	BB	SO	AVG	OBP	SLG	PRO+	BR	/A	RC	SB	CS	SBR	FR	POS	TPR
1907	Pit-N	26	95	9	19	1	1	0	10	4		.200	.232	.232	46	-6	-6	6	1			-1	1	-0.8
1908	Pit-N	53	176	7	38	6	1	0	13	5		.216	.238	.261	61	-8	-8	12	4			-5	1	-1.5
1914	Bal-F	158	617	70	173	26	8	0	90	14	23	.280	.297	.348	82	-14	-16	72	15			10	*1	-0.3
1915	Bal-F	85	301	24	74	13	1	1	38	9	11	.246	.268	.306	67	-12	-13	29	9			6	1/2	-0.6
Total	4	322	1189	110	304	46	11	1	151	32	34	.256	.276	.315	73	-40	-43	118	29			10	1/2	-3.2

■ ANDY SWAN   Swan, Andrew J.   Deb: 7/23/1884

YEAR	TM/L	G	AB	R	H	2B	3B	HR	RBI	BB	SO	AVG	OBP	SLG	PRO+	BR	/A	RC	SB	CS	SBR	FR	POS	TPR
1884	Was-a	5	21	3	3	1	0	0		0		.143	.143	.190	10	-2	-2	1				-3	/13	-0.3
	Ric-a	3	10	2	5	0	0	0		0		.500	.500	.500	235	1	1	3				0	/1	0.1
	Yr	8	31	5	8	1	0	0		0		.258	.258	.290	88	-1	-0	2				-3		-0.2

■ MARTY SWANDELL   Swandell, John Martin (b: Martin Schwendel) b: 1845, Brooklyn, N.Y. d: 10/25/06, Brooklyn, N.Y. 5'10.5", 146 lbs. Deb: 5/07/1872

YEAR	TM/L	G	AB	R	H	2B	3B	HR	RBI	BB	SO	AVG	OBP	SLG	PRO+	BR	/A	RC	SB	CS	SBR	FR	POS	TPR
1872	Eck-n	14	55	8	11	0	0	0		0		.200	.228	.200	39	-4	-2	3					/3O12	-0.1
1873	Res-n	2	9	1	1	0	0	0		0		.111	.111	.111	-37	-1	-1	0					/1O	0.0
Total	2 n	16	64	9	12	0	0	0		0	2	.188	.212	.188	27	-6	-4	3					/3O12	-0.1

■ PINKY SWANDER   Swander, Edward O. b: 7/4/1880, Portsmouth, Ohio d: 10/24/44, Springfield, Mass. BL/TL, 5'9", 180 lbs. Deb: 9/18/03

YEAR	TM/L	G	AB	R	H	2B	3B	HR	RBI	BB	SO	AVG	OBP	SLG	PRO+	BR	/A	RC	SB	CS	SBR	FR	POS	TPR
1903	StL-A	14	51	9	14	2	2	0	6	10		.275	.393	.392	142	3	3	8	0			-2	O	0.1
1904	StL-A	1	1	0	0	0	0	0	0	0		.000	.000	.000	-99	-0	-0	0	0			0	H	0.0
Total	2	15	52	9	14	2	2	0	6	10		.269	.387	.385	138	3	3	8	0			-2	/O	0.1

■ EVAR SWANSON   Swanson, Ernest Evar b: 10/15/02, DeKalb, Ill. d: 7/17/73, Galesburg, Ill. BR/TR, 5'9", 170 lbs. Deb: 4/18/29

YEAR	TM/L	G	AB	R	H	2B	3B	HR	RBI	BB	SO	AVG	OBP	SLG	PRO+	BR	/A	RC	SB	CS	SBR	FR	POS	TPR
1929	Cin-N	148	574	100	172	35	12	4	43	41	47	.300	.353	.423	96	-8	-4	84	33			-2	*O	-1.6
1930	Cin-N	95	301	43	93	15	3	2	22	11	19	.309	.335	.399	81	-1	-9	39	4			3	O	-0.9
1932	Chi-A	14	52	9	16	3	1	0	8	3	8	.308	.400	.404	116	1	2	9	3	1	0	-3	O	0.0
1933	Chi-A	144	539	102	165	25	7	1	63	93	35	.306	.411	.384	117	14	17	92	19	11	-1	-8	*O	0.3
1934	Chi-A	117	426	71	127	9	5	0	34	59	31	.298	.385	.343	86	-4	-6	61	10	3	1	-6	*O	-1.1

YEAR	TM/L	G	AB	R	H	2B	3B	HR	RBI	BB	SO	AVG	OBP	SLG	PRO+	BR	/A	RC	SB	CS	SBR	FR	POS	TPR
Total	5	518	1892	325	573	87	28	7	170	212	133	.303	.376	.390	98	-9	-0	285	69	15		-16	O	-3.3

■ KARL SWANSON
Swanson, Karl Edward b: 12/17/03, N.Henderson, Ill.   BL/TR, 5'10", 155 lbs.   Deb: 8/12/28

YEAR	TM/L	G	AB	R	H	2B	3B	HR	RBI	BB	SO	AVG	OBP	SLG	PRO+	BR	/A	RC	SB	CS	SBR	FR	POS	TPR
1928	Chi-A	22	64	2	9	1	0	0	6	4	7	.141	.191	.156	-8	-10	-10	3	3	0	1	1	2	-0.5
1929	Chi-A	2	1	0	0	0	0	0	0	0	0	.000	.000	.000	-99	-0	-0	0	0	0	0	0	H	0.0
Total	2	24	65	2	9	1	0	0	6	4	7	.138	.188	.154	-9	-10	-10	3	3	0	1	1	/2	-0.5

■ STAN SWANSON
Swanson, Stanley Lawrence b: 5/19/44, Yuba City, Cal.   BR/TR, 5'11", 168 lbs.   Deb: 6/23/71

YEAR	TM/L	G	AB	R	H	2B	3B	HR	RBI	BB	SO	AVG	OBP	SLG	PRO+	BR	/A	RC	SB	CS	SBR	FR	POS	TPR
1971	Mon-N	49	106	14	26	3	0	2	11	10	13	.245	.310	.330	81	-3	-3	11	1	3	-2	-1	O	-0.6

■ BILL SWANSON
Swanson, William Andrew b: 10/12/1888, New York, N.Y. d: 10/14/54, New York, N.Y.   BB/TR, 5'6", 156 lbs.   Deb: 9/02/14

YEAR	TM/L	G	AB	R	H	2B	3B	HR	RBI	BB	SO	AVG	OBP	SLG	PRO+	BR	/A	RC	SB	CS	SBR	FR	POS	TPR
1914	Bos-A	11	20	0	4	2	0	0	0	3	4	.200	.304	.300	82	-0	-0	2	0	1	-1	-3	/23S	-0.4

■ ED SWARTWOOD
Swartwood, Cyrus Edward b: 1/12/1859, Rockford, Ill. d: 5/15/24, Pittsburgh, Pa.   TR , 198 lbs.   Deb: 8/11/1881   U

YEAR	TM/L	G	AB	R	H	2B	3B	HR	RBI	BB	SO	AVG	OBP	SLG	PRO+	BR	/A	RC	SB	CS	SBR	FR	POS	TPR
1881	Buf-N	1	3	0	1	0	0	0	0	1	0	.333	.500	.333	170	0	0	1				-0	/O	0.0
1882	Pit-a	76	325	86	107	18	11	4		21		.329	.370	.489	197	29	32	60				-8	*O/1	2.0
1883	Pit-a	94	413	86	147	24	8	3		24		.356	.391	.475	186	35	38	79				3	1O/C	3.1
1884	Pit-a	102	399	74	115	19	6	0		33		.288	.365	.366	140	20	19	55				-3	*O1/3P	1.2
1885	Bro-a	99	399	80	106	8	9	0		36		.266	.334	.331	113	7	7	45				-9	*O/1SC	-0.6
1886	Bro-a	122	471	95	132	13	10	3		70		.280	.377	.369	135	23	22	82	37			7	O/C	2.2
1887	Bro-a	91	363	72	92	14	8	1		46		.253	.342	.344	93	-2	-3	54	29			2	O	-0.3
1890	Tol-a	126	462	106	151	23	11	3		80		.327	.442	.444	160	42	40	117	53			8	*O/P	3.5
1892	Pit-N	13	42	8	10	1	0	0	4	13	11	.238	.418	.262	109	2	2	5	1			4	O	0.5
Total	9	724	2877	607	861	120	63	14	4	324	11	.299	.378	.399	144	156	156	497	120			2	O/1CPS3	11.6

■ CHARLIE SWEASY
Sweasy, Charles James (b: Charles James Swasey)
b: 11/2/1847, Newark, N.J. d: 3/30/08, Newark, N.J.   BR/TR, 5'9", 172 lbs.   Deb: 5/19/1871   M

YEAR	TM/L	G	AB	R	H	2B	3B	HR	RBI	BB	SO	AVG	OBP	SLG	PRO+	BR	/A	RC	SB	CS	SBR	FR	POS	TPR
1871	Oly-n	5	19	5	4	1	0	0	4	1	0	.211	.250	.263	50	-1	-1	1	0				/2	0.0
1872	Cle-n	12	52	8	16	0	0	0		2		.308	.333	.308	104	0	1	5					2/O	0.0
1873	Bos-n	1	5	0	1	0	0	0		0		.200	.200	.200	17	-0	-1	0					/2	0.0
1874	Bal-n	8	33	2	8	0	0	0		2		.242	.286	.242	70	-1	-1	2					/2O	0.0
	Atl-n	10	44	4	5	1	0	0		0		.114	.114	.136	-24	-6	-5	1					2	-0.3
	Yr	18	77	6	13	1	0	0		2		.169	.190	.182	20	-7	-6	3						-0.3
1875	RS-n	19	76	7	13	0	0	0		4		.171	.213	.171	38	-5	-4	3					2M	-0.3
1876	Cin-N	56	225	18	46	5	2	0	10	2	5	.204	.211	.244	60	-11	-6	12	2				*2/O	-0.3
1878	Pro-N	55	212	29	37	3	0	0	8	7	23	.175	.201	.189	29	-16	-16	8				-8	*2	-1.8
Total	5 n	55	229	26	47	2	0	0	4	9		.205	.235	.214	49	-13	-10	13					/2O	-0.6
Total	2	111	437	41	83	8	2	0	18	9	28	.190	.206	.217	44	-27	-22	20				-6	2/O	-2.1

■ BUCK SWEENEY
Sweeney, Charles Francis b: 4/15/1890, Pittsburgh, Pa8 d: 3/13/55, Pittsburgh, Pa.   Deb: 9/28/14

YEAR	TM/L	G	AB	R	H	2B	3B	HR	RBI	BB	SO	AVG	OBP	SLG	PRO+	BR	/A	RC	SB	CS	SBR	FR	POS	TPR
1914	Phi-A	1	1	0	0	0	0	0	0	0	1	.000	.000	.000	-99	-0	-0	0	0			-0	/O	0.0

■ CHARLIE SWEENEY
Sweeney, Charles J. b: 4/13/1863, San Francisco, Cal d: 4/4/02, San Francisco, Cal.   BR , 5'10.5", 181 lbs.   Deb: 5/11/1882

YEAR	TM/L	G	AB	R	H	2B	3B	HR	RBI	BB	SO	AVG	OBP	SLG	PRO+	BR	/A	RC	SB	CS	SBR	FR	POS	TPR
1882	Pro-N	1	4	0	0	0	0	0	0	0	1	.000	.000	.000	-99	-1	-1	0				0	/O	0.0
1883	Pro-N	22	87	9	19	3	0	0	15	2	10	.218	.236	.253	47	-5	-6	5				3	P/O	0.0
1884	Pro-N	41	168	24	50	9	0	1	19	11	17	.298	.341	.369	126	5	5	22				0	PO/1	0.0
	StL-U	45	171	31	54	14	2	1		10		.316	.354	.439	161	12	11	27	0			4	PO/1	0.0
1885	StL-N	71	267	27	55	7	1	0	24	12	33	.206	.240	.240	59	-13	-10	16				-1	OP	-0.6
1886	StL-N	17	64	4	16	2	0	0	7	3	10	.250	.284	.281	77	-2	-1	5	0			1	P/OS	0.0
1887	Cle-a	36	133	22	30	4	4	0		21		.226	.331	.316	85	-2	-2	18	11			-4	10/PS3	-0.4
Total	6	233	894	117	224	39	7	2	65	59	71	.251	.297	.317	95	-7	-4	93	11			2	P/O1S3	-1.0

■ DAN SWEENEY
Sweeney, Daniel J. b: 1/28/1868, Philadelphia, Pa. d: 7/13/13, Louisville, Ky.   5'5", 160 lbs.   Deb: 4/18/1895

YEAR	TM/L	G	AB	R	H	2B	3B	HR	RBI	BB	SO	AVG	OBP	SLG	PRO+	BR	/A	RC	SB	CS	SBR	FR	POS	TPR
1895	Lou-N	22	90	18	24	5	0	1	16	17	2	.267	.389	.356	101	0	1	14	2			-4	O	-0.3

■ JEFF SWEENEY
Sweeney, Edward Francis "Ed" b: 7/19/1888, Chicago, Ill. d: 7/4/47, Chicago, Ill.   BR/TR, 6'1", 200 lbs.   Deb: 5/16/08

YEAR	TM/L	G	AB	R	H	2B	3B	HR	RBI	BB	SO	AVG	OBP	SLG	PRO+	BR	/A	RC	SB	CS	SBR	FR	POS	TPR
1908	NY-A	32	82	4	12	2	0	0	2	5		.146	.195	.171	20	-7	-7	3	0			0	C/1O	-0.4
1909	NY-A	67	176	19	47	3	0	0	21	16		.267	.328	.284	93	-1	-1	18	3			3	C/1	0.8
1910	NY-A	78	215	25	43	4	4	0	13	17		.200	.271	.256	62	-9	-10	18	12			6	C	0.4
1911	NY-A	83	229	17	53	6	5	0	18	14		.231	.299	.301	63	-10	-12	24	8			-4	C	-0.5
1912	NY-A	110	351	37	94	12	1	0	30	27		.268	.325	.308	77	-8	-11	37	6			0	*C	0.0
1913	NY-A	117	351	35	93	10	2	2	40	37	41	.265	.348	.322	96	-0	-1	42	11			9	*C/1O	1.8
1914	NY-A	87	258	25	55	8	1	1	22	35	30	.213	.316	.264	75	-7	-7	26	19	6	2	1	C	0.2
1915	NY-A	53	137	12	26	2	0	0	5	25	12	.190	.319	.204	57	-6	-6	11	3	3	-1	-6	C	-0.8
1919	Pit-N	17	42	0	4	1	0	0	0	5	6	.095	.191	.119	-5	-5	-5	1	1			-3	C	-0.7
Total	9	644	1841	174	427	48	13	3	151	181	89	.232	.310	.277	73	-53	-60	180	63	9		8	C/1O	0.8

■ HANK SWEENEY
Sweeney, Henry Leon b: 12/28/15, Franklin, Tenn. d: 5/6/80, Columbia, Tenn.   BL/TL, 6', 185 lbs.   Deb: 10/01/44

YEAR	TM/L	G	AB	R	H	2B	3B	HR	RBI	BB	SO	AVG	OBP	SLG	PRO+	BR	/A	RC	SB	CS	SBR	FR	POS	TPR
1944	Pit-N	1	2	0	0	0	0	0	0	0	1	.000	.000	.000	-96	-1	-1	0				0	/1	0.0

■ JERRY SWEENEY
Sweeney, Jeremiah H. b: 1860, Boston, Mass. d: 8/25/1891, Boston, Mass.   5'9.5", 157 lbs.   Deb: 8/22/1884

YEAR	TM/L	G	AB	R	H	2B	3B	HR	RBI	BB	SO	AVG	OBP	SLG	PRO+	BR	/A	RC	SB	CS	SBR	FR	POS	TPR
1884	KC-U	31	129	16	34	3	0	0		4		.264	.286	.287	108	-1	2	11	0			3	1	0.3

■ ROONEY SWEENEY
Sweeney, John J. b: 1860,   d: 6/1/1889, New York, N.Y.   5'8", 155 lbs.   Deb: 7/25/1883

YEAR	TM/L	G	AB	R	H	2B	3B	HR	RBI	BB	SO	AVG	OBP	SLG	PRO+	BR	/A	RC	SB	CS	SBR	FR	POS	TPR
1883	Bal-a	25	101	13	21	5	2	0		4		.208	.238	.297	69	-3	-4	7				3	C/O	0.1
1884	Bal-U	48	186	37	42	7	1	0		15		.226	.284	.274	81	-2	-5	15	0			-10	CO3	-1.0
1885	StL-N	3	11	1	1	0	0	0	0	0	4	.091	.091	.091	-44	-2	-2	0				0	/OC	0.0
Total	3	76	298	51	64	12	3	0	0	19	4	.215	.262	.275	73	-6	-10	22				-7	/CO3	-0.9

■ PETE SWEENEY
Sweeney, Peter Jay b: 12/31/1863, California d: 8/22/01, San Francisco, Cal   BR/TR,   Deb: 9/28/1888

YEAR	TM/L	G	AB	R	H	2B	3B	HR	RBI	BB	SO	AVG	OBP	SLG	PRO+	BR	/A	RC	SB	CS	SBR	FR	POS	TPR
1888	Was-N	11	44	3	8	0	0	0	5	0	4	.182	.182	.227	33	-3	-3	2	0			-0	/3O	-0.2
1889	Was-N	49	193	13	44	7	3	1	23	11	26	.228	.284	.311	72	-9	-7	20	8			-11	3/2O	-1.1
	StL-a	9	38	8	14	2	0	0	8	1	5	.368	.415	.421	125	2	1	8	2			-2	/3O	0.0
1890	StL-a	49	190	23	34	3	2	0		17		.179	.271	.216	40	-12	-17	14	8			-5	23/1O	-1.8
	Lou-a	2	7	1	1	1	0	0		1		.143	.250	.286	61	-0	-0	1				-1	/S	0.0
	Phi-a	14	49	5	8	1	1	0		7		.163	.281	.224	52	-3	-3	3	0			-6	/2O3	-0.6
	Yr	65	246	29	43	5	3	0		25		.175	.272	.220	43	-15	-19	18	9			-12		-2.4
Total	3	134	521	53	109	14	7	1	36	37	35	.209	.280	.269	59	-25	-28	47	19			-25	/3201S	-3.7

■ BILL SWEENEY
Sweeney, William John b: 3/6/1886, Covington, Ky. d: 5/26/48, Cambridge, Mass.   BR/TR, 5'11", 175 lbs.   Deb: 6/14/07

YEAR	TM/L	G	AB	R	H	2B	3B	HR	RBI	BB	SO	AVG	OBP	SLG	PRO+	BR	/A	RC	SB	CS	SBR	FR	POS	TPR
1907	Chi-N	3	10	1	1	0	0	0	1	1		.100	.182	.100	-10	-1	-1	0				-4	/S	-0.5
	Bos-N	58	191	24	50	2	0	0	18	15		.262	.316	.272	87	-3	-3	19	8			0	3SO/21	-0.1
	Yr	61	201	25	51	2	0	0	19	16		.254	.309	.264	81	-4	-4	20	9			-3		-0.6
1908	Bos-N	127	418	44	102	15	3	0	40	45		.244	.317	.294	99	0	1	45	17			12	*3/S2	1.8
1909	Bos-N	138	493	44	120	19	3	0	36	37		.243	.296	.300	81	-9	-12	50	25			7	*3S	-0.1
1910	Bos-N	150	499	43	133	22	4	5	46	61	28	.267	.349	.357	101	4	1	71	25			-1	*S31	0.4

YEAR	TM/L	G	AB	R	H	2B	3B	HR	RBI	BB	SO	AVG	OBP	SLG	PRO+	BR	/A	RC	SB	CS	SBR	FR	POS	TPR
1911	Bos-N	137	523	92	164	33	6	3	63	77	26	.314	.404	.417	120	23	17	101	33			11	*2	2.5
1912	Bos-N	153	593	84	204	31	13	1	100	68	34	.344	.416	.445	133	31	30	123	27			27	*2	4.9
1913	Bos-N	139	502	65	129	17	6	0	47	66	50	.257	.347	.315	88	-4	-6	59	18			1	*2	-0.8
1914	Chi-N	134	463	45	101	14	5	1	38	53	15	.218	.298	.276	71	-16	-15	44	18			15	*2	-0.1
Total	8	1039	3692	442	1004	153	40	11	389	423	153	.272	.349	.344	101	25	12	513	172			68	23S/10	8.0

■ BILL SWEENEY

Sweeney, William Joseph b: 12/29/04, Cleveland, Ohio d: 4/18/57, San Diego, Cal. BR/TR, 5'11", 180 lbs. Deb: 4/13/28

YEAR	TM/L	G	AB	R	H	2B	3B	HR	RBI	BB	SO	AVG	OBP	SLG	PRO+	BR	/A	RC	SB	CS	SBR	FR	POS	TPR
1928	Det-A	89	309	47	78	15	5	0	19	15	28	.252	.287	.333	62	-17	-18	28	12	9	-2	4	1/O	-1.9
1930	Bos-A	88	243	32	75	13	0	4	30	9	15	.309	.333	.412	91	-5	-4	32	5	3	-0	-0	1/3	-0.9
1931	Bos-A	131	498	48	147	30	3	1	58	20	30	.295	.322	.373	87	-13	-10	56	5	12	-6	10	*1	-1.5
Total	3	308	1050	127	300	58	8	5	107	44	73	.286	.314	.370	80	-36	-31	117	22	24	-8	13	1/O3	-4.3

■ RICK SWEET

Sweet, Ricky Joe b: 9/7/52, Longview, Wash. BB/TR, 6'1", 200 lbs. Deb: 4/08/78 C

YEAR	TM/L	G	AB	R	H	2B	3B	HR	RBI	BB	SO	AVG	OBP	SLG	PRO+	BR	/A	RC	SB	CS	SBR	FR	POS	TPR
1978	SD-N	88	226	15	50	8	0	1	11	27	22	.221	.307	.270	68	-11	-9	19	1	4	-2	3	C	-0.5
1982	NY-N	3	3	0	1	0	0	0	0	0	1	.333	.333	.333	88	-0	-0	0	0	0	0	0	/H	0.0
	Sea-A	88	258	29	66	6	1	4	24	20	24	.256	.314	.333	76	-8	-8	29	3	0	1	-6	C	-0.8
1983	Sea-A	93	249	18	55	9	0	1	22	13	26	.221	.260	.269	44	-18	-19	15	2	2	-1	-3	C	-1.8
Total	3	272	736	62	172	23	1	6	57	60	73	.234	.294	.292	63	-37	-37	63	6	6	-2	-5	C	-3.1

■ HAM SWEIGERT

Sweigert, Hampton Deb: 10/12/1890

YEAR	TM/L	G	AB	R	H	2B	3B	HR	RBI	BB	SO	AVG	OBP	SLG	PRO+	BR	/A	RC	SB	CS	SBR	FR	POS	TPR
1890	Phi-a	1	1	0	0	0	0	0	0	0	1	.000	.500	.000	53	0	0	1	1			1	/O	0.1

■ AUGIE SWENTOR

Swentor, August William b: 11/21/1899, Seymour, Conn. d: 11/10/69, Waterbury, Conn. BR/TR, 6', 185 lbs. Deb: 9/12/22

YEAR	TM/L	G	AB	R	H	2B	3B	HR	RBI	BB	SO	AVG	OBP	SLG	PRO+	BR	/A	RC	SB	CS	SBR	FR	POS	TPR
1922	Chi-A	1	1	0	0	0	0	0	0	0	1	.000	.000	.000	-99	-0	-0	0	0	0	0	0	H	0.0

■ STEVE SWETONIC

Swetonic, Stephen Albert b: 8/13/03, Mt.Pleasant, Pa. d: 4/22/74, Canonsburg, Pa. BR/TR, 5'11", 185 lbs. Deb: 4/17/29

YEAR	TM/L	G	AB	R	H	2B	3B	HR	RBI	BB	SO	AVG	OBP	SLG	PRO+	BR	/A	RC	SB	CS	SBR	FR	POS	TPR
1929	Pit-N	42	48	11	13	3	1	0	2	2	6	.271	.314	.375	68	-2	-3	6	0			2	P	0.0
1930	Pit-N	23	36	2	4	2	0	0	2	1	5	.111	.135	.167	-27	-8	-8	1	0			-1	P	0.0
1931	Pit-N	14	7	0	1	0	0	0		1	3	.143	.250	.143	8	-1	-1	0	0			-0	P	0.0
1932	Pit-N	24	54	1	5	1	0	0	2	2	7	.093	.125	.111	-37	-10	-10	1	0			-1	P	0.0
1933	Pit-N	31	55	3	11	0	2	0	4	1	7	.200	.214	.273	38	-4	-4	3	0			-1	P	0.0
1935	Pit-N	1	0	1	0	0	0	0	0	0	0	—	—	—		0	0	0	0			0	R	0.0
Total	6	135	200	18	34	6	3	0	10	7	28	.170	.202	.230	13	-25	-26	11	0			-1	P	0.0

■ POP SWETT

Swett, William E. b: 4/16/1870, San Francisco, Cal d: 11/22/37, San Francisco, Cal Deb: 5/03/1890

YEAR	TM/L	G	AB	R	H	2B	3B	HR	RBI	BB	SO	AVG	OBP	SLG	PRO+	BR	/A	RC	SB	CS	SBR	FR	POS	TPR
1890	Bos-P	37	94	16	18	4	3	1	12	16	26	.191	.321	.330	71	-3	-4	12	4			-8	C/O	-0.8

■ BOB SWIFT

Swift, Robert Virgil b: 3/6/15, Salina, Kan. d: 10/17/66, Detroit, Mich. BR/TR, 5'11.5", 180 lbs. Deb: 4/16/40 MC

YEAR	TM/L	G	AB	R	H	2B	3B	HR	RBI	BB	SO	AVG	OBP	SLG	PRO+	BR	/A	RC	SB	CS	SBR	FR	POS	TPR
1940	StL-A	130	398	37	97	20	1	0	39	28	39	.244	.295	.299	53	-27	-28	36	1	0	0	-20	*C	-3.6
1941	StL-A	63	170	13	44	7	0	0	21	22	11	.259	.344	.300	69	-6	-7	19	2	0	1	-4	C	-0.6
1942	StL-A	29	76	3	15	4	0	1	8	3	5	.197	.228	.289	44	-6	-6	5	0	2	-1	-1	C	-0.4
	Phi-A	60	192	9	44	3	0	0	15	13	17	.229	.278	.245	48	-13	-13	13	1	2	-1	2	C	-0.4
	Yr	89	268	12	59	7	0	1	23	16	22	.220	.264	.257	47	-19	-19	18	1	4	-2	1		-0.8
1943	Phi-A	77	224	16	43	5	1	1	11	35	16	.192	.301	.237	58	-11	-11	17	0	0	0	-3	C	-1.0
1944	Det-A	80	247	15	63	11	1	1	19	27	27	.255	.331	.320	82	-4	-6	22	2	0	1	1	C	0.1
1945	*Det-A	95	279	19	65	5	0	1	24	26	22	.233	.298	.251	56	-14	-16	22	1	0	0	1	C	-0.6
1946	Det-A	42	107	13	25	2	0	2	10	14	7	.234	.322	.308	72	-3	-4	11	0	0	0	-4	C	-0.6
1947	Det-A	97	279	23	70	11	0	1	21	33	16	.251	.350	.301	74	-8	-9	29	2	2	-1	0	C	-0.1
1948	Det-A	113	292	23	65	6	0	4	33	51	29	.223	.338	.284	65	-13	-14	32	1	0	0	7	*C	0.1
1949	Det-A	74	189	16	45	6	1	0	18	26	20	.238	.330	.302	68	-9	-9	21	0	0	0	1	C	-0.3
1950	Det-A	67	132	14	30	4	0	2	9	25	6	.227	.350	.303	66	-6	-6	15	0	0	0	8	C	0.4
1951	Det-A	44	104	8	20	0	0	0	5	12	10	.192	.276	.192	28	-10	-10	7	0	0	0	2	C	-0.4
1952	Det-A	28	58	3	8	1	0	0	4	7	7	.138	.242	.155	12	-7	-7	2	0	0	0	6	C	0.0
1953	Det-A	2	3	0	1	1	0	0	0	1	2	.333	.500	.667	245	1	1	2	0	0	0	1	/C	0.2
Total	14	1001	2750	212	635	86	3	14	238	324	233	.231	.313	.280	61	-135	-144	256	10	6	-1	-4	C	-7.2

■ JOSH SWINDELL

Swindell, Joshua Ernest b: 7/5/1883, Rose Hill, Kan. d: 3/19/69, Fruita, Colo. TR, 6', 180 lbs. Deb: 9/16/11

YEAR	TM/L	G	AB	R	H	2B	3B	HR	RBI	BB	SO	AVG	OBP	SLG	PRO+	BR	/A	RC	SB	CS	SBR	FR	POS	TPR
1911	Cle-A	4	4	0	1	0	0	0	0	0		.250	.250	.250	39	-0	-0	0	0			-0	/P	0.0
1913	Cle-A	1	0	0	0	0	0	0	0	0	0	—	—	—	—	0	0	0	0			0	H	0.0
Total	2	5	4	0	1	0	0	0	0	0	0	.250	.250	.250	39	-0	-0	0	0			-0	/P	0.0

■ CHARLIE SWINDELLS

Swindells, Charles Jay "Swin" b: 10/26/1878, Rockford, Ill. d: 7/22/40, Portland, Ore. TR, 5'11.5", 180 lbs. Deb: 9/07/04

YEAR	TM/L	G	AB	R	H	2B	3B	HR	RBI	BB	SO	AVG	OBP	SLG	PRO+	BR	/A	RC	SB	CS	SBR	FR	POS	TPR
1904	StL-N	3	8	0	1	0	0	0	0	0		.125	.125	.125	-23	-1	-1	0	0			-0	/C	0.0

■ STEVE SWISHER

Swisher, Steven Eugene b: 8/9/51, Parkersburg, W.Va. BR/TR, 6'2", 205 lbs. Deb: 6/14/74

YEAR	TM/L	G	AB	R	H	2B	3B	HR	RBI	BB	SO	AVG	OBP	SLG	PRO+	BR	/A	RC	SB	CS	SBR	FR	POS	TPR
1974	Chi-N	90	280	21	60	5	0	5	27	37	63	.214	.310	.286	65	-11	-13	25	0	3	-2	-1	C	-1.2
1975	Chi-N	93	254	20	54	16	2	1	22	30	57	.213	.306	.303	66	-10	-12	22	1	0	0	-8	C	-1.6
1976	Chi-N	109	377	25	89	13	3	5	42	20	82	.236	.278	.326	65	-15	-19	33	2	1	0	-3	*C	-1.7
1977	Chi-N	74	205	21	39	7	0	5	15	9	47	.190	.231	.298	37	-18	-20	14	0	0	0	10	C	-2.5
1978	StL-N	45	115	11	32	5	1	1	10	8	14	.278	.331	.365	96	-1	-1	13	1	0	0	6	C	0.7
1979	StL-N	38	73	4	11	1	1	1	3	6	17	.151	.215	.233	22	-8	-8	4	0	0	0	1	C	-0.6
1980	StL-N	18	24	2	6	1	0	0	2	1	7	.250	.280	.292	58	-1	-1	1	0	0	0	0	/C	0.0
1981	SD-N	16	28	2	4	0	0	0	0	2	11	.143	.200	.143	-2	-4	-3	1	0	0	0	-0	C	-0.3
1982	SD-N	26	58	2	10	1	0	2	3	5	24	.172	.238	.293	50	-4	-4	4	0	0	0	1	C	-0.1
Total	9	509	1414	108	305	49	7	20	124	118	322	.216	.281	.303	59	-72	-81	117	4	4	-1	-7	C	-7.3

■ RON SWOBODA

Swoboda, Ronald Alan "Rocky" b: 6/30/44, Baltimore, Md. BR/TR, 6'2", 195 lbs. Deb: 4/12/65

YEAR	TM/L	G	AB	R	H	2B	3B	HR	RBI	BB	SO	AVG	OBP	SLG	PRO+	BR	/A	RC	SB	CS	SBR	FR	POS	TPR
1965	NY-N	135	399	52	91	15	3	19	50	33	102	.228	.292	.424	102	-2	-0	47	2	3	-1	-2	*O	-0.6
1966	NY-N	112	342	34	76	9	4	8	50	31	76	.222	.296	.342	79	-11	-10	34	4	2	0	-4	O	-1.6
1967	NY-N	134	449	47	126	17	3	13	53	41	96	.281	.342	.419	119	10	10	65	3	1	0	3	*O1	0.8
1968	NY-N	132	450	46	109	14	6	11	59	52	113	.242	.326	.373	109	6	6	55	8	1	2	-2	*O	0.6
1969	*NY-N	109	327	38	77	10	2	9	52	43	90	.235	.328	.361	91	-3	-4	39	1	1	-0	-2	O	-1.0
1970	NY-N	115	245	29	57	8	2	9	40	40	72	.233	.343	.392	96	-1	-1	33	2	4	-2	-14	*O	-2.0
1971	Mon-N	39	75	7	19	4	3	0	6	11	16	.253	.364	.387	112	2	2	10	0	1	-1	2	O	0.2
	NY-A	54	138	17	36	2	1	2	20	27	35	.261	.393	.333	114	3	4	20	0	0	0	-2	O	0.0
1972	NY-A	63	113	9	28	8	0	1	12	17	29	.248	.346	.345	110	1	2	14	0	1	0	0	O/1	0.0
1973	NY-A	35	43	6	5	0	0	1	2	4	18	.116	.191	.186	7	-5	-5	2	0	0	0	0	O/D	-0.3
Total	9	928	2581	285	624	87	24	73	344	299	647	.242	.325	.379	101	0	4	320	20	14	-2	-13	O/1D	-3.9

■ LOU SYLVESTER

Sylvester, Louis J. b: 2/14/1855, Springfield, Ill. BR/TR, 5'3", 165 lbs. Deb: 4/18/1884

YEAR	TM/L	G	AB	R	H	2B	3B	HR	RBI	BB	SO	AVG	OBP	SLG	PRO+	BR	/A	RC	SB	CS	SBR	FR	POS	TPR
1884	Cin-U	82	333	67	89	13	8	2	18			.267	.305	.372	119	10	5	39	0			0	*O/PS	0.4
1886	Lou-a	45	154	41	35	5	3	0	29			.227	.350	.299	100	2	1	18	3			0	O	0.0
	Cin-a	17	55	10	10	0	0	3	7			.182	.286	.345	96	-0	-0	6	2			1	O	0.0
	Yr	62	209	51	45	5	3	3	36			.215	.333	.311	99	2	1	24	5			1		0.0
1887	StL-a	29	112	20	25	4	3	1	13			.223	.310	.339	75	-2	-5	16	13			2	O/2	-0.2
Total	3	173	654	138	159	22	14	6	67			.243	.315	.347	104	10	1	79	18			4	O/PS2	0.2

YEAR	TM/L	G	AB	R	H	2B	3B	HR	RBI	BB	SO	AVG	OBP	SLG	PRO+	BR	/A	RC	SB	CS	SBR	FR	POS	TPR

■ JOE SZEKELY Szekely, Joseph b: 2/2/25, Cleveland, Ohio BR/TR, 5'11", 180 lbs. Deb: 9/13/53

1953	Cin-N	5	13	0	1	0	0	0	0	0	3	.077	.077	.077	-59	-3	-3	0	0	0	0	1	/O	-0.1

■ KEN SZOTKIEWICZ Szotkiewicz, Kenneth John b: 2/25/47, Wilmington, Del. BL/TR, 6', 165 lbs. Deb: 4/07/70

1970	Det-A	47	84	9	9	1	0	3	9	12	29	.107	.219	.226	23	-9	-9	5	0	0	0	9	S	0.4

■ JERRY TABB Tabb, Jerry Lynn b: 3/17/52, Altus, Okla. BL/TR, 6'2", 195 lbs. Deb: 9/08/76

1976	Chi-N	11	24	2	7	0	0	0	0	3	2	.292	.370	.292	82	-0	-0	3	0	0	0	-0	/1	0.0
1977	Oak-A	51	144	8	32	3	0	6	19	10	26	.222	.273	.368	74	-6	-5	13	0	1	-1	-2	1/D	-0.9
1978	Oak-A	12	9	0	1	0	0	0	1	2	5	.111	.273	.111	12	-1	-1	0	0	0	0	0	/1D	0.0
Total	3	74	177	10	40	3	0	6	20	15	33	.226	.286	.345	72	-7	-7	16	0	1	-1	-2	/1D	-0.9

■ PAT TABLER Tabler, Patrick Sean b: 2/2/58, Hamilton, Ohio BR/TR, 6'3", 175 lbs. Deb: 8/21/81

1981	Chi-N	35	101	11	19	3	1	1	5	13	26	.188	.281	.267	54	-6	-6	7	0	1	-1	1	2	-0.3
1982	Chi-N	25	85	9	20	4	2	1	7	6	20	.235	.293	.365	81	-2	-2	9	0	0	0	-5	3	-0.7
1983	Cle-A	124	430	56	125	23	5	6	65	56	63	.291	.374	.409	111	11	8	63	2	4	-2	-6	O3/2D	0.0
1984	Cle-A	144	473	66	137	21	3	10	68	47	62	.290	.358	.410	110	8	7	68	3	1	0	-11	103/2D	-0.8
1985	Cle-A	117	404	47	111	18	3	5	59	27	55	.275	.323	.371	90	-6	-5	43	0	6	-4	4	1D/32	-1.0
1986	Cle-A	130	473	61	154	29	2	6	48	29	75	.326	.368	.433	119	11	12	74	3	1	0	3	*1D	0.8
1987	Cle-A	151	553	66	170	34	3	11	86	51	84	.307	.372	.439	113	12	12	93	5	2	0	6	1D	0.9
1988	Cle-A	41	143	16	32	5	1	1	17	23	27	.224	.335	.294	76	-3	-4	15	1	0	0	0	D1	-0.3
	KC-A	89	301	37	93	17	2	1	49	23	41	.309	.362	.389	109	4	4	42	2	3	-1	-4	DO/13	-0.1
	Yr	130	444	53	125	22	3	2	66	46	68	.282	.353	.358	98	1	0	57	3	3	-1	-3		-0.4
1989	KC-A	123	390	36	101	11	1	2	42	37	42	.259	.326	.308	80	-10	-9	39	0	0	0	0	OD1/23	-1.0
1990	KC-A	75	195	12	53	14	0	1	19	20	21	.272	.343	.359	99	-1	-0	22	0	2	-1	1	OD/31	0.0
	NY-N	17	43	6	12	1	1	1	0	3	8	.279	.340	.419	110	0	1	6	0	0	0	1	O	0.1
Total	10	1071	3591	423	1027	180	24	46	475	335	524	.286	.351	.388	102	20	17	482	16	20	-7	-10	10D/32	-2.4

■ GREG TABOR Tabor, Gregory Steven b: 5/21/61, Castro Valley, Cal. BR/TR, 6' ", 165 lbs. Deb: 9/10/87

1987	Tex-A	9	9	4	1	1	0	0	1	0	4	.111	.111	.222	-15	-1	-1	0	0	0	0	4	/2D	0.2

■ JIM TABOR Tabor, James Reubin "Rawhide" b: 11/5/16, New Hope, Ala. d: 8/22/53, Sacramento, Cal. BR/TR, 6'2", 175 lbs. Deb: 8/02/38

1938	Bos-A	19	57	8	18	3	2	1	8	1	6	.316	.328	.491	98	-0	-1	8	0	1	-1	1	3/S	0.0
1939	Bos-A	149	577	76	167	33	8	14	95	40	54	.289	.337	.447	95	-3	-6	82	16	10	-1	7	*3	-0.3
1940	Bos-A	120	459	73	131	28	6	21	81	42	58	.285	.345	.510	114	11	8	81	14	10	-2	5	*3	1.7
1941	Bos-A	126	498	65	139	29	3	16	101	36	48	.279	.328	.446	100	-0	-2	69	17	9	-0	2	*3	0.6
1942	Bos-A	139	508	56	128	18	2	12	75	37	47	.252	.303	.366	85	-10	-12	53	6	13	-6	-8	*3	-2.5
1943	Bos-A	137	537	57	130	26	3	13	85	43	54	.242	.299	.374	95	-4	-5	59	7	7	-2	-8	*3/O	-1.4
1944	Bos-A	116	438	58	125	25	3	13	72	31	38	.285	.334	.445	123	10	11	63	4	4	-1	3	*3	1.3
1946	Phi-N	124	463	53	124	15	2	10	50	36	51	.268	.322	.374	100	-3	-1	56	3			-3	*3	-0.3
1947	Phi-N	75	251	27	59	14	0	4	31	20	21	.235	.297	.339	71	-12	-11	25	2			-17	3	-2.9
Total	9	1005	3788	473	1021	191	29	104	598	286	377	.270	.322	.418	99	-12	-19	496	69	54		-18	3/OS	-3.8

■ DOUG TAITT Taitt, Douglas John "Poco" b: 8/3/02, Bay City, Mich. d: 12/12/70, Portland, Ore. BL/TR, 6', 176 lbs. Deb: 4/10/28

1928	Bos-A	143	482	51	144	28	14	3	61	36	32	.299	.350	.434	107	2	4	74	13	6	0	5	*O/P	0.1
1929	Bos-A	26	65	6	18	4	0	0	6	8	5	.277	.365	.338	84	-1	-1	8	0	1	-1	0	O	-0.2
	Chi-A	47	124	11	21	7	0	0	12	8	13	.169	.220	.226	15	-16	-16	7	0	0	0	0	O	-1.5
	Yr	73	189	17	39	11	0	0	18	16	18	.206	.272	.265	39	-17	-17	14	0	1	-1	0		-1.7
1931	Phi-N	38	151	13	34	4	2	1	15	4	14	.225	.245	.298	42	-12	-13	11	0			3	O	-1.2
1932	Phi-N	4	2	0	0	0	0	0	1	2	0	.000	.500	.000	43	0	0	0	0			0	H	0.0
Total	4	258	824	81	217	43	16	4	95	58	64	.263	.314	.369	79	-27	-26	100	13	7		7	O/P	-2.8

■ BOB TALBOT Talbot, Robert Dale b: 6/6/27, Visalia, Cal. BR/TR, 6', 170 lbs. Deb: 9/16/53

1953	Chi-N	8	30	5	10	0	1	0	0	0	4	.333	.333	.400	88	-0	-1	3	1	0	0	3	/O	0.2
1954	Chi-N	114	403	45	97	15	4	1	19	16	25	.241	.275	.305	50	-29	-30	32	3	6	-3	-10	*O	-4.5
Total	2	122	433	50	107	15	5	1	19	16	29	.247	.279	.312	53	-30	-30	36	4	6	-2	-7	O	-4.3

■ TIM TALTON Talton, Marion Lee b: 1/14/39, Pikeville, N.C. BL/TR, 6'3", 200 lbs. Deb: 7/08/66

1966	KC-A	37	53	8	18	3	1	2	6	1	5	.340	.364	.547	163	4	4	10	0	1	-1	-1	C/1	0.3
1967	KC-A	46	59	7	15	3	1	0	5	7	13	.254	.333	.339	102	0	0	6	0	0	0	-5	C/1	-0.3
Total	2	83	112	15	33	6	2	2	11	8	18	.295	.347	.438	131	4	4	16	0	1	-1	-6	/C1	0.0

■ JOHN TAMARGO Tamargo, John Felix b: 11/7/51, Tampa, Fla. BB/TR, 5'10", 170 lbs. Deb: 9/03/76

1976	StL-N	10	10	2	3	0	0	0	1	3	0	.300	.462	.300	118	1	1	2	0	0	0	-1	/C	0.0
1977	StL-N	4	4	0	0	0	0	0	0	0	2	.000	.000	.000	-99	-1	-1	0	0	0	0	0	/C	0.0
1978	StL-N	6	6	0	0	0	0	0	0	0	2	.000	.000	.000	-99	-2	-2	0	0	0	0	0	/C	-0.1
	SF-N	36	92	6	22	4	1	1	8	18	7	.239	.364	.337	101	0	1	12	1	1	-0	-3	C	-0.1
	Yr	42	98	6	22	4	1	1	8	18	9	.224	.345	.316	89	-1	-1	12	1	1	-0	-3		-0.2
1979	SF-N	30	60	7	12	3	0	2	6	4	8	.200	.250	.350	66	-3	-3	6	0	0	0	-6	C	-0.8
	Mon-N	12	21	0	8	2	0	0	5	3	3	.381	.458	.476	157	2	2	5	0	0	0	-1	/C	0.1
	Yr	42	81	7	20	5	0	2	11	7	11	.247	.307	.383	92	-2	-1	10	0	0	0	-7		-0.7
1980	Mon-N	37	51	4	14	3	0	1	13	6	5	.275	.351	.392	107	1	1	8	0	0	0	-2	C	0.0
Total	5	135	244	19	59	12	1	4	33	34	27	.242	.335	.348	92	-3	-2	32	1	1	-0	-12	/C	-0.9

■ LEO TANKERSLEY Tankersley, Lawrence William b: 6/8/01, Terrell, Tex. d: 9/18/80, Dallas, Tex. BR/TR, 6', 176 lbs. Deb: 7/02/25

1925	Chi-A	1	3	0	0	0	0	0	0	0	0	.000	.000	.000	-99	-1	-1	0	0	0	0	-1	/C	0.0

■ JESSE TANNEHILL Tannehill, Jesse Niles "Powder" b: 7/14/1874, Dayton, Ky. d: 9/22/56, Dayton, Ky. BB/TL, 5'8", 150 lbs. Deb: 6/17/1894 C

1894	Cin-N	5	11	0	0	0	0	0	1	1	2	.000	.083	.000	-75	-3	-3	0	0			-1	/P	0.0
1897	Pit-N	56	184	22	49	8	2	0	22	18		.266	.338	.332	82	-5	-4	23	4			7	OP	0.4
1898	Pit-N	60	152	25	44	9	3	1	17	7		.289	.321	.408	113	1	2	22	4			3	P/O	0.0
1899	Pit-N	47	132	17	34	5	3	0	10	8		.258	.310	.341	81	-4	-3	15	2			3	P/O	0.0
1900	Pit-N	34	110	19	37	7	0	0	17	5		.336	.365	.400	113	2	2	17	2			2	P/O	0.0
1901	Pit-N	42	135	19	33	3	3	1	12	6		.244	.277	.333	76	-4	-4	13	0			-3	PO	0.0
1902	Pit-N	44	148	27	43	6	1	1	17	12		.291	.352	.365	119	4	4	21	3			-3	PO	0.0
1903	NY-A	40	111	18	26	6	2	1	13	8		.234	.286	.351	87	-1	-2	12	1			1	P/O	0.0
1904	Bos-A	45	122	14	24	2	6	0	6	9		.197	.252	.311	75	-3	-4	10	1			3	P/O	0.0
1905	Bos-A	37	93	11	21	2	0	1	12	16		.226	.339	.280	98	1	1	10	1			3	P	0.0
1906	Bos-A	31	79	12	22	2	2	0	4	6		.278	.329	.354	116	1	1	10	1			0	P	0.0
1907	Bos-A	21	51	2	10	3	1	0	6	2		.196	.226	.294	68	-2	-2	4	0			1	P	0.0
1908	Bos-A	1	2	0	1	0	0	0	0	0		.500	.500	.500	223	0	0	0	0			0	/P	0.0
	Was-A	26	43	1	11	1	0	0	3	2		.256	.289	.279	95	-1	-0	3	0			2	P	0.3
	Yr	27	45	1	12	1	0	0	3	2		.267	.298	.289	101	-0	-0	4	0			2		0.3
1909	Was-A	16	36	2	6	1	0	0	1	5		.167	.286	.194	55	-2	-2	2	0			0	/OP	-0.1
1911	Cin-N	1	1	0	0	0	0	0	0	0	1	.000	.000	.000	-99	-0	-0	0	0			0	/P	0.0

YEAR	TM/L	G	AB	R	H	2B	3B	HR	RBI	BB	SO	AVG	OBP	SLG	PRO+	BR	/A	RC	SB	CS	SBR	FR	POS	TPR
Total	15	506	1410	189	361	55	23	5	141	105	3	.256	.311	.338	91	-14	-15	161	19			18	P/O	0.6

■ **LEE TANNEHILL**　　Tannehill, Lee Ford　b: 10/26/1880, Dayton, Ky.　d: 2/16/38, Live Oak, Fla.　BR/TR, 5'11", 170 lbs.　Deb: 4/22/03

YEAR	TM/L	G	AB	R	H	2B	3B	HR	RBI	BB	SO	AVG	OBP	SLG	PRO+	BR	/A	RC	SB	CS	SBR	FR	POS	TPR
1903	Chi-A	138	503	48	113	14	3	2	50	25		.225	.261	.276	66	-22	-19	42	10			-4	*S	-1.7
1904	Chi-A	153	547	50	125	31	5	0	61	20		.229	.256	.303	81	-14	-12	49	14			28	*3	2.4
1905	Chi-A	142	480	38	96	17	2	0	39	45		.200	.269	.244	67	-18	-16	37	8			28	*3	1.9
1906	*Chi-A	116	378	26	69	8	3	0	33	31		.183	.244	.220	48	-22	-21	24	7			40	3S	2.8
1907	Chi-A	33	108	9	26	2	0	0	11	8		.241	.293	.259	81	-2	-2	10	3			5	3/S	0.5
1908	Chi-A	141	482	44	104	15	3	0	35	25		.216	.254	.259	70	-16	-15	34	6			18	*3/S	1.3
1909	Chi-A	155	531	39	118	21	5	0	47	31		.222	.269	.281	77	-17	-14	44	12			7	3S	-0.1
1910	Chi-A	67	230	17	51	10	0	1	21	11		.222	.263	.278	73	-9	-7	18	3			3	S1/3	-0.2
1911	Chi-A	141	516	60	131	17	6	0	49	32		.254	.300	.310	73	-21	-19	49	0			43	*S2/31	3.2
1912	Chi-A	4	3	0	0	0	0	0	0	1		.000	.400	.000	18	-0	-0	0	0			-1	/3S	0.0
Total	10	1090	3778	331	833	135	27	3	346	229		.220	.267	.273	70	-141	-126	307	63			166	3S/12	10.1

■ **CHUCK TANNER**　　Tanner, Charles William　b: 7/4/29, New Castle, Pa.　BL/TL, 6', 185 lbs.　Deb: 4/12/55　M

YEAR	TM/L	G	AB	R	H	2B	3B	HR	RBI	BB	SO	AVG	OBP	SLG	PRO+	BR	/A	RC	SB	CS	SBR	FR	POS	TPR
1955	Mil-N	97	243	27	60	9	3	6	27	27	32	.247	.322	.383	91	-5	-3	28	0	0	0	-5	O	-0.8
1956	Mil-N	60	63	6	15	2	0	1	4	10	10	.238	.342	.317	84	-2	-1	7	0	0	0	-2	/O	-0.2
1957	Mil-N	22	69	5	17	3	0	2	6	5	4	.246	.297	.377	86	-2	-1	8	0	0	0	-1	O	-0.3
	Chi-N	95	318	42	91	16	2	7	42	23	20	.286	.338	.415	103	0	1	44	0	2	-1	-11	O	-1.3
	Yr	117	387	47	108	19	2	9	48	28	24	.279	.331	.408	100	-2	-0	51	0	2	-1	-13		-1.6
1958	Chi-N	73	103	10	27	6	0	4	17	9	10	.262	.321	.437	100	-0	-0	14	1	0	0	-2	O	-0.2
1959	Cle-A	14	48	6	12	2	0	1	5	2	9	.250	.280	.354	76	-2	-2	4	0	0	0	-1	O	-0.3
1960	Cle-A	21	25	2	7	1	0	0	4	4	6	.280	.379	.320	94	-0	-0	3	1	0	0	-0	/O	0.0
1961	LA-A	7	8	0	1	0	0	0	0	2	2	.125	.300	.125	16	-1	-1	0	0	0	0	0	/O	0.0
1962	LA-A	7	8	0	1	0	0	0	0	0	0	.125	.125	.125	-34	-1	-1	0	0	0	0	-0	/O	-0.1
Total	8	396	885	98	231	39	5	21	105	82	93	.261	.325	.388	93	-13	-9	109	2	2	-1	-23	O	-3.2

■ **WALTER TAPPAN**　　Tappan, Walter Van Dorn "Tap"　b: 10/8/1890, Carlinville, Ill.　d: 12/19/67, Lynwood, Cal.　BR/TR, 5'8", 158 lbs.　Deb: 4/16/14

YEAR	TM/L	G	AB	R	H	2B	3B	HR	RBI	BB	SO	AVG	OBP	SLG	PRO+	BR	/A	RC	SB	CS	SBR	FR	POS	TPR
1914	KC-F	18	39	1	8	1	0	1	3	1	0	.205	.225	.308	54	-3	-2	3	1			-2	/S32	-0.3

■ **EL TAPPE**　　Tappe, Elvin Walter　b: 5/21/27, Quincy, Ill.　BR/TR, 5'11", 180 lbs.　Deb: 4/24/54　MC

YEAR	TM/L	G	AB	R	H	2B	3B	HR	RBI	BB	SO	AVG	OBP	SLG	PRO+	BR	/A	RC	SB	CS	SBR	FR	POS	TPR
1954	Chi-N	46	119	5	22	3	0	0	4	10	9	.185	.248	.210	21	-14	-14	7	0	0	0	5	C	-0.7
1955	Chi-N	2	0	0	0	0	0	0	0	0	0	—	—	—	—	0	0	0	0	0	0	1	/C	0.1
1956	Chi-N	3	1	0	0	0	0	0	0	1	0	.000	.500	.000	51	0	0	0	0	0	0	0	/C	0.0
1958	Chi-N	17	28	2	6	0	0	0	4	3	1	.214	.290	.214	37	-2	-2	1	0	0	0	-0	C	-0.1
1960	Chi-N	51	103	11	24	7	0	0	3	11	12	.233	.313	.301	70	-4	-4	10	0	1	-1	9	C	0.7
1962	Chi-N	26	53	3	11	0	0	0	6	4	3	.208	.288	.208	34	-5	-5	3	0	0	0	4	CM	0.0
Total	6	145	304	21	63	10	0	0	17	29	25	.207	.283	.240	41	-25	-25	22	0	1	-1	18	C	0.0

■ **TED TAPPE**　　Tappe, Theodore Nash　b: 2/2/31, Seattle, Wash.　BL/TR, 6'3", 185 lbs.　Deb: 9/14/50

YEAR	TM/L	G	AB	R	H	2B	3B	HR	RBI	BB	SO	AVG	OBP	SLG	PRO+	BR	/A	RC	SB	CS	SBR	FR	POS	TPR
1950	Cin-N	7	5	1	1	0	0	1	1	1	1	.200	.333	.800	187	1	1	1				0	H	0.1
1951	Cin-N	4	3	0	1	0	0	0	0	0	0	.333	.333	.333	79	-0	-0	0	0	0	0	0	H	0.0
1955	Chi-N	23	50	12	13	2	0	4	10	11	11	.260	.413	.540	151	4	4	12	0	0	0	-2	O	0.2
Total	3	34	58	13	15	2	0	5	11	12	12	.259	.403	.552	151	5	5	14	0	0		-2	/O	0.3

■ **ARLIE TARBERT**　　Tarbert, Wilbur Arlington　b: 9/10/04, Cleveland, Ohio　d: 11/27/46, Cleveland, Ohio　BR/TR, 6', 160 lbs.　Deb: 6/18/27

YEAR	TM/L	G	AB	R	H	2B	3B	HR	RBI	BB	SO	AVG	OBP	SLG	PRO+	BR	/A	RC	SB	CS	SBR	FR	POS	TPR
1927	Bos-A	33	69	5	13	1	0	0	5	3	12	.188	.253	.203	20	-8	-8	4	0	0	0	-4	O	-1.2
1928	Bos-A	6	17	1	3	1	0	0	2	1	1	.176	.222	.235	21	-2	-2	1	1	0	0	-0	/O	-0.1
Total	2	39	86	6	16	2	0	0	7	4	13	.186	.247	.209	20	-10	-10	5	1	0	0	-4	/O	-1.3

■ **DAN TARTABULL**　　Tartabull, Danilo (Mora)　b: 10/30/62, San Juan, P.R.　BR/TR, 6'1.5", 185 lbs.　Deb: 9/07/84

YEAR	TM/L	G	AB	R	H	2B	3B	HR	RBI	BB	SO	AVG	OBP	SLG	PRO+	BR	/A	RC	SB	CS	SBR	FR	POS	TPR
1984	Sea-A	10	20	3	6	1	0	2	7	2	3	.300	.391	.650	185	2	2	5	0	0	0	2	/S2	0.4
1985	Sea-A	19	61	8	20	7	1	1	7	8	14	.328	.406	.525	152	5	4	14	1	0	0	-3	S/3	0.3
1986	Sea-A	137	511	76	138	25	6	25	96	61	157	.270	.349	.489	124	17	17	85	4	8	-4	-6	*O2/3D	0.7
1987	KC-A	158	582	95	180	27	3	34	101	79	136	.309	.393	.541	141	38	36	124	9	4	0	-11	*O/D	2.0
1988	KC-A	146	507	80	139	38	3	26	102	76	119	.274	.373	.515	145	32	31	99	8	5	-1	-7	*OD	2.1
1989	KC-A	133	441	54	118	22	0	18	62	69	123	.268	.370	.440	128	17	18	74	4	2	0	-7	OD	1.0
1990	KC-A	88	313	41	84	19	0	15	60	36	93	.268	.344	.473	129	10	11	50	1	1	-0	-7	OD	0.4
Total	7	691	2435	357	685	139	13	121	435	331	645	.281	.370	.498	135	121	119	451	27	20	-4	-39	OD/2S3	6.9

■ **JOSE TARTABULL**　　Tartabull, Jose Milages (Guzman)　b: 11/27/38, Cienfuegos, Cuba　BL/TL, 5'11", 165 lbs.　Deb: 4/10/62

YEAR	TM/L	G	AB	R	H	2B	3B	HR	RBI	BB	SO	AVG	OBP	SLG	PRO+	BR	/A	RC	SB	CS	SBR	FR	POS	TPR
1962	KC-A	107	310	49	86	6	5	0	22	20	19	.277	.323	.329	74	-10	-11	36	19	5	3	7	O	-0.3
1963	KC-A	79	242	27	58	8	5	1	19	17	17	.240	.290	.326	69	-9	-10	26	16	1	4	-1	O	-0.9
1964	KC-A	104	100	9	20	2	0	0	3	5	12	.200	.238	.220	28	-10	-10	6	4	0	1	4	O	-0.6
1965	KC-A	68	218	28	68	11	4	1	19	18	20	.312	.364	.413	122	6	6	33	11	5	0	7	O	1.2
1966	KC-A	37	127	13	30	2	3	0	4	11	13	.236	.297	.299	74	-4	-4	13	8	1	2	-0	O	-0.3
	Bos-A	68	195	28	54	7	4	0	11	6	11	.277	.299	.354	79	-4	-6	20	11	3	2	-0	O	-0.6
	Yr	105	322	41	84	9	7	0	15	17	24	.261	.298	.332	77	-8	-10	34	19	4	3	-0		-0.9
1967	*Bos-A	115	247	36	55	1	2	0	10	23	26	.223	.289	.243	54	-12	-14	18	6	6	-2	-5	O	-2.5
1968	Bos-A	72	139	24	39	6	0	0	6	6	11	.281	.310	.324	87	-1	-2	14	2	3	-1	0	O	-0.5
1969	Oak-A	75	266	28	71	11	1	0	11	9	11	.267	.291	.316	73	-11	-10	24	3	4	-2	-1	O	-1.4
1970	Oak-A	24	13	5	3	2	0	0	2	0	2	.231	.231	.385	69	-1	-1	1	1	0	0	1	/O	0.1
Total	9	749	1857	247	484	56	24	2	107	115	136	.261	.304	.320	75	-56	-62	192	81	28	8	13	O	-5.8

■ **LA SCHELLE TARVER**　　Tarver, La Schelle　b: 1/30/59, Modesto, Cal.　BL/TL, 5'11", 165 lbs.　Deb: 7/12/86

YEAR	TM/L	G	AB	R	H	2B	3B	HR	RBI	BB	SO	AVG	OBP	SLG	PRO+	BR	/A	RC	SB	CS	SBR	FR	POS	TPR
1986	Bos-A	13	25	3	3	0	0	0	1	1	4	.120	.154	.120	-24	-4	-4	0	0	1	-1	1	/O	-0.3

■ **WILLIE TASBY**　　Tasby, Willie　b: 1/8/33, Shreveport, La.　BR/TR, 5'11", 170 lbs.　Deb: 9/09/58

YEAR	TM/L	G	AB	R	H	2B	3B	HR	RBI	BB	SO	AVG	OBP	SLG	PRO+	BR	/A	RC	SB	CS	SBR	FR	POS	TPR
1958	Bal-A	18	50	6	10	3	0	1	1	7	15	.200	.310	.320	78	-2	-1	5	1	1	-0	-0	O	-0.2
1959	Bal-A	142	505	69	126	16	5	13	48	34	80	.250	.305	.378	88	-10	-9	57	3	5	-2	-3	*O	-2.0
1960	Bal-A	39	85	9	18	2	1	0	3	9	12	.212	.295	.259	52	-6	-6	7	1	0	-0	-0	O	-0.6
	Bos-A	105	385	68	108	17	1	7	37	51	54	.281	.372	.384	101	4	2	58	3	1	0	-2	*O	-0.2
	Yr	144	470	77	126	19	2	7	40	60	66	.268	.358	.362	93	-1	-3	64	4	1	1	-2		-0.8
1961	Was-A	141	494	54	124	13	2	17	63	58	94	.251	.332	.389	93	-6	-5	60	4	10	-5	-5	*O	-1.9
1962	Was-A	11	34	4	7	0	0	0	0	2	6	.206	.250	.206	24	-4	-4	2	0	0	0	-1	O	-0.4
	Cle-A	75	199	25	48	7	0	4	17	25	41	.241	.326	.337	81	-6	-5	22	0	2	-1	-1	O/3	-0.9
	Yr	86	233	29	55	7	0	4	17	27	47	.236	.315	.318	73	-9	-8	23	0	2	-1	-2		-1.3
1963	Cle-A	52	116	11	26	3	1	4	5	15	25	.224	.318	.371	93	-1	-1	13	0	1	-1	-3	O/2	-0.5
Total	6	583	1868	246	467	61	10	46	174	201	327	.250	.328	.367	89	-29	-27	224	12	20	-8	-14	O/23	-6.7

■ **POP TATE**　　Tate, Edward Christopher "Dimples"　b: 12/22/1860, Richmond, Va.　d: 6/25/32, Richmond, Va.　BR/TL, Deb: 9/26/1885

YEAR	TM/L	G	AB	R	H	2B	3B	HR	RBI	BB	SO	AVG	OBP	SLG	PRO+	BR	/A	RC	SB	CS	SBR	FR	POS	TPR
1885	Bos-N	4	13	1	2	0	0	0	2	1	3	.154	.214	.154	21	-1	-1	0				3	/C	0.2
1886	Bos-N	31	106	13	24	3	1	0	3	7	17	.226	.274	.274	70	-4	-3	8	0			-4	C	-0.4
1887	Bos-N	60	231	34	60	5	3	0	27	8	9	.260	.296	.307	69	-9	-9	24	7			10	C/O	0.6

YEAR	TM/L	G	AB	R	H	2B	3B	HR	RBI	BB	SO	AVG	OBP	SLG	PRO+	BR	/A	RC	SB	CS	SBR	FR	POS	TPR
1888	Bos-N	41	148	18	34	7	1	1	6	8	7	.230	.278	.311	88	-2	-2	14	3			-4	C/O	-0.4
1889	Bal-a	72	253	28	46	6	3	1	27	13	37	.182	.236	.241	37	-21	-21	16	4			-3	C1	-1.5
1890	Bal-a	19	71	7	13	1	1	0		4		.183	.284	.225	50	-4	-4	6	3			-2	C/1	-0.4
Total	6	227	822	101	179	22	9	2	65	41	73	.218	.269	.274	60	-40	-41	68	17			0	C/1O	-1.9

■ BENNIE TATE
Tate, Henry Bennett b: 12/3/01, Whitwell, Tenn. d: 10/27/73, W.Frankfort, Ill. BL/TR, 5'8", 165 lbs. Deb: 4/29/24

YEAR	TM/L	G	AB	R	H	2B	3B	HR	RBI	BB	SO	AVG	OBP	SLG	PRO+	BR	/A	RC	SB	CS	SBR	FR	POS	TPR
1924	*Was-A	21	43	2	13	2	0	0	7	1	2	.302	.318	.349	74	-2	-2	5	0	0	0	-3	C	-0.3
1925	Was-A	16	27	0	13	3	0	0	7	2	2	.481	.517	.593	185	3	3	8	0	1	-1	2	C	0.5
1926	Was-A	59	142	17	38	5	2	1	13	15	1	.268	.338	.352	82	-4	-4	18	0	0	0	-5	C	-0.5
1927	Was-A	61	131	12	41	5	1	1	24	8	4	.313	.357	.389	95	-1	-1	17	0	3	-2	4	C	0.3
1928	Was-A	57	122	10	30	6	0	0	15	10	4	.246	.303	.295	58	-7	-7	10	0	4	-2	2	C	-0.4
1929	Was-A	81	265	26	78	12	3	0	30	16	8	.294	.335	.362	79	-8	-8	31	2	5	-2	-2	C	-0.5
1930	Was-A	14	20	1	5	0	0	0	2	0	1	.250	.250	.250	27	-2	-2	1	0	0	0	-1	/C	-0.1
	Chi-A	72	230	26	73	11	2	0	27	18	10	.317	.367	.383	94	-3	-2	33	2	1	0	-10	C	-0.4
	Yr	86	250	27	78	11	2	0	29	18	11	.312	.358	.372	88	-5	-4	34	2	1	0	-10		-0.5
1931	Chi-A	89	273	27	73	12	3	0	22	26	10	.267	.331	.333	80	-10	-7	31	1	1	-0	7	C	0.5
1932	Chi-A	4	10	1	1	0	0	0	0	1	0	.100	.182	.100	-27	-2	-2	0	0	0	0	0	/C	0.0
	Bos-A	81	273	21	67	12	5	2	26	20	6	.245	.297	.348	68	-14	-13	28	0	1	-1	-6	C	-1.3
	Yr	85	283	22	68	12	5	2	26	21	6	.240	.293	.339	65	-16	-15	28	0	1	-1	-6		-1.3
1934	Chi-N	11	24	1	3	0	0	0	1	3		.125	.160	.125	-23	-4	-4	0	0			-3	/C	-0.6
Total	10	566	1560	144	435	68	16	4	173	118	51	.279	.330	.351	78	-54	-48	182	5	16		-14	C	-2.8

■ HUGHIE TATE
Tate, Hugh Henry b: 5/19/1880, Everett, Pa. d: 8/7/56, Greenville, Pa. BR/TR, 5'11", 190 lbs. Deb: 9/21/05

YEAR	TM/L	G	AB	R	H	2B	3B	HR	RBI	BB	SO	AVG	OBP	SLG	PRO+	BR	/A	RC	SB	CS	SBR	FR	POS	TPR
1905	Was-A	4	13	1	4	0	1	0	2	0		.308	.308	.462	151	1	1	2	1			0	/O	0.1

■ LEE TATE
Tate, Lee Willie "Skeeter" b: 3/18/32, Black Rock, Ark. BR/TR, 5'10", 165 lbs. Deb: 9/12/58

YEAR	TM/L	G	AB	R	H	2B	3B	HR	RBI	BB	SO	AVG	OBP	SLG	PRO+	BR	/A	RC	SB	CS	SBR	FR	POS	TPR
1958	StL-N	10	35	4	7	2	0	0	1	4	3	.200	.282	.257	42	-3	-3	3	0	0	0	-4	/S	-0.6
1959	StL-N	41	50	5	7	1	1	1	4	5	7	.140	.232	.260	29	-5	-5	3	0	0	0	1	S/23	-0.2
Total	2	51	85	9	14	3	1	1	5	9	10	.165	.253	.259	34	-8	-8	5	0	0	0	-4	/S32	-0.8

■ JARVIS TATUM
Tatum, Jarvis b: 10/11/46, Fresno, Cal. BR/TR, 6', 185 lbs. Deb: 9/07/68

YEAR	TM/L	G	AB	R	H	2B	3B	HR	RBI	BB	SO	AVG	OBP	SLG	PRO+	BR	/A	RC	SB	CS	SBR	FR	POS	TPR
1968	Cal-A	17	51	7	9	1	0	0	2	0	9	.176	.176	.196	13	-5	-5	2	0	0	0	0	/O	-0.5
1969	Cal-A	10	22	2	7	0	0	0	0	0	6	.318	.318	.318	83	-1	-1	2	0	1	-1	-1	/O	-0.1
1970	Cal-A	75	181	28	43	7	0	0	6	17	35	.238	.303	.276	63	-9	-9	15	1	0	0	3	O	-0.7
Total	3	102	254	37	59	8	0	0	8	17	50	.232	.280	.264	56	-15	-14	18	1	1	-0	2	/O	-1.3

■ TOMMY TATUM
Tatum, V T b: 7/16/19, Decatur, Tex. d: 11/89, Oklahoma City, Okla. BR/TR, 6', 185 lbs. Deb: 8/01/41

YEAR	TM/L	G	AB	R	H	2B	3B	HR	RBI	BB	SO	AVG	OBP	SLG	PRO+	BR	/A	RC	SB	CS	SBR	FR	POS	TPR
1941	Bro-N	8	12	1	2	1	0	0	1	1	3	.167	.231	.250	34	-1	-1	1	0			-0	/O	-0.1
1947	Bro-N	4	6	0	0	0	0	0	0	0	1	.000	.000	.000	-96	-2	-2	0	0			-0	/O	-0.1
	Cin-N	69	176	19	48	5	2	1	16	16	16	.273	.333	.341	80	-5	-5	21	7			8	O/2	0.1
	Yr	73	182	19	48	5	2	1	16	16	17	.264	.323	.330	74	-7	-7	20	7			8		0.0
Total	2	81	194	20	50	6	2	1	17	17	20	.258	.318	.325	72	-8	-8	22	7			8	/O2	-0.1

■ FRED TAUBY
Tauby, Fred Joseph (b: Fred Joseph Taubensee) b: 3/27/06, Canton, Ohio d: 11/23/55, Concordia, Cal. BR/TR, 5'9.5", 168 lbs. Deb: 9/01/35

YEAR	TM/L	G	AB	R	H	2B	3B	HR	RBI	BB	SO	AVG	OBP	SLG	PRO+	BR	/A	RC	SB	CS	SBR	FR	POS	TPR
1935	Chi-A	13	32	5	4	1	0	0	2	2	3	.125	.176	.156	-13	-5	-6	1	0	0	0	1	/O	-0.3
1937	Phi-N	11	20	2	0	0	0	0	3	0	5	.000	.000	.000	-93	-6	-6	0	1			-0	/O	-0.5
Total	2	24	52	7	4	1	0	0	5	2	8	.077	.111	.096	-43	-11	-11	1	1	0		1	/O	-0.8

■ DON TAUSSIG
Taussig, Donald Franklin b: 2/19/32, New York, N.Y. BR/TR, 6', 180 lbs. Deb: 4/23/58

YEAR	TM/L	G	AB	R	H	2B	3B	HR	RBI	BB	SO	AVG	OBP	SLG	PRO+	BR	/A	RC	SB	CS	SBR	FR	POS	TPR
1958	SF-N	39	50	10	10	0	0	1	4	3	8	.200	.245	.260	35	-5	-5	3	0	0	0	0	O	-0.5
1961	StL-N	98	188	27	54	14	5	2	25	16	34	.287	.343	.447	98	2	-1	28	2	2	-1	8	O	0.2
1962	Hou-N	16	25	1	5	0	0	1	1	2	11	.200	.259	.320	59	-2	-1	2	0	0	0	1	/O	0.0
Total	3	153	263	38	69	14	5	4	30	21	53	.262	.317	.399	84	-5	-7	33	2	2	-1	8	O	-0.3

■ JACKIE TAVENER
Tavener, John Adam "Rabbit" b: 12/27/1897, Celina, Ohio d: 9/14/69, Fort Worth, Tex. BL/TR, 5'5", 138 lbs. Deb: 9/24/21

YEAR	TM/L	G	AB	R	H	2B	3B	HR	RBI	BB	SO	AVG	OBP	SLG	PRO+	BR	/A	RC	SB	CS	SBR	FR	POS	TPR
1921	Det-A	2	4	0	0	0	0	0	0	0	1	.000	.000	.000	-99	-1	-1	0	0	0	0	1	/S	0.0
1925	Det-A	134	453	45	111	11	11	0	47	39	60	.245	.309	.318	60	-28	-27	47	5	4	-1	7	*S	0.0
1926	Det-A	156	532	65	141	22	14	1	58	52	53	.265	.332	.365	80	-15	-16	66	8	7	-2	9	*S	0.3
1927	Det-A	116	419	60	115	22	9	5	59	36	38	.274	.333	.406	90	-7	-7	53	20	8	1	4	*S	0.7
1928	Det-A	132	473	59	123	24	15	5	52	33	51	.260	.314	.406	86	-10	-11	60	13	8	-1	14	*S	1.4
1929	Cle-A	92	250	25	53	9	4	2	27	26	28	.212	.286	.304	50	-18	-20	22	1	4	-2	23	S	0.9
Total	6	632	2131	254	543	88	53	13	243	186	231	.255	.317	.364	75	-79	-82	249	47	31	-5	58	S	3.3

■ ALEX TAVERAS
Taveras, Alejandro Antonio (Betances) b: 10/9/55, Santiago, D.R. BR/TR, 5'10", 155 lbs. Deb: 9/09/76

YEAR	TM/L	G	AB	R	H	2B	3B	HR	RBI	BB	SO	AVG	OBP	SLG	PRO+	BR	/A	RC	SB	CS	SBR	FR	POS	TPR
1976	Hou-N	14	46	3	10	0	0	0	2	1	11	.217	.250	.217	37	-4	-4	2	1	2	-1	1	/2S	-0.1
1982	LA-N	11	3	1	1	1	0	0	2	0	1	.333	.333	.667	178	0	0	1	0	0	0	4	/23S	0.4
1983	LA-N	10	4	0	0	0	0	0	0	0	1	.000	.000	.000	-99	-1	-1	0	0	0	0	2	/S23	0.1
Total	3	35	53	4	11	1	0	0	4	2	3	.208	.236	.226	34	-5	-4	3	1	2	-1	7	/2S3	0.4

■ FRANK TAVERAS
Taveras, Franklin Crisostomo (Fabian) b: 12/24/49, Las Matas De Santa Cruz, D.R. BR/TR, 6', 155 lbs. Deb: 9/25/71

YEAR	TM/L	G	AB	R	H	2B	3B	HR	RBI	BB	SO	AVG	OBP	SLG	PRO+	BR	/A	RC	SB	CS	SBR	FR	POS	TPR
1971	Pit-N	1	0	0	0	0	0	0	0	0	0	—	—	—	—	—	0	0	0	0	0	0	R	0.0
1972	Pit-N	4	3	0	0	0	0	0	0	1	1	.000	.250	.000	-24	-0	-0	0	0	0	0	-1	/S	0.0
1974	*Pit-N	126	333	33	82	4	2	0	26	25	41	.246	.303	.270	63	-17	-15	29	13	4	2	-17	*S	-1.7
1975	*Pit-N	134	378	44	80	9	4	0	23	37	42	.212	.285	.257	52	-24	-24	32	17	6	2	-14	*S	-2.2
1976	Pit-N	144	519	76	134	8	6	0	24	44	79	.258	.321	.297	75	-15	-16	56	58	11	11	-5	*S	0.4
1977	Pit-N	147	544	72	137	20	10	1	29	38	71	.252	.308	.331	69	-22	-24	61	**70**	18	**10**	-22	*S	-1.5
1978	Pit-N	157	654	81	182	31	9	0	38	29	60	.278	.314	.353	82	-13	-16	72	46	25	-1	-29	*S	-3.5
1979	Pit-N	11	45	4	11	3	0	0	1	0	2	.244	.244	.311	48	-3	-3	3	2	1	0	-4	S	-0.6
	NY-N	153	635	89	167	26	9	1	33	33	72	.263	.301	.337	77	-23	-20	63	42	19	1	-22	*S	-2.6
	Yr	164	680	93	178	29	9	1	34	33	74	.262	.298	.335	75	-26	-24	66	44	20	1	-26		-3.2
1980	NY-N	141	562	65	157	27	0	0	25	23	64	.279	.309	.327	80	-17	-15	53	32	18	-1	-39	*S	-4.2
1981	NY-N	84	283	30	65	11	3	0	11	12	36	.230	.266	.290	58	-16	-16	23	16	4	2	-22	S	-2.8
1982	Mon-N	48	87	9	14	5	1	0	4	7	6	.161	.223	.241	29	-8	-8	5	4	0	1	-1	S2	-0.4
Total	11	1150	4043	503	1029	144	44	2	214	249	474	.255	.302	.313	71	-159	-158	395	300	106	26	-174	*S/2	-19.1

■ TAYLOR
Taylor Deb: 9/10/1874

YEAR	TM/L	G	AB	R	H	2B	3B	HR	RBI	BB	SO	AVG	OBP	SLG	PRO+	BR	/A	RC	SB	CS	SBR	FR	POS	TPR
1874	Bal-n	13	48	3	13	1	0	0	0			.271	.271	.292	80	-1	-1	4				1		0.0

■ TAYLOR
Taylor b: Brooklyn, N.Y. Deb: 8/21/1877

YEAR	TM/L	G	AB	R	H	2B	3B	HR	RBI	BB	SO	AVG	OBP	SLG	PRO+	BR	/A	RC	SB	CS	SBR	FR	POS	TPR
1877	Har-N	2	8	0	3	0	0	0		0	2	.375	.375	.375	153	0	0	1				-0	/O	0.0

■ TONY TAYLOR
Taylor, Antonio Nemesio (Sanchez) b: 12/19/35, Central Alara, Cuba BR/TR, 5'9", 170 lbs. Deb: 4/15/58 C

YEAR	TM/L	G	AB	R	H	2B	3B	HR	RBI	BB	SO	AVG	OBP	SLG	PRO+	BR	/A	RC	SB	CS	SBR	FR	POS	TPR
1958	Chi-N	140	497	63	117	15	5	6	27	40	93	.235	.301	.314	64	-26	-25	50	21	6	3	9	*2/3	-0.4
1959	Chi-N	150	624	96	175	30	8	8	38	45	86	.280	.335	.393	94	-6	-5	84	23	9	2	10	*2/S	1.8
1960	Chi-N	19	76	14	20	3	3	1	9	8	12	.263	.341	.421	108	1	1	12	2	0	1	-2	2	0.1
	Phi-N	127	505	66	145	22	4	4	35	33	86	.287	.333	.370	92	-5	-5	62	24	11	1	-6	*2/3	0.0

YEAR	TM/L	G	AB	R	H	2B	3B	HR	RBI	BB	SO	AVG	OBP	SLG	PRO+	BR	/A	RC	SB	CS	SBR	FR	POS	TPR
	Yr	146	581	80	165	25	7	5	44	41	98	.284	.334	.377	94	-4	-4	73	26	11	1	-8		0.1
1961	Phi-N	106	400	47	100	17	3	2	26	29	59	.250	.304	.322	67	-19	-18	38	11	5	0	0	2/3	-0.6
1962	Phi-N	152	625	87	162	21	5	7	43	68	82	.259	.337	.342	85	-14	-11	76	20	9	1	-15	*2/S	-1.2
1963	Phi-N	157	640	102	180	20	10	5	49	42	99	.281	.332	.367	102	1	2	79	23	9	2	-9	*23	0.4
1964	Phi-N	154	570	62	143	13	6	4	46	46	74	.251	.321	.316	81	-14	-13	60	13	7	-0	-20	*2	-2.1
1965	Phi-N	106	323	41	74	14	3	3	27	22	58	.229	.303	.319	77	-10	-10	32	5	4	-1	-2	2/3	-0.8
1966	Phi-N	125	434	47	105	14	8	5	40	31	56	.242	.294	.346	77	-13	-14	42	8	4	0	4	23	-0.9
1967	Phi-N	132	462	55	110	16	6	2	34	42	74	.238	.308	.312	77	-12	-13	42	10	9	-2	-8	132/S	-2.7
1968	Phi-N	145	547	59	137	20	2	3	38	39	60	.250	.304	.311	85	-10	-10	54	22	5	4	16	*3/21	1.1
1969	Phi-N	138	557	68	146	24	5	3	30	42	62	.262	.318	.339	87	-12	-10	60	19	10	-0	-2	321	-0.8
1970	Phi-N	124	439	74	132	26	9	9	55	50	67	.301	.376	.462	127	15	16	71	9	11	-4	-0	230/S	1.7
1971	Phi-N	36	107	9	25	2	1	1	5	9	10	.234	.293	.299	68	-4	-4	9	2	2	-1	5	23/1	0.0
	Det-A	55	181	27	52	10	2	3	19	12	11	.287	.335	.414	107	2	1	25	5	1	1	1	2/3	0.6
1972	*Det-A	78	228	33	69	12	4	1	20	14	34	.303	.348	.404	119	6	5	31	5	1	1	-8	2/31	0.3
1973	Det-A	84	275	35	63	9	3	5	24	17	29	.229	.276	.338	68	-11	-13	24	9	5	-0	-13	2/130D	-2.4
1974	Phi-N	62	64	5	21	4	0	2	13	6	6	.328	.394	.484	139	4	3	12	0	0	0	-1	/132	0.3
1975	Phi-N	79	103	13	25	5	1	1	17	17	18	.243	.355	.340	90	-0	-1	12	3	3	-1	1	3/12	0.0
1976	Phi-N	26	23	2	6	1	0	0	3	1	7	.261	.320	.304	76	-1	-1	2	0	0	0	-0	/23	0.0
Total	19	2195	7680	1005	2007	298	86	75	598	613	1083	.261	.322	.352	88	-128	-122	876	234	111	4	-39	*23/10SD	-5.2

■ BEN TAYLOR
Taylor, Benjamin Eugene b: 9/30/27, Metropolis, Ill. BL/TL, 6', 175 lbs. Deb: 7/29/51

YEAR	TM/L	G	AB	R	H	2B	3B	HR	RBI	BB	SO	AVG	OBP	SLG	PRO+	BR	/A	RC	SB	CS	SBR	FR	POS	TPR
1951	StL-A	33	93	14	24	2	1	3	6	9	22	.258	.337	.398	95	-0	-1	12	1	1	-0	-2	1	-0.2
1952	Det-A	7	18	0	3	0	0	0	0	0	5	.167	.167	.167	-7	-3	-3	0	0	0	0	0	/1	-0.2
1955	Mil-N	12	10	2	1	0	0	0	0	2	4	.100	.250	.100	-3	-1	-1	0	0	0	0	0	/1	-0.1
Total	3	52	121	16	28	2	1	3	6	11	31	.231	.306	.339	73	-4	-5	13	1	1	-0	-2	/1	-0.5

■ CHINK TAYLOR
Taylor, C L b: 2/9/1898, Burnet, Tex. d: 7/7/80, Temple, Tex. BR/TR, 5'9", 160 lbs. Deb: 4/18/25

YEAR	TM/L	G	AB	R	H	2B	3B	HR	RBI	BB	SO	AVG	OBP	SLG	PRO+	BR	/A	RC	SB	CS	SBR	FR	POS	TPR
1925	Chi-N	8	6	2	0	0	0	0	0	0	0	.000	.000	.000	-99	-2	-2	0	0	0	0	0	/O	0.0

■ CARL TAYLOR
Taylor, Carl Means b: 1/20/44, Sarasota, Fla. BR/TR, 6'2", 200 lbs. Deb: 4/11/68

YEAR	TM/L	G	AB	R	H	2B	3B	HR	RBI	BB	SO	AVG	OBP	SLG	PRO+	BR	/A	RC	SB	CS	SBR	FR	POS	TPR
1968	Pit-N	44	71	5	15	1	0	0	7	10	10	.211	.309	.225	63	-3	-3	5	1	0	0	-5	C/O	-0.6
1969	Pit-N	104	221	30	77	10	1	4	33	31	36	.348	.435	.457	153	16	17	45	0	1	-1	0	O1	1.3
1970	StL-N	104	245	39	61	12	2	6	45	41	30	.249	.359	.388	98	1	0	34	5	2	0	-3	O1/3	-0.5
1971	Pit-N	7	12	1	2	0	1	0	0	0	5	.167	.167	.333	39	-1	-1	0	0	0	0	-0	/O	-0.1
	KC-A	20	39	3	7	0	0	0	3	5	13	.179	.273	.179	30	-3	-3	2	0	1	-1	1	O	-0.3
1972	KC-A	63	113	17	30	2	1	0	11	17	16	.265	.366	.301	101	1	1	14	4	1	1	-3	C/O13	-0.1
1973	KC-A	69	145	18	33	6	1	0	16	32	20	.228	.367	.283	79	-1	-3	17	2	2	-1	1	C/1D	0.0
Total	6	411	846	113	225	31	6	10	115	136	130	.266	.371	.352	103	10	8	117	12	7	-1	-8	CO/13D	-0.3

■ DANNY TAYLOR
Taylor, Daniel Turney b: 12/23/1900, Lash, Pa. d: 10/11/72, Latrobe, Pa. BR/TR, 5'10", 190 lbs. Deb: 6/30/26

YEAR	TM/L	G	AB	R	H	2B	3B	HR	RBI	BB	SO	AVG	OBP	SLG	PRO+	BR	/A	RC	SB	CS	SBR	FR	POS	TPR
1926	Was-A	21	50	10	15	0	1	1	5	5	7	.300	.364	.400	102	-0	0	7	1	2	-1	-1	O	-0.2
1929	Chi-N	2	3	0	0	0	0	0	0	1	1	.000	.250	.000	-32	-1	-1	0	0			-0	/O	0.0
1930	Chi-N	74	219	43	62	14	3	2	37	27	34	.283	.364	.402	84	-5	-5	32	6			-5	O	-1.1
1931	Chi-N	88	270	48	81	13	6	5	41	31	46	.300	.372	.448	117	8	7	47	4			-5	O	-0.1
1932	Chi-N	6	22	3	5	2	0	0	3	3	1	.227	.320	.318	73	-1	-1	2	1			0	/O	0.0
	Bro-N	105	395	84	128	22	7	11	48	33	41	.324	.378	.499	136	18	19	76	13			-1	O	1.1
	Yr	111	417	87	133	24	7	11	51	36	42	.319	.374	.489	133	18	19	78	14			-1		1.1
1933	Bro-N	103	358	75	102	21	9	9	40	47	45	.285	.368	.469	144	18	20	64	11			-0	O	1.5
1934	Bro-N	120	405	62	121	24	6	7	57	63	47	.299	.396	.440	130	16	19	74	12			-9	*O	0.4
1935	Bro-N	112	352	51	102	19	5	7	59	46	32	.290	.372	.432	118	8	10	60	6			-6	O	0.0
1936	Bro-N	43	116	12	34	6	0	2	15	11	14	.293	.359	.397	102	1	1	16	2			-2	O	-0.2
Total	9	674	2190	388	650	121	37	44	305	267	268	.297	.374	.446	121	62	68	379	56	2		-29	O	1.4

■ DWIGHT TAYLOR
Taylor, Dwight Bernard b: 3/24/60, Los Angeles, Cal. BL/TL, 5'9", 166 lbs. Deb: 4/14/86

YEAR	TM/L	G	AB	R	H	2B	3B	HR	RBI	BB	SO	AVG	OBP	SLG	PRO+	BR	/A	RC	SB	CS	SBR	FR	POS	TPR
1986	KC-A	4	2	1	0	0	0	0	0	0	0	.000	.000	.000	-98	-1	-1	0	0	0	0	0	/OD	0.0

■ ED TAYLOR
Taylor, Edward James b: 11/17/01, Chicago, Ill. BR/TR, 5'6.5", 160 lbs. Deb: 4/14/26

YEAR	TM/L	G	AB	R	H	2B	3B	HR	RBI	BB	SO	AVG	OBP	SLG	PRO+	BR	/A	RC	SB	CS	SBR	FR	POS	TPR
1926	Bos-N	92	272	37	73	8	2	0	33	38	26	.268	.368	.313	93	-4	-0	34	4			-1	3S	0.2

■ FRED TAYLOR
Taylor, Frederick Rankin b: 12/3/24, Zanesville, Ohio BL/TR, 6'3", 201 lbs. Deb: 9/12/50

YEAR	TM/L	G	AB	R	H	2B	3B	HR	RBI	BB	SO	AVG	OBP	SLG	PRO+	BR	/A	RC	SB	CS	SBR	FR	POS	TPR
1950	Was-A	6	16	1	2	0	0	0	0	0	2	.125	.176	.125	-23	-3	-3	0	0	0	0	0	/1	-0.2
1951	Was-A	6	12	1	2	1	0	0	0	0	4	.167	.167	.250	12	-2	-1	1	0	0	0	-0	/1	-0.1
1952	Was-A	10	19	3	5	1	0	0	4	3	2	.263	.364	.316	93	-0	-0	3	0	0	0	1	/1	0.1
Total	3	22	47	5	9	2	0	0	4	4	8	.191	.255	.234	33	-5	-4	3	0	0	0	1	/1	-0.2

■ GEORGE TAYLOR
Taylor, George Edward "Live" b: 2/3/1855, Belfast, Me. d: 2/19/1888, San Francisco, Cal Deb: 5/01/1884

YEAR	TM/L	G	AB	R	H	2B	3B	HR	RBI	BB	SO	AVG	OBP	SLG	PRO+	BR	/A	RC	SB	CS	SBR	FR	POS	TPR
1884	Pit-a	41	152	22	32	4	1	0		6		.211	.255	.250	67	-5	-5	10				-1	O	-0.5

■ HARRY TAYLOR
Taylor, Harry Leonard b: 4/4/1866, Halsey Valley, N.Y. d: 7/12/55, Buffalo, N.Y. BL , 6'2", 160 lbs. Deb: 4/18/1890

YEAR	TM/L	G	AB	R	H	2B	3B	HR	RBI	BB	SO	AVG	OBP	SLG	PRO+	BR	/A	RC	SB	CS	SBR	FR	POS	TPR
1890	*Lou-a	134	553	115	169	7	7	0		68		.306	.382	.344	119	14	16	92	45			5	*1S/2C	1.5
1891	Lou-a	93	356	81	105	7	4	2	37	55	33	.295	.397	.354	120	11	12	57	15			3	1/32C	0.9
1892	Lou-N	125	493	66	128	7	1	0	34	58	23	.260	.342	.278	98	-3	3	56	24			-8	012/3S	-0.8
1893	Bal-N	88	360	50	102	9	1	1	54	32	11	.283	.347	.322	78	-9	-11	50	24			-3	*1	-1.0
Total	4	440	1762	312	504	30	13	3	125	213	67	.286	.367	.323	105	12	20	256	108			-2	1/O2S3C	0.6

■ HARRY TAYLOR
Taylor, Harry Warren b: 12/26/07, McKeesport, Pa. d: 4/27/69, Toledo, Ohio BL/TL, 6'1.5", 185 lbs. Deb: 4/14/32

YEAR	TM/L	G	AB	R	H	2B	3B	HR	RBI	BB	SO	AVG	OBP	SLG	PRO+	BR	/A	RC	SB	CS	SBR	FR	POS	TPR
1932	Chi-N	10	8	1	1	0	0	0	0	1	1	.125	.222	.125	-4	-1	-1	0	0			0	/1	0.0

■ SANDY TAYLOR
Taylor, James B. 5'10.5", 175 lbs. Deb: 8/11/1879

YEAR	TM/L	G	AB	R	H	2B	3B	HR	RBI	BB	SO	AVG	OBP	SLG	PRO+	BR	/A	RC	SB	CS	SBR	FR	POS	TPR
1879	Tro-N	24	97	10	21	4	0	0	8	1	8	.216	.224	.258	63	-4	-3	6				-3	O	-0.6

■ ZACK TAYLOR
Taylor, James Wren b: 7/27/1898, Yulee, Fla. d: 9/19/74, Orlando, Fla. BR/TR, 5'11.5", 180 lbs. Deb: 6/15/20 MC

YEAR	TM/L	G	AB	R	H	2B	3B	HR	RBI	BB	SO	AVG	OBP	SLG	PRO+	BR	/A	RC	SB	CS	SBR	FR	POS	TPR
1920	Bro-N	9	13	3	5	2	0	0	5	0	2	.385	.385	.538	158	1	1	2	0	1	-1	-1	/C	0.0
1921	Bro-N	30	102	6	20	0	2	0	8	1	8	.196	.212	.235	17	-12	-12	5	2	0	1	-0	C	-0.9
1922	Bro-N	7	14	0	3	0	0	0	2	1	1	.214	.267	.214	26	-2	-2	1	0	0	0	-1	/C	-0.1
1923	Bro-N	96	337	29	97	11	6	0	46	9	13	.288	.312	.356	78	-12	-11	36	2	5	-2	15	C	0.6
1924	Bro-N	99	345	36	100	9	4	1	39	14	14	.290	.319	.348	81	-10	-9	38	0	1	-1	-9	C	-1.6
1925	Bro-N	109	352	33	109	16	4	0	44	17	19	.310	.343	.403	92	-5	-4	48	0	0	0	-9	C	-0.7
1926	Bos-N	125	432	36	110	22	3	0	42	28	27	.255	.303	.319	74	-20	-15	41	1			2	*C	-0.7
1927	Bos-N	30	96	8	23	2	1	1	14	8	5	.240	.298	.313	69	-5	-4	9	0			12	C	0.9
	NY-N	83	258	18	60	7	3	0	21	17	20	.233	.283	.283	52	-17	-17	21	2			-3	C	-1.4
	Yr	113	354	26	83	9	4	1	35	25	25	.234	.287	.291	56	-22	-21	30	2			8		-0.5
1928	Bos-N	125	399	36	100	15	1	2	30	33	29	.251	.313	.308	66	-21	-18	39	2			-11	*C	-2.0
1929	Bos-N	34	101	8	25	7	0	0	10	7	9	.248	.303	.317	56	-7	-7	10	0			7	C	0.2
	*Chi-N	64	215	29	59	16	3	1	31	19	18	.274	.336	.391	79	-7	-7	28	0			-1	C	-0.2
	Yr	98	316	37	84	23	3	1	41	26	27	.266	.326	.367	72	-14	-14	38	0			5		0.0

YEAR	TM/L	G	AB	R	H	2B	3B	HR	RBI	BB	SO	AVG	OBP	SLG	PRO+	BR	/A	RC	SB	CS	SBR	FR	POS	TPR
1930	Chi-N	32	95	12	22	2	1	1	11	2	12	.232	.255	.305	34	-10	-10	7	0			-0	C	-0.7
1931	Chi-N	8	4	0	1	0	0	0	0	2	1	.250	.500	.250	106	0	0	1	0			1	/C	0.1
1932	Chi-N	21	30	2	6	1	0	0	3	1	4	.200	.226	.233	24	-3	-3	2	0			3	C	0.1
1933	Chi-N	16	11	0	0	0	0	0	0	0	1	.000	.000	.000	-99	-3	-3	0	0			-0	C	-0.2
1934	NY-A	4	7	0	1	0	0	0	0	0	1	.143	.143	.143	-28	-1	-1	0	0	0	0	-0	/C	0.0
1935	Bro-N	26	54	2	7	3	0	0	5	2	8	.130	.175	.185	-3	-8	-8	1	0			1	C	-0.6
Total	16	918	2865	258	748	113	28	9	311	161	192	.261	.304	.329	68	-143	-130	289	9	7		5	C	-7.2

■ JOE TAYLOR
Taylor, Joe Cephus b: 3/2/26, Chapman, Ala. BR/TR, 6'1", 185 lbs. Deb: 8/26/54

YEAR	TM/L	G	AB	R	H	2B	3B	HR	RBI	BB	SO	AVG	OBP	SLG	PRO+	BR	/A	RC	SB	CS	SBR	FR	POS	TPR
1954	Phi-A	18	58	5	13	1	1	1	8	2	9	.224	.250	.328	57	-4	-4	4	0	1	-1	-0	O	-0.4
1957	Cin-N	33	107	14	28	7	0	4	9	6	24	.262	.301	.439	89	-1	-2	13	0	1	-1	3	O	0.0
1958	StL-N	18	23	2	7	3	0	1	3	2	4	.304	.360	.565	135	1	1	5	0	0	0	0	/O	0.1
	Bal-A	36	77	11	21	4	0	2	9	7	19	.273	.333	.403	107	0	1	9	0	0	0	0	O	0.0
1959	Bal-A	14	32	2	5	1	0	1	2	11	5	.156	.372	.281	84	0	-0	4	0	0	0	-2	O	-0.2
Total	4	119	297	34	74	16	1	9	31	28	61	.249	.314	.401	92	-4	-4	35	0	2	-1	1	/O	-0.5

■ LEO TAYLOR
Taylor, Leo Thomas "Chink" b: 5/13/01, Walla Walla, Wash. d: 5/20/82, Seattle, Wash. BR/TR, 5'10.5", 150 lbs. Deb: 5/03/23

YEAR	TM/L	G	AB	R	H	2B	3B	HR	RBI	BB	SO	AVG	OBP	SLG	PRO+	BR	/A	RC	SB	CS	SBR	FR	POS	TPR
1923	Chi-A	1	0	0	0	0	0	0	0	0	0	—	—	—		0	0	0	0	0	0	0	R	0.0

■ HAWK TAYLOR
Taylor, Robert Dale b: 4/3/39, Metropolis, Ill. BR/TR, 6'1", 187 lbs. Deb: 6/09/57

YEAR	TM/L	G	AB	R	H	2B	3B	HR	RBI	BB	SO	AVG	OBP	SLG	PRO+	BR	/A	RC	SB	CS	SBR	FR	POS	TPR
1957	Mil-N	7	1	2	0	0	0	0	0	0	0	.000	.000	.000	-99	-0	-0	0	0	0	0	0	/C	0.0
1958	Mil-N	4	8	1	1	1	0	0	0	0	3	.125	.125	.250	-4	-1	-1	0	0	0	0	0	/O	0.0
1961	Mil-N	20	26	1	5	0	0	1	1	3	11	.192	.276	.308	58	-2	-2	2	0	1	-1	0	/OC	-0.1
1962	Mil-N	20	47	3	12	0	0	0	2	2	10	.255	.286	.255	48	-3	-3	3	0	1	-1	1	O	-0.3
1963	Mil-N	16	29	1	2	0	0	0	0	1	12	.069	.100	.069	-51	-6	-6	0	0	0	0	1	O	-0.5
1964	NY-N	92	225	20	54	8	0	4	23	8	33	.240	.272	.329	70	-10	-9	19	0	0	0	0	CO	-0.7
1965	NY-N	25	46	5	7	0	0	4	10	1	8	.152	.170	.413	61	-3	-3	2	0	0	0	-2	C/1	-0.4
1966	NY-N	53	109	5	19	2	0	3	12	3	19	.174	.204	.275	32	-10	-10	4	0	1	-1	-4	C1	-1.4
1967	NY-N	13	37	3	9	3	0	0	4	2	8	.243	.282	.324	74	-1	-1	3	0	0	0	6	C	0.5
	Cal-A	23	52	5	16	3	0	1	3	4	8	.308	.357	.423	135	2	2	8	0	0	0	2	C	0.6
1969	KC-A	64	89	7	24	5	0	3	21	6	18	.270	.316	.427	105	0	0	11	0	0	0	-1	O/C	-0.4
1970	KC-A	57	55	3	9	3	0	0	6	6	16	.164	.258	.218	33	-5	-5	3	0	0	0	0	/C1	-0.4
Total	11	394	724	56	158	25	0	16	82	36	146	.218	.259	.319	62	-39	-37	57	0	3	-2	3	C/O1	-2.7

■ BOB TAYLOR
Taylor, Robert Lee b: 3/20/44, Leland, Miss. BL/TR, 5'9", 170 lbs. Deb: 4/09/70

YEAR	TM/L	G	AB	R	H	2B	3B	HR	RBI	BB	SO	AVG	OBP	SLG	PRO+	BR	/A	RC	SB	CS	SBR	FR	POS	TPR
1970	SF-N	63	84	12	16	0	0	2	10	12	13	.190	.320	.262	58	-5	-4	8	0	0	0	-0	O/C	-0.5

■ SAMMY TAYLOR
Taylor, Samuel Douglas b: 2/27/33, Woodruff, S.C. BL/TR, 6'2", 185 lbs. Deb: 4/27/58

YEAR	TM/L	G	AB	R	H	2B	3B	HR	RBI	BB	SO	AVG	OBP	SLG	PRO+	BR	/A	RC	SB	CS	SBR	FR	POS	TPR
1958	Chi-N	96	301	30	78	12	2	6	36	27	46	.259	.320	.372	84	-8	-7	35	2	1	0	-11	C	-1.3
1959	Chi-N	110	353	41	95	13	2	13	43	35	47	.269	.337	.428	103	1	1	51	1	0	0	-15	*C	-0.6
1960	Chi-N	74	150	14	31	9	0	3	17	6	18	.207	.242	.327	55	-10	-10	10	0	1	-1	-9	C	-1.7
1961	Chi-N	89	235	26	56	8	2	8	23	23	39	.238	.317	.391	86	-5	-5	29	0	0	0	-8	C	-0.6
1962	Chi-N	7	15	0	2	1	0	0	1	3	3	.133	.278	.200	30	-1	-2	1	0	0	0	-1	/C	-0.2
	NY-N	68	158	12	35	4	2	3	20	23	17	.222	.328	.329	76	-5	-5	18	0	0	0	-9	C	-1.3
	Yr	75	173	12	37	5	2	3	21	26	20	.214	.323	.318	72	-6	-7	19	0	0	0	-11		-1.5
1963	NY-N	22	35	3	9	0	1	0	6	5	7	.257	.350	.314	91	-0	-0	3	0	0	0	0	C	0.0
	Cin-N	3	6	0	0	0	0	0	0	0	2	.000	.000	.000	-97	-2	-2	0	0	0	0	-1	/C	-0.2
	Yr	25	41	3	9	0	1	0	6	5	9	.220	.304	.268	65	-2	-2	3	0	0	0	-1		-0.2
	Cle-A	4	10	1	3	0	0	0	1	0	2	.300	.300	.300	69	-0	-0	1	0	0	0	-1	/C	0.0
Total	6	473	1263	127	309	47	9	33	147	122	181	.245	.315	.375	84	-29	-29	147	3	2	-0	-56	C	-5.9

■ TOMMY TAYLOR
Taylor, Thomas Livingstone Carlton b: 9/17/1892, Mexia, Tex. d: 4/5/56, Greenville, Miss. BR/TR, 5'8.5", 160 lbs. Deb: 7/09/24

YEAR	TM/L	G	AB	R	H	2B	3B	HR	RBI	BB	SO	AVG	OBP	SLG	PRO+	BR	/A	RC	SB	CS	SBR	FR	POS	TPR
1924	*Was-A	26	73	11	19	3	1	0	10	2	8	.260	.289	.329	61	-5	-4	7	2	0	1	-5	3/2O	-0.6

■ BILLY TAYLOR
Taylor, William H. b: 1872, Butler, Ky. d: 9/12/05, Cincinnati, Ohio Deb: 9/19/1898

YEAR	TM/L	G	AB	R	H	2B	3B	HR	RBI	BB	SO	AVG	OBP	SLG	PRO+	BR	/A	RC	SB	CS	SBR	FR	POS	TPR
1898	Lou-N	9	24	2	6	1	0	0		2	1	.250	.308	.292	76	-1	-1	3	1			-1	/32	0.0

■ BILLY TAYLOR
Taylor, William Henry "Bollicky Bill" b: 1855, Washington, D.C. d: 5/14/1900, Jacksonville, Fla. TR, 5'11.5", 204 lbs. Deb: 5/21/1881

YEAR	TM/L	G	AB	R	H	2B	3B	HR	RBI	BB	SO	AVG	OBP	SLG	PRO+	BR	/A	RC	SB	CS	SBR	FR	POS	TPR
1881	Wor-N	6	28	3	3	1	0	0	2	0	2	.107	.107	.143	-21	-4	-4	0				0	/OP	-0.2
	Det-N	1	4	0	2	2	0	0	1	0	0	.500	.500	1.000	346	1	1	2				-0	/3	0.1
	Cle-N	24	103	6	25	1	0	0	12	0	8	.243	.243	.252	59	-5	-4	6				-3	O/P3	-0.6
	Yr	31	135	9	30	4	0	0	15	0	10	.222	.222	.252	50	-8	-7	8				-2		-0.7
1882	Pit-a	70	299	40	84	16	13	3			7	.281	.297	.452	157	14	16	41				-12	C13/OP	0.4
1883	Pit-a	83	369	43	96	13	7	2			9	.260	.278	.350	106	-0	3	37				-13	OCP/1	-0.4
1884	StL-U	43	186	44	68	23	1	3			7	.366	.389	.548	206	21	20	41	0			1	P1/O	0.0
	Phi-a	30	111	8	28	6	2	0			2	.252	.272	.342	95	-0	-1	11				2	P	0.0
1885	Phi-a	6	21	0	4	0	0	0			0	.190	.190	.190	21	-2	-2	1				-1	/P	0.0
1886	Bal-A	10	39	4	12	0	1	0			1	.308	.325	.359	119	1	1	5	1			0	/P1C	0.0
1887	Phi-a	1	4	0	1	0	0	0			0	.250	.250	.250	41	-0	-0	0				-0	/P	0.0
Total	7	274	1164	148	323	62	24	8	15	26	10	.277	.294	.393	125	26	29	144	1			-25	P/OC13	-0.7

■ BILL TAYLOR
Taylor, William Michael b: 12/30/29, Alhambra, Cal. BL/TR, 6'3", 212 lbs. Deb: 4/14/54

YEAR	TM/L	G	AB	R	H	2B	3B	HR	RBI	BB	SO	AVG	OBP	SLG	PRO+	BR	/A	RC	SB	CS	SBR	FR	POS	TPR
1954	NY-N	55	65	4	12	1	0	2	10	3	15	.185	.243	.292	38	-6	-6	5	0	0	0	-2	/O	-0.7
1955	NY-N	65	64	9	17	4	0	4	12	1	16	.266	.277	.516	104	0	-0	8	0	0	0	0	/O	0.0
1956	NY-N	1	4	0	1	1	0	0	0	0	1	.250	.250	.500	96	-0	-0	1	0	0	0	-0	/O	0.0
1957	NY-N	11	9	0	0	0	0	0	0	1	2	.000	.100	.000	-70	-2	-2	0	0	0	0	0	H	-0.1
	Det-A	9	23	4	8	2	0	1	3	0	3	.348	.348	.565	142	1	1	5	0	0	0	-1	/O	0.0
1958	Det-A	8	8	0	3	0	0	0	1	0	2	.375	.375	.375	100	0	0	1	0	0	0	0	/O	0.0
Total	5	149	173	17	41	8	0	7	26	5	39	.237	.267	.405	74	-7	-7	19	0	0	0	-3	/O	-0.8

■ BIRDIE TEBBETTS
Tebbetts, George Robert b: 11/10/12, Burlington, Vt. BR/TR, 5'11.5", 170 lbs. Deb: 9/16/36 M

YEAR	TM/L	G	AB	R	H	2B	3B	HR	RBI	BB	SO	AVG	OBP	SLG	PRO+	BR	/A	RC	SB	CS	SBR	FR	POS	TPR
1936	Det-A	10	33	7	10	1	2	1	4	5	3	.303	.395	.545	129	1	1	7	0	0	0	2	C	0.4
1937	Det-A	50	162	15	31	4	3	2	16	10	13	.191	.238	.290	32	-17	-18	12	0	0	0	-4	C	-1.6
1938	Det-A	53	143	16	42	6	2	1	25	12	13	.294	.348	.385	79	-4	-5	19	1	2	-1	-4	C	-0.7
1939	Det-A	106	341	37	89	22	4	4	53	25	20	.261	.315	.372	70	-13	-17	40	2	1	0	15	*C	0.4
1940	*Det-A	111	379	46	112	24	4	4	46	35	14	.296	.357	.412	90	-1	-6	55	4	5	-2	18	*C	1.7
1941	Det-A	110	359	28	102	19	4	2	47	38	29	.284	.354	.376	85	-3	-8	50	1	2	-1	6	C	0.3
1942	Det-A	99	308	24	76	11	0	1	27	39	17	.247	.335	.292	71	-8	-11	33	4	0	1	6	C	0.8
1946	Det-A	87	280	20	68	11	2	1	34	28	23	.243	.312	.307	69	-10	-12	26	1	3	-2	-1	C	-1.0
1947	Det-A	20	53	1	5	1	0	0	2	3	3	.094	.143	.113	-27	-9	-9	1	0	1	-1	8	C	0.0
	Bos-A	90	291	20	87	10	1	1	28	21	30	.299	.346	.344	86	-3	-6	34	2	4	-2	-2	C	-0.1
	Yr	110	344	23	92	11	1	1	30	24	33	.267	.315	.308	69	-12	-15	32	2	5	-3	6		-0.1
1948	Bos-A	128	446	54	125	26	2	5	68	62	32	.280	.371	.381	95	1	-2	63	5	2	0	-9	*C	-0.2
1949	Bos-A	122	403	42	109	14	0	5	48	62	22	.270	.369	.342	83	-5	-9	55	8	1	2	-6	*C	-0.6
1950	Bos-A	79	268	33	83	10	1	8	45	29	26	.310	.377	.444	100	4	-0	43	1	1	-0	-6	C	-0.2

YEAR	TM/L	G	AB	R	H	2B	3B	HR	RBI	BB	SO	AVG	OBP	SLG	PRO+	BR	/A	RC	SB	CS	SBR	FR	POS	TPR
1951	Cle-A	55	137	8	36	6	0	2	18	8	7	.263	.308	.350	82	-5	-4	14	0	0	0	-1	C	-0.1
1952	Cle-A	42	101	4	25	4	0	1	8	12	9	.248	.339	.317	89	-2	-1	11	0	1	-1	-4	C	-0.3
Total	14	1162	3704	357	1000	169	22	38	469	389	261	.270	.341	.358	81	-73	-106	461	29	23	-5	18	*C	-1.2

■ PUSSY TEBEAU   Tebeau, Charles Alston   b: 2/22/1870, Worcester, Mass.   d: 3/25/50, Pittsfield, Mass.   BR/TR, 5'10", 175 lbs.   Deb: 7/22/1895

YEAR	TM/L	G	AB	R	H	2B	3B	HR	RBI	BB	SO	AVG	OBP	SLG	PRO+	BR	/A	RC	SB	CS	SBR	FR	POS	TPR
1895	Cle-N	2	6	3	3	0	0	0	1	2	1	.500	.625	.500	185	1	1	3	1			1	/O	0.1

■ GEORGE TEBEAU   Tebeau, George E. "White Wings"   b: 12/26/1861, St.Louis, Mo.   d: 2/4/23, Denver, Colo.   BR/TR, 5'9", 175 lbs.   Deb: 4/16/1887

YEAR	TM/L	G	AB	R	H	2B	3B	HR	RBI	BB	SO	AVG	OBP	SLG	PRO+	BR	/A	RC	SB	CS	SBR	FR	POS	TPR
1887	Cin-a	85	318	57	94	12	5	4		31		.296	.364	.403	114	7	6	62	37			4	O/P	0.6
1888	Cin-a	121	411	72	94	12	12	3	51	61		.229	.338	.338	115	12	9	61	37			4	*O	0.7
1889	Cin-a	135	496	110	125	21	11	7	70	69	62	.252	.350	.381	107	8	5	90	61			-5	*O/1	-0.4
1890	Tol-a	94	381	71	102	16	10	1		51		.268	.359	.370	114	9	7	72	55			3	*O/P	0.5
1894	Was-N	61	222	41	50	10	6	0	28	37	20	.225	.341	.324	65	-13	-12	31	17			-9	O	-1.8
	Cle-N	40	150	32	47	9	4	0	25	25	18	.313	.411	.427	100	2	1	31	9			-5	O1/3	-0.4
	Yr	101	372	73	97	19	10	0	53	62	38	.261	.369	.366	80	-11	-11	61	26			-14		-2.2
1895	Cle-N	91	337	57	110	16	6	0	68	50	28	.326	.415	.409	109	10	6	64	12			-9	O1	-0.4
Total	6	627	2315	440	622	96	54	15	242	324	128	.269	.364	.376	105	35	23	410	228			-18	O/1P3	-1.2

■ PATSY TEBEAU   Tebeau, Oliver Wendell   b: 12/5/1864, St.Louis, Mo.   d: 5/15/18, St.Louis, Mo.   BR/TR, 5'8", 163 lbs.   Deb: 9/20/1887   M

YEAR	TM/L	G	AB	R	H	2B	3B	HR	RBI	BB	SO	AVG	OBP	SLG	PRO+	BR	/A	RC	SB	CS	SBR	FR	POS	TPR
1887	Chi-N	20	68	8	11	3	0	0	10	4	4	.162	.208	.206	15	-8	-9	5	8			-3	3	-0.9
1889	Cle-N	136	521	72	147	20	6	6	76	37	41	.282	.332	.390	105	1	3	78	26			-1	*3	0.9
1890	Cle-P	110	450	86	135	26	6	5	74	34	20	.300	.353	.418	117	4	10	73	14			13	*3M	2.5
1891	Cle-N	61	249	38	65	8	3	1	41	16	13	.261	.313	.329	86	-4	-5	30	12			6	3/OM	0.3
1892	*Cle-N	86	340	47	83	13	3	2	49	23	34	.244	.307	.318	87	-4	-6	36	6			-2	3/21SM	-0.2
1893	Cle-N	116	486	90	160	32	8	2	102	32	11	.329	.375	.440	112	11	6	90	19			6	13/2M	1.0
1894	Cle-N	125	523	82	158	23	7	3	89	35	35	.302	.347	.390	76	-18	-22	83	30			-4	*12/3SM	-1.8
1895	*Cle-N	63	264	50	84	13	2	2	52	16	18	.318	.362	.405	94	-0	-3	43	8			6	1/23M	0.4
1896	*Cle-N	132	543	56	146	22	6	2	94	21	22	.269	.300	.343	67	-24	-29	63	20			7	*1/32SPM	-1.4
1897	Cle-N	109	412	62	110	15	9	0	59	30		.267	.323	.347	75	-12	-16	51	11			0	*12/3SM	-1.2
1898	Cle-N	131	477	53	123	11	4	1	63	53		.258	.341	.304	89	-5	-4	52	5			3	12/S3M	0.1
1899	StL-N	77	281	27	69	10	3	1	26	18		.246	.303	.313	70	-11	-12	29	5			-3	1S/32M	-1.1
1900	StL-N	1	4	0	0	0	0	0	0	0		.000	.000	.000	-99	-1	-1	0	0			-0	/SM	0.0
Total	13	1167	4618	671	1291	196	57	27	735	319	198	.280	.332	.364	88	-70	-87	633	164			28	13/2SPO	-1.4

■ DICK TEED   Teed, Richard Leroy   b: 3/8/26, Springfield, Mass.   BB/TR, 5'11", 180 lbs.   Deb: 7/24/53

YEAR	TM/L	G	AB	R	H	2B	3B	HR	RBI	BB	SO	AVG	OBP	SLG	PRO+	BR	/A	RC	SB	CS	SBR	FR	POS	TPR
1953	Bro-N	1	1	0	0	0	0	0	0	0	1	.000	.000	.000	-98	-0	-0	0	0	0	0	0	H	0.0

■ WILFREDO TEJADA   Tejada, Wilfredo Aristides (Andujar)   b: 11/12/62, Santo Domingo, D.R.   BR/TR, 6', 175 lbs.   Deb: 9/09/86

YEAR	TM/L	G	AB	R	H	2B	3B	HR	RBI	BB	SO	AVG	OBP	SLG	PRO+	BR	/A	RC	SB	CS	SBR	FR	POS	TPR
1986	Mon-N	10	25	1	6	1	0	0	2	2	8	.240	.296	.280	60	-1	-1	2	0	0	0	0	C	0.0
1988	Mon-N	8	15	1	4	2	0	0	2	0	4	.267	.267	.400	85	-0	-0	2	0	0	0	3	/C	0.3
Total	2	18	40	2	10	3	0	0	4	2	12	.250	.286	.325	70	-2	-2	4	0	0	0	3	/C	0.3

■ JOHNNY TEMPLE   Temple, John Ellis   b: 8/8/28, Lexington, N.C.   BR/TR, 5'11", 175 lbs.   Deb: 4/15/52   C

YEAR	TM/L	G	AB	R	H	2B	3B	HR	RBI	BB	SO	AVG	OBP	SLG	PRO+	BR	/A	RC	SB	CS	SBR	FR	POS	TPR
1952	Cin-N	30	97	8	19	3	0	1	5	5	1	.196	.235	.258	37	-8	-8	5	2	1	0	-1	2	-0.8
1953	Cin-N	63	110	14	29	4	0	1	9	7	12	.264	.314	.327	67	-5	-5	12	1	0	0	10	2	0.6
1954	Cin-N	146	505	60	155	14	8	0	44	62	24	.307	.385	.366	94	0	-1	77	21	7	2	-10	*2	0.0
1955	Cin-N	150	588	94	165	20	3	0	50	80	32	.281	.368	.325	81	-9	-13	79	19	4	3	-3	*2/S	0.0
1956	Cin-N	154	632	88	180	18	3	2	41	58	40	.285	.346	.332	78	-13	-18	76	14	4	2	-6	*2/O	-0.9
1957	Cin-N	145	557	85	158	24	4	0	37	94	34	.284	.391	.341	92	4	-1	86	19	5	3	-21	*2	-0.7
1958	Cin-N	141	542	82	166	31	6	3	47	91	41	.306	.406	.402	109	16	12	96	15	8	-0	-19	*2/1	0.1
1959	Cin-N	149	598	102	186	35	6	8	67	72	40	.311	.387	.430	114	17	14	104	14	3	-0	-26	*2	0.3
1960	Cle-A	98	381	50	102	13	1	2	19	32	20	.268	.326	.323	79	-12	-11	41	11	5	0	-30	23	-3.5
1961	Cle-A	129	518	73	143	22	3	3	30	61	36	.276	.352	.347	90	-7	-6	65	9	5	-0	-30	*2	-1.9
1962	Bal-A	78	270	28	71	8	1	1	17	36	22	.263	.352	.311	84	-6	-4	33	7	4	-0	-19	2	-1.8
	Hou-N	31	95	14	25	4	0	0	12	7	11	.263	.314	.305	72	-4	-3	10	1	0	0	-8	2/3	-0.8
1963	Hou-N	100	322	32	85	12	1	1	17	41	24	.264	.347	.317	99	-2	1	40	7	2	1	-20	23	-1.5
1964	Cin-N	6	3	0	0	0	0	0	0	2	1	.000	.400	.000	23	-0	-0	0	0	0	0	0	H	0.0
Total	13	1420	5218	720	1484	208	36	22	395	648	338	.284	.365	.351	91	-30	-45	725	140	48	13	-181	*2/310S	-10.9

■ GARRY TEMPLETON   Templeton, Garry Lewis   b: 3/24/56, Lockney, Tex.   BB/TR, 5'11", 175 lbs.   Deb: 8/09/76

YEAR	TM/L	G	AB	R	H	2B	3B	HR	RBI	BB	SO	AVG	OBP	SLG	PRO+	BR	/A	RC	SB	CS	SBR	FR	POS	TPR
1976	StL-N	53	213	32	62	8	2	1	17	7	33	.291	.317	.362	91	-3	-3	24	11	7	-1	1	S	0.2
1977	StL-N	153	621	94	200	19	18	8	79	15	70	.322	.339	.449	111	6	8	85	28	24	-6	-2	*S	2.0
1978	StL-N	155	647	82	181	31	13	2	47	22	87	.280	.304	.377	91	-11	-10	74	34	11	4	23	*S	3.1
1979	StL-N	154	672	105	211	32	19	9	62	18	91	.314	.333	.458	113	10	9	100	26	10	2	18	*S	4.4
1980	StL-N	118	504	83	161	19	9	4	43	18	43	.319	.343	.417	108	6	4	66	31	15	0	28	*S	4.7
1981	StL-N	80	333	47	96	16	8	1	33	14	55	.288	.317	.393	98	-1	-2	37	8	12	-5	5	S	0.7
1982	SD-N	141	563	76	139	25	8	6	64	26	82	.247	.281	.352	80	-19	-16	49	27	16	-2	-24	*S	-3.2
1983	SD-N	126	460	39	121	20	2	3	40	21	57	.263	.295	.335	77	-17	-15	42	16	6	1	-14	*S	-1.7
1984	*SD-N	148	493	40	127	19	3	2	35	39	81	.258	.313	.320	79	-14	-14	48	8	3	1	-23	*S	-2.0
1985	SD-N	148	546	63	154	30	2	6	55	41	88	.282	.333	.377	100	-1	-0	69	16	6	1	-7	*S	0.6
1986	SD-N	147	510	42	126	21	2	2	44	35	86	.247	.297	.308	68	-23	-22	44	10	5	0	-28	*S	-3.7
1987	SD-N	148	510	42	113	13	5	5	48	42	92	.222	.282	.296	55	-34	-32	42	14	3	2	9	*S	-0.3
1988	SD-N	110	362	35	90	15	7	3	36	20	50	.249	.288	.354	85	-8	-8	36	8	2	1	15	*S/3	1.7
1989	SD-N	142	506	43	129	26	3	6	40	23	80	.255	.287	.354	82	-13	-13	47	1	3	-2	13	*S	0.8
1990	SD-N	144	505	45	125	25	3	9	59	24	59	.248	.282	.362	75	-18	-19	46	1	4	-2	-9	*S	-1.8
Total	15	1967	7445	868	2035	319	104	67	702	365	1054	.273	.308	.371	88	-139	-130	810	239	127	-5	4	*S/3	5.5

■ GENE TENACE   Tenace, Fury Gene (b: Fiore Gino Tennaci)   b: 10/10/46, Russellton, Pa.   BR/TR, 6', 190 lbs.   Deb: 5/29/69   C

YEAR	TM/L	G	AB	R	H	2B	3B	HR	RBI	BB	SO	AVG	OBP	SLG	PRO+	BR	/A	RC	SB	CS	SBR	FR	POS	TPR
1969	Oak-A	16	38	1	6	0	0	1	2	1	15	.158	.200	.237	23	-4	-4	2	0	0	0	0	C	-0.2
1970	Oak-A	38	105	19	32	6	0	7	20	23	30	.305	.430	.562	178	11	11	26	0	2	-1	3	C	1.4
1971	*Oak-A	65	179	26	49	7	0	7	25	29	34	.274	.381	.430	132	8	8	31	2	1	0	-6	C/O	0.5
1972	*Oak-A	82	227	22	51	5	3	5	32	24	42	.225	.307	.339	97	-2	-1	24	0	0	0	-7	C/O123	-0.8
1973	*Oak-A	160	510	83	132	18	2	24	84	101	94	.259	.391	.443	142	27	31	94	2	2	-1	-11	*1C/2D	1.3
1974	*Oak-A	158	484	71	102	17	1	26	73	110	105	.211	.370	.411	133	19	24	78	2	9	-5	-9	*1C/2	0.8
1975	*Oak-A	158	498	83	127	17	0	29	87	106	127	.255	.398	.464	146	32	34	100	7	4	-0	-15	*C1/D	1.9
1976	Oak-A	128	417	64	104	19	1	22	66	81	91	.249	.376	.458	150	25	27	76	5	4	-1	-20	1C/D	0.5
1977	SD-N	147	437	66	102	24	4	15	61	125	119	.233	.417	.410	137	21	28	87	5	3	-0	-6	C13	1.9
1978	SD-N	142	401	60	90	18	4	16	61	101	98	.224	.394	.409	135	18	22	73	6	5	-1	-3	C1/3	1.8
1979	SD-N	151	463	61	122	16	4	20	67	105	106	.263	.407	.445	141	25	29	91	2	6	-3	-2	C1	2.4
1980	SD-N	133	316	46	70	11	1	17	50	92	63	.222	.403	.424	139	18	20	58	4	2	-0	-7	*C1	1.4
1981	StL-N	58	129	26	30	7	0	5	22	38	26	.233	.421	.403	131	8	8	26	0	0	0	-6	C/1	0.2
1982	*StL-N	66	124	18	32	9	0	7	18	36	31	.258	.439	.500	160	13	12	26	1	1	-0	2	C/1	1.4
1983	Pit-N	53	62	7	11	5	0	0	6	12	17	.177	.346	.258	68	-2	-2	7	0	1	-1	-1	1/CO	-0.4
Total	15	1555	4390	653	1060	179	20	201	674	984	998	.241	.391	.429	137	219	250	805	36	42	-14	-88	C1/3OD2	14.1

YEAR	TM/L	G	AB	R	H	2B	3B	HR	RBI	BB	SO	AVG	OBP	SLG	PRO+	BR	/A	RC	SB	CS	SBR	FR	POS	TPR

■ JOHN TENER Tener, John Kinley b: 7/25/1863, County Tyrone, Ireland d: 5/19/46, Pittsburgh, Pa. BR/TR, 6'4", 180 lbs. Deb: 6/08/1885

YEAR	TM/L	G	AB	R	H	2B	3B	HR	RBI	BB	SO	AVG	OBP	SLG	PRO+	BR	/A	RC	SB	CS	SBR	FR	POS	TPR
1885	Bal-a	1	4	0	0	0	0	0		0	0	.000	.000	.000	-99	-1	-1	0				-1	/O	-0.1
1888	Chi-N	12	46	4	9	1	0	0	1	1	15	.196	.229	.217	42	-3	-3	3	1			1	P/O	0.0
1889	Chi-N	42	150	18	41	4	2	1	19	7	22	.273	.306	.347	79	-4	-5	17	2			3	P/O1	0.0
1890	Pit-P	18	63	7	12	0	0	2	5	7	10	.190	.301	.286	64	-4	-3	6	1			2	P/O3	0.0
Total	4	73	263	29	62	5	2	3	25	15	47	.236	.287	.304	67	-11	-11	25	4			6	/PO31	-0.1

■ TOM TENNANT Tennant, Thomas Francis b: 7/3/1882, Monroe, Wis. d: 2/15/55, San Carlos, Cal. BL/TL, 5'11", 165 lbs. Deb: 4/18/12

YEAR	TM/L	G	AB	R	H	2B	3B	HR	RBI	BB	SO	AVG	OBP	SLG	PRO+	BR	/A	RC	SB	CS	SBR	FR	POS	TPR
1912	StL-A	2	2	1	0	0	0	0	0	0	0	.000	.000	.000	-99	-1	-1	0	0			0	H	0.0

■ FRED TENNEY Tenney, Fred Clay b: 7/9/1859, Marlborough, N.H. d: 6/15/19, Fall River, Mass. Deb: 4/28/1884

YEAR	TM/L	G	AB	R	H	2B	3B	HR	RBI	BB	SO	AVG	OBP	SLG	PRO+	BR	/A	RC	SB	CS	SBR	FR	POS	TPR
1884	Was-U	32	119	17	28	3	1	0		6		.235	.272	.277	89	-2	-1	9	0			-0	O/1	-0.1
	Bos-U	4	17	1	2	0	0	0		0		.118	.118	.118	-21	-2	-2	0	0			-1	/P	0.0
	Wil-U	1	3	0	0	0	0	0		0		.000	.000	.000	-97	-1	-1	0	0			0	/P	0.0
	Yr	37	139	18	30	3	1	0		6		.216	.248	.252	72	-4	-4	9	0			-1		-0.1

■ FRED TENNEY Tenney, Frederick b: 11/26/1871, Georgetown, Mass. d: 7/3/52, Boston, Mass. BL/TL, 5'9", 155 lbs. Deb: 6/16/1894 M

YEAR	TM/L	G	AB	R	H	2B	3B	HR	RBI	BB	SO	AVG	OBP	SLG	PRO+	BR	/A	RC	SB	CS	SBR	FR	POS	TPR
1894	Bos-N	27	86	23	34	7	1	2	21	12	9	.395	.469	.570	140	8	6	26	6			-0	C/O1	0.5
1895	Bos-N	49	173	35	47	9	1	1	21	24	5	.272	.360	.353	80	-3	-5	25	6			-3	OC	-0.6
1896	Bos-N	88	348	64	117	14	3	2	49	36	12	.336	.400	.411	110	9	6	66	18			0	OC	0.4
1897	*Bos-N	132	566	125	180	24	3	1	85	49		.318	.376	.376	95	3	-3	95	34			5	*1/O	0.0
1898	Bos-N	117	488	106	160	25	5	0	62	33		.328	.370	.400	117	14	11	83	23			5	*1/C	1.5
1899	Bos-N	150	603	115	209	19	17	1	67	63		.347	.411	.439	124	31	22	123	28			10	*1	3.2
1900	Bos-N	112	437	77	122	13	5	1	56	39		.279	.346	.339	82	-4	-12	59	17			9	*1	-0.1
1901	Bos-N	115	451	66	127	13	1	1	22	37		.282	.340	.322	87	-2	-7	58	15			7	*1/C	0.1
1902	Bos-N	134	489	88	154	18	3	2	30	73		.315	.410	.376	144	30	30	90	21			13	*1	3.8
1903	Bos-N	122	447	79	140	22	3	3	41	70		.313	.406	.396	137	21	24	85	21			8	*1	2.7
1904	Bos-N	147	533	76	144	17	9	1	37	57		.270	.341	.341	117	9	12	72	17			8	*1/O	2.7
1905	Bos-N	149	549	84	158	18	3	0	28	67		.288	.365	.332	113	10	11	76	17			21	*1/PM	2.7
1906	Bos-N	143	544	61	154	12	8	1	28	58		.283	.352	.340	121	13	14	75	17			10	*1M	2.0
1907	Bos-N	150	554	83	151	18	8	0	26	82		.273	.366	.334	122	17	17	78	15			9	*1M	2.5
1908	NY-N	156	583	**101**	149	20	1	2	49	72		.256	.337	.304	102	7	4	67	17			10	*1	1.2
1909	NY-N	101	375	43	88	8	2	3	30	52		.235	.333	.291	92	-1	-2	39	8			8	1	0.5
1911	Bos-N	102	369	52	97	13	4	1	36	50	17	.263	.352	.328	84	-3	-7	45	5			3	1/OM	-0.7
Total	17	1994	7595	1278	2231	270	77	22	688	874	43	.294	.369	.358	110	161	121	1164	285			123	*1O/CP	21.1

■ FRANK TEPEDINO Tepedino, Frank Ronald b: 11/23/47, Brooklyn, N.Y. BL/TL, 5'11", 185 lbs. Deb: 5/12/67

YEAR	TM/L	G	AB	R	H	2B	3B	HR	RBI	BB	SO	AVG	OBP	SLG	PRO+	BR	/A	RC	SB	CS	SBR	FR	POS	TPR
1967	NY-A	9	5	0	2	0	0	0	0	1	1	.400	.500	.400	175	1	1	1	0	0	0	0	/1	0.1
1969	NY-A	13	39	6	9	0	0	0	4	4	4	.231	.302	.231	53	-2	-2	3	1	0	0	-1	O	-0.3
1970	NY-A	16	19	2	6	2	0	0	2	1	2	.316	.350	.421	118	0	0	2	0	1	-1	-0	/1O	0.0
1971	NY-A	6	6	0	0	0	0	0	0	0	0	.000	.000	.000	-99	-2	-2	0	0	0	0	0	/O	-0.1
	Mil-A	53	106	11	21	1	0	2	7	4	17	.198	.234	.264	41	-8	-8	6	2	2	-1	3	1	-0.7
	Yr	59	112	11	21	1	0	2	7	4	17	.188	.222	.250	34	-10	-10	6	2	2	-1	3		-0.8
1972	NY-A	8	8	0	0	0	0	0	0	0	1	.000	.000	.000	-99	-2	-2	0	0	0	0	0	H	-0.1
1973	Atl-N	74	148	20	45	5	0	4	29	13	21	.304	.360	.419	107	3	2	21	0	0	0	2	1	0.1
1974	Atl-N	78	169	11	39	5	1	0	16	9	13	.231	.274	.272	51	-11	-11	11	1	2	-1	1	1	-1.3
1975	Atl-N	8	7	0	0	0	0	0	0	1	2	.000	.125	.000	-61	-2	-2	0	0	0	0	0	H	-0.1
Total	8	265	507	50	122	13	1	6	58	33	61	.241	.290	.306	65	-23	-24	44	4	5	-2	5	1/O	-2.4

■ JOE TEPSIC Tepsic, Joseph John b: 9/18/23, Slovan, Pa. BR/TR, 5'9", 170 lbs. Deb: 7/12/46

YEAR	TM/L	G	AB	R	H	2B	3B	HR	RBI	BB	SO	AVG	OBP	SLG	PRO+	BR	/A	RC	SB	CS	SBR	FR	POS	TPR
1946	Bro-N	15	5	2	0	0	0	0	0	0	1	.000	.167	.000	-50	-1	-1	0	0			1	/O	0.0

■ JERRY TERRELL Terrell, Jerry Wayne b: 7/13/46, Waseca, Minn. BR/TR, 5'11", 165 lbs. Deb: 4/14/73

YEAR	TM/L	G	AB	R	H	2B	3B	HR	RBI	BB	SO	AVG	OBP	SLG	PRO+	BR	/A	RC	SB	CS	SBR	FR	POS	TPR
1973	Min-A	124	438	43	116	15	2	1	32	21	56	.265	.300	.315	71	-16	-18	42	13	7	-0	-13	S32/OD	-2.0
1974	Min-A	116	229	43	56	4	6	0	19	11	27	.245	.279	.314	68	-9	-10	19	3	2	-0	**31**	S23D/O1	2.6
1975	Min-A	108	385	48	110	16	2	0	36	19	27	.286	.324	.345	87	-6	-7	41	4	4	-1	-4	S213/OD	-0.6
1976	Min-A	89	171	29	42	3	1	0	8	9	15	.246	.287	.275	63	-7	-8	14	11	2	2	11	23SD/O	0.8
1977	Min-A	93	214	32	48	6	0	1	20	11	21	.224	.265	.266	46	-16	-16	13	10	4	1	5	32/S10D	-0.9
1978	KC-A	73	133	14	27	1	0	0	8	4	13	.203	.226	.211	23	-13	-14	6	8	4	0	6	23S/1	-0.5
1979	KC-A	31	40	5	12	3	0	1	2	1	1	.300	.317	.450	102	-0	-0	5	1	0	0	2	3/2PS	0.3
1980	KC-A	23	16	4	1	0	0	0	0	0	0	.063	.063	.063	-65	-4	-4	0	0	0	0	4	/O12PD	0.0
Total	8	657	1626	218	412	48	11	4	125	76	160	.253	.289	.304	66	-71	-75	141	50	23	1	42	3S2/D10P	-0.3

■ TOM TERRELL Terrell, John Thomas b: 1866, Louisville, Ky. d: 7/9/1893, Louisville, Ky. Deb: 10/05/1886

YEAR	TM/L	G	AB	R	H	2B	3B	HR	RBI	BB	SO	AVG	OBP	SLG	PRO+	BR	/A	RC	SB	CS	SBR	FR	POS	TPR
1886	Lou-a	1	4	0	1	0	0	0		0		.250	.250	.250	55	-0	-0	0	0			-1	/OC	0.0

■ TERRY Terry Deb: 4/26/1875

YEAR	TM/L	G	AB	R	H	2B	3B	HR	RBI	BB	SO	AVG	OBP	SLG	PRO+	BR	/A	RC	SB	CS	SBR	FR	POS	TPR
1875	Was-n	6	22	0	4	0	1	0		0		.182	.182	.273	57	-1	-1	1					/O1	0.0

■ ADONIS TERRY Terry, William H b: 8/7/1864, Westfield, Mass. d: 2/24/15, Milwaukee, Wis. BR/TR, 5'11.5", 168 lbs. Deb: 5/01/1884 U

YEAR	TM/L	G	AB	R	H	2B	3B	HR	RBI	BB	SO	AVG	OBP	SLG	PRO+	BR	/A	RC	SB	CS	SBR	FR	POS	TPR
1884	Bro-a	67	236	15	55	10	3	0		8		.233	.258	.301	84	-4	-4	19				-2	PO	0.0
1885	Bro-a	71	264	23	45	1	3	1		10		.170	.201	.208	31	-20	-20	11				2	OP/3	-1.4
1886	Bro-a	75	299	34	71	8	9	2		10		.237	.265	.344	91	-4	-4	33	17			3	POS	0.2
1887	Bro-a	86	352	56	103	6	10	3		16		.293	.323	.392	100	-0	-1	55	27			2	OP/S	0.5
1888	Bro-a	30	115	13	29	6	0	0	8	5		.252	.283	.304	91	-1	-1	12	7			0	P/O1	0.0
1889	*Bro-a	49	160	29	48	6	6	2	26	14	14	.300	.356	.450	131	6	6	29	8			4	P1	0.0
1890	*Bro-N	99	363	63	101	17	9	6	59	40	34	.278	.356	.408	124	11	11	66	32			-2	OP/1	1.4
1891	Bro-N	30	91	10	19	7	1	0	6	9	26	.209	.301	.308	80	-2	-2	10	4			-2	P/O	0.0
1892	Bal-N	1	4	0	0	0	0	0	0	0	1	.000	.000	.000	-97	-1	-1	0	0			0	/P	0.0
	Pit-N	31	100	10	16	0	4	0	11	10	11	.160	.236	.300	63	-5	-5	8	2			-0	P/O	0.0
	Yr	32	104	10	16	0	4	0	11	10	12	.154	.228	.288	57	-6	-6	7	2			-0		0.0
1893	Pit-N	26	71	9	18	4	3	0	11	3	11	.254	.293	.394	85	-2	-2	9	1			0	P	0.0
1894	Pit-N	1	0	0	0	0	0	0	0	0	0	—			—	0	0	0	0			0	/P	0.0
	Chi-N	30	95	19	33	4	2	0	17	11	12	.347	.415	.432	101	1	0	19	3			-2	P/O1	0.0
	Yr	31	95	19	33	4	2	0	17	11	12	.347	.415	.432	101	1	0	19	3			-2		0.0
1895	Chi-N	40	137	18	30	3	2	1	10	2	11	.219	.236	.292	35	-13	-15	10	1			2	P/OS	0.0
1896	Chi-N	30	99	14	26	4	2	0	15	8	12	.263	.324	.343	75	-3	-4	13	4			-2	P	0.0
1897	Chi-N	1	3	1	0	0	0	0	0	0		.000	.000	.000	-96	-1	-1	0	0			0	/P	0.0
Total	14	667	2389	314	594	76	54	15	163	146	138	.249	.295	.344	87	-38	-43	292	106			4	PO/S13	0.7

■ BILL TERRY Terry, William Harold "Memphis Bill" b: 10/30/1898, Atlanta, Ga. d: 1/9/89, Jacksonville, Fla. BL/TL, 6'1", 200 lbs. Deb: 9/24/23 MH

YEAR	TM/L	G	AB	R	H	2B	3B	HR	RBI	BB	SO	AVG	OBP	SLG	PRO+	BR	/A	RC	SB	CS	SBR	FR	POS	TPR
1923	NY-N	3	7	1	1	0	0	0	0	0	1	.143	.333	.143	30	-1	-1	0	0	0	0	0	/1	0.0
1924	*NY-N	77	163	26	39	7	2	5	24	17	18	.239	.311	.399	91	-3	-2	21	1	1	-0	-1	1	-0.5
1925	NY-N	133	489	75	156	31	6	11	70	42	52	.319	.374	.474	120	11	14	86	4	5	-2	4	*1	0.2
1926	NY-N	98	225	26	65	12	5	5	43	22	17	.289	.352	.453	117	4	5	35	3			4	1O	0.7

YEAR	TM/L	G	AB	R	H	2B	3B	HR	RBI	BB	SO	AVG	OBP	SLG	PRO+	BR	/A	RC	SB	CS	SBR	FR	POS	TPR
1927	NY-N	150	580	101	189	32	13	20	121	46	53	.326	.377	.529	141	31	31	112	1			5	*1	2.6
1928	NY-N	149	568	100	185	36	11	17	101	64	36	.326	.394	.518	136	30	29	114	7			-1	*1	1.1
1929	NY-N	150	607	103	226	39	5	14	117	48	35	.372	.418	.522	132	30	31	128	10			7	*1/O	2.7
1930	NY-N	154	633	139	**254**	39	15	23	129	57	33	**.401**	.452	.619	159	58	60	170	8			13	*1	5.7
1931	NY-N	153	611	**121**	213	43	**20**	9	112	47	36	.349	.397	.529	150	39	41	130	8			9	*1	**3.7**
1932	NY-N	154	643	124	225	42	11	28	117	32	23	.350	.382	.580	158	46	48	142	4			14	*1M	5.2
1933	*NY-N	123	475	68	153	20	5	6	58	40	23	.322	.375	.423	129	17	18	77	3			1	*1M	1.7
1934	NY-N	153	602	109	213	30	6	8	83	60	47	.354	.414	.463	138	31	33	122	0			6	*1M	2.5
1935	NY-N	145	596	91	203	32	8	6	64	41	55	.341	.383	.451	126	20	21	104	7			6	*1M	2.4
1936	*NY-N	79	229	36	71	10	5	2	39	19	19	.310	.363	.424	112	4	4	35	0			3	1M	0.2
Total	14	1721	6428	1120	2193	373	112	154	1078	537	449	.341	.393	.506	137	318	332	1275	56	6		68	*1/O	28.2

■ ZEB TERRY
Terry, Zebulon Alexander b: 6/17/1891, Denison, Tex. d: 3/14/88, Los Angeles, Cal. BR/TR, 5'8", 129 lbs. Deb: 4/12/16

YEAR	TM/L	G	AB	R	H	2B	3B	HR	RBI	BB	SO	AVG	OBP	SLG	PRO+	BR	/A	RC	SB	CS	SBR	FR	POS	TPR
1916	Chi-A	94	269	20	51	8	4	0	17	33	36	.190	.292	.249	62	-12	-12	23	4			-10	S	-1.5
1917	Chi-A	2	1	0	0	0	0	0	0	2	0	.000	.667	.000	102	0	0	0	0			-0	/S	0.0
1918	Bos-N	28	105	17	32	2	2	0	8	8	14	.305	.360	.362	126	3	3	14	1			8	S	1.3
1919	Pit-N	129	472	46	107	12	6	0	27	31	26	.227	.280	.278	65	-18	-20	39	12			-31	*S	-5.2
1920	Chi-N	133	496	56	139	26	9	0	52	44	22	.280	.341	.369	102	3	2	61	12	16	-6	14	S2	1.6
1921	Chi-N	123	488	59	134	18	1	2	45	27	19	.275	.318	.328	71	-20	-20	49	1	13	-8	6	*2	-2.0
1922	Chi-N	131	496	56	142	24	2	0	67	34	16	.286	.335	.343	74	-18	-19	56	2	11	-6	9	*2/S3	-1.6
Total	7	640	2327	254	605	90	24	2	216	179	133	.260	.318	.322	78	-61	-66	243	32	40		-5	S2/3	-7.4

■ WAYNE TERWILLIGER
Terwilliger, Willard Wayne "Twig" b: 6/27/25, Clare, Mich. BR/TR, 5'11", 165 lbs. Deb: 8/06/49 C

YEAR	TM/L	G	AB	R	H	2B	3B	HR	RBI	BB	SO	AVG	OBP	SLG	PRO+	BR	/A	RC	SB	CS	SBR	FR	POS	TPR
1949	Chi-N	36	112	11	25	2	1	2	10	16	22	.223	.326	.313	74	-4	-4	13	0			4	2	0.1
1950	Chi-N	133	480	63	116	22	3	10	32	43	63	.242	.311	.363	77	-17	-16	56	13			-8	*2/13O	-2.0
1951	Chi-N	50	192	26	41	6	0	0	10	29	21	.214	.317	.245	52	-12	-12	17	3	1	0	-4	2	-1.3
	Bro-N	37	50	11	14	1	0	0	4	8	7	.280	.390	.300	87	-0	-0	7	1	0	0	6	2/3	0.7
	Yr	87	242	37	55	7	0	0	14	37	28	.227	.332	.256	59	-12	-13	23	4	1	1	3		-0.6
1953	Was-A	134	464	62	117	24	4	4	46	64	65	.252	.343	.347	89	-8	-6	58	7	4	-0	5	*2	0.6
1954	Was-A	106	337	42	70	10	1	3	24	32	40	.208	.282	.270	55	-22	-20	27	3	3	-1	13	23/S	-0.4
1955	NY-N	80	257	29	66	16	1	1	18	36	42	.257	.350	.339	84	-5	-5	30	2	4	-2	26	2/S3	2.5
1956	NY-N	14	18	0	4	1	0	0	0	0	5	.222	.222	.278	34	-2	-2	1	0	0	0	2	/2	0.1
1959	KC-A	74	180	27	48	11	0	2	18	19	31	.267	.337	.361	90	-2	-2	23	2	2	-1	20	2/S3	1.9
1960	KC-A	2	1	0	0	0	0	0	0	0	0	.000	.000	.000	-99	-0	-0	0	0	0	0	0	/2	0.0
Total	9	666	2091	271	501	93	10	22	162	247	296	.240	.323	.325	76	-72	-68	230	31	14		65	2/3SO1	2.2

■ AL TESCH
Tesch, Albert John "Tiny" b: 1/27/1891, Jersey City, N.J. d: 8/3/47, Jersey City, N.J. BB/TR, 5'10", 155 lbs. Deb: 8/21/15

YEAR	TM/L	G	AB	R	H	2B	3B	HR	RBI	BB	SO	AVG	OBP	SLG	PRO+	BR	/A	RC	SB	CS	SBR	FR	POS	TPR
1915	Bro-F	8	7	2	2	1	0	0	2	0	0	.286	.286	.429	111	0	0	1	0			3	/2	0.4

■ NICK TESTA
Testa, Nicholas b: 6/29/28, New York, N.Y. BR/TR, 5'8", 180 lbs. Deb: 4/23/58 C

YEAR	TM/L	G	AB	R	H	2B	3B	HR	RBI	BB	SO	AVG	OBP	SLG	PRO+	BR	/A	RC	SB	CS	SBR	FR	POS	TPR
1958	SF-N	1	0	0	0	0	0	0	0	0	0	—	—	—	—	0	0	0	0	0	0	-0	/C	0.0

■ DICK TETTELBACH
Tettelbach, Richard Morley "Tut" b: 6/26/29, New Haven, Conn. BR/TR, 6', 195 lbs. Deb: 9/25/55

YEAR	TM/L	G	AB	R	H	2B	3B	HR	RBI	BB	SO	AVG	OBP	SLG	PRO+	BR	/A	RC	SB	CS	SBR	FR	POS	TPR
1955	NY-A	2	5	0	0	0	0	0	0	0	0	.000	.000	.000	-99	-1	-1	0	0	0	0	0	/O	0.0
1956	Was-A	18	64	10	10	1	2	1	9	14	15	.156	.308	.281	56	-4	-4	7	0	1	-1	0	O	-0.4
1957	Was-A	9	11	2	2	0	0	0	1	4	2	.182	.400	.182	65	-0	-1	0	0	0	0	0	/O	0.0
Total	3	29	80	12	12	1	2	1	10	18	17	.150	.306	.250	49	-6	-6	8	0	1	-1	1	/O	-0.4

■ MICKEY TETTLETON
Tettleton, Mickey Lee b: 9/16/60, Oklahoma City, Okla. BB/TR, 6'2", 200 lbs. Deb: 6/30/84

YEAR	TM/L	G	AB	R	H	2B	3B	HR	RBI	BB	SO	AVG	OBP	SLG	PRO+	BR	/A	RC	SB	CS	SBR	FR	POS	TPR
1984	Oak-A	33	76	10	20	2	1	1	5	11	21	.263	.356	.355	105	0	1	10	0	0	0	0	C	0.3
1985	Oak-A	78	211	23	53	12	0	3	15	28	59	.251	.344	.351	98	-2	0	26	2	2	-1	0	C/D	0.3
1986	Oak-A	90	211	26	43	9	0	10	35	39	51	.204	.331	.389	103	-1	1	31	7	1	2	-2	C	0.7
1987	Oak-A	82	211	19	41	3	0	8	26	30	65	.194	.295	.322	68	-11	-9	22	1	1	0	3	C/1D	0.1
1988	Bal-A	86	283	31	74	11	1	11	37	28	70	.261	.332	.424	113	4	5	38	0	1	-1	-9	C	-0.1
1989	Bal-A	117	411	72	106	21	2	26	65	73	117	.258	.371	.509	150	26	27	80	3	2	-0	-2	CD	2.8
1990	Bal-A	135	444	68	99	21	2	15	51	106	160	.223	.378	.381	115	12	13	71	2	4	-2	-14	CD/1O	0.0
Total	7	621	1847	249	436	79	6	74	234	315	543	.236	.351	.406	114	27	39	278	15	11	-2	-23	C/D1O	4.1

■ TIM TEUFEL
Teufel, Timothy Shawn b: 7/7/58, Greenwich, Conn. BR/TR, 6', 175 lbs. Deb: 9/03/83

YEAR	TM/L	G	AB	R	H	2B	3B	HR	RBI	BB	SO	AVG	OBP	SLG	PRO+	BR	/A	RC	SB	CS	SBR	FR	POS	TPR
1983	Min-A	21	78	11	24	7	1	3	6	2	8	.308	.325	.538	128	3	3	13	0	0	0	-1	2/SD	0.2
1984	Min-A	157	568	76	149	30	3	14	61	76	73	.262	.351	.400	103	7	4	79	1	3	-2	-11	*2	-0.1
1985	Min-A	138	434	58	113	24	3	10	50	48	70	.260	.338	.399	95	1	-2	58	4	2	0	-33	*2/D	-2.9
1986	*NY-N	93	279	35	69	20	1	4	31	32	42	.247	.327	.369	94	-3	-2	34	1	2	-1	-18	2/13	-2.0
1987	NY-N	97	299	55	92	29	0	14	61	44	53	.308	.400	.545	155	21	23	66	3	2	-0	-11	2/1	1.3
1988	*NY-N	90	273	35	64	20	0	4	31	29	41	.234	.310	.352	94	-4	-2	30	0	1	-1	12	2/1	1.2
1989	NY-N	83	219	27	56	7	2	2	15	32	50	.256	.353	.333	102	0	2	27	1	3	-2	-0	21	-0.2
1990	NY-N	80	175	28	43	11	0	10	24	15	33	.246	.305	.480	115	2	3	24	0	0	0	-4	123	-0.1
Total	8	759	2325	325	610	148	10	61	279	278	370	.262	.344	.413	108	28	27	331	10	13	-5	-68	2/13DS	-2.6

■ GEORGE TEXTOR
Textor, George Bernhardt b: 12/27/1888, Newport, Ky. d: 3/10/54, Massillon, Ohio BB/TR, 5'10.5", 174 lbs. Deb: 4/19/14

YEAR	TM/L	G	AB	R	H	2B	3B	HR	RBI	BB	SO	AVG	OBP	SLG	PRO+	BR	/A	RC	SB	CS	SBR	FR	POS	TPR
1914	Ind-F	22	57	2	10	0	0	0	4	2	9	.175	.230	.175	15	-6	-7	2	0			-4	C	-0.9
1915	New-F	3	6	1	2	0	0	0	0	0	0	.333	.333	.333	104	-0	0	1	0			-1	/C	-0.1
Total	2	25	63	3	12	0	0	0	4	2	9	.190	.239	.190	22	-6	-7	3	0			-5	/C	-1.0

■ MOE THACKER
Thacker, Morris Benton b: 5/21/34, Louisville, Ky. BR/TR, 6'3", 205 lbs. Deb: 4/20/58

YEAR	TM/L	G	AB	R	H	2B	3B	HR	RBI	BB	SO	AVG	OBP	SLG	PRO+	BR	/A	RC	SB	CS	SBR	FR	POS	TPR
1958	Chi-N	11	24	4	6	1	0	0	3	1	7	.250	.280	.542	113	0	0	3	0	0	0	0	/C	0.1
1960	Chi-N	54	90	5	14	1	0	0	6	14	20	.156	.269	.167	23	-9	-9	4	1	1	-0	5	C	-0.2
1961	Chi-N	25	35	3	6	0	0	0	2	11	11	.171	.383	.171	53	-2	-2	3	0	0	0	-0	C	0.0
1962	Chi-N	65	107	8	20	5	0	0	9	14	40	.187	.287	.234	40	-9	-9	8	0	1	-1	14	C	0.5
1963	StL-N	3	4	0	0	0	0	0	0	0	3	.000	.000	.000	-91	-1	-1	0	0	0	0	1	/C	0.0
Total	5	158	260	20	46	7	0	2	20	40	81	.177	.291	.227	41	-20	-21	18	1	2	-1	19	C	0.4

■ AL THAKE
Thake, Albert b: 9/21/1849, Wymondham, England d: 9/1/1872, Hamilton, N.Y. 6', Deb: 6/13/1872

YEAR	TM/L	G	AB	R	H	2B	3B	HR	RBI	BB	SO	AVG	OBP	SLG	PRO+	BR	/A	RC	SB	CS	SBR	FR	POS	TPR
1872	Atl-n	18	80	14	23	2	2	0		0		.287	.287	.363	84	-0	-3	9					O/2	-0.1

■ RON THEOBALD
Theobald, Ronald Merrill b: 7/28/43, Oakland, Cal. BR/TR, 5'8", 165 lbs. Deb: 4/12/71

YEAR	TM/L	G	AB	R	H	2B	3B	HR	RBI	BB	SO	AVG	OBP	SLG	PRO+	BR	/A	RC	SB	CS	SBR	FR	POS	TPR
1971	Mil-A	126	388	50	107	12	2	1	23	38	39	.276	.345	.325	92	-4	-3	46	11	8	-2	1	*2/S3	0.1
1972	Mil-A	125	391	45	86	11	0	1	19	68	38	.220	.343	.256	80	-6	-6	37	0	7	-4	-13	*2	-1.7
Total	2	251	779	95	193	23	2	2	42	106	77	.248	.344	.290	87	-10	-9	83	11	15	-6	-12	2/3S	-1.6

■ GEORGE THEODORE
Theodore, George Basil b: 11/13/47, Salt Lake City, Ut. BR/TR, 6'4", 190 lbs. Deb: 4/14/73

YEAR	TM/L	G	AB	R	H	2B	3B	HR	RBI	BB	SO	AVG	OBP	SLG	PRO+	BR	/A	RC	SB	CS	SBR	FR	POS	TPR
1973	*NY-N	45	116	14	30	4	0	1	15	10	13	.259	.323	.319	80	-3	-3	11	1	0	0	2	O/1	-0.2
1974	NY-N	60	76	7	12	1	0	1	1	8	14	.158	.247	.211	29	-7	-7	3	0	0	0	-2	1O	-1.0
Total	2	105	192	21	42	5	0	2	16	18	27	.219	.292	.276	60	-10	-10	14	1	0	0	-0	/O1	-1.2

YEAR	TM/L	G	AB	R	H	2B	3B	HR	RBI	BB	SO	AVG	OBP	SLG	PRO+	BR	/A	RC	SB	CS	SBR	FR	POS	TPR

■ TOMMY THEVENOW
Thevenow, Thomas Joseph b: 9/6/03, Madison, Ind. d: 7/29/57, Madison, Ind. BR/TR, 5'10", 155 lbs. Deb: 9/04/24

YEAR	TM/L	G	AB	R	H	2B	3B	HR	RBI	BB	SO	AVG	OBP	SLG	PRO+	BR	/A	RC	SB	CS	SBR	FR	POS	TPR
1924	StL-N	23	89	4	18	4	1	0	7	1	6	.202	.211	.270	28	-9	-9	4	1	3	-2	8	S	0.0
1925	StL-N	50	175	17	47	7	2	0	17	7	12	.269	.301	.331	60	-9	-11	18	3	0	1	3	S	-0.2
1926	*StL-N	156	563	64	144	15	5	2	63	27	26	.256	.291	.311	60	-30	-33	50	8			18	*S	-0.3
1927	StL-N	59	191	23	37	6	1	0	4	14	8	.194	.249	.236	29	-19	-20	11	2			7	S	-0.6
1928	*StL-N	69	171	11	35	8	3	0	13	20	12	.205	.288	.287	50	-12	-13	15	0			-4	S/31	-0.7
1929	Phi-N	90	317	30	72	11	0	0	35	25	25	.227	.288	.262	35	-31	-34	25	3			3	S	-1.6
1930	Phi-N	156	573	57	164	21	1	0	78	23	26	.286	.316	.326	52	-40	-47	58	1			-2	*S	-3.0
1931	Pit-N	120	404	35	86	12	1	0	38	28	22	.213	.266	.248	39	-34	-34	28	0			9	*S	-1.5
1932	Pit-N	59	194	12	46	3	3	0	26	7	12	.237	.264	.284	48	-14	-14	15	0			-1	S3	-0.9
1933	Pit-N	73	253	20	79	5	1	0	34	3	5	.312	.320	.340	89	-4	-4	25	2			-13	2/S3	-1.2
1934	Pit-N	122	446	37	121	16	2	0	54	20	20	.271	.306	.316	65	-21	-22	41	0			-18	23/S	-2.8
1935	Pit-N	110	408	38	97	9	9	0	47	12	23	.238	.261	.304	50	-28	-30	30	1			4	3S/2	-2.0
1936	Cin-N	106	321	25	75	7	2	0	36	15	23	.234	.268	.268	48	-25	-22	21	2			-8	S23	-2.3
1937	Bos-N	21	34	5	4	0	1	0	2	4	2	.118	.211	.176	7	-4	-4	2	0			1	S/32	-0.1
1938	Pit-N	15	25	2	5	0	0	0	2	4	0	.200	.333	.200	49	-1	-2	2	0			3	/2S3	0.2
Total	15	1229	4164	380	1030	124	32	2	456	210	222	.247	.285	.294	52	-284	-297	346	23	3		9	S23/1	-17.0

■ HENRY THIELMAN
Thielman, Henry Joseph b: 10/3/1880, St.Cloud, Minn. d: 9/2/42, New York, N.Y. BR/TR, 5'11", 175 lbs. Deb: 4/17/02

YEAR	TM/L	G	AB	R	H	2B	3B	HR	RBI	BB	SO	AVG	OBP	SLG	PRO+	BR	/A	RC	SB	CS	SBR	FR	POS	TPR
1902	NY-N	6	9	0	1	0	0	0	0	0	2	.111	.273	.111	21	-1	-1	1	1			1	/PO	0.0
	Cin-N	28	91	6	12	0	2	0	4	5		.132	.186	.176	12	-9	-10	3	0			-1	P/O	0.0
	Yr	34	100	6	13	0	2	0	4	7		.130	.194	.170	13	-10	-11	4	1			-1		0.0
1903	Bro-N	9	23	3	5	1	0	1	2	5		.217	.357	.391	119	1	1	3	0			-0	/OP	0.1
Total	2	43	123	9	18	1	2	1	6	12		.146	.228	.211	33	-9	-10	7	1			-1	/PO	0.1

■ ANDRES THOMAS
Thomas, Andres Perez (b: Andres Perez (Thomas)) b: 11/10/63, Boca Chica, D.R. BR/TR, 6'1", 170 lbs. Deb: 9/03/85

YEAR	TM/L	G	AB	R	H	2B	3B	HR	RBI	BB	SO	AVG	OBP	SLG	PRO+	BR	/A	RC	SB	CS	SBR	FR	POS	TPR
1985	Atl-N	15	18	6	5	0	0	0	2	0	2	.278	.278	.278	53	-1	-1	1	0	0	0	3	S	0.2
1986	Atl-N	102	323	26	81	17	2	6	32	8	49	.251	.269	.372	71	-12	-14	26	4	6	-2	26	S	1.9
1987	Atl-N	82	324	29	75	11	0	5	39	14	50	.231	.268	.312	50	-22	-24	25	6	5	-1	9	S	-0.6
1988	Atl-N	153	606	54	153	22	2	13	68	14	95	.252	.271	.360	76	-18	-21	54	7	3	0	-8	*S	-2.0
1989	Atl-N	141	554	41	118	18	0	13	57	12	62	.213	.230	.316	53	-34	-36	35	3	3	-1	6	*S	-2.3
1990	Atl-N	84	278	26	61	8	0	5	30	11	43	.219	.249	.302	50	-19	-20	18	2	1	0	3	S/3	-1.0
Total	6	577	2103	182	493	76	4	42	228	59	301	.234	.256	.334	61	-106	-116	159	22	18	-4	38	S/3	-3.8

■ PINCH THOMAS
Thomas, Chester David b: 1/24/1888, Camp Point, Ill. d: 12/24/53, Modesto, Cal. BL/TR, 5'9.5", 173 lbs. Deb: 4/24/12

YEAR	TM/L	G	AB	R	H	2B	3B	HR	RBI	BB	SO	AVG	OBP	SLG	PRO+	BR	/A	RC	SB	CS	SBR	FR	POS	TPR
1912	Bos-A	13	30	0	6	0	0	0	5	2		.200	.250	.200	28	-3	-3	2	1			2	/C	0.0
1913	Bos-A	38	91	6	26	1	2	1	15	2	11	.286	.309	.374	97	-1	-1	10	1			2	C	0.3
1914	Bos-A	66	130	9	25	1	0	0	5	18	17	.192	.291	.200	48	-8	-8	8	1			-2	C/1	-0.4
1915	*Bos-A	86	203	21	48	4	4	0	21	13	20	.236	.286	.296	76	-7	-6	18	3	2	-0	4	C	0.4
1916	*Bos-A	99	216	21	57	10	1	1	21	33	13	.264	.364	.333	109	4	4	30	4			-8	C	0.0
1917	Bos-A	83	202	24	48	7	0	0	24	27	9	.238	.333	.272	86	-3	-2	19	2			4	C	0.8
1918	Cle-A	32	73	2	18	0	1	0	5	6	6	.247	.304	.274	68	-2	-3	6	0			0	C	0.0
1919	Cle-A	34	46	2	5	0	0	0	2	4	3	.109	.180	.109	-17	-7	-8	1	0			-2	C	-0.8
1920	*Cle-A	9	9	2	3	1	0	0	0	3	1	.333	.500	.444	147	1	1	2	0	0	0	1	/C	0.2
1921	Cle-A	21	35	1	9	3	0	0	4	10	2	.257	.422	.343	96	0	0	6	0	0	0	-7	C	-0.4
Total	10	481	1035	88	245	27	8	2	102	118	82	.237	.318	.284	78	-25	-26	104	12	2		-5	C/1	0.1

■ DAN THOMAS
Thomas, Danny Lee b: 5/9/51, Birmingham, Ala. d: 6/12/80, Mobile, Ala. BR/TR, 6'2", 190 lbs. Deb: 9/02/76

YEAR	TM/L	G	AB	R	H	2B	3B	HR	RBI	BB	SO	AVG	OBP	SLG	PRO+	BR	/A	RC	SB	CS	SBR	FR	POS	TPR
1976	Mil-A	32	105	13	29	5	1	4	15	14	28	.276	.372	.457	145	6	6	18	1	2	-1	-2	O	0.2
1977	Mil-A	22	70	11	19	3	2	2	11	8	11	.271	.354	.457	119	2	2	11	0	2	-1	-0	/OD	0.0
Total	2	54	175	24	48	8	3	6	26	22	39	.274	.365	.457	134	8	8	29	1	4	-2	-2	/OD	0.2

■ DERREL THOMAS
Thomas, Derrel Osbon b: 1/14/51, Los Angeles, Cal. BB/TR, 6', 160 lbs. Deb: 9/14/71

YEAR	TM/L	G	AB	R	H	2B	3B	HR	RBI	BB	SO	AVG	OBP	SLG	PRO+	BR	/A	RC	SB	CS	SBR	FR	POS	TPR
1971	Hou-N	5	5	0	0	0	0	0	0	0	2	.000	.000	.000	-99	-1	-1	-0	0	1	-1	1	/2	0.0
1972	SD-N	130	500	48	115	15	5	5	36	41	73	.230	.291	.310	76	-19	-15	45	9	9	-3	-18	2S/O	-2.5
1973	SD-N	113	404	41	96	7	1	0	22	34	52	.238	.300	.260	61	-23	-19	35	15	5	2	-14	S2	-1.9
1974	SD-N	141	523	48	129	24	6	3	41	51	58	.247	.315	.333	85	-13	-10	54	7	8	-3	6	*23O/S	-0.2
1975	SF-N	144	540	99	149	21	9	6	48	57	56	.276	.348	.381	98	-2	-1	75	28	13	1	-7	*2/O	0.0
1976	SF-N	81	272	38	63	5	4	2	19	29	26	.232	.315	.301	73	-8	-9	26	10	11	-4	2	2/OS3	-0.7
1977	SF-N	148	506	75	135	13	10	4	44	46	70	.267	.330	.379	90	-7	-7	63	15	13	-3	5	O2S/31	-0.2
1978	SD-N	128	352	36	80	10	2	3	26	35	37	.227	.303	.293	73	-15	-12	34	11	6	-0	22	O231	0.9
1979	LA-N	141	406	47	104	15	4	5	44	41	49	.256	.332	.350	87	-7	-6	49	18	5	2	-3	*03/2S1	-1.0
1980	LA-N	117	297	32	79	18	3	1	22	26	48	.266	.327	.357	93	-3	-3	33	7	9	-3	11	OS2/C3	1.0
1981	*LA-N	80	218	25	54	4	0	4	24	25	23	.248	.325	.321	87	-4	-3	25	7	2	1	-5	2SO3	-0.3
1982	LA-N	66	98	13	26	2	1	0	2	10	12	.265	.333	.306	82	-2	-2	10	2	3	-1	2	O23/S	-0.0
1983	*LA-N	118	192	38	48	6	6	2	8	27	36	.250	.348	.375	101	1	1	27	9	3	1	7	OS/23	0.9
1984	Mon-N	108	243	26	62	12	2	0	20	20	33	.255	.312	.321	82	-7	-6	23	0	4	-2	-26	SO2/31	-2.9
	Cal-A	14	29	3	4	0	1	0	2	3	4	.138	.219	.207	19	-3	-3	1	0	0	0	-4	/OS3	-0.6
1985	Phi-N	63	92	16	19	2	0	4	12	11	14	.207	.291	.359	79	-2	-3	10	2	0	1	-7	S/OC23	-0.7
Total	15	1597	4677	585	1163	154	54	43	370	456	593	.249	.319	.332	83	-114	-99	509	140	92	-13	-27	2OS3/1C	-8.2

■ FRANK THOMAS
Thomas, Frank Edward b: 5/27/68, Columbus, Ga. BR/TR, 6'5", 240 lbs. Deb: 8/02/90

YEAR	TM/L	G	AB	R	H	2B	3B	HR	RBI	BB	SO	AVG	OBP	SLG	PRO+	BR	/A	RC	SB	CS	SBR	FR	POS	TPR
1990	Chi-A	60	191	39	63	11	3	7	31	44	54	.330	.460	.529	180	22	23	49	0	1	-1	-4	1/D	1.4

■ FRANK THOMAS
Thomas, Frank Joseph b: 6/11/29, Pittsburgh, Pa. BR/TR, 6'3", 200 lbs. Deb: 8/17/51

YEAR	TM/L	G	AB	R	H	2B	3B	HR	RBI	BB	SO	AVG	OBP	SLG	PRO+	BR	/A	RC	SB	CS	SBR	FR	POS	TPR
1951	Pit-N	39	148	21	39	9	2	2	16	9	15	.264	.306	.392	84	-3	-4	16	0	2	-1	3	O	-0.2
1952	Pit-N	6	21	1	2	0	0	0	1	1		.095	.136	.095	-34	-4	-4	0	0	0	0	0	/O	-0.3
1953	Pit-N	128	455	68	116	22	1	30	102	50	93	.255	.331	.505	115	8	8	76	1	2	-1	21	*O	2.2
1954	Pit-N	153	577	81	172	32	7	23	94	51	74	.298	.365	.497	124	18	19	106	3	2	-0	3	*O	1.6
1955	Pit-N	142	510	72	125	16	2	25	72	60	76	.245	.327	.431	101	-1	-0	72	2	0	1	6	*O	0.3
1956	Pit-N	157	588	69	166	24	3	25	80	36	61	.282	.329	.461	112	7	8	80	0	5	-3	-8	*3O/2	-0.4
1957	Pit-N	151	594	72	172	30	1	23	89	44	66	.290	.342	.460	116	10	12	90	3	1	0	1	1O3	0.6
1958	Pit-N	149	562	89	158	26	4	35	109	42	79	.281	.339	.528	129	18	20	95	0	1	-1	-32	*3/O1	-1.2
1959	Cin-N	108	374	41	84	18	2	12	47	27	56	.225	.280	.380	72	-15	-16	37	0	2	-1	-10	3O1	-3.0
1960	Chi-N	135	479	54	114	12	1	21	64	28	58	.238	.280	.399	84	-12	-12	51	1	0	0	-9	1O3	-2.5
1961	Chi-N	15	50	7	13	2	0	2	6	2	8	.260	.288	.420	84	-1	-1	5	0	0	0	-0	O/1	-0.2
	Mil-N	124	423	58	120	13	3	25	67	29	70	.284	.338	.506	128	11	14	66	2	4	-2	-5	*O1	-0.0
	Yr	139	473	65	133	15	3	27	73	31	78	.281	.333	.497	123	10	13	70	2	4	-2	-6		-0.2
1962	NY-N	156	571	69	152	23	3	34	94	48	95	.266	.332	.496	117	13	12	91	2	1	0	-1	*O13	0.3
1963	NY-N	126	420	34	109	9	1	15	60	33	48	.260	.318	.393	102	2	2	46	0	0	0	-1	O1/3	-0.5
1964	NY-N	60	197	19	50	6	1	3	19	10	29	.254	.297	.340	81	-6	-5	19	1	1	-0	-1	O1/3	-0.6
	Phi-N	39	143	20	42	11	0	7	26	5	12	.294	.318	.517	132	5	5	22	0	1	-1	1	1	0.4
	Yr	99	340	39	92	17	1	10	45	15	41	.271	.305	.415	103	-1	-1	41	1	2	-1	1		-0.2
1965	Phi-N	35	77	7	20	4	0	1	7	4	10	.260	.296	.351	83	-2	-2	7	0	0	0	-1	O1/3	-0.3

YEAR	TM/L	G	AB	R	H	2B	3B	HR	RBI	BB	SO	AVG	OBP	SLG	PRO+	BR	/A	RC	SB	CS	SBR	FR	POS	TPR
	Hou-N	23	58	7	10	2	0	3	9	3	15	.172	.213	.362	63	-3	-3	5	0	0	0	-1	1/3O	-0.5
	Mil-N	15	33	3	7	3	0	0	1	2	11	.212	.257	.303	57	-2	-2	3	0	0	0	-0	/1O	-0.2
	Yr	73	168	17	37	9	0	4	17	9	36	.220	.260	.345	71	-7	-7	15	0	0	0	-2		-1.0
1966	Chi-N	5	5	0	0	0	0	0	0	0	1	.000	.000	.000	-99	-1	-1	0	0	0	0	0	H	0.0
Total	16	1766	6285	792	1671	262	31	286	962	484	894	.266	.323	.454	108	40	50	886	15	22	-9	-34	*O31/2	-4.5

■ FRED THOMAS
Thomas, Frederick Harvey "Tommy" b: 12/19/1892, Milwaukee, Wis. d: 1/15/86, Rice Lake, Wis. BR/TR, 5'10", 160 lbs. Deb: 4/22/18

YEAR	TM/L	G	AB	R	H	2B	3B	HR	RBI	BB	SO	AVG	OBP	SLG	PRO+	BR	/A	RC	SB	CS	SBR	FR	POS	TPR
1918	*Bos-A	44	144	19	37	2	1	1	11	15	20	.257	.331	.306	94	-1	-1	16	4			5	3/S	0.5
1919	Phi-A	124	453	42	96	11	10	2	23	43	52	.212	.283	.294	61	-23	-24	41	12			-5	*3	-2.0
1920	Phi-A	76	255	27	59	6	3	1	11	26	17	.231	.307	.290	58	-15	-15	25	8	4	0	1	3S	-0.8
	Was-A	3	7	0	1	0	0	0	0	0	1	.143	.143	.143	-25	-1	-1	0	0	1	-1	2	/3	0.0
	Yr	79	262	27	60	6	3	1	11	26	18	.229	.303	.286	56	-16	-16	24	8	5	-1	3		-0.8
Total	3	247	859	88	193	19	14	4	45	84	90	.225	.297	.293	65	-40	-41	81	24	5		3	3/S	-2.3

■ GEORGE THOMAS
Thomas, George Edward b: 11/29/37, Minneapolis, Minn. BR/TR, 6'3.5", 190 lbs. Deb: 9/11/57 C

YEAR	TM/L	G	AB	R	H	2B	3B	HR	RBI	BB	SO	AVG	OBP	SLG	PRO+	BR	/A	RC	SB	CS	SBR	FR	POS	TPR
1957	Det-A	1	1	0	0	0	0	0	0	0	1	.000	.000	.000	-97	-0	-0	0	0	0	0	-0	/3	0.0
1958	Det-A	1	0	0	0	0	0	0	0	0	0	—	—	—	—	0	0	0	0	0	0	0	/O	0.0
1961	Det-A	17	6	2	0	0	0	0	0	0	4	.000	.000	.000	-97	-2	-2	0	0	0	0	4	/OS	0.3
	LA-A	79	282	39	79	12	1	13	59	21	66	.280	.337	.468	101	4	0	43	3	6	-3	-10	O3	-1.1
	Yr	96	288	41	79	12	1	13	59	21	70	.274	.330	.458	99	2	-1	42	3	6	-3	-5		-0.8
1962	LA-A	56	181	13	43	10	2	4	12	21	37	.238	.320	.381	91	-3	-2	23	0	0	0	3	O	0.0
1963	LA-A	53	167	14	35	7	1	4	15	9	32	.210	.254	.335	68	-8	-7	14	0	0	0	-1	O3/1	-0.9
	Det-A	49	109	13	26	4	1	1	11	11	22	.239	.314	.321	76	-3	-3	12	2	1	0	4	O/2	0.0
	Yr	102	276	27	61	11	2	5	26	20	54	.221	.279	.330	71	-11	-11	25	2	1	0	3		-0.9
1964	Det-A	105	308	39	88	15	2	12	44	18	53	.286	.331	.464	117	7	6	47	4	1	1	4	O/3	0.8
1965	Det-A	79	169	19	36	5	1	3	10	12	39	.213	.273	.308	64	-8	-8	13	2	3	-1	3	O/2	-0.8
1966	Bos-A	69	173	25	41	4	0	5	20	23	33	.237	.333	.347	87	-0	-3	20	1	0	0	3	O/3C1	0.0
1967	*Bos-A	65	89	10	19	2	0	1	6	3	23	.213	.255	.270	51	-5	-6	6	0	1	-1	1	O/1C	-0.7
1968	Bos-A	12	10	3	2	0	0	1	1	1	3	.200	.273	.500	122	0	0	2	1	0	0	1	/O	0.1
1969	Bos-A	29	51	9	18	3	1	0	8	3	11	.353	.400	.451	131	3	2	10	0	0	0	-0	O1/C3	0.1
1970	Bos-A	38	99	13	34	8	0	2	13	11	12	.343	.420	.485	139	7	6	20	0	0	0	-5	O/3	0.0
1971	Bos-A	9	13	0	1	0	0	0	1	1	4	.077	.143	.077	-34	-2	-2	0	0	0	0	-1	/O	-0.3
	Min-A	23	30	4	8	1	0	0	2	4	3	.267	.353	.300	84	-0	-0	4	0	0	0	-1	O/13	-0.2
	Yr	32	43	4	9	1	0	0	3	5	7	.209	.292	.233	48	-3	-3	3	0	0	0	-2		-0.5
Total	13	685	1688	203	430	71	9	46	202	138	343	.255	.318	.389	92	-12	-19	213	13	12	-3	5	O/31C2S	-2.7

■ HERB THOMAS
Thomas, Herbert Mark b: 5/26/02, Sampson City, Fla. BR/TR, 5'4.5", 157 lbs. Deb: 8/28/24

YEAR	TM/L	G	AB	R	H	2B	3B	HR	RBI	BB	SO	AVG	OBP	SLG	PRO+	BR	/A	RC	SB	CS	SBR	FR	POS	TPR
1924	Bos-N	32	127	12	28	4	1	1	8	9	8	.220	.288	.291	58	-8	-7	11	5	2	0	9	O	0.2
1925	Bos-N	5	17	2	4	0	1	0	0	2	0	.235	.350	.353	88	-0	-0	2	0	1	-1	-1	/2	-0.1
1927	Bos-N	24	74	11	17	6	1	0	6	3	9	.230	.269	.338	67	-4	-3	7	2			-11	2/S	-1.4
	NY-N	13	17	2	3	1	1	0	1	1	1	.176	.263	.353	64	-1	-1	2	0			0	/OS	0.0
	Yr	37	91	13	20	7	2	0	7	4	10	.220	.268	.341	65	-5	-5	8	2			-10		-1.4
Total	3	74	235	27	52	11	4	1	15	15	18	.221	.285	.315	63	-14	-12	21	7	3		-2	/O2S	-1.3

■ IRA THOMAS
Thomas, Ira Felix b: 1/22/1881, Ballston Spa, N.Y. d: 10/11/58, Philadelphia, Pa. BR/TR, 6'2", 200 lbs. Deb: 5/18/06 C

YEAR	TM/L	G	AB	R	H	2B	3B	HR	RBI	BB	SO	AVG	OBP	SLG	PRO+	BR	/A	RC	SB	CS	SBR	FR	POS	TPR
1906	NY-A	44	115	12	23	1	2	0	15	8		.200	.252	.243	52	-6	-7	8	2			-5	C	-0.9
1907	NY-A	80	208	20	40	5	4	1	24	10		.192	.229	.269	56	-9	-11	15	5			9	C/1	0.3
1908	*Det-A	40	101	6	31	1	0	0	8	5		.307	.340	.317	111	2	1	11	0			-6	C	-0.1
1909	Phi-A	84	256	22	57	9	3	0	31	18		.223	.292	.281	79	-5	-6	22	4			11	C	1.3
1910	*Phi-A	60	180	14	50	8	2	1	19	6		.278	.301	.361	108	1	1	20	2			8	C	1.7
1911	*Phi-A	103	297	33	81	14	3	0	39	23		.273	.341	.340	92	-4	-3	36	4			6	*C	1.5
1912	Phi-A	48	139	14	30	4	2	1	13	8		.216	.268	.295	63	-7	-7	12	3			-1	C	-0.2
1913	Phi-A	22	53	3	15	4	1	0	6	4	8	.283	.333	.396	116	1	1	7	0			3	C	0.5
1914	Phi-A	2	3	0	0	0	0	0	0	0		.000	.000	.000	-99	-1	-1	0	0			1	/C	0.0
1915	Phi-A	1	0	0	0	0	0	0	0	0	0	—	—	—	—	0	0	0	0			0	/C	0.0
Total	10	484	1352	124	327	46	17	3	155	82	8	.242	.294	.308	81	-29	-31	129	20			25	C/1	4.1

■ GORMAN THOMAS
Thomas, James Gorman b: 12/12/50, Charleston, S.C. BR/TR, 6'2", 210 lbs. Deb: 4/06/73

YEAR	TM/L	G	AB	R	H	2B	3B	HR	RBI	BB	SO	AVG	OBP	SLG	PRO+	BR	/A	RC	SB	CS	SBR	FR	POS	TPR
1973	Mil-A	59	155	16	29	7	1	2	11	14	61	.187	.254	.284	53	-10	-10	11	5	5	-2	-1	O/3D	-1.4
1974	Mil-A	17	46	10	12	4	0	2	11	8	15	.261	.370	.478	143	3	3	9	4	0	1	-1	O/D	0.3
1975	Mil-A	121	240	34	43	12	2	10	28	31	84	.179	.273	.371	94	-2	-7	25	4	2	0	-8	O/3D	-1.7
1976	Mil-A	99	227	27	45	9	2	8	36	31	67	.198	.297	.361	94	-2	-2	24	2	3	-1	-1	O/3D	-0.6
1978	Mil-A	137	452	70	111	24	1	32	86	73	133	.246	.353	.515	141	24	24	85	3	4	-2	-9	*O	1.1
1979	Mil-A	156	557	97	136	29	0	45	123	98	175	.244	.359	.539	138	30	30	110	1	5	-3	-3	*O	1.8
1980	Mil-A	162	628	78	150	26	3	38	105	58	170	.239	.305	.471	113	5	8	91	8	5	-1	-2	*O/D	0.3
1981	*Mil-A	103	363	54	94	22	0	21	65	50	85	.259	.352	.493	149	19	21	63	4	5	-2	-6	O/D	1.2
1982	*Mil-A	158	567	96	139	29	1	39	112	84	143	.245	.347	.506	139	24	28	100	3	7	-3	3	*O	2.3
1983	Mil-A	46	164	21	30	6	1	5	18	23	50	.183	.287	.323	73	-7	-5	15	2	1	0	-0	O	-0.5
	Cle-A	106	371	51	82	17	0	17	51	57	98	.221	.326	.404	96	0	-2	51	8	3	1	8	*O	0.6
	Yr	152	535	72	112	23	1	22	69	80	148	.209	.314	.379	90	-7	-7	66	10	4	1	8		0.1
1984	Sea-A	35	108	6	17	3	0	1	13	28	27	.157	.336	.213	56	-5	-5	9	0	3	-2	-6	O/D	-1.4
1985	Sea-A	135	484	76	104	16	1	32	87	84	126	.215	.332	.450	111	8	8	74	3	2	0	0	*D	0.7
1986	Sea-A	57	170	24	33	4	0	10	26	27	55	.194	.308	.394	89	-3	-3	21	1	2	-1	0	D	-0.3
	Mil-A	44	145	21	26	4	1	6	10	31	50	.179	.324	.345	80	-3	-4	17	2	2	-1	-1	D/1	-0.5
	Yr	101	315	45	59	8	1	16	36	58	105	.187	.316	.371	85	-6	-6	39	3	4	-2	-1		-0.8
Total	13	1435	4677	681	1051	212	13	268	782	697	1339	.225	.328	.448	114	75	85	706	50	49	-14	-26	*OD/13	1.9

■ LEE THOMAS
Thomas, James Leroy b: 2/5/36, Peoria, Ill. BL/TR, 6'2", 195 lbs. Deb: 4/22/61 C

YEAR	TM/L	G	AB	R	H	2B	3B	HR	RBI	BB	SO	AVG	OBP	SLG	PRO+	BR	/A	RC	SB	CS	SBR	FR	POS	TPR
1961	NY-A	2	2	0	1	0	0	0	0	0	0	.500	.500	.500	177	0	0	1	0	0	0	0	H	0.0
	LA-A	130	450	77	128	11	5	24	70	47	74	.284	.355	.491	111	14	7	75	0	5	-3	-4	O1	-0.6
	Yr	132	452	77	129	11	5	24	70	47	74	.285	.355	.491	111	14	8	75	0	5	-3	-4		-0.6
1962	LA-A	160	583	88	169	21	2	26	104	55	74	.290	.357	.467	124	16	18	96	6	1	1	-9	1O	0.1
1963	LA-A	149	528	52	116	12	6	9	55	53	82	.220	.302	.316	78	-18	-14	52	6	0	2	4	*1O	-1.3
1964	LA-A	47	172	14	47	8	1	2	24	18	22	.273	.342	.366	108	-0	2	23	1	0	0	-3	O1	-0.2
	Bos-A	107	401	44	103	19	2	13	42	34	29	.257	.321	.411	97	1	-2	50	2	1	0	2	*O/1	-0.3
	Yr	154	573	58	150	27	3	15	66	52	51	.262	.328	.398	100	0	0	73	3	1	0	-2		-0.5
1965	Bos-A	151	521	74	141	27	4	22	75	72	42	.271	.362	.464	126	23	20	87	6	2	1	8	*1O	2.2
1966	Atl-N	39	126	11	25	1	4	1	6	15	10	.198	.263	.365	71	-5	-5	13	1	1	-0	2	1	-0.5
	Chi-N	75	149	15	36	4	0	1	9	14	15	.242	.319	.289	70	-5	-6	14	0	0	0	-2	1O	-0.9
	Yr	114	275	26	61	5	4	2	24	24	30	.222	.294	.324	71	-10	-11	27	1	1	-0	-0		-1.4
1967	Chi-N	77	191	16	42	4	1	7	23	15	22	.220	.287	.283	64	-9	-10	16	1	1	-0	-0	O1	-0.9
1968	Hou-N	90	201	14	39	4	0	1	11	14	22	.194	.250	.229	45	-13	-13	11	2	1	0	-0	O/1	-1.7
Total	8	1027	3324	405	847	111	22	106	428	332	397	.255	.328	.397	99	3	-2	438	25	11	1	-8	O1	-4.8

YEAR	TM/L	G	AB	R	H	2B	3B	HR	RBI	BB	SO	AVG	OBP	SLG	PRO+	BR	/A	RC	SB	CS	SBR	FR	POS	TPR
■ BUD THOMAS Thomas, John Tillman b: 3/10/29, Sedalia, Mo. BR/TR, 6', 180 lbs. Deb: 9/02/51																								
1951	StL-A	14	20	3	7	0	0	1	1	0	3	.350	.350	.500	124	1	1	4	2	0	1	1	S	0.3
■ KITE THOMAS Thomas, Keith Marshall b: 4/27/24, Kansas City, Kan. BR/TR, 6'1.5", 195 lbs. Deb: 4/19/52																								
1952	Phi-A	75	116	24	29	6	1	6	18	20	27	.250	.365	.474	124	5	4	20	0	1	-1	-2	O	0.1
1953	Phi-A	24	49	1	6	0	0	0	2	3	6	.122	.173	.122	-18	-8	-8	1	0	0	0	1	O	-0.7
	Was-A	38	58	10	17	3	2	1	12	11	7	.293	.414	.466	141	3	4	11	0	0	0	-2	/OC	0.1
	Yr	62	107	11	23	3	2	1	14	14	13	.215	.311	.308	68	-5	-5	10	0	0	0	-1		-0.6
Total	2	137	223	35	52	9	3	7	32	34	40	.233	.340	.395	98	0	-1	32	0	1	-1	-3	/OC	-0.5
■ LEO THOMAS Thomas, Leo Raymond "Tommy" b: 7/26/23, Turlock, Cal. BR/TR, 5'11.5", 178 lbs. Deb: 4/29/50																								
1950	StL-A	35	121	19	24	6	0	1	9	20	14	.198	.312	.273	49	-9	-10	11	0	1	-1	-4	3	-1.3
1952	StL-A	41	124	12	29	5	1	0	12	17	7	.234	.336	.290	73	-4	-4	13	2	0	1	4	3/S2	0.0
	Chi-A	19	24	1	4	0	0	0	6	6	4	.167	.333	.167	42	-2	-2	2	0	0	0	0	/3	0.0
	Yr	60	148	13	33	5	1	0	18	23	11	.223	.335	.270	68	-5	-6	15	2	0	1	4		0.0
Total	2	95	269	32	57	11	1	1	27	43	25	.212	.325	.271	59	-14	-15	27	2	1	0	1	/3S2	-1.3
■ RAY THOMAS Thomas, Raymond Joseph b: 7/9/10, Dover, N.H. BR/TR, 5'10.5", 175 lbs. Deb: 7/21/38																								
1938	Bro-N	1	3	1	1	0	0	0	0	0	0	.333	.333	.333	82	-0	-0	0	0			0	/C	0.0
■ RED THOMAS Thomas, Robert William b: 4/25/1898, Hargrove, Ala. d: 3/29/62, Fremont, Ohio BR/TR, 5'11", 165 lbs. Deb: 9/13/21																								
1921	Chi-N	8	30	5	8	3	0	1	5	4	5	.267	.371	.467	120	1	1	5	0	1	-1	1	/O	0.1
■ ROY THOMAS Thomas, Roy Allen b: 3/24/1874, Norristown, Pa. d: 11/20/59, Norristown, Pa. BL/TL, 5'11", 150 lbs. Deb: 4/14/1899 C																								
1899	Phi-N	150	547	137	178	12	4	0	47	115		.325	.457	.362	134	33	36	112	42			4	*O1	2.8
1900	Phi-N	140	531	**132**	168	4	3	0	33	**115**		.316	.447	.335	122	26	26	99	37			-2	*O/P	1.1
1901	Phi-N	129	479	102	148	5	2	1	28	**100**		.309	**.436**	.334	125	26	24	86	27			-2	*O	0.8
1902	Phi-N	138	500	89	143	4	7	0	24	**107**		.286	**.415**	.322	130	26	26	79	17			5	*O	2.2
1903	Phi-N	130	477	88	156	11	2	1	27	**107**		.327	**.450**	.365	140	31	33	92	17			14	*O	3.8
1904	Phi-N	139	496	92	144	6	6	3	29	**102**		.290	.411	.345	142	28	31	85	28			15	*O	4.2
1905	Phi-N	147	562	118	178	11	6	0	31	93		.317	.414	.358	138	29	31	98	23			19	*O	4.1
1906	Phi-N	142	493	81	125	10	7	0	16	**107**		.254	.387	.302	117	17	17	70	22			10	*O	2.6
1907	Phi-N	121	419	70	102	15	3	1	23	**83**		.243	.369	.301	114	11	11	54	11			5	*O	1.3
1908	Phi-N	6	24	2	4	0	0	0	0	2		.167	.231	.167	28	-2	-2	1	0			-1	/O	-0.2
	Pit-N	102	386	52	99	11	10	1	24	49		.256	.340	.345	121	10	10	49	11			5	*O	1.6
	Yr	108	410	54	103	11	10	1	24	51		.251	.334	.334	116	9	8	49	11			5		1.4
1909	Bos-N	82	281	36	74	9	1	0	11	47		.263	.369	.302	104	5	4	34	5			-1	O	0.0
1910	Bos-N	23	71	7	13	0	2	0	4	7	5	.183	.266	.239	46	-5	-5	6	4			0	O	-0.5
1911	Phi-N	21	30	5	5	2	0	0	2	8	6	.167	.342	.233	61	-1	-1	3	0			1	O	0.0
Total	13	1470	5296	1011	1537	100	53	7	299	1042	11	.290	.411	.333	126	233	242	867	244			74	*O/1P	23.8
■ VALMY THOMAS Thomas, Valmy b: 10/21/28, Santurce, P.R. BR/TR, 5'9", 165 lbs. Deb: 4/16/57																								
1957	NY-N	88	241	30	60	10	3	6	31	16	29	.249	.298	.390	83	-6	-6	28	0	0	0	2	C	0.1
1958	SF-N	63	143	14	37	5	0	3	16	13	24	.259	.325	.357	82	-4	-4	17	1	0	0	2	C	0.2
1959	Phi-N	66	140	5	28	2	0	1	7	9	19	.200	.253	.236	31	-14	-14	7	1	0	0	16	C/3	0.6
1960	Bal-A	8	16	0	1	0	0	0	0	1	0	.063	.118	.063	-51	-3	-3	-0	0	1	-1	1	/C	-0.2
1961	Cle-A	27	86	7	18	3	0	2	6	6	7	.209	.261	.314	54	-6	-6	5	0	0	0	9	C	0.3
Total	5	252	626	56	144	20	3	12	60	45	79	.230	.285	.329	64	-33	-32	57	2	1	0	30	C/3	1.0
■ BILL THOMAS Thomas, William Miskey b: 12/8/1877, Norristown, Pa. d: 1/14/50, Evansburg, Pa. TR , 5'10", 190 lbs. Deb: 5/01/02																								
1902	Phi-N	6	17	1	2	0	0	0	0	1		.118	.167	.118	-11	-2	-2	0	0			-1	/O12	-0.3
■ WALT THOMAS Thomas, William Walter "Tommy" b: 4/28/1884, Foot-Of-Ten, Pa. d: 6/6/50, Altoona, Pa. BR/TR, 5'8", Deb: 9/18/08																								
1908	Bos-N	5	13	2	2	0	0	0	1	3		.154	.313	.154	53	-1	-0	1	2			-1	/S	-0.1
■ ART THOMASON Thomason, Arthur Wilson b: 2/12/1889, Liberty, Mo. d: 5/2/44, Kansas City, Mo. BL/TL, 5'8", 150 lbs. Deb: 8/10/10																								
1910	Cle-A	20	70	4	12	0	1	0	2	5		.171	.227	.200	33	-5	-5	4	3			2	O	-0.4
■ GARY THOMASSON Thomasson, Gary Leah b: 7/29/51, San Diego, Cal. BL/TL, 6'1", 180 lbs. Deb: 9/05/72																								
1972	SF-N	10	27	5	9	1	1	0	1	1	7	.333	.357	.444	125	1	1	4	0	0	0	-1	/1O	0.0
1973	SF-N	112	235	35	67	10	4	4	30	22	43	.285	.346	.413	105	3	3	36	2	0	1	0	1O	-0.1
1974	SF-N	120	315	41	77	14	3	2	29	38	56	.244	.326	.327	79	-7	-8	35	7	1	2	3	O1	-0.7
1975	SF-N	114	326	44	74	12	3	7	32	37	48	.227	.308	.347	78	-8	-10	38	9	3	1	9	O1	-0.3
1976	SF-N	103	328	45	85	20	5	8	38	30	45	.259	.323	.424	107	4	3	45	8	3	1	-4	O1	-0.4
1977	SF-N	145	446	63	114	24	6	17	71	75	102	.256	.364	.451	118	12	12	78	16	4	2	1	*O1	1.0
1978	Oak-A	47	154	17	31	4	1	5	16	15	24	.201	.272	.338	74	-6	-5	14	4	1	1	-1	O/1	-0.6
	*NY-A	55	116	20	32	4	1	3	20	13	22	.276	.349	.405	114	2	2	17	0	2	-1	8	O/D	0.8
	Yr	102	270	37	63	8	2	8	36	28	66	.233	.305	.367	92	-4	-3	31	4	3	-1	7		0.2
1979	LA-N	115	315	39	78	11	1	14	50	43	70	.248	.340	.422	108	3	4	47	4	2	0	-1	*O/1	0.9
1980	LA-N	80	111	6	24	3	0	1	12	17	26	.216	.326	.270	69	-4	-4	10	0	0	0	-1	O/1	-0.6
Total	9	901	2373	315	591	103	25	61	294	291	463	.249	.332	.391	98	-2	-5	324	50	16	5	12	O1/D	-0.9
■ ANDREW THOMPSON Thompson, Andrew M. b: 1845, Illinois Non-Playing Manager Stp(U) 1884 Deb: 4/26/1875 M																								
1875	Was-n	11	41	3	4	0	1	0		0		.098	.098	.146	-17	-5	-4	1					C/O	-0.3
■ BOBBY THOMPSON Thompson, Bobby La Rue b: 11/3/53, Charlotte, N.C. BB/TR, 5'11", 175 lbs. Deb: 4/16/78																								
1978	Tex-A	64	120	23	27	3	3	2	12	9	26	.225	.290	.350	79	-3	-3	13	7	2	1	7	O/D	0.3
■ TIM THOMPSON Thompson, Charles Lemoine b: 3/1/24, Coalport, Pa. BL/TR, 5'11", 190 lbs. Deb: 4/28/54 C																								
1954	Bro-N	10	13	2	2	1	0	0	1	1	1	.154	.214	.231	15	-2	-2	1	0	0	0	-0	/CO	-0.1
1956	KC-A	92	268	21	73	13	2	1	27	17	23	.272	.321	.347	76	-9	-9	29	2	4	-2	-3	C	-0.6
1957	KC-A	81	230	25	47	10	2	0	7	19	18	26	.204	.262	.339	62	-12	-13	20	0	0	0	-3	C	-1.2
1958	Det-A	4	6	1	1	0	0	0	0	3	2	.167	.444	.167	70	0	-0	1	0	0	0	-1	/C	0.0
Total	4	187	517	49	123	24	2	8	47	39	52	.238	.294	.338	68	-23	-24	51	2	4	-2	-1	C/O	-1.9
■ DANNY THOMPSON Thompson, Danny Leon b: 2/1/47, Wichita, Kan. d: 12/10/76, Rochester, Minn. BR/TR, 6', 183 lbs. Deb: 6/25/70																								
1970	*Min-A	96	302	25	66	9	0	0	22	7	39	.219	.236	.248	33	-27	-28	17	0	0	0	-12	23/S	-3.2
1971	Min-A	48	57	10	15	2	0	0	7	7	12	.263	.344	.298	81	-1	-1	5	0	0	0	1	3/2S	0.0
1972	Min-A	144	573	54	158	22	6	4	48	34	57	.276	.319	.356	96	-0	-3	63	3	4	-2	-9	*S	0.2
1973	Min-A	99	347	29	78	13	2	1	36	16	41	.225	.263	.282	52	-22	-23	24	1	0	0	7	S/3D	-0.3
1974	Min-A	97	264	25	66	6	1	4	25	22	29	.250	.313	.326	81	-5	-7	24	1	1	-0	-24	S/3D	-2.4
1975	Min-A	112	355	25	96	11	2	5	37	18	30	.270	.306	.355	84	-7	-8	37	0	3	-2	-21	*S/32D	-2.1
1976	Min-A	34	124	9	29	4	0	0	6	3	8	.234	.258	.266	52	-7	-8	8	1	2	-0	-2	S	-0.7
	Tex-A	64	196	12	42	3	0	1	13	13	19	.214	.267	.245	49	-12	-13	13	2	1	-2	-7	32S/D	-2.0
	Yr	98	320	21	71	7	0	1	19	16	27	.222	.263	.253	50	-19	-20	21	3	3	-1	-9		-2.7
Total	7	694	2218	189	550	70	11	15	194	120	235	.248	.289	.310	70	-82	-90	192	8	11	-4	-67	S3/2D	-10.5

YEAR	TM/L	G	AB	R	H	2B	3B	HR	RBI	BB	SO	AVG	OBP	SLG	PRO+	BR	/A	RC	SB	CS	SBR	FR	POS	TPR

■ DON THOMPSON
Thompson, Donald Newlin b: 12/28/23, Swepsonville, N.C. BL/TL, 6′, 185 lbs. Deb: 4/24/49

YEAR	TM/L	G	AB	R	H	2B	3B	HR	RBI	BB	SO	AVG	OBP	SLG	PRO+	BR	/A	RC	SB	CS	SBR	FR	POS	TPR
1949	Bos-N	7	11	0	2	0	0	0	0	0	2	.182	.182	.182	-2	-2	-2	0	0			0	/O	-0.1
1951	Bro-N	80	118	25	27	3	0	0	6	12	12	.229	.305	.254	51	-8	-8	8	2	8	-4	4	O	-0.9
1953	*Bro-N	96	153	25	37	5	0	1	12	14	13	.242	.310	.294	57	-9	-10	13	2	3	-1	3	O	-1.0
1954	Bro-N	34	25	2	1	0	0	0	1	5	5	.040	.226	.040	-25	-5	-5	1	0	0	0	1	O	-0.4
Total	4	217	307	52	67	8	0	1	19	31	32	.218	.296	.254	46	-23	-24	22	4	11		7	O	-2.4

■ FRANK THOMPSON
Thompson, Frank Deb: 9/11/1875

YEAR	TM/L	G	AB	R	H	2B	3B	HR	RBI	BB	SO	AVG	OBP	SLG	PRO+	BR	/A	RC	SB	CS	SBR	FR	POS	TPR
1875	Atl-n	1	5	1	2	0	0	0		0		.400	.400	.400	204	0	0	1				O		0.0

■ FRANK THOMPSON
Thompson, Frank E b: 7/2/1895, Springfield, Mo. d: 6/27/40, Jasper Co., Mo. BR/TR, 5′8″, 155 lbs. Deb: 5/06/20

YEAR	TM/L	G	AB	R	H	2B	3B	HR	RBI	BB	SO	AVG	OBP	SLG	PRO+	BR	/A	RC	SB	CS	SBR	FR	POS	TPR
1920	StL-A	22	53	7	9	0	0	0	5	13	10	.170	.343	.170	38	-4	-4	4	1	1	-0	-4	3/2	-0.6

■ HANK THOMPSON
Thompson, Henry Curtis b: 12/8/25, Oklahoma City, Okla d: 9/30/69, Fresno, Cal. BL/TR, 5′9″, 174 lbs. Deb: 7/17/47

YEAR	TM/L	G	AB	R	H	2B	3B	HR	RBI	BB	SO	AVG	OBP	SLG	PRO+	BR	/A	RC	SB	CS	SBR	FR	POS	TPR
1947	StL-A	27	78	10	20	1	1	0	5	10	7	.256	.341	.295	76	-2	-2	8	2	1	0	1	2	0.0
1949	NY-N	75	275	51	77	10	4	9	34	42	30	.280	.377	.444	120	8	8	50	5			-7	2/3	0.3
1950	NY-N	148	512	82	148	17	6	20	91	83	60	.289	.391	.463	123	20	19	97	8			5	*3O	2.3
1951	*NY-N	87	264	37	62	8	4	8	33	43	23	.235	.342	.386	95	-1	-1	36	1	2	-1	-14	3	-1.6
1952	NY-N	128	423	67	110	13	9	17	67	50	38	.260	.344	.454	119	11	10	68	4	4	-1	5	O3/2	1.3
1953	NY-N	114	388	60	117	15	8	24	74	60	39	.302	.400	.567	146	28	27	93	6	5	-1	-2	*3/O2	2.0
1954	*NY-N	136	448	76	118	18	1	26	86	90	58	.263	.392	.482	126	20	19	92	3	0	1	-3	*3/2O	1.7
1955	NY-N	135	432	65	106	13	1	17	63	84	56	.245	.373	.398	105	6	5	71	2	2	-1	2	*3/2S	0.7
1956	NY-N	83	183	24	43	9	0	8	29	31	26	.235	.349	.415	105	2	2	29	2	1	0	1	3O/S	0.3
Total	9	933	3003	492	801	104	34	129	482	493	337	.267	.374	.453	118	90	88	545	33	15		-13	3O2/S	7.0

■ SHAG THOMPSON
Thompson, James Alfred b: 4/29/1893, Haw River, N.C. d: 1/7/90, Black Mountain, N.C BL/TR, 5′8.5″, 165 lbs. Deb: 6/08/14

YEAR	TM/L	G	AB	R	H	2B	3B	HR	RBI	BB	SO	AVG	OBP	SLG	PRO+	BR	/A	RC	SB	CS	SBR	FR	POS	TPR
1914	Phi-A	16	29	3	5	0	1	0	2	7	8	.172	.351	.241	81	-0	-0	3	1			1	/O	0.1
1915	Phi-A	17	33	5	11	2	0	0	2	4	6	.333	.405	.394	143	2	2	5	0	1	-1	0	/O	0.1
1916	Phi-A	15	17	4	0	0	0	0	0	7	6	.000	.292	.000	-12	-2	-2	0	1			-1	/O	-0.2
Total	3	48	79	12	16	2	1	0	4	18	20	.203	.357	.253	86	-1	-0	8	2	1		1	/O	0.0

■ JASON THOMPSON
Thompson, Jason Dolph b: 7/6/54, Hollywood, Cal. BL/TL, 6′4″, 200 lbs. Deb: 4/23/76

YEAR	TM/L	G	AB	R	H	2B	3B	HR	RBI	BB	SO	AVG	OBP	SLG	PRO+	BR	/A	RC	SB	CS	SBR	FR	POS	TPR
1976	Det-A	123	412	45	90	12	1	17	54	68	72	.218	.331	.376	103	4	2	53	2	4	-2	2	*1	-0.3
1977	Det-A	158	585	87	158	24	5	31	105	73	91	.270	.352	.487	120	21	16	100	0	1	-1	-7	*1	0.0
1978	Det-A	153	589	79	169	25	3	26	96	74	96	.287	.367	.472	130	27	25	104	0	0	0	-5	*1	1.4
1979	Det-A	145	492	58	121	16	1	20	79	70	90	.246	.341	.404	97	1	-1	68	2	0	1	-1	*1	-0.8
1980	Det-A	36	126	10	27	5	0	4	20	13	26	.214	.293	.349	73	-4	-5	12	0	1	-1	4	1	-0.3
	Cal-A	102	312	59	99	14	0	17	70	70	60	.317	.442	.526	168	31	32	76	2	0	1	-3	1D	2.6
	Yr	138	438	69	126	19	0	21	90	83	86	.288	.402	.475	141	27	27	88	2	1	0	1		2.3
1981	Pit-N	86	223	36	54	13	0	15	42	59	49	.242	.401	.502	150	18	17	48	0	0	0	-1	1	1.4
1982	Pit-N	156	550	87	156	32	0	31	101	101	107	.284	.397	.511	148	41	39	117	1	0	0	-1	*1	3.0
1983	Pit-N	152	517	70	134	20	1	18	76	99	128	.259	.379	.406	115	16	14	84	1	0	0	-6	*1	0.1
1984	Pit-N	154	543	61	138	22	0	17	74	87	73	.254	.359	.389	110	9	9	78	0	0	0	-10	*1	-0.5
1985	Pit-N	123	402	42	97	17	1	12	61	84	58	.241	.372	.378	111	9	9	61	0	0	0	2	*1	0.8
1986	Mon-N	30	51	6	10	4	0	0	4	18	12	.196	.406	.275	92	1	1	7	0	1	-1	-3	1	-0.3
Total	11	1418	4802	640	1253	204	12	208	782	816	862	.261	.369	.438	121	172	158	809	8	7	-2	-28	*1/D	7.1

■ TUG THOMPSON
Thompson, John P. b: London, Ontario, Canada BL, 160 lbs. Deb: 8/31/1882

YEAR	TM/L	G	AB	R	H	2B	3B	HR	RBI	BB	SO	AVG	OBP	SLG	PRO+	BR	/A	RC	SB	CS	SBR	FR	POS	TPR
1882	Cin-a	1	5	0	1	0	0	0		0		.200	.200	.200	33	-0	-0	0				-1	/O	0.0
1884	Ind-a	24	97	10	20	3	0	0		2		.206	.222	.237	54	-5	-4	5				-10	OC	-1.2
Total	2	25	102	10	21	3	0	0		2		.206	.221	.235	53	-5	-5	5				-11	/OC	-1.2

■ FRESCO THOMPSON
Thompson, Lafayette Fresco "Tommy" b: 6/6/02, Centerville, Ala. d: 11/20/68, Fullerton, Cal. BR/TR, 5′8″, 150 lbs. Deb: 9/05/25

YEAR	TM/L	G	AB	R	H	2B	3B	HR	RBI	BB	SO	AVG	OBP	SLG	PRO+	BR	/A	RC	SB	CS	SBR	FR	POS	TPR
1925	Pit-N	14	37	4	9	2	1	0	8	4	1	.243	.317	.351	66	-2	-2	4	2	1	0	-2	2	-0.3
1926	NY-N	2	8	1	5	0	0	0	1	2	0	.625	.700	.625	262	2	2	4	1			-1	/2	0.1
1927	Phi-N	153	597	78	181	32	14	1	70	34	36	.303	.343	.409	99	-0	-1	81	19			-5	*2	-0.7
1928	Phi-N	152	634	99	182	34	11	3	50	42	27	.287	.332	.390	85	-12	-15	80	19			9	*2	-0.3
1929	Phi-N	148	623	115	202	41	3	4	53	75	34	.324	.398	.419	96	5	-1	104	16			12	*2	1.3
1930	Phi-N	122	478	77	135	34	4	4	46	35	29	.282	.331	.395	70	-20	-25	61	7			1	*2	-0.9
1931	Bro-N	74	181	26	48	6	1	1	21	23	16	.265	.351	.326	84	-3	-3	22	5			-3	2S/3	-0.3
1932	Bro-N	3	1	0	0	0	0	0	0	0	0	.000	.000	.000	-99	-0	-0	0	0			0	H	0.0
1934	NY-N	1	1	0	0	0	0	0	0	0	0	.000	.000	.000	-99	-0	-0	0	0			0	H	0.0
Total	9	669	2560	400	762	149	34	13	249	215	143	.298	.353	.398	88	-30	-46	357	69	1		11	2/S3	-1.1

■ MILT THOMPSON
Thompson, Milton Bernard b: 1/5/59, Washington, D.C. BL/TR, 5′11″, 170 lbs. Deb: 9/04/84

YEAR	TM/L	G	AB	R	H	2B	3B	HR	RBI	BB	SO	AVG	OBP	SLG	PRO+	BR	/A	RC	SB	CS	SBR	FR	POS	TPR
1984	Atl-N	25	99	16	30	1	0	2	4	11	11	.303	.373	.374	103	2	1	16	14	2	3	-0	O	0.3
1985	Atl-N	73	182	17	55	7	2	0	6	7	36	.302	.339	.363	91	-1	-2	23	9	4	0	-2	O	-0.4
1986	Phi-N	96	299	38	75	7	1	6	23	26	62	.251	.313	.341	78	-8	-9	34	19	4	3	-0	O	-0.7
1987	Phi-N	150	527	86	159	26	9	7	43	42	87	.302	.353	.425	102	4	2	85	46	10	8	2	*O	0.5
1988	Phi-N	122	378	53	109	16	2	2	33	39	59	.288	.356	.357	103	4	3	48	17	9	-0	2	*O	0.1
1989	StL-N	155	545	60	158	28	8	4	68	39	91	.290	.342	.393	106	6	4	73	27	8	3	-7	*O	-0.1
1990	StL-N	135	418	42	91	14	7	6	30	39	60	.218	.292	.328	68	-17	-19	44	25	5	5	-4	*O	-2.1
Total	7	756	2448	312	677	99	29	27	207	203	406	.277	.335	.374	93	-10	-20	324	157	42	22	-10	O	-2.4

■ ROBBY THOMPSON
Thompson, Robert Randall b: 5/10/62, W.Palm Beach, Fla. BR/TR, 5′11″, 165 lbs. Deb: 4/08/86

YEAR	TM/L	G	AB	R	H	2B	3B	HR	RBI	BB	SO	AVG	OBP	SLG	PRO+	BR	/A	RC	SB	CS	SBR	FR	POS	TPR
1986	SF-N	149	549	73	149	27	3	7	47	42	112	.271	.329	.370	97	-6	-2	64	12	15	-5	1	*2/S	-0.4
1987	*SF-N	132	420	62	110	26	5	10	44	40	91	.262	.338	.419	104	-1	2	58	16	11	-2	6	*2	0.8
1988	SF-N	138	477	66	126	24	6	7	48	40	111	.264	.326	.384	108	2	4	62	14	5	1	-9	*2	0.0
1989	*SF-N	148	547	91	132	26	11	13	50	51	133	.241	.321	.400	108	3	5	75	12	2	2	5	*2	1.5
1990	SF-N	144	498	67	122	22	3	15	56	34	96	.245	.301	.392	90	-9	-8	59	14	4	2	28	*2	2.3
Total	5	711	2491	359	639	125	28	52	245	207	543	.257	.323	.392	101	-10	1	318	68	37	-2	30	2/S	4.2

■ TOMMY THOMPSON
Thompson, Rupert Lockhart b: 5/19/10, Elkhart, Ill. d: 5/24/71, Auburn, Cal. BL/TR, 5′9.5″, 155 lbs. Deb: 9/03/33

YEAR	TM/L	G	AB	R	H	2B	3B	HR	RBI	BB	SO	AVG	OBP	SLG	PRO+	BR	/A	RC	SB	CS	SBR	FR	POS	TPR
1933	Bos-N	24	97	6	18	1	0	0	6	4	6	.186	.218	.196	21	-10	-9	4	0			2	O	-0.8
1934	Bos-N	105	343	40	91	12	3	0	37	13	19	.265	.300	.318	71	-17	-13	34	2			9	O	-0.7
1935	Bos-N	112	297	34	81	7	1	4	30	36	17	.273	.353	.343	96	-4	-0	36	2			1	O	-0.2
1936	Bos-N	106	266	37	76	9	0	4	36	31	12	.286	.362	.365	103	-0	2	38	3			1	O1	0.0
1938	Chi-A	19	18	2	2	0	0	0	2	1	2	.111	.158	.111	-31	-4	-4	0	0	0	0	0	/1	-0.3
1939	Chi-A	1	0	0	0	0	0	0	0	1	0	—	—	—		-0	-0	0	0	0	0	0	H	0.0
	StL-A	30	86	23	26	5	0	1	7	23	7	.302	.455	.395	117	4	4	18	0	0	0	-2	O	0.1
	Yr	31	86	23	26	5	0	1	8	23	7	.302	.455	.395	117	4	4	19	0	0	0	-2		0.1
Total	6	397	1107	142	294	34	4	9	119	108	63	.266	.335	.328	84	-30	-21	130	7	0		11	O/1	-1.9

■ SAM THOMPSON
Thompson, Samuel Luther "Big Sam" b: 3/5/1860, Danville, Ind. d: 11/7/22, Detroit, Mich. BL/TL, 6′2″, 207 lbs. Deb: 7/02/1885

YEAR	TM/L	G	AB	R	H	2B	3B	HR	RBI	BB	SO	AVG	OBP	SLG	PRO+	BR	/A	RC	SB	CS	SBR	FR	POS	TPR
1885	Det-N	63	254	58	77	11	9	7	44	16	22	.303	.344	.500	170	19	19	45				7	O/3	2.2

YEAR	TM/L	G	AB	R	H	2B	3B	HR	RBI	BB	SO	AVG	OBP	SLG	PRO+	BR	/A	RC	SB	CS	SBR	FR	POS	TPR
1886	Det-N	122	503	101	156	18	13	8	89	35	31	.310	.355	.445	138	25	22	86	13			9	*O	3.0
1887	*Det-N	127	545	118	203	29	23	11	166	32	19	.372	.416	.571	168	53	50	142	22			3	*O	4.4
1888	Det-N	56	238	51	67	10	8	6	40	23	10	.282	.352	.466	162	17	17	42	5			-7	O	0.9
1889	Phi-N	128	533	103	158	36	4	20	111	36	22	.296	.348	.492	124	22	14	102	24			-8	*O	0.1
1890	Phi-N	132	549	116	172	41	9	4	102	42	29	.313	.371	.443	136	26	24	102	25			2	*O	2.0
1891	Phi-N	133	554	108	163	23	10	7	90	52	20	.294	.363	.410	124	19	17	95	29			19	*O	2.5
1892	Phi-N	153	609	109	186	28	11	9	104	59	19	.305	.377	.432	147	34	34	112	28			4	*O	3.1
1893	Phi-N	131	600	130	222	37	13	11	126	50	17	.370	.424	.530	155	45	46	146	18			-11	*O/1	2.4
1894	Phi-N	99	437	108	178	29	27	13	141	40	13	.407	.458	.686	179	51	53	152	24			-4	*O	3.2
1895	Phi-N	119	538	131	211	45	21	18	165	31	11	.392	.430	.654	179	59	58	167	27			12	*O	4.8
1896	Phi-N	119	517	103	154	28	7	12	100	28	13	.298	.341	.449	110	5	6	85	12			18	*O	1.3
1897	Phi-N	3	13	2	3	0	1	0	3	1		.231	.286	.385	80	-0	-0	1	0			0	/O	0.0
1898	Phi-N	14	63	14	22	5	3	1	15	4		.349	.388	.571	185	6	6	15	2			2	/O	0.7
1906	Det-A	8	31	4	7	0	1	0	3	1		.226	.250	.290	69	-1	-1	2	0			-0	/O	-0.1
Total	15	1407	5984	1256	1979	340	160	127	1299	450	226	.331	.384	.505	148	376	363	1296	229			46	*O/13	30.5

■ HOMER THOMPSON
Thompson, Thomas Homer b: 6/1/1892, Spring City, Tenn. d: 9/12/57, Atlanta, Ga. BR/TR, 5'9", 160 lbs. Deb: 10/05/12

YEAR	TM/L	G	AB	R	H	2B	3B	HR	RBI	BB	SO	AVG	OBP	SLG	PRO+	BR	/A	RC	SB	CS	SBR	FR	POS	TPR
1912	NY-A	1	0	0	0	0	0	0	0	0	0	—	—	—	—	0	0	0	0			-0	/C	0.0

■ SCOT THOMPSON
Thompson, Vernon Scot b: 12/7/55, Grove City, Pa. BL/TL, 6'3", 195 lbs. Deb: 9/03/78

YEAR	TM/L	G	AB	R	H	2B	3B	HR	RBI	BB	SO	AVG	OBP	SLG	PRO+	BR	/A	RC	SB	CS	SBR	FR	POS	TPR
1978	Chi-N	19	36	7	15	3	0	0	2	2	4	.417	.447	.500	147	3	3	8	0	0	0	-1	/O1	0.1
1979	Chi-N	128	346	36	100	13	5	2	29	17	37	.289	.324	.373	82	-5	-9	40	4	3	-1	-4	*O	-1.6
1980	Chi-N	102	226	26	48	10	1	2	13	28	31	.212	.302	.292	62	-10	-12	19	6	6	-2	-2	O1	-1.9
1981	Chi-N	57	115	8	19	5	0	0	8	7	8	.165	.213	.209	19	-12	-13	6	2	0	1	-2	O/1	-1.5
1982	Chi-N	49	74	11	27	5	1	0	7	5	4	.365	.405	.459	138	4	4	13	0	1	-1	3	O/1	0.6
1983	Chi-N	53	88	4	17	3	1	0	10	3	14	.193	.220	.250	28	-8	-9	4	0	0	0	-2	O/1	-1.1
1984	SF-N	120	245	30	75	7	1	1	31	30	26	.306	.382	.355	112	4	5	32	5	3	-0	-0	1/O	0.1
1985	SF-N	64	111	8	23	5	0	0	6	2	10	.207	.221	.252	34	-10	-10	5	0	0	0	2	1	-0.8
	Mon-N	34	32	2	9	1	0	0	4	3	7	.281	.343	.313	90	-1	-0	3	0	0	0	1	/1O	0.0
	Yr	98	143	10	32	6	0	0	10	5	17	.224	.250	.266	47	-11	-10	8	0	0	0	2		-0.8
Total	8	626	1273	132	333	52	9	5	110	97	141	.262	.315	.328	76	-35	-41	131	17	13	-3	-5	O1	-6.1

■ BOBBY THOMSON
Thomson, Robert Brown "The Staten Island Scot" b: 10/25/23, Glasgow, Scotland BR/TR, 6'2", 180 lbs. Deb: 9/09/46

YEAR	TM/L	G	AB	R	H	2B	3B	HR	RBI	BB	SO	AVG	OBP	SLG	PRO+	BR	/A	RC	SB	CS	SBR	FR	POS	TPR
1946	NY-N	18	54	8	17	4	1	2	9	4	5	.315	.362	.537	152	3	3	10	0			0	3	0.4
1947	NY-N	138	545	105	154	26	5	29	85	40	78	.283	.336	.508	121	13	13	92	1			6	*O/2	1.5
1948	NY-N	138	471	75	117	20	2	16	63	30	77	.248	.296	.401	87	-10	-11	53	2			9	*O	-0.9
1949	NY-N	156	641	99	198	35	9	27	109	44	45	.309	.355	.518	132	25	25	115	10			14	*O	3.0
1950	NY-N	149	563	79	142	22	7	25	85	55	45	.252	.324	.449	101	-1	-1	81	3			5	*O	0.0
1951	*NY-N	148	518	89	152	27	8	32	101	73	57	.293	.385	.562	150	37	36	113	5	5	-2	-8	O3	2.4
1952	NY-N	153	608	89	164	29	14	24	108	52	74	.270	.331	.482	122	16	16	97	5	2	0	1	3O	1.8
1953	NY-N	154	608	80	175	22	6	26	106	43	57	.288	.338	.472	106	6	6	95	4	2	0	-1	*O	-0.2
1954	Mil-N	43	99	7	23	3	0	2	15	12	29	.232	.315	.323	71	-5	-4	10	0	0	0	1	O	-0.3
1955	Mil-N	101	343	40	88	12	3	12	56	34	52	.257	.324	.414	99	-3	-1	45	2	1	0	-2	O	-0.3
1956	Mil-N	142	451	59	106	10	4	20	74	43	75	.235	.304	.408	95	-8	-4	55	2	4	-2	-3	*O/3	-1.3
1957	Mil-N	41	148	15	35	5	3	4	23	8	27	.236	.285	.392	86	-5	-3	17	2	1	0	-2	O	-0.5
	NY-N	81	215	24	52	7	4	8	38	19	39	.242	.303	.423	93	-3	-3	26	1	2	-1	1	O/3	-0.4
	Yr	122	363	39	87	12	7	12	61	27	66	.240	.296	.410	90	-7	-6	43	3	3	-1	-1		-0.9
1958	Chi-N	152	547	67	155	27	5	21	82	56	76	.283	.354	.466	117	11	13	87	0	2	-1	-3	*O/3	0.4
1959	Chi-N	122	374	55	97	15	2	11	52	35	50	.259	.326	.398	93	-5	-4	48	1	0	0	3	*O	-0.1
1960	Bos-A	40	114	12	30	3	1	5	20	11	15	.263	.328	.439	102	1	0	15	0	1	-1	1	O/1	0.0
	Bal-A	3	6	0	0	0	0	0	0	0	3	.000	.000	.000	-99	-2	-2	0	0	0	0	0	/O	-0.1
	Yr	43	120	12	30	3	1	5	20	11	18	.250	.313	.417	93	-1	-2	14	0	1	-1	1		-0.1
Total	15	1779	6305	903	1705	267	74	264	1026	559	804	.270	.333	.462	111	73	79	958	38	20		23	*O3/21	5.4

■ DICKIE THON
Thon, Richard William b: 6/20/58, South Bend, Ind BR/TR, 5'11", 160 lbs. Deb: 5/22/79

YEAR	TM/L	G	AB	R	H	2B	3B	HR	RBI	BB	SO	AVG	OBP	SLG	PRO+	BR	/A	RC	SB	CS	SBR	FR	POS	TPR
1979	*Cal-A	35	56	6	19	3	0	0	8	5	10	.339	.393	.393	117	1	1	8	0	0	0	1	2/S3	0.4
1980	Cal-A	80	267	32	68	12	2	0	15	10	28	.255	.284	.315	65	-13	-13	23	7	5	-1	-12	S2D3/1	-2.2
1981	*Hou-N	49	95	13	26	6	0	0	3	9	13	.274	.337	.337	96	-1	-0	11	6	1	1	-5	2S/3	0.0
1982	Hou-N	136	496	73	137	31	10	3	36	37	48	.276	.328	.397	110	1	5	69	37	8	6	5	*S/32	2.6
1983	Hou-N	154	619	81	177	28	9	20	79	54	73	.286	.345	.457	128	16	20	95	34	16	1	21	*S	5.7
1984	Hou-N	5	17	3	6	0	1	0	1	0	4	.353	.389	.471	151	1	1	2	0	1	-1	-0	/S	0.1
1985	Hou-N	84	251	26	63	6	1	6	29	18	50	.251	.301	.355	85	-6	-5	27	8	3	1	7	*S	0.9
1986	*Hou-N	106	278	24	69	13	1	3	21	29	49	.248	.319	.335	83	-7	-6	28	6	5	-1	-2	*S	0.0
1987	Hou-N	32	66	6	14	1	0	1	3	16	13	.212	.366	.273	75	-2	-2	8	3	0	1	-8	S	-0.4
1988	SD-N	95	258	36	68	12	2	1	18	33	49	.264	.349	.337	100	0	1	34	19	4	3	-20	S/23	-1.1
1989	Phi-N	136	435	45	118	18	4	15	60	33	81	.271	.323	.434	115	7	7	61	6	3	0	16	*S	3.2
1990	Phi-N	149	552	54	141	20	4	8	48	37	77	.255	.306	.350	80	-16	-15	57	12	5	1	3	*S	0.2
Total	12	1061	3390	399	906	150	34	57	321	281	495	.267	.325	.382	100	-19	-5	425	138	51	11	-6	S/23D1	9.4

■ JACK THONEY
Thoney, John "Bullet Jack" (b: John Thoeny) b: 12/8/1879, Ft.Thomas, Ky. d: 10/24/48, Covington, Ky. BR/TR, 5'10", 175 lbs. Deb: 4/26/02

YEAR	TM/L	G	AB	R	H	2B	3B	HR	RBI	BB	SO	AVG	OBP	SLG	PRO+	BR	/A	RC	SB	CS	SBR	FR	POS	TPR
1902	Cle-A	28	105	14	30	7	1	0	11		9	.286	.342	.371	104	0	1	15	4			-15	2S/O	-1.2
	Bal-A	3	11	1	0	0	0	0	0		1	.000	.083	.000	-72	-3	-3	0	1			-1	/3	-0.3
	Yr	31	116	15	30	7	1	0	11		10	.259	.317	.336	86	-3	-2	14	5			-17		-1.5
1903	Cle-A	32	122	10	25	3	0	1	9		2	.205	.218	.254	43	-8	-8	8	7			1	O/23	-0.8
1904	Was-A	17	70	6	21	3	0	0	6		1	.300	.310	.343	110	0	1	8	2			2	O	0.2
	NY-A	36	128	17	24	4	2	0	12		8	.188	.235	.250	53	-6	-7	10	9			1	3O	-0.5
	Yr	53	198	23	45	7	2	0	18		9	.227	.261	.283	72	-6	-6	18	11			3		-0.3
1908	Bos-A	109	416	58	106	5	9	2	30		13	.255	.277	.325	95	-2	-3	41	16			8	*O	-0.4
1909	Bos-A	13	40	1	5	1	0	0	3		2	.125	.167	.150	0	-5	-5	1	2			1	O	-0.4
1911	Bos-A	26	20	5	5	0	0	0	2		0	.250	.250	.250	40	-2	-2	1	1			0	H	-0.1
Total	6	264	912	112	216	23	12	3	73		36	.237	.266	.298	76	-25	-26	86	42			-3	O/32S	-3.1

■ ANDY THORNTON
Thornton, Andre b: 8/13/49, Tuskegee, Ala. BR/TR, 6'3", 200 lbs. Deb: 7/28/73

YEAR	TM/L	G	AB	R	H	2B	3B	HR	RBI	BB	SO	AVG	OBP	SLG	PRO+	BR	/A	RC	SB	CS	SBR	FR	POS	TPR
1973	Chi-N	17	35	3	7	3	0	0	2	7	9	.200	.333	.286	68	-1	-1	4	0	0	0	2	/1	0.0
1974	Chi-N	107	303	41	79	16	4	10	46	48	50	.261	.369	.439	120	11	9	51	2	1	0	8	1/3	1.4
1975	Chi-N	120	372	70	109	21	4	18	60	88	63	.293	.433	.516	156	35	33	89	3	2	-0	3	*1/3	3.0
1976	Chi-N	27	85	8	17	6	0	2	14	20	14	.200	.340	.341	93	1	-0	13	2	0	1	1	1	0.0
	Mon-N	69	183	20	35	5	2	9	24	28	32	.191	.308	.388	93	-1	-2	24	2	1	0	0	1O	-0.4
	Yr	96	268	28	52	11	2	11	38	48	46	.194	.327	.373	93	0	-2	37	4	1	1	1		-0.4
1977	Cle-A	131	433	77	114	20	5	28	70	70	82	.263	.379	.527	149	27	29	89	3	4	-2	-2	*1/D	1.8
1978	Cle-A	145	508	97	133	22	4	33	105	93	72	.262	.382	.516	152	36	36	99	4	7	-3	4	*1	3.2
1979	Cle-A	143	515	89	120	31	4	26	93	90	93	.233	.351	.449	114	11	11	86	5	4	-1	-2	*1D	0.0
1981	Cle-A	69	226	22	54	12	0	6	30	23	37	.239	.309	.372	97	-1	-1	23	3	1	0	-0	D1	-0.1
1982	Cle-A	161	589	90	161	26	1	32	116	109	81	.273	.389	.484	139	34	34	109	6	7	-2	0	*D/1	3.1

YEAR	TM/L	G	AB	R	H	2B	3B	HR	RBI	BB	SO	AVG	OBP	SLG	PRO+	BR	/A	RC	SB	CS	SBR	FR	POS	TPR
1983	Cle-A	141	508	78	143	27	1	17	77	87	72	.281	.389	.439	123	22	19	90	4	2	0	2	*D1	2.0
1984	Cle-A	155	587	91	159	26	0	33	99	91	79	.271	.371	.484	132	29	27	108	6	5	-1	0	*D1	2.5
1985	Cle-A	124	461	49	109	13	0	22	88	47	75	.236	.307	.408	94	-5	-4	56	3	2	-0	0	*D	-0.3
1986	Cle-A	120	401	49	92	14	0	17	66	65	67	.229	.338	.392	100	-0	1	55	4	1	1	0	*D	0.1
1987	Cle-A	36	85	8	10	2	0	0	5	10	25	.118	.211	.141	-4	-13	-13	3	1	0	0	0	D	-1.1
Total	14	1565	5291	792	1342	244	22	253	895	876	851	.254	.364	.452	123	184	179	900	48	37	-8	14	D1/O3	15.2

■ JOHN THORNTON
Thornton, John b: 1870, Washington, D.C. d: 8/31/1893, Pensacola, Fla. 5'10.5", 175 lbs. Deb: 8/14/1889

YEAR	TM/L	G	AB	R	H	2B	3B	HR	RBI	BB	SO	AVG	OBP	SLG	PRO+	BR	/A	RC	SB	CS	SBR	FR	POS	TPR
1889	Was-N	1	4	0	0	0	0	0	1	0	1	.000	.000	.000	-99	-1	-1	0	0			-0	/P	0.0
1891	Phi-N	39	123	7	17	3	0	0	6	2	10	.138	.152	.163	-7	-17	-17	3	1			0	P/O	0.0
1892	Phi-N	5	13	1	5	0	0	0	2	0	0	.385	.385	.385	135	0	0	2	0			-1	/PO	0.0
	StL-N	1	3	0	0	0	0	0	0	0	2	.000	.000	.000	-99	-1	-1	0	0			-0	/O	0.0
	Yr	6	16	1	5	0	0	0	2	0	2	.313	.313	.313	92	-0	-0	2	0			-1		0.0
Total	3	46	143	8	22	3	0	0	9	2	13	.154	.166	.175	0	-18	-18	5	1			-1	/PO	0.0

■ LOU THORNTON
Thornton, Louis b: 4/26/63, Montgomery, Ala. BL/TR, 6'2", 185 lbs. Deb: 4/08/85

YEAR	TM/L	G	AB	R	H	2B	3B	HR	RBI	BB	SO	AVG	OBP	SLG	PRO+	BR	/A	RC	SB	CS	SBR	FR	POS	TPR
1985	*Tor-A	56	72	18	17	1	1	1	8	2	24	.236	.267	.319	58	-4	-4	6	1	0	0	3	OD	0.0
1987	Tor-A	12	2	5	1	0	0	0	0	1	0	.500	.667	.500	212	0	0	0	0	1	-1	0	/OD	0.0
1988	Tor-A	11	2	1	0	0	0	0	0	0	0	.000	.000	.000	-99	-1	-1	0	0	0	0	0	O/D	0.0
1989	NY-N	13	13	5	4	1	0	0	1	0	1	.308	.308	.385	102	-0	-0	2	2	0	1	1	/O	0.2
1990	NY-N	3	0	0	0	0	0	0	0	0	0	—	—	—	—	0	0	0	0	0	0	0	/O	0.0
Total	5	95	89	29	22	2	1	1	9	3	25	.247	.280	.326	65	-4	-4	8	3	1	0	5	/OD	0.2

■ OTIS THORNTON
Thornton, Otis Benjamin b: 6/30/45, Docena, Ala. BR/TR, 6'1", 186 lbs. Deb: 7/06/73

YEAR	TM/L	G	AB	R	H	2B	3B	HR	RBI	BB	SO	AVG	OBP	SLG	PRO+	BR	/A	RC	SB	CS	SBR	FR	POS	TPR
1973	Hou-N	2	3	0	0	0	0	0	1	0	2	.000	.000	.000	-99	-1	-1	0	0	0	0	0	/C	0.0

■ WALTER THORNTON
Thornton, Walter Miller b: 2/18/1875, Lewiston, Maine d: 7/14/60, Los Angeles, Cal. TL, 6'1", 180 lbs. Deb: 7/01/1895

YEAR	TM/L	G	AB	R	H	2B	3B	HR	RBI	BB	SO	AVG	OBP	SLG	PRO+	BR	/A	RC	SB	CS	SBR	FR	POS	TPR
1895	Chi-N	8	22	4	7	1	0	1	7	3	1	.318	.400	.500	125	1	1	5	0			-1	/P1	0.0
1896	Chi-N	9	22	6	8	0	1	0	1	5	2	.364	.481	.455	144	2	2	6	2			-1	/PO	0.0
1897	Chi-N	75	265	39	85	9	6	0	55	30		.321	.402	.400	110	7	5	49	13			-11	OP	-0.5
1898	Chi-N	62	210	34	62	5	2	0	14	22		.295	.362	.338	104	2	2	29	8			-2	OP	0.2
Total	4	154	519	83	162	15	9	1	77	60	3	.312	.390	.382	110	12	10	89	23			-15	/OP1	-0.3

■ BOB THORPE
Thorpe, Benjamin Robert b: 11/19/26, Caryville, Fla. BR/TR, 6'1.5", 190 lbs. Deb: 4/19/51

YEAR	TM/L	G	AB	R	H	2B	3B	HR	RBI	BB	SO	AVG	OBP	SLG	PRO+	BR	/A	RC	SB	CS	SBR	FR	POS	TPR
1951	Bos-N	2	2	1	1	0	1	0	1	0	0	.500	.500	1.500	448	1	1	2	0	0	0	0	H	0.1
1952	Bos-N	81	292	20	76	8	2	3	26	5	42	.260	.275	.332	70	-13	-12	26	3	1	0	2	O	-1.2
1953	Mil-N	27	37	1	6	1	0	0	5	1	6	.162	.184	.189	-3	-6	-5	1	0	1	-1	-1	O	-0.7
Total	3	110	331	22	83	9	3	3	32	6	48	.251	.266	.323	64	-18	-17	28	3	2	-0	0	/O	-1.8

■ JIM THORPE
Thorpe, James Francis b: 5/28/1887, Prague, Okla. d: 3/28/53, Long Beach, Cal. BR/TR, 6'1", 185 lbs. Deb: 4/14/13

YEAR	TM/L	G	AB	R	H	2B	3B	HR	RBI	BB	SO	AVG	OBP	SLG	PRO+	BR	/A	RC	SB	CS	SBR	FR	POS	TPR
1913	NY-N	19	35	6	5	0	0	1	2	1	9	.143	.167	.229	12	-4	-4	1	2			1	/O	-0.2
1914	NY-N	30	31	5	6	1	0	0	2	0	4	.194	.194	.226	25	-3	-3	1	1			-0	/O	-0.2
1915	NY-N	17	52	8	12	3	1	0	1	2	16	.231	.259	.327	82	-2	-1	5	4	2	0	-1	O	-0.2
1917	Cin-N	77	251	29	62	2	8	4	36	6	35	.247	.267	.367	98	-3	-2	26	11			0	O	-0.4
	*NY-N	26	57	12	11	3	2	0	4	8	10	.193	.303	.316	93	-1	-0	6	1			-1	O	-0.2
	Yr	103	308	41	73	5	10	4	40	14	45	.237	.275	.357	97	-4	-2	32	12			-1		-0.6
1918	NY-N	58	113	15	28	4	4	1	11	4	18	.248	.286	.381	105	-0	-0	12	3			1	O	-0.1
1919	NY-N	2	3	0	1	0	0	0	1	0	0	.333	.333	.333	102	-0	-0	0	0			0	/O	0.0
	Bos-N	60	156	16	51	7	3	1	25	6	30	.327	.360	.429	143	7	7	25	7			-4	O/1	0.2
	Yr	62	159	16	52	7	3	1	26	6	30	.327	.359	.428	142	6	7	26	7			-4		0.2
Total	6	289	698	91	176	20	18	7	82	27	122	.252	.286	.362	99	-6	-3	77	29	2		-4	O/1	-1.1

■ BUCK THRASHER
Thrasher, Frank Edward b: 8/6/1889, Watkinsville, Ga. d: 6/12/38, Cleveland, Ohio BL/TR, 5'11", 182 lbs. Deb: 9/27/16

YEAR	TM/L	G	AB	R	H	2B	3B	HR	RBI	BB	SO	AVG	OBP	SLG	PRO+	BR	/A	RC	SB	CS	SBR	FR	POS	TPR
1916	Phi-A	7	29	4	9	2	1	0	4	2	1	.310	.355	.448	147	1	1	5	0			-1	/O	0.0
1917	Phi-A	23	77	5	18	2	1	0	2	3	12	.234	.272	.286	71	-3	-3	6	0			-3	O	-0.7
Total	2	30	106	9	27	4	2	0	6	5	13	.255	.295	.330	92	-2	-1	11	0			-4	/O	-0.7

■ MARV THRONEBERRY
Throneberry, Marvin Eugene "Marvelous Marv" b: 9/2/33, Collierville, Tenn. BL/TL, 6'1", 190 lbs. Deb: 9/25/55

YEAR	TM/L	G	AB	R	H	2B	3B	HR	RBI	BB	SO	AVG	OBP	SLG	PRO+	BR	/A	RC	SB	CS	SBR	FR	POS	TPR
1955	NY-A	1	2	1	2	1	0	0	3	0	0	1.000	1.000	1.500	574	1	1	3	0	0		0	/1	0.2
1958	*NY-A	60	150	30	34	5	2	7	19	19	40	.227	.318	.427	107	0	1	21	1	1	-0	-0	1/O	0.0
1959	NY-A	80	192	27	46	5	0	8	22	18	51	.240	.305	.391	93	-3	-2	24	0	0	0	2	1O	-0.1
1960	KC-A	104	236	29	59	9	2	11	41	23	60	.250	.317	.445	103	0	0	32	0	0	0	1	O	-0.3
1961	KC-A	40	130	17	31	2	1	6	24	19	30	.238	.336	.408	97	-0	-0	18	0	0	0	1	1O	-0.1
	Bal-A	56	96	9	20	3	0	5	11	12	20	.208	.296	.396	85	-3	-2	11	0	0	0	-1	O1	-0.4
	Yr	96	226	26	51	5	1	11	35	31	50	.226	.319	.403	93	-3	-3	29	0	0		2		-0.5
1962	Bal-A	9	9	1	0	0	0	0	0	4	6	.000	.308	.000	-9	-1	-1	0	0	0	0	0	/O	0.0
	NY-N	116	357	29	87	11	3	16	49	34	83	.244	.309	.426	94	-3	-4	46	1	3	-2	4	1	-0.4
1963	NY-N	14	14	0	2	1	0	0	1	1	5	.143	.200	.214	19	-1	-1	0	0	0	0	-0	/1	-0.1
Total	7	480	1186	143	281	37	8	53	170	130	295	.237	.313	.416	96	-10	-9	155	3	4	-2	7	1/O	-1.2

■ FAYE THRONEBERRY
Throneberry, Maynard Faye b: 6/22/31, Memphis, Tenn. BL/TR, 5'11", 185 lbs. Deb: 4/15/52

YEAR	TM/L	G	AB	R	H	2B	3B	HR	RBI	BB	SO	AVG	OBP	SLG	PRO+	BR	/A	RC	SB	CS	SBR	FR	POS	TPR
1952	Bos-A	98	310	38	80	11	3	5	23	33	67	.258	.331	.361	86	-3	-6	41	16	7	1	-4	O	-1.1
1955	Bos-A	60	144	20	37	7	3	6	27	14	31	.257	.327	.472	104	2	2	23	0	0	0	-0	O	-0.1
1956	Bos-A	24	50	6	11	2	0	1	3	3	16	.220	.264	.320	48	-4	-4	4	0	0	0	-1	O	-0.5
1957	Bos-A	1	1	0	0	0	0	0	0	0	1	.000	.000	.000	-95	-0	-0	0	0	0	0	0	H	0.0
	Was-A	68	195	21	36	8	2	2	12	17	37	.185	.254	.277	45	-15	-15	14	0	1	-1	0	O	-1.8
	Yr	69	196	21	36	8	2	2	12	17	38	.184	.252	.276	45	-15	-15	14	0	1	-1	0		-1.8
1958	Was-A	44	87	12	16	1	1	4	7	4	28	.184	.245	.356	64	-5	-5	8	0	1	-1	0	O	-0.7
1959	Was-A	117	327	36	82	11	2	10	42	33	61	.251	.325	.388	95	-2	-2	42	6	4	-1	-4	O	-1.0
1960	Was-A	85	157	18	39	7	1	1	23	18	33	.248	.330	.325	78	-5	-4	17	1	1	-0	-3	O	-0.8
1961	LA-A	24	31	1	6	1	0	0	0	5	10	.194	.306	.226	40	-2	-3	2	0	0	0	1	/O	-0.1
Total	8	521	1302	152	307	48	12	29	137	127	284	.236	.309	.358	79	-34	-39	151	23	14	-2	-12	O	-6.1

■ GARY THURMAN
Thurman, Gary Montez b: 11/12/64, Indianapolis, Ind. BR/TR, 5'10", 170 lbs. Deb: 8/30/87

YEAR	TM/L	G	AB	R	H	2B	3B	HR	RBI	BB	SO	AVG	OBP	SLG	PRO+	BR	/A	RC	SB	CS	SBR	FR	POS	TPR
1987	KC-A	27	81	12	24	2	0	0	5	8	20	.296	.360	.321	81	-2	-2	10	7	2	1	5	O	0.3
1988	KC-A	35	66	6	11	1	0	0	2	4	20	.167	.214	.182	12	-8	-8	3	5	1	1	-0	O/D	-0.7
1989	KC-A	72	87	24	17	2	1	0	5	15	26	.195	.314	.241	59	-4	-4	11	16	0	5	2	O/D	0.1
1990	KC-A	23	60	5	14	3	0	0	3	2	12	.233	.258	.283	52	-4	-4	4	1	1	-0	-1	O	-0.4
Total	4	157	294	47	66	8	1	0	15	29	78	.224	.294	.259	54	-18	-18	28	29	4	6	6	O/D	-0.7

■ BOB THURMAN
Thurman, Robert Burns b: 5/14/17, Wichita, Kan. BL/TL, 6'1", 205 lbs. Deb: 4/14/55

YEAR	TM/L	G	AB	R	H	2B	3B	HR	RBI	BB	SO	AVG	OBP	SLG	PRO+	BR	/A	RC	SB	CS	SBR	FR	POS	TPR
1955	Cin-N	82	152	19	33	2	3	7	22	17	26	.217	.296	.408	80	-4	-5	16	0	2	-1	-3	O	-0.8
1956	Cin-N	80	139	25	41	5	2	8	22	10	14	.295	.342	.532	123	5	4	25	0	0	0	-2	O	0.1
1957	Cin-N	74	190	38	47	4	2	16	40	15	33	.247	.306	.542	114	5	3	31	0	0	0	-2	O	0.0
1958	Cin-N	94	178	23	41	7	4	4	20	20	38	.230	.322	.382	81	-4	-5	21	1	2	-1	0	O	-0.6

YEAR	TM/L	G	AB	R	H	2B	3B	HR	RBI	BB	SO	AVG	OBP	SLG	PRO+	BR	/A	RC	SB	CS	SBR	FR	POS	TPR
1959	Cin-N	4	4	1	1	0	0	0	2	0	1	.250	.250	.250	33	-0	-0	0	0	0	0	0	H	0.0
Total	5	334	663	106	163	18	11	35	106	62	112	.246	.315	.465	99	2	-3	94	1	4	-2	-7	O	-1.3

■ **EDDIE TIEMEYER**   Tiemeyer, Edward Carl b: 5/9/1885, Cincinnati, Ohio   d: 9/27/46, Cincinnati, Ohio   BR/TR, 5'11.5", 185 lbs.   Deb: 8/19/06

YEAR	TM/L	G	AB	R	H	2B	3B	HR	RBI	BB	SO	AVG	OBP	SLG	PRO+	BR	/A	RC	SB	CS	SBR	FR	POS	TPR
1906	Cin-N	5	11	3	2	0	0	0	0	1		.182	.250	.182	35	-1	-1	1	0			0	/3P	0.0
1907	Cin-N	1	0	1	0	0	0	0	0	1		—	1.000	—	212	0	0	0	0			0	H	0.0
1909	NY-A	3	8	1	3	1	0	0	0	1		.375	.444	.375	197	1	1	2	0			-1	/1	0.0
Total	3	9	19	5	5	1	0	0	0	3		.263	.364	.316	111	0	0	2	0			-0	/13P	0.0

■ **MIKE TIERNAN**   Tiernan, Michael Joseph "Silent Mike" b: 1/21/1867, Trenton, N.J.   d: 11/9/18, New York, N.Y.   BL/TL, 5'11", 165 lbs.   Deb: 4/30/1887

YEAR	TM/L	G	AB	R	H	2B	3B	HR	RBI	BB	SO	AVG	OBP	SLG	PRO+	BR	/A	RC	SB	CS	SBR	FR	POS	TPR
1887	NY-N	103	407	82	117	13	12	10	62	32	31	.287	.344	.452	127	11	14	75	28			-8	*O/P	0.7
1888	*NY-N	113	443	75	130	16	8	9	52	42	42	.293	.364	.427	156	28	28	90	52			-0	*O	2.6
1889	*NY-N	122	499	147	167	23	14	10	73	96	32	.335	.447	.497	165	48	48	129	33			-4	*O	3.4
1890	NY-N	133	553	132	168	25	21	13	59	68	53	.304	.385	.495	158	40	40	130	56			-16	*O	1.9
1891	NY-N	134	542	111	166	30	12	16	73	69	32	.306	.388	.494	165	39	43	128	53			-9	*O	2.4
1892	NY-N	116	450	79	129	16	10	5	66	57	46	.287	.369	.400	137	20	21	76	20			-3	*O	1.2
1893	NY-N	125	511	114	158	19	12	14	102	72	24	.309	.399	.476	133	25	25	110	26			-9	*O	0.9
1894	*NY-N	112	424	84	117	19	13	5	77	54	21	.276	.359	.417	89	-8	-8	75	28			-11	*O	-1.9
1895	NY-N	120	476	127	165	23	21	7	70	66	19	.347	.427	.527	151	34	37	126	36			-5	*O	1.7
1896	NY-N	133	521	132	192	24	16	7	89	77	18	.369	.452	.516	162	46	48	141	35			-2	*O	3.1
1897	NY-N	127	528	123	174	29	10	5	72	61		.330	.400	.451	130	21	24	114	40			-11	*O	0.3
1898	NY-N	103	415	90	116	15	11	5	49	43		.280	.357	.405	125	11	13	68	19			-12	*O	-0.3
1899	NY-N	35	137	17	35	4	2	0	7	10		.255	.306	.314	75	-5	-4	14	2			-4	O	-0.9
Total	13	1476	5906	1313	1834	256	162	106	851	747	318	.311	.392	.463	141	310	329	1275	428			-92	*O/P	15.1

■ **COTTON TIERNEY**   Tierney, James Arthur b: 2/10/1894, Kansas City, Kan.   d: 4/18/53, Kansas City, Mo.   BR/TR, 5'8", 175 lbs.   Deb: 9/23/20

YEAR	TM/L	G	AB	R	H	2B	3B	HR	RBI	BB	SO	AVG	OBP	SLG	PRO+	BR	/A	RC	SB	CS	SBR	FR	POS	TPR
1920	Pit-N	12	46	4	11	5	0	0	8	3	4	.239	.286	.348	79	-1	-1	5	1	1	-0	-2	2/S	-0.2
1921	Pit-N	117	442	49	132	22	8	3	52	24	31	.299	.338	.405	93	-3	-5	59	4	6	-2	-27	23/OS	-3.2
1922	Pit-N	122	441	58	152	26	14	7	86	22	40	.345	.378	.515	127	17	16	82	7	8	-3	-35	*2/OS3	-2.1
1923	Pit-N	29	120	22	35	5	2	2	23	2	10	.292	.309	.417	88	-2	-3	15	2	1	0	-3	2	-0.4
	Phi-N	121	480	68	152	31	1	11	65	24	42	.317	.352	.454	100	6	-1	75	3	4	-2	19	*2/O3	1.6
	Yr	150	600	90	187	36	3	13	88	26	52	.312	.343	.447	97	4	-4	90	5	5	-2	16		1.2
1924	Bos-N	136	505	38	131	16	1	6	58	22	37	.259	.296	.331	71	-23	-21	49	11	8	-2	-1	*23	-2.7
1925	Bro-N	93	265	27	68	14	4	2	39	12	23	.257	.294	.362	68	-14	-13	27	0	3	-2	-1	3/12	-1.0
Total	6	630	2299	266	681	119	30	31	331	109	187	.296	.332	.415	93	-20	-27	312	28	31	-10	-49	23/OS1	-8.0

■ **BILL TIERNEY**   Tierney, William J. b: 5/14/1858, Boston, Mass.   d: 9/21/1898, Boston, Mass.   Deb: 5/02/1882

YEAR	TM/L	G	AB	R	H	2B	3B	HR	RBI	BB	SO	AVG	OBP	SLG	PRO+	BR	/A	RC	SB	CS	SBR	FR	POS	TPR
1882	Cin-a	1	5	1	0	0	0	0		0		.000	.000	.000	-94	-1	-1	0				0	/1	0.0
1884	Bal-U	1	3	0	1	0	0	0		1		.333	.500	.333	169	0	0	1	0			-0	/O	0.0
Total	2	2	8	1	1	0	0	0		1		.125	.222	.125	19	-1	-1	1	0			0	/O1	0.0

■ **JOHN TILLEY**   Tilley, John C. b: 1856, New York, N.Y.   Deb: 8/23/1882

YEAR	TM/L	G	AB	R	H	2B	3B	HR	RBI	BB	SO	AVG	OBP	SLG	PRO+	BR	/A	RC	SB	CS	SBR	FR	POS	TPR
1882	Cle-N	15	56	2	5	1	1	0	4	2	11	.089	.121	.143	-16	-7	-7	1				2	O	-0.4
1884	Tol-a	17	56	5	10	2	0	0		4		.179	.246	.214	52	-3	-3	3				-4	O	-0.6
	StP-U	9	26	2	4	1	0	0		3		.154	.241	.192	89	-1	1	1	0			0	/O	0.1
Total	2	41	138	9	19	4	1	0	4	9	11	.138	.196	.181	27	-11	-9	5	0			-2	/O	-0.9

■ **BOB TILLMAN**   Tillman, John Robert b: 3/24/37, Nashville, Tenn.   BR/TR, 6'4", 205 lbs.   Deb: 4/15/62

YEAR	TM/L	G	AB	R	H	2B	3B	HR	RBI	BB	SO	AVG	OBP	SLG	PRO+	BR	/A	RC	SB	CS	SBR	FR	POS	TPR
1962	Bos-A	81	249	28	57	6	4	14	38	19	65	.229	.286	.454	93	-3	-4	31	0	0	0	-4	C	-0.3
1963	Bos-A	96	307	24	69	10	2	8	32	34	64	.225	.304	.349	80	-7	-8	33	0	0	0	1	C	-0.5
1964	Bos-A	131	425	43	118	18	1	17	61	49	74	.278	.352	.445	114	12	9	65	0	0	0	-9	*C	0.5
1965	Bos-A	111	368	20	79	10	3	6	35	40	69	.215	.292	.307	66	-14	-17	32	0	0	0	-8	*C	-1.8
1966	Bos-A	78	204	12	47	8	0	3	24	22	35	.230	.305	.314	71	-5	-8	20	0	0	0	-3	C	-0.8
1967	Bos-A	30	64	4	12	1	0	1	4	3	18	.188	.224	.250	37	-5	-5	3	0	0	0	2	C	-0.1
	NY-A	22	63	5	16	1	0	2	9	7	17	.254	.329	.365	109	0	1	7	0	0	0	-0	C	0.2
	Yr	52	127	9	28	2	0	3	13	10	35	.220	.277	.307	70	-4	-5	10	0	0	0	1		0.1
1968	Atl-N	86	236	16	52	4	0	5	20	16	55	.220	.278	.301	74	-7	-8	19	1	0	0	4	C	0.0
1969	*Atl-N	69	190	18	37	5	0	12	29	18	47	.195	.264	.411	86	-4	-5	19	0	0	0	-10	C	-1.0
1970	Atl-N	71	223	19	53	5	0	11	30	20	66	.238	.300	.408	83	-5	-6	28	0	0	0	-1	C	-0.4
Total	9	775	2329	189	540	68	10	79	282	228	510	.232	.302	.371	85	-39	-50	258	1	0	0	-29	C	-4.2

■ **RUSTY TILLMAN**   Tillman, Kerry Jerome b: 8/29/60, Jacksonville, Fla.   BR/TR, 6', 185 lbs.   Deb: 6/06/82

YEAR	TM/L	G	AB	R	H	2B	3B	HR	RBI	BB	SO	AVG	OBP	SLG	PRO+	BR	/A	RC	SB	CS	SBR	FR	POS	TPR
1982	NY-N	12	13	4	2	1	0	0	0	0	4	.154	.154	.231	6	-2	-2	1	1	0	0	0	/O	0.0
1986	Oak-A	22	39	6	10	1	0	1	6	3	11	.256	.310	.359	88	-1	-1	5	2	0	1	-1	O	0.0
1988	SF-N	4	4	1	1	0	0	1	3	2	1	.250	.500	1.000	335	1	1	2	0	0	0	0	/O	0.1
Total	3	38	56	11	13	2	0	2	9	5	16	.232	.295	.375	88	-1	-1	8	3	0	1	-1	/O	0.1

■ **BEN TINCUP**   Tincup, Austin Ben b: 12/14/1890, Adair, Okla.   d: 7/5/80, Claremore, Okla.   BL/TR, 6'1", 180 lbs.   Deb: 5/22/14 C

YEAR	TM/L	G	AB	R	H	2B	3B	HR	RBI	BB	SO	AVG	OBP	SLG	PRO+	BR	/A	RC	SB	CS	SBR	FR	POS	TPR
1914	Phi-N	31	53	3	9	1	1	0	1	0	18	.170	.170	.226	16	-6	-6	2	0			0	P	0.0
1915	Phi-N	11	9	1	0	0	0	0	0	0	3	.000	.000	.000	-99	-2	-2	0	0			1	P	0.0
1916	Phi-N	1	1	0	0	0	0	0	0	0		.000	.000	.000	-97	-0	-0	0	0			0	H	0.0
1918	Phi-N	11	8	0	1	1	0	0	0	0	4	.125	.125	.250	13	-1	-1	0	0			0	/PO	0.0
1928	Chi-N	2	3	0	0	0	0	0	0	0		.000	.000	.000	-99	-1	-1	0	0			0	/P	0.0
Total	5	56	74	4	10	2	1	0	1	0	25	.135	.135	.189	-4	-10	-10	2	0			2	/PO	0.0

■ **RON TINGLEY**   Tingley, Ronald Irvin b: 5/27/59, Presque Isle, Maine   BR/TR, 6'2", 160 lbs.   Deb: 9/25/82

YEAR	TM/L	G	AB	R	H	2B	3B	HR	RBI	BB	SO	AVG	OBP	SLG	PRO+	BR	/A	RC	SB	CS	SBR	FR	POS	TPR
1982	SD-N	8	20	0	2	0	0	0	0	0	7	.100	.100	.100	-46	-4	-4	0	0	0	0	3	/C	0.0
1988	Cle-A	9	24	1	4	0	0	1	2	2	8	.167	.231	.292	44	-2	-2	1	0	0	0	3	/C	0.2
1989	Cal-A	4	3	0	1	0	0	0	0	1	0	.333	.500	.333	142	0	0	1	0	0	0	0	/C	0.1
1990	Cal-A	5	3	0	0	0	0	0	0	1	1	.000	.250	.000	-24	-0	-0	0	0	0	0	1	/C	0.1
Total	4	26	50	1	7	0	0	1	2	4	16	.140	.204	.200	14	-6	-6	2	0	0	0	7	/C	0.4

■ **JOE TINKER**   Tinker, Joseph Bert b: 7/27/1880, Muscotah, Kan.   d: 7/27/48, Orlando, Fla.   BR/TR, 5'9", 175 lbs.   Deb: 4/17/02 MH

YEAR	TM/L	G	AB	R	H	2B	3B	HR	RBI	BB	SO	AVG	OBP	SLG	PRO+	BR	/A	RC	SB	CS	SBR	FR	POS	TPR
1902	Chi-N	131	494	55	129	19	5	2	54	26		.261	.298	.332	99	-3	-1	60	27			4	*S/3	0.9
1903	Chi-N	124	460	67	134	21	7	2	70	37		.291	.344	.380	111	5	7	73	27			0	*S3	1.2
1904	Chi-N	141	488	55	108	12	13	3	41	29		.221	.265	.318	81	-11	-11	54	41			19	*S/O	0.8
1905	Chi-N	149	547	70	135	18	8	2	66	34		.247	.291	.320	81	-11	-14	65	31			17	*S	0.6
1906	*Chi-N	148	523	75	122	18	4	1	64	43		.233	.292	.289	78	-10	-14	58	30			4	*S/3	-0.1
1907	*Chi-N	117	402	36	89	11	3	1	36	25		.221	.267	.271	66	-14	-17	37	20			15	*S	0.3
1908	*Chi-N	157	548	67	146	22	14	6	68	32		.266	.307	.391	119	13	10	75	30			30	*S	4.4
1909	Chi-N	143	516	56	132	26	11	4	57	30		.256	.280	.372	100	-2	-4	59	23			16	*S	1.5
1910	*Chi-N	134	473	48	136	25	9	3	69	24	35	.288	.322	.397	110	3	3	66	20			16	*S	2.5
1911	Chi-N	144	536	61	149	24	12	4	69	39	21	.278	.327	.390	100	-2	-2	77	30			23	*S	2.6
1912	Chi-N	142	550	80	155	24	7	0	75	38	21	.282	.331	.351	87	-11	-11	73	25			25	*S	2.7
1913	Cin-N	110	382	47	121	20	13	1	57	20	26	.317	.352	.445	127	12	12	61	10			17	*S/3M	3.6

YEAR	TM/L	G	AB	R	H	2B	3B	HR	RBI	BB	SO	AVG	OBP	SLG	PRO+	BR	/A	RC	SB	CS	SBR	FR	POS	TPR
1914	Chi-F	126	438	50	112	21	7	2	46	38	30	.256	.317	.349	96	-5	-2	58	19			19	*SM	2.6
1915	Chi-F	31	67	7	18	2	1	0	9	13	5	.269	.387	.328	120	2	2	10	3			-2	S/23M	0.2
1916	Chi-N	7	10	0	1	0	0	0	1	1	1	.100	.182	.100	-11	-1	-1	0	0			-0	/S3M	-0.1
Total	15	1804	6434	774	1687	263	114	31	782	416	149	.262	.307	.353	96	-37	-42	828	336			203	*S/32O	23.7

■ JIM TIPPER
Tipper, James b: 6/18/1849, Middletown, Conn. d: 4/21/1895, New Haven, Conn. 5'5.5", 148 lbs. Deb: 4/26/1872

YEAR	TM/L	G	AB	R	H	2B	3B	HR	RBI	BB	SO	AVG	OBP	SLG	PRO+	BR	/A	RC	SB	CS	SBR	FR	POS	TPR
1872	Man-n	24	113	23	33	2	0	0		0		.292	.292	.310	91	-2	-1	10					O/3	0.0
1874	Har-n	45	197	35	60	10	0	0		0		.305	.305	.355	104	2	0	22					*O	0.1
1875	NH-n	41	158	10	25	0	0	0		0		.158	.158	.158	11	-14	-10	4					O	-0.7
Total	3 n	110	468	68	118	12	0	0		0		.252	.252	.278	75	-14	-11	36					O/3	-0.6

■ ERIC TIPTON
Tipton, Eric Gordon "Dukie" or "Blue Devil" b: 4/20/15, Petersburg, Va. BR/TR, 5'11", 190 lbs. Deb: 6/09/39

YEAR	TM/L	G	AB	R	H	2B	3B	HR	RBI	BB	SO	AVG	OBP	SLG	PRO+	BR	/A	RC	SB	CS	SBR	FR	POS	TPR
1939	Phi-A	47	104	12	24	4	2	1	14	13	7	.231	.316	.337	68	-5	-5	11	2	0	1	-1	O	-0.5
1940	Phi-A	2	8	2	1	0	1	0	0	1	1	.125	.222	.375	53	-1	-1	1	0	0	0	-0	/O	0.0
1941	Phi-A	1	4	0	2	0	0	0	0	0	0	.500	.500	.500	169	0	0	1	0	0	0	0	/O	0.0
1942	Cin-N	63	207	22	46	5	5	4	18	25	14	.222	.309	.353	94	-2	-2	22	1			1	O	-0.2
1943	Cin-N	140	493	82	142	26	7	9	49	85	36	.288	.395	.424	138	26	27	88	1			-4	*O	1.9
1944	Cin-N	140	479	62	144	28	3	3	36	59	32	.301	.380	.390	121	13	15	71	5			-1	*O	0.3
1945	Cin-N	108	331	32	80	17	1	5	34	40	37	.242	.327	.344	89	-6	-5	40	11			-3	O	-1.0
Total	7	501	1626	212	439	80	19	22	151	223	127	.270	.360	.383	112	25	30	234	20	0		-8	O	0.5

■ JOE TIPTON
Tipton, Joe Hicks b: 2/18/23, McCaysville, Ga. BR/TR, 5'11", 185 lbs. Deb: 5/02/48

YEAR	TM/L	G	AB	R	H	2B	3B	HR	RBI	BB	SO	AVG	OBP	SLG	PRO+	BR	/A	RC	SB	CS	SBR	FR	POS	TPR
1948	*Cle-A	47	90	11	26	3	0	1	13	4	10	.289	.333	.356	85	-2	-2	12	0	0	0	0	C	0.1
1949	Chi-A	67	191	20	39	5	3	3	19	27	17	.204	.306	.309	65	-11	-10	19	1	1	-0	2	C	-0.4
1950	Phi-A	64	184	15	49	5	1	6	20	19	16	.266	.335	.402	90	-4	-3	26	0	0	0	-4	C	-0.4
1951	Phi-A	72	213	23	51	9	0	3	20	51	25	.239	.389	.324	92	1	0	32	1	1	-0	2	C	0.6
1952	Phi-A	23	68	6	13	4	0	3	8	15	10	.191	.337	.382	94	0	-0	10	0	0	0	-2	C	-0.1
	Cle-A	43	105	15	26	2	0	6	22	21	21	.248	.383	.438	137	5	5	19	1	0	0	-8	C	0.0
	Yr	66	173	21	39	6	0	9	30	36	31	.225	.365	.416	119	5	5	29	1	0	0	-11		-0.1
1953	Cle-A	47	109	17	25	2	0	6	13	19	13	.229	.359	.413	111	2	2	16	0	0	0	-7	C	-0.3
1954	Was-A	54	157	9	35	6	1	1	10	30	30	.223	.354	.293	83	-3	-2	18	0	1	-1	4	C	0.4
Total	7	417	1117	116	264	36	5	29	125	186	142	.236	.351	.355	91	-13	-10	152	3	3	-1	-14	C	-0.1

■ TOM TISCHINSKI
Tischinski, Thomas Arthur b: 7/12/44, Kansas City, Mo. BR/TR, 5'10", 190 lbs. Deb: 4/11/69

YEAR	TM/L	G	AB	R	H	2B	3B	HR	RBI	BB	SO	AVG	OBP	SLG	PRO+	BR	/A	RC	SB	CS	SBR	FR	POS	TPR
1969	Min-A	37	47	2	9	0	0	0	2	8	8	.191	.309	.191	42	-3	-3	4	0	0	0	0	C	0.0
1970	Min-A	24	46	6	9	0	0	1	2	9	6	.196	.327	.261	63	-2	-2	4	0	0	0	1	C	0.0
1971	Min-A	21	23	0	3	2	0	0	2	1	4	.130	.200	.217	18	-3	-3	1	0	0	0	3	C	0.2
Total	3	82	116	8	21	2	0	1	6	18	18	.181	.296	.224	46	-8	-8	9	0	0	0	4	/C	0.2

■ JOHN TITUS
Titus, John Franklin "Silent John" b: 2/21/1876, St.Clair, Pa. d: 1/8/43, St.Clair, Pa. BL/TL, 5'9", 156 lbs. Deb: 6/08/03

YEAR	TM/L	G	AB	R	H	2B	3B	HR	RBI	BB	SO	AVG	OBP	SLG	PRO+	BR	/A	RC	SB	CS	SBR	FR	POS	TPR
1903	Phi-N	72	280	38	80	15	6	2	34	19		.286	.331	.404	115	3	4	41	5			3	O	0.3
1904	Phi-N	146	504	60	148	25	5	4	55	46		.294	.353	.387	135	18	20	77	15			8	*O	2.4
1905	Phi-N	147	548	99	169	36	14	3	89	69		.308	.386	.436	153	33	35	100	11			8	*O	3.4
1906	Phi-N	145	484	67	129	22	5	1	57	78		.267	.368	.339	123	16	16	69	12			7	*O	2.2
1907	Phi-N	145	523	72	144	23	12	3	63	47		.275	.335	.382	129	15	16	73	9			-4	*O	0.7
1908	Phi-N	149	539	75	154	24	5	2	48	53		.286	.360	.360	125	18	16	79	27			-3	*O	1.4
1909	Phi-N	151	540	69	146	22	6	3	46	66		.270	.367	.350	121	17	16	79	23			5	*O	1.9
1910	Phi-N	143	535	91	129	26	5	3	35	93	44	.241	.358	.325	96	3	0	70	20			-3	*O	-0.7
1911	Phi-N	76	236	35	67	14	1	8	26	32	16	.284	.372	.453	129	9	9	40	3			-2	O	0.5
1912	Phi-N	45	157	43	43	9	5	3	22	33	14	.274	.403	.452	125	8	7	31	6			-10	O	-0.4
	Bos-N	96	345	56	112	23	6	2	48	49	20	.325	.422	.443	134	20	19	67	5			-10	O	0.6
	Yr	141	502	99	155	32	11	5	70	82	34	.309	.416	.446	131	28	26	98	11			-20		0.2
1913	Bos-N	87	269	33	80	14	2	5	38	35	22	.297	.392	.420	129	12	12	45	4			-11	O	0.0
Total	11	1402	4960	738	1401	253	72	38	561	620	116	.282	.367	.385	126	173	172	770	140			-12	*O	12.3

■ JIM TOBIN
Tobin, James Anthony "Abba Dabba" b: 12/27/12, Oakland, Cal. d: 5/19/69, Oakland, Cal. BR/TR, 6', 185 lbs. Deb: 4/30/37

YEAR	TM/L	G	AB	R	H	2B	3B	HR	RBI	BB	SO	AVG	OBP	SLG	PRO+	BR	/A	RC	SB	CS	SBR	FR	POS	TPR
1937	Pit-N	21	34	7	15	4	0	0	6	4	3	.441	.500	.559	187	4	4	9	0			-2	P	0.0
1938	Pit-N	56	103	8	25	6	1	0	11	9	12	.243	.310	.320	73	-4	-4	11	0			-1	P	0.0
1939	Pit-N	43	74	9	18	3	1	2	11	2	12	.243	.263	.392	75	-3	-3	8	0			-1	P	0.0
1940	Bos-N	20	43	5	12	3	0	0	3	1	10	.279	.295	.349	82	-1	-1	4	0			-1	P	0.0
1941	Bos-N	43	103	6	19	5	0	1	9	10	31	.184	.257	.233	40	-8	-8	6	1			5	P	0.0
1942	Bos-N	47	114	14	28	2	0	6	15	16	23	.246	.344	.421	126	3	4	17	0			6	P	0.0
1943	Bos-N	46	107	8	30	4	0	2	12	6	16	.280	.319	.374	101	-0	-0	12	0			2	P/1	0.0
1944	Bos-N	62	116	13	22	5	1	2	18	16	28	.190	.288	.302	63	-5	-6	11	0			7	P	0.0
1945	Bos-N	41	77	9	11	3	0	3	12	15	22	.143	.290	.299	64	-4	-4	7	0			3	P	0.0
	*Det-A	17	25	2	3	0	0	2	5	1	5	.120	.154	.360	44	-2	-2	1	0	0	0	1	P	0.0
Total	9	396	796	81	183	35	3	17	102	80	162	.230	.303	.345	82	-20	-20	85	1	0		19	P/1	0.0

■ TIP TOBIN
Tobin, John Martin "Johnny" b: 9/15/06, Jamaica Plain, d: 8/6/83, Rhinebeck, N.Y. Mass. BR/TR, 6'3", 187 lbs. Deb: 9/22/32

YEAR	TM/L	G	AB	R	H	2B	3B	HR	RBI	BB	SO	AVG	OBP	SLG	PRO+	BR	/A	RC	SB	CS	SBR	FR	POS	TPR
1932	NY-N	1	1	0	0	0	0	0	0	0	0	.000	.000	.000	-99	-0	-0	0				0	H	0.0

■ JACKIE TOBIN
Tobin, John Patrick b: 1/8/21, Oakland, Cal. d: 1/18/82, Oakland, Cal. BL/TR, 6', 165 lbs. Deb: 4/20/45

YEAR	TM/L	G	AB	R	H	2B	3B	HR	RBI	BB	SO	AVG	OBP	SLG	PRO+	BR	/A	RC	SB	CS	SBR	FR	POS	TPR
1945	Bos-A	84	278	25	70	6	2	0	21	26	24	.252	.320	.288	75	-8	-8	26	2	6	-3	9	3/2O	0.0

■ JACK TOBIN
Tobin, John Thomas b: 5/4/1892, St.Louis, Mo. d: 12/10/69, St.Louis, Mo. BL/TL, 5'8", 142 lbs. Deb: 4/16/14 C

YEAR	TM/L	G	AB	R	H	2B	3B	HR	RBI	BB	SO	AVG	OBP	SLG	PRO+	BR	/A	RC	SB	CS	SBR	FR	POS	TPR
1914	StL-F	139	529	81	143	24	10	7	35	51	53	.270	.340	.393	104	7	3	81	20			5	*O	0.1
1915	StL-F	158	625	92	184	26	13	6	51	68	42	.294	.366	.406	122	23	19	109	31			3	*O	1.6
1916	StL-A	77	150	16	32	4	1	0	10	12	13	.213	.272	.253	61	-8	-7	13	7			-9	O	-1.9
1918	StL-A	122	480	59	133	19	5	0	36	48	26	.277	.349	.338	111	5	6	60	13			-1	*O	-0.1
1919	StL-A	127	486	54	159	22	7	6	57	36	24	.327	.376	.438	125	17	16	82	8			2	*O	1.0
1920	StL-A	147	593	94	202	34	10	4	62	39	23	.341	.383	.452	117	17	14	101	21	13	-2	4	*O	0.4
1921	StL-A	150	671	132	236	31	18	8	59	45	22	.352	.395	.487	117	23	18	125	7	12	-5	8	*O	0.8
1922	StL-A	146	625	122	207	34	8	13	66	56	22	.331	.388	.474	119	21	18	113	7	9	-3	-8	*O	-0.3
1923	StL-A	151	637	91	202	32	15	13	73	42	13	.317	.363	.476	113	15	10	108	8	7	-2	-9	*O	-1.3
1924	StL-A	136	569	87	170	30	8	2	48	50	12	.299	.352	.390	87	-6	-11	79	6	10	-4	-2	*O	-2.1
1925	StL-A	77	193	25	58	11	0	2	27	9	5	.301	.335	.389	79	-5	-7	26	8	2	1	-5	O/1	-1.3
1926	Was-A	27	33	5	7	0	1	0	3	0	0	.212	.212	.273	26	-4	-4	2	0	0	0	-2	/O	-0.5
	Bos-A	51	209	26	57	9	0	1	14	16	3	.273	.324	.330	73	-9	-8	22	6	5	-1	-3	O	-1.5
	Yr	78	242	31	64	9	1	1	17	16	3	.264	.310	.322	67	-13	-12	24	6	5	-1	-5		-2.0
1927	Bos-A	111	374	52	116	18	3	2	40	36	9	.310	.371	.390	100	-1	0	52	5	4	-1	-5	O	-1.0
Total	13	1619	6174	936	1906	294	99	64	581	508	267	.309	.364	.420	108	95	68	973	147	62		-15	*O/1	-6.0

■ BILL TOBIN
Tobin, William F. b: 10/10/1854, Hartford, Conn. d: 10/10/12, Hartford, Conn. BL, Deb: 7/21/1880

YEAR	TM/L	G	AB	R	H	2B	3B	HR	RBI	BB	SO	AVG	OBP	SLG	PRO+	BR	/A	RC	SB	CS	SBR	FR	POS	TPR
1880	Wor-N	5	16	1	2	0	0	0	3	0	5	.125	.125	.125	-14	-2	-2	0				0	/1	-0.1
	Tro-N	33	136	14	22	1	1	0	8	4	20	.162	.186	.184	24	-10	-11	5				-0	1	-1.2

YEAR	TM/L	G	AB	R	H	2B	3B	HR	RBI	BB	SO	AVG	OBP	SLG	PRO+	BR	/A	RC	SB	CS	SBR	FR	POS	TPR
	Yr	38	152	15	24	1	1	0	11	4	25	.158	.179	.178	20	-12	-13	5				-0		-1.3

■ AL TODD Todd, Alfred Chester b: 1/7/02, Troy, N.Y. d: 3/8/85, Elmira, N.Y. BR/TR, 6'1", 198 lbs. Deb: 4/25/32

YEAR	TM/L	G	AB	R	H	2B	3B	HR	RBI	BB	SO	AVG	OBP	SLG	PRO+	BR	/A	RC	SB	CS	SBR	FR	POS	TPR
1932	Phi-N	33	70	8	16	5	0	0	9	1	9	.229	.260	.300	45	-5	-6	6	1			-4	C	-0.9
1933	Phi-N	73	136	13	28	4	0	0	10	4	18	.206	.239	.235	32	-11	-13	8	1			5	C/O	-0.7
1934	Phi-N	91	302	33	96	22	2	4	41	10	39	.318	.344	.444	96	3	-2	44	3			-2	C	0.0
1935	Phi-N	107	328	40	95	18	3	3	42	19	35	.290	.334	.390	85	-3	-7	42	3			-13	C	-1.9
1936	Pit-N	76	267	28	73	10	5	2	28	11	24	.273	.307	.371	80	-7	-8	31	4			1	C	-0.4
1937	Pit-N	133	514	51	158	18	10	8	86	16	36	.307	.330	.428	104	1	1	69	2			-3	*C	0.2
1938	Pit-N	133	491	52	130	19	7	7	75	18	31	.265	.296	.375	83	-12	-13	48	2			9	*C	0.1
1939	Bro-N	86	245	28	68	10	0	5	32	13	16	.278	.317	.380	83	-5	-6	28	1			8	C	0.4
1940	Chi-N	104	381	31	97	13	2	6	42	11	29	.255	.283	.346	74	-15	-14	36	1			-6	*C	-1.5
1941	Chi-N	6	6	1	1	0	0	0	0	0	1	.167	.167	.167	-6	-1	-1	0	0			0	H	0.0
1943	Chi-N	21	45	1	6	0	0	0	1	1	5	.133	.152	.133	-17	-7	-7	1	0			4	C	-0.1
Total	11	863	2785	286	768	119	29	35	366	104	243	.276	.307	.377	82	-62	-75	312	18			-2	C/O	-4.8

■ PHIL TODT Todt, Philip Julius "Hook" b: 8/9/01, St.Louis, Mo. d: 11/15/73, St.Louis, Mo. BL/TL, 6', 175 lbs. Deb: 4/25/24

YEAR	TM/L	G	AB	R	H	2B	3B	HR	RBI	BB	SO	AVG	OBP	SLG	PRO+	BR	/A	RC	SB	CS	SBR	FR	POS	TPR
1924	Bos-A	52	103	17	27	8	2	1	14	6	9	.262	.309	.408	84	-3	-3	13	0	1	-1	-3	1/O	-0.6
1925	Bos-A	141	544	62	151	29	13	11	75	44	29	.278	.343	.439	97	-4	-4	83	3	2	-0	3	*1	-0.4
1926	Bos-A	154	599	56	153	19	12	7	69	40	38	.255	.306	.362	76	-25	-22	68	3	2	-0	10	*1	-1.8
1927	Bos-A	140	516	55	122	22	6	6	52	28	23	.236	.280	.337	61	-33	-31	47	6	2	1	9	*1	-2.5
1928	Bos-A	144	539	61	136	31	8	12	73	26	47	.252	.290	.406	83	-17	-16	63	6	5	-1	3	*1	-2.0
1929	Bos-A	153	534	49	140	38	10	4	64	31	28	.262	.305	.393	80	-19	-17	63	6	7	-2	3	*1	-3.6
1930	Bos-A	111	383	49	103	22	5	11	62	24	33	.269	.312	.439	92	-9	-6	53	4	1	1	3	*1	-1.3
1931	*Phi-A	62	197	23	48	14	2	5	44	8	22	.244	.273	.411	73	-8	-9	22	1	1	-0	-4	1	-1.7
Total	8	957	3415	372	880	183	58	57	453	207	229	.258	.305	.395	81	-117	-109	411	29	21	-4	24	1/O	-13.9

■ BOBBY TOLAN Tolan, Robert b: 11/19/45, Los Angeles, Cal. BL/TL, 5'11", 170 lbs. Deb: 9/03/65 C

YEAR	TM/L	G	AB	R	H	2B	3B	HR	RBI	BB	SO	AVG	OBP	SLG	PRO+	BR	/A	RC	SB	CS	SBR	FR	POS	TPR
1965	StL-N	17	69	8	13	2	0	0	6	0	4	.188	.200	.217	16	-7	-8	3	2	1	0	-1	O	-1.0
1966	StL-N	43	93	10	16	5	1	1	6	6	15	.172	.238	.280	43	-7	-7	6	1	2	-1	-1	O/1	-1.0
1967	*StL-N	110	265	35	67	7	3	6	32	19	43	.253	.313	.370	96	-2	-2	30	12	7	-1	4	O1	-0.2
1968	*StL-N	92	278	28	64	12	1	5	17	13	42	.230	.272	.335	82	-7	-6	23	9	5	-0	1	O/1	-1.0
1969	Cin-N	152	637	104	194	25	10	21	93	27	92	.305	.348	.474	122	22	18	103	26	12	1	1	*O	1.1
1970	*Cin-N	152	589	112	186	34	6	16	80	62	94	.316	.388	.475	130	26	26	113	57	20	5	3	*O	2.6
1972	*Cin-N	149	604	88	171	28	5	8	82	44	88	.283	.338	.386	112	4	8	78	42	15	4	6	*O	1.1
1973	Cin-N	129	457	42	94	14	2	9	51	27	68	.206	.255	.304	57	-29	-26	33	15	10	-2	-1	O	-3.6
1974	SD-N	95	357	45	95	16	1	8	40	20	41	.266	.321	.384	101	-2	-1	42	7	9	-3	-2	O	-0.9
1975	SD-N	147	506	58	129	19	4	5	43	28	45	.255	.307	.338	84	-15	-11	48	11	13	-5	-1	*O1	-2.3
1976	*Phi-N	110	272	32	71	7	0	5	35	7	39	.261	.290	.342	76	-8	-9	25	10	5	0	-6	1O	-2.0
1977	Phi-N	15	16	1	2	0	0	0	1	1	4	.125	.176	.125	-17	-3	-3	0	0	0	-0	-0	/1	-0.2
	Pit-N	49	74	7	15	4	0	2	9	4	10	.203	.244	.338	53	-5	-5	6	1	1	-0	1	1/O	-0.6
	Yr	64	90	8	17	4	0	2	10	5	14	.189	.232	.300	40	-8	-8	6	1	1	-0	-0		-0.8
1979	SD-N	22	21	2	4	0	1	0	1	3	4	.190	.190	.286	30	-2	-2	1	0	0	0	0	/1O	-0.1
Total	13	1282	4238	572	1121	173	34	86	497	258	587	.265	.317	.382	96	-37	-30	511	193	100	-2	1	*O1	-8.1

■ WAYNE TOLLESON Tolleson, Jimmy Wayne b: 11/22/55, Spartanburg, S.C. BB/TR, 5'9", 160 lbs. Deb: 9/01/81

YEAR	TM/L	G	AB	R	H	2B	3B	HR	RBI	BB	SO	AVG	OBP	SLG	PRO+	BR	/A	RC	SB	CS	SBR	FR	POS	TPR
1981	Tex-A	14	24	6	4	0	0	0	1	1	5	.167	.200	.167	7	-3	-3	1	2	0	1	-1	/3S	-0.2
1982	Tex-A	38	70	6	8	1	0	0	2	5	14	.114	.173	.129	-16	-11	-11	2	1	1	-0	5	S/32	-0.3
1983	Tex-A	134	470	64	122	13	2	3	20	40	68	.260	.320	.315	77	-15	-14	51	33	10	4	-10	*2S/D	-1.4
1984	Tex-A	118	338	35	72	9	2	0	9	27	47	.213	.277	.251	46	-24	-25	25	22	4	4	-6	*2/S30D	-2.1
1985	Tex-A	123	323	45	101	9	5	1	18	21	46	.313	.355	.381	100	1	0	43	21	12	-1	-2	S23/D	0.4
1986	Chi-A	81	260	39	65	7	3	3	29	38	43	.250	.346	.335	84	-4	-5	33	13	6	0	-9	3S/OD	-1.4
	NY-A	60	215	22	61	9	2	0	14	14	33	.284	.344	.344	86	-4	-4	25	4	4	-1	6	S/32	0.4
	Yr	141	475	61	126	16	5	3	43	52	76	.265	.340	.339	85	-8	-9	58	17	10	-1	-3		-1.0
1987	NY-A	121	349	48	77	4	0	1	22	43	72	.221	.306	.241	48	-25	-24	29	5	3	-0	-3	*S/3	-1.9
1988	NY-A	21	59	8	15	2	0	0	5	8	12	.254	.343	.288	79	-1	-1	7	1	0	0	6	23/S	0.5
1989	NY-A	80	140	16	23	5	2	1	9	16	23	.164	.255	.250	43	-11	-10	10	5	1	1		3S2D	0.3
1990	NY-A	73	74	12	11	1	1	0	4	6	21	.149	.213	.189	13	-9	-9	4	1	0	0	15	S2/3D	1.1
Total	10	863	2322	301	559	60	17	9	133	219	384	.241	.308	.293	66	-105	-105	228	108	41	8	11	S23/DO	-4.6

■ TIM TOLMAN Tolman, Timothy Lee b: 4/20/56, Santa Monica, Cal. BR/TR, 6', 190 lbs. Deb: 9/09/81

YEAR	TM/L	G	AB	R	H	2B	3B	HR	RBI	BB	SO	AVG	OBP	SLG	PRO+	BR	/A	RC	SB	CS	SBR	FR	POS	TPR
1981	Hou-N	4	8	0	1	0	0	0	0	0	0	.125	.125	.125	-30	-1	-1	0	0	0	0	-0	/O	-0.1
1982	Hou-N	15	26	4	5	2	0	1	3	4	3	.192	.300	.385	98	-0	-0	3	0	0	0	-0	/O1	0.0
1983	Hou-N	43	56	4	11	4	0	2	10	6	9	.196	.274	.375	83	-2	-1	5	0	1	-1	-0	/1O	-0.3
1984	Hou-N	14	17	2	3	1	0	0	0	0	3	.176	.176	.235	16	-2	-2	1	0	0	0	0	/O1	-0.1
1985	Hou-N	31	43	4	6	1	0	2	8	1	10	.140	.178	.302	33	-4	-4	2	0	1	-0	0	/O1	-0.4
1986	Det-A	16	34	4	6	1	0	0	2	6	4	.176	.300	.206	41	-3	-3	3	1	1	-0	0	/O1D	-0.3
1987	Det-A	9	12	3	1	1	0	0	1	7	2	.083	.450	.167	77	0	0	2	0	0	0	0	/OD	0.0
Total	7	132	196	21	33	10	0	5	24	24	31	.168	.266	.296	58	-12	-11	16	1	3	-2	-2	/O1D	-1.2

■ CHICK TOLSON Tolson, Charles Julius "Toby" b: 11/6/1898, Washington, D.C. d: 4/16/65, Washington, D.C. BR/TR, 6', 185 lbs. Deb: 7/03/25

YEAR	TM/L	G	AB	R	H	2B	3B	HR	RBI	BB	SO	AVG	OBP	SLG	PRO+	BR	/A	RC	SB	CS	SBR	FR	POS	TPR
1925	Cle-A	3	12	0	3	0	0	0		2	1	.250	.357	.250	56	-1	-1	1	0	0	0	0	/1	0.0
1926	Chi-N	57	80	4	25	6	1	1	8	5	8	.313	.353	.450	113	1	1	12	0			0	1	0.1
1927	Chi-N	39	54	6	16	4	0	2	17	4	9	.296	.345	.481	119	1	1	9	0			0	1/O	0.1
1929	*Chi-N	32	109	13	28	5	0	1	19	9	16	.257	.325	.330	63	-6	-6	12	0			-2	1	-0.8
1930	Chi-N	13	20	0	6	1	0	0	1	6	5	.300	.462	.350	99	0	0	4	1			1	1	0.1
Total	5	144	275	23	78	16	1	4	45	26	39	.284	.350	.393	90	-4	-4	38	1	0		-1	/1	-0.5

■ GEORGE TOMER Tomer, George Clarence b: 11/26/1895, Perry, Iowa d: 12/15/84, Perry, Iowa BL/TR, 6', 180 lbs. Deb: 9/17/13

YEAR	TM/L	G	AB	R	H	2B	3B	HR	RBI	BB	SO	AVG	OBP	SLG	PRO+	BR	/A	RC	SB	CS	SBR	FR	POS	TPR
1913	StL-A	1	1	0	0	0	0	0	0	0	1	.000	.000	.000	-99	-0	-0	0				0	H	0.0

■ PHIL TOMNEY Tomney, Philip Howard "Buster" b: 7/17/1863, Reading, Pa. d: 3/18/1892, Reading, Pa. BR/TR, 5'7", 155 lbs. Deb: 9/07/1888

YEAR	TM/L	G	AB	R	H	2B	3B	HR	RBI	BB	SO	AVG	OBP	SLG	PRO+	BR	/A	RC	SB	CS	SBR	FR	POS	TPR
1888	Lou-a	34	120	15	18	3	0	0	4	7		.150	.197	.175	22	-10	-10	6	11			6	S	-0.1
1889	Lou-a	112	376	61	80	8	5	4	38	46	47	.213	.304	.293	73	-13	-11	42	26			27	*S	2.0
1890	*Lou-a	108	386	72	107	21	7	1			43	.277	.357	.376	121	9	11	63	27			18	*S	3.0
Total	3	254	882	148	205	32	12	5	42	96	47	.232	.313	.313	88	-14	-10	112	64			50	S	4.9

■ TONY TONNEMAN Tonneman, Charles Richard b: 9/10/1881, Chicago, Ill. d: 8/7/51, Prescott, Ariz. BR/TR, 5'10.5", 175 lbs. Deb: 9/19/11

YEAR	TM/L	G	AB	R	H	2B	3B	HR	RBI	BB	SO	AVG	OBP	SLG	PRO+	BR	/A	RC	SB	CS	SBR	FR	POS	TPR
1911	Bos-A	2	5	0	1	0	0	0	3	1		.200	.333	.400	105	0	0	1				1	/C	0.1

■ BERT TOOLEY Tooley, Albert R. b: 8/30/1886, Howell, Mich. d: 8/17/76, Marshall, Mich. BR/TR, 5'10", 155 lbs. Deb: 4/12/11

YEAR	TM/L	G	AB	R	H	2B	3B	HR	RBI	BB	SO	AVG	OBP	SLG	PRO+	BR	/A	RC	SB	CS	SBR	FR	POS	TPR
1911	Bro-N	119	433	55	89	11	5	3	29	53	63	.206	.295	.252	56	-26	-24	37	18			-8	*S	-2.7
1912	Bro-N	77	265	34	62	6	5	2	37	19	21	.234	.285	.317	67	-14	-12	28	12			-15	S	-1.9
Total	2	196	698	89	151	17	8	3	66	72	84	.216	.291	.277	60	-40	-36	64	30			-24	S	-4.6

■ SPECS TOPORCER

Toporcer, George b: 2/9/1899, New York, N.Y. d: 5/17/89, Huntington Station, N.Y. BL/TR, 5'10.5", 165 lbs. Deb: 4/13/21

YEAR	TM/L	G	AB	R	H	2B	3B	HR	RBI	BB	SO	AVG	OBP	SLG	PRO+	BR	/A	RC	SB	CS	SBR	FR	POS	TPR
1921	StL-N	22	53	4	14	1	0	0	2	3	4	.264	.304	.283	57	-3	-3	5	1	0	0	0	2/S	-0.1
1922	StL-N	116	352	56	114	25	6	3	36	24	18	.324	.370	.455	117	6	8	60	2	1	0	-23	S/32O	-0.7
1923	StL-N	97	303	45	77	11	3	3	35	41	14	.254	.349	.340	84	-7	-6	38	4	3	-1	-13	2S/13	-1.4
1924	StL-N	70	198	30	62	10	3	1	24	11	14	.313	.362	.409	108	2	2	29	2	3	-1	-15	3S/2	-0.9
1925	StL-N	83	268	38	76	13	4	2	26	36	15	.284	.373	.384	92	-1	-2	41	7	2	1	-3	S/2	0.1
1926	*StL-N	64	88	13	22	3	2	0	9	8	9	.250	.327	.330	74	-3	-3	10	1			-9	2/S3	-1.0
1927	StL-N	86	290	37	72	13	4	0	19	27	16	.248	.314	.321	68	-12	-13	30	5			-11	3S/21	-1.7
1928	StL-N	8	14	0	0	0	0	0	0	0	3	.000	.000	.000	-98	-4	-4	0	0			0	/12	-0.3
Total	8	546	1566	223	437	76	22	9	151	150	93	.279	.347	.373	90	-22	-21	212	22	9		-73	S2/310	-6.0

■ JEFF TORBORG

Torborg, Jeffrey Allen b: 11/26/41, Plainfield, N.J. BR/TR, 6'0.5", 195 lbs. Deb: 5/10/64 MC

YEAR	TM/L	G	AB	R	H	2B	3B	HR	RBI	BB	SO	AVG	OBP	SLG	PRO+	BR	/A	RC	SB	CS	SBR	FR	POS	TPR
1964	LA-N	28	43	4	10	1	1	0	4	3	8	.233	.298	.302	75	-2	-1	4	0	0	0	-2	C	-0.1
1965	LA-N	56	150	8	36	5	1	3	13	10	26	.240	.292	.347	85	-4	-3	14	0	0	0	4	C	0.2
1966	LA-N	46	120	4	27	3	0	1	13	10	23	.225	.285	.275	61	-7	-6	9	0	0	0	6	C	0.2
1967	LA-N	76	196	11	42	4	1	2	12	13	31	.214	.267	.276	60	-11	-9	13	1	3	-2	11	C	0.5
1968	LA-N	37	93	2	15	2	0	0	4	6	10	.161	.212	.183	21	-9	-8	4	0	0	0	10	C	0.4
1969	LA-N	51	124	7	23	4	0	0	7	9	17	.185	.241	.218	31	-12	-11	7	1	0	0	11	C	0.4
1970	LA-N	64	134	11	31	8	0	1	17	14	15	.231	.304	.313	69	-6	-6	13	1	1	0	9	C	0.6
1971	Cal-A	55	123	6	25	5	0	0	5	3	6	.203	.222	.244	34	-11	-10	6	0	0	0	5	C	-0.2
1972	Cal-A	59	153	5	32	3	0	0	8	14	21	.209	.280	.229	56	-9	-8	9	0	0	0	15	C	0.9
1973	Cal-A	102	255	20	56	7	0	1	18	21	32	.220	.279	.259	57	-16	-13	18	0	2	-1	8	*C	-0.4
Total	10	574	1391	78	297	42	3	8	101	103	189	.214	.270	.265	56	-87	-75	97	3	6	-3	78	C	2.5

■ EARL TORGESON

Torgeson, Clifford Earl "The Earl Of Snohomish" b: 1/1/24, Snohomish, Wash. BL/TL, 6'3", 180 lbs. Deb: 4/15/47

YEAR	TM/L	G	AB	R	H	2B	3B	HR	RBI	BB	SO	AVG	OBP	SLG	PRO+	BR	/A	RC	SB	CS	SBR	FR	POS	TPR
1947	Bos-N	128	399	73	112	20	6	16	78	82	59	.281	.403	.481	137	22	23	83	11			-0	*1	1.5
1948	*Bos-N	134	438	70	111	23	5	10	67	81	54	.253	.372	.397	110	7	8	71	19			1	*1	0.8
1949	Bos-N	25	100	17	26	5	1	4	19	13	4	.260	.345	.450	118	2	2	15	4			-3	1	0.0
1950	Bos-N	156	576	120	167	30	3	23	87	119	69	.290	.412	.472	141	31	37	121	15			0	*1	2.9
1951	Bos-N	155	581	99	153	21	4	24	92	102	70	.263	.375	.437	127	17	22	99	20	11	-1	-1	*1	1.8
1952	Bos-N	122	382	49	88	17	0	5	34	81	38	.230	.366	.314	94	-2	0	51	11	7	-1	-0	*1/O	-0.4
1953	Phi-N	111	379	58	104	25	8	11	64	53	57	.274	.366	.470	117	9	10	70	7	1	2	-3	*1	0.6
1954	Phi-N	135	490	63	133	22	6	5	54	75	52	.271	.368	.371	93	-3	-3	71	7	1	2	-10	*1	-1.5
1955	Phi-N	47	150	29	40	5	3	1	17	32	20	.267	.396	.360	104	2	2	22	2	3	-1	-1	1	-0.2
	Det-A	89	300	58	85	10	1	9	50	61	29	.283	.404	.413	123	11	12	56	9	0	3	-0	1	1.0
1956	Det-A	117	318	61	84	9	3	12	42	78	47	.264	.409	.425	120	13	12	61	6	4	-1	-6	1	0.2
1957	Det-A	30	50	5	12	2	1	1	5	12	10	.240	.387	.380	108	1	1	8	0	0	0	0	1	0.1
	Chi-A	86	251	53	74	11	2	7	46	49	44	.295	.410	.438	131	13	13	47	7	3	0	-5	1/O	0.8
	Yr	116	301	58	86	13	3	8	51	61	54	.286	.406	.429	127	14	14	56	7	3	0	-5		0.9
1958	Chi-A	96	188	37	50	8	0	10	30	48	29	.266	.415	.468	146	13	14	39	7	2	1	-2	1	1.1
1959	*Chi-A	127	277	40	61	5	3	9	45	62	55	.220	.363	.357	100	1	2	39	7	6	-2	-6	*1	-0.5
1960	Chi-A	68	57	12	15	2	0	2	9	21	8	.263	.462	.404	137	4	5	13	1	0	0	0	1	0.5
1961	Chi-A	20	15	1	1	0	0	0	1	3	5	.067	.222	.067	-19	-3	-2	0	0	0	0	0	/1	-0.2
	NY-A	22	18	3	2	0	0	0	0	8	3	.111	.385	.111	42	-1	-1	1	0	1	-1	-0	/1	-0.1
	Yr	42	33	4	3	0	0	0	1	11	8	.091	.318	.091	16	-4	-3	2	0	1	-1	-0		-0.3
Total	15	1668	4969	848	1318	215	46	149	740	980	653	.265	.387	.417	118	139	157	870	133	39		-36	*1/O	8.4

■ RED TORPHY

Torphy, Walter Anthony b: 11/6/1891, Fall River, Mass. d: 2/11/80, Fall River, Mass. BR/TR, 5'11", 169 lbs. Deb: 9/25/20

YEAR	TM/L	G	AB	R	H	2B	3B	HR	RBI	BB	SO	AVG	OBP	SLG	PRO+	BR	/A	RC	SB	CS	SBR	FR	POS	TPR
1920	Bos-N	3	15	1	3	2	0	0	2	0	1	.200	.200	.333	54	-1	-1	1	0	0	0	-1	/1	-0.1

■ FRANK TORRE

Torre, Frank Joseph b: 12/30/31, Brooklyn, N.Y. BL/TL, 6'4", 200 lbs. Deb: 4/20/56

YEAR	TM/L	G	AB	R	H	2B	3B	HR	RBI	BB	SO	AVG	OBP	SLG	PRO+	BR	/A	RC	SB	CS	SBR	FR	POS	TPR
1956	Mil-N	111	159	17	41	6	0	0	16	11	4	.258	.306	.296	67	-8	-7	14	1	0	0	6	1	-0.4
1957	*Mil-N	129	364	46	99	19	5	5	40	29	19	.272	.341	.393	104	-1	2	49	0	0	0	1	*1	-0.6
1958	*Mil-N	138	372	41	115	22	5	6	55	42	14	.309	.390	.444	131	12	16	63	2	0	1	6	*1	1.5
1959	Mil-N	115	263	23	60	15	1	1	33	35	12	.228	.326	.304	75	-11	-8	28	0	0	1	-0	1	-1.4
1960	Mil-N	21	44	2	9	1	0	0	5	5	2	.205	.255	.227	36	-4	-4	3	0	0	0	-1	1	-0.5
1962	Phi-N	108	168	13	52	8	2	0	20	24	6	.310	.408	.381	117	5	5	26	1	1	-0	3	1	0.6
1963	Phi-N	92	112	8	28	7	2	1	10	11	7	.250	.333	.375	105	1	1	15	0	0	0	5	1	0.5
Total	7	714	1482	150	404	78	15	13	179	155	64	.273	.352	.372	101	-7	-6	197	4	1	1	20	1	-0.3

■ JOE TORRE

Torre, Joseph Paul b: 7/18/40, Brooklyn, N.Y. BR/TR, 6'2", 212 lbs. Deb: 9/25/60 M

YEAR	TM/L	G	AB	R	H	2B	3B	HR	RBI	BB	SO	AVG	OBP	SLG	PRO+	BR	/A	RC	SB	CS	SBR	FR	POS	TPR
1960	Mil-N	2	2	0	1	0	0	0	0	0	1	.500	.500	.500	189	0	0	1	0	0	0	0	H	0.0
1961	Mil-N	113	406	40	113	21	4	10	42	28	60	.278	.331	.424	105	-1	2	54	3	5	-2	-9	*C	0.0
1962	Mil-N	80	220	23	62	8	1	5	26	24	24	.282	.358	.395	105	1	2	31	1	0	0	5	C	0.0
1963	Mil-N	142	501	57	147	19	4	14	71	42	79	.293	.354	.431	126	16	16	71	1	5	-3	-6	*C1/O	1.1
1964	Mil-N	154	601	87	193	36	5	20	109	36	67	.321	.366	.498	140	31	31	99	2	4	-2	-7	C1	2.3
1965	Mil-N	148	523	68	152	21	1	27	80	61	79	.291	.373	.489	140	29	29	91	0	1	-1	-4	*C1	2.6
1966	Atl-N	148	546	83	172	20	3	36	101	60	61	.315	.385	.560	157	43	42	112	0	4		-3	*C1	3.9
1967	Atl-N	135	477	67	132	18	1	20	68	49	75	.277	.348	.444	127	15	16	68	2	2	-1	-4	*C1	1.8
1968	Atl-N	115	424	45	115	11	2	10	55	34	72	.271	.333	.377	112	7	7	51	1	0	0	-15	C1	-0.6
1969	StL-N	159	602	72	174	29	6	18	101	66	85	.289	.364	.447	126	21	21	99	0	0		-3	*1C	0.7
1970	StL-N	161	624	89	203	27	9	21	100	70	91	.325	.399	.498	136	35	34	120	2	2	-1	-9	C3/1	2.5
1971	StL-N	161	634	97	230	34	8	24	137	63	70	.363	.424	.555	169	62	60	145	4	1	1	-17	*3	4.5
1972	StL-N	149	544	71	157	26	6	11	81	54	64	.289	.361	.419	123	16	16	80	3	0	1	-15	*31	0.0
1973	StL-N	141	519	67	149	17	2	13	69	65	78	.287	.377	.403	116	13	14	78	2	0	1	-12	*13	-0.4
1974	StL-N	147	529	59	149	28	1	11	70	69	88	.282	.373	.401	117	13	14	80	1	2	-1	3	*13	1.0
1975	NY-N	114	361	33	89	16	3	6	35	35	55	.247	.317	.357	91	-7	-5	36	0	0	0	-1	31	-0.7
1976	NY-N	114	310	36	95	10	3	5	31	21	35	.306	.360	.406	124	7	9	44	1	3	-2	3	1/3	0.7
1977	NY-N	26	51	2	9	3	0	1	9	2	10	.176	.208	.294	34	-5	-5	2	0	0	0	-1	1/3M	-0.6
Total	18	2209	7874	996	2342	344	59	252	1185	779	1094	.297	.367	.452	129	298	302	1258	23	29	-11	-95	C13/O	19.6

■ GIL TORRES

Torres, Don Gilberto (Nunez) b: 8/23/15, Regla, Cuba d: 1/11/83, Regla, Cuba BR/TR, 6', 155 lbs. Deb: 4/25/40

YEAR	TM/L	G	AB	R	H	2B	3B	HR	RBI	BB	SO	AVG	OBP	SLG	PRO+	BR	/A	RC	SB	CS	SBR	FR	POS	TPR
1940	Was-A	2	0	0	0	0	0	0	0	0	0	—	—	—	—	0	0	0	0	0	0	0	/P	0.0
1944	Was-A	134	524	42	140	20	6	0	58	21	24	.267	.297	.328	82	-16	-13	47	10	7	-1	9	*32/1	-0.6
1945	Was-A	147	562	39	133	12	5	0	48	21	29	.237	.264	.276	62	-32	-27	40	7	4	-0	-21	*S/3	-4.5
1946	Was-A	63	185	18	47	8	0	0	13	11	12	.254	.296	.297	70	-8	-7	16	3	2	-0	2	S3/2P	-0.2
Total	4	346	1271	99	320	40	11	0	119	53	65	.252	.282	.301	72	-56	-47	102	20	13	-2	-10	S3/2P1	-5.3

■ FELIX TORRES

Torres, Felix (Sanchez) b: 5/1/32, Ponce, P.R. BR/TR, 5'11", 165 lbs. Deb: 4/10/62

YEAR	TM/L	G	AB	R	H	2B	3B	HR	RBI	BB	SO	AVG	OBP	SLG	PRO+	BR	/A	RC	SB	CS	SBR	FR	POS	TPR
1962	LA-A	127	451	44	117	19	4	11	74	28	73	.259	.308	.392	90	-9	-7	50	0	0	0	-3	*3	-0.8
1963	LA-A	138	463	40	121	32	1	4	51	30	73	.261	.310	.361	93	-8	-5	48	1	0	0	-4	*3/1	-0.7
1964	LA-A	100	277	25	64	10	0	12	28	13	56	.231	.268	.397	91	-8	-4	25	1	3	-2	0	3/1	-0.4
Total	3	365	1191	109	302	61	5	27	153	71	202	.254	.300	.381	91	-24	-16	123	2	3	-1	-8	3/1	-1.9

YEAR	TM/L	G	AB	R	H	2B	3B	HR	RBI	BB	SO	AVG	OBP	SLG	PRO+	BR	/A	RC	SB	CS	SBR	FR	POS	TPR

■ HECTOR TORRES
Torres, Hector Epitacio (Marroquin) b: 9/16/45, Monterrey, Mexico BR/TR, 6', 175 lbs. Deb: 4/10/68

YEAR	TM/L	G	AB	R	H	2B	3B	HR	RBI	BB	SO	AVG	OBP	SLG	PRO+	BR	/A	RC	SB	CS	SBR	FR	POS	TPR
1968	Hou-N	128	466	44	104	11	1	1	24	18	64	.223	.252	.258	54	-27	-26	29	2	3	-1	-4	*S/2	-1.7
1969	Hou-N	34	69	5	11	1	0	1	8	2	12	.159	.183	.217	12	-8	-8	2	0	0	0	0	S	-0.5
1970	Hou-N	31	65	6	16	1	2	0	5	6	8	.246	.310	.323	73	-3	-2	6	0	0	0	1	S/2	0.2
1971	Chi-N	31	58	4	13	3	0	0	2	4	10	.224	.274	.276	49	-3	-4	4	0	0	0	1	S/2	0.0
1972	Mon-N	83	181	14	28	4	1	2	7	13	26	.155	.215	.221	24	-18	-18	8	0	2	-1	15	2S/OP3	0.1
1973	Hou-N	38	66	3	6	1	0	0	2	7	13	.091	.189	.106	-16	-10	-10	1	0	1	-1	7	S2	0.0
1975	SD-N	112	352	31	91	12	0	5	26	22	32	.259	.302	.335	82	-12	-9	34	2	3	-1	11	S32	1.0
1976	SD-N	74	215	8	42	6	0	4	15	16	31	.195	.254	.279	56	-14	-12	14	2	1	0	-16	S/32	-2.3
1977	Tor-A	91	266	33	64	7	3	5	26	16	33	.241	.286	.346	70	-11	-11	24	1	1	-0	-2	S2/3	-0.3
Total	9	622	1738	148	375	46	7	18	115	104	229	.216	.262	.281	55	-106	-101	123	7	11	-5	13	S2/3OP	-3.5

■ RICARDO TORRES
Torres, Ricardo J. b: 1894, Cuba d: Havana, Cuba BR/TR, 5'11", 160 lbs. Deb: 5/18/20

YEAR	TM/L	G	AB	R	H	2B	3B	HR	RBI	BB	SO	AVG	OBP	SLG	PRO+	BR	/A	RC	SB	CS	SBR	FR	POS	TPR
1920	Was-A	16	30	8	10	1	0	0	3	1	4	.333	.355	.367	94	-0	-0	4	0	0	0	-1	/1C	0.0
1921	Was-A	2	3	1	1	0	0	0	0	1	1	.333	.500	.333	122	0	0	1	0	0	0	-1	/C	0.0
1922	Was-A	4	4	0	0	0	0	0	0	0	1	.000	.000	.000	-99	-1	-1	0	0	0	0	1	/C	0.0
Total	3	22	37	9	11	1	0	0	3	2	6	.297	.333	.324	76	-1	-1	4	0	0	0	-1	/C1	0.0

■ RUSTY TORRES
Torres, Rosendo (Hernandez) b: 9/30/48, Aquadilla, P.R. BB/TR, 5'10", 175 lbs. Deb: 9/20/71

YEAR	TM/L	G	AB	R	H	2B	3B	HR	RBI	BB	SO	AVG	OBP	SLG	PRO+	BR	/A	RC	SB	CS	SBR	FR	POS	TPR
1971	NY-A	9	26	5	10	3	0	2	3	0	8	.385	.385	.731	223	3	4	7	0	1	-1	0	/O	0.3
1972	NY-A	80	199	15	42	7	0	3	13	18	44	.211	.280	.291	73	-7	-7	16	0	4	-2	-4	O	-1.6
1973	Cle-A	122	312	31	64	8	1	7	28	50	62	.205	.321	.304	76	-8	-9	32	6	5	-1	-4	*O	-1.8
1974	Cle-A	108	150	19	28	2	0	3	12	13	24	.187	.252	.260	48	-10	-10	10	2	1	0	7	O/D	-0.4
1976	Cal-A	120	264	37	54	16	3	6	27	36	39	.205	.300	.356	98	-3	-1	29	4	4	-1	-5	*O/3D	-0.9
1977	Cal-A	58	77	9	12	1	1	3	10	10	18	.156	.253	.312	55	-5	-5	6	0	1	-1	3	O	-0.4
1978	Chi-A	16	44	7	14	3	0	3	6	6	7	.318	.400	.591	174	4	4	10	0	1	-1	-1	O	0.2
1979	Chi-A	90	170	26	43	5	0	8	24	23	37	.253	.349	.424	107	2	2	26	0	0	0	-13	O	-1.3
1980	KC-A	51	72	10	12	0	0	0	3	8	7	.167	.250	.167	16	-8	-8	3	1	3	-2	6	O/D	-0.3
Total	9	654	1314	159	279	45	5	35	126	164	246	.212	.303	.334	82	-32	-29	139	13	20	-8	-11	O/D3	-6.2

■ KELVIN TORVE
Torve, Kelvin Curtis b: 1/10/60, Rapid City, S.Dak. BL/TR, 6'3", 205 lbs. Deb: 6/25/88

YEAR	TM/L	G	AB	R	H	2B	3B	HR	RBI	BB	SO	AVG	OBP	SLG	PRO+	BR	/A	RC	SB	CS	SBR	FR	POS	TPR
1988	Min-A	12	16	1	3	1	0	0	2	1	2	.188	.235	.375	66	-1	-1	1	0	1	-1	0	/1D	-0.1
1990	NY-N	20	38	0	11	4	0	0	2	4	9	.289	.386	.395	118	1	1	6	0	0	0	-2	/1O	0.0
Total	2	32	54	1	14	4	0	0	4	5	11	.259	.344	.389	103	0	0	7	0	1	-1	-2	/1OD	-0.1

■ CESAR TOVAR
Tovar, Cesar Leonardo "Pepito" (b: Cesar Leonard Perez (Tovar)) b: 7/3/40, Caracas, Venez. BR/TR, 5'9", 155 lbs. Deb: 4/12/65

YEAR	TM/L	G	AB	R	H	2B	3B	HR	RBI	BB	SO	AVG	OBP	SLG	PRO+	BR	/A	RC	SB	CS	SBR	FR	POS	TPR
1965	Min-A	18	25	3	5	1	0	0	2	2	3	.200	.259	.240	41	-2	-2	2	2	0	1	1	/23OS	0.0
1966	Min-A	134	465	57	121	19	5	2	41	44	50	.260	.329	.335	86	-4	-8	54	16	6	1	-9	2SO	-0.8
1967	Min-A	164	649	98	173	32	7	6	47	46	51	.267	.328	.365	97	4	-2	80	19	11	-1	-4	O32/S	-0.6
1968	Min-A	157	613	89	167	31	6	6	47	34	41	.272	.328	.372	106	8	5	80	35	13	3	-0	O3S2/PC1	1.1
1969	*Min-A	158	535	99	154	25	5	11	52	37	37	.288	.344	.415	109	7	6	80	45	12	6	2	*O23	1.4
1970	*Min-A	161	650	120	195	36	13	10	54	52	47	.300	.359	.442	118	17	16	103	30	15	0	3	*O/23	1.3
1971	Min-A	157	657	94	204	29	3	1	45	45	39	.311	.357	.368	103	5	3	87	18	14	-3	14	*O/32	1.0
1972	Min-A	141	548	86	145	20	6	2	31	39	39	.265	.329	.334	93	-1	-4	63	21	10	0	6	*O	0.0
1973	Phi-N	97	328	49	88	18	4	1	21	29	35	.268	.337	.357	90	-3	-4	41	6	4	-1	-16	3O2	-2.2
1974	Tex-A	138	562	78	164	24	6	4	58	47	33	.292	.356	.377	114	9	11	79	13	9	-2	16	*O/D	2.2
1975	Tex-A	102	427	53	110	16	0	3	28	27	25	.258	.306	.316	77	-13	-12	40	16	11	-2	-5	DO/2	-2.0
	*Oak-A	19	26	5	6	1	0	0	3	3	3	.231	.310	.269	66	-1	-1	3	4	0	1	0	/23SD	0.0
	Yr	121	453	58	116	17	0	3	31	30	28	.256	.307	.313	76	-15	-14	43	20	11	-1	-5		-2.0
1976	Oak-A	29	45	1	8	0	0	0	4	4	4	.178	.275	.178	36	-4	-3	2	1	2	-1	-0	O/D	-0.4
	NY-A	13	39	2	6	1	0	0	2	4	3	.154	.250	.179	27	-3	-3	2	0	1	-1	1	D/2	-0.2
	Yr	42	84	3	14	1	0	0	6	8	7	.167	.263	.179	32	-7	-7	4	1	3	-2	1		-0.6
Total	12	1488	5569	834	1546	253	55	46	435	413	410	.278	.337	.368	99	19	1	717	226	108	3	8	O32/DS1C	0.8

■ BABE TOWNE
Towne, Jay King b: 3/12/1880, Coon Rapid, Iowa d: 10/29/38, Des Moines, Iowa BL/TR, 5'10", 180 lbs. Deb: 8/01/06

YEAR	TM/L	G	AB	R	H	2B	3B	HR	RBI	BB	SO	AVG	OBP	SLG	PRO+	BR	/A	RC	SB	CS	SBR	FR	POS	TPR
1906	*Chi-A	14	36	3	10	0	0	0	6	7		.278	.395	.278	117	1	1	4	0			-4	C	-0.1

■ GEORGE TOWNSEND
Townsend, George Hodgson "Sleepy" b: 6/4/1867, Hartsdale, N.Y. d: 3/15/30, New Haven, Conn. BR/TR, 5'7.5", 180 lbs. Deb: 6/25/1887

YEAR	TM/L	G	AB	R	H	2B	3B	HR	RBI	BB	SO	AVG	OBP	SLG	PRO+	BR	/A	RC	SB	CS	SBR	FR	POS	TPR
1887	Phi-a	31	109	12	21	3	0	0		3		.193	.214	.220	23	-11	-11	7	8			-6	C/O	-1.0
1888	Phi-a	42	161	13	25	6	0	0	12	4		.155	.181	.193	22	-14	-14	6	2			1	C	-0.7
1890	Bal-a	18	67	6	16	4	1	0		4		.239	.282	.328	78	-2	-2	7	3			2	C	0.1
1891	Bal-a	61	204	29	39	5	4	0	18	20	21	.191	.279	.255	55	-11	-12	16	3			-11	C/O	-1.8
Total	4	152	541	60	101	18	5	0	30	31	21	.187	.239	.238	42	-38	-39	36	16			-16	C/O	-3.4

■ JIM TOY
Toy, James Madison b: 2/20/1858, Beaver Falls, Pa. d: 3/13/19, Beaver Falls, Pa. 5'6", 160 lbs. Deb: 4/20/1887

YEAR	TM/L	G	AB	R	H	2B	3B	HR	RBI	BB	SO	AVG	OBP	SLG	PRO+	BR	/A	RC	SB	CS	SBR	FR	POS	TPR
1887	Cle-a	109	423	56	94	20	5	1		17		.222	.256	.300	58	-25	-23	35	8			4	1OC/3S	-1.5
1890	Bro-a	44	160	11	29	3	0	0		11		.181	.238	.200	32	-13	-13	8	2			-3	C	-0.8
Total	2	153	583	67	123	23	5	1		28		.211	.251	.273	51	-39	-36	44	10			1	/1CO3S	-2.3

■ JIM TRABER
Traber, James Joseph b: 12/26/61, Columbus, Ohio BL/TL, 6', 194 lbs. Deb: 9/21/84

YEAR	TM/L	G	AB	R	H	2B	3B	HR	RBI	BB	SO	AVG	OBP	SLG	PRO+	BR	/A	RC	SB	CS	SBR	FR	POS	TPR
1984	Bal-A	10	21	3	5	0	0	0	2	2	4	.238	.304	.238	54	-1	-1	2	0	0	0	0	/D	0.0
1986	Bal-A	65	212	28	54	7	0	13	44	18	31	.255	.328	.472	116	4	4	32	0	0	0	0	1D/O	0.2
1988	Bal-A	103	352	25	78	6	0	10	45	19	42	.222	.263	.324	65	-18	-16	28	1	2	-1	8	1DO	-1.3
1989	Bal-A	86	234	14	49	8	0	4	26	19	41	.209	.269	.295	61	-13	-12	18	4	3	-1	6	1/D	-1.0
Total	4	264	819	70	186	21	0	27	117	58	118	.227	.283	.352	77	-28	-25	79	5	5	-2	14	1/DO	-2.1

■ DICK TRACEWSKI
Tracewski, Richard Joseph b: 2/3/35, Eynon, Pa. BR/TR, 5'11", 160 lbs. Deb: 4/12/62 MC

YEAR	TM/L	G	AB	R	H	2B	3B	HR	RBI	BB	SO	AVG	OBP	SLG	PRO+	BR	/A	RC	SB	CS	SBR	FR	POS	TPR
1962	LA-N	15	2	3	0	0	0	0	0	2	0	.000	.500	.000	50	0	0	0	0	0	0	4	/S	0.5
1963	*LA-N	104	217	23	49	2	1	1	10	19	39	.226	.288	.258	63	-11	-9	16	2	3	-1	19	S2	1.9
1964	LA-N	106	304	31	75	13	4	1	26	31	61	.247	.316	.326	88	-7	-4	33	3	3	-1	-0	23S	0.0
1965	*LA-N	78	186	17	40	6	0	1	20	25	30	.215	.315	.263	69	-8	-6	15	2	6	-3	8	32/S	-0.1
1966	Det-A	81	124	15	24	1	0	1	9	7	32	.194	.254	.218	36	-10	-10	7	1	1	-0	11	2/S	0.7
1967	Det-A	74	107	19	30	4	2	1	9	8	20	.280	.330	.383	107	1	1	14	1	1	-0	9	S23	1.5
1968	*Det-A	90	212	30	33	3	1	4	15	24	51	.156	.242	.236	44	-14	-14	13	3	0	1	15	S32	-1.6
1969	Det-A	66	79	10	11	2	0	0	4	15	20	.139	.277	.165	25	-7	-8	5	3	0	1	16	S2/3	1.2
Total	8	614	1231	148	262	31	9	8	91	134	253	.213	.291	.272	65	-56	-52	104	15	14	-4	63	S23	4.1

■ JIM TRACY
Tracy, James Edwin b: 12/31/55, Hamilton, Ohio BL/TR, 6', 185 lbs. Deb: 7/20/80

YEAR	TM/L	G	AB	R	H	2B	3B	HR	RBI	BB	SO	AVG	OBP	SLG	PRO+	BR	/A	RC	SB	CS	SBR	FR	POS	TPR
1980	Chi-N	42	122	12	31	3	3	3	9	13	37	.254	.326	.402	95	0	-1	16	2	2	-1	-7	O/1	-1.0
1981	Chi-N	45	63	6	15	2	1	0	5	12	14	.238	.360	.302	85	-0	-1	8	1	0	0	-2	O	-0.2
Total	2	87	185	18	46	5	4	3	14	25	51	.249	.338	.368	92	-0	-2	24	3	2	-1	-9	/O1	-1.2

■ JOHN TRAFFLEY
Traffley, John b: 1862, Chicago, Ill. d: 7/13/1900, Baltimore, Md. 5'9", 180 lbs. Deb: 6/15/1889

YEAR	TM/L	G	AB	R	H	2B	3B	HR	RBI	BB	SO	AVG	OBP	SLG	PRO+	BR	/A	RC	SB	CS	SBR	FR	POS	TPR
1889	Lou-a	1	2	0	1	0	0	0	0	0	0	.500	.500	.500	192	0	0	1	0			-1	/O	0.0

YEAR	TM/L	G	AB	R	H	2B	3B	HR	RBI	BB	SO	AVG	OBP	SLG	PRO+ BR	/A	RC	SB	CS	SBR	FR	POS	TPR

■ BILL TRAFFLEY   Traffley, William F. b: 12/21/1859, Staten Island, N.Y   d: 6/24/08, Denver, Colo.   BR/TR, 5'11.5", 185 lbs.   Deb: 7/27/1878

YEAR	TM/L	G	AB	R	H	2B	3B	HR	RBI	BB	SO	AVG	OBP	SLG	PRO+ BR	/A	RC	SB	CS	SBR	FR	POS	TPR
1878	Chi-N	2	9	1	1	0	0	0	1	0	1	.111	.111	.111	-25	-1	-1	0				1	/C	0.0
1883	Cin-a	30	105	17	21	5	0	0		4		.200	.229	.248	51	-5	-6	6				2	C/S	-0.1
1884	Bal-a	53	210	25	37	4	6	0		3		.176	.192	.252	44	-12	-13	10				-6	C/O1	-1.3
1885	Bal-a	69	254	27	39	4	5	1		17		.154	.215	.220	40	-17	-16	12				8	CO/2	0.0
1886	Bal-a	25	85	15	18	0	1	0		10		.212	.295	.235	70	-3	-2	8	8			0	C	0.0
Total	5	179	663	85	116	13	12	1	1	34	1	.175	.220	.235	46	-38	-39	37	8			5	C/O2S1	-1.4

■ WALT TRAGESSER   Tragesser, Walter Joseph b: 6/14/1887, Lafayette, Ind.   d: 12/14/70, Lafayette, Ind.   BR/TR, 6', 175 lbs.   Deb: 7/30/13

YEAR	TM/L	G	AB	R	H	2B	3B	HR	RBI	BB	SO	AVG	OBP	SLG	PRO+ BR	/A	RC	SB	CS	SBR	FR	POS	TPR
1913	Bos-N	2	0	0	0	0	0	0	0	0	0	—	—	—	—	0	0	0	0			0	/C	0.0
1915	Bos-N	7	7	1	0	0	0	0	0	0	2	.000	.000	.000	-99	-2	-2	0	0			1	/C	0.0
1916	Bos-N	41	54	3	11	1	0	0	4	5	10	.204	.283	.222	59	-3	-2	4	0			4	C	0.4
1917	Bos-N	98	297	23	66	10	2	0	25	15	36	.222	.264	.269	68	-13	-11	22	5			-1	C	-0.7
1918	Bos-N	7	1	0	0	0	0	0	0	0	0	.000	.000	.000	-99	-0	-0	0	0			1	/C	0.1
1919	Bos-N	20	40	3	7	2	0	0	3	2	10	.175	.233	.225	39	-3	-3	2	1			0	C	-0.1
	Phi-N	35	114	7	27	7	0	0	8	9	31	.237	.298	.298	74	-3	-4	10	4			4	C	0.3
	Yr	55	154	10	34	9	0	0	11	11	41	.221	.281	.279	67	-6	-6	13	5			4		0.2
1920	Phi-N	62	176	17	37	11	1	6	26	4	36	.210	.236	.386	73	-6	-7	16	4	0	1	-12	C	-1.5
Total	7	272	689	54	148	31	3	6	66	35	125	.215	.260	.295	67	-29	-29	54	14	0		-3	C	-1.5

■ RED TRAMBACK   Tramback, Stephen Joseph b: 11/1/15, Iselin, Pa.   d: 12/28/79, Buffalo, N.Y.   BL/TL, 6', 175 lbs.   Deb: 9/15/40

YEAR	TM/L	G	AB	R	H	2B	3B	HR	RBI	BB	SO	AVG	OBP	SLG	PRO+ BR	/A	RC	SB	CS	SBR	FR	POS	TPR
1940	NY-N	2	4	0	1	0	0	0	0	1	1	.250	.400	.250	82	-0	-0	1	1			-0	/O	0.0

■ ALAN TRAMMELL   Trammell, Alan Stuart b: 2/21/58, Garden Grove, Cal.   BR/TR, 6', 165 lbs.   Deb: 9/09/77

YEAR	TM/L	G	AB	R	H	2B	3B	HR	RBI	BB	SO	AVG	OBP	SLG	PRO+ BR	/A	RC	SB	CS	SBR	FR	POS	TPR
1977	Det-A	19	43	6	8	0	0	0	0	4	12	.186	.255	.186	21	-5	-5	2	0	0	0	-7	S	-0.9
1978	Det-A	139	448	49	120	14	6	2	34	45	56	.268	.337	.339	88	-5	-6	52	3	1	0	6	*S	1.1
1979	Det-A	142	460	68	127	11	4	6	50	43	55	.276	.338	.357	85	-7	-9	56	17	14	-3	-13	*S	-0.8
1980	Det-A	146	560	107	168	21	5	9	65	69	63	.300	.380	.404	112	14	12	87	12	12	-4	-27	*S	-0.7
1981	Det-A	105	392	52	101	15	3	2	31	49	31	.258	.345	.327	91	-1	-3	47	10	3	1	6	*S	1.2
1982	Det-A	157	489	66	126	34	3	9	57	52	47	.258	.329	.395	97	-1	-2	67	19	8	1	-8	*S	0.5
1983	Det-A	142	505	83	161	31	2	14	66	57	64	.319	.388	.471	139	25	27	96	30	10	3	-17	*S	2.0
1984	*Det-A	139	555	85	174	34	5	14	69	60	63	.314	.383	.468	135	27	27	100	19	13	-2	-12	*SD	2.2
1985	Det-A	149	605	79	156	21	7	13	57	50	71	.258	.317	.380	90	-9	-8	76	14	5	1	-16	*S	-1.1
1986	Det-A	151	574	107	159	33	7	21	75	59	57	.277	.350	.469	121	16	16	95	25	12	0	6	*S/D	3.0
1987	*Det-A	151	597	109	205	34	3	28	105	60	47	.343	.406	.551	157	44	47	137	21	2	5	-10	*S	4.7
1988	Det-A	128	466	73	145	24	1	15	69	46	46	.311	.378	.464	140	22	24	79	7	4	-0	-7	*S	2.3
1989	Det-A	121	449	54	109	20	3	5	43	45	45	.243	.317	.334	86	-9	-8	50	10	2	2	12	*S/D	1.6
1990	Det-A	146	559	71	170	37	1	14	89	68	55	.304	.381	.449	132	24	25	95	12	10	-2	1	*S/D	3.2
Total	14	1835	6702	1009	1929	329	50	152	810	707	712	.288	.358	.420	114	134	137	1039	199	96	2	-86	*S/D	18.3

■ CECIL TRAVIS   Travis, Cecil Howell b: 8/8/13, Riverdale, Ga.   BL/TR, 6'1.5", 185 lbs.   Deb: 5/16/33

YEAR	TM/L	G	AB	R	H	2B	3B	HR	RBI	BB	SO	AVG	OBP	SLG	PRO+ BR	/A	RC	SB	CS	SBR	FR	POS	TPR
1933	Was-A	18	43	7	13	1	0	0	2	2	5	.302	.348	.326	80	-1	-1	5	0	0	0	4	3	0.4
1934	Was-A	109	392	48	125	22	4	1	53	24	37	.319	.361	.403	101	-2	0	56	1	5	-3	3	3	0.1
1935	Was-A	138	534	85	170	27	8	0	61	41	28	.318	.377	.399	104	1	4	82	4	2	0	22	*3O	2.5
1936	Was-A	138	517	77	164	34	10	2	92	39	21	.317	.366	.433	102	-3	1	82	4	4	-1	-12	SO/23	-0.6
1937	Was-A	135	526	72	181	27	7	3	66	39	34	.344	.395	.439	115	9	12	92	3	2	-0	-11	*S	0.7
1938	Was-A	146	567	96	190	30	5	5	67	58	22	.335	.401	.432	117	9	15	100	6	5	-1	3	*S	2.3
1939	Was-A	130	476	55	139	20	9	5	63	34	25	.292	.342	.403	97	-8	-3	65	0	3	-2	-4	*S	0.0
1940	Was-A	136	528	60	170	37	11	2	76	48	23	.322	.381	.445	121	11	16	94	0	1	-1	16	*3S	3.7
1941	Was-A	152	608	106	**218**	39	19	7	101	52	25	.359	.410	.520	152	38	42	131	2	2	-1	2	*S3	4.5
1945	Was-A	15	54	4	13	2	1	0	10	4	5	.241	.293	.315	83	-2	-1	4	0	1	-1	0	3	0.0
1946	Was-A	137	465	45	117	22	3	1	56	45	47	.252	.323	.318	85	-12	-9	47	2	4	-2	-19	S3	-2.4
1947	Was-A	74	204	10	44	4	1	1	10	16	19	.216	.273	.260	50	-14	-14	14	1	3	-2	-2	3S	-1.6
Total	12	1328	4914	665	1544	265	78	27	657	402	291	.314	.370	.416	109	26	63	772	23	32	-12	2	S3/O2	9.9

■ BRIAN TRAXLER   Traxler, Brian Lee b: 9/26/67, Waukegan, Ill.   BL/TL, 5'10", 200 lbs.   Deb: 4/24/90

YEAR	TM/L	G	AB	R	H	2B	3B	HR	RBI	BB	SO	AVG	OBP	SLG	PRO+ BR	/A	RC	SB	CS	SBR	FR	POS	TPR
1990	LA-N	9	11	0	1	1	0	0	0	0	4	.091	.091	.182	-29	-2	-2	0	0	0	0	1	/1	-0.1

■ JIM TRAY   Tray, James b: 2/14/1860, Jackson, Mich.   d: 7/28/05, Jackson, Mich.   5'8", 144 lbs.   Deb: 9/06/1884

YEAR	TM/L	G	AB	R	H	2B	3B	HR	RBI	BB	SO	AVG	OBP	SLG	PRO+ BR	/A	RC	SB	CS	SBR	FR	POS	TPR
1884	Ind-a	6	21	2	6	0	0	0		2		.286	.348	.286	116	0	0	2				-0	/C1	0.0

■ PIE TRAYNOR   Traynor, Harold Joseph b: 11/11/1899, Framingham, Mass.   d: 3/16/72, Pittsburgh, Pa.   BR/TR, 6', 170 lbs.   Deb: 9/15/20   MH

YEAR	TM/L	G	AB	R	H	2B	3B	HR	RBI	BB	SO	AVG	OBP	SLG	PRO+ BR	/A	RC	SB	CS	SBR	FR	POS	TPR
1920	Pit-N	17	52	6	11	3	1	0	2	3	6	.212	.268	.308	63	-2	-3	4	1	3	-2	-6	S	-0.9
1921	Pit-N	7	19	0	5	0	0	0	2	1	2	.263	.300	.263	49	-1	-1	2	0	0	0	1	/3S	0.0
1922	Pit-N	142	571	89	161	17	12	4	81	27	28	.282	.319	.375	77	-19	-20	70	17	3	3	-4	*3S	-0.8
1923	Pit-N	153	616	108	208	19	**19**	12	101	34	19	.338	.377	.489	124	22	20	112	28	13	1	8	*3/S	3.1
1924	Pit-N	142	545	86	160	26	13	5	82	37	26	.294	.340	.417	100	-1	-1	74	24	18	-4	9	*3	1.4
1925	*Pit-N	150	591	114	189	39	14	6	106	52	19	.320	.377	.464	106	12	6	103	15	9	-1	23	*3/S	3.5
1926	Pit-N	152	574	83	182	25	17	3	92	38	14	.317	.361	.436	108	10	6	88	8			7	*3/S	1.4
1927	*Pit-N	149	573	93	196	32	9	5	106	22	11	.342	.370	.455	112	15	9	92	11			13	*3/S	3.0
1928	Pit-N	144	569	91	192	38	12	3	124	28	10	.337	.370	.462	112	12	9	93	12			4	*3	1.5
1929	Pit-N	130	540	94	192	27	12	4	108	30	7	.356	.393	.472	111	11	9	96	13			-1	*3	1.6
1930	Pit-N	130	497	90	182	22	11	9	119	48	19	.366	.423	.509	104	21	21	104	7			5	*3	2.4
1931	Pit-N	155	615	81	183	37	15	2	103	54	28	.298	.354	.416	107	6	6	93	6			-9	*3	0.7
1932	Pit-N	135	513	74	169	27	10	2	68	32	20	.329	.373	.433	118	12	13	84	6			-3	*3	2.1
1933	Pit-N	154	624	85	190	27	6	1	82	35	24	.304	.342	.372	104	3	3	80	5			-1	*3	0.7
1934	Pit-N	119	444	62	137	22	10	1	61	21	27	.309	.341	.410	98	-0	-2	56	3			-10	*3M	-0.2
1935	Pit-N	57	204	24	57	10	3	1	36	10	17	.279	.323	.373	84	-4	-5	23	2			-3	*3/1M	-0.5
1937	Pit-N	5	12	3	2	0	0	0	0	0	1	.167	.167	.167	-9	-2	-2	0	0			1	/3M	0.0
Total	17	1941	7559	1183	2416	371	164	58	1273	472	278	.320	.362	.435	107	96	71	1174	158	46		34	*3/S1	19.0

■ FRED TREACEY   Treacey, Frederick S. b: 1847, Brooklyn, N.Y.   5'9.5", 145 lbs.   Deb: 5/16/1871

YEAR	TM/L	G	AB	R	H	2B	3B	HR	RBI	BB	SO	AVG	OBP	SLG	PRO+ BR	/A	RC	SB	CS	SBR	FR	POS	TPR
1871	Chi-n	25	124	39	42	7	5	**4**	33	2	5	.339	.349	.573	144	9	6	30	13				*O	0.4
1872	Ath-n	47	236	53	64	7	2	2		5		.271	.286	.343	93	-2	-2	24					*O	0.0
1873	Phi-n	51	244	49	63	7	2	1		4		.258	.270	.316	69	-8	-10	21					*O	-0.5
1874	Chi-n	35	146	18	28	6	0	0		3		.192	.208	.233	40	-9	-10	7					O	-0.6
1875	Cen-n	11	46	9	12	2	0	0		2		.261	.292	.304	116	0	1	4					O	0.1
	Phi-n	43	179	24	38	3	3	0		1		.212	.217	.263	62	-6	-7	10					O	-0.5
	Yr	54	225	33	50	5	3	0		3		.222	.232	.271	73	-6	-6	15						-0.4
1876	NY-N	57	256	47	54	5	1	0	18	1	5	.211	.214	.238	58	-13	-8	13				11	*O	0.2
Total	5 n	212	975	192	247	32	12	7	33	17	5	.253	.266	.332	82	-16	-22	97					O	-1.1

■ PETE TREACEY   Treacey, Peter b: 1852, Brooklyn, N.Y.   Deb: 8/05/1876

YEAR	TM/L	G	AB	R	H	2B	3B	HR	RBI	BB	SO	AVG	OBP	SLG	PRO+ BR	/A	RC	SB	CS	SBR	FR	POS	TPR
1876	NY-N	2	5	1	0	0	0	0	0	1	0	.000	.167	.000	-46	-1	-1	0				-1	/S	-0.1

YEAR	TM/L	G	AB	R	H	2B	3B	HR	RBI	BB	SO	AVG	OBP	SLG	PRO+	BR	/A	RC	SB	CS	SBR	FR	POS	TPR

■ RAY TREADAWAY   Treadaway, Edgar Raymond b: 10/31/07, Ragland, Ala.   d: 10/12/35, Chattanooga, Tenn.   BL/TR, 5′7″, 150 lbs. Deb: 9/17/30

YEAR	TM/L	G	AB	R	H	2B	3B	HR	RBI	BB	SO	AVG	OBP	SLG	PRO+	BR	/A	RC	SB	CS	SBR	FR	POS	TPR
1930	Was-A	6	19	1	4	2	0	0	1	0	3	.211	.211	.316	31	-2	-2	1	0	0	0	-1	/3	-0.2

■ GEORGE TREADAWAY   Treadaway, George B. BL , Deb: 4/27/1893

1893	Bal-N	115	458	78	119	16	17	1	67	57	50	.260	.347	.376	92	-4	-6	70	24			8	*O	-0.1
1894	Bro-N	123	479	124	157	27	26	4	102	72	43	.328	.418	.518	136	21	28	118	27			1	*O/1	1.6
1895	Bro-N	86	339	54	87	14	3	7	54	33	22	.257	.326	.378	90	-9	-4	46	9			-9	O	-1.6
1896	Lou-N	2	7	0	1	0	0	0	1	1	0	.143	.250	.143	7	-1	-1	0	0			-1	/O1	0.0
Total	4	326	1283	256	364	57	46	12	224	163	115	.284	.368	.428	108	7	18	233	60			-1	O/1	-0.1

■ JEFF TREADAWAY   Treadaway, Hugh Jeffery b: 1/22/63, Columbus, Ga.   BL/TR, 5′10″, 170 lbs.   Deb: 9/04/87

1987	Cin-N	23	84	9	28	4	0	2	4	2	6	.333	.356	.452	108	1	1	14	1	0	0	-7	2	-0.5
1988	Cin-N	103	301	30	76	19	4	2	23	27	30	.252	.320	.362	92	-2	-3	36	2	0	1	3	2/3	0.3
1989	Atl-N	134	473	58	131	18	3	8	40	30	38	.277	.320	.378	96	-1	-3	56	3	2	-0	3	*2/3	0.2
1990	Atl-N	128	474	56	134	20	2	11	59	25	42	.283	.323	.403	97	-2	-3	59	3	4	-2	10	*2	0.6
Total	4	388	1332	153	369	61	9	23	126	84	116	.277	.323	.388	96	-3	-8	165	9	6	-1	8	2/3	0.6

■ RED TREADAWAY   Treadaway, Thadford Leon b: 4/28/20, Athalone, N.C.   BL/TR, 5′10″, 175 lbs.   Deb: 7/25/44

1944	NY-N	50	170	23	51	5	2	0	5	13	11	.300	.350	.353	98	-0	-0	22	2			-1	O	-0.3
1945	NY-N	88	224	31	54	4	2	4	23	20	13	.241	.303	.330	75	-7	-8	24	3			-4	O	-1.3
Total	2	138	394	54	105	9	4	4	28	33	24	.266	.323	.340	85	-8	-8	46	5			-5	/O	-1.6

■ FRANK TRECHOCK   Trechock, Frank Adam b: 12/24/15, Windber, Pa.   d: 1/16/89, Minneapolis, Minn.   BR/TR, 5′10″, 175 lbs.   Deb: 9/19/37

| 1937 | Was-A | 1 | 4 | 0 | 2 | 0 | 0 | 0 | 0 | 0 | 1 | .500 | .500 | .500 | 160 | 0 | 0 | 1 | 0 | 0 | 0 | 0 | /S | 0.1 |

■ NICK TREMARK   Tremark, Nicholas Joseph b: 10/15/12, Yonkers, N.Y.   BL/TL, 5′5″, 150 lbs.   Deb: 8/09/34

1934	Bro-N	17	28	3	7	1	0	0	6	2	2	.250	.300	.286	61	-2	-1	2	0			1	/O	0.0
1935	Bro-N	10	13	1	3	1	0	0	3	1	1	.231	.286	.308	61	-1	-1	1	0			0	/O	0.0
1936	Bro-N	8	32	6	8	2	0	0	1	3	2	.250	.333	.313	74	-1	-1	3	0			1	/O	0.0
Total	3	35	73	10	18	4	0	0	10	6	5	.247	.313	.301	67	-3	-3	7	0			2	/O	0.0

■ OVERTON TREMPER   Tremper, Carlton Overton b: 3/22/06, Brooklyn, N.Y.   BR/TR, 5′10″, 163 lbs.   Deb: 6/16/27

1927	Bro-N	26	60	4	14	0	0	0	4	0	2	.233	.246	.233	29	-6	-6	3	0			-3	O	-0.9
1928	Bro-N	10	31	1	6	2	1	0	1	0	1	.194	.194	.323	33	-3	-3	2	0			0	/O	-0.2
Total	2	36	91	5	20	2	1	0	5	0	3	.220	.228	.264	30	-9	-9	5	0			-3	/O	-1.1

■ GEORGE TRENWITH   Trenwith, George b: Philadelphia, Pa.   d: 2/1/1890, Philadelphia, Pa.   Deb: 4/30/1875

1875	Cen-n	10	45	5	8	0	0	0			1	.178	.196	.178	33	-3	-2	2				3		-0.1
	NH-n	6	25	1	6	2	0	0			0	.240	.240	.320	107	-0	-0	2				/3		0.1
	Yr	16	70	6	14	2	0	0			1	.200	.211	.229	58	-3	-2	3						0.0

■ MIKE TRESH   Tresh, Michael b: 2/23/14, Hazleton, Pa.   d: 10/4/66, Detroit, Mich.   BR/TR, 5′11″, 170 lbs.   Deb: 9/04/38

1938	Chi-A	10	29	3	7	2	0	0	2	8	4	.241	.405	.310	80	-0	-1	4	0	0	0	2	C	0.1
1939	Chi-A	119	352	49	91	5	2	0	38	64	30	.259	.377	.284	70	-12	-13	43	3	2	-0	2	*C	-0.3
1940	Chi-A	135	480	62	135	15	5	1	64	49	40	.281	.349	.340	78	-13	-14	56	3	10	-5	8	*C	-0.1
1941	Chi-A	115	390	38	98	10	1	0	33	38	27	.251	.319	.282	61	-21	-21	36	1	0	0	11	*C	-0.2
1942	Chi-A	72	233	21	54	8	1	0	15	28	24	.232	.314	.275	68	-10	-9	22	2	0	1	-5	C	-0.4
1943	Chi-A	86	279	20	60	3	0	0	20	37	20	.215	.307	.226	57	-14	-14	22	2	1	0	-0	C	-1.0
1944	Chi-A	93	312	22	81	8	1	0	25	37	15	.260	.342	.292	83	-6	-5	32	0	3	-2	-2	C	-0.2
1945	Chi-A	150	458	50	114	12	0	0	47	65	37	.249	.342	.275	82	-9	-8	48	6	3	0	-3	*C	0.1
1946	Chi-A	80	217	28	47	5	2	0	21	36	24	.217	.336	.258	70	-8	-7	21	0	2	-1	14	C	0.9
1947	Chi-A	90	274	19	66	6	2	0	20	26	26	.241	.309	.277	66	-13	-12	24	2	0	1	-7	C	-1.1
1948	Chi-A	39	108	10	27	1	0	1	11	9	9	.250	.308	.287	61	-6	-6	10	0	0	0	-0	C	-0.3
1949	Cle-A	38	37	4	8	0	0	0	1	5	7	.216	.310	.216	41	-3	-3	3	0	0	0	6	C	0.4
Total	12	1027	3169	326	788	75	14	2	297	402	263	.249	.335	.283	71	-116	-112	322	19	21	-7	22	*C	-2.1

■ TOM TRESH   Tresh, Thomas Michael b: 9/20/37, Detroit, Mich.   BB/TR, 6′1″, 180 lbs.   Deb: 9/03/61

1961	NY-A	9	8	1	2	0	0	0	0	0	1	.250	.250	.250	36	-1	-1	0	0	0	0	3	/S	0.2
1962	*NY-A	157	622	94	178	26	5	20	93	67	74	.286	.363	.441	119	14	16	103	4	8	-4	-15	*SO	0.3
1963	*NY-A	145	520	91	140	28	5	25	71	83	79	.269	.374	.487	140	29	29	100	3	3	-1	-7	*O	1.7
1964	*NY-A	153	533	75	131	25	5	16	73	73	110	.246	.344	.402	105	6	5	78	13	0	4	-0	*O	0.3
1965	NY-A	156	602	94	168	29	6	26	74	59	92	.279	.348	.477	133	24	25	101	5	2	0	6	*O	2.6
1966	NY-A	151	537	76	125	12	4	27	68	86	89	.233	.345	.421	123	15	17	81	5	4	-1	27	O3	4.0
1967	NY-A	130	448	45	98	23	3	14	53	50	86	.219	.303	.377	104	-0	2	51	1	0	0	-1	*O	-0.2
1968	NY-A	152	507	60	99	18	3	11	52	76	97	.195	.305	.308	89	-7	-5	51	10	5	0	8	*SO	1.1
1969	NY-A	45	143	13	26	5	2	1	9	17	23	.182	.269	.266	52	-10	-9	11	2	1	0	5	S	-0.6
	Det-A	94	331	46	74	13	1	13	37	39	47	.224	.309	.387	90	-3	-5	41	2	2	-1	-19	SO/3	-2.2
	Yr	139	474	59	100	18	3	14	46	56	70	.211	.297	.350	79	-13	-14	51	4	3	-1	-18		-2.8
Total	9	1192	4251	595	1041	179	34	153	530	550	698	.245	.327	.411	113	66	74	618	45	25	-2	2	OS/3	7.2

■ ALEX TREVINO   Trevino, Alejandro (Castro) b: 8/26/57, Monterrey, Mex.   BR/TR, 5′10″, 165 lbs.   Deb: 9/11/78

1978	NY-N	6	12	3	3	0	0	0	2	1	2	.250	.308	.250	60	-1	-1	1	0	0	0	0	/C3	0.0
1979	NY-N	79	207	24	56	11	1	0	20	20	27	.271	.338	.333	87	-4	-3	22	2	2	-1	11	C3/2	0.7
1980	NY-N	106	355	26	91	11	2	0	37	13	41	.256	.285	.299	65	-18	-17	27	0	3	-2	-6	C3/2	-2.3
1981	NY-N	56	149	17	39	2	0	0	10	13	19	.262	.325	.275	73	-5	-5	14	3	0	1	3	C/2O3	0.0
1982	Cin-N	120	355	24	89	10	1	3	33	34	34	.251	.321	.304	74	-11	-11	33	3	1	0	4	*C/3	-0.5
1983	Cin-N	74	167	14	36	8	1	1	13	17	20	.216	.288	.293	59	-9	-9	14	0	0	0	11	C/32	0.3
1984	Cin-N	6	6	0	1	0	0	0	0	0	2	.167	.167	.167	-6	-1	-1	0	0	0	0	-0	/C	0.0
	Atl-N	79	266	36	65	16	0	3	28	16	27	.244	.290	.338	71	-9	-11	26	5	2	0	6	C	-0.1
	Yr	85	272	36	66	16	0	3	28	16	29	.243	.287	.335	69	-10	-12	26	5	2	0	6		-0.1
1985	SF-N	57	157	17	34	10	1	6	19	20	24	.217	.305	.408	103	-1	0	19	0	0	0	0	C/3	0.2
1986	LA-N	89	202	31	53	13	0	4	26	27	35	.262	.352	.386	111	1	3	28	0	0	0	-4	C/1	0.0
1987	LA-N	72	144	16	32	7	1	3	16	6	28	.222	.273	.347	65	-8	-7	12	1	0	0	-2	C/O3	-0.5
1988	Hou-N	78	193	19	48	17	0	2	13	24	29	.249	.341	.368	108	1	2	24	5	2	0	-8	C/O	-0.1
1989	Hou-N	59	131	15	38	7	1	2	16	7	18	.290	.331	.405	113	1	2	17	0	0	0	-3	C/13	0.1
1990	Hou-N	42	69	3	13	3	0	1	10	6	11	.188	.273	.275	52	-5	-4	5	0	1	-1	6	C/1	0.2
	NY-N	9	10	0	3	1	0	0	2	1	0	.300	.364	.400	112	0	0	2	0	0	0	1	/C	0.1
	Cin-N	7	7	0	3	1	0	0	1	0	0	.429	.500	.571	189	1	1	2	0	0	0	1	/C	0.2
	Yr	58	86	3	19	5	0	1	13	7	11	.221	.302	.314	71	-3	-3	8	0	1	-1	8		0.5
Total	13	939	2430	245	604	117	10	23	244	205	317	.249	.312	.333	81	-65	-61	247	19	11	-1	19	C/3201	-1.7

■ BOBBY TREVINO   Trevino, Carlos (Castro) b: 8/15/43, Monterrey, Mexico   BR/TR, 6′2″, 185 lbs.   Deb: 5/22/68

| 1968 | Cal-A | 17 | 40 | 1 | 9 | 1 | 0 | 1 | 2 | 9 | .225 | .262 | .250 | 58 | -2 | -2 | 3 | 0 | 1 | -1 | 2 | O | -0.1 |

■ GUS TRIANDOS
Triandos, Gus b: 7/30/30, San Francisco, Cal   BR/TR, 6'3", 205 lbs.   Deb: 8/13/53

YEAR	TM/L	G	AB	R	H	2B	3B	HR	RBI	BB	SO	AVG	OBP	SLG	PRO+	BR	/A	RC	SB	CS	SBR	FR	POS	TPR
1953	NY-A	18	51	5	8	2	0	1	6	3	9	.157	.204	.255	24	-6	-5	3	0	0	0	0	1/C	-0.4
1954	NY-A	2	1	0	0	0	0	0	0	0	1	.000	.000	.000	-99	-0	-0	0	0	0	0	0	/C	0.0
1955	Bal-A	140	481	47	133	17	3	12	65	40	55	.277	.335	.399	104	-3	1	64	0	0	0	1	*1C/3	-0.1
1956	Bal-A	131	452	47	126	18	1	21	88	48	73	.279	.351	.462	122	7	12	68	0	0	0	9	C1	2.0
1957	Bal-A	129	418	44	106	21	1	19	72	38	73	.254	.320	.445	114	3	6	58	0	0	0	-2	*C	0.9
1958	Bal-A	137	474	59	116	10	0	30	79	60	65	.245	.331	.456	120	8	12	67	1	0	0	1	*C	1.4
1959	Bal-A	126	393	43	85	7	1	25	73	65	56	.216	.332	.430	110	4	5	57	0	0	0	5	*C	1.7
1960	Bal-A	109	364	36	98	18	0	12	54	41	62	.269	.345	.418	107	3	3	52	0	0	0	-6	*C	0.3
1961	Bal-A	115	397	35	97	21	0	17	63	44	60	.244	.321	.426	100	-2	-1	52	0	0	0	7	*C	0.5
1962	Bal-A	66	207	20	33	7	0	6	23	29	43	.159	.263	.280	48	-16	-15	15	0	0	0	0	C	-1.0
1963	Det-A	106	327	28	78	13	0	14	41	32	67	.239	.318	.407	98	-1	-1	41	0	0	0	-4	C	-0.3
1964	Phi-N	73	188	17	47	9	0	8	33	26	41	.250	.344	.426	117	4	4	27	0	0	0	3	C/1	1.0
1965	Phi-N	30	82	3	14	2	0	0	4	9	17	.171	.253	.195	29	-8	-7	4	0	0	0	-4	C	-1.1
	Hou-N	24	52	5	13	2	0	2	7	5	14	.181	.244	.292	54	-5	-4	5	0	0	0	-2	C	-0.5
	Yr	54	154	8	27	4	0	2	11	14	31	.175	.249	.240	40	-12	-12	9	0	0	0	-6		-1.6
Total	13	1206	3907	389	954	147	6	167	608	440	636	.244	.324	.413	103	-10	9	514	1	0	0	8	C1/3	4.4

■ MANNY TRILLO
Trillo, Jesus Manuel Marcano (b: Jesus Manuel Marcano (Trillo)) b: 12/25/50, Caripito, Ven.   BR/TR, 6'1", 150 lbs.   Deb: 6/28/73

YEAR	TM/L	G	AB	R	H	2B	3B	HR	RBI	BB	SO	AVG	OBP	SLG	PRO+	BR	/A	RC	SB	CS	SBR	FR	POS	TPR
1973	Oak-A	17	12	0	3	2	0	0	3	0	4	.250	.250	.417	90	-0	-0	1	0	0	0	5	2	0.5
1974	*Oak-A	21	33	3	5	0	0	0	2	2	8	.152	.222	.152	10	-4	-4	1	0	0	0	6	2	0.3
1975	Chi-N	154	545	55	135	12	2	7	70	45	78	.248	.309	.316	70	-19	-22	53	1	7	-4	16	*2/S	-0.2
1976	Chi-N	158	582	42	139	24	3	4	59	53	70	.239	.306	.311	69	-18	-25	55	17	6	2	18	*2/S	0.3
1977	Chi-N	152	504	51	141	18	5	7	57	44	58	.280	.344	.377	84	-4	-11	62	3	5	-2	30	*2	2.6
1978	Chi-N	152	552	53	144	17	5	4	55	50	67	.261	.325	.332	75	-11	-19	59	0	7	-4	29	*2	1.5
1979	Phi-N	118	431	40	112	22	1	6	42	20	59	.260	.299	.357	76	-14	-15	42	4	7	-3	6	*2	-0.4
1980	*Phi-N	141	531	68	155	25	9	7	43	32	46	.292	.336	.412	102	5	1	70	8	3	1	19	*2	3.1
1981	*Phi-N	94	349	37	100	14	3	6	36	26	37	.287	.341	.395	104	4	2	48	10	4	1	11	2	2.1
1982	Phi-N	149	549	52	149	24	1	0	39	33	53	.271	.316	.319	76	-16	-17	52	8	10	-4	5	*2	-0.9
1983	Cle-A	88	320	33	87	13	1	1	29	21	46	.272	.317	.328	75	-9	-11	30	1	3	-2	3	*2	-0.5
	Mon-N	31	121	16	32	8	0	2	16	10	18	.264	.331	.380	97	-1	-0	16	0	0	0	-6	2	-0.5
1984	SF-N	98	401	45	102	21	1	4	36	25	55	.254	.303	.342	84	-11	-9	41	0	0	0	-8	2/3	-1.4
1985	SF-N	125	451	36	101	16	2	3	25	40	44	.224	.289	.288	65	-23	-20	40	2	0	1	4	*2/3	-1.5
1986	Chi-N	81	152	22	45	10	0	1	19	16	21	.296	.363	.382	98	1	0	21	0	2	-1	0	31/2	-0.2
1987	Chi-N	108	214	27	63	8	0	8	26	25	37	.294	.368	.444	110	5	3	34	0	3	-2	-4	132/S	-0.4
1988	Chi-N	76	164	15	41	5	0	1	14	8	32	.250	.285	.299	65	-7	-8	15	2	0	1	1	132/S	-0.6
1989	Cin-N	17	39	3	8	0	0	0	0	2	9	.205	.262	.205	34	-3	-3	2	0	0	0	-4	2/1S	-0.7
Total	17	1780	5950	598	1562	239	33	61	571	452	742	.263	.318	.345	80	-126	-159	641	56	57	-17	130	*23/1S	3.1

■ COAKER TRIPLETT
Triplett, Herman Coaker b: 12/18/11, Boone, N.C.   BR/TR, 5'11", 185 lbs.   Deb: 4/19/38

YEAR	TM/L	G	AB	R	H	2B	3B	HR	RBI	BB	SO	AVG	OBP	SLG	PRO+	BR	/A	RC	SB	CS	SBR	FR	POS	TPR
1938	Chi-N	12	36	4	9	2	1	0	2	0	1	.250	.250	.361	65	-2	-2	3	0			0	/O	-0.1
1941	StL-N	76	185	29	53	6	3	3	21	18	27	.286	.350	.400	104	3	1	25	0			-1	O	-0.1
1942	StL-N	64	154	18	42	7	4	1	23	17	15	.273	.345	.390	107	3	2	20	1			1	O	0.1
1943	StL-N	9	25	1	2	0	0	1	4	1	6	.080	.115	.200	-9	-4	-4	0	0			0	/O	-0.3
	Phi-N	105	360	45	98	16	4	14	52	28	28	.272	.325	.456	129	9	11	52	2			-0	O	0.7
	Yr	114	385	46	100	16	4	15	56	29	34	.260	.312	.439	120	5	7	51	2			-0		0.4
1944	Phi-N	84	184	15	43	5	1	1	25	19	10	.234	.305	.288	70	-8	-7	15	1			-0	O	-1.0
1945	Phi-N	120	363	36	87	11	1	7	46	40	27	.240	.315	.333	83	-10	-8	39	6			-4	O	-1.6
Total	6	470	1307	148	334	47	14	27	173	123	114	.256	.320	.375	97	-8	-8	155	10			-5	O	-2.3

■ HAL TROSKY
Trosky, Harold Arthur Sr. (b: Harold Arthur Troyavesky Sr.)
b: 11/11/12, Norway, Iowa   d: 6/18/79, Cedar Rapids, Ia.   BL/TR, 6'2", 207 lbs.   Deb: 9/11/33

YEAR	TM/L	G	AB	R	H	2B	3B	HR	RBI	BB	SO	AVG	OBP	SLG	PRO+	BR	/A	RC	SB	CS	SBR	FR	POS	TPR
1933	Cle-A	11	44	6	13	1	2	1	8	2	12	.295	.340	.477	110	1	0	7	0	0	0	-1	1	0.0
1934	Cle-A	154	625	117	206	45	9	35	142	58	49	.330	.388	.598	149	44	42	145	2	2	-1	0	*1	1.3
1935	Cle-A	154	632	84	171	33	7	26	113	46	60	.271	.321	.468	100	-2	-4	94	1	2	-1	1	*1	-1.8
1936	Cle-A	151	629	124	216	45	9	42	**162**	36	58	.343	.382	.644	148	42	41	150	6	5	-1	1	*1/2	1.8
1937	Cle-A	153	601	104	179	36	4	32	128	65	60	.298	.367	.547	127	22	22	122	3	1	0	-2	*1	0.1
1938	Cle-A	150	554	106	185	40	9	19	110	67	40	.334	.407	.542	130	31	31	125	5	1	1	4	*1	1.4
1939	Cle-A	122	448	89	150	31	4	25	104	52	28	.335	.405	.589	157	33	35	108	2	3	-1	11	*1	3.1
1940	Cle-A	140	522	85	154	39	4	25	93	79	45	.295	.392	.529	140	28	31	116	1	2	-1	-7	*1	1.5
1941	Cle-A	89	310	43	91	17	0	11	51	44	21	.294	.383	.455	127	10	12	57	1	2	-1	-2	1	0.6
1944	Chi-A	135	497	55	120	32	2	10	70	62	30	.241	.327	.374	101	-0	-1	62	3	2	-0	-9	*1	-1.7
1946	Chi-A	88	299	22	76	12	3	2	31	34	37	.254	.330	.334	89	-5	-4	33	4	3	-1	-8	1	-1.7
Total	11	1347	5161	835	1561	331	58	228	1012	545	440	.302	.371	.522	130	202	208	1018	28	23	-5	-11	*1/2	4.6

■ MIKE TROST
Trost, Michael J. b: 1866, Philadelphia, Pa.   d: 3/24/01, Philadelphia, Pa.   TR , 6'0.5", 180 lbs.   Deb: 8/21/1890

YEAR	TM/L	G	AB	R	H	2B	3B	HR	RBI	BB	SO	AVG	OBP	SLG	PRO+	BR	/A	RC	SB	CS	SBR	FR	POS	TPR
1890	StL-a	17	51	10	13	2	0	1	6			.255	.345	.353	95	1	-1	8	4			0	C/O	0.1
1895	Lou-N	3	12	1	1	0	0	0	1	0	1	.083	.083	.083	-60	-3	-3	0	1			-0	/1	-0.2
Total	2	20	63	11	14	2	0	1	1	6	1	.222	.300	.302	68	-2	-3	8	5			-0	/CO1	-0.1

■ SAM TROTT
Trott, Samuel W. b: 3/1859, Maryland   d: 6/5/25, Catonsville, Md.   BL/TL, 5'9", 190 lbs.   Deb: 5/29/1880 M

YEAR	TM/L	G	AB	R	H	2B	3B	HR	RBI	BB	SO	AVG	OBP	SLG	PRO+	BR	/A	RC	SB	CS	SBR	FR	POS	TPR
1880	Bos-N	39	125	14	26	4	1	0	9	3	5	.208	.227	.256	65	-5	-4	7	4			4	C/O	0.3
1881	Det-N	6	25	3	5	2	1	0	2	1	3	.200	.231	.360	80	-1	-1	2				-3	/C	-0.3
1882	Det-N	32	129	11	31	7	1	0	12	0	13	.240	.240	.310	75	-4	-4	10				7	C/S2103	0.4
1883	Det-N	75	295	27	72	14	1	0	29	10	23	.244	.269	.298	76	-10	-7	24				-12	2C/O1	-1.7
1884	Bal-a	71	284	36	73	17	9	3		4		.257	.272	.412	118	6	5	33				14	C/2O	2.1
1885	Bal-a	21	88	12	24	2	2	0		5		.273	.312	.341	110	1	1	10				-6	C/O2S	-0.1
1887	Bal-a	85	300	44	77	16	3	0		27		.257	.322	.330	89	-6	-3	35	8			4	C2/01S	1.0
1888	Bal-a	31	108	19	30	11	4	0	22	4		.278	.304	.454	148	5	5	16	1			-6	C/O21	0.2
Total	8	360	1354	166	338	73	22	3	74	54	44	.250	.280	.343	95	-12	-8	137	9			3	C/201S3	1.9

■ QUINCY TROUPPE
Trouppe, Quincy Thomas b: 12/25/12, Dublin, Ga.   BB/TR, 6'2.5", 225 lbs.   Deb: 4/30/52

YEAR	TM/L	G	AB	R	H	2B	3B	HR	RBI	BB	SO	AVG	OBP	SLG	PRO+	BR	/A	RC	SB	CS	SBR	FR	POS	TPR
1952	Cle-A	6	10	1	1	0	0	0	0	1	3	.100	.182	.100	-22	-2	-2	0	0	0	0	2	/C	0.1

■ DASHER TROY
Troy, John Joseph b: 5/8/1856, New York, N.Y.   d: 3/30/38, Ozone Park, N.Y.   BR/TR,   Deb: 8/23/1881

YEAR	TM/L	G	AB	R	H	2B	3B	HR	RBI	BB	SO	AVG	OBP	SLG	PRO+	BR	/A	RC	SB	CS	SBR	FR	POS	TPR
1881	Det-N	11	44	2	15	3	0	0	4	3	8	.341	.383	.409	143	3	2	7				-4	/32	0.0
1882	Det-N	40	152	22	37	7	2	0	14	5	10	.243	.268	.316	86	-2	-2	13				-20	2S	-1.8
	Pro-N	4	17	1	4	0	0	0	1	0	1	.235	.235	.235	52	-1	-1	1				-1	/S	-0.1
	Yr	44	169	23	41	7	2	0	15	5	11	.243	.264	.308	83	-3	-3	14				-21		-1.9
1883	NY-N	85	316	37	68	7	5	0	20	9	33	.215	.237	.269	54	-17	-17	21				-16	*2S	-3.1
1884	*NY-a	107	421	80	111	22	10	2		19		.264	.300	.378	126	10	12	49				-21	*2	-0.5
1885	NY-a	45	177	24	39	3	3	2		5		.220	.258	.305	86	-4	-2	14				-12	2/OS	-1.0
Total	5	292	1127	166	274	42	20	4	39	41	52	.243	.274	.327	93	-12	-8	105				-74	2/S3O	-6.5

YEAR	TM/L	G	AB	R	H	2B	3B	HR	RBI	BB	SO	AVG	OBP	SLG	PRO+	BR	/A	RC	SB	CS	SBR	FR	POS	TPR

■ FRED TRUAX Truax, Frederick W. b: 1868, d: 12/18/1899, Omaha, Neb. Deb: 8/18/1890

YEAR	TM/L	G	AB	R	H	2B	3B	HR	RBI	BB	SO	AVG	OBP	SLG	PRO+	BR	/A	RC	SB	CS	SBR	FR	POS	TPR
1890	Pit-N	1	3	0	1	0	0	0	1	1	1	.333	.500	.333	167	0	0	1	0			0	/O	0.0

■ HARRY TRUBY Truby, Harry Garvin "Bird Eye" b: 5/12/1870, Ironton, Ohio d: 3/21/53, Ironton, Ohio TR , 5'11", 185 lbs. Deb: 8/21/1895 U

YEAR	TM/L	G	AB	R	H	2B	3B	HR	RBI	BB	SO	AVG	OBP	SLG	PRO+	BR	/A	RC	SB	CS	SBR	FR	POS	TPR
1895	Chi-N	33	119	17	40	3	0	0	16	10	7	.336	.402	.361	94	1	-1	21	7			0	2	0.1
1896	Chi-N	29	109	13	28	2	2	2	31	6	5	.257	.314	.367	78	-3	-4	14	4			0	2	-0.2
	Pit-N	8	32	1	5	0	0	0	3	2	4	.156	.206	.156	-3	-5	-4	1	1			-3	/2	-0.6
	Yr	37	141	14	33	2	2	2	34	8	9	.234	.289	.319	61	-8	-8	15	5			-3		-0.8
Total	2	70	260	31	73	5	2	2	50	18	16	.281	.342	.338	76	-7	-9	36	12			-3	/2	-0.7

■ FRANK TRUESDALE Truesdale, Frank Day b: 3/31/1884, St.Louis, Mo. d: 8/27/43, Albuquerque, N.M. BB/TR, 5'8", 145 lbs. Deb: 4/27/10

YEAR	TM/L	G	AB	R	H	2B	3B	HR	RBI	BB	SO	AVG	OBP	SLG	PRO+	BR	/A	RC	SB	CS	SBR	FR	POS	TPR
1910	StL-A	123	415	39	91	7	2	1	25	48		.219	.303	.253	79	-11	-8	40	29			-8	*2	-2.6
1911	StL-A	1	0	1	0	0	0	0	0	0		—	—	—	—	0	0	0	0			0	R	0.0
1914	NY-A	77	217	23	46	4	0	0	13	39	35	.212	.340	.230	72	-5	-5	18	11	11	-3	-1	2/3	-1.1
1918	Bos-A	15	36	6	10	1	0	0	2	4	5	.278	.350	.306	100	0	0	4	1			-1	2	0.0
Total	4	216	668	69	147	12	2	1	40	91	40	.220	.318	.249	78	-16	-13	63	41	11		-10	2/3	-3.7

■ ED TRUMBULL Trumbull, Edward J. (b: Edward J. Trembly) b: 11/3/1860, Chicopee, Mass. Deb: 5/10/1884

YEAR	TM/L	G	AB	R	H	2B	3B	HR	RBI	BB	SO	AVG	OBP	SLG	PRO+	BR	/A	RC	SB	CS	SBR	FR	POS	TPR
1884	Was-a	25	86	5	10	2	0	0		2		.116	.136	.140	-10	-10	-8	2				-0	OP	-0.6

■ OLLIE TUCKER Tucker, Oliver Dinwiddie b: 1/27/02, Radiant, Va. d: 7/13/40, Radiant, Va. BL/TR, 5'11", 180 lbs. Deb: 4/17/27

YEAR	TM/L	G	AB	R	H	2B	3B	HR	RBI	BB	SO	AVG	OBP	SLG	PRO+	BR	/A	RC	SB	CS	SBR	FR	POS	TPR
1927	Was-A	20	24	1	5	2	0	0	8	4	2	.208	.321	.292	61	-1	-1	3	0	0	0	-0	/O	-0.1
1928	Cle-A	14	47	5	6	0	0	1	2	7	3	.128	.255	.191	19	-6	-6	2	0	2	-1	-0	O	-0.7
Total	2	34	71	6	11	2	0	1	10	11	5	.155	.277	.225	33	-7	-7	5	0	2	-1	-0	/O	-0.8

■ TOMMY TUCKER Tucker, Thomas Joseph "Foghorn" b: 10/28/1863, Holyoke, Mass. d: 10/22/35, Montague, Mass. BB/TR, 5'11", 165 lbs. Deb: 4/16/1887

YEAR	TM/L	G	AB	R	H	2B	3B	HR	RBI	BB	SO	AVG	OBP	SLG	PRO+	BR	/A	RC	SB	CS	SBR	FR	POS	TPR
1887	Bal-a	136	524	114	144	15	9	6	29			.275	.347	.372	109	3	9	100	85			4	*1	0.8
1888	Bal-a	136	520	74	149	17	12	6	61	16		.287	.330	.400	141	20	22	85	43			4	*1/OP	1.6
1889	Bal-a	134	527	103	**196**	22	11	5	99	42	26	**.372**	**.450**	**.484**	**166**	50	48	147	63			-1	*1O	3.0
1890	Bos-N	132	539	104	159	17	8	1	62	56	22	.295	.387	.362	112	18	10	94	43			-2	*1	0.0
1891	Bos-N	140	548	103	148	16	5	2	69	37	30	.270	.349	.328	89	2	-9	74	26			-3	*1/P	-1.3
1892	*Bos-N	149	542	85	153	15	7	1	62	45	35	.282	.365	.341	106	13	5	78	22			-12	*1	-1.6
1893	Bos-N	121	486	83	138	13	2	7	91	27	31	.284	.347	.362	84	-7	-13	65	8			-11	*1	-2.0
1894	Bos-N	123	500	112	165	24	6	3	100	53	21	.330	.412	.420	95	5	-3	96	18			2	*1/O	0.0
1895	Bos-N	125	462	87	115	19	6	3	73	61	29	.249	.360	.335	76	-10	-17	63	15			6	*1	-0.6
1896	Bos-N	122	474	74	144	27	5	2	72	30	29	.304	.363	.395	96	1	-3	72	6			3	*1	0.3
1897	Bos-N	4	14	0	3	2	0	0	4	2		.214	.313	.357	74	-0	-1	2	0			1	/1	0.0
	Was-N	93	352	52	119	18	5	5	61	27		.338	.403	.460	131	16	16	74	18			-3	*1	1.0
	Yr	97	366	52	122	20	5	5	65	29		.333	.399	.456	128	15	15	76	18			-2		1.0
1898	Bro-N	73	283	35	79	9	4	1	34	12		.279	.325	.350	96	-2	-2	33	1			7	1	0.5
	StL-N	72	252	18	60	7	2	0	20	18		.238	.319	.282	73	-7	-8	24	1			-0	1	-0.6
	Yr	145	535	53	139	16	6	1	54	30		.260	.322	.318	85	-9	-10	57	2			7		-0.1
1899	Cle-N	127	456	40	110	19	3	0	40	24		.241	.297	.296	70	-21	-16	42	3			-1	*1	-1.2
Total	13	1687	6479	1084	1882	240	85	42	848	479	223	.290	.364	.373	104	80	39	1048	352			-7	*1/OP	-0.1

■ THURMAN TUCKER Tucker, Thurman Lowell "Joe E." b: 9/26/17, Gordon, Tex. BL/TR, 5'10.5", 165 lbs. Deb: 4/14/42

YEAR	TM/L	G	AB	R	H	2B	3B	HR	RBI	BB	SO	AVG	OBP	SLG	PRO+	BR	/A	RC	SB	CS	SBR	FR	POS	TPR
1942	Chi-A	7	24	2	3	0	1	0	1	0	4	.125	.125	.208	-7	-3	-3	1	0	0	0	-0	/O	-0.4
1943	Chi-A	139	528	81	124	15	6	3	39	79	72	.235	.336	.303	87	-6	-6	60	29	17	-2	13	*O	0.1
1944	Chi-A	124	446	59	128	15	6	2	46	57	40	.287	.368	.361	110	7	7	63	13	12	-3	16	*O	1.7
1946	Chi-A	121	438	62	126	20	3	1	36	54	45	.288	.367	.354	106	3	5	61	9	10	-3	-1	*O	-0.5
1947	Chi-A	89	254	28	60	9	4	1	17	38	25	.236	.336	.315	85	-6	-4	31	10	4	1	4	O	-0.2
1948	*Cle-A	83	242	52	63	13	2	1	19	31	17	.260	.347	.343	86	-5	-4	33	11	2	2	-3	O	-0.7
1949	Cle-A	80	197	28	48	5	2	0	14	18	19	.244	.307	.289	59	-12	-11	19	4	2	0	3	O	-0.8
1950	Cle-A	57	101	13	18	2	0	1	7	14	14	.178	.284	.228	34	-10	-10	8	1	0	0	2	O	-0.6
1951	Cle-A	1	1	0	0	0	0	0	0	0	1	.000	.000	.000	-99	-0	-0	0	0	0	0	0	H	0.0
Total	9	701	2231	325	570	79	24	9	179	291	237	.255	.342	.325	89	-33	-28	275	77	47	-5	33	O	-1.4

■ JERRY TURBIDY Turbidy, Jeremiah b: 7/4/1852, Dudley, Mass. d: 9/5/20, Webster, Mass. 5'8", 165 lbs. Deb: 7/27/1884

YEAR	TM/L	G	AB	R	H	2B	3B	HR	RBI	BB	SO	AVG	OBP	SLG	PRO+	BR	/A	RC	SB	CS	SBR	FR	POS	TPR
1884	KC-U	13	49	5	11	4	0	0		3		.224	.269	.306	108	-0	1	4	0			6	S	0.6

■ EDDIE TURCHIN Turchin, Edward Lawrence "Smiley" b: 2/10/17, New York, N.Y. d: 2/8/82, Brookhaven, N.Y. BR/TR, 5'10", 165 lbs. Deb: 5/09/43

YEAR	TM/L	G	AB	R	H	2B	3B	HR	RBI	BB	SO	AVG	OBP	SLG	PRO+	BR	/A	RC	SB	CS	SBR	FR	POS	TPR
1943	Cle-A	11	13	4	3	0	0	0	1	3	1	.231	.375	.231	84	-0	-0	1	0	0	0	1	/3S	0.2

■ PETE TURGEON Turgeon, Eugene Joseph b: 1/3/1897, Minneapolis, Minn. d: 1/24/77, Wichita Falls, Tex BR/TR, 5'6", 145 lbs. Deb: 9/20/23

YEAR	TM/L	G	AB	R	H	2B	3B	HR	RBI	BB	SO	AVG	OBP	SLG	PRO+	BR	/A	RC	SB	CS	SBR	FR	POS	TPR
1923	Chi-N	3	6	1	1	0	0	0	0	0	0	.167	.167	.167	-12	-1	-1	0	0	0	0	0	/S	0.0

■ EARL TURNER Turner, Earl Edwin b: 5/6/23, Pittsfield, Mass. BR/TR, 5'9", 170 lbs. Deb: 9/25/48

YEAR	TM/L	G	AB	R	H	2B	3B	HR	RBI	BB	SO	AVG	OBP	SLG	PRO+	BR	/A	RC	SB	CS	SBR	FR	POS	TPR
1948	Pit-N	2	1	0	0	0	0	0	0	0	0	.000	.000	.000	-98	-0	-0	0	0			0	/C	0.0
1950	Pit-N	40	74	10	18	0	0	3	5	4	13	.243	.282	.365	66	-4	-4	7	1			2	C	0.0
Total	2	42	75	10	18	0	0	3	5	4	13	.240	.278	.360	64	-4	-4	7	1			2	/C	0.0

■ TUCK TURNER Turner, George A. b: 2/13/1873, W.New Brighton, N.Y. d: 7/16/45, Staten Island, N.Y. BB/TL, Deb: 8/18/1893

YEAR	TM/L	G	AB	R	H	2B	3B	HR	RBI	BB	SO	AVG	OBP	SLG	PRO+	BR	/A	RC	SB	CS	SBR	FR	POS	TPR
1893	Phi-N	36	155	32	50	4	3	1	13	9	19	.323	.364	.406	107	1	1	26	7			-2	O	-0.1
1894	Phi-N	80	339	91	141	21	9	1	82	23	13	.416	.456	.540	145	23	25	91	11			-9	O/P	0.8
1895	Phi-N	59	210	51	81	8	6	2	43	25	11	.386	.453	.510	150	17	16	56	14			-8	O	0.3
1896	Phi-N	13	32	12	7	2	0	0	0	8	5	.219	.375	.281	77	-1	-1	6	6			2	/O	0.0
	StL-N	51	203	30	50	7	8	1	27	14	21	.246	.298	.374	82	-7	-6	25	6			-5	O	-1.1
	Yr	64	235	42	57	9	8	1	27	22	26	.243	.310	.362	81	-8	-6	31	12			-4		-1.1
1897	StL-N	103	416	58	121	17	12	2	41	35		.291	.350	.404	103	0	2	63	8			-7	*O	-1.1
1898	StL-N	35	141	20	28	8	0	0	7	14		.199	.280	.255	55	-8	-8	11	1			-3	O	-1.2
Total	6	377	1496	294	478	67	38	7	213	128	69	.320	.377	.429	113	26	30	278	53			-32	O/P	-2.4

■ JERRY TURNER Turner, John Webber b: 1/17/54, Texarkana, Ark. BL/TL, 5'9", 180 lbs. Deb: 9/02/74

YEAR	TM/L	G	AB	R	H	2B	3B	HR	RBI	BB	SO	AVG	OBP	SLG	PRO+	BR	/A	RC	SB	CS	SBR	FR	POS	TPR
1974	SD-N	17	48	4	14	1	0	0	2	3	5	.292	.333	.313	85	-1	-1	5	2	1	0	-2	O	-0.2
1975	SD-N	11	22	1	6	0	0	0	0	2	1	.273	.333	.273	74	-1	-1	2	0	0	0	-0	/O	0.0
1976	SD-N	105	281	41	75	16	5	5	37	32	38	.267	.342	.413	123	5	8	41	12	6	0	-8	O	-0.2
1977	SD-N	118	289	43	71	16	1	10	48	31	43	.246	.319	.412	105	-3	-1	38	12	4	1	-0	O	0.0
1978	SD-N	106	225	28	63	9	1	8	37	21	32	.280	.349	.436	128	5	7	34	6	4	-1	-1	O	0.4
1979	SD-N	138	448	55	111	23	2	9	61	34	58	.248	.304	.368	88	-11	-8	50	4	2	0	-7	*O	-1.8
1980	SD-N	85	153	22	44	5	0	5	18	10	18	.288	.339	.379	106	0	1	20	8	3	1	-3	O	-0.2
1981	SD-N	33	31	5	7	0	0	2	6	4	3	.226	.314	.419	115	0	0	4	1	0	-1	0	/O	0.0
	Chi-A	10	12	1	2	0	0	0	2	1	2	.167	.231	.167	16	-1	-1	1	0	0	0	0	/O	0.0
1982	Det-A	85	210	21	52	3	0	8	27	20	24	.248	.313	.376	88	-3	-4	25	1	3	-2	0	DO	-0.5
1983	SD-N	25	23	1	3	0	0	0	1		8	.130	.167	.130	-17	-4	-4	0	0	0	0	-0	O/D	-0.3
Total	10	733	1742	222	448	73	9	45	238	159	245	.257	.322	.387	101	-14	-1	220	45	24	-1	-20	O/D	-2.8

YEAR	TM/L	G	AB	R	H	2B	3B	HR	RBI	BB	SO	AVG	OBP	SLG	PRO+ BR	/A	RC	SB	CS	SBR	FR	POS	TPR

■ SHANE TURNER   Turner, Shane Lee b: 1/8/63, Los Angeles, Cal. BL/TR, 5′10″, 180 lbs. Deb: 8/19/88

| 1988 | Phi-N | 18 | 35 | 1 | 6 | 0 | 0 | 0 | 1 | 5 | 9 | .171 | .275 | .171 | 30 | -3 | -3 | 2 | 0 | 0 | 0 | -2 | /3S | -0.5 |

■ TERRY TURNER   Turner, Terrence Lamont "Cotton Top" b: 2/28/1881, Sandy Lake, Pa. d: 7/18/60, Cleveland, Ohio BR/TR, 5′8″, 149 lbs. Deb: 8/25/01 C

1901	Pit-N	2	7	0	3	0	0	0	1	0		.429	.429	.429	147	0	0	1	0			1	/3	0.2
1904	Cle-A	111	404	41	95	9	6	1	45	11		.235	.255	.295	76	-12	-11	35	5			3	*S	-0.7
1905	Cle-A	155	586	49	155	16	14	4	72	14		.265	.282	.360	104	1	0	67	17			-25	*S	-2.1
1906	Cle-A	147	584	85	170	27	7	2	62	35		.291	.331	.372	123	14	15	85	27			24	*S	4.3
1907	Cle-A	140	524	57	127	20	7	0	46	19		.242	.269	.307	85	-10	-10	53	27			-3	*S	-1.0
1908	Cle-A	60	201	21	48	11	1	0	19	15		.239	.292	.303	95	-1	-1	23	18			-4	OS	-0.7
1909	Cle-A	53	208	25	52	7	4	0	16	14		.250	.304	.322	94	-1	-2	24	14			10	2S	1.0
1910	Cle-A	150	574	71	132	14	6	0	33	53		.230	.301	.275	79	-12	-13	57	31			2	S3/2	-0.8
1911	Cle-A	117	417	59	105	16	9	0	28	34		.252	.310	.333	78	-12	-13	52	29			2	32S	-0.9
1912	Cle-A	103	370	54	114	14	4	0	33	31		.308	.363	.368	106	5	3	57	19			-3	*3	-0.1
1913	Cle-A	120	388	60	96	13	4	0	44	55	35	.247	.348	.302	88	-3	-4	48	13			16	32S	1.6
1914	Cle-A	121	428	43	105	14	9	1	33	44	36	.245	.319	.327	91	-3	-5	50	17	13	-3	21	*32	1.7
1915	Cle-A	75	262	35	66	14	1	0	14	29	13	.252	.329	.313	90	-2	-3	29	12	11	-3	-9	23	-1.4
1916	Cle-A	124	428	52	112	15	3	0	38	40	29	.262	.325	.311	86	-5	-8	52	15			5	32	0.2
1917	Cle-A	69	180	16	37	7	0	0	15	14	19	.206	.263	.244	51	-10	-11	13	4			-2	32/S	-1.1
1918	Cle-A	74	233	24	58	7	2	0	23	22	15	.249	.316	.296	77	-4	-7	24	6			-3	32/S	-0.9
1919	Phi-A	38	127	7	24	3	0	0	6	5	9	.189	.220	.213	21	-13	-13	6	2			1	S2/3	-0.9
Total	17	1659	5921	699	1499	207	77	8	528	435	156	.253	.306	.318	89	-68	-83	676	256	24		37	S32/O	-1.6

■ TOM TURNER   Turner, Thomas Richard b: 9/8/16, Custer Co., Okla. d: 5/14/86, Kennewick, Wash. BR/TR, 6′2″, 195 lbs. Deb: 4/25/40

1940	Chi-A	37	96	11	20	1	2	0	6	3	12	.208	.240	.260	29	-10	-10	6	1	0	0	2	C	-0.5
1941	Chi-A	38	126	7	30	5	0	0	8	9	15	.238	.289	.278	51	-9	-9	10	2	0	1	5	C	0.0
1942	Chi-A	56	182	18	44	9	1	3	21	19	15	.242	.313	.352	89	-3	-3	21	0	1	-1	-1	C	0.2
1943	Chi-A	51	154	16	37	7	1	2	11	13	21	.240	.299	.338	86	-3	-3	15	1	0	0	6	C	0.6
1944	Chi-A	36	113	9	26	6	0	2	13	5	16	.230	.263	.336	71	-5	-5	8	0	1	-1	-2	C	-0.4
	*StL-A	15	25	2	8	1	0	0	4	2	5	.320	.370	.360	103	0	0	3	0	0	0	-1	C	0.0
	Yr	51	138	11	34	7	0	2	17	7	21	.246	.283	.341	77	-4	-5	11	0	1	-1	-2		-0.4
Total	5	233	696	63	165	29	4	7	63	51	84	.237	.290	.320	70	-30	-29	63	4	2	0	9	C	-0.1

■ BILL TUTTLE   Tuttle, William Robert b: 7/4/29, Elwood, Ill. BR/TR, 6′, 190 lbs. Deb: 9/10/52

1952	Det-A	7	25	2	6	0	0	0	2	0	1	.240	.240	.240	34	-2	-2	1	0	0	0	1	/O	0.0
1954	Det-A	147	530	64	141	20	11	7	58	62	60	.266	.345	.385	102	-0	1	69	5	8	-3	-1	*O	-0.6
1955	Det-A	154	603	102	168	23	4	14	78	76	54	.279	.360	.400	107	4	6	85	6	3	0	9	*O	0.7
1956	Det-A	140	546	61	138	22	4	9	65	38	48	.253	.303	.357	73	-22	-22	55	5	4	-1	5	*O	-2.4
1957	Det-A	133	451	49	113	12	4	4	47	44	41	.251	.319	.328	75	-14	-15	45	2	6	-3	-3	*O	-2.9
1958	KC-A	148	511	77	118	14	9	11	51	74	58	.231	.329	.358	88	-7	-8	59	7	9	-3	-2	*O	-2.3
1959	KC-A	126	463	74	139	19	6	7	43	48	38	.300	.371	.413	113	10	9	71	10	6	-1	6	*O	0.9
1960	KC-A	151	559	75	143	21	3	8	40	66	52	.256	.337	.347	85	-10	-11	64	1	5	0	10	*O	-0.8
1961	KC-A	25	84	15	22	2	2	0	8	9	9	.262	.333	.333	79	-2	-2	10	0	0	0	-0	O	-0.3
	Min-A	113	370	38	91	12	3	5	38	43	41	.246	.324	.335	73	-12	-15	39	1	3	-2	5	30/2	-0.7
	Yr	138	454	53	113	14	5	5	46	52	50	.249	.326	.335	74	-14	-17	49	1	3	-2	5		-1.0
1962	Min-A	110	123	21	26	4	1	1	13	19	14	.211	.322	.285	62	-6	-6	12	1	0	0	1	*O	-0.8
1963	Min-A	16	3	0	0	0	0	0	0	1	0	.000	.250	.000	-22	-0	-0	0	0	0	0	2	O	0.1
Total	11	1270	4268	578	1105	149	47	67	443	480	416	.259	.336	.363	88	-61	-66	509	38	44	-15	34	*O/32	-9.1

■ GUY TUTWILER   Tutwiler, Guy Isbell "King Tut" b: 7/17/1889, Coalburg, Ala. d: 8/15/30, Birmingham, Ala. BL/TR, 6′, 175 lbs. Deb: 8/29/11

1911	Det-A	13	32	3	6	2	0	0	3	2		.188	.235	.250	34	-3	-3	2	0			-4	/2O	-0.7
1913	Det-A	14	47	4	10	0	1	0	7	4	12	.213	.275	.255	56	-3	-3	4	2			1	1	-0.1
Total	2	27	79	7	16	2	1	0	10	6	12	.203	.259	.253	47	-6	-6	5	2			-3	/12O	-0.8

■ ART TWINEHAM   Twineham, Arthur W. "Old Hoss" b: 11/26/1866, Galesburg, Ill. BL/TL, 6′1.5″, 190 lbs. Deb: 9/11/1893

1893	StL-N	14	48	8	15	2	0	0	11	1	2	.313	.340	.354	86	-1	-1	6	0			3	C	0.3
1894	StL-N	38	127	22	40	4	1	1	16	9	11	.315	.387	.386	89	-2	-2	20	2			5	C	0.5
Total	2	52	175	30	55	6	1	1	27	10	13	.314	.375	.377	88	-3	-3	26	2			9	/C	0.8

■ LARRY TWITCHELL   Twitchell, Lawrence Grant b: 2/18/1864, Cleveland, Ohio d: 8/23/30, Cleveland, Ohio BR/TR, 6′, 185 lbs. Deb: 4/30/1886

1886	Det-N	4	16	0	1	0	0	0	0	0	2	.063	.063	.063	-60	-3	-3	0	0			1	/PO	0.0
1887	*Det-N	65	264	44	88	14	6	0	51	8	19	.333	.358	.432	116	7	5	46	12			-6	OP	0.2
1888	Det-N	131	524	71	128	19	4	5	67	28	45	.244	.286	.324	97	-2	-2	54	14			-8	*O/P	-1.0
1889	Cle-N	134	549	73	151	16	11	6	95	29	37	.275	.315	.366	93	-7	-6	70	17			-11	*O/P	-1.8
1890	Cle-P	56	233	33	52	6	3	2	36	17	17	.223	.279	.300	61	-15	-11	21	4			-9	O	-1.7
	Buf-P	44	172	24	38	3	1	2	17	23	12	.221	.316	.285	68	-9	-6	17	4			-1	OP/1	-0.3
	Yr	100	405	57	90	9	4	4	53	40	29	.222	.295	.294	64	-23	-17	38	8			-10		-2.0
1891	Col-a	57	224	32	62	9	4	0	35	20	28	.277	.341	.379	116	2	4	33	10			-9	O/P	-0.5
1892	Was-N	51	192	20	42	9	5	0	20	11	31	.219	.275	.318	83	-5	-4	19	4			-5	O/S3	-0.9
1893	Lou-N	45	187	37	58	11	3	2	31	17	20	.310	.377	.433	127	4	7	34	7			-2	O	0.3
1894	Lou-N	52	210	28	56	16	3	2	32	15	20	.267	.316	.400	78	-10	-7	30	8			6	O/P	-0.2
Total	9	639	2571	362	676	103	40	19	384	168	231	.263	.313	.356	93	-37	-23	325	84			-45	O/PS13	-5.9

■ BABE TWOMBLY   Twombly, Clarence Edward b: 1/18/1896, Jamaica Plain, Mass. d: 11/23/74, San Clemente, Cal. BL/TR, 5′10″, 165 lbs. Deb: 4/14/20

1920	Chi-N	78	183	25	43	1	1	2	14	17	20	.235	.303	.284	68	-7	-7	15	5	9	-4	1	O/2	-1.3
1921	Chi-N	87	175	22	66	8	1	1	18	11	10	.377	.414	.451	129	8	8	31	4	6	-2	6	O	0.8
Total	2	165	358	47	109	9	2	3	32	28	30	.304	.360	.366	98	1	0	46	9	15	-6	7	O/2	-0.5

■ GEORGE TWOMBLY   Twombly, George Frederick "Silent George" b: 6/4/1892, Boston, Mass. d: 2/17/75, Lexington, Mass. BR/TR, 5′9″, 165 lbs. Deb: 7/09/14

1914	Cin-N	68	240	22	56	0	5	0	19	14	27	.233	.284	.275	64	-10	-11	21	12			-1	O	-1.4
1915	Cin-N	46	66	5	13	0	1	0	5	8	8	.197	.293	.227	57	-3	-3	5	5	3	-0	1	O	-0.2
1916	Cin-N	3	5	0	0	0	0	0	0	1	1	.000	.167	.000	-48	-1	-1	0	0			0	/O	0.0
1917	Bos-N	32	102	8	19	1	1	0	9	18	5	.186	.314	.216	68	-3	-3	9	4			-4	O/1	-0.8
1919	Was-A	1	4	0	0	0	0	0	0	0	0	.000	.000	.000	-99	-1	-1	0	0			-0	/O	-0.1
Total	5	150	417	35	88	1	7	0	33	41	41	.211	.289	.247	62	-18	-19	35	21	3		-4	O/1	-2.5

■ JIM TYACK   Tyack, James Frederick b: 1/9/11, Florence, Mont. BL/TR, 6′2″, 195 lbs. Deb: 4/20/43

| 1943 | Phi-A | 54 | 155 | 11 | 40 | 8 | 1 | 0 | 23 | 14 | 9 | .258 | .320 | .323 | 88 | -2 | -2 | 17 | 1 | * | | | | |

■ FRED TYLER   Tyler, Frederick Franklin "Clancy" b: 12/16/1891, Derry, N.H. d: 10/14/45, E.Derry, N.H. TR, 5′10.5″, 180 lbs. Deb: 4/14

| 1914 | Bos-N | 6 | 19 | 2 | 2 | 0 | 0 | 0 | 2 | 1 | 5 | .105 | .150 | .105 | -24 | -3 | -3 | 0 | 0 | | | | | |

■ JOHNNIE TYLER   Tyler, John Anthony "Ty Ty" or "Katz" (b: John Tylka)
b: 7/30/06, Mt.Pleasant, Pa. d: 7/11/72, Mt.Pleasant, Pa. BB/TR, 6′, 175 lbs. Deb: 9/16/34

| 1934 | Bos-N | 3 | 6 | 0 | 1 | 0 | 0 | 0 | 1 | 0 | 3 | .167 | .167 | .167 | -11 | -1 | -1 | 0 | 0 | | | | | |

YEAR	TM/L	G	AB	R	H	2B	3B	HR	RBI	BB	SO	AVG	OBP	SLG	PRO+	BR	/A	RC	SB	CS	SBR	FR	POS	TPR
1935	Bos-N	13	47	7	16	2	1	2	11	4	3	.340	.404	.553	168	4	4	11	0			-1	O	0.3
Total	2	16	53	7	17	2	1	2	12	4	6	.321	.379	.509	148	3	3	11	0			0	/O	0.3

■ EARL TYREE Tyree, Earl Carlton "Ty" b: 3/4/1890, Huntsville, Ill. d: 5/17/54, Rushville, Ill. BR/TR, 5'8", 160 lbs. Deb: 10/05/14

YEAR	TM/L	G	AB	R	H	2B	3B	HR	RBI	BB	SO	AVG	OBP	SLG	PRO+	BR	/A	RC	SB	CS	SBR	FR	POS	TPR
1914	Chi-N	1	4	1	0	0	0	0	0	0	0	.000	.000	.000	-99	-1	-1	0	0			-1	/C	-0.1

■ JIM TYRONE Tyrone, James Vernon b: 1/29/49, Alice, Tex. BR/TR, 6'1", 185 lbs. Deb: 8/27/72

YEAR	TM/L	G	AB	R	H	2B	3B	HR	RBI	BB	SO	AVG	OBP	SLG	PRO+	BR	/A	RC	SB	CS	SBR	FR	POS	TPR
1972	Chi-N	13	8	1	0	0	0	0	0	0	3	.000	.000	.000	-90	-2	-2	0	1	0	0	2	/O	0.0
1974	Chi-N	57	81	19	15	0	1	3	3	6	8	.185	.241	.321	54	-5	-5	6	1	1	-0	-1	O/3	-0.8
1975	Chi-N	11	22	0	5	0	1	0	3	1	4	.227	.261	.318	58	-1	-1	2	1	1	-0	0	/O	-0.1
1977	Oak-A	96	294	32	72	11	1	5	26	25	62	.245	.304	.340	76	-10	-9	31	3	1	0	-1	O/1SD	-1.1
Total	4	177	405	52	92	11	3	8	32	32	77	.227	.284	.328	67	-18	-18	39	6	3	0	0	O/DS13	-2.0

■ WAYNE TYRONE Tyrone, Oscar Wayne b: 8/1/50, Alice, Tex. BR/TR, 6'1", 185 lbs. Deb: 7/15/76

YEAR	TM/L	G	AB	R	H	2B	3B	HR	RBI	BB	SO	AVG	OBP	SLG	PRO+	BR	/A	RC	SB	CS	SBR	FR	POS	TPR
1976	Chi-N	30	57	3	13	1	0	1	8	3	21	.228	.267	.298	55	-3	-4	5	0	0	0	-1	/O13	-0.5

■ TY TYSON Tyson, Albert Thomas b: 6/1/1892, Wilkes-Barre, Pa. d: 8/16/53, Buffalo, N.Y. BR/TR, 5'11", 169 lbs. Deb: 4/13/26

YEAR	TM/L	G	AB	R	H	2B	3B	HR	RBI	BB	SO	AVG	OBP	SLG	PRO+	BR	/A	RC	SB	CS	SBR	FR	POS	TPR
1926	NY-N	97	335	40	98	16	1	3	35	15	28	.293	.329	.373	90	-6	-5	40	6			2	O	-0.6
1927	NY-N	43	159	24	42	7	2	1	17	10	19	.264	.308	.352	76	-5	-5	17	5			-4	O	-1.0
1928	Bro-N	59	210	25	57	11	1	1	21	10	14	.271	.317	.348	75	-8	-8	23	3			4	O	-0.5
Total	3	199	704	89	197	34	4	5	73	35	61	.280	.320	.361	82	-19	-18	79	14			1	O	-2.1

■ TURKEY TYSON Tyson, Cecil Washington "Slim" b: 12/6/14, Elm City, N.C. BL/TR, 6'5.5", 225 lbs. Deb: 4/23/44

YEAR	TM/L	G	AB	R	H	2B	3B	HR	RBI	BB	SO	AVG	OBP	SLG	PRO+	BR	/A	RC	SB	CS	SBR	FR	POS	TPR
1944	Phi-N	1	1	0	0	0	0	0	0	0	0	.000	.000	.000	-99	-0	-0	0	0			0	H	0.0

■ MIKE TYSON Tyson, Michael Ray b: 1/13/50, Rocky Mount, N.C. BR/TR, 5'9", 170 lbs. Deb: 9/05/72

YEAR	TM/L	G	AB	R	H	2B	3B	HR	RBI	BB	SO	AVG	OBP	SLG	PRO+	BR	/A	RC	SB	CS	SBR	FR	POS	TPR
1972	StL-N	13	37	1	7	1	0	0	0	1	9	.189	.211	.216	22	-4	-4	2	0	1	-1	4	2/S	0.1
1973	StL-N	144	469	48	114	15	4	1	33	23	66	.243	.281	.299	61	-25	-25	37	2	5	-2	-18	*S2	-2.8
1974	StL-N	151	422	35	94	14	5	1	37	22	70	.223	.266	.287	55	-26	-26	29	4	2	0	15	*S2	0.6
1975	StL-N	122	368	45	98	16	3	2	37	24	39	.266	.316	.342	80	-9	-10	40	5	2	0	-12	S2/3	-1.0
1976	StL-N	76	245	26	70	12	9	3	28	16	34	.286	.330	.445	117	5	5	34	3	1	0	8	2	1.7
1977	StL-N	138	418	42	103	15	2	7	57	30	48	.246	.300	.342	73	-17	-16	41	3	4	-2	22	*2	1.3
1978	StL-N	125	377	26	88	16	0	3	26	24	41	.233	.279	.300	63	-19	-19	29	2	0	1	0	*2	-1.0
1979	StL-N	75	190	18	42	8	2	5	20	13	28	.221	.275	.363	72	-8	-8	18	2	1	0	8	2	0.5
1980	Chi-N	123	341	34	81	19	3	3	23	15	61	.238	.274	.337	65	-15	-17	31	1	2	-1	9	*2	0.0
1981	Chi-N	50	92	6	17	2	0	2	8	7	15	.185	.250	.272	46	-6	-7	7	1	0	0	-3	2/S	-0.3
Total	10	1017	2959	281	714	118	28	27	269	175	411	.241	.287	.327	69	-124	-127	268	23	18	-4	36	2S/3	-0.9

■ BOB UECKER Uecker, Robert George b: 1/26/35, Milwaukee, Wis. BR/TR, 6'1", 190 lbs. Deb: 4/13/62

YEAR	TM/L	G	AB	R	H	2B	3B	HR	RBI	BB	SO	AVG	OBP	SLG	PRO+	BR	/A	RC	SB	CS	SBR	FR	POS	TPR
1962	Mil-N	33	64	5	16	2	0	1	8	7	15	.250	.324	.328	78	-2	-2	6	0	0	0	5	C	0.3
1963	Mil-N	13	16	3	4	2	0	0	0	2	5	.250	.333	.375	105	0	0	2	0	0	0	1	/C	0.1
1964	StL-N	40	106	8	21	1	0	1	6	17	24	.198	.315	.236	53	-5	-6	9	0	1	-1	4	C	0.0
1965	StL-N	53	145	17	33	7	0	2	10	24	27	.228	.345	.317	80	-1	-3	18	0	1	-1	-1	C	-0.2
1966	Phi-N	78	207	15	43	6	0	7	30	22	36	.208	.284	.338	72	-8	-8	19	0	0	0	1	C	-0.4
1967	Phi-N	18	35	3	6	2	0	0	7	5	9	.171	.275	.229	45	-2	-2	2	0	0	0	0	C	0.0
	Atl-N	62	158	14	23	2	0	3	13	19	51	.146	.237	.215	31	-14	-14	8	0	1	-1	9	C	-0.1
	Yr	80	193	17	29	4	0	3	20	24	60	.150	.244	.218	33	-16	-16	11	0	1	-1	9		-0.1
Total	6	297	731	65	146	22	0	14	74	96	167	.200	.295	.287	63	-33	-35	64	0	3	-2	19	C	-0.3

■ FRENCHY UHALT Uhalt, Bernard Bartholomew b: 4/27/10, Bakersfield, Cal. BL/TR, 5'10", 180 lbs. Deb: 4/17/34

YEAR	TM/L	G	AB	R	H	2B	3B	HR	RBI	BB	SO	AVG	OBP	SLG	PRO+	BR	/A	RC	SB	CS	SBR	FR	POS	TPR
1934	Chi-A	57	165	28	40	5	1	0	16	29	12	.242	.359	.285	66	-7	-7	19	6	5	-1	-2	O	-1.0

■ TED UHLAENDER Uhlaender, Theodore Otto b: 10/21/40, Chicago, Heights, Ill. BL/TR, 6'2", 190 lbs. Deb: 9/04/65

YEAR	TM/L	G	AB	R	H	2B	3B	HR	RBI	BB	SO	AVG	OBP	SLG	PRO+	BR	/A	RC	SB	CS	SBR	FR	POS	TPR
1965	Min-A	13	22	1	4	0	0	0	1	0	2	.182	.182	.182	3	-3	-3	1	1	0	0	1	/O	-0.1
1966	Min-A	105	367	39	83	12	2	2	22	27	33	.226	.281	.286	60	-17	-20	32	10	2	2	9	*O	-1.3
1967	Min-A	133	415	41	107	19	7	6	49	13	45	.258	.285	.381	88	-4	-7	44	4	4	-1	3	*O	-0.9
1968	Min-A	140	488	52	138	21	5	7	52	28	46	.283	.326	.389	110	8	6	63	16	7	1	-6	*O	-0.4
1969	*Min-A	152	554	93	151	18	2	8	62	44	52	.273	.331	.356	90	-6	-7	68	15	9	-1	-1	*O	-1.3
1970	Cle-A	141	473	56	127	21	2	11	46	39	44	.268	.326	.391	92	-3	-5	60	3	6	-3	-15	*O	-2.9
1971	Cle-A	141	500	52	144	20	3	2	47	38	44	.288	.338	.352	88	-3	-8	59	3	6	-3	-9	*O	-2.5
1972	*Cin-N	73	113	9	18	3	0	0	6	13	11	.159	.246	.186	26	-11	-10	5	0	1	-1	0	O	-1.2
Total	8	898	2932	343	772	114	21	36	285	202	277	.263	.313	.353	86	-38	-55	330	52	35	-5	-17	O	-10.6

■ GEORGE UHLE Uhle, George Ernest "The Bull" b: 9/18/1898, Cleveland, Ohio d: 2/26/85, Lakewood, Ohio BR/TR, 6', 190 lbs. Deb: 4/30/19 C

YEAR	TM/L	G	AB	R	H	2B	3B	HR	RBI	BB	SO	AVG	OBP	SLG	PRO+	BR	/A	RC	SB	CS	SBR	FR	POS	TPR
1919	Cle-A	26	43	7	13	2	1	0	6	1	5	.302	.318	.395	94	-0	-1	5	0			0	P	0.0
1920	*Cle-A	27	32	4	11	0	0	0	2	2	2	.344	.382	.344	91	-0	-0	4	1	0	0	0	P	0.0
1921	Cle-A	48	94	21	23	2	3	1	18	6	9	.245	.290	.362	64	-5	-5	10	0	0	0	-2	P	0.0
1922	Cle-A	56	109	21	29	8	2	0	14	13	6	.266	.350	.376	88	-2	-2	15	1	2	-1	-3	P	0.0
1923	Cle-A	58	144	23	52	10	3	0	22	7	10	.361	.391	.472	127	5	5	26	2	1	0	0	P	0.2
1924	Cle-A	59	107	10	33	6	1	1	19	4	8	.308	.339	.411	92	-2	-2	14	0	1	-1	1	P	0.2
1925	Cle-A	55	101	10	29	3	3	0	13	7	7	.287	.339	.376	81	-3	-3	13	0	0	0	-2	P	0.0
1926	Cle-A	50	132	16	30	3	0	1	11	10	12	.227	.287	.273	46	-10	-11	11	2	2	-1	-2	P	0.0
1927	Cle-A	43	79	4	21	7	1	0	14	5	12	.266	.310	.380	78	-3	-3	9	0	1	-1	-1	P	0.0
1928	Cle-A	55	98	9	28	3	2	1	17	8	4	.286	.340	.388	90	-1	-2	13	0	0	0	2	P	0.0
1929	Det-A	40	108	18	37	1	1	0	13	6	6	.343	.377	.370	93	-1	-1	15	0	0		-3	P	0.0
1930	Det-A	59	117	15	36	4	2	2	21	8	13	.308	.352	.427	95	-1	-1	18	0	0		-3	P	0.0
1931	Det-A	53	90	8	22	6	0	2	7	8	8	.244	.306	.378	76	-3	-3	10	0	1	-1	-1	P	0.0
1932	Det-A	38	55	2	10	3	1	0	4	6	5	.182	.262	.273	37	-5	-5	4	0	0	0	-1	P	0.0
1933	Det-A	1	0	0	0	0	0	0	0	0	0	—	—	—	—	0	0	0	0	0	0	0	/P	0.0
	NY-N	8	5	1	0	0	0	0	0	1	3	.000	.167	.000	-50	-1	-1	0	0	0	0	0	/P	0.0
	NY-A	12	20	1	8	0	0	0	1	4	2	.400	.500	.450	163	2	2	5	0	0	0	-1	P	0.0
1934	NY-A	10	5	1	3	0	1	0	1	0	0	.600	.600	1.000	329	1	1	3	0	0	0	-0	P	0.0
1936	Cle-A	24	21	1	8	1	0	1	4	2	0	.381	.435	.571	145	2	1	5	0	0	0	-0	/P	0.2
Total	17	722	1360	172	393	60	21	9	187	98	112	.289	.339	.384	86	-27	-29	181	6	8		-16	P	0.4

■ MAURY UHLER Uhler, Maurice William b: 12/14/1886, Pikesville, Md. d: 5/4/18, Baltimore, Md. BR/TR, 5'11", 165 lbs. Deb: 4/14/14

YEAR	TM/L	G	AB	R	H	2B	3B	HR	RBI	BB	SO	AVG	OBP	SLG	PRO+	BR	/A	RC	SB	CS	SBR	FR	POS	TPR
1914	Cin-N	46	56	12	12	2	0	0	3	5	11	.214	.279	.250	56	-3	-3	5	4			2	O	-0.1

■ CHARLIE UHLIR Uhlir, Charles Karel b: 7/30/12, Chicago, Ill. BL/TL, 5'7.5", 150 lbs. Deb: 8/03/34

YEAR	TM/L	G	AB	R	H	2B	3B	HR	RBI	BB	SO	AVG	OBP	SLG	PRO+	BR	/A	RC	SB	CS	SBR	FR	POS	TPR
1934	Chi-A	14	27	3	4	0	0	0	3	2	6	.148	.207	.148	-7	-4	-4	1	0	0	0	-1	/O	-0.4

■ MIKE ULISNEY Ulisney, Michael Edward "Slugs" b: 9/28/17, Greenwald, Pa. BR/TR, 5'9", 165 lbs. Deb: 5/05/45

YEAR	TM/L	G	AB	R	H	2B	3B	HR	RBI	BB	SO	AVG	OBP	SLG	PRO+	BR	/A	RC	SB	CS	SBR	FR	POS	TPR
	Bos-N	11	18	4	7	1	0	1	4	1	0	.389	.421	.611	184	2	2	5	0			-2	/C	0.0

■ SCOTT ULLGER Ullger, Scott Matthew b: 6/10/56, New York, N.Y. BR/TR, 6'2", 186 lbs. Deb: 4/17/83

YEAR	TM/L	G	AB	R	H	2B	3B	HR	RBI	BB	SO	AVG	OBP	SLG	PRO+	BR	/A	RC	SB	CS	SBR	FR	POS	TPR
	-A	35	79	8	15	4	0	0	5	5	21	.190	.247	.241	34	-7	-7	3	0	2	-1	-1	1/3D	-1.1

GEORGE ULRICH
Ulrich, George F. b: Philadelphia, Pa. Deb: 5/01/1892

YEAR	TM/L	G	AB	R	H	2B	3B	HR	RBI	BB	SO	AVG	OBP	SLG	PRO+	BR	/A	RC	SB	CS	SBR	FR	POS	TPR
1892	Was-N	6	24	1	7	1	0	0	0	0	4	.292	.292	.333	93	-0	-0	3	2			-1	/3SC	0.0
1893	Cin-N	1	3	0	0	0	0	0	0	0	0	.000	.250	.000	-29	-1	-1	0	1			-0	/O	0.0
1896	NY-N	14	45	4	8	1	0	0	1	1	1	.178	.229	.200	15	-5	-5	2	0			0	O/3	-0.4
Total	3	21	72	5	15	2	0	0	1	1	5	.208	.250	.236	36	-6	-6	5	3			-1	/O3CS	-0.4

TOM UMPHLETT
Umphlett, Thomas Mullen b: 5/12/30, Scotland Neck, N.C BR/TR, 6'2", 180 lbs. Deb: 4/16/53

YEAR	TM/L	G	AB	R	H	2B	3B	HR	RBI	BB	SO	AVG	OBP	SLG	PRO+	BR	/A	RC	SB	CS	SBR	FR	POS	TPR
1953	Bos-A	137	495	53	140	27	5	3	59	34	30	.283	.331	.376	86	-7	-10	62	4	2	0	1	*O	-1.3
1954	Was-A	114	342	21	75	8	3	1	33	17	42	.219	.256	.269	46	-27	-25	21	1	2	-1	-3	*O	-3.1
1955	Was-A	110	323	34	70	10	0	2	19	24	35	.217	.271	.266	47	-25	-23	24	2	1	0	-5	*O	-3.2
Total	3	361	1160	108	285	45	8	6	111	75	107	.246	.293	.314	65	-59	-58	107	7	5	-1	-6	O	-7.6

BOB UNGLAUB
Unglaub, Robert Alexander b: 7/31/1881, Baltimore, Md. d: 11/29/16, Baltimore, Md. BR/TR, 5'11", 178 lbs. Deb: 4/15/04 M

YEAR	TM/L	G	AB	R	H	2B	3B	HR	RBI	BB	SO	AVG	OBP	SLG	PRO+	BR	/A	RC	SB	CS	SBR	FR	POS	TPR
1904	NY-A	6	19	2	4	0	0	0	2	0		.211	.211	.211	33	-1	-1	1	0			-1	/3S	-0.2
	Bos-A	9	13	1	2	1	0	0	2	1		.154	.214	.231	40	-1	-1	1	0			-2	/23S	-0.2
	Yr	15	32	3	6	1	0	0	4	1		.188	.212	.219	36	-2	-2	2	0			-3		-0.4
1905	Bos-A	43	121	18	27	5	1	0	11	6		.223	.260	.281	73	-4	-4	10	2			1	3/21	-0.1
1907	Bos-A	139	544	49	138	17	13	1	62	23		.254	.284	.338	101	-1	-1	59	14			-1	*1M	-0.3
1908	Bos-A	72	266	23	70	11	3	1	25	7		.263	.282	.338	101	0	-1	27	6			2	1	0.0
	Was-A	72	276	23	85	10	5	0	29	8		.308	.327	.380	144	9	11	36	8			11	32/1	2.6
	Yr	144	542	46	155	21	8	1	54	15		.286	.305	.360	122	9	10	63	14			13		2.6
1909	Was-A	130	480	43	127	14	9	3	41	22		.265	.301	.350	111	1	4	54	15			1	1O2/3	0.2
1910	Was-A	124	431	29	101	9	4	0	44	21		.234	.270	.274	74	-16	-13	37	21			6	*1	-0.2
Total	6	595	2150	188	554	67	35	5	216	88		.258	.288	.328	100	-13	-7	226	66			17	1/320S	1.8

AL UNSER
Unser, Albert Bernard b: 10/12/12, Morrisonville, Ill BR/TR, 6'1", 175 lbs. Deb: 9/14/42

YEAR	TM/L	G	AB	R	H	2B	3B	HR	RBI	BB	SO	AVG	OBP	SLG	PRO+	BR	/A	RC	SB	CS	SBR	FR	POS	TPR
1942	Det-A	4	8	2	3	0	0	0	0	0	2	.375	.375	.375	103	0	0	1	0	0	0	1	/C	0.1
1943	Det-A	38	101	14	25	5	0	0	4	15	15	.248	.350	.297	84	-1	-2	11	0	1	-1	-3	C	-0.3
1944	Det-A	11	25	2	3	0	1	1	5	3	2	.120	.214	.320	49	-2	-2	2	0	0	0	-4	/2C	-0.5
1945	Cin-N	67	204	23	54	10	3	3	21	14	24	.265	.318	.387	98	-2	-1	25	0			0	C	0.0
Total	4	120	338	41	85	15	4	4	30	32	43	.251	.322	.355	90	-4	-5	39	0	1		-7	C/2	-0.7

DEL UNSER
Unser, Delbert Bernard b: 12/9/44, Decatur, Ill. BL/TL, 6'1", 180 lbs. Deb: 4/10/68 C

YEAR	TM/L	G	AB	R	H	2B	3B	HR	RBI	BB	SO	AVG	OBP	SLG	PRO+	BR	/A	RC	SB	CS	SBR	FR	POS	TPR
1968	Was-A	156	635	66	146	13	7	1	30	46	66	.230	.284	.277	73	-22	-20	52	11	6	-0	13	*O/1	-1.4
1969	Was-A	153	581	69	166	19	8	1	57	58	54	.286	.351	.382	111	4	8	79	8	10	-4	-2	*O	0.0
1970	Was-A	119	322	37	83	5	1	5	30	30	29	.258	.321	.326	83	-9	-7	35	1	1	-0	-12	*O	-2.4
1971	Was-A	153	581	63	148	19	6	9	41	59	68	.255	.326	.355	98	-5	-2	70	11	6	-0	19	*O	1.2
1972	Cle-A	132	383	29	91	12	0	1	17	28	46	.238	.291	.277	67	-14	-15	31	5	9	-4	-4	*O	-2.9
1973	Phi-N	136	440	64	127	20	4	11	52	47	55	.289	.359	.427	114	10	9	68	5	8	-3	12	*O	1.2
1974	Phi-N	142	454	72	120	18	5	11	61	50	62	.264	.339	.399	101	3	1	62	6	4	-1	2	*O	-0.3
1975	NY-N	147	531	65	156	18	2	10	53	37	76	.294	.340	.392	107	1	4	70	4	3	-1	9	*O	0.7
1976	NY-N	77	276	28	63	13	2	5	25	18	40	.228	.278	.344	80	-9	-8	26	4	4	-1	0	O	-1.1
	Mon-N	69	220	29	50	6	2	7	15	11	44	.227	.264	.368	75	-7	-8	21	3	3	-1	-3	O	-1.5
	Yr	146	496	57	113	19	4	12	40	29	84	.228	.272	.355	78	-17	-16	47	7	7	-2	-3		-2.6
1977	Mon-N	113	289	33	79	14	1	12	40	33	41	.273	.348	.453	116	5	6	45	2	5	-2	-2	O1	-0.1
1978	Mon-N	130	179	16	35	5	0	2	15	24	29	.196	.294	.257	56	-10	-10	15	2	0	1	3	1O	-1.0
1979	Phi-N	95	141	26	42	8	0	6	29	14	33	.298	.361	.482	124	5	5	24	2	0	1	-1	O1	0.3
1980	*Phi-N	96	110	15	29	6	4	0	10	10	21	.264	.325	.391	94	-0	-1	14	0	1	-1	7	1O	0.3
1981	Phi-N	62	59	5	9	3	0	0	6	13	9	.153	.306	.203	45	-4	-4	4	0	0	0	2	1O	-0.3
1982	Phi-N	19	14	0	0	0	0	0	0	3	2	.000	.176	.000	-46	-3	-3	0	0	0	0	0	/1O	-0.2
Total	15	1799	5215	617	1344	179	42	87	481	481	675	.258	.321	.358	93	-56	-46	616	64	60	-17	42	*O1	-7.5

JOHN UPHAM
Upham, John Leslie b: 12/29/41, Windsor, Ont., Can. BL/TL, 6', 180 lbs. Deb: 4/16/67

YEAR	TM/L	G	AB	R	H	2B	3B	HR	RBI	BB	SO	AVG	OBP	SLG	PRO+	BR	/A	RC	SB	CS	SBR	FR	POS	TPR
1967	Chi-N	8	3	1	2	0	0	0	0	0	0	.667	.667	.667	270	1	1	1	0	0	0	0	/P	0.0
1968	Chi-N	13	10	0	2	0	0	0	0	0	3	.200	.200	.200	19	-1	-1	0	0	0	0	0	/PO	0.0
Total	2	21	13	1	4	0	0	0	0	0	3	.308	.308	.308	78	-0	-0	2	0	0	0	0	/PO	0.0

DIXIE UPRIGHT
Upright, R T b: 5/30/26, Kannapolis, N.C. d: 11/13/86, Concord, N.C. BL/TL, 6', 175 lbs. Deb: 4/18/53

YEAR	TM/L	G	AB	R	H	2B	3B	HR	RBI	BB	SO	AVG	OBP	SLG	PRO+	BR	/A	RC	SB	CS	SBR	FR	POS	TPR
1953	StL-A	9	8	3	2	0	0	1	1	1	3	.250	.333	.625	151	1	0	2	0	0	0	0	H	0.0

WILLIE UPSHAW
Upshaw, Willie Clay b: 4/27/57, Blanco, Tex. BL/TL, 6', 185 lbs. Deb: 4/09/78

YEAR	TM/L	G	AB	R	H	2B	3B	HR	RBI	BB	SO	AVG	OBP	SLG	PRO+	BR	/A	RC	SB	CS	SBR	FR	POS	TPR
1978	Tor-A	95	224	26	53	8	2	1	17	21	35	.237	.302	.304	69	-8	-9	20	4	6	-2	4	OD1	-0.8
1980	Tor-A	34	61	10	13	3	1	1	5	6	14	.213	.284	.344	68	-2	-3	7	1	0	0	1	1D/O	-0.2
1981	Tor-A	61	111	15	19	3	1	4	10	11	16	.171	.252	.324	61	-5	-6	9	2	1	0	1	D1O	-0.5
1982	Tor-A	160	580	77	155	25	7	21	75	52	91	.267	.329	.443	100	7	-0	82	8	8	-2	-2	*1/D	-0.7
1983	Tor-A	160	579	99	177	26	7	27	104	61	98	.306	.377	.515	134	34	29	113	10	7	-1	3	*1/D	2.4
1984	Tor-A	152	569	79	158	31	9	19	84	55	86	.278	.347	.464	118	16	14	92	10	4	-1	-3	*1/D	0.2
1985	*Tor-A	148	501	79	138	31	5	15	65	48	71	.275	.344	.447	112	10	8	76	8	8	-2	1	*1/D	-0.2
1986	Tor-A	155	573	85	144	28	6	9	60	78	87	.251	.343	.368	91	-4	-5	80	23	5	4	5	*1/D	-0.5
1987	Tor-A	150	512	68	125	22	4	15	58	58	78	.244	.325	.391	87	-8	-10	65	10	11	-4	12	*1	-1.4
1988	Cle-A	149	493	58	121	22	3	11	50	62	66	.245	.332	.369	94	-2	-3	61	12	9	-2	0	*1	-1.3
Total	10	1264	4203	596	1103	199	45	123	528	452	642	.262	.337	.419	102	37	14	605	88	59	-9	22	*1/OD	-3.0

TOM UPTON
Upton, Thomas Herbert "Muscles" b: 12/29/26, Ester, Mo. BR/TR, 6', 160 lbs. Deb: 4/19/50

YEAR	TM/L	G	AB	R	H	2B	3B	HR	RBI	BB	SO	AVG	OBP	SLG	PRO+	BR	/A	RC	SB	CS	SBR	FR	POS	TPR
1950	StL-A	124	389	50	92	5	6	2	30	52	45	.237	.328	.296	58	-22	-25	42	7	2	1	-10	*S/23	-2.6
1951	StL-A	52	131	9	26	4	3	0	12	12	22	.198	.271	.275	46	-10	-10	10	1	1	-0	-4	S	-1.1
1952	Was-A	5	5	1	0	0	0	0	0	1	0	.000	.167	.000	-53	-1	-1	0	0	0	0	2	/S	0.1
Total	3	181	525	60	118	9	9	2	42	65	67	.225	.313	.288	55	-33	-36	51	8	3	1	-12	S/23	-3.6

LUKE URBAN
Urban, Louis John b: 3/22/1898, Fall River, Mass. d: 12/7/80, Somerset, Mass. BR/TR, 5'8", 168 lbs. Deb: 7/19/27

YEAR	TM/L	G	AB	R	H	2B	3B	HR	RBI	BB	SO	AVG	OBP	SLG	PRO+	BR	/A	RC	SB	CS	SBR	FR	POS	TPR
1927	Bos-N	35	111	11	32	5	0	0	10	3	6	.288	.313	.333	79	-4	-3	11	1			-7	C	-0.7
1928	Bos-N	15	17	0	3	0	0	0	2	0	1	.176	.222	.176	6	-2	-2	1	0			1	C	0.0
Total	2	50	128	11	35	5	0	0	12	3	7	.273	.301	.313	69	-7	-5	12	1			-7	/C	-0.7

BILLY URBANSKI
Urbanski, William Michael b: 6/5/03, Linoleumville, N.Y d: 7/12/73, Perth Amboy, N.J. BR/TR, 5'8", 165 lbs. Deb: 7/04/31

YEAR	TM/L	G	AB	R	H	2B	3B	HR	RBI	BB	SO	AVG	OBP	SLG	PRO+	BR	/A	RC	SB	CS	SBR	FR	POS	TPR
1931	Bos-N	82	303	22	72	13	4	0	17	10	32	.238	.274	.307	58	-19	-18	27	3			11	3S	0.0
1932	Bos-N	136	563	80	153	25	8	8	46	28	60	.272	.307	.387	89	-12	-9	68	8			1	*S	0.3
1933	Bos-N	144	566	65	142	21	4	0	35	33	48	.251	.298	.302	78	-20	-15	52	4			-4	*S	-0.9
1934	Bos-N	146	605	104	177	30	6	7	53	56	37	.293	.357	.397	90	12	9	90	4			-10	*S	0.1
1935	Bos-N	132	514	53	118	17	0	4	30	40	32	.230	.286	.286	59	-32	-27	42	3			-27	*S	-4.7
1936	Bos-N	122	494	55	129	17	5	0	26	31	42	.261	.310	.316	74	-21	-17	48	2			-18	S3	-2.6
1937	Bos-N	1	1	0	0	0	0	0	0	0	1	.000	.000	.000	-99	-0	-0	0	0			0	H	0.0
Total	7	763	3046	379	791	123	27	19	207	198	252	.260	.309	.337	81	-103	-78	327	24			-47	S3	-7.8

YEAR	TM/L	G	AB	R	H	2B	3B	HR	RBI	BB	SO	AVG	OBP	SLG	PRO+	BR	/A	RC	SB	CS	SBR	FR	POS	TPR

■ JOSE URIBE
Uribe, Jose Altagracia (Player Under Real Name Of Jose Altagracia Gonzalez (Uribe) In 1984) b: 1/21/59, San Cristobal, D.R. BB/TR, 5'10", 155 lbs. Deb: 9/13/84

YEAR	TM/L	G	AB	R	H	2B	3B	HR	RBI	BB	SO	AVG	OBP	SLG	PRO+	BR	/A	RC	SB	CS	SBR	FR	POS	TPR
1984	StL-N	8	19	4	4	0	0	0	3	0	2	.211	.211	.211	19	-2	-2	1	1	0	0	0	/S2	0.0
1985	SF-N	147	476	46	113	20	4	3	26	30	57	.237	.285	.315	71	-21	-18	44	8	2	1	-2	*S/2	-0.7
1986	SF-N	157	453	46	101	15	1	3	43	61	76	.223	.315	.280	69	-20	-17	43	22	11	0	12	*S	1.0
1987	*SF-N	95	309	44	90	16	5	5	30	24	35	.291	.344	.424	107	1	3	48	12	2	2	11	S	2.6
1988	SF-N	141	493	47	124	10	7	3	35	36	69	.252	.302	.318	82	-14	-11	48	14	10	-2	-3	*S	-0.6
1989	*SF-N	151	453	34	100	12	6	1	30	34	54	.221	.275	.280	61	-24	-22	34	6	6	-2	8	*S	-0.6
1990	SF-N	138	415	35	103	8	6	1	24	29	49	.248	.297	.304	66	-19	-19	35	5	9	-4	16	*S	0.5
Total	7	837	2618	256	635	81	29	16	191	214	362	.243	.301	.314	74	-99	-87	253	68	40	-4	42	S/2	2.2

■ LON URY
Ury, Louis Newton "Old Sleep" b: 1877, Ft.Scott, Kan. d: 3/4/18, Kansas City, Mo. TR, 6', Deb: 9/09/03

YEAR	TM/L	G	AB	R	H	2B	3B	HR	RBI	BB	SO	AVG	OBP	SLG	PRO+	BR	/A	RC	SB	CS	SBR	FR	POS	TPR
1903	StL-N	2	7	0	1	0	0	0	0	0		.143	.143	.143	-18	-1	-1	0	0			0	/1	0.0

■ BOB USHER
Usher, Robert Royce b: 3/1/25, San Diego, Cal. BR/TR, 6'1.5", 180 lbs. Deb: 4/16/46

YEAR	TM/L	G	AB	R	H	2B	3B	HR	RBI	BB	SO	AVG	OBP	SLG	PRO+	BR	/A	RC	SB	CS	SBR	FR	POS	TPR
1946	Cin-N	92	152	16	31	5	1	1	14	13	27	.204	.271	.270	56	-9	-9	12	2			7	O/3	-0.3
1947	Cin-N	9	22	2	4	0	0	1	1	2	2	.182	.250	.318	50	-2	-2	2	0			1	/O	0.0
1950	Cin-N	106	321	51	83	17	0	6	35	27	38	.259	.316	.368	79	-10	-10	37	3			3	O	-0.9
1951	Cin-N	114	303	27	63	12	2	5	25	19	36	.208	.257	.310	51	-21	-22	23	4	5	-2	10	O	-1.6
1952	Chi-N	1	0	0	0	0	0	0	0	1	0	—	1.000	—	197	0	0	0	0	0	0	0	H	0.0
1957	Cle-A	10	8	1	1	0	0	0	0	1	3	.125	.222	.125	-3	-1	-1	0	0	0	0	-0	/O3	-0.1
	Was-A	96	295	36	77	7	1	5	27	27	30	.261	.327	.342	84	-7	-6	34	0	0	0	-2	O	-1.3
	Yr	106	303	37	78	7	1	5	27	28	33	.257	.324	.337	82	-8	-7	34	0	0	0	-2		-1.4
Total	6	428	1101	133	259	41	4	18	102	90	136	.235	.295	.329	69	-49	-49	107	9	5		19	O/3	-4.2

■ DUTCH USSAT
Ussat, William August b: 4/11/04, Dayton, Ohio d: 5/29/59, Dayton, Ohio BR/TR, 6'1", 170 lbs. Deb: 9/13/25

YEAR	TM/L	G	AB	R	H	2B	3B	HR	RBI	BB	SO	AVG	OBP	SLG	PRO+	BR	/A	RC	SB	CS	SBR	FR	POS	TPR
1925	Cle-A	1	1	0	0	0	0	0	0	0	0	.000	.000	.000	-99	-0	-0	0	0	0	0	0	/2	0.0
1927	Cle-A	4	16	4	3	0	1	0	2	0	1	.188	.278	.313	53	-1	-1	1	0	0	0	-1	/3	-0.1
Total	2	5	17	4	3	0	1	0	2	0	1	.176	.263	.294	44	-1	-1	1	0	0	0	-1	/32	-0.1

■ TEX VACHE
Vache, Ernest Lewis b: 11/17/1894, Santa Monica, Cal. d: 6/11/53, Los Angeles, Cal. BR/TR, 6'1", 200 lbs. Deb: 4/16/25

YEAR	TM/L	G	AB	R	H	2B	3B	HR	RBI	BB	SO	AVG	OBP	SLG	PRO+	BR	/A	RC	SB	CS	SBR	FR	POS	TPR
1925	Bos-A	110	252	41	79	15	7	3	48	21	33	.313	.382	.464	114	5	5	45	2	2	-1	-12	O	-1.0

■ GENE VADEBONCOEUR
Vadeboncoeur, Eugene F. b: 7/15/1858, Louiseville, Que. d: 10/16/35, Haverhill, Mass. 5'6", 150 lbs. Deb: 7/11/1884

YEAR	TM/L	G	AB	R	H	2B	3B	HR	RBI	BB	SO	AVG	OBP	SLG	PRO+	BR	/A	RC	SB	CS	SBR	FR	POS	TPR
1884	Phi-N	4	14	1	3	0	0	0	3	1	2	.214	.267	.214	56	-1	-1	1				0	/C	0.0

■ HARRY VAHRENHORST
Vahrenhorst, Harry Henry "Van" b: 2/13/1885, St.Louis, Mo. d: 10/10/43, St.Louis, Mo. BR/TR, 6'1", 175 lbs. Deb: 9/21/04

YEAR	TM/L	G	AB	R	H	2B	3B	HR	RBI	BB	SO	AVG	OBP	SLG	PRO+	BR	/A	RC	SB	CS	SBR	FR	POS	TPR
1904	StL-A	1	1	0	0	0	0	0	0	0	0	.000	.000	.000	-99	-0	-0	0	0			0	H	0.0

■ MIKE VAIL
Vail, Michael Lewis b: 11/10/51, San Francisco, Cal. BR/TR, 6'1", 180 lbs. Deb: 8/18/75

YEAR	TM/L	G	AB	R	H	2B	3B	HR	RBI	BB	SO	AVG	OBP	SLG	PRO+	BR	/A	RC	SB	CS	SBR	FR	POS	TPR
1975	NY-N	38	162	17	49	8	1	3	17	9	37	.302	.339	.420	115	2	2	23	0	0	0	8	O	1.0
1976	NY-N	53	143	8	31	5	1	0	9	6	19	.217	.248	.266	49	-10	-9	9	0	1	-1	-2	O	-1.3
1977	NY-N	108	279	29	73	12	1	8	35	19	58	.262	.313	.398	94	-5	-3	30	0	7	-4	-0	O	-1.0
1978	Cle-A	14	34	2	8	2	1	0	2	1	9	.235	.257	.353	71	-1	-1	3	1	1	-0	0	/OD	-0.1
	Chi-N	74	180	15	60	6	2	4	33	3	24	.333	.344	.456	109	4	2	25	0	1	-1	-8	O/3	-0.7
1979	Chi-N	87	179	28	60	8	2	7	35	14	27	.335	.383	.520	131	10	8	34	0	2	-1	-5	O/3	0.1
1980	Chi-N	114	312	30	93	17	2	6	47	14	77	.298	.330	.423	101	3	0	40	2	5	-2	-5	O	-1.0
1981	Cin-N	31	31	1	5	0	0	0	3	0	9	.161	.161	.161	-8	-4	-4	1	0	0	0	0	/O	-0.4
1982	Cin-N	78	189	9	48	10	1	4	29	6	33	.254	.277	.381	81	-5	-6	18	0	0	0	1	O	-0.4
1983	SF-N	18	26	1	4	1	0	0	3	0	7	.154	.185	.192	5	-3	-3	1	0	0	0	-1	/1O	-0.4
	Mon-N	34	53	5	15	2	0	2	4	8	10	.283	.387	.434	128	2	2	9	0	0	0	2	O/13	0.4
	Yr	52	79	6	19	3	0	2	7	8	17	.241	.326	.354	90	-1	-1	10	0	0	0	1		0.0
1984	LA-N	16	16	1	1	0	0	0	2	1	7	.063	.118	.063	-49	-3	-3	0	0	0	0	0	/O	-0.2
Total	10	665	1604	146	447	71	11	34	219	81	317	.279	.315	.400	95	-11	-15	192	3	17	-9	-9	O/13D	-4.0

■ ROY VALDES
Valdes, Rogelio Lazaro (Rojas) b: 2/20/20, Havana, Cuba BR/TR, 5'11", 185 lbs. Deb: 5/03/44

YEAR	TM/L	G	AB	R	H	2B	3B	HR	RBI	BB	SO	AVG	OBP	SLG	PRO+	BR	/A	RC	SB	CS	SBR	FR	POS	TPR
1944	Was-A	1	1	0	0	0	0	0	0	0	0	.000	.000	.000	-99	-0	-0	0	0	0	0	0	H	0.0

■ SANDY VALDESPINO
Valdespino, Hilario (Borroto) b: 1/14/39, San Jose De Las Lajas, Cuba BL/TL, 5'8", 170 lbs. Deb: 4/12/65

YEAR	TM/L	G	AB	R	H	2B	3B	HR	RBI	BB	SO	AVG	OBP	SLG	PRO+	BR	/A	RC	SB	CS	SBR	FR	POS	TPR
1965	*Min-A	108	245	38	64	8	2	1	22	20	28	.261	.322	.322	80	-5	-6	26	7	4	-0	-0	O	-0.9
1966	Min-A	52	108	11	19	1	1	2	9	4	24	.176	.212	.259	33	-9	-10	5	2	2	-1	-2	O	-1.4
1967	Min-A	99	97	9	16	2	0	1	3	5	22	.165	.206	.216	23	-9	-10	4	3	1	0	3	O	-0.8
1968	Atl-N	36	86	8	20	1	0	1	4	10	20	.233	.320	.279	81	-2	-2	8	0	0	0	-1	O	-0.4
1969	Hou-N	41	119	17	29	4	0	0	12	15	19	.244	.328	.277	73	-4	-4	12	2	2	-1	-2	O	-0.8
	Sea-A	20	38	3	8	1	0	0	2	1	7	.211	.250	.237	37	-3	-3	2	0	1	-1	2	/O	-0.1
1970	Mil-A	8	9	0	0	0	0	0	0	0	4	.000	.000	.000	-99	-2	-2	0	0	0	0	0	O	-0.2
1971	KC-A	18	63	10	20	6	0	2	15	2	5	.317	.338	.508	138	3	3	10	0	0	0	-3	O	0.0
Total	7	382	765	96	176	23	3	7	67	57	129	.230	.288	.295	66	-32	-34	67	14	10	-2	-3	O	-4.6

■ JULIO VALDEZ
Valdez, Julio Julian (b: Julio Julian Castillo (Valdez) b: 6/3/56, San Cristobal, D.R. BB/TR, 6'2", 160 lbs. Deb: 9/02/80

YEAR	TM/L	G	AB	R	H	2B	3B	HR	RBI	BB	SO	AVG	OBP	SLG	PRO+	BR	/A	RC	SB	CS	SBR	FR	POS	TPR
1980	Bos-A	8	19	4	5	1	0	1	4	0	5	.263	.300	.474	103	-0	-0	3	2	0	1	7	/S	0.8
1981	Bos-A	17	23	1	5	0	0	0	3	0	2	.217	.217	.217	24	-2	-2	1	0	1	-1	3	S	0.1
1982	Bos-A	28	20	3	5	1	0	0	1	0	7	.250	.250	.300	48	-1	-2	2	1	0	0	7	S/D	0.7
1983	Bos-A	12	25	3	3	0	0	0	0	1	4	.120	.185	.120	-13	-4	-4	1	0	0	0	-1	/2SD	-0.4
Total	4	65	87	11	18	2	0	1	8	1	18	.207	.233	.264	36	-7	-8	6	3	1	0	16	/S2D	1.2

■ JOSE VALDIVIELSO
Valdivielso, Jose (Lopez) (b: Jose Martinez De Valdivielso (Lopez)) b: 5/22/34, Matanzas, Cuba BR/TR, 6'1", 175 lbs. Deb: 6/21/55

YEAR	TM/L	G	AB	R	H	2B	3B	HR	RBI	BB	SO	AVG	OBP	SLG	PRO+	BR	/A	RC	SB	CS	SBR	FR	POS	TPR
1955	Was-A	94	294	32	65	12	5	2	28	21	38	.221	.280	.316	63	-17	-15	26	1	2	-1	9	S	0.3
1956	Was-A	90	246	18	58	8	2	4	29	29	36	.236	.319	.333	72	-10	-10	26	3	1	0	16	S	1.4
1959	Was-A	24	14	1	4	0	0	0	0	1	3	.286	.333	.286	72	-1	-0	1	0	0	0	5	S	0.6
1960	Was-A	117	268	23	57	1	1	2	19	20	36	.213	.277	.246	43	-21	-21	19	1	2	-1	-9	*S/3	-0.4
1961	Min-A	76	149	15	29	5	0	1	9	8	19	.195	.236	.248	28	-15	-16	8	1	1	-0	-2	S23	-1.2
Total	5	401	971	89	213	26	8	9	85	79	132	.219	.284	.290	55	-64	-62	80	6	6	-2	38	S/23	0.7

■ ELLIS VALENTINE
Valentine, Ellis Clarence b: 7/30/54, Helena, Ark. BR/TR, 6'4", 205 lbs. Deb: 9/03/75

YEAR	TM/L	G	AB	R	H	2B	3B	HR	RBI	BB	SO	AVG	OBP	SLG	PRO+	BR	/A	RC	SB	CS	SBR	FR	POS	TPR
1975	Mon-N	12	33	2	12	4	0	1	3	2	4	.364	.400	.576	161	3	3	7	0	0	0	-1	O	0.1
1976	Mon-N	94	305	36	85	15	2	7	39	30	51	.279	.343	.410	108	5	3	46	14	1	4	4	O	0.8
1977	Mon-N	127	508	63	149	28	2	25	76	30	58	.293	.333	.504	124	13	14	78	13	5	1	-3	*O	0.8
1978	Mon-N	151	570	75	165	35	4	25	76	35	88	.289	.333	.489	129	18	19	90	13	8	-1	11	*O	2.5
1979	Mon-N	146	548	73	151	29	3	21	82	22	74	.276	.305	.454	105	1	1	65	11	9	-2	1	*O	-0.3
1980	Mon-N	86	311	40	98	22	2	13	67	25	44	.315	.372	.524	147	19	19	60	5	5	-2	1	O	1.2
1981	Mon-N	22	76	8	16	3	0	3	15	6	11	.211	.268	.368	78	-2	-2	7	0	1	-1	-2	O	-0.5
	NY-N	48	169	15	35	8	1	5	21	5	38	.207	.230	.355	65	-9	-8	12	0	3	-1	0	O	-1.2
	Yr	70	245	23	51	11	1	8	36	11	49	.208	.242	.359	69	-11	-11	19	0	4	-2	-2		-1.7
1982	NY-N	111	337	33	97	14	2	8	48	5	38	.288	.300	.407	97	-3	-3	36	1	3	-2	-2	O	-0.7

YEAR	TM/L	G	AB	R	H	2B	3B	HR	RBI	BB	SO	AVG	OBP	SLG	PRO+	BR	/A	RC	SB	CS	SBR	FR	POS	TPR
1983	Cal-A	86	271	30	65	10	2	13	43	18	48	.240	.287	.435	97	-3	-2	33	2	1	0	-5	O	-0.7
1985	Tex-A	11	38	5	8	1	0	2	4	2	8	.211	.250	.395	72	-2	-2	3	0	1	-1	-1	/OD	-0.2
Total	10	894	3166	380	881	169	15	123	474	180	462	.278	.319	.458	113	39	42	437	59	37	-5	1	O/D	1.8

■ FRED VALENTINE
Valentine, Fred Lee "Squeaky"   b: 1/19/35, Clarksdale, Miss.   BB/TR, 6'1", 190 lbs.   Deb: 9/07/59

YEAR	TM/L	G	AB	R	H	2B	3B	HR	RBI	BB	SO	AVG	OBP	SLG	PRO+	BR	/A	RC	SB	CS	SBR	FR	POS	TPR
1959	Bal-A	12	19	0	6	0	0	0	1	3	4	.316	.409	.316	104	0	0	2	0	1	-1	0	/O	0.0
1963	Bal-A	26	41	5	11	1	0	0	1	8	5	.268	.388	.293	96	0	0	5	0	0	0	-1	O	0.0
1964	Was-A	102	212	20	48	5	0	4	20	21	44	.226	.305	.307	71	-8	-8	20	4	2	0	-3	O	-1.3
1965	Was-A	12	29	6	7	0	0	0	1	4	5	.241	.353	.241	73	-1	-1	3	3	0	1	1	O	0.1
1966	Was-A	146	508	77	140	29	7	16	59	51	63	.276	.353	.455	132	20	21	81	22	10	1	6	*O/1	2.3
1967	Was-A	151	457	52	107	16	1	11	44	56	76	.234	.331	.346	104	1	3	58	17	3	3	-10	*O	-0.7
1968	Was-A	37	101	11	24	2	0	3	7	6	11	.238	.294	.347	96	-1	-1	9	1	0	0	-2	O	-0.3
	Bal-A	47	91	9	17	3	2	2	5	7	20	.187	.253	.330	75	-3	-3	8	0	0	0	0	O	-0.3
	Yr	84	192	20	41	5	2	5	12	13	31	.214	.274	.339	86	-4	-4	17	1	0	0	-2		-0.6
Total	7	533	1458	180	360	56	10	36	138	156	228	.247	.331	.373	106	9	13	187	47	16	5	-8	O/1	-0.2

■ BOB VALENTINE
Valentine, Robert   Deb: 5/20/1876

YEAR	TM/L	G	AB	R	H	2B	3B	HR	RBI	BB	SO	AVG	OBP	SLG	PRO+	BR	/A	RC	SB	CS	SBR	FR	POS	TPR
1876	NY-N	1	3	0	0	0	0	0	0	0	0	.000	.000	.000	-99	-1	-1	0				-0	/C	0.0

■ BOBBY VALENTINE
Valentine, Robert John   b: 5/13/50, Stamford, Conn.   BR/TR, 5'10", 189 lbs.   Deb: 9/02/69   MC

YEAR	TM/L	G	AB	R	H	2B	3B	HR	RBI	BB	SO	AVG	OBP	SLG	PRO+	BR	/A	RC	SB	CS	SBR	FR	POS	TPR
1969	LA-N	5	0	3	0	0	0	0	0	0	0	—	—	—	—	0	0	0	0	0	0	0	R	0.0
1971	LA-N	101	281	32	70	10	2	1	25	15	20	.249	.292	.310	75	-11	-9	24	5	3	-0	1	S32O	-0.2
1972	LA-N	119	391	42	107	11	2	3	32	27	33	.274	.324	.335	90	-6	-5	41	5	5	-2	3	23OS	0.3
1973	Cal-A	32	126	12	38	5	2	1	13	5	9	.302	.328	.397	112	0	1	17	6	1	1	0	S/O	0.6
1974	Cal-A	117	371	39	97	10	3	3	39	25	25	.261	.313	.329	90	-7	-5	39	8	5	-1	-11	OS3/2D	-1.5
1975	Cal-A	26	57	5	16	2	0	0	5	4	3	.281	.339	.316	92	-1	-0	6	0	2	-1	-1	D/13O	-0.2
	SD-N	7	15	1	2	0	0	1	1	4	0	.133	.316	.333	86	-0	-0	2	1	0	0	-1	/O	0.0
1976	SD-N	15	49	3	18	4	0	0	4	6	2	.367	.436	.449	165	4	4	9	0	1	-1	1	O/1	0.5
1977	SD-N	44	67	5	12	3	0	1	10	7	10	.179	.257	.269	46	-6	-5	4	0	0	0	-1	S3/1	-0.4
	NY-N	42	83	8	11	1	0	1	3	6	9	.133	.191	.181	0	-12	-11	2	0	0	0	-1	1S/3	-1.0
	Yr	86	150	13	23	4	0	2	13	13	19	.153	.221	.220	20	-17	-16	7	0	0	0	-2		-1.4
1978	NY-N	69	160	17	43	7	0	1	18	19	18	.269	.350	.331	95	-1	-1	18	1	1	-0	-9	2/3	-0.7
1979	Sea-A	62	98	9	27	6	0	0	7	22	5	.276	.408	.337	102	2	2	14	1	2	-1	-6	SO/23C	-0.2
Total	10	639	1698	176	441	59	9	12	157	140	134	.260	.319	.326	86	-39	-29	177	27	20	-4	-25	SO23/1DC	-3.1

■ BENNY VALENZUELA
Valenzuela, Benjamin Beltran "Papelero"   b: 6/2/33, Los Mochis, Mexico   BR/TR, 5'10", 175 lbs.   Deb: 4/27/58

YEAR	TM/L	G	AB	R	H	2B	3B	HR	RBI	BB	SO	AVG	OBP	SLG	PRO+	BR	/A	RC	SB	CS	SBR	FR	POS	TPR
1958	StL-N	10	14	0	3	1	0	0	2	1	1	.214	.266	.286	45	-1	-1	1	0	0	0	0	/3	0.0

■ DAVE VALLE
Valle, David   b: 10/30/60, Bayside, N.Y.   BR/TR, 6'2", 200 lbs.   Deb: 9/07/84

YEAR	TM/L	G	AB	R	H	2B	3B	HR	RBI	BB	SO	AVG	OBP	SLG	PRO+	BR	/A	RC	SB	CS	SBR	FR	POS	TPR
1984	Sea-A	13	27	4	8	1	0	1	4	1	5	.296	.321	.444	111	0	0	4	0	0	0	2	C	0.3
1985	Sea-A	31	70	2	11	1	0	0	4	1	17	.157	.181	.171	-3	-10	-10	2	0	0	0	-1	C	-0.9
1986	Sea-A	22	53	10	18	3	0	5	15	7	7	.340	.417	.679	191	7	7	14	0	0	0	-4	C/1	0.3
1987	Sea-A	95	324	40	83	16	3	12	53	15	46	.256	.295	.435	86	-5	-8	38	2	0	1	1	CD/1O	0.1
1988	Sea-A	93	290	29	67	15	2	10	50	18	38	.231	.297	.400	89	-3	-5	31	0	1	-1	6	C/1D	0.4
1989	Sea-A	94	316	32	75	10	3	7	34	29	32	.237	.313	.354	85	-5	-6	34	0	0	0	-3	C	-0.5
1990	Sea-A	107	308	37	66	15	0	7	33	45	48	.214	.328	.331	84	-5	-6	34	1	2	-1	0	*C/1	-0.3
Total	7	455	1388	154	328	61	8	42	193	116	193	.236	.307	.383	86	-22	-27	157	3	3	-1	1	C/D1O	-0.7

■ HECTOR VALLE
Valle, Hector Jose   b: 10/27/40, Vega Baja, P.R.   BR/TR, 5'9", 180 lbs.   Deb: 6/06/65

YEAR	TM/L	G	AB	R	H	2B	3B	HR	RBI	BB	SO	AVG	OBP	SLG	PRO+	BR	/A	RC	SB	CS	SBR	FR	POS	TPR
1965	LA-N	9	13	1	4	0	0	0	2	2	3	.308	.400	.308	110	0	0	2	0	0	0	-0	/C	0.0

■ ELMER VALO
Valo, Elmer William   b: 3/5/21, Ribnik, Czech.   BL/TR, 5'11", 190 lbs.   Deb: 9/22/40   C

YEAR	TM/L	G	AB	R	H	2B	3B	HR	RBI	BB	SO	AVG	OBP	SLG	PRO+	BR	/A	RC	SB	CS	SBR	FR	POS	TPR
1940	Phi-A	6	23	6	8	1	0	0	0	3	0	.348	.423	.348	104	0	0	4	2	0	1	1	/O	0.1
1941	Phi-A	15	50	13	21	0	1	2	6	4	2	.420	.463	.580	179	5	5	14	0	0	0	-1	O	0.4
1942	Phi-A	133	459	64	115	13	10	2	40	70	21	.251	.355	.336	95	-1	-1	58	13	8	-1	-2	*O	-1.1
1943	Phi-A	77	249	31	55	6	2	3	18	35	13	.221	.319	.297	81	-5	-5	24	2	6	-3	-4	O	-1.4
1946	Phi-A	108	348	59	107	21	6	1	31	60	18	.307	.411	.411	131	17	17	64	9	8	-2	-1	O	1.0
1947	Phi-A	112	370	60	111	12	6	5	36	64	21	.300	.406	.405	123	16	15	69	11	3	2	-3	*O	0.9
1948	Phi-A	113	383	72	117	17	4	3	46	81	13	.305	.432	.394	120	16	16	72	10	6	-1	-5	*O	0.6
1949	Phi-A	150	547	86	155	27	12	5	85	119	32	.283	.413	.404	121	18	20	101	14	11	-2	8	*O	2.2
1950	Phi-A	129	446	62	125	16	5	10	46	82	22	.280	.400	.406	109	7	9	81	12	7	-1	2	*O	0.7
1951	Phi-A	123	444	75	134	27	8	7	55	75	20	.302	.412	.446	129	23	21	87	11	6	-0	-2	*O	1.4
1952	Phi-A	129	388	69	109	26	4	5	47	101	16	.281	.432	.407	126	24	21	76	12	11	-3	-6	*O	0.9
1953	Phi-A	50	85	15	19	3	0	0	9	22	7	.224	.383	.259	73	-2	-2	10	0	1	-1	0	O	-0.2
1954	Phi-A	95	224	28	48	11	6	1	33	51	18	.214	.360	.330	90	-1	-1	31	2	1	0	-2	O	-0.4
1955	KC-A	112	283	50	103	17	4	3	37	52	18	.364	.463	.484	153	25	24	67	5	3	-0	-2	O	1.8
1956	KC-A	9	9	1	2	0	0	0	2	1	1	.222	.300	.222	40	-1	-1	1	0	0	0	0	/O	0.0
	Phi-N	98	291	40	84	13	3	5	37	48	21	.289	.395	.405	118	9	9	48	7	6	-2	-1	O	0.3
1957	Bro-N	81	161	14	44	10	1	4	26	25	16	.273	.374	.422	104	4	2	24	0	1	-1	-4	O	-0.3
1958	LA-N	65	101	9	25	2	1	1	14	12	11	.248	.327	.317	69	-4	-4	11	0	1	-1	-4	O	-0.9
1959	Cle-A	34	24	3	7	0	0	0	5	7	0	.292	.452	.292	113	1	1	3	0	0	0	0	/O	0.1
1960	NY-A	8	5	1	0	0	0	0	0	2	1	.000	.286	.000	-17	-1	-1	0	0	0	0	0	/O	0.0
	Was-A	76	64	6	18	3	0	0	16	17	4	.281	.439	.328	112	2	2	11	0	0	0	0	O	0.2
	Yr	84	69	7	18	3	0	0	16	19	5	.261	.427	.304	103	2	2	11	0	0	0	0		0.2
1961	Min-A	33	32	0	5	2	0	0	4	3	3	.156	.250	.219	25	-3	-4	2	0	0	0	0	/O	-0.3
	Phi-N	50	43	4	8	2	0	1	8	8	6	.186	.327	.302	69	-2	-2	5	0	0	0	0	/O	-0.1
Total	20	1806	5029	768	1420	228	73	58	601	942	284	.282	.399	.391	114	147	143	864	110	79	-14	-26	*O	5.9

■ DEACON Van BUREN
Van Buren, Edward Eugene   b: 12/14/1870, LaSalle Co., Ill.   d: 6/29/57, Portland, Ore.   BL/TR, 5'10", 175 lbs.   Deb: 4/21/04

YEAR	TM/L	G	AB	R	H	2B	3B	HR	RBI	BB	SO	AVG	OBP	SLG	PRO+	BR	/A	RC	SB	CS	SBR	FR	POS	TPR
1904	Bro-N	1	1	0	1	0	0	0	0	0	0	1.000	1.000	1.000	538	0	0	1	0			0	H	0.0
	Phi-N	12	43	2	10	2	0	0	3		3	.233	.283	.279	78	-1	-1	4	2			1	O	0.0
	Yr	13	44	2	11	2	0	0	3		3	.250	.298	.295	88	-1	-1	5	2			1		0.0

■ AL Van CAMP
Van Camp, Albert Joseph   b: 9/7/03, Moline, Ill.   d: 2/2/81, Davenport, Iowa   BR/TR, 5'11.5", 175 lbs.   Deb: 9/11/28

YEAR	TM/L	G	AB	R	H	2B	3B	HR	RBI	BB	SO	AVG	OBP	SLG	PRO+	BR	/A	RC	SB	CS	SBR	FR	POS	TPR
1928	Cle-A	5	17	0	4	1	0	0	2	0	1	.235	.235	.294	38	-2	-2	1	1	0	0	-1	/1	-0.1
1931	Bos-A	101	324	34	89	15	4	0	33	20	24	.275	.319	.346	79	-12	-10	36	3	2	-0	-5	O1	-1.9
1932	Bos-A	34	103	10	23	4	2	0	6	4	17	.223	.252	.301	44	-9	-9	8	0	0	0	1	1	-0.9
Total	3	140	444	44	116	20	6	0	41	24	42	.261	.301	.333	69	-23	-20	45	4	2	0	-5	/O1	-2.9

■ CARL VANDAGRIFT
Vandagrift, Carl William   b: 4/22/1883, Cantrall, Ill.   d: 10/9/20, Fort Wayne, Ind.   BR/TR, 5'8", 155 lbs.   Deb: 5/19/14

YEAR	TM/L	G	AB	R	H	2B	3B	HR	RBI	BB	SO	AVG	OBP	SLG	PRO+	BR	/A	RC	SB	CS	SBR	FR	POS	TPR
1914	Ind-F	43	136	25	34	4	0	0	9	9	15	.250	.306	.279	62	-5	-7	17	7			-7	23/S	-1.3

■ FRED Van DUSEN
Van Dusen, Frederick William   b: 7/31/37, Jackson Heights, N.Y.   BL, 6'3", 180 lbs.   Deb: 9/11/55

YEAR	TM/L	G	AB	R	H	2B	3B	HR	RBI	BB	SO	AVG	OBP	SLG	PRO+	BR	/A	RC	SB	CS	SBR	FR	POS	TPR
1955	Phi-N	1	0	0	0	0	0	0	0	0	0	—	1.000	—	199	0	0	0	0	0	0	0	H	0.0

YEAR	TM/L	G	AB	R	H	2B	3B	HR	RBI	BB	SO	AVG	OBP	SLG	PRO+	BR	/A	RC	SB	CS	SBR	FR	POS	TPR

■ BILL Van DYKE   Van Dyke, William Jennings b: 12/15/1863, Paris, Ill. d: 5/5/33, ElPaso, Tex. BR/TR, 5′8″, 170 lbs. Deb: 4/17/1890

YEAR	TM/L	G	AB	R	H	2B	3B	HR	RBI	BB	SO	AVG	OBP	SLG	PRO+	BR	/A	RC	SB	CS	SBR	FR	POS	TPR
1890	Tol-a	129	502	74	129	14	11	2		25		.257	.294	.341	87	-9	-11	73	73			-6	*O3/2C	-1.9
1892	StL-N	4	16	2	2	0	0	0	1	0	1	.125	.125	.125	-25	-2	-2	0	0			-1	/O	-0.2
1893	Bos-N	3	12	2	3	1	0	0	1	0	1	.250	.250	.333	52	-1	-1	1	1			-1	/O	-0.1
Total	3	136	530	78	134	15	11	2	2	25	2	.253	.288	.334	83	-12	-14	75	74			-7	O/32C	-2.2

■ DAVE Van GORDER   Van Gorder, David Thomas b: 3/27/57, Los Angeles, Cal. BR/TR, 6′2″, 205 lbs. Deb: 6/15/82

YEAR	TM/L	G	AB	R	H	2B	3B	HR	RBI	BB	SO	AVG	OBP	SLG	PRO+	BR	/A	RC	SB	CS	SBR	FR	POS	TPR
1982	Cin-N	51	137	4	25	3	1	0	7	14	19	.182	.263	.219	35	-11	-12	8	1	0	0	-1	C	-1.2
1984	Cin-N	38	101	10	23	2	0	0	6	12	17	.228	.310	.248	56	-5	-6	8	0	0	0	1	C/1	-0.2
1985	Cin-N	73	151	12	36	7	0	2	24	9	19	.238	.286	.325	67	-6	-7	13	0	0	0	-4	C	-0.8
1986	Cin-N	9	10	0	0	0	0	0	0	1	2	.000	.091	.000	-70	-2	-2	0	0	0	0	1	/C	-0.1
1987	Bal-A	12	21	4	5	0	0	1	1	3	6	.238	.333	.381	91	-0	-0	3	0	0	0	0	C	0.1
Total	5	183	420	30	89	12	1	3	38	39	63	.212	.282	.267	52	-25	-27	32	1	0	0	-3	C/1	-2.2

■ GEORGE Van HALTREN   Van Haltren, George Edward Martin "Rip"
b: 3/30/1866, St.Louis, Mo. d: 9/29/45, Oakland, Cal. BL/TL, 5′11″, 170 lbs. Deb: 6/27/1887 M

YEAR	TM/L	G	AB	R	H	2B	3B	HR	RBI	BB	SO	AVG	OBP	SLG	PRO+	BR	/A	RC	SB	CS	SBR	FR	POS	TPR
1887	Chi-N	45	172	30	35	4	0	3	17	15	15	.203	.271	.279	48	-10	-14	17	12			-4	OP	-1.1
1888	Chi-N	81	318	46	90	9	14	4	34	22	34	.283	.329	.437	135	16	12	54	21			-1	OP	1.7
1889	Chi-N	134	543	126	168	20	10	9	81	82	41	.309	.405	.433	129	29	24	109	28			-2	*O/S2	1.5
1890	Bro-P	92	376	84	126	8	9	5	54	41	23	.335	.405	.444	121	16	12	84	35			5	OP/S	1.6
1891	Bal-a	139	566	136	180	14	15	9	83	71	46	.318	.398	.443	142	33	31	133	75			-12	OS/P2	1.7
1892	Bal-N	135	556	105	168	20	12	7	57	70	34	.302	.382	.419	140	31	28	110	49			0	*O/P31SM	2.3
	Pit-N	13	55	10	11	2	2	0	5	6	0	.200	.279	.309	79	-1	-1	7	6			-2	O	-0.3
	Yr	148	611	115	179	22	14	7	62	76	34	.293	.373	.409	134	29	26	117	55			-2		2.0
1893	Pit-N	124	529	129	179	14	11	3	79	75	25	.338	.422	.423	130	24	25	113	37			-6	*OS/2	1.2
1894	*NY-N	137	519	109	172	22	4	7	104	55	22	.331	.400	.430	103	3	4	109	43			-2	*O	-0.5
1895	NY-N	131	521	113	177	23	19	8	103	57	29	.340	.408	.503	140	28	30	123	32			-3	*O/P	1.3
1896	NY-N	133	562	136	197	18	21	5	74	55	36	.351	.410	.484	141	30	33	131	39			4	*O/P	2.4
1897	NY-N	129	564	117	186	22	9	2	64	40		.330	.375	.417	114	9	12	110	50			9	*O	0.9
1898	NY-N	156	654	129	204	28	16	2	68	59		.312	.372	.413	132	23	26	117	36			-2	*O	1.3
1899	NY-N	151	604	117	182	21	3	2	58	74		.301	.378	.356	108	7	10	95	31			3	*O	0.3
1900	NY-N	141	571	114	180	30	7	1	51	50		.315	.371	.398	120	12	16	104	**45**			10	*O/P	1.2
1901	NY-N	135	543	82	182	23	6	1	47	51		.335	.394	.405	140	25	28	100	24			4	*O/P	1.8
1902	NY-N	24	88	14	23	1	2	0	7	17		.261	.381	.318	119	3	3	13	6			2	O	0.3
1903	NY-N	84	280	42	72	6	1	0	28	28		.257	.325	.286	74	-8	-9	32	14			-6	O	-1.8
Total	17	1984	8021	1639	2532	285	161	69	1014	868	305	.316	.385	.417	124	269	271	1560	583			-2	*O/PS231	15.8

■ JOHN VANN   Vann, John Silas b: 6/7/1893, Fairland, Okla. d: 6/10/58, Shreveport, La. BR/TR, Deb: 6/11/13

YEAR	TM/L	G	AB	R	H	2B	3B	HR	RBI	BB	SO	AVG	OBP	SLG	PRO+	BR	/A	RC	SB	CS	SBR	FR	POS	TPR
1913	StL-N	1	1	0	0	0	0	0	0	0	1	.000	.000	.000	-99	-0	-0	0	0			0	H	0.0

■ JAY Van NOY   Van Noy, Jay Lowell b: 11/4/28, Garland, Utah BL/TR, 6′1″, 200 lbs. Deb: 6/18/51

YEAR	TM/L	G	AB	R	H	2B	3B	HR	RBI	BB	SO	AVG	OBP	SLG	PRO+	BR	/A	RC	SB	CS	SBR	FR	POS	TPR
1951	StL-N	6	7	1	0	0	0	0	0	1	6	.000	.125	.000	-63	-2	-2	0	0	0	0	0	/O	-0.1

■ MAURICE Van ROBAYS   Van Robays, Maurice Rene "Bomber" b: 11/15/14, Detroit, Mich. d: 3/1/65, Detroit, Mich. BR/TR, 6′0.5″, 190 lbs. Deb: 9/07/39

YEAR	TM/L	G	AB	R	H	2B	3B	HR	RBI	BB	SO	AVG	OBP	SLG	PRO+	BR	/A	RC	SB	CS	SBR	FR	POS	TPR
1939	Pit-N	27	105	13	33	9	0	2	16	6	10	.314	.351	.457	118	2	2	16	0			-4	O/3	-0.1
1940	Pit-N	145	572	82	156	27	7	11	116	33	58	.273	.316	.402	98	-4	-3	69	2			-5	*O/1	-1.3
1941	Pit-N	129	457	62	129	23	5	4	78	41	29	.282	.343	.381	104	2	2	57	0			6	*O	0.3
1942	Pit-N	100	328	29	76	13	5	1	46	30	24	.232	.298	.311	76	-9	-10	30	0			6	O	-0.6
1943	Pit-N	69	236	32	68	17	7	1	35	18	19	.288	.344	.432	119	6	5	34	0			-5	O	-0.1
1946	Pit-N	59	146	14	31	5	3	1	12	11	15	.212	.272	.308	63	-7	-8	11	0			-4	O/1	-1.3
Total	6	529	1844	232	493	94	27	20	303	139	155	.267	.321	.380	97	-10	-11	218	2			-6	O/13	-3.1

■ ANDY Van SLYKE   Van Slyke, Andrew James b: 12/21/60, Utica, N.Y. BL/TR, 6′1″, 190 lbs. Deb: 6/17/83

YEAR	TM/L	G	AB	R	H	2B	3B	HR	RBI	BB	SO	AVG	OBP	SLG	PRO+	BR	/A	RC	SB	CS	SBR	FR	POS	TPR
1983	StL-N	101	309	51	81	15	5	8	38	46	64	.262	.360	.421	115	7	7	50	21	7	2	-2	O3/1	0.5
1984	StL-N	137	361	45	88	16	4	7	50	63	71	.244	.356	.368	107	4	5	54	28	5	5	0	O31	0.6
1985	*StL-N	146	424	61	110	25	6	13	55	47	54	.259	.336	.439	116	8	9	66	34	6	7	-4	*O/1	0.7
1986	StL-N	137	418	48	113	23	7	13	61	47	85	.270	.345	.452	119	10	10	68	21	8	2	3	*O1	1.2
1987	Pit-N	157	564	93	165	36	11	21	82	56	122	.293	.361	.507	126	21	20	108	34	8	5	1	*O/1	2.0
1988	Pit-N	154	587	101	169	23	**15**	25	100	57	126	.288	.352	.506	146	31	32	107	30	9	4	10	*O	4.4
1989	Pit-N	130	476	64	113	18	9	9	53	47	100	.237	.310	.370	97	-4	-2	55	16	4	2	7	*O/1	0.5
1990	*Pit-N	136	493	67	140	26	6	17	77	66	89	.284	.370	.465	133	19	22	89	14	4	2	-4	*O	1.5
Total	8	1098	3632	530	979	182	63	113	516	429	711	.270	.349	.448	122	96	103	597	198	51	29	10	O/13	11.4

■ IKE Van ZANDT   Van Zandt, Charles Isaac b: 1877, Brooklyn, N.Y. d: 9/14/08, Nashua, N.H. BL , Deb: 8/05/01

YEAR	TM/L	G	AB	R	H	2B	3B	HR	RBI	BB	SO	AVG	OBP	SLG	PRO+	BR	/A	RC	SB	CS	SBR	FR	POS	TPR
1901	NY-N	3	6	1	1	0	0	0	0	0		.167	.167	.167	-2	-1	-1	0	0			-1	/PO	0.0
1904	Chi-N	3	11	0	0	0	0	0	0	0		.000	.000	.000	-99	-2	-2	0	0			0	/O	-0.2
1905	StL-A	94	322	31	75	15	1	1	20	7		.233	.249	.295	78	-10	-8	27	7			-11	O/P1	-2.5
Total	3	100	339	32	76	15	1	1	20	7		.224	.240	.283	71	-13	-11	27	7			-12	/OP1	-2.7

■ DICK Van ZANT   Van Zant, Richard "Foghorn Dick" b: 11/1864, Indiana d: 8/6/12, Wayne Co., Ind. Deb: 10/04/1888

YEAR	TM/L	G	AB	R	H	2B	3B	HR	RBI	BB	SO	AVG	OBP	SLG	PRO+	BR	/A	RC	SB	CS	SBR	FR	POS	TPR
1888	Cle-a	10	31	1	8	1	0	0	1	1		.258	.303	.290	96	-0	-0	3	1			0	3	0.0

■ EDDIE VARGAS   Vargas, Hediberto (Rodriguez) b: 2/23/59, Guanica, P.R. BR/TR, 6′4″, 205 lbs. Deb: 9/08/82

YEAR	TM/L	G	AB	R	H	2B	3B	HR	RBI	BB	SO	AVG	OBP	SLG	PRO+	BR	/A	RC	SB	CS	SBR	FR	POS	TPR
1982	Pit-N	8	8	1	3	1	0	0	3	0	2	.375	.375	.500	139	0	0	2	0	0	0	0	/1	0.0
1984	Pit-N	18	31	3	7	2	0	0	2	3	5	.226	.294	.290	65	-1	-1	3	0	0	0	-0	1	-0.1
Total	2	26	39	4	10	3	0	0	5	3	7	.256	.310	.333	80	-1	-1	4	0	0	0	-0	/1	-0.1

■ BUCK VARNER   Varner, Glen Gann b: 8/17/30, Hixson, Tenn. BL/TR, 5′10″, 170 lbs. Deb: 9/19/52

YEAR	TM/L	G	AB	R	H	2B	3B	HR	RBI	BB	SO	AVG	OBP	SLG	PRO+	BR	/A	RC	SB	CS	SBR	FR	POS	TPR
1952	Was-A	2	4	0	0	0	0	0	0	1	1	.000	.200	.000	-43	-1	-1	0	0	0	0	-0	/O	0.0

■ PETE VARNEY   Varney, Richard Fred b: 4/10/49, Roxbury, Mass. BR/TR, 6′3″, 235 lbs. Deb: 8/26/73

YEAR	TM/L	G	AB	R	H	2B	3B	HR	RBI	BB	SO	AVG	OBP	SLG	PRO+	BR	/A	RC	SB	CS	SBR	FR	POS	TPR
1973	Chi-A	5	4	0	0	0	0	0	0	1	0	.000	.200	.000	-38	-1	-1	0	0	0	0	0	/C	0.0
1974	Chi-A	9	28	1	7	0	0	0	2	1	8	.250	.276	.250	51	-2	-2	2	0	0	0	1	/C	0.0
1975	Chi-A	36	107	12	29	5	1	2	8	6	28	.271	.316	.393	98	-0	-1	14	2	0	1	-1	C/D	0.0
1976	Chi-A	14	41	5	10	2	0	3	5	2	9	.244	.279	.512	128	1	1	5	0	0	0	2	C	0.3
	Atl-N	5	10	0	1	0	0	0	0	0	2	.100	.100	.100	-41	-2	-2	0	0	0	0	0	/C	-0.1
Total	4	69	190	18	47	7	1	5	15	10	47	.247	.289	.374	86	-4	-4	21	2	0	1	2	/CD	0.2

■ GARY VARSHO   Varsho, Gary Andrew b: 6/20/61, Marshfield, Wis. BL/TR, 5′11″, 190 lbs. Deb: 7/06/88

YEAR	TM/L	G	AB	R	H	2B	3B	HR	RBI	BB	SO	AVG	OBP	SLG	PRO+	BR	/A	RC	SB	CS	SBR	FR	POS	TPR
1988	Chi-N	46	73	6	20	3	0	0	5	1	6	.274	.284	.315	69	-3	-3	7	5	0	2	0	O	-0.1
1989	Chi-N	61	87	10	16	4	2	0	6	4	13	.184	.220	.276	38	-7	-8	6	3	0	1	-0	O	-0.7
1990	Chi-N	46	48	10	12	4	0	0	1	1	6	.250	.265	.333	58	-2	-3	4	2	0	1	-0	O	-0.2
Total	3	153	208	26	48	11	2	0	12	6	25	.231	.252	.303	53	-12	-14	17	10	0	3	-1	/O	-1.0

■ JIM VATCHER   Vatcher, James Ernest b: 5/27/66, Santa Monica, Cal. BR/TR, 5′9″, 165 lbs. Deb: 5/30/90

YEAR	TM/L	G	AB	R	H	2B	3B	HR	RBI	BB	SO	AVG	OBP	SLG	PRO+	BR	/A	RC	SB	CS	SBR	FR	POS	TPR
1990	Phi-N	36	46	5	12	1	0	1	4	4	6	.261	.320	.348	84	-1	-1	5	0	0	0	-1	O	-0.2

YEAR	TM/L	G	AB	R	H	2B	3B	HR	RBI	BB	SO	AVG	OBP	SLG	PRO+	BR	/A	RC	SB	CS	SBR	FR	POS	TPR
	Atl-N	21	27	2	7	1	1	0	3	1	9	.259	.286	.370	78	-1	-1	3	0	0	0	0	/O	0.0
	Yr	57	73	7	19	2	1	1	7	5	15	.260	.308	.356	82	-2	-2	8	0	0	0	-1		-0.2

■ GLENN VAUGHAN
Vaughan, Glenn Edward "Sparky" b: 2/15/44, Compton, Cal. BB/TR, 5'11", 170 lbs. Deb: 9/20/63

YEAR	TM/L	G	AB	R	H	2B	3B	HR	RBI	BB	SO	AVG	OBP	SLG	PRO+	BR	/A	RC	SB	CS	SBR	FR	POS	TPR
1963	Hou-N	9	30	1	5	0	0	0	0	2	5	.167	.219	.167	14	-3	-3	1	1	0	0	-3	/S3	-0.5

■ ARKY VAUGHAN
Vaughan, Joseph Floyd b: 3/9/12, Clifty, Ark. d: 8/30/52, Eagleville, Cal. BL/TR, 5'10.5", 175 lbs. Deb: 4/17/32 H

YEAR	TM/L	G	AB	R	H	2B	3B	HR	RBI	BB	SO	AVG	OBP	SLG	PRO+	BR	/A	RC	SB	CS	SBR	FR	POS	TPR
1932	Pit-N	129	497	71	158	15	10	4	61	39	26	.318	.375	.412	113	9	10	79	10			-20	*S	0.1
1933	Pit-N	152	573	85	180	29	19	9	97	64	23	.314	.388	.478	146	35	35	112	3			-9	*S	3.7
1934	Pit-N	149	558	115	186	41	11	12	94	94	38	.333	.431	.511	148	44	42	135	10			3	*S	4.6
1935	Pit-N	137	499	108	192	34	10	19	99	97	18	.385	.491	.607	187	72	70	163	4			-11	*S	6.1
1936	Pit-N	156	568	122	190	30	11	9	78	118	21	.335	.453	.474	146	47	45	137	6			-11	*S	4.1
1937	Pit-N	126	469	71	151	17	17	5	72	54	22	.322	.394	.463	132	22	22	91	7			-0	*SO	2.9
1938	Pit-N	148	541	88	174	35	5	7	68	104	21	.322	.433	.444	140	36	36	115	14			18	*S	6.3
1939	Pit-N	152	595	94	182	30	11	6	62	70	20	.306	.385	.424	119	16	17	103	12			9	*S	3.5
1940	Pit-N	156	594	113	178	40	15	7	95	88	25	.300	.393	.453	134	29	29	113	12			8	*S/3	5.2
1941	Pit-N	106	374	69	118	20	7	6	38	50	13	.316	.399	.455	141	21	21	72	8			-12	S/3	1.7
1942	Bro-N	128	495	82	137	18	4	2	49	51	17	.277	.348	.341	100	2	1	63	8			-10	*3/S2	-0.8
1943	Bro-N	149	610	112	186	39	6	5	66	60	13	.305	.370	.413	126	20	20	96	20			-24	S3	0.5
1947	*Bro-N	64	126	24	41	5	2	2	25	27	11	.325	.444	.444	132	8	8	27	4			1	O3	0.7
1948	Bro-N	65	123	19	30	3	0	3	22	21	8	.244	.354	.341	86	-1	-2	15	0			2	O/3	-0.1
Total	14	1817	6622	1173	2103	356	128	96	926	937	276	.318	.406	.453	136	361	356	1323	118			-58	*S3/O2	38.5

■ FRED VAUGHN
Vaughn, Frederick Thomas "Muscles" b: 10/18/18, Coalinga, Cal. d: 3/2/64, Near Lake Wales, Fla. BR/TR, 5'10", 185 lbs. Deb: 8/20/44

YEAR	TM/L	G	AB	R	H	2B	3B	HR	RBI	BB	SO	AVG	OBP	SLG	PRO+	BR	/A	RC	SB	CS	SBR	FR	POS	TPR
1944	Was-A	30	109	10	28	2	1	1	21	9	24	.257	.319	.321	87	-2	-2	11	2	2	-1	-2	2/3	-0.2
1945	Was-A	80	268	28	63	7	4	1	25	23	48	.235	.298	.302	81	-9	-6	25	0	3	-2	-4	2/S	-1.1
Total	2	110	377	38	91	9	5	2	46	32	72	.241	.304	.308	83	-11	-8	36	2	5	-2	-6	2/3S	-1.3

■ GREG VAUGHN
Vaughn, Gregory Lamont b: 7/3/65, Sacramento, Cal. BR/TR, 6', 195 lbs. Deb: 8/10/89

YEAR	TM/L	G	AB	R	H	2B	3B	HR	RBI	BB	SO	AVG	OBP	SLG	PRO+	BR	/A	RC	SB	CS	SBR	FR	POS	TPR
1989	Mil-A	38	113	18	30	3	0	5	23	13	23	.265	.341	.425	116	2	2	18	4	1	1	-2	OD	0.1
1990	Mil-A	120	382	51	84	26	2	17	61	33	91	.220	.284	.432	101	-3	-2	44	7	4	-0	-5	*O/D	-0.7
Total	2	158	495	69	114	29	2	22	84	46	114	.230	.297	.430	104	-1	1	62	11	5	0	-7	O/D	-0.6

■ FARMER VAUGHN
Vaughn, Harry Francis b: 3/1/1864, Rural Dale, Ohio d: 2/21/14, Cincinnati, Ohio BR/TR, 6'3", 177 lbs. Deb: 10/07/1886

YEAR	TM/L	G	AB	R	H	2B	3B	HR	RBI	BB	SO	AVG	OBP	SLG	PRO+	BR	/A	RC	SB	CS	SBR	FR	POS	TPR
1886	Cin-a	1	3	0	0	0	0	0		0		.000	.250	.000	-17	-0	-0	0	0			1	/C	0.1
1888	Lou-a	51	189	15	37	4	2	1	21	4		.196	.216	.254	54	-10	-9	12	4			-1	OC	-0.7
1889	Lou-a	90	360	39	86	11	5	3	45	7	41	.239	.253	.322	66	-17	-16	34	13			6	CO1/3	-0.5
1890	NY-P	44	166	27	44	7	0	1	22	10	9	.265	.307	.325	65	-7	-10	19	6			-24	CO/32	-2.6
1891	Cin-a	51	175	21	45	7	1	1	14	14	15	.257	.316	.326	79	-3	-6	21	7			7	C/O13P	0.2
	Mil-a	25	99	13	33	7	0	0	9	4	5	.333	.359	.404	101	2	-1	15	1			2	C/1O	0.1
	Yr	76	274	34	78	14	1	1	23	18	20	.285	.331	.354	88	-1	-6	36	8			9		0.3
1892	Cin-N	91	346	45	88	10	5	2	50	16	13	.254	.295	.329	92	-5	-4	38	10			-14	C1O/3	-1.3
1893	Cin-N	121	483	68	135	17	12	1	108	35	17	.280	.332	.371	86	-9	-11	66	16			1	CO1	-0.2
1894	Cin-N	72	284	50	88	15	5	8	64	12	11	.310	.338	.482	94	-3	-5	49	5			-2	C1/OS	-0.1
1895	Cin-N	92	334	60	102	23	5	1	48	17	10	.305	.339	.413	91	-3	-6	53	15			10	C1/32	0.9
1896	Cin-N	114	433	71	127	20	9	2	66	16	7	.293	.320	.395	84	-8	-12	58	7			1	1C	-0.3
1897	Cin-N	54	199	21	58	13	5	0	30	2		.291	.299	.407	82	-5	-7	25	2			-0	1C	-0.4
1898	Cin-N	78	275	35	84	12	4	1	46	11		.305	.332	.389	102	2	-0	38	4			-3	1C	0.0
1899	Cin-N	31	108	9	19	1	0	0	2	3		.176	.198	.185	7	-13	-14	4	2			3	1/CO	-0.9
Total	13	915	3454	474	946	147	53	21	525	151	128	.274	.306	.365	82	-79	-101	432	92			-13	C1O/3S2P	-5.6

■ BOBBY VAUGHN
Vaughn, Robert b: 6/4/1885, Stamford, N.Y. d: 4/11/65, Seattle, Wash. BR/TR, 5'9", 150 lbs. Deb: 6/12/09

YEAR	TM/L	G	AB	R	H	2B	3B	HR	RBI	BB	SO	AVG	OBP	SLG	PRO+	BR	/A	RC	SB	CS	SBR	FR	POS	TPR
1909	NY-A	5	14	1	2	0	0	0	0	1		.143	.200	.143	8	-1	-1	1	1			-3	/2S	-0.4
1915	StL-F	144	521	69	146	19	9	0	32	58	38	.280	.356	.351	104	8	4	81	24			-8	*2S/3	-0.1
Total	2	149	535	70	148	19	9	0	32	59	38	.277	.352	.346	102	6	3	81	25			-11	2/S3	-0.5

■ BOBBY VEACH
Veach, Robert Hayes b: 6/29/1888, Island, Ky. d: 8/7/45, Detroit, Mich. BL/TR, 5'11", 160 lbs. Deb: 8/06/12

YEAR	TM/L	G	AB	R	H	2B	3B	HR	RBI	BB	SO	AVG	OBP	SLG	PRO+	BR	/A	RC	SB	CS	SBR	FR	POS	TPR
1912	Det-A	23	79	8	27	5	1	0	15	5		.342	.388	.430	138	5	3	14	2			2	O	0.4
1913	Det-A	137	491	54	132	22	10	0	64	53	31	.269	.346	.354	107	4	4	66	22			-5	*O	-0.7
1914	Det-A	149	531	56	146	19	14	1	72	50	29	.275	.341	.369	110	8	6	68	20	20	-6	3	*O	-0.5
1915	Det-A	152	569	81	178	40	14	3	112	68	43	.313	.390	.434	140	32	29	97	16	19	-7	2	*O	1.7
1916	Det-A	150	566	92	173	33	15	3	91	52	41	.306	.367	.433	135	26	24	94	24	15	-2	4	*O	1.9
1917	Det-A	154	571	79	182	31	12	8	103	61	44	.319	.393	.457	160	40	40	108	21			4	*O	3.9
1918	Det-A	127	499	59	139	21	13	3	78	35	23	.279	.331	.391	123	8	11	69	21			3	*O/P	0.8
1919	Det-A	139	538	87	191	45	17	3	101	33	33	.355	.398	.519	160	38	39	115	19			11	*O	4.2
1920	Det-A	154	612	92	188	39	15	11	113	36	22	.307	.353	.474	121	13	15	101	11	7	-1	15	*O	1.4
1921	Det-A	150	612	110	207	43	13	16	128	48	31	.338	.387	.529	133	27	28	123	14	10	-2	15	*O	2.7
1922	Det-A	155	618	96	202	34	13	9	126	42	27	.327	.377	.468	123	16	19	111	9	1	2	8	*O	1.7
1923	Det-A	114	293	45	94	13	3	2	39	29	21	.321	.388	.406	111	5	5	49	10	3	-2	-14	O	-1.4
1924	Bos-A	142	519	77	153	35	9	5	99	47	18	.295	.359	.426	102	0	0	81	5	5	-2	-1	*O	-1.0
1925	Bos-A	1	5	0	1	0	0	0	2	1	1	.200	.333	.200	38	-0	-0	0	0	0	0	0	/O	0.0
	NY-A	56	116	13	41	10	2	0	15	8	0	.353	.400	.474	123	4	4	20	1	4	-2	-7	O	-0.6
	*Was-A	18	37	4	9	3	0	0	8	3	3	.243	.300	.324	60	-2	-2	4	0	0	0	-3	O	-0.5
	Yr	75	158	17	51	13	2	0	25	12	4	.323	.374	.430	106	1	1	24	1	4	-2	-9		-1.1
Total	14	1821	6656	953	2063	393	147	64	1166	571	367	.310	.370	.442	127	221	225	1120	195	84		39	*O/P	14.0

■ PEEK-A-BOO VEACH
Veach, William Walter b: 6/15/1862, Indianapolis, Ind d: 11/12/37, Indianapolis, Ind. Deb: 8/24/1884

YEAR	TM/L	G	AB	R	H	2B	3B	HR	RBI	BB	SO	AVG	OBP	SLG	PRO+	BR	/A	RC	SB	CS	SBR	FR	POS	TPR
1884	KC-U	27	82	9	11	1	0	1		9		.134	.220	.183	43	-5	-3	3	0			-1	OP/21	-0.2
1887	Lou-a	1	3	0	0	0	0	0		1		.000	.250	.000	-25	-0	-0	0	0			0	/P	0.0
1890	Cle-N	64	238	24	56	10	5	0	32	33	28	.235	.336	.319	95	-1	-0	29	9			6	1	0.1
	Pit-N	8	30	6	9	1	1	2	5	8	3	.300	.447	.600	235	4	5	8	0			0	/1	0.4
	Yr	72	268	30	65	11	6	2	37	41	31	.243	.349	.351	110	3	5	37	9			7		0.5
Total	3	100	353	39	76	12	6	3	37	51	31	.215	.319	.309	96	-2	2	41	9			6	/1OP2	0.3

■ COOT VEAL
Veal, Orville Inman b: 7/9/32, Sandersville, Ga. BR/TR, 6'1", 165 lbs. Deb: 7/30/58

YEAR	TM/L	G	AB	R	H	2B	3B	HR	RBI	BB	SO	AVG	OBP	SLG	PRO+	BR	/A	RC	SB	CS	SBR	FR	POS	TPR
1958	Det-A	58	207	29	53	10	2	0	16	14	21	.256	.306	.324	69	-7	-9	19	1	1	-0	-8	S	-0.9
1959	Det-A	77	89	12	18	1	0	1	15	8	7	.202	.276	.247	42	-7	-7	7	0	0	0	10	S	0.8
1960	Det-A	27	64	8	19	5	1	0	8	11	7	.297	.400	.406	115	2	2	11	0	0	0	-2	S/32	0.2
1961	Was-A	69	218	21	44	10	0	0	8	19	29	.202	.275	.248	41	-18	-18	15	1	8	-5	0	S	-1.7
1962	Pit-N	1	1	0	0	0	0	0	0	0	1	.000	.000	.000	-99	-0	-0	0	0	0	0	0	H	0.0
1963	Det-A	15	32	5	7	0	0	0	4	4	4	.219	.306	.219	48	-2	-2	2	0	0	0	4	S	0.2
Total	6	247	611	75	141	26	3	1	51	56	69	.231	.301	.288	59	-32	-35	53	2	9	-5	4	S/32	-1.4

■ JESUS VEGA
Vega, Jesus Anthony (Morales) b: 10/14/55, Bayamon, PR. BR/TR, 6'1", 176 lbs. Deb: 9/05/79

YEAR	TM/L	G	AB	R	H	2B	3B	HR	RBI	BB	SO	AVG	OBP	SLG	PRO+	BR	/A	RC	SB	CS	SBR	FR	POS	TPR
1979	Min-A	4	7	0	0	0	0	0	0	0	2	.000	.000	.000	-96	-2	-2	0	0	0	0	0	/H	-0.1

YEAR	TM/L	G	AB	R	H	2B	3B	HR	RBI	BB	SO	AVG	OBP	SLG	PRO+	BR	/A	RC	SB	CS	SBR	FR	POS	TPR
1980	Min-A	12	30	3	5	0	0	0	4	3	7	.167	.242	.167	13	-3	-4	1	1	0	0	0	/1D	-0.2
1982	Min-A	71	199	23	53	6	0	5	29	8	19	.266	.295	.372	80	-5	-6	21	6	1	1	-1	D1/O	-0.5
Total	3	87	236	26	58	6	0	5	33	11	28	.246	.279	.335	65	-11	-12	23	7	1	2	-1	/D1O	-0.8

■ RANDY VELARDE
Velarde, Randy Lee   b: 11/24/62, Midland, Tex.   BR/TR, 6′, 185 lbs.   Deb: 8/20/87

YEAR	TM/L	G	AB	R	H	2B	3B	HR	RBI	BB	SO	AVG	OBP	SLG	PRO+	BR	/A	RC	SB	CS	SBR	FR	POS	TPR
1987	NY-A	8	22	1	4	0	0	0	1	0	6	.182	.182	.182	-3	-3	-3	1	0	0	0	0	/S	-0.2
1988	NY-A	48	115	18	20	6	0	5	12	8	24	.174	.240	.357	65	-6	-6	9	1	1	-0	8	2S3	0.5
1989	NY-A	33	100	12	34	4	2	2	11	7	14	.340	.389	.480	145	6	6	18	0	3	-2	2	3/S	0.6
1990	NY-A	95	229	21	48	6	2	5	19	20	53	.210	.276	.319	66	-11	-11	19	0	3	-2	10	3S/O2D	0.0
Total	4	184	466	52	106	16	4	12	43	35	97	.227	.287	.356	79	-14	-14	47	1	7	-4	20	3/S2OD	0.9

■ FREDDIE VELAZQUEZ
Velazquez, Federico Antonio (Velasquez)   b: 12/6/37, Santo Domingo, D.R.   BR/TR, 6′1″, 185 lbs.   Deb: 4/20/69

YEAR	TM/L	G	AB	R	H	2B	3B	HR	RBI	BB	SO	AVG	OBP	SLG	PRO+	BR	/A	RC	SB	CS	SBR	FR	POS	TPR
1969	Sea-A	6	16	1	2	2	0	0	2	1	3	.125	.176	.250	18	-2	-2	0	0	0	0	-0	/C	-0.1
1973	Atl-N	15	23	2	8	1	0	0	3	1	3	.348	.375	.391	105	-0	0	3	0	0	0	2	C	0.3
Total	2	21	39	3	10	3	0	0	5	2	6	.256	.293	.333	71	-1	-2	4	0	0	0	2	/C	0.2

■ OTTO VELEZ
Velez, Otoniel (Franceschi)   b: 11/29/50, Ponce, PR.   BR/TR, 6′, 170 lbs.   Deb: 9/04/73

YEAR	TM/L	G	AB	R	H	2B	3B	HR	RBI	BB	SO	AVG	OBP	SLG	PRO+	BR	/A	RC	SB	CS	SBR	FR	POS	TPR
1973	NY-A	23	77	9	15	4	0	2	7	15	24	.195	.326	.325	87	-1	-1	9	0	1	-1	-1	O	-0.3
1974	NY-A	27	67	9	14	1	1	2	10	15	24	.209	.354	.343	104	1	1	9	0	0	0	-3	1/O3	-0.2
1975	NY-A	6	8	0	2	0	0	0	1	2	0	.250	.400	.250	90	0	0	1	0	0	0	-0	/1D	0.0
1976	*NY-A	49	94	11	25	6	0	2	10	23	26	.266	.410	.394	137	6	6	17	0	0	0	-0	O/13D	0.5
1977	Tor-A	120	360	50	92	19	3	16	62	65	87	.256	.371	.458	123	14	13	64	4	2	0	-5	OD	0.5
1978	Tor-A	91	248	29	66	14	2	9	38	45	41	.266	.383	.448	130	12	11	43	1	3	-2	5	O/1D	1.3
1979	Tor-A	99	274	45	79	21	0	15	48	46	45	.288	.396	.529	145	19	19	58	0	1	-1	3	O/1D	1.7
1980	Tor-A	104	357	54	96	12	3	20	62	54	86	.269	.368	.487	126	16	14	65	0	0	0	0	D/1	1.4
1981	Tor-A	80	240	32	51	9	2	11	28	55	60	.213	.366	.404	114	9	7	38	0	3	-2	-0	D/1	0.5
1982	Tor-A	28	52	4	10	1	0	1	5	13	15	.192	.354	.269	68	-1	-2	6	1	0	0	0	D	-0.1
1983	Cle-A	10	25	1	2	0	0	0	1	3	6	.080	.179	.080	-25	-4	-4	0	0	0	0	0	/D	-0.4
Total	11	637	1802	244	452	87	11	78	272	336	414	.251	.372	.441	122	69	63	311	6	10	-4	-2	OD/13	4.9

■ PAT VELTMAN
Veltman, Arthur Patrick   b: 3/24/06, Mobile, Ala.   d: 10/1/80, San Antonio, Tex.   BR/TR, 6′, 175 lbs.   Deb: 4/17/26

YEAR	TM/L	G	AB	R	H	2B	3B	HR	RBI	BB	SO	AVG	OBP	SLG	PRO+	BR	/A	RC	SB	CS	SBR	FR	POS	TPR
1926	Chi-A	5	4	1	1	0	0	0	0	1	1	.250	.400	.250	75	-0	-0	0	0	0	0	0	/S	0.0
1928	NY-N	1	3	1	1	0	1	0	0	1	0	.333	.500	1.000	282	1	1	2				0	/O	0.1
1929	NY-N	2	1	1	0	0	0	0	0	2	0	.000	.667	.000	81	0	0	0				-0	/C	0.0
1931	Bos-N	1	1	0	0	0	0	0	0	0	0	.000	.000	.000	-99	-0	-0	0				0	H	0.0
1932	NY-N	2	1	0	0	0	0	0	0	0	1	.000	.000	.000	-99	-0	-0	0				0	H	0.0
1934	Pit-N	12	28	1	3	0	0	0	2	0	1	.107	.107	.107	-41	-6	-6	0				-1	C	-0.6
Total	6	23	38	4	5	0	1	0	2	4	3	.132	.214	.184	7	-5	-5	3	0	0		-1	/COS	-0.5

■ MAX VENABLE
Venable, William McKinley   b: 6/6/57, Phoenix, Ariz.   BL/TR, 5′10″, 185 lbs.   Deb: 4/08/79

YEAR	TM/L	G	AB	R	H	2B	3B	HR	RBI	BB	SO	AVG	OBP	SLG	PRO+	BR	/A	RC	SB	CS	SBR	FR	POS	TPR
1979	SF-N	55	85	12	14	1	1	0	3	10	18	.165	.260	.200	29	-8	-8	5	3	3	-1	-0	O	-0.9
1980	SF-N	64	138	13	37	5	0	0	10	15	22	.268	.340	.304	83	-3	-3	16	8	2	1	-3	O	-0.5
1981	SF-N	18	32	2	6	0	2	0	1	4	3	.188	.278	.313	68	-1	-1	3	3	1	0	-0	/O	-0.1
1982	SF-N	71	125	17	28	2	1	1	7	7	16	.224	.265	.280	53	-8	-8	9	9	3	1	5	O	-0.2
1983	SF-N	94	228	28	50	7	4	6	27	22	34	.219	.296	.364	85	-6	-5	27	15	2	3	6	O	0.3
1984	Mon-N	38	71	7	17	2	0	2	7	3	7	.239	.280	.352	80	-2	-2	7	1	0	0	-1	O	-0.3
1985	Cin-N	77	135	21	39	12	3	0	10	6	17	.289	.319	.422	101	1	-0	18	11	3	2	3	O	0.3
1986	Cin-N	108	147	17	31	7	1	2	15	17	24	.211	.293	.313	64	-7	-7	15	7	2	1	-1	O	-0.8
1987	Cin-N	7	7	2	1	0	0	0	2	0	0	.143	.143	.143	-23	-1	-1	0	0	0	0	0	/O	0.0
1989	Cal-A	20	53	7	19	4	0	0	4	1	16	.358	.370	.434	128	2	2	9	0	0	0	-3	O	-0.1
1990	Cal-A	93	189	26	49	9	3	4	21	24	31	.259	.343	.402	107	2	2	28	5	1	1	-2	O	0.0
Total	11	645	1210	152	291	49	15	15	107	109	188	.240	.306	.343	81	-32	-32	138	62	17	8	5	O	-2.3

■ ROBIN VENTURA
Ventura, Robin Mark   b: 7/14/67, Santa Maria, Cal.   BL/TR, 6′1″, 185 lbs.   Deb: 9/12/89

YEAR	TM/L	G	AB	R	H	2B	3B	HR	RBI	BB	SO	AVG	OBP	SLG	PRO+	BR	/A	RC	SB	CS	SBR	FR	POS	TPR
1989	Chi-A	16	45	5	8	3	0	0	7	8	6	.178	.315	.244	61	-2	-2	4	0	0	0	2	3	0.0
1990	Chi-A	150	493	48	123	17	1	5	54	55	53	.249	.326	.318	83	-11	-10	54	1	4	-2	0	*3/1	-1.0
Total	2	166	538	53	131	20	1	5	61	63	59	.243	.325	.312	81	-14	-12	58	1	4	-2	2	3/1	-1.0

■ VINCE VENTURA
Ventura, Vincent   b: 4/18/17, New York, N.Y.   BR/TR, 6′1.5″, 190 lbs.   Deb: 5/08/45

YEAR	TM/L	G	AB	R	H	2B	3B	HR	RBI	BB	SO	AVG	OBP	SLG	PRO+	BR	/A	RC	SB	CS	SBR	FR	POS	TPR
1945	Was-A	18	58	4	12	0	0	0	2	4	4	.207	.258	.207	39	-5	-4	3	0	0	0	-1	O	-0.6

■ EMIL VERBAN
Verban, Emil Matthew "Dutch" or "Antelope"   b: 8/27/15, Lincoln, Ill.   d: 6/8/89, Quincy, Ill.   BR/TR, 5′11″, 165 lbs.   Deb: 4/18/44

YEAR	TM/L	G	AB	R	H	2B	3B	HR	RBI	BB	SO	AVG	OBP	SLG	PRO+	BR	/A	RC	SB	CS	SBR	FR	POS	TPR
1944	*StL-N	146	498	51	128	14	2	0	43	19	14	.257	.287	.293	62	-24	-25	43	0			-6	*2	-1.6
1945	StL-N	155	597	59	166	22	8	0	72	19	15	.278	.304	.342	77	-18	-20	61	4			-19	*2	-2.5
1946	StL-N	1	1	0	0	0	0	0	0	0	0	.000	.000	.000	-96	-0	-0	0	0			0	H	0.0
	Phi-N	138	473	44	130	17	5	0	34	21	18	.275	.306	.332	83	-13	-11	48	5			-3	*2	-1.0
	Yr	139	474	44	130	17	5	0	34	21	18	.274	.305	.331	83	-13	-12	48	5			-3		-1.0
1947	Phi-N	155	540	50	154	14	8	0	42	23	8	.285	.316	.341	77	-20	-18	56	5			17	*2	1.6
1948	Phi-N	55	169	14	39	5	1	0	11	11	5	.231	.282	.272	51	-12	-11	14	0			-4	2	-1.0
	Chi-N	56	248	37	73	15	1	0	16	4	7	.294	.308	.375	88	-6	-5	28	4			6	2	0.5
	Yr	111	417	51	112	20	2	1	27	15	12	.269	.297	.333	72	-18	-16	41	4			2		-0.5
1949	Chi-N	98	343	38	99	11	1	0	22	8	2	.289	.309	.327	72	-14	-13	34	3			3	2	-0.6
1950	Chi-N	45	37	7	4	1	0	0	1	3	5	.108	.175	.135	-17	-6	-6	1	0			6	/2S3O	0.0
	Bos-N	4	5	1	0	0	0	0	0	0	0	.000	.000	.000	-99	-1	-1	0	0			1	/2	0.0
	Yr	49	42	8	4	1	0	0	1	3	5	.095	.156	.119	-27	-8	-8	1	0			7		0.0
Total	7	853	2911	301	793	99	26	1	241	108	74	.272	.301	.325	73	-116	-112	286	21			2	2/SO3	-4.6

■ GENE VERBLE
Verble, Gene Kermit "Satchel"   b: 6/29/28, Concord, N.C.   BR/TR, 5′10″, 163 lbs.   Deb: 4/17/51

YEAR	TM/L	G	AB	R	H	2B	3B	HR	RBI	BB	SO	AVG	OBP	SLG	PRO+	BR	/A	RC	SB	CS	SBR	FR	POS	TPR
1951	Was-A	68	177	16	36	3	0	0	15	18	10	.203	.277	.243	42	-14	-14	12	1	1	-0	-1	S2/3	-1.2
1953	Was-A	13	21	4	4	0	0	0	2	2	1	.190	.261	.190	24	-2	-2	1	0	0	0	2	/S	0.1
Total	2	81	198	20	40	3	0	0	17	20	11	.202	.275	.237	40	-17	-16	13	1	1	-0	1	/S23	-1.1

■ FRANK VERDI
Verdi, Frank Michael   b: 6/2/26, Brooklyn, N.Y.   BR/TR, 5′10.5″, 170 lbs.   Deb: 5/10/53

YEAR	TM/L	G	AB	R	H	2B	3B	HR	RBI	BB	SO	AVG	OBP	SLG	PRO+	BR	/A	RC	SB	CS	SBR	FR	POS	TPR
1953	NY-A	1	0	0	0	0	0	0	0	0	0	—	—	—	—	0	0	0	0	0	0	0	/S	0.0

■ JOHNNY VERGEZ
Vergez, John Louis   b: 7/9/06, Oakland, Cal.   BR/TR, 5′8″, 165 lbs.   Deb: 4/14/31

YEAR	TM/L	G	AB	R	H	2B	3B	HR	RBI	BB	SO	AVG	OBP	SLG	PRO+	BR	/A	RC	SB	CS	SBR	FR	POS	TPR
1931	NY-N	152	565	67	157	24	2	13	81	29	65	.278	.320	.396	94	-8	-6	73	11			-3	*3	0.0
1932	NY-N	118	376	42	98	21	3	6	43	25	36	.261	.310	.380	86	-8	-7	45	1			5	*3/S	0.7
1933	NY-N	123	458	57	124	21	6	16	72	39	66	.271	.332	.448	123	12	12	66	1			-14	*3	0.2
1934	NY-N	108	320	31	64	18	1	7	27	28	55	.200	.269	.328	60	-19	-18	29	1			10	*3	0.0
1935	Phi-N	148	546	65	136	27	4	9	63	46	67	.249	.312	.363	73	-15	-22	64	8			-7	*3/S	-2.2
1936	Phi-N	15	40	4	11	2	0	1	5	3	11	.275	.326	.400	86	-0	-1	6	0			0	3	0.0
	StL-N	8	18	1	3	1	0	0	1	1	3	.167	.211	.222	17	-2	-2	1	0			0	/3	-0.1
	Yr	23	58	5	14	3	0	1	6	4	14	.241	.290	.345	66	-2	-3	6	0			0		-0.1
Total	6	672	2323	258	593	114	16	52	292	171	303	.255	.311	.385	87	-41	-45	285	22			-8	3/S	-1.4

YEAR	TM/L	G	AB	R	H	2B	3B	HR	RBI	BB	SO	AVG	OBP	SLG	PRO+	BR	/A	RC	SB	CS	SBR	FR	POS	TPR

■ MICKEY VERNON   Vernon, James Barton   b: 4/22/18, Marcus Hook, Pa.   BL/TL, 6'2", 170 lbs.   Deb: 7/08/39   MC

YEAR	TM/L	G	AB	R	H	2B	3B	HR	RBI	BB	SO	AVG	OBP	SLG	PRO+	BR	/A	RC	SB	CS	SBR	FR	POS	TPR
1939	Was-A	76	276	23	71	15	4	1	30	24	28	.257	.317	.351	76	-12	-9	31	1	1	-0	-3	1	-1.8
1940	Was-A	5	19	0	3	0	0	0	0	0	3	.158	.158	.158	-19	-3	-3	0	0	0	0	-0	/1	-0.2
1941	Was-A	138	531	73	159	27	11	9	93	43	51	.299	.352	.443	114	6	9	84	9	3	1	-6	*1	0.0
1942	Was-A	151	621	76	168	34	6	9	86	59	63	.271	.337	.388	104	2	3	87	25	6	4	-8	*1	-0.2
1943	Was-A	145	553	89	148	29	8	7	70	67	55	.268	.357	.387	122	13	16	83	24	8	2	-11	*1	0.4
1946	Was-A	148	587	88	207	51	8	8	85	49	64	**.353**	.403	.508	163	40	44	120	14	10	-2	-1	*1	3.4
1947	Was-A	154	600	77	159	29	12	7	85	49	42	.265	.320	.388	99	-5	-3	73	12	12	-4	-4	*1	-1.3
1948	Was-A	150	558	78	135	27	7	3	48	54	43	.242	.310	.332	73	-24	-22	56	15	11	-2	5	*1	-1.1
1949	Cle-A	153	584	72	170	27	4	18	83	58	51	.291	.357	.443	113	7	8	96	9	7	-2	19	*1	2.6
1950	Cle-A	28	90	8	17	0	0	0	10	12	10	.189	.284	.189	24	-10	-10	6	2	0	1	1	1	-0.8
	Was-A	90	327	47	100	17	3	9	65	50	29	.306	.404	.459	127	11	13	67	6	1	1	1	1	1.1
	Yr	118	417	55	117	17	3	9	75	62	39	.281	.379	.400	104	1	4	72	8	1	2	3		0.3
1951	Was-A	141	546	69	160	30	7	9	87	53	45	.293	.358	.423	112	7	9	84	7	6	-2	-4	*1	0.1
1952	Was-A	154	569	71	143	33	9	10	80	89	66	.251	.353	.394	111	7	9	84	7	7	-2	1	*1	-0.1
1953	Was-A	152	608	101	205	**43**	11	15	115	63	57	**.337**	.403	.518	151	40	42	127	4	6	-2	-3	*1	3.3
1954	Was-A	151	597	90	173	**33**	14	20	97	61	61	.290	.360	.492	140	24	28	106	1	4	-2	-9	*1	1.3
1955	Was-A	150	538	74	162	23	8	14	85	74	50	.301	.389	.452	133	20	24	93	0	4	-2	-8	*1	0.6
1956	Bos-A	119	403	67	125	28	4	15	84	57	40	.310	.405	.511	125	24	17	84	1	0	0	-3	*1	1.0
1957	Bos-A	102	270	36	65	18	1	7	38	41	35	.241	.351	.393	97	2	-0	38	0	0	0	4	1	0.3
1958	Cle-A	119	355	49	104	22	3	8	55	44	56	.293	.374	.439	126	12	13	58	0	4	-2	-2	1	0.6
1959	Mil-N	74	91	8	20	4	0	3	14	7	20	.220	.283	.363	77	-4	-3	9	0	0	0	0	1/O	-0.3
1960	Pit-N	9	8	0	1	0	0	0	1	1	0	.125	.222	.125	-2	-1	-1	0	0	0	0	0	H	0.0
Total	20	2409	8731	1196	2495	490	120	172	1311	955	869	.286	.359	.428	116	155	183	1387	137	90	-13	-31	*1/O	8.9

■ ZOILO VERSALLES   Versalles, Zoilo Casanova (Rodriguez) "Zorro"   b: 12/18/39, Veldado, Cuba   BR/TR, 5'10", 146 lbs.   Deb: 8/01/59

YEAR	TM/L	G	AB	R	H	2B	3B	HR	RBI	BB	SO	AVG	OBP	SLG	PRO+	BR	/A	RC	SB	CS	SBR	FR	POS	TPR
1959	Was-A	29	59	4	9	0	0	1	1	4	15	.153	.219	.203	17	-7	-7	3	1	0	0	3	S	-0.1
1960	Was-A	15	45	2	6	2	2	0	4	2	5	.133	.170	.267	16	-5	-5	2	0	0	0	-1	S	-0.4
1961	Min-A	129	510	65	143	25	5	7	53	25	61	.280	.315	.390	83	-10	-14	61	16	9	-1	-2	*S	-0.6
1962	Min-A	160	568	69	137	18	3	17	67	37	71	.241	.290	.373	74	-20	-22	59	5	5	-2	32	*S	1.7
1963	Min-A	159	621	74	162	31	**13**	10	54	33	66	.261	.303	.401	94	-5	-6	74	7	4	-0	-2	*S	0.0
1964	Min-A	160	659	94	171	33	**10**	20	64	42	88	.259	.312	.431	103	2	2	91	14	4	2	-17	*S	-1.3
1965	*Min-A	160	666	**126**	182	**45**	12	19	77	41	122	.273	.322	.462	115	15	12	102	27	5	**5**	2	*S	2.7
1966	Min-A	137	543	73	135	20	6	7	36	40	85	.249	.308	.346	82	-8	-12	55	10	12	-4	-17	*S	-2.8
1967	Min-A	160	581	63	116	16	7	6	50	33	113	.200	.250	.282	53	-32	-37	39	5	3	-0	2	*S	-2.6
1968	LA-N	122	403	29	79	16	3	2	24	26	84	.196	.245	.266	57	-23	-20	26	6	4	-1	8	*S	0.2
1969	Cle-A	72	217	21	49	11	1	1	13	21	47	.226	.300	.300	66	-9	-10	19	3	1	0	-11	23/S	-1.9
	Was-A	31	75	9	20	2	1	0	6	3	13	.267	.304	.320	79	-3	-2	7	1	0	0	-1	S/23	-0.2
	Yr	103	292	30	69	13	2	1	19	24	60	.236	.301	.305	69	-12	-12	27	4	1	1	-12		-2.1
1971	Atl-N	66	194	21	37	11	0	5	22	11	40	.191	.234	.325	53	-12	-13	13	2	1	0	-14	3S/2	-2.5
Total	12	1400	5141	650	1246	230	63	95	471	318	810	.242	.292	.367	82	-116	-135	552	97	48	0	-19	*S/32	-7.8

■ TOM VERYZER   Veryzer, Thomas Martin   b: 2/11/53, Port Jefferson, N.Y   BR/TR, 6'1.5", 175 lbs.   Deb: 8/14/73

YEAR	TM/L	G	AB	R	H	2B	3B	HR	RBI	BB	SO	AVG	OBP	SLG	PRO+	BR	/A	RC	SB	CS	SBR	FR	POS	TPR
1973	Det-A	18	20	1	6	0	1	0	2	2	4	.300	.364	.400	108	0	0	3	0	0	0	-5	S	-0.1
1974	Det-A	22	55	4	13	2	0	2	9	5	8	.236	.300	.382	92	-0	-1	7	1	0	0	-10	S	-0.8
1975	Det-A	128	404	37	102	13	1	5	48	23	76	.252	.301	.327	74	-12	-14	38	2	6	-3	-4	*S	-0.8
1976	Det-A	97	354	31	83	8	2	1	25	21	44	.234	.289	.277	64	-15	-17	27	1	4	-2	-1	S	-1.4
1977	Det-A	125	350	31	69	12	1	2	28	16	44	.197	.232	.254	31	-35	-35	21	0	1	-1	10	*S	-1.0
1978	Cle-A	130	421	48	114	18	4	1	32	13	36	.271	.301	.340	81	-12	-11	42	1	2	-1	-5	*S	-0.6
1979	Cle-A	149	449	41	99	9	3	0	34	34	54	.220	.281	.254	45	-34	-34	32	2	5	-2	4	*S	-1.4
1980	Cle-A	109	358	28	97	12	0	2	28	10	25	.271	.306	.321	72	-14	-14	32	0	5	-3	-1	*S	-0.8
1981	Cle-A	75	221	13	54	4	0	0	14	10	10	.244	.280	.262	58	-12	-12	16	1	0	0	-7	S	-1.2
1982	NY-N	40	54	6	18	2	0	0	4	3	4	.333	.368	.370	108	1	1	7	1	0	0	-2	2S	0.2
1983	Chi-N	59	88	5	18	3	0	1	3	3	13	.205	.231	.273	37	-7	-8	5	0	0	0	7	S3	0.1
1984	*Chi-N	44	74	5	14	1	0	0	4	3	11	.189	.259	.203	29	-7	-7	4	0	0	0	-2	S/32	-0.5
Total	12	996	2848	250	687	84	12	14	231	143	329	.241	.285	.294	61	-144	-152	235	9	23	-11	-14	S/23	-8.3

■ ERNIE VICK   Vick, Henry Arthur   b: 7/2/1900, Toledo, Ohio   d: 7/16/80, Ann Arbor, Mich.   BR/TR, 5'9.5", 185 lbs.   Deb: 6/29/22

YEAR	TM/L	G	AB	R	H	2B	3B	HR	RBI	BB	SO	AVG	OBP	SLG	PRO+	BR	/A	RC	SB	CS	SBR	FR	POS	TPR
1922	StL-N	3	6	1	2	2	0	0	0	0	0	.333	.333	.667	159	0	0	1	0	0	0	-0	/C	0.0
1924	StL-N	16	23	2	8	1	0	0	0	3	3	.348	.423	.391	122	1	1	4	0	0	0	2	C	0.3
1925	StL-N	14	32	3	6	2	1	0	3	3	1	.188	.257	.313	44	-3	-3	3	0	0	0	0	/C	-0.1
1926	StL-N	24	51	6	10	2	0	0	4	3	4	.196	.241	.235	27	-5	-5	3	0			-1	C	-0.4
Total	4	57	112	12	26	7	1	0	7	9	8	.232	.289	.313	58	-7	-7	11	0	0		2	/C	-0.2

■ SAMMY VICK   Vick, Samuel Bruce   b: 4/12/1895, Batesville, Miss.   d: 8/17/86, Memphis, Tenn.   BR/TR, 5'10.5", 163 lbs.   Deb: 9/20/17

YEAR	TM/L	G	AB	R	H	2B	3B	HR	RBI	BB	SO	AVG	OBP	SLG	PRO+	BR	/A	RC	SB	CS	SBR	FR	POS	TPR
1917	NY-A	10	36	4	10	3	0	0	2	1	6	.278	.297	.361	100	-0	-0	4	2			-1	O	-0.1
1918	NY-A	2	3	1	2	0	0	0	1	0	0	.667	.667	.667	296	1	1	1	0			-0	/O	0.0
1919	NY-A	106	407	59	101	15	9	4	27	35	55	.248	.308	.344	82	-10	-10	44	9			-4	*O	-2.2
1920	NY-A	51	118	21	26	7	1	0	11	14	20	.220	.313	.297	60	-6	-7	12	1	1	-0	-4	O	-1.3
1921	Bos-A	44	77	5	20	3	1	0	9	1	10	.260	.269	.325	52	-6	-6	6	0	1	-1	-1	O	-0.7
Total	5	213	641	90	159	28	11	2	50	51	91	.248	.305	.335	76	-22	-22	67	12	2		-11	O	-4.3

■ SAM VICO   Vico, George Steve   b: 8/9/23, San Fernando, Cal.   BL/TR, 6'4", 200 lbs.   Deb: 4/20/48

YEAR	TM/L	G	AB	R	H	2B	3B	HR	RBI	BB	SO	AVG	OBP	SLG	PRO+	BR	/A	RC	SB	CS	SBR	FR	POS	TPR
1948	Det-A	144	521	50	139	23	9	8	58	39	39	.267	.326	.392	88	-9	-11	63	2	2	-1	-3	*1	-0.6
1949	Det-A	67	142	15	27	5	2	4	18	21	17	.190	.311	.338	72	-6	-6	16	0	0	0	2	1	-0.3
Total	2	211	663	65	166	28	11	12	76	60	56	.250	.323	.380	85	-15	-17	79	2	2	-1	-1	1	-0.9

■ JOSE VIDAL   Vidal, Jose (Nicolas) "Papito"   b: 4/3/40, Batey Lechugas, D.R.   BR/TR, 6', 190 lbs.   Deb: 9/05/66

YEAR	TM/L	G	AB	R	H	2B	3B	HR	RBI	BB	SO	AVG	OBP	SLG	PRO+	BR	/A	RC	SB	CS	SBR	FR	POS	TPR
1966	Cle-A	17	32	4	6	1	1	0	3	5	11	.188	.297	.281	67	-1	-1	3	0	1	-1	0	O	-0.1
1967	Cle-A	16	34	4	4	0	0	0	0	7	12	.118	.268	.118	17	-3	-3	1	0	1	-1	1	O	-0.2
1968	Cle-A	37	54	5	9	0	0	2	5	2	15	.167	.196	.278	43	-4	-4	3	3	0	1	-0	O/1	-0.4
1969	Sea-A	18	26	7	5	0	1	1	2	4	8	.192	.323	.385	99	-0	-0	3	1	1	-0	0	/O	0.0
Total	4	88	146	20	24	1	2	3	10	18	46	.164	.261	.260	53	-8	-8	11	4	3	-1	1	/O1	-0.7

■ HECTOR VILLANUEVA   Villanueva, Hector (Balasquide)   b: 10/2/64, San Juan, P.R.   BR/TR, 6'1", 220 lbs.   Deb: 6/01/90

YEAR	TM/L	G	AB	R	H	2B	3B	HR	RBI	BB	SO	AVG	OBP	SLG	PRO+	BR	/A	RC	SB	CS	SBR	FR	POS	TPR
1990	Chi-N	52	114	14	31	4	1	7	18	4	27	.272	.308	.509	111	3	1	17	1	0	0	-4	C1	-0.1

■ CHARLIE VINSON   Vinson, Charles Anthony "Chuck"   b: 1/5/44, Washington, D.C.   BL/TL, 6'3", 207 lbs.   Deb: 9/19/66

YEAR	TM/L	G	AB	R	H	2B	3B	HR	RBI	BB	SO	AVG	OBP	SLG	PRO+	BR	/A	RC	SB	CS	SBR	FR	POS	TPR
1966	Cal-A	13	22	3	4	2	0	1	6	5	9	.182	.357	.409	123	1	1	4	0	0	0	-1	1	0.0

■ RUBE VINSON   Vinson, Ernest Augustus   b: 3/20/1879, Dover, Del.   d: 10/12/51, Chester, Pa.   5'9", 168 lbs.   Deb: 9/27/04

YEAR	TM/L	G	AB	R	H	2B	3B	HR	RBI	BB	SO	AVG	OBP	SLG	PRO+	BR	/A	RC	SB	CS	SBR	FR	POS	TPR
1904	Cle-A	15	49	12	15	1	0	0	2	10		.306	.424	.327	143	3	3	8	2			3	O	0.6
1905	Cle-A	39	134	12	26	3	1	0	9	7		.194	.234	.231	49	-8	-8	9	4			-3	O	-1.3
1906	Chi-A	10	24	2	6	0	0	0	3	2		.250	.308	.250	79	-1	-0	2	1			-3	/O	-0.3
Total	3	64	207	26	47	4	1	0	14	19		.227	.292	.256	76	-5	-5	19	7			-2	/O	-1.0

YEAR	TM/L	G	AB	R	H	2B	3B	HR	RBI	BB	SO	AVG	OBP	SLG	PRO+	BR	/A	RC	SB	CS	SBR	FR	POS	TPR

■ JIM VIOX   Viox, James Harry b: 12/30/1890, Lockland, Ohio d: 1/6/69, Erlanger, Ky. BR/TR, 5'7", 150 lbs. Deb: 5/09/12

YEAR	TM/L	G	AB	R	H	2B	3B	HR	RBI	BB	SO	AVG	OBP	SLG	PRO+	BR	/A	RC	SB	CS	SBR	FR	POS	TPR
1912	Pit-N	33	70	8	13	2	3	1	7	3	9	.186	.219	.343	53	-5	-5	6	2			-4	3/SO2	-0.7
1913	Pit-N	137	492	86	156	32	8	2	65	64	28	.317	.399	.427	142	25	28	88	14			-43	*2S	-1.7
1914	Pit-N	143	506	52	134	18	5	1	57	63	33	.265	.351	.326	106	3	6	60	9			-25	*2/SO	-2.2
1915	Pit-N	150	503	56	129	17	8	2	45	75	31	.256	.357	.334	111	9	10	63	12	8	-1	-22	*23/O	-1.3
1916	Pit-N	43	132	12	33	7	0	1	17	17	11	.250	.340	.326	104	1	1	16	2			-16	23	-1.5
Total	5	506	1703	214	465	76	24	7	191	222	112	.273	.361	.358	116	33	39	233	39	8		-110	2/3SO	-7.4

■ BILL VIRDON   Virdon, William Charles b: 6/9/31, Hazel Park, Mich. BL/TR, 6', 175 lbs. Deb: 4/12/55 MC

YEAR	TM/L	G	AB	R	H	2B	3B	HR	RBI	BB	SO	AVG	OBP	SLG	PRO+	BR	/A	RC	SB	CS	SBR	FR	POS	TPR
1955	StL-N	144	534	58	150	18	6	17	68	36	64	.281	.327	.433	100	-1	-1	73	2	4	-2	-8	*O	-1.2
1956	StL-N	24	71	10	15	2	0	2	9	5	8	.211	.273	.324	60	-4	-4	6	0	1	-1	2	O	-0.3
	Pit-N	133	509	67	170	21	10	8	37	33	63	.334	.376	.462	126	17	18	84	6	6	-2	0	*O	1.2
	Yr	157	580	77	185	23	10	10	46	38	71	.319	.363	.445	118	13	14	90	6	7	-2	3		0.9
1957	Pit-N	144	561	59	141	28	11	8	50	33	69	.251	.293	.383	82	-17	-15	62	3	3	-1	6	*O	-1.4
1958	Pit-N	144	604	75	161	24	11	9	46	52	70	.267	.326	.387	90	-11	-9	78	5	3	-0	4	*O	-0.8
1959	Pit-N	144	519	67	132	24	2	8	41	55	65	.254	.328	.355	83	-13	-12	62	7	4	-0	16	*O	0.2
1960	*Pit-N	120	409	60	108	16	9	8	40	40	44	.264	.330	.406	99	-0	-0	57	8	2	1	3	*O	0.0
1961	Pit-N	146	599	81	156	22	8	9	58	49	45	.260	.316	.369	81	-16	-17	71	5	8	-3	5	*O	-2.2
1962	Pit-N	156	663	82	164	27	10	6	47	36	65	.247	.287	.345	69	-30	-30	62	5	13	-6	-1	*O	-4.6
1963	Pit-N	142	554	58	149	22	6	8	53	43	55	.269	.322	.374	99	-0	-1	68	1	2	-1	1	*O	-0.8
1964	Pit-N	145	473	59	115	11	3	3	27	30	48	.243	.288	.298	66	-21	-21	38	1	5	-3	-12	*O	-4.1
1965	Pit-N	135	481	58	134	22	5	4	24	30	49	.279	.322	.370	94	-4	-4	58	4	3	-1	-8	*O	-1.6
1968	Pit-N	6	3	1	1	0	0	1	2	0	2	.333	.333	1.333	388	1	1	1	0	0	0	0	/O	0.1
Total	12	1583	5980	735	1596	237	81	91	502	442	647	.267	.318	.379	89	-100	-95	721	47	54	-18	9	*O	-15.5

■ OZZIE VIRGIL   Virgil, Osvaldo Jose Jr. b: 12/7/56, Mayaguez, P.R. BR/TR, 6'1", 180 lbs. Deb: 10/05/80

YEAR	TM/L	G	AB	R	H	2B	3B	HR	RBI	BB	SO	AVG	OBP	SLG	PRO+	BR	/A	RC	SB	CS	SBR	FR	POS	TPR
1980	Phi-N	1	5	1	1	1	0	0	0	0	1	.200	.200	.400	60	-0	-0	0	0	0	0	-1	/C	0.0
1981	Phi-N	6	6	0	0	0	0	0	0	0	2	.000	.000	.000	-96	-2	-2	0	0	0	0	0	/C	-0.1
1982	Phi-N	49	101	11	24	6	0	3	8	10	26	.238	.306	.386	91	-1	-1	11	0	1	-1	4	C	0.2
1983	*Phi-N	55	140	11	30	7	0	6	23	8	34	.214	.272	.393	83	-4	-4	12	0	2	-1	-5	C	-0.7
1984	Phi-N	141	456	61	119	21	2	18	68	45	91	.261	.334	.434	113	8	7	62	1	1	-0	-4	*C	0.7
1985	Phi-N	131	426	47	105	16	3	19	55	49	85	.246	.331	.432	109	6	5	59	0	0	0	-4	*C	0.6
1986	Atl-N	114	359	45	80	9	0	15	48	63	73	.223	.345	.373	93	0	-2	49	1	0	0	14	*C	1.5
1987	Atl-N	123	429	57	106	13	1	27	72	47	81	.247	.331	.471	104	5	2	63	0	1	-1	-2	*C	0.9
1988	Atl-N	107	320	23	82	10	0	9	31	22	54	.256	.314	.372	92	-2	-4	36	2	0	1	-11	C	-0.9
1989	Tor-A	9	11	2	2	1	0	1	2	4	3	.182	.400	.545	167	1	1	3	0	0	0	0	/CD	0.1
1990	Tor-A	3	5	0	0	0	0	0	0	0	0	.000	.000	.000	-99	-1	-1	0	0	0	0	0	/CD	0.0
Total	11	739	2258	258	549	84	6	98	307	248	453	.243	.326	.416	101	11	1	296	4	5	-2	-8	C/D	2.3

■ OZZIE VIRGIL   Virgil, Osvaldo Jose Sr. (Pichardo) b: 5/17/33, Montecristi, D.R. BR/TR, 6'1", 174 lbs. Deb: 9/23/56 C

YEAR	TM/L	G	AB	R	H	2B	3B	HR	RBI	BB	SO	AVG	OBP	SLG	PRO+	BR	/A	RC	SB	CS	SBR	FR	POS	TPR
1956	NY-N	3	12	2	5	1	1	0	2	0	2	.417	.417	.667	186	1	1	4	1	0	0	-2	/3	0.0
1957	NY-N	96	226	26	53	0	2	4	24	14	27	.235	.279	.305	57	-14	-14	17	2	3	-1	11	3O/S	-0.2
1958	Det-A	49	193	19	47	10	2	3	19	8	20	.244	.274	.363	69	-7	-9	18	1	0	0	3	3	-0.3
1960	Det-A	62	132	16	30	4	2	3	13	4	14	.227	.250	.356	60	-7	-8	11	1	1	-0	8	3/2SC	0.2
1961	Det-A	20	30	1	4	0	0	1	1	1	5	.133	.161	.233	4	-4	-4	1	0	0	0	-1	/3C2S	-0.4
	KC-A	11	21	1	3	0	0	0	0	0	3	.143	.143	.143	-23	-4	-4	-0	0	0	0	0	/3C	-0.2
	Yr	31	51	2	7	0	0	1	1	1	8	.137	.154	.196	-7	-8	-8	0	0	0	0	-1		-0.6
1962	Bal-A	1	0	0	0	0	0	0	0	1	0	—	1.000	—	206	0	0	0	0	0	0	0	H	0.0
1965	Pit-N	39	49	3	13	2	0	1	5	2	10	.265	.294	.367	85	-1	-1	5	0	0	0	2	C/32	0.1
1966	SF-N	42	89	7	19	2	0	2	9	4	12	.213	.247	.303	51	-6	-6	6	1	1	-0	1	C3/120	-0.4
1969	SF-N	1	1	0	0	0	0	0	0	0	0	.000	.000	.000	-99	-0	-0	0	0	0	0	0	H	0.0
Total	9	324	753	75	174	19	7	14	73	34	91	.231	.264	.331	59	-42	-44	61	6	5	-1	23	3/CO2S1	-1.2

■ JAKE VIRTUE   Virtue, Jacob Kitchline "Guesses" b: 3/2/1865, Philadelphia, Pa. d: 2/3/43, Camden, N.J. BB/TR, 5'9.5", 165 lbs. Deb: 7/21/1890

YEAR	TM/L	G	AB	R	H	2B	3B	HR	RBI	BB	SO	AVG	OBP	SLG	PRO+	BR	/A	RC	SB	CS	SBR	FR	POS	TPR
1890	Cle-N	62	223	39	68	6	5	2	25	49	15	.305	.432	.404	150	16	17	44	9			0	1	1.1
1891	Cle-N	139	517	82	135	19	14	2	72	75	40	.261	.363	.364	110	12	8	76	15			-10	*1	-0.5
1892	*Cle-N	147	557	98	157	15	20	2	89	84	68	.282	.380	.391	130	26	23	90	14			-4	*1	0.7
1893	Cle-N	97	378	87	100	16	10	1	60	54	14	.265	.358	.368	89	-2	-6	55	11			1	10/S3P	-0.4
1894	Cle-N	29	89	15	23	4	1	0	10	13	3	.258	.359	.326	65	-4	-5	11	1			-2	O/21P	-0.5
Total	5	474	1764	321	483	60	50	7	256	275	140	.274	.376	.376	113	48	37	276	50			-14	1/O3S2P	0.4

■ JOE VISNER   Visner, Joseph Paul (b: Joseph Paul Vezina) b: 9/27/1859, Minneapolis, Minn. BL/TR, 5'11", 180 lbs. Deb: 7/04/1885

YEAR	TM/L	G	AB	R	H	2B	3B	HR	RBI	BB	SO	AVG	OBP	SLG	PRO+	BR	/A	RC	SB	CS	SBR	FR	POS	TPR
1885	Bal-a	4	13	2	3	0	0	0		2		.231	.333	.231	85	-0	-0	1				-1	/O	0.0
1889	*Bro-a	80	295	56	76	12	10	8	68	36	36	.258	.346	.447	127	10	10	51	13			-17	CO	-0.2
1890	Pit-P	127	521	110	138	15	22	3	71	76	44	.265	.367	.395	115	5	14	84	18			-6	*O	0.2
1891	Was-a	18	68	13	19	2	3	1	7	8	7	.279	.355	.441	137	2	3	12	2			-2	O/C3	0.0
	StL-a	6	27	2	4	0	1	0	1	0	3	.148	.148	.222	6	-3	-4	1	0			0	/O	-0.3
	Yr	24	95	15	23	2	4	1	8	8	10	.242	.301	.379	97	-1	-1	12	2			-2		-0.3
Total	4	235	924	183	240	29	36	12	147	122	90	.260	.353	.408	116	14	23	149	33			-26	O/C3	-0.3

■ JOE VITELLI   Vitelli, Antonio Joseph b: 4/12/08, Mckees Rocks, Pa. d: 2/7/67, Pittsburgh, Pa. BR/TR, 6'1", 195 lbs. Deb: 5/30/44

YEAR	TM/L	G	AB	R	H	2B	3B	HR	RBI	BB	SO	AVG	OBP	SLG	PRO+	BR	/A	RC	SB	CS	SBR	FR	POS	TPR
1944	Pit-N	4	3	0	0	0	0	0	0	0	0	.000	.000	.000	-96	-1	-1	0	0			0	/P	0.0
1945	Pit-N	1	0	0	0	0	0	0	0	0	0	—	—	—	—	0	0	0	0			0	R	0.0
Total	2	5	3	1	0	0	0	0	0	0	0	.000	.000	.000	-96	-1	-1	0	0			0	/P	0.0

■ OSSIE VITT   Vitt, Oscar Joseph b: 1/4/1890, San Francisco, Cal. d: 1/31/63, Oakland, Cal. BR/TR, 5'10", 150 lbs. Deb: 4/11/12 M

YEAR	TM/L	G	AB	R	H	2B	3B	HR	RBI	BB	SO	AVG	OBP	SLG	PRO+	BR	/A	RC	SB	CS	SBR	FR	POS	TPR
1912	Det-A	76	273	39	67	4	4	0	19	18		.245	.297	.289	70	-12	-10	28	17			0	O32	-1.2
1913	Det-A	99	359	45	86	11	3	2	33	31	18	.240	.304	.304	79	-10	-10	36	5			5	23/O	-0.6
1914	Det-A	66	195	35	49	7	0	0	8	31	8	.251	.354	.287	90	-0	-1	24	10	8	-2	2	23/OS	-0.8
1915	Det-A	152	560	116	140	18	13	1	48	80	22	.250	.348	.334	99	4	4	74	26	18	-3	14	*3/2	2.0
1916	Det-A	153	597	88	135	17	12	0	42	75	28	.226	.314	.295	80	-12	-14	65	18			28	*3/S	2.2
1917	Det-A	140	512	65	130	13	6	0	47	56	15	.254	.329	.303	93	-4	-3	58	18			-17	*3	-1.5
1918	Det-A	81	267	29	64	5	2	0	17	32	6	.240	.321	.273	88	-6	-5	27	5			4	3/2O	0.0
1919	Bos-A	133	469	64	114	10	3	0	40	44	11	.243	.309	.277	69	-21	-17	47	9			14	*3	0.7
1920	Bos-A	87	296	50	65	10	4	1	28	43	10	.220	.321	.291	66	-15	-13	31	5	4	-1	-6	32	-1.4
1921	Bos-A	78	232	29	44	11	1	0	16	45	9	.190	.321	.246	48	-18	-17	22	1			-4	3/O1	-1.4
Total	10	1065	3760	560	894	106	48	4	295	455	131	.238	.322	.295	80	-92	-90	412	114	32		41	32/OS1	-1.2

■ JOSE VIZCAINO   Vizcaino, Jose Luis (Pimental) b: 3/26/68, San Cristobal, D.R. BB/TR, 6'1", 150 lbs. Deb: 9/10/89

YEAR	TM/L	G	AB	R	H	2B	3B	HR	RBI	BB	SO	AVG	OBP	SLG	PRO+	BR	/A	RC	SB	CS	SBR	FR	POS	TPR
1989	LA-N	7	10	2	2	0	0	0	0	0	1	.200	.200	.200	15	-1	-1	0	0	0	0	2	/S	0.1
1990	LA-N	37	51	3	14	1	1	0	2	4	8	.275	.327	.333	87	-1	-1	5	1	1	-0	3	S/2	0.3
Total	2	44	61	5	16	1	1	0	2	4	9	.262	.308	.311	76	-2	-2	6	1	1	-0	4	/S2	0.4

■ OMAR VIZQUEL   Vizquel, Omar Enrique (Gonzalez) b: 4/24/67, Caracas, Venez. BB/TR, 5'9", 155 lbs. Deb: 4/03/89

YEAR	TM/L	G	AB	R	H	2B	3B	HR	RBI	BB	SO	AVG	OBP	SLG	PRO+	BR	/A	RC	SB	CS	SBR	FR	POS	TPR
1989	Sea-A	143	387	45	85	7	3	1	20	28	40	.220	.274	.261	50	-24	-26	28	1	4	-2	11	*S	-0.5

YEAR	TM/L	G	AB	R	H	2B	3B	HR	RBI	BB	SO	AVG	OBP	SLG	PRO+	BR	/A	RC	SB	CS	SBR	FR	POS	TPR
1990	Sea-A	81	255	19	63	3	2	2	18	18	22	.247	.297	.298	66	-11	-12	23	4	1	1	-2	S	-0.7
Total	2	224	642	64	148	10	5	3	38	46	62	.231	.283	.276	56	-36	-38	51	5	5	-2	9	S	-1.2

■ OTTO VOGEL

Vogel, Otto Henry   b: 10/26/1899, Mendota, Ill.   d: 7/19/69, Iowa City, Iowa   BR/TR, 6', 195 lbs.   Deb: 6/05/23

YEAR	TM/L	G	AB	R	H	2B	3B	HR	RBI	BB	SO	AVG	OBP	SLG	PRO+	BR	/A	RC	SB	CS	SBR	FR	POS	TPR
1923	Chi-N	41	81	10	17	0	1	1	6	7	11	.210	.297	.272	51	-6	-6	7	2	3	-1	-1	O/3	-0.7
1924	Chi-N	70	172	28	46	11	2	1	24	10	26	.267	.319	.372	84	-4	-4	20	4	4	-1	3	O/3	-0.2
Total	2	111	253	38	63	11	3	2	30	17	37	.249	.312	.340	73	-9	-10	27	6	7	-2	2	/O3	-0.9

■ CLYDE VOLLMER

Vollmer, Clyde Frederick   b: 9/24/21, Cincinnati, Ohio   BR/TR, 6'1", 185 lbs.   Deb: 5/31/42

YEAR	TM/L	G	AB	R	H	2B	3B	HR	RBI	BB	SO	AVG	OBP	SLG	PRO+	BR	/A	RC	SB	CS	SBR	FR	POS	TPR
1942	Cin-N	12	43	2	4	0	0	1	4	1	5	.093	.114	.163	-20	-7	-7	1	0			1	O	-0.5
1946	Cin-N	9	22	1	4	0	0	0	1	1	3	.182	.217	.182	14	-2	-2	1	2			-1	/O	-0.3
1947	Cin-N	78	155	19	34	10	0	1	13	9	18	.219	.267	.303	51	-11	-11	13	0			7	O	-0.5
1948	Cin-N	7	9	0	1	0	0	0	0	1	1	.111	.200	.111	-14	-1	-1	0	0			0	/O	-0.1
	Was-A	1	5	1	2	0	0	0	0	0	1	.400	.400	.400	116	0	0	1	0	0	0	0	/O	0.0
1949	Was-A	129	443	58	112	17	1	14	59	53	62	.253	.335	.391	94	-7	-5	59	1	2	-1	1	*O	-0.7
1950	Was-A	6	14	4	4	0	0	0	1	2	3	.286	.375	.286	75	-1	-0	2	1	0	0	0	/O	0.0
	Bos-A	57	169	35	48	10	0	7	37	21	35	.284	.363	.467	102	2	0	29	1	0	0	-2	O	-0.2
	Yr	63	183	39	52	10	0	7	38	23	38	.284	.364	.454	100	2	-0	31	2	0	1	-2		-0.2
1951	Bos-A	115	386	66	97	9	2	22	85	55	66	.251	.346	.456	105	7	2	59	0	0	0	-4	*O	-0.5
1952	Bos-A	90	250	35	66	12	4	11	50	39	47	.264	.370	.476	124	12	9	42	2	2	-1	0	O	0.7
1953	Bos-A	1	0	0	0	0	0	0	0	1	0	—	1.000	—	180	0	0	0	0	0	0	0	H	0.0
	Was-A	118	408	54	106	15	3	11	74	48	59	.260	.342	.392	100	-1	0	58	0	2	-1	3	*O	-0.1
	Yr	119	408	54	106	15	3	11	74	49	59	.260	.343	.392	101	-1	0	58	0	2	-1	3		-0.1
1954	Was-A	62	117	8	30	4	0	2	15	12	28	.256	.331	.342	89	-2	-2	13	0	0	0	-3	O	-0.5
Total	10	685	2021	283	508	77	10	69	339	243	328	.251	.335	.402	95	-11	-17	278	7	6		2	O	-2.7

■ FRITZ Von KOLNITZ

Von Kolnitz, Alfred Holmes   b: 5/20/1893, Charleston, S.C.   d: 3/18/48, Mount Pleasant, S.C.   BR/TR, 5'10.5", 175 lbs.   Deb: 4/18/14

YEAR	TM/L	G	AB	R	H	2B	3B	HR	RBI	BB	SO	AVG	OBP	SLG	PRO+	BR	/A	RC	SB	CS	SBR	FR	POS	TPR
1914	Cin-N	41	104	8	23	2	0	0	6	6	16	.221	.270	.240	51	-6	-6	7	4			-1	3O/C1	-0.7
1915	Cin-N	50	78	6	15	4	1	0	6	7	11	.192	.259	.269	59	-4	-4	5	1	3	-2	-6	3/S1C0	-1.1
1916	Chi-A	24	44	1	10	3	0	0	7	2	6	.227	.261	.295	66	-2	-2	3	0			-5	3	-0.6
Total	3	115	226	15	48	9	1	0	19	15	33	.212	.264	.261	56	-12	-12	16	5	3		-12	/3OS1C	-2.4

■ JOE VOSMIK

Vosmik, Joseph Franklin   b: 4/4/10, Cleveland, Ohio   d: 1/27/62, Cleveland, Ohio   BR/TR, 6', 185 lbs.   Deb: 9/13/30

YEAR	TM/L	G	AB	R	H	2B	3B	HR	RBI	BB	SO	AVG	OBP	SLG	PRO+	BR	/A	RC	SB	CS	SBR	FR	POS	TPR
1930	Cle-A	9	26	1	6	2	0	0	4	1	1	.231	.259	.308	42	-2	-2	2	0	0	0	1	/O	-0.1
1931	Cle-A	149	591	80	189	36	14	7	117	38	30	.320	.363	.464	110	12	7	97	7	7	-2	6	*O	0.2
1932	Cle-A	153	621	106	194	39	12	10	97	58	42	.312	.376	.462	109	14	8	109	2	3	-1	22	*O	2.1
1933	Cle-A	119	438	53	115	20	10	4	56	42	13	.263	.331	.381	84	-8	-10	56	0	2	-1	6	*O	-0.8
1934	Cle-A	104	405	71	138	33	2	6	78	35	10	.341	.393	.477	122	14	13	76	1	1	-0	-2	*O	0.9
1935	Cle-A	152	620	93	216	47	20	10	110	59	30	.348	.408	.537	140	38	37	137	2	1	0	2	*O	3.5
1936	Cle-A	138	506	76	145	29	7	7	94	79	21	.287	.383	.413	96	-1	-2	85	5	1	1	-4	*O	-0.7
1937	StL-A	144	594	81	193	47	9	4	93	49	38	.325	.377	.455	108	8	7	102	2	3	-1	7	*O	0.6
1938	Bos-A	146	621	121	201	37	6	9	86	59	26	.324	.384	.446	103	7	3	107	0	3	-2	5	*O	0.4
1939	Bos-A	145	554	89	153	29	6	7	84	66	33	.276	.356	.388	87	-7	-11	73	4	3	-1	-4	*O	-1.8
1940	Bro-N	116	404	45	114	14	6	1	42	22	21	.282	.321	.354	81	-8	-11	45	0			-1	O	-1.4
1941	Bro-N	25	56	0	11	0	0	0	4	4	4	.196	.250	.196	26	-5	-6	3	0			-4	O	-1.0
1944	Was-A	14	36	2	7	2	0	0	9	2	3	.194	.237	.250	41	-3	-3	2	0	0	0	-1	O	-0.4
Total	13	1414	5472	818	1682	335	92	65	874	514	272	.307	.369	.438	104	58	30	895	23	24		31	*O	1.5

■ ALEX VOSS

Voss, Alexander   b: 1855, Roswell, Ga.   d: 8/31/06, Cincinnati, Ohio   BR/TR, 6'1", 180 lbs.   Deb: 4/17/1884

YEAR	TM/L	G	AB	R	H	2B	3B	HR	RBI	BB	SO	AVG	OBP	SLG	PRO+	BR	/A	RC	SB	CS	SBR	FR	POS	TPR
1884	Was-U	63	245	33	47	9	0	0			5	.192	.208	.229	49	-13	-12	12	0			5	P310/S	-0.4
	KC-U	14	45	1	4	0	0	0			0	.089	.089	.089	-46	-6	-5	0	0			1	/OP	-0.3
	Yr	77	290	34	51	9	0	0			5	.176	.190	.207	36	-19	-17	12	0			6		-0.7

■ BILL VOSS

Voss, William Edward   b: 10/31/43, Glendale, Cal.   BL/TL, 6'2", 160 lbs.   Deb: 9/14/65

YEAR	TM/L	G	AB	R	H	2B	3B	HR	RBI	BB	SO	AVG	OBP	SLG	PRO+	BR	/A	RC	SB	CS	SBR	FR	POS	TPR
1965	Chi-A	11	33	4	6	0	1	1	3	3	5	.182	.250	.333	68	-2	-1	3	0	0	0	-1	O	-0.2
1966	Chi-A	2	2	0	0	0	0	0	0	0	2	.000	.000	.000	-99	-1	-0	0	0	0	0	0	/O	0.0
1967	Chi-A	13	22	4	2	0	0	0	0	0	1	.091	.091	.091	-48	-4	-4	0	1	1	-0	1	O	-0.3
1968	Chi-A	61	167	14	26	2	1	2	15	16	34	.156	.238	.216	38	-12	-12	9	5	3	-0	-2	O	-1.9
1969	Cal-A	133	349	33	91	11	4	2	40	35	40	.261	.328	.332	90	-7	-4	38	5	3	-0	-1	*O/1	-0.8
1970	Cal-A	80	181	21	44	4	3	3	30	23	18	.243	.335	.348	92	-2	-2	22	2	1	0	2	O	-0.1
1971	Mil-A	97	275	31	69	4	0	10	30	24	45	.251	.313	.375	95	-3	-2	33	2	2	-1	-3	O	-0.8
1972	Mil-A	27	36	1	3	1	0	0	1	5	4	.083	.195	.111	-7	-5	-5	1	0	1	-1	-1	O	-0.6
	Oak-A	40	97	10	22	5	1	1	5	9	16	.227	.299	.330	92	-2	-1	10	0	0	0	2	O	0.0
	Yr	67	133	11	25	6	1	1	6	14	20	.188	.270	.271	64	-6	-6	9	0	1	-1	2		-0.6
	StL-N	11	15	1	4	2	0	0	3	2	2	.267	.353	.400	115	0	0	2	0	0	0	-0	/O	0.0
Total	8	475	1177	119	267	29	10	19	127	117	167	.227	.300	.317	78	-36	-32	117	15	11	-2	-3	O/1	-4.7

■ PHIL VOYLES

Voyles, Philip Vance   b: 5/12/1900, Murphy, N.C.   d: 11/3/72, Marlboro, Mass.   BL/TR, 5'11.5", 175 lbs.   Deb: 9/04/29

YEAR	TM/L	G	AB	R	H	2B	3B	HR	RBI	BB	SO	AVG	OBP	SLG	PRO+	BR	/A	RC	SB	CS	SBR	FR	POS	TPR
1929	Bos-N	20	68	9	16	0	2	0	14	6	8	.235	.297	.294	49	-6	-5	2				-0	O	-0.6

■ GEORGE VUKOVICH

Vukovich, George Stephen   b: 6/24/56, Chicago, Ill.   BL/TR, 6', 198 lbs.   Deb: 4/13/80

YEAR	TM/L	G	AB	R	H	2B	3B	HR	RBI	BB	SO	AVG	OBP	SLG	PRO+	BR	/A	RC	SB	CS	SBR	FR	POS	TPR
1980	*Phi-N	78	58	6	13	1	1	0	8	6	9	.224	.297	.276	58	-3	-3	5	0	0	0	1	O	-0.3
1981	*Phi-N	20	26	5	10	0	0	1	4	1	0	.385	.407	.500	150	2	2	6	1	0	0	0	/O	0.2
1982	Phi-N	123	335	42	91	18	2	6	42	32	47	.272	.335	.391	100	1	0	41	2	9	-5	-1	*O	-0.6
1983	Cle-A	124	312	31	77	13	2	3	44	24	37	.247	.305	.330	72	-11	-12	30	3	4	-2	-15	*O	-2.9
1984	Cle-A	134	437	38	133	22	5	9	60	34	61	.304	.356	.439	117	11	10	66	1	4	-2	14	*O	1.7
1985	Cle-A	149	434	43	106	22	0	8	45	30	75	.244	.295	.350	76	-15	-14	43	2	2	-1	-11	*O	-2.7
Total	6	628	1602	164	430	76	10	27	203	127	229	.268	.324	.379	92	-15	-18	191	9	19	-9	-12	O	-4.6

■ JOHN VUKOVICH

Vukovich, John Christopher   b: 7/31/47, Sacramento, Cal.   BR/TR, 6'1", 187 lbs.   Deb: 9/11/70   MC

YEAR	TM/L	G	AB	R	H	2B	3B	HR	RBI	BB	SO	AVG	OBP	SLG	PRO+	BR	/A	RC	SB	CS	SBR	FR	POS	TPR
1970	Phi-N	3	8	1	1	0	0	0	0	1	0	.125	.222	.125	-5	-1	-1	0	0	0	0	1	/S3	0.0
1971	Phi-N	74	217	11	36	5	0	6	14	12	34	.166	.213	.189	15	-24	-24	9	2	1	0	10	3	-1.4
1973	Mil-A	55	128	10	16	3	0	2	9	9	40	.125	.182	.195	7	-16	-16	5	0	2	-1	-4	31/S	-2.2
1974	Mil-A	38	80	5	15	1	0	3	11	1	16	.188	.198	.313	45	-6	-6	4	2	1	0	2	S32/1	0.5
1975	Cin-N	31	38	4	8	3	0	0	2	4	5	.211	.286	.289	59	-2	-2	4	0	0	0	7	3	0.5
1976	Phi-N	4	8	2	1	0	0	1	2	0	2	.125	.125	.500	69	-0	-0	1	0	0	0	-0	/31	0.0
1977	Phi-N	2	2	0	0	0	0	0	0	0	1	.000	.000	.000	-96	-1	-1	0	0	0	0	0	H	0.0
1979	Phi-N	10	15	0	3	1	0	0	1	0	3	.200	.200	.267	25	-2	-2	1	0	0	0	2	/32	0.0
1980	Phi-N	49	62	4	10	1	1	0	5	2	7	.161	.200	.210	14	-7	-8	2	0	1	-1	0	3/2S1	-0.6
1981	Phi-N	11	1	0	0	0	0	0	0	0	1	.000	.000	.000	-96	-0	-0	0	0	0	0	1	/312	0.0
Total	10	277	559	37	90	14	1	6	44	29	109	.161	.205	.222	20	-59	-59	25	4	5	-2	18	3/21S	-3.8

■ FRANK WADDEY

Waddey, Frank Orum   b: 8/21/05, Memphis, Tenn.   BL/TL, 5'10.5", 185 lbs.   Deb: 4/16/31

YEAR	TM/L	G	AB	R	H	2B	3B	HR	RBI	BB	SO	AVG	OBP	SLG	PRO+	BR	/A	RC	SB	CS	SBR	FR	POS	TPR
1931	StL-A	14	22	3	6	1	0	0	2	2	3	.273	.333	.318	70	-1	-1	2	0	0	0	-2	/O	-0.3

YEAR	TM/L	G	AB	R	H	2B	3B	HR	RBI	BB	SO	AVG	OBP	SLG	PRO+	BR	/A	RC	SB	CS	SBR	FR	POS	TPR

■ HAM WADE
Wade, Abraham Lincoln b: 12/20/1880, Spring City, Pa. d: 7/21/68, Riverside, N.J. BR/TR, 5'8", 155 lbs. Deb: 9/09/07

YEAR	TM/L	G	AB	R	H	2B	3B	HR	RBI	BB	SO	AVG	OBP	SLG	PRO+	BR	/A	RC	SB	CS	SBR	FR	POS	TPR
1907	NY-N	1	0	0	0	0	0	0	0	0		—	—	—	—	0	0	0	0			0	/O	0.0

■ GALE WADE
Wade, Galeard Lee b: 1/20/29, Hollister, Mo. BL/TR, 6'1.5", 185 lbs. Deb: 4/11/55

YEAR	TM/L	G	AB	R	H	2B	3B	HR	RBI	BB	SO	AVG	OBP	SLG	PRO+	BR	/A	RC	SB	CS	SBR	FR	POS	TPR
1955	Chi-N	9	33	5	6	1	0	1	1	4	3	.182	.270	.303	52	-2	-2	3	0	0	0	-2	/O	-0.3
1956	Chi-N	10	12	0	0	0	0	0	0	1	0	.000	.077	.000	-78	-3	-3	-0	0	0	0	1	/O	-0.2
Total	2	19	45	5	6	1	0	1	1	5	3	.133	.220	.222	18	-5	-5	3	0	0	0	-1	/O	-0.5

■ RIP WADE
Wade, Richard Frank b: 1/12/1898, Duluth, Minn. d: 6/16/57, Sandstone, Minn. BL/TR, 5'11", 174 lbs. Deb: 4/19/23

YEAR	TM/L	G	AB	R	H	2B	3B	HR	RBI	BB	SO	AVG	OBP	SLG	PRO+	BR	/A	RC	SB	CS	SBR	FR	POS	TPR
1923	Was-A	33	69	8	16	2	2	2	14	5	10	.232	.284	.406	84	-2	-2	8	0	0	0	-2	O	-0.5

■ WOODY WAGENHORST
Wagenhorst, Elwood Otto b: 6/3/1863, Kutztown, Pa. d: 2/12/46, Deb: 6/25/1888

YEAR	TM/L	G	AB	R	H	2B	3B	HR	RBI	BB	SO	AVG	OBP	SLG	PRO+	BR	/A	RC	SB	CS	SBR	FR	POS	TPR
1888	Phi-N	2	8	2	1	0	0	0	0	0	1	.125	.125	.125	-18	-1	-1	0				-1	/3	-0.1

■ BUTTS WAGNER
Wagner, Albert b: 9/17/1869, Mansfield, Pa. d: 11/26/28, Pittsburgh, Pa. 5'10", 170 lbs. Deb: 4/27/1898

YEAR	TM/L	G	AB	R	H	2B	3B	HR	RBI	BB	SO	AVG	OBP	SLG	PRO+	BR	/A	RC	SB	CS	SBR	FR	POS	TPR
1898	Was-N	63	223	20	50	11	2	1	31	14		.224	.279	.305	70	-9	-9	21	4			-10	3O/S2	-1.6
	Bro-N	11	38	2	9	1	1	0	3	2		.237	.275	.316	72	-1	-1	3	0			-3	3	-0.3
	Yr	74	261	22	59	12	3	1	34	16		.226	.279	.307	70	-10	-10	24	4			-13		-1.9

■ HEINIE WAGNER
Wagner, Charles F. b: 9/23/1880, New York, N.Y. d: 3/20/43, New Rochelle, N.Y. BR/TR, 5'9", 183 lbs. Deb: 7/01/02 MC

YEAR	TM/L	G	AB	R	H	2B	3B	HR	RBI	BB	SO	AVG	OBP	SLG	PRO+	BR	/A	RC	SB	CS	SBR	FR	POS	TPR
1902	NY-N	17	56	4	12	1	0	0	2	0		.214	.214	.232	39	-4	-4	4	3			-3	S	-0.5
1906	Bos-A	9	32	1	9	0	0	0	4	1		.281	.303	.281	85	-1	-1	4	2			1	/2	0.0
1907	Bos-A	111	385	29	82	10	4	2	21	31		.213	.272	.275	77	-10	-10	36	20			5	*S/23	-0.1
1908	Bos-A	153	526	62	130	11	5	1	46	27		.247	.284	.293	87	-6	-8	50	20			32	*S	3.1
1909	Bos-A	124	430	53	110	16	7	1	49	35		.256	.316	.333	103	2	1	50	18			14	*S/2	2.0
1910	Bos-A	142	491	61	134	26	7	1	52	44		.273	.335	.360	115	10	8	68	26			-12	*S	0.0
1911	Bos-A	80	261	34	67	13	8	1	38	29		.257	.340	.379	101	0	0	38	15			-4	2S	0.0
1912	*Bos-A	144	504	75	138	25	6	2	68	62		.274	.358	.359	100	5	1	72	21			-13	*S	0.1
1913	Bos-A	110	365	43	83	14	8	2	34	40	29	.227	.316	.326	86	-6	-7	38	9			4	*S/2	0.6
1915	Bos-A	84	267	38	64	11	2	0	29	37	34	.240	.339	.296	93	-2	-1	30	8	4	0	-16	2/3O	-1.8
1916	Bos-A	6	8	2	4	1	0	0	0	3	0	.500	.636	.625	278	2	2	4	2			2	/32S	0.5
1918	Bos-A	3	8	0	1	0	0	0	0	1	0	.125	.222	.125	5	-1	-1	0	0			-0	/23	0.0
Total	12	983	3333	402	834	128	47	10	343	310	63	.250	.318	.326	95	-11	-17	395	144	4		11	S2/3O	3.9

■ HAL WAGNER
Wagner, Harold Edward b: 7/2/15, E.Riverton, N.J. d: 8/7/79, Riverside, N.J. BL/TR, 6', 165 lbs. Deb: 10/03/37

YEAR	TM/L	G	AB	R	H	2B	3B	HR	RBI	BB	SO	AVG	OBP	SLG	PRO+	BR	/A	RC	SB	CS	SBR	FR	POS	TPR
1937	Phi-A	1	0	0	0	0	0	0	0	0	0	—	—	—		0	0	0	0	0	0	0	/C	0.0
1938	Phi-A	33	88	10	20	2	1	0	8	8	9	.227	.299	.273	45	-8	-7	8	0	0	0	-1	C	-0.6
1939	Phi-A	5	8	0	1	0	0	0	0	0	3	.125	.125	.125	-37	-2	-2	0	0	0	0	2	/C	0.0
1940	Phi-A	34	75	9	19	5	1	0	10	11	6	.253	.356	.347	85	-2	-1	10	0	0	0	2	C	0.3
1941	Phi-A	46	131	18	29	8	2	1	15	19	9	.221	.320	.336	75	-5	-4	16	1	0	0	2	C	0.0
1942	Phi-A	104	288	26	68	17	1	1	30	24	29	.236	.304	.313	74	-10	-10	28	1	0	0	-1	C	0.1
1943	Phi-A	111	289	22	69	17	1	1	26	36	17	.239	.327	.315	89	-4	-3	31	3	3	-1	-7	C	-0.6
1944	Phi-A	5	4	0	1	0	0	0	0	0	0	.250	.250	.250	44	-0	-0	0	0	0	0	0	/C	0.0
	Bos-A	66	223	21	74	13	4	1	38	29	14	.332	.418	.439	147	14	15	45	1	1	-0	-0	C	1.9
	Yr	71	227	21	75	13	4	1	38	29	14	.330	.415	.436	145	14	14	45	1	1	-0	0		1.9
1946	*Bos-A	117	370	39	85	12	2	6	52	69	32	.230	.354	.322	85	-3	-5	48	3	1	0	-9	*C	-0.8
1947	Bos-A	21	65	5	15	3	0	0	6	9	5	.231	.324	.277	63	-3	-3	7	0	0	0	-1	C	-0.2
	Det-A	71	191	19	55	10	0	5	33	28	16	.288	.382	.419	119	6	6	33	0	0	1	-4	C	0.7
	Yr	92	256	24	70	13	0	5	39	37	21	.273	.367	.383	105	4	2	39	0	0	1	-5		0.5
1948	Det-A	54	109	10	22	3	0	0	10	20	11	.202	.326	.229	48	-7	-8	10	1	0	0	-4	C	-0.6
	Phi-N	3	4	0	0	0	0	0	0	0	0	.000	.000	.000	-99	-1	-1	0	0			1	/C	0.0
1949	Phi-N	1	4	0	0	0	0	0	0	0	0	.000	.000	.000	-99	-1	-1	0	0			-1	/C	-0.1
Total	12	672	1849	179	458	90	12	15	228	253	152	.248	.343	.334	87	-24	-27	235	10	6		-20	C	0.1

■ HONUS WAGNER
Wagner, John Peter "The Flying Dutchman"
b: 2/24/1874, Mansfield, Pa. d: 12/6/55, Carnegie, Pa. BR/TR, 5'11", 200 lbs. Deb: 7/19/1897 MCH

YEAR	TM/L	G	AB	R	H	2B	3B	HR	RBI	BB	SO	AVG	OBP	SLG	PRO+	BR	/A	RC	SB	CS	SBR	FR	POS	TPR
1897	Lou-N	61	237	37	80	17	4	2	39	15		.338	.379	.468	130	8	9	51	19			3	O/2	0.8
1898	Lou-N	151	588	80	176	29	3	10	105	31		.299	.340	.410	119	11	12	93	27			-5	132	0.9
1899	Lou-N	147	571	98	192	43	13	7	113	40		.336	.391	.494	145	33	33	128	37			2	3O/21	2.8
1900	*Pit-N	135	527	107	201	45	22	4	100	41		.381	.431	.573	178	54	54	150	38			-7	*O/321P	3.3
1901	Pit-N	140	549	101	194	37	11	6	126	53		.353	.415	.494	161	46	44	137	49			9	SO3/2	5.0
1902	Pit-N	136	534	105	176	30	16	3	91	43		.330	.391	.463	160	41	38	117	42			8	OS1/P2	4.4
1903	*Pit-N	129	512	97	182	30	19	5	101	44		.355	.406	.518	160	41	39	130	46			25	*SO/1	6.5
1904	Pit-N	132	490	97	171	44	14	4	75	59		.349	.419	.520	187	53	51	133	53			-6	*S/O12	4.7
1905	Pit-N	147	548	114	199	32	14	6	101	54		.363	.420	.505	174	52	50	144	57			20	*S/O	7.4
1906	Pit-N	142	516	103	175	38	9	2	71	58		.339	.406	.459	165	43	40	121	53			24	*S/O3	7.6
1907	Pit-N	142	515	98	180	38	14	6	82	46		.350	.403	.513	187	50	50	135	61			4	*S/1	6.6
1908	Pit-N	151	568	100	201	39	19	10	109	54		.354	.410	.542	206	65	65	146	53			-7	*S	6.3
1909	*Pit-N	137	495	92	168	39	10	5	100	66		.339	.420	.489	168	48	43	117	35			6	*S/O	5.5
1910	Pit-N	150	556	90	178	34	8	4	81	59	47	.320	.390	.432	132	28	24	103	24			3	*S1/2	3.4
1911	Pit-N	130	473	87	158	23	16	9	89	67	34	.334	.423	.507	154	39	36	109	20			4	*S1/O	4.2
1912	Pit-N	145	558	91	181	35	20	7	102	59	38	.324	.395	.496	145	32	33	118	26			23	*S	6.7
1913	Pit-N	114	413	51	124	18	4	3	56	26	40	.300	.349	.385	114	5	7	60	21			13	*S	2.8
1914	Pit-N	150	552	60	139	15	9	1	50	51	51	.252	.317	.317	93	-7	-5	60	23			7	*S3/1	0.8
1915	Pit-N	156	566	68	155	32	17	6	78	39	64	.274	.325	.422	127	15	16	79	22	15	-2	-5	*S21	1.2
1916	Pit-N	123	432	45	124	15	9	1	39	34	36	.287	.350	.370	120	11	11	61	11			-15	S1/2	0.0
1917	Pit-N	74	230	15	61	7	1	0	24	24	17	.265	.337	.304	94	0	-1	25	5			-4	13/2SM	-0.6
Total	21	2792	10430	1736	3415	640	252	101	1732	963	327	.327	.388	.466	151	669	652	2218	722	15		102	*SO13/2P	80.3

■ JOE WAGNER
Wagner, Joseph Bernard b: 4/24/1889, New York, N.Y. d: 11/15/48, Bronx, N.Y. 5'11", 165 lbs. Deb: 4/25/15

YEAR	TM/L	G	AB	R	H	2B	3B	HR	RBI	BB	SO	AVG	OBP	SLG	PRO+	BR	/A	RC	SB	CS	SBR	FR	POS	TPR
1915	Cin-N	75	197	17	35	5	2	0	13	8	35	.178	.210	.223	31	-17	-17	9	4	6	-2	6	2S/3	-1.3

■ LEON WAGNER
Wagner, Leon Lamar b: 5/13/34, Chattanooga, Tenn. BL/TR, 6'1", 195 lbs. Deb: 6/22/58

YEAR	TM/L	G	AB	R	H	2B	3B	HR	RBI	BB	SO	AVG	OBP	SLG	PRO+	BR	/A	RC	SB	CS	SBR	FR	POS	TPR
1958	SF-N	74	221	33	70	9	6	13	35	18	34	.317	.371	.534	139	11	12	45	1	0	0	-4	O	0.6
1959	SF-N	87	129	20	29	4	3	5	22	25	24	.225	.363	.419	110	2	2	20	0	0	0	-1	O	0.0
1960	StL-N	39	98	12	21	2	0	4	11	17	17	.214	.336	.357	83	-1	-2	12	0	1	-1	0	O	-0.3
1961	LA-A	133	453	74	127	19	2	28	79	48	65	.280	.353	.517	116	17	11	85	5	1	1	-2	*O	0.5
1962	LA-A	160	612	96	164	21	5	37	107	50	87	.268	.328	.500	123	14	17	101	7	5	-1	-6	*O	0.4
1963	LA-A	149	550	73	160	11	4	26	90	49	73	.291	.356	.456	134	19	23	90	5	7	-3	-6	*O	1.0
1964	Cle-A	163	641	94	162	19	2	31	100	56	121	.253	.319	.434	108	5	6	89	14	2	3	-7	*O	-0.5
1965	Cle-A	144	591	91	152	18	1	28	79	60	52	.294	.371	.495	148	30	29	99	12	2		-12	*O	1.5
1966	Cle-A	150	549	70	153	20	2	23	66	46	69	.279	.336	.441	121	14	14	80	5	2	0	-13	*O	-0.4
1967	Cle-A	135	433	56	105	15	1	15	54	37	76	.242	.320	.386	107	4	4	55	3	3	-1	-12	*O	-1.3
1968	Cle-A	38	49	5	9	4	0	1	6	6	6	.184	.273	.265	65	-2	-2	3	0	0	0	-3	O	-0.5
	Chi-A	69	162	14	46	8	0	2	18	21	31	.284	.366	.352	117	4	4	22	2	1	0	-9	O	-0.7

YEAR	TM/L	G	AB	R	H	2B	3B	HR	RBI	BB	SO	AVG	OBP	SLG	PRO+	BR	/A	RC	SB	CS	SBR	FR	POS	TPR
	Yr	107	211	19	55	12	0	1	24	27	37	.261	.345	.332	106	2	2	25	2	1	0	-12		-1.2
1969	SF-N	11	12	0	4	0	0	0	2	2	1	.333	.467	.333	130	1	1	2	0	0	0	0	/O	0.1
Total	12	1352	4426	636	1202	150	15	211	669	435	656	.272	.343	.455	121	118	117	703	54	24	2	-75	*O	0.4

■ MARK WAGNER
Wagner, Mark Duane b: 3/4/54, Conneaut, Ohio BR/TR, 6', 165 lbs. Deb: 8/20/76

YEAR	TM/L	G	AB	R	H	2B	3B	HR	RBI	BB	SO	AVG	OBP	SLG	PRO+	BR	/A	RC	SB	CS	SBR	FR	POS	TPR
1976	Det-A	39	115	9	30	2	3	0	12	6	18	.261	.298	.330	81	-3	-3	11	0	2	-1	9	S	0.8
1977	Det-A	22	48	4	7	0	1	1	3	4	12	.146	.226	.250	28	-5	-5	3	0	1	-1	-1	S/2	-0.3
1978	Det-A	39	109	10	26	1	2	0	6	3	11	.239	.272	.284	55	-6	-7	8	1	0	0	-7	S/2	-1.0
1979	Det-A	75	146	16	40	3	0	1	13	16	25	.274	.346	.315	77	-4	-4	17	3	2	-0	7	S2/3	0.8
1980	Det-A	45	72	5	17	1	0	0	3	7	11	.236	.304	.250	52	-4	-5	6	0	1	-1	2	S/32	0.0
1981	Tex-A	50	85	15	22	4	1	1	14	8	13	.259	.323	.365	103	-0	0	10	1	1	-0	21	S/23	2.4
1982	Tex-A	60	179	14	43	4	1	0	8	10	28	.240	.280	.274	56	-11	-10	13	1	0	0	-1	S	-0.4
1983	Tex-A	2	2	0	0	0	0	0	0	0	1	.000	.000	.000	-99	-1	-1	0	0	0	0	1	/S	0.1
1984	Oak-A	82	87	8	20	5	1	0	12	7	11	.230	.287	.310	70	-4	-3	7	2	0	1	12	S3/2PD	1.4
Total	9	414	843	81	205	20	9	3	71	61	130	.243	.297	.299	66	-38	-37	76	8	7	-2	43	S/23DP	3.8

■ BILL WAGNER
Wagner, William Joseph b: 1/2/1894, Jessup, Iowa d: 1/11/51, Waterloo, Iowa BR/TR, 6', 187 lbs. Deb: 7/16/14

YEAR	TM/L	G	AB	R	H	2B	3B	HR	RBI	BB	SO	AVG	OBP	SLG	PRO+	BR	/A	RC	SB	CS	SBR	FR	POS	TPR
1914	Pit-N	3	1	0	0	0	0	0	0	0	0	.000	.000	.000	-99	-0	-0	0	0			0	/C	0.0
1915	Pit-N	5	5	0	0	0	0	0	0	1	2	.000	.167	.000	-48	-1	-1	0	0			2	/C	0.1
1916	Pit-N	19	38	2	9	0	2	0	2	5	8	.237	.326	.342	104	0	0	4	0			2	C	0.3
1917	Pit-N	53	151	15	31	7	2	0	9	11	22	.205	.264	.278	64	-6	-7	11	1			-4	C1	-0.9
1918	Bos-N	13	47	2	10	0	0	1	7	4	5	.213	.275	.277	71	-2	-2	3	0			-5	C	-0.5
Total	5	93	242	19	50	7	4	1	18	21	37	.207	.273	.281	69	-9	-9	19	1			-5	/C1	-1.0

■ KERMIT WAHL
Wahl, Kermit Emerson b: 11/18/22, Columbia, S.Dak. d: 9/16/87, Tucson, Ariz. BR/TR, 5'11", 170 lbs. Deb: 6/23/44

YEAR	TM/L	G	AB	R	H	2B	3B	HR	RBI	BB	SO	AVG	OBP	SLG	PRO+	BR	/A	RC	SB	CS	SBR	FR	POS	TPR
1944	Cin-N	4	1	0	0	0	0	0	0	0	0	.000	.000	.000	-99	-0	-0	0	0			0	/3	0.0
1945	Cin-N	71	194	18	39	8	2	0	10	23	22	.201	.286	.263	54	-12	-12	16	2			5	2S/3	0.0
1947	Cin-N	39	81	8	14	0	0	1	4	6	12	.173	.239	.210	20	-9	-9	4	0			6	3/S2	-0.2
1950	Phi-A	89	280	26	72	12	3	2	27	30	30	.257	.331	.343	74	-12	-11	32	1	1	-0	11	3S/2	0.0
1951	Phi-A	20	59	4	11	2	0	0	6	9	5	.186	.294	.220	40	-5	-5	4	0	0	0	2	3	-0.2
	StL-A	8	27	2	9	1	1	0	3	0	3	.333	.333	.444	106	0	0	4	0	0	0	1	/3	0.0
	Yr	28	86	6	20	3	1	0	9	9	8	.233	.305	.291	60	-5	-5	8	0	0	0	3		-0.2
Total	5	231	642	58	145	23	6	3	50	68	72	.226	.302	.294	60	-38	-37	60	3	1		25	3/S2	-0.4

■ EDDIE WAITKUS
Waitkus, Edward Stephen b: 9/4/19, Cambridge, Mass. d: 9/15/72, Jamaica Plain, Mass. BL/TL, 6', 170 lbs. Deb: 4/15/41

YEAR	TM/L	G	AB	R	H	2B	3B	HR	RBI	BB	SO	AVG	OBP	SLG	PRO+	BR	/A	RC	SB	CS	SBR	FR	POS	TPR
1941	Chi-N	12	28	1	5	0	0	0	0	3	3	.179	.207	.179	10	-3	-3	1	0			-1	/1	-0.5
1946	Chi-N	113	441	50	134	24	5	4	55	23	14	.304	.340	.408	114	5	6	60	3			4	*1	0.1
1947	Chi-N	130	514	60	150	28	6	2	35	32	17	.292	.336	.381	94	-8	-5	66	3			8	*1	-0.3
1948	Chi-N	139	562	87	166	27	10	7	44	43	19	.295	.348	.416	110	4	7	81	11			5	*1O	1.0
1949	Phi-N	54	209	41	64	16	3	1	28	33	12	.306	.403	.426	126	8	9	38	3			1	1	0.9
1950	*Phi-N	154	641	102	182	32	5	2	44	55	29	.284	.341	.359	86	-14	-12	79	3			-2	*1	-2.0
1951	Phi-N	145	610	65	157	27	4	1	46	53	22	.257	.317	.320	73	-24	-23	64	0	3	-2	-2	*1	-2.9
1952	Phi-N	146	499	51	144	29	4	2	49	64	23	.289	.371	.375	108	7	7	75	2	2	-1	-2	*1	0.1
1953	Phi-N	81	247	24	72	9	2	1	16	13	23	.291	.330	.356	79	-8	-7	30	1	1	-0	-1	1	-0.9
1954	Bal-A	95	311	35	88	17	4	2	33	28	25	.283	.344	.383	107	-1	2	41	0	1	-1	1	1	0.0
1955	Bal-A	38	85	2	22	1	1	0	9	11	10	.259	.344	.294	78	-3	-2	9	2	0	-1	-2	1	-0.4
	Phi-N	33	107	10	30	5	0	2	14	17	7	.280	.379	.383	105	1	1	15	0	1	-1	0	1	0.1
Total	11	1140	4254	528	1214	215	44	24	373	372	204	.285	.344	.374	96	-35	-20	560	28	8		10	*1/O	-5.0

■ CHARLIE WAITT
Waitt, Charles C. b: 10/14/1853, Hallowell, Me. d: 10/21/12, San Francisco, Cal. 5'11", 165 lbs. Deb: 5/25/1875

YEAR	TM/L	G	AB	R	H	2B	3B	HR	RBI	BB	SO	AVG	OBP	SLG	PRO+	BR	/A	RC	SB	CS	SBR	FR	POS	TPR
1875	StL-n	31	118	14	25	9	0	0		2		.212	.225	.288	84	-3	-1	8					O/1	0.0
1877	Chi-N	10	41	2	4	0	0	0	2	0	3	.098	.098	.098	-34	-6	-7	0				1	O	-0.5
1882	Bal-a	72	250	19	39	4	0	0		13		.156	.198	.172	28	-19	-16	9				0	*O	-1.5
1883	Phi-N	1	3	0	1	0	0	0	0	0	1	.333	.333	.333	114	0	0	0				-1	/O	0.0
Total	3	83	294	21	44	4	0	0	2	13	4	.150	.186	.163	18	-25	-23	9				1	/O	-2.0

■ HOWARD WAKEFIELD
Wakefield, Howard John b: 4/2/1884, Bucyrus, Ohio d: 4/16/41, Chicago, Ill. BR/TR, 6'1", 205 lbs. Deb: 9/18/05

YEAR	TM/L	G	AB	R	H	2B	3B	HR	RBI	BB	SO	AVG	OBP	SLG	PRO+	BR	/A	RC	SB	CS	SBR	FR	POS	TPR
1905	Cle-A	10	26	3	4	0	0	0	1	0		.154	.154	.154	-1	-3	-3	1	0			-3	/C	-0.5
1906	Was-A	77	211	17	59	9	2	1	21	7		.280	.303	.355	113	1	2	25	6			-15	C	-0.8
1907	Cle-A	26	37	4	5	2	0	0	3	3		.135	.200	.189	25	-3	-3	1	0			-0	C	-0.2
Total	3	113	274	24	68	11	2	1	25	10		.248	.275	.314	90	-5	-4	27	6			-18	/C	-1.5

■ DICK WAKEFIELD
Wakefield, Richard Cummings b: 5/6/21, Chicago, Ill. d: 8/26/85, Wayne Co., Mich. BL/TR, 6'4", 210 lbs. Deb: 6/26/41

YEAR	TM/L	G	AB	R	H	2B	3B	HR	RBI	BB	SO	AVG	OBP	SLG	PRO+	BR	/A	RC	SB	CS	SBR	FR	POS	TPR
1941	Det-A	7	7	0	1	0	0	0	0	0	1	.143	.143	.143	-22	-1	-1	0	0	0	0	0	/O	0.0
1943	Det-A	155	633	91	200	38	8	7	79	62	60	.316	.377	.434	127	29	23	101	4	5	-2	-7	*O	1.1
1944	Det-A	78	276	53	98	15	5	12	53	55	29	.355	.464	.576	186	37	35	79	2	2	-1	-4	O	2.9
1946	Det-A	111	396	64	106	11	5	12	59	59	55	.268	.364	.412	110	10	7	63	3	5	-2	-1	*O	-0.1
1947	Det-A	112	368	59	104	15	5	8	51	80	44	.283	.412	.416	127	19	17	69	1	4	-2	-1	*O	1.0
1948	Det-A	110	322	50	89	20	5	11	53	70	55	.276	.406	.472	129	17	15	67	0	1	-1	-0	O	1.1
1949	Det-A	59	126	17	26	3	1	6	19	32	24	.206	.367	.389	100	0	0	20	0	0	0	1	O	0.1
1950	NY-A	3	2	0	1	0	0	0	1	1	1	.500	.667	.500	208	0	0	1	0	0	0	0	H	0.0
1952	NY-N	3	2	0	0	0	0	0	0	1	1	.000	.333	.000	-0	-0	-0	0	0	0	0	0	H	0.0
Total	9	638	2132	334	625	102	29	56	315	360	270	.293	.396	.447	130	110	97	401	10	17	-7	-11	O	6.1

■ ED WALCZAK
Walczak, Edwin Joseph "Husky" b: 9/21/18, Artic, R.I. BR/TR, 5'11", 180 lbs. Deb: 9/03/45

YEAR	TM/L	G	AB	R	H	2B	3B	HR	RBI	BB	SO	AVG	OBP	SLG	PRO+	BR	/A	RC	SB	CS	SBR	FR	POS	TPR
1945	Phi-N	20	57	6	12	3	0	0	2	6	9	.211	.286	.263	55	-4	-3	4	0			1	2/S	0.0

■ FRED WALDEN
Walden, Thomas Fred b: 6/25/1890, Fayette, Mo. d: 9/27/55, Jefferson Barracks, Mo. BR/TR, Deb: 6/03/12

YEAR	TM/L	G	AB	R	H	2B	3B	HR	RBI	BB	SO	AVG	OBP	SLG	PRO+	BR	/A	RC	SB	CS	SBR	FR	POS	TPR
1912	StL-A	1	0	0	0	0	0	0	0	0		—	—	—	—	0	0	0	0			-1	/C	0.0

■ IRV WALDRON
Waldron, Irving J. b: 1/21/1876, Hillside, N.Y. d: 7/22/44, Worcester, Mass. BR/TR, Deb: 4/25/01

YEAR	TM/L	G	AB	R	H	2B	3B	HR	RBI	BB	SO	AVG	OBP	SLG	PRO+	BR	/A	RC	SB	CS	SBR	FR	POS	TPR
1901	Mil-A	62	266	48	79	8	6	0	29	16		.297	.342	.372	105	0	2	39	12			-2	O	0.0
	Was-A	79	332	54	107	14	3	0	23	22		.322	.366	.383	112	5	6	51	8			-5	O	0.0
	Yr	141	598	102	186	22	9	0	52	38		.311	.355	.378	109	5	8	91	20			-7		0.0

■ JIM WALEWANDER
Walewander, James b: 5/2/62, Chicago, Ill. BB/TR, 5'10", 160 lbs. Deb: 5/31/87

YEAR	TM/L	G	AB	R	H	2B	3B	HR	RBI	BB	SO	AVG	OBP	SLG	PRO+	BR	/A	RC	SB	CS	SBR	FR	POS	TPR
1987	Det-A	53	54	24	13	3	1	1	4	7	6	.241	.328	.389	93	-1	-0	7	2	1	0	15	23/SD	1.5
1988	Det-A	88	175	23	37	5	0	0	6	12	26	.211	.262	.240	43	-13	-13	13	11	4	1	14	2/S3D	0.7
1990	NY-A	9	5	1	1	1	0	0	1	0	0	.200	.200	.400	64	-0	-0	0	1	1	-0	1	/23S	0.1
Total	3	150	234	48	51	9	1	1	11	19	32	.218	.277	.278	56	-15	-13	19	14	6	1	31	/23DS	2.3

■ RUBE WALKER
Walker, Albert Bluford b: 5/16/26, Lenoir, N.C. BL/TR, 6', 175 lbs. Deb: 4/20/48 C

YEAR	TM/L	G	AB	R	H	2B	3B	HR	RBI	BB	SO	AVG	OBP	SLG	PRO+	BR	/A	RC	SB	CS	SBR	FR	POS	TPR
1948	Chi-N	79	171	17	47	8	0	5	26	24	17	.275	.371	.409	115	3	4	25	0			-3	C	0.4
1949	Chi-N	56	172	11	42	4	1	3	22	9	18	.244	.282	.331	66	-9	-9	15	0			-4	C	-1.1
1950	Chi-N	74	213	19	49	7	1	6	16	18	34	.230	.290	.357	70	-10	-10	22	0			1	C	-0.6
1951	Chi-N	37	107	9	25	4	0	2	5	12	13	.234	.311	.327	71	-4	-4	11	0	0	0	-4	C	-0.8

YEAR	TM/L	G	AB	R	H	2B	3B	HR	RBI	BB	SO	AVG	OBP	SLG	PRO+	BR	/A	RC	SB	CS	SBR	FR	POS	TPR
	Bro-N	36	74	6	18	4	0	2	9	6	14	.243	.300	.378	80	-2	-2	8	0	0	0	-5	C	-0.6
	Yr	73	181	15	43	8	0	4	14	18	27	.238	.307	.348	74	-6	-7	19	0	0	0	-9		-1.4
1952	Bro-N	46	139	9	36	8	0	1	19	8	17	.259	.304	.338	77	-4	-4	14	0	0	0	6	C	0.2
1953	Bro-N	43	95	5	23	6	0	3	9	7	11	.242	.301	.400	79	-3	-3	12	0	0	0	1	C	0.0
1954	Bro-N	50	155	12	28	7	0	5	23	24	17	.181	.294	.323	59	-9	-10	15	0	0	0	1	C	-0.7
1955	Bro-N	48	103	6	26	5	0	2	13	15	11	.252	.347	.359	86	-1	-2	11	1	0	0	1	C	0.1
1956	*Bro-N	54	146	5	31	6	1	3	20	7	18	.212	.248	.329	50	-10	-11	11	0	1	-1	-2	C	-1.2
1957	Bro-N	60	166	12	30	8	0	2	23	15	33	.181	.249	.265	35	-15	-17	10	2	0	1	-6	C	-1.9
1958	LA-N	25	44	3	5	2	0	1	7	5	10	.114	.204	.227	14	-6	-6	2	0	0	0	-1	C	-0.5
Total	11	608	1585	114	360	69	3	35	192	150	213	.227	.296	.341	68	-70	-74	158	3	1		-16	C	-6.7

■ TONY WALKER
Walker, Anthony Bruce b: 7/1/59, San Diego, Cal. BR/TR, 6'2", 205 lbs. Deb: 4/08/86

YEAR	TM/L	G	AB	R	H	2B	3B	HR	RBI	BB	SO	AVG	OBP	SLG	PRO+	BR	/A	RC	SB	CS	SBR	FR	POS	TPR
1986	Hou-N	84	90	19	20	7	0	2	10	11	15	.222	.307	.367	87	-2	-2	10	11	3	2	5	O	0.4

■ FRANK WALKER
Walker, Charles Franklin b: 9/22/1894, Enoree, S.C. d: 9/16/74, Bristol, Tenn. BR/TR, 5'11", 165 lbs. Deb: 9/06/17

YEAR	TM/L	G	AB	R	H	2B	3B	HR	RBI	BB	SO	AVG	OBP	SLG	PRO+	BR	/A	RC	SB	CS	SBR	FR	POS	TPR
1917	Det-A	2	2	0	0	0	0	0	0	0	1	.000	.000	.000	-99	-0	-0	0				0	H	0.0
1918	Det-A	55	167	10	33	10	3	1	20	7	29	.198	.234	.311	67	-8	-8	12	3			-2	O	-1.2
1920	Phi-A	24	91	10	21	2	2	0	10	5	14	.231	.286	.297	54	-6	-6	7	0	2	-1	-1	O	-1.0
1921	Phi-A	19	66	6	15	3	0	1	6	8	11	.227	.311	.318	60	-4	-4	7	1	0	0	1	O	-0.3
1925	NY-N	39	81	12	18	1	0	1	5	9	11	.222	.308	.272	51	-6	-6	7	1	1	-0	2	O	-0.4
Total	5	139	407	38	87	16	5	3	41	29	66	.214	.273	.300	58	-25	-24	34	5	3		-1	O	-2.9

■ TILLY WALKER
Walker, Clarence William b: 9/4/1887, Telford, Tenn. d: 9/20/59, Chattanooga, Tenn BR/TR, 5'11", 165 lbs. Deb: 4/12/11

YEAR	TM/L	G	AB	R	H	2B	3B	HR	RBI	BB	SO	AVG	OBP	SLG	PRO+	BR	/A	RC	SB	CS	SBR	FR	POS	TPR
1911	Was-A	95	356	44	99	6	4	2	39	15		.278	.311	.334	82	-10	-9	41	12			-1	O	-1.7
1912	Was-A	39	110	22	30	2	1	0	9	8		.273	.333	.309	83	-2	-2	15	11			-3	O/2	-0.6
1913	StL-A	23	85	7	25	4	1	0	11	2	9	.294	.310	.365	100	-1	-0	11	5			-0	O	-0.1
1914	StL-A	151	517	67	154	24	16	6	78	51	72	.298	.365	.441	148	25	27	87	29	17	-2	16	*O	3.6
1915	StL-A	144	510	53	137	20	7	5	49	36	77	.269	.323	.365	110	2	4	62	20	17	-4	15	*O	0.8
1916	*Bos-A	128	467	68	124	29	11	3	46	23	45	.266	.303	.394	109	2	2	61	14			-3	*O	-0.9
1917	Bos-A	106	337	41	83	18	7	2	37	25	38	.246	.300	.359	102	-1	-1	38	6			6	O	0.0
1918	Phi-A	114	414	56	122	20	0	**11**	48	41	44	.295	.360	.423	135	17	16	64	8			5	*O	1.7
1919	Phi-A	125	456	47	133	30	6	10	64	26	41	.292	.330	.450	116	8	7	68	8			4	*O	-0.4
1920	Phi-A	149	585	79	157	23	7	17	82	41	59	.268	.321	.419	94	-7	-8	80	8	3	1	6	*O	-1.3
1921	Phi-A	142	556	89	169	32	5	23	101	73	41	.304	.389	.504	125	21	21	111	3	4	-2	9	*O	1.6
1922	Phi-A	153	565	111	160	31	4	37	99	61	64	.283	.357	.549	130	24	22	110	4	6	-2	-2	*O	0.7
1923	Phi-A	52	109	12	30	5	2	2	16	14	11	.275	.368	.413	104	1	1	7	1	2	-1	-2	O	-0.3
Total	13	1421	5067	696	1423	244	71	118	679	416	501	.281	.339	.427	115	79	80	762	129	49		42	*O/2	3.1

■ CHICO WALKER
Walker, Cleotha b: 11/25/57, Jackson, Miss. BB/TR, 5'9", 170 lbs. Deb: 9/02/80

YEAR	TM/L	G	AB	R	H	2B	3B	HR	RBI	BB	SO	AVG	OBP	SLG	PRO+	BR	/A	RC	SB	CS	SBR	FR	POS	TPR
1980	Bos-A	19	57	3	12	0	0	1	5	6	10	.211	.297	.263	52	-3	-4	5	3	2	-0	1	2/D	-0.2
1981	Bos-A	6	17	3	6	0	0	0	2	1	2	.353	.389	.353	108	0	0	2	0	2	-1	-2	/2	-0.2
1983	Bos-A	4	5	2	2	0	2	0	1	0	0	.400	.400	1.200	299	1	1	2	0	0	0	1	/O	0.2
1984	Bos-A	3	2	0	0	0	0	0	1	0	1	.000	.000	.000	-96	-1	-1	0	0	0	0	0	/2	0.0
1985	Chi-N	21	12	3	1	0	0	0	0	0	5	.083	.083	.083	-48	-2	-3	0	1	0	0	1	/O2	-0.1
1986	Chi-N	28	101	21	28	3	2	1	7	10	20	.277	.342	.376	91	-0	-1	14	15	4		-3	O	-0.2
1987	Chi-N	47	105	15	21	4	0	0	7	12	23	.200	.282	.238	38	-9	-9	8	11	4	1	-4	O/3	-1.3
1988	Cal-A	33	78	8	12	1	0	0	2	6	15	.154	.214	.167	8	-9	-9	3	2	1	0	-3	O/23	-1.1
Total	8	161	377	55	82	8	4	2	25	35	76	.218	.286	.276	52	-23	-25	34	32	13	2	-9	/O2D3	-2.9

■ DUANE WALKER
Walker, Duane Allen b: 3/13/57, Pasadena, Tex. BL/TL, 6', 185 lbs. Deb: 5/25/82

YEAR	TM/L	G	AB	R	H	2B	3B	HR	RBI	BB	SO	AVG	OBP	SLG	PRO+	BR	/A	RC	SB	CS	SBR	FR	POS	TPR
1982	Cin-N	86	239	26	52	10	0	5	22	27	58	.218	.302	.322	73	-8	-8	26	9	3	1	-1	O	-0.9
1983	Cin-N	109	225	14	53	12	1	2	29	20	43	.236	.298	.324	70	-8	-9	23	6	3	0	2	O	-0.8
1984	Cin-N	83	195	35	57	10	3	10	28	33	35	.292	.395	.528	150	15	14	43	7	3	0	0	O	1.2
1985	Cin-N	37	48	5	8	2	1	2	6	6	18	.167	.259	.375	72	-2	-2	5	1	0	0	-0	O	-0.1
	Tex-A	53	132	14	23	2	0	5	11	15	29	.174	.264	.303	54	-8	-9	11	2	1	0	3	OD	-0.5
1988	StL-N	24	22	1	4	1	0	0	3	2	7	.182	.250	.227	38	-2	-2	1	0	0	0	-0	/O1	-0.2
Total	5	392	861	95	197	37	5	24	99	103	190	.229	.313	.367	86	-13	-16	109	25	10	2	4	O/D1	-1.3

■ ERNIE WALKER
Walker, Ernest Robert b: 9/17/1890, Blossburg, Ala. d: 4/1/65, Pell City, Ala. BL/TR, 6', 165 lbs. Deb: 4/13/13

YEAR	TM/L	G	AB	R	H	2B	3B	HR	RBI	BB	SO	AVG	OBP	SLG	PRO+	BR	/A	RC	SB	CS	SBR	FR	POS	TPR
1913	StL-A	7	14	0	3	0	0	0	2	0	5	.214	.214	.214	26	-1	-1	1	0			0	/O	-0.1
1914	StL-A	74	131	19	39	5	3	1	14	13	26	.298	.366	.405	137	5	5	20	6	4	-1	-6	/O	-0.3
1915	StL-A	50	109	15	23	4	2	0	9	23	32	.211	.348	.284	93	-0	0	10	5	8	-3	-6	/O	-1.1
Total	3	131	254	34	65	9	5	1	25	36	63	.256	.351	.343	112	3	4	31	11	12		-12	/O	-1.5

■ DIXIE WALKER
Walker, Fred "The People's Cherce" b: 9/24/10, Villa Rica, Ga. d: 5/17/82, Birmingham, Ala. BL/TR, 6'1", 175 lbs. Deb: 4/28/31 C

YEAR	TM/L	G	AB	R	H	2B	3B	HR	RBI	BB	SO	AVG	OBP	SLG	PRO+	BR	/A	RC	SB	CS	SBR	FR	POS	TPR
1931	NY-A	2	10	1	3	2	0	0	1	0	4	.300	.300	.500	113	0	0	1	0	0	0	-0	/O	0.0
1933	NY-A	98	328	68	90	15	7	15	51	26	28	.274	.330	.500	125	6	9	54	2	2	-1	8	O	1.2
1934	NY-A	17	17	2	2	0	0	0	0	1	3	.118	.167	.118	-27	-3	-3	0	0	0	0	-0	/O	-0.2
1935	NY-A	8	13	1	2	1	0	0	1	0	1	.154	.154	.231	-2	-2	-2	0	0	0	0	-0	/O	-0.1
1936	NY-A	6	20	3	7	0	2	1	5	1	3	.350	.381	.700	167	2	2	5	1	1	-0	-0	/O	0.1
	Chi-A	26	70	12	19	2	0	0	11	14	6	.271	.400	.300	73	-2	-2	10	1	0	0	2	O	0.0
	Yr	32	90	15	26	2	2	1	16	15	9	.289	.396	.389	92	-0	-1	15	2	1	0	2		0.1
1937	Chi-A	154	593	105	179	28	**16**	9	95	78	26	.302	.383	.449	109	9	9	105	1	2	-1	-13	*O	-0.9
1938	Det-A	127	454	84	140	27	6	6	43	65	32	.308	.396	.434	102	7	3	81	5	4	-1	-3	*O	0.0
1939	Det-A	43	154	30	47	4	5	4	19	15	8	.305	.367	.474	106	3	1	26	4	1	1	3	O	0.3
	Bro-N	61	225	27	63	6	4	2	38	20	10	.280	.339	.369	87	-3	-4	28	1			0	O	-0.4
1940	Bro-N	143	556	75	171	37	8	6	66	42	21	.308	.357	.435	111	13	8	88	3			2	*O	0.6
1941	*Bro-N	148	531	88	165	32	8	9	71	70	18	.311	.391	.452	131	27	24	99	4			7	*O	2.6
1942	Bro-N	118	393	57	114	28	1	6	54	47	15	.290	.367	.412	126	14	13	64	1			-1	*O	1.0
1943	Bro-N	138	540	83	163	32	6	5	71	49	24	.302	.363	.411	123	16	16	82	3			2	*O	1.3
1944	Bro-N	147	535	77	191	37	8	13	91	72	27	**.357**	.434	.529	173	51	52	128				-4	*O	3.8
1945	Bro-N	154	607	102	182	42	9	8	**124**	75	16	.300	.381	.438	128	23	24	105	6			10	*O	2.7
1946	Bro-N	150	576	80	184	29	9	9	116	67	28	.319	.391	.448	136	29	28	104	14			-12	*O	1.4
1947	*Bro-N	148	529	77	162	31	3	9	94	97	26	.306	.415	.427	119	22	20	101	6			-14	*O	0.0
1948	Pit-N	129	408	39	129	19	3	2	54	52	18	.316	.393	.392	111	9	8	66	1			-18	*O	-1.7
1949	Pit-N	88	181	26	51	4	1	1	18	26	11	.282	.372	.331	88	-1	-2	24	0			-5	O/1	-0.2
Total	18	1905	6740	1037	2064	376	96	105	1023	817	325	.306	.383	.437	121	220	204	1171	59	10		-37	*O/1	10.9

■ GEE WALKER
Walker, Gerald Holmes b: 3/19/08, Gulfport, Miss. d: 3/20/81, Whitfield, Miss. BR/TR, 5'11", 188 lbs. Deb: 4/14/31 C

YEAR	TM/L	G	AB	R	H	2B	3B	HR	RBI	BB	SO	AVG	OBP	SLG	PRO+	BR	/A	RC	SB	CS	SBR	FR	POS	TPR
1931	Det-A	59	189	20	56	17	2	1	28	14	21	.296	.345	.423	98	-0	-1	26	10	7	-1	-3	O	-0.7
1932	Det-A	127	480	71	155	32	6	8	78	13	38	.323	.345	.465	104	4	1	78	30	6	**5**	-3	*O	0.0
1933	Det-A	127	483	68	135	29	7	9	64	15	44	.280	.304	.424	90	-9	-10	61	26	9	**2**	-1	*O	-1.1
1934	*Det-A	98	347	54	104	19	2	6	39	19	20	.300	.340	.418	94	-4	-4	49	20	9	1	4	O	0.0
1935	*Det-A	98	362	52	109	22	3	7	53	15	21	.301	.329	.453	104	-2	0	52	6	4	-1	-0	O	-0.1
1936	Det-A	134	550	105	194	55	5	12	93	23	30	.353	.387	.536	125	20	20	112	17	8	0	6	*O	1.9

YEAR	TM/L	G	AB	R	H	2B	3B	HR	RBI	BB	SO	AVG	OBP	SLG	PRO+	BR	/A	RC	SB	CS	SBR	FR	POS	TPR
1937	Det-A	151	635	105	213	42	4	18	113	41	74	.335	.380	.499	117	18	16	121	23	7	3	-6	*O	0.6
1938	Chi-A	120	442	69	135	23	6	16	87	38	32	.305	.360	.493	109	6	5	79	9	4	0	-11	*O	-0.5
1939	Chi-A	149	598	95	174	30	11	13	111	28	43	.291	.330	.443	94	-6	-8	84	17	6	2	9	*O	-0.1
1940	Was-A	140	595	87	175	29	7	13	96	24	58	.294	.325	.432	101	-7	-2	84	21	4	4	-2	*O	-0.8
1941	Cle-A	121	445	56	126	26	11	6	48	18	46	.283	.313	.431	100	-5	-3	56	12	6	0	7	*O	-0.1
1942	Cin-N	119	422	40	97	20	2	5	50	31	44	.230	.290	.322	79	-12	-12	40	11			-1	*O	-1.5
1943	Cin-N	114	429	48	105	23	2	3	54	12	38	.245	.270	.329	74	-17	-16	35	6			-11	*O	-3.3
1944	Cin-N	121	478	56	133	21	3	5	62	23	48	.278	.318	.366	96	-6	-4	53	7			-2	*O	-1.4
1945	Cin-N	106	316	28	80	11	2	2	21	16	38	.253	.289	.320	71	-14	-13	29	8			-11	O/3	-2.6
Total	15	1784	6771	954	1991	399	76	124	997	330	600	.294	.331	.430	99	-33	-30	959	223	70		-25	*O/3	-9.7

■ GREG WALKER

Walker, Gregory Lee b: 10/6/59, Douglas, Ga. BL/TR, 6'3", 205 lbs. Deb: 9/18/82

YEAR	TM/L	G	AB	R	H	2B	3B	HR	RBI	BB	SO	AVG	OBP	SLG	PRO+	BR	/A	RC	SB	CS	SBR	FR	POS	TPR
1982	Chi-A	11	17	3	7	2	1	2	7	2	3	.412	.474	1.000	292	4	4	8	0	0	0	0	/D	0.4
1983	*Chi-A	118	307	32	83	16	3	10	55	28	57	.270	.335	.440	107	4	3	46	2	1	0	-7	1D	-0.6
1984	Chi-A	136	442	62	130	29	2	24	75	35	66	.294	.349	.532	134	22	20	79	8	5	-1	-2	*1D	1.1
1985	Chi-A	163	601	77	155	38	4	24	92	44	100	.258	.311	.454	102	3	1	81	5	2	0	-3	*1/D	-1.1
1986	Chi-A	78	282	37	78	10	6	13	51	29	44	.277	.348	.493	122	10	8	48	1	2	0	-1	1/D	0.2
1987	Chi-A	157	566	85	145	33	2	27	94	75	112	.256	.348	.465	110	11	9	93	2	1	0	-14	*1/D	-1.8
1988	Chi-A	99	377	45	93	22	1	8	42	29	77	.247	.306	.374	90	-6	-6	43	0	1	-1	-14	1	-2.5
1989	Chi-A	77	233	25	49	14	0	5	26	23	50	.210	.290	.335	77	-8	-7	22	0			-5	1D	-1.5
1990	Chi-A	2	5	0	1	0	0	0	0	0	0	.200	.200	.200	12	-1	-1	0	0	0	0	0	/1D	-0.0
	Bal-A	14	34	2	5	0	0	0	2	3	9	.147	.237	.147	10	-4	-4	1	1	0	0		D	-0.3
	Yr	16	39	2	6	0	0	0	2	3	11	.154	.233	.154	10	-5	-4	1	1	0	0			-0.3
Total	9	855	2864	368	746	164	19	113	444	268	520	.260	.328	.449	108	37	28	422	19	12	-2	-46	1/D	-6.1

■ HARRY WALKER

Walker, Harry William "Harry The Hat" b: 10/22/16, Pascagoula, Miss. BL/TR, 6'2", 175 lbs. Deb: 9/25/40 MC

YEAR	TM/L	G	AB	R	H	2B	3B	HR	RBI	BB	SO	AVG	OBP	SLG	PRO+	BR	/A	RC	SB	CS	SBR	FR	POS	TPR
1940	StL-N	7	27	2	5	2	0	0	6	0	2	.185	.185	.259	20	-3	-3	1	0			3	/O	0.0
1941	StL-N	7	15	3	4	1	0	0	1	2	1	.267	.353	.333	88	-0	-0	2	0			-0	/O	0.0
1942	*StL-N	74	191	38	60	12	2	0	16	11	14	.314	.355	.398	112	4	3	28	2			6	O/2	0.8
1943	*StL-N	148	564	76	166	28	6	2	53	40	24	.294	.341	.376	102	4	1	76	5			-11	*O/2	-1.5
1946	*StL-N	112	346	53	82	14	6	3	27	30	29	.237	.300	.338	77	-9	-11	37	12			7	O/1	-0.6
1947	StL-N	10	25	2	5	1	0	0	0	4	2	.200	.310	.240	46	-2	-2	2	0			-1	O	-0.2
	Phi-N	130	488	79	181	28	16	1	41	59	37	.371	.443	.500	156	37	40	111	13			10	*O/1	4.3
	Yr	140	513	81	186	29	**16**	1	41	63	39	**.363**	.436	.487	150	35	38	112	13			10		4.1
1948	Phi-N	112	332	34	97	11	2	2	23	33	30	.292	.358	.355	95	-2	-1	44	4			4	O/13	-0.2
1949	Chi-N	42	159	20	42	6	3	1	14	11	6	.264	.312	.358	81	-5	-4	18	2			-5	O	-1.1
	Cin-N	86	314	53	100	15	2	1	23	34	17	.318	.385	.389	107	5	4	48	4			-3	O/1	-0.2
	Yr	128	473	73	142	21	5	2	37	45	23	.300	.361	.378	99	-0	-0	66	6			-8		-1.3
1950	StL-N	60	150	17	31	5	0	0	7	18	12	.207	.292	.240	40	-12	-13	11	0			2	O/1	-1.2
1951	StL-N	8	26	6	8	1	0	0	2	2	1	.308	.357	.346	90	-0	-0	3	0	0	0	-1	/O1	0.0
1955	StL-N	11	14	2	5	2	0	0	1	1	0	.357	.400	.500	137	1	1	3	0	0	0	1	/OM	0.2
Total	11	807	2651	385	786	126	37	10	214	245	175	.296	.358	.383	103	17	13	386	42	0		13	O/123	0.3

■ HUB WALKER

Walker, Harvey Willos b: 8/17/06, Gulfport, Miss. d: 11/26/82, San Jose, Cal. BL/TR, 5'10.5", 175 lbs. Deb: 4/15/31

YEAR	TM/L	G	AB	R	H	2B	3B	HR	RBI	BB	SO	AVG	OBP	SLG	PRO+	BR	/A	RC	SB	CS	SBR	FR	POS	TPR
1931	Det-A	90	252	27	72	13	1	0	16	23	25	.286	.355	.345	82	-5	-6	34	10	1	2	-0	O	-0.7
1935	Det-A	9	25	4	4	3	0	0	1	3	4	.160	.250	.280	38	-2	-2	2	0	0	0	1	/O	0.0
1936	Cin-N	92	258	49	71	18	1	4	23	35	32	.275	.366	.399	113	3	5	41	8			2	O/C1	0.4
1937	Cin-N	78	221	33	55	9	4	1	19	34	24	.249	.349	.339	92	-3	-1	28	7			0	O/2	-0.3
1945	*Det-A	28	23	4	3	0	0	0	1	9	4	.130	.375	.130	46	-1	-1	2	1	0	0	-0	O	0.0
Total	5	297	779	117	205	43	6	5	60	104	89	.263	.354	.353	92	-8	-6	106	26	1		2	O/21C	-0.6

■ JOHNNY WALKER

Walker, John Miles b: 12/11/1896, Toulon, Ill. d: 8/19/76, Hollywood, Fla. BR/TR, 6', 175 lbs. Deb: 9/19/19

YEAR	TM/L	G	AB	R	H	2B	3B	HR	RBI	BB	SO	AVG	OBP	SLG	PRO+	BR	/A	RC	SB	CS	SBR	FR	POS	TPR
1919	Phi-A	3	9	0	0	0	0	0	0	0	0	.000	.000	.000	-99	-2	-2	0	0			0	/C	-0.2
1920	Phi-A	9	22	0	5	1	0	0	5	0	1	.227	.227	.273	32	-2	-1	1	0	0	0	-1	/C	-0.1
1921	Phi-A	113	423	41	109	14	5	2	46	9	29	.258	.278	.329	54	-30	-30	39	5	0	2	-6	1/C	-3.3
Total	3	125	454	41	114	15	5	2	51	9	32	.251	.270	.319	50	-35	-35	40	5	0		-7	/1C	-3.6

■ SPEED WALKER

Walker, Joseph Richard b: 1/23/1898, Munhall, Pa. d: 6/20/59, W.Mifflin, Pa. BR/TR, 6', 170 lbs. Deb: 9/15/23

YEAR	TM/L	G	AB	R	H	2B	3B	HR	RBI	BB	SO	AVG	OBP	SLG	PRO+	BR	/A	RC	SB	CS	SBR	FR	POS	TPR
1923	StL-N	2	7	1	2	0	0	0	0	0	0	.286	.286	.286	52	-0	-1	1	0	0	0	-0	/1	0.0

■ LARRY WALKER

Walker, Larry Kenneth Robert b: 12/1/66, Maple River, B.C., Canada BL/TR, 6'2", 185 lbs. Deb: 8/16/89

YEAR	TM/L	G	AB	R	H	2B	3B	HR	RBI	BB	SO	AVG	OBP	SLG	PRO+	BR	/A	RC	SB	CS	SBR	FR	POS	TPR
1989	Mon-N	20	47	4	8	0	0	0	4	5	13	.170	.264	.170	26	-4	-4	3	1	1	-0	0	O	-0.4
1990	Mon-N	133	419	59	101	18	3	19	51	49	112	.241	.328	.434	108	4	4	61	21	7	2	5	*O	0.8
Total	2	153	466	63	109	18	3	19	55	54	125	.234	.321	.408	100	-0	-0	64	22	8	2	5	O	0.4

■ FLEET WALKER

Walker, Moses Fleetwood b: 10/7/1856, Mt.Pleasant, Ohio d: 5/11/24, Cleveland, Ohio BR/TR, Deb: 5/01/1884

YEAR	TM/L	G	AB	R	H	2B	3B	HR	RBI	BB	SO	AVG	OBP	SLG	PRO+	BR	/A	RC	SB	CS	SBR	FR	POS	TPR
1884	Tol-a	42	152	23	40	2	3	0	8			.263	.325	.316	109	3	2	16				-2	C/O	0.3

■ OSCAR WALKER

Walker, Oscar b: 3/18/1854, Brooklyn, N.Y. d: 5/20/1889, Brooklyn, N.Y. BL/TL, 5'10", 166 lbs. Deb: 9/17/1875

YEAR	TM/L	G	AB	R	H	2B	3B	HR	RBI	BB	SO	AVG	OBP	SLG	PRO+	BR	/A	RC	SB	CS	SBR	FR	POS	TPR
1875	Atl-n	1	2	0	0	0	0	0			1	.000	.333	.000	30	-0	-0	0					/O	0.0
1879	Buf-N	72	287	35	79	15	6	1	35	8	38	.275	.295	.380	118	6	5	33				3	*1	0.2
1880	Buf-N	34	126	12	29	4	2	1	15	6	18	.230	.265	.317	95	-0	-1	11				-1	1O	-0.3
1882	StL-a	76	318	48	76	15	7	7		10		.239	.262	.396	115	6	4	34				8	*O/21	1.0
1884	Bro-a	95	382	59	103	12	8	2		9		.270	.292	.359	113	5	5	41				0	O1	0.2
Total	4	277	1113	154	287	46	23	11	50	33	56	.258	.281	.370	113	17	14	119				10	O1/2	1.1

■ WALT WALKER

Walker, Walter S. b: Ionia, Mich. Deb: 9/02/1885

YEAR	TM/L	G	AB	R	H	2B	3B	HR	RBI	BB	SO	AVG	OBP	SLG	PRO+	BR	/A	RC	SB	CS	SBR	FR	POS	TPR
1885	Bal-a	4	13	1	0	0	0	0				.000	.000	.000	-99	-3	-3	0				-1	/O	-0.3

■ WELDAY WALKER

Walker, Welday Wilberforce b: 6/1859, Steubenville, Ohio d: 11/23/37, Steubenville, Ohio Deb: 7/15/1884

YEAR	TM/L	G	AB	R	H	2B	3B	HR	RBI	BB	SO	AVG	OBP	SLG	PRO+	BR	/A	RC	SB	CS	SBR	FR	POS	TPR
1884	Tol-a	5	18	1	4	1	0	0				.222	.222	.278	62	-1	-1	1				-1	/O	-0.1

■ CURT WALKER

Walker, William Curtis b: 7/3/1896, Beeville, Tex. d: 12/9/55, Beeville, Tex. BL/TR, 5'9.5", 170 lbs. Deb: 9/17/19

YEAR	TM/L	G	AB	R	H	2B	3B	HR	RBI	BB	SO	AVG	OBP	SLG	PRO+	BR	/A	RC	SB	CS	SBR	FR	POS	TPR
1919	NY-A	1	1	0	0	0	0	0	0	0	0	.000	.000	.000	-99	-0	-0	0	0			0	H	0.0
1920	NY-N	8	14	0	1	0	0	0	0	1	3	.071	.133	.071	-41	-3	-2	0	0	0	0	-0	/O	-0.2
1921	NY-N	64	192	30	55	13	5	3	35	15	8	.286	.338	.453	107	2	2	29	4	3	-1	7	O	0.5
	Phi-N	21	77	11	26	2	1	0	8	5	5	.338	.378	.390	96	1	-0	11	0	2	-1	-4	O	-0.5
	Yr	85	269	41	81	15	6	3	43	20	13	.301	.349	.435	104	2	1	40	4	5	-2	3		0.0
1922	Phi-N	148	581	102	196	36	11	12	89	56	46	.337	.399	.499	119	26	18	118	11	4	1	2	*O	1.5
1923	Phi-N	140	527	66	148	26	5	6	66	45	15	.281	.337	.378	79	-9	-17	66	6	12	-4	3	*O/1	-2.1
1924	Phi-N	24	71	11	21	6	1	1	8	7	4	.296	.359	.451	103	1	0	11	0	1	-4	-4	O	-0.3
	Cin-N	109	397	55	119	21	10	4	46	44	15	.300	.371	.433	117	9	10	65	7	5	-1	2	*O	0.8
	Yr	133	468	66	140	27	11	5	54	51	19	.299	.364	.436	114	10	10	76	7	6	-2	2		0.5
1925	Cin-N	145	509	86	162	22	16	4	71	57	31	.318	.387	.460	118	13	14	91	14	11	-2	1	*O	0.8
1926	Cin-N	155	571	83	175	24	20	6	78	60	31	.306	.372	.450	124	16	18	95	3			2	*O	1.4

YEAR	TM/L	G	AB	R	H	2B	3B	HR	RBI	BB	SO	AVG	OBP	SLG	PRO+	BR	/A	RC	SB	CS	SBR	FR	POS	TPR
1927	Cin-N	146	527	60	154	16	10	6	80	47	19	.292	.350	.395	102	-0	2	72	5			2	*O	-0.1
1928	Cin-N	123	427	64	119	15	12	6	73	49	14	.279	.354	.412	101	-0	1	63	19			4	*O	0.0
1929	Cin-N	141	492	76	154	28	15	7	83	85	17	.313	.416	.474	126	18	22	99	17			-2	*O	0.7
1930	Cin-N	134	472	74	145	26	11	8	51	64	30	.307	.391	.460	110	5	9	85	4			-9	*O	-0.7
Total	12	1359	4858	718	1475	235	117	64	688	535	254	.304	.374	.440	110	79	76	805	96	38		3	*O/1	1.8

■ HOWARD WALL   Wall, Howard   Deb: 9/13/1873

YEAR	TM/L	G	AB	R	H	2B	3B	HR	RBI	BB	SO	AVG	OBP	SLG	PRO+	BR	/A	RC	SB	CS	SBR	FR	POS	TPR
1873	Was-n	1	4	1	1	0	0	0		0		.250	.250	.250	49	-0	-0	0					/S	0.0

■ JOE WALL   Wall, Joseph Francis "Gummy"   b: 7/24/1873, Brooklyn, N.Y.   d: 7/17/36, Brooklyn, N.Y.   BL/TL,   Deb: 9/22/01

YEAR	TM/L	G	AB	R	H	2B	3B	HR	RBI	BB	SO	AVG	OBP	SLG	PRO+	BR	/A	RC	SB	CS	SBR	FR	POS	TPR
1901	NY-N	4	8	0	4	0	0	0	1	0		.500	.500	.500	201	1	1	2	0			-3	/CO	-0.1
1902	NY-N	6	14	2	5	2	0	0	2	2		.357	.438	.500	193	2	2	3	0			0	/O	0.1
	Bro-N	5	18	0	3	0	0	0	0	3		.167	.318	.167	52	-1	-1	1	0			-3	/C	-0.2
	Yr	11	32	2	8	2	0	0	0	5		.250	.368	.313	113	1	1	4	0			-3		-0.1
Total	2	15	40	2	12	2	0	0	1	5		.300	.391	.350	129	2	2	6	0			-5	/CO	-0.2

■ JACK WALLACE   Wallace, Clarence Eugene   b: 8/6/1890, Winnfield, La.   d: 10/15/60, Winnfield, La.   BR/TR, 5'10.5", 175 lbs.   Deb: 9/27/15

YEAR	TM/L	G	AB	R	H	2B	3B	HR	RBI	BB	SO	AVG	OBP	SLG	PRO+	BR	/A	RC	SB	CS	SBR	FR	POS	TPR
1915	Chi-N	2	7	1	2	0	0	0	1	0	2	.286	.375	.286	101	0	0	1	0			2	/C	0.2

■ DON WALLACE   Wallace, Donald Allen   b: 8/25/40, Sapulpa, Okla.   BL/TR, 5'8", 165 lbs.   Deb: 4/12/67

YEAR	TM/L	G	AB	R	H	2B	3B	HR	RBI	BB	SO	AVG	OBP	SLG	PRO+	BR	/A	RC	SB	CS	SBR	FR	POS	TPR
1967	Cal-A	23	6	2	0	0	0	0	0	3	2	.000	.333	.000	6	-1	-0	0	0	1	-1	5	/213	0.4

■ DOC WALLACE   Wallace, Frederick Renshaw "Jesse"   b: 9/30/1893, Church Hill, Md.   d: 12/31/64, Haverford, Pa.   TR, 5'6.5", 135 lbs.   Deb: 5/02/19

YEAR	TM/L	G	AB	R	H	2B	3B	HR	RBI	BB	SO	AVG	OBP	SLG	PRO+	BR	/A	RC	SB	CS	SBR	FR	POS	TPR
1919	Phi-N	2	4	0	1	0	0	0	0	0	1	.250	.250	.250	47	-0	-0	0	0			0	/S	0.0

■ JIM WALLACE   Wallace, James L.   b: 11/14/1881, Boston, Mass.   d: 5/16/53, Revere, Mass.   BL/TL,   Deb: 8/24/05

YEAR	TM/L	G	AB	R	H	2B	3B	HR	RBI	BB	SO	AVG	OBP	SLG	PRO+	BR	/A	RC	SB	CS	SBR	FR	POS	TPR
1905	Pit-N	7	29	3	6	1	0	0	3	3		.207	.281	.241	57	-1	-1	3	2			1	/O	0.0

■ BOBBY WALLACE   Wallace, Roderick John   b: 11/4/1873, Pittsburgh, Pa.   d: 11/3/60, Torrance, Cal.   BR/TR, 5'8", 170 lbs.   Deb: 9/15/1894   MUCH

YEAR	TM/L	G	AB	R	H	2B	3B	HR	RBI	BB	SO	AVG	OBP	SLG	PRO+	BR	/A	RC	SB	CS	SBR	FR	POS	TPR
1894	Cle-N	4	13	0	2	1	0	0	1	0	1	.154	.154	.231	-7	-2	-2	0	0			1	/P	0.0
1895	Cle-N	30	98	16	21	2	3	0	10	6	17	.214	.274	.296	46	-8	-9	8	0			3	P	0.0
1896	*Cle-N	45	149	19	35	6	3	1	17	11	21	.235	.287	.336	62	-8	-9	15	2			-2	OP/1	-0.7
1897	Cle-N	130	516	99	173	33	21	4	112	48		.335	.394	.504	132	27	23	111	14			4	*3/O	2.2
1898	Cle-N	154	593	81	160	25	13	3	99	63		.270	.343	.371	109	6	7	80	7			17	*32	2.7
1899	StL-N	151	577	91	170	28	14	12	108	54		.295	.357	.454	122	18	16	102	17			38	*S3	5.3
1900	StL-N	126	485	70	130	25	9	4	70	40		.268	.328	.381	98	-2	-1	64	7			3	*S/3	1.3
1901	StL-N	134	550	69	178	34	15	2	91	20		.324	.347	.451	140	20	24	95	15			30	*S	5.8
1902	StL-A	133	494	71	141	32	9	1	63	45		.285	.350	.393	109	5	6	77	18			11	*S/PO	2.7
1903	StL-A	135	511	63	136	21	7	1	54	28		.266	.304	.341	98	-3	-1	58	10			18	*S	2.4
1904	StL-A	139	541	57	149	29	4	2	69	42		.275	.328	.355	126	11	15	72	20			8	*S	2.7
1905	StL-A	156	587	67	159	25	9	1	59	45		.271	.323	.349	122	10	13	73	13			19	*S	4.1
1906	StL-A	139	476	64	123	21	7	2	67	58		.258	.339	.345	121	10	13	67	24			3	*S	1.9
1907	StL-A	147	538	56	138	20	7	0	70	54		.257	.324	.320	108	6	6	64	16			8	*S	1.9
1908	StL-A	137	487	59	123	24	4	1	60	52		.253	.325	.324	113	8	8	54	5			18	*S	3.3
1909	StL-A	116	403	36	96	12	2	0	35	38		.238	.310	.278	92	-5	-2	36	7			11	S3	1.3
1910	StL-A	138	508	47	131	19	7	0	37	49		.258	.324	.323	110	2	6	57	12			21	S3	3.2
1911	StL-A	125	410	35	95	12	2	0	31	46		.232	.312	.271	66	-19	-17	37	8			2	*S/2M	-0.3
1912	StL-A	100	323	39	78	14	5	0	31	43		.241	.332	.316	89	-5	-4	35	3			8	S3/2M	1.2
1913	StL-A	55	147	11	31	5	0	0	21	14	16	.211	.293	.245	59	-8	-7	11	1			-5	S/3	-0.8
1914	StL-A	26	73	3	16	2	1	0	5	5	13	.219	.269	.274	66	-3	-3	6	1	1	-0	-11	S/3	-1.4
1915	StL-A	9	13	1	3	0	1	0	4	5	0	.231	.444	.385	154	1	1	2	0	1	-1	1	/S	0.3
1916	StL-A	14	18	0	5	0	0	0	1	2	1	.278	.350	.278	93	-0	-0	2	0			5	/3S	0.7
1917	StL-N	8	10	0	1	0	0	0	2	0	1	.100	.100	.100	-40	-2	-2	0	0			-1	/3S	-0.2
1918	StL-N	32	98	3	15	1	0	0	4	6	9	.153	.202	.163	12	-10	-10	4	1			2	2S/3	-0.7
Total	25	2383	8618	1057	2309	391	143	34	1121	774	79	.268	.330	.358	107	50	70	1130	201	2		211	*S3/P201	38.9

■ TIM WALLACH   Wallach, Timothy Charles   b: 9/14/57, Huntington Park, Cal.   BR/TR, 6'3", 220 lbs.   Deb: 9/06/80

YEAR	TM/L	G	AB	R	H	2B	3B	HR	RBI	BB	SO	AVG	OBP	SLG	PRO+	BR	/A	RC	SB	CS	SBR	FR	POS	TPR
1980	Mon-N	5	11	1	2	0	0	1	2	1	5	.182	.250	.455	93	-0	-0	1	0	0	0	-0	/O1	0.0
1981	*Mon-N	71	212	19	50	9	1	4	13	15	37	.236	.299	.344	81	-5	-5	22	0	1	-1	-3	O13	-1.1
1982	Mon-N	158	596	89	160	31	3	28	97	36	81	.268	.314	.471	115	11	9	84	6	4	-1	-5	*3/O1	0.1
1983	Mon-N	156	581	54	156	33	3	19	70	55	97	.269	.338	.434	113	9	9	85	0	3	-2	-7	*3	-0.4
1984	Mon-N	160	582	55	143	25	4	18	72	50	101	.246	.313	.395	102	-3	0	70	3	7	-3	16	3/S	1.3
1985	Mon-N	155	569	70	148	36	3	22	81	38	79	.260	.312	.450	117	6	10	73	9	9	-3	37	*3	4.6
1986	Mon-N	134	480	50	112	22	1	18	71	44	72	.233	.311	.396	94	-5	-4	57	8	4	0	15	*3	0.8
1987	Mon-N	153	593	89	177	**42**	4	26	123	37	98	.298	.347	.514	121	19	17	105	9	5	-0	-0	*3/P	1.5
1988	Mon-N	159	592	52	152	32	5	12	69	38	88	.257	.305	.389	93	-3	-6	64	2	6	-3	12	*3/2	0.3
1989	Mon-N	154	573	76	159	**42**	0	13	77	58	81	.277	.345	.419	116	13	12	77	3	7	-3	6	*3/P	1.5
1990	Mon-N	161	626	69	185	37	5	21	98	42	80	.296	.343	.471	122	17	17	96	6	9	-4	4	*3	2.3
Total	11	1466	5415	624	1444	309	29	182	773	414	819	.267	.325	.435	110	58	58	733	46	55	-19	75	*3/O1P2S	10.9

■ JACK WALLAESA   Wallaesa, John   b: 8/31/19, Easton, Pa.   d: 12/27/86, Easton, Pa.   BB/TR, 6'3", 191 lbs.   Deb: 9/22/40

YEAR	TM/L	G	AB	R	H	2B	3B	HR	RBI	BB	SO	AVG	OBP	SLG	PRO+	BR	/A	RC	SB	CS	SBR	FR	POS	TPR
1940	Phi-A	6	20	0	3	0	0	0	2	0	2	.150	.150	.150	-22	-4	-4	0	0	0	0	1	/S	-0.1
1942	Phi-A	36	117	13	30	4	1	2	13	8	26	.256	.315	.359	90	-2	-2	14	0	1	-1	-7	S	-0.7
1946	Phi-A	63	194	16	38	4	2	5	11	14	47	.196	.250	.314	57	-12	-12	16	1	0	0	-16	S	-2.8
1947	Chi-A	81	205	25	40	9	1	7	32	23	51	.195	.279	.351	78	-8	-7	20	2	2	-1	12	SO/3	0.4
1948	Chi-A	33	48	2	9	0	0	1	3	1	12	.188	.204	.250	21	-6	-5	2	0	0	0	0	/SO	-0.4
Total	5	219	584	56	120	17	4	15	61	46	138	.205	.267	.325	65	-31	-29	52	3	3	-1	-10	S/O3	-3.6

■ NORM WALLEN   Wallen, Norman Edward (b: Norman Edward Walentoski)   b: 2/13/17, Milwaukee, Wis.   BR/TR, 5'11.5", 175 lbs.   Deb: 4/20/45

YEAR	TM/L	G	AB	R	H	2B	3B	HR	RBI	BB	SO	AVG	OBP	SLG	PRO+	BR	/A	RC	SB	CS	SBR	FR	POS	TPR
1945	Bos-N	4	15	1	2	1	0	1	1	1	1	.133	.188	.267	25	-2	-2	1	0			-2	/3	-0.2

■ TY WALLER   Waller, Elliott Tyrone   b: 3/14/57, Fresno, Cal.   BR/TR, 6', 180 lbs.   Deb: 9/06/80

YEAR	TM/L	G	AB	R	H	2B	3B	HR	RBI	BB	SO	AVG	OBP	SLG	PRO+	BR	/A	RC	SB	CS	SBR	FR	POS	TPR
1980	StL-N	5	12	3	1	0	0	0	0	1	5	.083	.154	.083	-31	-2	-2	0	0	0	0	-2	/3	-0.4
1981	Chi-N	30	71	10	19	2	1	3	13	4	18	.268	.307	.451	108	1	0	10	2	0	1	-1	3/2O	0.0
1982	Chi-N	17	21	4	5	0	0	1	1	2	5	.238	.304	.238	52	-1	-1	2	0	0	0	0	/O3	0.0
1987	Hou-N	11	6	1	1	1	0	0	0	0	3	.167	.167	.333	30	-1	-1	0	0	0	0	1	/O	0.0
Total	4	63	110	18	26	3	1	3	14	7	31	.236	.282	.364	78	-3	-4	13	2	0	1	-3	/3O2	-0.4

■ DENNIS WALLING   Walling, Dennis Martin   b: 4/17/54, Neptune, N.J.   BL/TR, 6', 180 lbs.   Deb: 9/07/75

YEAR	TM/L	G	AB	R	H	2B	3B	HR	RBI	BB	SO	AVG	OBP	SLG	PRO+	BR	/A	RC	SB	CS	SBR	FR	POS	TPR
1975	Oak-A	6	8	0	1	0	0	0	2	0	4	.125	.125	.250	4	-1	-1	0	0	0	0	0	/O	0.0
1976	Oak-A	3	11	1	3	0	0	0	0	0	3	.273	.273	.273	63	-1	-1	1	0	0	0	0	/O	0.0
1977	Hou-N	6	21	1	6	0	1	0	6	2	2	.286	.348	.381	105	-0	0	3	0	1	-1	0	/O	0.0
1978	Hou-N	120	247	30	62	11	3	3	36	30	24	.251	.335	.356	101	-2	0	32	9	2	2	3	O	0.2
1979	Hou-N	82	147	21	48	8	4	3	31	17	21	.327	.396	.497	151	9	10	29	3	2	-0	-0	O	0.8
1980	*Hou-N	100	284	30	85	6	5	3	29	35	26	.299	.376	.387	123	6	9	43	4	3	-1	-4	1O	0.1
1981	*Hou-N	65	158	23	37	6	0	5	23	28	17	.234	.349	.367	109	1	2	22	2	1	0	-4	1O	-0.2

YEAR	TM/L	G	AB	R	H	2B	3B	HR	RBI	BB	SO	AVG	OBP	SLG	PRO+	BR	/A	RC	SB	CS	SBR	FR	POS	TPR
1982	Hou-N	85	146	22	30	4	1	1	14	23	19	.205	.314	.267	69	-6	-5	12	4	2	0	0	O1	-0.6
1983	Hou-N	100	135	24	40	5	3	3	19	15	16	.296	.367	.444	132	4	5	22	2	2	-1	-1	13O	0.1
1984	Hou-N	87	249	37	70	11	5	3	31	16	28	.281	.327	.402	112	1	3	33	7	1	2	0	31/O	0.4
1985	Hou-N	119	345	44	93	20	1	7	45	25	26	.270	.319	.394	101	-1	-0	42	5	2	0	0	31O	-0.1
1986	*Hou-N	130	382	54	119	23	1	13	58	36	31	.312	.371	.479	136	16	18	67	1	1	-0	2	*3O/1	1.7
1987	Hou-N	110	325	45	92	21	4	5	33	39	37	.283	.360	.418	110	3	5	50	5	1	1	-3	31/O	0.0
1988	Hou-N	65	176	19	43	10	2	1	20	15	18	.244	.304	.341	88	-3	-3	19	1	0	0	9	3/1O	0.6
	StL-N	19	58	3	13	3	0	0	1	2	7	.224	.250	.276	50	-4	-4	4	1	0	0	-1	O/31	-0.5
	Yr	84	234	22	56	13	2	1	21	17	25	.239	.291	.325	79	-7	-6	23	2	0	1	7		0.1
1989	StL-N	69	79	9	24	7	0	1	11	14	12	.304	.409	.430	136	5	4	15	0	0	0	-2	1/3O	0.1
1990	StL-N	78	127	7	28	5	0	1	19	8	15	.220	.267	.283	50	-8	-9	9	0	0	0	2	13/O	-0.7
Total	16	1244	2898	370	794	141	30	49	378	305	308	.274	.344	.394	109	19	35	404	44	18	2	0	3O1	1.9

■ JOE WALLIS
Wallis, Harold Joseph   b: 1/9/52, E.St.Louis, Ill.   BB/TR, 5'11", 180 lbs.   Deb: 9/02/75

YEAR	TM/L	G	AB	R	H	2B	3B	HR	RBI	BB	SO	AVG	OBP	SLG	PRO+	BR	/A	RC	SB	CS	SBR	FR	POS	TPR
1975	Chi-N	16	56	9	16	2	2	1	4	5	14	.286	.344	.446	113	1	1	9	2	0	1	0	O	0.1
1976	Chi-N	121	338	51	86	11	5	5	21	33	62	.254	.323	.361	86	-3	-6	39	3	9	-5	7	O	-0.6
1977	Chi-N	56	80	14	20	3	0	2	8	16	25	.250	.375	.363	89	0	-1	12	0	1	-1	0	O	-0.1
1978	Chi-N	28	55	7	17	2	1	1	6	5	13	.309	.367	.436	110	2	1	8	0	2	-1	2	O	0.0
	Oak-A	85	279	28	66	16	1	6	26	26	42	.237	.302	.366	91	-5	-3	31	1	4	-2	4	O/D	-0.2
1979	Oak-A	23	78	6	11	2	0	1	3	10	18	.141	.247	.205	25	-8	-8	5	1	0	0	-3	O	-1.0
Total	5	329	886	115	216	36	9	16	68	95	174	.244	.318	.359	86	-13	-16	104	7	16	-8	11	O/D	-1.8

■ LEE WALLS
Walls, Ray Lee   b: 1/6/33, San Diego, Cal.   BR/TR, 6'3", 205 lbs.   Deb: 4/21/52   C

YEAR	TM/L	G	AB	R	H	2B	3B	HR	RBI	BB	SO	AVG	OBP	SLG	PRO+	BR	/A	RC	SB	CS	SBR	FR	POS	TPR
1952	Pit-N	32	80	6	15	0	1	2	5	8	22	.188	.261	.287	51	-5	-6	6	0	0	0	2	O	-0.4
1956	Pit-N	143	474	72	130	20	11	11	54	50	83	.274	.346	.432	110	5	7	70	3	5	-2	6	*O/3	0.6
1957	Pit-N	8	22	3	4	1	0	0	0	2	5	.182	.250	.227	30	-2	-2	2	1	0	0	1	/O	0.0
	Chi-N	117	366	42	88	10	5	6	33	27	67	.240	.294	.344	72	-15	-14	36	5	3	-0	-0	O/3	-1.7
	Yr	125	388	45	92	11	5	6	33	29	72	.237	.292	.338	70	-17	-17	38	6	3	0	1		-1.7
1958	Chi-N	136	513	80	156	19	3	24	72	47	62	.304	.371	.493	128	19	20	94	4	4	-1	1	*O	1.6
1959	Chi-N	120	354	43	91	18	3	8	33	42	73	.257	.344	.393	97	-2	-1	49	0	2	-1	-10	*O	-1.3
1960	Cin-N	29	84	12	23	3	2	1	7	17	20	.274	.396	.393	115	3	3	14	2	0	1	-1	O/1	0.2
	Phi-N	65	181	19	36	6	1	3	19	14	32	.199	.256	.293	50	-13	-13	13	3	2	-0	-8	3O/1	-2.3
	Yr	94	265	31	59	9	3	4	26	31	52	.223	.304	.325	72	-10	-10	26	5	2	0	-9		-2.1
1961	Phi-N	91	261	32	73	6	4	3	30	19	48	.280	.329	.425	99	-1	-1	34	2	2	-1	-4	13O	-0.8
1962	LA-N	60	109	9	29	3	1	0	17	10	21	.266	.328	.312	77	-4	-3	12	1	0	0	-1	O1/3	-0.4
1963	LA-N	64	86	12	20	1	0	3	11	7	25	.233	.290	.349	89	-2	-1	8	0	0	0	2	O/13	0.0
1964	LA-N	37	28	1	5	1	0	0	3	2	12	.179	.233	.214	29	-3	-2	1	0	0	0	-0	/OC	-0.2
Total	10	902	2558	331	670	88	31	66	284	245	470	.262	.330	.398	96	-19	-14	338	21	18	-5	-13	O/31C	-4.7

■ AUSTIN WALSH
Walsh, Austin Edward   b: 9/1/1891, Cambridge, Mass.   d: 1/26/55, Glendale, Cal.   BL/TL, 5'11", 175 lbs.   Deb: 4/19/14

YEAR	TM/L	G	AB	R	H	2B	3B	HR	RBI	BB	SO	AVG	OBP	SLG	PRO+	BR	/A	RC	SB	CS	SBR	FR	POS	TPR
1914	Chi-F	57	121	14	29	6	1	1	10	4	25	.240	.264	.331	74	-5	-4	11	0			-3	O	-0.8

■ JIMMY WALSH
Walsh, James Charles   b: 9/22/1885, Kaliila, Ireland   d: 7/3/62, Syracuse, N.Y.   BL/TR, 5'10.5", 170 lbs.   Deb: 8/26/12

YEAR	TM/L	G	AB	R	H	2B	3B	HR	RBI	BB	SO	AVG	OBP	SLG	PRO+	BR	/A	RC	SB	CS	SBR	FR	POS	TPR
1912	Phi-A	31	107	11	27	8	2	0	15	12		.252	.328	.364	102	-0	-1	15	7			0	O	-0.1
1913	Phi-A	97	303	56	77	16	5	0	27	38	40	.254	.341	.340	102	0	1	39	15			1	O	-0.2
1914	NY-A	43	136	13	26	1	3	1	11	29	21	.191	.333	.265	80	-2	-2	12	6	9	-4	-1	O	-0.9
	*Phi-A	68	216	35	51	11	6	3	36	30	27	.236	.340	.384	122	5	6	29	6	12	-5	0	O/13S	-0.2
	Yr	111	352	48	77	12	9	4	47	59	48	.219	.337	.338	105	3	4	41	12	21	-9	-1		-1.1
1915	Phi-A	117	417	48	86	15	6	1	20	57	64	.206	.306	.278	77	-12	-11	40	22	12	-1	7	*O/31	-0.9
1916	Phi-A	114	390	42	91	13	6	1	27	54	36	.233	.330	.305	95	-3	-1	45	27	14	-0	-0	*O/1	-0.9
	*Bos-A	14	17	5	3	1	0	0	2	4	2	.176	.333	.235	71	-0	-0	2	3	2	-0	-3	/O3	-0.3
	Yr	128	407	47	94	14	6	1	29	58	38	.231	.330	.302	93	-4	-2	47	30	16	-1	-3		-1.2
1917	Bos-A	57	185	25	49	6	3	0	12	25	14	.265	.352	.330	109	2	3	22	6			0	O	0.0
Total	6	541	1771	235	410	71	31	6	150	249	204	.232	.330	.317	96	-11	-5	203	92	49		5	O/31S	-3.5

■ JOHN WALSH
Walsh, John Gabriel   b: 3/25/1879, Wilkes-Barre, Pa.   d: 4/25/47, Jamaica, N.Y.   BR/TR, 5'8.5", 162 lbs.   Deb: 6/22/03

YEAR	TM/L	G	AB	R	H	2B	3B	HR	RBI	BB	SO	AVG	OBP	SLG	PRO+	BR	/A	RC	SB	CS	SBR	FR	POS	TPR
1903	Phi-N	1	3	0	0	0	0	0	0	0		.000	.000	.000	-99	-1	-1	0	0			-0	/3	0.0

■ JOE WALSH
Walsh, Joseph Francis   b: 10/14/1886, Minersville, Pa.   d: 1/6/67, Buffalo, N.Y.   BR/TR, 6'2", 170 lbs.   Deb: 10/08/10

YEAR	TM/L	G	AB	R	H	2B	3B	HR	RBI	BB	SO	AVG	OBP	SLG	PRO+	BR	/A	RC	SB	CS	SBR	FR	POS	TPR
1910	NY-A	1	4	0	2	1	0	0	2	0		.500	.500	.750	275	1	1	1	0			-1	/C	0.0
1911	NY-A	4	9	2	2	1	0	0	0	0		.222	.222	.333	51	-1	-1	1	0			-3	/C	-0.2
Total	2	5	13	2	4	2	0	0	2	0		.308	.308	.462	114	0	0	2	0			-3	/C	-0.2

■ JOE WALSH
Walsh, Joseph Patrick "Tweet"   b: 3/13/17, Roxbury, Mass.   BR/TR, 5'10", 155 lbs.   Deb: 7/01/38

YEAR	TM/L	G	AB	R	H	2B	3B	HR	RBI	BB	SO	AVG	OBP	SLG	PRO+	BR	/A	RC	SB	CS	SBR	FR	POS	TPR
1938	Bos-N	4	8	0	0	0	0	0	0	0	2	.000	.000	.000	-99	-2	-2	0	0			-1	/S	-0.2

■ JOE WALSH
Walsh, Joseph R. "Reddy"   b: 11/5/1864, Chicago, Ill.   d: 8/8/11, Omaha, Neb.   BL/TR,   Deb: 9/03/1891

YEAR	TM/L	G	AB	R	H	2B	3B	HR	RBI	BB	SO	AVG	OBP	SLG	PRO+	BR	/A	RC	SB	CS	SBR	FR	POS	TPR
1891	Bal-a	26	100	14	21	0	1	1	10	6	18	.210	.255	.260	49	-7	-7	8	4			6	S2	0.1

■ DEE WALSH
Walsh, Leo Thomas   b: 3/28/1890, St.Louis, Mo.   d: 7/14/71, St.Louis, Mo.   BB/TR, 5'9.5", 165 lbs.   Deb: 4/10/13

YEAR	TM/L	G	AB	R	H	2B	3B	HR	RBI	BB	SO	AVG	OBP	SLG	PRO+	BR	/A	RC	SB	CS	SBR	FR	POS	TPR
1913	StL-A	23	53	8	9	0	1	0	5	6	11	.170	.302	.208	51	-3	-3	4	3			2	S/3	0.1
1914	StL-A	7	23	1	2	0	0	0	1	2	4	.087	.160	.087	-27	-3	-3	0	1	1	-0	-0	/S	-0.3
1915	StL-A	59	150	13	33	5	0	0	6	14	25	.220	.308	.253	71	-5	-5	12	6	6	-2	1	O/3P2S	-0.7
Total	3	89	226	22	44	5	1	0	12	22	40	.195	.292	.226	56	-12	-11	17	10	7		3	/OS32P	-0.9

■ JIMMY WALSH
Walsh, Michael Timothy "Runt"   b: 3/25/1886, Lima, Ohio   d: 1/21/47, Baltimore, Md.   BR/TR, 5'9", 174 lbs.   Deb: 4/25/10

YEAR	TM/L	G	AB	R	H	2B	3B	HR	RBI	BB	SO	AVG	OBP	SLG	PRO+	BR	/A	RC	SB	CS	SBR	FR	POS	TPR
1910	Phi-N	88	242	28	60	8	3	0	31	25	38	.248	.323	.343	91	-2	-3	29	5			-1	2O/S3	-0.3
1911	Phi-N	94	289	29	78	20	3	1	31	21	30	.270	.324	.370	93	-3	-4	36	5			-4	O2/S3CP1	-0.8
1912	Phi-N	51	150	16	40	6	3	2	19	8	20	.267	.304	.387	83	-3	-4	18	3			1	23/C	-0.3
1913	Phi-N	26	30	3	10	4	0	0	5	1	5	.333	.355	.467	128	1	1	5	1			-0	/2S3O	0.1
1914	Bal-F	120	428	54	132	25	4	10	65	22	56	.308	.345	.456	124	14	12	76	18			3	*3/2SO	1.7
1915	Bal-F	106	401	43	121	20	1	9	60	21	44	.302	.340	.424	121	11	10	65	12			-9	*3	0.3
	StL-F	17	31	5	6	1	0	0	1	3	4	.194	.306	.226	55	-1	-2	3	1			-1	/3	-0.1
	Yr	123	432	48	127	21	1	9	61	24	48	.294	.337	.410	116	10	8	67	13			-10		0.2
Total	6	502	1571	178	447	84	14	25	212	101	197	.285	.332	.404	107	16	10	232	45			-12	3/2OSC1P	0.6

■ TOM WALSH
Walsh, Thomas Joseph   b: 2/28/1885, Davenport, Iowa   d: 3/16/63, Naples, Fla.   TR, 5'11", 170 lbs.   Deb: 8/15/06

YEAR	TM/L	G	AB	R	H	2B	3B	HR	RBI	BB	SO	AVG	OBP	SLG	PRO+	BR	/A	RC	SB	CS	SBR	FR	POS	TPR
1906	Chi-N	2	1	0	0	0	0	0	0	0		.000	.000	.000	-95	-0	-0	0	0			0	/C	0.0

■ WALT WALSH
Walsh, Walter William   b: 4/30/1897, Newark, N.J.   d: 1/15/66, Avon By The Sea, N.J.   BR/TR, 5'11", 170 lbs.   Deb: 5/04/20

YEAR	TM/L	G	AB	R	H	2B	3B	HR	RBI	BB	SO	AVG	OBP	SLG	PRO+	BR	/A	RC	SB	CS	SBR	FR	POS	TPR
1920	Phi-N	2	0	0	0	0	0	0	0	0	0	—	—	—	—	0	0	0	0	0	0	0	R	0.0

■ ROXY WALTERS
Walters, Alfred John   b: 11/5/1892, San Francisco, Cal.   d: 6/3/56, Almeda, Cal.   BR/TR, 5'8.5", 160 lbs.   Deb: 9/16/15

YEAR	TM/L	G	AB	R	H	2B	3B	HR	RBI	BB	SO	AVG	OBP	SLG	PRO+	BR	/A	RC	SB	CS	SBR	FR	POS	TPR
1915	NY-A	2	3	0	1	0	0	0	0	0	0	.333	.333	.333	100	-0	-0	0	0			2	/C	0.2
1916	NY-A	66	203	13	54	9	3	0	23	14	42	.266	.320	.340	96	-1	-1	24	2			16	C	2.0
1917	NY-A	61	171	16	45	2	0	0	14	9	22	.263	.304	.275	76	-5	-5	15	2			11	C	1.1

YEAR	TM/L	G	AB	R	H	2B	3B	HR	RBI	BB	SO	AVG	OBP	SLG	PRO+	BR	/A	RC	SB	CS	SBR	FR	POS	TPR
1918	NY-A	64	191	18	38	5	1	0	12	9	18	.199	.239	.236	42	-14	-14	11	3			-5	C/O	-1.6
1919	Bos-A	48	135	7	26	2	0	0	9	7	15	.193	.259	.207	33	-12	-11	8	1			5	C	-0.3
1920	Bos-A	88	258	25	51	11	1	0	28	30	21	.198	.303	.248	49	-19	-17	22	2	2	-1	8	C/1	-0.2
1921	Bos-A	54	169	17	34	4	1	0	14	10	11	.201	.254	.237	27	-19	-18	11	3	0	1	15	C	0.0
1922	Bos-A	38	98	4	19	2	0	0	6	6	8	.194	.240	.214	19	-12	-11	6	0	0	0	6	C	-0.4
1923	Bos-A	40	104	9	26	4	0	0	5	2	6	.250	.264	.288	45	-8	-8	8	0	2	-1	7	C/2	-0.2
1924	Cle-A	32	74	10	19	2	0	0	5	10	6	.257	.345	.284	63	-4	-4	8	0	1	-1	6	C/2	0.3
1925	Cle-A	5	20	0	4	0	0	0	0	0	2	.200	.200	.200	2	-3	-3	1	0	0	0	0	/C	-0.2
Total	11	498	1426	119	317	41	6	0	116	97	151	.222	.281	.259	51	-96	-94	113	13	5		70	C/O21	0.9

■ FRED WALTERS
Walters, Fred James "Whale" b: 9/4/12, Laurel, Miss. d: 2/1/80, Laurel, Miss. BR/TR, 6'1", 210 lbs. Deb: 4/17/45

YEAR	TM/L	G	AB	R	H	2B	3B	HR	RBI	BB	SO	AVG	OBP	SLG	PRO+	BR	/A	RC	SB	CS	SBR	FR	POS	TPR
1945	Bos-A	40	93	2	16	2	0	0	5	10	9	.172	.252	.194	29	-8	-8	4	1	1	-0	6	C	0.0

■ KEN WALTERS
Walters, Kenneth Rogers b: 11/11/33, Fresno, Cal. BR/TR, 6'1", 180 lbs. Deb: 4/12/60

YEAR	TM/L	G	AB	R	H	2B	3B	HR	RBI	BB	SO	AVG	OBP	SLG	PRO+	BR	/A	RC	SB	CS	SBR	FR	POS	TPR
1960	Phi-N	124	426	42	102	10	6	8	37	16	50	.239	.269	.319	60	-24	-24	34	4	3	-1	6	*O	-2.2
1961	Phi-N	86	180	23	41	8	2	2	14	5	25	.228	.253	.328	53	-12	-12	13	2	2	-1	1	O/13	-1.5
1963	Cin-N	49	75	6	14	2	0	1	7	4	14	.187	.237	.253	40	-6	-6	4	0	2	-1	-2	O/1	-1.1
Total	3	259	681	71	157	20	2	11	58	25	89	.231	.261	.314	56	-42	-42	51	6	7	-2	4	O/13	-4.8

■ BUCKY WALTERS
Walters, William Henry b: 4/19/09, Philadelphia, Pa. BR/TR, 6'1", 180 lbs. Deb: 9/18/31 MC

YEAR	TM/L	G	AB	R	H	2B	3B	HR	RBI	BB	SO	AVG	OBP	SLG	PRO+	BR	/A	RC	SB	CS	SBR	FR	POS	TPR
1931	Bos-N	9	38	2	8	2	0	0	0	0	3	.211	.211	.263	28	-4	-4	2	0			0	/32	-0.2
1932	Bos-N	22	75	8	14	3	1	0	4	2	18	.187	.208	.253	24	-8	-8	4	0			2	3	-0.3
1933	Bos-A	52	195	27	50	8	3	3	28	19	24	.256	.326	.390	90	-3	-3	26	1	1	-0	1	3/2	0.1
1934	Bos-A	23	88	10	19	4	4	4	18	3	12	.216	.242	.489	79	-3	-4	10	0	0	0	6	3	0.2
	Phi-N	83	300	36	78	20	3	4	38	19	54	.260	.308	.387	75	-7	-12	34	1			-7	3/2P	-1.1
1935	Phi-N	49	96	14	24	2	1	0	6	9	12	.250	.314	.292	58	-5	-6	9	0			2	P/O23	0.0
1936	Phi-N	64	121	12	29	10	1	1	16	7	15	.240	.281	.364	66	-5	-7	12	0			9	P/23	0.0
1937	Phi-N	56	137	15	38	6	0	1	16	5	16	.277	.303	.343	69	-5	-6	14	1			5	P/3	0.0
1938	Phi-N	15	35	6	10	2	0	1	3	1	5	.286	.306	.429	103	-0	-0	4	1			0	P	0.0
	Cin-N	36	64	10	9	1	0	0	5	7	18	.141	.236	.156	10	-8	-8	3	0			3	P	0.0
	Yr	51	99	16	19	3	0	1	8	8	23	.192	.259	.253	42	-8	-8	7	1			3		0.0
1939	*Cin-N	40	120	16	39	8	1	1	16	5	12	.325	.357	.433	111	2	2	18	1			4	P	0.0
1940	*Cin-N	37	117	11	24	3	0	1	18	4	14	.205	.231	.256	36	-11	-11	6	2			-1	P	0.0
1941	Cin-N	39	106	6	20	6	0	0	9	7	13	.189	.239	.245	36	-9	-9	6	0			2	P	0.0
1942	Cin-N	40	99	13	24	6	1	2	13	3	13	.242	.265	.384	89	-2	-2	10	0			1	P/O	0.0
1943	Cin-N	37	90	11	24	7	1	1	12	6	15	.267	.313	.400	107	0	0	12	1			1	P	0.0
1944	Cin-N	37	107	9	30	4	0	0	13	8	18	.280	.330	.318	86	-2	-2	12	0			0	P	0.0
1945	Cin-N	24	61	11	14	3	0	3	8	3	14	.230	.266	.426	93	-1	-1	6	2			0	P	0.0
1946	Cin-N	24	55	6	7	2	0	0	5	4	12	.127	.186	.164	-0	-7	-7	2	0			2	P	0.0
1947	Cin-N	20	45	3	12	2	0	0	4	2	13	.267	.298	.311	62	-2	-2	4	0			-1	P	0.0
1948	Cin-N	7	15	1	4	0	0	0	2	0	2	.267	.267	.267	46	-1	-1	1	0			1	/PM	0.0
1950	Bos-N	1	2	0	0	0	0	0	0	0	0	.000	.000	.000	-99	-1	-1	0	0			0	/P	0.0
Total	19	715	1966	227	477	99	16	23	234	114	303	.243	.286	.344	69	-83	-91	198	12	1		31	P3/2O	-1.3

■ DANNY WALTON
Walton, Daniel James "Mickey" b: 7/14/47, Los Angeles, Cal. BR/TR, 6', 195 lbs. Deb: 4/20/68

YEAR	TM/L	G	AB	R	H	2B	3B	HR	RBI	BB	SO	AVG	OBP	SLG	PRO+	BR	/A	RC	SB	CS	SBR	FR	POS	TPR
1968	Hou-N	2	2	0	0	0	0	0	0	0	1	.000	.000	.000	-99	-0	-0	0	0	0	0	0	H	0.0
1969	Sea-A	23	92	12	20	1	2	3	10	5	26	.217	.280	.370	82	-3	-3	9	2	0	1	-3	O	-0.5
1970	Mil-A	117	397	32	102	20	1	17	66	51	126	.257	.350	.441	116	9	9	63	2	3	-1	-11	*O	-0.8
1971	Mil-A	30	69	5	14	3	0	2	9	7	22	.203	.286	.333	76	-2	-2	6	0	0	0	-3	O/3	-0.6
	NY-A	5	14	1	2	0	0	0	2	0	7	.143	.143	.357	40	-1	-1	1	0	0	0	-1	/O	-0.1
	Yr	35	83	6	16	3	0	3	11	7	29	.193	.264	.337	71	-4	-3	7	0	0	0	-4		-0.7
1973	Min-A	37	96	13	17	1	1	4	8	17	28	.177	.301	.333	75	-3	-3	10	0	0	0	3	OD/3	0.0
1975	Min-A	42	63	4	11	2	0	1	8	4	18	.175	.224	.254	34	-6	-6	3	0	0	0	0	/1CD	-0.5
1976	LA-N	18	15	0	2	0	0	0	2	1	2	.133	.188	.133	-8	-2	-2	0	0	0	0	0	H	-0.1
1977	Hou-N	13	21	0	4	0	0	0	1	0	5	.190	.190	.190	3	-3	-3	1	0	0	0	-0	/1	-0.2
1980	Tex-A	10	10	2	2	0	0	0	1	3	5	.200	.385	.200	67	-0	-0	1	0	0	0	0	/D	0.0
Total	9	297	779	69	174	27	4	28	107	88	240	.223	.310	.376	90	-11	-11	94	4	3	-1	-16	O/D1C3	-2.8

■ JEROME WALTON
Walton, Jerome O'Terrell b: 7/8/65, Newnan, Ga. BR/TR, 6'1", 175 lbs. Deb: 4/04/89

YEAR	TM/L	G	AB	R	H	2B	3B	HR	RBI	BB	SO	AVG	OBP	SLG	PRO+	BR	/A	RC	SB	CS	SBR	FR	POS	TPR
1989	*Chi-N	116	475	64	139	23	3	5	46	27	77	.293	.339	.385	99	4	-0	64	24	7	3	-2	*O	0.0
1990	Chi-N	101	392	63	103	16	2	2	21	50	70	.263	.352	.329	81	-4	-9	49	14	7	0	-2	O	-1.4
Total	2	217	867	127	242	39	5	7	67	77	147	.279	.345	.360	91	-1	-9	113	38	14	3	-5	O	-1.4

■ REGGIE WALTON
Walton, Reginald Sherard b: 10/24/52, Kansas City, Mo. BR/TR, 6'3", 205 lbs. Deb: 6/13/80

YEAR	TM/L	G	AB	R	H	2B	3B	HR	RBI	BB	SO	AVG	OBP	SLG	PRO+	BR	/A	RC	SB	CS	SBR	FR	POS	TPR
1980	Sea-A	31	83	8	23	6	0	2	9	3	10	.277	.310	.422	98	-0	-1	10	2	2	-1	1	OD	0.0
1981	Sea-A	12	6	1	0	0	0	0	0	0	1	.000	.143	.000	-54	-1	-1	0	0	0	0	0	/OD	-0.1
1982	Pit-N	13	15	1	3	1	0	0	0	1	1	.200	.294	.267	56	-1	-1	1	0	0	0	0	/O	0.0
Total	3	56	104	10	26	7	0	2	9	5	13	.250	.297	.375	83	-2	-3	12	2	2	-1	1	/OD	-0.1

■ BILL WAMBSGANSS
Wambsganss, William Adolph b: 3/19/1894, Cleveland, Ohio d: 12/8/85, Lakewood, Ohio BR/TR, 5'11", 175 lbs. Deb: 8/04/14

YEAR	TM/L	G	AB	R	H	2B	3B	HR	RBI	BB	SO	AVG	OBP	SLG	PRO+	BR	/A	RC	SB	CS	SBR	FR	POS	TPR
1914	Cle-A	43	143	12	31	6	2	0	12	8	24	.217	.277	.287	67	-6	-6	10	2	7	-4	-1	S/2	-0.7
1915	Cle-A	121	375	30	73	4	4	0	21	36	50	.195	.272	.227	48	-23	-24	24	8	9	-3	7	23	-1.9
1916	Cle-A	136	475	57	117	14	4	0	45	41	40	.246	.313	.293	77	-10	-14	52	13			-8	*S2/3	-1.3
1917	Cle-A	141	499	52	127	17	6	0	43	37	42	.255	.315	.313	85	-5	-9	54	16			15	*2/1	1.6
1918	Cle-A	87	315	34	93	15	2	0	40	21	21	.295	.345	.356	102	4	0	44	16			-2	2	0.3
1919	Cle-A	139	526	60	146	17	6	2	60	32	24	.278	.323	.344	82	-9	-13	63	18			11	*2	1.0
1920	*Cle-A	153	565	83	138	16	11	0	55	54	26	.244	.316	.317	66	-26	-28	57	9	18	-8	8	*2	-2.3
1921	Cle-A	107	410	80	117	28	5	2	47	44	27	.285	.359	.393	90	-5	-6	61	13	7	-0	-18	*2/3	-1.9
1922	Cle-A	142	538	89	141	22	6	0	47	60	26	.262	.341	.325	74	-19	-19	64	17	10	-2	-27	*2S	-3.5
1923	Cle-A	101	345	59	100	20	4	1	59	43	15	.290	.373	.380	99	0	0	51	12	9	-2	5	2/3S	0.7
1924	Bos-A	156	632	93	174	41	5	0	49	54	33	.275	.336	.356	79	-20	-21	79	14	8	-1	15	*2	-0.1
1925	Bos-A	111	360	50	83	14	1	1	41	52	21	.231	.329	.294	59	-22	-21	38	3	5	-2	4	*2/1	-1.3
1926	Phi-A	54	54	11	19	3	0	0	1	8	8	.352	.444	.407	116	2	2	10	1	1	-0	0	S/2	0.3
Total	13	1491	5237	710	1359	215	59	7	520	490	357	.259	.328	.327	78	-139	-159	608	142	74		9	*2S/31	-9.1

■ LLOYD WANER
Waner, Lloyd James "Little Poison" b: 3/16/06, Harrah, Okla. d: 7/22/82, Oklahoma City, Okla. BL/TR, 5'9", 150 lbs. Deb: 4/12/27 H

YEAR	TM/L	G	AB	R	H	2B	3B	HR	RBI	BB	SO	AVG	OBP	SLG	PRO+	BR	/A	RC	SB	CS	SBR	FR	POS	TPR
1927	*Pit-N	150	629	133	223	17	6	2	27	37	23	.355	.396	.410	108	16	10	99	14			-11	*O/2	-0.6
1928	Pit-N	152	659	121	221	22	14	5	61	40	13	.335	.377	.434	107	11	7	104	8			3	*O	0.5
1929	Pit-N	151	662	134	234	28	20	5	74	29	20	.353	.395	.479	113	16	14	121	6			11	*O	1.0
1930	Pit-N	68	260	32	94	8	3	1	36	5	5	.362	.376	.427	93	-2	-2	39	3			1	O	-0.5
1931	Pit-N	154	681	90	214	13	4	5	57	39	16	.314	.352	.407	104	3	4	99	7			11	*O/2	0.8
1932	Pit-N	134	565	90	188	27	11	2	38	31	11	.333	.367	.430	116	11	12	90	6			5	*O	0.8
1933	Pit-N	121	500	59	138	14	5	0	26	22	8	.276	.307	.324	80	-13	-13	52	3			3	*O	-1.7
1934	Pit-N	140	611	95	173	27	14	2	48	38	12	.283	.326	.352	80	-16	-17	73	6			8	*O	-1.4
1935	Pit-N	122	537	83	166	22	14	0	46	22	10	.309	.336	.402	95	-2	-5	73	1			4	*O	-0.5

YEAR	TM/L	G	AB	R	H	2B	3B	HR	RBI	BB	SO	AVG	OBP	SLG	PRO+	BR	/A	RC	SB	CS	SBR	FR	POS	TPR
1936	Pit-N	106	414	67	133	13	8	1	31	31	5	.321	.369	.399	104	4	3	62	1			-3	O	-0.3
1937	Pit-N	129	537	80	177	23	4	1	45	34	12	.330	.370	.393	107	6	6	81	3			2	*O	0.2
1938	Pit-N	147	619	79	194	25	7	5	57	28	11	.313	.343	.401	103	2	2	85	5			-3	*O	-0.3
1939	Pit-N	112	379	49	108	15	3	0	24	17	13	.285	.321	.340	79	-12	-11	42	0			4	O/3	-0.8
1940	Pit-N	72	166	30	43	3	0	0	3	5	5	.259	.285	.277	56	-10	-10	13	2			4	O	-0.6
1941	Pit-N	3	4	2	1	0	0	0	1	2	0	.250	.500	.250	116	0	0	1	0			0	/O	0.1
	Bos-N	19	51	7	21	1	0	0	4	2	0	.412	.434	.431	151	3	3	10	1			1	O	0.4
	Cin-N	55	164	17	42	4	1	0	6	8	0	.256	.291	.293	64	-8	-8	14	0			-3	O	-1.2
	Yr	77	219	26	64	5	1	0	11	12	0	.292	.329	.324	85	-4	-4	24	1			-2		-0.7
1942	Phi-N	101	287	23	75	7	3	0	10	16	6	.261	.300	.307	82	-8	-7	27	1			-4	O	-1.2
1944	Bro-N	15	14	3	4	0	0	0	1	3	0	.286	.412	.286	101	0	0	2	0			0	/O	0.0
	Pit-N	19	14	2	5	0	0	0	2	2	0	.357	.438	.357	120	1	1	2	0			1	/O	0.1
	Yr	34	28	5	9	0	0	0	3	5	0	.321	.424	.321	110	1	1	4	0			1		0.1
1945	Pit-N	23	19	5	5	0	0	0	1	1	3	.263	.300	.263	55	-1	-1	2	0			1	/O	0.0
Total	18	1993	7772	1201	2459	281	118	27	598	420	173	.316	.353	.393	99	1	-12	1092	67			34	*O/23	-5.2

■ PAUL WANER

Waner, Paul Glee "Big Poison"   b: 4/16/03, Harrah, Okla.   d: 8/29/65, Sarasota, Fla.   BL/TL, 5'8.5", 153 lbs.   Deb: 4/13/26   CH

YEAR	TM/L	G	AB	R	H	2B	3B	HR	RBI	BB	SO	AVG	OBP	SLG	PRO+	BR	/A	RC	SB	CS	SBR	FR	POS	TPR
1926	Pit-N	144	536	101	180	35	**22**	8	79	66	19	**.336**	**.413**	.528	144	**39**	36	**115**	11			6	*O	**3.5**
1927	*Pit-N	155	623	114	**237**	42	18	9	**131**	60	14	**.380**	.437	.549	152	56	50	145	5			7	*O1	4.9
1928	Pit-N	152	602	**142**	223	**50**	19	6	86	77	16	.370	.446	.547	152	53	50	145	6			4	*O1	4.5
1929	Pit-N	151	596	131	200	43	15	15	100	89	24	.336	.424	.534	132	35	33	135	15			6	*O/1	2.3
1930	Pit-N	145	589	117	217	32	18	8	77	57	18	.368	.428	.525	128	29	29	129	18			2	*O	1.8
1931	Pit-N	150	559	88	180	35	10	6	70	73	21	.322	.404	.453	131	26	27	108	6			**19**	*O1	3.7
1932	Pit-N	154	630	107	215	**62**	10	8	82	56	24	.341	.397	.510	144	37	39	130	13			2	*O	3.0
1933	Pit-N	154	618	101	191	38	16	7	70	60	20	.309	.372	.456	136	29	29	109	3			3	*O	2.4
1934	Pit-N	146	599	**122**	**217**	32	16	14	90	68	24	**.362**	.429	.539	154	50	48	122	8			6	*O	4.5
1935	Pit-N	139	549	98	176	29	12	11	78	61	22	.321	.392	.477	128	26	24	105	2			0	*O	1.7
1936	Pit-N	148	585	107	218	53	9	5	94	74	29	**.373**	.446	.520	156	51	50	140	7			7	*O	4.8
1937	Pit-N	154	619	94	219	30	9	2	74	63	34	.354	.413	.441	132	30	30	118	4			-2	*O/1	2.1
1938	Pit-N	148	625	77	175	31	6	6	69	47	28	.280	.331	.378	94	-5	-6	79	2			-4	*O	-1.2
1939	Pit-N	125	461	62	151	30	6	3	45	35	18	.328	.375	.438	120	11	12	74	0			1	*O	1.1
1940	Pit-N	89	238	32	69	16	1	1	32	23	14	.290	.352	.378	102	1	1	32	0			-5	O/1	-0.6
1941	Bro-N	11	35	5	6	0	0	0	4	8	0	.171	.326	.171	41	-2	-2	2	0			-2	O/1	-0.5
	Bos-N	95	294	40	82	10	2	2	46	47	14	.279	.378	.347	110	4	6	41	1			-7	O/1	-0.5
	Yr	106	329	45	88	10	2	2	50	55	14	.267	.372	.328	102	2	3	42	1			-9		-1.0
1942	Bos-N	114	333	43	86	17	1	1	39	62	20	.258	.376	.324	108	6	6	45	2			-9	O	-0.4
1943	Bro-N	82	225	29	70	16	0	1	26	35	9	.311	.406	.396	132	11	11	37	0			-2	O	0.7
1944	Bro-N	83	136	16	39	4	1	0	16	27	7	.287	.405	.331	111	3	4	20	0			0	O	0.1
	NY-A	9	7	1	1	0	0	0	1	2	1	.143	.333	.143	37	-0	-0	1	1	0	0	0	H	0.0
1945	NY-A	1	0	0	0	0	0	0	0	1	0	—	1.000	—	191	0	0	0	0	0	0	0	H	0.0
Total	20	2549	9459	1627	3152	605	191	113	1309	1091	376	.333	.404	.473	133	491	474	1853	104	0		34	*O/1	37.9

■ JACK WANNER

Wanner, Clarence Curtis "Johnny"   b: 11/29/1885, Geneseo, Ill.   d: 5/28/19, Geneseo, Ill.   BR/TR, 5'11.5", 190 lbs.   Deb: 9/28/09

YEAR	TM/L	G	AB	R	H	2B	3B	HR	RBI	BB	SO	AVG	OBP	SLG	PRO+	BR	/A	RC	SB	CS	SBR	FR	POS	TPR
1909	NY-A	3	8	0	1	0	0	0	0	0	2	.125	.300	.125	35	-0	-0	1	1			-2	/S	-0.2

■ PEE-WEE WANNINGER

Wanninger, Paul Louis   b: 12/12/02, Birmingham, Ala.   d: 3/7/81, N.Augusta, S.C.   BL/TR, 5'7", 150 lbs.   Deb: 4/22/25

YEAR	TM/L	G	AB	R	H	2B	3B	HR	RBI	BB	SO	AVG	OBP	SLG	PRO+	BR	/A	RC	SB	CS	SBR	FR	POS	TPR
1925	NY-A	117	403	35	95	13	6	1	22	11	34	.236	.256	.305	43	-37	-36	30	3	5	-2	-6	*S/32	-2.4
1927	Bos-A	18	60	4	12	0	0	0	1	6	2	.200	.284	.200	28	-6	-6	3	2	4	-2	-1	S	-0.7
	Cin-N	28	93	14	23	2	2	0	8	6	7	.247	.293	.312	64	-5	-5	9	0			6	S	0.4
Total	2	163	556	53	130	15	8	1	31	23	43	.234	.266	.295	45	-48	-47	42	5	9		-1	S/32	-2.7

■ AARON WARD

Ward, Aaron Lee   b: 8/28/1896, Booneville, Ark.   d: 1/30/61, New Orleans, La.   BR/TR, 5'10.5", 160 lbs.   Deb: 8/14/17

YEAR	TM/L	G	AB	R	H	2B	3B	HR	RBI	BB	SO	AVG	OBP	SLG	PRO+	BR	/A	RC	SB	CS	SBR	FR	POS	TPR
1917	NY-A	8	26	0	3	0	0	0	1	1	5	.115	.148	.115	-19	-4	-4	0				-2	/S	-0.6
1918	NY-A	20	32	2	4	1	0	0	1	2	7	.125	.176	.156	0	-4	-4	1	1			4	S/O2	0.1
1919	NY-A	27	34	5	7	2	0	0	2	5	6	.206	.308	.265	61	-2	-2	3	0			2	/13S2	0.0
1920	NY-A	127	496	62	127	18	7	11	54	33	84	.256	.304	.387	79	-15	-17	58	7	5	-1	22	*3S	1.2
1921	*NY-A	153	556	77	170	30	10	5	75	42	68	.306	.363	.423	98	-0	-2	85	6	8	-3	19	*23	1.9
1922	*NY-A	154	558	69	149	19	5	7	68	45	64	.267	.328	.357	77	-18	-19	68	7	4	-0	3	*2/3	-0.5
1923	*NY-A	152	567	79	161	26	11	10	82	56	65	.284	.351	.422	101	1	-0	84	8	8	-2	14	*2	1.6
1924	NY-A	120	400	42	101	13	10	4	66	40	45	.253	.324	.395	85	-11	-11	52	1	4	-2	8	*2/S	-0.1
1925	NY-A	125	439	41	108	22	3	4	38	49	49	.246	.326	.337	70	-21	-20	50	1	4	-2	-11	*23	-2.5
1926	NY-A	22	31	5	10	2	0	0	3	2	6	.323	.364	.387	97	-0	-0	4	0			-4	/23	-0.3
1927	Chi-A	145	463	75	125	25	8	5	56	63	56	.270	.360	.391	97	-3	-1	65	6	5	-1	-19	*2/3	-1.3
1928	Cle-A	6	9	0	1	0	0	0	0	1	2	.111	.200	.111	-16	-2	-2	0	0	0	0	2	/3S2	0.1
Total	12	1059	3611	457	966	158	54	50	446	339	457	.268	.335	.383	85	-77	-82	472	37	38		36	23/S10	-0.4

■ CHUCK WARD

Ward, Charles William   b: 7/30/1894, St.Louis, Mo.   d: 4/4/69, Indian Rocks, Fla.   BR/TR, 5'11.5", 170 lbs.   Deb: 4/11/17

YEAR	TM/L	G	AB	R	H	2B	3B	HR	RBI	BB	SO	AVG	OBP	SLG	PRO+	BR	/A	RC	SB	CS	SBR	FR	POS	TPR
1917	Pit-N	125	423	25	100	12	3	0	43	32	43	.236	.302	.279	76	-10	-11	38	5			-27	*S/23	-4.1
1918	Bro-N	2	6	0	2	0	0	0	3	0	0	.333	.333	.333	104	0	0	1	0			-1	/3	0.0
1919	Bro-N	45	150	7	35	1	2	0	8	7	11	.233	.277	.267	62	-6	-7	11	0			-6	3	-1.3
1920	Bro-N	19	71	7	11	1	0	0	4	3	3	.155	.200	.169	6	-8	-9	3	1	0	0	-9	S	-1.7
1921	Bro-N	12	28	1	2	1	0	0	0	4	2	.071	.188	.107	-19	-5	-5	1	0	0	0	4	S	0.0
1922	Bro-N	33	91	12	25	5	1	0	14	5	8	.275	.320	.352	74	-4	-4	10	1	1	-0	-3	S/3	-0.4
Total	6	236	769	52	175	20	6	0	72	51	67	.228	.286	.269	63	-33	-35	64	7	1		-41	S/32	-7.5

■ CHRIS WARD

Ward, Chris Gilbert   b: 5/18/49, Oakland, Cal.   BL/TL, 6', 180 lbs.   Deb: 9/10/72

YEAR	TM/L	G	AB	R	H	2B	3B	HR	RBI	BB	SO	AVG	OBP	SLG	PRO+	BR	/A	RC	SB	CS	SBR	FR	POS	TPR
1972	Chi-N	1	1	0	0	0	0	0	0	0	0	.000	.000	.000	-90	-0	-0	0	0	0	0	0	H	0.0
1974	Chi-N	92	137	8	28	4	0	1	15	18	13	.204	.297	.255	53	-8	-9	10	0	2	-1	2	O/1	-0.8
Total	2	93	138	8	28	4	0	1	15	18	13	.203	.295	.254	52	-8	-9	10	0	2	-1	2	/O1	-0.8

■ PIGGY WARD

Ward, Frank Gray   b: 4/16/1867, Chambersburg, Pa.   d: 10/24/12, Altoona, Pa.   5'9.5", 196 lbs.   Deb: 6/12/1883

YEAR	TM/L	G	AB	R	H	2B	3B	HR	RBI	BB	SO	AVG	OBP	SLG	PRO+	BR	/A	RC	SB	CS	SBR	FR	POS	TPR
1883	Phi-N	1	5	0	0	0	0	0	0	0	2	.000	.000	.000	-99	-1	-1	0				-0	/3	0.0
1889	Phi-N	7	25	0	4	1	0	0	4	0	7	.160	.160	.200	1	-3	-4	1	1			-2	/2O	-0.4
1891	Pit-N	6	18	3	6	0	0	0	2	3	3	.333	.455	.333	137	1	1	4	3			-1	/O	0.0
1892	Bal-N	56	186	28	54	6	5	1	33	31	18	.290	.403	.392	138	11	10	34	10			1	O/2SC	0.9
1893	Bal-N	11	49	11	12	1	3	0	5	5	2	.245	.327	.388	90	-1	-1	8	4			-1	/O1	-0.1
	Cin-N	42	150	44	42	4	1	0	10	37	10	.280	.440	.320	103	5	4	34	27			-2	O/1	0.0
	Yr	53	199	55	54	5	4	0	15	42	12	.271	.415	.337	101	4	3	42	31			-3		-0.1
1894	Was-N	98	347	86	105	11	7	0	36	80	31	.303	.447	.375	105	7	10	78	41			-22	2O/S3	-0.5
Total	6	221	780	172	223	23	16	1	90	156	73	.286	.419	.360	107	19	19	159	86			-28	O/2S13C	-0.1

■ GARY WARD

Ward, Gary Lamell   b: 12/6/53, Los Angeles, Cal.   BR/TR, 6'2", 195 lbs.   Deb: 9/03/79

YEAR	TM/L	G	AB	R	H	2B	3B	HR	RBI	BB	SO	AVG	OBP	SLG	PRO+	BR	/A	RC	SB	CS	SBR	FR	POS	TPR
1979	Min-A	10	14	2	4	0	0	0	1	3	3	.286	.412	.286	89	0	-0	2	0	1	-1	0	/O	0.0
1980	Min-A	13	41	11	19	6	2	1	10	3	6	.463	.500	.780	228	8	8	16	0	0	0	-3	O	0.4
1981	Min-A	85	295	42	78	7	6	3	29	28	48	.264	.328	.359	92	-1	-3	34	5	2	0	6	O/D	0.1

YEAR	TM/L	G	AB	R	H	2B	3B	HR	RBI	BB	SO	AVG	OBP	SLG	PRO+	BR	/A	RC	SB	CS	SBR	FR	POS	TPR
1982	Min-A	152	570	85	165	33	7	28	91	37	105	.289	.334	.519	127	21	19	95	13	1	3	10	*O/D	2.8
1983	Min-A	157	623	76	173	34	5	19	88	44	98	.278	.328	.440	105	7	4	85	8	1	2	21	*O/D	2.5
1984	Tex-A	155	602	97	171	21	7	21	79	55	95	.284	.344	.447	113	13	11	87	7	5	-1	-4	*O/D	0.1
1985	Tex-A	154	593	77	170	28	7	15	70	39	97	.287	.332	.433	106	5	4	82	26	7	4	1	*O/D	0.6
1986	Tex-A	105	380	54	120	15	2	5	51	31	72	.316	.373	.405	109	7	6	56	12	8	-1	9	*O/D	1.1
1987	NY-A	146	529	65	131	22	1	16	78	33	101	.248	.293	.384	78	-18	-17	55	9	1	2	-1	OD1	-1.8
1988	NY-A	91	231	26	52	8	0	4	24	24	41	.225	.304	.312	73	-8	-8	21	0	1	-1	3	O1/3D	-0.6
1989	NY-A	8	17	3	5	1	0	0	1	3	5	.294	.400	.353	115	0	1	2	0	0	0	-1	/OD	0.0
	Det-A	105	275	24	69	10	2	9	29	21	54	.251	.304	.400	99	-2	-1	30	1	3	-2	3	O1D	-0.2
	Yr	113	292	27	74	11	2	9	30	24	59	.253	.310	.397	100	-1	-1	33	1	3	-2	2		-0.2
1990	Det-A	106	309	32	79	11	2	9	46	30	50	.256	.324	.392	100	-1	-0	38	2	0	1	-5	OD/1	-0.6
Total	12	1287	4479	594	1236	196	41	130	597	351	775	.276	.330	.425	104	33	23	602	83	30	7	38	*O/D13	4.4

■ JIM WARD
Ward, James H. b: 3/1855, Boston, Mass. d: 6/4/1886, Boston, Mass. Deb: 8/03/1876

YEAR	TM/L	G	AB	R	H	2B	3B	HR	RBI	BB	SO	AVG	OBP	SLG	PRO+	BR	/A	RC	SB	CS	SBR	FR	POS	TPR
1876	Phi-N	1	4	1	2	0	0	0	1	0	1	.500	.500	.500	236	1	1	1				0	/C	0.1

■ RUBE WARD
Ward, John Andrew b: 2/6/1879, New Lexington, Ohio d: 1/17/45, Akron, Ohio Deb: 4/28/02

YEAR	TM/L	G	AB	R	H	2B	3B	HR	RBI	BB	SO	AVG	OBP	SLG	PRO+	BR	/A	RC	SB	CS	SBR	FR	POS	TPR
1902	Bro-N	13	31	4	9	1	0	0	2	2		.290	.333	.323	104	0	0	3	0			-1	O	-0.1

■ JOHN WARD
Ward, John E. b: Washington, D.C. Deb: 5/23/1884

YEAR	TM/L	G	AB	R	H	2B	3B	HR	RBI	BB	SO	AVG	OBP	SLG	PRO+	BR	/A	RC	SB	CS	SBR	FR	POS	TPR
1884	Was-U	1	4	0	1	0	0	0				.250	.250	.250	72	-0	-0	0	0			-1	/O	0.0

■ JAY WARD
Ward, John Francis b: 9/9/38, Brookfield, Mo. BR/TR, 6'1", 185 lbs. Deb: 5/06/63 C

YEAR	TM/L	G	AB	R	H	2B	3B	HR	RBI	BB	SO	AVG	OBP	SLG	PRO+	BR	/A	RC	SB	CS	SBR	FR	POS	TPR
1963	Min-A	9	15	0	1	1	0	0	2	1	5	.067	.125	.133	-27	-3	-3	0	0	0	0	-0	/3O	-0.2
1964	Min-A	12	31	4	7	2	0	0	2	6	13	.226	.351	.290	80	-1	-1	4	0	0	0	1	/2O	0.1
1970	Cin-N	6	3	0	0	0	0	0	0	2	1	.000	.400	.000	17	-0	-0	0	0	0	0	0	/312	0.0
Total	3	27	49	4	8	3	0	0	4	9	19	.163	.293	.224	46	-3	-3	4	0	0	0		/23O1	-0.1

■ MONTE WARD
Ward, John Montgomery b: 3/3/1860, Bellefonte, Pa. d: 3/4/25, Augusta, Ga. BL/TR, 5'9", 165 lbs. Deb: 7/15/1878 MH

YEAR	TM/L	G	AB	R	H	2B	3B	HR	RBI	BB	SO	AVG	OBP	SLG	PRO+	BR	/A	RC	SB	CS	SBR	FR	POS	TPR
1878	Pro-N	37	138	14	27	5	4	1	15	2	13	.196	.207	.312	69	-5	-5	9				1	P	0.0
1879	Pro-N	83	364	71	104	9	4	2	41	7	14	.286	.299	.349	115	5	6	39				4	*P3/O	0.0
1880	Pro-N	86	356	53	81	12	2	0	27	6	16	.228	.240	.272	76	-10	-8	24				14	*P3/OM	0.0
1881	Pro-N	85	357	56	87	18	6	0	53	5	10	.244	.254	.328	83	-8	-7	30				5	OPS	0.4
1882	Pro-N	83	355	58	87	10	3	1	39	13	22	.245	.272	.299	83	-7	-6	30				10	OP/S	0.5
1883	NY-N	88	380	76	97	18	7	7	54	28	25	.255	.271	.395	100	-1	-0	42				16	OP/3S2	2.0
1884	NY-N	113	482	98	122	11	8	2	51	28	47	.253	.294	.322	91	-3	-5	47				5	O2/PM	0.2
1885	NY-N	111	446	72	101	8	9	0	37	17	39	.226	.255	.285	75	-13	-12	33				8	*S	0.2
1886	NY-N	122	491	82	134	17	5	2	81	19	46	.273	.300	.340	93	-4	-5	62	36			-10	*S	-1.4
1887	NY-N	129	545	114	184	16	5	1	53	29	12	.338	.375	.391	121	12	16	125	**111**	29			*S	3.4
1888	*NY-N	122	510	70	128	14	5	2	49	9	13	.251	.265	.310	86	-9	-8	53	38	-2			*S	-0.6
1889	*NY-N	114	479	87	143	13	4	1	67	27	7	.299	.339	.349	94	-4	-4	79	62	2			*S/2	0.2
1890	Bro-P	128	561	134	189	15	12	4	60	51	22	.337	.394	.428	115	18	11	122	63	21			*SM	3.2
1891	Bro-N	105	441	85	122	13	5	0	39	36	10	.277	.335	.329	96	-2	-1	69	57	-0			S2M	0.3
1892	Bro-N	148	614	109	163	13	3	1	47	82	19	.265	.355	.301	105	4	8	99	**88**	3			*2M	1.0
1893	NY-N	135	588	129	193	27	9	2	77	47	5	.328	.379	.415	112	10	10	113	46	7			*2M	1.3
1894	*NY-N	136	540	100	143	12	5	0	77	34	6	.265	.310	.306	50	-43	-42	65	39	5			*2M	-2.1
Total	17	1825	7647	1408	2105	231	96	26	867	420	326	.275	.314	.341	94	-59	-54	1042	540	119			S2PO/3	8.6

■ JOE WARD
Ward, Joseph A. b: 9/2/1884, Philadelphia, Pa. d: 8/11/34, Philadelphia, Pa. TR, Deb: 4/24/06

YEAR	TM/L	G	AB	R	H	2B	3B	HR	RBI	BB	SO	AVG	OBP	SLG	PRO+	BR	/A	RC	SB	CS	SBR	FR	POS	TPR
1906	Phi-N	35	129	12	38	8	6	0	11	5		.295	.321	.450	142	5	5	20	2			-6	3/2S	-0.1
1909	NY-A	9	28	3	5	0	0	0	0	1		.179	.233	.179	30	-2	-2	2	2			-5	/21	-0.8
	Phi-N	74	184	21	49	8	2	0	23	9		.266	.304	.332	96	-1	-1	21	7			-10	2/S1O	-1.2
1910	Phi-N	48	124	11	18	2	1	0	13	3	11	.145	.178	.177	4	-15	-16	5	1			2	1/S3	-1.5
Total	3	166	465	47	110	18	9	0	47	18	_11_	.237	.271	.314	78	-13	-14	47	12			-19	/213SO	-3.6

■ HAP WARD
Ward, Joseph Nichols b: 11/15/1885, Leesburg, N.J. d: 9/13/79, Elmer, N.J. Deb: 5/18/12

YEAR	TM/L	G	AB	R	H	2B	3B	HR	RBI	BB	SO	AVG	OBP	SLG	PRO+	BR	/A	RC	SB	CS	SBR	FR	POS	TPR
1912	Det-A	1	2	0	0	0	0	0				.000	.000	.000	-99	-1	-1	0	0			0	/O	0.0

■ PETE WARD
Ward, Peter Thomas b: 7/26/39, Montreal, Que., Can BL/TR, 6'1", 185 lbs. Deb: 9/21/62 C

YEAR	TM/L	G	AB	R	H	2B	3B	HR	RBI	BB	SO	AVG	OBP	SLG	PRO+	BR	/A	RC	SB	CS	SBR	FR	POS	TPR
1962	Bal-A	8	21	1	3	2	0	0	2	4	5	.143	.280	.238	43	-2	-2	2	0	0	0	-0	/O	-0.1
1963	Chi-A	157	600	80	177	34	6	22	84	52	77	.295	.356	.482	135	25	26	104	7	6	-2	-5	*3/2S	2.2
1964	Chi-A	144	539	61	152	28	3	23	94	56	76	.282	.352	.473	131	19	21	91	1	1	-0	13	*3	3.7
1965	Chi-A	138	507	62	125	25	3	10	57	56	83	.247	.329	.367	104	-1	3	61	2	4	-2	9	*3/2	1.1
1966	Chi-A	84	251	22	55	7	1	3	28	24	49	.219	.295	.291	74	-10	-8	23	3	1	0	-2	O3/1	-1.3
1967	Chi-A	146	467	49	109	16	2	18	62	61	109	.233	.336	.392	119	9	11	65	3	2	-0	-17	O13	-1.2
1968	Chi-A	125	399	43	86	15	0	15	50	76	85	.216	.355	.366	117	12	12	58	4	3	-1	-14	31O	-0.3
1969	Chi-A	105	199	22	49	7	0	6	32	33	38	.246	.362	.372	101	2	1	30	0	0	0	-2	13/O	-0.2
1970	NY-A	66	77	5	20	2	2	1	18	9	17	.260	.337	.377	102	-0	0	10	0	0	0	-1	1	0.0
Total	9	973	3060	345	776	136	17	98	427	371	539	.254	.342	.405	116	56	65	443	20	17	-4	-20	3O1/2S	3.9

■ PRESTON WARD
Ward, Preston Meyer b: 7/24/27, Columbia, Mo. BL/TR, 6'4", 190 lbs. Deb: 4/20/48

YEAR	TM/L	G	AB	R	H	2B	3B	HR	RBI	BB	SO	AVG	OBP	SLG	PRO+	BR	/A	RC	SB	CS	SBR	FR	POS	TPR
1948	Bro-N	42	146	9	38	9	2	1	21	15	23	.260	.329	.370	86	-2	-3	19	0			-2	1	-0.4
1950	Chi-N	80	285	31	72	11	2	6	33	27	42	.253	.317	.368	81	-9	-8	34	3			10	1	-0.1
1953	Chi-N	33	100	10	23	5	0	4	12	18	21	.230	.347	.400	92	-1	-1	15	3	1	0	-3	O/1	-0.4
	Pit-N	88	281	35	59	7	1	8	27	44	39	.210	.319	.327	69	-12	-12	31	1	3	-2	4	1	-0.9
	Yr	121	381	45	82	12	1	12	39	62	60	.215	.327	.346	76	-13	-13	46	4	4	-1	1		-1.3
1954	Pit-N	117	360	37	97	16	2	7	48	39	61	.269	.341	.383	90	-6	-6	49	0	0	0	2	1O3	-0.5
1955	Pit-N	84	179	16	38	7	4	5	25	22	28	.212	.299	.380	80	-6	-5	21	0	0	0	2	1/O	-0.6
1956	Pit-N	16	30	3	10	0	1	1	11	6	4	.333	.444	.500	157	3	3	7	0	0	0	-4	/3O	0.0
	Cle-A	87	150	18	38	10	0	6	21	16	20	.253	.325	.440	98	-1	-1	23	0	0	0	3	1O	0.0
1957	Cle-A	10	11	2	2	1	0	0	0	0	2	.182	.182	.273	23	-1	-1	1	0	0	0	0	/1	0.0
1958	Cle-A	48	148	22	50	3	1	4	21	10	27	.338	.384	.453	133	6	6	26	0	1	-1	-3	31	0.3
	KC-A	81	268	28	68	10	1	6	24	27	36	.254	.322	.366	87	-4	-5	33	0	1	-1	-7	13/O	-1.2
	Yr	129	416	50	118	13	2	10	45	37	63	.284	.344	.397	103	2	2	58	0	2	-1	-10		-0.9
1959	KC-A	58	109	8	27	4	1	2	19	7	12	.248	.293	.358	76	-4	-4	11	0	0	0	-3	1/O	-0.6
Total	9	744	2067	219	522	83	15	50	262	231	315	.253	.328	.380	88	-36	-36	269	7	_6_		1	1/O3	-4.4

■ TURNER WARD
Ward, Turner Max b: 4/11/65, Orlando, Fla. BB/TR, 6'2", 200 lbs. Deb: 9/10/90

YEAR	TM/L	G	AB	R	H	2B	3B	HR	RBI	BB	SO	AVG	OBP	SLG	PRO+	BR	/A	RC	SB	CS	SBR	FR	POS	TPR
1990	Cle-A	14	46	10	16	2	1	1	10	3	8	.348	.388	.500	144	3	3	9	3	0	1	0	O/D	0.3

■ BUZZY WARES
Wares, Clyde Ellsworth b: 5/23/1886, Vandalia, Mich. d: 5/26/64, South Bend, Ind. BR/TR, 5'10", 150 lbs. Deb: 9/15/13 C

YEAR	TM/L	G	AB	R	H	2B	3B	HR	RBI	BB	SO	AVG	OBP	SLG	PRO+	BR	/A	RC	SB	CS	SBR	FR	POS	TPR
1913	StL-A	11	35	5	10	2	0	0	1	3		.286	.306	.343	92	-1	-0	4	2			-4	/2	-0.4
1914	StL-A	81	215	20	45	10	1	0	23	28	35	.209	.300	.265	73	-7	-6	19	10	10	-3	-2	S/2	-0.5
Total	2	92	250	25	55	12	1	0	24	29	38	.220	.301	.276	76	-8	-7	23	12	_10_		-6	/S2	-0.9

YEAR	TM/L	G	AB	R	H	2B	3B	HR	RBI	BB	SO	AVG	OBP	SLG	PRO+	BR	/A	RC	SB	CS	SBR	FR	POS	TPR

■ FRED WARNER   Warner, Frederick John Rodney   b: 1855, Philadelphia, Pa.   d: 2/13/1886, Philadelphia, Pa.   5'7", 155 lbs.   Deb: 4/30/1875

YEAR	TM/L	G	AB	R	H	2B	3B	HR	RBI	BB	SO	AVG	OBP	SLG	PRO+	BR	/A	RC	SB	CS	SBR	FR	POS	TPR
1875	Cen-n	14	57	11	14	1	0	0		1		.246	.259	.263	88	-1	-0	4					O	0.0
1876	Phi-N	1	3	0	0	0	0	0	0	0	0	.000	.000	.000	-99	-1	-1	0				-0	/O	0.0
1878	Ind-N	43	165	19	41	4	0	0	10	2	15	.248	.257	.273	86	-4	-1	12				-3	*S/O	-0.1
1879	Cle-N	76	316	32	77	11	4	0	22	2	20	.244	.248	.304	82	-6	-6	24				-0	3O/1	-0.4
1883	Phi-N	39	141	13	32	6	1	0	13	5	21	.227	.253	.284	69	-6	-4	10				-9	3/O	-1.0
1884	Bro-a	84	352	40	78	4	0	1		17		.222	.259	.241	66	-12	-12	23				-6	*3	-1.5
Total	5	243	977	104	228	25	5	1	45	26	56	.233	.254	.272	74	-30	-24	69				-18	3/SO1	-3.0

■ HOOKS WARNER   Warner, Hoke Hayden   b: 5/22/1894, Del Rio, Tex.   d: 2/19/47, San Francisco, Cal   BL/TR, 5'10.5", 170 lbs.   Deb: 8/21/16

YEAR	TM/L	G	AB	R	H	2B	3B	HR	RBI	BB	SO	AVG	OBP	SLG	PRO+	BR	/A	RC	SB	CS	SBR	FR	POS	TPR
1916	Pit-N	44	168	12	40	1	1	2	14	6	19	.238	.264	.292	70	-6	-6	15	6			-11	3/2	-1.9
1917	Pit-N	3	5	0	1	0	0	0	0	0	1	.200	.200	.200	22	-0	-0	0	0			1	/3	0.1
1919	Pit-N	6	8	0	1	0	0	0	2	3	1	.125	.364	.125	48	-0	-0	0	0			1	/3	0.0
1921	Chi-N	14	38	4	8	1	0	0	3	2	1	.211	.268	.237	35	-3	-4	2	1	1	-0	-1	3	-0.4
Total	4	67	219	16	50	2	1	2	19	11	22	.228	.268	.274	61	-10	-11	18	7	1		-10	/32	-2.2

■ JOHN WARNER   Warner, John Joseph   b: 8/15/1872, New York, N.Y.   d: 12/21/43, Far Rockaway, N.Y.   BL/TR, 5'11", 165 lbs.   Deb: 4/23/1895

YEAR	TM/L	G	AB	R	H	2B	3B	HR	RBI	BB	SO	AVG	OBP	SLG	PRO+	BR	/A	RC	SB	CS	SBR	FR	POS	TPR
1895	Bos-N	3	7	2	1	0	0	0	1	1	0	.143	.333	.143	25	-1	-1	0	0			0	/C	0.0
	Lou-N	67	232	20	62	4	2	1	20	11	16	.267	.320	.315	70	-11	-9	27	10			-11	C/12	-1.1
	Yr	70	239	22	63	4	2	1	21	12	16	.264	.320	.310	69	-12	-10	28	10			-11		-1.1
1896	Lou-N	33	110	9	25	1	1	0	10	10	10	.227	.303	.255	52	-8	-7	10	3			9	C/1	0.4
	NY-N	19	54	9	14	1	0	0	3	3	7	.259	.310	.278	59	-3	-3	5	1			2	C	0.1
	Yr	52	164	18	39	2	1	0	13	13	17	.238	.306	.262	54	-11	-10	15	4			10		0.5
1897	NY-N	110	397	50	109	6	3	2	51	26		.275	.344	.320	80	-11	-9	48	8			16	*C	1.9
1898	NY-N	110	373	40	96	14	5	0	42	22		.257	.316	.322	88	-7	-5	42	9			17	*C/O	1.8
1899	NY-N	88	293	38	78	8	1	0	19	15		.266	.313	.300	73	-11	-10	33	15			13	C/1	0.8
1900	NY-N	34	108	15	27	4	0	0	13	8		.250	.314	.287	72	-4	-4	10	1			2	C	0.1
1901	NY-N	87	291	19	70	6	1	0	20	3		.241	.261	.268	57	-16	-15	22	3			-3	C	-0.7
1902	Bos-A	65	222	19	52	5	7	0	12	13		.234	.283	.320	66	-10	-10	21	0			5	C	0.0
1903	NY-N	89	285	38	81	8	5	0	34	7		.284	.301	.347	83	-6	-7	33	5			10	C	1.0
1904	NY-N	86	287	29	57	5	1	1	15	14		.199	.236	.233	45	-18	-19	19	7			1	C	-1.0
1905	StL-N	41	137	9	35	2	2	1	12	6		.255	.287	.321	85	-3	-3	14	2			2	C	0.4
	Det-A	36	119	12	24	2	3	0	7	8		.202	.252	.269	66	-4	-4	9	2			1	C	0.0
1906	Det-A	50	153	15	37	4	2	0	10	12		.242	.297	.294	85	-2	-3	15	4			8	C	1.0
	Was-A	32	103	5	21	4	1	1	9	2		.204	.219	.291	64	-5	-4	8	3			9	C	0.8
	Yr	82	256	20	58	8	3	1	19	14		.227	.267	.293	77	-7	-7	23	7			16		1.8
1907	Was-A	72	207	11	53	5	0	0	17	12		.256	.297	.280	93	-3	-1	19	3			-9	C	-0.4
1908	Was-A	51	116	8	28	2	1	0	8	8		.241	.290	.276	94	-2	-1	11	7			1	C/1	0.5
Total	14	1073	3494	348	870	81	35	6	303	181	33	.249	.296	.297	73	-125	-114	345	83			74	*C/1O2	5.6

■ JACKIE WARNER   Warner, John Joseph   b: 8/1/43, Monrovia, Cal.   BR/TR, 6', 180 lbs.   Deb: 4/12/66

YEAR	TM/L	G	AB	R	H	2B	3B	HR	RBI	BB	SO	AVG	OBP	SLG	PRO+	BR	/A	RC	SB	CS	SBR	FR	POS	TPR
1966	Cal-A	45	123	22	26	4	1	7	16	9	55	.211	.265	.431	99	-1	-1	14	0	0	0	-1	O	-0.3

■ JACK WARNER   Warner, John Ralph   b: 8/29/03, Evansville, Ind.   d: 3/13/86, Mt.Vernon, Ill.   BR/TR, 5'9.5", 165 lbs.   Deb: 9/24/25

YEAR	TM/L	G	AB	R	H	2B	3B	HR	RBI	BB	SO	AVG	OBP	SLG	PRO+	BR	/A	RC	SB	CS	SBR	FR	POS	TPR
1925	Det-A	10	39	7	13	0	0	0	2	3	6	.333	.381	.333	84	-1	-1	5	0	0	0	-2	3	-0.1
1926	Det-A	100	311	41	78	8	6	0	34	38	24	.251	.342	.315	71	-12	-12	37	8	4	0	-3	3/S	-0.6
1927	Det-A	139	559	78	149	22	9	0	45	47	45	.267	.330	.343	74	-21	-22	63	15	4	2	-5	*3	-1.3
1928	Det-A	75	206	33	44	4	4	0	13	16	15	.214	.274	.272	43	-17	-17	16	4	4	-1	6	3/S	-1.0
1929	Bro-N	17	62	3	17	2	0	0	4	7	6	.274	.348	.306	65	-3	-3	7	3			-2	S	-0.2
1930	Bro-N	21	25	4	8	1	0	0	0	2	7	.320	.370	.360	79	-1	-1	3	1			2	/3	0.1
1931	Bro-N	9	4	2	2	0	0	0	0	1	1	.500	.600	.500	200	1	1	1	0			3	/S3	0.3
1933	Phi-N	107	340	31	76	15	1	0	22	28	33	.224	.285	.274	53	-17	-22	26	1			3	23/S	-1.3
Total	8	478	1546	199	387	52	20	1	120	142	137	.250	.319	.312	65	-71	-77	158	32	12		1	3/2S	-4.1

■ HAL WARNOCK   Warnock, Harold Charles   b: 1/6/12, New York, N.Y.   BL/TR, 6'2", 180 lbs.   Deb: 9/02/35

YEAR	TM/L	G	AB	R	H	2B	3B	HR	RBI	BB	SO	AVG	OBP	SLG	PRO+	BR	/A	RC	SB	CS	SBR	FR	POS	TPR
1935	StL-A	6	7	1	2	0	0	0	0	0	3	.286	.286	.571	112	0	0	1	0	0	0	-0	/O	0.0

■ BENNIE WARREN   Warren, Bennie Louis   b: 3/2/12, Elk City, Okla.   BR/TR, 6'1", 184 lbs.   Deb: 9/13/39

YEAR	TM/L	G	AB	R	H	2B	3B	HR	RBI	BB	SO	AVG	OBP	SLG	PRO+	BR	/A	RC	SB	CS	SBR	FR	POS	TPR
1939	Phi-N	18	56	4	13	0	0	1	7	7	7	.232	.317	.286	65	-3	-3	6	0			-4	C	-0.5
1940	Phi-N	106	289	33	71	6	1	12	34	40	46	.246	.339	.398	107	1	3	39	1			-3	C/1	0.4
1941	Phi-N	121	345	34	74	13	2	9	35	44	66	.214	.309	.342	86	-8	-6	36	0			-4	*C	0.0
1942	Phi-N	90	225	19	47	6	3	7	20	24	36	.209	.288	.356	92	-4	-3	22	0			-2	C/1	-0.3
1946	NY-N	39	69	7	11	1	1	4	8	14	21	.159	.301	.377	91	-1	-1	9	0			1	C	0.1
1947	NY-N	3	5	0	1	0	0	0	0	0	1	.200	.200	.200	6	-1	-1	0	0			-1	/C	-0.1
Total	6	377	989	97	217	26	7	33	104	129	177	.219	.313	.360	92	-15	-10	111	1			-12	C/1	-0.4

■ BILL WARREN   Warren, William Hackney "Hack"   b: 2/11/1883, Missouri   d: 1/28/60, Whiteville, Tenn.   BR/TR, 5'8", 165 lbs.   Deb: 4/30/14

YEAR	TM/L	G	AB	R	H	2B	3B	HR	RBI	BB	SO	AVG	OBP	SLG	PRO+	BR	/A	RC	SB	CS	SBR	FR	POS	TPR
1914	Ind-F	26	50	5	12	2	0	0	5	5	7	.240	.309	.280	63	-2	-3	5	2			-10	C	-1.1
1915	New-F	5	3	0	1	0	0	0	1	0	0	.333	.333	.333	104	-0	-0	0	0			-0	/C1	0.0
Total	2	31	53	5	13	2	0	0	6	5	7	.245	.310	.283	65	-2	-3	6	2			-10	/C1	-1.1

■ RABBIT WARSTLER   Warstler, Harold Burton   b: 9/13/03, N.Canton, Ohio   d: 5/31/64, N.Canton, Ohio   BR/TR, 5'7.5", 150 lbs.   Deb: 7/24/30

YEAR	TM/L	G	AB	R	H	2B	3B	HR	RBI	BB	SO	AVG	OBP	SLG	PRO+	BR	/A	RC	SB	CS	SBR	FR	POS	TPR
1930	Bos-A	54	162	16	30	2	3	1	13	20	21	.185	.275	.253	36	-16	-15	12	0	2	-1	-3	S	-1.2
1931	Bos-A	66	181	20	44	5	3	0	10	15	27	.243	.308	.304	65	-10	-9	17	2	3	-1	1	2S/3	-0.3
1932	Bos-A	115	388	26	82	15	5	0	34	22	43	.211	.259	.276	40	-36	-34	28	9	6	-1	28	*S	0.1
1933	Bos-A	92	322	44	70	13	1	1	17	42	36	.217	.308	.273	55	-20	-20	29	2	4	-2	1	S	-1.2
1934	Phi-A	117	419	56	99	19	3	1	36	51	30	.236	.321	.303	64	-23	-21	45	9	3	1	16	*2/S	0.1
1935	Phi-A	138	496	62	124	20	7	3	59	56	53	.250	.326	.337	72	-21	-20	58	8	4	0	2	*2/3	-1.1
1936	Phi-A	66	236	27	59	8	6	1	24	36	16	.250	.354	.347	75	-9	-8	32	0	0	0	11	2	0.6
	Bos-N	74	304	27	64	6	0	0	17	22	33	.211	.266	.230	37	-27	-25	19	2			13	S	-0.7
1937	Bos-N	149	555	57	124	20	4	3	36	51	62	.223	.291	.276	60	-34	-27	48	4			-11	*S	-2.6
1938	Bos-N	142	467	37	108	10	4	0	40	48	38	.231	.303	.270	65	-25	-19	39	3			-7	*S/2	-1.6
1939	Bos-N	114	342	34	83	11	3	0	24	24	31	.243	.292	.292	62	-20	-17	29	2			1	S23	-1.0
1940	Bos-N	33	57	6	12	0	0	0	4	10	5	.211	.328	.211	54	-3	-3	4	1			-1	2/3S	-0.1
	Chi-N	45	159	19	36	4	1	1	18	8	19	.226	.263	.283	52	-11	-10	12	1			-1	S2	-0.7
	Yr	78	216	25	48	4	1	1	22	18	24	.222	.282	.264	53	-14	-13	16	1			-2		-0.8
Total	11	1205	4088	431	935	133	36	11	332	405	414	.229	.300	.287	59	-256	-229	372	42	22		50	S2/3	-9.7

■ CARL WARWICK   Warwick, Carl Wayne   b: 2/27/37, Dallas, Tex.   BR/TL, 5'10", 170 lbs.   Deb: 4/11/61

YEAR	TM/L	G	AB	R	H	2B	3B	HR	RBI	BB	SO	AVG	OBP	SLG	PRO+	BR	/A	RC	SB	CS	SBR	FR	POS	TPR
1961	LA-N	19	11	2	1	0	0	0	1	2	3	.091	.231	.091	-9	-2	-2	0	0	0	0	-0	O	-0.2
	StL-N	55	152	27	38	6	2	4	16	18	33	.250	.329	.395	83	-2	-4	21	3	0	1	1	O	-0.3
	Yr	74	163	29	39	6	2	4	17	20	36	.239	.322	.374	77	-4	-6	21	3	0	1	1		-0.5
1962	StL-N	13	23	4	8	0	0	1	4	2	2	.348	.400	.478	123	1	1	4	2	0	0	0	O	0.1
	Hou-N	130	477	63	124	17	1	16	60	38	77	.260	.315	.400	98	-7	-3	59	2	3	-1	-2	*O	-1.2
	Yr	143	500	67	132	17	1	17	64	40	79	.264	.319	.404	98	-6	-2	63	4	3	-1	-2		-1.1

YEAR	TM/L	G	AB	R	H	2B	3B	HR	RBI	BB	SO	AVG	OBP	SLG	PRO+	BR	/A	RC	SB	CS	SBR	FR	POS	TPR
1963	Hou-N	150	528	49	134	19	5	7	47	49	70	.254	.320	.348	98	-5	-1	58	3	3	-1	-2	*O/1	-1.2
1964	*StL-N	88	158	14	41	7	1	3	15	11	30	.259	.308	.373	83	-2	-4	19	2	0	1	-1	O	-0.5
1965	StL-N	50	77	3	12	2	1	0	6	4	18	.156	.198	.208	13	-9	-10	3	1	0	0	-0	O/1	-1.0
	Bal-A	9	14	3	0	0	0	0	0	3	2	.000	.176	.000	-44	-3	-3	0	0	0	0	-0	/O	-0.3
1966	Chi-N	16	22	3	5	0	0	0	0	0	6	.227	.227	.227	27	-2	-2	1	0	0	0	1	O	-0.1
Total	6	530	1462	168	363	51	10	31	149	127	241	.248	.309	.360	87	-30	-27	165	13	6	0	-3	O/1	-4.7

■ BILL WARWICK
Warwick, Firmin Newton b: 11/26/1897, Philadelphia, Pa. d: 12/19/84, San Antonio, Tex. BR/TR, 6'0.5", 180 lbs. Deb: 7/18/21

YEAR	TM/L	G	AB	R	H	2B	3B	HR	RBI	BB	SO	AVG	OBP	SLG	PRO+	BR	/A	RC	SB	CS	SBR	FR	POS	TPR
1921	Pit-N	1	1	0	0	0	0	0	0	0	0	.000	.000	.000	-97	-0	-0	0	0	0	0	0	/C	0.0
1925	StL-N	13	41	8	12	1	2	1	6	5	5	.293	.370	.488	114	1	1	7	0	1	-1	-4	C	-0.2
1926	StL-N	9	14	0	5	0	0	0	2	0	2	.357	.357	.357	89	-0	-0	2	0			2	/C	0.2
Total	3	23	56	8	17	1	2	1	8	5	7	.304	.361	.446	105	1	0	9	0	1		-2	/C	0.0

■ JIMMY WASDELL
Wasdell, James Charles b: 5/15/14, Cleveland, Ohio d: 8/6/83, New Port Richey, Fla. BL/TL, 5'11", 185 lbs. Deb: 9/03/37

YEAR	TM/L	G	AB	R	H	2B	3B	HR	RBI	BB	SO	AVG	OBP	SLG	PRO+	BR	/A	RC	SB	CS	SBR	FR	POS	TPR
1937	Was-A	32	110	13	28	4	4	2	12	7	13	.255	.299	.418	82	-4	-3	13	0	1	-1	0	1/O	-0.5
1938	Was-A	53	140	19	33	2	1	2	16	12	12	.236	.296	.307	55	-11	-9	13	5	2	0	-2	1/O	-1.2
1939	Was-A	29	109	12	33	5	1	0	13	9	16	.303	.361	.367	94	-2	-1	15	3	1	0	-2	1	-0.4
1940	Was-A	10	35	3	3	1	0	0	0	2	7	.086	.135	.114	-37	-7	-7	1	0	0	0	-1	/1	-0.7
	Bro-N	77	230	35	64	14	4	3	37	18	24	.278	.333	.413	99	1	-1	32	4			-7	O1	-1.0
1941	*Bro-N	94	265	39	79	14	3	4	48	16	15	.298	.345	.419	110	4	3	40	2			-6	O1	-0.7
1942	Pit-N	122	409	44	106	11	2	3	38	47	22	.259	.337	.318	90	-3	-4	46	1			-8	O/1	-1.6
1943	Pit-N	4	2	0	1	0	0	0	1	2	0	.500	.750	.500	256	1	1	1	0			0	H	0.1
	Phi-N	141	522	54	136	19	6	4	67	46	22	.261	.323	.343	96	-5	-3	58	6			-1	1O	-0.9
	Yr	145	524	54	137	19	6	4	68	48	22	.261	.326	.344	97	-4	-2	59	6			-1		-0.8
1944	Phi-N	133	451	47	125	20	3	3	40	45	11	.277	.344	.355	100	-1	1	55	0			-9	*O/1	-1.8
1945	Phi-N	134	500	65	150	19	8	7	60	32	11	.300	.346	.412	113	6	7	72	7			-1	O1	0.1
1946	Phi-N	26	51	7	13	0	2	1	5	3	2	.255	.309	.392	101	-0	-0	6	0			-2	O/1	-0.2
	Cle-A	32	41	1	11	0	0	0	4	4	4	.268	.333	.268	74	-2	-1	4	1	0	0	-1	/1O	-0.1
1947	Cle-A	1	1	0	0	0	0	0	0	0	0	.000	.000	.000	-99	-0	-0	0	0	0	0	0	H	0.0
Total	11	888	2866	339	782	109	34	29	341	243	165	.273	.332	.365	96	-23	-18	355	29	4		-40	O1	-8.9

■ LINK WASEM
Wasem, Lincoln William b: 1/30/11, Birmingham, Ohio d: 3/6/79, S.Laguna, Cal. BR/TR, 5'9.5", 180 lbs. Deb: 5/05/37

YEAR	TM/L	G	AB	R	H	2B	3B	HR	RBI	BB	SO	AVG	OBP	SLG	PRO+	BR	/A	RC	SB	CS	SBR	FR	POS	TPR
1937	Bos-N	2	1	0	0	0	0	0	0	0	0	.000	.000	.000	-99	-0	-0	0	0			0	/C	0.0

■ LIBE WASHBURN
Washburn, Libeus b: 6/16/1874, Lyme, N.H. d: 3/22/40, Malone, N.Y. BB/TL, 5'10", 180 lbs. Deb: 5/30/02

YEAR	TM/L	G	AB	R	H	2B	3B	HR	RBI	BB	SO	AVG	OBP	SLG	PRO+	BR	/A	RC	SB	CS	SBR	FR	POS	TPR
1902	NY-N	6	9	1	4	0	0	0	0	0	2	.444	.615	.444	233	2	2	3	1			-1	/O	0.1
1903	Phi-N	8	18	1	3	0	0	0	1	1	1	.167	.211	.167	9	-2	-2	1	0			-1	/PO	-0.1
Total	2	14	27	2	7	0	0	0	1	1	3	.259	.375	.259	91	-0	-0	4	1			-1	/OP	0.0

■ CLAUDELL WASHINGTON
Washington, Claudell b: 8/31/54, Los Angeles, Cal. BL/TL, 6', 190 lbs. Deb: 7/05/74

YEAR	TM/L	G	AB	R	H	2B	3B	HR	RBI	BB	SO	AVG	OBP	SLG	PRO+	BR	/A	RC	SB	CS	SBR	FR	POS	TPR
1974	*Oak-A	73	221	16	63	10	5	0	19	13	44	.285	.328	.376	109	0	2	24	6	8	-3	1	DO	0.0
1975	*Oak-A	148	590	86	182	24	7	10	77	32	80	.308	.349	.424	120	12	14	85	40	15	3	-2	*O	1.2
1976	Oak-A	134	490	65	126	20	6	5	53	30	90	.257	.304	.353	96	-6	-3	49	37	20	-1	0	*O/D	-0.6
1977	Tex-A	129	521	63	148	31	2	12	68	25	112	.284	.321	.420	99	-1	-2	68	21	8	2	3	*O/D	-0.1
1978	Tex-A	12	42	1	7	0	0	0	2	1	12	.167	.186	.167	-0	-6	-6	1	0	1	-1	-1	/OD	-0.7
	Chi-A	86	314	33	83	16	5	6	31	12	57	.264	.294	.404	94	-3	-4	34	5	5	-2	-2	O/D	-0.9
	Yr	98	356	34	90	16	5	6	33	13	69	.253	.281	.376	83	-9	-9	34	5	6	-2	-3		-1.6
1979	Chi-A	131	471	79	132	33	5	13	66	28	93	.280	.325	.454	108	4	4	65	19	11	-1	1	*O	-0.1
1980	Chi-A	32	90	15	26	4	2	1	12	5	19	.289	.333	.411	103	0	0	11	4	2	0	-2	O/D	-0.1
	NY-N	79	284	38	78	16	4	10	42	20	63	.275	.325	.465	121	6	7	42	17	5	2	0	O	0.7
1981	Atl-N	85	320	37	93	22	3	5	37	15	47	.291	.330	.425	110	4	4	44	12	6	0	-4	O	-0.2
1982	*Atl-N	150	563	94	150	24	6	16	80	50	107	.266	.333	.416	104	6	3	80	33	10	4	-10	*O	-0.4
1983	Atl-N	134	496	75	138	24	8	9	44	35	103	.278	.326	.413	96	1	-3	67	31	9	4	-4	*O	-0.5
1984	Atl-N	120	416	62	119	21	2	17	61	59	77	.286	.376	.469	127	21	17	73	21	9	1	-9	*O	0.5
1985	Atl-N	122	398	62	110	14	6	15	43	40	66	.276	.344	.455	115	11	8	61	14	4	2	-20	*O	-1.2
1986	Atl-N	40	137	17	37	11	0	5	14	14	26	.270	.338	.460	112	3	2	18	4	7	-3	-7	O	-0.8
	NY-A	54	135	19	32	5	0	6	16	7	33	.237	.285	.407	87	-3	-3	16	6	1	1	-2	O	-0.4
1987	NY-A	102	312	42	87	17	0	9	44	27	54	.279	.336	.420	100	-1	-0	46	10	1	2	3	OD	0.3
1988	NY-A	126	455	62	140	22	3	11	64	24	74	.308	.345	.442	120	10	11	68	15	6	1	-2	*O	0.8
1989	Cal-A	110	418	53	114	18	4	13	42	27	84	.273	.320	.428	111	4	5	57	13	5	1	-4	*O/D	0.0
1990	Cal-A	12	34	3	6	1	0	1	3	2	8	.176	.222	.294	43	-3	-3	2	1	0	0	0	/O	-0.1
	NY-A	33	80	4	13	1	1	0	6	2	17	.162	.183	.200	7	-10	-10	3	3	1	0	1	O	-0.8
	Yr	45	114	7	19	2	1	1	9	4	25	.167	.195	.228	18	-13	-13	5	4	1	1	2		-0.9
Total	17	1912	6787	926	1884	334	69	164	824	468	1266	.278	.328	.420	106	50	42	914	312	134	13	-57	*O/D	-3.4

■ HERB WASHINGTON
Washington, Herbert Lee b: 11/16/51, Belzonia, Miss. BR/TR, 6', 170 lbs. Deb: 4/04/74

YEAR	TM/L	G	AB	R	H	2B	3B	HR	RBI	BB	SO	AVG	OBP	SLG	PRO+	BR	/A	RC	SB	CS	SBR	FR	POS	TPR
1974	*Oak-A	92	0	29	0	0	0	0	0	0	0	—	—	—	—	0	0	0	29	16	-1	0	R	0.0
1975	Oak-A	13	0	4	0	0	0	0	0	0	0	—	—	—	—	0	0	0	2	1	0	0	R	0.0
Total	2	105	0	33	0	0	0	0	0	0	0	—	—	—	—	0	0	0	31	17	-1	0		0.0

■ LA RUE WASHINGTON
Washington, La Rue b: 9/7/53, Long Beach, Cal. BR/TR, 6', 170 lbs. Deb: 9/07/78

YEAR	TM/L	G	AB	R	H	2B	3B	HR	RBI	BB	SO	AVG	OBP	SLG	PRO+	BR	/A	RC	SB	CS	SBR	FR	POS	TPR
1978	Tex-A	3	3	0	0	0	0	0	0	0	1	.000	.000	.000	-99	-1	-1	0	0	0	0	2	/2D	0.1
1979	Tex-A	25	18	5	5	0	0	0	2	4	0	.278	.409	.278	90	0	0	3	2	1	0	2	O/3	0.2
Total	2	28	21	5	5	0	0	0	2	4	1	.238	.360	.238	67	-1	-1	3	2	1	0	4	/O23D	0.3

■ RON WASHINGTON
Washington, Ronald b: 4/29/52, New Orleans, La. BR/TR, 5'11", 155 lbs. Deb: 9/10/77

YEAR	TM/L	G	AB	R	H	2B	3B	HR	RBI	BB	SO	AVG	OBP	SLG	PRO+	BR	/A	RC	SB	CS	SBR	FR	POS	TPR
1977	LA-N	10	19	4	7	0	0	0	1	0	2	.368	.400	.368	108	0	0	2	1	1	-0	-1	S	0.0
1981	Min-A	28	84	8	19	3	1	0	5	0	14	.226	.270	.286	56	-4	-5	7	4	1	1	2	S/O	0.0
1982	Min-A	119	451	48	122	17	6	5	39	14	79	.271	.292	.368	78	-13	-15	45	3	3	-1	-44	S2/3	-5.0
1983	Min-A	99	317	28	78	7	3	4	26	22	50	.246	.297	.325	69	-12	-14	30	10	5	0	-17	S2/3D	-2.5
1984	Min-A	88	197	25	58	11	5	4	23	4	31	.294	.312	.447	102	1	0	26	1	1	-0	-16	S/23D	-0.9
1985	Min-A	70	135	24	37	6	4	1	14	8	15	.274	.315	.400	89	-1	-2	17	5	1	1	-4	S2/31D	-0.1
1986	Min-A	48	74	15	19	3	0	4	11	3	21	.257	.286	.459	96	-0	-1	9	1	2	-1	1	2D/S3	0.0
1987	Bal-A	26	79	7	16	3	1	1	6	1	15	.203	.213	.304	36	-7	-7	4	0	1	-1	3	3/2OSD	-0.4
1988	Cle-A	69	223	30	57	14	2	2	21	9	35	.256	.300	.363	82	-5	-6	24	3	3	-1	-14	S/32D	-1.7
1989	Hou-N	7	7	1	1	1	0	0	0	0	4	.143	.143	.286	20	-1	-1	0	0	0	0	-0	/23	0.0
Total	10	564	1586	190	414	65	22	20	146	65	266	.261	.294	.368	79	-43	-50	165	28	18	-2	-90	S2/3DO1	-10.6

■ GEORGE WASHINGTON
Washington, Sloan Vernon "Vern" b: 6/4/07, Linden, Tex. d: 2/17/85, Linden, Tex. BL/TL, 5'11.5", 190 lbs. Deb: 4/17/35

YEAR	TM/L	G	AB	R	H	2B	3B	HR	RBI	BB	SO	AVG	OBP	SLG	PRO+	BR	/A	RC	SB	CS	SBR	FR	POS	TPR
1935	Chi-A	108	339	40	96	22	3	8	47	10	18	.283	.310	.437	89	-6	-7	45	1	0	-3	O	-0.9
1936	Chi-A	20	49	6	8	2	0	1	5	1	4	.163	.180	.265	8	-7	-8	2	0	0		-1	O	-0.7
Total	2	128	388	46	104	24	3	9	52	11	22	.268	.294	.415	78	-14	-15	48	1	0	0	-3	/O	-1.6

■ U L WASHINGTON
Washington, U L b: 10/27/53, Stringtown, Okla. BB/TR, 5'11", 175 lbs. Deb: 9/06/77

YEAR	TM/L	G	AB	R	H	2B	3B	HR	RBI	BB	SO	AVG	OBP	SLG	PRO+	BR	/A	RC	SB	CS	SBR	FR	POS	TPR
1977	KC-A	10	20	0	4	1	1	0	1	5	4	.200	.360	.350	94	0	-0	3	1	0	0	0	/S	0.1

YEAR	TM/L	G	AB	R	H	2B	3B	HR	RBI	BB	SO	AVG	OBP	SLG	PRO+	BR	/A	RC	SB	CS	SBR	FR	POS	TPR
1978	KC-A	69	129	10	34	2	1	0	9	10	20	.264	.317	.295	71	-4	-5	12	12	6	0	-10	S2/D	-1.0
1979	KC-A	101	268	32	68	12	5	2	25	20	44	.254	.306	.358	77	-8	-9	30	10	7	-1	1	S2/3	0.0
1980	*KC-A	153	549	79	150	16	11	6	53	53	78	.273	.337	.375	94	-3	-4	70	20	7	2	-26	*S	-1.6
1981	KC-A	98	339	40	77	19	1	2	29	41	43	.227	.311	.307	79	-9	-8	32	10	10	-3	-21	S	-2.6
1982	KC-A	119	437	64	125	19	3	10	60	38	48	.286	.343	.412	106	4	4	65	23	7	3	-11	*S/D	0.6
1983	KC-A	144	547	76	129	19	6	5	41	48	78	.236	.299	.320	70	-22	-22	40	7	8		-10	*S/D	-1.5
1984	*KC-A	63	170	18	38	6	0	1	10	14	31	.224	.283	.276	55	-10	-10	13	4	6	-2	0	S	-0.7
1985	Mon-N	68	193	24	48	9	4	1	17	15	33	.249	.303	.352	88	-5	-3	21	6	3	0	-9	2/S3	-1.2
1986	Pit-N	72	135	14	27	0	4	0	10	15	27	.200	.280	.259	49	-9	-9	12	6	0	2	-8	S/2	-1.0
1987	Pit-N	10	10	1	3	0	0	0	0	2	3	.300	.417	.300	93	0	0	2	0	0	0	-0	/S3	0.0
Total	11	907	2797	358	703	103	36	27	255	261	409	.251	.315	.343	82	-67	-67	320	132	53	8	-94	S2/3D	-8.9

■ MARK WASINGER
Wasinger, Mark Thomas b: 8/4/61, Monterey, Cal. BR/TR, 6', 165 lbs. Deb: 5/27/86

YEAR	TM/L	G	AB	R	H	2B	3B	HR	RBI	BB	SO	AVG	OBP	SLG	PRO+	BR	/A	RC	SB	CS	SBR	FR	POS	TPR
1986	SD-N	3	8	0	0	0	0	0	1	0	2	.000	.000	.000	-99	-2	-2	0	0	0	0	-1	/32	-0.3
1987	SF-N	44	80	16	22	3	0	1	3	8	14	.275	.341	.350	88	-2	-1	10	2	0	1	3	32/S	0.3
1988	SF-N	3	2	1	0	0	0	0	0	0	0	.000	.000	.000	-99	-1	-0	0	0	0	0	0	/3	0.0
Total	3	50	90	17	22	3	0	1	4	8	16	.244	.306	.311	68	-4	-4	10	2	0	1	2	/32S	0.0

■ FRED WATERMAN
Waterman, Frederick A. b: 12/1845, New York, N.Y. d: 12/16/1899, Cincinnati, Ohio 5'7.5", 148 lbs. Deb: 5/05/1871

YEAR	TM/L	G	AB	R	H	2B	3B	HR	RBI	BB	SO	AVG	OBP	SLG	PRO+	BR	/A	RC	SB	CS	SBR	FR	POS	TPR
1871	Oly-n	32	158	46	50	7	4	0	17	10	0	.316	.357	.411	127	4	6	28	11				*3/C	0.2
1872	Oly-n	9	44	13	18	1	1	0			1	.409	.422	.477	186	4	4	9					/3C	0.3
1873	Was-n	15	78	20	27	3	3	0			1	.346	.354	.462	143	4	4	13					/SO3	0.3
1875	Chi-n	5	20	2	6	0	0	0			0	.300	.300	.300	107	0	0	2					/32	0.0
Total	4 n	61	300	81	101	11	8	0			12	.337	.362	.427	138	12	15	52					/3SCO2	0.8

■ JOHN WATHAN
Wathan, John David b: 10/4/49, Cedar Rapids, Iowa BR/TR, 6'2", 205 lbs. Deb: 5/26/76 MC

YEAR	TM/L	G	AB	R	H	2B	3B	HR	RBI	BB	SO	AVG	OBP	SLG	PRO+	BR	/A	RC	SB	CS	SBR	FR	POS	TPR
1976	*KC-A	27	42	5	12	1	0	0	5	2	5	.286	.333	.310	88	-1	-1	4	0	2	-1	-1	C/1	-0.1
1977	*KC-A	55	119	18	39	5	3	2	21	5	8	.328	.354	.471	122	3	3	20	2	0	1	-2	C/1D	0.2
1978	*KC-A	67	190	19	57	10	1	2	28	3	12	.300	.325	.395	99	-0	-1	23	2	1	0	1	1C	0.2
1979	KC-A	90	199	26	41	7	3	2	28	7	24	.206	.233	.302	42	-16	-17	13	2	1	0	-2	1CD/O	-1.9
1980	*KC-A	126	453	57	138	14	7	6	58	50	42	.305	.377	.406	114	11	10	69	17	3	3	-11	CO1	0.5
1981	KC-A	89	301	24	76	9	3	1	19	19	23	.252	.301	.312	78	-9	-9	27	11	6	-0	-7	CO/1	-1.3
1982	KC-A	121	448	79	121	11	3	3	51	48	46	.270	.343	.328	85	-7	-7	49	36	9	5	-18	*C/1	-1.3
1983	KC-A	128	437	49	107	18	3	2	32	27	56	.245	.290	.314	66	-20	-20	40	28	7	4	-9	C1/O	-2.2
1984	KC-A	97	171	17	31	7	1	2	10	21	34	.181	.271	.269	50	-11	-12	12	6	6	-2	6	C1/OD	-0.5
1985	*KC-A	60	145	11	34	8	1	1	9	17	15	.234	.319	.324	76	-4	-4	15	1	1	-0	20	C/1D	1.6
Total	10	860	2505	305	656	90	25	21	261	199	265	.262	.320	.343	83	-55	-57	271	105	36	10	-22	C1/OD	-5.0

■ DAVE WATKINS
Watkins, David Roger b: 3/15/44, Owensboro, Ky. BR/TR, 5'10", 185 lbs. Deb: 4/09/69

YEAR	TM/L	G	AB	R	H	2B	3B	HR	RBI	BB	SO	AVG	OBP	SLG	PRO+	BR	/A	RC	SB	CS	SBR	FR	POS	TPR
1969	Phi-N	69	148	17	26	2	1	4	12	22	53	.176	.291	.284	63	-7	-7	13	2	3	-1	-2	C/O3	-0.6

■ GEORGE WATKINS
Watkins, George Archibald b: 6/4/1900, Freesrone Co., Tex d: 6/1/70, Houston, Tex. BL/TR, 6', 175 lbs. Deb: 4/15/30

YEAR	TM/L	G	AB	R	H	2B	3B	HR	RBI	BB	SO	AVG	OBP	SLG	PRO+	BR	/A	RC	SB	CS	SBR	FR	POS	TPR
1930	*StL-N	119	391	85	146	32	7	17	87	24	49	.373	.415	.621	141	28	26	96	5			-3	O1/2	1.4
1931	*StL-N	131	503	93	145	30	13	13	51	31	66	.288	.336	.461	112	9	7	81	15			-1	*O	0.0
1932	StL-N	127	458	67	143	35	3	9	63	45	46	.312	.384	.461	122	18	16	84	18			2	*O	0.9
1933	StL-N	138	525	66	146	24	5	5	62	39	62	.278	.342	.371	98	3	0	71	11			-0	*O	-0.8
1934	NY-N	105	296	38	73	18	3	6	33	24	34	.247	.316	.389	90	-5	-5	40	2			-12	O	-2.0
1935	Phi-N	150	600	80	162	25	5	17	76	40	78	.270	.320	.413	87	-5	-13	82	3			5	*O	-1.3
1936	Phi-N	19	70	7	17	4	0	2	5	5	13	.243	.293	.386	74	-2	-3	8	2			-3	O	-0.6
	Bro-N	105	364	54	93	24	6	4	43	38	34	.255	.334	.387	93	-3	-4	51	5			-5	O	-1.2
	Yr	124	434	61	110	28	6	6	48	43	47	.253	.328	.387	90	-5	-7	59	7			-8		-1.8
Total	7	894	3207	490	925	192	42	73	420	246	382	.288	.347	.443	105	43	25	513	61			-19	O/12	-3.6

■ ED WATKINS
Watkins, James Edward b: 6/21/1877, Philadelphia, Pa. d: 3/29/33, Kelvin, Ariz. Deb: 9/06/02

YEAR	TM/L	G	AB	R	H	2B	3B	HR	RBI	BB	SO	AVG	OBP	SLG	PRO+	BR	/A	RC	SB	CS	SBR	FR	POS	TPR
1902	Phi-N	1	3	0	0	0	0	0	0	0	1	.000	.250	.000	-20	-0	-0	0	0			-0	/O	0.0

■ BILL WATKINS
Watkins, William Henry b: 5/5/1858, Brantford, Ont., Can d: 6/9/37, Port Huron, Mich. 5'10", 156 lbs. Deb: 8/01/1884 M

YEAR	TM/L	G	AB	R	H	2B	3B	HR	RBI	BB	SO	AVG	OBP	SLG	PRO+	BR	/A	RC	SB	CS	SBR	FR	POS	TPR
1884	Ind-a	34	127	16	26	4	0	0			5	.205	.241	.236	60	-5	-5	7				-6	3/2SM	-0.9

■ NEAL WATLINGTON
Watlington, Julius Neal b: 12/25/22, Yanceyville, N.C. BL/TR, 6', 195 lbs. Deb: 7/10/53

YEAR	TM/L	G	AB	R	H	2B	3B	HR	RBI	BB	SO	AVG	OBP	SLG	PRO+	BR	/A	RC	SB	CS	SBR	FR	POS	TPR
1953	Phi-A	21	44	4	7	1	0	0	3	3	8	.159	.213	.182	7	-6	-6	2	0	1	-1	0	/C	-0.5

■ ART WATSON
Watson, Arthur Stanhope "Watty" b: 1/11/1884, Jeffersonville, Ind. d: 5/9/50, Buffalo, N.Y. BL/TR, 5'10", 175 lbs. Deb: 5/19/14

YEAR	TM/L	G	AB	R	H	2B	3B	HR	RBI	BB	SO	AVG	OBP	SLG	PRO+	BR	/A	RC	SB	CS	SBR	FR	POS	TPR
1914	Bro-F	22	46	7	13	4	1	1	3	1	6	.283	.298	.478	121	1	1	7	0			-1	C	0.0
1915	Bro-F	9	19	4	5	0	3	0	1	3	4	.263	.364	.579	178	2	2	4	0			-5	/C	-0.2
	Buf-F	22	30	6	14	1	0	1	13	0	4	.467	.467	.600	210	4	4	9	0			-4	/CO	0.0
	Yr	31	49	10	19	1	3	1	14	3	8	.388	.423	.592	196	6	6	13	0			-9		-0.2
Total	2	53	95	17	32	5	4	2	17	4	14	.337	.364	.537	160	6	6	20	0			-10	/CO	-0.2

■ JOHHNY WATSON
Watson, John Thomas b: 1/16/08, Tazewell, Va. d: 4/29/65, Huntington, W.Va. BL/TR, 6', 175 lbs. Deb: 9/26/30

YEAR	TM/L	G	AB	R	H	2B	3B	HR	RBI	BB	SO	AVG	OBP	SLG	PRO+	BR	/A	RC	SB	CS	SBR	FR	POS	TPR
1930	Det-A	4	12	1	3	2	0	0	3	1	2	.250	.308	.417	80	-0	-0	2	0	0	0	-1	/S	0.0

■ BOB WATSON
Watson, Robert Jose "Bull" b: 4/10/46, Los Angeles, Cal. BR/TR, 6'0.5", 201 lbs. Deb: 9/09/66 C

YEAR	TM/L	G	AB	R	H	2B	3B	HR	RBI	BB	SO	AVG	OBP	SLG	PRO+	BR	/A	RC	SB	CS	SBR	FR	POS	TPR
1966	Hou-N	1	1	0	0	0	0	0	0	0	0	.000	.000	.000	-99	-0	-0	0	0	0	0	0	H	0.0
1967	Hou-N	6	14	1	3	0	0	1	2	0	3	.214	.214	.429	82	-0	-0	1	0	0	0	0	/1	0.0
1968	Hou-N	45	140	13	32	7	0	2	8	13	32	.229	.299	.321	88	-2	-2	13	1	0	0	-8	O	-1.2
1969	Hou-N	20	40	3	11	3	0	0	3	6	5	.275	.396	.350	113	1	1	6	0	0	0	-0	/O1C	0.0
1970	Hou-N	97	327	48	89	19	2	11	61	24	59	.272	.330	.443	110	1	3	46	1	1	-0	-7	1/CO	-1.1
1971	Hou-N	129	468	49	135	17	3	9	67	41	56	.288	.348	.395	113	6	8	62	0	3	-2	-14	O1	-1.5
1972	Hou-N	147	548	74	171	27	4	16	86	53	83	.312	.381	.464	142	28	29	100	1	1	-0	-10	*O/1	1.3
1973	Hou-N	158	573	97	179	24	3	16	94	85	73	.312	.405	.449	137	31	31	104	1	4	-2	-7	*O1/C	1.5
1974	Hou-N	150	524	69	156	19	4	11	67	60	61	.298	.373	.412	125	14	17	80	3	4	-2	-17	*O1	-0.8
1975	Hou-N	132	485	67	157	27	1	18	85	40	50	.324	.379	.495	152	25	30	87	3	5	-2	-1	*1/O	2.0
1976	Hou-N	157	585	76	183	31	3	16	102	62	64	.313	.382	.458	151	29	35	102	3	3	-1	-2	*1	2.6
1977	Hou-N	151	554	77	160	38	6	22	110	57	69	.289	.362	.498	141	21	28	102	5	0	2	12	*1	3.4
1978	Hou-N	139	461	51	133	25	4	14	79	51	57	.289	.364	.451	137	17	21	72	3	1	0	10	*1	2.7
1979	Hou-N	49	163	15	39	4	0	3	18	16	23	.239	.307	.319	75	-6	-5	16	0	0	0	3	1	-0.4
	Bos-A	84	312	48	105	19	4	13	53	29	33	.337	.402	.548	145	23	21	66	3	2	-0	2	1D	1.9
1980	*NY-A	130	469	62	144	25	3	13	68	48	56	.307	.373	.464	128	17	18	75	2	1	-0	-2	*1D	0.9
1981	*NY-A	59	156	15	33	3	3	6	12	24	17	.212	.317	.385	103	0	1	17	0	0	0	-1	1/D	0.0
1982	NY-A	7	17	3	4	3	0	0	3	3	0	.235	.350	.412	110	0	0	2	0	0	0	-1	/1D	0.0
	Atl-N	57	114	16	28	3	1	5	22	14	20	.246	.328	.421	104	1	1	15	1	1	-0	-3	1/O	-0.4
1983	Atl-N	65	149	14	46	9	0	6	37	18	23	.309	.383	.490	131	8	7	26	0	2	-1	3	1	0.1
1984	Atl-N	49	85	4	18	4	0	2	12	9	12	.212	.287	.329	68	-3	-4	8	0	0	0	1	1	-0.3
Total	19	1832	6185	802	1826	307	41	184	989	653	796	.295	.367	.447	130	213	239	1001	27	28	-9	-47	*1O/DC	10.7

YEAR	TM/L	G	AB	R	H	2B	3B	HR	RBI	BB	SO	AVG	OBP	SLG	PRO+	BR	/A	RC	SB	CS	SBR	FR	POS	TPR

■ ALLIE WATT   Watt, Albert Bailey   b: 12/12/1899, Philadelphia, Pa.   d: 3/15/68, Norfolk, Va.   BR/TR, 5'8", 154 lbs.   Deb: 10/03/20

YEAR	TM/L	G	AB	R	H	2B	3B	HR	RBI	BB	SO	AVG	OBP	SLG	PRO+	BR	/A	RC	SB	CS	SBR	FR	POS	TPR
1920	Was-A	1	1	0	1	1	0	0	1	0	0	1.000	1.000	2.000	700	1	1	2	0	0	0	0	/2	0.1

■ JOHNNY WATWOOD   Watwood, John Clifford "Lefty"   b: 8/17/05, Alexander City, Ala.   d: 3/1/80, Goodwater, Ala.   BL/TL, 6'1", 186 lbs.   Deb: 4/16/29

YEAR	TM/L	G	AB	R	H	2B	3B	HR	RBI	BB	SO	AVG	OBP	SLG	PRO+	BR	/A	RC	SB	CS	SBR	FR	POS	TPR
1929	Chi-A	85	278	33	84	12	6	2	28	22	21	.302	.355	.410	98	-1	-1	41	6	3	0	-2	O	-0.5
1930	Chi-A	133	427	75	129	25	4	2	51	52	35	.302	.382	.393	100	-0	2	66	5	7	-3	3	1O	-0.6
1931	Chi-A	128	367	51	104	16	6	1	47	56	30	.283	.380	.368	103	1	4	56	9	3	1	3	*O/1	0.1
1932	Chi-A	13	49	5	15	2	0	0	0	1	3	.306	.333	.347	82	-2	-1	6	0	0	0	-1	O	-0.2
	Bos-A	95	266	26	66	11	0	0	30	20	11	.248	.301	.289	55	-18	-17	24	7	4	-0	-1	O1	-2.0
	Yr	108	315	31	81	13	0	0	30	21	14	.257	.306	.298	59	-20	-18	30	7	4	-0	-2		-2.2
1933	Bos-A	13	30	2	4	0	0	0	2	3	3	.133	.212	.133	-7	-5	-5	1	0	0	0	0	/O	-0.4
1939	Phi-N	2	6	0	1	0	0	0	0	0	0	.167	.167	.167	-11	-1	-1	0	0			-1	/1	-0.1
Total	6	469	1423	192	403	66	16	5	158	154	103	.283	.356	.363	89	-26	-19	193	27	17		2	O/1	-3.7

■ BOB WAY   Way, Robert Clinton   b: 4/2/06, Emlenton, Pa.   d: 6/20/74, Pittsburgh, Pa.   BR/TR, 5'10.5", 168 lbs.   Deb: 4/12/27

YEAR	TM/L	G	AB	R	H	2B	3B	HR	RBI	BB	SO	AVG	OBP	SLG	PRO+	BR	/A	RC	SB	CS	SBR	FR	POS	TPR
1927	Chi-A	5	3	3	1	0	0	0	1	0	0	.333	.333	.333	75	-0	-0	0	0	0	0	1	/2	0.1

■ ROY WEATHERLY   Weatherly, Cyril Roy "Stormy"   b: 2/25/15, Warren, Tex.   BL/TR, 5'6.5", 170 lbs.   Deb: 6/27/36

YEAR	TM/L	G	AB	R	H	2B	3B	HR	RBI	BB	SO	AVG	OBP	SLG	PRO+	BR	/A	RC	SB	CS	SBR	FR	POS	TPR
1936	Cle-A	84	349	64	117	28	6	8	53	16	29	.335	.364	.519	115	7	6	61	3	8	-4	5	O	0.4
1937	Cle-A	53	134	19	27	4	0	5	13	6	14	.201	.246	.343	47	-12	-12	11	1	1	-0	-1	O/3	-1.3
1938	Cle-A	83	210	32	55	14	3	2	18	14	14	.262	.308	.386	74	-10	-9	24	8	5	-1	5	O	-0.3
1939	Cle-A	95	323	43	100	16	6	1	32	19	23	.310	.348	.406	95	-4	-3	47	7	2	1	-6	O	-0.9
1940	Cle-A	135	578	90	175	35	11	12	59	27	26	.303	.335	.464	108	2	4	88	9	8	-2	5	*O	-0.1
1941	Cle-A	102	363	59	105	21	5	3	37	32	20	.289	.350	.399	103	-1	1	52	2	5	-2	-10	O	-1.5
1942	Cle-A	128	473	61	122	23	7	5	39	35	25	.258	.310	.368	96	-7	-4	54	8	13	-5	0	*O	-1.7
1943	*NY-A	77	280	37	74	8	3	7	28	18	9	.264	.311	.389	104	0	0	34	4	7	-3	-3	O	-0.7
1946	NY-A	2	2	0	1	0	0	0	0	0	0	.500	.500	.500	178	0	0	1	0	0	0	0	H	0.0
1950	NY-N	52	69	10	18	3	3	0	11	13	10	.261	.378	.391	102	1	1	10	0			1	O	0.1
Total	10	811	2781	415	794	152	44	43	290	180	170	.286	.331	.418	99	-25	-15	382	42	49		-3	O/3	-6.0

■ ART WEAVER   Weaver, Arthur Coggshall "Six O'Clock"   b: 4/7/1879, Wichita, Kan.   d: 3/23/17, Denver, Colo.   TR , 6'1",   Deb: 9/14/02

YEAR	TM/L	G	AB	R	H	2B	3B	HR	RBI	BB	SO	AVG	OBP	SLG	PRO+	BR	/A	RC	SB	CS	SBR	FR	POS	TPR
1902	StL-N	11	33	2	6	2	0	0	3	1		.182	.206	.242	41	-2	-2	2	0			2	C	0.0
1903	StL-N	16	49	4	12	0	0	0	5	4		.245	.302	.245	60	-2	-2	4	1			2	C	0.1
	Pit-N	16	48	8	11	0	1	0	3	2		.229	.260	.271	51	-3	-3	3	0			-0	C/1	-0.2
	Yr	32	97	12	23	0	1	0	8	6		.237	.282	.258	56	-5	-5	8	1			2		-0.1
1905	StL-N	28	92	5	11	2	1	0	3	1		.120	.129	.163	-7	-11	-10	2	0			5	C	-0.2
1908	Chi-A	15	35	1	7	1	0	0	1	1		.200	.222	.229	49	-2	-2	2	0			-5	C	-0.6
Total	4	86	257	20	47	5	2	0	15	9		.183	.211	.218	32	-21	-20	13	1			3	/C1	-0.9

■ BUCK WEAVER   Weaver, George Daniel   b: 8/18/1890, Pottstown, Pa.   d: 1/31/56, Chicago, Ill.   BR/TR, 5'11", 170 lbs.   Deb: 4/11/12

YEAR	TM/L	G	AB	R	H	2B	3B	HR	RBI	BB	SO	AVG	OBP	SLG	PRO+	BR	/A	RC	SB	CS	SBR	FR	POS	TPR
1912	Chi-A	147	523	55	117	21	8	1	43	9		.224	.245	.300	57	-32	-30	41	12			-6	*S	-2.2
1913	Chi-A	151	533	51	145	17	8	4	52	15	60	.272	.302	.356	94	-7	-7	61	20			34	*S	4.2
1914	Chi-A	136	541	64	133	20	9	2	28	20	40	.246	.279	.327	83	-14	-13	47	14	20	-8	5	*S	-0.3
1915	Chi-A	148	563	83	151	18	11	3	49	32	58	.268	.316	.355	98	-2	-4	68	24	20	-5	1	*S	0.5
1916	Chi-A	151	582	78	132	27	6	3	38	30	48	.227	.280	.309	76	-18	-19	57	22	13	-1	7	3S	-0.4
1917	*Chi-A	118	447	64	127	16	5	3	32	27	29	.284	.332	.362	110	5	4	61	19			9	*3S	2.0
1918	Chi-A	112	420	37	126	12	5	0	29	11	24	.300	.323	.352	103	-0	-0	53	20			-0	S3/2	0.6
1919	*Chi-A	140	571	89	169	33	9	3	75	11	21	.296	.315	.401	100	-3	-3	77	22			0	3S	0.8
1920	Chi-A	151	630	104	210	35	8	2	75	28	23	.333	.367	.424	109	7	7	94	19	17	-5	-10	*3S	0.4
Total	9	1254	4810	625	1310	199	69	21	421	183	303	.272	.307	.356	92	-65	-66	558	172	70		39	S3/2	5.6

■ JIM WEAVER   Weaver, James Francis   b: 10/10/59, Kingston, N.Y.   BL/TL, 6'3", 190 lbs.   Deb: 4/10/85

YEAR	TM/L	G	AB	R	H	2B	3B	HR	RBI	BB	SO	AVG	OBP	SLG	PRO+	BR	/A	RC	SB	CS	SBR	FR	POS	TPR
1985	Det-A	12	7	2	1	1	0	0	0	1	4	.143	.250	.286	47	-1	-1	0	0	1	-1	0	/OD	0.0
1987	Sea-A	7	4	2	0	0	0	0	0	2	3	.000	.333	.000	-1	-1	-1	0	1	1	-0	1	/O	0.0
1989	SF-N	12	20	2	4	3	0	0	2	0	7	.200	.200	.350	56	-1	-1	2	1	0	0	-0	/O	-0.1
Total	3	31	31	6	5	4	0	0	2	3	14	.161	.235	.290	47	-2	-2	2	2	2	-1	1	/OD	-0.1

■ FARMER WEAVER   Weaver, William B.   b: 3/23/1865, Parkersburg, W.Va.   d: 1/23/43, Akron, Ohio   BL ,   Deb: 9/16/1888

YEAR	TM/L	G	AB	R	H	2B	3B	HR	RBI	BB	SO	AVG	OBP	SLG	PRO+	BR	/A	RC	SB	CS	SBR	FR	POS	TPR
1888	Lou-a	26	112	12	28	1	1	0	8	3		.250	.276	.277	82	-2	-2	12	12			-2	O	-0.3
1889	Lou-a	124	499	62	145	17	6	0	60	40	22	.291	.352	.349	104	2	4	70	21			-0	*O/C32	0.0
1890	*Lou-a	130	557	101	161	27	9	3		29		.289	.332	.386	117	8	10	89	45			-1	*O/S3	0.2
1891	Lou-a	135	565	76	160	25	7	1	55	33	23	.283	.335	.358	102	-0	1	80	30			17	*O/C	1.0
1892	Lou-N	138	551	58	140	15	4	0	57	40	17	.254	.315	.296	94	-8	-2	62	30			-11	*OC/1	-1.4
1893	Lou-N	106	439	79	128	17	7	2	49	27	12	.292	.348	.376	102	-4	2	65	17			-1	OC	0.0
1894	Lou-N	64	244	19	54	5	2	3	24	7	11	.221	.249	.295	34	-28	-24	19	3			1	OC1/2	-1.8
	Pit-N	30	115	16	40	7	2	0	24	6	1	.348	.405	.443	107	1	2	23	4			-9	CS/3O	-0.3
	Yr	94	359	35	94	12	4	3	48	13	12	.262	.301	.343	59	-26	-23	40	7			-8		-2.1
Total	7	753	3082	423	856	114	38	9	277	185	86	.278	.330	.348	97	-31	-10	420	162			-6	O/CS132	-2.5

■ SKEETER WEBB   Webb, James Laverne   b: 11/4/09, Meridian, Miss.   d: 7/8/86, Meridian, Miss.   BR/TR, 5'9.5", 150 lbs.   Deb: 7/20/32

YEAR	TM/L	G	AB	R	H	2B	3B	HR	RBI	BB	SO	AVG	OBP	SLG	PRO+	BR	/A	RC	SB	CS	SBR	FR	POS	TPR
1932	StL-N	1	0	0	0	0	0	0	0	0	0	—	—	—		0	0	0	0			0	/S	0.0
1938	Cle-A	20	58	11	16	2	0	0	2	8	7	.276	.364	.310	72	-2	-2	7	1	0	0	-2	S/32	-0.2
1939	Cle-A	81	269	28	71	14	1	2	26	15	24	.264	.305	.346	68	-14	-13	28	1	1	-0	-8	S	-1.2
1940	Chi-A	84	334	33	79	11	2	1	29	30	33	.237	.299	.290	53	-23	-23	30	3	6	-3	-9	2/S3	-2.9
1941	Chi-A	29	84	7	16	2	0	0	6	3	9	.190	.227	.214	18	-10	-10	4	1	0	0	6	2S/3	-0.1
1942	Chi-A	32	94	5	16	2	1	0	4	4	13	.170	.204	.213	18	-10	-10	4	1	2	-1	2	2	-0.8
1943	Chi-A	58	213	15	50	5	2	0	22	6	19	.235	.256	.277	56	-12	-12	14	5	4	-1	-3	2	-1.4
1944	Chi-A	139	513	44	108	19	6	0	30	20	39	.211	.242	.271	47	-37	-36	33	7	3	0	-5	*S/2	-3.4
1945	*Det-A	118	407	43	81	12	2	0	21	30	35	.199	.254	.238	41	-30	-33	25	8	7	-2	23	*S2	-0.7
1946	Det-A	64	169	12	37	1	1	0	17	9	18	.219	.258	.237	37	-14	-15	10	3	3	-1	15	2/S	0.3
1947	Det-A	50	79	13	16	3	0	0	6	7	9	.203	.267	.241	41	-6	-6	6	3	0	1	12	2/S	0.8
1948	Phi-A	23	54	5	8	2	0	0	3	0	9	.148	.148	.185	-12	-9	-9	1	0	0	0	3	/2S	-0.5
Total	12	699	2274	216	498	73	15	3	166	132	215	.219	.263	.268	46	-167	-169	163	33	26		32	S2/3	-10.1

■ EARL WEBB   Webb, William Earl   b: 9/17/1898, Bon Air, Tenn.   d: 5/23/65, Jamestown, Tenn.   BL/TR, 6'1", 185 lbs.   Deb: 8/13/25

YEAR	TM/L	G	AB	R	H	2B	3B	HR	RBI	BB	SO	AVG	OBP	SLG	PRO+	BR	/A	RC	SB	CS	SBR	FR	POS	TPR
1925	NY-N	4	3	0	0	0	0	0	1	1		.000	.250	.000	-31	-1	-1	0	0	0	0	0	H	0.0
1927	Chi-N	102	332	58	100	18	4	14	52	48	31	.301	.391	.506	138	18	18	66	3			1	O	1.6
1928	Chi-N	62	140	22	35	7	3	3	23	14	17	.250	.318	.407	90	-3	-3	18	0			1	O	-0.2
1930	Bos-A	127	449	61	145	30	6	16	66	44	56	.323	.385	.523	133	18	21	91	2	1	0	-5	*O	1.0
1931	Bos-A	151	589	96	196	67	3	14	103	70	51	.333	.404	.528	151	37	41	127	2	2	-1	-2	*O	2.7
1932	Bos-A	52	192	23	54	9	1	5	27	25	15	.281	.364	.417	105	1	2	30	0	0	0	-6	O/1	-0.5
	Det-A	88	338	49	97	19	8	3	51	39	18	.287	.361	.417	97	-1	-1	52	1	1	0	-2	O	-0.6
	Yr	140	530	72	151	28	9	8	78	64	33	.285	.362	.417	100	1	1	82	1	1	-0	-8		-1.1
1933	Det-A	6	11	1	3	0	0	0	3	3	0	.273	.429	.273	87	0	0	2	0	0	0	-1	/O	0.0
	Chi-A	58	107	16	31	5	0	1	8	16	13	.290	.382	.364	103	0	1	16	0	0	0	-2	O1	-0.1

YEAR	TM/L	G	AB	R	H	2B	3B	HR	RBI	BB	SO	AVG	OBP	SLG	PRO+	BR	/A	RC	SB	CS	SBR	FR	POS	TPR
	Yr	64	118	17	34	5	0	1	11	19	13	.288	.387	.356	102	0	1	18	0	0	0	-2	O/1	-0.1
Total	7	650	2161	326	661	155	25	56	333	260	202	.306	.381	.478	125	72	79	402	8	4		-16	O/1	3.9

■ BILL WEBB
Webb, William Joseph b: 6/25/1895, Chicago, Ill. d: 1/12/43, Chicago, Ill. BR/TR, 5'10", 161 lbs. Deb: 9/17/17 C

YEAR	TM/L	G	AB	R	H	2B	3B	HR	RBI	BB	SO	AVG	OBP	SLG	PRO+	BR	/A	RC	SB	CS	SBR	FR	POS	TPR
1917	Pit-N	5	15	1	3	0	0	0	0	2	3	.200	.294	.200	51	-1	-1	1	0			1	/2S	0.0

■ JOE WEBBER
Webber, Joseph Edward b: 1861, Hamilton, Ont., Canada d: 12/15/21, Hamilton, Ont., Can Deb: 7/22/1884

YEAR	TM/L	G	AB	R	H	2B	3B	HR	RBI	BB	SO	AVG	OBP	SLG	PRO+	BR	/A	RC	SB	CS	SBR	FR	POS	TPR
1884	Ind-a	3	8	0	0	0	0	0		0		.000	.111	.000	-62	-1	-1	0				3	/C	0.2

■ HARRY WEBER
Weber, Harry b: Indianapolis, Ind. Deb: 5/30/1884

YEAR	TM/L	G	AB	R	H	2B	3B	HR	RBI	BB	SO	AVG	OBP	SLG	PRO+	BR	/A	RC	SB	CS	SBR	FR	POS	TPR
1884	Det-N	2	8	0	0	0	0	0	0	0	2	.000	.000	.000	-99	-2	-2	0				0	/O	0.0

■ LENNY WEBSTER
Webster, Leonard Irell b: 2/10/65, New Orleans, La. BR/TR, 5'9", 185 lbs. Deb: 9/01/89

YEAR	TM/L	G	AB	R	H	2B	3B	HR	RBI	BB	SO	AVG	OBP	SLG	PRO+	BR	/A	RC	SB	CS	SBR	FR	POS	TPR
1989	Min-A	14	20	3	6	2	0	0	1	3	2	.300	.391	.400	116	1	1	3	0	0	0	-2	C	0.0
1990	Min-A	2	6	1	2	1	0	0	0	1	1	.333	.429	.500	148	1	0	1	0	0	0	-1	/C	0.0
Total	2	16	26	4	8	3	0	0	1	4	3	.308	.400	.423	123	1	1	5	0	0	0	-2	/C	0.0

■ MITCH WEBSTER
Webster, Mitchell Dean b: 5/16/59, Larned, Kan. BB/TL, 6', 185 lbs. Deb: 9/02/83

YEAR	TM/L	G	AB	R	H	2B	3B	HR	RBI	BB	SO	AVG	OBP	SLG	PRO+	BR	/A	RC	SB	CS	SBR	FR	POS	TPR
1983	Tor-A	11	11	2	2	0	0	0	0	1	1	.182	.250	.182	20	-1	-1	1	0	0	0	0	/OD	0.0
1984	Tor-A	26	22	9	5	2	1	0	4	1	7	.227	.261	.409	79	-1	-1	2	0	0	0	1	O/1D	0.0
1985	Tor-A	4	1	0	0	0	0	0	0	0	0	.000	.000	.000	-98	-0	-0	0	1	0	-1	0	/OD	0.0
	Mon-N	74	212	32	58	8	2	11	30	20	33	.274	.336	.486	135	7	8	33	15	9	-1	3	O	1.0
1986	Mon-N	151	576	89	167	31	13	8	49	57	78	.290	.358	.431	117	13	14	90	36	15	2	6	*O	1.9
1987	Mon-N	156	588	101	165	30	8	15	63	70	95	.281	.363	.435	107	10	7	99	33	10	4	-4	*O	0.1
1988	Chi-N	70	264	36	70	11	6	4	26	19	50	.265	.322	.398	101	2	0	35	10	4	1	0	O	0.0
	Mon-N	81	259	33	66	5	2	2	13	36	37	.255	.357	.313	90	-0	-2	31	12	10	-2	-1	O	-0.7
	Yr	151	523	69	136	16	8	6	39	55	87	.260	.340	.356	95	1	-2	66	22	14	-2	-1		-0.7
1989	*Chi-N	98	272	40	70	12	4	3	19	30	55	.257	.333	.364	92	0	-2	36	14	2	3	1	O	0.1
1990	Cle-A	128	437	58	110	20	6	12	55	20	61	.252	.289	.407	91	-6	-7	52	22	6	3	3	*O/1D	-0.1
Total	8	799	2642	400	713	119	42	55	259	254	417	.270	.339	.409	104	23	16	379	142	57	8	10	O/D1	2.3

■ RAY WEBSTER
Webster, Ramon Alberto b: 8/31/42, Colon, Panama BL/TL, 6', 185 lbs. Deb: 4/11/67

YEAR	TM/L	G	AB	R	H	2B	3B	HR	RBI	BB	SO	AVG	OBP	SLG	PRO+	BR	/A	RC	SB	CS	SBR	FR	POS	TPR
1967	KC-A	122	360	41	92	15	4	11	51	32	44	.256	.320	.411	118	6	7	46	5	3	-0	-2	1O	-0.2
1968	Oak-A	66	196	17	42	11	1	3	23	12	24	.214	.260	.327	81	-6	-5	16	3	0	1	-1	1	-0.8
1969	Oak-A	64	77	5	20	0	1	1	13	12	8	.260	.367	.325	99	-0	0	9	0	0	0	1	1	-0.1
1970	SD-N	95	116	12	30	3	0	2	11	11	12	.259	.323	.336	80	-4	-3	13	1	1	-0	-1	1/O	-0.5
1971	SD-N	10	8	0	1	0	0	0	0	2	1	.125	.300	.125	26	-1	-1	0	0	0	0	0	H	0.0
	Oak-A	7	5	0	0	0	0	0	0	0	2	.000	.000	.000	-99	-1	-1	0	0	0	0	0	/1	0.0
	Chi-N	16	16	1	5	2	0	0	0	1	3	.313	.353	.438	107	0	0	3	0	0	0	0	/1	0.0
Total	5	380	778	76	190	31	6	17	98	70	94	.244	.309	.365	99	-5	-2	87	9	4	0	-2	1/O	-1.5

■ RAY WEBSTER
Webster, Raymond George b: 11/15/37, Grass Valley, Cal. BR/TR, 6', 175 lbs. Deb: 4/17/59

YEAR	TM/L	G	AB	R	H	2B	3B	HR	RBI	BB	SO	AVG	OBP	SLG	PRO+	BR	/A	RC	SB	CS	SBR	FR	POS	TPR
1959	Cle-A	40	74	10	15	2	1	2	10	5	7	.203	.253	.338	63	-4	-4	6	1	0	0	0	2/3	-0.2
1960	Bos-A	7	3	1	0	0	0	0	1	1	0	.000	.250	.000	-25	-1	-1	0	0	0	0	1	/2	0.1
Total	2	47	77	11	15	2	1	2	11	6	7	.195	.253	.325	59	-5	-4	6	1	0	0	2	/23	-0.1

■ PETE WECKBECKER
Weckbecker, Peter b: 8/30/1864, Butler, Pa. d: 5/16/35, Hampton, Va. 5'7", 150 lbs. Deb: 10/05/1889

YEAR	TM/L	G	AB	R	H	2B	3B	HR	RBI	BB	SO	AVG	OBP	SLG	PRO+	BR	/A	RC	SB	CS	SBR	FR	POS	TPR
1889	Ind-N	1	1	0	0	0	0	0	2	0	0	.000	.000	.000	-98	-0	-0	0	0			0	/C	0.0
1890	*Lou-a	32	101	17	24	1	0	0		8		.238	.300	.248	65	-4	-4	10	7			1	C	0.0
Total	2	33	102	17	24	1	0	0	2	8	0	.235	.297	.245	63	-5	-4	10	7			1	/C	0.0

■ BERT WEEDEN
Weeden, Charles Albert b: 12/21/1882, Northwood, N.H. d: 1/7/39, Northwood, N.H. BL/TL, 6', 200 lbs. Deb: 6/04/11

YEAR	TM/L	G	AB	R	H	2B	3B	HR	RBI	BB	SO	AVG	OBP	SLG	PRO+	BR	/A	RC	SB	CS	SBR	FR	POS	TPR
1911	Bos-N	1	1	0	0	0	0	0	0	0	0	.000	.000	.000	-93	-0	-0	0	0			0	H	0.0

■ JOHNNY WEEKLY
Weekly, Johnny b: 6/14/37, Waterproof, La. d: 11/24/74, Walnut Creek, Cal. BR/TR, 6', 200 lbs. Deb: 4/13/62

YEAR	TM/L	G	AB	R	H	2B	3B	HR	RBI	BB	SO	AVG	OBP	SLG	PRO+	BR	/A	RC	SB	CS	SBR	FR	POS	TPR
1962	Hou-N	13	26	3	5	1	0	2	2	7	4	.192	.364	.462	129	1	1	5	0	0	0	-1	/O	0.0
1963	Hou-N	34	80	4	18	3	0	3	14	7	14	.225	.295	.375	98	-1	-0	9	0	0	0	1	O	0.0
1964	Hou-N	6	15	0	2	0	0	0	3	1	3	.133	.188	.133	-8	-2	-2	0	0	0	0	1	/O	0.0
Total	3	53	121	7	25	4	0	5	19	15	21	.207	.299	.364	92	-2	-1	14	0	0	0	0	/O	0.0

■ STUMP WEIDMAN
Weidman, George E. b: 2/17/1861, Rochester, N.Y. d: 3/2/05, New York, N.Y. BR/TR, Deb: 8/26/1880 U

YEAR	TM/L	G	AB	R	H	2B	3B	HR	RBI	BB	SO	AVG	OBP	SLG	PRO+	BR	/A	RC	SB	CS	SBR	FR	POS	TPR
1880	Buf-N	23	78	8	8	1	0	0	3	2	11	.103	.125	.115	-18	-9	-9	1				-0	PO	0.0
1881	Det-N	13	47	8	12	1	0	0	5	2	2	.255	.286	.277	75	-1	-1	4				-1	P	0.0
1882	Det-N	50	193	20	42	7	1	0	20	2	19	.218	.226	.264	57	-9	-9	12				1	P/OS	0.0
1883	Det-N	79	313	34	58	6	1	1	24	4	38	.185	.196	.220	27	-27	-25	14				-3	PO/2	0.0
1884	Det-N	81	300	24	49	6	0	0	26	13	41	.163	.198	.183	22	-27	-24	11				-3	OP/S2	-2.0
1885	Det-N	44	153	7	24	2	1	1	14	8	32	.157	.199	.203	30	-12	-12	6				-4	P/O2	0.0
1886	KC-N	51	179	13	30	2	0	0	7	5	46	.168	.190	.179	12	-18	-20	7	3			4	P/O	0.0
1887	Det-N	21	82	12	17	2	0	0	11	3	3	.207	.235	.232	30	-7	-8	6	6			-0	P/O	0.0
	NY-a	14	46	5	7	1	1	0	4			.152	.220	.217	25	-5	-4	3	2			2	P/O	0.0
	NY-N	1	3	0	1	0	0	0	0	0	0	.333	.333	.333	92	-0	-0	0	0			-0	/P	0.0
1888	NY-N	2	7	1	0	0	0	0	1	2	1	.000	.222	.000	-23	-1	-1	0	0			-0	/P	0.0
Total	9	379	1401	132	248	28	4	2	111	45	193	.177	.203	.207	28	-116	-113	64	11			-5	PO/2S	-2.0

■ RALPH WEIGEL
Weigel, Ralph Richard "Wig" b: 10/2/21, Coldwater, Ohio BR/TR, 6'1", 180 lbs. Deb: 9/18/46

YEAR	TM/L	G	AB	R	H	2B	3B	HR	RBI	BB	SO	AVG	OBP	SLG	PRO+	BR	/A	RC	SB	CS	SBR	FR	POS	TPR
1946	Cle-A	6	12	0	2	0	0	0	0	2	2	.167	.167	.167	-7	-2	-2	0	1	0	0	-1	/C	-0.1
1948	Chi-A	66	163	8	38	7	3	0	26	13	18	.233	.294	.313	64	-9	-9	14	1	2	-1	-6	C/O	-1.2
1949	Was-A	34	60	4	14	2	0	0	4	8	6	.233	.324	.267	58	-4	-3	5	0	1	-1	1	C	-0.1
Total	3	106	235	12	54	9	3	0	30	21	26	.230	.296	.294	59	-15	-14	20	2	3	-1	-6	/CO	-1.4

■ PODGE WEIHE
Weihe, John Garibaldi b: 11/13/1862, Cincinnati, Ohio d: 4/15/14, Cincinnati, Ohio BR/TR, 5'11", 175 lbs. Deb: 8/06/1883

YEAR	TM/L	G	AB	R	H	2B	3B	HR	RBI	BB	SO	AVG	OBP	SLG	PRO+	BR	/A	RC	SB	CS	SBR	FR	POS	TPR
1883	Cin-a	1	4	1	1	0	0	0		0		.250	.250	.250	58	-0	-0	0				0	/O	0.0
1884	Ind-a	63	256	29	65	13	2	4		9		.254	.279	.367	116	3	4	27				-0	O/21	0.3
Total	2	64	260	30	66	13	2	4		9		.254	.279	.365	115	3	4	27				0	/O21	0.3

■ DICK WEIK
Weik, Richard Henry "Legs" b: 11/17/27, Waterloo, Iowa BR/TR, 6'3.5", 184 lbs. Deb: 9/08/48

YEAR	TM/L	G	AB	R	H	2B	3B	HR	RBI	BB	SO	AVG	OBP	SLG	PRO+	BR	/A	RC	SB	CS	SBR	FR	POS	TPR
1948	Was-A	3	4	1	3	0	0	0	0	0	0	.750	.750	1.250	439	2	2	4	0	0	0	0	/P	0.0
1949	Was-A	28	28	3	5	0	0	0	2	1	8	.179	.207	.179	3	-4	-4	1	0	0	0	1	P	0.0
1950	Was-A	14	13	0	2	0	0	0	0	0	3	.154	.154	.154	-22	-2	-2	0	0	0	0	-1	P	0.0
	Cle-A	11	5	0	1	1	0	0	0	0	4	.200	.200	.400	52	-0	-0	0	0	0	0	0	P	0.0
	Yr	25	18	0	3	1	0	0	0	0	7	.167	.167	.222	-1	-3	-3	1	0	0	0	-1		0.0
1953	Cle-A	1	0	1	0	0	0	0	0	0	0	—	—	—	—	-0	-0	0	0	0	0	0	R	0.0
	Det-A	12	2	1	1	1	0	0	1	1	1	.500	.500	1.000	300	1	1	1	0	0	0	0	P	0.0
	Yr	13	2	2	1	1	0	0	1	1	1	.500	.500	1.000	301	1	1	1	0	0	0	0		0.0
1954	Det-A	9	1	0	0	0	0	0	0	0	0	.000	.000	.000	-99	-0	-0	0	0	0	0	-0	/P	0.0
Total	5	78	53	6	12	2	1	0	3	1	16	.226	.241	.302	43	-5	-5	6	0	0	0	0	/P	0.0

YEAR	TM/L	G	AB	R	H	2B	3B	HR	RBI	BB	SO	AVG	OBP	SLG	PRO+	BR	/A	RC	SB	CS	SBR	FR	POS	TPR

■ ELMER WEINGARTNER
Weingartner, Elmer William "Dutch" b: 8/13/18, Cleveland, Ohio BR/TR, 5'11", 178 lbs. Deb: 4/19/45

YEAR	TM/L	G	AB	R	H	2B	3B	HR	RBI	BB	SO	AVG	OBP	SLG	PRO+	BR	/A	RC	SB	CS	SBR	FR	POS	TPR
1945	Cle-A	20	39	5	9	1	0	0	1	4	11	.231	.302	.256	66	-2	-2	3	0	0	0	-2	S	-0.3

■ PHIL WEINTRAUB
Weintraub, Philip "Mickey" b: 10/12/07, Chicago, Ill. d: 6/21/87, Palm Springs, Cal BL/TL, 6'1", 195 lbs. Deb: 9/05/33

YEAR	TM/L	G	AB	R	H	2B	3B	HR	RBI	BB	SO	AVG	OBP	SLG	PRO+	BR	/A	RC	SB	CS	SBR	FR	POS	TPR
1933	NY-N	8	15	3	3	0	0	1	1	3	2	.200	.333	.400	110	0	1	2	0			-1	/O	-0.1
1934	NY-N	31	74	13	26	2	0	0	15	15	10	.351	.461	.378	130	4	4	15	0			-3	O	0.0
1935	NY-N	64	112	18	27	3	3	1	6	17	13	.241	.341	.348	87	-2	-2	14	0			-1	1/O	-0.2
1937	Cin-N	49	177	27	48	10	4	3	20	19	25	.271	.345	.424	113	2	3	25	1			-4	O	-0.2
	NY-N	6	9	3	3	2	0	0	1	1	1	.333	.400	.556	155	1	1	2	0			-0	/O	0.0
	Yr	55	186	30	51	12	4	3	21	20	26	.274	.348	.430	115	3	4	27	1			-4		-0.2
1938	Phi-N	100	351	51	109	23	2	4	45	64	43	.311	.422	.422	137	19	21	68	1			2	1	1.5
1944	NY-N	104	361	55	114	18	9	13	77	59	59	.316	.412	.524	162	31	31	82	0			3	1	2.6
1945	NY-N	82	283	45	77	9	1	10	42	54	29	.272	.389	.417	122	11	10	48	2			3	1	1.0
Total	7	444	1382	215	407	67	19	32	207	232	182	.295	.398	.440	133	66	68	256	4			-1	1/O	4.6

■ AL WEIS
Weis, Albert John b: 4/2/38, Franklin Square, N.Y. BB/TR, 6'", 160 lbs. Deb: 9/15/62

YEAR	TM/L	G	AB	R	H	2B	3B	HR	RBI	BB	SO	AVG	OBP	SLG	PRO+	BR	/A	RC	SB	CS	SBR	FR	POS	TPR
1962	Chi-A	7	12	2	1	0	0	0	0	2	3	.083	.267	.083	-1	-2	-2	1	1	0	0	-1	/S23	-0.1
1963	Chi-A	99	210	41	57	9	0	0	18	18	37	.271	.335	.314	85	-4	-4	26	15	1	4	14	2S/3	2.0
1964	Chi-A	133	328	36	81	4	4	2	23	22	41	.247	.300	.302	70	-14	-13	32	22	7	2	13	*2/SO	1.5
1965	Chi-A	103	135	29	40	4	3	1	12	12	22	.296	.362	.393	122	3	4	20	4	1	1	26	2/S3O	3.6
1966	Chi-A	129	187	20	29	4	1	0	9	17	50	.155	.233	.187	24	-18	-17	8	3	5	2	37	2S	2.9
1967	Chi-A	50	53	9	13	2	0	0	4	1	7	.245	.273	.283	67	-2	-2	3	3	3	-1	11	2S	1.1
1968	NY-N	90	274	15	47	6	0	1	14	21	63	.172	.236	.204	33	-22	-22	14	3	1	0	7	S2/3	-0.6
1969	*NY-N	103	247	20	53	9	2	2	23	15	51	.215	.260	.291	53	-15	-16	19	3	3	-1	13	S2/3	0.6
1970	NY-N	75	121	20	25	7	1	1	11	7	21	.207	.256	.306	50	-9	-9	8	1	1	-0	2	2S	0.0
1971	NY-N	11	11	3	0	0	0	0	1	2	4	.000	.154	.000	-54	-2	-2	0	0	0	0	1	/23	0.0
Total	10	800	1578	195	346	45	11	7	115	117	299	.219	.279	.275	59	-86	-83	132	55	22	3	123	2S/3O	11.0

■ BUTCH WEIS
Weis, Arthur John b: 3/2/03, St.Louis, Mo. BL/TL, 5'11", 180 lbs. Deb: 4/15/22

YEAR	TM/L	G	AB	R	H	2B	3B	HR	RBI	BB	SO	AVG	OBP	SLG	PRO+	BR	/A	RC	SB	CS	SBR	FR	POS	TPR
1922	Chi-N	2	2	2	1	0	0	0	0	0	0	.500	.500	.500	156	0	0	0	0	0	0	0	H	0.0
1923	Chi-N	22	26	2	6	1	0	0	2	5	8	.231	.355	.269	67	-1	-1	3	0	1	-1	-0	/O	-0.1
1924	Chi-N	37	133	19	37	8	1	0	23	15	14	.278	.356	.353	90	-1	-1	17	4	5	-2	3	O	0.0
1925	Chi-N	67	180	16	48	5	3	2	25	23	22	.267	.350	.361	81	-4	-5	23	2	4	-2	-6	O	-1.3
Total	4	128	341	39	92	14	4	2	50	43	44	.270	.353	.352	84	-7	-7	43	6	10	-4	-4	/O	-1.4

■ BUD WEISER
Weiser, Harry Budson b: 1/8/1891, Shamokin, Pa. d: 7/31/61, Shamokin, Pa. BR/TR, 5'11", 165 lbs. Deb: 4/29/15

YEAR	TM/L	G	AB	R	H	2B	3B	HR	RBI	BB	SO	AVG	OBP	SLG	PRO+	BR	/A	RC	SB	CS	SBR	FR	POS	TPR
1915	Phi-N	37	64	6	9	2	0	0	8	7	12	.141	.236	.172	24	-6	-6	3	2	2	-1	-2	O	-1.0
1916	Phi-N	4	10	1	3	1	0	0	1	0	3	.300	.300	.400	110	0	0	1	0			-0	/O	0.0
Total	2	41	74	7	12	3	0	0	9	7	15	.162	.244	.203	36	-6	-6	5	2	2		-2	/O	-1.0

■ GARY WEISS
Weiss, Gary Lee b: 12/27/55, Brenham, Tex. BB/TR, 5'10", 170 lbs. Deb: 9/13/80

YEAR	TM/L	G	AB	R	H	2B	3B	HR	RBI	BB	SO	AVG	OBP	SLG	PRO+	BR	/A	RC	SB	CS	SBR	FR	POS	TPR
1980	LA-N	8	0	2	0	0	0	0	0	0	0	—	—	—	—	0	0	0	0	0	0	0	/R	0.0
1981	LA-N	14	19	2	2	0	0	0	1	1	4	.105	.150	.105	-28	-3	-3	0	0	0	0	-1	S	-0.2
Total	2	22	19	4	2	0	0	0	1	1	4	.105	.150	.105	-28	-3	-3	0	0	0	0	-1	/S	-0.2

■ JOE WEISS
Weiss, Joseph Harold b: 1/27/1894, Chicago, Ill. d: 7/7/67, Cedar Rapids, Iowa BR/TR, 6', 165 lbs. Deb: 8/29/15

YEAR	TM/L	G	AB	R	H	2B	3B	HR	RBI	BB	SO	AVG	OBP	SLG	PRO+	BR	/A	RC	SB	CS	SBR	FR	POS	TPR
1915	Chi-F	29	85	6	19	1	2	0	11	3	24	.224	.250	.282	61	-5	-4	6	0			-1	1	-0.4

■ WALT WEISS
Weiss, Walter William b: 11/28/63, Tuxedo, N.Y. BB/TR, 6', 175 lbs. Deb: 7/12/87

YEAR	TM/L	G	AB	R	H	2B	3B	HR	RBI	BB	SO	AVG	OBP	SLG	PRO+	BR	/A	RC	SB	CS	SBR	FR	POS	TPR
1987	Oak-A	16	26	3	12	4	0	0	1	2	2	.462	.500	.615	208	4	4	7	1	2	-1	5	S/D	0.7
1988	*Oak-A	147	452	44	113	17	3	3	39	35	56	.250	.317	.321	82	-12	-10	47	4	4	-1	10	*S	0.6
1989	*Oak-A	84	236	30	55	11	0	3	21	21	39	.233	.298	.318	76	-8	-7	23	6	1	1	-14	*S	-1.2
1990	*Oak-A	138	445	50	118	17	1	2	35	46	53	.265	.339	.321	88	-7	-5	51	9	3	1	-26	*S	-2.1
Total	4	385	1159	127	298	49	4	8	96	104	150	.257	.326	.327	86	-24	-19	129	20	10	0	-26	S/D	-2.0

■ JOHNNY WELAJ
Welaj, John Ludwig b: 5/27/14, Moss Creek, Pa. BR/TR, 6', 164 lbs. Deb: 5/02/39

YEAR	TM/L	G	AB	R	H	2B	3B	HR	RBI	BB	SO	AVG	OBP	SLG	PRO+	BR	/A	RC	SB	CS	SBR	FR	POS	TPR
1939	Was-A	63	201	23	55	11	2	1	33	13	20	.274	.318	.363	80	-8	-6	25	13	2	3	-1	O	-0.4
1940	Was-A	88	215	31	55	9	0	3	21	19	20	.256	.322	.340	77	-9	-7	23	8	7	-2	4	O	-0.7
1941	Was-A	49	96	16	20	4	0	0	5	6	16	.208	.255	.250	36	-9	-9	6	3	1	0	1	O	-0.7
1943	Phi-A	93	281	45	68	16	1	0	15	15	17	.242	.280	.306	72	-11	-11	24	12	5	1	2	O	-1.0
Total	4	293	793	115	198	40	3	4	74	53	73	.250	.298	.323	71	-37	-32	79	36	15	2	5	O	-2.8

■ CURT WELCH
Welch, Curtis Benton b: 2/11/1862, E.Liverpool, Ohio d: 8/29/1896, E.Liverpool, Ohio BR , 5'10", 175 lbs. Deb: 5/01/1884

YEAR	TM/L	G	AB	R	H	2B	3B	HR	RBI	BB	SO	AVG	OBP	SLG	PRO+	BR	/A	RC	SB	CS	SBR	FR	POS	TPR
1884	Tol-a	109	425	61	95	24	5	0			10	.224	.248	.304	79	-8	-11	33				16	*O/2C1	0.4
1885	*StL-a	112	432	84	117	18	8	3			23	.271	.318	.370	114	10	6	52				14	*O	1.3
1886	*StL-a	138	563	114	158	31	13	2			29	.281	.332	.393	123	17	13	95	59			14	*O/2	2.0
1887	*StL-a	131	544	98	151	32	7	3			25	.278	.322	.379	88	-3	-13	97	89			19	*O/21	0.1
1888	Phi-a	136	549	125	155	22	8	1	61	33		.282	.355	.357	133	21	22	106	95			4	*O/2	1.9
1889	Phi-a	125	516	134	140	39	6	0	39	67	30	.271	.375	.370	117	13	14	99	66			8	*O	1.5
1890	Phi-a	103	396	100	106	21	4	2		49		.268	.391	.356	126	15	17	82	64			14	*O/P	2.2
	Bal-a	19	68	16	9	4	0	0		9		.132	.244	.191	29	-6	-6	5	8			2	O/1	-0.4
	Yr	122	464	116	115	25	4	2		58		.248	.370	.332	111	9	11	86	72			16		1.8
1891	Bal-a	132	514	122	138	22	10	3	55	77	42	.268	.400	.368	122	21	20	98	50			19	*O2/S	3.0
1892	Bal-N	63	237	42	56	1	3	1	22	36	9	.236	.363	.278	93	2	0	30	14			-4	O	-0.4
	Cin-N	25	94	14	19	0	2	1	7	7	8	.202	.299	.277	77	-2	-2	10	7			-0	O	-0.2
	Yr	88	331	56	75	1	5	2	29	43	17	.227	.345	.278	89	-1	-2	40	21			-4		-0.6
1893	Lou-N	14	47	5	8	1	0	0	2	16	4	.170	.400	.191	66	-1	-0	4	1			0	O	0.0
Total	10	1107	4385	915	1152	215	66	16	186	381	93	.263	.345	.353	110	78	60	712	453			107	*O/21SCP	11.4

■ FRANK WELCH
Welch, Frank Tiguer "Bugger" b: 8/10/1897, Birmingham, Ala. d: 7/25/57, Birmingham, Ala. BR/TR, 5'9", 175 lbs. Deb: 9/09/19

YEAR	TM/L	G	AB	R	H	2B	3B	HR	RBI	BB	SO	AVG	OBP	SLG	PRO+	BR	/A	RC	SB	CS	SBR	FR	POS	TPR
1919	Phi-A	15	54	5	9	1	1	2	7	7	10	.167	.262	.333	66	-3	-3	5	0			-0	O	-0.3
1920	Phi-A	100	360	43	93	17	5	4	40	26	41	.258	.312	.367	78	-12	-12	39	2	9	-5	-5	O	-2.9
1921	Phi-A	115	403	48	115	18	6	7	45	34	43	.285	.347	.412	92	-5	-5	60	6	0	2	3	*O	-0.8
1922	Phi-A	114	375	43	97	17	3	11	49	40	40	.259	.335	.408	90	-5	-6	52	3	4	-2	-0	*O	-1.4
1923	Phi-A	125	421	56	125	19	9	4	55	48	40	.297	.374	.413	106	5	4	67	1	4	-2	4	*O	-0.4
1924	Phi-A	94	293	47	85	13	2	5	31	35	27	.290	.372	.399	98	-0	-1	45	2	3	-1	1	O	-0.5
1925	Phi-A	85	202	40	56	5	4	4	41	29	14	.277	.373	.401	90	-1	-3	33	2	1	0	-3	O	-0.9
1926	Phi-A	75	174	26	49	8	1	4	23	26	9	.282	.381	.408	100	2	1	28	2	5	-2	-5	O	-1.0
1927	Bos-A	15	28	2	5	2	0	0	4	5	1	.179	.303	.250	46	-2	-2	2	0	2	-1	2	/O	-0.1
Total	9	738	2310	310	634	100	31	41	295	250	225	.274	.350	.398	92	-20	-27	330	18	28		-4	O	-8.3

■ HERB WELCH
Welch, Herbert M. "Dutch" b: 10/19/1898, RoEllen, Tenn. d: 4/13/67, Memphis, Tenn. BL/TR, 5'6", 154 lbs. Deb: 9/15/25

YEAR	TM/L	G	AB	R	H	2B	3B	HR	RBI	BB	SO	AVG	OBP	SLG	PRO+	BR	/A	RC	SB	CS	SBR	FR	POS	TPR
1925	Bos-A	13	38	2	11	0	1	0	2	0	6	.289	.289	.342	60	-2	-2	4	0	0	0	5	S	0.4

YEAR	TM/L	G	AB	R	H	2B	3B	HR	RBI	BB	SO	AVG	OBP	SLG	PRO+	BR	/A	RC	SB	CS	SBR	FR	POS	TPR

■ MILT WELCH   Welch, Milton Edward   b: 7/26/24, Farmersville, Ill   BR/TR, 5'10", 175 lbs.   Deb: 6/05/45

| 1945 | Det-A | 1 | 2 | 0 | 0 | 0 | 0 | 0 | 0 | 0 | 1 | .000 | .000 | .000 | -94 | -1 | -1 | 0 | 0 | 0 | 0 | 1 | /C | 0.0 |

■ HARRY WELCHONCE   Welchonce, Harry Monroe "Welch"   b: 11/20/1883, North Point, Pa.   d: 2/26/77, Arcadia, Cal.   BL/TR, 6', 170 lbs.   Deb: 4/17/11

| 1911 | Phi-N | 26 | 66 | 9 | 14 | 4 | 0 | 0 | 6 | 7 | 8 | .212 | .288 | .273 | 56 | -4 | -4 | 5 | 0 | | | -2 | O | -0.6 |

■ MIKE WELDAY   Welday, Lyndon Earl   b: 12/19/1879, Conway, Iowa   d: 5/28/42, Leavenworth, Kan.   BL/TL,   Deb: 4/21/07

1907	Chi-A	24	35	2	8	1	1	0		6		.229	.341	.314	115	1	1	4	0			-3	O	-0.2
1909	Chi-A	29	74	3	14	0	0	0	5	4		.189	.231	.189	34	-6	-5	4	2			1	O	-0.5
Total	2	53	109	5	22	1	1	0	5	10		.202	.269	.229	61	-5	-4	8	2			-2	/O	-0.7

■ OLLIE WELF   Welf, Oliver Henry   b: 1/17/1889, Cleveland, Ohio   d: 6/15/67, Cleveland, Ohio   BR/TL, 5'9", 160 lbs.   Deb: 8/30/16

| 1916 | Cle-A | 1 | 0 | 0 | 0 | 0 | 0 | 0 | 0 | 0 | 0 | — | — | — | — | 0 | 0 | 0 | 0 | | | 0 | R | 0.0 |

■ BRAD WELLMAN   Wellman, Brad Eugene   b: 8/17/59, Lodi, Cal.   BR/TR, 6', 170 lbs.   Deb: 9/04/82

1982	SF-N	6	4	1	1	0	0	0	0	0	1	.250	.250	.250	40	-0	-0	0	0	0	0	0	/2	0.0
1983	SF-N	82	182	15	39	3	0	1	16	22	39	.214	.299	.247	55	-11	-10	14	5	3	-0	2	2/S	-0.5
1984	SF-N	93	265	23	60	9	1	2	25	19	41	.226	.278	.291	62	-14	-13	21	10	5	0	16	2S/3	0.8
1985	SF-N	71	174	16	41	11	1	0	16	4	33	.236	.269	.310	65	-9	-8	14	5	2	0	-2	23/S	-0.9
1986	SF-N	12	13	0	2	0	0	0	1	1	2	.154	.214	.154	3	-2	-2	0	0	0	0	0	/S23	0.0
1987	LA-N	3	4	1	1	0	0	0	1	0	1	.250	.250	.250	34	-0	-0	0	0	0	0	1	/2S3	0.1
1988	KC-A	71	107	11	29	3	0	1	6	6	23	.271	.322	.327	81	-2	-3	11	1	2	-1	15	2S/3D	1.5
1989	KC-A	103	178	30	41	4	0	2	12	7	36	.230	.263	.287	55	-11	-11	12	5	3	-0	19	2S/3D	1.2
Total	8	441	927	97	214	30	2	6	77	59	176	.231	.282	.287	61	-50	-47	73	26	15	-1	50	2/S3D	2.2

■ BOB WELLMAN   Wellman, Robert Joseph   b: 7/15/25, Norwood, Ohio   BR/TR, 6'4", 210 lbs.   Deb: 9/23/48

1948	Phi-A	4	10	1	2	0	1	0	0	3	2	.200	.385	.400	109	0	0	2	0	0	0	0	/1O	0.0
1950	Phi-A	11	15	1	5	0	0	1	1	0	3	.333	.333	.533	121	0	0	3	0	0	0	0	/O	0.0
Total	2	15	25	2	7	0	1	1	1	3	5	.280	.357	.480	117	0	1	5	0	0	0	0	/O1	0.0

■ GREG WELLS   Wells, Gregory De Wayne   b: 4/25/54, McIntosh, Ala.   BR/TR, 6'5", 218 lbs.   Deb: 8/10/81

1981	Tor-A	32	73	7	18	5	0	0	5	5	12	.247	.295	.315	71	-2	-3	6	0	2	-1	-0	1/D	-0.4
1982	Min-A	15	54	5	11	1	2	0	3	1	8	.204	.218	.296	39	-5	-5	4	0	0	0	-2	1/D	-0.6
Total	2	47	127	12	29	6	2	0	8	6	20	.228	.263	.307	58	-7	-8	10	0	2	-1	-2	/1D	-1.0

■ JAKE WELLS   Wells, Jacob   b: 8/9/1863, Memphis, Tenn.   d: 3/16/27, Hendersonville, N.C.   BR/TR,   Deb: 8/10/1888

1888	Det-N	16	57	5	9	1	0	0	2	0	5	.158	.158	.175	7	-6	-6	2	0			4	C	0.0
1890	StL-a	30	105	17	25	3	0	0		10		.238	.333	.267	70	-2	-5	10	1			-0	C/O	-0.1
Total	2	46	162	22	34	4	0	0	2	10	5	.210	.277	.235	52	-8	-10	12	1			4	/CO	-0.1

■ LEO WELLS   Wells, Leo Donald   b: 7/18/17, Kansas City, Kan.   BR/TR, 5'9", 170 lbs.   Deb: 4/16/42

1942	Chi-A	35	62	8	12	2	0	1	4	4	5	.194	.242	.274	46	-5	-5	4	1	0	0	11	S/3	0.7
1946	Chi-A	45	127	11	24	4	1	1	11	12	34	.189	.259	.260	47	-9	-9	8	3	4	-2	8	3/S	0.0
Total	2	80	189	19	36	6	1	2	15	16	39	.190	.254	.265	47	-14	-13	13	4	4	-1	19	/3S	0.7

■ JIMMY WELSH   Welsh, James Daniel   b: 10/9/02, Denver, Colo.   d: 10/30/70, Oakland, Cal.   BL/TR, 6'1", 174 lbs.   Deb: 4/14/25

1925	Bos-N	122	484	69	151	25	8	7	63	20	24	.312	.350	.440	110	-0	5	74	7	4	-0	4	*O/2	0.6
1926	Bos-N	134	490	69	136	18	11	3	57	33	28	.278	.333	.378	100	-6	0	62	6			8	*O	0.3
1927	Bos-N	131	497	72	143	26	7	9	54	23	27	.288	.330	.423	109	-1	4	67	11			10	*O/1	0.8
1928	NY-N	124	476	77	146	22	5	9	54	29	30	.307	.357	.431	104	3	3	71	4			-3	*O	-0.4
1929	NY-N	38	129	25	32	7	0	2	8	9	3	.248	.331	.349	69	-6	-6	15	3			-6	O	-1.4
	Bos-N	53	186	24	54	8	7	2	16	13	9	.290	.350	.441	98	-2	-1	28	1			13	O	0.7
	Yr	91	315	49	86	15	7	4	24	22	12	.273	.342	.403	86	-8	-7	43	4			6		-0.7
1930	Bos-N	113	422	51	116	21	9	3	36	29	23	.275	.327	.389	75	-19	-17	53	5			10	*O	-1.3
Total	6	715	2684	387	778	127	47	35	288	156	144	.290	.340	.411	98	-33	-12	370	37	4		35	O/21	-0.7

■ TUB WELSH   Welsh, James J.   b: 7/3/1866, St.Louis, Mo.   TR, 5'11", 230 lbs.   Deb: 6/12/1890

1890	Tol-a	35	108	15	31	3	1	1		8		.287	.353	.361	110	2	1	17	7			3	C1	0.6
1895	Lou-N	47	153	18	37	4	1	1	8	13	7	.242	.310	.301	63	-9	-7	15	2			-0	C1	-0.3
Total	2	82	261	33	68	7	2	2	8	21	7	.261	.328	.326	82	-7	-6	32	9			3	/C1	0.3

■ LEW WENDELL   Wendell, Lewis Charles   b: 3/22/1892, New York, N.Y.   d: 7/11/53, Brooklyn, N.Y.   BR/TR, 5'11", 178 lbs.   Deb: 6/10/15

1915	NY-N	20	36	0	8	1	1	0	5	2	7	.222	.263	.306	76	-1	-1	3	0			-5	C	-0.4
1916	NY-N	2	2	0	0	0	0	0	0	0	2	.000	.000	.000	-99	-0	-0	0	0			0	H	0.0
1924	Phi-N	21	32	3	8	1	0	0	2	3	5	.250	.314	.281	54	-2	-2	3	0	0	0	-1	C	-0.2
1925	Phi-N	18	26	0	2	0	0	0	3	1	3	.077	.111	.077	-47	-6	-6	0	0	0	0	-1	/C	-0.5
1926	Phi-N	1	4	0	0	0	0	0	0	0	0	.000	.000	.000	-95	-1	-1	0	0			-1	/C	-0.1
Total	5	62	100	3	18	2	1	0	10	6	17	.180	.226	.220	23	-10	-11	6	0	0		-7	/C	-1.2

■ JACK WENTZ   Wentz, John George (b: John George Wernz)   b: 3/4/1863, Louisville, Ky.   d: 9/14/07, Louisville, Ky.   5'10.5", 175 lbs.   Deb: 4/15/1891

| 1891 | Lou-a | 1 | 4 | 0 | 1 | 0 | 0 | 0 | 0 | 0 | 0 | .250 | .250 | .250 | 46 | -0 | -0 | 0 | 0 | | | -1 | /2 | 0.0 |

■ STAN WENTZEL   Wentzel, Stanley Aaron   b: 1/13/17, Lorane, Pa.   BR/TR, 6'1", 200 lbs.   Deb: 9/23/45

| 1945 | Bos-N | 4 | 19 | 3 | 4 | 0 | 1 | 0 | 6 | 0 | 3 | .211 | .211 | .316 | 45 | -1 | -2 | 1 | 1 | | | -1 | /O | -0.2 |

■ JULIE WERA   Wera, Julian Valentine   b: 2/9/02, Winona, Minn.   d: 12/12/75, Rochester, Minn.   BR/TR, 5'8", 164 lbs.   Deb: 4/14/27

1927	NY-A	38	42	7	10	3	0	1	8	1	5	.238	.273	.381	70	-2	-2	4	0	0	0	3	3	0.2
1929	NY-A	5	12	1	5	0	0	0	2	1	1	.417	.462	.417	137	1	1	2	0	0	0	-1	/3	0.0
Total	2	43	54	8	15	3	0	1	10	2	6	.278	.316	.389	85	-2	-1	7	0	0	0	2	/3	0.2

■ BILLY WERBER   Werber, William Murray   b: 6/20/08, Berwyn, Md.   BR/TR, 5'10", 170 lbs.   Deb: 6/25/30

1930	NY-A	4	14	5	4	0	0	0	2	3	1	.286	.412	.286	84	-0	-0	2	0	0	0	1	/S3	0.1
1933	NY-A	3	2	0	0	0	0	0	0	0	0	.000	.000	.000	-99	-1	-1	0	0	0	0	0	/3	0.0
	Bos-A	108	425	64	110	30	6	3	39	33	39	.259	.312	.379	83	-12	-12	52	15	5	2	-16	S3/2	-1.6
	Yr	111	427	64	110	30	6	3	39	33	39	.258	.311	.377	82	-12	-12	52	15	5	2	-16		-1.6
1934	Bos-A	152	623	129	200	41	10	11	67	77	37	.321	.397	.472	115	22	16	121	**40**	15	3	20	*3S	3.7
1935	Bos-A	124	462	84	118	30	3	14	61	69	41	.255	.357	.424	95	1	-4	76	**29**	7	5	17	*3	1.7
1936	Bos-A	145	535	89	147	29	6	10	67	89	37	.275	.382	.407	90	-2	-8	89	23	13	-1	-14	*3O/2	-1.9
1937	Phi-A	128	493	85	144	31	4	7	70	74	39	.292	.386	.414	103	3	4	84	**35**	13	3	0	*3/O	0.9
1938	Phi-A	134	499	92	129	22	7	11	69	93	37	.259	.377	.397	96	-3	-1	79	19	15	-3	0	*3	0.0
1939	*Cin-N	147	599	**115**	173	35	5	9	57	91	46	.289	.388	.389	109	12	11	96	15			13	*3	2.8
1940	*Cin-N	143	584	105	162	35	5	12	48	68	40	.277	.361	.416	113	12	11	92	16			3	*3	1.3
1941	Cin-N	109	418	56	100	9	2	4	46	53	24	.239	.328	.299	77	-11	-11	43	14			13	*3	0.2
1942	NY-N	98	370	51	76	9	2	1	13	51	22	.205	.308	.249	64	-15	-15	30	9			10	3	-0.5
Total	11	1295	5024	875	1363	271	50	78	539	701	363	.271	.364	.392	97	5	-9	765	215	<u>68</u>		47	*3/SO2	6.7

YEAR	TM/L	G	AB	R	H	2B	3B	HR	RBI	BB	SO	AVG	OBP	SLG	PRO+	BR	/A	RC	SB	CS	SBR	FR	POS	TPR

■ PERRY WERDEN Werden, Percival Wheritt b: 7/21/1865, St.Louis, Mo. d: 1/9/34, Minneapolis, Minn. BR/TR, 6'2", 220 lbs. Deb: 4/24/1884

1884	StL-U	18	76	7	18	2	0	0		2		.237	.256	.263	73	-2	-2	5	0			-0	P/O	0.0
1888	Was-N	3	10	0	3	0	0	0	2	1	4	.300	.364	.300	123	0	0	1	0			-0	/O	0.0
1890	Tol-a	128	498	113	147	22	**20**	6		78		.295	.403	.456	152	37	34	118	59			6	*1/O	3.1
1891	Bal-a	139	552	102	160	20	18	6	104	52	59	.290	.363	.424	126	19	18	104	46			1	*1	1.0
1892	StL-N	149	598	73	154	22	6	8	84	59	52	.258	.328	.355	114	6	10	78	20			12	*1	1.0
1893	StL-N	125	500	73	138	22	**29**	1	94	49	25	.276	.349	.442	111	6	6	83	11			3	*1/O	0.6
1897	Lou-N	131	506	76	153	21	14	5	83	40		.302	.366	.429	116	8	11	87	14			18	*1	2.3
Total	7	693	2740	444	773	109	87	26	367	281	140	.282	.358	.414	122	74	78	476	150			39	1/PO	8.0

■ JOHNNY WERHAS Werhas, John Charles "Peaches" b: 2/7/38, Highland Park, Mich. BR/TR, 6'2", 200 lbs. Deb: 4/14/64

1964	LA-N	29	83	6	16	2	1	0	8	13	12	.193	.302	.241	59	-5	-4	6	0	0	0	4	3	-0.1
1965	LA-N	4	3	1	0	0	0	0	0	1	2	.000	.250	.000	-24	-0	-0	0	0	0	0	-36	/1	-3.8
1967	LA-N	7	7	0	1	0	0	0	0	0	3	.143	.143	.143	-20	-1	-1	0	0	0	0	0	H	0.0
	Cal-A	49	75	8	12	1	1	2	6	10	22	.160	.267	.280	64	-3	-3	5	0	0	0	0	3/1O	-0.2
Total	3	89	168	15	29	3	2	2	14	24	39	.173	.280	.250	57	-10	-8	12	0	0	0	-32	/31O	-4.1

■ DON WERNER Werner, Donald Paul b: 3/8/53, Appleton, Wis. BR/TR, 6'1", 175 lbs. Deb: 9/02/75

1975	Cin-N	7	8	0	1	0	0	0	0	0	0	.125	.222	.125	-2	-1	-1	0	0	0	0	1	/C	0.0
1976	Cin-N	3	4	0	2	1	0	0	1	1	1	.500	.600	.750	275	1	1	2	0	0	0	1	/C	0.2
1977	Cin-N	10	23	3	4	0	0	2	4	2	3	.174	.240	.435	75	-1	-1	2	0	1	-1	1	C	0.0
1978	Cin-N	50	113	7	17	2	1	0	11	14	30	.150	.250	.186	23	-11	-11	6	1	0	0	5	C	-0.5
1980	Cin-N	24	64	2	11	2	0	0	5	7	10	.172	.264	.203	32	-6	-6	4	1	0	0	1	C	-0.3
1981	Tex-A	2	8	1	2	0	0	0	0	0	2	.250	.250	.250	47	-1	-1	0	0	1	-1	0	/D	0.0
1982	Tex-A	22	59	4	12	2	0	0	3	3	7	.203	.242	.237	34	-5	-5	4	0	0	0	1	C	-0.2
Total	7	118	279	17	49	7	1	2	24	27	53	.176	.256	.229	36	-24	-24	18	2	2	-1	9	C/D	-0.8

■ JOE WERRICK Werrick, Joseph Abraham b: 10/25/1861, St.Paul, Minn. d: 5/10/43, St.Peter, Minn. BR/TR, 5'9", 151 lbs. Deb: 9/27/1884

1884	StP-U	9	27	3	2	0	0	0		1		.074	.107	.074	-70	-4	-2	0	0			-0	/S	-0.1
1886	Lou-a	136	561	75	140	20	14	3		33		.250	.294	.351	98	1	-4	65	19			-1	*3	0.1
1887	Lou-a	136	533	90	152	21	13	7		38		.285	.336	.413	108	6	4	93	49			0	*3	0.0
1888	Lou-a	111	413	49	89	12	7	0	51	30		.215	.274	.278	82	-9	-7	36	15			-12	3S/2O	-1.7
Total	4	392	1534	217	383	53	34	10	51	102		.250	.300	.348	96	-5	-9	194	83			-13	3/S2O	-1.7

■ DON WERT Wert, Donald Ralph b: 7/29/38, Strasburg, Pa. BR/TR, 5'10", 162 lbs. Deb: 5/11/63

1963	Det-A	78	251	31	65	6	2	7	25	24	51	.259	.329	.382	95	-0	-1	31	3	3	-1	3	32/S	0.4
1964	Det-A	148	525	63	135	18	5	9	55	50	74	.257	.329	.362	91	-5	-6	63	3	4	-2	0	*3/S	-0.4
1965	Det-A	162	609	81	159	22	2	12	54	73	71	.261	.343	.363	100	2	1	76	5	6	-2	5	*3/S2	0.6
1966	Det-A	150	559	56	150	20	2	11	70	64	69	.268	.346	.370	103	5	4	71	6	3	0	-18	*3	-1.9
1967	Det-A	142	534	60	137	23	2	6	40	44	59	.257	.321	.341	93	-2	-4	58	1	1	-0	-5	*3/S	-0.6
1968	*Det-A	150	536	44	107	15	1	12	37	37	79	.200	.258	.299	66	-21	-23	40	0	3	-2	-6	*3/S	-3.0
1969	Det-A	132	423	46	95	11	1	14	50	49	60	.225	.307	.355	81	-9	-11	45	3	1	0	-0	*3	-0.9
1970	Det-A	128	363	34	79	13	0	6	33	44	56	.218	.309	.303	69	-14	-15	33	1	3	-2	-2	*3/2	-1.8
1971	Was-A	20	40	2	2	1	0	0	2	4	10	.050	.156	.075	-35	-7	-7	0	0	0	0	-3	/S32	-1.0
Total	9	1110	3840	417	929	129	15	77	366	389	529	.242	.317	.343	87	-52	-62	417	22	24	-8	-27	*3/S2	-8.6

■ DENNIS WERTH Werth, Dennis Dean b: 12/29/52, Lincoln, Ill. BR/TR, 6'1", 200 lbs. Deb: 9/17/79

1979	NY-A	3	4	1	1	0	0	0	0	0	0	.250	.250	.250	36	-0	-0	0	0	0	0	0	/1	0.0
1980	NY-A	39	65	15	20	3	0	3	12	12	19	.308	.416	.492	150	5	5	13	0	1	-1	-1	1/OC3D	0.2
1981	NY-A	34	55	7	6	1	0	0	1	12	12	.109	.269	.127	18	-5	-5	2	1	0	0	2	1/OCD	-0.3
1982	KC-A	41	15	5	2	0	0	0	2	4	2	.133	.316	.133	29	-1	-1	1	0	0	0	2	1/C	0.0
Total	4	117	139	28	29	4	0	3	15	28	33	.209	.341	.302	82	-2	-2	16	1	1	-0	4	/1ODC3	-0.1

■ DEL WERTZ Wertz, Dwight Lyman Moody b: 10/11/1888, Canton, Ohio d: 5/26/58, Sarasota, Fla. BR/TR, 5'10", 160 lbs. Deb: 5/23/14

| 1914 | Buf-F | 3 | 0 | 1 | 0 | 0 | 0 | 0 | 0 | 0 | 0 | — | — | — | — | 0 | 0 | 0 | 0 | | | 1 | /S | 0.1 |

■ VIC WERTZ Wertz, Victor Woodrow b: 2/9/25, York, Pa. d: 7/7/83, Detroit, Mich. BL/TR, 6', 186 lbs. Deb: 4/15/47

1947	Det-A	102	333	50	96	22	4	6	44	47	66	.288	.376	.432	121	11	10	56	2	0	1	-7	O	0.0
1948	Det-A	119	391	49	97	19	9	7	67	48	70	.248	.335	.396	92	-4	-6	56	0	0	0	-4	O	-1.2
1949	Det-A	155	608	96	185	26	6	20	133	80	61	.304	.385	.465	124	20	20	110	2	3	-1	-5	*O	0.9
1950	Det-A	149	559	99	172	37	4	27	123	91	55	.308	.408	.533	135	33	31	128	0	1	-1	-12	*O	1.4
1951	Det-A	138	501	56	143	24	4	27	94	78	61	.285	.383	.511	139	28	27	101	0	3	-2	-4	*O	1.6
1952	Det-A	85	285	46	70	15	3	17	51	46	44	.246	.352	.498	134	13	12	53	1	0	0	-1	O	1.0
	StL-A	37	130	22	45	5	0	6	19	23	20	.346	.444	.523	164	13	12	33	0	0	0	-6	O	0.5
	Yr	122	415	68	115	20	3	23	70	69	64	.277	.381	.506	143	25	25	85	1	0	0	-7		1.5
1953	StL-A	128	440	61	118	18	6	19	70	72	44	.268	.376	.466	124	17	16	79	1	4	-2	6	*O	1.6
1954	Bal-A	29	94	5	19	1	0	1	13	11	17	.202	.286	.245	50	-7	-6	7	0	0	0	1	O	-0.5
	*Cle-A	94	295	33	81	14	2	14	48	34	40	.275	.350	.478	123	9	8	50	0	2	-1	1	1/O	0.6
	Yr	123	389	38	100	15	2	15	61	45	57	.257	.337	.422	106	2	2	56	0	2	-1	2		0.1
1955	Cle-A	74	257	30	65	11	2	14	55	32	33	.253	.338	.475	112	5	4	41	1	1	-0	-3	1/O	-0.2
1956	Cle-A	136	481	65	127	22	0	32	106	75	87	.264	.369	.509	127	20	18	93	0	0	0	1	*1	1.3
1957	Cle-A	144	515	84	145	21	0	28	105	78	88	.282	.378	.485	136	25	26	97	2	3	-1	-2	*1	2.2
1958	Cle-A	25	43	5	12	1	0	3	12	5	7	.279	.354	.512	139	2	2	7	0	0	0	0	/1	0.2
1959	Bos-A	94	247	38	68	13	0	7	49	29	32	.275	.339	.413	101	2	0	34	0	0	0	2	1	0.2
1960	Bos-A	131	443	45	125	22	0	19	103	37	54	.282	.339	.460	110	7	6	66	0	2	-1	3	*1	0.0
1961	Bos-A	99	317	33	83	16	2	11	60	38	43	.262	.345	.429	103	2	1	46	0	0	0	4	1	-0.2
	Det-A	8	6	0	1	0	0	0	1	0	1	.167	.167	.167	-10	-1	-1	0	0	0	0	0	H	0.0
	Yr	107	323	33	84	16	2	11	61	38	44	.260	.342	.424	101	1	0	46	0	0	0	4		-0.2
1962	Det-A	74	105	7	34	2	0	5	18	5	13	.324	.360	.486	121	3	3	18	0	0	0	0	1	0.2
1963	Det-A	6	5	0	0	0	0	0	0	0	1	.000	.000	.000	-97	-1	-1	0	0	0	0	0	H	0.0
	Min-A	35	44	3	6	0	0	3	7	6	5	.136	.240	.341	59	-2	-3	4	0	0	0	1	/1	-0.1
	Yr	41	49	3	6	0	0	3	7	6	6	.122	.218	.306	44	-4	-4	3	0	0	0	1		-0.1
Total	17	1862	6099	867	1692	289	42	266	1178	828	842	.277	.366	.469	121	195	180	1079	9	19	-9	-25	O1	9.5

■ JIM WESSINGER Wessinger, James Michael b: 9/25/55, Utica, N.Y. BR/TR, 5'10", 165 lbs. Deb: 8/04/79

| 1979 | Atl-N | 10 | 7 | 2 | 0 | 0 | 0 | 0 | 0 | 1 | 4 | .000 | .125 | .000 | -59 | -2 | -2 | 0 | 0 | 0 | 0 | 1 | /2 | 0.0 |

■ MAX WEST West, Max Edward b: 11/28/16, Dexter, Mo. BL/TR, 6'1.5", 182 lbs. Deb: 4/19/38

1938	Bos-N	123	418	47	98	16	5	10	63	38	38	.234	.300	.368	92	-11	-5	46	5			-8	*O/1	-1.5
1939	Bos-N	130	449	67	128	26	6	19	82	51	55	.285	.364	.497	139	18	22	82	1			3	*O	2.3
1940	Bos-N	139	524	72	137	27	5	7	72	65	54	.261	.344	.372	103	-1	3	72	2			8	*O1	0.4
1941	Bos-N	138	484	63	134	28	4	12	68	72	68	.277	.373	.426	130	17	20	80	5			6	*O	2.1
1942	Bos-N	134	452	54	115	22	4	16	56	68	59	.254	.354	.409	126	14	15	71	4			-1	1O	0.6
1946	Bos-N	1	1	0	0	0	0	0	0	0	1	.000	.000	.000	-99	-0	-0	0	0			0	/1	0.0
	Cin-N	72	202	16	43	13	0	5	18	32	36	.213	.323	.351	95	-2	-1	24	1			-3	O	-0.5

YEAR	TM/L	G	AB	R	H	2B	3B	HR	RBI	BB	SO	AVG	OBP	SLG	PRO+	BR	/A	RC	SB	CS	SBR	FR	POS	TPR
	Yr	73	203	16	43	13	0	5	18	32	37	.212	.322	.350	94	-2	-1	24	1			-3		-0.5
1948	Pit-N	87	146	19	26	4	0	8	21	27	29	.178	.310	.370	82	-3	-4	18	1			0	1O	-0.4
Total	7	824	2676	338	681	136	20	77	380	353	340	.254	.344	.407	114	31	49	392	19			6	O1	3.0

■ BUCK WEST
West, Milton Douglas   b: 8/29/1860, Spring Mill, Ohio   d: 1/13/29, Mansfield, Ohio   BL/TR, 5'10", 200 lbs.   Deb: 8/24/1884

YEAR	TM/L	G	AB	R	H	2B	3B	HR	RBI	BB	SO	AVG	OBP	SLG	PRO+	BR	/A	RC	SB	CS	SBR	FR	POS	TPR
1884	Cin-a	33	131	20	32	2	8	1		2		.244	.256	.405	109	2	1	14				-5	O	-0.4
1890	Cle-N	37	151	20	37	6	1	2	29	7	11	.245	.283	.338	84	-4	-3	16	4			-1	O	-0.3
Total	2	70	282	40	69	8	9	3	29	9	11	.245	.271	.369	96	-2	-2	30	4			-6	/O	-0.7

■ DICK WEST
West, Richard Thomas   b: 11/24/15, Louisville, Ky.   BR/TR, 6'2", 180 lbs.   Deb: 9/28/38

YEAR	TM/L	G	AB	R	H	2B	3B	HR	RBI	BB	SO	AVG	OBP	SLG	PRO+	BR	/A	RC	SB	CS	SBR	FR	POS	TPR
1938	Cin-N	1	1	0	0	0	0	0	0	0	0	.000	.000	.000	-99	-0	-0	0	0			0	H	0.0
1939	Cin-N	8	19	1	4	0	0	0	4	1	4	.211	.250	.211	25	-2	-2	1	0			-0	/OC	-0.1
1940	Cin-N	7	28	4	11	2	0	1	6	0	2	.393	.393	.571	161	2	2	6	1			-3	/C	0.0
1941	Cin-N	67	172	15	37	5	2	1	17	6	23	.215	.246	.285	49	-12	-12	12	4			-3	C	-0.8
1942	Cin-N	33	79	9	14	3	0	1	8	5	13	.177	.226	.253	40	-6	-6	5	1			3	C/O	-0.2
1943	Cin-N	3	0	1	0	0	0	0	0	0	0	—	—	—	-99	-0	-0	0	0			0	R	0.0
Total	6	119	299	30	66	10	2	3	35	12	42	.221	.253	.298	55	-18	-18	24	6			-2	/CO	-1.1

■ SAM WEST
West, Samuel Filmore   b: 10/5/04, Longview, Tex.   d: 11/23/85, Lubbock, Tex.   BL/TL, 5'11", 165 lbs.   Deb: 4/17/27   C

YEAR	TM/L	G	AB	R	H	2B	3B	HR	RBI	BB	SO	AVG	OBP	SLG	PRO+	BR	/A	RC	SB	CS	SBR	FR	POS	TPR
1927	Was-A	38	67	9	16	4	1	0	6	8	8	.239	.320	.328	69	-3	-3	7	1	0	0	-1	O	-0.4
1928	Was-A	125	378	59	114	30	7	3	40	20	23	.302	.338	.442	104	1	1	54	5	6	-2	-10	*O	-1.6
1929	Was-A	142	510	60	136	16	8	3	75	45	41	.267	.326	.347	73	-20	-21	59	9	8	-2	15	*O	-1.2
1930	Was-A	120	411	75	135	22	10	6	67	37	34	.328	.385	.474	116	11	10	75	5	5	-2	3	*O	0.7
1931	Was-A	132	526	77	175	43	13	3	91	30	37	.333	.369	.481	121	15	15	90	6	8	-3	21	*O	2.3
1932	Was-A	146	554	88	159	27	12	6	83	48	57	.287	.345	.412	96	-5	-3	79	4	5	-2	14	*O	0.3
1933	StL-A	133	517	93	155	25	12	11	48	59	49	.300	.373	.458	112	14	9	89	10	8	-2	7	*O	0.9
1934	StL-A	122	482	90	157	22	10	9	55	62	55	.326	.403	.469	115	18	12	92	3	5	-2	5	*O	1.2
1935	StL-A	138	527	93	158	37	4	10	70	75	46	.300	.388	.442	109	12	9	92	1	6	-3	13	*O	1.5
1936	StL-A	152	533	78	148	26	4	7	70	94	70	.278	.386	.381	87	-6	-8	85	2	0	1	4	*O	-0.6
1937	StL-A	122	457	68	150	37	4	7	58	46	28	.328	.390	.473	115	11	11	85	1	1	-0	8	*O	1.3
1938	StL-A	44	165	17	51	8	2	1	27	14	9	.309	.363	.400	91	-2	-2	25	1	0	-0	0	O	-0.1
	Was-A	92	344	51	104	19	5	5	47	33	21	.302	.363	.430	105	-1	2	55	1	1	-0	-5	O	-0.2
	Yr	136	509	68	155	27	7	6	74	47	30	.305	.363	.420	100	-4	0	79	2	1	-0	-5		-0.3
1939	Was-A	115	390	52	110	20	8	3	52	67	29	.282	.387	.397	109	3	7	65	1	1	-0	-4	O1	-0.1
1940	Was-A	57	99	7	25	6	1	1	18	16	13	.253	.357	.364	93	-2	-1	14	0	2	-1	-0	1/O	-0.2
1941	Was-A	26	37	3	10	0	0	0	6	11	2	.270	.438	.270	95	0	1	6	1	0	0	0	/O	0.1
1942	Chi-A	49	151	14	35	5	0	0	25	31	18	.232	.363	.265	80	-3	-2	18	2	0	1	0	O	-0.4
Total	16	1753	6148	934	1838	347	101	75	838	696	540	.299	.371	.425	103	44	37	991	53	56	-18	69	*O/1	3.5

■ MAX WEST
West, Walter Maxwell   b: 7/14/04, Sunset, Tex.   d: 4/25/71, Houston, Tex.   BR/TR, 5'11", 165 lbs.   Deb: 9/18/28

YEAR	TM/L	G	AB	R	H	2B	3B	HR	RBI	BB	SO	AVG	OBP	SLG	PRO+	BR	/A	RC	SB	CS	SBR	FR	POS	TPR
1928	Bro-N	7	21	4	6	1	1	0	1	4	1	.286	.400	.429	118	1	1	4	0			2	/O	0.2
1929	Bro-N	5	8	1	2	1	0	0	1	1	0	.250	.333	.375	77	-0	-0	1	0			-0	/O	0.0
Total	2	12	29	5	8	2	1	0	2	5	1	.276	.382	.414	107	0	0	5	0			1	/O	0.2

■ BILLY WEST
West, William Nelson   b: 8/21/1840, Philadelphia, Pa.   Deb: 5/22/1874

YEAR	TM/L	G	AB	R	H	2B	3B	HR	RBI	BB	SO	AVG	OBP	SLG	PRO+	BR	/A	RC	SB	CS	SBR	FR	POS	TPR
1874	Atl-n	9	35	4	7	1	0	0			1	.200	.222	.229	50	-2	-1	2				2		0.0
1876	NY-N	1	4	0	0	0	0	0	0	0	0	.000	.000	.000	-99	-1	-1	0				0	/2	0.0

■ OSCAR WESTERBERG
Westerberg, Oscar William   b: 7/8/1882, Alameda, Cal.   d: 4/17/09, Alameda, Cal.   BB/TR,   Deb: 9/05/07

YEAR	TM/L	G	AB	R	H	2B	3B	HR	RBI	BB	SO	AVG	OBP	SLG	PRO+	BR	/A	RC	SB	CS	SBR	FR	POS	TPR
1907	Bos-N	2	6	0	2	0	0	0	1	1		.333	.429	.333	142	0	0	1	0			-1	/S	0.0

■ JIM WESTLAKE
Westlake, James Patrick   b: 7/3/30, Sacramento, Cal.   BL/TL, 6'1", 190 lbs.   Deb: 4/16/55

YEAR	TM/L	G	AB	R	H	2B	3B	HR	RBI	BB	SO	AVG	OBP	SLG	PRO+	BR	/A	RC	SB	CS	SBR	FR	POS	TPR
1955	Phi-N	1	1	0	0	0	0	0	0	0	1	.000	.000	.000	-99	-0	-0	0	0	0	0	0	H	0.0

■ WALLY WESTLAKE
Westlake, Waldon Thomas   b: 11/8/20, Gridley, Cal.   BR/TR, 6', 186 lbs.   Deb: 4/15/47

YEAR	TM/L	G	AB	R	H	2B	3B	HR	RBI	BB	SO	AVG	OBP	SLG	PRO+	BR	/A	RC	SB	CS	SBR	FR	POS	TPR
1947	Pit-N	112	407	59	111	17	4	17	69	27	63	.273	.324	.459	103	2	0	56	5			-6	*O	-0.8
1948	Pit-N	132	428	78	122	10	4	17	65	46	40	.285	.360	.456	117	11	10	71	2			1	*O	0.2
1949	Pit-N	147	525	77	148	24	8	23	104	45	69	.282	.345	.490	118	14	12	86	6			3	*O	0.7
1950	Pit-N	139	477	69	136	15	6	24	95	48	78	.285	.359	.493	118	14	12	83	1			-1	*O	0.6
1951	Pit-N	50	181	28	51	4	0	16	45	9	26	.282	.323	.569	131	7	7	32	0	1	-1	6	3O	1.1
	StL-N	73	267	36	68	8	5	6	39	24	42	.255	.325	.390	91	-3	-4	34	1	2	-1	0	O	-0.6
	Yr	123	448	64	119	12	5	22	84	33	68	.266	.324	.462	107	4	3	66	1	3	-2	6		0.5
1952	StL-N	21	74	7	16	3	0	0	10	8	11	.216	.293	.257	53	-4	-5	5	1	1	-0	7	O	0.2
	Cin-N	59	183	29	37	4	0	3	14	31	29	.202	.324	.273	67	-7	-7	16	0	2	-1	4	O	-0.5
	Yr	80	257	36	53	7	0	3	24	39	40	.206	.315	.268	63	-12	-12	22	1	3	-2	11		-0.3
	Cle-A	29	69	11	16	4	1	1	9	8	16	.232	.312	.362	93	-1	-1	8	1	0	0	3	O	0.2
1953	Cle-A	82	218	42	72	7	1	9	46	35	29	.330	.427	.495	153	16	17	49	2	0	1	-5	O	1.0
1954	*Cle-A	85	240	36	63	9	2	11	42	26	37	.262	.340	.454	114	4	4	36	0	1	-1	-5	O	-0.2
1955	Cle-A	16	20	2	5	1	0	0	1	3	5	.250	.348	.300	73	-1	-1	2	0	0	0	1	/O	0.0
	Bal-A	8	24	0	3	1	0	0	0	6	5	.125	.300	.167	30	-2	-2	1	0	0	0	-2	/O	-0.3
	Yr	24	44	2	8	2	0	0	1	9	10	.182	.321	.227	49	-3	-3	3	0	0	0	-1		-0.3
1956	Phi-N	5	4	0	0	0	0	0	0	1	3	.000	.200	.000	-41	-1	-1	0	0	0	0	0	H	0.0
Total	10	958	3117	474	848	107	33	127	539	317	453	.272	.346	.450	111	49	42	480	19	7		6	O/3	1.6

■ AL WESTON
Weston, Alfred John   b: 12/11/05, Lynn, Mass.   BR/TR, 6', 195 lbs.   Deb: 7/07/29

YEAR	TM/L	G	AB	R	H	2B	3B	HR	RBI	BB	SO	AVG	OBP	SLG	PRO+	BR	/A	RC	SB	CS	SBR	FR	POS	TPR
1929	Bos-N	3	3	0	0	0	0	0	0	0	2	.000	.000	.000	-99	-1	-1	0	0			0	H	0.0

■ WES WESTRUM
Westrum, Wesley Noreen   b: 11/28/22, Clearbrook, Minn.   BR/TR, 5'11", 185 lbs.   Deb: 9/17/47   MC

YEAR	TM/L	G	AB	R	H	2B	3B	HR	RBI	BB	SO	AVG	OBP	SLG	PRO+	BR	/A	RC	SB	CS	SBR	FR	POS	TPR
1947	NY-N	6	12	1	5	1	0	0	2	0	2	.417	.417	.500	142	1	1	3	0			0	/C	0.1
1948	NY-N	66	125	14	20	3	1	4	16	20	36	.160	.276	.296	54	-8	-8	11	3			8	C	0.4
1949	NY-N	64	169	23	41	4	1	7	28	37	39	.243	.385	.402	111	4	4	28	1			-0	C	0.6
1950	NY-N	140	437	68	103	13	3	23	71	92	73	.236	.371	.437	111	9	9	74	2			10	*C	2.3
1951	*NY-N	124	361	59	79	12	0	20	70	104	93	.219	.400	.418	119	15	15	70	1	0	0	8	*C	2.3
1952	NY-N	114	322	47	71	11	0	14	43	76	68	.220	.374	.385	110	8	7	53	1	2	-1	-3	*C	0.5
1953	NY-N	107	290	40	65	5	0	12	30	56	73	.224	.352	.366	86	-4	-5	41	2	0	1	4	*C/3	0.6
1954	*NY-N	98	246	25	46	3	1	8	27	45	60	.187	.320	.305	63	-13	-13	27	0	1	-1	12	C	0.0
1955	NY-N	69	137	11	29	1	0	4	18	24	18	.212	.333	.307	71	-5	-5	14	0	1	-1	10	C	0.6
1956	NY-N	68	132	10	29	5	2	3	8	25	28	.220	.348	.356	91	-1	-1	16	0	0	0	15	C	1.6
1957	NY-N	63	91	4	15	1	0	1	2	10	24	.165	.255	.209	27	-9	-9	5	0	1	-1	2	C	-0.4
Total	11	919	2322	302	503	59	8	96	315	489	514	.217	.357	.373	95	-4	-6	342	10	5		66	C/3	8.6

■ JEFF WETHERBY
Wetherby, Jeffrey Barrett   b: 10/18/63, Granada Hills, Cal.   BL/TL, 6'2", 195 lbs.   Deb: 6/07/89

YEAR	TM/L	G	AB	R	H	2B	3B	HR	RBI	BB	SO	AVG	OBP	SLG	PRO+	BR	/A	RC	SB	CS	SBR	FR	POS	TPR
1989	Atl-N	52	48	5	10	2	1	1	7	4	6	.208	.269	.354	75	-2	-2	4	1	0	0	0	/O	0.0

■ DUTCH WETZEL
Wetzel, Franklin Burton   b: 7/7/1893, Columbus, Ind.   d: 3/5/42, Hollywood, Cal.   BR/TR, 5'9.5", 177 lbs.   Deb: 9/15/20

YEAR	TM/L	G	AB	R	H	2B	3B	HR	RBI	BB	SO	AVG	OBP	SLG	PRO+	BR	/A	RC	SB	CS	SBR	FR	POS	TPR
1920	StL-A	7	21	5	9	1	1	0	5	4	1	.429	.520	.571	183	3	3	6	0	1	-1	0	/O	0.2

YEAR	TM/L	G	AB	R	H	2B	3B	HR	RBI	BB	SO	AVG	OBP	SLG	PRO+	BR	/A	RC	SB	CS	SBR	FR	POS	TPR
1921	StL-A	61	119	16	25	2	0	2	10	9	20	.210	.271	.277	38	-11	-12	9	0	0	0	-2	O	-1.4
Total	2	68	140	21	34	3	1	2	15	13	21	.243	.312	.321	59	-8	-9	15	0	1	-1	-2	/O	-1.2

■ BILL WHALEY
Whaley, William Carl b: 2/10/1899, Indianapolis, Ind. d: 3/3/43, Indianapolis, Ind.   BR/TR, 5'11", 178 lbs.   Deb: 4/18/23

YEAR	TM/L	G	AB	R	H	2B	3B	HR	RBI	BB	SO	AVG	OBP	SLG	PRO+	BR	/A	RC	SB	CS	SBR	FR	POS	TPR
1923	StL-A	23	50	5	12	2	1	0	1	4	2	.240	.309	.320	62	-3	-3	5	0	0	0	-0	O	-0.3

■ BERT WHALING
Whaling, Albert James b: 6/22/1888, Los Angeles, Cal. d: 1/21/65, Sawtelle, Cal.   BR/TR, 6', 185 lbs.   Deb: 4/22/13

YEAR	TM/L	G	AB	R	H	2B	3B	HR	RBI	BB	SO	AVG	OBP	SLG	PRO+	BR	/A	RC	SB	CS	SBR	FR	POS	TPR
1913	Bos-N	79	211	22	51	8	2	0	25	10	32	.242	.283	.299	65	-10	-10	19	3			2	C	-0.2
1914	Bos-N	60	172	18	36	7	0	0	12	21	28	.209	.303	.250	65	-7	-7	13	2			11	C	0.7
1915	Bos-N	72	190	10	42	6	2	0	13	8	38	.221	.264	.274	66	-9	-8	14	0	1	-1	1	C	-0.3
Total	3	211	573	50	129	21	4	0	50	39	98	.225	.283	.276	65	-25	-24	46	5	1		14	C	0.2

■ MACK WHEAT
Wheat, McKinley Davis b: 6/9/1893, Polo, Mo. d: 8/14/79, Los Banos, Cal.   BR/TR, 5'11.5", 167 lbs.   Deb: 4/14/15

YEAR	TM/L	G	AB	R	H	2B	3B	HR	RBI	BB	SO	AVG	OBP	SLG	PRO+	BR	/A	RC	SB	CS	SBR	FR	POS	TPR
1915	Bro-N	8	14	0	1	0	0	0	0	0	5	.071	.071	.071	-56	-3	-3	0	0			0	/C	-0.2
1916	Bro-N	2	2	0	0	0	0	0	0	0	1	.000	.000	.000	-97	-0	-0	0	0			0	/C	0.0
1917	Bro-N	29	60	2	8	1	0	0	0	1	12	.133	.161	.150	-4	-7	-7	1	1			4	C/O	-0.3
1918	Bro-N	57	157	11	34	7	1	1	3	8	24	.217	.255	.293	67	-7	-6	12	2			-1	C/O	-0.5
1919	Bro-N	41	112	5	23	3	0	0	8	2	22	.205	.246	.232	43	-8	-8	7	1			-4	C	-0.9
1920	Phi-N	78	230	15	52	10	3	3	20	8	35	.226	.261	.335	67	-9	-11	20	3	1	0	9	C	0.4
1921	Phi-N	10	27	1	5	2	1	0	4	0	3	.185	.241	.333	47	-2	-2	2	0	0	0	4	/C	0.3
Total	7	225	602	34	123	23	5	4	35	19	102	.204	.241	.279	52	-36	-38	42	7	1		12	C/O	-1.2

■ ZACH WHEAT
Wheat, Zachary Davis "Buck" b: 5/23/1888, Hamilton, Mo. d: 3/11/72, Sedalia, Mo.   BL/TR, 5'10", 170 lbs.   Deb: 9/11/09

YEAR	TM/L	G	AB	R	H	2B	3B	HR	RBI	BB	SO	AVG	OBP	SLG	PRO+	BR	/A	RC	SB	CS	SBR	FR	POS	TPR
1909	Bro-N	26	102	15	31	7	3	0	4	6		.304	.343	.431	145	4	5	15	1			2	O	0.6
1910	Bro-N	156	606	78	172	36	15	2	55	47	80	.284	.341	.403	120	11	13	87	16			11	*O	2.0
1911	Bro-N	140	534	55	153	26	13	5	76	29	58	.287	.332	.412	112	3	6	79	21			-1	*O	0.1
1912	Bro-N	123	453	70	138	28	7	8	65	39	40	.305	.367	.450	128	13	16	79	16			6	*O	1.8
1913	Bro-N	138	535	64	161	28	10	7	58	25	45	.301	.335	.430	114	10	8	79	19			13	*O	1.9
1914	Bro-N	145	533	66	170	26	9	9	89	47	50	.319	.377	.452	143	29	28	95	20			13	*O	3.9
1915	Bro-N	146	528	64	136	15	12	5	66	52	42	.258	.330	.360	107	6	5	65	21	14	-2	15	*O	1.5
1916	*Bro-N	149	568	76	177	32	13	9	73	43	49	.312	.366	**.461**	149	**34**	**33**	**103**	19			9	*O	4.1
1917	Bro-N	109	362	38	113	15	11	1	41	20	18	.312	.352	.423	133	15	14	53	5			7	O	2.0
1918	Bro-N	105	409	39	137	15	3	0	51	16	17	**.335**	.369	.386	131	14	14	59	9			2	*O	1.2
1919	Bro-N	137	536	70	159	23	11	5	62	33	27	.297	.344	.409	123	16	15	76	15			-1	*O	0.9
1920	*Bro-N	148	583	89	191	26	13	9	73	48	21	.328	.385	.463	138	32	30	102	8	10	-4	-6	*O	1.3
1921	Bro-N	148	568	91	182	31	10	14	85	44	19	.320	.372	.484	121	20	17	101	11	8	-2	-5	*O	0.4
1922	Bro-N	152	600	92	201	29	12	16	112	45	22	.335	.388	.503	129	24	25	116	9	6	-1	-1	*O	1.6
1923	Bro-N	98	349	63	131	13	5	8	65	23	12	.375	.417	.510	148	22	23	73	3	3	-1	-15	O	0.4
1924	Bro-N	141	566	92	212	41	8	14	97	49	18	.375	.428	.549	165	48	51	132	3	4	-2	4	*O	4.9
1925	Bro-N	150	616	125	221	42	14	14	103	45	22	.359	.403	.541	143	35	37	134	3	1	0	-8	*O	2.3
1926	Bro-N	111	411	68	119	31	2	5	35	21	14	.290	.326	.411	99	-3	-2	53	4			-4	*O	-0.9
1927	Phi-A	88	247	34	80	12	1	1	35	9	9	.324	.379	.393	95	1	-1	35	2	3	-1	-3	O	-0.8
Total	19	2410	9106	1289	2884	476	172	132	1248	650	559	.317	.367	.450	129	334	335	1539	205	49		40	*O	29.2

■ WOODY WHEATON
Wheaton, Elwood Pierce b: 10/3/14, Philadelphia, Pa.   BL/TL, 5'8.5", 160 lbs.   Deb: 9/28/43

YEAR	TM/L	G	AB	R	H	2B	3B	HR	RBI	BB	SO	AVG	OBP	SLG	PRO+	BR	/A	RC	SB	CS	SBR	FR	POS	TPR
1943	Phi-A	7	30	2	6	2	0	0	2	3	2	.200	.294	.267	65	-1	-1	2	0	0	0	1	/O	0.0
1944	Phi-A	30	59	1	11	2	0	0	5	5	3	.186	.250	.220	35	-5	-5	3	1	2	-1	2	P/O	-0.1
Total	2	37	89	3	17	4	0	0	7	8	5	.191	.265	.236	45	-6	-6	5	1	2	-1	3	/OP	-0.1

■ DON WHEELER
Wheeler, Donald Wesley "Scott" b: 9/29/22, Minneapolis, Minn   BR/TR, 5'10", 175 lbs.   Deb: 4/23/49

YEAR	TM/L	G	AB	R	H	2B	3B	HR	RBI	BB	SO	AVG	OBP	SLG	PRO+	BR	/A	RC	SB	CS	SBR	FR	POS	TPR
1949	Chi-A	67	192	17	46	9	2	1	22	27	19	.240	.333	.323	76	-7	-6	22	2	0	1	3	C	0.0

■ ED WHEELER
Wheeler, Edward b: 6/15/1878, Sherman, Mich. d: 8/15/60, Ft.Worth, Tex.   BB/TR, 5'10", 160 lbs.   Deb: 5/10/02

YEAR	TM/L	G	AB	R	H	2B	3B	HR	RBI	BB	SO	AVG	OBP	SLG	PRO+	BR	/A	RC	SB	CS	SBR	FR	POS	TPR
1902	Bro-N	30	96	4	12	0	0	0	5		3	.125	.152	.125	-14	-12	-12	2	1			-3	32/S	-1.4

■ ED WHEELER
Wheeler, Edward Raymond b: 5/24/17, Los Angeles, Cal.   BR/TR, 5'9", 160 lbs.   Deb: 4/19/45

YEAR	TM/L	G	AB	R	H	2B	3B	HR	RBI	BB	SO	AVG	OBP	SLG	PRO+	BR	/A	RC	SB	CS	SBR	FR	POS	TPR
1945	Cle-A	46	72	12	14	2	0	0	1	8	13	.194	.275	.222	47	-5	-5	5	1	1	-0	-6	3S/2	-1.0

■ GEORGE WHEELER
Wheeler, George Harrison "Heavy" b: 11/10/1881, Shelburn, Ind. d: 6/14/18, Clinton, Ind.   BL/TR, 5'9.5", 180 lbs.   Deb: 7/27/10

YEAR	TM/L	G	AB	R	H	2B	3B	HR	RBI	BB	SO	AVG	OBP	SLG	PRO+	BR	/A	RC	SB	CS	SBR	FR	POS	TPR
1910	Cin-N	3	3	0	0	0	0	0	0	0	2	.000	.000	.000	-99	-1	-1	0	0			0	H	0.0

■ HARRY WHEELER
Wheeler, Harry Eugene b: 3/3/1858, Versailles, Ind. d: 10/9/1900, Cincinnati, Ohio   BR/TR, 5'11", 165 lbs.   Deb: 6/19/1878 M

YEAR	TM/L	G	AB	R	H	2B	3B	HR	RBI	BB	SO	AVG	OBP	SLG	PRO+	BR	/A	RC	SB	CS	SBR	FR	POS	TPR
1878	Pro-N	7	27	7	4	0	0	0	1	2	15	.148	.207	.148	18	-2	-2	1				-2	/P	0.0
1879	Cin-N	1	3	0	0	0	0	0	0	0	0	.000	.000	.000	-99	-1	-1	0				0	/OP	0.0
1880	Cle-N	1	4	0	1	0	0	0	0	0	0	.250	.250	.250	72	-0	-0	0				0	/O	0.0
	Cin-N	17	65	1	6	2	0	0	2	0	15	.092	.092	.123	-28	-8	-8	1				1	O	-0.7
	Yr	18	69	1	7	2	0	0	2	0	15	.101	.101	.130	-22	-8	-8	1				1		-0.7
1882	Cin-a	76	344	59	86	11	11	1		7		.250	.265	.355	101	2	-1	33				-5	*O1/P	-0.5
1883	Col-a	82	371	42	84	6	7	0		6		.226	.239	.280	72	-14	-9	25				-2	*O/2P	-0.8
1884	StL-a	5	19	0	5	2	0	0		1		.263	.300	.368	115	0	0	2				-1	/O	0.0
	KC-U	14	62	11	16	1	0	0		3		.258	.292	.274	106	-0	1	5	0			0	O/PM	0.1
	CP-U	37	158	29	36	5	3	1		4		.228	.247	.316	90	-2	-2	13	0			-5	O	-0.5
	Bal-U	17	69	3	18	2	0	0		0		.261	.261	.290	78	-1	-2	5	0			-0	O	-0.2
	Yr	68	289	43	70	8	3	1		7		.242	.260	.301	90	-3	-3	23	0			-5	O	-0.6
Total	6	257	1122	152	256	29	21	2	3	23	32	.228	.244	.297	79	-26	-24	86	0			-14	O/P12	-2.6

■ DICK WHEELER
Wheeler, Richard (b: Richard Wheeler Maynard) b: 1/14/1898, Keene, N.H. d: 2/12/62, Lexington, Mass.   BR/TR, 5'11", 185 lbs.   Deb: 6/17/18

YEAR	TM/L	G	AB	R	H	2B	3B	HR	RBI	BB	SO	AVG	OBP	SLG	PRO+	BR	/A	RC	SB	CS	SBR	FR	POS	TPR
1918	StL-N	3	6	0	0	0	0	0	0	0	3	.000	.000	.000	-99	-1	-1	0	0			0	/O	-0.1

■ BOBBY WHEELOCK
Wheelock, Warren H. b: 8/6/1864, Charlestown, Mass. d: 3/13/28, Boston, Mass.   BR/TR, 5'8", 160 lbs.   Deb: 5/19/1887

YEAR	TM/L	G	AB	R	H	2B	3B	HR	RBI	BB	SO	AVG	OBP	SLG	PRO+	BR	/A	RC	SB	CS	SBR	FR	POS	TPR
1887	Bos-N	48	166	32	42	4	2	2	15	15	15	.253	.315	.337	83	-4	-4	25	20			-5	OS/2	-0.7
1890	Col-a	52	190	24	45	6	1	1		25		.237	.326	.295	92	-3	-1	30	34			-1	S	0.1
1891	Col-a	136	498	82	114	15	1	0	39	78	55	.229	.336	.263	79	-13	-8	63	52			19	*S	1.4
Total	3	236	854	138	201	25	4	3	54	118	70	.235	.330	.285	83	-20	-12	118	106			13	S/O2	0.8

■ JIMMY WHELAN
Whelan, James Francis b: 5/11/1890, Kansas City, Mo. d: 11/29/29, Dayton, Ohio   BR/TR, 5'8.5", 165 lbs.   Deb: 4/24/13

YEAR	TM/L	G	AB	R	H	2B	3B	HR	RBI	BB	SO	AVG	OBP	SLG	PRO+	BR	/A	RC	SB	CS	SBR	FR	POS	TPR
1913	StL-N	1	1	0	0	0	0	0	0	0	0	.000	.000	.000	-99	-0	-0	0	0			0	H	0.0

■ TOM WHELAN
Whelan, Thomas Joseph b: 1/3/1894, Lynn, Mass. d: 6/26/57, Boston, Mass.   BR/TR, 5'11", 175 lbs.   Deb: 8/13/20

YEAR	TM/L	G	AB	R	H	2B	3B	HR	RBI	BB	SO	AVG	OBP	SLG	PRO+	BR	/A	RC	SB	CS	SBR	FR	POS	TPR
1920	Bos-N	1	1	0	0	0	0	0	0	1	1	.000	.500	.000	54	0	0	0	0	0	0	0	/1	0.0

■ PETE WHISENANT
Whisenant, Thomas Peter b: 12/14/29, Asheville, N.C.   BR/TR, 6'2", 190 lbs.   Deb: 4/16/52 C

YEAR	TM/L	G	AB	R	H	2B	3B	HR	RBI	BB	SO	AVG	OBP	SLG	PRO+	BR	/A	RC	SB	CS	SBR	FR	POS	TPR
1952	Bos-N	24	52	3	10	2	0	0	7	4	13	.192	.250	.231	35	-5	-4	3	1	1	-0	3	O	-0.1
1955	StL-N	58	115	10	22	5	1	2	9	5	29	.191	.225	.304	39	-10	-10	8	2	0	1	6	O	-0.3
1956	Chi-N	103	314	37	75	16	3	11	46	24	53	.239	.295	.414	89	-6	-5	38	8	2	1	0	O	-0.7
1957	Cin-N	67	90	18	19	3	2	5	11	5	24	.211	.253	.456	80	-2	-3	10	0	1	-1	2	O	-0.2

YEAR	TM/L	G	AB	R	H	2B	3B	HR	RBI	BB	SO	AVG	OBP	SLG	PRO+	BR	/A	RC	SB	CS	SBR	FR	POS	TPR
1958	Cin-N	85	203	33	48	9	2	11	40	18	37	.236	.299	.463	93	-1	-3	28	3	0	1	2	O/2	0.0
1959	Cin-N	36	71	13	17	2	0	5	11	8	18	.239	.316	.479	105	1	0	11	0	0	0	-1	O	0.0
1960	Cin-N	1	1	0	0	0	0	0	0	0	0	.000	.000	.000	-98	-0	-0	0	0	0	0	0	H	0.0
	Cle-A	7	6	0	1	0	0	0	0	0	2	.167	.167	.167	-10	-1	-1	0	0	0	0	0	/O	0.0
	Was-A	58	115	19	26	9	0	3	9	19	14	.226	.336	.383	95	-1	-1	15	2	1	0	2	O	0.0
	Yr	65	121	19	27	9	0	3	9	19	16	.223	.329	.372	90	-2	-2	15	2	1	0	2		0.0
1961	Min-A	10	6	1	0	0	0	0	0	1	2	.000	.143	.000	-55	-1	-1	0	0	0	0	0	/O	0.0
	Cin-N	26	15	6	3	0	0	0	1	2	4	.200	.294	.200	34	-1	-1	1	1	0	0	1	O/C3	0.0
Total	8	475	988	140	221	46	8	37	134	86	196	.224	.287	.399	80	-29	-30	114	17	5	2	16	O/3C2	-1.3

■ LARRY WHISENTON
Whisenton, Larry b: 7/3/56, St.Louis, Mo. BL/TL, 6'1", 190 lbs. Deb: 9/17/77

YEAR	TM/L	G	AB	R	H	2B	3B	HR	RBI	BB	SO	AVG	OBP	SLG	PRO+	BR	/A	RC	SB	CS	SBR	FR	POS	TPR
1977	Atl-N	4	4	1	1	0	0	0	1	0	3	.250	.250	.250	31	-0	-0	0	0	0	0	0	H	0.0
1978	Atl-N	6	16	1	3	1	0	0	2	1	2	.188	.235	.250	32	-1	-2	1	0	0	0	-1	/O	-0.2
1979	Atl-N	13	37	3	9	2	1	0	1	3	3	.243	.300	.351	72	-1	-2	4	1	0	0	3	O	0.2
1981	Atl-N	9	5	1	1	0	0	0	0	2	1	.200	.429	.200	81	0	0	1	0	0	0	-0	O	0.0
1982	*Atl-N	84	143	21	34	7	2	4	17	23	33	.238	.343	.399	103	2	1	20	2	2	-1	-2	O	-0.2
Total	5	116	205	27	48	10	3	4	21	29	42	.234	.329	.371	90	-1	-3	26	3	2	-0	-0	/O	-0.2

■ LEW WHISTLER
Whistler, Lewis (b: Lewis Wissler) b: 3/10/1868, St.Louis, Mo. d: 12/30/59, St.Louis, Mo. TR, Deb: 8/07/1890

YEAR	TM/L	G	AB	R	H	2B	3B	HR	RBI	BB	SO	AVG	OBP	SLG	PRO+	BR	/A	RC	SB	CS	SBR	FR	POS	TPR
1890	NY-N	45	170	27	49	9	7	2	29	20	37	.288	.366	.459	142	9	9	32	8			-2	1	0.4
1891	NY-N	72	265	39	65	8	7	3	38	24	45	.245	.315	.362	103	-1	1	32	4			-16	SO/123	-1.2
1892	Bal-N	52	209	32	47	6	6	2	21	18	22	.225	.296	.340	91	-2	-3	25	12			-1	1/O	-0.7
	Lou-N	80	285	42	67	4	7	5	34	30	45	.235	.312	.351	111	1	4	36	14			-2	12	-0.2
	Yr	132	494	74	114	10	13	7	55	48	67	.231	.305	.346	102	-1	1	62	26			-3		-0.9
1893	Lou-N	13	47	5	10	1	1	0	9	5	5	.213	.302	.277	60	-3	-2	4	1			-0	1	-0.1
	StL-N	10	38	5	9	1	0	0	2	3	2	.237	.293	.263	50	-3	-3	3	0			-1	/O1	-0.3
	Yr	23	85	10	19	2	1	0	11	8	7	.224	.298	.271	55	-6	-5	7	1			-2		-0.4
Total	4	272	1014	150	247	29	28	12	133	100	156	.244	.318	.363	105	1	6	134	39			-21	1/SO23	-2.1

■ LOU WHITAKER
Whitaker, Louis Rodman b: 5/12/57, Brooklyn, N.Y. BL/TR, 5'11", 160 lbs. Deb: 9/09/77

YEAR	TM/L	G	AB	R	H	2B	3B	HR	RBI	BB	SO	AVG	OBP	SLG	PRO+	BR	/A	RC	SB	CS	SBR	FR	POS	TPR
1977	Det-A	11	32	5	8	1	0	0	2	4	6	.250	.333	.281	66	-1	-1	3	2	2	-1	-4	/2	-0.5
1978	Det-A	139	484	71	138	12	7	3	58	61	65	.285	.366	.357	101	5	3	66	7	7	-2	-11	*2/D	-0.2
1979	Det-A	127	423	75	121	14	8	3	42	78	66	.286	.398	.378	107	10	8	69	20	10	0	2	*2	1.5
1980	Det-A	145	477	68	111	19	1	1	45	73	79	.233	.335	.283	69	-16	-18	50	8	4	0	-3	*2	-1.2
1981	Det-A	109	335	48	88	14	4	5	36	40	42	.263	.343	.373	103	3	2	45	5	3	-0	5	*2	1.0
1982	Det-A	152	560	76	160	22	8	15	65	48	58	.286	.343	.434	111	9	8	85	11	3	2	12	*2/D	3.0
1983	Det-A	161	643	94	206	40	6	12	72	67	70	.320	.385	.457	134	28	30	114	17	10	-1	-13	*2	2.1
1984	*Det-A	143	558	90	161	25	1	13	56	62	63	.289	.360	.407	112	10	10	83	6	5	-1	-11	*2	0.5
1985	Det-A	152	609	102	170	29	8	21	73	80	56	.279	.365	.456	124	20	21	107	6	4	-1	-16	*2	1.0
1986	Det-A	144	584	95	157	26	6	20	73	63	70	.269	.340	.437	110	7	8	82	13	8	-1	-1	*2	1.4
1987	*Det-A	149	604	110	160	38	6	16	59	71	108	.265	.343	.427	107	3	6	93	13	5	1	-14	*2	0.4
1988	Det-A	115	403	54	111	18	2	12	55	66	61	.275	.377	.419	128	14	16	67	2	0	1	-23	*2	0.1
1989	Det-A	148	509	77	128	21	1	28	85	89	59	.251	.366	.462	135	23	25	91	6	3	0	-1	*2/D	2.6
1990	Det-A	132	472	75	111	22	2	18	60	74	71	.237	.341	.407	109	6	6	68	8	2	1	12	*2/D	2.6
Total	14	1827	6693	1040	1831	301	60	167	781	876	874	.274	.358	.411	112	121	125	1024	124	66	-2	-67	*2/D	14.3

■ STEVE WHITAKER
Whitaker, Stephen Edward b: 5/7/43, Tacoma, Wash. BL/TR, 6', 180 lbs. Deb: 8/23/66

YEAR	TM/L	G	AB	R	H	2B	3B	HR	RBI	BB	SO	AVG	OBP	SLG	PRO+	BR	/A	RC	SB	CS	SBR	FR	POS	TPR
1966	NY-A	31	114	15	28	3	2	7	15	9	24	.246	.306	.491	130	3	4	18	0	0	0	1	O	0.3
1967	NY-A	122	441	37	107	12	3	11	50	23	89	.243	.285	.358	92	-7	-5	43	2	5	-2	5	*O	-0.6
1968	NY-A	28	60	3	7	2	0	0	3	8	18	.117	.221	.150	14	-6	-6	2	0	1	-1	-1	O	-0.8
1969	Sea-A	69	116	15	29	2	1	6	13	12	29	.250	.326	.440	114	2	2	18	2	0	1	2	O	0.4
1970	SF-N	16	27	3	3	1	0	0	4	2	14	.111	.172	.148	-13	-4	-4	1	0	0	0	-1	/O	-0.5
Total	5	266	758	73	174	20	6	24	85	54	174	.230	.285	.367	92	-13	-10	82	4	6	-2	6	O	-1.2

■ FUZZ WHITE
White, Albert Eugene b: 6/27/18, Springfield, Mo. BL/TR, 6', 175 lbs. Deb: 9/17/40

YEAR	TM/L	G	AB	R	H	2B	3B	HR	RBI	BB	SO	AVG	OBP	SLG	PRO+	BR	/A	RC	SB	CS	SBR	FR	POS	TPR
1940	StL-A	2	2	0	0	0	0	0	0	0	0	.000	.000	.000	-98	-1	-1	0	0	0	0	0	H	0.0
1947	NY-N	7	13	3	3	0	0	0	0	0	0	.231	.231	.231	23	-1	-1	0	0			1	/O	0.0
Total	2	9	15	3	3	0	0	0	0	0	0	.200	.200	.200	6	-2	-2	0	0	0	0	1	/O	0.0

■ C. B. WHITE
White, C. B. b: Wakeman, Ohio Deb: 6/01/1883

YEAR	TM/L	G	AB	R	H	2B	3B	HR	RBI	BB	SO	AVG	OBP	SLG	PRO+	BR	/A	RC	SB	CS	SBR	FR	POS	TPR
1883	Phi-N	1	1	0	0	0	0	0	0	0	0	.000	.000	.000	-99	-0	-0	0				0	/S3	0.0

■ CHARLIE WHITE
White, Charles b: 8/12/28, Kinston, N.C. BL/TR, 5'11", 192 lbs. Deb: 4/18/54

YEAR	TM/L	G	AB	R	H	2B	3B	HR	RBI	BB	SO	AVG	OBP	SLG	PRO+	BR	/A	RC	SB	CS	SBR	FR	POS	TPR
1954	Mil-N	50	93	14	22	4	0	1	8	9	8	.237	.304	.312	65	-5	-5	8	0	0	0	-2	C	-0.5
1955	Mil-N	12	30	3	7	1	0	0	4	5	7	.233	.361	.267	74	-1	-1	3	0	0	0	-2	C	-0.1
Total	2	62	123	17	29	5	0	1	12	14	15	.236	.319	.301	67	-6	-5	11	0	0	0	-4	/C	-0.6

■ DEVON WHITE
White, Devon Markes b: 12/29/62, Kingston, Jamaica BB/TR, 6'1", 170 lbs. Deb: 9/02/85

YEAR	TM/L	G	AB	R	H	2B	3B	HR	RBI	BB	SO	AVG	OBP	SLG	PRO+	BR	/A	RC	SB	CS	SBR	FR	POS	TPR
1985	Cal-A	21	7	7	1	0	0	0	0	1	3	.143	.333	.143	37	-1	-1	1	3	1	0	2	O	0.2
1986	*Cal-A	29	51	8	12	1	1	1	3	6	8	.235	.316	.353	83	-1	-1	7	6	0	2	3	O	0.3
1987	Cal-A	159	639	103	168	33	5	24	87	39	135	.263	.307	.443	99	-6	-3	87	32	11	3	25	*O	2.1
1988	Cal-A	122	455	76	118	22	2	11	51	23	84	.259	.298	.389	93	-7	-5	52	17	8	0	10	*O	0.3
1989	Cal-A	156	636	86	156	18	13	12	56	31	129	.245	.283	.371	84	-16	-15	64	44	16	4	10	*O/D	-0.2
1990	Cal-A	125	443	57	96	17	3	11	44	44	116	.217	.292	.343	77	-14	-14	47	21	6	3	3	*O	-0.9
Total	6	612	2231	337	551	91	24	59	241	144	475	.247	.296	.389	89	-44	-38	258	123	42	12	54	O/D	1.8

■ DON WHITE
White, Donald William b: 1/8/19, Everett, Wash. d: 6/15/87, Carlsbad, Cal. BR/TR, 6'1", 195 lbs. Deb: 4/19/48

YEAR	TM/L	G	AB	R	H	2B	3B	HR	RBI	BB	SO	AVG	OBP	SLG	PRO+	BR	/A	RC	SB	CS	SBR	FR	POS	TPR
1948	Phi-A	86	253	29	62	14	2	1	28	19	16	.245	.303	.328	68	-12	-12	25	0	1	-1	-0	O3	-1.5
1949	Phi-A	57	169	12	36	6	0	0	10	14	12	.213	.273	.249	40	-15	-14	12	2	0	1	0	O/3	-1.4
Total	2	143	422	41	98	20	2	1	38	33	28	.232	.291	.296	57	-27	-27	38	2	1	0	-0	O/3	-2.9

■ ED WHITE
White, Edward Perry b: 4/6/26, Anniston, Ala. d: 9/28/82, Lakeland, Fla. BR/TR, 6'2", 200 lbs. Deb: 9/16/55

YEAR	TM/L	G	AB	R	H	2B	3B	HR	RBI	BB	SO	AVG	OBP	SLG	PRO+	BR	/A	RC	SB	CS	SBR	FR	POS	TPR
1955	Chi-A	3	4	0	2	0	0	0	0	1	1	.500	.600	.500	193	1	1	1	0	0	0	0	/O	0.0

■ ELDER WHITE
White, Elder Lafayette b: 12/23/34, Colerain, N.C. BR/TR, 5'11", 165 lbs. Deb: 4/10/62

YEAR	TM/L	G	AB	R	H	2B	3B	HR	RBI	BB	SO	AVG	OBP	SLG	PRO+	BR	/A	RC	SB	CS	SBR	FR	POS	TPR
1962	Chi-N	23	53	4	8	2	0	0	1	8	11	.151	.274	.189	26	-5	-6	4	3	0	1	0	S/3	-0.2

■ ELMER WHITE
White, Elmer b: 5/23/1850, Caton, N.Y. d: 3/17/1872, Caton, N.Y. Deb: 5/04/1871

YEAR	TM/L	G	AB	R	H	2B	3B	HR	RBI	BB	SO	AVG	OBP	SLG	PRO+	BR	/A	RC	SB	CS	SBR	FR	POS	TPR
1871	Cle-n	15	70	13	18	2	0	0	9	1	6	.257	.268	.286	63	-4	-3	5	0				O/C	0.0

■ FRANK WHITE
White, Frank b: 9/4/50, Greenville, Miss. BR/TR, 5'11", 165 lbs. Deb: 6/12/73

YEAR	TM/L	G	AB	R	H	2B	3B	HR	RBI	BB	SO	AVG	OBP	SLG	PRO+	BR	/A	RC	SB	CS	SBR	FR	POS	TPR
1973	KC-A	51	139	20	31	6	1	0	5	8	23	.223	.265	.281	50	-9	-10	11	3	1	0	7	S2	0.3
1974	KC-A	99	204	19	45	6	3	1	18	5	33	.221	.239	.294	40	-13	-14	13	3	4	-2	25	2S3/D	1.5
1975	KC-A	111	304	43	76	10	2	7	36	20	39	.250	.298	.365	84	-6	-7	34	11	3	2	15	2S/CD	1.6
1976	*KC-A	152	446	39	102	17	6	2	46	19	42	.229	.265	.307	67	-19	-20	37	20	11	-1	21	*2S	1.1
1977	*KC-A	152	474	59	116	21	5	5	50	25	67	.245	.285	.342	70	-20	-21	49	23	5	4	-3	*2/S	-0.6

YEAR	TM/L	G	AB	R	H	2B	3B	HR	RBI	BB	SO	AVG	OBP	SLG	PRO+	BR	/A	RC	SB	CS	SBR	FR	POS	TPR
1978	*KC-A	143	461	66	127	24	6	7	50	26	59	.275	.318	.399	98	-1	-2	59	13	10	-2	-17	*2	-1.3
1979	*KC-A	127	467	73	124	26	4	10	48	25	54	.266	.304	.403	87	-8	-10	56	28	8	4	-22	*2	-2.1
1980	*KC-A	154	560	70	148	23	4	7	60	19	69	.264	.291	.357	76	-19	-19	57	19	6	2	-7	*2	-1.6
1981	*KC-A	94	364	35	91	17	1	9	38	19	50	.250	.287	.376	91	-6	-5	37	4	2	0	-17	2	-2.0
1982	KC-A	145	524	71	156	45	6	11	56	16	65	.298	.321	.469	114	8	8	73	10	7	-1	-15	*2	0.0
1983	KC-A	146	549	52	143	35	6	11	77	20	51	.260	.286	.406	88	-10	-11	58	13	5	1	8	*2	0.2
1984	*KC-A	129	479	58	130	22	5	17	56	27	72	.271	.313	.445	106	3	3	63	5	5	-2	13	*2	2.0
1985	KC-A	149	563	62	140	25	1	22	69	28	86	.249	.285	.414	88	-10	-11	65	10	4	1	11	*2	0.6
1986	KC-A	151	566	76	154	37	3	22	84	43	88	.272	.326	.465	110	8	7	84	4	4	-1	-0	*2/S3	1.3
1987	KC-A	154	563	67	138	32	2	17	78	51	86	.245	.310	.400	84	-12	-14	67	1	3	-2	8	*2/D	0.4
1988	KC-A	150	537	48	126	25	1	8	58	21	67	.235	.269	.330	66	-25	-25	44	7	3	0	7	*2/D	-0.8
1989	KC-A	135	418	34	107	22	1	2	36	30	52	.256	.309	.328	80	-11	-11	43	3	2	-0	7	*2/O	-0.1
1990	KC-A	82	241	20	52	14	1	2	21	10	32	.216	.256	.307	58	-14	-14	18	1	0	0	3	2/O	-0.6
Total	18	2324	7859	912	2006	407	58	160	886	412	1035	.255	.295	.383	85	-164	-175	866	178	83	4	43	*2S/3DOC	-0.1

■ DOC WHITE
White, Guy Harris b: 4/9/1879, Washington, D.C. d: 2/19/69, Silver Spring, Md. BL/TL, 6'1", 150 lbs. Deb: 4/22/01

YEAR	TM/L	G	AB	R	H	2B	3B	HR	RBI	BB	SO	AVG	OBP	SLG	PRO+	BR	/A	RC	SB	CS	SBR	FR	POS	TPR
1901	Phi-N	31	98	15	27	3	1	1	10	2		.276	.297	.357	89	-1	-2	12	1			1	P/O	0.0
1902	Phi-N	61	179	17	47	3	1	1	15	11		.263	.305	.307	91	-2	-2	20	5			-3	P/O	0.0
1903	Chi-A	38	99	10	20	3	0	0	5	19		.202	.331	.232	77	-2	-2	8	1			2	P/O	0.0
1904	Chi-A	33	76	7	12	2	0	0	2	10		.158	.256	.184	44	-5	-4	5	3			0	P/O	0.0
1905	Chi-A	37	90	7	15	5	0	0	7	4		.167	.202	.222	37	-6	-6	5	3			1	P/O	0.0
1906	*Chi-A	29	65	11	12	1	1	0	3	13		.185	.321	.231	77	-1	-1	7	3			2	P/O	0.0
1907	Chi-A	48	90	12	20	1	0	0	2	12		.222	.314	.233	79	-2	-1	9	2			4	P/O2	0.0
1908	Chi-A	51	109	12	25	1	0	0	10	12		.229	.306	.239	81	-2	-2	10	4			6	P/O	0.0
1909	Chi-A	72	192	24	45	1	5	0	7	33		.234	.347	.292	106	2	3	23	7			-4	OP	0.2
1910	Chi-A	56	126	14	25	1	2	0	8	14		.198	.279	.238	65	-5	-5	10	2			2	PO	0.0
1911	Chi-A	39	78	12	20	1	1	0	6	7		.256	.318	.295	74	-3	-3	8	1			0	P/1O	0.0
1912	Chi-A	32	56	5	7	1	1	0	0	7		.125	.222	.179	15	-6	-6	2	0			-0	P	0.0
1913	Chi-A	20	25	1	3	0	0	0	0	3	1	.120	.214	.120	-2	-3	-3	1	0			3	P/1	0.0
Total	13	547	1283	147	278	23	12	2	75	147	1	.217	.298	.258	75	-37	-32	120	32			13	P/O12	0.2

■ DEACON WHITE
White, James Laurie b: 12/7/1847, Caton, N.Y. d: 7/7/39, Aurora, Ill. BL/TR, 5'11", 175 lbs. Deb: 5/04/1871 M

YEAR	TM/L	G	AB	R	H	2B	3B	HR	RBI	BB	SO	AVG	OBP	SLG	PRO+	BR	/A	RC	SB	CS	SBR	FR	POS	TPR
1871	Cle-n	29	146	40	47	6	5	1	21	4	1	.322	.340	.452	132	5	6	24	2				*C/2	0.4
1872	Cle-n	22	108	21	37	3	2	0		4		.343	.366	.407	146	5	6	17					C/2OM	0.3
1873	Bos-n	60	310	78	122	20	8	0		0		.394	.394	.510	151	23	18	64					*C/O	1.3
1874	Bos-n	70	350	75	106	4	7	3		4		.303	.311	.380	112	7	3	42					*CO/12	0.4
1875	Bos-n	80	372	77	136	20	4	1		2		**.366**	.369	.449	175	29	27	63					*C/O1	2.4
1876	Chi-N	66	303	66	104	18	1	1	**60**	7	3	.343	.358	.419	141	18	12	47	2				*C/O13P	1.6
1877	Bos-N	59	266	51	**103**	14	**11**	2	**49**	8	3	**.387**	**.405**	**.545**	**190**	**28**	**27**	**60**	1				1O/C	2.2
1878	Cin-N	61	258	41	81	4	1	0	29	10	5	.314	.340	.337	136	6	10	30				-7	*CO/3	0.3
1879	Cin-N	78	333	55	110	16	6	1	52	6		.330	.342	.423	159	17	20	49				-1	*CO/1M	1.6
1880	Cin-N	35	141	21	42	4	2	0	7	9	7	.298	.340	.355	137	5	6	17				-3	O/12	0.1
1881	Buf-N	78	319	58	99	24	4	0	53	9	8	.310	.329	.411	133	11	11	44				-8	120/3C	0.0
1882	Buf-N	83	337	51	95	17	0	1	33	15	16	.282	.313	.341	108	4	3	37				-7	*3C	-0.1
1883	Buf-N	94	391	62	114	14	5	0	47	23	18	.292	.331	.353	106	4	3	47				-5	*3C	0.0
1884	Buf-N	110	452	82	147	16	11	5	74	32	13	.325	.370	.442	150	28	26	76				-6	*3/C	1.3
1885	Buf-N	98	404	54	118	6	6	0	57	12	11	.292	.313	.337	107	4	2	44	1				*3	0.4
1886	Det-N	124	491	65	142	19	5	1	76	31	35	.289	.331	.354	105	5	3	62	9			-8	*3	0.0
1887	*Det-N	111	449	71	136	20	11	3	75	26	15	.303	.353	.416	111	9	7	75	20			-2	*3/O1	0.5
1888	Det-N	125	527	75	157	22	5	4	71	21	24	.298	.336	.381	131	18	18	73	12			-3	*3	1.9
1889	Pit-N	55	225	35	57	10	1	0	26	16	18	.253	.314	.307	83	-7	-4	23	2			-8	3/1	-0.6
1890	Buf-P	122	439	62	114	13	4	0	47	67	30	.260	.381	.308	95	-4	4	54	3			19	31/SP	1.7
Total	5 n	261	1286	291	448	53	26	5	21	14	1	.348	.355	.442	144	69	61	209	2				C/O21	4.8
Total	15	1299	5335	849	1619	217	73	18	756	292	215	.303	.344	.382	123	147	147	738	46			-34	3C10/2PS	10.9

■ JERRY WHITE
White, Jerome Cardell b: 8/23/52, Shirley, Mass. BB/TR, 5'10", 164 lbs. Deb: 9/16/74

YEAR	TM/L	G	AB	R	H	2B	3B	HR	RBI	BB	SO	AVG	OBP	SLG	PRO+	BR	/A	RC	SB	CS	SBR	FR	POS	TPR
1974	Mon-N	9	10	0	4	1	1	0	2	0	0	.400	.400	.700	193	1	1	3	3	0	1	0	/O	0.2
1975	Mon-N	39	97	14	29	4	1	2	7	10	7	.299	.364	.423	113	2	2	16	5	2	0	6	O	0.7
1976	Mon-N	114	278	32	68	11	1	2	21	27	31	.245	.316	.313	76	-7	-9	29	15	7	0	-6	O	-1.8
1977	Mon-N	16	21	4	4	0	0	0	1	1	3	.190	.227	.190	14	-3	-2	1	1	0	0	-1	/O	-0.2
1978	Mon-N	18	10	2	2	0	0	0	0	1	3	.200	.273	.200	34	-1	-1	1	1	0	0	0	/O	0.0
	Chi-N	59	136	22	37	6	0	1	10	23	16	.272	.377	.338	90	1	-1	18	4	3	-1	6	O	0.2
	Yr	77	146	24	39	6	0	1	10	24	19	.267	.371	.329	89	0	-1	19	5	3	-0	6		0.2
1979	Mon-N	88	138	30	41	7	1	3	18	21	23	.297	.394	.428	125	5	5	25	8	4	0	-1	O	0.3
1980	Mon-N	110	214	22	56	9	3	7	23	30	37	.262	.355	.430	118	6	5	34	8	7	-2	-2	O	-0.1
1981	*Mon-N	59	119	11	26	5	1	3	11	13	17	.218	.295	.353	82	-3	-3	14	5	2	-0	-1	O	-0.4
1982	Mon-N	69	115	13	28	6	1	2	13	8	26	.243	.304	.365	85	-2	-2	12	3	3	-1	-1	O	-0.4
1983	Mon-N	40	34	4	5	1	0	0	12	8		.147	.383	.176	60	-1	-1	4	4	0	1	0	O	-0.2
1986	StL-N	25	24	1	3	0	0	1	3	2	3	.125	.192	.250	21	-3	-3	1	0	0	0	0	/O	-0.2
Total	11	646	1196	155	303	50	9	21	109	148	174	.253	.339	.363	94	-4	-8	158	57	28	0	0	O	-1.7

■ JACK WHITE
White, John Peter b: 8/31/05, New York, N.Y. d: 6/19/71, Flushing, N.Y. BB/TR, 5'7.5", 150 lbs. Deb: 6/22/27

YEAR	TM/L	G	AB	R	H	2B	3B	HR	RBI	BB	SO	AVG	OBP	SLG	PRO+	BR	/A	RC	SB	CS	SBR	FR	POS	TPR
1927	Cin-N	5	4	1	0	0	0	0	0	0	0	.000	.000	.000	-99	-1	-1	0	0			0	/2S	0.0
1928	Cin-N	1	3	0	0	0	0	0	0	0	1	.000	.000	.000	-99	-1	-2	0	0			-0	/2	0.0
Total	2	6	7	1	0	0	0	0	0	0	1	.000	.000	.000	-99	-2	-2	0	0			0	/2S	0.0

■ JACK WHITE
White, John Wallace b: 1/19/1878, Indianapolis, Ind. d: 9/30/63, Indianapolis, Ind BR/TR, 5'6", Deb: 6/26/04

YEAR	TM/L	G	AB	R	H	2B	3B	HR	RBI	BB	SO	AVG	OBP	SLG	PRO+	BR	/A	RC	SB	CS	SBR	FR	POS	TPR
1904	Bos-N	1	5	1	0	0	0	0	0	0	0	.000	.000	.000	-99	-1	-1	0				1	/O	0.0

■ JO-JO WHITE
White, Joyner Clifford b: 6/1/09, Red Oak, Ga. d: 10/9/86, Tacoma, Wash. BL/TR, 5'11", 165 lbs. Deb: 4/15/32 MC

YEAR	TM/L	G	AB	R	H	2B	3B	HR	RBI	BB	SO	AVG	OBP	SLG	PRO+	BR	/A	RC	SB	CS	SBR	FR	POS	TPR
1932	Det-A	80	208	25	54	6	3	2	21	22	19	.260	.330	.346	73	-7	-9	23	6	8	-3	0	O	-1.1
1933	Det-A	91	234	43	59	9	5	2	34	27	26	.252	.337	.359	83	-5	-6	29	5	5	-2	0	O	-0.7
1934	*Det-A	115	384	97	120	18	5	0	44	69	39	.313	.419	.385	108	9	9	71	28	6	**5**	-3	*O	0.8
1935	*Det-A	114	412	82	99	13	12	2	32	68	42	.240	.348	.345	83	-11	-9	53	19	10	-0	-4	O	-1.3
1936	Det-A	58	51	11	14	3	0	0	6	9	10	.275	.383	.333	78	-1	-1	7	2	0	1	1	O	0.0
1937	Det-A	94	305	50	75	5	7	0	21	50	40	.246	.354	.308	67	-13	-14	37	12	7	-1	-7	O	-2.2
1938	Det-A	78	206	40	54	6	1	0	15	30	15	.262	.359	.301	63	-9	-11	24	3	4	-2	5	O	-0.6
1943	Phi-A	139	500	69	124	17	7	1	30	61	51	.248	.335	.316	91	-5	-4	59	12	4	1	-6	*O	-1.3
1944	Phi-A	85	267	30	59	4	2	1	21	40	27	.221	.329	.262	71	-9	-8	27	5	4	-1	-0	O/S	-1.1
	Cin-N	24	85	9	20	2	0	0	5	10	7	.235	.316	.259	65	-4	-3	8	0			2	O	-0.3
Total	9	878	2652	456	678	83	42	8	229	386	276	.256	.353	.328	82	-56	-58	337	92	<u>48</u>		-11	O/S	-7.8

■ MIKE WHITE
White, Joyner Michael b: 12/18/38, Detroit, Mich. BR/TR, 5'8", 160 lbs. Deb: 9/21/63

YEAR	TM/L	G	AB	R	H	2B	3B	HR	RBI	BB	SO	AVG	OBP	SLG	PRO+	BR	/A	RC	SB	CS	SBR	FR	POS	TPR
1963	Hou-N	3	7	0	2	0	0	0	0	0	0	.286	.286	.286	69	-0	-0	1	0	0	0	1	/2	0.1

YEAR	TM/L	G	AB	R	H	2B	3B	HR	RBI	BB	SO	AVG	OBP	SLG	PRO+	BR	/A	RC	SB	CS	SBR	FR	POS	TPR
1964	Hou-N	89	280	30	76	11	3	0	27	20	47	.271	.320	.332	89	-6	-4	28	1	1	-0	6	O2/3	0.1
1965	Hou-N	8	9	0	0	0	0	0	0	1	2	.000	.100	.000	-74	-2	-2	0	0	0	0	-0	/3	-0.1
Total	3	100	296	30	78	11	3	0	27	21	49	.264	.312	.321	84	-8	-6	29	1	1	-0	7	/O23	0.1

■ MYRON WHITE
White, Myron Alan   b: 8/1/57, Long Beach, Cal.   BL/TL, 5'11", 180 lbs.   Deb: 9/04/78

YEAR	TM/L	G	AB	R	H	2B	3B	HR	RBI	BB	SO	AVG	OBP	SLG	PRO+	BR	/A	RC	SB	CS	SBR	FR	POS	TPR
1978	LA-N	7	4	1	2	0	0	0	1	0	1	.500	.500	.500	181	0	0	1	0	1	-1	0	/O	0.0

■ ROY WHITE
White, Roy Hilton   b: 12/27/43, Los Angeles, Cal.   BB/TR, 5'10", 160 lbs.   Deb: 9/07/65   C

YEAR	TM/L	G	AB	R	H	2B	3B	HR	RBI	BB	SO	AVG	OBP	SLG	PRO+	BR	/A	RC	SB	CS	SBR	FR	POS	TPR
1965	NY-A	14	42	7	14	2	0	0	3	4	7	.333	.404	.381	125	2	2	7	2	1	0	-1	O/2	0.1
1966	NY-A	115	316	39	71	13	2	7	20	37	43	.225	.308	.345	91	-5	-3	35	14	7	0	-1	O/2	-0.7
1967	NY-A	70	214	22	48	8	0	2	18	19	25	.224	.291	.290	75	-7	-6	20	10	4	1	-9	O3	-1.6
1968	NY-A	159	577	89	154	20	7	17	62	73	50	.267	.352	.414	136	23	25	86	20	11	-1	8	*O	2.9
1969	NY-A	130	448	55	130	30	5	7	74	81	51	.290	.400	.426	136	22	24	81	18	10	-1	8	*O	2.9
1970	NY-A	162	609	109	180	30	6	22	94	95	66	.296	.391	.473	144	33	37	116	24	10	1	-1	*O	3.1
1971	NY-A	147	524	86	153	22	7	19	84	86	66	.292	.399	.469	154	34	38	103	14	7	0	2	*O	3.7
1972	NY-A	155	556	76	150	29	0	10	54	**99**	59	.270	.385	.376	131	23	25	88	23	7	3	3	*O	3.0
1973	NY-A	162	639	88	157	22	3	18	60	78	81	.246	.330	.374	101	-1	1	80	16	9	-1	-2	*O	-0.4
1974	NY-A	136	473	68	130	19	8	7	43	67	44	.275	.369	.393	123	14	16	73	15	6	1	-4	OD	1.1
1975	NY-A	148	556	81	161	32	5	12	59	72	50	.290	.373	.430	130	20	22	91	16	15	-4	6	*O/1D	2.0
1976	*NY-A	156	626	**104**	179	29	3	14	65	83	52	.286	.370	.409	129	23	24	98	31	13	2	5	*O	2.9
1977	*NY-A	143	519	72	139	25	2	14	52	75	58	.268	.360	.405	109	7	8	77	18	11	-1	5	*O/D	0.7
1978	*NY-A	103	346	44	93	13	3	8	43	42	35	.269	.351	.393	112	5	6	48	10	4	1	-8	OD	-0.2
1979	NY-A	81	205	24	44	6	0	3	27	23	21	.215	.294	.288	59	-12	-11	17	2	2	-1	-1	DO	-1.2
Total	15	1881	6650	964	1803	300	51	160	758	934	708	.271	.363	.404	122	180	206	1020	233	117	-0	11	*OD/312	18.3

■ SAM WHITE
White, Samuel Lambeth   b: 8/23/1892, Greater Preston, Yorkshire, England   d: 11/11/29, Philadelphia, Pa.   BL/TR, 6', 185 lbs.   Deb: 9/08/19

YEAR	TM/L	G	AB	R	H	2B	3B	HR	RBI	BB	SO	AVG	OBP	SLG	PRO+	BR	/A	RC	SB	CS	SBR	FR	POS	TPR
1919	Bos-N	1	1	0	0	0	0	0	0	0	0	.000	.000	.000	-99	-0	-0	0	0			2	/C	0.1

■ SAMMY WHITE
White, Samuel Charles   b: 7/7/28, Wenatchee, Wash.   BR/TR, 6'3", 195 lbs.   Deb: 9/26/51

YEAR	TM/L	G	AB	R	H	2B	3B	HR	RBI	BB	SO	AVG	OBP	SLG	PRO+	BR	/A	RC	SB	CS	SBR	FR	POS	TPR
1951	Bos-A	4	11	0	2	0	0	0	0	0	3	.182	.182	.182	-1	-2	-2	0	0	0	0	0	/C	0.0
1952	Bos-A	115	381	35	107	20	2	10	49	16	43	.281	.310	.423	95	-1	-4	46	2	3	-1	-2	*C	-0.1
1953	Bos-A	136	476	59	130	34	2	13	64	29	48	.273	.318	.435	96	-1	-4	63	3	2	-0	8	*C	0.8
1954	Bos-A	137	493	46	139	25	2	14	75	21	50	.282	.311	.426	90	-2	-9	60	1	3	-2	14	*C	1.0
1955	Bos-A	143	544	65	142	30	4	11	64	44	58	.261	.324	.392	84	-8	-14	64	1	2	-1	-1	*C	-1.0
1956	Bos-A	114	392	28	96	15	2	5	44	35	40	.245	.307	.332	61	-18	-24	37	2	1	-1	7	*C	-1.4
1957	Bos-A	111	340	24	73	10	1	3	31	25	38	.215	.268	.276	46	-24	-26	22	0	1	-1	-4	*C	-2.7
1958	Bos-A	102	328	25	85	15	3	6	35	21	37	.259	.306	.378	81	-6	-9	37	1	1	-0	-3	*C	-1.1
1959	Bos-A	119	377	34	107	13	4	1	42	23	39	.284	.327	.347	81	-8	-10	40	4	2	0	-1	*C	-0.3
1961	Mil-N	21	63	1	14	1	0	1	5	2	9	.222	.246	.286	43	-5	-5	4	0	0	0	4	C	0.0
1962	Phi-N	41	97	7	21	4	0	2	12	2	16	.216	.240	.320	50	-7	-7	6	0	0	0	5	C	-0.1
Total	11	1043	3502	324	916	167	20	66	421	218	381	.262	.307	.377	79	-82	-114	379	14	15	-5	26	*C	-4.9

■ BARNEY WHITE
White, William Barney "Bear"   b: 6/25/23, Paris, Tex.   BR/TR, 5'11", 186 lbs.   Deb: 6/05/45

YEAR	TM/L	G	AB	R	H	2B	3B	HR	RBI	BB	SO	AVG	OBP	SLG	PRO+	BR	/A	RC	SB	CS	SBR	FR	POS	TPR
1945	Bro-N	4	1	2	0	0	0	0	0	0	1	.000	.500	.000	46	0	0	0	0			0	/S3	0.0

■ BILL WHITE
White, William De Kova   b: 1/28/34, Lakewood, Fla.   BL/TL, 6', 185 lbs.   Deb: 5/07/56

YEAR	TM/L	G	AB	R	H	2B	3B	HR	RBI	BB	SO	AVG	OBP	SLG	PRO+	BR	/A	RC	SB	CS	SBR	FR	POS	TPR
1956	NY-N	138	508	63	130	23	7	22	59	47	72	.256	.324	.459	108	4	5	76	15	8	-0	3	*1/O	0.1
1958	SF-N	26	29	5	7	1	0	1	4	7	5	.241	.389	.379	107	0	1	5	1	0	0	-0	/1O	0.0
1959	StL-N	138	517	77	156	33	9	12	72	34	61	.302	.347	.455	108	10	6	83	15	10	-2	-3	O1	-0.4
1960	StL-N	144	554	81	157	27	10	16	79	42	83	.283	.336	.455	105	10	4	84	12	6	0	-5	*1O	-0.7
1961	StL-N	153	591	89	169	28	11	20	90	64	84	.286	.357	.472	107	15	7	96	8	11	-4	-2	*1	-0.8
1962	StL-N	159	614	93	199	31	3	20	102	58	69	.324	.388	.482	120	28	20	114	9	7	-2	2	*1O	1.4
1963	StL-N	162	658	106	200	26	8	27	109	59	100	.304	.361	.491	131	35	28	117	10	9	-2	-1	*1	2.3
1964	*StL-N	160	631	92	191	37	4	21	102	52	103	.303	.357	.474	121	26	19	107	7	6	-2	-0	*1	1.3
1965	StL-N	148	543	82	157	26	3	24	73	63	86	.289	.367	.481	125	27	21	97	3	3	-1	9	*1	2.2
1966	Phi-N	159	577	85	159	23	6	22	103	68	109	.276	.355	.451	122	18	18	96	16	6	1	7	*1	1.8
1967	Phi-N	110	308	29	77	6	2	8	33	52	61	.250	.364	.360	107	5	5	44	6	1	1	1	*1	0.0
1968	Phi-N	127	385	34	92	16	2	9	40	39	79	.239	.312	.361	102	1	1	44	0	1	-1	4	*1	0.0
1969	StL-N	49	57	7	12	1	0	0	4	11	15	.211	.338	.228	61	-2	-2	5	1	0	0	1	1	-0.2
Total	13	1673	5972	843	1706	278	65	202	870	596	927	.286	.353	.455	115	177	132	968	103	68	-10	14	*1O	7.2

■ BILL WHITE
White, William Dighton   b: 5/1/1860, Bridgeport, Ohio   d: 12/29/24, Bellaire, Ohio   TR   Deb: 5/03/1884

YEAR	TM/L	G	AB	R	H	2B	3B	HR	RBI	BB	SO	AVG	OBP	SLG	PRO+	BR	/A	RC	SB	CS	SBR	FR	POS	TPR
1884	Pit-a	74	291	25	66	7	10	0		13		.227	.262	.320	90	-3	-3	25				-11	S3/O	-1.3
1886	Lou-a	135	557	96	143	17	10	1		37		.257	.304	.329	94	-0	-6	61	14			17	*S/P	1.6
1887	Lou-a	132	512	85	129	7	9	2		47		.252	.315	.313	76	-15	-16	65	41			22	*S	0.2
1888	Lou-a	49	198	35	55	6	5	1	30	7		.278	.313	.374	125	4	5	29	15			-3	S3	0.4
	*StL-a	76	275	31	48	2	3	2	30	21		.175	.238	.225	46	-14	-19	17	6			-3	S/2	-1.6
Yr		125	473	66	103	8	8	3	60	28		.218	.269	.288	77	-10	-14	43	21			-5		-1.2
Total	4	466	1833	272	441	39	37	6	60	125		.241	.292	.312	84	-27	-39	196	76			22	S/302P	-0.7

■ BILL WHITE
White, William Edward   b: Milner, Ga.   Deb: 6/21/1879

YEAR	TM/L	G	AB	R	H	2B	3B	HR	RBI	BB	SO	AVG	OBP	SLG	PRO+	BR	/A	RC	SB	CS	SBR	FR	POS	TPR
1879	Pro-N	1	4	1	1	0	0	0	0	0	1	.250	.250	.250	66	-0	-0	0				0	/1	0.0

■ WILLIAM WHITE
White, William Warren (a.k.a. William Warren)   d: 3/3/1898,   Deb: 6/17/1871   M

YEAR	TM/L	G	AB	R	H	2B	3B	HR	RBI	BB	SO	AVG	OBP	SLG	PRO+	BR	/A	RC	SB	CS	SBR	FR	POS	TPR
1871	Oly-n	1	4	0	0	0	0	0	0	0	0	.000	.000	.000	-99	-1	-1	0	0				/2	0.0
1872	Nat-n	10	45	7	12	0	0	0		0	0	.267	.267	.267	55	-2	-3	3					3S	-0.2
1873	Was-n	39	158	29	44	3	5	0		0		.278	.278	.361	89	-3	-2	16					*3/S	-0.1
1874	Bal-n	45	212	20	56	1	0	0		1		.264	.268	.269	72	-7	-6	16					*3M	-0.4
1875	Chi-n	69	285	37	71	9	0	0		0		.249	.249	.281	82	-5	-5	20					*3/SO2	-0.2
1884	Was-U	4	18	2	1	0	0	0	0	0		.056	.056	.056	-64	-3	-3	0	0			-1	/3S2	-0.2
Total	5 n	164	704	93	183	13	5	0		1		.260	.261	.293	78	-17	-18	56	0				3/SO2	-0.9

■ ED WHITED
Whited, Edward Morris   b: 2/9/64, Bristol, Pa.   BR/TR, 6'3", 195 lbs.   Deb: 7/05/89

YEAR	TM/L	G	AB	R	H	2B	3B	HR	RBI	BB	SO	AVG	OBP	SLG	PRO+	BR	/A	RC	SB	CS	SBR	FR	POS	TPR
1989	Atl-N	36	74	5	12	3	0	1	4	6	15	.162	.225	.243	33	-6	-7	4	1	0	0	-0	3/1	-0.7

■ BURGESS WHITEHEAD
Whitehead, Burgess Urquhart "Whitey"   b: 6/29/10, Tarboro, N.C.   BR/TR, 5'10.5", 160 lbs.   Deb: 4/30/33

YEAR	TM/L	G	AB	R	H	2B	3B	HR	RBI	BB	SO	AVG	OBP	SLG	PRO+	BR	/A	RC	SB	CS	SBR	FR	POS	TPR
1933	StL-N	12	7	2	2	0	0	0	1	0	1	.286	.286	.286	60	-0	-0	0	0			0	/S2	0.1
1934	*StL-N	100	332	55	92	13	5	1	24	12	19	.277	.310	.355	73	-11	-13	38	5			-1	2S3	-0.5
1935	StL-N	107	338	45	89	10	2	0	33	11	14	.263	.289	.305	57	-19	-21	30	5			4	2/3S	-0.8
1936	*NY-N	154	632	99	176	31	3	4	47	29	32	.278	.317	.356	82	-17	-16	70	14			29	*2	2.2
1937	*NY-N	152	574	64	164	15	6	5	52	28	20	.286	.323	.359	84	-12	-13	67	7			26	*2	1.9
1939	NY-N	95	335	31	80	6	3	2	24	24	19	.239	.299	.293	59	-19	-19	28	1			21	2/S3	0.5
1940	NY-N	133	568	68	160	9	6	4	36	26	21	.282	.319	.340	81	-14	-15	59	9			13	32/S	0.1
1941	NY-N	116	403	41	92	15	4	1	23	14	10	.228	.258	.293	54	-25	-26	27	7			-0	*2/3	-1.9
1946	Pit-N	55	127	10	28	1	2	0	5	6	6	.220	.261	.260	47	-9	-9	8	3			-6	2/3S	-1.4

YEAR	TM/L	G	AB	R	H	2B	3B	HR	RBI	BB	SO	AVG	OBP	SLG	PRO+	BR	/A	RC	SB	CS	SBR	FR	POS	TPR
Total	9	924	3316	415	883	100	31	17	245	150	138	.266	.304	.331	72	-126	-132	328	51			86	23/S	0.2

■ MILT WHITEHEAD   Whitehead, Milton P.   b: 1862, Canada   d: 8/15/01, Highland Township San Bernardino County, Cal.   Deb: 4/20/1884

YEAR	TM/L	G	AB	R	H	2B	3B	HR	RBI	BB	SO	AVG	OBP	SLG	PRO+	BR	/A	RC	SB	CS	SBR	FR	POS	TPR
1884	StL-U	99	393	61	83	15	1	1		8		.211	.227	.262	63	-14	-16	24	0			-11	*S/OP23	-2.1
	KC-U	5	22	2	3	0	0	0		0		.136	.136	.136	-9	-2	-2	0	0			-1	/2CS3	-0.2
	Yr	104	415	63	86	15	1	1		8		.207	.222	.255	59	-16	-18	24	0			-12		-2.3

■ GIL WHITEHOUSE   Whitehouse, Gilbert Arthur   b: 10/15/1893, Somerville, Mass.   d: 2/14/26, Brewer, Me.   BB/TR, 5'10", 170 lbs.   Deb: 6/20/12

YEAR	TM/L	G	AB	R	H	2B	3B	HR	RBI	BB	SO	AVG	OBP	SLG	PRO+	BR	/A	RC	SB	CS	SBR	FR	POS	TPR
1912	Bos-N	2	3	0	0	0	0	0	0	0	3	.000	.000	.000	-98	-1	-1	0	0			-1	/C	-0.1
1915	New-F	35	120	16	27	6	2	0	9	6	16	.225	.268	.308	75	-5	-4	11	3			-1	O/PC	-0.6
Total	2	37	123	16	27	6	2	0	9	6	19	.220	.262	.301	70	-6	-5	11	3			-2	/OCP	-0.7

■ GURDON WHITELEY   Whiteley, Gurdon W.   b: 10/5/1859, Ashaway, R.I.   d: 11/24/24, Cranston, R.I.   5'11", 190 lbs.   Deb: 8/07/1884

YEAR	TM/L	G	AB	R	H	2B	3B	HR	RBI	BB	SO	AVG	OBP	SLG	PRO+	BR	/A	RC	SB	CS	SBR	FR	POS	TPR
1884	Cle-N	8	34	4	5	0	0	0	1		8	.147	.171	.147	1	-4	-4	1				0	/O	-0.2
1885	Bos-N	33	135	14	25	2	2	1	7	1	25	.185	.191	.252	44	-9	-8	7				-2	O/C	-0.9
Total	2	41	169	18	30	2	2	1	7	2	33	.178	.187	.231	35	-12	-12	8				-2	/OC	-1.1

■ GEORGE WHITEMAN   Whiteman, George "Lucky"   b: 12/23/1882, Peoria, Ill.   d: 2/10/47, Houston, Tex.   BR/TR, 5'7", 160 lbs.   Deb: 9/13/07

YEAR	TM/L	G	AB	R	H	2B	3B	HR	RBI	BB	SO	AVG	OBP	SLG	PRO+	BR	/A	RC	SB	CS	SBR	FR	POS	TPR
1907	Bos-A	4	12	0	2	0	0	0	1	0		.167	.167	.167	7	-1	-1	0	0			-0	/O	-0.1
1913	NY-A	11	32	8	11	3	1	0	2	7	2	.344	.462	.500	181	4	4	8	2			1	O	0.4
1918	*Bos-A	71	214	24	57	14	0	1	28	20	9	.266	.335	.346	107	1	2	28	9			-11	O	-1.4
Total	3	86	258	32	70	17	1	1	31	27	11	.271	.345	.357	113	4	4	36	11			-11	/O	-1.1

■ MARK WHITEN   Whiten, Mark Anthony   b: 11/25/66, Pensacola, Fla.   BR/TR, 6'3", 210 lbs.   Deb: 7/12/90

YEAR	TM/L	G	AB	R	H	2B	3B	HR	RBI	BB	SO	AVG	OBP	SLG	PRO+	BR	/A	RC	SB	CS	SBR	FR	POS	TPR
1990	Tor-A	33	88	12	24	1	1	2	7	7	14	.273	.326	.375	97	-1	-0	11	2	0	1	3	O/D	0.3

■ FRED WHITFIELD   Whitfield, Fred Dwight   b: 1/7/38, Vandiver, Ala.   BL/TL, 6'1", 190 lbs.   Deb: 5/27/62

YEAR	TM/L	G	AB	R	H	2B	3B	HR	RBI	BB	SO	AVG	OBP	SLG	PRO+	BR	/A	RC	SB	CS	SBR	FR	POS	TPR
1962	StL-N	73	158	20	42	7	1	8	34	7	30	.266	.301	.475	95	0	-2	21	1	0	0	1	1	0.0
1963	Cle-A	109	346	44	87	17	3	21	54	24	61	.251	.307	.500	123	9	9	54	0	1	-1	-3	1	0.3
1964	Cle-A	101	293	29	79	13	1	10	29	12	58	.270	.303	.423	100	-1	-1	34	0	5	-3	-2	1	-0.7
1965	Cle-A	132	468	49	137	23	1	26	90	16	42	.293	.319	.513	131	17	17	71	2	2	-1	6	*1	1.7
1966	Cle-A	137	502	59	121	15	2	27	78	27	76	.241	.285	.440	105	1	1	61	1	2	-1	-2	*1	-0.5
1967	Cle-A	100	257	24	56	10	0	9	31	25	45	.218	.290	.362	91	-3	-3	26	3	3	-1	4	1	-0.5
1968	Cin-N	87	171	15	44	8	0	6	32	9	29	.257	.302	.409	105	2	1	20	0	3	-2	-0	1	-0.3
1969	Cin-N	74	74	2	11	0	0	1	8	18	27	.149	.315	.189	42	-5	-5	6	0	0	0	1	1	-0.5
1970	Mon-N	4	15	0	1	0	0	0	0	1	3	.067	.125	.067	-47	-3	-3	0	0	0	0	2	/1	-0.1
Total	9	817	2284	242	578	93	8	108	356	139	371	.253	.301	.443	107	17	14	293	7	16	-8	7	1	-0.6

■ TERRY WHITFIELD   Whitfield, Terry Bertland   b: 1/12/53, Blythe, Cal.   BL/TR, 6'1", 197 lbs.   Deb: 9/29/74

YEAR	TM/L	G	AB	R	H	2B	3B	HR	RBI	BB	SO	AVG	OBP	SLG	PRO+	BR	/A	RC	SB	CS	SBR	FR	POS	TPR
1974	NY-A	2	5	0	1	0	0	0	0	0	1	.200	.200	.200	16	-1	-1	0	0	0	0	0	/O	0.0
1975	NY-A	28	81	9	22	1	1	0	7	1	17	.272	.280	.309	68	-4	-3	7	1	0	0	1	O/D	-0.2
1976	NY-A	1	0	0	0	0	0	0	0	0	0	—	—	—	—	0	0	0	0	0	0	0	/O	0.0
1977	SF-N	114	326	41	93	21	3	7	36	20	46	.285	.330	.433	103	1	1	46	2	3	-1	-0	O	-0.3
1978	SF-N	149	488	70	141	20	2	10	32	33	69	.289	.337	.400	109	3	5	62	5	11	-5	-6	*O	-1.2
1979	SF-N	133	394	52	113	20	4	5	44	36	47	.287	.353	.396	111	3	6	52	5	4	-1	-6	*O	-0.4
1980	SF-N	118	321	38	95	16	2	4	26	20	44	.296	.339	.396	107	2	2	42	4	2	0	-0	O	-0.1
1984	LA-N	87	180	15	44	8	0	4	18	17	35	.244	.313	.356	88	-3	-3	18	1	4	-2	-1	O	-0.7
1985	*LA-N	79	104	8	27	7	0	3	16	6	27	.260	.300	.413	101	-1	-0	12	0	0	0	-1	O	-0.1
1986	LA-N	19	14	0	1	0	0	0	0	5	2	.071	.316	.071	14	-1	-1	0	0	0	0	0	/O	0.0
Total	10	730	1913	233	537	93	12	33	179	138	288	.281	.332	.394	103	-2	6	241	18	24	-9	-13	O/D	-3.0

■ ED WHITING   Whiting, Edward C. (a.k.a. Harry Zieber)   b: 1860, Philadelphia, Pa.   BL/TR, 188 lbs.   Deb: 5/02/1882

YEAR	TM/L	G	AB	R	H	2B	3B	HR	RBI	BB	SO	AVG	OBP	SLG	PRO+	BR	/A	RC	SB	CS	SBR	FR	POS	TPR
1882	Bal-a	74	308	43	80	14	5	0		7		.260	.276	.338	115	2	5	29				-5	*C/1O	0.0
1883	Lou-a	58	240	35	70	16	4	2		9		.292	.317	.417	146	9	12	33				-5	C/O231	0.9
1884	Lou-a	42	157	16	35	7	3	0		9		.223	.274	.306	96	-1	-0	13				-1	C/O1	0.2
1886	Was-N	6	21	0	0	0	0	0	0	1	12	.000	.045	.000	-90	-5	-4	0	0			-1	/C	-0.4
Total	4	180	726	94	185	37	12	2	0	26	12	.255	.282	.347	114	5	12	75	0			-12	C/O123	0.7

■ DICK WHITMAN   Whitman, Dick Corwin   b: 11/9/20, Woodburn, Ore.   BL/TR, 5'11", 170 lbs.   Deb: 4/16/46

YEAR	TM/L	G	AB	R	H	2B	3B	HR	RBI	BB	SO	AVG	OBP	SLG	PRO+	BR	/A	RC	SB	CS	SBR	FR	POS	TPR
1946	Bro-N	104	265	39	69	15	3	2	31	22	19	.260	.317	.362	92	-3	-3	30	5			7	O	0.2
1947	Bro-N	4	10	1	4	0	0	0	2	1	0	.400	.455	.400	124	0	0	2	0			0	/O	0.0
1948	Bro-N	60	165	24	48	13	0	0	20	14	12	.291	.346	.370	91	-1	-2	22	4			1	O	-0.4
1949	*Bro-N	23	49	8	9	2	0	0	2	4	4	.184	.245	.224	26	-5	-5	2	0			-1	O	-0.6
1950	*Phi-N	75	132	21	33	7	0	0	12	10	10	.250	.317	.303	65	-7	-6	13	1			1	O	-0.6
1951	Phi-N	19	17	0	2	0	0	0	0	0	1	.118	.118	.118	-37	-3	-3	0	0	0	0	0	O	-0.2
Total	6	285	638	93	165	37	3	2	67	51	46	.259	.316	.335	78	-19	-20	69	10	0		7	O	-1.6

■ FRANK WHITMAN   Whitman, Walter Franklin "Hooker"   b: 8/15/24, Marengo, Ind.   BR/TR, 6'2", 175 lbs.   Deb: 6/30/46

YEAR	TM/L	G	AB	R	H	2B	3B	HR	RBI	BB	SO	AVG	OBP	SLG	PRO+	BR	/A	RC	SB	CS	SBR	FR	POS	TPR
1946	Chi-A	17	16	7	1	0	0	0	1	2	6	.063	.211	.063	-22	-3	-3	0	0	1	-1	4	/S12	0.1
1948	Chi-A	3	6	0	0	0	0	0	0	0	3	.000	.000	.000	-99	-2	-2	0	0	0	0	-1	/S	-0.2
Total	2	20	22	7	1	0	0	0	1	2	9	.045	.160	.045	-43	-4	-4	0	0	1	-1	3	/S21	-0.1

■ DAN WHITMER   Whitmer, Daniel Charles   b: 11/23/55, Redlands, Cal.   BR/TR, 6'3", 195 lbs.   Deb: 7/20/80

YEAR	TM/L	G	AB	R	H	2B	3B	HR	RBI	BB	SO	AVG	OBP	SLG	PRO+	BR	/A	RC	SB	CS	SBR	FR	POS	TPR
1980	Cal-A	48	87	8	21	3	0	0	7	4	21	.241	.275	.276	53	-6	-5	7	1	0	0	5	C	0.2
1981	Tor-A	7	9	0	1	1	0	0	0	1	2	.111	.200	.222	20	-1	-1	0	0	0	0	1	/C	0.0
Total	2	55	96	8	22	4	0	0	7	5	23	.229	.267	.271	49	-7	-6	7	1	0	0	6	/C	0.2

■ PINKY WHITNEY   Whitney, Arthur Carter   b: 1/2/05, San Antonio, Tex.   d: 9/1/87, Center, Tex.   BR/TR, 5'10", 165 lbs.   Deb: 4/11/28

YEAR	TM/L	G	AB	R	H	2B	3B	HR	RBI	BB	SO	AVG	OBP	SLG	PRO+	BR	/A	RC	SB	CS	SBR	FR	POS	TPR
1928	Phi-N	151	585	73	176	35	4	10	103	36	30	.301	.342	.426	96	-2	-4	83	3			3	*3	0.1
1929	Phi-N	154	612	89	200	43	14	8	115	61	35	.327	.390	.482	108	14	8	113	7			21	*3	3.7
1930	Phi-N	149	606	87	207	41	5	8	117	40	41	.342	.383	.465	97	4	-3	104	3			20	*3	1.7
1931	Phi-N	130	501	64	144	36	5	9	74	30	38	.287	.331	.433	96	2	-3	73	6			-6	*3	-0.1
1932	Phi-N	154	624	93	186	33	11	13	124	35	66	.298	.335	.449	97	6	-3	95	6			5	*3/2	1.5
1933	Phi-N	31	121	12	32	4	0	3	19	8	8	.264	.310	.372	83	-1	-3	12	1			-4	3	-0.6
	Bos-N	100	382	42	94	17	2	8	49	25	23	.246	.296	.364	95	-7	-3	40	2			1	32	0.1
	Yr	131	503	54	126	21	2	11	68	33	31	.250	.299	.366	92	-8	-6	52	3			-4		-0.5
1934	Bos-N	146	563	58	146	26	2	12	79	25	54	.259	.294	.377	85	-18	-13	61	7			3	*32/S	0.5
1935	Bos-N	126	458	41	125	23	4	4	60	24	36	.273	.312	.367	89	-12	-7	51	2			6	32	0.5
1936	Bos-N	10	40	1	7	0	0	0	5	2	4	.175	.233	.175	12	-5	-5	1	0			1	3	-0.2
	Phi-N	114	411	44	121	17	3	6	59	37	33	.294	.354	.394	92	1	-5	58	2			10	*3/2	1.4
	Yr	124	451	45	128	17	3	6	64	39	37	.284	.343	.375	86	-4	-9	59	2			11		1.2
1937	Phi-N	138	487	56	166	19	4	8	79	43	44	.341	.395	.446	118	20	15	84	6			4	*3	2.4
1938	Phi-N	102	300	27	83	9	1	3	38	27	22	.277	.336	.343	90	-5	-4	34	0			-2	3/12	-0.7
1939	Phi-N	34	75	9	14	0	1	1	6	7	4	.187	.256	.253	38	-7	-6	5	0			1	/23	-0.6
Total	12	1539	5765	696	1701	303	56	93	927	400	438	.295	.343	.415	96	-9	-36	815	45			63	*32/1S	9.4

YEAR	TM/L	G	AB	R	H	2B	3B	HR	RBI	BB	SO	AVG	OBP	SLG	PRO+	BR	/A	RC	SB	CS	SBR	FR	POS	TPR

■ ART WHITNEY
Whitney, Arthur Wilson b: 1/16/1858, Brockton, Mass. d: 8/15/43, Lowell, Mass. BR/TR, 5'8", 155 lbs. Deb: 5/01/1880

YEAR	TM/L	G	AB	R	H	2B	3B	HR	RBI	BB	SO	AVG	OBP	SLG	PRO+	BR	/A	RC	SB	CS	SBR	FR	POS	TPR
1880	Wor-N	76	302	38	67	13	5	1	36	9	15	.222	.244	.308	79	-4	-8	23				-1	*3	-0.8
1881	Det-N	58	214	23	39	7	5	0	9	7	15	.182	.208	.262	45	-13	-14	12				7	*3	-0.1
1882	Pro-N	11	40	2	3	0	0	0	1	2	11	.075	.119	.075	-36	-6	-6	0				-2	S	-0.5
	Det-N	31	115	10	21	0	0	0	4	1	12	.183	.190	.183	20	-10	-10	4				1	3/SP	-0.6
	Yr	42	155	12	24	0	0	0	5	3	23	.155	.171	.155	5	-16	-16	4				-1		-1.1
1884	Pit-a	23	94	10	28	4	0	0		1		.298	.305	.340	111	1	1	10				4	3/OS	0.4
1885	Pit-a	90	373	53	87	10	4	0		16		.233	.267	.282	77	-10	-9	29				-14	*S/32O	-1.9
1886	Pit-a	136	511	70	122	13	4	0		51		.239	.315	.280	89	-5	-4	51	15			11	*3S/P	1.2
1887	Pit-N	119	431	57	112	11	4	0	51	55	18	.260	.346	.304	89	-7	-2	50	10			-3	*3	-0.3
1888	*NY-N	90	328	28	72	1	4	1	28	8	22	.220	.240	.256	61	-14	-14	22	7			8	3	-0.2
1889	*NY-N	129	473	71	103	12	2	1	59	56	39	.218	.303	.258	59	-24	-24	44	19			-2	*3/P	-1.5
1890	NY-P	119	442	71	97	12	3	0	45	64	19	.219	.322	.260	53	-24	-32	41	8			-12	3S	-2.8
1891	Cin-a	93	347	42	69	6	1	3	33	31	20	.199	.270	.248	47	-22	-27	26	8			-5	3	-2.4
	StL-a	3	11	0	0	0	0	0	0	1	2	.000	.083	.000	-65	-2	-3	0	0			2	/3	0.0
	Yr	96	358	42	69	6	1	3	33	32	22	.193	.265	.240	43	-24	-30	25	8			-3		-2.4
Total	11	978	3681	475	820	89	32	6	266	302	173	.223	.285	.269	66	-140	-152	312	67			-6	3S/P2O	-9.5

■ FRANK WHITNEY
Whitney, Frank Thomas "Jumbo" b: 2/18/1856, Brockton, Mass. d: 10/30/43, Baltimore, Md. BR/TR, 5'7.5", 152 lbs. Deb: 5/17/1876

YEAR	TM/L	G	AB	R	H	2B	3B	HR	RBI	BB	SO	AVG	OBP	SLG	PRO+	BR	/A	RC	SB	CS	SBR	FR	POS	TPR
1876	Bos-N	34	139	27	33	7	1	0	15	1	3	.237	.243	.302	79	-3	-3	10				1	O/2	-0.1

■ JIM WHITNEY
Whitney, James Evans "Grasshopper Jim" b: 11/10/1857, Conklin, N.Y. d: 5/21/1891, Binghamton, N.Y. BL/TR, 6'2", 172 lbs. Deb: 5/02/1881

YEAR	TM/L	G	AB	R	H	2B	3B	HR	RBI	BB	SO	AVG	OBP	SLG	PRO+	BR	/A	RC	SB	CS	SBR	FR	POS	TPR
1881	Bos-N	75	282	37	72	17	3	0	32	19	18	.255	.302	.337	106	1	3	29				-5	*PO/1	0.0
1882	Bos-N	61	251	49	81	18	7	5	48	24	13	.323	.382	.510	183	24	24	50				-1	P/1	0.0
1883	Bos-N	96	409	78	115	27	10	5	57	25	29	.281	.323	.433	124	13	12	59				-6	PO/1	0.0
1884	Bos-N	66	270	41	70	17	5	3	40	16	38	.259	.301	.393	117	5	5	33				-0	PO1/3	0.0
1885	Bos-N	72	290	35	68	8	4	0	36	17	24	.234	.277	.290	87	-5	-4	24				6	PO/1	0.0
1886	KC-N	67	247	25	59	13	3	2	23	29	39	.239	.319	.340	94	1	-2	29	5			5	PO/3	0.0
1887	Was-N	54	201	29	53	9	6	2	22	18	24	.264	.324	.398	107	0	2	30	10			4	P/O	0.0
1888	Was-N	42	141	13	24	0	0	1	17	7	20	.170	.209	.191	32	-11	-10	6	3			-1	P/O1	0.0
1889	Ind-N	10	32	6	12	4	1	0	4	5	6	.375	.474	.563	188	4	4	10	2			-1	/PO	0.0
1890	Phi-a	7	21	3	5	0	0	0		1		.238	.273	.238	54	-1	-1	1	0			-0	/PO	0.0
Total	10	550	2144	316	559	113	39	18	279	161	211	.261	.313	.375	113	31	33	271	20			1	PO/13	0.0

■ ERNIE WHITT
Whitt, Leo Ernest b: 6/13/52, Detroit, Mich. BL/TR, 6'2", 200 lbs. Deb: 9/12/76

YEAR	TM/L	G	AB	R	H	2B	3B	HR	RBI	BB	SO	AVG	OBP	SLG	PRO+	BR	/A	RC	SB	CS	SBR	FR	POS	TPR
1976	Bos-A	8	18	4	4	2	0	1	3	2	2	.222	.300	.500	117	1	0	3	0	0	0	-1	/C	0.0
1977	Tor-A	23	41	4	7	3	0	0	6	2	12	.171	.209	.244	23	-4	-4	2	0	0	0	2	.C	-0.2
1978	Tor-A	2	4	0	0	0	0	0	0	1	1	.000	.200	.000	-38	-1	-1	0	0	0	0	1	/C	0.0
1980	Tor-A	106	295	23	70	12	2	6	34	22	30	.237	.290	.353	72	-10	-12	27	1	3	-2	5	*C	-0.3
1981	Tor-A	74	195	16	46	9	0	1	16	20	30	.236	.307	.297	70	-6	-7	19	5	2	0	9	C	0.5
1982	Tor-A	105	284	28	74	14	2	11	42	26	34	.261	.323	.440	98	2	-1	40	3	1	0	1	C/D	0.5
1983	Tor-A	123	344	53	88	15	2	17	56	50	55	.256	.350	.459	114	10	7	55	1	1	-0	6	*C	1.8
1984	Tor-A	124	315	35	75	12	1	15	46	43	49	.238	.331	.425	104	3	2	44	0	3	-2	12	*C	1.9
1985	*Tor-A	139	412	55	101	21	2	19	64	47	59	.245	.324	.444	105	4	3	58	3	6	-3	4	*C	1.0
1986	Tor-A	131	395	48	106	19	2	16	56	35	39	.268	.328	.448	106	4	3	56	0	1	-1	-5	*C	0.5
1987	Tor-A	135	446	57	120	24	1	19	75	44	50	.269	.336	.455	105	4	3	64	0	1	-1	5	*C	1.7
1988	Tor-A	127	398	63	100	11	2	16	70	61	38	.251	.352	.410	112	8	8	59	4	2	0	-5	*C	0.7
1989	*Tor-A	129	385	42	101	24	1	11	53	52	53	.262	.350	.416	117	8	9	56	5	4	-1	-1	*C/D	1.2
1990	Atl-N	67	180	14	31	8	0	2	10	23	27	.172	.266	.250	42	-14	-14	11	0	2	-1	2	C	-1.0
Total	14	1293	3712	442	923	174	15	134	531	428	479	.249	.327	.412	99	9	-6	496	22	26	-9	34	*C/D	8.3

■ POSSUM WHITTED
Whitted, George Bostic b: 2/4/1890, Durham, N.C. d: 10/16/62, Wilmington, N.C. BR/TR, 5'8.5", 168 lbs. Deb: 9/16/12

YEAR	TM/L	G	AB	R	H	2B	3B	HR	RBI	BB	SO	AVG	OBP	SLG	PRO+	BR	/A	RC	SB	CS	SBR	FR	POS	TPR
1912	StL-N	12	46	7	12	3	0	0	7	3	5	.261	.306	.326	75	-2	-2	5	1			-3	3	-0.4
1913	StL-N	123	404	44	89	10	5	0	38	31	44	.220	.282	.270	59	-22	-21	32	9			23	OS3/21	0.3
1914	StL-N	20	31	3	4	1	0	0	1	0	3	.129	.129	.161	-14	-4	-4	1	1			-1	/3O2	-0.5
	*Bos-N	66	218	36	57	11	4	2	31	18	18	.261	.326	.376	109	2	2	30	10			5	O2/13S	0.6
	Yr	86	249	39	61	12	4	2	32	18	21	.245	.304	.349	95	-2	-2	30	11			3		0.1
1915	*Phi-N	128	448	46	126	17	3	1	43	29	47	.281	.328	.339	101	1	0	55	24	15	-2	-3	*O/1	-0.9
1916	Phi-N	147	526	68	148	20	12	6	68	19	46	.281	.309	.399	113	8	6	69	29	17	-2	4	*O1	0.4
1917	Phi-N	149	553	69	155	24	9	3	70	30	56	.280	.317	.373	107	6	3	68	10			5	*O1/32	0.4
1918	Phi-N	24	86	7	21	4	0	0	3	4	10	.244	.278	.291	69	-3	-3	7	4			2	O/1	-0.2
1919	Phi-N	78	289	32	72	14	1	3	32	14	20	.249	.284	.336	80	-6	-8	28	5			-1	O2/1	-1.0
	Pit-N	35	131	15	51	7	7	0	21	6	4	.389	.420	.550	183	14	13	32	7			3	1/3O	1.7
	Yr	113	420	47	123	21	8	3	53	20	24	.293	.327	.402	112	8	5	57	12			2		0.7
1920	Pit-N	134	494	53	129	11	12	1	74	35	36	.261	.314	.338	85	-8	-10	52	11	11	-3	-3	*31/O	-1.0
1921	Pit-N	108	403	60	114	23	7	7	63	26	21	.283	.328	.427	96	-2	-3	54	5	10	-5	6	*O/1	-0.6
1922	Bro-N	1	1	0	0	0	0	0	0	0	0	.000	.000	.000	-99	-0	-0	0	0	0	0	0	H	0.0
Total	11	1025	3630	440	978	145	60	23	451	215	310	.269	.313	.361	95	-16	-26	433	116	53		35	O3/12S	-1.2

■ FLOYD WICKER
Wicker, Floyd Euliss b: 9/12/43, Burlington, N.C. BL/TR, 6'2", 175 lbs. Deb: 6/23/68

YEAR	TM/L	G	AB	R	H	2B	3B	HR	RBI	BB	SO	AVG	OBP	SLG	PRO+	BR	/A	RC	SB	CS	SBR	FR	POS	TPR
1968	StL-N	5	4	2	2	0	0	0	0	0	0	.500	.500	.500	204	0	0	1	0	0	0	0	H	0.1
1969	Mon-N	41	39	2	4	0	0	0	2	2	20	.103	.146	.103	-29	-7	-7	1	0	0	0	1	O	-0.6
1970	Mil-A	15	41	3	8	1	0	1	3	1	8	.195	.214	.293	38	-4	-4	2	0	0	0	-1	O	-0.4
1971	Mil-A	11	8	0	1	0	0	0	0	2	0	.125	.300	.125	24	-1	-1	0	0	0	0	0	H	0.0
	SF-N	9	21	3	3	0	0	0	1	2	5	.143	.250	.143	14	-2	-2	1	0	0	0	1	/O	-0.1
Total	4	81	113	10	18	1	0	1	6	7	33	.159	.215	.195	15	-13	-13	5	0	0	0	1	/O	-1.0

■ AL WICKLAND
Wickland, Albert b: 1/27/1888, Chicago, Ill. d: 3/14/80, Port Washington, Wis. BL/TL, 5'7", 155 lbs. Deb: 8/21/13

YEAR	TM/L	G	AB	R	H	2B	3B	HR	RBI	BB	SO	AVG	OBP	SLG	PRO+	BR	/A	RC	SB	CS	SBR	FR	POS	TPR
1913	Cin-N	26	79	7	17	5	5	0	8	6	19	.215	.279	.405	94	-1	-1	9	3			3	O	0.2
1914	Chi-F	157	536	74	148	31	10	6	68	81	58	.276	.375	.405	131	19	23	94	17			-1	*O	1.4
1915	Chi-F	30	86	11	21	2	2	1	5	13	11	.244	.343	.349	112	1	2	12	3			-2	O	-0.1
	Pit-F	110	389	63	117	12	8	1	30	52	47	.301	.386	.380	128	15	16	71	23			4	*O	1.5
	Yr	140	475	74	138	14	10	2	35	65	58	.291	.378	.375	126	16	17	83	26			2		1.4
1918	Bos-N	95	332	55	87	7	13	4	32	53	39	.262	.367	.398	129	15	16	52	12			-1	O	1.1
1919	NY-A	26	46	2	7	1	0	0	1	2	10	.152	.188	.174	2	-6	-6	1	0			-4	O	-1.1
Total	5	444	1468	212	397	58	38	12	144	207	184	.270	.364	.386	125	42	50	239	58			-1	O	3.0

■ TOM WIEDENBAUER
Wiedenbauer, Thomas John b: 11/5/58, Menomonie, Wis. BR/TR, 6'1", 180 lbs. Deb: 9/14/79

YEAR	TM/L	G	AB	R	H	2B	3B	HR	RBI	BB	SO	AVG	OBP	SLG	PRO+	BR	/A	RC	SB	CS	SBR	FR	POS	TPR
1979	Hou-N	4	6	0	4	1	0	0	2	0	2	.667	.667	.833	326	2	2	3	0	0	0	0	/O	0.2

■ TOM WIEGHAUS
Wieghaus, Thomas Robert b: 2/1/57, Chicago Heights, Ill BR/TR, 6', 195 lbs. Deb: 10/04/81

YEAR	TM/L	G	AB	R	H	2B	3B	HR	RBI	BB	SO	AVG	OBP	SLG	PRO+	BR	/A	RC	SB	CS	SBR	FR	POS	TPR
1981	Mon-N	1	1	0	0	0	0	0	0	0	0	.000	.000	.000	-99	-0	-0	0	0	0	0	1	/C	0.1
1983	Mon-N	1	0	0	0	0	0	0	0	0	0	—	—	—		0	0	0	0	0	0	0	/C	0.0
1984	Hou-N	6	10	0	0	0	0	0	1	1	3	.000	.091	.000	-78	-2	-2	0	0	0	0	3	/C	0.1

YEAR	TM/L	G	AB	R	H	2B	3B	HR	RBI	BB	SO	AVG	OBP	SLG	PRO+	BR	/A	RC	SB	CS	SBR	FR	POS	TPR
Total	3	8	11	0	0	0	0	0	1	1	3	.000	.083	.000	-80	-3	-2	0	0	0	0	4	/C	0.2

■ WHITEY WIETELMANN
Wietelmann, William Frederick b: 3/15/19, Zanesville, Ohio BB/TR, 6', 170 lbs. Deb: 9/06/39 C

YEAR	TM/L	G	AB	R	H	2B	3B	HR	RBI	BB	SO	AVG	OBP	SLG	PRO+	BR	/A	RC	SB	CS	SBR	FR	POS	TPR
1939	Bos-N	23	69	2	14	1	0	0	5	2	9	.203	.225	.217	21	-8	-7	3	1			2	S/2	-0.3
1940	Bos-N	35	41	3	8	1	0	0	1	5	5	.195	.283	.220	43	-3	-3	3	0			3	2/3S	0.1
1941	Bos-N	16	33	1	3	0	0	0	0	1	2	.091	.118	.091	-43	-6	-6	0	0			3	2/S3	-0.1
1942	Bos-N	13	34	4	7	2	0	0	0	4	5	.206	.289	.265	64	-2	-1	2	0			-0	S/2	0.0
1943	Bos-N	153	534	33	115	14	1	0	39	46	40	.215	.281	.245	53	-32	-31	39	9			20	*S	0.4
1944	Bos-N	125	417	46	100	18	1	2	32	33	25	.240	.300	.302	67	-16	-19	40	0			-6	*S2/3	-0.8
1945	Bos-N	123	428	53	116	15	3	4	33	39	27	.271	.335	.348	89	-6	-6	53	4			3	2S/3P	0.8
1946	Bos-N	44	78	7	16	0	0	0	5	14	8	.205	.326	.205	52	-4	-4	6	0			-5	S/32P	-0.8
1947	Pit-N	48	128	21	30	4	1	1	7	12	10	.234	.300	.305	59	-7	-8	11	0			-13	S2/31	-1.7
Total	9	580	1762	170	409	55	6	7	122	156	131	.232	.298	.282	63	-84	-85	157	14			5	S2/3P1	-2.4

■ AL WIGGINS
Wiggins, Alan Anthony b: 2/17/58, Los Angeles, Cal. BB/TR, 6'2", 160 lbs. Deb: 9/04/81

YEAR	TM/L	G	AB	R	H	2B	3B	HR	RBI	BB	SO	AVG	OBP	SLG	PRO+	BR	/A	RC	SB	CS	SBR	FR	POS	TPR
1981	SD-N	15	14	4	5	0	0	0	0	1	0	.357	.400	.357	125	0	0	3	2	0	1	0	/O	0.1
1982	SD-N	72	254	40	65	3	3	1	15	13	19	.256	.295	.303	71	-11	-9	25	33	6	6	2	O/2	-0.1
1983	SD-N	144	503	83	139	20	2	0	22	65	43	.276	.360	.324	94	-4	-1	72	66	13	12	8	*O1	1.5
1984	*SD-N	158	596	106	154	19	7	3	34	75	57	.258	.344	.329	90	-6	-6	79	70	21	8	-29	*2	-2.2
1985	SD-N	10	37	3	2	1	0	0	0	2	4	.054	.103	.081	-49	-7	-7	0	0	1	-1	-3	/2	-1.2
	Bal-A	76	298	43	85	11	4	0	21	29	16	.285	.353	.349	96	-2	-1	39	30	13	1	-24	2/D	-2.0
1986	Bal-A	71	239	30	60	3	1	0	11	22	20	.251	.314	.272	62	-12	-12	24	21	7	2	-19	2/D	-2.4
1987	Bal-A	85	306	37	71	4	2	1	15	28	34	.232	.299	.268	53	-21	-19	26	20	7	2	0	D2/O	-1.4
Total	7	631	2247	346	581	61	19	5	118	235	193	.259	.331	.308	80	-62	-55	269	242	68	32	-65	2O/D1	-7.7

■ DEL WILBER
Wilber, Delbert Quentin "Babe" b: 2/24/19, Lincoln Park, Mich BR/TR, 6'3", 200 lbs. Deb: 4/21/46 MC

YEAR	TM/L	G	AB	R	H	2B	3B	HR	RBI	BB	SO	AVG	OBP	SLG	PRO+	BR	/A	RC	SB	CS	SBR	FR	POS	TPR
1946	StL-N	4	4	0	0	0	0	0	0	1	0	.000	.200	.000	-39	-1	-1	0	0			1	/C	0.1
1947	StL-N	51	99	7	23	8	1	0	12	5	13	.232	.269	.333	57	-6	-7	8	0			1	C	-0.4
1948	StL-N	27	58	5	11	2	0	0	10	4	9	.190	.242	.224	25	-6	-6	3	0			-3	C	-0.7
1949	StL-N	2	4	0	1	0	0	0	0	0	0	.250	.250	.250	33	-0	-0	0	0			0	/C	0.0
1951	Phi-N	84	245	30	68	7	3	8	34	17	26	.278	.324	.429	102	-0	-0	33	0	1	-1	5	C	0.5
1952	Phi-N	2	2	0	0	0	0	0	0	0	1	.000	.000	.000	-99	-1	-1	0	0	0	0	0	H	0.0
	Bos-A	47	135	7	36	10	1	3	23	7	20	.267	.308	.422	94	-0	-0	17	1	0	1	1	C	0.2
1953	Bos-A	58	112	16	27	6	1	7	29	6	21	.241	.286	.500	103	-0	-0	14	0	0	0	-2	C/1	-0.1
1954	Bos-A	24	61	2	8	2	1	1	7	4	6	.131	.185	.246	15	-7	-8	3	0	0	0	-5	C	-1.2
Total	8	299	720	67	174	35	7	19	115	44	96	.242	.287	.389	79	-21	-25	78	1	1		-2	C/1	-1.6

■ CLAUDE WILBORN
Wilborn, Claude Edward b: 9/1/12, Woodsdale, N.C. BL/TR, 6'1", 180 lbs. Deb: 9/08/40

YEAR	TM/L	G	AB	R	H	2B	3B	HR	RBI	BB	SO	AVG	OBP	SLG	PRO+	BR	/A	RC	SB	CS	SBR	FR	POS	TPR
1940	Bos-N	5	7	0	0	0	0	0	0	0	1	.000	.000	.000	-99	-2	-2	0	0			-1	/O	-0.2

■ TED WILBORN
Wilborn, Thaddeaus Iglehart b: 12/16/58, Waco, Tex. BB/TR, 6', 165 lbs. Deb: 4/05/79

YEAR	TM/L	G	AB	R	H	2B	3B	HR	RBI	BB	SO	AVG	OBP	SLG	PRO+	BR	/A	RC	SB	CS	SBR	FR	POS	TPR
1979	Tor-A	22	12	3	0	0	0	0	0	1	7	.000	.077	.000	-76	-3	-3	0	0	1	-1	1	/O	-0.2
1980	NY-A	8	8	2	2	0	0	0	1	0	1	.250	.250	.250	38	-1	-1	1	0	0	0	2	/O	0.1
Total	2	30	20	5	2	0	0	0	1	1	8	.100	.143	.100	-33	-4	-4	1	0	1	-1	3	/O	-0.1

■ WILEY
Wiley Deb: 6/23/1884

YEAR	TM/L	G	AB	R	H	2B	3B	HR	RBI	BB	SO	AVG	OBP	SLG	PRO+	BR	/A	RC	SB	CS	SBR	FR	POS	TPR
1884	Was-U	1	4	0	0	0	0	0		0		.000	.000	.000	-99	-1	-1	0	0			-1	/3	0.0

■ ROB WILFONG
Wilfong, Robert Donald b: 9/1/53, Pasadena, Cal. BL/TR, 6'1", 180 lbs. Deb: 4/10/77

YEAR	TM/L	G	AB	R	H	2B	3B	HR	RBI	BB	SO	AVG	OBP	SLG	PRO+	BR	/A	RC	SB	CS	SBR	FR	POS	TPR
1977	Min-A	73	171	22	42	1	1	1	13	17	26	.246	.321	.281	67	-8	-7	17	10	4	1	4	2/D	0.2
1978	Min-A	92	199	23	53	8	0	1	11	19	27	.266	.336	.322	84	-3	-4	24	8	4	0	6	2/D	0.7
1979	Min-A	140	419	71	131	22	6	9	59	29	54	.313	.360	.458	115	11	8	72	11	4	1	22	*2/O	3.6
1980	Min-A	131	416	55	103	16	5	8	45	34	61	.248	.309	.368	79	-9	-13	47	10	6	-1	-3	*2/O	-1.0
1981	Min-A	93	305	32	75	11	3	3	19	29	43	.246	.311	.331	80	-6	-8	33	2	4	-2	0	2	-0.6
1982	Min-A	25	81	7	13	1	0	0	5	7	13	.160	.236	.173	14	-9	-10	3	0	2	-1	-0	2	-0.9
	*Cal-A	55	102	17	25	4	2	1	11	7	17	.245	.294	.353	77	-3	-3	11	4	0	1	20	2/3OSD	1.9
	Yr	80	183	24	38	5	2	1	16	14	30	.208	.268	.273	49	-13	-13	13	4	2	0	20		1.0
1983	Cal-A	65	177	17	45	7	1	2	17	10	25	.254	.294	.339	74	-6	-6	17	0	2	-1	11	23/SD	0.5
1984	Cal-A	108	307	31	76	13	2	6	33	20	53	.248	.298	.362	82	-8	-8	34	3	2	-0	3	2/SD	0.0
1985	Cal-A	83	217	16	41	3	0	4	13	16	32	.189	.245	.258	38	-19	-18	15	4	1	1	21	2/D	0.5
1986	*Cal-A	92	288	25	63	11	3	3	33	16	34	.219	.265	.309	56	-18	-18	23	1	4	-2	9	2	-0.5
1987	SF-N	2	8	2	1	0	0	1	2	1	5	.125	.222	.500	89	-0	-0	1	1	0	0	-2	/2	-0.1
Total	11	959	2690	318	668	97	23	39	261	205	387	.248	.305	.345	77	-79	-87	297	54	33	-4	90	2/3SOD	4.3

■ SPIDER WILHELM
Wilhelm, Charles Ernest b: 5/23/29, Baltimore, Md. BR/TR, 5'9", 170 lbs. Deb: 9/06/53

YEAR	TM/L	G	AB	R	H	2B	3B	HR	RBI	BB	SO	AVG	OBP	SLG	PRO+	BR	/A	RC	SB	CS	SBR	FR	POS	TPR
1953	Phi-A	7	7	1	2	1	0	0	3	0	3	.286	.286	.429	87	-0	-0	1	0	0	0	-0	/S	0.0

■ JIM WILHELM
Wilhelm, James Webster b: 9/20/52, Greenbrae, Cal. BR/TR, 6'3", 190 lbs. Deb: 9/04/78

YEAR	TM/L	G	AB	R	H	2B	3B	HR	RBI	BB	SO	AVG	OBP	SLG	PRO+	BR	/A	RC	SB	CS	SBR	FR	POS	TPR
1978	SD-N	10	19	2	7	2	0	0	4	0	2	.368	.400	.474	155	1	1	4	1	0	0	-1	O	0.1
1979	SD-N	39	103	8	25	4	3	0	8	2	12	.243	.257	.340	65	-6	-5	9	1	1	-0	4	O	-0.1
Total	2	49	122	10	32	6	3	0	12	2	14	.262	.280	.361	79	-5	-4	13	2	1	0	3	/O	0.0

■ JOE WILHOIT
Wilhoit, Joseph William b: 12/20/1891, Hiawatha, Kan. d: 9/25/30, Santa Barbara, Cal. BL/TR, 6'2", 175 lbs. Deb: 4/12/16

YEAR	TM/L	G	AB	R	H	2B	3B	HR	RBI	BB	SO	AVG	OBP	SLG	PRO+	BR	/A	RC	SB	CS	SBR	FR	POS	TPR
1916	Bos-N	116	383	44	88	13	4	2	38	27	45	.230	.282	.300	82	-10	-8	39	18			-3	*O	-1.6
1917	Bos-N	54	186	20	51	5	0	1	10	17	15	.274	.335	.317	107	1	2	21	5			-6	O	-0.6
	Pit-N	9	10	0	2	0	0	0	0	1	1	.200	.273	.200	44	-1	-1	1	0			0	/O1	0.0
	*NY-N	34	50	9	17	2	0	0	8	8	5	.340	.431	.460	179	5	5	10	0			-1	O	0.4
	Yr	97	246	29	70	7	2	1	18	26	21	.285	.353	.341	118	5	6	31	5			-6		-0.2
1918	NY-N	64	135	13	37	3	3	0	15	17	14	.274	.355	.341	115	3	3	17	4			3	O	0.3
1919	Bos-A	6	18	7	6	0	0	0	2	5	2	.333	.478	.333	138	1	1	3	1			-1	/O	0.0
Total	4	283	782	93	201	23	9	3	73	75	82	.257	.323	.321	101	-1	2	91	28			-7	O/1	-1.5

■ DENNEY WILIE
Wilie, Dennis Ernest b: 9/22/1890, Mt.Calm, Tex. d: 6/20/66, Hayward, Cal. BL/TL, 5'8", 155 lbs. Deb: 7/27/11

YEAR	TM/L	G	AB	R	H	2B	3B	HR	RBI	BB	SO	AVG	OBP	SLG	PRO+	BR	/A	RC	SB	CS	SBR	FR	POS	TPR
1911	StL-N	28	51	10	12	3	1	0	3	8	11	.235	.361	.333	97	-0	0	7	3			-1	O	0.0
1912	StL-N	30	48	2	11	0	1	0	6	7	9	.229	.351	.271	73	-2	-1	5	0			-1	O	-0.2
1915	Cle-A	45	131	14	33	4	1	2	10	26	18	.252	.384	.344	115	4	4	17	2	6	-3	-2	O	-0.3
Total	3	103	230	26	56	7	3	2	19	41	38	.243	.372	.326	102	3	3	28	5	6		-4	/O	-0.5

■ HARRY WILKE
Wilke, Henry Joseph b: 12/14/1900, Cincinnati, Ohio BR/TR, 5'10.5", 171 lbs. Deb: 5/12/27

YEAR	TM/L	G	AB	R	H	2B	3B	HR	RBI	BB	SO	AVG	OBP	SLG	PRO+	BR	/A	RC	SB	CS	SBR	FR	POS	TPR
1927	Chi-N	3	9	0	0	0	0	0	0	1	0	.000	.000	.000	-99	-3	-3	0	0			0	/3	-0.1

■ CURT WILKERSON
Wilkerson, Curtis Vernon b: 4/26/61, Petersburgh, Va. BB/TR, 5'9", 158 lbs. Deb: 9/10/83

YEAR	TM/L	G	AB	R	H	2B	3B	HR	RBI	BB	SO	AVG	OBP	SLG	PRO+	BR	/A	RC	SB	CS	SBR	FR	POS	TPR
1983	Tex-A	16	35	7	6	0	1	0	1	2	5	.171	.216	.229	23	-4	-4	2	3	0	1	2	/S23	0.0
1984	Tex-A	153	484	47	120	12	0	1	26	22	72	.248	.283	.279	55	-28	-30	38	12	10	-2	-28	*S2	-5.0
1985	Tex-A	129	360	35	88	11	6	0	22	22	63	.244	.295	.308	65	-17	-17	33	14	7	0	1	*S2/D	-0.7
1986	Tex-A	110	236	27	56	10	3	0	15	11	42	.237	.274	.305	56	-14	-15	19	9	7	-2	15	2S/D	0.5

YEAR	TM/L	G	AB	R	H	2B	3B	HR	RBI	BB	SO	AVG	OBP	SLG	PRO+	BR	/A	RC	SB	CS	SBR	FR	POS	TPR
1987	Tex-A	85	138	28	37	5	3	2	14	6	16	.268	.308	.391	84	-3	-3	16	6	3	0	11	S23/D	1.0
1988	Tex-A	117	338	41	99	12	5	0	28	26	43	.293	.347	.358	95	-0	-2	42	9	4	0	10	2S3/D	1.6
1989	Chi-N	77	160	18	39	4	2	1	10	8	33	.244	.280	.313	64	-7	-8	14	4	2	0	4	32/SO	-0.3
1990	Chi-N	77	186	21	41	5	1	0	16	7	36	.220	.249	.258	36	-15	-17	11	2	2	-1	-3	32/SO	-1.9
Total	8	764	1937	224	486	59	21	4	132	104	310	.251	.293	.309	64	-88	-96	175	59	35	-3	10	S23/DO	-4.8

■ BOBBY WILKINS
Wilkins, Robert Linwood b: 8/11/22, Denton, N.C. BR/TR, 5'9", 165 lbs. Deb: 4/18/44

YEAR	TM/L	G	AB	R	H	2B	3B	HR	RBI	BB	SO	AVG	OBP	SLG	PRO+	BR	/A	RC	SB	CS	SBR	FR	POS	TPR
1944	Phi-A	24	25	7	6	0	0	0	3	1	4	.240	.296	.240	55	-1	-1	2	0	0	0	5	/S	0.4
1945	Phi-A	62	154	22	40	6	0	0	4	10	17	.260	.305	.299	76	-5	-5	13	2	4	-2	1	S/O	-0.4
Total	2	86	179	29	46	6	0	0	7	11	21	.257	.304	.291	73	-6	-6	15	2	4	-2	6	/SO	0.0

■ ED WILKINSON
Wilkinson, Edward Henry b: 6/20/1890, Jacksonville, Ore d: 4/9/18, Tucson, Ariz. BR/TR, 6', 170 lbs. Deb: 7/04/11

YEAR	TM/L	G	AB	R	H	2B	3B	HR	RBI	BB	SO	AVG	OBP	SLG	PRO+	BR	/A	RC	SB	CS	SBR	FR	POS	TPR
1911	NY-A	10	13	2	3	0	0	0	1	0		.231	.231	.231	27	-1	-1	1	0			-1	/O2	-0.1

■ BOB WILL
Will, Robert Lee "Butch" b: 7/15/31, Berwyn, Ill. BL/TL, 5'10.5", 175 lbs. Deb: 4/16/57

YEAR	TM/L	G	AB	R	H	2B	3B	HR	RBI	BB	SO	AVG	OBP	SLG	PRO+	BR	/A	RC	SB	CS	SBR	FR	POS	TPR
1957	Chi-N	70	112	13	25	3	0	1	10	5	21	.223	.256	.277	44	-9	-9	8	1	0	0	1	O	-0.7
1958	Chi-N	6	4	1	1	0	0	0	0	0	2	.250	.500	.250	108	0	0	1	0	0	0	0	/O	0.0
1960	Chi-N	138	475	58	121	20	9	6	53	47	54	.255	.323	.373	91	-6	-6	56	1	5	-3	1	*O	-1.1
1961	Chi-N	86	113	9	29	9	0	0	8	15	19	.257	.344	.336	80	-3	-3	14	0	1	-1	-2	O/1	-0.6
1962	Chi-N	87	92	6	22	3	0	2	15	13	22	.239	.333	.337	78	-2	-3	11	0	0	0	-0	O	-0.3
1963	Chi-N	23	23	0	4	0	0	0	1	1	3	.174	.208	.174	11	-3	-3	1	0	0	0	0	/1	-0.2
Total	6	410	819	87	202	35	9	9	87	83	119	.247	.317	.344	80	-23	-22	91	2	6	-3	-0	O/1	-2.9

■ JERRY WILLARD
Willard, Gerald Duane b: 3/14/60, Oxnard, Cal. BL/TR, 6'2", 195 lbs. Deb: 4/11/84

YEAR	TM/L	G	AB	R	H	2B	3B	HR	RBI	BB	SO	AVG	OBP	SLG	PRO+	BR	/A	RC	SB	CS	SBR	FR	POS	TPR
1984	Cle-A	87	246	21	55	8	1	10	37	26	55	.224	.298	.386	86	-4	-5	28	1	0	0	0	C/D	0.0
1985	Cle-A	104	300	39	81	13	0	7	36	28	59	.270	.334	.383	97	-1	-1	40	0	0	0	1	C/D	0.3
1986	Oak-A	75	161	17	43	7	0	4	26	22	28	.267	.362	.385	112	1	3	23	0	1	-1	-12	C/D	-0.4
1987	Oak-A	7	6	1	1	0	0	0	0	2	1	.167	.375	.167	55	-0	-0	1	0	0	0	-0	/13D	0.0
1990	Chi-N	3	3	0	0	0	0	0	0	0	2	.000	.000	.000	-99	-1	-1	0	0	0	0	0	/C	0.0
Total	5	276	716	78	180	28	1	21	99	78	145	.251	.327	.381	95	-6	-4	92	1	1	-0	-11	C/D31	-0.1

■ RIP WILLIAMS
Williams, Alva Mitchel "Buff" b: 1/31/1882, Carthage, Ill. d: 7/23/33, Keokuk, Iowa BR/TR, 5'11.5", 187 lbs. Deb: 4/12/11

YEAR	TM/L	G	AB	R	H	2B	3B	HR	RBI	BB	SO	AVG	OBP	SLG	PRO+	BR	/A	RC	SB	CS	SBR	FR	POS	TPR
1911	Bos-A	95	284	36	68	8	5	0	31	24		.239	.314	.303	73	-10	-10	31	9			2	1C	-0.1
1912	Was-A	61	157	14	50	11	4	0	22	7		.318	.352	.439	125	4	4	24	2			4	C	1.2
1913	Was-A	66	106	9	30	6	2	1	12	9	16	.283	.339	.406	115	2	2	15	3			-4	C/1O	0.0
1914	Was-A	81	169	17	47	6	4	1	22	13	19	.278	.341	.379	113	3	2	22	2	2	-1	-4	C/1O	0.0
1915	Was-A	91	197	14	48	8	4	0	31	18	20	.244	.320	.325	92	-2	-2	23	4	3	-1	8	C1/3	0.8
1916	Was-A	76	202	16	54	10	2	0	20	15	19	.267	.324	.337	101	-1	-0	25	5			-8	1C/3	-0.8
1918	Cle-A	28	71	5	17	2	2	0	7	9	6	.239	.325	.324	87	-0	-1	9	2			-1	1/C	-0.3
Total	7	498	1186	111	314	51	23	2	145	95	80	.265	.328	.352	98	-4	-5	149	27	5		-5	C1/O3	0.8

■ ART WILLIAMS
Williams, Arthur Franklin b: 8/26/1877, Somerville, Mass. d: 5/16/41, Arlington, Va. TR , Deb: 5/07/02

YEAR	TM/L	G	AB	R	H	2B	3B	HR	RBI	BB	SO	AVG	OBP	SLG	PRO+	BR	/A	RC	SB	CS	SBR	FR	POS	TPR
1902	Chi-N	47	160	17	37	3	0	0	14	15		.231	.305	.250	76	-4	-4	16	9			-3	O1	-0.9

■ GUS WILLIAMS
Williams, August Joseph "Gloomy Gus" b: 5/7/1888, Omaha, Neb. d: 4/16/64, Sterling, Ill. BL/TL, 6', 185 lbs. Deb: 4/12/11

YEAR	TM/L	G	AB	R	H	2B	3B	HR	RBI	BB	SO	AVG	OBP	SLG	PRO+	BR	/A	RC	SB	CS	SBR	FR	POS	TPR
1911	StL-A	9	26	1	7	3	0	0	4	0		.269	.296	.385	93	-1	-0	3	0			-1	/O	-0.1
1912	StL-A	64	216	32	63	13	7	2	32	27		.292	.370	.444	138	9	10	41	18			2	O	0.8
1913	StL-A	148	538	72	147	21	16	5	53	57	87	.273	.346	.400	121	11	13	80	31			4	*O	1.0
1914	StL-A	144	499	51	126	19	6	4	47	36	120	.253	.308	.339	98	-5	-3	56	35	20	-2	2	*O	-1.1
1915	StL-A	45	119	15	24	2	2	1	11	6	16	.202	.246	.277	59	-7	-6	10	11	1	3	-5	O	-1.1
Total	5	410	1398	171	367	58	31	12	147	126	223	.263	.327	.374	110	8	14	191	95	21		1	O	-0.5

■ BERNIE WILLIAMS
Williams, Bernard b: 10/8/48, Alameda, Cal. BR/TR, 6'1", 175 lbs. Deb: 9/07/70

YEAR	TM/L	G	AB	R	H	2B	3B	HR	RBI	BB	SO	AVG	OBP	SLG	PRO+	BR	/A	RC	SB	CS	SBR	FR	POS	TPR
1970	SF-N	7	16	2	5	2	0	0	1	2	1	.313	.389	.438	122	1	1	2	1	1	-0	1	/O	0.1
1971	SF-N	35	73	8	13	1	0	1	5	12	24	.178	.294	.233	52	-4	-4	6	1	1	-0	-3	O	-0.9
1972	SF-N	46	68	12	13	3	1	3	9	7	22	.191	.267	.397	85	-2	-2	7	0	0	-0	3	O	0.0
1974	SD-N	14	15	1	2	0	0	0	0	0	6	.133	.133	.133	-26	-2	-2	0	0	0	0	0	/O	-0.2
Total	4	102	172	23	33	6	1	4	15	21	53	.192	.280	.308	66	-8	-8	15	2	2	-1	0	/O	-1.0

■ BILLY WILLIAMS
Williams, Billy Leo b: 6/15/38, Whistler, Ala. BL/TR, 6'1", 175 lbs. Deb: 8/06/59 CH

YEAR	TM/L	G	AB	R	H	2B	3B	HR	RBI	BB	SO	AVG	OBP	SLG	PRO+	BR	/A	RC	SB	CS	SBR	FR	POS	TPR
1959	Chi-N	18	33	0	5	0	1	0	2	1	7	.152	.176	.212	3	-5	-5	1	0	0	0	1	O	-0.3
1960	Chi-N	12	47	4	13	0	2	2	7	5	12	.277	.346	.489	127	2	2	8	0	0	0	-1	O	0.0
1961	Chi-N	146	529	75	147	20	7	25	86	45	70	.278	.340	.484	114	11	10	87	6	0	2	-6	*O	-0.1
1962	Chi-N	159	618	94	184	22	8	22	91	70	72	.298	.373	.466	119	21	18	107	9	9	-3	4	*O	1.1
1963	Chi-N	161	612	87	175	36	9	25	95	68	78	.286	.359	.497	136	34	30	108	7	6	-2	5	*O	2.7
1964	Chi-N	162	645	100	201	39	2	33	98	59	84	.312	.371	.532	145	42	39	125	10	7	-1	-10	*O	2.5
1965	Chi-N	164	645	115	203	39	6	34	108	65	76	.315	.380	.552	155	49	48	132	10	1	2	0	*O	4.6
1966	Chi-N	162	648	100	179	23	5	29	91	69	61	.276	.346	.461	122	20	19	104	6	3	0	8	*O	2.3
1967	Chi-N	162	634	92	176	21	12	28	84	68	67	.278	.349	.481	129	28	25	106	6	3	0	-8	*O	1.0
1968	Chi-N	163	642	91	185	30	8	30	98	48	59	.288	.340	.500	140	36	32	107	4	1	1	-12	*O	1.3
1969	Chi-N	163	642	103	188	33	10	21	95	59	70	.293	.356	.474	116	25	15	106	3	2	-0	-1	*O	0.6
1970	Chi-N	161	636	**137**	**205**	34	4	42	129	72	65	.322	.393	.586	142	51	41	**147**	7	1	2	-1	*O	3.3
1971	Chi-N	157	594	86	179	27	5	28	93	77	44	.301	.384	.505	131	39	29	112	7	5	-1	-3	*O	2.2
1972	Chi-N	150	574	95	191	34	6	37	122	62	59	**.333**	.403	**.606**	166	**61**	**54**	**137**	3	1	0	-6	*O/1	4.3
1973	Chi-N	156	576	72	166	22	2	20	86	76	72	.288	.372	.438	115	19	14	94	4	3	-1	6	*O1	1.3
1974	Chi-N	117	404	55	113	22	0	16	68	67	44	.280	.383	.453	128	19	17	71	4	5	-2	1	1O	1.2
1975	*Oak-A	155	520	68	127	20	1	23	81	76	68	.244	.343	.419	117	10	12	78	0	0	0	-0	*D/1	1.1
1976	Oak-A	120	351	36	74	12	0	11	41	58	44	.211	.323	.339	98	-2	-0	41	4	2	0	0	*D/O	0.0
Total	18	2488	9350	1410	2711	434	88	426	1475	1045	1046	.290	.364	.492	131	463	401	1671	90	49	-2	-24	*OD/1	29.1

■ DALLAS WILLIAMS
Williams, Dallas McKinley b: 2/28/58, Brooklyn, N.Y. BL/TL, 5'11", 165 lbs. Deb: 9/19/81

YEAR	TM/L	G	AB	R	H	2B	3B	HR	RBI	BB	SO	AVG	OBP	SLG	PRO+	BR	/A	RC	SB	CS	SBR	FR	POS	TPR
1981	Bal-A	2	2	0	1	0	0	0	0	0	0	.500	.500	.500	189	0	0	1	0	0	0	0	/O	0.0
1983	Cin-N	18	36	2	2	0	0	0	1	3	6	.056	.128	.056	-46	-7	-7	0	0	0	0	-0	O	-0.7
Total	2	20	38	2	3	0	0	0	1	3	6	.079	.146	.079	-35	-7	-7	1	0	0	0	0	/O	-0.7

■ DANA WILLIAMS
Williams, Dana Lamont b: 3/20/63, Weirton, W.Va. BR/TR, 5'10", 170 lbs. Deb: 6/21/89

YEAR	TM/L	G	AB	R	H	2B	3B	HR	RBI	BB	SO	AVG	OBP	SLG	PRO+	BR	/A	RC	SB	CS	SBR	FR	POS	TPR
1989	Bos-A	8	5	1	1	1	0	0	0	0	1	.200	.333	.400	100	0	0	1	0	0	0	1	/OD	0.1

■ DAVEY WILLIAMS
Williams, David Carlous b: 11/2/27, Dallas, Tex. BR/TR, 5'10", 160 lbs. Deb: 9/16/49 C

YEAR	TM/L	G	AB	R	H	2B	3B	HR	RBI	BB	SO	AVG	OBP	SLG	PRO+	BR	/A	RC	SB	CS	SBR	FR	POS	TPR
1949	NY-N	13	50	7	12	1	1	1	5	7	4	.240	.333	.360	86	-1	-1	7	0			-10	2	-1.0
1951	*NY-N	30	64	17	17	1	0	2	8	5	8	.266	.319	.375	85	-1	-1	7	1	1	-0	2	2	0.1
1952	NY-N	138	540	70	137	26	3	13	55	48	63	.254	.324	.385	95	-3	-4	71	2	3	-1	-15	*2	-1.4
1953	NY-N	112	340	51	101	11	2	3	34	44	19	.297	.382	.368	95	0	-1	50	2	5	-2	0	2	0.1
1954	*NY-N	142	544	65	121	18	3	9	46	43	33	.222	.285	.316	56	-35	-36	48	1	1	-0	-7	*2	-3.3
1955	NY-N	82	247	25	62	4	1	4	15	17	17	.251	.305	.324	67	-12	-12	24	0	2	-1	-8	2	-1.4
Total	6	517	1785	235	450	61	10	32	163	164	144	.252	.321	.351	79	-52	-54	207	6	12		-38	2	-6.9

YEAR	TM/L	G	AB	R	H	2B	3B	HR	RBI	BB	SO	AVG	OBP	SLG	PRO+	BR	/A	RC	SB	CS	SBR	FR	POS	TPR

■ DEWEY WILLIAMS
Williams, Dewey Edgar "Dee" b: 2/5/16, Durham, N.C.   BR/TR, 6', 160 lbs.   Deb: 6/28/44

1944	Chi-N	79	262	23	63	7	2	0	27	23	18	.240	.302	.282	65	-12	-12	22	2			3	C	-0.4
1945	*Chi-N	59	100	16	28	2	2	2	5	13	13	.280	.363	.400	114	2	2	14	0			2	C	0.5
1946	Chi-N	4	5	0	1	0	0	0	0	0	2	.200	.200	.200	14	-1	-1	0	0			0	/C	0.0
1947	Chi-N	3	2	0	0	0	0	0	0	0	1	.000	.000	.000	-99	-1	-1	0	0			0	/C	0.0
1948	Cin-N	48	95	9	16	2	0	1	5	10	18	.168	.248	.221	29	-10	-9	6	0			-3	C	-0.8
Total	5	193	464	48	108	11	4	3	37	46	52	.233	.302	.293	67	-21	-20	41	2			3	C	-0.7

■ EARL WILLIAMS
Williams, Earl Baxter b: 1/27/03, Cumberland Gap, Tenn.   d: 3/10/58, Knoxville, Tnnn.   BR/TR, 6'0.5", 185 lbs.   Deb: 5/27/28

| 1928 | Bos-N | 3 | 2 | 0 | 0 | 0 | 0 | 0 | 0 | 0 | 1 | .000 | .000 | .000 | -99 | -1 | -1 | 0 | 0 | | | 0 | /C | 0.0 |

■ EARL WILLIAMS
Williams, Earl Craig b: 7/14/48, Newark, N.J.   BR/TR, 6'3", 215 lbs.   Deb: 9/13/70

1970	Atl-N	10	19	4	7	4	0	0	5	3	4	.368	.455	.579	165	2	2	5	0	0	0	1	/13	0.3
1971	Atl-N	145	497	64	129	14	1	33	87	42	80	.260	.326	.491	121	17	13	78	0	1	-1	-7	C31	0.5
1972	Atl-N	151	565	72	146	24	2	28	87	62	118	.258	.338	.457	113	17	11	85	0	0	0	-16	*C31	0.0
1973	*Bal-A	132	459	58	109	18	1	22	83	66	107	.237	.337	.425	114	8	9	65	0	2	-1	-9	C1/D	-0.1
1974	*Bal-A	118	413	47	105	16	0	14	52	40	79	.254	.330	.395	111	4	6	54	0	2	-1	-14	C1/D	-0.8
1975	Atl-N	111	383	42	92	13	0	11	50	34	63	.240	.307	.360	82	-9	-10	40	0	0	0	-4	1C	-1.9
1976	Atl-N	61	184	18	39	3	0	9	26	19	33	.212	.289	.375	82	-4	-5	19	0	0	0	-8	C1	-1.2
	Mon-N	61	190	17	45	10	2	8	29	14	32	.237	.289	.437	100	-0	-1	22	0	0	0	6	1C	0.4
	Yr	122	374	35	84	13	2	17	55	33	65	.225	.289	.406	91	-4	-6	40	0	0	0	-2		-0.8
1977	Oak-A	100	348	39	84	13	0	13	38	18	58	.241	.288	.391	84	-9	-8	34	2	0	1	-4	DC1	-1.2
Total	8	889	3058	361	756	115	6	138	457	298	574	.247	.321	.424	105	27	16	401	2	5	-2	-54	C1/3D	-4.0

■ EDDIE WILLIAMS
Williams, Edward Laquan b: 11/1/64, Shreveport, La.   BR/TR, 6', 175 lbs.   Deb: 4/18/86

1986	Cle-A	5	7	2	1	0	0	0	1	0	3	.143	.143	.143	-22	-1	-1	0	0	0	0	0	/O	0.0
1987	Cle-A	22	64	9	11	4	0	1	4	9	19	.172	.284	.281	50	-5	-5	5	0	0	0	2	3	-0.2
1988	Cle-A	10	21	3	4	0	0	0	1	0	3	.190	.227	.190	18	-2	-2	1	0	0	0	3	3	0.1
1989	Chi-A	66	201	25	55	8	0	3	10	18	31	.274	.345	.358	101	0	1	25	1	2	-1	1	3	0.1
1990	SD-N	14	42	5	12	3	0	3	4	5	6	.286	.362	.571	150	3	3	8	0	1	-1	-1	3	0.2
Total	5	117	335	44	83	15	0	7	20	32	62	.248	.324	.355	89	-5	-5	39	1	3	-2	4	3/O	0.1

■ DIB WILLIAMS
Williams, Edwin Dibrell b: 1/19/10, Greenbrier, Ark.   BR/TR, 5'11.5", 175 lbs.   Deb: 4/27/30

1930	Phi-A	67	191	24	50	10	3	3	22	15	19	.262	.322	.393	77	-6	-7	25	2	1	0	4	2S/3	0.0
1931	*Phi-A	86	294	41	79	12	2	6	40	19	21	.269	.313	.384	78	-8	-11	36	2	0	1	7	S2/O	0.4
1932	Phi-A	62	215	30	54	10	1	4	24	22	23	.251	.329	.363	76	-7	-8	26	0	1	-1	7	2/S	0.1
1933	Phi-A	115	408	52	118	26	5	11	73	32	35	.289	.342	.444	106	3	2	63	1	0	0	-9	S2/1	0.0
1934	Phi-A	66	205	25	56	10	1	2	17	21	18	.273	.341	.361	84	-6	-5	26	0	1	-1	-0	2/S	-0.2
1935	Phi-A	4	10	0	1	0	0	0	0	0	1	.100	.100	.100	-49	-2	-2	0	0	0	0	-2	/2	-0.3
	Bos-A	75	251	26	63	12	0	3	25	24	23	.251	.319	.335	65	-12	-14	28	2	0	1	-5	32S/1	-1.5
	Yr	79	261	26	64	12	0	3	25	24	24	.245	.311	.326	61	-14	-16	28	2	0	1	-7		-1.8
Total	6	475	1574	198	421	74	12	29	201	133	140	.267	.327	.385	82	-37	-44	204	7	3	0	2	2S/310	-1.5

■ DENNY WILLIAMS
Williams, Evon Daniel b: 12/13/1899, Portland, Ore.   d: 3/23/29, San Clemente, Cal.   BL/TR, 5'8.5", 150 lbs.   Deb: 4/15/21

1921	Cin-N	10	7	0	0	0	0	0	0	0	2	.000	.000	.000	-99	-2	-2	0	0	1	-1	0	/O	-0.1
1924	Bos-A	25	85	17	31	3	0	0	4	10	5	.365	.438	.400	117	3	3	15	3	3	-1	-2	O	0.0
1925	Bos-A	69	218	28	50	1	3	0	13	17	11	.229	.285	.261	39	-20	-20	16	2	6	-3	-2	O	-2.7
1928	Bos-A	16	18	1	4	0	0	0	1	1	1	.222	.263	.222	29	-2	-2	1	0	0	0	-2	O	-0.3
Total	4	120	328	46	85	4	3	0	18	28	19	.259	.319	.290	56	-21	-21	32	5	10	-5	-6	/O	-3.1

■ CY WILLIAMS
Williams, Fred b: 12/21/1887, Wadena, Ind.   d: 4/23/74, Eagle River, Wis.   BL/TL, 6'2", 180 lbs.   Deb: 7/18/12

1912	Chi-N	28	62	3	15	1	1	0	1	6	14	.242	.309	.290	65	-3	-3	6	2			2	O	-0.1
1913	Chi-N	49	156	17	35	3	3	4	32	5	26	.224	.262	.359	76	-6	-6	15	5			-1	O	-0.7
1914	Chi-N	55	94	12	19	2	2	0	5	13	13	.202	.312	.266	73	-3	-3	8	2			1	O	-0.2
1915	Chi-N	151	518	59	133	22	6	13	64	26	49	.257	.305	.398	112	5	5	64	15	10	-2	-2	*O	-0.2
1916	Chi-N	118	405	55	113	19	9	12	66	51	64	.279	.372	.459	140	27	22	74	6			-8	*O	1.1
1917	Chi-N	138	468	53	113	22	4	5	42	38	78	.241	.308	.338	91	-1	-5	52	8			9	*O	0.0
1918	Phi-N	94	351	49	97	14	1	6	39	27	30	.276	.337	.373	109	7	4	47	10			-4	*O	-0.4
1919	Phi-N	109	435	54	121	21	1	9	39	30	43	.278	.335	.393	111	9	6	58	9			0	*O	0.2
1920	Phi-N	148	590	88	192	36	10	15	72	32	45	.325	.364	.497	139	32	29	103	6			6	*O	2.6
1921	Phi-N	146	562	67	180	28	6	18	75	30	32	.320	.357	.488	112	15	10	91	5	15	-8	10	*O	0.6
1922	Phi-N	151	584	98	180	30	6	26	92	74	49	.308	.392	.514	120	27	19	116	11	14	-5	-2	*O	0.6
1923	Phi-N	136	535	98	157	22	3	41	114	59	57	.293	.371	.552	131	33	25	112	11	10	-3	-7	*O	1.0
1924	Phi-N	148	558	101	183	31	11	24	93	67	49	.328	.403	.552	137	42	33	121	7	12	-5	-6	*O	1.9
1925	Phi-N	107	314	78	104	11	5	13	60	53	34	.331	.435	.522	132	23	19	72	4	9	-4	-1	O	1.0
1926	Phi-N	107	336	63	116	13	4	18	53	38	35	.345	.418	.568	155	30	27	78	2			-6	O	1.7
1927	Phi-N	131	492	86	135	18	2	30	98	61	57	.274	.365	.502	128	20	19	90	0			1	*O	1.4
1928	Phi-N	99	238	31	61	9	0	12	37	54	34	.256	.400	.445	117	9	8	45	0			-2	O	0.3
1929	Phi-N	66	65	11	19	2	0	5	21	22	9	.292	.471	.554	144	7	6	18	0			2	O	0.6
1930	Phi-N	21	17	1	8	2	0	2	4	3	2	.471	.571	.588	169	3	2	6	0			-0	/O	0.2
Total	19	2002	6780	1024	1981	306	74	251	1005	690	721	.292	.365	.470	123	278	218	1177	115	82		-9	*O	11.6

■ PAPA WILLIAMS
Williams, Fred b: 7/17/13, Meridian, Miss.   BR/TR, 6'1", 200 lbs.   Deb: 4/19/45

| 1945 | Cle-A | 16 | 19 | 0 | 4 | 0 | 0 | 0 | 1 | 2 | 2 | .211 | .250 | .211 | 36 | -2 | -1 | 1 | 0 | 0 | 0 | 0 | /1 | 0.0 |

■ GEORGE WILLIAMS
Williams, George b: 10/23/39, Detroit, Mich.   BR/TR, 5'11", 165 lbs.   Deb: 7/16/61

1961	Phi-N	17	36	4	9	0	0	0	1	4	4	.250	.325	.250	56	-2	-2	3	0	0	0	2	2	0.2
1962	Hou-N	5	8	1	3	1	0	0	2	0	1	.375	.375	.500	143	0	0	2	0	0	0	0	/2	0.1
1964	KC-A	37	91	10	19	6	0	0	2	6	12	.209	.265	.275	49	-6	-6	7	0	0	0	-2	2/S3O	-0.6
Total	3	59	135	15	31	7	0	0	5	10	17	.230	.288	.281	56	-8	-8	11	0	0	0	0	/2O3S	-0.3

■ HARRY WILLIAMS
Williams, Harry Peter b: 6/23/1890, Omaha, Neb.   d: 12/21/63, Huntington Park, Cal.   BR/TR, 6'1.5", 200 lbs.   Deb: 8/07/13

| 1913 | NY-A | 27 | 82 | 18 | 21 | 3 | 1 | 1 | 12 | 15 | 10 | .256 | .378 | .354 | 114 | 2 | 2 | 13 | 6 | | | -2 | 1 | 0.0 |

■ JIM WILLIAMS
Williams, James Alfred b: 4/29/47, Zachary, La.   BR/TR, 6'2", 190 lbs.   Deb: 9/08/69

1969	SD-N	13	25	4	7	1	0	0	2	3	11	.280	.357	.320	95	-0	-0	3	0	0	0	-1	/O	0.0
1970	SD-N	11	14	4	4	0	0	0	0	1	3	.286	.333	.286	70	-1	-1	2	1	0	0	0	/O	0.0
Total	2	24	39	8	11	1	0	0	2	4	14	.282	.349	.308	86	-1	-1	5	1	0	0	-1	/O	0.0

■ JIMY WILLIAMS
Williams, James Francis b: 10/4/43, Santa Maria, Cal.   BR/TR, 5'10", 170 lbs.   Deb: 4/26/66   MC

1966	StL-N	13	11	1	3	0	0	0	1	1	5	.273	.333	.273	71	-0	-0	1	0	0	0	-2	/S2	-0.1
1967	StL-N	1	2	0	0	0	0	0	0	0	1	.000	.000	.000	-99	-1	-1	0	0	0	0	1	/S	0.0
Total	2	14	13	1	3	0	0	0	1	1	6	.231	.286	.231	36	-1	-1	1	0	0	0	-1	/S2	-0.1

YEAR	TM/L	G	AB	R	H	2B	3B	HR	RBI	BB	SO	AVG	OBP	SLG	PRO+	BR	/A	RC	SB	CS	SBR	FR	POS	TPR

■ JIMMY WILLIAMS Williams, James Thomas b: 12/20/1876, St.Louis, Mo. d: 1/16/65, St.Petersburg, Fla BR/TR, 5'9", 175 lbs. Deb: 4/15/1899

YEAR	TM/L	G	AB	R	H	2B	3B	HR	RBI	BB	SO	AVG	OBP	SLG	PRO+	BR	/A	RC	SB	CS	SBR	FR	POS	TPR
1899	Pit-N	152	617	126	219	28	27	9	116	60		.355	.416	.532	162	51	51	151	26			7	*3	5.1
1900	*Pit-N	106	416	73	110	15	11	5	68	32		.264	.322	.389	97	-2	-2	59	18			6	*3/S	0.4
1901	Bal-A	130	501	113	159	26	21	7	96	56		.317	.388	.495	140	31	27	108	21			-2	*2	1.7
1902	Bal-A	125	498	83	156	27	21	8	83	36		.313	.364	.500	134	25	22	99	14			4	*23/1	2.7
1903	NY-A	132	502	60	134	30	12	3	82	39		.267	.320	.392	108	9	5	68	9			16	*2	2.4
1904	NY-A	146	559	62	147	31	7	2	74	38		.263	.310	.354	107	7	4	69	14			17	*2	2.4
1905	NY-A	129	470	54	107	20	8	6	62	50		.228	.302	.343	95	4	-2	55	14			5	*2	0.2
1906	NY-A	139	501	62	139	25	7	3	77	44		.277	.336	.373	112	14	8	70	8			11	*2	1.7
1907	NY-A	139	504	53	136	17	11	2	63	35		.270	.317	.359	109	9	5	65	14			-1	*2	0.4
1908	StL-A	148	539	63	127	20	7	4	53	55		.236	.306	.321	106	4	4	56	7			5	*2	0.7
1909	StL-A	110	374	32	73	3	6	0	22	29		.195	.257	.235	66	-19	-16	24	6			-6	*2	-2.7
Total	11	1456	5481	781	1507	242	138	49	796	474		.275	.334	.396	116	133	106	824	151			61	*23/S1	15.0

■ KEN WILLIAMS Williams, Kenneth Roy b: 6/28/1890, Grants Pass, Ore. d: 1/22/59, Grants Pass, Ore. BL/TR, 6', 170 lbs. Deb: 7/14/15

YEAR	TM/L	G	AB	R	H	2B	3B	HR	RBI	BB	SO	AVG	OBP	SLG	PRO+	BR	/A	RC	SB	CS	SBR	FR	POS	TPR
1915	Cin-N	71	219	22	53	10	4	0	16	15	20	.242	.297	.324	86	-3	-4	22	4	3	-1	4	O	-0.1
1916	Cin-N	10	27	1	3	0	0	0	1	2	5	.111	.172	.111	-12	-4	-3	1	1			2	O	-0.1
1918	StL-A	2	1	0	0	0	0	0	1	1	0	.000	.500	.000	53	0	0	0	0			0	H	0.0
1919	StL-A	65	227	32	68	10	5	6	35	26	25	.300	.376	.467	133	11	10	42	7			4	O	1.0
1920	StL-A	141	521	90	160	34	13	10	72	41	26	.307	.362	.480	118	14	12	91	18	8	1	8	*O	0.8
1921	StL-A	146	547	115	190	31	7	24	117	74	42	.347	.429	.561	142	42	38	130	20	17	-4	7	*O	2.6
1922	StL-A	153	585	128	194	34	11	39	155	74	31	.332	.413	.627	162	56	53	150	37	19	-0	7	*O	4.6
1923	StL-A	147	555	106	198	37	12	29	91	79	32	.357	.439	.623	168	61	57	148	18	17	-5	11	*O	4.7
1924	StL-A	114	398	78	129	21	4	18	84	69	17	.324	.425	.533	137	28	24	93	20	11	-1	6	*O	2.0
1925	StL-A	102	411	83	136	31	5	25	105	37	14	.331	.390	.613	144	29	26	97	10	5	0	5	*O	1.9
1926	StL-A	108	347	55	97	15	7	17	74	39	23	.280	.354	.510	118	10	8	63	5	4	-1	1	O/2	0.0
1927	StL-A	131	423	70	136	23	6	17	74	57	30	.322	.403	.525	135	24	22	86	9	7	-2	6	*O	1.9
1928	Bos-A	133	462	59	140	25	1	8	67	37	15	.303	.356	.413	104	1	2	66	4	9	-4	-3	O	-1.1
1929	Bos-A	74	139	21	48	14	2	3	21	15	7	.345	.409	.540	146	9	9	29	1	5	-3	-5	O/1	0.3
Total	14	1397	4862	860	1552	285	77	196	913	566	287	.319	.393	.530	136	278	253	1016	154	105		52	*O/12	18.2

■ KEN WILLIAMS Williams, Kenneth Royal b: 4/6/64, Berkeley, Cal. BR/TR, 6'2", 187 lbs. Deb: 9/02/86

YEAR	TM/L	G	AB	R	H	2B	3B	HR	RBI	BB	SO	AVG	OBP	SLG	PRO+	BR	/A	RC	SB	CS	SBR	FR	POS	TPR
1986	Chi-A	15	31	2	4	0	0	1	1	1	11	.129	.182	.226	10	-4	-4	1	1	1	-0	1	O/D	-0.2
1987	Chi-A	116	391	48	110	18	2	11	50	10	83	.281	.315	.422	91	-5	-6	50	21	10	0	2	*O	-0.5
1988	Chi-A	73	220	18	35	4	2	8	28	10	64	.159	.223	.305	46	-16	-16	15	6	5	-1	1	O3/D	-1.7
1989	Det-A	94	258	29	53	5	1	6	23	18	63	.205	.270	.302	63	-13	-13	21	9	4	0	5	O/1D	-0.8
1990	Det-A	57	83	10	11	2	0	0	5	3	24	.133	.172	.157	-7	-12	-12	2	2	2	-1	8	O/D	-0.4
	Tor-A	49	72	13	14	6	1	0	8	7	18	.194	.275	.306	63	-4	-4	7	7	2	1	1	O/D	-0.1
	Yr	106	155	23	25	8	1	0	13	10	42	.161	.222	.226	26	-16	-15	8	9	4	0	9		-0.5
Total	5	404	1055	120	227	35	6	26	115	49	263	.215	.267	.334	63	-54	-54	96	46	24	-1	19	O/3D1	-3.7

■ MARK WILLIAMS Williams, Mark Westley b: 7/28/53, Elmira, N.Y. BL/TL, 6', 180 lbs. Deb: 5/20/77

YEAR	TM/L	G	AB	R	H	2B	3B	HR	RBI	BB	SO	AVG	OBP	SLG	PRO+	BR	/A	RC	SB	CS	SBR	FR	POS	TPR
1977	Oak-A	3	2	0	0	0	0	0	1	1	1	.000	.333	.000	0	-0	-0	0	0	0	0	0	/O	0.0

■ MATT WILLIAMS Williams, Matthew Derrick b: 11/28/65, Bishop, Cal. BR/TR, 6'2", 205 lbs. Deb: 4/11/87

YEAR	TM/L	G	AB	R	H	2B	3B	HR	RBI	BB	SO	AVG	OBP	SLG	PRO+	BR	/A	RC	SB	CS	SBR	FR	POS	TPR
1987	SF-N	84	245	28	46	9	2	8	21	16	68	.188	.240	.339	54	-18	-16	19	4	3	-1	20	S3	1.1
1988	SF-N	52	156	17	32	6	1	8	19	8	41	.205	.253	.410	91	-3	-3	14	0	1	-1	10	3S	0.8
1989	*SF-N	84	292	31	59	18	1	18	50	14	72	.202	.244	.455	98	-4	-3	30	1	2	-1	6	3S	0.4
1990	SF-N	159	617	87	171	27	2	33	122	33	138	.277	.321	.488	121	13	14	92	7	4	-0	4	*3	2.3
Total	4	379	1310	163	308	60	6	67	212	71	319	.235	.281	.444	100	-12	-7	155	12	10	-2	40	3S	4.6

■ OTTO WILLIAMS Williams, Otto George b: 11/2/1877, Newark, N.J. d: 3/19/37, Omaha, Neb. BR/TR, 5'8", 165 lbs. Deb: 10/05/02 C

YEAR	TM/L	G	AB	R	H	2B	3B	HR	RBI	BB	SO	AVG	OBP	SLG	PRO+	BR	/A	RC	SB	CS	SBR	FR	POS	TPR
1902	StL-N	2	5	0	2	0	0	0	2	1		.400	.500	.400	189	1	1	2	1			1	/S	0.2
1903	StL-N	53	187	10	38	4	2	0	9	9		.203	.240	.246	41	-15	-14	13	6			-5	S/2	-1.4
	Chi-N	38	130	14	29	5	0	0	13	4		.223	.246	.262	47	-9	-9	11	8			5	S/213	-0.1
	Yr	91	317	24	67	9	2	0	22	13		.211	.242	.252	44	-24	-22	24	14			0		-1.5
1904	Chi-N	57	185	21	37	4	1	0	8	13		.200	.253	.232	52	-10	-10	14	9			-0	O1S/23	-1.1
1906	Was-A	20	51	3	7	0	0	0	2	2		.137	.170	.137	-3	-6	-6	1	0			0	/S213	-0.5
Total	4	170	558	48	113	13	3	0	34	29		.203	.242	.237	44	-39	-37	41	24			1	/SO213	-2.9

■ REGGIE WILLIAMS Williams, Reginald Dewayne b: 8/29/60, Memphis, Tenn. BR/TR, 5'11", 185 lbs. Deb: 9/02/85

YEAR	TM/L	G	AB	R	H	2B	3B	HR	RBI	BB	SO	AVG	OBP	SLG	PRO+	BR	/A	RC	SB	CS	SBR	FR	POS	TPR
1985	LA-N	22	9	4	3	0	0	0	0	0	4	.333	.333	.333	90	-0	-0	1	1	0	0	2	O	0.2
1986	LA-N	128	303	35	84	14	2	4	32	23	57	.277	.332	.376	102	-2	-0	37	9	3	1	-17	*O	-1.8
1987	LA-N	39	36	6	4	0	0	0	4	5	9	.111	.220	.111	-9	-6	-5	1	1	1	-0	0	O	-0.6
1988	Cle-A	11	31	7	7	2	0	1	3	0	6	.226	.226	.387	66	-1	-2	2	0	0	0	-1	O	-0.2
Total	4	200	379	52	98	16	2	5	39	28	76	.259	.313	.351	87	-9	-7	41	11	4	1	-16	O	-2.4

■ DICK WILLIAMS Williams, Richard Hirschfeld b: 5/7/28, St.Louis, Mo. BR/TR, 6', 190 lbs. Deb: 6/10/51 MC

YEAR	TM/L	G	AB	R	H	2B	3B	HR	RBI	BB	SO	AVG	OBP	SLG	PRO+	BR	/A	RC	SB	CS	SBR	FR	POS	TPR
1951	Bro-N	23	60	5	12	3	1	1	5	4	10	.200	.250	.333	54	-4	-4	5	0	0	0	-2	O	-0.5
1952	Bro-N	36	68	13	21	4	1	0	11	2	10	.309	.329	.397	99	-0	-0	8	0	0	0	3	O/13	0.2
1953	*Bro-N	30	55	4	12	2	0	2	5	3	10	.218	.271	.364	62	-3	-3	6	0	0	0	-2	O	-0.5
1954	Bro-N	16	34	5	5	0	0	1	2	2	7	.147	.194	.235	11	-5	-5	1	0	0	0	-2	O	-0.6
1956	Bro-N	7	7	0	2	0	0	0	0	0	1	.286	.286	.286	50	-0	-1	1	0	0	0	0	H	0.0
	Bal-A	87	353	45	101	18	4	11	37	30	40	.286	.342	.453	117	3	7	52	5	5	-2	-2	O12/3	0.0
1957	Bal-A	47	167	16	39	10	2	1	17	14	21	.234	.293	.335	76	-7	-6	15	0	1	-1	4	O31	-0.2
	Cle-A	67	205	33	58	7	0	6	17	12	19	.283	.326	.405	99	-1	-1	24	3	4	-2	-1	O3	-0.4
	Yr	114	372	49	97	17	2	7	34	26	40	.261	.311	.374	89	-8	-6	39	3	5	-2	4		-0.6
1958	Bal-A	128	409	36	113	17	0	4	32	37	47	.276	.339	.347	94	-5	-3	44	0	6	-4	-2	O31/2	-1.0
1959	KC-A	130	488	72	130	33	1	16	75	28	60	.266	.313	.436	102	1	-0	64	4	1	1	-6	31O/2	-0.6
1960	KC-A	127	420	47	121	31	0	12	65	39	68	.288	.350	.448	113	8	7	62	0	0	0	3	31O	0.8
1961	Bal-A	103	310	37	64	15	2	8	24	20	38	.206	.255	.345	60	-19	-18	25	0	4	-2	-9	O1/3	-3.3
1962	Bal-A	82	178	20	44	7	1	1	18	14	26	.247	.306	.315	71	-8	-7	16	0	0	0	-4	O1/3	-1.3
1963	Bos-A	79	136	15	35	8	0	2	12	15	25	.257	.331	.360	91	-1	-1	17	0	0	0	-4	31/O	-0.5
1964	Bos-A	61	69	10	11	2	0	5	11	7	10	.159	.247	.406	74	-2	-3	6	0	0	0	5	13/O	0.1
Total	13	1023	2959	358	768	157	12	70	331	227	392	.260	.315	.392	92	-44	-38	346	12	21	-9	-17	O31/2	-7.8

■ RINALDO WILLIAMS Williams, Rinaldo Lewis b: 12/18/1893, Santa Cruz, Cal. d: 4/24/66, Cottonwood, Ariz. BL/TR, Deb: 10/08/14

YEAR	TM/L	G	AB	R	H	2B	3B	HR	RBI	BB	SO	AVG	OBP	SLG	PRO+	BR	/A	RC	SB	CS	SBR	FR	POS	TPR
1914	Bro-F	4	15	1	4	2	0	0	0	0	0	.267	.267	.400	90	-0	-0	2	0			0	/3	0.0

■ BOB WILLIAMS Williams, Robert Elias b: 4/27/1884, Monday, Ohio d: 8/6/62, Nelsonville, Ohio BR/TR, 6', 190 lbs. Deb: 7/03/11

YEAR	TM/L	G	AB	R	H	2B	3B	HR	RBI	BB	SO	AVG	OBP	SLG	PRO+	BR	/A	RC	SB	CS	SBR	FR	POS	TPR
1911	NY-A	20	47	3	9	2	0	0	8	5		.191	.269	.234	38	-4	-4	3	1			1	C	0.0
1912	NY-A	20	44	7	6	1	0	0	3	9		.136	.283	.159	26	-4	-4	2	0			-2	C	-0.3
1913	NY-A	6	19	0	3	0	0	0	0	1	3	.158	.200	.158	5	-2	-2	1	0			0	/C	-0.1
1914	NY-A	59	178	9	29	5	2	1	17	26	26	.163	.287	.230	56	-9	-9	12	3	6	-3	-5	1	-1.8
Total	4	105	288	19	47	8	2	1	28	41	29	.163	.278	.215	45	-19	-19	18	4	6		-6	/1C	-2.2

YEAR	TM/L	G	AB	R	H	2B	3B	HR	RBI	BB	SO	AVG	OBP	SLG	PRO+	BR	/A	RC	SB	CS	SBR	FR	POS	TPR

■ **TED WILLIAMS**　Williams, Theodore Samuel "The Kid", "The Thumper" or "The Splendid Splinter"
b: 8/30/18, San Diego, Cal.　BL/TR, 6'3", 205 lbs.　Deb: 4/20/39　MH

YEAR	TM/L	G	AB	R	H	2B	3B	HR	RBI	BB	SO	AVG	OBP	SLG	PRO+	BR	/A	RC	SB	CS	SBR	FR	POS	TPR
1939	Bos-A	149	565	131	185	44	11	31	**145**	107	64	.327	.436	.609	158	56	53	**157**	2	1	0	-2	*O	4.2
1940	Bos-A	144	561	**134**	193	43	14	23	113	96	54	.344	**.442**	.594	159	57	54	154	4	4	-1	0	*O/P	4.0
1941	Bos-A	143	456	135	185	33	3	**37**	120	**145**	27	**.406**	**.551**	**.735**	232	102	100	202	2	4	-2	-5	*O	**8.0**
1942	Bos-A	150	522	**141**	186	34	5	**36**	137	**145**	51	.356	**.499**	.648	214	93	90	185	3	2	-0	4	*O	**8.3**
1946	*Bos-A	150	514	**142**	176	37	8	38	123	**156**	44	.342	**.497**	.667	211	94	90	188	0	0	0	-1	*O	**8.2**
1947	Bos-A	156	528	**125**	181	40	9	**32**	114	**162**	47	**.343**	**.499**	.634	199	91	86	186	0	1	-1	3	*O	**8.2**
1948	Bos-A	137	509	124	188	**44**	3	25	127	**126**	41	**.369**	**.497**	.615	185	76	72	172	4	0	1	-1	*O	6.3
1949	Bos-A	155	566	**150**	194	**39**	3	**43**	159	**162**	48	.343	**.490**	.650	187	89	83	193	1	1	-0	0	*O	**7.5**
1950	Bos-A	89	334	82	106	24	1	28	97	82	21	.317	.452	.647	163	41	36	103	3	0	1	-4	*O	2.8
1951	Bos-A	148	531	109	169	28	4	30	126	**144**	45	.318	**.464**	.556	159	63	55	152	1	1	-0	6	*O	**5.3**
1952	Bos-A	6	10	2	4	0	1	1	3	2	2	.400	.500	.900	264	2	2	5	0	0	0	0	/O	0.2
1953	Bos-A	37	91	17	37	6	0	13	34	19	10	.407	.509	.901	261	22	22	44	0	1	-1	-5	O	1.5
1954	Bos-A	117	386	93	133	23	1	29	89	**136**	32	**.345**	**.516**	.635	193	71	65	139	0	0	0	-7	*O	**5.5**
1955	Bos-A	98	320	77	114	21	3	28	83	91	24	.356	.501	.703	203	59	55	118	2	0	1	-4	*O	4.6
1956	Bos-A	136	400	71	138	28	2	24	82	102	39	.345	**.479**	.605	164	54	47	121	0	0	0	-10	*O	3.0
1957	Bos-A	132	420	96	163	28	1	38	87	119	43	**.388**	**.528**	**.731**	227	90	86	167	0	1	-1	-9	*O	7.0
1958	Bos-A	129	411	81	135	23	2	26	85	98	49	**.328**	**.462**	.584	174	54	50	112	1	0	0	-17	*O	2.6
1959	Bos-A	103	272	32	69	15	0	10	43	52	27	.254	.377	.419	113	8	7	45	0	0	0	-11	O	-0.8
1960	Bos-A	113	310	56	98	15	0	29	72	75	41	.316	.454	.645	187	43	42	95	1	1	-0	-4	O	3.4
Total	19	2292	7706	1798	2654	525	71	521	1839	2019	709	.344	.483	.634	186	1166	1093	2538	24	17	-3	-67	*O/P	89.8

■ **WALT WILLIAMS**　Williams, Walter Allen "No-Neck"　b: 12/19/43, Brownwood, Tex.　BR/TR, 5'6", 165 lbs.　Deb: 4/21/64　C

YEAR	TM/L	G	AB	R	H	2B	3B	HR	RBI	BB	SO	AVG	OBP	SLG	PRO+	BR	/A	RC	SB	CS	SBR	FR	POS	TPR
1964	Hou-N	10	9	1	0	0	0	0	0	0	2	.000	.000	.000	-99	-2	-2	0	1	0	0	0	/O	-0.1
1967	Chi-A	104	275	35	66	16	3	3	15	17	20	.240	.289	.353	92	-4	-3	27	3	2	-0	-2	O	-0.8
1968	Chi-A	63	133	6	32	6	0	1	8	4	17	.241	.273	.308	75	-4	-4	10	0	1	-1	-2	O	-0.8
1969	Chi-A	135	471	59	143	22	1	3	32	26	33	.304	.344	.374	96	0	-3	62	6	2	1	1	*O	-0.3
1970	Chi-A	110	315	43	79	18	1	3	15	19	30	.251	.298	.343	73	-11	-12	32	3	3	-1	-1	O	-1.7
1971	Chi-A	114	361	43	106	17	3	8	35	24	27	.294	.346	.424	114	7	6	52	5	5	-2	-3	O/3	0.0
1972	Chi-A	77	221	22	55	7	1	2	11	13	20	.249	.291	.317	79	-6	-6	21	6	1	1	-0	O/3	-0.6
1973	Cle-A	104	350	43	101	15	1	8	38	14	29	.289	.318	.406	101	0	-1	43	9	4	0	-0	OD	-0.2
1974	NY-A	43	53	5	6	0	0	0	3	1	10	.113	.130	.113	-31	-9	-9	1	1	0	0	1	O/D	-0.7
1975	NY-A	82	185	27	52	5	1	5	16	9	23	.281	.321	.400	106	0	1	23	0	1	-1	-1	OD/2	-0.1
Total	10	842	2373	284	640	106	11	33	173	126	211	.270	.311	.365	91	-28	-32	270	34	19	-1	-5	O/D23	-5.3

■ **WASH WILLIAMS**　Williams, Washington J.　b: Philadelphia, Pa.　d: 1/1890, Philadelphia, Pa.　5'11", 180 lbs.　Deb: 8/05/1884

YEAR	TM/L	G	AB	R	H	2B	3B	HR	RBI	BB	SO	AVG	OBP	SLG	PRO+	BR	/A	RC	SB	CS	SBR	FR	POS	TPR
1884	Ric-a	2	8	0	2	0	0	0		0		.250	.250	.250	67	-0	-0	1				-1	/O	0.0
1885	Chi-N	1	4	0	1	0	0	0	0	0	0	.250	.250	.250	54	-0	-0	0				-0	/OP	0.0
Total	2	3	12	0	3	0	0	0	0	0	0	.250	.250	.250	62	-0	-1	1				-1	/OP	0.0

■ **BILLY WILLIAMS**　Williams, William　b: 6/13/33, Newberry, S.C.　BL/TR, 6'3", 195 lbs.　Deb: 8/15/69

YEAR	TM/L	G	AB	R	H	2B	3B	HR	RBI	BB	SO	AVG	OBP	SLG	PRO+	BR	/A	RC	SB	CS	SBR	FR	POS	TPR
1969	Sea-A	4	10	1	0	0	0	0	0	1	3	.000	.167	.000	-51	-2	-2	0	0	0	0	1	/O	-0.1

■ **WOODY WILLIAMS**　Williams, Woodrow Wilson　b: 8/22/12, Pamplin, Va.　BR/TR, 5'11", 175 lbs.　Deb: 9/05/38

YEAR	TM/L	G	AB	R	H	2B	3B	HR	RBI	BB	SO	AVG	OBP	SLG	PRO+	BR	/A	RC	SB	CS	SBR	FR	POS	TPR
1938	Bro-N	20	51	6	17	1	1	0	6	4	1	.333	.382	.392	111	1	1	8	1			-7	S/3	-0.4
1943	Cin-N	30	69	8	26	2	1	0	11	1	3	.377	.386	.435	139	3	3	11	0			1	2/3S	0.5
1944	Cin-N	155	653	73	157	23	3	1	35	44	24	.240	.290	.289	66	-31	-28	56	7			15	*2	0.2
1945	Cin-N	133	482	46	114	14	0	0	27	39	24	.237	.296	.266	58	-27	-26	40	6			-10	*2	-2.5
Total	4	338	1255	133	314	40	5	1	79	88	52	.250	.301	.292	69	-55	-51	115	14			-1	2/S3	-2.2

■ **NED WILLIAMSON**　Williamson, Edward Nagle　b: 10/24/1857, Philadelphia, Pa.　d: 3/3/1894, Willow Springs, Ark　BR/TR, 5'11", 170 lbs.　Deb: 5/01/1878

YEAR	TM/L	G	AB	R	H	2B	3B	HR	RBI	BB	SO	AVG	OBP	SLG	PRO+	BR	/A	RC	SB	CS	SBR	FR	POS	TPR
1878	Ind-N	63	250	31	58	10	2	1	19	5	15	.232	.247	.300	91	-6	-1	19				-4	*3	-0.1
1879	Chi-N	80	320	66	94	20	13	1	36	24	31	.294	.343	.447	149	20	18	50				18	*3/1C	3.3
1880	Chi-N	75	311	65	78	20	2	0	31	15	26	.251	.285	.328	101	3	0	30				13	*3C/2	1.3
1881	Chi-N	82	343	56	92	12	6	1	48	19	19	.268	.307	.347	100	2	-0	37				22	*3/2PSC	2.7
1882	Chi-N	83	348	66	98	27	4	3	60	27	21	.282	.333	.408	130	15	12	49				15	*3/P	2.5
1883	Chi-N	98	402	83	111	**49**	5	2	59	22	48	.276	.314	.438	118	12	8	57				17	*3/CP	2.3
1884	Chi-N	107	417	84	116	18	8	**27**	84	42	56	.278	.344	.554	164	37	31	82				24	*3C/P	4.5
1885	*Chi-N	113	407	87	97	16	5	3	65	**75**	60	.238	.357	.324	106	14	4	48				11	*3/PC	1.6
1886	*Chi-N	121	430	69	93	17	8	6	58	80	71	.216	.339	.335	92	6	-5	55	13			-1	*S/CP	-0.5
1887	Chi-N	127	439	77	117	20	14	9	78	73	57	.267	.377	.437	113	19	8	92	45			-31	*S/P	-2.3
1888	Chi-N	132	452	75	113	9	14	8	73	65	71	.250	.352	.385	128	21	17	72	25			-11	*S	0.9
1889	Chi-N	47	173	16	41	3	1	1	30	23	22	.237	.340	.283	73	-4	-6	18	2			-24	S	-2.4
1890	Chi-P	73	261	34	51	7	3	2	26	36	35	.195	.311	.268	55	-15	-17	23	3			-20	3S	-2.5
Total	13	1201	4553	809	1159	228	85	64	667	506	532	.255	.332	.384	112	123	68	630	88			31	3S/CP21	11.3

■ **HOWIE WILLIAMSON**　Williamson, Nathaniel Howard　b: 12/23/04, Little Rock, Ark.　d: 8/15/69, Texarkana, Ark.　BL/TL, 6', 170 lbs.　Deb: 7/07/28

YEAR	TM/L	G	AB	R	H	2B	3B	HR	RBI	BB	SO	AVG	OBP	SLG	PRO+	BR	/A	RC	SB	CS	SBR	FR	POS	TPR
1928	StL-N	10	9	0	2	0	0	0	0	1	4	.222	.300	.222	38	-1	-1	1	0			0	H	0.0

■ **JULIUS WILLIGROD**　Willigrod, Julius　b: 1870, Iowa　d: 11/27/06, San Francisco, Cal　BL　Deb: 7/15/1882

YEAR	TM/L	G	AB	R	H	2B	3B	HR	RBI	BB	SO	AVG	OBP	SLG	PRO+	BR	/A	RC	SB	CS	SBR	FR	POS	TPR
1882	Det-N	1	3	0	1	0	0	0	1	0	1	.333	.333	.333	115	0	0	0				-1	/S	0.0
	Cle-N	9	36	5	5	1	1	0	2	3	7	.139	.205	.222	38	-2	-2	2				-2	/O	-0.3
	Yr	10	39	5	6	1	1	0	3	3	8	.154	.214	.231	44	-2	-2	2				-3		-0.3

■ **HUGH WILLINGHAM**　Willingham, Thomas Hugh　b: 5/30/06, Dalhart, Tex.　d: 6/15/88, ElReno, Okla.　BR/TR, 6', 180 lbs.　Deb: 9/13/30

YEAR	TM/L	G	AB	R	H	2B	3B	HR	RBI	BB	SO	AVG	OBP	SLG	PRO+	BR	/A	RC	SB	CS	SBR	FR	POS	TPR
1930	Chi-A	3	4	2	1	0	0	0	0	2	1	.250	.500	.250	100	0	0	1	0	0	0	-0	/2	0.0
1931	Phi-N	23	35	5	9	2	1	1	3	2	9	.257	.297	.457	93	-0	-1	5	0			1	/S3O	0.1
1932	Phi-N	4	2	0	0	0	0	0	0	0	0	.000	.000	.000	-89	-1	-1	0	0			0	H	0.0
1933	Phi-N	1	1	0	0	0	0	0	0	0	0	.000	.000	.000	-89	-0	-0	0	0			0	H	0.0
Total	4	31	42	7	10	2	1	1	3	4	10	.238	.304	.405	82	-1	-1	6	0	0		0	/S3O2	0.1

■ **WILLS**　Wills　Deb: 5/14/1884

YEAR	TM/L	G	AB	R	H	2B	3B	HR	RBI	BB	SO	AVG	OBP	SLG	PRO+	BR	/A	RC	SB	CS	SBR	FR	POS	TPR
1884	Was-a	4	15	1	2	2	0	0		0		.133	.133	.267	32	-1	-1	1				2	/O	0.1
	KC-U	5	21	2	3	1	0	0		0		.143	.143	.190	14	-2	-1	1	0			1	/O	0.0

■ **DAVE WILLS**　Wills, Davis Bowles　b: 1/26/1877, Charlottesville, Va.　d: 10/12/59, Washington, D.C.　BL/TL,　Deb: 6/08/1899

YEAR	TM/L	G	AB	R	H	2B	3B	HR	RBI	BB	SO	AVG	OBP	SLG	PRO+	BR	/A	RC	SB	CS	SBR	FR	POS	TPR
1899	Lou-N	24	94	15	21	3	1	0	12	2		.223	.240	.277	43	-7	-7	7	1			-3	1	-0.8

■ **BUMP WILLS**　Wills, Elliott Taylor　b: 7/27/52, Washington, D.C.　BB/TR, 5'9", 172 lbs.　Deb: 4/07/77

YEAR	TM/L	G	AB	R	H	2B	3B	HR	RBI	BB	SO	AVG	OBP	SLG	PRO+	BR	/A	RC	SB	CS	SBR	FR	POS	TPR
1977	Tex-A	152	541	87	155	28	6	9	62	65	96	.287	.363	.410	109	9	8	83	28	12	1	3	*2/S1D	2.4
1978	Tex-A	157	539	78	135	17	4	9	57	63	59	.250	.333	.347	91	-5	-5	68	52	14	7	21	*2	3.2
1979	Tex-A	146	543	90	148	21	3	5	46	53	58	.273	.342	.350	88	-9	-8	68	35	11	4	7	*2	0.9
1980	Tex-A	146	578	102	152	31	5	5	58	51	71	.263	.326	.360	90	-9	-7	73	34	9	5	19	*2	2.4
1981	Tex-A	102	410	51	103	13	2	2	41	32	49	.251	.307	.307	82	-12	-9	38	12	9	-2	8	*2/D	0.1

YEAR	TM/L	G	AB	R	H	2B	3B	HR	RBI	BB	SO	AVG	OBP	SLG	PRO+	BR	/A	RC	SB	CS	SBR	FR	POS	TPR
1982	Chi-N	128	419	64	114	18	4	6	38	46	76	.272	.351	.377	101	3	2	61	35	10	5	-18	*2	-0.7
Total	6	831	3030	472	807	128	24	36	302	310	441	.266	.338	.360	94	-22	-19	390	196	65	20	40	2/DS1	8.3

■ MAURY WILLS

Wills, Maurice Morning b: 10/2/32, Washington, D.C. BB/TR, 5'11", 170 lbs. Deb: 6/06/59 M

YEAR	TM/L	G	AB	R	H	2B	3B	HR	RBI	BB	SO	AVG	OBP	SLG	PRO+	BR	/A	RC	SB	CS	SBR	FR	POS	TPR
1959	*LA-N	83	242	27	63	5	2	0	7	13	27	.260	.298	.298	55	-14	-16	22	7	3	0	2	S	-1.0
1960	LA-N	148	516	75	152	15	2	0	27	35	47	.295	.343	.331	80	-9	-13	62	50	12	8	21	*S	2.1
1961	LA-N	148	613	105	173	12	10	1	31	59	50	.282	.346	.339	76	-13	-20	77	35	15	2	12	*S	0.7
1962	LA-N	165	695	130	208	13	10	6	48	51	57	.299	.349	.373	100	-5	0	106	104	13	23	-4	*S	3.4
1963	*LA-N	134	527	83	159	19	3	0	34	44	48	.302	.357	.349	112	4	8	69	40	19	1	-5	*S3	1.5
1964	LA-N	158	630	81	173	15	5	2	34	41	73	.275	.319	.324	88	-15	-9	70	53	17	6	-7	*S/3	0.0
1965	*LA-N	158	650	92	186	14	7	0	33	40	64	.286	.331	.329	93	-11	-6	77	94	31	10	21	*S	4.4
1966	*LA-N	143	594	60	162	14	2	1	39	34	60	.273	.314	.308	80	-20	-15	57	38	24	-3	9	*S/3	0.3
1967	Pit-N	149	616	92	186	12	9	3	45	31	44	.302	.336	.365	100	0	0	78	29	10	3	9	*3/S	0.5
1968	Pit-N	153	627	76	174	12	6	0	31	45	57	.278	.327	.316	95	-4	-3	67	52	21	3	-9	*3S	-0.9
1969	Mon-N	47	189	23	42	3	0	0	8	20	21	.222	.297	.238	51	-12	-12	15	15	6	1	-3	S/2	-0.8
	LA-N	104	434	57	129	7	8	4	39	39	40	.297	.357	.378	114	4	8	59	25	15	-1	7	*S	2.6
	Yr	151	623	80	171	10	8	4	47	59	61	.274	.338	.335	94	-8	-4	73	40	21	-1	5		1.8
1970	LA-N	132	522	77	141	19	3	0	34	50	34	.270	.334	.318	79	-17	-14	57	28	13	1	-19	*S/3	-1.6
1971	LA-N	149	601	73	169	14	3	3	44	40	44	.281	.326	.329	92	-11	-7	66	15	8	-0	1	*S/3	1.4
1972	LA-N	71	132	16	17	3	1	0	4	10	18	.129	.190	.167	2	-17	-17	5	1	1	-0	-4	S3	-1.8
Total	14	1942	7588	1067	2134	177	71	20	458	552	684	.281	.331	.331	88	-139	-115	885	586	208	51	31	*S3/2	10.8

■ KID WILLSON

Willson, Frank Hoxie b: 11/3/1895, Bloomington, Neb. d: 4/17/64, Union Gap, Wash. BL/TL, 6'1", 190 lbs. Deb: 7/02/18

YEAR	TM/L	G	AB	R	H	2B	3B	HR	RBI	BB	SO	AVG	OBP	SLG	PRO+	BR	/A	RC	SB	CS	SBR	FR	POS	TPR
1918	Chi-A	4	1	2	0	0	0	0	0	1	1	.000	.500	.000	50	0	0	0	0			0	H	0.0
1927	Chi-A	7	10	1	1	0	0	0	1	0	2	.100	.100	.100	-49	-2	-2	0	0	0	0	0	/O	-0.1
Total	2	11	11	3	1	0	0	0	1	1	3	.091	.167	.091	-31	-2	-2	0	0	0		0	/O	-0.1

■ WALT WILMOT

Wilmot, Walter Robert b: 10/18/1863, Plover, Wis. d: 2/1/29, Chicago, Ill. BB/TR, Deb: 4/20/1888

YEAR	TM/L	G	AB	R	H	2B	3B	HR	RBI	BB	SO	AVG	OBP	SLG	PRO+	BR	/A	RC	SB	CS	SBR	FR	POS	TPR
1888	Was-N	119	473	61	106	16	9	4	43	23	55	.224	.263	.321	93	-7	-3	53	46			11	*O	0.6
1889	Was-N	108	432	88	125	19	19	9	57	51	32	.289	.367	.484	147	21	26	94	40			14	*O	3.0
1890	Chi-N	139	571	114	159	15	12	13	99	64	44	.278	.353	.415	121	18	14	113	76			10	*O	1.9
1891	Chi-N	121	498	102	139	14	10	11	71	55	21	.279	.357	.414	127	16	17	91	42			-5	*O	0.5
1892	Chi-N	92	380	47	82	7	7	2	35	40	20	.216	.297	.287	78	-9	-10	43	31			2	O	-0.9
1893	Chi-N	94	392	69	118	14	14	3	61	40	8	.301	.367	.431	116	7	8	78	39			-0	*O	0.4
1894	Chi-N	133	597	134	197	45	12	5	130	35	23	.330	.368	.471	97	1	-6	134	74			-6	*O	-1.5
1895	Chi-N	108	466	86	132	16	6	8	72	30	19	.283	.327	.395	82	-10	-15	71	28			4	*O	-1.6
1897	NY-N	11	34	8	9	2	0	1	4	2		.265	.306	.412	93	-1	-0	5	1			0	O	0.0
1898	NY-N	35	138	16	33	4	2	2	22	9		.239	.286	.341	84	-4	-3	15	4			-5	O	-0.8
Total	10	960	3981	725	1100	152	91	58	594	349	222	.276	.337	.404	107	33	28	697	381			24	O	1.6

■ ARCHIE WILSON

Wilson, Archie Clifton b: 11/25/23, Los Angeles, Cal. BR/TR, 5'11", 175 lbs. Deb: 9/18/51

YEAR	TM/L	G	AB	R	H	2B	3B	HR	RBI	BB	SO	AVG	OBP	SLG	PRO+	BR	/A	RC	SB	CS	SBR	FR	POS	TPR
1951	NY-A	4	4	0	0	0	0	0	0	0	0	.000	.200	.000	-44	-1	-1	0	0	0	0	0	/O	0.0
1952	NY-A	3	2	0	1	0	0	0	1	0	0	.500	.500	.500	190	0	0	1	0	0	0	0	H	0.0
	Was-A	26	96	8	20	2	3	0	14	5	11	.208	.255	.292	54	-6	-6	5	0	0	0	1	O	-0.5
	Bos-A	18	38	1	10	3	0	0	2	2	3	.263	.300	.342	73	-1	-2	4	0	0	0	-0	O	-0.1
	Yr	47	136	9	31	5	3	0	17	7	14	.228	.271	.309	61	-7	-8	9	0	0	0	1		-0.6
Total	2	51	140	9	31	5	3	0	17	7	14	.221	.268	.300	58	-8	-8	9	0	0	0	1	/O	-0.6

■ ART WILSON

Wilson, Arthur Earl "Dutch" b: 12/11/1885, Macon, Ill. d: 6/12/60, Chicago, Ill. BR/TR, 5'8", 170 lbs. Deb: 9/29/08

YEAR	TM/L	G	AB	R	H	2B	3B	HR	RBI	BB	SO	AVG	OBP	SLG	PRO+	BR	/A	RC	SB	CS	SBR	FR	POS	TPR
1908	NY-N	1	0	0	0	0	0	0	0	0		—	—	—	—	—	0	0	0	0			0	R	0.0
1909	NY-N	19	42	4	10	2	1	0	5	4		.238	.304	.333	96	-0	-0	4	0			-4	C	-0.2
1910	NY-N	26	52	10	14	4	1	0	5	9	6	.269	.387	.385	125	2	2	9	2			-1	C/1	0.3
1911	*NY-N	66	109	17	33	9	1	1	17	19	12	.303	.411	.431	132	6	5	22	6			-6	C	0.4
1912	*NY-N	65	121	17	35	6	0	3	19	13	14	.289	.358	.413	107	2	1	19	2			1	C	0.5
1913	*NY-N	54	79	5	15	0	1	0	8	11	11	.190	.289	.215	45	-5	-5	5	1			7	C	0.4
1914	Chi-F	137	440	78	128	31	8	10	64	70	80	.291	.394	.466	155	28	32	90	13			15	*C	5.4
1915	Chi-F	96	269	44	82	11	2	7	31	65	38	.305	.442	.439	171	25	27	60	8			-6	C	2.4
1916	Pit-N	53	128	11	33	5	2	1	12	13	27	.258	.331	.352	109	2	2	17	4			-8	C	-0.4
	Chi-N	36	114	5	22	3	1	0	5	6	14	.193	.233	.237	40	-7	-9	7	1			-3	C	-1.1
	Yr	89	242	16	55	8	3	1	17	19	41	.227	.286	.298	76	-6	-7	23	5			-11		-1.5
1917	Chi-N	81	211	17	45	9	2	2	25	32	36	.213	.322	.303	86	-1	-3	22	6			8	C	1.0
1918	Bos-N	89	280	15	69	8	2	0	19	24	31	.246	.310	.289	87	-5	-4	26	5			-10	C	-0.7
1919	Bos-N	71	191	14	49	8	1	0	16	25	19	.257	.346	.309	102	1	1	22	2			-2	C/1	0.4
1920	Bos-N	16	19	0	1	0	0	0	0	1	1	.053	.143	.053	-44	-3	-3	0	0	0	0	-2	/3C	-0.4
1921	Cle-A	2	1	0	0	0	0	0	0	0	0	.000	.000	.000	-99	-0	-0	0	0	0	0	-0	/C	-0.0
Total	14	812	2056	237	536	96	22	24	226	292	289	.261	.357	.364	114	42	46	302	50	0		-10	C/31	8.0

■ ARTIE WILSON

Wilson, Arthur Lee b: 10/28/20, Springfield, Ala. BL/TR, 5'10", 162 lbs. Deb: 4/18/51

YEAR	TM/L	G	AB	R	H	2B	3B	HR	RBI	BB	SO	AVG	OBP	SLG	PRO+	BR	/A	RC	SB	CS	SBR	FR	POS	TPR
1951	NY-N	19	22	2	4	0	0	0	1	2	1	.182	.250	.182	18	-2	-3	1	2	0	1	3	/2S1	0.1

■ CHARLIE WILSON

Wilson, Charles Woodrow "Swamp Baby" b: 1/13/05, Clinton, S.C. d: 12/19/70, Rochester, N.Y. BB/TR, 5'10.5", 178 lbs. Deb: 4/14/31

YEAR	TM/L	G	AB	R	H	2B	3B	HR	RBI	BB	SO	AVG	OBP	SLG	PRO+	BR	/A	RC	SB	CS	SBR	FR	POS	TPR
1931	Bos-N	16	58	7	11	4	0	1	11	3	5	.190	.230	.310	45	-5	-5	4	0			-2	3	-0.5
1932	StL-N	24	96	7	19	3	3	1	2	3	8	.198	.222	.323	43	-8	-8	7	0			-7	S	-1.2
1933	StL-N	1	1	0	0	0	0	0	0	0	1	.000	.000	.000	-95	-0	-0	0	0			0	/S	0.0
1935	StL-N	16	31	1	10	0	0	0	1	2	2	.323	.364	.323	83	-0	-1	3	0			-1	/3	0.0
Total	4	57	186	15	40	7	3	2	14	8	16	.215	.247	.317	50	-13	-13	14	0			-9	/S3	-1.7

■ CRAIG WILSON

Wilson, Craig b: 11/28/64, Annapolis, Md. BR/TR, 5'11", 175 lbs. Deb: 9/06/89

YEAR	TM/L	G	AB	R	H	2B	3B	HR	RBI	BB	SO	AVG	OBP	SLG	PRO+	BR	/A	RC	SB	CS	SBR	FR	POS	TPR
1989	StL-N	6	4	1	1	0	0	0	1	1	2	.250	.400	.250	87	0	-0	1	0	0	0	-0	/3	0.0
1990	StL-N	55	121	13	30	2	0	0	7	8	14	.248	.295	.264	53	-7	-8	8	0	2	-1	0	3O/21	-0.8
Total	2	61	125	14	31	2	0	0	8	9	16	.248	.299	.264	55	-7	-8	8	0	2	-1	-0	/3O21	-0.8

■ EDDIE WILSON

Wilson, Edward Francis b: 9/7/09, Hamden, Conn. d: 4/11/79, Hamden, Conn. BL/TL, 5'11", 165 lbs. Deb: 6/21/36

YEAR	TM/L	G	AB	R	H	2B	3B	HR	RBI	BB	SO	AVG	OBP	SLG	PRO+	BR	/A	RC	SB	CS	SBR	FR	POS	TPR
1936	Bro-N	52	173	28	60	8	1	3	25	14	25	.347	.402	.457	129	8	8	34	3			-5	O	0.0
1937	Bro-N	36	54	11	12	4	1	1	8	17	14	.222	.408	.389	116	2	2	11	1			-0	O	0.1
Total	2	88	227	39	72	12	2	4	33	31	39	.317	.404	.441	126	10	10	44	4			-6	/O	0.1

■ FRANK WILSON

Wilson, Francis Edward "Squash" b: 4/20/01, Malden, Mass. d: 11/25/74, Leicester, Mass. BL/TR, 6', 185 lbs. Deb: 6/20/24

YEAR	TM/L	G	AB	R	H	2B	3B	HR	RBI	BB	SO	AVG	OBP	SLG	PRO+	BR	/A	RC	SB	CS	SBR	FR	POS	TPR
1924	Bos-N	61	215	20	51	7	0	1	15	23	22	.237	.311	.284	63	-11	-10	20	3	4	-2	2	O	-1.0
1925	Bos-N	12	31	3	13	1	1	0	0	4	1	.419	.486	.516	171	3	3	8	2	1	0	1	O	0.4
1926	Bos-N	87	236	22	56	11	3	0	23	20	21	.237	.300	.309	70	-12	-9	22	3			-1	O	-1.2
1928	Cle-A	2	2	1	0	0	0	0	0	0	1	.000	.500	.000	41	0	0	0	0	0	0	-0	H	0.0
	StL-A	6	5	1	0	0	0	0	0	0	0	.000	.000	.000	-97	-1	-1	0	0	0	0	-0	/O	-0.1
	Yr	8	6	1	0	0	0	0	0	1	0	.000	.143	.000	-58	-1	-1	0	0	0	0	-0		-0.1
Total	4	168	488	46	120	19	4	1	38	48	44	.246	.315	.307	72	-22	-17	50	8	5		2	O	-1.9

YEAR	TM/L	G	AB	R	H	2B	3B	HR	RBI	BB	SO	AVG	OBP	SLG	PRO+	BR	/A	RC	SB	CS	SBR	FR	POS	TPR

■ TUG WILSON
Wilson, George Archer b: 1860, Brooklyn, N.Y. d: 11/28/14, New York, N.Y. Deb: 5/09/1884

1884	Bro-a	24	82	13	19	4	0	0		5		.232	.276	.280	84	-1	-1	7				-2	OC/12	-0.2

■ SQUANTO WILSON
Wilson, George Francis b: 3/29/1889, Old Town, Me. d: 3/26/67, Winthrop, Maine BB/TR, 5'9.5", 170 lbs. Deb: 10/02/11

1911	Det-A	5	16	2	3	0	0	0	0	2		.188	.278	.188	29	-1	-2	1	0			-1	/C	-0.1
1914	Bos-A	1	0	0	0	0	0	0	0	0	0	—	—	—	—	0	0	0	0			0	/1	0.0
Total	2	6	16	2	3	0	0	0	0	2	0	.188	.278	.188	29	-1	-2	1	0			-1	/C1	-0.1

■ ICEHOUSE WILSON
Wilson, George Peacock b: 9/14/12, Maricopa, Cal. d: 10/13/73, Moraga, Cal. BR/TR, 6', 186 lbs. Deb: 5/31/34

1934	Det-A	1	1	0	0	0	0	0	0	0	0	.000	.000	.000	-99	-0	-0	0	0	0	0	0	H	0.0

■ GEORGE WILSON
Wilson, George Washington "Teddy" b: 8/30/25, Cherryville, N.C. d: 10/29/74, Gastonia, N.C. BL/TR, 6'1.5", 185 lbs. Deb: 4/15/52

1952	Chi-A	8	9	0	1	0	0	0	1	1	2	.111	.200	.111	-12	-1	-1	0	0	0	0	0	/O	0.0
	NY-N	62	112	9	27	7	0	2	16	3	14	.241	.261	.357	69	-5	-5	11	0	0	0	-2	O/1	-0.7
1953	NY-N	11	8	0	1	0	0	0	0	2	2	.125	.364	.125	34	-1	-1	1	0	0	0	0	H	0.0
1956	NY-N	53	68	5	9	1	0	1	2	5	14	.132	.192	.191	3	-9	-9	3	0	0	0	0	/O	-0.9
	*NY-A	11	12	1	2	0	0	0	0	3	0	.167	.333	.167	37	-1	-1	1	0	0	0	-1	/O	-0.1
Total	3	145	209	15	40	8	0	3	19	14	32	.191	.246	.273	41	-17	-17	15	0	0	0	-2	/O1	-1.7

■ GLENN WILSON
Wilson, Glenn Dwight b: 12/22/58, Baytown, Tex. BR/TR, 6'1", 190 lbs. Deb: 4/15/82

1982	Det-A	84	322	39	94	15	1	12	34	15	51	.292	.323	.457	111	4	4	44	2	3	-1	3	O/D	0.3
1983	Det-A	144	503	55	135	25	6	11	65	25	79	.268	.307	.408	97	-5	-3	61	1	1	-0	-12	*O	-1.6
1984	Phi-N	132	341	28	82	21	3	6	31	17	56	.240	.279	.372	80	-9	-10	33	7	1	2	-6	*O/3	-1.9
1985	Phi-N	161	608	73	167	39	5	14	102	35	117	.275	.314	.424	102	2	-0	73	7	4	-0	15	*O	1.1
1986	Phi-N	155	584	70	158	30	4	15	84	42	91	.271	.324	.413	98	0	-2	76	5	1	1	16	*O	1.2
1987	Phi-N	154	569	55	150	21	2	14	54	38	82	.264	.311	.381	80	-15	-17	62	3	6	-5	11	*O/P	-1.5
1988	Sea-A	78	284	28	71	10	1	3	17	15	52	.250	.288	.324	68	-11	-13	23	1	1	-0	-1	O/D	-1.5
	Pit-N	37	126	11	34	8	0	2	15	3	18	.270	.292	.381	93	-2	-2	13	0	0	0	-1	O	-0.2
1989	Pit-N	100	330	42	93	20	4	9	49	32	39	.282	.347	.448	130	11	12	49	1	4	-2	-4	O1	0.4
	Hou-N	28	102	8	22	6	0	2	15	5	14	.216	.252	.333	68	-5	-4	8	0	1	-1	3	O	-0.2
	Yr	128	432	50	115	26	4	11	64	37	53	.266	.326	.421	116	6	8	56	1	5	-3	-2		0.2
1990	Hou-N	118	368	42	90	14	0	10	55	26	64	.245	.296	.364	82	-10	-9	35	0	3	-2	6	*O/1	-0.8
Total	9	1191	4137	451	1096	209	26	98	521	253	663	.265	.309	.399	93	-41	-45	479	27	25	-7	30	*O/1D3P	-4.7

■ GRADY WILSON
Wilson, Grady Herbert b: 11/23/22, Columbus, Ga. BR/TR, 6'0.5", 170 lbs. Deb: 5/15/48

1948	Pit-N	12	10	1	1	1	0	0	1	0	3	.100	.100	.200	-20	-2	-2	0	0			1	/S	0.0

■ HENRY WILSON
Wilson, Henry C. b: Baltimore, Md. Deb: 10/12/1898

1898	Bal-N	1	2	0	0	0	0	0	0		1	.000	.333	.000	0	-0	-0	0	0			1	/C	0.0

■ JIMMY WILSON
Wilson, James "Ace" b: 7/23/1900, Philadelphia, Pa. d: 5/31/47, Bradenton, Fla. BR/TR, 6'1.5", 200 lbs. Deb: 4/17/23 MC

1923	Phi-N	85	252	27	66	9	0	1	25	4	17	.262	.276	.310	49	-17	-21	21	4	2	0	-2	C/O	-1.8
1924	Phi-N	95	280	32	78	16	3	6	39	17	12	.279	.322	.421	87	-2	-6	37	5	4	-1	6	C/1O	0.0
1925	Phi-N	108	335	42	110	19	3	3	54	32	25	.328	.390	.430	100	6	1	57	5	3	-0	-9	C/O	-0.2
1926	Phi-N	90	279	40	85	10	2	4	32	25	20	.305	.362	.398	99	2	0	40	3			1	C	0.3
1927	Phi-N	128	443	50	122	15	2	2	45	34	15	.275	.330	.332	77	-13	-14	48	13			-18	*C	-2.3
1928	Phi-N	21	70	11	21	4	1	0	13	9	8	.300	.380	.386	97	0	0	10	3			1	C	0.3
	*StL-N	120	411	45	106	26	2	2	50	45	24	.258	.333	.345	76	-13	-14	48	9			0	*C	-0.5
	Yr	141	481	56	127	30	3	2	63	54	32	.264	.340	.351	79	-13	-14	58	12			2		-0.2
1929	StL-N	120	394	59	128	27	8	4	71	43	19	.325	.394	.464	111	8	7	71	4			4	*C	1.9
1930	*StL-N	107	362	54	115	25	7	1	58	28	17	.318	.368	.434	90	-4	-6	57	8			10	C	0.8
1931	*StL-N	115	383	45	105	20	2	0	51	28	15	.274	.332	.337	77	-10	-12	45	5			10	*C	0.3
1932	StL-N	92	274	36	68	16	2	2	28	15	18	.248	.290	.343	67	-12	-13	28	9			2	C/12	-0.7
1933	StL-N	113	369	34	94	17	0	1	45	23	33	.255	.300	.309	71	-12	-14	34	6			2	*C	-0.8
1934	Phi-N	91	277	25	81	11	0	3	35	14	10	.292	.326	.365	75	-6	-11	31	1			2	C/12M	-0.5
1935	Phi-N	93	290	38	81	20	0	1	37	19	19	.279	.326	.359	76	-6	-10	35	4			7	C/2M	-0.2
1936	Phi-N	85	230	25	64	12	0	1	27	12	21	.278	.314	.343	70	-7	-10	24	5			-6	C/1M	-1.4
1937	Phi-N	39	87	15	24	3	0	1	8	6	4	.276	.323	.345	75	-2	-3	9	1			-1	C/1M	-0.3
1938	Phi-N	3	2	0	0	0	0	0	0	0	1	.000	.000	.000	-99	-1	-1	0	0			0	/CM	0.0
1939	Cin-N	4	3	0	1	0	0	0	0	0	1	.333	.333	.333	79	-0	-0	0	0			0	/C	0.0
1940	*Cin-N	16	37	2	9	2	0	0	3	2	1	.243	.282	.297	59	-2	-2	3	1			3	C	0.1
Total	18	1525	4778	580	1358	252	32	32	621	356	280	.284	.336	.370	82	-91	-128	600	86	9		13	*C/1O2	-5.0

■ GARY WILSON
Wilson, James Garrett b: 1/12/1877, Baltimore, Md. d: 5/1/69, Randallstown, Md. BR/TR, 5'7", 168 lbs. Deb: 9/27/02

1902	Bos-A	2	8	0	1	0	0	0	1	0		.125	.125	.125	-29	-1	-1	0	0			0	/2	0.0

■ JIM WILSON
Wilson, James George b: 12/29/60, Corvallis, Ore. BR/TR, 6'3", 230 lbs. Deb: 9/13/85

1985	Cle-A	4	14	2	5	0	0	0	4	1	3	.357	.400	.357	110	0	0	2	0	0	0	-0	/1D	0.0
1989	Sea-A	5	8	0	0	0	0	0	0	0	3	.000	.000	.000	-97	-2	-2	0	0	0	0	-0	/D	-0.1
Total	2	9	22	2	5	0	0	0	4	1	6	.227	.261	.227	36	-2	-2	2	0	0	0	-0	/D1	-0.1

■ CHIEF WILSON
Wilson, John Owen b: 8/21/1883, Austin, Tex. d: 2/22/54, Bertram, Tex. BL/TR, 6'2", 185 lbs. Deb: 4/15/08

1908	Pit-N	144	529	47	120	8	7	3	43	22		.227	.258	.285	75	-15	-15	42	12			1	*O	-1.8
1909	*Pit-N	154	569	64	155	22	12	4	59	19		.272	.303	.374	102	3	-2	69	17			6	*O	0.0
1910	Pit-N	146	536	59	148	14	13	4	50	21	68	.276	.312	.373	94	-3	-7	64	8			-1	*O	-1.3
1911	Pit-N	148	544	72	163	34	12	12	**107**	41	55	.300	.353	.472	125	19	16	93	10			3	*O	1.4
1912	Pit-N	152	583	80	175	19	**36**	11	95	35	67	.300	.342	.513	134	21	22	106	16			-5	*O	1.2
1913	Pit-N	155	580	71	154	12	14	10	73	32	62	.266	.307	.386	102	-4	-1	68	9			-4	*O	-0.7
1914	StL-N	154	580	64	150	27	12	9	73	32	66	.259	.302	.393	107	1	2	69	14			15	*O	1.3
1915	StL-N	107	348	33	96	13	6	3	39	19	43	.276	.321	.374	110	3	3	41	8	15	-7	4	*O	-0.2
1916	StL-N	120	355	30	85	8	2	3	32	20	46	.239	.289	.299	81	-8	-8	33	4			-7	*O	-2.1
Total	9	1280	4624	520	1246	157	114	59	571	241	407	.269	.311	.391	105	17	11	585	98	15		11	*O	-2.2

■ LES WILSON
Wilson, Lester Wilbur "Tug" b: 7/15/1885, Gratiot County, Mich. d: 4/4/69, Edmonds, Wash. BL/TR, 5'11", 170 lbs. Deb: 7/15/11

1911	Bos-A	5	7	0	0	0	0	0	0	0	2	.000	.222	.000	-36	-1	-1	0	0			-0	/O	-0.1

■ HACK WILSON
Wilson, Lewis Robert b: 4/26/1900, Ellwood City, Pa. d: 11/23/48, Baltimore, Md. BR/TR, 5'6", 190 lbs. Deb: 9/29/23 H

1923	NY-N	3	10	0	2	0	0	0	0	0	1	.200	.200	.200	6	-1	-1	0	0			-0	/O	-0.1
1924	*NY-N	107	383	62	113	19	12	10	57	44	46	.295	.369	.486	131	15	16	70	4	3	-1	-10	*O	0.3
1925	NY-N	62	180	28	43	7	4	6	30	21	33	.239	.322	.422	92	-4	-3	25	5	2	0	-8	*O	-1.0
1926	Chi-N	142	529	97	170	36	8	**21**	109	69	61	.321	.406	**.539**	150	39	38	115	10			-0	*O	3.2
1927	Chi-N	146	551	119	175	30	12	**30**	129	71	70	.318	.401	.579	160	46	46	126	13			-6	*O	3.3
1928	Chi-N	145	520	89	163	32	9	**31**	120	77	94	.313	.404	.588	159	42	43	122	4			-13	*O	2.4
1929	*Chi-N	150	574	135	198	30	5	39	**159**	78	83	.345	.425	.618	155	49	49	148	3			-7	*O	2.5
1930	Chi-N	155	585	146	208	35	6	**56**	**190**	**105**	84	.356	.454	**.723**	177	75	75	189	3			-10	*O	4.7

YEAR	TM/L	G	AB	R	H	2B	3B	HR	RBI	BB	SO	AVG	OBP	SLG	PRO+	BR	/A	RC	SB	CS	SBR	FR	POS	TPR
1931	Chi-N	112	395	66	103	22	4	13	61	63	69	.261	.362	.435	112	8	7	66	1			-1	*O	0.1
1932	Bro-N	135	481	77	143	37	5	23	123	51	85	.297	.366	.538	142	26	27	97	2			-10	*O	0.9
1933	Bro-N	117	360	41	96	13	2	9	54	52	50	.267	.359	.389	119	8	10	53	7			-6	O/2	-0.1
1934	Bro-N	67	172	24	45	5	0	6	27	40	33	.262	.401	.395	120	5	7	30	0			-4	O	0.0
	Phi-N	7	20	0	2	0	0	0	3	3	4	.100	.217	.100	-11	-3	-4	0	0			-0	/O	-0.3
	Yr	74	192	24	47	5	0	6	30	43	37	.245	.383	.365	105	2	3	29	0			-4		-0.3
Total	12	1348	4760	884	1461	266	67	244	1062	674	713	.307	.395	.545	145	305	310	1042	52	5		-74	*O/2	15.9

■ TACK WILSON
Wilson, Michael   b: 5/16/55, Shreveport, La.   BR/TR, 5'10", 185 lbs.   Deb: 4/09/83

YEAR	TM/L	G	AB	R	H	2B	3B	HR	RBI	BB	SO	AVG	OBP	SLG	PRO+	BR	/A	RC	SB	CS	SBR	FR	POS	TPR
1983	Min-A	5	4	4	1	1	0	0	1	0	0	.250	.250	.500	97	-0	-0	1	0	0	0	0	/OD	0.0
1987	Cal-A	7	2	5	1	0	0	0	0	1	0	.500	.667	.500	224	0	1	1	0	0	0	0	/OD	0.0
Total	2	12	6	9	2	1	0	0	1	1	0	.333	.429	.500	150	0	0	1	0	0	0	0	/OD	0.0

■ PARKE WILSON
Wilson, Parke Asel   b: 10/26/1867, Keithsburg, Ill.   d: 12/20/34, Hermosa Beach, Cal   BR/TR, 5'11", 166 lbs.   Deb: 7/19/1893

YEAR	TM/L	G	AB	R	H	2B	3B	HR	RBI	BB	SO	AVG	OBP	SLG	PRO+	BR	/A	RC	SB	CS	SBR	FR	POS	TPR
1893	NY-N	31	114	16	28	4	1	2	21	7	9	.246	.289	.351	71	-5	-5	13	5			-7	C	-0.7
1894	NY-N	49	175	35	58	5	5	1	32	14	5	.331	.387	.434	100	0	0	33	8			-8	C1	-0.2
1895	NY-N	67	238	32	56	9	0	0	30	14	16	.235	.281	.273	46	-19	-18	22	11			4	C1/3	-0.7
1896	NY-N	75	253	33	60	2	0	0	23	13	14	.237	.277	.245	41	-21	-20	20	9			-2	C/1	-1.2
1897	NY-N	46	154	29	46	9	3	0	22	15		.299	.365	.396	106	1	2	25	5			-0	C1/O2	0.4
1898	NY-N	1	4	0	0	0	0	0	0	0		.000	.000	.000	-99	-1	-1	0	0			-0	/O	0.0
1899	NY-N	97	328	49	88	8	6	0	42	43		.268	.360	.329	95	-2	0	46	16			-7	C1S3/O	-0.3
Total	7	366	1266	194	336	37	15	3	170	106	44	.265	.327	.325	75	-47	-42	159	54			-21	C/1S3O2	-2.7

■ BOB WILSON
Wilson, Robert   b: 2/22/25, Dallas, Tex.   d: 4/23/85, Dallas, Tex.   BR/TR, 5'11", 197 lbs.   Deb: 5/17/58

YEAR	TM/L	G	AB	R	H	2B	3B	HR	RBI	BB	SO	AVG	OBP	SLG	PRO+	BR	/A	RC	SB	CS	SBR	FR	POS	TPR
1958	LA-N	3	5	0	1	0	0	0	0	0	1	.200	.200	.200	6	-1	-1	0	0	0	0	0	/O	0.0

■ RED WILSON
Wilson, Robert James   b: 3/7/29, Milwaukee, Wis.   BR/TR, 5'10", 160 lbs.   Deb: 9/22/51

YEAR	TM/L	G	AB	R	H	2B	3B	HR	RBI	BB	SO	AVG	OBP	SLG	PRO+	BR	/A	RC	SB	CS	SBR	FR	POS	TPR
1951	Chi-A	4	11	1	3	1	0	0	0	1	2	.273	.333	.364	90	-0	-0	1	0	0	0	-1	/C	0.0
1952	Chi-A	2	3	0	0	0	0	0	0	0	1	.000	.000	.000	-99	-1	-1	0	0	0	0	1	/C	0.0
1953	Chi-A	71	164	21	41	6	1	0	10	26	12	.250	.353	.299	75	-4	-5	17	2	3	-1	10	C	0.6
1954	Chi-A	8	20	2	4	0	0	1	1	1	2	.200	.238	.350	58	-1	-1	2	0	0		4	C	0.3
	Det-A	54	170	22	48	11	1	2	22	27	12	.282	.381	.394	115	4	4	26	3	1	0	2	C	0.9
	Yr	62	190	24	52	11	1	3	23	28	14	.274	.367	.389	108	3	2	27	3	1	0	6		1.2
1955	Det-A	78	241	26	53	9	0	2	17	26	23	.220	.296	.282	57	-15	-14	18	1	2	-1	-6	C	-1.7
1956	Det-A	78	228	32	66	12	2	7	38	42	18	.289	.400	.452	124	9	9	43	2	1	0	4	C	1.4
1957	Det-A	60	180	21	43	8	1	3	13	25	19	.239	.341	.344	86	-2	-3	22	2	2	-1	2	C	0.0
1958	Det-A	103	298	31	89	13	1	3	29	35	30	.299	.376	.379	101	5	2	45	10	0	3	7	*C	1.3
1959	Det-A	67	228	28	60	17	2	4	35	10	23	.263	.300	.408	88	-3	-5	25	2	2	-1	2	C	0.0
1960	Det-A	45	134	17	29	4	0	1	14	16	14	.216	.300	.269	54	-8	-9	12	3	0	1	-0	C	-0.4
	Cle-A	32	88	5	19	3	0	1	10	6	7	.216	.274	.284	51	-6	-6	7	0	0	0	7	C	0.3
	Yr	77	222	22	48	7	0	2	24	22	21	.216	.290	.275	53	-14	-14	19	3	0	1	7		-0.1
Total	10	602	1765	206	455	84	8	24	189	215	163	.258	.341	.355	87	-24	-28	217	25	12	0	32	C	2.7

■ MIKE WILSON
Wilson, Samuel Marshall   b: 12/2/1896, Edge Hill, Pa.   d: 5/16/78, Boynton Beach, Fla   BR/TR, 5'10.5", 160 lbs.   Deb: 6/04/21

YEAR	TM/L	G	AB	R	H	2B	3B	HR	RBI	BB	SO	AVG	OBP	SLG	PRO+	BR	/A	RC	SB	CS	SBR	FR	POS	TPR
1921	Pit-N	5	4	0	0	0	0	0	0	0	0	.000	.000	.000	-97	-1	-1	0	0	0	0	0	/C	0.0

■ NEIL WILSON
Wilson, Samuel O'Neil   b: 6/14/35, Lexington, Tenn.   BL/TR, 6'1", 175 lbs.   Deb: 4/17/60

YEAR	TM/L	G	AB	R	H	2B	3B	HR	RBI	BB	SO	AVG	OBP	SLG	PRO+	BR	/A	RC	SB	CS	SBR	FR	POS	TPR
1960	SF-N	6	10	0	0	0	0	0	0	1	2	.000	.091	.000	-77	-2	-2	0	0	0	0	0	/C	-0.1

■ TOM WILSON
Wilson, Thomas G. "Slats"   b: 6/3/1890, Fleming, Kan.   d: 3/7/53, San Pedro, Cal.   BB/TR, 6'1.5", 160 lbs.   Deb: 9/08/14

YEAR	TM/L	G	AB	R	H	2B	3B	HR	RBI	BB	SO	AVG	OBP	SLG	PRO+	BR	/A	RC	SB	CS	SBR	FR	POS	TPR
1914	Was-A	1	1	0	0	0	0	0	0	0	0	.000	.000	.000	-97	-0	-0	0	0			0	/C	0.0

■ BILL WILSON
Wilson, William Donald   b: 11/6/28, Central City, Neb.   BR/TR, 6'2", 200 lbs.   Deb: 9/24/50

YEAR	TM/L	G	AB	R	H	2B	3B	HR	RBI	BB	SO	AVG	OBP	SLG	PRO+	BR	/A	RC	SB	CS	SBR	FR	POS	TPR
1950	Chi-A	3	6	0	0	0	0	0	0	2	2	.000	.250	.000	-33	-1	-1	0	0	0	0	-0	/O	0.0
1953	Chi-A	9	17	1	1	0	0	0	1	0	7	.059	.111	.059	-51	-4	-4	0	0	0	0	0	/O	-0.3
1954	Chi-A	20	35	4	6	1	0	2	5	7	5	.171	.310	.371	83	-1	-1	3	0	1	-1	1	O	0.0
	Phi-A	94	323	43	77	10	1	15	33	39	59	.238	.335	.415	104	2	1	47	1	1	-1	5	O	0.4
	Yr	114	358	47	83	11	1	17	38	46	64	.232	.333	.411	102	1	0	50	1	3	-2	6		0.4
1955	KC-A	98	273	39	61	12	0	15	38	24	63	.223	.289	.432	91	-5	-5	32	1	1	-0	2	O/P	-0.7
Total	4	224	654	87	145	23	1	32	77	72	136	.222	.308	.407	92	-9	-10	83	2	4	-2	8	O/P	-0.6

■ BILL WILSON
Wilson, William G.   b: 10/28/1867, Hannibal, Mo.   d: 5/9/24, St.Paul, Minn.   TR ,   Deb: 4/30/1890

YEAR	TM/L	G	AB	R	H	2B	3B	HR	RBI	BB	SO	AVG	OBP	SLG	PRO+	BR	/A	RC	SB	CS	SBR	FR	POS	TPR
1890	Pit-N	83	304	30	65	11	3	0	21	22	50	.214	.271	.270	67	-15	-10	24	5			3	CO1/S	-0.5
1897	Lou-N	105	381	43	81	12	4	1	41	18		.213	.257	.273	43	-32	-30	30	9			2	*C/3	-1.1
1898	Lou-N	29	102	5	17	1	2	1	13	5		.167	.213	.245	33	-9	-9	6	3			-4	C1/1	-0.9
Total	3	217	787	78	163	24	9	2	75	45	50	.207	.257	.268	50	-56	-49	60	17			1	C/O13S	-2.5

■ MOOKIE WILSON
Wilson, William Hayward   b: 2/9/56, Bamberg, S.C.   BB/TR, 5'10", 170 lbs.   Deb: 9/02/80

YEAR	TM/L	G	AB	R	H	2B	3B	HR	RBI	BB	SO	AVG	OBP	SLG	PRO+	BR	/A	RC	SB	CS	SBR	FR	POS	TPR
1980	NY-N	27	105	16	26	5	3	0	4	12	19	.248	.325	.352	91	-1	-1	12	7	7	-2	2	O	-0.1
1981	NY-N	92	328	49	89	8	8	3	14	20	59	.271	.317	.372	96	-3	-2	38	24	12	0	3	O	-0.1
1982	NY-N	159	639	90	178	25	9	5	55	32	102	.279	.315	.369	91	-9	-8	78	58	16	8	9	*O	0.7
1983	NY-N	152	638	91	176	25	6	7	51	18	103	.276	.300	.367	85	-15	-15	71	54	16	7	5	*O	-0.5
1984	NY-N	154	587	88	162	28	10	10	54	26	90	.276	.309	.409	102	-2	-1	78	46	9	8	11	*O	1.4
1985	NY-N	93	337	56	93	16	8	6	26	28	52	.276	.332	.424	113	4	5	46	24	9	2	-0	O	0.4
1986	*NY-N	123	381	61	110	17	5	9	45	32	72	.289	.345	.430	116	6	7	58	25	7	3	3	*O	1.2
1987	NY-N	124	385	58	115	19	7	9	34	35	85	.299	.360	.455	120	8	10	66	21	6	3	1	*O	0.9
1988	*NY-N	112	378	61	112	17	5	8	41	27	63	.296	.346	.431	128	10	12	55	15	4	2	2	*O	1.4
1989	NY-N	80	249	22	51	10	1	3	18	10	47	.205	.238	.289	53	-17	-15	17	7	4	0	4	O	-1.2
	*Tor-A	54	238	32	71	9	1	2	17	3	37	.298	.313	.370	93	-3	-3	28	12	1	3	-5	O	-0.4
1990	Tor-A	147	588	81	156	36	4	3	51	31	102	.265	.302	.355	85	-14	-13	64	23	4	5	1	*O/D	-0.7
Total	11	1317	4853	705	1339	215	67	65	410	274	831	.276	.317	.388	98	-36	-23	611	316	95	38	37	*O/D	3.0

■ WILLIE WILSON
Wilson, Willie James   b: 7/9/55, Montgomery, Ala.   BB/TR, 6'3", 190 lbs.   Deb: 9/04/76

YEAR	TM/L	G	AB	R	H	2B	3B	HR	RBI	BB	SO	AVG	OBP	SLG	PRO+	BR	/A	RC	SB	CS	SBR	FR	POS	TPR
1976	KC-A	12	6	0	1	0	0	0	0	0	2	.167	.167	.167	-2	-1	-1	0	2	1	0	2	/O	0.1
1977	KC-A	13	34	10	11	2	0	0	1	1	8	.324	.343	.382	97	-0	-0	4	6	3	0	1	/OD	0.1
1978	*KC-A	127	198	43	43	8	2	0	16	16	33	.217	.282	.278	57	-11	-11	18	46	12	7	-14	*O/D	-2.1
1979	KC-A	154	588	113	185	18	13	6	49	28	92	.315	.353	.420	106	6	4	99	**83**	12	**18**	14	*O	2.9
1980	*KC-A	161	705	**133**	**230**	28	**15**	3	49	28	81	.326	.357	.420	112	11	11	117	79	10	**18**	24	*O	4.9
1981	*KC-A	102	439	54	133	10	7	1	32	18	42	.303	.336	.364	103	1	1	56	34	8	5	22	*O	2.7
1982	KC-A	136	585	87	194	19	**15**	3	46	26	81	**.332**	.366	.431	118	14	14	96	37	11	5	13	*O	2.7
1983	KC-A	137	576	90	159	22	8	2	33	33	75	.276	.316	.356	84	-13	-13	72	59	8	13	-8	*O	-0.9
1984	*KC-A	128	541	81	163	24	9	2	44	39	56	.301	.352	.390	104	4	3	82	47	5	**11**	3	*O	1.3
1985	*KC-A	141	605	87	168	25	**21**	4	43	29	94	.278	.316	.408	96	-4	-4	80	43	15	6	-4	*O	-0.3
1986	KC-A	156	631	77	170	20	7	9	44	31	97	.269	.313	.366	82	-14	-16	76	34	8	5	-3	*O	-1.5
1987	KC-A	146	610	97	170	18	**15**	4	30	32	88	.279	.321	.377	82	-14	-16	78	59	11	**11**	-1	*O/D	-0.8

YEAR	TM/L	G	AB	R	H	2B	3B	HR	RBI	BB	SO	AVG	OBP	SLG	PRO+	BR	/A	RC	SB	CS	SBR	FR	POS	TPR
1988	KC-A	147	591	81	155	17	11	1	37	22	106	.262	.291	.333	74	-21	-21	61	35	7	6	-6	*O	-2.3
1989	KC-A	112	383	58	97	17	7	3	43	27	78	.253	.304	.358	86	-8	-7	43	24	6	4	-6	*O/D	-1.1
1990	KC-A	115	307	49	89	13	3	2	42	30	57	.290	.357	.371	106	2	3	44	24	6	4	-6	*O/D	0.0
Total	15	1787	6799	1060	1968	241	133	40	509	360	990	.289	.330	.382	95	-47	-53	926	612	119	112	31	*O/D	5.7

■ ED WINCENIAK   Winceniak, Edward Joseph b: 4/16/29, Chicago, Ill. BR/TR, 5'9", 165 lbs. Deb: 4/25/56

YEAR	TM/L	G	AB	R	H	2B	3B	HR	RBI	BB	SO	AVG	OBP	SLG	PRO+	BR	/A	RC	SB	CS	SBR	FR	POS	TPR
1956	Chi-N	15	17	1	2	0	0	0	0	1	3	.118	.167	.118	-22	-3	-3	0	0	0	0	0	/32	-0.2
1957	Chi-N	17	50	5	12	3	0	1	8	2	9	.240	.269	.360	68	-2	-2	4	0	0	0	-3	/S32	-0.4
Total	2	32	67	6	14	3	0	1	8	3	12	.209	.243	.299	45	-5	-5	5	0	0	0	-3	/3S2	-0.6

■ GORDIE WINDHORN   Windhorn, Gordon Ray b: 12/19/33, Watseka, Ill. BR/TR, 6'1", 185 lbs. Deb: 9/10/59

YEAR	TM/L	G	AB	R	H	2B	3B	HR	RBI	BB	SO	AVG	OBP	SLG	PRO+	BR	/A	RC	SB	CS	SBR	FR	POS	TPR
1959	NY-A	7	11	0	0	0	0	0	0	0	3	.000	.000	.000	-99	-3	-3	0	0	0	0	0	/O	-0.2
1961	LA-N	34	33	10	8	2	1	2	6	4	3	.242	.324	.545	115	1	1	5	0	1	-1	2	O	0.1
1962	KC-A	14	19	1	3	1	0	0	1	0	3	.158	.158	.211	-2	-3	-3	1	0	0	0	-0	/O	-0.2
	LA-A	40	45	9	8	6	0	0	1	7	10	.178	.288	.311	63	-2	-2	4	1	1	0	1	O	-0.2
	Yr	54	64	10	11	7	0	0	2	7	13	.172	.254	.281	44	-5	-5	5	1	1	-0	0		-0.4
Total	3	95	108	20	19	9	1	2	8	11	19	.176	.252	.333	55	-7	-7	10	1	2	-1	2	/O	-0.5

■ BILL WINDLE   Windle, Willis Brewer b: 12/13/04, Galena, Kan. d: 12/8/81, Corpus Christi, Tex BL/TL, 5'11.5", 170 lbs. Deb: 9/27/28

YEAR	TM/L	G	AB	R	H	2B	3B	HR	RBI	BB	SO	AVG	OBP	SLG	PRO+	BR	/A	RC	SB	CS	SBR	FR	POS	TPR
1928	Pit-N	1	1	1	1	1	0	0	0	0	0	1.000	1.000	2.000	641	1	1	2	0			0	/1	0.1
1929	Pit-N	2	1	0	0	0	0	0	0	0	1	.000	.000	.000	-98	-0	-0	0	0			0	/1	0.0
Total	2	3	2	1	1	1	0	0	0	0	1	.500	.500	1.000	264	0	0	2	0			0	/1	0.1

■ ROBBIE WINE   Wine, Robert Paul Jr. b: 7/13/62, Norristown, Pa. BR/TR, 6'2", 190 lbs. Deb: 9/02/86

YEAR	TM/L	G	AB	R	H	2B	3B	HR	RBI	BB	SO	AVG	OBP	SLG	PRO+	BR	/A	RC	SB	CS	SBR	FR	POS	TPR
1986	Hou-N	9	12	2	3	1	0	0	0	1	4	.250	.308	.333	79	-0	-0	1	0	0	0	3	/C	0.3
1987	Hou-N	14	29	1	3	1	0	0	0	1	10	.103	.133	.138	-29	-5	-5	1	0	0	0	-1	C	-0.4
Total	2	23	41	3	6	2	0	0	0	2	14	.146	.186	.195	2	-6	-6	2	0	0	0	2	/C	-0.1

■ BOBBY WINE   Wine, Robert Paul Sr. b: 9/17/38, New York, N.Y. BR/TR, 6'1", 187 lbs. Deb: 9/20/60 MC

YEAR	TM/L	G	AB	R	H	2B	3B	HR	RBI	BB	SO	AVG	OBP	SLG	PRO+	BR	/A	RC	SB	CS	SBR	FR	POS	TPR
1960	Phi-N	4	14	1	2	0	0	0	0	0	2	.143	.143	.143	-22	-2	-2	0	0	0	0	0	/S	-0.1
1962	Phi-N	112	311	30	76	15	0	4	25	11	49	.244	.270	.331	62	-18	-17	23	2	0	1	7	S3	0.0
1963	Phi-N	142	418	29	90	14	3	6	44	14	83	.215	.242	.306	58	-24	-23	28	1	3	-2	15	*S/3	0.3
1964	Phi-N	126	283	28	60	8	3	4	34	25	37	.212	.276	.304	64	-14	-13	23	1	0	0	11	*S3	0.5
1965	Phi-N	139	394	31	90	8	1	5	33	31	69	.228	.285	.292	64	-19	-18	30	0	0	0	22	*S/1	1.9
1966	Phi-N	46	89	8	21	5	0	0	5	6	13	.236	.292	.292	63	-4	-4	7	0	1	-1	13	S/O	1.1
1967	Phi-N	135	363	27	69	12	5	2	28	29	77	.190	.250	.267	48	-24	-25	23	3	2	-0	29	*S/1	2.0
1968	Phi-N	27	71	5	12	3	0	2	7	6	17	.169	.234	.296	58	-4	-4	4	0	0	0	3	S/3	0.3
1969	Mon-N	121	370	23	74	8	1	3	25	28	49	.200	.256	.251	43	-28	-28	23	0	0	0	17	*S/13	0.2
1970	Mon-N	159	501	40	116	21	3	3	51	39	94	.232	.288	.303	59	-29	-29	44	0	1	-1	20	*S	1.0
1971	Mon-N	119	340	25	68	9	0	1	16	25	46	.200	.255	.235	39	-27	-27	20	0	0	0	2	*S	-0.9
1972	Mon-N	34	18	2	4	1	0	0	0	0	2	.222	.222	.278	41	-1	-1	1	0	0	0	5	3/S2	0.4
Total	12	1164	3172	249	682	104	16	30	268	214	538	.215	.265	.286	54	-195	-193	227	7	7	-2	142	*S/3102	6.7

■ RALPH WINEGARNER   Winegarner, Ralph Lee b: 10/29/09, Benton, Kan. d: 88, Benton, Kan. BR/TR, 6', 182 lbs. Deb: 9/20/30 C

YEAR	TM/L	G	AB	R	H	2B	3B	HR	RBI	BB	SO	AVG	OBP	SLG	PRO+	BR	/A	RC	SB	CS	SBR	FR	POS	TPR
1930	Cle-A	5	22	5	10	1	0	0	2	1	7	.455	.478	.500	143	2	2	5	0	0	0	1	/3	0.2
1932	Cle-A	7	7	1	1	0	0	0	0	0	5	.143	.143	.143	-24	-1	-1	0	0	0	0	-0	/P	0.0
1934	Cle-A	32	51	9	10	2	0	1	5	3	11	.196	.241	.294	37	-5	-5	4	0	0	0	0	P/O	0.0
1935	Cle-A	65	84	11	26	4	1	3	17	9	12	.310	.376	.488	120	3	2	15	1	1	-0	1	P/O31	0.7
1936	Cle-A	18	16	0	2	0	0	0	2	1	6	.125	.176	.125	-24	-3	-3	0	0	0	0	0	/P	0.0
1949	StL-A	9	5	2	2	0	0	1	2	1	2	.400	.500	1.000	280	1	1	3	0	0	0	-0	/P	0.0
Total	6	136	185	28	51	7	1	5	28	15	43	.276	.330	.405	86	-4	-4	27	1	1	-0	2	/P3O1	0.9

■ DAVE WINFIELD   Winfield, David Mark b: 10/3/51, St.Paul, Minn. BR/TR, 6'6", 220 lbs. Deb: 6/19/73

YEAR	TM/L	G	AB	R	H	2B	3B	HR	RBI	BB	SO	AVG	OBP	SLG	PRO+	BR	/A	RC	SB	CS	SBR	FR	POS	TPR
1973	SD-N	56	141	9	39	4	1	3	12	12	19	.277	.333	.383	107	-0	1	17	0	0	0	-2	O/1	-0.2
1974	SD-N	145	498	57	132	18	4	20	75	40	96	.265	.321	.438	116	5	7	66	9	7	-2	7	*O	0.8
1975	SD-N	143	509	74	136	20	2	15	76	69	82	.267	.358	.403	118	8	12	77	23	4	5	5	*O	1.7
1976	SD-N	137	492	81	139	26	4	13	69	65	78	.283	.370	.431	138	18	23	80	26	7	4	12	*O	3.5
1977	SD-N	157	615	104	169	29	7	25	92	58	75	.275	.337	.467	126	10	18	95	16	7	1	16	*O	2.9
1978	SD-N	158	587	88	181	30	5	24	97	55	81	.308	.370	.499	153	31	36	105	21	9	1	0	*O/1	3.3
1979	SD-N	159	597	97	184	27	10	34	**118**	85	71	.308	.396	.558	**167**	**47**	**52**	132	15	9	-1	11	*O	5.8
1980	SD-N	162	558	89	154	25	6	20	87	79	83	.276	.368	.450	135	21	25	94	23	7	3	-2	*O	2.0
1981	*NY-A	105	388	52	114	25	1	13	68	43	41	.294	.366	.464	140	19	19	66	11	1	3	-6	*O/D	1.4
1982	NY-A	140	539	84	151	24	8	37	106	45	64	.280	.336	.560	143	28	29	93	5	3	-0	4	*O/D	3.1
1983	NY-A	152	598	99	169	26	8	32	116	58	77	.283	.348	.513	139	26	29	97	15	6	1	-4	*O	2.3
1984	NY-A	141	567	106	193	34	4	19	100	53	71	.340	.397	.515	156	38	41	113	6	4	-1	1	*O	3.7
1985	NY-A	155	633	105	174	34	6	26	114	52	96	.275	.330	.471	119	13	15	94	19	7	2	6	*O/D	1.1
1986	NY-A	154	565	90	148	31	5	24	104	77	106	.262	.352	.462	121	16	17	89	6	5	-1	-0	*O/3D	1.1
1987	NY-A	156	575	83	158	22	1	27	97	76	96	.275	.359	.457	116	13	14	91	5	6	-2	-10	*O/D	0.0
1988	NY-A	149	559	96	180	37	2	25	107	69	88	.322	.398	.530	159	43	44	115	9	4	0	-7	*O/D	3.5
1990	NY-A	20	61	7	13	3	0	2	6	4	13	.213	.273	.361	75	-2	-2	6	0	0	0	-2	O/D	-0.3
	Cal-A	112	414	63	114	18	2	19	72	48	68	.275	.352	.466	127	15	14	65	0	1	-1	-10	*O/D	0.3
	Yr	132	475	70	127	21	2	21	78	52	81	.267	.342	.453	120	12	12	71	0	1	-1	-11		0.0
Total	17	2401	8896	1384	2548	433	76	378	1516	988	1305	.286	.359	.480	135	347	394	1495	209	87	11	23	*O/D13	36.8

■ AL WINGO   Wingo, Absalom Holbrook "Red" b: 5/6/1898, Norcross, Ga. d: 10/9/64, Detroit, Mich. BL/TR, 5'11", 180 lbs. Deb: 9/09/19

YEAR	TM/L	G	AB	R	H	2B	3B	HR	RBI	BB	SO	AVG	OBP	SLG	PRO+	BR	/A	RC	SB	CS	SBR	FR	POS	TPR
1919	Phi-A	19	59	9	18	1	3	0	2	4	12	.305	.349	.424	115	1	1	8	0			-3	O	-0.2
1924	Det-A	78	150	21	43	12	2	1	26	21	13	.287	.374	.413	105	1	1	23	2	5	-2	-8	O	-1.1
1925	Det-A	130	440	104	163	34	10	5	68	69	31	.370	.456	.527	151	35	36	106	14	13	-4	8	*O	2.7
1926	Det-A	108	298	45	84	19	0	1	45	52	32	.282	.389	.356	94	-0	-1	45	4	2	0	4	O/3	-0.1
1927	Det-A	75	137	15	32	8	2	0	20	25	14	.234	.352	.321	74	-4	-5	17	1	0	0	-3	O	-0.8
1928	Det-A	87	242	30	69	13	2	2	30	40	17	.285	.389	.380	101	3	3	38	2	2	-1	-3	O	-0.5
Total	6	493	1326	224	409	87	19	9	191	211	119	.308	.404	.423	114	35	35	237	23	22		-6	O/3	-0.0

■ ED WINGO   Wingo, Edmond Armand (b: Edmond Armand La Riviere)
b: 10/8/1895, St.Anne De Bellevue, Que., Canada d: 12/5/64, Lachine, Que., Can. BR/TR, 5'6", 145 lbs. Deb: 10/02/20

YEAR	TM/L	G	AB	R	H	2B	3B	HR	RBI	BB	SO	AVG	OBP	SLG	PRO+	BR	/A	RC	SB	CS	SBR	FR	POS	TPR
1920	Phi-A	1	4	0	1	0	0	0	0	0	0	.250	.250	.250	32	-0	-0	0	0	0	0	1	/C	0.0

■ IVEY WINGO   Wingo, Ivey Brown b: 7/8/1890, Gainesville, Ga. d: 3/1/41, Waycross, Ga. BL/TL, 5'10", 160 lbs. Deb: 4/20/11 MC

YEAR	TM/L	G	AB	R	H	2B	3B	HR	RBI	BB	SO	AVG	OBP	SLG	PRO+	BR	/A	RC	SB	CS	SBR	FR	POS	TPR
1911	StL-N	25	57	4	12	0	3	3	9	3	7	.211	.250	.246	40	-5	-5	3	0			0	C	-0.2
1912	StL-N	100	310	38	82	18	8	2	44	23	45	.265	.317	.394	96	-4	-3	40	8			3	C	0.5
1913	StL-N	112	307	25	78	5	8	2	35	17	41	.254	.295	.342	83	-8	-7	34	18			1	C/1O	0.0
1914	StL-N	80	237	24	71	8	5	2	24	14	21	.300	.352	.426	132	8	9	38	15			0	C/O	0.9
1915	Cin-N	119	339	26	75	11	6	3	29	13	33	.221	.250	.316	69	-13	-14	27	10	11	-4	3	C/O	-0.9
1916	Cin-N	119	347	30	85	8	11	2	40	25	27	.245	.298	.349	100	-1	-0	40	4			7	*CM	1.4
1917	Cin-N	121	399	37	106	16	11	2	39	25	13	.266	.311	.376	115	4	6	47	9			-4	*C	0.8

YEAR	TM/L	G	AB	R	H	2B	3B	HR	RBI	BB	SO	AVG	OBP	SLG	PRO+	BR	/A	RC	SB	CS	SBR	FR	POS	TPR
1918	Cin-N	100	323	35	82	15	6	0	31	19	18	.254	.297	.337	95	-3	-3	33	6			-5	C/O	0.0
1919	*Cin-N	76	245	30	67	12	6	0	27	23	19	.273	.336	.371	115	4	5	30	4			4	C	1.5
1920	Cin-N	108	364	32	96	11	5	2	38	19	13	.264	.300	.338	84	-8	-8	37	6	4	-1	-11	*C/2	-1.2
1921	Cin-N	97	295	20	79	7	6	3	38	21	14	.268	.319	.363	84	-9	-7	35	3	2	-0	6	C/O	0.5
1922	Cin-N	80	260	24	74	13	3	3	45	23	11	.285	.343	.392	91	-4	-4	34	1	4	-2	3	C	-0.1
1923	Cin-N	61	171	10	45	9	2	1	24	9	11	.263	.304	.357	75	-7	-6	18	1	1	-0	4	C	0.0
1924	Cin-N	66	192	21	55	5	4	1	23	14	8	.286	.338	.370	91	-3	-2	24	1	1	-0	4	C/1	0.3
1925	Cin-N	55	146	6	30	7	0	0	12	11	8	.205	.261	.253	33	-15	-14	10	1	2	-1	3	C	-0.8
1926	Cin-N	7	10	0	2	0	0	0	1	1	0	.200	.333	.200	48	-1	-1	1	0			-0	/C	0.0
1929	Cin-N	1	1	0	0	0	0	0	0	0	0	.000	.000	.000	-99	-0	-0	0	0			0	/C	0.0
Total	17	1327	4003	362	1039	147	81	25	455	264	285	.260	.307	.355	91	-65	-55	452	87	25		16	*C/O12	2.7

■ GEORGE WINKELMAN

Winkelman, George Edward   b: 2/18/1865, Washington, D.C.   d: 5/19/60, Washington, D.C.   BL/TL,   Deb: 8/04/1883

YEAR	TM/L	G	AB	R	H	2B	3B	HR	RBI	BB	SO	AVG	OBP	SLG	PRO+	BR	/A	RC	SB	CS	SBR	FR	POS	TPR
1883	Lou-a	4	13	2	0	0	0	0		1		.000	.071	.000	-81	-2	-2	0				0	/O	-0.1
1886	Was-N	1	5	0	1	0	0	0	0	0	1	.200	.200	.200	23	-0	-0	0	0			-1	/OP	0.0
Total	2	5	18	2	1	0	0	0	0	1	1	.056	.105	.056	-51	-3	-3	0	0			-0	/OP	-0.1

■ HERM WINNINGHAM

Winningham, Herman Son   b: 12/1/61, Orangeburg, S.C.   BL/TR, 6'1", 170 lbs.   Deb: 9/01/84

YEAR	TM/L	G	AB	R	H	2B	3B	HR	RBI	BB	SO	AVG	OBP	SLG	PRO+	BR	/A	RC	SB	CS	SBR	FR	POS	TPR
1984	NY-N	14	27	5	11	1	1	0	5	1	7	.407	.429	.519	167	2	2	6	2	1	0	-1	O	0.1
1985	Mon-N	125	312	30	74	6	5	3	21	28	72	.237	.300	.317	77	-11	-9	32	20	9	1	-10	*O	-2.2
1986	Mon-N	90	185	23	40	6	3	4	11	18	51	.216	.286	.346	74	-7	-7	17	12	7	-1	2	O/S	-0.6
1987	Mon-N	137	347	34	83	20	3	4	41	34	68	.239	.307	.349	71	-13	-15	37	29	10	3	-14	*O	-3.1
1988	Mon-N	47	90	10	21	2	1	0	6	12	18	.233	.324	.278	71	-3	-3	8	4	5	-2	2	O	-0.4
	Cin-N	53	113	6	26	1	3	0	15	5	27	.230	.263	.292	57	-6	-7	9	8	3	1	3	O	-0.4
	Yr	100	203	16	47	3	4	0	21	17	45	.232	.291	.286	63	-9	-10	17	12	8	-1	4		-0.8
1989	Cin-N	115	251	40	63	11	3	3	13	24	50	.251	.316	.355	88	-3	-4	29	14	5	1	3	O	0.0
1990	*Cin-N	84	160	20	41	8	5	3	17	14	31	.256	.316	.425	100	0	-0	22	6	4	-1	2	O	0.0
Total	7	665	1485	168	359	55	24	17	129	136	324	.242	.305	.345	79	-41	-42	159	95	44	2	-14	O/S	-6.6

■ TOM WINSETT

Winsett, John Thomas "Long Tom"   b: 11/24/09, McKenzie, Tenn.   BL/TR, 6'2", 190 lbs.   Deb: 4/20/30

YEAR	TM/L	G	AB	R	H	2B	3B	HR	RBI	BB	SO	AVG	OBP	SLG	PRO+	BR	/A	RC	SB	CS	SBR	FR	POS	TPR
1930	Bos-A	1	1	0	0	0	0	0	0	0	1	.000	.000	.000	-99	-0	-0	0	0	0	0	0	H	0.0
1931	Bos-A	64	76	6	15	1	0	1	7	4	21	.197	.247	.250	33	-8	-7	5	0	0	0	-0	/O	-0.6
1933	Bos-A	6	12	1	1	0	0	0	0	1	6	.083	.154	.083	-36	-2	-2	0	0	0	0	-1	/O	-0.3
1935	StL-N	7	12	2	6	1	0	0	2	2	3	.500	.571	.583	203	2	2	4	0			0	/O	0.2
1936	Bro-N	22	85	13	20	7	0	1	18	11	14	.235	.330	.353	83	-2	-2	10	0			0	O	0.2
1937	Bro-N	118	350	32	83	15	5	5	42	45	64	.237	.329	.351	84	-7	-7	44	3			-1	*O/P	-1.2
1938	Bro-N	12	30	6	9	1	0	1	7	6	4	.300	.417	.433	131	2	2	6	0			-1	/O	0.0
Total	7	230	566	60	134	25	5	8	76	69	113	.237	.325	.341	79	-15	-15	69	3	0		-3	O/P	-2.1

■ MATT WINTERS

Winters, Matthew Littleton   b: 3/18/60, Buffalo, N.Y.   BL/TR, 6'3", 215 lbs.   Deb: 5/30/89

YEAR	TM/L	G	AB	R	H	2B	3B	HR	RBI	BB	SO	AVG	OBP	SLG	PRO+	BR	/A	RC	SB	CS	SBR	FR	POS	TPR
1989	KC-A	42	107	14	25	6	0	2	9	14	23	.234	.322	.346	89	-1	-1	12	0	0	0	-3	O/D	-0.4

■ KETTLE WIRTS

Wirts, Elwood Vernon   b: 10/31/1897, Consumnes, Cal.   d: 7/12/68, Sacramento, Cal.   BR/TR, 5'11", 170 lbs.   Deb: 7/20/21

YEAR	TM/L	G	AB	R	H	2B	3B	HR	RBI	BB	SO	AVG	OBP	SLG	PRO+	BR	/A	RC	SB	CS	SBR	FR	POS	TPR
1921	Chi-N	7	11	0	2	0	0	0	1	0	3	.182	.182	.182	-3	-2	-2	0	0	0	0	1	/C	0.0
1922	Chi-N	31	58	7	10	2	0	1	6	12	15	.172	.314	.259	48	-4	-4	5	0	0	0	-5	C	-0.8
1923	Chi-N	5	5	2	1	0	0	0	1	2	0	.200	.429	.200	71	-0	-0	1	0	0	0	1	/C	0.1
1924	Chi-A	6	12	0	1	0	0	0	0	2	2	.083	.214	.083	-22	-2	-2	0	0	0	0	1	/C	0.0
Total	4	49	86	9	14	2	0	1	8	16	20	.163	.294	.221	35	-8	-8	7	0	0	0	-2	/C	-0.7

■ HUGHIE WISE

Wise, Hugh Edward   b: 3/9/06, Campbellsville, Ky.   d: 7/21/87, Plantation, Fla.   BB/TR, 6', 178 lbs.   Deb: 9/26/30

YEAR	TM/L	G	AB	R	H	2B	3B	HR	RBI	BB	SO	AVG	OBP	SLG	PRO+	BR	/A	RC	SB	CS	SBR	FR	POS	TPR
1930	Det-A	2	6	0	2	0	0	0	0	0	0	.333	.333	.333	68	-0	-0	1	0	0	0	1	/C	0.1

■ CASEY WISE

Wise, Kendall Cole   b: 9/8/32, Lafayette, Ind.   BB/TR, 6', 170 lbs.   Deb: 4/16/57

YEAR	TM/L	G	AB	R	H	2B	3B	HR	RBI	BB	SO	AVG	OBP	SLG	PRO+	BR	/A	RC	SB	CS	SBR	FR	POS	TPR
1957	Chi-N	43	106	12	19	3	1	0	7	11	14	.179	.256	.226	32	-10	-10	6	0	0	0	3	2/S	-0.3
1958	*Mil-N	31	71	8	14	1	0	0	0	4	8	.197	.240	.211	23	-8	-7	3	1	1	-0	0	2/S3	-0.5
1959	Mil-N	22	76	11	13	2	0	1	5	10	5	.171	.267	.237	39	-7	-6	5	0	0	0	-7	2/S	-1.1
1960	Det-A	30	68	6	10	0	2	2	5	4	9	.147	.194	.294	29	-7	-7	3	1	0	0	3	2S/3	-0.1
Total	4	126	321	37	56	6	3	3	17	29	36	.174	.243	.240	31	-32	-30	17	2	1	0	-2	/2S3	-2.0

■ NICK WISE

Wise, Nicholas Joseph   b: 6/15/1866, Boston, Mass.   d: 1/15/23, Boston, Mass.   BR/TR, 5'11", 194 lbs.   Deb: 6/20/1888

YEAR	TM/L	G	AB	R	H	2B	3B	HR	RBI	BB	SO	AVG	OBP	SLG	PRO+	BR	/A	RC	SB	CS	SBR	FR	POS	TPR
1888	Bos-N	1	3	0	0	0	0	0	0	0	0	.000	.000	.000	-98	-1	-1	0	0			0	/OC	0.0

■ SAM WISE

Wise, Samuel Washington "Modoc"   b: 8/18/1857, Akron, Ohio   d: 1/22/10, Akron, Ohio   TR, 5'10.5", 170 lbs.   Deb: 7/30/1881

YEAR	TM/L	G	AB	R	H	2B	3B	HR	RBI	BB	SO	AVG	OBP	SLG	PRO+	BR	/A	RC	SB	CS	SBR	FR	POS	TPR
1881	Det-N	1	4	0	2	0	0	0		0	2	.500	.500	.500	207	0	0	1				-0	/3	0.0
1882	Bos-N	78	298	44	66	11	4	4	34	5	45	.221	.234	.326	77	-8	-8	23				-12	*S/3	-1.0
1883	Bos-N	96	406	73	110	25	7	4	58	13	74	.271	.294	.397	105	3	2	48				-2	*S	0.3
1884	Bos-N	114	426	60	91	15	9	4	41	25	104	.214	.257	.319	81	-10	-9	36				7	*S/2	0.7
1885	Bos-N	107	424	71	120	20	10	4	46	25	61	.283	.323	.406	140	15	18	57				14	S2/O	3.5
1886	Bos-N	96	387	71	112	19	12	4	72	35	61	.289	.345	.432	141	16	18	70	31			-23	12S	-1.2
1887	Bos-N	113	467	103	156	27	17	9	92	36	44	.334	.390	.522	153	33	33	115	43			-7	SO2	2.0
1888	Bos-N	105	417	66	100	19	12	4	40	34	66	.240	.306	.372	115	9	8	59	33			9	S/3102	1.9
1889	Was-N	121	472	79	118	15	8	4	62	61	62	.250	.341	.341	98	-3	1	65	24			-23	2S3O	-1.2
1890	Buf-P	119	505	95	148	29	11	6	102	46	45	.293	.359	.430	122	8	16	87	19			5	*2	2.1
1891	Bal-a	103	388	70	96	14	5	1	48	62	52	.247	.364	.317	97	2	1	58	33			-13	*2/S	-0.3
1893	Was-N	122	521	102	162	27	17	5	77	49	27	.311	.375	.457	126	15	18	99	20			14	*23	2.6
Total	12	1175	4715	834	1281	221	112	49	672	389	643	.272	.332	.397	116	81	98	718	203			-31	S2/130	9.4

■ PHIL WISNER

Wisner, Philip N.   b: 7/1869, Washington, D.C.   d: 7/5/36, Washington, D.C.   TR,   Deb: 8/30/1895

YEAR	TM/L	G	AB	R	H	2B	3B	HR	RBI	BB	SO	AVG	OBP	SLG	PRO+	BR	/A	RC	SB	CS	SBR	FR	POS	TPR
1895	Was-N	1	0	0	0	0	0	0	0	0	0	—	—	—	—	0	0	0	0			-1	/S	0.0

■ DAVE WISSMAN

Wissman, David Alvin   b: 2/17/41, Greenfield, Mass.   BL/TR, 6'2", 178 lbs.   Deb: 9/15/64

YEAR	TM/L	G	AB	R	H	2B	3B	HR	RBI	BB	SO	AVG	OBP	SLG	PRO+	BR	/A	RC	SB	CS	SBR	FR	POS	TPR
1964	Pit-N	16	27	2	4	0	0	0	1	9	.148	.179	.148	-7	-4	-4	1	0	0	0	0	O	-0.3

■ TEX WISTERZIL

Wisterzil, George John   b: 3/7/1891, Detroit, Mich.   d: 6/27/64, San Antonio, Tex.   BR/TR, 5'9.5", 150 lbs.   Deb: 4/14/14

YEAR	TM/L	G	AB	R	H	2B	3B	HR	RBI	BB	SO	AVG	OBP	SLG	PRO+	BR	/A	RC	SB	CS	SBR	FR	POS	TPR
1914	Bro-F	149	534	54	137	18	10	0	66	34	47	.257	.314	.328	85	-11	-10	64	17			15	*3	0.8
1915	Bro-F	36	106	13	33	3	3	0	21	21	7	.311	.438	.396	149	8	8	24	8			3	3	1.2
	Chi-F	7	20	3	4	1	0	0	0	3	2	.200	.304	.250	69	-1	-1	2	0			1	/3	0.0
	StL-F	8	24	1	5	1	0	0	4	2	2	.208	.296	.250	59	-1	-1	3	2			2	/3	0.1
	Chi-F	42	144	12	36	3	1	0	14	5	10	.250	.280	.285	71	-6	-5	13	2			9	3	0.5
	Yr	93	294	29	78	8	4	0	39	31	21	.265	.345	.320	100	0	1	40	12			15		1.8
Total	2	242	828	83	215	26	14	0	105	65	68	.260	.326	.325	90	-11	-9	105	29			30	3	2.6

■ MICKEY WITEK

Witek, Nicholas Joseph   b: 12/19/15, Luzerne, Pa.   d: 8/24/90, Kingston, Pa.   BR/TR, 5'10", 170 lbs.   Deb: 4/16/40

YEAR	TM/L	G	AB	R	H	2B	3B	HR	RBI	BB	SO	AVG	OBP	SLG	PRO+	BR	/A	RC	SB	CS	SBR	FR	POS	TPR
1940	NY-N	119	433	34	111	7	0	3	31	24	17	.256	.295	.293	62	-22	-22	36	2			19	S2	0.8
1941	NY-N	26	94	11	34	5	0	1	16	4	2	.362	.388	.447	132	4	4	16	0			2	2	0.7
1942	NY-N	148	553	72	144	19	6	5	48	36	20	.260	.306	.344	89	-8	-9	54	2			-1	*2	0.1

YEAR	TM/L	G	AB	R	H	2B	3B	HR	RBI	BB	SO	AVG	OBP	SLG	PRO+	BR	/A	RC	SB	CS	SBR	FR	POS	TPR
1943	NY-N	153	622	68	195	17	0	6	55	41	23	.314	.356	.370	109	7	7	78	1			16	*2	2.8
1946	NY-N	82	284	32	75	13	2	4	29	28	10	.264	.330	.366	97	-1	-1	34	1			-12	23	-1.2
1947	NY-N	51	160	22	35	4	1	3	17	15	12	.219	.286	.313	58	-10	-10	15	1			11	2/3	0.5
1949	NY-A	1	1	0	1	0	0	0	0	0	0	1.000	1.000	1.000	430	0	0	1	0	0	0	0	H	0.0
Total	7	580	2147	239	595	65	9	22	196	148	84	.277	.324	.347	90	-29	-31	235	7	0		34	2/S3	3.7

■ FRANK WITHROW
Withrow, Frank Blaine "Kid" b: 6/14/1891, Greenwood, Mo. d: 9/5/66, Omaha, Neb. BR/TR, 5'11.5", 187 lbs. Deb: 4/15/20

YEAR	TM/L	G	AB	R	H	2B	3B	HR	RBI	BB	SO	AVG	OBP	SLG	PRO+	BR	/A	RC	SB	CS	SBR	FR	POS	TPR
1920	Phi-N	48	132	8	24	4	1	0	12	8	26	.182	.239	.227	33	-11	-12	8	0	0	0	4	C	-0.4
1922	Phi-N	10	21	3	7	2	0	0	3	3	5	.333	.417	.429	108	1	0	4	0	0	0	1	/C	0.1
Total	2	58	153	11	31	6	1	0	15	11	31	.203	.265	.255	45	-10	-11	12	0	0	0	5	/C	-0.3

■ CORKY WITHROW
Withrow, Raymond Wallace b: 11/28/37, High Coal, W.Va. BR/TR, 6'3.5", 197 lbs. Deb: 9/06/63

YEAR	TM/L	G	AB	R	H	2B	3B	HR	RBI	BB	SO	AVG	OBP	SLG	PRO+	BR	/A	RC	SB	CS	SBR	FR	POS	TPR
1963	StL-N	6	9	0	0	0	0	0	1	0	2	.000	.000	.000	-91	-2	-2	0	0	0	0	0	/O	-0.2

■ WHITEY WITT
Witt, Lawton Walter (b: Ladislaw Waldemar Wittkowski) b: 9/28/1895, Orange, Mass. d: 7/14/88, Salem Co., N.J. BL/TR, 5'7", 150 lbs. Deb: 4/12/16

YEAR	TM/L	G	AB	R	H	2B	3B	HR	RBI	BB	SO	AVG	OBP	SLG	PRO+	BR	/A	RC	SB	CS	SBR	FR	POS	TPR
1916	Phi-A	143	563	64	138	16	15	2	36	55	71	.245	.315	.337	100	-4	-1	66	19			-1	*S	1.0
1917	Phi-A	128	452	62	114	13	4	0	28	65	45	.252	.346	.299	98	1	1	50	12			5	*S/O3	1.1
1919	Phi-A	122	460	56	123	15	6	0	33	46	26	.267	.334	.326	85	-8	-9	52	11			-3	O2/3	-1.0
1920	Phi-A	65	218	29	70	11	3	1	25	27	16	.321	.396	.413	113	5	5	36	2	3	-1	-8	O2/S	-0.7
1921	Phi-A	154	629	100	198	31	11	4	45	77	52	.315	.390	.418	106	8	7	104	16	15	-4	-2	*O	-1.4
1922	*NY-A	140	528	98	157	11	6	4	40	89	29	.297	.400	.364	98	5	3	81	5	8	-3	-5	*O	-1.4
1923	*NY-A	146	596	113	187	18	10	6	56	67	42	.314	.386	.408	107	9	8	95	2	7	-4	2	*O	-0.5
1924	NY-A	147	600	88	178	26	5	1	36	45	20	.297	.346	.362	83	-16	-15	76	9	7	-2	-1	*O	-2.6
1925	NY-A	31	40	9	8	2	1	0	0	6	2	.200	.304	.300	55	-3	-3	4	1	1	-0	-1	O	-0.4
1926	Bro-N	63	85	13	22	1	1	0	3	12	6	.259	.351	.294	76	-2	-2	9	1			3	O	0.0
Total	10	1139	4171	632	1195	144	62	18	302	489	309	.287	.362	.364	97	-5	-6	574	78	41		-10	OS/23	-5.5

■ JERRY WITTE
Witte, Jerome Charles b: 7/30/15, St.Louis, Mo. BR/TR, 6'1", 190 lbs. Deb: 9/10/46

YEAR	TM/L	G	AB	R	H	2B	3B	HR	RBI	BB	SO	AVG	OBP	SLG	PRO+	BR	/A	RC	SB	CS	SBR	FR	POS	TPR
1946	StL-A	18	73	7	14	2	0	2	4	0	18	.192	.192	.301	35	-7	-7	4	0	0	0	-2	1	-1.0
1947	StL-A	34	99	4	14	2	1	2	12	11	22	.141	.227	.242	30	-10	-10	6	0	0	0	-1	1	-1.2
Total	2	52	172	11	28	4	1	4	16	11	40	.163	.213	.267	32	-16	-17	10	0	0	0	-4	/1	-2.2

■ JOHN WOCKENFUSS
Wockenfuss, Johnny Bilton b: 2/27/49, Welch, W.Va. BR/TR, 6', 190 lbs. Deb: 8/11/74

YEAR	TM/L	G	AB	R	H	2B	3B	HR	RBI	BB	SO	AVG	OBP	SLG	PRO+	BR	/A	RC	SB	CS	SBR	FR	POS	TPR
1974	Det-A	13	29	1	4	1	0	0	2	3	2	.138	.219	.172	13	-3	-3	1	0	0	0	-1	C	-0.3
1975	Det-A	35	118	15	27	6	3	4	13	10	15	.229	.289	.432	97	-0	-1	13	0	0	0	5	C	0.5
1976	Det-A	60	144	18	32	7	2	3	10	17	14	.222	.309	.361	92	-1	-2	15	0	3	-2	-9	C	-1.0
1977	Det-A	53	164	26	45	8	1	9	25	14	18	.274	.331	.500	117	5	4	28	0	0	0	5	C/OD	0.9
1978	Det-A	71	187	23	53	5	0	7	22	21	14	.283	.359	.422	116	5	4	27	0	1	-1	4	O/D	0.6
1979	Det-A	87	231	27	61	9	1	15	46	18	40	.264	.323	.506	116	5	4	34	2	2	-1	7	1CD/O	0.9
1980	Det-A	126	372	56	102	13	2	16	65	68	64	.274	.391	.449	126	17	16	68	1	4	-2	3	1DCO	1.4
1981	Det-A	70	172	20	37	4	0	9	25	28	22	.215	.325	.395	103	2	1	23	0	0	0	-3	D1/CO	-0.2
1982	Det-A	70	193	28	58	9	0	8	32	29	21	.301	.382	.472	135	10	10	37	0	0	0	1	C1D0/3	1.2
1983	Det-A	92	245	32	66	8	1	9	44	31	37	.269	.351	.420	114	4	5	37	1	1	-0	1	DC1/30	1.0
1984	Phi-N	86	180	20	52	3	1	6	24	30	24	.289	.390	.417	125	7	7	31	1	0	0	-7	1C/3	0.0
1985	Phi-N	32	37	1	6	0	0	0	6	3	7	.162	.225	.162	35	-3	-3	2	0	0	0	-1	/1C	-0.3
Total	12	795	2072	267	543	73	11	86	310	277	278	.262	.351	.432	114	49	43	316	5	11	-5	9	C1D0/3	4.7

■ ANDY WOEHR
Woehr, Andrew Emil b: 2/4/1896, Fort Wayne, Ind. BR/TR, 5'11", 165 lbs. Deb: 9/15/23

YEAR	TM/L	G	AB	R	H	2B	3B	HR	RBI	BB	SO	AVG	OBP	SLG	PRO+	BR	/A	RC	SB	CS	SBR	FR	POS	TPR
1923	Phi-N	13	41	3	14	2	0	0	3	1	1	.341	.357	.390	87	-0	-1	6	0	0	0	3	3	0.2
1924	Phi-N	50	152	11	33	4	5	0	17	5	8	.217	.252	.309	44	-11	-13	12	2	2	-1	-5	3/2	-1.5
Total	2	63	193	14	47	6	5	0	20	6	9	.244	.274	.326	53	-11	-14	17	2	2	-1	-2	/32	-1.3

■ JOE WOERLIN
Woerlin, Joseph b: 10/9/1864, France d: 6/22/19, St.Louis, Mo. Deb: 7/21/1895

YEAR	TM/L	G	AB	R	H	2B	3B	HR	RBI	BB	SO	AVG	OBP	SLG	PRO+	BR	/A	RC	SB	CS	SBR	FR	POS	TPR
1895	Was-N	1	3	1	1	0	0	0	0	0	0	.333	.333	.333	75	-0	-0	0	0			0	/S	0.0

■ JIM WOHLFORD
Wohlford, James Eugene b: 2/28/51, Visalia, Cal. BR/TR, 5'11", 175 lbs. Deb: 9/01/72

YEAR	TM/L	G	AB	R	H	2B	3B	HR	RBI	BB	SO	AVG	OBP	SLG	PRO+	BR	/A	RC	SB	CS	SBR	FR	POS	TPR
1972	KC-A	15	25	3	6	1	0	0	2	2	6	.240	.321	.280	80	-1	-1	3	0	0	0	-2	/2	-0.2
1973	KC-A	45	109	21	29	1	3	2	10	11	12	.266	.333	.385	95	0	-1	14	1	1	-0	2	DO	-0.3
1974	KC-A	143	501	55	136	16	7	2	44	39	74	.271	.328	.343	88	-4	-7	55	16	13	-3	-6	*O/D	-2.0
1975	KC-A	116	353	45	90	10	5	0	30	34	37	.255	.322	.312	78	-9	-10	38	12	7	-1	-4	*O/D	-1.7
1976	*KC-A	107	293	47	73	10	2	1	24	29	24	.249	.319	.307	83	-5	-6	27	22	16	-3	-3	O/2D	-1.4
1977	Mil-A	129	391	41	97	16	3	2	36	21	49	.248	.288	.320	65	-19	-19	32	17	16	-5	-2	*O/2D	-2.9
1978	Mil-A	46	118	16	35	7	2	1	19	6	10	.297	.331	.415	108	1	1	16	3	2	-0	-2	O/D	-0.1
1979	Mil-A	63	175	19	46	13	1	1	17	8	28	.263	.295	.379	77	-6	-6	19	6	2	1	2	O/D	-0.5
1980	SF-N	91	193	17	54	6	4	1	24	13	23	.280	.329	.368	96	-2	-1	22	1	4	-2	0	O/3	-0.5
1981	SF-N	50	68	4	11	3	0	1	7	4	9	.162	.208	.250	30	-6	-6	3	0	0	0	-2	O	-0.9
1982	SF-N	97	250	37	64	12	1	2	25	30	36	.256	.336	.336	89	-3	-3	28	8	3	1	-2	O	-0.5
1983	Mon-N	83	141	7	39	8	0	1	14	5	14	.277	.301	.355	82	-4	-4	14	0	0	0	-5	O/3	-0.1
1984	Mon-N	95	213	20	64	13	2	5	29	14	19	.300	.344	.451	127	5	7	34	3	0	1	3	O/3	0.5
1985	Mon-N	70	125	7	24	5	1	1	15	16	19	.192	.284	.272	60	-7	-6	10	0	2	-1	-1	O	-0.9
1986	Mon-N	70	94	10	25	4	2	1	15	7	23	.266	.320	.383	97	-1	-0	11	0	2	-1	-0	O/3	-0.2
Total	15	1220	3049	349	793	125	33	21	305	241	376	.260	.316	.343	85	-59	-62	325	89	68	-14	-22	O/D23	-11.9

■ JOHN WOJCIK
Wojcik, John Joseph b: 4/6/42, Olean, N.Y. BL/TR, 6' ", 175 lbs. Deb: 9/09/62

YEAR	TM/L	G	AB	R	H	2B	3B	HR	RBI	BB	SO	AVG	OBP	SLG	PRO+	BR	/A	RC	SB	CS	SBR	FR	POS	TPR
1962	KC-A	16	43	8	13	4	0	0	9	13	4	.302	.474	.395	133	3	3	11	3	0	1	-1	O	0.3
1963	KC-A	19	59	7	11	0	0	0	2	8	8	.186	.284	.186	34	-5	-5	4	2	0	1	0	O	-0.4
1964	KC-A	6	22	1	3	0	0	0	0	2	8	.136	.208	.136	-2	-3	-3	1	0	0	0	-0	/O	-0.3
Total	3	41	124	16	27	4	0	0	11	23	20	.218	.345	.250	65	-4	-5	15	5	0	2	-1	/O	-0.4

■ RAY WOLF
Wolf, Raymond Bernard "Grandpa" b: 7/15/04, Chicago, Ill. d: 10/6/79, Fort Worth, Tex. BR/TR, 5'11", 175 lbs. Deb: 7/27/27

YEAR	TM/L	G	AB	R	H	2B	3B	HR	RBI	BB	SO	AVG	OBP	SLG	PRO+	BR	/A	RC	SB	CS	SBR	FR	POS	TPR
1927	Cin-N	1	1	0	0	0	0	0	0	0	0	.000	.000	.000	-99	-0	-0	0	0			0	/1	0.0

■ JIMMY WOLF
Wolf, William Van Winkle "Chicken" b: 5/12/1862, Louisville, Ky. d: 5/16/03, Louisville, Ky. BR, 5'9", 190 lbs. Deb: 5/02/1882 M

YEAR	TM/L	G	AB	R	H	2B	3B	HR	RBI	BB	SO	AVG	OBP	SLG	PRO+	BR	/A	RC	SB	CS	SBR	FR	POS	TPR
1882	Lou-a	78	318	46	95	11	8	0			9	.299	.318	.384	144	11	14	40				-2	*O/S1P	1.0
1883	Lou-a	98	389	59	102	17	9	1		5		.262	.272	.360	110	0	5	39				17	*OC/S2	2.1
1884	Lou-a	110	486	79	146	24	11	3		4		.300	.310	.414	144	18	21	64				2	*OC/S31	2.1
1885	Lou-a	112	483	79	141	23	17	1		11		.292	.309	.416	130	15	15	64				0	*O/C3P	0.8
1886	Lou-a	130	545	93	148	17	12	3		27		.272	.310	.363	106	6	1	70	23			12	*O/1C2P	0.8
1887	Lou-a	137	569	103	160	27	13	2		34		.281	.331	.385	99	0	-2	89	45			8	*O1	0.1
1888	Lou-a	128	538	80	154	28	11	0	67	26		.286	.320	.379	130	15	16	80	41			7	OS/3C1	0.5
1889	Lou-a	130	546	72	159	20	9	3	57	29	34	.291	.333	.377	106	2	4	76	18			-1	O12S/3M	0.0
1890	*Lou-a	134	543	100	197	29	11	4		43		.363	.419	.479	172	45	47	132	46			-2	*O3	3.3
1891	Lou-a	138	537	67	136	17	8	1	82	42	36	.253	.317	.320	86	-11	-9	60	13			5	*O/13	-0.8
1892	StL-N	3	14	1	2	0	0	0	1	0	1	.143	.143	.143	-13	-2	-2	0	0			-1	/O	-0.2

YEAR	TM/L	G	AB	R	H	2B	3B	HR	RBI	BB	SO	AVG	OBP	SLG	PRO+	BR	/A	RC	SB	CS	SBR	FR	POS	TPR
Total	11	1198	4968	779	1440	213	109	18	207	229	71	.290	.326	.387	121	100	110	715	186			46	*O/S1C32P	11.3

■ HARRY WOLFE
Wolfe, Harold "Whitey" b: 11/24/1890, Massachusetts d: 7/28/71, Fort Wayne, Ind. BR/TR, 5'8", 160 lbs. Deb: 4/15/17

YEAR	TM/L	G	AB	R	H	2B	3B	HR	RBI	BB	SO	AVG	OBP	SLG	PRO+	BR	/A	RC	SB	CS	SBR	FR	POS	TPR
1917	Chi-N	9	5	1	2	0	0	0	1	1	1	.400	.500	.400	164	1	1	1	0			1	/OS	0.1
	Pit-N	3	5	0	0	0	0	0	0	1	4	.000	.167	.000	-45	-1	-1	0	0			1	/2S	0.0
	Yr	12	10	1	2	0	0	0	1	2	5	.200	.333	.200	61	-0	-0	1	0			1		0.1

■ LARRY WOLFE
Wolfe, Laurence Marcy b: 3/2/53, Melbourne, Fla. BR/TR, 5'11", 170 lbs. Deb: 9/16/77

YEAR	TM/L	G	AB	R	H	2B	3B	HR	RBI	BB	SO	AVG	OBP	SLG	PRO+	BR	/A	RC	SB	CS	SBR	FR	POS	TPR
1977	Min-A	8	25	3	6	1	0	0	6	1	0	.240	.269	.280	51	-2	-2	2	0	0	0	0	/3	-0.1
1978	Min-A	88	235	25	55	10	1	3	25	36	27	.234	.336	.323	85	-3	-4	26	0	1	-1	6	3/S	0.1
1979	Bos-A	47	78	12	19	4	0	3	15	17	21	.244	.385	.410	109	2	2	14	0	0	0	6	2/3SC1	0.8
1980	Bos-A	18	23	3	3	1	0	1	4	0	5	.130	.130	.304	15	-3	-3	1	0	0	0	1	3/D	-0.1
Total	4	161	361	43	83	16	1	7	50	54	53	.230	.332	.338	84	-6	-7	43	0	1	-1	13	3/2SD1C	0.7

■ POLLY WOLFE
Wolfe, Roy Chamberlain b: 9/1/1888, Knoxville, Ill. d: 11/21/38, Morris, Ill. BL/TR, 5'10", 170 lbs. Deb: 9/22/12

YEAR	TM/L	G	AB	R	H	2B	3B	HR	RBI	BB	SO	AVG	OBP	SLG	PRO+	BR	/A	RC	SB	CS	SBR	FR	POS	TPR
1912	Chi-A	1	1	0	0	0	0	0	0	0		.000	.000	.000	-99	-0	-0	0	0			0	H	0.0
1914	Chi-A	8	28	0	6	0	0	0	0	3	6	.214	.290	.214	53	-1	-1	2	1	1	-0	-1	/O	-0.3
Total	2	9	29	0	6	0	0	0	0	3	6	.207	.281	.207	47	-2	-2	2	1	1		-1	/O	-0.3

■ ABE WOLSTENHOLME
Wolstenholme, Abraham Lincoln b: 3/4/1861, Philadelphia, Pa. d: 3/4/16, Philadelphia, Pa. Deb: 6/04/1883

YEAR	TM/L	G	AB	R	H	2B	3B	HR	RBI	BB	SO	AVG	OBP	SLG	PRO+	BR	/A	RC	SB	CS	SBR	FR	POS	TPR
1883	Phi-N	3	11	0	1	1	0	0	0	0	0	.091	.091	.182	-22	-2	-1	0				-1	/CO	-0.2

■ HARRY WOLTER
Wolter, Harry Meigs b: 7/11/1884, Monterey, Cal. d: 7/7/70, Palo Alto, Cal. BL/TL, 5'10", 175 lbs. Deb: 5/14/07

YEAR	TM/L	G	AB	R	H	2B	3B	HR	RBI	BB	SO	AVG	OBP	SLG	PRO+	BR	/A	RC	SB	CS	SBR	FR	POS	TPR
1907	Cin-N	4	15	1	2	0	0	0	1	0		.133	.133	.133	-15	-2	-2	0	0			-0	/O	-0.2
	Pit-N	1	1	0	0	0	0	0	0	0		.000	.000	.000	-99	-0	-0	0	0			0	/P	0.0
	StL-N	16	47	4	16	0	0	0	6	3		.340	.380	.340	133	2	2	7	1			3	O/P	0.5
	Yr	21	63	5	18	0	0	0	7	3		.286	.318	.286	93	-1	-1	6	1			3		0.3
1909	Bos-A	54	122	14	30	2	4	2	10	9		.246	.298	.377	110	1	1	14	2			-1	1P/O	0.2
1910	NY-A	135	479	84	128	15	9	4	42	66		.267	.364	.361	120	17	14	78	39			-3	*O/1	0.6
1911	NY-A	122	434	78	132	17	15	4	36	62		.304	.396	.440	125	21	16	86	28			4	*O/1	1.1
1912	NY-A	12	32	8	11	2	1	0	1	10		.344	.512	.469	171	4	4	10	5			-1	/O	0.2
1913	NY-A	127	425	53	108	18	6	2	43	80	50	.254	.377	.339	109	9	9	58	13			-7	*O	-0.5
1917	Chi-N	117	353	44	88	15	7	0	28	38	40	.249	.324	.331	94	1	-2	39	7			-7	O/1	-1.3
Total	7	588	1908	286	515	69	42	12	167	268	90	.270	.365	.369	114	53	42	292	95			-12	O/1P	0.6

■ HARRY WOLVERTON
Wolverton, Harry Sterling "Fighting Harry"
b: 12/6/1873, Mt.Vernon, Ohio d: 2/4/37, Oakland, Cal. BL/TR, 5'11", 205 lbs. Deb: 9/25/1898 M

YEAR	TM/L	G	AB	R	H	2B	3B	HR	RBI	BB	SO	AVG	OBP	SLG	PRO+	BR	/A	RC	SB	CS	SBR	FR	POS	TPR
1898	Chi-N	13	49	4	16	1	0	0	2	1		.327	.353	.347	104	0	0	7	1			3	3	0.3
1899	Chi-N	99	389	50	111	14	11	1	49	30		.285	.350	.386	107	3	4	59	14			-6	3/S	-0.1
1900	Chi-N	3	11	2	2	0	0	0	0	2		.182	.308	.182	40	-1	-1	1	1			-2	/3	-0.1
	Phi-N	101	383	42	108	10	8	3	58	20		.282	.323	.373	95	-4	-3	49	4			-9	*3	-1.0
	Yr	104	394	44	110	10	8	3	58	22		.279	.322	.368	93	-4	-4	50	5			-11		-1.1
1901	Phi-N	93	379	42	117	15	4	0	43	22		.309	.355	.369	110	6	5	56	13			3	3	1.4
1902	Was-A	59	249	35	62	8	3	1	23	13		.249	.294	.317	70	-10	-10	26	8			3	3	-0.7
	Phi-N	34	136	12	40	3	2	0	16	9		.294	.347	.346	116	3	3	18	3			9	3	1.4
1903	Phi-N	123	494	72	152	13	12	0	53	18		.308	.332	.383	109	2	4	70	10			1	*3	0.5
1904	Phi-N	102	398	43	106	15	5	0	49	26		.266	.311	.329	103	-0	1	49	18			1	*3	0.7
1905	Bos-N	122	463	38	104	15	7	2	55	23		.225	.261	.300	70	-18	-17	41	10			4	*3	-0.4
1912	NY-A	34	50	6	15	1	1	0	4	2		.300	.340	.360	94	-0	-0	6	1			-1	/3M	-0.1
Total	9	783	3001	346	833	95	53	7	352	166		.278	.321	.352	97	-19	-13	383	83			7	3/S	1.9

■ SID WOMACK
Womack, Sidney Kirk "Tex" b: 10/2/1896, Greensburg, La. d: 8/28/58, Jackson, Miss. BR/TR, 5'10.5", 185 lbs. Deb: 8/15/26

YEAR	TM/L	G	AB	R	H	2B	3B	HR	RBI	BB	SO	AVG	OBP	SLG	PRO+	BR	/A	RC	SB	CS	SBR	FR	POS	TPR
1926	Bos-N	1	3	0	0	0	0	0	1	0	0	.000	.000	.000	-99	-1	-1	0	0			0	/C	0.0

■ WOOD
Wood Deb: 9/30/1874

YEAR	TM/L	G	AB	R	H	2B	3B	HR	RBI	BB	SO	AVG	OBP	SLG	PRO+	BR	/A	RC	SB	CS	SBR	FR	POS	TPR
1874	Bal-n	1	6	0	0	0	0	0		0		.000	.000	.000	-99	-1	-1	0					/2	0.0

■ DOC WOOD
Wood, Charles Spencer b: 2/28/1900, Batesville, Miss. d: 11/3/74, New Orleans, La. BR/TR, 5'10", 150 lbs. Deb: 7/21/23

YEAR	TM/L	G	AB	R	H	2B	3B	HR	RBI	BB	SO	AVG	OBP	SLG	PRO+	BR	/A	RC	SB	CS	SBR	FR	POS	TPR
1923	Phi-A	3	3	0	1	0	0	0	0	0	0	.333	.333	.333	75	-0	-0	0	0	0	0	1	/S	0.1

■ FRED WOOD
Wood, Fred S. b: 1863, Hamilton, Ont., Canada d: 8/23/33, New York, N.Y. 5'5", 160 lbs. Deb: 5/14/1884

YEAR	TM/L	G	AB	R	H	2B	3B	HR	RBI	BB	SO	AVG	OBP	SLG	PRO+	BR	/A	RC	SB	CS	SBR	FR	POS	TPR
1884	Det-N	12	42	4	2	0	0	0	1	3	18	.048	.111	.048	-51	-7	-7	0				1	/COS	-0.3
1885	Buf-N	1	4	0	1	0	0	0	0	0	0	.250	.250	.250	60	-0	-0	0				-0	/C	0.0
Total	2	13	46	4	3	0	0	0	1	3	18	.065	.122	.065	-41	-7	-7	0				1	/COS	-0.3

■ GEORGE WOOD
Wood, George A. "Dandy" b: 11/9/1858, Boston, Mass. d: 4/4/24, Harrisburg, Pa. BL/TR, 5'10.5", 175 lbs. Deb: 5/01/1880 MU

YEAR	TM/L	G	AB	R	H	2B	3B	HR	RBI	BB	SO	AVG	OBP	SLG	PRO+	BR	/A	RC	SB	CS	SBR	FR	POS	TPR
1880	Wor-N	81	327	37	80	16	5	0	28	10	37	.245	.267	.324	91	-0	-4	29				-7	*O/31	-1.3
1881	Det-N	80	337	54	100	18	9	2	32	19	32	.297	.334	.421	131	14	12	49				-3	*O	0.7
1882	Det-N	84	375	69	101	12	12	7	29	14	30	.269	.296	.421	127	11	11	48				1	*O	1.0
1883	Det-N	99	441	81	133	26	11	5	47	25	37	.302	.339	.444	142	19	22	68				8	*O/P	2.8
1884	Det-N	114	473	79	119	16	10	8	29	39	75	.252	.309	.378	122	8	13	57				3	*O/3	1.3
1885	Det-N	82	362	62	105	19	8	5	28	13	19	.290	.315	.428	138	14	14	50				1	O3/SP	1.2
1886	Phi-N	106	450	81	123	18	15	4	66	23	75	.273	.309	.407	115	8	7	61	9			-6	*O/S3	0.2
1887	Phi-N	113	491	118	142	22	19	14	66	40	51	.289	.350	.497	122	22	17	94	19			-11	*O/S32	0.6
1888	Phi-N	106	433	67	99	19	6	6	15	39	44	.229	.303	.342	102	5	1	52	20			0	*O/3P	0.1
1889	Phi-N	97	422	77	106	21	4	5	53	53	33	.251	.336	.355	87	-2	-8	58	17			-5	O/SP	-1.3
	Bal-a	3	10	1	2	0	0	0	1	0	2	.200	.200	.200	55	-1	-1	1	1			-0	/O	0.0
1890	Phi-P	132	539	115	156	20	14	9	102	51	35	.289	.360	.429	109	8	6	92	20			14	*O/3	1.1
1891	Phi-a	132	528	105	163	18	14	3	61	72	52	.309	.399	.413	132	26	23	98	22			7	*O/3SM	2.2
1892	Bal-N	21	76	9	17	1	1	0	10	10	10	.224	.330	.263	79	-1	-2	7	1			2	O	0.0
	Cin-N	30	107	10	21	2	4	0	14	10	17	.196	.271	.290	72	-4	-4	10	4			-2	O	-0.5
	Yr	51	183	19	38	3	5	0	24	20	25	.208	.296	.279	75	-5	-5	17	5			1		-0.5
Total	13	1280	5371	965	1467	228	132	68	565	418	547	.273	.329	.403	117	125	107	773	113			3	*O/3SP21	8.1

■ HARRY WOOD
Wood, Harold Austin b: 2/10/1881, Waterville, Maine d: 5/18/55, Bethesda, Md. BL/TR, 5'10", 155 lbs. Deb: 4/19/03

YEAR	TM/L	G	AB	R	H	2B	3B	HR	RBI	BB	SO	AVG	OBP	SLG	PRO+	BR	/A	RC	SB	CS	SBR	FR	POS	TPR
1903	Cin-N	2	3	0	0	0	0	0	0	1		.000	.250	.000	-23	-0	-1	0	0			-1	/O	0.0

■ JAKE WOOD
Wood, Jacob b: 6/22/37, Elizabeth, N.J. BR/TR, 6'1", 163 lbs. Deb: 4/11/61

YEAR	TM/L	G	AB	R	H	2B	3B	HR	RBI	BB	SO	AVG	OBP	SLG	PRO+	BR	/A	RC	SB	CS	SBR	FR	POS	TPR
1961	Det-A	162	663	96	171	17	14	11	69	58	141	.258	.321	.376	83	-14	-16	84	30	9	4	-27	*2	-1.9
1962	Det-A	111	367	68	83	10	5	8	30	33	59	.226	.292	.346	68	-15	-17	40	24	3	5	-31	2	-3.6
1963	Det-A	85	351	50	95	11	2	11	27	24	61	.271	.330	.407	102	2	1	50	18	5	2	-11	2/3	-0.1
1964	Det-A	64	125	11	29	2	2	1	7	4	24	.232	.256	.304	54	-8	-8	10	0	0	0	-1	12/3O	-0.8
1965	Det-A	58	104	12	30	3	0	2	7	10	19	.288	.357	.375	107	1	1	12	3	3	1	-2	2/1S3	0.0
1966	Det-A	98	230	39	58	9	3	2	27	28	48	.252	.336	.343	94	-1	-1	27	4	3	-1	-13	2/31	-1.0
1967	Det-A	14	20	2	1	1	0	0	0	1	7	.050	.095	.100	-41	-4	-4	0	0	0	0	0	/12	-0.3
	Cin-N	16	17	1	2	0	0	0	1	1	3	.118	.167	.118	-15	-3	-3	0	0	0	0	0	/O	-0.2

YEAR	TM/L	G	AB	R	H	2B	3B	HR	RBI	BB	SO	AVG	OBP	SLG	PRO+	BR	/A	RC	SB	CS	SBR	FR	POS	TPR
Total	7	608	1877	279	469	53	26	35	168	159	362	.250	.313	.362	82	-40	-47	223	79	23	10	-84	2/130S	-7.9

■ JIMMY WOOD
Wood, James Leon b: 12/1/1844, Brooklyn, N.Y. d: 11/30/1886, 5'8.5", 150 lbs. Deb: 5/08/1871 M

YEAR	TM/L	G	AB	R	H	2B	3B	HR	RBI	BB	SO	AVG	OBP	SLG	PRO+	BR	/A	RC	SB	CS	SBR	FR	POS	TPR
1871	Chi-n	28	135	45	51	10	6	1	29	11	3	.378	.425	.563	163	14	10	41	18				*2M	0.7
1872	Tro-n	25	116	40	38	9	3	2		2		.328	.339	.509	155	7	7	21					2M	0.2
	Eck-n	7	30	10	6	1	1	0		4		.200	.294	.300	98	-0	1	3					2M	0.0
	Yr	32	146	50	44	10	4	2		6		.301	.329	.466	145	7	8	23						0.2
1873	Phi-n	42	211	67	67	10	1	0		7		.318	.339	.374	106	3	1	27					*2M	-0.1
Total	3 n	102	492	162	162	30	11	3		24		.329	.360	.453	134	24	19	92					2	0.8

■ JOE WOOD
Wood, Joseph "Smokey Joe" (b: Howard Ellsworth Wood)
b: 10/25/1889, Kansas City, Mo. d: 7/27/85, West Haven, Conn BR/TR, 5'11", 180 lbs. Deb: 8/24/08

YEAR	TM/L	G	AB	R	H	2B	3B	HR	RBI	BB	SO	AVG	OBP	SLG	PRO+	BR	/A	RC	SB	CS	SBR	FR	POS	TPR
1908	Bos-A	6	7	1	0	0	0	0	0	0		.000	.000	.000	-97	-1	-1	0	0			-0	/P	0.0
1909	Bos-A	24	55	4	9	0	1	0	3	2		.164	.207	.200	28	-4	-5	2	0			-4	P	0.0
1910	Bos-A	35	69	9	18	2	1	1	5	5		.261	.311	.362	108	1	0	8	0			1	P	0.0
1911	Bos-A	44	88	15	23	4	2	2	11	10		.261	.343	.420	114	1	1	13	1			0	P	0.0
1912	*Bos-A	43	124	16	36	13	1	1	13	11		.290	.348	.435	118	3	2	19	0			6	P	0.0
1913	Bos-A	24	56	10	15	5	0	0	10	4	7	.268	.317	.357	95	-0	-1	6	1			3	P	0.0
1914	Bos-A	21	43	2	6	1	0	0	1	3	14	.140	.213	.163	13	-5	-5	2	1			0	P	0.0
1915	Bos-A	29	54	6	14	1	1	1	7	5	10	.259	.322	.370	111	0	0	7	1	1	-0	0	P	0.0
1917	Cle-A	10	6	1	0	0	0	0	0	0	3	.000	.000	.000	-93	-1	-1	0	0			0	/P	0.0
1918	Cle-A	119	422	41	125	22	4	5	66	36	38	.296	.356	.403	118	14	9	63	8			0	O2/1	0.6
1919	Cle-A	72	192	30	49	10	5	1	27	32	21	.255	.367	.375	102	3	2	28	3			-8	O/P	-1.0
1920	*Cle-A	61	137	25	37	11	2	1	30	25	16	.270	.390	.401	107	3	2	24	1	1	-0	-6	O/P	-0.8
1921	Cle-A	66	194	32	71	16	5	4	60	25	17	.366	.438	.562	151	16	15	49	2	0	1	-13	O	-0.1
1922	Cle-A	142	505	74	150	33	8	8	92	50	63	.297	.367	.442	109	7	7	85	5	1	1	2	*O	0.0
Total	14	696	1952	266	553	118	30	24	325	208	189	.283	.357	.411	110	36	27	305	23	3		-18	OP/21	-1.3

■ JOE WOOD
Wood, Joseph Perry "Joe", "J.P." or "Little Joe" b: 10/3/19, Houston, Tex. d: 3/25/85, Houston, Tex. BR/TR, 5'9.5", 160 lbs. Deb: 5/02/43

YEAR	TM/L	G	AB	R	H	2B	3B	HR	RBI	BB	SO	AVG	OBP	SLG	PRO+	BR	/A	RC	SB	CS	SBR	FR	POS	TPR
1943	Det-A	60	164	22	53	4	4	1	17	6	13	.323	.347	.415	114	4	2	21	2	2	-1	-16	23	-1.3

■ KEN WOOD
Wood, Kenneth Lanier b: 7/1/24, Lincolnton, N.C. BR/TR, 6', 200 lbs. Deb: 4/28/48

YEAR	TM/L	G	AB	R	H	2B	3B	HR	RBI	BB	SO	AVG	OBP	SLG	PRO+	BR	/A	RC	SB	CS	SBR	FR	POS	TPR
1948	StL-A	10	24	2	2	0	1	0	2	1	4	.083	.120	.167	-24	-4	-4	0	0	0	0	0	/O	-0.3
1949	StL-A	7	6	0	0	0	0	0	0	1	2	.000	.143	.000	-58	-1	-1	0	0	0	0	0	/O	-0.1
1950	StL-A	128	369	42	83	24	0	13	62	38	58	.225	.299	.396	74	-15	-17	40	0	4	-2	-4	O	-2.3
1951	StL-A	109	333	40	79	19	0	15	44	27	49	.237	.296	.429	92	-5	-6	40	1	2	-1	-6	*O	-1.6
1952	Bos-A	15	20	0	2	0	0	0	0	3	4	.100	.217	.100	-9	-3	-3	1	0	0	0	-1	O	-0.4
	Was-A	61	210	26	50	8	6	6	32	30	21	.238	.333	.419	112	2	3	30	0	1	-1	7	O	0.8
	Yr	76	230	26	52	8	6	6	32	33	25	.226	.323	.391	99	-1	-1	30	0	1	-1	6		0.4
1953	Was-A	12	33	0	7	1	0	0	3	2	3	.212	.257	.242	36	-3	-3	2	0	0	0	-0	/O	-0.2
Total	6	342	995	110	223	52	7	34	143	102	141	.224	.298	.393	81	-30	-32	113	1	7	-4	-5	O	-4.1

■ BOB WOOD
Wood, Robert Lynn b: 7/28/1865, Thorn Hill, Ohio d: 5/22/43, Churchill, Ohio BR/TR, Deb: 5/02/1898

YEAR	TM/L	G	AB	R	H	2B	3B	HR	RBI	BB	SO	AVG	OBP	SLG	PRO+	BR	/A	RC	SB	CS	SBR	FR	POS	TPR
1898	Cin-N	39	109	14	30	6	0	0	16	9		.275	.331	.330	86	-1	-2	13	1			1	C/O1	0.1
1899	Cin-N	62	194	34	61	11	7	0	24	25		.314	.401	.443	132	10	9	37	3			-11	C/O31	0.1
1900	Cin-N	45	139	17	37	8	1	0	22	10		.266	.315	.338	85	-3	-3	16	3			-7	C3/O	-0.6
1901	Cle-A	98	346	45	101	23	3	1	49	12		.292	.329	.384	103	-1	1	47	6			-1	C/3O12S	0.7
1902	Cle-A	81	258	23	76	18	2	0	40	27		.295	.377	.380	117	5	7	39	1			-8	C1/O23	0.3
1904	Det-A	49	175	15	43	6	2	1	17	5		.246	.267	.320	90	-3	-2	16	1			9	C	1.3
1905	Det-A	8	24	1	2	1	0	0	0	1		.083	.120	.125	-21	-3	-3	0	0			-0	/C	-0.2
Total	7	382	1245	149	350	73	15	2	168	89		.281	.338	.369	104	4	7	167	15			-16	C/3102S	1.7

■ ROY WOOD
Wood, Roy Winton "Woody" b: 8/29/1892, Monticello, Ark. d: 4/6/74, Fayetteville, Ark. BR/TR, 6', 175 lbs. Deb: 6/16/13

YEAR	TM/L	G	AB	R	H	2B	3B	HR	RBI	BB	SO	AVG	OBP	SLG	PRO+	BR	/A	RC	SB	CS	SBR	FR	POS	TPR
1913	Pit-N	14	35	4	10	4	0	0	2	1	8	.286	.306	.400	105	-0	0	4	0			2	/O1	0.1
1914	Cle-A	72	220	24	52	6	3	1	15	13	26	.236	.300	.305	79	-5	-6	19	6	9	-4	-0	O1	-1.3
1915	Cle-A	33	78	5	15	2	1	0	3	2	13	.192	.232	.244	41	-6	-6	4	1	2	-1	-0	1/O	-0.9
Total	3	119	333	33	77	12	4	1	20	16	47	.231	.285	.300	73	-11	-12	27	7	11		-0	/O1	-2.1

■ LARRY WOODALL
Woodall, Charles Lawrence b: 7/26/1894, Staunton, Va. d: 5/16/63, Cambridge, Mass. BR/TR, 5'9", 165 lbs. Deb: 5/20/20 C

YEAR	TM/L	G	AB	R	H	2B	3B	HR	RBI	BB	SO	AVG	OBP	SLG	PRO+	BR	/A	RC	SB	CS	SBR	FR	POS	TPR
1920	Det-A	18	49	4	12	1	0	0	5	2	6	.245	.275	.265	45	-4	-4	4	0	0	0	2	C	0.0
1921	Det-A	46	80	10	29	4	1	0	14	6	7	.363	.407	.438	117	2	2	15	1	0	0	-7	C	-0.3
1922	Det-A	50	125	19	43	2	2	0	18	8	11	.344	.388	.392	107	1	2	19	0	1	-1	-10	C	-0.6
1923	Det-A	71	148	20	41	12	2	1	19	22	4	.277	.371	.405	106	1	2	24	2	1	0	-5	C	0.1
1924	Det-A	67	165	23	51	9	2	0	25	21	5	.309	.387	.388	102	1	1	26	0	0	0	0	C	0.5
1925	Det-A	75	171	20	35	4	1	0	13	24	8	.205	.303	.240	39	-16	-15	14	1	0	0	-7	C	-1.6
1926	Det-A	67	146	18	34	5	0	0	15	15	2	.233	.304	.267	49	-11	-11	12	0	0	0	-3	C	-0.9
1927	Det-A	88	246	28	69	8	6	0	39	37	9	.280	.375	.362	90	-2	-2	34	9	1	2	4	C	0.6
1928	Det-A	65	186	19	39	7	1	0	13	24	10	.210	.300	.258	47	-14	-14	16	3	1	0	5	C	-0.4
1929	Det-A	1	0	0	0	0	0	0	0	0	0	.000	.000	.000	-99	-0	-0	0	0	0	0	0	H	0.0
Total	10	548	1317	161	353	52	15	1	161	159	67	.268	.347	.333	77	-41	-40	164	16	4	2	-22	C	-2.6

■ DARRELL WOODARD
Woodard, Darrell Lee b: 12/10/56, Wilma, Ark. BR/TR, 5'11", 160 lbs. Deb: 8/06/78

YEAR	TM/L	G	AB	R	H	2B	3B	HR	RBI	BB	SO	AVG	OBP	SLG	PRO+	BR	/A	RC	SB	CS	SBR	FR	POS	TPR
1978	Oak-A	33	9	10	0	0	0	0	0	1	1	.000	.100	.000	-73	-2	-2	-1	3	4	-2	12	2/3D	0.9

■ MIKE WOODARD
Woodard, Michael Cary b: 3/2/60, Melrose Park, Ill. BL/TR, 5'9", 155 lbs. Deb: 9/11/85

YEAR	TM/L	G	AB	R	H	2B	3B	HR	RBI	BB	SO	AVG	OBP	SLG	PRO+	BR	/A	RC	SB	CS	SBR	FR	POS	TPR
1985	SF-N	24	82	12	20	1	0	0	9	5	3	.244	.287	.256	56	-5	-5	7	6	1	1	-5	2	-0.8
1986	SF-N	48	79	14	20	2	1	0	5	10	9	.253	.337	.342	92	-1	-1	11	7	2	1	-2	2/S3	0.0
1987	SF-N	10	19	0	4	1	0	0	1	0	1	.211	.211	.263	26	-2	-2	1	0	0	0	2	/2	-0.2
1988	Chi-A	18	45	3	6	0	1	0	4	1	5	.133	.170	.178	-2	-6	-6	1	1	1	-0	2	2/D	-0.1
Total	4	100	225	29	50	4	2	1	19	16	18	.222	.277	.271	55	-14	-13	20	14	4	2	-1	/2D3S	-0.9

■ RED WOODHEAD
Woodhead, James b: 7/1851, Chelsea, Mass. d: 9/7/1881, Boston, Mass. 5'6", 160 lbs. Deb: 4/15/1873

YEAR	TM/L	G	AB	R	H	2B	3B	HR	RBI	BB	SO	AVG	OBP	SLG	PRO+	BR	/A	RC	SB	CS	SBR	FR	POS	TPR
1873	Mar-n	1	5	1	0	0	0	0		0		.000	.000	.000	-99	-1	-1	0					/S	0.0
1879	Syr-N	34	131	4	21	1	0	0	2	0	23	.160	.160	.168	9	-12	-10	4				-7	3	-1.5

■ GENE WOODLING
Woodling, Eugene Richard b: 8/16/22, Akron, Ohio BL/TR, 5'9.5", 195 lbs. Deb: 9/23/43 C

YEAR	TM/L	G	AB	R	H	2B	3B	HR	RBI	BB	SO	AVG	OBP	SLG	PRO+	BR	/A	RC	SB	CS	SBR	FR	POS	TPR
1943	Cle-A	8	25	5	8	2	1	1	5	1	5	.320	.348	.600	186	2	2	5	0	0	0	-1	/O	0.1
1946	Cle-A	61	133	8	25	1	4	0	9	16	13	.188	.280	.256	54	-9	-8	11	1	2	-1	1	O	-0.9
1947	Pit-N	22	79	7	21	2	2	0	10	7	5	.266	.326	.342	75	-3	-3	9	0			2	O	-0.1
1949	*NY-A	112	296	60	80	13	7	5	44	52	21	.270	.381	.412	110	5	5	50	2	2	-1	-11	O	-0.8
1950	*NY-A	122	449	81	127	20	10	6	60	70	31	.283	.381	.412	106	3	5	75	5	3	-0	10	*O	1.2
1951	*NY-A	120	420	65	118	15	8	15	71	62	37	.281	.373	.462	130	15	17	75	0	4	-2	9	*O	1.5
1952	*NY-A	122	408	58	126	19	6	12	63	59	31	.309	.397	.473	151	24	27	81	1	4	-2	6	*O	2.8
1953	*NY-A	125	395	64	121	26	4	10	58	82	29	.306	**.429**	.468	147	27	29	82	2	7	-4	-1	*O	2.1
1954	NY-A	97	304	33	76	12	5	3	40	53	35	.250	.361	.352	99	-0	1	42	3	4	-2	-4	O	-0.6

YEAR	TM/L	G	AB	R	H	2B	3B	HR	RBI	BB	SO	AVG	OBP	SLG	PRO+	BR	/A	RC	SB	CS	SBR	FR	POS	TPR
1955	Bal-A	47	145	22	32	6	2	3	18	24	18	.221	.335	.352	91	-3	-1	18	1	1	-0	-4	O	-0.7
	Cle-A	79	259	33	72	15	1	5	35	36	15	.278	.372	.402	104	4	2	38	2	4	-2	-3	O	-0.5
	Yr	126	404	55	104	21	3	8	53	60	33	.257	.359	.384	100	1	1	57	3	5	-2	-7		-1.2
1956	Cle-A	100	317	56	83	17	0	8	38	69	29	.262	.398	.391	107	7	6	53	2	6	-3	-9	O	-0.9
1957	Cle-A	133	430	74	138	25	2	19	78	64	35	.321	.412	.521	155	33	34	94	0	5	-3	6	*O	3.0
1958	Bal-A	133	413	57	114	16	1	15	65	66	49	.276	.378	.429	128	14	17	68	4	2	0	-8	*O	0.1
1959	Bal-A	140	440	63	132	22	2	14	77	78	35	.300	.405	.455	139	24	26	87	1	1	-0	-10	*O	0.9
1960	Bal-A	140	435	68	123	18	3	11	62	84	40	.283	.403	.414	123	17	18	80	3	0	1	-4	*O	0.9
1961	Was-A	110	342	39	107	16	4	10	57	50	24	.313	.404	.471	135	17	18	66	1	0	0	-7	O	0.7
1962	Was-A	44	107	19	30	4	0	5	16	24	5	.280	.421	.458	138	7	7	23	1	0	0	-5	O	0.1
	NY-N	81	190	18	52	8	1	5	24	24	22	.274	.358	.405	103	2	1	28	0	0	0	-6	O	-0.7
Total	17	1796	5587	830	1585	257	63	147	830	921	479	.284	.388	.431	123	186	202	986	29	45		-42	*O	8.2

■ SAM WOODRUFF

Woodruff, Orville Francis   b: 12/27/1876, Chilo, Ohio   d: 7/22/37, Cincinnati, Ohio   BR/TR, 5'9", 160 lbs.   Deb: 4/14/04

YEAR	TM/L	G	AB	R	H	2B	3B	HR	RBI	BB	SO	AVG	OBP	SLG	PRO+	BR	/A	RC	SB	CS	SBR	FR	POS	TPR
1904	Cin-N	87	306	20	58	14	3	0	20	19		.190	.237	.255	49	-17	-20	22	9			-4	32/SO	-2.1
1910	Cin-N	21	61	6	9	1	0	0	2	7	8	.148	.235	.164	18	-6	-6	3	2			-1	3/2	-0.6
Total	2	108	367	26	67	15	3	0	22	26	8	.183	.237	.240	44	-23	-26	25	11			-4	/32SO	-2.7

■ PETE WOODRUFF

Woodruff, Peter Frank   b: Richmond, Va.   BR/TR,   Deb: 9/19/1899

YEAR	TM/L	G	AB	R	H	2B	3B	HR	RBI	BB	SO	AVG	OBP	SLG	PRO+	BR	/A	RC	SB	CS	SBR	FR	POS	TPR
1899	NY-N	20	61	11	15	1	1	2	7	9		.246	.343	.393	108	0	1	9	3			-1	O/1	0.0

■ AL WOODS

Woods, Alvis   b: 8/8/53, Oakland, Cal.   BL/TL, 6'3", 190 lbs.   Deb: 4/07/77

YEAR	TM/L	G	AB	R	H	2B	3B	HR	RBI	BB	SO	AVG	OBP	SLG	PRO+	BR	/A	RC	SB	CS	SBR	FR	POS	TPR
1977	Tor-A	122	440	58	125	17	4	6	35	36	38	.284	.338	.382	94	-2	-3	55	8	7	-2	-4	*O/D	-1.2
1978	Tor-A	62	220	19	53	12	3	3	25	11	23	.241	.280	.364	78	-6	-7	21	1	2	-1	-8	O	-1.7
1979	Tor-A	132	436	57	121	24	4	5	36	40	28	.278	.340	.385	94	-3	-3	58	6	4	-1	-1	*O	-0.9
1980	Tor-A	109	373	54	112	18	2	15	47	37	35	.300	.365	.480	124	15	13	66	4	4	-1	2	OD	1.2
1981	Tor-A	85	288	20	71	15	0	1	21	19	31	.247	.293	.309	69	-10	-12	25	3	4	-2	1	O/D	-1.4
1982	Tor-A	85	201	20	47	11	1	3	24	21	20	.234	.306	.343	71	-6	-8	21	1	3	-2	-3	OD	-1.5
1986	Min-A	23	28	5	9	1	0	2	8	3	5	.321	.387	.571	153	2	2	6	0	0	0	0	/D	0.2
Total	7	618	1986	233	538	98	14	35	196	167	180	.271	.328	.387	93	-10	-19	252	23	24	-8	-14	O/D	-5.3

■ GARY WOODS

Woods, Gary Lee   b: 7/20/54, Santa Barbara, Cal.   BR/TR, 6'2", 185 lbs.   Deb: 9/14/76

YEAR	TM/L	G	AB	R	H	2B	3B	HR	RBI	BB	SO	AVG	OBP	SLG	PRO+	BR	/A	RC	SB	CS	SBR	FR	POS	TPR
1976	Oak-A	6	8	0	1	0	0	0	0	0	3	.125	.125	.125	-28	-1	-1	0	0	0	0	1	/OD	0.0
1977	Tor-A	60	227	21	49	9	1	0	17	7	38	.216	.246	.264	38	-19	-19	14	5	4	-1	-0	O	-2.2
1978	Tor-A	8	19	1	3	1	0	0	0	1	1	.158	.200	.211	15	-2	-2	1	1	0	0	-0	/O	-0.1
1980	*Hou-N	19	53	8	20	5	0	2	15	2	9	.377	.400	.585	186	5	5	12	1	0	0	-1	O	0.4
1981	*Hou-N	54	110	10	23	4	1	0	12	11	22	.209	.281	.264	56	-6	-6	8	2	1	0	0	O	-0.6
1982	Chi-N	117	245	28	66	15	1	4	30	21	48	.269	.327	.388	97	-0	-1	31	3	3	-1	-7	*O	-1.0
1983	Chi-N	93	190	25	46	9	0	4	22	15	27	.242	.298	.353	76	-6	-7	18	5	3	-0	1	O/2	-0.7
1984	*Chi-N	87	98	13	23	4	1	3	10	15	21	.235	.336	.388	94	1	-1	13	2	1	0	3	O/2	0.0
1985	Chi-N	81	82	11	20	3	0	0	4	14	18	.244	.354	.280	72	-2	-3	9	0	1	-1	2	O	-0.2
Total	9	525	1032	117	251	50	4	13	110	86	187	.243	.303	.337	76	-31	-35	106	19	13	-2	-3	O/2D	-4.4

■ JIM WOODS

Woods, James Jerome "Woody"   b: 9/17/39, Chicago, Ill.   BR/TR, 6', 175 lbs.   Deb: 9/27/57

YEAR	TM/L	G	AB	R	H	2B	3B	HR	RBI	BB	SO	AVG	OBP	SLG	PRO+	BR	/A	RC	SB	CS	SBR	FR	POS	TPR
1957	Chi-N	2	0	1	0	0	0	0	0	0	0	—	—	—	—	0	0	0	0	0	0	0	R	0.0
1960	Phi-N	11	34	4	6	0	0	1	3	3	13	.176	.243	.265	39	-3	-3	2	0	0	0	2	3	-0.1
1961	Phi-N	23	48	6	11	3	0	2	9	4	15	.229	.302	.417	89	-1	-1	5	0	0	0	-0	3	-0.1
Total	3	36	82	11	17	3	0	3	12	7	28	.207	.278	.354	69	-4	-4	7	0	0	0	1	/3	-0.2

■ RON WOODS

Woods, Ronald Lawrence   b: 2/1/43, Hamilton, Ohio   BR/TR, 5'10", 168 lbs.   Deb: 4/22/69

YEAR	TM/L	G	AB	R	H	2B	3B	HR	RBI	BB	SO	AVG	OBP	SLG	PRO+	BR	/A	RC	SB	CS	SBR	FR	POS	TPR
1969	Det-A	17	15	3	4	0	0	1	3	2	3	.267	.353	.467	122	1	0	3	0	0	0	1	/O	0.1
	NY-A	72	171	18	30	5	2	1	7	22	29	.175	.273	.246	48	-12	-11	13	2	0	1	-6	O	-1.9
	Yr	89	186	21	34	5	2	2	10	24	32	.183	.280	.263	54	-12	-11	15	2	0	1	-6		-1.8
1970	NY-A	95	225	30	51	5	3	8	27	33	35	.227	.326	.382	100	-2	-0	27	4	2	0	-7	O	-1.0
1971	NY-A	25	32	4	8	1	0	1	2	4	2	.250	.333	.375	107	0	0	4	0	0	0	0	/O	0.0
	Mon-N	51	138	26	41	7	3	1	19	19	18	.297	.382	.413	125	5	5	21	0	2	-1	2	O	0.5
1972	Mon-N	97	221	21	57	5	1	10	31	22	33	.258	.325	.425	110	3	3	30	3	1	0	-2	O	-0.3
1973	Mon-N	135	318	45	73	11	3	3	31	56	34	.230	.345	.311	80	-5	-7	39	12	6	0	-11	*O	-2.3
1974	Mon-N	90	127	15	26	0	0	1	12	17	17	.205	.303	.228	48	-8	-9	9	6	5	-1	1	O	-1.1
Total	6	582	1247	162	290	34	12	26	130	175	171	.233	.328	.342	87	-18	-19	146	27	18	-3	-22	O	-6.0

■ TRACY WOODSON

Woodson, Tracy Michael   b: 10/5/62, Richmond, Va.   BR/TR, 6'3", 215 lbs.   Deb: 4/07/87

YEAR	TM/L	G	AB	R	H	2B	3B	HR	RBI	BB	SO	AVG	OBP	SLG	PRO+	BR	/A	RC	SB	CS	SBR	FR	POS	TPR
1987	LA-N	53	136	14	31	8	1	1	11	9	21	.228	.286	.324	63	-8	-7	12	1	1	-0	-1	3/1	-0.8
1988	*LA-N	65	173	15	43	4	1	3	15	7	32	.249	.282	.335	79	-6	-5	15	1	2	-1	-5	31	-1.2
1989	LA-N	4	6	0	0	0	0	0	0	0	1	.000	.000	.000	-99	-2	-2	0	0	0	0	0	/3	-0.1
Total	3	122	315	29	74	12	2	4	26	16	54	.235	.278	.324	68	-15	-14	28	2	3	-1	-6	/31	-2.1

■ WOODY WOODWARD

Woodward, William Frederick   b: 9/23/42, Miami, Fla.   BR/TR, 6'2", 180 lbs.   Deb: 9/09/63

YEAR	TM/L	G	AB	R	H	2B	3B	HR	RBI	BB	SO	AVG	OBP	SLG	PRO+	BR	/A	RC	SB	CS	SBR	FR	POS	TPR
1963	Mil-N	10	2	1	0	0	0	0	0	0	0	.000	.000	.000	-99	-1	-1	0	0	0	0	4	/S	0.4
1964	Mil-N	77	115	18	24	2	1	0	11	6	28	.209	.260	.243	43	-9	-9	7	0	1	-1	13	2S/31	0.8
1965	Mil-N	112	265	17	55	7	4	0	11	10	50	.208	.236	.264	41	-21	-21	16	2	2	-1	11	*S/2	0.1
1966	Atl-N	144	455	46	120	23	3	0	43	37	54	.264	.325	.327	81	-10	-11	49	2	2	-1	-6	2S	-0.6
1967	Atl-N	136	429	30	97	15	2	0	25	37	51	.226	.289	.270	62	-21	-20	32	0	6	-4	9	*2S	-0.5
1968	Atl-N	12	24	2	4	1	0	0	1	1	6	.167	.200	.208	23	-2	-2	1	1	0	0	3	/S32	0.2
	Cin-N	56	119	13	29	2	0	0	10	7	23	.244	.297	.261	64	-4	-5	10	1	0	0	-3	S/21	-0.2
	Yr	68	143	15	33	3	0	0	11	8	29	.231	.281	.252	58	-7	-7	10	2	0	1	-0		0.0
1969	Cin-N	97	241	36	63	12	0	0	15	24	40	.261	.333	.311	77	-5	-7	25	3	2	-0	2	S/2	-0.6
1970	*Cin-N	100	264	23	59	8	3	1	14	20	21	.223	.283	.288	53	-17	-17	21	1	2	-1	2	S32/1	-0.6
1971	Cin-N	136	273	22	66	9	1	0	18	27	28	.242	.310	.282	70	-11	-10	25	4	0	1	-5	S3/2	-0.1
Total	9	880	2187	208	517	79	14	1	148	169	301	.236	.295	.287	64	-101	-103	186	14	15	-5	25	S2/31	-0.3

■ JUNIOR WOOTEN

Wooten, Earl Hazwell   b: 1/16/24, Pelzer, S.C.   BR/TL, 5'11", 160 lbs.   Deb: 9/16/47

YEAR	TM/L	G	AB	R	H	2B	3B	HR	RBI	BB	SO	AVG	OBP	SLG	PRO+	BR	/A	RC	SB	CS	SBR	FR	POS	TPR
1947	Was-A	6	24	0	2	0	0	0	1	0	4	.083	.083	.083	-55	-5	-5	0	1	0	0	0	/O	-0.4
1948	Was-A	88	258	34	66	8	3	1	23	24	21	.256	.324	.322	74	-10	-9	29	2	1	0	12	O/1P	0.0
Total	2	94	282	34	68	8	3	1	24	24	25	.241	.305	.301	64	-15	-14	29	3	1	0	12	/O1P	-0.4

■ FAVEL WORDSWORTH

Wordsworth, Favel Perry   b: 12/22/1850, New York, N.Y.   d: 8/12/1888, New York, N.Y.   Deb: 4/28/1873

YEAR	TM/L	G	AB	R	H	2B	3B	HR	RBI	BB	SO	AVG	OBP	SLG	PRO+	BR	/A	RC	SB	CS	SBR	FR	POS	TPR
1873	Res-n	12	43	5	11	1	0	0		1		.256	.273	.279	68	-2	-1	3					S	0.0

■ CHUCK WORKMAN

Workman, Charles Thomas   b: 1/6/15, Leeton, Mo.   d: 1/3/53, Kansas City, Mo.   BL/TR, 6', 175 lbs.   Deb: 9/18/38

YEAR	TM/L	G	AB	R	H	2B	3B	HR	RBI	BB	SO	AVG	OBP	SLG	PRO+	BR	/A	RC	SB	CS	SBR	FR	POS	TPR
1938	Cle-A	2	5	1	2	0	0	0	0	0	0	.400	.400	.400	103	0	0	1	0	0	0	-0	/O	0.0
1941	Cle-A	9	4	2	0	0	0	0	0	1	1	.000	.200	.000	-45	-1	-1	0	0	0	0	0	H	0.0
1943	Bos-N	153	615	71	153	17	1	10	67	53	72	.249	.311	.328	86	-12	-11	66	12			4	*O/13	-1.3
1944	Bos-N	140	418	46	87	18	3	11	53	42	41	.208	.287	.344	74	-14	-16	43	1			-5	*O3	-2.8
1945	Bos-N	139	514	77	141	16	2	25	87	51	58	.274	.347	.459	122	14	14	84	9			-17	*3O	-0.5

YEAR	TM/L	G	AB	R	H	2B	3B	HR	RBI	BB	SO	AVG	OBP	SLG	PRO+	BR	/A	RC	SB	CS	SBR	FR	POS	TPR
1946	Bos-N	25	48	5	8	2	0	2	7	3	11	.167	.231	.333	58	-3	-3	4	0			0	O	-0.2
	Pit-N	58	145	11	32	4	1	2	16	11	19	.221	.280	.303	64	-7	-7	13	2			7	O/3	0.0
	Yr	83	193	16	40	6	1	4	23	14	30	.207	.268	.311	63	-10	-10	16	2			7		-0.2
Total	6	526	1749	213	423	57	7	50	230	161	202	.242	.311	.368	91	-22	-24	209	24	0		-11	O3/1	-4.8

■ HANK WORKMAN
Workman, Henry Kilgariff b: 2/5/26, Los Angeles, Cal. BL/TR, 6'1", 185 lbs. Deb: 9/04/50

YEAR	TM/L	G	AB	R	H	2B	3B	HR	RBI	BB	SO	AVG	OBP	SLG	PRO+	BR	/A	RC	SB	CS	SBR	FR	POS	TPR
1950	NY-A	2	5	1	1	0	0	0	0	0	1	.200	.200	.200	3	-1	-1	0	0	0	0	-0	/1	0.0

■ HERB WORTH
Worth, Herbert b: 5/2/1847, Brooklyn, N.Y. d: 4/27/14, Brooklyn, N.Y. Deb: 7/29/1872

YEAR	TM/L	G	AB	R	H	2B	3B	HR	RBI	BB	SO	AVG	OBP	SLG	PRO+	BR	/A	RC	SB	CS	SBR	FR	POS	TPR
1872	Atl-n	1	6	1	1	1	0	0		0		.167	.167	.333	43	-0	-1	0					/O	0.0

■ CRAIG WORTHINGTON
Worthington, Craig Richard b: 4/17/65, Los Angeles, Cal. BR/TR, 6', 160 lbs. Deb: 4/26/88

YEAR	TM/L	G	AB	R	H	2B	3B	HR	RBI	BB	SO	AVG	OBP	SLG	PRO+	BR	/A	RC	SB	CS	SBR	FR	POS	TPR
1988	Bal-A	26	81	5	15	2	0	2	4	9	24	.185	.267	.284	56	-5	-5	6	1	0	0	1	3	-0.2
1989	Bal-A	145	497	57	123	23	0	15	70	61	114	.247	.335	.384	105	2	4	65	1	2	-1	-10	*3	-0.6
1990	Bal-A	133	425	46	96	17	0	8	44	63	96	.226	.330	.322	85	-8	-7	47	1	2	-1	-12	*3/D	-1.8
Total	3	304	1003	108	234	42	0	25	118	133	234	.233	.327	.350	93	-11	-8	118	3	4	-2	-21	3/D	-2.6

■ RED WORTHINGTON
Worthington, Robert Lee b: 4/24/06, Alhambra, Cal. d: 12/8/63, Sepulveda, Cal. BR/TR, 5'11", 170 lbs. Deb: 4/14/31

YEAR	TM/L	G	AB	R	H	2B	3B	HR	RBI	BB	SO	AVG	OBP	SLG	PRO+	BR	/A	RC	SB	CS	SBR	FR	POS	TPR
1931	Bos-N	128	491	47	143	25	10	4	44	26	38	.291	.328	.407	100	-3	-1	66	1			-7	*O	-1.4
1932	Bos-N	105	435	62	132	35	8	8	61	15	24	.303	.330	.476	118	7	9	68	1			-5	*O	-0.2
1933	Bos-N	17	45	3	7	4	0	0	0	1	3	.156	.174	.244	20	-5	-4	1	0			-1	O	-0.6
1934	Bos-N	41	65	6	16	5	0	0	6	6	5	.246	.319	.323	78	-2	-2	6	0			-1	O	-0.2
	StL-N	1	1	0	0	0	0	0	0	0	1	.000	.000	.000	-94	-0	-0	0	0			0	H	0.0
	Yr	42	66	6	16	5	0	0	6	6	6	.242	.315	.318	75	-3	-2	6	0			-1		-0.2
Total	4	292	1037	118	298	69	18	12	111	48	71	.287	.321	.423	103	-4	1	142	2			-14	O	-2.4

■ CHUCK WORTMAN
Wortman, William Lewis b: 1/5/1892, Baltimore, Md. d: 8/19/77, Las Vegas, Nev. BR/TR, 5'7", 150 lbs. Deb: 7/20/16

YEAR	TM/L	G	AB	R	H	2B	3B	HR	RBI	BB	SO	AVG	OBP	SLG	PRO+	BR	/A	RC	SB	CS	SBR	FR	POS	TPR
1916	Chi-N	69	234	17	47	4	2	6	16	18	22	.201	.258	.261	54	-11	-14	17	4			-21	S	-3.5
1917	Chi-N	75	190	24	33	4	1	0	9	18	23	.174	.245	.205	36	-13	-15	12	6			-8	S/23	-2.5
1918	*Chi-N	17	17	4	2	0	0	1	3	1	2	.118	.167	.294	39	-1	-1	1	3			2	/2S	0.1
Total	3	161	441	45	82	8	3	3	28	37	47	.186	.249	.238	46	-26	-30	30	13			-27	S/23	-5.9

■ RON WOTUS
Wotus, Ronald Allan b: 3/3/61, Colchester, Conn. BR/TR, 6'1", 164 lbs. Deb: 9/03/83

YEAR	TM/L	G	AB	R	H	2B	3B	HR	RBI	BB	SO	AVG	OBP	SLG	PRO+	BR	/A	RC	SB	CS	SBR	FR	POS	TPR
1983	Pit-N	5	3	0	0	0	0	0	0	0	1	.000	.000	.000	-98	-1	-1	0	0	0	0	1	/S2	0.0
1984	Pit-N	27	55	4	12	6	0	0	2	6	8	.218	.295	.327	75	-2	-2	5	0	0	0	9	S/2	1.0
Total	2	32	58	4	12	6	0	0	2	6	9	.207	.281	.310	66	-3	-3	5	0	0	0	10	/S2	1.0

■ JIMMY WOULFE
Woulfe, James Joseph b: 11/25/1859, New Orleans, La. d: 12/20/24, New Orleans, La. TR, 5'11", Deb: 5/16/1884

YEAR	TM/L	G	AB	R	H	2B	3B	HR	RBI	BB	SO	AVG	OBP	SLG	PRO+	BR	/A	RC	SB	CS	SBR	FR	POS	TPR
1884	Cin-a	8	34	3	5	0	1	0			1	.147	.171	.206	23	-3	-3	1				-3	/O3	-0.5
	Pit-a	15	53	7	6	1	0	0			0	.113	.113	.132	-19	-7	-7	1				1	O	-0.5
	Yr	23	87	10	11	1	1	0			1	.126	.136	.161	-2	-9	-10	2				-2		-1.0

■ AL WRIGHT
Wright, Albert Edgar "A-1" b: 11/11/12, San Francisco, Cal BR/TR, 6'1.5", 170 lbs. Deb: 4/25/33

YEAR	TM/L	G	AB	R	H	2B	3B	HR	RBI	BB	SO	AVG	OBP	SLG	PRO+	BR	/A	RC	SB	CS	SBR	FR	POS	TPR
1933	Bos-N	4	1	0	1	0	0	0	0	0	0	1.000	1.000	1.000	515	0	0	1	0			-0	/2	0.0

■ AB WRIGHT
Wright, Albert Owen b: 11/16/05, Terlton, Okla. BR/TR, 6'1.5", 190 lbs. Deb: 4/20/35

YEAR	TM/L	G	AB	R	H	2B	3B	HR	RBI	BB	SO	AVG	OBP	SLG	PRO+	BR	/A	RC	SB	CS	SBR	FR	POS	TPR
1935	Cle-A	67	160	17	38	11	1	2	18	10	17	.237	.291	.356	65	-8	-9	17	2	1	0	-4	O	-1.1
1944	Bos-N	71	195	20	50	9	0	7	35	18	31	.256	.326	.410	102	1	0	26	0			-6	O	-0.9
Total	2	138	355	37	88	20	1	9	53	28	48	.248	.310	.386	85	-7	-9	43	2	1		-10	/O	-2.0

■ CY WRIGHT
Wright, Ceylon b: 8/16/1893, Minneapolis, Minn. d: 11/7/47, Hines, Ill. BL/TR, 5'9", 150 lbs. Deb: 6/30/16

YEAR	TM/L	G	AB	R	H	2B	3B	HR	RBI	BB	SO	AVG	OBP	SLG	PRO+	BR	/A	RC	SB	CS	SBR	FR	POS	TPR
1916	Chi-A	8	18	0	0	0	0	0	0	1	7	.000	.053	.000	-83	-4	-4	0	0			-0	/S	-0.3

■ GLENN WRIGHT
Wright, Forest Glenn "Buckshot" b: 2/6/01, Archie, Mo. d: 4/6/84, Olathe, Kan. BR/TR, 5'11", 170 lbs. Deb: 4/15/24

YEAR	TM/L	G	AB	R	H	2B	3B	HR	RBI	BB	SO	AVG	OBP	SLG	PRO+	BR	/A	RC	SB	CS	SBR	FR	POS	TPR
1924	Pit-N	153	616	80	177	28	18	7	111	27	52	.287	.318	.425	96	-4	-5	82	14	6	1	11	*S	1.8
1925	*Pit-N	153	614	97	189	32	10	18	121	31	32	.308	.341	.480	100	4	-1	97	3	7	-3	0	*S/3	0.8
1926	Pit-N	119	458	73	141	15	15	8	77	19	26	.308	.335	.459	106	6	3	67	6			-13	*S	-0.1
1927	*Pit-N	143	570	78	160	26	4	9	105	39	46	.281	.328	.388	85	-8	-13	71	4			-17	*S	-1.6
1928	Pit-N	108	407	63	126	20	8	6	66	21	53	.310	.343	.457	103	3	1	61	3			-24	*S/1O	-0.8
1929	Bro-N	24	25	4	5	0	0	1	6	3	6	.200	.286	.320	51	-2	-2	2	0			-3	/S	-0.3
1930	Bro-N	135	532	83	171	28	12	22	126	32	70	.321	.360	.543	116	10	11	99	2			-1	*S	1.9
1931	Bro-N	77	268	36	76	9	4	9	32	14	35	.284	.324	.448	106	1	1	39	1			6	S	1.3
1932	Bro-N	127	446	50	122	31	5	11	60	12	57	.274	.293	.439	96	-5	-4	57	4			8	*S/1	1.3
1933	Bro-N	71	192	19	49	13	0	1	18	11	24	.255	.299	.339	85	-5	-4	18	1			-4	S/13	-0.4
1935	Chi-A	9	25	1	3	1	0	0	1	0	6	.120	.120	.160	-27	-5	-5	1	0	0	0	0	/2	-0.3
Total	11	1119	4153	584	1219	203	76	94	723	209	407	.294	.328	.447	99	-5	-19	594	38	13		-36	*S/1230	3.6

■ GEORGE WRIGHT
Wright, George b: 1/28/1847, Yonkers, N.Y. d: 8/21/37, Boston, Mass. BR/TR, 5'9.5", 150 lbs. Deb: 5/05/1871 MH

YEAR	TM/L	G	AB	R	H	2B	3B	HR	RBI	BB	SO	AVG	OBP	SLG	PRO+	BR	/A	RC	SB	CS	SBR	FR	POS	TPR
1871	Bos-n	16	80	33	33	7	5	0	11	6	1	.412	.453	.625	200	11	10	27	9				S/1	0.7
1872	Bos-n	48	255	87	87	16	5	2		2		.341	.346	.467	140	14	11	42					*S	0.8
1873	Bos-n	59	327	99	124	13	7	3		8		.379	.394	.489	146	23	17	65					*S	1.2
1874	Bos-n	60	313	76	106	11	15	2		7		.339	.353	.489	156	22	19	55					*S	1.1
1875	Bos-n	79	406	105	135	18	7	1		2		.333	.336	.419	154	23	21	59					*S/P	1.6
1876	Bos-N	70	335	72	100	18	6	1	34	8	9	.299	.315	.397	134	12	11	43				13	*S/2P	2.0
1877	Bos-N	61	290	58	80	15	1	0	35	9	15	.276	.298	.334	95	-0	-2	30				9	*2/S	0.8
1878	Bos-N	59	267	35	60	5	1	0	12	6	22	.225	.242	.251	58	-11	-13	17				11	*S	0.1
1879	Pro-N	85	388	79	107	15	10	1	42	13	20	.276	.299	.374	122	8	9	44				20	*SM	3.2
1880	Bos-N	1	4	2	1	0	0	0	0	0	0	.250	.250	.250	72	-0	-0	0				-0	/S	0.0
1881	Bos-N	7	25	4	5	0	0	0	0	3	1	.200	.286	.200	58	-1	-1	1				-3	/S	-0.2
1882	Pro-N	46	185	14	30	1	2	0	9	4	36	.162	.180	.189	19	-16	-16	6				-6	S	-1.6
Total	5 n	262	1381	400	485	65	39	8	11	25	1	.351	.363	.472	153	93	78	248					S/P1	5.4
Total	7	329	1494	264	383	54	20	2	132	43	103	.256	.277	.323	93	-8	-12	142				44	S/2P	4.3

■ GEORGE WRIGHT
Wright, George De Witt b: 12/22/58, Oklahoma City, Okla BB/TR, 5'11", 180 lbs. Deb: 4/10/82

YEAR	TM/L	G	AB	R	H	2B	3B	HR	RBI	BB	SO	AVG	OBP	SLG	PRO+	BR	/A	RC	SB	CS	SBR	FR	POS	TPR
1982	Tex-A	150	557	69	147	20	5	11	50	30	78	.264	.305	.377	91	-11	-8	61	3	7	-3	5	*O	-1.0
1983	Tex-A	162	634	79	175	28	6	18	80	41	82	.276	.322	.424	106	2	3	84	8	7	-2	5	*O	0.5
1984	Tex-A	101	383	40	93	19	4	9	48	15	54	.243	.275	.384	78	-11	-13	39	0	2	-1	1	OD	-1.5
1985	Tex-A	109	363	21	69	13	0	2	18	25	49	.190	.242	.242	33	-33	-34	19	4	7	-3	4	*O/D	-3.3
1986	Tex-A	49	106	10	23	3	1	2	7	4	23	.217	.252	.321	53	-7	-7	7	3	5	-2	1	O	-0.8
	Mon-N	56	117	12	22	5	2	0	5	11	28	.188	.264	.265	47	-9	-8	8	1	1	-0	0	O	-0.9
Total	5	627	2160	231	529	88	18	42	208	126	314	.245	.289	.361	78	-69	-67	218	19	29	-12	15	O/D	-7.0

■ JOE WRIGHT
Wright, Joseph b: 1873, Pittsburgh, Pa. BL, 5'8", 175 lbs. Deb: 7/14/1895

YEAR	TM/L	G	AB	R	H	2B	3B	HR	RBI	BB	SO	AVG	OBP	SLG	PRO+	BR	/A	RC	SB	CS	SBR	FR	POS	TPR
1895	Lou-N	60	228	30	63	10	4	1	30	12	28	.276	.315	.368	83	-8	-5	29	7			-2	O	-1.0
1896	Lou-N	2	7	0	2	0	0	0	0	0	1	.286	.286	.286	55	-0	-0	1	0			-0	/O	0.0
	Pit-N	15	52	5	16	2	1	0	6	1	2	.308	.321	.385	91	-1	-1	7	1			-2	O/3	-0.2

YEAR	TM/L	G	AB	R	H	2B	3B	HR	RBI	BB	SO	AVG	OBP	SLG	PRO+	BR	/A	RC	SB	CS	SBR	FR	POS	TPR
	Yr	17	59	5	18	2	1	0	6	1	3	.305	.317	.373	87	-2	-1	7	1			-2		-0.2
Total	2	77	287	35	81	12	5	1	36	13	31	.282	.316	.369	84	-10	-7	37	8			-4	/O3	-1.2

■ PAT WRIGHT
Wright, Patrick Francis b: 7/5/1865, Pottsville, Pa. d: 5/29/43, Springfield, Ill. BB/TR, 6'2", 190 lbs. Deb: 7/11/1890

YEAR	TM/L	G	AB	R	H	2B	3B	HR	RBI	BB	SO	AVG	OBP	SLG	PRO+	BR	/A	RC	SB	CS	SBR	FR	POS	TPR
1890	Chi-N	1	2	0	0	0	0	0	0	0	1	.000	.333	.000	1	-0	-0	0	0			0	/2	0.0

■ SAM WRIGHT
Wright, Samuel b: 11/25/1848, New York, N.Y. d: 5/6/28, Boston, Mass. 5'7.5", 146 lbs. Deb: 4/21/1875

YEAR	TM/L	G	AB	R	H	2B	3B	HR	RBI	BB	SO	AVG	OBP	SLG	PRO+	BR	/A	RC	SB	CS	SBR	FR	POS	TPR
1875	NH-n	33	128	10	24	4	0	0			1	.188	.194	.219	50	-7	-4	6					S	-0.3
1876	Bos-N	2	8	0	1	0	0	0	0	0	0	.125	.125	.125	-16	-1	-1	0				-0	/S	0.0
1880	Cin-N	9	34	0	3	0	0	0	0	0	5	.088	.088	.088	-40	-5	-5	0				-2	/S	-0.5
1881	Bos-N	1	4	0	1	0	0	0	0	0	0	.250	.250	.250	60	-0	-0	0				-1	/S	0.0
Total	3	12	46	0	5	0	0	0	0	0	5	.109	.109	.109	-27	-6	-6	1				-2	/S	-0.5

■ TAFFY WRIGHT
Wright, Taft Shedron b: 8/10/11, Tabor City, N.C. d: 10/22/81, Orlando, Fla. BL/TR, 5'10", 180 lbs. Deb: 4/18/38

YEAR	TM/L	G	AB	R	H	2B	3B	HR	RBI	BB	SO	AVG	OBP	SLG	PRO+	BR	/A	RC	SB	CS	SBR	FR	POS	TPR
1938	Was-A	100	263	37	92	18	10	2	36	13	17	.350	.389	.517	134	9	12	52	1	2	-1	-3	O	0.7
1939	Was-A	129	499	77	154	29	11	4	93	38	19	.309	.359	.435	110	1	6	78	1	2	-1	-6	*O	-0.3
1940	Chi-A	147	581	79	196	31	9	5	88	43	25	.337	.385	.448	114	13	12	101	4	7	-3	-7	*O	-0.7
1941	Chi-A	136	513	71	165	35	5	10	97	60	27	.322	.399	.468	130	22	23	101	5	4	-1	-6	*O	0.7
1942	Chi-A	85	300	43	100	13	5	0	47	48	9	.333	.432	.410	141	18	19	55	1	8	-5	1	O	0.9
1946	Chi-A	115	422	46	116	19	4	7	52	42	17	.275	.342	.389	108	2	4	55	10	3	1	-5	*O	-0.5
1947	Chi-A	124	401	48	130	13	0	4	54	48	17	.324	.398	.387	123	12	14	64	8	6	-1	-5	*O	0.3
1948	Chi-A	134	455	50	127	15	6	4	61	39	18	.279	.341	.365	91	-8	-6	57	2	1	0	-4	*O	-1.3
1949	Phi-A	59	149	14	35	2	5	2	25	16	6	.235	.321	.356	82	-5	-4	16	0	0	0	-2	O	-0.6
Total	9	1029	3583	465	1115	175	55	38	553	347	155	.311	.376	.423	116	64	79	580	32	33	-10	-37	O	-0.8

■ TOM WRIGHT
Wright, Thomas Everette b: 9/22/23, Shelby, N.C. BL/TR, 5'11.5", 180 lbs. Deb: 9/15/48

YEAR	TM/L	G	AB	R	H	2B	3B	HR	RBI	BB	SO	AVG	OBP	SLG	PRO+	BR	/A	RC	SB	CS	SBR	FR	POS	TPR
1948	Bos-A	3	2	1	1	0	1	0	0	0	0	.500	.500	1.500	400	1	1	2	0	0	0	0	H	0.1
1949	Bos-A	5	4	1	1	1	0	0	1	1	1	.250	.400	.500	128	0	0	1	0	0	0	0	H	0.0
1950	Bos-A	54	107	17	34	7	0	0	20	6	18	.318	.360	.383	82	-2	-3	15	0	0	0	-1	O	-0.3
1951	Bos-A	28	63	8	14	1	1	1	9	11	8	.222	.347	.317	73	-1	-2	7	0	0	0	-4	O	-0.6
1952	StL-A	29	66	6	16	0	0	1	6	12	20	.242	.359	.288	79	-1	-1	7	1	1	-0	1	O	0.0
	Chi-A	60	132	15	34	10	2	1	21	16	16	.258	.342	.386	102	0	0	19	1	0	0	-1	O	-0.1
	Yr	89	198	21	50	10	2	2	27	28	36	.253	.348	.354	94	-1	-1	26	2	1	0	-0		-0.1
1953	Chi-A	77	132	14	33	5	3	2	25	12	21	.250	.322	.379	86	-2	-3	17	0	0	0	-3	O	-0.6
1954	Was-A	76	171	13	42	4	4	1	17	18	38	.246	.325	.333	85	-4	-3	20	0	0	0	-2	O	-0.6
1955	Was-A	7	7	0	0	0	0	0	0	0	1	.000	.000	.000	-99	-2	-2	0	0	0	0	0	H	-0.1
1956	Was-A	2	1	0	0	0	0	0	0	0	0	.000	.000	.000	-99	-0	-0	0	0	0	0	0	H	0.0
Total	9	341	685	75	175	28	11	6	99	76	123	.255	.336	.355	85	-12	-14	87	2	1	0	-11	O	-2.2

■ DICK WRIGHT
Wright, Willard James b: 5/5/1890, Worcester, N.Y. d: 1/24/52, Bethlehem, Pa. TR , 5'10", 170 lbs. Deb: 6/30/15

YEAR	TM/L	G	AB	R	H	2B	3B	HR	RBI	BB	SO	AVG	OBP	SLG	PRO+	BR	/A	RC	SB	CS	SBR	FR	POS	TPR
1915	Bro-F	4	5	0	0	0	0	0	0	0	0	.000	.000	.000	-99	-1	-1	0	0			-1	/C	-0.1

■ BILL WRIGHT
Wright, William H. Deb: 9/16/1887

YEAR	TM/L	G	AB	R	H	2B	3B	HR	RBI	BB	SO	AVG	OBP	SLG	PRO+	BR	/A	RC	SB	CS	SBR	FR	POS	TPR
1887	Was-N	1	3	0	2	0	0	0	0	0	0	.667	.667	.667	290	1	1	1	0			0	/C	0.1

■ HARRY WRIGHT
Wright, William Henry b: 1/10/1835, Sheffield, England d: 10/3/1895, Atlantic City, N.J. BR/TR, 5'9.5", 157 lbs. Deb: 5/05/1871 MH

YEAR	TM/L	G	AB	R	H	2B	3B	HR	RBI	BB	SO	AVG	OBP	SLG	PRO+	BR	/A	RC	SB	CS	SBR	FR	POS	TPR
1871	Bos-n	31	147	42	44	5	2	0	26	13	2	.299	.356	.361	103	2	1	22	7				*O/PSM	0.2
1872	Bos-n	48	208	39	54	6	0	0		8		.260	.287	.288	74	-5	-7	18					*O/PM	-0.2
1873	Bos-n	58	267	56	67	9	2	2		10		.251	.278	.322	70	-8	-12	25					*O/PM	-0.4
1874	Bos-n	40	184	44	56	9	2	2		4		.304	.319	.408	123	6	4	25					*O/PCM	0.4
1875	Bos-n	1	4	1	1	0	0	0		0		.250	.250	.250	71	-0	-0	0					/OM	0.0
1876	Bos-N	1	3	0	0	0	0	0	0	0	1	.000	.000	.000	-98	-1	-1	0	0				/OM	0.0
1877	Bos-N	1	4	0	0	0	0	0	0	0	1	.000	.000	.000	-97	-1	-1	0	0			1	/OM	0.0
Total	5 n	178	.810	182	222	29	6	4	26	35	2	.274	.304	.340	89	-5	-15	89					O/PCS	0.0
Total	2	2	7	0	0	0	0	0	0	0	2	.000	.000	.000	-97	-1	-2	0				1	/O	0.0

■ RASTY WRIGHT
Wright, William Smith b: 1/31/1863, Birmingham, Mich. d: 10/14/22, Duluth, Minn. 6'1", 258 lbs. Deb: 4/17/1890

YEAR	TM/L	G	AB	R	H	2B	3B	HR	RBI	BB	SO	AVG	OBP	SLG	PRO+	BR	/A	RC	SB	CS	SBR	FR	POS	TPR
1890	Syr-a	88	348	82	106	10	6	0		69		.305	.427	.368	152	21	27	69	30			4	O	2.3
	Cle-N	13	45	7	5	1	0	0	2	12	4	.111	.298	.133	29	-3	-3	3	3			-2	O	-0.4

■ RUSS WRIGHTSTONE
Wrightstone, Russell Guy b: 3/18/1893, Bowmansdale, Pa. d: 2/25/69, Harrisburg, Pa. BL/TR, 5'10.5", 176 lbs. Deb: 4/19/20

YEAR	TM/L	G	AB	R	H	2B	3B	HR	RBI	BB	SO	AVG	OBP	SLG	PRO+	BR	/A	RC	SB	CS	SBR	FR	POS	TPR
1920	Phi-N	76	206	23	54	6	1	3	17	10	25	.262	.303	.345	82	-4	-5	21	3	2	-0	6	3/S2	0.3
1921	Phi-N	109	372	59	110	13	4	9	51	18	20	.296	.332	.425	92	-1	-5	51	4	4	-1	3	3O/2	-0.4
1922	Phi-N	99	331	56	101	18	6	5	33	28	17	.305	.365	.441	98	3	-1	53	4	5	-2	13	3S/1	1.4
1923	Phi-N	119	392	59	107	21	7	7	57	21	19	.273	.315	.416	82	-6	-12	51	5	2	0	-4	3S/2	-1.1
1924	Phi-N	118	388	55	119	24	4	7	58	27	15	.307	.363	.443	102	8	2	62	5	4	-1	-8	3/2SO	0.0
1925	Phi-N	92	286	48	99	18	5	14	61	19	18	.346	.389	.591	135	19	15	63	0	3	-2	-17	OS32/1	-0.3
1926	Phi-N	112	368	55	113	23	1	7	57	27	11	.307	.356	.432	106	5	3	55	5			1	132/O	0.3
1927	Phi-N	141	533	62	163	24	5	6	75	48	20	.306	.365	.403	104	5	4	78	9			1	*1/23	-0.3
1928	Phi-N	33	91	7	19	5	1	1	11	14	5	.209	.321	.319	65	-4	-5	10	0			-3	O/1	-0.8
	NY-N	30	25	3	4	0	0	1	5	3	2	.160	.250	.280	38	-2	-2	2	0			0	/1	-0.2
	Yr	63	116	10	23	5	1	2	16	17	7	.198	.306	.310	60	-6	-7	12	0			-3		-1.0
Total	9	929	2992	427	889	152	34	60	425	215	152	.297	.349	.431	99	22	-7	447	35	20		-7	310/S2	-1.1

■ ZEKE WRIGLEY
Wrigley, George Watson b: 1/18/1874, Philadelphia, Pa. d: 9/28/52, Philadelphia, Pa. 5'8.5", 150 lbs. Deb: 8/31/1896

YEAR	TM/L	G	AB	R	H	2B	3B	HR	RBI	BB	SO	AVG	OBP	SLG	PRO+	BR	/A	RC	SB	CS	SBR	FR	POS	TPR
1896	Was-N	5	9	1	1	0	0	0	2	1	1	.111	.200	.111	-16	-1	-1	0	0			3	/2S	0.1
1897	Was-N	104	388	65	110	14	8	3	64	21		.284	.320	.384	88	-8	-8	51	5			-1	OS3/2	-0.8
1898	Was-N	111	400	50	98	9	10	2	39	20		.245	.283	.333	78	-12	-12	41	10			10	S2/O3	0.3
1899	NY-N	4	15	1	3	0	0	0	1	1		.200	.250	.200	27	-1	-1	1	1			-1	/3	-0.2
	Bro-N	15	49	4	10	2	2	0	11	3		.204	.250	.327	58	-3	-3	5	2			-5	S/3	-0.6
	Yr	19	64	5	13	2	2	0	12	4		.203	.250	.297	51	-4	-4	6	3			-6		-0.8
Total	4	239	861	121	222	25	20	5	117	46	1	.258	.296	.351	80	-26	-25	98	18			6	S/O32	-1.2

■ RICK WRONA
Wrona, Richard James b: 12/10/63, Tulsa, Okla. BR/TR, 6'1", 185 lbs. Deb: 9/03/88

YEAR	TM/L	G	AB	R	H	2B	3B	HR	RBI	BB	SO	AVG	OBP	SLG	PRO+	BR	/A	RC	SB	CS	SBR	FR	POS	TPR
1988	Chi-N	4	6	0	0	0	0	0	0	0	1	.000	.000	.000	-96	-2	-2	0	0	0	0	1	/C	0.0
1989	*Chi-N	38	92	11	26	2	1	2	14	2	21	.283	.305	.391	91	-1	-1	11	0	0	0	2	C	0.4
1990	Chi-N	16	29	3	5	0	0	0	0	2	11	.172	.226	.172	10	-3	-4	1	1	0	0	3	C	0.0
Total	3	58	127	14	31	2	1	2	14	4	33	.244	.273	.323	63	-6	-7	12	1	0	0	6	/C	0.4

■ YATS WUESTLING
Wuestling, George b: 10/18/03, St.Louis, Mo. d: 4/26/70, St.Louis, Mo. BR/TR, 5'11", 167 lbs. Deb: 6/15/29

YEAR	TM/L	G	AB	R	H	2B	3B	HR	RBI	BB	SO	AVG	OBP	SLG	PRO+	BR	/A	RC	SB	CS	SBR	FR	POS	TPR
1929	Det-A	54	150	13	30	4	1	0	16	9	24	.200	.250	.240	27	-16	-17	9	1	3	-2	-2	S/23	-1.4
1930	Det-A	4	9	0	0	0	0	0	0	2	3	.000	.182	.000	-48	-2	-2	0	0	0	0	-0	/S	0.0
	NY-A	25	58	5	11	0	1	0	3	4	14	.190	.242	.224	20	-7	-7	3	0	1	-1	4	S/3	0.0
	Yr	29	67	5	11	0	1	0	3	6	17	.164	.233	.194	10	-9	-9	3	0	1	-1	5		0.0
Total	2	83	217	18	41	4	2	0	19	15	41	.189	.245	.226	21	-26	-25	12	1	4	-2	2	/S32	-1.4

YEAR	TM/L	G	AB	R	H	2B	3B	HR	RBI	BB	SO	AVG	OBP	SLG	PRO+	BR	/A	RC	SB	CS	SBR	FR	POS	TPR

■ **JOE WYATT**   Wyatt, Loral John b: 4/6/1900, Petersburg, Ind.   d: 12/5/70, Oblong, Ill.   BR/TR, 6'1", 175 lbs.   Deb: 9/11/24

YEAR	TM/L	G	AB	R	H	2B	3B	HR	RBI	BB	SO	AVG	OBP	SLG	PRO+	BR	/A	RC	SB	CS	SBR	FR	POS	TPR
1924	Cle-A	4	12	1	2	0	0	0	1	2	1	.167	.286	.167	18	-1	-1	1	0	0	0	-1	/O	-0.2

■ **REN WYLIE**   Wylie, James Renwick b: 12/14/1861, Elizabeth, Pa.   d: 8/17/51, Wilkinsburg, Pa.   5'11", 155 lbs.   Deb: 8/11/1882

YEAR	TM/L	G	AB	R	H	2B	3B	HR	RBI	BB	SO	AVG	OBP	SLG	PRO+	BR	/A	RC	SB	CS	SBR	FR	POS	TPR
1882	Pit-a	1	3	0	0	0	0	0		0		.000	.000	.000	-99	-1	-1	0				0	/O	0.0

■ **FRANK WYMAN**   Wyman, Frank H. b: 5/10/1862, Haverhill, Mass.   d: 2/4/16, Everett, Mass.   Deb: 6/24/1884

YEAR	TM/L	G	AB	R	H	2B	3B	HR	RBI	BB	SO	AVG	OBP	SLG	PRO+	BR	/A	RC	SB	CS	SBR	FR	POS	TPR
1884	KC-U	30	124	16	27	4	0	0		3		.218	.236	.250	74	-4	-2	8	0			5	O/P13	0.2
	CP-U	2	8	1	3	0	0	0		0		.375	.375	.375	155	0	0	1	0			-0	/1	0.0
	Yr	32	132	17	30	4	0	0		3		.227	.244	.258	80	-4	-2	9	0			4		0.2

■ **BUTCH WYNEGAR**   Wynegar, Harold Delano b: 3/14/56, York, Pa.   BB/TR, 6'1", 190 lbs.   Deb: 4/09/76

YEAR	TM/L	G	AB	R	H	2B	3B	HR	RBI	BB	SO	AVG	OBP	SLG	PRO+	BR	/A	RC	SB	CS	SBR	FR	POS	TPR
1976	Min-A	149	534	58	139	21	2	10	69	79	63	.260	.358	.363	108	10	8	72	0	0	0	-9	*CD	0.4
1977	Min-A	144	532	76	139	22	3	10	79	68	61	.261	.347	.370	97	-2	-1	70	2	3	-1	-11	*C/3	-0.8
1978	Min-A	135	454	36	104	22	1	4	45	47	42	.229	.310	.308	73	-15	-16	46	1	0	0	-3	*C/3	-1.5
1979	Min-A	149	504	74	136	20	1	7	57	74	36	.270	.366	.351	91	-1	-4	68	2	2	-1	-6	*C	-0.3
1980	Min-A	146	486	61	124	18	3	5	57	63	36	.255	.343	.335	81	-7	-12	59	3	1	0	3	*C/D	-0.2
1981	Min-A	47	150	11	37	5	0	0	10	17	9	.247	.327	.280	72	-4	-5	13	0	1	-1	2	C/D	-0.2
1982	Min-A	24	86	9	18	4	0	1	8	10	12	.209	.292	.291	59	-5	-5	7	0	0	0	-2	C	-0.4
	NY-A	63	191	27	56	8	1	3	20	40	21	.293	.418	.393	126	9	9	33	0	1	-1	-1	C	1.1
	Yr	87	277	36	74	12	1	4	28	50	33	.267	.381	.361	106	4	4	40	0	1	-1	-2		0.7
1983	NY-A	94	301	40	89	18	2	6	42	52	29	.296	.401	.429	133	14	15	54	1	1	-0	-13	C	0.6
1984	NY-A	129	442	48	118	13	1	6	45	65	35	.267	.361	.342	99	-0	2	53	1	4	-2	-4	*C	0.4
1985	NY-A	102	309	27	69	15	0	5	32	64	43	.223	.357	.320	89	-3	-2	38	0	0	0	-6	C	-0.3
1986	NY-A	61	194	19	40	4	1	7	29	30	21	.206	.313	.345	80	-5	-5	20	0	0	0	-2	C	-0.2
1987	Cal-A	31	92	4	19	2	0	0	5	9	13	.207	.277	.228	37	-8	-8	6	0	0	0	2	C/D	-0.2
1988	Cal-A	27	55	8	14	4	1	1	8	8	7	.255	.349	.418	117	1	1	8	0	0	0	-1	C	0.2
Total	13	1301	4330	498	1102	176	15	65	506	626	428	.255	.351	.347	93	-17	-21	549	10	13	-5	-49	*C/D3	-1.4

■ **EARLY WYNN**   Wynn, Early "Gus" b: 1/6/20, Hartford, Ala.   BB/TR, 6', 190 lbs.   Deb: 9/13/39   CH

YEAR	TM/L	G	AB	R	H	2B	3B	HR	RBI	BB	SO	AVG	OBP	SLG	PRO+	BR	/A	RC	SB	CS	SBR	FR	POS	TPR
1939	Was-A	3	6	0	1	0	0	0	1	1	1	.167	.286	.167	20	-1	-1	0	0	0	0	-1	/P	0.0
1941	Was-A	5	15	1	2	1	0	0	0	0	5	.133	.133	.200	-14	-2	-2	0	0	0	0	0	/P	0.0
1942	Was-A	30	69	4	15	2	0	0	7	3	13	.217	.250	.246	40	-6	-5	4	0	0	0	-1	P	0.0
1943	Was-A	38	98	6	29	3	1	1	11	1	11	.296	.303	.378	102	1	-0	11	0	0	0	-2	P	0.0
1944	Was-A	43	92	4	19	2	0	1	6	3	21	.207	.232	.261	42	-7	-7	5	0	0	0	-2	P	0.0
1946	Was-A	25	47	4	15	2	0	1	9	5	7	.319	.385	.426	134	2	2	8	0	0	0	0	P	0.0
1947	Was-A	54	120	6	33	6	0	2	13	1	19	.275	.281	.375	84	-4	-3	13	0	0	0	-1	P	0.0
1948	Was-A	73	106	9	23	3	1	0	16	14	22	.217	.308	.264	55	-7	-7	9	0	0	0	-1	P	-0.2
1949	Cle-A	35	70	3	10	1	0	1	7	4	10	.143	.189	.200	3	-10	-10	2	0	0	0	1	P	0.0
1950	Cle-A	39	77	12	18	5	1	2	10	10	12	.234	.322	.403	87	-2	-2	11	0	0	0	-0	P	0.0
1951	Cle-A	41	108	8	20	8	1	1	13	7	9	.185	.235	.306	48	-9	-8	7	0	0	0	-1	P	0.0
1952	Cle-A	44	99	5	22	2	0	0	10	9	15	.222	.287	.242	52	-7	-6	7	0	0	0	-1	P	0.0
1953	Cle-A	37	91	11	25	2	0	3	10	7	17	.275	.327	.396	97	-1	-1	13	0	0	0	-1	P	0.0
1954	*Cle-A	40	93	10	17	3	0	0	4	7	13	.183	.240	.215	25	-10	-10	5	0	0	0	-4	P	0.0
1955	Cle-A	34	84	8	15	3	0	1	7	6	17	.179	.233	.250	29	-8	-9	5	0	0	0	-2	P	0.0
1956	Cle-A	38	101	5	23	5	0	1	15	7	22	.228	.278	.307	53	-7	-7	9	1	0	0	1	P	0.0
1957	Cle-A	40	86	4	10	0	0	0	4	11	23	.116	.216	.116	-7	-13	-12	3	0	0	0	-1	P	0.0
1958	Chi-A	40	75	7	15	1	0	0	11	10	25	.200	.294	.213	43	-6	-5	5	0	0	0	-3	P	0.0
1959	*Chi-A	37	90	11	22	7	0	2	8	9	18	.244	.320	.389	95	-1	-1	12	0	0	0	-2	P	0.0
1960	Chi-A	36	75	8	15	2	1	1	7	14	17	.200	.333	.293	72	-3	-3	9	0	0	0	-3	P	0.0
1961	Chi-A	17	37	4	6	0	0	0	2	3	11	.162	.225	.162	5	-5	-5	1	0	0	0	-2	P	0.0
1962	Chi-A	27	54	5	7	1	0	0	2	7	17	.130	.230	.148	4	-7	-7	2	0	0	0	-2	P	0.0
1963	Cle-A	20	11	1	3	0	0	0	0	2	5	.273	.385	.273	89	-0	-0	1	0	0	0	-0	P	0.0
Total	23	796	1704	136	365	59	5	17	173	141	330	.214	.275	.285	54	-113	-109	145	1	0	0	-25	P	-0.2

■ **JIM WYNN**   Wynn, James Sherman b: 3/12/42, Hamilton, Ohio   BR/TR, 5'10", 160 lbs.   Deb: 7/10/63

YEAR	TM/L	G	AB	R	H	2B	3B	HR	RBI	BB	SO	AVG	OBP	SLG	PRO+	BR	/A	RC	SB	CS	SBR	FR	POS	TPR
1963	Hou-N	70	250	31	61	10	5	4	27	30	53	.244	.325	.372	107	0	2	32	4	2	0	-7	OS/3	-0.5
1964	Hou-N	67	219	19	49	7	0	5	18	24	58	.224	.303	.324	81	-6	-5	21	5	5	-2	1	*O	-0.7
1965	Hou-N	157	564	90	155	30	7	22	73	84	126	.275	.374	.470	146	29	33	108	43	4	11	14	*O	5.4
1966	Hou-N	105	418	62	107	21	1	18	62	41	81	.256	.324	.440	118	5	9	58	13	10	-2	6	*O	1.0
1967	Hou-N	158	594	102	148	29	3	37	107	74	137	.249	.334	.495	139	25	28	102	16	4	2	6	*O	3.1
1968	Hou-N	156	542	85	146	23	5	26	67	90	131	.269	.378	.474	158	38	40	98	11	17	-7	17	*O	4.7
1969	Hou-N	149	495	113	133	17	1	33	87	**148**	142	.269	.440	.507	168	51	52	126	23	7	3	6	*O	5.4
1970	Hou-N	157	554	82	156	32	2	27	88	106	96	.282	.398	.493	143	32	35	114	24	5	4	8	*O	4.0
1971	Hou-N	123	404	38	82	16	0	7	45	56	63	.203	.303	.295	72	-15	-14	36	10	5	0	4	*O	-1.4
1972	Hou-N	145	542	117	148	29	3	24	90	103	99	.273	.391	.470	147	34	35	107	17	7	1	5	*O	3.7
1973	Hou-N	139	481	90	106	14	5	20	55	91	102	.220	.349	.395	106	6	8	68	14	11	-2	4	*O	0.1
1974	*LA-N	150	535	104	145	17	4	32	108	108	104	.271	.393	.497	154	36	39	109	18	15	-4	7	*O	3.8
1975	LA-N	130	412	80	102	16	0	18	58	110	77	.248	.407	.417	135	21	24	79	7	3	0	-2	*O	1.8
1976	Atl-N	148	449	75	93	19	1	17	66	**127**	111	.207	.382	.367	107	14	10	75	16	6	1	10	*O	1.7
1977	NY-A	30	77	7	11	2	1	1	3	15	16	.143	.283	.234	43	-6	-6	6	1	0	0	1	D/O	-0.4
	Mil-A	36	117	10	23	3	1	0	10	17	31	.197	.299	.239	49	-8	-8	10	3	0	1	-3	OD	-0.9
	Yr	66	194	17	34	5	2	1	13	32	47	.175	.292	.237	46	-14	-14	16	4	0	1	-2		-1.3
Total	15	1920	6653	1105	1665	285	39	291	964	1224	1427	.250	.369	.436	129	256	281	1148	225	101	7	75	*O/DS3	30.8

■ **MARVELL WYNNE**   Wynne, Marvell b: 12/17/59, Chicago, Ill.   BL/TL, 5'11", 175 lbs.   Deb: 6/15/83

YEAR	TM/L	G	AB	R	H	2B	3B	HR	RBI	BB	SO	AVG	OBP	SLG	PRO+	BR	/A	RC	SB	CS	SBR	FR	POS	TPR
1983	Pit-N	103	366	66	89	16	2	7	26	38	52	.243	.319	.355	85	-6	-8	43	12	10	-2	-5	*O	-1.7
1984	Pit-N	154	653	77	174	24	11	0	39	42	81	.266	.311	.337	82	-16	-16	67	24	19	-4	-1	*O	-2.7
1985	Pit-N	103	337	21	69	6	3	2	18	18	48	.205	.247	.258	42	-26	-26	21	10	5	0	2	O	-2.8
1986	SD-N	137	288	34	76	19	2	7	37	15	45	.264	.303	.417	98	-2	-2	32	11	11	-3	-9	*O	-1.7
1987	SD-N	98	188	17	47	8	2	2	24	20	37	.250	.327	.346	80	-6	-5	21	11	6	-0	1	O	-0.6
1988	SD-N	128	333	37	88	13	4	11	42	31	62	.264	.327	.426	117	6	6	47	3	4	-2	-11	*O	-0.9
1989	SD-N	105	294	19	74	11	1	6	35	12	41	.252	.283	.357	82	-8	-8	30	4	1	1	-4	O	-1.2
	*Chi-N	20	48	8	9	2	1	1	4	1	7	.188	.220	.333	52	-3	-3	4	2	0	1	-2	O	-0.4
	Yr	125	342	27	83	13	2	7	39	13	48	.243	.279	.354	77	-10	-11	34	6	1	1	-6		-1.6
1990	Chi-N	92	186	21	38	8	2	4	19	14	25	.204	.264	.333	58	-10	-12	16	3	2	-0	3	O	-1.0
Total	8	940	2693	300	664	107	28	40	244	191	398	.247	.298	.352	81	-72	-73	279	80	58	-11	-27	O	-13.0

■ **JOHNNY WYROSTEK**   Wyrostek, John Barney b: 7/12/19, Fairmont City, Ill.   d: 12/12/86, St.Louis, Mo.   BL/TR, 6'2", 180 lbs.   Deb: 9/10/42

YEAR	TM/L	G	AB	R	H	2B	3B	HR	RBI	BB	SO	AVG	OBP	SLG	PRO+	BR	/A	RC	SB	CS	SBR	FR	POS	TPR
1942	Pit-N	9	35	0	4	0	1	0	3	3	2	.114	.184	.171	4	-4	-4	1	0			0	/O	-0.4
1943	Pit-N	51	79	7	12	3	0	1	9	9	6	.152	.189	.190	7	-9	-10	3	0			-1	O/312	-1.2
1946	Phi-N	145	545	73	153	30	4	6	45	70	42	.281	.366	.383	116	10	12	82	7			12	*O	2.3
1947	Phi-N	128	454	68	124	24	7	5	51	61	45	.273	.364	.390	104	1	4	67	7			-2	*O	-0.2
1948	Cin-N	136	512	74	140	24	9	17	76	52	63	.273	.344	.455	119	9	11	83	7			-2	*O	0.0

YEAR	TM/L	G	AB	R	H	2B	3B	HR	RBI	BB	SO	AVG	OBP	SLG	PRO+	BR	/A	RC	SB	CS	SBR	FR	POS	TPR
1949	Cin-N	134	474	54	118	20	4	9	46	58	63	.249	.333	.365	86	-8	-9	60	7			-0	*O	-1.6
1950	Cin-N	131	509	70	145	34	5	8	76	52	38	.285	.357	.418	103	3	2	76	1			-2	*O/1	-0.4
1951	Cin-N	142	537	52	167	31	3	2	61	54	54	.311	.376	.391	105	7	6	83	2	1	0	-10	*O	-0.7
1952	Cin-N	30	106	12	25	1	3	1	10	18	7	.236	.347	.330	89	-1	-1	12	1	2	-1	4	O/1	0.1
	Phi-N	98	321	45	88	16	3	1	37	44	26	.274	.363	.352	100	1	2	42	1	7	-4	8	O	0.3
	Yr	128	427	57	113	17	6	2	47	62	33	.265	.359	.347	97	-0		54	2	9	-5	12		0.4
1953	Phi-N	125	409	42	111	14	2	6	47	38	43	.271	.339	.359	83	-10	-10	51	0	3	-2	-2	*O	-1.7
1954	Phi-N	92	259	28	62	12	4	3	28	29	39	.239	.318	.351	74	-10	-10	29	0	0	0	-3	O1	-1.4
Total	11	1221	4240	525	1149	209	45	58	481	482	437	.271	.349	.383	98	-11	-6	589	33	13		2	*O/132	-4.9

■ HENRY YAIK
Yaik, Henry   b: 3/1/1864, Detroit, Mich.   d: 9/21/35, Detroit, Mich.   5'11", 185 lbs.   Deb: 10/03/1888

YEAR	TM/L	G	AB	R	H	2B	3B	HR	RBI	BB	SO	AVG	OBP	SLG	PRO+	BR	/A	RC	SB	CS	SBR	FR	POS	TPR
1888	Pit-N	2	6	0	2	0	0	0	1	1	0	.333	.429	.333	161	0	0	1	0			2	/OC	0.2

■ AD YALE
Yale, William M.   b: 4/17/1870, Bristol, Conn.   d: 4/27/48, Bridgeport, Conn.   Deb: 9/18/05

YEAR	TM/L	G	AB	R	H	2B	3B	HR	RBI	BB	SO	AVG	OBP	SLG	PRO+	BR	/A	RC	SB	CS	SBR	FR	POS	TPR
1905	Bro-N	4	13	1	1	0	0	0	0	1	1	.077	.143	.077	-36	-2	-2	0	0			-0	/1	-0.2

■ HUGH YANCY
Yancy, Hugh   b: 10/16/49, Sarasota, Fla.   BR/TR, 5'11", 170 lbs.   Deb: 7/05/72

YEAR	TM/L	G	AB	R	H	2B	3B	HR	RBI	BB	SO	AVG	OBP	SLG	PRO+	BR	/A	RC	SB	CS	SBR	FR	POS	TPR
1972	Chi-A	3	9	0	1	0	0	0	0	0	0	.111	.111	.111	-33	-1	-1	-0	0	1	-1	0	/3	-0.1
1974	Chi-A	1	0	0	0	0	0	0	0	0	0	—	—	—	—	0	-0	0	0	0	0	0	/D	0.0
1976	Chi-A	3	10	0	1	1	0	0	0	0	3	.100	.100	.200	-14	-1	-1	0	0	0	0	-1	/2	-0.1
Total	3	7	19	0	2	1	0	0	0	0	3	.105	.105	.158	-23	-3	-3	0	0	1	-1	-0	/23D	-0.2

■ GEORGE YANKOWSKI
Yankowski, George Edward   b: 11/19/22, Cambridge, Mass.   BR/TR, 6', 180 lbs.   Deb: 8/17/42

YEAR	TM/L	G	AB	R	H	2B	3B	HR	RBI	BB	SO	AVG	OBP	SLG	PRO+	BR	/A	RC	SB	CS	SBR	FR	POS	TPR
1942	Phi-A	6	13	0	2	1	0	0	2	0	2	.154	.154	.231	7	-2	-2	0	0	0	0	0	/C	0.0
1949	Chi-A	12	18	0	3	1	0	0	2	0	2	.167	.167	.222	3	-3	-3	0	0	0	0	1	/C	0.0
Total	2	18	31	0	5	2	0	0	4	0	2	.161	.161	.226	5	-4	-4	0	0	0	0	1	/C	0.0

■ GEORGE YANTZ
Yantz, George Webb   b: 7/27/1886, Louisville, Ky.   d: 2/26/67, Louisville, Ky.   BR/TR, 5'6.5", 168 lbs.   Deb: 9/30/12

YEAR	TM/L	G	AB	R	H	2B	3B	HR	RBI	BB	SO	AVG	OBP	SLG	PRO+	BR	/A	RC	SB	CS	SBR	FR	POS	TPR
1912	Chi-N	1	1	0	1	0	0	0	0	0	0	1.000	1.000	1.000	449	0	0	1	0			0	/C	0.1

■ YAM YARYAN
Yaryan, Clarence Everett   b: 11/5/1892, Knowlton, Iowa   d: 11/16/64, Birmingham, Ala.   BR/TR, 5'10.5", 180 lbs.   Deb: 4/23/21

YEAR	TM/L	G	AB	R	H	2B	3B	HR	RBI	BB	SO	AVG	OBP	SLG	PRO+	BR	/A	RC	SB	CS	SBR	FR	POS	TPR
1921	Chi-A	45	102	11	31	8	2	0	15	9	16	.304	.366	.422	102	0	0	16	0	0	0	-7	C	-0.4
1922	Chi-A	36	71	9	14	2	0	2	9	6	10	.197	.269	.310	51	-5	-5	6	1	0	0	-1	C	-0.5
Total	2	81	173	20	45	10	2	2	24	15	26	.260	.326	.376	81	-5	-5	22	1	0	0	-8	/C	-0.9

■ CARL YASTRZEMSKI
Yastrzemski, Carl Michael "Yaz"   b: 8/22/39, Southampton, N.Y.   BL/TR, 5'11", 175 lbs.   Deb: 4/11/61   H

YEAR	TM/L	G	AB	R	H	2B	3B	HR	RBI	BB	SO	AVG	OBP	SLG	PRO+	BR	/A	RC	SB	CS	SBR	FR	POS	TPR
1961	Bos-A	148	583	71	155	31	6	11	80	50	96	.266	.327	.396	90	-7	-9	72	6	5	-1	-6	*O	-2.1
1962	Bos-A	160	646	99	191	43	6	19	94	66	82	.296	.364	.469	118	20	17	103	7	4	-0	12	*O	2.3
1963	Bos-A	151	570	91	**183**	40	3	14	68	95	72	.321	.419	.475	145	42	40	118	8	5	-1	8	*O	4.4
1964	Bos-A	151	567	77	164	29	9	15	67	75	90	.289	.374	.451	122	23	20	89	6	5	-1	18	*O/3	3.2
1965	Bos-A	133	494	78	154	**45**	3	20	72	70	58	.312	**.398**	**.536**	154	42	38	102	7	6	-2	5	*O	**3.8**
1966	Bos-A	160	594	81	165	**39**	2	16	80	84	60	.278	.368	.464	117	24	17	92	8	9	-3	11	*O	1.9
1967	*Bos-A	161	579	**112**	189	31	4	44	121	91	69	.326	.421	.622	189	76	71	155	10	8	-2	7	*O	7.7
1968	Bos-A	157	539	90	162	32	2	23	74	**119**	90	.301	.429	.495	168	58	53	121	13	6	0	12	*O/1	6.6
1969	Bos-A	162	603	96	154	28	2	40	111	101	91	.255	.363	.507	134	33	29	113	15	7	0	7	*O1	3.2
1970	Bos-A	161	566	**125**	186	29	0	40	102	128	66	.329	**.453**	**.592**	174	72	66	157	23	13	-1	-3	1O	5.6
1971	Bos-A	148	508	75	129	21	2	15	70	106	60	.254	.384	.392	112	18	13	80	8	7	-2	6	*O	1.4
1972	Bos-A	125	455	70	120	18	2	12	68	67	44	.264	.363	.391	118	16	13	66	5	4	-1	5	O1	1.2
1973	Bos-A	152	540	82	160	25	4	19	95	105	58	.296	.411	.463	138	37	32	103	9	7	-2		*13O	1.3
1974	Bos-A	148	515	**93**	155	25	2	15	79	104	48	.301	.421	.445	139	38	33	102	12	7	-1	-8	1O/D	2.0
1975	*Bos-A	149	543	91	146	30	1	14	60	87	67	.269	.372	.405	110	16	10	84	8	4	0	-1	*1/OD	0.1
1976	Bos-A	155	546	71	146	23	2	21	102	80	67	.267	.362	.432	118	23	14	86	5	6	-2	-8	1OD	0.0
1977	Bos-A	150	558	99	165	27	3	28	102	73	40	.296	.378	.505	124	30	21	110	11	1	3	9	*O/1D	2.7
1978	Bos-A	144	523	70	145	21	2	17	81	76	44	.277	.372	.423	111	18	11	85	4	5	-2	-1	O1D	0.4
1979	Bos-A	147	518	69	140	28	1	21	87	62	46	.270	.351	.450	108	10	6	81	3	3	-1	5	D1O	0.6
1980	Bos-A	105	364	49	100	21	1	15	50	44	38	.275	.353	.462	115	11	8	58	0	2	-1	-3	DO1	0.2
1981	Bos-A	91	338	36	83	14	1	7	53	49	28	.246	.341	.355	95	1	-1	41	0	1	-1	3	D1	0.1
1982	Bos-A	131	459	53	126	22	1	16	72	59	50	.275	.360	.431	110	11	7	72	0	1	-1	0	*D1/O	0.3
1983	Bos-A	119	380	38	101	24	0	10	56	54	29	.266	.360	.408	103	7	3	55	0	0	0	-0	*D/1O	0.3
Total	23	3308	11988	1816	3419	646	59	452	1844	1845	1393	.285	.382	.462	128	617	514	2147	168	116	-19	67	*O1D/3	47.5

■ AL YATES
Yates, Albert Arthur   b: 5/26/45, Jersey City, N.J.   BR/TR, 6'2", 210 lbs.   Deb: 5/13/71

YEAR	TM/L	G	AB	R	H	2B	3B	HR	RBI	BB	SO	AVG	OBP	SLG	PRO+	BR	/A	RC	SB	CS	SBR	FR	POS	TPR
1971	Mil-A	24	47	5	13	2	0	1	4	3	7	.277	.320	.383	100	-0	-0	5	1	0	0	1	O	0.1

■ BERT YEABSLEY
Yeabsley, Robert Watkins   b: 12/17/1893, Philadelphia, Pa.   d: 2/8/61, Philadelphia, Pa.   TR, 5'9.5", 175 lbs.   Deb: 5/28/19

YEAR	TM/L	G	AB	R	H	2B	3B	HR	RBI	BB	SO	AVG	OBP	SLG	PRO+	BR	/A	RC	SB	CS	SBR	FR	POS	TPR
1919	Phi-N	3	0	0	0	0	0	0	0	1	0	—	1.000	—	200	0	0	0	0			0	H	0.0

■ GEORGE YEAGER
Yeager, George J. "Doc"   b: 6/5/1874, Cincinnati, Ohio   d: 7/5/40, Cincinnati, Ohio   TR, 5'10", 190 lbs.   Deb: 9/25/1896

YEAR	TM/L	G	AB	R	H	2B	3B	HR	RBI	BB	SO	AVG	OBP	SLG	PRO+	BR	/A	RC	SB	CS	SBR	FR	POS	TPR
1896	Bos-N	2	5	1	1	0	0	0	0	0	1	.200	.200	.200	6	-1	-1	0	0			-0	/1	0.0
1897	*Bos-N	30	95	20	23	2	3	2	15	7		.242	.294	.389	77	-3	-4	12	2			1	CO/23	0.0
1898	Bos-N	68	221	37	59	13	1	3	24	16		.267	.328	.376	99	1	1	28	1			-3	C1/OS	-0.1
1899	Bos-N	3	8	1	1	0	0	0	0	1		.125	.222	.125	-2	-1	-1	0	0			0	/OC	0.0
1901	Cle-A	39	139	13	31	5	0	0	14	4		.223	.250	.259	45	-11	-10	10	2			4	C/1O2	-0.3
	Pit-N	26	91	9	24	2	1	0	10	4		.264	.302	.308	77	-2	-3	9	1			-1	C/31	0.0
1902	NY-N	38	108	6	22	2	1	0	9	11		.204	.277	.241	62	-4	-4	8	1			-1	C/1O	-0.2
	Bal-A	11	38	3	7	1	0	0	1	2		.184	.225	.211	21	-4	-4	2	0			2	C	-0.1
Total	6	217	705	90	168	25	6	5	73	45	1	.238	.290	.312	71	-25	-28	70	7			1	C/1023S	-0.7

■ JOE YEAGER
Yeager, Joseph F. "Little Joe"   b: 8/28/1875, Philadelphia, Pa.   d: 7/2/37, Detroit, Mich.   BR/TR,   Deb: 4/22/1898

YEAR	TM/L	G	AB	R	H	2B	3B	HR	RBI	BB	SO	AVG	OBP	SLG	PRO+	BR	/A	RC	SB	CS	SBR	FR	POS	TPR
1898	Bro-N	43	134	12	23	5	1	0	15	7		.172	.218	.224	29	-12	-12	7	1			5	P/OS2	0.0
1899	Bro-N	23	47	12	9	0	1	0	4	6		.191	.234	.234	58	-2	-2	4	0			3	SP/O3	0.3
1900	Bro-N	3	9	0	3	0	0	0	0	0		.333	.333	.333	82	-0	-0	1	0			-0	/P3	0.0
1901	Det-A	41	125	18	37	7	1	2	17	4		.296	.338	.416	106	2	1	19	3			5	PS/2	0.0
1902	Det-A	50	161	17	39	6	5	1	23	5		.242	.282	.360	77	-5	-5	17	0			-1	PO2/S3	-0.1
1903	Det-A	109	402	36	103	15	6	0	43	18		.256	.288	.323	87	-7	-6	42	9			-9	*3/PS	-1.5
1905	NY-A	115	401	53	107	16	7	0	42	25		.267	.310	.342	98	4	-2	47	8			-0	3S	0.2
1906	NY-A	57	123	20	37	6	1	0	12	13		.301	.368	.366	120	5	3	19	3			-1	S2/3	0.3
1907	StL-A	123	436	32	104	21	7	1	44	31		.239	.288	.326	98	-1	-1	46	11			7	32S	1.2
1908	StL-A	10	15	3	5	1	0	0	1	1		.333	.375	.400	154	1	1	3	2			0	/2S	0.1
Total	10	574	1853	203	467	77	29	4	201	110		.252	.299	.331	90	-18	-24	206	37			9	3/PS20	0.5

■ STEVE YEAGER
Yeager, Stephen Wayne   b: 11/24/48, Huntington, W.Va.   BR/TR, 6', 190 lbs.   Deb: 8/02/72

YEAR	TM/L	G	AB	R	H	2B	3B	HR	RBI	BB	SO	AVG	OBP	SLG	PRO+	BR	/A	RC	SB	CS	SBR	FR	POS	TPR
1972	LA-N	35	106	18	29	0	1	4	15	16	26	.274	.374	.406	124	3	4	16	0	0	0	8	C	1.5
1973	LA-N	54	134	18	34	5	0	2	10	15	33	.254	.342	.336	93	-2	-1	16	1	0	0	5	C	0.8
1974	*LA-N	94	316	41	84	16	1	12	41	32	77	.266	.337	.437	120	6	7	46	2	2	-1	14	C	2.5
1975	LA-N	135	452	34	103	16	1	12	54	40	75	.228	.302	.347	83	-13	-11	45	2	5	-2	11	*C	0.3

YEAR	TM/L	G	AB	R	H	2B	3B	HR	RBI	BB	SO	AVG	OBP	SLG	PRO+	BR	/A	RC	SB	CS	SBR	FR	POS	TPR
1976	LA-N	117	359	42	77	11	3	11	35	30	84	.214	.288	.354	83	-10	-9	38	3	1	0	8	*C	0.6
1977	*LA-N	125	387	53	99	21	2	16	55	43	84	.256	.336	.444	108	4	4	57	1	3	-2	11	*C	1.2
1978	*LA-N	94	228	19	44	7	0	4	23	36	41	.193	.303	.276	63	-11	-11	20	0	0	0	11	*C	0.2
1979	LA-N	105	310	33	67	9	2	13	41	29	68	.216	.283	.384	81	-9	-9	31	1	0	0	11	*C	0.5
1980	LA-N	96	227	20	48	8	0	2	20	20	54	.211	.275	.273	55	-14	-13	16	2	3	-1	4	C	-0.9
1981	*LA-N	42	86	5	18	2	0	3	7	6	14	.209	.261	.337	71	-4	-3	7	0	0	0	1	C	-0.1
1982	LA-N	82	196	13	48	5	2	2	18	13	28	.245	.295	.321	74	-7	-7	19	0	0	0	6	C	0.0
1983	*LA-N	113	335	31	68	8	3	15	41	23	57	.203	.256	.379	74	-13	-13	28	1	1	-0	-6	*C	-1.6
1984	LA-N	74	197	16	45	4	0	4	29	20	38	.228	.300	.310	72	-7	-7	19	1	2	-1	-6	C	-1.2
1985	*LA-N	53	121	4	25	4	1	0	9	7	24	.207	.250	.256	43	-9	-9	7	0	1	-1	9	C	0.1
1986	Sea-A	50	130	10	27	2	0	2	12	12	23	.208	.275	.269	48	-9	-9	9	0	0	0	0	C	-0.5
Total	15	1269	3584	357	816	118	16	102	410	342	726	.228	.300	.355	83	-96	-87	375	14	18	-7	88	*C	3.4

■ BILL YEATMAN   Yeatman, William Suter b: 1849, Alexandria, Va. d: 4/20/01, York, Pa. Deb: 4/20/1872

YEAR	TM/L	G	AB	R	H	2B	3B	HR	RBI	BB	SO	AVG	OBP	SLG	PRO+	BR	/A	RC	SB	CS	SBR	FR	POS	TPR
1872	Nat-n	1	4	0	0	0	0	0		0		.000	.000	.000	-86	-1	-1	0					/O	0.0

■ ERIC YELDING   Yelding, Eric Girard b: 2/22/65, Montrose, Ala. BR/TR, 6'1", 170 lbs. Deb: 4/09/89

YEAR	TM/L	G	AB	R	H	2B	3B	HR	RBI	BB	SO	AVG	OBP	SLG	PRO+	BR	/A	RC	SB	CS	SBR	FR	POS	TPR
1989	Hou-N	70	90	19	21	2	0	0	9	7	19	.233	.296	.256	61	-5	-4	7	11	5	0	8	S2/O	0.6
1990	Hou-N	142	511	69	130	9	5	1	28	39	87	.254	.307	.297	68	-22	-21	48	64	25	4	-10	OS2/3	-2.6
Total	2	212	601	88	151	11	5	1	37	46	106	.251	.306	.291	67	-27	-25	55	75	30	5	-1	O/S23	-2.0

■ ARCHIE YELLE   Yelle, Archie Joseph b: 6/11/1892, Saginaw, Mich. d: 5/2/83, Woodland, Cal. BR/TR, 5'10.5", 170 lbs. Deb: 5/12/17

YEAR	TM/L	G	AB	R	H	2B	3B	HR	RBI	BB	SO	AVG	OBP	SLG	PRO+	BR	/A	RC	SB	CS	SBR	FR	POS	TPR
1917	Det-A	25	51	4	7	1	0	0	0	5	4	.137	.214	.157	13	-5	-5	2	2			-1	C	-0.4
1918	Det-A	56	144	7	25	3	0	0	7	9	15	.174	.227	.194	28	-13	-12	6	0			8	C	0.1
1919	Det-A	6	4	1	0	0	0	0	0	1	0	.000	.200	.000	-42	-1	-1	0	0			-1	/C	0.0
Total	3	87	199	12	32	4	0	0	7	15	19	.161	.223	.181	23	-19	-18	8	2			6	/C	-0.3

■ STEVE YERKES   Yerkes, Stephen Douglas b: 5/15/1888, Hatboro, Pa. d: 1/31/71, Lansdale, Pa. BR/TR, 5'9", 165 lbs. Deb: 9/29/09

YEAR	TM/L	G	AB	R	H	2B	3B	HR	RBI	BB	SO	AVG	OBP	SLG	PRO+	BR	/A	RC	SB	CS	SBR	FR	POS	TPR
1909	Bos-A	5	7	0	2	0	0	0	0	0		.286	.286	.286	79	-0	-0	1	0			-1	/S	0.0
1911	Bos-A	142	502	70	140	24	3	1	57	52		.279	.354	.345	96	-2	-2	68	14			-20	*S23	-1.0
1912	*Bos-A	131	523	73	132	22	6	0	42	41		.252	.312	.317	76	-14	-18	54	4			-15	*2	-3.4
1913	Bos-A	137	483	67	129	29	6	1	48	50	32	.267	.338	.358	101	2	1	62	11			-19	*2	-2.2
1914	Bos-A	92	293	23	64	17	2	1	23	14	23	.218	.259	.300	68	-13	-13	24	5	6	-2	4	2	-1.2
	Pit-F	39	142	18	48	9	5	1	25	11	13	.338	.386	.493	152	9	9	29	2			8	S	1.9
1915	Pit-F	121	434	44	125	17	8	1	49	30	27	.288	.337	.371	110	5	5	63	17			-3	*2/S	0.4
1916	Chi-N	44	137	12	36	6	2	1	10	9	7	.263	.308	.358	94	0	-1	16	1			1	2	0.1
Total	7	711	2521	307	676	124	32	6	254	207	102	.268	.328	.350	95	-13	-18	317	54	6		-45	2S/3	-5.4

■ TOM YEWCIC   Yewcic, Thomas J. "Kibby" b: 5/9/32, Conemaugh, Pa. BR/TR, 5'11", 180 lbs. Deb: 6/27/57

YEAR	TM/L	G	AB	R	H	2B	3B	HR	RBI	BB	SO	AVG	OBP	SLG	PRO+	BR	/A	RC	SB	CS	SBR	FR	POS	TPR
1957	Det-A	1	1	0	0	0	0	0	0	0	0	.000	.000	.000	-97	-0	-0	0	0	0	0	1	/C	0.0

■ ED YEWELL   Yewell, Edwin Leonard b: 8/22/1862, Washington, D.C. d: 9/15/40, Washington, D.C. Deb: 5/12/1884

YEAR	TM/L	G	AB	R	H	2B	3B	HR	RBI	BB	SO	AVG	OBP	SLG	PRO+	BR	/A	RC	SB	CS	SBR	FR	POS	TPR
1884	Was-a	27	93	14	23	3	1	0		1		.247	.263	.301	97	-1	0	8				-2	2/O3S	-0.1
	Was-U	1	4	0	0	0	0	0		0		.000	.000	.000	-99	-1	-1	0	0			-0	/3	0.0

■ JOE YINGLING   Yingling, Joseph Granville b: 7/23/1866, Westminster, Md. d: 10/24/46, Manchester, Md. BR/TL, 5'7.5", 145 lbs. Deb: 5/28/1886

YEAR	TM/L	G	AB	R	H	2B	3B	HR	RBI	BB	SO	AVG	OBP	SLG	PRO+	BR	/A	RC	SB	CS	SBR	FR	POS	TPR
1886	Was-N	1	2	0	0	0	0	0	0	0	1	.000	.000	.000	-99	-0	-0	0	0			0	/P	0.0
1894	Phi-N	1	4	0	1	0	0	0	0	0	1	.250	.250	.250	23	-0	-0	0	0			-1	/S	0.0
Total	2	2	6	0	1	0	0	0	0	0	2	.167	.167	.167	-13	-1	-1	0	0			-0	/SP	0.0

■ BILL YOHE   Yohe, William Clyde b: 9/2/1878, Mt.Elere, Ill. d: 12/24/38, Bremerton, Wash. TR , 5'8", 180 lbs. Deb: 8/30/09

YEAR	TM/L	G	AB	R	H	2B	3B	HR	RBI	BB	SO	AVG	OBP	SLG	PRO+	BR	/A	RC	SB	CS	SBR	FR	POS	TPR
1909	Was-A	21	72	6	15	2	0	0	4	3		.208	.240	.236	53	-4	-4	5	2			3	3	0.0

■ TONY YORK   York, Anthony Batton b: 11/27/12, Irene, Tex. d: 4/18/70, Hillsboro, Tex. BR/TR, 5'10", 165 lbs. Deb: 4/18/44

YEAR	TM/L	G	AB	R	H	2B	3B	HR	RBI	BB	SO	AVG	OBP	SLG	PRO+	BR	/A	RC	SB	CS	SBR	FR	POS	TPR
1944	Chi-N	28	85	4	20	1	0	0	7	4	11	.235	.270	.247	46	-6	-6	6	0			10	S3	0.7

■ RUDY YORK   York, Preston Rudolph b: 8/17/13, Ragland, Ala. d: 2/5/70, Rome, Ga. BR/TR, 6'1", 209 lbs. Deb: 8/22/34 MC

YEAR	TM/L	G	AB	R	H	2B	3B	HR	RBI	BB	SO	AVG	OBP	SLG	PRO+	BR	/A	RC	SB	CS	SBR	FR	POS	TPR
1934	Det-A	3	6	0	1	0	0	0	0	1	3	.167	.286	.167	19	-1	-1	0	0	0	0	0	/C	0.0
1937	Det-A	104	375	72	115	18	3	35	103	41	52	.307	.375	.651	150	27	26	91	3	2	-0	-17	C3/1	1.2
1938	Det-A	135	463	85	138	27	2	33	127	92	74	.298	.417	.579	139	34	30	116	1	2	-1	-0	*CO/1	2.7
1939	Det-A	102	329	66	101	16	1	20	68	41	50	.307	.387	.544	126	17	13	70	5	0	2	-8	C1	0.9
1940	*Det-A	155	588	105	186	46	6	33	134	89	88	.316	.410	.583	141	47	39	147	3	2	-0	5	*1	3.3
1941	Det-A	155	590	91	153	29	3	27	111	92	88	.259	.360	.456	104	12	4	101	3	1	0	-1	*1	-0.1
1942	Det-A	153	577	81	150	26	4	21	90	73	71	.260	.343	.428	107	11	5	86	3	3	-1	15	*1	1.8
1943	Det-A	155	571	90	155	22	11	**34**	**118**	84	88	.271	.366	**.527**	148	41	36	108	5	5	-2	18	*1	5.1
1944	Det-A	151	583	77	161	27	7	18	98	68	73	.276	.353	.439	119	18	15	91	5	3	-0	5	*1	1.1
1945	*Det-A	155	595	71	157	25	5	18	87	60	85	.264	.331	.413	109	10	6	78	6	6	-2	-2	*1	-0.3
1946	*Bos-A	154	579	78	160	30	6	17	119	86	93	.276	.371	.437	118	20	16	98	3	2	-0	6	*1	1.4
1947	Bos-A	48	184	16	39	7	0	6	27	22	32	.212	.296	.348	73	-6	-7	18	0	0	0	1	1	-0.7
	Chi-A	102	400	40	97	18	4	15	64	36	55	.243	.305	.420	104	-2	-0	51	1	0	0	-1	*1	-0.3
	Yr	150	584	56	136	25	4	21	91	58	87	.233	.302	.397	94	-8	-8	68	1	0	0	0		-1.0
1948	Phi-A	31	51	4	8	0	0	0	6	7	15	.157	.259	.157	12	-6	-6	2	0	0	0	-0	1	-0.5
Total	13	1603	5891	876	1621	291	52	277	1152	792	867	.275	.362	.483	121	223	175	1057	38	26	-4	20	*1C/3O	15.6

■ TOM YORK   York, Thomas J. b: 7/13/1851, Brooklyn, N.Y. d: 2/17/36, New York, N.Y. BL , 5'9", 165 lbs. Deb: 5/09/1871 MU

YEAR	TM/L	G	AB	R	H	2B	3B	HR	RBI	BB	SO	AVG	OBP	SLG	PRO+	BR	/A	RC	SB	CS	SBR	FR	POS	TPR
1871	Tro-n	29	145	36	37	5	7	2	23	9	1	.255	.299	.428	104	1	0	20	2				*O	0.1
1872	Bal-n	51	249	65	64	8	4	1		3		.257	.266	.333	80	-5	-7	23					*O	-0.3
1873	Bal-n	57	279	70	83	14	3	2		3		.297	.305	.391	104	1	1	34					*O	0.2
1874	Phi-n	50	223	36	58	3	8	0		4		.260	.273	.345	92	-1	-2	22					*O	0.0
1875	Har-n	86	376	68	112	12	7	0		4		.298	.305	.367	125	11	8	43					*O	0.8
1876	Har-N	67	263	47	68	12	7	1	39	10	4	.259	.286	.369	108	5	1	28				2	*O	0.2
1877	Har-N	56	237	43	67	16	7	1	37	3	11	.283	.292	.422	137	5	9	30				-0	*O	0.6
1878	Pro-N	62	269	56	83	19	**10**	1	26	8	19	.309	.329	.465	159	16	16	42				3	*OM	1.3
1879	Pro-N	81	342	69	106	25	5	1	50	19	28	.310	.346	.421	154	19	20	51				-5	*O	1.2
1880	Pro-N	53	203	21	43	9	2	0	18	8	29	.212	.242	.276	77	-5	-4	14				-3	O	-0.8
1881	Pro-N	85	316	57	96	23	5	2	47	29	26	.304	.362	.427	150	18	19	50				-3	*OM	1.4
1882	Pro-N	81	321	48	86	23	7	1	40	19	14	.268	.309	.393	123	8	8	40				-3	*O	0.4
1883	Cle-N	100	381	56	99	29	5	2	46	**37**	55	.260	.325	.378	114	7	8	48				-1	*O	0.8
1884	Bal-a	83	314	64	70	14	7	1		34		.223	.318	.322	108	6	4	33				-5	*O	-0.1
1885	Bal-a	22	87	6	23	4	2	0		8		.264	.326	.356	120	2	2	10				1	O	0.2
Total	5 n	273	1272	275	354	42	29	5	23	23	1	.278	.291	.369	103	7	0	141					O	0.8
Total	10	690	2733	467	741	174	57	10	303	175	186	.271	.317	.387	127	81	83	347				-13	O	5.2

■ ED YOST   Yost, Edgar Frederick b: 8/19/55, Eureka, Cal. BR/TR, 6'1", 190 lbs. Deb: 4/12/80

YEAR	TM/L	G	AB	R	H	2B	3B	HR	RBI	BB	SO	AVG	OBP	SLG	PRO+	BR	/A	RC	SB	CS	SBR	FR	POS	TPR
1980	Mil-A	15	31	0	5	0	0	0	0	0	6	.161	.161	.161	-12	-5	-5	1	0	0	0	2	C	-0.1
1981	Mil-A	18	27	4	6	0	0	3	3	3	6	.222	.300	.556	150	1	1	5	0	0	0	2	C	0.4

YEAR	TM/L	G	AB	R	H	2B	3B	HR	RBI	BB	SO	AVG	OBP	SLG	PRO+	BR	/A	RC	SB	CS	SBR	FR	POS	TPR
1982	*Mil-A	40	98	13	27	6	3	1	8	7	20	.276	.324	.429	111	0	1	14	3	1	0	-1	C/D	0.3
1983	Mil-A	61	196	21	44	5	1	6	28	5	36	.224	.244	.352	67	-11	-9	15	1	0	0	-5	C	-1.0
1984	Tex-A	80	242	15	44	4	0	6	25	6	47	.182	.202	.273	29	-23	-24	12	1	2	-1	-4	C	-2.4
1985	Mon-N	5	11	1	2	0	0	0	0	0	2	.182	.182	.182	2	-1	-1	0	0	0	0	1	/C	0.0
Total	6	219	605	54	128	15	4	16	64	21	117	.212	.238	.329	56	-38	-36	47	5	3	-0	-5	C/D	-2.8

■ EDDIE YOST

Yost, Edward Frederick Joseph "The Walking Man" b: 10/13/26, Brooklyn, N.Y. BR/TR, 5'10", 170 lbs. Deb: 8/16/44 MC

YEAR	TM/L	G	AB	R	H	2B	3B	HR	RBI	BB	SO	AVG	OBP	SLG	PRO+	BR	/A	RC	SB	CS	SBR	FR	POS	TPR
1944	Was-A	7	14	3	2	0	0	0	0	1	2	.143	.200	.143	-1	-2	-2	1	0	0	0	-0	/3S	-0.1
1946	Was-A	8	25	2	2	1	0	0	1	5	5	.080	.233	.120	1	-3	-3	1	2	1	0	1	/3	-0.1
1947	Was-A	115	428	52	102	17	3	0	14	45	57	.238	.314	.292	71	-17	-16	41	3	5	-2	-9	*3	-2.4
1948	Was-A	145	555	74	138	32	11	2	50	82	51	.249	.349	.357	91	-9	-6	73	4	3	-1	-13	*3	-2.4
1949	Was-A	124	435	57	110	19	7	9	45	91	41	.253	.383	.391	107	5	7	71	3	3	-1	-2	*3	0.3
1950	Was-A	155	573	114	169	26	2	11	58	141	63	.295	.440	.405	123	24	28	116	6	6	-2	-2	*3	1.8
1951	Was-A	154	568	109	161	36	4	12	65	126	55	.283	.423	.424	132	30	32	117	6	4	-1	-26	*3/O	0.0
1952	Was-A	157	587	92	137	32	3	12	49	129	73	.233	.378	.359	110	10	13	93	4	3	-1	-35	*3	-2.3
1953	Was-A	152	577	107	157	30	7	9	45	123	59	.272	.403	.395	119	19	21	103	7	4	-0	-13	*3	0.0
1954	Was-A	155	539	101	138	26	4	11	47	131	71	.256	.406	.380	123	19	23	97	7	3	-0	3	*3	1.8
1955	Was-A	122	375	64	91	17	5	7	48	95	54	.243	.410	.371	117	11	14	66	4	3	-1	-6	*3	1.0
1956	Was-A	152	515	94	119	17	2	11	53	151	82	.231	.412	.336	100	9	9	86	8	5	-1	11	*3/O	2.1
1957	Was-A	110	414	47	104	13	5	9	38	73	49	.251	.370	.372	104	4	5	58	1	11	-6	-11	*3	-1.0
1958	Was-A	134	406	55	91	16	0	8	37	81	43	.224	.365	.323	93	-1	-0	52	3	6	-3	-15	*3/O1	-1.4
1959	Det-A	148	521	115	145	19	0	21	61	135	77	.278	**.437**	.436	133	38	34	115	9	2	2	-11	*3/2	2.3
1960	Det-A	143	497	78	129	23	2	14	47	125	69	.260	**.416**	.398	118	22	20	92	5	4	-1	-27	*3	-0.5
1961	LA-A	76	213	29	43	4	0	3	15	50	48	.202	.358	.263	62	-7	-11	24	0	1	-1	-10	3	-1.7
1962	LA-A	52	104	22	25	9	1	0	10	30	21	.240	.415	.346	111	3	3	17	0	2	-1	-3	3/1	0.0
Total	18	2109	7346	1215	1863	337	56	139	683	1614	920	.254	.395	.371	109	154	170	1225	72	66	-18	-168	*3/O1S2	-2.6

■ ELMER YOTER

Yoter, Elmer Elsworth b: 6/26/1900, Plainfield, Pa. d: 7/26/66, Camp Hill, Pa. BR/TR, 5'7", 155 lbs. Deb: 9/09/21

YEAR	TM/L	G	AB	R	H	2B	3B	HR	RBI	BB	SO	AVG	OBP	SLG	PRO+	BR	/A	RC	SB	CS	SBR	FR	POS	TPR
1921	Phi-A	3	3	0	0	0	0	0	0	0	0	.000	.000	.000	-99	-1	-1	0	0	0	0	0	H	0.0
1924	Cle-A	19	66	3	18	1	1	0	7	5	8	.273	.324	.318	65	-3	-3	7	0	0	0	-2	3	-0.3
1927	Chi-N	13	27	2	6	1	1	0	5	4	4	.222	.323	.333	76	-1	-1	3	0			0	3	0.0
1928	Chi-N	1	0	0	0	0	0	0	0	0	0	—	—	—	—	0	0	0	0			0	/3	0.0
Total	4	36	96	5	24	2	2	0	12	9	12	.250	.314	.313	63	-5	-5	10	0		0	-2	/3	-0.3

■ DEL YOUNG

Young, Delmer Edward b: 3/11/12, Cleveland, Ohio d: 12/8/79, San Francisco, Cal. BB/TR, 5'11", 168 lbs. Deb: 4/19/37

YEAR	TM/L	G	AB	R	H	2B	3B	HR	RBI	BB	SO	AVG	OBP	SLG	PRO+	BR	/A	RC	SB	CS	SBR	FR	POS	TPR
1937	Phi-N	109	360	36	70	9	2	0	24	18	55	.194	.235	.231	25	-36	-40	20	6			11	*2	-2.4
1938	Phi-N	108	340	27	78	13	2	0	31	20	35	.229	.276	.279	55	-22	-20	27	0			-2	S2	-1.5
1939	Phi-N	77	217	22	57	9	2	3	20	8	24	.263	.289	.364	77	-8	-8	22	1			-18	S2	-2.0
1940	Phi-N	15	33	2	8	0	1	0	1	2	1	.242	.286	.303	65	-2	-2	3	0			0	/S2	0.0
Total	4	309	950	87	213	31	7	3	76	48	115	.224	.264	.281	48	-68	-70	72	7			-9	S2	-5.9

■ DEL YOUNG

Young, Delmer John b: 10/24/1885, Macon City, Mo. d: 12/17/59, Cleveland, Ohio BL/TR, 5'11", 195 lbs. Deb: 9/24/09

YEAR	TM/L	G	AB	R	H	2B	3B	HR	RBI	BB	SO	AVG	OBP	SLG	PRO+	BR	/A	RC	SB	CS	SBR	FR	POS	TPR
1909	Cin-N	2	7	0	2	0	0	0	1	1		.286	.375	.286	106	0	0	1	0			0	/O	0.0
1914	Buf-F	80	174	17	48	5	5	4	22	3	13	.276	.288	.431	102	-0	-1	22	0			-6	O	-0.8
1915	Buf-F	12	15	0	2	0	0	0	0	1	0	.133	.188	.133	-4	-2	-2	1	1			-1	/O	-0.3
Total	3	94	196	17	52	5	5	4	23	5	13	.265	.284	.403	94	-2	-2	24	1			-7	/O	-1.1

■ DON YOUNG

Young, Donald Wayne b: 10/18/45, Houston, Tex. BR/TR, 6'2", 185 lbs. Deb: 9/09/65

YEAR	TM/L	G	AB	R	H	2B	3B	HR	RBI	BB	SO	AVG	OBP	SLG	PRO+	BR	/A	RC	SB	CS	SBR	FR	POS	TPR
1965	Chi-N	11	35	1	2	0	0	1	2	0	11	.057	.057	.143	-45	-7	-7	0	0	0	0	-1	O	-0.8
1969	Chi-N	101	272	36	65	12	3	6	27	38	74	.239	.343	.371	89	1	-4	35	1	5	-3	-6	*O	-1.8
Total	2	112	307	37	67	12	3	7	29	38	85	.218	.314	.345	76	-6	-10	36	1	5	-3	-7	O	-2.6

■ GEORGE YOUNG

Young, George Joseph b: 4/1/1890, Brooklyn, N.Y. d: 3/13/50, Brightwaters, N.Y. BL/TR, 6', 185 lbs. Deb: 8/10/13

YEAR	TM/L	G	AB	R	H	2B	3B	HR	RBI	BB	SO	AVG	OBP	SLG	PRO+	BR	/A	RC	SB	CS	SBR	FR	POS	TPR
1913	Cle-A	2	2	0	0	0	0	0	0	0	0	.000	.000	.000	-97	-0	-1	0	0			0	H	0.0

■ GERALD YOUNG

Young, Gerald Anthony b: 10/22/64, Tele, Honduras BB/TR, 6'2", 185 lbs. Deb: 7/08/87

YEAR	TM/L	G	AB	R	H	2B	3B	HR	RBI	BB	SO	AVG	OBP	SLG	PRO+	BR	/A	RC	SB	CS	SBR	FR	POS	TPR
1987	Hou-N	71	274	44	88	9	2	1	15	26	27	.321	.382	.380	107	2	3	44	26	9	2	2	O	0.5
1988	Hou-N	149	576	79	148	21	9	0	37	66	66	.257	.336	.325	94	-5	-3	67	65	27	3	6	*O	0.3
1989	Hou-N	146	533	71	124	17	3	0	38	74	60	.233	.328	.276	77	-15	-13	51	34	25	-5	19	*O	0.0
1990	Hou-N	57	154	15	27	4	1	1	4	20	23	.175	.270	.234	41	-12	-12	11	6	3	0	2	O	-1.1
Total	4	423	1537	209	387	51	15	2	94	186	176	.252	.335	.308	85	-31	-24	172	131	64	1	29	O	-0.3

■ HERMAN YOUNG

Young, Herman John b: 4/14/1886, Boston, Mass. d: 12/13/66, Ipswich, Mass. BR/TR, 5'8", 155 lbs. Deb: 6/11/11

YEAR	TM/L	G	AB	R	H	2B	3B	HR	RBI	BB	SO	AVG	OBP	SLG	PRO+	BR	/A	RC	SB	CS	SBR	FR	POS	TPR
1911	Bos-N	9	25	2	6	0	0	0	0	0	3	.240	.269	.240	40	-2	-2	2	0			4	/3S	0.2

■ JOHN YOUNG

Young, John Thomas b: 2/9/49, Los Angeles, Cal. BL/TL, 6'3", 210 lbs. Deb: 9/09/71

YEAR	TM/L	G	AB	R	H	2B	3B	HR	RBI	BB	SO	AVG	OBP	SLG	PRO+	BR	/A	RC	SB	CS	SBR	FR	POS	TPR
1971	Det-A	2	4	1	2	1	0	0	1	0	0	.500	.500	.750	241	1	1	2	0	0	0	-0	/1	0.1

■ PEP YOUNG

Young, Lemuel Floyd b: 8/29/07, Jamestown, N.C. d: 1/14/62, Jamestown, N.C. BR/TR, 5'9", 162 lbs. Deb: 4/25/33

YEAR	TM/L	G	AB	R	H	2B	3B	HR	RBI	BB	SO	AVG	OBP	SLG	PRO+	BR	/A	RC	SB	CS	SBR	FR	POS	TPR
1933	Pit-N	25	20	3	6	1	1	0	0	0	5	.300	.300	.450	112	0	0	3	0			2	/2S	0.2
1934	Pit-N	19	17	3	4	0	0	0	2	0	6	.235	.235	.235	26	-2	-2	1	0			2	/2S	0.1
1935	Pit-N	128	494	60	131	25	10	7	82	21	59	.265	.298	.399	83	-11	-13	58	2			-12	*2/3OS	-1.5
1936	Pit-N	125	475	47	118	23	10	6	77	29	52	.248	.293	.377	77	-15	-17	53	3			-24	*2	-3.1
1937	Pit-N	113	408	43	106	20	3	9	54	26	63	.260	.306	.390	88	-8	-8	49	4			18	S32	1.6
1938	Pit-N	149	562	58	156	36	5	4	79	40	64	.278	.329	.381	94	-5	-5	70	7			32	*2	3.7
1939	Pit-N	84	293	34	81	14	3	3	29	23	29	.276	.333	.375	92	-4	-4	37	1			3	2	0.3
1940	Pit-N	54	136	19	34	8	2	2	20	12	23	.250	.320	.382	94	-1	-1	18	1			-5	S3	-0.2
1941	Cin-N	4	12	2	2	0	0	0	0	0	1	.167	.231	.167	13	-1	-1	1	0			1	/3	0.0
	StL-N	2	2	0	0	0	0	0	0	0	2	.000	.000	.000	-94	-1	-1	0	0			0	H	0.0
	Yr	6	14	2	2	0	0	0	0	0	3	.143	.200	.143	-2	-2	-2	0	0			1		0.0
1945	StL-N	27	47	5	7	1	0	1	4	1	8	.149	.167	.234	10	-6	-6	2	0			1	S/32	-0.3
Total	10	730	2466	274	645	128	34	32	347	152	312	.262	.308	.380	85	-54	-57	291	18			18	2/S3O	0.8

■ MIKE YOUNG

Young, Michael Darren b: 3/20/60, Oakland, Cal. BB/TR, 6'2", 195 lbs. Deb: 9/14/82

YEAR	TM/L	G	AB	R	H	2B	3B	HR	RBI	BB	SO	AVG	OBP	SLG	PRO+	BR	/A	RC	SB	CS	SBR	FR	POS	TPR
1982	Bal-A	6	2	2	0	0	0	0	0	0	1	.000	.000	.000	-99	-1	-1	0	0	0	0	0	/OD	0.0
1983	Bal-A	25	36	5	6	2	1	0	2	2	8	.167	.231	.278	40	-3	-3	2	1	0	0	2	O/D	0.0
1984	Bal-A	123	401	59	101	17	2	17	52	58	110	.252	.356	.431	119	10	11	66	6	2	1	-8	*O/D	0.0
1985	Bal-A	139	450	72	123	22	1	28	81	48	104	.273	.349	.513	136	19	21	78	1	5	-3	1	OD	1.7
1986	Bal-A	117	369	43	93	15	1	9	42	49	90	.252	.344	.371	96	-2	-1	47	3	1	0	-2	OD	-0.4
1987	Bal-A	110	363	46	87	10	1	16	39	46	91	.240	.328	.405	96	-4	-2	48	10	7	-1	-5	OD	-0.9
1988	Phi-N	75	146	13	33	14	0	1	14	26	43	.226	.347	.342	96	1	0	19	0	0	0	-1	O	-0.2
	Mil-A	8	14	2	0	0	0	0	0	2	5	.000	.176	.000	-46	-3	-3	0	0	0	0	0	/OD	-0.2
1989	Cle-A	32	59	2	11	0	0	1	5	6	13	.186	.273	.237	44	-4	-4	4	1	2	-1	0	D/O	-0.4
Total	8	635	1840	244	454	80	6	72	235	237	465	.247	.339	.414	107	14	19	266	22	17	-4	-14	OD	-0.4

YEAR	TM/L	G	AB	R	H	2B	3B	HR	RBI	BB	SO	AVG	OBP	SLG	PRO+	BR	/A	RC	SB	CS	SBR	FR	POS	TPR

■ BABE YOUNG
Young, Norman Robert b: 7/1/15, Astoria, N.Y. d: 12/25/83, Everett, Mass. BL/TL, 6'2.5", 185 lbs. Deb: 9/26/36

1936	NY-N	1	1	0	0	0	0	0	0	0	0	.000	.000	.000	-99	-0	-0	0	0			0	H	0.0
1939	NY-N	22	75	8	23	4	0	3	14	5	6	.307	.373	.480	127	3	3	14	0			-2	1	-0.1
1940	NY-N	149	556	75	159	27	4	17	101	69	28	.286	.367	.441	121	17	17	92	4			-2	*1	0.1
1941	NY-N	152	574	90	152	28	5	25	104	66	28	.265	.346	.462	124	18	17	93	1			-3	*1	-0.7
1942	NY-N	101	287	37	80	17	1	11	59	34	22	.279	.365	.460	140	14	14	50	1			-3	O1	0.9
1946	NY-N	104	291	30	81	11	0	7	33	30	21	.278	.346	.388	107	3	3	40	3			-6	1O	-0.8
1947	NY-N	14	14	0	1	1	0	0	0	0	1	.071	.071	.143	-44	-3	-3	0	0			0	H	-0.2
	Cin-N	95	364	55	103	21	3	14	79	35	26	.283	.349	.473	117	7	8	60	0			-1	1	0.0
	Yr	109	378	55	104	22	3	14	79	35	27	.275	.340	.460	111	4	5	59	0			-1		-0.2
1948	Cin-N	49	130	11	30	7	2	1	12	19	12	.231	.329	.338	84	-3	-3	16	0			0	1/O	-0.2
	StL-N	41	111	14	27	5	2	1	13	16	6	.243	.339	.351	82	-2	-3	14	0			-4	1	-0.6
	Yr	90	241	25	57	12	4	2	25	35	18	.237	.333	.344	83	-5	-5	30	0			-4		-0.8
Total	8	728	2403	320	656	121	17	79	415	274	161	.273	.352	.436	117	55	53	379	9			-22	1/O	-1.6

■ RALPH YOUNG
Young, Ralph Stuart b: 9/19/1889, Philadelphia, Pa. d: 1/24/65, Philadelphia, Pa. BB/TR, 5'5", 165 lbs. Deb: 4/10/13

1913	NY-A	7	15	2	1	0	0	0	0	3	3	.067	.222	.067	-15	-2	-2	1	2			1	/S	0.0
1915	Det-A	123	378	44	92	6	5	0	31	53	31	.243	.339	.286	83	-4	-7	41	12	11	-3	8	*2	-0.2
1916	Det-A	153	528	60	139	16	6	1	45	62	43	.263	.342	.322	96	1	-2	61	20	20	-6	-1	*2/S3	-0.4
1917	Det-A	141	503	64	116	18	2	1	35	61	35	.231	.317	.280	83	-9	-9	49	8			8	*2	0.9
1918	Det-A	91	298	31	56	7	1	0	21	54	17	.188	.313	.218	63	-12	-11	26	15			-12	2	-1.9
1919	Det-A	125	456	63	96	13	5	1	25	53	32	.211	.294	.268	60	-25	-23	43	8			17	*2/S	0.5
1920	Det-A	150	594	84	173	21	6	0	33	85	30	.291	.382	.347	96	-1	1	82	8	13	-5	-11	*2	-1.1
1921	Det-A	107	401	70	120	8	3	0	29	69	23	.299	.406	.334	91	-1	-1	60	11	9	-2	-23	*2	-2.0
1922	Phi-A	125	470	62	105	19	2	1	35	55	21	.223	.309	.279	53	-31	-33	43	8	6	-1	-15	*2	-3.9
Total	9	1022	3643	480	898	108	30	4	254	495	235	.247	.339	.296	79	-85	-86	406	92	59		-27	2/S3	-8.1

■ DICK YOUNG
Young, Richard Ennis b: 6/3/28, Seattle, Wash. BL/TR, 5'11", 175 lbs. Deb: 9/11/51

1951	Phi-N	15	68	7	16	5	0	0	2	3	6	.235	.268	.309	55	-4	-4	5	0	1	-1	-9	2	-1.3
1952	Phi-N	5	9	3	2	1	0	0	0	1	3	.222	.300	.333	76	-0	-0	1	1	0	0	-0	/2	0.0
Total	2	20	77	10	18	6	0	0	2	4	9	.234	.272	.312	58	-5	-5	6	1	1	-0	-9	/2	-1.3

■ BOBBY YOUNG
Young, Robert George b: 1/22/25, Granite, Md. d: 1/28/85, Baltimore, Md. BL/TR, 6'1", 175 lbs. Deb: 7/28/48

1948	StL-N	3	1	0	0	0	0	0	0	0	1	.000	.000	.000	-95	-0	-0	0	0			1	/3	0.0
1951	StL-A	147	611	75	159	13	9	1	31	44	51	.260	.310	.316	67	-26	-29	60	8	7	-2	1	*2	-2.3
1952	StL-A	149	575	59	142	15	9	4	39	56	48	.247	.314	.325	76	-17	-19	62	3	3	-1	-9	*2	-2.3
1953	StL-A	148	537	48	137	22	2	4	25	41	40	.255	.309	.326	70	-22	-23	56	2	1	0	-17	*2	-3.1
1954	Bal-A	130	432	43	106	13	6	4	24	54	42	.245	.331	.331	88	-10	-6	49	4	4	-1	-14	*2	-1.6
1955	Bal-A	59	186	5	37	3	0	1	8	11	23	.199	.244	.231	30	-19	-17	10	1	4	-2	3	2	-1.3
	Cle-A	18	45	7	14	1	1	0	6	1	2	.311	.326	.378	86	-1	-1	6	0	0	0	7	2/3	0.6
	Yr	77	231	12	51	4	1	1	14	12	25	.221	.259	.260	42	-20	-18	15	1	4	-2	9		-0.7
1956	Cle-A	1	0	0	0	0	0	0	0	0	0	—	—	—	—	0	0	0	0	0	0	0	R	0.0
1958	Phi-N	32	60	7	14	1	1	0	4	1	5	.233	.246	.333	52	-4	-4	4	0	0	0	-2	2	-0.4
Total	8	687	2447	244	609	68	28	15	137	208	212	.249	.308	.318	71	-100	-100	247	18	19		-32	2/3	-10.4

■ RUSS YOUNG
Young, Russell Charles b: 9/15/02, Bryan, Ohio d: 5/13/84, Roseville, Cal. BB/TR, 6', 175 lbs. Deb: 4/16/31

1931	StL-A	16	34	2	4	0	0	1	2	2	4	.118	.167	.206	-3	-5	-5	1	0	0	0	2	C	-0.1

■ JOEL YOUNGBLOOD
Youngblood, Joel Randolph b: 8/28/51, Houston, Tex. BR/TR, 6', 180 lbs. Deb: 4/13/76

1976	Cin-N	55	57	8	11	1	1	0	1	2	8	.193	.233	.246	35	-5	-5	3	1	0	0	1	/O3C2	-0.3
1977	StL-N	25	27	1	5	2	0	0	1	3	5	.185	.267	.259	43	-2	-2	1	0	2	-1	-0	O/3	-0.3
	NY-N	70	182	16	46	11	1	0	11	13	40	.253	.303	.324	72	-8	-7	16	1	3	-2	5	2O3	-0.2
	Yr	95	209	17	51	13	1	0	12	16	45	.244	.298	.316	67	-10	-9	17	1	5	-3	5		-0.5
1978	NY-N	113	266	40	67	12	8	7	30	16	39	.252	.297	.436	106	-0	1	35	4	0	1	9	O2/3S	1.2
1979	NY-N	158	590	90	162	37	5	16	60	60	84	.275	.349	.436	117	10	13	90	18	13	-2	7	*O23	1.4
1980	NY-N	146	514	58	142	26	2	8	69	52	84	.276	.345	.381	105	2	4	67	14	11	-2	19	*O3/2	1.7
1981	NY-N	43	143	16	50	10	2	4	25	12	19	.350	.408	.531	167	12	12	28	2	5	-2	-1	O	0.9
1982	NY-N	80	202	21	52	12	0	3	21	8	37	.257	.302	.361	85	-4	-4	20	0	4	-2	-3	O/2S3	-1.0
	Mon-N	40	90	16	18	2	0	0	8	9	21	.200	.294	.222	45	-6	-6	6	2	1	-0	-0	O	-0.6
	Yr	120	292	37	70	14	0	3	29	17	58	.240	.300	.318	73	-10	-11	27	2	5	-2	-3		-1.0
1983	SF-N	124	373	59	109	20	3	17	53	33	59	.292	.358	.499	139	17	18	64	7	4	-0	-29	23O	-1.0
1984	SF-N	134	469	50	119	17	1	10	51	48	86	.254	.328	.358	96	-4	-2	56	5	6	-2	-23	*3O/2	-3.0
1985	SF-N	95	230	24	62	6	0	4	24	30	37	.270	.356	.348	103	0	2	29	3	2	-0	-1	O/3	0.0
1986	SF-N	97	184	20	47	12	0	5	28	18	34	.255	.325	.402	105	-0	1	25	1	1	-0	-4	O/132S	-0.1
1987	SF-N	69	91	9	23	3	0	3	11	5	13	.253	.299	.385	83	-3	-2	10	1	1	-0	1	O/3	-0.1
1988	SF-N	83	123	12	31	4	0	3	16	10	17	.252	.313	.285	76	-4	-3	11	1	1	-0	-2	O	-0.6
1989	Cin-N	76	118	13	25	5	0	3	13	13	21	.212	.301	.331	78	-3	-3	11	0	1	-1	-5	O	-0.9
Total	14	1408	3659	453	969	180	23	80	422	332	589	.265	.332	.392	103	1	14	471	60	55	-15	-25	O32/1SC	-3.2

■ HENRY YOUNGMAN
Youngman, Henry b: 1865, Indiana, Pa. d: 1/24/36, Pittsburgh, Pa. TR, Deb: 4/19/1890

1890	Pit-N	13	47	6	6	1	1	0	4	6	9	.128	.226	.191	27	-4	-4	2	1			-2	/32	-0.4

■ ROSS YOUNGS
Youngs, Ross Middlebrook "Pep" (b: Royce Middlebrook Youngs)
b: 4/10/1897, Shiner, Tex. d: 10/22/27, San Antonio, Tex. BL/TR, 5'8", 162 lbs. Deb: 9/25/17 H

1917	NY-N	7	26	5	9	2	3	0	1	1	5	.346	.370	.654	218	3	3	6	1			2	/O	0.5
1918	NY-N	121	474	70	143	16	8	1	25	44	49	.302	.368	.376	129	16	17	67	10			-11	*O/2	0.0
1919	NY-N	130	489	73	152	31	7	2	43	51	47	.311	.384	.415	142	25	26	84	24			-1	*O	2.2
1920	NY-N	153	581	92	204	27	14	6	78	75	55	.351	.427	.477	161	47	48	118	18	18	-5	0	*O	3.6
1921	*NY-N	141	504	90	165	24	16	3	102	71	47	.327	.411	.456	129	24	24	96	21	17	-4	-9	*O	0.5
1922	*NY-N	149	559	105	185	34	10	7	86	55	50	.331	.398	.465	121	19	18	105	17	9	-0	1	*O	1.3
1923	*NY-N	152	596	121	200	33	12	3	87	73	36	.336	.412	.446	128	26	27	108	13	19	-8	-1	*O	1.2
1924	*NY-N	133	526	112	187	33	12	10	74	77	31	.356	.441	.521	161	45	47	123	11	9	-2	-4	*O/2	3.8
1925	NY-N	130	500	82	132	24	6	6	53	66	51	.264	.354	.372	89	-9	-6	69	17	11	-2	-8	*O	-1.8
1926	NY-N	95	372	62	114	12	5	4	43	37	19	.306	.372	.398	109	5	5	55	21			-2	O	0.0
Total	10	1211	4627	812	1491	236	93	42	592	550	390	.322	.399	.441	131	201	210	831	153	83		-33	*O/2	11.3

■ EDDIE YOUNT
Yount, Floyd Edwin b: 12/19/16, Newton, N.C. d: 10/26/73, Newton, N.C. BR/TR, 6'1", 185 lbs. Deb: 9/09/37

1937	Phi-A	4	7	1	2	0	0	0	1	0	1	.286	.286	.286	45	-1	-1	1	0	0	0	0	/O	0.0
1939	Pit-N	2	2	0	0	0	0	0	0	0	2	.000	.000	.000	-99	-0	-0	0	0			0	H	0.0
Total	2	6	9	1	2	0	0	0	1	0	3	.222	.222	.222	14	-1	-1	1	0	0	0	0	/O	0.0

■ ROBIN YOUNT
Yount, Robin R b: 9/16/55, Danville, Ill. BR/TR, 6', 165 lbs. Deb: 4/05/74

1974	Mil-A	107	344	48	86	14	5	3	26	12	46	.250	.277	.346	79	-10	-10	31	7	7	-2	-11	*S	-1.5
1975	Mil-A	147	558	67	149	28	2	8	52	33	69	.267	.309	.367	90	-8	-8	64	12	4	1	-23	*S	-1.6
1976	Mil-A	161	638	59	161	19	3	2	54	38	69	.252	.294	.301	76	-21	-19	55	16	11	-2	-5	*S/O	-1.6

YEAR	TM/L	G	AB	R	H	2B	3B	HR	RBI	BB	SO	AVG	OBP	SLG	PRO+	BR	/A	RC	SB	CS	SBR	FR	POS	TPR
1977	Mil-A	154	605	66	174	34	4	4	49	41	80	.288	.335	.377	94	-5	-5	77	16	7	1	-9	*S	0.5
1978	Mil-A	127	502	66	147	23	9	9	71	24	43	.293	.326	.428	110	5	5	71	16	5	2	22	*S	3.9
1979	Mil-A	149	577	72	154	26	5	8	51	35	52	.267	.310	.371	83	-15	-15	63	11	8	-2	5	*S	0.7
1980	Mil-A	143	611	121	179	**49**	10	23	87	26	67	.293	.323	.519	131	19	21	101	20	5	3	0	*S/D	3.4
1981	*Mil-A	96	377	50	103	15	5	10	49	22	37	.273	.317	.419	116	4	6	51	4	1	1	28	S/D	4.2
1982	*Mil-A	156	635	129	**210**	46	12	29	114	54	63	.331	.384	**.578**	171	50	55	136	14	3	2	-4	*S/D	**6.5**
1983	Mil-A	149	578	102	178	42	**10**	17	80	72	58	.308	.387	.503	155	35	41	115	12	5	1	-4	*S/D	4.4
1984	Mil-A	160	624	105	186	27	7	16	80	67	67	.298	.367	.441	127	20	23	99	14	4	2	15	*SD	4.8
1985	Mil-A	122	466	76	129	26	3	15	68	49	56	.277	.348	.442	115	9	10	73	10	4	1	-11	*OD/1	-0.1
1986	Mil-A	140	522	82	163	31	7	9	46	62	73	.312	.389	.450	124	22	19	94	14	5	1	5	*O/1D	2.2
1987	Mil-A	158	635	99	198	25	9	21	103	76	94	.312	.386	.479	124	26	24	120	19	9	0	4	*O/D	2.3
1988	Mil-A	162	621	92	190	38	**11**	13	91	63	63	.306	.373	.465	132	28	27	106	22	4	4	8	*O/D	3.7
1989	Mil-A	160	614	101	195	38	9	21	103	63	71	.318	.387	.511	153	41	42	**125**	19	3	4	0	*OD	4.4
1990	Mil-A	158	587	98	145	17	5	17	77	78	89	.247	.341	.380	105	2	5	81	15	8	0	-1	*O/D	0.1
Total	17	2449	9494	1433	2747	498	116	225	1201	815	1097	.289	.348	.437	118	203	221	1461	241	93	17	19	*SOD/1	36.3

■ **JEFF YURAK**   Yurak, Jeffrey Lynn   b: 2/26/54, Pasadena, Cal.   BB/TR, 6'3", 195 lbs.   Deb: 9/15/78

YEAR	TM/L	G	AB	R	H	2B	3B	HR	RBI	BB	SO	AVG	OBP	SLG	PRO+	BR	/A	RC	SB	CS	SBR	FR	POS	TPR
1978	Mil-A	5	5	0	0	0	0	0	0	1	0	.000	.167	.000	-49	-1	-1	0	0	0	0	1	/O	0.0

■ **SAL YVARS**   Yvars, Salvador Anthony   b: 2/20/24, New York, N.Y.   BR/TR, 5'10", 187 lbs.   Deb: 9/27/47

YEAR	TM/L	G	AB	R	H	2B	3B	HR	RBI	BB	SO	AVG	OBP	SLG	PRO+	BR	/A	RC	SB	CS	SBR	FR	POS	TPR
1947	NY-N	1	5	0	1	0	0	0	0	0	2	.200	.200	.200	6	-1	-1	0	0			-0	/C	0.0
1948	NY-N	15	38	4	8	1	0	1	6	3	1	.211	.286	.316	62	-2	-2	3	0			2	C	0.1
1949	NY-N	3	8	0	0	0	0	0	0	1	1	.000	.111	.000	-68	-2	-2	0	0			1	/C	0.0
1950	NY-N	9	14	0	2	0	0	0	0	1	2	.143	.200	.143	-8	-2	-2	0	0			2	/C	0.0
1951	*NY-N	25	41	9	13	2	0	2	3	5	7	.317	.417	.512	147	3	3	10	0	0	0	-3	C	0.0
1952	NY-N	66	151	15	37	3	0	4	18	10	16	.245	.296	.344	77	-5	-5	14	0	0	0	8	C	0.4
1953	NY-N	23	47	1	13	0	0	0	1	7	1	.277	.370	.277	71	-2	-2	5	0	0	0	1	C	0.1
	StL-N	30	57	4	14	2	0	1	6	4	6	.246	.306	.333	67	-3	-3	5	0	1	-1	2	C	0.0
	Yr	53	104	5	27	2	0	1	7	11	7	.260	.336	.308	69	-4	-4	10	0	1	-1	3		0.1
1954	StL-N	38	57	8	14	4	0	2	8	6	5	.246	.328	.421	93	-1	-1	8	1	0	0	-2	C	-0.1
Total	8	210	418	41	102	12	0	10	42	37	41	.244	.315	.344	76	-14	-14	46	1	1		11	C	0.5

■ **ELMER ZACHER**   Zacher, Elmer Henry "Silver"   b: 9/17/1883, Buffalo, N.Y.   d: 12/20/44, Buffalo, N.Y.   BR/TR, 5'9", 190 lbs.   Deb: 4/30/10

YEAR	TM/L	G	AB	R	H	2B	3B	HR	RBI	BB	SO	AVG	OBP	SLG	PRO+	BR	/A	RC	SB	CS	SBR	FR	POS	TPR
1910	NY-N	1	0	0	0	0	0	0	0	0	0	—	—	—	—	0	0	0	0			0	/O	0.0
	StL-N	47	132	7	28	5	1	0	10	10	19	.212	.278	.265	61	-7	-6	11	3			3	O/2	-0.4
	Yr	48	132	7	28	5	1	0	10	10	19	.212	.278	.265	61	-7	-6	11	3			4		-0.4

■ **FRED ZAHNER**   Zahner, Frederick Joseph   b: 6/5/1870, Louisville, Ky.   d: 7/24/1900, Louisville, Ky.   Deb: 7/23/1894

YEAR	TM/L	G	AB	R	H	2B	3B	HR	RBI	BB	SO	AVG	OBP	SLG	PRO+	BR	/A	RC	SB	CS	SBR	FR	POS	TPR
1894	Lou-N	13	45	7	9	0	1	0	3	3	5	.200	.250	.244	22	-6	-5	3	2			-5	C/O1	-0.7
1895	Lou-N	21	49	7	11	1	1	0	6	6	4	.224	.321	.286	63	-3	-2	5	0			-6	C	-0.4
Total	2	34	94	14	20	1	2	0	9	9	9	.213	.288	.266	43	-9	-7	8	2			-11	/CO1	-1.1

■ **FRANKIE ZAK**   Zak, Frank Thomas   b: 2/22/22, Passaic, N.J.   d: 2/6/72, Passaic, N.J.   BR/TR, 5'10", 150 lbs.   Deb: 4/21/44

YEAR	TM/L	G	AB	R	H	2B	3B	HR	RBI	BB	SO	AVG	OBP	SLG	PRO+	BR	/A	RC	SB	CS	SBR	FR	POS	TPR
1944	Pit-N	87	160	33	48	3	1	0	11	22	18	.300	.385	.331	99	2	1	22	6			6	S	1.5
1945	Pit-N	15	28	2	4	2	0	0	3	3	5	.143	.226	.214	22	-3	-3	2	0			1	S/2	0.0
1946	Pit-N	21	20	8	4	0	0	0	0	1	0	.200	.238	.200	24	-2	-2	1	0			9	S	0.7
Total	3	123	208	43	56	5	1	0	14	26	23	.269	.350	.303	82	-3	-4	25	6			15	/S2	2.2

■ **JACK ZALUSKY**   Zalusky, John Francis   b: 6/22/1879, Minneapolis, Minn   d: 8/11/35, Minneapolis, Minn.   BR/TR, 5'11.5", 172 lbs.   Deb: 9/04/03

YEAR	TM/L	G	AB	R	H	2B	3B	HR	RBI	BB	SO	AVG	OBP	SLG	PRO+	BR	/A	RC	SB	CS	SBR	FR	POS	TPR
1903	NY-A	7	16	2	5	0	0	0	1	1		.313	.353	.313	97	0	-0	2	0			-1	/C1	0.0

■ **JOE ZAPUSTAS**   Zapustas, Joseph John   b: 7/25/07, Boston, Mass.   BR/TR, 6'1", 185 lbs.   Deb: 9/28/33

YEAR	TM/L	G	AB	R	H	2B	3B	HR	RBI	BB	SO	AVG	OBP	SLG	PRO+	BR	/A	RC	SB	CS	SBR	FR	POS	TPR
1933	Phi-A	2	5	0	1	0	0	0	0	0	0	.200	.200	.200	6	-1	-1	0	0	0	0	-0	/O	0.0

■ **JOSE ZARDON**   Zardon, Jose Antonio (Sanchez) "Guineo"   b: 5/20/23, Havana, Cuba   BR/TR, 6', 150 lbs.   Deb: 4/18/45

YEAR	TM/L	G	AB	R	H	2B	3B	HR	RBI	BB	SO	AVG	OBP	SLG	PRO+	BR	/A	RC	SB	CS	SBR	FR	POS	TPR
1945	Was-A	54	131	13	38	5	3	0	13	7	11	.290	.326	.374	112	0	1	15	3	1	0	5	O	0.5

■ **AL ZARILLA**   Zarilla, Allen Lee "Zeke"   b: 5/1/19, Los Angeles, Cal.   BL/TR, 5'11", 180 lbs.   Deb: 6/30/43   C

YEAR	TM/L	G	AB	R	H	2B	3B	HR	RBI	BB	SO	AVG	OBP	SLG	PRO+	BR	/A	RC	SB	CS	SBR	FR	POS	TPR
1943	StL-A	70	228	27	58	7	1	2	17	17	20	.254	.309	.320	82	-5	-5	23	1	1	-0	-2	O	-0.9
1944	*StL-A	100	288	43	86	13	6	6	45	29	33	.299	.375	.448	127	13	11	52	1	1	-0	-1	O	0.7
1946	StL-A	125	371	46	96	14	9	4	43	27	37	.259	.311	.377	87	-5	-7	43	3	5	-2	7	*O	-0.8
1947	StL-A	127	380	34	85	15	6	3	38	40	45	.224	.303	.318	71	-14	-15	39	3	6	-3	-6	*O	-2.9
1948	StL-A	144	529	77	174	39	3	12	74	48	48	.329	.389	.482	128	22	20	103	11	6	-0	-0	*O	1.4
1949	StL-A	15	56	10	14	1	0	1	6	8	2	.250	.354	.321	76	-1	-2	7	1	1	-0	-4	O	-0.6
	Bos-A	124	474	68	133	32	4	9	71	48	51	.281	.352	.422	97	1	-3	70	4	4	-1	-7	*O	-1.3
	Yr	139	530	78	147	33	4	10	77	56	53	.277	.352	.411	95	-0	-5	77	5	5	-2	-11		-1.9
1950	Bos-A	130	471	92	153	32	10	9	74	76	47	.325	.423	.493	122	26	19	106	2	3	-1	-7	*O	0.8
1951	Chi-A	120	382	56	98	21	2	10	60	60	57	.257	.363	.401	109	4	5	58	2	4	-2	-17	*O	-1.7
1952	Chi-A	39	99	14	23	4	1	2	7	14	6	.232	.333	.354	90	-1	-1	13	1	0	0	-4	O	-0.5
	StL-A	48	130	20	31	6	0	1	9	27	15	.238	.373	.308	88	-0	-1	17	2	1	0	2	O	0.0
	Bos-A	21	60	9	11	0	1	2	8	7	8	.183	.269	.317	58	-3	-4	6	2	0	1	0	O	-0.3
	Yr	108	289	43	65	10	2	5	24	48	29	.225	.339	.325	83	-5	-6	36	5	1	1	-2		-0.8
1953	Bos-A	57	67	11	13	2	0	0	4	14	13	.194	.333	.224	50	-4	-4	5	0	1	-1	-1	O	-0.6
Total	10	1120	3535	507	975	186	43	61	456	415	382	.276	.357	.405	102	32	12	543	33	33	-10	-41	O	-6.7

■ **NORM ZAUCHIN**   Zauchin, Norbert Henry   b: 11/17/29, Royal Oak, Mich.   BR/TR, 6'4.5", 220 lbs.   Deb: 9/23/51

YEAR	TM/L	G	AB	R	H	2B	3B	HR	RBI	BB	SO	AVG	OBP	SLG	PRO+	BR	/A	RC	SB	CS	SBR	FR	POS	TPR
1951	Bos-A	5	12	0	2	1	0	0	0	0	4	.167	.167	.250	11	-2	-2	0	0	1	-1	0	/1	-0.1
1955	Bos-A	130	477	65	114	10	0	27	93	69	105	.239	.339	.430	97	3	-3	73	3	0	1	1	*1	-0.6
1956	Bos-A	44	84	12	18	2	0	2	11	14	22	.214	.333	.310	63	-3	-5	9	0	0	0	-1	1	-0.6
1957	Bos-A	52	91	11	24	3	0	3	14	9	13	.264	.343	.396	96	-0	-0	11	0	0	0	0	1	0.0
1958	Was-A	96	303	35	69	8	2	15	37	38	68	.228	.316	.416	101	-1	-0	39	0	0	0	2	1	0.0
1959	Was-A	19	71	11	15	4	0	3	4	7	14	.211	.291	.394	87	-2	-1	7	2	0	1	-2	1	-0.2
Total	6	346	1038	134	242	28	2	50	159	137	226	.233	.327	.408	93	-4	-11	139	5	1	1	0	1	-1.5

■ **ZAY**   Zay   Deb: 10/07/1886

YEAR	TM/L	G	AB	R	H	2B	3B	HR	RBI	BB	SO	AVG	OBP	SLG	PRO+	BR	/A	RC	SB	CS	SBR	FR	POS	TPR
1886	Bal-a	1	1	0	0	0	0	0	0		0	.000	.000	.000	-99	-0	-0	0	0			-0	/OP	0.0

■ **JOE ZDEB**   Zdeb, Joseph Edmund   b: 6/27/53, Compton, Ill.   BR/TR, 5'11", 185 lbs.   Deb: 4/07/77

YEAR	TM/L	G	AB	R	H	2B	3B	HR	RBI	BB	SO	AVG	OBP	SLG	PRO+	BR	/A	RC	SB	CS	SBR	FR	POS	TPR
1977	*KC-A	105	195	26	58	5	2	2	23	16	23	.297	.351	.374	97	-0	-1	24	6	5	-1	-1	O/3D	-0.5
1978	KC-A	60	127	18	32	2	3	0	11	7	18	.252	.291	.315	69	-5	-5	12	3	0	1	-3	O/23D	-0.9
1979	KC-A	15	23	3	4	1	1	0	0	2	4	.174	.240	.304	45	-2	-2	2	1	0	0	0	/O	-0.1
Total	3	180	345	47	94	8	6	2	34	25	45	.272	.322	.348	83	-7	-8	38	10	5	0	-5	O/D32	-1.5

■ **DAVE ZEARFOSS**   Zearfoss, David William Tilden   b: 1/1/1868, Schenectady, N.Y.   d: 9/12/45, Wilmington, Del.   TR , 5'9",   Deb: 4/17/1896

YEAR	TM/L	G	AB	R	H	2B	3B	HR	RBI	BB	SO	AVG	OBP	SLG	PRO+	BR	/A	RC	SB	CS	SBR	FR	POS	TPR
1896	NY-N	19	60	5	13	1	1	0	6	5	5	.217	.288	.267	50	-4	-4	5	2			-5	C	-0.5
1897	NY-N	5	10	1	3	0	1	0	0	0		.300	.300	.500	114	0	0	2	0			3	/C	0.3

YEAR	TM/L	G	AB	R	H	2B	3B	HR	RBI	BB	SO	AVG	OBP	SLG	PRO+	BR	/A	RC	SB	CS	SBR	FR	POS	TPR
1898	NY-N	1	1	0	1	0	0	0	0	0		1.000	1.000	1.000	497	0	0	1	0			0	/C	0.1
1904	StL-N	27	80	7	17	2	0	0	9	10		.213	.300	.237	72	-2	-2	6	0			-1	C	0.0
1905	StL-N	20	51	2	8	0	1	0	2	4		.157	.218	.196	26	-5	-4	2	0			-0	C	-0.2
Total	5	72	202	15	42	3	3	0	17	19	5	.208	.279	.252	58	-11	-10	16	2			-4	/C	-0.3

■ GEORGE ZEBER
Zeber, George William b: 8/29/50, Ellwood City, Pa.   BB/TR, 5'11", 170 lbs.   Deb: 5/07/77

YEAR	TM/L	G	AB	R	H	2B	3B	HR	RBI	BB	SO	AVG	OBP	SLG	PRO+	BR	/A	RC	SB	CS	SBR	FR	POS	TPR
1977	*NY-A	25	65	8	21	3	0	3	10	9	11	.323	.405	.508	149	4	5	14	0	0	0	2	2/S3D	0.8
1978	NY-A	3	6	0	0	0	0	0	0	0	0	.000	.000	.000	-99	-2	-2	0	0	0	0	-1	/2	-0.2
Total	2	28	71	8	21	3	0	3	10	9	11	.296	.375	.465	129	3	3	14	0	0	0	0	/23SD	0.6

■ ROLLIE ZEIDER
Zeider, Rollie Hubert "Bunions" b: 11/16/1883, Auburn, Ind. d: 9/12/67, Garrett, Ind.   BR/TR, 5'10", 162 lbs.   Deb: 4/14/10

YEAR	TM/L	G	AB	R	H	2B	3B	HR	RBI	BB	SO	AVG	OBP	SLG	PRO+	BR	/A	RC	SB	CS	SBR	FR	POS	TPR
1910	Chi-A	136	498	57	108	9	2	0	31	62		.217	.305	.243	75	-14	-12	52	49			-1	2S/3	-1.9
1911	Chi-A	73	217	39	55	3	0	2	21	29		.253	.347	.295	82	-5	-4	32	28			-5	1S3/2	-0.6
1912	Chi-A	130	420	57	103	12	10	1	42	50		.245	.330	.329	91	-6	-4	62	47			6	13/S	0.2
1913	Chi-A	16	20	4	7	0	0	0	2	4	1	.350	.458	.350	139	1	1	4	3			2	/312	0.4
	NY-A	50	159	15	37	2	0	0	12	25	9	.233	.341	.245	72	-4	-4	14	3			-13	S2/13	-1.7
	Yr	66	179	19	44	2	0	0	14	29	10	.246	.354	.257	79	-3	-3	18	6			-11		-1.3
1914	Chi-F	119	452	60	124	13	2	1	36	44	28	.274	.344	.319	96	-4	-0	65	35			0	*3/S	0.1
1915	Chi-F	129	494	65	112	22	2	0	34	43	24	.227	.297	.279	75	-17	-14	49	16			0	23S	-1.0
1916	Chi-N	98	345	29	81	11	2	1	22	26	26	.235	.294	.287	71	-8	-12	32	9			-7	32/0S1	-2.0
1917	Chi-N	108	354	36	86	14	2	0	27	28	30	.243	.302	.294	77	-7	-10	35	17			-20	S32/10	-3.2
1918	*Chi-N	82	251	31	56	3	2	0	26	23	20	.223	.288	.251	63	-10	-11	23	16			-11	2/13	-1.9
Total	9	941	3210	393	769	89	22	5	253	334	138	.240	.315	.286	80	-74	-69	369	223			-50	23S1/O	-11.6

■ TODD ZEILE
Zeile, Todd Edward b: 9/9/65, Van Nuys, Cal.   BR/TR, 6'1", 190 lbs.   Deb: 8/18/89

YEAR	TM/L	G	AB	R	H	2B	3B	HR	RBI	BB	SO	AVG	OBP	SLG	PRO+	BR	/A	RC	SB	CS	SBR	FR	POS	TPR
1989	StL-N	28	82	7	21	3	1	1	8	9	14	.256	.330	.354	92	-0	-1	10	0	0	0	-1	C	0.0
1990	StL-N	144	495	62	121	25	3	15	57	67	77	.244	.337	.398	99	1	-0	67	2	4	-2	-9	*C31/O	-0.6
Total	2	172	577	69	142	28	4	16	65	76	91	.246	.336	.392	98	1	-1	77	2	4	-2	-11	C/31O	-0.6

■ BART ZELLER
Zeller, Barton Wallace b: 7/22/41, Chicago Heights, Ill.   BR/TR, 6'1", 185 lbs.   Deb: 5/21/70   C

YEAR	TM/L	G	AB	R	H	2B	3B	HR	RBI	BB	SO	AVG	OBP	SLG	PRO+	BR	/A	RC	SB	CS	SBR	FR	POS	TPR
1970	StL-N	1	0	0	0	0	0	0	0	0	0	—	—	—		0	0	0	0	0	0	0	/C	0.0

■ GUS ZERNIAL
Zernial, Gus Edward "Ozark Ike" b: 6/27/23, Beaumont, Tex.   BR/TR, 6'2.5", 210 lbs.   Deb: 4/19/49

YEAR	TM/L	G	AB	R	H	2B	3B	HR	RBI	BB	SO	AVG	OBP	SLG	PRO+	BR	/A	RC	SB	CS	SBR	FR	POS	TPR
1949	Chi-A	73	198	29	63	17	2	5	38	15	26	.318	.366	.500	132	7	7	37	0	1	-1	-4	O	0.1
1950	Chi-A	143	543	75	152	16	4	29	93	38	110	.280	.330	.484	110	1	3	84	0	2	-1	1	*O	0.0
1951	Chi-A	4	19	2	2	0	0	0	4	2	2	.105	.190	.105	-19	-3	-3	0	0	0	0	1	/O	-0.1
	Phi-A	139	552	90	151	30	5	33	125	61	99	.274	.350	.525	132	23	22	102	2	2	-1	12	*O	2.7
	Yr	143	571	92	153	30	5	33	129	63	101	.268	.345	.511	127	20	18	101	2	2	-1	13		2.6
1952	Phi-A	145	549	76	144	15	1	29	100	70	87	.262	.347	.452	114	14	10	89	5	1	1	-0	*O	0.7
1953	Phi-A	147	556	85	158	21	3	42	108	57	79	.284	.355	.559	138	30	28	113	4	0	1	7	*O	3.2
1954	Phi-A	97	336	42	84	8	2	14	62	30	60	.250	.319	.411	98	-2	-2	44	0	0	0	-8	O/1	-1.1
1955	KC-A	120	413	62	105	9	3	30	84	30	90	.254	.309	.508	116	6	6	59	1	0	0	6	*O	0.6
1956	KC-A	109	272	36	61	12	0	16	44	33	66	.224	.317	.445	99	-2	-2	40	2	0	1	-3	O	-0.6
1957	KC-A	131	437	56	103	20	1	27	69	34	84	.236	.292	.471	104	1	-0	57	1	1	-0	-5	*O/1	-1.2
1958	Det-A	66	124	8	40	7	1	5	23	6	25	.323	.354	.516	127	6	5	22	0	0	0	-4	O	0.0
1959	Det-A	60	132	11	30	4	0	7	26	7	27	.227	.266	.417	80	-3	-4	14	0	0	0	-3	1/O	-0.7
Total	11	1234	4131	572	1093	159	22	237	776	383	755	.265	.331	.486	115	78	69	661	15	7	0	1	*O/1	3.6

■ CHARLIE ZIEGLER
Ziegler, Charles W. b: 1/13/1875, Canton, Ohio d: 3/16/04, Canton, Ohio   Deb: 9/23/1899

YEAR	TM/L	G	AB	R	H	2B	3B	HR	RBI	BB	SO	AVG	OBP	SLG	PRO+	BR	/A	RC	SB	CS	SBR	FR	POS	TPR
1899	Cle-N	2	8	2	2	0	0	0	0	0		.250	.250	.250	42	-1	-1	1	0			-1	/S2	-0.1
1900	Phi-N	3	11	0	3	0	0	0	1	0		.273	.273	.273	53	-1	-1	1	0			-1	/3	-0.1
Total	2	5	19	2	5	0	0	0	1	0		.263	.263	.263	49	-1	-1	1	0			-2	/32S	-0.2

■ BENNY ZIENTARA
Zientara, Benedict Joseph b: 2/14/20, Chicago, Ill. d: 4/16/85, Lake Elsinore, Cal.   BR/TR, 5'9", 165 lbs.   Deb: 9/11/41

YEAR	TM/L	G	AB	R	H	2B	3B	HR	RBI	BB	SO	AVG	OBP	SLG	PRO+	BR	/A	RC	SB	CS	SBR	FR	POS	TPR
1941	Cin-N	9	21	3	6	0	0	0	2	1	3	.286	.318	.286	71	-1	-1	2	0			1	/2	0.1
1946	Cin-N	78	280	26	81	10	2	0	16	14	11	.289	.323	.339	91	-5	-4	30	3			24	23	2.3
1947	Cin-N	117	418	60	108	18	1	2	24	23	23	.258	.297	.321	64	-22	-21	39	2			-17	*23	-2.7
1948	Cin-N	74	187	17	35	1	2	0	7	12	11	.187	.236	.214	23	-20	-19	9	0			12	2/3S	-0.2
Total	4	278	906	106	230	29	5	2	49	50	48	.254	.293	.304	64	-48	-45	80	5			20	2/3S	-0.5

■ BILL ZIES
Zies, William BL,   Deb: 8/09/1891

YEAR	TM/L	G	AB	R	H	2B	3B	HR	RBI	BB	SO	AVG	OBP	SLG	PRO+	BR	/A	RC	SB	CS	SBR	FR	POS	TPR
1891	StL-a	2	3	0	1	0	0	0	0	0	0	.333	.333	.333	81	-0	-0	0	0			1	/C	0.0

■ CHIEF ZIMMER
Zimmer, Charles Louis b: 11/23/1860, Marietta, Ohio d: 8/22/49, Cleveland, Ohio   BR/TR, 6', 190 lbs.   Deb: 7/18/1884   MU

YEAR	TM/L	G	AB	R	H	2B	3B	HR	RBI	BB	SO	AVG	OBP	SLG	PRO+	BR	/A	RC	SB	CS	SBR	FR	POS	TPR
1884	Det-N	8	29	0	2	1	0	0		1	14	.069	.100	.103	-38	-4	-4	0				-1	/CO	-0.3
1886	NY-a	6	19	1	3	0	0	0		1		.158	.238	.158	28	-2	-1	1	0			3	/C	0.2
1887	Cle-a	14	52	9	12	5	0	0		4		.231	.298	.327	78	-2	-1	6	1			-4	C/1	-0.2
1888	Cle-a	65	212	27	51	11	4	0	22	18		.241	.312	.330	112	3	3	27	15			7	C/O1S	1.5
1889	Cle-N	84	259	47	67	9	9	1	21	44	35	.259	.368	.375	112	5	5	42	14			9	C/1	1.3
1890	Cle-N	125	444	54	95	16	6	2	57	46	54	.214	.303	.291	77	-13	-12	45	15			12	*C	0.8
1891	Cle-N	116	440	55	112	21	4	3	69	33	49	.255	.312	.341	88	-5	-8	53	15			16	*C/3	1.6
1892	*Cle-N	111	413	63	108	29	13	1	64	32	47	.262	.325	.402	117	9	7	61	18			6	*C	1.8
1893	Cle-N	57	227	27	70	13	7	2	41	16	15	.308	.357	.454	110	4	2	39	4			9	C/3	1.3
1894	Cle-N	90	341	55	97	20	5	4	65	17	31	.284	.328	.408	75	-13	-16	51	14			7	*C	0.0
1895	*Cle-N	88	315	60	107	21	2	5	56	33	30	.340	.417	.467	123	15	12	69	14			8	C/1	2.1
1896	*Cle-N	91	336	46	93	18	3	3	46	31	48	.277	.354	.375	89	-2	-6	47	4			9	*C/3	1.0
1897	Cle-N	80	294	50	93	22	3	0	40	25		.316	.378	.412	105	5	2	50	8			6	C	1.6
1898	Cle-N	20	63	5	15	2	0	0	4	5		.238	.304	.270	68	-2	-2	6	2			4	C	0.3
1899	Cle-N	20	73	9	25	2	1	2	14	5		.342	.407	.479	158	5	5	15	1			-1	C	0.5
	Lou-N	75	262	43	78	11	3	2	29	22		.298	.370	.385	110	4	4	42	9			-1	C1	0.7
	Yr	95	335	52	103	13	4	4	43	27		.307	.378	.406	120	9	10	57	10			-2		1.2
1900	*Pit-N	82	271	27	80	7	10	0	35	17		.295	.359	.395	110	4	4	41	4			6	C/1	1.5
1901	Pit-N	69	236	17	52	7	3	0	21	20		.220	.290	.275	64	-9	-10	22	6			-8	C	-0.9
1902	Pit-N	42	142	13	38	4	2	0	17	11		.268	.338	.324	103	1	1	18	4			-1	C/1	0.4
1903	Phi-N	37	118	9	26	3	1	1	19	9		.220	.276	.288	64	-6	-5	11	3			4	CM	0.1
Total	19	1280	4546	617	1224	222	76	26	620	390	323	.269	.339	.369	97	-3	-20	646	151			90	*C/103S	15.3

■ DON ZIMMER
Zimmer, Donald William b: 1/17/31, Cincinnati, Ohio   BR/TR, 5'9", 165 lbs.   Deb: 7/02/54   MC

YEAR	TM/L	G	AB	R	H	2B	3B	HR	RBI	BB	SO	AVG	OBP	SLG	PRO+	BR	/A	RC	SB	CS	SBR	FR	POS	TPR
1954	Bro-N	24	33	3	6	0	1	0	3		8	.182	.270	.242	34	-3	-3	2	2	0	1	3	S	0.1
1955	*Bro-N	88	280	38	67	10	1	15	50	19	66	.239	.292	.443	89	-4	-5	34	5	3	-0	9	2S/3	0.9
1956	Bro-N	17	20	9	6	1	0	0	2	1		.300	.333	.350	78	-0	-1	2	0	1	-1	2	/S32	-0.1
1957	Bro-N	84	269	23	59	9	1	6	19	16	63	.219	.263	.327	52	-16	-20	21	1	3	-2	9	3S/2	-0.8
1958	LA-N	127	455	52	119	15	2	17	60	40	92	.262	.306	.415	86	-9	-10	55	14	2	3	33	*S3/2O	3.3
1959	*LA-N	97	249	21	41	7	1	4	28	37	56	.165	.275	.249	38	-21	-23	18	3	1	0	2	S/32	-1.7
1960	Chi-N	132	368	37	95	16	7	6	35	27	56	.258	.309	.389	90	-6	-5	42	8	6	-1	7	23/SO	0.7

YEAR	TM/L	G	AB	R	H	2B	3B	HR	RBI	BB	SO	AVG	OBP	SLG	PRO+	BR	/A	RC	SB	CS	SBR	FR	POS	TPR
1961	Chi-N	128	477	57	120	25	4	13	40	25	70	.252	.292	.403	81	-14	-14	52	5	1	1	1	*2/3O	0.1
1962	NY-N	14	52	3	4	1	0	0	1	3	10	.077	.127	.096	-38	-10	-10	1	0	1	-1	5	3	-0.5
	Cin-N	63	192	16	48	11	2	2	16	14	30	.250	.304	.359	75	-6	-7	20	1	2	-1	-1	32/S	-0.5
	Yr	77	244	19	52	12	2	2	17	17	40	.213	.267	.303	51	-16	-17	18	1	3	-2	4		-1.0
1963	LA-N	22	23	4	5	1	0	1	2	3	10	.217	.308	.391	107	-0	-0	3	0	0	0	2	3/2S	0.2
	Was-A	83	298	37	74	12	1	13	44	18	57	.248	.296	.426	100	-1	-1	34	3	2	-0	3	3/2	0.2
1964	Was-A	121	341	38	84	16	2	12	38	27	94	.246	.302	.411	96	-3	-2	40	1	3	-2	-12	3/OC2	-1.5
1965	Was-A	95	226	20	45	6	0	2	17	26	59	.199	.287	.252	56	-13	-12	17	2	0	1	-7	C32	-1.6
Total	12	1095	3283	353	773	130	22	91	352	246	678	.235	.291	.372	76	-106	-115	340	45	25	-2	55	32S/CO	-1.0

■ EDDIE ZIMMERMAN
Zimmerman, Edward Desmond   b: 1/4/1883, Oceanic, N.J.   d: 5/6/45, Emmaus, Pa.   BR/TR, 5'9", 160 lbs.   Deb: 9/29/06

YEAR	TM/L	G	AB	R	H	2B	3B	HR	RBI	BB	SO	AVG	OBP	SLG	PRO+	BR	/A	RC	SB	CS	SBR	FR	POS	TPR
1906	StL-N	5	14	0	3	0	0	0	1	0		.214	.214	.214	36	-1	-1	1	0			-0	/3	-0.1
1911	Bro-N	122	417	31	77	10	7	3	36	34	37	.185	.249	.264	46	-33	-30	30	9			3	*3	-2.1
Total	2	127	431	31	80	10	7	3	37	34	37	.186	.248	.262	45	-34	-31	31	9			3	3	-2.2

■ JERRY ZIMMERMAN
Zimmerman, Gerald Robert   b: 9/21/34, Omaha, Neb.   BR/TR, 6'2", 185 lbs.   Deb: 4/14/61   C

YEAR	TM/L	G	AB	R	H	2B	3B	HR	RBI	BB	SO	AVG	OBP	SLG	PRO+	BR	/A	RC	SB	CS	SBR	FR	POS	TPR
1961	*Cin-N	76	204	8	42	5	0	0	10	11	21	.206	.253	.230	29	-20	-21	11	1	1	-0	3	C	-1.1
1962	Min-A	34	62	8	17	4	0	0	7	3	5	.274	.318	.339	74	-2	-2	7	0	0	0	2	C	0.1
1963	Min-A	39	56	3	13	1	0	0	3	2	8	.232	.259	.250	43	-4	-4	3	0	0	0	6	C	0.2
1964	Min-A	63	120	6	24	3	0	0	12	10	15	.200	.278	.225	42	-9	-9	7	0	0	0	6	C	0.0
1965	*Min-A	83	154	8	33	1	1	1	11	12	23	.214	.275	.253	49	-10	-10	10	0	0	0	12	C	0.8
1966	Min-A	60	119	11	30	4	1	1	15	15	23	.252	.341	.328	88	-1	-2	13	0	0	0	9	C	1.1
1967	Min-A	104	234	13	39	3	0	1	12	22	49	.167	.244	.192	28	-20	-22	11	0	1	-1	14	*C	-0.1
1968	Min-A	24	45	3	5	1	0	0	2	3	10	.111	.184	.133	-3	-6	-6	1	0	0	0	5	C	0.0
Total	8	483	994	60	203	22	2	3	72	78	154	.204	.270	.239	43	-71	-76	64	1	2	-1	55	C	1.0

■ HEINIE ZIMMERMAN
Zimmerman, Henry   b: 2/9/1887, New York, N.Y.   d: 3/14/69, New York, N.Y.   BR/TR, 5'11.5", 176 lbs.   Deb: 9/08/07

YEAR	TM/L	G	AB	R	H	2B	3B	HR	RBI	BB	SO	AVG	OBP	SLG	PRO+	BR	/A	RC	SB	CS	SBR	FR	POS	TPR
1907	*Chi-N	5	9	0	2	1	0	0	1		0	.222	.222	.333	71	-0	-0	1	0			1	/2SO	0.1
1908	Chi-N	46	113	17	33	4	1	0	9		1	.292	.298	.345	103	-0	-0	12	2			-10	2/OS3	-1.1
1909	Chi-N	65	183	23	50	9	2	0	21		3	.273	.285	.344	93	-2	-3	19	7			4	23S	0.2
1910	*Chi-N	99	335	35	95	16	6	3	38	20	36	.284	.326	.394	111	2	3	44	7			-9	2S3/01	-0.4
1911	Chi-N	143	535	80	164	22	17	9	85	25	50	.307	.343	.462	124	14	14	91	23			-1	*231	1.1
1912	Chi-N	145	557	95	207	41	14	14	99	38	60	.372	.418	.571	169	50	50	141	23			2	*31	5.0
1913	Chi-N	127	447	69	140	28	12	9	95	41	40	.313	.379	.490	147	26	26	87	18			4	*3	2.9
1914	Chi-N	146	564	75	167	36	12	4	87	20	46	.296	.326	.424	123	12	12	79	17			-21	*3S2	-0.3
1915	Chi-N	139	520	65	138	28	11	3	62	21	33	.265	.300	.379	105	1	1	61	19	13	-2	-9	*23/S	-0.8
1916	Chi-N	107	398	54	116	25	5	6	64	16	33	.291	.324	.425	116	12	7	55	15	12	-3	7	32/S	1.8
	NY-N	40	151	22	41	4	0	0	19	7	10	.272	.304	.298	90	-3	-2	14	9	8	-2	-3	3/2	-0.4
	Yr	147	549	76	157	29	5	6	83	23	43	.286	.318	.390	110	9	6	68	24	20	-5	4		1.4
1917	*NY-N	150	585	61	174	22	9	5	102	16	43	.297	.317	.391	121	9	11	74	13			13	*3/2	2.4
1918	NY-N	121	463	43	126	19	10	1	56	13	23	.272	.294	.363	102	-2	-1	51	14			-4	*31	-0.4
1919	NY-N	123	444	56	113	20	6	4	58	21	30	.255	.296	.354	96	-4	-3	48	8			-1	*3	-0.3
Total	13	1456	5304	695	1566	275	105	58	796	242	404	.295	.331	.419	121	116	115	776	175	33		-26	32/S10	9.8

■ ROY ZIMMERMAN
Zimmerman, Roy Franklin   b: 9/13/16, Pine Grove, Pa.   BL/TL, 6'2", 187 lbs.   Deb: 9/02/45

YEAR	TM/L	G	AB	R	H	2B	3B	HR	RBI	BB	SO	AVG	OBP	SLG	PRO+	BR	/A	RC	SB	CS	SBR	FR	POS	TPR
1945	NY-N	27	98	14	27	1	0	5	15	5	16	.276	.330	.439	111	1	1	14	1			-2	1/O	-0.1

■ BILL ZIMMERMAN
Zimmerman, William H.   b: 1/20/1889, Kengen, Germany   d: 10/4/52, Newark, N.J.   BR/TR, 5'8.5", 172 lbs.   Deb: 4/14/15

YEAR	TM/L	G	AB	R	H	2B	3B	HR	RBI	BB	SO	AVG	OBP	SLG	PRO+	BR	/A	RC	SB	CS	SBR	FR	POS	TPR
1915	Bro-N	22	57	3	16	2	0	0	7	4	8	.281	.328	.316	93	-0	-0	6	1			-4	O	-0.4

■ FRANK ZINN
Zinn, Frank   b: 12/21/1865, Phoenixville, Pa.   d: 5/12/36, Manayunk, Pa.   5'8", 150 lbs.   Deb: 4/18/1888

YEAR	TM/L	G	AB	R	H	2B	3B	HR	RBI	BB	SO	AVG	OBP	SLG	PRO+	BR	/A	RC	SB	CS	SBR	FR	POS	TPR
1888	Phi-a	2	7	0	0	0	0	0	0	0	1	.000	.125	.000	-58	-1	-1	0	0			0	/C	0.0

■ GUY ZINN
Zinn, Guy   b: 2/13/1887, Hallbrook, W.Va.   d: 10/6/49, Clarksburg, W.Va.   BL/TR, 5'10.5", 170 lbs.   Deb: 9/11/11

YEAR	TM/L	G	AB	R	H	2B	3B	HR	RBI	BB	SO	AVG	OBP	SLG	PRO+	BR	/A	RC	SB	CS	SBR	FR	POS	TPR
1911	NY-A	9	27	5	4	0	2	0	1	4		.148	.281	.296	57	-1	-2	2	0			-0	/O	-0.2
1912	NY-A	106	401	56	105	15	10	6	55	50		.262	.345	.394	105	6	2	60	17			-9	*O	-1.2
1913	Bos-N	36	138	15	41	8	2	1	15	4	23	.297	.322	.406	105	1	0	18	3			5	O	0.5
1914	Bal-F	61	225	30	63	10	6	3	25	16	26	.280	.336	.418	112	4	3	35	6			-5	O	-0.4
1915	Bal-F	102	312	30	84	18	3	5	43	35	28	.269	.343	.394	114	7	6	45	2			-5	O	-0.2
Total	5	314	1103	136	297	51	23	15	139	109	77	.269	.338	.398	108	16	9	160	28			-14	O	-1.5

■ BUD ZIPFEL
Zipfel, Marion Sylvester   b: 11/18/38, Belleville, Ill.   BL/TR, 6'3", 200 lbs.   Deb: 7/26/61

YEAR	TM/L	G	AB	R	H	2B	3B	HR	RBI	BB	SO	AVG	OBP	SLG	PRO+	BR	/A	RC	SB	CS	SBR	FR	POS	TPR
1961	Was-A	50	170	17	34	7	5	4	18	15	49	.200	.265	.371	69	-8	-8	17	1	1	-0	-4	1	-1.6
1962	Was-A	68	184	21	44	4	1	6	21	17	43	.239	.307	.370	82	-5	-5	21	1	2	-1	-3	1O	-1.0
Total	2	118	354	38	78	11	6	10	39	32	92	.220	.287	.370	76	-14	-13	38	2	3	-1	-7	/1O	-2.6

■ RICHIE ZISK
Zisk, Richard Walter   b: 2/6/49, Brooklyn, N.Y.   BR/TR, 6'1", 200 lbs.   Deb: 9/08/71

YEAR	TM/L	G	AB	R	H	2B	3B	HR	RBI	BB	SO	AVG	OBP	SLG	PRO+	BR	/A	RC	SB	CS	SBR	FR	POS	TPR
1971	Pit-N	7	15	2	3	1	0	1	2	4	7	.200	.368	.467	136	1	1	3	0	0	0	-0	/O	0.0
1972	Pit-N	17	37	4	7	3	0	0	4	7	10	.189	.318	.270	70	-1	-1	3	0	0	0	-1	O	-0.2
1973	Pit-N	103	333	44	108	23	7	10	54	21	63	.324	.364	.526	148	18	19	62	0	0	0	1	O	1.7
1974	*Pit-N	149	536	75	168	30	3	17	100	65	91	.313	.388	.476	146	29	32	96	1	1	-0	6	*O	3.3
1975	*Pit-N	147	504	69	146	27	3	20	75	68	109	.290	.376	.474	136	24	24	90	0	1	-1	-3	*O	1.6
1976	Pit-N	155	581	91	168	35	2	21	89	52	96	.289	.348	.465	128	20	20	90	1	0	0	0	*O	1.6
1977	Chi-A	141	531	78	154	17	6	30	101	55	98	.290	.360	.514	135	25	25	94	4	2	-2	2	*OD	2.0
1978	Tex-A	140	511	68	134	19	1	22	85	58	76	.262	.341	.432	116	11	11	74	3	3	-1	-10	OD	-0.2
1979	Tex-A	144	503	69	132	21	1	18	64	57	75	.262	.338	.416	103	1	2	69	1	1	-0	-5	*O	-0.7
1980	Tex-A	135	448	48	130	17	1	19	77	39	72	.290	.347	.460	123	11	13	66	0	2	-1	-2	DO	0.9
1981	Sea-A	94	357	42	111	12	1	16	43	28	63	.311	.366	.485	138	19	17	61	0	2	-1	0	D	1.7
1982	Sea-A	131	503	61	147	28	1	21	62	49	89	.292	.356	.477	123	18	16	86	2	1	0	0	*D	1.6
1983	Sea-A	90	285	30	69	12	0	12	36	30	61	.242	.314	.411	94	-1	-3	37	0	0	0	0	D	-0.2
Total	13	1453	5144	681	1477	245	26	207	792	533	910	.287	.355	.466	126	174	176	834	8	15	-7	-12	OD	13.1

■ BILLY ZITZMANN
Zitzmann, William Arthur   b: 11/19/1895, Long Island City, N.Y.   d: 5/29/85, Passaic, N.J.   BR/TR, 5'10.5", 175 lbs.   Deb: 4/17/19

YEAR	TM/L	G	AB	R	H	2B	3B	HR	RBI	BB	SO	AVG	OBP	SLG	PRO+	BR	/A	RC	SB	CS	SBR	FR	POS	TPR
1919	Pit-N	11	26	5	5	1	0	0	2	0	6	.192	.192	.231	26	-2	-2	1	2			-1	/O	-0.3
	Cin-N	2	1	0	0	0	0	0	0	0	0	.000	.000	.000	-99	-0	-0	0	0			0	/O	0.0
	Yr	13	27	5	5	1	0	0	2	0	6	.185	.185	.222	22	-3	-3	1	2			-1		-0.3
1925	Cin-N	104	301	53	76	13	3	0	21	35	22	.252	.342	.316	71	-13	-12	33	11	11	-3	-12	O/S	-2.7
1926	Cin-N	53	94	21	23	2	1	0	3	6	7	.245	.304	.287	61	-5	-5	8	3			0	O	-0.5
1927	Cin-N	88	232	47	66	10	4	0	24	20	18	.284	.352	.362	94	-2	-1	30	9			-4	O/S3	-0.6
1928	Cin-N	101	266	53	79	9	3	3	33	13	22	.297	.337	.387	90	-5	-4	34	13			-4	O/3	-1.0
1929	Cin-N	47	84	18	19	3	0	0	6	9	10	.226	.309	.262	45	-7	-7	7	4			-1	O	-0.4
Total	6	406	1004	197	268	38	11	3	89	83	85	.267	.333	.336	77	-35	-31	114	42	11		-21	O/S13	-5.9

■ FRANK ZUPO
Zupo, Frank Joseph "Noodles"   b: 8/29/39, San Francisco, Cal   BL/TR, 5'11", 182 lbs.   Deb: 7/01/57

YEAR	TM/L	G	AB	R	H	2B	3B	HR	RBI	BB	SO	AVG	OBP	SLG	PRO+	BR	/A	RC	SB	CS	SBR	FR	POS	TPR
1957	Bal-A	10	12	2	1	0	0	0	0	0	4	.083	.154	.083	-36	-2	-2	0	0	0	0	1	/C	0.0

YEAR	TM/L	G	AB	R	H	2B	3B	HR	RBI	BB	SO	AVG	OBP	SLG	PRO+	BR	/A	RC	SB	CS	SBR	FR	POS	TPR
1958	Bal-A	1	2	0	0	0	0	0	0	0	1	.000	.000	.000	-99	-1	-1	0	0	0	0	0	/C	0.0
1961	Bal-A	5	4	1	2	1	0	0	0	1	1	.500	.600	.750	264	1	1	2	0	0	0	0	/C	0.1
Total	3	16	18	3	3	1	0	0	0	2	6	.167	.250	.222	31	-2	-2	2	0	0	0	1	/C	0.1

■ **PAUL ZUVELLA**   Zuvella, Paul   b: 10/31/58, San Mateo, Cal.   BR/TR, 6', 173 lbs.   Deb: 9/04/82

YEAR	TM/L	G	AB	R	H	2B	3B	HR	RBI	BB	SO	AVG	OBP	SLG	PRO+	BR	/A	RC	SB	CS	SBR	FR	POS	TPR
1982	Atl-N	2	1	0	0	0	0	0	0	0	0	.000	.000	.000	-96	-0	-0	0	0	0	0	1	/S	0.1
1983	Atl-N	3	5	0	0	0	0	0	0	2	1	.000	.375	.000	11	-0	-0	0	0	0	0	-2	/S	-0.1
1984	Atl-N	11	25	2	5	1	0	0	1	2	3	.200	.259	.240	38	-2	-2	2	0	0	0	1	/2S	0.0
1985	Atl-N	81	190	16	48	8	1	0	4	16	14	.253	.311	.305	69	-7	-8	19	2	0	1	9	2S/3	0.4
1986	NY-A	21	48	2	4	1	0	0	2	5	4	.083	.170	.104	-24	-8	-8	1	0	0	0	4	S	-0.2
1987	NY-A	14	34	2	6	0	0	0	0	0	4	.176	.176	.176	-6	-5	-5	1	0	0	0	-1	/2S3	-0.4
1988	Cle-A	51	130	9	30	5	1	0	7	8	13	.231	.275	.285	56	-7	-8	10	0	0	0	-3	S	-0.8
1989	Cle-A	24	58	10	16	2	0	2	6	1	11	.276	.300	.414	98	-0	-0	7	0	0	0	-3	S/3D	-0.1
Total	8	207	491	41	109	17	2	2	20	34	50	.222	.275	.277	52	-30	-32	41	2	0	1	5	S/23D	-1.1

■ **DUTCH ZWILLING**   Zwilling, Edward Harrison   b: 11/2/1888, St.Louis, Mo.   d: 3/27/78, LaCrescenta, Cal.   BL/TL, 5'6.5", 160 lbs.   Deb: 8/14/10   C

YEAR	TM/L	G	AB	R	H	2B	3B	HR	RBI	BB	SO	AVG	OBP	SLG	PRO+	BR	/A	RC	SB	CS	SBR	FR	POS	TPR
1910	Chi-A	27	87	7	16	5	0	0	5	11		.184	.283	.241	67	-3	-3	6	1			-2	O	-0.6
1914	Chi-F	154	592	91	185	38	8	**16**	95	46	68	.313	.363	.485	150	30	34	116	21			2	*O	2.9
1915	Chi-F	150	548	65	157	32	7	13	**94**	67	65	.286	.366	.442	147	26	30	102	24			8	*O/1	3.3
1916	Chi-N	35	53	4	6	1	0	1	8	4	6	.113	.175	.189	11	-6	-6	2	0			-2	O	-0.9
Total	4	366	1280	167	364	76	15	30	202	128	<u>139</u>	.284	.351	.438	137	47	56	225	46			7	O/1	4.7

The Pitcher Register

The Pitcher Register

The Pitcher Register consists of the central pitching statistics of every man who has pitched in major league play since 1871, *without exception.* Pitcher batting is expressed in Batting Runs in the Pitcher Batting column, and in the newly added columns for base hits and batting average. Pitcher defense is expressed in Fielding Runs in the Pitcher Defense column.

The pitchers are listed alphabetically by surname and, when more than one pitcher bears the name, alphabetically by *given* name—not by "use name," by which we mean the name he may have had applied to him during his playing career. This is the standard method of alphabetizing used in other biographical reference works, and in the case of baseball it makes it easier to find a lesser-known player with a common surname like Smith or Johnson. This method also jibes with that employed in the Team Roster and Annual Record where, for example, Charles "Old Hoss" Radbourn is shown not as the puzzling O. Radbourn or H. Radbourn, as some reference books have it, but as C. Radbourn. On the whole, we have been conservative in ascribing nicknames, doing so only when the player was in fact known by that name during his playing days.

Each page of the Pitcher Register is topped at the corner by a finding aid: in capital letters, the surname of, first, the pitcher whose entry heads up the page and, second, the pitcher whose entry concludes it. Another finding aid is the use of boldface numerals indicating a league leading total in those categories in which a pitcher is truly attempting to excel. No boldface is given to the "leaders" in losses; in games started (innings pitched is the better category to highlight endurance); in hits allowed (the most would produce an absurd leader, while the fewest would tend to reward a man for pitching fewer innings—hits per nine innings is the better category in which to cite leaders); or (using the same reasoning as for hits allowed) in home runs allowed or bases on balls. Pitcher batting and pitcher defense, because the win-denominated numbers they produce are so small, are also not sorted for single-season leaders (although the all-time leaders in these categories, single season and lifetime, will be found in the separate section called "All-Time Leaders"). Condensed type will appear occasionally throughout this section; it has no special significance but is designed to accommodate unusually wide figures, such as the 108.00 ERA of Harry Heitmann, who allowed four earned runs in his career of one-third of an inning's work.

The record of a man who pitched in more than one season is given in one line for each season, plus a career total line. If he pitched for more than one team in a given year, his totals for each team are given on separate lines; and if the teams for which he pitched in his "traded year"

are in the same league, then his full record is stated in both separate and combined fashion. (In the odd case of a man playing for three or more clubs in one year, with some of these clubs being in the same league, the combined total line will reflect only his play in that one league.) A man who pitched in only one year has no additional career total line since it would be identical to his seasonal listing.

In *Total Baseball 1,* fractional innings were calculated for teams in the Annual Record but were rounded off to the nearest whole inning for individuals, in accordance with baseball scoring practice from 1976 through 1981 (for the previous century, fractional innings pitched were simply lopped off). In 1981, this rounding-off procedure cost Sammy Stewart of Baltimore an ERA title, as Oakland's Steve McCatty won the crown despite having a higher ERA when fractional innings were counted; this singular occurrence led to a change in baseball scoring practice. In the first edition our data base conformed to the 1976–1982 practice for all of pitching history, excepting those men who pitched only one-third of an inning in an entire season. For this second edition of *Total Baseball* we have recalculated all fractional innings pitched: look for a superscript figure, either a one or a two, in the IP column to indicate thirds of innings.

Pitching records for the National Association are included in the Pitcher Register because the editors, like most baseball historians, regard it as a major league, inasmuch as it was the only professional league of its day and supplied the National League of 1876 with most of its personnel. In this second edition of *Total Baseball,* we benefit from the SABR research project referred to in the Introduction to the Annual Record—which to date has produced games started, complete games, shutouts, saves, innings pitched, hits, and bases on balls and, for 1871 only, earned runs and ERA. For the years 1872–1875 we have estimated ERA based on the teams' average of 40 percent of runs allowed being earned. For *Total Baseball 3* we expect to have actual earned-run data, but for now this estimation produces reasonable results. Until Major League Baseball reverses the position it adopted in 1969 and restores the NA to official major league status, we will reluctantly continue the practice of carrying separate totals for the National Association rather than integrating them into the career marks of those pitchers whose major league tenures began before 1876 and concluded in that year or after it.

Gaps remain elsewhere in the official record of baseball and in the ongoing process of sabermetric reconstruction. The reader will note occasional blank elements in biographical lines; these are not typographical lapses but signs that the information does not exist or has not yet been found. However, unlike the case of batting records, there are no incomplete statistical columns for pitchers except in the National Association years of 1871–1875. Where official statistics did not exist or the raw data have not survived, as with batters facing pitchers before 1908 in the American League and before 1903 in the National, we have constructed figures from the available raw data. For example, to obtain a pitcher's BFP—Batters Facing Pitchers—for calculating Opponents' On Base Percentage or Batting Average, we have subtracted league base hits from league at-bats, divided by league innings pitched, multiplied by the pitcher's innings and added his hits and walks allowed and hit-by-pitch, if available. Research in this area continues, and we hope one day to

eliminate the need for inferential data all the way back to 1871. (In this edition, incidentally, we correct an error in Opponents' Batting Average and Opponents' On Base Percentage for pre-1909 pitchers in which the estimated at-bats mistakenly subtracted pitcher batting from league batting, resulting in a figure that was about 10 percent too high.)

For a key to the team and league abbreviations used in the Pitcher Register, flip to the last page of this volume. For a guide to the other procedures and abbreviations employed in the Pitcher Register, review the comments on the prodigiously extended pitching record below.

YEAR	TM/L	W	L	PCT	G	GS	CG	SH	SV	IP	H	HR	BB	SO	RAT	ERA	ERA+	OAV	OOB	BH	AVG	PB	PR	/A	PD	TPI
■ **RIP VAN WINKLE**					Van Winkle, Rip "Half Moon" (Also Played in 1874 as Geoffrey Crayon)																					
					b: 4/30/1820, Plattekill, N.Y.				d: 12/12/80, Hudson, N.Y.		BL/TL, 5'5", 145 lbs.		Deb: 5/7/1874 MUCH ♦													
1874	Bos-n	27	30	.474	57	57	56	1	0	498	502		18		9.4	3.90	104			40	.167	-3	5	3		-0.1
1875	Wes-n	29	22	.569	52	51	50	2	1	450	491		25		10.3	4.02	106			50	.200	1	7	7		0.5
1883	Bal-a	5	18	.217	27	23	19	0	1	196	207	7	76	77	13.0	3.44	101	.274	.340	18	.180	-0	-3	1	0	-0.1
1884	Was-U	0	1	.000	1	1	1	0	0	8	10	0	2	3	13.5	4.50	110	.309	.349	0	.000	1	-0	-0	.0	0.0
	KC-U	5	2	.714	8	6	5	0	0	52	66	0	9	14	13.0	4.33	104	.312	.340	9	.250	2	3	1	0	0.1
	Yr	5	3	.625	7	7	6	0	0	60	76	0	11	17	13.0	4.35	104	.311	.341	9	.225	2	3	1	0	0.1
1890	Cin-P	0	0	—	1	1	1	0	0	0	5	2	2	0	∞	∞	-97	1.000	1.000	1	.250	0	-2	-2	0	-0.2
1907	NY-N	16	13	.552	35	34	18	0	2	251	224	19	78	170	10.8	2.76	126	.236	.293	30	.250	1	17	20	2	2.2
1908	NY-N	16	12	.571	36	35	14	1	5	278	224	15	48	205	8.8	2.20	130	.215	.250	25	.200	1	24	20	-3	2.2
1909	NY-N	25	7	.781	36	35	18	0	5	273	202	24	82	208		2.21	164	.201	.261	20	.147	-1	42	43	1	4.2
1910	NY-N	18	12	.600	37	36	19	0	2	291	230	21	83	283	9.4	2.81	135	.211	.267	38	.277	4	40	32	1	3.6
1911	NY-N	20	10	.667	36	35	21	0	4	286	214	18	61	289	8.6	1.76	188	.202	.246	40	.296	4	54	49	-1	5.5
1912	NY-N	21	12	.636	35	35	13	0	3	262	215	23	77	249	10.0	2.92	116	.219	.275	34	.281	3	16	14	1	1.7
1913	NY-N	19	10	.655	36	36	18	0	3	290	219	23	64	251	8.8	2.08	184	.202	.247	31	.263	3	51	56	2	5.9
1914	Ind-F	11	11	.500	32	32	12	0	5	236	199	19	75	201	10.4	3.20	126	.226	.287	22	.227	-1	11	22	1	2.2
1915	NY-N	22	9	.710	36	36	15	0	5	280	217	11	88	243	9.8	2.38	155	.211	.274	33	.311	3	39	41	1	4.2
1916	NY-N	7	3	.700	13	13	5	0	3	96	79	7	28	72	10.0	3.00	140	.218	.274	11	.196	1	10	13	3	1.5
	Bos-A	5	7	.417	16	16	1	0	0	104	114	8	29	72	12.4	3.81	112	.271	.318	20	.189	0	4	5	-2	0.7
1917	Bos-A	0	1	.000	1	1	0	0	0	1/3	5	2	1	1	180.0	108.00	1200	.833	.857	0	.000	0	-2	-2	0	-0.2
Total	2 n	56	52	.519	109	108	106	3	1	948	993		43		9.8	3.96	105			90	.184	-2	12	7		0.4
Total	14	190	128	.597	384	375	180	1	38	2903	2486	199	803	2338	10.2	2.76	134	.226	.285	294	.224	23	304	313	6	33.6

Looking at the biographical line for any pitcher, we see first his use name in full capitals, then his given name and nickname (and any other name he may have used or been born with, such as the matronymic of a Latin American player). His date and place of birth follow "b" and his date and place of death follow "d"; years through 1900 are expressed fully, in four digits, and years after 1900 are expressed in only their last two digits. Then come his manner of batting and throwing, abbreviated for a left-handed batter who throws right as BL/TR (a switch-hitter would be shown as BB for "bats both" and a switch thrower as TB for "throws both"). Next, and for most pitchers last, is the pitcher's debut date in the major leagues, if known at this point. While we, thanks to SABR research, are able to report most of these, for some individuals we have had to list only the two digits representing their rookie year.

Some pitchers continue in major league baseball after their pitching days are through, as managers, coaches, or even umpires. A pitcher whose biographical line concludes with an M can also be located in the Manager Roster; one whose line bears a C will be listed in the Coach Roster; and one with a U occupies a place in the Umpire Roster. (In the last case we have placed a U on the biographical line only for those pitchers who were employed as umpires by a league, for in the nineteenth century—and especially in the years of the National Association—there were literally hundreds of players who were pressed into service as umpires for a game or two; it

would be misleading to accord such pitchers the same code we give to Bob Emslie or Bill Dinneen.) The select few who have been enshrined in the Baseball Hall of Fame are noted with an H. They are also listed in the Hall of Fame Roster found toward the end of Bill Deane's "Awards and Honors" essay in Part One. A new feature is a black diamond at the end of the biographical line for pitchers who also appear in the Player Register by virtue of their having played in 100 or more games at another position, including pinch hitter, or having played more than half of their total major league games at another position, or having played more games at a position other than pitcher in at least one year.

The explanations for the statistical column heads follow; for more technical information about formulas and calculations, see the Glossary. The vertical rules in the column-header line separate the stats into six logical groupings: year, team, league; wins and losses; game-related counting stats; inning-related counting stats; basic calculated averages; pitcher batting; sabermetric figures of more complex calculation; and run-denominated Linear Weights stats for pitching, fielding, and Total Pitcher Index.

Absent from the Pitcher Register in this edition are some statistics present in the original: Hits Per Game and Bases on Balls Per Game (still available in the Annual Record and Leaders sections, and now stated in combined fashion as Ratio); Strikeouts Per Game (still available in the Annual Record and Leaders sections and, in any event, fairly evident from a glance at the SO and IP columns); Park Factor for pitchers (still available from the Annual Record); Clutch Pitching Index, newly developed for *Total Baseball* but which we have judged to be of lesser interest and value than the more established sabermetric measures (still, it is present in the Annual Record and Leaders sections); and Wins Above Team, a stat that has so many cautions associated with it that we judged it to be of little value when applied to all 6,156 pitchers shown in the Register.

YEAR   Year in which a man pitched (When a space in the column is blank, this indicates that the man pitched for two or more clubs in the last year stated in the column; if those clubs were in the same league, then the man will also have a combined total line, beginning with the abbreviation "Yr" placed in the TM/L column.)

Yr   Year's totals for pitching with two or more clubs in same league (see comments for YEAR)

TM/L   Team and League (see comments for YEAR)

W   Wins

L   Losses

PCT   Win Percentage (Wins divided by decisions)

G   Games pitched

GS   Games Started

CG   Complete Games

SH   Shutouts (Complete-game shutouts only)

SV   Saves (Employing definition in force at the time, and 1969 definition for years prior to 1969)

IP   Innings Pitched (Fractional innings included, as discussed above)

H   Hits allowed

HR   Home Runs allowed

BB   Bases on Balls allowed

SO   Strikeouts

RAT   Ratio (Hits allowed plus walks allowed per nine innings)

ERA   Earned Run Average (In a handful of cases, a pitcher will have faced one or more batters for his full season's work yet failed to retire any of them [thus having an innings-pitched figure of zero]; if any of the men he put on base came around to score earned runs, these runs produced an infinite ERA, expressed in the pitcher's record as ∞. (see Van Winkle's 1890 season)

ERA   Adjusted Earned Run Average normalized to league average and adjusted for home-park factor. (See comments for /A.)

OAV   Opponents' Batting Average

OOB   Opponents' On Base Percentage

BH   Base Hits (as a batter)

AVG   Batting Average

PB   Pitcher Batting (Expressed in Batting Runs. Pitcher Batting is park-adjusted and weighted, for those who played primarily at other positions, by the ratio of games pitched to games played. For more technical data about Runs Per Win and Batting Run formulas, see Glossary.)

PR   Pitching Runs (Linear Weights measure of runs saved *beyond* what a league-average pitcher might have saved, defined as zero. Occasionally the curious figure of −0 will appear in this column, or in the columns of other Linear Weights measures of batting, fielding, and the TPI. This "negative zero" figure signifies a run contribution that falls below the league average, but to so small a degree that it cannot be said to have cost the team a run. Also, this column and the Adjusted one to its right will each contain a pair of single-season leaders, the figures shown in boldface: the top mark in Starters' Runs and the top mark in Relievers' Runs. The former category is reserved for men who averaged more than three innings per game pitched, while the latter category is for those who averaged less than three innings per game pitched.)

/A   Adjusted (This signifies that the stat to the immediate left, in this instance Pitching Runs, is here normalized to league average and adjusted for home-park factor. A mark of 100 is a league-average performance, and superior marks exceed 100. An innovation for this edition is to use three-year averages for pitching park factors. If a team moved, or the park changed dramatically, then two-year averages are employed; if the park was used for only one year, then of course only that run-scoring data is used.)

PD   Pitcher Defense (Expressed in Fielding Runs. See comment above on PB and see Glossary.)

TPI   Total Pitcher Index (The sum, expressed in wins beyond league average, of a pitcher's Pitching Runs, Batting Runs [in the AL since 1973, 0], and Fielding Runs, all divided by the Runs Per Win factor for that year—generally around 10, historically in the 9–11 range; see Glossary.)

Total   For players whose careers include play in the National Association as well as other major leagues, two totals are given, as described above and as illustrated in Rip Van Winkle's record, where the record of his years in the National Association is shown alongside the notation "Total 2 n," where *2* stands for the number of years totaled and *n* stands for National Association. For players whose careers began in 1876 or later, the lifetime record is shown alongside the notation "Total x," where *x* stands for the number of post-1875 years totaled.

YEAR	TM/L	W	L	PCT	G	GS	CG	SH	SV	IP	H	HR	BB	SO	RAT	ERA	ERA+	OAV	OOB	BH	AVG	PB	PR	/A	PD	TPI

■ DON AASE
Aase, Donald William b: 9/8/54, Orange, Cal. BR/TR, 6'3", 190 lbs. Deb: 7/26/77

YEAR	TM/L	W	L	PCT	G	GS	CG	SH	SV	IP	H	HR	BB	SO	RAT	ERA	ERA+	OAV	OOB	BH	AVG	PB	PR	/A	PD	TPI
1977	Bos-A	6	2	.750	13	13	4	2	0	92¹	85	6	19	49	10.2	3.12	144	.244	.285	0	—	0	10	14	-0	1.4
1978	Cal-A	11	8	.579	29	29	6	1	0	178²	185	14	80	93	13.4	4.03	90	.270	.348	0	—	0	-5	-8	1	-0.7
1979	*Cal-A	9	10	.474	37	28	7	1	2	185¹	200	19	77	96	13.5	4.81	85	.277	.347	0	—	0	-12	-15	-2	-1.5
1980	Cal-A	8	13	.381	40	21	5	1	2	175	193	13	66	74	13.4	4.06	97	.287	.351	0	—	0	-1	-3	-1	-0.3
1981	Cal-A	4	4	.500	39	0	0	0	11	65¹	56	4	24	38	11.0	2.34	156	.234	.304	0	—	0	10	9	-0	1.0
1982	Cal-A	3	3	.500	24	0	0	0	4	52	45	5	23	40	11.8	3.46	117	.243	.327	0	—	0	4	3	-0	0.3
1984	Cal-A	4	1	.800	23	0	0	0	8	39	30	1	19	28	11.3	1.62	246	.221	.316	0	—	0	10	10	-0	1.0
1985	Bal-A	10	6	.625	54	0	0	0	14	88	83	6	35	67	12.2	3.78	106	.258	.332	0	—	0	4	2	-0	0.2
1986	Bal-A	6	7	.462	66	0	0	0	34	81²	71	6	28	67	10.9	2.98	139	.234	.298	0	—	0	11	11	0	1.1
1987	Bal-A	1	0	1.000	7	0	0	0	2	8	8	1	4	3	13.5	2.25	195	.276	.364	0	—	0	2	2	0	0.2
1988	Bal-A	0	0	—	35	0	0	0	0	46²	40	4	37	28	14.9	4.05	96	.240	.377	0	—	0	-0	-1	-1	0.0
1989	NY-N	1	5	.167	49	0	0	0	2	59¹	56	5	26	34	12.6	3.94	83	.245	.324	0	.000	-1	-3	-4	0	-0.4
1990	LA-N	3	1	.750	32	0	0	0	3	38	33	5	19	24	12.3	4.97	72	.232	.323	0	—	0	-5	-6	-0	-0.6
Total	13	66	60	.524	448	91	22	5	82	1109¹	1085	89	457	641	12.6	3.80	103	.259	.333	0	.000	-1	23	14	-4	1.7

■ BERT ABBEY
Abbey, Bert Wood b: 11/29/1869, Essex, Vt. d: 6/11/62, Essex Junction, Vt. BR/TR, 5'11", 175 lbs. Deb: 6/14/1892

YEAR	TM/L	W	L	PCT	G	GS	CG	SH	SV	IP	H	HR	BB	SO	RAT	ERA	ERA+	OAV	OOB	BH	AVG	PB	PR	/A	PD	TPI
1892	Was-N	5	18	.217	27	23	19	0	1	195²	207	7	76	77	13.0	3.45	94	.261	.325	9	.120	-3	-4	-4	2	-0.4
1893	Chi-N	2	4	.333	7	7	5	0	0	56	74	1	20	6	15.1	5.46	84	.309	.362	6	.231	-0	-5	-5	0	-0.3
1894	Chi-N	2	7	.222	11	11	10	0	0	92	119	3	37	24	15.3	5.18	108	.310	.371	5	.128	-5	1	4	-1	0.0
1895	Chi-N	0	1	.000	1	1	1	0	0	8	10	0	2	3	13.5	4.50	113	.301	.341	1	.333	0	0	1	0	0.1
	Bro-N	5	2	.714	8	6	5	0	0	52	66	0	9	14	13.0	4.33	102	.304	.332	5	.263	1	3	0	1	0.1
	Yr	5	3	.625	9	7	6	0	0	60	76	0	11	17	13.1	4.35	103	.304	.333	2	.091	1	3	1	1	0.2
1896	Bro-N	8	8	.500	25	18	12	0	0	164¹	210	7	48	37	14.1	5.15	80	.308	.354	12	.190	-0	-14	-19	-1	-1.6
Total	5	22	40	.355	79	66	52	0	1	568	686	18	192	161	13.9	4.52	92	.292	.346	38	.169	-8	-18	-23	0	-2.1

■ CHARLIE ABBEY
Abbey, Charles S. b: 10/1868, Falls City, Neb. BL, 5'8.5", 169 lbs. Deb: 8/16/1893 ♦

YEAR	TM/L	W	L	PCT	G	GS	CG	SH	SV	IP	H	HR	BB	SO	RAT	ERA	ERA+	OAV	OOB	BH	AVG	PB	PR	/A	PD	TPI
1896	Was-N	0	0	—	1	0	0	0	0	2	6	0	0	0	27.0	4.50	98	.511	.511	79	.262	0	-0	-0	0	0.0

■ JIM ABBOTT
Abbott, James Anthony b: 9/19/67, Flint, Mich. BL/TL, 6'3", 200 lbs. Deb: 4/08/89

YEAR	TM/L	W	L	PCT	G	GS	CG	SH	SV	IP	H	HR	BB	SO	RAT	ERA	ERA+	OAV	OOB	BH	AVG	PB	PR	/A	PD	TPI
1989	Cal-A	12	12	.500	29	29	4	2	0	181¹	190	13	74	115	13.3	3.92	97	.274	.347	0	—	0	-1	-2	-1	-0.2
1990	Cal-A	10	14	.417	33	33	4	1	0	211²	246	16	72	105	13.7	4.51	87	.295	.355	0	—	0	-14	-14	1	-1.2
Total	2	22	26	.458	62	62	8	3	0	393	436	29	146	220	13.5	4.24	91	.286	.351	0	—	0	-15	-16	1	-1.4

■ DAN ABBOTT
Abbott, Leander Franklin "Big Dan" b: 3/16/1862, Portage, Ohio d: 2/13/30, Ottawa Lake, Mich. BR/TR, 5'11", 190 lbs. Deb: 4/19/1890

YEAR	TM/L	W	L	PCT	G	GS	CG	SH	SV	IP	H	HR	BB	SO	RAT	ERA	ERA+	OAV	OOB	BH	AVG	PB	PR	/A	PD	TPI
1890	Tol-a	0	2	.000	3	1	1	0	1	13	19	0	8	1	18.7	6.23	63	.330	.412	1	.143	0	-3	-3	1	-0.1

■ PAUL ABBOTT
Abbott, Paul David b: 9/15/67, Van Nuys, Cal. BR/TR, 6'3", 185 lbs. Deb: 8/21/90

YEAR	TM/L	W	L	PCT	G	GS	CG	SH	SV	IP	H	HR	BB	SO	RAT	ERA	ERA+	OAV	OOB	BH	AVG	PB	PR	/A	PD	TPI
1990	Min-A	0	5	.000	7	7	0	0	0	34²	37	0	28	25	17.1	5.97	70	.282	.412	0	—	0	-8	-7	-0	-0.6

■ GLENN ABBOTT
Abbott, William Glenn b: 2/16/51, Little Rock, Ark. BR/TR, 6'6", 200 lbs. Deb: 7/29/73

YEAR	TM/L	W	L	PCT	G	GS	CG	SH	SV	IP	H	HR	BB	SO	RAT	ERA	ERA+	OAV	OOB	BH	AVG	PB	PR	/A	PD	TPI
1973	Oak-A	1	0	1.000	5	3	1	0	0	18²	16	3	7	6	11.1	3.86	92	.225	.295	0	—	0	-0	-1	-0	0.0
1974	Oak-A	5	7	.417	19	17	3	0	0	96	89	4	34	38	11.8	3.00	111	.247	.317	0	—	0	7	3	-0	0.3
1975	*Oak-A	5	5	.500	30	15	3	1	0	114¹	109	12	50	51	12.7	4.25	85	.253	.333	0	—	0	-6	-8	-0	-0.7
1976	Oak-A	2	4	.333	19	10	0	0	0	62¹	87	6	16	27	15.0	5.49	61	.333	.374	0	—	0	-14	-15	-0	-1.4
1977	Sea-A	12	13	.480	36	34	7	0	, 0	204¹	212	32	56	100	12.3	4.45	92	.270	.328	0	—	0	-9	-8	-0	-0.7
1978	Sea-A	7	15	.318	29	28	8	1	0	155¹	191	22	44	67	13.7	5.27	72	.303	.350	0	—	0	-26	-25	0	-2.4
1979	Sea-A	4	10	.286	23	19	3	0	0	116²	138	19	38	25	13.8	5.17	84	.301	.358	0	—	0	-12	-11	0	-0.9
1980	Sea-A	12	12	.500	31	31	7	2	0	215	228	27	49	78	11.7	4.10	101	.272	.315	0	—	0	-2	1	3	0.3
1981	Sea-A	4	9	.308	22	20	1	0	0	130¹	127	14	28	35	10.7	3.94	98	.258	.298	0	—	0	-4	-1	-0	-0.2
1983	Sea-A	5	3	.625	14	14	2	0	0	82¹	103	9	15	38	13.3	4.59	93	.311	.349	0	—	0	-5	-3	-0	-0.2
	Det-A	2	1	.667	7	7	1	1	0	46²	43	5	7	11	9.6	1.93	203	.244	.273	0	—	0	11	10	-0	1.1
	Yr	7	4	.636	21	21	3	1	0	129	146	14	22	49	11.7	3.63	114	.285	.314	0	—	0	6	7	-1	0.9
1984	Det-A	3	4	.429	13	8	1	0	0	44	62	9	8	8	14.7	5.93	66	.326	.360	0	—	0	-9	-10	1	-0.8
Total	11	62	83	.428	248	206	37	5	0	1286	1405	162	352	484	12.5	4.39	89	.280	.331	0	—	0	-69	-67	3	-5.4

■ AL ABER
Aber, Albert Julius "Lefty" b: 7/31/27, Cleveland, Ohio BL/TL, 6'2", 195 lbs. Deb: 9/15/50

YEAR	TM/L	W	L	PCT	G	GS	CG	SH	SV	IP	H	HR	BB	SO	RAT	ERA	ERA+	OAV	OOB	BH	AVG	PB	PR	/A	PD	TPI
1950	Cle-A	1	0	1.000	1	1	1	0	0	9	5	0	4	4	9.0	2.00	217	.167	.265	0	.000	0	3	2	0	0.2
1953	Cle-A	1	1	.500	6	0	0	0	0	6	6	0	9	4	22.5	7.50	50	.240	.441	0	—	1	-2	-2	0	-0.1
	Det-A	4	3	.571	17	10	2	0	0	66²	63	3	41	34	14.0	4.45	91	.260	.367	3	.130	-1	-3	-3	1	-0.2
	Yr	5	4	.556	23	10	2	0	0	72²	69	3	50	38	14.7	4.71	86	.258	.375	3	.130	-1	-6	-5	1	-0.3
1954	Det-A	5	11	.313	32	18	4	0	3	124²	121	8	40	54	11.8	3.97	93	.257	.320	5	.128	-1	-3	-4	1	-0.4
1955	Det-A	6	3	.667	39	1	0	0	9	80	86	9	28	37	12.8	3.37	114	.275	.334	1	.059	-2	5	4	1	0.3
1956	Det-A	4	4	.500	42	0	0	0	7	63	65	1	25	21	13.1	3.43	120	.270	.343	3	.300	1	5	5	0	0.6
1957	Det-A	3	3	.500	28	0	0	0	1	37	46	6	11	15	14.1	6.81	57	.315	.367	1	.125	-0	-12	-12	1	-1.1
	KC-A	0	0	—	3	0	0	0	0	3	6	2	2	0	24.0	12.00	33	.400	.471	1	1.000	0	-3	-3	0	-0.1
	Yr	3	3	.500	31	0	0	0	1	40	52	8	13	15	14.6	7.20	54	.317	.367	1	.111	0	-15	-15	1	-1.2
Total	6	24	25	.490	168	30	7	0	14	389¹	398	29	160	169	13.0	4.18	93	.269	.342	14	.140	-3	-11	-13	3	-0.8

■ BILL ABERNATHIE
Abernathie, William Edward b: 1/30/29, Torrance, Cal. BR/TR, 5'10", 190 lbs. Deb: 9/27/52

YEAR	TM/L	W	L	PCT	G	GS	CG	SH	SV	IP	H	HR	BB	SO	RAT	ERA	ERA+	OAV	OOB	BH	AVG	PB	PR	/A	PD	TPI
1952	Cle-A	0	0	—	1	0	0	0	1	2	4	1	1	0	22.5	13.50	25	.444	.500	0	.000	-0	-2	-2	0	-0.1

■ TED ABERNATHY
Abernathy, Talmadge Lafayette b: 10/30/21, Bynum, N.C. BR/TL, 6'2", 210 lbs. Deb: 9/19/42

YEAR	TM/L	W	L	PCT	G	GS	CG	SH	SV	IP	H	HR	BB	SO	RAT	ERA	ERA+	OAV	OOB	BH	AVG	PB	PR	/A	PD	TPI
1942	Phi-A	0	0	—	1	0	0	0	0	2²	2	0	3	1	16.9	10.13	37	.222	.417	0	—	0	-2	-2	0	0.0
1943	Phi-A	0	3	.000	5	2	1	0	0	14²	24	0	13	10	22.7	12.89	26	.353	.457	1	.250	0	-16	-15	0	-1.3
1944	Phi-A	0	0	—	1	0	0	0	0	3	5	0	1	2	18.0	3.00	116	.417	.462	0	.000	-0	0	0	0	0.0
Total	3	0	3	.000	7	2	1	0	0	20¹	31	0	17	13	21.2	11.07	31	.348	.453	1	.200	0	-17	-17	0	-1.3

■ TED ABERNATHY
Abernathy, Theodore Wade b: 3/6/33, Stanley, N.C. BR/TR, 6'4", 215 lbs. Deb: 4/13/55

YEAR	TM/L	W	L	PCT	G	GS	CG	SH	SV	IP	H	HR	BB	SO	RAT	ERA	ERA+	OAV	OOB	BH	AVG	PB	PR	/A	PD	TPI
1955	Was-A	5	9	.357	40	14	3	2	0	119¹	136	9	67	79	15.8	5.96	64	.294	.392	4	.154	-1	-26	-28	1	-2.7
1956	Was-A	1	3	.250	5	4	2	0	0	30¹	35	2	10	18	13.6	4.15	104	.292	.351	2	.182	-0	0	1	2	0.0
1957	Was-A	2	10	.167	26	16	2	0	0	85	100	9	65	50	17.9	6.78	57	.314	.437	4	.167	0	-28	-27	1	-2.4
1960	Was-A	0	0	—	2	0	0	0	0	3	4	0	4	1	24.0	12.00	32	.308	.471	1	1.000	0	-3	-3	0	-0.1
1963	Cle-A	7	2	.778	43	0	0	0	12	59¹	54	3	29	47	12.6	2.88	126	.251	.340	2	.400	1	5	5	2	0.8
1964	Cle-A	2	6	.250	53	0	0	0	11	72²	66	5	46	57	14.1	4.33	83	.247	.362	0	.000	0	-6	-6	3	-0.3
1965	Chi-N	4	6	.400	84	0	0	0	31	136¹	113	7	56	104	11.5	2.57	143	.227	.311	3	.167	0	15	17	4	2.3
1966	Chi-N	1	3	.250	20	0	0	0	4	27²	26	4	17	18	14.6	6.18	60	.255	.372	0	.000	-0	-8	-8	2	-0.6
	Atl-N	4	4	.500	38	0	0	0	4	65¹	58	5	36	42	12.9	3.86	94	.247	.347	2	.250	1	-2	-2	1	-0.1
	Yr	5	7	.417	58	0	0	0	8	93	84	9	53	60	13.3	4.55	80	.248	.349	2	.083	1	-10	-9	2	-0.6
1967	Cin-N	6	3	.667	70	0	0	0	28	106¹	63	1	41	88	9.2	1.27	295	.170	.261	1	.059	-1	25	29	1	3.3
1968	Cin-N	10	7	.588	78	0	0	0	13	134²	111	9	55	64	11.4	2.47	128	.228	.312	0	.000	-1	8	10	4	1.5
1969	Chi-N	4	3	.571	56	0	0	0	0	85¹	75	9	42	55	12.4	3.16	127	.234	.325	2	.250	0	4	8	2	1.2
1970	Chi-N	0	0	—	11	0	0	0	1	9	9	0	5	2	15.0	2.00	225	.281	.395	0	—	0	2	3	0	0.3
	StL-N	1	0	1.000	11	0	0	0	1	18¹	15	0	12	8	14.7	2.95	140	.246	.395	0	.000	-0	2	1	1	0.3
	Yr	1	0	1.000	22	0	0	0	2	27¹	24	0	17	10	14.5	2.63	161	.255	.386	0	.000	-0	4	5	2	0.6

YEAR	TM/L	W	L	PCT	G	GS	CG	SH	SV	IP	H	HR	BB	SO	RAT	ERA	ERA+	OAV	OOB	BH	AVG	PB	PR	/A	PD	TPI
	KC-A	9	3	.750	36	0	0	0	12	55²	41	3	38	49	12.9	2.59	144	.209	.340	3	.214	0	7	7	0	0.8
1971	KC-A	4	6	.400	63	0	0	0	23	81	60	3	50	55	12.9	2.56	134	.210	.339	1	.077	-1	8	8	2	0.9
1972	KC-A	3	4	.429	45	0	0	0	5	58¹	44	2	19	28	10.2	1.70	179	.210	.284	0	.000	-1	9	9	1	1.0
Total	14	63	69	.477	681	34	7	2	148	1147²	1010	70	592	765	12.9	3.46	106	.241	.341	25	.138	-4	12	26	26	6.5

■ WOODY ABERNATHY
Abernathy, Virgil Woodrow b: 2/1/15, Forest City, N.C. BL/TL, 6', 170 lbs. Deb: 7/28/46

YEAR	TM/L	W	L	PCT	G	GS	CG	SH	SV	IP	H	HR	BB	SO	RAT	ERA	ERA+	OAV	OOB	BH	AVG	PB	PR	/A	PD	TPI
1946	NY-N	1	1	.500	15	1	0	0	1	40	32	5	10	6	9.4	3.37	102	.232	.284	0	.000	-1	0	0	-0	0.0
1947	NY-N	0	0	—	1	0	0	0	0	2	4	0	1	0	22.5	9.00	45	.400	.455	0	—	0	-1	-1	0	0.0
Total	2	1	1	.500	16	1	0	0	1	42	36	5	11	6	10.1	3.64	95	.243	.296	0	.000	-1	-1	-1	-0	0.0

■ HARRY ABLES
Ables, Harry Terrell "Hans" b: 10/4/1884, Terrell, Tex. d: 2/8/51, San Antonio, Tex. BR/TL, 6'2.5", 200 lbs. Deb: 9/04/05

YEAR	TM/L	W	L	PCT	G	GS	CG	SH	SV	IP	H	HR	BB	SO	RAT	ERA	ERA+	OAV	OOB	BH	AVG	PB	PR	/A	PD	TPI
1905	StL-A	0	3	.000	6	3	1	0	0	30²	37	0	13	11	14.7	3.82	67	.299	.366	0	.000	-1	-4	-4	-1	-0.6
1909	Cle-A	1	1	.500	5	3	3	0	0	29²	26	1	10	24	11.2	2.12	120	.226	.294	0	.000	-2	1	1	-1	0.0
1911	NY-A	0	1	.000	3	2	0	0	0	11	16	0	7	6	18.8	9.82	37	.333	.418	0	.000	-1	-8	-8	-0	-0.6
Total	3	1	5	.167	14	8	4	0	0	71¹	79	1	30	41	13.9	4.04	67	.276	.346	0	.000	-4	-11	-11	-2	-1.2

■ GEORGE ABRAMS
Abrams, George Allen b: 11/9/1899, Seattle, Wash. d: 12/5/86, Clearwater, Fla. BR/TR, 5'9", 170 lbs. Deb: 4/19/23

YEAR	TM/L	W	L	PCT	G	GS	CG	SH	SV	IP	H	HR	BB	SO	RAT	ERA	ERA+	OAV	OOB	BH	AVG	PB	PR	/A	PD	TPI
1923	Cin-N	0	0	—	3	0	0	0	0	4²	10	0	3	1	27.0	9.64	40	.500	.583	1	1.000	0	-3	-3	0	-0.1

■ JOHNNY ABREGO
Abrego, Johnny Ray b: 7/4/62, Corpus Christi, Tex. BR/TR, 6', 185 lbs. Deb: 9/04/85

YEAR	TM/L	W	L	PCT	G	GS	CG	SH	SV	IP	H	HR	BB	SO	RAT	ERA	ERA+	OAV	OOB	BH	AVG	PB	PR	/A	PD	TPI
1985	Chi-N	1	1	.500	6	5	0	0	0	24	32	3	12	13	16.5	6.38	63	.352	.427	0	.000	-1	-7	-6	0	-0.6

■ JIM ACKER
Acker, James Justin b: 9/24/58, Freer, Tex. BR/TR, 6'2", 210 lbs. Deb: 4/07/83

YEAR	TM/L	W	L	PCT	G	GS	CG	SH	SV	IP	H	HR	BB	SO	RAT	ERA	ERA+	OAV	OOB	BH	AVG	PB	PR	/A	PD	TPI
1983	Tor-A	5	1	.833	38	5	0	0	1	97²	103	7	38	44	13.7	4.33	99	.273	.352	0	—	0	-3	-0	1	0.1
1984	Tor-A	3	5	.375	32	3	0	0	1	72	79	3	25	33	13.8	4.38	94	.286	.358	0	—	0	-3	-2	-0	-0.1
1985	*Tor-A	7	2	.778	61	0	0	0	10	86¹	86	7	43	42	13.8	3.23	130	.268	.360	0	—	0	9	9	1	1.1
1986	Tor-A	2	4	.333	23	5	0	0	0	60	63	6	22	32	13.1	4.35	97	.281	.351	0	—	0	-1	-1	1	0.0
	Atl-N	3	8	.273	21	14	0	0	0	95	100	7	26	37	12.0	3.79	105	.274	.324	3	.107	-1	-1	2	1	0.2
1987	Atl-N	4	9	.308	68	0	0	0	14	114²	109	11	51	68	12.9	4.16	104	.253	.338	3	.214	-1	-1	1	0	0.4
1988	Atl-N	0	4	.000	21	1	0	0	0	42	45	6	14	25	12.9	4.71	78	.280	.341	2	.400	1	-6	-5	0	-0.3
1989	Atl-N	0	6	.000	59	0	0	0	2	97²	84	5	20	68	9.7	2.67	137	.237	.280	1	.143	-0	9	11	1	1.2
	*Tor-A	2	1	.667	14	0	0	0	0	28¹	24	1	12	24	11.8	1.59	237	.235	.322	0	—	0	7	7	1	0.8
1990	Tor-A	4	4	.500	59	0	0	0	1	91²	103	9	30	54	13.4	3.83	99	.281	.341	0	—	0	1	-0	1	0.1
Total	8	30	44	.405	396	28	0	0	29	785¹	796	62	281	427	12.7	3.78	107	.267	.337	9	.167	-1	11	23	9	3.5

■ TOM ACKER
Acker, Thomas James b: 3/7/30, Paterson, N.J. BR/TR, 6'4", 215 lbs. Deb: 4/20/56

YEAR	TM/L	W	L	PCT	G	GS	CG	SH	SV	IP	H	HR	BB	SO	RAT	ERA	ERA+	OAV	OOB	BH	AVG	PB	PR	/A	PD	TPI
1956	Cin-N	4	3	.571	29	7	1	1	1	83²	60	7	29	54	9.8	2.37	168	.201	.277	1	.053	-1	13	15	1	1.5
1957	Cin-N	10	5	.667	49	6	1	0	4	108²	122	16	41	67	14.2	4.97	83	.293	.368	1	.053	-1	-13	-10	-0	-1.0
1958	Cin-N	4	3	.571	38	10	3	0	1	124²	126	10	43	90	12.4	4.55	91	.266	.331	2	.067	-1	-8	-6	-2	-0.8
1959	Cin-N	1	2	.333	37	0	0	0	2	63¹	57	10	37	45	13.9	4.12	98	.246	.359	1	.111	-0	-1	-0	-1	-0.1
Total	4	19	13	.594	153	23	5	1	8	380¹	365	43	150	256	12.6	4.12	99	.257	.335	5	.065	-3	-10	-1	-3	-0.4

■ FRITZ ACKLEY
Ackley, Florian Frederick b: 4/10/37, Hayward, Wis. BL/TR, 6'1.5", 202 lbs. Deb: 9/21/63

YEAR	TM/L	W	L	PCT	G	GS	CG	SH	SV	IP	H	HR	BB	SO	RAT	ERA	ERA+	OAV	OOB	BH	AVG	PB	PR	/A	PD	TPI
1963	Chi-A	1	0	1.000	2	2	0	0	0	13	7	2	7	11	9.7	2.08	169	.167	.286	1	.200	0	2	2	0	0.3
1964	Chi-A	0	0	—	3	2	0	0	0	6¹	10	2	4	6	19.9	8.53	41	.345	.424	1	1.000	1	-3	-4	0	-0.1
Total	2	1	0	1.000	5	4	0	0	0	19¹	17	4	11	17	13.0	4.19	83	.239	.341	2	.333	1	-1	-2	1	0.2

■ CY ACOSTA
Acosta, Cecilio (Miranda) b: 11/22/46, Sabino, Mexico BR/TR, 5'10", 165 lbs. Deb: 6/04/72

YEAR	TM/L	W	L	PCT	G	GS	CG	SH	SV	IP	H	HR	BB	SO	RAT	ERA	ERA+	OAV	OOB	BH	AVG	PB	PR	/A	PD	TPI
1972	Chi-A	3	0	1.000	26	0	0	0	5	34²	25	2	17	28	10.9	1.56	201	.210	.309	0	.000	-0	6	6	-0	0.6
1973	Chi-A	10	6	.625	48	0	0	0	18	97	66	8	39	60	10.4	2.23	178	.193	.289	0	.000	0	17	19	-1	1.8
1974	Chi-A	0	3	.000	27	0	0	0	3	45²	43	3	18	19	13.0	3.74	100	.256	.346	0	.000	-1	-0	0	0	0.0
1975	Phi-N	0	0	—	6	0	0	0	1	8²	9	2	3	2	12.5	6.23	60	.273	.333	0	—	0	-3	-2	-0	-0.2
Total	4	13	9	.591	107	0	0	0	27	186	143	15	77	109	11.2	2.66	140	.216	.309	0	.000	-0	20	22	-2	2.2

■ ED ACOSTA
Acosta, Eduardo Elixbet b: 3/9/44, Boquete, Panama BB/TR, 6'5", 215 lbs. Deb: 9/07/70

YEAR	TM/L	W	L	PCT	G	GS	CG	SH	SV	IP	H	HR	BB	SO	RAT	ERA	ERA+	OAV	OOB	BH	AVG	PB	PR	/A	PD	TPI
1970	Pit-N	0	0	—	3	0	0	0	1	2²	5	1	2	1	27.0	13.50	29	.417	.533	0	—	0	-3	-3	0	-0.2
1971	SD-N	3	3	.500	8	6	3	1	0	46	43	4	7	16	9.8	2.74	120	.246	.275	0	.000	-2	4	3	-0	0.1
1972	SD-N	3	6	.333	46	2	0	0	0	89	105	7	30	53	14.0	4.45	74	.302	.362	1	.083	-0	-10	-11	-1	-1.2
Total	3	6	9	.400	57	8	3	1	1	137²	153	12	39	70	12.8	4.05	81	.286	.339	1	.034	-2	-9	-11	-1	-1.3

■ JOSE ACOSTA
Acosta, Jose "Acostica" b: 3/4/1891, Havana, Cuba d: 11/16/77, Havana, Cuba BR/TR, 5'6", 134 lbs. Deb: 7/28/20

YEAR	TM/L	W	L	PCT	G	GS	CG	SH	SV	IP	H	HR	BB	SO	RAT	ERA	ERA+	OAV	OOB	BH	AVG	PB	PR	/A	PD	TPI
1920	Was-A	5	4	.556	17	5	4	1	1	82²	92	1	26	9	12.8	4.03	93	.290	.344	6	.240	1	-2	-3	-2	-0.3
1921	Was-A	5	4	.556	33	7	2	0	3	115²	148	4	36	30	14.3	4.36	94	.317	.366	2	.067	-2	-1	-3	-1	-0.5
1922	Chi-A	0	2	.000	5	1	0	0	0	15	25	4	6	6	18.6	8.40	48	.417	.470	1	.200	0	-7	-7	-0	-0.6
Total	3	10	10	.500	55	13	6	1	4	213¹	265	9	68	45	14.0	4.51	88	.314	.365	9	.150	-1	-10	-13	-4	-1.4

■ ACE ADAMS
Adams, Ace Townsend b: 3/2/12, Willows, Cal. BR/TR, 5'10.5", 182 lbs. Deb: 4/15/41

YEAR	TM/L	W	L	PCT	G	GS	CG	SH	SV	IP	H	HR	BB	SO	RAT	ERA	ERA+	OAV	OOB	BH	AVG	PB	PR	/A	PD	TPI
1941	NY-N	4	1	.800	38	0	0	0	1	71	84	3	35	18	15.2	4.82	77	.304	.385	1	.083	-1	-9	-9	-1	-1.0
1942	NY-N	7	4	.636	61	0	0	0	11	88	69	1	31	33	10.2	1.84	183	.223	.293	1	.100	-1	14	15	0	1.6
1943	NY-N	11	7	.611	70	3	1	0	9	140¹	121	6	55	46	11.4	2.82	122	.236	.311	4	.125	1	9	10	-0	0.9
1944	NY-N	8	11	.421	65	4	1	0	13	137²	149	8	58	32	13.8	4.25	86	.279	.354	3	.103	-2	-10	-9	-1	-1.1
1945	NY-N	11	9	.550	65	0	0	0	15	113	109	7	44	39	12.3	3.42	114	.252	.324	3	.188	0	5	6	1	0.8
1946	NY-N	0	1	.000	3	0	0	0	0	2²	9	2	1	3	33.8	16.88	30	.500	.526	0	—	0	-4	-4	0	-0.3
Total	6	41	33	.554	302	7	2	0	49	552²	541	26	224	171	12.6	3.47	104	.260	.334	12	.121	-5	5	9	-1	1.9

■ BABE ADAMS
Adams, Charles Benjamin b: 5/18/1882, Tipton, Ind. d: 7/27/68, Silver Spring, Md BL/TR, 5'11.5", 185 lbs. Deb: 4/18/06

YEAR	TM/L	W	L	PCT	G	GS	CG	SH	SV	IP	H	HR	BB	SO	RAT	ERA	ERA+	OAV	OOB	BH	AVG	PB	PR	/A	PD	TPI
1906	StL-N	0	1	.000	1	1	0	0	0	4	9	0	2	0	24.8	13.50	19	.474	.524	0	.000	-0	-5	-5	0	-0.3
1907	Pit-N	0	2	.000	4	3	1	0	0	22	40	1	3	11	18.8	6.95	35	.408	.442	2	.286	0	-11	-11	0	-0.9
1909	*Pit-N	12	3	.800	25	12	7	3	2	130	88	0	23	65	7.9	1.11	196	.196	.240	2	.051	-3	22	23	-1	2.3
1910	Pit-N	18	9	.667	34	30	16	3	0	245	217	4	60	101	10.4	2.24	138	.240	.291	16	.193	1	22	23	-5	2.1
1911	Pit-N	22	12	.647	40	37	24	6	0	293¹	253	5	42	133	9.3	2.33	147	.237	.271	26	.252	4	35	36	-8	3.4
1912	Pit-N	11	8	.579	28	21	11	2	0	170¹	169	4	35	63	10.9	2.91	122	.254	.294	12	.226	4	10	7	-1	0.8
1913	Pit-N	21	10	.677	43	37	24	4	0	313²	271	8	49	144	9.2	2.15	140	.235	.267	33	.289	8	37	30	-1	4.0
1914	Pit-N	13	16	.448	40	35	19	3	1	283	253	5	39	91	9.5	2.51	105	.244	.276	16	.165	1	9	4	-2	0.3
1915	Pit-N	14	14	.500	40	30	17	2	2	245	229	6	34	62	9.7	2.87	95	.252	.280	12	.141	-2	-3	-4	-1	-0.5
1916	Pit-N	2	9	.182	16	10	4	1	0	72¹	91	2	12	22	13.2	5.72	48	.320	.355	6	.223	2	-25	-24	0	-2.2
1918	Pit-N	1	1	.500	3	3	2	0	0	22²	15	0	4	6	7.5	1.19	241	.197	.237	3	.333	1	4	4	-1	0.6
1919	Pit-N	17	10	.630	34	29	23	6	1	263¹	213	1	23	92	8.2	1.98	152	.220	.241	17	.185	-0	27	30	-5	3.0
1920	Pit-N	17	13	.567	35	33	19	8	2	263	240	6	18	84	8.9	2.16	149	.244	.259	13	.146	-5	29	31	-2	2.7
1921	Pit-N	14	5	.737	25	20	11	2	0	160	155	4	18	55	9.7	2.64	145	.251	.272	16	.254	-2	20	21	-2	2.4
1922	Pit-N	8	11	.421	27	19	12	4	0	171¹	191	1	15	39	11.0	3.57	114	.287	.307	16	.286	4	10	10	1	1.4
1923	Pit-N	13	7	.650	26	22	11	0	1	158²	196	8	25	38	12.6	4.42	91	.309	.336	15	.273	4	-7	-7	-2	-0.4
1924	Pit-N	3	1	.750	9	3	2	0	1	39²	31	4	3	5	7.7	1.36	299	.210	.226	2	.182	-0	12	12	-1	1.5
1925	*Pit-N	6	5	.545	33	10	3	0	3	101¹	129	7	17	18	13.2	5.42	82	.306	.338	7	.226	0	-13	-11	-2	-1.0
1926	Pit-N	2	3	.400	19	0	0	0	3	36²	51	7	8	7	14.5	6.14	64	.347	.381	2	.222	-0	-9	-9	-1	-0.8
Total	19	194	140	.581	482	355	206	44	15	2995¹	2841	68	430	1036	10.0	2.76	118	.253	.283	216	.212	23	161	161	-30	18.0

YEAR TM/L	W	L	PCT	G	GS	CG	SH	SV	IP	H	HR	BB	SO	RAT	ERA	ERA+	OAV	OOB	BH	AVG	PB	PR	/A	PD	TPI

■ RED ADAMS   Adams, Charles Dwight   b: 10/7/21, Parlier, Cal.   BR/TR, 6', 185 lbs.   Deb: 5/05/46   C

| 1946 Chi-N | 0 | 1 | .000 | 8 | 0 | 0 | 0 | 0 | 12 | 18 | 1 | 7 | 8 | 18.8 | 8.25 | 40 | .353 | .431 | 0 | .000 | -0 | -6 | -7 | 1 | -0.5 |

■ DAN ADAMS   Adams, Daniel Leslie "Rube"   b: 6/19/1887, St.Louis, Mo.   d: 10/6/64, St.Louis, Mo.   BR/TR, 5'11.5", 165 lbs.   Deb: 5/22/14

1914 KC-F	4	9	.308	36	14	6	0	3	136	141	3	52	38	13.2	3.51	88	.273	.347	7	.152	-1	-5	-6	-0	-0.7
1915 KC-F	0	2	.000	11	2	0	0	0	35	41	2	13	16	14.1	4.63	63	.300	.365	1	.111	-0	-6	-7	0	-0.6
Total 2	4	11	.267	47	16	6	0	3	171	182	5	65	54	13.4	3.74	82	.278	.351	8	.145	-1	-11	-13	0	-1.3

■ JOE ADAMS   Adams, Joseph Edward   b: 10/28/1877, Cowden, Ill.   d: 10/8/52, Montgomery City, Mo   TL , 6', 190 lbs.   Deb: 4/26/02

| 1902 StL-N | 0 | 0 | — | 1 | 0 | 0 | 0 | 0 | 4 | 9 | 0 | 2 | 0 | 27.0 | 9.00 | 30 | .442 | .513 | 0 | .000 | -0 | -3 | -3 | 1 | -0.1 |

■ KARL ADAMS   Adams, Karl Tutwiler "Rebel"   b: 8/11/1891, Columbus, Ga.   d: 9/17/67, Everett, Wash.   BR/TR, 6'2", 170 lbs.   Deb: 4/19/14

1914 Cin-N	0	0	—	4	0	0	0	0	8	14	0	5	5	21.4	9.00	33	.424	.500	1	.500	0	-6	-5	0	-0.4
1915 Chi-N	1	9	.100	26	12	3	0	0	107	105	5	43	57	12.6	4.71	59	.267	.342	0	.000	-4	-23	-23	0	-2.7
Total 2	1	9	.100	30	12	3	0	0	115	119	5	48	62	13.2	5.01	56	.279	.355	1	.031	-4	-29	-28	0	-3.1

■ RICK ADAMS   Adams, Reuben Alexander   b: 12/23/1878, Paris, Tex.   d: 3/10/55, Paris, Tex.   BL/TL, 6', 165 lbs.   Deb: 7/13/05

| 1905 Was-A | 2 | 5 | .286 | 11 | 6 | 3 | 1 | 0 | 62² | 63 | 1 | 24 | 25 | 12.5 | 3.59 | 74 | .263 | .330 | 4 | .174 | 1 | -6 | -7 | 0 | -0.5 |

■ BOB ADAMS   Adams, Robert Andrew   b: 1/20/07, Birmingham, Ala.   d: 3/6/70, Jacksonville, Fla.   BR/TR, 6'0.5", 165 lbs.   Deb: 9/27/31

1931 Phi-N	0	1	.000	1	1	0	0	0	6	14	0	1	3	22.5	9.00	47	.424	.441	0	.000	-0	-3	-3	-0	-0.2
1932 Phi-N	0	0	—	4	0	0	0	0	6	7	0	2	2	13.5	1.50	294	.318	.375	0	—	0	2	2	0	0.2
Total 2	0	1	.000	5	1	0	0	0	12	21	0	3	5	18.0	5.25	82	.382	.414	0	.000	-0	-2	-1	0	0.0

■ BOB ADAMS   Adams, Robert Burdette   b: 7/24/01, Holyoke, Mass.   BR/TR, 5'11", 168 lbs.   Deb: 9/22/25

| 1925 Bos-A | 0 | 0 | — | 2 | 0 | 0 | 0 | 0 | 5² | 10 | 1 | 3 | 1 | 20.6 | 7.94 | 57 | .417 | .481 | 1 | .333 | 0 | -2 | -2 | 1 | 0.0 |

■ WILLIE ADAMS   Adams, William John Irvin   b: 9/27/1890, Clearfield, Pa.   d: 6/18/37, Albany, N.Y.   BR/TR, 6'4", 180 lbs.   Deb: 6/30/12

1912 StL-A	2	3	.400	13	5	0	0	0	46¹	50	0	19	16	13.8	3.88	85	.284	.360	0	.000	-2	-3	-3	-1	-0.5
1913 StL-A	0	0	—	4	0	0	0	0	9	12	1	4	5	19.0	10.00	29	.286	.388	0	.000	0	-7	-7	-0	-0.6
1914 Pit-F	1	1	.500	15	2	1	0	2	55¹	70	4	22	14	15.1	3.74	85	.326	.391	1	.067	-1	-3	-3	-1	-0.5
1918 Phi-A	5	12	.294	32	14	7	0	0	169	164	2	97	39	14.5	4.42	66	.272	.383	8	.140	-3	-31	-28	1	-3.1
1919 Phi-A	0	0	—	1	0	0	0	0	4²	7	1	2	0	19.3	3.86	89	.389	.476	0	.000	-0	-0	-0	0	0.0
Total 5	8	16	.333	65	21	8	0	2	284¹	303	8	144	74	14.8	4.37	70	.287	.383	9	.102	-6	-44	-41	-2	-4.7

■ MIKE ADAMSON   Adamson, John Michael   b: 9/13/47, San Diego, Cal.   BR/TR, 6'2", 185 lbs.   Deb: 7/01/67

1967 Bal-A	0	1	.000	3	2	0	0	0	9²	9	1	8	12	19.6	8.38	38	.257	.447	1	.500	1	-6	-6	-0	-0.4
1968 Bal-A	0	2	.000	2	2	0	0	0	7²	9	2	4	4	15.3	9.39	31	.281	.361	1	.333	0	-5	-6	-0	-0.4
1969 Bal-A	0	1	.000	6	0	0	0	0	8	10	0	6	2	18.0	4.50	79	.357	.471	0	.000	-0	-1	-1	1	0.0
Total 3	0	4	.000	11	4	0	0	0	25¹	28	3	22	14	17.8	7.46	43	.295	.427	2	.333	1	-12	-12	0	-0.8

■ GRADY ADKINS   Adkins, Grady Emmett "Butcher Boy"   b: 6/29/1897, Jacksonville, Ark   d: 3/31/66, Little Rock, Ark.   BR/TR, 5'11", 175 lbs.   Deb: 4/13/28

1928 Chi-A	10	16	.385	36	27	14	0	1	224²	235	12	89	54	13.2	3.73	109	.278	.351	10	.143	-3	8	8	-0	0.4
1929 Chi-A	2	11	.154	31	15	5	0	0	138¹	168	12	67	24	15.4	5.33	80	.303	.379	11	.239	3	-17	-16	2	-1.0
Total 2	12	27	.308	67	42	19	0	1	363	403	24	156	78	14.0	4.34	95	.288	.363	21	.181	-1	-9	-8	1	-0.6

■ DEWEY ADKINS   Adkins, John Dewey   b: 5/11/18, Norcatur, Kan.   BR/TR, 6'2", 195 lbs.   Deb: 9/19/42

1942 Was-A	0	0	—	1	1	0	0	0	6¹	7	0	6	3	18.5	9.95	37	.259	.394	1	.500	0	-4	-4	-0	-0.3
1943 Was-A	0	0	—	7	0	0	0	0	10¹	9	0	5	1	12.2	2.61	123	.250	.341	0	—	0	1	1	-0	0.0
1949 Chi-N	2	4	.333	30	5	1	0	0	82¹	98	10	39	43	15.0	5.68	71	.298	.372	4	.200	1	-15	-15	1	-1.2
Total 3	2	4	.333	38	6	1	0	0	99	114	10	50	47	14.9	5.64	70	.291	.371	5	.227	1	-19	-19	1	-1.5

■ DOC ADKINS   Adkins, Merle Theron   b: 8/5/1872, Troy, Wis.   d: 2/21/34, Durham, N.C.   TR , 5'10.5", 220 lbs.   Deb: 6/24/02

1902 Bos-A	1	1	.500	4	2	1	0	0	20	30	2	7	3	16.6	4.05	88	.346	.395	2	.222	-0	-1	-1	0	0.0
1903 NY-A	0	0	—	2	1	0	0	1	7	10	0	5	0	19.3	7.71	40	.334	.429	0	.000	-0	-4	-4	-0	-0.3
Total 2	1	1	.500	6	3	1	0	1	27	40	2	12	3	17.3	5.00	69	.343	.404	2	.167	-1	-5	-5	0	-0.3

■ STEVE ADKINS   Adkins, Steven Thomas   b: 10/26/64, Chicago, Ill.   BR/TL, 6'6", 210 lbs.   Deb: 9/12/90

| 1990 NY-A | 1 | 2 | .333 | 5 | 5 | 0 | 0 | 0 | 24 | 19 | 4 | 29 | 14 | 18.0 | 6.38 | 62 | .226 | .425 | 0 | — | 0 | -7 | -6 | -0 | -0.5 |

■ JUAN AGOSTO   Agosto, Juan Roberto (Gonzalez)   b: 2/23/58, Rio Piedras, P.R.   BL/TL, 6', 175 lbs.   Deb: 9/07/81

1981 Chi-A	0	0	—	2	0	0	0	0	5²	5	1	0	3	9.5	4.76	75	.238	.273	0	—	0	-1	-1	0	0.0
1982 Chi-A	0	0	—	1	0	0	0	0	2	7	0	1	0	31.5	18.00	22	.538	.538	0	—	0	-3	-3	0	-0.2
1983 *Chi-A	2	2	.500	39	0	0	0	7	41²	41	2	11	29	11.4	4.10	102	.283	.338	0	—	0	-0	0	0	0.1
1984 Chi-A	2	1	.667	49	0	0	0	7	55¹	54	2	34	26	14.8	3.09	135	.270	.384	0	—	0	6	7	3	0.9
1985 Chi-A	4	3	.571	54	0	0	0	1	60¹	45	3	23	39	10.6	3.58	121	.210	.296	0	—	0	4	5	2	0.7
1986 Chi-A	0	2	.000	9	0	0	0	0	4²	6	0	4	3	19.3	7.71	56	.300	.417	0	—	0	-2	-2	-0	-0.1
Min-A	1	2	.333	17	1	0	0	1	20¹	43	1	14	9	26.1	8.85	49	.443	.522	0	—	0	-11	-10	-0	-0.9
Yr	1	4	.200	26	1	0	0	1	25	49	1	18	12	24.8	8.64	50	.419	.504	0	—	0	-12	-12	0	-1.0
1987 Hou-N	1	1	.500	27	0	0	0	2	27¹	26	1	10	6	11.9	2.63	149	.248	.313	0	.000	-0	4	4	1	0.5
1988 Hou-N	10	2	.833	75	0	0	0	4	91²	74	6	30	33	10.2	2.26	147	.226	.291	0	.000	0	12	11	5	1.6
1989 Hou-N	4	5	.444	71	0	0	0	1	83	81	3	32	46	12.5	2.93	116	.256	.329	1	.200	0	5	4	1	0.6
1990 Hou-N	9	8	.529	82	0	0	0	4	92¹	91	4	39	50	13.4	4.29	87	.261	.347	0	.000	-0	-5	-6	2	-0.3
Total 10	33	26	.559	426	1	0	0	27	484¹	473	23	197	245	12.8	3.62	105	.262	.341	1	.077	-1	10	9	14	2.9

■ RICK AGUILERA   Aguilera, Richard Warren   b: 12/31/61, San Gabriel, Cal.   BR/TR, 6'4", 195 lbs.   Deb: 6/12/85

1985 NY-N	10	7	.588	21	19	2	0	0	122¹	118	8	37	74	11.6	3.24	107	.258	.317	10	.278	3	5	3	-0	0.6
1986 *NY-N	10	7	.588	28	20	2	0	0	141²	145	15	36	104	11.9	3.88	91	.263	.316	8	.157	2	-2	-5	2	-0.1
1987 NY-N	11	3	.786	18	17	1	0	0	115	124	12	33	77	12.5	3.60	105	.276	.330	9	.225	3	6	2	2	0.7
1988 *NY-N	0	4	.000	11	3	0	0	0	24²	29	2	10	16	14.6	6.93	46	.296	.367	1	.250	0	-10	-10	0	-0.9
1989 NY-N	6	6	.500	36	0	0	0	7	69¹	59	3	21	80	10.6	2.34	140	.231	.295	0	.000	-0	9	7	-1	0.7
Min-A	3	5	.375	11	11	3	0	0	75²	71	5	17	57	10.6	3.21	129	.245	.289	0	—	0	6	8	1	0.9
1990 Min-A	5	3	.625	56	0	0	0	32	65¹	55	5	19	61	10.7	2.76	152	.224	.291	0	—	0	8	10	-1	1.0
Total 6	45	35	.563	181	70	8	0	39	614	601	50	173	469	11.6	3.44	106	.256	.313	28	.203	8	22	15	3	2.9

■ HANK AGUIRRE   Aguirre, Henry John   b: 1/31/32, Azusa, Cal.   BR/TL, 6'4", 205 lbs.   Deb: 9/10/55   C

1955 Cle-A	2	0	1.000	4	1	1	1	0	12²	6	0	12	6	12.8	1.42	281	.143	.333	0	.000	-1	4	4	-0	0.3
1956 Cle-A	3	5	.375	16	9	2	1	1	65¹	63	7	31	12.5	3.72	113	.253	.329	2	.111	-2	3	4	-1	0.1
1957 Cle-A	1	1	.500	10	1	0	0	0	20¹	26	0	13	9	17.3	5.75	65	.317	.411	0	.000	-1	-4	-5	-0	-0.4
1958 Det-A	3	4	.429	44	3	0	0	5	69²	67	5	27	38	12.3	3.75	108	.255	.326	3	.214	0	0	2	1	0.4
1959 Det-A	0	0	—	3	0	0	0	0	2²	4	0	3	2	23.6	3.38	120	.364	.500	0	—	0	0	0	0	0.0
1960 Det-A	5	3	.625	37	6	1	0	10	94²	75	7	30	80	10.3	2.85	139	.217	.286	1	.036	-3	11	12	-2	0.7
1961 Det-A	4	4	.500	45	0	0	0	8	55¹	44	5	38	32	13.7	3.25	126	.224	.356	0	.000	-1	5	5	-1	0.3
1962 Det-A	16	8	.667	42	22	11	2	3	216	162	14	65	156	9.7	2.21	184	.205	.269	2	.027	-8	42	45	-4	3.5
1963 Det-A	14	15	.483	38	33	14	3	0	225²	222	25	68	134	11.9	3.67	102	.256	.316	10	.132	-2	-1	2	-3	-0.2
1964 Det-A	5	10	.333	32	27	3	0	1	161²	134	15	59	88	11.2	3.79	97	.223	.301	3	.057	-4	-3	-2	-3	-0.8

YEAR	TM/L	W	L	PCT	G	GS	CG	SH	SV	IP	H	HR	BB	SO	RAT	ERA	ERA+	OAV	OOB	BH	AVG	PB	PR	/A	PD	TPI
1965	Det-A	14	10	.583	32	32	10	2	0	208^1	185	24	60	141	11.0	3.59	97	.236	.298	6	.086	-3	-3	-3	-1	-0.5
1966	Det-A	3	9	.250	30	14	2	0	0	103^2	104	14	26	50	11.5	3.82	91	.260	.310	3	.120	0	-4	-4	-1	-0.4
1967	Det-A	0	1	.000	31	1	0	0	0	41^1	34	2	17	33	11.1	2.40	136	.219	.297	1	.500	1	4	4	0	0.6
1968	LA-N	1	2	.333	25	0	0	0	0	39^1	32	0	13	25	11.0	0.69	403	.227	.306	0	.000	-0	10	9	-1	0.9
1969	Chi-N	1	0	1.000	41	0	0	0	1	45	45	2	12	19	11.8	2.60	155	.269	.326	2	.400	1	5	7	1	0.9
1970	Chi-N	3	0	1.000	17	0	0	0	1	14	13	3	9	11	14.8	4.50	100	.250	.371	0	.000	-0	-1	0	-0	0.0
Total 16		75	72	.510	447	149	44	9	33	1375^2	1216	123	479	856	11.4	3.24	116	.236	.307	33	.085	-21	67	79	-14	5.4

■ EDDIE AINSMITH   Ainsmith, Edward Wilbur "Dorf"   b: 2/4/1892, Cambridge, Mass.   d: 9/6/81, Ft.Lauderdale, Fla   BR/TR, 5'11", 180 lbs.   Deb: 8/09/10 ♦

YEAR	TM/L	W	L	PCT	G	GS	CG	SH	SV	IP	H	HR	BB	SO	RAT	ERA	ERA+	OAV	OOB	BH	AVG	PB	PR	/A	PD	TPI
1913	Was-A	0	0	—	1	0	0	0	0	0^1	2	0	0	0	54.0	54.00	5	.667	.667	49	.214	0	-2	-2	0	-0.1

■ RALEIGH AITCHISON   Aitchison, Raleigh Leonidas   b: 12/5/1887, Tyndall, S.D.   d: 9/26/58, Columbus, Kan.   BR/TL, 5'11.5", 175 lbs.   Deb: 4/19/11

YEAR	TM/L	W	L	PCT	G	GS	CG	SH	SV	IP	H	HR	BB	SO	RAT	ERA	ERA+	OAV	OOB	BH	AVG	PB	PR	/A	PD	TPI
1911	Bro-N	0	1	.000	1	0	0	0	0	1^1	1	0	1	0	13.5	0.00	—	.200	.333	0	—	0	1	0	0	0.0
1914	Bro-N	12	7	.632	26	17	8	3	0	172^1	156	4	60	87	11.4	2.66	107	.244	.312	10	.196	1	2	4	-3	0.2
1915	Bro-N	0	4	.000	7	5	2	0	0	32^2	36	3	6	14	12.1	4.96	56	.267	.308	0	.000	-0	-8	-8	0	-0.7
Total 3		12	12	.500	34	22	10	3	0	206^1	193	7	67	101	11.6	3.01	95	.247	.311	10	.169	1	-5	-4	-3	-0.5

■ JACK AKER   Aker, Jackie Delane   b: 7/13/40, Tulare, Cal.   BR/TR, 6'2", 190 lbs.   Deb: 5/03/64   C

YEAR	TM/L	W	L	PCT	G	GS	CG	SH	SV	IP	H	HR	BB	SO	RAT	ERA	ERA+	OAV	OOB	BH	AVG	PB	PR	/A	PD	TPI
1964	KC-A	0	1	.000	9	0	0	0	0	16^1	17	6	10	7	18.2	8.82	43	.266	.412	0	.000	-0	-9	-9	1	-0.8
1965	KC-A	4	3	.571	34	0	0	0	3	51^1	45	3	18	26	11.6	3.16	111	.242	.319	0	.000	-1	2	2	1	0.2
1966	KC-A	8	4	.667	66	0	0	0	**32**	113	81	9	28	68	8.9	1.99	171	.201	.258	2	.095	-1	**18**	**18**	3	2.2
1967	KC-A	3	8	.273	57	0	0	0	12	88	87	9	32	65	12.5	4.30	74	.264	.334	1	.125	-0	-10	-11	2	-0.9
1968	Oak-A	4	4	.500	54	0	0	0	11	74^2	72	6	33	44	13.4	4.10	69	.258	.349	1	.143	-0	-9	-11	0	-1.1
1969	Sea-A	0	2	.000	15	0	0	0	3	16^2	25	4	13	7	21.1	7.56	48	.357	.464	0	.000	0	-7	-7	1	-0.6
	NY-A	8	4	.667	38	0	0	0	11	65^2	51	4	22	40	10.6	2.06	169	.217	.295	1	.111	-0	11	10	2	1.2
	Yr	8	6	.571	53	0	0	0	14	82^1	76	8	35	47	12.6	3.17	111	.248	.333	1	.100	-0	4	3	2	0.6
1970	NY-A	4	2	.667	41	0	0	0	16	70	57	3	20	36	10.4	2.06	171	.226	.293	1	.063	-0	13	11	0	1.1
1971	NY-A	4	4	.500	41	0	0	0	4	55^2	48	5	26	24	12.0	2.59	125	.238	.325	0	.000	-0	5	4	1	0.5
1972	NY-A	0	0	—	4	0	0	0	0	6	5	0	3	1	13.5	3.00	98	.238	.360	0	—	0	-0	-1	0	0.1
	Chi-N	6	6	.500	48	0	0	0	17	67	65	4	23	36	12.5	2.96	129	.259	.333	0	.000	-0	4	6	2	0.8
1973	Chi-N	4	5	.444	47	0	0	0	12	63^2	76	4	23	25	14.3	4.10	96	.308	.371	0	.000	-1	-3	-1	2	0.0
1974	Atl-N	0	1	.000	17	0	0	0	0	16^2	17	3	9	7	14.0	3.78	100	.298	.394	0	.000	-0	-0	-0	0	0.0
	NY-N	2	1	.667	24	0	0	0	2	41^1	33	4	14	18	10.7	3.48	102	.213	.287	1	.500	-0	1	0	-1	0.0
	Yr	2	2	.500	41	0	0	0	2	58	50	7	23	25	11.6	3.57	102	.234	.314	1	.000	1	0	-0	-0	0.0
Total 11		47	45	.511	495	0	0	0	123	746	679	64	274	404	12.0	3.28	105	.247	.324	7	.076	-5	14	13	14	2.7

■ DARREL AKERFELDS   Akerfelds, Darrel Wayne   b: 6/12/62, Denver, Colo.   BR/TR, 6'2", 210 lbs.   Deb: 8/01/86

YEAR	TM/L	W	L	PCT	G	GS	CG	SH	SV	IP	H	HR	BB	SO	RAT	ERA	ERA+	OAV	OOB	BH	AVG	PB	PR	/A	PD	TPI
1986	Oak-A	0	0	—	2	0	0	0	0	5^1	7	2	3	5	16.9	6.75	57	.304	.385	0	—	0	-2	-2	0	0.0
1987	Cle-A	2	6	.250	16	13	1	0	0	74^2	84	18	38	42	15.5	6.75	67	.284	.378	0	—	0	-19	-18	-0	-1.6
1989	Tex-A	0	1	.000	6	0	0	0	0	11	11	1	5	9	13.1	3.27	121	.250	.327	0	—	0	1	1	0	0.1
1990	Phi-N	5	2	.714	71	0	0	0	3	93	65	10	54	42	11.8	3.77	101	.201	.320	1	.167	-0	0	0	0	0.0
Total 4		7	9	.438	95	13	1	0	3	184	167	31	100	98	13.5	5.04	82	.243	.348	1	.167	-0	-20	-19	-0	-1.5

■ JERRY AKERS   Akers, Albert Earl   b: 11/1/1887, Shelbyville, Ind.   d: 5/15/79, Bay Pines, Fla.   BR/TR, 5'11", 175 lbs.   Deb: 5/04/12

YEAR	TM/L	W	L	PCT	G	GS	CG	SH	SV	IP	H	HR	BB	SO	RAT	ERA	ERA+	OAV	OOB	BH	AVG	PB	PR	/A	PD	TPI
1912	Was-A	1	1	.500	5	1	0	0	0	20^1	24	1	15	11	18.1	4.87	68	.300	.423	2	.333	0	-4	-3	-1	-0.3

■ GIBSON ALBA   Alba, Gibson Alberto (Rosado)   b: 1/18/60, Santiago, D.R.   BL/TL, 6'2", 160 lbs.   Deb: 5/03/88

YEAR	TM/L	W	L	PCT	G	GS	CG	SH	SV	IP	H	HR	BB	SO	RAT	ERA	ERA+	OAV	OOB	BH	AVG	PB	PR	/A	PD	TPI
1988	StL-N	0	0	—	3	0	0	0	0	3^1	1	0	2	3	8.1	2.70	129	.091	.231	0	—	0	0	0	0	0.0

■ JOE ALBANESE   Albanese, Joseph Peter   b: 6/26/33, New York, N.Y.   BR/TR, 6'3", 215 lbs.   Deb: 7/18/58

YEAR	TM/L	W	L	PCT	G	GS	CG	SH	SV	IP	H	HR	BB	SO	RAT	ERA	ERA+	OAV	OOB	BH	AVG	PB	PR	/A	PD	TPI
1958	Was-A	0	0	—	6	0	0	0	0	6	8	1	2	3	15.0	4.50	85	.348	.400	0	—	0	-0	-0	0	0.0

■ CY ALBERTS   Alberts, Frederick Joseph   b: 1/14/1882, Grand Rapids, Mich.   d: 8/27/17, Fort Wayne, Ind.   6', 230 lbs.   Deb: 9/17/10

YEAR	TM/L	W	L	PCT	G	GS	CG	SH	SV	IP	H	HR	BB	SO	RAT	ERA	ERA+	OAV	OOB	BH	AVG	PB	PR	/A	PD	TPI
1910	StL-N	1	2	.333	4	3	2	0	0	27^2	35	1	20	10	17.9	6.18	48	.330	.437	0	.000	-0	-10	-10	-1	-0.9

■ ED ALBOSTA   Albosta, Edward John "Rube"   b: 10/27/18, Saginaw, Mich.   BR/TR, 6'1", 175 lbs.   Deb: 9/03/41

YEAR	TM/L	W	L	PCT	G	GS	CG	SH	SV	IP	H	HR	BB	SO	RAT	ERA	ERA+	OAV	OOB	BH	AVG	PB	PR	/A	PD	TPI
1941	Bro-N	0	2	.000	2	2	0	0	0	13	11	1	8	5	13.2	6.23	58	.239	.352	0	.000	-1	-4	-4	0	-0.3
1946	Pit-N	0	6	.000	17	6	0	0	0	39^2	41	3	35	19	17.5	6.13	58	.266	.405	1	.125	-1	-12	-11	0	-1.1
Total 2		0	8	.000	19	8	0	0	0	52^2	52	4	43	24	16.4	6.15	58	.260	.393	1	.083	-1	-16	-15	0	-1.4

■ ED ALBRECHT   Albrecht, Edward Arthur   b: 2/28/29, Affton, Mo.   d: 12/29/79, Cahokia, Ill.   BR/TR, 5'10.5", 165 lbs.   Deb: 10/02/49

YEAR	TM/L	W	L	PCT	G	GS	CG	SH	SV	IP	H	HR	BB	SO	RAT	ERA	ERA+	OAV	OOB	BH	AVG	PB	PR	/A	PD	TPI
1949	StL-A	1	0	1.000	1	1	1	0	0	5	1	0	4	1	9.0	5.40	84	.063	.250	0	.000	-0	-1	-0	0	0.0
1950	StL-A	0	1	.000	2	1	0	0	0	6^2	6	0	7	1	17.6	5.40	92	.250	.419	0	.000	-0	-1	-0	0	0.0
Total 2		1	1	.500	3	2	1	0	0	11^2	7	0	11	2	13.1	5.40	88	.175	.353	0	.000	-0	-1	-1	0	0.0

■ VIC ALBURY   Albury, Victor   b: 5/12/47, Key West, Fla.   BL/TL, 6', 190 lbs.   Deb: 8/07/73

YEAR	TM/L	W	L	PCT	G	GS	CG	SH	SV	IP	H	HR	BB	SO	RAT	ERA	ERA+	OAV	OOB	BH	AVG	PB	PR	/A	PD	TPI
1973	Min-A	1	0	1.000	14	0	0	0	0	23^1	13	1	19	13	12.3	2.70	147	.169	.333	0	—	0	3	3	-1	0.3
1974	Min-A	8	9	.471	32	22	4	1	0	164	159	19	80	85	13.4	4.12	91	.259	.350	0	—	0	-9	-7	-0	-0.6
1975	Min-A	6	7	.462	32	15	2	0	1	135	115	16	97	72	14.4	4.53	85	.237	.368	0	.000	0	-11	-10	1	-0.9
1976	Min-A	3	1	.750	23	0	0	0	0	50^1	51	0	24	23	13.8	3.58	101	.271	.360	0	—	0	-0	0	0	0.0
Total 4		18	17	.514	101	37	6	1	1	372^2	338	36	220	193	13.8	4.11	92	.248	.357	0	.000	-1	-18	-13	-1	-1.2

■ SANTO ALCALA   Alcala, Santo (b: Santo Anibal (Alcala))   b: 12/23/52, San Pedro De Macoris, D.R.   BR/TR, 6'5", 195 lbs.   Deb: 4/10/76

YEAR	TM/L	W	L	PCT	G	GS	CG	SH	SV	IP	H	HR	BB	SO	RAT	ERA	ERA+	OAV	OOB	BH	AVG	PB	PR	/A	PD	TPI
1976	Cin-N	11	4	.733	30	21	3	1	0	132	131	12	67	67	13.7	4.70	74	.261	.352	6	.140	-0	-18	-18	-1	-1.8
1977	Cin-N	1	1	.500	7	2	0	0	0	15^2	22	1	7	9	17.2	5.74	68	.349	.423	0	.000	-0	-3	-3	0	-0.2
	Mon-N	2	6	.250	31	10	0	0	2	101^2	104	12	47	64	13.5	4.69	81	.263	.344	2	.080	-1	-9	-10	-1	-1.1
	Yr	3	7	.300	38	12	0	0	2	117^1	126	13	54	73	14.0	4.83	79	.273	.352	2	.080	-1	-12	-13	-1	-1.3
Total 2		14	11	.560	68	33	3	1	2	249^1	257	25	121	140	13.9	4.76	77	.268	.353	8	.113	-2	-30	-31	-2	-3.1

■ DALE ALDERSON   Alderson, Dale Leonard   b: 3/9/18, Belden, Neb.   d: 2/12/82, Garden Grove, Cal.   BR/TR, 5'10", 190 lbs.   Deb: 9/18/43

YEAR	TM/L	W	L	PCT	G	GS	CG	SH	SV	IP	H	HR	BB	SO	RAT	ERA	ERA+	OAV	OOB	BH	AVG	PB	PR	/A	PD	TPI
1943	Chi-N	0	1	.000	4	2	0	0	0	14	21	2	3	4	15.4	6.43	52	.356	.387	0	.000	-0	-5	-5	0	-0.4
1944	Chi-N	0	0	—	12	1	0	0	0	21^2	31	2	9	7	16.6	6.65	53	.344	.404	0	.000	-1	-7	-7	1	-0.6
Total 2		0	1	.000	16	3	0	0	0	35^2	52	4	12	11	16.6	6.56	53	.349	.398	0	.000	-1	-12	-12	1	-1.0

■ SCOTT ALDRED   Aldred, Scott Phillip   b: 6/12/68, Flint, Mich.   BL/TL, 6'4", 195 lbs.   Deb: 9/09/90

YEAR	TM/L	W	L	PCT	G	GS	CG	SH	SV	IP	H	HR	BB	SO	RAT	ERA	ERA+	OAV	OOB	BH	AVG	PB	PR	/A	PD	TPI
1990	Det-A	1	2	.333	4	3	0	0	0	14^1	13	0	10	7	15.1	3.77	104	.265	.400	0	—	0	0	0	0	0.0

■ JAY ALDRICH   Aldrich, Jay Robert   b: 4/14/61, Alexandria, La.   BR/TR, 6'3", 210 lbs.   Deb: 6/05/87

YEAR	TM/L	W	L	PCT	G	GS	CG	SH	SV	IP	H	HR	BB	SO	RAT	ERA	ERA+	OAV	OOB	BH	AVG	PB	PR	/A	PD	TPI
1987	Mil-A	3	1	.750	31	0	0	0	0	58^1	71	8	13	22	13.3	4.94	93	.306	.348	0	—	0	-3	-2	-0	-0.2
1989	Mil-A	1	0	1.000	16	0	0	0	1	26	24	3	13	12	13.2	3.81	101	.253	.349	0	—	0	0	0	0	0.0
	Atl-N	1	2	.333	8	0	0	0	0	12^1	16	1	6	7	9.5	2.19	167	.167	.271	0	—	0	2	2	-0	0.2
1990	Bal-A	1	2	.333	7	0	0	0	0	12	17	1	7	5	18.0	8.25	46	.327	.407	0	—	0	-6	-6	0	-0.5
Total 3		6	5	.545	62	0	0	0	2	108^2	119	12	39	46	13.3	4.72	89	.283	.348	0	.000	-0	-7	-6	-0	-0.5

■ VIC ALDRIDGE   Aldridge, Victor Eddington   b: 10/25/1893, Indian Sprgs., Ind   d: 4/17/73, Terre Haute, Ind.   BR/TR, 5'9.5", 175 lbs.   Deb: 4/15/17

YEAR	TM/L	W	L	PCT	G	GS	CG	SH	SV	IP	H	HR	BB	SO	RAT	ERA	ERA+	OAV	OOB	BH	AVG	PB	PR	/A	PD	TPI
1917	Chi-N	6	6	.500	30	5	1	1	2	106^2	100	1	37	44	11.7	3.12	93	.252	.319	4	.138	-2	-5	-3	3	-0.1

YEAR	TM/L	W	L	PCT	G	GS	CG	SH	SV	IP	H	HR	BB	SO	RAT	ERA	ERA+	OAV	OOB	BH	AVG	PB	PR	/A	PD	TPI
1918	Chi-N	0	1	.000	3	0	0	0	0	12¹	11	0	6	10	12.4	1.46	191	.275	.370	1	.333	0	2	2	-0	0.2
1922	Chi-N	16	15	.516	36	34	20	2	0	258¹	287	14	56	66	12.4	3.52	119	.286	.332	26	.260	3	17	20	1	2.3
1923	Chi-N	16	9	.640	30	30	15	2	0	217	209	17	67	64	11.5	3.48	115	.251	.307	19	.268	3	12	12	-1	1.5
1924	Chi-N	15	12	.556	32	32	20	0	0	244¹	261	10	80	74	12.8	3.50	112	.279	.341	15	.176	-3	10	11	-0	0.7
1925	*Pit-N	15	7	.682	30	26	14	1	0	213¹	218	15	74	88	12.5	3.63	123	.269	.334	20	.233	-1	15	20	-4	1.5
1926	Pit-N	10	13	.435	30	26	12	1	1	190	204	7	73	61	13.3	4.07	97	.279	.348	16	.225	-1	-5	-3	-2	-0.4
1927	*Pit-N	15	10	.600	35	34	17	1	1	239¹	248	16	74	86	12.3	4.25	97	.270	.328	21	.219	-0	-9	-4	-4	-0.6
1928	NY-N	4	7	.364	22	17	3	0	2	119¹	133	7	45	33	13.7	4.83	81	.285	.352	11	.275	2	-11	-12	-1	-0.9
Total	9	97	80	.548	248	204	102	8	6	1600²	1671	87	512	526	12.5	3.76	107	.273	.333	133	.229	2	26	44	-7	4.2

■ DOYLE ALEXANDER

Alexander, Doyle Lafayette b: 9/4/50, Cordova, Ala.   BR/TR, 6'3", 190 lbs.   Deb: 6/26/71

YEAR	TM/L	W	L	PCT	G	GS	CG	SH	SV	IP	H	HR	BB	SO	RAT	ERA	ERA+	OAV	OOB	BH	AVG	PB	PR	/A	PD	TPI
1971	LA-N	6	6	.500	17	12	4	0	0	92¹	105	6	18	30	12.1	3.80	85	.282	.317	9	.273	3	-3	-6	-0	-0.3
1972	Bal-A	6	8	.429	35	9	2	2	2	106¹	78	5	30	49	9.2	2.45	125	.203	.262	2	.080	-1	7	7	2	0.9
1973	*Bal-A	12	8	.600	29	26	10	0	0	174²	169	19	52	63	11.7	3.86	97	.258	.319	0	—	0	-1	-3	2	0.0
1974	Bal-A	6	9	.400	30	12	0	0	0	114¹	127	7	43	40	13.7	4.01	86	.290	.359	0	—	0	-5	-7	4	-0.3
1975	Bal-A	8	8	.500	32	11	3	1	1	133¹	127	7	47	46	11.8	3.04	116	.251	.316	0	—	0	11	7	2	1.0
1976	Bal-A	3	4	.429	11	6	2	1	0	64¹	58	3	24	17	11.5	3.50	94	.247	.317	0	—	0	0	-2	2	0.0
	*NY-A	10	5	.667	19	19	5	2	0	136²	114	9	39	41	10.3	3.29	104	.229	.289	0	—	0	3	2	-2	0.0
	Yr	13	9	.591	30	25	7	3	0	201	172	12	63	58	10.7	3.36	100	.234	.297	0	—	0	4	0	-0	0.0
1977	Tex-A	17	11	.607	34	34	12	1	0	237	221	24	82	82	11.6	3.65	112	.246	.311	0	—	0	11	11	2	1.4
1978	Tex-A	9	10	.474	31	28	7	1	0	191	198	18	71	81	12.7	3.86	97	.270	.336	0	—	0	-2	-3	2	0.0
1979	Tex-A	5	7	.417	23	18	0	0	0	113¹	114	3	69	50	14.6	4.45	93	.268	.371	0	—	0	-3	-4	2	-0.1
1980	Atl-N	14	11	.560	35	35	7	1	0	231²	227	20	74	114	11.8	4.20	89	.256	.316	15	.181	0	-15	-12	3	-0.7
1981	SF-N	11	7	.611	24	24	1	1	0	152¹	156	11	44	77	11.9	2.89	118	.263	.316	9	.176	1	10	9	-1	1.0
1982	NY-A	1	7	.125	16	11	0	0	0	66²	81	14	14	26	12.8	6.08	66	.298	.332	0	—	0	-15	-15	0	-1.4
1983	NY-A	0	2	.000	8	5	0	0	0	28¹	31	6	7	17	12.1	6.35	61	.277	.319	0	—	0	-7	-8	-0	-0.7
	Tor-A	7	6	.538	17	15	5	0	0	116²	126	14	26	46	11.8	3.93	109	.279	.319	0	—	0	2	5	1	0.5
	Yr	7	8	.467	25	20	5	0	0	145	157	20	33	63	11.9	4.41	96	.278	.319	0	—	0	-6	-3	-0	-0.2
1984	Tor-A	17	6	**.739**	36	35	11	2	0	261²	238	21	59	139	10.3	3.13	131	.242	.287	0	—	0	25	28	0	3.0
1985	*Tor-A	17	10	.630	36	36	6	1	0	260²	268	28	67	142	11.8	3.45	122	.266	.315	0	—	0	20	22	1	2.3
1986	Tor-A	5	4	.556	17	17	3	0	0	111	120	18	20	65	11.7	4.46	95	.273	.310	0	—	0	-3	-3	-1	-0.3
	Atl-N	6	6	.500	17	17	2	0	0	117¹	135	9	17	74	11.7	3.84	104	.287	.312	8	.211	1	-2	2	-0	0.0
1987	Atl-N	5	10	.333	16	16	3	0	0	117²	115	21	27	64	11.0	4.13	105	.257	.302	1	.029	-3	-1	3	-2	-0.1
	*Det-A	9	0	1.000	11	11	3	3	0	88¹	63	3	26	44	9.1	1.53	270	.201	.263	0	—	0	29	26	0	2.9
1988	Det-A	14	11	.560	34	34	5	1	0	229	260	30	46	126	12.2	4.32	88	.282	.320	0	—	0	-9	-13	-2	-1.4
1989	Det-A	6	18	.250	33	33	5	1	0	223	245	28	76	95	13.2	4.44	86	.280	.341	0	—	0	-14	-15	1	-1.3
Total	19	194	174	.527	561	464	98	18	3	3367²	3376	324	978	1528	11.8	3.76	102	.261	.316	44	.166	1	38	32	13	6.6

■ GERALD ALEXANDER

Alexander, Gerald Paul b: 3/26/68, Baton Rouge, La.   BR/TR, 5'11", 190 lbs.   Deb: 9/09/90

YEAR	TM/L	W	L	PCT	G	GS	CG	SH	SV	IP	H	HR	BB	SO	RAT	ERA	ERA+	OAV	OOB	BH	AVG	PB	PR	/A	PD	TPI
1990	Tex-A	0	0	—	3	2	0	0	0	7	14	0	5	8	25.7	7.71	52	.438	.526	0	—	0	-3	-3	0	-0.2

■ PETE ALEXANDER

Alexander, Grover Cleveland b: 2/26/1887, Elba, Neb. d: 11/4/50, St.Paul, Neb.   BR/TR, 6'1", 185 lbs.   Deb: 4/15/11 H

YEAR	TM/L	W	L	PCT	G	GS	CG	SH	SV	IP	H	HR	BB	SO	RAT	ERA	ERA+	OAV	OOB	BH	AVG	PB	PR	/A	PD	TPI
1911	Phi-N	**28**	13	.683	48	37	31	7	3	367	285	5	129	227	10.3	2.57	134	.219	.293	24	.174	-2	34	35	-0	3.4
1912	Phi-N	19	17	.528	46	34	26	3	3	310¹	289	11	105	**195**	11.6	2.81	129	.245	.310	19	.186	0	21	28	-0	2.9
1913	Phi-N	22	8	.733	47	35	23	**9**	2	306¹	288	9	75	159	10.8	2.79	120	.254	.302	13	.126	-4	14	19	1	1.6
1914	Phi-N	27	15	.643	46	39	**32**	6	1	355	327	6	76	**214**	10.5	2.38	123	.244	.290	32	.234	2	16	22	3	1.6
1915	*Phi-N	31	10	.756	**49**	42	**36**	**12**	3	**376¹**	253	3	64	**241**	**7.8**	**1.22**	**225**	**.191**	**.234**	22	.169	0	**64**	**64**	6	**8.5**
1916	Phi-N	**33**	12	.733	48	45	38	**16**	3	388²	323	6	50	**167**	8.9	**1.55**	**171**	.230	.262	33	.239	8	46	48	1	7.1
1917	Phi-N	**30**	13	.698	45	44	34	8	0	**387²**	336	4	56	**200**	9.2	1.83	153	.234	.266	30	.216	4	38	42	1	5.9
1918	Chi-N	2	1	.667	3	3	3	0	0	26	19	0	3	15	8.0	1.73	161	.207	.240	1	.100	-1	3	3	0	0.3
1919	Chi-N	16	11	.593	30	27	20	**9**	1	235	180	3	38	121	8.3	**1.72**	**167**	.211	.245	12	.171	1	31	30	4	4.2
1920	Chi-N	27	14	.659	46	40	33	7	5	**363¹**	335	6	69	**173**	10.0	**1.91**	**168**	.248	.285	27	.229	4	**50**	**52**	1	**6.8**
1921	Chi-N	15	13	.536	31	29	21	**3**	1	252	286	10	33	77	11.4	3.39	113	.296	.320	29	.305	6	11	12	-0	1.8
1922	Chi-N	16	13	.552	33	31	20	1	1	245²	283	8	34	48	11.7	3.63	116	.295	.321	15	.176	-2	13	16	3	1.7
1923	Chi-N	22	12	.647	39	36	26	3	2	305	308	11	30	72	**10.0**	3.19	126	.259	**.277**	24	.216	0	28	28	4	3.2
1924	Chi-N	12	5	.706	21	20	12	0	0	169¹	183	7	25	33	11.1	3.03	129	.272	.299	15	.231	1	16	16	2	2.0
1925	Chi-N	15	11	.577	32	30	20	1	0	236	270	14	29	63	11.5	3.39	127	.288	.312	19	.241	3	23	24	-2	2.4
1926	Chi-N	3	3	.500	7	7	4	0	0	52	55	0	7	12	10.7	3.46	111	.270	.294	7	.467	5	3	2	1	0.6
	*StL-N	9	7	.563	23	16	11	2	2	148¹	136	8	24	35	9.8	2.91	134	.242	.276	6	.120	-4	15	16	0	1.3
	Yr	12	10	.545	30	23	15	2	2	200¹	191	8	31	47	10.1	3.05	120	.250	.281	2	.031	-1	17	19	1	1.9
1927	StL-N	21	10	.677	37	30	22	2	3	268	261	11	38	48	10.1	2.52	157	.258	.286	23	.245	3	**42**	**43**	1	**5.0**
1928	*StL-N	16	9	.640	34	31	18	1	2	243²	262	15	37	59	11.1	3.36	119	.277	.306	25	.291	6	17	17	-1	2.2
1929	StL-N	9	8	.529	22	19	8	0	0	132	149	10	23	33	11.8	3.89	120	.285	.317	2	.049	-4	12	11	2	0.9
1930	Phi-N	0	3	.000	9	3	0	0	0	21²	40	5	6	6	19.1	9.14	60	.396	.430	0	.000	-0	-10	-9	-1	-0.7
Total	20	373	208	.642	696	598	438	90	32	5189¹	4868	164	951	2198	10.2	2.56	135	.250	.287	378	.209	25	484	522	27	64.3

■ BOB ALEXANDER

Alexander, Robert Somerville b: 8/7/22, Vancouver, B.C., Can   BR/TR, 6'2.5", 205 lbs.   Deb: 4/11/55

YEAR	TM/L	W	L	PCT	G	GS	CG	SH	SV	IP	H	HR	BB	SO	RAT	ERA	ERA+	OAV	OOB	BH	AVG	PB	PR	/A	PD	TPI
1955	Bal-A	1	0	1.000	4	0	0	0	0	4	8	0	2	1	24.8	13.50	28	.444	.524	0	—	0	-4	-4	-0	-0.3
1957	Cle-A	0	1	.000	5	0	0	0	0	7	10	0	5	1	20.6	9.00	41	.357	.471	0	.000	-0	-4	-4	-0	-0.3
Total	2	1	1	.500	9	0	0	0	0	11	18	0	7	2	22.1	10.64	35	.391	.491	0	.000	-0	-8	-8	-0	-0.6

■ BRIAN ALLARD

Allard, Brian Marshall b: 1/3/58, Spring Valley, Ill.   BR/TR, 6'1", 175 lbs.   Deb: 8/08/79

YEAR	TM/L	W	L	PCT	G	GS	CG	SH	SV	IP	H	HR	BB	SO	RAT	ERA	ERA+	OAV	OOB	BH	AVG	PB	PR	/A	PD	TPI
1979	Tex-A	1	3	.250	7	4	2	0	0	33¹	36	4	13	14	13.2	4.32	96	.283	.350	0	—	0	-0	-1	0	0.0
1980	Tex-A	0	1	.000	5	2	0	0	0	14¹	13	0	10	10	15.1	5.65	69	.236	.364	0	—	0	-3	-3	-0	-0.2
1981	Sea-A	3	2	.600	7	7	1	0	0	48	48	5	8	20	10.5	3.75	103	.265	.296	0	—	0	-0	1	-0	0.0
Total	3	4	6	.400	19	13	3	0	0	95²	97	9	31	44	12.1	4.23	94	.267	.327	0	—	0	-3	-3	-0	-0.2

■ FRANK ALLEN

Allen, Frank Leon b: 8/26/1889, Newbern, Ala. d: 7/30/33, Gainesville, Ala.   BR/TL, 5'9", 175 lbs.   Deb: 5/18/12

YEAR	TM/L	W	L	PCT	G	GS	CG	SH	SV	IP	H	HR	BB	SO	RAT	ERA	ERA+	OAV	OOB	BH	AVG	PB	PR	/A	PD	TPI
1912	Bro-N	3	9	.250	20	15	5	1	0	109	119	1	57	58	14.6	3.63	92	.272	.358	6	.167	2	-3	-3	0	-0.1
1913	Bro-N	4	18	.182	34	25	11	0	2	174²	144	6	81	82	12.1	2.83	116	.231	.329	7	.137	-1	7	9	-3	0.5
1914	Bro-N	8	14	.364	36	21	10	1	0	171¹	165	6	57	68	11.8	3.10	92	.265	.330	6	.128	0	-6	-5	-1	-0.5
	Pit-F	1	0	1.000	1	1	1	0	0	7	9	0	0	3	11.6	5.14	62	.320	.320	1	.500	1	-2	-2	-0	0.0
1915	Pit-F	23	13	.639	41	37	24	6	0	283¹	230	9	100	127	10.8	2.51	120	.227	.304	7	.079	-4	16	16	-1	1.1
1916	Bos-N	8	3	.800	19	14	7	2	1	113	102	1	31	63	10.9	2.07	120	.244	.302	7	.206	3	7	5	-1	0.8
1917	Bos-N	3	11	.214	29	14	2	0	0	112	124	3	47	56	14.2	3.94	65	.297	.376	5	.172	1	-15	-17	-2	-1.9
Total	6	50	67	.427	180	127	60	10	3	970¹	893	26	373	457	12.1	2.93	101	.251	.328	39	.135	3	5	3	-9	-0.1

■ JOHN ALLEN

Allen, John Marshall b: 10/27/1890, Berkeley Springs, W.Va. d: 9/24/67, Hagerstown, Md.   BR/TR, 6'1", 170 lbs.   Deb: 6/02/14

YEAR	TM/L	W	L	PCT	G	GS	CG	SH	SV	IP	H	HR	BB	SO	RAT	ERA	ERA+	OAV	OOB	BH	AVG	PB	PR	/A	PD	TPI
1914	Bal-F	0	0	—	1	0	0	0	0	2	2	0	2	2	22.5	18.00	19	.268	.478	0	—	0	-3	-3	-0	-0.2

■ JOHNNY ALLEN

Allen, John Thomas b: 9/30/05, Lenoir, N.C. d: 3/29/59, St.Petersburg, Fla   BR/TR, 6', 180 lbs.   Deb: 4/19/32

YEAR	TM/L	W	L	PCT	G	GS	CG	SH	SV	IP	H	HR	BB	SO	RAT	ERA	ERA+	OAV	OOB	BH	AVG	PB	PR	/A	PD	TPI
1932	*NY-A	17	4	**.810**	33	21	13	3	4	192	162	10	76	109	11.4	3.70	110	.228	.306	8	.123	-1	17	8	-1	0.4
1933	NY-A	15	7	.682	25	24	10	1	2	184²	171	9	87	119	12.8	4.39	89	.242	.328	13	.181	0	-2	-10	-1	-1.0
1934	NY-A	5	2	.714	13	10	4	0	0	71²	62	3	32	54	12.1	2.89	141	.227	.313	5	.192	1	13	9	-0	0.9
1935	NY-A	13	6	.684	23	23	12	2	0	167	149	11	58	113	11.4	3.61	112	**.238**	.307	15	.224	1	16	8	1	0.9

YEAR TM/L	W	L	PCT	G	GS	CG	SH	SV	IP	H	HR	BB	SO	RAT	ERA	ERA+	OAV	OOB	BH	AVG	PB	PR	/A	PD	TPI
1936 Cle-A	20	10	.667	36	31	19	4	1	243	234	5	97	165	12.3	3.44	146	.256	.328	14	.161	-3	43	43	1	3.9
1937 Cle-A	15	1	**.938**	24	20	14	0	0	173	157	4	60	87	11.5	2.55	181	.244	.313	6	.090	-7	40	40	1	3.4
1938 Cle-A	14	8	.636	30	27	13	0	0	200	189	15	81	112	12.3	4.18	111	.246	.321	20	.253	4	13	10	2	1.5
1939 Cle-A	9	7	.563	28	26	9	2	0	175	199	9	56	79	13.3	4.58	96	.291	.347	16	.225	1	1	-3	3	0.0
1940 Cle-A	9	8	.529	32	17	5	3	5	138^{2}	126	3	48	62	11.5	3.44	123	.243	.311	10	.208	0	15	12	-0	1.1
1941 StL-A	2	5	.286	20	9	2	0	1	67	89	4	29	27	16.1	6.58	65	.319	.387	3	.136	0	-18	-17	-0	-1.5
*Bro-N	3	0	1.000	11	4	1	0	0	57^{1}	38	6	12	21	7.8	2.51	146	.188	.234	1	.050	-2	7	7	0	0.6
1942 Bro-N	10	6	.625	27	15	5	1	3	118	106	11	39	50	11.2	3.20	102	.238	.302	7	.179	-0	1	1	0	0.0
1943 Bro-N	5	1	.833	17	1	0	0	1	38	42	3	25	15	16.3	4.26	79	.280	.390	3	.429	2	-4	-4	-0	-0.1
NY-N	1	3	.250	15	0	0	0	2	41	37	4	14	24	11.2	3.07	112	.245	.309	0	.000	-2	1	2	1	0.1
Yr	6	4	.600	32	1	0	0	3	79	79	7	39	39	13.4	3.65	93	.261	.345	2	.095	-0	-2	-2	1	0.0
1944 NY-N	4	7	.364	18	13	2	1	0	84	88	7	24	33	12.2	4.07	90	.260	.313	2	.083	-2	-4	-4	-1	-0.6
Total 13	142	75	.654	352	241	109	17	18	1950^{1}	1849	104	738	1070	12.1	3.75	113	.249	.321	124	.173	-8	138	102	4	9.6

■ LLOYD ALLEN
Allen, Lloyd Cecil b: 5/8/50, Merced, Cal. BR/TR, 6'1", 185 lbs. Deb: 9/01/69

YEAR TM/L	W	L	PCT	G	GS	CG	SH	SV	IP	H	HR	BB	SO	RAT	ERA	ERA+	OAV	OOB	BH	AVG	PB	PR	/A	PD	TPI
1969 Cal-A	0	1	.000	4	1	0	0	0	10	5	1	10	5	13.5	5.40	65	.147	.341	1	.500	1	-2	-2	1	0.0
1970 Cal-A	1	1	.500	8	2	0	0	0	24	23	0	11	12	13.1	2.63	138	.261	.350	0	.000	-0	3	3	-0	0.2
1971 Cal-A	4	6	.400	54	1	0	0	15	94	75	4	40	72	11.0	2.49	130	.221	.303	5	.294	2	10	8	0	1.1
1972 Cal-A	3	7	.300	42	6	0	0	5	85^{1}	76	7	55	53	14.1	3.48	84	.240	.357	2	.118	-1	-4	-5	-0	-0.6
1973 Cal-A	0	0	—	5	0	0	0	1	8^{2}	15	0	5	4	20.8	10.38	34	.417	.488	0	—	0	-6	-7	0	-0.5
Tex-A	0	6	.000	23	5	0	0	1	41	58	3	39	25	22.4	9.22	40	.326	.459	0	—	0	-25	-25	1	-2.2
Yr	0	6	.000	28	5	0	0	2	49^{2}	73	3	44	29	22.1	9.42	39	.338	.460	0	—	0	-31	-32	1	-2.7
1974 Tex-A	0	1	.000	14	0	0	0	0	22	24	2	18	18	17.6	6.55	54	.276	.406	0	—	0	-7	-7	-0	-0.7
Chi-A	0	1	.000	6	2	0	0	0	7	7	0	12	3	25.7	10.29	36	.259	.500	0	—	0	-5	-5	0	-0.4
Yr	0	2	.000	20	2	0	0	0	29	31	2	30	21	19.2	7.45	48	.265	.419	0	—	0	-12	-12	-0	-1.1
1975 Chi-A	0	2	.000	3	2	0	0	0	5^{1}	8	2	6	2	23.6	11.81	33	.348	.483	0	—	0	-5	-5	0	-0.3
Total 7	8	25	.242	159	19	0	0	22	297^{1}	291	19	196	194	15.1	4.69	70	.258	.373	8	.200	2	-41	-46	1	-3.4

■ MYRON ALLEN
Allen, Myron Smith "Zeke" b: 3/22/1854, Kingston, N.Y. d: 3/8/24, Kingston, N.Y. 5'8", 150 lbs. Deb: 7/19/1883 ♦

YEAR TM/L	W	L	PCT	G	GS	CG	SH	SV	IP	H	HR	BB	SO	RAT	ERA	ERA+	OAV	OOB	BH	AVG	PB	PR	/A	PD	TPI
1883 NY-N	0	1	.000	1	1	1	0	0	8	8	0	3	0	12.4	1.13	275	.245	.309	0	.000	-1	2	2	0	0.1
1887 Cle-a	1	0	1.000	2	0	0	0	0	9^{2}	9	0	3	1	11.2	0.93	468	.238	.294	128	.276	0	4	4	-0	0.3
1888 KC-a	0	2	.000	2	2	2	0	0	18	17	0	1	2	9.0	2.50	137	.240	.251	29	.213	0	1	2	1	0.2
Total 3	1	3	.250	5	3	3	0	0	35^{2}	34	0	7	3	10.3	1.77	205	.241	.277	157	.259	-0	7	7	1	0.6

■ NEIL ALLEN
Allen, Neil Patrick b: 1/24/58, Kansas City, Kan. BR/TR, 6'3", 185 lbs. Deb: 4/15/79

YEAR TM/L	W	L	PCT	G	GS	CG	SH	SV	IP	H	HR	BB	SO	RAT	ERA	ERA+	OAV	OOB	BH	AVG	PB	PR	/A	PD	TPI
1979 NY-N	6	10	.375	50	5	0	0	8	99	100	4	47	65	13.4	3.55	103	.268	.350	0	.000	-2	2	1	0	0.0
1980 NY-N	7	10	.412	59	0	0	0	22	97^{1}	87	7	40	79	11.7	3.70	96	.244	.320	2	.143	-0	-1	-2	-1	-0.2
1981 NY-N	7	6	.538	43	0	0	0	18	66^{2}	64	4	26	50	12.2	2.97	117	.259	.330	1	.200	1	4	4	1	0.5
1982 NY-N	3	7	.300	50	0	0	0	19	64^{2}	65	5	30	59	13.4	3.06	119	.266	.349	1	.167	1	4	4	-1	0.4
1983 NY-N	2	7	.222	21	4	1	1	2	54	57	6	36	32	15.5	4.50	81	.278	.386	0	.000	-1	-5	-5	-0	-0.6
StL-N	10	6	.625	25	18	4	2	0	121^{2}	122	6	48	74	12.6	3.70	98	.265	.335	5	.128	-1	-1	-1	-1	-0.1
Yr	12	13	.480	46	22	5	3	2	175^{2}	179	12	84	106	13.5	3.94	92	.268	.351	0	.000	-2	-6	-6	-1	-0.7
1984 StL-N	9	6	.600	57	1	0	0	3	119	105	6	49	66	11.6	3.55	98	.239	.315	6	.240	1	0	-1	1	0.1
1985 StL-N	1	4	.200	23	1	0	0	2	29	32	3	17	10	15.5	5.59	63	.283	.382	0	.000	-0	-6	-7	0	-0.6
NY-A	1	0	1.000	17	0	0	0	1	29^{1}	26	1	13	16	12.0	2.76	145	.234	.315	0	—	0	5	4	0	0.4
1986 Chi-A	7	2	.778	22	17	2	2	0	113	101	8	38	57	11.2	3.82	113	.244	.311	0	—	0	4	6	-0	0.2
1987 Chi-A	0	7	.000	15	10	0	0	0	49^{2}	74	6	26	26	18.5	7.07	65	.365	.442	0	—	0	-14	-14	-0	-1.2
NY-A	0	1	.000	8	1	0	0	0	24^{2}	23	2	10	16	12.0	3.65	120	.242	.314	0	—	0	2	2	-0	0.2
Yr	0	8	.000	23	11	0	0	0	74^{1}	97	8	36	42	16.1	5.93	76	.321	.393	0	—	0	-12	-12	-0	-1.0
1988 NY-A	5	3	.625	41	2	0	1	0	117^{1}	121	14	37	61	12.3	3.84	103	.268	.326	0	—	0	2	1	-2	0.0
1989 Cle-A	0	1	.000	3	0	0	0	0	3	8	1	0	0	24.0	15.00	26	.500	.500	0	—	0	-4	-4	0	-0.2
Total 11	58	70	.453	434	59	7	6	75	988^{1}	985	73	417	611	12.8	3.88	97	.264	.339	15	.130	-1	-9	-11	-3	-0.7

■ BOB ALLEN
Allen, Robert Earl "Thin Man" b: 7/2/14, Smithville, Tenn. BR/TR, 6'1", 165 lbs. Deb: 9/19/37

YEAR TM/L	W	L	PCT	G	GS	CG	SH	SV	IP	H	HR	BB	SO	RAT	ERA	ERA+	OAV	OOB	BH	AVG	PB	PR	/A	PD	TPI
1937 Phi-N	0	1	.000	3	1	0	0	0	12	18	2	8	8	19.5	6.75	64	.321	.406	1	.333	0	-4	-3	-1	-0.3

■ BOB ALLEN
Allen, Robert Gray b: 10/23/37, Tatum, Tex. BL/TL, 6'2", 175 lbs. Deb: 4/14/61

YEAR TM/L	W	L	PCT	G	GS	CG	SH	SV	IP	H	HR	BB	SO	RAT	ERA	ERA+	OAV	OOB	BH	AVG	PB	PR	/A	PD	TPI
1961 Cle-A	3	2	.600	48	0	0	0	3	81^{2}	96	7	40	42	15.1	3.75	105	.294	.373	2	.167	0	3	2	0	0.2
1962 Cle-A	1	1	.500	30	0	0	0	4	30^{2}	29	5	25	23	15.8	5.87	66	.250	.383	0	.000	-1	-6	-7	0	-0.6
1963 Cle-A	1	3	.333	43	0	0	0	2	56	58	5	29	51	14.1	4.66	78	.266	.355	1	.200	-0	-6	-6	0	-0.6
1966 Cle-A	2	2	.500	36	0	0	0	5	51^{1}	56	2	13	33	12.4	4.21	82	.273	.323	1	.111	-0	-4	-4	-0	-0.3
1967 Cle-A	0	5	.000	47	0	0	0	5	54^{1}	49	4	25	50	12.4	2.98	110	.243	.329	0	—	0	2	2	1	0.2
Total 5	7	12	.368	204	0	0	0	19	274	288	23	132	199	14.0	4.11	89	.270	.353	4	.129	-1	-13	-14	2	-1.1

■ DOUG ALLISON
Allison, Douglas b: 1846, Philadelphia, Pa. d: 12/19/16, Washington, D.C. BR/TR, 5'10.5", 160 lbs. Deb: 5/05/1871 ♦

YEAR TM/L	W	L	PCT	G	GS	CG	SH	SV	IP	H	HR	BB	SO	RAT	ERA	ERA+	OAV	OOB	BH	AVG	PB	PR	/A	PD	TPI
1878 Pro-N	0	0	—	1	0	0	0	0	5	11	0	1	0	21.6	1.80	122	.420	.441	22	.289	0	0	0	-0	0.0

■ MACK ALLISON
Allison, Mack Pendleton b: 1/23/1887, Owensboro, Ky. d: 3/13/64, St.Joseph, Mo. BR/TR, 6'1", 185 lbs. Deb: 9/13/11

YEAR TM/L	W	L	PCT	G	GS	CG	SH	SV	IP	H	HR	BB	SO	RAT	ERA	ERA+	OAV	OOB	BH	AVG	PB	PR	/A	PD	TPI
1911 StL-A	2	1	.667	3	3	3	0	0	26^{1}	24	0	5	2	10.6	2.05	165	.253	.304	2	.200	-0	4	4	-0	0.3
1912 StL-A	6	17	.261	31	20	11	1	1	169	171	4	49	43	12.0	3.62	92	.269	.327	7	.135	-3	-6	-6	-1	-0.8
1913 StL-A	1	3	.250	11	4	3	0	0	51^{1}	52	0	13	12	11.9	2.28	129	.287	.345	0	.000	-2	4	4	-1	0.0
Total 3	9	21	.300	45	27	17	1	1	246^{2}	247	4	67	57	11.9	3.17	102	.271	.328	9	.118	-6	2	2	-3	-0.5

■ LUIS ALOMA
Aloma, Luis (Barba) "Witto" b: 7/23/23, Havana, Cuba BR/TR, 6'2", 195 lbs. Deb: 4/19/50

YEAR TM/L	W	L	PCT	G	GS	CG	SH	SV	IP	H	HR	BB	SO	RAT	ERA	ERA+	OAV	OOB	BH	AVG	PB	PR	/A	PD	TPI
1950 Chi-A	7	2	.778	42	0	0	0	4	87^{2}	77	6	53	49	13.4	3.80	118	.234	.342	1	.067	-2	8	7	-1	0.4
1951 Chi-A	6	0	1.000	25	1	1	1	3	69^{1}	52	3	24	25	10.1	1.82	222	.215	.291	7	.350	2	18	17	-1	1.8
1952 Chi-A	3	1	.750	25	0	0	0	6	40	42	5	11	18	12.1	4.27	85	.278	.331	0	.000	-1	-3	-3	0	-0.3
1953 Chi-A	2	0	1.000	24	0	0	0	2	38^{1}	41	7	23	23	15.0	4.70	86	.283	.381	0	.000	-1	-3	-3	-0	-0.3
Total 4	18	3	.857	116	1	1	1	15	235^{1}	212	21	111	115	12.5	3.44	120	.245	.333	8	.167	-2	20	18	-2	1.6

■ MATTY ALOU
Alou, Mateo Rojas (b: Mateo Rojas (Alou)) b: 12/22/38, Haina, D.R. BL/TL, 5'9", 160 lbs. Deb: 9/26/60 ♦

YEAR TM/L	W	L	PCT	G	GS	CG	SH	SV	IP	H	HR	BB	SO	RAT	ERA	ERA+	OAV	OOB	BH	AVG	PB	PR	/A	PD	TPI
1965 SF-N	0	0	—	1	0	0	0	0	2	3	0	1	3	18.0	0.00	—	.333	.400	75	.231	0	1	1	0	0.1

■ PORFI ALTAMIRANO
Altamirano, Porfirio (Ramirez) b: 5/17/52, Darillo, Nic. BR/TR, 6', 175 lbs. Deb: 5/09/82

YEAR TM/L	W	L	PCT	G	GS	CG	SH	SV	IP	H	HR	BB	SO	RAT	ERA	ERA+	OAV	OOB	BH	AVG	PB	PR	/A	PD	TPI
1982 Phi-N	5	1	.833	29	0	0	0	2	39	41	2	14	26	12.9	4.15	88	.281	.348	1	.250	-0	-2	-2	0	-0.1
1983 Phi-N	2	3	.400	31	0	0	0	0	41^{1}	38	9	15	24	12.0	3.70	96	.255	.331	0	.000	-0	-0	-1	0	0.0
1984 Chi-N	0	0	—	5	0	0	0	0	11^{1}	8	2	1	7	7.1	4.76	82	.195	.214	0	.000	-0	-1	-1	0	0.0
Total 3	7	4	.636	65	0	0	0	2	91^{2}	87	13	30	57	11.8	4.03	91	.259	.325	1	.125	-0	-4	-4	1	-0.1

■ ERNIE ALTEN
Alten, Ernest Matthias "Lefty" b: 12/1/1894, Avon, Ohio d: 9/9/81, Napa, Cal. BR/TL, 6', 175 lbs. Deb: 4/17/20

YEAR TM/L	W	L	PCT	G	GS	CG	SH	SV	IP	H	HR	BB	SO	RAT	ERA	ERA+	OAV	OOB	BH	AVG	PB	PR	/A	PD	TPI
1920 Det-A	0	1	.000	14	1	0	0	0	23	40	2	9	4	19.6	9.00	41	.392	.446	0	.000	-1	-13	-13	0	-1.2

■ NICK ALTROCK
Altrock, Nicholas b: 9/15/1876, Cincinnati, Ohio d: 1/20/65, Washington, D.C. BB/TL, 5'10", 197 lbs. Deb: 7/14/1898 C♦

YEAR TM/L	W	L	PCT	G	GS	CG	SH	SV	IP	H	HR	BB	SO	RAT	ERA	ERA+	OAV	OOB	BH	AVG	PB	PR	/A	PD	TPI
1898 Lou-N	3	3	.500	11	7	6	0	0	70	89	2	21	13	14.1	4.50	79	.307	.354	7	.241	0	-7	-7	2	-0.3
1902 Bos-A	0	2	.000	3	2	1	0	1	18	19	0	7	5	13.0	2.00	179	.271	.338	0	.000	-1	3	3	1	0.2
1903 Bos-A	0	1	.000	1	1	1	0	0	8	13	0	4	3	19.1	9.00	34	.363	.427	2	.667	1	-5	-5	1	-0.2

YEAR	TM/L	W	L	PCT	G	GS	CG	SH	SV	IP	H	HR	BB	SO	RAT	ERA	ERA+	OAV	OOB	BH	AVG	PB	PR	/A	PD	TPI
	Chi-A	4	3	.571	12	8	6	1	0	71	59	4	19	19	9.9	2.15	130	.226	.278	9	.300	2	6	5	3	1.1
	Yr	4	4	.500	13	9	7	1	0	79	72	4	23	22	10.8	2.85	99	.242	.297	4	.121	3	1	-0	4	0.9
1904	Chi-A	19	14	.576	38	36	31	6	1	307	274	2	48	87	9.4	2.96	83	.240	.270	22	.198	1	-12	-17	5	-1.2
1905	Chi-A	23	12	.657	38	34	31	3	0	315²	274	3	63	97	9.6	1.88	131	.235	.274	14	.125	-4	27	21	10	2.9
1906	*Chi-A	20	13	.606	38	30	25	4	0	287²	269	0	42	99	9.7	2.06	123	.251	.279	16	.160	-1	20	15	4	2.1
1907	Chi-A	7	13	.350	30	21	15	1	2	213²	210	3	31	61	10.2	2.57	93	.259	.286	13	.181	0	-0	-4	6	0.1
1908	Chi-A	5	7	.417	23	13	8	1	2	136	127	2	18	21	9.7	2.71	85	.248	.276	10	.204	0	-5	-6	6	0.0
1909	Chi-A	0	1	.000	1	1	1	0	0	9	16	1	0	2	17.0	5.00	47	.485	.500	0	.000	0	-3	-3	0	-0.2
	Was-A	1	3	.250	9	5	2	0	0	38	55	0	5	9	14.4	5.45	45	.333	.357	1	.053	-1	-13	-13	1	-1.3
	Yr	1	4	.200	10	6	3	0	0	47	71	0	6	11	14.9	5.36	45	.359	.380	2	.091	-1	-15	-15	1	-1.5
1912	Was-A	1	0	1.000	1	0	0	0	0	1	1	0	2	0	27.0	18.00	19	.200	.429	0	.000	-0	-2	-2	0	-0.1
1913	Was-A	0	0	—	4	0	0	0	0	9	7	0	4	2	12.0	5.00	59	.184	.279	0	.000	-0	-2	-2	0	-0.1
1914	Was-A	0	0	—	1	0	0	0	0	1	3	0	0	0	27.0	0.00	—	.750	.750	0	—	0	0	0	0	0.0
1915	Was-A	0	0	—	1	0	0	0	1	3	7	0	1	2	24.0	9.00	33	.438	.471	0	.000	-0	-2	-2	-0	-0.1
1918	Was-A	1	2	.333	5	3	1	0	0	24	24	1	6	5	11.6	3.00	91	.279	.333	1	.125	0	-1	-1	1	0.0
1919	Was-A	0	0	—	1	0	0	0	0	0	4	0	0	0	—	∞	—	1.000	1.000	0	—	0	-4	-4	0	-0.2
1924	Was-A	0	0	—	1	0	0	0	0	2	4	0	0	0	18.0	0.00	—	.500	.500	1	1.000	1	1	1	0	0.2
Total 16		83	75	.525	218	161	128	16	7	1514	1455	17	272	425	10.3	2.67	95	.254	.289	97	.176	-1	3	-20	40	2.9

■ JOSE ALVAREZ
Alvarez, Jose Lino b: 4/12/56, Tampa, Fla. BR/TR, 5'10", 170 lbs. Deb: 10/01/81

YEAR	TM/L	W	L	PCT	G	GS	CG	SH	SV	IP	H	HR	BB	SO	RAT	ERA	ERA+	OAV	OOB	BH	AVG	PB	PR	/A	PD	TPI
1981	Atl-N	0	0	—	1	0	0	0	0	2	0	0	0	2	0.0	0.00	—	.000	.000	0	—	0	1	1	0	0.1
1982	Atl-N	0	0	—	7	0	0	0	0	7²	8	1	2	6	11.7	4.70	79	.308	.357	0	—	0	-1	-1	0	0.0
1988	Atl-N	5	6	.455	60	0	0	0	3	102¹	88	7	53	81	12.9	2.99	123	.240	.346	3	.375	1	5	8	1	1.1
1989	Atl-N	3	3	.500	30	0	0	0	2	50¹	44	4	24	45	12.3	2.86	128	.237	.327	0	.000	-0	4	4	1	0.5
Total 4		8	9	.471	98	0	0	0	5	162¹	140	12	79	134	12.5	2.99	123	.240	.337	3	.273	1	9	12	2	1.7

■ WILSON ALVAREZ
Alvarez, Wilson Eduardo (Fuenmayor) b: 3/24/70, Maracaibo, Venez. BL/TL, 6'1", 175 lbs. Deb: 7/24/89

YEAR	TM/L	W	L	PCT	G	GS	CG	SH	SV	IP	H	HR	BB	SO	RAT	ERA	ERA+	OAV	OOB	BH	AVG	PB	PR	/A	PD	TPI
1989	Tex-A	0	1	.000	1	1	0	0	0	0	3	2	2	0	—	∞	—	1.000	1.000	0	—	0	-3	-3	0	-0.2

■ RED AMES
Ames, Leon Kessling b: 8/2/1882, Warren, Ohio d: 10/8/36, Warren, Ohio BB/TR, 5'10.5", 185 lbs. Deb: 9/14/03

YEAR	TM/L	W	L	PCT	G	GS	CG	SH	SV	IP	H	HR	BB	SO	RAT	ERA	ERA+	OAV	OOB	BH	AVG	PB	PR	/A	PD	TPI
1903	NY-N	2	0	1.000	2	2	2	1	0	14	5	0	8	14	8.4	1.29	260	.114	.250	0	.000	-1	3	3	-1	0.2
1904	NY-N	4	6	.400	16	13	11	1	3	115	94	2	38	93	10.6	2.27	120	.222	.291	5	.125	-1	6	6	-1	0.4
1905	*NY-N	22	8	.733	34	31	21	2	0	263	220	2	105	198	11.2	2.74	107	.230	.308	14	.144	-1	8	6	0	0.5
1906	NY-N	12	10	.545	31	25	15	1	1	203¹	166	1	93	156	11.6	2.66	98	.223	.312	4	.066	-3	-0	-1	2	-0.2
1907	NY-N	10	12	.455	39	26	17	2	1	233¹	184	4	108	146	11.6	2.16	115	.219	.315	12	.174	2	8	8	2	1.4
1908	NY-N	7	4	.636	18	15	5	0	1	114¹	96	0	27	81	9.8	1.81	133	.232	.281	7	.194	0	7	8	0	0.9
1909	NY-N	15	10	.600	34	26	20	2	1	244	217	3	81	156	11.1	2.69	95	.241	.306	6	.074	-5	-2	-4	6	-0.2
1910	NY-N	12	11	.522	33	23	13	3	0	190¹	161	3	63	94	10.9	2.22	133	.237	.308	11	.177	-1	17	16	4	2.0
1911	*NY-N	11	10	.524	34	23	13	1	2	205	170	0	54	118	10.0	2.68	126	.223	.277	6	.094	-3	16	16	3	1.5
1912	*NY-N	11	5	.688	33	22	9	2	2	179	194	3	35	83	11.7	2.46	137	.275	.313	13	.224	1	19	18	2	2.2
1913	NY-N	2	1	.667	8	5	2	0	1	41²	35	1	8	30	9.5	2.16	144	.241	.286	2	.154	-1	5	4	2	0.6
	Cin-N	11	13	.458	31	24	12	1	2	187¹	185	7	70	80	12.5	2.88	113	.265	.336	6	.102	-4	7	8	0	0.3
	Yr	13	14	.481	39	29	14	1	3	229	220	7	78	110	11.9	2.75	117	.261	.327	1	.014	-5	12	12	2	0.9
1914	Cin-N	15	23	.395	47	36	18	3	**6**	297	274	8	94	128	11.3	2.64	111	.248	.311	12	.128	-4	5	10	4	1.1
1915	Cin-N	2	4	.333	17	7	4	1	1	68	82	2	24	26	14.0	4.50	64	.311	.368	1	.050	-1	-13	-12	1	-1.2
	StL-N	9	3	.750	15	14	8	2	1	113¹	93	1	32	48	9.9	2.46	113	.226	.282	4	.114	-2	4	4	1	0.4
	Yr	11	7	.611	32	21	12	3	2	181¹	175	3	56	74	11.5	3.23	87	.259	.316	4	.073	-3	-10	-8	2	-0.8
1916	StL-N	11	16	.407	45	22	10	2	**8**	228	225	3	57	98	11.3	2.64	100	.263	.313	12	.176	-0	-1	0	-2	-0.1
1917	StL-N	15	10	.600	43	19	10	2	3	209	189	2	57	62	10.7	2.71	99	.249	.304	12	.188	2	-0	-0	5	0.7
1918	StL-N	9	14	.391	27	25	17	0	1	206²	192	1	52	68	10.8	2.31	117	.252	.304	10	.156	-1	10	9	-1	0.8
1919	StL-N	3	5	.375	23	7	1	0	1	70	88	1	25	19	14.7	4.89	57	.314	.373	4	.222	-0	-15	-16	-2	-1.8
	Phi-N	0	2	.000	3	2	1	0	1	16	26	0	3	4	16.3	6.19	52	.400	.426	2	.400	1	-6	-5	0	-0.3
	Yr	3	7	.300	26	9	2	0	2	86	114	1	28	23	14.9	5.13	56	.329	.380	0	.000	1	-21	-22	-1	-2.1
Total 17		183	167	.523	533	367	209	26	36	3198¹	2896	43	1034	1702	11.2	2.63	108	.245	.309	143	.141	-21	77	77	26	9.2

■ DOC AMOLE
Amole, Morris George b: 7/5/1878, Coatesville, Pa. d: 3/7/12, Wilmington, Del. BR/TL, 5'9", 165 lbs. Deb: 8/19/1897

YEAR	TM/L	W	L	PCT	G	GS	CG	SH	SV	IP	H	HR	BB	SO	RAT	ERA	ERA+	OAV	OOB	BH	AVG	PB	PR	/A	PD	TPI
1897	Bal-N	4	4	.500	11	7	6	0	0	70	67	0	17	19	10.8	2.57	162	.250	.295	3	.107	-3	14	12	0	0.9
1898	Was-N	0	6	.000	7	5	4	0	0	49¹	83	0	22	11	19.2	7.84	47	.370	.426	2	.100	-2	-23	-23	1	-1.8
Total 2		4	10	.286	18	12	10	0	0	119¹	150	0	39	30	14.3	4.75	84	.305	.356	5	.104	-5	-10	-10	1	-0.9

■ VICENTE AMOR
Amor, Vicente (Alvarez) b: 8/8/32, Havana, Cuba BR/TR, 6'3", 182 lbs. Deb: 4/16/55

YEAR	TM/L	W	L	PCT	G	GS	CG	SH	SV	IP	H	HR	BB	SO	RAT	ERA	ERA+	OAV	OOB	BH	AVG	PB	PR	/A	PD	TPI
1955	Chi-N	0	1	.000	4	0	0	0	0	6	11	0	3	3	21.0	4.50	91	.407	.467	0	—	0	-0	-0	1	0.0
1957	Cin-N	1	2	.333	9	4	1	0	0	27¹	39	2	10	9	16.8	5.93	69	.345	.408	1	.167	-0	-6	-6	-0	-0.5
Total 2		1	3	.250	13	4	1	0	0	33¹	50	2	13	12	17.6	5.67	72	.357	.419	1	.167	-0	-7	-6	0	-0.5

■ WALTER ANCKER
Ancker, Walter b: 4/10/1894, New York, N.Y. d: 2/13/54, Englewood, N.J. BR/TR, 6'1", 190 lbs. Deb: 9/03/15

YEAR	TM/L	W	L	PCT	G	GS	CG	SH	SV	IP	H	HR	BB	SO	RAT	ERA	ERA+	OAV	OOB	BH	AVG	PB	PR	/A	PD	TPI
1915	Phi-A	0	0	—	4	1	0	0	0	17²	19	1	17	4	19.9	3.57	83	.279	.443	0	.000	-1	-1	-1	0	-0.1

■ LARRY ANDERSEN
Andersen, Larry Eugene b: 5/6/53, Portland, Ore. BR/TR, 6'3", 200 lbs. Deb: 9/05/75

YEAR	TM/L	W	L	PCT	G	GS	CG	SH	SV	IP	H	HR	BB	SO	RAT	ERA	ERA+	OAV	OOB	BH	AVG	PB	PR	/A	PD	TPI
1975	Cle-A	0	0	—	3	0	0	0	0	5²	4	0	2	4	9.5	4.76	79	.200	.273	0	—	0	-1	-1	0	0.0
1977	Cle-A	0	1	.000	11	0	0	0	0	14¹	10	1	9	8	11.9	3.14	126	.200	.322	0	—	0	1	1	1	0.2
1979	Cle-A	0	0	—	8	0	0	0	0	16²	25	3	4	7	15.7	7.56	56	.357	.392	0	—	0	-6	-6	0	-0.4
1981	Sea-A	3	3	.500	41	0	0	0	0	67²	57	4	18	40	10.2	2.66	145	.228	.285	0	—	0	7	9	-0	0.9
1982	Sea-A	0	0	—	40	1	0	0	1	79²	100	16	23	32	14.3	5.99	71	.311	.364	0	—	0	-17	-15	1	-1.3
1983	*Phi-N	1	0	1.000	17	0	0	0	0	26¹	19	0	9	14	9.6	2.39	149	.200	.269	0	.000	-0	4	3	1	0.4
1984	Phi-N	3	7	.300	64	0	0	0	4	90²	85	5	25	54	10.9	2.38	152	.248	.299	0	.000	-0	12	13	0	1.3
1985	Phi-N	3	3	.500	57	0	0	0	3	73	78	5	26	50	13.2	4.32	85	.274	.341	0	.000	-0	-6	-5	2	-0.3
1986	Phi-N	0	0	—	10	0	0	0	0	12²	19	0	3	9	15.6	4.26	90	.388	.423	0	—	0	-1	-1	0	0.0
	*Hou-N	2	1	.667	38	0	0	0	1	64²	64	2	23	33	12.2	2.78	129	.276	.344	0	.000	-1	7	6	1	0.6
	Yr	2	1	.667	48	0	0	0	1	77¹	83	2	26	42	12.8	3.03	120	.294	.356	0	.000	-1	6	5	1	0.6
1987	Hou-N	9	5	.643	67	0	0	0	5	101²	95	7	41	94	12.2	3.45	113	.246	.322	1	.167	0	7	5	-1	0.5
1988	Hou-N	2	4	.333	53	0	0	0	5	82²	82	3	20	66	11.2	2.94	113	.254	.299	2	.333	1	5	3	-0	0.4
1989	Hou-N	4	4	.500	60	0	0	0	3	87²	63	2	24	85	8.9	1.54	220	.198	.254	1	.333	0	**19**	18	0	2.0
1990	Hou-N	5	2	.714	50	0	0	0	6	73²	61	2	24	69	10.5	1.95	191	.229	.296	0	.000	-0	15	15	1	1.6
	*Bos-A	0	0	—	15	0	0	0	1	22	18	0	3	25	9.0	1.23	332	.220	.256	0	—	0	7	7	-1	0.7
Total 13		32	30	.516	534	1	0	0	34	819	780	50	254	589	11.5	3.15	118	.252	.312	4	.118	-1	53	52	6	6.6

■ ALLAN ANDERSON
Anderson, Allan Lee b: 1/7/64, Lancaster, Ohio BL/TL, 5'11.5", 178 lbs. Deb: 6/11/86

YEAR	TM/L	W	L	PCT	G	GS	CG	SH	SV	IP	H	HR	BB	SO	RAT	ERA	ERA+	OAV	OOB	BH	AVG	PB	PR	/A	PD	TPI
1986	Min-A	3	6	.333	21	10	1	0	0	84¹	106	11	30	51	14.6	5.55	78	.316	.374	0	—	0	-13	-12	0	-1.0
1987	Min-A	1	0	1.000	4	2	0	0	0	12¹	20	3	10	3	21.9	10.95	42	.392	.492	0	—	0	-9	-9	-0	-0.7
1988	Min-A	16	9	.640	30	30	3	1	0	202¹	199	14	37	83	10.8	**2.45**	**166**	.261	.301	0	—	0	34	36	1	4.1
1989	Min-A	17	10	.630	33	33	4	1	0	196²	214	15	53	69	12.5	3.80	109	.275	.327	0	.000	0	2	7	0	0.8
1990	Min-A	7	18	.280	31	31	4	1	0	188²	214	20	39	82	12.3	4.53	92	.289	.329	0	—	0	-13	-7	2	-0.4
Total 5		44	43	.506	119	106	13	3	0	684¹	753	63	169	288	12.4	3.95	106	.282	.330	0	.000	0	1	17	4	2.8

RED ANDERSON
Anderson, Arnold Revola b: 6/19/12, Lawton, Iowa d: 8/7/72, Sioux City, Iowa BR/TR, 6'3", 210 lbs. Deb: 9/19/37

YEAR	TM/L	W	L	PCT	G	GS	CG	SH	SV	IP	H	HR	BB	SO	RAT	ERA	ERA+	OAV	OOB	BH	AVG	PB	PR	/A	PD	TPI
1937	Was-A	0	1	.000	2	1	0	0	0	10²	11	0	11	3	19.4	6.75	66	.282	.451	0	.000	-0	-3	-3	0	-0.2
1940	Was-A	1	1	.500	2	2	2	0	0	14	12	0	5	3	10.9	3.86	108	.245	.315	3	.600	1	1	0	0	0.2
1941	Was-A	4	6	.400	32	6	1	0	0	112	127	7	53	34	14.7	4.18	97	.296	.377	8	.258	2	-0	-2	-1	0.0
Total 3		5	8	.385	36	9	3	0	0	136²	150	7	69	40	14.7	4.35	94	.290	.378	11	.282	3	-2	-4	-0	0.0

DAVE ANDERSON
Anderson, David S. b: 10/10/1868, Chester, Pa. d: 3/22/1897, Chester, Pa. TL, Deb: 8/24/1889

YEAR	TM/L	W	L	PCT	G	GS	CG	SH	SV	IP	H	HR	BB	SO	RAT	ERA	ERA+	OAV	OOB	BH	AVG	PB	PR	/A	PD	TPI
1889	Phi-N	0	1	.000	5	2	1	0	0	23	30	2	14	8	17.2	7.43	59	.305	.392	2	.182	-0	-9	-8	0	-0.5
1890	Phi-N	1	1	.500	3	2	1	0	0	19¹	31	0	11	7	19.6	7.45	49	.352	.424	1	.111	-1	-8	-8	0	-0.6
	Pit-N	2	11	.154	13	13	13	0	0	108	116	2	49	41	13.8	4.67	70	.267	.341	3	.071	-5	-13	-17	4	-1.4
	Yr	3	12	.200	16	15	14	0	0	127¹	147	2	60	48	14.6	5.09	66	.281	.355	1	.020	-6	-22	-25	4	-2.0
Total 2		3	13	.188	21	17	15	0	0	150¹	177	4	74	56	15.0	5.45	64	.285	.361	6	.097	-6	-30	-33	4	-2.5

JOHN ANDERSON
Anderson, John Charles b: 11/23/32, St.Paul, Minn. BR/TR, 6'1", 190 lbs. Deb: 8/17/58

YEAR	TM/L	W	L	PCT	G	GS	CG	SH	SV	IP	H	HR	BB	SO	RAT	ERA	ERA+	OAV	OOB	BH	AVG	PB	PR	/A	PD	TPI
1958	Phi-N	0	0	—	5	1	0	0	0	16	26	5	4	9	17.4	7.88	50	.361	.403	0	.000	-0	-7	-7	-0	-0.6
1960	Bal-A	0	0	—	4	0	0	0	0	4²	8	0	4	1	23.1	13.50	28	.444	.545	0	—	0	-5	-5	-0	-0.3
1962	StL-N	0	0	—	5	0	0	0	1	6¹	4	0	3	3	9.9	1.42	300	.182	.280	0	—	0	2	2	-0	0.2
	Hou-N	0	0	—	10	0	0	0	0	17²	26	1	3	6	14.8	5.09	73	.338	.363	0	.000	-0	-2	-3	1	-0.1
	Yr	0	0	—	15	0	0	0	1	24	30	1	6	9	13.5	4.13	94	.300	.340	0	.000	-0	-0	-1	1	0.1
Total 3		0	0	—	24	1	0	0	1	44²	64	6	14	19	15.9	6.45	60	.339	.387	0	.000	-0	-12	-13	1	-0.8

FRED ANDERSON
Anderson, John Frederick b: 12/11/1885, Calahan, N.C. d: 11/8/57, Winston-Salem, N.C. BR/TR, 6'2", 180 lbs. Deb: 9/25/09

YEAR	TM/L	W	L	PCT	G	GS	CG	SH	SV	IP	H	HR	BB	SO	RAT	ERA	ERA+	OAV	OOB	BH	AVG	PB	PR	/A	PD	TPI
1909	Bos-A	0	0	—	1	1	0	0	0	8	3	0	1	5	4.5	1.13	222	.115	.148	0	.000	-0	1	1	0	0.1
1913	Bos-A	0	6	.000	10	8	4	0	0	57¹	84	0	21	32	16.6	5.97	49	.350	.405	1	.050	-2	-19	-19	-0	-2.0
1914	Buf-F	13	15	.464	37	28	21	2	0	260¹	243	8	64	144	10.7	3.08	107	.249	.297	17	.189	-1	4	6	-2	0.4
1915	Buf-F	19	13	.594	36	28	14	5	0	240	192	5	72	142	10.0	2.51	124	.222	.285	12	.150	-3	14	16	-2	1.2
1916	NY-N	9	13	.409	38	27	13	2	2	188	206	7	38	98	11.9	3.40	72	.277	.316	8	.138	-0	-16	-20	-3	-2.5
1917	*NY-N	8	8	.500	38	18	8	1	3	162	122	1	34	69	**8.8**	**1.44**	**177**	**.209**	**.255**	3	.071	-3	23	20	-1	1.9
1918	NY-N	4	2	.667	18	4	2	1	**3**	70²	62	1	17	24	10.3	2.67	98	.246	.299	0	.000	-3	1	-0	3	0.0
Total 7		53	57	.482	178	114	62	11	8	986¹	912	22	247	514	10.7	2.86	101	.248	.298	41	.131	-13	7	3	-4	-0.9

BUD ANDERSON
Anderson, Karl Adam b: 5/27/56, Westbury, N.Y. BR/TR, 6'3", 210 lbs. Deb: 6/11/82

YEAR	TM/L	W	L	PCT	G	GS	CG	SH	SV	IP	H	HR	BB	SO	RAT	ERA	ERA+	OAV	OOB	BH	AVG	PB	PR	/A	PD	TPI
1982	Cle-A	3	4	.429	25	5	1	0	0	80²	84	4	30	44	12.8	3.35	122	.268	.334	0	—	0	7	7	-0	0.6
1983	Cle-A	1	6	.143	39	1	0	0	7	68¹	64	8	32	32	12.6	4.08	104	.255	.339	0	—	0	-0	1	-1	0.0
Total 2		4	10	.286	64	6	1	0	7	149	148	12	62	76	12.7	3.68	113	.262	.337	0	—	0	6	8	-1	0.6

LARRY ANDERSON
Anderson, Lawrence Dennis b: 12/3/52, Maywood, Cal. BR/TR, 6'3", 190 lbs. Deb: 9/25/74

YEAR	TM/L	W	L	PCT	G	GS	CG	SH	SV	IP	H	HR	BB	SO	RAT	ERA	ERA+	OAV	OOB	BH	AVG	PB	PR	/A	PD	TPI
1974	Mil-A	0	0	—	2	0	0	0	0	2¹	2	0	1	3	11.6	0.00	—	.250	.333	0	—	0	1	1	0	0.1
1975	Mil-A	1	0	1.000	8	1	1	1	0	30¹	36	3	6	13	12.5	5.04	76	.298	.331	0	—	0	-4	-4	0	-0.3
1977	Chi-A	1	3	.250	6	0	0	0	0	8²	10	1	15	7	26.0	9.35	44	.286	.500	0	—	0	-5	-5	-0	-0.4
Total 3		2	3	.400	16	1	1	1	0	41¹	48	4	22	23	15.2	5.66	68	.293	.376	0	—	0	-8	-8	0	-0.6

MIKE ANDERSON
Anderson, Michael Allen b: 6/22/51, Florence, S.C. BR/TR, 6'2", 200 lbs. Deb: 9/02/71 ♦

YEAR	TM/L	W	L	PCT	G	GS	CG	SH	SV	IP	H	HR	BB	SO	RAT	ERA	ERA+	OAV	OOB	BH	AVG	PB	PR	/A	PD	TPI
1979	Phi-N	0	0	—	1	0	0	0	0	1	2	0	0	2	18.0	0.00	—	.400	.400	18	.231	0	0	0	0	0.0

CRAIG ANDERSON
Anderson, Norman Craig b: 7/1/38, Washington, D.C. BR/TR, 6'2", 205 lbs. Deb: 6/23/61

YEAR	TM/L	W	L	PCT	G	GS	CG	SH	SV	IP	H	HR	BB	SO	RAT	ERA	ERA+	OAV	OOB	BH	AVG	PB	PR	/A	PD	TPI
1961	StL-N	4	3	.571	25	0	0	0	1	38²	38	3	12	21	11.9	3.26	135	.255	.315	3	.333	1	3	5	0	0.6
1962	NY-N	3	17	.150	50	14	2	0	4	131¹	150	18	63	62	14.9	5.35	78	.278	.359	3	.094	-2	-20	-17	3	-1.5
1963	NY-N	0	2	.000	3	2	0	0	0	9¹	17	0	3	6	19.3	8.68	40	.362	.400	1	.333	-0	-6	-5	0	-0.4
1964	NY-N	0	1	.000	4	1	0	0	0	13	21	0	3	5	16.6	5.54	65	.382	.414	0	.000	-0	-3	-3	0	-0.2
Total 4		7	23	.233	82	17	2	0	5	192¹	226	21	81	94	14.6	5.10	81	.286	.357	7	.149	-1	-26	-20	3	-1.5

RICK ANDERSON
Anderson, Richard Arlen b: 11/29/56, Everett, Wash. BR/TR, 6', 175 lbs. Deb: 6/09/86

YEAR	TM/L	W	L	PCT	G	GS	CG	SH	SV	IP	H	HR	BB	SO	RAT	ERA	ERA+	OAV	OOB	BH	AVG	PB	PR	/A	PD	TPI
1986	NY-N	2	1	.667	15	5	0	0	1	49²	45	3	11	21	10.1	2.72	130	.245	.287	1	.091	-1	6	5	-0	0.4
1987	KC-A	0	2	.000	6	2	0	0	0	13	26	3	9	12	25.6	13.85	33	.394	.481	0	—	0	-14	-13	0	-1.0
1988	KC-A	2	1	.667	7	3	0	0	0	34	41	3	9	9	13.5	4.24	94	.308	.357	0	—	0	-1	-1	-0	-0.6
Total 3		4	4	.500	28	10	0	0	1	96²	112	9	29	42	13.4	4.75	81	.292	.347	1	.091	-1	-9	-10	-0	-0.6

RICK ANDERSON
Anderson, Richard Lee b: 12/25/53, Inglewood, Cal. d: 6/23/89, Wilmington, Cal. BR/TR, 6'2", 210 lbs. Deb: 9/18/79

YEAR	TM/L	W	L	PCT	G	GS	CG	SH	SV	IP	H	HR	BB	SO	RAT	ERA	ERA+	OAV	OOB	BH	AVG	PB	PR	/A	PD	TPI
1979	NY-A	0	0	—	1	0	0	0	0	2¹	1	0	4	0	19.3	3.86	106	.167	.500	0	—	0	0	0	1	0.1
1980	Sea-A	0	0	—	5	2	0	0	0	9²	8	1	10	7	16.8	3.72	110	.229	.400	0	—	0	0	0	-0	0.0
Total 2		0	0	—	6	2	0	0	0	12	9	1	14	7	17.3	3.75	110	.220	.418	0	—	0	0	0	1	0.1

BOB ANDERSON
Anderson, Robert Carl b: 9/29/35, E.Chicago, Ind. BR/TR, 6'4.5", 210 lbs. Deb: 7/31/57

YEAR	TM/L	W	L	PCT	G	GS	CG	SH	SV	IP	H	HR	BB	SO	RAT	ERA	ERA+	OAV	OOB	BH	AVG	PB	PR	/A	PD	TPI
1957	Chi-N	0	1	.000	8	0	0	0	0	16¹	20	2	8	7	16.0	7.71	50	.317	.403	0	.000	-1	-7	-7	0	-0.6
1958	Chi-N	3	3	.500	17	8	2	0	0	65²	61	3	29	51	12.5	3.97	99	.255	.338	2	.118	-1	-0	-0	0	0.0
1959	Chi-N	12	13	.480	37	36	7	1	0	235¹	245	21	77	113	12.5	4.13	96	.272	.333	6	.075	-4	-5	-5	1	-0.7
1960	Chi-N	9	11	.450	38	30	5	0	1	203²	201	26	68	115	12.2	4.11	92	.255	.320	12	.169	-0	-8	-8	1	-0.6
1961	Chi-N	7	10	.412	57	12	1	0	8	152	162	14	56	96	13.0	4.26	98	.275	.340	6	.143	0	-4	-1	3	0.2
1962	Chi-N	2	7	.222	57	4	0	0	4	107²	111	9	60	82	14.7	5.02	83	.286	.364	3	.130	0	-13	-10	-1	-1.0
1963	Det-A	3	1	.750	32	3	0	0	0	60	58	5	21	38	12.8	3.30	113	.258	.337	4	.444	2	2	3	-0	0.4
Total 7		36	46	.439	246	93	15	1	13	840²	858	80	319	502	12.9	4.26	93	.266	.337	33	.134	-4	-34	-29	5	-2.3

SCOTT ANDERSON
Anderson, Scott Richard b: 8/1/62, Corvallis, Ore. BR/TR, 6'6", 190 lbs. Deb: 4/08/87

YEAR	TM/L	W	L	PCT	G	GS	CG	SH	SV	IP	H	HR	BB	SO	RAT	ERA	ERA+	OAV	OOB	BH	AVG	PB	PR	/A	PD	TPI
1987	Tex-A	0	1	.000	8	0	0	0	0	11¹	17	0	8	6	20.6	9.53	47	.347	.448	0	—	0	-6	-6	1	-0.4
1990	Mon-N	0	1	.000	4	3	0	0	0	18	12	1	5	16	8.5	3.00	125	.188	.246	0	.000	-0	2	2	-0	0.1
Total 2		0	2	.000	12	3	0	0	0	29¹	29	1	13	22	13.2	5.52	73	.257	.339	0	.000	-0	-5	-5	0	-0.3

VARNEY ANDERSON
Anderson, Varney Samuel "Varn" b: 6/18/1866, Geneva, Ill. d: 11/5/41, Rockford, Ill. BR/TR, 5'10", 165 lbs. Deb: 8/01/1889

YEAR	TM/L	W	L	PCT	G	GS	CG	SH	SV	IP	H	HR	BB	SO	RAT	ERA	ERA+	OAV	OOB	BH	AVG	PB	PR	/A	PD	TPI
1889	Ind-N	0	1	.000	2	1	1	0	0	12	13	0	9	3	16.5	4.50	93	.267	.382	0	.000	-1	-1	-0	0	0.0
1894	Was-N	0	2	.000	2	2	2	0	0	14	15	0	6	3	13.5	7.07	74	.271	.342	3	.429	1	-3	-3	-0	-0.1
1895	Was-N	9	16	.360	29	25	18	0	0	204²	288	13	97	35	16.9	5.89	81	.327	.394	28	.289	3	-25	-25	1	-1.5
1896	Was-N	0	1	.000	2	2	1	0	0	9	23	0	3	0	26.0	13.00	34	.471	.502	3	.600	1	-9	-9	-1	-0.5
Total 4		9	20	.310	35	30	22	0	0	239²	339	13	115	41	17.0	6.16	78	.328	.395	34	.298	4	-37	-37	1	-2.1

WALTER ANDERSON
Anderson, Walter Carl "Lefty" b: 9/25/1897, Grand Rapids, Mich BL/TL, 6'2", 160 lbs. Deb: 5/14/17

YEAR	TM/L	W	L	PCT	G	GS	CG	SH	SV	IP	H	HR	BB	SO	RAT	ERA	ERA+	OAV	OOB	BH	AVG	PB	PR	/A	PD	TPI
1917	Phi-A	0	0	—	14	2	0	0	0	38²	32	0	21	10	12.6	3.03	91	.246	.355	3	.429	1	-2	-1	-0	0.0
1919	Phi-A	1	0	1.000	3	0	0	0	0	14	13	0	8	10	14.1	3.86	89	.245	.355	0	.000	-1	-1	-1	0	0.0
Total 2		1	0	1.000	17	2	0	0	0	52²	45	0	29	20	13.0	3.25	90	.246	.355	3	.273	0	-3	-2	0	0.0

BILL ANDERSON
Anderson, William Edward "Lefty" b: 11/28/1895, Boston, Mass. d: 3/13/83, Medford, Mass. BR/TL, 6'1", 165 lbs. Deb: 9/10/25

YEAR	TM/L	W	L	PCT	G	GS	CG	SH	SV	IP	H	HR	BB	SO	RAT	ERA	ERA+	OAV	OOB	BH	AVG	PB	PR	/A	PD	TPI
1925	Bos-N	0	0	—	2	0	0	0	0	2²	5	0	2	1	23.6	10.13	40	.500	.583	0	.000	-0	-2	-2	-0	-0.1

WINGO ANDERSON
Anderson, Wingo Charlie b: 8/13/1886, Alvarado, Tex. d: 12/19/50, Fort Worth, Tex. BL/TL, 5'10.5", 150 lbs. Deb: 4/16/10

YEAR	TM/L	W	L	PCT	G	GS	CG	SH	SV	IP	H	HR	BB	SO	RAT	ERA	ERA+	OAV	OOB	BH	AVG	PB	PR	/A	PD	TPI
1910	Cin-N	0	0	—	7	2	0	0	0	17¹	16	0	17	11	17.7	4.67	62	.258	.425	1	.200	-0	-3	-3	-1	-0.3

YEAR	TM/L	W	L	PCT	G	GS	CG	SH	SV	IP	H	HR	BB	SO	RAT	ERA	ERA+	OAV	OOB	BH	AVG	PB	PR	/A	PD	TPI

■ JOHN ANDRE Andre, John Edward b: 1/3/23, Brockton, Mass. d: 11/25/76, Centerville, Mass. BL/TR, 6'4", 200 lbs. Deb: 4/16/55

| | 1955 | Chi-N | 0 | 1 | .000 | 22 | 3 | 0 | 0 | 1 | 45 | 45 | 7 | 28 | 19 | 14.8 | 5.80 | 70 | .259 | .365 | 1 | .111 | -1 | -9 | -9 | -0 | -0.8 |

■ ELBERT ANDREWS Andrews, Elbert De Vore b: 12/11/01, Greenwood, S.C. d: 11/25/79, Greenwood, S.C. BL/TR, 6', 175 lbs. Deb: 5/01/25

| | 1925 | Phi-A | 0 | 0 | — | 6 | 0 | 0 | 0 | 0 | 8 | 12 | 0 | 11 | 0 | 25.9 | 10.13 | 46 | .375 | .535 | 0 | — | 0 | -5 | -5 | 0 | -0.3 |

■ HUB ANDREWS Andrews, Herbert Carl b: 8/31/22, Burbank, Okla. BR/TR, 6', 170 lbs. Deb: 4/20/47

	1947	NY-N	0	0	—	7	0	0	0	0	8²	14	1	4	2	18.7	6.23	65	.368	.429	0	—	0	-2	-2	0	-0.1
	1948	NY-N	0	0	—	1	0	0	0	0	3	3	0	0	0	9.0	0.00	—	.300	.300	0	—	0	1	1	0	0.2
	Total	2	0	0	—	8	0	0	0	0	11²	17	1	4	2	16.2	4.63	87	.354	.404	0	—	0	-1	-1	0	0.1

■ IVY ANDREWS Andrews, Ivy Paul "Poison" b: 5/6/07, Dora, Ala. d: 11/24/70, Birmingham, Ala. BR/TR, 6'1", 200 lbs. Deb: 8/15/31

	1931	NY-A	2	0	1.000	7	3	1	0	0	34¹	36	3	8	10	11.5	4.19	95	.273	.314	2	.182	0	1	-1	0	0.0
	1932	NY-A	2	1	.667	4	1	1	0	0	24²	20	0	9	7	10.6	1.82	223	.215	.284	2	.222	1	7	6	0	0.8
		Bos-A	8	6	.571	25	19	8	0	0	141²	144	4	53	30	12.6	3.81	118	.262	.329	7	.137	-3	11	11	-1	0.6
		Yr	10	7	.588	29	20	9	0	0	166¹	164	4	62	37	12.3	3.52	126	.255	.322	2	.033	-2	18	17	-0	1.4
	1933	Bos-A	7	13	.350	34	17	5	0	1	140	157	8	61	37	14.1	4.95	88	.279	.350	9	.214	-0	-10	-9	-1	-0.8
	1934	StL-A	4	11	.267	43	13	2	0	3	139	166	7	65	51	15.0	4.66	107	.301	.375	14	.350	4	-3	5	-2	0.7
	1935	StL-A	13	7	.650	50	20	10	0	1	213¹	231	10	53	43	12.0	3.54	135	.273	.317	9	.132	-6	22	30	-2	2.1
	1936	StL-A	7	12	.368	36	25	11	0	1	191¹	221	15	50	33	12.7	4.84	111	.286	.330	10	.169	-1	4	11	-2	0.8
	1937	Cle-A	3	4	.429	20	4	1	1	0	59²	76	3	9	16	12.8	4.37	105	.311	.336	3	.250	1	2	2	-1	0.1
	*NY-A		3	2	.600	11	5	3	1	1	49	49	2	17	17	12.1	3.12	142	.259	.320	1	.067	-1	8	7	1	0.6
		Yr	6	6	.500	31	9	4	2	1	108²	125	5	26	33	12.5	3.81	119	.289	.329	4	.137	-1	10	9	-0	0.7
	1938	NY-A	1	3	.250	19	1	1	0	1	48	51	3	17	13	12.8	3.00	151	.268	.329	2	.167	-0	10	8	0	0.8
	Total	8	50	59	.459	249	108	43	2	8	1041	1151	59	342	257	12.9	4.14	115	.279	.335	59	.185	-6	51	70	-6	5.7

■ JOHN ANDREWS Andrews, John Richard b: 2/9/49, Monterey Park, Cal. BL/TL, 5'10", 175 lbs. Deb: 4/08/73

| | 1973 | StL-N | 1 | 1 | .500 | 16 | 0 | 0 | 0 | 0 | 18¹ | 16 | 3 | 11 | 5 | 13.3 | 4.42 | 82 | .235 | .342 | 1 | .500 | 0 | -2 | -2 | -0 | -0.1 |

■ NATE ANDREWS Andrews, Nathan Hardy b: 9/30/13, Pembroke, N.C. BR/TR, 6', 195 lbs. Deb: 5/01/37

	1937	StL-N	0	0	—	4	0	0	0	0	9	12	1	3	6	15.0	4.00	100	.324	.375	0	—	0	-0	-0	0	0.1
	1939	StL-N	1	2	.333	11	1	0	0	0	16	24	0	12	6	20.3	6.75	61	.343	.439	0	.000	-0	-5	-5	0	-0.3
	1940	Cle-A	0	1	.000	6	0	0	0	0	12	16	1	6	3	16.5	6.00	70	.327	.400	0	.000	-0	-2	-2	1	0.0
	1941	Cle-A	0	0	—	2	0	0	0	0	2¹	3	0	2	1	19.3	11.57	34	.300	.417	0	.000	-0	-2	-2	0	-0.1
	1943	Bos-N	14	20	.412	36	34	23	3	0	283²	253	11	75	80	10.6	2.57	133	.238	.291	14	.156	-0	26	27	2	3.2
	1944	Bos-N	16	15	.516	37	34	16	2	2	257¹	263	14	74	76	11.9	3.22	119	.261	.312	10	.114	-4	11	17	2	1.6
	1945	Bos-N	7	12	.368	21	19	8	0	0	137²	160	9	52	26	13.9	4.58	84	.295	.356	9	.209	-1	-12	-11	0	-1.0
	1946	Cin-N	2	4	.333	7	7	3	0	0	43¹	50	2	8	13	12.3	3.95	85	.281	.316	1	.071	-1	-3	-3	-0	-0.3
		NY-N	1	0	1.000	3	2	0	0	0	12	17	2	4	5	15.8	6.00	57	.362	.412	1	.500	1	-3	-3	-0	-0.2
		Yr	3	4	.429	10	9	3	0	0	55¹	67	4	12	18	12.8	4.39	77	.296	.332	2	.125	0	-6	-6	-0	-0.5
	Total	8	41	54	.432	127	97	50	5	2	773¹	798	40	236	216	12.1	3.46	106	.265	.321	35	.146	-4	10	17	5	3.0

■ FRED ANDRUS Andrus, Frederick Hotham b: 8/23/1850, Washington, Mich. d: 11/10/37, Detroit, Mich. BR/TR, 6'2", 185 lbs. Deb: 7/25/1876 ♦

| | 1884 | Chi-N | 1 | 0 | 1.000 | 1 | 1 | 1 | 0 | 0 | 9 | 11 | 1 | 2 | 2 | 13.0 | 2.00 | 157 | .285 | .321 | 1 | .200 | 0 | 1 | 1 | 0 | 0.1 |

■ JOAQUIN ANDUJAR Andujar, Joaquin b: 12/21/52, San Pedro De Macoris, D.R. BB/TR, 6', 170 lbs. Deb: 4/08/76

	1976	Hou-N	9	10	.474	28	25	9	4	0	172¹	163	8	75	59	12.5	3.60	89	.255	.334	8	.140	-0	-2	-8	-0	-0.8
	1977	Hou-N	11	8	.579	26	25	4	1	0	158²	149	11	64	69	12.3	3.69	97	.251	.328	10	.189	1	4	-2	3	0.1
	1978	Hou-N	5	7	.417	35	13	2	0	1	110²	88	3	58	55	12.2	3.42	97	.224	.330	3	.130	-2	-1	2	0.1
	1979	Hou-N	12	12	.500	46	23	8	0	4	194	168	7	88	77	12.0	3.43	102	.233	.319	5	.088	-0	6	2	5	0.6
	1980	*Hou-N	3	8	.273	35	14	0	0	2	122	132	8	43	75	12.9	3.91	84	.277	.337	5	.172	2	-4	-8	1	-0.4
	1981	Hou-N	2	3	.400	9	3	0	0	0	23²	29	2	12	18	15.6	4.94	67	.296	.373	0	.000	-0	-4	-4	-1	-0.4
		StL-N	6	1	.857	11	8	1	0	0	55¹	56	4	11	19	10.9	3.74	95	.265	.302	0	.000	-2	-2	-1	-0	-0.2
		Yr	8	4	.667	20	11	1	0	0	79	85	6	23	37	12.3	4.10	85	.273	.323	1	.043	-2	-5	-5	-0	-0.6
	1982	*StL-N	15	10	.600	38	37	9	5	0	265²	237	11	50	137	10.0	2.47	146	.240	.282	15	.158	-1	33	34	1	3.8
	1983	StL-N	6	16	.273	39	34	5	2	1	225	215	23	75	125	11.7	4.16	87	.253	.316	6	.082	-3	-13	-14	5	-1.1
	1984	StL-N	**20**	14	.588	36	36	12	**4**	0	**261¹**	218	20	70	147	10.2	3.34	104	.229	.286	11	.131	3	7	4	3	0.9
	1985	*StL-N	21	12	.636	38	38	10	2	0	269²	265	15	82	112	11.9	3.40	104	.260	.322	10	.106	-0	6	4	0	0.2
	1986	Oak-A	12	7	.632	28	26	7	1	1	155¹	139	23	56	72	11.5	3.82	101	.239	.310	0	—	0	6	1	1	0.2
	1987	Oak-A	3	5	.375	13	13	1	0	0	60²	63	11	26	32	13.6	6.08	68	.269	.350	0	—	0	-11	-13	0	-1.1
	1988	Hou-N	2	5	.286	23	10	0	0	0	78²	94	9	21	35	13.7	4.00	83	.297	.350	4	.211	2	-5	-6	0	-0.3
	Total	13	127	118	.518	405	305	68	19	9	2153	2016	155	731	1032	11.7	3.58	98	.250	.316	77	.127	-1	24	-13	21	1.6

■ NORM ANGELINI Angelini, Norman Stanley b: 9/24/47, San Francisco, Cal. BL/TL, 5'11", 175 lbs. Deb: 7/22/72

	1972	KC-A	2	1	.667	21	0	0	0	2	16	13	1	12	16	14.6	2.25	135	.228	.371	0	.000	-0	1	1	-0	0.1
	1973	KC-A	0	0	—	7	0	0	0	1	3²	2	0	7	3	22.1	4.91	84	.200	.529	0	—	0	-0	-0	0	0.0
	Total	2	2	1	.667	28	0	0	0	3	19²	15	1	19	19	16.0	2.75	117	.224	.402	0	.000	-0	1	1	-0	0.1

■ CAP ANSON Anson, Adrian Constantine b: 4/11/1852, Marshalltown, Iowa d: 4/14/22, Chicago, Ill. BR/TR, 6', 227 lbs. Deb: 5/06/1871 MH♦

	1883	Chi-N	0	0	—	2	0	0	0	1	3	1	0	1	0	6.0	0.00	—	.098	.178	127	.308	1	1	1	0	0.1
	1884	Chi-N	0	1	.000	1	0	0	0	0	1	3	2	1	1	36.0	18.00	17	.495	.567	159	.335	1	-2	-2	0	0.0
	Total	2	0	1	.000	3	0	0	0	1	4	4	2	2	1	13.5	4.50	71	.246	.328	2995	.329	1	-1	-1	0	0.1

■ JOHNNY ANTONELLI Antonelli, John August b: 4/12/30, Rochester, N.Y. BL/TL, 6'1.5", 185 lbs. Deb: 7/04/48

	1948	Bos-N	0	0	—	4	0	0	0	0	4	2	0	3	0	11.3	2.25	170	.143	.294	0	—	0	1	1	0	0.1
	1949	Bos-N	3	7	.300	22	10	3	1	0	96	99	6	42	48	13.4	3.56	106	.273	.351	3	.120	-1	5	2	-1	0.0
	1950	Bos-N	2	3	.400	20	6	2	1	0	57²	81	2	33	33	16.7	5.93	65	.335	.399	2	.125	-1	-11	-13	0	-1.2
	1953	Mil-N	12	12	.500	31	26	11	2	1	175¹	167	15	71	131	12.3	3.18	123	.242	.314	11	.177	0	22	14	1	1.5
	1954	*NY-N	21	7	**.750**	39	37	18	**6**	2	258²	209	22	94	152	10.7	**2.30**	**176**	**.219**	.293	16	.163	0	**51**	**50**	2	**5.5**
	1955	NY-N	14	16	.467	38	34	14	2	1	235¹	206	24	82	143	11.4	3.33	121	.234	.307	17	.207	3	19	18	1	2.3
	1956	NY-N	20	13	.606	41	36	15	5	1	258¹	225	20	75	145	10.6	2.86	132	.234	.292	14	.157	1	26	27	1	3.1
	1957	NY-N	12	18	.400	40	30	8	3	0	212¹	228	19	67	114	12.6	3.77	104	.276	.333	11	.153	1	3	4	-2	0.5
	1958	SF-N	16	13	.552	41	34	13	0	3	241²	216	31	87	143	11.4	3.28	116	.239	.308	19	.226	4	18	14	-3	1.5
	1959	SF-N	19	10	.655	40	38	17	**4**	1	282	247	29	76	165	10.4	3.10	123	.233	.286	16	.158	1	27	22	-1	2.3
	1960	SF-N	6	7	.462	41	10	1	1	11	112¹	106	7	47	57	12.4	3.77	92	.253	.331	8	.235	2	-0	-4	-0	-0.1
	1961	Cle-A	0	4	.000	11	7	0	0	0	48	68	8	18	23	16.3	6.56	60	.338	.395	4	.267	1	-14	-14	1	-1.1
		Mil-N	1	0	1.000	9	0	0	0	0	10²	16	2	3	8	16.0	7.59	49	.340	.380	0	.000	-0	-4	-5	0	-0.4
	Total	12	126	110	.534	377	268	102	25	21	1992¹	1870	185	687	1162	11.7	3.34	116	.247	.313	121	.178	15	141	118	-1	14.0

■ BOB APODACA Apodaca, Robert John b: 1/31/50, Los Angeles, Cal. BR/TR, 5'11", 170 lbs. Deb: 9/18/73

	1973	NY-N	-0	0	—	1	0	0	0	0	1	1	0	0	0	9.0	∞	—	1.000	0	—	0	-1	-1	0	0.0
	1974	NY-N	6	6	.500	35	8	1	0	3	103	92	7	42	54	11.9	3.50	102	.241	.319	3	.120	0	1	1	-0	0.1
	1975	NY-N	3	4	.429	46	0	0	0	13	84²	66	4	28	51	10.0	1.49	232	.222	.289	4	.364	1	20	18	2	2.4
	1976	NY-N	3	7	.300	43	0	0	0	5	89²	71	4	29	45	10.3	2.81	117	.223	.293	2	.125	0	7	5	1	0.7
	1977	NY-N	4	8	.333	59	0	0	0	5	84	83	7	30	53	12.2	3.43	109	.255	.319	1	.167	-0	4	3	1	0.4

YEAR	TM/L	W	L	PCT	G	GS	CG	SH	SV	IP	H	HR	BB	SO	RAT	ERA	ERA+	OAV	OOB	BH	AVG	PB	PR	/A	PD	TPI
Total	5	16	25	.390	184	11	1	0	26	361¹	312	22	131	197	11.2	2.86	123	.236	.307	10	.172	2	32	26	4	3.6

■ LUIS APONTE
Aponte, Luis Eduardo (Yuripe)   b: 6/14/53, ElTigre, Venez.   BR/TR, 6′, 185 lbs.   Deb: 9/04/80

YEAR	TM/L	W	L	PCT	G	GS	CG	SH	SV	IP	H	HR	BB	SO	RAT	ERA	ERA+	OAV	OOB	BH	AVG	PB	PR	/A	PD	TPI
1980	Bos-A	0	0	—	4	0	0	0	0	7	6	0	2	1	10.3	1.29	328	.250	.308	0	—	0	2	2	0	0.3
1981	Bos-A	1	0	1.000	7	0	0	0	1	15²	11	0	3	11	8.0	0.57	674	.208	.250	0	—	0	5	6	1	0.7
1982	Bos-A	2	2	.500	40	0	0	0	3	85	78	5	25	44	10.9	3.18	136	.246	.301	0	—	0	8	11	2	1.3
1983	Bos-A	5	4	.556	34	0	0	0	3	62	74	7	23	32	14.4	3.63	120	.301	.365	0	—	0	3	5	1	0.6
1984	Cle-A	1	0	1.000	25	0	0	0	0	50¹	53	5	15	25	12.3	4.11	99	.269	.324	0	—	0	-1	-0	-1	0.0
Total	5	9	6	.600	110	0	0	0	7	220	222	17	68	113	12.0	3.27	129	.265	.323	0	—	0	18	23	3	2.9

■ KEVIN APPIER
Appier, Robert Kevin   b: 12/6/67, Lancaster, Cal.   BR/TR, 6′2″, 180 lbs.   Deb: 6/14/89

YEAR	TM/L	W	L	PCT	G	GS	CG	SH	SV	IP	H	HR	BB	SO	RAT	ERA	ERA+	OAV	OOB	BH	AVG	PB	PR	/A	PD	TPI
1989	KC-A	1	4	.200	6	5	0	0	0	21²	34	3	12	10	19.1	9.14	42	.374	.447	0	—	0	-13	-13	-1	-1.1
1990	KC-A	12	8	.600	32	24	3	3	0	185²	179	13	54	127	11.6	2.76	138	.252	.310	0	—	0	24	21	0	2.3
Total	2	13	12	.520	38	29	3	3	0	207¹	213	16	66	137	12.4	3.43	111	.266	.326	0	—	0	11	9	-1	1.2

■ FRED APPLEGATE
Applegate, Frederick Romaine   b: 5/9/1879, Williamsport, Pa.   d: 4/21/68, Williamsport, Pa.   BR/TR, 6′2″, 180 lbs.   Deb: 9/30/04

YEAR	TM/L	W	L	PCT	G	GS	CG	SH	SV	IP	H	HR	BB	SO	RAT	ERA	ERA+	OAV	OOB	BH	AVG	PB	PR	/A	PD	TPI
1904	Phi-A	1	2	.333	3	3	3	0	0	21	29	0	8	12	15.9	6.43	42	.328	.384	2	.286	0	-9	-9	0	-0.7

■ ED APPLETON
Appleton, Edward Samuel "Whitey"   b: 2/29/1892, Arlington, Tex.   d: 1/27/32, Arlington, Tex.   BR/TR, 6′0.5″, 173 lbs.   Deb: 4/16/15

YEAR	TM/L	W	L	PCT	G	GS	CG	SH	SV	IP	H	HR	BB	SO	RAT	ERA	ERA+	OAV	OOB	BH	AVG	PB	PR	/A	PD	TPI
1915	Bro-N	4	10	.286	34	10	5	0	1	138¹	133	3	66	50	13.5	3.32	84	.263	.357	7	.159	-0	-9	-8	-1	-0.9
1916	Bro-N	1	2	.333	14	3	1	0	1	47	49	1	18	14	13.0	3.06	88	.278	.349	2	.167	-0	-2	-2	-1	-0.3
Total	2	5	12	.294	48	13	6	0	1	185¹	182	4	84	64	13.4	3.25	85	.267	.355	9	.161	-1	-11	-10	-1	-1.2

■ PETE APPLETON
Appleton, Peter William "Jake" (a.k.a. Jablonowski In 1927-33)   b: 5/20/04, Terryville, Conn.   d: 1/18/74, Trenton, N.J.   BR/TR, 5′11″, 180 lbs.   Deb: 9/14/27

YEAR	TM/L	W	L	PCT	G	GS	CG	SH	SV	IP	H	HR	BB	SO	RAT	ERA	ERA+	OAV	OOB	BH	AVG	PB	PR	/A	PD	TPI
1927	Cin-N	2	1	.667	6	2	2	1	0	29²	29	0	17	3	14.0	1.82	208	.261	.359	6	.545	2	7	6	1	1.0
1928	Cin-N	3	4	.429	31	1	0	0	0	82²	101	7	22	20	13.6	4.68	84	.311	.358	10	.323	3	-6	-7	2	-0.1
1930	Cle-A	8	7	.533	39	7	2	0	1	118²	122	8	53	45	13.7	4.02	120	.274	.357	8	.200	-1	8	11	2	1.0
1931	Cle-A	4	4	.500	29	4	3	0	0	79²	100	2	29	25	14.7	4.63	100	.293	.350	5	.208	0	-2	-0	0	0.0
1932	Cle-A	0	0	—	4	0	0	0	0	5	11	1	3	1	25.2	16.20	29	.407	.467	0	—	0	-7	-6	0	-0.5
	Bos-A	0	3	.000	11	3	0	0	0	46	49	2	26	15	15.1	4.11	109	.265	.362	3	.176	-0	2	2	2	0.3
	Yr	0	3	.000	15	3	0	0	0	51	60	3	29	16	16.1	5.29	85	.283	.374	0	—	-0	-5	-4	2	-0.2
1933	NY-A	0	0	—	1	0	0	0	0	2	3	0	1	0	18.0	0.00	—	.375	.444	0	—	0	1	1	0	0.1
1936	Was-A	14	9	.609	38	20	12	1	3	201²	199	4	77	77	12.5	3.53	135	.254	.324	19	.250	2	34	28	1	2.8
1937	Was-A	8	15	.348	35	18	7	4	2	168	167	16	72	62	13.1	4.39	101	.260	.339	11	.186	-1	4	1	3	0.1
1938	Was-A	7	9	.438	43	10	5	0	5	164¹	175	12	61	62	13.0	4.60	98	.270	.333	15	.254	0	3	-2	-0	-0.2
1939	Was-A	5	10	.333	40	4	2	0	6	102²	104	7	48	50	13.7	4.56	95	.265	.351	4	.160	-1	1	-2	-0	-0.2
1940	Chi-A	4	0	1.000	25	0	0	0	5	57²	54	8	28	21	13.0	5.62	79	.248	.336	3	.176	-0	-8	-8	-0	-0.7
1941	Chi-A	0	3	.000	13	0	0	0	1	27¹	27	4	17	12	15.1	5.27	78	.257	.371	1	.250	0	-3	-4	0	-0.2
1942	Chi-A	0	0	—	4	0	0	0	1	4²	2	0	3	2	9.6	3.86	93	.133	.278	0	—	0	-0	-0	0	0.0
	StL-A	1	1	.500	14	0	0	0	2	27¹	25	1	11	12	11.9	2.96	125	.243	.316	1	.167	1	2	2	1	0.4
	Yr	1	1	.500	18	0	0	0	2	32	27	1	14	14	11.5	3.09	119	.229	.311	1	.167	1	2	2	1	0.4
1945	StL-A	0	0	—	2	0	0	0	0	2¹	3	0	7	1	38.6	15.43	23	.273	.556	0	—	0	-3	-3	0	-0.2
	Was-A	1	0	1.000	6	2	1	0	1	21¹	16	1	11	12	11.4	3.38	92	.211	.310	1	.200	-0	-0	-1	-0	0.0
	Yr	1	0	1.000	8	2	1	0	1	23²	19	1	18	13	14.1	4.56	69	.218	.352	0	.000	-0	-3	-4	0	-0.2
Total	14	57	66	.463	341	71	34	6	26	1141	1187	76	486	420	13.4	4.30	104	.268	.343	87	.233	6	33	19	12	3.8

■ LUIS AQUINO
Aquino, Luis Antonio (Colon)   b: 5/19/64, Santurce, P.R.   BR/TR, 6′, 155 lbs.   Deb: 8/08/86

YEAR	TM/L	W	L	PCT	G	GS	CG	SH	SV	IP	H	HR	BB	SO	RAT	ERA	ERA+	OAV	OOB	BH	AVG	PB	PR	/A	PD	TPI
1986	Tor-A	1	1	.500	7	0	0	0	0	11¹	14	2	3	5	13.5	6.35	66	.304	.347	0	—	0	-3	-3	0	-0.2
1988	KC-A	1	0	1.000	7	5	1	1	0	29	33	1	17	11	15.8	2.79	143	.282	.378	0	—	0	4	4	-0	0.4
1989	KC-A	6	8	.429	34	16	2	1	0	141¹	148	6	35	68	11.9	3.50	110	.271	.320	0	—	0	6	5	1	0.7
1990	KC-A	4	1	.800	20	3	1	0	0	68¹	59	6	27	28	11.9	3.16	120	.237	.321	0	—	0	6	5	1	0.6
Total	4	12	10	.545	68	24	4	2	0	250	254	15	82	112	12.4	3.46	112	.265	.329	0	—	0	13	11	2	1.5

■ FRED ARCHER
Archer, Frederick Marvin "Lefty"   b: 3/7/10, Johnson City, Tenn.   d: 10/31/81, Charlotte, N.C.   BL/TL, 6′, 193 lbs.   Deb: 9/05/36

YEAR	TM/L	W	L	PCT	G	GS	CG	SH	SV	IP	H	HR	BB	SO	RAT	ERA	ERA+	OAV	OOB	BH	AVG	PB	PR	/A	PD	TPI
1936	Phi-A	2	3	.400	6	5	2	0	0	36²	41	3	15	9	14.5	6.38	80	.289	.369	4	.267	0	-5	-5	0	-0.3
1937	Phi-A	0	0	—	1	0	0	0	0	3	4	0	0	2	12.0	6.00	79	.333	.333	0	—	0	-0	-0	0	0.0
Total	2	2	3	.400	7	5	2	0	0	39²	45	3	15	11	14.3	6.35	80	.292	.366	4	.267	1	-6	-6	0	-0.3

■ JIM ARCHER
Archer, James William   b: 5/25/32, Max Meadows, Va.   BR/TL, 6′, 190 lbs.   Deb: 4/30/61

YEAR	TM/L	W	L	PCT	G	GS	CG	SH	SV	IP	H	HR	BB	SO	RAT	ERA	ERA+	OAV	OOB	BH	AVG	PB	PR	/A	PD	TPI
1961	KC-A	9	15	.375	39	27	9	2	5	205¹	204	11	60	110	11.8	3.20	129	.257	.313	4	.063	-5	19	21	-0	1.6
1962	KC-A	0	1	.000	18	1	0	0	0	27²	40	8	10	12	16.3	9.43	44	.342	.394	1	1.000	0	-17	-16	-0	-1.4
Total	2	9	16	.360	57	28	9	2	5	233	244	19	70	122	12.3	3.94	105	.268	.323	5	.078	-4	2	5	-0	0.2

■ RUGGER ARDIZOIA
Ardizoia, Rinaldo Joseph   b: 11/20/19, Oleggio, Italy   BR/TR, 5′11″, 180 lbs.   Deb: 4/30/47

YEAR	TM/L	W	L	PCT	G	GS	CG	SH	SV	IP	H	HR	BB	SO	RAT	ERA	ERA+	OAV	OOB	BH	AVG	PB	PR	/A	PD	TPI
1947	NY-A	0	0	—	1	0	0	0	0	2	4	1	1	0	22.5	9.00	39	.500	.556	0	—	0	-1	-1	0	0.0

■ FRANK ARELLANES
Arellanes, Frank Julian   b: 1/28/1882, Santa Cruz, Cal.   d: 12/13/18, San Jose, Cal.   BR/TR, 6′, 180 lbs.   Deb: 7/28/08

YEAR	TM/L	W	L	PCT	G	GS	CG	SH	SV	IP	H	HR	BB	SO	RAT	ERA	ERA+	OAV	OOB	BH	AVG	PB	PR	/A	PD	TPI
1908	Bos-A	4	3	.571	11	8	6	1	0	79	60	1	18	33	9.2	1.82	135	.213	.267	5	.167	0	5	6	-1	0.5
1909	Bos-A	16	12	.571	45	28	17	1	8	230²	192	3	43	82	9.4	2.18	114	.229	.270	13	.167	-1	8	8	1	0.8
1910	Bos-A	4	7	.364	18	13	2	0	0	100	106	1	24	33	12.0	2.88	89	.283	.332	6	.176	-0	-4	-4	1	-0.2
Total	3	24	22	.522	74	49	25	2	8	409²	358	5	85	148	10.0	2.28	110	.239	.285	24	.169	-1	9	10	-0	1.1

■ RUDY ARIAS
Arias, Rodolfo (Martinez)   b: 6/6/31, Las Villas, Cuba   BL/TL, 5′10″, 165 lbs.   Deb: 4/10/59

YEAR	TM/L	W	L	PCT	G	GS	CG	SH	SV	IP	H	HR	BB	SO	RAT	ERA	ERA+	OAV	OOB	BH	AVG	PB	PR	/A	PD	TPI
1959	Chi-A	2	0	1.000	34	0	0	0	2	44	49	7	20	28	14.3	4.09	92	.277	.354	0	.000	-1	-1	-2	1	-0.1

■ DON ARLICH
Arlich, Donald Louis   b: 2/15/43, Wayne, Mich.   BL/TL, 6′2″, 185 lbs.   Deb: 10/02/65

YEAR	TM/L	W	L	PCT	G	GS	CG	SH	SV	IP	H	HR	BB	SO	RAT	ERA	ERA+	OAV	OOB	BH	AVG	PB	PR	/A	PD	TPI
1965	Hou-N	0	0	—	1	1	0	0	0	6	5	0	1	0	9.0	3.00	112	.227	.261	0	.000	-0	0	0	0	0.0
1966	Hou-N	0	1	.000	7	0	0	0	0	4	11	0	4	1	36.0	15.75	22	.478	.571	0	.000	-0	-5	-5	-0	-0.5
Total	2	0	1	.000	8	1	0	0	0	10	16	0	5	1	19.8	8.10	42	.356	.431	0	.000	-0	-5	-5	-0	-0.5

■ STEVE ARLIN
Arlin, Stephen Ralph   b: 9/25/45, Seattle, Wash.   BR/TR, 6′3.5″, 195 lbs.   Deb: 6/17/69

YEAR	TM/L	W	L	PCT	G	GS	CG	SH	SV	IP	H	HR	BB	SO	RAT	ERA	ERA+	OAV	OOB	BH	AVG	PB	PR	/A	PD	TPI
1969	SD-N	0	1	.000	4	1	0	0	0	10²	13	2	9	9	18.6	9.28	38	.289	.407	0	.000	-0	-7	-7	-0	-0.6
1970	SD-N	1	0	1.000	2	2	1	1	0	12²	11	0	8	3	13.5	2.84	140	.244	.358	0	.000	-1	2	2	0	0.1
1971	SD-N	9	19	.321	36	34	10	4	0	227²	211	8	103	156	12.7	3.48	95	.244	.329	9	.123	-1	-0	-5	-1	-0.7
1972	SD-N	10	21	.323	38	37	12	3	0	250	217	19	122	159	12.5	3.60	91	.237	.332	11	.153	2	-4	-9	-0	-0.6
1973	SD-N	11	14	.440	34	27	7	3	0	180	196	26	72	98	13.4	5.10	68	.278	.346	10	.167	1	-29	-33	-1	-3.1
1974	SD-N	1	7	.125	16	12	1	0	0	64	85	5	37	18	17.4	5.91	60	.326	.413	2	.111	-1	-16	-17	-0	-1.6
	Cle-A	2	5	.286	11	10	1	0	0	43²	54	1	22	20	16.7	6.60	55	.333	.407	0	—	0	-14	-14	-1	-1.4
Total	6	34	67	.337	141	123	32	11	1	788²	792	61	373	463	13.5	4.33	78	.263	.348	32	.139	1	-69	-82	-2	-7.9

■ ORVILLE ARMBRUST
Armbrust, Orville Martin   b: 3/2/10, Beirne, Ark.   d: 10/2/67, Mobile, Ala.   BR/TR, 5′10″, 195 lbs.   Deb: 9/18/34

YEAR	TM/L	W	L	PCT	G	GS	CG	SH	SV	IP	H	HR	BB	SO	RAT	ERA	ERA+	OAV	OOB	BH	AVG	PB	PR	/A	PD	TPI
1934	Was-A	1	0	1.000	3	2	0	0	0	12²	10	1	3	3	9.2	2.13	203	.208	.255	0	.000	-1	3	3	1	0.3

■ HOWARD ARMSTRONG
Armstrong, Howard Elmer   b: 12/2/1889, E.Claridon, Ohio   d: 3/8/26, Canisteo, N.Y.   TR , 5′9″, 165 lbs.   Deb: 9/30/11

YEAR	TM/L	W	L	PCT	G	GS	CG	SH	SV	IP	H	HR	BB	SO	RAT	ERA	ERA+	OAV	OOB	BH	AVG	PB	PR	/A	PD	TPI
1911	Phi-A	0	1	.000	1	0	0	0	0	3	3	0	1	0	12.0	0.00	—	.273	.333	0	.000	-0	1	1	0	0.1

YEAR TM/L	W	L	PCT	G	GS	CG	SH	SV	IP	H	HR	BB	SO	RAT	ERA	ERA+	OAV	OOB	BH	AVG	PB	PR	/A	PD	TPI

■ JACK ARMSTRONG
Armstrong, Jack William b: 3/7/65, Englewood, N.J. BR/TR, 6'5", 220 lbs. Deb: 6/21/88

YEAR TM/L	W	L	PCT	G	GS	CG	SH	SV	IP	H	HR	BB	SO	RAT	ERA	ERA+	OAV	OOB	BH	AVG	PB	PR	/A	PD	TPI
1988 Cin-N	4	7	.364	14	13	0	0	0	65¹	63	8	38	45	13.9	5.79	62	.256	.356	2	.095	-1	-17	-16	1	-1.6
1989 Cin-N	2	3	.400	9	8	0	0	0	42²	40	5	21	23	12.9	4.64	78	.245	.332	0	.000	-1	-5	-5	0	-0.4
1990 •Cin-N	12	9	.571	29	27	2	1	0	166	151	9	59	110	11.7	3.42	113	.241	.313	5	.106	-1	7	8	0	0.8
Total 3	18	19	.486	52	48	2	1	0	274	254	22	118	178	12.4	4.17	90	.245	.326	7	.092	-3	-15	-12	1	-1.2

■ MIKE ARMSTRONG
Armstrong, Michael Dennis b: 3/7/54, Glen Cove, N.Y. BR/TR, 6'3", 193 lbs. Deb: 8/12/80

YEAR TM/L	W	L	PCT	G	GS	CG	SH	SV	IP	H	HR	BB	SO	RAT	ERA	ERA+	OAV	OOB	BH	AVG	PB	PR	/A	PD	TPI
1980 SD-N	0	0	—	11	0	0	0	0	14¹	16	3	13	14	18.2	5.65	61	.296	.433	0	.000	-0	-3	-4	-0	-0.4
1981 SD-N	0	2	.000	10	0	0	0	0	12	14	1	11	9	18.8	6.00	54	.311	.446	0	—	0	-3	-4	-0	-0.3
1982 KC-A	5	5	.500	52	0	0	0	6	112²	88	9	43	75	10.7	3.20	128	.215	.295	0	—	0	11	11	-1	1.0
1983 KC-A	10	7	.588	58	0	0	0	3	102²	86	11	45	52	11.7	3.86	106	.228	.315	0	—	0	2	2	-0	0.2
1984 NY-A	3	2	.600	36	0	0	0	1	54¹	47	6	26	43	12.1	3.48	109	.239	.327	0	—	0	3	2	-0	0.2
1985 NY-A	0	0	—	9	0	0	0	0	14²	9	4	2	11	6.8	3.07	130	.173	.204	0	—	0	2	2	-0	0.1
1986 NY-A	0	1	.000	7	1	0	0	0	8²	13	4	5	8	18.7	9.35	44	.351	.429	0	—	0	-5	-5	-0	-0.4
1987 Cle-A	1	0	1.000	14	0	0	0	1	18²	27	4	10	9	17.8	8.68	52	.333	.407	0	—	0	-9	-9	-0	-0.7
Total 8	19	17	.528	197	1	0	0	11	338	300	42	155	221	12.3	4.10	97	.240	.326	0	.000	-0	-2	-4	-3	-0.3

■ SCOTT ARNOLD
Arnold, Scott Gentry b: 8/18/62, Lexington, Ky. BR/TR, 6'2", 210 lbs. Deb: 4/07/88

YEAR TM/L	W	L	PCT	G	GS	CG	SH	SV	IP	H	HR	BB	SO	RAT	ERA	ERA+	OAV	OOB	BH	AVG	PB	PR	/A	PD	TPI
1988 StL-N	0	0	—	6	0	0	0	0	6²	9	0	4	8	17.6	5.40	64	.321	.406	0	—	0	-1	-1	0	-0.1

■ TONY ARNOLD
Arnold, Tony Dale b: 5/3/59, ElPaso, Tex. BR/TR, 5'11", 170 lbs. Deb: 8/09/86

YEAR TM/L	W	L	PCT	G	GS	CG	SH	SV	IP	H	HR	BB	SO	RAT	ERA	ERA+	OAV	OOB	BH	AVG	PB	PR	/A	PD	TPI
1986 Bal-A	0	2	.000	11	0	0	0	0	25¹	25	0	11	7	12.8	3.55	116	.278	.356	0	—	0	2	2	1	0.3
1987 Bal-A	0	0	—	27	0	0	0	0	53	71	8	17	18	15.3	5.77	76	.330	.385	0	—	0	-8	-8	2	-0.4
Total 2	0	2	.000	38	0	0	0	0	78¹	96	8	28	25	14.5	5.06	85	.315	.376	0	—	0	-6	-6	4	-0.1

■ BRAD ARNSBERG
Arnsberg, Bradley James b: 8/20/63, Seattle, Wash. BR/TR, 6'4", 205 lbs. Deb: 9/06/86

YEAR TM/L	W	L	PCT	G	GS	CG	SH	SV	IP	H	HR	BB	SO	RAT	ERA	ERA+	OAV	OOB	BH	AVG	PB	PR	/A	PD	TPI
1986 NY-A	0	0	—	2	1	0	0	0	8	13	1	1	3	15.8	3.38	121	.342	.359	0	—	0	1	1	-0	0.0
1987 NY-A	1	3	.250	6	2	0	0	0	19¹	22	5	13	14	16.3	5.59	78	.289	.393	0	—	0	-2	-3	0	-0.1
1989 Tex-A	2	1	.667	16	1	0	0	1	48	45	6	22	26	13.1	4.13	96	.247	.338	0	—	0	-1	-1	1	0.0
1990 Tex-A	6	1	.857	53	0	0	0	5	62²	56	4	33	44	13.1	2.15	185	.235	.333	0	—	0	12	13	1	1.4
Total 4	9	5	.643	77	4	0	0	6	138	136	16	69	87	13.7	3.39	119	.255	.345	0	—	0	9	10	2	1.3

■ ORIE ARNTZEN
Arntzen, Orie Edgar "Old Folks" b: 10/18/09, Beverly, Ill. d: 1/28/70, Cedar Rapids, Iowa BR/TR, 6'1", 200 lbs. Deb: 4/20/43

YEAR TM/L	W	L	PCT	G	GS	CG	SH	SV	IP	H	HR	BB	SO	RAT	ERA	ERA+	OAV	OOB	BH	AVG	PB	PR	/A	PD	TPI
1943 Phi-A	4	13	.235	32	20	9	0	0	164¹	172	5	69	66	13.5	4.22	81	.277	.354	8	.160	-1	-17	-15	-3	-1.9

■ GERRY ARRIGO
Arrigo, Gerald William b: 6/12/41, Chicago, Ill. BL/TL, 6'1", 185 lbs. Deb: 6/12/61

YEAR TM/L	W	L	PCT	G	GS	CG	SH	SV	IP	H	HR	BB	SO	RAT	ERA	ERA+	OAV	OOB	BH	AVG	PB	PR	/A	PD	TPI
1961 Min-A	0	1	.000	7	2	0	0	0	9²	9	0	10	6	19.6	10.24	41	.265	.457	1	.500	0	-7	-6	0	-0.5
1962 Min-A	0	0	—	1	0	0	0	0	1	3	0	1	1	36.0	18.00	23	.600	.667	0	—	0	-2	-2	0	0.0
1963 Min-A	1	2	.333	5	1	0	0	0	15²	12	2	4	13	9.2	2.87	127	.211	.262	0	.000	-0	1	1	0	0.1
1964 Min-A	7	4	.636	41	12	2	1	1	105¹	97	11	45	96	12.3	3.84	93	.244	.324	5	.172	1	-3	-3	0	-0.2
1965 Cin-N	2	4	.333	27	5	0	0	2	54	75	4	30	43	17.8	6.17	61	.342	.426	2	.167	1	-16	-15	-1	-1.4
1966 Cin-N	0	0	—	3	0	0	0	0	7¹	7	2	3	3	12.3	4.91	79	.250	.323	0	.000	-0	-1	-1	-0	0.0
NY-N	3	3	.500	17	5	0	0	0	43¹	47	5	16	28	13.1	3.74	97	.276	.339	5	.500	3	-1	-0	0	0.3
Yr	3	3	.500	20	5	0	0	0	50²	54	7	19	31	13.0	3.91	94	.273	.336	2	.182	3	-2	-1	0	0.3
1967 Cin-N	6	6	.500	32	5	1	1	1	74	61	6	35	56	12.2	3.16	119	.232	.331	4	.211	1	2	5	-2	0.4
1968 Cin-N	12	10	.545	36	31	5	1	0	205¹	181	13	77	140	11.5	3.33	95	.237	.310	5	.075	-2	-8	-4	1	-0.4
1969 Cin-N	4	7	.364	20	16	1	0	0	91	89	6	61	35	15.6	4.15	91	.256	.379	5	.161	-0	-6	-4	-2	-0.5
1970 Chi-A	0	3	.000	5	3	0	0	0	13¹	24	4	9	12	22.3	12.83	30	.393	.471	0	.000	-0	-13	-13	-0	-1.2
Total 10	35	40	.467	194	80	9	3	4	620	605	56	291	433	13.3	4.14	85	.258	.345	27	.151	2	-52	-42	-3	-3.4

■ FERNANDO ARROYO
Arroyo, Fernando b: 3/21/52, Sacramento, Cal. BR/TR, 6'2", 180 lbs. Deb: 6/28/75

YEAR TM/L	W	L	PCT	G	GS	CG	SH	SV	IP	H	HR	BB	SO	RAT	ERA	ERA+	OAV	OOB	BH	AVG	PB	PR	/A	PD	TPI
1975 Det-A	2	1	.667	14	2	1	0	0	53¹	56	5	22	25	13.3	4.56	88	.272	.345	0	—	0	-5	-3	1	-0.1
1977 Det-A	8	18	.308	38	28	8	1	0	209¹	227	23	52	60	12.0	4.17	103	.278	.321	0	—	0	-3	3	7	0.9
1978 Det-A	0	0	—	2	0	0	0	0	4¹	8	1	0	1	18.7	8.31	47	.400	.429	0	—	0	-2	-2	0	-0.1
1979 Det-A	1	1	.500	6	0	0	0	0	12	17	3	4	7	15.8	8.25	52	.340	.389	0	—	0	-5	-5	0	-0.4
1980 Min-A	6	6	.500	21	11	1	1	0	92¹	97	7	32	27	12.8	4.68	93	.273	.337	0	—	0	-7	-3	-1	-0.3
1981 Min-A	7	10	.412	23	19	2	0	0	128¹	144	11	34	39	12.8	3.93	100	.290	.342	0	—	0	-4	0	1	-0.3
1982 Min-A	0	1	.000	13	2	0	0	0	13²	17	2	6	4	15.1	5.27	81	.321	.390	0	—	0	-2	-2	0	0.0
Oak-A	0	0	—	10	0	0	0	0	22¹	23	4	7	9	12.5	5.24	75	.271	.333	0	—	0	-3	-0	0	-0.2
Yr	0	1	.000	16	0	0	0	0	36	40	6	13	13	13.5	5.25	77	.288	.353	0	—	0	-5	-5	1	-0.2
1986 Oak-A	0	0	—	1	0	0	0	0	0	0	0	3	0	—	—	—	—	1.000	0	—	0	0	0	0	0.0
Total 8	24	37	.393	121	60	12	2	0	535²	589	56	160	172	12.8	4.44	94	.283	.337	0	—	0	-30	-16	9	-0.1

■ LUIS ARROYO
Arroyo, Luis Enrique b: 2/18/27, Penuelas, P.R. BL/TL, 5'8.5", 178 lbs. Deb: 4/20/55

YEAR TM/L	W	L	PCT	G	GS	CG	SH	SV	IP	H	HR	BB	SO	RAT	ERA	ERA+	OAV	OOB	BH	AVG	PB	PR	/A	PD	TPI
1955 StL-N	11	8	.579	35	24	9	1	0	159	162	23	63	68	12.8	4.19	97	.261	.331	13	.232	1	-3	-2	-2	-0.2
1956 Pit-N	3	3	.500	18	2	1	0	0	28²	36	5	12	17	15.1	4.71	80	.298	.361	2	.500	1	-3	-3	0	-0.1
1957 Pit-N	3	11	.214	54	10	0	0	1	130²	151	19	31	101	13.0	4.68	81	.282	.329	5	.156	-1	-12	-13	-3	-1.5
1959 Cin-N	1	0	1.000	10	0	0	0	0	13²	17	0	11	8	18.4	3.95	103	.321	.438	0	.000	-0	-0	0	0	0.0
1960 •NY-A	5	1	.833	29	0	0	0	7	40²	30	2	22	29	11.5	2.88	125	.207	.311	0	.000	-0	5	3	0	0.3
1961 •NY-A	15	5	.750	**65**	0	0	0	29	119	83	5	49	87	12.6	2.19	169	.199	.288	7	.280	2	24	20	-1	2.1
1962 NY-A	1	3	.250	27	0	0	0	7	33²	33	5	17	21	13.6	4.81	78	.262	.354	2	.500	1	-3	-4	-1	-0.3
1963 NY-A	1	1	.500	6	0	0	0	0	6	12	0	3	5	22.5	13.50	26	.444	.500	0	—	0	-7	-7	-0	-0.6
Total 8	40	32	.556	244	36	10	1	44	531¹	524	58	208	336	12.6	3.93	98	.256	.329	29	.227	3	2	-5	-6	-0.3

■ RUDY ARROYO
Arroyo, Rudolph b: 6/19/50, New York, N.Y. BL/TL, 6'2", 195 lbs. Deb: 6/01/71

YEAR TM/L	W	L	PCT	G	GS	CG	SH	SV	IP	H	HR	BB	SO	RAT	ERA	ERA+	OAV	OOB	BH	AVG	PB	PR	/A	PD	TPI
1971 StL-N	0	1	.000	9	0	0	0	0	11²	18	2	5	5	17.7	5.40	67	.375	.434	0	.000	-0	-3	-2	-0	-0.2

■ HARRY ARUNDEL
Arundel, Harry b: 1854, Philadelphia, Pa. d: 3/25/04, Cleveland, Ohio Deb: 7/19/1875

YEAR TM/L	W	L	PCT	G	GS	CG	SH	SV	IP	H	HR	BB	SO	RAT	ERA	ERA+	OAV	OOB	BH	AVG	PB	PR	/A	PD	TPI
1875 Atl-n	0	1	.000	1	1	0	0	0	1¹	6	0	1		47.3	13.50	17	.429	.467	0	.000	-1	-2	-2		-0.1
1882 Pit-a	4	10	.286	14	14	13	0	0	120	155	3	23	47	13.4	4.65	56	.293	.323	10	.189	0	-26	-27	5	-1.8
1884 Pro-N	1	0	1.000	1	1	1	0	0	9	8	0	4	4	12.0	1.00	283	.225	.304	1	.333	0	2	2	-0	0.2
Total 2	5	10	.333	15	15	14	0	0	129	163	3	27	51	13.3	4.40	60	.289	.322	11	.196	0	-24	-25	5	-1.6

■ KEN ASH
Ash, Kenneth Lowther b: 9/16/01, Anmoore, W.Va. d: 11/15/79, Clarksburg, W.Va. BR/TR, 5'11", 165 lbs. Deb: 4/17/25

YEAR TM/L	W	L	PCT	G	GS	CG	SH	SV	IP	H	HR	BB	SO	RAT	ERA	ERA+	OAV	OOB	BH	AVG	PB	PR	/A	PD	TPI
1925 Chi-A	0	0	—	2	0	0	0	0	4	7	2	0	0	15.8	9.00	46	.389	.389	—		0	-2	-2	-0	-0.1
1928 Cin-N	3	3	.500	8	5	2	0	0	36	43	1	13	6	14.3	6.50	61	.314	.377	1	.071	-1	-10	-10	0	-0.9
1929 Cin-N	1	5	.167	29	7	2	0	2	82	91	2	30	26	13.8	4.83	95	.292	.363	3	.143	-0	-1	-2	-0	-0.2
1930 Cin-N	2	0	1.000	16	1	1	0	0	39¹	37	1	16	15	12.1	3.43	141	.268	.344	2	.182	-1	7	6	1	0.6
Total 4	6	8	.429	55	13	5	0	2	161¹	178	6	59	47	13.6	4.96	90	.294	.363	6	.130	-3	-6	-6	1	-0.6

■ PAUL ASSENMACHER
Assenmacher, Paul Andre b: 12/10/60, Detroit, Mich. BL/TL, 6'3", 195 lbs. Deb: 4/12/86

YEAR TM/L	W	L	PCT	G	GS	CG	SH	SV	IP	H	HR	BB	SO	RAT	ERA	ERA+	OAV	OOB	BH	AVG	PB	PR	/A	PD	TPI
1986 Atl-N	7	3	.700	61	0	0	0	7	68¹	61	5	26	56	11.5	2.50	159	.241	.312	0	.000	-0	9	11	1	1.3
1987 Atl-N	1	1	.500	52	0	0	0	2	54²	58	8	24	39	13.7	5.10	85	.260	.335	0	.000	-0	-6	-5	-1	-0.5
1988 Atl-N	8	7	.533	64	0	0	0	5	79¹	72	4	32	71	11.9	3.06	120	.251	.328	1	.333	1	3	5	0	0.6
1989 Atl-N	1	3	.250	49	0	0	0	0	57²	55	2	16	64	11.2	3.59	102	.249	.303	0	.000	-0	-1	0	0	0.0

YEAR TM/L	W	L	PCT	G	GS	CG	SH	SV	IP	H	HR	BB	SO	RAT	ERA	ERA+	OAV	OOB	BH	AVG	PB	PR	/A	PD	TPI
*Chi-N	2	1	.667	14	0	0	0	0	19	19	1	12	15	14.7	5.21	72	.275	.383	0	.000	-0	-4	-3	0	-0.2
Yr	3	4	.429	63	0	0	0	0	76²	74	3	28	79	12.0	3.99	92	.253	.318	0	.000	-1	-4	-3	0	-0.2
1990 Chi-N	7	2	.778	74	1	0	0	10	103	90	10	36	95	11.1	2.80	148	.239	.308	0	.000	-1	11	15	0	1.5
Total 5	26	17	.605	314	1	0	0	24	382	355	30	146	340	11.9	3.37	117	.248	.320	1	.038	-1	14	24	0	2.7

■ KEITH ATHERTON
Atherton, Keith Rowe b: 2/19/59, Mathews, Va. BR/TR, 6'4", 200 lbs. Deb: 7/14/83

YEAR TM/L	W	L	PCT	G	GS	CG	SH	SV	IP	H	HR	BB	SO	RAT	ERA	ERA+	OAV	OOB	BH	AVG	PB	PR	/A	PD	TPI
1983 Oak-A	2	5	.286	29	0	0	0	4	68¹	53	7	23	40	10.1	2.77	139	.215	.285	0	.000	0	10	8	-1	0.7
1984 Oak-A	7	6	.538	57	0	0	0	2	104	110	13	39	58	13.1	4.33	86	.274	.341	0	—	0	-4	-7	-2	-0.8
1985 Oak-A	4	7	.364	56	0	0	0	3	104²	89	17	42	77	11.3	4.30	90	.231	.306	0	—	0	-2	-5	-2	-0.6
1986 Oak-A	1	2	.333	13	0	0	0	0	15¹	18	2	11	8	17.0	5.87	66	.295	.403	0	—	0	-3	-3	-0	-0.2
Min-A	5	8	.385	47	0	0	0	10	81²	82	9	35	59	13.0	3.75	115	.264	.340	0	—	0	4	5	-0	0.5
Yr	6	10	.375	60	0	0	0	10	97	100	11	46	67	13.6	4.08	104	.267	.349	0	—	0	1	2	-0	0.3
1987 *Min-A	7	5	.583	59	0	0	0	2	79¹	81	10	30	51	13.0	4.54	102	.262	.335	0	—	0	-1	1	0	0.1
1988 Min-A	7	5	.583	49	0	0	0	3	74	65	10	22	43	10.8	3.41	119	.235	.296	0	—	0	5	5	-0	0.5
1989 Cle-A	0	3	.000	32	0	0	0	2	39	48	7	13	13	14.1	4.15	95	.293	.345	0	—	0	-1	-1	-1	-0.1
Total 7	33	41	.446	342	0	0	0	26	566¹	546	75	215	349	12.3	3.99	101	.253	.324	0	.000	0	8	3	-6	0.1

■ TOMMY ATKINS
Atkins, Francis Montgomery b: 12/9/1887, Ponca, Neb. d: 5/7/56, Cleveland, Ohio BL/TL, 5'10.5", 165 lbs. Deb: 10/02/09

YEAR TM/L	W	L	PCT	G	GS	CG	SH	SV	IP	H	HR	BB	SO	RAT	ERA	ERA+	OAV	OOB	BH	AVG	PB	PR	/A	PD	TPI
1909 Phi-A	0	0	—	1	1	0	0	0	6	6	0	5	4	16.5	4.50	53	.261	.393	0	.000	-0	-1	-1	0	0.0
1910 Phi-A	3	2	.600	15	3	2	0	2	57	53	0	23	29	12.2	2.68	88	.254	.330	2	.118	-1	-1	-2	0	-0.3
Total 2	3	2	.600	16	4	2	0	2	63	59	0	28	33	12.6	2.86	83	.254	.337	2	.105	-1	-2	-3	0	-0.3

■ JAMES ATKINS
Atkins, James Curtis b: 3/10/21, Birmingham, Ala. BL/TR, 6'3", 205 lbs. Deb: 9/29/50

YEAR TM/L	W	L	PCT	G	GS	CG	SH	SV	IP	H	HR	BB	SO	RAT	ERA	ERA+	OAV	OOB	BH	AVG	PB	PR	/A	PD	TPI
1950 Bos-A	0	0	—	1	0	0	0	0	4²	4	1	4	0	17.4	3.86	127	.235	.409	0	.000	-0	0	1	0	0.0
1952 Bos-A	0	1	.000	3	1	0	0	0	10¹	11	0	7	2	15.7	3.48	113	.275	.383	2	.667	1	0	1	0	0.2
Total 2	0	1	.000	4	1	0	0	0	15	15	1	11	2	16.2	3.60	118	.263	.391	2	.400	0	1	1	0	0.2

■ AL ATKINSON
Atkinson, Albert Wright b: 3/9/1861, Clinton, Ill. d: 6/17/52, Elkhorn Township Mo. BR/TR, 5'11.5", 165 lbs. Deb: 5/01/1884

YEAR TM/L	W	L	PCT	G	GS	CG	SH	SV	IP	H	HR	BB	SO	RAT	ERA	ERA+	OAV	OOB	BH	AVG	PB	PR	/A	PD	TPI
1884 Phi-a	11	11	.500	22	22	20	1	0	184	186	3	21	93	10.1	4.21	81	.248	.269	16	.193	-1	-20	-17	0	-1.3
CP-U	6	10	.375	16	16	16	1	0	140	127	1	21	104	9.5	2.76	109	.226	.254	14	.206	-3	4	4	1	0.2
Bal-U	3	5	.375	8	8	8	0	0	69²	60	4	12	50	9.3	2.33	143	.217	.249	4	.138	-2	5	8	0	0.5
Yr	9	15	.375	24	24	24	1	0	209²	187	5	33	154	9.4	2.62	119	.223	.252	1	.010	-5	9	12	1	0.7
1886 Phi-a	25	17	.595	45	45	44	1	0	396²	414	11	101	154	11.7	3.95	89	.256	.300	18	.122	-6	-22	-20	-2	-2.3
1887 Phi-a	6	8	.429	15	15	11	0	0	124²	156	2	54	34	15.2	5.92	72	.295	.361	12	.203	-0	-22	-23	1	-1.6
Total 3	51	51	.500	106	106	99	3	0	915	943	21	209	435	11.3	3.96	88	.253	.292	64	.165	-12	-55	-47	0	-4.5

■ BILL ATKINSON
Atkinson, William Cecil Glenn b: 10/4/54, Chatham, Ont., Can. BL/TR, 5'7", 165 lbs. Deb: 9/18/76

YEAR TM/L	W	L	PCT	G	GS	CG	SH	SV	IP	H	HR	BB	SO	RAT	ERA	ERA+	OAV	OOB	BH	AVG	PB	PR	/A	PD	TPI
1976 Mon-N	0	0	—	4	0	0	0	0	5	3	0	1	4	7.2	0.00	—	.176	.222	0	—	0	2	2	0	0.2
1977 Mon-N	7	2	.778	55	0	0	0	7	83¹	72	12	29	56	10.9	3.35	114	.234	.300	1	.200	-0	5	4	1	0.5
1978 Mon-N	2	2	.500	29	0	0	0	3	45¹	45	5	28	32	14.7	4.37	81	.268	.376	2	.500	1	-4	-4	0	-0.2
1979 Mon-N	2	0	1.000	10	0	0	0	1	13²	9	0	4	7	8.6	1.98	186	.170	.228	0	.000	-0	3	3	-0	0.2
Total 4	11	4	.733	98	0	0	0	11	147¹	129	17	62	99	11.7	3.42	108	.236	.315	3	.300	1	6	5	1	0.7

■ DON AUGUST
August, Donald Glenn b: 7/3/63, Inglewood, Cal. BR/TR, 6'3", 190 lbs. Deb: 6/02/88

YEAR TM/L	W	L	PCT	G	GS	CG	SH	SV	IP	H	HR	BB	SO	RAT	ERA	ERA+	OAV	OOB	BH	AVG	PB	PR	/A	PD	TPI
1988 Mil-A	13	7	.650	24	22	6	1	0	148¹	137	12	48	66	11.2	3.09	129	.245	.305	0	—	0	14	15	2	1.8
1989 Mil-A	12	12	.500	31	25	2	1	0	142¹	175	17	58	51	14.9	5.31	72	.302	.368	0	—	0	-23	-23	2	-2.0
1990 Mil-A	0	3	.000	5	0	0	0	0	11	13	0	5	2	14.7	6.55	58	.295	.367	0	—	0	-3	-3	0	-0.2
Total 3	25	22	.532	60	47	8	2	0	301²	325	29	111	119	13.1	4.27	91	.275	.338	0	—	0	-11	-12	4	-0.4

■ JERRY AUGUSTINE
Augustine, Gerald Lee b: 7/24/52, Kewaunee, Wis. BL/TL, 6', 183 lbs. Deb: 9/09/75

YEAR TM/L	W	L	PCT	G	GS	CG	SH	SV	IP	H	HR	BB	SO	RAT	ERA	ERA+	OAV	OOB	BH	AVG	PB	PR	/A	PD	TPI
1975 Mil-A	2	0	1.000	5	3	1	0	0	26²	26	2	12	8	13.2	3.04	126	.274	.361	0	—	0	2	2	-0	0.2
1976 Mil-A	9	12	.429	39	24	5	3	0	171²	167	9	56	59	11.9	3.30	106	.261	.324	0	—	0	4	4	-2	0.2
1977 Mil-A	12	18	.400	33	33	10	1	0	209	222	23	72	68	12.8	4.48	91	.277	.339	0	—	0	-10	-10	1	-0.8
1978 Mil-A	13	12	.520	35	30	9	2	0	188¹	204	14	61	59	12.9	4.54	83	.280	.339	0	—	0	-16	-16	2	-1.3
1979 Mil-A	9	6	.600	43	2	0	0	5	85²	95	6	30	41	13.2	3.47	120	.284	.344	0	—	0	7	7	-2	0.5
1980 Mil-A	4	3	.571	39	1	0	0	2	69²	83	5	36	22	15.6	4.52	86	.301	.385	0	—	0	-4	-5	0	-0.4
1981 Mil-A	2	2	.500	27	2	0	0	2	61¹	75	4	18	24	13.8	4.26	80	.300	.349	0	—	0	-4	-6	0	-0.5
1982 Mil-A	1	3	.250	20	2	1	0	2	62	63	13	26	22	13.2	5.08	74	.267	.345	0	—	0	-7	-9	-1	-0.9
1983 Mil-A	3	3	.500	34	7	1	0	2	64¹	89	11	25	40	16.1	5.74	65	.328	.387	0	—	0	-12	-14	-0	-1.3
1984 Mil-A	0	0	—	4	0	0	0	0	5¹	4	0	4	3	15.2	0.00	—	.211	.375	0	—	0	2	2	0	0.3
Total 10	55	59	.482	279	104	27	6	11	944	1028	87	340	348	13.2	4.23	90	.281	.346	0	—	0	-37	-45	-1	-4.0

■ ELDON AUKER
Auker, Eldon Le Roy "Submarine" b: 9/21/10, Norcatur, Kan. BR/TR, 6'2", 194 lbs. Deb: 8/10/33

YEAR TM/L	W	L	PCT	G	GS	CG	SH	SV	IP	H	HR	BB	SO	RAT	ERA	ERA+	OAV	OOB	BH	AVG	PB	PR	/A	PD	TPI
1933 Det-A	3	3	.500	15	6	2	1	0	55	63	3	25	17	14.7	5.24	82	.285	.363	2	.118	-1	-6	-6	-1	-0.6
1934 *Det-A	15	7	.682	43	18	10	2	1	205	234	9	56	86	12.9	3.42	128	.288	.336	11	.149	-2	24	22	3	2.2
1935 *Det-A	18	7	.720	36	25	13	2	0	195	213	13	61	63	13.1	3.83	109	.279	.340	16	.216	1	14	7	2	0.9
1936 Det-A	13	16	.448	35	31	14	2	0	215¹	263	11	83	66	14.6	4.89	101	.302	.365	24	.308	7	4	1	5	1.2
1937 Det-A	17	9	.654	39	32	19	1	1	252²	250	13	97	73	12.6	3.88	120	.260	.331	18	.198	4	21	22	5	3.1
1938 Det-A	11	10	.524	27	24	12	1	0	160²	184	14	56	46	13.7	5.27	95	.284	.346	5	.088	-4	-9	-5	3	-0.4
1939 Bos-A	9	10	.474	31	25	6	1	0	151	183	8	61	43	14.6	5.36	88	.294	.358	12	.226	2	-12	-11	2	-0.5
1940 StL-A	16	11	.593	38	35	20	2	0	263²	299	17	96	78	13.6	3.96	116	.281	.342	19	.213	3	12	18	2	2.3
1941 StL-A	14	15	.483	34	31	13	0	0	216	268	20	85	60	14.8	5.50	78	.303	.365	10	.125	-3	-32	-29	1	-2.7
1942 StL-A	14	13	.519	35	34	17	2	0	249	273	16	86	62	13.1	4.08	91	.277	.337	14	.161	-1	-12	-11	1	-0.9
Total 10	130	101	.563	333	261	126	14	2	1963¹	2230	129	706	594	13.6	4.42	101	.285	.347	131	.187	5	3	11	23	4.6

■ DENNIS AUST
Aust, Dennis Kay b: 11/25/40, Tecumseh, Neb. BR/TR, 5'11", 180 lbs. Deb: 9/06/65

YEAR TM/L	W	L	PCT	G	GS	CG	SH	SV	IP	H	HR	BB	SO	RAT	ERA	ERA+	OAV	OOB	BH	AVG	PB	PR	/A	PD	TPI
1965 StL-N	0	0	—	6	0	0	0	1	7¹	6	0	2	7	9.8	4.91	78	.214	.267	0	.000	-0	-1	-1	0	0.0
1966 StL-N	0	1	.000	9	0	0	0	1	9²	12	1	6	7	16.8	6.52	55	.308	.400	0	.000	-0	-3	-3	0	-0.2
Total 2	0	1	.000	15	0	0	0	2	17	18	1	8	14	13.8	5.82	64	.269	.347	0	.000	-0	-4	-4	0	-0.2

■ RICK AUSTIN
Austin, Rick Gerald b: 10/27/46, Seattle, Was. BR/TL, 6'4", 190 lbs. Deb: 6/21/70

YEAR TM/L	W	L	PCT	G	GS	CG	SH	SV	IP	H	HR	BB	SO	RAT	ERA	ERA+	OAV	OOB	BH	AVG	PB	PR	/A	PD	TPI
1970 Cle-A	2	5	.286	31	8	1	1	3	67²	74	10	26	53	13.7	4.79	83	.281	.353	2	.111	0	-8	-6	1	-0.4
1971 Cle-A	0	0	—	23	0	0	0	1	23	25	3	20	20	18.8	5.09	75	.291	.440	0	.000	-0	-4	-3	0	-0.2
1975 Mil-A	2	3	.400	32	0	0	0	2	40	42	3	32	30	14.6	4.05	95	.222	.361	0	—	0	-1	-1	-1	-0.1
1976 Mil-A	0	0	—	3	0	0	0	0	5¹	10	1	0	3	18.6	5.06	69	.435	.458	0	—	0	-1	-1	0	0.0
Total 4	4	8	.333	89	8	1	1	6	136	141	17	78	106	15.0	4.63	84	.273	.377	2	.105	0	-14	-11	1	-0.7

■ AL AUTRY
Autry, Albert b: 2/29/52, Modesto, Cal. BR/TR, 6'5", 225 lbs. Deb: 9/14/76

YEAR TM/L	W	L	PCT	G	GS	CG	SH	SV	IP	H	HR	BB	SO	RAT	ERA	ERA+	OAV	OOB	BH	AVG	PB	PR	/A	PD	TPI
1976 Atl-N	1	0	1.000	1	1	0	0	0	5	4	2	3	3	12.6	5.40	70	.222	.333	0	.000	-0	-1	-1	-0	0.0

■ STEVE AVERY
Avery, Steven Thomas b: 4/14/70, Trenton, Mich. BL/TL, 6'4", 180 lbs. Deb: 6/13/90

YEAR TM/L	W	L	PCT	G	GS	CG	SH	SV	IP	H	HR	BB	SO	RAT	ERA	ERA+	OAV	OOB	BH	AVG	PB	PR	/A	PD	TPI
1990 Atl-N	3	11	.214	21	20	1	1	0	99	121	7	45	75	15.3	5.64	69	.302	.375	4	.133	-1	-20	-19	1	-1.7

■ JAY AVREA
Avrea, James Epherium b: 7/6/20, Cleburne, Tex. BR/TR, 6'1.5", 175 lbs. Deb: 4/22/50

YEAR TM/L	W	L	PCT	G	GS	CG	SH	SV	IP	H	HR	BB	SO	RAT	ERA	ERA+	OAV	OOB	BH	AVG	PB	PR	/A	PD	TPI
1950 Cin-N	0	0	—	2	0	0	0	0	5¹	6	0	3	2	15.2	3.38	125	.273	.360	0	.000	-0	0	1	0	0.0

YEAR TM/L	W	L	PCT	G	GS	CG	SH	SV	IP	H	HR	BB	SO	RAT	ERA	ERA+	OAV	OOB	BH	AVG	PB	PR	/A	PD	TPI

■ JAKE AYDELOTT
Aydelott, Jacob Stuart b: 7/6/1861, N.Manchester, Ind. d: 10/22/26, Detroit, Mich. 6', 180 lbs. Deb: 5/15/1884

YEAR TM/L	W	L	PCT	G	GS	CG	SH	SV	IP	H	HR	BB	SO	RAT	ERA	ERA+	OAV	OOB	BH	AVG	PB	PR	/A	PD	TPI
1884 Ind-a	5	7	.417	12	12	11	0	0	106	129	0	29	30	13.4	4.92	66	.285	.328	5	.114	-3	-20	-20	-1	-1.9
1886 Phi-a	0	2	.000	2	2	2	0	0	18	21	0	12	5	16.5	4.00	88	.278	.377	0	.000	-1	-1	-1	0	-0.1
Total 2	5	9	.357	14	14	13	0	0	124	150	0	41	35	13.9	4.79	69	.284	.335	5	.100	-4	-21	-21	-1	-2.0

■ BILL AYERS
Ayers, William Oscar b: 9/27/19, Newnan, Ga. d: 9/24/80, Newnan, Ga. BR/TR, 6'3", 185 lbs. Deb: 4/17/47

YEAR TM/L	W	L	PCT	G	GS	CG	SH	SV	IP	H	HR	BB	SO	RAT	ERA	ERA+	OAV	OOB	BH	AVG	PB	PR	/A	PD	TPI
1947 NY-N	0	3	.000	13	4	0	0	1	35¹	46	7	14	22	15.5	8.15	50	.322	.386	2	.250	0	-16	-16	0	-1.3

■ DOC AYERS
Ayers, Yancy Wyatt b: 5/20/1890, Fancy Gap, Va. d: 5/26/68, Pulaski, Va. BR/TR, 6'1", 185 lbs. Deb: 9/09/13

YEAR TM/L	W	L	PCT	G	GS	CG	SH	SV	IP	H	HR	BB	SO	RAT	ERA	ERA+	OAV	OOB	BH	AVG	PB	PR	/A	PD	TPI
1913 Was-A	1	1	.500	4	2	1	1	1	17²	12	0	4	17	8.7	1.53	193	.182	.239	0	.000	-1	3	3	0	0.2
1914 Was-A	12	15	.444	49	32	8	3	3	265¹	221	5	54	148	9.6	2.54	109	.238	.286	14	.169	0	6	7	-2	0.5
1915 Was-A	14	9	.609	40	16	8	2	3	211¹	178	1	38	96	9.5	2.21	132	.234	.276	12	.190	-1	17	17	-3	1.1
1916 Was-A	5	9	.357	43	17	7	0	2	157	173	4	52	69	13.1	3.78	73	.285	.346	6	.140	-2	-17	-18	-4	-2.4
1917 Was-A	11	10	.524	40	15	12	3	1	207²	192	3	59	78	11.2	2.17	121	.256	.317	13	.206	-0	12	11	0	1.1
1918 Was-A	10	12	.455	40	24	11	4	3	219²	215	2	63	67	11.7	2.83	96	.261	.319	10	.152	-2	-1	-2	1	-0.4
1919 Was-A	0	6	.000	11	5	0	0	1	43²	52	0	17	12	15.0	2.89	111	.317	.395	5	.417	2	2	2	1	0.4
Det-A	5	3	.625	24	5	3	1	0	93²	88	2	31	32	11.7	2.69	119	.254	.320	3	.125	-1	6	5	-0	0.4
Yr	5	9	.357	35	10	3	1	1	137¹	140	2	48	44	12.5	2.75	116	.272	.337	2	.056	-1	7	7	1	0.8
1920 Det-A	7	14	.333	46	23	8	3	1	208²	217	6	62	103	12.4	3.88	96	.280	.340	9	.153	-2	-2	-4	-1	-0.6
1921 Det-A	0	0	—	2	1	0	0	0	4	9	0	2	0	24.8	9.00	47	.450	.500	0	—	0	-2	-2	-0	-0.1
Total 9	65	79	.451	299	140	58	17	15	1428²	1357	23	382	622	11.3	2.84	104	.259	.315	72	.171	-8	22	18	-8	0.2

■ BOB BABCOCK
Babcock, Robert Ernest b: 8/25/49, New Castle, Pa. BR/TR, 6'5", 210 lbs. Deb: 7/22/79

YEAR TM/L	W	L	PCT	G	GS	CG	SH	SV	IP	H	HR	BB	SO	RAT	ERA	ERA+	OAV	OOB	BH	AVG	PB	PR	/A	PD	TPI
1979 Tex-A	0	0	—	4	0	0	0	0	5¹	7	1	7	6	23.6	10.13	41	.318	.483	0	—	0	-4	-4	-0	-0.2
1980 Tex-A	1	2	.333	19	0	0	0	0	23¹	20	3	8	15	11.6	4.63	84	.238	.319	0	—	0	-2	-2	-0	-0.1
1981 Tex-A	1	1	.500	16	0	0	0	0	28²	21	2	16	18	11.9	2.20	158	.219	.336	0	—	0	5	4	0	0.4
Total 3	2	3	.400	39	0	0	0	0	57¹	48	6	31	39	12.9	3.92	94	.238	.347	0	—	0	-0	-1	-0	0.1

■ JOHNNY BABICH
Babich, John Charles b: 5/14/13, Albion, Cal. BR/TR, 6'1.5", 185 lbs. Deb: 6/19/34

YEAR TM/L	W	L	PCT	G	GS	CG	SH	SV	IP	H	HR	BB	SO	RAT	ERA	ERA+	OAV	OOB	BH	AVG	PB	PR	/A	PD	TPI
1934 Bro-N	7	11	.389	25	19	7	0	1	135	148	5	51	62	13.4	4.20	93	.281	.347	7	.140	-3	-2	-4	1	-0.5
1935 Bro-N	7	14	.333	37	24	7	2	0	143¹	191	7	52	55	15.4	6.66	60	.317	.373	9	.184	-0	-42	-43	0	-3.9
1936 Bos-N	0	0	—	3	0	0	0	0	6	11	1	6	1	27.0	10.50	37	.440	.563	0	.000	-0	-4	-4	0	-0.3
1940 Phi-A	14	13	.519	31	30	16	1	0	229¹	222	16	80	94	11.9	3.73	119	.248	.310	10	.116	-6	17	18	0	1.3
1941 Phi-A	2	7	.222	16	14	4	0	0	78¹	85	9	31	19	13.7	6.09	69	.281	.353	10	.400	4	-17	-17	1	-1.0
Total 5	30	45	.400	112	87	34	3	1	592	657	38	220	231	13.5	4.93	85	.279	.343	36	.171	-5	-49	-50	3	-4.4

■ LES BACKMAN
Backman, Lester John b: 3/20/1888, Cleves, Ohio d: 11/8/75, Cincinnati, Ohio TR, 6'0.5", 195 lbs. Deb: 7/03/09

YEAR TM/L	W	L	PCT	G	GS	CG	SH	SV	IP	H	HR	BB	SO	RAT	ERA	ERA+	OAV	OOB	BH	AVG	PB	PR	/A	PD	TPI
1909 StL-N	3	11	.214	21	14	8	0	0	128¹	146	1	39	35	13.2	4.14	61	.302	.357	4	.103	-1	-22	-23	-0	-2.4
1910 StL-N	6	7	.462	26	11	4	0	2	116	117	4	53	41	13.3	3.03	98	.265	.346	4	.114	0	0	-1	-0	0.0
Total 2	9	18	.333	47	25	12	0	2	244¹	263	5	92	76	13.3	3.61	76	.284	.352	8	.108	-1	-22	-24	-1	-2.4

■ EDDIE BACON
Bacon, Edgar Suter b: 4/8/1895, Franklin Co., Ky. d: 10/2/63, Frankfort, Ky. Deb: 8/13/17 ♦

YEAR TM/L	W	L	PCT	G	GS	CG	SH	SV	IP	H	HR	BB	SO	RAT	ERA	ERA+	OAV	OOB	BH	AVG	PB	PR	/A	PD	TPI
1917 Phi-A	0	0	—	1	0	0	0	0	6	5	0	9	2	18.0	6.00	46	.238	.429	3	.500	1	-2	-2	1	-0.1

■ MIKE BACSIK
Bacsik, Michael James b: 4/1/52, Dallas, Tex. BR/TR, 6'2", 180 lbs. Deb: 6/15/75

YEAR TM/L	W	L	PCT	G	GS	CG	SH	SV	IP	H	HR	BB	SO	RAT	ERA	ERA+	OAV	OOB	BH	AVG	PB	PR	/A	PD	TPI
1975 Tex-A	1	2	.333	7	3	0	0	0	26²	28	1	9	13	12.8	3.71	101	.275	.339	0	—	0	0	-0	-0	0.0
1976 Tex-A	3	2	.600	23	0	0	0	0	55	66	3	26	21	15.4	4.25	84	.308	.388	0	—	0	-4	-4	-1	-0.4
1977 Tex-A	0	0	—	2	0	0	0	0	2¹	9	1	0	1	34.7	19.29	21	.563	.563	0	—	0	-4	-4	0	-0.2
1979 Min-A	4	2	.667	31	0	0	0	0	65²	61	6	29	33	12.3	4.39	100	.249	.328	0	—	0	-1	-0	-0	0.0
1980 Min-A	0	0	—	10	0	0	0	0	23	26	1	11	9	14.5	4.30	101	.286	.363	0	—	0	-1	0	0	0.0
Total 5	8	6	.571	73	3	0	0	0	172²	190	12	75	77	14.0	4.43	91	.284	.359	0	—	0	-10	-8	-0	-0.6

■ FRED BACZEWSKI
Baczewski, Frederic John "Lefty" b: 5/15/26, St.Paul, Minn. d: 11/14/76, Culver City, Cal. BL/TL, 6'2.5", 185 lbs. Deb: 4/26/53

YEAR TM/L	W	L	PCT	G	GS	CG	SH	SV	IP	H	HR	BB	SO	RAT	ERA	ERA+	OAV	OOB	BH	AVG	PB	PR	/A	PD	TPI
1953 Chi-N	0	0	—	9	0	0	0	0	10	20	1	6	3	24.3	6.30	71	.435	.509	1	.500	0	-2	-2	0	-0.1
Cin-N	11	4	.733	24	18	10	1	1	138¹	125	13	52	58	11.6	3.45	126	.244	.315	8	.178	-0	13	14	-3	1.1
Yr	11	4	.733	33	18	10	1	1	148¹	145	14	58	61	12.4	3.64	120	.259	.330	1	.021	0	11	12	-3	1.0
1954 Cin-N	6	6	.500	29	22	4	1	0	130	159	22	53	43	14.7	5.26	80	.305	.370	3	.071	-4	-17	-15	-1	-1.8
1955 Cin-N	0	0	—	1	0	0	0	0	1	2	2	0	0	18.0	18.00	24	.400	.400	0	—	0	-2	-2	0	0.0
Total 3	17	10	.630	63	40	14	2	1	279¹	306	38	111	104	13.5	4.45	96	.282	.351	12	.135	-3	-8	-5	-4	-0.8

■ LORE BADER
Bader, Lore Verne "King" b: 4/27/1888, Bader, Ill. d: 6/2/73, LeRoy, Kan. BL/TR, 6', 175 lbs. Deb: 9/30/12 C

YEAR TM/L	W	L	PCT	G	GS	CG	SH	SV	IP	H	HR	BB	SO	RAT	ERA	ERA+	OAV	OOB	BH	AVG	PB	PR	/A	PD	TPI
1912 NY-N	2	0	1.000	2	1	1	0	0	10	9	0	6	3	14.4	0.90	376	.231	.348	0	.000	-0	3	3	0	0.3
1917 Bos-A	2	0	1.000	15	1	0	0	0	38¹	48	1	18	14	15.7	2.35	110	.306	.381	3	.300	1	1	1	1	0.3
1918 Bos-A	1	3	.250	5	4	2	1	0	27	26	1	12	10	13.7	3.33	81	.271	.369	1	.111	-1	-2	-2	-1	-0.3
Total 3	5	3	.625	22	6	3	1	1	75¹	83	2	36	27	14.8	2.51	109	.284	.372	4	.182	0	2	2	-0	0.3

■ ED BAECHT
Baecht, Edward Joseph b: 5/15/07, Paden, Okla. d: 8/15/57, Grafton, Ill. BR/TR, 6'3", 195 lbs. Deb: 4/24/26

YEAR TM/L	W	L	PCT	G	GS	CG	SH	SV	IP	H	HR	BB	SO	RAT	ERA	ERA+	OAV	OOB	BH	AVG	PB	PR	/A	PD	TPI
1926 Phi-N	2	0	1.000	28	1	1	0	0	56	73	4	28	14	16.4	6.11	68	.324	.402	2	.143	-1	-14	-12	2	-1.0
1927 Phi-N	0	1	.000	1	1	0	0	0	6	12	0	2	0	21.0	12.00	34	.429	.467	0	.000	-0	-5	-5	0	-0.3
1928 Phi-N	1	1	.500	9	1	0	0	0	24	37	1	9	10	17.3	6.00	71	.385	.438	1	.143	-0	-5	-5	0	-0.3
1931 Chi-N	2	4	.333	22	6	2	0	0	67	64	1	32	34	14.0	3.76	103	.250	.351	5	.278	1	1	1	1	0.2
1932 Chi-N	0	0	—	1	0	0	0	0	1	1	0	1	0	18.0	0.00	—	.333	.500	0	—	0	0	0	0	0.0
1937 StL-A	0	0	—	3	0	0	0	0	6¹	13	3	6	3	29.8	12.79	38	.419	.538	0	.000	-0	-6	-6	0	-0.4
Total 6	5	6	.455	64	9	3	0	0	160¹	200	9	78	61	16.2	5.56	73	.313	.397	8	.190	-2	-29	-27	3	-1.8

■ JIM BAGBY
Bagby, James Charles Jacob Jr. b: 9/8/16, Cleveland, Ohio d: 9/2/88, Marietta, Ga. BR/TR, 6'2", 170 lbs. Deb: 4/18/38

YEAR TM/L	W	L	PCT	G	GS	CG	SH	SV	IP	H	HR	BB	SO	RAT	ERA	ERA+	OAV	OOB	BH	AVG	PB	PR	/A	PD	TPI
1938 Bos-A	15	11	.577	43	25	10	1	2	198²	218	9	90	73	14.1	4.21	117	.283	.360	13	.191	-1	13	16	2	1.6
1939 Bos-A	5	5	.500	21	11	3	0	0	80	119	7	36	35	17.7	7.09	67	.347	.412	10	.294	3	-22	-21	-0	-1.5
1940 Bos-A	10	16	.385	36	21	6	1	2	182²	217	15	83	57	14.8	4.73	95	.296	.368	15	.203	-0	-7	-5	0	-0.3
1941 Cle-A	9	15	.375	33	27	12	0	0	200²	214	10	76	53	13.3	4.04	98	.273	.341	18	.243	2	2	2	2	0.2
1942 Cle-A	17	9	.654	38	35	16	4	1	270²	267	19	64	54	11.0	2.96	117	.258	.302	18	.189	1	21	15	1	1.7
1943 Cle-A	17	14	.548	36	33	16	3	1	273	248	15	80	70	10.9	3.10	100	.240	.296	30	.268	4	6	0	3	0.8
1944 Cle-A	4	5	.444	13	10	2	0	0	79	101	4	34	12	15.8	4.33	76	.312	.384	7	.226	1	-8	-9	1	-0.7
1945 Cle-A	8	11	.421	25	19	11	3	1	159¹	171	3	59	38	13.1	3.73	87	.279	.344	17	.293	3	-6	-8	4	-0.1
1946 *Bos-A	7	6	.538	21	11	6	1	0	106²	117	4	49	16	14.1	3.71	99	.279	.356	5	.119	-2	-2	-1	0	-0.2
1947 Pit-N	5	4	.556	37	6	2	0	0	115²	143	14	37	23	14.4	4.67	90	.304	.361	7	.219	1	-8	-6	1	-0.2
Total 10	97	96	.503	303	198	84	13	9	1666¹	1815	98	608	431	13.2	3.96	97	.278	.342	140	.226	12	-11	-23	14	1.4

■ JIM BAGBY
Bagby, James Charles Jacob Sr. "Sarge" b: 10/5/1889, Barnett, Ga. d: 7/28/54, Marietta, Ga. BB/TR, 6', 170 lbs. Deb: 4/22/12

YEAR TM/L	W	L	PCT	G	GS	CG	SH	SV	IP	H	HR	BB	SO	RAT	ERA	ERA+	OAV	OOB	BH	AVG	PB	PR	/A	PD	TPI
1912 Cin-N	2	1	.667	5	1	0	0	0	17¹	17	2	9	10	13.5	3.12	108	.266	.356	0	.000	-1	1	0	0	0.0
1916 Cle-A	16	16	.500	48	27	14	3	5	272²	253	2	67	88	10.8	2.61	115	.251	.303	15	.167	-1	7	12	-2	1.1
1917 Cle-A	23	13	.639	49	37	26	8	7	320²	277	6	73	83	10.0	1.96	144	.235	.283	25	.231	3	25	31	-2	3.7
1918 Cle-A	17	16	.515	45	31	23	2	6	271¹	274	0	78	74	11.7	2.69	112	.276	.330	21	.212	-0	3	10	-1	1.0
1919 Cle-A	17	11	.607	35	32	21	0	3	241¹	258	4	44	61	11.4	2.80	120	.275	.310	23	.258	5	12	15	0	2.2
1920 *Cle-A	31	12	.721	48	38	30	3	0	339²	338	9	79	73	11.2	2.89	132	.266	.311	33	.252	6	34	34	-6	3.4

YEAR	TM/L	W	L	PCT	G	GS	CG	SH	SV	IP	H	HR	BB	SO	RAT	ERA	ERA+	OAV	OOB	BH	AVG	PB	PR	/A	PD	TPI
1921	Cle-A	14	12	.538	40	26	13	0	4	191²	238	14	44	37	13.4	4.70	91	.308	.348	15	.197	-1	-9	-9	-1	-1.0
1922	Cle-A	4	5	.444	25	10	4	0	1	98¹	134	5	39	25	16.1	6.32	63	.340	.404	11	.262	3	-25	-25	1	-1.9
1923	Pit-N	3	2	.600	21	6	2	0	3	68²	95	6	25	16	15.9	5.24	76	.336	.392	1	.050	-2	-9	-9	-1	-1.0
Total	9	127	88	.591	316	208	133	16	29	1821²	1884	47	458	450	11.7	3.11	110	.273	.321	144	.218	11	38	62	-11	7.5

■ STAN BAHNSEN
Bahnsen, Stanley Raymond   b: 12/15/44, Council Bluffs, Ia.   BR/TR, 6'2", 185 lbs.   Deb: 9/09/66

YEAR	TM/L	W	L	PCT	G	GS	CG	SH	SV	IP	H	HR	BB	SO	RAT	ERA	ERA+	OAV	OOB	BH	AVG	PB	PR	/A	PD	TPI
1966	NY-A	1	1	.500	4	3	1	0	1	23	15	3	7	16	8.6	3.52	94	.181	.244	1	.143	-0	-0	-1	-0	0.0
1968	NY-A	17	12	.586	37	34	10	1	0	267¹	216	14	68	162	9.6	2.05	141	.221	.273	4	.049	-4	27	25	-2	2.2
1969	NY-A	9	16	.360	40	33	5	2	1	220²	222	28	90	130	12.7	3.83	91	.260	.331	5	.083	-3	-5	-9	1	-1.1
1970	NY-A	14	11	.560	36	35	6	2	0	232²	227	23	75	116	11.8	3.33	106	.256	.316	11	.149	-0	10	5	1	0.5
1971	NY-A	14	12	.538	36	34	14	3	0	242	221	20	72	110	11.1	3.35	97	.248	.308	12	.152	0	3	-3	3	0.0
1972	Chi-A	21	16	.568	43	41	5	1	0	252¹	263	22	73	157	12.2	3.60	87	.268	.323	14	.152	-15	-13	3	-1.2
1973	Chi-A	18	21	.462	42	42	14	4	0	282¹	290	20	117	120	13.1	3.57	111	.269	.343	0	—	0	8	12	3	1.5
1974	Chi-A	12	15	.444	38	35	10	1	0	216¹	230	17	116	102	14.3	4.70	79	.277	.364	0	—	0	-26	-23	1	-2.2
1975	Chi-A	4	6	.400	12	12	2	0	0	67¹	78	9	40	31	16.2	6.01	64	.291	.389	0	—	0	-17	-16	0	-1.4
	Oak-A	6	7	.462	21	16	2	0	0	100	88	2	37	49	11.5	3.24	112	.238	.313	0	.000	0	6	4	0	0.5
	Yr	10	13	.435	33	28	4	0	0	167¹	166	11	77	80	13.2	4.36	85	.259	.342	0	.000	0	-11	-12	0	-0.9
1976	Oak-A	8	7	.533	35	14	1	1	0	143	124	13	43	82	10.6	3.34	101	.232	.292	0	—	0	3	0	1	0.1
1977	Oak-A	1	2	.333	11	2	0	0	1	22	24	5	13	21	15.5	6.14	66	.286	.388	0	—	0	-5	-5	-1	-0.5
	Mon-N	8	9	.471	23	22	3	1	0	127¹	142	14	38	58	12.7	4.81	79	.283	.333	5	.119	-1	-13	-14	0	-1.4
1978	Mon-N	1	5	.167	44	1	0	0	7	75	74	9	31	44	12.6	3.84	92	.261	.334	1	.091	-1	-2	-3	-0	-0.3
1979	Mon-N	3	1	.750	55	0	0	0	5	94¹	80	10	42	71	11.6	3.15	116	.236	.320	1	.071	-0	6	5	-0	0.5
1980	Mon-N	7	6	.538	57	0	0	0	4	91¹	80	7	33	48	11.1	3.05	117	.235	.302	1	.111	1	6	5	-0	0.6
1981	*Mon-N	2	1	.667	25	3	0	0	1	49	45	7	24	28	12.9	4.96	70	.247	.338	1	.111	-0	-8	-8	-1	-0.9
1982	Cal-A	0	1	.000	7	0	0	0	0	9²	13	0	8	5	16.6	4.66	87	.310	.420	0	—	0	-1	-1	-0	0.0
	Phi-N	0	0	—	8	0	0	0	0	13¹	9	0	3	9	7.4	1.35	271	.182	.234	0	—	0	3	3	-0	0.4
Total	16	146	149	.495	574	327	73	16	20	2529	2440	223	924	1359	12.1	3.60	97	.255	.323	56	.117	-8	-20	-35	6	-2.7

■ ED BAHR
Bahr, Edson Garfield   b: 10/16/19, Rouleau, Sask., Canada   BR/TR, 6'1.5", 172 lbs.   Deb: 5/01/46

YEAR	TM/L	W	L	PCT	G	GS	CG	SH	SV	IP	H	HR	BB	SO	RAT	ERA	ERA+	OAV	OOB	BH	AVG	PB	PR	/A	PD	TPI
1946	Pit-N	8	6	.571	27	14	7	0	0	136²	128	8	52	44	12.2	2.63	134	.254	.330	8	.178	-1	12	14	0	1.4
1947	Pit-N	3	5	.375	19	11	1	0	0	82¹	82	5	43	25	14.0	4.59	92	.263	.358	2	.087	-2	-5	-3	-1	-0.5
Total	2	11	11	.500	46	25	8	0	0	219	210	13	95	69	12.9	3.37	112	.257	.341	10	.147	-3	7	10	-1	0.9

■ GROVER BAICHLEY
Baichley, Grover Cleveland   b: 1/7/1890, Toledo, Ill.   d: 6/30/56, San Jose, Cal.   BR/TR, 5'9.5", 165 lbs.   Deb: 8/24/14

YEAR	TM/L	W	L	PCT	G	GS	CG	SH	SV	IP	H	HR	BB	SO	RAT	ERA	ERA+	OAV	OOB	BH	AVG	PB	PR	/A	PD	TPI
1914	StL-A	0	0	—	4	0	0	0	0	7	9	0	3	3	15.4	5.14	53	.346	.414	0	.000	-0	-2	-2	0	-0.1

■ SCOTT BAILES
Bailes, Scott Alan   b: 12/18/61, Chillicothe, Ohio   BL/TL, 6'2", 170 lbs.   Deb: 4/09/86

YEAR	TM/L	W	L	PCT	G	GS	CG	SH	SV	IP	H	HR	BB	SO	RAT	ERA	ERA+	OAV	OOB	BH	AVG	PB	PR	/A	PD	TPI
1986	Cle-A	10	10	.500	62	10	0	0	7	112²	123	12	43	60	13.3	4.95	84	.276	.342	0	—	0	-10	-10	-1	-1.0
1987	Cle-A	7	8	.467	39	17	0	0	6	120¹	145	21	47	65	14.7	4.64	98	.296	.362	0	—	0	-2	-2	0	0.0
1988	Cle-A	9	14	.391	37	21	5	2	0	145	149	22	46	53	12.2	4.90	84	.266	.324	0	—	0	-15	-13	0	-1.1
1989	Cle-A	5	9	.357	34	11	0	0	0	113²	116	7	29	47	11.7	4.28	93	.269	.320	0	—	0	-5	-4	0	-0.3
1990	Cal-A	2	0	1.000	27	0	0	0	0	35¹	46	8	20	16	17.1	6.37	61	.315	.401	0	—	0	-10	-10	1	-0.8
Total	5	33	41	.446	199	59	5	2	13	527	579	70	185	241	13.2	4.82	87	.279	.342	0	—	0	-42	-38	1	-3.2

■ SWEETBREADS BAILEY
Bailey, Abraham Lincoln   b: 2/12/1895, Joliet, Ill.   d: 9/27/39, Joliet, Ill.   BR/TR, 6', 184 lbs.   Deb: 5/23/19

YEAR	TM/L	W	L	PCT	G	GS	CG	SH	SV	IP	H	HR	BB	SO	RAT	ERA	ERA+	OAV	OOB	BH	AVG	PB	PR	/A	PD	TPI
1919	Chi-N	3	5	.375	21	5	0	0	0	71¹	75	2	20	19	12.4	3.15	91	.288	.346	7	.389	3	-2	-2	2	0.3
1920	Chi-N	1	2	.333	21	1	0	0	0	36²	55	1	11	8	16.7	7.12	45	.359	.410	1	.143	-0	-16	-16	1	-1.5
1921	Chi-N	0	0	—	3	0	0	0	0	5	6	0	2	2	16.2	3.60	106	.300	.391	0	0	0	0	0	0.0
	Bro-N	0	0	—	7	0	0	0	0	24¹	35	1	7	6	15.9	5.18	75	.368	.417	0	.000	-0	-4	-3	0	-0.3
	Yr	0	0	—	10	0	0	0	0	29¹	41	1	9	8	15.6	4.91	79	.353	.405	1	.200	-0	-4	-3	0	-0.3
Total	3	4	7	.364	52	6	0	0	0	137¹	171	4	40	35	14.3	4.59	69	.324	.379	8	.267	2	-22	-22	3	-1.5

■ HARVEY BAILEY
Bailey, Harvey Francis   b: 11/24/1876, Adrian, Mich.   d: 7/10/22, Toledo, Ohio   TL, 6',   Deb: 6/30/1899

YEAR	TM/L	W	L	PCT	G	GS	CG	SH	SV	IP	H	HR	BB	SO	RAT	ERA	ERA+	OAV	OOB	BH	AVG	PB	PR	/A	PD	TPI
1899	Bos-N	6	4	.600	12	11	8	0	0	86²	83	7	35	26	12.3	3.95	105	.252	.324	8	.235	0	-1	2	-1	0.2
1900	Bos-N	0	0	—	4	1	0	0	0	20	24	0	11	9	15.7	4.95	83	.296	.381	2	.222	0	-3	-2	1	0.0
Total	2	6	4	.600	16	12	8	0	0	106²	107	7	46	35	12.9	4.13	100	.261	.335	10	.233	0	-4	0	-0	0.2

■ HOWARD BAILEY
Bailey, Howard L   b: 7/31/57, Grand Haven, Mich.   BR/TL, 6', 195 lbs.   Deb: 4/12/81

YEAR	TM/L	W	L	PCT	G	GS	CG	SH	SV	IP	H	HR	BB	SO	RAT	ERA	ERA+	OAV	OOB	BH	AVG	PB	PR	/A	PD	TPI
1981	Det-A	1	4	.200	9	5	0	0	0	36²	45	4	13	17	15.0	7.36	51	.308	.377	0	—	0	-15	-15	1	-1.2
1982	Det-A	0	0	—	8	0	0	0	1	10	6	0	2	3	7.2	0.00	—	.182	.229	0	—	0	5	5	0	0.5
1983	Det-A	5	5	.500	33	3	0	0	0	72	69	11	25	21	12.0	4.88	80	.255	.322	0	—	0	-7	-8	0	-0.6
Total	3	6	9	.400	50	8	0	0	1	118²	120	15	40	41	12.5	5.23	74	.267	.333	0	—	0	-17	-18	2	-1.3

■ JAMES BAILEY
Bailey, James Hopkins   b: 12/16/34, Strawberry Plains, Tenn.   BB/TL, 6'2.5", 210 lbs.   Deb: 9/10/59

YEAR	TM/L	W	L	PCT	G	GS	CG	SH	SV	IP	H	HR	BB	SO	RAT	ERA	ERA+	OAV	OOB	BH	AVG	PB	PR	/A	PD	TPI
1959	Cin-N	0	1	.000	3	1	0	0	0	11²	17	1	6	7	18.5	6.17	66	.333	.414	0	.000	-0	-3	-3	-0	-0.2

■ KING BAILEY
Bailey, Leonard C.   b: 11/1870, Virginia   BL/TL, 6' ", 185 lbs.   Deb: 9/21/1895

YEAR	TM/L	W	L	PCT	G	GS	CG	SH	SV	IP	H	HR	BB	SO	RAT	ERA	ERA+	OAV	OOB	BH	AVG	PB	PR	/A	PD	TPI
1895	Cin-N	1	0	1.000	1	1	1	0	0	8	13	0	0	0	14.6	5.63	88	.359	.359	2	.500	1	-1	-1	0	0.0

■ STEVE BAILEY
Bailey, Steven John   b: 2/12/42, Bronx, N.Y.   BR/TR, 6'1", 194 lbs.   Deb: 4/14/67

YEAR	TM/L	W	L	PCT	G	GS	CG	SH	SV	IP	H	HR	BB	SO	RAT	ERA	ERA+	OAV	OOB	BH	AVG	PB	PR	/A	PD	TPI
1967	Cle-A	2	5	.286	32	1	0	0	2	64²	62	5	42	46	14.9	3.90	84	.259	.377	0	.000	-1	-5	-5	0	-0.5
1968	Cle-A	0	1	.000	2	1	0	0	0	5	4	1	2	1	10.8	3.60	82	.235	.316	0	—	0	-0	-0	-0	-0.0
Total	2	2	6	.250	34	2	0	0	2	69²	66	6	44	47	14.6	3.88	84	.258	.373	0	.000	-1	-5	-5	0	-0.5

■ BILL BAILEY
Bailey, William F.   b: 4/12/1889, Ft.Smith, Ark.   d: 11/2/26, Houston, Tex.   BL/TL, 5'11", 165 lbs.   Deb: 9/17/07

YEAR	TM/L	W	L	PCT	G	GS	CG	SH	SV	IP	H	HR	BB	SO	RAT	ERA	ERA+	OAV	OOB	BH	AVG	PB	PR	/A	PD	TPI
1907	StL-A	4	1	.800	6	5	3	0	0	48¹	39	0	15	17	10.1	2.42	104	.223	.284	3	.150	-1	1	1	-1	-0.1
1908	StL-A	3	5	.375	22	12	7	0	0	106²	85	2	50	42	11.6	3.04	79	.220	.314	3	.088	-2	-8	-8	-2	-1.2
1909	StL-A	9	10	.474	32	20	17	1	0	199	174	2	75	114	11.5	2.44	99	.248	.325	22	.286	5	1	-1	-2	0.3
1910	StL-A	3	18	.143	34	20	13	0	0	192¹	186	6	97	90	13.7	3.32	74	.262	.359	13	.206	-0	-17	-18	-2	-2.0
1911	StL-A	0	3	.000	7	2	2	0	0	31²	42	1	16	8	17.1	4.55	74	.339	.423	0	.000	-2	-4	-4	1	-0.4
1912	StL-A	0	1	.000	3	2	0	0	0	10²	15	0	10	2	21.1	9.28	36	.341	.463	1	.500	1	-7	-7	-0	-0.5
1914	Bal-F	7	9	.438	19	18	10	1	0	128²	106	2	68	131	12.7	3.08	110	.230	.338	7	.163	-0	2	4	0	0.6
1915	Bal-F	6	19	.240	36	23	11	2	0	190¹	179	8	115	98	14.3	4.63	69	.255	.366	15	.231	1	-34	-31	-2	-3.1
	Chi-F	3	1	.750	5	5	3	3	0	33¹	23	1	10	24	8.9	2.16	129	.202	.266	2	.222	0	3	2	0	0.3
	Yr	9	20	.310	41	28	14	5	0	223²	202	9	125	122	13.2	4.27	73	.245	.344	17	.190	1	-31	-28	-1	-2.8
1918	Det-A	1	2	.333	8	4	1	0	0	37²	53	0	26	13	19.1	5.97	45	.368	.468	1	.077	-1	-13	-14	1	-1.3
1921	StL-N	2	5	.286	19	6	3	1	0	74	95	1	22	20	14.5	4.26	86	.330	.381	2	.091	-2	-4	-5	1	-0.4
1922	StL-N	0	2	.000	10	1	0	0	0	31²	38	1	23	11	17.3	5.40	72	.325	.436	2	.286	0	-5	-5	1	-0.3
Total	11	38	76	.333	203	117	70	8	0	1084¹	1035	20	527	570	13.3	3.57	80	.261	.353	71	.194	-1	-85	-85	-3	-8.1

■ BOB BAILOR
Bailor, Robert Michael   b: 7/10/51, Connellsville, Pa.   BR/TR, 5'11", 170 lbs.   Deb: 9/06/75 ♦

YEAR	TM/L	W	L	PCT	G	GS	CG	SH	SV	IP	H	HR	BB	SO	RAT	ERA	ERA+	OAV	OOB	BH	AVG	PB	PR	/A	PD	TPI
1980	Tor-A	0	0	—	3	0	0	0	0	2¹	4	0	1	0	19.3	7.71	56	.364	.417	82	.236	2	-1	-1	0	0.0

■ LOREN BAIN
Bain, Herbert Loren   b: 7/4/22, Staples, Minn.   BR/TR, 6', 190 lbs.   Deb: 6/23/45

YEAR	TM/L	W	L	PCT	G	GS	CG	SH	SV	IP	H	HR	BB	SO	RAT	ERA	ERA+	OAV	OOB	BH	AVG	PB	PR	/A	PD	TPI
1945	NY-N	0	0	—	3	0	0	0	0	8	10	1	4	1	16.9	7.88	50	.323	.417	1	.333	0	-4	-4	0	-0.2

■ DOUG BAIR
Bair, Charles Douglas b: 8/22/49, Defiance, Ohio   BR/TR, 6', 170 lbs.   Deb: 9/13/76

YEAR	TM/L	W	L	PCT	G	GS	CG	SH	SV	IP	H	HR	BB	SO	RAT	ERA	ERA+	OAV	OOB	BH	AVG	PB	PR	/A	PD	TPI
1976	Pit-N	0	0	—	4	0	0	0	0	6¹	4	0	5	4	12.8	5.68	61	.174	.321	0	—	0	-2	-2	0	-0.1
1977	Oak-A	4	6	.400	45	0	0	0	8	83¹	78	11	57	68	14.6	3.46	116	.253	.370	0	—	0	6	5	1	0.6
1978	Cin-N	7	6	.538	70	0	0	0	28	100¹	87	6	38	91	11.2	1.97	180	.236	.307	2	.143	-0	18	18	-1	1.7
1979	*Cin-N	11	7	.611	65	0	0	0	16	94¹	93	7	51	86	14.0	4.29	87	.256	.353	0	.000	-1	-6	-6	-1	-0.7
1980	Cin-N	3	6	.333	61	0	0	0	6	85	91	7	39	62	13.9	4.24	84	.277	.355	0	.000	-0	-6	-6	2	-0.4
1981	Cin-N	2	2	.500	24	0	0	0	0	39	42	5	17	16	13.6	5.77	62	.271	.343	1	.333	1	-10	-10	-0	-0.8
	StL-N	2	0	1.000	11	0	0	0	1	15²	13	0	2	14	8.6	3.45	103	.224	.250	0	.000	-0	0	0	-0	0.0
	Yr	4	2	.667	35	0	0	0	1	54²	55	5	19	30	12.2	5.10	70	.258	.319	0	—	1	-10	-9	-1	-0.8
1982	*StL-N	5	3	.625	63	0	0	0	8	91²	69	7	36	68	10.4	2.55	142	.211	.291	1	.077	-1	11	11	0	1.0
1983	StL-N	1	1	.500	26	0	0	0	1	29²	24	4	13	21	11.2	3.03	119	.224	.308	0	.000	-0	2	2	-0	0.1
	Det-A	7	3	.700	27	1	0	0	4	55²	51	8	19	39	11.5	3.88	101	.242	.307	0	—	0	1	0	0	0.0
1984	Det-A	5	3	.625	47	1	0	0	4	93²	82	10	36	57	11.3	3.75	105	.238	.310	0	—	0	3	2	1	0.2
1985	Det-A	2	0	1.000	21	3	0	0	0	49	54	3	25	30	14.7	6.24	65	.281	.367	0	—	0	-11	-12	1	-1.0
	StL-N	0	0	—	2	0	0	0	0	2	1	0	2	0	13.5	0.00	—	.167	.375	0	—	0	1	1	0	0.1
1986	Oak-A	2	3	.400	31	0	0	0	0	45	37	5	18	40	11.0	3.00	129	.224	.301	0	—	0	6	4	0	0.5
1987	Phi-N	2	0	1.000	11	0	0	0	0	13²	17	4	5	10	14.5	5.93	72	.309	.367	0	.000	-0	-3	-3	-0	-0.2
1988	Tor-A	0	0	—	10	0	0	0	0	13¹	14	2	3	8	11.5	4.05	97	.280	.321	0	—	0	-0	-0	0	0.0
1989	Pit-N	2	3	.400	44	0	0	0	1	67¹	52	4	28	56	10.7	2.27	148	.211	.292	1	.200	0	9	8	0	0.9
1990	Pit-N	0	0	—	22	0	0	0	0	24¹	30	3	11	19	15.2	4.81	75	.306	.376	0	.000	-0	-3	-3	-0	-0.2
Total 15		55	43	.561	584	5	0	0	81	909¹	839	86	405	689	12.4	3.63	103	.246	.328	5	.096	-2	15	10	1	1.7

■ BOB BAIRD
Baird, Robert Allen b: 1/16/40, Knoxville, Tenn. d: 4/11/74, Chattanooga, Tenn.   BL/TL, 6'4", 195 lbs.   Deb: 9/03/62

YEAR	TM/L	W	L	PCT	G	GS	CG	SH	SV	IP	H	HR	BB	SO	RAT	ERA	ERA+	OAV	OOB	BH	AVG	PB	PR	/A	PD	TPI
1962	Was-A	0	1	.000	3	3	0	0	0	10²	13	0	8	3	17.7	6.75	60	.310	.420	0	.000	-0	-3	-3	0	-0.2
1963	Was-A	0	3	.000	5	3	0	0	0	11²	12	1	7	7	15.4	7.71	48	.261	.370	1	.333	-0	-5	-5	-0	-0.4
Total 2		0	4	.000	8	6	0	0	0	22¹	25	1	15	10	16.5	7.25	53	.284	.394	1	.167	-0	-9	-8	-0	-0.6

■ JERSEY BAKELY
Bakely, Edward Enoch (b: Edward Enoch Bakley) b: 4/17/1864, Blackwood, N.J. d: 2/17/15, Philadelphia, Pa.   BR/TR,   Deb: 5/11/1883

YEAR	TM/L	W	L	PCT	G	GS	CG	SH	SV	IP	H	HR	BB	SO	RAT	ERA	ERA+	OAV	OOB	BH	AVG	PB	PR	/A	PD	TPI
1883	Phi-a	5	3	.625	8	8	7	0	0	61¹	65	0	12	14	11.3	3.23	108	.255	.288	5	.192	1	1	2	0	0.3
1884	Phi-U	14	25	.359	39	38	38	1	0	344²	390	0	76	204	12.6	4.47	64	.267	.303	22	.132	-7	-55	-61	-3	-5.9
	Wil-U	0	2	.000	2	2	2	0	0	17	24	0	1	9	13.2	4.24	78	.312	.321	0	.000	-1	-2	-2	0	-0.1
	KC-U	2	3	.400	5	5	3	0	0	33	29	0	4	13	9.0	2.45	113	.220	.243	3	.150	-1	2	1	-0	0.0
	Yr	16	30	.348	46	45	43	1	0	394²	443	0	81	226	11.9	4.29	67	.265	.299	13	.068	-8	-56	-62	-4	-6.0
1888	Cle-a	25	33	.431	61	61	60	4	0	532²	518	14	128	212	10.9	2.97	105	.246	.289	26	.134	-5	5	8	-1	0.2
1889	Cle-N	12	22	.353	36	34	33	2	0	304¹	296	9	106	105	11.9	2.96	136	.247	.308	15	.135	-1	36	36	2	3.4
1890	Cle-P	12	25	.324	43	38	32	0	0	326¹	412	13	147	67	15.4	4.47	89	.295	.362	28	.203	-2	-9	-18	-3	-1.7
1891	Was-a	2	10	.167	13	12	11	0	0	104¹	127	6	60	32	16.1	5.35	70	.290	.376	10	.222	-0	-19	-19	-2	-1.6
	Bal-a	4	2	.667	8	6	5	0	0	59	48	1	30	13	11.9	2.29	163	.215	.308	2	.095	0	9	10	-0	0.9
	Yr	6	12	.333	21	18	16	0	0	163¹	175	7	90	45	14.6	4.24	88	.262	.353	10	.152	-0	-9	-9	-2	-0.7
Total 6		76	125	.378	215	204	191	7	0	1782²	1909	43	564	669	12.5	3.66	94	.262	.315	111	.153	-16	-32	-41	-8	-4.5

■ DAVE BAKENHASTER
Bakenhaster, David Lee b: 3/5/45, Columbus, O.   BR/TR, 5'10", 168 lbs.   Deb: 6/20/64

YEAR	TM/L	W	L	PCT	G	GS	CG	SH	SV	IP	H	HR	BB	SO	RAT	ERA	ERA+	OAV	OOB	BH	AVG	PB	PR	/A	PD	TPI
1964	StL-N	0	0	—	2	0	0	0	0	3	9	1	1	0	30.0	6.00	63	.474	.500	0	—	0	-1	-1	0	0.0

■ AL BAKER
Baker, Albert Jones b: 2/28/06, Batesville, Miss. d: 11/6/82, Kenedy, Tex.   BR/TR, 5'11", 170 lbs.   Deb: 8/20/38

YEAR	TM/L	W	L	PCT	G	GS	CG	SH	SV	IP	H	HR	BB	SO	RAT	ERA	ERA+	OAV	OOB	BH	AVG	PB	PR	/A	PD	TPI
1938	Bos-A	0	0	—	3	0	0	0	0	7²	13	2	2	2	18.8	9.39	53	.371	.421	0	.000	-1	-4	-4	0	-0.3

■ BOCK BAKER
Baker, Charles "Smiling Bock" b: 7/17/1878, Troy, N.Y. d: 8/17/40, New York, N.Y.   TL,   Deb: 4/28/01

YEAR	TM/L	W	L	PCT	G	GS	CG	SH	SV	IP	H	HR	BB	SO	RAT	ERA	ERA+	OAV	OOB	BH	AVG	PB	PR	/A	PD	TPI
1901	Cle-A	0	1	.000	1	1	0	0	0	8	23	0	6	0	32.6	5.63	63	.499	.557	0	.000	-1	-2	-2	0	-0.1
	Phi-A	0	1	.000	1	1	0	0	0	6	6	0	6	1	18.0	10.50	36	.257	.409	1	.333	0	-5	-4	-0	-0.3
	Yr	0	2	.000	2	2	1	0	0	14	29	0	12	1	26.4	7.71	47	.418	.504	0	.000	-1	-6	-6	-0	-0.4

■ ERNIE BAKER
Baker, Earnest Gould b: 8/8/1875, Concord, Mich. d: 10/25/45, Homer, Mich.   5'10", 160 lbs.   Deb: 8/18/05

YEAR	TM/L	W	L	PCT	G	GS	CG	SH	SV	IP	H	HR	BB	SO	RAT	ERA	ERA+	OAV	OOB	BH	AVG	PB	PR	/A	PD	TPI
1905	Cin-N	0	0	—	1	0	0	0	0	4	7	1	0	1	18.0	4.50	73	.412	.444	0	.000	-0	-1	-1	-0	0.0

■ JESSE BAKER
Baker, Jesse Ormond b: 6/3/1888, Anderson Island, Wash. d: 9/26/72, Tacoma, Wash.   BL/TL, 5'11", 188 lbs.   Deb: 4/23/11

YEAR	TM/L	W	L	PCT	G	GS	CG	SH	SV	IP	H	HR	BB	SO	RAT	ERA	ERA+	OAV	OOB	BH	AVG	PB	PR	/A	PD	TPI
1911	Chi-A	2	7	.222	22	8	3	0	1	94	101	3	30	51	12.9	3.93	82	.288	.351	3	.103	-2	-6	-7	1	-0.7

■ KIRTLEY BAKER
Baker, Kirtley "Whitey" b: 6/24/1869, Aurora, Ind. d: 4/15/27, Covington, Ky.   BR/TR, 5'9", 160 lbs.   Deb: 5/07/1890 ◆

YEAR	TM/L	W	L	PCT	G	GS	CG	SH	SV	IP	H	HR	BB	SO	RAT	ERA	ERA+	OAV	OOB	BH	AVG	PB	PR	/A	PD	TPI
1890	Pit-N	3	19	.136	25	21	19	2	0	178¹	209	11	86	76	14.9	5.60	59	.284	.359	10	.147	-2	-40	-46	-0	-3.9
1893	Bal-N	3	8	.273	15	12	8	0	0	91²	138	5	58	26	19.2	8.44	56	.337	.419	17	.298	3	-38	-37	3	-2.3
1894	Bal-N	0	1	.000	1	0	0	0	0	0	1	0	2	0	—	∞	—	1.000	1.000	0	.000	-0	-5	-5	0	-0.2
1898	Was-N	3	4	.400	6	5	4	0	0	47	56	1	18	7	14.2	3.06	119	.293	.354	5	.278	2	3	3	-0	0.4
1899	Was-N	1	7	.125	11	6	3	0	0	54	79	3	22	6	16.8	6.83	57	.340	.397	3	.158	-1	-18	-18	2	-1.3
Total 5		9	38	.191	58	44	34	2	0	371	483	20	186	115	16.2	6.28	60	.308	.381	35	.211	1	-99	-103	4	-7.3

■ NEAL BAKER
Baker, Neal Vernon b: 4/30/04, Laporte, Tex. d: 1/5/82, Houston, Tex.   BR/TR, 6'1", 175 lbs.   Deb: 6/26/27

YEAR	TM/L	W	L	PCT	G	GS	CG	SH	SV	IP	H	HR	BB	SO	RAT	ERA	ERA+	OAV	OOB	BH	AVG	PB	PR	/A	PD	TPI
1927	Phi-A	0	0	—	5	2	0	0	0	17¹	27	2	7	3	17.7	5.71	75	.365	.420	1	.167	-0	-3	-3	0	-0.2

■ NORM BAKER
Baker, Norman Leslie b: 10/14/1863, Philadelphia, Pa. d: 2/20/49, Hurffville, N.J.   Deb: 5/21/1883

YEAR	TM/L	W	L	PCT	G	GS	CG	SH	SV	IP	H	HR	BB	SO	RAT	ERA	ERA+	OAV	OOB	BH	AVG	PB	PR	/A	PD	TPI
1883	Pit-a	0	2	.000	3	3	2	0	0	19	24	0	11	5	16.6	3.32	97	.289	.372	0	.000	-1	-0	-0	-1	-0.2
1885	Lou-a	13	12	.520	25	24	24	1	0	217	210	3	69	79	11.6	3.40	95	.243	.299	18	.207	-1	-4	-4	-1	-0.5
1890	Bal-a	1	1	.500	2	2	2	0	0	17	16	0	6	10	11.6	3.71	109	.241	.304	0	.000	-1	0	1	0	0.0
Total 3		14	15	.483	30	29	28	1	0	253	250	3	86	94	12.0	3.42	96	.247	.306	18	.170	-4	-3	-4	-2	-0.7

■ STEVE BAKER
Baker, Steven Byrne b: 8/30/56, Eugene, Ore.   BR/TR, 6', 185 lbs.   Deb: 5/25/78

YEAR	TM/L	W	L	PCT	G	GS	CG	SH	SV	IP	H	HR	BB	SO	RAT	ERA	ERA+	OAV	OOB	BH	AVG	PB	PR	/A	PD	TPI
1978	Det-A	2	4	.333	15	10	0	0	0	63¹	66	6	42	39	15.3	4.55	85	.276	.384	0	—	0	-6	-5	-1	-0.5
1979	Det-A	1	7	.125	21	12	0	0	1	84	97	13	51	54	16.5	6.64	65	.296	.400	0	—	0	-23	-22	-1	-2.0
1982	Oak-A	1	1	.500	5	3	0	0	0	25²	30	3	14	11	11.9	4.56	86	.288	.315	0	—	0	-1	-2	-0	-0.1
1983	Oak-A	3	3	.500	35	1	0	0	5	54	59	4	26	23	14.5	4.33	89	.282	.367	0	—	0	-2	-3	-1	-0.3
	StL-N	0	1	.000	8	0	0	0	0	10	10	0	4	1	13.5	1.80	201	.286	.375	0	—	0	2	2	0	0.2
Total 4		7	16	.304	84	26	0	0	6	237	262	26	127	131	15.1	5.13	78	.286	.379	0	—	0	-29	-29	-3	-2.7

■ TOM BAKER
Baker, Thomas Calvin "Rattlesnake" b: 6/11/13, Nursery, Tex.   BR/TR, 6'1.5", 180 lbs.   Deb: 8/15/35

YEAR	TM/L	W	L	PCT	G	GS	CG	SH	SV	IP	H	HR	BB	SO	RAT	ERA	ERA+	OAV	OOB	BH	AVG	PB	PR	/A	PD	TPI
1935	Bro-N	1	0	1.000	11	1	1	0	0	42	48	2	20	10	14.6	4.29	93	.277	.352	9	.474	3	-1	-1	-1	0.1
1936	Bro-N	1	8	.111	35	8	2	0	2	87²	98	3	48	35	15.2	4.72	88	.288	.379	7	.233	1	-7	-6	0	-0.3
1937	Bro-N	0	1	.000	7	0	0	0	0	8¹	14	1	5	2	21.6	8.64	47	.378	.465	0	—	0	-4	-4	0	-0.3
	NY-N	1	0	1.000	13	0	0	0	0	31	30	0	16	11	13.4	4.06	96	.268	.359	2	.222	-0	-1	-1	-0	0.0
	Yr	1	1	.500	20	0	0	0	0	39¹	44	1	21	13	14.9	5.03	78	.293	.380	2	.000	-0	-5	-5	-0	-0.3
1938	NY-N	0	0	—	2	0	0	0	0	4	5	0	3	0	18.0	6.75	56	.313	.421	0	—	0	-1	-1	0	-0.1
Total 4		3	9	.250	68	9	3	0	2	173	195	6	92	58	15.1	4.73	85	.288	.375	18	.310	5	-14	-13	-1	-0.5

■ TOM BAKER
Baker, Thomas Henry b: 5/6/34, Port Townsend, Wash. d: 3/9/80, Port Townsend, Wash   BL/TL, 6', 195 lbs.   Deb: 8/02/63

YEAR	TM/L	W	L	PCT	G	GS	CG	SH	SV	IP	H	HR	BB	SO	RAT	ERA	ERA+	OAV	OOB	BH	AVG	PB	PR	/A	PD	TPI
1963	Chi-N	0	1	.000	10	1	0	0	0	18	20	2	7	14	14.0	3.00	117	.282	.354	0	.000	-0	1	1	0	0.1

YEAR TM/L	W	L	PCT	G	GS	CG	SH	SV	IP	H	HR	BB	SO	RAT	ERA	ERA+	OAV	OOB	BH	AVG	PB	PR	/A	PD	TPI

■ MIKE BALAS
Balas, Mitchell Francis (b: Mitchell Francis Balaski) b: 5/17/10, Lowell, Mass. BR/TR, 6', 195 lbs. Deb: 4/27/38

YEAR TM/L	W	L	PCT	G	GS	CG	SH	SV	IP	H	HR	BB	SO	RAT	ERA	ERA+	OAV	OOB	BH	AVG	PB	PR	/A	PD	TPI
1938 Bos-N	0	0	—	1	0	0	0	0	1¹	3	0	0	0	20.3	6.75	51	.375	.375	0	—	0	-0	-0	0	0.0

■ JACK BALDSCHUN
Baldschun, Jack Edward b: 10/16/36, Greenville, O. BR/TR, 6'1", 175 lbs. Deb: 4/28/61

YEAR TM/L	W	L	PCT	G	GS	CG	SH	SV	IP	H	HR	BB	SO	RAT	ERA	ERA+	OAV	OOB	BH	AVG	PB	PR	/A	PD	TPI
1961 Phi-N	5	3	.625	65	0	0	0	3	99²	90	7	49	59	13.0	3.88	105	.243	.339	0	.000	-1	2	2	0	0.1
1962 Phi-N	12	7	.632	67	0	0	0	13	112²	95	6	58	95	12.4	2.96	131	.231	.328	1	.063	-1	12	11	0	1.1
1963 Phi-N	11	7	.611	65	0	0	0	16	113²	99	7	42	89	11.4	2.30	141	.232	.306	0	.000	-2	13	12	1	1.2
1964 Phi-N	6	9	.400	71	0	0	0	21	118¹	111	8	40	96	11.7	3.12	111	.246	.312	4	.250	1	6	5	1	0.8
1965 Phi-N	5	8	.385	65	0	0	0	6	99	102	4	42	81	13.5	3.82	91	.273	.352	0	.000	-1	-3	-4	1	-0.3
1966 Cin-N	1	5	.167	42	0	0	0	0	57¹	71	4	25	44	15.7	5.49	71	.318	.397	1	.333	0	-12	-10	0	-0.9
1967 Cin-N	0	0	—	9	0	0	0	0	13	15	0	9	12	16.6	4.15	90	.283	.387	0	.000	-0	-1	-1	0	0.0
1969 SD-N	7	2	.778	61	0	0	0	1	77	80	7	29	67	13.0	4.79	74	.264	.332	1	.250	0	-10	-11	-0	-1.0
1970 SD-N	1	0	1.000	12	0	0	0	0	13¹	24	2	4	12	18.9	10.13	39	.375	.412	0	—	0	-9	-9	-0	-0.8
Total 9	48	41	.539	457	0	0	0	60	704	687	45	298	555	12.9	3.69	98	.257	.336	7	.090	-3	-3	-5	3	0.2

■ LADY BALDWIN
Baldwin, Charles Busted b: 4/8/1859, Ormel, N.Y. d: 3/7/37, Hastings, Mich. BL/TL, 5'11", 160 lbs. Deb: 9/30/1884 ♦

YEAR TM/L	W	L	PCT	G	GS	CG	SH	SV	IP	H	HR	BB	SO	RAT	ERA	ERA+	OAV	OOB	BH	AVG	PB	PR	/A	PD	TPI
1884 Mil-U	1	1	.500	2	2	2	0	0	17	7	0	1	21	4.2	2.65	62	.117	.131	6	.222	1	1	-2	0	-0.1
1885 Det-N	11	9	.550	21	20	19	1	1	179¹	137	2	28	135	8.3	1.86	153	.202	.233	30	.242	3	19	20	1	2.5
1886 Det-N	42	13	.764	56	56	55	7	0	487	371	11	100	323	8.7	2.24	148	.202	.244	41	.201	3	58	58	2	6.1
1887 *Det-N	13	10	.565	24	24	24	1	0	211	225	8	61	60	12.2	3.84	105	.265	.315	23	.271	3	5	4	1	0.7
1888 Det-N	3	3	.500	6	6	5	0	0	53	76	5	15	26	15.5	5.43	51	.325	.365	6	.261	2	-15	-16	-1	-1.2
1890 Bro-N	1	0	1.000	2	1	0	0	0	7²	15	0	4	4	22.3	7.04	49	.398	.456	0	.000	-0	-3	-3	0	-0.1
Buf-P	2	5	.286	7	7	7	0	0	62	90	5	24	13	16.5	4.50	91	.325	.379	8	.286	1	-2	-3	0	-0.1
Total 6	73	41	.640	118	116	112	9	1	1017	921	31	233	582	10.2	2.85	118	.232	.275	114	.231	12	62	58	4	7.8

■ KID BALDWIN
Baldwin, Clarence Geoghan b: 11/1/1864, Newport, Ky. d: 7/12/1897, Cincinnati, Ohio BR/TR, 5'6", 147 lbs. Deb: 7/27/1884 ♦

YEAR TM/L	W	L	PCT	G	GS	CG	SH	SV	IP	H	HR	BB	SO	RAT	ERA	ERA+	OAV	OOB	BH	AVG	PB	PR	/A	PD	TPI
1885 Cin-a	0	0	—	2	1	0	0	0	4	5	0	6	1	24.8	9.00	36	.293	.477	17	.135	-0	-3	-3	0	-0.1

■ DAVE BALDWIN
Baldwin, David George b: 3/30/38, Tucson, Ariz. BR/TR, 6'2", 200 lbs. Deb: 9/06/66

YEAR TM/L	W	L	PCT	G	GS	CG	SH	SV	IP	H	HR	BB	SO	RAT	ERA	ERA+	OAV	OOB	BH	AVG	PB	PR	/A	PD	TPI
1966 Was-A	0	0	—	4	0	0	0	0	7	8	0	1	4	11.6	3.86	90	.267	.290	0	—	0	-0	-0	-0	0.0
1967 Was-A	2	4	.333	58	0	0	0	12	68²	53	2	20	52	10.1	1.70	186	.215	.285	0	.000	-0	12	11	1	1.3
1968 Was-A	0	2	.000	40	0	0	0	5	42	40	7	12	30	11.1	4.07	72	.260	.313	0	.000	0	-5	-5	0	-0.4
1969 Was-A	2	4	.333	43	0	0	0	4	66²	57	4	34	51	13.0	4.05	86	.236	.342	0	.000	-1	-3	-4	-1	-0.5
1970 Mil-A	2	1	.667	28	0	0	0	1	35¹	25	4	18	26	11.0	2.55	149	.205	.307	1	.500	0	5	5	2	0.8
1973 Chi-A	0	0	—	3	0	0	0	0	5	7	0	4	1	19.8	3.60	110	.368	.478	0	—	0	0	0	0	0.0
Total 6	6	11	.353	176	0	0	0	22	224²	190	17	89	164	11.5	3.08	108	.234	.316	1	.067	-1	8	6	3	1.2

■ HARRY BALDWIN
Baldwin, Howard Edward b: 6/3/1900, Baltimore, Md. d: 1/23/58, Baltimore, Md. BR/TR, 5'11", 160 lbs. Deb: 5/04/24

YEAR TM/L	W	L	PCT	G	GS	CG	SH	SV	IP	H	HR	BB	SO	RAT	ERA	ERA+	OAV	OOB	BH	AVG	PB	PR	/A	PD	TPI
1924 *NY-N	3	1	.750	10	2	1	0	0	33²	42	5	11	5	14.2	4.28	86	.309	.361	4	.364	1	-2	-2	0	-0.1
1925 NY-N	0	0	—	1	0	0	0	0	1	3	0	1	0	36.0	9.00	45	.500	.571	0	—	0	-1	-1	0	0.0
Total 2	3	1	.750	11	2	1	0	0	34²	45	5	12	5	14.8	4.41	83	.317	.370	4	.364	1	-2	-3	0	-0.1

■ MARK BALDWIN
Baldwin, Marcus Elmore "Fido" b: 10/29/1863, Pittsburgh, Pa. d: 11/10/29, Pittsburgh, Pa. BR/TR, 6', 190 lbs. Deb: 5/02/1887

YEAR TM/L	W	L	PCT	G	GS	CG	SH	SV	IP	H	HR	BB	SO	RAT	ERA	ERA+	OAV	OOB	BH	AVG	PB	PR	/A	PD	TPI
1887 Chi-N	18	17	.514	40	39	35	1	1	334	329	23	122	164	12.2	3.40	131	.250	.314	26	.187	-4	24	40	-3	3.1
1888 Chi-N	13	15	.464	30	30	27	2	0	251	241	13	99	157	12.2	2.76	109	.243	.312	16	.151	-1	2	7	2	0.8
1889 Col-a	27	34	.443	63	59	54	6	1	513²	458	9	274	368	12.8	3.61	100	.231	.325	39	.188	1	14	1	-1	0.0
1890 Chi-P	34	24	.586	59	57	54	1	0	501	498	10	249	211	13.4	3.31	131	.248	.331	45	.209	-1	52	58	4	5.1
1891 Pit-N	22	28	.440	53	50	48	2	0	437²	385	10	227	197	12.6	2.76	119	.227	.319	27	.153	-3	29	26	0	2.0
1892 Pit-N	26	27	.491	56	53	45	0	0	440¹	447	11	194	157	13.1	3.47	95	.253	.327	18	.101	-12	-9	-9	-2	-1.9
1893 Pit-N	0	0	—	1	1	0	0	0	2¹	6	0	1	0	27.0	11.57	39	.465	.503	0	.000	-0	-2	-2	0	-0.1
NY-N	16	20	.444	45	39	33	2	2	331¹	335	6	141	100	12.9	4.10	114	.255	.327	8	.127	-10	21	21	-3	0.6
Yr	16	20	.444	46	40	33	2	2	333²	341	6	142	100	13.0	4.15	112	.257	.328	8	.059	-10	19	19	-3	0.5
Total 7	156	165	.486	347	328	296	14	4	2811¹	2699	82	1307	1354	12.8	3.36	113	.244	.323	188	.162	-30	130	141	-3	9.6

■ O. F. BALDWIN
Baldwin, Orson F. b: Youngstown, Ohio Deb: 9/06/08

YEAR TM/L	W	L	PCT	G	GS	CG	SH	SV	IP	H	HR	BB	SO	RAT	ERA	ERA+	OAV	OOB	BH	AVG	PB	PR	/A	PD	TPI
1908 StL-N	1	3	.250	4	4	0	0	0	14²	16	0	11	5	18.4	6.14	38	.302	.448	0	.000	-1	-6	-6	0	-0.6

■ RICK BALDWIN
Baldwin, Rickey Alan b: 6/1/53, Fresno, Cal. BL/TR, 6'3", 180 lbs. Deb: 4/10/75

YEAR TM/L	W	L	PCT	G	GS	CG	SH	SV	IP	H	HR	BB	SO	RAT	ERA	ERA+	OAV	OOB	BH	AVG	PB	PR	/A	PD	TPI
1975 NY-N	3	5	.375	54	0	0	0	6	97¹	97	4	34	54	12.5	3.33	104	.263	.332	3	.200	0	3	1	1	0.2
1976 NY-N	0	0	—	11	0	0	0	0	22¹	14	0	10	9	10.3	2.38	138	.189	.302	1	.333	0	3	2	0	0.3
1977 NY-N	1	2	.333	40	0	0	0	1	62²	62	6	31	23	14.1	4.45	84	.265	.363	2	.500	1	-4	-5	1	-0.2
Total 3	4	7	.364	105	0	0	0	7	182²	173	10	75	86	12.8	3.60	98	.256	.339	6	.273	1	2	-1	2	0.3

■ JEFF BALLARD
Ballard, Jeffrey Scott b: 8/13/63, Billings, Mont. BL/TL, 6'3", 195 lbs. Deb: 5/09/87

YEAR TM/L	W	L	PCT	G	GS	CG	SH	SV	IP	H	HR	BB	SO	RAT	ERA	ERA+	OAV	OOB	BH	AVG	PB	PR	/A	PD	TPI
1987 Bal-A	2	8	.200	14	14	0	0	0	69²	100	15	35	27	17.4	6.59	67	.344	.414	0	—	0	-17	-17	0	-1.4
1988 Bal-A	8	12	.400	25	25	6	1	0	153¹	167	15	42	41	12.6	4.40	89	.278	.332	0	—	0	-7	-9	-1	-0.9
1989 Bal-A	18	8	.692	35	35	4	1	0	215¹	240	16	57	62	12.6	3.43	111	.287	.336	0	—	0	11	9	5	1.4
1990 Bal-A	2	11	.154	44	17	0	0	0	133¹	152	22	42	50	13.3	4.93	78	.289	.345	0	—	0	-15	-16	1	-1.5
Total 4	30	39	.435	118	91	10	2	0	571²	659	68	176	180	13.4	4.42	88	.292	.347	0	—	0	-28	-33	4	-2.4

■ JAY BALLER
Baller, Jay Scot b: 10/6/50, Stayton, Ohio BR/TR, 6'6", 215 lbs. Deb: 9/19/82

YEAR TM/L	W	L	PCT	G	GS	CG	SH	SV	IP	H	HR	BB	SO	RAT	ERA	ERA+	OAV	OOB	BH	AVG	PB	PR	/A	PD	TPI
1982 Phi-N	0	0	—	4	1	0	0	0	8	7	1	2	7	11.3	3.38	109	.226	.294	0	—	0	0	0	0	0.1
1985 Chi-N	2	3	.400	20	4	0	0	1	52	52	8	17	31	12.1	3.46	115	.260	.321	0	.000	-1	1	3	-0	0.2
1986 Chi-N	2	4	.333	36	0	0	0	5	53²	58	7	28	42	14.8	5.37	75	.275	.365	0	.000	-1	-10	-8	-1	-0.9
1987 Chi-N	0	1	.000	23	0	0	0	0	29¹	38	4	20	27	17.8	6.75	63	.325	.423	1	1.000	0	-9	-8	-0	-0.7
1990 KC-A	0	1	.000	3	0	0	0	0	2¹	4	1	2	1	27.0	15.43	25	.364	.500	0	—	0	-3	-3	0	-0.2
Total 5	4	9	.308	86	5	0	0	6	145¹	159	21	69	108	14.4	5.02	81	.279	.362	1	.071	-1	-21	-16	-2	-1.5

■ MARK BALLINGER
Ballinger, Mark Alan b: 1/31/49, Glendale, Cal. BR/TR, 6'6", 205 lbs. Deb: 8/06/71

YEAR TM/L	W	L	PCT	G	GS	CG	SH	SV	IP	H	HR	BB	SO	RAT	ERA	ERA+	OAV	OOB	BH	AVG	PB	PR	/A	PD	TPI
1971 Cle-A	1	2	.333	18	0	0	0	0	34²	30	3	13	25	11.4	4.67	82	.233	.308	1	.200	-0	-5	-3	-0	-0.3

■ WIN BALLOU
Ballou, Noble Winfield b: 11/30/1897, Mount Morgan, Ky. d: 1/30/63, San Francisco, Cal BR/TL, 5'10.5", 170 lbs. Deb: 8/24/25

YEAR TM/L	W	L	PCT	G	GS	CG	SH	SV	IP	H	HR	BB	SO	RAT	ERA	ERA+	OAV	OOB	BH	AVG	PB	PR	/A	PD	TPI
1925 *Was-A	1	1	.500	10	1	1	0	0	27²	38	1	13	13	16.6	4.55	93	.342	.411	1	.143	-0	-0	-1	0	0.0
1926 StL-A	11	10	.524	43	14	5	0	2	154	186	12	71	59	15.3	4.79	90	.311	.387	2	.048	-3	-13	-9	2	-0.8
1927 StL-A	5	6	.455	21	11	4	0	0	90¹	105	4	46	17	15.1	4.78	91	.309	.393	1	.036	-0	-6	-4	0	-0.6
1929 Bro-N	2	3	.400	25	1	0	0	0	57²	69	5	38	20	16.7	6.71	69	.304	.404	1	.063	-2	-13	-13	2	-1.1
Total 4	19	20	.487	99	27	10	0	2	329²	398	22	168	109	15.6	5.11	86	.312	.394	5	.054	-9	-33	-27	4	-2.5

■ TONY BALSAMO
Balsamo, Anthony Fred b: 11/21/37, Brooklyn, N.Y. BR/TR, 6'2", 185 lbs. Deb: 4/14/62

YEAR TM/L	W	L	PCT	G	GS	CG	SH	SV	IP	H	HR	BB	SO	RAT	ERA	ERA+	OAV	OOB	BH	AVG	PB	PR	/A	PD	TPI
1962 Chi-N	0	1	.000	18	0	0	0	0	29¹	34	1	20	27	16.9	6.44	64	.293	.401	1	.200	0	-8	-7	0	-0.6

■ GEORGE BAMBERGER
Bamberger, George Irvin b: 8/1/25, Staten Island, N.Y. BR/TR, 6', 175 lbs. Deb: 4/19/51 MC

YEAR TM/L	W	L	PCT	G	GS	CG	SH	SV	IP	H	HR	BB	SO	RAT	ERA	ERA+	OAV	OOB	BH	AVG	PB	PR	/A	PD	TPI
1951 NY-N	0	0	—	2	0	0	0	0	2	4	2	2	1	27.0	18.00	22	.444	.545	0	—	0	-3	-3	0	-0.2
1952 NY-N	0	0	—	5	0	0	0	0	4	6	1	6	0	27.0	9.00	41	.353	.522	0	—	0	-2	-2	0	-0.1
1959 Bal-A	0	0	—	3	1	0	0	1	8¹	15	1	2	2	18.4	7.56	50	.405	.436	0	.000	-0	-3	-3	0	-0.2
Total 3	0	0	—	10	1	0	0	1	14¹	25	4	10	3	22.0	9.42	40	.397	.479	0	.000	-0	-9	-9	0	-0.5

YEAR TM/L	W	L	PCT	G	GS	CG	SH	SV	IP	H	HR	BB	SO	RAT	ERA	ERA+	OAV	OOB	BH	AVG	PB	PR	/A	PD	TPI

■ SAL BANDO
Bando, Salvatore Leonard b: 2/13/44, Cleveland, O. BR/TR, 6', 195 lbs. Deb: 9/03/66 C♦

| 1979 Mil-A | 0 | 0 | — | 1 | 0 | 0 | 0 | 0 | 3 | 3 | 0 | 0 | 0 | 9.0 | 6.00 | 69 | .231 | .231 | 117 | .246 | 1 | -1 | -1 | 0 | 0.0 |

■ EDDIE BANE
Bane, Edward Norman b: 3/22/52, Chicago, Ill. BR/TL, 5'9", 160 lbs. Deb: 7/04/73

1973 Min-A	0	5	.000	23	6	0	0	2	60¹	62	5	30	42	14.0	4.92	80	.270	.359	0	—	0	-7	-6	1	-0.4
1975 Min-A	3	1	.750	4	4	0	0	0	28¹	28	2	15	14	14.0	2.86	135	.262	.358	0	—	0	3	3	-1	0.3
1976 Min-A	4	7	.364	17	15	1	0	0	79¹	92	6	39	24	14.9	5.11	71	.290	.368	0	—	0	-14	-13	-2	-1.4
Total 3	7	13	.350	44	25	1	0	2	168	182	13	84	80	14.4	4.66	81	.278	.363	0	—	0	-19	-17	-1	-1.5

■ DICK BANEY
Baney, Richard Lee b: 11/1/46, Fullerton, Cal. BR/TR, 6', 185 lbs. Deb: 7/11/69

1969 Sea-A	1	0	1.000	9	1	0	0	0	18²	21	2	7	9	13.5	3.86	94	.292	.354	0	.000	-0	-0	-0	-0	0.0
1973 Cin-N	2	1	.667	11	1	0	0	2	30²	26	1	6	17	10.6	2.93	116	.234	.298	2	.222	1	2	2	-1	0.1
1974 Cin-N	1	0	1.000	22	1	0	0	1	41	51	4	17	12	14.9	5.49	64	.305	.370	0	.000`	-1	-9	-9	-1	-1.0
Total 3	4	1	.800	42	3	0	0	3	90¹	98	7	30	38	13.2	4.28	81	.280	.344	2	.125	-0	-7	-8	-2	-0.9

■ DAN BANKHEAD
Bankhead, Daniel Robert b: 5/3/20, Empire, Ala. d: 5/2/76, Houston, Tex. BR/TR, 6'1", 184 lbs. Deb: 8/26/47

1947 *Bro-N	0	0	—	4	0	0	0	1	10	15	1	8	6	21.6	7.20	57	.341	.453	1	.250	1	-3	-3	-0	-0.1
1950 Bro-N	9	4	.692	41	12	2	1	3	129¹	119	16	88	96	14.5	5.50	75	.252	.371	9	.231	1	-19	-20	-1	-1.8
1951 Bro-N	0	1	.000	7	1	0	0	0	14	27	5	14	9	26.4	15.43	25	.422	.526	0	.000	-0	-18	-18	-0	-1.5
Total 3	9	5	.643	52	13	2	1	4	153¹	161	22	110	111	16.1	6.52	63	.277	.395	10	.222	2	-41	-41	-1	-3.4

■ SCOTT BANKHEAD
Bankhead, Michael Scott b: 7/31/63, Raleigh, N.C. BR/TR, 5'10", 175 lbs. Deb: 5/25/86

1986 KC-A	8	9	.471	24	17	0	0	0	121	121	14	37	94	12.0	4.61	92	.259	.318	0	—	0	-6	-5	-1	-0.4
1987 Sea-A	9	8	.529	27	25	2	0	0	149	168	35	37	95	12.5	5.42	87	.283	.329	0	—	0	-16	-12	-2	-1.2
1988 Sea-A	7	9	.438	21	21	2	1	0	135	115	8	38	102	10.3	3.07	136	.224	.278	0	—	0	13	16	-1	1.6
1989 Sea-A	14	6	.700	33	33	3	2	0	210¹	187	19	63	140	10.8	3.34	121	.239	.298	0	—	0	13	16	-2	1.5
1990 Sea-A	0	2	.000	4	4	0	0	0	13	18	2	7	10	17.3	11.08	36	.333	.410	0	—	0	-10	-10	-0	-0.9
Total 5	38	34	.528	109	100	7	3	0	628²	609	78	182	441	11.5	4.18	102	.252	.308	0	—	0	-6	6	-6	0.6

■ BILL BANKS
Banks, William John (b: William John Yerrick) b: 2/26/1874, Danville, Pa. d: 9/8/36, Danville, Pa. 5'11", 150 lbs. Deb: 9/27/1895

1895 Bos-N	1	0	1.000	1	1	1	0	0	7	7	0	4	4	14.1	0.00	—	.256	.352	0	.000	-1	4	4	0	0.3
1896 Bos-N	0	3	.000	4	3	2	0	0	23	42	2	13	6	21.5	10.57	43	.389	.454	3	.273	0	-16	-15	-1	-1.1
Total 2	1	3	.250	5	4	3	0	0	30	49	2	17	10	19.8	8.10	58	.362	.433	3	.214	-1	-12	-11	-0	-0.8

■ FLOYD BANNISTER
Bannister, Floyd Franklin b: 6/10/55, Pierre, S.D. BL/TL, 6'1", 190 lbs. Deb: 4/19/77

1977 Hou-N	8	9	.471	24	23	4	1	0	142²	138	11	68	112	13.2	4.04	88	.254	.341	9	.188	0	-2	-7	-2	-0.8
1978 Hou-N	3	9	.250	28	16	2	2	0	110¹	120	13	63	94	15.0	4.81	69	.280	.374	5	.161	0	-15	-18	-2	-2.0
1979 Sea-A	10	15	.400	30	30	6	2	0	182¹	185	25	68	115	12.7	4.05	108	.260	.328	0	—	0	3	6	-2	0.4
1980 Sea-A	9	13	.409	32	32	8	0	0	217²	200	24	66	155	11.1	3.47	119	.239	.296	0	—	0	14	16	-1	1.5
1981 Sea-A	9	9	.500	21	20	5	2	0	121¹	128	14	39	85	12.6	4.45	87	.268	.327	0	—	0	-11	-8	-1	-0.8
1982 Sea-A	12	13	.480	35	35	5	3	0	247	225	32	77	**209**	11.1	3.43	124	.243	.303	0	—	0	18	22	-1	2.2
1983 *Chi-A	16	10	.615	34	34	5	2	0	217¹	191	19	71	193	10.9	3.35	125	.233	.295	0	—	0	17	20	-2	1.9
1984 Chi-A	14	11	.560	34	33	4	0	0	218	211	30	80	152	12.3	4.83	86	.252	.322	0	.000	0	-20	-16	-2	-1.7
1985 Chi-A	10	14	.417	34	34	4	1	0	210²	211	30	100	198	13.5	4.87	89	.261	.346	0	—	0	-17	-13	-2	-1.4
1986 Chi-A	10	14	.417	28	27	6	1	0	165¹	162	17	48	92	11.5	3.54	122	.259	.314	0	—	0	12	14	-1	1.3
1987 Chi-A	16	11	.593	34	34	11	2	0	228²	216	38	49	124	10.4	3.58	128	.246	.286	0	—	0	22	25	-3	2.2
1988 KC-A	12	13	.480	31	31	2	0	0	189¹	182	22	68	113	12.1	4.33	92	.248	.316	0	—	0	-8	-7	-0	-0.6
1989 KC-A	4	1	.800	14	14	0	0	0	75¹	87	8	18	35	12.7	4.66	83	.290	.332	0	—	0	-7	-7	1	-0.5
Total 13	133	142	.484	379	363	62	16	0	2326	2256	283	815	1677	12.0	4.03	103	.253	.318	14	.175	1	7	26	-18	1.7

■ JIMMY BANNON
Bannon, James Henry "Foxy Grandpa" b: 5/5/1871, Amesbury, Mass. d: 3/24/48, Glen Rock, N.J. BR , 5'5", 160 lbs. Deb: 6/15/1893 ♦

1893 StL-N	0	1	.000	1	1	0	0	0	4	10	1	5	1	33.8	22.50	21	.458	.559	36	.336	0	-8	-8	-0	-0.4
1894 Bos-N	0	0	—	1	0	0	0	0	2	4	1	1	0	22.5	0.00	—	.410	.465	166	.336	0	1	1	0	0.1
1895 Bos-N	0	0	—	1	0	0	0	0	3	4	0	2	1	18.0	6.00	85	.315	.408	171	.350	0	-0	-0	0	0.0
Total 3	0	1	.000	3	1	0	0	0	9	18	2	8	2	26.0	12.00	42	.406	.497	459	.320	1	-7	-7	0	-0.3

■ JACK BANTA
Banta, John Kay b: 6/24/25, Hutchinson, Kan. BL/TR, 6'2.5", 175 lbs. Deb: 9/18/47

1947 Bro-N	0	1	.000	3	1	0	0	0	7²	7	1	4	3	14.1	7.04	59	.226	.333	0	.000	-0	-3	-2	1	-0.1
1948 Bro-N	0	1	.000	2	1	0	0	0	3¹	5	0	5	1	27.0	8.10	49	.385	.556	0	.000	-0	-2	-2	0	-0.1
1949 *Bro-N	10	6	.625	48	12	2	1	3	152¹	125	12	68	97	11.8	3.37	122	.223	.314	5	.109	-2	11	12	0	1.1
1950 Bro-N	4	4	.500	16	5	1	0	2	41¹	39	2	36	15	17.0	4.35	94	.252	.402	2	.167	-0	-1	-1	-1	-0.1
Total 4	14	12	.538	69	19	3	1	5	204²	176	15	113	116	13.1	3.78	108	.232	.339	7	.115	-2	6	7	1	0.8

■ STEVE BARBER
Barber, Stephen David b: 2/22/39, Takoma Park, Md. BL/TL, 6', 195 lbs. Deb: 4/21/60

1960 Bal-A	10	7	.588	36	27	6	1	2	181²	148	10	113	112	13.1	3.22	118	.226	.343	3	.056	-3	13	12	0	0.8
1961 Bal-A	18	12	.600	37	34	14	**8**	1	248¹	194	13	130	150	11.8	3.33	117	.218	.319	13	.162	2	19	16	4	2.2
1962 Bal-A	9	6	.600	28	19	5	2	0	140¹	145	9	61	89	13.3	3.46	109	.262	.337	3	.071	-2	8	5	1	0.3
1963 Bal-A	20	13	.606	39	36	11	2	0	258²	253	12	92	180	12.1	2.75	128	.258	.324	12	.138	-0	25	22	1	2.5
1964 Bal-A	9	13	.409	36	26	4	0	1	157	144	15	81	118	13.3	3.84	93	.248	.347	7	.149	1	-4	-5	3	-0.1
1965 Bal-A	15	10	.600	37	32	7	2	0	220²	177	16	81	130	10.6	2.69	129	.224	.297	5	.077	-2	19	19	1	2.1
1966 Bal-A	10	5	.667	25	22	5	3	0	133¹	104	6	49	91	10.5	2.30	145	.218	.294	3	.068	-3	17	15	2	1.5
1967 Bal-A	4	9	.308	15	15	1	1	0	74²	47	5	61	48	13.6	4.10	77	.185	.353	2	.091	-1	-7	-8	0	-0.8
NY-A	6	9	.400	17	17	3	1	0	97²	103	4	54	70	14.7	4.05	77	.278	.375	1	.172	1	-9	-10	-1	-1.0
Yr	10	18	.357	32	32	4	2	0	172¹	150	9	115	118	14.0	4.07	77	.238	.358	3	.059	1	-16	-18	-1	-1.8
1968 NY-A	6	5	.545	20	19	3	1	0	128¹	127	7	64	87	13.6	3.23	90	.256	.345	2	.051	-1	-4	-5	0	-0.5
1969 Sea-A	4	7	.364	25	16	0	0	0	86¹	99	9	48	69	15.4	4.80	76	.292	.381	5	.200	1	-11	-11	0	-1.0
1970 Chi-N	0	1	.000	5	0	0	0	0	5²	10	0	6	3	25.4	9.53	47	.417	.533	0	—	0	-3	-3	-0	-0.2
Atl-N	0	1	.000	5	2	0	0	0	14²	17	3	5	11	14.1	4.91	87	.288	.354	1	.250	0	-1	-1	0	-0.1
Yr	0	2	.000	10	2	0	0	0	20¹	27	3	11	14	17.3	6.20	70	.325	.411	0	.000	0	-5	-4	-0	-0.2
1971 Atl-N	3	1	.750	39	3	0	0	2	75	92	6	25	40	14.4	4.80	77	.301	.357	2	.154	-0	-11	-9	0	-0.8
1972 Atl-N	0	0	—	5	0	0	0	0	15²	18	1	6	6	14.4	5.74	66	.290	.362	1	.200	-0	-4	-3	1	-0.2
Cal-A	4	4	.500	34	3	0	0	2	58	37	4	30	34	10.6	2.02	144	.188	.298	1	.143	1	7	6	-1	0.7
1973 Cal-A	3	2	.600	50	1	0	0	4	89¹	90	5	39	58	12.6	3.53	101	.265	.333	0	—	0	3	0	0	0.0
1974 SF-N	0	0	—	13	0	0	0	1	13²	13	0	12	13	16.5	5.27	72	.255	.397	0	—	0	-3	-2	-1	-0.2
Total 15	121	106	.533	466	272	59	21	13	1999	1818	125	950	1309	12.7	3.36	105	.245	.334	65	.115	-6	54	38	10	5.3

■ STEVE BARBER
Barber, Steven Lee b: 3/13/48, Grand Rapids, Mich. BR/TR, 6'1", 190 lbs. Deb: 4/09/70

1970 Min-A	0	0	—	18	0	0	0	0	27¹	26	1	18	14	15.1	4.61	81	.263	.387	0	.000	-0	-3	-3	-0	-0.2
1971 Min-A	1	0	1.000	4	2	0	0	0	11²	8	2	13	4	16.2	6.17	58	.190	.382	0	.000	-1	-4	-3	-0	-0.3
Total 2	1	0	1.000	22	2	0	0	0	39	34	3	31	18	15.5	5.08	72	.241	.385	0	.000	-1	-6	-6	-0	-0.5

■ FRANK BARBERICH
Barberich, Frank Frederick b: 2/3/1882, New Town, N.Y. d: 5/1/65, Ocala, Fla. BB/TR, 5'10.5", 175 lbs. Deb: 9/17/07

1907 Bos-A	1	1	.500	2	2	1	0	0	12¹	19	0	5	1	17.5	5.84	44	.358	.414	0	.000	-1	-5	-5	-0	-0.4
1910 Bos-A	0	0	—	2	0	0	0	0	5	7	0	2	0	16.2	7.20	35	.350	.409	0	.000	-0	-3	-3	-0	-0.2
Total 2	1	1	.500	4	2	1	0	0	17¹	26	0	7	1	17.1	6.23	41	.356	.412	0	.000	-1	-7	-7	0	-0.6

YEAR	TM/L	W	L	PCT	G	GS	CG	SH	SV	IP	H	HR	BB	SO	RAT	ERA	ERA+	OAV	OOB	BH	AVG	PB	PR	/A	PD	TPI
■ CURT BARCLAY										Barclay, Curtis Cordell b: 8/22/31, Chicago, Ill. d: 3/25/85, Missoula, Montana BR/TR, 6'3", 210 lbs. Deb: 4/21/57																
1957	NY-N	9	9	.500	37	28	5	2	0	183	196	21	48	67	12.1	3.44	114	.274	.321	11	.190	0	9	10	3	1.4
1958	SF-N	1	0	1.000	6	1	0	0	0	16	16	3	5	6	13.5	2.81	136	.258	.343	4	.667	2	2	2	0	0.4
1959	SF-N	0	0	—	1	0	0	0	0	0¹	2	0	2	0	108.0	54.00	7	.500	.667	0	—	0	-2	-2	0	-0.1
Total	3	10	9	.526	44	29	5	2	0	199¹	214	24	55	73	12.4	3.48	113	.274	.325	15	.234	2	9	10	3	1.7
■ RAY BARE										Bare, Raymond Douglas b: 4/15/49, Miami, Fla. BR/TR, 6'2", 185 lbs. Deb: 7/30/72																
1972	StL-N	0	1	.000	14	0	0	0	1	16²	18	0	6	5	13.0	0.54	630	.281	.343	0	—	0	5	5	-0	0.6
1974	StL-N	1	2	.333	10	3	0	0	0	24¹	25	2	9	6	12.6	5.92	60	.281	.347	1	.200	-0	-6	-6	1	-0.5
1975	Det-A	8	13	.381	29	21	6	1	0	150²	174	10	47	71	13.3	4.48	90	.293	.346	0	—	0	-12	-8	2	-0.5
1976	Det-A	7	8	.467	30	21	3	2	0	134	157	13	51	59	14.0	4.63	80	.293	.354	0	—	0	-17	-14	1	-1.2
1977	Det-A	0	2	.000	5	4	0	0	0	14¹	24	3	7	4	19.5	12.56	34	.381	.443	0	—	0	-14	-13	1	-1.0
Total	5	16	26	.381	88	49	9	3	1	340	398	28	120	145	13.7	4.79	80	.296	.354	1	.200	-0	-43	-36	5	-2.6
■ JOHN BARFIELD										Barfield, John David b: 10/15/64, Pine Bluff, Ark. BL/TL, 6'1", 185 lbs. Deb: 9/07/89																
1989	Tex-A	0	1	.000	4	2	0	0	0	11²	15	0	4	9	14.7	6.17	64	.319	.373	0	—	0	-3	-3	0	-0.2
1990	Tex-A	4	3	.571	33	0	0	0	1	44¹	42	2	13	17	11.4	4.67	85	.268	.327	0	—	0	-4	-3	0	-0.2
Total	2	4	4	.500	37	2	0	0	1	56	57	2	17	26	12.1	4.98	80	.279	.338	0	—	0	-7	-6	0	-0.4
■ CLYDE BARFOOT										Barfoot, Clyde Raymond "Foots" b: 7/8/1891, Richmond, Va. d: 3/11/71, Highland Park, Cal BR/TR, 6', 170 lbs. Deb: 4/13/22																
1922	StL-N	4	5	.444	42	2	1	0	2	117²	139	2	30	19	13.7	4.21	92	.307	.363	12	.353	5	-1	-4	1	0.1
1923	StL-N	3	3	.500	33	2	1	1	1	101¹	112	7	27	23	12.4	3.73	105	.289	.337	7	.189	-1	3	2	0	0.1
1926	Det-A	1	2	.333	11	1	0	0	2	31¹	42	4	9	7	14.6	4.88	83	.318	.362	1	.200	-0	-3	-3	1	-0.1
Total	3	8	10	.444	86	5	2	1	5	250¹	293	13	66	49	13.3	4.10	95	.301	.353	20	.263	4	-1	-5	2	0.1
■ GREG BARGAR										Bargar, Greg Robert b: 1/27/59, Inglewood, Cal. BR/TR, 6'2", 185 lbs. Deb: 7/17/83																
1983	Mon-N	2	0	1.000	8	3	0	0	0	20	23	6	8	9	14.4	6.75	53	.271	.340	1	.167	-0	-7	-7	-0	-0.6
1984	Mon-N	0	1	.000	3	1	0	0	0	8	8	1	7	2	16.9	7.88	43	.286	.429	0	—	-0	-4	-4	0	-0.3
1986	StL-N	0	2	.000	22	0	0	0	0	27¹	36	3	10	12	16.1	5.60	65	.330	.402	0	.000	-0	-6	-6	1	-0.5
Total	3	2	3	.400	33	4	0	0	0	55¹	67	10	25	23	15.6	6.34	57	.302	.382	1	.111	-0	-16	-17	0	-1.4
■ CY BARGER										Barger, Eros Bolivar b: 5/18/1885, Jamestown, Ky. d: 9/23/64, Columbia, Ky. BL/TR, 6', 160 lbs. Deb: 8/30/06																
1906	NY-A	0	0	—	2	1	0	0	1	5¹	7	0	3	3	16.9	10.13	29	.319	.401	1	.333	0	-4	-4	0	-0.3
1907	NY-A	0	0	—	1	0	0	0	0	6	10	0	1	0	16.5	3.00	93	.372	.394	0	.000	-0	-0	-0	0	0.0
1910	Bro-N	15	15	.500	35	30	25	2	1	271²	267	2	107	87	12.6	2.88	105	.275	.351	24	.231	3	5	5	2	1.0
1911	Bro-N	11	15	.423	30	30	21	1	0	217¹	224	4	71	60	12.5	3.52	95	.279	.342	33	.228	1	-3	-4	2	0.0
1912	Bro-N	1	9	.100	16	11	6	0	0	94	120	4	42	30	15.9	5.46	61	.316	.390	7	.189	-0	-21	-22	1	-1.9
1914	Pit-F	10	16	.385	33	26	18	1	1	228¹	252	7	63	70	12.7	4.34	73	.290	.342	17	.205	0	-29	-29	-2	-2.9
1915	Pit-F	9	8	.529	34	13	8	1	6	153	130	1	47	47	10.6	2.29	131	.238	.303	15	.278	2	13	12	-1	1.5
Total	7	46	63	.422	151	111	78	5	9	975²	1010	18	334	297	12.6	3.56	89	.279	.344	97	.227	7	-40	-43	2	-2.6
■ LEN BARKER										Barker, Leonard Harold b: 7/7/55, Fort Knox, Ky. BR/TR, 6'5", 225 lbs. Deb: 9/14/76																
1976	Tex-A	1	0	1.000	2	2	1	1	0	15	7	0	6	7	9.0	2.40	141	.149	.273	0	—	0	2	2	0	0.2
1977	Tex-A	4	1	.800	15	3	0	0	1	47¹	36	1	24	51	11.6	2.66	153	.217	.319	0	—	0	7	7	0	0.8
1978	Tex-A	1	5	.167	29	0	0	0	4	52¹	63	6	29	33	16.2	4.82	78	.304	.395	0	—	0	-6	-6	0	-0.5
1979	Cle-A	6	6	.500	29	19	2	0	0	137¹	146	6	70	93	14.3	4.92	87	.277	.364	0	—	0	-11	-10	-1	-1.0
1980	Cle-A	19	12	.613	36	36	8	1	0	246¹	237	17	92	187	12.1	4.17	98	.252	.320	0	—	0	-4	-3	-2	-0.4
1981	Cle-A	8	7	.533	22	22	9	3	0	154¹	150	7	46	127	11.5	3.91	93	.249	.303	0	—	0	-4	-5	-1	-0.5
1982	Cle-A	15	11	.577	33	33	10	1	0	244²	211	17	88	187	11.1	3.90	105	.232	.301	0	—	0	5	5	-1	0.4
1983	Cle-A	8	13	.381	24	24	4	1	0	149²	150	16	52	105	12.3	5.11	83	.266	.330	0	—	0	-17	-15	-1	-1.4
	Atl-N	1	3	.250	6	6	0	0	0	33	31	0	14	21	12.3	3.82	102	.248	.324	1	.125	-0	-1	0	1	0.1
1984	Atl-N	7	8	.467	21	20	1	0	0	126¹	120	10	38	95	11.4	3.85	100	.254	.312	2	.053	-1	-4	-4	3	0.2
1985	Atl-N	2	9	.182	20	18	0	0	0	73²	84	10	37	47	14.9	6.35	61	.288	.370	0	.000	-2	-23	-21	-1	-2.2
1987	Mil-A	2	1	.667	11	11	0	0	0	43²	54	6	17	22	15.0	5.36	85	.303	.371	0	—	0	-4	-4	0	-0.3
Total	11	74	76	.493	248	194	35	7	5	1323²	1289	96	513	975	12.4	4.34	93	.256	.327	3	.048	-3	-59	-48	-3	-4.6
■ JEFF BARKLEY										Barkley, Jeffrey Carver b: 11/21/59, Hickory, N.C. BB/TR, 6'3", 185 lbs. Deb: 9/16/84																
1984	Cle-A	0	0	—	3	0	0	0	0	4	6	0	1	4	15.8	6.75	61	.353	.389	0	—	0	-1	-1	0	0.0
1985	Cle-A	0	3	.000	21	0	0	0	1	41	37	5	15	30	11.4	5.27	78	.243	.311	0	—	0	-5	-5	0	-0.4
Total	2	0	3	.000	24	0	0	0	1	45	43	5	16	34	11.8	5.40	76	.254	.319	0	—	0	-6	-6	0	-0.4
■ MIKE BARLOW										Barlow, Michael Roswell b: 4/30/48, Stamford, N.Y. BL/TR, 6'6", 210 lbs. Deb: 6/18/75																
1975	StL-N				9	0	0	0	0	7²	11	0	3	2	17.6	4.70	80	.355	.429	0	—	0	-1	-1	-0	0.0
1976	Hou-N	2	2	.500	16	0	0	0	0	22	27	0	17	11	18.0	4.50	71	.318	.431	0	.000	-0	-2	-3	1	-0.2
1977	Cal-A	4	2	.667	20	1	0	0	1	59	53	3	27	25	12.8	4.58	86	.249	.344	0	—	0	-3	-4	0	-0.3
1978	Cal-A	0	0	—	1	0	0	0	0	2	3	0	0	1	13.5	4.50	80	.375	.375	0	—	0	-0	-0	0	0.0
1979	*Cal-A	1	1	.500	35	0	0	0	0	85²	106	8	30	33	14.7	5.15	79	.314	.376	0	—	0	-9	-10	-0	-0.9
1980	Tor-A	3	1	.750	40	1	0	0	5	55	57	4	21	19	13.1	4.09	105	.273	.345	0	—	0	-0	1	0	0.1
1981	Tor-A	0	0	—	12	0	0	0	0	15	22	1	6	5	19.2	4.20	94	.338	.427	0	—	0	-1	-0	0	0.0
Total	7	10	6	.625	133	2	0	0	6	246¹	279	16	104	96	14.5	4.64	86	.294	.373	0	.000	-0	-17	-18	1	-1.3
■ CHARLIE BARNABE										Barnabe, Charles Edward b: 6/12/1900, Russell Gulch, Colo. d: 8/16/77, Waco, Tex. BL/TL, 5'11.5", 164 lbs. Deb: 4/14/27																
1927	Chi-A	0	5	.000	17	4	1	0	0	61	86	2	20	5	16.4	5.31	76	.351	.411	3	.158	1	-8	-9	1	-0.5
1928	Chi-A	0	2	.000	7	2	0	0	0	9²	17	0	0	3	16.8	6.52	62	.395	.409	4	.500	2	-3	-3	1	0.1
Total	2	0	7	.000	24	6	1	0	0	70²	103	2	20	8	16.4	5.48	74	.358	.411	7	.259	3	-11	-11	2	-0.4
■ BRIAN BARNES										Barnes, Brian Keith b: 3/25/67, Roanoke Rapids, N.C. BL/TL, 5'9", 170 lbs. Deb: 9/14/90																
1990	Mon-N	1	1	.500	4	4	1	0	0	28	25	2	7	23	10.3	2.89	130	.236	.283	0	.000	-1	3	3	0	0.2
■ FRANK BARNES										Barnes, Frank b: 8/26/28, Longwood, Miss. BR/TR, 6', 170 lbs. Deb: 9/22/57																
1957	StL-N	0	1	.000	3	1	0	0	0	10	13	0	9	5	19.8	4.50	88	.317	.440	0	.000	-0	-1	-1	-0	0.0
1958	StL-N	1	1	.500	8	1	0	0	0	19	19	3	16	17	17.5	7.58	54	.260	.407	1	.167	0	-8	-7	-0	-0.7
1960	StL-N	0	1	.000	4	1	0	0	1	7²	8	1	9	8	21.1	3.52	116	.267	.450	0	.000	-0	0	0	-0	0.0
Total	3	1	3	.250	15	3	0	0	1	36²	40	4	34	30	18.9	5.89	69	.278	.425	1	.100	-1	-8	-7	-1	-0.7
■ FRANK BARNES										Barnes, Frank Samuel "Lefty" b: 1/9/1900, Dallas, Tex. d: 9/27/67, Houston, Tex. BL/TL, 6'2.5", 195 lbs. Deb: 4/18/29																
1929	Det-A	0	1	.000	4	1	0	0	0	5	10	0	3	0	25.2	7.20	60	.400	.483	0	.000	-0	-2	-2	0	0.0
1930	NY-A	0	1	.000	2	2	0	0	0	12¹	13	0	13	2	19.7	8.03	54	.283	.450	2	.333	1	-5	-5	2	-0.1
Total	2	0	2	.000	6	3	0	0	0	17¹	23	0	16	2	21.3	7.79	55	.324	.461	2	.286	1	-6	-7	2	-0.1
■ JESS BARNES										Barnes, Jesse Lawrence "Nubby" b: 8/26/1892, Perkins, Okla. d: 9/9/61, Santa Rosa, N.Mex. BL/TR, 6', 170 lbs. Deb: 7/30/15																
1915	Bos-N	3	0	1.000	9	3	2	0	0	45¹	41	1	10	16	10.9	1.39	186	.244	.302	3	.176	0	7	6	-0	0.6
1916	Bos-N	6	15	.286	33	18	9	3	1	163	154	3	37	55	10.8	2.37	105	.254	.302	9	.188	0	4	2	4	0.7
1917	Bos-N	13	21	.382	50	33	27	2	1	295	261	3	50	107	9.6	2.68	95	.241	.277	24	.238	4	1	-4	3	0.3
1918	NY-N	6	1	.857	9	9	4	2	0	54²	53	0	13	12	10.9	1.81	145	.255	.299	4	.222	-0	6	5	2	0.8

YEAR TM/L	W	L	PCT	G	GS	CG	SH	SV	IP	H	HR	BB	SO	RAT	ERA	ERA+	OAV	OOB	BH	AVG	PB	PR	/A	PD	TPI
1919 NY-N	25	9	.735	38	34	23	4	1	295²	263	8	35	92	9.1	2.40	117	.236	.260	32	.267	5	17	13	2	2.3
1920 NY-N	20	15	.571	43	35	23	2	0	292²	271	9	56	63	10.1	2.64	113	.250	.288	22	.204	-2	16	11	3	1.3
1921 *NY-N	15	9	.625	42	31	15	1	6	258²	298	13	44	56	12.0	3.10	118	.299	.331	19	.207	-1	20	16	2	1.6
1922 *NY-N	13	8	.619	37	30	14	2	0	212²	236	10	38	52	11.7	3.51	114	.278	.311	14	.182	-1	14	12	3	1.3
1923 NY-N	3	1	.750	12	4	1	0	1	36	48	1	13	12	15.3	6.25	61	.329	.384	3	.273	0	-9	-10	1	-0.7
Bos-N	10	14	.417	31	23	12	5	2	195¹	204	8	43	41	11.4	2.76	144	.270	.310	10	.147	-4	27	27	3	2.6
Yr	13	15	.464	43	27	13	5	3	231¹	252	9	56	53	12.0	3.31	120	.280	.322	2	.025	-4	18	17	5	1.9
1924 Bos-N	15	20	.429	37	32	21	4	0	267²	292	7	53	49	11.6	3.23	118	.284	.319	20	.222	-1	19	18	1	1.7
1925 Bos-N	11	16	.407	32	28	17	0	0	216¹	255	14	63	55	13.3	4.53	88	.297	.346	16	.198	-0	-6	-13	-2	-1.4
1926 Bro-N	10	11	.476	31	24	10	1	1	158	204	6	35	29	13.7	5.24	73	.321	.358	14	.237	-0	-25	-25	0	-2.3
1927 Bro-N	2	10	.167	18	10	2	0	0	78²	106	5	25	14	15.0	5.72	69	.331	.380	5	.217	-0	-16	-15	0	-1.4
Total 13	152	150	.503	422	314	180	26	13	2569²	2686	88	515	653	11.3	3.22	104	.273	.310	195	.214	0	74	41	23	7.4

■ JUNIE BARNES
Barnes, Junie Shoaf "Lefty" b: 12/1/11, Linwood, N.C. d: 12/31/63, Jacksonville, N.C. BL/TL, 5'11.5", 170 lbs. Deb: 9/12/34

YEAR TM/L	W	L	PCT	G	GS	CG	SH	SV	IP	H	HR	BB	SO	RAT	ERA	ERA+	OAV	OOB	BH	AVG	PB	PR	/A	PD	TPI
1934 Cin-N	0	0	—	2	0	0	0	0	0¹	0	0	1	0	27.0	0.00	—	.000	.500	0	—	0	0	0	0	0.0

■ RICH BARNES
Barnes, Richard Monroe b: 7/21/59, Palm Beach, Fla. BR/TL, 6'4", 186 lbs. Deb: 7/18/82

YEAR TM/L	W	L	PCT	G	GS	CG	SH	SV	IP	H	HR	BB	SO	RAT	ERA	ERA+	OAV	OOB	BH	AVG	PB	PR	/A	PD	TPI
1982 Chi-A	0	2	.000	6	2	0	0	1	17	21	1	4	6	14.3	4.76	85	.292	.346	0	—	0	-1	-1	0	-0.2
1983 Cle-A	1	1	.500	4	2	0	0	0	11²	18	0	10	2	21.6	6.94	61	.375	.483	0	—	0	-4	-4	0	-0.2
Total 2	1	3	.250	10	4	0	0	1	28²	39	1	14	8	17.3	5.65	73	.325	.404	0	—	0	-5	-5	0	-0.2

■ BOB BARNES
Barnes, Robert Avery "Lefty" b: 1/6/02, Washburn, Ill. BL/TL, 5'11.5", 150 lbs. Deb: 7/08/24

YEAR TM/L	W	L	PCT	G	GS	CG	SH	SV	IP	H	HR	BB	SO	RAT	ERA	ERA+	OAV	OOB	BH	AVG	PB	PR	/A	PD	TPI
1924 Chi-A	0	0	—	2	0	0	0	0	4²	14	1	0	1	27.0	19.29	21	.519	.519	0	.000	-0	-8	-8	0	-0.5

■ ROSS BARNES
Barnes, Roscoe Charles b: 5/8/1850, Lima, N.Y. d: 2/5/15, Chicago, Ill. BR/TR, 5'8.5", 145 lbs. Deb: 5/05/1871 U♦

YEAR TM/L	W	L	PCT	G	GS	CG	SH	SV	IP	H	HR	BB	SO	RAT	ERA	ERA+	OAV	OOB	BH	AVG	PB	PR	/A	PD	TPI
1876 Chi-N	0	0	—	1	0	0	0	0	1¹	7	0	0	0	47.3	20.25	12	.627	.627	138	.429	1	-3	-3	0	-0.1

■ VIRGIL BARNES
Barnes, Virgil Jennings "Zeke" b: 3/5/1897, Ontario, Kan. d: 7/24/58, Wichita, Kan. BR/TR, 6', 165 lbs. Deb: 9/25/19

YEAR TM/L	W	L	PCT	G	GS	CG	SH	SV	IP	H	HR	BB	SO	RAT	ERA	ERA+	OAV	OOB	BH	AVG	PB	PR	/A	PD	TPI
1919 NY-N	0	0	—	1	0	0	0	0	2	6	0	1	1	31.5	18.00	16	.545	.583	0	—	-0	-3	-3	0	-0.2
1920 NY-N	0	1	.000	1	1	0	0	0	7	9	0	1	2	12.9	3.86	78	.310	.333	0	—	-0	-1	-1	0	0.0
1922 NY-N	1	0	1.000	22	3	1	0	2	51²	46	1	11	16	9.9	3.48	115	.243	.285	2	.167	-1	4	3	0	0.3
1923 *NY-N	2	3	.400	22	2	0	0	1	53	59	2	19	6	13.2	3.91	98	.285	.345	0	.000	-2	1	-0	1	-0.1
1924 *NY-N	16	10	.615	35	29	15	1	3	229¹	239	10	57	59	11.6	3.06	120	.270	.294	14	.182	-2	21	15	2	1.5
1925 NY-N	15	11	.577	32	27	17	1	2	221²	242	9	53	53	12.0	3.53	114	.281	.323	9	.101	-8	18	12	1	0.4
1926 NY-N	8	13	.381	31	25	9	2	1	185	183	4	56	54	11.8	2.87	131	.261	.318	3	.054	-7	20	18	-0	1.0
1927 NY-N	14	11	.560	35	29	12	2	2	228²	251	14	51	66	12.0	3.98	97	.283	.325	9	.108	-7	-1	-3	-1	-1.0
1928 NY-N	3	3	.500	10	9	3	1	0	55¹	71	3	18	11	14.5	5.04	77	.330	.382	2	.091	-2	-6	-7	-0	-0.8
Bos-N	2	7	.222	16	10	1	0	0	60¹	86	3	26	7	16.7	5.82	67	.344	.406	1	.059	-1	-12	-13	-1	-1.3
Yr	5	10	.333	26	19	4	1	0	115²	157	6	44	18	15.6	5.45	72	.338	.395	1	.026	-3	-19	-20	-1	-2.1
Total 9	61	59	.508	205	135	58	7	11	1094	1192	46	293	275	12.3	3.66	105	.282	.329	40	.108	-30	38	22	2	-0.2

■ REX BARNEY
Barney, Rex Edward b: 12/19/24, Omaha, Neb. BR/TR, 6'3", 185 lbs. Deb: 8/18/43

YEAR TM/L	W	L	PCT	G	GS	CG	SH	SV	IP	H	HR	BB	SO	RAT	ERA	ERA+	OAV	OOB	BH	AVG	PB	PR	/A	PD	TPI
1943 Bro-N	2	2	.500	9	8	1	0	0	45¹	36	4	41	23	15.7	6.35	53	.217	.378	1	.056	-2	-15	-15	-0	-1.5
1946 Bro-N	2	5	.286	16	9	1	0	0	53²	46	2	51	36	16.3	5.87	58	.240	.399	4	.235	1	-15	-15	-1	-1.4
1947 *Bro-N	5	2	.714	28	9	0	0	0	77²	66	4	59	36	14.7	4.75	87	.240	.378	3	.111	-1	-6	-5	-0	-0.6
1948 Bro-N	15	13	.536	44	34	12	4	0	246²	193	17	122	138	11.7	3.10	129	.217	.315	14	.167	-2	23	25	-4	1.9
1949 *Bro-N	9	8	.529	38	20	6	2	1	140²	108	15	89	80	12.8	4.41	93	.216	.338	10	.213	-0	-6	-5	-3	-0.7
1950 Bro-N	2	1	.667	20	1	0	0	0	33²	25	6	48	23	20.0	6.42	64	.214	.449	1	.125	0	-9	-9	-1	-0.8
Total 6	35	31	.530	155	81	20	6	1	597²	474	48	410	336	13.5	4.31	91	.221	.350	33	.164	-4	-26	-24	-9	-3.1

■ EDGAR BARNHART
Barnhart, Edgar Vernon b: 9/16/04, Providence, Mo. d: 9/14/84, Columbia, Mo. BL/TR, 5'10", 160 lbs. Deb: 9/23/24

YEAR TM/L	W	L	PCT	G	GS	CG	SH	SV	IP	H	HR	BB	SO	RAT	ERA	ERA+	OAV	OOB	BH	AVG	PB	PR	/A	PD	TPI
1924 StL-A	0	0	—	1	0	0	0	0	1	0	0	2	0	18.0	0.00	—	.000	.400	0	—	0	0	1	0	0.1

■ LES BARNHART
Barnhart, Leslie Earl "Barney" b: 2/23/05, Hoxie, Kan. d: 10/7/71, Scottsdale, Ariz. BR/TR, 6', 180 lbs. Deb: 9/22/28

YEAR TM/L	W	L	PCT	G	GS	CG	SH	SV	IP	H	HR	BB	SO	RAT	ERA	ERA+	OAV	OOB	BH	AVG	PB	PR	/A	PD	TPI
1928 Cle-A	0	1	.000	2	1	0	0	0	9	13	1	4	1	17.0	7.00	59	.325	.386	1	.500	-0	-3	-3	-0	-0.2
1930 Cle-A	1	0	1.000	1	1	0	0	0	8¹	12	0	4	1	17.0	6.48	74	.364	.432	0	—	-1	-2	-2	0	-0.1
Total 2	1	1	.500	3	2	0	0	0	17¹	25	1	8	2	17.1	6.75	66	.342	.407	1	.200	-0	-5	-4	-0	-0.3

■ GEORGE BARNICLE
Barnicle, George Bernard "Barney" b: 8/26/17, Fitchburg, Mass. d: 10/10/90, Largo, Fla. BR/TR, 6'2", 175 lbs. Deb: 9/06/39

YEAR TM/L	W	L	PCT	G	GS	CG	SH	SV	IP	H	HR	BB	SO	RAT	ERA	ERA+	OAV	OOB	BH	AVG	PB	PR	/A	PD	TPI
1939 Bos-N	2	2	.500	6	1	0	0	0	18¹	16	1	8	15	11.8	4.91	75	.235	.316	0	.000	-1	-2	-2	0	-0.2
1940 Bos-N	1	0	1.000	13	2	1	0	0	32²	28	1	31	11	17.9	7.44	50	.233	.414	0	.000	-1	-13	-14	1	-1.3
1941 Bos-N	0	1	.000	1	1	0	0	0	6²	5	0	4	2	13.5	6.75	53	.264	.385	0	.000	-0	-2	-2	0	-0.1
Total 3	3	3	.500	20	4	1	0	0	57²	49	2	43	28	15.5	6.55	56	.234	.382	0	.000	-2	-17	-18	1	-1.6

■ ED BARNOWSKI
Barnowski, Edward Anthony b: 8/23/43, Scranton, Pa. BR/TR, 6'2", 195 lbs. Deb: 9/08/65

YEAR TM/L	W	L	PCT	G	GS	CG	SH	SV	IP	H	HR	BB	SO	RAT	ERA	ERA+	OAV	OOB	BH	AVG	PB	PR	/A	PD	TPI
1965 Bal-A	0	0	—	4	0	0	0	0	4¹	3	0	7	6	20.8	2.08	167	.200	.455	0	—	0	1	1	-0	0.1
1966 Bal-A	0	0	—	2	0	0	0	0	3	4	0	1	2	15.0	3.00	111	.364	.417	0	—	0	0	0	0	0.0
Total 2	0	0	—	6	0	0	0	0	7¹	7	0	8	8	18.4	2.45	139	.269	.441	0	—	0	1	1	0	0.1

■ SALOME BAROJAS
Barojas, Salome (Romero) b: 6/16/57, Cordoba, Mex. BR/TR, 5'9", 160 lbs. Deb: 4/11/82

YEAR TM/L	W	L	PCT	G	GS	CG	SH	SV	IP	H	HR	BB	SO	RAT	ERA	ERA+	OAV	OOB	BH	AVG	PB	PR	/A	PD	TPI
1982 Chi-A	6	6	.500	61	0	0	0	21	106²	96	9	46	56	12.1	3.54	114	.244	.324	0	—	0	6	6	3	0.9
1983 *Chi-A	3	3	.500	52	0	0	0	12	87¹	70	2	32	38	11.0	2.47	169	.224	.306	0	—	0	15	17	0	1.7
1984 Chi-A	3	2	.600	24	0	0	0	1	39¹	48	3	19	18	15.3	4.58	91	.310	.385	0	—	0	-3	-2	1	0.0
Sea-A	6	5	.545	19	14	0	0	1	95¹	88	12	41	37	12.5	3.97	101	.249	.332	0	—	0	0	0	1	0.1
Yr	9	7	.563	43	14	0	0	2	134²	136	15	60	55	13.3	4.14	97	.268	.349	0	—	0	-2	-2	2	0.1
1985 Sea-A	0	5	.000	17	4	0	0	0	52²	65	6	33	27	16.7	5.98	70	.305	.398	0	—	0	-11	-10	0	-0.9
1988 Phi-N	0	0	—	6	0	0	0	0	8²	7	1	8	1	15.6	8.31	43	.250	.417	0	—	0	-5	-5	0	-0.4
Total 5	18	21	.462	179	18	0	0	35	390	374	33	179	177	13.0	3.95	103	.257	.342	0	—	0	4	6	6	1.4

■ JIM BARR
Barr, James Leland b: 2/10/48, Lynwood, Cal. BR/TR, 6'3", 205 lbs. Deb: 7/31/71

YEAR TM/L	W	L	PCT	G	GS	CG	SH	SV	IP	H	HR	BB	SO	RAT	ERA	ERA+	OAV	OOB	BH	AVG	PB	PR	/A	PD	TPI
1971 *SF-N	1	1	.500	17	0	0	0	0	35¹	33	3	5	16	9.9	3.57	95	.254	.287	0	.000	-0	-0	-1	1	0.0
1972 SF-N	8	10	.444	44	18	8	2	2	166	166	16	41	86	10.6	2.87	122	.246	.292	9	.184	1	12	12	1	1.5
1973 SF-N	11	17	.393	41	33	8	3	2	231¹	240	24	49	88	11.4	3.81	100	.268	.310	10	.152	-1	-4	0	0	0.0
1974 SF-N	13	9	.591	44	27	11	5	2	239²	223	17	47	84	10.2	2.74	139	.265	.290	18	.254	5	23	28	1	3.8
1975 SF-N	13	14	.481	35	33	12	2	0	244	244	17	58	77	11.3	3.06	124	.265	.310	9	.118	-3	15	20	4	2.3
1976 SF-N	15	12	.556	37	37	8	3	0	252¹	260	17	60	75	11.5	2.89	126	.266	.310	12	.162	-2	17	21	4	3.0
1977 SF-N	12	16	.429	38	38	9	1	0	234¹	286	18	56	97	13.3	4.76	82	.306	.347	10	.132	-2	-22	-22	3	-2.0
1978 SF-N	8	11	.421	32	25	5	2	1	163	180	7	34	44	11.9	3.53	98	.281	.319	5	.100	-2	1	-2	2	-0.2
1979 Cal-A	10	12	.455	36	25	5	0	0	197	217	22	55	69	12.6	4.20	97	.287	.338	0	—	0	-3	2	0	0.0
1980 Cal-A	1	4	.200	24	7	0	0	1	68	90	12	23	22	15.4	5.56	71	.323	.380	0	—	0	-12	-12	-0	-1.1
1982 SF-N	4	3	.571	53	9	1	1	2	128²	125	9	20	36	10.4	3.29	109	.262	.297	8	.250	1	4	4	1	0.7
1983 SF-N	5	3	.625	53	0	0	0	2	92²	106	7	20	47	12.3	3.98	89	.294	.332	2	.133	-0	-4	-5	0	-0.4
Total 12	101	112	.474	454	252	64	20	12	2065¹	2170	161	469	741	11.6	3.56	105	.273	.316	83	.162	0	31	42	18	7.6

■ BOB BARR
Barr, Robert Alexander b: 3/12/08, Newton, Mass. BR/TR, 6', 175 lbs. Deb: 9/11/35

YEAR TM/L	W	L	PCT	G	GS	CG	SH	SV	IP	H	HR	BB	SO	RAT	ERA	ERA+	OAV	OOB	BH	AVG	PB	PR	/A	PD	TPI
1935 Bro-N	0	0	—	2	0	0	0	0	2¹	5	0	2	0	27.0	3.86	103	.385	.467	0	—	0	0	0	0	0.0

YEAR TM/L	W	L	PCT	G	GS	CG	SH	SV	IP	H	HR	BB	SO	RAT	ERA	ERA+	OAV	OOB	BH	AVG	PB	PR	/A	PD	TPI

■ BOB BARR   Barr, Robert McClelland b: 1856, Washington, D.C. d: 3/11/30, Washington, D.C.   BR/TR, 6'1", 192 lbs. Deb: 6/23/1883

1883 Pit-a	6	18	.250	26	23	19	0	1	203¹	263	5	28	81	12.9	4.38	73	.294	.316	35	.246	3	-24	-26	1	-1.8
1884 Was-a	9	23	.281	32	32	32	2	0	281	311	9	31	138	11.0	3.46	88	.266	.285	20	.148	-2	-7	-13	-1	-1.5
Ind-a	3	11	.214	16	16	15	0	0	132	160	2	19	69	12.2	4.98	66	.284	.307	12	.185	0	-25	-25	-1	-2.1
Yr	12	34	.261	48	48	47	2	0	413	471	11	50	207	11.4	3.94	79	.272	.292	8	.040	-2	-32	-38	-2	-3.6
1886 Was-N	3	18	.143	22	22	21	1	0	190²	216	7	54	80	12.7	4.30	76	.274	.320	13	.165	-2	-21	-22	-1	-2.1
1890 Roc-a	28	24	.538	57	54	52	3	0	493¹	458	7	219	209	12.4	3.25	110	.239	.317	36	.179	-1	34	17	3	1.5
1891 NY-N	0	4	.000	5	4	2	0	0	27	47	1	12	11	19.7	5.33	60	.368	.422	1	.091	-0	-6	-6	0	-0.5
Total 5	49	98	.333	158	151	141	6	1	1327¹	1455	31	363	588	12.3	3.83	87	.266	.312	117	.185	-3	-49	-75	1	-6.5

■ STEVE BARR   Barr, Steven Charles b: 9/8/51, St.Louis, Mo. BL/TL, 6'4", 200 lbs. Deb: 10/01/74

1974 Bos-A	1	0	1.000	1	1	1	0	0	9	7	0	6	3	13.0	4.00	96	.212	.333	0	—	0	-0	-0	0	0.0
1975 Bos-A	0	1	.000	3	2	0	0	0	7	11	1	7	2	23.1	2.57	158	.367	.486	0	—	0	1	1	0	0.1
1976 Tex-A	2	6	.250	20	10	3	0	0	67²	70	10	44	27	15.2	5.59	64	.269	.375	0	—	0	-16	-15	0	-1.4
Total 3	3	7	.300	24	13	4	0	0	83²	88	11	57	32	15.6	5.16	71	.272	.382	0	—	0	-15	-14	1	-1.3

■ RED BARRETT   Barrett, Charles Henry b: 2/14/15, Santa Barbara, Cal d: 7/28/90, Wilson, N.C. BR/TR, 5'11", 183 lbs. Deb: 9/15/37

1937 Cin-N	0	0	—	1	0	0	0	0	6¹	5	0	2	1	9.9	1.42	263	.227	.292	0	.000	-0	2	2	-0	0.1
1938 Cin-N	2	0	1.000	6	2	2	0	0	28²	28	2	15	5	13.5	3.14	116	.257	.347	1	.143	-0	2	2	-0	0.1
1939 Cin-N	0	0	—	2	0	0	0	0	5¹	5	0	1	1	10.1	1.69	227	.263	.300	0	.000	-0	1	1	0	0.1
1940 Cin-N	1	0	1.000	3	0	0	0	0	2²	5	0	1	0	20.3	6.75	56	.455	.500	0	—	0	-1	-1	0	0.0
1943 Bos-N	12	18	.400	38	31	14	3	0	255	240	11	63	64	10.8	3.18	107	.250	.298	11	.136	-4	6	7	1	0.4
1944 Bos-N	9	16	.360	42	30	11	1	2	230¹	257	13	63	54	12.6	4.06	94	.279	.327	13	.173	-1	-12	-6	2	-0.4
1945 Bos-N	2	3	.400	9	5	2	0	2	38	43	6	16	13	14.2	4.74	81	.281	.353	2	.222	-0	-4	-4	1	-0.2
StL-N	21	9	.700	36	29	22	3	0	246²	244	12	38	63	10.3	2.74	137	.256	.285	10	.112	-5	29	28	-1	2.3
Yr	23	12	.657	45	34	24	3	2	284²	287	18	54	76	10.8	3.00	125	.259	.294	1	.010	-5	25	24	1	2.1
1946 StL-N	3	2	.600	23	9	1	1	2	67	75	5	24	22	13.6	4.03	86	.282	.346	1	.059	-1	-5	-4	1	-0.4
1947 Bos-N	11	12	.478	36	30	12	3	1	210²	200	16	53	53	10.9	3.55	110	.244	.292	8	.111	-2	12	8	0	0.6
1948 *Bos-N	7	8	.467	34	13	3	0	0	128¹	132	9	26	40	11.1	3.65	105	.268	.305	7	.179	-1	4	3	1	0.3
1949 Bos-N	1	1	.500	23	0	0	0	0	44¹	58	4	10	17	14.2	5.68	66	.326	.368	1	.200	-0	-8	-9	1	-0.7
Total 11	69	69	.500	253	149	67	11	7	1263¹	1292	78	312	333	11.5	3.53	105	.264	.309	54	.136	-16	28	26	7	2.2

■ FRANK BARRETT   Barrett, Francis Joseph "Red" b: 7/1/13, Ft.Lauderdale, Fla BR/TR, 6'2", 173 lbs. Deb: 10/01/39

1939 StL-N	0	1	.000	1	0	0	0	0	1²	1	0	1	3	10.8	5.40	76	.167	.286	0	—	0	-0	-0	0	0.0
1944 Bos-A	8	7	.533	38	2	0	0	8	90¹	93	5	42	40	13.5	3.69	92	.271	.352	4	.143	-1	-3	-3	-0	-0.3
1945 Bos-A	4	3	.571	37	0	0	0	3	86	77	0	29	35	11.1	2.62	130	.249	.314	5	.250	1	7	8	-1	0.8
1946 Bos-N	2	4	.333	23	0	0	0	1	35¹	35	2	17	12	13.5	5.09	67	.252	.338	0	.000	-1	-7	-7	1	-0.5
1950 Pit-N	1	2	.333	5	0	0	0	0	4¹	5	1	1	0	12.5	4.15	106	.357	.400	0	—	0	-0	-0	0	0.1
Total 5	15	17	.469	104	2	0	0	12	217²	211	8	90	90	12.5	3.51	98	.260	.336	9	.167	-1	-2	-2	1	0.1

■ TIM BARRETT   Barrett, Timothy Wayne b: 1/24/61, Huntingburg, Ind. BL/TR, 6'1", 185 lbs. Deb: 7/18/88

| 1988 Mon-N | 0 | 0 | — | 4 | 0 | 0 | 0 | 1 | 9¹ | 10 | 2 | 2 | 5 | 11.6 | 5.79 | 62 | .270 | .308 | 0 | .000 | 0 | -2 | -2 | 0 | -0.1 |

■ DICK BARRETT   Barrett, Tracy Souter "Kewpie Dick" (a.k.a. Richard Oliver 1933 And Richard Oliver Barrett 1934-43)
b: 9/28/06, Montoursville, Pa d: 10/30/66, Seattle, Wash. BR/TR, 5'9", 175 lbs. Deb: 6/27/33

1933 Phi-A	4	4	.500	15	7	3	0	0	70¹	74	2	49	26	15.9	5.76	74	.272	.385	6	.286	2	-12	-12	0	-0.8
1934 Bos-N	1	3	.250	15	3	0	0	0	32¹	50	2	12	14	17.3	6.68	57	.365	.416	1	.143	-0	-9	-10	1	-0.8
1943 Chi-N	0	4	.000	15	4	0	0	0	45	52	2	28	20	16.2	4.80	70	.291	.389	1	.111	-1	-7	-7	-0	-0.7
Phi-N	10	9	.526	23	20	10	2	1	169¹	137	5	51	65	10.1	2.39	141	.221	.282	7	.143	-1	19	18	0	2.1
Yr	10	13	.435	38	24	10	2	1	214¹	189	7	79	85	11.3	2.90	116	.236	.306	7	.121	-1	12	11	0	1.4
1944 Phi-N	12	18	.400	37	27	11	1	0	221¹	223	7	88	74	12.8	3.86	94	.262	.333	16	.216	-2	-6	-6	2	-0.1
1945 Phi-N	8	20	.286	36	30	8	0	1	190²	217	11	92	72	14.9	5.38	71	.281	.363	9	.145	-1	-33	-33	0	-3.1
Total 5	35	58	.376	141	91	32	3	2	729	753	29	320	271	13.4	4.28	86	.266	.343	40	.180	1	-49	-50	4	-3.4

■ BILL BARRETT   Barrett, William Joseph "Whispering Bill" b: 5/28/1900, Cambridge, Mass. d: 1/26/51, Cambridge, Mass. BR/TR, 6', 175 lbs. Deb: 5/13/21 ♦

| 1921 Phi-A | 1 | 0 | 1.000 | 4 | 0 | 0 | 0 | 0 | 5 | 2 | 0 | 9 | 2 | 19.8 | 7.20 | 62 | .133 | .458 | 7 | .233 | 0 | -2 | -2 | 0 | 0.0 |

■ FRANCISCO BARRIOS   Barrios, Francisco Javier (Jimenez)
b: 6/10/53, Hermosillo, Mex. d: 4/9/82, Hermosillo, Mexico BR/TR, 5'11", 155 lbs. Deb: 8/18/74

1974 Chi-A	0	0	—	2	0	0	0	0	2	7	0	2	2	40.5	27.00	14	.538	.600	0	—	0	-5	-5	0	-0.4
1976 Chi-A	5	9	.357	35	14	6	0	3	141²	136	13	46	81	11.8	4.32	83	.255	.318	0	—	0	-13	-12	-1	-1.2
1977 Chi-A	14	7	.667	33	31	9	0	0	231¹	241	22	58	119	11.8	4.12	99	.267	.315	0	—	0	-2	-1	-0	-0.1
1978 Chi-A	9	15	.375	33	32	9	2	0	195²	180	13	85	79	12.5	4.05	94	.246	.330	0	—	0	-6	-5	3	-0.2
1979 Chi-A	8	3	.727	15	15	2	0	0	94²	88	9	33	28	12.0	3.61	118	.242	.314	0	—	0	6	7	-1	0.6
1980 Chi-A	1	1	.500	3	3	0	0	0	16¹	21	4	8	2	16.5	4.96	81	.323	.405	0	—	0	-2	-2	0	-0.1
1981 Chi-A	1	3	.250	8	7	1	0	0	36¹	45	3	14	12	14.9	3.96	90	.292	.355	0	—	0	-1	-2	0	-0.1
Total 7	38	38	.500	129	102	27	2	3	718	718	64	246	323	12.4	4.15	94	.260	.326	0	—	0	-22	-20	0	-1.5

■ FRANK BARRON   Barron, Frank John b: 8/6/1890, St.Mary's, W.Va. d: 9/18/64, St.Mary's, W.Va. BL/TL, 6'1", 175 lbs. Deb: 8/19/14

| 1914 Was-A | 0 | 0 | — | 1 | 0 | 0 | 0 | 0 | 1 | 1 | 0 | 1 | 0 | 9.0 | 0.00 | — | .333 | .333 | 0 | — | 0 | 0 | 0 | 0 | 0.0 |

■ ED BARRY   Barry, Edward "Jumbo" b: 10/2/1882, Madison, Wis. d: 6/19/20, Montague, Mass. TL, 6'3", 185 lbs. Deb: 8/21/05

1905 Bos-A	1	2	.333	7	5	2	0	0	40²	38	2	15	18	11.7	2.88	94	.249	.316	1	.091	-0	-1	-1	-2	-0.2
1906 Bos-A	0	3	.000	3	3	3	0	0	21	23	2	5	10	12.0	6.00	46	.281	.323	1	.111	-0	-8	-8	0	-0.6
1907 Bos-A	0	1	.000	2	2	1	0	0	17¹	13	1	5	6	9.3	2.08	124	.210	.270	0	.000	-0	1	1	-0	0.0
Total 3	1	6	.143	12	10	6	0	0	79	74	5	25	34	11.3	3.53	76	.250	.308	2	.087	-1	-8	-7	-2	-0.8

■ HARDIN BARRY   Barry, Hardin "Finn" b: 3/26/1891, Susanville, Cal. d: 11/5/69, Carson City, Nev. BR/TR, 6', 185 lbs. Deb: 6/21/12

| 1912 Phi-A | 0 | 0 | — | 3 | 0 | 0 | 0 | 0 | 13 | 18 | 0 | 4 | 3 | 15.9 | 7.62 | 40 | .360 | .418 | 0 | .000 | -0 | -6 | -7 | -0 | -0.5 |

■ TOM BARRY   Barry, Thomas Arthur b: 4/10/1879, St.Louis, Mo. d: 6/4/46, St.Louis, Mo. TR, 5'9", 155 lbs. Deb: 4/15/04

| 1904 Phi-N | 0 | 1 | .000 | 1 | 0 | 0 | 0 | 0 | 0² | 6 | 0 | 1 | 1 | 94.5 | 40.50 | 7 | .667 | .700 | 0 | — | 0 | -3 | -3 | 0 | -0.2 |

■ BOB BARTHELSON   Barthelson, Robert Edward b: 7/15/24, New Haven, Conn. BR/TR, 6', 185 lbs. Deb: 7/04/44

| 1944 NY-N | 1 | 1 | .500 | 7 | 1 | 0 | 0 | 0 | 9² | 13 | 2 | 5 | 4 | 16.8 | 4.66 | 78 | .310 | .383 | 0 | — | 0 | -1 | -1 | -0 | -0.1 |

■ JOHN BARTHOLD   Barthold, John Francis "Hans" b: 4/14/1882, Philadelphia, Pa. d: 11/4/46, Fairview Village, Pa. BB/TR, 5'11", 180 lbs. Deb: 5/17/04

| 1904 Phi-A | 0 | 0 | — | 4 | 0 | 0 | 0 | 0 | 10² | 12 | 0 | 8 | 5 | 16.9 | 5.06 | 53 | .284 | .399 | 1 | .333 | 1 | -3 | -3 | 0 | -0.1 |

■ LES BARTHOLOMEW   Bartholomew, Lester Justin b: 4/4/03, Madison, Wis. d: 9/19/72, Barrington, Ill. BR/TL, 5'11.5", 195 lbs. Deb: 4/11/28

1928 Pit-N	0	0	—	6	0	0	0	0	22²	31	2	9	6	15.9	7.15	57	.356	.417	1	.143	-0	-8	-8	-0	-0.6
1932 Chi-A	0	0	—	3	0	0	0	0	5¹	5	0	6	1	18.6	5.06	85	.250	.423	0	.000	-0	-0	-0	0	0.0
Total 2	0	0	—	9	0	0	0	0	28	36	2	15	7	16.4	6.75	61	.336	.418	1	.125	-0	-8	-8	-0	-0.6

■ BILL BARTLEY   Bartley, William Jackson b: 1/8/1885, Cincinnati, Ohio d: 5/17/65, Cincinnati, Ohio BR/TR, 5'11.5", 190 lbs. Deb: 9/15/03

| 1903 NY-N | 0 | 0 | — | 1 | 0 | 0 | 0 | 0 | 3 | 3 | 0 | 4 | 2 | 21.0 | 0.00 | — | .273 | .467 | 0 | .000 | -0 | 1 | 1 | 0 | 0.1 |

YEAR TM/L	W	L	PCT	G	GS	CG	SH	SV	IP	H	HR	BB	SO	RAT	ERA	ERA+	OAV	OOB	BH	AVG	PB	PR	/A	PD	TPI
1906 Phi-A	0	0	—	3	0	0	0	1	8²	10	0	6	6	16.6	9.35	29	.292	.398	1	.333	1	-6	-6	1	-0.4
1907 Phi-A	0	1	.000	15	3	2	0	0	56¹	44	0	19	16	10.1	2.24	117	.217	.284	2	.095	-1	2	2	0	0.1
Total 3	0	1	.000	19	3	2	1	1	68	57	0	29	24	11.4	3.04	87	.230	.311	3	.120	-1	-3	-3	1	-0.2

■ CHARLIE BARTSON
Bartson, Charles Franklin b: 3/13/1865, Peoria, Ill. d: 6/9/36, Peoria, Ill. 6', 170 lbs. Deb: 5/14/1890

YEAR TM/L	W	L	PCT	G	GS	CG	SH	SV	IP	H	HR	BB	SO	RAT	ERA	ERA+	OAV	OOB	BH	AVG	PB	PR	/A	PD	TPI
1890 Chi-P	8	10	.444	25	19	16	0	1	188	222	8	66	47	13.8	4.26	102	.281	.337	13	.173	-2	-1	2	5	0.4

■ JIM BASKETTE
Baskette, James Blaine "Big Jim" b: 12/10/1887, Athens, Tenn. d: 7/30/42, Athens, Tenn. BR/TR, 6'2", 185 lbs. Deb: 9/22/11

YEAR TM/L	W	L	PCT	G	GS	CG	SH	SV	IP	H	HR	BB	SO	RAT	ERA	ERA+	OAV	OOB	BH	AVG	PB	PR	/A	PD	TPI
1911 Cle-A	1	2	.333	4	2	2	0	0	21¹	21	0	9	8	13.1	3.38	101	.273	.356	2	.333	1	-0	0	-0	0.0
1912 Cle-A	8	4	.667	29	11	7	1	1	116	109	2	46	51	12.6	3.18	107	.252	.334	5	.125	-1	2	3	-3	0.0
1913 Cle-A	0	0	—	2	1	0	0	0	4²	8	1	2	0	19.3	5.79	53	.400	.455	1	1.000	1	-1	-1	1	0.0
Total 3	9	6	.600	35	14	9	1	1	142	138	3	57	59	12.9	3.30	103	.261	.342	8	.170	1	0	2	-2	0.0

■ NORM BASS
Bass, Norman Delaney b: 1/21/39, Laurel, Miss. BR/TR, 6'3", 205 lbs. Deb: 4/23/61

YEAR TM/L	W	L	PCT	G	GS	CG	SH	SV	IP	H	HR	BB	SO	RAT	ERA	ERA+	OAV	OOB	BH	AVG	PB	PR	/A	PD	TPI
1961 KC-A	11	11	.500	40	23	6	2	0	170²	164	17	82	74	13.2	4.69	88	.255	.343	7	.119	-2	-13	-11	-3	-1.4
1962 KC-A	2	6	.250	22	10	0	0	0	75¹	96	7	46	33	17.0	6.09	68	.317	.407	1	.045	-2	-18	-16	2	-1.5
1963 KC-A	0	0	—	3	1	0	0	0	7²	11	2	9	4	23.5	11.74	33	.333	.476	0	.000	-0	-7	-7	-0	-0.6
Total 3	13	17	.433	65	34	6	2	0	253²	271	26	137	111	14.6	5.32	77	.277	.368	8	.098	-4	-37	-34	-1	-3.5

■ DICK BASS
Bass, Richard William b: 7/7/06, Rogersville, Tenn. d: 2/3/89, Graceville, Fla. BR/TR, 6'2", 175 lbs. Deb: 9/21/39

YEAR TM/L	W	L	PCT	G	GS	CG	SH	SV	IP	H	HR	BB	SO	RAT	ERA	ERA+	OAV	OOB	BH	AVG	PB	PR	/A	PD	TPI
1939 Was-A	0	1	.000	1	1	0	0	0	8	7	0	6	1	15.8	6.75	64	.241	.389	0	.000	-0	-2	-2	0	-0.1

■ CHARLIE BASTIAN
Bastian, Charles J. b: 7/4/1860, Philadelphia, Pa. d: 1/18/32, Pennsauken, N.J. BR/TR, 5'6.5", 145 lbs. Deb: 8/18/1884 ♦

YEAR TM/L	W	L	PCT	G	GS	CG	SH	SV	IP	H	HR	BB	SO	RAT	ERA	ERA+	OAV	OOB	BH	AVG	PB	PR	/A	PD	TPI
1884 Wil-U	0	0	—	1	0	0	0	0	6	6	0	0	2	9.0	3.00	110	.243	.243	12	.200	0	0	0	-0	0.0

■ JOE BATCHELDER
Batchelder, Joseph Edmund "Win" b: 7/11/1898, Wenham, Mass. d: 5/5/89, Beverly, Mass. BR/TL, 5'7", 165 lbs. Deb: 9/29/23

YEAR TM/L	W	L	PCT	G	GS	CG	SH	SV	IP	H	HR	BB	SO	RAT	ERA	ERA+	OAV	OOB	BH	AVG	PB	PR	/A	PD	TPI
1923 Bos-N	1	0	1.000	4	1	0	0	0	9	12	1	2	2	14.0	7.00	57	.353	.389	0	.000	0	-3	-3	-0	-0.2
1924 Bos-N	0	0	—	3	0	0	0	0	4²	4	0	2	2	11.6	3.86	99	.235	.316	0	.000	-0	0	-0	-0	0.0
1925 Bos-N	0	0	—	4	0	0	0	0	7	10	1	1	2	14.1	5.14	78	.357	.379	0	.000	-0	-1	-1	0	0.0
Total 3	1	0	1.000	11	1	1	0	0	20²	26	2	4	6	13.5	5.66	70	.329	.369	0	.000	-0	-4	-4	-0	-0.2

■ BUSH BATES
Bates, Bush Deb: 8/25/1889

YEAR TM/L	W	L	PCT	G	GS	CG	SH	SV	IP	H	HR	BB	SO	RAT	ERA	ERA+	OAV	OOB	BH	AVG	PB	PR	/A	PD	TPI
1889 KC-a	0	1	.000	1	1	0	0	0	8	15	0	5	3	22.5	13.50	31	.387	.458	0	.000	-1	-9	-8	-0	-0.5

■ DICK BATES
Bates, Charles Richard b: 10/7/45, McArthur, Ohio BL/TR, 6', 190 lbs. Deb: 4/27/69

YEAR TM/L	W	L	PCT	G	GS	CG	SH	SV	IP	H	HR	BB	SO	RAT	ERA	ERA+	OAV	OOB	BH	AVG	PB	PR	/A	PD	TPI
1969 Sea-A	0	0	—	1	0	0	0	0	1²	3	1	3	3	32.4	27.00	13	.375	.545	0	—	0	-4	-4	0	-0.3

■ FRANK BATES
Bates, Creed Frank b: Chattanooga, Tenn. Deb: 10/07/1898

YEAR TM/L	W	L	PCT	G	GS	CG	SH	SV	IP	H	HR	BB	SO	RAT	ERA	ERA+	OAV	OOB	BH	AVG	PB	PR	/A	PD	TPI
1898 Cle-N	2	1	.667	4	4	4	0	0	29	30	0	11	5	12.7	3.10	117	.265	.330	1	.111	0	2	2	0	0.2
1899 StL-N	0	0	—	2	0	0	0	0	8²	7	0	5	0	12.5	1.04	383	.221	.327	1	.333	1	3	3	-0	0.3
Cle-N	1	18	.053	20	19	17	0	0	153	239	6	105	13	20.2	7.24	51	.355	.441	14	.215	1	-57	-60	0	-4.7
Yr	1	18	.053	22	19	17	0	0	161²	246	6	110	13	19.8	6.90	54	.349	.436	15	.132	1	-55	-58	0	-4.4
Total 2	3	19	.136	26	23	21	0	0	190²	276	6	121	18	18.7	6.33	58	.337	.422	16	.208	1	-53	-56	0	-4.2

■ JOE BATTIN
Battin, Joseph V. b: 11/11/1851, Philadelphia, Pa. d: 12/10/37, Akron, Ohio BR/TR, Deb: 8/11/1871 MU♦

YEAR TM/L	W	L	PCT	G	GS	CG	SH	SV	IP	H	HR	BB	SO	RAT	ERA	ERA+	OAV	OOB	BH	AVG	PB	PR	/A	PD	TPI
1877 StL-N	0	0	—	1	0	0	0	0	3²	3	0	1	1	9.8	4.91	53	.210	.262	45	.199	0	-1	-1	-0	0.0
1883 Pit-a	0	0	—	2	0	0	0	0	4	9	0	1	0	22.5	2.25	143	.420	.446	83	.214	0	0	0	-0	0.0
Total 2	0	0	—	3	0	0	0	0	7²	12	0	2	1	16.4	3.52	83	.336	.372	313	.218	0	-1	-0	0	0.0

■ CHRIS BATTON
Batton, Christopher Sean b: 8/24/54, Los Angeles, Cal. BR/TR, 6'4", 195 lbs. Deb: 9/19/76

YEAR TM/L	W	L	PCT	G	GS	CG	SH	SV	IP	H	HR	BB	SO	RAT	ERA	ERA+	OAV	OOB	BH	AVG	PB	PR	/A	PD	TPI
1976 Oak-A	0	0	—	2	1	0	0	0	4	5	1	3	4	18.0	9.00	37	.313	.421	0	—	0	-2	-3	0	-0.2

■ LOU BAUER
Bauer, Louis Walter b: 11/30/1898, Egg Harbor City, N.J. d: 2/4/79, Pomona, N.J. 6', 175 lbs. Deb: 8/13/18

YEAR TM/L	W	L	PCT	G	GS	CG	SH	SV	IP	H	HR	BB	SO	RAT	ERA	ERA+	OAV	OOB	BH	AVG	PB	PR	/A	PD	TPI
1918 Phi-A	0	0	—	1	0	0	0	0	0	0	0	2	0	—	∞	—	—	1.000	0	—	0	-1	-1	0	0.0

■ AL BAUERS
Bauers, Albert J. b: 1850, Columbus, Ohio d: 9/6/13, Wilkes-Barre, Pa. TL, Deb: 9/22/1884 U

YEAR TM/L	W	L	PCT	G	GS	CG	SH	SV	IP	H	HR	BB	SO	RAT	ERA	ERA+	OAV	OOB	BH	AVG	PB	PR	/A	PD	TPI
1884 Col-a	1	2	.333	3	3	3	0	0	25	22	1	14	13	13.0	4.68	65	.223	.320	3	.273	0	-4	-5	0	-0.3
1886 StL-N	0	4	.000	4	4	3	0	0	28²	31	1	27	13	18.2	5.97	54	.265	.403	2	.167	-1	-8	-9	-1	-0.7
Total 2	1	6	.143	7	7	6	0	0	53²	53	2	41	26	15.8	5.37	58	.246	.366	5	.217	-0	-12	-13	-1	-1.0

■ RUSS BAUERS
Bauers, Russell Lee b: 5/10/14, Townsend, Wis. BL/TR, 6'3", 195 lbs. Deb: 8/20/36

YEAR TM/L	W	L	PCT	G	GS	CG	SH	SV	IP	H	HR	BB	SO	RAT	ERA	ERA+	OAV	OOB	BH	AVG	PB	PR	/A	PD	TPI
1936 Pit-N	0	0	—	1	1	0	0	0	1¹	2	0	4	0	47.3	33.75	12	.500	.778	0	—	0	-4	-4	0	-0.3
1937 Pit-N	13	6	.684	34	19	11	2	1	187²	174	9	80	118	12.4	2.88	134	.245	.325	15	.217	1	22	21	3	2.4
1938 Pit-N	13	14	.481	40	34	12	2	3	243	207	7	99	117	11.6	3.07	124	.233	.314	21	.239	4	19	20	-3	2.0
1939 Pit-N	2	4	.333	15	8	1	0	1	53²	46	4	25	12	12.1	3.35	114	.240	.330	4	.211	-0	3	3	-1	0.2
1940 Pit-N	0	2	.000	15	2	0	0	0	30²	42	2	18	11	18.2	7.63	50	.323	.413	2	.286	0	-13	-13	0	-1.1
1941 Pit-N	1	3	.250	8	5	1	0	0	37¹	40	1	25	20	15.7	5.54	65	.267	.371	5	.357	1	-8	-8	-1	-0.7
1946 Chi-N	2	1	.667	15	2	0	0	1	43¹	45	1	19	22	13.5	3.53	94	.273	.351	3	.300	1	-1	-1	-0	0.0
1950 StL-A	0	0	—	1	0	0	0	0	2	6	0	1	0	31.5	4.50	110	.600	.636	0	—	0	0	0	0	0.0
Total 8	31	30	.508	129	71	27	4	6	599	562	17	271	300	12.7	3.53	107	.250	.334	50	.242	7	19	17	-2	2.5

■ FRANK BAUMANN
Baumann, Frank Matt "The Beau" b: 7/1/33, St.Louis, Mo. BL/TL, 6', 205 lbs. Deb: 7/31/55

YEAR TM/L	W	L	PCT	G	GS	CG	SH	SV	IP	H	HR	BB	SO	RAT	ERA	ERA+	OAV	OOB	BH	AVG	PB	PR	/A	PD	TPI
1955 Bos-A	2	1	.667	7	5	0	0	0	34	38	2	17	27	14.8	5.82	74	.281	.366	3	.231	-0	-7	-6	0	-0.5
1956 Bos-A	2	1	.667	7	1	0	0	0	24²	22	3	14	18	13.1	3.28	141	.234	.333	3	.333	1	2	4	-1	0.4
1957 Bos-A	1	0	1.000	4	1	0	0	0	12	13	1	3	7	12.8	3.75	106	.277	.333	1	.500	0	0	0	-0	0.0
1958 Bos-A	2	2	.500	10	7	2	0	0	52¹	56	4	27	31	15.0	4.47	90	.276	.372	3	.214	1	-4	-3	-0	-0.1
1959 Bos-A	6	4	.600	26	10	2	0	1	95²	96	11	55	48	14.3	4.05	100	.259	.357	6	.207	1	-2	0	1	0.2
1960 Chi-A	13	6	.684	47	20	7	2	3	185¹	169	11	53	71	10.8	**2.67**	142	.247	.302	8	.154	1	25	23	-2	2.3
1961 Chi-A	10	13	.435	53	23	5	1	3	187²	249	22	59	75	14.9	5.61	70	.318	.368	16	.262	6	-33	-35	2	-2.6
1962 Chi-A	7	6	.538	40	10	3	1	4	119²	117	10	36	55	11.7	3.38	115	.258	.316	8	.267	4	8	7	1	1.2
1963 Chi-A	2	1	.667	24	1	0	0	1	50¹	52	2	17	31	12.3	3.04	115	.265	.324	1	.091	-0	3	3	0	0.3
1964 Chi-A	0	3	.000	22	0	0	0	1	32	40	4	16	19	15.8	6.19	56	.320	.397	0	.000	-0	-9	-10	-0	-1.0
1965 Chi-N	0	1	.000	4	0	0	0	0	3²	4	1	3	2	17.2	7.36	50	.286	.412	0	—	0	-2	-1	0	-0.1
Total 11	45	38	.542	244	78	19	4	13	797¹	856	70	300	384	13.2	4.11	95	.276	.342	49	.218	14	-19	-19	-0	0.1

■ GEORGE BAUMGARDNER
Baumgardner, George Washington b: 7/22/1891, Barboursville, W.Va. d: 12/13/70, Barbourville, W.Va. BL/TR, 5'11", 178 lbs. Deb: 4/14/12

YEAR TM/L	W	L	PCT	G	GS	CG	SH	SV	IP	H	HR	BB	SO	RAT	ERA	ERA+	OAV	OOB	BH	AVG	PB	PR	/A	PD	TPI
1912 StL-A	11	13	.458	30	27	18	2	0	218¹	222	1	79	102	12.9	3.38	98	.274	.346	11	.145	-2	-2	-2	-0	-0.1
1913 StL-A	10	19	.345	38	31	23	2	1	253¹	267	6	84	78	12.3	3.13	94	.283	.348	13	.167	2	-5	-5	-1	-0.4
1914 StL-A	14	13	.519	45	18	9	3	3	183²	152	3	84	93	12.0	2.79	97	.229	.323	7	.132	-1	-1	-2	-1	-0.4
1915 StL-A	0	2	.000	7	1	1	0	0	22¹	29	0	11	6	16.1	4.43	65	.358	.435	0	.000	-1	-4	-4	1	-0.3
1916 StL-A	1	0	1.000	4	2	0	0	0	8	12	0	5	4	19.1	7.88	35	.364	.447	0	.000	-0	-4	-4	-0	-0.1
Total 5	36	47	.434	124	79	51	7	4	685²	682	10	263	283	12.8	3.22	93	.269	.345	31	.144	-0	-16	-17	-1	-1.6

■ ROSS BAUMGARTEN
Baumgarten, Ross b: 5/27/55, Highland Park, Ill. BL/TL, 6'1", 180 lbs. Deb: 8/16/78

YEAR TM/L	W	L	PCT	G	GS	CG	SH	SV	IP	H	HR	BB	SO	RAT	ERA	ERA+	OAV	OOB	BH	AVG	PB	PR	/A	PD	TPI
1978 Chi-A	2	2	.500	7	4	1	1	0	23	29	3	9	15	15.3	5.87	65	.315	.382	0	—	0	-5	-5	-0	-0.5
1979 Chi-A	13	8	.619	28	28	4	3	0	190²	175	18	83	72	12.2	3.54	120	.243	.322	0	—	0	14	15	0	1.5

YEAR TM/L	W	L	PCT	G	GS	CG	SH	SV	IP	H	HR	BB	SO	RAT	ERA	ERA+	OAV	OOB	BH	AVG	PB	PR	/A	PD	TPI
1980 Chi-A	2	12	.143	24	23	3	1	0	136	127	10	52	66	11.9	3.44	117	.256	.327	0	—	0	9	9	2	1.1
1981 Chi-A	5	9	.357	19	19	2	1	0	101²	101	9	40	52	12.6	4.07	88	.260	.331	0	—	0	-5	-6	0	-0.5
1982 Pit-N	0	5	.000	12	10	0	0	0	44	60	3	27	17	17.8	6.75	55	.347	.435	1	.083	-1	-15	-15	0	-1.4
Total 5	22	36	.379	90	84	10	6	0	495¹	492	43	211	222	12.8	4.02	99	.263	.339	1	.083	-1	-2	-2	3	0.2

■ HARRY BAUMGARTNER
Baumgartner, Harry E.   b: 10/8/1892, S.Pittsburg, Tenn.   d: 12/3/30, Augusta, Ga.   BL, 5'11", 175 lbs.   Deb: 9/06/20

YEAR TM/L	W	L	PCT	G	GS	CG	SH	SV	IP	H	HR	BB	SO	RAT	ERA	ERA+	OAV	OOB	BH	AVG	PB	PR	/A	PD	TPI
1920 Det-A	0	1	.000	9	0	0	0	0	18	18	1	6	7	12.0	4.00	93	.273	.333	1	.250	0	-0	-1	0	0.0

■ STAN BAUMGARTNER
Baumgartner, Stanwood Fulton   b: 12/14/1894, Houston, Tex.   d: 10/4/55, Philadelphia, Pa.   BL/TL, 6', 175 lbs.   Deb: 6/26/14

YEAR TM/L	W	L	PCT	G	GS	CG	SH	SV	IP	H	HR	BB	SO	RAT	ERA	ERA+	OAV	OOB	BH	AVG	PB	PR	/A	PD	TPI
1914 Phi-N	2	2	.500	15	3	2	1	0	60¹	60	0	16	24	11.6	3.28	90	.270	.325	1	.053	-1	-3	-2	-1	-0.4
1915 Phi-N	0	2	.000	16	1	0	0	0	48¹	38	2	23	27	11.5	2.42	113	.226	.323	1	.083	-1	2	2	1	0.2
1916 Phi-N	0	0	—	1	0	0	0	0	4	5	0	1	0	13.5	2.25	118	.333	.375	0	.000	-0	0	0	0	0.0
1921 Phi-N	3	6	.333	22	7	2	0	0	66²	103	8	22	13	17.1	7.02	60	.355	.404	6	.200	0	-24	-21	-1	-1.8
1922 Phi-N	1	1	.500	6	1	0	0	0	9²	18	1	5	2	21.4	6.52	72	.409	.469	1	.333	0	-3	-2	0	0.0
1924 Phi-A	13	6	.684	36	16	12	1	4	181	181	6	73	45	12.8	2.88	**149**	.271	.347	13	.217	-0	27	28	-2	2.5
1925 Phi-A	6	3	.667	37	11	2	1	3	113¹	120	2	35	18	12.9	3.57	130	.275	.338	7	.233	-0	10	14	-0	1.3
1926 Phi-A	1	1	.500	10	0	0	0	0	22¹	28	0	10	0	15.3	4.03	103	.326	.396	1	.333	-0	-0	0	1	0.1
Total 8	26	21	.553	143	40	18	3	7	505²	553	19	185	129	13.4	3.70	109	.287	.354	30	.190	-1	9	19	-1	1.9

■ GEORGE BAUSEWINE
Bausewine, George W.   b: 3/22/1869, Philadelphia, Pa.   d: 7/29/47, Norristown, Pa.   6'2",   Deb: 9/14/1889   U

YEAR TM/L	W	L	PCT	G	GS	CG	SH	SV	IP	H	HR	BB	SO	RAT	ERA	ERA+	OAV	OOB	BH	AVG	PB	PR	/A	PD	TPI
1889 Phi-a	1	4	.200	7	6	6	0	0	55¹	64	1	33	18	15.8	3.90	97	.281	.372	1	.048	-2	-0	-1	0	-0.1

■ ED BAUTA
Bauta, Eduardo (Galvez)   b: 1/6/35, Florida Camaguey, Cuba   BR/TR, 6'3", 200 lbs.   Deb: 7/06/60

YEAR TM/L	W	L	PCT	G	GS	CG	SH	SV	IP	H	HR	BB	SO	RAT	ERA	ERA+	OAV	OOB	BH	AVG	PB	PR	/A	PD	TPI
1960 StL-N	0	0	—	9	0	0	0	1	15²	14	4	11	6	14.9	6.32	65	.237	.366	0	.000	-0	-4	-4	-0	-0.3
1961 StL-N	2	0	1.000	13	0	0	0	5	19¹	12	2	5	12	7.9	1.40	315	.171	.227	2	.500	1	6	6	-0	0.7
1962 StL-N	1	0	1.000	20	0	0	0	1	32¹	28	5	21	25	13.9	5.01	85	.239	.360	1	.250	0	-4	-3	0	-0.1
1963 StL-N	3	4	.429	38	0	0	0	3	52²	55	2	21	30	13.3	3.93	90	.279	.355	0	.000	-1	-4	-4	-1	-0.3
NY-N	0	0	—	9	0	0	0	0	19	22	0	9	13	14.7	5.21	67	.289	.365	0	.000	-0	-4	-4	-0	-0.3
Yr	3	4	.429	47	0	0	0	3	71²	77	2	30	43	13.4	4.27	83	.278	.349	0	.000	-1	-8	-6	-1	-0.6
1964 NY-N	0	2	.000	8	0	0	0	1	10	17	1	3	3	18.0	5.40	66	.395	.435	0	—	0	-2	-2	1	-0.1
Total 5	6	6	.500	97	0	0	0	11	149	148	14	70	89	13.4	4.35	89	.263	.349	3	.176	-0	-13	-8	-1	-0.4

■ JOSE BAUTISTA
Bautista, Jose Joaquin (Arias)   b: 7/25/64, Bani, D.R.   BR/TR, 6'1", 177 lbs.   Deb: 4/09/88

YEAR TM/L	W	L	PCT	G	GS	CG	SH	SV	IP	H	HR	BB	SO	RAT	ERA	ERA+	OAV	OOB	BH	AVG	PB	PR	/A	PD	TPI
1988 Bal-A	6	15	.286	33	25	3	0	0	171²	171	21	45	76	11.7	4.30	91	.258	.311	0	—	0	-6	-8	-1	-0.7
1989 Bal-A	3	4	.429	15	10	0	0	0	78	84	17	15	30	11.5	5.31	71	.274	.310	0	—	0	-12	-13	-1	-1.2
1990 Bal-A	1	0	1.000	22	0	0	0	0	26²	28	4	7	15	11.8	4.05	94	.272	.318	0	—	0	-0	-1	-0	0.0
Total 3	10	19	.345	70	35	3	0	0	276¹	283	42	67	121	11.7	4.56	85	.264	.312	0	—	0	-19	-21	-2	-1.9

■ BILL BAYNE
Bayne, William Lear "Beverly"   b: 4/18/1899, Pittsburgh, Pa.   d: 5/22/81, St.Louis, Mo.   BL/TL, 5'9", 160 lbs.   Deb: 9/20/19

YEAR TM/L	W	L	PCT	G	GS	CG	SH	SV	IP	H	HR	BB	SO	RAT	ERA	ERA+	OAV	OOB	BH	AVG	PB	PR	/A	PD	TPI
1919 StL-A	1	1	.500	2	2	1	0	0	12	16	0	6	0	16.5	5.25	63	.320	.393	2	.400	0	-3	-3	0	-0.1
1920 StL-A	5	6	.455	18	13	6	1	0	99²	102	3	41	38	13.5	3.70	106	.279	.363	6	.171	-2	1	2	-2	-0.1
1921 StL-A	11	5	.688	47	14	6	1	3	164	167	8	80	82	13.8	4.72	95	.270	.358	18	.300	5	-8	-4	-1	0.0
1922 StL-A	4	5	.444	26	9	3	0	2	92²	86	5	37	38	12.8	4.56	91	.249	.338	7	.233	-1	-5	-4	-2	-0.6
1923 StL-A	2	2	.500	19	2	0	0	0	46	49	4	31	15	16.2	4.50	93	.287	.405	3	.231	-0	-3	-2	-1	-0.2
1924 StL-A	1	3	.250	22	3	0	0	0	50²	47	4	29	20	14.9	4.44	102	.250	.373	6	.429	3	-1	0	-1	0.2
1928 Cle-A	2	5	.286	37	6	3	0	3	108²	128	3	43	39	15.0	5.13	81	.309	.388	11	.367	3	-13	-12	2	-0.7
1929 Bos-A	5	5	.500	27	6	2	0	0	84¹	111	9	29	26	15.8	6.72	64	.326	.392	8	.320	2	-23	-23	1	-1.7
1930 Bos-A	0	0	—	1	0	0	0	0	4	5	1	1	1	13.5	4.50	102	.294	.333	1	.500	1	0	0	0	0.0
Total 9	31	32	.492	199	55	21	2	8	662	711	37	297	259	14.4	4.84	87	.283	.370	62	.290	11	-55	-45	-4	-3.2

■ WALTER BEALL
Beall, Walter Esau   b: 7/29/1899, Washington, D.C.   d: 1/28/59, Suitland, Md.   BR/TR, 5'10", 178 lbs.   Deb: 9/03/24

YEAR TM/L	W	L	PCT	G	GS	CG	SH	SV	IP	H	HR	BB	SO	RAT	ERA	ERA+	OAV	OOB	BH	AVG	PB	PR	/A	PD	TPI
1924 NY-A	2	0	1.000	4	2	0	0	0	23	19	2	17	18	14.1	3.52	118	.237	.371	1	.143	-1	2	2	-1	0.0
1925 NY-A	0	1	.000	8	1	0	0	0	11¹	11	0	19	8	26.2	12.71	34	.282	.541	0	.000	-1	-10	-11	0	-0.9
1926 NY-A	2	4	.333	20	9	1	0	1	81²	71	2	68	56	16.0	3.53	109	.240	.392	3	.136	-1	4	3	0	0.3
1927 NY-A	0	0	—	1	0	0	0	0	1	1	0	0	0	9.0	9.00	43	.333	.333	0	—	0	-1	-1	0	0.0
1929 Was-A	1	0	1.000	3	0	0	0	0	7	8	0	7	3	19.3	3.86	110	.348	.500	0	.000	-1	0	0	0	0.0
Total 5	5	5	.500	36	12	1	0	1	124	110	4	111	85	16.7	4.43	90	.249	.410	4	.114	-1	-4	-6	-1	-0.6

■ ALEX BEAM
Beam, Alexander Rodger   b: 11/21/1870, Johnstown, Pa.   d: 4/17/38, Nogales, Ariz.   Deb: 5/25/1889

YEAR TM/L	W	L	PCT	G	GS	CG	SH	SV	IP	H	HR	BB	SO	RAT	ERA	ERA+	OAV	OOB	BH	AVG	PB	PR	/A	PD	TPI
1889 Pit-N	1	1	.500	2	2	2	0	0	18	11	0	15	1	13.0	6.50	58	.171	.327	1	.167	0	-5	-5	-0	-0.3

■ ERNIE BEAM
Beam, Ernest Joseph   b: 3/17/1867, Mansfield, Ohio   d: 9/12/18, Mansfield, Ohio   185 lbs.   Deb: 5/02/1895

YEAR TM/L	W	L	PCT	G	GS	CG	SH	SV	IP	H	HR	BB	SO	RAT	ERA	ERA+	OAV	OOB	BH	AVG	PB	PR	/A	PD	TPI
1895 Phi-N	0	2	.000	9	1	1	0	3	24²	33	1	25	3	21.2	11.31	42	.316	.448	2	.182	-1	-18	-18	-0	-1.3

■ CHARLIE BEAMON
Beamon, Charles Alfonzo Sr.   b: 12/25/34, Oakland, Cal.   BR/TR, 5'11", 195 lbs.   Deb: 9/26/56

YEAR TM/L	W	L	PCT	G	GS	CG	SH	SV	IP	H	HR	BB	SO	RAT	ERA	ERA+	OAV	OOB	BH	AVG	PB	PR	/A	PD	TPI
1956 Bal-A	2	0	1.000	2	1	1	1	0	13	9	0	8	14	11.8	1.38	283	.191	.309	0	.000	-1	4	4	0	0.3
1957 Bal-A	0	0	—	4	1	0	0	0	8²	8	1	7	5	16.6	5.19	69	.229	.372	0	.000	-0	-1	-2	0	-0.1
1958 Bal-A	1	3	.250	21	3	0	0	0	49²	47	3	21	26	13.4	4.35	83	.266	.363	0	.000	-1	-3	-4	2	-0.2
Total 3	3	3	.500	27	5	1	1	0	71¹	64	4	36	45	13.5	3.91	93	.247	.354	0	.000	-2	-1	-2	2	0.0

■ BELVE BEAN
Bean, Beveric Benton "Bill"   b: 4/23/05, Mullin, Tex.   d: 6/1/88, Comanche, Tex.   BR/TR, 6'1.5", 197 lbs.   Deb: 5/30/30

YEAR TM/L	W	L	PCT	G	GS	CG	SH	SV	IP	H	HR	BB	SO	RAT	ERA	ERA+	OAV	OOB	BH	AVG	PB	PR	/A	PD	TPI
1930 Cle-A	3	3	.500	23	3	1	0	2	74¹	99	7	32	19	15.9	5.45	89	.331	.396	9	.346	2	-7	-5	0	-0.2
1931 Cle-A	0	1	.000	4	0	0	0	0	7	11	0	4	3	20.6	6.43	72	.379	.471	0	.000	-0	-2	-1	0	0.0
1933 Cle-A	1	2	.333	27	2	0	0	0	70¹	80	6	20	41	12.9	5.25	85	.300	.351	4	.182	-1	-8	-6	0	-0.5
1934 Cle-A	5	1	.833	21	1	0	0	0	51¹	53	2	21	20	13.5	3.86	118	.265	.344	3	.200	0	4	4	1	0.4
1935 Cle-A	0	0	—	1	0	0	0	0	1	2	1	0	0	18.0	9.00	50	.400	.400	0	—	0	-1	-0	0	0.0
Was-A	2	0	1.000	10	2	0	0	0	31	43	5	19	6	18.0	7.26	60	.339	.425	3	.375	2	-10	-10	-1	-0.6
Yr	2	0	1.000	11	2	0	0	0	32	45	6	19	6	18.0	7.31	59	.341	.424	3	.125	2	-10	-11	-1	-0.6
Total 5	11	7	.611	86	8	1	0	2	235	288	21	96	89	14.9	5.32	86	.311	.378	19	.264	4	-22	-19	1	-0.9

■ DAVE BEARD
Beard, Charles David   b: 10/2/59, Atlanta, Ga.   BL/TR, 6'5", 190 lbs.   Deb: 7/16/80

YEAR TM/L	W	L	PCT	G	GS	CG	SH	SV	IP	H	HR	BB	SO	RAT	ERA	ERA+	OAV	OOB	BH	AVG	PB	PR	/A	PD	TPI
1980 Oak-A	0	1	.000	13	0	0	0	1	16	12	0	7	12	11.3	3.38	112	.218	.317	0	—	0	1	1	-0	0.1
1981 *Oak-A	1	1	.500	8	0	0	0	3	13	9	1	4	15	9.7	2.77	126	.191	.269	0	—	0	1	1	0	0.1
1982 Oak-A	10	9	.526	54	2	0	0	11	91²	85	9	35	73	11.9	3.44	114	.244	.315	0	—	0	6	5	-1	0.4
1983 Oak-A	5	5	.500	43	0	0	0	10	61	55	8	36	40	13.7	5.61	69	.246	.355	0	—	0	-10	-12	-1	-1.2
1984 Sea-A	3	2	.600	43	0	0	0	5	76	88	15	33	40	14.8	5.80	69	.291	.369	0	—	0	-15	-15	-0	-1.4
1985 Chi-N	0	0	—	9	0	0	0	0	12²	16	2	7	4	16.3	6.39	62	.314	.397	0	—	0	-4	-3	0	-0.3
1989 Det-A	0	2	.000	2	1	0	0	0	5¹	9	2	2	1	20.3	5.06	75	.375	.444	0	—	0	-1	-1	0	0.0
Total 7	19	20	.487	172	3	0	0	30	275²	274	37	124	185	13.3	4.70	83	.261	.344	0	—	0	-21	-25	-2	-2.3

■ MIKE BEARD
Beard, Michael Richard   b: 6/21/50, Little Rock, Ark.   BL/TL, 6'1", 185 lbs.   Deb: 9/07/74

YEAR TM/L	W	L	PCT	G	GS	CG	SH	SV	IP	H	HR	BB	SO	RAT	ERA	ERA+	OAV	OOB	BH	AVG	PB	PR	/A	PD	TPI
1974 Atl-N	0	0	—	6	0	0	0	0	9¹	5	1	1	7	6.8	2.89	131	.156	.206	0	—	0	1	1	0	0.1
1975 Atl-N	4	0	1.000	34	2	0	0	0	70¹	71	4	28	27	12.9	3.20	118	.265	.339	1	.111	-0	3	4	0	0.5
1976 Atl-N	0	2	.000	30	0	0	0	1	33²	38	1	14	8	13.9	4.28	89	.293	.369	0	.000	-0	-3	-2	1	0.0
1977 Atl-N	0	0	—	4	0	0	0	0	4²	14	3	2	1	30.9	9.64	46	.452	.485	0	—	0	-3	-3	0	-0.2
Total 4	4	2	.667	74	2	0	0	1	118	128	9	45	43	13.4	3.74	102	.279	.348	1	.100	-0	-2	1	2	0.4

YEAR TM/L	W	L	PCT	G	GS	CG	SH	SV	IP	H	HR	BB	SO	RAT	ERA	ERA+	OAV	OOB	BH	AVG	PB	PR	/A	PD	TPI

■ RALPH BEARD Beard, Ralph William b: 2/11/29, Cincinnati, Ohio BR/TR, 6'5", 200 lbs. Deb: 6/29/54

| 1954 StL-N | 0 | 4 | .000 | 13 | 10 | 0 | 0 | 0 | 58 | 62 | 2 | 28 | 17 | 14.3 | 3.72 | 110 | .278 | .364 | 1 | .059 | -1 | 2 | 2 | -1 | 0.0 |

■ GENE BEARDEN Bearden, Henry Eugene b: 9/5/20, Lexa, Ark. BL/TL, 6'3", 198 lbs. Deb: 5/10/47

1947 Cle-A	0	0	—	1	0	0	0	0	0¹	2	0	1	0	81.0	81.00	4	.667	.750	0	—	0	-3	-3	0	-0.2
1948 •Cle-A	20	7	.741	37	29	15	6	1	229²	187	9	106	80	11.6	**2.43**	**167**	.229	.320	23	.256	5	47	**42**	4	5.2
1949 Cle-A	8	8	.500	32	19	5	0	0	127	140	6	92	41	16.6	5.10	78	.286	.401	5	.111	-3	-13	-16	4	-1.3
1950 Cle-A	1	3	.250	14	3	0	0	0	45¹	57	5	32	10	17.7	6.15	70	.328	.432	2	.154	1	-8	-9	-0	-0.7
Was-A	3	5	.375	12	9	4	0	0	68¹	81	1	33	20	15.3	4.21	107	.297	.377	3	.227	1	3	2	0	0.3
Yr	4	8	.333	26	12	4	0	0	113²	138	6	65	30	16.2	4.99	89	.309	.399	5	.143	2	-5	-7	0	-0.4
1951 Was-A	0	0	—	1	1	0	0	0	2²	6	0	2	1	27.0	16.88	24	.429	.500	0	—	0	-4	-4	0	-0.2
Det-A	3	4	.429	37	4	2	1	0	106	112	6	58	38	14.5	4.33	96	.275	.366	6	.188	1	-2	-2	0	0.0
Yr	3	4	.429	38	5	2	1	0	108²	118	6	60	39	14.8	4.64	90	.280	.371	6	.000	1	-6	-6	0	-0.2
1952 StL-A	7	8	.467	34	16	3	0	0	150²	158	13	78	45	14.2	4.30	91	.270	.357	23	.354	6	-10	-6	1	0.1
1953 Chi-A	3	3	.500	25	3	0	0	0	58¹	48	8	33	24	12.5	2.93	137	.223	.327	4	.190	-1	7	7	0	0.7
Total 7	45	38	.542	193	84	29	7	1	788¹	791	48	435	259	14.1	3.96	103	.266	.361	68	.236	10	17	12	9	3.9

■ GARY BEARE Beare, Gary Ray b: 8/22/52, San Diego, Cal. BR/TR, 6'4", 205 lbs. Deb: 9/07/76

1976 Mil-A	2	3	.400	6	5	2	0	0	41	43	4	15	32	12.7	3.29	106	.274	.337	0	—	0	1	1	-0	0.0
1977 Mil-A	3	3	.500	17	6	0	0	0	58²	63	6	38	32	15.6	6.44	63	.276	.382	0	—	0	-16	-15	2	-1.2
Total 2	5	6	.455	23	11	2	0	0	99²	106	10	53	64	14.4	5.15	74	.275	.364	0	—	0	-15	-15	1	-1.2

■ LARRY BEARNARTH Bearnarth, Lawrence Donald b: 9/11/41, New York, N.Y. BR/TR, 6'2", 203 lbs. Deb: 4/16/63 C

1963 NY-N	3	8	.273	58	2	0	0	4	126¹	127	7	47	48	12.8	3.42	102	.268	.340	6	.200	1	-2	-1	3	0.6
1964 NY-N	5	5	.500	44	1	0	0	3	78	79	6	38	31	13.7	4.15	86	.271	.360	2	.143	-0	-5	-5	3	-0.1
1965 NY-N	3	5	.375	40	3	0	0	1	60²	75	6	28	16	15.9	4.60	77	.304	.384	1	.111	-0	-7	-7	1	-0.6
1966 NY-N	2	3	.400	29	1	0	0	0	54²	59	11	20	27	13.2	4.45	82	.281	.346	1	.111	-0	-5	-5	1	-0.3
1971 Mil-A	0	0	—	2	0	0	0	0	3	10	1	2	2	36.0	18.00	19	.556	.600	0	—	0	-5	-5	0	-0.3
Total 5	13	21	.382	173	7	0	0	8	322²	350	31	135	124	13.9	4.13	86	.282	.358	10	.161	1	-24	-21	8	-0.7

■ KEVIN BEARSE Bearse, Kevin Gerard b: 11/7/65, Jersey City, N.J. BL/TL, 6'2", 195 lbs. Deb: 4/15/90

| 1990 Cle-A | 0 | 2 | .000 | 3 | 3 | 0 | 0 | 0 | 7² | 16 | 2 | 5 | 2 | 27.0 | 12.91 | 31 | .421 | .511 | 0 | — | 0 | -8 | -8 | 0 | -0.6 |

■ ED BEATIN Beatin, Ebenezer Ambrose b: 8/10/1866, Baltimore, Md. d: 5/9/25, Baltimore, Md. BR/TL, 5'9", 162 lbs. Deb: 8/02/1887

1887 Det-N	1	1	.500	2	2	2	0	0	18	13	2	8	6	10.5	4.00	101	.197	.283	0	.000	-1	0	0	-0	0.0
1888 Det-N	5	7	.417	12	12	12	1	0	107	111	6	16	44	10.7	2.86	96	.258	.285	14	.250	5	-0	-1	0	0.5
1889 Cle-N	20	15	.571	36	36	35	3	0	317²	316	12	141	126	12.9	3.57	113	.251	.327	14	.116	-5	16	16	-2	0.8
1890 Cle-N	22	30	.423	54	54	53	1	0	474¹	518	11	186	155	13.4	3.83	93	.270	.334	27	.141	-9	-14	-14	2	-1.7
1891 Cle-N	0	3	.000	5	4	2	0	0	29	39	1	21	4	18.6	5.28	66	.310	.409	1	.077	-2	-6	-6	0	-0.5
Total 5	48	56	.462	109	108	104	5	0	946	997	32	372	335	13.0	3.68	99	.262	.328	56	.144	-12	-5	-5	1	-0.9

■ JIM BEATTIE Beattie, James Louis b: 7/4/54, Hampton, Va. BR/TR, 6'5", 210 lbs. Deb: 4/25/78

1978 •NY-A	6	9	.400	25	22	0	0	0	128	123	8	51	65	12.8	3.73	97	.255	.336	0	—	0	1	-2	1	0.0
1979 NY-A	3	6	.333	15	13	1	1	0	76	85	5	41	32	14.9	5.21	78	.294	.382	0	—	0	-8	-10	1	-0.7
1980 Sea-A	5	15	.250	33	29	3	0	0	187¹	205	19	98	67	14.7	4.85	85	.286	.375	0	—	0	-17	-15	0	-1.3
1981 Sea-A	3	2	.600	13	9	0	0	1	66²	59	2	18	36	10.7	2.97	130	.232	.288	0	—	0	5	7	0	0.7
1982 Sea-A	8	12	.400	28	26	6	1	0	172¹	149	13	65	140	11.2	3.34	127	.233	.305	0	—	0	14	17	0	1.8
1983 Sea-A	10	15	.400	30	29	8	2	0	196²	197	12	66	132	12.2	3.84	111	.259	.321	0	—	0	5	9	3	1.3
1984 Sea-A	12	16	.429	32	32	12	2	0	211	206	13	75	119	12.2	3.41	117	.260	.328	0	—	0	14	13	1	1.5
1985 Sea-A	5	6	.455	18	15	1	1	0	70¹	93	9	33	45	16.5	7.29	58	.316	.391	0	—	0	-25	-24	-1	-2.2
1986 Sea-A	0	6	.000	9	7	0	0	0	40¹	57	7	14	24	16.5	6.02	70	.341	.402	0	—	0	-8	-8	1	-0.6
Total 9	52	87	.374	203	182	31	7	1	1148²	1174	88	461	660	13.0	4.17	98	.267	.341	0	—	0	-20	-12	8	0.5

■ BLAINE BEATTY Beatty, Gordon Blaine b: 4/25/64, Victoria, Tex. BL/TL, 6'2", 185 lbs. Deb: 9/16/89

| 1989 NY-N | 0 | 0 | — | 2 | 1 | 0 | 0 | 0 | 6 | 5 | 1 | 2 | 3 | 10.5 | 1.50 | 218 | .217 | .280 | 1 | .500 | 0 | 1 | 1 | 0 | 0.2 |

■ JOHNNY BEAZLEY Beazley, John Andrew "Nig" b: 5/25/18, Nashville, Tenn. d: 4/21/90, Nashville, Tenn. BR/TR, 6'1.5", 190 lbs. Deb: 9/28/41

1941 StL-N	1	0	1.000	1	1	1	0	0	9	10	0	3	4	13.0	1.00	376	.294	.351	0	.000	-0	3	3	-0	0.3
1942 •StL-N	21	6	.778	43	23	13	3	3	215¹	181	4	73	91	10.7	2.13	161	.226	.293	10	.137	-1	28	31	1	3.5
1946 •StL-N	7	5	.583	19	18	5	0	0	103	109	6	55	36	14.7	4.46	77	.275	.368	8	.242	1	-12	-11	-0	-1.0
1947 Bos-N	2	0	1.000	9	2	2	0	0	28²	30	1	19	12	15.4	4.40	89	.273	.380	0	.000	-1	-1	-2	0	-0.2
1948 Bos-N	0	1	.000	3	2	0	0	0	16	19	2	7	4	14.6	4.50	85	.284	.351	0	.000	-0	-1	-1	-0	-0.1
1949 Bos-N	0	0	—	1	0	0	0	0	2	0	0	0	0	0.0	0.00	—	.000	.000	0	—	0	1	1	0	0.1
Total 6	31	12	.721	76	46	21	3	3	374	349	13	157	147	12.3	3.01	116	.247	.325	18	.150	-1	18	20	0	2.6

■ BUCK BECANNON Becannon, James Melvin b: 8/22/1859, New York, N.Y. d: 11/5/23, New York, N.Y. 5'10", 165 lbs. Deb: 10/15/1884 ◆

1884 •NY-a	1	0	1.000	1	1	0	0	0	6	2	0	2	2	6.0	1.50	208	.098	.179	0	.000	-0	1	1	0	0.1
1885 NY-a	2	8	.200	10	10	10	0	0	85	108	5	24	13	14.0	6.25	47	.297	.340	10	.303	2	-28	-31	1	-2.2
Total 2	3	8	.273	11	11	11	0	0	91	110	5	26	15	13.5	5.93	50	.286	.331	10	.244	1	-27	-30	1	-2.1

■ GEORGE BECHTEL Bechtel, George A. b: 1848, Philadelphia, Pa. 5'11", 165 lbs. Deb: 5/20/1871 ◆

1871 Ath-n	1	2	.333	3	3	2	0	0	26	43	0	11	1	18.7	7.96	51	.319	.370	33	.351	1	-11	-11		-0.6
1873 Phi-n	0	2	.000	3	2	1	0	0	16	27	0	2		16.3	5.63	65	.318	.333	61	.237	0	-4	-4		-0.1
1874 Phi-n	1	3	.250	6	4	4	0	0	42	64	0	0		13.7	3.86	79	.320	.320	44	.291	1	-4	-4		-0.2
1875 Cen-n	2	12	.143	14	14	14	0	0	126	170	0	3		12.4	3.93	61	.277	.281	17	.274	3	-21	-21		-1.4
Ath-n	3	1	.750	4	4	4	0	0	36	45	0	3		12.0	2.25	117	.298	.312	46	.280	0	1	2		0.1
Yr	5	13	.278	18	18	18	0	0	162	215	0	6		12.3	3.56	69	.281	.287	1	.004	3	-20	-20		-1.3
Total 4 n	7	20	.259	30	27	25	0	0	246	349	0	19	1	13.5	4.21	58	.295	.306	275	.282	6	-48	-48		-2.2

■ GEORGE BECK Beck, Ernest George B. b: 2/21/1890, South Bend, Ind. d: 10/29/73, South Bend, Ind. BR/TR, 5'11", 165 lbs. Deb: 5/15/14

| 1914 Cle-A | 0 | 0 | — | 1 | 0 | 0 | 0 | 0 | 1 | 1 | 0 | 0 | 0 | 18.0 | 0.00 | — | .250 | .400 | 0 | — | 0 | 0 | 0 | 0 | 0.0 |

■ FRANK BECK Beck, Frank J. b: 1862, Poughkeepsie, N.Y. TR , Deb: 5/02/1884 ◆

| 1884 Pit-a | 0 | 3 | .000 | 3 | 3 | 3 | 0 | 0 | 25 | 33 | 0 | 6 | 11 | 14.0 | 6.12 | 55 | .301 | .338 | 4 | .333 | 1 | -8 | -8 | 0 | -0.5 |
| Bal-U | 0 | 2 | .000 | 2 | 2 | 1 | 0 | 0 | 9 | 17 | 0 | 4 | 7 | 21.0 | 8.00 | 41 | .378 | .429 | 2 | .100 | -1 | -5 | -5 | 0 | -0.3 |

■ RICH BECK Beck, Richard Henry b: 1/21/41, Pasco, Wash. BB/TR, 6'3", 190 lbs. Deb: 9/14/65

| 1965 NY-A | 2 | 1 | .667 | 3 | 3 | 1 | 1 | 0 | 21 | 22 | 1 | 7 | 10 | 12.4 | 2.14 | 159 | .275 | .333 | 0 | .000 | -0 | 3 | 3 | 1 | 0.3 |

■ BOOM-BOOM BECK Beck, Walter William b: 10/16/04, Decatur, Ill. d: 5/7/87, Champaign, Ill. BR/TR, 6'2", 200 lbs. Deb: 9/22/24 C

1924 StL-A	0	0	—	1	0	0	0	0	1	2	0	1	0	27.0	0.00	—	.667	.750	0	—	0	0	1	0	0.1
1927 StL-A	1	0	1.000	3	1	1	0	0	11¹	15	0	5	6	16.7	5.56	78	.333	.412	1	.250	-0	-2	-2	0	-0.1
1928 StL-A	2	3	.400	16	4	2	0	0	49	52	4	20	17	14.0	4.41	95	.289	.373	6	.429	1	-2	-1	0	0.0
1933 Bro-N	12	20	.375	43	35	15	3	1	257	270	9	69	89	12.3	3.54	91	.267	.321	18	.189	-0	-6	-9	-1	-0.9
1934 Bro-N	2	6	.250	22	9	2	0	0	57	72	6	32	24	17.2	7.42	53	.301	.395	4	.235	1	-21	-22	1	-1.8
1939 Phi-N	7	14	.333	34	16	12	0	3	182²	203	11	64	77	13.3	4.73	85	.284	.345	9	.132	-3	-16	-15	-0	-1.6

YEAR TM/L	W	L	PCT	G	GS	CG	SH	SV	IP	H	HR	BB	SO	RAT	ERA	ERA+	OAV	OOB	BH	AVG	PB	PR	/A	PD	TPI
1940 Phi-N	4	9	.308	29	15	4	0	0	129¹	147	13	41	38	13.7	4.31	90	.286	.349	2	.056	-3	-7	-6	1	-0.7
1941 Phi-N	1	9	.100	34	7	2	0	0	95¹	104	8	35	34	13.3	4.63	80	.276	.341	3	.120	-2	-11	-10	-3	-1.3
1942 Phi-N	0	1	.000	26	1	0	0	0	53	69	4	17	10	14.8	4.75	70	.325	.378	4	.333	1	-8	-9	-0	-0.7
1943 Phi-N	0	0	—	4	0	0	0	0	13²	24	1	5	3	20.4	9.88	34	.393	.456	2	.500	1	-10	-10	-0	-0.8
1944 Det-A	1	2	.333	28	2	0	0	1	74	67	5	27	25	11.8	3.89	92	.243	.317	7	.318	2	-4	-3	-2	-0.2
1945 Cin-N	2	4	.333	11	5	2	0	1	47²	42	0	12	9	10.4	3.40	111	.236	.288	3	.214	-0	2	2	0	0.2
Pit-N	6	1	.857	14	5	4	0	0	63	54	2	14	20	9.7	2.14	184	.234	.278	2	.125	-1	12	13	-0	1.2
Yr	8	5	.615	25	10	6	0	1	110²	96	2	26	29	9.9	2.68	144	.234	.280	1	.033	-1	14	15	-0	1.4
Total 12	38	69	.355	265	100	44	3	6	1034	1121	63	342	352	13.1	4.30	86	.277	.340	61	.187	-2	-72	-71	-3	-6.6

■ CHARLIE BECKER
Becker, Charles S. "Buck" b: 10/14/1888, Washington, D.C. d: 7/30/28, Washington, D. C. BL/TL, 6'2", 180 lbs. Deb: 8/02/11

YEAR TM/L	W	L	PCT	G	GS	CG	SH	SV	IP	H	HR	BB	SO	RAT	ERA	ERA+	OAV	OOB	BH	AVG	PB	PR	/A	PD	TPI
1911 Was-A	3	5	.375	11	5	5	1	0	71¹	80	2	23	31	13.9	4.04	81	.268	.335	5	.227	-0	-5	-6	-0	-0.5
1912 Was-A	0	0	—	4	0	0	0	0	9	8	0	6	5	14.0	3.00	111	.258	.378	1	.500	0	0	0	-0	0.0
Total 2	3	5	.375	15	5	5	1	0	80¹	88	2	29	36	13.9	3.92	84	.267	.340	6	.250	0	-5	-6	-0	-0.5

■ BOB BECKER
Becker, Robert Charles b: 8/15/1875, Syracuse, N.Y. d: 10/11/51, Syracuse, N.Y. Deb: 9/06/1897

YEAR TM/L	W	L	PCT	G	GS	CG	SH	SV	IP	H	HR	BB	SO	RAT	ERA	ERA+	OAV	OOB	BH	AVG	PB	PR	/A	PD	TPI
1897 Phi-N	0	2	.000	5	2	2	0	0	24	32	0	7	10	14.6	5.63	75	.317	.361	1	.111	-0	-3	-4	-0	-0.3
1898 Phi-N	0	0	—	1	0	0	0	0	5	6	0	5	0	19.8	10.80	32	.295	.434	0	.000	-0	-4	-4	0	-0.2
Total 2	0	2	.000	6	2	2	0	0	29	38	0	12	10	15.5	6.52	62	.313	.375	1	.100	-0	-7	-8	-0	-0.5

■ JAKE BECKLEY
Beckley, Jacob Peter "Eagle Eye" b: 8/4/1867, Hannibal, Mo. d: 6/25/18, Kansas City, Mo. BL/TL, 5'10", 200 lbs. Deb: 6/20/1888 H♦

YEAR TM/L	W	L	PCT	G	GS	CG	SH	SV	IP	H	HR	BB	SO	RAT	ERA	ERA+	OAV	OOB	BH	AVG	PB	PR	/A	PD	TPI
1902 Cin-N	0	1	.000	1	1	0	0	0	4	9	0	1	2	22.5	6.75	44	.442	.468	175	.330	0	-2	-2	1	-0.1

■ JIM BECKMAN
Beckman, James Joseph b: 3/1/05, Cincinnati, Ohio BR/TR, 5'10", 172 lbs. Deb: 7/27/27

YEAR TM/L	W	L	PCT	G	GS	CG	SH	SV	IP	H	HR	BB	SO	RAT	ERA	ERA+	OAV	OOB	BH	AVG	PB	PR	/A	PD	TPI
1927 Cin-N	0	1	.000	4	1	0	0	0	12¹	18	2	6	0	18.2	5.84	65	.340	.417	0	.000	0	-3	-3	-1	-0.2
1928 Cin-N	0	1	.000	6	0	0	0	0	15¹	19	1	9	4	16.4	5.87	67	.306	.394	0	.000	-0	-3	-3	-0	-0.3
Total 2	0	2	.000	10	1	0	0	0	27²	37	3	15	4	17.2	5.86	66	.322	.405	0	.000	-0	-6	-6	-1	-0.5

■ BILL BECKMANN
Beckmann, William Aloysius b: 12/8/07, Clayton, Mo. d: 1/2/90, Florissant, Mo. BR/TR, 6', 175 lbs. Deb: 5/02/39

YEAR TM/L	W	L	PCT	G	GS	CG	SH	SV	IP	H	HR	BB	SO	RAT	ERA	ERA+	OAV	OOB	BH	AVG	PB	PR	/A	PD	TPI
1939 Phi-A	7	11	.389	27	19	7	2	0	155¹	198	4	41	20	13.9	5.39	87	.312	.355	13	.250	0	-13	-12	-1	-1.0
1940 Phi-A	8	4	.667	34	19	6	2	1	127¹	132	11	35	47	11.9	4.17	107	.265	.314	8	.205	-1	3	4	-2	0.1
1941 Phi-A	5	9	.357	22	15	4	0	1	130	141	11	33	28	12.2	4.57	92	.270	.315	9	.191	0	-6	-6	-3	-0.7
1942 Phi-A	0	1	.000	5	1	0	0	0	20¹	24	1	9	10	14.6	7.08	53	.289	.359	2	.500	1	-8	-7	-0	-0.5
StL-N	1	0	1.000	2	0	0	0	0	7	4	0	1	3	6.4	0.00	—	.200	.238	0	.000	-0	3	3	0	0.3
Total 4	21	25	.457	90	44	17	4	2	440	499	38	119	108	12.7	4.79	92	.284	.330	32	.224	1	-22	-18	-6	-1.8

■ JOE BECKWITH
Beckwith, Thomas Joseph b: 1/28/55, Opelika, Ala. BL/TR, 6'3", 200 lbs. Deb: 7/21/79

YEAR TM/L	W	L	PCT	G	GS	CG	SH	SV	IP	H	HR	BB	SO	RAT	ERA	ERA+	OAV	OOB	BH	AVG	PB	PR	/A	PD	TPI
1979 LA-N	1	2	.333	17	0	0	0	2	37¹	42	4	15	28	13.7	4.34	84	.284	.350	0	.000	-1	-3	-3	0	-0.3
1980 LA-N	3	3	.500	38	0	0	0	0	59²	60	1	23	40	12.7	1.96	178	.263	.333	0	.000	0	11	10	-1	1.0
1982 LA-N	2	1	.667	19	1	0	0	1	40	38	2	14	33	11.7	2.70	128	.252	.315	0	.000	-1	4	3	-1	0.2
1983 *LA-N	3	4	.429	42	3	0	0	1	71	73	5	35	50	13.8	3.55	101	.264	.348	1	.200	-1	1	0	1	0.1
1984 KC-A	8	4	.667	49	1	0	0	2	100²	92	13	25	75	10.6	3.40	119	.247	.298	0	—	0	7	7	0	0.7
1985 *KC-A	1	5	.167	49	0	0	0	1	95	99	9	32	80	12.7	4.07	102	.269	.333	0	—	0	1	1	-0	0.1
1986 LA-N	0	0	—	15	0	0	0	0	18¹	28	5	6	13	16.7	6.87	50	.350	.395	0	—	0	-6	-7	-0	-0.7
Total 7	18	19	.486	229	5	0	0	7	422	432	39	150	319	12.6	3.54	107	.266	.331	1	.053	-1	14	12	-1	1.1

■ JULIO BECQUER
Becquer, Julio (Villegas) b: 12/20/31, Havana, Cuba BL/TL, 5'11.5", 178 lbs. Deb: 9/13/55 ♦

YEAR TM/L	W	L	PCT	G	GS	CG	SH	SV	IP	H	HR	BB	SO	RAT	ERA	ERA+	OAV	OOB	BH	AVG	PB	PR	/A	PD	TPI
1960 Was-A	0	0	—	1	0	0	0	0	1	1	1	0	0	9.0	9.00	43	.250	.250	75	.252	0	-1	-1	0	0.0
1961 Min-A	0	0	—	1	0	0	0	0	1¹	4	0	1	0	33.8	20.25	21	.500	.556	20	.238	0	-2	-2	0	-0.1
Total 2	0	0	—	2	0	0	0	0	2¹	5	1	1	0	23.1	15.43	26	.417	.462	238	.244	0	-3	-3	0	-0.1

■ PHIL BEDGOOD
Bedgood, Phillip Burlette b: 3/8/1898, Harrison, Ga. d: 11/8/27, Fort Pierce, Fla. BR/TR, 6'3", 218 lbs. Deb: 9/20/22

YEAR TM/L	W	L	PCT	G	GS	CG	SH	SV	IP	H	HR	BB	SO	RAT	ERA	ERA+	OAV	OOB	BH	AVG	PB	PR	/A	PD	TPI
1922 Cle-A	1	0	1.000	1	1	0	0	0	9	7	0	4	5	14.0	4.00	100	.233	.378	0	.000	-0	0	0	-0	0.0
1923 Cle-A	0	2	.000	9	2	0	0	0	18²	16	0	14	7	15.4	5.30	75	.246	.395	1	.250	0	-3	-3	0	-0.1
Total 2	1	2	.333	10	3	1	0	0	27²	23	0	18	12	15.0	4.88	82	.242	.390	1	.167	0	-3	-3	-0	-0.1

■ HUGH BEDIENT
Bedient, Hugh Carpenter b: 10/23/1889, Gerry, N.Y. d: 7/21/65, Jamestown, N.Y. BR/TR, 6', 185 lbs. Deb: 4/26/12

YEAR TM/L	W	L	PCT	G	GS	CG	SH	SV	IP	H	HR	BB	SO	RAT	ERA	ERA+	OAV	OOB	BH	AVG	PB	PR	/A	PD	TPI
1912 *Bos-A	20	9	.690	41	28	19	0	2	231	206	6	55	122	10.3	2.92	116	.240	.288	14	.192	1	10	12	0	1.4
1913 Bos-A	15	14	.517	43	28	15	1	5	259	255	0	67	122	11.4	2.78	106	.261	.312	10	.125	-3	4	5	-4	-0.1
1914 Bos-A	8	12	.400	42	16	7	1	2	177¹	187	4	45	70	12.0	3.60	75	.281	.331	5	.100	-2	-17	-18	-0	-2.1
1915 Buf-F	16	18	.471	53	30	16	2	10	269¹	284	5	69	106	11.9	3.17	98	.274	.321	9	.108	-4	-4	-2	-2	-0.7
Total 4	59	53	.527	179	102	57	4	19	936²	932	15	236	420	11.4	3.08	99	.263	.312	38	.133	-8	-7	-3	-6	-1.5

■ ANDY BEDNAR
Bednar, Andrew Jackson b: 8/16/08, Streator, Ill. d: 11/26/37, Graham, Tex. BR/TR, 5'10.5", 180 lbs. Deb: 9/06/30

YEAR TM/L	W	L	PCT	G	GS	CG	SH	SV	IP	H	HR	BB	SO	RAT	ERA	ERA+	OAV	OOB	BH	AVG	PB	PR	/A	PD	TPI
1930 Pit-N	0	0	—	2	0	0	0	0	1¹	4	0	1	1	33.8	27.00	18	.500	.556	0	—	0	-3	-3	0	-0.2
1931 Pit-N	0	0	—	3	0	0	0	0	4	10	1	0	2	22.5	11.25	34	.476	.476	0	—	0	-3	-3	0	-0.2
Total 2	0	0	—	5	0	0	0	0	5¹	14	1	1	3	25.3	15.19	27	.483	.500	0	—	0	-7	-7	0	-0.4

■ STEVE BEDROSIAN
Bedrosian, Stephen Wayne b: 12/6/57, Methuen, Mass. BR/TR, 6'3", 200 lbs. Deb: 8/14/81

YEAR TM/L	W	L	PCT	G	GS	CG	SH	SV	IP	H	HR	BB	SO	RAT	ERA	ERA+	OAV	OOB	BH	AVG	PB	PR	/A	PD	TPI
1981 Atl-N	1	2	.333	15	1	0	0	0	24¹	15	2	15	9	11.5	4.44	81	.169	.295	0	.000	-0	-3	-2	-0	-0.2
1982 *Atl-N	8	6	.571	64	3	0	0	11	137²	102	7	57	123	10.7	2.42	154	.206	.293	1	.038	-2	18	20	-1	1.8
1983 Atl-N	9	10	.474	70	1	0	0	19	120	100	11	51	114	11.6	3.60	108	.229	.315	2	.105	-1	0	4	-0	0.2
1984 Atl-N	9	6	.600	40	4	0	0	11	83²	65	5	33	81	10.6	2.37	163	.210	.289	2	.118	-1	11	14	-1	1.3
1985 Atl-N	7	15	.318	37	37	0	0	0	206²	198	17	111	134	13.7	3.83	100	.254	.351	5	.078	-4	-6	-0	-2	-0.5
1986 Phi-N	8	6	.571	68	0	0	0	29	90¹	79	12	34	82	11.3	3.39	114	.232	.301	1	.200	0	3	5	-1	0.4
1987 Phi-N	5	3	.625	65	0	0	0	**40**	89	79	11	28	74	10.9	2.83	150	.237	.298	0	.000	-0	12	14	-2	1.2
1988 Phi-N	6	6	.500	57	0	0	0	28	74¹	75	6	27	61	12.3	3.75	95	.257	.320	0	.000	-0	-3	-2	-0	-0.1
1989 Phi-N	2	3	.400	28	0	0	0	6	33²	21	7	17	24	10.4	3.21	110	.183	.293	0	—	0	1	1	-0	0.1
*SF-N	1	4	.200	40	0	0	0	17	51	35	5	22	34	10.1	2.65	127	.192	.279	1	.167	-0	5	4	-1	0.3
Yr	3	7	.300	68	0	0	0	23	84²	56	12	39	58	10.1	2.87	120	.187	.280	0	.000	-0	6	5	-2	0.4
1990 SF-N	9	9	.500	68	0	0	0	17	79¹	72	6	44	43	13.4	4.20	89	.241	.342	2	.500	1	-4	-4	0	-0.2
Total 10	65	70	.481	552	46	0	0	178	990	841	89	439	779	11.8	3.31	115	.229	.315	14	.094	-8	37	54	-9	4.3

■ FRED BEEBE
Beebe, Frederick Leonard b: 12/31/1880, Lincoln, Neb. d: 10/30/57, Elgin, Ill. BR/TR, 6'1", 190 lbs. Deb: 4/17/06

YEAR TM/L	W	L	PCT	G	GS	CG	SH	SV	IP	H	HR	BB	SO	RAT	ERA	ERA+	OAV	OOB	BH	AVG	PB	PR	/A	PD	TPI
1906 Chi-N	6	1	.857	14	6	4	0	1	70	56	1	32	55	12.0	2.70	98	.210	.306	3	.103	-1	-1	-0	-2	-0.3
StL-N	9	9	.500	20	19	16	1	0	160²	115	1	68	116	10.8	3.02	87	.208	.305	10	.172	0	-7	-7	-1	-0.8
Yr	15	10	.600	34	25	20	1	1	230²	171	2	100	**171**	10.9	2.93	90	.207	.300	3	.034	-1	-7	-8	-3	-1.1
1907 StL-N	7	19	.269	31	29	24	4	0	238¹	192	1	109	141	11.7	2.72	92	.230	.326	11	.128	-3	-7	-6	-0	-0.8
1908 StL-N	5	13	.278	29	19	12	0	1	174¹	134	3	66	72	10.5	2.63	90	**.193**	.267	7	.125	-2	-5	-5	2	-0.6
1909 StL-N	15	21	.417	44	34	18	1	1	287²	256	5	104	105	11.5	2.82	90	.229	.299	18	.167	-2	-7	-9	0	-1.1
1910 Cin-N	12	14	.462	35	26	11	2	0	214¹	193	3	94	93	12.3	3.07	95	.246	.333	12	.164	-2	-4	4	3	-0.3
1911 Phi-N	3	3	.500	9	8	3	0	0	48¹	52	1	24	20	14.7	4.47	77	.297	.391	5	.263	2	-6	-6	1	-0.2
1916 Cle-A	5	3	.625	20	12	5	1	2	100²	92	1	37	32	11.6	2.41	125	.251	.321	6	.214	1	5	7	-0	0.8
Total 7	62	83	.428	202	153	93	9	4	1294¹	1090	17	534	634	11.6	2.86	93	.227	.311	72	.158	-8	-28	-30	3	-3.3

YEAR TM/L	W	L	PCT	G	GS	CG	SH	SV	IP	H	HR	BB	SO	RAT	ERA	ERA+	OAV	OOB	BH	AVG	PB	PR	/A	PD	TPI

■ ED BEECHER
Beecher, Edward H. b: 7/2/1860, Guilford, Conn. d: 9/12/35, Hartford, Conn. BL/TL, 5'10", 185 lbs. Deb: 6/28/1887 ♦

| 1890 Buf-P | 0 | 0 | — | 1 | 0 | 0 | 0 | 0 | 6 | 10 | 0 | 3 | 0 | 19.5 | 12.00 | 34 | .356 | .418 | 159 | .297 | 0 | -5 | -5 | -0 | -0.3 |

■ ROY BEECHER
Beecher, Leroy "Colonel" b: 5/10/1884, Swanton, Ohio d: 10/11/52, Toledo, Ohio BL/TR, 6'2", 180 lbs. Deb: 9/29/07

1907 NY-N	0	2	.000	2	2	2	0	0	14	17	0	6	5	14.8	2.57	96	.293	.359	-1	.000	-1	-0	-0	-0	0.0
1908 NY-N	0	0	—	2	0	0	0	1	5²	11	0	3	0	22.2	7.94	30	.440	.500	1	.333	1	-4	-3	0	-0.2
Total 2	0	2	.000	4	2	2	0	1	19²	28	0	9	5	16.9	4.12	60	.337	.402	1	.125	-0	-4	-4	0	-0.2

■ FRED BEENE
Beene, Freddy Ray b: 11/24/42, Angleton, Tex. BB/TR, 5'9", 155 lbs. Deb: 9/18/68

1968 Bal-A	0	0	—	1	0	0	0	0	1	2	0	1	1	27.0	9.00	33	.500	.600	0	—	0	-1	-1	0	0.0
1969 Bal-A	0	0	—	2	0	0	0	0	2²	2	0	1	0	10.1	0.00	—	.200	.273	0	—	0	1	1	0	0.1
1970 Bal-A	0	0	—	4	0	0	0	0	6	8	1	5	4	19.5	6.00	61	.320	.433	0	—	0	-2	-2	0	-0.1
1972 NY-A	1	3	.250	29	1	0	0	3	57²	55	3	24	37	12.5	2.34	126	.256	.333	0	.000	-1	5	4	-0	0.3
1973 NY-A	6	0	1.000	19	4	0	0	1	91	67	5	27	49	9.4	1.68	218	.209	.273	0	—	0	22	20	1	2.3
1974 NY-A	0	0	—	6	0	0	0	1	10	9	1	2	10	10.8	2.70	129	.231	.286	0	—	0	1	1	0	0.1
Cle-A	4	4	.500	32	0	0	0	2	73	68	7	26	35	11.7	4.93	73	.247	.315	0	—	0	-11	-11	1	-0.9
Yr	4	4	.500	38	0	0	0	3	83	77	8	28	45	11.5	4.66	77	.244	.308	0	—	0	-10	-10	1	-0.8
1975 Cle-A	1	0	1.000	19	1	0	0	1	46²	63	4	25	20	17.6	6.94	54	.323	.408	0	—	0	-16	-16	0	-1.5
Total 7	12	7	.632	112	6	0	0	8	288	274	21	111	156	12.3	3.63	97	.253	.326	0	.000	-1	-1	-4	2	0.3

■ ANDY BEENE
Beene, Ramon Andrew b: 10/13/56, Freeport, Tex. BR/TR, 6'3", 205 lbs. Deb: 9/22/83

1983 Mil-A	0	0	—	1	0	0	0	0	2	3	0	1	0	18.0	4.50	83	.333	.400	0	—	0	-0	-0	0	0.0
1984 Mil-A	0	2	.000	5	3	0	0	0	18²	28	1	9	11	18.8	11.09	35	.350	.429	0	—	0	-15	-15	0	-1.2
Total 2	0	2	.000	6	3	0	0	0	20²	31	1	10	11	18.7	10.45	37	.348	.426	0	—	0	-15	-15	0	-1.2

■ CLARENCE BEERS
Beers, Clarence Scott b: 12/9/18, ElDorado, Kan. BR/TR, 6', 175 lbs. Deb: 5/02/48

| 1948 StL-N | 0 | 0 | — | 1 | 0 | 0 | 0 | 0 | 0² | 3 | 0 | 1 | 0 | 54.0 | 13.50 | 30 | .500 | .571 | 0 | — | 0 | -1 | -1 | 0 | 0.0 |

■ JOE BEGGS
Beggs, Joseph Stanley "Fireman" b: 11/4/10, Rankin, Pa. d: 7/19/83, Indianapolis, Ind BR/TR, 6'1", 182 lbs. Deb: 4/19/38

1938 NY-A	3	2	.600	14	9	4	0	0	58¹	69	7	20	8	13.7	5.40	84	.299	.355	5	.250	1	-4	-6	2	-0.2
1940 *Cin-N	12	3	.800	37	1	0	0	7	76²	68	1	21	25	10.6	2.00	190	.243	.298	4	.190	-0	16	15	1	1.7
1941 Cin-N	4	3	.571	37	0	0	0	5	57	57	2	27	19	13.3	3.79	95	.313	.402	3	.300	1	-1	-1	0	0.0
1942 Cin-N	6	5	.545	38	0	0	0	8	88²	65	4	33	24	10.0	2.13	154	.206	.283	0	.000	-3	12	11	3	1.2
1943 Cin-N	7	6	.538	39	4	4	2	6	115¹	120	0	25	28	11.3	2.34	142	.274	.313	5	.143	-1	13	12	1	1.4
1944 Cin-N	1	0	1.000	1	1	1	0	0	9	8	0	0	2	8.0	2.00	174	.222	.222	0	.000	-1	2	1	0	0.1
1946 Cin-N	12	10	.545	28	22	14	2	1	190	175	15	39	38	10.2	2.32	144	.247	.287	14	.222	2	23	22	1	2.8
1947 Cin-N	0	3	.000	11	4	0	0	0	32¹	42	4	6	11	13.4	5.29	78	.316	.345	1	.091	-1	-4	-4	1	-0.3
NY-N	3	3	.500	32	0	0	0	2	66	81	6	18	23	13.6	4.23	96	.300	.346	1	.077	-1	-1	-1	0	-0.1
Yr	3	6	.333	43	4	0	0	2	98¹	123	10	24	34	13.5	4.58	89	.305	.346	0	.000	-2	-6	-5	1	-0.4
1948 NY-N	0	0	—	1	0	0	0	0	0¹	2	0	0	0	54.0	0.00	—	.667	.667	0	—	0	0	0	0	0.0
Total 9	48	35	.578	238	41	23	4	29	693²	687	39	189	178	11.4	2.96	122	.265	.315	33	.167	-3	55	50	10	6.6

■ ED BEGLEY
Begley, Edward N. (b: Edward N. Bagley) b: 1863, New York, N.Y. d: 7/24/19, Waterbury, Conn. Deb: 5/03/1884

1884 NY-N	12	18	.400	31	30	30	0	0	266	296	9	99	104	13.4	4.16	71	.267	.327	22	.182	-3	-35	-35	-1	-3.2
1885 NY-a	4	9	.308	15	14	10	0	0	115	131	5	48	44	14.0	4.93	60	.274	.341	9	.173	-0	-21	-25	1	-2.0
Total 2	16	27	.372	46	44	40	0	0	381	427	14	147	148	13.6	4.39	68	.269	.331	31	.179	-3	-56	-60	-0	-5.2

■ PETIE BEHAN
Behan, Charles Frederick b: 12/11/1887, Dallas City, Pa. d: 1/22/57, Bradford, Pa. BR/TR, 5'10", 160 lbs. Deb: 9/16/21

1921 Phi-N	0	1	.000	2	2	1	0	0	10²	17	0	1	3	15.2	5.91	72	.354	.367	0	.000	-1	-3	-2	-0	-0.2
1922 Phi-N	4	2	.667	7	5	3	1	0	47¹	49	3	14	13	12.2	2.47	189	.259	.314	5	.250	0	9	12	-1	1.1
1923 Phi-N	3	12	.200	31	17	5	0	2	131	182	11	57	27	16.5	5.50	84	.336	.401	8	.186	-2	-22	-13	-1	-1.3
Total 3	7	15	.318	40	24	9	1	2	189	248	14	72	43	15.3	4.76	97	.319	.378	13	.194	-3	-16	-3	-2	-0.4

■ RICK BEHENNA
Behenna, Richard Kipp b: 3/6/60, Miami, Fla. BR/TR, 6'2", 170 lbs. Deb: 4/12/83

1983 Atl-N	3	3	.500	14	6	0	0	0	37¹	37	7	12	17	12.1	4.58	85	.255	.316	4	.333	2	-4	-3	-0	0.0
Cle-A	0	2	.000	5	4	0	0	0	26	22	0	14	9	12.8	4.15	102	.232	.336	0	—	0	-0	0	0	0.1
1984 Cle-A	0	3	.000	3	3	0	0	0	9²	17	5	8	6	24.2	13.97	29	.386	.491	0	—	0	-11	-11	-0	-0.8
1985 Cle-A	0	2	.000	4	4	0	0	0	19²	29	3	8	4	16.9	7.78	53	.354	.411	0	—	0	-8	-8	-0	-0.7
Total 3	3	10	.231	26	17	0	0	0	92²	105	15	42	36	14.6	6.12	66	.287	.365	4	.333	2	-23	-21	-0	-1.4

■ MEL BEHNEY
Behney, Melvin Brian b: 9/2/47, Newark, N.J. BL/TL, 6'2", 180 lbs. Deb: 8/14/70

| 1970 Cin-N | 0 | 2 | .000 | 5 | 1 | 0 | 0 | 0 | 10 | 15 | 1 | 8 | 2 | 20.7 | 4.50 | 90 | .341 | .442 | 0 | .000 | -0 | -1 | -1 | -0 | 0.0 |

■ HANK BEHRMAN
Behrman, Henry Bernard b: 6/27/21, Brooklyn, N.Y. d: 1/20/87, New York, N.Y. BR/TR, 5'11", 174 lbs. Deb: 4/17/46

1946 Bro-N	11	5	.688	47	11	2	0	4	150²	138	3	69	78	12.5	2.93	115	.241	.325	4	.095	-3	8	8	-2	0.3
1947 *Bro-N	0	0	—	2	0	0	0	0	3²	3	1	4	2	17.2	9.82	42	.231	.412	0	—	0	-2	-2	0	-0.1
Pit-N	0	2	.000	10	2	0	0	0	24²	33	6	17	11	19.0	9.12	46	.347	.456	0	.000	-1	-14	-13	-1	-1.3
*Bro-N	5	3	.625	38	6	0	0	8	88¹	94	9	44	31	14.1	5.30	78	.274	.357	6	.231	-1	-12	-11	-1	-1.0
Yr	5	5	.500	50	8	0	0	8	116²	130	16	65	44	15.0	6.25	66	.287	.376	1	.031	-1	-28	-27	-2	-2.4
1948 Bro-N	5	4	.556	34	4	2	1	7	91	95	7	42	42	13.8	4.05	99	.268	.350	3	.107	-2	-1	-1	-0	-0.1
1949 NY-N	3	3	.500	43	4	1	1	0	71¹	64	5	52	25	14.6	4.92	81	.239	.363	1	.077	-1	-7	-7	0	-0.7
Total 4	24	17	.585	174	27	5	2	19	429²	427	31	228	189	13.9	4.40	87	.259	.352	14	.122	-5	-28	-28	-5	-2.9

■ TIM BELCHER
Belcher, Timothy Wayne b: 10/19/61, Mount Gilead, Ohio BR/TR, 6'3", 210 lbs. Deb: 9/06/87

1987 LA-N	4	2	.667	6	5	0	0	0	34	30	2	7	23	9.8	2.38	166	.240	.280	2	.200	0	6	6	0	0.6
1988 *LA-N	12	6	.667	36	27	4	1	4	179²	143	8	51	152	9.8	2.91	115	.217	.275	4	.071	-1	11	8	-1	0.6
1989 LA-N	15	12	.556	39	30	10	8	1	230	182	20	80	200	10.5	2.82	121	.217	.291	7	.100	-2	17	15	-2	1.2
1990 LA-N	9	9	.500	24	24	5	2	0	153	136	17	48	102	10.9	4.00	89	.240	.302	7	.163	1	-4	-7	-1	-0.8
Total 4	40	29	.580	105	86	19	11	5	596²	491	47	186	477	10.4	3.12	111	.224	.288	20	.112	-3	31	22	-5	1.6

■ STAN BELINDA
Belinda, Stanley Peter b: 8/6/66, Huntingdon, Pa. BR/TR, 6'3", 185 lbs. Deb: 9/08/89

1989 Pit-N	0	1	.000	8	0	0	0	0	10¹	13	0	2	10	13.1	6.10	55	.295	.326	0	—	0	-3	-3	-0	-0.3
1990 *Pit-N	3	4	.429	55	0	0	0	8	58¹	48	4	29	55	12.0	3.55	102	.227	.324	0	.000	-0	2	0	-1	0.0
Total 2	3	5	.375	63	0	0	0	8	68²	61	4	31	65	12.2	3.93	91	.239	.324	0	.000	-0	-1	-3	-1	-0.3

■ BO BELINSKY
Belinsky, Robert b: 12/7/36, New York, N.Y. BL/TL, 6'2", 191 lbs. Deb: 4/18/62

1962 LA-A	10	11	.476	33	31	5	3	1	187¹	149	12	122	145	13.6	3.56	109	.216	.344	10	.167	1	9	6	-1	0.6
1963 LA-A	2	9	.182	16	13	2	0	0	76²	78	12	35	60	13.5	5.75	60	.262	.347	2	.074	-2	-18	-20	1	-1.9
1964 LA-A	9	8	.529	23	22	4	1	0	135¹	120	8	49	91	11.6	2.86	115	.240	.315	4	.095	-1	11	6	-0	0.4
1965 Phi-N	4	9	.308	30	14	3	0	1	109²	103	13	48	71	12.9	4.84	71	.248	.334	6	.188	1	-16	-17	-1	-1.7
1966 Phi-N	0	0	—	9	0	0	0	0	15¹	14	3	5	8	12.9	2.93	123	.250	.344	1	.333	0	1	1	0	0.1
1967 Hou-N	3	9	.250	27	18	0	0	0	115¹	112	12	54	80	13.6	4.68	71	.255	.347	2	.077	-2	-17	-18	-2	-2.1
1969 Pit-N	0	3	.000	8	3	0	0	0	17²	17	1	14	15	16.8	4.58	76	.266	.412	0	.000	-0	-2	-2	0	-0.1
1970 Cin-N	0	0	—	3	0	0	0	0	8	10	0	6	6	18.0	4.50	90	.294	.400	1	1.000	1	-0	-0	-0	0.0
Total 8	28	51	.354	146	102	14	4	2	665¹	603	61	333	476	13.2	4.10	86	.241	.340	27	.131	-2	-32	-43	-4	-4.7

YEAR TM/L	W	L	PCT	G	GS	CG	SH	SV	IP	H	HR	BB	SO	RAT	ERA	ERA+	OAV	OOB	BH	AVG	PB	PR	/A	PD	TPI

■ CHARLIE BELL   Bell, Charles C.   b: 8/12/1868, Cincinnati, Ohio   d: 2/7/37, Cincinnati, Ohio   TR,   Deb: 10/13/1889 ◆

1889 KC-a	1	0	1.000	1	1	1	0	0	9	4	0	3	3	7.0	1.00	418	.130	.208	1	.167	0	3	3	1	0.3
1891 Lou-a	2	6	.250	10	9	8	0	0	77	93	4	20	16	13.2	4.68	78	.289	.330	1	.036	-2	-8	-9	-1	-0.9
Cin-a	1	0	1.000	1	1	1	0	0	9	2	0	3	1	5.0	0.00	—	.070	.157	2	.500	1	4	4	0	0.6
Yr	3	6	.333	11	10	9	0	0	86	95	4	23	17	12.3	4.19	88	.271	.316	6	.188	-2	-4	-5	-1	-0.3
Total 2	4	6	.400	12	11	10	0	0	95	99	4	26	20	11.8	3.88	97	.259	.307	4	.105	-2	-2	-1	-0	0.0

■ ERIC BELL   Bell, Eric Alvin   b: 10/27/63, Modesto, Cal.   BL/TL, 6'3", 195 lbs.   Deb: 9/24/85

1985 Bal-A	0	0	—	4	0	0	0	0	5^2	4	1	4	4	12.7	4.76	85	.200	.333	0	—	0	-0	-0	0	0.0
1986 Bal-A	1	2	.333	4	4	0	0	0	23^1	23	4	14	18	14.3	5.01	82	.258	.359	0	—	0	-2	-2	-1	-0.2
1987 Bal-A	10	13	.435	33	29	2	0	0	165	174	32	78	111	13.9	5.45	81	.271	.351	0	—	0	-18	-19	-1	-1.8
Total 3	11	15	.423	41	33	2	0	0	194	201	37	96	133	13.8	5.38	81	.267	.352	0	—	0	-21	-22	-2	-2.0

■ GARY BELL   Bell, Gary   b: 11/17/36, San Antonio, Tex.   BR/TR, 6'1", 196 lbs.   Deb: 6/01/58

1958 Cle-A	12	10	.545	33	23	10	0	1	182	141	17	73	110	10.8	3.31	110	.213	.296	11	.196	2	9	7	-2	0.6
1959 Cle-A	16	11	.593	44	28	12	1	5	234	208	28	105	136	12.2	4.04	91	.238	.323	18	.240	3	-5	-9	-2	-0.8
1960 Cle-A	9	10	.474	28	23	6	2	1	154^2	139	15	82	109	13.3	4.13	90	.242	.344	7	.149	-0	-4	-7	1	-0.5
1961 Cle-A	12	16	.429	34	34	11	2	0	228^1	214	32	100	163	12.6	4.10	96	.245	.326	16	.198	1	-2	-4	-1	-0.4
1962 Cle-A	10	9	.526	57	6	1	0	12	107^2	104	14	52	80	13.3	4.26	91	.264	.354	5	.208	1	-4	-5	-1	-0.4
1963 Cle-A	8	5	.615	58	7	0	0	5	119	91	13	52	98	11.1	2.95	123	.208	.298	3	.115	-1	9	9	0	0.9
1964 Cle-A	8	6	.571	56	2	0	0	4	106	106	15	53	89	13.4	4.33	83	.260	.351	6	.375	2	-8	-9	-1	-0.7
1965 Cle-A	6	5	.545	60	0	0	0	17	103^2	86	7	50	86	12.0	3.04	115	.226	.319	1	.063	-0	5	5	1	0.4
1966 Cle-A	14	15	.483	40	37	12	0	0	254^1	211	19	79	194	10.4	3.22	107	.228	.291	10	.132	-1	6	6	2	0.8
1967 Cle-A	1	5	.167	9	9	1	0	0	60^2	50	7	24	39	11.1	3.71	88	.234	.314	0	.000	-2	-3	-3	1	-0.3
*Bos-A	12	8	.600	29	24	8	0	3	165^1	143	16	47	115	10.6	3.16	110	.231	.290	12	.203	1	1	6	-0	0.8
Yr	13	13	.500	38	33	9	0	3	226	193	23	71	154	10.7	3.31	104	.231	.295	0	.000	-0	-2	3	1	0.5
1968 Bos-A	11	11	.500	35	27	9	3	1	199^1	177	7	68	103	11.3	3.12	101	.239	.308	13	.220	2	-3	1	1	0.4
1969 Sea-A	2	6	.250	13	11	1	1	2	61^1	76	8	34	30	16.4	4.70	77	.305	.393	3	.214	1	-7	-7	-0	-0.5
Chi-A	0	0	—	23	2	0	0	0	38^2	48	8	23	26	17.0	6.28	61	.308	.403	0	.000	-0	-11	-10	0	-1.0
Yr	2	6	.250	36	13	1	1	2	100	124	16	57	56	16.5	5.31	70	.302	.390	3	.158	1	-19	-18	0	-1.5
Total 12	121	117	.508	519	233	71	9	51	2015	1794	206	842	1378	12.0	3.68	98	.239	.320	105	.185	9	-17	-18	-4	-0.7

■ GEORGE BELL   Bell, George Glenn "Farmer"   b: 11/2/1874, Greenwood, N.Y.   d: 12/25/41, New York, N.Y.   BR/TR, 6', 195 lbs.   Deb: 4/17/07

1907 Bro-N	8	16	.333	35	27	20	3	1	263^2	222	1	77	88	10.4	2.25	104	.238	.300	8	.095	-3	6	3	2	0.2
1908 Bro-N	4	15	.211	29	21	12	2	1	155^1	162	3	45	63	12.1	3.59	65	.270	.324	8	.170	1	-21	-22	1	-2.1
1909 Bro-N	16	15	.516	33	30	29	6	1	256	236	5	73	95	11.0	2.71	96	.251	.307	15	.167	1	-3	-3	2	0.0
1910 Bro-N	10	27	.270	44	36	25	4	1	310	267	4	82	102	10.2	2.64	115	.241	.296	13	.134	-4	13	13	-3	0.7
1911 Bro-N	5	6	.455	19	12	6	2	0	101	123	2	28	28	13.6	4.28	78	.315	.364	4	.121	-1	-10	-11	2	-0.9
Total 5	43	79	.352	160	126	92	17	4	1086	1010	15	305	376	11.0	2.85	94	.254	.310	48	.137	-6	-14	-20	5	-2.1

■ HI BELL   Bell, Herman S   b: 7/16/1897, Mt.Sherman, Ky.   d: 6/7/49, Glendale, Cal.   BR/TR, 6', 185 lbs.   Deb: 4/16/24

1924 StL-N	3	8	.273	28	11	5	0	1	113^1	124	5	29	29	12.5	4.92	77	.292	.344	2	.065	-2	-13	-14	0	-1.5
1926 *StL-N	6	6	.500	27	7	3	0	2	85	82	1	17	27	10.7	3.18	123	.255	.296	3	.120	-1	6	7	-1	0.4
1927 StL-N	1	3	.250	25	1	0	0	0	57^1	71	5	22	31	14.8	3.92	101	.317	.381	1	.091	-1	-0	0	0	0.0
1929 StL-N	0	2	.000	7	0	0	0	0	13	19	1	4	4	15.9	6.92	67	.339	.383	0	.000	-0	-3	-3	-0	-0.3
1930 *StL-N	4	3	.571	39	9	2	0	**8**	115^1	143	4	23	42	13.1	3.90	129	.299	.334	2	.077	-3	**14**	14	1	1.1
1932 NY-N	8	4	.667	35	10	3	0	2	120	132	12	16	25	11.3	3.68	101	.280	.307	3	.088	-2	3	0	-0	-0.1
1933 *NY-N	6	5	.545	38	7	1	1	5	105^1	100	4	20	24	10.4	2.05	157	.246	.285	4	.138	-1	**15**	14	1	1.3
1934 NY-N	4	3	.571	22	2	0	0	6	54	72	2	12	9	14.3	3.67	105	.319	.358	2	.105	-1	2	1	-1	0.0
Total 8	32	34	.485	221	47	14	1	24	663^1	743	34	143	191	12.2	3.69	107	.285	.326	17	.096	-12	23	19	-2	0.9

■ JERRY BELL   Bell, Jerry Houston   b: 10/6/47, Madison, Tenn.   BB/TR, 6'4", 190 lbs.   Deb: 9/06/71

1971 Mil-A	2	1	.667	8	0	0	0	0	14^2	10	0	6	8	9.8	3.07	113	.200	.286	0	—	0	1	1	-0	0.0
1972 Mil-A	5	1	.833	25	3	0	0	0	70^2	50	1	33	20	11.0	1.66	183	.209	.313	1	.071	-1	11	11	1	1.2
1973 Mil-A	9	9	.500	31	25	8	0	1	183^2	185	14	70	57	12.7	3.97	95	.263	.334	0	—	0	-3	-4	1	-0.2
1974 Mil-A	1	0	1.000	5	0	0	0	0	14	17	2	5	4	14.1	2.57	141	.315	.373	0	—	0	2	2	0	0.2
Total 4	17	11	.607	69	28	8	0	1	283	262	17	114	89	12.2	3.28	109	.250	.329	1	.071	-1	10	9	2	1.2

■ RALPH BELL   Bell, Ralph Albert "Lefty"   b: 11/6/1890, Kokoka, Mo.   d: 10/18/59, Burlington, Iowa   BL/TL, 5'11.5", 170 lbs.   Deb: 7/16/12

| 1912 Chi-A | 0 | 0 | — | 3 | 0 | 0 | 0 | 0 | 6 | 8 | 1 | 8 | 5 | 24.0 | 9.00 | 36 | .333 | .500 | 0 | .000 | -0 | -4 | -4 | 0 | -0.3 |

■ BILL BELL   Bell, William Samuel "Ding Dong"   b: 10/24/33, Goldsboro, N.C.   d: 10/11/62, Durham, N.C.   BR/TR, 6'3", 200 lbs.   Deb: 9/05/52

1952 Pit-N	0	1	.000	4	1	0	0	0	15^2	16	3	13	4	16.7	4.60	87	.254	.382	0	.000	-0	-2	-1	0	0.0
1955 Pit-N	0	0	—	1	0	0	0	0	1	0	0	1	0	9.0	0.00	—	.000	.250	0	—	0	0	0	0	0.0
Total 2	0	1	.000	5	1	0	0	0	16^2	16	3	14	4	16.2	4.32	93	.242	.375	0	.000	-0	-1	-1	0	0.0

■ CHIEF BENDER   Bender, Charles Albert   b: 5/5/1884, Crow Wing Co., Minn   d: 5/22/54, Philadelphia, Pa.   BR/TR, 6'2", 185 lbs.   Deb: 4/20/03   CH

1903 Phi-A	17	14	.548	36	33	29	2	0	270	239	6	65	127	10.1	3.07	100	.237	.283	22	.183	-1	-3	-0	0	0.0
1904 Phi-A	10	11	.476	29	20	18	4	0	203^2	167	1	59	149	10.0	2.87	93	.225	.282	18	.228	3	-6	-4	-3	-0.3
1905 *Phi-A	18	11	.621	35	28	18	4	0	229	193	5	90	142	11.1	2.83	94	.230	.304	20	.217	3	-4	-4	3	0.1
1906 Phi-A	15	10	.600	36	27	24	0	3	238^1	208	5	48	159	9.7	2.53	108	.238	.277	25	.253	7	4	5	-2	1.3
1907 Phi-A	16	8	.667	33	24	20	4	3	219^1	185	1	34	112	9.0	2.05	127	.231	.262	23	.230	3	12	14	-1	1.8
1908 Phi-A	8	9	.471	18	17	14	2	1	138^2	121	1	21	85	9.4	1.75	146	.236	.270	11	.220	3	10	13	-2	1.6
1909 Phi-A	18	8	.692	34	29	24	5	1	250	196	1	45	161	8.9	1.66	145	.214	.254	20	.215	4	23	21	1	3.0
1910 *Phi-A	23	5	**.821**	30	25	25	3	0	250	182	1	47	155	8.6	1.58	150	.207	.255	25	.269	8	26	22	2	3.6
1911 *Phi-A	17	5	**.773**	31	24	16	2	3	216^1	198	2	58	114	10.8	2.16	146	.252	.307	13	.165	-3	28	24	1	2.1
1912 Phi-A	13	8	.619	27	19	12	1	2	171	169	1	33	90	10.7	2.74	112	.277	.315	9	.150	-1	11	6	-2	0.3
1913 *Phi-A	21	10	.677	48	21	14	2	**13**	236^2	208	2	59	135	10.3	2.21	125	.228	.277	12	.154	-0	19	15	-2	1.3
1914 *Phi-A	17	3	**.850**	28	23	14	7	2	179	159	4	55	107	10.8	2.26	116	.240	.299	9	.145	-1	10	7	-1	0.8
1915 Bal-F	4	16	.200	26	23	15	0	1	178^1	198	5	37	89	12.2	3.99	80	.298	.342	16	.267	4	-19	-16	-1	-1.2
1916 Phi-N	7	7	.500	27	13	4	0	3	122^2	137	3	34	43	13.3	3.74	71	.287	.347	12	.279	4	-15	-15	2	-1.0
1917 Phi-N	8	2	.800	20	10	8	4	2	113	84	1	26	43	9.3	1.67	168	.215	.277	8	.205	1	13	14	-1	1.6
1925 Chi-A	0	0	—	1	0	0	0	0	1	1	0	1	0	18.0	18.00	23	.333	.500	0	—	0	-2	-2	0	0.0
Total 16	212	127	.625	459	331	255	40	34	3017	2645	40	712	1711	10.2	2.46	112	.239	.288	243	.212	34	107	100	-7	15.0

■ ANDY BENES   Benes, Andrew Charles   b: 8/20/67, Evansville, Ind.   BR/TR, 6'6", 235 lbs.   Deb: 8/11/89

1989 SD-N	6	3	.667	10	10	0	0	0	66^2	51	7	31	66	11.2	3.51	100	.213	.305	6	.250	2	-0	-0	-0	0.2
1990 SD-N	10	11	.476	32	31	2	0	0	192^1	177	18	69	140	11.6	3.60	107	.242	.309	6	.100	-2	4	5	-3	0.0
Total 2	16	14	.533	42	41	2	0	0	259	228	25	100	206	11.5	3.58	105	.235	.308	12	.143	-0	4	5	-3	0.2

■ RAY BENGE   Benge, Raymond Adelphia   b: 4/22/02, Jacksonville, Tex.   BR/TR, 5'9.5", 160 lbs.   Deb: 9/26/25

1925 Cle-A	1	0	1.000	2	2	1	0	0	11^2	9	0	3	3	9.3	1.54	286	.205	.255	2	.400	0	4	4	-0	0.4
1926 Cle-A	1	0	1.000	8	0	0	0	0	11^2	15	0	4	3	14.7	3.86	105	.313	.365	1	.333	0	0	0	0	0.1
1928 Phi-N	8	18	.308	40	28	12	1	1	201^2	219	15	88	68	13.9	4.55	94	.286	.363	12	.207	0	-13	-6	-2	-0.6
1929 Phi-N	11	15	.423	38	27	9	2	4	199	255	24	77	78	15.2	6.29	83	.322	.385	15	.203	-3	-35	-24	-3	-2.5

YEAR	TM/L	W	L	PCT	G	GS	CG	SH	SV	IP	H	HR	BB	SO	RAT	ERA	ERA+	OAV	OOB	BH	AVG	PB	PR	/A	PD	TPI
1930	Phi-N	11	15	.423	38	29	14	0	1	225²	305	22	81	70	15.4	5.70	96	.328	.382	18	.205	-4	-18	-6	-1	-0.7
1931	Phi-N	14	18	.438	38	31	16	2	2	247	251	12	61	117	11.6	3.17	134	.262	.310	18	.205	-2	19	30	-2	2.7
1932	Phi-N	13	12	.520	41	28	13	2	6	222¹	247	15	58	89	12.5	4.05	109	.281	.329	13	.173	-3	-4	9	-1	0.6
1933	Bro-N	10	17	.370	37	30	16	2	1	228²	238	11	55	74	11.8	3.42	94	.268	.315	14	.184	0	-2	-5	-0	-0.8
1934	Bro-N	14	12	.538	36	32	14	1	0	227	252	11	61	64	12.5	4.32	90	.272	.319	15	.169	-2	-7	-11	-0	-1.2
1935	Bro-N	9	9	.500	23	17	5	1	1	124²	142	12	47	39	13.7	4.48	89	.289	.353	9	.191	-1	-6	-7	-2	-0.8
1936	Bos-N	7	9	.438	21	19	2	0	0	115	161	6	38	32	15.7	5.79	66	.333	.382	6	.140	-3	-23	-25	-2	-2.6
	Phi-N	1	4	.200	15	6	0	0	1	45²	70	3	19	13	17.5	4.73	96	.350	.406	0	.000	-2	-4	-1	-2	-0.3
	Yr	8	13	.381	36	25	2	0	1	160²	231	9	57	45	16.1	5.49	73	.337	.388	0	.000	-4	-26	-26	-4	-2.9
1938	Cin-N	1	1	.500	9	0	0	0	2	15¹	13	1	6	5	11.2	4.11	89	.228	.302	1	.333	0	-1	-1	-0	0.0
Total 12		101	130	.437	346	249	102	12	19	1875¹	2177	132	598	655	13.5	4.52	95	.292	.347	124	.188	-17	-89	-46	-18	-5.7

■ HENRY BENN
Benn, Henry Omer b: 1/25/1890, Viola, Wis. d: 6/4/67, Madison, Wis. BR/TR, 6', 190 lbs. Deb: 9/24/14

YEAR	TM/L	W	L	PCT	G	GS	CG	SH	SV	IP	H	HR	BB	SO	RAT	ERA	ERA+	OAV	OOB	BH	AVG	PB	PR	/A	PD	TPI
1914	Cle-A	0	0	—	1	0	0	0	0	1	0	0	0	1	0.0	0.00	—	.000	.000	0	—	0	0	0	0	0.0

■ DAVE BENNETT
Bennett, David Hans b: 11/7/45, Berkeley, Cal. BR/TR, 6'5", 195 lbs. Deb: 6/12/64

YEAR	TM/L	W	L	PCT	G	GS	CG	SH	SV	IP	H	HR	BB	SO	RAT	ERA	ERA+	OAV	OOB	BH	AVG	PB	PR	/A	PD	TPI
1964	Phi-N	0	0	—	1	0	0	0	0	1	2	0	0	1	18.0	9.00	39	.400	.400	0	—	0	-1	-1	0	0.0

■ DENNIS BENNETT
Bennett, Dennis John b: 10/5/39, Oakland, Cal. BL/TL, 6'3", 192 lbs. Deb: 5/12/62

YEAR	TM/L	W	L	PCT	G	GS	CG	SH	SV	IP	H	HR	BB	SO	RAT	ERA	ERA+	OAV	OOB	BH	AVG	PB	PR	/A	PD	TPI
1962	Phi-N	9	9	.500	31	24	7	2	3	174²	144	17	68	149	11.2	3.81	102	.224	.304	8	.127	-1	3	1	-1	0.0
1963	Phi-N	9	5	.643	23	16	6	1	1	119¹	102	13	33	82	10.5	2.64	122	.231	.290	9	.225	3	9	8	0	1.2
1964	Phi-N	12	14	.462	41	32	7	2	1	208	222	23	58	125	12.3	3.68	94	.280	.333	13	.197	3	-3	-5	-0	-0.1
1965	Bos-A	5	7	.417	34	18	3	0	0	141²	152	15	53	85	13.4	4.38	85	.279	.350	7	.179	2	-15	-10	-0	-0.8
1966	Bos-A	3	3	.500	16	13	0	0	0	75	75	9	23	47	11.9	3.24	117	.261	.318	3	.130	1	2	5	-1	0.5
1967	Bos-A	4	3	.571	13	11	4	1	0	69²	72	12	22	34	12.4	3.88	90	.268	.328	3	.120	-0	-5	-3	0	-0.2
	NY-N	1	1	.500	8	6	0	0	0	26¹	37	4	7	14	15.4	5.13	66	.336	.381	2	.250	1	-5	-5	-0	-0.4
1968	Cal-A	0	5	.000	16	7	1	0	1	48¹	46	6	17	36	12.5	3.54	82	.260	.327	1	.077	-1	-3	-3	0	-0.3
Total 7		43	47	.478	182	127	28	6	6	863	850	98	281	572	12.1	3.69	96	.260	.324	46	.166	7	-18	-13	-2	-0.1

■ FRANK BENNETT
Bennett, Francis Allen "Chip" b: 10/27/04, Mardela Springs, Md. d: 3/18/66, New Castle, Del. BR/TR, 5'10.5", 163 lbs. Deb: 9/17/27

YEAR	TM/L	W	L	PCT	G	GS	CG	SH	SV	IP	H	HR	BB	SO	RAT	ERA	ERA+	OAV	OOB	BH	AVG	PB	PR	/A	PD	TPI
1927	Bos-A	0	1	.000	4	1	0	0	0	12¹	15	0	6	1	15.3	2.92	145	.333	.412	0	.000	-1	2	2	0	0.1
1928	Bos-A	0	0	—	1	0	0	0	0	1	1	0	0	0	9.0	0.00	—	.250	.250	0	—	0	0	0	0	0.1
Total 2		0	1	.000	5	1	0	0	0	13¹	16	0	6	1	14.9	2.70	156	.327	.400	0	.000	-1	2	2	0	0.2

■ ALLEN BENSON
Benson, Allen Wilbert "Bullet Ben" b: 7/12/08, Hurley, S.Dak. BR/TR, 6'1", 185 lbs. Deb: 8/19/34

YEAR	TM/L	W	L	PCT	G	GS	CG	SH	SV	IP	H	HR	BB	SO	RAT	ERA	ERA+	OAV	OOB	BH	AVG	PB	PR	/A	PD	TPI
1934	Was-A	0	1	.000	2	2	0	0	0	9²	19	0	5	4	24.2	12.10	36	.413	.491	0	.000	-0	-8	-8	-0	-0.6

■ CY BENTLEY
Bentley, Clytus G. b: 11/23/1850, East Haven, Conn. d: 2/26/1873, Middletown, Conn. Deb: 4/26/1872

YEAR	TM/L	W	L	PCT	G	GS	CG	SH	SV	IP	H	HR	BB	SO	RAT	ERA	ERA+	OAV	OOB	BH	AVG	PB	PR	/A	PD	TPI
1872	Man-n	2	15	.118	18	17	16	0	0	154	273	4	11		16.6	6.14	60	.319	.328	27	.235	-0	-41	-42		-2.7

■ JACK BENTLEY
Bentley, John Needles b: 3/8/1895, Sandy Spring, Md. d: 10/24/69, Olney, Md. BL/TL, 5'11.5", 200 lbs. Deb: 9/06/13 ♦

YEAR	TM/L	W	L	PCT	G	GS	CG	SH	SV	IP	H	HR	BB	SO	RAT	ERA	ERA+	OAV	OOB	BH	AVG	PB	PR	/A	PD	TPI
1913	Was-A	1	0	1.000	3	1	0	1	0	11	5	0	2	5	5.7	0.00	—	.147	.194	0	.000	-0	4	4	0	0.4
1914	Was-A	5	7	.417	30	11	3	2	4	125¹	110	3	53	55	11.9	2.37	117	.249	.334	11	.275	2	5	6	-0	0.8
1915	Was-A	0	2	.000	4	2	0	0	0	11¹	8	0	3	0	8.7	0.79	369	.200	.256	0	.000	-0	3	3	-0	0.2
1916	Was-A	0	0	—	2	0	0	0	0	1¹	1	0	1	1	6.8	0.00	—	.250	.250	0	—	0	0	0	0	0.1
1923	*NY-N	13	8	.619	31	26	12	1	3	183	198	10	67	80	13.3	4.48	85	.277	.343	38	.427	15	-10	-13	-1	0.0
1924	*NY-N	16	5	.762	28	24	13	1	1	188	196	11	56	60	12.3	3.78	97	.273	.329	26	.265	4	2	-2	-1	0.0
1925	NY-N	11	9	.550	28	22	11	0	0	157	200	10	59	47	14.9	5.04	80	.323	.383	30	.303	5	-14	-18	-1	-1.5
1926	Phi-N	0	2	.000	7	3	0	0	0	25¹	37	2	10	7	16.7	8.17	51	.327	.382	62	.258	1	-12	-11	-0	-0.9
	NY-N	0	0	—	1	0	0	0	0	2	0	0	2	1	9.0	0.00	—	.000	.250	1	.250	-0	1	1	0	0.1
	Yr	0	2	.000	8	3	0	0	0	27¹	37	2	12	8	16.1	7.57	54	.311	.374	5	.020	1	-11	-11	-0	-0.8
1927	NY-N	0	0	—	4	0	0	0	0	9²	7	1	10	3	16.8	2.79	138	.206	.400	2	.222	1	1	1	0	0.1
Total 9		46	33	.582	138	89	39	4	9	714	761	37	263	259	13.1	4.01	91	.280	.346	170	.291	27	-20	-29	-2	-0.7

■ AL BENTON
Benton, John Alton b: 3/18/11, Noble, Okla. d: 4/14/68, Lynwood, Cal. BR/TR, 6'4", 215 lbs. Deb: 4/18/34

YEAR	TM/L	W	L	PCT	G	GS	CG	SH	SV	IP	H	HR	BB	SO	RAT	ERA	ERA+	OAV	OOB	BH	AVG	PB	PR	/A	PD	TPI
1934	Phi-A	7	9	.438	32	21	7	0	1	155	145	7	88	58	13.6	4.88	90	.249	.349	6	.109	-4	-7	-9	0	-1.1
1935	Phi-A	3	4	.429	27	9	0	0	0	78¹	110	7	47	42	18.2	7.70	59	.328	.413	1	.040	-3	-28	-27	-1	-2.7
1938	Det-A	5	3	.625	19	10	6	0	0	95¹	93	10	39	33	12.6	3.30	151	.259	.333	4	.121	-3	16	18	1	1.6
1939	Det-A	6	8	.429	37	16	3	0	5	150	182	11	58	67	14.5	4.56	107	.294	.355	4	.091	-4	1	5	-0	0.2
1940	Det-A	6	10	.375	42	0	0	0	17	79¹	93	5	36	50	14.6	4.42	107	.294	.366	0	.000	-3	-0	3	-0	-0.0
1941	Det-A	15	6	.714	38	14	7	1	7	157²	130	11	65	63	11.3	2.97	153	.221	.302	3	.060	-5	21	28	0	2.3
1942	Det-A	7	13	.350	35	30	9	1	2	226²	210	9	84	110	11.7	2.90	136	.246	.314	5	.075	-6	19	26	-1	2.2
1945	*Det-A	13	8	.619	31	27	12	5	3	191²	175	7	63	76	11.3	2.02	174	.241	.303	4	.063	-6	29	32	2	3.1
1946	Det-A	11	7	.611	28	15	6	1	1	140²	132	9	58	60	12.2	3.65	100	.245	.319	9	.184	-1	-2	0	1	0.1
1947	Det-A	6	7	.462	36	14	4	0	7	133	147	11	61	33	14.1	4.40	86	.288	.365	6	.154	-2	-10	-9	-0	-0.5
1948	Det-A	2	2	.500	30	0	0	0	3	44¹	45	4	36	18	16.6	5.68	77	.273	.406	2	.182	-0	-7	-6	-0	-0.5
1949	Cle-A	9	6	.600	40	11	4	2	10	135²	116	7	51	41	11.1	2.12	188	.238	.312	5	.132	-2	31	28	-2	2.4
1950	Cle-A	4	2	.667	36	0	0	0	4	63	57	7	30	26	12.6	3.57	121	.243	.331	1	.083	-1	7	5	-0	0.4
1952	Bos-A	4	3	.571	24	0	0	0	6	37²	37	1	17	20	12.9	2.39	165	.268	.348	0	.000	-1	5	6	-0	0.5
Total 14		98	88	.527	455	167	58	10	66	1688¹	1672	106	733	697	12.9	3.66	115	.259	.336	50	.098	-41	74	102	1	7.5

■ RUBE BENTON
Benton, John Clebon b: 6/27/1887, Clinton, N.C. d: 12/12/37, Dothan, Ala. BL/TL, 6'1", 190 lbs. Deb: 6/28/10

YEAR	TM/L	W	L	PCT	G	GS	CG	SH	SV	IP	H	HR	BB	SO	RAT	ERA	ERA+	OAV	OOB	BH	AVG	PB	PR	/A	PD	TPI
1910	Cin-N	0	1	.000	12	2	0	0	0	38	44	1	23	15	16.1	4.74	62	.282	.378	1	.091	-1	-7	-8	1	-0.7
1911	Cin-N	3	3	.500	6	6	5	0	0	44²	44	0	23	28	14.1	2.01	164	.270	.370	2	.143	-0	7	6	-1	0.5
1912	Cin-N	18	20	.474	50	39	22	2	2	302	316	2	118	162	13.5	3.10	108	.271	.347	14	.135	-6	10	9	1	0.3
1913	Cin-N	11	7	.611	23	22	9	1	0	144¹	140	4	60	68	13.0	3.49	93	.265	.350	10	.208	1	5	-4	-1	-0.3
1914	Cin-N	16	18	.471	41	31	16	5	2	271	223	3	95	121	10.9	2.96	99	.228	.303	13	.143	-3	-5	-1	0	-0.3
1915	Cin-N	6	13	.316	35	21	6	2	4	176¹	165	2	67	83	12.6	3.32	86	.257	.340	11	.208	-0	-11	-9	2	-0.7
	NY-N	3	5	.375	10	7	3	0	1	60²	57	0	9	26	10.5	2.82	91	.253	.297	5	.217	1	-0	-2	-0	0.0
	Yr	9	18	.333	45	28	9	2	5	237	222	2	76	109	11.5	3.19	87	.252	.315	0	.000	1	-12	-11	2	-0.7
1916	NY-N	16	8	.667	38	30	15	3	2	238²	210	5	58	115	10.5	2.87	85	.241	.296	7	.090	-4	-7	-11	-1	-1.8
1917	*NY-N	15	9	.625	35	25	14	3	3	215	190	5	41	70	10.0	2.72	94	.238	.281	12	.167	-1	-0	-4	-1	-0.6
1918	NY-N	1	2	.333	3	3	2	0	0	24	17	0	9	9	7.5	1.88	140	.202	.230	1	.143	1	2	2	0	0.3
1919	NY-N	17	11	.607	35	28	11	1	2	209	181	5	52	53	10.2	2.63	107	.237	.289	13	.194	-1	7	4	-1	0.3
1920	NY-N	9	16	.360	33	25	12	4	2	193²	222	8	31	52	11.9	3.03	99	.291	.321	6	.092	-6	2	-1	-4	-0.2
1921	NY-N	5	2	.714	18	9	3	1	0	72	72	2	17	11	11.1	2.88	128	.266	.309	3	.143	-1	7	6	-1	0.5
1923	Cin-N	14	10	.583	33	26	15	0	1	219	243	11	57	59	12.5	3.66	106	.284	.333	23	.287	4	5	5	1	0.9
1924	Cin-N	7	9	.438	32	15	6	1	1	162²	166	2	24	42	10.7	2.77	136	.266	.297	12	.261	2	20	18	1	2.2
1925	Cin-N	9	10	.474	33	16	6	1	1	146²	155	2	34	36	13.3	4.05	102	.301	.340	9	.200	1	4	1	-1	0.0
Total 15		150	144	.510	437	305	145	24	21	2517¹	2472	53	712	950	11.7	3.09	104	.260	.318	142	.172	-14	33	13	4	0.4

■ LARRY BENTON
Benton, Lawrence James b: 11/20/1897, St.Louis, Mo. d: 4/3/53, Amberly Village, O. BR/TR, 5'11", 165 lbs. Deb: 4/25/23

YEAR	TM/L	W	L	PCT	G	GS	CG	SH	SV	IP	H	HR	BB	SO	RAT	ERA	ERA+	OAV	OOB	BH	AVG	PB	PR	/A	PD	TPI
1923	Bos-N	5	9	.357	35	9	1	0	0	128	141	4	57	42	14.2	4.99	80	.293	.373	5	.161	-1	-14	-14	0	-1.3
1924	Bos-N	5	7	.417	30	13	4	0	1	128	129	4	64	41	13.8	4.15	92	.274	.365	3	.091	-3	-4	-5	-0	-0.7
1925	Bos-N	14	7	.667	31	21	16	2	1	183¹	170	6	70	49	11.9	3.09	130	.249	.320	14	.241	2	24	19	-1	1.8

YEAR	TM/L	W	L	PCT	G	GS	CG	SH	SV	IP	H	HR	BB	SO	RAT	ERA	ERA+	OAV	OOB	BH	AVG	PB	PR	/A	PD	TPI
1926	Bos-N	14	14	.500	43	27	12	1	1	231²	244	10	81	103	12.9	3.85	92	.280	.346	12	.154	-3	-1	-8	-3	-1.4
1927	Bos-N	4	2	.667	11	10	3	0	1	60¹	72	3	27	25	15.1	4.48	83	.310	.387	4	.222	1	-4	-5	-1	-0.4
	NY-N	13	5	.722	29	23	8	1	2	173	183	9	54	65	12.4	3.95	98	.275	.331	8	.160	-2	-1	-2	-0	-0.3
	Yr	17	7	**.708**	40	33	11	1	2	233¹	255	12	81	90	13.0	4.09	93	.284	.344	3	.044	-1	-4	-7	-1	-0.7
1928	NY-N	**25**	9	**.735**	42	35	**28**	2	4	310¹	299	14	71	90	10.7	2.73	143	.258	.300	16	.143	-3	43	41	0	3.8
1929	NY-N	11	17	.393	39	30	14	3	3	237	276	16	61	63	12.8	4.14	111	.297	.340	9	.105	-6	15	12	1	0.6
1930	NY-N	1	3	.250	8	4	1	0	1	30	42	8	14	16	16.8	7.80	61	.323	.389	3	.300	1	-9	-10	-0	-0.7
	Cin-N	7	12	.368	35	22	9	0	1	177²	246	7	45	47	14.7	5.12	94	.337	.375	11	.177	-2	-3	-6	-3	-0.8
	Yr	8	15	.348	43	26	10	0	2	207²	288	15	59	63	15.0	5.50	87	.334	.377	4	.056	-0	-12	-16	-3	-1.5
1931	Cin-N	10	15	.400	38	23	12	2	2	204¹	240	6	53	35	12.9	3.35	112	.299	.343	11	.167	-1	12	9	1	0.9
1932	Cin-N	6	13	.316	35	21	7	0	2	179²	201	10	27	35	11.4	4.31	90	.285	.311	11	.204	0	-9	-9	-0	-0.8
1933	Cin-N	10	11	.476	34	19	7	2	2	152²	160	5	36	33	11.7	3.71	91	.271	.316	9	.170	-1	-6	-5	-2	-0.8
1934	Cin-N	0	1	.000	16	1	0	0	2	29	53	1	7	5	18.6	6.52	63	.393	.423	2	.286	0	-8	-8	-0	-0.6
1935	Bos-N	2	3	.400	29	0	0	0	0	72	103	6	24	21	16.0	6.88	55	.338	.388	4	.200	0	-23	-25	-1	-2.2
Total	13	127	128	.498	455	258	122	13	22	2297	2559	109	691	670	12.8	4.03	98	.288	.341	122	.165	-17	13	-16	-8	-2.9

■ SID BENTON

Benton, Sidney Wright   b: 8/4/1895, Buckner, Ark.   d: 3/8/77, Fayetteville, Ark.   BR/TR, 6'1", 170 lbs.   Deb: 4/18/22

YEAR	TM/L	W	L	PCT	G	GS	CG	SH	SV	IP	H	HR	BB	SO	RAT	ERA	ERA+	OAV	OOB	BH	AVG	PB	PR	/A	PD	TPI
1922	StL-N	0	0	—	1	0	0	0	0	0	0	0	2	0	—	—	—	—	1.000	0	—	0	0	0	0	0.0

■ JOE BENZ

Benz, Joseph Louis "Blitzen" or "Butcher Boy"   b: 1/21/1886, New Alsace, Ind.   d: 4/22/57, Chicago, Ill.   BR/TR, 6'1.5", 196 lbs.   Deb: 8/16/11

YEAR	TM/L	W	L	PCT	G	GS	CG	SH	SV	IP	H	HR	BB	SO	RAT	ERA	ERA+	OAV	OOB	BH	AVG	PB	PR	/A	PD	TPI
1911	Chi-A	3	2	.600	12	6	2	0	0	55²	52	0	13	28	10.8	2.26	142	.251	.302	1	.059	-2	7	6	1	0.5
1912	Chi-A	13	17	.433	42	31	12	3	0	238²	231	5	70	97	11.7	2.90	110	.259	.319	10	.132	-5	11	8	1	0.4
1913	Chi-A	7	10	.412	33	17	6	1	1	151	146	1	59	79	12.3	2.74	107	.254	.325	9	.180	-1	3	3	4	0.7
1914	Chi-A	14	19	.424	48	35	16	4	2	283¹	245	4	66	142	9.9	2.26	119	.236	.282	12	.130	-3	15	14	6	1.9
1915	Chi-A	15	11	.577	39	28	17	2	0	238¹	209	4	43	81	9.6	2.11	141	.238	.276	10	.127	-5	22	23	3	2.3
1916	Chi-A	9	5	.643	28	16	6	4	0	142	108	0	32	57	9.1	2.03	136	.214	.265	3	.065	-3	13	12	1	1.0
1917	Chi-A	7	3	.700	19	13	7	2	0	94²	76	1	23	25	9.6	2.47	108	.220	.272	5	.167	-1	2	2	0	0.1
1918	Chi-A	8	8	.500	29	17	10	1	0	154	156	1	28	30	10.9	2.63	104	.269	.304	11	.216	-1	3	2	4	0.5
1919	Chi-A	0	0	—	1	0	0	0	0	2	2	0	0	0	9.0	0.00	—	.250	.250	0	—	0	1	1	0	0.1
Total	9	76	75	.503	251	163	76	17	3	1359²	1225	16	334	539	10.5	2.43	119	.243	.294	61	.138	-20	76	70	20	7.5

■ JUAN BERENGUER

Berenguer, Juan Bautista   b: 11/30/54, Aguadulce, Pan.   BR/TR, 5'11", 186 lbs.   Deb: 8/17/78

YEAR	TM/L	W	L	PCT	G	GS	CG	SH	SV	IP	H	HR	BB	SO	RAT	ERA	ERA+	OAV	OOB	BH	AVG	PB	PR	/A	PD	TPI
1978	NY-N	0	2	.000	5	3	0	0	0	13	17	1	11	8	20.1	8.31	42	.327	.453	0	.000	-0	-7	-7	0	-0.6
1979	NY-N	1	1	.500	5	5	0	0	0	30²	28	2	12	25	12.0	2.93	124	.252	.331	1	.143	0	3	2	-1	0.2
1980	NY-N	0	1	.000	6	0	0	0	0	9¹	9	1	10	7	18.3	5.79	61	.250	.413	0	—	0	-2	-2	-0	-0.1
1981	KC-A	0	4	.000	8	3	0	0	0	19²	22	4	16	20	18.3	8.69	41	.289	.426	0	—	0	-11	-11	-1	-1.0
	Tor-A	2	9	.182	12	11	1	0	0	71	62	7	35	29	12.7	4.31	91	.235	.331	0	—	0	-5	-3	-1	-0.3
	Yr	2	13	.133	20	14	1	0	0	90²	84	11	51	49	13.7	5.26	73	.243	.346	0	—	0	-16	-14	-1	-1.3
1982	Det-A	0	0	—	2	1	0	0	0	6²	5	0	9	8	18.9	6.75	60	.200	.412	0	—	0	-2	-2	-0	-0.1
1983	Det-A	9	5	.643	37	19	2	1	1	157²	110	19	71	129	10.7	3.14	124	.193	.289	0	—	0	16	13	-2	1.1
1984	Det-A	11	10	.524	31	27	2	1	0	168¹	146	14	79	118	12.3	3.48	113	.232	.323	0	—	0	10	8	-2	0.7
1985	Det-A	5	6	.455	31	13	0	0	0	95	96	12	48	82	13.7	5.59	73	.259	.346	0	—	0	-15	-16	-0	-1.4
1986	SF-N	2	3	.400	46	4	0	0	4	73¹	64	4	44	72	13.5	2.70	130	.242	.354	1	.143	-0	8	7	-1	0.6
1987	*Min-A	8	1	.889	47	6	0	0	4	112	100	10	47	110	11.8	3.94	117	.238	.315	0	—	0	6	8	-2	0.6
1988	Min-A	8	4	.667	57	1	0	0	2	100	74	7	61	99	12.2	3.96	103	.207	.325	0	—	0	1	1	-0	0.1
1989	Min-A	9	3	.750	56	0	0	0	3	106	96	11	47	93	12.3	3.48	119	.246	.330	0	—	0	5	8	-1	0.7
1990	Min-A	8	5	.615	51	0	0	0	0	100¹	85	9	58	77	13.0	3.41	123	.232	.340	0	—	0	6	9	-2	0.7
Total	13	63	54	.538	394	93	5	2	14	1063	914	101	548	877	12.6	3.89	103	.232	.330	2	.118	-0	11	16	-12	1.2

■ BRUCE BERENYI

Berenyi, Bruce Michael   b: 8/21/54, Bryan, Ohio   BR/TR, 6'3", 205 lbs.   Deb: 7/05/80

YEAR	TM/L	W	L	PCT	G	GS	CG	SH	SV	IP	H	HR	BB	SO	RAT	ERA	ERA+	OAV	OOB	BH	AVG	PB	PR	/A	PD	TPI
1980	Cin-N	2	2	.500	6	6	0	0	0	27²	34	1	23	19	18.5	7.81	46	.318	.438	0	.000	-1	-13	-13	-0	-1.2
1981	Cin-N	9	6	.600	21	20	5	3	0	126	97	3	77	106	12.4	3.50	101	.211	.324	8	.190	1	-0	1	-1	0.1
1982	Cin-N	9	18	.333	34	34	4	1	0	222¹	208	8	96	157	12.4	3.36	110	.255	.335	15	.242	3	6	8	2	1.4
1983	Cin-N	9	14	.391	32	31	4	1	0	186¹	173	9	102	151	13.4	3.86	98	.247	.345	12	.218	2	-5	-1	2	0.3
1984	Cin-N	3	7	.300	13	11	0	0	0	51	63	0	42	53	18.5	6.00	63	.306	.423	1	.063	-0	-14	-13	-0	-1.3
	NY-N	9	6	.600	19	19	0	0	0	115	100	6	53	81	12.1	3.76	94	.238	.325	9	.243	2	-2	-3	-1	-0.1
	Yr	12	13	.480	32	30	0	0	0	166	163	6	95	134	14.0	4.45	81	.260	.358	0	.000	0	-16	-15	-1	-1.4
1985	NY-N	1	0	1.000	3	3	0	0	0	13²	11	0	8	10	12.5	2.63	131	.170	.328	1	.250	0	1	1	1	0.2
1986	NY-N	2	2	.500	14	7	0	0	0	39²	47	5	22	30	15.9	6.35	56	.299	.389	0	.000	-1	-12	-12	-0	-1.2
Total	7	44	55	.444	142	131	13	5	0	781²	730	32	425	607	13.4	4.03	91	.251	.347	46	.197	5	-38	-32	2	-1.8

■ HEINIE BERGER

Berger, Charles   b: 1/7/1882, Lasalle, Ill.   d: 2/10/54, Lakewood, Ohio   TR, 5'9",   Deb: 5/06/07

YEAR	TM/L	W	L	PCT	G	GS	CG	SH	SV	IP	H	HR	BB	SO	RAT	ERA	ERA+	OAV	OOB	BH	AVG	PB	PR	/A	PD	TPI
1907	Cle-A	3	3	.500	14	7	5	1	0	87¹	74	0	20	50	9.7	2.99	84	.231	.277	5	.179	0	-4	-5	-2	-0.6
1908	Cle-A	13	8	.619	29	24	16	0	0	199¹	152	1	66	101	10.0	2.12	113	.219	.290	8	.108	-4	6	6	-1	0.1
1909	Cle-A	13	14	.481	34	29	19	4	1	247	221	2	58	162	10.6	2.73	94	.256	.312	11	.133	-1	-7	-5	-1	-0.7
1910	Cle-A	3	4	.429	13	8	2	0	0	65¹	57	0	32	24	12.7	3.03	85	.243	.341	3	.143	-1	-4	-3	-0	-0.4
Total	4	32	29	.525	90	68	42	5	1	599	504	3	176	337	10.5	2.60	96	.238	.303	27	.131	-6	-9	-7	-4	-1.6

■ JACK BERLY

Berly, John Chambers   b: 5/24/03, Natchitoches, La.   d: 6/26/77, Houston, Tex.   BR/TR, 5'11.5", 190 lbs.   Deb: 4/22/24

YEAR	TM/L	W	L	PCT	G	GS	CG	SH	SV	IP	H	HR	BB	SO	RAT	ERA	ERA+	OAV	OOB	BH	AVG	PB	PR	/A	PD	TPI
1924	StL-N	0	0	—	4	0	0	0	0	8	8	1	4	2	13.5	5.63	67	.267	.353	0	.000	-0	-2	-2	0	-0.1
1931	NY-N	7	8	.467	27	11	4	1	0	111¹	114	6	51	45	13.7	3.88	95	.270	.354	6	.171	-1	-0	-2	1	-0.1
1932	Phi-N	1	2	.333	21	1	1	0	2	46	61	4	21	15	16.2	7.63	58	.333	.405	0	.000	-2	-19	-16	1	-1.5
1933	Phi-N	2	3	.400	13	6	1	1	0	50	62	5	22	4	15.5	5.04	76	.307	.381	4	.308	0	-9	-7	1	-0.5
Total	4	10	13	.435	65	18	6	2	2	215¹	245	16	98	66	14.6	5.02	78	.292	.371	10	.167	-2	-30	-27	3	-2.2

■ VICTOR BERNAL

Bernal, Victor Hugo   b: 10/6/53, Los Angeles, Cal.   BR/TR, 6'1", 175 lbs.   Deb: 4/06/77

YEAR	TM/L	W	L	PCT	G	GS	CG	SH	SV	IP	H	HR	BB	SO	RAT	ERA	ERA+	OAV	OOB	BH	AVG	PB	PR	/A	PD	TPI
1977	SD-N	1	1	.500	15	0	0	0	0	20¹	23	4	9	6	14.2	5.31	67	.287	.360	0	.000	-0	-3	-4	-0	-0.3

■ DWIGHT BERNARD

Bernard, Dwight Vern   b: 5/31/52, Mt.Vernon, Ill.   BR/TR, 6'2", 170 lbs.   Deb: 6/29/78

YEAR	TM/L	W	L	PCT	G	GS	CG	SH	SV	IP	H	HR	BB	SO	RAT	ERA	ERA+	OAV	OOB	BH	AVG	PB	PR	/A	PD	TPI
1978	NY-N	1	4	.200	30	1	0	0	0	48	54	4	27	26	15.2	4.31	81	.297	.388	1	.200	0	-4	-4	0	-0.3
1979	NY-N	0	3	.000	32	1	0	0	0	44	59	2	26	20	17.4	4.70	77	.331	.417	0	—	0	-5	-5	0	-0.4
1981	*Mil-A	0	0	—	6	0	0	0	0	5	5	0	6	1	19.8	3.60	95	.263	.440	0	—	0	0	-0	-0	0.0
1982	*Mil-A	3	1	.750	47	0	0	0	6	79	78	4	27	45	12.1	3.76	101	.263	.326	0	—	0	3	0	-1	0.0
Total	4	4	8	.333	115	2	0	0	6	176	196	10	86	92	14.5	4.14	88	.290	.371	1	.200	1	-6	-9	-1	-0.7

■ JOE BERNARD

Bernard, Joseph Carl "J.C."   b: 3/24/1882, Brighton, Ill.   d: 9/22/60, Springfield, Ill   BR/TR, 6'1", 175 lbs.   Deb: 9/23/09

YEAR	TM/L	W	L	PCT	G	GS	CG	SH	SV	IP	H	HR	BB	SO	RAT	ERA	ERA+	OAV	OOB	BH	AVG	PB	PR	/A	PD	TPI
1909	StL-N	0	0	—	1	0	0	0	0	1	1	0	2	1	27.0	0.00	—	.250	.500	0	—	0	0	0	0	0.0

■ BILL BERNHARD

Bernhard, William Henry "Strawberry Bill"   b: 3/16/1871, Clarence, N.Y.   d: 3/30/49, San Diego, Cal.   BB/TR, 6'1", 205 lbs.   Deb: 4/24/1899

YEAR	TM/L	W	L	PCT	G	GS	CG	SH	SV	IP	H	HR	BB	SO	RAT	ERA	ERA+	OAV	OOB	BH	AVG	PB	PR	/A	PD	TPI
1899	Phi-N	6	6	.500	21	12	10	1	0	132¹	120	3	36	23	10.6	2.65	139	.242	.293	13	.241	0	18	15	0	1.4
1900	Phi-N	15	10	.600	32	27	20	0	2	218²	284	3	74	49	14.7	4.77	76	.313	.365	14	.154	-5	-26	-28	1	-2.7
1901	Phi-A	17	10	.630	28	27	21	1	0	257	328	6	50	58	13.2	4.52	84	.307	.338	20	.187	-1	-24	-21	4	-1.5
1902	Phi-A	1	0	1.000	1	1	1	0	0	9	7	0	3	1	10.0	1.00	367	.215	.282	0	.000	0	3	3	-0	0.2
	Cle-A	17	5	.773	27	24	22	3	1	217	169	4	34	57	8.4	2.20	157	.216	.248	18	.200	-1	33	30	1	3.0
	Yr	18	5	**.783**	28	25	23	3	1	226	176	4	37	58	**8.5**	2.15	161	**.216**	**.250**	1	.011	-1	36	33	1	3.2

YEAR TM/L	W	L	PCT	G	GS	CG	SH	SV	IP	H	HR	BB	SO	RAT	ERA	ERA+	OAV	OOB	BH	AVG	PB	PR	/A	PD	TPI
1903 Cle-A	14	6	.700	20	19	18	3	0	165²	151	1	21	60	9.3	2.12	135	.242	.267	12	.185	-0	16	14	1	1.5
1904 Cle-A	23	13	.639	38	37	35	4	0	320²	323	1	55	137	10.6	2.13	119	.263	.294	22	.177	-1	17	14	-1	1.4
1905 Cle-A	7	13	.350	22	19	17	0	0	174¹	185	5	34	56	11.3	3.36	79	.273	.308	6	.087	-6	-13	-14	0	-1.9
1906 Cle-A	16	15	.516	31	30	23	2	0	255¹	235	1	47	85	9.9	2.54	103	.248	.283	21	.212	2	4	2	2	0.7
1907 Cle-A	0	4	.000	8	4	3	0	0	42	58	0	11	19	14.8	3.21	78	.329	.369	3	.200	0	-3	-3	0	-0.2
Total 9	116	82	.586	231	200	175	14	3	1792	1860	26	365	545	11.2	3.04	102	.268	.304	129	.180	-11	23	11	8	1.9

■ WALTER BERNHARDT
Bernhardt, Walter Jacob b: 5/20/1893, Pleasant Village, Pa. d: 7/26/58, Watertown, N.Y. BR/TR, 6'2", 175 lbs. Deb: 7/16/18

YEAR TM/L	W	L	PCT	G	GS	CG	SH	SV	IP	H	HR	BB	SO	RAT	ERA	ERA+	OAV	OOB	BH	AVG	PB	PR	/A	PD	TPI
1918 NY-A	0	0	—	1	0	0	0	0	0²	0	0	0	1	0.0	0.00	—	.000	.000	0	—	0	0	0	0	0.0

■ JOE BERRY
Berry, Jonas Arthur "Jittery Joe" b: 12/16/04, Huntsville, Ark. d: 9/27/58, Anaheim, Cal. BL/TR, 5'10.5", 145 lbs. Deb: 9/06/42

YEAR TM/L	W	L	PCT	G	GS	CG	SH	SV	IP	H	HR	BB	SO	RAT	ERA	ERA+	OAV	OOB	BH	AVG	PB	PR	/A	PD	TPI
1942 Chi-N	0	0	—	2	0	0	0	0	2	7	0	2	1	40.5	18.00	18	.538	.600	0	—	0	-3	-3	0	-0.2
1944 Phi-A	10	8	.556	53	0	0	0	12	111¹	78	4	23	44	8.3	1.94	179	.192	.238	3	.120	-1	18	19	2	2.1
1945 Phi-A	8	7	.533	52	0	0	0	5	130¹	114	5	38	51	10.5	2.35	146	.232	.287	5	.143	-1	15	16	1	1.7
1946 Phi-A	0	1	.000	5	0	0	0	0	13	15	1	3	5	13.2	2.77	128	.288	.339	1	.333	0	1	1	0	0.2
Cle-A	3	6	.333	21	0	0	0	1	37¹	32	4	21	16	12.8	3.38	98	.235	.338	2	.286	0	1	-0	-1	0.0
Yr	3	7	.300	26	0	0	0	1	50¹	47	5	24	21	12.7	3.22	105	.249	.333	0	.000	1	2	1	-0	0.2
Total 4	21	22	.488	133	0	0	0	18	294	246	14	87	117	10.3	2.45	140	.224	.282	11	.157	-2	31	32	3	3.8

■ FRANK BERTAINA
Bertaina, Frank Louis b: 4/14/44, San Francisco, Cal. BL/TL, 5'11", 177 lbs. Deb: 8/01/64

YEAR TM/L	W	L	PCT	G	GS	CG	SH	SV	IP	H	HR	BB	SO	RAT	ERA	ERA+	OAV	OOB	BH	AVG	PB	PR	/A	PD	TPI
1964 Bal-A	1	0	1.000	6	4	1	1	0	26	18	3	13	18	10.7	2.77	129	.198	.298	0	.000	-1	2	2	0	0.2
1965 Bal-A	0	0	—	2	1	0	0	0	6	9	0	4	5	19.5	6.00	58	.360	.448	0	.000	-0	-2	-2	0	-0.1
1966 Bal-A	2	5	.286	16	9	0	0	0	63¹	52	3	36	46	13.1	3.13	107	.226	.341	2	.105	-1	2	1	-2	0.0
1967 Bal-A	1	1	.500	5	2	0	0	0	21²	14	4	14	19	12.9	3.32	95	.224	.344	1	.111	-0	-0	-0	0	0.0
Was-A	6	5	.545	18	17	4	4	0	95²	90	8	37	67	11.9	2.92	108	.251	.322	2	.057	-2	3	3	-1	0.0
Yr	7	6	.538	23	19	4	4	0	117¹	107	12	51	86	12.1	2.99	106	.246	.325	0	.000	-3	3	2	-1	0.0
1968 Was-A	7	13	.350	27	23	1	0	0	127¹	133	15	69	81	14.7	4.66	63	.273	.369	5	.132	-0	-24	-25	-0	-2.6
1969 Was-A	1	3	.250	14	5	0	0	0	35²	43	8	23	25	16.7	6.56	53	.291	.386	4	.364	2	-12	-12	0	-1.2
Bal-A	0	0	—	3	0	0	0	0	6	1	0	3	5	6.0	0.00	—	.063	.211	1	1.000	1	2	2	0	0.3
Yr	1	3	.250	17	5	0	0	0	41²	44	8	26	30	15.1	5.62	62	.267	.366	5	.083	3	-9	-10	-0	-0.6
1970 StL-N	1	2	.333	8	5	0	0	0	31¹	36	1	15	14	14.6	3.16	130	.293	.370	1	.143	0	3	3	0	0.4
Total 7	19	29	.396	99	66	6	5	0	413	399	42	214	280	13.6	3.84	85	.257	.350	16	.127	-1	-24	-27	-2	-2.7

■ LEFTY BERTRAND
Bertrand, Roman Mathias b: 2/28/09, Cobden, Minn. BR/TL, 6', 180 lbs. Deb: 4/15/36

YEAR TM/L	W	L	PCT	G	GS	CG	SH	SV	IP	H	HR	BB	SO	RAT	ERA	ERA+	OAV	OOB	BH	AVG	PB	PR	/A	PD	TPI
1936 Phi-N	0	0	—	1	0	0	0	0	2	3	1	2	1	22.5	9.00	50	.333	.455	0	—	0	-1	-1	0	0.0

■ FRED BESANA
Besana, Frederick Cyril b: 4/5/31, Lincoln, Cal. BR/TL, 6'3.5", 200 lbs. Deb: 4/18/56

YEAR TM/L	W	L	PCT	G	GS	CG	SH	SV	IP	H	HR	BB	SO	RAT	ERA	ERA+	OAV	OOB	BH	AVG	PB	PR	/A	PD	TPI
1956 Bal-A	1	0	1.000	7	2	0	0	0	17²	22	0	14	7	19.4	5.60	70	.310	.437	0	.000	-0	-3	-3	1	-0.2

■ HERMAN BESSE
Besse, Herman A. b: 8/16/11, St.Louis, Mo. d: 8/13/72, Los Angeles, Cal. BL/TL, 6'2", 190 lbs. Deb: 4/19/40

YEAR TM/L	W	L	PCT	G	GS	CG	SH	SV	IP	H	HR	BB	SO	RAT	ERA	ERA+	OAV	OOB	BH	AVG	PB	PR	/A	PD	TPI
1940 Phi-A	0	3	.000	17	5	0	0	0	53	70	10	34	19	18.2	8.83	50	.315	.413	5	.263	2	-26	-26	-1	-2.1
1941 Phi-A	2	0	1.000	6	2	1	0	0	19²	28	4	12	8	18.3	10.07	42	.329	.412	1	.200	-0	-13	-13	0	-1.0
1942 Phi-A	2	9	.182	30	14	4	0	1	133	163	7	69	78	16.0	6.16	61	.300	.383	12	.226	2	-37	-35	-2	-3.3
1943 Phi-A	1	1	.500	5	1	0	0	0	16¹	18	2	4	3	12.7	3.31	103	.295	.348	0	.000	-1	-0	0	0	0.0
1946 Phi-A	0	2	.000	7	3	0	0	1	20²	19	1	9	10	12.2	5.23	68	.247	.326	0	.000	-0	-4	-4	-0	-0.3
Total 5	5	15	.250	65	25	5	0	2	242²	298	24	128	118	16.1	6.79	58	.302	.386	18	.200	2	-80	-77	-3	-6.7

■ DON BESSENT
Bessent, Fred Donald b: 3/13/31, Jacksonville, Fla. d: 7/7/90, Jacksonville, Fla. BR/TR, 6', 175 lbs. Deb: 7/17/55

YEAR TM/L	W	L	PCT	G	GS	CG	SH	SV	IP	H	HR	BB	SO	RAT	ERA	ERA+	OAV	OOB	BH	AVG	PB	PR	/A	PD	TPI
1955 *Bro-N	8	1	.889	24	2	1	0	3	63¹	51	7	21	29	10.2	2.70	150	.220	.285	2	.100	-2	9	10	0	0.8
1956 *Bro-N	4	3	.571	38	0	0	0	9	79¹	63	5	31	52	10.7	2.50	159	.221	.297	2	.111	-1	11	13	-1	1.1
1957 Bro-N	1	3	.250	27	0	0	0	0	44	58	5	19	24	15.8	5.73	73	.328	.393	1	.250	0	-9	-8	-0	-0.7
1958 LA-N	1	0	1.000	19	0	0	0	0	24¹	24	3	17	13	15.5	3.33	123	.270	.393	0	.000	-0	2	2	1	0.3
Total 4	14	7	.667	108	2	1	0	12	211	196	20	88	118	12.2	3.33	122	.250	.327	5	.114	-3	13	17	-1	1.5

■ KARL BEST
Best, Karl Jon b: 3/6/59, Aberdeen, Was. BR/TR, 6'4", 190 lbs. Deb: 8/19/83

YEAR TM/L	W	L	PCT	G	GS	CG	SH	SV	IP	H	HR	BB	SO	RAT	ERA	ERA+	OAV	OOB	BH	AVG	PB	PR	/A	PD	TPI
1983 Sea-A	0	1	.000	4	0	0	0	0	5¹	14	2	5	3	35.4	13.50	32	.483	.583	0	—	0	-6	-5	-0	-0.4
1984 Sea-A	1	1	.500	5	0	0	0	0	6	7	0	0	6	10.5	3.00	133	.292	.292	0	—	0	1	1	-0	0.0
1985 Sea-A	2	1	.667	15	0	0	0	4	32¹	25	1	6	32	8.9	1.95	216	.207	.250	0	—	0	8	8	-1	0.8
1986 Sea-A	2	3	.400	26	0	0	0	1	35²	35	3	21	23	14.4	4.04	105	.255	.358	0	—	0	1	1	-0	0.0
1988 Min-A	0	0	—	11	0	0	0	0	12	15	1	7	9	16.5	6.00	68	.306	.393	0	—	0	-3	-3	-0	-0.2
Total 5	5	6	.455	61	0	0	0	5	91¹	96	7	39	73	13.7	4.04	104	.267	.345	0	—	0	1	2	-1	0.2

■ JIM BETHKE
Bethke, James Charles b: 11/5/46, Falls City, Neb. BR/TR, 6'3", 185 lbs. Deb: 4/12/65

YEAR TM/L	W	L	PCT	G	GS	CG	SH	SV	IP	H	HR	BB	SO	RAT	ERA	ERA+	OAV	OOB	BH	AVG	PB	PR	/A	PD	TPI
1965 NY-N	2	0	1.000	25	0	0	0	0	40	41	3	22	19	15.5	4.27	83	.266	.379	0	.000	-0	-3	-3	1	-0.2

■ JEFF BETTENDORF
Bettendorf, Jeffrey Allen b: 12/10/60, Lompoc, Cal. BR/TR, 6'3", 180 lbs. Deb: 4/08/84

YEAR TM/L	W	L	PCT	G	GS	CG	SH	SV	IP	H	HR	BB	SO	RAT	ERA	ERA+	OAV	OOB	BH	AVG	PB	PR	/A	PD	TPI
1984 Oak-A	0	0	—	3	0	0	0	1	9²	9	3	5	5	13.0	4.66	80	.243	.333	0	—	0	-1	-1	-0	0.0

■ HARRY BETTS
Betts, Harold Matthew "Chubby" or "Ginger" b: 6/19/1881, Alliance, Ohio d: 5/22/46, San Antonio, Tex. BR/TR, 5'10", 200 lbs. Deb: 9/22/03

YEAR TM/L	W	L	PCT	G	GS	CG	SH	SV	IP	H	HR	BB	SO	RAT	ERA	ERA+	OAV	OOB	BH	AVG	PB	PR	/A	PD	TPI
1903 StL-N	0	1	.000	1	1	1	0	0	9	11	0	5	2	18.0	10.00	33	.297	.409	0	.000	-0	-7	-7	0	-0.4
1913 Cin-N	0	0	—	1	0	0	0	0	3¹	1	0	3	0	13.5	2.70	120	.143	.455	0	.000	-0	0	0	0	0.0
Total 2	0	1	.000	2	1	1	0	0	12¹	12	0	8	2	16.8	8.03	41	.273	.418	0	.000	-1	-7	-7	-0	-0.4

■ HUCK BETTS
Betts, Walter Martin b: 2/18/1897, Millsboro, Del. d: 6/13/87, Millsboro, Del. BR/TR, 5'11", 170 lbs. Deb: 4/26/20

YEAR TM/L	W	L	PCT	G	GS	CG	SH	SV	IP	H	HR	BB	SO	RAT	ERA	ERA+	OAV	OOB	BH	AVG	PB	PR	/A	PD	TPI
1920 Phi-N	1	1	.500	27	4	1	0	0	88¹	86	3	33	18	12.3	3.57	96	.261	.332	2	.080	-2	-4	-1	-0	-0.3
1921 Phi-N	3	7	.300	32	2	1	0	4	100²	141	8	14	28	14.2	4.47	95	.337	.365	8	.267	0	-8	-3	0	-0.1
1922 Phi-N	1	0	1.000	7	0	0	0	0	15	23	3	8	4	18.6	9.60	49	.348	.419	0	.000	-0	-9	-8	-0	-0.7
1923 Phi-N	2	4	.333	19	4	3	0	1	84¹	100	7	14	18	12.6	3.09	149	.314	.351	3	.097	-4	9	14	0	1.1
1924 Phi-N	7	10	.412	37	9	2	0	2	144¹	160	8	42	46	12.9	4.30	104	.286	.341	7	.156	-3	-7	3	-2	0.0
1925 Phi-N	4	5	.444	35	7	1	0	1	97¹	146	10	38	28	17.3	5.55	86	.342	.400	10	.294	2	-14	-8	1	-0.4
1932 Bos-N	13	11	.542	31	27	16	3	1	221²	229	9	35	32	10.7	2.80	134	.267	.295	19	.241	2	27	24	-1	2.4
1933 Bos-N	11	11	.500	35	26	17	2	4	242	225	9	55	40	10.4	2.79	110	.248	.290	17	.224	5	15	7	5	1.5
1934 Bos-N	17	10	.630	40	27	10	2	3	213	258	17	42	69	12.8	4.06	94	.296	.330	13	.188	1	0	-6	-2	-0.6
1935 Bos-N	2	9	.182	44	19	2	1	0	159²	213	9	40	44	14.4	5.47	69	.321	.362	7	.159	-4	-26	-30	1	-2.7
Total 10	61	68	.473	307	125	53	8	16	1366¹	1581	83	321	323	12.7	3.93	98	.292	.334	86	.197	-3	-18	-9	2	0.2

■ BILL BEVENS
Bevens, Floyd Clifford b: 10/21/16, Hubbard, Ore. BR/TR, 6'3.5", 210 lbs. Deb: 5/12/44

YEAR TM/L	W	L	PCT	G	GS	CG	SH	SV	IP	H	HR	BB	SO	RAT	ERA	ERA+	OAV	OOB	BH	AVG	PB	PR	/A	PD	TPI
1944 NY-A	4	1	.800	8	5	3	0	0	43²	44	4	13	16	12.0	2.68	130	.273	.331	1	.063	-2	4	4	-0	0.2
1945 NY-A	13	9	.591	29	25	14	2	0	184	174	12	68	76	11.9	3.67	94	.254	.322	7	.111	-4	-6	-4	1	-0.8
1946 NY-A	16	13	.552	31	31	18	3	0	249²	213	11	78	105	10.5	2.23	154	.232	.293	7	.083	-4	35	34	-4	2.8
1947 *NY-A	7	13	.350	28	23	11	1	0	165	167	13	77	77	13.4	3.82	93	.264	.345	7	.121	-3	-2	-5	-0	-0.8
Total 4	40	36	.526	96	84	46	6	0	642¹	598	40	236	289	11.7	3.08	113	.250	.318	22	.100	-13	31	29	-4	1.4

■ LOU BEVIL
Bevil, Louis Eugene (b: Louis Eugene Bevilacqua) b: 11/27/22, Nelson, Ill. d: 2/1/73, Dixon, Ill. BB/TR, 5'11.5", 190 lbs. Deb: 9/02/42

YEAR TM/L	W	L	PCT	G	GS	CG	SH	SV	IP	H	HR	BB	SO	RAT	ERA	ERA+	OAV	OOB	BH	AVG	PB	PR	/A	PD	TPI
1942 Was-A	0	1	.000	4	1	0	0	0	9²	9	0	11	2	19.6	6.52	56	.265	.457	0	.000	-0	-3	-3	-0	-0.3

YEAR TM/L	W	L	PCT	G	GS	CG	SH	SV	IP	H	HR	BB	SO	RAT	ERA	ERA+	OAV	OOB	BH	AVG	PB	PR	/A	PD	TPI

■ BEN BEVILLE
Beville, Clarence Benjamin b: 8/28/1877, Colusa, Cal. d: 1/5/37, Yountville, Cal. 5'9", 190 lbs. Deb: 5/24/01

YEAR TM/L	W	L	PCT	G	GS	CG	SH	SV	IP	H	HR	BB	SO	RAT	ERA	ERA+	OAV	OOB	BH	AVG	PB	PR	/A	PD	TPI
1901 Bos-A	0	2	.000	2	2	1	0	0	9	8	0	9	1	17.0	4.00	88	.235	.396	2	.286	0	-0	-0	0	0.0

■ JIM BIBBY
Bibby, James Blair b: 10/29/44, Franklinton, N.C. BR/TR, 6'5", 235 lbs. Deb: 9/04/72

YEAR TM/L	W	L	PCT	G	GS	CG	SH	SV	IP	H	HR	BB	SO	RAT	ERA	ERA+	OAV	OOB	BH	AVG	PB	PR	/A	PD	TPI
1972 StL-N	1	3	.250	6	6	0	0	0	40^1	29	4	19	28	10.9	3.35	102	.206	.304	1	.125	0	0	0	0	0.1
1973 StL-N	0	2	.000	6	3	0	0	0	16	19	2	17	12	21.4	9.56	38	.306	.469	0	.000	0	-10	-11	0	-0.9
Tex-A	9	10	.474	26	23	11	2	1	180^1	121	14	106	155	11.6	3.24	115	**.192**	.314	0	—	0	11	10	-2	0.8
1974 Tex-A	19	19	.500	41	41	11	5	0	264	255	25	113	149	12.9	4.74	75	.255	.336	0	—	0	-33	-34	1	-3.3
1975 Tex-A	2	6	.250	12	12	4	1	0	68^1	73	2	28	31	13.6	5.00	75	.274	.348	0	—	0	-9	-9	-0	-0.9
Cle-A	5	9	.357	24	12	2	0	1	112^2	99	7	50	62	11.9	3.20	118	.235	.316	0	—	0	7	7	1	0.8
Yr	7	15	.318	36	24	6	1	1	181	172	9	78	93	12.4	3.88	97	.248	.324	0	—	0	-2	-2	0	-0.1
1976 Cle-A	13	7	.650	34	21	4	3	1	163^1	162	6	56	84	12.1	3.20	109	.266	.329	0	—	0	6	5	-1	0.5
1977 Cle-A	12	13	.480	37	30	9	2	2	206^2	197	17	73	141	11.9	3.57	110	.250	.317	0	—	0	11	9	-2	0.6
1978 Pit-N	8	7	.533	34	14	3	2	1	107	100	10	39	72	11.9	3.53	105	.246	.315	4	.129	1	1	2	0	0.3
1979 *Pit-N	12	4	.750	34	17	4	1	0	137^2	110	9	47	103	10.5	2.81	138	.218	.290	8	.178	2	14	16	-2	1.8
1980 Pit-N	19	6	**.760**	35	34	6	1	0	238^1	210	20	88	144	11.5	3.32	110	.238	.312	12	.156	2	7	8	-2	0.9
1981 Pit-N	6	3	.667	14	14	2	2	0	93^2	79	4	26	48	10.3	2.50	144	.225	.282	4	.143	1	10	11	-1	1.3
1983 Pit-N	5	12	.294	29	12	0	0	2	78	92	10	51	44	16.6	6.69	55	.297	.398	2	.111	-1	-27	-26	-0	-2.6
1984 Tex-A	0	0	—	8	0	0	0	0	16^1	19	1	10	6	16.0	4.41	94	.297	.392	0	—	0	-1	-0	0	0.0
Total 12	111	101	.524	340	239	56	19	8	1722^2	1565	131	723	1079	12.2	3.76	98	.243	.323	31	.148	5	-11	-11	-8	-0.6

■ VERN BICKFORD
Bickford, Vernon Edgell b: 8/17/20, Hellier, Ky. d: 5/6/60, Concord, Va. BR/TR, 6', 180 lbs. Deb: 4/24/48

YEAR TM/L	W	L	PCT	G	GS	CG	SH	SV	IP	H	HR	BB	SO	RAT	ERA	ERA+	OAV	OOB	BH	AVG	PB	PR	/A	PD	TPI
1948 *Bos-N	11	5	.688	33	22	10	1	1	146	125	9	63	60	11.8	3.27	117	.226	.309	10	.204	1	11	9	-1	0.9
1949 Bos-N	16	11	.593	37	36	15	2	0	230^2	246	20	106	101	14.0	4.25	89	.273	.354	15	.185	-0	-5	-12	2	-1.0
1950 Bos-N	19	14	.576	40	39	**27**	2	0	311^2	293	25	122	126	12.2	3.47	111	.248	.321	16	.138	-4	23	13	-1	0.7
1951 Bos-N	11	9	.550	25	20	12	3	0	164^2	146	7	76	76	12.5	3.12	118	.240	.330	6	.115	-2	15	10	2	1.1
1952 Bos-N	7	12	.368	26	22	7	1	0	161^1	165	7	64	62	12.9	3.74	97	.279	.340	9	.176	-0	-0	-2	1	-0.1
1953 Mil-N	2	5	.286	20	9	2	0	1	58	60	8	35	25	15.1	5.28	74	.279	.385	1	.067	-0	-6	-9	1	-0.7
1954 Bal-A	0	1	.000	1	1	0	0	0	4	5	0	1	0	13.5	9.00	40	.333	.375	0	.000	-0	-2	-2	0	-0.1
Total 7	66	57	.537	182	149	73	9	2	1076^1	1040	76	467	450	12.8	3.71	102	.254	.335	57	.156	-6	36	7	4	0.8

■ DAN BICKHAM
Bickham, Daniel Denison b: 10/31/1864, Dayton, Ohio d: 3/3/51, Dayton, Ohio 5'10", 160 lbs. Deb: 8/13/1886

YEAR TM/L	W	L	PCT	G	GS	CG	SH	SV	IP	H	HR	BB	SO	RAT	ERA	ERA+	OAV	OOB	BH	AVG	PB	PR	/A	PD	TPI
1886 Cin-a	1	0	1.000	1	1	1	0	0	9	13	0	6	3	16.0	3.00	117	.323	.370	1	.333	0	0	1	0	0.1

■ CHARLIE BICKNELL
Bicknell, Charles Stephen "Bud" b: 7/27/28, Plainfield, N.J. BR/TR, 5'11", 170 lbs. Deb: 4/22/48

YEAR TM/L	W	L	PCT	G	GS	CG	SH	SV	IP	H	HR	BB	SO	RAT	ERA	ERA+	OAV	OOB	BH	AVG	PB	PR	/A	PD	TPI
1948 Phi-N	0	1	.000	17	1	0	0	0	25^2	29	5	17	5	16.1	5.96	66	.287	.390	0	.000	-1	-6	-6	-0	-0.6
1949 Phi-N	0	0	—	13	0	0	0	0	28^1	32	3	17	4	16.2	7.62	52	.291	.395	0	.000	0	-11	-12	0	-0.9
Total 2	0	1	.000	30	1	0	0	0	54	61	8	34	9	16.2	6.83	58	.289	.393	0	.000	-0	-17	-17	-0	-1.5

■ MIKE BIELECKI
Bielecki, Michael Joseph b: 7/31/59, Baltimore, Md. BR/TR, 6'3", 200 lbs. Deb: 9/14/84

YEAR TM/L	W	L	PCT	G	GS	CG	SH	SV	IP	H	HR	BB	SO	RAT	ERA	ERA+	OAV	OOB	BH	AVG	PB	PR	/A	PD	TPI
1984 Pit-N	0	0	—	4	0	0	0	0	4^1	4	0	1	0	8.3	0.00	—	.250	.250	0	—	0	2	2	0	0.2
1985 Pit-N	2	3	.400	12	7	0	0	0	45^2	45	5	31	22	15.2	4.53	79	.257	.372	0	.000	-1	-5	-5	1	-0.4
1986 Pit-N	6	11	.353	31	27	0	0	0	148^2	149	10	83	83	14.2	4.66	82	.262	.358	3	.063	-3	-16	-14	-1	-1.6
1987 Pit-N	2	3	.400	8	8	2	0	0	45^2	43	6	12	25	11.0	4.73	87	.250	.303	1	.063	-1	-3	-3	-0	-0.3
1988 Chi-N	2	2	.500	19	5	0	0	0	48^1	55	4	16	33	13.2	3.35	108	.284	.338	1	.100	-0	1	1	-0	0.1
1989 *Chi-N	18	7	**.720**	33	33	4	3	0	212^1	187	16	81	147	11.4	3.14	120	.237	.308	3	.043	-5	8	15	-1	0.9
1990 Chi-N	8	11	.421	36	29	0	0	1	168	188	13	70	103	14.1	4.93	84	.287	.361	1	.163	-0	-21	-15	3	-1.1
Total 7	38	37	.507	143	109	6	3	1	673	671	54	293	414	13.0	4.12	94	.261	.339	15	.076	-11	-34	-19	1	-2.2

■ HARRY BIEMILLER
Biemiller, Harry Lee b: 10/9/1897, Baltimore, Md. d: 5/25/65, Orlando, Fla. BR/TR, 6'1", 171 lbs. Deb: 8/26/20

YEAR TM/L	W	L	PCT	G	GS	CG	SH	SV	IP	H	HR	BB	SO	RAT	ERA	ERA+	OAV	OOB	BH	AVG	PB	PR	/A	PD	TPI
1920 Was-A	1	0	1.000	5	2	1	0	0	17	21	1	13	10	18.0	4.76	78	.318	.430	0	.000	-1	-2	-2	1	-0.1
1925 Cin-N	0	1	.000	23	1	0	0	2	47	45	2	21	9	14.0	4.02	102	.280	.386	0	.000	-0	1	0	2	0.1
Total 2	1	1	.500	28	3	1	0	2	64	66	3	34	19	15.0	4.22	95	.291	.399	0	.000	-1	-1	-1	2	0.0

■ LOU BIERBAUER
Bierbauer, Louis W. b: 9/28/1865, Erie, Pa. d: 1/31/26, Erie, Pa. BL/TR, 5'8", 140 lbs. Deb: 4/17/1886 ♦

YEAR TM/L	W	L	PCT	G	GS	CG	SH	SV	IP	H	HR	BB	SO	RAT	ERA	ERA+	OAV	OOB	BH	AVG	PB	PR	/A	PD	TPI
1886 Phi-a	0	0	—	2	0	0	0	0	10^2	8	0	5	4	11.0	4.22	83	.199	.287	118	.226	-0	-1	-1	-0	0.0
1887 Phi-a	0	0	—	1	0	0	0	1	1	0	0	0	1	0.0	0.00	—	.000	.000	144	.272	0	0	0	0	0.0
1888 Phi-a	0	0	—	1	0	0	0	0	3	5	0	0	3	15.0	0.00	—	.358	.358	143	.267	0	1	1	0	0.1
Total 3	0	0	—	4	0	0	0	1	14^2	13	0	5	5	11.0	3.07	112	.227	.289	1521	.267	1	1	1	-0	0.1

■ LYLE BIGBEE
Bigbee, Lyle Randolph "Al" b: 8/22/1893, Sweet Home, Ore. d: 8/5/42, Portland, Ore. BL/TR, 6', 180 lbs. Deb: 4/15/20 ♦

YEAR TM/L	W	L	PCT	G	GS	CG	SH	SV	IP	H	HR	BB	SO	RAT	ERA	ERA+	OAV	OOB	BH	AVG	PB	PR	/A	PD	TPI
1920 Phi-A	0	3	.000	12	2	0	0	0	45	66	5	29	12	18.2	8.00	50	.369	.446	14	.187	0	-21	-20	0	-1.7
1921 Pit-N	0	0	—	5	0	0	0	0	8	4	0	4	1	9.0	1.13	341	.154	.267	0	.000	-0	2	2	0	0.2
Total 2	0	3	.000	17	2	0	0	0	53	70	5	29	13	16.8	6.96	57	.341	.423	14	.182	-0	-19	-17	0	-1.5

■ CHARLIE BIGGS
Biggs, Charles Orval b: 9/15/06, French Lick, Ind. d: 5/24/54, French Lick, Ind. BR/TR, 6'1", 185 lbs. Deb: 9/03/32

YEAR TM/L	W	L	PCT	G	GS	CG	SH	SV	IP	H	HR	BB	SO	RAT	ERA	ERA+	OAV	OOB	BH	AVG	PB	PR	/A	PD	TPI
1932 Chi-A	1	1	.500	6	4	0	0	0	24^2	32	2	12	1	17.1	6.93	62	.314	.402	1	.111	-0	-7	-7	0	-0.6

■ LARRY BIITTNER
Biittner, Lawrence David b: 7/27/45, Pocahontas, Ia. BL/TL, 6'2", 205 lbs. Deb: 7/17/70 ♦

YEAR TM/L	W	L	PCT	G	GS	CG	SH	SV	IP	H	HR	BB	SO	RAT	ERA	ERA+	OAV	OOB	BH	AVG	PB	PR	/A	PD	TPI
1977 Chi-N	0	0	—	1	0	0	0	0	1^1	5	3	1	3	40.5	40.50	11	.556	.600	147	.298	0	-5	-5	0	-0.3

■ JIM BILBREY
Bilbrey, James Melvin b: 4/20/24, Rickman, Tenn. d: 12/26/85, Toledo, Ohio BR/TR, 6'2.5", 205 lbs. Deb: 5/17/49

YEAR TM/L	W	L	PCT	G	GS	CG	SH	SV	IP	H	HR	BB	SO	RAT	ERA	ERA+	OAV	OOB	BH	AVG	PB	PR	/A	PD	TPI
1949 StL-A	0	0	—	1	0	0	0	0	1	1	0	3	0	36.0	18.00	25	.250	.571	0	—	0	-2	-1	0	0.0

■ EMIL BILDILLI
Bildilli, Emil "Hill Billy" b: 9/16/12, Diamond, Ind. d: 9/16/46, Hartford City, Ind. BR/TL, 5'10", 170 lbs. Deb: 8/24/37

YEAR TM/L	W	L	PCT	G	GS	CG	SH	SV	IP	H	HR	BB	SO	RAT	ERA	ERA+	OAV	OOB	BH	AVG	PB	PR	/A	PD	TPI
1937 StL-A	0	1	.000	4	1	0	0	0	8	12	1	3	2	16.9	10.13	48	.353	.405	0	.000	-0	-5	-5	1	-0.3
1938 StL-A	1	2	.333	5	3	2	0	0	21^2	33	3	11	11	18.3	7.06	70	.359	.427	2	.250	-0	-5	-5	-0	-0.3
1939 StL-A	1	1	.500	2	2	2	0	0	19	21	0	6	8	12.8	3.32	147	.266	.318	0	.000	-1	3	3	0	0.3
1940 StL-A	2	4	.333	28	11	3	0	1	97	113	12	52	32	15.5	5.57	82	.298	.386	6	.200	-1	-13	-11	3	-0.7
1941 StL-A	0	0	—	2	0	0	0	0	2^1	5	0	3	2	30.9	11.57	37	.417	.533	0	—	0	-2	-2	0	-0.1
Total 5	4	8	.333	41	17	7	0	1	148	184	16	75	55	15.9	5.84	80	.309	.388	8	.178	-2	-22	-19	4	-1.1

■ HARRY BILLIARD
Billiard, Harry Pree "Pree" b: 11/11/1883, Monroe, Ind. d: 6/3/23, Wooster, Ohio BR/TR, 6', 190 lbs. Deb: 7/31/08

YEAR TM/L	W	L	PCT	G	GS	CG	SH	SV	IP	H	HR	BB	SO	RAT	ERA	ERA+	OAV	OOB	BH	AVG	PB	PR	/A	PD	TPI
1908 NY-A	0	0	—	6	0	0	0	0	17	15	1	14	10	18.0	2.65	94	.234	.410	0	.200	-0	-0	-0	-1	0.0
1914 Ind-F	8	7	.533	32	16	5	0	2	125^2	117	4	63	45	13.4	3.72	93	.257	.356	7	.184	-1	-7	-4	-1	-0.5
1915 New-F	0	1	.000	14	2	0	0	1	28^1	32	0	28	7	20.0	5.72	50	.292	.448	2	.333	0	-8	-9	1	-0.7
Total 3	8	8	.500	52	18	5	0	3	171	164	5	105	62	14.9	3.95	83	.261	.379	10	.204	-0	-16	-13	-1	-1.2

■ JACK BILLINGHAM
Billingham, John Eugene b: 2/21/43, Orlando, Fla. BR/TR, 6'4", 195 lbs. Deb: 4/11/68

YEAR TM/L	W	L	PCT	G	GS	CG	SH	SV	IP	H	HR	BB	SO	RAT	ERA	ERA+	OAV	OOB	BH	AVG	PB	PR	/A	PD	TPI
1968 LA-N	3	0	1.000	50	1	0	0	8	70^2	54	0	30	46	11.0	2.17	128	.215	.304	0	.000	0	6	5	1	0.6
1969 Hou-N	6	7	.462	52	4	0	0	2	82^2	92	12	29	71	13.7	4.25	83	.290	.359	1	.071	0	-6	-6	-0	-0.6
1970 Hou-N	13	9	.591	46	24	8	2	0	187^2	190	10	63	134	12.6	3.98	97	.259	.326	6	.103	-2	1	-2	1	-0.3
1971 Hou-N	10	16	.385	33	33	8	3	0	228^1	205	9	68	137	11.0	3.39	99	.243	.311	9	.123	-3	2	-1	0	-0.3
1972 *Cin-N	12	12	.500	36	31	8	4	1	217^2	197	18	64	137	11.1	3.18	101	.241	.301	5	.070	-4	7	1	-0	-0.4
1973 *Cin-N	19	10	.655	40	40	16	**7**	0	293^1	257	20	95	155	11.1	3.04	112	.236	.303	6	.065	-5	20	12	2	0.9
1974 Cin-N	19	11	.633	36	35	8	3	0	212^1	233	16	64	103	12.8	3.94	88	.288	.345	5	.075	-5	-8	-11	1	-1.4

YEAR TM/L	W	L	PCT	G	GS	CG	SH	SV	IP	H	HR	BB	SO	RAT	ERA	ERA+	OAV	OOB	BH	AVG	PB	PR	/A	PD	TPI
1975 *Cin-N	15	10	.600	33	32	5	0	0	208	222	22	76	79	13.3	4.11	87	.279	.348	7	.108	-1	-11	-12	-2	-1.4
1976 *Cin-N	12	10	.545	34	29	5	2	1	177	190	17	62	76	13.0	4.32	81	.279	.343	14	.237	3	-16	-16	-0	-1.3
1977 Cin-N	10	10	.500	36	23	3	2	0	161²	195	16	56	76	14.5	5.23	75	.306	.371	9	.161	-1	-24	-23	2	-2.0
1978 Det-A	15	8	.652	30	30	10	4	0	201²	218	16	65	59	13.0	3.88	100	.284	.346	0	—	0	-3	-0	-1	0.0
1979 Det-A	10	7	.588	35	19	2	0	3	158	163	13	60	59	13.1	3.30	131	.275	.348	0	—	0	16	18	-1	1.7
1980 Det-A	0	0	—	8	0	0	0	0	7¹	11	1	6	3	20.9	7.36	56	.355	.459	0	—	0	-3	-3	0	-0.1
Bos-A	1	3	.250	7	4	0	0	0	24¹	45	6	12	4	22.6	11.10	38	.413	.488	0	—	0	-19	-19	-0	-1.5
Yr	1	3	.250	15	4	0	0	0	31²	56	7	18	7	22.2	10.23	41	.397	.479	0	—	0	-22	-21	0	-1.6
Total 13	145	113	.562	476	305	74	27	15	2230²	2272	176	750	1141	12.6	3.83	94	.268	.335	62	.111	-16	-37	-59	3	-6.1

■ JOSH BILLINGS — Billings, Haskell Clark b: 9/27/07, New York, N.Y. d: 12/26/83, Greenbrae, Cal. BR/TR, 5'11", 180 lbs. Deb: 8/17/27

YEAR TM/L	W	L	PCT	G	GS	CG	SH	SV	IP	H	HR	BB	SO	RAT	ERA	ERA+	OAV	OOB	BH	AVG	PB	PR	/A	PD	TPI
1927 Det-A	5	4	.556	10	9	5	0	0	67	64	3	39	18	14.6	4.84	87	.259	.373	7	.259	0	-5	-5	-0	-0.3
1928 Det-A	5	10	.333	21	16	3	1	0	110²	118	4	59	48	14.8	5.12	80	.276	.371	10	.286	3	-13	-12	-1	-0.9
1929 Det-A	0	1	.000	8	0	0	0	0	19¹	27	0	9	1	17.2	5.12	84	.365	.440	0	.000	-1	-2	-2	1	0.0
Total 3	10	15	.400	39	25	8	1	0	197	209	7	107	67	15.0	5.03	83	.279	.378	17	.250	2	-20	-19	0	-1.2

■ DOUG BIRD — Bird, James Douglas b: 3/5/50, Corona, Cal. BR/TR, 6'4", 180 lbs. Deb: 4/29/73

YEAR TM/L	W	L	PCT	G	GS	CG	SH	SV	IP	H	HR	BB	SO	RAT	ERA	ERA+	OAV	OOB	BH	AVG	PB	PR	/A	PD	TPI
1973 KC-A	4	4	.500	54	0	0	0	20	102¹	81	10	30	83	9.9	2.99	137	.217	.279	0	—	0	9	13	-2	1.1
1974 KC-A	7	6	.538	55	1	1	0	10	92¹	100	6	27	62	12.5	2.73	140	.286	.339	0	—	0	9	11	0	1.2
1975 KC-A	9	6	.600	51	4	0	0	11	105¹	100	7	40	81	12.1	3.25	119	.258	.331	0	—	0	6	7	-1	0.6
1976 *KC-A	12	10	.545	39	27	2	1	2	197²	191	17	31	107	10.2	3.37	104	.251	.283	0	—	0	3	3	-2	0.1
1977 *KC-A	11	4	.733	53	5	0	0	14	118¹	120	14	29	83	11.6	3.88	104	.270	.319	0	—	0	2	2	-1	0.1
1978 *KC-A	6	6	.500	40	6	0	0	1	98²	110	8	31	48	13.0	5.29	72	.284	.340	0	—	0	-17	-16	-0	-1.6
1979 Phi-N	2	0	1.000	32	1	1	0	0	61	73	7	16	33	13.4	5.16	74	.305	.354	1	.167	0	-10	-9	-1	-0.9
1980 NY-A	3	0	1.000	22	1	0	0	1	50²	47	3	14	17	11.0	2.66	147	.257	.313	0	—	0	8	7	1	0.8
1981 NY-A	5	1	.833	17	4	0	0	0	53¹	58	5	16	28	12.5	2.70	132	.280	.332	0	—	0	6	5	0	0.6
Chi-N	4	5	.444	12	12	2	1	0	75¹	72	5	16	34	10.6	3.58	103	.254	.297	2	.100	-1	-1	-1	-3	-0.3
1982 Chi-N	9	14	.391	35	33	2	1	0	191	230	26	30	71	12.4	5.14	73	.297	.325	8	.143	-2	-33	-30	-1	-3.1
1983 Bos-A	1	4	.200	22	6	0	0	1	67²	91	14	16	33	14.5	6.65	65	.324	.365	0	—	0	-19	-17	0	-1.6
Total 11	73	60	.549	432	100	8	3	60	1213²	1273	122	296	680	11.8	3.99	96	.272	.319	11	.134	-2	-36	-23	-8	-2.7

■ RED BIRD — Bird, James Edward b: 4/25/1890, Stephenville, Tex. d: 3/23/72, Murfreesboro, Ark. BL/TL, 5'11", 170 lbs. Deb: 9/17/21

YEAR TM/L	W	L	PCT	G	GS	CG	SH	SV	IP	H	HR	BB	SO	RAT	ERA	ERA+	OAV	OOB	BH	AVG	PB	PR	/A	PD	TPI
1921 Was-A	0	0	—	1	0	0	0	0	5	5	0	1	2	12.6	5.40	76	.294	.368	0	.000	-0	-1	-1	0	0.0

■ MIKE BIRKBECK — Birkbeck, Michael Lawrence b: 3/10/61, Orrville, Ohio BR/TR, 6'1", 190 lbs. Deb: 8/17/86

YEAR TM/L	W	L	PCT	G	GS	CG	SH	SV	IP	H	HR	BB	SO	RAT	ERA	ERA+	OAV	OOB	BH	AVG	PB	PR	/A	PD	TPI
1986 Mil-A	1	1	.500	7	4	0	0	0	22	24	0	12	13	14.7	4.50	96	.282	.371	0	—	0	-1	-0	-0	0.0
1987 Mil-A	1	4	.200	10	10	1	0	0	45	43	8	19	25	16.4	6.20	74	.335	.396	0	—	0	-9	-8	1	-0.5
1988 Mil-A	10	8	.556	23	23	0	0	0	124	141	10	37	64	13.0	4.72	84	.285	.336	0	—	0	-10	-10	2	-0.7
1989 Mil-A	0	4	.000	9	9	1	0	0	44²	57	4	22	31	16.5	5.44	71	.310	.392	0	—	0	-8	-8	-0	-0.7
Total 4	12	17	.414	49	46	2	0	0	235²	285	22	90	133	14.5	5.12	80	.300	.363	0	—	0	-28	-27	3	-1.9

■ RALPH BIRKOFER — Birkofer, Ralph Joseph "Lefty" b: 11/5/08, Cincinnati, Ohio d: 3/16/71, Cincinnati, Ohio BL/TL, 5'11", 213 lbs. Deb: 4/25/33

YEAR TM/L	W	L	PCT	G	GS	CG	SH	SV	IP	H	HR	BB	SO	RAT	ERA	ERA+	OAV	OOB	BH	AVG	PB	PR	/A	PD	TPI
1933 Pit-N	4	2	.667	9	8	3	1	0	50²	43	1	17	20	10.8	2.31	144	.229	.296	7	.318	1	6	6	-0	0.7
1934 Pit-N	11	12	.478	41	24	11	0	1	204	227	11	66	71	13.1	4.10	100	.277	.335	17	.227	1	-1	0	-1	0.0
1935 Pit-N	9	7	.563	37	18	8	1	1	150¹	173	5	42	80	13.2	4.07	101	.283	.335	14	.241	2	-1	1	-3	-0.3
1936 Pit-N	7	5	.583	34	13	2	0	0	109¹	130	4	41	44	14.5	4.69	86	.295	.362	9	.220	-0	-8	-8	-3	-0.9
1937 Bro-N	0	2	.000	11	1	0	0	0	29²	45	3	9	9	16.4	6.67	60	.341	.383	3	.273	1	-9	-9	-0	-0.7
Total 5	31	28	.525	132	64	24	2	2	544	618	24	175	224	13.4	4.19	96	.282	.340	50	.242	5	-13	-10	-8	-0.9

■ BABE BIRRER — Birrer, Werner Joseph b: 7/4/28, Buffalo, N.Y. BR/TR, 6', 195 lbs. Deb: 6/05/55

YEAR TM/L	W	L	PCT	G	GS	CG	SH	SV	IP	H	HR	BB	SO	RAT	ERA	ERA+	OAV	OOB	BH	AVG	PB	PR	/A	PD	TPI
1955 Det-A	4	3	.571	36	3	1	0	3	80¹	77	9	29	28	11.9	4.15	93	.248	.313	3	.158	2	-2	-3	-1	0.0
1956 Bal-A	0	0	—	4	0	0	0	0	5¹	9	0	1	1	16.9	6.75	58	.360	.385	0	.000	-0	-2	-2	-0	-0.1
1958 LA-N	0	0	—	16	0	0	0	1	34	43	4	7	16	13.5	4.50	91	.309	.347	4	.571	2	-2	-2	-1	0.0
Total 3	4	3	.571	56	3	1	0	4	119²	129	13	37	45	12.6	4.36	90	.272	.326	7	.259	4	-5	-6	-2	-0.1

■ TIM BIRTSAS — Birtsas, Timothy Dean b: 9/5/60, Pontiac, Mich. BL/TL, 6'7", 240 lbs. Deb: 5/03/85

YEAR TM/L	W	L	PCT	G	GS	CG	SH	SV	IP	H	HR	BB	SO	RAT	ERA	ERA+	OAV	OOB	BH	AVG	PB	PR	/A	PD	TPI
1985 Oak-A	10	6	.625	29	25	2	0	0	141¹	124	18	91	94	13.9	4.01	96	.238	.354	0	—	0	2	-2	-3	-0.4
1986 Oak-A	0	0	—	2	0	0	0	0	2	2	1	4	1	27.0	22.50	17	.286	.545	0	—	0	-4	-4	0	-0.3
1988 Cin-N	1	3	.250	36	4	0	0	0	64¹	61	6	24	38	12.3	4.20	85	.250	.325	0	.000	-1	-5	-4	-1	-0.6
1989 Cin-N	2	2	.500	42	1	0	0	1	69²	68	5	27	57	12.7	3.75	96	.261	.337	1	.250	1	-2	-1	-1	0.0
1990 Cin-N	1	3	.250	29	0	0	0	1	51¹	69	7	24	41	16.5	3.86	100	.325	.397	0	.000	-0	-0	0	0	0.0
Total 5	14	14	.500	138	30	2	0	1	328²	324	37	170	231	13.8	4.08	92	.260	.354	1	.056	-0	-10	-11	-4	-1.3

■ FRANK BISCAN — Biscan, Frank Stephen "Porky" b: 3/13/20, Mt.Olive, Ill. d: 5/22/59, St.Louis, Mo. BL/TL, 5'11", 190 lbs. Deb: 5/03/42

YEAR TM/L	W	L	PCT	G	GS	CG	SH	SV	IP	H	HR	BB	SO	RAT	ERA	ERA+	OAV	OOB	BH	AVG	PB	PR	/A	PD	TPI
1942 StL-A	0	1	.000	11	0	0	0	1	27	13	1	11	10	8.0	2.33	159	.143	.235	0	.000	-0	4	4	0	0.4
1946 StL-A	1	1	.500	16	0	0	0	0	22²	28	0	22	9	19.9	5.16	72	.318	.455	0	.000	-0	-4	-4	-0	-0.3
1948 StL-A	6	7	.462	47	4	1	0	2	98²	129	3	71	45	19.1	6.11	75	.322	.435	5	.192	1	-20	-17	0	-1.4
Total 3	7	9	.438	74	4	1	0	4	148¹	170	4	104	64	17.2	5.28	81	.294	.409	5	.143	-0	-20	-17	0	-1.3

■ CHARLIE BISHOP — Bishop, Charles Tuller b: 1/1/24, Atlanta, Ga. BR/TR, 6'2", 195 lbs. Deb: 8/22/52

YEAR TM/L	W	L	PCT	G	GS	CG	SH	SV	IP	H	HR	BB	SO	RAT	ERA	ERA+	OAV	OOB	BH	AVG	PB	PR	/A	PD	TPI
1952 Phi-A	2	2	.500	6	5	1	0	0	30²	29	2	24	17	15.6	6.46	61	.238	.363	1	.111	-0	-9	-9	-0	-0.7
1953 Phi-A	3	14	.176	39	20	1	1	2	160²	174	15	86	66	14.8	5.66	76	.282	.375	5	.089	-4	-30	-24	2	-2.5
1954 Phi-A	4	6	.400	20	12	4	0	1	96	98	10	50	34	14.3	4.41	89	.275	.372	4	.121	-2	-7	-5	-1	-0.7
1955 KC-A	1	0	1.000	4	0	0	0	0	6²	6	1	8	4	23.0	5.40	77	.261	.500	1	.500	0	-1	-1	0	0.0
Total 4	10	22	.313	69	37	6	1	3	294	307	28	168	121	14.9	5.33	77	.275	.376	11	.110	-6	-47	-39	1	-3.9

■ JIM BISHOP — Bishop, James Morton b: 1/28/1898, Montgomery City, Mo. d: 9/20/73, Montgomery City, Mo. BR/TR, 6', 195 lbs. Deb: 4/26/23

YEAR TM/L	W	L	PCT	G	GS	CG	SH	SV	IP	H	HR	BB	SO	RAT	ERA	ERA+	OAV	OOB	BH	AVG	PB	PR	/A	PD	TPI
1923 Phi-N	0	3	.000	15	0	0	0	1	32²	48	2	11	5	17.1	6.34	73	.353	.413	0	.000	-0	-8	-6	1	-0.6
1924 Phi-N	0	1	.000	7	1	0	0	0	16²	24	3	7	3	16.7	6.48	69	.348	.408	1	.200	-0	-5	-4	0	-0.2
Total 2	0	4	.000	22	1	0	0	1	49¹	72	5	18	8	17.0	6.39	71	.351	.412	1	.067	-2	-13	-10	1	-0.8

■ LLOYD BISHOP — Bishop, Lloyd Clifton b: 4/25/1890, Conway Springs, Kan. d: 6/18/68, Wichita, Kan. BR/TR, 6', 180 lbs. Deb: 9/05/14

YEAR TM/L	W	L	PCT	G	GS	CG	SH	SV	IP	H	HR	BB	SO	RAT	ERA	ERA+	OAV	OOB	BH	AVG	PB	PR	/A	PD	TPI
1914 Cle-A	0	1	.000	3	1	0	0	0	8	14	0	3	1	19.1	5.63	51	.389	.436	0	.000	-0	-3	-2	-0	-0.2

■ BILL BISHOP — Bishop, William Henry "Lefty" b: 10/22/1900, Houtzdale, Pa. d: 2/14/56, St.Joseph, Mo. BL/TL, 5'8", 170 lbs. Deb: 9/15/21

YEAR TM/L	W	L	PCT	G	GS	CG	SH	SV	IP	H	HR	BB	SO	RAT	ERA	ERA+	OAV	OOB	BH	AVG	PB	PR	/A	PD	TPI
1921 Phi-A	0	0	—	2	0	0	0	0	7	8	0	10	4	23.1	9.00	50	.267	.450	0	.000	-1	-4	-4	0	-0.2

■ BILL BISHOP — Bishop, William Robinson b: 12/27/1869, Adamsburg, Pa. d: 12/15/32, Pittsburgh, Pa. Deb: 7/13/1886

YEAR TM/L	W	L	PCT	G	GS	CG	SH	SV	IP	H	HR	BB	SO	RAT	ERA	ERA+	OAV	OOB	BH	AVG	PB	PR	/A	PD	TPI
1886 Pit-a	0	1	.000	2	2	2	0	0	17	17	0	11	4	14.8	3.18	107	.248	.352	1	.143	-1	1	0	-0	0.0
1887 Pit-N	0	3	.000	3	3	3	0	0	27	45	2	22	4	13.33	13.33	29	.361	.457	0	.000	-0	-28	-28	-1	-1.8
1889 Chi-N	0	0	—	2	0	0	0	2	3	6	0	6	1	36.0	18.00	23	.403	.574	0	.000	0	-5	-5	-0	-0.3
Total 3	0	4	.000	7	5	5	0	2	47	68	2	39	9	20.5	9.96	37	.327	.433	1	.059	-2	-32	-33	-0	-2.1

■ HI BITHORN — Bithorn, Hiram Gabriel (Sosa) b: 3/18/16, Santurce, P.R. d: 1/1/52, ElMante, Mex. BR/TR, 6'1", 200 lbs. Deb: 4/15/42

YEAR TM/L	W	L	PCT	G	GS	CG	SH	SV	IP	H	HR	BB	SO	RAT	ERA	ERA+	OAV	OOB	BH	AVG	PB	PR	/A	PD	TPI
1942 Chi-N	9	14	.391	38	16	9	0	2	171¹	191	8	81	65	14.3	3.68	87	.296	.374	7	.123	-1	-7	-9	-1	-1.1
1943 Chi-N	18	12	.600	39	30	19	7	2	249²	226	8	65	86	10.6	2.60	129	.242	.293	16	.174	-0	22	21	1	2.4

YEAR TM/L	W	L	PCT	G	GS	CG	SH	SV	IP	H	HR	BB	SO	RAT	ERA	ERA+	OAV	OOB	BH	AVG	PB	PR	/A	PD	TPI
1946 Chi-N	6	5	.545	26	7	2	1	1	86²	97	5	25	34	12.7	3.84	86	.283	.332	5	.179	-0	-4	-5	-0	-0.5
1947 Chi-A	1	0	1.000	2	0	0	0	0	2	2	0	0	0	9.0	0.00	—	.286	.286	0	—	0	1	1	0	0.1
Total 4	34	31	.523	105	53	30	8	5	509²	516	21	171	185	12.2	3.16	104	.268	.328	28	.158	-2	12	7	0	0.9

■ JOE BITKER
Bitker, Joseph Anthony b: 2/12/64, Glendale, Cal. BR/TR, 6'1", 175 lbs. Deb: 7/31/90

YEAR TM/L	W	L	PCT	G	GS	CG	SH	SV	IP	H	HR	BB	SO	RAT	ERA	ERA+	OAV	OOB	BH	AVG	PB	PR	/A	PD	TPI
1990 Oak-A	0	0	—	1	0	0	0	0	3	1	0	1	2	6.0	0.00	—	.111	.200	0	—	0	1	1	0	0.2
Tex-A	0	0	—	5	0	0	0	0	9	7	0	3	6	11.0	3.00	133	.212	.297	0	—	0	1	1	0	0.1
Yr	0	0	—	6	0	0	0	0	12	8	0	4	8	9.8	2.25	174	.190	.277	0	—	0	2	2	0	0.3

■ JEFF BITTIGER
Bittiger, Jeffrey Scott b: 4/13/62, Jersey City, N.J. BR/TR, 5'10", 175 lbs. Deb: 9/02/86

YEAR TM/L	W	L	PCT	G	GS	CG	SH	SV	IP	H	HR	BB	SO	RAT	ERA	ERA+	OAV	OOB	BH	AVG	PB	PR	/A	PD	TPI
1986 Phi-N	1	1	.500	3	3	0	0	0	14²	16	2	7	8	14.7	5.52	70	.271	.358	1	.333	1	-3	-3	0	-0.1
1987 Min-A	1	0	1.000	3	1	0	0	0	8¹	11	2	0	5	13.0	5.40	85	.314	.333	0	—	0	-1	-1	0	0.0
1988 Chi-A	2	4	.333	25	7	0	0	0	61²	59	11	29	33	12.8	4.23	94	.255	.338	0	—	0	-2	-2	-1	-0.2
1989 Chi-A	0	1	.000	2	1	0	0	0	9²	9	2	6	7	14.0	6.52	58	.257	.366	0	—	0	-3	-3	-0	-0.2
Total 4	4	6	.400	33	12	0	0	0	94¹	95	17	42	53	13.3	4.77	84	.264	.344	1	.333	1	-8	-8	-1	-0.5

■ JIM BIVIN
Bivin, James Nathaniel b: 12/11/09, Jackson, Miss. d: 11/7/82, Pueblo, Colo. BR/TR, 6', 155 lbs. Deb: 4/16/35

YEAR TM/L	W	L	PCT	G	GS	CG	SH	SV	IP	H	HR	BB	SO	RAT	ERA	ERA+	OAV	OOB	BH	AVG	PB	PR	/A	PD	TPI
1935 Phi-N	2	9	.182	47	14	0	0	1	161²	220	20	65	54	16.0	5.79	78	.316	.377	7	.146	-1	-32	-23	-1	-2.1

■ DAVE BLACK
Black, David b: 4/19/1892, Chicago, Ill. d: 10/27/36, Pittsburgh, Pa. TR, 6'2", 175 lbs. Deb: 5/02/14

YEAR TM/L	W	L	PCT	G	GS	CG	SH	SV	IP	H	HR	BB	SO	RAT	ERA	ERA+	OAV	OOB	BH	AVG	PB	PR	/A	PD	TPI
1914 Chi-F	1	0	1.000	8	1	1	0	0	25	28	1	4	19	11.5	6.12	48	.291	.319	2	.286	1	-8	-9	-0	-0.7
1915 Chi-F	6	7	.462	25	10	2	0	0	121¹	104	3	33	43	10.6	2.45	114	.241	.304	4	.108	-2	8	5	2	0.4
Bal-F	1	3	.250	8	4	1	0	0	34	32	2	15	10	13.0	3.71	86	.260	.350	2	.250	0	-3	-2	1	0.0
Yr	7	10	.412	33	14	3	0	0	155¹	136	5	48	53	10.8	2.72	106	.243	.305	3	.061	-2	5	3	2	0.4
1923 Bos-A	0	0	—	2	0	0	0	0	1	2	0	0	0	18.0	0.00	—	.500	.500	0	—	0	0	0	0	0.0
Total 3	8	10	.444	43	15	4	0	0	181¹	166	6	52	72	11.2	3.18	91	.254	.316	9	.161	-1	-2	-6	2	-0.3

■ DON BLACK
Black, Donald Paul b: 7/20/16, Salix, Iowa d: 4/21/59, Cuyahoga Falls, O. BR/TR, 6', 185 lbs. Deb: 4/24/43

YEAR TM/L	W	L	PCT	G	GS	CG	SH	SV	IP	H	HR	BB	SO	RAT	ERA	ERA+	OAV	OOB	BH	AVG	PB	PR	/A	PD	TPI
1943 Phi-A	6	16	.273	33	26	12	1	1	208	193	8	110	65	13.4	4.20	81	.247	.344	13	.188	-1	-21	-19	0	-1.9
1944 Phi-A	10	12	.455	29	27	8	0	0	177¹	177	6	75	78	13.0	4.06	86	.259	.336	11	.186	-1	-12	-11	-0	-1.2
1945 Phi-A	5	11	.313	26	18	8	0	0	125¹	154	5	69	47	16.0	5.17	66	.307	.391	6	.162	-2	-25	-24	-1	-2.7
1946 Cle-A	1	2	.333	18	4	0	0	0	43²	45	5	21	15	13.8	4.53	73	.273	.358	2	.200	0	-5	-6	1	-0.4
1947 Cle-A	10	12	.455	30	28	8	3	0	190²	177	17	85	72	12.4	3.92	89	.249	.330	12	.182	-1	-5	-9	1	-0.9
1948 Cle-A	2	2	.500	18	10	1	0	0	52	57	5	40	16	17.0	5.37	76	.282	.403	3	.200	-0	-6	-8	1	-0.6
Total 6	34	55	.382	154	113	37	4	1	797	803	46	400	293	13.7	4.35	80	.264	.352	47	.184	-4	-74	-76	1	-7.7

■ BUD BLACK
Black, Harry Ralston b: 6/30/57, San Mateo, Cal. BL/TL, 6'2", 180 lbs. Deb: 9/05/81

YEAR TM/L	W	L	PCT	G	GS	CG	SH	SV	IP	H	HR	BB	SO	RAT	ERA	ERA+	OAV	OOB	BH	AVG	PB	PR	/A	PD	TPI
1981 Sea-A	0	0	—	2	0	0	0	0	1	2	0	3	0	45.0	0.00	—	.500	.714	0	—	0	0	0	0	0.1
1982 KC-A	4	6	.400	22	14	0	0	0	88¹	92	10	34	40	13.1	4.58	89	.269	.340	0	—	0	-5	-5	0	-0.4
1983 KC-A	10	7	.588	24	24	3	0	0	161¹	159	19	43	58	11.4	3.79	107	.257	.308	0	—	0	5	5	2	0.7
1984 *KC-A	17	12	.586	35	35	8	1	0	257	226	22	64	140	**10.3**	3.12	129	.233	**.283**	0	—	0	25	26	3	3.0
1985 *KC-A	10	15	.400	33	33	5	2	0	205²	216	17	59	122	12.4	4.33	96	.268	.324	0	—	0	-4	-4	-1	-0.4
1986 KC-A	5	10	.333	56	4	0	0	9	121	100	14	43	68	11.2	3.20	133	.225	.303	0	—	0	13	14	1	1.5
1987 KC-A	8	6	.571	29	18	0	0	1	122¹	126	16	35	61	12.2	3.60	126	.265	.322	0	—	0	12	13	0	1.3
1988 KC-A	2	1	.667	17	0	0	0	0	22	23	2	11	19	13.9	4.91	81	.267	.351	0	—	0	-2	-2	-0	-0.2
Cle-A	2	3	.400	16	7	0	0	1	59	59	6	23	44	13.1	5.03	82	.262	.341	0	—	0	-7	-6	1	-0.4
Yr	4	4	.500	33	7	0	0	1	81	82	8	34	63	13.3	5.00	82	.264	.344	0	—	0	-9	-8	0	-0.6
1989 Cle-A	12	11	.522	33	32	6	3	0	222¹	213	14	52	88	10.8	3.36	118	.252	.296	0	—	0	13	15	0	1.6
1990 Cle-A	11	10	.524	29	29	5	2	0	191	171	17	58	103	11.0	3.53	113	.236	.296	0	—	0	8	9	1	1.0
Tor-A	2	1	.667	3	2	0	0	0	15²	10	2	3	3	8.0	4.02	94	.189	.246	0	—	0	-0	-0	1	0.0
Yr	13	11	.542	32	31	5	2	0	206²	181	19	61	106	10.6	3.57	111	.230	.286	0	—	0	8	9	1	1.0
Total 10	83	82	.503	299	198	27	8	11	1466²	1397	139	428	746	11.4	3.70	111	.250	.307	0	—	0	57	65	6	7.8

■ JOE BLACK
Black, Joseph b: 2/8/24, Plainfield, N.J. BR/TR, 6'2", 220 lbs. Deb: 5/01/52

YEAR TM/L	W	L	PCT	G	GS	CG	SH	SV	IP	H	HR	BB	SO	RAT	ERA	ERA+	OAV	OOB	BH	AVG	PB	PR	/A	PD	TPI
1952 *Bro-N	15	4	.789	56	2	1	0	15	142¹	102	9	41	85	9.1	2.15	169	.201	.262	5	.139	-1	**25**	**24**	-2	2.2
1953 *Bro-N	6	3	.667	34	3	0	0	5	72²	74	12	27	42	12.6	5.33	80	.259	.325	4	.235	4	-8	-9	-0	-0.7
1954 Bro-N	0	0	—	5	0	0	0	0	7	11	3	5	5	20.6	11.57	35	.355	.444	0	—	0	-6	-6	-0	-0.5
1955 Bro-N	1	0	1.000	6	0	0	0	0	15¹	15	1	5	9	11.7	2.93	138	.273	.333	1	.333	0	2	2	-0	0.2
Cin-N	5	2	.714	32	11	1	0	3	102¹	106	13	25	54	11.5	4.22	100	.263	.306	3	.100	-3	-2	-0	-0	-0.2
Yr	6	2	.750	38	11	1	0	3	117²	121	14	30	63	11.5	4.05	104	.264	.309	1	.030	-2	-0	2	-1	-0.2
1956 Cin-N	3	2	.600	32	0	0	0	2	61²	61	11	25	27	12.6	4.52	88	.256	.327	0	.000	-1	-5	-4	-0	-0.5
1957 Was-A	0	1	.000	7	0	0	0	0	12²	22	4	1	2	16.3	7.11	55	.393	.404	0	—	0	-5	-5	-0	-0.3
Total 6	30	12	.714	172	16	2	0	25	414	391	53	129	222	11.3	3.91	102	.248	.306	13	.135	-5	1	3	-3	0.2

■ BOB BLACK
Black, Robert Benjamin b: 12/10/1862, Cincinnati, Ohio d: 3/21/33, Sioux City, Iowa Deb: 8/17/1884 ♦

YEAR TM/L	W	L	PCT	G	GS	CG	SH	SV	IP	H	HR	BB	SO	RAT	ERA	ERA+	OAV	OOB	BH	AVG	PB	PR	/A	PD	TPI
1884 KC-U	4	9	.308	16	15	13	0	0	123	127	1	17	93	10.5	3.22	86	.249	.273	36	.247	4	-3	-6	1	-0.4

■ BUD BLACK
Black, William Carroll b: 7/9/32, St.Louis, Mo. BR/TR, 6'3", 197 lbs. Deb: 9/13/52

YEAR TM/L	W	L	PCT	G	GS	CG	SH	SV	IP	H	HR	BB	SO	RAT	ERA	ERA+	OAV	OOB	BH	AVG	PB	PR	/A	PD	TPI
1952 Det-A	0	1	.000	2	2	0	0	0	8	14	0	5	0	21.4	10.13	38	.389	.463	0	.000	-0	-6	-6	0	-0.4
1955 Det-A	1	1	.500	3	2	1	1	0	14	12	0	8	7	14.1	1.29	299	.231	.355	1	.250	0	4	4	0	0.4
1956 Det-A	1	1	.500	5	1	0	0	0	10	10	2	5	7	13.5	3.60	114	.256	.341	0	.000	-0	1	1	0	0.0
Total 3	2	3	.400	10	5	1	1	0	32	36	2	18	14	15.8	4.22	93	.283	.381	1	.111	-1	-1	-1	0	0.0

■ CHARLIE BLACKBURN
Blackburn, Foster Edwin b: 1/6/1895, Chicago, Ill. d: 3/9/84, New Port Richey, Fla. 6'1", 165 lbs. Deb: 4/17/15

YEAR TM/L	W	L	PCT	G	GS	CG	SH	SV	IP	H	HR	BB	SO	RAT	ERA	ERA+	OAV	OOB	BH	AVG	PB	PR	/A	PD	TPI
1915 KC-F	0	1	.000	7	2	0	0	0	15²	19	2	13	7	18.4	8.62	34	.307	.428	0	.000	-1	-10	-10	0	-0.9
1921 Chi-A	0	0	—	1	0	0	0	0	1	0	0	1	0	9.0	0.00	—	.000	.333	0	—	0	0	0	0	0.0
Total 2	0	1	.000	8	2	0	0	0	16²	19	2	14	7	17.8	8.10	37	.298	.424	0	.000	-1	-9	-9	0	-0.9

■ GEORGE BLACKBURN
Blackburn, George W. "Smiling George" b: 9/21/1871, Ozark, Mo. 5'11", 184 lbs. Deb: 7/06/1897

YEAR TM/L	W	L	PCT	G	GS	CG	SH	SV	IP	H	HR	BB	SO	RAT	ERA	ERA+	OAV	OOB	BH	AVG	PB	PR	/A	PD	TPI
1897 Bal-N	2	2	.500	5	4	3	0	0	33	34	2	12	1	12.5	6.82	61	.264	.327	1	.077	-2	-9	-10	0	-0.8

■ JIM BLACKBURN
Blackburn, James Ray "Bones" b: 6/19/24, Warsaw, Ky. d: 10/26/69, Cincinnati, Ohio BR/TR, 6'4", 175 lbs. Deb: 7/24/48

YEAR TM/L	W	L	PCT	G	GS	CG	SH	SV	IP	H	HR	BB	SO	RAT	ERA	ERA+	OAV	OOB	BH	AVG	PB	PR	/A	PD	TPI
1948 Cin-N	0	2	.000	16	0	0	0	0	32¹	38	1	14	10	14.5	4.18	94	.302	.371	0	.000	-0	-1	-1	0	-0.1
1951 Cin-N	0	0	—	2	0	0	0	0	3²	8	3	2	1	29.5	17.18	24	.444	.545	0	—	0	-5	-5	0	-0.3
Total 2	0	2	.000	18	0	0	0	0	36	46	4	16	11	16.0	5.50	71	.319	.395	0	.000	-0	-6	-6	0	-0.4

■ RON BLACKBURN
Blackburn, Ronald Hamilton b: 4/23/35, Mt.Airy, N.C. BR/TR, 6'0.5", 160 lbs. Deb: 4/15/58

YEAR TM/L	W	L	PCT	G	GS	CG	SH	SV	IP	H	HR	BB	SO	RAT	ERA	ERA+	OAV	OOB	BH	AVG	PB	PR	/A	PD	TPI
1958 Pit-N	2	1	.667	38	2	0	0	3	63²	61	7	27	31	12.9	3.39	114	.261	.345	2	.286	1	4	3	1	0.5
1959 Pit-N	1	1	.500	26	0	0	0	1	44¹	50	5	15	19	13.6	3.65	106	.286	.349	1	.200	1	1	1	-1	0.1
Total 2	3	2	.600	64	2	0	0	4	108	111	12	42	50	13.2	3.50	110	.271	.346	3	.250	2	5	4	0	0.6

■ LENA BLACKBURNE
Blackburne, Russell Aubrey "Slats"
b: 10/23/1886, Clifton Heights, Pa. d: 2/29/68, Riverside, N.J. BR/TR, 5'11", 160 lbs. Deb: 4/14/10 MC♦

YEAR TM/L	W	L	PCT	G	GS	CG	SH	SV	IP	H	HR	BB	SO	RAT	ERA	ERA+	OAV	OOB	BH	AVG	PB	PR	/A	PD	TPI
1929 Chi-A	0	0	—	1	0	0	0	0	0¹	1	0	0	0	27.0	0.00	—	1.000	1.000	0	—	0	0	0	0	0.0

YEAR TM/L	W	L	PCT	G	GS	CG	SH	SV	IP	H	HR	BB	SO	RAT	ERA	ERA+	OAV	OOB	BH	AVG	PB	PR	/A	PD	TPI

■ EWELL BLACKWELL
Blackwell, Ewell "The Whip" b: 10/23/22, Fresno, Cal. BR/TR, 6'6", 195 lbs. Deb: 4/21/42

YEAR TM/L	W	L	PCT	G	GS	CG	SH	SV	IP	H	HR	BB	SO	RAT	ERA	ERA+	OAV	OOB	BH	AVG	PB	PR	/A	PD	TPI
1942 Cin-N	0	0	—	2	0	0	0	0	3	3	0	3	1	18.0	6.00	55	.231	.375	0	.000	-0	-1	-1	0	0.0
1946 Cin-N	9	13	.409	33	25	10	5	0	194¹	160	1	79	100	11.3	2.45	136	.226	.307	6	.107	-3	21	19	4	2.2
1947 Cin-N	22	8	.733	33	33	23	6	0	273	227	10	95	193	10.7	2.47	166	.234	.304	13	.123	-5	48	49	4	5.2
1948 Cin-N	7	9	.438	22	20	4	1	1	138²	134	12	52	114	12.3	4.54	86	.251	.323	11	.229	1	-9	-10	3	-0.4
1949 Cin-N	5	5	.500	30	4	0	0	1	76²	80	7	34	55	13.7	4.23	99	.271	.352	4	.211	-0	-2	-0	1	0.0
1950 Cin-N	17	15	.531	40	32	18	1	4	261	203	12	112	188	11.3	2.97	143	.210	.301	13	.146	-2	34	37	1	3.6
1951 Cin-N	16	15	.516	38	32	11	2	2	232²	204	16	97	120	12.0	3.44	118	.233	.315	24	.293	8	13	16	0	2.5
1952 Cin-N	3	12	.200	23	17	3	0	0	102	107	6	60	48	15.2	5.38	70	.275	.379	5	.156	-0	-19	-18	-0	-1.8
*NY-A	1	0	1.000	5	2	0	0	1	16	12	0	12	7	13.5	0.56	591	.203	.338	1	.200	-0	6	5	-0	0.5
1953 NY-A	2	0	1.000	8	4	0	0	1	19²	17	2	13	11	14.2	3.66	101	.233	.356	0	.000	-1	1	0	-0	0.0
1955 KC-A	0	1	.000	2	0	0	0	0	4	3	1	5	2	20.3	6.75	62	.250	.500	0	—	0	-1	-1	-0	0.0
Total 10	82	78	.512	236	169	69	15	10	1321	1150	67	562	839	12.0	3.30	120	.235	.319	77	.174	-3	91	96	12	11.8

■ GEORGE BLAEHOLDER
Blaeholder, George Franklin b: 1/26/04, Orange, Cal. d: 12/29/47, Garden Grove, Cal. BR/TR, 5'11", 175 lbs. Deb: 4/20/25

YEAR TM/L	W	L	PCT	G	GS	CG	SH	SV	IP	H	HR	BB	SO	RAT	ERA	ERA+	OAV	OOB	BH	AVG	PB	PR	/A	PD	TPI
1925 StL-A	0	0	—	2	0	0	0	0	2	6	3	1	1	36.0	31.50	15	.600	.667	0	—	-0	-6	-6	0	-0.4
1927 StL-A	0	1	.000	1	1	1	0	0	9	8	1	4	2	13.0	5.00	87	.258	.361	1	.333	0	-1	-1	0	0.0
1928 StL-A	10	15	.400	38	26	9	1	3	214¹	235	23	52	87	12.1	4.37	96	.280	.324	15	.211	2	-8	-4	4	0.2
1929 StL-A	14	15	.483	42	24	13	4	2	222	237	18	61	72	12.1	4.18	106	.275	.323	9	.122	-4	2	6	6	0.8
1930 StL-A	11	13	.458	37	23	10	1	4	191¹	235	20	46	70	13.3	4.61	106	.303	.343	12	.185	-1	1	6	-1	0.3
1931 StL-A	11	15	.423	35	32	13	1	0	226¹	280	15	56	79	13.4	4.53	102	.295	.335	11	.143	-3	-4	3	3	0.4
1932 StL-A	14	14	.500	42	36	16	1	0	258¹	304	19	76	80	13.3	4.70	103	.290	.340	12	.136	-4	-6	4	1	0.2
1933 StL-A	15	19	.441	38	36	14	3	0	255²	283	24	69	63	12.4	4.72	99	.280	.326	14	.182	-1	-12	-2	3	0.2
1934 StL-A	14	18	.438	39	33	14	1	3	234¹	276	16	68	66	13.2	4.22	118	.296	.343	7	.093	-6	7	20	1	1.5
1935 StL-A	1	1	.500	6	2	0	0	0	17²	25	3	6	0	15.8	7.13	67	.342	.392	0	.000	-1	-5	-5	1	-0.3
Phi-A	6	10	.375	23	22	10	1	0	149	173	10	49	22	13.4	3.99	114	.289	.343	2	.043	-6	8	9	2	0.5
Yr	7	11	.389	29	24	10	1	0	166²	198	13	55	22	13.7	4.32	106	.295	.348	2	.040	-7	3	5	3	0.2
1936 Cle-A	8	4	.667	35	16	6	1	0	134¹	158	21	47	30	13.9	5.09	99	.295	.356	6	.130	-3	-1	-1	2	0.0
Total 11	104	125	.454	338	251	106	14	12	1914¹	2220	173	535	572	13.0	4.54	103	.290	.337	89	.142	-26	-26	30	21	3.4

■ DENNIS BLAIR
Blair, Dennis Herman b: 6/5/54, Middletown, Ohio BR/TR, 6'5", 182 lbs. Deb: 5/26/74

YEAR TM/L	W	L	PCT	G	GS	CG	SH	SV	IP	H	HR	BB	SO	RAT	ERA	ERA+	OAV	OOB	BH	AVG	PB	PR	/A	PD	TPI
1974 Mon-N	11	7	.611	22	22	4	1	0	146	113	7	72	76	11.7	3.27	117	.210	.308	6	.118	-2	6	9	3	1.1
1975 Mon-N	8	15	.348	30	27	1	0	0	163¹	150	14	106	82	14.3	3.80	101	.251	.366	7	.143	-1	-3	0	-1	0.0
1976 Mon-N	0	2	.000	5	4	1	0	0	15²	21	1	11	9	19.5	4.02	92	.300	.410	0	.000	-0	-1	-1	0	0.0
1980 SD-N	0	1	.000	5	1	0	0	0	14	18	3	3	11	13.5	6.43	53	.310	.344	1	.200	0	-4	-5	-0	-0.4
Total 4	19	25	.432	62	54	6	1	0	339	302	25	192	178	13.4	3.69	103	.239	.344	14	.128	-4	-3	4	2	0.7

■ WILLIE BLAIR
Blair, William Allen b: 12/18/65, Paintsville, Ky. BR/TR, 6'1", 185 lbs. Deb: 4/11/90

YEAR TM/L	W	L	PCT	G	GS	CG	SH	SV	IP	H	HR	BB	SO	RAT	ERA	ERA+	OAV	OOB	BH	AVG	PB	PR	/A	PD	TPI
1990 Tor-A	3	5	.375	27	6	0	0	0	68²	66	4	28	43	12.5	4.06	93	.250	.324	0	—	0	-1	-2	-1	-0.2

■ BILL BLAIR
Blair, William Ellsworth b: 9/17/1863, Pittsburgh, Pa. d: 2/22/1890, Pittsburgh, Pa. BL/TL, 5'8.5", 172 lbs. Deb: 7/19/1888

YEAR TM/L	W	L	PCT	G	GS	CG	SH	SV	IP	H	HR	BB	SO	RAT	ERA	ERA+	OAV	OOB	BH	AVG	PB	PR	/A	PD	TPI
1888 Phi-a	1	3	.250	4	4	3	0	0	31	29	0	8	16	10.7	2.61	114	.239	.286	4	.308	1	2	1	1	0.3

■ DICK BLAISDELL
Blaisdell, Howard Carleton b: 6/18/1862, Bradford, Mass. d: 8/20/1886, Malden, Mass. Deb: 7/09/1884

YEAR TM/L	W	L	PCT	G	GS	CG	SH	SV	IP	H	HR	BB	SO	RAT	ERA	ERA+	OAV	OOB	BH	AVG	PB	PR	/A	PD	TPI
1884 KC-U	0	3	.000	3	3	3	0	0	26	49	0	4	8	18.3	8.65	32	.377	.396	5	.313	1	-16	-17	-0	-1.1

■ ED BLAKE
Blake, Edward James b: 12/23/25, E.St.Louis, Ill. BR/TR, 5'11", 175 lbs. Deb: 5/01/51

YEAR TM/L	W	L	PCT	G	GS	CG	SH	SV	IP	H	HR	BB	SO	RAT	ERA	ERA+	OAV	OOB	BH	AVG	PB	PR	/A	PD	TPI
1951 Cin-N	0	0	—	3	0	0	0	0	4	10	3	1	1	24.8	11.25	36	.476	.500	0	—	0	-3	-3	0	-0.2
1952 Cin-N	0	0	—	2	0	0	0	0	3	3	0	0	0	9.0	0.00	—	.250	.250	0	—	0	1	1	0	0.2
1953 Cin-N	0	0	—	1	0	0	0	0	0	1	0	1	0	—	∞	—	1.000	1.000	0	—	0	-2	-2	0	-0.1
1957 KC-A	0	0	—	2	0	0	0	0	1²	1	1	2	0	16.2	5.40	73	.167	.375	0	—	0	-0	-0	0	0.0
Total 4	0	0	—	8	0	0	0	0	8²	15	4	4	1	19.7	8.31	48	.375	.432	0	—	0	-4	-4	1	-0.1

■ SHERIFF BLAKE
Blake, John Frederick b: 9/17/1899, Ansted, W.Va. d: 10/31/82, Beckley, W.Va. BB/TR, 6', 180 lbs. Deb: 6/29/20

YEAR TM/L	W	L	PCT	G	GS	CG	SH	SV	IP	H	HR	BB	SO	RAT	ERA	ERA+	OAV	OOB	BH	AVG	PB	PR	/A	PD	TPI
1920 Pit-N	0	0	—	6	0	0	0	0	13¹	21	0	6	17	18.9	8.10	40	.368	.438	1	.250	-0	-7	-7	-0	-0.4
1924 Chi-N	6	6	.500	29	11	4	0	1	106¹	123	3	44	42	14.3	4.57	85	.299	.370	9	.290	1	-8	-8	1	-0.5
1925 Chi-N	10	18	.357	36	31	14	0	2	231¹	260	17	114	93	14.7	4.86	89	.287	.370	12	.152	-4	-15	-14	0	-1.6
1926 Chi-N	11	12	.478	39	27	11	4	1	197²	204	7	92	95	13.8	3.60	107	.280	.366	14	.215	-1	5	5	2	0.6
1927 Chi-N	13	14	.481	32	27	13	2	0	224¹	238	3	82	64	13.0	3.29	117	.282	.348	16	.193	-2	16	14	3	1.5
1928 Chi-N	17	11	.607	34	29	16	4	1	240²	209	4	101	78	11.7	2.47	156	.240	.321	19	.216	0	41	37	-2	3.6
1929 *Chi-N	14	13	.519	35	30	13	1	1	218¹	244	8	103	70	14.4	4.29	108	.291	.370	14	.173	-2	10	8	-1	0.4
1930 Chi-N	10	14	.417	34	24	7	0	0	186²	213	14	99	80	15.2	4.82	101	.291	.378	15	.227	-1	3	1	3	0.3
1931 Chi-N	0	4	.000	16	5	0	0	0	50	64	4	26	29	16.4	5.22	74	.312	.392	8	.500	3	-8	-8	-0	-0.3
Phi-N	4	5	.444	14	9	1	0	1	71	90	2	35	31	16.2	5.58	76	.305	.384	6	.240	0	-13	-11	2	-0.7
Yr	4	9	.308	30	14	1	0	1	121	154	6	61	60	16.2	5.43	75	.307	.386	1	.024	3	-21	-18	3	-1.0
1937 StL-A	2	2	.500	15	1	0	0	1	36²	55	5	20	12	18.4	7.61	63	.350	.424	1	.100	-1	-12	-11	0	-1.0
StL-N	0	3	.000	14	2	2	0	0	43²	45	1	18	20	13.0	3.71	107	.271	.342	3	.300	1	1	-1	0	0.2
Total 10	87	102	.460	304	196	81	11	8	1620	1766	68	740	631	14.1	4.13	101	.284	.363	118	.211	-6	12	9	9	1.9

■ AL BLANCHE
Blanche, Prosby Albert (b: Prosper Belangio) b: 9/21/09, Somerville, Mass. BR/TR, 6', 178 lbs. Deb: 8/23/35

YEAR TM/L	W	L	PCT	G	GS	CG	SH	SV	IP	H	HR	BB	SO	RAT	ERA	ERA+	OAV	OOB	BH	AVG	PB	PR	/A	PD	TPI
1935 Bos-N	0	0	—	6	0	0	0	0	17¹	14	0	5	4	9.9	1.56	243	.230	.288	1	.167	-0	5	4	0	0.4
1936 Bos-N	0	1	.000	11	0	0	0	1	16	20	1	8	4	16.3	6.19	62	.303	.387	1	.250	-0	-4	-4	1	-0.2
Total 2	0	1	.000	17	0	0	0	1	33¹	34	1	13	8	13.0	3.78	101	.268	.340	2	.200	-0	1	0	1	0.2

■ GIL BLANCO
Blanco, Gilbert Henry b: 12/15/45, Phoenix, Ariz. BL/TL, 6'5", 205 lbs. Deb: 4/24/65

YEAR TM/L	W	L	PCT	G	GS	CG	SH	SV	IP	H	HR	BB	SO	RAT	ERA	ERA+	OAV	OOB	BH	AVG	PB	PR	/A	PD	TPI
1965 NY-A	1	1	.500	17	1	0	0	0	20¹	16	1	12	14	12.8	3.98	85	.232	.354	0	—	0	-1	-1	-1	-0.1
1966 KC-A	2	4	.333	11	8	0	0	0	38¹	31	3	36	21	16.7	4.70	72	.237	.415	2	.167	-0	-5	-6	0	-0.5
Total 2	3	5	.375	28	9	0	0	0	58²	47	4	48	35	15.3	4.45	76	.235	.395	2	.167	-0	-7	-7	-0	-0.6

■ FRED BLANDING
Blanding, Frederick James "Fritz" b: 2/8/1888, Redlands, Cal. d: 7/16/50, Salem, Va. BR/TR, 6', 185 lbs. Deb: 9/15/10

YEAR TM/L	W	L	PCT	G	GS	CG	SH	SV	IP	H	HR	BB	SO	RAT	ERA	ERA+	OAV	OOB	BH	AVG	PB	PR	/A	PD	TPI
1910 Cle-A	2	2	.500	6	5	4	1	0	45¹	43	0	12	25	11.7	2.78	93	.254	.319	2	.111	-1	-1	-1	-1	-0.2
1911 Cle-A	7	11	.389	29	16	11	0	2	176	190	4	60	80	13.1	3.68	93	.283	.347	17	.262	2	-7	-5	1	-0.2
1912 Cle-A	18	14	.563	39	31	23	1	1	262	259	4	79	75	11.7	2.92	117	.267	.324	21	.226	1	12	14	1	1.8
1913 Cle-A	15	10	.600	41	22	14	3	0	215	234	4	72	63	12.9	2.55	119	.282	.341	21	.244	4	9	12	-1	1.6
1914 Cle-A	3	9	.250	29	12	5	0	1	116	133	0	54	35	14.6	3.96	73	.301	.378	4	.103	-2	-16	-14	2	-1.4
Total 5	45	46	.495	144	86	57	5	4	814¹	859	14	277	278	12.7	3.13	102	.279	.341	65	.216	4	-3	6	1	1.6

■ FRED BLANK
Blank, Frederick August b: 6/18/1874, Desoto, Mo. d: 2/5/36, St.Louis, Mo. BL/TL, 6'0.5", 175 lbs. Deb: 6/20/1894

YEAR TM/L	W	L	PCT	G	GS	CG	SH	SV	IP	H	HR	BB	SO	RAT	ERA	ERA+	OAV	OOB	BH	AVG	PB	PR	/A	PD	TPI
1894 Cin-N	0	1	.000	1	1	1	0	0	8	5	0	9	1	15.8	4.50	124	.178	.378	0	.000	-1	1	1	1	0.1

■ HOMER BLANKENSHIP
Blankenship, Homer "Si" b: 8/4/02, Bonham, Tex. d: 6/22/74, Longview, Tex. BR/TR, 6', 185 lbs. Deb: 9/06/22

YEAR TM/L	W	L	PCT	G	GS	CG	SH	SV	IP	H	HR	BB	SO	RAT	ERA	ERA+	OAV	OOB	BH	AVG	PB	PR	/A	PD	TPI
1922 Chi-A	0	0	—	4	0	0	0	0	13	21	1	5	3	18.0	4.85	84	.389	.441	0	.000	-1	-1	-1	-0	-0.1
1923 Chi-A	1	1	.500	4	0	0	0	1	5	9	0	1	4	18.0	3.60	110	.429	.455	0	—	0	0	0	0	0.0
1928 Pit-N	0	2	.000	5	2	1	0	0	21²	27	1	9	6	15.0	5.82	70	.321	.387	3	.375	1	-4	-4	1	-0.2
Total 3	1	3	.250	13	2	1	0	1	39²	57	2	15	10	16.3	5.22	78	.358	.414	3	.250	0	-5	-5	1	-0.3

YEAR	TM/L	W	L	PCT	G	GS	CG	SH	SV	IP	H	HR	BB	SO	RAT	ERA	ERA+	OAV	OOB	BH	AVG	PB	PR	/A	PD	TPI

■ KEVIN BLANKENSHIP   Blankenship, Kevin De Wayne b: 1/26/63, Anaheim, Cal. BR/TR, 6′, 180 lbs. Deb: 9/20/88

1988	Atl-N	0	1	.000	2	2	0	0	0	10²	7	0	7	5	12.7	3.38	109	.194	.341	0	.000	-0	0	0	-0	0.0
	Chi-N	1	0	1.000	1	1	0	0	0	5	7	2	1	4	14.4	7.20	50	.318	.348	0	.000	-0	-2	-2	-0	-0.1
	Yr	1	1	.500	3	3	0	0	0	15²	14	2	8	9	12.6	4.60	79	.237	.328	0	.000	-1	-2	-2	-0	-0.1
1989	Chi-N	0	0	—	2	0	0	0	0	5¹	4	0	2	2	10.1	1.69	223	.200	.273	0	.000	-0	1	1	0	0.1
1990	Chi-N	0	2	.000	3	2	0	0	0	12¹	13	1	6	5	13.9	5.84	71	.265	.345	0	.000	-0	-3	-2	-0	-0.2
Total	3	1	3	.250	8	5	0	0	0	33¹	31	3	16	16	13.0	4.59	84	.244	.333	0	.000	-1	-4	-3	-0	-0.2

■ TED BLANKENSHIP   Blankenship, Theodore b: 5/10/01, Bonham, Tex. d: 1/14/45, Atoka, Okla. BR/TR, 6′1″, 170 lbs. Deb: 7/02/22

1922	Chi-A	8	10	.444	24	15	7	0	1	127²	124	4	47	42	12.2	3.81	107	.266	.335	7	.171	-1	3	4	0	0.3
1923	Chi-A	9	14	.391	44	23	9	1	0	204²	219	8	100	57	14.2	4.35	91	.287	.372	16	.211	2	-8	-9	-1	-0.7
1924	Chi-A	7	6	.538	25	11	7	0	1	129¹	167	1	38	36	14.3	5.01	82	.317	.364	15	.326	5	-11	-13	-2	-0.8
1925	Chi-A	17	8	.680	40	23	16	3	1	232	218	11	69	81	11.1	3.03	137	.253	.308	18	.205	2	35	29	-5	2.4
1926	Chi-A	13	10	.565	29	26	15	1	1	209¹	217	13	65	66	12.2	3.61	107	.273	.328	10	.132	-2	10	6	-2	0.1
1927	Chi-A	12	17	.414	37	34	11	3	0	236²	280	14	74	51	13.5	5.06	80	.299	.352	15	.188	3	-24	-27	-2	-2.3
1928	Chi-A	9	11	.450	27	22	8	0	0	158	186	9	80	36	15.3	4.61	88	.306	.388	10	.169	-2	-10	-10	-1	-1.1
1929	Chi-A	0	2	.000	8	1	0	0	0	18¹	28	3	9	7	18.2	8.84	48	.359	.425	1	.250	-0	-9	-9	-1	-0.8
1930	Chi-A	2	1	.667	7	1	0	0	0	14²	23	0	7	2	19.0	9.20	50	.371	.443	1	.200	-0	-7	-7	-0	-0.6
Total	9	77	79	.494	241	156	73	8	4	1330²	1462	63	489	378	13.3	4.29	94	.287	.351	93	.196	7	-22	-36	-14	-3.5

■ CY BLANTON   Blanton, Darrell Elijah b: 7/6/08, Waurika, Okla. d: 9/13/45, Norman, Okla. BL/TR, 5′11.5″, 180 lbs. Deb: 9/23/34

1934	Pit-N	0	1	.000	1	1	0	0	0	8	5	1	4	5	11.3	3.38	122	.161	.278	0	.000	0	1	1	0	0.1
1935	Pit-N	18	13	.581	35	31	23	**4**	1	254¹	220	3	55	142	**9.8**	**2.58**	**159**	**.229**	**.272**	13	.134	-4	**41**	**43**	1	**4.2**
1936	Pit-N	13	15	.464	44	32	15	**4**	3	235²	235	9	55	127	11.2	3.51	115	.257	.301	13	.155	-3	13	14	0	1.1
1937	Pit-N	14	12	.538	36	34	14	4	0	242²	250	6	73	76	12.3	3.30	117	.266	.324	14	.165	-0	17	15	-1	1.4
1938	Pit-N	11	7	.611	29	25	10	1	0	172²	190	13	46	80	12.4	3.70	103	.281	.329	13	.203	-1	2	2	2	0.3
1939	Pit-N	2	3	.400	10	6	1	0	0	42	45	4	10	11	11.8	4.29	90	.266	.307	4	.286	1	-2	-2	0	0.0
1940	Phi-N	4	3	.571	13	10	5	0	0	77	82	7	21	24	12.2	4.32	90	.272	.322	2	.083	-1	-4	-4	0	-0.4
1941	Phi-N	6	13	.316	28	25	7	1	0	163²	186	11	57	64	13.5	4.51	82	.284	.344	6	.118	-2	-16	-15	-3	-1.9
1942	Phi-N	0	4	.000	6	3	0	0	0	22¹	30	3	13	15	17.7	5.64	59	.345	.436	1	.125	-0	-6	-6	-0	-0.5
Total	9	68	71	.489	202	167	75	14	4	1218¹	1243	64	337	611	11.8	3.55	110	.262	.314	66	.154	-12	45	49	-0	4.3

■ WADE BLASINGAME   Blasingame, Wade Allen b: 11/22/43, Deming, N.Mex. BL/TL, 6′1″, 185 lbs. Deb: 9/17/63

1963	Mil-N	0	0	—	2	0	0	0	0	3	7	0	2	6	27.0	12.00	37	.467	.529	0	—	0	-3	-3	0	-0.2
1964	Mil-N	9	5	.643	28	13	3	1	2	116²	113	15	51	70	12.7	4.24	83	.257	.334	7	.175	3	-9	-9	1	-0.5
1965	Mil-N	16	10	.615	38	36	10	1	1	224²	200	17	116	117	12.9	3.77	94	.244	.341	15	.185	3	-6	-6	2	0.0
1966	Atl-N	3	7	.300	16	12	0	0	0	67²	71	5	25	34	13.0	5.32	68	.272	.340	5	.217	1	-13	-13	-0	-1.1
1967	Atl-N	1	0	1.000	10	4	0	0	0	25¹	27	1	21	20	17.4	4.62	72	.287	.422	1	.143	0	-4	-4	0	-0.2
	Hou-N	4	7	.364	15	14	0	0	0	77	91	9	27	46	14.0	5.96	56	.298	.359	4	.182	2	-22	-23	-2	-2.0
	Yr	5	7	.417	25	18	0	0	0	102¹	118	10	48	66	14.8	5.63	59	.295	.373	6	.207	2	-26	-26	0	-2.2
1968	Hou-N	1	2	.333	22	2	0	0	1	36	45	3	10	22	13.8	4.75	62	.308	.353	0	.000	-0	-7	-7	1	-0.6
1969	Hou-N	0	5	.000	26	5	0	0	1	52	66	4	33	33	17.5	5.37	66	.306	.402	0	.000	-1	-10	-11	0	-1.1
1970	Hou-N	3	3	.500	13	13	1	0	0	77²	76	4	23	55	11.7	3.48	112	.261	.320	2	.083	-0	5	3	0	0.3
1971	Hou-N	9	11	.450	30	28	2	0	0	158¹	177	11	45	93	13.4	4.60	73	.285	.346	10	.204	4	-20	-22	1	-1.6
1972	Hou-N	0	0	—	10	0	0	0	0	8¹	4	1	8	9	15.1	8.64	39	.148	.378	0	—	0	-5	-5	0	-0.4
	NY-A	0	1	.000	12	1	0	0	0	17	14	5	11	7	13.8	4.24	70	.250	.382	0	.000	0	-2	-2	1	-0.1
Total	10	46	51	.474	222	128	16	2	5	863²	891	75	372	512	13.5	4.52	77	.271	.350	44	.166	13	-96	-101	6	-7.5

■ STEVE BLASS   Blass, Stephen Robert b: 4/18/42, Canaan, Conn. BR/TR, 6′, 165 lbs. Deb: 5/10/64

1964	Pit-N	5	8	.385	24	13	3	1	0	104²	107	9	45	67	13.2	4.04	87	.266	.341	2	.067	-1	-6	-6	0	-0.6
1966	Pit-N	11	7	.611	34	25	1	0	0	155²	173	12	46	76	12.8	3.87	92	.284	.336	12	.231	1	-5	-5	-2	-0.6
1967	Pit-N	6	8	.429	32	16	2	0	0	126²	126	12	47	72	12.4	3.55	95	.261	.329	5	.128	1	-3	-3	0	-0.2
1968	Pit-N	18	6	**.750**	33	31	12	7	0	220¹	191	13	57	132	10.3	2.12	138	.234	.288	11	.138	-1	21	20	-1	2.1
1969	Pit-N	16	10	.615	38	32	9	0	2	210	207	21	86	147	12.8	4.46	78	.258	.335	21	.250	6	-20	-23	3	-1.4
1970	Pit-N	10	12	.455	31	31	6	1	0	196²	187	14	73	120	12.1	3.52	111	.254	.326	8	.114	-2	11	8	0	0.6
1971	*Pit-N	15	8	.652	33	33	12	**5**	0	240	226	16	68	136	11.1	2.85	119	.249	.303	10	.120	-3	16	14	1	1.3
1972	*Pit-N	19	8	.704	33	32	11	2	0	249²	227	18	84	117	11.4	2.49	134	.246	.311	15	.183	1	27	23	2	3.0
1973	Pit-N	3	9	.250	23	18	1	0	0	88²	109	11	84	27	20.8	9.85	36	.313	.462	10	.417	4	-61	-62	1	-5.1
1974	Pit-N	0	0	—	1	1	0	0	0	5	5	2	7	2	21.6	9.00	38	.238	.429	0	.000	-0	-3	-3	0	-0.2
Total	10	103	76	.575	282	231	57	16	2	1597¹	1558	128	597	896	12.4	3.63	94	.258	.328	94	.172	4	-21	-37	5	-1.1

■ STEVE BLATERIC   Blateric, Stephen Lawrence b: 3/20/44, Denver, Colo. BR/TR, 6′3″, 200 lbs. Deb: 9/17/71

1971	Cin-N	0	0	—	2	0	0	0	0	2²	5	2	0	4	20.3	13.50	25	.385	.429	0	—	0	-3	-3	0	-0.2
1972	NY-A	0	0	—	1	0	0	0	0	4	2	0	4	4	4.5	0.00	—	.143	.143	0	.000	-0	1	1	0	0.2
1975	Cal-A	0	0	—	2	0	0	0	0	4¹	9	0	1	5	20.8	6.23	57	.429	.455	0	—	0	-1	-1	0	0.0
Total	3	0	0	—	5	0	0	0	0	11	16	2	1	13	14.7	5.73	57	.333	.360	0	.000	-0	-3	-3	0	0.0

■ HENRY BLAUVELT   Blauvelt, Henry Russell b: 4/8/1873, Nyack, N.Y. d: 12/28/26, Portland, Ore. Deb: 6/22/1890

| 1890 | Roc-a | 0 | 0 | — | 2 | 0 | 0 | 0 | 0 | 12¹ | 19 | 0 | 8 | 5 | 19.7 | 10.22 | 35 | .342 | .425 | 3 | .500 | 1 | -9 | -9 | 0 | -0.5 |

■ GARY BLAYLOCK   Blaylock, Gary Nelson b: 10/11/31, Clarkton, Mo. BR/TR, 6′, 196 lbs. Deb: 4/10/59 C

| 1959 | StL-N | 4 | 5 | .444 | 26 | 12 | 3 | 0 | 0 | 100 | 117 | 14 | 43 | 61 | 14.6 | 5.13 | 83 | .298 | .371 | 4 | .118 | 0 | -13 | -10 | 1 | -0.8 |
| | NY-A | 0 | 1 | .000 | 15 | 1 | 0 | 0 | 0 | 25² | 30 | 0 | 15 | 20 | 16.1 | 3.51 | 104 | .306 | .404 | 1 | .500 | 1 | 1 | 0 | -0 | 0.1 |

■ BOB BLAYLOCK   Blaylock, Robert Edward b: 6/28/35, Chattanooga, Okla BR/TR, 6′1″, 185 lbs. Deb: 7/22/56

1956	StL-N	1	6	.143	14	6	0	0	0	41	45	7	24	39	15.1	6.37	59	.276	.369	1	.091	-1	-12	-12	0	-1.1
1959	StL-N	0	1	.000	3	1	0	0	0	9	8	1	3	3	11.0	4.00	106	.229	.289	0	.000	-0	-0	0	0	0.0
Total	2	1	7	.125	17	7	0	0	0	50	53	8	27	42	14.4	5.94	65	.268	.356	1	.083	-1	-12	-12	0	-1.1

■ RAY BLEMKER   Blemker, Ray b: 8/9/37, Huntingburg, Ind. BR/TL, 5′11″, 190 lbs. Deb: 7/03/60

| 1960 | KC-A | 0 | 0 | — | 1 | 0 | 0 | 0 | 0 | 1² | 3 | 1 | 2 | 0 | 32.4 | 27.00 | 15 | .375 | .545 | 0 | — | 0 | -4 | -4 | 0 | -0.3 |

■ CLARENCE BLETHEN   Blethen, Clarence Waldo "Climax" b: 7/11/1893, Dover-Foxcroft, Maine d: 4/11/73, Frederick, Md. BL/TR, 5′11″, 165 lbs. Deb: 9/17/23

1923	Bos-A	0	0	—	5	0	0	0	0	17²	29	0	7	2	18.3	7.13	58	.382	.434	0	.000	-1	-6	-6	-1	-0.6
1929	Bro-N	0	0	—	2	0	0	0	0	2	4	0	3	0	31.5	9.00	51	.444	.583	0	—	0	-1	-1	0	0.0
Total	2	0	0	—	7	0	0	0	0	19²	33	0	10	2	19.7	7.32	57	.388	.453	0	.000	-1	-7	-7	-0	-0.6

■ BOB BLEWETT   Blewett, Robert Lawrence b: 6/28/1877, Fond Du Lac, Wis. d: 3/17/58, Sedro Woolley, Wash. BL/TL, 5′11″, 170 lbs. Deb: 6/17/02

| 1902 | NY-N | 0 | 2 | .000 | 5 | 3 | 2 | 0 | 0 | 28 | 39 | 0 | 7 | 8 | 15.1 | 4.82 | 58 | .329 | .371 | 0 | .000 | -1 | -6 | -6 | -1 | -0.7 |

■ ELMER BLISS   Bliss, Elmer Ward b: 3/9/1875, Penfield, Pa. d: 3/18/62, Bradford, Pa. BL/TR, 6′, 180 lbs. Deb: 9/28/03 ♦

| 1903 | NY-A | 1 | 0 | 1.000 | 1 | 0 | 0 | 0 | 0 | 7 | 4 | 0 | 3 | 3 | 5.1 | 0.00 | — | .167 | .167 | 0 | .000 | -0 | 2 | 2 | -0 | 0.2 |

■ TERRY BLOCKER   Blocker, Terry Fennell b: 8/18/59, Columbia, S.C. BL/TL, 6′2″, 195 lbs. Deb: 4/11/85 ♦

| 1989 | Atl-N | 0 | 0 | — | 1 | 0 | 0 | 0 | 0 | 1 | 0 | 0 | 2 | 0 | 18.0 | 0.00 | — | .000 | .500 | 7 | .226 | 0 | 0 | 0 | 0 | 0.0 |

YEAR TM/L	W	L	PCT	G	GS	CG	SH	SV	IP	H	HR	BB	SO	RAT	ERA	ERA+	OAV	OOB	BH	AVG	PB	PR	/A	PD	TPI
■ **JOE BLONG**				Blong, Joseph Myles b: 9/17/1853, St.Louis, Mo. d: 9/22/1892, St.Louis, Mo. BR/TR, Deb: 5/04/1875 ♦																				
1875 RS-n	3	12	.200	15	15	12	1	0	129	169	0	2		11.9	3.35	72	.285	.287	10	.147	-3	-13	-13		-1.3
1876 StL-N	0	0	—	1	0	0	0	0	4	2	0	1	0	6.8	0.00	—	.138	.194	62	.235	0	1	1	0	0.1
1877 StL-N	10	9	.526	25	21	17	0	0	187¹	203	0	38	51	11.6	2.74	95	.261	.295	47	.216	0	1	-3	-2	-0.2
Total 2	10	9	.526	26	21	17	0	0	191¹	205	0	39	51	11.5	2.68	97	.258	.293	109	.226	0	2	-2	-1	-0.1
■ **VIDA BLUE**				Blue, Vida Rochelle b: 7/28/49, Mansfield, La. BB/TL, 6', 189 lbs. Deb: 7/20/69																				
1969 Oak-A	1	1	.500	12	4	0	0	1	42	49	13	18	24	14.4	6.64	52	.290	.358	0	.000	-0	-14	-15	-1	-1.5
1970 Oak-A	2	0	1.000	6	6	2	2	0	38²	20	0	12	35	7.7	2.09	169	.152	.228	3	.200	2	7	6	0	0.9
1971 *Oak-A	24	8	.750	39	39	24	**8**	0	312	209	19	88	301	**8.7**	**1.82**	183	**.189**	**.252**	12	.118	-2	57	53	-5	5.2
1972 *Oak-A	6	10	.375	25	23	5	4	0	151	117	11	48	111	9.9	2.80	101	.215	.280	2	.044	-2	4	1	-2	-0.4
1973 *Oak-A	20	9	.690	37	37	13	4	0	263²	214	26	105	158	11.0	3.28	108	.224	.303	0	.000	0	16	8	-3	0.5
1974 *Oak-A	17	15	.531	40	40	12	1	0	282¹	246	17	98	174	11.0	3.25	102	.236	.303	0	—	0	11	2	-6	-0.3
1975 *Oak-A	22	11	.667	39	38	13	2	1	278	243	21	99	189	11.2	3.01	120	.236	.307	0	—	0	24	19	-3	1.7
1976 Oak-A	18	13	.581	37	37	20	6	0	298¹	268	9	63	166	10.0	2.35	143	.239	.280	0	—	0	**39**	33	-4	3.3
1977 Oak-A	14	19	.424	38	38	16	1	0	279²	284	23	86	157	11.9	3.83	105	.264	.319	0	.000	0	7	6	-1	0.5
1978 SF-N	18	10	.643	35	35	9	4	0	258	233	12	70	171	10.6	2.79	124	.246	.298	6	.076	2	23	19	-2	2.0
1979 SF-N	14	14	.500	34	34	10	0	0	237	246	23	111	138	13.6	5.01	77	.272	.352	10	.120	0	-34	-40	2	-3.6
1980 SF-N	14	10	.583	31	31	10	3	0	224	202	14	61	129	10.6	2.97	119	.242	.294	5	.074	-4	16	14	2	1.3
1981 SF-N	8	6	.571	18	18	1	0	0	124²	97	7	54	63	11.0	2.45	140	.217	.303	7	.200	2	14	14	2	2.0
1982 KC-A	13	12	.520	31	31	6	2	0	181	163	20	80	103	12.1	3.78	108	.238	.318	0	—	0	6	6	-1	0.5
1983 KC-A	0	5	.000	19	14	1	0	0	85¹	96	12	35	53	14.0	6.01	68	.286	.357	0	—	0	-18	-18	-1	-1.7
1985 SF-N	8	8	.500	33	20	1	0	0	131	115	17	80	103	13.5	4.47	77	.240	.350	4	.133	1	-13	-15	0	-1.4
1986 SF-N	10	10	.500	28	28	0	0	0	156²	137	19	77	121	12.3	3.27	107	.239	.329	4	.093	1	8	4	-1	0.5
Total 17	209	161	.565	502	473	143	37	2	3343¹	2939	263	1185	2175	11.2	3.27	108	.237	.305	53	.104	-1	152	95	-20	9.5
■ **JIM BLUEJACKET**				Bluejacket, James (b: James Smith) b: 7/8/1887, Adair, Okla. d: 3/26/47, Pekin, Ill. BR/TR, 6'2.5", 200 lbs. Deb: 8/06/14																				
1914 Bro-F	4	5	.444	17	7	3	1	1	67	77	2	19	29	12.9	3.76	85	.302	.350	3	.136	-0	-4	-4	1	-0.3
1915 Bro-F	10	11	.476	24	21	10	2	0	162²	155	2	75	48	12.7	3.15	96	.258	.340	8	.131	-4	-2	-2	-3	-0.8
1916 Cin-N	0	1	.000	3	2	0	0	0	7	12	0	3	1	19.3	7.71	34	.400	.455	0	.000	-0	-4	-4	-0	-0.4
Total 3	14	17	.452	44	30	13	3	1	236²	244	4	97	78	13.0	3.46	88	.275	.347	11	.129	-4	-10	-11	-2	-1.5
■ **CLINT BLUME**				Blume, Clinton Willis b: 10/17/1898, Brooklyn, N.Y. d: 6/12/73, Islip, L.I., N.Y. BR/TR, 5'11", 175 lbs. Deb: 9/30/22																				
1922 NY-N	1	0	1.000	1	1	1	0	0	9	7	0	1	2	8.0	1.00	400	.212	.235	1	1.000	1	3	3	-1	0.4
1923 NY-N	2	0	1.000	12	1	0	0	0	24	22	0	20	2	16.5	3.75	102	.265	.419	0	.000	-0	1	0	-0	0.0
Total 2	3	0	1.000	13	2	1	0	0	33	29	0	21	4	14.2	3.00	129	.250	.374	1	.167	1	4	3	-1	0.4
■ **BERT BLYLEVEN**				Blyleven, Rik Aalbert b: 4/6/51, Zeist, Holland BR/TR, 6'3", 200 lbs. Deb: 6/05/70																				
1970 *Min-A	10	9	.526	27	25	5	1	0	164	143	17	47	135	10.5	3.18	117	.232	.289	7	.140	-1	10	10	-2	0.7
1971 Min-A	16	15	.516	38	38	17	5	0	278¹	267	21	59	224	10.7	2.81	126	.255	.286	12	.132	-3	20	23	-1	2.2
1972 Min-A	17	17	.500	39	38	11	3	0	287¹	247	22	69	228	10.2	2.73	118	.233	.286	15	.160	-1	11	15	0	1.8
1973 Min-A	20	17	.541	40	40	25	**9**	0	325	296	16	67	258	10.3	2.52	**157**	.242	.287	0	—	-1	**47**	52	-3	**5.4**
1974 Min-A	17	17	.500	37	37	19	3	0	281	244	14	77	249	10.6	2.66	141	.233	.292	0	—	0	30	34	-1	3.7
1975 Min-A	15	10	.600	35	35	20	3	0	275²	219	24	84	233	10.0	3.00	128	.219	.283	0	—	0	24	26	2	3.0
1976 Min-A	4	5	.444	12	12	4	0	0	95¹	101	3	35	75	13.2	3.12	116	.283	.354	0	—	0	4	5	-0	0.5
Tex-A	9	11	.450	24	24	14	6	0	202¹	182	11	46	144	10.5	2.76	130	.242	.293	0	—	0	17	19	1	2.2
Yr	13	16	.448	36	36	18	6	0	297²	283	14	81	219	11.2	2.87	125	.254	.309	0	—	0	21	24	1	2.7
1977 Tex-A	14	12	.538	30	30	15	5	0	234²	181	20	69	182	**9.9**	2.72	150	.214	.279	0	—	0	35	35	-0	3.7
1978 Pit-N	14	10	.583	34	34	11	4	0	243²	217	17	66	182	10.7	3.03	122	.235	.290	11	.129	-2	15	18	1	1.8
1979 *Pit-N	12	5	.706	37	37	4	0	0	237¹	238	21	92	172	12.7	3.60	108	.265	.338	9	.129	-3	3	7	-3	0.2
1980 Pit-N	8	13	.381	34	32	5	2	0	216²	219	20	59	168	11.5	3.82	95	.262	.311	5	.082	-4	-5	-4	-1	-0.8
1981 Cle-A	11	7	.611	20	20	9	1	0	159¹	145	9	40	107	10.7	2.88	126	.245	.298	0	—	0	14	13	-2	1.3
1982 Cle-A	2	2	.500	4	4	0	0	0	20¹	16	2	11	19	12.0	4.87	84	.211	.310	0	—	0	-2	-2	0	-0.1
1983 Cle-A	7	10	.412	24	24	5	0	0	156¹	160	8	44	123	12.3	3.91	108	.267	.328	0	—	0	3	6	1	0.7
1984 Cle-A	19	7	.731	33	32	12	4	0	245	204	19	74	170	10.4	2.87	143	.224	.287	0	—	0	31	33	0	3.5
1985 Cle-A	9	11	.450	23	23	15	4	0	179²	163	14	49	129	11.0	3.26	127	.240	.298	0	—	0	18	18	-1	1.7
Min-A	8	5	.615	14	14	9	1	0	114	101	9	26	77	10.2	3.00	147	.237	.284	0	—	0	15	18	-0	1.8
Yr	17	16	.515	37	37	**24**	5	0	293²	264	23	75	**206**	10.5	3.16	134	.236	.286	0	—	0	32	35	-2	3.5
1986 Min-A	17	14	.548	36	36	16	3	0	271²	262	50	58	215	10.9	4.01	107	.250	.295	0	—	0	5	9	-1	0.8
1987 *Min-A	15	12	.556	37	37	8	1	0	267	249	46	101	196	12.1	4.01	115	.249	.323	0	—	0	13	18	1	1.9
1988 Min-A	10	17	.370	33	33	7	0	0	207¹	240	21	51	145	13.3	5.43	75	.287	.348	0	—	0	-34	-31	-1	-3.0
1989 Cal-A	17	5	.773	33	33	8	**5**	0	241	225	14	44	131	10.3	2.73	140	.248	.289	0	—	0	31	29	1	3.3
1990 Cal-A	8	7	.533	23	23	2	0	0	134	163	15	25	69	13.1	5.24	74	.303	.342	0	—	0	-20	-20	1	-1.8
Total 21	279	238	.540	667	661	241	60	0	4837	4482	413	1293	3631	11.0	3.27	119	.246	.302	59	.131	-14	283	331	-7	34.5
■ **MIKE BLYZKA**				Blyzka, Michael John b: 12/25/28, Hamtramck, Mich. BR/TR, 5'11.5", 190 lbs. Deb: 4/21/53																				
1953 StL-A	2	6	.250	33	9	2	0	1	94¹	110	6	56	23	15.8	6.39	66	.292	.383	0	.000	-3	-25	-23	-0	-2.4
1954 Bal-A	1	5	.167	37	0	0	0	0	86¹	83	2	51	35	14.0	4.69	76	.258	.354	2	.133	-1	-9	-11	0	-1.0
Total 2	3	11	.214	70	9	2	0	1	180²	193	8	107	58	14.9	5.58	70	.274	.370	2	.053	-4	-34	-34	0	-3.4
■ **CHARLIE BOARDMAN**				Boardman, Charles Louis b: 4/27/1893, Seneca Falls, N.Y. d: 8/10/68, Sacramento, Cal. BL/TL, 6'2.5", 194 lbs. Deb: 9/26/13																				
1913 Phi-A	0	2	.000	2	2	1	0	0	9	10	0	6	4	16.0	2.00	138	.294	.400	0	.000	-0	1	1	-0	0.0
1914 Phi-A	0	0	—	2	0	0	0	0	7¹	10	0	4	2	17.2	4.91	54	.357	.438	0	.000	-0	-2	-2	0	-0.1
1915 StL-N	1	0	1.000	3	1	1	0	0	19	12	0	15	7	12.8	2.84	98	.188	.342	2	.286	-0	-0	-0	-0	0.0
Total 3	1	2	.333	7	3	2	0	0	35¹	32	0	25	13	14.5	3.06	90	.254	.377	2	.167	-0	-1	-1	-0	-0.1
■ **RANDY BOCKUS**				Bockus, Randy Walter b: 10/5/60, Canton, Ohio BL/TR, 6'2", 190 lbs. Deb: 9/10/86																				
1986 SF-N	0	0	—	5	0	0	0	0	7	7	1	6	4	16.7	2.57	137	.241	.371	0	.000	-0	1	1	1	0.1
1987 SF-N	1	0	1.000	12	0	0	0	0	17¹	17	2	4	9	10.9	3.63	106	.266	.309	0	.000	-0	1	0	0	0.0
1988 SF-N	1	1	.500	20	0	0	0	0	32	35	2	13	18	13.8	4.78	68	.297	.371	1	.167	-0	-5	-5	-0	-0.4
1989 Det-A	0	0	—	2	0	0	0	0	5¹	7	0	2	2	15.2	5.06	75	.333	.391	0	—	0	-1	-1	-0	0.0
Total 4	2	1	.667	39	0	0	0	0	61²	66	5	25	33	13.4	4.23	83	.284	.357	1	.125	-0	-4	-5	1	-0.3
■ **MIKE BODDICKER**				Boddicker, Michael James b: 8/23/57, Cedar Rapids, Iowa BR/TR, 5'11", 172 lbs. Deb: 10/04/80																				
1980 Bal-A	0	1	.000	1	1	0	0	0	7¹	6	1	5	4	13.5	6.14	64	.207	.324	0	—	0	-2	-2	-0	-0.1
1981 Bal-A	0	0	—	2	0	0	0	0	5²	6	1	2	2	12.7	4.76	76	.261	.300	0	—	0	-1	-1	-0	0.0
1982 Bal-A	1	0	1.000	7	0	0	0	0	25²	25	2	12	20	13.0	3.51	115	.258	.339	0	—	0	2	2	-0	0.2
1983 *Bal-A	16	8	.667	27	26	10	**5**	0	179	141	13	52	120	9.7	2.77	143	**.216**	.274	0	—	0	26	24	3	2.8
1984 Bal-A	**20**	11	.645	34	34	16	4	0	261¹	218	23	81	128	10.5	**2.79**	139	.228	.292	0	—	0	**35**	31	6	4.0
1985 Bal-A	12	17	.414	32	32	9	2	0	203¹	227	13	89	135	14.2	4.07	99	.286	.361	0	—	0	-2	-1	5	-0.4
1986 Bal-A	14	12	.538	33	33	7	0	0	218¹	214	30	74	175	12.3	4.70	88	.255	.323	0	—	0	-13	-14	-1	-0.9
1987 Bal-A	10	12	.455	33	33	7	2	0	226	212	29	78	152	11.8	4.18	105	.248	.316	0	—	0	7	5	4	0.9
1988 Bal-A	6	12	.333	21	21	4	0	0	147	149	14	51	100	12.9	3.86	101	.265	.338	0	—	0	2	1	-1	0.0
*Bos-A	7	3	.700	15	14	1	1	0	89	85	3	26	56	11.5	2.63	156	.257	.317	0	—	0	13	15	2	1.8

YEAR	TM/L	W	L	PCT	G	GS	CG	SH	SV	IP	H	HR	BB	SO	RAT	ERA	ERA+	OAV	OOB	BH	AVG	PB	PR	/A	PD	TPI
	Yr	13	15	.464	36	35	5	1	0	236	234	17	77	156	12.0	3.39	117	.256	.316	0	—	0	15	15	1	1.8
1989	Bos-A	15	11	.577	34	34	3	2	0	211²	217	19	71	145	12.7	4.00	103	.267	.333	0	—	0	-3	2	1	0.4
1990	*Bos-A	17	8	.680	34	34	4	0	0	228	225	16	69	143	12.0	3.36	122	.258	.319	0	—	0	14	18	2	2.1
Total	11	118	95	.554	273	262	61	16	0	1802¹	1725	164	610	1180	12.0	3.66	111	.253	.320	0	—	0	82	81	24	11.6

■ GEORGE BOEHLER
Boehler, George Henry   b: 1/2/1892, Lawrenceburg, Ind.   d: 6/23/58, Lawrenceburg, Ind   BR/TR, 6'2", 180 lbs.   Deb: 9/13/12

YEAR	TM/L	W	L	PCT	G	GS	CG	SH	SV	IP	H	HR	BB	SO	RAT	ERA	ERA+	OAV	OOB	BH	AVG	PB	PR	/A	PD	TPI
1912	Det-A	0	2	.000	5	4	2	0	0	32	50	0	14	15	18.6	6.47	50	.365	.431	1	.100	-1	-11	-11	1	-0.9
1913	Det-A	0	1	.000	1	1	1	0	0	8	11	0	6	2	21.4	6.75	43	.355	.487	1	.333	1	-3	-3	1	-0.1
1914	Det-A	2	3	.400	18	6	2	0	0	63	54	1	48	37	15.7	3.57	79	.242	.394	3	.176	1	-6	-5	-1	-0.7
1915	Det-A	1	1	.500	8	0	0	0	0	15	19	0	4	7	14.4	1.80	168	.328	.381	3	.750	2	2	2	-0	0.4
1916	Det-A	1	1	.500	5	2	1	0	0	13¹	12	0	9	8	15.5	4.73	61	.261	.404	0	.000	0	-3	-3	0	-0.1
1920	StL-A	0	1	.000	3	1	0	0	0	7	10	1	4	2	18.0	7.71	51	.303	.378	0	.000	0	-3	-3	-0	-0.2
1921	StL-A	0	0	—	1	0	0	0	0	1	1	0	0	0	9.0	0.00	—	.500	.500	0	—	0	0	0	0	0.0
1923	Pit-N	1	3	.250	10	3	1	0	0	28¹	33	1	26	12	19.1	6.04	66	.314	.455	3	.300	1	-6	-6	-0	-0.5
1926	Bro-N	1	0	1.000	10	1	0	0	0	34²	42	1	23	10	17.7	4.41	87	.302	.412	3	.250	0	-2	-2	-0	-0.1
Total	9	6	12	.333	61	18	7	0	0	202¹	232	4	134	93	17.1	4.71	70	.300	.415	14	.233	3	-33	-32	1	-1.9

■ JOE BOEHLING
Boehling, John Joseph   b: 3/20/1891, Richmond, Va.   d: 9/8/41, Richmond, Va.   BL/TL, 5'11", 168 lbs.   Deb: 6/20/12

YEAR	TM/L	W	L	PCT	G	GS	CG	SH	SV	IP	H	HR	BB	SO	RAT	ERA	ERA+	OAV	OOB	BH	AVG	PB	PR	/A	PD	TPI
1912	Was-A	0	0	—	3	0	0	0	0	5	4	0	6	2	21.6	7.20	46	.235	.480	0	—	0	-2	-2	0	-0.1
1913	Was-A	17	7	.708	38	25	18	3	4	235¹	197	3	82	110	11.0	2.14	138	.229	.303	19	.221	1	21	21	3	2.7
1914	Was-A	12	8	.600	27	24	14	2	1	196	180	3	76	91	12.2	3.03	92	.258	.339	17	.239	4	-6	-6	3	0.1
1915	Was-A	14	13	.519	40	32	14	2	0	229¹	217	5	119	108	13.5	3.22	91	.255	.352	13	.173	1	-7	-7	2	-0.4
1916	Was-A	9	11	.450	27	19	7	2	0	139²	134	1	54	52	12.3	3.09	89	.260	.333	7	.171	1	-4	-5	4	0.0
	Cle-A	2	4	.333	12	9	3	0	0	60²	63	0	23	18	13.1	2.67	113	.281	.353	5	.263	1	1	2	1	0.4
	Yr	11	15	.423	39	28	10	2	0	200¹	197	1	77	70	12.4	2.97	96	.265	.336	4	.067	2	-3	-3	5	0.4
1917	Cle-A	1	6	.143	12	7	1	0	0	46¹	50	1	16	11	13.4	4.66	61	.291	.361	3	.188	-0	-10	-9	0	-0.9
1920	Cle-A	0	1	.000	3	2	0	0	0	13	16	0	10	4	18.0	4.85	78	.333	.448	2	.500	1	-2	-2	0	-0.1
Total	7	55	50	.524	162	118	57	9	5	925¹	861	13	386	396	12.5	2.97	97	.254	.337	66	.212	8	-10	-8	13	1.8

■ LARRY BOERNER
Boerner, Lawrence Hyer   b: 1/21/05, Staunton, Va.   d: 10/16/69, Staunton, Va.   BR/TR, 6'4.5", 175 lbs.   Deb: 6/30/32

YEAR	TM/L	W	L	PCT	G	GS	CG	SH	SV	IP	H	HR	BB	SO	RAT	ERA	ERA+	OAV	OOB	BH	AVG	PB	PR	/A	PD	TPI
1932	Bos-A	0	4	.000	21	5	0	0	0	61	71	2	37	19	16.4	5.02	90	.302	.404	0	.000	-3	-4	-4	0	-0.4

■ JOE BOEVER
Boever, Joseph Martin   b: 10/4/60, Kirkwood, Mo.   BR/TR, 6'1", 200 lbs.   Deb: 7/19/85

YEAR	TM/L	W	L	PCT	G	GS	CG	SH	SV	IP	H	HR	BB	SO	RAT	ERA	ERA+	OAV	OOB	BH	AVG	PB	PR	/A	PD	TPI
1985	StL-N	0	0	—	13	0	0	0	0	16¹	17	3	4	20	11.6	4.41	80	.270	.313	0	—	0	-1	-2	-1	-0.1
1986	StL-N	0	1	.000	11	0	0	0	0	21²	19	2	11	8	12.5	1.66	219	.232	.323	1	.500	0	5	5	-0	0.5
1987	Atl-N	1	0	1.000	14	0	0	0	0	18¹	29	4	12	18	20.1	7.36	59	.367	.451	0	—	0	-7	-6	-0	-0.5
1988	Atl-N	0	2	.000	16	0	0	0	1	20¹	12	1	1	7	6.2	1.77	208	.182	.206	0	—	0	4	4	0	0.5
1989	Atl-N	4	11	.267	66	0	0	0	21	82¹	78	6	34	68	12.4	3.94	93	.252	.328	0	.000	-0	-4	-3	1	-0.1
1990	Atl-N	1	3	.250	33	0	0	0	8	42¹	40	6	35	35	15.9	4.68	84	.252	.387	0	.000	-0	-4	-4	-1	-0.4
	Phi-N	2	3	.400	34	0	0	0	6	46	37	0	16	40	10.4	2.15	177	.215	.282	0	.000	-0	8	9	0	0.9
	Yr	3	6	.333	67	0	0	0	14	88¹	77	6	51	75	13.0	3.36	115	.231	.333	0	.000	-0	4	5	-1	0.5
Total	6	8	20	.286	187	0	0	0	36	247¹	232	22	113	196	12.6	3.64	104	.249	.332	1	.167	-0	1	4	-1	0.8

■ JOHN BOGART
Bogart, John Renzie "Big John"   b: 9/21/1900, Bloomsburg, Pa.   d: 12/7/86, Clarence, N.Y.   BR/TR, 6'2", 195 lbs.   Deb: 9/17/20

YEAR	TM/L	W	L	PCT	G	GS	CG	SH	SV	IP	H	HR	BB	SO	RAT	ERA	ERA+	OAV	OOB	BH	AVG	PB	PR	/A	PD	TPI
1920	Det-A	2	1	.667	4	3	0	0	0	23²	16	0	18	5	12.9	3.04	122	.195	.340	2	.250	-0	2	2	-1	0.1

■ RAY BOGGS
Boggs, Raymond Joseph "Lefty"   b: 12/12/04, Reamsville, Kan.   BL/TL, 6'0.5", 170 lbs.   Deb: 9/01/28

YEAR	TM/L	W	L	PCT	G	GS	CG	SH	SV	IP	H	HR	BB	SO	RAT	ERA	ERA+	OAV	OOB	BH	AVG	PB	PR	/A	PD	TPI
1928	Bos-N	0	0	—	4	0	0	0	0	5	2	0	7	0	21.6	5.40	72	.167	.545	0	—	0	-1	-1	0	0.0

■ TOMMY BOGGS
Boggs, Thomas Winton   b: 10/25/55, Poughkeepsie, N.Y.   BR/TR, 6'2", 195 lbs.   Deb: 7/19/76

YEAR	TM/L	W	L	PCT	G	GS	CG	SH	SV	IP	H	HR	BB	SO	RAT	ERA	ERA+	OAV	OOB	BH	AVG	PB	PR	/A	PD	TPI
1976	Tex-A	1	7	.125	13	13	3	0	0	90¹	87	7	34	36	12.2	3.49	103	.257	.326	0	—	0	0	1	-0	0.1
1977	Tex-A	0	3	.000	6	6	0	0	0	27¹	40	1	12	15	17.5	5.93	69	.351	.417	0	—	0	-6	-6	-0	-0.5
1978	Atl-N	2	8	.200	16	12	1	1	0	59	80	8	26	21	16.3	6.71	60	.323	.389	3	.167	0	-21	-17	-1	-1.7
1979	Atl-N	0	2	.000	3	3	0	0	0	12²	21	0	4	1	18.5	6.39	63	.362	.413	1	.250	0	-4	-3	0	-0.2
1980	Atl-N	12	9	.571	32	26	4	3	0	192¹	180	14	46	84	10.8	3.42	109	.249	.298	10	.159	-2	4	7	-2	0.3
1981	Atl-N	3	13	.188	25	24	2	0	0	142²	140	11	54	81	12.4	4.10	87	.265	.336	7	.152	-1	-10	-8	-1	-0.9
1982	Atl-N	2	2	.500	10	10	0	0	0	46¹	43	2	22	29	13.0	3.30	113	.253	.345	4	.235	0	2	2	-0	0.3
1983	Atl-N	0	0	—	5	0	0	0	0	6¹	8	1	5	4	18.5	5.68	68	.320	.346	0	—	0	-1	-1	-0	-0.0
1985	Tex-A	0	0	—	4	0	0	0	0	7	13	3	2	6	19.3	11.57	37	.382	.417	0	—	0	-6	-6	0	-0.4
Total	9	20	44	.313	114	94	10	4	0	584	612	47	201	278	12.7	4.22	89	.273	.337	25	.169	-2	-41	-31	-4	-3.0

■ WARREN BOGLE
Bogle, Warren Frederick   b: 10/19/46, Passaic, N.J.   BL/TL, 6'4", 220 lbs.   Deb: 7/31/68

YEAR	TM/L	W	L	PCT	G	GS	CG	SH	SV	IP	H	HR	BB	SO	RAT	ERA	ERA+	OAV	OOB	BH	AVG	PB	PR	/A	PD	TPI
1968	Oak-A	0	0	—	16	1	0	0	0	23	26	3	8	26	13.3	4.30	65	.283	.340	0	.000	-0	-3	-4	0	-0.3

■ BRIAN BOHANON
Bohanon, Brian Edward   b: 8/1/68, Denton, Tex.   BL/TL, 6'2", 210 lbs.   Deb: 4/10/90

YEAR	TM/L	W	L	PCT	G	GS	CG	SH	SV	IP	H	HR	BB	SO	RAT	ERA	ERA+	OAV	OOB	BH	AVG	PB	PR	/A	PD	TPI
1990	Tex-A	0	3	.000	11	6	0	0	0	34	40	6	18	15	15.9	6.62	60	.296	.387	0	—	0	-10	-10	1	-0.7

■ PAT BOHEN
Bohen, Leo Ignatius   b: 9/30/1891, Oakland, Iowa   d: 4/8/42, Napa, Cal.   BR/TR, 5'10.5", 155 lbs.   Deb: 10/01/13

YEAR	TM/L	W	L	PCT	G	GS	CG	SH	SV	IP	H	HR	BB	SO	RAT	ERA	ERA+	OAV	OOB	BH	AVG	PB	PR	/A	PD	TPI
1913	Phi-A	0	1	.000	1	1	0	0	0	8	3	0	2	5	5.6	1.13	245	.115	.179	0	.000	-0	2	1	0	0.1
1914	Pit-N	0	0	—	1	0	0	0	0	1	2	0	2	0	45.0	18.00	15	.500	.714	0	.000	-0	-2	-2	0	-0.1
Total	2	0	1	.000	2	1	0	0	0	9	5	0	4	5	10.0	3.00	92	.167	.286	0	.000	-1	-0	-0	0	0.0

■ CHARLIE BOHN
Bohn, Charles   b: 1857, Cleveland, Ohio   d: 8/1/03, Cleveland, Ohio   Deb: 6/20/1882 ♦

YEAR	TM/L	W	L	PCT	G	GS	CG	SH	SV	IP	H	HR	BB	SO	RAT	ERA	ERA+	OAV	OOB	BH	AVG	PB	PR	/A	PD	TPI
1882	Lou-a	1	1	.500	2	2	2	0	0	18	21	0	3	1	12.0	3.00	82	.273	.300	2	.154	-0	-1	-1	0	0.0

■ JOHN BOHNET
Bohnet, John Kelly   b: 1/18/61, Pasadena, Cal.   BB/TL, 6', 175 lbs.   Deb: 5/10/82

YEAR	TM/L	W	L	PCT	G	GS	CG	SH	SV	IP	H	HR	BB	SO	RAT	ERA	ERA+	OAV	OOB	BH	AVG	PB	PR	/A	PD	TPI
1982	Cle-A	0	0	—	3	3	0	0	0	11²	11	4	7	4	14.7	6.94	59	.250	.365	0	—	0	-4	-4	0	-0.2

■ DAN BOITANO
Boitano, Danny Jon   b: 3/22/53, Sacramento, Cal.   BR/TR, 6', 185 lbs.   Deb: 10/01/78

YEAR	TM/L	W	L	PCT	G	GS	CG	SH	SV	IP	H	HR	BB	SO	RAT	ERA	ERA+	OAV	OOB	BH	AVG	PB	PR	/A	PD	TPI
1978	Phi-N	0	0	—	1	0	0	0	0	1	0	0	1	0	9.0	0.00	—	.000	.250	0	—	0	0	0	0	0.0
1979	Mil-A	0	0	—	5	0	0	0	0	6	6	1	3	5	13.5	1.50	278	.273	.360	0	—	0	2	2	0	0.2
1980	Mil-A	0	1	.000	11	0	0	0	0	17²	26	7	6	11	16.8	8.15	47	.342	.398	0	—	0	-8	-8	0	-0.7
1981	NY-N	2	1	.667	15	0	0	0	0	16¹	21	2	5	8	15.4	5.51	63	.309	.373	0	—	0	-4	-4	0	-0.3
1982	Tex-A	0	0	—	19	0	0	0	0	30¹	33	5	13	28	14.2	5.34	72	.280	.361	0	—	0	-4	-5	-0	-0.4
Total	5	2	2	.500	51	0	0	0	0	71¹	86	15	28	52	15.0	5.68	67	.300	.372	0	—	0	-14	-15	-0	-1.2

■ DICK BOKELMANN
Bokelmann, Richard Werner   b: 10/26/26, Arlington Heights, Ill.   BR/TR, 6'0.5", 180 lbs.   Deb: 8/03/51

YEAR	TM/L	W	L	PCT	G	GS	CG	SH	SV	IP	H	HR	BB	SO	RAT	ERA	ERA+	OAV	OOB	BH	AVG	PB	PR	/A	PD	TPI
1951	StL-N	3	3	.500	20	1	0	0	3	52¹	49	2	31	22	13.9	3.78	105	.245	.349	0	.000	-2	1	1	-1	-0.1
1952	StL-N	0	1	.000	11	0	0	0	0	12²	20	0	7	5	19.2	9.24	40	.357	.429	0	—	0	-8	-8	1	-0.6
1953	StL-N	0	0	—	3	0	0	0	0	3	4	0	0	0	12.0	6.00	71	.308	.308	0	—	0	-1	-1	0	0.0
Total	3	3	4	.429	34	1	0	0	3	68	73	2	38	27	14.8	4.90	80	.271	.364	0	.000	-2	-7	-7	1	-0.7

■ JOE BOKINA
Bokina, Joseph   b: 4/4/10, Northampton, Mass.   BR/TR, 6', 184 lbs.   Deb: 4/16/36

YEAR	TM/L	W	L	PCT	G	GS	CG	SH	SV	IP	H	HR	BB	SO	RAT	ERA	ERA+	OAV	OOB	BH	AVG	PB	PR	/A	PD	TPI
1936	Was-A	0	2	.000	5	1	0	0	0	8¹	15	0	6	5	22.7	8.64	55	.395	.477	0	.000	-0	-3	-4	0	-0.2

YEAR	TM/L	W	L	PCT	G	GS	CG	SH	SV	IP	H	HR	BB	SO	RAT	ERA	ERA+	OAV	OOB	BH	AVG	PB	PR	/A	PD	TPI

BERNIE BOLAND — Boland, Bernard Anthony b: 1/21/1892, Rochester, N.Y. d: 9/12/73, Detroit, Mich. BR/TR, 5'8.5", 168 lbs. Deb: 4/14/15

1915	Det-A	13	7	.650	45	18	8	1	2	202²	167	2	75	72	11.0	3.11	98	.230	.307	11	.175	-1	-4	-2	0	-0.1
1916	Det-A	10	3	.769	46	9	5	1	3	130¹	111	1	73	59	13.0	3.94	73	.240	.349	8	.250	2	-16	-15	-3	-1.7
1917	Det-A	16	11	.593	43	28	13	3	6	238	192	0	95	89	11.1	2.68	99	.226	.308	4	.056	-5	-0	-1	0	-0.6
1918	Det-A	14	10	.583	29	25	14	4	0	204	176	1	67	63	11.0	2.65	101	.236	.304	12	.174	0	3	0	-1	0.0
1919	Det-A	14	16	.467	35	30	18	1	1	242²	222	7	80	71	11.3	3.04	105	.253	.318	8	.108	-3	5	4	-1	0.0
1920	Det-A	0	2	.000	4	3	1	0	0	17¹	23	1	14	4	20.3	7.79	48	.348	.476	1	.143	-0	-8	-8	0	-0.6
1921	StL-A	1	4	.200	7	6	0	0	0	27	34	2	28	6	21.0	9.33	48	.309	.453	1	.100	-1	-15	-15	0	-1.2
Total	7	68	53	.562	209	119	59	10	12	1062	925	13	432	364	11.7	3.25	91	.241	.322	45	.138	-8	-35	-36	-5	-4.2

BILL BOLDEN — Bolden, William Horace "Big Bill" b: 5/9/1893, Dandridge, Tenn. d: 12/8/66, Jefferson City, Tenn. BR/TR, 6'4", 200 lbs. Deb: 6/27/19

| 1919 | StL-N | 0 | 1 | .000 | 3 | 1 | 0 | 0 | 0 | 12 | 17 | 0 | 4 | 4 | 16.5 | 5.25 | 53 | .340 | .400 | 1 | .333 | 0 | -3 | -3 | 0 | -0.2 |

STEW BOLEN — Bolen, Stewart O'Neal b: 10/12/02, Jackson, Ala. d: 8/30/69, Mobile, Ala. BL/TL, 5'11", 180 lbs. Deb: 4/15/26

1926	StL-A	0	0	—	5	0	0	0	0	14²	21	2	6	7	16.6	6.14	70	.356	.415	2	.500	1	-3	-3	-0	-0.1
1927	StL-A	0	1	.000	3	1	1	0	0	9²	14	0	5	7	17.7	8.38	52	.368	.442	1	.333	0	-5	-4	0	-0.3
1931	Phi-N	3	12	.200	28	16	2	0	0	98¹	117	5	63	55	16.8	6.39	66	.297	.399	5	.156	-1	-28	-23	0	-2.2
1932	Phi-N	0	0	—	5	0	0	0	0	16	18	0	10	3	16.9	2.81	157	.281	.395	1	.143	-0	2	3	-0	0.2
Total	4	3	13	.188	41	17	3	0	0	139	170	7	84	72	16.8	6.09	70	.306	.403	9	.196	-0	-34	-28	-0	-2.4

BOBBY BOLIN — Bolin, Bobby Donald b: 1/29/39, Hickory Grove, S.C. BR/TR, 6'4", 185 lbs. Deb: 4/18/61

1961	SF-N	2	2	.500	37	1	0	0	5	48	37	6	37	48	14.4	3.19	120	.210	.356	2	.286	0	5	3	-1	0.2
1962	*SF-N	7	3	.700	41	5	2	0	5	92	84	10	35	74	12.1	3.62	105	.243	.321	6	.261	2	3	2	-1	0.2
1963	SF-N	10	6	.625	47	12	2	0	7	137¹	128	13	57	134	12.6	3.28	98	.242	.324	5	.143	2	-0	-1	-3	-0.2
1964	SF-N	6	9	.400	38	23	5	3	1	174²	143	16	77	146	11.9	3.25	110	.220	.313	5	.100	0	6	6	-1	0.6
1965	SF-N	14	6	.700	45	13	2	0	2	163	125	17	56	135	10.2	2.76	130	.214	.288	9	.167	1	14	15	-2	1.6
1966	SF-N	11	10	.524	36	34	10	4	1	224¹	174	25	70	143	10.2	2.89	127	.211	.281	13	.171	3	18	19	-2	2.3
1967	SF-N	6	8	.429	37	15	0	0	0	120	120	16	50	69	13.0	4.88	67	.258	.333	8	.242	2	-20	-21	-1	-2.0
1968	SF-N	10	5	.667	34	19	6	3	0	176²	128	9	46	126	9.1	1.99	148	.200	.258	5	.091	-1	20	19	-1	2.0
1969	SF-N	7	7	.500	30	22	2	0	0	146¹	149	17	49	102	12.6	4.43	79	.260	.326	6	.154	3	-14	-15	-1	-1.2
1970	Mil-A	5	11	.313	32	20	3	0	1	132	131	20	67	81	13.8	4.91	77	.256	.346	7	.194	2	-18	-16	-1	-1.5
	Bos-A	2	0	1.000	6	0	0	0	2	8	2	0	5	8	9.0	0.00	—	.080	.258	0	.000	-0	3	4	0	0.4
	Yr	7	11	.389	38	20	3	0	3	140	133	20	72	89	13.2	4.63	82	.243	.332	3	.081	2	-14	-13	-1	-1.1
1971	Bos-A	5	3	.625	52	0	0	0	6	69²	74	7	24	51	12.7	4.26	87	.273	.332	3	.250	1	-6	-4	-1	-0.4
1972	Bos-A	0	1	.000	21	0	0	0	5	30²	24	3	11	27	10.6	2.93	109	.209	.283	0	.000	-0	0	1	-0	0.1
1973	Bos-A	3	4	.429	39	0	0	0	15	53¹	45	5	13	31	10.0	2.70	149	.232	.284	0	—	0	7	8	1	0.9
Total	13	88	75	.540	495	164	32	10	50	1576	1364	164	597	1175	11.5	3.40	103	.231	.308	69	.163	15	18	19	-14	3.0

GREG BOLLO — Bollo, Gregory Gene b: 11/16/43, Detroit, Mich. BR/TR, 6'4", 183 lbs. Deb: 5/09/65

1965	Chi-A	0	0	—	15	0	0	0	0	22²	12	5	9	16	9.1	3.57	89	.152	.256	0	—	-0	-0	-1	0	0.0
1966	Chi-A	0	1	.000	3	1	0	0	0	7	7	0	3	4	14.1	2.57	123	.269	.367	0	.000	-0	1	0	0	0.0
Total	2	0	1	.000	18	1	0	0	0	29²	19	5	12	20	10.3	3.34	96	.181	.283	0	.000	-0	0	-0	0	0.0

TOM BOLTON — Bolton, Thomas Edward b: 5/6/62, Nashville, Tenn. BL/TL, 6'2", 172 lbs. Deb: 5/17/87

1987	Bos-A	1	0	1.000	29	0	0	0	0	61²	83	5	27	49	16.3	4.38	104	.329	.399	0	—	0	1	1	0	0.1
1988	Bos-A	1	3	.250	28	0	0	0	1	30¹	35	1	14	21	14.5	4.75	87	.285	.358	0	—	0	-3	-2	1	0.0
1989	Bos-A	0	4	.000	4	4	0	0	0	17¹	21	1	10	9	16.1	8.31	49	.292	.378	0	—	0	-9	-8	0	-0.6
1990	*Bos-A	10	5	.667	21	16	3	0	0	119²	111	6	47	65	12.1	3.38	120	.251	.327	0	—	0	7	9	1	1.1
Total	4	12	12	.500	82	20	3	0	1	229	250	13	98	144	13.9	4.21	100	.281	.355	0	—	0	-4	0	2	0.6

MARK BOMBACK — Bomback, Mark Vincent b: 4/14/53, Portsmouth, Va. BR/TR, 5'11", 170 lbs. Deb: 9/12/78

1978	Mil-A	0	0	—	2	1	0	0	0	1²	5	1	1	1	32.4	16.20	23	.500	.545	0	—	0	-2	-2	0	-0.1
1980	NY-N	10	8	.556	36	25	2	1	0	162²	191	17	49	68	13.5	4.09	87	.297	.350	10	.233	3	-9	-10	3	-0.3
1981	Tor-A	5	5	.500	20	11	0	0	0	90¹	84	6	35	33	12.0	3.89	101	.251	.323	0	—	0	-2	1	0	0.1
1982	Tor-A	1	5	.167	16	8	0	0	0	59²	87	10	25	22	17.3	6.03	74	.343	.408	0	—	0	-13	-10	0	-0.9
Total	4	16	18	.471	74	45	2	1	0	314¹	367	34	110	124	13.9	4.47	86	.295	.356	10	.233	3	-27	-22	3	-1.2

TOMMY BOND — Bond, Thomas Henry b: 4/2/1856, Granard, Ireland d: 1/24/41, Boston, Mass. BR/TR, 5'7.5", 160 lbs. Deb: 5/05/1874 MU♦

1874	Atl-n	22	32	.407	55	55	55	1	0	497	609	16	10		11.2	3.19	88	.268	.271	54	.219	-1	-10	-21		-1.8
1875	Har-n	19	16	.543	40	39	37	6	0	352	301	3	10		8.0	1.56	166	.215	.220	78	.270	4	35	40		4.4
1876	Har-N	31	13	.705	45	45	45	6	0	408	355	2	13	88	8.1	1.68	141	.218	.224	50	.275	1	29	32	5	3.5
1877	Bos-N	40	17	.702	58	58	58	6	0	521	530	5	36	170	9.8	2.11	133	.249	.261	59	.228	-4	41	41	3	3.7
1878	Bos-N	40	19	.678	59	59	57	9	0	532²	571	6	33	182	10.2	2.06	114	.261	.272	50	.212	-4	14	18	2	1.6
1879	Bos-N	43	19	.694	64	64	60	12	0	555¹	543	8	24	155	9.2	1.96	127	.240	.248	62	.241	2	33	32	8	3.9
1880	Bos-N	26	29	.473	63	57	49	3	0	493	559	4	45	118	11.0	2.67	85	.271	.287	62	.220	-2	-16	-22	10	-1.4
1881	Bos-N	0	3	.000	3	3	2	0	0	25¹	40	3	2	2	14.9	4.26	62	.344	.355	2	.200	-0	-4	-5	1	-0.3
1882	Wor-N	0	1	.000	2	2	0	0	0	12¹	12	0	7	2	13.9	4.38	71	.241	.334	4	.133	-1	-2	-2	-0	-0.1
1884	Bos-U	13	9	.591	23	21	19	0	0	189	185	3	14	128	9.5	3.00	98	.239	.253	48	.296	4	0	-1	3	0.7
	Ind-a	0	5	.000	5	5	5	0	0	43	62	5	4	15	13.8	5.65	58	.320	.334	3	.130	-1	-11	-11	-1	-1.0
Total	2 n		41	48	.461	95	94	92	7	0	849	910	19	20		9.9	2.51	109	.248	.252	132	.246	2	25	21		2.6
Total	8	193	115	.627	322	314	295	36	0	2779²	2857	32	178	860	9.8	2.25	112	.250	.262	340	.236	2	83	82	31	10.6

JULIO BONETTI — Bonetti, Julio Giacomo b: 7/14/11, Genoa, Italy d: 6/17/52, Belmont, Cal. BR/TR, 6', 180 lbs. Deb: 4/22/37

1937	StL-A	4	11	.267	28	16	7	0	1	143¹	190	13	60	43	15.8	5.84	83	.321	.385	7	.149	-2	-19	-16	2	-1.3
1938	StL-A	2	3	.400	17	0	0	0	0	28¹	41	1	13	7	17.2	6.35	78	.350	.415	0	.000	-1	-5	-4	1	-0.4
1940	Chi-N	0	0	—	1	0	0	0	0	1¹	3	0	4	0	47.3	20.25	19	.429	.636	0	—	0	-2	-2	0	-0.1
Total	3	6	14	.300	46	16	7	0	1	173	234	14	77	50	16.3	6.03	80	.327	.394	7	.127	-3	-27	-23	3	-1.8

HANK BONEY — Boney, Henry Tate "Haney" b: 10/28/03, Wallace, N.C. BR/TR, 5'11", 176 lbs. Deb: 6/28/27

| 1927 | NY-N | 0 | 0 | — | 3 | 0 | 0 | 0 | 0 | 4 | 4 | 0 | 2 | 0 | 13.5 | 2.25 | 171 | .267 | .353 | 0 | — | 0 | 1 | 1 | -0 | 0.1 |

TINY BONHAM — Bonham, Ernest Edward b: 8/16/13, Ione, Cal. d: 9/15/49, Pittsburgh, Pa. BR/TR, 6'2", 215 lbs. Deb: 8/08/40

1940	NY-A	9	3	.750	12	12	10	3	0	99¹	83	4	13	37	8.7	1.90	212	.224	.250	7	.189	0	27	24	-2	2.2
1941	*NY-A	9	6	.600	23	14	7	1	2	126²	118	12	31	43	10.7	2.98	132	.246	.294	8	.160	-1	16	13	-2	1.0
1942	*NY-A	21	5	.808	28	27	22	6	0	226	199	11	24	71	8.9	2.27	152	.237	.259	9	.122	-2	35	29	-3	2.5
1943	*NY-A	15	8	.652	28	26	17	4	1	225²	197	13	52	71	10.0	2.27	142	.236	.282	15	.197	-2	26	24	-4	2.2
1944	NY-A	12	9	.571	26	25	17	1	0	213²	228	14	41	54	11.3	2.99	116	.273	.307	10	.133	-3	10	12	-3	0.7
1945	NY-A	8	11	.421	23	23	12	0	0	180²	186	11	22	42	10.4	3.29	105	.265	.288	15	.238	3	2	4	-3	0.4
1946	NY-A	5	8	.385	18	14	6	2	3	104²	97	6	23	30	10.5	3.70	93	.243	.284	4	.129	-0	-2	-3	-1	-0.4
1947	Pit-N	11	8	.579	33	18	7	3	3	149²	167	17	35	63	12.3	3.85	110	.277	.319	7	.156	-0	3	6	-3	0.3
1948	Pit-N	6	10	.375	22	20	7	0	0	135²	145	18	23	42	11.3	4.31	94	.276	.310	8	.163	-2	-5	-4	-3	-0.7
1949	Pit-N	7	4	.636	18	14	5	1	0	89	81	11	23	25	10.5	4.25	99	.246	.295	1	.045	-2	-2	-0	-1	-0.2
Total	10	103	72	.589	231	193	110	21	9	1551	1501	117	287	478	10.4	3.06	120	.254	.289	84	.161	-7	110	105	-26	8.0

YEAR	TM/L	W	L	PCT	G	GS	CG	SH	SV	IP	H	HR	BB	SO	RAT	ERA	ERA+	OAV	OOB	BH	AVG	PB	PR	/A	PD	TPI
■ **BILL BONHAM**					Bonham, William Gordon				b: 10/1/48, Glendale, Cal.			BR/TR, 6'3", 190 lbs.			Deb: 4/07/71										
1971	Chi-N	2	1	.667	33	2	0	0	0	60	63	6	36	41	15.6	4.65	85	.281	.392	2	.167	-0	-8	-5	1	-0.3
1972	Chi-N	1	1	.500	19	4	0	0	0	57²	56	4	25	49	12.8	3.12	122	.260	.340	4	.286	1	2	4	0	0.6
1973	Chi-N	7	5	.583	44	15	3	0	6	152	126	10	64	121	11.5	3.02	131	.230	.315	4	.093	-3	11	16	4	1.8
1974	Chi-N	11	22	.333	44	36	10	2	1	242²	246	13	109	191	13.4	3.86	99	.263	.343	12	.143	-3	-6	-1	4	0.0
1975	Chi-N	13	15	.464	38	36	7	2	0	229¹	254	15	109	165	14.4	4.71	82	.281	.361	15	.183	-0	-28	-22	1	-2.0
1976	Chi-N	9	13	.409	32	31	3	0	0	196	215	11	96	110	14.4	4.27	90	.283	.365	13	.200	1	-17	-9	0	-0.6
1977	Chi-N	10	13	.435	34	34	1	0	0	214²	207	15	82	134	12.2	4.36	101	.254	.324	15	.231	1	-11	1	3	0.6
1978	Cin-N	11	5	.688	23	23	1	0	0	140¹	151	9	50	83	13.0	3.53	101	.276	.337	8	.186	2	1	0	3	0.6
1979	Cin-N	9	7	.563	29	29	2	0	0	175²	173	14	60	78	12.3	3.79	98	.261	.330	8	.140	-1	-1	-1	1	-0.1
1980	Cin-N	2	1	.667	4	4	0	0	0	19	21	1	5	13	12.3	4.74	75	.276	.321	0	.000	-0	-2	-2	-0	-0.2
Total	10	75	83	.475	300	214	27	4	11	1487¹	1512	98	636	985	13.2	4.01	97	.266	.343	81	.172	-2	-59	-20	17	0.4
■ **JOE BONIKOWSKI**					Bonikowski, Joseph Peter				b: 1/16/41, Philadelphia, Pa.			BR/TR, 6', 175 lbs.			Deb: 4/12/62										
1962	Min-A	5	7	.417	30	13	3	0	2	99²	95	6	38	45	12.1	3.88	105	.255	.325	4	.148	-1	1	2	1	0.3
■ **BILL BONNESS**					Bonness, William John "Lefty"				b: 12/15/23, Cleveland, Ohio			d: 12/3/77, Detroit, Mich.			BR/TL, 6'4", 200 lbs.			Deb: 9/26/44						
1944	Cle-A	0	1	.000	2	1	0	0	0	7	11	0	5	1	23.1	7.71	43	.367	.486	0	.000	-0	-3	-3	0	-0.3
■ **GUS BONO**					Bono, Adlai Wendell				b: 8/29/1894, Doe Run, Mo.			d: 12/3/48, Dearborn, Mich.			BR/TR, 5'11", 175 lbs.			Deb: 9/13/20						
1920	Was-A	0	2	.000	4	1	0	0	0	12¹	17	0	6	4	16.8	8.76	43	.315	.383	0	.000	-0	-7	-7	0	-0.5
■ **GREG BOOKER**					Booker, Gregory Scott				b: 6/22/60, Lynchburg, Va.			BR/TR, 6'6", 230 lbs.			Deb: 9/11/83								
1983	SD-N	0	1	.000	6	1	0	0	0	11²	18	2	9	5	20.8	7.71	45	.375	.474	0	.000	-0	-5	-5	0	-0.4
1984	•SD-N	1	1	.500	32	1	0	0	0	57¹	67	4	27	28	14.8	3.30	108	.295	.370	2	.286	1	2	2	0	0.3
1985	SD-N	0	1	.000	17	0	0	0	0	22¹	20	3	17	7	15.3	6.85	52	.247	.384	0	.000	-0	-8	-8	-0	-0.8
1986	SD-N	1	0	1.000	9	0	0	0	0	11	10	0	4	7	11.5	1.64	223	.233	.298	0	—	0	3	2	-0	0.2
1987	SD-N	1	1	.500	44	0	0	0	1	68¹	62	5	30	17	12.5	3.16	125	.246	.333	0	.000	-1	7	6	0	0.5
1988	SD-N	2	2	.500	34	2	0	0	1	64¹	68	5	19	43	12.3	3.36	101	.278	.332	2	.250	1	1	0	1	0.2
1989	SD-N	0	1	.000	11	0	0	0	0	19	15	2	10	8	11.8	4.26	82	.224	.325	0	—	0	-2	-2	0	-0.1
	Min-A	0	0	—	6	0	0	0	0	8²	11	1	2	3	13.5	4.15	100	.306	.342	0	—	0	-0	-0	1	0.1
1990	SF-N	0	0	—	2	0	0	0	0	2	7	0	0	1	31.5	13.50	28	.538	.538	0	—	0	-2	-2	-0	-0.1
Total	8	5	7	.417	161	4	0	0	1	264²	278	22	118	119	13.6	3.88	94	.275	.353	4	.174	1	-5	-7	2	-0.1
■ **RED BOOLES**					Booles, Seabron Jesse				b: 7/14/1880, Bernice, La.			d: 3/16/55, Monroe, La.			BL/TL, 5'10", 150 lbs.			Deb: 7/30/09				
1909	Cle-A	0	1	.000	4	1	0	0	0	22²	20	0	8	6	11.5	1.99	129	.235	.309	1	.167	0	1	1	0	0.2
■ **DANNY BOONE**					Boone, Daniel Hugh				b: 1/14/54, Long Beach, Cal.			BL/TL, 5'8", 150 lbs.			Deb: 4/11/81						
1981	SD-N	1	0	1.000	37	0	0	0	2	63¹	63	2	21	43	12.1	2.84	115	.267	.329	2	.500	1	5	3	1	0.5
1982	SD-N	1	0	1.000	10	0	0	0	1	16	21	2	3	8	13.5	5.63	61	.323	.353	1	.200	1	-4	-4	0	-0.3
	Hou-N	0	1	.000	10	0	0	0	1	12²	7	1	4	4	7.8	3.55	93	.171	.244	0	.000	-0	0	-0	0	0.0
	Yr	1	1	.500	20	0	0	0	2	28²	28	3	7	12	11.0	4.71	72	.264	.310	0	.000	0	-4	-4	0	-0.3
1990	Bal-A	0	0	—	4	1	0	0	0	9²	12	1	3	2	14.9	2.79	137	.308	.372	0	—	0	1	1	0	0.1
Total	3	2	1	.667	61	1	0	0	4	101²	103	6	31	57	12.0	3.36	99	.270	.329	3	.300	1	2	-0	1	0.3
■ **GEORGE BOONE**					Boone, George Morris				b: 3/1/1871, Louisville, Ky.			d: 9/24/10, Louisville, Ky.			Deb: 4/23/1891					
1891	Lou-a	0	0	—	4	1	0	0	1	15	15	0	9	4	14.4	7.80	47	.252	.350	2	.333	0	-7	-7	0	-0.4
■ **DAN BOONE**					Boone, James Albert				b: 1/19/1895, Samantha, Ala.			d: 5/11/68, Tuscaloosa, Ala.			BR/TR, 6'2", 190 lbs.			Deb: 9/10/19				
1919	Phi-A	0	1	.000	3	2	0	0	0	14²	24	0	10	1	20.9	6.75	51	.375	.459	0	.000	-1	-6	-5	1	-0.4
1921	Det-A	0	0	—	1	0	0	0	0	2	1	0	2	0	13.5	0.00	—	.200	.429	0	.000	-0	1	1	0	0.1
1922	Cle-A	4	6	.400	11	10	4	2	0	75¹	87	3	19	9	12.8	4.06	99	.298	.343	5	.192	-1	-0	-0	1	0.0
1923	Cle-A	4	6	.400	27	4	2	0	0	70¹	93	3	31	15	16.3	6.01	66	.322	.393	4	.211	0	-16	-16	3	-1.1
Total	4	8	13	.381	42	16	6	2	0	162¹	205	6	62	25	15.0	5.10	77	.315	.378	9	.180	-1	-21	-21	5	-1.4
■ **AMOS BOOTH** •					Booth, Amos Smith "Darling"				b: 9/14/1853, Cincinnati, O.			d: 7/1/21, Miamisburg, Ohio			BR/TR,			Deb: 4/25/1876 ♦				
1876	Cin-N	0	1	.000	3	1	0	0	0	9²	22	0	0	0	20.5	9.31	24	.422	.422	71	.261	0	-8	-8	-0	-0.5
1877	Cin-N	1	7	.125	12	8	6	0	0	86	114	1	13	18	13.3	3.56	74	.301	.325	27	.172	-1	-7	-9	-1	-0.7
Total	2	1	8	.111	15	9	6	0	0	95²	136	1	13	18	14.0	4.14	63	.316	.336	98	.224	-1	-15	-16	-1	-1.2
■ **EDDIE BOOTH**					Booth, Edward H.				b: Brooklyn, N.Y.			Deb: 4/26/1872 ♦											
1876	NY-N	0	0	—	1	0	0	0	0	5	16	0	0	0	28.8	10.80	20	.506	.506	49	.215	-0	-5	-5	-0	-0.3
■ **JOHN BOOZER**					Boozer, John Morgan				b: 7/6/38, Columbia, S.C.			d: 1/24/86, Lexington, S.C.			BR/TR, 6'3", 205 lbs.			Deb: 7/22/62				
1962	Phi-N	0	0	—	9	0	0	0	0	20¹	22	3	10	13	14.2	5.75	67	.282	.364	0	.000	-0	-4	-4	0	-0.3
1963	Phi-N	3	4	.429	26	8	2	0	1	83	67	11	33	69	11.0	2.93	110	.227	.307	3	.143	-0	3	3	0	0.1
1964	Phi-N	3	1	.120	22	0	0	0	2	60¹	64	6	18	51	12.5	5.07	68	.271	.328	1	.077	-1	-10	-11	1	-1.0
1966	Phi-N	0	0	—	2	2	0	0	0	5¹	8	1	3	5	18.6	6.75	53	.348	.423	0	.000	-0	-2	-2	0	-0.1
1967	Phi-N	5	4	.556	28	7	1	0	1	74²	86	6	24	48	13.4	4.10	83	.292	.347	4	.211	1	-6	-6	0	-0.4
1968	Phi-N	2	2	.500	38	0	0	0	5	68²	76	3	15	49	12.2	3.67	82	.279	.322	1	.111	-0	-5	-5	0	-0.5
1969	Phi-N	1	2	.333	46	2	0	0	6	82	91	12	36	47	13.9	4.28	83	.283	.356	3	.333	1	-6	-7	-1	-0.6
Total	7	14	16	.467	171	22	3	0	15	394¹	414	42	139	282	12.8	4.09	82	.272	.336	12	.162	-0	-30	-31	-1	-2.8
■ **PEDRO BORBON**					Borbon, Pedro (Rodriguez)				b: 12/2/46, Valverde, Mao, D.R.			BR/TR, 6'2", 185 lbs.			Deb: 4/09/69					
1969	Cal-A	2	3	.400	22	0	0	0	0	41	55	5	11	20	15.4	6.15	57	.324	.378	0	.000	-0	-12	-12	-0	-1.2
1970	Cin-N	0	2	.000	12	1	0	0	0	17¹	21	2	6	6	15.6	6.75	60	.309	.390	0	.000	-0	-5	-5	2	-0.3
1971	Cin-N	0	0	—	3	0	0	0	0	4¹	3	1	1	4	8.3	4.15	81	.200	.250	0	—	0	-0	-0	-0	-0.0
1972	•Cin-N	8	3	.727	62	2	0	0	11	122	115	5	32	48	11.1	3.17	101	.254	.307	1	.048	-1	4	1	0	0.0
1973	•Cin-N	11	4	.733	80	0	0	0	14	121	137	4	35	60	12.9	2.16	158	.298	.349	5	.333	1	20	17	0	1.9
1974	Cin-N	10	7	.588	73	0	0	0	14	139	133	11	32	53	10.9	3.24	108	.255	.303	5	.192	-0	6	4	0	0.3
1975	•Cin-N	9	5	.643	67	0	0	0	5	125	145	6	21	29	12.2	2.95	122	.301	.334	7	.292	2	9	9	-0	1.1
1976	•Cin-N	4	3	.571	69	1	0	0	8	121	135	4	31	53	12.6	3.35	105	.292	.342	4	.222	0	2	2	-0	0.2
1977	Cin-N	10	5	.667	73	0	0	0	18	127	131	7	24	48	11.2	3.19	123	.268	.307	4	.182	-0	10	10	-1	0.9
1978	Cin-N	8	2	.800	62	0	0	0	4	99¹	102	6	27	35	12.0	4.98	71	.274	.328	2	.182	-0	-16	-16	0	-1.5
1979	Cin-N	2	2	.500	30	0	0	0	2	44²	48	2	8	23	11.3	3.43	109	.277	.309	2	.333	0	2	2	0	0.2
	SF-N	4	3	.571	30	0	0	0	3	46	56	7	13	26	13.5	4.89	71	.303	.348	1	.333	0	-6	-7	-1	-0.7
	Yr	6	5	.545	60	0	0	0	5	90²	104	9	21	49	12.4	4.17	87	.287	.326	3	.333	1	-4	-6	-0	-0.5
1980	StL-N	1	0	1.000	19	0	0	0	0	17	19	1	3	10	14.8	3.79	97	.250	.346	1	.250	-0	-0	-0	-0	-0.0
Total	12	69	39	.639	593	4	0	0	80	1026²	1098	63	251	409	12.1	3.52	101	.280	.328	32	.205	2	14	3	-1	0.9
■ **GEORGE BORCHERS**					Borchers, George Benard "Chief"				b: 4/18/1869, Sacramento, Cal.			d: 10/24/38, Sacramento, Cal.			BB/TR, 5'10", 180 lbs.			Deb: 5/18/1888	
1888	Chi-N	4	4	.500	10	10	7	1	0	67	67	2	29	26	12.9	3.49	86	.251	.324	2	.061	-3	-5	-4	0	-0.5
1895	Lou-N	0	1	.000	1	1	0	0	0	0²	1	0	3	0	54.0	27.00	17	.341	.674	0	—	0	-2	-2	0	0.0
Total	2	4	5	.444	11	11	7	1	0	67²	68	2	32	26	13.3	3.72	81	.252	.331	2	.061	-3	-7	-5	0	-0.5

YEAR	TM/L	W	L	PCT	G	GS	CG	SH	SV	IP	H	HR	BB	SO	RAT	ERA	ERA+	OAV	OOB	BH	AVG	PB	PR	/A	PD	TPI

■ JOE BORDEN Borden, Joseph Emley (a.k.a. Joseph Emley Josephs In 1875) b: 5/9/1854, Jacobstown, N.J. d: 10/14/29, Yeadon, Pa. BR/TR, 5'9", 140 lbs. Deb: 7/24/1875

YEAR	TM/L	W	L	PCT	G	GS	CG	SH	SV	IP	H	HR	BB	SO	RAT	ERA	ERA+	OAV	OOB	BH	AVG	PB	PR	/A	PD	TPI
1875	Phi-n	2	4	.333	7	7	7	2	0	66	47	0	7		7.4	1.64	154	.181	.203	3	.107	-3	6	6		0.3
1876	Bos-N	11	12	.478	29	24	16	2	1	218¹	257	4	51	34	12.7	2.89	78	.274	.311	25	.207	-3	-14	-15	-2	-1.7

■ RICH BORDI Bordi, Richard Albert b: 4/18/59, San Francisco, Cal. BR/TR, 6'7", 210 lbs. Deb: 7/16/80

YEAR	TM/L	W	L	PCT	G	GS	CG	SH	SV	IP	H	HR	BB	SO	RAT	ERA	ERA+	OAV	OOB	BH	AVG	PB	PR	/A	PD	TPI
1980	Oak-A	0	0	—	1	0	0	0	0	2	4	0	0	0	18.0	4.50	84	.400	.400	0	—	0	-0	-0	0	0.0
1981	Oak-A	0	0	—	2	0	0	0	0	2	1	0	1	0	9.0	0.00	—	.143	.250	0	—	0	1	1	0	0.1
1982	Sea-A	0	2	.000	7	2	0	0	0	13	18	4	1	10	13.8	8.31	51	.310	.333	0	—	0	-6	-6	0	-0.5
1983	Chi-N	0	2	.000	11	1	0	0	1	25¹	34	2	12	20	16.3	4.97	76	.321	.390	0	.000	-0	-4	-3	0	-0.3
1984	Chi-N	5	2	.714	31	7	0	0	4	83¹	78	11	20	41	10.6	3.46	113	.242	.287	1	.053	-1	1	4	-1	0.2
1985	NY-A	6	8	.429	51	3	0	0	2	98	95	5	29	64	11.5	3.21	124	.253	.308	0	—	0	10	9	1	0.8
1986	Bal-A	6	4	.600	52	1	0	0	3	107	105	13	41	83	12.6	4.46	93	.254	.327	0	—	0	-3	-4	0	-0.2
1987	NY-A	3	1	.750	16	1	0	0	0	33	42	7	12	23	14.7	7.64	57	.309	.365	0	—	0	-12	-12	-1	-1.1
1988	Oak-A	0	1	.000	2	2	0	0	0	7²	6	0	5	6	12.9	4.70	80	.214	.333	0	—	0	-1	-1	-0	0.0
Total	9	20	20	.500	173	17	0	0	10	371¹	383	42	121	247	12.4	4.34	93	.263	.322	1	.043	-2	-13	-12	-2	-1.0

■ BILL BORDLEY Bordley, William Clarke b: 1/9/58, Los Angeles, Cal. BR/TL, 6'3", 185 lbs. Deb: 6/30/80

YEAR	TM/L	W	L	PCT	G	GS	CG	SH	SV	IP	H	HR	BB	SO	RAT	ERA	ERA+	OAV	OOB	BH	AVG	PB	PR	/A	PD	TPI
1980	SF-N	2	3	.400	8	6	0	0	0	30²	34	3	21	11	16.1	4.70	75	.288	.396	1	.167	0	-4	-4	1	-0.2

■ PAUL BORIS Boris, Paul Stanley b: 12/13/55, Irvington, N.J. BR/TR, 6'2", 200 lbs. Deb: 5/21/82

YEAR	TM/L	W	L	PCT	G	GS	CG	SH	SV	IP	H	HR	BB	SO	RAT	ERA	ERA+	OAV	OOB	BH	AVG	PB	PR	/A	PD	TPI
1982	Min-A	1	2	.333	23	0	0	0	0	49²	46	8	19	30	12.1	3.99	106	.246	.322	0	—	0	0	1	-1	0.1

■ FRANK BORK Bork, Frank Bernard b: 7/13/40, Buffalo, N.Y. BR/TL, 6'2", 175 lbs. Deb: 4/15/64

YEAR	TM/L	W	L	PCT	G	GS	CG	SH	SV	IP	H	HR	BB	SO	RAT	ERA	ERA+	OAV	OOB	BH	AVG	PB	PR	/A	PD	TPI
1964	Pit-N	2	2	.500	33	2	0	0	2	42	51	6	11	31	13.5	4.07	86	.295	.341	1	.200	0	-2	-3	0	-0.1

■ TOM BORLAND Borland, Thomas Bruce "Spike" b: 2/14/33, ElDorado, Kan. BL/TL, 6'3", 172 lbs. Deb: 5/15/60

YEAR	TM/L	W	L	PCT	G	GS	CG	SH	SV	IP	H	HR	BB	SO	RAT	ERA	ERA+	OAV	OOB	BH	AVG	PB	PR	/A	PD	TPI
1960	Bos-A	0	4	.000	26	4	0	0	3	51	67	4	23	32	15.9	6.53	62	.322	.390	0	.000	-2	-15	-14	0	-1.4
1961	Bos-A	0	0		1	0	0	0	0	1	3	0	0	0	27.0	18.00	23	.500	.500	0	—	0	-2	-2	0	0.0
Total	2	0	4	.000	27	4	0	0	3	52	70	4	23	32	16.1	6.75	60	.327	.392	0	.000	-2	-17	-16	0	-1.4

■ HANK BOROWY Borowy, Henry Ludwig b: 5/12/16, Bloomfield, N.J. BR/TR, 6', 175 lbs. Deb: 4/18/42

YEAR	TM/L	W	L	PCT	G	GS	CG	SH	SV	IP	H	HR	BB	SO	RAT	ERA	ERA+	OAV	OOB	BH	AVG	PB	PR	/A	PD	TPI
1942	*NY-A	15	4	.789	25	21	13	4	1	178¹	157	6	66	85	11.3	2.52	136	.233	.301	11	.157	-1	22	18	1	1.9
1943	*NY-A	14	9	.609	29	27	14	3	0	217¹	195	11	72	113	11.1	2.82	114	.241	.305	15	.203	3	12	10	1	1.4
1944	NY-A	17	12	.586	35	30	19	3	2	252²	224	15	88	107	11.1	2.64	132	.236	.301	12	.133	-3	22	24	0	2.3
1945	NY-A	10	5	.667	18	18	7	1	0	132¹	107	6	58	35	11.3	3.13	111	.221	.305	11	.220	1	3	5	1	0.8
	*Chi-N	11	2	.846	15	14	11	1	1	122¹	105	2	47	47	11.2	2.13	171	.231	.303	7	.171	0	23	21	-1	2.2
1946	Chi-N	12	10	.545	32	28	8	1	0	201	220	9	61	95	12.6	3.76	88	.274	.326	13	.181	1	-8	-10	0	-0.9
1947	Chi-N	8	12	.400	40	25	7	1	2	183	190	19	63	75	12.5	4.38	90	.267	.328	7	.125	-1	-6	-9	0	-0.8
1948	Chi-N	5	10	.333	39	17	2	1	1	127	156	9	49	50	14.5	4.89	80	.308	.369	8	.222	2	-13	-14	3	-0.9
1949	Phi-N	12	12	.500	28	28	12	1	0	193¹	188	19	63	43	11.7	4.19	94	.259	.319	13	.213	3	-3	-5	-1	-0.2
1950	Phi-N	0	0	—	3	0	0	0	0	6¹	5	0	4	3	12.8	5.68	71	.250	.375	0	—	0	-1	-1	-0	0.0
	Pit-N	1	3	.250	11	3	0	0	0	25¹	32	6	9	9	14.9	6.39	69	.311	.372	1	.167	-0	-6	-6	0	-0.4
	Yr	1	3	.250	14	3	0	0	0	31²	37	6	13	12	14.5	6.25	69	.301	.372	0	.000	-0	-7	-7	0	-0.4
	Det-A	1	1	.500	13	2	1	0	0	32²	23	3	16	12	10.7	3.31	142	.205	.305	1	.143	-1	5	5	0	0.4
1951	Det-A	2	2	.500	26	1	0	0	0	45¹	58	3	27	16	17.1	6.95	60	.314	.404	0	.000	-1	-14	-14	1	-1.3
Total	10	108	82	.568	314	214	94	16	7	1717	1660	108	623	690	12.0	3.50	104	.254	.320	99	.173	3	35	24	6	4.5

■ CHRIS BOSIO Bosio, Christopher Louis b: 4/3/63, Carmichael, Cal. BR/TR, 6'3", 220 lbs. Deb: 8/03/86

YEAR	TM/L	W	L	PCT	G	GS	CG	SH	SV	IP	H	HR	BB	SO	RAT	ERA	ERA+	OAV	OOB	BH	AVG	PB	PR	/A	PD	TPI
1986	Mil-A	0	4	.000	10	4	0	0	0	34²	41	9	13	29	14.0	7.01	62	.293	.353	0	—	0	-11	-10	0	-0.8
1987	Mil-A	11	8	.579	46	19	2	1	2	170	187	18	50	150	12.6	5.24	87	.276	.327	0	—	0	-15	-13	1	-1.0
1988	Mil-A	7	15	.318	38	22	9	1	6	182	190	13	38	84	11.4	3.36	118	.268	.307	0	—	0	12	12	3	1.6
1989	Mil-A	15	10	.600	33	33	8	2	0	234²	225	16	48	173	10.7	2.95	130	.249	.291	0	—	0	24	23	0	2.5
1990	Mil-A	4	9	.308	20	20	4	1	0	132²	131	15	38	76	11.7	4.00	94	.258	.313	0	—	0	-1	-3	2	-0.1
Total	5	37	46	.446	147	98	23	5	8	754	774	71	187	512	11.6	3.94	103	.263	.310	0	—	0	9	9	6	2.2

■ SHAWN BOSKIE Boskie, Shawn Kealoha b: 3/28/67, Hawthorne, Nev. BR/TR, 6'3", 205 lbs. Deb: 5/20/90

YEAR	TM/L	W	L	PCT	G	GS	CG	SH	SV	IP	H	HR	BB	SO	RAT	ERA	ERA+	OAV	OOB	BH	AVG	PB	PR	/A	PD	TPI
1990	Chi-N	5	6	.455	15	15	1	0	0	97²	99	8	31	49	12.1	3.69	112	.265	.323	8	.222	1	1	5	1	0.8

■ DICK BOSMAN Bosman, Richard Allen b: 2/17/44, Kenosha, Wis. BR/TR, 6'2", 195 lbs. Deb: 6/01/66 C

YEAR	TM/L	W	L	PCT	G	GS	CG	SH	SV	IP	H	HR	BB	SO	RAT	ERA	ERA+	OAV	OOB	BH	AVG	PB	PR	/A	PD	TPI
1966	Was-A	2	6	.250	13	7	0	0	0	39	60	4	12	20	16.6	7.62	45	.361	.404	3	.250	0	-18	-18	-1	-1.7
1967	Was-A	3	1	.750	7	7	2	1	0	51¹	38	3	10	25	8.4	1.75	180	.204	.245	3	.200	0	8	8	-0	0.7
1968	Was-A	2	9	.182	46	10	0	0	1	139	139	9	35	63	11.5	3.69	79	.262	.312	6	.200	1	-11	-12	0	-1.1
1969	Was-A	14	5	.737	31	26	5	2	1	193	156	11	39	99	9.2	**2.19**	**158**	.220	.262	6	.094	-1	31	27	1	3.0
1970	Was-A	16	12	.571	36	34	7	3	0	230²	212	16	71	134	11.1	3.00	118	.245	.304	11	.138	-2	18	14	0	1.3
1971	Was-A	12	16	.429	35	35	7	1	0	236²	245	29	71	113	12.2	3.73	89	.272	.329	7	.093	-1	-7	-11	-2	-1.4
1972	Tex-A	8	10	.444	29	29	1	1	0	173¹	183	11	48	105	12.3	3.63	83	.273	.327	5	.094	-2	-11	-12	1	-1.3
1973	Tex-A	2	5	.286	7	7	1	1	0	40¹	42	6	17	14	13.4	4.24	88	.268	.343	0	—	0	-2	-2	-0	-0.2
	Cle-A	1	8	.111	22	17	2	0	0	97	130	19	29	41	15.3	6.22	63	.320	.374	0	—	0	-26	-25	-0	-2.3
	Yr	3	13	.188	29	24	3	1	0	137¹	172	25	46	55	14.7	5.64	69	.304	.363	0	—	0	-28	-27	-1	-2.5
1974	Cle-A	7	5	.583	25	18	2	1	0	127¹	126	13	29	56	11.0	4.10	88	.255	.298	0	—	0	-7	-7	-2	-0.9
1975	Cle-A	0	2	.000	6	3	0	0	0	28²	33	3	8	11	13.8	4.08	93	.292	.355	0	—	0	-1	-1	0	0.0
	*Oak-A	11	4	.733	22	21	2	0	0	122²	112	12	24	42	10.2	3.52	103	.240	.281	0	—	0	3	1	-1	0.1
	Yr	11	6	.647	28	24	2	0	0	151¹	145	15	32	53	10.7	3.63	101	.248	.290	0	—	0	3	0	-1	0.1
1976	Oak-A	4	2	.667	27	15	0	0	0	112	112	18	13	19	12.4	4.10	82	.274	.306	0	—	0	-7	-9	1	-0.8
Total	11	82	85	.491	306	229	29	10	2	1591	1594	149	412	757	11.5	3.67	93	.261	.312	41	.125	-4	-29	-46	-3	-4.3

■ MEL BOSSER Bosser, Melvin Edward b: 2/8/20, Johnstown, Pa. BR/TR, 6', 173 lbs. Deb: 4/29/45

YEAR	TM/L	W	L	PCT	G	GS	CG	SH	SV	IP	H	HR	BB	SO	RAT	ERA	ERA+	OAV	OOB	BH	AVG	PB	PR	/A	PD	TPI
1945	Cin-N	2	0	1.000	7	2	0	0	0	16	9	0	17	3	14.6	3.38	111	.158	.351	0	.000	-1	1	1	-0	0.0

■ ANDY BOSWELL Boswell, Andrew Cottrell b: 9/5/1874, New Gretna, N.J. d: 2/3/36, Ocean City, N.J. 6'1", 165 lbs. Deb: 5/10/1895

YEAR	TM/L	W	L	PCT	G	GS	CG	SH	SV	IP	H	HR	BB	SO	RAT	ERA	ERA+	OAV	OOB	BH	AVG	PB	PR	/A	PD	TPI
1895	NY-N	2	2	.500	5	4	3	0	0	34	41	1	22	18	16.7	5.82	80	.294	.390	3	.188	-1	-4	-4	-0	-0.4
	Was-N	1	2	.333	6	3	3	0	0	30	44	1	19	12	18.9	6.00	80	.336	.420	4	.286	0	-4	-4	-0	-0.2
	Yr	3	4	.429	11	7	6	0	0	64	85	2	41	30	17.7	5.91	80	.314	.404	2	.067	-1	-8	-8	-1	-0.6

■ DAVE BOSWELL Boswell, David Wilson b: 1/20/45, Baltimore, Md. BR/TR, 6'3", 185 lbs. Deb: 9/18/64

YEAR	TM/L	W	L	PCT	G	GS	CG	SH	SV	IP	H	HR	BB	SO	RAT	ERA	ERA+	OAV	OOB	BH	AVG	PB	PR	/A	PD	TPI
1964	Min-A	2	0	1.000	4	4	0	0	0	23¹	21	4	12	25	12.7	4.24	84	.236	.327	2	.222	0	-2	-2	0	0.0
1965	*Min-A	6	5	.545	27	12	1	0	0	106	77	20	46	85	10.9	3.40	105	.204	.298	12	.316	4	1	2	-1	0.5
1966	Min-A	12	5	.706	28	21	8	1	0	169¹	120	19	65	173	10.1	3.14	115	.197	.280	9	.143	-1	6	9	0	0.9
1967	Min-A	14	12	.538	37	32	11	3	0	222²	162	14	107	204	11.2	3.27	106	.202	.302	16	.219	4	-1	5	-2	0.8
1968	Min-A	10	13	.435	34	28	7	2	0	190	148	19	87	143	11.5	3.32	93	.213	.307	14	.233	5	-7	-5	-2	-0.1
1969	*Min-A	20	12	.625	39	38	10	0	0	256¹	215	18	99	190	11.3	3.23	113	.226	.304	16	.170	3	11	12	-1	1.3
1970	Min-A	3	7	.300	18	15	0	0	0	68²	80	12	44	45	16.5	6.42	58	.292	.394	4	.160	-0	-21	-21	-1	-2.0
1971	Det-A	0	0	—	3	0	0	0	0	4¹	3	0	6	3	18.7	6.23	58	.200	.429	0	—	0	-1	-1	0	0.0
	Bal-A	1	2	.333	15	1	0	0	0	24²	32	4	15	14	17.1	4.38	77	.305	.392	1	.200	0	-3	-3	-0	-0.2

YEAR	TM/L	W	L	PCT	G	GS	CG	SH	SV	IP	H	HR	BB	SO	RAT	ERA	ERA+	OAV	OOB	BH	AVG	PB	PR	/A	PD	TPI
	Yr	1	2	.333	18	1	0	0	0	29	35	4	21	17	17.4	4.66	73	.289	.394	0	.000	0	-4	-4	0	-0.2
Total	8	68	56	.548	205	151	37	6	0	1065¹	858	110	481	882	11.6	3.52	99	.219	.310	74	.202	14	-17	-4	-6	1.2

■ DEREK BOTELHO
Botelho, Derek Wayne b: 8/2/56, Long Beach, Cal. BR/TR, 6'2", 180 lbs. Deb: 7/18/82

YEAR	TM/L	W	L	PCT	G	GS	CG	SH	SV	IP	H	HR	BB	SO	RAT	ERA	ERA+	OAV	OOB	BH	AVG	PB	PR	/A	PD	TPI
1982	KC-A	2	1	.667	8	4	0	0	0	24	25	4	8	12	12.4	4.13	99	.275	.333	0	—	0	-0	-0	-0	0.0
1985	Chi-N	1	3	.250	11	7	1	0	0	44	52	8	23	23	15.8	5.32	75	.299	.387	2	.143	-0	-8	-6	-0	-0.6
Total	2	3	4	.429	19	11	1	0	0	68	77	12	31	35	14.6	4.90	82	.291	.369	2	.143	-0	-9	-7	-1	-0.6

■ RALPH BOTTING
Botting, Ralph Wayne b: 5/12/55, Houlton, Maine BL/TL, 6', 195 lbs. Deb: 6/28/79

YEAR	TM/L	W	L	PCT	G	GS	CG	SH	SV	IP	H	HR	BB	SO	RAT	ERA	ERA+	OAV	OOB	BH	AVG	PB	PR	/A	PD	TPI
1979	Cal-A	2	0	1.000	12	1	0	0	0	29²	46	6	15	22	18.8	8.80	46	.362	.434	0	—	0	-15	-16	-0	-1.3
1980	Cal-A	0	3	.000	6	6	0	0	0	26¹	40	1	13	12	18.1	5.81	68	.348	.414	0	—	0	-5	-6	-0	-0.5
Total	2	2	3	.400	18	7	0	0	0	56	86	7	28	34	18.5	7.39	54	.355	.424	0	—	0	-20	-21	-0	-1.8

■ BOB BOTZ
Botz, Robert Allen b: 4/28/35, Milwaukee, Wis. BR/TR, 5'11", 170 lbs. Deb: 5/08/62

YEAR	TM/L	W	L	PCT	G	GS	CG	SH	SV	IP	H	HR	BB	SO	RAT	ERA	ERA+	OAV	OOB	BH	AVG	PB	PR	/A	PD	TPI
1962	LA-A	2	1	.667	35	0	0	0	2	63	71	7	11	24	12.0	3.43	113	.285	.321	0	.000	-1	4	3	-1	0.1

■ CARL BOULDIN
Bouldin, Carl Edward b: 9/17/39, Germantown, Ky. BB/TR, 6'2", 180 lbs. Deb: 9/02/61

YEAR	TM/L	W	L	PCT	G	GS	CG	SH	SV	IP	H	HR	BB	SO	RAT	ERA	ERA+	OAV	OOB	BH	AVG	PB	PR	/A	PD	TPI
1961	Was-A	0	1	.000	2	1	0	0	0	3¹	9	0	2	2	29.7	16.20	25	.500	.550	0	.000	-0	-5	-5	0	-0.3
1962	Was-A	1	2	.333	6	3	1	0	0	20	26	0	9	12	16.2	5.85	69	.321	.396	0	.000	-1	-4	-4	-0	-0.4
1963	Was-A	2	2	.500	10	3	0	0	0	23¹	31	3	8	10	15.0	5.79	64	.307	.358	0	.000	-1	-6	-5	-0	-0.5
1964	Was-A	0	3	.000	9	3	0	0	0	25	30	2	11	12	15.5	5.40	69	.294	.374	0	.000	-0	-5	-5	0	-0.5
Total	4	3	8	.273	27	10	1	0	0	71²	96	5	30	36	16.2	6.15	62	.318	.385	0	.000	-2	-19	-19	0	-1.7

■ JAKE BOULTES
Boultes, Jacob John b: 8/6/1884, St.Louis, Mo. d: 12/24/55, St.Louis, Mo. TR, 6'3", Deb: 4/18/07

YEAR	TM/L	W	L	PCT	G	GS	CG	SH	SV	IP	H	HR	BB	SO	RAT	ERA	ERA+	OAV	OOB	BH	AVG	PB	PR	/A	PD	TPI
1907	Bos-N	5	9	.357	24	12	11	0	0	139²	140	1	50	49	12.8	2.71	94	.266	.338	9	.132	-2	-4	-2	4	0.0
1908	Bos-N	3	5	.375	17	5	1	0	0	74²	80	7	8	28	10.7	3.01	80	.274	.296	3	.143	-1	-5	-5	-1	-0.6
1909	Bos-N	0	0	—	1	0	0	0	0	8	9	2	0	1	11.3	6.75	42	.290	.313	1	.333	0	-4	-3	0	-0.2
Total	3	8	14	.364	42	17	12	0	0	222¹	229	10	58	78	12.0	2.96	85	.269	.324	13	.141	-2	-13	-11	3	-0.8

■ JIM BOUTON
Bouton, James Alan b: 3/8/39, Newark, N.J. BR/TR, 6', 170 lbs. Deb: 4/22/62

YEAR	TM/L	W	L	PCT	G	GS	CG	SH	SV	IP	H	HR	BB	SO	RAT	ERA	ERA+	OAV	OOB	BH	AVG	PB	PR	/A	PD	TPI
1962	NY-A	7	7	.500	36	16	3	1	2	133	124	9	59	71	12.4	3.99	94	.254	.334	2	.063	-2	-0	-4	0	-0.4
1963	*NY-A	21	7	.750	40	30	12	6	1	249¹	191	18	87	148	10.1	2.53	139	.212	.284	6	.072	-6	31	27	-1	2.3
1964	*NY-A	18	13	.581	38	37	11	4	0	271¹	227	32	60	125	9.7	3.02	120	.225	.273	13	.130	-3	18	18	-2	1.4
1965	NY-A	4	15	.211	30	25	2	0	0	151¹	158	23	60	97	13.3	4.82	71	.269	.342	4	.093	-0	-23	-24	0	-2.4
1966	NY-A	3	8	.273	24	19	3	0	1	120¹	117	13	38	65	11.7	2.69	123	.257	.315	4	.105	-1	10	8	1	0.9
1967	NY-A	1	0	1.000	17	1	0	0	0	44¹	47	5	18	31	13.4	4.67	67	.275	.347	0	.000	-0	-7	-8	0	-0.8
1968	NY-A	1	1	.500	12	3	1	0	0	44	49	5	9	24	12.3	3.68	79	.287	.330	0	.000	-0	-3	-4	1	-0.2
1969	Sea-A	2	1	.667	57	1	0	0	1	92	77	12	38	68	11.4	3.91	93	.219	.299	0	.000	-1	-3	-3	1	-0.2
	Hou-N	0	2	.000	16	1	1	0	1	30²	32	1	12	32	13.5	4.11	86	.267	.343	0	.000	-0	-2	-2	0	-0.1
1970	Hou-N	4	6	.400	29	6	1	0	0	73¹	84	5	33	49	14.5	5.40	72	.285	.359	6	.353	2	-11	-12	-0	-0.9
1978	Atl-N	1	3	.250	5	5	0	0	0	29	25	4	21	10	14.3	4.97	82	.234	.359	0	.000	-1	-4	-3	-0	-0.3
Total	10	62	63	.496	304	144	34	11	6	1238²	1131	127	435	720	11.5	3.57	99	.243	.311	35	.101	-13	5	-5	1	-0.7

■ CY BOWEN
Bowen, Sutherland McCoy b: 2/17/1871, Kingston, Ind. d: 1/25/25, Greensburg, Ind. BR/TR, 6', 175 lbs. Deb: 4/28/1896

YEAR	TM/L	W	L	PCT	G	GS	CG	SH	SV	IP	H	HR	BB	SO	RAT	ERA	ERA+	OAV	OOB	BH	AVG	PB	PR	/A	PD	TPI
1896	NY-N	0	1	.000	2	1	1	0	0	12	12	0	9	3	15.8	6.00	70	.258	.379	1	.333	0	-2	-2	0	0.0

■ FRANK BOWERMAN
Bowerman, Frank Eugene "Mike" b: 12/5/1868, Romeo, Mich. d: 11/30/48, Romeo, Mich. BR/TR, 6'2", 190 lbs. Deb: 8/24/1895 M♦

YEAR	TM/L	W	L	PCT	G	GS	CG	SH	SV	IP	H	HR	BB	SO	RAT	ERA	ERA+	OAV	OOB	BH	AVG	PB	PR	/A	PD	TPI
1904	NY-N	0	0	—	1	0	0	0	0	1	3	0	1	0	36.0	9.00	30	.429	.500	67	.232	0	-1	-1	0	0.0

■ STEW BOWERS
Bowers, Stewart Cole "Doc" b: 2/26/15, New Freedom, Pa. BB/TR, 6', 170 lbs. Deb: 8/05/35 ♦

YEAR	TM/L	W	L	PCT	G	GS	CG	SH	SV	IP	H	HR	BB	SO	RAT	ERA	ERA+	OAV	OOB	BH	AVG	PB	PR	/A	PD	TPI
1935	Bos-A	2	1	.667	10	1	0	0	0	23²	26	1	17	5	16.4	3.42	139	.283	.394	1	.200	0	3	3	0	0.4
1936	Bos-A	0	0	—	5	0	0	0	0	5²	10	1	2	0	19.1	9.53	56	.370	.414	0	—	0	-3	-3	-0	-0.1
Total	2	2	1	.667	15	2	0	0	0	29¹	36	2	19	5	16.9	4.60	106	.303	.399	1	.200	0	-0	1	0	0.3

■ GRANT BOWLER
Bowler, Grant Tierney "Moose" b: 10/24/07, Denver, Col. d: 6/25/68, Denver, Colo. BR/TR, 6', 190 lbs. Deb: 8/21/31

YEAR	TM/L	W	L	PCT	G	GS	CG	SH	SV	IP	H	HR	BB	SO	RAT	ERA	ERA+	OAV	OOB	BH	AVG	PB	PR	/A	PD	TPI
1931	Chi-A	0	1	.000	13	3	1	0	0	35¹	40	1	24	15	16.3	5.35	80	.288	.393	1	.100	-0	-4	-4	-1	-0.4
1932	Chi-A	0	0	—	4	0	0	0	0	6¹	15	1	3	2	25.6	15.63	28	.484	.529	0	.000	-0	-8	-8	0	-0.6
Total	2	0	1	.000	17	3	1	0	0	41²	55	2	27	17	17.7	6.91	62	.324	.416	1	.083	-1	-12	-12	-1	-1.0

■ CHARLIE BOWLES
Bowles, Charles James b: 3/15/17, Norwood, Mass. BR/TR, 6'3", 180 lbs. Deb: 9/25/43

YEAR	TM/L	W	L	PCT	G	GS	CG	SH	SV	IP	H	HR	BB	SO	RAT	ERA	ERA+	OAV	OOB	BH	AVG	PB	PR	/A	PD	TPI
1943	Phi-A	1	1	.500	2	2	2	0	0	18	17	0	4	6	10.5	3.00	113	.258	.300	1	.125	-1	1	1	0	0.0
1945	Phi-A	0	3	.000	8	4	1	0	0	33¹	35	3	23	11	15.7	5.13	67	.273	.384	5	.238	0	-7	-6	0	-0.5
Total	2	1	4	.200	10	6	3	0	0	51¹	52	3	27	17	13.9	4.38	78	.268	.357	6	.207	-0	-6	-5	0	-0.5

■ EMMETT BOWLES
Bowles, Emmett Jerome "Chief" b: 8/2/1898, Wanette, Okla. d: 9/3/59, Flagstaff, Ariz. BR/TR, 6', 180 lbs. Deb: 9/12/22

YEAR	TM/L	W	L	PCT	G	GS	CG	SH	SV	IP	H	HR	BB	SO	RAT	ERA	ERA+	OAV	OOB	BH	AVG	PB	PR	/A	PD	TPI
1922	Chi-A	0	0	—	1	0	0	0	0	1	2	0	1	0	27.0	27.00	15	.500	.600	0	—	0	-3	-3	0	-0.1

■ ABE BOWMAN
Bowman, Alvah Edson b: 1/25/1893, Greenup, Ill. d: 10/11/79, Longview, Tex. BR/TR, 6'1", 190 lbs. Deb: 5/19/14

YEAR	TM/L	W	L	PCT	G	GS	CG	SH	SV	IP	H	HR	BB	SO	RAT	ERA	ERA+	OAV	OOB	BH	AVG	PB	PR	/A	PD	TPI
1914	Cle-A	2	7	.222	22	10	2	1	0	72²	74	0	45	27	15.2	4.46	65	.277	.389	1	.048	-2	-14	-13	0	-1.5
1915	Cle-A	0	1	.000	2	1	0	0	0	1¹	1	0	3	0	27.0	20.25	15	.250	.571	0	—	0	-3	-3	1	-0.1
Total	2	2	8	.200	24	11	2	1	0	74	75	0	48	27	15.4	4.74	61	.277	.393	1	.048	-2	-16	-15	1	-1.6

■ JOE BOWMAN
Bowman, Joseph Emil b: 6/17/10, Argentine, Kan. BL/TR, 6'2", 190 lbs. Deb: 4/18/32 ♦

YEAR	TM/L	W	L	PCT	G	GS	CG	SH	SV	IP	H	HR	BB	SO	RAT	ERA	ERA+	OAV	OOB	BH	AVG	PB	PR	/A	PD	TPI
1932	Phi-A	0	1	.000	7	0	0	0	0	11	14	2	6	4	18.8	8.18	55	.318	.434	1	1.000	0	-5	-4	1	-0.2
1934	NY-N	5	4	.556	30	10	3	0	3	107¹	119	9	36	36	13.2	3.61	107	.279	.338	5	.172	0	5	3	-0	0.3
1935	Phi-N	7	10	.412	33	17	6	1	1	148¹	157	13	56	58	13.2	4.25	107	.269	.337	13	.194	-0	-4	5	-0	0.6
1936	Phi-N	9	20	.310	40	28	12	0	1	203²	243	14	53	80	13.4	5.04	90	.289	.336	15	.195	-1	-23	-11	-3	-1.3
1937	Pit-N	8	8	.500	30	19	7	0	1	128	161	11	35	38	13.9	4.57	85	.306	.351	10	.213	1	-9	-10	1	-0.7
1938	Pit-N	3	4	.429	17	1	0	0	1	60	68	2	20	25	13.2	4.65	82	.285	.340	7	.333	-2	-6	-6	-1	-0.3
1939	Pit-N	10	14	.417	37	27	10	1	1	184²	217	15	43	58	13.0	4.48	86	.292	.336	33	.344	12	-12	-13	0	0.0
1940	Pit-N	9	10	.474	32	24	10	0	2	187²	209	10	66	57	13.5	4.46	85	.274	.337	22	.244	9	-13	-14	0	-0.3
1941	Pit-N	3	2	.600	18	7	1	1	1	69¹	77	3	28	22	13.8	2.99	121	.278	.346	8	.258	1	5	5	0	0.6
1944	Bos-A	12	8	.600	26	24	10	1	0	168¹	175	14	64	53	12.9	4.81	71	.269	.336	20	.200	3	-26	-26	-2	-2.5
1945	Bos-A	0	2	.000	3	3	0	0	0	11²	18	1	9	0	20.8	9.26	37	.360	.458	2	.222	0	-8	-8	0	-0.6
	Cin-N	11	13	.458	25	24	15	1	0	185²	198	8	68	71	13.2	3.59	105	.270	.338	5	.070	-5	4	4	-2	-0.2
Total	11	77	96	.445	298	184	74	5	11	1465²	1656	102	484	502	13.4	4.40	89	.282	.341	141	.221	24	-89	-77	-6	-4.6

■ BOB BOWMAN
Bowman, Robert James b: 10/3/10, Keystone, W.Va. d: 9/4/72, Bluefield, W.Va. BR/TR, 5'10.5", 160 lbs. Deb: 4/21/39

YEAR	TM/L	W	L	PCT	G	GS	CG	SH	SV	IP	H	HR	BB	SO	RAT	ERA	ERA+	OAV	OOB	BH	AVG	PB	PR	/A	PD	TPI
1939	StL-N	13	5	.722	51	15	4	2	9	169¹	141	8	60	78	10.7	2.60	158	.232	.302	4	.085	-3	25	28	-1	2.5
1940	StL-N	7	5	.583	28	17	7	0	0	114¹	118	9	43	43	13.0	4.33	92	.267	.337	2	.061	-2	-6	-4	-0	-0.6
1941	NY-N	6	7	.462	29	6	2	0	1	80¹	100	10	36	25	15.3	5.71	65	.302	.372	1	.048	-1	-19	-18	1	-1.7
1942	Chi-N	0	0	—	1	0	0	0	0	1	1	0	0	0	0.00	—	.250	.250	0	—	0	0	0	0	0.0
Total	4	26	17	.605	109	38	13	2	10	365	360	27	139	146	12.5	3.82	104	.260	.330	7	.069	-6	0	6	0	0.2

■ BOB BOWMAN
Bowman, Robert Leroy b: 5/10/31, Laytonville, Cal. BR/TR, 6'1", 195 lbs. Deb: 4/16/55 ♦

YEAR	TM/L	W	L	PCT	G	GS	CG	SH	SV	IP	H	HR	BB	SO	RAT	ERA	ERA+	OAV	OOB	BH	AVG	PB	PR	/A	PD	TPI
1959	Phi-N	0	1	.000	5	0	0	0	0	6	5	1	5	0	15.0	6.00	67	.227	.370	10	.127	-0	-1	-1	0	0.0

YEAR TM/L	W	L	PCT	G	GS	CG	SH	SV	IP	H	HR	BB	SO	RAT	ERA	ERA+	OAV	OOB	BH	AVG	PB	PR	/A	PD	TPI

■ ROGER BOWMAN Bowman, Roger Clinton b: 8/18/27, Amsterdam, N.Y. BR/TL, 6', 175 lbs. Deb: 9/22/49

YEAR TM/L	W	L	PCT	G	GS	CG	SH	SV	IP	H	HR	BB	SO	RAT	ERA	ERA+	OAV	OOB	BH	AVG	PB	PR	/A	PD	TPI
1949 NY-N	0	0	—	2	2	0	0	0	6¹	6	1	7	4	18.5	4.26	93	.261	.433	0	.000	-0	-0	-0	1	0.0
1951 NY-N	2	4	.333	9	5	0	0	0	26¹	35	2	22	24	19.8	6.15	64	.297	.411	0	.000	-0	-6	-7	-1	-0.6
1952 NY-N	0	0	—	2	1	0	0	0	3	6	0	3	3	30.0	12.00	31	.429	.556	0	.000	-0	-3	-3	0	-0.2
1953 Pit-N	0	4	.000	30	2	0	0	0	65¹	65	9	29	36	13.1	4.82	93	.261	.341	2	.286	1	-4	-3	0	-0.1
1955 Pit-N	0	3	.000	7	2	0	0	0	16²	25	2	10	8	19.4	8.64	48	.347	.434	1	.500	0	-9	-8	0	-0.6
Total 5	2	11	.154	50	12	0	0	0	117²	137	14	71	75	16.2	5.81	73	.288	.385	3	.167	0	-22	-20	1	-1.5

■ SUMNER BOWMAN Bowman, Sumner Sallade b: 2/9/1867, Millersburg, Pa. d: 1/11/54, Millersburg, Pa. BL/TL, 6', 160 lbs. Deb: 6/11/1890

YEAR TM/L	W	L	PCT	G	GS	CG	SH	SV	IP	H	HR	BB	SO	RAT	ERA	ERA+	OAV	OOB	BH	AVG	PB	PR	/A	PD	TPI
1890 Phi-N	0	0	—	1	1	0	0	0	8	11	0	2	2	14.6	7.88	46	.318	.355	2	.500	1	-4	-4	0	-0.2
Pit-N	2	5	.286	9	7	6	0	0	70²	100	1	50	22	19.1	6.62	50	.324	.418	10	.278	2	-24	-26	-0	-1.9
Yr	2	5	.286	10	8	6	0	0	78²	111	1	52	24	18.6	6.75	49	.323	.412	4	.100	3	-28	-30	-0	-2.1
1891 Phi-a	2	5	.286	8	8	8	0	0	68	73	0	37	22	14.6	3.44	111	.265	.352	13	.241	0	2	3	-1	0.2
Total 2	4	10	.286	18	16	14	0	0	146²	184	1	89	46	16.8	5.22	68	.297	.386	25	.266	3	-26	-27	-1	-1.9

■ TED BOWSFIELD Bowsfield, Edward Oliver b: 1/10/35, Vernon, B.C., Canada BR/TL, 6'1", 190 lbs. Deb: 7/20/58

YEAR TM/L	W	L	PCT	G	GS	CG	SH	SV	IP	H	HR	BB	SO	RAT	ERA	ERA+	OAV	OOB	BH	AVG	PB	PR	/A	PD	TPI
1958 Bos-A	4	2	.667	16	10	2	0	0	65²	58	3	36	38	13.0	3.84	104	.233	.332	4	.154	-1	-1	1	1	0.1
1959 Bos-A	0	1	.000	5	2	0	0	0	9	16	2	9	4	25.0	15.00	27	.390	.500	0	.000	-0	-11	-11	-0	-0.9
1960 Bos-A	1	2	.333	17	2	0	0	2	21	20	1	13	18	14.6	5.14	79	.260	.374	1	.250	-0	-3	-3	1	-0.1
Cle-A	3	4	.429	11	6	1	1	0	40²	47	1	20	14	14.8	5.09	73	.296	.374	1	.100	-0	-5	-6	1	-0.5
Yr	4	6	.400	28	8	1	1	2	61²	67	2	33	32	14.6	5.11	75	.280	.368	1	.071	-0	-8	-9	2	-0.6
1961 LA-A	11	8	.579	41	21	4	1	0	157	154	18	63	88	12.5	3.73	121	.255	.327	7	.137	-1	5	14	-1	1.3
1962 LA-A	9	8	.529	34	25	1	0	1	139	154	12	40	52	12.7	4.40	88	.277	.328	6	.162	1	-7	-8	-2	-0.8
1963 KC-A	5	7	.417	41	11	2	1	3	111¹	115	14	47	67	13.3	4.45	86	.269	.345	1	.043	-1	-10	-7	2	-0.6
1964 KC-A	4	7	.364	50	9	2	1	0	118²	135	12	31	45	12.9	4.10	93	.285	.334	2	.095	-1	-6	-4	1	-0.3
Total 7	37	39	.487	215	86	12	4	6	662¹	699	63	259	326	13.2	4.35	92	.270	.339	22	.127	-4	-38	-24	3	-1.8

■ OIL CAN BOYD Boyd, Dennis Ray b: 10/6/59, Meridian, Miss. BR/TR, 6'1", 155 lbs. Deb: 9/13/82

YEAR TM/L	W	L	PCT	G	GS	CG	SH	SV	IP	H	HR	BB	SO	RAT	ERA	ERA+	OAV	OOB	BH	AVG	PB	PR	/A	PD	TPI
1982 Bos-A	0	1	.000	3	1	0	0	0	8¹	11	2	2	2	14.0	5.40	80	.314	.351	0	—	0	-1	-1	0	0.0
1983 Bos-A	4	8	.333	15	13	5	0	0	98²	103	9	23	43	11.6	3.28	132	.269	.312	0	—	0	9	12	-1	1.1
1984 Bos-A	12	12	.500	29	26	10	3	0	197²	207	18	53	134	11.9	4.37	95	.269	.317	0	—	0	-8	-5	2	-0.2
1985 Bos-A	15	13	.536	35	35	13	3	0	272¹	273	26	67	154	11.4	3.70	116	.261	.308	0	—	0	13	18	3	2.1
1986 *Bos-A	16	10	.615	30	30	10	0	0	214¹	222	32	45	129	11.3	3.78	110	.265	.304	0	—	0	9	9	1	1.0
1987 Bos-A	1	3	.250	7	7	0	0	0	36²	47	6	9	12	14.2	5.89	77	.315	.363	0	—	0	-6	-6	1	-0.3
1988 Bos-A	9	7	.563	23	23	1	0	0	129²	147	25	41	71	13.2	5.34	77	.289	.344	0	—	0	-20	-18	-0	-1.7
1989 Bos-A	3	2	.600	10	10	0	0	0	59	57	8	19	26	11.6	4.42	93	.253	.311	0	—	0	-4	-2	1	0.0
1990 Mon-N	10	6	.625	31	31	3	3	0	190²	164	19	52	113	10.3	2.93	128	.233	.289	3	.051	-4	18	18	-1	1.3
Total 9	70	62	.530	183	176	42	9	0	1207¹	1231	145	311	684	11.6	3.96	105	.264	.313	3	.051	-4	11	25	7	3.3

■ JAKE BOYD Boyd, Jacob Henry b: 1/19/1874, Martinsburg, W.Va. d: 8/12/32, Gettysburg, Pa. TL, 160 lbs. Deb: 9/20/1894 ♦

YEAR TM/L	W	L	PCT	G	GS	CG	SH	SV	IP	H	HR	BB	SO	RAT	ERA	ERA+	OAV	OOB	BH	AVG	PB	PR	/A	PD	TPI
1894 Was-N	0	3	.000	3	3	3	0	0	19	37	1	14	3	24.2	8.53	62	.403	.482	3	.143	-1	-7	-7	0	-0.4
1895 Was-N	2	11	.154	14	12	8	0	0	85¹	126	1	35	16	17.0	7.07	68	.337	.394	42	.268	1	-22	-21	1	-1.6
1896 Was-N	1	2	.333	4	2	2	0	0	32	45	0	15	6	16.9	6.75	65	.329	.395	1	.077	-2	-8	-8	0	-0.6
Total 3	3	16	.158	21	17	13	0	0	136¹	208	2	64	25	18.0	7.20	66	.346	.408	46	.241	-2	-37	-37	2	-2.6

■ GARY BOYD Boyd, Gary Lee b: 8/22/46, Pasadena, Cal. BR/TR, 6'4", 200 lbs. Deb: 8/01/69

YEAR TM/L	W	L	PCT	G	GS	CG	SH	SV	IP	H	HR	BB	SO	RAT	ERA	ERA+	OAV	OOB	BH	AVG	PB	PR	/A	PD	TPI
1969 Cle-A	0	2	.000	8	3	0	0	0	11	8	1	14	9	18.0	9.00	42	.205	.415	0	.000	-0	-7	-6	-0	-0.6

■ RAY BOYD Boyd, Raymond C. b: 2/11/1887, Hortonville, Ind. d: 2/11/20, Hortonville, Ind. BR/TR, 5'10", 160 lbs. Deb: 9/24/10

YEAR TM/L	W	L	PCT	G	GS	CG	SH	SV	IP	H	HR	BB	SO	RAT	ERA	ERA+	OAV	OOB	BH	AVG	PB	PR	/A	PD	TPI
1910 StL-A	0	2	.000	3	2	1	0	0	14¹	16	0	5	6	13.8	4.40	56	.286	.355	1	.200	-0	-3	-3	-1	-0.3
1911 Cin-N	2	2	.500	7	4	3	0	1	44	34	0	19	20	11.3	2.66	124	.206	.296	1	.083	-0	4	3	-0	0.3
Total 2	2	4	.333	10	6	4	0	1	58¹	50	0	24	26	11.9	3.09	101	.226	.310	2	.118	-0	1	0	-1	0.0

■ BILL BOYD Boyd, William J. b: 12/22/1852, New York, N.Y. d: 9/30/12, Jamaica, N.Y. Deb: 4/22/1872 M♦

YEAR TM/L	W	L	PCT	G	GS	CG	SH	SV	IP	H	HR	BB	SO	RAT	ERA	ERA+	OAV	OOB	BH	AVG	PB	PR	/A	PD	TPI
1875 Atl-n	0	0	—	1	0	0	0	0	1²	4	0	0		21.6	5.40	43	.444	.444	44	.297	0	-1	-1		0.0

■ CLOYD BOYER Boyer, Cloyd Victor "Junior" b: 9/1/27, Alba, Mo. BR/TR, 6'1", 188 lbs. Deb: 4/23/49 C

YEAR TM/L	W	L	PCT	G	GS	CG	SH	SV	IP	H	HR	BB	SO	RAT	ERA	ERA+	OAV	OOB	BH	AVG	PB	PR	/A	PD	TPI
1949 StL-N	0	0	—	4	1	0	0	0	3¹	5	0	7	0	32.4	10.80	39	.357	.571	0	—	0	-3	-2	0	-0.1
1950 StL-N	7	7	.500	36	14	6	1	1	120¹	105	15	49	82	11.7	3.52	122	.233	.312	6	.182	0	8	10	-0	1.0
1951 StL-N	2	5	.286	19	8	1	0	1	63¹	68	9	46	40	16.6	5.26	75	.286	.408	4	.200	0	-9	-9	-2	-1.0
1952 StL-N	6	6	.500	23	14	4	2	0	110¹	108	11	47	44	13.0	4.24	88	.258	.338	8	.211	2	-6	-6	-2	-0.5
1955 KC-A	5	5	.500	30	11	2	0	0	98¹	107	21	69	32	16.7	6.22	67	.282	.402	2	.069	-2	-25	-22	-1	-2.3
Total 5	20	23	.465	112	48	13	3	2	395²	393	56	218	198	14.3	4.73	86	.262	.362	20	.167	-0	-34	-30	-4	-2.9

■ HENRY BOYLE Boyle, Henry J. "Handsome Henry" b: 9/20/1860, Philadelphia, Pa. d: 5/25/32, Philadelphia, Pa. TR, Deb: 7/09/1884 ♦

YEAR TM/L	W	L	PCT	G	GS	CG	SH	SV	IP	H	HR	BB	SO	RAT	ERA	ERA+	OAV	OOB	BH	AVG	PB	PR	/A	PD	TPI
1884 StL-U	15	3	.833	19	16	16	2	1	150	118	3	10	88	7.7	1.74	170	.202	.215	68	.260	3	21	20	-1	1.9
1885 StL-N	16	24	.400	42	39	39	1	0	366²	346	2	100	133	10.9	2.75	100	.238	.287	52	.202	1	3	-0	-1	0.0
1886 StL-N	9	15	.375	25	24	23	2	0	165	183	5	46	101	12.5	2.40	134	.270	.316	27	.250	4	17	15	1	1.9
1887 Ind-N	13	24	.351	38	38	37	0	0	328	356	6	69	85	11.7	3.65	113	.269	.305	27	.191	-1	14	17	-4	1.1
1888 Ind-N	15	22	.405	37	37	36	3	0	323	315	6	58	98	10.4	3.26	90	.246	.279	18	.144	-3	-15	-11	3	-0.9
1889 Ind-N	21	23	.477	46	45	38	2	0	378²	422	14	95	97	12.3	3.92	107	.273	.315	38	.245	5	4	11	-4	1.1
Total 6	89	111	.445	207	199	189	10	1	1711¹	1740	46	378	602	11.1	3.16	108	.253	.292	230	.219	8	44	50	-6	5.1

■ HARRY BOYLES Boyles, Harry "Stretch" b: 11/29/11, Granite City, Ill. BR/TR, 6'5", 185 lbs. Deb: 8/03/38

YEAR TM/L	W	L	PCT	G	GS	CG	SH	SV	IP	H	HR	BB	SO	RAT	ERA	ERA+	OAV	OOB	BH	AVG	PB	PR	/A	PD	TPI
1938 Chi-A	0	4	.000	9	2	1	0	1	29¹	31	2	25	18	17.8	5.22	94	.263	.400	1	.125	-1	-1	-1	1	0.0
1939 Chi-A	0	0	—	2	0	0	0	0	3¹	4	0	6	1	27.0	10.80	44	.308	.526	0	.000	-0	-2	-2	0	-0.1
Total 2	0	4	.000	11	2	1	0	1	32²	35	2	31	19	18.7	5.79	84	.267	.415	1	.111	-1	-4	-3	1	-0.1

■ GENE BRABENDER Brabender, Eugene Mathew b: 8/16/41, Madison, Wis. BR/TR, 6'5.5", 225 lbs. Deb: 5/11/66

YEAR TM/L	W	L	PCT	G	GS	CG	SH	SV	IP	H	HR	BB	SO	RAT	ERA	ERA+	OAV	OOB	BH	AVG	PB	PR	/A	PD	TPI
1966 Bal-A	4	3	.571	31	1	0	0	2	71	57	4	29	62	11.0	3.55	94	.229	.312	1	.077	-1	-1	-2	0	-0.1
1967 Bal-A	6	4	.600	14	14	3	1	0	94	77	6	23	71	9.7	3.35	94	.220	.270	2	.071	-1	-2	-0	-0.3
1968 Bal-A	6	7	.462	37	15	3	2	3	125	116	9	48	92	12.0	3.31	88	.248	.322	3	.086	-1	-5	-5	-1	-0.6
1969 Sea-A	13	14	.481	40	29	7	1	0	202¹	193	26	103	139	13.7	4.36	83	.254	.353	9	.129	-1	-17	-16	-3	-1.9
1970 Mil-A	6	15	.286	29	21	2	0	1	128²	127	8	79	76	14.5	6.02	63	.255	.359	4	.098	-2	-33	-32	0	-3.2
Total 5	35	43	.449	151	80	15	4	6	621	570	53	282	440	12.6	4.25	80	.245	.332	19	.102	-5	-56	-58	-3	-6.1

■ JACK BRACKEN Bracken, John James b: 4/14/1881, Cleveland, Ohio d: 7/16/54, Highland Park, Mich. BR/TR, 5'11", 175 lbs. Deb: 8/07/01

YEAR TM/L	W	L	PCT	G	GS	CG	SH	SV	IP	H	HR	BB	SO	RAT	ERA	ERA+	OAV	OOB	BH	AVG	PB	PR	/A	PD	TPI
1901 Cle-A	4	8	.333	12	12	12	0	0	100	137	4	31	18	15.1	6.21	57	.322	.368	10	.227	-0	-28	-30	-1	-2.4

■ JOHN BRACKENRIDGE Brackenridge, John Givler b: 12/24/1880, Harrisburg, Pa. d: 3/20/53, Harrisburg, Pa. BR/TR, 6'. Deb: 4/15/04

YEAR TM/L	W	L	PCT	G	GS	CG	SH	SV	IP	H	HR	BB	SO	RAT	ERA	ERA+	OAV	OOB	BH	AVG	PB	PR	/A	PD	TPI
1904 Phi-N	0	1	.000	7	1	0	0	0	34	37	4	16	11	15.1	5.56	48	.298	.396	2	.154	-0	-11	-11	2	-0.8

■ DON BRADEY Bradey, Donald Eugene b: 10/4/34, Charlotte, N.C. BR/TR, 5'9", 180 lbs. Deb: 9/25/64

YEAR TM/L	W	L	PCT	G	GS	CG	SH	SV	IP	H	HR	BB	SO	RAT	ERA	ERA+	OAV	OOB	BH	AVG	PB	PR	/A	PD	TPI
1964 Hou-N	0	2	.000	3	1	0	0	0	2¹	6	0	3	2	34.7	19.29	18	.429	.529	0	—	0	-4	-4	0	-0.3

YEAR	TM/L	W	L	PCT	G	GS	CG	SH	SV	IP	H	HR	BB	SO	RAT	ERA	ERA+	OAV	OOB	BH	AVG	PB	PR	/A	PD	TPI

■ LARRY BRADFORD   Bradford, Larry   b: 12/21/49, Chicago, Ill.   BR/TL, 6'1", 200 lbs.   Deb: 9/24/77

1977	Atl-N	0	0	—	2	0	0	0	0	2²	3	1	0	1	10.1	3.38	132	.273	.273	0	—	0	0	0	0	0.0
1979	Atl-N	1	0	1.000	21	0	0	0	2	19	11	0	10	11	10.4	0.95	427	.172	.293	0	.000	-0	6	7	0	0.7
1980	Atl-N	3	4	.429	56	0	0	0	4	55¹	49	3	22	32	11.7	2.44	153	.243	.320	0	.000	-0	7	8	0	0.8
1981	Atl-N	2	0	1.000	25	0	0	0	1	26²	26	1	12	14	12.8	3.71	96	.268	.349	1	1.000	0	-1	-0	0	0.0
Total 4		6	4	.600	104	0	0	0	7	103²	89	5	44	58	11.7	2.52	150	.238	.321	1	.200	-0	13	14	1	1.5

■ BILL BRADFORD   Bradford, William D   b: 8/28/21, Choctaw, Ark.   BR/TR, 6'2", 180 lbs.   Deb: 4/24/56

| 1956 | KC-A | 0 | 0 | — | 1 | 0 | 0 | 0 | 0 | 2 | 2 | 2 | 1 | 0 | 13.5 | 9.00 | 48 | .250 | .333 | 0 | — | 0 | -1 | -1 | 0 | 0.0 |

■ FRED BRADLEY   Bradley, Fred Langdon   b: 7/31/20, Parsons, Kan.   BR/TR, 6'1", 180 lbs.   Deb: 5/01/48

1948	Chi-A	0	0	—	8	0	0	0	0	15²	11	2	4	2	9.2	4.60	93	.190	.254	0	.000	-0	-1	-1	0	0.0
1949	Chi-A	0	0	—	1	1	0	0	0	2	4	0	3	0	31.5	13.50	31	.444	.583	0	.000	-0	-2	-2	0	-0.1
Total 2		0	0	—	9	1	0	0	0	17²	15	2	7	2	11.7	5.60	76	.224	.307	0	.000	-0	-3	-3	0	-0.1

■ FOGHORN BRADLEY   Bradley, George H.   b: 7/1/1855, Milford, Mass.   d: 4/3/1900, Philadelphia, Pa.   BR/TR,   Deb: 8/23/1876   U

| 1876 | Bos-N | 9 | 10 | .474 | 22 | 21 | 16 | 1 | 1 | 173¹ | 201 | 1 | 16 | 16 | 11.3 | 2.49 | 91 | .271 | .286 | 19 | .232 | -1 | -4 | -5 | -1 | -0.4 |

■ GEORGE BRADLEY   Bradley, George Washington "Grin"   b: 7/13/1852, Reading, Pa.   d: 10/2/31, Philadelphia, Pa.   BR/TR, 5'10.5", 175 lbs.   Deb: 5/04/1875   ♦

1875	StL-n	33	26	.559	60	60	57	4	0	535²	538	3	16		9.3	2.05	108	.240	.245	62	.244	7	24	10		1.2
1876	StL-N	45	19	.703	64	64	63	**16**	0	573	470	3	38	103	8.0	**1.23**	**174**	**.208**	**.221**	66	.249	6	**69**	58	1	5.5
1877	Chi-N	18	23	.439	50	44	35	2	0	394	452	4	39	59	11.2	3.31	90	.272	.288	52	.243	0	-22	-15	1	-1.0
1879	Tro-N	13	40	.245	54	54	53	3	0	487	590	12	26	133	11.4	2.85	88	.281	.290	62	.247	4	-19	-19	5	-0.7
1880	Pro-N	13	8	.619	28	20	16	4	1	196	158	2	6	54	**7.5**	1.38	160	.209	**.216**	70	.227	1	22	18	1	1.8
1881	Cle-N	2	4	.333	6	6	5	0	0	51	70	2	3	6	12.9	3.88	67	.313	.322	60	.249	0	-6	-7	-0	-0.5
1882	Cle-N	6	9	.400	18	16	15	0	0	147	164	5	22	32	11.4	3.73	75	.267	.292	21	.183	-3	-14	-15	3	-1.4
1883	Phi-a	16	7	.696	26	23	22	0	0	214¹	215	7	22	56	10.0	3.15	111	.244	.263	73	.234	-0	4	8	-1	0.7
1884	Cin-U	25	15	.625	41	38	36	3	0	342	350	7	23	168	9.8	2.71	117	.248	.260	43	.190	-4	12	17	2	1.3
Total 8		138	125	.525	287	265	245	28	1	2404¹	2469	42	179	611	9.9	2.50	106	.249	.262	456	.228	3	45	41	13	5.7

■ HERB BRADLEY   Bradley, Herbert Theodore   b: 1/3/03, Agenda, Kan.   d: 10/16/59, Clay Center, Kan.   BR/TR, 6', 170 lbs.   Deb: 5/09/27

1927	Bos-A	1	1	.500	6	2	2	0	0	23	16	0	7	6	9.8	3.13	135	.198	.278	3	.429	1	3	3	-0	0.3
1928	Bos-A	0	3	.000	15	5	1	1	0	47¹	64	2	16	14	15.6	7.23	57	.339	.396	2	.154	-0	-17	-16	1	-1.4
1929	Bos-A	0	0	—	3	0	0	0	0	4	7	1	2	0	20.3	6.75	63	.438	.500	0	.000	-0	-1	-1	0	-0.0
Total 3		1	4	.200	24	7	3	1	0	74¹	87	3	25	20	14.0	5.93	70	.304	.368	5	.238	-0	-15	-15	1	-1.1

■ BERT BRADLEY   Bradley, Steven Bert   b: 12/23/56, Athens, Ga.   BB/TR, 6'1", 190 lbs.   Deb: 9/03/83

| 1983 | Oak-A | 0 | 0 | — | 6 | 0 | 0 | 0 | 0 | 8¹ | 14 | 1 | 4 | 3 | 19.4 | 6.48 | 59 | .400 | .462 | 0 | — | 0 | -2 | -2 | 1 | -0.1 |

■ TOM BRADLEY   Bradley, Thomas William   b: 3/16/47, Asheville, N.C.   BR/TR, 6'2.5", 180 lbs.   Deb: 9/09/69

1969	Cal-A	0	1	.000	3	0	0	0	0	2	9	1	0	2	40.5	27.00	13	.600	.600	0	—	0	-5	-5	0	-0.4
1970	Cal-A	2	5	.286	17	11	1	1	0	69²	71	3	33	53	13.6	4.13	87	.270	.354	3	.167	-1	-3	-4	-0	-0.3
1971	Chi-A	15	15	.500	45	39	7	6	2	285²	273	16	74	206	11.0	2.96	121	.248	.297	15	.156	-1	16	20	-2	1.9
1972	Chi-A	15	14	.517	40	40	11	2	0	260	225	19	65	209	10.1	2.98	105	.231	.280	12	.132	-2	2	4	-1	0.1
1973	SF-N	13	12	.520	35	34	6	1	0	224	212	26	69	136	11.4	3.90	98	.246	.304	15	.195	1	-6	-2	-2	-0.2
1974	SF-N	8	11	.421	30	21	2	0	0	134¹	152	15	52	72	13.7	5.16	74	.282	.346	3	.075	-2	-23	-20	-1	-2.3
1975	SF-N	2	3	.400	13	6	0	0	0	42	57	6	18	13	16.3	6.21	61	.326	.392	0	.000	-1	-12	-11	1	-1.1
Total 7		55	61	.474	183	151	27	10	2	1017²	999	86	311	691	11.7	3.72	96	.254	.311	48	.145	-5	-31	-19	-6	-2.3

■ BILL BRADLEY   Bradley, William Joseph   b: 2/13/1878, Cleveland, Ohio   d: 3/11/54, Cleveland, Ohio   BR/TR, 6', 185 lbs.   Deb: 8/26/1899   M♦

| 1901 | Cle-A | 0 | 0 | — | 1 | 0 | 0 | 0 | 0 | 1 | 4 | 0 | 0 | 0 | 36.0 | 0.00 | — | .581 | .581 | 151 | .293 | 0 | 0 | 0 | 0 | 0.0 |

■ JOE BRADSHAW   Bradshaw, Joe Siah   b: 8/17/1897, Roellen, Tenn.   d: 1/30/85, Tavares, Fla.   BR/TR, 6'2.5", 200 lbs.   Deb: 5/09/29

| 1929 | Bro-N | 0 | 0 | — | 2 | 0 | 0 | 0 | 0 | 4 | 3 | 0 | 4 | 1 | 20.3 | 4.50 | 102 | .231 | .474 | 0 | — | 0 | 0 | 0 | 0 | 0.0 |

■ NEAL BRADY   Brady, Cornelius Joseph   b: 3/4/1897, Covington, Ky.   d: 6/19/47, Fort Mitchell, Ky   BR/TR, 6'0.5", 197 lbs.   Deb: 9/25/15

1915	NY-A	0	0	—	2	1	0	0	0	8²	9	0	7	6	16.6	3.12	94	.281	.410	0	.000	-1	-0	-0	-0	0.0
1917	NY-A	1	0	1.000	2	1	0	0	0	9	6	0	5	4	11.0	2.00	134	.188	.297	1	.500	0	1	1	0	0.2
1925	Cin-N	1	3	.250	20	3	2	0	1	63²	73	4	20	12	13.7	4.66	88	.289	.350	6	.240	1	-3	-4	1	-0.2
Total 3		2	3	.400	24	5	2	0	1	81¹	88	4	32	22	13.7	4.20	91	.278	.351	7	.226	1	-2	-3	1	0.0

■ JIM BRADY   Brady, James Joseph "Diamond Jim"   b: 3/2/36, Jersey City, N.J.   BL/TL, 6'2", 185 lbs.   Deb: 5/12/56

| 1956 | Det-A | 0 | 0 | — | 6 | 0 | 0 | 0 | 0 | 6¹ | 15 | 3 | 11 | 3 | 36.9 | 28.42 | 14 | .484 | .619 | 0 | — | 0 | -17 | -17 | 0 | -1.3 |

■ KING BRADY   Brady, James Ward   b: 5/28/1881, Elmer, N.J.   d: 8/21/47, Albany, N.Y.   BR/TR, 6', 190 lbs.   Deb: 9/21/05

1905	Phi-N	1	1	.500	2	2	2	0	0	13	19	0	2	3	14.5	3.46	84	.333	.356	1	.200	-0	-1	-1	0	0.0
1906	Pit-N	1	1	.500	3	2	1	0	0	23	30	0	4	14	13.3	2.35	114	.313	.340	1	.100	-1	1	1	-1	0.0
1907	Pit-N	0	0	—	1	0	0	0	0	2	2	0	1	0	13.5	0.00	—	.286	.375	0	—	-0	1	1	-0	0.0
1908	Bos-A	1	0	1.000	1	1	1	1	0	9	8	0	0	3	8.0	0.00	—	.242	.242	0	.000	-0	2	2	-0	0.2
1912	Bos-N	0	0	—	1	0	0	0	0	2²	5	0	3	0	27.0	20.25	18	.313	.421	0	.000	-0	-5	-5	0	-0.3
Total 5		3	2	.600	8	5	4	1	0	49²	64	0	10	20	13.4	3.08	89	.306	.338	2	.111	-1	-2	-2	-1	-0.1

■ BILL BRADY   Brady, William A. "King"   b: 1888,   TR, 6'2",   Deb: 4/13/12

| 1912 | Bos-N | 0 | 0 | — | 1 | 0 | 0 | 0 | 0 | 1 | 2 | 0 | 0 | 0 | 18.0 | 0.00 | — | .500 | .500 | 0 | — | 0 | 0 | 0 | -0 | 0.0 |

■ DICK BRAGGINS   Braggins, Richard Realf   b: 12/25/1879, Mercer, Pa.   d: 8/16/63, Lake Wales, Fla.   BR/TR, 5'11", 170 lbs.   Deb: 5/16/01

| 1901 | Cle-A | 1 | 2 | .333 | 4 | 3 | 2 | 0 | 0 | 32 | 44 | 1 | 15 | 1 | 16.6 | 4.78 | 74 | .323 | .390 | 2 | .154 | -1 | -4 | -4 | 0 | -0.3 |

■ ASA BRAINARD   Brainard, Asa "Count"   b: 1841, Albany, N.Y.   d: 12/29/1888, Denver, Colo.   TR, 5'8.5", 150 lbs.   Deb: 5/05/1871   ♦

1871	Oly-n	12	15	.444	30	30	30	0	0	264	361	4	37	13	13.6	4.50	93	.288	.308	30	.224	-6	-8	-10		-0.9
1872	Oly-n	2	7	.222	9	9	9	0	0	79	147	0	5		17.3	6.38	58	.332	.339	16	.390	4	-23	-24		-1.2
	Man-n	0	2	.000	2	2	1	0	0	8	14	1	0		15.8	7.88	47	.286	.286	5	.200	-0	-4	-4		-0.1
	Yr	2	9	.182	11	11	10	0	0	87	161	1	5		17.2	6.52	56	.327	.334	21	.030	4	-27	-28		-1.3
1873	Bal-n	5	7	.417	14	14	12	0	0	109¹	182	0	10		15.8	4.61	78	.326	.338	18	.261	1	-12	-12		-0.7
1874	Bal-n	5	22	.185	29	27	25	0	0	239	403	1	27		16.2	4.93	62	.326	.341	50	.253	-0	-51	-50		-3.6
Total 4 n		24	53	.312	84	82	77	0	0	699¹	1107	6	79	<u>13</u>	15.3	4.92	62	.313	.328	119	.255	-2	-149	-145		-6.5

■ AL BRAITHWOOD   Braithwood, Alfred   b: 2/15/1892, Braceville, Ill.   d: 11/24/60, Rowlesburg, W.Va.   6'1.5", 145 lbs.   Deb: 9/01/15

| 1915 | Pit-F | 0 | 0 | — | 2 | 0 | 0 | 0 | 0 | 3 | 0 | 0 | 2 | 0 | 6.0 | 0.00 | — | .000 | .000 | 0 | — | 0 | 1 | 1 | -0 | 0.1 |

■ ERV BRAME   Brame, Ervin Beckham   b: 10/12/01, Big Rock, Tenn.   d: 11/22/49, Hopkinsville, Ky.   BL/TR, 6'2", 190 lbs.   Deb: 4/14/28

1928	Pit-N	7	4	.636	24	11	6	0	0	95¹	110	5	40	22	14.6	5.08	80	.291	.366	13	.265	4	-12	-11	-1	-0.6
1929	Pit-N	16	11	.593	37	28	19	1	0	229²	250	17	71	68	12.6	4.55	105	.278	.331	36	.310	12	4	6	-4	1.3
1930	Pit-N	17	8	.680	32	29	**22**	0	1	235²	291	21	56	55	13.4	4.70	106	.305	.346	41	.353	11	7	7	-3	1.4
1931	Pit-N	9	13	.409	26	21	15	2	0	179²	211	14	45	33	12.8	4.21	91	.295	.336	26	.274	6	-7	-7	-2	-0.2
1932	Pit-N	3	1	.750	23	3	0	0	0	51	84	6	16	10	17.6	7.41	51	.365	.407	5	.250	1	-20	-20	-0	-1.8

YEAR TM/L	W	L	PCT	G	GS	CG	SH	SV	IP	H	HR	BB	SO	RAT	ERA	ERA+	OAV	OOB	BH	AVG	PB	PR	/A	PD	TPI
Total 5	52	37	.584	142	92	62	3	1	791²	946	63	232	188	13.5	4.76	94	.298	.347	121	.306	33	-27	-25	-9	0.1

■ RALPH BRANCA   Branca, Ralph Theodore Joseph "Hawk"   b: 1/6/26, Mt.Vernon, N.Y.   BR/TR, 6'3", 220 lbs.   Deb: 6/12/44

YEAR TM/L	W	L	PCT	G	GS	CG	SH	SV	IP	H	HR	BB	SO	RAT	ERA	ERA+	OAV	OOB	BH	AVG	PB	PR	/A	PD	TPI
1944 Bro-N	0	2	.000	21	1	0	0	1	44²	46	2	32	16	16.7	7.05	50	.274	.405	0	.000	-1	-17	-17	0	-1.7
1945 Bro-N	5	6	.455	16	15	7	0	1	109²	73	4	79	69	12.5	3.04	124	.189	.327	4	.100	-3	9	9	0	0.6
1946 Bro-N	3	1	.750	24	10	2	2	3	67¹	62	4	41	42	13.8	3.88	87	.246	.352	2	.111	0	-3	-4	-1	-0.4
1947 *Bro-N	21	12	.636	43	36	15	4	1	280	251	22	98	148	11.4	2.67	155	.240	.309	12	.124	-3	43	46	-4	4.0
1948 Bro-N	14	9	.609	36	28	11	1	1	215²	189	24	80	122	11.4	3.51	114	.232	.304	15	.203	1	11	12	-4	0.9
1949 *Bro-N	13	5	.722	34	27	9	2	1	186²	181	21	91	109	13.2	4.39	93	.253	.339	5	.081	-2	-7	-6	-4	-1.1
1950 Bro-N	7	9	.438	43	15	5	0	7	142	152	24	55	100	13.1	4.69	87	.271	.336	4	.118	1	-9	-9	-1	-0.8
1951 Bro-N	13	12	.520	42	27	13	3	3	204	180	19	85	118	11.8	3.26	120	.237	.316	11	.175	-1	16	15	-3	1.1
1952 Bro-N	4	2	.667	16	7	2	0	0	61	52	8	21	26	11.4	3.84	95	.232	.309	3	.158	-0	-1	-1	-1	-0.1
1953 Bro-N	0	0	—	7	0	0	0	0	11	15	4	5	5	18.0	9.82	43	.341	.431	0	—	0	-7	-7	0	-0.5
Det-A	4	7	.364	17	14	7	0	1	102	98	7	31	50	11.6	4.15	98	.253	.311	4	.118	-1	-2	-1	-1	-0.2
1954 Det-A	3	3	.500	17	5	0	0	0	45¹	63	10	30	15	18.9	5.76	64	.330	.426	4	.308	2	-10	-10	-0	-0.8
NY-A	1	0	1.000	5	3	0	0	0	12²	9	0	13	7	16.3	2.84	121	.209	.404	2	.500	1	1	1	0	0.2
Yr	4	3	.571	22	8	0	0	0	58	72	10	43	22	18.0	5.12	71	.305	.414	2	.118	2	-9	-10	-0	-0.6
1956 Bro-N	0	0	—	1	0	0	0	0	2	1	0	2	2	13.5	0.00	—	.143	.333	0	—	0	1	1	0	0.1
Total 12	88	68	.564	322	188	71	12	19	1484	1372	149	663	829	12.5	3.79	104	.245	.328	66	.142	-6	25	27	-19	1.3

■ HARVEY BRANCH   Branch, Harvey Alfred   b: 2/8/39, Memphis, Tenn.   BR/TL, 6', 175 lbs.   Deb: 9/18/62

YEAR TM/L	W	L	PCT	G	GS	CG	SH	SV	IP	H	HR	BB	SO	RAT	ERA	ERA+	OAV	OOB	BH	AVG	PB	PR	/A	PD	TPI
1962 StL-N	0	1	.000	1	1	0	0	0	5	5	1	5	2	18.0	5.40	79	.263	.417	0	.000	-0	-1	-1	0	0.0

■ NORM BRANCH   Branch, Norman Downs "Red"   b: 3/22/15, Spokane, Wash.   d: 11/21/71, Navasota, Tex.   BR/TR, 6'3", 200 lbs.   Deb: 5/05/41

YEAR TM/L	W	L	PCT	G	GS	CG	SH	SV	IP	H	HR	BB	SO	RAT	ERA	ERA+	OAV	OOB	BH	AVG	PB	PR	/A	PD	TPI
1941 NY-A	5	1	.833	27	0	0	0	2	47	37	2	26	28	12.1	2.87	137	.224	.330	0	.000	-1	7	6	0	0.5
1942 NY-A	0	1	.000	10	0	0	0	2	15²	18	3	16	13	19.5	6.32	54	.290	.436	1	.333	0	-5	-5	0	-0.4
Total 2	5	2	.714	37	0	0	0	4	62²	55	5	42	41	13.9	3.73	102	.242	.361	1	.077	-1	2	1	1	0.1

■ ROY BRANCH   Branch, Roy   b: 7/12/53, St.Louis, Mo.   BR/TR, 6', 175 lbs.   Deb: 9/11/79

YEAR TM/L	W	L	PCT	G	GS	CG	SH	SV	IP	H	HR	BB	SO	RAT	ERA	ERA+	OAV	OOB	BH	AVG	PB	PR	/A	PD	TPI
1979 Sea-A	0	1	.000	2	2	0	0	0	11¹	12	2	7	6	15.1	7.94	55	.273	.373	0	—	0	-5	-5	-0	-0.3

■ CHICK BRANDOM   Brandom, Chester Milton   b: 3/31/1887, Coldwater, Kan.   d: 10/7/58, Santa Ana, Cal.   TR, 5'8", 161 lbs.   Deb: 9/03/08

YEAR TM/L	W	L	PCT	G	GS	CG	SH	SV	IP	H	HR	BB	SO	RAT	ERA	ERA+	OAV	OOB	BH	AVG	PB	PR	/A	PD	TPI
1908 Pit-N	1	0	1.000	3	1	1	0	1	17	13	0	4	8	9.5	0.53	434	.228	.290	1	.143	-0	3	3	0	0.4
1909 Pit-N	1	0	1.000	13	2	0	0	2	40²	33	0	10	21	9.7	1.11	246	.239	.295	1	.100	-1	7	7	1	0.9
1915 New-F	1	1	.500	16	1	1	0	0	50¹	55	0	15	15	12.7	3.40	84	.293	.348	2	.200	1	-2	-3	1	-0.1
Total 3	3	1	.750	32	4	2	0	3	108	101	0	29	44	11.1	2.08	131	.264	.320	4	.148	-0	8	8	2	1.2

■ BUCKY BRANDON   Brandon, Darrell G   b: 7/8/40, Nacogdoches, Tex.   BR/TR, 6'2", 200 lbs.   Deb: 4/19/66

YEAR TM/L	W	L	PCT	G	GS	CG	SH	SV	IP	H	HR	BB	SO	RAT	ERA	ERA+	OAV	OOB	BH	AVG	PB	PR	/A	PD	TPI
1966 Bos-A	8	8	.500	40	17	5	2	2	157²	129	13	70	101	11.6	3.31	115	.222	.310	8	.182	2	2	9	0	1.2
1967 Bos-A	5	11	.313	39	19	2	0	3	157¹	147	21	59	96	12.2	4.17	84	.245	.320	8	.186	1	-16	-12	-0	-1.1
1968 Bos-A	0	0	—	8	0	0	0	0	12²	19	1	9	10	20.6	6.39	49	.333	.433	0	.000	-0	-5	-5	0	-0.4
1969 Sea-A	0	1	.000	8	1	0	0	0	15	15	4	16	10	19.8	8.40	43	.250	.423	0	—	0	-8	-8	0	-0.7
Min-A	0	0	—	3	0	0	0	0	3¹	5	1	3	1	21.6	2.70	135	.357	.471	0	.000	0	0	0	-0	-0.0
Yr	0	1	.000	11	1	0	0	0	18¹	20	5	19	11	19.1	7.36	49	.263	.411	1	1.000	0	-8	-8	-0	-0.7
1971 Phi-N	6	6	.500	52	0	0	0	4	83	81	5	47	44	13.9	3.90	90	.266	.362	2	.154	-0	-4	-4	-0	-0.4
1972 Phi-N	7	7	.500	42	6	0	0	2	104¹	106	9	46	67	13.6	3.45	104	.268	.353	1	.067	-1	0	2	-2	0.0
1973 Phi-N	2	4	.333	36	0	0	0	2	56¹	54	5	25	25	13.1	5.43	70	.261	.349	1	.200	0	-11	-10	0	-0.9
Total 7	28	37	.431	228	43	7	2	13	590	556	59	275	354	13.0	4.04	90	.250	.339	20	.164	1	-42	-27	-2	-2.3

■ ED BRANDT   Brandt, Edward Arthur "Big Ed"   b: 2/17/05, Spokane, Wash.   d: 11/1/44, Spokane, Wash.   BL/TL, 6'1", 190 lbs.   Deb: 4/26/28

YEAR TM/L	W	L	PCT	G	GS	CG	SH	SV	IP	H	HR	BB	SO	RAT	ERA	ERA+	OAV	OOB	BH	AVG	PB	PR	/A	PD	TPI
1928 Bos-N	9	21	.300	38	31	12	1	0	225¹	234	22	109	84	14.0	5.07	77	.273	.359	17	.243	5	-27	-29	1	-2.1
1929 Bos-N	8	13	.381	26	21	13	0	0	167²	196	12	83	50	15.2	5.53	85	.302	.385	15	.234	2	-15	-16	2	-1.0
1930 Bos-N	4	11	.267	41	13	4	1	1	147¹	168	15	59	65	13.9	5.01	99	.291	.356	12	.240	1	-1	-1	1	0.1
1931 Bos-N	18	11	.621	33	29	23	3	2	250	228	11	77	112	11.1	2.92	130	.244	.304	21	.256	5	26	24	2	3.3
1932 Bos-N	16	16	.500	35	31	19	2	1	254	271	11	57	79	11.8	3.97	95	.273	.318	19	.207	-0	-3	-6	1	-0.4
1933 Bos-N	18	14	.563	41	32	23	4	4	287²	256	10	77	104	10.5	2.60	118	.245	.298	30	.309	9	24	15	-1	2.4
1934 Bos-N	16	14	.533	40	28	20	3	5	255	249	16	83	106	11.9	3.53	108	.254	.315	23	.240	4	15	8	-3	0.9
1935 Bos-N	5	19	.208	29	25	12	0	1	174²	224	12	66	61	15.0	5.00	76	.319	.378	13	.210	-0	-19	-24	1	-2.1
1936 Bro-N	11	13	.458	38	29	12	1	2	234	246	14	65	104	12.1	3.50	118	.268	.319	16	.190	-0	14	16	-2	1.5
1937 Pit-N	11	10	.524	33	25	7	2	2	176¹	177	11	67	74	12.6	3.11	124	.263	.332	10	.169	1	16	15	1	1.7
1938 Pit-N	5	4	.556	24	14	5	1	0	96¹	93	3	35	38	12.0	3.46	110	.250	.314	11	.297	3	4	4	-0	0.6
Total 11	121	146	.453	378	278	150	18	17	2268¹	2342	134	778	877	12.5	3.86	101	.269	.332	187	.236	29	34	5	4	4.9

■ BILL BRANDT   Brandt, William George   b: 3/21/15, Aurora, Ind.   d: 5/16/68, Fort Wayne, Ind.   BR/TR, 5'8.5", 170 lbs.   Deb: 9/20/41

YEAR TM/L	W	L	PCT	G	GS	CG	SH	SV	IP	H	HR	BB	SO	RAT	ERA	ERA+	OAV	OOB	BH	AVG	PB	PR	/A	PD	TPI
1941 Pit-N	0	1	.000	2	1	0	0	0	7	5	0	3	0	10.3	3.86	94	.200	.286	0	.000	-0	-0	-0	0	0.0
1942 Pit-N	1	1	.500	3	3	1	0	0	16¹	23	1	5	4	15.4	4.96	68	.343	.389	1	.143	-0	-3	-3	-0	-0.3
1943 Pit-N	4	1	.800	29	3	0	0	0	57¹	57	3	19	17	12.1	3.14	111	.248	.308	1	.143	-0	2	2	-0	0.2
Total 3	5	3	.625	34	7	1	0	0	80²	85	4	27	21	12.6	3.57	97	.264	.323	2	.133	-1	-2	-1	-0	-0.1

■ JEFF BRANTLEY   Brantley, Jeffrey Hoke   b: 9/5/63, Florence, Ala.   BR/TR, 5'11", 180 lbs.   Deb: 8/05/88

YEAR TM/L	W	L	PCT	G	GS	CG	SH	SV	IP	H	HR	BB	SO	RAT	ERA	ERA+	OAV	OOB	BH	AVG	PB	PR	/A	PD	TPI
1988 SF-N	0	1	.000	9	1	0	0	1	20²	22	2	6	11	12.6	5.66	58	.275	.333	1	.500	0	-5	-6	1	-0.4
1989 *SF-N	7	1	.875	59	1	0	0	0	97¹	101	10	37	69	12.9	4.07	83	.271	.340	1	.083	-1	-6	-8	0	-0.8
1990 SF-N	5	3	.625	55	0	0	0	19	86²	77	3	33	61	11.7	1.56	239	.240	.317	2	.286	1	22	21	-0	2.3
Total 3	12	5	.706	123	2	0	0	20	204²	200	15	76	141	12.4	3.17	111	.258	.329	4	.190	0	10	8	1	1.1

■ ROY BRASHEAR   Brashear, Roy Parks   b: 1/3/1874, Ashtabula, Ohio   d: 4/20/51, Los Angeles, Cal.   TR,   Deb: 6/25/1899   ♦

YEAR TM/L	W	L	PCT	G	GS	CG	SH	SV	IP	H	HR	BB	SO	RAT	ERA	ERA+	OAV	OOB	BH	AVG	PB	PR	/A	PD	TPI
1899 Lou-N	1	0	1.000	3	0	0	0	0	8	8	0	2	5	11.3	4.50	86	.260	.305	1	.500	0	-1	-1	0	0.0

■ JOHN BRAUN   Braun, John Paul   b: 12/26/39, Madison, Wis.   BR/TR, 6'5", 218 lbs.   Deb: 10/02/64

YEAR TM/L	W	L	PCT	G	GS	CG	SH	SV	IP	H	HR	BB	SO	RAT	ERA	ERA+	OAV	OOB	BH	AVG	PB	PR	/A	PD	TPI
1964 Mil-N	0	0	—	1	0	0	0	0	2	2	0	1	1	13.5	0.00	—	.286	.375	0	—	0	1	1	0	0.1

■ GARLAND BRAXTON   Braxton, Edgar Garland   b: 6/10/1900, Snow Camp, N.C.   d: 2/25/66, Norfolk, Va.   BB/TL, 5'11", 152 lbs.   Deb: 5/27/21

YEAR TM/L	W	L	PCT	G	GS	CG	SH	SV	IP	H	HR	BB	SO	RAT	ERA	ERA+	OAV	OOB	BH	AVG	PB	PR	/A	PD	TPI
1921 Bos-N	1	3	.250	17	2	0	0	0	37¹	44	0	17	16	15.2	4.82	76	.310	.391	0	.000	-1	-4	-5	1	-0.4
1922 Bos-N	1	2	.333	25	2	0	0	0	66²	75	3	24	15	13.9	3.38	118	.286	.355	1	.063	-2	5	5	0	-0.2
1925 NY-A	1	1	.500	3	2	0	0	0	19¹	26	1	5	11	14.9	6.52	65	.338	.386	2	.333	0	-5	-5	0	-0.3
1926 NY-A	5	1	.833	37	1	0	0	2	67¹	71	1	19	30	12.0	2.67	144	.275	.325	6	.300	1	10	9	0	1.0
1927 Was-A	10	9	.526	58	2	0	0	13	155¹	144	5	33	96	10.4	2.95	138	.246	.289	9	.231	0	20	19	-3	1.6
1928 Was-A	13	11	.542	38	24	15	2	6	218¹	177	7	44	94	9.3	2.51	160	.222	.267	9	.125	-1	37	36	0	3.2
1929 Was-A	12	10	.545	37	20	9	0	4	182	219	6	51	59	13.5	4.85	88	.299	.346	8	.148	-1	-12	-12	-1	-1.2
1930 Was-A	3	2	.600	15	0	0	0	5	27¹	23		9	7	10.2	3.29	140	.222	.287	0	.000	-1	4	4	-1	0.2
Chi-A	4	10	.286	19	10	2	0	1	90²	127	9	33	44	16.0	6.45	81	.333	.388	2	.087	-2	-18	-18	-1	-1.8
Yr	7	12	.368	34	10	2	0	6	118	149	12	42	51	14.6	5.72	81	.310	.367	5	.179	-2	-14	-14	-2	-1.6
1931 Chi-A	0	3	.000	17	3	0	0	0	47¹	71	1	23	28	18.3	6.85	62	.338	.409	1	.091	-1	-13	-14	0	-1.2
StL-A	0	0	—	11	1	0	0	0	18	27	2	10	7	19.0	10.50	44	.370	.452	2	.667	1	-12	-12	-0	-0.9
Yr	0	3	.000	28	4	0	0	0	65¹	98	3	33	35	18.2	7.85	56	.344	.414	2	.143	0	-25	-25	-0	-2.1
1933 StL-A	0	1	.000	5	1	0	0	0	8¹	11	0	8	5	21.6	9.72	48	.289	.426	0	.000	-0	-5	-5	-0	-0.4

YEAR TM/L	W	L	PCT	G	GS	CG	SH	SV	IP	H	HR	BB	SO	RAT	ERA	ERA+	OAV	OOB	BH	AVG	PB	PR	/A	PD	TPI
Total 10	50	53	.485	282	70	28	2	32	938	1014	38	276	412	12.6	4.13	101	.278	.332	40	.156	-8	8	2	-6	0.0

■ **AL BRAZLE**   Brazle, Alpha Eugene "Cotton" b: 10/19/13, Loyal, Okla. d: 10/24/73, Grand Junction, Colo. BL/TL, 6'2", 185 lbs. Deb: 7/25/43

YEAR TM/L	W	L	PCT	G	GS	CG	SH	SV	IP	H	HR	BB	SO	RAT	ERA	ERA+	OAV	OOB	BH	AVG	PB	PR	/A	PD	TPI
1943 *StL-N	8	2	.800	13	9	8	1	0	88	74	0	29	26	10.5	1.53	219	.231	.295	9	.281	2	18	18	1	2.4
1946 *StL-N	11	10	.524	37	15	6	2	0	153¹	152	1	55	58	12.3	3.29	105	.261	.327	11	.212	-0	2	3	0	0.3
1947 StL-N	14	8	.636	44	19	7	0	4	168	186	7	48	85	12.6	2.84	146	.284	.335	14	.219	1	23	24	3	2.8
1948 StL-N	10	6	.625	42	23	6	2	1	156¹	171	8	50	55	12.7	3.80	108	.281	.335	8	.145	-2	3	5	3	0.7
1949 StL-N	14	8	.636	39	25	9	1	0	206¹	208	18	61	75	12.0	3.18	131	.263	.321	11	.134	-5	20	22	-0	1.8
1950 StL-N	11	9	.550	46	12	3	0	6	164²	188	12	80	47	14.9	4.10	105	.296	.378	13	.213	-1	1	4	0	0.3
1951 StL-N	6	5	.545	56	8	5	0	7	154¹	139	13	60	66	11.9	3.09	128	.245	.322	5	.109	-3	15	15	-2	1.0
1952 StL-N	12	5	.706	46	6	3	1	16	109¹	75	7	42	55	9.7	2.72	137	.198	.280	4	.125	-1	12	12	-1	1.0
1953 StL-N	6	7	.462	60	0	0	0	18	92	101	8	43	57	14.3	4.21	101	.280	.360	5	.333	1	1	1	2	0.3
1954 StL-N	5	4	.556	58	0	0	0	8	84¹	93	10	24	30	12.8	4.16	99	.288	.343	0	.000	-2	-1	-0	-0	-0.2
Total 10	97	64	.602	441	117	47	7	60	1376²	1387	84	492	554	12.6	3.31	120	.266	.332	80	.177	-9	93	103	4	10.4

■ **HARRY BRECHEEN**   Brecheen, Harry David "Harry The Cat" b: 10/14/14, Broken Bow, Okla. BL/TL, 5'10", 160 lbs. Deb: 4/22/40 C

YEAR TM/L	W	L	PCT	G	GS	CG	SH	SV	IP	H	HR	BB	SO	RAT	ERA	ERA+	OAV	OOB	BH	AVG	PB	PR	/A	PD	TPI
1940 StL-N	0	0	—	3	0	0	0	0	3¹	2	0	2	4	10.8	0.00	—	.167	.286	0	—	0	1	1	0	0.2
1943 *StL-N	9	6	.600	29	13	8	1	4	135¹	98	4	39	68	9.3	2.26	149	.206	.270	8	.190	1	17	17	1	2.0
1944 *StL-N	16	5	.762	30	22	13	3	0	189¹	174	8	46	88	10.6	2.85	124	.242	.290	11	.162	-1	16	14	-0	1.5
1945 StL-N	15	4	.789	24	18	13	3	2	157¹	136	5	44	63	10.6	2.52	149	.238	.298	7	.123	-1	22	21	-1	2.0
1946 *StL-N	15	15	.500	36	30	14	5	3	231¹	212	8	67	117	11.0	2.49	139	.244	.301	11	.133	-3	24	25	1	2.5
1947 StL-N	16	11	.593	29	28	18	1	1	223¹	220	20	66	89	11.6	3.30	125	.260	.316	20	.241	5	19	21	1	2.8
1948 StL-N	20	7	.741	33	30	21	7	1	233¹	193	6	49	149	9.4	2.24	183	.222	.265	12	.146	-1	45	48	0	5.2
1949 StL-N	14	11	.560	32	31	14	2	1	214²	207	18	65	88	11.7	3.35	124	.252	.312	21	.273	6	16	19	-1	2.4
1950 StL-N	8	11	.421	27	23	12	2	1	163¹	151	18	45	80	11.0	3.80	113	.244	.298	14	.241	4	6	9	-1	1.2
1951 StL-N	8	4	.667	24	16	5	0	2	138²	134	11	54	57	12.3	3.25	122	.256	.327	12	.218	2	11	11	-0	1.3
1952 StL-N	7	5	.583	25	13	4	1	2	100¹	82	12	28	54	10.1	3.32	112	.223	.283	6	.207	1	5	4	2	0.8
1953 StL-A	5	13	.278	26	16	3	0	1	117¹	122	7	31	44	12.0	3.07	137	.269	.320	7	.179	-1	12	15	2	1.6
Total 12	133	92	.591	318	240	125	25	18	1907²	1731	117	536	901	10.9	2.92	133	.242	.298	129	.192	11	194	205	5	23.5

■ **BILL BRECKINRIDGE**   Breckinridge, William Robertson b: 10/16/07, Tulsa, Okla. d: 8/23/58, Tulsa, Okla. BR/TR, 5'11", 175 lbs. Deb: 6/30/29

YEAR TM/L	W	L	PCT	G	GS	CG	SH	SV	IP	H	HR	BB	SO	RAT	ERA	ERA+	OAV	OOB	BH	AVG	PB	PR	/A	PD	TPI
1929 Phi-A	0	0	—	3	1	0	0	0	10	10	0	16	2	23.4	8.10	52	.270	.491	0	.000	-1	-4	-4	-0	-0.4

■ **FRED BREINING**   Breining, Fred Lawrence b: 11/15/55, San Francisco, Cal. BR/TR, 6'4", 185 lbs. Deb: 9/04/80

YEAR TM/L	W	L	PCT	G	GS	CG	SH	SV	IP	H	HR	BB	SO	RAT	ERA	ERA+	OAV	OOB	BH	AVG	PB	PR	/A	PD	TPI
1980 SF-N	0	0	—	5	0	0	0	0	6²	8	0	4	3	17.6	5.40	65	.333	.448	0	—	0	-1	-1	0	0.0
1981 SF-N	5	2	.714	45	1	0	0	1	77²	66	4	38	37	12.3	2.55	135	.243	.340	0	.000	-1	8	8	-0	0.7
1982 SF-N	11	6	.647	54	9	2	0	0	143¹	146	6	52	98	12.5	3.08	117	.269	.334	6	.207	1	8	8	1	1.1
1983 SF-N	11	12	.478	32	32	6	0	0	202²	202	15	60	117	11.9	3.82	93	.259	.316	10	.149	1	-4	-6	-0	-0.5
1984 Mon-N	0	0	—	4	0	0	0	0	6²	4	0	5	5	12.2	1.35	254	.190	.346	0	.000	-0	2	2	-0	0.1
Total 5	27	20	.574	140	42	8	0	1	437	426	25	159	260	12.2	3.34	106	.260	.329	16	.148	1	12	10	-0	1.4

■ **ALONZO BREITENSTEIN**   Breitenstein, Alonzo b: 11/9/1857, Utica, N.Y. d: 6/19/32, Utica, N.Y. Deb: 7/07/1883

YEAR TM/L	W	L	PCT	G	GS	CG	SH	SV	IP	H	HR	BB	SO	RAT	ERA	ERA+	OAV	OOB	BH	AVG	PB	PR	/A	PD	TPI
1883 Phi-N	0	1	.000	1	1	0	0	0	5	8	0	2	0	18.0	9.00	34	.342	.394	0	.000	-0	-3	-3	0	-0.2

■ **TED BREITENSTEIN**   Breitenstein, Theodore P. "Theo" b: 6/1/1869, St.Louis, Mo. d: 5/3/35, St.Louis, Mo. BL/TL, 5'9", 167 lbs. Deb: 4/28/1891

YEAR TM/L	W	L	PCT	G	GS	CG	SH	SV	IP	H	HR	BB	SO	RAT	ERA	ERA+	OAV	OOB	BH	AVG	PB	PR	/A	PD	TPI
1891 StL-a	2	0	1.000	6	1	1	1	1	28²	15	2	14	13	9.1	2.20	191	.150	.254	0	.000	-2	5	6	-1	0.4
1892 StL-N	9	19	.321	39	32	28	1	0	282¹	280	8	148	126	13.6	4.69	68	.248	.336	16	.122	-4	-44	-47	2	-4.2
1893 StL-N	19	24	.442	48	42	38	1	1	382²	359	8	156	102	12.1	3.18	149	.241	.313	29	.181	-5	64	66	2	5.5
1894 StL-N	27	23	.540	56	50	46	1	0	447¹	497	21	191	100	13.8	4.79	113	.220	.348	40	.220	-1	27	31	3	2.6
1895 StL-N	19	30	.388	54	50	46	1	1	429²	458	16	178	127	13.3	4.44	109	.269	.338	42	.193	-7	16	19	3	1.1
1896 StL-N	18	26	.409	44	43	37	1	0	339²	376	12	138	114	13.6	4.48	97	.278	.345	42	.259	3	-4	-5	4	0.1
1897 Cin-N	23	12	.657	40	39	32	2	0	320¹	345	3	91	98	12.2	3.62	126	.273	.322	24	.266	4	25	33	-1	3.3
1898 Cin-N	20	14	.588	39	37	32	3	0	315²	313	2	123	62	12.4	3.42	112	.257	.325	26	.215	1	7	15	3	1.9
1899 Cin-N	13	9	.591	26	24	21	0	0	210²	219	2	71	59	12.4	3.59	109	.268	.326	37	.352	9	6	8	-0	1.8
1900 Cin-N	10	10	.500	24	20	18	1	0	192¹	205	4	79	39	13.3	3.65	101	.272	.341	24	.190	-0	1	0	3	0.3
1901 StL-N	0	3	.000	3	3	3	1	0	15	24	1	14	3	22.8	6.60	48	.358	.469	2	.333	0	-5	-6	1	-0.3
Total 11	160	170	.485	379	341	300	12	3	2964¹	3091	79	1203	889	13.0	4.04	109	.265	.333	291	.216	-2	96	121	18	12.5

■ **AD BRENNAN**   Brennan, Addison Foster b: 7/18/1881, Laharpe, Kan. d: 1/7/62, Kansas City, Mo. BL/TL, 5'11", 170 lbs. Deb: 5/19/10

YEAR TM/L	W	L	PCT	G	GS	CG	SH	SV	IP	H	HR	BB	SO	RAT	ERA	ERA+	OAV	OOB	BH	AVG	PB	PR	/A	PD	TPI
1910 Phi-N	2	0	1.000	19	5	2	0	0	73¹	72	2	28	28	12.6	2.33	134	.264	.339	7	.280	1	6	6	-1	0.7
1911 Phi-N	2	1	.667	5	3	1	0	0	22²	22	0	12	12	13.9	3.57	96	.259	.357	2	.222	-0	-0	-0	0	0.0
1912 Phi-N	11	9	.550	27	19	13	1	2	174	185	4	49	78	12.3	3.57	102	.268	.319	15	.254	-1	3	1	2	0.8
1913 Phi-N	14	12	.538	40	25	12	1	1	207	204	5	46	94	11.1	2.39	139	.268	.314	11	.164	-2	19	22	0	2.1
1914 Chi-F	5	5	.500	16	11	5	1	0	85²	84	6	21	31	11.2	3.57	83	.256	.305	8	.250	1	-3	-6	-1	-0.5
1915 Chi-F	3	9	.250	19	13	7	2	0	106	117	4	30	40	13.1	3.74	75	.230	.283	5	.185	-1	-8	-11	-2	-1.2
1918 Was-A	0	0	—	2	1	0	0	0	5¹	7	0	5	0	21.9	5.06	54	.241	.371	0	.000	-0	-1	-1	-0	-0.1
Cle-A	0	0	—	1	0	0	0	0	3	3	0	3	0	18.0	3.00	100	.333	.500	0	—	0	0	-0	-0	-0.0
Yr	0	0	—	3	1	0	0	0	8¹	10	0	8	0	19.4	4.32	65	.256	.383	0	.000	-0	-1	-1	-0	-0.1
Total 7	37	36	.507	129	77	40	5	3	677	694	21	194	283	12.1	3.11	104	.258	.314	48	.218	5	8	10	-1	1.8

■ **DON BRENNAN**   Brennan, James Donald b: 12/2/03, Augusta, Maine d: 4/26/53, Boston, Mass. BR/TR, 6', 210 lbs. Deb: 4/16/33

YEAR TM/L	W	L	PCT	G	GS	CG	SH	SV	IP	H	HR	BB	SO	RAT	ERA	ERA+	OAV	OOB	BH	AVG	PB	PR	/A	PD	TPI
1933 NY-A	5	1	.833	18	10	3	0	3	85	92	4	47	46	14.7	4.98	78	.275	.365	7	.259	2	-7	-10	1	-0.6
1934 Cin-N	4	3	.571	28	7	2	0	2	78	89	4	35	31	14.4	3.81	107	.290	.364	5	.227	0	2	2	-1	0.2
1935 Cin-N	5	5	.500	38	5	2	1	5	114¹	101	4	44	48	11.7	3.15	126	.242	.320	3	.100	-1	11	11	-2	0.7
1936 Cin-N	5	2	.714	41	4	0	0	9	94¹	117	2	35	40	14.6	4.39	87	.305	.364	2	.080	-2	-4	-6	-0	-0.8
1937 Cin-N	1	1	.500	10	0	0	0	0	16	25	1	10	0	19.7	6.75	55	.347	.427	0	.000	-1	-5	-5	-0	-0.5
*NY-N	1	0	1.000	6	0	0	0	0	9¹	12	0	9	1	21.2	6.75	58	.316	.458	0	.000	0	-3	-3	-0	-0.2
Yr	2	1	.667	16	0	0	0	0	25¹	37	1	19	7	20.3	6.75	56	.336	.438	1	.167	-0	-8	-8	-0	-0.7
Total 5	21	12	.636	141	26	7	1	19	397	436	14	180	172	14.1	4.19	94	.281	.358	17	.155	-2	-5	-12	-2	-1.2

■ **TOM BRENNAN**   Brennan, Thomas Martin b: 10/30/52, Chicago, Ill. BR/TR, 6'1", 180 lbs. Deb: 9/05/81

YEAR TM/L	W	L	PCT	G	GS	CG	SH	SV	IP	H	HR	BB	SO	RAT	ERA	ERA+	OAV	OOB	BH	AVG	PB	PR	/A	PD	TPI
1981 Cle-A	2	2	.500	7	6	1	0	0	48¹	49	5	14	15	11.7	3.17	114	.259	.310	0	—	0	3	2	1	0.4
1982 Cle-A	4	2	.667	30	4	0	0	2	92²	112	9	10	46	12.0	4.27	95	.300	.322	0	—	0	-2	-2	1	0.0
1983 Cle-A	2	2	.500	11	5	1	1	0	39²	45	3	8	21	12.3	3.86	110	.288	.327	0	—	0	1	2	-0	0.1
1984 Chi-A	0	1	.000	4	1	0	0	0	6²	8	1	3	3	14.9	4.05	103	.308	.379	0	—	0	-0	-0	0	0.0
1985 LA-N	1	3	.250	12	4	0	0	0	31²	41	2	11	17	14.8	7.39	47	.333	.388	1	.125	-0	-13	-14	2	-1.1
Total 5	9	10	.474	64	20	2	1	2	219	255	20	46	102	12.5	4.40	89	.294	.332	1	.125	-0	-12	-12	4	-0.6

■ **BILL BRENNAN**   Brennan, William Raymond b: 1/15/63, Tampa, Fla. BR/TR, 6'3", 200 lbs. Deb: 7/19/88

YEAR TM/L	W	L	PCT	G	GS	CG	SH	SV	IP	H	HR	BB	SO	RAT	ERA	ERA+	OAV	OOB	BH	AVG	PB	PR	/A	PD	TPI
1988 LA-N	0	1	.000	4	2	0	0	0	9¹	13	0	6	7	18.3	6.75	49	.342	.432	0	.000	-0	-3	-4	0	-0.3

■ **JIM BRENNEMAN**   Brenneman, James Leroy b: 2/13/41, San Diego, Cal. BR/TR, 6'2", 180 lbs. Deb: 7/09/65

YEAR TM/L	W	L	PCT	G	GS	CG	SH	SV	IP	H	HR	BB	SO	RAT	ERA	ERA+	OAV	OOB	BH	AVG	PB	PR	/A	PD	TPI
1965 NY-A	0	0	—	3	0	0	0	0	2	5	1	3	2	36.0	18.00	19	.455	.571	0	—	0	-3	-3	-0	-0.2

■ **BERT BRENNER**   Brenner, Delbert Henry "Dutch" b: 7/18/1887, Minneapolis, Minn d: 4/11/71, St.Louis Park, Minn. BR/TR, 6', 175 lbs. Deb: 9/21/12

YEAR TM/L	W	L	PCT	G	GS	CG	SH	SV	IP	H	HR	BB	SO	RAT	ERA	ERA+	OAV	OOB	BH	AVG	PB	PR	/A	PD	TPI
1912 Cle-A	1	0	1.000	2	1	1	0	0	13	14	0	4	3	12.5	2.77	123	.286	.340	0	.000	-1	1	1	0	0.0

YEAR TM/L	W	L	PCT	G	GS	CG	SH	SV	IP	H	HR	BB	SO	RAT	ERA	ERA+	OAV	OOB	BH	AVG	PB	PR	/A	PD	TPI
■ **LYNN BRENTON**								Brenton, Lynn Davis "Buck" or "Herb" b: 10/7/1890, Peoria, Ill. d: 10/14/68, Los Angeles, Cal. BR/TR, 5'10", 165 lbs. Deb: 8/09/13																
1913 Cle-A	0	0	—	1	0	0	0	0	2	4	0	2	2	18.0	9.00	34	.400	.400	0	—	0	-1	-1	0	0.0
1915 Cle-A	2	3	.400	11	5	1	1	0	51	60	1	20	18	14.5	3.35	91	.308	.378	2	.118	-1	-2	-2	-1	-0.3
1920 Cin-N	2	1	.667	5	1	1	0	1	18¹	17	0	4	13	10.3	4.91	62	.236	.276	2	.250	-0	-4	-4	1	-0.1
1921 Cin-N	1	8	.111	17	9	2	0	1	60	80	0	17	19	14.7	4.05	88	.342	.389	2	.133	-0	-2	-3	2	0.0
Total 4	5	12	.294	34	15	4	1	2	131¹	161	1	41	52	14.0	3.97	83	.315	.369	6	.150	-1	-9	-10	3	-0.4
■ **ROGER BRESNAHAN**								Bresnahan, Roger Philip "The Duke Of Tralee"																	
									b: 6/11/1879, Toledo, Ohio d: 12/4/44, Toledo, Ohio BR/TR, 5'9", 200 lbs. Deb: 8/27/1897 MCH♦																
1897 Was-N	4	0	1.000	6	5	3	1	0	41	52	1	10	12	13.6	3.95	110	.306	.345	6	.375	1	2	2	-0	0.2
1901 Bal-A	0	1	.000	2	1	0	0	0	6	10	0	4	3	21.0	6.00	64	.366	.447	79	.268	0	-2	-1	0	0.0
1910 StL-N	0	0	—	1	0	0	0	0	3¹	6	0	1	0	18.9	0.00	—	.400	.438	65	.278	0	1	1	1	0.1
Total 3	4	1	.800	9	6	3	1	0	50¹	68	1	15	15	14.8	3.93	107	.321	.366	1252	.279	2	1	1	0	0.3
■ **RUBE BRESSLER**								Bressler, Raymond Bloom b: 10/23/1894, Coder, Pa. d: 11/7/66, Cincinnati, Ohio BR/TL, 6', 187 lbs. Deb: 4/24/14 ♦																
1914 Phi-A	10	4	.714	29	10	8	1	2	147²	112	1	56	96	10.5	1.77	149	.220	.302	11	.216	4	16	14	-3	1.7
1915 Phi-A	4	17	.190	32	20	7	1	0	178¹	183	3	118	69	15.5	5.20	57	.283	.399	8	.145	1	-45	-45	1	-4.1
1916 Phi-A	0	2	.000	4	2	0	0	0	15	16	0	14	8	19.2	6.60	44	.296	.457	1	.200	1	-6	-6	-0	-0.5
1917 Cin-N	0	0	—	2	1	0	0	0	9	15	0	5	2	20.0	6.00	44	.429	.500	1	.200	-0	-3	-3	-0	-0.3
1918 Cin-N	8	5	.615	17	13	10	0	0	128	124	3	39	37	11.5	2.46	108	.261	.318	17	.274	4	4	3	1	1.2
1919 Cin-N	2	4	.333	13	4	1	0	0	41²	37	1	8	13	9.7	3.46	80	.248	.287	34	.206	2	-3	-3	1	-0.2
1920 Cin-N	2	0	1.000	10	2	1	1	0	20¹	24	0	2	4	11.5	1.77	172	.300	.317	8	.267	0	3	3	0	0.3
Total 7	26	32	.448	107	52	27	3	2	540	511	8	242	229	12.8	3.40	82	.262	.348	1170	.301	11	-34	-37	1	-1.9
■ **DUKE BRETT**								Brett, Herbert James "Herb" b: 5/23/1900, Lawrenceville, Va. d: 11/25/74, St.Petersburg, Fla BR/TR, 6', 175 lbs. Deb: 8/08/24																
1924 Chi-N	0	0	—	1	1	0	0	0	5¹	6	0	7	1	21.9	5.06	77	.300	.481	0	.000	-0	-1	-1	-0	0.0
1925 Chi-N	1	1	.500	10	1	0	0	0	17¹	12	0	3	6	8.3	3.63	119	.194	.242	0	.000	-0	1	1	0	0.2
Total 2	1	1	.500	11	2	0	0	0	22²	18	0	10	7	11.5	3.97	106	.220	.312	0	.000	-1	1	1	0	0.2
■ **KEN BRETT**								Brett, Kenneth Alven b: 9/18/48, Brooklyn, N.Y. BL/TL, 6', 190 lbs. Deb: 9/27/67																
1967 *Bos-A	0	0	—	1	0	0	0	0	2	3	0	2	2	13.5	4.50	77	.375	.375	0	—	0	-0	-0	0	0.0
1969 Bos-A	2	3	.400	8	8	0	0	0	39¹	41	6	22	23	15.1	5.26	72	.275	.379	3	.300	2	-7	-6	0	-0.3
1970 Bos-A	8	9	.471	41	14	1	0	2	139¹	118	17	79	155	12.9	4.07	97	.237	.327	13	.317	6	-6	-2	0	0.5
1971 Bos-A	0	3	.000	29	2	0	0	1	59	57	7	35	57	14.2	5.34	69	.253	.356	2	.200	-0	-12	-11	-1	-1.1
1972 Mil-A	7	12	.368	26	22	2	1	0	133	121	13	49	74	11.6	4.53	67	.242	.311	10	.227	2	-22	-22	-1	-2.3
1973 Phi-N	13	9	.591	31	25	10	1	0	211²	206	19	74	111	11.9	3.44	110	.259	.322	20	.250	9	5	8	2	2.1
1974 *Pit-N	13	9	.591	27	27	10	3	0	191	192	9	52	96	11.6	3.30	104	.257	.308	27	.310	10	7	3	0	1.4
1975 *Pit-N	9	5	.643	23	16	4	1	0	118	110	10	43	47	11.8	3.36	106	.250	.320	12	.231	4	3	2	1	0.7
1976 NY-A	0	0	—	2	0	0	0	1	2¹	2	0	0	1	7.7	0.00	—	.222	.222	0	—	0	1	1	0	0.1
Chi-A	10	12	.455	27	26	16	1	1	200²	171	5	76	91	11.2	3.32	107	.234	.308	1	.083	2	4	5	1	0.6
Yr	10	12	.455	29	26	16	1	2	203	173	5	76	92	11.2	3.28	109	.233	.307	0	.000	2	5	6	1	0.7
1977 Chi-A	6	4	.600	13	13	2	0	0	82²	101	10	15	39	12.7	5.01	82	.305	.337	0	—	0	-9	-8	0	-0.7
Cal-A	7	10	.412	21	21	5	0	0	142	157	15	38	41	12.5	4.25	92	.287	.337	0	—	0	-3	-5	3	-0.1
Yr	13	14	.481	34	34	7	0	0	224²	258	25	53	80	12.6	4.53	88	.293	.335	0	—	0	-12	-14	3	-0.8
1978 Cal-A	3	5	.375	31	10	1	1	1	100	100	12	42	43	12.9	4.95	73	.262	.336	0	—	0	-13	-15	2	-1.2
1979 Min-A	0	0	—	9	0	0	0	0	12²	16	1	6	3	15.6	4.97	88	.320	.393	0	—	0	-1	-1	0	0.0
LA-N	4	3	.571	30	0	0	0	2	47	52	1	12	13	12.4	3.45	105	.277	.323	3	.273	1	1	1	2	0.4
1980 KC-A	0	0	—	8	0	0	0	1	13¹	8	0	5	4	9.5	0.00	—	.174	.269	0	—	0	6	6	0	0.6
1981 KC-A	1	1	.500	22	0	0	0	2	32¹	35	2	14	7	13.9	4.18	86	.282	.360	0	—	0	-2	-2	1	-0.1
Total 14	83	85	.494	349	184	51	8	11	1526¹	1490	127	562	807	12.2	3.93	93	.257	.325	91	.262	36	-47	-46	10	0.6
■ **MARV BREUER**								Breuer, Marvin Howard "Baby Face" b: 4/29/14, Rolla, Mo. BR/TR, 6'2", 185 lbs. Deb: 5/04/39																
1939 NY-A	0	0	—	1	0	0	0	0	1	2	0	1	0	27.0	9.00	48	.667	.750	0	—	0	-0	-1	0	0.0
1940 NY-A	8	9	.471	27	22	10	0	0	164	175	20	61	71	13.0	4.55	89	.267	.329	2	.037	-4	-3	-10	-1	-1.3
1941 *NY-A	9	7	.563	26	18	7	1	2	141	131	10	49	77	11.6	4.09	96	.243	.308	4	.087	-3	1	-2	-1	-0.5
1942 *NY-A	8	9	.471	27	19	6	0	1	164¹	157	11	37	72	10.7	3.07	112	.252	.295	3	.056	-3	11	7	-2	0.1
1943 NY-A	0	1	.000	5	1	0	0	0	14	22	0	6	6	18.0	8.36	39	.349	.406	1	.333	-0	-8	-8	0	-0.6
Total 5	25	26	.490	86	60	23	1	3	484¹	487	41	154	226	12.0	4.03	94	.258	.315	10	.064	-10	0	-13	-4	-2.3
■ **JIM BREWER**								Brewer, James Thomas b: 11/17/37, Merced, Cal. d: 11/16/87, Tyler, Tex. BL/TL, 6'1", 186 lbs. Deb: 7/17/60 C																
1960 Chi-N	0	3	.000	5	4	0	0	0	21²	25	2	6	7	13.3	5.82	65	.272	.323	1	.167	0	-5	-5	0	-0.3
1961 Chi-N	1	7	.125	36	11	0	0	0	86²	116	17	21	57	14.3	5.82	72	.321	.360	4	.182	0	-17	-16	-2	-1.6
1962 Chi-N	0	1	.000	6	1	0	0	0	5²	10	2	3	1	20.6	9.53	44	.435	.500	0	—	0	-4	-3	0	-0.2
1963 Chi-N	3	2	.600	29	1	0	0	0	49²	59	10	15	35	13.4	4.89	72	.294	.343	0	.000	0	-9	-8	-1	-0.8
1964 LA-N	4	3	.571	34	5	1	1	1	93	79	5	25	63	10.1	3.00	108	.232	.284	6	.273	2	6	2	-1	0.3
1965 *LA-N	3	2	.600	19	2	0	0	2	49¹	33	1	28	31	11.1	1.82	179	.196	.311	0	.000	-1	9	8	1	0.8
1966 *LA-N	0	2	.000	13	0	0	0	2	22	17	0	11	8	11.5	3.68	90	.221	.318	0	—	0	-1	0	0	0.0
1967 LA-N	5	4	.556	30	11	0	0	1	100²	78	8	31	74	9.8	2.68	116	.218	.283	1	.045	-1	8	5	-1	0.3
1968 LA-N	8	3	.727	54	0	0	0	14	76¹	59	5	33	75	10.8	2.48	112	.219	.304	2	.222	0	4	2	0	0.3
1969 LA-N	7	6	.538	59	0	0	0	20	88¹	71	5	41	92	11.8	2.55	131	.221	.317	1	.091	0	10	8	0	0.8
1970 LA-N	7	6	.538	58	0	0	0	24	89	66	10	33	91	10.0	3.13	122	.207	.281	1	.083	-0	9	7	-0	0.6
1971 LA-N	6	5	.545	55	0	0	0	22	81¹	55	4	24	66	8.7	1.88	172	.194	.257	3	.333	1	14	12	0	1.4
1972 LA-N	8	7	.533	51	0	0	0	17	78¹	41	6	25	69	7.8	1.26	264	.157	.236	0	.000	0	19	18	-0	2.0
1973 LA-N	6	8	.429	56	0	0	0	20	71²	58	8	25	56	10.4	3.01	114	.229	.299	2	.400	1	5	3	-0	0.4
1974 *LA-N	4	4	.500	24	0	0	0	0	39¹	29	5	10	26	8.9	2.52	135	.207	.260	0	.000	-0	5	4	-1	0.3
1975 LA-N	3	1	.750	21	0	0	0	2	33	44	2	12	21	15.5	5.18	66	.333	.393	0	.000	-0	-6	-7	0	-0.6
Cal-A	1	0	1.000	21	0	0	0	5	34²	38	2	11	22	12.7	1.82	195	.281	.336	0	—	0	8	7	0	0.6
1976 Cal-A	3	1	.750	13	0	0	0	2	20	20	0	6	16	11.7	2.70	123	.256	.310	0	—	0	2	1	0	0.1
Total 17	69	65	.515	584	35	1	1	132	1040²	898	92	360	810	11.0	3.07	111	.236	.303	21	.150	1	59	38	-5	4.3
■ **JACK BREWER**								Brewer, John Herndon "Buddy" b: 7/21/19, Los Angeles, Cal. BR/TR, 6'2", 170 lbs. Deb: 7/15/44																
1944 NY-N	1	4	.200	14	7	2	0	0	55	66	8	16	21	13.9	5.56	66	.288	.343	4	.211	0	-12	-12	-1	-1.1
1945 NY-N	8	6	.571	28	21	8	0	0	159²	162	14	58	49	12.6	3.83	102	.260	.326	10	.179	-1	1	1	-2	-0.1
1946 NY-N	0	0	—	1	0	0	0	0	2	3	0	2	3	22.5	13.50	35	.333	.455	0	—	0	-2	-2	0	-0.1
Total 3	9	10	.474	43	28	10	0	0	216²	231	22	76	73	13.0	4.36	88	.268	.332	14	.187	-1	-15	-12	-3	-1.3
■ **TOM BREWER**								Brewer, Thomas Austin b: 9/3/31, Wadesboro, S.C. BR/TR, 6'1", 175 lbs. Deb: 4/18/54																
1954 Bos-A	10	9	.526	33	23	7	0	0	162²	152	15	95	69	14.1	4.65	88	.249	.356	16	.267	3	-17	-10	-2	-0.7
1955 Bos-A	11	10	.524	31	28	9	2	0	192²	198	21	87	91	13.7	4.20	102	.263	.346	11	.151	-2	-5	2	3	0.3
1956 Bos-A	19	9	.679	32	32	15	4	0	244¹	200	14	112	127	11.7	3.50	132	.220	.309	28	.298	5	18	30	4	4.3
1957 Bos-A	16	13	.552	32	32	15	2	0	238¹	225	24	93	128	12.3	3.85	103	.250	.325	19	.202	-1	-2	4	6	0.9
1958 Bos-A	12	12	.500	33	32	10	1	0	227¹	227	21	93	124	13.0	3.72	108	.259	.335	16	.195	-0	1	7	4	1.2
1959 Bos-A	10	12	.455	36	32	11	3	2	215¹	219	14	88	121	13.2	3.76	108	.265	.338	8	.111	-4	2	7	4	0.8
1960 Bos-A	10	15	.400	34	29	8	1	1	186²	220	13	72	60	14.4	4.82	84	.301	.368	12	.194	-0	-20	-16	4	-1.1

YEAR	TM/L	W	L	PCT	G	GS	CG	SH	SV	IP	H	HR	BB	SO	RAT	ERA	ERA+	OAV	OOB	BH	AVG	PB	PR	/A	PD	TPI
1961	Bos-A	3	2	.600	10	9	0	0	0	42	37	4	29	13	14.1	3.43	122	.242	.363	4	.286	1	3	3	1	0.6
Total	8	91	82	.526	241	217	75	13	3	1509¹	1478	126	669	733	13.1	4.00	104	.257	.338	114	.207	2	-19	27	23	6.3

■ ALAN BRICE
Brice, Alan Healey b: 10/1/37, New York, N.Y. BR/TR, 6'5", 215 lbs. Deb: 9/22/61

YEAR	TM/L	W	L	PCT	G	GS	CG	SH	SV	IP	H	HR	BB	SO	RAT	ERA	ERA+	OAV	OOB	BH	AVG	PB	PR	/A	PD	TPI
1961	Chi-A	0	1	.000	3	0	0	0	0	3¹	4	0	3	3	18.9	0.00	—	.308	.438	0	—	0	1	1	0	0.1

■ RALPH BRICKNER
Brickner, Ralph Harold "Brick" b: 5/2/25, Cincinnati, Ohio BR/TR, 6'3.5", 215 lbs. Deb: 5/04/52

YEAR	TM/L	W	L	PCT	G	GS	CG	SH	SV	IP	H	HR	BB	SO	RAT	ERA	ERA+	OAV	OOB	BH	AVG	PB	PR	/A	PD	TPI
1952	Bos-A	3	1	.750	14	1	0	0	1	33	32	1	11	9	11.7	2.18	181	.264	.326	2	.250	0	5	6	-0	0.7

■ MARSHALL BRIDGES
Bridges, Marshall "Sheriff" b: 6/2/31, Jackson, Miss. d: 9/3/90, Jackson, Miss. BB/TL, 6'1", 165 lbs. Deb: 6/17/59

YEAR	TM/L	W	L	PCT	G	GS	CG	SH	SV	IP	H	HR	BB	SO	RAT	ERA	ERA+	OAV	OOB	BH	AVG	PB	PR	/A	PD	TPI
1959	StL-N	6	3	.667	27	4	1	0	1	76	67	10	37	76	12.3	4.26	99	.240	.329	5	.217	2	-3	-0	-2	0.0
1960	StL-N	2	2	.500	20	1	0	0	1	31¹	33	2	16	27	14.4	3.45	119	.266	.355	0	.000	-0	1	2	-0	0.1
	Cin-N	4	0	1.000	14	0	0	0	2	25¹	14	1	7	26	7.5	1.07	359	.161	.223	1	.250	0	8	8	-0	0.8
	Yr	6	2	.750	34	1	0	0	3	56²	47	3	23	53	11.1	2.38	167	.220	.295	2	.200	-0	9	10	-1	0.9
1961	Cin-N	0	1	.000	13	0	0	0	0	20²	26	4	11	17	16.5	7.84	52	.317	.404	0	.000	-0	-9	-9	-0	-0.8
1962	*NY-A	8	4	.667	52	0	0	0	18	71²	49	4	48	66	12.2	3.14	119	.194	.323	0	.000	-2	7	5	1	0.5
1963	NY-A	2	0	1.000	23	0	0	0	1	33	27	2	30	35	15.8	3.82	92	.237	.400	0	—	0	-1	-1	2	0.0
1964	Was-A	0	3	.000	17	0	0	0	2	30	37	3	17	16	16.2	5.70	65	.303	.388	0	.000	-0	-7	-7	0	-0.6
1965	Was-A	1	2	.333	40	0	0	0	0	57¹	62	3	25	39	13.7	2.67	130	.268	.340	1	.143	0	5	5	-0	0.6
Total	7	23	15	.605	206	5	1	0	25	345¹	315	29	191	302	13.3	3.75	102	.244	.343	7	.119	0	1	3	-0	0.6

■ TOMMY BRIDGES
Bridges, Thomas Jefferson Davis b: 12/28/06, Gordonsville, Tenn. d: 4/19/68, Nashville, Tenn. BR/TR, 5'10.5", 155 lbs. Deb: 8/13/30 C

YEAR	TM/L	W	L	PCT	G	GS	CG	SH	SV	IP	H	HR	BB	SO	RAT	ERA	ERA+	OAV	OOB	BH	AVG	PB	PR	/A	PD	TPI
1930	Det-A	3	2	.600	8	5	2	0	0	37²	28	4	23	17	12.2	4.06	118	.215	.333	3	.300	1	2	3	-0	0.3
1931	Det-A	8	16	.333	35	23	8	2	0	173	182	13	108	105	15.1	4.99	92	.263	.363	8	.148	-2	-12	-8	-2	-1.0
1932	Det-A	14	12	.538	34	26	10	4	1	201	174	14	119	108	13.2	3.36	140	.233	.339	11	.164	-1	25	30	-2	2.7
1933	Det-A	14	12	.538	33	28	17	2	2	233	192	8	110	120	11.9	3.09	140	**.226**	.319	16	.205	2	31	32	0	3.4
1934	*Det-A	22	11	.667	36	35	23	3	1	275	249	16	104	151	11.7	3.67	120	.241	.312	12	.122	-4	25	22	-2	1.5
1935	*Det-A	21	10	.677	36	34	23	4	1	274¹	277	22	113	**163**	12.9	3.51	119	.259	.332	26	.239	3	29	20	-2	1.9
1936	Det-A	**23**	11	.676	39	38	26	5	0	294²	289	21	115	**175**	12.5	3.60	137	.255	.326	25	.212	0	47	44	1	4.2
1937	Det-A	15	12	.556	34	31	18	3	0	245¹	267	15	91	138	13.2	4.07	115	.274	.338	23	.240	1	15	16	0	1.8
1938	Det-A	13	9	.591	25	20	13	0	1	151	171	14	58	101	13.8	4.59	109	.287	.353	7	.130	-1	3	7	-2	0.4
1939	Det-A	17	7	.708	29	26	16	2	2	198	186	11	61	129	11.5	3.50	140	.243	.304	14	.197	0	25	31	-1	2.9
1940	*Det-A	12	9	.571	29	28	12	2	0	197²	171	11	88	133	11.8	3.37	141	.229	.311	12	.176	-2	22	30	-1	2.8
1941	Det-A	9	12	.429	25	22	10	1	0	147²	128	9	70	102	12.1	3.41	133	.233	.320	4	.085	-3	12	19	2	1.8
1942	Det-A	9	7	.563	23	22	11	2	1	174	164	6	61	97	11.8	2.74	144	.246	.313	6	.095	-3	18	23	0	2.4
1943	Det-A	12	7	.632	25	22	11	3	0	191²	159	9	61	124	10.3	2.39	147	.226	.287	14	.219	2	19	24	-1	2.9
1945	*Det-A	1	0	1.000	4	1	0	0	0	11	14	2	2	6	13.1	3.27	107	.311	.340	0	.000	-0	0	0	1	0.0
1946	Det-A	1	1	.500	9	1	0	0	1	21¹	24	5	8	17	13.9	5.91	62	.279	.347	0	.000	0	-6	-5	0	-0.4
Total	16	194	138	.584	424	362	200	33	10	2826¹	2675	181	1192	1674	12.4	3.57	126	.248	.325	181	.180	-6	256	291	-10	27.6

■ BUTTONS BRIGGS
Briggs, Herbert Theodore b: 7/8/1875, Poughkeepsie, N.Y. d: 2/18/11, Cleveland, Ohio BR/TR, 6'1", 180 lbs. Deb: 4/23/1896

YEAR	TM/L	W	L	PCT	G	GS	CG	SH	SV	IP	H	HR	BB	SO	RAT	ERA	ERA+	OAV	OOB	BH	AVG	PB	PR	/A	PD	TPI
1896	Chi-N	12	8	.600	26	21	19	0	1	194	202	6	108	84	14.4	4.31	105	.266	.358	10	.128	-6	1	5	-4	-0.3
1897	Chi-N	4	17	.190	22	22	21	0	0	186²	246	6	85	60	16.0	5.26	85	.315	.382	13	.160	-6	-20	-16	-1	-1.8
1898	Chi-N	1	3	.250	4	4	3	0	0	30	38	0	10	14	14.4	5.70	63	.306	.358	6	.429	2	-7	-7	-0	-0.4
1904	Chi-N	19	11	.633	34	30	28	3	3	277	252	2	77	112	10.9	2.05	130	.246	.304	16	.170	-0	21	19	-3	1.6
1905	Chi-N	8	8	.500	20	20	13	5	0	168	141	1	52	68	10.7	2.14	139	.237	.304	3	.053	-4	16	16	-2	1.0
Total	5	44	47	.484	106	97	84	8	4	855²	879	15	332	338	12.9	3.41	104	.268	.337	48	.148	-14	12	14	-10	0.1

■ JOHN BRIGGS
Briggs, Jonathan Tift b: 1/24/34, Natoma, Cal. BR/TR, 5'10", 175 lbs. Deb: 4/17/56

YEAR	TM/L	W	L	PCT	G	GS	CG	SH	SV	IP	H	HR	BB	SO	RAT	ERA	ERA+	OAV	OOB	BH	AVG	PB	PR	/A	PD	TPI
1956	Chi-N	0	0	—	3	0	0	0	0	5¹	5	1	4	1	20.3	1.69	223	.238	.429	0	—	0	1	1	0	0.1
1957	Chi-N	0	1	.000	3	0	0	0	0	4¹	7	2	3	1	20.8	12.46	31	.368	.455	0	—	0	-4	-4	-0	-0.3
1958	Chi-N	5	5	.500	20	17	3	1	0	95²	99	12	45	46	13.6	4.52	87	.270	.352	9	.257	-2	-6	-6	-1	-0.4
1959	Cle-A	0	1	.000	4	1	0	0	0	12²	12	1	3	5	10.7	2.13	173	.245	.288	0	.000	-0	2	2	0	0.2
1960	Cle-A	4	2	.667	21	2	0	0	1	36¹	32	4	15	19	11.9	4.46	84	.250	.333	1	.125	-0	-2	-3	-1	-0.3
	KC-A	2	2	.000	8	1	0	0	0	11¹	19	3	12	8	24.6	12.71	30	.380	.500	0	.000	-0	-11	-11	-0	-1.0
	Yr	4	4	.500	29	3	0	0	1	47²	51	7	27	27	14.7	6.42	59	.282	.375	0	.000	-1	-13	-14	-1	-1.3
Total	5	9	11	.450	59	21	3	1	1	165²	174	23	82	80	14.2	5.00	77	.275	.363	10	.208	1	-20	-21	-2	-1.7

■ NELSON BRILES
Briles, Nelson Kelley b: 8/5/43, Dorris, Cal. BR/TR, 5'11", 195 lbs. Deb: 4/19/65

YEAR	TM/L	W	L	PCT	G	GS	CG	SH	SV	IP	H	HR	BB	SO	RAT	ERA	ERA+	OAV	OOB	BH	AVG	PB	PR	/A	PD	TPI
1965	StL-N	3	3	.500	37	2	0	0	4	82¹	79	4	26	52	12.1	3.50	110	.258	.328	2	.133	-0	0	3	-1	0.2
1966	StL-N	4	15	.211	49	17	0	0	6	154	162	14	54	100	13.0	3.21	112	.279	.348	3	.079	-2	7	6	1	0.6
1967	*StL-N	14	5	.737	49	14	4	2	6	155¹	139	8	40	94	10.7	2.43	135	.236	.290	6	.150	0	16	15	-2	1.5
1968	*StL-N	19	11	.633	33	33	13	4	0	243²	251	18	55	141	11.6	2.81	103	.266	.311	11	.138	1	5	2	-2	0.1
1969	StL-N	15	13	.536	36	33	10	3	0	227²	218	17	63	126	11.2	3.52	102	.251	.303	8	.105	-1	2	1	-0	0.0
1970	StL-N	6	7	.462	30	19	1	1	0	106²	129	14	36	59	14.1	6.24	66	.297	.353	5	.179	1	-26	-25	-2	-2.3
1971	*Pit-N	8	4	.667	37	14	4	2	1	136	131	12	35	76	11.2	3.04	111	.250	.301	10	.256	4	6	5	-1	0.9
1972	*Pit-N	14	11	.560	28	27	9	2	0	195²	185	14	43	120	10.5	3.08	108	.249	.291	11	.157	-0	8	5	-0	0.5
1973	Pit-N	14	13	.519	33	33	7	1	0	218²	201	19	51	94	10.4	2.84	124	.244	.288	14	.194	3	20	16	1	2.1
1974	KC-A	5	7	.417	18	17	3	0	0	103	118	9	21	41	12.3	4.02	95	.293	.331	0	—	0	-5	-5	-2	-0.2
1975	KC-A	6	6	.500	24	16	3	0	2	112	127	6	19	73	12.6	4.26	90	.285	.330	0	—	0	-6	-5	-0	-0.4
1976	Tex-A	11	9	.550	32	31	7	1	1	210	224	17	47	98	11.7	3.26	110	.273	.314	0	—	0	6	8	-3	0.5
1977	Tex-A	6	4	.600	28	15	2	1	1	108¹	114	13	30	57	12.5	4.24	96	.275	.333	0	—	0	-2	-2	-1	-0.2
	Bal-A	0	0	—	2	0	0	0	0	4	5	2	0	2	11.3	6.75	56	.294	.294	0	—	0	-1	-1	-0	0.0
	Yr	6	4	.600	30	15	2	1	2	112¹	119	15	30	59	11.9	4.33	94	.271	.318	0	—	0	-3	-3	-1	-0.2
1978	Bal-A	4	4	.500	30	8	1	0	0	54¹	56	6	21	30	13.4	4.64	75	.279	.351	0	—	0	-5	-7	-1	-0.7
Total	14	129	112	.535	452	279	64	17	22	2111²	2141	186	547	1163	11.7	3.44	102	.264	.314	72	.154	5	25	19	-11	2.6

■ FRANK BRILL
Brill, Francis Hasbrouck (b: Francis Hasbrouck Briell) b: 3/30/1864, Astoria, L.I., N.Y. d: 11/19/44, Flushing, N.Y. BR/TR, 5'8", 155 lbs. Deb: 6/23/1884

YEAR	TM/L	W	L	PCT	G	GS	CG	SH	SV	IP	H	HR	BB	SO	RAT	ERA	ERA+	OAV	OOB	BH	AVG	PB	PR	/A	PD	TPI
1884	Det-N	2	10	.167	12	12	12	1	0	103	148	7	26	18	15.2	5.50	53	.320	.356	6	.136	-3	-29	-30	-1	-2.6

■ JIM BRILLHEART
Brillheart, James Benson b: 9/28/03, Dublin, Va. d: 9/2/72, Radford, Va. BR/TL, 5'11", 170 lbs. Deb: 4/17/22

YEAR	TM/L	W	L	PCT	G	GS	CG	SH	SV	IP	H	HR	BB	SO	RAT	ERA	ERA+	OAV	OOB	BH	AVG	PB	PR	/A	PD	TPI
1922	Was-A	4	6	.400	31	10	3	0	1	119²	120	3	72	47	15.0	3.61	107	.275	.388	3	.083	-3	6	3	-2	-0.1
1923	Was-A	0	1	.000	12	0	0	0	0	18	27	1	12	8	20.0	7.00	54	.360	.455	0	.000	-0	-6	-6	-0	-0.5
1927	Chi-N	4	2	.667	32	12	4	0	0	128²	140	4	38	36	12.7	4.13	94	.286	.343	1	.023	-5	-3	-4	-1	-0.9
1931	Bos-A	0	0	—	11	1	0	0	0	19²	27	2	15	7	19.2	5.49	78	.325	.429	2	.500	2	-2	-3	1	0.0
Total	4	8	9	.471	86	23	7	0	1	286	314	10	137	98	14.6	4.19	93	.290	.376	6	.070	-8	-6	-9	-2	-1.5

■ LOU BRISSIE
Brissie, Leland Victor b: 6/5/24, Anderson, S.C. BL/TL, 6'4.5", 210 lbs. Deb: 9/28/47

YEAR	TM/L	W	L	PCT	G	GS	CG	SH	SV	IP	H	HR	BB	SO	RAT	ERA	ERA+	OAV	OOB	BH	AVG	PB	PR	/A	PD	TPI
1947	Phi-A	0	1	.000	1	1	0	0	0	7	9	1	5	4	18.0	6.43	59	.310	.412	0	.000	-0	-2	-2	0	-0.1
1948	Phi-A	14	10	.583	39	25	11	0	5	194	202	6	95	127	13.9	4.13	104	.269	.352	18	.237	0	3	3	-3	0.1
1949	Phi-A	16	11	.593	34	29	18	0	3	229¹	220	20	118	118	13.5	4.28	96	.251	.344	24	.267	3	-2	-4	-5	-0.5
1950	Phi-A	7	19	.269	46	31	15	2	8	246	237	22	117	101	13.1	4.02	113	.253	.338	15	.172	-3	15	14	-1	1.0
1951	Phi-A	0	2	.000	2	2	0	0	0	13¹	20	0	4	3	18.9	6.75	63	.357	.438	1	.200	-0	-4	-4	-0	-0.3
	Cle-A	4	3	.571	54	4	1	0	9	112¹	90	5	61	50	12.3	3.20	118	.223	.329	6	.261	0	11	7	-2	0.6

YEAR	TM/L	W	L	PCT	G	GS	CG	SH	SV	IP	H	HR	BB	SO	RAT	ERA	ERA+	OAV	OOB	BH	AVG	PB	PR	/A	PD	TPI
	Yr	4	5	.444	56	6	1	0	9	125²	110	5	69	53	13.0	3.58	107	.239	.342	0	.000	0	8	4	-2	0.3
1952	Cle-A	3	2	.600	42	1	0	0	2	82²	68	5	34	28	11.1	3.48	96	.221	.299	3	.250	1	2	-1	1	0.0
1953	Cle-A	0	0	—	16	0	0	0	2	13	21	2	13	5	23.5	7.62	49	.389	.507	0	—	0	-5	-6	0	-0.5
Total 7		44	48	.478	234	93	45	2	29	897²	867	61	451	436	13.4	4.07	102	.254	.343	67	.227	1	19	8	-8	0.3

■ JIM BRITT   Britt, James Edward b: 2/25/1856, Brooklyn, N.Y. d: 2/28/23, San Francisco, Cal   Deb: 5/02/1872

YEAR	TM/L	W	L	PCT	G	GS	CG	SH	SV	IP	H	HR	BB	SO	RAT	ERA	ERA+	OAV	OOB	BH	AVG	PB	PR	/A	PD	TPI
1872	Atl-n	9	28	.243	37	37	37	0	0	336	561	6	17		15.5	5.06	91	.323	.330	39	.248	-8	-50	-17		-1.1
1873	Atl-n	17	36	.321	54	54	51	1	0	481	694	5	38		13.7	3.89	86	.299	.310	46	.193	-3	-16	-29		-2.3
Total 2 n		26	64	.289	91	91	88	1	0	817	1255	11	55		14.4	4.37	77	.309	.318	85	.215	-11	-70	-92		-3.4

■ JACK BRITTIN   Brittin, John Albert b: 3/4/24, Athens, Ill. BR/TR, 5'11", 175 lbs. Deb: 9/15/50

YEAR	TM/L	W	L	PCT	G	GS	CG	SH	SV	IP	H	HR	BB	SO	RAT	ERA	ERA+	OAV	OOB	BH	AVG	PB	PR	/A	PD	TPI
1950	Phi-N	0	0	—	3	0	0	0	0	4	2	0	3	3	11.3	4.50	90	.143	.294	0	—	0	-0	-0	0	0.0
1951	Phi-N	0	0	—	3	0	0	0	0	4	5	0	6	3	24.8	9.00	43	.294	.478	0	—	0	-2	-2	0	-0.1
Total 2		0	0	—	6	0	0	0	0	8	7	0	9	6	18.0	6.75	58	.226	.400	0	—	0	-2	-2	0	-0.1

■ JIM BRITTON   Britton, James Allan b: 3/25/44, N.Tonawanda, N.Y. BR/TR, 6'5", 225 lbs. Deb: 9/20/67

YEAR	TM/L	W	L	PCT	G	GS	CG	SH	SV	IP	H	HR	BB	SO	RAT	ERA	ERA+	OAV	OOB	BH	AVG	PB	PR	/A	PD	TPI
1967	Atl-N	0	2	.000	2	2	0	0	0	13¹	15	2	2	4	11.5	6.08	55	.278	.304	0	.000	-0	-4	-4	-0	-0.3
1968	Atl-N	4	6	.400	34	9	2	2	3	90	81	1	34	61	11.7	3.10	97	.245	.320	3	.143	-0	-1	-1	0	-0.1
1969	*Atl-N	7	5	.583	24	13	2	1	1	88	69	10	49	60	12.1	3.78	95	.218	.323	4	.190	0	-2	-2	-1	-0.2
1971	Mon-N	2	3	.400	16	6	0	0	0	45²	49	10	27	23	15.4	5.72	62	.274	.375	0	.000	-1	-11	-11	-1	-1.2
Total 4		13	16	.448	76	30	4	3	4	237	214	23	112	148	12.5	4.03	83	.243	.332	7	.127	-2	-18	-18	-2	-1.8

■ TONY BRIZZOLARA   Brizzolara, Anthony John b: 1/14/57, Santa Monica, Cal. BR/TR, 6'5", 215 lbs. Deb: 5/19/79

YEAR	TM/L	W	L	PCT	G	GS	CG	SH	SV	IP	H	HR	BB	SO	RAT	ERA	ERA+	OAV	OOB	BH	AVG	PB	PR	/A	PD	TPI
1979	Atl-N	6	9	.400	20	19	2	0	0	107¹	133	6	33	64	14.2	5.28	77	.303	.356	1	.029	-3	-18	-15	0	-1.6
1983	Atl-N	1	0	1.000	14	0	0	0	1	20¹	22	2	6	17	12.4	3.54	109	.278	.329	0	—	0	1	-0	0	0.0
1984	Atl-N	1	2	.333	10	4	0	0	0	29	33	4	13	17	14.3	5.28	73	.284	.357	0	.000	-1	-5	-5	-0	-0.4
Total 3		8	11	.421	44	23	2	0	1	156²	188	12	52	98	14.0	5.06	79	.297	.353	1	.024	-4	-24	-19	-0	-2.0

■ JOHNNY BROACA   Broaca, John Joseph b: 10/3/09, Lawrence, Mass. d: 5/16/85, Lawrence, Mass. BR/TR, 5'11", 190 lbs. Deb: 6/02/34

YEAR	TM/L	W	L	PCT	G	GS	CG	SH	SV	IP	H	HR	BB	SO	RAT	ERA	ERA+	OAV	OOB	BH	AVG	PB	PR	/A	PD	TPI
1934	NY-A	12	9	.571	26	24	13	1	0	177¹	203	9	65	74	13.7	4.16	98	.284	.344	2	.030	-6	7	-2	-2	-0.9
1935	NY-A	15	7	.682	29	27	14	2	0	201	199	16	79	78	12.4	3.58	113	.254	.323	12	.150	-4	19	10	-2	0.3
1936	NY-A	12	7	.632	37	27	12	1	3	206	235	16	66	84	13.2	4.24	110	.284	.337	9	.110	-6	18	10	-2	0.0
1937	NY-A	1	4	.200	7	6	3	0	0	44	58	5	17	9	15.3	4.70	94	.324	.383	0	.000	-2	-0	-1	-1	-0.3
1939	Cle-A	4	2	.667	22	2	0	0	0	46	53	5	28	13	15.8	4.70	94	.288	.382	0	.000	-1	-0	-1	0	-0.2
Total 5		44	29	.603	121	86	42	4	3	674¹	748	51	255	258	13.4	4.08	105	.278	.341	23	.091	-19	44	15	-7	-1.1

■ PETE BROBERG   Broberg, Peter Sven b: 3/2/50, W.Palm Beach, Fla. BR/TR, 6'3", 205 lbs. Deb: 6/20/71

YEAR	TM/L	W	L	PCT	G	GS	CG	SH	SV	IP	H	HR	BB	SO	RAT	ERA	ERA+	OAV	OOB	BH	AVG	PB	PR	/A	PD	TPI
1971	Was-A	5	9	.357	18	18	7	1	0	124²	104	10	53	89	12.1	3.47	95	.228	.322	5	.114	0	-0	-2	-1	-0.3
1972	Tex-A	5	12	.294	39	25	3	2	1	176¹	153	14	85	133	12.8	4.29	70	.237	.338	4	.078	-2	-24	-25	1	-2.8
1973	Tex-A	5	9	.357	22	20	6	1	0	118²	130	8	66	57	15.2	5.61	66	.283	.379	0	—	0	-24	-25	0	-2.3
1974	Tex-A	0	4	.000	12	2	0	0	0	29	29	7	13	15	13.3	8.07	44	.264	.347	0	—	0	-14	-15	0	-1.3
1975	Mil-A	14	16	.467	38	32	7	2	0	220¹	219	17	106	100	13.9	4.13	93	.263	.357	0	—	0	-9	-7	0	-0.6
1976	Mil-A	1	7	.125	20	11	1	0	0	92¹	99	5	72	28	17.1	4.97	70	.281	.409	0	—	0	-15	-15	-1	-1.5
1977	Chi-N	1	2	.333	22	0	0	0	0	36	34	8	18	20	13.0	4.75	92	.256	.344	0	.000	-1	-3	-1	0	-0.1
1978	Oak-A	10	12	.455	35	26	2	0	0	165²	174	16	65	94	13.1	4.62	79	.269	.338	0	—	0	-16	-18	1	-1.6
Total 8		41	71	.366	206	134	26	6	1	963	942	85	478	536	13.8	4.56	78	.259	.353	9	.089	-3	-105	-109	0	-10.5

■ LEW BROCKETT   Brockett, Lewis Albert "King" b: 7/23/1880, Brownsville, Ill. d: 9/19/60, Norris City, Ill. TR , 5'10.5", 168 lbs. Deb: 4/25/07

YEAR	TM/L	W	L	PCT	G	GS	CG	SH	SV	IP	H	HR	BB	SO	RAT	ERA	ERA+	OAV	OOB	BH	AVG	PB	PR	/A	PD	TPI
1907	NY-A	1	2	.333	8	4	1	0	0	46¹	58	1	26	13	16.3	6.22	45	.308	.392	4	.182	-1	-19	-18	-1	-1.7
1909	NY-A	10	8	.556	26	18	10	3	1	170	148	3	59	70	11.3	2.12	119	.245	.318	17	.283	3	7	8	4	1.8
1911	NY-A	2	4	.333	16	8	2	0	0	75¹	73	3	39	25	14.0	4.66	77	.256	.356	12	.308	2	-11	-9	1	-0.4
Total 3		13	14	.481	50	30	13	3	1	291²	279	7	124	108	12.8	3.43	83	.259	.341	33	.273	5	-23	-19	4	-0.3

■ DICK BRODOWSKI   Brodowski, Richard Stanley b: 7/26/32, Bayonne, N.J. BR/TR, 6'1", 182 lbs. Deb: 6/15/52

YEAR	TM/L	W	L	PCT	G	GS	CG	SH	SV	IP	H	HR	BB	SO	RAT	ERA	ERA+	OAV	OOB	BH	AVG	PB	PR	/A	PD	TPI
1952	Bos-A	5	5	.500	20	12	4	0	0	114²	111	12	50	42	12.9	4.40	90	.252	.333	8	.205	1	-9	-6	0	-0.3
1955	Bos-A	1	0	1.000	16	0	0	0	0	32	36	5	25	10	17.4	5.63	76	.295	.419	5	.500	3	-6	-5	1	0.0
1956	Was-A	0	3	.000	7	3	1	0	0	17²	31	5	12	8	21.9	9.17	47	.397	.478	0	.000	-1	-10	-10	0	-0.8
1957	Was-A	0	1	.000	6	0	0	0	0	11¹	12	2	10	4	18.3	11.12	35	.261	.404	0	.000	-0	-9	-9	0	-0.8
1958	Cle-A	1	0	1.000	5	0	0	0	0	10	3	0	6	12	8.1	0.00	—	.100	.250	0	.000	-0	4	4	-0	0.4
1959	Cle-A	2	2	.500	18	0	0	0	5	30	19	3	21	9	12.9	1.80	205	.181	.333	2	.333	0	7	6	-0	0.7
Total 6		9	11	.450	72	15	5	0	5	215²	212	27	124	85	14.4	4.76	84	.258	.361	15	.242	3	-23	-19	1	-0.8

■ ERNIE BROGLIO   Broglio, Ernest Gilbert b: 8/27/35, Berkeley, Cal. BR/TR, 6'2", 200 lbs. Deb: 4/11/59

YEAR	TM/L	W	L	PCT	G	GS	CG	SH	SV	IP	H	HR	BB	SO	RAT	ERA	ERA+	OAV	OOB	BH	AVG	PB	PR	/A	PD	TPI
1959	StL-N	7	12	.368	35	25	6	3	0	181¹	174	20	89	133	13.1	4.72	90	.250	.335	6	.098	-3	-15	-10	1	-1.0
1960	StL-N	21	9	.700	52	24	9	3	0	226¹	172	18	100	188	10.9	2.74	149	.213	.301	14	.206	3	26	34	0	4.1
1961	StL-N	9	12	.429	29	26	7	2	0	174²	166	19	75	113	12.5	4.12	107	.248	.325	9	.145	-2	-2	5	-1	0.3
1962	StL-N	12	9	.571	34	30	11	4	0	222¹	193	22	93	132	11.7	3.00	143	.237	.316	10	.139	-2	23	31	1	3.2
1963	StL-N	18	8	.692	39	35	11	5	0	250	202	24	90	145	10.7	2.99	119	.216	.287	10	.112	-3	8	16	0	1.6
1964	StL-N	3	5	.375	11	11	3	1	0	69¹	65	7	26	56	11.9	3.50	109	.247	.317	2	.095	-0	0	2	-0	0.2
	Chi-N	4	7	.364	18	16	3	0	1	100¹	111	12	30	46	12.6	4.04	92	.281	.332	10	.286	3	-6	-4	-1	-0.1
	Yr	7	12	.368	29	27	6	1	1	169²	176	19	56	82	12.3	3.82	98	.267	.324	3	.054	-5	-1	-1	-1	0.1
1965	Chi-N	1	6	.143	26	6	0	0	0	50²	63	7	46	22	19.4	6.93	53	.313	.441	0	.000	-0	-19	-18	-1	-1.8
1966	Chi-N	2	6	.250	15	11	2	0	1	62¹	70	14	38	34	15.6	6.35	58	.290	.387	7	.368	3	-19	-19	2	-1.3
Total 8		77	74	.510	259	184	52	18	2	1337¹	1216	143	587	849	12.2	3.74	107	.242	.322	68	.158	-2	-3	39	1	5.2

■ KEN BRONDELL   Brondell, Kenneth Leroy b: 10/17/21, Bradshaw, Neb. BR/TR, 6'1", 195 lbs. Deb: 5/03/44

YEAR	TM/L	W	L	PCT	G	GS	CG	SH	SV	IP	H	HR	BB	SO	RAT	ERA	ERA+	OAV	OOB	BH	AVG	PB	PR	/A	PD	TPI
1944	NY-N	0	1	.000	7	2	1	0	0	19	27	3	8	1	16.3	8.38	44	.329	.389	0	.000	-1	-10	-10	-0	-0.9

■ JIM BRONSTAD   Bronstad, James Warren b: 6/22/36, Ft.Worth, Tex. BR/TR, 6'3", 196 lbs. Deb: 6/07/59

YEAR	TM/L	W	L	PCT	G	GS	CG	SH	SV	IP	H	HR	BB	SO	RAT	ERA	ERA+	OAV	OOB	BH	AVG	PB	PR	/A	PD	TPI
1959	NY-A	0	3	.000	16	3	0	0	2	29¹	34	2	13	14	14.7	5.22	70	.288	.364	0	.000	-0	-4	-5	0	-0.4
1963	Was-A	1	3	.250	25	0	0	0	1	57¹	66	9	22	22	14.0	5.65	66	.297	.363	0	.000	-1	-13	-12	2	-1.2
1964	Was-A	0	1	.000	4	0	0	0	0	7	10	0	2	9	15.4	5.14	72	.345	.387	0	—	0	-1	-1	-0	0.0
Total 3		1	7	.125	45	3	0	0	3	93²	110	11	37	45	14.3	5.48	67	.298	.365	0	.000	-2	-18	-19	2	-1.6

■ IKE BROOKENS   Brookens, Edward Dwain b: 1/3/49, Chambersburg, Pa. BR/TR, 6'5", 170 lbs. Deb: 6/17/75

YEAR	TM/L	W	L	PCT	G	GS	CG	SH	SV	IP	H	HR	BB	SO	RAT	ERA	ERA+	OAV	OOB	BH	AVG	PB	PR	/A	PD	TPI
1975	Det-A	0	0	—	3	0	0	0	0	10¹	11	3	5	8	14.8	5.23	77	.282	.378	0	—	0	-2	-1	0	0.0

■ HARRY BROOKS   Brooks, Harry Frank b: 11/30/1865, Philadelphia d: 12/5/45, Philadelphia, Pa. Deb: 7/24/1886 ♦

YEAR	TM/L	W	L	PCT	G	GS	CG	SH	SV	IP	H	HR	BB	SO	RAT	ERA	ERA+	OAV	OOB	BH	AVG	PB	PR	/A	PD	TPI
1886	NY-a	0	1	.000	1	1	0	0	0	7	9	0	2	0	49.5	36.00	9	.598	.645	0	.000	-0	-7	-7	0	-0.4

■ JIM BROSNAN   Brosnan, James Patrick b: 10/24/29, Cincinnati, O. BR/TR, 6'4", 197 lbs. Deb: 4/15/54

YEAR	TM/L	W	L	PCT	G	GS	CG	SH	SV	IP	H	HR	BB	SO	RAT	ERA	ERA+	OAV	OOB	BH	AVG	PB	PR	/A	PD	TPI
1954	Chi-N	1	0	1.000	18	0	0	0	0	33¹	44	9	18	17	17.0	9.45	44	.331	.414	1	.125	-0	-20	-19	1	-1.7
1956	Chi-N	5	9	.357	30	10	1	1	1	95	95	9	45	51	13.3	3.79	100	.270	.353	4	.182	-0	-0	-0	-1	0.0
1957	Chi-N	5	5	.500	41	5	1	0	0	98²	79	11	46	73	11.5	3.38	115	.219	.310	5	.250	2	6	5	0	0.8
1958	Chi-N	3	4	.429	8	8	2	0	0	51²	41	3	29	24	12.2	3.14	125	.225	.332	2	.105	-1	5	4	1	0.5
	StL-N	8	4	.667	33	12	2	0	7	115	107	10	50	65	12.4	3.44	120	.250	.330	3	.097	-1	6	9	0	0.8

YEAR TM/L	W	L	PCT	G	GS	CG	SH	SV	IP	H	HR	BB	SO	RAT	ERA	ERA+	OAV	OOB	BH	AVG	PB	PR	/A	PD	TPI
Yr	11	8	.579	41	20	4	0	7	166^2	148	13	79	89	12.3	3.35	121	.241	.329	3	.060	-2	11	13	1	1.3
1959 StL-N	1	3	.250	20	1	0	0	2	33	34	5	15	18	13.6	4.91	86	.276	.360	2	.286	1	-4	-2	1	0.0
Cin-N	8	3	.727	26	9	1	1	2	83^1	79	7	26	56	11.9	3.35	121	.248	.314	1	.043	-2	6	7	0	0.5
Yr	9	6	.600	46	10	1	1	4	116^1	113	12	41	74	12.3	3.79	108	.255	.324	1	.033	-1	2	4	1	0.5
1960 Cin-N	7	2	.778	57	2	0	0	12	99	79	4	22	62	9.2	2.36	162	.225	.271	3	.200	2	15	16	-0	1.8
1961 *Cin-N	10	4	.714	53	0	0	0	16	80	77	7	18	40	10.7	3.04	134	.249	.291	2	.154	-0	9	9	1	1.0
1962 Cin-N	4	4	.500	48	0	0	0	13	64^2	76	6	18	51	13.1	3.34	120	.292	.338	0	.000	-1	4	5	-1	0.4
1963 Cin-N	0	1	.000	6	0	0	0	0	4^2	8	2	3	4	21.2	7.71	43	.421	.500	0	—	0	-2	-2	0	-0.1
Chi-A	3	8	.273	45	0	0	0	14	73	71	7	22	46	11.5	2.84	124	.263	.318	4	.308	1	6	5	-0	0.6
Total 9	55	47	.539	385	47	7	2	67	831^1	790	80	312	507	12.0	3.54	111	.254	.324	27	.153	1	31	36	4	4.6

■ FRANK BROSSEAU
Brosseau, Franklin Lee b: 7/31/44, Drayton, N.D. BR/TR, 6'1", 180 lbs. Deb: 9/10/69

YEAR TM/L	W	L	PCT	G	GS	CG	SH	SV	IP	H	HR	BB	SO	RAT	ERA	ERA+	OAV	OOB	BH	AVG	PB	PR	/A	PD	TPI
1969 Pit-N	0	0	—	2	0	0	0	0	1^2	2	0	2	2	21.6	10.80	32	.286	.444	0	—	0	-1	-1	0	0.0
1971 Pit-N	0	0	—	1	0	0	0	0	2	1	0	0	4	4.5	0.00	—	.200	.200	0	—	0	1	1	0	0.1
Total 2	0	0	—	3	0	0	0	0	3^2	3	0	2	2	12.3	4.91	70	.250	.357	0	—	0	-1	-1	0	0.1

■ DAN BROUTHERS
Brouthers, Dennis Joseph "Big Dan" b: 5/8/1858, Sylvan Lake, N.Y. d: 8/2/32, E.Orange, N.J. BL/TL, 6'2", 207 lbs. Deb: 6/23/1879 H◆

YEAR TM/L	W	L	PCT	G	GS	CG	SH	SV	IP	H	HR	BB	SO	RAT	ERA	ERA+	OAV	OOB	BH	AVG	PB	PR	/A	PD	TPI
1879 Tro-N	0	2	.000	3	2	2	0	0	21	35	0	8	6	18.4	5.57	45	.349	.398	46	.274	1	-7	-7	-1	-0.5
1883 Buf-N	0	0	—	1	0	0	0	0	2	9	0	3	2	54.0	31.50	10	.594	.661	159	.374	1	-6	-6	0	-0.3
Total 2	0	2	.000	4	2	2	0	0	23	44	0	11	8	21.5	7.83	33	.382	.435	2296	.342	1	-13	-13	-1	-0.8

■ FRANK BROWER
Brower, Frank Willard "Turkeyfoot" b: 3/26/1893, Gainesville, Va. d: 11/20/60, Baltimore, Md. BL/TR, 6'2", 180 lbs. Deb: 8/14/20 ◆

YEAR TM/L	W	L	PCT	G	GS	CG	SH	SV	IP	H	HR	BB	SO	RAT	ERA	ERA+	OAV	OOB	BH	AVG	PB	PR	/A	PD	TPI
1924 Cle-A	0	0	—	4	0	0	0	0	9^2	7	0	4	0	11.2	0.93	459	.212	.316	30	.280	1	4	4	-0	0.4

■ ALTON BROWN
Brown, Alton Leo "Deacon" b: 4/16/25, Norfolk, Va. BR/TR, 6'2", 195 lbs. Deb: 4/21/51

YEAR TM/L	W	L	PCT	G	GS	CG	SH	SV	IP	H	HR	BB	SO	RAT	ERA	ERA+	OAV	OOB	BH	AVG	PB	PR	/A	PD	TPI
1951 Was-A	0	0	—	7	0	0	0	0	11^2	14	1	12	7	20.8	9.26	44	.298	.450	0	.000	-0	-7	-7	-0	-0.6

■ BOARDWALK BROWN
Brown, Carroll William b: 2/20/1887, Woodbury, N.J. d: 2/8/77, Burlington, N.J. BR/TR, 6'1.5", 178 lbs. Deb: 9/27/11

YEAR TM/L	W	L	PCT	G	GS	CG	SH	SV	IP	H	HR	BB	SO	RAT	ERA	ERA+	OAV	OOB	BH	AVG	PB	PR	/A	PD	TPI
1911 Phi-A	0	1	.000	2	1	1	0	0	12	12	0	2	6	10.5	4.50	70	.267	.298	0	.000	-1	-2	-2	0	-0.1
1912 Phi-A	13	11	.542	34	24	15	3	0	199	204	2	87	64	13.6	3.66	84	.283	.367	11	.145	-3	-8	-13	3	-1.2
1913 Phi-A	17	11	.607	43	35	11	3	1	235^1	200	6	87	70	11.4	2.94	94	.219	.294	13	.159	-1	-0	-5	-1	-0.7
1914 Phi-A	1	6	.143	15	8	2	0	0	66	64	1	26	20	12.3	4.09	64	.268	.340	0	.000	-2	-10	-11	0	-1.2
NY-A	5	5	.500	20	14	8	0	1	122^1	123	2	42	57	12.2	3.24	85	.271	.334	8	.182	1	-7	-6	3	-0.2
Yr	6	11	.353	35	22	10	0	1	188^1	187	3	68	77	12.2	3.54	77	.270	.336	4	.063	-0	-17	-17	3	-1.4
1915 NY-A	2	6	.250	19	11	5	0	1	96^2	95	4	47	34	13.7	4.10	72	.275	.370	6	.188	-1	-12	-13	-0	-1.3
Total 5	38	40	.487	133	93	42	6	3	731^1	698	15	291	251	12.5	3.47	83	.257	.334	38	.147	-6	-39	-49	6	-4.7

■ CHARLIE BROWN
Brown, Charles E. b: 1878, Baltimore, Md. TL, 6', 180 lbs. Deb: 8/04/1897

YEAR TM/L	W	L	PCT	G	GS	CG	SH	SV	IP	H	HR	BB	SO	RAT	ERA	ERA+	OAV	OOB	BH	AVG	PB	PR	/A	PD	TPI
1897 Cle-N	1	2	.333	4	4	2	0	0	24^1	30	2	17	8	17.4	7.77	58	.300	.402	3	.273	0	-9	-9	0	-0.6

■ BUSTER BROWN
Brown, Charles Edward "Yank" b: 8/31/1881, Boone, Iowa d: 2/9/14, Sioux City, Iowa BR/TR, 6', 180 lbs. Deb: 6/22/05

YEAR TM/L	W	L	PCT	G	GS	CG	SH	SV	IP	H	HR	BB	SO	RAT	ERA	ERA+	OAV	OOB	BH	AVG	PB	PR	/A	PD	TPI
1905 StL-N	8	11	.421	23	21	17	3	0	179	172	5	62	57	12.3	2.97	100	.260	.332	6	.092	-3	1	0	2	0.0
1906 StL-N	8	16	.333	32	27	21	0	0	238^1	208	2	112	109	12.5	2.64	99	.234	.327	14	.165	1	-0	-0	1	0.1
1907 StL-N	1	6	.143	9	8	6	0	0	63^2	57	2	45	17	15.1	3.39	74	.263	.401	7	.269	2	-7	-6	2	-0.2
Phi-N	9	6	.600	21	16	13	4	0	130	118	3	56	38	12.5	2.42	100	.246	.333	10	.189	2	1	-0	-0	0.1
Yr	10	12	.455	30	24	19	4	0	193^2	175	5	101	55	13.1	2.74	89	.250	.349	1	.013	4	-6	-6	2	-0.1
1908 Phi-N	0	0	—	3	0	0	0	0	7	9	0	5	3	19.3	2.57	94	.346	.469	1	.200	-0	-0	-0	1	0.1
1909 Phi-N	0	0	—	7	1	0	0	0	25	22	1	16	10	14.0	3.24	80	.259	.382	0	.000	-1	-2	-2	0	-0.2
Bos-N	4	8	.333	18	17	8	2	0	123^1	108	1	56	32	12.5	3.14	90	.244	.339	7	.146	-2	-7	-4	1	-0.5
Yr	4	8	.333	25	18	8	2	0	148^1	130	2	72	42	12.7	3.16	88	.246	.344	2	.035	-3	-9	-6	1	-0.7
1910 Bos-N	9	23	.281	46	29	16	1	2	263	251	4	94	88	11.9	2.67	125	.268	.337	16	.198	0	11	19	1	2.3
1911 Bos-N	8	18	.308	42	25	13	0	2	241	259	11	116	76	14.4	4.29	89	.285	.372	21	.250	4	-24	-13	-0	-0.6
1912 Bos-N	4	15	.211	31	21	13	0	0	168^1	146	7	66	68	11.4	4.01	89	.228	.302	13	.213	1	-11	-8	0	-0.6
1913 Bos-N	0	0	—	2	0	0	0	0	13^1	19	0	3	3	16.2	4.73	70	.396	.453	0	.000	-0	-2	-2	0	-0.1
Total 9	51	103	.331	234	165	107	10	4	1452	1369	36	631	501	12.8	3.20	96	.257	.342	95	.182	4	-41	-18	9	0.4

■ CURLY BROWN
Brown, Charles Roy "Lefty" b: 12/9/1888, Spring Hill, Kan. d: 6/10/68, Spring Hill, Kan. BL/TL, 5'10.5", 165 lbs. Deb: 9/08/11

YEAR TM/L	W	L	PCT	G	GS	CG	SH	SV	IP	H	HR	BB	SO	RAT	ERA	ERA+	OAV	OOB	BH	AVG	PB	PR	/A	PD	TPI
1911 StL-A	1	2	.333	3	2	2	0	0	23	22	0	5	8	11.0	2.74	123	.247	.295	0	.000	-1	2	2	0	0.0
1912 StL-A	1	3	.250	16	4	2	1	0	64^2	69	0	35	28	14.9	4.87	68	.277	.373	5	.208	-0	-11	-11	-3	-1.2
1913 StL-A	1	1	.500	2	2	2	0	0	14	12	0	4	3	10.3	2.57	114	.245	.302	2	.400	1	1	1	0	0.1
1915 Cin-N	0	2	.000	7	3	0	0	0	27	26	2	6	13	11.3	4.67	61	.245	.298	4	.364	1	-6	-5	-1	-0.5
Total 4	3	8	.273	28	11	6	1	0	128^2	129	2	50	52	12.9	4.20	76	.262	.337	11	.224	0	-15	-14	-4	-1.6

■ CLINT BROWN
Brown, Clinton Harold b: 7/8/03, Blackash, Pa. d: 12/31/55, Rocky River, Ohio BL/TR, 6'1", 190 lbs. Deb: 9/27/28

YEAR TM/L	W	L	PCT	G	GS	CG	SH	SV	IP	H	HR	BB	SO	RAT	ERA	ERA+	OAV	OOB	BH	AVG	PB	PR	/A	PD	TPI
1928 Cle-A	0	1	.000	2	1	1	0	0	11	14	0	2	2	13.1	4.91	84	.304	.333	1	.200	-0	-1	-1	0	0.0
1929 Cle-A	0	2	.000	3	1	1	0	0	16^1	18	0	6	1	13.2	3.31	134	.286	.348	0	.000	-1	2	2	1	0.2
1930 Cle-A	11	13	.458	35	31	16	3	1	213^2	271	14	51	54	13.7	4.97	99	.314	.356	18	.247	2	-8	-3	3	0.1
1931 Cle-A	11	15	.423	39	33	12	2	0	233^1	284	10	55	50	13.1	4.71	98	.295	.333	15	.172	-2	-8	-2	4	0.1
1932 Cle-A	15	12	.556	37	32	21	1	1	262^2	298	14	50	59	12.1	4.08	116	.279	.314	25	.250	6	12	19	2	2.7
1933 Cle-A	11	12	.478	33	23	10	2	1	185	202	10	34	47	11.6	3.41	130	.276	.310	9	.145	-3	18	21	3	2.2
1934 Cle-A	4	3	.571	17	2	0	0	1	50^1	83	3	14	15	17.3	5.90	84	.359	.396	5	.294	2	-8	-8	-0	-0.5
1935 Cle-A	4	3	.571	23	5	1	0	2	49	61	3	14	20	14.0	5.14	88	.300	.349	2	.200	2	-4	-3	1	-0.1
1936 Chi-A	6	2	.750	38	2	0	0	5	83	106	5	24	19	14.4	4.99	104	.315	.366	4	.160	-0	0	2	0	0.2
1937 Chi-A	7	7	.500	53	0	0	0	18	100	92	7	36	51	11.6	3.42	135	.242	.309	4	.222	1	13	13	1	1.4
1938 Chi-A	1	3	.250	8	0	0	0	0	13^2	16	0	9	2	16.5	4.61	106	.333	.439	1	.500	1	0	1	0	0.2
1939 Chi-A	11	10	.524	61	0	0	0	18	118^1	127	8	27	41	11.7	3.88	122	.281	.322	4	.211	1	10	11	2	1.3
1940 Chi-A	4	6	.400	37	0	0	0	10	66	75	5	23	12	12.7	3.68	120	.284	.330	1	.071	-1	5	5	0	0.5
1941 Cle-A	3	3	.500	41	0	0	0	5	74^1	77	3	28	22	12.8	3.27	120	.279	.348	2	.118	0	7	6	3	0.8
1942 Cle-A	1	1	.500	7	0	0	0	0	9	16	2	2	4	19.0	6.00	57	.356	.396	0	.000	-0	-2	-3	-0	-0.2
Total 15	89	93	.489	434	130	62	8	64	1485^2	1740	84	368	410	12.9	4.26	109	.291	.335	91	.199	6	37	60	22	8.9

■ CURT BROWN
Brown, Curtis Steven b: 1/15/60, Ft.Lauderdale, Fla. BR/TR, 6'5", 200 lbs. Deb: 6/10/83

YEAR TM/L	W	L	PCT	G	GS	CG	SH	SV	IP	H	HR	BB	SO	RAT	ERA	ERA+	OAV	OOB	BH	AVG	PB	PR	/A	PD	TPI
1983 Cal-A	1	1	.500	10	0	0	0	0	16	25	1	4	7	16.3	7.31	55	.368	.403	0	—	0	-6	-6	-0	-0.5
1984 NY-A	1	1	.500	13	0	0	0	0	16^2	18	1	4	10	11.9	2.70	140	.281	.324	0	—	0	2	2	0	0.2
1986 Mon-N	0	1	.000	6	0	0	0	0	12	15	0	2	4	12.8	3.00	123	.319	.347	0	.000	0	1	1	0	0.1
1987 Mon-N	0	1	.000	5	0	0	0	0	7	10	2	4	6	18.0	7.71	54	.333	.412	0	—	0	-3	-3	0	-0.2
Total 4	2	4	.333	34	0	0	0	0	51^2	68	4	14	27	14.3	4.88	80	.325	.368	0	.000	-0	-5	-6	0	-0.4

■ ED BROWN
Brown, Edward P. b: Chicago, Ill. TR, Deb: 8/19/1882 ◆

YEAR TM/L	W	L	PCT	G	GS	CG	SH	SV	IP	H	HR	BB	SO	RAT	ERA	ERA+	OAV	OOB	BH	AVG	PB	PR	/A	PD	TPI
1882 StL-a	0	0	—	1	0	0	0	0	2	2	0	0	1	9.0	0.00	—	.243	.243	11	.183	-0	1	1	0	0.1
1884 Tol-a	0	1	.000	1	1	1	0	0	9	19	0	4	1	23.0	9.00	38	.408	.455	27	.176	0	-6	-6	-0	-0.3
Total 2	0	1	.000	2	1	1	0	0	11	21	0	4	2	20.5	7.36	45	.384	.426	38	.178	-0	-5	-5	0	-0.2

■ ELMER BROWN
Brown, Elmer Young "Shook" b: 3/25/1883, Southport, Ind. d: 1/23/55, Indianapolis, Ind. BL/TR, 5'11.5", 172 lbs. Deb: 9/16/11

YEAR TM/L	W	L	PCT	G	GS	CG	SH	SV	IP	H	HR	BB	SO	RAT	ERA	ERA+	OAV	OOB	BH	AVG	PB	PR	/A	PD	TPI
1911 StL-A	1	1	.500	5	3	1	1	0	16^2	16	0	14	5	16.2	6.48	52	.242	.375	1	.125	-1	-6	-6	1	-0.5
1912 StL-A	5	8	.385	23	13	2	1	0	120^1	122	2	42	45	13.2	2.99	111	.280	.359	6	.167	-1	4	4	-1	0.3

YEAR TM/L	W	L	PCT	G	GS	CG	SH	SV	IP	H	HR	BB	SO	RAT	ERA	ERA+	OAV	OOB	BH	AVG	PB	PR	/A	PD	TPI
1913 Bro-N	0	0	—	3	1	0	0	0	13	6	0	10	6	11.8	2.08	159	.158	.347	0	.000	-1	2	2	0	0.1
1914 Bro-N	1	2	.333	11	4	1	0	0	36²	33	2	23	22	15.5	3.93	73	.402	.563	1	.083	-1	-5	-4	1	-0.4
1915 Bro-N	0	0	—	1	0	0	0	0	2	4	0	3	1	31.5	9.00	31	.500	.636	0	—	0	-1	-1	0	0.0
Total 5	7	11	.389	43	21	4	2	0	188²	181	4	92	79	14.0	3.48	93	.287	.395	8	.133	-3	-6	-5	1	-0.5

■ HAL BROWN

Brown, Hector Harold "Skinny"   b: 12/11/24, Greensboro, N.C.   BR/TR, 6'2", 180 lbs.   Deb: 4/19/51

YEAR TM/L	W	L	PCT	G	GS	CG	SH	SV	IP	H	HR	BB	SO	RAT	ERA	ERA+	OAV	OOB	BH	AVG	PB	PR	/A	PD	TPI
1951 Chi-A	0	0	—	3	0	0	0	1	8²	15	3	4	4	19.7	9.35	43	.385	.442	2	1.000	1	-5	-5	0	-0.2
1952 Chi-A	2	3	.400	24	8	1	0	0	72¹	82	8	21	31	12.8	4.23	86	.284	.332	3	.158	1	-4	-5	0	-0.4
1953 Bos-A	11	6	.647	30	25	6	1	0	166¹	177	16	57	62	12.7	4.65	90	.269	.327	17	.293	5	-12	-8	0	-0.2
1954 Bos-A	1	8	.111	40	5	1	0	0	118	126	6	41	66	13.0	4.12	100	.269	.331	3	.125	-0	-5	-0	1	0.0
1955 Bos-A	1	0	1.000	2	0	0	0	0	4	2	0	2	2	9.0	2.25	191	.143	.250	1	1.000	0	1	1	-0	0.1
Bal-A	0	4	.000	15	5	1	0	0	57	51	5	26	26	12.2	4.11	93	.241	.324	0	.000	-1	-1	-2	-1	-0.3
Yr	1	4	.200	17	5	1	0	0	61	53	5	28	28	12.0	3.98	97	.235	.319	2	.118	-1	-0	-1	-1	-0.2
1956 Bal-A	9	7	.563	35	14	4	1	2	151²	142	18	37	57	10.7	4.04	97	.247	.294	8	.190	1	-2	-2	0	-0.0
1957 Bal-A	7	8	.467	25	20	7	2	1	150	132	17	37	62	10.3	3.90	92	.236	.285	10	.208	2	-2	-5	-1	-0.3
1958 Bal-A	7	5	.583	19	17	4	2	1	96²	96	9	20	44	10.8	3.07	117	.259	.297	4	.148	-0	7	6	-0	0.5
1959 Bal-A	11	9	.550	31	21	2	0	3	164	158	16	32	81	10.5	3.79	100	.252	.290	2	.048	-2	1	-0	-1	-0.2
1960 Bal-A	12	5	.706	30	20	6	1	0	159	155	14	22	66	**10.1**	3.06	125	.258	**.286**	8	.182	3	14	13	-1	1.5
1961 Bal-A	10	6	.625	27	23	6	3	1	166²	153	14	33	61	10.1	3.19	123	.247	.286	7	.140	-0	16	13	0	1.3
1962 Bal-A	6	4	.600	22	11	0	0	1	85²	88	12	21	25	11.8	4.10	92	.268	.318	8	.286	1	-1	-3	-1	-0.2
NY-A	0	1	.000	2	1	0	0	0	6²	9	3	2	2	14.9	6.75	56	.333	.379	0	.000	0	-2	-2	0	-0.1
Yr	6	5	.545	24	12	0	0	1	92¹	97	15	23	27	11.7	4.29	88	.270	.314	0	.000	1	-3	-5	-1	-0.3
1963 Hou-N	5	11	.313	26	20	6	3	0	141¹	137	14	8	68	9.2	3.31	95	.255	.266	4	.093	-2	-0	-2	-2	-0.6
1964 Hou-N	3	15	.167	27	21	3	0	1	132	154	18	26	53	12.4	3.95	86	.292	.327	5	.128	-1	-6	-8	-1	-0.3
Total 14	85	92	.480	358	211	47	13	11	1680	1677	173	389	710	11.1	3.81	99	.260	.303	82	.169	8	2	-10	-5	-0.0

■ JACKIE BROWN

Brown, Jackie Gene   b: 5/31/43, Holdenville, Okla.   BR/TR, 6'1", 195 lbs.   Deb: 7/02/70 C

YEAR TM/L	W	L	PCT	G	GS	CG	SH	SV	IP	H	HR	BB	SO	RAT	ERA	ERA+	OAV	OOB	BH	AVG	PB	PR	/A	PD	TPI
1970 Was-A	2	2	.500	24	5	1	0	0	57	49	8	37	47	13.6	3.95	90	.231	.345	2	.154	-0	-1	-2	-1	-0.3
1971 Was-A	3	4	.429	14	9	0	0	0	47	60	9	27	21	16.9	5.94	56	.316	.404	2	.133	-0	-13	-14	1	-1.3
1973 Tex-A	5	5	.500	25	3	2	1	2	66²	82	7	25	45	14.7	3.92	95	.309	.373	0	—	0	-1	-1	-1	-0.1
1974 Tex-A	13	12	.520	35	26	9	2	0	216²	219	13	74	134	12.3	3.57	100	.265	.329	0	—	1	1	-0	-0	0.0
1975 Tex-A	5	5	.500	17	7	2	1	0	70¹	70	7	35	35	13.7	4.22	89	.266	.357	0	—	0	-3	-4	-2	-0.4
Cle-A	1	2	.333	25	3	1	0	1	69¹	72	9	29	41	13.1	4.28	88	.276	.348	0	—	0	-4	-4	-0	-0.3
Yr	6	7	.462	42	10	3	1	1	139²	142	16	64	76	13.3	4.25	89	.269	.349	0	—	0	-7	-8	-2	-0.7
1976 Cle-A	9	11	.450	32	27	5	2	0	180	193	14	55	104	12.8	4.25	82	.276	.335	0	—	0	-15	-15	-0	-1.5
1977 Mon-N	9	12	.429	42	25	6	2	0	185²	189	15	71	89	12.8	4.51	84	.264	.334	7	.125	-2	-12	-14	-2	-1.7
Total 7	47	53	.470	214	105	26	8	3	892²	934	82	353	516	13.2	4.18	87	.272	.343	11	.131	-3	-48	-55	-6	-5.6

■ KEVIN BROWN

Brown, James Kevin   b: 3/14/65, Milledgeville, Ga.   BR/TR, 6'4", 195 lbs.   Deb: 9/30/86

YEAR TM/L	W	L	PCT	G	GS	CG	SH	SV	IP	H	HR	BB	SO	RAT	ERA	ERA+	OAV	OOB	BH	AVG	PB	PR	/A	PD	TPI
1986 Tex-A	1	0	1.000	1	1	0	0	0	5	6	0	4	4	10.8	3.60	119	.316	.316	0	—	0	0	0	0	0.0
1988 Tex-A	1	1	.500	4	4	1	0	0	23¹	33	2	8	12	16.2	4.24	96	.330	.385	0	—	0	-1	-0	0	0.0
1989 Tex-A	12	9	.571	28	28	7	0	0	191	167	10	70	104	11.4	3.35	118	.234	.305	0	—	0	11	13	4	1.8
1990 Tex-A	12	10	.545	26	26	6	2	0	180	175	13	60	88	11.9	3.60	111	.255	.318	0	.000	0	6	8	0	0.8
Total 4	26	20	.565	59	59	14	2	0	399¹	381	25	138	208	11.9	3.52	113	.251	.317	0	.000	0	17	21	4	2.6

■ JIM BROWN

Brown, James W. H.   b: 12/12/1860, Clinton Co., Pa.   d: 4/6/08, Williamsport, Pa.   Deb: 4/17/1884 ♦

YEAR TM/L	W	L	PCT	G	GS	CG	SH	SV	IP	H	HR	BB	SO	RAT	ERA	ERA+	OAV	OOB	BH	AVG	PB	PR	/A	PD	TPI
1884 Alt-U	1	9	.100	11	11	7	0	0	74	99	0	36	39	16.4	5.35	61	.301	.370	22	.250	0	-19	-17	0	-1.2
NY-N	0	1	.000	1	1	1	0	0	9	10	0	8	2	18.0	5.00	59	.266	.395	0	.000	-1	-2	-2	-0	-0.1
StP-U	1	4	.200	6	6	4	1	0	36	43	1	14	20	14.3	3.75	44	.277	.337	5	.313	3	-3	-8	-0	-0.4
1886 Phi-a	0	1	.000	1	1	1	0	0	8¹	9	0	3	4	13.0	3.24	108	.263	.322	0	.000	-1	0	0	0	0.0
Total 2	2	15	.118	19	19	13	1	0	127¹	161	1	61	65	15.7	4.74	59	.290	.360	27	.245	2	-24	-27	0	-1.7

■ JOHN BROWN

Brown, John J. "Ad"   b: Trenton, N.J.   Deb: 8/11/1897

YEAR TM/L	W	L	PCT	G	GS	CG	SH	SV	IP	H	HR	BB	SO	RAT	ERA	ERA+	OAV	OOB	BH	AVG	PB	PR	/A	PD	TPI
1897 Bro-N	0	1	.000	1	1	0	0	0	5	7	0	4	0	19.8	7.20	57	.328	.434	1	.500	0	-2	-2	0	0.0

■ JOPHERY BROWN

Brown, Jophery Clifford   b: 1/22/45, Grambling, La.   BL/TR, 6'2", 190 lbs.   Deb: 9/21/68

YEAR TM/L	W	L	PCT	G	GS	CG	SH	SV	IP	H	HR	BB	SO	RAT	ERA	ERA+	OAV	OOB	BH	AVG	PB	PR	/A	PD	TPI
1968 Chi-N	0	0	—	1	0	0	0	0	2	2	0	1	0	13.5	4.50	70	.286	.375	0	—	0	-0	-0	0	0.0

■ JOE BROWN

Brown, Joseph E.   b: 4/4/1859, Warren, Pa.   d: 6/28/1888, Warren, Pa.   Deb: 8/16/1884 ♦

YEAR TM/L	W	L	PCT	G	GS	CG	SH	SV	IP	H	HR	BB	SO	RAT	ERA	ERA+	OAV	OOB	BH	AVG	PB	PR	/A	PD	TPI
1884 Chi-N	4	2	.667	7	6	5	0	0	50	56	4	7	27	11.3	4.68	67	.268	.292	13	.213	-1	-9	-9	-0	-0.6
1885 Bal-a	0	4	.000	4	4	4	0	0	38	52	0	4	9	13.3	5.68	62	.312	.329	3	.158	-1	-10	-10	-0	-0.8
Total 2	4	6	.400	11	10	9	0	0	88	108	4	11	36	12.2	5.11	62	.288	.308	16	.200	-2	-20	-19	-0	-1.4

■ JOE BROWN

Brown, Joseph Henry   b: 7/3/1900, Little Rock, Ark.   d: 3/7/50, Los Angeles, Cal.   BR/TR, 6', 176 lbs.   Deb: 5/17/27

YEAR TM/L	W	L	PCT	G	GS	CG	SH	SV	IP	H	HR	BB	SO	RAT	ERA	ERA+	OAV	OOB	BH	AVG	PB	PR	/A	PD	TPI
1927 Chi-A	0	0	—	1	1	0	0	0	2	0	1	0	0	—	∞		1.000	1.000	0	—	0	-3	-3	0	-0.1

■ KEITH BROWN

Brown, Keith Edward   b: 2/14/64, Flagstaff, Ariz.   BB/TR, 6'4", 215 lbs.   Deb: 8/25/88

YEAR TM/L	W	L	PCT	G	GS	CG	SH	SV	IP	H	HR	BB	SO	RAT	ERA	ERA+	OAV	OOB	BH	AVG	PB	PR	/A	PD	TPI
1988 Cin-N	2	1	.667	4	3	0	0	0	16¹	14	1	4	6	9.9	2.76	130	.237	.286	0	.000	-0	1	1	0	0.1
1990 Cin-N	0	0	—	8	0	0	0	0	11¹	12	2	3	8	11.9	4.76	81	.286	.333	0	—	0	-1	-1	0	0.0
Total 2	2	1	.667	12	3	0	0	0	27²	26	3	7	14	10.7	3.58	103	.257	.306	0	.000	-0	0	0	0	0.1

■ KEVIN BROWN

Brown, Kevin Dewayne   b: 3/5/66, Oroville, Cal.   BL/TL, 6'1", 185 lbs.   Deb: 7/27/90

YEAR TM/L	W	L	PCT	G	GS	CG	SH	SV	IP	H	HR	BB	SO	RAT	ERA	ERA+	OAV	OOB	BH	AVG	PB	PR	/A	PD	TPI
1990 NY-N	0	0	—	2	0	0	0	0	2	2	0	1	0	13.5	0.00	—	.250	.333	0	—	0	1	1	0	0.1
Mil-A	1	1	.500	5	3	0	0	0	21	14	1	7	12	9.4	2.57	147	.182	.259	0	—	0	3	3	1	0.4

■ LEW BROWN

Brown, Lewis J. "Blower"   b: 2/1/1858, Leominster, Mass.   d: 1/16/1889, Boston, Mass.   BR/TR, 5'10.5", 185 lbs.   Deb: 6/17/1876 ♦

YEAR TM/L	W	L	PCT	G	GS	CG	SH	SV	IP	H	HR	BB	SO	RAT	ERA	ERA+	OAV	OOB	BH	AVG	PB	PR	/A	PD	TPI
1878 Pro-N	0	0	—	1	0	0	0	0	1	0	0	4	0	36.0	18.00	12	.000	.568	74	.305	0	-2	-2	0	-0.1
1884 Bos-U	0	0	—	1	0	0	0	1	1	6	0	1	0	63.0	36.00	8	.659	.692	75	.231	0	-4	-4	0	-0.2
Total 2	0	0	—	2	0	0	0	1	2	6	0	5	0	49.5	27.00	10	.494	.641	379	.248	0	-5	-5	0	-0.3

■ LLOYD BROWN

Brown, Lloyd Andrew "Gimpy"   b: 12/25/04, Beeville, Tex.   d: 1/14/74, Opalocka, Fla.   BL/TL, 5'9", 170 lbs.   Deb: 7/17/25

YEAR TM/L	W	L	PCT	G	GS	CG	SH	SV	IP	H	HR	BB	SO	RAT	ERA	ERA+	OAV	OOB	BH	AVG	PB	PR	/A	PD	TPI
1925 Bro-N	0	3	.000	17	5	1	0	0	63¹	79	1	25	23	15.1	4.12	101	.319	.385	2	.087	-2	1	0	0	-0.1
1928 Was-A	4	4	.500	27	10	2	0	1	107	112	7	40	38	13.0	4.04	99	.273	.341	5	.161	0	0	-0	3	0.3
1929 Was-A	8	7	.533	40	15	7	1	0	168	186	7	69	48	13.7	4.18	101	.297	.368	11	.220	3	1	1	2	0.6
1930 Was-A	16	12	.571	38	22	10	1	0	197	220	6	65	59	13.2	4.25	108	.293	.354	14	.215	2	9	8	4	1.2
1931 Was-A	15	14	.517	42	32	15	1	0	258²	256	13	79	79	11.7	3.20	134	.257	.311	22	.229	3	34	31	2	3.5
1932 Was-A	15	12	.556	46	24	10	2	5	202²	239	11	55	53	13.1	4.44	97	.296	.342	7	.100	-5	1	-3	1	-0.5
1933 StL-A	1	6	.143	8	6	0	0	0	39	57	1	17	7	17.1	7.15	65	.350	.411	3	.273	1	-12	-11	1	-0.7
Bos-A	8	11	.421	33	21	9	2	1	163¹	180	4	64	37	13.4	4.02	109	.281	.347	16	.281	6	5	6	5	1.7
Yr	9	17	.346	41	27	9	2	1	202¹	237	5	81	44	14.1	4.63	96	.295	.360	5	.074	-8	-8	-4	6	1.0
1934 Cle-A	5	10	.333	38	15	5	0	6	117	116	7	51	39	13.0	3.85	118	.263	.342	7	.233	1	8	9	0	1.0
1935 Cle-A	8	7	.533	42	8	4	2	4	122	123	6	37	45	12.0	3.61	125	.265	.323	4	.108	-2	**11**	**12**	1	1.0
1936 Cle-A	8	10	.444	24	16	12	1	1	140¹	166	13	46	34	13.0	4.17	121	.294	.349	10	.222	2	14	14	1	1.5
1937 Cle-A	2	6	.250	31	5	2	0	0	77	107	4	27	32	16.0	6.55	70	.329	.386	4	.167	-1	-16	-17	1	-1.4
1940 Phi-N	1	3	.250	18	2	0	0	3	37²	58	3	16	16	17.7	6.21	63	.354	.411	1	.077	-1	-10	-10	0	-1.0
Total 12	91	105	.464	404	181	77	10	21	1693	1899	83	590	510	13.3	4.20	105	.288	.348	106	.192	7	45	42	21	7.1

YEAR	TM/L	W	L	PCT	G	GS	CG	SH	SV	IP	H	HR	BB	SO	RAT	ERA	ERA+	OAV	OOB	BH	AVG	PB	PR	/A	PD	TPI
■ **MACE BROWN**				Brown, Mace Stanley		b: 5/21/09, North English, Ia.			BR/TR, 6'1", 190 lbs.		Deb: 5/21/35	C													
1935	Pit-N	4	1	.800	18	5	2	0	0	72²	84	5	22	28	13.1	3.59	114	.287	.337	4	.167	-0	3	4	2	0.5
1936	Pit-N	10	11	.476	47	10	3	0	3	165	178	8	55	56	12.8	3.87	105	.275	.332	10	.167	-2	3	3	1	0.3
1937	Pit-N	7	2	.778	50	2	0	0	7	107²	109	2	45	60	13.0	4.18	92	.261	.334	9	.300	-2	-3	-4	-1	-0.2
1938	Pit-N	15	9	.625	51	2	0	0	5	132²	155	5	44	55	13.5	3.80	100	.294	.349	5	.132	-2	-0	-0	-0	-0.1
1939	Pit-N	9	13	.409	47	19	8	1	7	200¹	232	8	52	71	12.8	3.37	114	.293	.338	7	.109	-4	12	10	0	0.7
1940	Pit-N	10	9	.526	48	17	5	1	7	173	181	5	49	73	12.1	3.49	109	.267	.318	6	.115	-1	7	6	1	0.6
1941	Pit-N	0	0	—	1	0	0	0	0	1¹	2	0	0	0	13.5	0.00	—	.333	.333	0	—	0	1	1	0	0.1
	Bro-N	3	2	.600	24	0	0	0	3	42²	31	3	26	22	12.2	3.16	116	.208	.330	0	.000	-1	2	2	1	0.2
	Yr	3	2	.600	25	0	0	0	3	44	33	3	26	22	12.3	3.07	119	.213	.330	0	.000	-1	3	3	1	0.3
1942	Bos-A	9	3	.750	34	0	0	0	6	60¹	56	4	28	20	12.5	3.43	109	.255	.339	1	.067	-1	2	2	1	0.2
1943	Bos-A	6	6	.500	49	0	0	0	9	93¹	71	2	51	40	11.8	2.12	156	.222	.329	1	.059	-1	12	12	0	1.2
1946	*Bos-A	3	1	.750	18	0	0	0	1	26¹	26	2	16	10	14.4	2.05	179	.268	.372	0	.000	-1	4	5	1	0.5
Total	10	76	57	.571	387	55	18	2	48	1075¹	1125	44	388	435	12.7	3.46	110	.271	.335	43	.137	-11	43	43	6	4.0
■ **MARK BROWN**				Brown, Mark Anthony		b: 7/13/59, Bellows Falls, Vt.			BB/TR, 6'2", 190 lbs.		Deb: 8/09/84														
1984	Bal-A	1	2	.333	9	0	0	0	0	23	22	2	7	10	11.7	3.91	99	.256	.319	0	—	0	0	-0	-0	0.0
1985	Min-A	0	0	—	6	0	0	0	0	15²	21	1	7	5	16.1	6.89	64	.333	.400	0	—	0	-5	-4	-0	-0.3
Total	2	1	2	.333	15	0	0	0	0	38²	43	3	14	15	13.5	5.12	80	.289	.354	0	—	0	-5	-4	-1	-0.3
■ **MIKE BROWN**				Brown, Michael Gary		b: 3/4/59, Camden County, N.J.			BR/TR, 6'2", 195 lbs.		Deb: 9/16/82														
1982	Bos-A	1	0	1.000	3	0	0	0	0	6	7	0	1	4	12.0	0.00	—	.304	.333	0	—	0	3	3	-0	0.3
1983	Bos-A	6	6	.500	19	18	3	1	0	104	110	12	43	35	13.4	4.67	93	.276	.350	0	—	0	-7	-4	-0	-0.3
1984	Bos-A	1	8	.111	15	11	0	0	0	67	104	9	19	32	16.9	6.85	61	.347	.391	0	—	0	-21	-20	1	-1.7
1985	Bos-A	0	0	—	2	1	0	0	0	3¹	9	0	3	3	32.4	21.60	20	.500	.571	0	—	0	-6	-6	-0	-0.5
1986	Bos-A	4	4	.500	15	10	0	0	0	57¹	72	10	25	32	15.4	5.34	78	.316	.386	0	—	0	-7	-7	1	-0.6
	Sea-A	0	2	.000	6	2	0	0	0	15²	19	4	11	9	17.2	7.47	57	.302	.405	0	—	0	-6	-6	0	-0.4
	Yr	4	6	.400	21	12	0	0	0	73	91	14	36	41	15.7	5.79	72	.308	.384	0	—	0	-13	-13	1	-1.0
1987	Sea-A	0	0	—	1	0	0	0	0	0¹	3	0	0	0	81.0	54.00	9	.750	.750	0	—	0	-2	-2	0	-0.1
Total	6	12	20	.375	61	42	3	1	0	253²	324	35	102	115	15.3	5.75	74	.313	.378	0	—	0	-47	-42	1	-3.3
■ **MORDECAI BROWN**				Brown, Mordecai Peter Centennial "Three Finger" or "Miner"																					
				b: 10/19/1876, Nyesville, Ind.		d: 2/14/48, Terre Haute, Ind.			BB/TR, 5'10", 175 lbs.		Deb: 4/19/03	MH													
1903	StL-N	9	13	.409	26	24	19	1	0	201	231	7	59	83	13.3	2.60	126	.293	.347	15	.195	-1	15	15	2	1.6
1904	Chi-N	15	10	.600	26	23	21	4	1	212¹	155	1	50	81	8.9	1.86	143	.199	.253	19	.213	1	21	19	-0	2.2
1905	Chi-N	18	12	.600	30	24	24	4	0	249	219	3	44	89	9.5	2.17	138	.235	.271	13	.140	-1	23	23	0	2.3
1906	*Chi-N	26	6	.813	36	32	27	9	3	277¹	198	1	61	144	8.5	1.04	254	.202	.252	20	.204	2	49	49	2	6.5
1907	*Chi-N	20	6	.769	34	27	20	6	3	233	180	2	40	107	8.7	1.39	180	.221	.262	13	.153	-0	28	29	4	3.9
1908	*Chi-N	29	9	.763	44	31	27	9	5	312¹	214	1	49	123	7.7	1.47	160	.195	.232	25	.207	1	31	31	-0	3.8
1909	*Chi-N	27	9	.750	50	34	32	8	7	342²	246	1	53	172	8.0	1.31	194	.202	.239	22	.176	1	49	47	-1	5.5
1910	*Chi-N	25	14	.641	46	31	27	6	7	295¹	256	3	64	143	9.9	1.86	155	.232	.277	18	.175	-0	39	34	3	3.9
1911	Chi-N	21	11	.656	53	27	21	0	13	270	267	5	55	129	10.9	2.80	118	.262	.303	23	.253	5	18	15	-4	1.6
1912	Chi-N	5	6	.455	15	8	5	2	0	88²	92	2	20	34	11.5	2.64	126	.267	.309	8	.290	2	8	7	-2	0.7
1913	Cin-N	11	12	.478	39	16	11	1	6	173¹	174	7	44	41	11.4	2.91	112	.277	.325	11	.204	0	6	7	-1	0.6
1914	StL-F	12	6	.667	26	18	13	2	0	175	172	7	43	81	11.2	3.29	103	.254	.302	15	.254	2	-2	2	-2	0.2
	Bro-F	2	5	.286	9	8	5	0	0	57²	63	1	18	32	12.6	4.21	76	.276	.329	4	.211	-0	-6	-7	-0	-0.6
	Yr	14	11	.560	35	26	18	2	0	232²	235	8	61	113	11.4	3.52	95	.259	.306	4	.051	2	-8	-5	-3	-0.4
1915	Chi-F	17	8	.680	35	25	17	3	4	236¹	189	4	64	95	9.9	2.09	133	.220	.279	24	.293	6	25	18	3	3.0
1916	Chi-N	2	3	.400	12	4	2	0	0	48¹	52	0	9	21	12.1	3.91	74	.289	.337	4	.250	0	-7	-5	-0	-0.5
Total	14	239	130	.648	481	332	271	55	49	3172¹	2708	43	673	1375	9.8	2.06	139	.232	.278	235	.206	17	295	283	2	34.7
■ **MYRL BROWN**				Brown, Myrl Lincoln		b: 10/10/1894, Waynesboro, Pa.		d: 2/23/81, Harrisburg, Pa.		BR/TR, 5'11", 172 lbs.		Deb: 8/19/22													
1922	Pit-N	3	1	.750	7	5	2	0	0	34²	42	2	13	9	14.3	5.97	68	.296	.355	3	.273	1	-7	-7	1	-0.4
■ **NORM BROWN**				Brown, Norman		b: 2/1/19, Evergreen, N.C.			BB/TR, 6'3", 180 lbs.		Deb: 10/03/43														
1943	Phi-A	0	0	—	1	1	0	0	0	7	5	0	1	6.4	10.0		—	.185	.185	0	.000	-0	3	3	0	0.3
1946	Phi-A	0	1	.000	4	0	0	0	0	7¹	8	2	6	3	17.2	6.14	58	.267	.389	0	—	0	-2	-2	0	-0.1
Total	2	0	1	.000	5	1	0	0	0	14¹	13	2	6	4	11.9	3.14	111	.228	.302	0	.000	-0	0	1	0	0.2
■ **PAUL BROWN**				Brown, Paul Dwayne		b: 6/18/41, Ft.Smith, Ark.			BR/TR, 6'1", 190 lbs.		Deb: 7/23/61														
1961	Phi-N	0	1	.000	5	1	0	0	0	10	13	3	8	1	19.8	8.10	50	.325	.449	1	.500	0	-5	-4	0	-0.3
1962	Phi-N	0	6	.000	23	9	0	0	1	63²	74	9	33	29	15.5	5.94	65	.298	.387	2	.154	0	-14	-15	-0	-1.3
1963	Phi-N	0	1	.000	6	2	0	0	0	15¹	15	2	5	11	12.9	4.11	79	.238	.314	1	.500	0	-1	-1	0	0.0
1968	Phi-N	0	0	—	2	0	0	0	0	4	6	0	1	4	15.8	9.00	33	.353	.389	0	—	0	-3	-3	-0	-0.2
Total	4	0	8	.000	36	12	0	0	1	93	108	14	47	45	15.6	6.00	63	.293	.382	4	.235	1	-23	-23	0	-1.8
■ **RAY BROWN**				Brown, Paul Percival		b: 1/31/1889, Chicago, Ill.		d: 5/29/55, Los Angeles, Cal.			Deb: 9/29/09														
1909	Chi-N	1	0	1.000	1	1	1	0	0	9	5	0	4	2	9.0	2.00	127	.172	.273	0	.000	-1	1	1	-0	0.0
■ **STUB BROWN**				Brown, Richard P.		b: 8/3/1870, Baltimore, Md.		d: 3/11/48, Baltimore, Md.		TL, 6'2", 220 lbs.		Deb: 8/15/1893													
1893	Bal-N	0	0	—	2	0	0	0	0	9	13	0	5	0	18.0	6.00	79	.328	.403	1	.200	-0	-1	-1	-0	-0.1
1894	Bal-N	4	0	1.000	9	6	3	0	0	49²	59	3	24	8	15.0	4.89	112	.292	.367	2	.087	-4	2	3	-1	0.0
1897	Cin-N	0	1	.000	2	1	1	0	0	13	17	1	8	2	17.3	4.15	110	.313	.401	0	.000	-1	0	1	0	0.0
Total	3	4	1	.800	13	7	4	0	0	71²	89	4	37	10	15.8	4.90	106	.301	.378	3	.091	-5	1	3	-1	-0.1
■ **BOB BROWN**				Brown, Robert M.		b: 1891,		BR/TR, 5'6", 165 lbs.		Deb: 5/02/14															
1914	Buf-F	0	0	—	15	1	0	0	3	36²	39	3	16	13	14.0	3.44	96	.280	.363	2	.222	1	-1	-1	1	0.1
■ **BOB BROWN**				Brown, Robert Murray		b: 4/1/11, Dorchester, Mass.		d: 8/30/90, Pembroke, Mass.		BR/TR, 6'0.5", 190 lbs.		Deb: 4/21/30												
1930	Bos-N	0	0	—	3	0	0	0	0	6	10	0	8	1	27.0	10.50	47	.417	.563	0	.000	-0	-4	-4	0	-0.2
1931	Bos-N	0	1	.000	3	1	0	0	0	6¹	9	0	3	2	17.1	8.53	64	.375	.444	1	.500	-0	-3	-3	0	-0.3
1932	Bos-N	14	7	.667	35	28	9	0	1	213	187	6	104	110	12.4	3.30	114	.238	.329	13	.194	-0	14	11	-1	0.9
1933	Bos-N	0	0	—	5	0	0	0	0	6²	6	0	3	3	12.2	2.70	114	.250	.333	0	.000	-0	0	0	0	0.0
1934	Bos-N	1	3	.250	16	8	2	1	0	58¹	59	2	36	21	15.5	5.71	67	.262	.371	5	.238	-0	-11	-12	-1	-1.1
1935	Bos-N	1	8	.111	15	10	2	1	0	65	79	3	36	17	15.9	6.37	59	.302	.386	2	.105	-1	-17	-19	-1	-1.8
1936	Bos-N	0	2	.000	2	2	0	0	0	8¹	10	1	3	5	14.0	5.40	71	.278	.333	0	.000	-0	-1	-1	0	-0.1
Total	7	16	21	.432	79	49	13	2	1	363²	360	11	193	159	13.8	4.48	84	.261	.354	21	.183	-1	-22	-28	-3	-2.4
■ **SCOTT BROWN**				Brown, Scott Edward		b: 8/30/56, DeQuincy, La.			BR/TR, 6'2", 220 lbs.		Deb: 8/11/81													
1981	Cin-N	1	0	1.000	10	0	0	0	0	13	16	0	1	7	11.8	2.77	128	.314	.327	0	.000	-0	1	1	0	0.1
■ **STEVE BROWN**				Brown, Steven Elbert		b: 2/12/57, San Francisco, Cal.			BR/TR, 6'5", 200 lbs.		Deb: 8/01/83												
1983	Cal-A	2	3	.400	12	4	2	1	0	46	45	4	16	23	11.9	3.52	114	.256	.318	0	—	0	3	3	0	0.2
1984	Cal-A	0	1	.000	3	3	0	0	0	11	16	0	9	5	20.5	9.00	44	.340	.446	0	—	0	-6	-6	-0	-0.5
Total	2	2	4	.333	15	7	2	1	0	57	61	4	25	28	13.6	4.58	87	.274	.347	0	—	0	-3	-4	-0	-0.3

YEAR TM/L	W	L	PCT	G	GS	CG	SH	SV	IP	H	HR	BB	SO	RAT	ERA	ERA+	OAV	OOB	BH	AVG	PB	PR	/A	PD	TPI
■ TOM BROWN Brown, Thomas Dale b: 8/10/49, Lafayette, La. BR/TR, 6'1", 170 lbs. Deb: 9/14/78																									
1978 Sea-A	0	0	—	6	0	0	0	0	13	14	2	4	8	12.5	4.15	92	.286	.340	0	—	0	-1	-1	0	0.0
■ TOM BROWN Brown, Thomas T. b: 9/21/1860, Liverpool, England d: 10/25/27, Washington, D.C. BL/TR, 5'10", 168 lbs. Deb: 7/06/1882 MU♦																									
1882 Bal-a	0	0	—	2	0	0	0	0	8¹	13	0	6	2	20.5	1.08	255	.334	.423	55	.304	1	1	2	-1	0.1
1883 Col-a	0	1	.000	3	1	1	0	0	14	14	0	10	6	15.4	5.79	53	.244	.356	115	.274	1	-4	-4	-1	-0.3
1884 Col-a	2	1	.667	4	0	0	0	0	19	27	0	7	5	16.1	7.11	43	.317	.369	123	.273	1	-8	-9	-1	-0.6
1885 Pit-a	0	0	—	2	0	0	0	0	6	0	0	3	2	4.5	3.00	107	.000	.142	134	.307	1	0	0	-0	0.0
1886 Pit-a	0	0	—	1	0	0	0	0	2	2	0	5	1	31.5	9.00	38	.248	.536	131	.285	0	-1	-1	0	0.0
Total 5	2	2	.500	12	1	1	0	0	49¹	56	0	31	16	15.9	5.29	57	.270	.365	1952	.265	4	-12	-12	-2	-0.8
■ JUMBO BROWN Brown, Walter George b: 4/30/07, Greene, R.I. d: 10/2/66, Freeport, N.Y. BR/TR, 6'4", 295 lbs. Deb: 8/26/25																									
1925 Chi-N	0	0	—	2	0	0	0	0	6	5	0	4	0	13.5	3.00	144	.217	.333	0	.000	-0	1	1	0	0.1
1927 Cle-A	0	2	.000	8	0	0	0	0	18²	19	3	26	8	22.2	6.27	67	.284	.489	2	.667	1	-4	-4	0	-0.2
1928 Cle-A	0	1	.000	5	0	0	0	0	14²	19	0	15	12	20.9	6.75	61	.365	.507	2	.667	1	-4	-4	-0	-0.2
1932 NY-A	5	2	.714	19	3	3	1	1	55²	58	1	30	31	14.6	4.53	90	.270	.364	4	.174	-1	-0	-3	1	-0.1
1933 NY-A	7	5	.583	21	8	1	0	0	74	78	3	52	55	15.8	5.23	74	.269	.380	5	.179	-0	-8	-11	-0	-1.0
1935 NY-A	6	5	.545	20	8	3	1	0	87¹	94	2	37	41	13.5	3.61	112	.279	.350	10	.313	3	8	4	0	0.7
1936 NY-A	1	4	.200	20	3	0	0	1	64	66	4	29	19	17.2	5.91	79	.352	.416	0	.000	-3	-6	-9	1	-0.8
1937 Cin-N	1	0	1.000	4	1	0	0	0	9²	16	0	3	4	17.7	8.38	45	.390	.482	0	.000	-0	-5	-5	-0	-0.4
NY-N	1	0	1.000	4	0	0	0	0	8²	5	0	5	4	10.4	1.04	374	.172	.294	0	—	0	3	3	1	0.3
Yr	2	0	1.000	8	1	0	0	0	18¹	21	0	8	8	14.2	4.91	78	.300	.372	1	.500	0	-2	-2	0	-0.1
1938 NY-N	5	3	.625	43	0	0	0	5	90	65	5	28	42	9.4	1.80	209	.204	.271	3	.188	1	**20**	**20**	-1	1.9
1939 NY-N	4	0	1.000	31	0	0	0	7	56¹	69	1	25	24	15.2	4.15	95	.304	.375	4	.364	1	-1	-1	0	0.0
1940 NY-N	2	4	.333	41	0	0	0	7	55¹	49	5	25	31	12.0	3.42	114	.232	.314	1	.100	-1	3	3	-1	0.1
1941 NY-N	1	5	.167	31	0	0	0	8	57	49	2	21	30	11.1	3.32	111	.238	.308	1	.111	-1	2	2	-1	0.1
Total 12	33	31	.516	249	23	7	2	29	597¹	619	26	300	301	13.9	4.07	99	.271	.357	32	.204	2	7	-4	-0	0.5
■ WALTER BROWN Brown, Walter Irving b: 4/23/15, Jamestown, N.Y. BR/TR, 5'11", 175 lbs. Deb: 5/16/47																									
1947 StL-A	1	0	1.000	19	0	0	0	0	46	50	3	28	10	15.3	4.89	79	.294	.394	0	.000	-1	-6	-5	0	-0.5
■ CAL BROWNING Browning, Calvin Duane b: 3/16/38, Burns Flat, Okla. BL/TL, 5'11", 190 lbs. Deb: 6/12/60																									
1960 StL-N	0	0	—	1	0	0	0	0	0²	5	1	1	0	81.0	40.50	10	.714	.750	0	—	0	-3	-3	0	-0.1
■ FRANK BROWNING Browning, Frank "Dutch" b: 10/29/1882, Falmouth, Ky. d: 5/19/48, San Antonio, Tex. BR/TR, 5'5", 145 lbs. Deb: 4/16/10																									
1910 Det-A	2	2	.500	11	6	2	0	3	49	51	0	16	11	11.2	2.57	102	.262	.298	0	.000	-2	-0	0	1	0.0
■ PETE BROWNING Browning, Louis Rogers "The Gladiator" b: 6/17/1861, Louisville, Ky. d: 9/10/05, Louisville, Ky. BR/TR, 6', 180 lbs. Deb: 5/02/1882 ♦																									
1884 Lou-a	0	1	.000	1	1	0	0	0	0¹	2	0	2	0	108.0	54.00	6	.662	.797	150	.336	0	-2	-2	0	-0.1
■ TOM BROWNING Browning, Thomas Leo b: 4/28/60, Casper, Wyoming BL/TL, 6'1", 190 lbs. Deb: 9/09/84																									
1984 Cin-N	1	0	1.000	3	3	0	0	0	23¹	27	0	5	14	12.3	1.54	245	.303	.340	1	.143	-0	5	6	0	0.7
1985 Cin-N	20	9	.690	38	38	6	4	0	261¹	242	29	73	155	11.0	3.55	107	.245	.299	17	.193	2	1	7	-1	0.9
1986 Cin-N	14	13	.519	39	39	4	2	0	243¹	225	26	70	147	10.9	3.81	102	.245	.299	14	.163	-1	-3	2	-3	0.0
1987 Cin-N	10	13	.435	32	31	2	0	0	183	201	27	61	117	13.1	5.02	85	.284	.345	8	.154	0	-19	-16	-2	-1.5
1988 Cin-N	18	5	.783	36	36	5	2	0	250²	205	36	64	124	9.9	3.41	105	.224	.280	12	.145	1	1	5	-0	0.4
1989 Cin-N	15	12	.556	37	37	9	2	0	249²	241	31	64	118	11.1	3.39	106	.255	.304	7	.090	-3	3	6	-0	0.2
1990 *Cin-N	15	9	.625	35	35	2	1	0	227²	235	24	52	99	11.5	3.80	102	.266	.311	7	.093	-3	-0	2	-1	-0.1
Total 7	93	61	.604	220	219	28	11	0	1439	1376	173	389	774	11.2	3.73	102	.253	.305	66	.141	-4	-11	11	-10	0.6
■ BRUCE BRUBAKER Brubaker, Bruce Ellsworth b: 12/29/41, Harrisburg, Pa. BR/TR, 6'1", 198 lbs. Deb: 4/15/67																									
1967 LA-N	0	0	—	1	0	0	0	0	1¹	3	1	0	2	20.3	20.25	15	.429	.429	0	—	0	-3	-3	0	-0.1
1970 Mil-A	0	0	—	1	0	0	0	0	2	2	1	1	0	13.5	9.00	42	.250	.333	0	—	0	-1	-1	0	0.0
Total 2	0	0	—	2	0	0	0	0	3¹	5	2	1	2	16.2	13.50	26	.333	.375	0	—	0	-4	-4	0	-0.1
■ LOU BRUCE Bruce, Louis R. b: 1/16/1877, St.Regis, N.Y. d: 2/9/68, Ilion, N.Y. BL/TR, 5'5", 145 lbs. Deb: 6/22/04 ♦																									
1904 Phi-A	0	0	—	2	0	0	0	0	11	11	1	2	2	10.6	4.91	55	.261	.295	27	.267	0	-3	-3	1	-0.2
■ BOB BRUCE Bruce, Robert James b: 5/16/33, Detroit, Mich. BR/TR, 6'3", 200 lbs. Deb: 9/14/59																									
1959 Det-A	0	1	.000	2	1	0	0	0	2	2	1	3	1	22.5	9.00	45	.250	.455	0	—	0	-1	-1	0	0.0
1960 Det-A	4	7	.364	34	15	1	0	0	130	127	16	56	76	13.0	3.74	106	.250	.331	7	.179	0	2	3	1	0.4
1961 Det-A	1	2	.333	14	6	0	0	0	44²	57	6	24	25	16.7	4.43	92	.320	.407	1	.111	0	-2	-2	-1	-0.1
1962 Hou-N	10	9	.526	32	27	6	0	0	175	164	16	82	135	13.3	4.06	92	.248	.342	11	.200	5	-2	-0	-1	-0.1
1963 Hou-N	5	9	.357	30	25	1	1	0	170¹	162	7	60	123	12.2	3.59	88	.250	.321	7	.127	2	-6	-8	-1	-0.8
1964 Hou-N	15	9	.625	35	29	9	4	0	202¹	191	8	33	135	10.1	2.76	124	.246	.279	12	.190	2	18	15	-0	1.8
1965 Hou-N	9	18	.333	35	34	7	1	0	229²	241	22	38	145	11.3	3.72	90	.270	.307	9	.122	-1	-5	-9	0	-1.0
1966 Hou-N	3	13	.188	25	23	1	0	0	129²	160	16	29	71	13.7	5.34	64	.301	.346	3	.077	-2	-25	-28	-0	-2.8
1967 Atl-N	2	3	.400	12	7	1	0	0	38²	42	3	15	22	13.5	4.89	68	.269	.337	2	.167	0	-7	-7	-0	-0.6
Total 9	49	71	.408	219	167	26	6	1	1122¹	1146	95	340	733	12.3	3.85	91	.263	.323	52	.150	6	-28	-43	-2	-3.2
■ FRED BRUCKBAUER Bruckbauer, Frederick John b: 5/27/38, New Ulm, Minn. BR/TR, 6'1", 185 lbs. Deb: 4/25/61																									
1961 Min-A	0	0	—	1	0	0	0	0	0	3	0	1	0	—	∞	—	1.000	1.000	0	—	0	-3	-3	0	-0.2
■ ANDY BRUCKMILLER Bruckmiller, Andrew b: 1/1/1882, McKeesport, Pa. d: 1/12/70, McKeesport, Pa. BR/TR, 5'11", 175 lbs. Deb: 6/26/05																									
1905 Det-A	0	0	—	1	0	0	0	0	1	4	0	1	1	45.0	27.00	10	.586	.639	0	.000	-0	-3	-3	0	-0.2
■ MIKE BRUHERT Bruhert, Michael Edwin b: 6/24/51, Jamaica, N.Y. BR/TR, 6'6", 220 lbs. Deb: 4/09/78																									
1978 NY-N	4	11	.267	27	22	1	1	0	133²	171	6	34	56	13.9	4.78	73	.317	.359	3	.075	-3	-18	-19	0	-2.1
■ JACK BRUNER Bruner, Jack Raymond b: 7/1/24, Waterloo, Iowa BL/TL, 6'1", 185 lbs. Deb: 9/16/49																									
1949 Chi-A	1	2	.333	4	2	0	0	0	7²	10	0	8	4	21.1	8.22	51	.357	.500	0	.000	-0	-3	-3	-0	-0.3
1950 Chi-A	0	0	—	9	0	0	0	0	12¹	7	0	14	8	16.1	3.65	123	.184	.415	0	—	0	1	1	-0	0.1
StL-A	1	2	.333	13	1	0	0	1	35	36	4	23	16	15.7	4.63	107	.267	.381	0	.000	-1	-0	1	-1	0.0
Yr	1	2	.333	22	1	0	0	1	47¹	43	4	37	24	15.6	4.37	110	.247	.385	2	.200	-1	1	2	-1	0.1
Total 2	2	4	.333	26	3	0	0	1	55	53	4	45	28	16.5	4.91	96	.264	.406	0	.000	-1	-2	-1	-1	-0.2
■ ROY BRUNER Bruner, Walter Roy b: 2/10/17, Cecilia, Ky. d: 11/30/86, St.Matthews, Ky. BR/TR, 6', 165 lbs. Deb: 9/14/39																									
1939 Phi-N	0	4	.000	4	4	2	0	0	27	38	3	13	11	17.0	6.67	60	.339	.408	1	.111	-1	-8	-8	-0	-0.7
1940 Phi-N	0	0	—	2	0	0	0	0	6¹	5	2	6	4	15.6	5.68	69	.227	.393	1	.500	0	-1	-1	0	-0.1
1941 Phi-N	0	3	.000	13	1	0	0	0	29¹	37	1	25	13	19.0	4.91	75	.336	.459	0	.000	-0	-4	-4	-0	-0.4
Total 3	0	7	.000	19	5	2	0	0	62²	80	6	44	28	17.8	5.74	67	.328	.431	2	.118	-1	-14	-13	-1	-1.1
■ GEORGE BRUNET Brunet, George Stuart "Lefty" b: 6/8/35, Houghton, Mich. BR/TL, 6'1", 195 lbs. Deb: 9/14/56																									
1956 KC-A	0	0	—	6	1	0	0	0	9	10	1	11	5	21.0	7.00	62	.286	.457	0	.000	-0	-3	-3	0	-0.2
1957 KC-A	0	1	.000	4	2	0	0	0	11¹	13	2	4	3	13.5	5.56	71	.277	.333	0	.000	-0	-2	-2	0	-0.1
1959 KC-A	0	0	—	2	0	0	0	0	4²	10	2	7	7	34.7	11.57	35	.435	.581	0	—	0	-4	-4	1	-0.2

YEAR	TM/L	W	L	PCT	G	GS	CG	SH	SV	IP	H	HR	BB	SO	RAT	ERA	ERA+	OAV	OOB	BH	AVG	PB	PR	/A	PD	TPI
1960	KC-A	0	2	.000	3	2	0	0	0	10¹	12	0	10	4	20.0	4.35	91	.308	.460	0	.000	-0	-1	-0	1	0.0
	Mil-N	2	0	1.000	17	6	0	0	0	49²	53	6	22	39	13.8	5.07	68	.275	.352	1	.091	-1	-7	-9	0	-0.9
1961	Mil-N	0	0	—	5	0	0	0	0	5	7	1	2	0	16.2	5.40	69	.412	.474	0	—	0	-1	-1	0	0.0
1962	Hou-N	2	4	.333	17	11	2	0	0	54	62	2	21	36	13.8	4.50	83	.291	.355	1	.059	-1	-3	-5	1	-0.4
1963	Hou-N	0	3	.000	5	2	0	0	0	12²	24	2	6	11	21.3	7.11	44	.393	.448	0	.000	-0	-5	-6	0	-0.5
	Bal-A	0	1	.000	16	0	0	0	1	20	25	3	9	13	15.7	5.40	65	.301	.376	0	.000	-0	-4	-4	0	-0.3
1964	LA-A	2	2	.500	10	7	0	0	0	42¹	38	2	25	36	13.4	3.61	91	.237	.341	2	.182	0	0	-2	-0	-0.1
1965	Cal-A	9	11	.450	41	26	8	3	2	197	149	9	69	141	10.1	2.56	133	.209	.282	3	.054	-2	20	18	-2	1.5
1966	Cal-A	13	13	.500	41	32	8	2	0	212	183	21	106	148	12.5	3.31	101	.234	.329	7	.103	-2	3	1	-0	0.0
1967	Cal-A	11	19	.367	40	37	7	2	1	250	203	19	90	165	10.7	3.31	95	.223	.295	6	.077	-4	-2	-5	-2	-1.1
1968	Cal-A	13	17	.433	39	36	8	5	0	245¹	191	23	68	132	9.6	2.86	102	.215	.273	6	.081	-3	3	1	-2	-0.4
1969	Cal-A	6	7	.462	23	19	2	2	0	100²	98	15	39	56	12.3	3.84	91	.255	.325	1	.037	-1	-2	-4	-1	-0.5
	Sea-A	2	5	.286	12	11	2	0	0	63²	70	11	28	37	13.9	5.37	68	.280	.353	3	.150	1	-12	-12	1	-1.0
	Yr	8	12	.400	35	30	4	2	0	164¹	168	26	67	93	12.9	4.44	80	.264	.334	4	.085	-0	-15	-16	0	-1.5
1970	Was-A	8	6	.571	24	20	2	1	0	118	124	10	48	67	13.2	4.42	80	.275	.346	6	.158	1	-9	-11	-1	-1.0
	Pit-N	1	1	.500	12	1	0	0	0	16²	19	1	9	17	15.7	2.70	144	.311	.408	0	.000	-0	2	2	0	0.2
1971	StL-N	0	1	.000	12	1	0	0	0	9¹	12	3	7	4	18.3	5.79	62	.316	.422	1	.333	0	-2	-2	-0	-0.1
Total	15	69	93	.426	324	213	39	15	4	1431²	1303	133	581	921	12.0	3.62	92	.244	.320	37	.089	-13	-31	-46	-3	-5.1

■ TOM BRUNO
Bruno, Thomas Michael b: 1/26/53, Chicago, Ill. BR/TR, 6'5", 210 lbs. Deb: 8/01/76

YEAR	TM/L	W	L	PCT	G	GS	CG	SH	SV	IP	H	HR	BB	SO	RAT	ERA	ERA+	OAV	OOB	BH	AVG	PB	PR	/A	PD	TPI
1976	KC-A	1	0	1.000	12	0	0	0	0	17¹	20	3	9	11	15.1	6.75	52	.290	.372	0	—	0	-6	-6	-0	-0.6
1977	Tor-A	0	1	.000	12	0	0	0	0	18¹	30	4	13	9	21.6	7.85	53	.366	.458	0	—	0	-8	-7	0	-0.6
1978	StL-N	4	3	.571	18	3	0	0	1	49²	38	3	17	33	10.0	1.99	176	.209	.276	1	.083	-1	9	8	-1	0.8
1979	StL-N	2	3	.400	27	1	0	0	0	38¹	37	1	22	27	14.3	4.23	89	.253	.359	1	.200	0	-2	-2	-0	-0.1
Total	4	7	7	.500	69	4	0	0	1	123²	125	11	61	80	13.8	4.22	87	.261	.348	2	.118	-1	-7	-7	-1	-0.5

■ WARREN BRUSSTAR
Brusstar, Warren Scott b: 2/2/52, Oakland, Cal. BR/TR, 6'3", 200 lbs. Deb: 5/06/77

YEAR	TM/L	W	L	PCT	G	GS	CG	SH	SV	IP	H	HR	BB	SO	RAT	ERA	ERA+	OAV	OOB	BH	AVG	PB	PR	/A	PD	TPI
1977	*Phi-N	7	2	.778	46	0	0	0	3	71¹	64	7	24	46	11.2	2.65	151	.250	.317	0	.000	-1	10	11	1	1.1
1978	*Phi-N	6	3	.667	58	0	0	0	0	88²	74	0	30	60	10.9	2.33	153	.239	.312	1	.143	0	12	12	2	1.5
1979	Phi-N	1	0	1.000	13	0	0	0	1	14¹	23	1	4	3	17.0	6.91	55	.383	.422	0	—	0	-5	-5	0	-0.4
1980	*Phi-N	2	2	.500	26	0	0	0	0	38²	42	3	13	21	12.8	3.72	102	.286	.344	0	.000	-0	-1	-0	0	0.0
1981	*Phi-N	0	1	.000	14	0	0	0	0	12¹	12	0	10	8	16.8	4.38	83	.250	.390	0	—	0	-1	-1	0	-0.1
1982	Phi-N	2	3	.400	22	0	0	0	2	22²	31	2	5	11	14.7	4.76	77	.348	.389	0	.000	-0	-3	-3	0	-0.2
	Chi-A	2	0	1.000	10	0	0	0	0	18¹	19	2	3	8	11.3	3.44	117	.257	.295	0	—	0	1	1	1	0.2
1983	Chi-N	3	1	.750	59	0	0	0	1	80¹	67	1	37	46	11.9	2.35	161	.234	.326	0	.000	-0	11	13	1	1.3
1984	*Chi-N	1	1	.500	41	0	0	0	3	63²	57	4	21	36	11.2	3.11	126	.247	.312	1	.200	1	3	6	0	0.7
1985	Chi-N	4	3	.571	51	0	0	0	0	74¹	87	8	36	34	15.3	6.05	66	.292	.374	1	.143	0	-20	-17	-2	-1.8
Total	9	28	16	.636	340	0	0	0	14	484²	476	28	183	273	12.5	3.51	109	.265	.337	3	.094	-1	8	17	3	2.4

■ CLAY BRYANT
Bryant, Claiborne Henry b: 11/16/11, Madison Heights, Va. BR/TR, 6'2.5", 195 lbs. Deb: 4/19/35 C

YEAR	TM/L	W	L	PCT	G	GS	CG	SH	SV	IP	H	HR	BB	SO	RAT	ERA	ERA+	OAV	OOB	BH	AVG	PB	PR	/A	PD	TPI
1935	Chi-N	1	2	.333	9	1	0	0	2	22²	34	1	7	13	16.3	5.16	76	.358	.402	2	.333	2	-3	-3	-0	0.0
1936	Chi-N	1	2	.333	26	0	0	0	0	57¹	57	0	24	35	13.0	3.30	121	.259	.337	5	.417	1	5	4	0	0.6
1937	Chi-N	9	3	.750	38	10	4	1	3	135¹	117	1	78	75	13.0	4.26	94	.232	.336	14	.311	5	-5	-4	-3	-0.1
1938	*Chi-N	19	11	.633	44	30	17	3	2	270¹	235	6	125	**135**	12.0	3.10	124	.235	.321	24	.226	4	21	22	-3	2.4
1939	Chi-N	2	1	.667	4	4	2	0	0	31¹	42	3	14	9	16.4	5.74	69	.307	.375	3	.214	0	-6	-6	-1	-0.5
1940	Chi-N	0	1	.000	8	0	0	0	0	26¹	26	2	14	5	13.7	4.78	78	.265	.357	3	.333	1	-3	-3	0	-0.2
Total	6	32	20	.615	129	45	23	4	7	543¹	511	13	262	272	12.9	3.73	104	.249	.335	51	.266	13	8	10	-7	2.2

■ RON BRYANT
Bryant, Ronald Raymond b: 11/12/47, Redlands, Cal. BB/TL, 6', 190 lbs. Deb: 9/29/67

YEAR	TM/L	W	L	PCT	G	GS	CG	SH	SV	IP	H	HR	BB	SO	RAT	ERA	ERA+	OAV	OOB	BH	AVG	PB	PR	/A	PD	TPI
1967	SF-N	0	0	—	1	0	0	0	0	4	3	0	2	9	9.0	4.50	73	.200	.250	0	.000	-0	-1	-1	-0	0.0
1969	SF-N	4	3	.571	16	8	0	0	1	57²	60	8	25	30	13.6	4.37	80	.271	.351	3	.188	1	-5	-6	0	-0.4
1970	SF-N	5	8	.385	34	11	1	0	0	96	103	7	38	66	13.4	4.78	83	.274	.344	3	.111	-1	-8	-9	1	-0.8
1971	*SF-N	7	10	.412	27	22	3	2	0	140	146	9	49	79	12.7	3.79	90	.272	.336	10	.200	1	-5	-6	0	-0.5
1972	SF-N	14	7	.667	35	28	11	4	0	214	176	20	77	107	10.7	2.90	120	.224	.295	12	.171	1	13	14	-4	1.1
1973	SF-N	**24**	12	.667	41	39	8	0	0	270	240	23	115	143	12.1	3.53	108	.234	.316	16	.168	1	4	9	0	1.1
1974	SF-N	3	15	.167	41	23	0	0	0	126²	142	11	68	75	15.2	5.61	68	.286	.376	4	.129	-1	-28	-26	-0	-2.6
1975	StL-N	0	1	.000	10	1	0	0	0	8²	20	2	7	7	28.0	16.62	23	.444	.519	0	.000	-0	-13	-12	0	-1.1
Total	8	57	56	.504	205	132	23	6	1	917	890	80	379	509	12.7	4.02	91	.254	.331	48	.165	0	-42	-36	-3	-3.2

■ T.R. BRYDEN
Bryden, Thomas Ray b: 1/17/59, Moses Lake, Wash. BR/TR, 6'4", 190 lbs. Deb: 4/10/86

YEAR	TM/L	W	L	PCT	G	GS	CG	SH	SV	IP	H	HR	BB	SO	RAT	ERA	ERA+	OAV	OOB	BH	AVG	PB	PR	/A	PD	TPI
1986	Cal-A	2	1	.667	16	0	0	0	0	34¹	38	4	21	25	16.0	6.55	63	.290	.396	0	—	0	-9	-9	0	-0.8

■ TOD BRYNAN
Brynan, Charles Ruley b: 7/1863, Philadelphia, Pa. d: 5/10/25, Philadelphia, Pa. BR/TR, Deb: 6/22/1888

YEAR	TM/L	W	L	PCT	G	GS	CG	SH	SV	IP	H	HR	BB	SO	RAT	ERA	ERA+	OAV	OOB	BH	AVG	PB	PR	/A	PD	TPI
1888	Chi-N	2	1	.667	3	3	2	0	0	25	29	2	7	11	13.0	6.48	46	.280	.326	2	.182	0	-10	-10	-0	-0.7
1891	Bos-N	0	1	.000	1	1	0	0	0	1	4	0	3	0	63.0	54.00	7	.572	.701	0	—	0	-6	-6	0	-0.3
Total	2	2	2	.500	4	4	2	0	0	26	33	2	10	11	14.9	8.31	37	.298	.357	2	.182	0	-16	-15	-0	-1.0

■ JIM BUCHANAN
Buchanan, James Forrest b: 7/1/1876, Chatham Hill, Va. d: 6/15/49, Norfolk, Neb. BL/TR, 5'10", 165 lbs. Deb: 4/16/05

YEAR	TM/L	W	L	PCT	G	GS	CG	SH	SV	IP	H	HR	BB	SO	RAT	ERA	ERA+	OAV	OOB	BH	AVG	PB	PR	/A	PD	TPI
1905	StL-A	5	9	.357	22	15	12	1	**2**	141¹	149	2	27	54	11.2	3.50	73	.272	.306	7	.152	-0	-13	-15	-0	-1.5

■ BOB BUCHANAN
Buchanan, Robert Gordon b: 5/3/61, Ridley Park, Pa. BL/TL, 6'1", 185 lbs. Deb: 7/13/85

YEAR	TM/L	W	L	PCT	G	GS	CG	SH	SV	IP	H	HR	BB	SO	RAT	ERA	ERA+	OAV	OOB	BH	AVG	PB	PR	/A	PD	TPI
1985	Cin-N	1	0	1.000	14	0	0	0	0	16	25	4	9	3	19.1	8.44	45	.368	.442	0	.000	-0	-9	-8	0	-0.7
1989	KC-A	0	0	—	2	0	0	0	0	3¹	5	1	3	3	21.6	16.20	24	.333	.444	0	—	0	-5	-5	0	-0.3
Total	2	1	0	1.000	16	0	0	0	0	19¹	30	5	12	6	19.6	9.78	39	.361	.442	0	.000	-0	-13	-13	0	-1.0

■ GARLAND BUCKEYE
Buckeye, Garland Maiers "Gob" b: 10/16/1897, Heron Lake, Minn. d: 11/14/75, Stone Lake, Wis. BB/TL, 6', 260 lbs. Deb: 6/19/18

YEAR	TM/L	W	L	PCT	G	GS	CG	SH	SV	IP	H	HR	BB	SO	RAT	ERA	ERA+	OAV	OOB	BH	AVG	PB	PR	/A	PD	TPI
1918	Was-A	0	0	—	1	0	0	0	0	2	3	0	6	2	40.5	18.00	15	.333	.600	0	—	0	-3	-3	0	-0.2
1925	Cle-A	13	8	.619	30	18	11	1	0	153	161	3	58	49	13.2	3.65	121	.267	.338	14	.226	2	13	13	-1	1.4
1926	Cle-A	6	9	.400	32	18	5	1	0	165²	160	3	69	36	12.8	3.10	131	.264	.345	12	.200	2	17	18	-1	1.8
1927	Cle-A	10	17	.370	35	25	13	2	1	204²	231	6	74	38	13.6	3.96	106	.296	.360	19	.268	3	4	6	-0	0.7
1928	Cle-A	1	5	.167	9	6	0	0	0	35	58	2	5	6	16.7	6.69	62	.389	.417	1	.111	-1	-10	-10	-0	-0.9
	NY-N	0	0	—	1	0	0	0	0	3²	9	1	2	3	27.0	14.73	27	.409	.458	1	.500	1	-4	-4	0	-0.2
Total	5	30	39	.435	108	67	29	4	1	564	622	15	214	134	13.6	3.91	108	.287	.356	47	.230	7	16	19	-2	2.6

■ ED BUCKINGHAM
Buckingham, Edward Taylor b: 5/12/1874, Metuchen, N.J. d: 7/30/42, Bridgeport, Conn. Deb: 8/30/1895

YEAR	TM/L	W	L	PCT	G	GS	CG	SH	SV	IP	H	HR	BB	SO	RAT	ERA	ERA+	OAV	OOB	BH	AVG	PB	PR	/A	PD	TPI
1895	Was-N	0	0	—	1	1	0	0	0	3	6	0	2	1	24.0	6.00	80	.408	.479	0	.000	-0	-0	-0	0	0.0

■ JESS BUCKLES
Buckles, Jesse Robert "Jim" b: 5/20/1890, LaVerne, Cal. d: 8/2/75, Westminster, Cal. BL/TL, 6'2.5", 205 lbs. Deb: 9/17/16

YEAR	TM/L	W	L	PCT	G	GS	CG	SH	SV	IP	H	HR	BB	SO	RAT	ERA	ERA+	OAV	OOB	BH	AVG	PB	PR	/A	PD	TPI
1916	NY-A	0	0	—	2	0	0	0	0	4	3	0	1	2	9.0	2.25	128	.188	.235	0	.000	-0	0	0	0	0.0

■ JOHN BUCKLEY
Buckley, John Edward b: 3/20/1869, Marlboro, Mass. d: 5/3/42, Westborough, Mass. TR, 6'1", 200 lbs. Deb: 7/15/1890

YEAR	TM/L	W	L	PCT	G	GS	CG	SH	SV	IP	H	HR	BB	SO	RAT	ERA	ERA+	OAV	OOB	BH	AVG	PB	PR	/A	PD	TPI
1890	Buf-P	1	3	.250	4	4	4	0	0	34	49	5	16	4	17.2	7.68	53	.323	.388	0	.000	-2	-13	-14	1	-1.0

■ MIKE BUDNICK
Budnick, Michael Joe b: 9/15/19, Astoria, Ore. BR/TR, 6'1", 200 lbs. Deb: 4/18/46

YEAR	TM/L	W	L	PCT	G	GS	CG	SH	SV	IP	H	HR	BB	SO	RAT	ERA	ERA+	OAV	OOB	BH	AVG	PB	PR	/A	PD	TPI
1946	NY-N	2	3	.400	35	7	1	1	3	88¹	75	13	48	36	12.5	3.16	109	.231	.330	6	.300	3	2	3	1	0.7
1947	NY-N	0	0	—	7	1	0	0	0	12	16	0	10	6	19.5	10.50	39	.314	.426	1	.250	0	-9	-9	-0	-0.7

YEAR TM/L	W	L	PCT	G	GS	CG	SH	SV	IP	H	HR	BB	SO	RAT	ERA	ERA+	OAV	OOB	BH	AVG	PB	PR	/A	PD	TPI
Total 2	2	3	.400	42	8	1	1	3	100¹	91	13	58	42	13.4	4.04	87	.242	.343	7	.292	3	-6	-6	1	0.0

■ CHARLIE BUFFINTON
Buffinton, Charles G.   b: 6/14/1861, Fall River, Mass.   d: 9/23/07, Fall River, Mass.   BR/TR, 6'1", 180 lbs.   Deb: 5/17/1882   M♦

YEAR TM/L	W	L	PCT	G	GS	CG	SH	SV	IP	H	HR	BB	SO	RAT	ERA	ERA+	OAV	OOB	BH	AVG	PB	PR	/A	PD	TPI
1882 Bos-N	2	3	.400	5	5	4	1	0	42	53	2	14	17	14.4	4.07	70	.291	.342	13	.260	0	-6	-6	1	-0.4
1883 Bos-N	25	14	.641	43	41	34	4	1	333	346	4	51	188	10.7	3.03	103	.252	.279	81	.238	0	4	3	-0	0.2
1884 Bos-N	48	16	.750	67	67	63	8	0	587	506	15	76	417	8.9	2.15	134	.220	.245	94	.267	12	54	48	3	6.1
1885 Bos-N	22	27	.449	51	50	49	6	0	434¹	425	10	112	242	11.1	2.88	93	.244	.290	81	.240	5	-3	-10	5	0.0
1886 Bos-N	7	10	.412	18	17	16	0	0	151	203	4	39	47	14.4	4.59	69	.309	.348	51	.290	4	-22	-24	-0	-1.9
1887 Phi-N	21	17	.553	40	38	35	1	0	332¹	352	16	92	160	12.0	3.66	115	.264	.312	72	.268	2	14	20	7	2.9
1888 Phi-N	28	17	.622	46	46	43	6	0	400¹	324	6	59	199	8.6	1.91	154	.213	.243	29	.181	-1	41	46	9	5.8
1889 Phi-N	28	16	.636	47	43	37	2	0	380	390	10	121	153	12.1	3.24	134	.257	.312	32	.208	-3	33	47	1	4.3
1890 Phi-P	19	15	.559	36	33	28	0	1	283¹	312	8	126	89	13.9	3.81	112	.268	.339	41	.273	4	13	15	1	1.6
1891 Bos-a	29	9	.763	48	43	33	2	3	363²	303	8	120	158	10.5	2.55	137	.253	.281	34	.188	0	47	38	6	3.8
1892 Bal-N	4	8	.333	13	13	9	0	0	97	130	4	46	30	16.3	4.92	70	.309	.377	15	.349	4	-18	-16	2	-0.8
Total 11	233	152	.605	414	396	351	30	5	3404	3344	87	856	1700	11.1	2.96	114	.246	.291	543	.245	27	160	158	34	21.6

■ BOB BUHL
Buhl, Robert Ray   b: 8/12/28, Saginaw, Mich.   BR/TR, 6'2", 180 lbs.   Deb: 4/17/53

YEAR TM/L	W	L	PCT	G	GS	CG	SH	SV	IP	H	HR	BB	SO	RAT	ERA	ERA+	OAV	OOB	BH	AVG	PB	PR	/A	PD	TPI
1953 Mil-N	13	8	.619	30	18	8	3	0	154¹	133	9	73	83	12.2	2.97	132	.235	.326	6	.113	-2	23	16	1	1.4
1954 Mil-N	2	7	.222	31	14	2	1	3	110¹	117	5	65	57	15.0	4.00	93	.277	.376	1	.032	-2	1	-3	-0	-0.5
1955 Mil-N	13	11	.542	38	27	11	1	1	201²	168	13	109	117	12.4	3.21	117	.227	.327	6	.105	-3	18	12	-1	0.7
1956 Mil-N	18	8	.692	38	33	13	2	0	216²	190	18	105	86	12.3	3.32	104	.236	.326	7	.096	-3	11	3	0	0.0
1957 *Mil-N	18	7	.720	34	31	14	2	0	216²	191	15	121	117	13.0	2.74	128	.241	.341	6	.082	-3	27	18	-2	1.3
1958 Mil-N	5	2	.714	11	10	3	0	1	73	74	5	30	27	12.9	3.45	102	.260	.332	5	.200	0	4	1	1	0.2
1959 Mil-N	15	9	.625	31	25	12	4	0	198	181	19	74	105	11.7	2.86	124	.243	.313	4	.057	-4	24	15	3	1.4
1960 Mil-N	16	9	.640	36	33	11	2	0	238²	202	23	103	121	11.6	3.09	111	.229	.312	14	.157	-2	18	9	3	1.0
1961 Mil-N	9	10	.474	32	28	9	1	0	188¹	180	23	98	77	13.5	4.11	91	.256	.312	4	.067	-3	-2	-8	1	-1.0
1962 Mil-N	0	1	.000	1	1	0	0	0	2	6	0	4	1	45.0	22.50	17	.545	.667	0	.000	-0	-4	-4	0	-0.3
Chi-N	12	13	.480	34	30	8	1	0	212	204	23	94	109	12.9	3.69	112	.255	.338	0	.000	-6	6	11	-1	0.3
Yr	12	14	.462	35	31	8	1	0	214	210	23	98	110	13.2	3.87	107	.259	.343	7	.100	-6	2	7	-1	0.0
1963 Chi-N	11	14	.440	37	34	6	0	0	226	219	24	62	108	11.3	3.38	104	.255	.312	8	.108	-3	-2	3	1	0.2
1964 Chi-N	15	14	.517	36	35	11	3	0	227²	208	22	68	107	11.1	3.83	97	.244	.303	7	.096	-2	-8	-3	2	-0.1
1965 Chi-N	13	11	.542	32	31	2	0	0	184¹	207	26	57	92	12.9	4.39	84	.284	.335	4	.060	-4	-17	-15	0	-1.8
1966 Chi-N	0	0	—	1	1	0	0	0	2¹	4	1	1	1	19.3	15.43	24	.400	.455	0	.000	-0	-3	-3	0	-0.2
Phi-N	6	8	.429	32	18	1	0	1	132	156	10	39	59	13.6	4.77	75	.298	.351	4	.098	-1	-17	-17	1	-1.7
Yr	6	8	.429	33	19	1	0	1	134¹	160	11	40	60	13.7	4.96	73	.299	.352	3	.071	-2	-20	-20	1	-1.9
1967 Phi-N	0	0	—	3	0	0	0	0	3	6	2	2	1	24.0	12.00	28	.462	.533	0	—	0	-3	-3	0	-0.2
Total 15	166	132	.557	457	369	111	20	6	2587	2446	238	1105	1268	12.5	3.55	103	.251	.330	76	.089	-41	75	36	10	0.7

■ DE WAYNE BUICE
Buice, De Wayne Allison   b: 8/20/57, Lynwood, Cal.   BR/TR, 6', 170 lbs.   Deb: 4/25/87

YEAR TM/L	W	L	PCT	G	GS	CG	SH	SV	IP	H	HR	BB	SO	RAT	ERA	ERA+	OAV	OOB	BH	AVG	PB	PR	/A	PD	TPI
1987 Cal-A	6	7	.462	57	0	0	0	17	114	87	12	40	109	10.2	3.39	127	.213	.287	0	—	0	13	11	-0	1.1
1988 Cal-A	2	4	.333	32	0	0	0	3	41¹	45	5	19	38	13.9	5.88	65	.287	.364	0	—	0	-9	-9	-0	-0.8
1989 Tor-A	1	0	1.000	7	0	0	0	0	17	13	2	13	10	13.8	5.82	65	.220	.361	0	—	0	-4	-4	0	-0.3
Total 3	9	11	.450	96	0	0	0	20	172¹	145	19	72	157	11.4	4.23	98	.232	.314	0	—	0	1	-2	-0	0.0

■ CY BUKER
Buker, Cyril Owen   b: 2/5/19, Greenwood, Wis.   BL/TR, 5'11", 190 lbs.   Deb: 5/17/45

YEAR TM/L	W	L	PCT	G	GS	CG	SH	SV	IP	H	HR	BB	SO	RAT	ERA	ERA+	OAV	OOB	BH	AVG	PB	PR	/A	PD	TPI
1945 Bro-N	7	2	.778	42	4	0	0	5	87¹	90	2	45	48	14.0	3.30	114	.268	.356	3	.188	-0	5	4	-1	0.3

■ RED BULLOCK
Bullock, Malton Joseph   b: 10/12/11, Biloxi, Miss.   d: 6/27/88, Pascagoula, Miss.   BL/TL, 6'1", 192 lbs.   Deb: 5/19/36

YEAR TM/L	W	L	PCT	G	GS	CG	SH	SV	IP	H	HR	BB	SO	RAT	ERA	ERA+	OAV	OOB	BH	AVG	PB	PR	/A	PD	TPI
1936 Phi-A	0	2	.000	12	2	0	0	0	16²	19	0	37	7	30.2	14.04	36	.271	.523	0	.000	-1	-17	-17	0	-1.3

■ WALLY BUNKER
Bunker, Wallace Edward   b: 1/25/45, Seattle, Wash.   BR/TR, 6'2", 197 lbs.   Deb: 9/29/63

YEAR TM/L	W	L	PCT	G	GS	CG	SH	SV	IP	H	HR	BB	SO	RAT	ERA	ERA+	OAV	OOB	BH	AVG	PB	PR	/A	PD	TPI
1963 Bal-A	0	1	.000	1	1	0	0	0	4	10	1	3	1	29.3	13.50	26	.476	.542	1	.500	0	-4	-4	-0	-0.3
1964 Bal-A	19	5	.792	29	29	12	1	0	214	161	17	62	96	9.5	2.69	133	.207	.269	5	.069	-2	22	21	1	2.2
1965 Bal-A	10	8	.556	34	27	4	1	2	189	170	16	58	84	11.0	3.38	103	.242	.303	4	.073	-1	2	2	-0	0.0
1966 *Bal-A	10	6	.625	29	24	3	0	0	142²	151	16	48	89	12.7	4.29	78	.269	.329	5	.104	-0	-14	-15	-0	-1.5
1967 Bal-A	3	7	.300	29	9	1	0	1	88	83	7	31	51	11.9	4.09	77	.254	.322	2	.077	-2	-8	-9	1	-0.9
1968 Bal-A	2	0	1.000	18	10	2	1	0	71	59	4	14	44	9.4	2.41	121	.225	.267	2	.111	-0	5	4	0	0.4
1969 KC-A	12	11	.522	35	31	10	1	2	222²	198	29	62	130	10.7	3.23	114	.238	.294	10	.143	0	10	11	3	1.6
1970 KC-A	2	11	.154	24	15	2	1	0	121²	109	16	50	59	11.8	4.22	89	.238	.313	2	.065	-0	-7	-6	-1	-0.7
1971 KC-A	2	3	.400	7	6	0	0	0	32¹	35	7	6	15	11.4	5.01	68	.271	.304	0	.000	-1	-6	-6	0	-0.6
Total 9	60	52	.536	206	152	34	5	5	1085¹	976	113	334	569	11.0	3.51	99	.240	.300	31	.094	-5	-1	-3	4	0.2

■ JIM BUNNING
Bunning, James Paul David   b: 10/23/31, Southgate, Ky.   BR/TR, 6'3", 190 lbs.   Deb: 7/20/55

YEAR TM/L	W	L	PCT	G	GS	CG	SH	SV	IP	H	HR	BB	SO	RAT	ERA	ERA+	OAV	OOB	BH	AVG	PB	PR	/A	PD	TPI
1955 Det-A	3	5	.375	15	8	0	0	1	51	59	8	32	37	16.6	6.35	60	.291	.395	3	.200	-0	-14	-14	0	-1.3
1956 Det-A	5	1	.833	15	3	0	0	1	53¹	55	6	28	34	14.0	3.71	111	.257	.343	6	.333	2	3	2	-1	0.3
1957 Det-A	20	8	.714	45	30	14	1	1	267¹	214	33	72	182	10.0	2.69	143	.218	.279	20	.213	3	33	35	-6	3.5
1958 Det-A	14	12	.538	35	34	10	3	0	219²	188	28	79	177	10.9	3.52	115	.228	.296	14	.187	-1	6	12	-4	0.9
1959 Det-A	17	13	.567	40	35	14	1	1	249²	220	37	75	201	11.0	3.89	104	.234	.298	17	.191	1	-1	5	-5	0.1
1960 Det-A	11	14	.440	36	34	10	3	0	252	217	20	64	201	10.4	2.79	142	.236	.293	13	.160	-2	30	33	-2	3.0
1961 Det-A	17	11	.607	38	37	12	4	1	268	232	25	71	194	10.5	3.19	128	.229	.285	13	.130	-4	25	27	-2	2.2
1962 Det-A	19	10	.655	41	35	12	2	6	258	262	24	74	184	12.2	3.59	113	.261	.320	23	.242	4	11	14	-6	1.3
1963 Det-A	12	13	.480	39	35	6	2	1	248¹	245	38	69	196	11.6	3.88	97	.254	.307	13	.155	-1	-7	-4	-2	-0.6
1964 Phi-N	19	8	.704	41	39	13	5	2	284¹	248	23	46	219	9.7	2.63	132	.233	.274	12	.121	-2	29	27	-4	2.1
1965 Phi-N	19	9	.679	39	39	15	7	0	291	253	23	62	268	10.1	2.60	133	.232	.281	22	.214	4	30	28	-1	3.4
1966 Phi-N	19	14	.576	43	41	16	5	1	314	260	26	55	252	9.6	2.41	149	.223	.270	19	.179	1	42	41	-4	4.2
1967 Phi-N	17	15	.531	40	40	16	6	0	302¹	241	18	73	253	9.7	2.29	149	.217	.273	17	.163	2	36	38	-3	4.2
1968 Pit-N	4	14	.222	27	26	3	1	0	160	168	14	48	95	12.6	3.88	75	.272	.333	5	.098	-2	-16	-17	-2	-2.2
1969 Pit-N	10	9	.526	25	25	4	0	0	156	147	16	49	124	11.7	3.81	92	.249	.313	2	.043	-3	-4	-6	-3	-1.1
LA-N	3	1	.750	9	9	1	0	0	56¹	65	5	10	33	12.1	3.36	99	.288	.321	2	.111	-1	1	-0	-1	-0.1
Yr	13	10	.565	34	34	5	0	0	212¹	212	15	59	157	11.5	3.69	93	.257	.307	3	.046	-4	-2	-6	-4	-1.2
1970 Phi-N	10	15	.400	34	33	4	0	0	219	233	19	56	147	12.2	4.11	97	.274	.325	9	.127	-2	-2	-3	-1	-0.5
1971 Phi-N	5	12	.294	29	16	1	0	1	110	126	11	37	58	13.8	5.48	64	.297	.362	3	.120	0	-25	-24	-0	-2.4
Total 17	224	184	.549	591	519	151	40	16	3760¹	3433	372	1000	2855	11.0	3.27	114	.242	.299	213	.167	-1	179	192	-47	17.0

■ DAVE BURBA
Burba, David Allen   b: 7/7/66, Dayton, Ohio   BR/TR, 6'4", 220 lbs.   Deb: 9/08/90

YEAR TM/L	W	L	PCT	G	GS	CG	SH	SV	IP	H	HR	BB	SO	RAT	ERA	ERA+	OAV	OOB	BH	AVG	PB	PR	/A	PD	TPI
1990 Sea-A	0	0	—	6	0	0	0	0	8	8	0	2	4	12.4	4.50	88	.267	.333	0	—	0	-1	-0	0	0.0

■ BILL BURBACH
Burbach, William David   b: 8/22/47, Dickeyville, Wis.   BR/TR, 6'4", 215 lbs.   Deb: 4/11/69

YEAR TM/L	W	L	PCT	G	GS	CG	SH	SV	IP	H	HR	BB	SO	RAT	ERA	ERA+	OAV	OOB	BH	AVG	PB	PR	/A	PD	TPI
1969 NY-A	6	8	.429	31	24	2	1	0	140²	112	15	102	82	13.8	3.65	95	.219	.351	4	.100	-1	-0	-3	-1	-0.4
1970 NY-A	0	2	.000	4	4	0	0	0	16²	23	2	9	10	17.8	10.26	34	.324	.407	0	.000	-1	-12	-12	-0	-1.1
1971 NY-A	0	1	.000	2	0	0	0	0	3¹	6	0	5	3	29.7	10.80	30	.400	.550	0	.000	-0	-3	-3	-0	-0.2
Total 3	6	11	.353	37	28	2	1	0	160²	141	17	116	95	14.6	4.48	78	.236	.363	4	.085	-2	-15	-18	-1	-1.7

■ LARRY BURCHART
Burchart, Larry Wayne   b: 2/8/46, Tulsa, Okla.   BR/TR, 6'3", 205 lbs.   Deb: 4/10/69

YEAR TM/L	W	L	PCT	G	GS	CG	SH	SV	IP	H	HR	BB	SO	RAT	ERA	ERA+	OAV	OOB	BH	AVG	PB	PR	/A	PD	TPI
1969 Cle-A	0	2	.000	29	0	0	0	0	42¹	42	2	24	26	14.2	4.25	89	.266	.366	0	—	0	-3	-2	-1	-0.2

YEAR	TM/L	W	L	PCT	G	GS	CG	SH	SV	IP	H	HR	BB	SO	RAT	ERA	ERA+	OAV	OOB	BH	AVG	PB	PR	/A	PD	TPI

■ FRED BURCHELL Burchell, Frederick Duff b: 7/14/1879, Perth Amboy, N.J. d: 11/20/51, Jordan, N.Y. BR/TL, 5'11", 190 lbs. Deb: 4/17/03

YEAR	TM/L	W	L	PCT	G	GS	CG	SH	SV	IP	H	HR	BB	SO	RAT	ERA	ERA+	OAV	OOB	BH	AVG	PB	PR	/A	PD	TPI
1903	Phi-N	0	3	.000	6	3	2	0	0	44	48	0	14	12	13.1	2.86	114	.293	.356	3	.188	-1	2	2	-0	0.1
1907	Bos-A	0	1	.000	2	1	0	0	0	10	8	0	2	6	9.0	2.70	96	.221	.262	1	.200	-0	-0	-0	-0	0.0
1908	Bos-A	10	8	.556	31	19	9	0	0	179²	161	2	65	94	11.9	2.96	83	.247	.326	17	.246	1	-11	-10	-2	-1.1
1909	Bos-A	3	3	.500	10	5	1	0	0	52	51	1	11	12	11.1	2.94	85	.271	.318	3	.158	-0	-3	-3	1	-0.1
Total	4	13	15	.464	49	28	12	0	0	285²	268	3	92	124	11.8	2.93	89	.258	.327	24	.220	-0	-12	-10	-2	-1.1

■ FREDDIE BURDETTE Burdette, Freddie Thomason b: 9/15/36, Moultrie, Ga. BR/TR, 6'1", 170 lbs. Deb: 9/05/62

YEAR	TM/L	W	L	PCT	G	GS	CG	SH	SV	IP	H	HR	BB	SO	RAT	ERA	ERA+	OAV	OOB	BH	AVG	PB	PR	/A	PD	TPI
1962	Chi-N	0	0	—	8	0	0	0	1	9²	5	2	8	5	12.1	3.72	111	.161	.333	0	.000	-0	0	0	0	0.0
1963	Chi-N	0	0	—	4	0	0	0	0	4²	5	1	2	1	13.5	3.86	91	.313	.389	0	—	0	-0	-0	0	0.0
1964	Chi-N	1	0	1.000	18	0	0	0	0	20	17	2	10	4	12.6	3.15	118	.243	.346	1	1.000	0	1	1	-0	0.2
Total	3	1	0	1.000	30	0	0	0	1	34¹	27	5	20	10	12.6	3.41	112	.231	.348	1	.500	0	1	2	0	0.2

■ LEW BURDETTE Burdette, Selva Lewis b: 11/22/26, Nitro, W.Va. BR/TR, 6'2", 180 lbs. Deb: 9/26/50 C

YEAR	TM/L	W	L	PCT	G	GS	CG	SH	SV	IP	H	HR	BB	SO	RAT	ERA	ERA+	OAV	OOB	BH	AVG	PB	PR	/A	PD	TPI
1950	NY-A	0	0	—	2	0	0	0	0	1¹	3	0	0	0	20.3	6.75	64	.500	.500	0	—	0	-0	-0	0	0.0
1951	Bos-N	0	0	—	3	0	0	0	0	4¹	6	0	5	1	24.9	6.23	59	.375	.545	0	.000	-0	-1	-1	0	0.0
1952	Bos-N	6	11	.353	45	9	5	0	7	137	138	8	47	47	12.3	3.61	100	.265	.328	4	.114	-0	2	-0	1	0.1
1953	Mil-N	15	5	.750	46	13	6	1	8	175	177	7	56	58	12.2	3.24	121	.264	.326	9	.170	-1	20	13	2	1.3
1954	Mil-N	15	14	.517	38	32	13	4	0	238	224	17	62	79	11.0	2.76	135	.251	.302	7	.089	-4	35	26	2	2.3
1955	Mil-N	13	8	.619	42	33	11	2	0	230	253	25	73	70	13.0	4.03	93	.280	.337	20	.233	3	0	-7	3	-0.2
1956	Mil-N	19	10	.655	39	35	16	**6**	1	256¹	234	22	52	110	10.1	**2.70**	128	.241	.282	16	.186	1	30	22	1	2.4
1957	*Mil-N	17	9	.654	37	33	14	1	0	256²	260	25	59	78	11.3	3.72	94	.264	.307	13	.148	1	5	-6	2	-0.3
1958	*Mil-N	20	10	**.667**	40	36	19	3	0	275¹	279	18	50	113	10.9	2.91	121	.264	.301	24	.242	8	**32**	19	3	3.0
1959	Mil-N	**21**	15	.583	41	39	20	4	1	289²	312	38	38	105	10.9	4.07	87	.273	.297	21	.202	6	-4	-17	1	-1.1
1960	Mil-N	19	13	.594	45	32	**18**	4	4	275²	277	19	35	83	10.3	3.36	102	.260	.287	16	.176	5	12	2	6	1.2
1961	Mil-N	18	11	.621	40	36	14	3	0	**272¹**	295	31	33	92	10.9	4.00	94	.273	.296	21	.204	5	1	-8	3	0.0
1962	Mil-N	10	9	.526	37	19	6	1	2	143²	172	26	23	59	12.3	4.89	78	.298	.327	9	.176	-0	-15	-17	2	-1.5
1963	Mil-N	6	5	.545	15	13	4	1	0	84	71	15	24	28	10.3	3.64	88	.228	.285	1	.038	-0	-3	-4	0	-0.4
	StL-N	3	8	.273	21	14	3	0	2	98	106	6	16	45	11.8	3.77	94	.278	.319	3	.097	-1	-5	-2	-1	-0.4
	Yr	9	13	.409	36	27	7	1	2	182	177	21	40	73	11.1	3.71	92	.255	.302	3	.053	-2	-9	-6	-1	-0.8
1964	StL-N	1	0	1.000	8	0	0	0	0	10	10	1	3	3	11.7	1.80	211	.256	.310	0	.000	-0	2	2	0	0.2
	Chi-N	9	9	.500	28	17	8	2	0	131	152	15	19	40	11.8	4.88	76	.292	.319	12	.279	6	-20	-17	2	-0.8
	Yr	10	9	.526	36	17	8	2	0	141	162	16	22	43	11.8	4.66	80	.289	.317	4	.091	6	-18	-15	2	-0.6
1965	Chi-N	0	2	.000	7	3	0	0	0	20¹	26	3	4	5	13.7	5.31	69	.299	.337	2	.333	1	-4	-4	0	-0.2
	Phi-N	3	3	.500	19	9	1	1	0	70²	95	5	17	23	14.9	5.48	63	.329	.376	6	.300	1	-15	-16	1	-1.3
	Yr	3	5	.375	26	12	1	1	0	91	121	8	21	28	14.5	5.44	65	.321	.365	0	.000	2	-19	-20	1	-1.5
1966	Cal-A	7	2	.778	54	0	0	0	5	79²	80	4	12	27	10.5	3.39	99	.268	.298	1	.125	-0	0	-0	-0	0.0
1967	Cal-A	1	0	1.000	19	0	0	1	0	18¹	16	4	0	8	8.3	4.91	64	.232	.243	0	—	0	-3	-4	0	-0.3
Total	18	203	144	.585	626	373	158	33	31	3067¹	3186	289	628	1074	11.4	3.66	99	.268	.308	185	.183	29	68	-18	28	4.0

■ BILL BURDICK Burdick, William Byron b: 10/11/1859, Austin, Minn. d: 10/23/49, Spokane, Wash. BR/TR, Deb: 7/23/1888

YEAR	TM/L	W	L	PCT	G	GS	CG	SH	SV	IP	H	HR	BB	SO	RAT	ERA	ERA+	OAV	OOB	BH	AVG	PB	PR	/A	PD	TPI
1888	Ind-N	10	10	.500	20	20	20	0	0	176	168	12	43	55	10.8	2.81	105	.242	.287	10	.147	-3	0	3	-0	0.0
1889	Ind-N	2	4	.333	10	4	2	0	1	45²	58	7	13	16	14.0	4.53	92	.300	.344	2	.118	-0	-3	-2	0	-0.1
Total	2	12	14	.462	30	24	22	0	1	221²	226	19	56	71	11.4	3.17	101	.255	.299	12	.141	-3	-2	1	-0	-0.1

■ TOM BURGMEIER Burgmeier, Thomas Henry b: 8/2/43, St.Paul, Minn. BL/TL, 5'11", 185 lbs. Deb: 4/10/68

YEAR	TM/L	W	L	PCT	G	GS	CG	SH	SV	IP	H	HR	BB	SO	RAT	ERA	ERA+	OAV	OOB	BH	AVG	PB	PR	/A	PD	TPI
1968	Cal-A	1	4	.200	56	2	0	0	5	72²	65	5	24	33	11.0	4.33	67	.250	.313	0	.000	0	-11	-12	4	-0.7
1969	KC-A	3	1	.750	31	0	0	0	1	54	67	5	21	23	14.8	4.17	88	.316	.380	3	.167	-0	-3	-3	2	-0.4
1970	KC-A	6	6	.500	41	0	0	0	1	68¹	59	6	23	43	10.8	3.16	118	.236	.300	2	.143	-0	4	4	3	0.6
1971	KC-A	9	7	.563	67	0	0	0	17	88¹	71	3	30	44	11.0	1.73	198	.223	.303	5	.250	2	17	17	3	2.4
1972	KC-A	6	2	.750	51	0	0	0	9	55¹	67	0	33	18	16.4	4.23	72	.313	.407	4	.333	1	-7	-7	1	-0.5
1973	KC-A	0	0	—	6	0	0	0	1	10	13	2	4	4	16.2	5.40	76	.310	.383	0	—	0	-2	-1	-0	-0.1
1974	Min-A	5	3	.625	50	0	0	0	4	91²	92	7	26	34	11.8	4.52	83	.270	.325	0	—	0	-9	-8	3	-0.4
1975	Min-A	5	8	.385	46	0	0	0	11	75²	76	7	23	41	11.9	3.09	126	.264	.321	0	—	0	6	6	1	0.7
1976	Min-A	8	1	.889	57	0	0	0	7	115¹	95	11	29	45	9.8	2.50	144	.226	.279	0	—	0	13	14	2	1.8
1977	Min-A	6	4	.600	61	0	0	0	7	97¹	113	6	33	56	13.7	5.09	78	.299	.358	0	—	0	-11	-12	1	-1.0
1978	Bos-A	2	1	.667	35	1	0	0	4	61¹	74	7	23	24	14.7	4.40	93	.302	.369	0	—	0	-4	-2	1	0.0
1979	Bos-A	3	2	.600	44	0	0	0	4	88²	89	8	16	60	11.1	2.74	161	.263	.304	0	—	0	15	16	1	1.7
1980	Bos-A	5	4	.556	62	0	0	0	24	99	87	3	20	54	9.9	2.00	211	.241	.285	0	—	0	22	24	3	2.8
1981	Bos-A	4	5	.444	32	0	0	0	6	59²	61	5	17	35	12.4	2.87	135	.268	.329	0	—	0	5	7	1	0.8
1982	Bos-A	7	0	1.000	40	0	0	0	2	102¹	98	6	22	44	10.7	2.29	188	.259	.303	0	—	0	20	23	3	2.6
1983	Oak-A	6	7	.462	49	0	0	0	4	96	89	4	32	39	11.3	2.81	137	.244	.305	0	—	0	13	11	2	1.3
1984	Oak-A	3	0	1.000	17	0	0	0	2	23	15	2	8	8	9.0	2.35	159	.190	.264	0	—	0	4	4	0	0.4
Total	17	79	55	.590	745	3	0	0	102	1258²	1231	94	384	584	11.8	3.23	118	.261	.321	14	.212	2	72	81	29	12.4

■ SANDY BURK Burk, Charles Sanford b: 4/22/1887, Columbus, Ohio d: 10/11/34, Brooklyn, N.Y. BR/TR, 5'8", 155 lbs. Deb: 9/12/10

YEAR	TM/L	W	L	PCT	G	GS	CG	SH	SV	IP	H	HR	BB	SO	RAT	ERA	ERA+	OAV	OOB	BH	AVG	PB	PR	/A	PD	TPI
1910	Bro-N	0	3	.000	4	3	1	0	0	19¹	17	0	27	14	21.4	6.05	50	.258	.484	0	.000	-1	-6	-6	0	-0.6
1911	Bro-N	1	3	.250	13	7	1	0	0	58	54	1	47	15	16.1	5.12	65	.261	.405	2	.105	-1	-11	-12	0	-1.1
1912	Bro-N	0	0	—	2	0	0	0	0	8¹	9	0	3	2	13.0	3.24	103	.273	.333	1	.250	0	0	0	0	0.0
	StL-N	1	3	.250	12	4	2	0	1	44²	37	0	12	17	10.1	2.42	142	.226	.282	0	.000	-2	5	5	-1	0.2
	Yr	1	3	.250	14	4	2	0	1	53	46	0	15	19	10.5	2.55	134	.234	.291	1	.000	-1	5	5	-1	0.2
1913	StL-N	0	2	.000	19	5	0	0	0	70	81	1	33	29	15.4	5.14	63	.290	.377	2	.091	-2	-15	-15	-0	-1.6
1915	Pit-F	2	0	1.000	2	2	1	0	0	18	8	0	11	9	9.5	1.00	301	.140	.278	1	.167	-0	4	4	-1	0.4
Total	5	4	11	.267	52	21	5	0	2	218¹	206	2	133	86	14.5	4.25	77	.256	.369	6	.090	-5	-23	-24	-1	-2.7

■ ELMER BURKART Burkart, Elmer Robert "Swede" b: 2/1/17, Torresdale, Pa. BR/TR, 6'2", 190 lbs. Deb: 9/14/36

YEAR	TM/L	W	L	PCT	G	GS	CG	SH	SV	IP	H	HR	BB	SO	RAT	ERA	ERA+	OAV	OOB	BH	AVG	PB	PR	/A	PD	TPI
1936	Phi-N	0	0	—	2	2	0	0	0	7²	4	0	12	2	18.8	3.52	129	.160	.432	0	.000	-0	0	1	0	0.1
1937	Phi-N	0	0	—	7	0	0	0	0	16	20	0	9	4	16.3	6.19	70	.323	.408	0	.000	-1	-4	-3	0	-0.3
1938	Phi-N	0	1	.000	2	1	0	0	0	10	12	0	3	1	14.4	4.50	86	.286	.348	0	.000	-0	-1	-1	-0	0.0
1939	Phi-N	1	0	1.000	5	0	0	0	0	8¹	11	0	2	2	14.0	4.32	93	.344	.382	1	1.000	1	-0	-0	-0	0.0
Total	4	1	1	.500	16	3	1	0	0	42	47	0	26	9	15.9	4.93	85	.292	.394	1	.083	-1	-5	-3	-0	-0.2

■ JOHN BURKE Burke, John Patrick b: 1/27/1877, Hazelton, Pa. d: 8/4/50, Jersey City, N.J. BR/TR, Deb: 6/27/02 ◆

YEAR	TM/L	W	L	PCT	G	GS	CG	SH	SV	IP	H	HR	BB	SO	RAT	ERA	ERA+	OAV	OOB	BH	AVG	PB	PR	/A	PD	TPI
1902	NY-N	0	1	.000	2	1	1	0	0	14	21	0	3	3	15.4	5.79	48	.345	.376	2	.154	-0	-5	-5	0	-0.3

■ BOBBY BURKE Burke, Robert James "Lefty" b: 1/23/07, Joliet, Ill. d: 2/8/71, Joliet, Ill. BL/TL, 6'0.5", 150 lbs. Deb: 4/16/27

YEAR	TM/L	W	L	PCT	G	GS	CG	SH	SV	IP	H	HR	BB	SO	RAT	ERA	ERA+	OAV	OOB	BH	AVG	PB	PR	/A	PD	TPI
1927	Was-A	3	2	.600	36	6	1	0	0	100	91	6	32	20	11.7	3.96	103	.245	.316	3	.125	-2	2	1	0	0.0
1928	Was-A	2	4	.333	26	7	2	1	0	85¹	87	1	18	27	11.3	3.90	103	.277	.320	5	.250	1	1	1	0	0.2
1929	Was-A	6	8	.429	37	17	4	0	0	141	154	6	55	51	13.6	4.79	89	.279	.349	6	.140	-3	-8	-9	-2	-1.1
1930	Was-A	3	4	.429	24	4	2	0	0	74¹	64	2	29	35	11.4	3.63	127	.229	.310	4	.174	-1	8	8	-1	0.5
1931	Was-A	8	3	.727	30	13	3	1	2	128²	124	6	50	38	12.3	4.27	101	.255	.327	10	.213	-0	2	1	1	0.5
1932	Was-A	3	6	.333	22	10	2	0	0	91	98	4	44	32	14.1	5.14	84	.272	.353	5	.200	1	-7	-8	-1	-0.7
1933	Was-A	4	3	.571	25	6	4	1	0	64	64	1	31	28	13.6	3.23	129	.256	.343	4	.235	0	7	7	0	0.7
1934	Was-A	8	8	.500	37	15	7	1	0	168	155	2	72	52	12.2	3.21	134	.245	.323	13	.228	2	24	21	0	2.2

YEAR TM/L	W	L	PCT	G	GS	CG	SH	SV	IP	H	HR	BB	SO	RAT	ERA	ERA+	OAV	OOB	BH	AVG	PB	PR	/A	PD	TPI
1935 Was-A	1	8	.111	15	10	2	0	0	66¹	90	7	27	16	16.1	7.46	58	.327	.391	4	.182	-0	-22	-23	1	-1.9
1937 Phi-N	0	0	—	2	0	0	0	0	0	1	0	2	0	—	∞	—	.500	.750	0	—	0	-1	-1	0	0.0
Total 10	38	46	.452	254	88	27	4	5	918²	926	35	360	299	12.8	4.29	99	.263	.336	54	.194	-3	6	-3	-2	0.0

■ STEVE BURKE
Burke, Steven Michael b: 3/5/55, Stockton, Cal. BB/TR, 6'2", 200 lbs. Deb: 9/10/77

YEAR TM/L	W	L	PCT	G	GS	CG	SH	SV	IP	H	HR	BB	SO	RAT	ERA	ERA+	OAV	OOB	BH	AVG	PB	PR	/A	PD	TPI
1977 Sea-A	0	1	.000	6	0	0	0	0	15²	12	0	7	6	10.9	2.87	143	.226	.317	0	—	0	2	2	0	0.2
1978 Sea-A	0	1	.000	18	0	0	0	0	49	46	2	24	16	13.0	3.49	109	.258	.350	0	—	0	1	2	0	0.2
Total 2	0	2	.000	24	0	0	0	0	64²	58	2	31	22	12.5	3.34	116	.251	.342	0	—	0	4	4	0	0.4

■ TIM BURKE
Burke, Timothy Philip b: 2/19/59, Omaha, Neb. BR/TR, 6'3", 205 lbs. Deb: 4/08/85

YEAR TM/L	W	L	PCT	G	GS	CG	SH	SV	IP	H	HR	BB	SO	RAT	ERA	ERA+	OAV	OOB	BH	AVG	PB	PR	/A	PD	TPI
1985 Mon-N	9	4	.692	**78**	0	0	0	8	120¹	86	9	44	87	10.2	2.39	142	.204	.290	1	.100	-0	**16**	13	0	1.4
1986 Mon-N	9	7	.563	68	2	0	0	4	101¹	103	7	46	82	13.6	2.93	126	.262	.345	0	.000	-0	9	9	1	1.0
1987 Mon-N	7	0	1.000	55	0	0	0	18	91	64	3	17	58	8.0	1.19	354	.196	.235	0	.000	-1	**29**	**30**	1	3.1
1988 Mon-N	3	5	.375	61	0	0	0	18	82	84	7	25	42	12.3	3.40	106	.272	.332	0	.000	-0	0	2	1	0.2
1989 Mon-N	9	3	.750	68	0	0	0	28	84²	68	6	22	54	9.6	2.55	138	.225	.278	0	.000	-0	9	9	1	1.1
1990 Mon-N	3	3	.500	58	0	0	0	20	75	71	6	21	47	11.3	2.52	149	.247	.303	1	.167	0	11	10	2	1.3
Total 6	40	22	.645	388	2	0	0	96	554¹	476	38	175	370	10.8	2.48	148	.233	.299	2	.053	-2	74	74	5	8.1

■ WALTER BURKE
Burke, Walter R. b: California d: 3/3/11, Memphis, Tenn. 6', 200 lbs. Deb: 6/10/1882 ♦

YEAR TM/L	W	L	PCT	G	GS	CG	SH	SV	IP	H	HR	BB	SO	RAT	ERA	ERA+	OAV	OOB	BH	AVG	PB	PR	/A	PD	TPI
1882 Buf-N	0	1	.000	1	1	0	0	0	4	10	0	0	0	22.5	11.25	26	.449	.449	0	.000	-1	-4	-4	1	-0.2
1883 Buf-N	0	0	—	1	1	0	0	0	8	8	0	3	1	13.5	5.63	56	.268	.328	1	.200	-0	-2	-2	0	-0.1
1884 Bos-U	19	15	.559	38	36	34	0	0	322	326	10	31	255	10.0	2.85	103	.246	.263	41	.223	1	6	3	-4	0.0
1887 Det-N	0	1	.000	2	2	1	0	0	15	21	0	5	3	15.6	6.00	67	.322	.370	2	.250	-0	-3	-3	0	-0.2
Total 4	19	17	.528	42	40	35	0	0	349	366	10	39	259	10.4	3.15	95	.253	.272	44	.219	-1	-3	-6	-3	-0.5

■ BILLY BURKE
Burke, William Ignatius b: 7/11/1889, Clinton, Mass. d: 2/9/67, Worcester, Mass. BL/TL, 5'10", 165 lbs. Deb: 4/30/10

YEAR TM/L	W	L	PCT	G	GS	CG	SH	SV	IP	H	HR	BB	SO	RAT	ERA	ERA+	OAV	OOB	BH	AVG	PB	PR	/A	PD	TPI
1910 Bos-N	1	0	1.000	19	1	0	0	0	64	68	1	29	22	13.9	4.08	82	.302	.387	4	.190	-1	-7	-5	-1	-0.6
1911 Bos-N	0	1	.000	2	1	0	0	0	3¹	6	0	5	1	29.7	18.90	20	.429	.579	1	1.000	0	-6	-6	-0	-0.4
Total 2	1	1	.500	21	2	1	0	0	67¹	74	1	34	23	14.7	4.81	70	.310	.400	5	.227	-1	-13	-11	-1	-1.0

■ JESSE BURKETT
Burkett, Jesse Cail "Crab" b: 12/4/1868, Wheeling, W.Va. d: 5/27/53, Worcester, Mass. BL/TL, 5'8", 155 lbs. Deb: 4/22/1890 CH♦

YEAR TM/L	W	L	PCT	G	GS	CG	SH	SV	IP	H	HR	BB	SO	RAT	ERA	ERA+	OAV	OOB	BH	AVG	PB	PR	/A	PD	TPI
1890 NY-N	3	10	.231	21	12	6	0	0	118	134	3	92	82	17.2	5.57	63	.278	.393	124	.309	8	-26	-27	2	-2.2
1894 Cle-N	0	0	—	1	0	0	0	0	4	6	0	1	0	15.8	4.50	121	.342	.378	187	.358	0	-1	-1	0	0.0
1902 StL-A	0	1	.000	1	0	0	0	0	1	4	0	1	2	45.0	9.00	39	.585	.638	169	.306	0	-1	-1	0	0.0
Total 3	3	11	.214	23	12	6	0	0	123	144	3	94	84	17.4	5.56	64	.284	.396	2850	.338	9	-27	-27	2	-2.2

■ JOHN BURKETT
Burkett, John David b: 11/28/64, New Brighton, Pa. BR/TR, 6'2", 175 lbs. Deb: 9/15/87

YEAR TM/L	W	L	PCT	G	GS	CG	SH	SV	IP	H	HR	BB	SO	RAT	ERA	ERA+	OAV	OOB	BH	AVG	PB	PR	/A	PD	TPI
1987 SF-N	0	0	—	3	0	0	0	0	6	7	2	3	5	16.5	4.50	85	.304	.407	0	.000	-0	-0	-0	0	0.0
1990 SF-N	14	7	.667	33	32	2	0	1	204	201	18	61	118	11.7	3.79	98	.257	.314	3	.048	-3	-0	-2	-1	-0.5
Total 2	14	7	.667	36	32	2	0	1	210	208	20	64	123	11.9	3.81	98	.259	.317	3	.047	-3	-0	-2	-1	-0.5

■ KEN BURKHART
Burkhart, Kenneth William (b: Kenneth William Burkhardt) b: 11/18/16, Knoxville, Tenn. BR/TR, 6'1", 190 lbs. Deb: 4/21/45 U

YEAR TM/L	W	L	PCT	G	GS	CG	SH	SV	IP	H	HR	BB	SO	RAT	ERA	ERA+	OAV	OOB	BH	AVG	PB	PR	/A	PD	TPI
1945 StL-N	18	8	.692	42	22	12	4	2	217¹	206	9	66	67	11.4	2.90	129	.251	.309	13	.181	1	22	20	-1	2.1
1946 StL-N	6	3	.667	25	13	5	2	2	100	111	4	36	32	13.4	2.88	120	.282	.346	5	.147	-0	6	6	-1	0.5
1947 StL-N	3	6	.333	34	6	1	0	1	95	108	13	23	44	12.8	5.21	79	.292	.340	3	.125	-1	-12	-11	1	-1.1
1948 StL-N	0	0	—	20	0	0	0	1	37¹	50	4	14	16	15.9	5.54	74	.331	.395	1	.250	0	-7	-6	1	-0.4
Cin-N	0	3	.000	16	0	0	0	0	41²	42	3	16	14	12.7	6.91	57	.255	.324	3	.333	2	-14	-14	-0	-1.1
Yr	0	3	.000	36	0	0	0	1	79	92	7	30	30	14.0	6.27	64	.289	.352	1	.077	2	-20	-20	0	-1.5
1949 Cin-N	0	0	—	11	0	0	0	1	28¹	29	2	10	8	12.4	3.18	132	.282	.345	2	.286	0	3	3	0	0.1
Total 5	27	20	.574	148	41	18	6	7	519²	546	35	165	181	12.5	3.84	99	.273	.332	27	.180	2	-2	-1	-1	0.4

■ WALLY BURNETTE
Burnette, Wallace Harper b: 6/20/29, Blairs, Va. BR/TR, 6'0.5", 178 lbs. Deb: 7/15/56

YEAR TM/L	W	L	PCT	G	GS	CG	SH	SV	IP	H	HR	BB	SO	RAT	ERA	ERA+	OAV	OOB	BH	AVG	PB	PR	/A	PD	TPI
1956 KC-A	6	8	.429	18	14	4	1	0	121¹	115	13	39	54	11.6	2.89	150	.252	.314	2	.051	-5	17	19	-1	1.5
1957 KC-A	7	12	.368	38	9	1	0	1	113	115	8	44	57	12.7	4.30	92	.268	.338	8	.250	1	-6	-4	2	0.0
1958 KC-A	1	1	.500	12	4	0	0	0	28¹	29	2	14	11	13.7	3.49	112	.264	.347	1	.167	-0	1	1	-0	0.1
Total 3	14	21	.400	68	27	5	1	1	262²	259	23	97	122	12.3	3.56	116	.260	.328	11	.143	-4	11	16	1	1.6

■ DENNIS BURNS
Burns, Dennis b: 5/24/1898, Tiff City, Mo. d: 5/21/69, Tulsa, Okla. BR/TR, 5'10", 180 lbs. Deb: 9/22/23

YEAR TM/L	W	L	PCT	G	GS	CG	SH	SV	IP	H	HR	BB	SO	RAT	ERA	ERA+	OAV	OOB	BH	AVG	PB	PR	/A	PD	TPI
1923 Phi-A	2	1	.667	4	3	2	0	0	27	21	1	7	8	9.3	2.00	205	.210	.262	1	.111	-1	6	6	0	0.6
1924 Phi-A	6	8	.429	37	17	7	0	1	154	191	3	68	26	15.2	5.08	84	.314	.384	6	.143	-2	-15	-14	0	-1.3
Total 2	8	9	.471	41	20	9	0	1	181	212	4	75	34	14.3	4.62	92	.299	.367	7	.137	-3	-9	-7	0	-0.7

■ FARMER BURNS
Burns, James "Slab" b: Ashtabula, Ohio TR, 5'7", 168 lbs. Deb: 7/06/01

YEAR TM/L	W	L	PCT	G	GS	CG	SH	SV	IP	H	HR	BB	SO	RAT	ERA	ERA+	OAV	OOB	BH	AVG	PB	PR	/A	PD	TPI
1901 StL-N	0	0	—	1	0	0	0	0	1	2	0	1	0	36.0	9.00	35	.411	.583	0	—	0	-1	-1	0	0.0

■ DICK BURNS
Burns, Richard Simon b: 12/26/1863, Holyoke, Mass. d: 11/11/37, Holyoke, Mass. BL, 140 lbs. Deb: 5/03/1883 ♦

YEAR TM/L	W	L	PCT	G	GS	CG	SH	SV	IP	H	HR	BB	SO	RAT	ERA	ERA+	OAV	OOB	BH	AVG	PB	PR	/A	PD	TPI
1883 Det-N	2	12	.143	17	13	13	0	0	127²	172	8	33	30	14.5	4.51	69	.305	.343	26	.186	-2	-19	-20	-0	-1.6
1884 Cin-U	23	15	.605	40	40	34	1	0	329²	298	7	47	167	9.4	2.46	129	.225	.252	107	.306	11	21	26	1	4.8
1885 StL-N	0	0	—	1	0	0	0	0	3	3	0	0	2	9.0	9.00	30	.248	.248	12	.222	0	-2	-2	1	-0.1
Total 3	25	27	.481	58	53	47	1	0	460¹	473	15	80	199	10.8	3.07	103	.249	.279	145	.267	10	-1	4	1	3.1

■ BRITT BURNS
Burns, Robert Britt b: 6/8/59, Houston, Tex. BL/TL, 6'5", 215 lbs. Deb: 8/05/78

YEAR TM/L	W	L	PCT	G	GS	CG	SH	SV	IP	H	HR	BB	SO	RAT	ERA	ERA+	OAV	OOB	BH	AVG	PB	PR	/A	PD	TPI
1978 Chi-A	0	2	.000	2	2	0	0	0	7²	14	2	3	3	20.0	12.91	29	.378	.425	0	—	0	-8	-8	0	-0.6
1979 Chi-A	0	0	—	6	0	0	0	0	5	10	1	1	2	19.8	5.40	79	.435	.458	0	—	0	-1	-1	-0	0.0
1980 Chi-A	15	13	.536	34	32	11	1	0	238	213	17	63	133	10.6	2.84	142	.241	.295	0	—	0	32	31	-1	3.2
1981 Chi-A	10	6	.625	24	23	5	1	0	156²	139	14	49	108	11.1	2.64	135	.238	.303	0	—	0	18	16	-4	1.3
1982 Chi-A	13	5	.722	28	28	5	1	0	169¹	168	12	67	116	12.6	4.04	100	.257	.329	0	—	0	1	-0	-3	-0.2
1983 •Chi-A	10	11	.476	29	26	8	4	0	173²	165	14	55	115	11.7	3.58	117	.249	.311	0	—	0	9	12	-3	0.9
1984 Chi-A	4	12	.250	34	16	2	0	3	117	130	7	45	85	13.8	5.00	83	.280	.349	0	—	0	-13	-11	-0	-1.0
1985 Chi-A	18	11	.621	36	34	8	4	0	227	206	26	79	172	11.4	3.96	109	.242	.308	0	—	0	5	9	-1	0.7
Total 8	70	60	.538	193	161	39	11	3	1094¹	1045	93	362	734	11.8	3.66	111	.251	.315	0	—	0	42	49	-12	4.3

■ TOM BURNS
Burns, Thomas Everett b: 3/30/1857, Honesdale, Pa. d: 3/19/02, Jersey City, N.J. BR/TR, 5'7", 152 lbs. Deb: 5/01/1880 MU♦

YEAR TM/L	W	L	PCT	G	GS	CG	SH	SV	IP	H	HR	BB	SO	RAT	ERA	ERA+	OAV	OOB	BH	AVG	PB	PR	/A	PD	TPI
1880 Chi-N	0	0	—	1	0	0	0	0	1¹	2	0	2	1	27.0	0.00	—	.330	.496	103	.309	0	0	0	0	0.0

■ OYSTER BURNS
Burns, Thomas P. b: 9/6/1864, Philadelphia, Pa. d: 11/11/28, Brooklyn, N.Y. BR/TR, 5'8", 183 lbs. Deb: 8/18/1884 ♦

YEAR TM/L	W	L	PCT	G	GS	CG	SH	SV	IP	H	HR	BB	SO	RAT	ERA	ERA+	OAV	OOB	BH	AVG	PB	PR	/A	PD	TPI
1884 Bal-a	0	0	—	2	0	0	0	1	9	12	0	2	6	14.0	3.00	116	.304	.337	39	.298	1	0	0	0	0.0
1885 Bal-a	7	4	.636	15	11	10	1	3	105²	112	2	21	30	11.3	3.58	91	.260	.295	74	.231	2	-4	-4	-1	-0.2
1887 Bal-a	1	0	1.000	3	0	0	0	0	11¹	16	0	4	2	15.9	9.53	43	.321	.371	188	.341	2	-7	-7	-0	-0.4
1888 Bal-a	0	1	.000	5	0	0	0	0	12²	12	0	3	2	10.7	4.26	70	.241	.284	97	.298	2	-2	-2	0	-0.1
Total 4	8	5	.615	25	11	10	1	4	138²	152	2	30	40	11.8	4.09	81	.267	.304	1389	.300	7	-12	-12	-1	-0.7

■ TODD BURNS
Burns, Todd Edward b: 7/6/63, Maywood, Cal. BR/TR, 6'2", 186 lbs. Deb: 5/31/88

YEAR TM/L	W	L	PCT	G	GS	CG	SH	SV	IP	H	HR	BB	SO	RAT	ERA	ERA+	OAV	OOB	BH	AVG	PB	PR	/A	PD	TPI
1988 •Oak-A	8	2	.800	17	14	2	0	1	102²	93	8	34	57	11.2	3.16	120	.241	.304	0	—	0	9	7	-1	0.7
1989 •Oak-A	6	5	.545	50	2	0	0	8	96¹	66	3	28	49	8.9	2.24	164	.196	.260	0	—	0	18	15	-1	1.5
1990 •Oak-A	3	3	.500	43	2	0	0	3	78²	78	8	32	43	12.6	2.97	126	.263	.334	0	—	0	8	7	-1	0.6

YEAR	TM/L	W	L	PCT	G	GS	CG	SH	SV	IP	H	HR	BB	SO	RAT	ERA	ERA+	OAV	OOB	BH	AVG	PB	PR	/A	PD	TPI
Total	3	17	10	.630	110	18	2	0	12	277²	237	19	94	149	10.8	2.79	134	.232	.298	0	—	0	35	29	-2	2.8

■ BILL BURNS
Burns, William Thomas "Sleepy Bill" b: 1/29/1880, San Saba, Tex. d: 6/6/53, Ramona, Cal. BB/TL, 6'2″, 195 lbs. Deb: 4/18/08

YEAR	TM/L	W	L	PCT	G	GS	CG	SH	SV	IP	H	HR	BB	SO	RAT	ERA	ERA+	OAV	OOB	BH	AVG	PB	PR	/A	PD	TPI
1908	Was-A	6	11	.353	23	19	11	2	0	165	135	3	18	55	8.6	1.69	135	.229	.257	8	.148	-1	13	11	3	1.5
1909	Was-A	1	1	.500	6	4	1	0	0	29¹	25	0	7	13	10.7	1.23	198	.229	.294	2	.182	-0	4	4	0	0.5
	Chi-A	7	13	.350	23	19	10	3	0	168	161	2	34	50	10.9	2.04	115	.264	.312	10	.172	2	8	6	1	1.0
	Yr	8	14	.364	29	23	11	3	0	197¹	186	2	41	63	10.7	1.92	123	.258	.305	5	.072	1	12	10	2	1.5
1910	Chi-A	0	0	—	1	0	0	0	0	0¹	0	0	1	0	27.0	0.00	—	.000	.500	0	—	0	0	0	0	0.0
	Cin-N	8	13	.381	31	21	13	2	0	178²	183	3	49	57	12.3	3.48	84	.273	.333	16	.262	2	-9	-11	1	-0.8
1911	Cin-N	1	0	1.000	6	3	0	0	1	17²	17	1	3	5	11.7	3.06	108	.254	.315	3	.429	2	1	0	1	0.3
	Phi-N	6	10	.375	21	14	8	3	1	121	132	5	26	47	12.2	3.42	101	.287	.333	6	.150	-1	-0	0	2	0.1
	Yr	7	10	.412	27	17	8	3	2	138²	149	6	29	52	11.9	3.38	102	.281	.326	9	.064	1	0	1	3	0.4
1912	Det-A	1	4	.200	6	5	2	0	0	38²	52	0	9	6	14.7	5.35	61	.338	.382	3	.231	1	-9	-9	0	-0.6
Total	5	30	52	.366	117	85	45	10	2	718²	705	14	147	233	11.1	2.72	100	.265	.313	48	.197	5	8	1	9	2.0

■ PETE BURNSIDE
Burnside, Peter Willits b: 7/2/30, Evanston, Ill. BR/TL, 6'2″, 180 lbs. Deb: 9/20/55

YEAR	TM/L	W	L	PCT	G	GS	CG	SH	SV	IP	H	HR	BB	SO	RAT	ERA	ERA+	OAV	OOB	BH	AVG	PB	PR	/A	PD	TPI
1955	NY-N	1	0	1.000	2	1	0	0	0	12¹	10	1	9	2	13.5	2.84	142	.204	.328	1	.200	0	2	2	0	0.2
1957	NY-N	1	4	.200	10	9	1	1	0	30²	47	5	13	18	17.9	8.80	45	.356	.418	0	.000	-1	-17	-17	-0	-1.6
1958	SF-N	0	0	—	6	1	0	0	0	10²	20	3	5	4	21.1	6.75	56	.400	.455	0	—	0	-3	-3	0	-0.2
1959	Det-A	1	3	.250	30	0	0	0	1	62	55	7	25	49	11.9	3.77	108	.237	.317	0	.000	-1	1	2	0	0.1
1960	Det-A	7	7	.500	31	15	2	0	2	113²	122	14	50	71	13.9	4.28	93	.277	.356	4	.148	-4	-5	-4	-1	-0.5
1961	Was-A	4	9	.308	33	16	4	2	2	113¹	106	11	51	56	12.7	4.53	89	.251	.335	2	.059	-3	-6	-6	-1	-0.9
1962	Was-A	5	11	.313	40	20	6	0	12	149²	152	20	51	74	12.3	4.45	91	.263	.325	2	.057	-3	-8	-7	-2	-1.0
1963	Bal-A	0	1	.000	6	0	0	0	0	7¹	11	0	2	6	17.2	4.91	72	.344	.400	0	.000	-0	-1	-1	-0	-0.1
	Was-A	0	1	.000	38	1	0	0	0	67¹	84	12	24	23	14.4	6.15	60	.308	.364	1	.091	-0	-19	-18	-1	-1.9
	Yr	0	2	.000	44	1	0	0	0	74²	95	12	26	29	14.6	6.03	61	.310	.364	1	.083	-1	-20	-19	-1	-2.0
Total	8	19	36	.345	196	64	14	3	7	567¹	607	73	230	303	13.5	4.81	82	.275	.347	10	.076	-8	-57	-53	-5	-5.9

■ SHELDON BURNSIDE
Burnside, Sheldon John b: 12/22/54, South Bend, Ind. BR/TL, 6'5″, 200 lbs. Deb: 9/04/78

YEAR	TM/L	W	L	PCT	G	GS	CG	SH	SV	IP	H	HR	BB	SO	RAT	ERA	ERA+	OAV	OOB	BH	AVG	PB	PR	/A	PD	TPI
1978	Det-A	0	0	—	2	0	0	0	0	4	4	0	2	3	13.5	9.00	43	.250	.333	0	—	0	-2	-2	-0	-0.1
1979	Det-A	1	1	.500	10	0	0	0	0	21¹	28	2	8	13	15.6	6.33	68	.333	.398	0	—	0	-5	-5	0	-0.3
1980	Cin-N	1	0	1.000	7	0	0	0	0	4²	6	1	1	2	13.5	1.93	185	.333	.368	0	.000	-0	1	1	1	0.1
Total	3	2	1	.667	19	0	0	0	0	30	38	3	11	18	15.0	6.00	69	.322	.385	0	.000	-0	-6	-6	1	-0.3

■ GEORGE BURPO
Burpo, George Harvie b: 6/19/22, Jenkins, Ky. BR/TL, 6', 195 lbs. Deb: 6/09/46

YEAR	TM/L	W	L	PCT	G	GS	CG	SH	SV	IP	H	HR	BB	SO	RAT	ERA	ERA+	OAV	OOB	BH	AVG	PB	PR	/A	PD	TPI
1946	Cin-N	0	0	—	2	0	0	0	0	2¹	4	0	5	1	34.7	15.43	22	.400	.600	0	—	0	-3	-3	0	-0.2

■ HARRY BURRELL
Burrell, Harry J. b: 1866, Vermont d: 12/11/14, Omaha, Neb. Deb: 9/13/1891

YEAR	TM/L	W	L	PCT	G	GS	CG	SH	SV	IP	H	HR	BB	SO	RAT	ERA	ERA+	OAV	OOB	BH	AVG	PB	PR	/A	PD	TPI
1891	StL-a	4	2	.667	7	4	3	0	0	43	51	4	21	19	15.1	4.81	87	.285	.360	5	.227	-0	-5	-3	-0	-0.2

■ AL BURRIS
Burris, Alva Burton b: 1/28/1874, Warwick, Md. d: 3/24/38, Salisbury, Md. BR/TR, Deb: 6/22/1894

YEAR	TM/L	W	L	PCT	G	GS	CG	SH	SV	IP	H	HR	BB	SO	RAT	ERA	ERA+	OAV	OOB	BH	AVG	PB	PR	/A	PD	TPI
1894	Phi-N	0	0	—	1	0	0	0	0	5	14	0	2	0	28.8	18.00	28	.493	.526	2	.500	1	-7	-7	0	-0.3

■ RAY BURRIS
Burris, Bertram Ray b: 8/22/50, Idabel, Okla. BR/TR, 6'5″, 200 lbs. Deb: 4/08/73 C

YEAR	TM/L	W	L	PCT	G	GS	CG	SH	SV	IP	H	HR	BB	SO	RAT	ERA	ERA+	OAV	OOB	BH	AVG	PB	PR	/A	PD	TPI
1973	Chi-N	1	1	.500	31	1	0	0	0	64²	65	2	27	57	12.8	2.92	135	.261	.333	1	.143	0	5	7	1	0.8
1974	Chi-N	3	5	.375	40	5	0	0	0	75	91	8	26	40	14.5	6.60	58	.300	.363	1	.077	-1	-25	-23	-0	-2.4
1975	Chi-N	15	10	.600	36	35	8	2	0	238¹	259	25	73	108	12.7	4.12	93	.281	.337	15	.183	1	-13	-7	-4	-0.9
1976	Chi-N	15	13	.536	37	36	10	4	0	249	251	22	70	112	11.8	3.11	124	.263	.317	9	.111	-5	11	21	1	2.0
1977	Chi-N	14	16	.467	39	39	5	1	0	221	270	29	67	105	13.8	4.72	93	.305	.356	12	.174	1	-20	-8	3	-0.2
1978	Chi-N	7	13	.350	40	32	4	1	1	198²	210	15	79	94	13.5	4.76	85	.274	.349	7	.115	-1	-26	-16	2	-1.4
1979	Chi-N	0	0	—	14	0	0	0	0	21²	23	0	15	14	16.2	6.23	66	.284	.402	0	.000	0	-6	-5	0	-0.4
	NY-A	1	3	.250	15	0	0	0	0	27²	40	5	10	19	16.3	6.18	66	.342	.394	0	—	0	-6	-6	-0	-0.5
	NY-N	0	2	.000	4	4	0	0	0	21²	21	2	6	10	11.6	3.32	109	.247	.304	1	.167	-0	1	1	0	0.1
1980	NY-N	7	13	.350	29	29	1	0	0	170¹	181	20	54	83	12.6	4.02	88	.277	.336	5	.098	-2	-8	-9	-0	-1.2
1981	*Mon-N	9	7	.563	22	21	4	0	0	135²	117	9	41	52	10.7	3.05	114	.235	.297	7	.189	1	7	7	-1	0.7
1982	Mon-N	4	14	.222	37	15	2	0	2	123²	143	14	53	55	14.4	4.73	77	.297	.369	5	.179	1	-16	-15	-0	-1.4
1983	Mon-N	4	7	.364	40	17	2	1	0	154	139	14	56	100	11.5	3.68	97	.244	.314	9	.231	3	-1	-2	0	0.2
1984	Oak-A	13	10	.565	34	28	5	1	0	211²	193	15	90	93	12.4	3.15	119	.244	.327	0	—	0	20	14	-3	1.1
1985	Mil-A	9	13	.409	29	28	6	0	0	170¹	182	25	53	81	12.6	4.81	87	.272	.328	0	—	0	-13	-12	-0	-1.1
1986	StL-N	4	5	.444	23	10	0	0	0	82	92	13	32	34	14.0	5.60	65	.287	.359	4	.148	0	-17	-18	-1	-1.7
1987	Mil-A	2	2	.500	10	2	0	0	0	23	33	4	12	8	17.6	5.87	78	.351	.425	0	—	0	-4	-3	0	-0.2
Total	15	108	134	.446	480	302	47	10	4	2188¹	2310	221	764	1065	12.9	4.17	93	.274	.338	76	.151	-1	-110	-75	-2	-6.5

■ JOHN BURROWS
Burrows, John b: 10/30/13, Winnfield, La. d: 4/27/87, Coal Run, Ohio BR/TL, 5'10″, 200 lbs. Deb: 4/25/43

YEAR	TM/L	W	L	PCT	G	GS	CG	SH	SV	IP	H	HR	BB	SO	RAT	ERA	ERA+	OAV	OOB	BH	AVG	PB	PR	/A	PD	TPI
1943	Phi-A	0	1	.000	4	1	0	0	0	7²	8	0	9	3	21.1	8.22	41	.276	.462	0	.000	-0	-4	-4	0	-0.3
	Chi-N	0	2	.000	23	1	0	0	2	32²	25	0	16	18	11.8	3.86	87	.205	.307	2	.667	1	-2	-2	0	0.0
1944	Chi-N	0	0	—	3	0	0	0	0	3	7	0	3	1	30.0	18.00	20	.467	.556	0	—	0	-5	-5	0	-0.4
Total	2	0	3	.000	30	2	0	0	2	43¹	40	0	28	22	14.7	5.61	60	.241	.360	2	.500	1	-11	-11	0	-0.7

■ JIM BURTON
Burton, Jim Scott b: 10/27/49, Royal Oak, Mich. BR/TL, 6'3″, 195 lbs. Deb: 6/10/75

YEAR	TM/L	W	L	PCT	G	GS	CG	SH	SV	IP	H	HR	BB	SO	RAT	ERA	ERA+	OAV	OOB	BH	AVG	PB	PR	/A	PD	TPI
1975	*Bos-A	1	2	.333	29	4	0	0	1	53	58	6	19	39	13.1	2.89	141	.276	.336	0	—	0	5	7	-0	0.7
1977	Bos-A	0	0	—	1	0	0	0	0	2²	2	0	1	3	10.1	0.00	—	.200	.273	0	—	0	1	1	0	0.1
Total	2	1	2	.333	30	4	0	0	1	55²	60	6	20	42	12.9	2.75	149	.273	.333	0	—	0	6	8	-0	0.8

■ MOE BURTSCHY
Burtschy, Edward Frank b: 4/18/22, Cincinnati, Ohio BR/TR, 6'3″, 208 lbs. Deb: 6/17/50

YEAR	TM/L	W	L	PCT	G	GS	CG	SH	SV	IP	H	HR	BB	SO	RAT	ERA	ERA+	OAV	OOB	BH	AVG	PB	PR	/A	PD	TPI
1950	Phi-A	0	1	.000	9	1	0	0	0	19	22	2	21	12	20.8	7.11	64	.289	.449	0	.000	-0	-5	-5	0	-0.4
1951	Phi-A	0	0	—	7	0	0	0	0	17	18	0	12	4	16.4	5.29	81	.277	.397	1	.333	0	-2	-2	0	-0.1
1954	Phi-A	5	4	.556	46	0	0	0	4	94²	80	7	53	54	13.4	3.80	103	.234	.350	2	.118	-1	-1	1	-0	0.0
1955	KC-A	2	0	1.000	7	0	0	0	0	11¹	17	0	10	9	22.2	10.32	40	.354	.475	1	.333	0	-8	-8	-0	-0.7
1956	KC-A	3	1	.750	21	0	0	0	0	43¹	41	6	30	18	15.4	3.95	110	.263	.392	1	.125	-1	1	2	2	0.3
Total	5	10	6	.625	90	1	0	0	4	185¹	178	15	126	97	15.4	4.71	88	.259	.385	5	.139	-1	-15	-12	1	-0.9

■ DENNIS BURTT
Burtt, Dennis Allen b: 11/29/57, San Diego, Cal. BB/TR, 6', 180 lbs. Deb: 9/04/85

YEAR	TM/L	W	L	PCT	G	GS	CG	SH	SV	IP	H	HR	BB	SO	RAT	ERA	ERA+	OAV	OOB	BH	AVG	PB	PR	/A	PD	TPI
1985	Min-A	2	2	.500	5	2	0	0	0	28¹	20	2	9	8	8.6	3.81	116	.200	.252	0	—	0	1	2	0	0.2
1986	Min-A	0	0	—	3	0	0	0	0	2	7	1	3	1	45.0	31.50	14	.538	.625	0	—	0	-6	-6	0	-0.4
Total	2	2	2	.500	8	2	0	0	0	30¹	27	3	10	10	11.0	5.64	78	.239	.301	0	—	0	-5	-4	0	-0.2

■ DICK BURWELL
Burwell, Richard Matthew b: 1/23/40, Alton, Ill. BR/TR, 6'1″, 190 lbs. Deb: 9/13/60

YEAR	TM/L	W	L	PCT	G	GS	CG	SH	SV	IP	H	HR	BB	SO	RAT	ERA	ERA+	OAV	OOB	BH	AVG	PB	PR	/A	PD	TPI
1960	Chi-N	0	0	—	3	1	0	0	0	9²	11	2	7	1	17.7	5.59	68	.306	.432	1	.333	0	-2	-2	0	-0.1
1961	Chi-N	0	0	—	2	0	0	0	0	4	6	0	4	0	22.5	9.00	46	.375	.500	0	.000	-0	-2	-2	0	-0.1
Total	2	0	0	—	5	1	0	0	0	13²	17	2	11	1	19.1	6.59	59	.327	.453	1	.250	-0	-4	-4	0	-0.2

■ BILL BURWELL
Burwell, William Edwin b: 3/27/1895, Jarbalo, Kan. d: 6/11/73, Ormond Beach, Fla BL/TR, 5'11″, 175 lbs. Deb: 5/01/20 MC

YEAR	TM/L	W	L	PCT	G	GS	CG	SH	SV	IP	H	HR	BB	SO	RAT	ERA	ERA+	OAV	OOB	BH	AVG	PB	PR	/A	PD	TPI
1920	StL-A	6	4	.600	33	2	0	0	4	113¹	133	5	42	30	14.2	3.65	107	.303	.369	7	.167	-2	2	3	0	0.1
1921	StL-A	2	4	.333	33	3	1	0	2	84¹	102	2	29	17	14.2	5.12	87	.309	.368	6	.240	-0	-8	-6	-1	-0.5
1928	Pit-N	1	0	1.000	4	1	0	0	0	20²	18	2	8	2	11.3	5.23	78	.234	.306	2	.222	-0	-3	-3	1	-0.1

YEAR TM/L	W	L	PCT	G	GS	CG	SH	SV	IP	H	HR	BB	SO	RAT	ERA	ERA+	OAV	OOB	BH	AVG	PB	PR	/A	PD	TPI
Total 3	9	8	.529	70	6	1	0	6	218¹	253	9	79	49	13.9	4.37	95	.299	.363	15	.197	-2	-9	-5	0	-0.5

■ STEVE BUSBY
Busby, Steven Lee b: 9/29/49, Burbank, Cal. BR/TR, 6'2", 205 lbs. Deb: 9/08/72

YEAR TM/L	W	L	PCT	G	GS	CG	SH	SV	IP	H	HR	BB	SO	RAT	ERA	ERA+	OAV	OOB	BH	AVG	PB	PR	/A	PD	TPI
1972 KC-A	3	1	.750	5	5	3	0	0	40	28	1	8	31	8.1	1.57	192	.200	.243	3	.200	0	7	6	-1	0.8
1973 KC-A	16	15	.516	37	37	7	1	0	238¹	246	18	105	174	13.5	4.23	97	.271	.350	0	—	0	-11	-3	2	-0.1
1974 KC-A	22	14	.611	38	38	20	3	0	292¹	284	14	92	198	11.9	3.39	113	.258	.320	0	—	0	8	14	2	1.7
1975 KC-A	18	12	.600	34	34	18	3	0	260¹	233	18	81	160	11.0	3.08	125	.242	.303	0	—	0	20	22	3	2.7
1976 KC-A	3	3	.500	13	13	1	0	0	71²	58	7	49	29	13.8	4.40	80	.218	.346	0	—	0	-7	-7	0	-0.6
1978 KC-A	1	0	1.000	7	5	0	0	0	21¹	24	2	15	10	17.3	7.59	50	.282	.402	0	—	0	-9	-9	0	-0.7
1979 KC-A	6	6	.500	22	12	4	0	0	94¹	71	10	64	45	12.9	3.63	118	.220	.349	0	—	0	6	7	2	0.8
1980 KC-A	1	3	.250	11	6	0	0	0	42¹	53	7	19	12	15.3	6.17	66	.335	.406	0	—	0	-10	-10	-0	-0.9
Total 8	70	54	.565	167	150	53	7	0	1060²	1003	73	433	659	12.4	3.72	105	.253	.330	3	.200	0	4	20	8	3.7

■ DON BUSCHHORN
Buschhorn, Donald Lee b: 4/29/46, Independence, Mo. BR/TR, 6', 170 lbs. Deb: 5/15/65

YEAR TM/L	W	L	PCT	G	GS	CG	SH	SV	IP	H	HR	BB	SO	RAT	ERA	ERA+	OAV	OOB	BH	AVG	PB	PR	/A	PD	TPI
1965 KC-A	0	1	.000	12	3	0	0	0	31	36	7	8	9	13.1	4.35	80	.295	.344	2	.500	1	-3	-3	0	-0.1

■ GUY BUSH
Bush, Guy Terrell "The Mississippi Mudcat" b: 8/23/01, Aberdeen, Miss. d: 7/2/85, Shannon, Miss. BR/TR, 6', 175 lbs. Deb: 9/17/23

YEAR TM/L	W	L	PCT	G	GS	CG	SH	SV	IP	H	HR	BB	SO	RAT	ERA	ERA+	OAV	OOB	BH	AVG	PB	PR	/A	PD	TPI
1923 Chi-N	0	0	—	1	0	0	0	0	1	1	0	0	2	9.0	0.00	—	.250	.250	0	—	0	0	0	0	0.0
1924 Chi-N	2	5	.286	16	8	4	0	0	80²	91	7	24	36	13.1	4.02	97	.285	.339	4	.154	-1	-1	-1	-2	-0.3
1925 Chi-N	6	13	.316	42	15	5	0	4	182	213	15	52	76	13.3	4.30	101	.300	.350	11	.193	-2	-1	0	3	0.2
1926 Chi-N	13	9	.591	35	16	7	2	2	157¹	149	3	42	32	11.1	2.86	134	.258	.311	8	.167	-3	17	17	0	1.5
1927 Chi-N	10	10	.500	36	22	9	1	2	193¹	177	3	79	62	12.2	3.03	128	.250	.330	8	.123	-4	19	18	0	1.4
1928 Chi-N	15	6	.714	42	24	9	2	2	204¹	229	10	86	61	14.1	3.83	100	.293	.367	6	.082	-6	4	0	-0	-0.5
1929 *Chi-N	18	7	.720	50	29	18	2	8	270²	277	16	107	82	12.9	3.66	126	.265	.335	15	.165	-4	32	29	1	2.4
1930 Chi-N	15	10	.600	46	25	11	0	3	225	291	22	86	75	15.2	6.20	79	.316	.376	22	.282	3	-31	-33	2	-2.3
1931 Chi-N	16	8	.667	39	24	14	1	2	180¹	190	9	66	54	12.9	4.49	86	.268	.332	7	.123	-2	-13	-13	4	-0.9
1932 *Chi-N	19	11	.633	40	30	15	1	0	238²	262	13	70	73	12.8	3.21	118	.278	.332	15	.179	0	18	15	1	1.6
1933 Chi-N	20	12	.625	41	32	20	4	2	259	261	9	68	84	11.5	2.75	119	.257	.304	11	.125	-1	17	15	4	1.9
1934 Chi-N	18	10	.643	40	27	15	1	2	209¹	213	15	54	75	11.5	3.83	101	.262	.309	16	.229	1	5	1	1	0.3
1935 Pit-N	11	11	.500	41	25	8	1	2	204¹	237	16	40	42	12.4	4.32	95	.285	.321	8	.127	-1	-7	-5	0	-0.5
1936 Pit-N	1	3	.250	16	0	0	0	2	34²	49	3	11	10	15.6	5.97	68	.336	.382	3	.333	1	-8	-7	1	-0.5
Bos-N	4	5	.444	15	11	5	0	0	90¹	98	2	20	28	11.8	3.39	113	.281	.320	3	.120	-1	6	4	0	0.4
Yr	5	8	.385	31	11	5	0	2	125	147	5	31	38	12.8	4.10	95	.297	.338	3	.088	-1	-1	-3	1	-0.1
1937 Bos-N	8	15	.348	32	20	11	1	1	180²	201	8	46	56	12.4	3.54	101	.282	.328	6	.111	-2	8	1	1	0.0
1938 StL-N	0	1	.000	6	0	0	0	0	6	6	1	3	1	13.5	4.50	88	.286	.375	0	—	0	-0	-0	-0	0.0
1945 Cin-N	0	0	—	4	0	0	0	1	4¹	5	0	3	1	16.6	8.31	45	.278	.381	0	—	0	-2	-2	-0	-0.1
Total 17	176	136	.564	542	308	151	16	34	2722	2950	152	859	850	12.7	3.86	103	.277	.334	143	.161	-21	64	40	15	4.6

■ JOE BUSH
Bush, Leslie Ambrose "Bullet Joe" b: 11/27/1892, Brainerd, Minn. d: 11/1/74, Ft.Lauderdale, Fla. BR/TR, 5'9", 173 lbs. Deb: 9/30/12

YEAR TM/L	W	L	PCT	G	GS	CG	SH	SV	IP	H	HR	BB	SO	RAT	ERA	ERA+	OAV	OOB	BH	AVG	PB	PR	/A	PD	TPI
1912 Phi-A	0	0	—	1	1	0	0	0	8	14	0	4	3	20.3	7.88	39	.368	.429	2	.500	1	-4	-4	-0	-0.2
1913 *Phi-A	15	6	.714	39	16	6	1	3	200¹	199	3	66	81	12.1	3.82	72	.248	.310	11	.157	-0	-20	-24	5	-2.0
1914 *Phi-A	16	12	.571	38	22	14	2	3	206	184	2	81	109	11.9	3.06	86	.242	.322	14	.189	2	-7	-10	-0	-0.8
1915 Phi-A	5	15	.250	25	18	8	0	0	145²	137	3	89	89	14.2	4.14	71	.263	.375	7	.143	-3	-19	-19	-0	-2.2
1916 Phi-A	15	24	.385	40	33	25	8	0	286²	222	4	130	157	11.1	2.57	112	.219	.310	14	.140	-4	8	10	4	1.1
1917 Phi-A	11	17	.393	37	31	17	4	2	233¹	207	3	111	121	12.3	2.47	112	.241	.328	16	.200	1	5	7	-1	0.9
1918 *Bos-A	15	15	.500	36	31	26	7	2	272²	241	3	91	125	11.1	2.11	127	.242	.307	27	.276	6	20	17	3	3.0
1919 Bos-A	0	0	—	3	2	0	0	0	9	11	0	4	3	15.0	5.00	60	.324	.395	2	.400	1	-2	-2	-0	-0.1
1920 Bos-A	15	15	.500	35	32	18	0	1	243²	287	6	94	88	14.4	4.25	86	.300	.369	25	.245	2	-12	-16	3	-1.2
1921 Bos-A	16	9	.640	37	32	21	3	1	254¹	244	10	93	96	12.1	3.50	121	.260	.330	39	.325	6	22	20	1	2.9
1922 *NY-A	26	7	.788	39	30	20	0	3	255¹	240	16	85	92	11.5	3.31	124	.252	.314	31	.326	8	21	20	1	2.8
1923 *NY-A	19	15	.559	37	30	22	3	0	275²	263	7	117	125	12.6	3.43	115	.260	.340	31	.274	7	17	16	1	2.4
1924 NY-A	17	16	.515	39	31	19	3	1	252	262	9	109	80	13.5	3.57	116	.273	.352	42	.339	13	18	16	2	3.1
1925 StL-A	14	14	.500	33	28	15	2	0	208²	230	18	91	63	13.9	5.09	92	.284	.357	26	.255	3	-16	-10	2	0.0
1926 Was-A	1	8	.111	12	11	3	0	0	71¹	83	6	35	27	15.5	6.69	58	.292	.380	7	.233	1	-21	-22	0	-1.9
Pit-N	6	6	.500	19	11	9	2	3	110²	97	7	35	38	10.9	3.01	131	.236	.299	13	.265	3	10	11	-1	1.3
1927 Pit-N	1	2	.333	5	3	0	0	0	6²	14	1	5	1	25.7	13.50	30	.412	.487	3	.600	1	-7	-7	0	-0.4
NY-N	1	1	.500	3	2	1	0	0	12	18	1	5	6	17.0	7.50	51	.340	.397	2	.500	1	-5	-5	-0	-0.3
Yr	2	3	.400	8	5	1	0	0	18²	32	2	10	7	20.3	9.64	41	.368	.433	1	.111	2	-12	-12	0	-0.7
1928 Phi-A	2	1	.667	11	2	1	0	1	35¹	39	1	18	15	14.8	5.09	79	.300	.389	1	.067	-1	-4	-4	1	-0.4
Total 17	195	183	.516	489	366	225	35	20	3087¹	2992	96	1263	1319	12.6	3.51	99	.259	.335	313	.253	48	4	-6	18	8.0

■ JACK BUSHELMAN
Bushelman, John Francis b: 8/29/1885, Cincinnati, Ohio d: 10/26/55, Roanoke, Va. BR/TR, 6'2", 175 lbs. Deb: 10/05/09

YEAR TM/L	W	L	PCT	G	GS	CG	SH	SV	IP	H	HR	BB	SO	RAT	ERA	ERA+	OAV	OOB	BH	AVG	PB	PR	/A	PD	TPI
1909 Cin-N	0	1	.000	1	1	1	0	0	7	7	1	4	3	14.1	2.57	101	.241	.333	0	.000	-0	0	0	-0	0.0
1911 Bos-A	0	1	.000	3	1	1	0	0	12	8	0	10	5	14.3	3.00	109	.186	.352	0	.000	-0	0	0	-0	0.0
1912 Bos-A	1	0	1.000	3	0	0	0	0	7²	9	0	5	5	16.4	4.70	72	.310	.412	0	.000	-0	-1	-1	-0	0.0
Total 3	1	2	.333	7	2	2	0	0	26²	24	1	19	13	14.9	3.38	93	.238	.364	0	.000	-1	-1	-1	-0	0.0

■ FRANK BUSHEY
Bushey, Francis Clyde b: 8/1/06, Wheaton, Kan. d: 3/18/72, Topeka, Kan. BR/TR, 6', 180 lbs. Deb: 9/17/27

YEAR TM/L	W	L	PCT	G	GS	CG	SH	SV	IP	H	HR	BB	SO	RAT	ERA	ERA+	OAV	OOB	BH	AVG	PB	PR	/A	PD	TPI
1927 Bos-A	0	0	—	1	0	0	0	0	1¹	2	0	2	0	27.0	6.75	63	.500	.667	0	—	0	-0	-0	-0	0.0
1930 Bos-A	0	1	.000	11	0	0	0	0	30	34	1	15	4	15.3	6.30	73	.306	.398	1	.111	-1	-6	-6	0	-0.5
Total 2	0	1	.000	12	0	0	0	0	31¹	36	1	17	4	15.8	6.32	73	.313	.410	1	.111	-1	-6	-6	0	-0.5

■ TOM BUSKEY
Buskey, Thomas William b: 2/20/47, Harrisburg, Pa. BR/TR, 6'3", 200 lbs. Deb: 8/05/73

YEAR TM/L	W	L	PCT	G	GS	CG	SH	SV	IP	H	HR	BB	SO	RAT	ERA	ERA+	OAV	OOB	BH	AVG	PB	PR	/A	PD	TPI
1973 NY-A	0	1	.000	8	0	0	0	0	16²	18	2	4	8	12.4	5.40	68	.286	.338	0	—	0	-3	-3	0	-0.2
1974 NY-A	0	1	.000	4	0	0	0	1	5²	10	1	3	3	22.2	6.35	55	.400	.483	0	—	0	-2	-2	-0	-0.1
Cle-A	2	6	.250	51	0	0	0	17	93	93	10	33	40	12.3	3.19	113	.263	.327	0	—	0	4	4	1	0.6
Yr	2	7	.222	55	0	0	0	18	98²	103	11	36	43	12.8	3.38	107	.271	.336	0	—	0	3	3	1	0.5
1975 Cle-A	5	3	.625	50	0	0	0	7	77	69	7	29	29	11.6	2.57	147	.252	.326	0	—	0	10	10	2	1.3
1976 Cle-A	5	4	.556	39	0	0	0	3	94¹	88	9	34	32	11.9	3.63	96	.256	.328	0	—	0	-1	-1	1	0.0
1977 Cle-A	0	0	—	21	0	0	0	0	34	45	6	8	15	14.3	5.29	74	.313	.353	0	—	0	-5	-5	-0	-0.1
1978 Tor-A	0	1	.000	8	0	0	0	0	13¹	14	1	5	7	12.8	3.38	116	.275	.339	0	—	0	1	1	0	0.1
1979 Tor-A	6	10	.375	44	0	0	0	7	78²	74	9	25	44	11.4	3.43	126	.249	.310	0	—	0	7	8	1	0.9
1980 Tor-A	3	1	.750	33	0	0	0	0	66²	68	11	26	34	12.7	4.45	97	.278	.347	0	—	0	-3	-1	0	0.0
Total 8	21	27	.438	258	0	0	0	34	479¹	479	57	167	212	12.3	3.66	105	.267	.332	0	—	0	9	11	6	2.2

■ MAX BUTCHER
Butcher, Albert Maxwell b: 9/21/10, Holden, W.Va. d: 9/15/57, Man, W.Va. BR/TR, 6'2", 220 lbs. Deb: 4/20/36

YEAR TM/L	W	L	PCT	G	GS	CG	SH	SV	IP	H	HR	BB	SO	RAT	ERA	ERA+	OAV	OOB	BH	AVG	PB	PR	/A	PD	TPI
1936 Bro-N	6	6	.500	38	15	5	0	2	147²	154	11	59	55	13.0	3.96	104	.268	.337	6	.125	-3	1	3	-1	0.0
1937 Bro-N	11	15	.423	39	24	8	1	0	191²	203	12	75	55	13.4	4.27	94	.280	.354	10	.161	-1	-8	-5	4	-0.1
1938 Bro-N	5	4	.556	24	8	3	0	2	72²	104	9	39	21	17.8	6.56	59	.334	.410	4	.160	0	-22	-21	2	-1.8
Phi-N	4	8	.333	12	12	11	0	0	98¹	94	6	31	29	11.6	2.93	133	.253	.314	9	.257	-1	9	10	-1	1.2
Yr	9	12	.429	36	20	14	0	2	171	198	15	70	50	14.2	4.47	87	.290	.358	1	.017	1	-13	-11	2	-0.6
1939 Phi-N	2	13	.133	19	16	3	0	0	104¹	131	10	51	29	15.8	5.61	71	.308	.383	7	.184	-1	-20	-19	-2	-1.9
Pit-N	4	4	.500	14	12	5	2	0	86²	104	2	23	21	13.2	3.43	112	.297	.340	3	.097	-2	5	4	2	0.4
Yr	6	17	.261	33	28	8	2	0	191	235	12	74	48	14.6	4.62	85	.302	.363	10	.014	-3	-15	-15	0	-1.5
1940 Pit-N	8	9	.471	35	24	6	2	2	136¹	161	13	46	40	13.7	6.01	63	.290	.346	15	.300	4	-33	-33	1	-2.6

YEAR	TM/L	W	L	PCT	G	GS	CG	SH	SV	IP	H	HR	BB	SO	RAT	ERA	ERA+	OAV	OOB	BH	AVG	PB	PR	/A	PD	TPI
1941	Pit-N	17	12	.586	33	32	19	0	0	236	249	11	66	61	12.1	3.05	118	.265	.314	15	.183	-1	15	15	1	1.5
1942	Pit-N	5	8	.385	24	18	9	0	1	150²	144	7	44	49	11.3	2.93	116	.247	.303	7	.143	-2	6	8	0	0.6
1943	Pit-N	10	8	.556	33	21	10	2	1	193²	191	4	57	45	11.6	2.60	134	.262	.317	10	.164	-1	17	19	0	2.0
1944	Pit-N	13	11	.542	35	27	13	5	1	199	216	8	46	43	11.9	3.12	116	.273	.314	12	.190	-0	11	13	3	1.7
1945	Pit-N	10	8	.556	28	20	12	2	0	169¹	184	7	46	37	12.4	3.03	130	.277	.328	12	.222	1	15	17	1	1.9
Total 10		95	106	.473	334	229	104	14	9	1786¹	1935	100	583	485	12.8	3.73	101	.276	.333	110	.184	-6	-3	11	10	2.9

■ JOHN BUTCHER
Butcher, John Daniel b: 3/8/57, Glendale, Cal. BR/TR, 6'4", 185 lbs. Deb: 9/08/80

YEAR	TM/L	W	L	PCT	G	GS	CG	SH	SV	IP	H	HR	BB	SO	RAT	ERA	ERA+	OAV	OOB	BH	AVG	PB	PR	/A	PD	TPI
1980	Tex-A	3	3	.500	6	6	1	0	0	35¹	34	2	13	27	12.0	4.08	96	.248	.313	0	—	0	-0	-1	0	0.0
1981	Tex-A	1	2	.333	5	3	1	1	0	27²	18	0	8	19	8.5	1.63	213	.186	.248	0	—	0	6	6	0	0.7
1982	Tex-A	1	5	.167	18	13	2	0	1	94¹	102	10	34	39	13.2	4.87	80	.280	.345	0	—	0	-8	-10	2	-0.8
1983	Tex-A	6	6	.500	38	6	1	1	5	123	128	8	41	58	12.4	3.51	114	.270	.329	0	—	0	8	7	0	0.7
1984	Min-A	13	11	.542	34	34	8	1	0	225	242	18	53	83	12.0	3.44	122	.276	.320	0	—	0	14	19	-1	1.9
1985	Min-A	11	14	.440	34	33	8	2	0	207²	239	24	41	92	12.5	4.98	88	.289	.328	0	—	0	-19	-13	1	-1.1
1986	Min-A	0	3	.000	16	10	1	0	0	70	82	11	24	29	13.8	6.30	68	.294	.352	0	—	0	-17	-16	-1	-1.3
	Cle-A	1	5	.167	13	8	1	1	0	50²	86	6	13	16	18.1	6.93	60	.381	.421	0	—	0	-15	-16	-0	-1.4
	Yr	1	8	.111	29	18	2	1	0	120²	168	17	37	45	15.5	6.56	65	.330	.379	0	—	0	-32	-31	-0	-2.7
Total 7		36	49	.424	164	113	23	6	6	833²	931	79	229	363	12.7	4.42	94	.284	.334	0	—	0	-32	-24	2	-1.3

■ SAL BUTERA
Butera, Salvatore Philip b: 9/25/52, Richmond Hill, N.Y BR/TR, 6', 190 lbs. Deb: 4/10/80 ♦

YEAR	TM/L	W	L	PCT	G	GS	CG	SH	SV	IP	H	HR	BB	SO	RAT	ERA	ERA+	OAV	OOB	BH	AVG	PB	PR	/A	PD	TPI
1985	Mon-N	0	0	—	1	0	0	0	0	1	0	0	0	0	0.0	0.00	—	.000	.000	24	.200	0	0	0	0	0.0
1986	Cin-N	0	0	—	1	0	0	0	0	1	0	0	1	1	9.0	0.00	—	.000	.250	27	.239	0	0	0	0	0.0
Total 2		0	0	—	2	0	0	0	0	2	0	0	1	1	4.5	0.00	—	.000	.143	182	.227	0	1	1	0	0.0

■ BILL BUTLAND
Butland, Wilburn Rue b: 3/22/18, Terre Haute, Ind. BR/TL, 6'5", 185 lbs. Deb: 5/29/40

YEAR	TM/L	W	L	PCT	G	GS	CG	SH	SV	IP	H	HR	BB	SO	RAT	ERA	ERA+	OAV	OOB	BH	AVG	PB	PR	/A	PD	TPI
1940	Bos-A	1	2	.333	3	3	1	0	0	21	27	0	10	5	15.9	5.57	81	.307	.378	0	.000	-1	-3	-3	1	-0.2
1942	Bos-A	7	1	.875	23	10	6	2	1	111¹	85	8	33	46	9.8	2.51	149	.206	.270	1	.036	-1	14	15	0	1.6
1946	Bos-A	1	0	1.000	5	2	0	0	0	16¹	23	3	13	10	19.8	11.02	33	.343	.450	1	.250	0	-14	-13	0	-1.1
1947	Bos-A	0	0	—	1	0	0	0	0	2	3	0	0	1	13.5	4.50	86	.333	.333	0	—	0	-0	-0	0	0.0
Total 4		9	3	.750	32	15	7	2	1	150²	138	11	56	62	11.8	3.88	99	.240	.310	2	.051	-2	-2	-1	1	0.3

■ CECIL BUTLER
Butler, Cecil Dean "Slewfoot" b: 10/23/37, Dallas, Ga. BR/TR, 6'4", 195 lbs. Deb: 4/23/62

YEAR	TM/L	W	L	PCT	G	GS	CG	SH	SV	IP	H	HR	BB	SO	RAT	ERA	ERA+	OAV	OOB	BH	AVG	PB	PR	/A	PD	TPI
1962	Mil-N	2	0	1.000	9	2	1	0	0	31	36	4	9	22	10.2	2.61	145	.217	.271	0	.000	-1	5	4	0	0.4
1964	Mil-N	0	0	—	2	0	0	0	0	4¹	7	2	0	2	14.5	8.31	42	.368	.368	0	—	0	-2	-2	0	-0.1
Total 2		2	0	1.000	11	2	1	0	0	35¹	33	6	9	24	10.7	3.31	114	.237	.284	0	.000	-1	2	2	0	0.3

■ CHARLIE BUTLER
Butler, Charles Thomas b: 5/12/06, Green Cove Springs, Fla. d: 5/10/64, Brunswick, Ga. BR/TL, 6'1.5", 210 lbs. Deb: 5/01/33

YEAR	TM/L	W	L	PCT	G	GS	CG	SH	SV	IP	H	HR	BB	SO	RAT	ERA	ERA+	OAV	OOB	BH	AVG	PB	PR	/A	PD	TPI
1933	Phi-N	0	0	—	1	0	0	0	0	1	1	0	2	0	27.0	9.00	42	.250	.500	0	—	0	-1	-1	0	0.0

■ IKE BUTLER
Butler, Isaac Burr b: 8/22/1873, Langston, Mich. d: 3/17/48, Oakland, Cal. TR, 6', 175 lbs. Deb: 8/05/02

YEAR	TM/L	W	L	PCT	G	GS	CG	SH	SV	IP	H	HR	BB	SO	RAT	ERA	ERA+	OAV	OOB	BH	AVG	PB	PR	/A	PD	TPI
1902	Bal-A	1	10	.091	16	14	12	0	0	116¹	168	1	45	13	16.5	5.34	71	.338	.392	6	.113	-3	-23	-20	-0	-2.0

■ BILL BUTLER
Butler, William Franklin b: 3/12/47, Hyattsville, Md. BL/TL, 6'2", 210 lbs. Deb: 4/09/69

YEAR	TM/L	W	L	PCT	G	GS	CG	SH	SV	IP	H	HR	BB	SO	RAT	ERA	ERA+	OAV	OOB	BH	AVG	PB	PR	/A	PD	TPI
1969	KC-A	9	10	.474	34	29	5	4	0	193²	174	15	91	156	12.5	3.90	94	.240	.328	3	.050	-4	-6	-5	-3	-1.1
1970	KC-A	4	12	.250	25	25	2	1	0	140²	117	17	87	75	13.1	3.77	99	.229	.342	2	.045	-3	-1	-1	-2	-0.4
1971	KC-A	1	2	.333	14	6	0	0	0	44¹	45	6	18	32	12.8	3.45	99	.268	.339	1	.083	-1	0	-0	-0	0.0
1972	Cle-A	0	0	—	6	2	0	0	0	11²	9	1	10	6	14.7	1.54	208	.220	.373	0	.000	-0	2	2	0	0.2
1974	Min-A	4	6	.400	26	12	2	0	1	98²	91	9	56	79	13.5	4.10	91	.251	.353	0	—	0	-5	-4	-2	-0.5
1975	Min-A	5	4	.556	23	8	1	0	0	81²	100	12	35	55	14.4	5.95	65	.301	.368	0	—	0	-20	-19	-0	-1.8
1977	Min-A	0	1	.000	6	4	0	0	0	21	19	5	15	5	15.0	6.86	58	.244	.372	0	—	0	-7	-7	-1	-0.6
Total 7		23	35	.397	134	86	10	5	1	591²	555	65	312	408	13.3	4.21	88	.250	.345	6	.051	-7	-37	-33	-8	-4.2

■ TOM BUTTERS
Butters, Thomas Arden b: 4/8/38, Delaware, O. BR/TR, 6'2", 195 lbs. Deb: 9/08/62

YEAR	TM/L	W	L	PCT	G	GS	CG	SH	SV	IP	H	HR	BB	SO	RAT	ERA	ERA+	OAV	OOB	BH	AVG	PB	PR	/A	PD	TPI
1962	Pit-N	0	0	—	4	0	0	0	0	6	5	0	6	10	18.0	1.50	262	.238	.429	0	—	0	2	2	0	0.2
1963	Pit-N	0	0	—	6	1	0	0	0	16¹	15	1	8	11	13.8	4.41	75	.259	.368	1	.333	0	-2	-2	-0	-0.1
1964	Pit-N	2	2	.500	28	4	0	0	0	64¹	52	3	37	58	12.5	2.38	148	.221	.327	2	.182	0	8	8	1	0.8
1965	Pit-N	0	1	.000	5	0	0	0	0	9	9	2	5	6	14.0	7.00	50	.250	.341	0	.000	-0	-3	-3	0	-0.3
Total 4		2	3	.400	43	5	0	0	0	95²	81	6	56	85	13.2	3.10	113	.231	.342	3	.200	0	4	4	-1	0.6

■ FRANK BUTTERY
Buttery, Frank b: 5/13/1851, Silver Mine, Conn. d: 12/16/02, Silver Mine, Conn. Deb: 4/26/1872 ♦

YEAR	TM/L	W	L	PCT	G	GS	CG	SH	SV	IP	H	HR	BB	SO	RAT	ERA	ERA+	OAV	OOB	BH	AVG	PB	PR	/A	PD	TPI
1872	Man-n	3	2	.600	6	5	5	0	0	49	81	0	1		15.1	*5.14*	71	.331	.333	25	.269	-0	-8	-8		-0.4

■ RALPH BUXTON
Buxton, Ralph Stanley "Buck" b: 6/7/11, Weyburn, Sask., Can BR/TR, 5'11.5", 163 lbs. Deb: 9/11/38

YEAR	TM/L	W	L	PCT	G	GS	CG	SH	SV	IP	H	HR	BB	SO	RAT	ERA	ERA+	OAV	OOB	BH	AVG	PB	PR	/A	PD	TPI
1938	Phi-A	0	1	.000	5	0	0	0	0	9¹	12	1	5	9	16.4	4.82	100	.324	.405	0	—	0	-0	-0	-0	0.0
1949	NY-A	0	1	.000	14	0	0	0	2	26²	22	3	16	14	12.8	4.05	100	.229	.339	0	.000	-0	0	-0	0	0.0
Total 2		0	2	.000	19	0	0	0	2	36	34	4	21	23	13.8	4.25	100	.256	.357	0	.000	-1	0	-0	-0	0.0

■ JOHN BUZHARDT
Buzhardt, John William b: 8/17/36, Prosperity, S.C. BR/TR, 6'2.5", 195 lbs. Deb: 9/10/58

YEAR	TM/L	W	L	PCT	G	GS	CG	SH	SV	IP	H	HR	BB	SO	RAT	ERA	ERA+	OAV	OOB	BH	AVG	PB	PR	/A	PD	TPI
1958	Chi-N	3	0	1.000	6	2	1	0	0	24¹	16	2	7	9	8.5	1.85	212	.184	.245	1	.125	-0	6	6	1	0.6
1959	Chi-N	4	5	.444	31	10	1	1	0	101¹	107	12	29	33	12.2	4.97	79	.271	.322	2	.069	-1	-12	-12	1	-1.1
1960	Phi-N	5	16	.238	30	29	5	0	0	200¹	198	14	68	73	12.0	3.86	100	.259	.321	10	.161	-1	-2	0	0	0.0
1961	Phi-N	6	18	.250	41	27	6	1	0	202¹	200	28	65	92	12.1	4.49	91	.263	.326	6	.105	-2	-10	-9	0	-1.0
1962	Chi-A	8	12	.400	28	25	8	2	0	152¹	156	16	59	64	12.9	4.19	93	.264	.335	6	.118	-2	-4	-5	2	-0.4
1963	Chi-A	9	4	.692	19	18	6	3	0	126¹	100	8	31	59	9.7	2.42	145	.216	.273	4	.083	-3	17	15	1	1.5
1964	Chi-A	10	8	.556	31	25	8	3	0	160	150	13	35	97	10.6	2.98	116	.250	.295	11	.204	2	11	8	1	1.1
1965	Chi-A	13	8	.619	32	30	4	1	1	188²	167	12	56	108	11.0	3.01	106	.242	.305	7	.125	0	10	4	-1	0.3
1966	Chi-A	6	11	.353	33	22	5	4	1	150¹	144	13	30	66	10.7	3.83	83	.248	.289	5	.116	-1	-7	-11	3	-0.9
1967	Chi-A	3	9	.250	28	7	0	0	0	88²	100	11	37	33	14.5	3.96	78	.294	.373	4	.200	0	-7	-8	-1	-0.7
	Bal-A	0	1	.000	7	1	0	0	0	11²	14	1	5	7	14.7	4.63	68	.298	.365	0	.000	-0	-2	-2	0	-0.1
	Yr	3	10	.231	35	8	0	0	0	100¹	114	12	42	40	14.0	4.04	77	.288	.356	0	.000	-0	-9	-10	1	-0.8
	Hou-N	0	0	—	1	0	0	0	0	0²	0	0	0	0	0.0	0.00	—	.000	.000	0	—	0	0	0	0	0.0
1968	Hou-N	4	4	.500	39	4	0	0	5	83²	73	0	35	37	12.0	3.12	95	.239	.325	4	.250	1	-1	-2	1	0.1
Total 11		71	96	.425	326	200	44	15	7	1490¹	1425	130	457	678	11.6	3.66	97	.253	.314	60	.135	-7	-1	-16	11	-0.6

■ BUD BYERLY
Byerly, Eldred William b: 10/26/20, Webster Groves, Mo BR/TR, 6'2.5", 185 lbs. Deb: 9/26/43

YEAR	TM/L	W	L	PCT	G	GS	CG	SH	SV	IP	H	HR	BB	SO	RAT	ERA	ERA+	OAV	OOB	BH	AVG	PB	PR	/A	PD	TPI
1943	StL-N	1	0	1.000	2	2	0	0	0	13	14	0	5	6	13.2	3.46	97	.280	.345	0	.000	-0	-0	-0	-0	0.0
1944	*StL-N	2	2	.500	9	4	2	0	0	42¹	37	2	20	13	12.1	3.40	104	.228	.313	2	.167	-0	1	1	1	0.1
1945	StL-N	4	5	.444	33	8	2	0	0	95	111	3	41	39	14.5	4.74	79	.288	.358	5	.217	1	-10	-10	2	-0.6
1950	Cin-N	0	1	.000	4	1	0	0	0	14²	12	1	4	5	9.8	2.45	173	.218	.271	0	.000	-0	3	3	-0	0.2
1951	Cin-N	2	1	.667	40	0	0	0	0	66	69	6	25	28	13.1	3.27	125	.267	.337	0	.000	-0	5	6	1	0.6
1952	Cin-N	0	1	.000	12	2	0	0	1	24¹	29	0	7	14	13.1	5.11	74	.309	.356	1	.200	0	-4	-4	-0	-0.2
1956	Was-A	2	4	.333	25	0	0	0	4	51²	45	6	14	19	10.6	2.96	146	.243	.303	1	.091	-1	7	8	0	0.7
1957	Was-A	6	6	.500	47	0	0	0	6	95	94	6	22	39	11.1	3.13	125	.264	.309	1	.067	-1	7	8	1	0.8
1958	Was-A	2	0	1.000	17	0	0	0	1	24	34	4	11	13	17.3	6.75	58	.347	.418	0	.000	-0	-8	-8	-0	-0.7
	Bos-A	1	2	.333	18	0	0	0	0	30¹	31	1	7	16	11.6	1.78	225	.272	.320	0	.000	-1	7	7	0	0.1
	Yr	3	2	.600	35	0	0	0	1	54¹	65	5	18	29	13.9	3.98	99	.302	.359	0	.000	-1	-1	-0	0	0.0

YEAR TM/L	W	L	PCT	G	GS	CG	SH	SV	IP	H	HR	BB	SO	RAT	ERA	ERA+	OAV	OOB	BH	AVG	PB	PR	/A	PD	TPI
1959 SF-N	1	0	1.000	11	0	0	0	0	13	11	2	5	4	11.1	1.38	275	.234	.308	0	—	0	4	4	1	0.4
1960 SF-N	1	0	1.000	19	0	0	0	2	22	32	3	6	13	16.0	5.32	65	.340	.386	0	.000	-0	-4	-4	-0	-0.4
Total 11	22	22	.500	237	17	4	0	14	491²	519	34	167	209	12.7	3.70	105	.273	.335	10	.118	-4	8	10	5	1.6

■ HARRY BYRD
Byrd, Harry Gladwin b: 2/3/25, Darlington, S.C. d: 5/14/85, Darlington, S.C. BR/TR, 6'1", 188 lbs. Deb: 4/21/50

YEAR TM/L	W	L	PCT	G	GS	CG	SH	SV	IP	H	HR	BB	SO	RAT	ERA	ERA+	OAV	OOB	BH	AVG	PB	PR	/A	PD	TPI
1950 Phi-A	0	0	—	6	0	0	0	0	10²	25	3	9	2	30.4	16.88	27	.481	.571	0	.000	-0	-15	-15	0	-1.2
1952 Phi-A	15	15	.500	37	28	15	3	2	228¹	244	12	98	116	13.8	3.31	120	.274	.351	10	.133	-3	9	16	-0	1.4
1953 Phi-A	11	20	.355	40	37	11	2	0	236²	279	23	115	122	15.5	5.51	78	.294	.379	18	.222	-1	-40	-32	-2	-3.2
1954 NY-A	9	7	.563	25	21	5	1	0	132¹	131	10	43	52	12.3	2.99	115	.258	.324	9	.196	1	11	7	-0	0.6
1955 Bal-A	3	2	.600	14	8	1	1	1	65¹	64	7	28	25	13.6	4.55	84	.261	.354	3	.158	-0	-4	-5	-1	-0.5
Chi-A	4	6	.400	25	12	1	1	1	91	85	10	30	44	11.6	4.65	85	.251	.315	2	.067	-3	-7	-7	-0	-0.9
Yr	7	8	.467	39	20	2	2	2	156¹	149	17	58	69	12.0	4.61	85	.251	.320	1	.020	-3	-11	-12	-0	-1.4
1956 Chi-A	0	1	.000	3	1	0	0	0	4¹	9	0	4	0	27.0	10.38	39	.474	.565	0	.000	-0	-3	-3	0	-0.2
1957 Det-A	4	3	.571	37	1	0	0	5	59	53	9	20	38	12.7	3.36	115	.249	.342	0	.000	-1	3	3	-0	0.2
Total 7	46	54	.460	187	108	33	8	9	827²	890	71	355	381	14.0	4.35	91	.277	.356	42	.160	-8	-46	-36	-2	-3.8

■ JEFF BYRD
Byrd, Jeffrey Alan b: 11/11/56, LaMesa, Cal. BR/TR, 6'3", 195 lbs. Deb: 6/20/77

YEAR TM/L	W	L	PCT	G	GS	CG	SH	SV	IP	H	HR	BB	SO	RAT	ERA	ERA+	OAV	OOB	BH	AVG	PB	PR	/A	PD	TPI
1977 Tor-A	2	13	.133	17	17	1	0	0	87¹	98	5	68	40	17.1	6.18	68	.286	.404	0	—	0	-21	-19	1	-1.7

■ JERRY BYRNE
Byrne, Gerald Wilford b: 2/2/07, Parnell, Mich. d: 8/11/55, Lansing, Mich. BR/TR, 6', 170 lbs. Deb: 8/31/29

YEAR TM/L	W	L	PCT	G	GS	CG	SH	SV	IP	H	HR	BB	SO	RAT	ERA	ERA+	OAV	OOB	BH	AVG	PB	PR	/A	PD	TPI
1929 Chi-A	0	1	.000	3	1	0	0	0	7¹	11	0	6	1	20.9	7.36	58	.379	.486	0	.000	-0	-3	-3	-0	-0.2

■ TOMMY BYRNE
Byrne, Thomas Joseph b: 12/31/19, Baltimore, Md. BL/TL, 6'1", 182 lbs. Deb: 4/27/43

YEAR TM/L	W	L	PCT	G	GS	CG	SH	SV	IP	H	HR	BB	SO	RAT	ERA	ERA+	OAV	OOB	BH	AVG	PB	PR	/A	PD	TPI
1943 NY-A	2	1	.667	11	2	0	0	0	31²	28	1	35	22	18.8	6.54	49	.248	.437	1	.091	-0	-11	-12	0	-1.1
1946 NY-A	0	1	.000	4	1	0	0	0	9¹	7	1	8	5	15.4	5.79	60	.194	.356	2	.222	0	-2	-2	0	-0.1
1947 NY-A	0	0	—	4	1	0	0	0	4	5	0	6	2	22.8	4.15	85	.294	.478	0	—	-0	-0	-0	0	0.0
1948 NY-A	8	5	.615	31	11	5	1	2	133²	79	8	101	93	12.7	3.30	124	.172	.332	15	.326	5	15	12	-1	1.5
1949 *NY-A	15	7	.682	32	30	12	3	0	196	125	11	179	129	14.6	3.72	109	.183	.362	16	.193	1	10	7	-3	0.4
1950 NY-A	15	9	.625	31	31	10	2	0	203¹	188	23	160	118	16.2	4.74	91	.245	.387	22	.272	7	-4	-10	-2	-0.4
1951 NY-A	2	1	.667	9	3	0	0	0	21	16	0	36	14	23.6	6.86	56	.213	.482	2	.222	1	-6	-7	-0	-0.5
StL-A	4	10	.286	19	17	7	2	0	122²	104	5	114	57	16.9	3.82	115	.235	.404	16	.281	3	4	8	-1	1.1
Yr	6	11	.353	28	20	7	2	0	143²	120	5	150	71	17.7	4.26	101	.230	.413	4	.061	4	-2	-1	-1	0.6
1952 StL-A	7	14	.333	29	24	14	0	0	196	182	16	112	91	14.0	4.68	84	.247	.354	21	.250	5	-22	-17	-4	-1.4
1953 Chi-A	2	0	1.000	6	6	0	0	0	16	18	0	26	4	24.8	10.13	40	.295	.506	3	.167	1	-11	-11	0	-0.9
Was-A	0	5	.000	6	5	2	0	0	33²	35	3	22	22	15.5	4.28	91	.276	.387	1	.059	-1	-1	-1	0	0.0
Yr	2	5	.286	12	11	2	0	0	49²	53	3	48	26	18.5	6.16	64	.282	.430	5	.143	-0	-12	-12	1	-0.9
1954 NY-A	3	2	.600	5	5	4	1	0	40	36	1	19	24	12.4	2.70	127	.240	.325	7	.368	4	5	3	0	0.8
1955 *NY-A	16	5	.762	27	22	9	3	2	160	137	12	87	76	13.0	3.15	119	.237	.344	16	.205	4	14	11	-1	1.3
1956 NY-A	7	3	.700	37	8	1	0	6	109²	108	9	72	52	14.9	3.36	115	.262	.344	14	.269	6	10	6	1	1.2
1957 *NY-A	4	6	.400	30	4	1	0	2	84²	70	8	60	57	14.6	4.36	82	.227	.364	7	.189	4	-5	-7	-1	-0.4
Total 13	85	69	.552	281	170	65	12	12	1362	1138	98	1037	766	14.9	4.11	97	.229	.371	143	.238	40	-5	-20	-12	1.5

■ MARTY BYSTROM
Bystrom, Martin Eugene b: 7/26/58, Coral Gables, Fla. BR/TR, 6'5", 200 lbs. Deb: 9/07/80

YEAR TM/L	W	L	PCT	G	GS	CG	SH	SV	IP	H	HR	BB	SO	RAT	ERA	ERA+	OAV	OOB	BH	AVG	PB	PR	/A	PD	TPI
1980 *Phi-N	5	0	1.000	6	5	1	1	0	36	26	1	9	21	8.8	1.50	252	.195	.246	1	.071	-1	8	9	1	1.1
1981 Phi-N	4	3	.571	9	9	1	0	0	53²	55	3	16	24	12.1	3.35	108	.264	.320	2	.118	-1	1	2	1	0.1
1982 Phi-N	5	6	.455	19	16	1	0	0	89	93	2	35	50	13.4	4.85	76	.277	.354	3	.125	-0	-12	-12	-1	-1.2
1983 Phi-N	6	9	.400	24	23	1	1	0	119¹	136	6	44	87	14.1	4.60	85	.285	.353	9	.237	2	-13	-14	-1	-1.2
1984 Phi-N	4	4	.500	11	11	0	0	0	56²	66	5	22	36	14.0	5.08	71	.283	.345	3	.158	-0	-9	-9	-0	-0.9
NY-A	2	2	.500	7	7	0	0	0	39¹	34	3	13	24	11.0	2.97	127	.230	.296	0	—	0	4	4	-0	0.3
1985 NY-A	3	2	.600	8	8	0	0	0	41	44	8	19	16	14.0	5.71	70	.280	.362	0	—	0	-7	-8	0	-0.6
Total 6	29	26	.527	84	79	4	2	0	435	454	28	158	258	13.0	4.26	86	.268	.336	18	.161	-0	-28	-28	-0	-2.4

■ GREG CADARET
Cadaret, Gregory James b: 2/27/62, Detroit, Mich. BL/TL, 6'3", 200 lbs. Deb: 7/05/87

YEAR TM/L	W	L	PCT	G	GS	CG	SH	SV	IP	H	HR	BB	SO	RAT	ERA	ERA+	OAV	OOB	BH	AVG	PB	PR	/A	PD	TPI
1987 Oak-A	6	2	.750	29	0	0	0	0	39²	37	6	24	30	14.1	4.54	91	.252	.360	0	—	0	-0	-2	1	0.0
1988 *Oak-A	5	2	.714	58	0	0	0	3	71²	60	2	36	64	12.2	2.89	131	.226	.320	0	—	0	9	7	-0	0.7
1989 Oak-A	0	0	—	26	0	0	0	0	27²	21	0	19	14	13.0	2.28	162	.214	.342	0	—	0	5	4	1	0.5
NY-A	5	5	.500	20	13	3	1	0	92¹	109	7	38	66	14.5	4.58	84	.298	.367	0	—	0	-7	-7	-0	-0.6
Yr	5	5	.500	46	13	3	1	0	120	130	7	57	80	14.2	4.05	94	.279	.360	0	—	0	-2	-3	1	-0.1
1990 NY-A	5	4	.556	54	6	0	0	3	121¹	120	8	64	80	13.7	4.15	96	.268	.361	0	—	0	-3	-2	2	0.0
Total 4	21	13	.618	187	19	3	1	6	352²	347	23	181	254	13.6	3.90	100	.262	.353	0	—	0	-3	-0	4	0.6

■ LEON CADORE
Cadore, Leon Joseph "Caddy" b: 11/20/1890, Chicago, Ill. d: 3/16/58, Spokane, Wash. BR/TR, 6'1", 190 lbs. Deb: 4/28/15

YEAR TM/L	W	L	PCT	G	GS	CG	SH	SV	IP	H	HR	BB	SO	RAT	ERA	ERA+	OAV	OOB	BH	AVG	PB	PR	/A	PD	TPI
1915 Bro-N	0	2	.000	7	2	1	0	0	21	28	0	8	12	16.3	5.57	50	.337	.409	0	.000	-1	-7	-7	0	-0.7
1916 Bro-N	0	0	—	1	0	0	0	0	6	10	0	0	2	15.0	4.50	60	.370	.370	0	.000	-0	-1	-1	1	0.0
1917 Bro-N	13	13	.500	37	30	21	1	3	264	231	3	63	115	10.3	2.45	114	.241	.292	24	.261	5	8	10	-2	1.5
1918 Bro-N	1	0	1.000	2	1	1	0	0	17	6	0	2	6	4.8	0.53	526	.115	.164	0	.000	-0	4	4	0	0.5
1919 Bro-N	14	12	.538	35	27	16	3	0	250²	228	5	39	94	9.8	2.37	125	.245	.280	14	.161	-3	15	17	-3	1.2
1920 *Bro-N	15	14	.517	35	30	16	4	0	254¹	256	4	56	79	11.1	2.62	122	.270	.313	20	.220	2	15	17	2	2.3
1921 Bro-N	13	14	.481	35	30	12	1	0	211²	243	17	46	79	12.5	4.17	93	.292	.334	14	.187	-1	-9	-7	-1	-0.8
1922 Bro-N	8	15	.348	29	21	13	0	0	190¹	224	15	57	49	13.3	4.35	94	.299	.349	19	.268	4	-5	-6	-2	-0.3
1923 Bro-N	4	1	.800	8	4	3	0	0	36	39	2	13	5	13.0	3.25	119	.291	.354	1	.077	-1	3	3	-1	0.0
Chi-A	0	1	.000	1	1	0	0	0	2¹	6	0	2	3	30.9	23.14	17	.500	.571	0	—	0	-5	-5	0	-0.3
1924 NY-N	0	0	—	2	0	0	0	0	4	2	0	3	2	11.3	0.00	—	.154	.313	0	—	0	2	2	0	0.2
Total 10	68	72	.486	192	147	83	10	3	1257¹	1273	44	289	445	11.4	3.14	106	.269	.314	92	.208	5	19	27	-7	3.6

■ CHARLIE CADY
Cady, Charles B. b: 12/1865, Chicago, Ill. d: 6/7/09, Kankakee, Ill. 5'11", 180 lbs. Deb: 9/05/1883 ♦

YEAR TM/L	W	L	PCT	G	GS	CG	SH	SV	IP	H	HR	BB	SO	RAT	ERA	ERA+	OAV	OOB	BH	AVG	PB	PR	/A	PD	TPI
1883 Cle-N	0	1	.000	1	1	1	0	0	8	13	0	4	5	19.1	7.88	40	.346	.409	0	.000	-1	-4	-4	0	-0.2
1884 CP-U	3	1	.750	4	4	4	0	0	35	37	0	13	15	12.9	2.83	107	.254	.315	2	.100	-1	1	1	0	0.0
Total 2	3	2	.600	5	5	5	0	0	43	50	0	17	20	14.0	3.77	81	.272	.334	2	.059	-1	-3	-3	0	-0.2

■ JOHN CAHILL
Cahill, John Patrick Francis "Patsy" b: 1864, San Francisco, Cal. d: 11/1/01, Pleasanton, Cal. BR/TR, 5'7.5", 168 lbs. Deb: 5/31/1884 ♦

YEAR TM/L	W	L	PCT	G	GS	CG	SH	SV	IP	H	HR	BB	SO	RAT	ERA	ERA+	OAV	OOB	BH	AVG	PB	PR	/A	PD	TPI
1884 Col-a	1	0	1.000	2	1	1	0	0	16	15	0	4	1	10.7	5.06	60	.235	.280	46	.219	-0	-3	-4	0	-0.2
1886 StL-N	1	0	1.000	2	0	0	0	0	12	11	0	3	2	10.5	3.00	107	.234	.280	92	.199	-0	0	0	0	0.0
1887 Ind-N	0	2	.000	6	1	1	0	0	22	40	2	19	5	24.1	14.32	29	.381	.476	54	.205	-1	-25	-25	-1	-1.7
Total 3	2	2	.500	10	2	2	0	0	-50	66	2	26	8	16.6	8.64	41	.306	.380	192	.205	-1	-28	-28	-1	-1.9

■ LES CAIN
Cain, Leslie b: 1/13/48, San Luis Obispo, Cal. BL/TL, 6'1", 200 lbs. Deb: 4/28/68

YEAR TM/L	W	L	PCT	G	GS	CG	SH	SV	IP	H	HR	BB	SO	RAT	ERA	ERA+	OAV	OOB	BH	AVG	PB	PR	/A	PD	TPI
1968 Det-A	1	0	1.000	8	4	0	0	0	24	25	1	20	13	16.9	3.00	100	.269	.398	1	.143	0	-0	0	0	0.1
1970 Det-A	12	7	.632	29	29	5	0	0	180²	167	15	98	156	13.5	3.84	97	.247	.349	11	.162	0	-2	-2	-1	-0.2
1971 Det-A	10	9	.526	26	26	3	1	0	144²	121	14	91	118	13.6	4.35	82	.228	.348	8	.145	-0	-14	-12	-1	-1.3
1972 Det-A	0	3	.000	5	5	0	0	0	23²	18	2	16	16	12.9	3.80	83	.209	.333	1	.143	-0	-2	-2	-0	-0.2
Total 4	23	19	.548	68	64	8	1	0	373	331	32	225	303	13.7	3.98	90	.239	.351	21	.153	-0	-19	-16	-1	-1.6

■ SUGAR CAIN
Cain, Merritt Patrick b: 4/5/07, Macon, Ga. d: 4/3/75, Atlanta, Ga. BL/TR, 5'11", 190 lbs. Deb: 4/15/32

YEAR TM/L	W	L	PCT	G	GS	CG	SH	SV	IP	H	HR	BB	SO	RAT	ERA	ERA+	OAV	OOB	BH	AVG	PB	PR	/A	PD	TPI
1932 Phi-A	3	4	.429	10	6	3	0	0	45	42	1	28	24	14.0	5.00	90	.256	.365	3	.250	1	-3	-2	-0	-0.1

YEAR TM/L	W	L	PCT	G	GS	CG	SH	SV	IP	H	HR	BB	SO	RAT	ERA	ERA+	OAV	OOB	BH	AVG	PB	PR	/A	PD	TPI
1933 Phi-A	13	12	.520	38	32	16	1	1	218	244	18	137	43	15.9	4.25	101	.280	.379	16	.200	-1	1	1	-0	0.0
1934 Phi-A	9	17	.346	36	32	15	0	0	230²	235	15	128	66	14.3	4.41	99	.266	.360	13	.159	-3	2	-1	-0	-0.3
1935 Phi-A	0	5	.000	6	5	0	0	0	26	39	1	19	5	20.1	6.58	69	.382	.479	0	.000	-1	-6	-6	0	-0.5
StL-A	9	8	.529	31	24	8	0	0	167²	197	7	104	68	16.4	5.26	91	.290	.388	11	.193	-3	-15	-9	-3	-1.2
Yr	9	13	.409	37	29	8	0	0	193²	236	8	123	73	16.9	5.44	88	.302	.400	11	.015	-6	-21	-15	-3	-1.7
1936 StL-A	1	1	.500	4	3	1	0	0	16¹	20	0	9	8	16.0	6.61	81	.286	.367	2	.286	0	-3	-2	-0	-0.1
Chi-A	14	10	.583	30	26	14	1	0	195¹	228	18	75	42	14.2	4.75	110	.293	.359	7	.103	-4	6	10	-2	0.3
Yr	15	11	.577	34	29	15	1	0	211²	248	18	84	50	14.3	4.89	107	.292	.360	7	.093	-4	3	8	-3	0.2
1937 Chi-A	4	2	.667	18	6	1	0	0	68²	88	7	51	17	18.2	6.16	75	.325	.432	4	.182	-1	-12	-12	0	-1.0
1938 Chi-A	0	1	.000	5	3	0	0	0	19²	26	0	18	6	20.1	4.58	107	.321	.444	0	.000	-1	0	1	-1	0.0
Total 7	53	60	.469	178	137	58	2	1	987¹	1119	67	569	279	15.5	4.83	96	.287	.380	56	.163	-13	-29	-21	-7	-2.9

■ BOB CAIN
Cain, Robert Max "Sugar" b: 10/16/24, Longford, Kan. BL/TL, 6', 165 lbs. Deb: 9/18/49 ♦

YEAR TM/L	W	L	PCT	G	GS	CG	SH	SV	IP	H	HR	BB	SO	RAT	ERA	ERA+	OAV	OOB	BH	AVG	PB	PR	/A	PD	TPI
1949 Chi-A	0	0	—	6	0	0	0	1	11	7	0	5	5	9.8	2.45	170	.179	.273	0	.000	-0	2	2	-0	0.1
1950 Chi-A	9	12	.429	34	23	11	1	2	171²	153	12	109	77	14.0	3.93	114	.244	.361	12	.197	-0	12	11	0	1.0
1951 Chi-A	1	2	.333	4	4	1	0	0	26¹	25	3	13	13	14.0	3.76	107	.248	.350	3	.333	1	1	1	0	0.1
Det-A	11	10	.524	35	22	6	1	2	149¹	135	12	82	58	13.7	4.70	89	.239	.347	13	.245	2	-10	-9	0	-0.5
Yr	12	12	.500	39	26	7	1	2	175²	160	15	95	61	13.6	4.56	91	.240	.344	6	.097	3	-9	-8	0	-0.4
1952 StL-A	12	10	.545	29	27	8	1	2	170	169	15	62	70	12.3	4.13	95	.264	.331	8	.138	-1	-9	-4	-2	-0.7
1953 StL-A	4	10	.286	32	13	1	0	1	99²	129	8	45	36	15.8	6.23	67	.310	.379	6	.200	0	-25	-22	-1	-2.2
Total 5	37	44	.457	140	89	27	3	8	628	618	50	316	249	13.7	4.50	93	.259	.351	42	.196	0	-27	-21	-4	-2.2

■ CHARLIE CALDWELL
Caldwell, Charles William "Chuck" b: 8/2/01, Bristol, Va. d: 11/1/57, Princeton, N.J. BR/TR, 5'10", 180 lbs. Deb: 7/07/25

YEAR TM/L	W	L	PCT	G	GS	CG	SH	SV	IP	H	HR	BB	SO	RAT	ERA	ERA+	OAV	OOB	BH	AVG	PB	PR	/A	PD	TPI
1925 NY-A	0	0	—	3	0	0	0	0	2²	7	0	3	1	33.8	16.88	25	.467	.556	0	.000	-0	-4	-4	-0	-0.3

■ EARL CALDWELL
Caldwell, Earl Welton "Teach" b: 4/9/05, Sparks, Tex. d: 9/15/81, Mission, Tex. BR/TR, 6'1", 178 lbs. Deb: 9/08/28

YEAR TM/L	W	L	PCT	G	GS	CG	SH	SV	IP	H	HR	BB	SO	RAT	ERA	ERA+	OAV	OOB	BH	AVG	PB	PR	/A	PD	TPI
1928 Phi-N	1	4	.200	5	5	1	1	0	34²	46	5	17	6	16.4	5.71	75	.348	.423	1	.111	-0	-7	-6	0	-0.4
1935 StL-A	3	2	.600	6	5	2	1	0	36²	34	2	17	5	12.5	3.68	130	.245	.327	2	.182	-0	3	5	1	0.5
1936 StL-A	7	16	.304	41	25	10	2	2	189	252	15	83	59	16.7	6.00	90	.319	.394	11	.190	-1	-20	-13	-1	-1.2
1937 StL-A	0	0	—	9	2	0	0	0	29	39	3	13	8	16.8	6.83	71	.317	.391	2	.222	0	-7	-6	-0	-0.5
1945 Chi-A	6	7	.462	27	11	5	1	4	105¹	108	8	37	45	12.6	3.59	92	.265	.331	8	.216	-0	-3	-3	3	0.0
1946 Chi-A	13	4	.765	39	0	0	0	8	90²	60	2	29	42	8.9	2.08	164	.186	.255	3	.167	1	**14**	**13**	1	1.6
1947 Chi-A	1	4	.200	40	0	0	0	8	54¹	53	4	30	22	13.9	3.64	100	.261	.359	0	.000	-1	0	0	-1	-0.1
1948 Chi-A	1	5	.167	25	1	0	0	3	39	53	3	22	10	17.8	5.31	80	.335	.423	0	.000	-0	-4	-5	-0	-0.4
Bos-A	1	1	.500	8	0	0	0	0	9	11	2	11	5	23.0	13.00	34	.333	.511	1	.333	-0	-9	-9	-0	-0.7
Yr	2	6	.250	33	1	0	0	3	48	64	5	33	15	18.4	6.75	63	.332	.432	2	.250	-0	-13	-13	-1	-1.1
Total 8	33	43	.434	200	49	18	5	25	587²	656	44	259	202	14.4	4.69	92	.284	.363	28	.178	-2	-32	-25	3	-1.2

■ RALPH CALDWELL
Caldwell, Ralph Grant "Lefty" b: 1/18/1884, Philadelphia, Pa. d: 8/5/69, W.Trenton, N.J. BL/TL, 5'9", 155 lbs. Deb: 9/10/04

YEAR TM/L	W	L	PCT	G	GS	CG	SH	SV	IP	H	HR	BB	SO	RAT	ERA	ERA+	OAV	OOB	BH	AVG	PB	PR	/A	PD	TPI
1904 Phi-N	2	2	.500	6	5	5	0	0	41	40	1	15	30	12.5	4.17	64	.242	.313	8	.444	3	-7	-7	-0	-0.3
1905 Phi-N	1	3	.250	7	2	1	0	1	34	44	1	7	29	14.3	4.24	69	.321	.367	0	.000	-2	-5	-5	-1	-0.7
Total 2	3	5	.375	13	7	6	0	1	75	84	2	22	59	13.3	4.20	66	.278	.337	8	.242	1	-11	-12	-1	-1.0

■ MIKE CALDWELL
Caldwell, Ralph Michael b: 1/22/49, Tarboro, N.C. BR/TL, 6', 185 lbs. Deb: 9/04/71

YEAR TM/L	W	L	PCT	G	GS	CG	SH	SV	IP	H	HR	BB	SO	RAT	ERA	ERA+	OAV	OOB	BH	AVG	PB	PR	/A	PD	TPI
1971 SD-N	1	0	1.000	6	0	0	0	0	6²	4	0	3	5	9.5	0.00	—	.174	.269	1	1.000	1	3	2	0	0.4
1972 SD-N	7	11	.389	42	20	4	2	2	163²	183	10	49	102	13.0	4.01	82	.282	.337	7	.140	-1	-10	-13	5	-0.9
1973 SD-N	5	14	.263	55	13	3	1	10	149	146	8	53	86	12.1	3.74	93	.260	.326	5	.143	-1	-1	-5	2	-0.3
1974 SF-N	14	5	.737	31	27	6	2	0	189¹	176	17	63	83	11.6	2.95	129	.249	.314	9	.143	-2	14	18	5	2.2
1975 SF-N	7	13	.350	38	21	4	0	1	163¹	194	16	48	57	13.6	4.79	79	.296	.348	7	.159	-0	-21	-18	2	-1.5
1976 SF-N	1	7	.125	50	9	0	0	2	107¹	145	5	20	55	14.0	4.86	75	.324	.356	3	.158	-0	-16	-15	1	-1.3
1977 Cin-N	0	0	—	14	0	0	0	1	24²	25	1	8	11	12.0	4.01	98	.260	.317	2	.500	2	-0	-0	0	0.1
Mil-A	5	8	.385	21	12	2	0	0	94¹	101	6	36	38	13.3	4.58	89	.271	.338	0	—	0	-5	-5	3	-0.1
1978 Mil-A	22	9	.710	37	34	23	6	1	293	258	14	54	131	9.8	2.37	159	.234	.274	0	—	0	45	45	1	5.2
1979 Mil-A	16	6	**.727**	30	30	16	4	0	235	252	18	39	89	11.3	3.29	126	.278	.311	0	—	0	24	23	5	2.8
1980 Mil-A	13	11	.542	34	33	11	2	1	225¹	248	29	56	74	12.2	4.03	96	.285	.330	0	—	0	-0	-4	0	-0.3
1981 *Mil-A	11	9	.550	24	23	8	0	0	144¹	151	8	38	41	11.8	3.93	87	.272	.319	0	—	0	-4	-8	0	-0.7
1982 *Mil-A	17	13	.567	35	34	12	3	0	258	269	30	58	75	11.4	3.91	97	.271	.311	0	—	0	5	-4	2	0.0
1983 Mil-A	12	11	.522	32	32	10	2	0	228¹	269	35	51	58	12.7	4.53	82	.296	.334	0	—	0	-12	-20	-1	-1.8
1984 Mil-A	6	13	.316	26	19	4	1	0	126	160	11	21	34	13.0	4.64	83	.314	.343	0	—	0	-9	-11	1	-0.9
Total 14	137	130	.513	475	307	98	23	18	2408¹	2581	218	597	939	12.0	3.81	99	.276	.322	34	.157	-2	11	-14	28	2.9

■ RAY CALDWELL
Caldwell, Raymond Benjamin "Rube" or "Slim" b: 4/26/1888, Corydon, Pa. d: 8/17/67, Salamanca, N.Y. BL/TR, 6'2", 190 lbs. Deb: 9/09/10 ♦

YEAR TM/L	W	L	PCT	G	GS	CG	SH	SV	IP	H	HR	BB	SO	RAT	ERA	ERA+	OAV	OOB	BH	AVG	PB	PR	/A	PD	TPI
1910 NY-A	1	0	1.000	6	2	1	0	1	19¹	19	1	9	17	13.0	3.72	71	.260	.341	0	.000	-1	-3	-2	-0	-0.3
1911 NY-A	14	14	.500	41	27	19	1	1	255	240	7	79	145	11.7	3.35	107	.260	.327	40	.272	4	-0	7	-3	1.0
1912 NY-A	8	16	.333	30	26	13	3	0	183¹	196	1	67	95	13.2	4.47	80	.277	.344	18	.237	4	-23	-18	2	-1.2
1913 NY-A	9	8	.529	27	16	15	2	1	164¹	131	5	60	87	11.0	2.41	124	.219	.299	28	.289	3	10	11	-1	1.1
1914 NY-A	17	9	.654	31	23	22	5	1	213	153	5	51	92	8.8	1.94	142	.205	.260	22	.195	1	19	19	-3	2.2
1915 NY-A	19	16	.543	36	35	31	3	0	305	266	6	107	130	11.2	2.89	101	.244	.315	35	.243	8	2	1	-3	0.1
1916 NY-A	5	12	.294	21	18	14	1	0	165²	142	6	65	76	11.7	2.99	97	.243	.327	19	.204	-0	-3	-2	-1	-0.1
1917 NY-A	13	16	.448	32	29	21	1	0	236	199	8	76	102	10.7	2.86	94	.234	.302	32	.258	5	-5	-5	-2	0.6
1918 NY-A	9	8	.529	24	21	14	1	1	176²	173	2	62	59	12.0	3.06	93	.261	.325	44	.291	5	-5	-4	-3	-0.4
1919 Bos-A	7	4	.636	18	12	6	1	0	86¹	92	1	31	23	13.1	3.96	76	.279	.346	13	.271	1	-7	-9	-1	-0.8
Cle-A	5	1	.833	6	6	4	1	0	52²	33	1	19	24	9.2	1.71	196	.181	.266	8	.348	3	9	10	-1	1.3
Yr	12	5	.706	24	18	10	2	0	139	125	2	50	47	11.5	3.11	101	.243	.312	0	.000	4	2	1	-3	0.5
1920 *Cle-A	20	10	.667	34	33	20	1	0	237²	286	9	63	80	13.4	3.86	98	.303	.350	19	.213	1	-2	-3	-3	-0.4
1921 Cle-A	6	6	.500	37	12	4	1	4	147	159	7	49	76	12.9	4.90	87	.275	.333	11	.208	0	-10	-10	-1	-0.9
Total 12	133	120	.526	343	260	184	21	9	2242	2089	59	738	1006	11.6	3.22	99	.253	.319	289	.248	32	-20	-4	-19	2.2

■ JEFF CALHOUN
Calhoun, Jeffrey Wilton b: 4/11/58, LaGrange, Ga. BL/TL, 6'2", 190 lbs. Deb: 9/02/84

YEAR TM/L	W	L	PCT	G	GS	CG	SH	SV	IP	H	HR	BB	SO	RAT	ERA	ERA+	OAV	OOB	BH	AVG	PB	PR	/A	PD	TPI
1984 Hou-N	0	1	.000	9	0	0	0	0	15¹	9	0	2	11	4.1	1.17	283	.100	.135	0	—	0	4	4	0	0.4
1985 Hou-N	2	5	.286	44	0	0	0	4	63²	56	2	24	47	11.3	2.54	136	.243	.315	0	.000	-0	7	6	0	0.7
1986 *Hou-N	1	0	1.000	20	0	0	0	0	26²	28	3	12	14	13.5	3.71	97	.264	.339	0	—	0	0	-0	-0	0.0
1987 Phi-N	3	1	.750	42	0	0	0	0	42²	25	1	26	31	11.0	1.48	287	.168	.295	0	.000	-0	12	13	0	1.4
1988 Phi-N	0	0	—	3	0	0	0	0	2¹	6	2	1	1	27.0	15.43	23	.462	.500	0	—	0	-3	-3	0	-0.2
Total 5	6	7	.462	118	0	0	0	5	150²	120	8	65	104	11.1	2.51	147	.219	.303	0	.000	-0	21	20		2.3

■ FRED CALIGIURI
Caligiuri, Frederick John b: 10/22/18, W.Hickory, Pa. BR/TR, 6', 190 lbs. Deb: 9/03/41

YEAR TM/L	W	L	PCT	G	GS	CG	SH	SV	IP	H	HR	BB	SO	RAT	ERA	ERA+	OAV	OOB	BH	AVG	PB	PR	/A	PD	TPI
1941 Phi-A	2	2	.500	5	5	4	0	0	43	45	2	14	7	12.3	2.93	143	.257	.312	4	.200	1	6	6	-1	0.6
1942 Phi-A	0	3	.000	13	2	0	0	1	36²	45	2	18	20	16.0	6.38	59	.300	.382	1	.083	-0	-11	-11	-0	-1.0
Total 2	2	5	.286	18	7	4	0	1	79²	90	4	32	27	14.0	4.52	89	.277	.345	5	.156	1	-5	-5	-1	-0.4

■ WILL CALIHAN
Calihan, William T. b: 1867, Oswego, N.Y. d: 12/20/17, Rochester, N.Y. 5'8", 150 lbs. Deb: 4/17/1890

YEAR TM/L	W	L	PCT	G	GS	CG	SH	SV	IP	H	HR	BB	SO	RAT	ERA	ERA+	OAV	OOB	BH	AVG	PB	PR	/A	PD	TPI
1890 Roc-a	18	15	.545	37	36	31	0	0	296¹	276	4	125	127	12.2	3.28	109	.306	.314	23	.145	-3	19	9	3	0.5
1891 Phi-a	6	6	.500	13	11	11	0	0	112	151	7	47	28	15.9	6.43	59	.312	.373	11	.196	-1	-34	-32	2	-2.4
Total 2	24	21	.533	50	47	42	0	0	408¹	427	11	172	155	13.2	4.14	88	.261	.331	34	.158	-4	-14	-23	5	-1.9

YEAR TM/L	W	L	PCT	G	GS	CG	SH	SV	IP	H	HR	BB	SO	RAT	ERA	ERA+	OAV	OOB	BH	AVG	PB	PR	/A	PD	TPI

■ BEN CALLAHAN
Callahan, Benjamin Franklin b: 5/19/57, Mt.Airy, N.C. BR/TR, 6'7", 230 lbs. Deb: 6/22/83

| 1983 Oak-A | 1 | 2 | .333 | 4 | 2 | 0 | 0 | 0 | 9¹ | 18 | 0 | 5 | 2 | 22.2 | 12.54 | 31 | .400 | .460 | 0 | — | 0 | -9 | -9 | 0 | -0.7 |

■ NIXEY CALLAHAN
Callahan, James Joseph b: 3/18/1874, Fitchburg, Mass. d: 10/4/34, Boston, Mass. BR/TR, 5'10.5", 180 lbs. Deb: 5/12/1894 M♦

1894 Phi-N	1	2	.333	9	2	1	0	2	33²	64	3	17	9	21.7	9.89	52	.398	.455	5	.238	-1	-17	-18	1	-1.2
1897 Chi-N	12	9	.571	23	22	21	1	0	189²	221	6	55	52	13.1	4.03	111	.289	.336	105	.292	3	6	9	1	0.8
1898 Chi-N	20	10	.667	31	31	30	2	0	274¹	267	2	71	73	11.1	2.46	146	.253	.300	43	.262	4	35	34	1	4.1
1899 Chi-N	21	12	.636	35	34	33	3	0	294¹	327	5	76	77	12.3	3.06	123	.281	.325	39	.260	4	26	23	5	3.1
1900 Chi-N	13	16	.448	32	32	32	2	0	285¹	347	5	74	77	13.3	3.82	94	.299	.341	27	.235	2	-4	-7	6	0.1
1901 Chi-A	15	8	.652	27	22	20	1	0	215¹	195	4	50	70	10.2	2.42	144	.239	.283	39	.331	8	30	25	6	4.3
1902 Chi-A	16	14	.533	35	31	29	2	0	282¹	287	8	89	75	12.0	3.60	94	.264	.320	51	.234	2	-1	-7	6	-0.6
1903 Chi-A	1	2	.333	3	3	3	0	0	28	40	0	5	12	14.5	4.50	62	.334	.360	128	.292	1	-5	-5	1	-0.4
Total 8	99	73	.576	195	177	169	11	2	1603	1748	33	437	445	12.3	3.39	109	.276	.323	901	.273	24	70	54	26	10.2

■ JIM CALLAHAN
Callahan, James W. b: Moberly, Mo. Deb: 9/03/1898

| 1898 StL-N | 0 | 2 | .000 | 2 | 2 | 1 | 0 | 0 | 8¹ | 18 | 2 | 7 | 2 | 27.0 | 16.20 | 23 | .430 | .511 | 0 | .000 | -1 | -12 | -11 | 0 | -0.8 |

■ JOE CALLAHAN
Callahan, Joseph Thomas b: 10/8/16, E.Boston, Mass. d: 5/24/49, S.Boston, Mass. BR/TR, 6'2", 170 lbs. Deb: 9/13/39

1939 Bos-N	1	0	1.000	4	1	1	0	0	17¹	17	0	3	8	10.9	3.12	119	.250	.292	0	.000	-1	2	1	0	0.1
1940 Bos-N	0	2	.000	6	2	0	0	0	15	20	1	13	3	19.8	10.20	36	.351	.471	0	.000	-1	-11	-11	1	-0.9
Total 2	1	2	.333	10	3	1	0	0	32¹	37	1	16	11	15.0	6.40	58	.296	.380	0	.000	-1	-9	-10	1	-0.8

■ RAY CALLAHAN
Callahan, Raymond James "Pat" b: 8/29/1891, Ashland, Wis. d: 1/23/73, Olympia, Wash. BL/TL, 5'10.5", 170 lbs. Deb: 9/12/15

| 1915 Cin-N | 0 | 0 | — | 3 | 0 | 0 | 0 | 0 | 6¹ | 12 | 1 | 1 | 4 | 18.5 | 8.53 | 34 | .364 | .382 | 1 | .333 | 0 | -4 | -4 | -0 | -0.3 |

■ DICK CALMUS
Calmus, Richard Lee b: 1/7/44, Los Angeles, Cal. BR/TR, 6'4", 187 lbs. Deb: 4/22/63

1963 LA-N	3	1	.750	21	1	0	0	0	44	32	3	16	25	9.8	2.66	114	.204	.277	0	.000	-1	3	2	-0	0.1
1967 Chi-N	0	0	—	1	1	0	0	0	4¹	5	2	0	1	10.4	8.31	43	.278	.278	1	.500	0	-2	-2	-0	-0.1
Total 2	3	1	.750	22	2	0	0	0	48¹	37	5	16	26	9.9	3.17	97	.211	.277	1	.125	-0	1	-1	-0	0.0

■ MARK CALVERT
Calvert, Mark b: 9/29/56, Tulsa, Okla. BR/TR, 6'1", 195 lbs. Deb: 4/17/83

1983 SF-N	1	4	.200	18	4	0	0	0	37¹	46	2	34	14	20.0	6.27	56	.307	.444	0	.000	-1	-11	-11	1	-1.0
1984 SF-N	2	4	.333	10	5	1	0	0	32	40	4	9	5	14.1	5.06	69	.303	.352	0	.000	-1	-5	-6	1	-0.5
Total 2	3	8	.273	28	9	1	0	0	69¹	86	6	43	19	17.3	5.71	62	.305	.404	0	.000	-1	-16	-17	1	-1.5

■ PAUL CALVERT
Calvert, Paul Leo Emile b: 10/6/17, Montreal, Que., Can. BR/TR, 6', 175 lbs. Deb: 9/24/42

1942 Cle-A	0	0	—	1	0	0	0	0	2	0	0	2	2	9.0	0.00	—	.000	.286	0	—	0	1	1	0	0.1
1943 Cle-A	0	0	—	5	0	0	0	0	8¹	6	0	6	2	14.0	4.32	72	.200	.351	0	.000	-0	-1	-1	0	0.0
1944 Cle-A	1	3	.250	35	4	0	0	0	77	89	4	38	31	14.8	4.56	72	.289	.367	4	.267	1	-10	-11	2	-0.7
1945 Cle-A	0	0	—	1	0	0	0	0	1¹	3	0	1	1	27.0	13.50	24	.429	.500	0	—	0	-2	-2	0	-0.1
1949 Was-A	6	17	.261	34	23	5	0	1	160²	175	11	86	52	14.7	5.43	78	.279	.368	7	.137	-2	-22	-21	3	-1.8
1950 Det-A	2	2	.500	32	0	0	0	4	51¹	71	7	25	14	17.2	6.31	74	.324	.398	0	.000	-1	-10	-9	1	-0.7
1951 Det-A	0	0	—	1	0	0	0	0	1	1	0	0	0	9.0	0.00	—	.250	.250	0	—	0	0	0	0	0.1
Total 7	9	22	.290	109	27	5	0	5	301²	345	22	158	102	15.2	5.31	76	.287	.373	11	.149	-2	-43	-43	6	-3.1

■ ERNIE CAMACHO
Camacho, Ernest Carlos b: 2/1/55, Salinas, Cal. BR/TR, 6'1", 180 lbs. Deb: 5/22/80

1980 Oak-A	0	0	—	5	0	0	0	0	11²	20	2	5	9	20.1	6.94	54	.364	.426	0	—	0	-4	-4	-0	-0.3
1981 Pit-N	0	1	.000	7	3	0	0	0	21²	23	0	15	11	15.8	4.98	72	.295	.409	0	.000	-0	-4	-3	-0	-0.3
1983 Cle-A	0	1	.000	4	0	0	0	0	5¹	5	1	2	2	13.5	5.06	84	.250	.348	0	—	0	-1	-0	-0	0.0
1984 Cle-A	5	9	.357	69	0	0	0	23	100	83	6	37	48	10.9	2.43	168	.229	.303	0	—	0	17	18	0	1.9
1985 Cle-A	0	1	.000	2	0	0	0	0	3¹	4	0	1	2	13.5	8.10	51	.333	.385	0	—	0	-1	-1	0	0.0
1986 Cle-A	2	4	.333	51	0	0	0	20	57¹	60	1	31	36	14.6	4.08	101	.269	.363	0	—	0	1	0	1	0.1
1987 Cle-A	0	1	.000	15	0	0	0	1	13²	21	1	5	9	19.1	9.22	49	.350	.426	0	—	0	-7	-7	1	-0.5
1988 Hou-N	0	3	.000	13	0	0	0	1	17²	25	1	12	13	18.8	7.64	43	.352	.446	0	.000	-0	-8	-8	0	-0.8
1989 SF-N	3	0	1.000	13	0	0	0	0	16¹	10	1	11	14	11.6	2.76	122	.175	.309	0	.000	-0	1	1	1	0.2
1990 SF-N	0	0	—	8	0	0	0	0	10	10	1	3	8	11.7	3.60	103	.256	.370	0	—	0	-0	-0	-0	0.0
StL-N	0	0	—	6	0	0	0	0	5²	7	2	6	7	20.6	7.94	49	.318	.464	0	—	0	-3	-3	0	-0.2
Yr	0	0	—	14	0	0	0	0	15²	17	3	9	15	14.9	5.17	73	.279	.371	0	—	0	-2	-2	-0	-0.2
Total 10	10	20	.333	193	3	0	0	45	262²	268	16	128	159	13.8	4.21	94	.268	.356	0	.000	-1	-8	-8	1	0.1

■ FRED CAMBRIA
Cambria, Frederick Dennis b: 1/22/48, Cambria Heights, N.Y. BR/TR, 6'2", 195 lbs. Deb: 8/26/70

| 1970 Pit-N | 1 | 2 | .333 | 6 | 5 | 0 | 0 | 0 | 33¹ | 37 | 2 | 12 | 14 | 13.5 | 3.51 | 111 | .272 | .336 | 2 | .200 | 1 | 2 | 1 | 0 | 0.2 |

■ JACK CAMERON
Cameron, John William "Happy Jack" b: 1885, Canada d: 8/17/51, Boston, Mass. Deb: 9/13/06 ♦

| 1906 Bos-N | 0 | 0 | — | 2 | 1 | 0 | 0 | 0 | 6 | 4 | 0 | 6 | 2 | 15.0 | 0.00 | — | .211 | .400 | 11 | .180 | -0 | 2 | 2 | 0 | 0.2 |

■ HARRY CAMNITZ
Camnitz, Henry Richardson b: 10/26/1884, McKinney, Ky. d: 1/6/51, Louisville, Ky. BR/TR, 6'1", 168 lbs. Deb: 4/14/09

1909 Pit-N	0	0	—	1	0	0	0	0	4	6	0	1	1	15.8	4.50	61	.353	.389	0	.000	-0	-1	-1	0	0.0
1911 StL-N	1	0	1.000	2	0	0	0	0	2	0	0	1	2	4.5	0.00	—	.000	.143	0	—	0	1	1	0	0.1
Total 2	1	0	1.000	3	0	0	0	0	6	6	0	2	3	12.0	3.00	98	.261	.320	0	.000	-0	-0	-0	0	0.1

■ HOWIE CAMNITZ
Camnitz, Samuel Howard "Red" b: 8/22/1881, Covington, Ky. d: 3/2/60, Louisville, Ky. BR/TR, 5'9", 169 lbs. Deb: 4/22/04

1904 Pit-N	1	4	.200	10	2	2	0	0	49	48	0	20	21	13.0	4.22	65	.259	.341	1	.063	-1	-8	-8	-1	-0.9
1906 Pit-N	1	0	1.000	2	1	1	0	0	9	6	0	5	5	11.0	2.00	134	.188	.297	0	.000	-0	1	1	-0	0.0
1907 Pit-N	13	8	.619	31	19	15	4	1	180	135	0	59	85	9.9	2.15	113	.211	.281	3	.050	-5	6	6	-0	0.0
1908 Pit-N	16	9	.640	38	26	17	3	2	236²	182	6	69	118	9.7	1.56	148	.210	.272	6	.083	-3	21	19	-2	1.7
1909 *Pit-N	25	6	**.806**	41	30	20	6	3	283	207	1	68	133	9.0	1.62	168	.211	.267	12	.138	-0	31	35	-3	3.6
1910 Pit-N	12	13	.480	38	31	16	1	2	260	246	6	61	120	11.0	3.22	96	.256	.308	11	.125	-3	-5	-3	-3	-0.9
1911 Pit-N	20	15	.571	40	33	18	1	1	267²	245	8	84	139	11.2	3.13	110	.248	.309	12	.143	-3	8	9	-3	0.2
1912 Pit-N	22	12	.647	41	32	22	2	2	276²	256	8	82	121	11.4	2.83	115	.245	.307	23	.235	1	18	13	-2	1.1
1913 Pit-N	6	17	.261	36	22	5	1	2	192¹	203	7	84	64	13.8	3.74	81	.282	.363	9	.153	-1	-12	-16	-1	-1.6
Phi-N	3	3	.500	9	5	1	0	1	49	49	1	23	21	13.6	3.67	91	.268	.356	1	.063	-1	-3	-2	-1	-0.4
Yr	9	20	.310	45	27	6	1	3	241¹	252	8	107	85	13.5	3.73	83	.277	.354	1	.013	-3	-14	-17	0	-1.9
1914 Pit-F	14	19	.424	36	34	20	1	1	262	256	8	90	82	12.2	3.23	99	.258	.324	14	.161	-3	-1	-1	-4	-0.8
1915 Pit-F	0	0	—	4	2	0	0	0	20	19	1	11	6	13.5	4.50	67	.258	.354	0	.000	-1	-3	-3	-1	-0.4
Total 11	133	106	.556	326	237	137	20	15	2085¹	1852	41	656	915	11.1	2.75	108	.241	.306	92	.136	-22	54	50	-19	1.7

■ RICK CAMP
Camp, Rick Lamar b: 6/10/53, Trion, Ga. BR/TR, 6'1", 185 lbs. Deb: 9/15/76

1976 Atl-N	0	1	.000	5	1	0	0	0	11¹	13	0	2	6	11.9	6.35	60	.302	.333	0	.000	-0	-4	-3	1	-0.2
1977 Atl-N	6	3	.667	54	0	0	0	10	78²	89	6	47	51	15.7	4.00	111	.283	.377	0	.000	-1	-1	4	-0	0.3
1978 Atl-N	2	4	.333	42	4	0	0	0	74¹	99	5	32	23	16.2	3.75	108	.329	.399	0	.000	-1	2	0	0	0.2
1980 Atl-N	6	4	.600	77	0	0	0	22	108¹	92	3	29	33	10.4	1.91	196	.235	.294	1	.111	-0	20	22	4	2.8
1981 Atl-N	9	3	.750	48	0	0	0	17	76	68	5	12	47	9.6	1.78	202	.239	.272	0	.000	-1	14	**15**	0	1.5
1982 *Atl-N	11	13	.458	51	21	3	0	5	177¹	199	18	52	68	12.8	3.65	102	.291	.342	1	.024	-3	-1	1	1	0.0
1983 Atl-N	10	9	.526	40	16	1	0	1	140	146	16	38	61	12.1	3.79	102	.270	.323	3	.077	-2	-3	1	1	0.0

YEAR	TM/L	W	L	PCT	G	GS	CG	SH	SV	IP	H	HR	BB	SO	RAT	ERA	ERA+	OAV	OOB	BH	AVG	PB	PR	/A	PD	TPI
1984	Atl-N	8	6	.571	31	21	1	0	0	148²	134	11	63	69	12.0	3.27	118	.245	.325	5	.111	-2	5	10	1	0.9
1985	Atl-N	4	6	.400	66	2	0	0	3	127²	130	8	61	49	13.8	3.95	97	.263	.349	3	.231	1	-5	-1	-2	-0.1
Total	9	56	49	.533	414	65	5	0	57	942¹	970	72	336	407	12.7	3.37	114	.269	.335	13	.074	-9	25	51	5	5.4

■ KID CAMP
Camp, Winfield Scott   b: 1870, Columbus, Ohio   d: 3/2/1895, Omaha, Neb.   6', 160 lbs.   Deb: 5/03/1892

YEAR	TM/L	W	L	PCT	G	GS	CG	SH	SV	IP	H	HR	BB	SO	RAT	ERA	ERA+	OAV	OOB	BH	AVG	PB	PR	/A	PD	TPI
1892	Pit-N	0	1	.000	4	1	1	0	0	23	31	4	9	6	15.7	6.26	53	.310	.367	1	.091	-1	-8	-8	-1	-0.7
1894	Chi-N	0	1	.000	3	2	2	0	0	22	34	0	12	6	18.8	6.55	86	.349	.421	0	.000	-3	-3	-2	0	-0.2
Total	2	0	2	.000	7	3	3	0	0	45	65	4	21	12	17.2	6.40	69	.329	.394	1	.045	-4	-11	-10	-1	-0.9

■ BERT CAMPANERIS
Campaneris, Dagoberto (Blanco) "Campy" (b: Dagoberto Campaneria (Blanco))   b: 3/9/42, Pueblo Nuevo, Cuba   BR/TR, 5'10", 160 lbs.   Deb: 7/23/64 ♦

YEAR	TM/L	W	L	PCT	G	GS	CG	SH	SV	IP	H	HR	BB	SO	RAT	ERA	ERA+	OAV	OOB	BH	AVG	PB	PR	/A	PD	TPI
1965	KC-A	0	0	—	1	0	0	0	0	1	1	0	2	1	27.0	9.00	39	.333	.600	156	.270	0	-1	-1	0	0.0

■ ARCHIE CAMPBELL
Campbell, Archibald Stewart "Iron Man"   b: 10/20/03, Maplewood, N.J.   BR/TR, 6', 180 lbs.   Deb: 4/21/28

YEAR	TM/L	W	L	PCT	G	GS	CG	SH	SV	IP	H	HR	BB	SO	RAT	ERA	ERA+	OAV	OOB	BH	AVG	PB	PR	/A	PD	TPI
1928	NY-A	0	1	.000	13	1	0	0	2	24	30	0	11	9	15.4	5.25	72	.288	.357	1	.250	0	-3	-4	-0	-0.3
1929	Was-A	0	1	.000	4	0	0	0	0	4	10	1	5	1	33.8	15.75	27	.500	.600	0	—	0	-5	-5	0	-0.3
1930	Cin-N	2	4	.333	23	3	1	0	4	58	71	2	31	19	16.0	5.43	89	.311	.396	4	.267	0	-3	-4	2	-0.1
Total	3	2	6	.250	40	4	1	0	6	86	111	3	47	29	16.6	5.86	77	.315	.398	5	.263	0	-11	-13	2	-0.7

■ DAVE CAMPBELL
Campbell, David Alan   b: 9/3/51, Princeton, Ind.   BR/TR, 6'3", 210 lbs.   Deb: 5/06/77

YEAR	TM/L	W	L	PCT	G	GS	CG	SH	SV	IP	H	HR	BB	SO	RAT	ERA	ERA+	OAV	OOB	BH	AVG	PB	PR	/A	PD	TPI
1977	Atl-N	0	6	.000	65	0	0	0	13	88²	78	7	33	42	11.6	3.05	146	.239	.315	1	.083	-1	9	14	-1	1.2
1978	Atl-N	4	4	.500	53	0	0	0	1	69¹	67	10	49	45	15.7	4.80	84	.258	.385	0	—	0	-9	-6	0	-0.5
Total	2	4	10	.286	118	0	0	0	14	158	145	17	82	87	13.4	3.82	112	.247	.348	1	.083	-1	-1	8	-1	0.7

■ HUGH CAMPBELL
Campbell, Hugh F.   d: 1881, Elizabeth, N.J.   Deb: 4/28/1873

YEAR	TM/L	W	L	PCT	G	GS	CG	SH	SV	IP	H	HR	BB	SO	RAT	ERA	ERA+	OAV	OOB	BH	AVG	PB	PR	/A	PD	TPI
1873	Res-n	2	16	.111	19	18	18	0	0	165	247	7	7		13.9	4.64	80	.294	.300	13	.153	-6	-19	-17		-1.4

■ JIM CAMPBELL
Campbell, James Marcus   b: 5/19/66, Santa Monica, Cal.   BL/TL, 5'11", 175 lbs.   Deb: 8/21/90

YEAR	TM/L	W	L	PCT	G	GS	CG	SH	SV	IP	H	HR	BB	SO	RAT	ERA	ERA+	OAV	OOB	BH	AVG	PB	PR	/A	PD	TPI
1990	KC-A	1	0	1.000	2	2	0	0	0	9²	15	1	1	2	14.9	8.38	45	.349	.364	0	—	0	-5	-5	-0	-0.4

■ JOHN CAMPBELL
Campbell, John Millard   b: 9/13/07, Washington, D.C.   BR/TR, 6'1.5", 184 lbs.   Deb: 7/23/33

YEAR	TM/L	W	L	PCT	G	GS	CG	SH	SV	IP	H	HR	BB	SO	RAT	ERA	ERA+	OAV	OOB	BH	AVG	PB	PR	/A	PD	TPI
1933	Was-A	0	0	—	1	0	0	0	0	1	1	0	1	0	18.0	0.00	—	.200	.333	0	—	0	0	0	0	0.0

■ MIKE CAMPBELL
Campbell, Michael Thomas   b: 2/17/64, Seattle, Wash.   BR/TR, 6'3", 210 lbs.   Deb: 7/04/87

YEAR	TM/L	W	L	PCT	G	GS	CG	SH	SV	IP	H	HR	BB	SO	RAT	ERA	ERA+	OAV	OOB	BH	AVG	PB	PR	/A	PD	TPI
1987	Sea-A	1	4	.200	9	9	1	0	0	49¹	41	9	25	35	12.4	4.74	99	.224	.324	0	—	0	-2	-0	0	0.0
1988	Sea-A	6	10	.375	20	20	2	0	0	114²	128	18	43	63	13.4	5.89	71	.280	.342	0	—	0	-24	-22	-0	-2.0
1989	Sea-A	1	2	.333	5	5	0	0	0	21	28	4	10	6	16.3	7.29	55	.301	.369	0	—	0	-8	-8	-0	-0.6
Total	3	8	16	.333	34	34	3	0	0	185	197	31	78	104	13.5	5.74	75	.269	.341	0	—	0	-34	-30	-1	-2.6

■ BILLY CAMPBELL
Campbell, William James   b: 11/5/1873, Pittsburgh, Pa.   d: 10/6/57, Cincinnati, Ohio   BL/TL, 5'10", 165 lbs.   Deb: 4/17/05

YEAR	TM/L	W	L	PCT	G	GS	CG	SH	SV	IP	H	HR	BB	SO	RAT	ERA	ERA+	OAV	OOB	BH	AVG	PB	PR	/A	PD	TPI
1905	StL-N	1	1	.500	2	2	2	0	0	17	27	0	7	2	18.0	7.41	40	.365	.420	1	.143	-0	-8	-8	1	-0.6
1907	Cin-N	3	0	1.000	3	3	3	0	0	21	19	0	3	4	9.4	2.14	121	.244	.272	2	.250	0	1	1	1	0.2
1908	Cin-N	12	13	.480	35	24	19	2	2	221¹	203	3	44	73	10.5	2.60	89	.252	.299	6	.083	-3	-6	-7	4	-0.7
1909	Cin-N	7	11	.389	30	15	7	0	2	148¹	162	0	39	37	12.7	2.67	97	.288	.344	6	.140	-1	-1	-1	3	0.1
Total	4	23	25	.479	70	44	31	2	4	407²	411	3	93	116	11.5	2.80	88	.270	.320	15	.115	-4	-15	-16	9	-1.0

■ BILL CAMPBELL
Campbell, William Richard   b: 8/9/48, Highland Park, Mich.   BL/TR, 6'3", 185 lbs.   Deb: 7/14/73

YEAR	TM/L	W	L	PCT	G	GS	CG	SH	SV	IP	H	HR	BB	SO	RAT	ERA	ERA+	OAV	OOB	BH	AVG	PB	PR	/A	PD	TPI
1973	Min-A	3	3	.500	28	2	0	0	7	51²	44	5	20	42	11.3	3.14	126	.226	.301	0	—	0	4	5	0	0.5
1974	Min-A	8	7	.533	63	0	0	0	19	120¹	109	4	55	89	12.4	2.62	143	.242	.327	0	—	0	13	15	0	1.6
1975	Min-A	4	6	.400	47	7	2	1	5	121	119	13	46	76	12.4	3.79	102	.262	.333	0	.000	-0	-0	1	1	0.1
1976	Min-A	17	5	.773	78	0	0	0	20	167²	145	9	62	115	11.4	3.01	120	.234	.309	0	—	0	10	11	-1	1.1
1977	Bos-A	13	9	.591	69	0	0	0	31	140	112	13	60	114	11.4	2.96	152	.224	.313	0	—	0	17	24	1	2.5
1978	Bos-A	7	5	.583	29	0	0	0	4	50²	62	3	17	47	14.0	3.91	105	.308	.362	0	—	0	-1	1	0	0.1
1979	Bos-A	3	4	.429	41	0	0	0	9	54²	55	5	23	25	13.0	4.28	103	.262	.338	0	—	0	-0	1	1	0.2
1980	Bos-A	4	0	1.000	23	0	0	0	0	41¹	44	1	22	17	14.4	4.79	88	.284	.373	0	—	0	-3	-3	-1	-0.2
1981	Bos-A	1	1	.500	30	0	0	0	7	48¹	45	5	20	37	12.1	3.17	122	.245	.319	0	—	0	3	4	0	0.4
1982	Chi-N	3	6	.333	62	0	0	0	8	100	89	6	40	71	11.6	3.69	101	.245	.319	1	.143	-0	-1	0	2	0.2
1983	Chi-N	6	8	.429	82	0	0	0	8	122¹	128	4	49	97	13.1	4.49	84	.275	.346	1	.100	-1	-12	-9	2	-0.8
1984	Phi-N	6	5	.545	57	0	0	0	1	81¹	68	2	35	52	11.4	3.43	106	.222	.302	0	.000	-0	1	2	-1	0.0
1985	*StL-N	5	3	.625	50	0	0	0	4	64¹	55	5	21	41	10.9	3.50	101	.230	.298	2	.333	1	1	0	-1	0.1
1986	Det-A	3	6	.333	34	0	0	0	3	55²	46	5	21	37	11.0	3.88	106	.230	.306	0	—	0	2	1	-1	0.1
1987	Mon-N	0	0	—	7	0	0	0	0	10	18	2	4	4	19.8	8.10	52	.360	.407	0	.000	0	-4	-4	0	-0.3
Total	15	83	68	.550	700	9	2	1	126	1229¹	1139	82	495	864	12.1	3.54	110	.248	.324	4	.154	1	28	49	3	5.5

■ CARDELL CAMPER
Camper, Cardell   b: 7/6/52, Boley, Okla.   BR/TR, 6'3", 208 lbs.   Deb: 9/11/77

YEAR	TM/L	W	L	PCT	G	GS	CG	SH	SV	IP	H	HR	BB	SO	RAT	ERA	ERA+	OAV	OOB	BH	AVG	PB	PR	/A	PD	TPI
1977	Cle-A	1	0	1.000	3	1	0	0	0	9¹	7	0	4	9	10.6	3.86	102	.200	.282	0	—	0	0	0	-0	0.0

■ SAL CAMPFIELD
Campfield, William Holton   b: 2/19/1868, Meadville, Pa.   d: 5/16/52, Meadville, Pa.   BR/TR, 6'0.5",   Deb: 5/15/1896

YEAR	TM/L	W	L	PCT	G	GS	CG	SH	SV	IP	H	HR	BB	SO	RAT	ERA	ERA+	OAV	OOB	BH	AVG	PB	PR	/A	PD	TPI
1896	NY-N	1	1	.500	6	2	2	0	0	27	31	1	6	6	12.3	4.00	105	.286	.323	2	.167	-0	1	1	-0	0.0

■ SAL CAMPISI
Campisi, Salvatore John   b: 8/11/42, Brooklyn, N.Y.   BR/TR, 6'2", 210 lbs.   Deb: 8/15/69

YEAR	TM/L	W	L	PCT	G	GS	CG	SH	SV	IP	H	HR	BB	SO	RAT	ERA	ERA+	OAV	OOB	BH	AVG	PB	PR	/A	PD	TPI
1969	StL-N	1	0	1.000	7	0	0	0	0	9²	4	0	6	7	9.3	0.93	384	.121	.256	0	—	0	3	3	0	0.3
1970	StL-N	2	2	.500	37	0	0	0	4	49¹	53	2	37	26	17.0	2.92	141	.282	.408	0	.000	-0	6	7	0	0.6
1971	Min-A	0	0	—	6	0	0	0	0	4¹	5	1	4	2	18.7	4.15	86	.294	.429	0	—	0	-0	-0	0	0.0
Total	3	3	2	.600	50	0	0	0	4	63¹	62	3	47	35	15.9	2.70	148	.261	.389	0	.000	-0	9	9	0	0.9

■ HUGH CANAVAN
Canavan, Hugh Edward "Hugo"   b: 5/13/1897, Worcester, Mass.   d: 9/4/67, Boston, Mass.   BL/TL, 5'8", 160 lbs.   Deb: 4/23/18

YEAR	TM/L	W	L	PCT	G	GS	CG	SH	SV	IP	H	HR	BB	SO	RAT	ERA	ERA+	OAV	OOB	BH	AVG	PB	PR	/A	PD	TPI
1918	Bos-N	0	4	.000	11	3	3	0	0	46²	70	0	15	18	17.4	6.36	42	.366	.427	2	.095	-0	-19	-19	1	-1.8

■ JOHN CANDELARIA
Candelaria, John Robert "Candy Man"   b: 11/6/53, New York, N.Y.   BL/TL, 6'7", 205 lbs.   Deb: 6/08/75

YEAR	TM/L	W	L	PCT	G	GS	CG	SH	SV	IP	H	HR	BB	SO	RAT	ERA	ERA+	OAV	OOB	BH	AVG	PB	PR	/A	PD	TPI
1975	*Pit-N	8	6	.571	18	18	4	1	0	120²	95	8	36	95	9.9	2.76	128	.212	.273	6	.140	-0	12	10	-2	0.9
1976	Pit-N	16	7	.696	32	31	11	4	1	220	173	22	60	138	9.6	3.15	111	.216	.273	14	.184	3	9	8	-1	1.1
1977	Pit-N	20	5	.800	33	33	6	1	0	230²	197	29	50	133	9.7	2.34	170	.232	.276	18	.225	4	40	42	-1	4.9
1978	Pit-N	12	11	.522	30	29	3	1	1	189	191	11	49	94	11.7	3.24	114	.261	.312	9	.173	4	7	10	1	1.3
1979	*Pit-N	14	9	.609	33	30	8	0	0	207	201	25	41	101	10.7	3.22	121	.253	.292	9	.132	-1	12	15	1	1.6
1980	Pit-N	11	14	.440	35	34	7	0	0	233¹	246	14	50	97	11.5	4.01	91	.276	.317	15	.195	2	-11	-10	-2	-0.7
1981	Pit-N	2	2	.500	6	6	0	0	0	40²	42	3	11	14	11.7	3.54	101	.271	.319	3	.231	0	-0	0	0	0.1
1982	Pit-N	12	7	.632	31	30	1	1	1	174²	166	13	37	133	10.7	2.94	126	.255	.299	12	.222	3	13	15	-2	1.8
1983	Pit-N	15	8	.652	33	32	2	0	0	197²	191	15	45	157	10.8	3.23	115	.257	.302	9	.138	-0	9	10	-2	0.9
1984	Pit-N	12	11	.522	33	28	3	1	2	185¹	179	19	34	133	10.4	2.72	132	.256	.291	8	.129	1	18	18	-2	1.8
1985	Pit-N	2	4	.333	37	0	0	0	9	54¹	57	7	14	47	11.9	3.64	98	.275	.324	0	.000	0	-0	0	-0	0.0
	Cal-A	7	3	.700	13	13	1	1	0	71	70	7	24	53	12.3	3.80	108	.262	.330	0	—	0	2	3	0	0.1
1986	*Cal-A	10	2	.833	16	16	1	1	0	91²	68	4	26	81	9.5	2.55	161	.206	.270	0	—	0	17	16	-1	1.6
1987	Cal-A	8	6	.571	20	20	1	0	0	116²	127	17	20	74	11.4	4.71	91	.279	.311	0	—	0	-3	-5	1	-0.3
	NY-N	2	0	1.000	3	3	0	0	0	12¹	17	1	3	10	14.6	5.84	65	.333	.370	1	.200	0	-2	-3	0	-0.2
1988	NY-A	13	7	.650	25	24	6	2	1	157	150	18	23	121	10.0	3.38	116	.248	.278	0		0	10	10	-0	1.0

YEAR	TM/L	W	L	PCT	G	GS	CG	SH	SV	IP	H	HR	BB	SO	RAT	ERA	ERA+	OAV	OOB	BH	AVG	PB	PR	/A	PD	TPI
1989	NY-A	3	3	.500	10	6	1	0	0	49	49	8	12	37	11.2	5.14	75	.258	.302	0	—	0	-7	-7	-0	-0.6
	Mon-N	0	2	.000	12	0	0	0	0	16¹	17	3	4	14	11.6	3.31	107	.283	.328	0	—	0	0	0	-0	0.0
1990	Min-A	7	3	.700	34	1	0	0	4	58¹	55	9	9	44	9.9	3.39	123	.244	.274	0	—	0	3	5	-1	0.4
	Tor-A	0	3	.000	13	2	0	0	1	21¹	32	2	11	19	19.0	5.48	69	.356	.437	0	—	0	-4	-4	-1	-0.2
	Yr	7	6	.538	47	3	0	0	5	79²	87	11	20	63	12.3	3.95	103	.274	.321	0	—	0	-1	1	-0	0.2
Total 16		174	113	.606	467	356	54	13	21	2447	2323	239	559	1595	10.7	3.29	115	.251	.297	104	.174	15	124	134	-12	15.6

■ MILO CANDINI
Candini, Mario Cain   b: 8/3/17, Manteca, Cal.   BR/TR, 6', 187 lbs.   Deb: 5/01/43

YEAR	TM/L	W	L	PCT	G	GS	CG	SH	SV	IP	H	HR	BB	SO	RAT	ERA	ERA+	OAV	OOB	BH	AVG	PB	PR	/A	PD	TPI
1943	Was-A	11	7	.611	28	21	8	3	1	166	144	3	65	67	11.4	2.49	128	.238	.313	9	.161	-1	15	13	1	1.4
1944	Was-A	6	7	.462	28	10	4	2	1	103	110	3	49	31	14.0	4.11	79	.276	.357	10	.313	3	-8	-10	-0	-0.6
1946	Was-A	2	0	1.000	9	0	0	0	1	21²	15	1	4	6	7.9	2.08	161	.192	.232	2	.333	1	3	3	-0	0.4
1947	Was-A	3	4	.429	38	2	0	0	1	87	96	5	35	31	13.6	5.17	72	.273	.339	3	.167	-0	-14	-14	1	-1.3
1948	Was-A	2	3	.400	35	4	1	0	3	94¹	96	1	63	23	15.3	5.15	84	.267	.378	8	.364	3	-9	-8	0	-0.4
1949	Was-A	0	0	—	3	0	0	0	1	5²	4	0	1	1	7.9	4.76	89	.200	.238	1	1.000	0	-0	-0	-0	0.0
1950	Phi-N	1	0	1.000	18	0	0	0	1	30	32	2	15	10	14.1	2.70	150	.281	.364	1	.167	-0	5	4	1	0.5
1951	Phi-N	1	0	1.000	15	0	0	0	0	30	33	3	18	14	15.3	6.00	64	.275	.370	1	.333	1	-7	-7	0	-0.5
Total 8		26	21	.553	174	37	13	5	8	537²	530	18	250	183	13.1	3.92	92	.259	.341	35	.243	6	-15	-19	1	-0.5

■ TOM CANDIOTTI
Candiotti, Thomas Caesar   b: 8/31/57, Walnut Creek, Cal.   BR/TR, 6'3", 205 lbs.   Deb: 8/08/83

YEAR	TM/L	W	L	PCT	G	GS	CG	SH	SV	IP	H	HR	BB	SO	RAT	ERA	ERA+	OAV	OOB	BH	AVG	PB	PR	/A	PD	TPI
1983	Mil-A	4	4	.500	10	8	2	1	0	55²	62	4	16	21	12.9	3.23	116	.291	.346	0	—	0	5	3	-0	0.3
1984	Mil-A	2	2	.500	8	6	0	0	0	32¹	38	5	10	23	13.4	5.29	73	.277	.327	0	—	0	-5	-5	-1	-0.5
1986	Cle-A	16	12	.571	36	34	**17**	3	0	252²	234	18	106	167	12.4	3.57	116	.246	.326	0	—	0	17	16	3	1.9
1987	Cle-A	7	18	.280	32	32	7	2	0	201²	193	28	93	111	12.9	4.78	95	.250	.333	0	—	0	-7	-6	1	-0.4
1988	Cle-A	14	8	.636	31	31	11	1	0	216²	225	15	53	137	11.8	3.28	125	.272	.321	0	—	0	16	20	2	2.3
1989	Cle-A	13	10	.565	31	31	4	0	0	206	188	10	55	124	10.8	3.10	128	.242	.295	0	—	0	18	20	4	2.5
1990	Cle-A	15	11	.577	31	29	3	1	0	202	207	23	55	128	11.9	3.65	109	.263	.316	0	—	0	6	7	3	1.1
Total 7		71	65	.522	179	171	44	8	0	1166²	1147	103	388	711	12.1	3.69	112	.257	.320	0	—	0	50	56	11	7.2

■ JOHN CANEIRA
Caneira, John Cascaes   b: 10/7/52, Waterbury, Conn.   BR/TR, 6'3", 180 lbs.   Deb: 9/10/77

YEAR	TM/L	W	L	PCT	G	GS	CG	SH	SV	IP	H	HR	BB	SO	RAT	ERA	ERA+	OAV	OOB	BH	AVG	PB	PR	/A	PD	TPI
1977	Cal-A	2	2	.500	6	4	0	0	0	28²	27	5	16	17	13.5	4.08	96	.252	.350	0	—	0	-0	-1	-1	0.0
1978	Cal-A	0	0	—	2	2	0	0	0	7²	8	2	3	0	12.9	7.04	51	.286	.355	0	—	0	-3	-3	-0	-0.2
Total 2		2	2	.500	8	6	0	0	0	36¹	35	7	19	17	13.4	4.71	82	.259	.351	0	—	0	-3	-3	-1	-0.2

■ JOHN CANGELOSI
Cangelosi, John Anthony   b: 3/10/63, Brooklyn, N.Y.   BB/TL, 5'8", 150 lbs.   Deb: 6/03/85 ♦

YEAR	TM/L	W	L	PCT	G	GS	CG	SH	SV	IP	H	HR	BB	SO	RAT	ERA	ERA+	OAV	OOB	BH	AVG	PB	PR	/A	PD	TPI
1988	Pit-N	0	0	—	1	0	0	0	0	2	1	0	0	0	4.5	0.00	—	.143	.143	30	.254	0	1	1	0	0.1

■ JOSE CANO
Cano, Joselito (Soriano)   b: 3/7/62, Boca De Soco, D.R.   BR/TR, 6'3", 175 lbs.   Deb: 8/28/89

YEAR	TM/L	W	L	PCT	G	GS	CG	SH	SV	IP	H	HR	BB	SO	RAT	ERA	ERA+	OAV	OOB	BH	AVG	PB	PR	/A	PD	TPI
1989	Hou-N	1	1	.500	6	3	1	0	0	23	24	2	7	8	12.1	5.09	67	.267	.320	0	.000	-1	-4	-4	-0	-0.4

■ GUY CANTRELL
Cantrell, Guy Dewey "Gunner"   b: 4/9/04, Clarita, Okla.   d: 1/31/61, McAlester, Okla.   BR/TR, 6', 190 lbs.   Deb: 8/18/25

YEAR	TM/L	W	L	PCT	G	GS	CG	SH	SV	IP	H	HR	BB	SO	RAT	ERA	ERA+	OAV	OOB	BH	AVG	PB	PR	/A	PD	TPI
1925	Bro-N	1	0	1.000	14	3	1	0	0	36	42	0	14	13	14.3	3.00	139	.294	.361	0	.000	-1	5	5	1	0.4
1927	Bro-N	0	0	—	6	0	0	0	0	10	10	0	6	5	14.4	2.70	147	.250	.348	1	.333	1	1	1	0	0.2
	Phi-A	0	2	.000	2	2	2	0	0	18	25	0	7	7	16.0	5.00	85	.338	.395	1	.167	-0	-2	-1	0	-0.1
1930	Det-A	1	5	.167	16	2	1	0	0	35	38	5	20	20	15.2	5.66	85	.271	.366	0	.000	-2	-4	-3	1	-0.3
Total 3		2	7	.222	38	7	4	0	0	99	115	5	47	45	14.9	4.27	103	.290	.368	2	.074	-3	1	1	2	0.2

■ BEN CANTWELL
Cantwell, Benjamin Caldwell   b: 4/13/02, Milan, Tenn.   d: 12/4/62, Salem, Mo.   BR/TR, 6'1", 168 lbs.   Deb: 8/19/27

YEAR	TM/L	W	L	PCT	G	GS	CG	SH	SV	IP	H	HR	BB	SO	RAT	ERA	ERA+	OAV	OOB	BH	AVG	PB	PR	/A	PD	TPI
1927	NY-N	1	1	.500	5	2	1	0	0	19²	26	1	2	6	13.3	4.12	94	.313	.337	2	.250	-0	-0	-1	-0	0.0
1928	NY-N	1	0	1.000	7	1	0	0	1	18¹	20	1	4	0	12.3	4.42	88	.282	.329	2	.500	1	-1	-1	1	0.0
	Bos-N	3	3	.500	22	9	3	0	0	90	112	7	36	18	15.0	5.10	77	.304	.369	5	.172	-1	-11	-12	1	-1.0
	Yr	4	3	.571	29	10	3	0	1	108¹	132	8	40	18	14.5	4.98	78	.300	.361	0	.000	-0	-12	-13	2	-1.0
1929	Bos-N	4	13	.235	27	20	8	0	2	157	171	11	52	25	12.9	4.47	105	.280	.338	9	.180	-0	4	4	0	0.7
1930	Bos-N	9	15	.375	31	21	10	0	2	173¹	213	15	45	43	13.4	4.88	101	.312	.355	19	.302	2	2	1	4	0.7
1931	Bos-N	7	9	.438	33	16	9	2	2	156¹	160	4	34	32	11.2	3.63	104	.262	.301	13	.228	0	4	3	3	0.6
1932	Bos-N	13	11	.542	37	9	3	1	5	146	133	6	33	33	10.5	2.96	127	.247	.296	14	.280	2	15	13	3	1.8
1933	Bos-N	20	10	**.667**	40	29	18	2	2	254²	242	12	54	57	10.6	2.62	117	.249	.291	12	.141	-1	20	13	4	1.7
1934	Bos-N	5	11	.313	27	19	6	1	5	143¹	163	8	45	45	12.5	4.33	88	.285	.327	12	.279	1	-4	-8	2	-0.4
1935	Bos-N	4	25	.138	39	24	13	0	0	210²	235	15	44	34	12.0	4.61	82	.282	.320	19	.284	4	-14	-19	2	-1.2
1936	Bos-N	9	9	.500	34	12	4	0	2	133¹	127	8	35	42	11.2	3.04	126	.252	.306	8	.195	-1	15	12	3	1.4
1937	NY-N	0	1	.000	1	1	0	0	0	4	6	1	1	1	15.8	9.00	43	.375	.412	0	—	0	-2	-2	0	-0.1
	Bro-N	0	0	—	13	0	0	0	0	27¹	32	1	8	12	13.2	4.61	88	.288	.336	1	.167	-0	-2	-2	2	0.0
	Yr	0	1	.000	14	1	0	0	0	31¹	38	2	9	13	13.5	5.17	78	.299	.346	1	.167	-0	-4	-4	2	-0.1
Total 11		76	108	.413	316	163	75	6	21	1534	1640	90	382	348	12.0	3.91	100	.275	.321	116	.231	8	25	-2	31	4.2

■ MIKE CANTWELL
Cantwell, Michael Joseph   b: 1/15/1896, Washington, D.C.   d: 1/5/53, Oteen, N.C.   BL/TL, 5'10", 155 lbs.   Deb: 8/17/16

YEAR	TM/L	W	L	PCT	G	GS	CG	SH	SV	IP	H	HR	BB	SO	RAT	ERA	ERA+	OAV	OOB	BH	AVG	PB	PR	/A	PD	TPI
1916	NY-A	0	0	—	1	0	0	0	0	2	0	0	2	0	9.0	0.00	—	.000	.333	0	—	0	1	1	0	0.1
1919	Phi-N	1	3	.250	5	3	2	0	0	27¹	36	1	9	6	15.5	5.60	58	.343	.405	2	.222	-0	-8	-7	-1	-0.7
1920	Phi-N	0	3	.000	5	1	0	0	0	23¹	25	1	15	8	16.6	3.86	89	.284	.406	1	.143	-1	-2	-1	0	0.0
Total 3		1	6	.143	11	4	2	0	0	52²	61	2	26	14	15.7	4.61	71	.310	.404	3	.188	-0	-9	-8	-0	-0.6

■ TOM CANTWELL
Cantwell, Thomas Aloysius   b: 12/23/1888, Washington, D.C.   d: 4/1/68, Washington, D.C.   BL/TR, 6', 170 lbs.   Deb: 5/19/09

YEAR	TM/L	W	L	PCT	G	GS	CG	SH	SV	IP	H	HR	BB	SO	RAT	ERA	ERA+	OAV	OOB	BH	AVG	PB	PR	/A	PD	TPI
1909	Cin-N	1	0	1.000	6	1	1	0	0	21²	16	0	7	7	10.0	1.66	157	.205	.279	3	.600	1	2	2	-0	0.4
1910	Cin-N	0	0	—	2	0	0	0	0	1¹	2	0	3	0	33.8	13.50	22	.400	.625	0	—	0	-2	-2	0	-0.1
Total 2		1	0	1.000	8	1	1	0	0	23	18	0	10	7	11.3	2.35	112	.217	.309	3	.600	1	1	1	-0	0.3

■ MIKE CAPEL
Capel, Michael Lee   b: 10/13/61, Marshall, Tex.   BR/TR, 6'1", 175 lbs.   Deb: 5/07/88

YEAR	TM/L	W	L	PCT	G	GS	CG	SH	SV	IP	H	HR	BB	SO	RAT	ERA	ERA+	OAV	OOB	BH	AVG	PB	PR	/A	PD	TPI
1988	Chi-N	2	1	.667	22	0	0	0	0	29¹	34	5	13	19	15.3	4.91	73	.293	.379	0	.000	-0	-5	-4	-0	-0.4
1990	Mil-A	0	0	—	2	0	0	0	0	0¹	6	0	1	1	216.0	135.00	3	.857	.889	0	—	0	-5	-5	0	-0.3
Total 2		2	1	.667	24	0	0	0	0	29²	40	5	14	20	17.6	6.37	57	.325	.411	0	.000	-0	-10	-9	-0	-0.7

■ DOUG CAPILLA
Capilla, Douglas Edmund   b: 1/7/52, Honolulu, Hawaii   BL/TL, 5'11", 160 lbs.   Deb: 9/12/76

YEAR	TM/L	W	L	PCT	G	GS	CG	SH	SV	IP	H	HR	BB	SO	RAT	ERA	ERA+	OAV	OOB	BH	AVG	PB	PR	/A	PD	TPI
1976	StL-N	1	0	1.000	7	0	0	0	0	8¹	8	0	4	5	13.0	5.40	65	.242	.324	0	—	0	-2	-2	0	-0.1
1977	StL-N	0	0	—	2	0	0	0	0	2¹	2	0	2	1	15.4	15.43	25	.222	.364	0	—	0	-3	-3	0	-0.2
	Cin-N	7	8	.467	22	16	1	0	0	106¹	94	10	59	74	13.1	4.23	93	.237	.338	2	.059	-3	-4	-4	-1	-0.6
	Yr	7	8	.467	24	16	1	0	0	108²	96	10	61	75	13.2	4.47	88	.236	.339	1	.029	-3	-7	-7	-1	-0.8
1978	Cin-N	0	1	.000	6	3	0	0	0	11	14	1	11	9	20.5	9.82	36	.318	.455	0	.000	-0	-8	-8	0	-0.7
1979	Cin-N	1	0	1.000	5	0	0	0	0	6¹	7	1	5	0	18.5	8.53	44	.269	.406	1	1.000	0	-3	-3	0	-0.2
	Chi-N	0	1	.000	13	1	0	0	0	17¹	14	1	7	10	10.9	2.60	159	.206	.280	0	—	0	2	3	0	0.3
	Yr	1	1	.500	18	1	0	0	0	23²	21	2	12	10	12.5	4.18	96	.221	.308	0	.000	-0	-1	-0	1	0.1
1980	Chi-N	2	8	.200	39	11	0	0	0	89²	82	7	51	51	13.7	4.12	95	.253	.360	4	.190	-0	-5	-2	1	0.0
1981	Chi-N	1	0	1.000	42	0	0	0	0	51	52	3	26	18	15.5	3.18	116	.284	.402	0	—	0	2	3	0	0.3
Total 6		12	18	.400	136	31	1	0	0	292¹	273	21	173	178	14.0	4.34	89	.252	.359	7	.115	-3	-21	-15	1	-1.2

■ GEORGE CAPPUZZELLO
Cappuzzello, George Angelo   b: 1/15/54, Youngstown, Ohio   BR/TL, 6', 175 lbs.   Deb: 5/31/81

YEAR	TM/L	W	L	PCT	G	GS	CG	SH	SV	IP	H	HR	BB	SO	RAT	ERA	ERA+	OAV	OOB	BH	AVG	PB	PR	/A	PD	TPI
1981	Det-A	1	1	.500	18	3	0	0	1	33²	28	2	18	19	12.8	3.48	108	.222	.329	0	—	0	1	1	-0	0.1
1982	Hou-N	0	1	.000	17	0	0	0	0	19¹	16	2	7	13	12.1	2.79	119	.232	.329	0	.000	-0	2	1	0	0.1

YEAR	TM/L	W	L	PCT	G	GS	CG	SH	SV	IP	H	HR	BB	SO	RAT	ERA	ERA+	OAV	OOB	BH	AVG	PB	PR	/A	PD	TPI
Total	2	1	2	.333	35	3	0	0	1	53	44	4	25	32	12.6	3.23	112	.226	.329	0	.000	-0	2	2	0	0.2

■ BUZZ CAPRA
Capra, Lee William   b: 10/1/47, Chicago, Ill.   BR/TR, 5'10", 168 lbs.   Deb: 9/15/71

YEAR	TM/L	W	L	PCT	G	GS	CG	SH	SV	IP	H	HR	BB	SO	RAT	ERA	ERA+	OAV	OOB	BH	AVG	PB	PR	/A	PD	TPI
1971	NY-N	0	1	.000	3	0	0	0	0	5¹	3	0	5	6	13.5	8.44	40	.167	.348	0	.000	-0	-3	-3	0	-0.2
1972	NY-N	3	2	.600	14	6	0	0	0	53	50	7	27	45	13.1	4.58	73	.253	.342	3	.250	1	-7	-7	1	-0.4
1973	NY-N	2	7	.222	24	0	0	0	4	42	35	4	28	35	13.9	3.86	94	.233	.361	0	.000	0	-1	-1	0	0.0
1974	Atl-N	16	8	.667	39	27	11	5	1	217	163	13	84	137	10.4	**2.28**	**166**	**.208**	.287	11	.164	0	32	36	-3	3.7
1975	Atl-N	4	7	.364	12	12	5	0	0	78¹	77	8	28	35	12.2	4.25	89	.257	.322	1	.043	-0	-5	-4	1	-0.5
1976	Atl-N	0	1	.000	5	0	0	0	0	9¹	9	0	6	4	14.5	8.68	44	.265	.375	0	—	0	-5	-5	0	-0.4
1977	Atl-N	6	11	.353	45	16	0	0	0	139¹	142	28	80	100	14.6	5.36	83	.263	.362	4	.111	-2	-22	-14	-1	-1.5
Total	7	31	37	.456	142	61	16	5	5	544¹	479	60	258	362	12.4	3.87	100	.237	.326	19	.135	-2	-12	1	-1	0.7

■ PAT CARAWAY
Caraway, Cecil Bradford Patrick   b: 9/26/05, Erath Co., Tex.   d: 6/9/74, ElPaso, Tex.   BL/TL, 6'4", 175 lbs.   Deb: 4/19/30

YEAR	TM/L	W	L	PCT	G	GS	CG	SH	SV	IP	H	HR	BB	SO	RAT	ERA	ERA+	OAV	OOB	BH	AVG	PB	PR	/A	PD	TPI
1930	Chi-A	10	10	.500	38	21	9	1	1	193¹	194	11	57	83	11.8	3.86	120	.267	.323	11	.172	-1	17	16	3	1.6
1931	Chi-A	10	24	.294	51	32	11	1	2	220	268	17	101	55	15.4	6.22	68	.295	.370	14	.194	-1	-45	-48	-1	-4.3
1932	Chi-A	2	6	.250	19	9	1	0	0	64²	80	6	37	13	16.7	6.82	63	.304	.396	3	.143	-1	-17	-18	0	-1.6
Total	3	22	40	.355	108	62	21	2	3	478	542	34	195	151	14.1	5.35	83	.286	.356	28	.178	-3	-45	-50	2	-4.3

■ JOHN CARDEN
Carden, John Bruton   b: 5/19/21, Killeen, Tex.   d: 2/8/49, Mexia, Tex.   BR/TR, 6'5", 210 lbs.   Deb: 5/18/46

YEAR	TM/L	W	L	PCT	G	GS	CG	SH	SV	IP	H	HR	BB	SO	RAT	ERA	ERA+	OAV	OOB	BH	AVG	PB	PR	/A	PD	TPI
1946	NY-N	0	0	—	1	0	0	0	0	2	4	0	4	1	40.5	22.50	15	.400	.600	0	—	0	-4	-4	-0	-0.3

■ CONRAD CARDINAL
Cardinal, Conrad Seth   b: 3/30/42, Brooklyn, N.Y.   BR/TR, 6'1", 190 lbs.   Deb: 4/11/63

YEAR	TM/L	W	L	PCT	G	GS	CG	SH	SV	IP	H	HR	BB	SO	RAT	ERA	ERA+	OAV	OOB	BH	AVG	PB	PR	/A	PD	TPI
1963	Hou-N	0	1	.000	6	1	0	0	0	13¹	15	0	7	7	14.9	6.08	52	.283	.367	0	.000	-0	-4	-4	0	-0.3

■ BEN CARDONI
Cardoni, Armand Joseph "Big Ben"   b: 8/21/20, Jessup, Pa.   d: 4/2/69, Jessup, Pa.   BR/TR, 6'3", 195 lbs.   Deb: 8/22/43

YEAR	TM/L	W	L	PCT	G	GS	CG	SH	SV	IP	H	HR	BB	SO	RAT	ERA	ERA+	OAV	OOB	BH	AVG	PB	PR	/A	PD	TPI
1943	Bos-N	0	0	—	11	0	0	0	1	28	38	1	14	5	17.0	6.43	53	.336	.414	0	.000	-1	-9	-9	0	-0.9
1944	Bos-N	0	6	.000	22	5	1	0	0	75²	83	5	37	24	14.4	3.93	97	.284	.367	4	.235	-0	-3	-1	-1	-0.1
1945	Bos-N	0	0	—	3	0	0	0	0	4	6	0	3	5	22.5	9.00	43	.300	.417	0	—	0	-2	-2	-0	-0.1
Total	3	0	6	.000	36	5	1	0	1	107²	127	6	54	34	15.4	4.76	78	.299	.382	4	.167	-1	-14	-13	-1	-1.1

■ DON CARDWELL
Cardwell, Donald Eugene   b: 12/7/35, Winston-Salem, N.C.   BR/TR, 6'4", 210 lbs.   Deb: 4/21/57

YEAR	TM/L	W	L	PCT	G	GS	CG	SH	SV	IP	H	HR	BB	SO	RAT	ERA	ERA+	OAV	OOB	BH	AVG	PB	PR	/A	PD	TPI
1957	Phi-N	4	8	.333	30	15	5	1	1	128¹	122	17	42	92	11.8	4.91	78	.251	.316	7	.200	1	-15	-16	-0	-1.4
1958	Phi-N	3	6	.333	16	14	3	0	0	107²	99	16	37	77	11.5	4.51	88	.241	.307	8	.211	1	-7	-7	-0	-0.5
1959	Phi-N	9	10	.474	25	22	5	1	0	153	135	22	65	106	12.0	4.06	101	.238	.320	3	.055	-3	-2	1	-3	-0.4
1960	Phi-N	1	2	.333	5	4	0	0	0	28¹	28	4	11	21	12.7	4.45	87	.262	.336	2	.250	2	-2	-2	-1	0.0
	Chi-N	8	14	.364	31	26	6	1	0	177	166	19	68	129	12.2	4.37	86	.249	.323	14	.203	3	-12	-12	-2	-0.9
	Yr	9	16	.360	36	30	6	1	0	205¹	194	23	79	150	12.2	4.38	87	.250	.324	16	.209	5	-14	-13	-2	-0.9
1961	Chi-N	15	14	.517	39	38	13	3	0	259¹	243	22	88	156	11.8	3.82	110	.246	.314	10	.105	-1	6	10	2	1.2
1962	Chi-N	7	16	.304	41	29	6	1	4	195²	205	27	60	104	12.6	4.92	84	.267	.327	9	.148	0	-21	-17	-1	-1.4
1963	Pit-N	13	15	.464	33	32	7	2	0	213²	195	21	52	112	11.1	3.07	107	.245	.305	6	.085	-2	5	5	0	0.3
1964	Pit-N	1	2	.333	4	4	1	1	0	19¹	15	1	7	10	11.6	2.79	126	.217	.316	1	.143	-0	2	2	0	0.2
1965	Pit-N	13	10	.565	37	34	12	2	0	240¹	214	21	59	107	10.7	3.18	110	.239	.295	12	.162	3	10	9	3	1.6
1966	Pit-N	6	6	.500	32	14	1	0	1	101²	112	15	27	60	12.8	4.60	78	.282	.337	3	.103	-1	-11	-12	2	-0.9
1967	NY-N	5	9	.357	26	16	3	3	0	118¹	112	8	39	71	12.0	3.57	95	.249	.319	6	.158	2	-3	-2	2	-0.2
1968	NY-N	7	13	.350	29	25	5	1	1	179²	156	9	50	82	10.8	2.96	102	.233	.296	3	.049	-4	1	1	3	0.0
1969	*NY-N	8	10	.444	30	21	4	0	0	152¹	145	15	47	60	11.6	3.01	121	.252	.314	8	.170	1	10	11	3	1.6
1970	NY-N	0	2	.000	16	1	0	0	0	25	31	3	6	14	14.4	6.48	62	.316	.374	0	.000	-1	-7	-7	-0	-0.6
	Atl-N	2	1	.667	16	2	1	1	0	23	31	5	13	16	17.6	9.00	48	.326	.413	2	.400	1	-13	-12	1	-1.0
	Yr	2	3	.400	32	3	1	1	0	48	62	8	19	24	15.4	7.69	54	.312	.374	2	.000	-0	-19	-19	1	-1.6
Total	14	102	138	.425	410	301	72	17	7	2122²	2009	225	671	1211	11.8	3.92	95	.250	.315	94	.135	2	-59	-47	12	-2.0

■ TEX CARLETON
Carleton, James Otto   b: 8/19/06, Comanche, Tex.   d: 1/11/77, Fort Worth, Tex.   BB/TR, 6'1.5", 180 lbs.   Deb: 4/17/32

YEAR	TM/L	W	L	PCT	G	GS	CG	SH	SV	IP	H	HR	BB	SO	RAT	ERA	ERA+	OAV	OOB	BH	AVG	PB	PR	/A	PD	TPI
1932	StL-N	10	13	.435	44	22	9	3	0	196¹	198	12	70	113	12.4	4.08	96	.261	.326	9	.150	-2	-4	-3	2	-0.2
1933	StL-N	17	11	.607	44	33	15	4	3	277	263	15	97	147	11.8	3.38	103	.249	.315	17	.187	1	-1	3	-1	0.3
1934	*StL-N	16	11	.593	40	31	16	0	2	240²	260	14	52	103	11.9	4.26	99	.271	.314	17	.193	1	-5	-1	0	0.1
1935	*Chi-N	11	8	.579	31	22	8	0	1	171	169	17	60	84	12.2	3.89	101	.257	.322	8	.129	-3	2	1	2	0.0
1936	Chi-N	14	10	.583	35	26	12	**4**	1	197¹	204	14	67	88	12.6	3.65	109	.268	.332	14	.233	6	8	7	2	1.5
1937	Chi-N	16	8	.667	32	27	18	4	0	208¹	183	10	94	105	12.1	3.15	126	.236	.321	12	.169	1	18	19	1	2.2
1938	*Chi-N	10	9	.526	33	24	9	0	0	167²	213	11	74	80	15.8	5.42	71	.307	.381	15	.231	4	-30	-30	-0	-2.5
1940	Bro-N	6	6	.500	34	17	4	1	2	149	140	12	47	88	11.5	3.81	105	.245	.305	8	.186	-0	1	3	-2	0.1
Total	8	100	76	.568	293	202	91	16	9	1607¹	1630	105	561	808	12.5	3.91	100	.261	.326	100	.185	6	-13	-0	4	1.6

■ CISCO CARLOS
Carlos, Francisco Manuel   b: 9/17/40, Monrovia, Cal.   BR/TR, 6'3", 205 lbs.   Deb: 8/25/67

YEAR	TM/L	W	L	PCT	G	GS	CG	SH	SV	IP	H	HR	BB	SO	RAT	ERA	ERA+	OAV	OOB	BH	AVG	PB	PR	/A	PD	TPI
1967	Chi-A	2	0	1.000	8	7	1	1	0	41²	23	0	9	27	7.1	0.86	359	.161	.216	1	.063	-1	11	10	0	1.1
1968	Chi-A	4	14	.222	29	21	0	0	0	122¹	121	13	37	57	12.4	3.90	78	.258	.326	2	.065	-1	-13	-12	2	-1.1
1969	Chi-A	4	3	.571	25	4	0	0	0	49¹	52	4	23	28	14.6	5.66	68	.274	.367	0	.000	-1	-11	-10	1	-0.9
	Was-A	1	1	.500	6	4	0	0	0	17²	23	2	6	5	14.8	4.58	76	.348	.403	1	.200	1	-2	-2	0	0.0
	Yr	5	4	.556	31	8	0	0	0	67	75	6	29	33	14.0	5.37	70	.287	.359	2	.133	-0	-13	-12	1	-0.9
1970	Was-A	0	0	—	5	0	0	0	0	6	3	0	4	2	10.5	1.50	237	.150	.292	0	—	0	1	1	0	0.2
Total	4	11	18	.379	73	36	1	1	0	237	222	19	79	119	12.0	3.72	88	.250	.326	4	.065	-3	-13	-12	4	-0.7

■ DON CARLSEN
Carlsen, Donald Herbert   b: 10/15/26, Chicago, Ill.   BR/TR, 6'1", 175 lbs.   Deb: 4/28/48

YEAR	TM/L	W	L	PCT	G	GS	CG	SH	SV	IP	H	HR	BB	SO	RAT	ERA	ERA+	OAV	OOB	BH	AVG	PB	PR	/A	PD	TPI
1948	Chi-N	0	0	—	1	0	0	0	0	1	5	0	2	1	63.0	36.00	11	.625	.700	0	—	0	-4	-4	0	-0.2
1951	Pit-N	2	3	.400	7	6	2	0	0	43	50	4	14	20	13.6	4.19	101	.292	.349	4	.250	0	-1	0	-1	0.0
1952	Pit-N	0	1	.000	5	1	0	0	0	10	20	1	5	2	22.5	10.80	37	.417	.472	1	.333	0	-8	-8	1	-0.5
Total	3	2	4	.333	13	7	2	0	0	54	75	5	21	23	16.2	6.00	70	.330	.390	5	.263	0	-12	-11	0	-0.7

■ HAL CARLSON
Carlson, Harold Gust   b: 5/17/1892, Rockford, Ill.   d: 5/28/30, Chicago, Ill.   BR/TR, 6', 180 lbs.   Deb: 4/13/17

YEAR	TM/L	W	L	PCT	G	GS	CG	SH	SV	IP	H	HR	BB	SO	RAT	ERA	ERA+	OAV	OOB	BH	AVG	PB	PR	/A	PD	TPI
1917	Pit-N	7	11	.389	34	17	9	1	1	161¹	140	0	49	68	10.8	2.90	98	.241	.304	6	.122	-2	-3	-1	2	-0.1
1918	Pit-N	0	1	.000	3	2	0	0	0	12	12	1	5	5	12.8	3.75	77	.286	.362	1	.200	-0	-1	-1	-0	-0.1
1919	Pit-N	8	10	.444	22	14	7	1	0	141	114	0	39	49	9.9	2.23	135	.243	.303	7	.163	-1	11	12	1	1.5
1920	Pit-N	14	13	.519	39	31	16	3	3	246²	262	4	63	62	12.1	3.36	96	.281	.331	23	.271	3	-6	-4	-4	-0.4
1921	Pit-N	4	8	.333	31	10	3	0	4	109²	121	6	23	37	12.0	4.27	90	.290	.330	10	.294	3	-6	-5	1	-0.2
1922	Pit-N	9	12	.429	39	18	6	0	2	145¹	193	10	58	64	15.8	5.70	72	.323	.386	15	.268	-1	-26	-26	2	-1.8
1923	Pit-N	0	0	—	4	0	0	0	0	13¹	19	2	2	4	14.9	4.73	85	.358	.393	0	—	-1	-1	0	0.0
1924	Phi-N	8	17	.320	38	24	12	1	2	203²	267	9	55	66	14.4	4.86	92	.329	.374	21	.276	2	-22	-9	-2	-0.4
1925	Phi-N	13	14	.481	35	32	18	**4**	0	234	281	19	52	80	13.0	4.23	113	.298	.338	17	.183	-2	1	14	-1	1.1
1926	Phi-N	17	12	.586	35	34	20	3	0	267¹	293	6	47	55	11.5	3.23	128	.281	.313	23	.240	2	18	27	-3	2.8
1927	Phi-N	4	5	.444	11	9	4	0	1	63²	80	7	18	13	13.9	5.23	79	.316	.362	6	.240	-0	-9	-8	-0	-0.7
	Chi-N	12	8	.600	27	22	15	2	0	184¹	201	9	27	27	11.2	3.17	122	.280	.307	11	.164	-3	15	14	1	1.1
	Yr	16	13	.552	38	31	19	2	1	248	281	16	45	40	11.9	3.70	106	.289	.322	1	.011	-3	6	6	0	0.4
1928	Chi-N	4	2	.667	20	5	2	0	4	56¹	74	6	11	11	15.0	5.91	65	.329	.371	5	.263	0	-12	-13	1	-1.1
1929	*Chi-N	11	5	.688	31	14	6	2	2	111²	131	6	31	35	13.1	5.16	90	.231	—	9	.231	1	-5	-7	2	-0.3
1930	Chi-N	4	2	.667	8	6	3	0	0	51²	68	5	14	14	14.5	5.05	97	.313	.358	5	.250	0	-0	-1	2	0.1
Total	14	114	120	.487	377	238	121	17	19	2002	2256	93	498	590	12.5	3.97	99	.291	.337	159	.223	5	-49	-8	1	1.5

YEAR TM/L	W	L	PCT	G	GS	CG	SH	SV	IP	H	HR	BB	SO	RAT	ERA	ERA+	OAV	OOB	BH	AVG	PB	PR	/A	PD	TPI
■ LEON CARLSON Carlson, Leon Alton "Swede" b: 2/17/1895, Jamestown, N.Y. d: 9/15/61, Jamestown, N.Y. BR/TR, 6'3", 195 lbs. Deb: 5/31/20																								
1920 Was-A	0	0	—	3	0	0	0	0	12¹	14	1	2	3	11.7	3.65	102	.292	.320	1	.167	-0	0	0	-0	0.0
■ STEVE CARLTON Carlton, Steven Norman "Lefty" b: 12/22/44, Miami, Fla. BL/TL, 6'4", 210 lbs. Deb: 4/12/65																								
1965 StL-N	0	0	—	15	2	0	0	0	25	27	3	8	21	13.0	2.52	153	.287	.350	0	.000	-0	3	4	0	0.4
1966 StL-N	3	3	.500	9	9	2	1	0	52	56	2	18	25	12.8	3.12	115	.280	.339	4	.267	1	3	3	0	0.4
1967 *StL-N	14	9	.609	30	28	11	2	1	193	173	10	62	168	11.1	2.98	110	.238	.300	11	.153	1	8	6	-1	0.7
1968 *StL-N	13	11	.542	34	33	10	5	0	231²	214	11	61	162	10.8	2.99	97	.246	.298	12	.164	2	-0	-2	-1	-0.1
1969 StL-N	17	11	.607	31	31	12	2	0	236¹	185	15	93	210	10.7	2.17	165	.216	.295	17	.213	5	37	37	-2	4.5
1970 StL-N	10	19	.345	34	33	13	2	0	253²	239	25	109	193	12.4	3.73	110	.251	.329	16	.200	2	9	11	-1	1.2
1971 StL-N	20	9	.690	37	36	18	4	0	273¹	275	23	98	172	12.4	3.56	101	.262	.328	17	.177	1	-3	1	-0	0.2
1972 Phi-N	27	10	.730	41	41	30	8	0	346¹	257	17	87	310	9.0	1.97	182	.206	.259	23	.197	4	57	62	-3	7.6
1973 Phi-N	13	20	.394	40	40	18	3	0	293¹	293	29	113	223	12.5	3.90	97	.260	.329	16	.160	0	-8	-3	-2	-0.3
1974 Phi-N	16	13	.552	39	39	17	1	0	291	249	21	136	240	12.1	3.22	117	.234	.323	25	.245	2	13	18	-1	2.0
1975 Phi-N	15	14	.517	37	37	14	3	0	255¹	217	24	104	192	11.4	3.56	105	.233	.312	14	.156	-0	2	5	-1	0.4
1976 *Phi-N	20	7	.741	35	35	13	2	0	252²	224	19	72	195	10.6	3.13	113	.237	.291	20	.217	2	10	12	-4	1.1
1977 *Phi-N	23	10	.697	36	36	17	2	0	283	229	25	89	198	10.2	2.64	151	.223	.287	26	.268	8	40	43	1	5.7
1978 Phi-N	16	13	.552	34	34	12	3	0	247¹	228	30	63	161	10.7	2.84	126	.246	.297	25	.291	7	20	20	1	3.1
1979 Phi-N	18	11	.621	35	35	13	4	0	251	202	25	89	213	10.6	3.62	106	.219	.292	21	.223	4	3	6	-2	0.8
1980 *Phi-N	24	9	.727	38	38	13	3	0	304	243	15	90	286	9.9	2.34	162	.218	.278	19	.188	-1	43	49	-2	5.3
1981 *Phi-N	13	4	.765	24	24	10	1	0	190	152	9	62	179	10.2	2.42	150	.222	.288	9	.134	-0	23	26	-2	2.7
1982 *Phi-N	23	11	.676	38	38	19	6	0	295¹	253	17	86	286	10.3	3.10	118	.232	.289	22	.218	4	16	18	-3	2.2
1983 *Phi-N	15	16	.484	37	37	8	3	0	283²	277	20	84	275	11.5	3.11	115	.258	.314	19	.196	3	16	14	-2	1.6
1984 Phi-N	13	7	.650	33	33	1	0	0	229	214	14	79	163	11.5	3.58	102	.246	.309	16	.190	2	0	1	-3	0.1
1985 Phi-N	1	8	.111	16	16	0	0	0	92	84	6	53	48	13.4	3.33	111	.249	.305	5	.179	0	3	4	1	0.5
1986 Phi-N	4	8	.333	16	16	0	0	0	83	102	15	45	62	15.9	6.18	62	.297	.379	7	.206	1	-23	-21	-1	-2.0
SF-N	1	3	.250	6	6	0	0	0	30	36	4	16	18	15.9	5.10	69	.303	.390	2	.182	1	-5	-5	1	-0.3
Yr	5	11	.313	22	22	0	0	0	113	138	19	61	80	15.9	5.89	64	.297	.380	1	.022	2	-27	-27	-1	-2.3
Chi-A	4	3	.571	10	10	0	0	0	63¹	58	6	25	40	11.8	3.69	117	.252	.325	0	—	0	3	4	-0	0.4
1987 Cle-A	5	9	.357	23	14	3	0	0	109	111	17	63	71	14.5	5.37	84	.266	.364	0	—	0	-11	-10	-0	-0.9
Min-A	1	5	.167	9	7	0	0	0	43	54	7	23	20	16.5	6.70	69	.310	.397	0	—	0	-11	-10	0	-0.8
Yr	6	14	.300	32	21	3	0	1	152	165	24	86	91	15.5	5.74	79	.276	.369	0	—	0	-22	-20	0	-1.7
1988 Min-A	0	1	.000	4	1	0	0	0	9²	20	5	5	5	23.3	16.76	24	.408	.463	0	—	0	-14	-14	0	-1.1
Total 24	329	244	.574	741	709	254	55	2	5217¹	4672	414	1833	4136	11.3	3.22	115	.240	.308	346	.201	50	236	277	-28	35.4
■ DON CARMAN Carman, Donald Wayne b: 8/14/59, Oklahoma City, Okla BL/TL, 6'3", 195 lbs. Deb: 10/01/83																								
1983 Phi-N	0	0	—	1	0	0	0	1	1	0	0	0	0	0.0	0.00	—	.000	.000	0	—	0	0	0	0	0.1
1984 Phi-N	0	1	.000	11	0	0	0	0	13¹	14	2	6	16	13.5	5.40	67	.255	.328	0	.000	-0	-3	-3	-0	-0.2
1985 Phi-N	9	4	.692	71	0	0	0	7	86¹	52	6	38	87	9.6	2.08	177	.178	.277	0	.000	-0	14	15	-0	1.6
1986 Phi-N	10	5	.667	50	14	2	1	1	134¹	113	11	52	98	11.3	3.22	120	.234	.313	0	.000	-3	7	9	2	0.8
1987 Phi-N	13	11	.542	35	35	3	2	0	211	194	34	69	125	11.4	4.22	100	.244	.308	5	.082	-3	-3	-0	-3	-0.5
1988 Phi-N	10	14	.417	36	32	2	0	0	201¹	211	20	70	116	12.7	4.29	83	.270	.333	3	.048	-5	-19	-16	-2	-2.3
1989 Phi-N	5	15	.250	49	20	0	0	0	149¹	152	21	86	81	14.5	5.24	68	.260	.358	1	.029	-3	-29	-28	-1	-3.2
1990 Phi-N	6	2	.750	59	1	0	0	1	86²	69	13	38	58	11.5	4.15	92	.218	.310	3	.273	1	-3	-3	0	-0.2
Total 8	53	52	.505	312	102	7	3	10	883¹	805	107	359	581	12.1	4.06	94	.243	.321	12	.059	-14	-35	-25	-5	-3.9
■ CHET CARMICHAEL Carmichael, Chester Keller b: 1/9/1888, Muncie, Ind. d: 8/22/60, Rochester, N.Y. BR/TR, 5'11.5", 200 lbs. Deb: 9/05/09																								
1909 Cin-N	0	0	—	2	0	0	0	0	7	9	0	3	2	18.0	0.00	—	.321	.424	0	.000	-0	2	2	-0	0.2
■ EDDIE CARNETT Carnett, Edwin Elliott "Lefty" b: 10/21/16, Springfield, Mo. BL/TL, 6', 185 lbs. Deb: 4/19/41 ♦																								
1941 Bos-N	0	0	—	2	0	0	0	0	1¹	4	0	3	2	47.3	20.25	18	.500	.636	0	—	0	-2	-2	0	-0.1
1944 Chi-A	0	0	—	2	0	0	0	0	2	3	1	0	1	13.5	9.00	38	.333	.333	126	.276	1	-1	-1	0	0.0
1945 Cle-A	0	0	—	2	0	0	0	0	2	0	0	0	1	0.0	0.00	—	.000	.000	16	.219	0	1	1	0	0.1
Total 3	0	0	—	6	0	0	0	0	5¹	7	1	3	4	16.9	8.44	40	.304	.385	142	.268	1	-3	-3	0	0.0
■ PAT CARNEY Carney, Patrick Joseph "Doc" b: 8/7/1876, Holyoke, Mass. d: 1/9/53, Worcester, Mass. BL/TL, 6', 200 lbs. Deb: 9/20/01 ♦																								
1902 Bos-N	0	1	.000	2	1	0	0	0	5	6	1	3	3	18.0	9.00	31	.297	.413	141	.270	-0	-3	-3	-0	-0.2
1903 Bos-N	4	5	.444	10	9	9	0	0	78	93	2	31	29	14.5	4.04	79	.284	.349	94	.240	2	-7	-7	-0	-0.6
1904 Bos-N	0	4	.000	4	2	1	0	0	26¹	40	1	12	5	18.1	5.81	47	.364	.431	57	.204	0	-9	-9	-0	-0.7
Total 3	4	10	.286	16	12	10	0	0	109¹	139	4	46	37	15.6	4.69	66	.303	.372	308	.247	2	-19	-20	-1	-1.5
■ CRIS CARPENTER Carpenter, Cris Howell b: 4/5/65, St.Augustine, Fla. BR/TR, 6'1", 195 lbs. Deb: 5/14/88																								
1988 StL-N	2	3	.400	8	8	1	0	0	47²	56	3	9	24	12.5	4.72	74	.298	.333	2	.143	-0	-7	-7	-0	-0.6
1989 StL-N	4	4	.500	36	5	0	0	0	68	70	4	26	35	13.0	3.18	114	.262	.332	4	.444	1	2	3	0	0.5
1990 StL-N	0	0	—	4	0	0	0	0	8	5	2	2	6	7.9	4.50	87	.167	.219	0	.000	-0	-1	-1	-0	-0.1
Total 3	6	7	.462	48	13	1	0	0	123²	131	9	37	65	12.4	3.86	93	.270	.326	6	.250	1	-5	-4	-1	-0.1
■ LEW CARPENTER Carpenter, Lewis Emmett b: 8/16/13, Woodstock, Ga. d: 4/25/79, Marietta, Ga. BR/TR, 6'2", 195 lbs. Deb: 5/01/43																								
1943 Was-A	0	0	—	4	0	0	0	0	3¹	1	0	4	1	16.2	0.00	—	.125	.462	0	—	0	1	1	0	0.1
■ PAUL CARPENTER Carpenter, Paul Calvin b: 8/12/1894, Granville, Ohio d: 3/14/68, Newark, Ohio BR/TR, 5'11", 165 lbs. Deb: 7/26/16																								
1916 Pit-N	0	0	—	5	0	0	0	0	7²	8	0	4	5	14.1	1.17	229	.258	.343	0	.000	-0	1	1	0	0.1
■ BOB CARPENTER Carpenter, Robert Louis b: 12/12/17, Chicago, Ill. BR/TR, 6'3", 195 lbs. Deb: 9/12/40																								
1940 NY-N	2	0	1.000	5	3	2	0	0	33	29	2	14	25	11.7	2.73	142	.238	.316	1	.100	-0	4	4	-0	0.4
1941 NY-N	11	6	.647	29	19	8	1	2	131²	138	15	42	42	12.4	3.83	97	.265	.323	7	.156	-0	-3	-2	-2	-0.3
1942 NY-N	11	10	.524	28	25	12	2	0	185²	192	13	51	53	11.8	3.15	107	.263	.312	12	.185	-1	3	4	-3	0.1
1946 NY-N	1	3	.250	12	6	1	1	0	39	37	7	18	13	12.7	4.85	71	.245	.325	1	.100	-0	-6	-6	-0	-0.6
1947 NY-N	0	0	—	2	0	0	0	0	3	5	0	3	0	24.0	12.00	34	.385	.500	—	-0	-3	-3	0	-0.1	
Chi-N	0	1	.000	4	1	0	0	0	7¹	10	1	4	1	17.2	4.91	80	.323	.400	1	1.000	-0	-1	-1	-0	-0.0
Yr	0	1	.000	6	1	0	0	0	10¹	15	1	7	1	19.2	6.97	57	.341	.431	0	.000	0	-3	-3	0	-0.1
Total 5	25	20	.556	80	54	23	4	2	399²	411	38	132	134	12.3	3.60	98	.262	.321	22	.168	-1	-5	-3	-5	-0.5
■ FRANK CARPIN Carpin, Frank Dominic b: 9/14/38, Brooklyn, N.Y. BL/TL, 5'10", 172 lbs. Deb: 5/25/65																								
1965 Pit-N	3	1	.750	39	0	0	0	4	39²	35	0	24	27	14.1	3.18	111	.243	.363	0	.000	-0	2	1	1	0.3
1966 Hou-N	1	0	1.000	10	0	0	0	0	6	9	0	6	2	22.5	7.50	46	.346	.469	0	—	0	-3	-3	-0	-0.2
Total 2	4	1	.800	49	0	0	0	4	45²	44	0	30	29	15.2	3.74	93	.259	.379	0	.000	-0	-1	-1	1	0.1
■ ALEX CARRASQUEL Carrasquel, Alejandro Eloy (Aparicio) b: 7/24/12, Caracas, Venez. d: 8/19/69, Caracas, Venez. BR/TR, 6'1", 182 lbs. Deb: 4/23/39																								
1939 Was-A	5	9	.357	40	17	2	0	2	159¹	165	7	68	41	13.2	4.69	93	.266	.340	7	.167	1	-1	-6	1	-0.4
1940 Was-A	6	2	.750	28	0	0	0	0	48	42	4	29	19	13.3	4.88	86	.240	.348	0	.000	-1	-3	-4	0	-0.3
1941 Was-A	7	7	.500	35	5	0	0	0	96²	103	7	49	30	14.2	3.44	117	.278	.364	2	.095	0	8	6	4	1.0
1942 Was-A	7	7	.500	35	15	3	1	4	152¹	161	7	53	40	12.7	3.43	107	.267	.327	6	.136	-0	4	4	2	0.5
1943 Was-A	11	7	.611	39	13	4	1	5	144¹	160	3	54	48	13.4	3.68	87	.279	.342	8	.186	1	-6	-8	1	-0.6
1944 Was-A	8	7	.533	43	7	3	0	2	134	143	8	50	35	13.1	3.43	95	.273	.339	7	.194	1	0	-3	1	0.0

YEAR	TM/L	W	L	PCT	G	GS	CG	SH	SV	IP	H	HR	BB	SO	RAT	ERA	ERA+	OAV	OOB	BH	AVG	PB	PR	/A	PD	TPI
1945	Was-A	7	5	.583	35	7	5	2	1	122²	105	5	40	38	10.6	2.71	114	.228	.289	3	.083	-1	9	5	0	0.4
1949	Chi-A	0	0	—	3	0	0	0	0	3²	8	1	4	1	29.5	14.73	28	.421	.522	0	—	0	-4	-4	0	-0.3
Total	8	50	39	.562	258	64	30	4	16	861	887	42	347	252	13.0	3.73	98	.265	.335	33	.144	0	6	-9	9	0.3

■ BILL CARRICK
Carrick, William Martin "Doughnut Bill" b: 9/5/1873, Erie, Pa. d: 3/7/32, Philadelphia, Pa. TR , Deb: 7/30/1898

YEAR	TM/L	W	L	PCT	G	GS	CG	SH	SV	IP	H	HR	BB	SO	RAT	ERA	ERA+	OAV	OOB	BH	AVG	PB	PR	/A	PD	TPI
1898	NY-N	5	4	.556	5	4	4	0	0	39²	39	0	21	10	13.6	3.40	102	.255	.345	1	.167	-0	1	0	1	0.0
1899	NY-N	16	27	.372	44	43	40	3	0	361²	485	4	122	60	15.1	4.65	81	.320	.371	18	.138	-6	-32	-36	3	-3.3
1900	NY-N	19	22	.463	45	41	32	1	0	341²	415	7	92	63	13.4	3.53	102	.299	.343	20	.174	-2	6	3	0	0.0
1901	Was-A	14	24	.368	42	37	34	0	0	324	367	12	93	70	12.8	3.75	98	.282	.330	20	.159	-5	-3	-3	0	-0.6
1902	Was-A	11	17	.393	31	30	28	0	0	257²	344	10	72	36	14.5	4.86	76	.320	.363	20	.185	-2	-37	-33	-2	-3.1
Total	5	63	91	.409	167	155	138	4	0	1324²	1650	33	400	239	13.9	4.14	89	.304	.352	81	.163	-15	-64	-68	2	-7.0

■ DON CARRITHERS
Carrithers, Donald George b: 9/15/49, Lynwood, Cal. BR/TR, 6'2", 180 lbs. Deb: 8/01/70

YEAR	TM/L	W	L	PCT	G	GS	CG	SH	SV	IP	H	HR	BB	SO	RAT	ERA	ERA+	OAV	OOB	BH	AVG	PB	PR	/A	PD	TPI
1970	SF-N	2	1	.667	11	2	0	0	0	22	31	5	14	14	18.4	7.36	54	.333	.421	0	.000	-0	-8	-8	0	-0.7
1971	*SF-N	5	3	.625	22	12	2	1	1	80¹	77	6	37	41	13.0	4.03	84	.254	.339	3	.176	0	-5	-6	-0	-0.5
1972	SF-N	4	8	.333	25	14	2	0	1	90	108	10	42	42	15.5	5.80	60	.296	.376	6	.207	1	-23	-23	0	-2.2
1973	SF-N	1	2	.333	25	3	0	0	0	58	64	2	35	36	16.0	4.81	79	.278	.383	4	.250	0	-7	-6	1	-0.4
1974	Mon-N	5	2	.714	22	3	0	0	1	60	56	6	17	31	11.4	3.00	128	.249	.310	4	.286	1	4	6	1	0.8
1975	Mon-N	5	3	.625	19	14	5	2	0	101	90	7	38	37	11.8	3.30	116	.240	.317	6	.176	0	4	6	2	0.9
1976	Mon-N	6	12	.333	34	19	2	0	0	140¹	153	9	78	71	15.3	4.43	84	.286	.384	4	.108	-1	-14	-11	1	-1.0
1977	Min-A	0	1	.000	7	0	0	0	0	14¹	16	2	6	3	14.4	6.91	58	.271	.348	0	—	0	-5	-5	0	-0.3
Total	8	28	32	.467	165	67	11	3	3	566	595	47	267	275	14.1	4.45	83	.272	.358	27	.176	0	-55	-48	6	-3.4

■ CLAY CARROLL
Carroll, Clay Palmer "Hawk" b: 5/2/41, Clanton, Ala. BR/TR, 6'1", 178 lbs. Deb: 9/02/64

YEAR	TM/L	W	L	PCT	G	GS	CG	SH	SV	IP	H	HR	BB	SO	RAT	ERA	ERA+	OAV	OOB	BH	AVG	PB	PR	/A	PD	TPI
1964	Mil-N	2	0	1.000	11	1	0	0	1	20¹	15	1	3	17	8.0	1.77	199	.200	.231	0	.000	-0	4	4	1	0.5
1965	Mil-N	0	1	.000	19	1	0	0	1	34²	35	3	13	16	12.7	4.41	80	.269	.340	0	.000	-1	-3	-3	0	-0.3
1966	Atl-N	8	7	.533	73	3	0	0	11	144¹	127	8	29	67	10.0	2.37	154	.236	.280	3	.100	-2	20	20	2	2.1
1967	Atl-N	6	12	.333	42	7	1	0	0	93	111	6	29	35	13.8	5.52	60	.304	.360	1	.063	-1	-22	-23	1	-2.2
1968	Atl-N	0	1	.000	10	0	0	0	0	22¹	26	1	6	10	12.9	4.84	62	.310	.356	0	.000	-1	-5	-5	0	-0.4
	Cin-N	7	7	.500	58	1	0	0	17	121²	102	3	32	61	10.4	2.29	138	.230	.290	6	.250	1	9	12	2	1.7
	Yr	7	8	.467	68	1	0	0	17	144	128	4	38	71	10.8	2.69	117	.242	.300	1	.034	1	5	7	2	1.3
1969	Cin-N	12	6	.667	71	4	0	0	7	150²	149	9	78	90	14.0	3.52	107	.262	.358	6	.207	2	1	4	3	1.0
1970	*Cin-N	9	4	.692	65	0	0	0	16	104¹	104	4	31	63	11.5	2.59	156	.259	.309	1	.071	-1	17	17	1	1.8
1971	Cin-N	10	4	.714	61	0	0	0	15	93²	78	5	42	64	11.7	2.50	134	.234	.324	1	.100	-1	10	9	3	1.3
1972	*Cin-N	6	4	.600	65	0	0	0	37	96	89	5	32	51	11.4	2.25	143	.256	.321	2	.182	0	13	10	1	1.2
1973	*Cin-N	8	8	.500	53	5	0	0	14	92²	111	5	34	41	14.6	3.69	92	.307	.374	3	.214	0	-3	1	-0	-0.1
1974	Cin-N	12	5	.706	57	0	0	0	6	100²	96	3	30	46	11.3	2.15	163	.256	.311	3	.167	-0	16	15	2	1.7
1975	*Cin-N	7	5	.583	56	2	0	0	7	96¹	93	2	32	44	12.0	2.62	137	.255	.320	0	.000	-2	11	10	-0	0.8
1976	Chi-A	4	4	.500	29	0	0	0	6	77¹	67	1	24	38	10.8	2.56	139	.242	.307	0	—	0	8	9	1	1.0
1977	StL-N	4	2	.667	51	1	0	0	4	90	77	8	24	34	10.2	2.50	154	.238	.293	1	.091	-1	14	13	1	1.4
	Chi-A	1	3	.250	8	0	0	0	1	11¹	14	3	4	4	14.3	4.76	86	.311	.367	0	—	0	-1	-1	0	0.0
1978	Pit-N	0	0	—	2	0	0	0	0	4	2	0	3	0	11.3	2.25	164	.143	.294	0	—	0	1	1	0	0.1
Total	15	96	73	.568	731	28	1	0	143	1353¹	1296	67	442	681	11.8	2.94	120	.257	.321	27	.130	-5	93	90	19	11.6

■ ED CARROLL
Carroll, Edgar Fleischer b: 7/27/07, Baltimore, Md. d: 10/13/84, Rossville, Md. BR/TR, 6'3", 185 lbs. Deb: 5/01/29

YEAR	TM/L	W	L	PCT	G	GS	CG	SH	SV	IP	H	HR	BB	SO	RAT	ERA	ERA+	OAV	OOB	BH	AVG	PB	PR	/A	PD	TPI
1929	Bos-A	1	0	1.000	24	3	0	0	0	67¹	77	6	20	13	13.5	5.61	76	.291	.349	1	.063	-2	-10	-10	1	-1.0

■ OWNIE CARROLL
Carroll, Owen Thomas b: 11/11/02, Kearny, N.J. d: 6/8/75, Orange, N.J. BR/TR, 5'10.5", 165 lbs. Deb: 6/20/25

YEAR	TM/L	W	L	PCT	G	GS	CG	SH	SV	IP	H	HR	BB	SO	RAT	ERA	ERA+	OAV	OOB	BH	AVG	PB	PR	/A	PD	TPI
1925	Det-A	2	2	.500	10	4	1	0	0	40²	46	1	28	12	16.8	3.76	114	.293	.406	3	.375	1	3	2	-2	0.2
1927	Det-A	10	6	.625	31	15	8	0	0	172	186	1	73	41	13.9	3.98	106	.281	.358	12	.174	-2	3	4	2	0.4
1928	Det-A	16	12	.571	34	28	19	2	2	231	219	6	87	51	12.2	3.27	126	.262	.337	19	.194	-0	20	21	2	2.2
1929	Det-A	9	17	.346	34	26	12	0	1	202	249	10	86	54	15.3	4.63	93	.310	.383	17	.230	2	-9	-8	2	-0.2
1930	Det-A	0	5	.000	6	3	0	0	0	20¹	30	3	9	4	17.3	10.62	45	.333	.394	1	.143	-1	-13	-13	0	-1.0
	NY-A	0	1	.000	10	1	0	0	0	32²	49	2	18	8	19.6	6.61	65	.374	.464	2	.200	0	-7	-8	1	-0.6
	Yr	0	6	.000	16	4	0	0	0	53	79	5	27	12	18.7	8.15	55	.357	.437	2	.118	-1	-21	-22	1	-1.6
	Cin-N	0	1	.000	3	2	1	0	0	14	17	3	3	0	12.9	4.50	107	.309	.345	1	.200	-0	1	1	0	0.0
1931	Cin-N	3	9	.250	29	12	4	0	0	107¹	135	6	51	24	15.9	5.53	67	.314	.392	7	.206	0	-20	-21	1	-1.8
1932	Cin-N	10	19	.345	32	26	15	0	1	210	245	7	44	55	12.8	4.50	80	.286	.328	16	.208	2	-14	-15	-1	-1.3
1933	Bro-N	13	15	.464	33	31	11	0	0	226¹	248	9	54	45	12.3	3.78	85	.281	.327	11	.149	-1	-11	-14	4	-1.1
1934	Bro-N	1	3	.250	26	5	0	0	1	74¹	108	9	33	17	17.2	6.42	61	.342	.406	6	.240	1	-19	-21	3	-1.5
Total	9	64	90	.416	248	153	71	2	5	1330²	1532	61	486	311	14.0	4.43	89	.294	.359	98	.200	2	-68	-72	13	-4.7

■ DICK CARROLL
Carroll, Richard Thomas "Shadow" b: 7/21/1884, Cleveland, Ohio d: 11/22/45, Cleveland, Ohio BR/TR, 6'2", Deb: 9/25/09

YEAR	TM/L	W	L	PCT	G	GS	CG	SH	SV	IP	H	HR	BB	SO	RAT	ERA	ERA+	OAV	OOB	BH	AVG	PB	PR	/A	PD	TPI
1909	NY-A	0	0	—	2	1	0	0	0	5	7	1	1	1	14.4	3.60	70	.292	.320	1	.500	0	-1	-1	-0	0.0

■ TOM CARROLL
Carroll, Thomas Michael b: 11/5/52, Utica, N.Y. BL/TR, 6'3", 190 lbs. Deb: 7/07/74

YEAR	TM/L	W	L	PCT	G	GS	CG	SH	SV	IP	H	HR	BB	SO	RAT	ERA	ERA+	OAV	OOB	BH	AVG	PB	PR	/A	PD	TPI
1974	Cin-N	4	3	.571	16	13	0	0	0	78¹	68	11	44	37	12.9	3.68	95	.231	.331	4	.154	-1	-1	-2	-1	-0.2
1975	Cin-N	4	1	.800	12	7	0	0	0	47	52	1	26	14	15.3	4.98	72	.284	.379	0	.000	-2	-7	-7	-1	-0.9
Total	2	8	4	.667	28	20	0	0	0	125¹	120	12	70	51	13.8	4.16	85	.252	.350	4	.100	-2	-9	-9	-1	-1.1

■ KID CARSEY
Carsey, Wilfred b: 10/22/1870, New York, N.Y. d: 3/29/60, Miami, Fla. BL/TR, 5'7", 168 lbs. Deb: 4/08/1891 ◆

YEAR	TM/L	W	L	PCT	G	GS	CG	SH	SV	IP	H	HR	BB	SO	RAT	ERA	ERA+	OAV	OOB	BH	AVG	PB	PR	/A	PD	TPI
1891	Was-a	14	37	.275	54	53	46	1	0	415	513	17	161	174	14.6	4.99	75	.294	.353	28	.150	-6	-58	-57	6	-4.6
1892	Phi-N	19	16	.543	43	36	30	1	1	317²	320	6	104	76	12.0	3.12	104	.251	.308	20	.153	-3	6	5	3	0.3
1893	Phi-N	20	15	.571	39	35	30	1	0	318¹	375	7	124	50	14.1	4.81	95	.285	.346	28	.186	-8	-5	-8	2	-1.0
1894	Phi-N	18	12	.600	35	31	26	0	0	277	349	22	102	41	14.7	5.56	92	.304	.361	34	.272	3	-7	-14	2	-0.7
1895	Phi-N	24	16	.600	44	40	35	0	1	342¹	460	14	118	64	15.2	4.92	97	.317	.368	41	.291	3	-5	-5	-1	-0.7
1896	Phi-N	11	11	.500	27	21	18	1	1	187¹	273	4	72	36	16.6	5.62	77	.337	.391	18	.222	2	-26	-27	1	-1.9
1897	Phi-N	2	1	.667	4	4	2	0	0	28	35	0	16	1	16.4	5.14	82	.303	.383	3	.231	0	-3	-3	0	-0.2
	StL-N	3	8	.273	12	11	11	0	0	99	133	5	31	14	14.9	6.00	73	.319	.366	13	.302	2	-19	-18	1	-1.1
	Yr	5	9	.357	16	15	13	0	0	127	168	5	47	15	15.2	5.81	75	.315	.371	1	.018	2	-21	-20	1	-1.3
1898	StL-N	2	12	.143	20	13	10	0	0	123¹	177	2	37	10	15.6	6.33	60	.333	.376	21	.200	-0	-37	-35	2	-2.8
1899	Cle-N	1	8	.111	10	9	8	0	0	77²	109	2	24	11	15.4	5.68	65	.330	.376	10	.278	1	-16	-17	1	-1.2
	Was-N	1	2	.333	4	3	2	0	0	29	27	0	4	3	9.6	3.72	105	.247	.273	0	.000	-2	1	1	0	0.0
	Yr	2	10	.167	14	12	10	0	0	106²	136	2	28	14	13.8	5.15	73	.310	.351	3	.064	-1	-15	-17	2	-1.2
1901	Bro-N	1	0	1.000	2	0	0	0	0	2	3	0	2	3	16.7	10.29	33	.310	.393	0	—	-0	-5	-4	-0	-0.4
Total	10	116	138	.457	294	256	218	4	3	2222	2780	80	796	484	14.5	4.95	85	.300	.355	221	.213	-8	-175	-183	17	-13.7

■ AL CARSON
Carson, Albert James "Soldier" b: 8/22/1882, Chicago, Ill. d: 11/26/62, San Diego, Cal. TR , Deb: 5/06/10

YEAR	TM/L	W	L	PCT	G	GS	CG	SH	SV	IP	H	HR	BB	SO	RAT	ERA	ERA+	OAV	OOB	BH	AVG	PB	PR	/A	PD	TPI
1910	Chi-N	0	0	—	2	0	0	0	0	6²	6	0	1	2	9.5	4.05	71	.240	.269	0	.000	0	-1	-1	0	0.0

■ ARNOLD CARTER
Carter, Arnold Lee "Hook" or "Lefty" b: 3/14/18, Rainelle, W.Va. BL/TL, 5'10", 170 lbs. Deb: 4/29/44

YEAR	TM/L	W	L	PCT	G	GS	CG	SH	SV	IP	H	HR	BB	SO	RAT	ERA	ERA+	OAV	OOB	BH	AVG	PB	PR	/A	PD	TPI
1944	Cin-N	11	7	.611	33	18	9	3	3	148²	143	1	40	33	11.3	2.60	134	.256	.309	12	.250	5	17	15	1	2.2
1945	Cin-N	2	4	.333	13	6	2	1	0	46²	54	2	13	4	13.3	3.09	122	.286	.338	3	.176	0	4	3	0	0.4
Total	2	13	11	.542	46	24	11	4	3	195¹	197	3	53	37	11.7	2.72	131	.264	.317	15	.231	5	20	18	2	2.6

YEAR TM/L	W	L	PCT	G	GS	CG	SH	SV	IP	H	HR	BB	SO	RAT	ERA	ERA+	OAV	OOB	BH	AVG	PB	PR	/A	PD	TPI

■ NICK CARTER   Carter, Conrad Powell b: 5/19/1879, Oatlands, Va.   d: 11/23/61, Grasonville, Md.   TR , 5'8", 126 lbs.   Deb: 4/14/08

| 1908 Phi-A | 2 | 5 | .286 | 14 | 5 | 2 | 0 | 0 | 60² | 58 | 1 | 17 | 17 | 11.4 | 2.97 | 86 | .270 | .329 | 2 | .100 | -2 | -4 | -3 | 1 | -0.2 |

■ PAUL CARTER   Carter, Paul Warren "Nick" b: 5/1/1894, Lake Park, Ga.   d: 9/11/84, Lake Park, Ga.   BL/TR, 6'3", 175 lbs.   Deb: 9/15/14

1914 Cle-A	1	3	.250	5	4	1	0	0	24²	35	0	5	9	14.6	2.92	99	.340	.370	0	.000	-1	-0	-0	-0	0.0
1915 Cle-A	1	1	.500	11	2	2	0	0	42	44	1	18	14	13.3	3.21	95	.272	.344	3	.214	1	-1	-1	1	0.1
1916 Chi-N	2	2	.500	8	5	2	0	0	36	26	1	17	14	10.8	2.75	106	.203	.297	2	.167	-0	-1	1	1	0.2
1917 Chi-N	5	8	.385	23	13	6	0	2	113¹	115	2	19	34	10.9	3.26	89	.276	.313	6	.171	-0	-7	-5	-0	-0.5
1918 Chi-N	3	2	.600	21	4	1	0	2	73	78	2	19	13	12.1	2.71	103	.290	.339	6	.240	0	0	1	2	0.3
1919 Chi-N	5	4	.556	28	7	2	0	1	85	81	1	28	17	11.8	2.65	109	.252	.316	7	.269	1	3	2	0	0.3
1920 Chi-N	3	6	.333	31	8	2	0	0	106	131	3	36	14	14.6	4.67	69	.324	.387	6	.171	-1	-18	-17	-1	-1.9
Total 7	20	26	.435	127	43	16	0	7	480	510	10	142	115	12.4	3.32	89	.283	.339	30	.195	-1	-24	-19	3	-1.5

■ SOL CARTER   Carter, Solomon Mobley "Buck" b: 12/23/08, Picayune, Miss.   BR/TR, 6', 178 lbs.   Deb: 4/15/31

| 1931 Phi-A | 0 | 0 | — | 2 | 0 | 0 | 0 | 0 | 2¹ | 1 | 0 | 4 | 1 | 19.3 | 19.29 | 23 | .143 | .455 | 0 | — | 0 | -4 | -4 | 1 | -0.2 |

■ BOB CARUTHERS   Caruthers, Robert Lee "Parisian Bob" b: 1/5/1864, Memphis, Tenn.   d: 8/5/11, Peoria, Ill.   BL/TR, 5'7", 138 lbs.   Deb: 9/07/1884   MU♦

1884 StL-a	7	2	.778	13	7	7	0	0	82²	61	1	15	58	8.3	2.61	125	.194	.231	21	.256	2	6	6	-1	0.8
1885 *StL-a	40	13	.755	53	53	53	6	0	482¹	430	3	57	190	9.1	2.07	158	.228	.251	50	.225	7	63	65	0	7.0
1886 *StL-a	30	14	.682	44	43	42	2	0	387¹	323	8	86	166	9.5	2.32	148	.216	.259	106	.334	26	49	48	-2	9.5
1887 *StL-a	29	9	.763	39	39	39	2	0	341	337	6	61	74	10.5	3.30	138	.249	.281	130	.357	21	38	47	8	4.0
1888 Bro-a	29	15	.659	44	43	42	4	0	391²	337	4	53	140	9.0	2.39	125	.224	.250	77	.230	10	29	26	2	2.4
1889 *Bro-a	40	11	.784	56	50	46	7	1	445	444	16	104	118	11.1	3.13	119	.252	.294	43	.250	17	35	29	3	4.3
1890 *Bro-N	23	11	.676	37	33	30	1	0	300	292	9	87	64	11.4	3.09	111	.248	.300	63	.265	11	16	11	4	3.3
1891 Bro-N	18	14	.563	38	32	29	2	1	297	323	7	107	69	13.0	3.12	106	.267	.326	48	.281	11	7	6	1	2.1
1892 StL-N	2	10	.167	16	10	10	0	1	101²	131	10	27	21	14.0	5.84	55	.301	.341	142	.277	5	-29	-30	1	-2.5
Total 9	218	99	.688	340	310	298	24	3	2828²	2678	59	597	900	10.4	2.83	123	.240	.279	694	.282	110	214	207	15	30.9

■ CHUCK CARY   Cary, Charles Douglas b: 3/3/60, Whittier, Cal.   BL/TL, 6'4", 210 lbs.   Deb: 8/22/85

1985 Det-A	0	1	.000	16	0	0	0	2	23²	16	2	8	22	9.9	3.42	119	.190	.277	0	—	0	2	2	-0	0.1
1986 Det-A	1	2	.333	22	0	0	0	0	31²	33	3	15	21	13.6	3.41	121	.273	.353	0	—	0	3	3	-0	0.2
1987 Atl-N	1	1	.500	13	0	0	0	1	16²	17	3	4	15	11.9	3.78	115	.266	.319	0	.000	-0	1	1	0	0.1
1988 Atl-N	0	0	—	7	0	0	0	0	8¹	8	1	4	7	14.0	6.48	57	.250	.351	0	—	0	-3	-3	-0	-0.2
1989 NY-A	4	4	.500	22	11	2	0	0	99¹	78	13	29	79	9.7	3.26	119	.209	.266	0	—	0	7	7	-2	0.4
1990 NY-A	6	12	.333	28	27	2	0	0	156²	155	21	55	134	12.1	4.19	95	.260	.323	0	—	0	-5	-4	-2	-0.5
Total 6	12	20	.375	108	38	4	0	3	336¹	307	43	115	278	11.4	3.83	104	.242	.307	0	.000	-0	4	5	-5	0.1

■ SCOTT CARY   Cary, Scott Russell "Red" b: 4/11/23, Kendallville, Ind.   BL/TL, 5'11.5", 168 lbs.   Deb: 5/01/47

| 1947 Was-A | 3 | 1 | .750 | 23 | 3 | 1 | 0 | 0 | 54² | 73 | 5 | 20 | 25 | 15.5 | 5.93 | 63 | .312 | .369 | 1 | .077 | -1 | -13 | -13 | -1 | -1.4 |

■ JERRY CASALE   Casale, Jerry Joseph b: 9/27/33, Brooklyn, N.Y.   BR/TR, 6'2", 200 lbs.   Deb: 9/14/9158

1958 Bos-A	0	0	—	2	0	0	0	0	3	1	0	2	3	9.0	0.00	—	.111	.273	0	—	0	1	1	0	0.1
1959 Bos-A	13	8	.619	31	26	9	3	0	179²	162	20	89	93	12.8	4.31	94	.238	.331	10	.169	3	-9	-5	-4	-0.5
1960 Bos-A	2	9	.182	29	14	1	0	0	96¹	113	14	67	54	16.9	6.17	66	.294	.400	9	.273	3	-25	-23	-0	-1.9
1961 LA-A	1	5	.167	13	7	0	0	1	42²	52	9	25	35	16.5	6.54	69	.297	.388	6	.462	1	-12	-10	-0	-0.5
Det-A	0	0	—	3	1	0	0	0	12	15	3	3	6	13.5	5.25	78	.313	.353	0	.000	-0	-2	-2	0	-0.1
Yr	1	5	.167	16	8	0	0	1	54²	67	12	28	41	15.6	6.26	71	.298	.375	1	.063	3	-14	-11	-0	-0.6
1962 Det-A	1	2	.333	18	1	0	0	0	36²	33	5	18	16	12.5	4.66	87	.236	.323	0	.000	-1	-3	-2	0	-0.2
Total 5	17	24	.415	96	49	10	3	1	370¹	376	51	204	207	14.3	5.08	81	.262	.356	25	.216	8	-49	-40	-4	-3.1

■ JOE CASCARELLA   Cascarella, Joseph Thomas "Crooning Joe" b: 6/28/07, Philadelphia, Pa.   BR/TR, 5'10.5", 175 lbs.   Deb: 4/17/34

1934 Phi-A	12	15	.444	42	22	9	2	1	194¹	214	8	104	71	14.9	4.68	94	.288	.377	6	.094	-4	-4	-6	2	-0.7
1935 Phi-A	1	6	.143	9	3	1	0	0	32¹	29	1	22	15	14.2	5.29	86	.252	.372	1	.125	-1	-3	-3	2	-0.1
Bos-A	0	3	.000	6	4	0	0	0	17	25	3	11	9	19.1	6.88	69	.329	.414	0	.000	-0	-5	-4	0	-0.3
Yr	1	9	.100	15	7	1	0	0	49¹	54	4	33	24	15.9	5.84	79	.283	.388	1	.000	-1	-8	-7	2	-0.4
1936 Bos-A	0	2	.000	10	1	0	0	0	20²	27	0	9	7	15.7	6.97	76	.329	.396	0	.000	-1	-4	-4	0	-0.3
Was-A	9	8	.529	22	16	7	1	1	139¹	147	7	54	34	13.4	4.07	117	.276	.349	7	.143	-2	15	11	-2	0.6
Yr	9	10	.474	32	17	7	1	1	160	174	7	63	41	13.7	4.44	109	.283	.355	2	.038	-3	11	7	-2	0.3
1937 Was-A	0	5	.000	10	4	1	0	1	32¹	50	3	23	10	20.6	8.07	55	.347	.440	2	.222	-1	-12	-13	1	-1.0
Cin-N	1	2	.333	11	3	2	0	1	43²	44	1	22	16	13.6	3.92	95	.263	.349	1	.091	-1	-0	-1	0	-0.1
1938 Cin-N	4	7	.364	33	1	0	0	4	61	66	2	22	30	13.0	4.57	80	.275	.336	3	.167	-1	-5	-6	-0	-0.6
Total 5	27	48	.360	143	54	20	3	8	540²	602	25	267	192	14.6	4.84	91	.287	.370	20	.121	-9	-19	-26	2	-2.5

■ CHARLIE CASE   Case, Charles Emmett b: 9/7/1879, Smith Landing, O.   d: 4/16/64, Clairmont, Ohio   BR/TR, 6', 170 lbs.   Deb: 7/05/01

1901 Cin-N	1	2	.333	3	3	3	0	0	27	34	0	6	5	13.3	4.67	69	.305	.341	1	.100	-1	-4	-4	0	-0.4
1904 Pit-N	10	5	.667	18	17	14	3	0	141	129	0	31	49	10.5	2.94	93	.243	.290	9	.170	0	-3	-3	1	-0.1
1905 Pit-N	11	11	.500	31	24	18	3	1	217	202	2	66	57	11.7	2.57	117	.251	.319	7	.103	-2	10	10	-3	0.6
1906 Pit-N	1	1	.500	2	2	1	0	0	11	8	0	5	3	11.5	5.73	47	.190	.292	1	.500	1	-4	-4	0	-0.2
Total 4	23	19	.548	54	46	36	6	1	396	373	2	108	114	11.4	2.93	99	.250	.310	18	.135	-2	-0	-1	-2	-0.1

■ DAN CASEY   Casey, Daniel Maurice b: 11/20/1862, Binghamton, N.Y.   d: 2/8/43, Washington, D.C.   BR/TL, 6', 180 lbs.   Deb: 8/18/1884

1884 Wil-U	1	1	.500	2	2	2	0	0	18	23	0	4	10	13.5	1.00	329	.291	.325	1	.167	-1	4	5	0	0.4
1885 Det-N	4	8	.333	12	12	12	1	0	104	105	1	35	79	12.1	3.29	86	.250	.308	5	.116	-3	-5	-5	0	-0.6
1886 Phi-N	24	18	.571	44	44	39	4	0	369	326	8	104	193	10.5	2.41	137	.227	.280	23	.152	-5	37	36	-1	2.8
1887 Phi-N	28	13	.683	45	45	43	4	0	390¹	377	15	115	119	11.3	2.86	147	.247	.289	27	.165	-11	52	58	-1	4.2
1888 Phi-N	14	18	.438	33	33	31	2	0	285²	298	6	48	108	10.9	3.15	94	.259	.289	18	.153	-3	-10	-6	1	-0.7
1889 Phi-N	6	10	.375	20	20	15	1	0	152²	170	4	72	65	14.3	3.77	115	.273	.348	15	.221	-2	4	10	0	0.8
1890 Syr-a	19	22	.463	45	42	40	2	0	360²	365	8	165	169	13.2	4.14	86	.255	.332	26	.162	-3	-11	-23	2	-2.2
Total 7	96	90	.516	201	198	182	14	0	1680¹	1664	42	543	743	11.8	3.18	113	.250	.306	115	.162	-27	70	75	1	4.7

■ HUGH CASEY   Casey, Hugh Thomas b: 10/14/13, Atlanta, Ga.   d: 7/3/51, Atlanta, Ga.   BR/TR, 6'1", 207 lbs.   Deb: 4/29/35

1935 Chi-N	0	0	—	13	0	0	0	0	25²	29	2	14	10	15.1	3.86	102	.279	.364	1	.167	-0	0	0	0	0.0
1939 Bro-N	15	10	.600	40	25	15	0	1	227¹	228	13	54	79	11.6	2.93	137	.260	.311	15	.203	0	25	28	2	3.2
1940 Bro-N	11	8	.579	44	10	5	2	2	154	136	13	51	53	11.3	3.62	110	.237	.306	9	.250	2	4	6	2	1.0
1941 *Bro-N	14	11	.560	45	18	4	1	7	162	155	8	57	61	11.8	3.89	94	.251	.316	6	.120	-1	-5	-4	2	-0.2
1942 Bro-N	6	3	.667	50	2	0	0	13	112	91	3	44	54	11.0	2.25	145	.221	.300	4	.148	-0	13	13	-1	1.3
1946 Bro-N	11	5	.688	46	1	0	0	5	99²	101	2	33	31	12.3	1.99	170	.267	.329	3	.136	-1	16	15	3	2.0
1947 *Bro-N	10	4	.714	46	0	0	0	18	76²	75	7	29	40	12.4	3.99	104	.260	.331	1	.056	-1	1	0	0	0.0
1948 Bro-N	3	0	1.000	22	0	0	0	0	36	59	6	17	7	19.5	8.00	50	.391	.459	1	.000	-1	-16	-16	0	-1.5
1949 Pit-N	4	1	.800	33	0	0	0	5	38²	50	4	14	9	15.1	4.66	90	.314	.374	1	.333	0	-3	-2	-1	-0.2
NY-A	1	0	1.000	4	0	0	0	0	7²	11	0	8	5	22.3	8.22	49	.324	.452	0	.000	-0	-3	-4	0	-0.3
Total 9	75	42	.641	343	56	24	3	55	939²	935	58	321	291	12.3	3.45	110	.260	.325	40	.164	-2	32	38	7	5.3

■ BILL CASEY   Casey, William B. b: St.Louis, Mo.   Deb: 8/17/1887

| 1887 Phi-a | 0 | 0 | — | 1 | 0 | 0 | 0 | 0 | 1 | 4 | 0 | 1 | 0 | 45.0 | 18.00 | 24 | .573 | .626 | 0 | — | 0 | -2 | -2 | 0 | -0.3 |

YEAR TM/L	W	L	PCT	G	GS	CG	SH	SV	IP	H	HR	BB	SO	RAT	ERA	ERA+	OAV	OOB	BH	AVG	PB	PR	/A	PD	TPI

■ CARL CASHION
Cashion, Jay Carl b: 6/6/1891, Mecklenburg, N.C. d: 11/17/35, Lake Millicent, Wis. BL/TR, 6'2", 200 lbs. Deb: 8/04/11

YEAR TM/L	W	L	PCT	G	GS	CG	SH	SV	IP	H	HR	BB	SO	RAT	ERA	ERA+	OAV	OOB	BH	AVG	PB	PR	/A	PD	TPI
1911 Was-A	1	5	.167	11	9	5	0	0	71¹	67	4	47	26	15.3	4.16	79	.220	.338	12	.324	2	-6	-7	1	-0.3
1912 Was-A	10	6	.625	26	17	13	1	1	170¹	150	4	103	84	13.6	3.17	105	.250	.365	22	.214	2	3	3	-0	0.7
1913 Was-A	1	1	.500	4	3	0	0	0	9	7	0	14	3	24.0	6.00	49	.269	.558	3	.250	0	-3	-3	1	-0.1
1914 Was-A	0	1	.000	2	1	0	0	0	5	4	0	6	1	19.8	10.80	24	.250	.478	0	.000	-0	-4	-4	0	-0.3
Total 4	12	13	.480	43	30	18	1	1	255²	228	8	170	114	14.6	3.70	89	.241	.366	37	.242	5	-11	-11	1	-0.0

■ LARRY CASIAN
Casian, Lawrence Paul b: 10/28/65, Lynwood, Cal. BR/TL, 6', 170 lbs. Deb: 90

YEAR TM/L	W	L	PCT	G	GS	CG	SH	SV	IP	H	HR	BB	SO	RAT	ERA	ERA+	OAV	OOB	BH	AVG	PB	PR	/A	PD	TPI
1990 Min-A	2	1	.667	5	3	0	0	0	22¹	26	2	4	11	12.1	3.22	130	.306	.337	0	—	0	2	2	0	0.2

■ CRAIG CASKEY
Caskey, Craig Douglas b: 12/11/49, Visalia, Cal. BB/TL, 5'11", 185 lbs. Deb: 7/19/73

YEAR TM/L	W	L	PCT	G	GS	CG	SH	SV	IP	H	HR	BB	SO	RAT	ERA	ERA+	OAV	OOB	BH	AVG	PB	PR	/A	PD	TPI
1973 Mon-N	0	0	—	9	1	0	0	0	14¹	15	3	4	6	12.6	5.65	67	.278	.339	0	.000	-0	-3	-3	0	-0.2

■ ED CASSIAN
Cassian, Edwin b: Connecticut 5'8", 160 lbs. Deb: 6/26/1891

YEAR TM/L	W	L	PCT	G	GS	CG	SH	SV	IP	H	HR	BB	SO	RAT	ERA	ERA+	OAV	OOB	BH	AVG	PB	PR	/A	PD	TPI
1891 Phi-N	1	3	.250	6	4	3	0	0	38	40	0	16	10	13.3	2.84	120	.260	.330	2	.118	-1	2	2	1	0.1
Was-a	2	4	.333	7	5	5	0	0	53	73	4	35	14	18.3	5.60	67	.316	.407	9	.346	2	-11	-11	0	-0.6

■ JOHN CASSIDY
Cassidy, John P. b: 1857, Brooklyn, N.Y. d: 7/2/1891, Brooklyn, N.Y. TL, 5'8", 168 lbs. Deb: 4/24/1875 ♦

YEAR TM/L	W	L	PCT	G	GS	CG	SH	SV	IP	H	HR	BB	SO	RAT	ERA	ERA+	OAV	OOB	BH	AVG	PB	PR	/A	PD	TPI
1875 Atl-n	1	20	.048	30	22	18	0	0	214²	278	6	12		12.2	3.98	58	.276	.284	29	.176	-2	-36	-40		-3.5
1877 Har-N	1	1	.500	2	2	2	0	0	18	24	0	1	2	12.5	5.00	49	.303	.311	95	.378	1	-4	-5	-0	-0.3

■ GEORGE CASTER
Caster, George Jasper "Ug" b: 8/4/07, Colton, Cal. d: 12/18/55, Lakewood, Cal. BR/TR, 6'1.5", 180 lbs. Deb: 9/10/34

YEAR TM/L	W	L	PCT	G	GS	CG	SH	SV	IP	H	HR	BB	SO	RAT	ERA	ERA+	OAV	OOB	BH	AVG	PB	PR	/A	PD	TPI
1934 Phi-A	3	2	.600	5	3	2	0	0	37	32	3	14	15	11.9	3.41	129	.235	.320	4	.267	0	4	4	1	0.5
1935 Phi-A	1	4	.200	25	1	0	0	1	63¹	86	8	37	24	17.8	6.25	73	.322	.408	5	.227	0	-13	-12	2	-0.9
1937 Phi-A	12	19	.387	34	33	19	3	0	231²	227	23	107	100	13.1	4.43	106	.258	.339	19	.211	-1	5	7	0	0.6
1938 Phi-A	16	20	.444	42	40	20	2	1	281¹	310	25	117	112	13.8	4.35	111	.277	.347	20	.198	1	14	15	-2	1.4
1939 Phi-A	9	9	.500	28	17	7	1	0	136	144	16	45	59	12.7	4.90	96	.276	.337	9	.209	-1	-4	-3	0	-0.3
1940 Phi-A	4	19	.174	36	24	11	0	2	178¹	234	18	69	75	15.4	6.56	68	.312	.372	8	.129	-3	-43	-42	-1	-4.0
1941 StL-A	3	7	.300	32	9	3	0	3	104¹	105	12	37	36	12.4	5.00	86	.259	.324	3	.103	-2	-10	-8	1	-0.8
1942 StL-A	8	2	.800	39	0	0	0	5	80	62	3	39	34	11.7	2.81	132	.217	.317	1	.067	-1	8	8	1	0.8
1943 StL-A	6	8	.429	35	0	0	0	8	76¹	69	4	41	43	13.1	2.12	157	.246	.345	10	.136	-1	10	10	0	1.1
1944 StL-A	6	6	.500	42	0	0	0	12	81	91	5	33	46	13.8	2.44	147	.284	.351	5	.250	0	9	10	-1	1.1
1945 StL-A	1	2	.333	10	0	0	0	1	15²	20	0	7	9	15.5	6.89	51	.308	.375	1	.333	0	-6	-6	-0	-0.5
*Det-A	5	1	.833	22	0	0	0	2	51¹	47	3	27	23	13.3	3.86	91	.250	.350	2	.182	0	-3	-2	0	-0.1
Yr	6	3	.667	32	0	0	0	3	67	67	3	34	32	13.8	4.57	77	.265	.356	2	.143	0	-9	-8	-0	-0.6
1946 Det-A	2	1	.667	26	0	0	0	1	41¹	42	1	24	19	14.6	5.66	65	.264	.364	1	.143	-0	-10	-9	1	-0.8
Total 12	76	100	.432	376	127	62	6	39	1377²	1469	121	597	595	13.7	4.54	96	.273	.349	81	.184	-7	-39	-27	1	-1.9

■ TONY CASTILLO
Castillo, Antonio Jose b: 3/1/63, Quibor, Venez. BL/TL, 5'10", 177 lbs. Deb: 8/14/88

YEAR TM/L	W	L	PCT	G	GS	CG	SH	SV	IP	H	HR	BB	SO	RAT	ERA	ERA+	OAV	OOB	BH	AVG	PB	PR	/A	PD	TPI
1988 Tor-A	1	0	1.000	14	0	0	0	0	15	10	2	2	14	7.2	3.00	131	.200	.231	0	—	0	2	2	0	0.2
1989 Tor-A	1	1	.500	17	0	0	0	1	17²	23	0	10	10	17.3	6.11	62	.333	.425	0	—	0	-4	-5	-0	-0.4
Atl-N	0	1	.000	12	0	0	0	0	9¹	8	0	4	5	11.6	4.82	76	.222	.300	0	.000	-0	-1	-1	0	0.0
1990 Atl-N	5	1	.833	52	3	0	0	1	76²	93	5	20	64	13.4	4.23	93	.302	.347	1	.143	0	-4	-3	1	-0.1
Total 3	7	3	.700	95	3	0	0	2	118²	134	7	36	93	13.0	4.40	88	.289	.343	1	.125	0	-8	-7	1	-0.3

■ MANNY CASTILLO
Castillo, Esteban Manuel Antonio (Cabrera) b: 4/1/57, Santo Domingo, D.R. BB/TR, 5'9", 160 lbs. Deb: 9/01/80 ♦

YEAR TM/L	W	L	PCT	G	GS	CG	SH	SV	IP	H	HR	BB	SO	RAT	ERA	ERA+	OAV	OOB	BH	AVG	PB	PR	/A	PD	TPI
1983 Sea-A	0	0	—	1	0	0	0	0	2²	8	3	3	2	40.5	23.63	18	.533	.632	42	.207	1	-6	-6	0	-0.3

■ ROBERT CASTILLO
Castillo, Robert Ernie b: 4/18/55, Los Angeles, Cal. BR/TR, 5'10", 170 lbs. Deb: 9/10/77

YEAR TM/L	W	L	PCT	G	GS	CG	SH	SV	IP	H	HR	BB	SO	RAT	ERA	ERA+	OAV	OOB	BH	AVG	PB	PR	/A	PD	TPI
1977 LA-N	1	0	1.000	6	1	0	0	0	11¹	12	2	2	7	11.1	3.97	96	.279	.311	0	.000	-0	-0	-0	0	0.0
1978 LA-N	0	4	.000	18	0	0	0	1	34	28	2	33	30	16.1	3.97	88	.239	.407	0	.000	-1	-1	-2	0	-0.2
1979 LA-N	2	0	1.000	19	0	0	0	7	24¹	26	0	13	25	14.8	1.11	328	.277	.370	0	.000	-0	7	7	0	0.7
1980 LA-N	8	6	.571	61	0	0	0	0	98¹	70	4	45	60	10.6	2.75	127	.206	.301	1	.111	-0	9	8	1	0.9
1981 *LA-N	2	4	.333	34	1	0	0	5	50²	50	5	24	35	13.1	5.33	62	.262	.344	4	.444	2	-10	-11	-1	-1.0
1982 Min-A	13	11	.542	40	25	6	1	0	218²	194	26	85	123	11.5	3.66	116	.241	.313	0	—	0	10	14	-2	1.3
1983 Min-A	8	12	.400	27	25	3	0	0	158	170	17	65	90	13.4	4.78	89	.278	.348	0	—	0	-13	-9	0	-0.8
1984 Min-A	2	1	.667	10	2	0	0	0	25¹	14	2	19	7	11.7	1.78	237	.177	.337	0	—	0	6	7	-0	0.7
1985 *LA-N	2	2	.500	35	5	0	0	0	68	59	9	41	57	13.4	5.43	64	.230	.339	1	.100	-0	-14	-15	0	-1.4
Total 9	38	40	.487	250	59	9	1	18	688²	623	67	327	434	12.5	3.95	99	.246	.333	6	.154	0	-6	-2	-1	-0.3

■ SLICK CASTLEMAN
Castleman, Clydell b: 9/8/13, Donelson, Tenn. BR/TR, 6', 185 lbs. Deb: 5/09/34

YEAR TM/L	W	L	PCT	G	GS	CG	SH	SV	IP	H	HR	BB	SO	RAT	ERA	ERA+	OAV	OOB	BH	AVG	PB	PR	/A	PD	TPI
1934 NY-N	1	0	1.000	7	1	0	0	0	16²	14	1	10	5	15.1	5.40	72	.277	.373	1	.250	1	-2	-3	1	-0.1
1935 NY-N	15	6	.714	29	25	9	1	0	173²	186	14	64	64	13.0	4.09	94	.268	.330	12	.179	-0	-1	-5	1	-0.3
1936 *NY-N	4	7	.364	29	12	2	1	1	111²	148	6	56	54	16.8	5.64	69	.323	.403	5	.128	-1	-20	-22	0	-2.0
1937 NY-N	11	6	.647	23	23	10	2	0	160¹	148	19	33	78	10.2	3.31	117	.247	.287	4	.070	-5	11	10	-3	0.3
1938 NY-N	4	5	.444	21	14	4	0	0	90²	108	4	37	18	14.7	4.17	90	.296	.365	3	.097	-1	-4	-4	-1	-0.5
1939 NY-N	1	2	.333	12	4	0	0	0	33²	36	1	23	6	15.8	4.54	86	.286	.396	3	.333	1	-2	-2	-0	-0.1
Total 6	36	26	.581	121	79	25	4	1	586²	644	45	223	225	13.4	4.25	91	.279	.345	28	.135	-6	-19	-25	-1	-2.7

■ ROY CASTLETON
Castleton, Royal Eugene b: 7/26/1885, Salt Lake City, Utah d: 6/24/67, Los Angeles, Cal. BR/TL, 5'11", 167 lbs. Deb: 4/16/07

YEAR TM/L	W	L	PCT	G	GS	CG	SH	SV	IP	H	HR	BB	SO	RAT	ERA	ERA+	OAV	OOB	BH	AVG	PB	PR	/A	PD	TPI
1907 NY-A	1	1	.500	3	2	1	0	0	16	11	1	3	3	7.9	2.81	100	.196	.237	0	.000	-1	-0	-0	0	0.0
1909 Cin-N	1	1	.500	4	1	1	0	0	14	14	0	6	5	14.1	1.93	135	.275	.373	2	.667	1	1	1	0	0.3
1910 Cin-N	1	2	.333	4	2	1	0	0	13²	15	0	6	5	14.5	3.29	89	.288	.373	0	.000	-1	-0	-1	0	0.0
Total 3	3	4	.429	11	5	3	0	0	43²	40	1	15	13	12.0	2.68	104	.252	.328	2	.154	-0	0	0	0	0.3

■ PAUL CASTNER
Castner, Paul Henry "Lefty" b: 2/16/1897, St.Paul, Minn. d: 3/3/86, St.Paul, Minn. BL/TL, 5'11", 187 lbs. Deb: 8/06/23

YEAR TM/L	W	L	PCT	G	GS	CG	SH	SV	IP	H	HR	BB	SO	RAT	ERA	ERA+	OAV	OOB	BH	AVG	PB	PR	/A	PD	TPI
1923 Chi-A	0	0	—	6	0	0	0	0	10	14	0	5	0	17.1	6.30	63	.326	.396	0	.000	-0	-3	-3	0	-0.2

■ BILL CASTRO
Castro, William Radhames (Checo) b: 12/13/53, Santiago, D.R. BR/TR, 5'11", 170 lbs. Deb: 8/20/74

YEAR TM/L	W	L	PCT	G	GS	CG	SH	SV	IP	H	HR	BB	SO	RAT	ERA	ERA+	OAV	OOB	BH	AVG	PB	PR	/A	PD	TPI
1974 Mil-A	0	0	—	8	0	0	0	0	18	19	2	5	10	12.0	4.50	80	.264	.312	0	—	0	-2	-2	0	-0.1
1975 Mil-A	3	2	.600	18	5	0	0	1	75	78	3	17	25	11.6	2.52	152	.272	.317	0	—	0	10	11	0	1.2
1976 Mil-A	4	6	.400	39	0	0	0	8	70¹	70	4	19	23	11.8	3.45	101	.265	.322	0	—	0	1	1	0	0.0
1977 Mil-A	8	6	.571	51	0	0	0	13	69¹	76	7	23	28	13.1	4.15	98	.293	.356	0	—	0	-1	-1	1	-0.1
1978 Mil-A	5	4	.556	42	0	0	0	8	49²	43	2	14	17	11.4	1.81	204	.234	.309	0	—	0	11	11	0	1.2
1979 Mil-A	3	1	.750	39	0	0	0	6	44¹	40	4	17	21	10.8	2.03	205	.244	.299	0	—	0	11	11	-0	1.1
1980 Mil-A	2	4	.333	56	0	0	0	8	84¹	89	2	17	32	11.5	2.77	139	.274	.314	0	—	0	12	10	1	1.2
1981 NY-A	1	1	.500	11	0	0	0	0	19	26	2	5	4	14.7	3.79	94	.329	.369	0	—	0	-0	-0	0	0.0
1982 KC-A	3	2	.600	21	4	0	0	1	75²	72	8	20	37	11.2	3.45	118	.243	.296	0	—	0	5	5	1	0.4
1983 KC-A	2	0	1.000	18	0	0	0	0	40²	51	4	12	17	15.0	6.64	61	.300	.364	0	—	0	-12	-12	0	-1.0
Total 10	31	26	.544	303	9	0	0	45	546¹	564	36	145	203	12.0	3.33	117	.269	.322	0	—	0	35	34	1	3.8

■ ELI CATES
Cates, Eli Eldo b: 1/26/1877, Greensfork, Ind. d: 5/29/64, Richmond, Ind. BR/TR, 5'9.5", 175 lbs. Deb: 4/20/08 ♦

YEAR TM/L	W	L	PCT	G	GS	CG	SH	SV	IP	H	HR	BB	SO	RAT	ERA	ERA+	OAV	OOB	BH	AVG	PB	PR	/A	PD	TPI
1908 Was-A	4	8	.333	19	10	7	0	0	114²	112	1	32	33	11.4	2.51	91	.261	.314	11	.186	1	-1	-3	1	-0.2

■ TED CATHER
Cather, Theodore P b: 5/20/1889, Chester, Pa. d: 4/9/45, Elkton, Md. BR/TR, 5'10.5", 178 lbs. Deb: 9/23/12 ♦

YEAR TM/L	W	L	PCT	G	GS	CG	SH	SV	IP	H	HR	BB	SO	RAT	ERA	ERA+	OAV	OOB	BH	AVG	PB	PR	/A	PD	TPI
1913 StL-N	0	0	—	1	0	0	0	0	0¹	1	0	2	0	108.0	54.00	6	.500	.800	39	.213	0	-2	-2	0	-0.1

YEAR TM/L	W	L	PCT	G	GS	CG	SH	SV	IP	H	HR	BB	SO	RAT	ERA	ERA+	OAV	OOB	BH	AVG	PB	PR	/A	PD	TPI

■ HARDIN CATHEY Cathey, Hardin "Lil Abner" b: 7/6/19, Burns, Tenn. BR/TR, 6'4", 190 lbs. Deb: 4/16/42

| 1942 Was-A | 1 | 1 | .500 | 12 | 2 | 0 | 0 | 0 | 30¹ | 44 | 4 | 16 | 8 | 17.8 | 7.42 | 49 | .341 | .414 | 3 | .375 | 1 | -13 | -13 | -0 | -1.1 |

■ KEEFE CATO Cato, John Keefe b: 5/6/58, Yonkers, N.Y. BR/TR, 6'1", 185 lbs. Deb: 6/13/83

1983 Cin-N	1	0	1.000	4	0	0	0	0	3²	2	0	1	3	7.4	2.45	155	.154	.214	0	—	0	0	1	0	0.0
1984 Cin-N	0	1	.000	8	0	0	0	1	15²	22	5	4	12	14.9	8.04	47	.344	.382	2	.500	1	-8	-7	0	-0.5
Total 2	1	1	.500	12	0	0	0	1	19¹	24	5	5	15	13.5	6.98	54	.312	.354	2	.500	1	-7	-7	0	-0.5

■ JOHN CATTANACH Cattanach, John Leckie b: 5/10/1863, Providence, R.I. d: 11/10/26, Providence, R.I. 5'10", 190 lbs. Deb: 6/05/1884

| 1884 Pro-N | 0 | 0 | — | 1 | 1 | 0 | 0 | 0 | 5 | 2 | 0 | 4 | 2 | 10.8 | 9.00 | 31 | .116 | .282 | 0 | .000 | -1 | -3 | -3 | -0 | -0.2 |
| StL-U | 1 | 1 | .500 | 2 | 2 | 2 | 0 | 0 | 17 | 12 | 0 | 4 | 13 | 8.5 | 2.12 | 140 | .185 | .232 | 0 | .000 | -1 | 2 | 2 | 0 | 0.0 |

■ BILL CAUDILL Caudill, William Holland b: 7/13/56, Santa Monica, Cal. BR/TR, 6'1", 190 lbs. Deb: 5/12/79

1979 Chi-N	1	7	.125	29	12	0	0	0	90	89	16	41	104	13.4	4.80	86	.255	.340	1	.059	-2	-11	-7	-0	-0.7
1980 Chi-N	4	6	.400	72	2	0	0	1	127²	100	6	59	112	11.3	2.19	179	.223	.314	2	.222	0	20	25	-2	2.5
1981 Chi-N	1	5	.167	30	10	0	0	0	71	87	9	31	45	15.2	5.83	63	.301	.373	2	.143	-1	-18	-17	-1	-1.7
1982 Sea-A	12	9	.571	70	0	0	0	26	95²	65	9	35	111	9.5	2.35	180	.192	.270	0	—	0	18	20	-2	1.9
1983 Sea-A	2	8	.200	63	0	0	0	26	72²	70	10	38	73	13.6	4.71	90	.257	.353	0	—	0	-5	-4	-1	-0.4
1984 Oak-A	9	7	.563	68	0	0	0	36	96¹	77	9	31	89	10.1	2.71	138	.218	.281	0	.000	0	14	11	-2	0.9
1985 Tor-A	4	6	.400	67	0	0	0	14	69¹	53	9	35	44	11.7	2.99	141	.209	.310	0	—	0	9	9	-1	0.8
1986 Tor-A	2	4	.333	40	0	0	0	2	36¹	36	6	17	32	13.6	6.19	68	.254	.342	0	—	0	-8	-8	-1	-0.7
1987 Oak-A	0	0	—	6	0	0	0	1	8	10	3	1	8	12.4	9.00	46	.294	.314	0	—	0	-4	-4	-0	-0.3
Total 9	35	52	.402	445	24	0	0	106	667	587	81	288	620	12.0	3.68	110	.237	.320	5	.122	-1	14	26	-9	2.3

■ RED CAUSEY Causey, Cecil Algernon b: 8/11/1893, Georgetown, Fla. d: 11/11/60, Avon Park, Fla. BR/TR, 6'1", 160 lbs. Deb: 4/26/18

1918 NY-N	11	6	.647	29	18	10	2	2	158¹	143	2	42	48	10.9	2.79	94	.245	.304	6	.125	-3	-0	-3	-1	-0.6
1919 NY-N	9	3	.750	19	16	6	0	0	105	99	5	38	25	11.9	3.69	76	.251	.320	5	.132	-1	-9	-10	-0	-1.2
Bos-N	4	5	.444	10	10	3	0	0	69	81	1	20	14	13.3	4.57	63	.308	.359	2	.095	-2	-13	-13	0	-1.4
Yr	13	8	.619	29	26	9	0	0	174	180	6	58	39	12.4	4.03	70	.273	.333	2	.034	-3	-22	-23	-0	-2.6
1920 Phi-N	7	14	.333	35	26	11	1	3	181¹	203	4	79	30	14.2	4.32	79	.299	.376	11	.186	-2	-24	-18	-1	-2.1
1921 Phi-N	3	3	.500	7	7	4	0	0	50²	58	4	11	8	12.4	2.84	149	.294	.335	3	.150	-1	5	8	0	0.7
NY-N	1	1	.500	7	1	0	0	0	14²	13	0	6	1	11.7	2.45	149	.228	.302	1	.333	0	2	2	-0	0.2
Yr	4	4	.500	14	8	4	0	0	65¹	71	4	17	9	12.1	2.76	149	.278	.324	4	.000	-1	7	10	-0	0.9
1922 NY-N	4	3	.571	24	2	1	0	1	70²	69	2	34	13	13.1	3.18	126	.262	.347	5	.238	1	7	6	1	0.7
Total 5	39	35	.527	131	80	35	3	6	649²	666	18	230	139	12.6	3.59	89	.273	.340	33	.157	-9	-31	-29	-1	-3.7

■ PUG CAVET Cavet, Tiller H. b: 12/26/1889, Mcgregor, Tex. d: 8/4/66, San Luis Obispo, Cal. TL, 6'3", 176 lbs. Deb: 4/25/11

1911 Det-A	0	0	—	1	1	0	0	0	4	6	0	1	1	15.8	4.50	77	.316	.350	0	.000	-0	-1	-0	0	0.0
1914 Det-A	7	7	.500	31	14	6	1	2	151¹	129	2	44	51	10.8	2.44	115	.238	.306	5	.106	-2	5	6	1	0.6
1915 Det-A	4	2	.667	17	7	2	0	1	71	83	1	22	26	13.6	4.06	75	.300	.355	6	.250	2	-9	-8	0	-0.6
Total 3	11	9	.550	49	22	8	1	3	226¹	218	3	67	78	11.8	2.98	97	.260	.323	11	.153	-0	-4	-2	1	0.0

■ JOSE CECENA Cecena, Jose Isabel (Lugo) b: 8/20/63, Ciudad Obregon, Mexico BR/TR, 5'11", 180 lbs. Deb: 4/06/88

| 1988 Tex-A | 0 | 0 | — | 22 | 0 | 0 | 0 | 1 | 26¹ | 20 | 2 | 23 | 27 | 15.4 | 4.78 | 85 | .213 | .378 | 0 | — | 0 | -2 | -2 | -0 | -0.1 |

■ ART CECCARELLI Ceccarelli, Arthur Edward "Chic" b: 4/2/30, New Haven, Conn. BR/TL, 6', 190 lbs. Deb: 5/03/55

1955 KC-A	4	7	.364	31	16	3	1	0	123²	123	20	71	68	14.1	5.31	79	.258	.354	3	.079	-3	-19	-16	-2	-1.9
1956 KC-A	0	1	.000	3	2	0	0	0	10	13	3	4	2	16.2	7.20	60	.317	.391	0	.000	-0	-3	-3	1	-0.2
1957 Bal-A	0	5	.000	20	8	1	0	0	58	62	3	31	30	14.7	4.50	80	.278	.371	0	.000	-1	-5	-6	-1	-0.7
1959 Chi-N	5	5	.500	18	15	4	2	0	102	95	19	37	56	11.7	4.76	83	.245	.312	3	.091	-1	-9	-9	-1	-1.0
1960 Chi-N	0	0	—	7	1	0	0	0	13	16	1	4	10	13.8	5.54	68	.296	.345	0	—	0	-3	-3	0	-0.2
Total 5	9	18	.333	79	42	8	3	0	306²	309	46	147	166	13.5	5.05	79	.261	.345	6	.068	-6	-38	-37	-3	-4.0

■ REX CECIL Cecil, Rex Rolston b: 10/8/16, Lindsay, Okla. d: 10/30/66, Long Beach, Cal. BL/TR, 6'3", 195 lbs. Deb: 8/13/44

1944 Bos-A	4	5	.444	11	9	4	0	0	61	72	5	33	33	15.6	5.16	66	.286	.371	5	.278	1	-12	-12	-0	-1.0
1945 Bos-A	2	5	.286	7	7	1	0	0	45	46	4	27	30	14.6	5.20	66	.261	.360	6	.300	1	-9	-9	1	-0.7
Total 2	6	10	.375	18	16	5	0	0	106	118	9	60	63	15.2	5.18	66	.276	.366	11	.289	2	-21	-21	0	-1.7

■ PETE CENTER Center, Marvin Earl b: 4/22/12, Hazel Green, Ky. BR/TR, 6'4", 190 lbs. Deb: 9/11/42

1942 Cle-A	0	0	—	1	0	0	0	0	3¹	7	0	4	0	32.4	16.20	21	.438	.571	0	.000	-0	-5	-5	0	-0.3
1943 Cle-A	1	2	.333	24	1	0	0	1	42¹	29	3	18	10	10.0	2.76	112	.201	.290	0	.000	-1	3	2	-0	0.1
1945 Cle-A	6	3	.667	31	8	2	0	1	85²	89	2	28	34	12.4	3.99	81	.270	.329	2	.091	-2	-6	-7	-2	-1.0
1946 Cle-A	0	2	.000	21	0	0	0	1	29	29	2	20	6	15.5	4.97	67	.269	.388	0	.000	-0	-5	-5	0	-0.5
Total 4	7	7	.500	77	9	2	0	3	160¹	154	7	70	50	12.7	4.10	79	.258	.338	2	.065	-3	-13	-16	-2	-1.7

■ RICK CERONE Cerone, Richard Aldo b: 5/19/54, Newark, N.J. BR/TR, 5'11", 192 lbs. Deb: 8/17/75 ♦

| 1987 NY-A | 0 | 0 | — | 2 | 0 | 0 | 0 | 0 | 2 | 0 | 0 | 1 | 1 | 4.5 | 0.00 | — | .000 | .143 | 69 | .243 | 1 | 1 | 1 | 0 | 0.1 |

■ JOHN CERUTTI Cerutti, John Joseph b: 4/28/60, Albany, N.Y. BL/TL, 6'2", 195 lbs. Deb: 9/01/85

1985 Tor-A	0	2	.000	4	1	0	0	0	6²	10	1	4	5	20.3	5.40	78	.323	.417	0	—	0	-1	-1	0	0.0
1986 Tor-A	9	4	.692	34	20	2	1	1	145¹	150	25	47	89	12.3	4.15	102	.268	.326	0	—	0	1	0	0	0.1
1987 Tor-A	11	4	.733	44	21	2	0	0	151¹	144	30	59	92	12.1	4.40	102	.251	.322	0	—	0	1	2	-1	0.0
1988 Tor-A	6	7	.462	46	12	0	0	1	123²	120	12	42	65	12.0	3.13	126	.256	.322	0	—	0	11	11	3	1.4
1989 •Tor-A	11	11	.500	33	31	3	1	0	205¹	214	19	53	69	12.0	3.07	123	.273	.323	0	—	0	19	16	4	2.1
1990 Tor-A	9	9	.500	30	23	0	0	0	140	162	23	49	49	13.8	4.76	80	.297	.359	0	—	0	-13	-15	0	-1.4
Total 6	46	37	.554	191	108	7	2	2	772¹	800	110	254	369	12.5	3.87	104	.270	.331	0	—	0	17	13	6	2.2

■ RAY CHADWICK Chadwick, Ray Charles b: 11/17/62, Durham, N.C. BB/TR, 6'2", 180 lbs. Deb: 7/29/86

| 1986 Cal-A | 0 | 5 | .000 | 7 | 7 | 0 | 0 | 0 | 27¹ | 39 | 5 | 15 | 9 | 18.1 | 7.24 | 57 | .336 | .417 | 0 | — | 0 | -9 | -10 | 0 | -0.8 |

■ LEON CHAGNON Chagnon, Leon Wilbur "Shag" b: 9/28/02, Pittsfield, N.H. d: 7/30/53, Amesbury, Mass. BR/TR, 6', 182 lbs. Deb: 10/05/29

1929 Pit-N	0	0	—	1	1	0	0	0	7	11	1	1	4	15.4	9.00	53	.333	.353	0	.000	-0	-3	-3	0	-0.2
1930 Pit-N	0	3	.000	18	4	3	0	0	62	92	9	23	27	17.4	6.82	73	.355	.418	4	.200	-1	-13	-13	0	-1.0
1932 Pit-N	9	6	.600	30	10	4	1	0	128	140	10	34	52	12.4	3.94	97	.276	.324	9	.225	2	-1	-2	-0	-0.1
1933 Pit-N	6	4	.600	39	5	1	0	1	100	100	8	17	35	10.8	3.69	90	.259	.296	1	.048	-2	-4	-4	-1	-0.6
1934 Pit-N	4	1	.800	33	1	0	0	0	58	68	5	24	19	14.4	4.81	86	.288	.356	3	.231	0	-5	-4	1	-0.2
1935 NY-N	0	2	.000	14	1	0	0	1	38¹	32	7	5	16	8.7	3.52	109	.232	.259	0	.000	-1	2	1	0	0.0
Total 6	19	16	.543	135	22	8	1	3	393¹	443	34	104	153	12.8	4.51	87	.284	.333	17	.162	-2	-24	-25	-1	-2.1

■ BOB CHAKALES Chakales, Robert Edward "Chick" b: 8/10/27, Asheville, N.C. BR/TR, 6'1", 185 lbs. Deb: 4/21/51

1951 Cle-A	3	4	.429	17	10	2	1	0	68¹	80	3	43	32	16.2	4.74	80	.292	.388	7	.350	2	-5	-7	-0	-0.4
1952 Cle-A	1	2	.333	5	1	0	0	0	12	19	2	8	7	20.3	9.75	34	.388	.474	2	.500	1	-8	-9	-0	-0.7
1953 Cle-A	0	2	.000	7	3	1	0	0	27	28	2	10	6	13.0	2.67	141	.283	.355	2	.500	0	4	3	0	0.4
1954 Cle-A	2	0	1.000	9	1	0	0	0	10¹	4	0	12	9	13.9	0.87	422	.114	.340	1	.333	1	3	3	-0	0.4
Bal-A	3	7	.300	38	6	0	0	3	89¹	81	8	43	44	12.6	3.73	96	.245	.333	8	.364	2	-0	-1	0	0.1
Yr	5	7	.417	41	6	0	0	3	99²	85	8	55	47	12.7	3.43	105	.232	.334	1	.040	3	3	2	-0	0.5

YEAR	TM/L	W	L	PCT	G	GS	CG	SH	SV	IP	H	HR	BB	SO	RAT	ERA	ERA+	OAV	OOB	BH	AVG	PB	PR	/A	PD	TPI
1955	Chi-A	0	0	—	7	0	0	0	0	12¹	11	2	6	6	12.4	1.46	271	.256	.347	0	.000	-0	3	3	0	0.3
	Was-A	2	3	.400	29	0	0	0	0	54²	55	4	25	28	13.3	5.27	73	.263	.345	0	.000	-1	-8	-9	1	-0.8
	Yr	2	3	.400	36	0	0	0	0	67	66	6	31	34	13.2	4.57	84	.262	.345	0	.000	-1	-5	-5	1	-0.5
1956	Was-A	4	4	.500	43	1	0	0	4	96	94	3	57	33	14.4	4.03	107	.268	.375	3	.150	-1	1	3	2	0.4
1957	Was-A	0	1	.000	4	2	0	0	0	18¹	20	2	10	12	14.7	5.40	72	.274	.361	1	.143	0	-3	-3	0	-0.1
	Bos-A	0	2	.000	18	0	0	0	3	32	53	5	11	16	18.3	8.16	49	.379	.428	2	.667	1	-16	-15	-1	-1.3
	Yr	0	3	.000	22	2	0	0	3	50¹	73	7	21	28	17.0	7.15	55	.341	.403	0	.000	1	-19	-18	-0	-1.4
Total	7	15	25	.375	171	23	3	1	10	420¹	445	31	225	187	14.5	4.54	85	.277	.369	26	.271	4	-28	-31	1	-1.7

■ GEORGE CHALMERS

Chalmers, George W. "Dut"   b: 6/7/1888, Edinburgh, Scot.   d: 8/5/60, Bronx, N.Y.   BR/TR, 6'1", 189 lbs.   Deb: 9/21/10

YEAR	TM/L	W	L	PCT	G	GS	CG	SH	SV	IP	H	HR	BB	SO	RAT	ERA	ERA+	OAV	OOB	BH	AVG	PB	PR	/A	PD	TPI
1910	Phi-N	1	1	.500	4	3	2	0	0	22	21	0	11	12	13.5	5.32	59	.280	.379	1	.143	-0	-6	-5	1	-0.3
1911	Phi-N	13	10	.565	38	22	11	3	4	208²	196	5	101	101	13.0	3.11	111	.256	.346	13	.178	-1	7	8	-1	0.6
1912	Phi-N	3	4	.429	12	8	3	0	0	57²	64	4	37	22	16.1	3.28	111	.288	.395	3	.188	-0	1	2	-2	0.1
1913	Phi-N	3	10	.231	26	13	4	0	1	116	133	3	51	46	14.7	4.81	69	.296	.374	7	.212	-1	-21	-19	1	-1.8
1914	Phi-N	0	3	.000	3	2	1	0	0	18	23	0	15	6	19.5	5.50	53	.324	.448	0	.000	-1	-5	-5	0	-0.5
1915	*Phi-N	8	9	.471	26	20	13	1	1	170¹	159	3	45	82	10.8	2.48	110	.255	.305	10	.169	-0	5	5	1	0.5
1916	Phi-N	1	4	.200	12	8	2	0	0	53²	49	2	19	21	11.7	3.19	83	.244	.315	0	.000	-2	-3	-3	0	-0.4
Total	7	29	41	.414	121	76	36	4	6	646¹	645	17	279	290	13.1	3.41	93	.268	.348	34	.163	-5	-22	-18	1	-1.8

■ CRAIG CHAMBERLAIN

Chamberlain, Craig Philip   b: 2/2/57, Hollywood, Cal.   BR/TR, 6'1", 190 lbs.   Deb: 8/12/79

YEAR	TM/L	W	L	PCT	G	GS	CG	SH	SV	IP	H	HR	BB	SO	RAT	ERA	ERA+	OAV	OOB	BH	AVG	PB	PR	/A	PD	TPI
1979	KC-A	4	4	.500	10	10	4	0	0	69²	68	7	18	30	11.2	3.75	114	.261	.311	0	—	0	4	4	-2	0.2
1980	KC-A	0	1	.000	5	0	0	0	0	9¹	10	3	5	3	14.5	6.75	60	.270	.357	0	—	0	-3	-3	0	-0.2
Total	2	4	5	.444	15	10	4	0	0	79	78	10	23	33	11.6	4.10	103	.262	.317	0	—	0	1	1	-2	0.0

■ ELTON CHAMBERLAIN

Chamberlain, Elton P. "Icebox"   b: 11/5/1867, Buffalo, N.Y.   d: 9/22/29, Baltimore, Md.   BR/TR, 5'9", 168 lbs.   Deb: 9/13/1886

YEAR	TM/L	W	L	PCT	G	GS	CG	SH	SV	IP	H	HR	BB	SO	RAT	ERA	ERA+	OAV	OOB	BH	AVG	PB	PR	/A	PD	TPI
1886	Lou-a	0	3	.000	4	4	4	0	0	31¹	39	0	17	18	16.1	6.61	55	.291	.371	3	.158	-0	-11	-10	0	-0.7
1887	Lou-a	18	16	.529	36	36	35	1	0	309	340	8	117	118	13.3	3.79	116	.269	.331	26	.198	-3	17	21	1	1.6
1888	Lou-a	14	9	.609	24	24	21	1	0	196	177	2	59	119	10.8	2.53	122	.232	.287	18	.191	1	12	12	1	1.3
	*StL-a	11	2	.846	14	14	13	1	0	112	61	1	27	57	7.1	1.61	203	.154	.208	5	.100	-3	18	21	-1	1.7
	Yr	25	11	.694	38	38	34	2	0	308	238	3	86	176	9.5	2.19	143	.206	.261	9	.063	-3	30	33	-0	3.0
1889	StL-a	32	15	.681	53	51	44	3	1	421²	376	8	165	202	11.5	2.97	142	.231	.302	34	.199	-2	41	59	-3	5.1
1890	StL-a	3	1	.750	5	5	3	0	0	35	47	1	26	14	18.8	5.91	73	.312	.413	2	.133	-1	-8	-6	0	-0.5
	Col-a	12	6	.667	25	21	19	6	0	175	128	2	70	114	10.2	2.21	162	.198	.276	15	.231	3	32	27	-2	2.5
	Yr	15	7	.682	30	26	22	6	0	210	175	3	96	128	11.6	2.83	131	.220	.303	7	.087	1	24	21	-2	2.0
1891	Phi-a	22	23	.489	49	46	44	0	0	405²	397	10	206	204	13.4	4.22	91	.248	.333	33	.188	2	-22	-18	-0	-1.6
1892	Cin-N	19	23	.452	52	49	43	2	0	406¹	391	8	170	169	12.4	3.39	96	.243	.315	36	.225	3	-5	-5	-5	-0.6
1893	Cin-N	16	12	.571	34	27	19	1	0	241	248	3	112	59	13.4	3.73	128	.258	.335	19	.196	-4	25	28	-2	2.0
1894	Cin-N	10	9	.526	23	22	18	1	0	177²	220	10	91	57	15.8	5.77	96	.301	.378	22	.314	5	-9	-4	-1	0.0
1896	Cle-N	0	1	.000	2	2	1	0	0	11	21	0	5	2	21.3	7.36	62	.399	.452	0	.000	-0	-4	-3	-0	-0.2
Total	10	157	120	.567	321	301	264	16	1	2521²	2445	63	1065	1133	12.5	3.57	112	.246	.319	213	.203	-2	88	119	-12	11.0

■ BILL CHAMBERLAIN

Chamberlain, William Vincent   b: 4/21/09, Stoughton, Mass.   BR/TL, 5'10.5", 173 lbs.   Deb: 8/02/32

YEAR	TM/L	W	L	PCT	G	GS	CG	SH	SV	IP	H	HR	BB	SO	RAT	ERA	ERA+	OAV	OOB	BH	AVG	PB	PR	/A	PD	TPI
1932	Chi-A	0	5	.000	12	5	0	0	0	41¹	39	3	25	11	13.9	4.57	95	.250	.354	1	.100	-1	-0	-1	-1	-0.1

■ CLIFF CHAMBERS

Chambers, Clifford Day "Lefty"   b: 1/10/22, Portland, Ore.   BL/TL, 6'3", 208 lbs.   Deb: 4/24/48

YEAR	TM/L	W	L	PCT	G	GS	CG	SH	SV	IP	H	HR	BB	SO	RAT	ERA	ERA+	OAV	OOB	BH	AVG	PB	PR	/A	PD	TPI
1948	Chi-N	2	9	.182	29	12	3	1	0	103²	100	4	48	51	13.1	4.43	88	.254	.339	4	.133	-1	-5	-6	0	-0.6
1949	Pit-N	13	7	.650	34	21	10	1	0	177¹	186	15	58	93	12.6	3.96	106	.268	.329	13	.236	3	2	5	0	0.8
1950	Pit-N	12	15	.444	37	33	11	2	0	249¹	262	18	92	93	13.0	4.30	102	.265	.332	26	.289	7	-4	2	-2	0.8
1951	Pit-N	3	6	.333	10	10	2	1	0	59²	64	5	31	19	14.9	5.58	76	.276	.371	7	.333	2	-11	-9	-2	-0.7
	StL-N	11	6	.647	21	16	9	1	0	129¹	120	13	56	45	12.2	3.83	104	.251	.329	8	.163	0	2	2	-1	0.1
	Yr	14	12	.538	31	26	11	2	0	189	184	18	87	64	12.9	4.38	92	.257	.338	4	.057	2	-9	-7	-3	-0.6
1952	StL-N	4	4	.500	26	13	2	1	1	98¹	110	8	33	47	13.3	4.12	90	.285	.344	9	.281	3	-4	-4	0	0.0
1953	StL-N	3	6	.333	32	8	0	0	0	79²	82	7	43	26	14.2	4.86	88	.266	.358	2	.118	-1	-5	-5	0	-0.4
Total	6	48	53	.475	189	113	37	7	1	897¹	924	70	361	374	13.1	4.29	96	.266	.338	69	.235	14	-26	-16	-4	0.0

■ ROME CHAMBERS

Chambers, Jerome   b: 8/1874, Weaverville, N.C.   BL/TL, 6'2", 173 lbs.   Deb: 5/07/00

YEAR	TM/L	W	L	PCT	G	GS	CG	SH	SV	IP	H	HR	BB	SO	RAT	ERA	ERA+	OAV	OOB	BH	AVG	PB	PR	/A	PD	TPI
1900	Bos-N	0	0	—	1	0	0	0	1	4	5	0	5	2	22.5	11.25	37	.305	.467	0	.000	-0	-3	-3	-0	-0.2

■ JOHNNIE CHAMBERS

Chambers, Johnnie Monroe   b: 9/10/11, Copper Hill, Tenn   d: 5/11/77, Palatka, Fla.   BL/TR, 6', 185 lbs.   Deb: 5/04/37

YEAR	TM/L	W	L	PCT	G	GS	CG	SH	SV	IP	H	HR	BB	SO	RAT	ERA	ERA+	OAV	OOB	BH	AVG	PB	PR	/A	PD	TPI
1937	StL-N	0	0	—	2	0	0	0	0	2	5	0	2	1	31.5	18.00	22	.455	.538	0	—	0	-3	-3	-0	-0.2

■ BILL CHAMBERS

Chambers, William Christopher   b: 9/13/1889, Cameron, W.Va.   d: 3/27/62, Fort Wayne, Ind.   5'9", 185 lbs.   Deb: 7/11/10

YEAR	TM/L	W	L	PCT	G	GS	CG	SH	SV	IP	H	HR	BB	SO	RAT	ERA	ERA+	OAV	OOB	BH	AVG	PB	PR	/A	PD	TPI
1910	StL-N	0	0	—	1	0	0	0	0	1	1	0	0	0	9.0	0.00	—	.250	.250	0	—	0	0	0	0	0.00

■ BILL CHAMPION

Champion, Buford Billy   b: 9/18/47, Shelby, N.C.   BR/TR, 6'4", 188 lbs.   Deb: 6/04/69

YEAR	TM/L	W	L	PCT	G	GS	CG	SH	SV	IP	H	HR	BB	SO	RAT	ERA	ERA+	OAV	OOB	BH	AVG	PB	PR	/A	PD	TPI
1969	Phi-N	5	10	.333	23	20	4	2	1	116²	130	7	63	70	15.1	5.01	71	.286	.376	6	.171	0	-18	-19	1	-1.7
1970	Phi-N	0	2	.000	7	1	0	0	0	14	21	3	10	12	20.6	9.00	44	.375	.478	0	.000	-0	-8	-8	0	-0.7
1971	Phi-N	3	5	.375	37	9	0	0	0	108²	100	10	48	49	12.5	4.39	80	.249	.334	3	.111	-1	-11	-10	1	-1.0
1972	Phi-N	4	14	.222	30	22	2	0	0	132²	155	11	54	54	14.2	5.09	71	.301	.368	5	.147	0	-24	-22	1	-1.0
1973	Mil-A	5	8	.385	37	11	2	0	1	136¹	139	10	62	67	13.5	3.70	102	.267	.350	0	—	0	2	1	2	0.3
1974	Mil-A	11	4	.733	31	23	2	0	0	161²	168	12	49	65	12.1	3.62	100	.270	.323	0	—	0	-0	-0	-1	0.0
1975	Mil-A	6	6	.500	27	13	3	1	0	110	125	11	55	40	14.7	5.89	65	.290	.370	0	—	0	-26	-25	1	-2.3
1976	Mil-A	0	1	.000	10	3	0	0	0	24¹	35	0	13	8	18.1	7.03	56	.361	.441	0	—	0	-9	-10	1	-0.7
Total	8	34	50	.405	202	102	13	3	2	804¹	873	64	354	360	13.9	4.69	78	.282	.358	14	.141	-1	-95	-93	5	-8.2

■ DEAN CHANCE

Chance, Wilmer Dean   b: 6/1/41, Wayne, O.   BR/TR, 6'3", 200 lbs.   Deb: 9/11/61

YEAR	TM/L	W	L	PCT	G	GS	CG	SH	SV	IP	H	HR	BB	SO	RAT	ERA	ERA+	OAV	OOB	BH	AVG	PB	PR	/A	PD	TPI
1961	LA-A	0	2	.000	5	4	0	0	0	18¹	33	0	5	11	19.1	6.87	66	.412	.453	0	.000	-1	-6	-5	1	-0.3
1962	LA-A	14	10	.583	50	24	6	2	8	206²	195	14	66	127	11.6	2.96	130	.250	.313	4	.062	-4	23	21	1	1.7
1963	LA-A	13	18	.419	45	35	6	2	3	248	229	10	90	168	11.9	3.19	107	.243	.316	12	.150	-1	12	6	1	0.6
1964	LA-A	**20**	9	.690	46	35	**15**	**11**	4	278¹	194	7	86	207	9.1	**1.65**	**199**	.195	.261	7	.079	-5	**61**	**51**	-3	4.8
1965	Cal-A	15	10	.600	36	33	10	4	0	225²	197	12	101	164	12.2	3.15	108	.238	.328	7	.093	-2	8	6	3	0.7
1966	Cal-A	12	17	.414	41	37	11	2	1	259²	206	18	114	180	11.3	3.08	109	.222	.312	2	.026	-6	10	8	2	0.4
1967	Min-A	20	14	.588	41	39	**18**	5	1	283²	244	17	68	220	10.1	2.73	127	.229	.279	3	.033	-6	16	23	1	2.2
1968	Min-A	16	16	.500	43	39	15	6	1	292	224	19	63	234	9.2	2.53	122	.211	.261	5	.054	-6	15	18	3	1.8
1969	*Min-A	5	4	.556	20	15	1	0	0	88¹	76	6	35	50	11.7	2.95	124	.233	.315	1	.042	-1	7	7	-1	0.5
1970	Cle-A	9	8	.529	45	19	1	1	4	155	172	18	59	109	13.8	4.24	93	.287	.357	3	.071	-3	-9	-5	-1	-0.7
	NY-N	0	1	.000	3	0	0	0	1	2	3	0	2	0	22.5	13.50	30	.500	.625	0	—	0	-2	-2	0	-0.1
1971	Det-A	4	6	.400	31	14	0	0	3	89²	91	5	50	64	14.6	3.51	102	.265	.364	0	.000	-2	-1	1	0	-0.1
Total	11	128	115	.527	406	294	83	33	23	2147¹	1864	122	739	1534	11.2	2.92	119	.234	.305	44	.066	-37	134	131	6	11.5

■ ED CHANDLER

Chandler, Edward Oliver   b: 2/17/22, Pinson, Ala.   BR/TR, 6'2", 190 lbs.   Deb: 4/18/47

YEAR	TM/L	W	L	PCT	G	GS	CG	SH	SV	IP	H	HR	BB	SO	RAT	ERA	ERA+	OAV	OOB	BH	AVG	PB	PR	/A	PD	TPI
1947	Bro-N	0	1	.000	15	1	0	0	1	29²	31	7	12	8	13.0	6.37	65	.263	.331	0	.000	0	-8	-7	0	-0.6

■ SPUD CHANDLER

Chandler, Spurgeon Ferdinand   b: 9/12/07, Commerce, Ga.   d: 1/9/90, S.Pasadena, Fla.   BR/TR, 6', 181 lbs.   Deb: 5/06/37   C

YEAR	TM/L	W	L	PCT	G	GS	CG	SH	SV	IP	H	HR	BB	SO	RAT	ERA	ERA+	OAV	OOB	BH	AVG	PB	PR	/A	PD	TPI
1937	NY-A	7	4	.636	12	10	6	2	0	82¹	79	8	20	31	10.9	2.84	156	.253	.300	4	.133	-2	16	15	2	1.4
1938	NY-A	14	5	.737	23	23	14	2	0	172	183	7	47	36	12.1	4.03	113	.271	.320	14	.203	2	15	10	5	1.5

YEAR TM/L	W	L	PCT	G	GS	CG	SH	SV	IP	H	HR	BB	SO	RAT	ERA	ERA+	OAV	OOB	BH	AVG	PB	PR	/A	PD	TPI
1939 NY-A	3	0	1.000	11	0	0	0	0	19	26	0	9	4	16.6	2.84	153	.329	.398	2	.400	1	4	3	1	0.5
1940 NY-A	8	7	.533	27	24	6	1	0	172	184	12	60	56	13.1	4.60	88	.275	.341	9	.150	1	-4	-11	4	-0.6
1941 *NY-A	10	4	.714	28	20	11	4	4	163²	146	5	60	60	11.3	3.19	123	.239	.307	11	.183	-1	17	13	3	1.5
1942 *NY-A	16	5	.762	24	24	17	3	0	200²	176	13	74	74	11.4	2.38	145	.237	.309	4	.211	4	29	24	3	3.3
1943 *NY-A	20	4	.833	30	30	20	5	0	253	197	5	54	134	9.1	1.64	197	.215	**.261**	25	.258	7	47	44	2	6.5
1944 NY-A	0	0	—	1	1	0	0	0	6	6	1	1	4		4.50	77	.300	.364	0	.000	-0	-1	-1	0	-0.2
1945 NY-A	2	1	.667	4	4	2	1	0	31	30	2	7	12	10.7	4.65	75	.250	.291	4	.333	1	-4	-4	0	-0.2
1946 NY-A	20	8	.714	34	32	20	6	2	257¹	200	7	90	138	10.2	2.10	164	.218	.288	14	.149	-0	40	39	4	4.8
1947 *NY-A	9	5	.643	17	16	13	2	0	128	100	4	41	68	9.9	2.46	144	.214	.277	12	.245	4	18	15	3	2.5
Total 11	109	43	.717	211	184	109	26	6	1485	1327	64	463	614	11.0	2.84	132	.240	.301	110	.201	16	176	149	28	21.2

■ ESTY CHANEY
Chaney, Esty Clyon b: 1/29/1891, Hadley, Pa. d: 2/5/52, Cleveland, Ohio BR/TR, 5'11", 170 lbs. Deb: 8/02/13

YEAR TM/L	W	L	PCT	G	GS	CG	SH	SV	IP	H	HR	BB	SO	RAT	ERA	ERA+	OAV	OOB	BH	AVG	PB	PR	/A	PD	TPI
1913 Bos-A	0	0	—	1	0	0	0	0	1	1	0	2	0	27.0	9.00	33	.200	.429	0	—	0	-1	-1	0	0.0
1914 Bro-F	0	0	—	1	0	0	0	0	4	7	0	2	1	20.3	6.75	47	.391	.452	0	.000	-0	-2	-2	0	-0.1
Total 2	0	0	—	2	0	0	0	0	5	8	0	4	1	21.6	7.20	44	.349	.446	0	.000	-0	-2	-2	0	-0.1

■ TINY CHAPLIN
Chaplin, James Bailey b: 7/13/05, Los Angeles, Cal. d: 3/25/39, National City, Cal BR/TR, 6'1", 195 lbs. Deb: 4/13/28

YEAR TM/L	W	L	PCT	G	GS	CG	SH	SV	IP	H	HR	BB	SO	RAT	ERA	ERA+	OAV	OOB	BH	AVG	PB	PR	/A	PD	TPI
1928 NY-N	0	2	.000	12	1	0	0	0	24	27	0	8	5	13.1	4.50	87	.284	.340	0	.000	-1	-1	-2	-0	-0.2
1930 NY-N	2	6	.250	19	8	3	0	1	73	89	8	16	20	13.4	5.18	91	.305	.349	2	.105	-0	-2	-4	-0	-0.2
1931 NY-N	3	0	1.000	16	3	1	0	1	42¹	39	2	16	7	12.1	3.19	116	.242	.318	2	.182	0	3	2	-1	0.2
1936 Bos-N	10	15	.400	40	31	14	0	2	231²	273	21	62	86	13.1	4.12	93	.294	.340	17	.202	-0	-3	-7	1	-0.6
Total 4	15	23	.395	87	43	18	0	4	371	428	31	102	118	13.1	4.25	94	.290	.340	21	.176	-1	-2	-10	-1	-0.8

■ ED CHAPMAN
Chapman, Edwin Volney b: 11/28/05, Courtland, Miss. BB/TR, 6'1", 185 lbs. Deb: 8/06/33

YEAR TM/L	W	L	PCT	G	GS	CG	SH	SV	IP	H	HR	BB	SO	RAT	ERA	ERA+	OAV	OOB	BH	AVG	PB	PR	/A	PD	TPI
1933 Was-A	0	0	—	6	1	0	0	0	9	10	2	2	4	12.0	8.00	52	.270	.308	0	.000	-0	-4	-4	-0	-0.3

■ FRED CHAPMAN
Chapman, Frederick Joseph b: 11/24/1872, Little Cooley, Pa. d: 12/14/57, Union City, Pa. BR/TR, 5'8", 165 lbs. Deb: 7/22/1887

YEAR TM/L	W	L	PCT	G	GS	CG	SH	SV	IP	H	HR	BB	SO	RAT	ERA	ERA+	OAV	OOB	BH	AVG	PB	PR	/A	PD	TPI
1887 Phi-a	0	0	—	1	1	1	0	0	5	8	0	2	4	18.0	7.20	60	.349	.401	0	.000	-0	-2	-2	-0	-0.1

■ BEN CHAPMAN
Chapman, William Benjamin b: 12/25/08, Nashville, Tenn. BR/TR, 6', 190 lbs. Deb: 4/15/30 MC♦

YEAR TM/L	W	L	PCT	G	GS	CG	SH	SV	IP	H	HR	BB	SO	RAT	ERA	ERA+	OAV	OOB	BH	AVG	PB	PR	/A	PD	TPI
1944 Bro-N	5	3	.625	11	9	6	0	0	79¹	75	4	33	37	12.6	3.40	104	.242	.321	14	.368	6	2	1	-2	0.6
1945 Bro-N	3	3	.500	10	7	2	0	0	53²	64	3	32	23	16.6	5.53	68	.296	.394	4	.136	-1	-10	-11	1	-0.9
Phi-N	0	0	—	3	0	0	0	0	7	7	0	6	4	16.7	7.71	50	.259	.394	16	.314	-0	-3	-3	0	-0.2
Yr	3	3	.500	13	7	2	0	0	60²	71	3	38	27	16.2	5.79	65	.289	.384	4	.055	-0	-13	-14	1	-1.1
1946 Phi-N	0	0	—	1	0	0	0	0	1	1	0	1	0	9.0	0.00		.200	.200	0	.000	-0	0	0	0	0.0
Total 3	8	6	.571	25	16	8	0	0	141	147	7	71	65	14.3	4.40	83	.263	.353	1958	.302	6	-11	-12	-1	-0.5

■ BILL CHAPPELLE
Chappelle, William Hogan "Big Bill" b: 3/22/1884, Waterloo, N.Y. d: 12/31/44, Mineola, N.Y. BR/TR, 6'2", 206 lbs. Deb: 8/20/08

YEAR TM/L	W	L	PCT	G	GS	CG	SH	SV	IP	H	HR	BB	SO	RAT	ERA	ERA+	OAV	OOB	BH	AVG	PB	PR	/A	PD	TPI
1908 Bos-N	2	4	.333	13	7	3	1	0	70¹	60	0	17	23	10.4	1.79	135	.233	.290	1	.048	-1	4	5	1	0.5
1909 Bos-N	1	1	.500	5	3	2	0	0	29	31	0	11	8	13.3	1.86	152	.279	.350	4	.364	-1	2	3	1	0.8
Cin-N	0	0	—	1	0	0	0	1	4	5	0	2	0	18.0	2.25	116	.278	.381	0	.000	-0	0	0	0	0.0
Yr	1	1	.500	6	3	2	0	1	33	36	0	13	8	13.6	1.91	146	.277	.347	0	.000	-1	2	3	1	0.8
1914 Bro-F	4	2	.667	16	6	4	0	0	74¹	71	1	29	31	12.5	3.15	101	.255	.332	0	.000	-3	0	-0	-1	-0.3
Total 3	7	7	.500	35	16	9	1	1	177²	167	1	59	62	11.9	2.38	118	.251	.321	5	.089	-3	7	9	1	1.0

■ NORM CHARLTON
Charlton, Norman Wood b: 1/6/63, Fort Polk, La. BB/TL, 6'3", 195 lbs. Deb: 8/19/88

YEAR TM/L	W	L	PCT	G	GS	CG	SH	SV	IP	H	HR	BB	SO	RAT	ERA	ERA+	OAV	OOB	BH	AVG	PB	PR	/A	PD	TPI
1988 Cin-N	4	5	.444	10	10	0	0	0	61¹	60	6	20	39	12.0	3.96	90	.256	.320	0	.000	-1	-4	-3	-0	-0.3
1989 Cin-N	8	3	.727	69	0	0	0	0	95¹	67	5	40	98	10.3	2.93	123	.197	.285	0	.000	-1	6	7	-1	0.6
1990 *Cin-N	12	9	.571	56	16	1	1	2	154¹	131	10	70	117	12.0	2.74	141	.231	.320	5	.135	1	18	19	0	2.1
Total 3	24	17	.585	135	26	1	1	2	311	258	21	130	254	11.5	3.04	123	.226	.310	5	.088	-1	21	24	-0	2.4

■ PETE CHARTON
Charton, Frank Lane b: 12/21/42, Jackson, Tenn. BL/TR, 6'2", 190 lbs. Deb: 4/19/64

YEAR TM/L	W	L	PCT	G	GS	CG	SH	SV	IP	H	HR	BB	SO	RAT	ERA	ERA+	OAV	OOB	BH	AVG	PB	PR	/A	PD	TPI
1964 Bos-A	0	2	.000	25	5	0	0	0	65	67	12	24	37	12.7	5.26	73	.275	.342	1	.100	-0	-12	-10	2	-0.8

■ KEN CHASE
Chase, Kendall Fay "Lefty" b: 10/6/13, Oneonta, N.Y. d: 1/16/85, Oneonta, N.Y. BL/TL, 6'2", 210 lbs. Deb: 4/23/36

YEAR TM/L	W	L	PCT	G	GS	CG	SH	SV	IP	H	HR	BB	SO	RAT	ERA	ERA+	OAV	OOB	BH	AVG	PB	PR	/A	PD	TPI
1936 Was-A	0	0	—	1	0	0	0	0	2¹	2	0	4	1	23.1	11.57	41	.250	.500	1	1.000	0	-2	-2	0	0.0
1937 Was-A	4	3	.571	14	9	4	0	0	76¹	74	4	60	43	15.8	4.13	107	.257	.385	1	.034	-4	4	3	-1	-0.1
1938 Was-A	9	10	.474	32	21	7	0	1	150	151	4	113	64	16.1	5.58	81	.268	.394	10	.208	-1	-13	-18	1	-1.4
1939 Was-A	10	19	.345	32	31	15	1	0	232	215	10	114	118	12.8	3.80	114	.243	.330	15	.169	-3	21	14	0	1.0
1940 Was-A	15	17	.469	35	34	20	1	0	261²	260	14	143	129	14.0	3.23	129	.261	.357	15	.163	-0	33	27	-1	2.5
1941 Was-A	6	18	.250	33	30	8	1	0	205²	228	11	115	98	15.1	5.08	80	.280	.371	4	.149	-2	-21	-24	1	-2.2
1942 Bos-A	5	1	.833	13	10	4	0	0	80¹	82	5	41	34	13.8	3.81	98	.263	.348	6	.182	-1	-1	-1	-0	0.0
1943 Bos-A	0	4	.000	7	5	0	0	0	27¹	36	0	30	9	21.7	6.91	48	.316	.458	1	.091	-1	-11	-11	0	-1.0
NY-N	4	12	.250	21	20	4	1	0	129¹	140	7	74	86	15.0	4.11	84	.275	.369	9	.214	0	-10	-9	-1	-1.0
Total 8	53	84	.387	188	160	62	4	1	1165	1188	55	694	582	14.7	4.27	97	.265	.365	69	.165	-8	-0	-19	-2	-2.2

■ JIM CHATTERTON
Chatterton, James M. b: 10/14/1864, Brooklyn, N.Y. d: 12/15/44, Tewksbury, Mass. Deb: 6/07/1884 ♦

YEAR TM/L	W	L	PCT	G	GS	CG	SH	SV	IP	H	HR	BB	SO	RAT	ERA	ERA+	OAV	OOB	BH	AVG	PB	PR	/A	PD	TPI
1884 KC-U	0	1	.000	1	1	0	0	0	5	11	0	2	2	23.4	3.60	77	.414	.455	2	.133	-0	-0	0	0	0.0

■ NESTOR CHAVEZ
Chavez, Nestor Isais (Silva) b: 7/6/47, Chacao, Venez. d: 3/16/69, Maracaibo, Venez. BR/TR, 6', 170 lbs. Deb: 9/09/67

YEAR TM/L	W	L	PCT	G	GS	CG	SH	SV	IP	H	HR	BB	SO	RAT	ERA	ERA+	OAV	OOB	BH	AVG	PB	PR	/A	PD	TPI
1967 SF-N	1	0	1.000	2	0	0	0	0	5	4	0	3	3	12.6	0.00	—	.211	.318	0	.000	-0	2	2	0	0.2

■ DAVE CHEADLE
Cheadle, David Baird b: 2/19/52, Greensboro, N.C. BL/TL, 6'2", 203 lbs. Deb: 9/16/73

YEAR TM/L	W	L	PCT	G	GS	CG	SH	SV	IP	H	HR	BB	SO	RAT	ERA	ERA+	OAV	OOB	BH	AVG	PB	PR	/A	PD	TPI
1973 Atl-N	0	1	.000	2	0	0	0	0	2	5	0	5	2		18.00	22	.250	.455	0	—	0	-3	-3	0	-0.2

■ CHARLIE CHECH
Chech, Charles William b: 4/27/1878, Madison, Wis. d: 1/31/38, Los Angeles, Cal. BR/TR, 5'11.5", 190 lbs. Deb: 4/14/05

YEAR TM/L	W	L	PCT	G	GS	CG	SH	SV	IP	H	HR	BB	SO	RAT	ERA	ERA+	OAV	OOB	BH	AVG	PB	PR	/A	PD	TPI
1905 Cin-N	14	14	.500	39	25	20	1	0	268	300	4	77	79	13.0	2.89	114	.288	.344	17	.191	1	3	12	0	1.5
1906 Cin-N	1	4	.200	11	5	5	0	3	66	59	1	24	17	12.1	2.32	119	.243	.326	5	.200	1	2	3	0	0.5
1908 Cle-A	11	7	.611	27	20	14	4	0	165²	136	2	34	51	9.6	1.74	138	.229	.279	5	.104	-1	12	12	2	1.5
1909 Bos-A	7	5	.583	17	13	6	1	0	106²	107	3	27	40	11.7	2.95	85	.260	.314	3	.083	-1	-6	-5	-0	-0.8
Total 4	33	30	.524	94	63	45	6	3	606¹	602	10	162	187	11.8	2.52	113	.263	.320	30	.152	-1	12	21	2	2.7

■ VIRGIL CHEEVES
Cheeves, Virgil Earl "Chief" b: 2/12/01, Oklahoma City, Okla. d: 5/5/79, Dallas, Tex. BR/TR, 6', 195 lbs. Deb: 9/07/20

YEAR TM/L	W	L	PCT	G	GS	CG	SH	SV	IP	H	HR	BB	SO	RAT	ERA	ERA+	OAV	OOB	BH	AVG	PB	PR	/A	PD	TPI
1920 Chi-N	0	0	—	5	2	0	0	0	18	16	0	7	3	11.5	3.50	92	.250	.324	0	.000	-0	-1	-1	-1	-0.1
1921 Chi-N	11	12	.478	37	22	9	1	0	163	192	8	47	39	13.7	4.64	82	.309	.366	8	.167	-2	-15	-15	-2	-1.7
1922 Chi-N	12	11	.522	39	23	9	1	2	182²	195	9	76	40	13.8	4.09	103	.281	.360	13	.210	2	0	-2	-1	0.2
1923 Chi-N	3	4	.429	19	8	0	0	0	71¹	89	6	37	13	16.3	6.18	65	.314	.399	4	.174	-1	-17	-17	-1	-1.6
1924 Cle-A	0	0	—	8	1	0	0	0	17¹	26	2	17	2	22.8	7.79	55	.388	.518	1	.250	0	-7	-7	0	-0.5
1927 NY-N	0	0	—	3	0	0	0	0	6¹	8	1	4	1	17.1	4.26	90	.333	.429	0	—	0	-0	-0	0	0.0
Total 6	26	27	.491	111	56	18	2	2	458²	526	28	188	98	14.5	4.73	84	.300	.375	26	.184	-1	-40	-38	-4	-3.7

■ ITALO CHELINI
Chelini, Italo Vincent "Chilly" or "Lefty" b: 10/10/14, San Francisco, Cal d: 8/25/72, San Francisco, Cal BL/TL, 5'10.5", 175 lbs. Deb: 9/12/35

YEAR TM/L	W	L	PCT	G	GS	CG	SH	SV	IP	H	HR	BB	SO	RAT	ERA	ERA+	OAV	OOB	BH	AVG	PB	PR	/A	PD	TPI
1935 Chi-A	0	0	—	2	0	0	0	0	5	7	1	4	1	21.6	12.60	37	.350	.480	1	.500	0	-5	-4	0	-0.3
1936 Chi-A	4	3	.571	18	6	5	0	0	83²	100	8	30	16	14.0	4.95	105	.291	.348	5	.156	-1	1	2	-1	0.0
1937 Chi-A	0	1	.000	4	0	0	0	0	8²	15	2	0	3	16.6	10.38	44	.405	.421	0	.000	0	-6	-6	-0	-0.4

YEAR TM/L	W	L	PCT	G	GS	CG	SH	SV	IP	H	HR	BB	SO	RAT	ERA	ERA+	OAV	OOB	BH	AVG	PB	PR	/A	PD	TPI
Total 3	4	4	.500	24	6	5	0	0	97¹	122	11	34	20	14.6	5.83	88	.304	.362	6	.171	-1	-9	-8	-1	-0.7

■ LARRY CHENEY
Cheney, Laurance Russell   b: 5/2/1886, Belleville, Kan.   d: 1/6/69, Daytona Beach, Fla.   BR/TR, 6'1.5", 185 lbs.   Deb: 9/09/11

YEAR TM/L	W	L	PCT	G	GS	CG	SH	SV	IP	H	HR	BB	SO	RAT	ERA	ERA+	OAV	OOB	BH	AVG	PB	PR	/A	PD	TPI
1911 Chi-N	1	0	1.000	3	1	0	0	0	10	8	0	3	11	9.9	0.00	—	.229	.289	1	.250	0	4	4	0	0.5
1912 Chi-N	26	10	.722	42	37	28	4	0	303¹	262	5	111	140	11.3	2.85	117	.228	.300	24	.226	5	19	16	-2	1.8
1913 Chi-N	21	14	.600	54	36	25	2	11	305	271	7	98	136	11.1	2.57	124	.241	.306	20	.192	2	22	21	-0	2.3
1914 Chi-N	20	18	.526	50	40	21	6	5	311¹	239	9	140	157	11.2	2.54	109	.215	.308	18	.180	3	9	8	1	1.2
1915 Chi-N	8	9	.471	25	18	6	2	0	131¹	120	1	55	68	12.3	3.56	78	.246	.327	6	.150	-1	-12	-11	2	-1.1
Bro-N	0	2	.000	5	4	1	0	0	27	16	0	17	11	11.7	1.67	167	.174	.315	1	.143	0	3	3	0	0.4
Yr	8	11	.421	30	22	7	2	0	158¹	136	1	72	79	11.9	3.24	86	.233	.319	4	.085	-1	-9	-8	2	-0.7
1916 *Bro-N	18	12	.600	41	32	15	5	0	253	178	5	105	166	10.4	1.92	140	.198	.289	9	.114	-3	20	21	-2	2.0
1917 Bro-N	8	12	.400	35	24	14	1	2	210¹	185	4	73	102	11.3	2.35	119	.239	.309	14	.206	2	8	10	-1	1.3
1918 Bro-N	11	13	.458	32	21	15	0	1	200²	177	2	74	83	11.7	3.00	93	.241	.319	16	.242	2	-5	-5	1	-0.1
1919 Bro-N	1	3	.250	9	4	2	0	0	39	45	1	14	14	14.1	4.15	72	.300	.367	2	.182	-0	-5	-5	-0	-0.5
Bos-N	0	2	.000	8	2	0	0	0	33	35	0	15	13	13.6	3.55	81	.294	.373	2	.182	-0	-2	-3	0	-0.1
Phi-N	2	5	.286	9	6	5	0	0	57¹	69	2	28	25	15.4	4.55	71	.315	.395	2	.095	-2	-10	-8	-1	-1.1
Yr	3	10	.231	26	12	7	0	0	129¹	149	3	57	52	14.4	4.18	73	.304	.378	2	.047	-2	-18	-16	-1	-1.7
Total 9	116	100	.537	313	225	132	20	19	1881¹	1605	36	733	926	11.5	2.70	109	.233	.312	115	.186	9	49	52	-3	6.6

■ TOM CHENEY
Cheney, Thomas Edgar   b: 10/14/34, Morgan, Ga.   BR/TR, 5'11", 170 lbs.   Deb: 4/21/57

YEAR TM/L	W	L	PCT	G	GS	CG	SH	SV	IP	H	HR	BB	SO	RAT	ERA	ERA+	OAV	OOB	BH	AVG	PB	PR	/A	PD	TPI
1957 StL-N	0	1	.000	4	3	0	0	0	9	6	0	15	10	21.0	5.00	79	.207	.477	0	.000	-0	-1	-1	0	0.0
1959 StL-N	0	1	.000	11	2	0	0	0	11²	17	2	11	8	23.1	6.94	61	.354	.492	0	—	0	-4	-4	0	-0.3
1960 *Pit-N	2	2	.500	11	8	1	1	0	52	44	5	33	35	13.3	3.98	94	.238	.353	3	.176	0	-1	-1	-1	-0.2
1961 Pit-N	0	0	—	1	0	0	0	0	0	1	1	4	0	—	∞	—	.500	.833	0	—	0	-4	-4	0	-0.2
Was-A	1	3	.250	10	7	0	0	0	29²	32	8	26	20	17.6	8.80	46	.283	.417	4	.500	2	-16	-16	-1	-1.3
1962 Was-A	7	9	.438	37	23	4	3	1	173¹	134	12	97	147	12.1	3.17	127	.213	.320	3	.063	-3	15	17	-1	1.3
1963 Was-A	8	9	.471	23	21	7	4	0	136¹	99	14	40	97	9.2	2.71	137	.202	.264	5	.109	-3	14	15	-3	1.1
1964 Was-A	1	3	.250	15	6	1	0	1	48²	45	10	13	25	10.7	3.70	100	.245	.294	3	.250	0	0	0	-0	0.0
1966 Was-A	0	1	.000	3	1	0	0	0	5¹	4	1	6	3	18.6	5.06	68	.222	.440	0	—	0	-1	-1	0	0.0
Total 8	19	29	.396	115	71	13	8	2	466	382	53	245	345	12.2	3.77	103	.225	.325	18	.135	-4	2	5	-5	0.4

■ JACK CHESBRO
Chesbro, John Dwight "Happy Jack"   b: 6/5/1874, N.Adams, Mass.   d: 11/6/31, Conway, Mass.   BR/TR, 5'9", 180 lbs.   Deb: 7/12/1899   CH

YEAR TM/L	W	L	PCT	G	GS	CG	SH	SV	IP	H	HR	BB	SO	RAT	ERA	ERA+	OAV	OOB	BH	AVG	PB	PR	/A	PD	TPI
1899 Pit-N	6	9	.400	19	17	15	0	0	149	165	3	59	28	13.5	4.11	93	.280	.346	9	.155	-3	-4	-5	-2	-0.8
1900 Pit-N	15	13	.536	32	26	20	3	1	215²	220	4	79	56	12.5	3.67	99	.264	.327	15	.176	-1	-1	-1	-2	-0.3
1901 Pit-N	21	10	.677	36	28	26	6	1	287²	261	4	52	129	10.2	2.38	137	.240	.283	25	.216	2	30	28	-3	2.8
1902 Pit-N	28	6	.824	35	33	31	8	1	286¹	242	1	62	136	10.2	2.17	126	.229	.285	20	.179	-2	19	18	-2	1.5
1903 NY-A	21	15	.583	40	36	33	1	0	324²	300	7	74	147	10.4	2.77	113	.245	.288	23	.185	-1	7	13	1	1.5
1904 NY-A	41	12	.774	55	51	48	6	0	454²	338	4	88	239	8.4	1.82	149	.208	.249	41	.236	6	39	45	4	6.8
1905 NY-A	19	15	.559	41	38	24	3	0	303¹	262	5	71	156	9.9	2.20	134	.234	.280	21	.188	0	16	25	1	3.1
1906 NY-A	24	17	.585	49	42	24	4	1	325	314	2	75	152	10.8	2.96	100	.257	.300	26	.208	-1	-10	0	-0	0.0
1907 NY-A	10	10	.500	30	25	17	1	0	206	192	0	46	78	10.4	2.53	110	.249	.291	15	.197	-0	0	6	-0	0.7
1908 NY-A	14	20	.412	45	31	21	3	1	289	271	6	67	124	11.0	2.93	85	.250	.303	18	.176	-2	-17	-14	1	-1.6
1909 NY-A	0	4	.000	9	4	2	0	0	49²	70	2	13	17	15.6	6.34	40	.347	.394	3	.176	-0	-21	-21	1	-1.9
Bos-A	0	1	.000	1	1	0	0	0	6	7	1	4	3	16.5	4.50	56	.318	.423	1	.500	0	-1	-1	-0	0.0
Yr	0	5	.000	10	5	2	0	0	55²	77	3	17	20	15.2	6.14	41	.339	.385	1	.053	-0	-23	-22	1	-1.9
Total 11	199	132	.601	392	332	261	35	5	2897	2642	39	690	1265	10.5	2.68	111	.244	.292	217	.197	0	59	97	-3	11.8

■ BOB CHESNES
Chesnes, Robert Vincent   b: 5/6/21, Oakland, Cal.   d: 5/23/79, Everett, Wash.   BB/TR, 6', 180 lbs.   Deb: 5/06/48

YEAR TM/L	W	L	PCT	G	GS	CG	SH	SV	IP	H	HR	BB	SO	RAT	ERA	ERA+	OAV	OOB	BH	AVG	PB	PR	/A	PD	TPI
1948 Pit-N	14	6	.700	25	23	15	0	0	194¹	180	13	90	69	12.7	3.57	114	.247	.333	25	.275	7	8	11	3	2.2
1949 Pit-N	7	13	.350	27	25	8	1	1	145¹	153	15	82	49	14.9	5.88	71	.276	.374	17	.250	6	-30	-27	3	-1.6
1950 Pit-N	3	3	.500	9	7	2	0	0	39	44	7	17	12	14.8	5.54	79	.293	.376	2	.154	-0	-6	-5	2	-0.2
Total 3	24	22	.522	61	55	25	1	1	378²	377	35	189	130	13.7	4.66	89	.263	.354	44	.256	13	-27	-21	8	0.4

■ MITCH CHETKOVICH
Chetkovich, Mitchell   b: 7/21/17, Fairpoint, Ohio   d: 8/24/71, Grass Valley, Cal.   BR/TR, 6'3.5", 208 lbs.   Deb: 4/19/45

YEAR TM/L	W	L	PCT	G	GS	CG	SH	SV	IP	H	HR	BB	SO	RAT	ERA	ERA+	OAV	OOB	BH	AVG	PB	PR	/A	PD	TPI
1945 Phi-N	0	0	—	4	0	0	0	0	3	2	0	3	0	15.0	0.00	—	.182	.357	0	—	0	1	1	-0	0.1

■ TONY CHEVEZ
Chevez, Silvio Antonio (b: Silvio Antonio Aguilera (Chevez))   b: 6/20/54, Telica, Nicaragua   BR/TR, 5'11", 177 lbs.   Deb: 5/31/77

YEAR TM/L	W	L	PCT	G	GS	CG	SH	SV	IP	H	HR	BB	SO	RAT	ERA	ERA+	OAV	OOB	BH	AVG	PB	PR	/A	PD	TPI
1977 Bal-A	0	0	—	4	0	0	0	0	8	10	3	8	7	22.5	12.38	31	.294	.455	0	—	0	-7	-8	-0	-0.6

■ SCOTT CHIAMPARINO
Chiamparino, Scott Michael   b: 8/22/66, San Mateo, Cal.   BR/TR, 6'2", 190 lbs.   Deb: 9/05/90

YEAR TM/L	W	L	PCT	G	GS	CG	SH	SV	IP	H	HR	BB	SO	RAT	ERA	ERA+	OAV	OOB	BH	AVG	PB	PR	/A	PD	TPI
1990 Tex-A	1	2	.333	6	6	0	0	0	37²	36	1	12	19	11.9	2.63	152	.250	.316	0	—	0	5	6	-1	0.5

■ FLOYD CHIFFER
Chiffer, Floyd John   b: 4/20/56, Glen Cove, N.Y.   BR/TR, 6'2", 185 lbs.   Deb: 4/07/82

YEAR TM/L	W	L	PCT	G	GS	CG	SH	SV	IP	H	HR	BB	SO	RAT	ERA	ERA+	OAV	OOB	BH	AVG	PB	PR	/A	PD	TPI
1982 SD-N	4	3	.571	51	0	0	0	4	79¹	73	9	34	48	12.6	2.95	116	.247	.333	0	.000	-1	6	4	-0	0.3
1983 SD-N	0	2	.000	15	0	0	0	1	22²	17	0	10	15	10.7	3.18	110	.210	.297	0	.000	-0	1	1	0	0.1
1984 SD-N	1	0	1.000	15	1	0	0	0	28	42	1	16	20	18.6	7.71	46	.347	.423	0	.000	-0	-13	-13	-1	-1.3
Total 3	5	5	.500	81	1	0	0	5	130	132	10	60	83	13.6	4.02	86	.266	.349	0	.000	-1	-6	-8	-1	-0.9

■ HARRY CHILD
Child, Harry Stephen Patrick (b: Harry Stephen Patrick Chesley)
b: 5/23/05, Baltimore, Md.   d: 11/8/72, Alexandria, Va.   BB/TR, 5'11", 187 lbs.   Deb: 7/16/30

YEAR TM/L	W	L	PCT	G	GS	CG	SH	SV	IP	H	HR	BB	SO	RAT	ERA	ERA+	OAV	OOB	BH	AVG	PB	PR	/A	PD	TPI
1930 Was-A	0	0	—	5	0	0	0	0	10	10	1	5	5	13.5	6.30	73	.263	.349	1	.250	-0	-2	-2	0	-0.1

■ CHILDERS
Childers   b: St.Louis, Mo.   Deb: 7/27/1895

YEAR TM/L	W	L	PCT	G	GS	CG	SH	SV	IP	H	HR	BB	SO	RAT	ERA	ERA+	OAV	OOB	BH	AVG	PB	PR	/A	PD	TPI
1895 Lou-N	0	0	—	1	0	0	0	0	0	2	0	6	0	—	∞	—	1.000	1.000	0	—	0	-6	-6	0	-0.3

■ ROCKY CHILDRESS
Childress, Rodney Osborne   b: 2/18/62, Santa Rosa, Cal.   BR/TR, 6'2", 195 lbs.   Deb: 5/17/85

YEAR TM/L	W	L	PCT	G	GS	CG	SH	SV	IP	H	HR	BB	SO	RAT	ERA	ERA+	OAV	OOB	BH	AVG	PB	PR	/A	PD	TPI
1985 Phi-N	0	1	.000	16	1	0	0	0	33¹	45	3	9	14	14.6	6.21	59	.326	.367	1	.167	-0	-10	-9	-0	-0.9
1986 Phi-N	0	0	—	2	0	0	0	0	2²	4	0	1	1	16.9	6.75	57	.364	.417	0	—	0	-1	-1	0	0.0
1987 Hou-N	1	2	.333	32	0	0	0	0	48¹	46	4	18	26	11.9	2.98	131	.260	.328	0	.000	-0	6	5	-0	0.5
1988 Hou-N	1	0	1.000	11	0	0	0	0	23¹	26	3	9	24	13.9	6.17	54	.280	.350	1	.250	-0	-7	-7	-1	-0.7
Total 4	2	3	.400	61	1	0	0	0	107²	121	10	37	65	13.3	4.76	78	.289	.348	2	.167	-0	-12	-13	-1	-1.1

■ BOB CHIPMAN
Chipman, Robert Howard "Mr. Chips"   b: 10/11/18, Brooklyn, N.Y.   d: 11/8/73, Huntington, N.Y.   BL/TL, 6'2", 190 lbs.   Deb: 9/28/41

YEAR TM/L	W	L	PCT	G	GS	CG	SH	SV	IP	H	HR	BB	SO	RAT	ERA	ERA+	OAV	OOB	BH	AVG	PB	PR	/A	PD	TPI
1941 Bro-N	1	0	1.000	1	0	0	0	0	5	3	0	1	3	7.2	0.00	—	.150	.190	0	.000	-0	2	2	0	0.2
1942 Bro-N	0	0	—	2	0	0	0	0	1¹	1	0	2	1	20.3	0.00	—	.250	.500	0	—	0	0	0	0	0.0
1943 Bro-N	0	0	—	1	0	0	0	0	1²	2	0	2	0	21.6	0.00	—	.400	.571	0	—	0	1	1	0	0.1
1944 Bro-N	3	1	.750	11	3	1	0	0	36¹	38	1	24	20	15.4	4.21	84	.270	.376	2	.182	-0	-2	-3	0	-0.2
Chi-N	9	9	.500	26	21	8	1	2	129	147	9	40	41	13.6	3.49	101	.288	.340	5	.104	-2	2	1	-0	-0.1
Yr	12	10	.545	37	24	9	1	2	165¹	185	10	64	61	13.6	3.65	97	.284	.348	3	.051	-3	-1	-2	0	-0.3
1945 *Chi-N	4	5	.444	25	10	3	1	0	72	63	4	34	29	12.3	3.50	104	.230	.317	3	.176	1	2	1	1	0.2
1946 Chi-N	6	5	.545	34	10	5	3	2	109¹	103	8	54	42	13.0	3.13	106	.255	.344	2	.061	-3	3	2	-1	0.0
1947 Chi-N	7	6	.538	32	17	5	1	0	134²	135	6	66	51	13.4	3.68	107	.264	.348	4	.091	-3	6	4	2	0.3
1948 Chi-N	2	1	.667	34	3	0	0	4	60¹	73	5	24	16	14.5	3.58	109	.293	.355	4	.250	1	3	2	1	0.5
1949 Chi-N	7	8	.467	38	11	5	1	0	113¹	117	7	63	46	13.9	3.97	102	.284	.344	3	.125	-0	1	1	-0	0.0
1950 Bos-N	7	7	.500	27	12	4	0	1	124	127	10	37	40	12.2	4.43	87	.262	.319	6	.154	-1	-4	-8	-2	-1.0
1951 Bos-N	4	3	.571	33	0	0	0	4	52	59	5	19	17	13.8	4.85	76	.284	.349	1	.100	-1	-5	-7	-0	-0.7

YEAR TM/L	W	L	PCT	G	GS	CG	SH	SV	IP	H	HR	BB	SO	RAT	ERA	ERA+	OAV	OOB	BH	AVG	PB	PR	/A	PD	TPI
1952 Bos-N	1	1	.500	29	0	0	0	0	41²	28	5	20	16	10.4	2.81	129	.188	.284	2	.400	1	4	4	0	0.5
Total 12	51	46	.526	293	87	29	7	14	880²	889	60	386	322	13.1	3.72	100	.261	.338	32	.128	-8	13	1	-1	-0.2

■ **STEVE CHITREN** Chitren, Stephen Vincent b: 6/8/67, Tokyo, Japan BR/TR, 6', 180 lbs. Deb: 9/15/90

YEAR TM/L	W	L	PCT	G	GS	CG	SH	SV	IP	H	HR	BB	SO	RAT	ERA	ERA+	OAV	OOB	BH	AVG	PB	PR	/A	PD	TPI
1990 Oak-A	1	0	1.000	8	0	0	0	0	17²	7	0	4	19	5.6	1.02	366	.117	.172	0	—	0	6	5	0	0.6

■ **NELSON CHITTUM** Chittum, Nelson Boyd b: 3/25/33, Harrisonburg, Va. BR/TR, 6'1", 180 lbs. Deb: 8/17/58

YEAR TM/L	W	L	PCT	G	GS	CG	SH	SV	IP	H	HR	BB	SO	RAT	ERA	ERA+	OAV	OOB	BH	AVG	PB	PR	/A	PD	TPI
1958 StL-N	0	1	.000	13	2	0	0	0	29¹	31	5	7	13	12.0	6.44	64	.265	.312	1	.250	0	-8	-8	0	-0.6
1959 Bos-A	3	0	1.000	21	0	0	0	0	30¹	29	0	11	12	11.9	1.19	342	.266	.333	1	.200	0	9	10	1	1.1
1960 Bos-A	0	0	—	6	0	0	0	0	8¹	8	0	6	5	15.1	4.32	94	.242	.359	0	.000	-0	-0	-0	0	0.0
Total 3	3	1	.750	40	2	0	0	0	68	68	5	24	30	12.3	3.84	106	.263	.327	2	.200	0	0	2	1	0.5

■ **BOB CHLUPSA** Chlupsa, Robert Joseph b: 9/16/45, New York, N.Y. BR/TR, 6'7", 215 lbs. Deb: 7/16/70

YEAR TM/L	W	L	PCT	G	GS	CG	SH	SV	IP	H	HR	BB	SO	RAT	ERA	ERA+	OAV	OOB	BH	AVG	PB	PR	/A	PD	TPI
1970 StL-N	0	2	.000	14	0	0	0	0	16¹	26	2	9	10	19.3	8.82	47	.366	.438	0	—	0	-9	-9	1	-0.7
1971 StL-N	0	0	—	1	0	0	0	0	2	3	0	0	1	13.5	9.00	40	.333	.333	0	—	0	-1	-1	0	0.0
Total 2	0	2	.000	15	0	0	0	0	18¹	29	2	9	11	18.7	8.84	46	.363	.427	0	—	0	-10	-10	1	-0.7

■ **DON CHOATE** Choate, Donald Leon b: 7/2/38, Potosi, Mo. BR/TR, 6', 185 lbs. Deb: 9/12/60

YEAR TM/L	W	L	PCT	G	GS	CG	SH	SV	IP	H	HR	BB	SO	RAT	ERA	ERA+	OAV	OOB	BH	AVG	PB	PR	/A	PD	TPI
1960 SF-N	0	0	—	4	0	0	0	0	8	7	0	4	7	12.4	2.25	155	.233	.324	0	—	0	1	1	0	0.2

■ **CHIEF CHOUNEAU** Chouneau, William (b: William Cadreau) b: 9/2/1889, Cloquet, Minn. d: 9/17/48, Cloquet, Minn. TR, 5'9", 150 lbs. Deb: 10/09/10

YEAR TM/L	W	L	PCT	G	GS	CG	SH	SV	IP	H	HR	BB	SO	RAT	ERA	ERA+	OAV	OOB	BH	AVG	PB	PR	/A	PD	TPI
1910 Chi-A	0	1	.000	1	1	0	0	0	5¹	7	0	0	1	11.8	3.38	71	.292	.292	0	.000	0	-1	-1	-0	0.0

■ **MIKE CHRIS** Chris, Michael b: 10/8/57, Santa Monica, Cal. BL/TL, 6'3", 180 lbs. Deb: 7/31/79

YEAR TM/L	W	L	PCT	G	GS	CG	SH	SV	IP	H	HR	BB	SO	RAT	ERA	ERA+	OAV	OOB	BH	AVG	PB	PR	/A	PD	TPI
1979 Det-A	3	3	.500	13	8	0	0	0	39	46	3	21	31	15.5	6.92	62	.297	.381	0	—	0	-12	-11	0	-0.9
1982 SF-N	0	2	.000	9	6	0	0	0	26	23	2	26	10	17.3	4.85	74	.245	.413	1	.143	-0	-4	-4	1	-0.2
1983 SF-N	0	0	—	7	0	0	0	0	13¹	16	1	16	5	23.0	8.10	44	.308	.486	0	.000	-0	-7	-7	-0	-0.6
Total 3	3	5	.375	29	14	0	0	0	78¹	85	6	63	46	17.3	6.43	61	.282	.411	1	.111	-0	-22	-22	1	-1.7

■ **GARY CHRISTENSON** Christenson, Gary Richard b: 5/5/53, Mineola, N.Y. BL/TL, 6'5", 200 lbs. Deb: 9/01/79

YEAR TM/L	W	L	PCT	G	GS	CG	SH	SV	IP	H	HR	BB	SO	RAT	ERA	ERA+	OAV	OOB	BH	AVG	PB	PR	/A	PD	TPI
1979 KC-A	0	0	—	6	0	0	0	0	10²	10	1	2	4	10.1	3.38	126	.250	.286	0	—	0	1	1	0	0.1
1980 KC-A	3	0	1.000	24	0	0	0	1	31¹	35	4	18	16	15.8	5.17	78	.278	.377	0	—	0	-4	-4	1	-0.2
Total 2	3	0	1.000	30	0	0	0	1	42	45	5	20	20	14.4	4.71	87	.271	.356	0	—	0	-3	-3	1	-0.1

■ **LARRY CHRISTENSON** Christenson, Larry Richard b: 11/10/53, Everett, Wash. BR/TR, 6'4", 215 lbs. Deb: 4/13/73

YEAR TM/L	W	L	PCT	G	GS	CG	SH	SV	IP	H	HR	BB	SO	RAT	ERA	ERA+	OAV	OOB	BH	AVG	PB	PR	/A	PD	TPI
1973 Phi-N	1	4	.200	10	9	1	0	0	34¹	53	3	20	11	19.4	6.55	58	.366	.446	0	.000	-1	-11	-11	0	-1.0
1974 Phi-N	1	1	.500	10	1	0	0	2	23	20	2	15	18	13.7	4.30	88	.241	.357	0	.000	-1	-2	-1	-0	-0.1
1975 Phi-N	11	6	.647	29	26	5	2	1	171²	149	12	45	88	10.2	3.67	102	.236	.288	14	.246	1	-1	-1	-2	0.5
1976 Phi-N	13	8	.619	32	29	2	0	0	168²	199	8	42	54	12.9	3.68	96	.297	.339	10	.196	4	-3	-3	-2	-0.1
1977 *Phi-N	19	6	.760	34	34	5	1	0	219¹	229	21	69	118	12.5	4.06	98	.268	.327	10	.135	1	-4	-2	-1	-0.1
1978 *Phi-N	13	14	.481	33	33	9	3	0	228	209	16	47	130	10.1	3.24	110	.244	.284	5	.075	-2	9	8	-0	0.6
1979 Phi-N	5	10	.333	19	17	2	0	0	106	118	9	30	53	12.7	4.50	85	.291	.342	9	.290	5	-9	-8	-0	-0.2
1980 *Phi-N	5	1	.833	14	14	0	0	0	73²	62	4	27	49	11.2	4.03	94	.227	.304	7	.368	4	-4	-2	1	0.3
1981 *Phi-N	4	7	.364	20	15	0	0	1	106²	108	8	30	70	11.7	3.54	102	.267	.319	3	.100	-2	-1	-1	-1	0.0
1982 Phi-N	9	10	.474	33	33	3	0	0	223	212	15	53	145	10.8	3.47	106	.253	.300	5	.075	-3	3	5	-1	0.2
1983 Phi-N	2	4	.333	9	9	0	0	0	48¹	42	2	17	44	11.2	3.91	91	.233	.303	1	.059	-1	-2	-2	1	-0.1
Total 11	83	71	.539	243	220	27	6	4	1402²	1401	100	395	781	11.7	3.79	98	.262	.315	64	.150	10	-24	-12	-7	0.1

■ **CLAY CHRISTIANSEN** Christiansen, Clay C. b: 6/28/58, Wichita, Kan. BR/TR, 6'5", 205 lbs. Deb: 5/10/84

YEAR TM/L	W	L	PCT	G	GS	CG	SH	SV	IP	H	HR	BB	SO	RAT	ERA	ERA+	OAV	OOB	BH	AVG	PB	PR	/A	PD	TPI
1984 NY-A	2	4	.333	24	1	0	0	2	38²	50	4	12	27	14.7	6.05	63	.309	.360	0	—	0	-9	-10	-0	-0.9

■ **RUSS CHRISTOPHER** Christopher, Russell Ormand b: 9/12/17, Richmond, Cal. d: 12/5/54, Richmond, Cal. BR/TR, 6'3.5", 170 lbs. Deb: 4/14/42

YEAR TM/L	W	L	PCT	G	GS	CG	SH	SV	IP	H	HR	BB	SO	RAT	ERA	ERA+	OAV	OOB	BH	AVG	PB	PR	/A	PD	TPI
1942 Phi-A	4	13	.235	30	18	10	0	1	165	154	8	99	58	14.0	3.82	99	.254	.362	5	.089	-3	-3	-1	6	0.2
1943 Phi-A	5	8	.385	24	15	5	0	2	133	120	3	58	56	12.2	3.45	98	.242	.325	7	.156	-1	-2	-1	8	0.6
1944 Phi-A	14	14	.500	35	24	13	1	1	215¹	200	6	63	84	11.4	2.97	117	.245	.306	18	.222	3	11	12	5	2.3
1945 Phi-A	13	13	.500	33	27	17	2	2	227¹	213	9	75	100	11.8	3.17	108	.251	.319	13	.171	-1	5	7	7	1.5
1946 Phi-A	5	7	.417	30	13	1	0	0	119¹	119	5	44	79	12.5	4.30	82	.254	.322	5	.139	-0	-11	-10	4	-0.6
1947 Phi-A	10	7	.588	44	0	0	0	12	80²	70	4	33	49	11.5	2.90	131	.236	.313	2	.125	-1	7	8	0	0.9
1948 *Cle-A	3	2	.600	45	0	0	0	17	59	55	3	27	14	12.5	2.90	140	.247	.328	0	.000	-0	9	8	0	0.8
Total 7	54	64	.458	241	97	46	3	35	999²	931	38	399	424	12.2	3.37	106	.248	.325	50	.158	-3	17	24	30	5.7

■ **BUBBA CHURCH** Church, Emory Nicholas b: 9/12/24, Birmingham, Ala. BR/TR, 6', 180 lbs. Deb: 4/30/50

YEAR TM/L	W	L	PCT	G	GS	CG	SH	SV	IP	H	HR	BB	SO	RAT	ERA	ERA+	OAV	OOB	BH	AVG	PB	PR	/A	PD	TPI
1950 Phi-N	8	6	.571	31	18	8	2	1	142	113	12	56	50	10.7	2.73	149	.225	.303	8	.182	-0	22	22	0	2.1
1951 Phi-N	15	11	.577	38	33	15	4	1	247	246	17	90	104	12.3	3.53	109	.261	.326	22	.256	5	12	9	-2	1.1
1952 Phi-N	0	0	—	2	1	0	0	0	5	11	0	1	3	23.4	10.80	34	.440	.481	0	.000	-0	-4	-4	0	-0.3
Cin-N	5	9	.357	29	22	5	1	0	153¹	173	21	48	47	13.1	4.34	87	.301	.358	12	.240	3	-10	-10	-0	-0.6
Yr	5	9	.357	31	23	5	1	0	158¹	184	21	49	50	13.4	4.55	83	.306	.361	12	1.020	3	-14	-14	-0	-0.9
1953 Cin-N	3	3	.500	11	7	2	0	0	43²	55	6	19	12	15.7	5.98	73	.318	.392	4	.267	1	-8	-8	-0	-0.5
Chi-N	4	5	.444	27	11	1	0	1	104¹	115	16	49	47	14.3	5.00	89	.276	.355	7	.212	1	-8	-6	-1	-0.5
Yr	7	8	.467	38	18	3	0	1	148	170	25	68	59	14.6	5.29	84	.288	.363	2	.042	-1	-17	-14	-1	-1.0
1954 Chi-N	1	3	.250	7	3	1	0	0	14²	21	8	13	8	20.9	9.82	43	.350	.466	0	.000	-1	-9	-9	0	-0.8
1955 Chi-N	0	0	—	2	0	0	0	1	3¹	4	1	1	3	13.5	5.40	76	.286	.333	0	.000	-0	-1	-0	0	-0.1
Total 6	36	37	.493	147	95	32	7	4	713¹	738	84	277	274	12.9	4.10	97	.272	.342	53	.226	9	-7	-8	-3	0.5

■ **LEN CHURCH** Church, Leonard b: 3/21/42, Chicago, Ill. d: 4/22/88, Richardson, Tex. BB/TR, 6', 190 lbs. Deb: 8/27/66

YEAR TM/L	W	L	PCT	G	GS	CG	SH	SV	IP	H	HR	BB	SO	RAT	ERA	ERA+	OAV	OOB	BH	AVG	PB	PR	/A	PD	TPI
1966 Chi-N	0	1	.000	4	0	0	0	0	6	10	1	7	3	25.5	7.50	49	.400	.531	0	.000	-0	-3	-3	0	-0.2

■ **CHUCK CHURN** Churn, Clarence Nottingham b: 2/1/30, Bridgetown, Va. BR/TR, 6'3", 205 lbs. Deb: 4/18/57

YEAR TM/L	W	L	PCT	G	GS	CG	SH	SV	IP	H	HR	BB	SO	RAT	ERA	ERA+	OAV	OOB	BH	AVG	PB	PR	/A	PD	TPI
1957 Pit-N	0	0	—	5	0	0	0	0	8¹	9	1	4	4	14.0	4.32	88	.333	.419	0	.000	-0	-0	-0	1	0.0
1958 Cle-A	0	0	—	6	0	0	0	0	8²	12	1	5	4	17.7	6.23	59	.343	.425	0	—	0	-2	-2	0	-0.2
1959 *LA-N	3	2	.600	14	0	0	0	1	30²	28	2	10	24	11.4	4.99	85	.255	.322	1	.167	0	-4	-3	0	-0.1
Total 3	3	2	.600	25	0	0	0	1	47²	49	4	19	32	13.0	5.10	79	.285	.359	1	.143	0	-6	-6	1	-0.3

■ **MARK CIARDI** Ciardi, Mark Thomas b: 8/19/61, New Brunswick, N.J. BR/TR, 6'1", 180 lbs. Deb: 4/09/87

YEAR TM/L	W	L	PCT	G	GS	CG	SH	SV	IP	H	HR	BB	SO	RAT	ERA	ERA+	OAV	OOB	BH	AVG	PB	PR	/A	PD	TPI
1987 Mil-A	1	1	.500	4	3	0	0	0	16¹	26	5	9	8	19.3	9.37	49	.361	.432	0	—	0	-9	-9	0	-0.6

■ **AL CICOTTE** Cicotte, Alva Warren "Bozo" b: 12/23/29, Melvindale, Mich. d: 11/29/82, Westland, Mich. BR/TR, 6'3", 185 lbs. Deb: 4/22/57

YEAR TM/L	W	L	PCT	G	GS	CG	SH	SV	IP	H	HR	BB	SO	RAT	ERA	ERA+	OAV	OOB	BH	AVG	PB	PR	/A	PD	TPI
1957 NY-A	2	2	.500	20	2	0	0	2	65¹	57	5	30	36	12.1	3.03	118	.237	.325	3	.150	-0	6	4	0	0.4
1958 Was-A	0	3	.000	8	4	0	0	0	28	36	3	14	14	16.1	4.82	79	.316	.391	2	.200	-0	-3	-3	-1	-0.3
Det-A	3	1	.750	14	2	0	0	0	43	50	1	15	21	13.6	3.56	113	.307	.365	1	.176	-1	1	2	1	0.3
Yr	3	4	.429	22	6	0	0	0	71	86	4	29	35	14.6	4.06	97	.309	.375	0	.000	-1	-2	-1	1	0.0
1959 Cle-A	3	1	.750	26	1	0	0	0	44	46	4	25	29	14.9	5.32	69	.299	.403	6	.333	1	-7	-8	-0	-0.6
1961 StL-N	2	6	.250	29	7	0	0	0	75	83	16	34	51	14.3	5.28	83	.283	.362	6	.286	1	-10	-7	-0	-0.5
1962 Hou-N	0	0	—	5	0	0	0	0	4²	8	1	4	2	17.4	3.86	97	.381	.409	0	—	0	-0	-0	0	0.0
Total 5	10	13	.435	102	16	0	0	4	260	280	30	119	149	14.0	4.36	90	.284	.364	15	.211	0	-14	-12	1	-0.7

YEAR TM/L	W	L	PCT	G	GS	CG	SH	SV	IP	H	HR	BB	SO	RAT	ERA	ERA+	OAV	OOB	BH	AVG	PB	PR	/A	PD	TPI

■ EDDIE CICOTTE   Cicotte, Edward Victor "Knuckles"   b: 6/19/1884, Detroit, Mich.   d: 5/5/69, Detroit, Mich.   BB/TR, 5'9", 175 lbs.   Deb: 9/03/05

YEAR TM/L	W	L	PCT	G	GS	CG	SH	SV	IP	H	HR	BB	SO	RAT	ERA	ERA+	OAV	OOB	BH	AVG	PB	PR	/A	PD	TPI
1905 Det-A	1	1	.500	3	1	1	0	0	18	25	0	5	6	15.0	3.50	78	.330	.371	3	.429	1	-2	-2	-1	0.0
1908 Bos-A	11	12	.478	39	24	17	2	2	207¹	198	0	59	95	11.5	2.43	101	.260	.320	17	.236	3	-1	1	0	0.4
1909 Bos-A	13	5	.722	27	17	10	1	2	159²	117	3	56	82	9.8	1.97	127	.210	.283	11	.224	3	9	9	-1	1.3
1910 Bos-A	15	11	.577	36	30	20	3	0	250	213	4	86	104	11.2	2.74	93	.233	.308	12	.141	-1	-6	-5	3	-0.2
1911 Bos-A	11	15	.423	35	25	16	1	0	220	236	2	73	106	12.8	2.82	116	.282	.342	10	.141	-2	13	11	1	0.9
1912 Bos-A	1	3	.250	9	6	2	0	0	46	58	0	15	20	14.5	5.67	60	.319	.374	2	.154	0	-12	-12	1	-0.9
Chi-A	9	7	.563	20	18	13	1	0	152	159	3	37	70	11.6	2.84	113	.277	.320	13	.245	1	8	6	2	1.0
Yr	10	10	.500	29	24	15	1	0	198	217	3	52	90	12.2	3.50	93	.286	.332	6	.091	1	-4	-6	3	0.1
1913 Chi-A	18	12	.600	41	30	18	3	1	268	224	2	73	121	10.1	1.58	185	.226	.281	13	.143	-3	40	40	7	5.1
1914 Chi-A	11	16	.407	45	30	15	4	3	269¹	220	0	72	122	9.9	2.04	132	.232	.288	14	.163	-1	21	19	7	2.9
1915 Chi-A	13	12	.520	39	26	15	1	3	223¹	216	2	48	106	10.9	3.02	99	.261	.306	14	.209	1	-2	-1	0	0.0
1916 Chi-A	15	7	.682	44	19	11	2	5	187	138	1	70	91	10.1	1.78	155	.218	.296	12	.211	2	22	20	1	2.6
1917 *Chi-A	**28**	12	.700	49	35	29	7	4	**346²**	246	2	70	150	**8.3**	**1.53**	174	.203	**.248**	20	.179	1	**44**	44	-2	**5.0**
1918 Chi-A	12	19	.387	38	30	24	1	2	266	275	2	40	104	10.7	2.77	99	.271	.300	14	.163	2	0	-1	-1	0.0
1919 *Chi-A	29	7	.806	40	35	**30**	5	1	306²	256	5	49	110	**9.0**	1.82	175	.228	.261	20	.202	1	48	46	-4	4.8
1920 Chi-A	21	10	.677	37	35	28	4	2	303¹	316	6	74	87	11.6	3.26	115	.275	.320	22	.196	-3	18	17	1	1.5
Total 14	208	149	.583	502	361	249	35	25	3223¹	2897	32	827	1374	10.5	2.38	123	.245	.298	197	.186	4	200	195	15	24.4

■ PETE CIMINO   Cimino, Peter William   b: 10/17/42, Philadelphia, Pa.   BR/TR, 6'2", 195 lbs.   Deb: 9/22/65

YEAR TM/L	W	L	PCT	G	GS	CG	SH	SV	IP	H	HR	BB	SO	RAT	ERA	ERA+	OAV	OOB	BH	AVG	PB	PR	/A	PD	TPI
1965 Min-A	0	0	—	1	0	0	0	0	1	0	0	0	0	0.0	0.00	—	.000	.000	0	—	0	0	0	0	0.0
1966 Min-A	2	5	.286	35	0	0	0	4	64²	67	5	30	57	11.7	2.92	123	.222	.311	0	.000	-0	4	5	-1	0.4
1967 Cal-A	3	3	.500	46	1	0	0	1	88¹	73	12	31	80	10.8	3.26	96	.229	.301	5	.417	2	-0	-1	-2	-0.1
1968 Cal-A	0	0	—	4	0	0	0	0	7	7	0	4	2	14.1	2.57	113	.259	.355	0	—	0	0	0	0	0.0
Total 4	5	8	.385	86	1	0	0	5	161	133	16	65	139	11.2	3.07	108	.226	.306	5	.278	1	4	4	-3	0.3

■ LOU CIOLA   Ciola, Louis Alexander   b: 9/6/22, Norfolk, Va.   BR/TR, 5'9", 165 lbs.   Deb: 7/25/43

YEAR TM/L	W	L	PCT	G	GS	CG	SH	SV	IP	H	HR	BB	SO	RAT	ERA	ERA+	OAV	OOB	BH	AVG	PB	PR	/A	PD	TPI
1943 Phi-A	1	3	.250	12	3	2	0	0	43²	48	2	22	7	14.6	5.56	61	.273	.357	3	.167	-1	-11	-11	-0	-1.1

■ GALEN CISCO   Cisco, Galen Bernard   b: 3/7/36, St. Mary's, Ohio   BR/TR, 6', 200 lbs.   Deb: 6/11/61   C

YEAR TM/L	W	L	PCT	G	GS	CG	SH	SV	IP	H	HR	BB	SO	RAT	ERA	ERA+	OAV	OOB	BH	AVG	PB	PR	/A	PD	TPI
1961 Bos-A	2	4	.333	17	8	0	0	0	52¹	67	5	28	26	16.3	6.71	62	.325	.406	1	.100	-0	-16	-15	-0	-1.3
1962 Bos-A	4	7	.364	23	9	1	0	0	83	95	11	50	43	16.0	6.72	61	.292	.392	2	.080	-1	-25	-24	1	-2.1
NY-N	1	1	.500	4	2	1	0	0	19¹	15	0	11	13	13.5	3.26	128	.208	.337	0	.000	-1	1	2	-0	0.1
1963 NY-N	7	15	.318	51	17	1	0	0	155²	165	15	64	81	13.6	4.34	80	.273	.349	5	.132	0	-18	-15	-0	-1.4
1964 NY-N	6	19	.240	36	25	5	2	0	191²	182	17	54	78	11.4	3.62	99	.256	.313	6	.111	-0	-2	-1	2	0.1
1965 NY-N	4	8	.333	35	17	1	1	0	112¹	119	12	51	58	13.7	4.49	79	.272	.349	7	.259	2	-12	-12	-1	-1.1
1967 Bos-A	0	1	.000	11	0	0	0	0	22¹	21	4	8	8	11.7	3.63	96	.266	.333	0	.000	-0	-1	-0	0	0.0
1969 KC-A	1	1	.500	15	0	0	0	0	22¹	17	4	15	18	12.9	3.63	102	.215	.340	0	—	0	-0	0	0	0.0
Total 7	25	56	.309	192	78	9	3	2	659	681	68	281	325	13.4	4.56	81	.271	.349	21	.128	-0	-72	-64	2	-5.7

■ RALPH CITARELLA   Citarella, Ralph Alexander   b: 2/7/58, East Orange, N.J.   BR/TR, 6', 180 lbs.   Deb: 9/13/83

YEAR TM/L	W	L	PCT	G	GS	CG	SH	SV	IP	H	HR	BB	SO	RAT	ERA	ERA+	OAV	OOB	BH	AVG	PB	PR	/A	PD	TPI
1983 StL-N	0	0	—	6	0	0	0	0	11	8	0	3	4	9.0	1.64	221	.205	.262	0	.000	-0	2	2	0	0.2
1984 StL-N	0	1	.000	10	2	0	0	0	22¹	20	0	7	15	12.1	3.63	96	.238	.319	1	.250	0	-0	-0	-0	0.0
1987 Chi-A	0	0	—	5	0	0	0	0	11	13	4	4	9	15.5	7.36	62	.302	.388	0	—	0	-4	-3	-0	-0.2
Total 3	0	1	.000	21	2	0	0	0	44¹	41	4	14	28	12.2	4.06	93	.247	.324	1	.200	0	-1	-1	0	0.0

■ BOBBY CLACK   Clack, Robert S. "Gentlemanly Bob" (b: Robert S. Clark)   b: 1851, Brooklyn, N.Y.   d: 10/22/33, Danvers, Mass.   BR/TR, 5'9", 153 lbs.   Deb: 5/15/1874 ♦

YEAR TM/L	W	L	PCT	G	GS	CG	SH	SV	IP	H	HR	BB	SO	RAT	ERA	ERA+	OAV	OOB	BH	AVG	PB	PR	/A	PD	TPI
1876 Cin-N	0	0	—	1	0	0	0	0	2	2	0	0	0	9.0	4.50	49	.243	.243	19	.161	-0	-0	-1	0	0.0

■ JIM CLANCY   Clancy, James   b: 12/18/55, Chicago, Ill.   BR/TR, 6'2", 185 lbs.   Deb: 7/26/77

YEAR TM/L	W	L	PCT	G	GS	CG	SH	SV	IP	H	HR	BB	SO	RAT	ERA	ERA+	OAV	OOB	BH	AVG	PB	PR	/A	PD	TPI
1977 Tor-A	4	9	.308	13	13	4	1	0	76²	80	7	47	44	14.9	5.05	83	.280	.381	0	—	0	-8	-7	1	-0.5
1978 Tor-A	10	12	.455	31	30	7	0	0	193²	199	10	91	106	13.5	4.09	96	.270	.351	0	—	0	-7	-4	1	-0.2
1979 Tor-A	2	7	.222	12	11	2	0	0	63²	65	9	31	33	13.6	5.51	79	.272	.356	0	—	0	-9	-8	0	-0.7
1980 Tor-A	13	16	.448	34	34	15	2	0	250²	217	19	128	152	12.5	3.30	130	.233	.327	0	—	0	20	28	-1	2.8
1981 Tor-A	6	12	.333	22	22	2	0	0	125	126	12	64	56	14.0	4.90	80	.262	.355	0	—	0	-17	-13	-3	-1.5
1982 Tor-A	16	14	.533	40	40	11	3	0	266²	251	26	77	139	11.1	3.71	121	.248	.302	0	—	0	11	23	-2	2.1
1983 Tor-A	15	11	.577	34	34	11	1	0	223	238	23	61	99	12.1	3.91	110	.271	.319	0	—	0	4	10	2	0.8
1984 Tor-A	13	15	.464	36	36	5	0	0	219²	249	25	88	118	13.9	5.12	80	.287	.355	0	—	0	-28	-25	1	-2.3
1985 *Tor-A	9	6	.600	23	23	1	0	0	128²	117	15	37	66	10.8	3.78	111	.241	.295	0	—	0	5	6	1	0.5
1986 Tor-A	14	14	.500	34	34	6	3	0	219¹	202	24	63	126	11.0	3.94	107	.243	.299	0	—	0	6	7	1	0.8
1987 Tor-A	15	11	.577	37	37	5	1	0	241¹	234	24	80	180	11.7	3.54	127	.255	.315	0	—	0	24	25	2	2.7
1988 Tor-A	11	13	.458	36	31	4	0	1	196¹	207	26	47	118	12.1	4.49	87	.272	.322	0	—	0	-11	-12	-1	-1.2
1989 Hou-N	7	14	.333	33	26	1	0	0	147	155	13	66	91	13.5	5.08	67	.269	.344	6	.146	-0	-26	-28	-3	-3.0
1990 Hou-N	2	8	.200	33	10	0	0	1	76	100	4	33	44	16.1	6.51	57	.322	.392	3	.214	0	-23	-23	1	-2.1
Total 14	137	162	.458	418	381	74	11	2	2427²	2440	236	913	1372	12.5	4.24	98	.262	.330	9	.164	0	-60	-23	-5	-1.8

■ BRYAN CLARK   Clark, Bryan Donald   b: 7/12/56, Madera, Cal.   BL/TL, 6'2", 185 lbs.   Deb: 4/11/81

YEAR TM/L	W	L	PCT	G	GS	CG	SH	SV	IP	H	HR	BB	SO	RAT	ERA	ERA+	OAV	OOB	BH	AVG	PB	PR	/A	PD	TPI
1981 Sea-A	2	5	.286	29	9	1	0	2	93¹	92	3	55	52	14.3	4.34	89	.261	.363	0	—	0	-7	-5	1	-0.4
1982 Sea-A	5	2	.714	37	5	1	1	0	114²	104	6	58	70	12.7	2.75	154	.241	.331	0	—	0	17	19	1	2.1
1983 Sea-A	7	10	.412	41	17	2	0	0	162¹	160	14	72	76	13.0	3.94	108	.261	.342	0	—	0	2	6	3	0.9
1984 Tor-A	1	2	.333	20	3	0	0	0	45²	66	6	22	21	17.5	5.91	69	.342	.412	0	—	0	-10	-9	1	-0.7
1985 Cle-A	3	4	.429	31	3	0	0	2	62²	78	8	34	24	16.1	6.32	65	.311	.393	0	—	0	-15	-15	1	-1.3
1986 Chi-A	0	0	—	5	0	0	0	0	8	8	0	2	5	11.3	4.50	96	.276	.323	0	—	0	-0	-0	0	0.0
1987 Chi-A	0	0	—	11	0	0	0	0	18²	19	1	8	8	13.0	2.41	190	.297	.375	0	—	0	4	4	-0	0.4
1990 Sea-A	2	0	1.000	12	0	0	0	0	11	9	0	10	3	15.5	3.27	121	.237	.396	0	—	0	1	1	1	0.1
Total 8	20	23	.465	186	37	4	1	4	516¹	536	38	261	259	14.0	4.15	100	.272	.359	0	—	0	-8	1	8	1.1

■ ED CLARK   Clark, Edward C.   b: Cincinnati, Ohio   Deb: 7/04/1886

YEAR TM/L	W	L	PCT	G	GS	CG	SH	SV	IP	H	HR	BB	SO	RAT	ERA	ERA+	OAV	OOB	BH	AVG	PB	PR	/A	PD	TPI
1886 Phi-a	0	1	.000	1	1	1	0	0	8	10	2	2	2	13.5	6.75	52	.292	.331	0	.000	-0	-3	-3	-0	-0.2
1891 Col-a	0	0	—	1	0	0	0	0	2	2	0	0	1	9.0	0.00	—	.252	.252	0	.000	-0	1	1	0	0.1
Total 2	0	1	.000	2	1	1	0	0	10	12	2	2	3	12.6	5.40	65	.285	.317	0	.000	-0	-2	-2	0	-0.1

■ GEORGE CLARK   Clark, George Myron   b: 5/19/1891, Smithland, Iowa   d: 11/14/40, Sioux City, Iowa   BR/TL, 6', 190 lbs.   Deb: 5/16/13

YEAR TM/L	W	L	PCT	G	GS	CG	SH	SV	IP	H	HR	BB	SO	RAT	ERA	ERA+	OAV	OOB	BH	AVG	PB	PR	/A	PD	TPI
1913 NY-A	0	1	.000	11	1	0	0	0	19	22	1	19	5	20.8	9.00	33	.272	.427	2	.500	1	-13	-13	0	-1.1

■ GINGER CLARK   Clark, Harvey Daniel   b: 3/7/1879, Wooster, Ohio   d: 5/10/43, Lake Charles, La.   BR/TR, 5'11", 165 lbs.   Deb: 8/11/02

YEAR TM/L	W	L	PCT	G	GS	CG	SH	SV	IP	H	HR	BB	SO	RAT	ERA	ERA+	OAV	OOB	BH	AVG	PB	PR	/A	PD	TPI
1902 Cle-A	1	0	1.000	1	0	0	0	0	6	10	0	3	1	19.5	6.00	57	.370	.433	2	.500	1	-2	-2	0	0.0

■ MIKE CLARK   Clark, Michael John   b: 2/12/22, Camden, N.J.   BR/TR, 6'4", 190 lbs.   Deb: 7/27/52

YEAR TM/L	W	L	PCT	G	GS	CG	SH	SV	IP	H	HR	BB	SO	RAT	ERA	ERA+	OAV	OOB	BH	AVG	PB	PR	/A	PD	TPI
1952 StL-N	2	0	1.000	12	4	0	0	0	25¹	32	2	14	10	16.3	6.04	61	.311	.393	0	.000	-1	-6	-7	0	-0.6
1953 StL-N	1	0	1.000	23	2	0	0	1	35²	46	2	21	17	17.4	4.79	89	.315	.408	0	.000	-1	-2	-2	1	-0.1
Total 2	3	0	1.000	35	6	0	0	1	61	78	4	35	27	17.0	5.31	76	.313	.402	0	.000	-1	-9	-9	1	-0.7

SPIDER CLARK — Clark, Owen F. b: 9/16/1867, Brooklyn, N.Y. d: 2/8/1892, Brooklyn, N.Y. TR, 5'10", 150 lbs. Deb: 5/02/1889 ◆

YEAR TM/L	W	L	PCT	G	GS	CG	SH	SV	IP	H	HR	BB	SO	RAT	ERA	ERA+	OAV	OOB	BH	AVG	PB	PR	/A	PD	TPI
1890 Buf-P	0	0	—	1	0	0	0	0	4	8	0	2	2	22.5	6.75	61	.399	.453	69	.265	0	-1	-1	-0	0.0

PHIL CLARK — Clark, Philip James b: 10/3/32, Albany, Ga. BR/TR, 6'3", 210 lbs. Deb: 4/15/58

YEAR TM/L	W	L	PCT	G	GS	CG	SH	SV	IP	H	HR	BB	SO	RAT	ERA	ERA+	OAV	OOB	BH	AVG	PB	PR	/A	PD	TPI
1958 StL-N	0	1	.000	7	0	0	0	1	7²	11	2	3	1	16.4	3.52	117	.355	.412	0	.000	-0	0	1	-0	0.0
1959 StL-N	0	1	.000	7	0	0	0	1	7	8	0	8	5	20.6	12.86	33	.286	.444	0	—	0	-7	-7	0	-0.5
Total 2	0	2	.000	14	0	0	0	1	14²	19	2	11	6	18.4	7.98	52	.322	.429	0	.000	-0	-7	-6	0	-0.5

RICKEY CLARK — Clark, Rickey Charles b: 3/21/46, Mt.Clemens, Mich. BR/TR, 6'2", 170 lbs. Deb: 4/22/67

YEAR TM/L	W	L	PCT	G	GS	CG	SH	SV	IP	H	HR	BB	SO	RAT	ERA	ERA+	OAV	OOB	BH	AVG	PB	PR	/A	PD	TPI
1967 Cal-A	12	11	.522	32	30	1	1	0	174	144	15	69	81	11.3	2.59	121	.224	.305	2	.040	-4	12	11	1	0.9
1968 Cal-A	1	11	.083	21	17	0	0	0	94¹	74	4	54	60	12.3	3.53	82	.217	.326	3	.107	-1	-6	-6	1	-0.7
1969 Cal-A	0	0	—	6	1	0	0	0	9²	12	2	7	6	17.7	5.59	62	.300	.404	1	.500	0	-2	-2	-0	-0.1
1971 Cal-A	2	1	.667	11	7	1	1	1	44	36	6	28	28	13.5	2.86	113	.220	.340	4	.267	1	3	2	-1	0.2
1972 Cal-A	4	9	.308	26	15	2	0	1	109²	105	10	55	61	13.3	4.51	64	.261	.352	3	.097	-1	-18	-20	1	-2.1
Total 5	19	32	.373	96	70	4	2	2	431²	371	37	213	236	12.4	3.38	90	.233	.328	13	.103	-5	-10	-16	2	-1.8

BOB CLARK — Clark, Robert William b: 8/22/1897, Newport, Pa. d: 5/18/44, Carlsbad, N.Mex. BR/TR, 6'3", 188 lbs. Deb: 5/26/20

YEAR TM/L	W	L	PCT	G	GS	CG	SH	SV	IP	H	HR	BB	SO	RAT	ERA	ERA+	OAV	OOB	BH	AVG	PB	PR	/A	PD	TPI
1920 Cle-A	1	2	.333	11	2	2	1	0	42	59	0	13	8	15.6	3.43	111	.383	.435	2	.200	-0	2	2	-0	0.1
1921 Cle-A	0	0	—	5	0	0	0	0	9¹	23	2	6	2	28.9	14.46	29	.511	.577	0	.000	-1	-11	-11	0	-0.9
Total 2	1	2	.333	16	2	2	1	0	51¹	82	2	19	10	18.1	5.44	71	.412	.468	2	.154	-1	-9	-9	-0	-0.8

TERRY CLARK — Clark, Terry Lee b: 10/18/60, Los Angeles, Cal. BR/TR, 6'2", 190 lbs. Deb: 7/07/88

YEAR TM/L	W	L	PCT	G	GS	CG	SH	SV	IP	H	HR	BB	SO	RAT	ERA	ERA+	OAV	OOB	BH	AVG	PB	PR	/A	PD	TPI
1988 Cal-A	6	6	.500	15	15	2	1	0	94	120	8	31	39	14.5	5.07	76	.323	.375	0	—	0	-12	-13	0	-1.1
1989 Cal-A	0	2	.000	4	2	0	0	0	11	13	0	3	7	13.1	4.91	78	.310	.356	0	—	0	-1	-1	0	0.0
1990 Hou-N	0	0	—	1	1	0	0	0	4	9	0	3	2	27.0	13.50	28	.429	.500	1	.500	0	-4	-4	0	-0.2
Total 3	6	8	.429	20	18	2	1	0	109	142	8	37	48	14.8	5.37	72	.326	.379	1	.500	0	-17	-18	0	-1.3

OTIE CLARK — Clark, William Otis b: 5/22/18, Boscobel, Wis. BR/TR, 6'1.5", 190 lbs. Deb: 4/17/45

YEAR TM/L	W	L	PCT	G	GS	CG	SH	SV	IP	H	HR	BB	SO	RAT	ERA	ERA+	OAV	OOB	BH	AVG	PB	PR	/A	PD	TPI
1945 Bos-A	4	4	.500	12	9	4	1	0	82	86	6	19	20	11.6	3.07	111	.268	.311	5	.208	0	3	3	-2	0.1

WATTY CLARK — Clark, William Watson "Lefty" b: 5/16/02, St.Joseph, La. d: 3/4/72, Clearwater, Fla. BL/TL, 6'0.5", 175 lbs. Deb: 5/28/24

YEAR TM/L	W	L	PCT	G	GS	CG	SH	SV	IP	H	HR	BB	SO	RAT	ERA	ERA+	OAV	OOB	BH	AVG	PB	PR	/A	PD	TPI
1924 Cle-A	1	3	.250	12	1	0	0	0	25²	38	0	14	6	18.9	7.01	61	.345	.429	2	.222	1	-8	-8	-0	-0.6
1927 Bro-N	7	2	.778	27	3	1	0	2	73²	74	2	19	32	11.4	2.32	171	.265	.312	3	.143	-1	**13**	**13**	0	2.7
1928 Bro-N	12	9	.571	40	19	10	2	3	194²	193	4	50	85	11.3	2.68	148	.259	.306	10	.152	-2	28	28	0	2.7
1929 Bro-N	16	19	.457	41	36	19	3	1	**279**	295	14	71	140	11.9	3.74	123	.270	.316	16	.165	-3	30	27	-1	2.1
1930 Bro-N	13	13	.500	44	24	9	1	6	200	209	20	38	61	11.1	4.18	117	.276	.306	14	.206	-0	17	16	0	1.5
1931 Bro-N	14	10	.583	34	28	16	3	1	233¹	243	4	52	96	11.4	3.20	119	.267	.308	21	.250	4	17	16	-3	1.7
1932 Bro-N	20	12	.625	40	36	19	2	0	273	282	10	49	99	11.0	3.49	109	.264	.299	21	.216	1	12	10	1	1.2
1933 Bro-N	2	4	.333	11	8	4	1	1	50²	61	2	6	14	12.4	4.80	67	.303	.333	2	.154	-0	-8	-9	-0	-0.9
NY-N	3	4	.429	16	5	0	0	0	44	58	3	11	11	14.3	4.70	68	.317	.359	3	.273	1	-7	-7	1	-0.6
Yr	5	8	.385	27	13	4	1	1	94²	119	5	17	25	13.0	4.75	68	.307	.338	2	.083	1	-15	-16	1	-1.4
1934 NY-N	1	2	.333	5	4	1	0	0	18²	23	5	5	6	13.5	6.75	57	.295	.337	1	.167	0	-6	-6	0	-0.4
Bro-N	2	0	1.000	17	1	0	0	0	25¹	40	0	9	10	17.8	5.33	73	.345	.397	1	.125	-1	-4	-4	-0	-0.8
Yr	3	2	.600	22	5	1	0	0	44	63	5	14	16	16.0	5.93	66	.325	.373	1	.071	0	-9	-10	0	-0.8
1935 Bro-N	13	8	.619	33	25	11	1	0	207	215	11	28	35	10.6	3.30	120	.264	.289	14	.177	-0	16	15	3	1.8
1936 Bro-N	7	11	.389	33	16	1	1	2	120	162	11	28	28	14.3	4.43	93	.316	.351	9	.231	0	-5	-4	1	-0.2
1937 Bro-N	0	0	—	2	0	0	0	0	2¹	4	0	3	0	27.0	7.71	52	.308	.438	0	—	0	-1	-1	0	0.0
Total 12	111	97	.534	355	206	91	14	16	1747¹	1897	86	383	643	11.8	3.66	112	.275	.315	117	.196	1	96	87	2	9.3

LEFTY CLARKE — Clarke, Alan Thomas b: 3/8/1896, Clarksville, Md. d: 3/11/75, Cheverly, Md. BB/TL, 5'11", 180 lbs. Deb: 10/02/21

YEAR TM/L	W	L	PCT	G	GS	CG	SH	SV	IP	H	HR	BB	SO	RAT	ERA	ERA+	OAV	OOB	BH	AVG	PB	PR	/A	PD	TPI
1921 Cin-N	0	1	.000	1	1	1	0	0	5	7	0	2	1	16.2	5.40	66	.304	.360	0	.000	-0	-1	-1	-0	0.0

HENRY CLARKE — Clarke, Henry Tefft b: 8/28/1875, Bellevue, Neb. d: 3/28/50, Colorado Springs, Colo. BR/TR, Deb: 6/26/1897 ◆

YEAR TM/L	W	L	PCT	G	GS	CG	SH	SV	IP	H	HR	BB	SO	RAT	ERA	ERA+	OAV	OOB	BH	AVG	PB	PR	/A	PD	TPI
1897 Cle-N	0	4	.000	5	4	3	0	0	30²	32	4	12	3	12.9	6.16	73	.267	.333	7	.280	0	-6	-6	-1	-0.4
1898 Chi-N	1	0	1.000	1	1	1	0	0	9	8	0	5	1	13.0	2.00	179	.237	.335	1	.250	0	2	2	-0	0.2
Total 2	1	4	.200	6	5	4	0	0	39²	40	4	17	4	12.9	5.22	82	.260	.334	8	.276	0	-5	-4	-1	-0.2

RUFE CLARKE — Clarke, Rufus Rivers b: 4/13/1900, Estill, S.C. d: 2/8/83, Columbia, S.C. BR/TR, 6'1", 203 lbs. Deb: 9/03/23

YEAR TM/L	W	L	PCT	G	GS	CG	SH	SV	IP	H	HR	BB	SO	RAT	ERA	ERA+	OAV	OOB	BH	AVG	PB	PR	/A	PD	TPI
1923 Det-A	1	1	.500	5	0	0	0	0	6	6	0	6	2	19.5	4.50	86	.300	.481	0	—	0	-0	-0	0	0.0
1924 Det-A	0	0	—	2	0	0	0	0	5¹	3	0	5	1	15.2	3.38	122	.158	.360	0	.000	-0	1	0	0	0.0
Total 2	1	1	.500	7	0	0	0	0	11¹	9	0	11	3	17.5	3.97	100	.231	.423	0	.000	-0	0	0	0	0.0

STAN CLARKE — Clarke, Stanley Martin b: 8/9/60, Toledo, Ohio BL/TL, 6'1", 180 lbs. Deb: 6/07/83

YEAR TM/L	W	L	PCT	G	GS	CG	SH	SV	IP	H	HR	BB	SO	RAT	ERA	ERA+	OAV	OOB	BH	AVG	PB	PR	/A	PD	TPI
1983 Tor-A	1	1	.500	10	0	0	0	0	11	10	2	5	7	12.3	3.27	131	.256	.341	0	—	0	1	1	0	0.1
1985 Tor-A	0	0	—	4	0	0	0	0	4	3	1	2	2	11.3	4.50	94	.214	.313	0	—	0	-0	-0	0	0.0
1986 Tor-A	0	1	.000	10	0	0	0	0	12²	18	4	10	9	19.9	9.24	46	.375	.483	0	—	0	-7	-7	0	-0.6
1987 Sea-A	2	2	.500	22	0	0	0	0	23	31	7	10	13	16.0	5.48	86	.333	.398	0	—	0	-3	-2	-0	-0.1
1989 KC-A	0	2	.000	2	0	0	0	0	7	14	2	4	2	23.1	15.43	25	.438	.500	0	—	0	-9	-9	0	-0.6
1990 StL-N	0	0	—	2	0	0	0	0	3¹	2	0	3	5	5.4	2.70	145	.167	.167	0	—	0	0	0	0	0.0
Total 6	3	6	.333	50	2	0	0	0	61	78	16	31	36	16.1	6.79	64	.328	.405	0	—	0	-18	-16	0	-1.2

WEBBO CLARKE — Clarke, Vibert Ernesto b: 6/8/28, Colon, Panama d: 6/14/70, Cristobal, C.Z. BL/TL, 6', 165 lbs. Deb: 9/04/55

YEAR TM/L	W	L	PCT	G	GS	CG	SH	SV	IP	H	HR	BB	SO	RAT	ERA	ERA+	OAV	OOB	BH	AVG	PB	PR	/A	PD	TPI
1955 Was-A	0	0	—	7	2	0	0	0	21¹	17	2	14	9	13.1	4.64	83	.221	.341	1	.167	-0	-2	-2	0	-0.1

DAD CLARKE — Clarke, William H. b: 1/7/1865, Oswego, N.Y. d: 6/3/11, Lorain, Ohio BB/TR, Deb: 4/23/1888

YEAR TM/L	W	L	PCT	G	GS	CG	SH	SV	IP	H	HR	BB	SO	RAT	ERA	ERA+	OAV	OOB	BH	AVG	PB	PR	/A	PD	TPI
1888 Chi-N	1	0	1.000	2	2	1	0	0	16	23	2	6	6	16.3	5.06	59	.325	.378	2	.286	2	-4	-4	0	0.0
1891 Col-a	1	2	.333	4	3	2	0	0	21	30	0	16	2	19.7	6.86	50	.324	.424	1	.111	-0	-7	-8	0	-0.5
1894 NY-N	3	4	.429	15	6	5	0	0	84	114	3	26	15	15.0	4.93	106	.320	.367	8	.216	-0	4	3	0	0.4
1895 NY-N	18	15	.545	37	30	27	1	1	281²	336	5	60	67	12.7	3.39	137	.292	.327	29	.240	-2	44	39	-2	2.9
1896 NY-N	17	24	.415	48	40	33	1	1	351	431	9	60	66	12.6	4.26	99	.300	.328	30	.204	-3	4	-2	-3	-0.7
1897 NY-N	2	1	.667	6	4	2	0	0	31	41	1	11	10	15.7	6.10	68	.320	.378	3	.167	-1	-6	-7	0	-0.5
Lou-N	2	4	.333	7	6	6	0	0	54²	74	3	10	7	13.8	3.95	108	.320	.349	5	.227	-1	2	2	1	0.2
Yr	4	5	.444	13	10	8	0	0	85²	117	4	21	17	14.5	4.73	89	.322	.359	1	.025	-2	-4	-5	1	-0.3
1898 Lou-N	0	1	.000	1	1	1	0	0	9	10	1	2	1	12.0	5.00	72	.279	.317	1	.025	-0	-1	-1	0	-0.1
Total 7	44	51	.463	120	92	77	2	3	848¹	1061	24	191	174	13.3	4.17	106	.302	.338	78	.214	-6	35	23	-3	1.5

DAD CLARKSON — Clarkson, Arthur Hamilton b: 8/31/1866, Cambridge, Mass. d: 2/5/11, Somerville, Mass. 5'10", 165 lbs. Deb: 8/20/1891

YEAR TM/L	W	L	PCT	G	GS	CG	SH	SV	IP	H	HR	BB	SO	RAT	ERA	ERA+	OAV	OOB	BH	AVG	PB	PR	/A	PD	TPI
1891 NY-N	1	2	.333	5	2	1	0	0	28	24	0	18	11	13.5	2.89	111	.223	.334	4	.444	2	1	1	0	0.2
1892 Bos-N	1	0	1.000	1	1	1	0	0	7	5	0	3	0	10.3	1.29	273	.192	.276	0	.000	-1	2	2	0	0.1
1893 StL-N	12	9	.571	24	21	17	1	0	186¹	194	4	79	37	13.2	3.48	136	.260	.331	10	.133	-5	25	26	1	1.8
1894 StL-N	8	17	.320	32	32	24	1	0	233¹	318	9	117	46	16.8	6.36	85	.321	.393	16	.182	-4	-27	-25	1	-1.9
1895 StL-N	1	6	.143	7	7	7	0	0	61	91	7	26	9	17.3	7.38	66	.340	.398	1	.043	-3	-18	-17	-1	-1.5
Bal-N	12	3	.800	20	14	10	0	0	142	169	5	64	23	14.8	3.87	123	.291	.361	8	.140	-4	14	14	2	1.0
Yr	13	9	.591	27	21	17	0	0	203	260	12	90	32	15.5	4.92	97	.306	.373	8	.100	-7	-3	-3	1	-0.5
1896 Bal-N	4	2	.667	7	4	3	0	0	47	72	1	18	7	17.2	4.98	86	.348	.400	5	.278	0	-3	-4	-0	-0.2

YEAR TM/L	W	L	PCT	G	GS	CG	SH	SV	IP	H	HR	BB	SO	RAT	ERA	ERA+	OAV	OOB	BH	AVG	PB	PR	/A	PD	TPI
Total 6	39	39	.500	96	81	63	2	0	704²	873	26	325	133	15.3	4.90	99	.299	.369	44	.161	-14	-6	-3	3	-0.5

■ JOHN CLARKSON
Clarkson, John Gibson b: 7/1/1861, Cambridge, Mass. d: 2/4/09, Belmont, Mass. BR/TR, 5'10", 155 lbs. Deb: 5/02/1882 H

YEAR TM/L	W	L	PCT	G	GS	CG	SH	SV	IP	H	HR	BB	SO	RAT	ERA	ERA+	OAV	OOB	BH	AVG	PB	PR	/A	PD	TPI
1882 Wor-N	1	2	.333	3	3	2	0	0	24	49	0	2	3	19.1	4.50	69	.399	.409	4	.364	1	-4	-4	0	-0.1
1884 Chi-N	10	3	.769	14	13	12	0	0	118	94	10	25	102	9.1	2.14	147	.207	.248	22	.262	4	11	13	2	2.1
1885 *Chi-N	53	16	.768	70	70	68	10	0	623	497	21	97	308	8.6	1.85	164	.209	.240	61	.216	2	67	82	7	9.5
1886 *Chi-N	36	17	.679	55	55	50	3	0	466²	419	20	86	313	9.7	2.41	151	.230	.265	49	.233	1	46	64	4	6.9
1887 Chi-N	38	21	.644	60	59	56	2	0	523	513	20	92	237	10.4	3.08	145	.250	.282	52	.242	3	56	80	9	8.7
1888 Bos-N	33	20	.623	54	54	53	3	0	483¹	448	17	119	223	10.6	2.76	103	.237	.282	40	.195	3	4	4	2	0.9
1889 Bos-N	49	19	.721	73	72	68	8	1	620	589	16	203	284	11.5	2.73	153	.243	.301	54	.206	1	89	99	11	10.4
1890 Bos-N	26	18	.591	44	44	43	2	0	383	370	14	140	138	12.0	3.27	115	.246	.311	43	.249	4	13	20	-1	2.3
1891 Bos-N	33	19	.635	55	51	47	3	3	460²	435	18	154	141	11.5	2.79	131	.240	.299	42	.225	4	28	44	5	5.2
1892 Bos-N	8	6	.571	16	16	15	4	0	145²	115	4	60	48	10.8	2.35	150	.208	.286	13	.228	1	15	19	0	2.1
*Cle-N	17	10	.630	29	28	27	1	1	243¹	235	4	72	91	11.4	2.55	133	.244	.296	14	.139	-5	20	23	-1	1.6
Yr	25	16	.610	45	44	42	5	1	389	350	8	132	139	11.2	2.48	139	.231	.292	11	.070	-4	35	41	-1	3.7
1893 Cle-N	16	17	.485	36	35	31	0	0	295	358	11	95	62	13.8	4.45	110	.291	.342	27	.206	-4	7	14	3	1.2
1894 Cle-N	8	10	.444	22	18	13	1	0	150²	173	6	46	28	13.1	4.42	124	.285	.335	11	.200	-2	15	17	2	1.3
Total 12	328	178	.648	531	518	485	37	5	4536¹	4295	161	1191	1978	10.9	2.81	134	.241	.289	432	.219	13	368	477	44	52.1

■ WALTER CLARKSON
Clarkson, Walter Hamilton b: 11/3/1878, Cambridge, Mass. d: 10/10/46, Cambridge, Mass. TR, 5'10", 150 lbs. Deb: 7/02/04

YEAR TM/L	W	L	PCT	G	GS	CG	SH	SV	IP	H	HR	BB	SO	RAT	ERA	ERA+	OAV	OOB	BH	AVG	PB	PR	/A	PD	TPI
1904 NY-A	1	2	.333	13	4	2	0	1	66¹	63	3	25	43	11.9	5.02	54	.251	.319	7	.269	2	-18	-17	-2	-1.6
1905 NY-A	3	3	.500	9	4	3	0	0	46	40	1	13	35	10.4	3.91	75	.235	.290	1	.053	-2	-6	-5	-1	-0.7
1906 NY-A	9	4	.692	32	16	9	3	0	151	135	6	55	64	11.3	2.32	128	.242	.310	8	.157	-1	6	11	-1	1.0
1907 NY-A	1	1	.500	5	2	0	0	0	17¹	19	1	8	3	14.0	6.23	45	.280	.356	2	.286	0	-7	-7	0	-0.5
Cle-A	4	6	.400	17	10	9	1	0	90²	77	1	29	32	10.5	1.99	127	.232	.294	1	.036	-3	6	5	-0	0.3
Yr	5	7	.417	22	12	9	1	0	108	96	2	37	35	11.1	2.67	96	.240	.304	3	.000	-3	-1	-1	0	-0.3
1908 Cle-A	0	0	—	2	1	0	0	0	3¹	6	0	2	1	27.0	10.80	22	.400	.526	1	1.000	0	-3	-3	-0	-0.2
Total 5	18	16	.529	78	37	23	4	1	374²	340	12	132	178	11.4	3.17	88	.244	.310	20	.152	-4	-23	-16	-4	-1.8

■ BILL CLARKSON
Clarkson, William Henry "Blackie" b: 9/27/1898, Portsmouth, Va. d: 8/27/71, Raleigh, N.C. BR/TR, 5'11", 160 lbs. Deb: 5/02/27

YEAR TM/L	W	L	PCT	G	GS	CG	SH	SV	IP	H	HR	BB	SO	RAT	ERA	ERA+	OAV	OOB	BH	AVG	PB	PR	/A	PD	TPI
1927 NY-N	3	9	.250	26	7	2	0	2	86²	92	3	52	28	15.1	4.36	88	.280	.380	1	.050	-1	-4	-5	0	-0.5
1928 NY-N	0	0	—	4	0	0	0	0	5²	10	0	1	3	17.5	7.94	49	.455	.478	0	—	-0	-2	-3	0	-0.2
Bos-N	0	2	.000	19	1	0	0	0	34²	53	2	22	8	19.7	6.75	58	.349	.434	0	.000	-0	-11	-11	1	-0.9
Yr	0	2	.000	23	1	0	0	0	40¹	63	2	23	11	19.4	6.92	56	.362	.439	0	.000	-0	-13	-13	1	-1.1
1929 Bos-N	0	1	.000	2	1	0	0	0	7	16	0	4	0	25.7	10.29	45	.485	.541	1	.500	0	-4	-4	0	-0.2
Total 3	3	12	.200	51	9	2	0	2	134	171	5	79	39	16.9	5.44	72	.319	.408	2	.080	-1	-22	-23	1	-1.8

■ MARTY CLARY
Clary, Martin Keith b: 4/3/62, Detroit, Mich. BR/TR, 6'4", 190 lbs. Deb: 9/05/87

YEAR TM/L	W	L	PCT	G	GS	CG	SH	SV	IP	H	HR	BB	SO	RAT	ERA	ERA+	OAV	OOB	BH	AVG	PB	PR	/A	PD	TPI
1987 Atl-N	0	1	.000	7	1	0	0	0	14²	20	2	4	7	15.3	6.14	71	.328	.379	0	.000	-0	-3	-3	-0	-0.2
1989 Atl-N	4	3	.571	18	17	2	1	0	108²	103	6	31	30	11.2	3.15	116	.249	.303	5	.161	0	4	6	1	0.8
1990 Atl-N	1	10	.091	33	14	0	0	0	101²	128	9	39	44	14.9	5.67	69	.308	.368	0	.000	-3	-21	-20	1	-2.0
Total 3	5	14	.263	58	32	2	1	0	225	251	17	74	81	13.1	4.48	85	.282	.339	5	.083	-2	-20	-17	2	-1.4

■ GOWELL CLASET
Claset, Gowell Sylvester "Lefty" b: 11/26/07, Battle Creek, Mich d: 3/8/81, St.Petersburg, Fla. BB/TL, 6'3.5", 210 lbs. Deb: 4/12/33

YEAR TM/L	W	L	PCT	G	GS	CG	SH	SV	IP	H	HR	BB	SO	RAT	ERA	ERA+	OAV	OOB	BH	AVG	PB	PR	/A	PD	TPI
1933 Phi-A	2	0	1.000	8	1	0	0	0	11¹	23	1	11	1	27.0	9.53	45	.426	.523	1	.500	1	-7	-7	0	-0.4

■ FRITZ CLAUSEN
Clausen, Frederick William b: 4/26/1869, New York, N.Y. d: 2/11/60, Memphis, Tenn. BR/TL, 5'11", 190 lbs. Deb: 7/23/1892

YEAR TM/L	W	L	PCT	G	GS	CG	SH	SV	IP	H	HR	BB	SO	RAT	ERA	ERA+	OAV	OOB	BH	AVG	PB	PR	/A	PD	TPI
1892 Lou-N	9	13	.409	24	24	24	2	0	200	181	3	87	94	12.1	3.06	100	.232	.309	13	.155	-3	5	0	-2	-0.3
1893 Lou-N	1	4	.200	5	5	3	0	0	33	41	2	22	4	17.2	6.00	73	.296	.392	3	.214	-1	-5	-6	0	-0.4
Chi-N	6	2	.750	10	9	8	0	1	76	71	1	39	31	13.0	3.08	150	.240	.328	4	.121	-3	13	13	0	0.8
Yr	7	6	.538	15	14	11	0	1	109	112	3	61	35	14.3	3.96	115	.258	.349	7	.043	-4	9	7	0	0.4
1894 Chi-N	0	1	.000	1	1	0	0	0	4¹	5	0	3	1	16.6	10.38	54	.286	.391	0	.000	-0	-2	-2	0	-0.1
1896 Lou-N	0	2	.000	2	2	1	0	0	11	17	1	6	4	18.8	6.55	66	.350	.421	0	.000	-1	-3	-3	0	-0.2
Total 4	16	22	.421	42	41	36	2	1	324¹	315	7	157	134	13.1	3.58	101	.246	.328	20	.147	-9	9	2	-1	-0.2

■ AL CLAUSS
Clauss, Albert Stanley "Lefty" b: 6/24/1891, New Haven, Conn. d: 9/13/52, New Haven, Conn. BR/TL, 5'10.5", 178 lbs. Deb: 4/22/13

YEAR TM/L	W	L	PCT	G	GS	CG	SH	SV	IP	H	HR	BB	SO	RAT	ERA	ERA+	OAV	OOB	BH	AVG	PB	PR	/A	PD	TPI
1913 Det-A	0	1	.000	5	1	0	0	0	13¹	11	0	12	1	16.9	4.73	62	.220	.391	0	.000	-1	-3	-3	0	-0.2

■ DANNY CLAY
Clay, Danny Bruce b: 10/24/61, Sun Walley, Cal. BR/TR, 6'1", 190 lbs. Deb: 5/01/88

YEAR TM/L	W	L	PCT	G	GS	CG	SH	SV	IP	H	HR	BB	SO	RAT	ERA	ERA+	OAV	OOB	BH	AVG	PB	PR	/A	PD	TPI
1988 Phi-N	0	1	.000	17	0	0	0	0	24	27	5	21	12	18.0	6.00	59	.303	.436	0	.000	-0	-7	-7	0	-0.7

■ KEN CLAY
Clay, Kenneth Earl b: 4/6/54, Lynchburg, Va. BR/TR, 6'3", 185 lbs. Deb: 6/07/77

YEAR TM/L	W	L	PCT	G	GS	CG	SH	SV	IP	H	HR	BB	SO	RAT	ERA	ERA+	OAV	OOB	BH	AVG	PB	PR	/A	PD	TPI
1977 *NY-A	2	3	.400	21	3	0	0	1	55²	53	6	24	20	12.6	4.37	90	.251	.331	0	—	0	-2	-3	0	-0.1
1978 *NY-A	3	4	.429	28	6	0	0	0	75²	89	3	21	32	13.3	4.28	85	.291	.340	0	—	0	-4	-6	-0	-0.5
1979 NY-A	1	7	.125	32	5	0	0	2	78¹	88	12	25	28	13.2	5.40	75	.291	.350	0	—	0	-10	-12	0	-1.0
1980 Tex-A	2	3	.400	8	8	0	0	0	43	43	4	29	17	15.7	4.60	85	.256	.375	0	—	0	-3	-3	-0	-0.3
1981 Sea-A	2	7	.222	22	14	0	0	0	101	116	10	42	32	14.3	4.63	83	.294	.366	0	—	0	-11	-9	-1	-0.9
Total 5	10	24	.294	111	36	0	0	3	353²	389	35	141	129	13.8	4.68	83	.281	.353	0	—	0	-30	-32	-1	-2.8

■ MARK CLEAR
Clear, Mark Alan b: 5/27/56, Los Angeles, Cal. BR/TR, 6'4", 200 lbs. Deb: 4/04/79

YEAR TM/L	W	L	PCT	G	GS	CG	SH	SV	IP	H	HR	BB	SO	RAT	ERA	ERA+	OAV	OOB	BH	AVG	PB	PR	/A	PD	TPI
1979 *Cal-A	11	5	.688	52	0	0	0	14	109	87	6	68	98	13.0	3.63	112	.219	.337	0	—	0	7	5	-2	0.4
1980 Cal-A	11	11	.500	58	0	0	0	9	106¹	82	2	65	105	12.9	3.30	119	.216	.338	0	—	0	9	7	-1	0.6
1981 Bos-A	8	3	.727	34	0	0	0	9	76²	69	11	51	82	14.3	4.11	94	.239	.357	0	—	0	-4	-2	-2	-0.3
1982 Bos-A	14	9	.609	55	0	0	0	14	105	92	11	61	109	13.7	3.00	144	.238	.352	0	—	0	13	15	-1	1.5
1983 Bos-A	4	5	.444	48	0	0	0	4	96	101	10	68	81	16.1	6.28	69	.273	.390	0	—	0	-24	-21	-1	-2.1
1984 Bos-A	8	3	.727	47	0	0	0	8	67	47	2	70	76	16.0	4.03	103	.198	.385	0	—	0	-0	1	0	0.1
1985 Bos-A	1	3	.250	41	0	0	0	3	55²	45	1	50	55	16.2	3.72	115	.225	.392	0	—	0	3	3	1	0.4
1986 Mil-A	5	5	.500	59	0	0	0	16	73²	53	4	36	85	11.0	2.20	197	.201	.299	0	—	0	16	17	-1	1.6
1987 Mil-A	8	5	.615	58	1	0	0	6	78¹	70	9	55	81	14.9	4.48	102	.239	.368	0	—	0	-0	1	1	0.1
1988 Mil-A	1	0	1.000	25	0	0	0	0	29	23	4	21	26	13.7	2.79	142	.215	.344	0	—	0	4	4	-1	0.3
1990 Cal-A	0	0	—	4	0	0	0	0	7²	5	0	9	6	18.8	5.87	66	.200	.444	0	—	0	-2	-2	-0	-0.1
Total 11	71	49	.592	481	1	0	0	83	804¹	674	60	554	804	14.1	3.85	109	.228	.357	0	—	0	21	30	-7	2.5

■ JOE CLEARY
Cleary, Joseph Christopher "Fire" b: 12/3/18, Cork City, Eire, Ireland BR/TR, 5'9", 150 lbs. Deb: 8/04/45

YEAR TM/L	W	L	PCT	G	GS	CG	SH	SV	IP	H	HR	BB	SO	RAT	ERA	ERA+	OAV	OOB	BH	AVG	PB	PR	/A	PD	TPI
1945 Was-A	0	0	—	1	0	0	0	0	0	5	0	3	1	—	∞	—	.833	.889	0	—	0	-7	-7	0	-0.4

■ ROGER CLEMENS
Clemens, William Roger b: 8/4/62, Dayton, Ohio BR/TR, 6'4", 205 lbs. Deb: 5/15/84

YEAR TM/L	W	L	PCT	G	GS	CG	SH	SV	IP	H	HR	BB	SO	RAT	ERA	ERA+	OAV	OOB	BH	AVG	PB	PR	/A	PD	TPI
1984 Bos-A	9	4	.692	21	20	5	1	0	133¹	146	13	29	126	11.9	4.32	96	.271	.311	0	—	0	-5	-2	-0	-0.2
1985 Bos-A	7	5	.583	15	15	3	1	0	98¹	83	5	37	74	11.3	3.29	130	.228	.304	0	—	0	9	11	-0	1.1
1986 *Bos-A	24	4	.857	33	33	10	1	0	254	179	21	67	238	8.9	2.48	168	.195	.253	0	—	0	48	48	-2	4.9
1987 Bos-A	20	9	.690	36	36	18	7	0	281²	248	19	83	256	10.9	2.97	153	.235	.296	0	—	0	46	49	-3	4.7
1988 *Bos-A	18	12	.600	35	35	14	8	0	264	217	17	62	291	9.7	2.93	140	.220	.270	0	—	0	30	35	-3	3.4
1989 Bos-A	17	11	.607	35	35	8	3	0	253¹	215	20	93	230	11.2	3.13	131	.231	.307	0	—	0	21	27	-1	2.8
1990 *Bos-A	21	6	.778	31	31	7	4	0	228¹	193	7	54	209	10.0	1.93	211	.228	.280	0	—	0	50	54	0	6.2
Total 7	116	51	.695	206	205	65	25	0	1513	1281	102	425	1424	10.4	2.89	146	.227	.286	0	—	0	200	222	-8	22.9

YEAR TM/L	W	L	PCT	G	GS	CG	SH	SV	IP	H	HR	BB	SO	RAT	ERA	ERA+	OAV	OOB	BH	AVG	PB	PR	/A	PD	TPI
■ BILL CLEMENSEN								Clemensen, William Melville b: 6/20/19, New Brunswick, N.J. BR/TR, 6'1", 193 lbs. Deb: 5/22/39																
1939 Pit-N	0	1	.000	12	1	0	0	0	27	32	0	20	13	18.3	7.33	52	.311	.437	2	.333	1	-10	-10	1	-0.7
1941 Pit-N	1	0	1.000	2	1	1	0	0	13	7	0	7	4	9.7	2.77	130	.159	.275	0	.000	-1	1	1	-0	0.0
1946 Pit-N	0	0	—	1	0	0	0	0	2	0	0	0	2	0.0	0.00	—	.000	.000	0	—	0	1	1	0	0.1
Total 3	1	1	.500	15	2	1	0	0	42	39	0	27	19	14.8	5.57	67	.255	.377	2	.200	0	-8	-8	1	-0.6
■ PAT CLEMENTS								Clements, Patrick Brian b: 2/2/62, McCloud, Cal. BR/TL, 6', 175 lbs. Deb: 4/09/85																
1985 Cal-A	5	0	1.000	41	0	0	0	1	62	47	4	25	19	10.7	3.34	123	.218	.305	0	—	0	6	5	1	0.6
Pit-N	0	2	.000	27	0	0	0	2	34¹	39	2	15	17	14.2	3.67	97	.289	.360	1	.333	0	-0	-0	-1	0.0
1986 Pit-N	0	4	.000	65	0	0	0	2	61	53	1	32	31	12.8	2.80	137	.251	.355	0	.000	-1	6	7	1	0.7
1987 NY-A	3	3	.500	55	0	0	0	7	80	91	4	30	36	13.9	4.95	89	.299	.368	0	—	0	-4	-5	1	-0.3
1988 NY-A	0	0	—	6	1	0	0	0	8¹	12	1	4	3	17.3	6.48	61	.343	.410	0	—	0	-2	-2	-0	-0.1
1989 SD-N	4	1	.800	23	0	0	0	0	39	39	4	15	18	12.5	3.92	89	.267	.335	0	.000	-1	-2	-2	0	-0.1
1990 SD-N	0	0	—	9	0	0	0	0	13	20	1	7	6	18.7	4.15	93	.357	.429	0	—	0	-1	-0	0	0.0
Total 6	12	10	.545	226	2	0	0	12	297²	301	17	128	130	13.2	3.90	102	.273	.352	1	.067	-1	2	2	3	0.8
■ LANCE CLEMONS								Clemons, Lance Levis b: 7/6/47, Philadelphia, Pa. BL/TL, 6'2", 205 lbs. Deb: 8/12/71																
1971 KC-A	1	0	1.000	10	3	0	0	0	24	26	2	12	20	14.6	4.13	83	.263	.348	2	.286	2	-2	-2	0	0.0
1972 StL-N	0	1	.000	3	1	0	0	0	5¹	8	1	5	2	23.6	10.13	34	.364	.500	0	.000	-0	-4	-4	0	-0.3
1974 Bos-A	1	0	1.000	6	0	0	0	0	6¹	8	1	4	1	18.5	9.95	39	.296	.406	0	—	0	-4	-4	0	-0.3
Total 3	2	1	.667	19	4	0	0	0	35²	42	4	21	23	16.7	6.06	58	.284	.384	2	.250	2	-10	-10	0	-0.6
■ REGGIE CLEVELAND								Cleveland, Reginald Leslie b: 5/23/48, Swift Current, Sask., Canada BR/TR, 6'1", 195 lbs. Deb: 10/01/69																
1969 StL-N	0	0	—	1	1	0	0	0	4	7	0	1	3	18.0	9.00	40	.368	.400	0	.000	-0	-2	-2	-0	-0.1
1970 StL-N	0	4	.000	16	1	0	0	0	26	31	3	18	22	17.0	7.62	54	.298	.402	1	.250	0	-10	-10	-1	-0.9
1971 StL-N	12	12	.500	34	34	10	2	0	222	238	20	53	148	12.0	4.01	90	.271	.317	14	.171	-1	-14	-10	-0	-1.1
1972 StL-N	14	15	.483	33	33	11	3	0	230²	229	21	60	153	11.5	3.94	86	.258	.308	17	.239	3	-13	-14	-1	-1.2
1973 StL-N	14	10	.583	32	32	6	3	0	224	211	13	61	122	11.1	3.01	121	.246	.300	17	.230	4	16	16	-2	1.9
1974 Bos-A	12	14	.462	41	27	10	0	0	221¹	234	25	69	103	12.7	4.31	89	.271	.332	0	—	0	-17	-12	1	-1.0
1975 *Bos-A	13	9	.591	31	20	3	1	0	170²	173	19	52	78	12.0	4.43	92	.263	.320	0	—	0	-12	-7	0	-0.6
1976 Bos-A	10	9	.526	41	14	3	0	2	170	159	3	61	76	11.9	3.07	127	.246	.315	0	—	0	8	16	-1	1.7
1977 Bos-A	11	8	.579	36	27	9	1	2	190¹	211	20	43	85	12.2	4.26	105	.281	.323	0	—	0	-4	5	-1	0.4
1978 Bos-A	0	1	.000	1	0	0	0	0	0¹	1	0	0	0	27.0	0.00	—	.333	.333	0	—	0	0	0	0	0.0
Tex-A	5	7	.417	53	0	0	0	12	75²	65	5	23	46	10.8	3.09	121	.236	.301	0	—	0	6	5	0	0.6
Yr	5	8	.385	54	0	0	0	12	76	66	5	23	46	10.9	3.08	122	.237	.302	0	—	0	6	5	0	0.6
1979 Mil-A	1	5	.167	29	1	0	0	4	55	77	9	23	22	16.4	6.71	62	.344	.405	0	—	0	-15	-16	-1	-1.5
1980 Mil-A	11	9	.550	45	13	5	2	4	154¹	150	9	49	54	11.9	3.73	104	.254	.317	0	—	0	5	2	-1	0.2
1981 Mil-A	2	3	.400	35	0	0	0	1	64²	57	9	30	18	12.2	5.15	66	.239	.327	0	—	0	-11	-12	-1	-1.3
Total 13	105	106	.498	428	203	57	12	25	1809	1843	152	543	930	12.1	4.01	95	.264	.321	49	.211	6	-63	-38	-7	-2.9
■ TEX CLEVENGER								Clevenger, Truman Eugene b: 7/9/32, Visalia, Cal. BR/TR, 6'1", 180 lbs. Deb: 4/18/54																
1954 Bos-A	2	4	.333	23	8	1	0	0	67²	67	9	29	43	13.0	4.79	86	.262	.341	3	.214	0	-8	-5	0	-0.4
1956 Was-A	0	0	—	20	1	0	0	0	31²	33	4	21	17	15.3	5.40	80	.264	.370	0	.000	-0	-4	-4	0	-0.3
1957 Was-A	7	6	.538	52	9	2	0	8	139²	139	11	47	75	12.2	4.19	93	.261	.326	7	.212	1	-6	-5	1	-0.1
1958 Was-A	9	9	.500	55	4	0	0	6	124	119	12	50	70	12.3	4.35	88	.251	.324	3	.136	0	-8	-7	3	-0.4
1959 Was-A	8	5	.615	50	7	2	2	8	117¹	114	9	51	71	12.8	3.91	100	.256	.335	4	.174	1	-1	0	4	0.5
1960 Was-A	5	11	.313	53	11	1	0	7	128²	150	10	49	49	14.1	4.20	93	.298	.363	2	.091	-1	-5	-4	0	-0.5
1961 LA-A	2	1	.667	12	0	0	0	1	16	13	1	13	11	14.6	1.69	267	.220	.361	0	.000	-0	4	5	1	0.5
NY-A	1	1	.500	21	0	0	0	0	31²	35	3	21	14	16.2	4.83	77	.287	.396	1	.250	0	-3	-4	1	-0.2
Yr	3	2	.600	33	0	0	0	1	47²	48	4	34	25	15.7	3.78	105	.265	.384	1	.167	0	1	1	1	0.3
1962 NY-A	2	0	1.000	21	0	0	0	0	38	36	3	17	11	12.8	2.84	132	.248	.331	0	.000	-0	5	4	0	0.4
Total 8	36	37	.493	307	40	6	2	30	694²	706	62	298	361	13.2	4.18	94	.265	.342	20	.157	1	-26	-20	9	-0.5
■ STEW CLIBURN								Cliburn, Stewart Walker b: 12/19/56, Jackson, Miss. BR/TR, 6', 195 lbs. Deb: 9/17/84																
1984 Cal-A	0	0	—	1	0	0	0	0	2	3	0	1	1	18.0	13.50	29	.333	.400	0	—	0	-2	-2	0	-0.1
1985 Cal-A	9	3	.750	44	0	0	0	6	99	87	5	26	48	10.4	2.09	197	.241	.294	0	—	0	23	22	1	2.4
1988 Cal-A	4	2	.667	40	1	0	0	0	84	83	11	32	42	13.0	4.07	95	.266	.346	0	—	0	-1	-2	0	-0.1
Total 3	13	5	.722	85	1	0	0	6	185	173	16	59	91	11.6	3.11	128	.254	.320	0	—	0	20	18	2	2.2
■ JIM CLINTON								Clinton, James Lawrence "Big Jim" b: 8/10/1850, New York, N.Y. d: 9/3/21, Brooklyn, N.Y. BR/TR, 5'8.5", 174 lbs. Deb: 5/21/1872 MU♦																
1875 Atl-n	1	14	.067	17	14	9	0	0	123	146	0	8		11.3	3.22	71	.268	.279	10	.123	-4	-10	-13		-1.5
1876 Lou-N	0	1	.000	1	1	1	0	0	9	12	0	1	1	12.0	6.00	45	.299	.299	22	.338	0	-4	-3	0	-0.2
■ TONY CLONINGER								Cloninger, Tony Lee b: 8/13/40, Lincoln, N.C. BR/TR, 6', 210 lbs. Deb: 6/15/61																
1961 Mil-N	7	2	.778	19	10	3	0	0	84	84	16	33	51	12.6	5.25	71	.258	.328	5	.167	-0	-11	-14	1	-1.3
1962 Mil-N	8	3	.727	24	15	4	1	0	111	113	10	46	69	13.0	4.30	88	.264	.337	4	.103	-2	-4	-6	0	-0.7
1963 Mil-N	9	11	.450	41	18	4	2	1	145¹	131	17	63	100	12.1	3.78	85	.239	.320	5	.135	-0	-8	-9	-2	-1.1
1964 Mil-N	19	14	.576	38	34	15	3	2	242²	206	20	82	163	10.8	3.56	99	.231	.298	21	.241	3	-1	-1	-0	-0.2
1965 Mil-N	24	11	.686	40	38	16	1	1	279	247	20	119	211	11.9	3.29	107	.236	.316	17	.162	2	8	7	-2	0.8
1966 Atl-N	14	11	.560	39	38	11	1	1	257²	253	29	116	178	13.1	4.12	88	.258	.316	26	.234	10	-15	-14	-1	-0.4
1967 Atl-N	4	7	.364	16	16	1	0	0	76²	85	13	31	55	13.6	5.17	64	.285	.353	5	.200	1	-15	-16	-1	-1.5
1968 Atl-N	1	3	.250	8	1	0	0	0	19	15	0	11	7	12.3	4.26	70	.227	.338	0	.000	-0	-3	-3	0	-0.1
Cin-N	4	3	.571	17	17	2	2	0	91¹	81	7	48	65	13.0	4.04	78	.233	.331	7	.206	3	-11	-9	-0	-0.6
Yr	5	6	.455	25	18	2	2	0	110¹	96	7	59	72	12.9	4.08	77	.233	.331	1	.026	3	-13	-12	-0	-0.8
1969 Cin-N	11	17	.393	35	34	6	2	0	189²	184	24	103	103	13.9	5.03	75	.250	.346	12	.167	1	-30	-27	-2	-2.6
1970 *Cin-N	9	7	.563	30	18	0	0	1	148	136	10	78	56	13.3	3.83	105	.249	.347	10	.213	3	4	3	3	0.9
1971 Cin-N	3	6	.333	28	8	1	1	0	97¹	79	12	49	51	12.2	3.88	86	.230	.332	7	.259	1	-5	-6	-0	-0.4
1972 StL-N	0	2	.000	17	0	0	0	0	26	29	2	19	14	16.5	5.19	66	.293	.412	0	.000	-0	-5	-5	1	-0.4
Total 12	113	97	.538	352	247	63	13	6	1767²	1643	180	798	1120	12.6	4.07	88	.247	.330	119	.192	21	-96	-98	-3	-7.3
■ AL CLOSTER								Closter, Alan Edward b: 6/15/43, Creighton, Neb. BL/TL, 6'2", 190 lbs. Deb: 4/19/66																
1966 Was-A	0	0	—	1	0	0	0	0	0¹	1	0	2	0	81.0	0.00	—	.500	.750	0	—	0	0	0	0	0.0
1971 NY-A	2	2	.500	14	1	0	0	0	28¹	33	4	13	22	15.2	5.08	64	.289	.372	0	.000	-1	-5	-6	0	-0.5
1972 NY-A	0	0	—	2	0	0	0	0	2¹	2	1	4	2	23.1	11.57	25	.250	.500	0	.000	-0	-2	-2	0	-0.1
1973 Atl-N	0	0	—	4	0	0	0	0	4¹	7	1	4	2	22.8	14.54	27	.389	.500	0	—	0	-5	-5	0	-0.1
Total 4	2	2	.500	21	1	0	0	0	35¹	43	6	23	26	17.3	6.62	50	.303	.407	0	.000	-1	-12	-13	1	-1.0
■ ED CLOUGH								Clough, Edgar George "Big Ed" or "Spec" b: 10/28/06, Wiconisco, Pa. d: 1/30/44, Harrisburg, Pa. BL/TL, 6', 188 lbs. Deb: 8/28/24 ♦																
1925 StL-N	0	1	.000	3	1	0	0	0	10	11	1	5	3	15.3	8.10	53	.289	.386	1	.250	-0	-4	-4	-0	-0.3
1926 StL-N	0	0	—	1	0	0	0	0	2	5	0	3	0	40.5	22.50	17	.556	.692	0	.000	-0	-4	-4	-0	-0.3
Total 2	0	1	.000	4	1	0	0	0	12	16	1	8	3	19.5	10.50	40	.340	.456	2	.105	-0	-8	-8	-0	-0.6
■ BILL CLOWERS								Clowers, William Perry b: 8/14/1898, San Marcos, Tex. d: 1/13/78, Sweeny, Tex. BL/TL, 5'11", 175 lbs. Deb: 7/20/26																
1926 Bos-A	0	0	—	2	0	0	0	0	1²	2	0	0	0	10.8	0.00	—	.333	.333	0	—	0	1	1	0	0.1

YEAR	TM/L	W	L	PCT	G	GS	CG	SH	SV	IP	H	HR	BB	SO	RAT	ERA	ERA+	OAV	OOB	BH	AVG	PB	PR	/A	PD	TPI

■ BRYAN CLUTTERBUCK Clutterbuck, Bryan Richard b: 12/17/59, Detroit, Mich. BR/TR, 6'4", 223 lbs. Deb: 7/18/86

1986	Mil-A	0	1	.000	20	0	0	0	0	56²	68	8	16	38	13.7	4.29	101	.296	.347	0	—	0	-1	0	-0	0.0
1989	Mil-A	2	5	.286	14	11	1	0	0	67¹	73	11	16	29	11.9	4.14	93	.269	.310	0	—	0	-2	-2	-2	-0.3
Total	2	2	6	.250	34	11	1	0	0	124	141	19	32	67	12.7	4.21	96	.281	.327	0	—	0	-3	-2	-2	-0.3

■ DAVID CLYDE Clyde, David Eugene b: 4/22/55, Kansas City, Kan. BL/TL, 6'1.5", 180 lbs. Deb: 6/27/73

1973	Tex-A	4	8	.333	18	18	0	0	0	93¹	106	8	54	74	15.8	5.01	74	.293	.390	0	—	0	-12	-13	-0	-1.3
1974	Tex-A	3	9	.250	28	21	4	0	0	117	129	14	47	52	13.8	4.38	81	.286	.359	0	—	0	-10	-11	-1	-1.1
1975	Tex-A	0	1	.000	1	1	0	0	0	7	6	0	6	2	15.4	2.57	146	.273	.429	0	—	0	1	1	-0	0.1
1978	Cle-A	8	11	.421	28	25	5	0	0	153¹	166	4	60	83	13.4	4.28	87	.280	.350	0	—	0	-9	-9	-1	-0.9
1979	Cle-A	3	4	.429	9	8	1	0	0	45²	50	7	13	17	12.6	5.91	72	.279	.332	0	—	0	-9	-8	-0	-0.7
Total	5	18	33	.353	84	73	10	0	0	416¹	457	33	180	228	14.0	4.63	81	.285	.361	0	—	0	-39	-41	-3	-3.9

■ TOM CLYDE Clyde, Thomas Knox b: 8/17/23, Wachapreague, Va. BR/TR, 6'3", 195 lbs. Deb: 5/31/43

| 1943 | Phi-A | 0 | 0 | — | 4 | 0 | 0 | 0 | 0 | 6 | 7 | 1 | 4 | 0 | 18.0 | 9.00 | 38 | .304 | .429 | 0 | .000 | -0 | -4 | -4 | -0 | -0.3 |

■ ANDY COAKLEY Coakley, Andrew James (a.k.a. Jack McAllister In 1902)
b: 11/20/1882, Providence, R.I. d: 9/27/63, New York, N.Y. BL/TR, 6', 165 lbs. Deb: 9/17/02

1902	Phi-A	2	1	.667	3	3	3	0	0	27	25	0	9	9	11.3	2.67	138	.246	.308	3	.375	2	3	3	0	0.5
1903	Phi-A	0	3	.000	6	3	2	0	0	37²	48	2	11	20	14.1	5.50	56	.309	.355	3	.200	-0	-11	-10	0	-0.9
1904	Phi-A	4	3	.571	8	8	7	2	0	62	48	1	23	33	10.3	1.89	142	.215	.288	2	.087	-2	5	5	-0	0.4
1905	*Phi-A	18	8	.692	35	31	21	3	0	255	227	1	73	145	10.6	1.84	145	.240	.294	13	.138	-3	23	23	-1	2.2
1906	Phi-A	7	8	.467	22	16	10	0	0	149	144	0	44	59	11.4	3.14	87	.257	.311	7	.143	-1	-7	-7	-2	-1.0
1907	Cin-N	17	16	.515	37	30	21	1	1	265¹	269	1	79	89	12.0	2.34	111	.274	.332	6	.071	-6	4	8	-3	0.0
1908	Cin-N	8	18	.308	32	28	20	4	2	242¹	219	3	64	61	10.7	1.86	124	.249	.303	7	.092	-4	14	12	-4	0.4
	Chi-N	2	0	1.000	4	3	2	1	0	20¹	14	0	6	7	8.9	0.89	266	.192	.253	0	.000	-1	3	3	-0	0.3
	Yr	10	18	.357	36	31	22	5	2	262²	233	3	70	68	10.4	1.78	130	.244	.295	2	.024	-5	17	15	-4	0.7
1909	Chi-N	0	1	.000	1	0	0	0	0	2	7	0	3	1	45.0	18.00	14	.583	.667	0	—	0	-3	-3	0	-0.2
1911	NY-A	0	1	.000	2	1	1	0	0	11²	20	0	2	4	17.0	5.40	67	.377	.400	1	.250	0	-3	-2	-0	-0.1
Total	9	58	59	.496	150	124	87	11	3	1072¹	1021	9	314	428	11.3	2.35	111	.256	.312	42	.117	-16	28	32	-9	1.6

■ JIM COATES Coates, James Alton b: 8/4/32, Farnham, Va. BR/TR, 6'4", 192 lbs. Deb: 9/21/56

1956	NY-A	0	0	—	2	0	0	0	0	2	1	0	4	0	27.0	13.50	29	.167	.545	0	—	0	-2	-2	0	-0.1
1959	NY-A	6	1	.857	37	4	2	0	0	100¹	89	10	36	64	11.5	2.87	127	.234	.305	2	.095	-1	11	9	0	0.7
1960	*NY-A	13	3	.813	35	18	6	2	1	149¹	139	16	66	73	12.5	4.28	84	.248	.330	12	.250	4	-7	-12	-2	-0.9
1961	*NY-A	11	5	.688	43	11	4	1	5	141¹	128	15	53	80	12.0	3.44	108	.243	.321	1	.029	-3	9	4	-0	0.1
1962	*NY-A	7	6	.538	50	6	0	0	6	117²	119	9	50	67	13.3	4.44	84	.263	.343	4	.125	-1	-6	-9	-2	-1.1
1963	Was-A	2	4	.333	20	2	0	0	0	44¹	51	4	21	31	15.2	5.28	70	.297	.383	0	.000	-1	-8	-8	0	-0.8
	Cin-N	0	0	—	9	0	0	0	0	16¹	21	2	7	11	15.4	5.51	61	.313	.378	0	.000	-0	-4	-4	0	-0.3
1965	Cal-A	2	0	1.000	17	0	0	0	3	28	23	1	16	15	12.5	3.54	96	.228	.333	0	.000	-0	-0	-0	0	0.0
1966	Cal-A	1	1	.500	9	4	1	1	0	31²	32	3	10	16	11.9	3.98	84	.258	.313	1	.091	-1	-2	-2	-0	-0.2
1967	Cal-A	1	2	.333	25	1	0	0	0	52¹	47	5	23	39	12.7	4.30	73	.244	.336	1	.333	1	-6	-7	0	-0.3
Total	9	43	22	.662	247	46	13	4	15	683¹	650	65	286	396	12.7	4.00	90	.252	.332	21	.131	-3	-15	-30	-4	-3.1

■ GEORGE COBB Cobb, George Washington b: San Francisco, Cal. Deb: 4/15/1892

| 1892 | Bal-N | 10 | 37 | .213 | 53 | 47 | 42 | 0 | 0 | 394¹ | 495 | 21 | 140 | 159 | 14.5 | 4.86 | 71 | .295 | .349 | 36 | .209 | 6 | -69 | -62 | 1 | -4.6 |

■ HERB COBB Cobb, Herbert Edward b: 8/6/04, Pinetops, N.C. d: 1/8/80, Tarboro, N.C. BR/TR, 5'11", 150 lbs. Deb: 4/21/29

| 1929 | StL-A | 0 | 0 | — | 1 | 0 | 0 | 0 | 0 | 1 | 3 | 1 | 1 | 0 | 36.0 | 36.00 | 12 | .600 | .667 | 0 | — | 0 | -4 | -4 | 0 | -0.2 |

■ TY COBB Cobb, Tyrus Raymond "The Georgia Peach" b: 12/18/1886, Narrows, Ga. d: 7/17/61, Atlanta, Ga. BL/TR, 6'1", 175 lbs. Deb: 8/30/05 MH♦

1918	Det-A	0	0	—	2	0	0	0	0	4	6	0	2	0	18.0	4.50	59	.400	.471	161	.382	1	-1	-1	0	0.0
1925	Det-A	0	0	—	1	0	0	0	1	1	0	0	0	0	0.00	0.00	—	.000	.000	157	.378	1	0	0	0	0.0
Total	2	0	0	—	3	0	0	0	1	5	6	0	2	0	14.4	3.60	83	.333	.400	4190	.366	2	-0	-0	0	0.0

■ JAIME COCANOWER Cocanower, James Stanley b: 2/14/57, San Juan, P.R. BR/TR, 6'4", 200 lbs. Deb: 9/07/83

1983	Mil-A	2	0	1.000	5	3	1	0	0	30	21	1	12	8	10.2	1.80	208	.200	.288	0	—	0	8	6	1	0.7
1984	Mil-A	8	16	.333	33	27	1	0	0	174²	188	13	78	65	14.2	4.02	96	.279	.362	0	—	0	-1	-3	2	-0.1
1985	Mil-A	6	8	.429	24	15	3	1	0	116¹	122	6	73	44	15.7	4.33	96	.274	.386	0	—	0	-2	-2	0	-0.1
1986	Mil-A	0	1	.000	17	2	0	0	0	44²	40	1	38	22	16.1	4.43	98	.248	.398	0	—	0	-1	-1	1	0.1
Total	4	16	25	.390	79	47	5	1	0	365²	371	21	201	139	14.6	3.99	100	.268	.369	0	—	0	3	0	4	0.6

■ GOAT COCHRAN Cochran, Alvah Jackson "Al" or "Goat" b: 1/31/1891, Concord, Ga. d: 5/23/47, Atlanta, Ga. BR/TR, 5'10", 175 lbs. Deb: 8/25/15

| 1915 | Cin-N | 0 | 0 | — | 1 | 0 | 0 | 0 | 0 | 2 | 5 | 0 | 0 | 1 | 22.5 | 9.00 | 32 | .455 | .455 | 0 | — | 0 | -1 | -1 | 0 | 0.0 |

■ GENE COCREHAM Cocreham, Eugene b: 11/14/1884, Luling, Tex. d: 12/27/45, Luling, Tex. BR/TR, 6'3.5", 192 lbs. Deb: 9/25/13

1913	Bos-N	0	1	.000	1	1	0	0	0	8¹	13	0	4	3	19.4	7.56	43	.371	.450	0	.000	-1	-4	-4	0	-0.3
1914	Bos-N	3	4	.429	15	3	1	0	0	44²	48	2	27	15	15.1	4.84	57	.296	.397	1	.100	-0	-10	-10	-1	-1.1
1915	Bos-N	0	0	—	1	0	0	0	0	1²	3	0	0	0	16.2	5.40	48	.429	.429	0	—	0	-0	-1	0	0.0
Total	3	3	5	.375	17	4	1	0	0	54²	64	2	31	18	15.8	5.27	54	.314	.407	1	.071	-1	-15	-15	-1	-1.4

■ CHRIS CODIROLI Codiroli, Christopher Allen b: 3/26/58, Oxnard, Cal. BR/TR, 6'1", 160 lbs. Deb: 9/11/82

1982	Oak-A	1	2	.333	3	3	0	0	0	16²	16	1	4	5	10.8	4.32	90	.246	.290	0	—	0	-0	-1	0	0.0
1983	Oak-A	12	12	.500	37	31	7	2	1	205²	208	17	72	85	12.6	4.46	86	.264	.331	0	—	0	-9	-14	-2	-1.4
1984	Oak-A	6	4	.600	28	14	1	0	1	89¹	111	16	34	44	14.9	5.84	64	.304	.368	0	—	0	-18	-21	-0	-1.9
1985	Oak-A	14	14	.500	37	37	4	0	0	226	228	23	78	111	12.3	4.46	86	.259	.321	0	—	0	-8	-15	-1	-1.5
1986	Oak-A	5	8	.385	16	16	1	0	0	91²	91	15	38	43	12.9	4.03	96	.250	.324	0	—	0	2	-2	1	0.0
1987	Oak-A	0	2	.000	3	3	0	0	0	11¹	12	1	8	4	16.7	8.74	47	.273	.396	0	—	0	-5	-6	0	-0.4
1988	Cle-A	0	4	.000	14	2	0	0	1	19¹	32	2	10	12	20.9	9.31	44	.372	.455	0	—	0	-11	-11	0	-1.0
1990	KC-A	0	1	.000	6	2	0	0	0	10¹	13	1	17	8	29.6	9.58	40	.325	.557	0	—	0	-7	-7	-0	-0.6
Total	8	38	47	.447	144	108	13	2	3	670¹	711	76	261	312	13.4	4.87	79	.270	.341	0	—	0	-58	-76	-1	-6.8

■ SLICK COFFMAN Coffman, George David b: 12/11/10, Veto, Ala. BR/TR, 6', 155 lbs. Deb: 5/21/37

1937	Det-A	7	5	.583	28	5	1	0	0	101	121	8	39	22	14.5	4.37	107	.295	.361	5	.172	3	3	3	-1	0.3
1938	Det-A	4	4	.500	39	6	1	0	2	95²	120	6	48	31	15.8	6.02	83	.310	.386	4	.167	-0	-13	-11	-0	-0.9
1939	Det-A	2	1	.667	23	1	0	0	0	42¹	51	4	22	10	15.7	6.38	77	.295	.378	0	.000	-1	-8	-7	-0	-0.6
1940	StL-A	2	2	.500	31	4	1	0	1	74²	108	5	23	26	15.8	6.27	73	.334	.379	3	.200	-0	-16	-14	1	-1.1
Total	4	15	12	.556	121	16	3	0	3	313²	400	23	132	89	15.4	5.60	85	.309	.375	12	.164	-0	-34	-28	0	-2.3

■ KEVIN COFFMAN Coffman, Kevin Reese b: 1/19/65, Austin, Tex. BR/TR, 6'2", 175 lbs. Deb: 9/05/87

1987	Atl-N	2	3	.400	5	5	0	0	0	25¹	31	2	14	19	19.9	4.62	94	.313	.452	1	.100	-0	-2	-1	1	0.0
1988	Atl-N	2	6	.250	18	11	0	0	0	67	62	3	54	24	16.1	5.78	64	.251	.393	5	.227	2	-17	-16	1	-1.2
1990	Chi-N	0	2	.000	8	2	0	0	0	18¹	26	0	19	9	22.1	11.29	37	.333	.464	1	.200	0	-15	-15	1	-1.2
Total	3	4	11	.267	31	18	0	0	0	110²	119	5	95	47	18.0	6.42	61	.281	.420	7	.189	2	-34	-31	2	-2.4

YEAR	TM/L	W	L	PCT	G	GS	CG	SH	SV	IP	H	HR	BB	SO	RAT	ERA	ERA+	OAV	OOB	BH	AVG	PB	PR	/A	PD	TPI

■ DICK COFFMAN   Coffman, Samuel Richard b: 12/18/06, Veto, Ala. d: 3/24/72, Athens, Ala.   BR/TR, 6'2", 195 lbs.   Deb: 4/28/27

1927	Was-A	0	1	.000	5	2	0	0	0	16	20	0	2	5	13.5	3.38	120	.313	.353	1	.333	0	1	1	0	0.2
1928	StL-A	4	5	.444	29	7	3	0	1	85²	122	7	37	25	16.8	6.09	69	.359	.423	1	.043	-3	-20	-18	0	-1.8
1929	StL-A	1	1	.500	27	3	1	1	1	52²	61	3	14	11	13.3	5.98	74	.295	.348	0	.000	-1	-10	-9	0	-0.7
1930	StL-A	8	18	.308	38	30	12	1	1	196	250	14	69	54	14.9	5.14	95	.311	.369	9	.136	-5	-11	-6	1	0.8
1931	StL-A	9	13	.409	32	17	11	2	1	169¹	159	10	51	39	11.3	3.88	119	.241	.298	4	.078	-5	9	14	-1	0.8
1932	StL-A	5	3	.625	9	6	3	0	0	61	66	3	21	14	13.1	3.10	157	.277	.341	1	.045	-2	9	12	-1	0.9
	Was-A	1	6	.143	22	9	2	1	0	76¹	92	2	31	17	14.6	4.83	89	.307	.373	2	.091	-1	-3	-4	-1	-0.4
	Yr	6	9	.400	31	15	5	1	0	137¹	158	5	52	31	13.8	4.06	112	.293	.356	4	.091	-3	6	7	-1	0.5
1933	StL-A	3	7	.300	21	13	3	1	1	81	114	9	39	19	17.2	5.89	79	.329	.399	1	.037	-3	-14	-11	0	-1.1
1934	StL-A	9	10	.474	40	21	6	1	3	173	212	11	59	55	14.2	4.53	110	.303	.358	11	.216	-1	-1	9	0	0.9
1935	StL-A	5	11	.313	41	18	5	0	2	143²	206	14	46	34	15.9	6.14	78	.335	.383	6	.146	-1	-27	-21	-1	-2.0
1936	*NY-N	7	5	.583	42	2	0	0	7	101²	119	7	23	26	12.7	3.90	100	.296	.337	4	.200	-0	1	0	2	0.1
1937	*NY-N	8	3	.727	42	1	0	0	3	80	93	4	31	30	14.4	3.04	128	.289	.359	7	.368	2	8	8	1	1.0
1938	NY-N	8	4	.667	**51**	3	1	1	**12**	111¹	116	3	21	21	11.3	3.48	108	.268	.306	2	.071	-3	4	4	-1	0.0
1939	NY-N	1	2	.333	28	0	0	0	3	38	50	1	6	9	14.0	3.08	128	.316	.353	0	.000	-1	4	4	-0	0.3
1940	Bos-N	1	5	.167	31	0	0	0	3	48¹	63	4	11	11	14.2	5.40	69	.323	.365	1	.083	-1	-8	-9	-0	-0.9
1945	Phi-N	2	1	.667	14	0	0	0	0	26¹	39	0	2	2	14.0	5.13	75	.351	.363	1	.250	0	-4	-4	1	-0.1
Total	15	72	95	.431	472	132	47	8	38	1460¹	1782	92	463	372	14.1	4.65	96	.302	.357	51	.127	-23	-61	-33	0	-3.7

■ DICK COGAN   Cogan, Richard Henry b: 12/5/1871, Paterson, N.J. d: 5/2/48, Paterson, N.J.   5'7", 150 lbs.   Deb: 5/10/1897

1897	Bal-N	0	0	—	1	0	0	0	0	2	4	0	2	0	27.0	13.50	31	.411	.511	0	.000	-0	-2	-2	0	-0.1
1899	Chi-N	2	3	.400	5	5	5	0	0	44	54	1	24	9	16.0	4.30	87	.301	.384	5	.200	1	-2	-3	-1	-0.1
1900	NY-N	0	0	—	2	0	0	0	0	8	10	0	6	1	18.0	6.75	54	.305	.413	1	.125	-0	-3	-3	-0	-0.2
Total	3		2	3	.400	8	5	5	0	0	54	68	1	32	10	16.7	5.00	75	.307	.394	6	.176	0	-7	-8	-1	-0.4

■ HY COHEN   Cohen, Hyman b: 1/29/31, Brooklyn, N.Y.   BR/TR, 6'5", 220 lbs.   Deb: 4/17/55

| 1955 | Chi-N | 0 | 0 | — | 7 | 1 | 0 | 0 | 0 | 17 | 28 | 2 | 10 | 4 | 20.6 | 7.94 | 51 | .378 | .459 | 0 | .000 | -0 | -7 | -7 | -0 | -0.6 |

■ SYD COHEN   Cohen, Sydney Harry b: 5/7/08, Baltimore, Md. d: 4/9/88, ElPaso, Tex.   BB/TL, 5'11", 180 lbs.   Deb: 9/18/34

1934	Was-A	1	1	.500	3	2	2	0	0	18	25	2	6	6	15.5	7.50	58	.333	.383	3	.273	0	-6	-6	1	-0.3
1936	Was-A	0	2	.000	19	1	0	0	1	36	44	4	14	21	15.3	5.25	91	.303	.377	0	.000	-1	-1	-2	2	0.0
1937	Was-A	2	4	.333	33	0	0	0	4	55	64	1	17	22	13.3	3.11	142	.299	.351	2	.143	-1	9	8	2	0.8
Total	3		3	7	.300	55	3	2	0	5	109	133	7	37	49	14.3	4.54	100	.306	.365	5	.152	-2	2	-0	5	0.5

■ ROCKY COLAVITO   Colavito, Rocco Domenico b: 8/10/33, New York, N.Y.   BR/TR, 6'3", 190 lbs.   Deb: 9/10/55 C♦

1958	Cle-A	0	0	—	1	0	0	0	0	3	0	0	3	1	9.0	0.00	—	.000	.273	148	.303	1	1	1	0	0.1
1968	NY-A	1	0	1.000	1	0	0	0	0	2²	1	0	2	1	10.1	0.00	—	.111	.273	20	.220	0	1	1	0	0.1
Total	2		1	0	1.000	2	0	0	0	0	5²	1	0	5	2	9.5	0.00	—	.059	.273	1730	.266	1	2	2	0	0.2

■ VINCE COLBERT   Colbert, Vincent Norman b: 12/20/45, Washington, D.C.   BR/TR, 6'4", 200 lbs.   Deb: 5/19/70

1970	Cle-A	1	1	.500	23	0	0	0	2	31	37	4	16	17	15.7	7.26	55	.298	.383	0	.000	-0	-12	-11	0	-1.0
1971	Cle-A	7	6	.538	50	10	2	0	2	142²	140	11	71	74	13.7	3.97	96	.265	.358	4	.138	-0	-8	-2	1	-0.1
1972	Cle-A	1	7	.125	22	11	1	1	0	74²	74	8	38	36	14.3	4.58	70	.267	.370	4	.200	1	-13	-11	1	-1.0
Total	3		9	14	.391	95	21	3	1	4	248¹	251	23	125	127	14.1	4.57	80	.270	.365	8	.157	0	-33	-25	2	-2.1

■ JIM COLBORN   Colborn, James William b: 5/22/46, Santa Paula, Cal.   BR/TR, 6', 185 lbs.   Deb: 7/13/69

1969	Chi-N	1	0	1.000	6	2	0	0	0	14²	15	2	9	4	15.3	3.07	131	.283	.397	0	.000	-0	1	2	0	0.2
1970	Chi-N	3	1	.750	34	5	0	0	4	72²	88	3	23	50	13.9	3.59	125	.298	.351	1	.067	-1	4	7	1	0.7
1971	Chi-N	0	1	.000	14	0	0	0	0	10¹	18	1	3	2	18.3	6.97	56	.383	.420	0	—	0	-4	-3	0	-0.2
1972	Mil-A	7	7	.500	39	12	4	1	0	147²	135	14	43	97	11.0	3.11	97	.245	.302	3	.081	-1	-1	-1	-1	-0.4
1973	Mil-A	20	12	.625	43	36	22	4	1	314¹	297	21	87	135	11.1	3.18	118	.251	.304	0	—	0	22	20	2	2.3
1974	Mil-A	10	13	.435	33	31	10	1	0	224	230	27	60	83	11.9	4.06	89	.268	.320	0	—	0	-11	-11	0	-1.0
1975	Mil-A	11	13	.458	36	29	8	1	2	206¹	215	18	65	79	12.4	4.27	90	.270	.329	0	—	0	-11	-10	1	-0.8
1976	Mil-A	9	15	.375	32	32	7	0	0	225²	232	20	54	101	11.5	3.71	94	.268	.312	0	—	0	-5	-5	-0	-0.5
1977	KC-A	18	14	.563	36	35	6	1	0	239	233	24	81	103	12.3	3.62	112	.255	.324	0	—	0	12	11	2	1.3
1978	KC-A	1	2	.333	8	3	0	0	0	28¹	31	4	12	8	14.3	4.76	80	.282	.363	0	—	0	-3	-3	1	-0.1
	Sea-A	3	10	.231	20	19	3	0	0	114¹	125	21	38	26	13.3	5.35	71	.279	.343	0	—	0	-20	-20	3	-1.5
	Yr	4	12	.250	28	22	3	0	0	142²	156	25	50	34	13.4	5.24	73	.279	.344	0	—	0	-23	-23	4	-1.6
Total	10	83	88	.485	301	204	60	8	7	1597¹	1619	153	475	688	12.0	3.80	98	.265	.322	4	.073	-3	-17	-14	8	-0.0

■ TOM COLCOLOUGH   Colcolough, Thomas Bernard b: 10/8/1870, Charleston, S.C. d: 12/10/19, Charleston, S.C.   BR/TR, 5'10.5", 180 lbs.   Deb: 8/01/1893

1893	Pit-N	1	0	1.000	8	3	1	0	**2**	43²	45	1	32	7	15.9	4.12	111	.258	.373	2	.143	0	3	2	0	0.1
1894	Pit-N	8	5	.615	22	14	11	0	0	148²	207	5	70	29	16.8	7.08	74	.326	.393	14	.200	-3	-29	-30	1	-2.3
1895	Pit-N	1	1	.500	6	5	2	0	0	35¹	38	1	21	15	15.0	5.60	81	.271	.365	5	.333	3	-3	-4	-1	-0.1
1899	NY-N	4	5	.444	11	8	7	0	0	81²	85	1	41	14	13.9	3.97	95	.268	.352	10	.270	1	-1	-2	1	0.0
Total	4		14	11	.560	47	30	21	0	2	309¹	375	8	164	65	15.7	5.67	82	.296	.377	31	.228	1	-31	-35	1	-2.3

■ BERT COLE   Cole, Albert George b: 7/1/1896, San Francisco, Cal. d: 5/30/75, San Mateo, Cal.   BL/TL, 6'1", 180 lbs.   Deb: 4/19/21

1921	Det-A	7	4	.636	20	11	7	1	1	109²	134	3	36	22	14.3	4.27	100	.305	.363	13	.283	3	0	0	-0	0.3
1922	Det-A	1	6	.143	23	5	2	1	0	79¹	105	4	39	21	16.4	4.88	80	.313	.387	4	.160	-1	-7	-9	1	-0.8
1923	Det-A	13	5	.722	52	13	6	1	5	163	183	9	61	32	13.7	4.14	93	.284	.351	14	.255	2	-3	-5	-1	-0.2
1924	Det-A	3	9	.250	28	11	2	1	2	109¹	135	4	35	16	14.3	4.69	88	.314	.371	10	.270	1	-6	-7	1	-0.4
1925	Det-A	2	3	.400	14	2	1	0	1	33²	44	2	15	7	16.0	5.88	73	.336	.408	3	.273	-0	-6	-6	1	-0.3
	Cle-A	1	1	.500	13	2	0	0	1	44	55	1	25	9	16.6	6.14	72	.322	.411	2	.154	-0	-9	-8	-0	-0.7
	Yr	3	4	.429	27	4	1	0	2	77²	99	3	40	16	16.2	6.03	73	.327	.407	4	.167	0	-14	-14	1	-1.0
1927	Chi-A	1	4	.200	27	2	0	0	0	66²	79	3	19	12	13.6	4.72	86	.309	.363	3	.167	-1	-4	-5	2	-0.3
Total	6		28	32	.467	177	46	18	4	10	605²	735	26	230	119	14.6	4.67	87	.305	.370	49	.239	5	-34	-40	3	-2.4

■ DAVE COLE   Cole, David Bruce b: 8/29/30, Williamsport, Md.   BR/TR, 6'2", 175 lbs.   Deb: 9/09/50

1950	Bos-N	0	1	.000	4	0	0	0	0	8	7	0	3	8	12.4	1.13	342	.259	.355	0	.000	-0	3	2	-0	0.2
1951	Bos-N	2	4	.333	23	7	1	0	0	67²	64	3	64	33	17.3	4.26	86	.254	.409	6	.353	3	-2	-4	0	0.0
1952	Bos-N	1	1	.500	22	3	0	0	0	44²	38	2	42	22	16.7	4.03	90	.241	.409	0	.000	-1	-1	-2	0	-0.1
1953	Mil-N	0	1	.000	10	0	0	0	0	14²	17	1	14	13	19.0	8.59	46	.279	.413	1	.500	1	-7	-8	0	-0.5
1954	Chi-N	3	8	.273	18	14	2	1	0	84	74	7	62	37	14.7	5.36	78	.241	.370	6	.214	1	-12	-11	-0	-0.8
1955	Phi-N	0	3	.000	7	3	0	0	0	18¹	21	3	14	6	16.2	6.38	62	.304	.422	1	.200	-0	-5	-5	0	-0.3
Total	6		6	18	.250	84	27	3	1	0	237¹	221	16	199	119	16.2	4.93	79	.253	.395	14	.230	5	-25	-27	1	-1.6

■ ED COLE   Cole, Edward William (b: Edward William Kisleauskas) b: 3/22/09, Wilkes-Barre, Pa.   BR/TR, 5'11", 170 lbs.   Deb: 4/22/38

1938	StL-A	1	5	.167	36	6	1	0	3	88²	116	8	48	26	17.2	5.18	96	.313	.399	3	.143	-1	-4	-2	-1	-0.3
1939	StL-A	0	2	.000	6	0	0	0	0	6¹	8	1	6	5	19.9	7.11	68	.308	.438	0	.000	-0	-2	-2	0	-0.1
Total	2		1	7	.125	42	6	1	0	3	95	124	9	54	31	17.3	5.31	94	.312	.401	3	.136	-2	-6	-4	-1	-0.4

■ KING COLE   Cole, Leonard Leslie b: 4/15/1886, Toledo, Iowa d: 1/6/16, Bay City, Mich.   BR/TR, 6'1", 170 lbs.   Deb: 10/06/09

| 1909 | Chi-N | 1 | 0 | 1.000 | 1 | 1 | 1 | 1 | 0 | 9 | 6 | 0 | 3 | 1 | 9.0 | 0.00 | — | .194 | .265 | 3 | .750 | 2 | 3 | 3 | -0 | 0.7 |

YEAR TM/L	W	L	PCT	G	GS	CG	SH	SV	IP	H	HR	BB	SO	RAT	ERA	ERA+	OAV	OOB	BH	AVG	PB	PR	/A	PD	TPI
1910 *Chi-N	20	4	**.833**	33	29	21	4	1	239²	174	2	130	114	11.8	**1.80**	**160**	**.211**	.325	21	.231	2	33	29	-1	3.3
1911 Chi-N	18	7	.720	32	27	13	2	0	221¹	188	3	99	101	12.0	3.13	106	.236	.328	12	.152	-2	7	4	-2	0.0
1912 Chi-N	1	2	.333	8	3	0	0	0	19	36	2	8	9	21.8	10.89	31	.400	.460	2	.400	1	-16	-16	0	-1.2
Pit-N	2	2	.500	12	4	2	0	0	49	61	1	18	11	14.9	6.43	51	.308	.372	2	.133	-1	-16	-17	0	-1.5
Yr	3	4	.429	20	7	2	0	0	68	97	3	26	20	16.5	7.68	43	.334	.393	1	.050	-1	-32	-33	1	-2.7
1914 NY-A	11	9	.550	33	15	8	2	0	141²	151	3	51	43	12.9	3.30	84	.288	.352	2	.048	-3	-9	-9	-3	-1.5
1915 NY-A	3	3	.500	10	6	2	0	1	51	41	2	22	19	11.6	3.18	92	.224	.317	1	.077	-1	-1	-1	-0	-0.2
Total 6	56	27	.675	129	85	47	9	2	730²	657	13	331	298	12.5	3.12	97	.248	.338	43	.173	-2	-0	-7	-5	-0.4

■ JOHN COLEMAN
Coleman, John   b: Bristol, Pa.   Deb: 6/23/1890

YEAR TM/L	W	L	PCT	G	GS	CG	SH	SV	IP	H	HR	BB	SO	RAT	ERA	ERA+	OAV	OOB	BH	AVG	PB	PR	/A	PD	TPI
1890 Phi-N	0	1	.000	1	1	0	0	0	1²	4	0	3	2	37.8	21.60	17	.448	.587	0	—	0	-3	-3	0	-0.2

■ JOHN COLEMAN
Coleman, John   b: Jefferson City, Mo.   TL,   Deb: 9/25/1895

YEAR TM/L	W	L	PCT	G	GS	CG	SH	SV	IP	H	HR	BB	SO	RAT	ERA	ERA+	OAV	OOB	BH	AVG	PB	PR	/A	PD	TPI
1895 StL-N	0	1	.000	1	1	0	0	0	8	12	1	8	5	22.5	13.50	36	.341	.463	1	.200	-0	-8	-8	0	-0.4

■ JOHN COLEMAN
Coleman, John Francis   b: 3/6/1863, Saratoga Spgs., N.Y.   d: 5/31/22, Detroit, Mich.   BL/TR, 5'9.5", 170 lbs.   Deb: 5/01/1883 ♦

YEAR TM/L	W	L	PCT	G	GS	CG	SH	SV	IP	H	HR	BB	SO	RAT	ERA	ERA+	OAV	OOB	BH	AVG	PB	PR	/A	PD	TPI
1883 Phi-N	12	48	.200	65	61	59	3	0	538¹	772	17	48	159	13.7	4.87	63	.318	.331	83	.234	4	-103	-106	1	-8.1
1884 Phi-N	5	15	.250	21	19	14	1	0	154¹	216	9	22	37	13.9	4.90	61	.314	.335	42	.246	2	-33	-33	2	-2.7
Phi-a	0	2	.000	3	2	2	0	0	21	28	0	2	5	12.9	3.43	99	.304	.318	22	.206	0	-0	-0	0	0.0
1885 Phi-a	2	2	.500	8	3	3	0	0	60¹	82	0	5	12	13.0	3.43	100	.311	.324	119	.299	3	-1	0	0	0.0
1886 Phi-a	1	1	.500	3	1	1	0	0	20²	18	1	5	2	10.0	2.61	134	.223	.269	121	.246	0	2	2	0	0.2
1889 Phi-a	3	2	.600	5	5	4	0	0	34	38	2	14	6	13.8	2.91	130	.274	.340	1	.053	-2	4	3	1	0.1
1890 Pit-N	0	2	.000	2	2	1	0	0	14	28	1	6	3	21.9	9.64	34	.404	.451	2	.182	0	-9	-10	-0	-0.6
Total 6	23	72	.242	107	93	84	4	0	842²	1182	30	102	224	13.7	4.68	67	.314	.332	645	.257	7	-142	-144	4	-11.1

■ JOE COLEMAN
Coleman, Joseph Howard   b: 2/3/47, Boston, Mass.   BR/TR, 6'3", 175 lbs.   Deb: 9/28/65   C

YEAR TM/L	W	L	PCT	G	GS	CG	SH	SV	IP	H	HR	BB	SO	RAT	ERA	ERA+	OAV	OOB	BH	AVG	PB	PR	/A	PD	TPI
1965 Was-A	2	0	1.000	2	2	2	0	0	18	9	0	8	7	8.5	1.50	232	.153	.254	0	.000	-1	4	4	1	0.5
1966 Was-A	1	0	1.000	1	1	1	0	0	9	6	0	2	4	8.0	2.00	173	.188	.235	0	.000	-0	1	1	0	0.2
1967 Was-A	8	9	.471	28	22	3	0	0	134	154	6	47	77	14.1	4.63	68	.291	.359	2	.056	-1	-21	-22	-2	-2.5
1968 Was-A	12	16	.429	33	33	12	2	0	223	212	19	51	139	11.1	3.27	89	.250	.302	9	.129	-1	-7	-9	-1	-1.1
1969 Was-A	12	13	.480	40	36	12	4	1	247²	222	26	100	182	11.9	3.27	106	.243	.322	9	.107	-2	10	5	0	0.3
1970 Was-A	8	12	.400	39	29	6	1	0	218²	190	25	89	152	11.6	3.58	99	.233	.311	8	.119	2	3	-1	0	0.1
1971 Det-A	20	9	.690	39	38	16	3	0	286	241	17	96	236	10.8	3.15	114	.229	.298	9	.094	-3	10	14	-2	0.9
1972 *Det-A	19	14	.576	40	39	9	3	0	280	216	23	110	222	10.8	2.80	112	.214	.297	9	.110	-3	8	11	-1	0.8
1973 Det-A	23	15	.605	40	40	13	2	0	288¹	283	32	93	202	12.0	3.53	116	.258	.322	0	—	0	9	18	-0	1.8
1974 Det-A	14	12	.538	41	41	11	2	0	285²	272	30	158	177	13.9	4.32	88	.254	.356	0	—	0	-22	-16	2	-1.4
1975 Det-A	10	18	.357	31	31	6	1	0	201	234	27	85	125	14.7	5.55	72	.291	.366	0	—	0	-40	-34	2	-3.2
1976 Det-A	2	5	.286	12	12	1	0	0	66²	80	1	34	38	16.1	4.86	76	.308	.398	0	—	0	-10	-9	2	-0.6
Chi-N	2	8	.200	39	4	0	0	4	79	72	9	35	66	12.4	4.10	94	.246	.330	2	.154	-0	-5	-2	0	-0.1
1977 Oak-A	4	4	.500	43	12	2	0	2	127²	114	11	49	55	11.6	2.96	136	.241	.314	0	—	0	16	15	0	1.5
1978 Oak-A	3	0	1.000	10	0	0	0	0	19²	12	1	5	4	7.8	1.37	265	.185	.243	0	—	0	5	5	0	0.6
Tor-A	2	0	1.000	31	0	0	0	0	60²	67	6	30	28	14.5	4.60	85	.286	.370	0	—	0	-6	-5	-1	-0.5
Yr	5	0	1.000	41	0	0	0	0	80¹	79	7	35	32	12.9	3.81	101	.263	.342	0	—	0	-0	-0	-0	0.1
1979 SF-N	0	0	—	5	0	0	0	0	3²	3	0	2	0	14.7	0.00	—	.231	.375	0	—	0	2	1	0	0.1
Pit-N	0	0	—	10	0	0	0	0	20²	29	1	9	14	17.0	6.10	64	.326	.394	1	.200	0	-5	-5	-1	-0.4
Yr	0	0	—	15	0	0	0	0	24¹	32	1	11	14	16.3	5.18	74	.308	.379	0	.000	0	-4	-4	-1	-0.3
Total 15	142	135	.513	484	340	94	18	7	2569¹	2416	234	1003	1728	12.3	3.70	97	.250	.327	49	.106	-10	-48	-28	-3	-3.0

■ JOE COLEMAN
Coleman, Joseph Patrick   b: 7/30/22, Medford, Mass.   BR/TR, 6'2.5", 200 lbs.   Deb: 9/19/42

YEAR TM/L	W	L	PCT	G	GS	CG	SH	SV	IP	H	HR	BB	SO	RAT	ERA	ERA+	OAV	OOB	BH	AVG	PB	PR	/A	PD	TPI
1942 Phi-A	0	1	.000	1	0	0	0	0	6	8	0	1	0	13.5	3.00	126	.308	.333	0	.000	-1	0	1	0	0.0
1946 Phi-A	0	2	.000	4	2	0	0	0	13	19	1	8	8	18.7	5.54	64	.345	.429	2	.400	1	-3	-3	-0	-0.2
1947 Phi-A	6	12	.333	32	21	9	2	1	160¹	171	17	62	65	13.1	4.32	88	.275	.341	7	.146	-1	-11	-9	-2	-1.1
1948 Phi-A	14	13	.519	33	29	13	3	0	215²	224	11	90	86	13.1	4.09	105	.269	.341	9	.122	-4	5	5	-2	0.0
1949 Phi-A	13	14	.481	33	30	18	1	1	240¹	249	12	127	109	14.2	3.86	107	.271	.361	14	.177	0	9	7	-5	0.2
1950 Phi-A	0	5	.000	15	6	2	0	0	54	74	9	50	12	20.7	8.50	54	.332	.454	1	.059	-1	-24	-24	-2	-2.1
1951 Phi-A	1	6	.143	28	9	1	0	1	96¹	117	12	59	34	16.7	5.98	72	.305	.402	7	.259	1	-20	-18	-1	-1.6
1953 Phi-A	3	4	.429	21	9	2	1	0	90	85	8	49	18	13.5	4.00	107	.254	.352	8	.286	2	-0	3	-1	0.3
1954 Bal-A	13	17	.433	33	32	15	4	0	221¹	184	16	96	103	11.5	3.50	102	.232	.317	13	.176	2	6	2	1	0.6
1955 Bal-A	0	1	.000	6	2	0	0	0	11²	19	5	10	4	23.1	10.80	35	.373	.484	2	.667	1	-9	-9	0	-0.6
Det-A	2	1	.667	17	0	0	0	3	25¹	22	1	14	5	13.1	3.20	120	.239	.346	1	.750	1	2	2	1	0.4
Yr	2	2	.500	23	2	0	0	3	37	41	6	24	9	16.1	5.59	69	.281	.386	0	.000	2	-7	-7	1	-0.2
Total 10	52	76	.406	223	140	60	11	6	1134	1172	92	566	444	13.9	4.38	92	.271	.357	66	.182	2	-44	-44	-11	-4.1

■ PERCY COLEMAN
Coleman, Pierce D.   b: 10/15/1876, Mason, Ohio   d: 2/16/48, Van Nuys, Cal.   Deb: 7/02/1897

YEAR TM/L	W	L	PCT	G	GS	CG	SH	SV	IP	H	HR	BB	SO	RAT	ERA	ERA+	OAV	OOB	BH	AVG	PB	PR	/A	PD	TPI
1897 StL-N	1	2	.333	12	4	2	0	0	57¹	99	0	32	10	20.6	8.16	54	.376	.443	6	.214	-1	-25	-24	1	-1.8
1898 Cin-N	0	1	.000	1	1	1	0	0	9	13	0	3	2	16.0	3.00	128	.335	.383	0	.000	-1	1	1	-0	0.0
Total 2	1	3	.250	13	5	3	0	0	66¹	112	0	35	12	19.9	7.46	58	.370	.436	6	.194	-2	-24	-23	0	-1.8

■ RIP COLEMAN
Coleman, Walter Gary   b: 7/31/31, Troy, N.Y.   BL/TL, 6'2", 185 lbs.   Deb: 8/15/55

YEAR TM/L	W	L	PCT	G	GS	CG	SH	SV	IP	H	HR	BB	SO	RAT	ERA	ERA+	OAV	OOB	BH	AVG	PB	PR	/A	PD	TPI
1955 *NY-A	2	1	.667	10	6	0	0	1	29	40	2	16	15	17.7	5.28	71	.331	.413	2	.200	1	-4	-5	0	-0.3
1956 NY-A	3	5	.375	29	9	0	0	2	88¹	97	6	42	42	14.3	3.67	105	.285	.366	1	.042	-3	5	2	0	0.0
1957 KC-A	0	7	.000	19	6	1	1	0	41	53	5	25	15	17.1	5.93	67	.325	.415	0	.000	-1	-10	-9	0	-0.9
1959 KC-A	2	10	.167	29	11	2	0	2	81	85	8	34	54	13.3	4.56	88	.273	.347	2	.080	-2	-6	-5	-0	-0.6
Bal-A	0	0	—	3	0	0	0	0	4	4	0	2	4	13.5	0.00	—	.267	.353	0	—	0	2	2	1	0.3
Yr	2	10	.167	32	11	2	0	2	85	89	8	36	58	13.2	4.34	92	.271	.342	2	.080	-2	-5	-3	-1	-0.3
1960 Bal-A	0	2	.000	5	1	0	0	0	4	8	0	5	0	31.5	11.25	34	.444	.583	0	.000	-0	-3	-3	0	-0.2
Total 5	7	25	.219	95	33	3	1	5	247¹	287	21	124	130	15.1	4.58	85	.296	.379	5	.072	-5	-17	-18	2	-1.7

■ ALLAN COLLAMORE
Collamore, Allan Edward   b: 6/5/1887, Worcester, Mass.   d: 8/8/80, Battle Creek, Mich.   BR/TR, 6', 170 lbs.   Deb: 4/15/11

YEAR TM/L	W	L	PCT	G	GS	CG	SH	SV	IP	H	HR	BB	SO	RAT	ERA	ERA+	OAV	OOB	BH	AVG	PB	PR	/A	PD	TPI
1911 Phi-A	0	1	.000	2	0	0	0	0	2	6	0	3	1	49.5	36.00	9	.600	.733	0	—	0	-7	-7	0	-0.5
1914 Cle-A	3	7	.300	27	8	3	0	0	105¹	100	1	49	32	13.2	3.25	89	.264	.357	3	.094	-2	-6	-4	0	-0.6
1915 Cle-A	2	5	.286	11	6	5	2	0	64¹	52	1	22	15	10.4	2.38	128	.235	.305	4	.174	0	4	5	1	0.7
Total 3	5	13	.278	40	14	8	2	0	171²	158	4	74	48	12.6	3.30	89	.259	.347	7	.127	-2	-9	-7	1	-0.4

■ HAP COLLARD
Collard, Earl Clinton   b: 8/29/1898, Williams, Ariz.   d: 7/9/68, Jamestown, Cal.   BR/TR, 6', 170 lbs.   Deb: 4/23/27

YEAR TM/L	W	L	PCT	G	GS	CG	SH	SV	IP	H	HR	BB	SO	RAT	ERA	ERA+	OAV	OOB	BH	AVG	PB	PR	/A	PD	TPI
1927 Cle-A	0	0	—	4	0	0	0	0	5¹	8	0	3	2	18.6	5.06	83	.333	.407	0	—	0	-1	-1	0	0.0
1928 Cle-A	0	0	—	1	0	0	0	0	4	4	0	4	1	18.0	2.25	184	.250	.400	1	1.000	0	1	1	-0	0.1
1930 Phi-N	6	12	.333	30	15	4	0	0	127	188	15	39	25	16.3	6.80	80	.350	.397	9	.205	-2	-26	-19	2	-1.5
Total 3	6	12	.333	35	15	4	0	0	136¹	200	15	46	28	16.4	6.60	81	.347	.398	10	.222	-1	-26	-19	2	-1.4

■ ORLIN COLLIER
Collier, Orlin Edward   b: 2/17/07, E.Prairie, Mo.   d: 9/9/44, Memphis, Tenn.   BR/TR, 5'11.5", 180 lbs.   Deb: 9/11/31

YEAR TM/L	W	L	PCT	G	GS	CG	SH	SV	IP	H	HR	BB	SO	RAT	ERA	ERA+	OAV	OOB	BH	AVG	PB	PR	/A	PD	TPI
1931 Det-A	0	1	.000	2	2	0	0	0	10¹	17	0	7	3	20.9	7.84	59	.362	.444	0	.000	-0	-4	-4	-0	-0.3

■ HARRY COLLIFLOWER
Colliflower, James Harry "Collie"
b: 3/11/1869, Petersville, Md.   d: 8/12/61, Washington, D.C.   BL/TL, 5'11.5", 175 lbs.   Deb: 7/21/1899   U

YEAR TM/L	W	L	PCT	G	GS	CG	SH	SV	IP	H	HR	BB	SO	RAT	ERA	ERA+	OAV	OOB	BH	AVG	PB	PR	/A	PD	TPI
1899 Cle-N	1	11	.083	14	12	11	0	0	98	152	6	41	8	17.7	8.17	45	.353	.409	23	.303	2	-47	-49	0	-3.5

YEAR TM/L	W	L	PCT	G	GS	CG	SH	SV	IP	H	HR	BB	SO	RAT	ERA	ERA+	OAV	OOB	BH	AVG	PB	PR	/A	PD	TPI
■ **DAN COLLINS** Collins, Daniel Thomas b: 7/12/1854, St.Louis, Mo. d: 9/21/1883, New Orleans, La. Deb: 6/08/1874 ♦																									
1874 Chi-n	1	1	.500	2	2	1	0	0	11	21	0	2		18.8	5.73	53	.368	.390	1	.083	-1	-3	-3		-0.2
■ **DON COLLINS** Collins, Donald Edward b: 9/15/52, Lyons, Ga. BR/TL, 6'2", 195 lbs. Deb: 5/04/77																									
1977 Atl-N	3	9	.250	40	6	0	0	2	70²	82	8	41	27	15.8	5.09	87	.299	.392	0	.000	-2	-9	-5	-1	-0.6
1980 Cle-A	0	0	—	4	0	0	0	0	6	9	0	7	0	24.0	7.50	54	.346	.485	0	—	0	-2	-2	0	-0.1
Total 2	3	9	.250	44	6	0	0	2	76²	91	8	48	27	16.4	5.28	84	.303	.401	0	.000	-2	-12	-7	-1	-0.7
■ **RIP COLLINS** Collins, Harry Warren b: 2/26/1896, Weatherford, Tex. d: 5/27/68, Bryan, Tex. BR/TR, 6'1", 205 lbs. Deb: 4/19/20																									
1920 NY-A	14	8	.636	36	18	10	2	1	187¹	171	6	79	66	12.7	3.22	119	.247	.337	8	.129	-4	12	13	-0	0.8
1921 *NY-A	11	5	.688	28	16	7	2	0	137¹	158	6	78	64	16.1	5.44	78	.293	.392	11	.196	-1	-18	-18	-1	-1.8
1922 Bos-A	14	11	.560	32	29	15	3	0	210²	219	4	103	69	14.2	3.76	109	.274	.364	12	.158	-3	7	8	-1	0.4
1923 Det-A	3	7	.300	17	14	3	1	0	92¹	104	3	22	25	13.3	4.87	79	.284	.342	3	.111	-2	-9	-10	0	-1.0
1924 Det-A	14	7	.667	34	30	11	1	0	216	199	6	63	75	11.1	3.21	128	.249	.307	11	.145	-4	25	22	0	1.6
1925 Det-A	6	11	.353	26	20	5	0	0	140	149	7	52	33	13.3	4.56	94	.281	.352	5	.119	-4	-3	-4	4	-0.3
1926 Det-A	8	8	.500	30	13	5	3	1	122	128	4	44	44	13.2	2.73	149	.278	.350	6	.154	-1	17	18	1	1.8
1927 Det-A	13	7	.650	30	25	10	1	0	172²	207	5	59	37	14.3	4.69	90	.312	.375	11	.204	0	-11	-9	5	-0.3
1929 StL-A	11	6	.647	26	20	10	1	1	155¹	162	16	73	47	14.0	4.00	111	.270	.355	17	.274	4	7	0	1	1.1
1930 StL-A	9	7	.563	35	20	6	1	2	171²	168	11	63	75	12.4	4.35	112	.259	.330	7	.130	-2	6	10	-1	0.7
1931 StL-A	5	5	.500	17	14	2	0	0	107	130	5	38	34	14.2	3.79	122	.307	.366	5	.147	-1	7	10	1	1.1
Total 11	108	82	.568	311	219	84	15	5	1712¹	1795	73	674	569	13.4	3.99	106	.275	.351	96	.165	-18	38	45	9	4.1
■ **ORTH COLLINS** Collins, Orth Stein "Buck" b: 4/27/1880, Lafayette, Ind. d: 12/13/49, Ft.Lauderdale, Fla BL/TR, 6', 150 lbs. Deb: 6/01/04 ♦																									
1909 Was-A	0	0	—	1	0	0	0	0	1	0	0	0	1	0.0	0.00	—	.000	.000	0	.000	-0	0	0	0	0.0
■ **PHIL COLLINS** Collins, Philip Eugene "Fidgety Phil" b: 8/27/01, Chicago, Ill. d: 8/14/48, Chicago, Ill. BR/TR, 5'11", 175 lbs. Deb: 10/07/23																									
1923 Chi-N	1	0	1.000	1	1	0	0	0	5	8	0	1	2	16.2	3.60	111	.400	.429	0	.000	-0	0	0	0	0.0
1929 Phi-N	9	7	.563	43	11	3	0	5	153¹	172	18	83	61	15.2	5.75	90	.284	.374	11	.190	-1	-18	-10	-1	-0.9
1930 Phi-N	16	11	.593	47	25	17	1	3	239	287	22	86	87	14.4	4.78	114	.299	.363	22	.253	3	5	18	-2	1.8
1931 Phi-N	12	16	.429	42	27	16	2	4	240¹	268	18	83	73	13.3	3.86	110	.283	.344	16	.168	-4	0	10	1	0.9
1932 Phi-N	14	12	.538	43	21	6	0	3	184¹	231	21	65	66	14.7	5.27	84	.314	.375	18	.265	3	-29	-18	-0	-1.3
1933 Phi-N	8	13	.381	42	13	5	1	**6**	151	178	9	57	40	14.4	4.11	93	.293	.360	7	.132	-3	-13	-5	-1	-0.8
1934 Phi-N	13	18	.419	45	32	15	0	1	254	277	30	87	72	13.0	4.18	113	.273	.333	15	.170	-5	-3	15	-3	0.9
1935 Phi-N	0	2	.000	3	3	0	0	0	14²	24	5	9	4	20.3	11.66	39	.348	.423	0	.000	-1	-12	-12	-0	-0.9
StL-N	7	6	.538	26	8	2	0	2	82²	96	6	26	18	13.6	4.57	90	.290	.347	4	.160	-1	-5	-4	-0	-0.4
Yr	7	8	.467	29	11	2	0	2	97¹	120	11	35	22	14.6	5.64	74	.300	.361	1	.032	-2	-18	-16	-0	-1.3
Total 8	80	85	.485	292	141	64	4	24	1324¹	1541	125	497	423	14.1	4.66	100	.291	.356	93	.193	-9	-75	-3	-7	-0.7
■ **RAY COLLINS** Collins, Raymond Williston b: 2/11/1887, Colchester, Vt. d: 1/9/70, Burlington, Vt. BL/TL, 6'1", 185 lbs. Deb: 7/19/09																									
1909 Bos-A	4	3	.571	12	8	4	2	0	73²	70	2	18	31	10.8	2.81	89	.269	.357	3	.130	-0	-3	-3	1	-0.1
1910 Bos-A	13	11	.542	35	26	18	4	1	244²	205	1	41	109	9.1	1.62	158	.229	.264	15	.179	-1	25	25	-3	2.5
1911 Bos-A	11	12	.478	31	24	14	0	1	194²	184	1	44	86	10.7	2.40	136	.256	.302	9	.150	0	20	19	-3	1.6
1912 *Bos-A	13	8	.619	27	24	17	4	0	199¹	192	4	42	82	10.7	2.53	134	.256	.297	11	.169	0	17	19	-2	1.9
1913 Bos-A	19	8	.704	30	30	19	3	0	246²	242	3	37	88	10.3	2.63	112	.263	.293	12	.150	2	8	9	-3	0.8
1914 Bos-A	20	13	.606	39	30	16	6	0	272¹	252	3	56	72	10.2	2.51	107	.258	.298	11	.139	-0	7	5	-4	0.0
1915 Bos-A	4	7	.364	25	9	2	0	2	104²	101	1	31	43	11.4	4.30	65	.261	.317	8	.286	4	-16	-18	-3	-1.6
Total 7	84	62	.575	199	151	90	19	4	1336	1246	15	269	511	10.3	2.51	115	.254	.294	69	.165	6	59	58	-18	5.1
■ **JACKIE COLLUM** Collum, Jack Dean b: 6/21/27, Victor, Ia. BL/TL, 5'7.5", 160 lbs. Deb: 9/21/51																									
1951 StL-N	2	1	.667	3	2	1	1	0	17	11	0	10	5	11.1	1.59	250	.204	.328	3	.429	1	4	4	0	0.6
1952 StL-N	0	0	—	2	0	0	0	0	3	2	0	1	0	9.0	0.00	—	.200	.273	0	—	0	1	1	0	0.2
1953 StL-N	0	0	—	7	0	0	0	0	11¹	15	1	4	5	15.1	6.35	67	.326	.380	0	.000	-0	-3	-3	1	-0.1
Cin-N	7	11	.389	30	12	4	1	3	124²	123	8	39	51	12.1	3.75	116	.263	.328	10	.278	3	7	8	1	1.1
Yr	7	11	.389	37	12	4	1	3	136	138	9	43	56	12.4	3.97	109	.269	.333	4	.103	3	5	6	2	1.0
1954 Cin-N	7	3	.700	36	2	1	0	0	79	86	8	32	28	14.0	3.76	112	.283	.361	3	.231	2	3	4	3	0.8
1955 Cin-N	9	8	.529	32	17	5	0	1	134	128	17	37	49	11.2	3.63	117	.254	.308	10	.250	2	6	9	-0	1.2
1956 StL-N	6	2	.750	38	1	0	0	7	60	63	6	27	17	13.8	4.20	90	.281	.364	3	.214	1	-3	-3	1	-0.1
1957 Chi-N	1	1	.500	9	0	0	0	1	10²	8	0	9	7	15.2	6.75	57	.211	.375	0	—	0	-3	-3	0	-0.2
Bro-N	0	0	—	3	0	0	0	0	4¹	7	1	1	3	16.6	8.31	50	.368	.400	0	—	0	-2	-2	-0	-0.1
Yr	1	1	.500	12	0	0	0	1	15	15	1	10	10	15.0	7.20	55	.254	.362	0	—	0	-6	-5	-0	-0.3
1958 LA-N	0	0	—	2	0	0	0	0	3¹	4	2	2	0	16.2	8.10	51	.308	.400	0	.000	-0	-2	-1	0	-0.1
1962 Min-A	0	2	.000	8	3	0	0	0	15¹	29	1	11	5	23.5	11.15	37	.414	.494	0	.000	-1	-12	-12	0	-1.0
Cle-A	0	0	—	1	0	0	0	0	1¹	4	0	1	1	27.0	13.50	29	.571	.571	0	—	0	-1	-1	0	0.0
Yr	0	2	.000	9	3	0	0	0	16²	33	1	11	6	23.8	11.34	36	.418	.489	0	.000	-1	-14	-13	0	-1.0
Total 9	32	28	.533	171	37	11	2	12	464	480	44	173	171	13.0	4.15	101	.273	.344	29	.246	8	-4	1	6	2.5
■ **DICK COLPAERT** Colpaert, Richard Charles b: 1/3/44, Fraser, Mich. BR/TR, 5'10", 182 lbs. Deb: 7/21/70																									
1970 Pit-N	1	0	1.000	8	0	0	0	0	10²	9	3	8	6	14.3	5.91	66	.237	.370	0	—	0	-2	-2	-0	-0.2
■ **LOYD COLSON** Colson, Loyd Albert b: 11/4/47, Wellington, Tex. BR/TR, 6'1", 190 lbs. Deb: 9/25/70																									
1970 NY-A	0	0	—	1	0	0	0	0	2	3	0	0	3	13.5	4.50	78	.333	.333	0	—	0	-0	-0	0	0.0
■ **LARRY COLTON** Colton, Lawrence Robert b: 6/8/42, Los Angeles, Cal. BL/TR, 6'3", 200 lbs. Deb: 5/06/68																									
1968 Phi-N	0	0	—	1	0	0	0	0	2	3	0	2	2	13.5	4.50	67	.333	.333	0	—	0	-0	-0	0	0.0
■ **GEOFF COMBE** Combe, Geoffrey Wade b: 2/1/56, Melrose, Mass. BR/TR, 6'2", 185 lbs. Deb: 9/02/80																									
1980 Cin-N	0	0	—	4	0	0	0	0	6²	9	0	4	10	17.6	10.80	33	.346	.433	0	—	0	-5	-5	0	-0.4
1981 Cin-N	1	0	1.000	14	0	0	0	0	17²	27	3	10	9	18.8	7.64	46	.370	.446	0	—	0	-8	-8	-0	-0.8
Total 2	1	0	1.000	18	0	0	0	0	24¹	36	3	14	19	18.5	8.51	42	.364	.442	0	—	0	-13	-13	-0	-1.2
■ **PAT COMBS** Combs, Patrick Dennis b: 10/29/66, Newport, R.I. BL/TL, 6'3", 200 lbs. Deb: 9/05/89																									
1989 Phi-N	4	0	1.000	6	6	1	1	0	38²	36	2	6	30	9.8	2.09	169	.248	.278	2	.167	0	6	6	-1	0.7
1990 Phi-N	10	10	.500	32	31	3	2	0	183¹	179	12	86	108	13.2	4.07	94	.257	.342	9	.150	0	-6	-5	-0	-0.4
Total 2	14	10	.583	38	37	4	3	0	222	215	14	92	138	12.6	3.73	101	.256	.332	11	.153	1	0	1	-1	0.3
■ **JORGE COMELLAS** Comellas, Jorge (Pous) "Pancho" b: 12/7/16, Havana, Cuba BR/TR, 6', 190 lbs. Deb: 4/19/45																									
1945 Chi-N	0	2	.000	7	1	0	0	0	12	11	1	6	6	12.8	4.50	81	.244	.333	0	.000	-0	-1	-1	1	0.0
■ **STEVE COMER** Comer, Steven Michael b: 1/13/54, Minneapolis, Minn. BB/TR, 6'3", 195 lbs. Deb: 4/15/78 C																									
1978 Tex-A	11	5	.688	30	11	3	2	1	117¹	107	5	37	65	11.1	2.30	163	.249	.310	0	—	0	19	19	1	2.1
1979 Tex-A	17	12	.586	36	36	6	1	0	242¹	230	24	84	86	12.0	3.68	113	.252	.320	0	—	0	14	13	1	1.3
1980 Tex-A	2	4	.333	12	11	0	0	0	41²	65	5	22	9	19.2	7.99	49	.367	.443	0	—	0	-18	-19	0	-1.6
1981 Tex-A	8	2	.800	36	1	0	0	6	77¹	70	1	31	22	11.9	2.56	135	.241	.317	0	—	0	9	8	1	1.0
1982 Tex-A	1	6	.143	37	3	1	0	6	97	133	11	36	23	15.9	5.10	76	.342	.400	0	—	0	-11	-13	0	-1.2

YEAR TM/L	W	L	PCT	G	GS	CG	SH	SV	IP	H	HR	BB	SO	RAT	ERA	ERA+	OAV	OOB	BH	AVG	PB	PR	/A	PD	TPI
1983 Phi-N	1	0	1.000	3	1	0	0	0	8²	11	0	3	1	14.5	5.19	69	.314	.368	0	.000	-0	-2	-2	0	-0.1
1984 Cle-A	4	8	.333	22	20	1	0	0	117¹	146	11	39	39	14.5	5.68	72	.309	.366	0	—	0	-22	-21	1	-1.8
Total 7	44	37	.543	176	83	11	3	13	701²	762	57	252	245	13.2	4.13	95	.281	.347	0	.000	-0	-10	-15	3	-0.3

■ CHARLIE COMISKEY
Comiskey, Charles Albert "Commy" or "The Old Roman"
b: 8/15/1859, Chicago, Ill. d: 10/26/31, Eagle River, Wis. BR/TR, 6', 180 lbs. Deb: 5/02/1882 MH♦

YEAR TM/L	W	L	PCT	G	GS	CG	SH	SV	IP	H	HR	BB	SO	RAT	ERA	ERA+	OAV	OOB	BH	AVG	PB	PR	/A	PD	TPI
1882 StL-a	0	1	.000	2	1	1	0	0	8	12	0	3	2	16.9	0.00	—	.325	.376	80	.243	0	2	2	0	0.2
1884 StL-a	0	0	—	1	0	0	0	0	4	1	0	0	4	2.3	2.25	145	.076	.076	110	.239	0	0	0	-0	0.0
1889 StL-a	0	0	—	1	0	0	0	0	0¹	0	0	0	0	0.0	0.00	—	.000	.000	168	.286	0	0	0	0	0.0
Total 3	0	1	.000	4	1	1	0	0	12¹	13	0	3	6	11.7	0.73	411	.254	.296	1531	.264	0	3	3	-0	0.2

■ JACK COMPTON
Compton, Harry Leroy b: 3/9/1882, Lancaster, Ohio d: 7/4/74, Lancaster, Ohio BR/TR, 5'9", 157 lbs. Deb: 9/07/11

YEAR TM/L	W	L	PCT	G	GS	CG	SH	SV	IP	H	HR	BB	SO	RAT	ERA	ERA+	OAV	OOB	BH	AVG	PB	PR	/A	PD	TPI
1911 Cin-N	0	1	.000	8	3	0	0	1	25¹	19	0	15	6	12.4	3.91	85	.204	.321	2	.333	0	-1	-2	0	0.0

■ CLINT COMPTON
Compton, Robert Clinton b: 11/1/50, Montgomery, Ala. BL/TL, 5'11", 185 lbs. Deb: 10/03/72

YEAR TM/L	W	L	PCT	G	GS	CG	SH	SV	IP	H	HR	BB	SO	RAT	ERA	ERA+	OAV	OOB	BH	AVG	PB	PR	/A	PD	TPI
1972 Chi-N	0	0	—	1	0	0	0	0	2	2	0	2	0	18.0	9.00	42	.286	.444	0	—	0	-1	-1	0	0.0

■ KEITH COMSTOCK
Comstock, Keith Martin b: 12/23/55, San Francisco, Cal. BL/TL, 6', 174 lbs. Deb: 4/03/84

YEAR TM/L	W	L	PCT	G	GS	CG	SH	SV	IP	H	HR	BB	SO	RAT	ERA	ERA+	OAV	OOB	BH	AVG	PB	PR	/A	PD	TPI
1984 Min-A	0	0	—	4	0	0	0	0	6¹	6	2	4	2	14.2	8.53	49	.261	.370	0	—	0	-3	-3	0	-0.2
1987 SF-N	2	0	1.000	15	0	0	0	1	20²	19	1	10	21	12.6	3.05	126	.253	.341	0	.000	-0	2	2	0	0.2
SD-N	0	1	.000	26	0	0	0	1	36	33	4	21	38	13.5	5.50	72	.252	.355	0	.000	-0	-6	-6	-1	-0.6
Yr	2	1	.667	41	0	0	0	2	56²	52	5	31	59	13.2	4.61	85	.251	.349	0	.000	-0	-3	-4	-1	-0.4
1988 SD-N	0	0	—	7	0	0	0	0	8	8	1	3	9	12.4	6.75	50	.250	.314	0	—	0	-3	-3	-0	-0.2
1989 Sea-A	1	2	.333	31	0	0	0	0	25²	26	2	10	22	12.6	2.81	144	.268	.336	0	—	0	3	3	-0	0.3
1990 Sea-A	7	4	.636	60	0	0	0	2	56	40	4	26	50	10.6	2.89	137	.206	.300	0	—	0	6	7	1	0.7
Total 5	10	7	.588	143	0	0	0	3	152²	132	14	74	142	12.1	3.95	100	.239	.329	0	.000	-0	-0	-0	0	0.2

■ RALPH COMSTOCK
Comstock, Ralph Remick "Commy" b: 11/24/1890, Sylvania, Ohio d: 9/13/66, Toledo, Ohio BR/TR, 5'10", 168 lbs. Deb: 8/26/13

YEAR TM/L	W	L	PCT	G	GS	CG	SH	SV	IP	H	HR	BB	SO	RAT	ERA	ERA+	OAV	OOB	BH	AVG	PB	PR	/A	PD	TPI
1913 Det-A	2	5	.286	10	7	1	0	1	60¹	90	0	16	37	16.0	5.37	54	.344	.384	5	.227	1	-16	-16	0	-1.4
1915 Bos-A	1	0	1.000	3	0	0	0	1	9	10	2	2	1	12.0	2.00	139	.294	.333	0	.000	0	1	1	0	0.1
Pit-F	3	3	.500	12	7	3	0	2	52²	44	3	7	18	8.9	3.25	93	.237	.268	0	.000	-2	-1	-1	-0	-0.3
1918 Pit-N	5	6	.455	15	8	6	0	1	81	78	0	14	44	10.4	3.00	96	.259	.297	5	.192	-0	-2	-1	-0	-0.1
Total 3	11	14	.440	40	22	10	0	4	203	222	5	39	100	11.7	3.72	78	.284	.321	10	.152	-1	-19	-18	-1	-1.7

■ DAVE CONCEPCION
Concepcion, David Ismael (Benitez) b: 6/17/48, Aragua, Venez. BR/TR, 6'2", 155 lbs. Deb: 4/06/70 ♦

YEAR TM/L	W	L	PCT	G	GS	CG	SH	SV	IP	H	HR	BB	SO	RAT	ERA	ERA+	OAV	OOB	BH	AVG	PB	PR	/A	PD	TPI
1988 Cin-N	0	0	—	1	0	0	0	0	1¹	2	0	1	1	13.5	0.00	—	.333	.333	39	.198	0	1	1	0	0.1

■ DAVID CONE
Cone, David Bryan b: 1/2/63, Kansas City, Mo. BL/TR, 6'1", 180 lbs. Deb: 6/08/86

YEAR TM/L	W	L	PCT	G	GS	CG	SH	SV	IP	H	HR	BB	SO	RAT	ERA	ERA+	OAV	OOB	BH	AVG	PB	PR	/A	PD	TPI
1986 KC-A	0	0	—	11	0	0	0	0	22²	29	2	13	21	17.1	5.56	76	.309	.398	0	—	0	-3	-3	-0	-0.3
1987 *NY-N	5	6	.455	21	13	1	0	1	99¹	87	11	44	68	12.3	3.71	102	.239	.329	2	.065	-1	4	1	-0	0.0
1988 *NY-N	20	3	**.870**	35	28	8	4	0	231¹	178	10	80	213	10.2	2.22	145	.213	.285	12	.150	1	32	26	-2	2.7
1989 NY-N	14	8	.636	34	33	7	2	0	219²	183	20	74	190	10.7	3.52	93	.223	.290	18	.234	4	-1	-6	-2	-0.5
1990 NY-N	14	10	.583	31	30	6	2	0	211²	177	21	65	**233**	10.3	3.23	113	.226	.286	14	.200	3	13	10	-1	1.2
Total 5	53	27	.663	132	104	22	8	1	784²	654	64	276	725	10.8	3.14	110	.226	.296	46	.178	7	45	26	-6	3.1

■ BOB CONE
Cone, Robert Earl b: 2/27/1894, Galveston, Tex. d: 5/24/55, Galveston, Tex. BR/TR, 6'2", 172 lbs. Deb: 7/25/15

YEAR TM/L	W	L	PCT	G	GS	CG	SH	SV	IP	H	HR	BB	SO	RAT	ERA	ERA+	OAV	OOB	BH	AVG	PB	PR	/A	PD	TPI
1915 Phi-A	0	0	—	1	1	0	0	0	0²	5	0	0	0	67.5	40.50	7	.714	.714	0	—	0	-3	-3	0	-0.2

■ DICK CONGER
Conger, Richard b: 4/3/21, Los Angeles, Cal. d: 2/16/70, Los Angeles, Cal. BR/TR, 6', 185 lbs. Deb: 4/22/40

YEAR TM/L	W	L	PCT	G	GS	CG	SH	SV	IP	H	HR	BB	SO	RAT	ERA	ERA+	OAV	OOB	BH	AVG	PB	PR	/A	PD	TPI
1940 Det-A	1	0	1.000	2	0	0	0	0	3	2	0	3	1	15.0	3.00	159	.200	.385	0	—	0	0	1	0	0.0
1941 Pit-N	0	0	—	2	1	0	0	0	4	3	0	3	2	13.5	0.00	—	.214	.353	0	—	0	2	2	-0	0.2
1942 Pit-N	0	0	—	2	1	0	0	0	8¹	9	0	5	3	15.1	2.16	157	.290	.389	0	.000	-0	1	1	1	0.1
1943 Phi-N	2	7	.222	13	10	2	0	0	54²	72	3	24	18	16.6	6.09	55	.327	.406	1	.063	-1	-16	-17	0	-1.6
Total 4	3	7	.300	19	12	2	0	0	70	86	3	35	24	16.2	5.14	67	.313	.400	1	.053	-1	-13	-13	0	-1.3

■ ALLEN CONKWRIGHT
Conkwright, Allen Howard "Red" b: 12/4/1896, Sedalia, Mo. BR/TR, 5'10", 170 lbs. Deb: 9/16/20

YEAR TM/L	W	L	PCT	G	GS	CG	SH	SV	IP	H	HR	BB	SO	RAT	ERA	ERA+	OAV	OOB	BH	AVG	PB	PR	/A	PD	TPI
1920 Det-A	2	1	.667	5	2	0	0	1	19¹	29	0	16	4	20.9	6.98	53	.397	.506	1	.200	1	-7	-7	0	-0.5

■ GENE CONLEY
Conley, Donald Eugene b: 11/10/30, Muskogee, Okla. BR/TR, 6'8", 225 lbs. Deb: 4/17/52

YEAR TM/L	W	L	PCT	G	GS	CG	SH	SV	IP	H	HR	BB	SO	RAT	ERA	ERA+	OAV	OOB	BH	AVG	PB	PR	/A	PD	TPI
1952 Bos-N	0	3	.000	4	3	0	0	0	12²	14	3	9	6	24.2	7.82	46	.397	.493	2	.400	1	-6	-6	0	-0.4
1954 Mil-N	14	9	.609	28	27	12	2	0	194¹	171	17	79	113	11.9	2.96	126	.240	.322	12	.156	-2	24	16	-1	1.3
1955 Mil-N	11	7	.611	22	21	10	0	0	158	152	23	52	107	11.7	4.16	90	.254	.315	11	.204	-1	-2	-7	-1	-0.8
1956 Mil-N	8	9	.471	31	19	5	1	3	158¹	169	13	52	68	12.7	3.13	111	.276	.335	7	.156	-0	11	6	-0	0.5
1957 *Mil-N	9	9	.500	35	18	6	1	1	148	133	9	64	61	12.1	3.16	111	.244	.325	9	.196	1	12	6	-0	0.6
1958 Mil-N	0	6	.000	26	7	0	0	2	72	89	8	17	53	13.8	4.88	72	.309	.356	3	.188	1	-7	-11	-0	-0.6
1959 Phi-N	12	7	.632	25	22	12	3	1	180	159	13	42	102	10.1	3.00	**137**	.235	.281	16	.239	2	19	22	0	2.6
1960 Phi-N	8	14	.364	29	25	9	2	0	183¹	192	10	42	117	11.6	3.68	105	.272	.314	8	.127	-1	2	4	-2	0.1
1961 Bos-A	11	14	.440	33	30	6	2	1	199²	229	33	65	113	13.4	4.91	85	.287	.343	16	.219	4	-20	-17	-1	-1.2
1962 Bos-A	15	14	.517	34	33	9	2	1	241²	238	28	68	134	11.6	3.95	105	.256	.310	18	.207	4	1	5	-1	0.8
1963 Bos-A	3	4	.429	9	9	0	0	0	40²	51	14	21	14	16.2	6.64	57	.305	.386	3	.200	0	-14	-13	-1	-1.2
Total 11	91	96	.487	276	214	69	13	9	1588²	1606	162	511	888	12.2	3.82	101	.264	.324	105	.192	8	20	6	-6	1.4

■ ED CONLEY
Conley, Edward J. b: 7/10/1864, Sandwich, Mass. d: 10/16/1894, Cumberland, R.I. 5'11.5", Deb: 7/20/1884

YEAR TM/L	W	L	PCT	G	GS	CG	SH	SV	IP	H	HR	BB	SO	RAT	ERA	ERA+	OAV	OOB	BH	AVG	PB	PR	/A	PD	TPI
1884 Pro-N	4	4	.500	8	8	8	1	0	71	63	4	22	33	10.8	2.15	131	.225	.281	4	.143	-2	7	5	-1	0.2

■ SNIPE CONLEY
Conley, James Patrick b: 4/25/1894, Cressona, Pa. d: 1/7/78, DeSoto, Tex. BR/TR, 5'11.5", 179 lbs. Deb: 5/20/14

YEAR TM/L	W	L	PCT	G	GS	CG	SH	SV	IP	H	HR	BB	SO	RAT	ERA	ERA+	OAV	OOB	BH	AVG	PB	PR	/A	PD	TPI
1914 Bal-F	4	6	.400	35	11	4	2	1	125	112	2	47	86	11.9	2.52	134	.259	.340	4	.114	-3	10	12	-1	0.9
1915 Bal-F	1	4	.200	25	6	4	0	0	86	97	5	32	40	13.9	4.29	74	.314	.386	6	.250	2	-12	-11	-1	-0.9
1918 Cin-N	2	0	1.000	5	0	0	0	1	13²	17	2	5	2	14.5	5.27	51	.321	.379	1	.250	0	-4	-4	0	-0.3
Total 3	7	10	.412	65	17	8	2	2	224²	226	9	84	128	12.8	3.36	97	.284	.360	11	.175	-1	-6	-3	-2	-0.3

■ BOB CONLEY
Conley, Robert Burns b: 2/1/34, Knott County, Va. BR/TR, 6'1", 188 lbs. Deb: 9/11/58

YEAR TM/L	W	L	PCT	G	GS	CG	SH	SV	IP	H	HR	BB	SO	RAT	ERA	ERA+	OAV	OOB	BH	AVG	PB	PR	/A	PD	TPI
1958 Phi-N	0	0	—	2	2	0	0	0	8¹	9	0	1	0	10.8	7.56	52	.273	.294	0	.000	-0	-3	-3	0	-0.2

■ BERT CONN
Conn, Albert Thomas b: 9/22/1879, Philadelphia, Pa. d: 11/2/44, Philadelphia, Pa. TR, Deb: 9/16/1898 ♦

YEAR TM/L	W	L	PCT	G	GS	CG	SH	SV	IP	H	HR	BB	SO	RAT	ERA	ERA+	OAV	OOB	BH	AVG	PB	PR	/A	PD	TPI
1898 Phi-N	0	1	.000	1	1	0	0	0	7	13	1	2	3	19.3	6.43	53	.393	.428	1	.333	1	-2	-2	-0	0.0
1900 Phi-N	0	2	.000	4	1	0	0	0	17¹	29	0	16	2	23.4	8.31	44	.370	.477	3	.333	1	-9	-9	-1	-0.6
Total 2	0	3	.000	5	2	0	0	0	24¹	42	1	18	5	22.2	7.77	46	.377	.464	8	.267	2	-11	-11	-1	-0.6

■ SARGE CONNALLY
Connally, George Walter b: 8/31/1898, Mcgregor, Tex. d: 1/27/78, Temple, Tex. BR/TR, 5'11", 170 lbs. Deb: 9/10/21

YEAR TM/L	W	L	PCT	G	GS	CG	SH	SV	IP	H	HR	BB	SO	RAT	ERA	ERA+	OAV	OOB	BH	AVG	PB	PR	/A	PD	TPI
1921 Chi-A	0	1	.000	5	2	0	0	0	22¹	29	0	10	6	16.1	6.45	66	.330	.404	4	.500	2	-5	-5	0	-0.2
1923 Chi-A	0	0	—	3	0	0	0	0	8²	7	0	12	3	20.8	6.23	64	.241	.476	1	.333	1	-2	-2	-0	-0.1
1924 Chi-A	7	13	.350	44	13	6	0	6	160	177	4	68	55	14.3	4.05	102	.290	.369	11	.220	-1	3	1	3	0.0
1925 Chi-A	6	7	.462	40	2	0	0	8	104²	122	2	58	45	15.6	4.64	89	.310	.402	7	.250	1	-3	-6	2	-0.1
1926 Chi-A	4	5	.545	31	8	5	0	0	108¹	128	0	35	47	13.7	3.16	122	.300	.356	5	.156	-1	10	9	2	0.9
1927 Chi-A	10	15	.400	43	18	11	1	5	198¹	217	8	83	58	14.0	4.08	99	.292	.370	22	.328	4	1	-1	1	0.3
1928 Chi-A	2	5	.286	28	5	1	0	2	74¹	89	1	29	28	14.8	4.84	84	.313	.385	2	.105	-2	-7	-7	-0	-0.7

YEAR	TM/L	W	L	PCT	G	GS	CG	SH	SV	IP	H	HR	BB	SO	RAT	ERA	ERA+	OAV	OOB	BH	AVG	PB	PR	/A	PD	TPI
1929	Chi-A	0	0	—	11	0	0	0	1	11¹	13	0	8	3	16.7	4.76	90	.317	.429	0	—	0	-1	-1	-0	0.0
1931	Cle-A	5	5	.500	17	9	5	0	1	85²	87	7	50	37	15.0	4.20	110	.256	.361	5	.185	1	2	4	-0	0.4
1932	Cle-A	8	6	.571	35	7	4	1	3	112¹	119	6	42	32	13.1	4.33	110	.266	.333	7	.175	-0	2	5	-0	0.5
1933	Cle-A	5	3	.625	41	3	1	0	1	103	112	4	49	30	14.3	4.89	91	.271	.353	6	.231	1	-7	-5	-2	-0.5
1934	Cle-A	0	0	—	5	0	0	0	1	5¹	4	0	5	1	15.2	5.06	90	.222	.391	0	.000	-0	-0	-0	0	0.0
Total	12	49	60	.450	303	67	33	2	31	994¹	1104	32	449	345	14.4	4.30	98	.288	.368	70	.233	5	-7	-8	5	0.8

■ BILL CONNELLY
Connelly, William Wirt "Wild Bill"   b: 6/29/25, Alberta, Va.   d: 11/27/80, Richmond, Va.   BL/TR, 6', 175 lbs.   Deb: 8/22/45

YEAR	TM/L	W	L	PCT	G	GS	CG	SH	SV	IP	H	HR	BB	SO	RAT	ERA	ERA+	OAV	OOB	BH	AVG	PB	PR	/A	PD	TPI
1945	Phi-A	1	1	.500	2	1	0	0	0	8	7	0	8	0	16.9	4.50	76	.259	.429	0	—	0	-1	-1	-0	0.0
1950	Chi-A	0	0	—	2	0	0	0	0	2¹	5	1	1	0	23.1	11.57	39	.455	.500	0	—	0	-2	-2	0	-0.1
	Det-A	0	0	—	2	0	0	0	0	4	4	1	2	1	13.5	6.75	69	.250	.333	0	.000	-0	-1	-1	0	0.0
	Yr	0	0	—	4	0	0	0	0	6¹	9	2	3	1	17.1	8.53	54	.333	.400	1	1.000	0	-3	-3	-0	-0.1
1952	NY-N	5	0	1.000	11	4	0	0	0	31²	22	4	25	22	13.4	4.55	81	.208	.359	4	.364	3	-3	-3	0	0.0
1953	NY-N	0	1	.000	8	2	0	0	0	20¹	33	4	17	11	22.1	11.07	39	.371	.472	0	.000	-1	-15	-15	-0	-1.3
Total	4	6	2	.750	25	7	0	0	0	66¹	71	10	53	34	16.8	6.92	57	.285	.411	4	.211	3	-22	-22	-0	-1.4

■ ED CONNOLLY
Connolly, Edward Joseph Jr.   b: 12/3/39, Brooklyn, N.Y.   BL/TL, 6'1", 190 lbs.   Deb: 4/19/64

YEAR	TM/L	W	L	PCT	G	GS	CG	SH	SV	IP	H	HR	BB	SO	RAT	ERA	ERA+	OAV	OOB	BH	AVG	PB	PR	/A	PD	TPI
1964	Bos-A	4	11	.267	27	15	1	1	0	80²	80	3	64	73	16.7	4.91	79	.261	.398	3	.167	0	-12	-9	-1	-1.0
1967	Cle-A	2	1	.667	15	4	0	0	0	49¹	63	6	34	45	17.9	7.48	44	.315	.417	2	.182	0	-23	-23	-0	-2.2
Total	2	6	12	.333	42	19	1	1	0	130	143	9	98	118	17.2	5.88	62	.282	.405	5	.172	0	-35	-33	-2	-3.2

■ JOHN CONNOR
Connor, John   b: 1853, Scotland   d: 10/13/32, Boston, Mass.   Deb: 7/26/1884

YEAR	TM/L	W	L	PCT	G	GS	CG	SH	SV	IP	H	HR	BB	SO	RAT	ERA	ERA+	OAV	OOB	BH	AVG	PB	PR	/A	PD	TPI
1884	Bos-N	1	4	.200	7	7	7	0	0	60	70	1	18	29	13.2	3.15	91	.276	.324	2	.080	-3	-1	-2	1	-0.2
1885	Buf-N	0	1	.000	1	1	1	0	0	9	14	0	2	0	16.0	4.00	74	.340	.370	0	.000	-0	-1	-1	-0	-0.1
	Lou-a	1	3	.250	4	4	4	0	0	35	43	0	12	19	14.1	4.89	66	.290	.343	2	.143	-1	-6	-6	-1	-0.6
Total	2	2	8	.200	12	12	12	0	0	104	127	1	32	48	13.8	3.81	79	.287	.335	4	.095	-4	-9	-9	-1	-0.9

■ JOE CONNORS
Connors, Joseph P.   b: Paterson, N.J.   Deb: 5/03/1884   ♦

YEAR	TM/L	W	L	PCT	G	GS	CG	SH	SV	IP	H	HR	BB	SO	RAT	ERA	ERA+	OAV	OOB	BH	AVG	PB	PR	/A	PD	TPI
1884	Alt-U	0	1	.000	1	1	1	0	0	9	18	0	5	0	23.0	7.00	47	.391	.451	1	.091	-0	-4	-4	0	-0.2
	KC-U	0	1	.000	2	1	1	0	0	12	24	1	0	1	18.0	4.50	61	.391	.391	1	.091	-1	-2	-2	-0	-0.2
	Yr	0	2	.000	3	2	2	0	0	21	42	1	5	1	20.1	5.57	54	.391	.418	2	.045	-1	-6	-6	0	-0.4

■ BILL CONNORS
Connors, William Joseph   b: 11/2/41, Schenectady, N.Y.   BR/TR, 6'1", 180 lbs.   Deb: 5/03/66 C

YEAR	TM/L	W	L	PCT	G	GS	CG	SH	SV	IP	H	HR	BB	SO	RAT	ERA	ERA+	OAV	OOB	BH	AVG	PB	PR	/A	PD	TPI
1966	Chi-N	0	1	.000	11	0	0	0	0	16	20	4	7	3	15.2	7.31	50	.308	.375	0	—	0	-7	-6	-0	-0.5
1967	NY-N	0	0	—	6	1	0	0	0	13	8	3	5	13	9.7	6.23	54	.170	.264	0	.000	-0	-4	-4	-0	-0.4
1968	NY-N	0	1	.000	9	0	0	0	0	14	21	0	7	8	18.6	9.00	34	.339	.414	1	1.000	1	-9	-9	0	-0.8
Total	3	0	2	.000	26	1	0	0	0	43	49	7	19	24	14.7	7.53	45	.282	.359	1	.500	1	-20	-20	-0	-1.7

■ TED CONOVAR
Conovar, Theodore "Huck"   b: 3/10/1868, Lexington, Ky.   d: 7/27/10, Paris, Ky.   5'10.5", 165 lbs.   Deb: 5/26/1889

YEAR	TM/L	W	L	PCT	G	GS	CG	SH	SV	IP	H	HR	BB	SO	RAT	ERA	ERA+	OAV	OOB	BH	AVG	PB	PR	/A	PD	TPI
1889	Cin-a	0	0	—	1	0	0	0	1	2	4	0	2	1	27.0	13.50	29	.403	.503	0	—	0	-2	-2	-0	-0.1

■ TIM CONROY
Conroy, Timothy James   b: 4/3/60, McKeesport, Pa.   BL/TL, 6', 178 lbs.   Deb: 6/23/78

YEAR	TM/L	W	L	PCT	G	GS	CG	SH	SV	IP	H	HR	BB	SO	RAT	ERA	ERA+	OAV	OOB	BH	AVG	PB	PR	/A	PD	TPI
1978	Oak-A	0	0	—	2	2	0	0	0	4²	3	0	9	0	25.1	7.71	47	.188	.500	0	—	0	-2	-2	-0	-0.1
1982	Oak-A	2	2	.500	5	5	1	0	0	25¹	20	1	18	17	13.5	3.55	110	.222	.352	0	—	0	1	1	-0	0.1
1983	Oak-A	7	10	.412	39	18	3	1	0	162¹	141	17	98	112	13.4	3.94	98	.232	.340	0	—	0	2	-1	-3	-0.3
1984	Oak-A	1	6	.143	38	14	0	0	0	93	82	11	63	69	14.2	5.32	70	.236	.356	0	—	0	-14	-16	-2	-1.7
1985	Oak-A	0	1	.000	16	2	0	0	0	25¹	22	3	15	8	13.5	4.26	90	.237	.349	0	—	0	-0	-1	-0	0.0
1986	StL-N	5	11	.313	25	21	1	0	0	115¹	122	15	56	79	14.1	5.23	70	.275	.360	4	.138	1	-19	-20	-1	-2.0
1987	StL-N	3	2	.600	10	9	0	0	0	40²	48	0	25	22	16.4	5.53	75	.306	.404	0	.000	-2	-7	-6	-0	-0.7
Total	7	18	32	.360	135	71	5	1	0	466²	438	47	284	307	14.1	4.71	81	.249	.357	4	.091	-1	-38	-47	-7	-4.7

■ JIM CONSTABLE
Constable, Jimmy Lee "Sheriff"   b: 6/14/33, Jonesboro, Tenn.   BB/TL, 6'1", 185 lbs.   Deb: 6/24/56

YEAR	TM/L	W	L	PCT	G	GS	CG	SH	SV	IP	H	HR	BB	SO	RAT	ERA	ERA+	OAV	OOB	BH	AVG	PB	PR	/A	PD	TPI
1956	NY-N	0	0	—	3	0	0	0	0	4¹	9	0	7	1	35.3	14.54	26	.429	.586	0	—	0	-5	-5	0	-0.4
1957	NY-N	1	1	.500	16	0	0	0	0	28¹	27	2	7	13	12.1	2.86	138	.262	.333	0	.000	-0	3	3	-0	0.3
1958	SF-N	1	0	1.000	9	0	0	0	1	8	10	1	3	4	14.6	5.63	68	.323	.382	1	1.000	1	-1	-2	1	0.0
	Cle-A	0	0	—	6	2	0	0	0	9¹	17	1	4	3	21.2	11.57	32	.415	.478	2	1.000	1	-8	-8	-0	-0.6
	Was-A	0	1	.000	15	2	0	0	0	27²	29	3	15	25	14.6	4.88	78	.271	.366	1	.250	1	-3	-3	-0	-0.3
	Yr	0	2	.000	21	4	0	0	0	37	46	4	19	28	16.1	6.57	57	.309	.391	0	.000	1	-12	-11	-0	-0.9
1962	Mil-N	1	1	.500	3	2	1	1	1	18	14	1	4	12	9.0	2.00	190	.222	.269	0	.000	-0	4	4	-0	0.3
1963	SF-N	0	0	—	4	0	0	0	0	2¹	3	0	1	1	15.4	3.86	83	.333	.400	0	—	0	-0	-0	-0	0.0
Total	5	3	4	.429	56	6	1	1	2	98	109	8	41	59	14.4	4.87	78	.291	.371	4	.235	2	-11	-11	-1	-0.7

■ SANDY CONSUEGRA
Consuegra, Sandalio Simeon (Castello)   b: 9/3/20, Potrerillos, Cuba   BR/TR, 5'10", 165 lbs.   Deb: 6/10/50

YEAR	TM/L	W	L	PCT	G	GS	CG	SH	SV	IP	H	HR	BB	SO	RAT	ERA	ERA+	OAV	OOB	BH	AVG	PB	PR	/A	PD	TPI
1950	Was-A	7	8	.467	21	18	8	2	2	124²	132	6	57	38	13.7	4.40	102	.270	.347	7	.175	-1	2	1	0	0.0
1951	Was-A	7	8	.467	40	12	5	0	3	146	140	10	63	31	12.5	4.01	102	.251	.325	10	.233	-0	2	1	0	0.2
1952	Was-A	6	0	1.000	30	2	0	0	5	73²	80	2	27	19	13.1	3.05	116	.276	.338	3	.176	-0	5	4	-1	0.3
1953	Was-A	0	0	—	4	0	0	0	0	5	9	0	4	0	23.4	10.80	36	.391	.481	0	—	0	-4	-4	0	-0.2
	Chi-A	7	5	.583	29	13	5	1	3	124	122	9	28	30	11.0	2.54	158	.258	.302	2	.057	-4	20	20	3	2.1
	Yr	7	5	.583	33	13	5	1	3	129	131	9	32	30	11.5	2.86	141	.264	.311	1	.029	-4	16	17	4	1.9
1954	Chi-A	16	3	.842	39	17	3	2	3	154	142	9	35	31	10.3	2.69	139	.248	.292	11	.229	1	18	18	2	2.2
1955	Chi-A	6	5	.545	44	7	3	0	7	126¹	120	4	18	35	10.0	2.64	150	.256	.286	3	.103	-2	19	18	0	1.7
1956	Chi-A	1	2	.333	28	1	0	0	3	38¹	45	0	11	7	13.4	5.17	79	.296	.348	0	.000	-1	-4	-5	0	-0.4
	Bal-A	1	1	.500	4	1	0	0	0	8²	10	2	2	1	12.5	4.15	94	.294	.333	1	.500	0	-0	-0	-0	0.0
	Yr	2	3	.400	32	2	0	0	3	47	55	2	13	8	13.0	4.98	82	.293	.338	0	.000	-0	-4	-5	0	-0.4
1957	Bal-A	0	0	—	5	0	0	0	0	5	4	0	0	0	7.2	1.80	200	.211	.211	0	—	0	1	1	0	0.1
	NY-N	0	0	—	4	0	0	0	0	4	3	0	1	1	9.0	2.45	160	.389	.421	0	—	0	1	1	0	0.1
Total	8	51	32	.614	248	71	24	5	26	809¹	811	43	246	193	11.8	3.37	119	.262	.318	37	.170	-5	59	57	6	6.1

■ NARDI CONTRERAS
Contreras, Arnaldo Juan   b: 9/19/51, Tampa, Fla.   BB/TR, 6'2", 193 lbs.   Deb: 5/23/80

YEAR	TM/L	W	L	PCT	G	GS	CG	SH	SV	IP	H	HR	BB	SO	RAT	ERA	ERA+	OAV	OOB	BH	AVG	PB	PR	/A	PD	TPI
1980	Chi-A	0	0	—	8	0	0	0	0	13²	18	1	7	8	17.8	5.93	68	.333	.429	0	—	0	-3	-3	0	-0.2

■ JIM CONWAY
Conway, James P.   b: Clifton, Pa.   TR,   Deb: 5/05/1884

YEAR	TM/L	W	L	PCT	G	GS	CG	SH	SV	IP	H	HR	BB	SO	RAT	ERA	ERA+	OAV	OOB	BH	AVG	PB	PR	/A	PD	TPI
1884	Bro-a	3	9	.250	13	13	10	0	0	105¹	132	4	15	25	12.6	4.44	75	.291	.313	6	.128	-4	-14	-13	-1	-1.5
1885	Phi-a	0	1	.000	2	2	1	0	0	12¹	19	0	2	0	15.3	7.30	47	.338	.361	0	.000	-1	-6	-5	0	-0.4
1889	KC-a	19	19	.500	41	37	33	0	0	335	334	12	90	115	11.4	3.25	129	.252	.299	31	.208	-6	22	35	1	2.8
Total	3	22	29	.431	56	52	44	0	0	452²	485	16	107	140	11.8	3.64	109	.264	.304	37	.183	-11	3	16	-0	0.9

■ JERRY CONWAY
Conway, Jerome Patrick   b: 6/7/01, Holyoke, Mass.   d: 4/16/80, Holyoke, Mass.   BL/TL, 6'2", 190 lbs.   Deb: 8/31/20

YEAR	TM/L	W	L	PCT	G	GS	CG	SH	SV	IP	H	HR	BB	SO	RAT	ERA	ERA+	OAV	OOB	BH	AVG	PB	PR	/A	PD	TPI
1920	Was-A	0	0	—	1	0	0	0	0	2	1	0	1	0	9.0	0.00	—	.167	.286	0	—	0	1	1	0	0.1

■ PETE CONWAY
Conway, Peter J.   b: 10/30/1866, Burmont, Pa.   d: 1/13/03, Clifton Heights, Pa.   BR/TR, 5'10.5",   Deb: 8/10/1885   ♦

YEAR	TM/L	W	L	PCT	G	GS	CG	SH	SV	IP	H	HR	BB	SO	RAT	ERA	ERA+	OAV	OOB	BH	AVG	PB	PR	/A	PD	TPI
1885	Buf-N	10	17	.370	27	27	26	1	0	210	256	1	44	94	12.9	4.67	63	.287	.321	10	.111	-4	-43	-40	1	-3.7
1886	KC-N	5	15	.250	23	20	19	0	0	180	236	6	61	81	14.9	5.75	66	.304	.355	47	.242	1	-49	-40	-2	-3.2
	Det-N	6	5	.545	11	11	11	0	0	91	93	1	25	35	11.7	3.36	98	.254	.302	8	.186	1	-1	-1	-0	0.0
	Yr	11	20	.355	34	31	30	0	0	271	329	7	86	116	13.4	4.95	73	.288	.338	6	.025	1	-49	-40	-2	-3.2
1887	•Det-N	8	9	.471	17	17	16	0	0	146	132	3	47	40	11.0	2.90	139	.235	.294	22	.232	0	19	18	3	1.9

YEAR	TM/L	W	L	PCT	G	GS	CG	SH	SV	IP	H	HR	BB	SO	RAT	ERA	ERA+	OAV	OOB	BH	AVG	PB	PR	/A	PD	TPI
1888	Det-N	30	14	.682	45	45	43	4	0	391	315	11	57	176	8.6	2.26	122	.213	.242	46	.275	14	25	21	2	3.9
1889	Pit-N	2	1	.667	3	3	2	0	0	22	26	1	16	2	17.2	4.91	76	.285	.391	1	.100	0	-2	-3	0	-0.1
Total	5	61	61	.500	126	123	117	5	0	1040	1058	32	250	428	11.3	3.59	90	.254	.296	134	.224	11	-51	-43	4	-1.2

■ DICK CONWAY
Conway, Richard Butler   b: 4/25/1865, Lowell, Mass.   d: 9/9/26, Lowell, Mass.   BL/TR, 5′7.5″, 140 lbs.   Deb: 7/22/1886

YEAR	TM/L	W	L	PCT	G	GS	CG	SH	SV	IP	H	HR	BB	SO	RAT	ERA	ERA+	OAV	OOB	BH	AVG	PB	PR	/A	PD	TPI
1886	Bal-a	2	7	.222	9	9	8	0	0	76²	106	6	43	64	17.5	6.81	50	.314	.391	7	.206	0	-29	-29	2	-2.0
1887	Bos-N	9	15	.375	26	26	25	0	0	222¹	249	10	86	45	13.6	4.66	87	.275	.338	36	.248	2	-15	-15	1	-0.8
1888	Bos-N	4	2	.667	6	6	6	0	0	53	49	2	8	12	9.7	2.38	119	.237	.265	4	.160	-1	3	3	-0	0.2
Total	3	15	24	.385	41	41	39	0	0	352	404	18	137	121	13.8	4.78	78	.279	.341	47	.230	2	-41	-42	2	-2.6

■ JOE CONZELMAN
Conzelman, Joseph Harrison   b: 7/14/1885, Bristol, Conn.   d: 4/17/79, Mountain Brook, Ala.   BR/TR, 6′, 170 lbs.   Deb: 5/01/13

YEAR	TM/L	W	L	PCT	G	GS	CG	SH	SV	IP	H	HR	BB	SO	RAT	ERA	ERA+	OAV	OOB	BH	AVG	PB	PR	/A	PD	TPI
1913	Pit-N	0	1	.000	3	2	1	0	0	15	13	0	5	9	11.4	1.20	251	.245	.322	0	.000	-1	3	3	0	0.3
1914	Pit-N	5	6	.455	33	9	4	1	2	101	88	2	40	39	11.7	2.94	90	.254	.337	3	.111	-2	-2	-3	1	-0.3
1915	Pit-N	1	1	.500	18	1	0	0	0	47¹	41	0	20	22	12.2	3.42	80	.248	.340	1	.091	-1	-4	-4	1	-0.3
Total	3	6	8	.429	54	12	5	1	2	163¹	142	2	65	70	11.8	2.92	93	.252	.336	4	.095	-3	-2	-4	2	-0.3

■ DENNIS COOK
Cook, Dennis Bryan   b: 10/4/62, LaMarque, Tex.   BL/TL, 6′3″, 185 lbs.   Deb: 9/12/88

YEAR	TM/L	W	L	PCT	G	GS	CG	SH	SV	IP	H	HR	BB	SO	RAT	ERA	ERA+	OAV	OOB	BH	AVG	PB	PR	/A	PD	TPI
1988	SF-N	2	1	.667	4	4	1	1	0	22	9	1	11	13	8.2	2.86	114	.125	.241	0	.000	1	1	1	-1	0.1
1989	SF-N	1	0	1.000	2	2	1	0	0	15	13	1	5	9	10.8	1.80	187	.245	.310	1	.167	1	3	3	0	0.4
	Phi-N	6	8	.429	21	16	1	1	0	106	97	17	33	58	11.2	3.99	89	.243	.304	8	.222	1	-6	-5	-1	-0.4
	Yr	7	8	.467	23	18	2	1	0	121	110	18	38	67	11.2	3.72	95	.243	.305	9	.000	2	-3	-3	-1	0.0
1990	Phi-N	8	3	.727	42	13	2	1	1	141²	132	13	54	58	11.9	3.56	107	.250	.322	13	.310	4	4	4	0	0.8
	LA-N	1	1	.500	5	3	0	0	0	14¹	23	7	2	6	15.7	7.53	47	.365	.385	2	.286	1	-6	-6	0	-0.4
	Yr	9	4	.692	47	16	2	1	1	156	155	20	56	64	12.2	3.92	97	.259	.323	0	.000	5	-2	-2	0	0.4
Total	3	18	13	.581	74	38	5	3	1	299	274	39	105	144	11.5	3.76	97	.246	.313	24	.253	7	-4	-4	-1	0.5

■ EARL COOK
Cook, Earl Davis   b: 12/10/08, Stouffville, Ont.,   BR/TR, 6′, 195 lbs.   Deb: 9/12/41

YEAR	TM/L	W	L	PCT	G	GS	CG	SH	SV	IP	H	HR	BB	SO	RAT	ERA	ERA+	OAV	OOB	BH	AVG	PB	PR	/A	PD	TPI
1941	Det-A	0	0	—	1	0	0	0	0	2	4	0	0	1	18.0	4.50	101	.400	.400	0	—	0	-0	0	0	0.0

■ GLEN COOK
Cook, Glen Patrick   b: 9/8/59, Buffalo, N.Y.   BR/TR, 5′11″, 180 lbs.   Deb: 6/23/85

YEAR	TM/L	W	L	PCT	G	GS	CG	SH	SV	IP	H	HR	BB	SO	RAT	ERA	ERA+	OAV	OOB	BH	AVG	PB	PR	/A	PD	TPI
1985	Tex-A	2	3	.400	9	7	0	0	0	40	53	12	18	19	16.6	9.45	45	.327	.404	0	—	0	-24	-23	-1	-2.0

■ MIKE COOK
Cook, Michael Horace   b: 8/14/63, Charleston, S.C.   BR/TR, 6′3″, 200 lbs.   Deb: 7/01/86

YEAR	TM/L	W	L	PCT	G	GS	CG	SH	SV	IP	H	HR	BB	SO	RAT	ERA	ERA+	OAV	OOB	BH	AVG	PB	PR	/A	PD	TPI
1986	Cal-A	0	2	.000	5	1	0	0	0	9	13	3	7	6	20.0	9.00	46	.333	.435	0	—	0	-5	-5	0	-0.3
1987	Cal-A	1	2	.333	16	1	0	0	0	34¹	34	7	18	27	13.6	5.50	78	.264	.354	0	—	0	-4	-5	1	-0.2
1988	Cal-A	0	1	.000	3	0	0	0	0	3²	4	0	1	2	14.7	4.91	79	.308	.400	0	—	0	-0	-0	0	0.0
1989	Min-A	0	1	.000	15	0	0	0	0	21¹	22	1	17	15	16.9	5.06	82	.268	.400	0	—	0	-3	-2	-0	-0.2
Total	4	1	6	.143	39	2	0	0	0	68¹	73	11	43	50	15.5	5.80	73	.278	.383	0	—	0	-12	-12	1	-0.7

■ ROLLIN COOK
Cook, Rollin Edward   b: 10/5/1890, Toledo, Ohio   d: 8/11/75, Toledo, Ohio   BR/TR, 5′9″, 152 lbs.   Deb: 7/06/15

YEAR	TM/L	W	L	PCT	G	GS	CG	SH	SV	IP	H	HR	BB	SO	RAT	ERA	ERA+	OAV	OOB	BH	AVG	PB	PR	/A	PD	TPI
1915	StL-A	0	0	—	5	0	0	0	0	13²	16	0	9	7	17.1	7.24	40	.276	.382	1	.250	0	-7	-7	0	-0.5

■ RON COOK
Cook, Ronald Wayne   b: 7/11/47, Jefferson, Tex.   BL/TL, 6′1″, 175 lbs.   Deb: 4/10/70

YEAR	TM/L	W	L	PCT	G	GS	CG	SH	SV	IP	H	HR	BB	SO	RAT	ERA	ERA+	OAV	OOB	BH	AVG	PB	PR	/A	PD	TPI
1970	Hou-N	4	4	.500	41	7	0	0	2	82¹	80	4	42	50	13.7	3.72	104	.274	.371	4	.235	2	3	1	0	0.3
1971	Hou-N	0	4	.000	5	4	0	0	0	25²	23	2	8	10	11.2	4.91	69	.237	.302	2	.250	0	-4	-4	0	-0.3
Total	2	4	8	.333	46	11	0	0	2	108	103	6	50	60	13.1	4.00	94	.265	.354	6	.240	2	-1	-3	0	0.0

■ DANNY COOMBS
Coombs, Daniel Bernard   b: 3/23/42, Lincoln, Me.   BR/TL, 6′4″, 200 lbs.   Deb: 9/27/63

YEAR	TM/L	W	L	PCT	G	GS	CG	SH	SV	IP	H	HR	BB	SO	RAT	ERA	ERA+	OAV	OOB	BH	AVG	PB	PR	/A	PD	TPI
1963	Hou-N	0	0	—	1	0	0	0	0	0¹	3	0	0	0	81.0	27.00	12	.750	.750	0	—	0	-1	-1	0	0.0
1964	Hou-N	1	1	.500	7	1	0	0	0	18	21	1	10	14	16.0	5.00	68	.300	.395	0	.000	-0	-3	-3	-0	-0.3
1965	Hou-N	0	2	.000	26	3	0	0	0	47	54	3	23	35	15.3	4.79	70	.292	.379	1	.111	-0	-7	-7	1	-0.6
1966	Hou-N	0	0	—	2	0	0	0	0	2²	4	0	0	3	13.5	3.38	101	.333	.333	0	.000	-0	0	0	0	0.0
1967	Hou-N	3	0	1.000	6	2	0	0	0	24¹	21	0	9	23	11.1	3.33	99	.233	.303	1	.125	0	0	-0	0	0.0
1968	Hou-N	4	3	.571	40	0	0	0	2	46²	52	0	17	29	13.5	3.28	90	.286	.350	4	.400	1	-2	-2	1	0.0
1969	Hou-N	0	1	.000	8	0	0	0	0	8	12	0	2	3	16.9	6.75	52	.364	.417	0	.000	-0	-3	-3	-0	-0.2
1970	SD-N	10	14	.417	35	27	5	1	0	188¹	185	12	76	105	12.6	3.30	121	.256	.329	5	.096	-2	16	14	-2	1.1
1971	SD-N	1	6	.143	19	7	0	0	0	57²	81	10	25	37	16.5	6.24	53	.327	.388	3	.214	1	-18	-19	1	-1.6
Total	9	19	27	.413	144	42	5	1	2	393	433	26	162	249	13.8	4.08	88	.280	.351	14	.140	-0	-17	-21	1	-1.6

■ JACK COOMBS
Coombs, John Wesley "Colby Jack"   b: 11/18/1882, LeGrand, Iowa   d: 4/15/57, Palestine, Tex.   BB/TR, 6′, 185 lbs.   Deb: 7/05/06   MC♦

YEAR	TM/L	W	L	PCT	G	GS	CG	SH	SV	IP	H	HR	BB	SO	RAT	ERA	ERA+	OAV	OOB	BH	AVG	PB	PR	/A	PD	TPI
1906	Phi-A	10	10	.500	23	18	13	1	0	173	144	0	68	90	11.0	2.50	109	.229	.305	16	.239	1	4	4	0	0.6
1907	Phi-A	6	9	.400	23	17	10	2	2	132²	109	2	64	73	11.7	3.12	84	.226	.317	8	.167	-1	-8	-8	0	-0.8
1908	Phi-A	7	5	.583	26	18	10	4	0	153	130	1	64	80	11.6	2.00	128	.233	.316	56	.255	4	7	10	0	1.1
1909	Phi-A	12	11	.522	30	25	18	6	1	205²	156	1	73	97	10.3	2.32	104	.213	.289	14	.169	1	4	2	0	0.3
1910	*Phi-A	31	9	.775	45	38	35	13	1	353	248	0	115	224	9.4	1.30	183	.201	.273	29	.220	3	48	42	-6	4.5
1911	*Phi-A	28	12	.700	47	40	26	1	2	336²	360	8	119	185	13.2	3.53	89	.280	.348	45	.319	14	-7	-14	-3	-0.4
1912	Phi-A	21	10	.677	40	32	23	1	2	262¹	227	5	94	120	11.4	3.29	93	.241	.316	28	.255	6	1	-6	-1	-0.4
1913	Phi-A	0	0	—	2	2	0	0	0	5¹	5	0	6	0	20.3	10.13	27	.250	.444	1	.333	1	-4	-4	-0	-0.3
1914	Phi-A	0	1	.000	2	2	0	0	0	8	8	0	3	1	13.5	4.50	58	.267	.353	3	.273	0	-2	-2	-0	-0.1
1915	Bro-N	15	10	.600	29	24	17	2	0	195²	166	1	91	56	12.6	2.58	108	.236	.337	21	.280	4	4	4	-3	0.5
1916	*Bro-N	14	8	.636	27	21	10	3	0	159	136	3	44	47	10.3	2.66	101	.239	.296	11	.180	-0	-1	0	-5	-0.4
1917	Bro-N	7	11	.389	31	14	9	0	0	141	147	7	49	44	13.0	3.96	71	.284	.355	10	.227	2	-20	-18	-2	-1.9
1918	Bro-N	8	14	.364	27	22	16	2	0	189	191	10	49	44	11.5	3.81	73	.266	.315	19	.168	-0	-22	-22	-2	-2.4
1920	Det-A	0	0	—	2	0	0	0	0	5²	7	0	2	1	14.3	3.18	117	.318	.375	0	.000	-0	0	0	0	0.0
Total	14	159	110	.591	354	273	187	35	8	2320	2034	38	841	1052	11.4	2.78	99	.241	.315	261	.235	35	4	-8	-23	0.7

■ BOBBY COOMBS
Coombs, Raymond Franklin   b: 2/2/08, Goodwins Mills, Me.   BR/TR, 5′9.5″, 160 lbs.   Deb: 6/08/33

YEAR	TM/L	W	L	PCT	G	GS	CG	SH	SV	IP	H	HR	BB	SO	RAT	ERA	ERA+	OAV	OOB	BH	AVG	PB	PR	/A	PD	TPI
1933	Phi-A	0	1	.000	21	0	0	0	2	31¹	47	4	20	8	19.2	7.47	57	.348	.432	2	.400	1	-11	-11	-0	-0.8
1943	NY-N	0	1	.000	9	0	0	0	0	16	33	1	8	5	23.1	12.94	27	.423	.477	0	.000	0	-17	-17	0	-1.5
Total	2	0	2	.000	30	0	0	0	2	47¹	80	5	28	13	20.5	9.32	43	.376	.448	2	.286	1	-28	-28	0	-2.3

■ WILLIAM COON
Coon, William K.   b: 3/21/1855, Pennsylvania   d: 8/30/15, Burlington, N.J.   Deb: 9/04/1875   ♦

YEAR	TM/L	W	L	PCT	G	GS	CG	SH	SV	IP	H	HR	BB	SO	RAT	ERA	ERA+	OAV	OOB	BH	AVG	PB	PR	/A	PD	TPI
1876	Phi-N	0	0	—	2	0	0	0	0	7	9	0	0	0	11.6	5.14	47	.292	.292	50	.227	-0	-2	-2	-0	-0.1

■ JOHNNY COONEY
Cooney, John Walter   b: 3/18/01, Cranston, R.I.   d: 7/8/86, Sarasota, Fla.   BR/TL, 5′10″, 165 lbs.   Deb: 4/19/21   MC♦

YEAR	TM/L	W	L	PCT	G	GS	CG	SH	SV	IP	H	HR	BB	SO	RAT	ERA	ERA+	OAV	OOB	BH	AVG	PB	PR	/A	PD	TPI
1921	Bos-N	0	1	.000	8	1	0	0	0	20²	19	3	10	9	12.6	3.92	93	.241	.326	1	.200	-0	-0	-1	0	0.0
1922	Bos-N	1	2	.333	4	3	1	0	0	25	19	0	6	7	9.4	2.16	185	.224	.283	0	.000	-1	5	5	0	0.4
1923	Bos-N	3	5	.375	23	8	5	2	0	98	92	3	22	23	10.7	3.31	121	.246	.293	25	.379	4	8	7	-2	1.2
1924	Bos-N	8	9	.471	34	19	12	2	2	181	176	4	50	67	11.4	3.18	120	.260	.314	33	.254	2	14	13	-1	1.2
1925	Bos-N	14	14	.500	31	29	20	2	0	245²	267	18	50	65	11.7	3.48	115	.274	.312	33	.320	5	22	14	1	2.3
1926	Bos-N	3	3	.500	19	8	3	1	0	83¹	106	0	29	26	15.3	4.00	89	.320	.387	38	.302	3	-2	-4	0	-0.3
1928	Bos-N	3	7	.300	24	6	2	0	1	89²	106	7	31	18	13.8	4.32	91	.303	.360	7	.171	-0	-3	-4	3	0.0
1929	Bos-N	2	3	.400	14	3	1	0	3	45	57	4	22	11	15.8	5.00	94	.315	.389	23	.319	2	-1	-2	1	0.0
1930	Bos-N	0	0	—	2	0	0	0	0	7	16	2	3	1	25.7	18.00	27	.471	.526	0	.000	-1	-10	-10	1	-0.6
Total	9	34	44	.436	159	76	44	7	6	795¹	858	41	223	224	12.4	3.72	106	.278	.331	965	.286	14	32	19	4	4.2

YEAR	TM/L	W	L	PCT	G	GS	CG	SH	SV	IP	H	HR	BB	SO	RAT	ERA	ERA+	OAV	OOB	BH	AVG	PB	PR	/A	PD	TPI

■ BOB COONEY
Cooney, Robert Daniel b: 7/12/07, Glens Falls, N.Y. d: 5/4/76, Glens Falls, N.Y. BR/TR, 5′11″, 160 lbs. Deb: 9/06/31

YEAR	TM/L	W	L	PCT	G	GS	CG	SH	SV	IP	H	HR	BB	SO	RAT	ERA	ERA+	OAV	OOB	BH	AVG	PB	PR	/A	PD	TPI
1931	StL-A	0	3	.000	5	4	1	0	0	39¹	46	1	20	13	15.3	4.12	113	.291	.374	5	.385	1	1	2	-0	0.3
1932	StL-A	1	2	.333	23	3	1	0	1	71	94	8	36	23	16.7	6.97	70	.324	.402	0	.000	-3	-20	-17	-2	-1.8
Total	2	1	5	.167	28	7	2	0	1	110¹	140	9	56	36	16.2	5.95	80	.313	.393	5	.143	-2	-19	-14	-2	-1.5

■ BILL COONEY
Cooney, William A. "Cush" b: 4/4/1887, Boston, Mass. d: 11/6/28, Roxbury, Mass. TR, Deb: 9/22/09 ♦

YEAR	TM/L	W	L	PCT	G	GS	CG	SH	SV	IP	H	HR	BB	SO	RAT	ERA	ERA+	OAV	OOB	BH	AVG	PB	PR	/A	PD	TPI
1909	Bos-N	0	0	—	3	0	0	0	0	6¹	4	0	2	3	8.5	1.42	199	.182	.250	3	.300	0	1	1	-0	0.1

■ WILBUR COOPER
Cooper, Arley Wilbur b: 2/24/1892, Bearsville, W.Va. d: 8/7/73, Encino, Cal. BR/TL, 5′11″, 175 lbs. Deb: 8/29/12

YEAR	TM/L	W	L	PCT	G	GS	CG	SH	SV	IP	H	HR	BB	SO	RAT	ERA	ERA+	OAV	OOB	BH	AVG	PB	PR	/A	PD	TPI
1912	Pit-N	3	0	1.000	6	4	3	2	0	38	32	1	15	30	11.1	1.66	197	.224	.297	2	.154	-0	7	7	-0	0.6
1913	Pit-N	5	3	.625	30	9	3	1	0	93	98	4	45	39	14.0	3.29	92	.276	.361	2	.077	-1	-1	-3	-1	-0.5
1914	Pit-N	16	15	.516	40	34	19	0	1	266²	246	4	79	102	11.1	2.13	125	.254	.313	19	.207	1	20	16	0	1.8
1915	Pit-N	5	16	.238	38	21	11	1	4	185²	180	4	52	71	11.7	3.30	83	.262	.323	7	.117	-3	-11	-12	1	-1.4
1916	Pit-N	12	11	.522	42	23	16	2	2	246	189	4	74	111	9.8	1.87	144	.215	.279	17	.215	0	21	22	-1	2.6
1917	Pit-N	17	11	.607	40	34	23	7	1	297²	276	6	54	99	10.1	2.36	120	.258	.297	21	.204	2	12	16	-3	2.1
1918	Pit-N	19	14	.576	38	29	26	2	3	273¹	219	2	65	117	9.7	2.11	136	.223	.279	23	.242	3	20	23	-3	2.7
1919	Pit-N	19	13	.594	35	32	27	4	1	286²	229	10	74	106	10.0	2.67	113	.225	.287	29	.287	6	8	11	-5	1.4
1920	Pit-N	24	15	.615	44	37	28	3	2	327	307	4	52	114	10.2	2.39	134	.253	.290	25	.221	1	27	30	-3	2.9
1921	Pit-N	**22**	14	.611	38	38	29	2	0	**327**	341	9	80	134	11.9	3.25	118	.272	.320	31	.254	4	19	21	-3	2.2
1922	Pit-N	23	14	.622	41	37	**27**	4	0	294²	330	13	61	129	12.2	3.18	128	.286	.326	29	.269	9	**30**	**29**	-2	**3.6**
1923	Pit-N	17	19	.472	39	38	26	1	0	294²	331	11	71	77	12.6	3.57	112	.288	.335	28	.262	4	14	14	-1	1.6
1924	Pit-N	20	14	.588	38	35	25	**4**	1	268²	296	13	40	62	11.4	3.28	117	.283	.313	36	.346	10	17	17	-4	2.3
1925	Chi-N	12	14	.462	32	26	13	0	0	212¹	249	18	61	41	13.3	4.28	101	.291	.341	17	.207	1	-0	1	-2	0.0
1926	Chi-N	2	1	.667	8	8	3	2	0	55	65	6	21	18	14.1	4.42	87	.311	.374	7	.389	3	-4	-4	-1	0.0
Det-A	0	4	.000	8	3	0	0	0	13²	27	0	9	2	25.7	11.20	36	.443	.534	0	.000	-1	-11	-11	0	-0.9
Total	15	216	178	.548	517	408	279	35	14	3480	3415	103	853	1252	11.3	2.89	116	.262	.312	293	.239	40	168	180	-27	20.7

■ CAL COOPER
Cooper, Calvin Asa b: 8/11/22, Great Falls, S.C. Deb: 9/14/48

YEAR	TM/L	W	L	PCT	G	GS	CG	SH	SV	IP	H	HR	BB	SO	RAT	ERA	ERA+	OAV	OOB	BH	AVG	PB	PR	/A	PD	TPI
1948	Was-A	0	0	—	1	0	0	0	0	1	5	1	1	0	54.0	45.00	10	.625	.667	0	—	0	-5	-5	0	-0.3

■ DON COOPER
Cooper, Donald James b: 1/15/56, New York, N.Y. BR/TR, 6′1″, 185 lbs. Deb: 4/09/81

YEAR	TM/L	W	L	PCT	G	GS	CG	SH	SV	IP	H	HR	BB	SO	RAT	ERA	ERA+	OAV	OOB	BH	AVG	PB	PR	/A	PD	TPI
1981	Min-A	1	5	.167	27	2	0	0	0	58²	61	9	32	33	14.4	4.30	92	.274	.367	0	—	0	-4	-2	-1	-0.2
1982	Min-A	0	1	.000	6	1	0	0	0	11¹	14	0	11	5	19.9	9.53	45	.311	.446	0	—	0	-7	-7	-0	-0.5
1983	Tor-A	0	0	—	4	0	0	0	0	5¹	8	3	0	5	13.5	6.75	64	.348	.348	0	—	0	-2	-1	-0	-0.1
1985	NY-A	0	0	—	7	0	0	0	0	10	12	2	3	4	13.5	5.40	74	.300	.349	0	—	0	-1	-2	-0	-0.1
Total	4	1	6	.143	44	3	0	0	0	85¹	95	14	46	47	15.0	5.27	76	.287	.376	0	—	0	-14	-12	-1	-0.9

■ GUY COOPER
Cooper, Guy Evans "Rebel" b: 1/28/1893, Rome, Ga. d: 8/2/51, Santa Monica, Cal. BB/TR, 6′1″, 185 lbs. Deb: 5/02/14

YEAR	TM/L	W	L	PCT	G	GS	CG	SH	SV	IP	H	HR	BB	SO	RAT	ERA	ERA+	OAV	OOB	BH	AVG	PB	PR	/A	PD	TPI
1914	NY-A	0	0	—	1	0	0	0	0	3	3	0	2	3	15.0	9.00	31	.273	.385	0	.000	-0	-2	-2	0	-0.1
Bos-A	1	0	1.000	9	1	0	0	0	22	23	1	9	5	14.3	5.32	51	.299	.393	0	.000	-1	-6	-6	-1	-0.8
Yr	1	0	1.000	10	1	0	0	0	25	26	1	11	8	14.4	5.76	47	.295	.392	0	.000	-1	-8	-8	-1	-0.9
1915	Bos-A	0	0	—	1	0	0	0	0	2	0	0	2	0	9.0	0.00	—	.000	.286	0	—	0	1	1	0	0.1
Total	2	1	0	1.000	11	1	0	0	0	27	26	1	13	8	14.0	5.33	51	.280	.385	0	.000	-1	-8	-8	-1	-0.8

■ MORT COOPER
Cooper, Morton Cecil b: 3/2/13, Atherton, Mo. d: 11/17/58, Little Rock, Ark. BR/TR, 6′2″, 210 lbs. Deb: 9/14/38

YEAR	TM/L	W	L	PCT	G	GS	CG	SH	SV	IP	H	HR	BB	SO	RAT	ERA	ERA+	OAV	OOB	BH	AVG	PB	PR	/A	PD	TPI
1938	StL-N	2	1	.667	4	3	1	0	1	23²	17	1	12	11	11.4	3.04	130	.195	.300	2	.222	0	2	2	1	0.3
1939	StL-N	12	6	.667	45	26	7	2	4	210²	208	6	97	130	13.1	3.25	127	.260	.342	16	.232	3	16	20	-3	2.0
1940	StL-N	11	12	.478	38	29	16	3	3	230²	225	12	86	95	12.3	3.63	110	.253	.321	13	.157	-2	6	9	-2	0.5
1941	StL-N	13	9	.591	29	25	12	0	0	186²	175	15	69	118	11.9	3.91	96	.244	.313	13	.186	-0	-6	-3	-1	-0.3
1942	*StL-N	22	7	.759	37	35	22	**10**	0	278²	207	9	68	152	**9.0**	**1.78**	**193**	**.204**	**.258**	19	.184	-1	**48**	**51**	-3	**5.5**
1943	*StL-N	**21**	8	**.724**	37	32	24	6	3	274	228	5	79	141	10.2	2.30	146	.226	.286	17	.170	-1	33	32	-2	3.3
1944	*StL-N	22	7	.759	34	33	22	**7**	1	252¹	227	6	60	97	10.4	2.46	143	.239	.288	19	.202	2	32	30	-4	2.9
1945	StL-N	2	0	1.000	4	3	1	0	0	23²	20	1	7	14	10.6	1.52	246	.227	.292	2	.333	1	6	6	-1	0.7
Bos-N	7	4	.636	20	11	4	1	1	78	77	4	27	45	12.1	3.35	115	.257	.320	6	.231	1	4	4	-0	0.5
Yr	9	4	.692	24	14	5	1	1	101²	97	5	34	59	11.7	2.92	130	.249	.311	8	.250	2	10	10	-1	1.2
1946	Bos-N	13	11	.542	28	27	15	4	1	199	181	16	39	83	**9.9**	3.12	110	.239	**.276**	14	.209	1	6	7	-3	0.5
1947	Bos-N	2	5	.286	10	7	2	0	0	46²	48	2	13	15	12.2	4.05	96	.271	.328	0	.000	-1	-1	-1	-0	-0.8
NY-N	1	5	.167	8	8	2	0	0	36²	51	7	13	12	15.7	7.12	57	.323	.374	6	.429	4	-12	-12	-1	-0.8
Yr	3	10	.231	18	15	4	0	0	83¹	99	9	26	27	13.5	5.40	74	.294	.344	2	.074	2	-12	-13	-1	-1.0
1949	Chi-N	0	0	—	1	0	0	0	0	0	2	1	1	0	∞	∞	0	1.000	1.000	0	—	0	-3	-3	-0	-0.2
Total	11	128	75	.631	295	239	128	33	14	1840²	1666	85	571	913	11.1	2.97	123	.240	.300	127	.194	6	132	143	-22	14.7

■ PAT COOPER
Cooper, Orge Patterson b: 11/26/17, Albemarle, N.C. BR/TR, 6′3″, 180 lbs. Deb: 5/11/46 ♦

YEAR	TM/L	W	L	PCT	G	GS	CG	SH	SV	IP	H	HR	BB	SO	RAT	ERA	ERA+	OAV	OOB	BH	AVG	PB	PR	/A	PD	TPI
1946	Phi-A	0	0	—	1	0	0	0	0	1	1	0	1	0	18.0	0.00	—	.250	.400	0	—	0	0	0	0	0.0

■ MAYS COPELAND
Copeland, Mays b: 8/31/13, Mountain View, Ark d: 11/29/82, Indio, Cal. BR/TR, 6′, 180 lbs. Deb: 4/27/35

YEAR	TM/L	W	L	PCT	G	GS	CG	SH	SV	IP	H	HR	BB	SO	RAT	ERA	ERA+	OAV	OOB	BH	AVG	PB	PR	/A	PD	TPI
1935	StL-N	0	0	—	1	0	0	0	0	0²	2	0	0	0	27.0	13.50	30	.667	.667	0	—	0	-1	-1	0	0.0

■ HENRY COPPOLA
Coppola, Henry Peter b: 8/6/12, E.Douglas, Mass. d: 7/10/90, Norfolk, Mass. BR/TR, 5′11″, 175 lbs. Deb: 4/19/35

YEAR	TM/L	W	L	PCT	G	GS	CG	SH	SV	IP	H	HR	BB	SO	RAT	ERA	ERA+	OAV	OOB	BH	AVG	PB	PR	/A	PD	TPI
1935	Was-A	3	4	.429	19	5	2	1	0	59¹	72	6	29	19	15.5	5.92	73	.300	.378	1	.071	-0	-10	-11	-0	-0.9
1936	Was-A	0	0	—	6	0	0	0	1	14	17	1	12	2	18.6	4.50	106	.315	.439	1	.333	0	1	0	0	0.1
Total	2	3	4	.429	25	5	2	1	1	73¹	89	7	41	21	16.1	5.65	78	.303	.390	2	.118	-0	-9	-10	-0	-0.8

■ DOUG CORBETT
Corbett, Douglas Mitchell b: 11/4/52, Sarasota, Fla. BR/TR, 6′1″, 185 lbs. Deb: 4/10/80

YEAR	TM/L	W	L	PCT	G	GS	CG	SH	SV	IP	H	HR	BB	SO	RAT	ERA	ERA+	OAV	OOB	BH	AVG	PB	PR	/A	PD	TPI
1980	Min-A	8	6	.571	73	0	0	0	23	136¹	102	7	42	89	9.6	1.98	220	.213	.278	0	—	0	**31**	**36**	3	4.0
1981	Min-A	2	6	.250	**54**	0	0	0	17	87²	80	5	34	60	11.7	2.57	154	.239	.309	0	—	0	11	13	2	1.6
1982	Min-A	0	2	.000	10	0	0	0	3	22	27	3	10	15	15.1	5.32	80	.300	.370	0	—	0	-3	-3	1	-0.1
Cal-A	1	7	.125	33	0	0	0	8	57	46	8	25	37	11.2	5.05	80	.223	.307	0	—	0	-6	-6	0	-0.5
Yr	1	9	.100	43	0	0	0	11	79	73	11	35	52	12.3	5.13	80	.247	.326	0	—	0	-9	-9	1	-0.6
1983	Cal-A	1	1	.500	11	0	0	0	0	17¹	26	1	4	18	16.1	3.63	110	.351	.392	0	—	0	1	1	-0	0.0
1984	Cal-A	5	1	.833	45	1	0	0	4	85	76	2	30	48	11.4	2.12	187	.244	.314	0	—	0	18	17	0	1.8
1985	Cal-A	3	3	.500	30	0	0	0	0	46	49	7	20	24	13.7	4.89	84	.274	.350	0	—	0	-4	-4	0	-0.3
1986	*Cal-A	4	2	.667	46	0	0	0	10	78²	66	11	22	36	10.2	3.66	112	.231	.288	0	—	0	5	4	2	0.5
1987	Bal-A	0	2	.000	11	0	0	0	1	23	25	5	13	16	14.9	7.83	56	.281	.373	0	—	0	-9	-9	1	-0.7
Total	8	24	30	.444	313	1	0	0	66	553	497	49	200	343	11.4	3.32	125	.242	.312	0	—	0	43	50	7	6.3

■ JOE CORBETT
Corbett, Joseph A. b: 12/4/1875, San Francisco, Cal. d: 5/2/45, San Francisco, Cal. BR/TR, 5′10″, Deb: 8/23/1895

YEAR	TM/L	W	L	PCT	G	GS	CG	SH	SV	IP	H	HR	BB	SO	RAT	ERA	ERA+	OAV	OOB	BH	AVG	PB	PR	/A	PD	TPI
1895	Was-N	0	2	.000	3	3	3	0	0	19	26	3	9	3	16.6	5.68	84	.321	.389	2	.133	-1	-2	-2	0	0.0
1896	*Bal-N	3	0	1.000	8	3	3	0	1	41	31	0	17	28	10.5	2.20	195	.208	.290	6	.273	1	10	9	-1	0.8
1897	*Bal-N	24	8	.750	37	37	34	1	0	313	330	2	115	149	12.8	3.11	134	.269	.331	37	.247	-0	42	37	1	3.3
1904	StL-N	5	8	.385	14	14	12	0	0	108²	110	2	51	68	14.0	4.39	61	.240	.327	9	.209	2	-20	-20	-0	-1.8
Total	4	32	18	.640	62	57	52	1	1	481²	497	7	192	248	13.0	3.42	113	.259	.329	54	.235	1	30	24	1	2.3

■ SHERM CORBETT
Corbett, Sherman Stanley b: 11/3/62, New Braunfels, Tex. BL/TL, 6′4″, 205 lbs. Deb: 5/29/88

YEAR	TM/L	W	L	PCT	G	GS	CG	SH	SV	IP	H	HR	BB	SO	RAT	ERA	ERA+	OAV	OOB	BH	AVG	PB	PR	/A	PD	TPI
1988	Cal-A	2	1	.667	34	0	0	0	1	45²	47	2	23	28	13.8	4.14	93	.273	.359	0	—	0	-1	-1	0	-0.1

YEAR	TM/L	W	L	PCT	G	GS	CG	SH	SV	IP	H	HR	BB	SO	RAT	ERA	ERA+	OAV	OOB	BH	AVG	PB	PR	/A	PD	TPI
1989	Cal-A	0	0	—	4	0	0	0	0	5¹	3	1	1	3	6.8	3.38	113	.158	.200	0	—	0	0	0	-0	0.0
1990	Cal-A	0	0	—	4	0	0	0	0	5	8	0	3	2	19.8	9.00	43	.364	.440	0	—	0	-3	-3	-0	-0.2
Total	3	2	1	.667	42	0	0	0	1	56	58	3	27	33	13.7	4.50	86	.272	.354	0	—	0	-3	-4	-0	-0.3

■ RAY CORBIN
Corbin, Alton Ray   b: 2/12/49, Live Oak, Fla.   BR/TR, 6'2", 200 lbs.   Deb: 4/06/71

YEAR	TM/L	W	L	PCT	G	GS	CG	SH	SV	IP	H	HR	BB	SO	RAT	ERA	ERA+	OAV	OOB	BH	AVG	PB	PR	/A	PD	TPI
1971	Min-A	8	11	.421	52	11	2	0	3	140¹	141	19	70	83	13.7	4.10	87	.265	.353	7	.206	1	-10	-9	1	-0.6
1972	Min-A	8	9	.471	31	19	5	3	0	161²	135	12	53	83	10.8	2.62	123	.230	.300	4	.082	-2	8	11	-2	0.8
1973	Min-A	8	5	.615	51	7	1	0	14	148¹	124	7	60	83	11.5	3.03	104	.229	.311	0	—	0	13	15	-1	1.5
1974	Min-A	7	6	.538	29	15	1	0	0	112¹	133	8	40	50	14.1	5.29	71	.294	.356	0	—	0	-21	-19	1	-1.7
1975	Min-A	5	7	.417	18	11	3	0	0	89²	105	13	38	49	14.6	5.12	75	.295	.366	0	—	0	-13	-13	1	-1.1
Total	5	36	38	.486	181	63	12	3	17	652¹	638	59	261	348	12.7	3.84	95	.258	.334	11	.133	-2	-23	-14	1	-1.1

■ JACK CORCORAN
Corcoran, John H.   b: 1860, Lowell, Mass.   Deb: 5/01/1884 ♦

YEAR	TM/L	W	L	PCT	G	GS	CG	SH	SV	IP	H	HR	BB	SO	RAT	ERA	ERA+	OAV	OOB	BH	AVG	PB	PR	/A	PD	TPI
1884	Bro-a	0	0	—	1	0	0	0	0	1	0	0	1	0	9.0	0.00	—	.000	.246	39	.211	0	0	0	0	0.0

■ LARRY CORCORAN
Corcoran, Lawrence J.   b: 8/10/1859, Brooklyn, N.Y.   d: 10/14/1891, Newark, N.J.   BL/TB, 120 lbs.   Deb: 5/01/1880 ♦

YEAR	TM/L	W	L	PCT	G	GS	CG	SH	SV	IP	H	HR	BB	SO	RAT	ERA	ERA+	OAV	OOB	BH	AVG	PB	PR	/A	PD	TPI
1880	Chi-N	43	14	.754	63	60	57	4	2	536¹	404	6	99	**268**	8.4	1.95	124	.198	.236	66	.231	-0	25	28	5	3.4
1881	Chi-N	**31**	14	.689	45	44	43	4	0	396²	380	10	78	150	10.4	2.31	118	.241	.277	42	.222	-1	20	19	-2	1.4
1882	Chi-N	27	12	**.692**	39	39	38	3	0	355²	281	5	63	170	**8.7**	**1.95**	**147**	**.205**	**.240**	35	.207	-2	37	36	0	3.2
1883	Chi-N	34	20	.630	56	53	51	3	0	473²	483	7	82	216	10.7	2.49	128	.249	.279	55	.209	-1	34	37	1	3.3
1884	Chi-N	35	23	.603	60	59	57	7	0	516²	473	35	116	272	10.3	2.40	131	.230	.271	61	.243	-2	33	42	6	4.9
1885	Chi-N	5	2	.714	7	7	6	1	0	59¹	63	2	24	10	13.2	3.64	83	.260	.326	6	.273	2	-5	-4	0	0.0
	NY-N	2	1	.667	3	3	2	0	0	25	24	1	11	10	12.6	2.88	93	.241	.316	5	.357	1	-0	-1	1	0.1
	Yr	7	3	.700	10	10	8	1	0	84¹	87	3	35	20	13.0	3.42	86	.254	.323	6	.167	3	-6	-5	1	0.1
1886	Was-N	0	1	.000	2	1	1	0	0	14	16	0	4	3	12.9	5.79	57	.276	.322	15	.185	0	-4	-4	-0	-0.2
1887	Ind-N	0	2	.000	2	2	1	0	0	15	23	3	19	4	25.2	12.60	33	.342	.487	2	.200	0	-14	-14	0	-0.8
Total	8	177	89	.665	277	268	256	22	2	2392¹	2147	69	496	1103	9.9	2.36	122	.227	.266	287	.223	1	126	140	12	15.3

■ MIKE CORCORAN
Corcoran, Michael   b: Brooklyn, N.Y.   Deb: 7/15/1884

YEAR	TM/L	W	L	PCT	G	GS	CG	SH	SV	IP	H	HR	BB	SO	RAT	ERA	ERA+	OAV	OOB	BH	AVG	PB	PR	/A	PD	TPI
1884	Chi-N	0	1	.000	1	1	1	0	0	9	16	1	7	2	23.0	4.00	79	.368	.455	0	.000	-0	-1	-1	-0	0.0

■ ED COREY
Corey, Edward Norman "Ike" (b: Abraham Simon Cohen)   b: 7/13/1899, Chicago, Ill.   d: 9/17/70, Kenosha, Wis.   BR/TR, 6', 170 lbs.   Deb: 7/02/18

YEAR	TM/L	W	L	PCT	G	GS	CG	SH	SV	IP	H	HR	BB	SO	RAT	ERA	ERA+	OAV	OOB	BH	AVG	PB	PR	/A	PD	TPI
1918	Chi-A	0	0	—	1	0	0	0	0	2	2	0	1	0	13.5	4.50	61	.333	.429	0	.000	-0	-0	-0	0	0.0

■ FRED COREY
Corey, Frederick Harrison   b: 1857, S.Kingston, R.I.   d: 11/27/12, Providence, R.I.   BR/TR,   Deb: 5/01/1878 ♦

YEAR	TM/L	W	L	PCT	G	GS	CG	SH	SV	IP	H	HR	BB	SO	RAT	ERA	ERA+	OAV	OOB	BH	AVG	PB	PR	/A	PD	TPI
1878	Pro-N	1	2	.333	5	5	2	0	0	23	22	0	7	11	11.3	2.35	94	.239	.293	3	.143	-1	-0	-0	-0	-0.1
1880	Wor-N	8	9	.471	25	17	9	2	0	148¹	131	6	16	47	8.9	2.43	107	.225	.246	24	.174	-3	-1	3	-3	-0.3
1881	Wor-N	6	15	.286	23	21	20	1	0	188²	231	3	31	33	12.5	3.72	81	.289	.316	45	.222	-1	-20	-15	-0	-1.2
1882	Wor-N	1	13	.071	21	14	12	0	0	139	180	5	19	36	12.9	3.56	87	.297	.318	63	.247	-1	-10	-7	1	-0.5
1883	Phi-a	10	7	.588	18	16	15	0	0	148¹	182	3	24	42	12.5	3.40	103	.283	.309	77	.258	2	-2	2	2	0.1
1885	Phi-a	1	0	1.000	1	1	1	0	0	9	18	2	1	3	19.0	7.00	49	.399	.412	94	.245	0	-4	-4	-0	-0.2
Total	6	27	46	.370	93	74	59	3	2	656¹	764	19	98	168	11.8	3.32	91	.276	.301	427	.246	-3	-37	-21	-1	-2.2

■ POP CORKHILL
Corkhill, John Stewart   b: 4/11/1858, Parkesburg, Pa.   d: 4/4/21, Pennsauken, N.J.   BL/TR, 5'10", 180 lbs.   Deb: 5/01/1883 ♦

YEAR	TM/L	W	L	PCT	G	GS	CG	SH	SV	IP	H	HR	BB	SO	RAT	ERA	ERA+	OAV	OOB	BH	AVG	PB	PR	/A	PD	TPI
1884	Cin-a	1	0	1.000	1	0	0	0	0	5	1	0	2	4	5.4	1.80	185	.061	.164	124	.274	0	1	1	-0	0.1
1885	Cin-a	1	4	.200	8	1	0	0	1	37	36	2	10	12	11.2	3.65	89	.244	.292	111	.252	1	-2	-2	0	0.0
1886	Cin-a	0	0	—	1	0	0	0	0	0²	1	0	0	1	13.5	13.50	26	.331	.331	143	.265	-0	-1	-1	0	0.0
1887	Cin-a	1	0	1.000	5	0	0	0	0	14²	22	0	5	3	16.6	5.52	78	.334	.381	168	.311	1	-2	-2	-0	-0.1
1888	Cin-a	0	0	—	2	0	0	0	1	5	8	1	0	1	14.4	10.80	29	.349	.349	133	.271	0	-4	-4	-0	-0.3
Total	5	3	4	.429	17	1	0	0	2	62¹	68	3	17	21	12.3	4.62	76	.266	.312	1120	.254	2	-8	-8	-0	-0.3

■ MIKE CORKINS
Corkins, Michael Patrick   b: 5/25/46, Riverside, Cal.   BR/TR, 6'1", 190 lbs.   Deb: 9/08/69

YEAR	TM/L	W	L	PCT	G	GS	CG	SH	SV	IP	H	HR	BB	SO	RAT	ERA	ERA+	OAV	OOB	BH	AVG	PB	PR	/A	PD	TPI
1969	SD-N	1	3	.250	6	4	0	0	0	17	27	3	8	13	18.5	8.47	42	.370	.432	0	.000	0	-9	-9	0	-0.8
1970	SD-N	5	6	.455	24	18	1	0	0	111	109	11	79	75	15.6	4.62	86	.258	.379	8	.216	2	-7	-8	-1	-0.6
1971	SD-N	0	0	—	8	0	0	0	0	13	14	1	6	16	13.8	3.46	95	.280	.357	0	—	0	0	-0	-0	0.0
1972	SD-N	6	9	.400	47	9	2	1	6	140	125	14	62	108	12.3	3.54	93	.240	.325	9	.237	2	-1	-4	0	0.0
1973	SD-N	5	8	.385	47	11	2	0	3	122	130	12	61	82	14.9	4.50	77	.274	.370	7	.212	4	-11	-14	-2	-1.2
1974	SD-N	2	2	.500	25	2	0	0	0	56¹	53	5	32	41	13.7	4.79	74	.255	.357	0	.000	-0	-7	-8	-1	-0.8
Total	6	19	28	.404	157	44	5	1	9	459¹	458	46	248	335	14.2	4.39	81	.262	.360	24	.202	9	-36	-43	-4	-3.4

■ MARDIE CORNEJO
Cornejo, Nieves Mardie   b: 8/5/51, Wellington, Kan.   BR/TR, 6'3", 200 lbs.   Deb: 4/08/78

YEAR	TM/L	W	L	PCT	G	GS	CG	SH	SV	IP	H	HR	BB	SO	RAT	ERA	ERA+	OAV	OOB	BH	AVG	PB	PR	/A	PD	TPI
1978	NY-N	4	2	.667	25	0	0	0	0	36²	37	1	14	17	13.3	2.45	142	.285	.367	0	—	0	5	4	-0	0.4

■ JEFF CORNELL
Cornell, Jeffery Ray   b: 2/10/57, Kansas City, Mo.   BB/TR, 5'11", 170 lbs.   Deb: 6/02/84

YEAR	TM/L	W	L	PCT	G	GS	CG	SH	SV	IP	H	HR	BB	SO	RAT	ERA	ERA+	OAV	OOB	BH	AVG	PB	PR	/A	PD	TPI
1984	SF-N	1	3	.250	23	0	0	0	0	38¹	51	4	22	19	17.4	6.10	57	.340	.428	0	.000	-0	-11	-11	-0	-1.1

■ TERRY CORNUTT
Cornutt, Terry Stanton   b: 10/2/52, Roseburg, Ore.   BR/TR, 6'2", 195 lbs.   Deb: 4/09/77

YEAR	TM/L	W	L	PCT	G	GS	CG	SH	SV	IP	H	HR	BB	SO	RAT	ERA	ERA+	OAV	OOB	BH	AVG	PB	PR	/A	PD	TPI
1977	SF-N	1	2	.333	28	1	0	0	0	44¹	38	4	22	23	12.2	3.86	101	.229	.319	0	.000	-0	0	0	-1	0.0
1978	SF-N	0	0	—	1	0	0	0	0	3	1	0	0	0	3.0	0.00	—	.100	.100	0	—	0	1	1	0	0.1
Total	2	1	2	.333	29	1	0	0	0	47¹	39	4	22	23	11.6	3.61	107	.222	.308	0	.000	-0	1	1	-1	0.1

■ ED CORREA
Correa, Edwin Josue (Andino)   b: 4/29/66, Hato Rey, P.R.   BR/TR, 6'2", 192 lbs.   Deb: 9/18/85

YEAR	TM/L	W	L	PCT	G	GS	CG	SH	SV	IP	H	HR	BB	SO	RAT	ERA	ERA+	OAV	OOB	BH	AVG	PB	PR	/A	PD	TPI
1985	Chi-A	1	0	1.000	5	1	0	0	0	10¹	11	2	11	10	19.2	6.97	62	.275	.431	0	—	0	-3	-3	-0	-0.2
1986	Tex-A	12	14	.462	32	32	4	2	0	202¹	167	15	126	189	13.2	4.23	102	.223	.337	0	—	0	-1	2	2	0.4
1987	Tex-A	3	5	.375	15	15	0	0	0	70	83	17	52	61	17.9	7.59	59	.296	.414	0	—	0	-24	-24	-0	-2.1
Total	3	16	19	.457	52	48	4	2	0	282²	261	34	189	260	14.6	5.16	84	.244	.361	0	—	0	-29	-26	2	-1.9

■ FRANK CORRIDON
Corridon, Frank J. "Fiddler"   b: 11/25/1880, Newport, R.I.   d: 2/21/41, Syracuse, N.Y.   BR/TR, 6', 170 lbs.   Deb: 4/15/04

YEAR	TM/L	W	L	PCT	G	GS	CG	SH	SV	IP	H	HR	BB	SO	RAT	ERA	ERA+	OAV	OOB	BH	AVG	PB	PR	/A	PD	TPI
1904	Chi-N	5	5	.500	12	10	9	0	0	100¹	88	2	37	34	11.8	3.05	87	.240	.321	13	.224	0	-3	-4	3	0.0
	Phi-N	6	5	.545	12	11	11	1	0	94¹	88	2	28	44	11.8	2.19	122	.250	.320	6	.171	-0	6	5	2	0.8
	Yr	11	10	.524	24	21	20	1	0	194²	176	4	65	78	11.5	2.64	101	.242	.312	2	.022	0	2	1	6	0.8
1905	Phi-N	10	12	.455	35	26	18	1	1	212	203	2	57	79	11.7	3.48	84	.257	.319	15	.208	4	-11	-13	2	-0.6
1907	Phi-N	18	14	.563	37	32	23	3	2	274	228	0	89	131	10.7	2.46	98	.230	.299	16	.165	-0	0	-1	5	0.3
1908	Phi-N	14	10	.583	27	24	18	2	1	208¹	178	0	48	50	10.0	2.51	97	.239	.290	9	.123	-2	-3	-2	4	0.0
1909	Phi-N	11	7	.611	27	19	11	3	0	171	147	0	61	69	11.3	2.11	124	.242	.318	11	.186	0	9	9	5	1.6
1910	StL-N	6	14	.300	30	18	9	0	3	156	168	1	55	51	13.4	3.81	78	.283	.353	10	.196	-0	-13	-14	3	-1.1
Total	6	70	67	.511	180	140	99	10	7	1216	1100	7	375	458	11.4	2.80	95	.247	.315	80	.180	2	-16	-20	24	1.0

■ JIM CORSI
Corsi, James Bernard   b: 9/9/61, Newton, Mass.   BR/TR, 6'1", 210 lbs.   Deb: 6/28/88

YEAR	TM/L	W	L	PCT	G	GS	CG	SH	SV	IP	H	HR	BB	SO	RAT	ERA	ERA+	OAV	OOB	BH	AVG	PB	PR	/A	PD	TPI
1988	Oak-A	0	1	.000	11	0	0	0	0	21¹	20	1	6	10	11.0	3.80	100	.260	.313	0	—	0	0	-0	-0	0.0
1989	Oak-A	1	2	.333	22	0	0	0	0	38¹	26	2	10	21	8.7	1.88	196	.194	.255	0	—	0	9	8	0	0.8
Total	2	1	3	.250	33	0	0	0	0	59²	46	3	16	31	9.5	2.56	145	.218	.276	0	—	0	9	8	-0	0.8

■ BARRY CORT
Cort, Barry Lee   b: 4/15/56, Toronto, Ont., Can.   BR/TR, 6'5", 210 lbs.   Deb: 4/22/77

YEAR	TM/L	W	L	PCT	G	GS	CG	SH	SV	IP	H	HR	BB	SO	RAT	ERA	ERA+	OAV	OOB	BH	AVG	PB	PR	/A	PD	TPI
1977	Mil-A	1	1	.500	7	3	1	0	0	24¹	25	1	9	17	12.9	3.33	122	.281	.354	0	—	0	2	2	0	0.2

YEAR TM/L	W	L	PCT	G	GS	CG	SH	SV	IP	H	HR	BB	SO	RAT	ERA	ERA+	OAV	OOB	BH	AVG	PB	PR	/A	PD	TPI
■ **AL CORWIN** Corwin, Elmer Nathan b: 12/3/26, Newburgh, N.Y. BR/TR, 6'1", 170 lbs. Deb: 7/25/51																									
1951 *NY-N	5	1	.833	15	8	3	1	1	59	49	7	21	30	10.7	3.66	107	.222	.289	1	.050	-2	2	2	-2	-0.1
1952 NY-N	6	1	.857	21	7	1	0	2	67²	58	5	36	36	12.5	2.66	139	.237	.335	2	.095	-1	8	8	-1	0.6
1953 NY-N	6	4	.600	48	7	2	1	2	106²	122	17	68	49	16.3	4.98	86	.290	.393	9	.281	4	-8	-8	-1	-0.4
1954 NY-N	1	3	.250	20	0	0	0	0	31¹	35	4	14	14	14.1	4.02	100	.297	.371	0	.000	-0	0	0	-1	0.0
1955 NY-N	0	1	.000	13	0	0	0	0	24²	25	3	17	13	15.3	4.01	100	.263	.375	0	.000	-0	0	0	-0	0.0
Total 5	18	10	.643	117	22	6	2	5	289¹	289	36	156	142	13.9	3.98	101	.263	.356	12	.152	0	2	1	-5	0.1
■ **MIKE COSGROVE** Cosgrove, Michael John b: 2/17/51, Phoenix, Ariz. BL/TL, 6'1", 170 lbs. Deb: 9/10/72																									
1972 Hou-N	0	1	.000	7	1	0	0	1	13²	16	2	3	7	12.5	4.61	73	.286	.322	0	.000	-0	-2	-2	-0	-0.2
1973 Hou-N	1	1	.500	13	0	0	0	0	10	11	1	8	2	17.1	1.80	202	.282	.404	0	—	0	2	2	-0	0.2
1974 Hou-N	7	3	.700	45	0	0	0	2	90	76	2	39	47	11.6	3.50	99	.232	.316	1	.056	-1	1	-0	-0	-0.1
1975 Hou-N	1	2	.333	32	3	1	0	5	71¹	62	2	37	32	12.5	3.03	111	.245	.341	2	.154	0	5	3	0	0.3
1976 Hou-N	3	4	.429	22	16	1	1	0	89²	106	6	58	34	16.7	5.52	58	.303	.405	2	.087	-1	-20	-23	0	-2.3
Total 5	12	11	.522	119	20	2	1	8	274²	271	13	145	122	13.7	4.03	83	.264	.357	5	.089	-2	-14	-21	-1	-2.1
■ **JIM COSMAN** Cosman, James Henry b: 2/19/43, Brockport, N.Y. BR/TR, 6'4.5", 211 lbs. Deb: 10/02/66																									
1966 StL-N	1	0	1.000	1	1	1	1	0	9	2	0	2	5	5.0	0.00	—	.074	.167	0	.000	-0	4	4	-0	0.4
1967 StL-N	1	0	1.000	10	5	0	0	0	31¹	21	2	24	11	14.4	3.16	104	.198	.370	1	.125	-0	1	0	-0	0.0
1970 Chi-N	0	0	—	1	0	0	0	0	1	3	1	1	0	36.0	27.00	17	.600	.667	0	—	0	-3	-2	0	-0.1
Total 3	2	0	1.000	12	6	1	1	0	41¹	26	3	27	16	12.8	3.05	111	.188	.345	1	.091	-1	2	2	-0	0.3
■ **JOHN COSTELLO** Costello, John Reilly b: 12/24/60, Bronx, N.Y. BR/TR, 6'1", 190 lbs. Deb: 6/02/88																									
1988 StL-N	5	2	.714	36	0	0	0	1	49²	44	3	25	38	12.5	1.81	192	.235	.325	0	.000	-0	9	9	-1	0.8
1989 StL-N	5	4	.556	48	0	0	0	3	62¹	44	5	20	40	10.1	3.32	109	.213	.283	0	.000	-1	1	2	-1	0.0
1990 StL-N	0	0	—	4	0	0	0	0	4¹	7	1	1	1	18.7	6.23	63	.368	.429	0	—	0	-1	-1	0	0.0
Mon-N	0	0	—	4	0	0	0	0	6¹	5	2	1	1	8.5	5.68	66	.208	.240	0	—	0	-1	-1	-0	-0.1
Yr	0	0	—	8	0	0	0	0	10²	12	3	2	2	11.8	5.91	65	.273	.304	0	—	0	-3	-2	-0	-0.1
Total 3	10	6	.625	92	0	0	0	4	122²	104	11	47	80	11.3	2.93	122	.229	.305	0	.000	-1	8	9	-2	0.7
■ **DAN COTTER** Cotter, Daniel Joseph b: 4/14/1867, Boston, Mass. d: 9/4/35, Boston, Mass. TR , Deb: 7/16/1890																									
1890 Buf-P	0	1	.000	1	1	1	0	0	9	18	1	7	0	25.0	14.00	29	.399	.480	0	.000	-1	-10	-10	-0	-0.6
■ **ENSIGN COTTRELL** Cottrell, Ensign Stover b: 8/29/1888, Hoosick Falls, N.Y. d: 2/27/47, Syracuse, N.Y. BL/TL, 5'9.5", 173 lbs. Deb: 6/21/11																									
1911 Pit-N	0	0	—	1	0	0	0	0	1	4	0	1	0	45.0	9.00	38	.667	.714	0	—	0	-1	-1	0	0.0
1912 Chi-N	0	0	—	1	0	0	0	0	4	8	0	1	1	20.3	9.00	37	.444	.474	0	.000	-0	-2	-3	-0	-0.1
1913 Phi-A	1	0	1.000	2	1	1	0	0	10	15	0	2	3	15.3	5.40	51	.326	.354	1	.250	1	-3	-3	-0	-0.1
1914 Bos-N	0	1	.000	1	1	0	0	0	1	2	0	3	1	45.0	9.00	31	.333	.556	0	—	0	-1	-1	0	0.0
1915 NY-A	0	1	.000	7	0	0	0	0	21¹	29	2	7	7	15.6	3.38	87	.330	.385	0	.000	-1	-1	-1	1	-0.1
Total 5	1	2	.333	12	2	1	0	0	37¹	58	2	14	12	17.6	4.82	61	.354	.408	1	.083	-0	-8	-8	0	-0.3
■ **JOHNNY COUCH** Couch, John Daniel b: 3/31/1891, Vaughn, Mont. d: 12/8/75, San Mateo, Cal. BL/TR, 6', 180 lbs. Deb: 4/11/17																									
1917 Det-A	0	0	—	3	0	0	0	0	13¹	13	0	1	1	9.5	2.70	98	.255	.269	0	.000	-0	-0	-0	0	0.0
1922 Cin-N	16	9	.640	43	34	18	2	1	264	301	13	56	45	12.3	3.89	103	.289	.328	12	.132	-3	6	3	1	0.1
1923 Cin-N	2	7	.222	19	8	1	0	0	69¹	98	2	15	14	14.7	5.97	65	.344	.377	4	.174	-1	-15	-16	-1	-1.5
Phi-N	2	4	.333	11	7	2	0	0	65	91	4	21	18	15.9	5.26	87	.335	.389	6	.250	-1	-9	-5	-0	-0.4
Yr	4	11	.267	30	15	3	0	0	134¹	189	6	36	32	15.3	5.63	75	.339	.383	2	.043	-1	-24	-21	-1	-1.9
1924 Phi-N	4	8	.333	37	6	3	0	3	137	170	13	39	23	13.8	4.73	94	.306	.352	10	.204	-1	-13	-4	1	-0.2
1925 Phi-N	5	6	.455	34	7	2	1	2	94¹	112	9	39	11	14.5	5.44	88	.298	.365	5	.161	-1	-12	-7	2	-0.5
Total 5	29	34	.460	147	62	26	3	6	643	785	41	171	112	13.5	4.63	91	.304	.350	37	.167	-6	-43	-29	3	-2.5
■ **MIKE COUCHEE** Couchee, Michael Eugene b: 12/4/57, San Jose, Cal. BR/TR, 6', 190 lbs. Deb: 4/05/83																									
1983 SD-N	0	1	.000	8	0	0	0	0	14	12	1	6	5	11.6	5.14	68	.214	.290	1	.500	0	-2	-3	-0	-0.1
■ **ED COUGHLIN** Coughlin, Edward E. b: 8/5/1861, Hartford, Conn. d: 12/25/52, Hartford, Conn. Deb: 5/15/1884 ♦																									
1884 Buf-N	0	0	—	1	0	0	0	0	3	5	0	0	0	∞	—	1.000	1.000	1	.250	-0	-3	-3	0	-0.1
■ **ROSCOE COUGHLIN** Coughlin, William Edward b: 3/15/1868, Walpole, Mass. d: 3/20/51, Chelsea, Mass. TR , 5'10", 160 lbs. Deb: 4/22/1890																									
1890 Chi-N	4	6	.400	11	10	10	0	0	95	102	3	40	29	13.5	4.26	86	.267	.336	10	.256	1	-7	-6	1	-0.3
1891 NY-N	3	4	.429	8	7	6	0	0	61	74	5	23	22	14.3	3.84	83	.289	.347	3	.130	1	-3	-4	1	-0.1
Total 2	7	10	.412	19	17	16	0	0	156	176	8	63	51	13.8	4.10	85	.275	.340	13	.210	2	-11	-11	2	-0.4
■ **FRITZ COUMBE** Coumbe, Frederick Nicholas b: 12/13/1889, Antrim, Pa. d: 3/21/78, Paradise, Cal. BL/TL, 6', 152 lbs. Deb: 4/22/14																									
1914 Bos-A	1	2	.333	17	5	1	0	1	62¹	49	0	16	17	9.4	1.44	186	.222	.274	2	.111	-1	9	9	1	1.0
Cle-A	1	5	.167	14	5	2	0	0	55¹	59	0	16	22	12.8	3.25	89	.261	.351	6	.261	1	-3	-2	1	0.0
Yr	2	7	.222	31	10	3	0	1	117²	108	0	32	39	11.0	2.29	121	.254	.312	0	.000	1	6	6	1	1.0
1915 Cle-A	4	7	.364	30	12	4	1	2	114	123	1	37	37	12.9	3.47	88	.294	.355	10	.270	1	-7	-5	3	-0.1
1916 Cle-A	7	5	.583	29	13	7	2	0	120¹	121	1	27	39	11.1	2.02	149	.279	.323	2	.057	-3	11	13	5	1.7
1917 Cle-A	8	7	.533	34	10	4	1	5	134¹	119	0	35	30	10.5	2.14	132	.251	.307	6	.154	-1	8	10	3	1.4
1918 Cle-A	13	7	.650	30	17	9	0	3	150	164	4	52	41	13.0	3.06	98	.286	.347	12	.214	-1	-5	-1	5	0.4
1919 Cle-A	1	1	.500	8	2	0	0	1	23²	32	2	9	7	15.6	5.32	63	.348	.406	3	.500	1	-6	-5	0	-0.3
1920 Cin-N	0	1	.000	3	0	0	0	0	14²	17	0	4	7	12.9	4.91	62	.304	.350	3	.231	1	-3	-3	0	0.0
1921 Cin-N	3	4	.429	28	6	3	0	1	86²	89	2	21	12	11.5	3.22	111	.280	.326	8	.320	1	5	3	3	0.8
Total 8	38	39	.494	193	70	30	4	13	761¹	773	10	217	212	11.9	2.80	108	.277	.332	52	.206	-1	10	20	21	4.9
■ **HARRY COURTNEY** Courtney, Henry Seymour b: 11/19/1898, Asheville, N.C. d: 12/11/54, Lyme, Conn. BB/TL, 6'4", 185 lbs. Deb: 9/13/19																									
1919 Was-A	3	0	1.000	4	3	2	1	0	26¹	25	0	19	6	15.0	2.73	117	.269	.393	2	.200	-0	1	1	-1	0.0
1920 Was-A	8	11	.421	37	24	10	1	0	188	223	6	77	48	14.8	4.74	79	.232	.371	16	.232	4	-20	-21	-3	-1.9
1921 Was-A	6	9	.400	30	15	3	0	1	132²	159	7	71	26	16.1	5.63	73	.305	.397	14	.298	2	-20	-22	1	-1.8
1922 Was-A	0	1	.000	5	0	0	0	0	10	11	0	9	4	18.0	3.60	107	.306	.444	0	.000	-1	0	0	0	0.0
Chi-A	5	6	.455	18	11	5	0	0	86²	100	5	37	28	14.3	4.98	82	.299	.371	9	.273	3	-9	-9	-0	-0.5
Yr	5	7	.417	23	11	5	0	0	96²	111	5	46	32	14.7	4.84	84	.300	.379	3	.081	2	-9	-8	-0	-0.5
Total 4	22	27	.449	94	53	20	2	1	443²	518	18	213	112	15.2	4.91	79	.299	.382	41	.252	7	-47	-50	-4	-4.2
■ **HARRY COVELESKI** Coveleski, Harry Frank "The Giant Killer" (b: Harry Frank Kowalewski) b: 4/23/1886, Shamokin, Pa. d: 8/4/50, Shamokin, Pa. BB/TL, 6', 180 lbs. Deb: 9/10/07																									
1907 Phi-N	1	0	1.000	4	0	0	0	0	20	10	0	3	6	6.3	0.00	—	.147	.194	0	.000	-0	5	5	0	0.6
1908 Phi-N	4	1	.800	6	5	5	2	0	43²	29	0	12	22	8.9	1.24	196	.196	.265	2	.133	-0	5	6	1	0.8
1909 Phi-N	6	10	.375	24	17	8	2	1	121²	109	0	49	56	12.1	2.74	95	.247	.329	4	.108	-2	-2	-2	1	-0.2
1910 Cin-N	1	1	.500	7	4	2	0	0	39¹	35	1	42	27	18.5	5.26	55	.246	.431	1	.063	-1	-10	-10	1	-1.0
1914 Det-A	22	12	.647	44	36	23	5	2	303¹	251	4	100	124	10.8	2.49	113	.227	.298	23	.242	5	8	11	7	2.4
1915 Det-A	22	13	.629	50	38	20	1	4	312²	251	7	87	150	10.9	2.45	124	.233	.298	18	.175	-2	17	20	3	2.3
1916 Det-A	21	11	.656	44	39	22	3	2	324¹	278	6	63	108	9.8	1.97	145	.237	.282	25	.212	1	31	32	4	4.4
1917 Det-A	4	6	.400	16	11	2	0	0	69	70	0	14	15	11.2	2.61	102	.265	.307	5	.227	-0	0	0	2	0.2
1918 Det-A	0	1	.000	3	1	1	0	0	14	17	0	6	3	14.8	3.86	69	.315	.383	1	.250	0	-2	-2	1	0.0

YEAR TM/L	W	L	PCT	G	GS	CG	SH	SV	IP	H	HR	BB	SO	RAT	ERA	ERA+	OAV	OOB	BH	AVG	PB	PR	/A	PD	TPI
Total 9	81	55	.596	198	151	83	13	9	1248	1070	13	376	511	10.8	2.39	118	.235	.301	79	.189	-0	55	61	19	9.5

■ STAN COVELESKI
Coveleski, Stanley Anthony (b: Stanislaus Kowalewski)
b: 7/13/1889, Shamokin, Pa. d: 3/20/84, South Bend, Ind. BR/TR, 5'11", 166 lbs. Deb: 9/10/12 H

YEAR TM/L	W	L	PCT	G	GS	CG	SH	SV	IP	H	HR	BB	SO	RAT	ERA	ERA+	OAV	OOB	BH	AVG	PB	PR	/A	PD	TPI
1912 Phi-A	2	1	.667	5	2	2	1	0	21	18	0	4	9	9.9	3.43	90	.231	.277	1	.143	-0	-0	-1	-0	0.0
1916 Cle-A	15	13	.536	45	27	11	1	3	232	247	6	58	76	11.9	3.41	88	.278	.323	13	.173	-6	-15	-10	2	-0.8
1917 Cle-A	19	14	.576	45	36	24	9	4	298¹	202	3	94	133	9.0	1.81	157	**.194**	.261	13	.134	-4	28	34	-5	3.0
1918 Cle-A	22	13	.629	38	33	25	2	1	311	261	2	76	87	9.9	1.82	165	.229	.279	21	.191	-3	33	41	0	4.7
1919 Cle-A	24	12	.667	43	34	24	4	4	286	286	2	60	118	11.0	2.61	128	.267	.308	20	.213	4	20	23	3	3.3
1920 *Cle-A	24	14	.632	41	38	26	3	2	315	284	6	65	**133**	**10.1**	2.49	153	**.243**	**.285**	25	.225	3	**46**	**46**	3	**5.4**
1921 Cle-A	23	13	.639	43	40	28	2	2	315	341	6	84	99	12.3	3.37	126	.280	.329	18	.155	-6	32	31	7	3.1
1922 Cle-A	17	14	.548	35	33	21	3	2	276²	292	14	64	98	11.6	3.32	121	.274	.316	10	.101	-7	22	21	1	1.5
1923 Cle-A	13	14	.481	33	31	17	**5**	2	228	251	8	42	54	11.6	**2.76**	**143**	.282	.316	7	.089	-8	**31**	30	3	2.6
1924 Cle-A	15	16	.484	37	33	18	2	0	240¹	286	6	73	58	13.6	4.04	106	.294	.346	11	.134	-5	5	6	-0	0.1
1925 *Was-A	20	5	**.800**	32	32	15	3	0	241	230	7	73	58	11.4	**2.84**	**149**	.255	.312	9	.111	-7	42	37	1	2.9
1926 Was-A	14	11	.560	36	34	11	3	1	245¹	272	1	81	50	12.9	3.12	124	.286	.342	17	.207	1	25	20	2	2.3
1927 Was-A	2	1	.667	5	4	0	0	0	14¹	13	0	8	3	13.2	3.14	129	.250	.350	2	.333	0	2	1	-0	0.1
1928 NY-A	5	1	.833	12	8	2	0	0	58	72	5	20	5	14.3	5.74	66	.323	.379	1	.053	-2	-11	-13	1	-1.2
Total 14	215	142	.602	450	385	224	38	21	3082	3055	66	802	981	11.4	2.89	128	.262	.311	168	.159	-34	259	276	17	27.0

■ CHET COVINGTON
Covington, Chester Rogers "Chesty" b: 11/6/10, Cairo, Ill. d: 6/11/76, Pembroke Park, Fla. BB/TL, 6'2", 195 lbs. Deb: 4/23/44

YEAR TM/L	W	L	PCT	G	GS	CG	SH	SV	IP	H	HR	BB	SO	RAT	ERA	ERA+	OAV	OOB	BH	AVG	PB	PR	/A	PD	TPI
1944 Phi-N	1	1	.500	19	0	0	0	0	38²	46	2	8	13	12.6	4.66	78	.297	.331	0	.000	-1	-4	-4	-0	-0.5

■ TEX COVINGTON
Covington, William Wilkes b: 3/19/1887, Henryville, Tenn. d: 12/10/31, Denison, Tex. BL/TR, 6'1", 175 lbs. Deb: 4/25/11

YEAR TM/L	W	L	PCT	G	GS	CG	SH	SV	IP	H	HR	BB	SO	RAT	ERA	ERA+	OAV	OOB	BH	AVG	PB	PR	/A	PD	TPI
1911 Det-A	7	1	.875	17	6	5	0	0	83²	94	2	33	29	14.7	4.09	85	.297	.381	6	.188	-1	-7	-6	-1	-0.6
1912 Det-A	3	4	.429	14	9	2	1	0	63¹	58	0	30	19	12.9	4.12	79	.253	.347	2	.133	-0	-6	-6	-0	-0.4
Total 2	10	5	.667	31	15	7	1	0	147	152	2	63	48	14.0	4.10	82	.278	.367	8	.170	-1	-13	-12	-1	-1.1

■ JOE COWLEY
Cowley, Joseph Alan b: 8/15/58, Lexington, Ky. BR/TR, 6'5", 210 lbs. Deb: 4/13/82

YEAR TM/L	W	L	PCT	G	GS	CG	SH	SV	IP	H	HR	BB	SO	RAT	ERA	ERA+	OAV	OOB	BH	AVG	PB	PR	/A	PD	TPI
1982 Atl-N	1	2	.333	17	8	0	0	0	52¹	53	6	16	27	12.0	4.47	83	.265	.323	3	.200	-0	-5	-4	0	-0.3
1984 NY-A	9	2	.818	16	11	3	1	0	83¹	75	12	31	71	11.7	3.56	106	.234	.305	0	—	0	4	2	0	0.2
1985 NY-A	12	6	.667	30	26	1	0	0	159²	132	29	85	97	12.6	3.95	101	.224	.328	0	—	0	4	1	-0	0.0
1986 Chi-A	11	11	.500	27	27	4	0	0	162¹	133	20	83	132	12.1	3.88	111	.223	.321	0	—	0	5	8	-1	0.7
1987 Phi-N	0	4	.000	5	4	0	0	0	11²	21	2	17	5	30.9	15.43	27	.389	.548	1	.333	1	-15	-15	-0	-1.1
Total 5	33	25	.569	95	76	8	1	0	469¹	414	69	232	332	12.7	4.20	96	.235	.329	4	.222	1	-7	-8	-1	-0.5

■ DANNY COX
Cox, Danny Bradford b: 9/21/59, Northampton, England BR/TR, 6'4", 235 lbs. Deb: 8/06/83

YEAR TM/L	W	L	PCT	G	GS	CG	SH	SV	IP	H	HR	BB	SO	RAT	ERA	ERA+	OAV	OOB	BH	AVG	PB	PR	/A	PD	TPI
1983 StL-N	3	6	.333	12	12	0	0	0	83	92	6	23	36	12.5	3.25	111	.286	.333	2	.074	-2	3	3	1	0.3
1984 StL-N	9	11	.450	29	27	1	1	0	156¹	171	9	54	70	13.4	4.03	86	.289	.355	7	.132	0	-8	-10	1	-0.8
1985 *StL-N	18	9	.667	35	35	10	4	0	241	226	19	64	131	10.9	2.88	123	.251	.303	12	.152	1	19	18	-1	1.9
1986 StL-N	12	13	.480	32	32	8	0	0	220	189	14	60	108	10.3	2.90	125	.234	.289	5	.077	-3	20	18	-5	1.1
1987 *StL-N	11	9	.550	31	31	2	0	0	199¹	224	17	71	101	13.5	3.88	107	.290	.352	8	.116	-2	4	6	-0	0.4
1988 StL-N	3	8	.273	13	13	0	0	0	86	89	6	25	47	12.0	3.98	87	.272	.326	1	.043	-2	-5	-5	-0	-0.5
Total 6	56	56	.500	152	150	21	5	0	985²	991	71	297	493	11.9	3.40	108	.266	.323	35	.111	-7	34	30	-3	2.4

■ ERNIE COX
Cox, Ernest Thompson b: 2/19/1894, Birmingham, Ala. d: 4/29/74, Birmingham, Ala. BL/TR, 6'1", 180 lbs. Deb: 5/05/22

YEAR TM/L	W	L	PCT	G	GS	CG	SH	SV	IP	H	HR	BB	SO	RAT	ERA	ERA+	OAV	OOB	BH	AVG	PB	PR	/A	PD	TPI
1922 Chi-A	0	0	—	1	0	0	0	0	1	1	0	2	0	27.0	18.00	23	.250	.500	0	—	0	-2	-2	0	0.0

■ GEORGE COX
Cox, George Melvin b: 11/15/04, Sherman, Tex. BR/TR, 6'1", 170 lbs. Deb: 4/12/28

YEAR TM/L	W	L	PCT	G	GS	CG	SH	SV	IP	H	HR	BB	SO	RAT	ERA	ERA+	OAV	OOB	BH	AVG	PB	PR	/A	PD	TPI
1928 Chi-A	1	2	.333	26	2	0	0	0	89	110	6	39	22	15.3	5.26	77	.313	.385	2	.077	-2	-12	-12	2	-1.1

■ GLENN COX
Cox, Glenn Melvin b: 2/3/31, Montebello, Cal. BR/TR, 6'2", 210 lbs. Deb: 9/20/55

YEAR TM/L	W	L	PCT	G	GS	CG	SH	SV	IP	H	HR	BB	SO	RAT	ERA	ERA+	OAV	OOB	BH	AVG	PB	PR	/A	PD	TPI
1955 KC-A	0	2	.000	2	2	0	0	0	2¹	11	0	1	2	46.3	30.86	14	.611	.632	0	.000	-0	-7	-7	-0	-0.5
1956 KC-A	0	2	.000	3	3	1	0	0	23¹	15	2	22	6	14.3	4.24	102	.203	.385	0	.000	-1	-0	0	-1	-0.1
1957 KC-A	1	0	1.000	10	0	0	0	0	14¹	18	1	9	8	17.0	5.02	79	.321	.415	0	.000	0	-2	-2	0	-0.1
1958 KC-A	0	0	—	2	0	0	0	0	3²	6	1	3	1	22.1	9.82	40	.400	.500	0	—	0	-2	-2	-0	-0.1
Total 4	1	4	.200	17	5	1	0	0	43²	50	4	35	17	17.5	6.39	65	.307	.429	0	.000	-1	-12	-11	-1	-0.7

■ CASEY COX
Cox, Joseph Casey b: 7/3/41, Long Beach, Cal. BR/TR, 6'5", 200 lbs. Deb: 4/15/66

YEAR TM/L	W	L	PCT	G	GS	CG	SH	SV	IP	H	HR	BB	SO	RAT	ERA	ERA+	OAV	OOB	BH	AVG	PB	PR	/A	PD	TPI
1966 Was-A	4	5	.444	66	0	0	0	7	113	104	6	35	46	11.4	3.50	99	.250	.314	0	.000	-1	-1	-1	1	0.0
1967 Was-A	7	4	.636	54	0	0	0	5	73	67	2	21	32	11.3	2.96	107	.250	.314	0	.000	-0	2	2	0	0.2
1968 Was-A	0	1	.000	4	0	0	0	0	7²	7	0	0	4	8.2	2.35	124	.250	.250	0	—	0	1	0	-0	0.0
1969 Was-A	12	7	.632	44	13	4	0	0	171²	161	15	64	73	11.8	2.78	125	.251	.320	5	.106	-2	16	13	-1	1.1
1970 Was-A	8	12	.400	37	30	4	0	1	192¹	211	27	44	68	12.1	4.45	80	.285	.329	7	.121	-2	-16	-19	-1	-2.1
1971 Was-A	5	7	.417	54	11	0	0	7	124¹	131	9	40	43	12.9	3.98	83	.273	.338	2	.077	-1	-7	-9	-1	-1.1
1972 Tex-A	3	5	.375	35	4	0	0	4	65¹	73	7	26	22	13.8	4.41	68	.277	.344	1	.111	1	-10	-10	0	-0.9
NY-A	0	1	.000	5	1	0	0	0	11²	13	0	3	4	13.9	4.63	64	.289	.360	2	.333	0	-2	-2	-0	-0.2
Yr	3	6	.333	40	5	0	0	4	77	86	7	29	31	13.7	4.44	68	.276	.341	3	.333	1	-12	-12	0	-1.1
1973 NY-A	0	0	—	1	0	0	0	0	3	5	0	1	0	24.0	6.00	61	.357	.471	0	—	0	-1	-1	0	0.0
Total 8	39	42	.481	308	59	5	0	20	762	772	66	234	297	12.2	3.70	91	.266	.327	15	.099	-6	-17	-27	-1	-3.0

■ LES COX
Cox, Leslie Warren b: 8/14/05, Junction, Tex. d: 10/14/34, San Angelo, Tex. BR/TR, 6', 164 lbs. Deb: 9/11/26

YEAR TM/L	W	L	PCT	G	GS	CG	SH	SV	IP	H	HR	BB	SO	RAT	ERA	ERA+	OAV	OOB	BH	AVG	PB	PR	/A	PD	TPI
1926 Chi-A	0	1	.000	2	0	0	0	0	5	6	2	5	3	19.8	5.40	72	.261	.393	1	.500	0	-1	-1	0	0.0

■ RED COX
Cox, Plateau Rex b: 2/16/1895, Laurel Springs, N.C. d: 10/15/84, Roanoke, Va. BL/TR, 6'2", 190 lbs. Deb: 4/17/20

YEAR TM/L	W	L	PCT	G	GS	CG	SH	SV	IP	H	HR	BB	SO	RAT	ERA	ERA+	OAV	OOB	BH	AVG	PB	PR	/A	PD	TPI
1920 Det-A	0	0	—	3	0	0	0	0	5	9	0	3	1	21.6	5.40	69	.375	.444	0	.000	-0	-1	-1	0	0.0

■ TERRY COX
Cox, Terry Lee b: 3/30/49, Odessa, Tex. BR/TR, 6'5", 215 lbs. Deb: 9/07/70

YEAR TM/L	W	L	PCT	G	GS	CG	SH	SV	IP	H	HR	BB	SO	RAT	ERA	ERA+	OAV	OOB	BH	AVG	PB	PR	/A	PD	TPI
1970 Cal-A	0	0	—	3	0	0	0	0	2¹	4	0	0	3	15.4	3.86	94	.400	.400	0	—	0	-0	-0	0	0.0

■ BILL COX
Cox, William Donald b: 6/23/13, Ashmore, Ill. BR/TR, 6'1", 185 lbs. Deb: 6/06/36

YEAR TM/L	W	L	PCT	G	GS	CG	SH	SV	IP	H	HR	BB	SO	RAT	ERA	ERA+	OAV	OOB	BH	AVG	PB	PR	/A	PD	TPI
1936 StL-N	0	0	—	2	0	0	0	0	2²	4	0	1	1	16.9	6.75	58	.333	.385	0	—	0	-1	-1	-0	0.0
1937 Chi-A	1	0	1.000	3	2	1	1	0	12¹	9	0	5	8	9.9	0.71	648	.200	.280	1	.250	0	6	5	0	0.5
1938 Chi-A	0	2	.000	7	1	0	0	0	11²	11	0	13	5	18.5	6.94	70	.244	.414	0	.000	-0	-3	-3	0	-0.2
StL-A	1	4	.200	22	7	1	0	0	63	81	8	35	16	16.6	7.00	71	.315	.397	1	.059	-1	-15	-14	1	-1.2
Yr	1	6	.143	29	8	1	0	0	74²	92	8	48	21	16.9	6.99	71	.305	.400	1	.053	-1	-18	-17	1	-1.4
1939 StL-A	0	2	.000	4	2	1	0	0	9¹	10	0	8	8	17.4	9.64	50	.256	.383	0	.000	-0	-5	-5	-0	-0.3
1940 StL-A	0	1	.000	12	0	0	0	0	17¹	23	3	12	7	18.2	7.27	63	.333	.432	0	.000	-0	-6	-5	0	-0.4
Total 5	2	9	.182	50	12	3	1	0	116²	138	11	74	45	16.4	6.56	74	.296	.392	2	.080	-2	-24	-22	1	-1.6

■ BILL COYLE
Coyle, William Claude b: Pittsburgh, Pa. TR d: 7/07/1893

YEAR TM/L	W	L	PCT	G	GS	CG	SH	SV	IP	H	HR	BB	SO	RAT	ERA	ERA+	OAV	OOB	BH	AVG	PB	PR	/A	PD	TPI
1893 Bos-N	0	1	.000	2	1	0	0	0	8	14	1	3	2	19.1	9.00	55	.372	.418	0	.000	-1	-4	-4	0	-0.2

■ CHARLIE COZART
Cozart, Charles Rhubin b: 10/17/19, Lenoir, N.C. BR/TL, 6', 190 lbs. Deb: 4/17/45

YEAR TM/L	W	L	PCT	G	GS	CG	SH	SV	IP	H	HR	BB	SO	RAT	ERA	ERA+	OAV	OOB	BH	AVG	PB	PR	/A	PD	TPI
1945 Bos-N	1	0	1.000	5	0	0	0	0	8	10	2	15	4	28.1	10.13	38	.303	.521	0	.000	-0	-6	-6	1	-0.4

YEAR TM/L	W	L	PCT	G	GS	CG	SH	SV	IP	H	HR	BB	SO	RAT	ERA	ERA+	OAV	OOB	BH	AVG	PB	PR	/A	PD	TPI

■ ROY CRABB
Crabb, James Roy b: 8/23/1890, Monticello, Iowa d: 3/30/40, Lewiston, Mont. BR/TR, 5'11", 160 lbs. Deb: 8/10/12

YEAR TM/L	W	L	PCT	G	GS	CG	SH	SV	IP	H	HR	BB	SO	RAT	ERA	ERA+	OAV	OOB	BH	AVG	PB	PR	/A	PD	TPI
1912 Chi-A	0	1	.000	2	1	0	0	0	8²	6	0	4	3	10.4	1.04	308	.214	.313	0	.000	-0	2	2	0	0.2
Phi-A	2	4	.333	7	7	3	0	0	43¹	48	0	17	12	14.3	3.74	82	.287	.367	0	.000	-2	-2	-3	0	-0.4
Yr	2	5	.286	9	8	3	0	0	52	54	0	21	15	13.7	3.29	94	.277	.359	0	.000	-3	0	-1	1	-0.2

■ GEORGE CRABLE
Crable, George E. b: 12/1885, Nebraska BL/TL, 6'1", 190 lbs. Deb: 8/03/10

YEAR TM/L	W	L	PCT	G	GS	CG	SH	SV	IP	H	HR	BB	SO	RAT	ERA	ERA+	OAV	OOB	BH	AVG	PB	PR	/A	PD	TPI
1910 Bro-N	0	0	—	2	1	1	0	0	7¹	5	0	5	3	14.7	4.91	62	.217	.400	0	.000	0	-2	-2	0	-0.1

■ WALT CRADDOCK
Craddock, Walter Anderson b: 3/25/32, Pax, W.Va. d: 7/6/80, Parma Heights, O. BR/TL, 5'11.5", 176 lbs. Deb: 9/03/55

YEAR TM/L	W	L	PCT	G	GS	CG	SH	SV	IP	H	HR	BB	SO	RAT	ERA	ERA+	OAV	OOB	BH	AVG	PB	PR	/A	PD	TPI
1955 KC-A	0	2	.000	4	2	0	0	0	15	18	3	10	9	16.8	7.80	54	.300	.400	0	.000	-1	-6	-6	-0	-0.5
1956 KC-A	0	2	.000	2	2	0	0	0	9¹	9	1	10	8	18.3	6.75	64	.265	.432	0	.000	-0	-3	-3	-0	-0.4
1958 KC-A	0	3	.000	23	1	0	0	0	36²	41	4	20	22	15.2	5.89	66	.289	.380	0	.000	-0	-9	-8	0	-0.7
Total 3	0	7	.000	29	5	0	0	0	61	68	8	40	39	16.1	6.49	62	.288	.394	0	.000	-1	-18	-17	0	-1.4

■ MOLLY CRAFT
Craft, Maurice Montague b: 11/28/1895, Portsmouth, Va. d: 10/25/78, Los Angeles, Cal. BR/TR, 6'2", 165 lbs. Deb: 8/08/16

YEAR TM/L	W	L	PCT	G	GS	CG	SH	SV	IP	H	HR	BB	SO	RAT	ERA	ERA+	OAV	OOB	BH	AVG	PB	PR	/A	PD	TPI
1916 Was-A	0	1	.000	2	1	1	0	0	11	12	0	6	9	14.7	3.27	84	.316	.409	0	.000	-0	-1	-1	0	0.0
1917 Was-A	0	0	—	8	0	0	0	1	14	17	0	8	2	16.1	3.86	68	.315	.403	1	.500	0	-2	-2	0	0.0
1918 Was-A	0	0	—	3	0	0	0	0	7	5	0	1	5	7.7	1.29	212	.208	.240	0	.000	-0	1	1	0	0.1
1919 Was-A	0	3	.000	16	2	0	0	1	48²	59	2	18	17	14.6	3.88	83	.309	.374	2	.111	-2	-4	-4	0	-0.4
Total 4	0	4	.000	29	3	1	0	2	80²	93	2	33	33	14.3	3.57	84	.303	.374	3	.115	-2	-5	-5	1	-0.3

■ HOWARD CRAGHEAD
Craghead, Howard Oliver "Judge" b: 5/25/08, Selma, Cal. d: 7/15/62, San Zieloe, Cal. BR/TR, 6'2", 200 lbs. Deb: 4/30/31

YEAR TM/L	W	L	PCT	G	GS	CG	SH	SV	IP	H	HR	BB	SO	RAT	ERA	ERA+	OAV	OOB	BH	AVG	PB	PR	/A	PD	TPI
1931 Cle-A	0	0	—	4	0	0	0	0	5²	8	0	2	2	15.9	6.35	73	.320	.370	0	—	0	-1	-1	0	0.0
1933 Cle-A	0	0	—	11	0	0	0	0	17¹	19	1	10	2	15.6	6.23	71	.292	.395	-0	.000	-0	-4	-3	0	-0.2
Total 2	0	0	—	15	0	0	0	0	23	27	1	12	4	15.7	6.26	72	.300	.388	0	.000	-0	-5	-5	0	-0.2

■ GEORGE CRAIG
Craig, George McCarthy "Lefty" b: 11/15/1887, Philadelphia, Pa. d: 4/23/11, Indianapolis, Ind. TL, Deb: 7/12/07

YEAR TM/L	W	L	PCT	G	GS	CG	SH	SV	IP	H	HR	BB	SO	RAT	ERA	ERA+	OAV	OOB	BH	AVG	PB	PR	/A	PD	TPI
1907 Phi-A	0	0	—	2	0	0	0	0	1²	5	0	3	0	27.0	10.80	24	.299	.516	0	.000	-0	-2	-2	0	-0.1

■ PETE CRAIG
Craig, Peter Joel b: 7/10/40, Lasalle, Ont., Can. BL/TR, 6'5", 220 lbs. Deb: 9/06/64

YEAR TM/L	W	L	PCT	G	GS	CG	SH	SV	IP	H	HR	BB	SO	RAT	ERA	ERA+	OAV	OOB	BH	AVG	PB	PR	/A	PD	TPI
1964 Was-A	0	0	—	2	1	0	0	0	1²	8	1	4	0	64.8	48.60	8	.667	.750	0	—	0	-8	-8	0	-0.6
1965 Was-A	0	3	.000	3	3	0	0	0	14¹	18	1	8	2	16.3	8.16	43	.321	.406	2	.667	1	-7	-7	1	-0.4
1966 Was-A	0	0	—	1	0	0	0	0	2	2	0	1	1	13.5	4.50	77	.250	.333	0	—	-0	-0	-0	0	0.0
Total 3	0	3	.000	6	4	0	0	0	18	28	2	13	3	20.5	11.50	30	.368	.461	2	.667	1	-16	-16	1	-1.0

■ ROGER CRAIG
Craig, Roger Lee b: 2/17/30, Durham, N.C. BR/TR, 6'4", 185 lbs. Deb: 7/17/55 MC

YEAR TM/L	W	L	PCT	G	GS	CG	SH	SV	IP	H	HR	BB	SO	RAT	ERA	ERA+	OAV	OOB	BH	AVG	PB	PR	/A	PD	TPI
1955 *Bro-N	5	3	.625	21	10	3	0	2	90²	81	8	43	48	12.4	2.78	146	.238	.325	2	.077	-2	13	13	-1	1.0
1956 *Bro-N	12	11	.522	35	32	8	2	1	199	169	25	87	109	11.8	3.71	107	.231	.316	1	.016	-6	1	6	-2	-0.1
1957 Bro-N	6	9	.400	32	13	1	0	0	111¹	102	18	47	69	12.2	4.61	90	.249	.329	4	.138	-1	-9	-5	-1	-0.4
1958 LA-N	2	1	.667	9	2	1	0	0	32	30	3	12	16	11.8	4.50	91	.242	.309	0	.000	-1	-2	-1	-1	-0.2
1959 *LA-N	11	5	.688	29	17	7	4	0	152²	122	13	45	76	9.9	2.06	205	.217	.276	3	.058	-4	32	37	0	3.6
1960 LA-N	8	3	.727	21	15	6	1	0	115²	99	8	43	69	11.3	3.27	121	.230	.305	2	.056	-2	6	9	0	0.8
1961 LA-N	5	6	.455	40	14	2	0	2	112²	130	22	52	63	14.9	6.15	71	.288	.367	4	.148	-0	-27	-23	-1	-2.2
1962 NY-N	10	24	.294	42	33	13	0	3	233¹	261	35	70	118	13.0	4.51	93	.288	.343	4	.053	-6	-15	-9	4	-0.9
1963 NY-N	5	22	.185	46	31	14	0	2	236	249	28	58	108	11.9	3.78	92	.267	.314	6	.087	-2	-13	-8	4	-0.6
1964 *StL-N	7	9	.438	39	19	3	0	5	166	180	16	35	84	11.9	3.25	117	.276	.317	10	.208	2	5	10	2	1.6
1965 Cin-N	1	4	.200	40	0	0	0	0	64¹	74	6	25	30	14.3	3.64	103	.289	.359	2	.182	-0	-1	1	0	0.1
1966 Phi-N	2	1	.667	14	0	0	0	1	22²	31	4	5	13	14.3	5.56	65	.326	.360	0	.000	-0	-5	-5	1	-0.4
Total 12	74	98	.430	368	186	58	7	19	1536¹	1528	186	522	803	12.2	3.83	104	.259	.323	38	.085	-23	-13	25	8	2.3

■ GERALD CRAM
Cram, Gerald Allen b: 12/9/47, Los Angeles, Cal. BR/TR, 6', 180 lbs. Deb: 9/03/69

YEAR TM/L	W	L	PCT	G	GS	CG	SH	SV	IP	H	HR	BB	SO	RAT	ERA	ERA+	OAV	OOB	BH	AVG	PB	PR	/A	PD	TPI
1969 KC-A	0	1	.000	5	2	0	0	0	16²	15	0	6	10	11.3	3.24	114	.231	.296	0	.000	-0	1	1	-0	0.6
1974 NY-N	0	1	.000	10	0	0	0	0	22¹	22	1	4	8	10.5	1.61	221	.275	.310	1	.333	0	5	5	0	0.6
1975 NY-N	0	1	.000	4	0	0	0	0	5	7	2	2	2	16.2	5.40	64	.333	.391	0	—	0	-1	-1	0	0.0
1976 KC-A	0	0	—	4	0	0	0	0	4¹	8	0	1	2	18.7	6.23	56	.421	.450	0	—	0	-1	-1	0	0.0
Total 4	0	3	.000	23	2	0	0	0	48¹	52	3	13	22	12.1	2.98	120	.281	.328	1	.167	-0	3	3	0	0.6

■ DOC CRAMER
Cramer, Roger Maxwell "Flit" b: 7/22/05, Beach Haven, N.J. d: 9/9/90, Manahawkin, N.J. BL/TL, 6'2", 185 lbs. Deb: 9/18/29 C♦

YEAR TM/L	W	L	PCT	G	GS	CG	SH	SV	IP	H	HR	BB	SO	RAT	ERA	ERA+	OAV	OOB	BH	AVG	PB	PR	/A	PD	TPI
1938 Bos-A	0	0	—	1	0	0	0	0	4	3	0	1	0	13.5	4.50	110	.214	.353	198	.301	0	0	0	0	0.0

■ BILL CRAMER
Cramer, William Wendell b: 5/21/1891, Bedford, Ind. d: 9/11/66, Fort Wayne, Ind. BR/TR, 6', 175 lbs. Deb: 6/25/12

YEAR TM/L	W	L	PCT	G	GS	CG	SH	SV	IP	H	HR	BB	SO	RAT	ERA	ERA+	OAV	OOB	BH	AVG	PB	PR	/A	PD	TPI
1912 Cin-N	0	0	—	1	0	0	0	0	2¹	6	0	0	2	23.1	0.00	—	.400	.400	0	.000	-0	1	1	-0	0.0

■ DOC CRANDALL
Crandall, James Otis b: 10/8/1887, Wadena, Ind. d: 8/17/51, Bell, Cal. BR/TR, 5'10.5", 180 lbs. Deb: 4/24/08 ♦

YEAR TM/L	W	L	PCT	G	GS	CG	SH	SV	IP	H	HR	BB	SO	RAT	ERA	ERA+	OAV	OOB	BH	AVG	PB	PR	/A	PD	TPI
1908 NY-N	12	12	.500	32	24	13	0	0	214²	198	3	59	77	11.2	2.93	82	.248	.307	16	.222	5	-14	-12	-1	-0.8
1909 NY-N	6	4	.600	30	7	4	0	6	122	117	5	33	55	11.3	2.88	89	.252	.305	10	.244	3	-4	-4	2	0.0
1910 NY-N	17	4	.810	42	18	13	2	5	207²	194	10	43	73	10.4	2.56	116	.246	.289	25	.342	10	11	9	-0	2.1
1911 *NY-N	15	5	.750	41	15	9	2	5	198²	199	10	51	94	11.6	2.63	128	.256	.307	27	.239	6	17	16	2	2.7
1912 *NY-N	13	7	.650	37	10	7	0	2	162	181	7	35	60	12.1	3.61	94	.278	.317	25	.313	6	-4	-4	0	0.4
1913 *NY-N	2	4	.333	24	0	1	0	0	55¹	61	3	13	28	12.2	3.09	101	.293	.338	-7	.280	2	1	0	0	0.3
*NY-N	2	0	1.000	11	0	1	0	0	42¹	41	1	11	14	11.1	2.55	122	.248	.295	8	.364	3	3	3	1	0.7
Yr	4	4	.500	35	0	2	0	0	97²	102	3	24	42	11.6	2.86	109	.273	.317	3	.064	5	4	3	1	1.0
1914 StL-F	13	9	.591	27	21	18	1	0	196	194	8	52	84	11.4	3.54	96	.256	.305	86	.309	9	-7	-3	-1	-0.3
1915 StL-F	21	15	.583	51	33	22	4	1	312²	307	5	77	117	11.3	2.59	123	.263	.314	40	.284	14	15	21	2	4.4
1916 StL-A	0	0	—	2	0	0	0	0	1¹	7	0	1	0	60.8	27.00	10	.636	.692	1	.083	-0	-4	-4	-0	-0.3
1918 Bos-N	1	2	.333	5	3	3	0	0	34	39	1	4	4	11.6	2.38	113	.307	.333	8	.286	1	1	1	0	0.1
Total 10	102	62	.622	302	131	91	9	19	1546²	1538	52	379	606	11.4	2.92	105	.260	.309	253	.285	57	17	23	5	9.3

■ ED CRANE
Crane, Edward Nicholas "Cannon-Ball" b: 5/1862, Boston, Mass. d: 9/19/1896, Rochester, N.Y. BR/TR, 5'10.5", 204 lbs. Deb: 4/17/1884 ♦

YEAR TM/L	W	L	PCT	G	GS	CG	SH	SV	IP	H	HR	BB	SO	RAT	ERA	ERA+	OAV	OOB	BH	AVG	PB	PR	/A	PD	TPI
1884 Bos-U	0	2	.000	4	2	1	0	0	18	17	1	6	13	11.5	4.00	74	.233	.291	122	.285	1	-2	-2	1	-0.1
1886 Was-N	1	7	.125	10	8	7	1	0	70	91	6	53	39	18.5	7.20	46	.302	.407	50	.171	-1	-30	-30	0	-2.3
1888 *NY-N	5	6	.455	12	11	11	2	1	92²	70	3	40	58	10.7	2.43	112	.202	.285	6	.162	1	4	3	1	0.5
1889 *NY-N	14	10	.583	29	25	23	0	0	230	221	10	136	130	14.0	3.68	107	.245	.343	21	.204	3	9	7	-5	0.5
1890 NY-P	16	19	.457	43	35	28	0	0	330¹	323	12	210	117	14.5	4.63	98	.245	.349	46	.315	8	-15	-3	-3	0.3
1891 Cin-a	14	14	.500	32	31	25	1	0	250	216	3	139	122	12.8	2.45	168	.225	.323	17	.155	-6	35	46	-2	3.5
Cin-N	4	8	.333	15	13	11	0	0	116²	134	3	64	51	15.3	4.09	83	.277	.362	5	.109	-3	-10	-9	0	-1.0
1892 NY-N	16	24	.400	47	43	35	2	1	364¹	350	10	189	174	13.3	3.80	85	.243	.330	40	.245	4	-21	-24	0	-0.3
1893 NY-N	2	4	.333	10	7	4	0	0	68¹	84	2	41	11	16.5	5.93	79	.293	.382	12	.462	4	-10	-10	0	-0.3
Bro-N	0	2	.000	2	2	1	0	0	10	19	2	9	5	25.2	13.50	33	.391	.486	2	.400	-0	-10	-10	0	-0.6
Yr	2	6	.250	12	9	5	0	0	78¹	103	4	50	16	17.6	6.89	67	.308	.398	7	.226	5	-19	-20	-1	-0.9
Total 8	72	96	.429	204	177	146	7	2	1550¹	1525	51	887	720	14.0	3.99	95	.247	.342	335	.238	12	-48	-34	-9	-1.2

■ LARRY CRAWFORD
Crawford, Charles Lowrie b: 4/27/14, Swissvale, Pa. BL/TL, 6'1", 165 lbs. Deb: 7/21/37

YEAR TM/L	W	L	PCT	G	GS	CG	SH	SV	IP	H	HR	BB	SO	RAT	ERA	ERA+	OAV	OOB	BH	AVG	PB	PR	/A	PD	TPI
1937 Phi-N	0	0	—	6	0	0	0	1	6	12	2	1	2	19.5	15.00	29	.387	.406	0	—	0	-7	-7	-0	-0.6

YEAR	TM/L	W	L	PCT	G	GS	CG	SH	SV	IP	H	HR	BB	SO	RAT	ERA	ERA+	OAV	OOB	BH	AVG	PB	PR	/A	PD	TPI

■ JIM CRAWFORD   Crawford, James Frederick "Catfish"   b: 9/29/50, Chicago, Ill.   BL/TL, 6'3", 200 lbs.   Deb: 4/06/73

1973	Hou-N	2	4	.333	48	0	0	0	6	70	69	7	33	56	13.4	4.50	81	.256	.341	3	.231	1	-7	-7	1	-0.5
1975	Hou-N	3	5	.375	44	2	0	0	4	86²	92	9	37	37	13.6	3.63	93	.280	.356	5	.294	2	-0	-3	0	0.0
1976	Det-A	1	8	.111	32	5	1	0	2	109¹	115	4	43	68	13.0	4.53	82	.275	.343	0	—	0	-12	-10	4	-0.5
1977	Det-A	7	8	.467	37	7	0	0	1	126	156	13	50	91	14.8	4.79	90	.310	.373	0	—	0	-10	-7	0	-0.6
1978	Det-A	2	3	.400	20	0	0	0	0	39¹	45	3	19	24	15.1	4.35	89	.292	.367	0	—	0	-3	-2	-0	-0.2
Total	5	15	28	.349	181	14	1	0	13	431¹	477	27	182	276	13.9	4.40	86	.285	.357	8	.267	3	-32	-29	5	-1.8

■ STEVE CRAWFORD   Crawford, Steven Ray   b: 4/29/58, Pryor, Okla.   BR/TR, 6'5", 225 lbs.   Deb: 9/02/80

1980	Bos-A	2	0	1.000	6	4	2	0	0	32¹	41	3	8	10	13.6	3.62	117	.306	.345	0	—	0	1	2	-0	0.2
1981	Bos-A	0	5	.000	14	11	0	0	0	57²	69	10	18	29	14.0	4.99	77	.301	.360	0	—	0	-9	-7	0	-0.6
1982	Bos-A	1	0	1.000	5	0	0	0	0	9	14	0	0	4	14.0	2.00	215	.341	.341	0	—	0	2	2	0	0.2
1984	Bos-A	5	0	1.000	35	0	0	0	1	62	69	6	21	21	13.2	3.34	125	.286	.346	0	—	0	4	6	0	0.6
1985	Bos-A	6	5	.545	44	1	0	0	12	91	103	5	28	58	13.0	3.76	114	.289	.340	0	—	0	4	5	1	0.6
1986	*Bos-A	0	2	.000	40	0	0	0	4	57¹	69	5	19	32	13.8	3.92	106	.308	.362	0	—	0	2	2	0	0.2
1987	Bos-A	5	4	.556	29	0	0	0	0	72²	91	13	32	43	15.5	5.33	85	.314	.386	0	—	0	-7	-6	1	-0.4
1989	KC-A	3	1	.750	25	0	0	0	0	54	48	2	19	33	11.7	2.83	136	.242	.318	0	—	0	6	6	2	0.8
1990	KC-A	5	4	.556	46	0	0	1	0	80	79	7	23	54	11.8	4.16	91	.254	.312	0	—	0	-2	-3	1	-0.1
Total	9	27	21	.563	244	16	2	0	18	516	583	51	168	282	13.3	4.01	103	.288	.346	0	—	0	2	6	4	1.5

■ JACK CREEL   Creel, Jack Dalton "Tex"   b: 4/23/16, Kyle, Tex.   BR/TR, 6', 165 lbs.   Deb: 4/22/45

| 1945 | StL-N | 5 | 4 | .556 | 26 | 8 | 2 | 0 | 2 | 87 | 78 | 5 | 45 | 34 | 13.3 | 4.14 | 90 | .245 | .349 | 2 | .077 | -2 | -3 | -4 | 0 | -0.4 |

■ KEITH CREEL   Creel, Steven Keith   b: 2/4/59, Dallas, Tex.   BR/TR, 6'2", 180 lbs.   Deb: 5/25/82

1982	KC-A	1	4	.200	9	6	0	0	0	41²	43	8	25	13	14.7	5.40	76	.267	.366	0	—	0	-6	-6	0	-0.5
1983	KC-A	2	5	.286	25	10	1	0	0	89¹	116	17	35	31	15.4	6.35	64	.320	.382	0	—	0	-23	-23	-1	-2.1
1985	Cle-A	2	5	.286	15	8	0	0	0	62	73	7	23	31	14.2	4.79	86	.296	.360	0	—	0	-4	-5	-1	-0.5
1987	Tex-A	0	0	—	6	0	0	0	0	9²	12	2	5	5	15.8	4.66	96	.293	.370	0	—	0	-0	-0	0	0.0
Total	4	5	14	.263	55	24	1	0	0	202²	244	34	88	80	14.9	5.60	74	.300	.372	0	—	0	-33	-33	-1	-3.1

■ BOB CREMINS   Cremins, Robert Anthony "Lefty" or "Crooked Arm"   b: 2/15/06, Pelham Manor, N.Y.   BL/TL, 5'11", 178 lbs.   Deb: 8/17/27

| 1927 | Bos-A | 0 | 0 | — | 4 | 0 | 0 | 0 | 0 | 5¹ | 5 | 0 | 3 | 0 | 13.5 | 5.06 | 83 | .250 | .348 | | | 0 | -1 | -0 | 0 | 0.0 |

■ WALKER CRESS   Cress, Walker James "Foots"   b: 3/6/17, Ben Hur, Va.   BR/TR, 6'5", 205 lbs.   Deb: 4/27/48

1948	Cin-N	0	1	.000	30	2	1	0	0	60	60	2	42	33	15.5	4.50	87	.271	.390	4	.500	2	-4	-4	-1	-0.2
1949	Cin-N	0	0	—	3	0	0	0	0	2	2	0	3	0	22.5	0.00	—	.286	.500	0	—	0	1	1	-0	0.1
Total	2	0	1	.000	33	2	1	0	0	62	62	2	45	33	15.7	4.35	90	.272	.394	4	.500	2	-3	-3	-1	-0.1

■ TIM CREWS   Crews, Stanley Timothy   b: 4/3/61, Tampa, Fla.   BR/TR, 6' ", 180 lbs.   Deb: 7/27/87

1987	LA-N	1	1	.500	20	0	0	0	3	29	30	2	8	20	12.4	2.48	160	.268	.328	0	.000	-0	5	5	0	0.5
1988	LA-N	4	0	1.000	42	0	0	0	0	71²	77	3	16	45	11.7	3.14	106	.278	.317	1	.200	0	2	2	-1	0.0
1989	LA-N	0	1	.000	44	0	0	0	1	61²	69	7	23	56	13.7	3.21	106	.284	.351	0	—	0	2	1	-0	0.1
1990	LA-N	4	5	.444	66	2	0	0	5	107¹	98	9	24	76	10.3	2.77	129	.238	.282	0	.000	-1	12	10	-1	0.8
Total	4	9	7	.563	172	2	0	0	9	269²	274	21	71	197	11.7	2.94	120	.263	.313	1	.071	-1	22	17	-3	1.4

■ JERRY CRIDER   Crider, Jerry Stephen   b: 9/2/41, Sioux Falls, S.D.   BR/TR, 6'2", 200 lbs.   Deb: 5/21/69

1969	Min-A	1	0	1.000	21	1	0	0	1	28²	31	3	15	16	15.1	4.71	78	.284	.381	4	.444	2	-3	-3	0	0.0
1970	Chi-A	4	7	.364	32	8	0	0	4	91	101	13	34	40	13.5	4.45	88	.288	.354	2	.083	-1	-7	-6	-2	-0.8
Total	2	5	7	.417	53	9	0	0	5	119²	132	16	49	56	13.9	4.51	85	.287	.361	6	.182	1	-11	-9	-2	-0.8

■ CHUCK CRIM   Crim, Charles Robert   b: 7/23/61, Van Nuys, Cal.   BR/TR, 6' ", 175 lbs.   Deb: 4/08/87

1987	Mil-A	6	8	.429	53	5	0	0	12	130	133	15	39	56	12.1	3.67	125	.266	.323	0	—	0	11	13	0	1.3
1988	Mil-A	7	6	.538	70	0	0	0	9	105	95	11	28	58	10.7	2.91	136	.247	.302	0	—	0	12	12	0	1.3
1989	Mil-A	9	7	.563	76	0	0	0	7	117²	114	7	36	59	11.6	2.83	136	.259	.318	0	—	0	14	13	-1	1.3
1990	Mil-A	3	5	.375	67	0	0	0	11	85²	88	7	23	39	11.9	3.47	109	.261	.312	0	—	0	4	3	1	0.4
Total	4	25	26	.490	266	5	0	0	39	438¹	430	40	126	212	11.6	3.22	126	.259	.315	0	—	0	42	41	0	4.3

■ JACK CRIMIAN   Crimian, John Melvin   b: 2/17/26, Philadelphia, Pa.   BR/TR, 5'10", 180 lbs.   Deb: 7/03/51

1951	StL-N	1	0	1.000	11	0	0	0	1	17	24	3	8	5	16.9	9.00	44	.338	.405	1	.333	0	-10	-10	-0	-0.8
1952	StL-N	0	0	—	5	0	0	0	0	8¹	15	4	4	4	20.5	9.72	38	.417	.475	0	.000	0	-6	-6	0	-0.4
1956	KC-A	4	8	.333	54	7	0	0	3	129	129	19	49	59	12.8	5.51	79	.265	.339	5	.227	1	-19	-17	-0	-1.5
1957	Det-A	0	1	.000	4	0	0	0	0	5²	9	1	4	1	20.6	12.71	30	.375	.464	0	—	0	-6	-6	0	-0.4
Total	4	5	9	.357	74	7	0	0	4	160	177	27	65	69	13.9	6.36	67	.287	.360	6	.231	1	-40	-38	-1	-3.1

■ DODE CRISS   Criss, Dode   b: 3/12/1885, Sherman, Miss.   d: 9/8/55, Sherman, Miss.   BL/TR, 6'2", 200 lbs.   Deb: 4/20/08 ♦

1908	StL-A	0	1	.000	9	1	0	0	0	18	15	1	13	9	15.5	6.50	37	.250	.408	28	.341	1	-8	-8	-1	-0.8
1909	StL-A	1	5	.167	11	6	3	0	0	55¹	53	0	32	43	14.2	3.42	71	.262	.369	14	.292	5	-6	-6	-1	-0.6
1910	StL-A	2	1	.667	6	0	0	0	0	19¹	12	0	9	9	11.6	1.40	177	.176	.309	21	.231	1	2	2	0	0.3
1911	StL-A	0	2	.000	4	2	0	0	0	18¹	24	0	10	9	17.7	8.35	40	.333	.429	21	.253	1	-10	-10	0	-0.8
Total	4	3	9	.250	30	9	3	0	0	111	104	1	64	70	14.5	4.38	59	.259	.375	84	.276	8	-22	-22	-2	-1.9

■ BILL CRISTALL   Cristall, William Arthur "Lefty"   b: 9/12/1878, Odessa, Russia   d: 1/28/39, Buffalo, N.Y.   BL/TL, 5'7", 145 lbs.   Deb: 9/03/01

| 1901 | Cle-A | 1 | 5 | .167 | 6 | 6 | 5 | 1 | 0 | 48¹ | 54 | 1 | 30 | 12 | 15.6 | 4.84 | 73 | .279 | .376 | 7 | .350 | 2 | -6 | -7 | 2 | -0.2 |

■ LEO CRISTANTE   Cristante, Dante Leo   b: 12/10/26, Detroit, Mich.   d: 8/24/77, Dearborn, Mich.   BR/TR, 6'1", 195 lbs.   Deb: 4/21/51

1951	Phi-N	1	1	.500	10	1	0	0	0	22	28	3	9	6	15.5	4.91	78	.318	.388	1	.167	-0	-2	-3	0	-0.2
1955	Det-A	0	1	.000	20	1	0	0	0	36²	37	1	14	9	12.5	3.19	120	.261	.327	0	.000	-1	3	3	-1	0.0
Total	2	1	2	.333	30	2	0	0	0	58²	65	4	23	15	13.7	3.84	100	.283	.350	1	.077	-1	1	0	-1	-0.2

■ MORRIE CRITCHLEY   Critchley, Morris Arthur   b: 3/26/1850, New London, Conn.   d: 3/6/10, Pittsburgh, Pa.   6'1", 190 lbs.   Deb: 5/08/1882

1882	Pit-a	1	0	1.000	1	1	1	1	0	9	7	0	1	3	8.0	0.00	—	.200	.222	0	—	-1	3	3	0	0.2
	StL-a	0	4	.000	4	4	4	0	0	34	43	3	7	2	13.2	4.24	66	.289	.321	3	.214	-0	-6	-5	-1	-0.5
	Yr	1	4	.200	5	5	5	1	0	43	50	3	8	5	12.1	3.35	83	.272	.303	0	.000	-1	-3	-3	-1	-0.3

■ CLAUDE CROCKER   Crocker, Claude Arthur   b: 7/20/24, Caroleen, N.C.   BR/TR, 6'2", 185 lbs.   Deb: 8/01/44

1944	Bro-N	0	0	—	2	0	0	0	0	3¹	6	0	5	1	29.7	10.80	33	.400	.550	1	1.000	0	-3	-3	0	-0.1
1945	Bro-N	0	0	—	1	0	0	0	1	2	2	0	1	1	13.5	0.00	—	.286	.375	0	—	0	1	1	0	0.1
Total	2	0	0	—	3	0	0	0	1	5¹	8	0	6	2	23.6	6.75	54	.364	.500	1	1.000	0	-2	-2	0	0.0

■ RAY CRONE   Crone, Raymond Hayes   b: 8/7/31, Memphis, Tenn.   BR/TR, 6'2", 165 lbs.   Deb: 4/13/54

1954	Mil-N	1	0	1.000	19	2	1	0	1	49	44	6	19	33	11.8	2.02	184	.247	.323	2	.200	-0	11	9	-0	0.9
1955	Mil-N	10	9	.526	33	15	6	1	0	140¹	117	11	42	76	10.2	3.46	108	.227	.285	7	.159	-1	9	5	0	0.3
1956	Mil-N	11	10	.524	35	21	6	0	2	169²	173	19	44	73	11.6	3.87	89	.263	.311	6	.122	-1	-2	-8	-1	-0.7
1957	Mil-N	3	1	.750	11	5	2	0	0	42¹	54	4	15	15	14.7	4.46	78	.312	.367	2	.182	1	-3	-5	1	-0.2
	NY-N	4	8	.333	25	17	2	0	1	120²	131	11	40	56	13.0	4.33	91	.272	.331	1	.025	-4	-6	-5	3	-0.5
	Yr	7	9	.438	36	22	4	0	1	163	185	19	55	71	13.4	4.36	88	.282	.340	5	.098	-3	-9	-10	3	-0.7

YEAR	TM/L	W	L	PCT	G	GS	CG	SH	SV	IP	H	HR	BB	SO	RAT	ERA	ERA+	OAV	OOB	BH	AVG	PB	PR	/A	PD	TPI
1958	SF-N	1	2	.333	14	1	0	0	0	24	35	5	13	7	18.0	6.75	56	.354	.429	0	.000	-0	-7	-8	0	-0.7
Total	5	30	30	.500	137	61	17	1	4	546	554	60	173	260	12.1	3.87	95	.263	.321	18	.115	-3	2	-12	2	-0.9

■ JACK CRONIN   Cronin, John J. b: 5/26/1874, W.New Brighton, S.I., N.Y. d: 7/12/29, Middletown, N.Y.   BR/TR, 6' ", 200 lbs.   Deb: 8/24/1895

YEAR	TM/L	W	L	PCT	G	GS	CG	SH	SV	IP	H	HR	BB	SO	RAT	ERA	ERA+	OAV	OOB	BH	AVG	PB	PR	/A	PD	TPI
1895	Bro-N	0	0	—	2	0	0	0	2	5	10	0	3	1	23.4	10.80	41	.408	.473	1	.500	1	-3	-4	-0	-0.1
1898	Pit-N	2	2	.500	4	4	2	1	0	28	35	0	8	9	13.8	3.54	101	.304	.349	1	.100	-0	0	0	0	0.0
1899	Cin-N	2	2	.500	5	5	5	0	0	41	56	2	16	9	15.8	5.49	71	.324	.382	2	.118	-1	-7	-7	-1	-0.7
1901	Det-A	13	15	.464	30	28	21	1	0	219¹	261	6	42	62	12.4	3.89	99	.292	.323	21	.247	2	-6	-1	-3	0.0
1902	Det-A	0	0	—	4	0	0	0	0	17¹	26	1	8	5	17.7	9.35	39	.346	.409	0	.000	-1	-11	-11	0	-0.9
	Bal-A	3	5	.375	10	8	8	0	0	75²	66	1	24	20	10.7	2.62	144	.235	.296	4	.148	-2	8	10	2	1.1
	Yr	3	5	.375	14	8	8	0	0	93	92	2	32	25	12.0	3.87	97	.259	.320	0	.000	-3	-3	-1	3	0.2
	NY-N	5	6	.455	13	12	11	0	0	114	105	3	18	52	9.7	2.45	115	.245	.275	11	.169	-1	4	5	0	0.3
1903	NY-N	6	4	.600	20	11	8	0	1	115²	130	5	37	50	13.5	3.81	88	.284	.345	9	.196	-0	-7	-6	-0	-0.5
1904	Bro-N	12	23	.343	40	34	33	4	0	307	284	10	79	110	11.0	2.70	102	.245	.300	17	.157	-3	1	2	0	0.0
Total	7	43	57	.430	128	102	88	6	3	923¹	973	28	235	318	12.0	3.40	96	.270	.317	66	.180	-5	-20	-13	-0	-0.8

■ GEORGE CROSBY   Crosby, George W. b: 1860, Iowa   d: 1/9/13, San Francisco, Cal.   Deb: 5/22/1884

YEAR	TM/L	W	L	PCT	G	GS	CG	SH	SV	IP	H	HR	BB	SO	RAT	ERA	ERA+	OAV	OOB	BH	AVG	PB	PR	/A	PD	TPI
1884	Chi-N	1	2	.333	3	3	3	0	0	28	27	3	12	11	12.5	3.54	89	.240	.313	4	.308	1	-2	-1	1	0.1

■ KEN CROSBY   Crosby, Kenneth Stewart b: 12/15/47, New Denver, B.C., Canada BR/TR, 6'2", 179 lbs. Deb: 8/05/75

YEAR	TM/L	W	L	PCT	G	GS	CG	SH	SV	IP	H	HR	BB	SO	RAT	ERA	ERA+	OAV	OOB	BH	AVG	PB	PR	/A	PD	TPI
1975	Chi-N	1	0	1.000	9	0	0	0	0	8¹	10	0	7	6	18.4	3.24	119	.294	.415	0	—	0	0	1	0	0.1
1976	Chi-N	0	0	—	7	1	0	0	0	12	20	3	8	5	21.0	12.00	32	.377	.459	1	.500	0	-11	-11	0	-0.9
Total	2	1	0	1.000	16	1	0	0	0	20¹	30	3	15	11	19.9	8.41	46	.345	.441	1	.500	1	-11	-10	0	-0.8

■ LEM CROSS   Cross, George Lewis b: 1/9/1872, Sanbornton, N.H. d: 10/9/30, Manchester, N.H. 5'9", 155 lbs. Deb: 8/06/1893

YEAR	TM/L	W	L	PCT	G	GS	CG	SH	SV	IP	H	HR	BB	SO	RAT	ERA	ERA+	OAV	OOB	BH	AVG	PB	PR	/A	PD	TPI
1893	Cin-N	0	2	.000	3	3	2	0	0	21	24	3	9	7	14.1	5.57	86	.279	.347	2	.333	1	-2	-2	0	0.0
1894	Cin-N	3	4	.429	8	7	3	0	0	53	94	8	21	11	19.5	8.49	65	.381	.430	6	.231	-1	-19	-17	-1	-1.2
Total	2	3	6	.333	11	10	5	0	0	74	118	11	30	18	18.0	7.66	70	.355	.408	8	.250	-0	-21	-19	-0	-1.2

■ DOUG CROTHERS   Crothers, Douglas b: 11/16/1859, Natchez, Miss. d: 3/29/07, St.Louis, Mo. BR/TR, Deb: 8/03/1884

YEAR	TM/L	W	L	PCT	G	GS	CG	SH	SV	IP	H	HR	BB	SO	RAT	ERA	ERA+	OAV	OOB	BH	AVG	PB	PR	/A	PD	TPI
1884	KC-U	1	2	.333	3	3	3	0	0	25	26	0	6	11	11.5	1.80	153	.251	.291	2	.133	-1	3	3	-0	0.1
1885	NY-a	7	11	.389	18	18	18	1	0	154	192	4	49	40	14.1	5.08	58	.293	.342	8	.157	0	-31	-36	1	-2.9
Total	2	8	13	.381	21	21	21	1	0	179	218	4	55	51	13.7	4.63	63	.287	.335	10	.152	-1	-28	-34	0	-2.8

■ BILL CROUCH   Crouch, Wilmer Elmer b: 8/20/10, Wilmington, Del. d: 12/26/80, Howell, Mich. BB/TR, 6'1", 180 lbs. Deb: 5/09/39

YEAR	TM/L	W	L	PCT	G	GS	CG	SH	SV	IP	H	HR	BB	SO	RAT	ERA	ERA+	OAV	OOB	BH	AVG	PB	PR	/A	PD	TPI
1939	Bro-N	4	0	1.000	6	3	3	0	0	38¹	37	3	14	10	12.0	2.58	156	.255	.321	2	.133	-1	6	6	-1	0.5
1941	Phi-N	2	3	.400	20	5	1	0	0	59	65	4	17	26	12.5	4.42	84	.286	.336	1	.091	-0	-5	-5	2	-0.3
	StL-N	1	2	.333	18	4	0	0	6	45	45	2	14	15	11.8	3.00	125	.271	.328	0	.000	-1	3	4	-1	0.2
	Yr	3	5	.375	38	9	1	0	7	104	110	6	31	41	12.2	3.81	98	.280	.333	3	.125	-2	-2	-1	1	-0.1
1945	StL-N	1	0	1.000	6	0	0	0	0	13¹	12	1	7	4	13.5	3.38	111	.255	.364	0	.000	-0	1	1	0	0.0
Total	3	8	5	.615	50	12	4	0	7	155²	159	10	52	55	12.3	3.47	110	.272	.332	3	.073	-3	4	6	1	0.4

■ BILL CROUCH   Crouch, William Henry "Skip" b: 12/3/1886, Marshallton, Del. d: 12/22/45, Highland Park, Mich. BL/TL, 6'1", 210 lbs. Deb: 7/12/10

YEAR	TM/L	W	L	PCT	G	GS	CG	SH	SV	IP	H	HR	BB	SO	RAT	ERA	ERA+	OAV	OOB	BH	AVG	PB	PR	/A	PD	TPI
1910	StL-A	0	0	—	1	1	1	0	0	8	6	0	7	2	14.6	3.38	73	.231	.394	0	.000	-0	-1	-1	-0	0.0

■ ZACH CROUCH   Crouch, Zachary Quinn b: 10/26/65, Folsom, Cal. BL/TL, 6'3", 180 lbs. Deb: 6/04/88

YEAR	TM/L	W	L	PCT	G	GS	CG	SH	SV	IP	H	HR	BB	SO	RAT	ERA	ERA+	OAV	OOB	BH	AVG	PB	PR	/A	PD	TPI
1988	Bos-A	0	0	—	3	0	0	0	0	1¹	4	0	2	0	40.5	6.75	61	.571	.667	0	—	0	-0	-0	0	0.0

■ GENERAL CROWDER   Crowder, Alvin Floyd b: 1/11/1899, Winston-Salem, N.C d: 4/3/72, Winston-Salem, N.C. BL/TR, 5'10", 170 lbs. Deb: 7/24/26

YEAR	TM/L	W	L	PCT	G	GS	CG	SH	SV	IP	H	HR	BB	SO	RAT	ERA	ERA+	OAV	OOB	BH	AVG	PB	PR	/A	PD	TPI
1926	Was-A	7	4	.636	19	12	6	0	1	100	97	3	60	26	14.3	3.96	98	.261	.367	9	.237	1	1	-1	1	0.1
1927	Was-A	4	7	.364	15	11	4	2	0	67¹	58	3	42	22	13.6	4.54	89	.232	.347	3	.136	-1	-3	-4	-1	-0.4
	StL-A	3	5	.375	21	8	2	1	3	73²	71	3	42	30	13.9	5.01	87	.260	.361	6	.261	0	-7	-5	-1	-0.5
	Yr	7	12	.368	36	19	6	3	3	141	129	6	84	52	13.7	4.79	88	.246	.351	1	.022	-1	-10	-9	-2	-0.9
1928	StL-A	21	5	.808	41	31	19	1	2	244	238	11	91	99	12.2	3.69	114	.258	.325	15	.188	-2	10	14	-5	0.7
1929	StL-A	17	15	.531	40	34	19	4	4	266²	272	22	93	79	12.3	3.92	113	.271	.332	18	.188	-3	10	15	-2	1.0
1930	StL-A	3	7	.300	13	10	5	1	0	77¹	85	11	27	42	13.2	4.66	105	.283	.345	4	.160	-2	-0	2	1	0.1
	Was-A	15	9	.625	27	25	20	0	1	202¹	191	6	69	64	11.6	3.60	128	.249	.312	13	.171	-2	24	22	-3	1.5
	Yr	18	16	.529	40	35	25	1	2	279²	276	17	96	107	12.0	3.89	120	.259	.320	5	.050	-4	23	24	-3	1.6
1931	Was-A	18	11	.621	44	26	13	1	2	234¹	255	13	72	85	12.6	3.88	111	.275	.328	19	.216	-1	13	11	-3	0.6
1932	Was-A	26	13	.667	50	39	21	3	1	327	319	17	77	103	10.9	3.33	130	.252	.295	27	.221	2	42	36	-2	3.2
1933	*Was-A	24	15	.615	52	35	17	0	4	299¹	311	14	81	110	11.9	3.97	105	.267	.316	19	.186	1	10	7	-4	0.0
1934	Was-A	4	10	.286	29	13	4	0	3	100²	142	9	38	39	16.1	6.79	64	.326	.380	7	.219	1	-26	-28	-1	-2.4
	*Det-A	5	1	.833	9	9	3	1	0	66²	81	3	20	30	13.6	4.18	105	.295	.342	4	.133	-2	2	2	-1	0.0
	Yr	9	11	.450	38	22	7	1	3	167¹	223	12	58	69	15.1	5.75	76	.314	.365	2	.032	-1	-23	-26	-2	-2.4
1935	*Det-A	16	10	.615	33	32	16	2	0	241	269	16	67	59	12.7	4.26	98	.285	.335	17	.183	-2	5	-2	-2	-0.6
1936	Det-A	4	3	.571	9	7	1	0	0	44	64	5	21	10	17.4	8.39	59	.342	.409	3	.150	-1	-16	-17	0	-1.3
Total	11	167	115	.592	402	292	150	16	22	2344¹	2453	136	800	799	12.5	4.12	105	.270	.330	164	.194	-12	64	52	-23	2.4

■ CAP CROWELL   Crowell, Minot Joy b: 9/5/1892, Roxbury, Mass. d: 9/30/62, Central Falls, R.I. BR/TR, 6'1", 178 lbs. Deb: 6/23/15

YEAR	TM/L	W	L	PCT	G	GS	CG	SH	SV	IP	H	HR	BB	SO	RAT	ERA	ERA+	OAV	OOB	BH	AVG	PB	PR	/A	PD	TPI
1915	Phi-A	2	6	.250	10	8	4	0	0	54¹	56	1	47	15	17.9	5.47	54	.292	.443	5	.227	-0	-15	-15	-0	-1.4
1916	Phi-A	0	5	.000	9	6	1	0	0	39²	43	0	34	15	17.9	4.99	58	.289	.427	0	.000	-2	-10	-9	-1	-1.1
Total	2	2	11	.154	19	14	5	0	0	94	99	1	81	30	17.9	5.27	55	.290	.436	5	.147	-2	-25	-25	-1	-2.5

■ BILLY CROWELL   Crowell, William Theodore b: 11/6/1865, Cincinnati, Ohio d: 7/24/35, Ft.Worth, Tex. BR/TR, 5'8.5", 160 lbs. Deb: 4/20/1887

YEAR	TM/L	W	L	PCT	G	GS	CG	SH	SV	IP	H	HR	BB	SO	RAT	ERA	ERA+	OAV	OOB	BH	AVG	PB	PR	/A	PD	TPI
1887	Cle-a	14	31	.311	45	45	45	1	0	389¹	541	9	138	72	15.7	4.88	89	.318	.369	22	.141	-13	-25	-22	-2	-2.8
1888	Cle-a	5	13	.278	18	18	16	0	0	150²	212	8	61	61	16.3	5.79	54	.320	.378	5	.086	-5	-46	-45	-0	-4.0
	Lou-a	0	1	.000	1	1	1	0	0	9	12	1	6	5	18.0	6.00	51	.309	.401	0	.000	-0	-3	-3	0	-0.1
	Yr	5	14	.263	19	19	17	0	0	159²	224	9	67	66	16.4	5.81	54	.320	.379	4	.066	-5	-49	-48	-0	-4.1
Total	2	19	45	.297	64	64	62	1	0	549	765	18	205	138	15.9	5.15	78	.318	.372	27	.124	-18	-74	-70	-3	-6.9

■ WOODY CROWSON   Crowson, Thomas Woodrow b: 9/9/18, Fuquay Sprgs., N.C d: 8/14/47, Mayodan, N.C. BR/TR, 6'2", 185 lbs. Deb: 4/17/45

YEAR	TM/L	W	L	PCT	G	GS	CG	SH	SV	IP	H	HR	BB	SO	RAT	ERA	ERA+	OAV	OOB	BH	AVG	PB	PR	/A	PD	TPI
1945	Phi-A	0	0	—	1	0	0	0	0	3	2	0	3	2	15.0	6.00	57	.200	.385	0	.000	-0	-1	-1	0	0.0

■ CAL CRUM   Crum, Calvin N. b: 7/27/1890, Cooks Mills, Ill. d: 12/7/45, Tulsa, Okla. Deb: 4/17/17

YEAR	TM/L	W	L	PCT	G	GS	CG	SH	SV	IP	H	HR	BB	SO	RAT	ERA	ERA+	OAV	OOB	BH	AVG	PB	PR	/A	PD	TPI
1917	Bos-N	0	0	—	1	0	0	0	0	1	1	0	1	0	18.0	0.00	—	.250	.400	0	—	0	0	0	0	0.1
1918	Bos-N	0	1	.000	1	1	0	0	0	2¹	6	0	3	0	38.6	15.43	17	.600	.714	0	.000	-0	-3	-3	0	-0.2
Total	2	0	1	.000	2	1	0	0	0	3¹	7	0	4	0	32.4	10.80	24	.500	.632	0	.000	-0	-3	-3	1	-0.1

■ ROY CRUMPLER   Crumpler, Roy Maxton b: 7/8/1896, Clinton, N.C. d: 10/6/69, Fayetteville, N.C. BL/TL, 6'1", 195 lbs. Deb: 9/16/20

YEAR	TM/L	W	L	PCT	G	GS	CG	SH	SV	IP	H	HR	BB	SO	RAT	ERA	ERA+	OAV	OOB	BH	AVG	PB	PR	/A	PD	TPI
1920	Det-A	1	0	1.000	2	2	1	0	0	13	17	2	11	2	20.1	5.54	67	.315	.439	3	.333	1	-3	-3	-0	-0.1
1925	Phi-N	0	0	—	3	1	0	0	0	4²	8	0	2	1	19.3	7.71	62	.381	.435	0	.000	-0	-2	-2	0	0.0
Total	2	1	0	1.000	5	3	1	0	0	17²	25	2	13	3	19.9	6.11	65	.333	.438	3	.273	1	-4	-4	0	-0.1

■ DICK CRUTCHER   Crutcher, Richard Louis b: 11/25/1889, Frankfort, Ky. d: 6/19/52, Frankfort, Ky. BR/TR, 5'9", 148 lbs. Deb: 4/14/14

YEAR	TM/L	W	L	PCT	G	GS	CG	SH	SV	IP	H	HR	BB	SO	RAT	ERA	ERA+	OAV	OOB	BH	AVG	PB	PR	/A	PD	TPI
1914	Bos-N	5	7	.417	33	15	5	1	0	158²	169	4	66	48	13.7	3.46	80	.293	.371	8	.148	-1	-12	-12	1	-1.2
1915	Bos-N	2	2	.500	14	4	1	0	2	43²	50	1	16	17	14.0	4.33	60	.309	.378	3	.231	1	-8	-8	1	-0.7

YEAR	TM/L	W	L	PCT	G	GS	CG	SH	SV	IP	H	HR	BB	SO	RAT	ERA	ERA+	OAV	OOB	BH	AVG	PB	PR	/A	PD	TPI
Total	2	7	9	.438	47	19	6	1	2	202¹	219	5	82	65	13.7	3.65	75	.296	.373	11	.164	-0	-19	-21	2	-1.9

■ TODD CRUZ   Cruz, Todd Ruben b: 11/23/55, Highland Park, Mich BR/TR, 6', 175 lbs. Deb: 9/04/78 ♦

| 1984 | Bal-A | 0 | 0 | — | 1 | 0 | 0 | 0 | 0 | 1 | 0 | 0 | 0 | 0 | 0.0 | 0.00 | — | .000 | .000 | 31 | .218 | 0 | 0 | 0 | 0 | 0.0 |

■ VICTOR CRUZ   Cruz, Victor Manuel (b: b: 12/24/57, Rancho Viejo La Vega, D.R. BR/TR, 5'9", 174 lbs. Deb: 6/24/78

1978	Tor-A	7	3	.700	32	0	0	0	9	47¹	28	0	35	51	12.2	1.71	229	.179	.333	0	—	0	11	12	-1	1.2
1979	Cle-A	3	9	.250	61	0	0	0	10	78²	70	10	44	63	13.2	4.23	100	.244	.346	0	—	0	-0	0	-2	-0.1
1980	Cle-A	6	7	.462	55	0	0	0	12	86	71	10	27	88	10.6	3.45	118	.229	.297	0	—	0	6	6	-2	0.4
1981	Pit-N	1	1	.500	22	0	0	0	1	34	33	6	15	28	13.0	2.65	136	.264	.348	0	.000	-0	3	4	0	0.3
1983	Tex-A	1	3	.250	17	0	0	0	5	25	16	2	10	18	9.7	1.44	278	.184	.276	0	—	0	7	7	-0	0.7
Total	5	18	23	.439	187	0	0	0	37	271	218	28	131	248	11.8	3.09	131	.226	.323	0	.000	-0	27	28	-5	2.5

■ COOKIE CUCCURULLO   Cuccurullo, Arthur Joseph b: 2/8/18, Asbury Park, N.J. d: 1/23/83, W.Orange, N.J. BL/LL, 5'10", 168 lbs. Deb: 10/03/43

1943	Pit-N	0	1	.000	1	1	0	0	0	7	10	0	3	3	16.7	6.43	54	.357	.419	0	—	1	-2	-2	0	0.0
1944	Pit-N	2	1	.667	32	4	0	0	4	106¹	110	5	44	31	13.3	4.06	91	.270	.346	14	.368	5	-5	-4	1	0.2
1945	Pit-N	1	3	.250	29	4	0	0	1	56²	68	2	34	17	16.4	5.24	75	.305	.399	3	.214	-0	-9	-8	0	-0.7
Total	3	3	5	.375	62	9	0	0	5	170	188	7	81	51	14.5	4.55	83	.286	.367	17	.327	5	-17	-15	1	-0.5

■ JIM CUDWORTH   Cudworth, James Alaric "Cuddy" b: 8/22/1858, Fairhaven, Mass. d: 12/21/43, Middleboro, Mass. BR/TR, 6', 165 lbs. Deb: 7/27/1884 ♦

| 1884 | KC-U | 0 | 0 | — | 2 | 1 | 1 | 0 | 0 | 17 | 19 | 1 | 3 | 6 | 11.6 | 4.24 | 65 | .264 | .294 | 17 | .147 | -0 | -2 | -3 | -0 | -0.1 |

■ CHARLIE CUELLAR   Cuellar, Jesus Patracis b: 9/24/17, Ybor City, Fla. BR/TR, 5'11", 183 lbs. Deb: 7/02/50

| 1950 | Chi-A | 0 | 0 | — | 2 | 0 | 0 | 0 | 0 | 1¹ | 6 | 0 | 3 | 1 | 60.8 | 33.75 | 13 | .600 | .692 | 0 | — | 0 | -4 | -4 | 0 | -0.3 |

■ MIKE CUELLAR   Cuellar, Miguel Angel (Santana) b: 5/8/37, Las Villas, Cuba BL/TL, 6', 165 lbs. Deb: 4/18/59

1959	Cin-N	0	0	—	2	0	0	0	0	4	7	1	4	5	24.8	15.75	26	.368	.478	0	.000	-0	-5	-5	-0	-0.4
1964	StL-N	5	5	.500	32	7	1	0	4	72	80	8	33	56	14.3	4.50	85	.288	.365	0	.000	-2	-8	-6	1	-0.6
1965	Hou-N	1	4	.200	25	4	0	0	2	56	55	3	21	46	12.4	3.54	95	.262	.332	0	.000	-1	0	-1	0	-0.1
1966	Hou-N	12	10	.545	38	28	11	1	2	227¹	193	10	52	175	9.7	2.22	154	.229	.274	8	.113	-1	35	30	0	3.1
1967	Hou-N	16	11	.593	36	32	16	3	1	246¹	233	16	63	203	10.9	3.03	109	.248	.296	13	.140	-1	9	8	-1	0.8
1968	Hou-N	8	11	.421	28	24	11	2	1	170²	152	8	45	133	10.4	2.74	108	.237	.289	11	.193	2	5	4	-1	0.7
1969	*Bal-A	23	11	.676	39	39	18	5	0	290²	213	18	79	182	9.1	2.38	149	.204	**.261**	12	.117	-3	**40**	38	-0	**3.9**
1970	*Bal-A	**24**	8	**.750**	40	40	21	4	0	297²	273	34	69	190	10.4	3.48	105	.242	.286	10	.089	-4	8	6	-3	-0.1
1971	*Bal-A	20	9	.690	38	38	21	4	0	292¹	250	30	78	124	10.1	3.08	109	.234	.287	11	.103	-3	12	9	1	0.7
1972	Bal-A	18	12	.600	35	35	17	4	0	248¹	197	21	71	132	9.7	2.57	119	.220	.277	11	.126	-1	13	14	1	1.5
1973	*Bal-A	18	13	.581	38	38	17	2	0	267	265	29	84	140	11.8	3.27	114	.258	.314	0	—	0	16	14	0	1.5
1974	*Bal-A	22	10	**.688**	38	38	20	5	0	269¹	253	17	86	106	11.4	3.11	111	.252	.312	0	—	0	15	10	-2	0.9
1975	Bal-A	14	12	.538	36	36	17	5	0	256	229	17	84	105	11.0	3.66	96	.249	.313	0	—	0	3	-4	2	-0.1
1976	Bal-A	4	13	.235	26	19	2	1	1	107	129	8	50	32	15.2	4.96	66	.307	.383	0	—	0	-17	-20	-0	-1.9
1977	Cal-A	0	1	.000	2	1	0	0	0	3¹	9	2	3	3	32.4	18.90	21	.500	.571	0	—	0	-5	-6	-0	-0.4
Total	15	185	130	.587	453	379	172	36	11	2808	2538	222	822	1632	10.8	3.14	109	.243	.299	76	.115	-13	122	92	-1	9.5

■ BOBBY CUELLAR   Cuellar, Robert b: 8/20/52, Alice, Tex. BR/TR, 5'11", 188 lbs. Deb: 9/09/77

| 1977 | Tex-A | 0 | 0 | — | 4 | 0 | 0 | 0 | 0 | 6² | 4 | 1 | 2 | 3 | 8.1 | 1.35 | 302 | .182 | .250 | 0 | — | 0 | 2 | 2 | -0 | 0.2 |

■ BERT CUETO   Cueto, Dagoberto (Concepcion) b: 8/14/37, San Luis, Pinar, Cuba BR/TR, 6'4", 170 lbs. Deb: 6/18/61

| 1961 | Min-A | 1 | 3 | .250 | 7 | 5 | 0 | 0 | 0 | 21¹ | 27 | 7 | 10 | 5 | 16.0 | 7.17 | 59 | .300 | .376 | 0 | .000 | -0 | -7 | -7 | 0 | -0.6 |

■ JACK CULLEN   Cullen, John Patrick b: 10/6/39, Newark, N.J. BR/TR, 5'11", 170 lbs. Deb: 9/09/62

1962	NY-A	0	0	—	2	0	0	0	1	3	2	0	2	2	12.0	0.00	—	.182	.308	0	—	0	1	1	0	0.1
1965	NY-A	3	4	.429	12	9	2	1	0	59	59	2	21	25	12.2	3.05	112	.262	.325	3	.150	-0	3	2	1	0.3
1966	NY-A	1	0	1.000	5	0	0	0	0	11¹	11	0	5	7	12.7	3.97	84	.256	.333	0	.000	-0	-1	-1	-0	-0.1
Total	3	4	4	.500	19	9	2	1	1	73¹	72	2	28	34	12.3	3.07	111	.258	.326	3	.130	-1	3	3	1	0.3

■ NICK CULLOP   Cullop, Henry Nicholas "Tomato Face" b: 10/16/1900, St.Louis, Mo. d: 12/8/78, Westerville, Ohio BR/TR, 6', 200 lbs. Deb: 4/14/26 ♦

| 1927 | Cle-A | 0 | 0 | — | 1 | 0 | 0 | 0 | 0 | 1 | 3 | 0 | 0 | 0 | 27.0 | 9.00 | 47 | .600 | .600 | 16 | .235 | -0 | -1 | -1 | 0 | 0.0 |

■ NICK CULLOP   Cullop, Norman Andrew b: 9/17/1887, Chilhowie, Va. d: 4/15/61, Tazewell, Va. BL/TL, 5'11.5", 172 lbs. Deb: 5/20/13

1913	Cle-A	3	7	.300	23	8	4	0	0	97²	105	3	35	30	13.2	4.42	69	.291	.358	4	.129	-1	-16	-15	1	-1.5
1914	Cle-A	0	1	.000	1	0	0	0	0	3¹	4	0	1	3	13.5	2.70	107	.364	.417	0	.000	-0	0	0	-0	0.0
	KC-F	14	19	.424	44	36	22	4	1	295²	256	6	87	149	10.8	2.34	132	.215	.275	14	.141	-3	28	24	0	2.2
1915	KC-F	22	11	.667	44	36	22	3	2	302¹	278	8	67	111	10.5	2.44	120	.249	.297	18	.188	1	20	16	6	2.5
1916	NY-A	13	6	.684	28	22	9	0	1	167	151	4	32	77	10.0	2.05	141	.243	.284	6	.109	-3	14	15	5	0.9
1917	NY-A	5	9	.357	30	18	5	2	1	146¹	161	2	31	27	11.9	3.32	81	.307	.348	7	.159	-1	-11	-10	0	-1.1
1921	StL-A	0	2	.000	4	1	0	0	0	11²	18	1	6	3	18.5	8.49	53	.340	.407	0	.000	-0	-5	-5	-0	-0.4
Total	6	57	55	.509	174	121	62	9	5	1024	973	24	259	400	11.1	2.73	108	.251	.303	49	.149	-8	31	26	3	2.6

■ BUD CULLOTON   Culloton, Bernard Aloysius b: 5/19/1897, Kingston, N.Y. d: 11/9/76, Kingston, N.Y. BR/TR, 5'11", 180 lbs. Deb: 4/16/25

1925	Pit-N	0	1	.000	9	1	0	0	0	21	19	1	1	3	8.6	2.57	173	.241	.250	0	.000	-1	4	4	-0	0.3
1926	Pit-N	0	0	—	4	0	0	0	0	3²	3	0	6	1	22.1	7.36	53	.214	.450	0	—	0	-1	-1	0	0.0
Total	2	0	1	.000	13	1	0	0	0	24²	22	1	7	4	10.6	3.28	133	.237	.290	0	.000	-1	3	3	-0	0.3

■ RAY CULP   Culp, Raymond Leonard b: 8/6/41, Elgin, Tex. BR/TR, 6', 200 lbs. Deb: 4/10/63

1963	Phi-N	14	11	.560	34	34	10	5	0	203¹	148	15	102	176	11.3	2.97	109	.206	.309	9	.136	-0	7	6	-1	0.5
1964	Phi-N	8	7	.533	30	19	3	1	0	135	139	15	56	96	13.3	4.13	84	.263	.340	5	.114	-1	-9	-10	-1	-1.1
1965	Phi-N	14	10	.583	33	30	11	2	0	204¹	188	14	78	134	12.2	3.22	108	.243	.322	6	.088	-2	7	6	-1	0.3
1966	Phi-N	7	4	.636	34	12	1	0	1	110²	106	19	53	100	13.5	5.04	71	.246	.338	2	.077	-2	-18	-18	-1	-2.0
1967	Chi-N	8	11	.421	30	22	4	1	0	152²	138	22	59	111	11.7	3.89	91	.239	.311	5	.098	-1	-9	-6	-1	-0.8
1968	Bos-A	16	6	.727	35	30	11	6	0	216¹	166	18	82	190	10.7	2.91	108	.210	.292	8	.114	-1	2	6	-1	0.4
1969	Bos-A	17	8	.680	32	32	9	2	0	227	195	36	79	172	11.1	3.81	100	.231	.302	12	.152	1	-5	-0	-1	0.0
1970	Bos-A	17	14	.548	33	33	15	1	0	251¹	216	22	91	197	11.2	3.04	130	.224	.300	12	.124	-4	19	26	-2	2.3
1971	Bos-A	14	16	.467	35	35	12	3	0	242¹	236	21	67	151	11.4	3.60	103	.253	.307	8	.118	-2	-4	-2	0	0.0
1972	Bos-A	5	8	.385	16	16	4	1	0	105	104	8	53	52	13.7	4.46	72	.260	.351	7	.212	1	-16	-15	-1	-1.3
1973	Bos-A	2	6	.250	10	9	0	0	0	50¹	46	9	32	32	14.7	4.47	90	.247	.369	0	—	0	-4	-3	0	-0.1
Total	11	122	101	.547	322	268	80	22	1	1898¹	1677	188	752	1411	11.8	3.58	99	.235	.314	74	.123	-11	-29	-5	-9	-1.8

■ BILL CULP   Culp, William Edward b: 6/11/1887, Bellaire, Ohio d: 9/3/69, Arnold, Pa. BB/TR, 6'1.5", 165 lbs. Deb: 9/08/10

| 1910 | Phi-N | 0 | 0 | — | 4 | 0 | 0 | 0 | 1 | 6² | 8 | 0 | 4 | 4 | 16.2 | 8.10 | 39 | .333 | .429 | 0 | .000 | -0 | -4 | -4 | 1 | -0.2 |

■ GEORGE CULVER   Culver, George Raymond b: 7/8/43, Salinas, Cal. BR/TR, 6'2", 185 lbs. Deb: 9/07/66

1966	Cle-A	0	2	.000	5	1	0	0	0	9²	15	1	7	6	21.4	8.38	41	.357	.460	0	.000	-0	-5	-5	0	-0.4
1967	Cle-A	7	3	.700	53	1	0	0	3	75	71	2	31	41	13.0	3.96	82	.258	.346	1	.250	0	-6	-6	1	-0.4
1968	Cin-N	11	16	.407	42	35	5	2	2	226¹	229	8	84	114	13.0	3.22	98	.264	.339	8	.121	-0	-6	-2	3	0.0
1969	Cin-N	5	7	.417	32	13	0	0	4	101¹	117	8	52	58	15.8	4.26	88	.291	.384	3	.097	-2	-8	-6	2	-0.5
1970	StL-N	3	3	.500	11	7	2	0	0	56²	64	6	24	23	14.1	4.61	89	.284	.356	3	.176	0	-4	-3	2	0.0

YEAR	TM/L	W	L	PCT	G	GS	CG	SH	SV	IP	H	HR	BB	SO	RAT	ERA	ERA+	OAV	OOB	BH	AVG	PB	PR	/A	PD	TPI
	Hou-N	3	3	.500	32	0	0	0	3	45	44	1	21	31	13.6	3.20	121	.254	.345	1	.250	0	4	3	-1	0.3
	Yr	6	6	.500	43	7	2	0	3	101²	108	7	45	54	13.8	3.98	101	.270	.348	0	.000	0	1	0	1	0.3
1971	Hou-N	5	8	.385	59	0	0	0	7	95¹	89	4	38	57	12.2	2.64	127	.257	.334	1	.091	-1	9	8	1	0.8
1972	Hou-N	6	2	.750	45	0	0	0	2	97¹	73	7	43	82	11.2	3.05	110	.212	.309	3	.158	-0	4	3	-0	0.4
1973	LA-N	4	4	.500	28	0	0	0	2	42	45	4	21	23	14.4	3.00	115	.292	.381	0	.000	-0	3	2	2	0.3
	Phi-N	3	1	.750	14	0	0	0	0	18²	26	0	15	7	19.8	4.82	79	.342	.451	0	—	0	-2	-2	1	0.0
	Yr	7	5	.583	42	0	0	0	2	60²	71	4	36	30	15.9	3.56	100	.305	.398	0	.000	-0	1	-0	3	0.3
1974	Phi-N	1	0	1.000	14	0	0	0	0	21²	20	1	16	9	15.4	6.65	57	.267	.402	0	.000	-0	-7	-7	-0	-0.7
Total	9	48	49	.495	335	57	7	2	23	789	793	42	352	451	13.6	3.62	96	.266	.352	20	.124	-4	-18	-13	9	-0.2

■ JOHN CUMBERLAND
Cumberland, John Sheldon b: 5/10/47, Westbrook, Me.   BR/TL, 6′, 185 lbs.   Deb: 9/27/68

YEAR	TM/L	W	L	PCT	G	GS	CG	SH	SV	IP	H	HR	BB	SO	RAT	ERA	ERA+	OAV	OOB	BH	AVG	PB	PR	/A	PD	TPI
1968	NY-A	0	0	—	1	0	0	0	0	2	3	1	1	1	18.0	9.00	32	.333	.400	0	—	0	-1	-1	0	0.0
1969	NY-A	0	0	—	2	0	0	0	0	4	3	0	4	0	15.8	4.50	77	.231	.412	0	—	0	-0	-0	0	0.0
1970	NY-A	3	4	.429	15	8	1	0	0	64	62	9	15	38	10.8	3.94	89	.252	.295	1	.059	-1	-2	-3	-1	-0.4
	SF-N	2	0	1.000	7	0	0	0	0	11	6	0	4	6	8.2	0.82	486	.158	.238	0	.000	-0	4	4	0	0.4
1971	*SF-N	9	6	.600	45	21	5	2	2	185	153	22	55	65	10.1	2.92	116	.223	.281	7	.119	-2	11	10	-2	0.6
1972	SF-N	0	4	.000	9	6	0	0	0	25	38	6	7	8	16.2	8.64	40	.336	.375	1	.111	-0	-14	-14	-1	-1.4
	StL-N	1	1	.500	14	1	0	0	0	21²	23	6	7	7	12.5	6.65	51	.291	.349	0	.000	-1	-8	-8	-1	-0.8
	Yr	1	5	.167	23	7	0	0	0	46²	61	12	14	15	14.5	7.71	45	.316	.362	0	.000	-1	-22	-22	-2	-2.2
1974	Cal-A	0	1	.000	17	0	0	0	0	21²	24	2	10	12	14.1	3.74	92	.289	.366	0	—	0	-0	-1	-0	0.0
Total	6	15	16	.484	110	36	6	2	2	334¹	312	46	103	137	11.2	3.82	90	.246	.303	9	.099	-5	-11	-14	-4	-1.6

■ STEVE CUMMINGS
Cummings, Steven Brent b: 7/15/64, Houston, Tex.   BB/TR, 6′2″, 200 lbs.   Deb: 6/24/89

YEAR	TM/L	W	L	PCT	G	GS	CG	SH	SV	IP	H	HR	BB	SO	RAT	ERA	ERA+	OAV	OOB	BH	AVG	PB	PR	/A	PD	TPI
1989	Tor-A	2	0	1.000	5	2	0	0	0	21	18	1	11	8	12.9	3.00	126	.237	.333	0	—	0	2	2	0	0.2
1990	Tor-A	0	0	—	6	2	0	0	0	12¹	22	4	5	4	20.4	5.11	74	.431	.491	0	—	0	-2	-2	0	-0.1
Total	2	2	0	1.000	11	4	0	0	0	33¹	40	5	16	12	15.7	3.78	100	.310	.395	0	—	0	0	-0	0	0.1

■ CANDY CUMMINGS
Cummings, William Arthur b: 10/18/1848, Ware, Mass.   d: 5/16/24, Toledo, Ohio   BR/TR, 5′9″, 120 lbs.   Deb: 4/22/1872   H

YEAR	TM/L	W	L	PCT	G	GS	CG	SH	SV	IP	H	HR	BB	SO	RAT	ERA	ERA+	OAV	OOB	BH	AVG	PB	PR	/A	PD	TPI
1872	Mut-n	33	20	.623	55	55	53	3	0	497	600	2	29		11.4	2.52	137	.270	.279	52	.206	-3	66	51		3.1
1873	Bal-n	28	14	.667	42	42	42	1	0	382	468	4	33		11.8	2.76	130	.271	.284	49	.254	2	36	36		2.7
1874	Phi-n	28	26	.519	54	54	52	3	0	482	602	4	21		11.6	2.88	106	.271	.278	54	.236	-1	7	9		0.6
1875	Har-n	35	12	.745	48	47	46	7	0	417	396	0	6		8.7	1.60	162	.235	.237	44	.199	-5	40	46		3.8
1876	Har-N	16	8	.667	24	24	24	5	0	216	215	0	14	26	9.5	1.67	142	.242	.254	17	.162	-8	15	17	-2	0.7
1877	Cin-N	5	14	.263	19	19	16	0	0	155²	219	2	13	11	13.4	4.34	61	.314	.327	14	.200	-1	-26	-29	-2	-2.3
Total	4 n	124	72	.633	199	198	193	14	0	1778	2066	10	89		10.9	2.45	130	.263	.271	199	.222	-8	148	145		10.2
Total	2	21	22	.488	43	43	40	5	0	371²	434	2	27	37	11.2	2.78	90	.274	.286	31	.177	-8	-11	-12	-1	-1.6

■ BRUCE CUNNINGHAM
Cunningham, Bruce Lee b: 9/29/05, San Francisco, Cal.   d: 3/8/84, Hayward, Cal.   BR/TR, 5′10.5″, 165 lbs.   Deb: 5/07/29

YEAR	TM/L	W	L	PCT	G	GS	CG	SH	SV	IP	H	HR	BB	SO	RAT	ERA	ERA+	OAV	OOB	BH	AVG	PB	PR	/A	PD	TPI
1929	Bos-N	4	6	.400	17	8	4	0	1	91²	100	7	32	22	13.2	4.52	104	.282	.344	4	.148	-0	2	1	2	0.2
1930	Bos-N	5	6	.455	36	6	2	0	0	106²	121	7	41	28	13.7	5.48	90	.289	.352	6	.194	0	-6	-6	3	-0.2
1931	Bos-N	3	12	.200	33	16	6	1	1	136²	157	7	54	32	14.0	4.48	85	.296	.363	3	.071	-4	-9	-10	5	-0.8
1932	Bos-N	1	0	1.000	18	3	0	0	0	47	50	1	19	21	14.0	3.45	109	.281	.363	2	.222	2	2	2	1	0.4
Total	4	13	24	.351	104	33	12	1	2	382	428	22	146	103	13.7	4.64	93	.289	.356	15	.138	-2	-11	-14	10	-0.4

■ BERT CUNNINGHAM
Cunningham, Ellsworth Elmer b: 11/25/1865, Wilmington, Del.   d: 5/14/52, Cragmere, Del.   BR/TR, 187 lbs.   Deb: 9/15/1887   U

YEAR	TM/L	W	L	PCT	G	GS	CG	SH	SV	IP	H	HR	BB	SO	RAT	ERA	ERA+	OAV	OOB	BH	AVG	PB	PR	/A	PD	TPI
1887	Bro-a	0	2	.000	3	3	3	0	0	23	26	0	13	8	15.3	5.09	85	.275	.362	0	.000	-1	-2	-2	-0	-0.1
1888	Bal-a	22	29	.431	51	51	50	0	0	453¹	412	8	157	186	11.3	3.39	88	.233	.296	33	.186	-2	-17	-21	1	-2.0
1889	Bal-a	16	19	.457	39	33	29	0	1	279¹	306	11	141	140	14.4	4.87	81	.270	.351	27	.206	-3	-32	-29	-0	-2.4
1890	Phi-P	3	9	.250	14	11	11	0	0	108²	133	0	67	33	16.6	5.22	82	.289	.379	6	.115	-4	-12	-11	1	-1.0
	Buf-P	9	15	.375	25	25	24	2	0	211	251	8	134	78	16.4	5.84	70	.283	.377	23	.228	1	-38	-41	-1	-3.0
	Yr	12	24	.333	39	36	35	2	0	319²	384	8	201	111	16.5	5.63	74	.285	.378	8	.052	-3	-50	-52	0	-4.0
1891	Bal-a	11	14	.440	30	25	21	0	0	237²	241	8	138	59	14.4	4.01	93	.254	.349	15	.150	-1	-8	-7	3	-0.4
1895	Lou-N	11	16	.407	31	28	24	1	0	231	299	6	104	49	15.7	4.75	97	.309	.376	30	.300	6	1	-3	2	0.3
1896	Lou-N	7	14	.333	27	20	17	0	1	189¹	242	6	74	37	15.0	5.09	85	.308	.368	22	.250	3	-15	-16	2	-0.8
1897	Lou-N	14	13	.519	29	27	25	0	0	234²	286	2	72	49	13.7	4.14	103	.298	.347	22	.237	-0	4	3	2	0.4
1898	Lou-N	28	15	.651	44	42	41	0	0	362	387	8	65	34	11.2	3.16	113	.271	.303	32	.229	2	18	17	-0	1.8
1899	Lou-N	17	17	.500	39	37	33	1	0	323²	385	4	75	36	12.8	3.84	101	.295	.333	40	.260	3	1	1	6	0.9
1900	Chi-N	4	3	.571	8	7	7	0	0	64	84	0	21	7	14.8	4.36	83	.315	.366	4	.148	-1	-5	-5	-1	-0.6
1901	Chi-N	0	1	.000	1	1	1	0	0	9	11	0	3	2	14.0	5.00	65	.299	.352	0	.000	0	-2	-2	1	0.0
Total	12	142	167	.460	341	310	286	4	2	2726²	3063	61	1064	718	13.6	4.22	91	.278	.341	254	.217	2	-105	-117	15	-6.9

■ GEORGE CUNNINGHAM
Cunningham, George Harold b: 7/13/1894, Sturgeon Lake, Minn.   d: 3/10/72, Chattanooga, Tenn.   BR/TR, 5′11″, 185 lbs.   Deb: 4/14/16   ◆

YEAR	TM/L	W	L	PCT	G	GS	CG	SH	SV	IP	H	HR	BB	SO	RAT	ERA	ERA+	OAV	OOB	BH	AVG	PB	PR	/A	PD	TPI
1916	Det-A	7	10	.412	35	14	5	0	2	150¹	146	0	74	68	13.4	2.75	104	.269	.360	11	.268	5	1	2	1	0.9
1917	Det-A	2	7	.222	44	8	4	0	4	139	113	2	51	49	10.9	2.91	91	.227	.304	6	.176	1	-4	-4	0	-0.3
1918	Det-A	6	7	.462	27	14	10	0	1	140	131	0	38	39	11.2	3.15	84	.255	.312	25	.223	3	-6	-8	1	-0.7
1919	Det-A	1	1	.500	17	0	0	0	1	47²	54	0	15	11	14.0	4.91	65	.292	.361	5	.217	2	-9	-9	0	-0.5
Total	4	16	25	.390	123	36	19	0	8	477	444	2	178	167	12.1	3.13	89	.255	.330	47	.224	11	-17	-19	2	-0.6

■ MIKE CUNNINGHAM
Cunningham, Mody b: 6/14/1882, Lancaster, S.C.   d: 12/10/69, Lancaster, S.C.   BR/TR, 5′10.5″, 175 lbs.   Deb: 8/31/06

YEAR	TM/L	W	L	PCT	G	GS	CG	SH	SV	IP	H	HR	BB	SO	RAT	ERA	ERA+	OAV	OOB	BH	AVG	PB	PR	/A	PD	TPI
1906	Phi-A	1	0	1.000	5	1	1	0	0	28	29	1	9	15	12.2	3.21	85	.270	.327	4	.333	1	-2	-2	-0	0.0

■ NIG CUPPY
Cuppy, George Joseph (b: George Koppe) b: 7/3/1869, Logansport, Ind.   d: 7/27/22, Elkhart, Ind.   TR , 5′7″, 160 lbs.   Deb: 4/16/1892

YEAR	TM/L	W	L	PCT	G	GS	CG	SH	SV	IP	H	HR	BB	SO	RAT	ERA	ERA+	OAV	OOB	BH	AVG	PB	PR	/A	PD	TPI
1892	*Cle-N	28	13	.683	47	42	38	1	1	376	333	9	121	103	10.9	2.51	135	.228	.287	36	.214	1	32	37	4	4.0
1893	Cle-N	17	10	.630	31	30	24	0	0	243²	316	6	75	39	14.4	4.47	109	.305	.352	27	.248	1	5	11	-1	1.0
1894	Cle-N	24	15	.615	43	33	29	3	0	316	381	11	128	65	14.5	4.56	120	.295	.359	35	.259	4	27	32	1	2.8
1895	*Cle-N	26	14	.650	47	40	36	1	2	353	384	9	95	91	12.2	3.54	141	.273	.319	40	.286	7	49	57	4	5.9
1896	*Cle-N	25	14	.641	46	40	35	1	1	358	388	8	75	86	11.6	3.12	146	.274	.311	38	.270	7	50	56	4	6.2
1897	Cle-N	10	6	.625	19	17	13	1	0	139¹	150	3	26	23	11.4	3.17	142	.273	.306	8	.145	-4	18	21	-0	1.5
1898	Cle-N	9	8	.529	18	15	13	1	0	128	147	4	25	27	12.1	3.30	109	.286	.319	5	.104	-4	4	4	-1	0.4
1899	StL-N	11	8	.579	21	21	18	1	0	171²	203	3	26	25	12.0	3.15	126	.294	.319	13	.186	-3	14	16	1	1.3
1900	Bos-N	8	4	.667	17	13	9	0	1	105¹	107	8	24	23	11.2	3.08	134	.263	.304	11	.262	1	7	12	-1	1.3
1901	Bos-A	4	6	.400	13	11	9	0	0	93¹	111	1	14	22	12.1	4.15	85	.292	.317	10	.204	0	-5	-6	-1	-0.6
Total	10	162	98	.623	302	262	224	9	5	2284¹	2520	62	609	504	12.3	3.48	127	.275	.320	223	.233	7	201	239	9	23.4

■ SAMMY CURRAN
Curran, Simon Francis b: 10/30/1874, Dorchester, Mass.   d: 5/19/36, Dorchester, Mass.   Deb: 8/01/02

YEAR	TM/L	W	L	PCT	G	GS	CG	SH	SV	IP	H	HR	BB	SO	RAT	ERA	ERA+	OAV	OOB	BH	AVG	PB	PR	/A	PD	TPI
1902	Bos-N	0	0	—	1	0	0	0	0	6²	6	0	0	3	8.1	1.35	209	.240	.240	0	.000	-0	1	1	-0	0.0

■ LAFAYETTE CURRENCE
Currence, Delancy Lafayette b: 12/3/51, Rock Hill, S.C.   BB/TL, 5′11″, 175 lbs.   Deb: 7/24/75

YEAR	TM/L	W	L	PCT	G	GS	CG	SH	SV	IP	H	HR	BB	SO	RAT	ERA	ERA+	OAV	OOB	BH	AVG	PB	PR	/A	PD	TPI
1975	Mil-A	0	2	.000	8	1	0	0	0	18²	25	5	14	7	18.8	7.71	50	.316	.419	0	—	0	-8	-8	-0	-0.7

■ CLARENCE CURRIE
Currie, Clarence Ffranklin b: 12/30/1878, Glencoe, Ont., Can.   d: 7/15/41, Little Chute, Wis   BR/TR,   Deb: 4/25/02

YEAR	TM/L	W	L	PCT	G	GS	CG	SH	SV	IP	H	HR	BB	SO	RAT	ERA	ERA+	OAV	OOB	BH	AVG	PB	PR	/A	PD	TPI
1902	Cin-N	3	4	.429	10	7	6	1	0	65¹	70	1	17	20	12.3	3.72	81	.274	.324	2	.083	-2	-7	-5	1	-0.6
	StL-N	7	5	.583	15	12	10	2	0	124²	125	0	35	30	11.9	2.60	105	.261	.318	9	.196	-0	3	2	2	0.5
	Yr	10	9	.526	25	19	16	3	0	190	195	1	52	50	11.9	2.98	95	.265	.317	2	.029	-3	-4	-3	3	-0.1

YEAR	TM/L	W	L	PCT	G	GS	CG	SH	SV	IP	H	HR	BB	SO	RAT	ERA	ERA+	OAV	OOB	BH	AVG	PB	PR	/A	PD	TPI
1903	StL-N	4	12	.250	22	16	13	1	1	148	155	7	60	52	13.7	4.01	81	.281	.362	4	.085	-3	-12	-12	4	-1.0
	Chi-N	1	2	.333	6	3	2	0	1	33¹	35	1	9	9	12.7	2.97	106	.254	.313	5	.417	2	1	1	1	0.3
	Yr	5	14	.263	28	19	15	1	2	181¹	190	8	69	61	13.0	3.82	85	.271	.339	4	.068	-1	-11	-12	5	-0.7
Total	2	15	23	.395	53	38	31	4	2	371¹	385	9	121	111	12.7	3.39	89	.270	.336	20	.155	-4	-15	-15	8	-0.8

■ MURPHY CURRIE

Currie, Murphy Archibald   b: 8/31/1893, Fayetteville, N.C.   d: 6/22/39, Asheboro, N.C.   BR/TR, 5'11.5", 185 lbs.   Deb: 8/31/16

YEAR	TM/L	W	L	PCT	G	GS	CG	SH	SV	IP	H	HR	BB	SO	RAT	ERA	ERA+	OAV	OOB	BH	AVG	PB	PR	/A	PD	TPI
1916	StL-N	0	0	—	6	0	0	0	0	14¹	7	1	9	8	10.0	1.88	140	.149	.286	0	.000	-0	1	1	-1	0.1

■ BILL CURRIE

Currie, William Cleveland   b: 11/29/28, Leary, Ga.   BR/TR, 6', 175 lbs.   Deb: 4/13/55

YEAR	TM/L	W	L	PCT	G	GS	CG	SH	SV	IP	H	HR	BB	SO	RAT	ERA	ERA+	OAV	OOB	BH	AVG	PB	PR	/A	PD	TPI
1955	Was-A	0	0	—	3	0	0	0	0	4¹	7	3	2	2	20.8	12.46	31	.350	.435	0	—	0	-4	-4	0	-0.3

■ GEORGE CURRY

Curry, George James "Soldier Boy"   b: 12/21/1888, Bridgeport, Conn.   d: 10/5/63, Stratford, Conn.   BR/TR, 6', 185 lbs.   Deb: 7/16/11

YEAR	TM/L	W	L	PCT	G	GS	CG	SH	SV	IP	H	HR	BB	SO	RAT	ERA	ERA+	OAV	OOB	BH	AVG	PB	PR	/A	PD	TPI
1911	StL-A	0	3	.000	3	3	0	0	0	15²	19	0	24	2	24.7	7.47	45	.339	.538	0	.000	-1	-7	-7	-0	-0.6

■ STEVE CURRY

Curry, Stephen Thomas   b: 9/13/65, Winter Park, Fla.   BR/TR, 6'6", 217 lbs.   Deb: 7/10/88

YEAR	TM/L	W	L	PCT	G	GS	CG	SH	SV	IP	H	HR	BB	SO	RAT	ERA	ERA+	OAV	OOB	BH	AVG	PB	PR	/A	PD	TPI
1988	Bos-A	0	1	.000	3	3	0	0	0	11	15	0	14	4	23.7	8.18	50	.357	.518	0	—	0	-5	-5	0	-0.3

■ WES CURRY

Curry, Wesley   b: 4/1/1860, Wilmington, Del.   d: 5/19/33, Philadelphia, Pa.   Deb: 8/06/1884   U

YEAR	TM/L	W	L	PCT	G	GS	CG	SH	SV	IP	H	HR	BB	SO	RAT	ERA	ERA+	OAV	OOB	BH	AVG	PB	PR	/A	PD	TPI
1884	Ric-a	0	2	.000	2	2	2	0	0	16	15	2	3	1	10.1	5.06	66	.235	.269	2	.250	-0	-3	-3	-0	-0.2

■ CLIFF CURTIS

Curtis, Clifton Garfield   b: 7/3/1883, Delaware, Ohio   d: 4/23/43, Newark, Ohio   BR/TR, 6'2", 180 lbs.   Deb: 8/23/09

YEAR	TM/L	W	L	PCT	G	GS	CG	SH	SV	IP	H	HR	BB	SO	RAT	ERA	ERA+	OAV	OOB	BH	AVG	PB	PR	/A	PD	TPI
1909	Bos-N	4	5	.444	10	9	8	2	0	83	53	1	30	22	9.2	1.41	200	.191	.275	1	.034	-3	11	13	1	1.3
1910	Bos-N	6	24	.200	43	37	12	2	2	251	251	9	124	75	13.9	3.55	94	.277	.371	12	.146	-5	-14	-6	6	-0.3
1911	Bos-N	1	8	.111	12	9	5	0	1	77	79	4	34	23	13.4	4.44	86	.265	.344	7	.250	-0	-9	-5	1	-0.3
	Chi-N	1	2	.333	4	1	0	0	0	7	7	0	5	4	19.3	3.86	86	.241	.405	1	.500	-0	-0	-0	0	0.0
	Phi-N	2	1	.667	8	5	3	1	0	45	45	0	15	13	12.2	2.60	132	.260	.323	4	.267	0	4	4	-0	0.4
	Yr	4	11	.267	24	15	8	1	1	129	131	4	54	40	13.0	3.77	97	.259	.332	0	.000	-0	-5	-1	1	0.1
1912	Phi-N	2	5	.286	10	8	2	0	0	50	55	3	17	20	13.7	3.24	112	.271	.339	0	.000	-2	1	2	1	0.1
	Bro-N	4	7	.364	19	9	3	0	1	80	72	4	37	22	12.9	3.94	85	.238	.332	8	.308	1	-5	-5	-0	-0.3
	Yr	6	12	.333	29	17	5	0	1	130	127	7	54	42	12.9	3.67	94	.249	.328	2	.049	-1	-4	-3	1	-0.2
1913	Bro-N	8	9	.471	30	16	5	0	2	151²	145	1	55	57	12.3	3.26	101	.255	.328	6	.122	-3	-1	1	2	0.0
Total	5	28	61	.315	136	94	38	5	6	744²	707	22	317	236	12.8	3.31	101	.256	.341	39	.159	-11	-13	3	10	0.9

■ JACK CURTIS

Curtis, Jack Patrick   b: 1/11/37, Rhodhiss, N.C.   BL/TL, 5'10", 175 lbs.   Deb: 4/22/61

YEAR	TM/L	W	L	PCT	G	GS	CG	SH	SV	IP	H	HR	BB	SO	RAT	ERA	ERA+	OAV	OOB	BH	AVG	PB	PR	/A	PD	TPI
1961	Chi-N	10	13	.435	31	27	6	0	0	180¹	220	23	51	57	13.6	4.89	85	.303	.350	10	.167	3	-17	-14	1	-0.8
1962	Chi-N	0	2	.000	4	3	0	0	0	18	18	2	6	8	12.0	3.50	118	.277	.338	1	.250	0	1	1	-0	0.1
	Mil-N	4	4	.500	30	5	0	0	1	75²	82	8	27	40	13.2	4.16	91	.282	.347	4	.222	2	-2	-3	-1	-0.1
	Yr	4	6	.400	34	8	0	0	1	93²	100	10	33	48	13.0	4.04	96	.280	.344	4	.182	2	-1	-2	-1	0.0
1963	Cle-A	0	0	—	4	0	0	0	0	5	8	0	5	3	25.2	18.00	20	.348	.483	0	—	0	-8	-8	0	-0.6
Total	3	14	19	.424	69	35	6	0	1	279	328	33	89	108	13.6	4.84	84	.297	.352	15	.183	5	-26	-24	1	-1.4

■ JACK CURTIS

Curtis, John Duffield   b: 3/9/48, Newton, Mass.   BL/TL, 6'1", 175 lbs.   Deb: 8/13/70

YEAR	TM/L	W	L	PCT	G	GS	CG	SH	SV	IP	H	HR	BB	SO	RAT	ERA	ERA+	OAV	OOB	BH	AVG	PB	PR	/A	PD	TPI
1970	Bos-A	0	0	—	1	0	0	0	0	2¹	4	1	1	1	19.3	11.57	34	.333	.385	0	—	0	-2	-2	0	-0.1
1971	Bos-A	2	2	.500	5	3	1	0	0	26	30	3	6	19	12.5	3.12	119	.291	.330	1	.111	-0	1	2	-1	0.1
1972	Bos-A	11	8	.579	26	21	8	3	0	154¹	161	8	50	106	12.3	3.73	86	.271	.328	5	.094	-3	-12	-9	-0	-1.2
1973	Bos-A	13	13	.500	35	30	10	4	0	221¹	225	24	83	101	12.6	3.58	112	.264	.331	0	—	0	6	11	-0	1.1
1974	StL-N	10	14	.417	33	29	5	2	1	195	199	15	83	89	13.1	3.78	94	.267	.342	10	.159	-0	-4	-5	0	-0.4
1975	StL-N	8	9	.471	39	18	4	0	1	146²	151	13	65	67	13.4	3.44	109	.268	.346	8	.211	2	3	5	2	1.0
1976	StL-N	6	11	.353	37	15	3	1	1	134	139	11	65	52	13.7	4.50	79	.276	.359	7	.200	2	-15	-14	0	-1.2
1977	SF-N	3	3	.500	43	9	1	1	1	77	95	5	48	47	16.8	5.49	71	.314	.409	3	.231	1	-14	-14	-1	-1.0
1978	SF-N	4	3	.571	46	0	0	0	1	63	60	1	29	38	12.7	3.71	93	.262	.345	0	.000	-0	-1	-2	0	-0.1
1979	SF-N	10	9	.526	27	18	3	2	0	120²	121	15	42	85	12.2	4.18	84	.257	.318	5	.147	1	-6	-9	-1	-0.9
1980	SD-N	10	8	.556	30	27	6	0	0	187	184	9	67	71	12.2	3.51	98	.262	.329	12	.194	1	2	-2	1	0.0
1981	SD-N	2	6	.250	28	8	0	0	0	66²	70	11	30	31	13.6	5.13	63	.275	.353	1	.077	-1	-12	-14	-0	-1.5
1982	SD-N	8	6	.571	26	18	1	1	0	116¹	121	15	46	54	13.0	4.10	83	.271	.341	11	.297	3	-6	-9	-1	-0.6
	Cal-A	0	1	.000	8	0	0	0	1	12	16	0	3	10	14.3	6.00	68	.320	.358	0	—	0	-3	-3	-0	-0.2
1983	Cal-A	1	2	.333	37	3	0	0	5	90	89	5	40	36	13.1	3.80	106	.258	.339	0	—	0	3	2	-1	0.1
1984	Cal-A	1	2	.333	17	0	0	0	0	28²	30	4	11	18	12.9	4.40	90	.263	.328	0	—	0	-1	-1	0	0.0
Total	15	89	97	.478	438	199	42	14	11	1641	1695	140	669	825	13.0	3.96	91	.270	.341	63	.175	4	-61	-63	1	-4.9

■ VERN CURTIS

Curtis, Vernon Eugene "Turk"   b: 5/24/20, Cairo, Ill.   BR/TR, 6', 170 lbs.   Deb: 9/06/43

YEAR	TM/L	W	L	PCT	G	GS	CG	SH	SV	IP	H	HR	BB	SO	RAT	ERA	ERA+	OAV	OOB	BH	AVG	PB	PR	/A	PD	TPI
1943	Was-A	0	0	—	2	0	0	0	0	4	3	0	6	1	20.3	6.75	47	.200	.429	0	—	0	-2	-2	0	-0.1
1944	Was-A	0	1	.000	3	1	0	0	0	9²	8	0	3	2	10.2	2.79	117	.235	.297	0	.000	-0	1	0	0	0.0
1946	Was-A	0	0	—	11	0	0	0	0	16¹	19	1	10	7	16.0	7.16	47	.297	.392	0	.000	-0	-7	-7	0	-0.6
Total	3	0	1	.000	16	1	0	0	0	30	30	1	19	10	14.7	5.70	58	.265	.371	0	.000	-1	-7	-8	0	-0.7

■ ED CUSHMAN

Cushman, Edgar Leander   b: 3/27/1852, Eaglesville, Ohio   d: 9/26/15, Erie, Pa.   BR/TL,   Deb: 7/06/1883

YEAR	TM/L	W	L	PCT	G	GS	CG	SH	SV	IP	H	HR	BB	SO	RAT	ERA	ERA+	OAV	OOB	BH	AVG	PB	PR	/A	PD	TPI
1883	Buf-N	3	3	.500	7	7	5	0	0	50¹	61	0	17	34	13.9	3.93	81	.283	.335	5	.217	-0	-4	-4	-1	-0.3
1884	Mil-U	4	0	1.000	4	4	4	2	0	36	10	0	3	47	3.3	1.00	164	.082	.104	1	.091	0	8	3	-0	0.1
1885	Phi-a	3	7	.300	10	10	10	0	0	87	101	1	17	37	12.2	3.52	98	.278	.311	7	.189	-1	-3	-1	-1	-0.1
	NY-a	8	14	.364	22	22	22	0	0	191	158	2	33	133	9.0	2.78	106	.216	.249	10	.145	-1	10	4	-2	0.0
	Yr	11	21	.344	32	32	32	0	0	278	259	3	50	170	10.0	3.01	103	.236	.270	10	.094	-2	7	3	-3	-0.1
1886	NY-a	17	20	.459	38	37	37	2	0	325²	278	6	99	167	10.4	3.12	109	.220	.277	19	.151	-7	12	11	0	0.3
1887	NY-a	10	15	.400	26	26	25	0	0	220	310	4	83	64	16.1	5.97	71	.321	.374	23	.247	3	-41	-42	-1	-3.0
1890	Tol-a	17	21	.447	40	38	34	0	1	315²	346	5	107	125	12.9	4.19	94	.270	.326	13	.100	-9	-11	-8	-4	-1.7
Total	6	62	80	.437	147	144	137	4	1	1225²	1264	23	359	607	11.9	3.86	92	.256	.306	78	.160	-15	-29	-40	-9	-4.7

■ HARVEY CUSHMAN

Cushman, Harvey Barnes   b: 7/10/1877, Rockland, Me.   d: 12/27/20, Emsworth, Pa.   Deb: 8/24/02

YEAR	TM/L	W	L	PCT	G	GS	CG	SH	SV	IP	H	HR	BB	SO	RAT	ERA	ERA+	OAV	OOB	BH	AVG	PB	PR	/A	PD	TPI
1902	Pit-N	0	4	.000	4	4	3	0	0	25²	30	0	31	12	22.1	7.36	37	.291	.463	2	.200	-0	-13	-13	-1	-1.1

■ MIKE CVENGROS

Cvengros, Michael John   b: 12/1/01, Pana, Ill.   d: 8/2/70, Hot Springs, Ark.   BL/TL, 5'8", 159 lbs.   Deb: 9/30/22

YEAR	TM/L	W	L	PCT	G	GS	CG	SH	SV	IP	H	HR	BB	SO	RAT	ERA	ERA+	OAV	OOB	BH	AVG	PB	PR	/A	PD	TPI
1922	NY-N	0	1	.000	1	1	0	0	0	9	6	1	3	3	10.0	4.00	100	.194	.286	0	.000	-0	0	0	0	0.0
1923	Chi-A	12	13	.480	40	26	14	0	3	214¹	216	6	107	86	14.1	4.41	90	.269	.364	15	.203	-1	-10	-11	-0	-1.1
1924	Chi-A	3	12	.200	26	15	2	0	0	105²	119	5	67	36	16.1	5.88	70	.300	.405	6	.200	2	-19	-21	0	-1.6
1925	Chi-A	3	9	.250	22	11	4	0	0	104²	109	7	55	32	14.4	4.30	97	.278	.371	5	.152	-1	1	-2	-0	-0.2
1927	•Pit-N	2	1	.667	23	4	0	0	1	53²	55	3	24	21	13.4	3.35	123	.271	.351	3	.158	-0	3	5	1	0.5
1929	Chi-N	5	4	.556	32	2	0	0	2	64	82	2	29	23	15.8	4.64	99	.319	.390	6	.400	2	1	-0	0	0.2
Total	6	25	40	.385	144	59	21	0	6	551¹	587	24	285	201	14.6	4.59	90	.282	.374	35	.201	1	-24	-28	1	-2.2

■ JOHN D'ACQUISTO

D'Acquisto, John Francis   b: 12/24/51, San Diego, Cal.   BR/TR, 6'2", 205 lbs.   Deb: 9/02/73

YEAR	TM/L	W	L	PCT	G	GS	CG	SH	SV	IP	H	HR	BB	SO	RAT	ERA	ERA+	OAV	OOB	BH	AVG	PB	PR	/A	PD	TPI
1973	SF-N	1	1	.500	7	3	1	0	0	27²	23	4	19	29	13.7	3.58	107	.219	.339	0	.000	-1	0	1	-1	0.0
1974	SF-N	12	14	.462	38	36	5	1	0	215	182	13	124	167	13.1	3.77	97	.227	.334	8	.113	-0	-4	1	-4	-0.4
1975	SF-N	2	4	.333	10	6	0	0	0	28	29	5	34	22	20.9	10.29	37	.264	.445	0	.000	-0	-21	-20	-1	-1.9
1976	SF-N	3	8	.273	28	19	0	0	0	106	93	6	102	53	16.8	5.35	68	.243	.406	7	.269	2	-22	-20	0	-1.8
1977	StL-N	0	0	—	3	2	0	0	0	8¹	5	0	10	9	17.3	4.32	89	.185	.421	0	.000	-1	-0	-0	-0	0.0
	SD-N	1	2	.333	17	12	0	0	0	44	49	3	47	45	19.8	6.95	51	.297	.455	0	.000	-0	-15	-17	0	-1.5

YEAR TM/L	W	L	PCT	G	GS	CG	SH	SV	IP	H	HR	BB	SO	RAT	ERA	ERA+	OAV	OOB	BH	AVG	PB	PR	/A	PD	TPI
Yr	1	2	.333	20	14	0	0	0	52¹	54	3	57	54	19.3	6.54	55	.278	.444	1	.125	-1	-15	-17	-0	-1.5
1978 SD-N	4	3	.571	45	3	0	0	10	93	60	2	56	104	11.3	2.13	156	.185	.307	4	.190	1	15	12	-2	1.2
1979 SD-N	9	13	.409	51	11	1	1	2	133²	140	15	86	97	15.4	4.92	72	.275	.383	4	.129	1	-18	-21	-3	-2.2
1980 SD-N	2	3	.400	39	0	0	0	1	67	67	2	36	44	14.0	3.76	91	.270	.365	0	.000	-1	-1	-2	-1	-0.3
Mon-N	0	2	.000	11	0	0	0	2	20²	14	0	9	15	10.0	2.18	164	.206	.299	0	—	0	3	3	0	0.3
Yr	2	5	.286	50	0	0	0	3	87²	81	2	45	59	12.9	3.39	102	.252	.343	1	.125	-1	2	1	-1	0.0
1981 Cal-A	0	0	—	6	0	0	0	0	19¹	26	2	12	8	18.2	10.71	34	.338	.433	0	—	0	-15	-15	-0	-1.3
1982 Oak-A	0	1	.000	11	0	0	0	0	17	20	1	9	7	15.4	5.29	74	.290	.372	0	—	0	-2	-3	-0	-0.2
Total 10	34	51	.400	266	92	7	2	15	779²	708	52	544	600	14.7	4.56	79	.245	.368	23	.127	0	-79	-81	-10	-8.1

■ JOHN DAGENHARD
Dagenhard, John Douglas b: 4/25/17, Magnolia, Ohio BR/TR, 6'2", 195 lbs. Deb: 9/28/43

YEAR TM/L	W	L	PCT	G	GS	CG	SH	SV	IP	H	HR	BB	SO	RAT	ERA	ERA+	OAV	OOB	BH	AVG	PB	PR	/A	PD	TPI
1943 Bos-N	1	0	1.000	2	1	1	0	0	11	9	0	4	2	12.3	0.00	—	.225	.326	0	.000	-0	4	4	1	0.6

■ PETE DAGLIA
Daglia, Peter George b: 2/28/06, Napa, Cal. d: 3/11/52, Willits, Cal. BR/TR, 6'1", 200 lbs. Deb: 6/08/32

YEAR TM/L	W	L	PCT	G	GS	CG	SH	SV	IP	H	HR	BB	SO	RAT	ERA	ERA+	OAV	OOB	BH	AVG	PB	PR	/A	PD	TPI
1932 Chi-A	2	4	.333	12	5	2	0	0	50	67	4	20	16	16.4	5.76	75	.324	.394	1	.077	-1	-7	-8	-1	-0.8

■ JAY DAHL
Dahl, Jay Steven b: 12/6/45, San Bernardino, Cal. d: 6/20/65, Salisbury, N.C. BB/TL, 5'10", 183 lbs. Deb: 9/27/63

YEAR TM/L	W	L	PCT	G	GS	CG	SH	SV	IP	H	HR	BB	SO	RAT	ERA	ERA+	OAV	OOB	BH	AVG	PB	PR	/A	PD	TPI
1963 Hou-N	0	1	.000	1	1	0	0	0	2²	7	0	0	0	23.6	16.88	19	.438	.438	0	—	0	-4	-4	0	-0.3

■ JERRY DAHLKE
Dahlke, Jerome Alexander "Joe" b: 6/8/30, Marathon, Wis. BR/TR, 6', 180 lbs. Deb: 5/06/56

YEAR TM/L	W	L	PCT	G	GS	CG	SH	SV	IP	H	HR	BB	SO	RAT	ERA	ERA+	OAV	OOB	BH	AVG	PB	PR	/A	PD	TPI
1956 Chi-A	0	0	—	5	0	0	0	0	2¹	5	0	6	1	42.4	19.29	21	.455	.647	0	—	0	-4	-4	0	-0.3

■ SAM DAILEY
Dailey, Samuel Laurence b: 3/31/04, Oakford, Ill. d: 12/2/79, Columbia, Mo. BL/TR, 5'11", 168 lbs. Deb: 7/04/29

YEAR TM/L	W	L	PCT	G	GS	CG	SH	SV	IP	H	HR	BB	SO	RAT	ERA	ERA+	OAV	OOB	BH	AVG	PB	PR	/A	PD	TPI
1929 Phi-N	2	2	.500	20	5	0	0	0	51¹	74	5	23	18	17.2	7.54	69	.349	.415	1	.059	-2	-16	-13	-1	-1.4

■ VINCE DAILEY
Dailey, Vincent Perry b: 12/25/1864, Osceola, Pa. d: 11/14/19, Hornell, N.Y. 6', 200 lbs. Deb: 4/21/1890 ♦

YEAR TM/L	W	L	PCT	G	GS	CG	SH	SV	IP	H	HR	BB	SO	RAT	ERA	ERA+	OAV	OOB	BH	AVG	PB	PR	/A	PD	TPI
1890 Cle-N	0	1	.000	2	1	0	0	0	7	12	0	7	0	24.4	7.71	46	.367	.479	71	.289	1	-3	-3	0	-0.2

■ BILL DAILEY
Dailey, William Garland b: 5/13/35, Arlington, Va. BR/TR, 6'3", 185 lbs. Deb: 8/17/61

YEAR TM/L	W	L	PCT	G	GS	CG	SH	SV	IP	H	HR	BB	SO	RAT	ERA	ERA+	OAV	OOB	BH	AVG	PB	PR	/A	PD	TPI
1961 Cle-A	1	0	1.000	12	0	0	0	0	19	16	0	6	7	10.4	0.95	415	.232	.293	0	.000	-0	6	6	1	0.7
1962 Cle-A	2	2	.500	27	0	0	0	1	42²	43	0	17	24	13.1	3.59	108	.270	.348	0	.000	-0	2	1	-0	0.1
1963 Min-A	6	3	.667	66	0	0	0	21	108²	80	9	19	72	8.2	1.99	183	.208	.246	5	.238	2	20	20	2	2.6
1964 Min-A	1	2	.333	14	0	0	0	0	15¹	23	3	17	6	25.8	8.22	44	.377	.537	0	—	0	-8	-8	0	-0.7
Total 4	10	7	.588	119	0	0	0	22	185²	162	12	59	109	11.0	2.76	135	.241	.308	5	.192	1	20	20	3	2.7

■ ED DAILY
Daily, Edward M. b: 9/7/1862, Providence, R.I. d: 10/21/1891, Washington, D.C. BR/TR, 5'10.5", 174 lbs. Deb: 5/04/1885 ♦

YEAR TM/L	W	L	PCT	G	GS	CG	SH	SV	IP	H	HR	BB	SO	RAT	ERA	ERA+	OAV	OOB	BH	AVG	PB	PR	/A	PD	TPI
1885 Phi-N	26	23	.531	50	50	49	4	0	440	370	12	90	140	9.4	2.21	126	.217	.257	38	.207	-0	30	28	-3	2.4
1886 Phi-N	16	9	.640	27	23	22	1	0	218	211	7	59	95	11.1	3.06	108	.244	.292	70	.227	2	6	6	2	0.5
1887 Phi-N	0	4	.000	6	5	4	0	0	41¹	52	2	25	7	16.8	7.19	59	.299	.387	30	.283	1	-14	-14	1	-1.0
Was-N	0	1	1.000	1	1	1	0	0	7	5	0	6	3	14.1	7.71	52	.195	.348	78	.251	0	-3	-3	0	-0.1
Yr	0	5	.000	7	6	5	0	0	48¹	57	2	31	10	16.4	7.26	58	.286	.382	17	.041	1	-17	-17	2	-1.1
1888 Was-N	2	7	.222	9	8	8	0	0	73²	88	7	19	20	13.1	4.89	57	.286	.327	102	.225	1	-17	-17	1	-1.4
1889 Col-a	0	0	—	2	0	0	0	1	1²	1	0	4	2	27.0	21.60	17	.168	.503	148	.256	0	-3	-3	-0	-0.2
1890 Bro-a	10	15	.400	27	27	27	0	0	235²	252	6	93	82	13.2	4.05	96	.265	.331	94	.239	4	-5	-4	1	-0.3
NY-N	2	0	1.000	2	1	1	0	0	16	6	0	6	0	6.8	2.25	155	.113	.202	2	.133	-1	2	2	1	0.2
*Lou-a	6	3	.667	12	10	9	1	0	93	83	2	30	31	10.9	1.94	199	.232	.291	20	.250	3	20	20	3	2.7
1891 Lou-a	4	8	.333	15	14	11	0	0	111¹	149	6	47	27	15.3	5.74	64	.310	.373	16	.250	2	-25	-26	1	-1.7
Total 7	66	70	.485	151	139	132	6	1	1237²	1217	39	380	407	11.6	3.39	98	.247	.301	616	.239	12	-9	-11	6	1.1

■ HUGH DAILY
Daily, Hugh Ignatius "One Arm" (b: Harry Criss) b: 1857, Baltimore, Md. BR/TR, 6'2", 180 lbs. Deb: 5/01/1882

YEAR TM/L	W	L	PCT	G	GS	CG	SH	SV	IP	H	HR	BB	SO	RAT	ERA	ERA+	OAV	OOB	BH	AVG	PB	PR	/A	PD	TPI
1882 Buf-N	15	14	.517	29	29	29	0	0	255²	246	6	70	116	11.1	2.99	98	.239	.287	18	.164	-6	-3	-2	-5	-1.0
1883 Cle-N	23	19	.548	45	43	40	4	1	378²	360	5	99	171	10.9	2.42	130	.236	.283	18	.127	-10	30	31	-1	1.8
1884 CP-U	27	27	.500	56	56	54	5	0	484²	430	11	71	469	9.3	2.43	124	.222	.249	43	.219	-2	32	32	0	2.6
Was-U	1	1	.500	2	2	2	0	0	16	16	0	1	14	9.6	2.25	132	.243	.255	0	.000	-1	1	1	-0	0.0
Yr	28	28	.500	58	58	56	5	0	500²	446	11	72	**483**	9.3	2.43	124	.223	.250	9	.045	-3	33	33	0	2.6
1885 StL-N	3	8	.273	11	11	10	1	0	91¹	92	5	44	31	13.4	3.94	70	.250	.330	3	.086	-3	-11	-12	0	-1.2
1886 Was-N	0	6	.000	6	6	6	0	0	49	69	2	40	15	20.0	7.35	45	.319	.426	2	.125	-1	-22	-22	-1	-1.7
1887 Cle-a	4	12	.250	16	16	16	0	0	139²	181	0	44	30	14.5	3.67	119	.303	.350	4	.069	-8	10	11	-1	0.2
Total 6	73	87	.456	165	163	157	10	1	1415	1394	30	369	846	11.2	2.92	108	.243	.288	88	.157	-30	36	37	-6	0.7

■ BRUCE DalCANTON
DalCanton, John Bruce b: 6/15/42, California, Pa. BR/TR, 6'2", 205 lbs. Deb: 9/03/67 C

YEAR TM/L	W	L	PCT	G	GS	CG	SH	SV	IP	H	HR	BB	SO	RAT	ERA	ERA+	OAV	OOB	BH	AVG	PB	PR	/A	PD	TPI
1967 Pit-N	2	1	.667	8	2	1	0	0	24	19	1	10	13	11.3	1.88	179	.211	.297	2	.333	1	4	4	-0	0.5
1968 Pit-N	1	1	.500	7	0	0	0	2	17	7	0	6	8	7.9	2.12	138	.127	.238	0	.000	-0	2	2	-0	0.1
1969 Pit-N	8	2	.800	57	0	0	0	0	86¹	79	3	49	56	13.3	3.34	105	.252	.353	3	.300	3	2	1	0	0.4
1970 Pit-N	9	4	.692	41	6	1	0	1	84²	94	7	39	53	14.2	4.57	85	.282	.359	0	.000	-1	-5	-6	-0	-0.7
1971 KC-A	8	6	.571	25	22	2	0	0	141¹	144	8	44	58	12.0	3.44	100	.262	.317	4	.087	-3	-0	-1	-3	-0.9
1972 KC-A	6	6	.500	35	16	1	0	2	132¹	135	7	29	75	11.2	3.40	89	.265	.306	2	.098	-2	-5	-5	-1	-0.9
1973 KC-A	4	3	.571	32	3	1	0	2	97¹	108	8	46	38	14.6	4.81	85	.284	.367	0	—	0	-11	-8	0	-0.6
1974 KC-A	8	10	.444	31	22	9	2	0	175¹	135	5	82	96	11.4	3.13	122	.211	.306	0	—	0	9	13	0	1.5
1975 KC-A	0	2	.000	4	2	0	0	0	8²	23	0	7	5	32.2	15.58	25	.479	.554	0	—	0	-11	-11	0	-0.9
Atl-N	2	7	.222	26	9	0	0	3	67	63	6	24	38	12.5	3.36	112	.248	.327	2	.105	-1	2	3	1	0.3
1976 Atl-N	3	5	.375	42	1	0	0	1	73¹	67	6	42	36	13.6	3.56	106	.244	.348	2	.222	1	-0	2	1	0.4
1977 Chi-N	0	2	.000	8	0	0	0	2	24	20	1	13	9	12.4	3.75	109	.230	.330	0	—	1	1	1	-0	0.2
Total 11	51	49	.510	316	83	15	2	19	931¹	894	48	391	485	12.6	3.67	99	.253	.331	17	.113	-3	-12	-5	-2	-0.2

■ GENE DALE
Dale, Emmett Eugene b: 6/16/1889, St.Louis, Mo. d: 3/20/58, St.Louis, Mo. BR/TR, 6'3", 179 lbs. Deb: 9/19/11

YEAR TM/L	W	L	PCT	G	GS	CG	SH	SV	IP	H	HR	BB	SO	RAT	ERA	ERA+	OAV	OOB	BH	AVG	PB	PR	/A	PD	TPI
1911 StL-N	0	2	.000	5	2	0	0	0	14²	13	0	16	13	19.0	6.75	50	.250	.443	2	.400	1	-5	-5	-0	-0.4
1912 StL-N	0	5	.000	19	3	1	0	0	61²	76	4	51	37	19.0	6.57	52	.292	.414	6	.273	1	-22	-22	-1	-1.9
1915 Cin-N	18	17	.514	49	35	20	4	3	296²	256	6	107	104	11.2	2.46	116	.243	.316	20	.222	2	10	13	-1	1.6
1916 Cin-N	3	4	.429	17	5	2	0	0	69²	80	3	33	23	14.9	5.17	50	.304	.386	3	.143	-0	-20	-20	2	-1.9
Total 4	21	28	.429	90	45	23	4	3	442²	425	13	207	177	13.1	3.60	81	.261	.349	31	.223	3	-37	-34	-1	-2.6

■ BUD DALEY
Daley, Leavitt Leo b: 10/7/32, Orange, Cal. BL/TL, 6'1", 185 lbs. Deb: 9/10/55

YEAR TM/L	W	L	PCT	G	GS	CG	SH	SV	IP	H	HR	BB	SO	RAT	ERA	ERA+	OAV	OOB	BH	AVG	PB	PR	/A	PD	TPI
1955 Cle-A	0	1	.000	2	1	0	0	0	7	10	1	1	2	14.1	6.43	62	.333	.355	0	.000	-0	-2	-2	0	-0.1
1956 Cle-A	1	0	1.000	14	0	0	0	0	20¹	21	2	14	13	17.7	6.20	68	.273	.417	0	.000	-0	-5	-5	1	-0.3
1957 Cle-A	2	8	.200	34	10	1	0	2	87¹	99	7	40	54	15.4	4.43	84	.279	.368	4	.200	-0	-6	-7	1	-0.5
1958 KC-A	3	2	.600	26	5	1	0	0	70²	67	5	19	39	11.7	3.31	118	.249	.313	2	.125	-1	4	5	1	0.5
1959 KC-A	16	13	.552	39	29	12	2	1	216¹	212	24	62	125	11.9	3.16	127	.257	.317	23	.295	5	17	20	-1	2.6
1960 KC-A	16	16	.500	37	35	13	1	0	231	234	27	96	126	13.2	4.56	87	.263	.341	12	.160	1	-18	-15	1	-1.2
1961 KC-A	4	8	.333	16	10	2	0	0	63²	84	6	22	36	15.7	4.95	83	.319	.383	2	.111	-1	-7	-6	0	-0.5
*NY-A	8	9	.471	23	17	7	0	0	129²	127	17	51	83	12.6	3.96	94	.257	.331	6	.133	-1	1	-3	-1	-0.5
Yr	12	17	.414	39	27	9	0	1	193¹	211	23	73	119	13.4	4.28	90	.275	.341	3	.048	-2	-6	-9	-0	-1.0
1962 *NY-A	7	5	.583	43	6	0	0	4	105¹	105	8	21	55	11.2	3.59	104	.258	.303	5	.185	-0	4	2	0	0.0
1963 NY-A	0	0	—	1	0	0	0	0	1	2	0	0	0	18.0	0.00	—	.667	.667	0	—	0	0	0	0	0.0
1964 NY-A	3	2	.600	13	0	0	0	0	35	37	3	25	16	17.0	4.63	78	.274	.402	2	.250	1	-4	-4	1	-0.2
Total 10	60	64	.484	248	116	36	3	10	967¹	998	100	351	549	13.1	4.03	97	.266	.339	56	.192	3	-15	-14	4	-0.1

YEAR TM/L	W	L	PCT	G	GS	CG	SH	SV	IP	H	HR	BB	SO	RAT	ERA	ERA+	OAV	OOB	BH	AVG	PB	PR	/A	PD	TPI

■ BILL DALEY
Daley, William b: 6/27/1868, Poughkeepsie, N.Y d: 5/4/22, Poughkeepsie, N.Y. TL, Deb: 7/17/1889

YEAR TM/L	W	L	PCT	G	GS	CG	SH	SV	IP	H	HR	BB	SO	RAT	ERA	ERA+	OAV	OOB	BH	AVG	PB	PR	/A	PD	TPI
1889 Bos-N	3	3	.500	9	7	4	0	0	48	34	1	43	40	14.4	4.31	97	.193	.351	3	.150	-1	-2	-1	3	0.1
1890 Bos-P	18	7	**.720**	34	25	19	2	2	235	246	7	167	110	15.8	3.60	122	.258	.368	17	.155	-5	17	21	-2	1.2
1891 Bos-a	8	6	.571	19	11	10	0	2	126²	119	6	81	68	14.2	2.98	117	.240	.347	10	.169	-2	10	7	0	0.4
Total 3	29	16	.644	62	43	33	2	4	409²	399	14	291	218	15.2	3.49	117	.245	.360	30	.159	-8	25	27	1	1.7

■ GEORGE DALY
Daly, George Josephs "Pecks" b: 7/28/1887, Buffalo, N.Y. d: 12/12/57, Buffalo, N.Y. BR/TR, 5'10.5", 175 lbs. Deb: 9/26/09

YEAR TM/L	W	L	PCT	G	GS	CG	SH	SV	IP	H	HR	BB	SO	RAT	ERA	ERA+	OAV	OOB	BH	AVG	PB	PR	/A	PD	TPI
1909 NY-N	0	3	.000	3	3	3	0	0	21	31	0	8	8	17.1	6.00	43	.341	.400	1	.111	-1	-8	-8	-1	-0.8

■ BILL DAMMANN
Dammann, William Henry "Wee Willie" b: 8/9/1872, Chicago, Ill. d: 12/6/48, Lynnhaven, Va. BL/TL, 5'7", 155 lbs. Deb: 4/24/1897

YEAR TM/L	W	L	PCT	G	GS	CG	SH	SV	IP	H	HR	BB	SO	RAT	ERA	ERA+	OAV	OOB	BH	AVG	PB	PR	/A	PD	TPI
1897 Cin-N	6	4	.600	16	11	7	1	0	95	122	1	37	21	15.1	4.74	96	.309	.368	5	.161	-1	-4	-2	1	0.0
1898 Cin-N	16	10	.615	35	22	16	2	2	224²	277	3	67	51	13.8	3.61	106	.301	.348	16	.195	1	0	6	-3	0.4
1899 Cin-N	2	1	.667	9	5	3	1	1	48	74	0	11	2	15.9	4.88	80	.351	.384	1	.056	-2	-5	-5	0	-0.5
Total 3	24	15	.615	60	38	26	4	3	367²	473	4	115	74	14.4	4.06	99	.310	.358	22	.168	-1	-10	-1	-1	-0.1

■ ART DANEY
Daney, Arthur Lee b: 7/9/04, Talihina, Okla. d: 3/11/88, Phoenix, Ariz. BR/TR, 5'11", 165 lbs. Deb: 5/25/28

YEAR TM/L	W	L	PCT	G	GS	CG	SH	SV	IP	H	HR	BB	SO	RAT	ERA	ERA+	OAV	OOB	BH	AVG	PB	PR	/A	PD	TPI
1928 Phi-A	0	0	—	1	0	0	0	0	1	1	0	0	0	9.0	0.00	—	.250	.250	0	—	0	0	0	0	0.1

■ DAVE DANFORTH
Danforth, David Charles "Dauntless Dave" b: 3/7/1890, Granger, Tex. d: 9/19/70, Baltimore, Md. BL/TL, 6', 167 lbs. Deb: 8/01/11

YEAR TM/L	W	L	PCT	G	GS	CG	SH	SV	IP	H	HR	BB	SO	RAT	ERA	ERA+	OAV	OOB	BH	AVG	PB	PR	/A	PD	TPI
1911 Phi-A	4	1	.800	14	2	1	0	1	33²	29	1	17	21	13.1	3.74	84	.240	.348	1	.167	0	-1	-2	-0	-0.1
1912 Phi-A	0	0	—	3	0	0	0	0	20¹	26	0	12	8	16.8	3.98	77	.338	.427	2	.250	0	-2	-2	0	-0.1
1916 Chi-A	6	5	.545	28	8	1	0	2	93²	87	1	37	49	12.2	3.27	85	.259	.338	2	.087	-1	-5	-5	1	-0.5
1917 *Chi-A	12	6	.667	**50**	9	1	1	9	173	155	1	74	79	12.1	2.65	100	.244	.325	6	.130	0	0	0	-3	-0.2
1918 Chi-A	6	15	.286	39	11	5	0	2	139	148	1	40	48	12.5	3.43	80	.288	.345	6	.143	-2	-10	-11	0	-1.2
1919 Chi-A	1	2	.333	15	1	0	0	1	41²	58	1	20	17	17.1	7.78	41	.333	.405	1	.111	0	-21	-21	-0	-2.0
1922 StL-A	5	2	.714	20	10	3	0	1	79²	93	1	38	48	14.9	3.28	127	.304	.383	2	.087	-2	7	8	-1	0.4
1923 StL-A	16	14	.533	38	26	16	0	1	226¹	221	4	87	96	12.7	3.94	106	.262	.340	15	.211	3	1	6	-1	0.8
1924 StL-A	15	12	.556	41	27	11	1	4	219²	246	16	69	65	13.0	4.51	100	.292	.348	13	.171	-2	-7	-0	-3	-0.3
1925 StL-A	7	9	.438	38	15	5	0	2	159	172	19	61	53	13.4	4.36	107	.284	.353	8	.174	-2	1	6	-4	0.0
Total 10	72	66	.522	286	109	43	2	23	1186	1235	45	455	484	13.1	3.89	95	.277	.349	56	.160	-6	-37	-25	-11	-3.2

■ CHUCK DANIEL
Daniel, Charles Edward b: 9/17/33, Bluffton, Ark. BR/TR, 6'2", 195 lbs. Deb: 9/21/57

YEAR TM/L	W	L	PCT	G	GS	CG	SH	SV	IP	H	HR	BB	SO	RAT	ERA	ERA+	OAV	OOB	BH	AVG	PB	PR	/A	PD	TPI
1957 Det-A	0	0	—	1	0	0	0	0	2¹	3	1	0	2	11.6	7.71	50	.333	.333	0	—	0	-1	-1	0	0.0

■ BENNIE DANIELS
Daniels, Bennie b: 6/17/32, Tuscaloosa, Ala. BL/TR, 6'1.5", 193 lbs. Deb: 9/24/57

YEAR TM/L	W	L	PCT	G	GS	CG	SH	SV	IP	H	HR	BB	SO	RAT	ERA	ERA+	OAV	OOB	BH	AVG	PB	PR	/A	PD	TPI
1957 Pit-N	0	1	.000	1	1	0	0	0	7	5	0	3	2	10.3	1.29	295	.208	.296	0	.000	-0	2	2	1	0.3
1958 Pit-N	0	3	.000	8	5	1	0	0	27²	31	3	15	7	15.3	5.53	70	.290	.382	1	.125	-0	-5	-5	1	-0.3
1959 Pit-N	7	9	.438	34	12	0	0	1	100²	115	9	39	67	13.9	5.45	71	.287	.353	9	.310	6	-17	-18	-1	-1.2
1960 Pit-N	1	3	.250	10	6	0	0	0	40¹	52	4	17	16	15.4	7.81	48	.311	.375	3	.188	0	-18	-18	1	-1.5
1961 Was-A	12	11	.522	32	28	12	1	0	212	184	14	80	110	11.3	3.44	117	.237	.311	15	.197	3	14	14	1	1.8
1962 Was-A	7	16	.304	44	21	3	1	2	161¹	172	14	66	66	13.5	4.85	83	.280	.354	6	.130	-1	-16	-15	5	-0.9
1963 Was-A	5	10	.333	35	24	6	1	1	168²	163	19	58	88	11.8	4.38	85	.250	.312	7	.152	1	-14	-12	3	-0.8
1964 Was-A	8	10	.444	33	24	3	2	0	163	147	20	64	73	11.7	3.70	100	.245	.317	6	.128	0	-1	0	3	0.3
1965 Was-A	5	13	.278	33	18	1	0	1	116¹	135	16	39	42	13.5	4.72	74	.290	.345	4	.133	0	-16	-16	0	-1.5
Total 9	45	76	.372	230	139	26	5	5	997	1004	99	383	471	12.6	4.44	86	.264	.332	51	.170	9	-72	-69	13	-3.8

■ CHARLIE DANIELS
Daniels, Charles L. b: 7/1/1861, Roxbury, Mass. d: 2/9/38, Boston, Mass. Deb: 4/18/1884

YEAR TM/L	W	L	PCT	G	GS	CG	SH	SV	IP	H	HR	BB	SO	RAT	ERA	ERA+	OAV	OOB	BH	AVG	PB	PR	/A	PD	TPI
1884 Bos-U	0	2	.000	2	2	1	0	0	16²	24	0	2	11	14.0	4.32	68	.278	.298	3	.273	0	-2	-3	-0	-0.1

■ PETE DANIELS
Daniels, Peter J. "Smiling Pete" b: 4/8/1864, County Cavan, Ireland d: 2/13/28, Indianapolis, Ind. BL/TL, Deb: 4/19/1890

YEAR TM/L	W	L	PCT	G	GS	CG	SH	SV	IP	H	HR	BB	SO	RAT	ERA	ERA+	OAV	OOB	BH	AVG	PB	PR	/A	PD	TPI
1890 Pit-N	1	2	.333	4	4	3	0	0	28	40	1	12	8	16.7	7.07	46	.326	.386	4	.333	1	-11	-12	-0	-0.8
1898 StL-N	1	6	.143	10	6	3	0	0	54²	62	0	14	13	12.5	3.62	105	.283	.326	3	.176	0	-0	1	0	0.1
Total 2	2	8	.200	14	10	6	0	0	82²	102	1	26	21	13.9	4.79	76	.299	.348	7	.241	1	-11	-11	-0	-0.7

■ GEORGE DARBY
Darby, George William "Deacon" b: 2/6/1869, Kansas City, Mo. d: 2/25/37, Sacramento, Cal. BR/TR, 5'10.5", 160 lbs. Deb: 4/28/1893

YEAR TM/L	W	L	PCT	G	GS	CG	SH	SV	IP	H	HR	BB	SO	RAT	ERA	ERA+	OAV	OOB	BH	AVG	PB	PR	/A	PD	TPI
1893 Cin-N	1	1	.500	4	3	2	0	0	29	41	2	18	6	18.3	7.76	62	.323	.407	3	.300	0	-10	-10	1	-0.5

■ PAT DARCY
Darcy, Patrick Leonard b: 5/12/50, Troy, Ohio BL/TR, 6'3", 175 lbs. Deb: 9/12/74

YEAR TM/L	W	L	PCT	G	GS	CG	SH	SV	IP	H	HR	BB	SO	RAT	ERA	ERA+	OAV	OOB	BH	AVG	PB	PR	/A	PD	TPI
1974 Cin-N	1	0	1.000	6	2	0	0	0	17	17	2	8	14	13.2	3.71	94	.262	.342	1	.333	0	-0	-0	-0	0.0
1975 *Cin-N	11	5	.688	27	22	1	0	1	130²	134	4	59	46	13.3	3.58	100	.269	.346	4	.085	-3	1	0	0	-0.2
1976 Cin-N	2	3	.400	11	4	0	0	2	39	41	2	22	15	14.5	6.23	56	.279	.373	2	.182	1	-12	-12	-0	-1.1
Total 3	14	8	.636	44	28	1	0	3	186²	192	8	89	75	13.5	4.15	86	.270	.352	7	.115	-2	-11	-12	-0	-1.3

■ AL DARK
Dark, Alvin Ralph "Blackie" b: 1/7/22, Comanche, Okla. BR/TR, 5'11", 185 lbs. Deb: 7/14/46 MC♦

YEAR TM/L	W	L	PCT	G	GS	CG	SH	SV	IP	H	HR	BB	SO	RAT	ERA	ERA+	OAV	OOB	BH	AVG	PB	PR	/A	PD	TPI
1953 NY-N	0	0	—	1	1	0	0	0	1	1	1	1	0	18.0	18.00	24	.250	.400	194	.300	1	-2	-2	0	0.0

■ RON DARLING
Darling, Ronald Maurice b: 8/19/60, Honolulu, Hawaii BR/TR, 6'3", 195 lbs. Deb: 9/06/83

YEAR TM/L	W	L	PCT	G	GS	CG	SH	SV	IP	H	HR	BB	SO	RAT	ERA	ERA+	OAV	OOB	BH	AVG	PB	PR	/A	PD	TPI
1983 NY-N	1	3	.250	5	5	1	0	0	35¹	31	0	17	23	13.0	2.80	129	.248	.352	1	.100	-1	3	3	0	0.3
1984 NY-N	12	9	.571	33	33	2	2	0	205²	179	17	104	136	12.6	3.81	93	.235	.331	10	.149	-1	-5	-6	2	-0.4
1985 NY-N	16	6	.727	36	35	4	2	0	248	214	21	114	167	12.0	2.90	119	.235	.323	13	.171	2	19	15	3	2.2
1986 *NY-N	15	6	.714	34	34	4	2	0	237	203	21	81	184	10.9	2.81	126	.234	.302	8	.099	-2	24	19	3	2.1
1987 NY-N	12	8	.600	32	32	2	0	0	207²	183	24	96	167	12.2	4.29	88	.233	.319	8	.123	1	-5	-12	3	-0.8
1988 *NY-N	17	9	.654	34	34	7	4	0	240²	218	24	60	161	10.6	3.25	99	.245	.297	18	.220	6	5	-1	-0	0.5
1989 NY-N	14	14	.500	33	33	4	0	0	217¹	214	19	70	153	11.9	3.52	93	.258	.318	9	.123	1	-1	-6	2	-0.3
1990 NY-N	7	9	.438	33	18	1	0	0	126	135	20	44	99	13.1	4.50	81	.273	.338	4	.129	0	-10	-12	1	-1.0
Total 8	94	64	.595	240	224	25	10	0	1517²	1377	146	586	1090	11.8	3.48	100	.243	.318	71	.146	6	31	1	15	2.6

■ BOB DARNELL
Darnell, Robert Jack b: 11/6/30, Wewoka, Okla. BR/TR, 5'10", 175 lbs. Deb: 8/10/54

YEAR TM/L	W	L	PCT	G	GS	CG	SH	SV	IP	H	HR	BB	SO	RAT	ERA	ERA+	OAV	OOB	BH	AVG	PB	PR	/A	PD	TPI
1954 Bro-N	0	0	—	6	1	0	0	0	14¹	15	2	7	5	13.8	3.14	130	.278	.361	0	.000	-0	1	1	0	0.2
1956 Bro-N	0	0	—	1	0	0	0	0	1¹	1	0	0	0	6.8	0.00	—	.200	.200	0	—	0	1	1	0	0.1
Total 2	0	0	—	7	1	0	0	0	15²	16	2	7	5	13.2	2.87	142	.271	.348	0	.000	-0	2	2	0	0.3

■ MIKE DARR
Darr, Michael Edward b: 3/23/56, Pomona, Cal. BR/TR, 6'4", 190 lbs. Deb: 9/06/77

YEAR TM/L	W	L	PCT	G	GS	CG	SH	SV	IP	H	HR	BB	SO	RAT	ERA	ERA+	OAV	OOB	BH	AVG	PB	PR	/A	PD	TPI
1977 Tor-A	0	1	.000	1	1	0	0	0	1¹	3	1	4	1	54.0	33.75	12	.429	.667	0	—	0	-4	-4	0	-0.3

■ GEORGE DARROW
Darrow, George Oliver b: 7/12/03, Beloit, Kan. d: 3/24/83, Sun City, Ariz. BL/TL, 6', 180 lbs. Deb: 4/22/34

YEAR TM/L	W	L	PCT	G	GS	CG	SH	SV	IP	H	HR	BB	SO	RAT	ERA	ERA+	OAV	OOB	BH	AVG	PB	PR	/A	PD	TPI
1934 Phi-N	2	6	.250	17	8	2	0	1	49	57	4	28	14	16.3	5.51	86	.302	.403	2	.133	1	-8	-4	0	-0.2

■ BOBBY DARWIN
Darwin, Arthur Bobby Lee b: 2/16/43, Los Angeles, Cal. BR/TR, 6'2", 190 lbs. Deb: 9/30/62 ♦

YEAR TM/L	W	L	PCT	G	GS	CG	SH	SV	IP	H	HR	BB	SO	RAT	ERA	ERA+	OAV	OOB	BH	AVG	PB	PR	/A	PD	TPI
1962 LA-A	0	1	.000	1	1	0	0	0	3¹	8	0	4	6	32.4	10.80	36	.421	.522	0	.000	-0	-3	-3	-0	-0.2
1969 LA-N	0	0	—	3	0	0	0	0	3²	4	0	5	0	27.0	9.82	36	.333	.579	0	—	-0	-3	-3	-0	-0.2
Total 2	0	1	.000	4	1	0	0	0	7	12	0	9	6	29.6	10.29	35	.387	.548	559	.251	-0	-5	-5	-0	-0.4

■ DANNY DARWIN
Darwin, Daniel Wayne b: 10/25/55, Bonham, Tex. BR/TR, 6'3", 185 lbs. Deb: 9/08/78

YEAR TM/L	W	L	PCT	G	GS	CG	SH	SV	IP	H	HR	BB	SO	RAT	ERA	ERA+	OAV	OOB	BH	AVG	PB	PR	/A	PD	TPI
1978 Tex-A	1	0	1.000	3	1	0	0	0	8²	11	0	1	8	12.5	4.15	90	.324	.343	0	—	0	-0	-0	0	0.0
1979 Tex-A	4	4	.500	20	6	1	0	0	78	50	5	30	58	9.8	4.04	103	.186	.280	0	—	0	2	1	-1	0.0

YEAR	TM/L	W	L	PCT	G	GS	CG	SH	SV	IP	H	HR	BB	SO	RAT	ERA	ERA+	OAV	OOB	BH	AVG	PB	PR	/A	PD	TPI
1980	Tex-A	13	4	.765	53	2	0	0	8	109²	98	4	50	104	12.3	2.63	148	.243	.329	0	—	0	17	15	-1	1.5
1981	Tex-A	9	9	.500	22	22	6	2	0	146	115	12	57	98	11.0	3.64	95	.218	.302	0	—	0	0	-3	-1	-0.3
1982	Tex-A	10	8	.556	56	1	0	0	7	89	95	6	37	61	13.6	3.44	113	.279	.354	0	—	0	6	4	1	0.6
1983	Tex-A	8	13	.381	28	26	9	2	0	183	175	9	62	92	11.8	3.49	115	.250	.313	0	—	0	12	10	-1	1.0
1984	Tex-A	8	12	.400	35	32	5	1	0	223²	249	19	54	123	12.4	3.94	105	.279	.323	0	—	0	1	5	-2	0.3
1985	Mil-A	8	18	.308	39	29	11	1	2	217²	212	34	65	125	11.6	3.80	109	.254	.311	0	—	0	8	9	-3	0.6
1986	Mil-A	6	8	.429	27	14	5	1	0	130¹	120	13	35	80	10.9	3.52	123	.246	.300	0	—	0	9	12	1	1.2
	Hou-N	5	2	.714	12	8	1	0	0	54¹	50	3	40	40	9.8	2.32	155	.239	.271	1	.063	-1	8	8	-0	0.7
1987	Hou-N	9	10	.474	33	30	3	1	0	195²	184	17	69	134	11.9	3.59	109	.246	.314	12	.182	2	11	7	-1	0.8
1988	Hou-N	8	13	.381	44	20	3	0	3	192	189	20	48	129	11.4	3.84	86	.259	.311	4	.071	-1	-8	-11	2	-1.0
1989	Hou-N	11	4	.733	68	0	0	0	7	122	92	8	33	104	9.4	2.36	143	.212	.271	2	.118	-1	15	14	-2	1.2
1990	Hou-N	11	4	.733	48	17	3	0	2	162²	136	11	31	109	9.5	2.21	169	.225	.267	5	.132	1	29	28	-1	2.8
Total	13	111	109	.505	488	208	47	8	29	1912²	1776	161	581	1265	11.3	3.40	114	.246	.307	24	.124	-0	110	98	-10	9.4

■ DOUG DASCENZO
Dascenzo, Douglas Craig b: 6/30/64, Cleveland, Ohio BB/TL, 5'7", 150 lbs. Deb: 9/02/88 ◆

YEAR	TM/L	W	L	PCT	G	GS	CG	SH	SV	IP	H	HR	BB	SO	RAT	ERA	ERA+	OAV	OOB	BH	AVG	PB	PR	/A	PD	TPI
1990	Chi-N	0	0	—	1	0	0	0	0	1	1	0	0	0	9.0	0.00	—	.333	.333	61	.253	0	0	0	0	0.0

■ LEE DASHNER
Dashner, Lee Claire "Lefty" b: 4/25/1887, Renault, Ill. d: 12/16/59, ElDorado, Kan. BB/TL, 5'11.5", 192 lbs. Deb: 8/04/13

YEAR	TM/L	W	L	PCT	G	GS	CG	SH	SV	IP	H	HR	BB	SO	RAT	ERA	ERA+	OAV	OOB	BH	AVG	PB	PR	/A	PD	TPI
1913	Cle-A	0	0	—	1	0	0	0	0	1²	0	0	0	2	0.0	5.40	56	.000	.000	0	—	0	-0	-0	0	0.0

■ FRANK DASSO
Dasso, Francis Joseph Nicholas b: 8/31/17, Chicago, Ill. BR/TR, 5'11.5", 185 lbs. Deb: 4/22/45

YEAR	TM/L	W	L	PCT	G	GS	CG	SH	SV	IP	H	HR	BB	SO	RAT	ERA	ERA+	OAV	OOB	BH	AVG	PB	PR	/A	PD	TPI
1945	Cin-N	4	5	.444	16	12	6	0	0	95²	89	9	53	39	13.4	3.67	102	.253	.351	5	.161	-1	1	1	0	0.1
1946	Cin-N	0	0	—	2	0	0	0	0	1	2	0	2	1	36.0	27.00	12	.400	.571	0	—	0	-3	-3	0	-0.2
Total	2	4	5	.444	18	12	6	0	0	96²	91	9	55	40	13.6	3.91	96	.255	.354	5	.161	-1	-1	-2	0	-0.1

■ DAN DAUB
Daub, Daniel William "Mickey" b: 1/12/1868, Middletown, Ohio d: 3/25/51, Bradenton, Fla. 5'10", 160 lbs. Deb: 8/31/1892

YEAR	TM/L	W	L	PCT	G	GS	CG	SH	SV	IP	H	HR	BB	SO	RAT	ERA	ERA+	OAV	OOB	BH	AVG	PB	PR	/A	PD	TPI
1892	Cin-N	1	2	.333	4	3	2	0	0	25	23	0	13	7	13.0	2.88	113	.235	.324	0	.000	-1	1	1	0	0.0
1893	Bro-N	6	6	.500	12	12	12	0	0	103	104	3	61	25	14.4	3.84	115	.254	.351	8	.190	-1	9	7	3	0.6
1894	Bro-N	9	12	.429	33	26	14	0	0	215	283	7	90	45	15.6	6.32	78	.314	.376	16	.174	-6	-24	-33	-0	-2.9
1895	Bro-N	10	10	.500	25	21	16	0	0	184²	212	4	51	36	12.8	4.29	102	.284	.329	14	.197	-2	10	2	2	0.1
1896	Bro-N	12	11	.522	32	24	18	0	0	225	255	4	63	53	12.7	3.60	115	.283	.330	19	.226	2	19	13	4	1.6
1897	Bro-N	6	11	.353	19	16	11	0	0	137²	180	8	48	19	14.9	6.08	67	.313	.366	11	.224	2	-27	-30	0	-2.2
Total	6	44	52	.458	125	102	73	0	0	890¹	1057	26	326	185	14.0	4.79	92	.291	.349	68	.197	-7	-11	-40	9	-2.8

■ HOOKS DAUSS
Dauss, George August (b: George August Daus) b: 9/22/1889, Indianapolis, Ind d: 7/27/63, St.Louis, Mo. BR/TR, 5'10.5", 168 lbs. Deb: 9/28/12

YEAR	TM/L	W	L	PCT	G	GS	CG	SH	SV	IP	H	HR	BB	SO	RAT	ERA	ERA+	OAV	OOB	BH	AVG	PB	PR	/A	PD	TPI
1912	Det-A	1	1	.500	2	2	2	0	0	17	11	0	9	7	12.2	3.18	103	.186	.324	1	.250	1	0	0	1	0.2
1913	Det-A	13	12	.520	33	29	22	2	1	225	188	4	82	107	11.3	2.48	118	.228	.308	14	.177	3	11	11	-1	1.4
1914	Det-A	18	15	.545	45	35	22	3	4	302	286	3	87	150	11.7	2.86	98	.257	.321	21	.216	6	-4	-2	-0	0.4
1915	Det-A	24	13	.649	46	35	27	1	2	309²	261	1	115	132	11.2	2.50	121	.235	.313	15	.146	5	15	18	9	3.1
1916	Det-A	19	12	.613	39	29	18	1	4	238²	220	2	90	95	12.3	3.21	89	.257	.339	16	.222	8	-10	-9	2	0.1
1917	Det-A	17	14	.548	37	31	22	6	2	270²	243	3	87	102	11.2	2.43	109	.245	.311	11	.126	-1	7	7	4	1.1
1918	Det-A	12	16	.429	33	26	21	1	3	249²	243	3	58	73	11.2	2.99	89	.263	.313	14	.182	3	-6	-9	2	-0.4
1919	Det-A	21	9	.700	34	32	22	2	0	256¹	262	9	63	73	11.6	3.55	90	.267	.315	14	.144	-3	-9	-10	6	-0.6
1920	Det-A	13	21	.382	38	32	18	0	0	270¹	308	11	84	82	13.3	3.56	105	.289	.345	14	.169	1	7	5	9	1.4
1921	Det-A	10	15	.400	32	28	16	0	1	233	275	11	81	68	14.3	4.33	99	.297	.362	23	.261	2	-1	-1	5	0.6
1922	Det-A	13	13	.500	39	25	12	1	1	218²	251	7	59	78	13.0	4.20	92	.289	.339	15	.208	3	-4	-8	1	-0.3
1923	Det-A	21	13	.618	50	39	22	4	3	316	331	10	78	105	11.8	3.62	107	.272	.319	24	.231	5	13	9	2	1.4
1924	Det-A	12	11	.522	40	10	5	0	6	131¹	155	6	40	44	13.4	4.59	90	.302	.354	5	.132	-2	-5	-7	-0	-0.7
1925	Det-A	16	11	.593	35	30	16	1	1	228	238	11	85	58	12.9	3.16	136	.272	.339	15	.185	1	31	29	17	2.8
1926	Det-A	12	6	.667	35	5	0	0	9	124¹	135	6	49	27	13.3	4.20	97	.287	.354	10	.238	4	-2	-2	0	0.2
Total	15	222	182	.550	538	388	245	22	40	3390²	3407	87	1067	1201	12.2	3.30	103	.266	.329	212	.189	32	44	34	38	10.7

■ VIC DAVALILLO
Davalillo, Victor Jose (Romero) b: 7/31/36, Cabimas, Venez. BL/TL, 5'7", 150 lbs. Deb: 4/09/63 ◆

YEAR	TM/L	W	L	PCT	G	GS	CG	SH	SV	IP	H	HR	BB	SO	RAT	ERA	ERA+	OAV	OOB	BH	AVG	PB	PR	/A	PD	TPI
1969	StL-N	0	0	—	2	0	0	0	0	0	2	0	2	0	—	∞	—	1.000	1.000	26	.265	0	-1	-1	0	0.0

■ CLAUDE DAVENPORT
Davenport, Claude Edwin "Big Dave" b: 5/28/1898, Runge, Tex. d: 6/13/76, Corpus Christi, Tex. BR/TR, 6'6", 193 lbs. Deb: 10/02/20

YEAR	TM/L	W	L	PCT	G	GS	CG	SH	SV	IP	H	HR	BB	SO	RAT	ERA	ERA+	OAV	OOB	BH	AVG	PB	PR	/A	PD	TPI
1920	NY-N	0	0	—	1	0	0	0	0	2	2	1	1	0	13.5	4.50	67	.250	.333	0	.000	-0	-0	-0	0	0.0

■ DAVE DAVENPORT
Davenport, David W. b: 2/20/1890, DeRidder, La. d: 10/16/54, ElDorado, Ark. BR/TR, 6'6", 220 lbs. Deb: 4/17/14

YEAR	TM/L	W	L	PCT	G	GS	CG	SH	SV	IP	H	HR	BB	SO	RAT	ERA	ERA+	OAV	OOB	BH	AVG	PB	PR	/A	PD	TPI
1914	Cin-N	2	2	.500	10	6	3	1	2	54	38	1	30	22	11.8	2.50	117	.202	.321	2	.111	-1	2	3	-0	0.1
	StL-F	8	13	.381	33	26	13	2	4	215²	204	3	80	142	12.1	3.46	98	.251	.324	6	.088	-6	-6	-2	-0	-0.6
1915	StL-F	22	18	.550	55	46	30	10	1	392²	300	5	96	229	9.2	2.20	145	.215	.268	12	.092	-9	36	43	-9	2.9
1916	StL-A	12	11	.522	59	31	13	1	2	290²	267	4	100	129	11.6	2.85	97	.256	.326	10	.137	3	-1	-3	-4	-0.4
1917	StL-A	17	17	.500	47	39	20	2	2	280²	273	5	105	100	12.4	3.08	84	.260	.331	9	.098	-6	-13	-15	-1	-2.3
1918	StL-A	10	11	.476	31	22	12	2	1	180	182	0	69	60	12.9	3.25	84	.273	.347	7	.135	1	-9	-10	2	-1.1
1919	StL-A	2	11	.154	24	16	5	0	0	123¹	135	4	41	37	13.0	3.94	84	.280	.339	3	.077	-4	-10	-9	1	-1.1
Total	6	73	83	.468	259	186	96	18	12	1537	1399	22	521	719	11.5	2.93	101	.248	.316	49	.104	-22	-1	6	-11	-2.2

■ LUM DAVENPORT
Davenport, Joubert Lum b: 6/27/1900, Tucson, Ariz. d: 4/21/61, Dallas, Tex. BL/TL, 6'1", 165 lbs. Deb: 5/02/21

YEAR	TM/L	W	L	PCT	G	GS	CG	SH	SV	IP	H	HR	BB	SO	RAT	ERA	ERA+	OAV	OOB	BH	AVG	PB	PR	/A	PD	TPI
1921	Chi-A	0	3	.000	13	2	0	0	0	35¹	41	1	9	18	18.8	6.88	62	.318	.457	7	.412	2	-10	-10	-0	-0.7
1922	Chi-A	1	1	.500	9	1	0	0	0	16²	14	2	13	9	14.6	10.80	38	.233	.370	0	.000	-0	-13	-12	0	-1.0
1923	Chi-A	0	0	—	2	0	0	0	0	4¹	7	0	4	1	22.8	6.23	64	.438	.550	1	1.000	0	-1	-1	0	0.1
1924	Chi-A	0	0	—	1	0	0	0	0	2	1	0	2	1	13.5	0.00	—	.125	.300	0	—	0	1	1	-0	0.1
Total	4	1	4	.200	25	3	0	0	0	58¹	63	3	51	20	17.7	7.71	54	.296	.434	8	.381	2	-23	-23	0	-1.6

■ MIKE DAVEY
Davey, Michael Gerard b: 6/2/52, Spokane, Wash. BR/TL, 6'2", 190 lbs. Deb: 8/13/77

YEAR	TM/L	W	L	PCT	G	GS	CG	SH	SV	IP	H	HR	BB	SO	RAT	ERA	ERA+	OAV	OOB	BH	AVG	PB	PR	/A	PD	TPI
1977	Atl-N	0	0	—	16	0	0	0	2	16	19	1	9	7	15.8	5.06	88	.302	.389	0	.000	-0	-2	-1	0	0.1
1978	Atl-N	0	0	—	3	0	0	0	0	2²	1	0	1	0	6.8	0.00	—	.125	.222	0	—	0	1	1	0	0.1
Total	2	0	0	—	19	0	0	0	2	18²	20	1	10	7	14.5	4.34	101	.282	.370	0	.000	-0	-1	0	0	0.1

■ RAY DAVIAULT
Daviault, Raymond Joseph Robert b: 5/27/34, Montreal, Que., Can BR/TR, 6'1", 170 lbs. Deb: 4/13/62

YEAR	TM/L	W	L	PCT	G	GS	CG	SH	SV	IP	H	HR	BB	SO	RAT	ERA	ERA+	OAV	OOB	BH	AVG	PB	PR	/A	PD	TPI
1962	NY-N	1	5	.167	36	3	0	0	0	81	92	14	48	51	16.0	6.22	67	.288	.388	1	.067	-1	-21	-18	-1	-1.9

■ BOB DAVIDSON
Davidson, Robert Banks b: 1/6/63, Bad Kurznach, W.Ger. BR/TR, 6', 185 lbs. Deb: 7/15/89

YEAR	TM/L	W	L	PCT	G	GS	CG	SH	SV	IP	H	HR	BB	SO	RAT	ERA	ERA+	OAV	OOB	BH	AVG	PB	PR	/A	PD	TPI
1989	NY-A	0	0	—	1	0	0	0	0	1	1	1	1	0	18.0	18.00	21	.250	.400	0	—	0	-2	-2	0	-0.1

■ TED DAVIDSON
Davidson, Thomas Eugene b: 10/4/39, Las Vegas, Nev. BR/TL, 6', 192 lbs. Deb: 7/24/65

YEAR	TM/L	W	L	PCT	G	GS	CG	SH	SV	IP	H	HR	BB	SO	RAT	ERA	ERA+	OAV	OOB	BH	AVG	PB	PR	/A	PD	TPI
1965	Cin-N	4	3	.571	24	1	0	0	1	68²	57	5	17	54	10.0	2.23	168	.233	.288	0	.000	-2	10	12	0	1.1
1966	Cin-N	5	4	.556	54	0	0	0	4	85¹	82	11	23	54	11.2	3.90	100	.253	.305	0	.000	-2	-3	-0	-0	-0.1
1967	Cin-N	1	0	1.000	9	0	0	0	0	13	13	0	3	6	11.1	4.15	90	.250	.291	0	—	0	-1	-1	0	0.0
1968	Cin-N	1	0	1.000	23	0	0	0	0	21²	27	3	7	7	14.1	6.23	51	.307	.358	0	.000	-0	-8	-7	0	-0.7
	Atl-N	0	0	—	4	0	0	0	0	6²	10	2	4	3	18.9	6.75	44	.345	.424	0	—	0	-3	-3	0	-0.2
	Yr	1	0	1.000	27	0	0	0	0	28¹	37	5	11	10	15.2	6.35	49	.316	.375	1	.500	0	-11	-10	0	-0.9
Total	4	11	7	.611	114	1	0	0	5	195¹	189	21	54	124	11.3	3.69	101	.256	.309	0	.000	-3	-5	1	1	0.1

YEAR TM/L	W	L	PCT	G	GS	CG	SH	SV	IP	H	HR	BB	SO	RAT	ERA	ERA+	OAV	OOB	BH	AVG	PB	PR	/A	PD	TPI

■ JERRY DAVIE Davie, Gerald Lee b: 2/10/33, Detroit, Mich. BR/TR, 6', 180 lbs. Deb: 4/14/59

| 1959 Det-A | 2 | 2 | .500 | 11 | 5 | 1 | 0 | 0 | 36² | 40 | 8 | 17 | 20 | 15.0 | 4.17 | 97 | .265 | .355 | 4 | .400 | 2 | -1 | -0 | 1 | 0.2 |

■ GEORGE DAVIES Davies, George Washington b: 2/22/1868, Portage, Wis. d: 9/22/06, Waterloo, Wis. 180 lbs. Deb: 8/18/1891

1891 Mil-a	7	5	.583	12	12	12	1	0	102	94	2	35	61	11.4	2.65	166	.237	.298	9	.243	1	12	20	-1	1.9
1892 Cle-N	10	16	.385	26	26	23	0	0	215²	201	4	69	95	11.3	2.59	131	.237	.294	12	.138	-5	17	19	2	1.5
1893 Cle-N	0	2	.000	3	3	1	0	0	15	28	1	10	3	22.8	11.40	41	.387	.461	2	.333	0	-11	-11	0	-0.7
NY-N	1	1	.500	5	1	1	0	0	36¹	41	1	13	7	13.4	6.19	75	.276	.334	4	.333	2	-6	-6	0	-0.2
Yr	1	3	.250	8	4	2	0	0	51¹	69	2	23	10	16.1	7.71	61	.312	.377	5	.278	2	-17	-17	1	-0.9
Total 3	18	24	.429	46	42	37	1	0	369	364	8	127	166	12.0	3.32	116	.248	.308	27	.190	-2	12	22	2	2.5

■ CHICK DAVIES Davies, Lloyd Garrison b: 3/6/1892, Peabody, Mass. d: 9/5/73, Middletown, Conn. BL/TL, 5'8", 145 lbs. Deb: 7/11/14 ♦

1914 Phi-A	1	0	1.000	1	1	1	0	0	9	8	0	3	4	11.0	1.00	263	.258	.324	11	.239	0	2	2	0	0.2
1915 Phi-A	1	2	.333	4	2	0	0	0	15¹	20	0	12	2	19.4	8.80	33	.339	.458	24	.182	0	-10	-10	1	-0.8
1925 NY-N	0	0	—	2	1	0	0	0	7¹	13	0	4	5	20.9	6.14	66	.361	.425	0	.000	-0	-2	-2	0	-0.1
1926 NY-N	2	4	.333	38	1	0	0	6	89	96	3	35	27	13.2	3.94	95	.277	.344	4	.222	1	-1	-2	1	0.0
Total 4	4	6	.400	45	5	1	0	6	120²	137	3	54	38	14.3	4.48	80	.290	.364	39	.193	1	-11	-12	2	-0.7

■ CURT DAVIS Davis, Curtis Benton "Coonskin" b: 9/7/03, Greenfield, Mo. d: 10/13/65, Covina, Cal. BR/TR, 6'2", 185 lbs. Deb: 4/21/34

1934 Phi-N	19	17	.528	51	31	18	3	5	274¹	283	14	60	99	11.5	2.95	160	.269	.313	20	.211	-2	34	54	9	**6.6**
1935 Phi-N	16	14	.533	44	27	19	3	2	231	264	14	47	74	12.4	3.66	124	.285	.324	13	.173	-1	9	22	2	2.5
1936 Phi-N	2	4	.333	10	8	3	0	0	60¹	71	6	19	18	13.6	4.62	98	.291	.345	4	.154	-2	-4	-1	0	-0.1
Chi-N	11	9	.550	24	20	10	0	1	153	146	11	31	52	10.5	3.00	133	.251	.290	8	.151	-2	17	17	3	1.8
Yr	13	13	.500	34	28	13	0	1	213¹	217	17	50	70	11.3	3.46	120	.263	.306	2	.025	-4	13	16	3	1.7
1937 Chi-N	10	5	.667	28	14	8	0	1	123²	138	7	30	32	12.6	4.08	98	.286	.334	12	.300	4	-2	-1	2	0.4
1938 StL-N	12	8	.600	40	21	8	2	3	173¹	187	9	27	36	11.2	3.63	109	.272	.301	13	.228	1	3	6	1	1.0
1939 StL-N	22	16	.579	49	31	13	3	7	248	279	18	48	70	12.0	3.63	113	.280	.315	40	.381	12	8	13	2	2.9
1940 StL-N	0	4	.000	14	7	0	0	0	54	73	4	19	12	15.5	5.17	77	.327	.383	0	.000	-3	-8	-7	1	-0.7
Bro-N	8	7	.533	22	18	9	0	2	137	135	13	19	46	10.2	3.81	105	.256	.283	6	.128	-1	1	3	2	0.4
Yr	8	11	.421	36	25	9	0	3	191	208	17	38	58	11.6	4.19	94	.277	.312	2	.030	-3	-7	-4	3	-0.3
1941 *Bro-N	13	7	.650	28	16	10	5	2	154¹	141	6	27	50	9.9	2.97	123	.244	.280	11	.186	2	11	12	4	1.9
1942 Bro-N	15	6	.714	32	26	13	5	2	206	179	10	51	60	10.4	2.36	138	.233	.287	12	.176	-0	22	21	4	2.7
1943 Bro-N	10	13	.435	31	21	8	2	3	164¹	182	8	39	47	12.2	3.78	89	.281	.324	9	.164	-1	-7	-8	3	-0.5
1944 Bro-N	10	11	.476	31	23	12	1	0	194	207	12	39	44	11.6	3.34	106	.270	.310	10	.159	-2	6	5	2	0.5
1945 Bro-N	10	10	.500	24	18	10	0	0	149²	171	9	21	39	11.7	3.25	116	.280	.308	7	.137	-1	9	8	1	0.8
1946 Bro-N	0	0	—	1	0	0	0	0	2	3	1	2	0	27.0	13.50	25	.375	.545	0	—	0	-2	-2	0	-0.1
Total 13	158	131	.547	429	281	141	24	33	2325	2459	142	479	684	11.6	3.42	116	.270	.310	165	.203	7	96	139	35	20.1

■ DIXIE DAVIS Davis, Frank Talmadge b: 10/12/1890, Wilson Mills, N.C. d: 2/4/44, Raleigh, N.C. BR/TR, 5'11", 155 lbs. Deb: 7/12/12

1912 Cin-N	0	1	.000	7	0	0	0	0	26²	25	0	16	12	14.2	2.70	124	.243	.350	2	.200	-0	2	2	-1	0.1
1915 Chi-A	0	0	—	2	0	0	0	0	3	2	0	2	2	15.0	0.00	—	.250	.455	0	—	0	1	1	0	0.1
1918 Phi-A	0	2	.000	17	2	1	0	0	47	43	1	30	18	14.0	3.06	98	.247	.358	0	.000	-0	-2	-0	-1	-0.1
1920 StL-A	18	12	.600	38	31	22	0	0	269¹	250	10	149	85	13.6	3.17	123	.256	.359	25	.266	3	19	22	-4	2.1
1921 StL-A	16	16	.500	40	36	20	2	0	265¹	279	12	123	100	14.0	4.44	101	.281	.366	20	.211	-3	-5	1	-1	-0.1
1922 StL-A	11	6	.647	25	25	7	2	0	174¹	162	10	87	65	13.3	4.08	102	.250	.345	8	.136	-3	-1	1	-0	-0.1
1923 StL-A	4	6	.400	19	17	5	1	0	109¹	106	4	63	36	14.3	3.62	115	.259	.365	10	.250	0	4	7	-2	0.5
1924 StL-A	11	13	.458	29	24	11	5	0	160¹	159	9	72	45	13.3	4.10	110	.263	.347	7	.152	-2	2	7	-1	0.5
1925 StL-A	12	7	.632	35	23	9	0	1	180¹	192	10	106	58	15.2	4.59	102	.279	.380	11	.172	-4	-4	2	1	0.0
1926 StL-A	3	8	.273	27	7	2	0	1	83	93	7	40	39	14.5	4.66	92	.292	.372	4	.167	-0	-6	-3	-1	-0.3
Total 10	75	71	.514	239	165	77	10	2	1318²	1311	63	688	460	14.0	3.97	107	.266	.362	87	.197	-10	12	39	-10	2.7

■ IRON DAVIS Davis, George Allen b: 3/9/1890, Lancaster, N.Y. d: 6/4/61, Buffalo, N.Y. BB/TR, 5'10.5", 175 lbs. Deb: 7/16/12

1912 NY-A	1	4	.200	10	7	5	0	0	54	61	3	28	22	15.3	6.50	55	.293	.385	2	.111	-1	-19	-17	-1	-1.7
1913 Bos-N	0	0	—	2	0	0	0	0	8	7	1	5	3	13.5	4.50	73	.241	.353	0	.000	-0	-1	-1	-0	-0.1
1914 Bos-N	3	3	.500	9	6	4	1	0	55²	42	1	26	26	11.5	3.40	81	.215	.317	3	.167	0	-4	-4	-2	-0.5
1915 Bos-N	3	3	.500	15	9	4	0	0	73¹	85	2	19	26	13.3	3.80	68	.304	.356	6	.261	1	-9	-10	0	-0.8
Total 4	7	10	.412	36	22	13	1	0	191	195	7	78	77	13.3	4.48	66	.274	.354	11	.180	-1	-33	-33	-3	-3.1

■ STORM DAVIS Davis, George Earl b: 12/26/61, Dallas, Tex. BR/TR, 6'4", 207 lbs. Deb: 4/29/82

1982 Bal-A	8	4	.667	29	8	1	0	0	100²	96	8	28	67	11.1	3.49	116	.257	.308	0	—	0	7	6	-1	0.6
1983 *Bal-A	13	7	.650	34	29	6	1	0	200¹	180	14	64	125	11.1	3.59	110	.238	.299	0	—	0	10	8	-2	0.6
1984 Bal-A	14	9	.609	35	31	10	2	1	225	205	7	71	105	11.2	3.12	124	.247	.310	0	—	0	22	19	-3	1.7
1985 Bal-A	10	8	.556	31	28	8	1	0	175	172	11	70	93	12.5	4.53	89	.256	.327	0	—	0	-7	-10	-0	-0.9
1986 Bal-A	9	12	.429	25	25	2	0	0	154	166	16	49	96	12.6	3.62	114	.275	.330	0	—	0	9	9	2	0.7
1987 SD-N	2	7	.222	21	10	0	0	0	62²	70	5	36	37	15.5	6.18	64	.280	.375	1	.063	-1	-15	-15	0	-1.5
Oak-A	1	1	.500	5	5	0	0	0	30¹	28	3	11	28	11.6	3.26	126	.241	.307	0	—	0	4	3	1	0.2
1988 *Oak-A	16	7	.696	33	33	1	0	0	201²	211	16	91	127	13.5	3.70	102	.274	.352	0	—	0	6	2	-2	0.0
1989 *Oak-A	19	7	.731	31	31	1	0	0	169¹	187	19	68	91	13.7	4.36	84	.288	.358	0	—	0	-9	-13	-1	-1.3
1990 KC-A	7	10	.412	21	20	0	0	0	112	129	9	35	62	13.4	4.74	80	.281	.332	0	—	0	-10	-12	-1	-1.1
Total 9	99	72	.579	265	220	29	4	1	1431	1444	108	523	831	12.5	3.93	99	.263	.329	1	.063	-1	17	-3	-8	-0.7

■ GEORGE DAVIS Davis, George Stacey b: 8/23/1870, Cohoes, N.Y. d: 10/17/40, Philadelphia, Pa. BB/TR, 5'9", 180 lbs. Deb: 4/19/1890 M♦

| 1891 Cle-N | 0 | 1 | .000 | 3 | 0 | 0 | 0 | 1 | 4 | 8 | 0 | 3 | 4 | 24.8 | 15.75 | 22 | .401 | .479 | 165 | .289 | 1 | -6 | -5 | -0 | -0.4 |

■ JIM DAVIS Davis, James Bennett b: 9/15/24, Red Bluff, Cal. BB/TL, 6', 180 lbs. Deb: 4/18/54

1954 Chi-N	11	7	.611	46	12	2	0	4	127²	114	12	51	58	11.8	3.52	119	.247	.326	2	.063	-1	8	10	1	1.0
1955 Chi-N	7	11	.389	42	16	0	0	3	133²	122	16	58	62	12.3	4.44	92	.246	.327	1	.027	-4	-6	-5	-0	-0.9
1956 Chi-N	5	7	.417	46	11	2	1	2	120¹	116	11	59	66	13.5	3.66	103	.256	.349	5	.179	-0	1	1	0	0.2
1957 StL-N	0	1	.000	10	0	0	0	1	13²	18	1	6	5	15.8	5.27	75	.340	.407	0	.000	-0	-2	-2	0	-0.1
NY-N	1	0	1.000	10	0	0	0	0	11	13	2	5	6	14.7	6.55	60	.283	.353	1	1.000	0	-3	-3	0	-0.2
Yr	1	1	.500	20	0	0	0	1	24²	31	3	11	11	15.3	5.84	68	.310	.378	0	.000	0	-5	-5	0	-0.3
Total 4	24	26	.480	154	39	4	1	10	406¹	383	42	179	197	12.7	4.01	100	.253	.337	9	.091	-5	-2	0	1	0.0

■ JOEL DAVIS Davis, Joel Clark b: 1/30/65, Jacksonville, Fla. BL/TR, 6'5", 205 lbs. Deb: 8/11/85

1985 Chi-A	3	3	.500	12	11	1	0	0	71¹	77	6	26	37	12.4	4.16	104	.256	.322	0	—	0	-0	1	-1	0.0
1986 Chi-A	4	5	.444	19	19	1	0	0	105¹	115	9	51	54	14.3	4.70	92	.280	.361	0	—	0	-6	-5	1	-0.3
1987 Chi-A	1	5	.167	13	9	1	0	0	55	56	7	29	25	13.9	5.73	80	.264	.353	0	—	0	-8	-7	-1	-0.7
1988 Chi-A	0	1	.000	5	2	0	0	0	16	21	4	5	10	14.6	6.75	58	.328	.377	0	—	0	-5	-5	-0	-0.4
Total 4	8	14	.364	49	41	3	0	0	247²	263	26	111	126	13.7	4.91	89	.273	.349	0	—	0	-19	-15	-2	-1.4

■ DAISY DAVIS Davis, John Henry Albert b: 11/28/1858, Boston, Mass. d: 11/5/02, Lynn, Mass. TR Deb: 5/06/1884

1884 StL-a	10	12	.455	25	24	20	1	0	198¹	196	1	35	143	10.5	2.90	113	.244	.276	15	.172	-2	8	8	-2	0.3
Bos-N	1	3	.250	4	4	3	0	0	31	50	1	8	13	16.8	7.84	37	.345	.380	0	.000	-3	-17	-17	0	-1.4
1885 Bos-N	5	6	.455	11	11	10	1	0	94¹	110	2	28	30	13.2	4.29	62	.278	.326	7	.189	-0	-15	-17	-1	-1.5
Total 2	16	21	.432	40	39	33	2	0	323²	356	5	71	186	11.9	3.78	81	.265	.302	22	.157	-5	-25	-26	-2	-2.6

YEAR TM/L	W	L	PCT	G	GS	CG	SH	SV	IP	H	HR	BB	SO	RAT	ERA	ERA+	OAV	OOB	BH	AVG	PB	PR	/A	PD	TPI

■ **JOHN DAVIS** Davis, John Kirk b: 1/5/63, Chicago, Ill. BR/TR, 6'7", 215 lbs. Deb: 7/24/87

YEAR TM/L	W	L	PCT	G	GS	CG	SH	SV	IP	H	HR	BB	SO	RAT	ERA	ERA+	OAV	OOB	BH	AVG	PB	PR	/A	PD	TPI
1987 KC-A	5	2	.714	27	0	0	0	2	43²	29	0	26	24	11.7	2.27	201	.195	.322	0	—	0	11	11	0	1.1
1988 Chi-A	2	5	.286	34	1	0	0	1	63²	77	5	50	37	18.5	6.64	60	.297	.419	0	—	0	-19	-19	-0	-1.8
1989 Chi-A	0	1	.000	4	0	0	0	1	6	5	2	2	5	10.5	4.50	85	.217	.280	0	—	0	-0	-0	0	0.0
1990 SD-N	0	1	.000	6	0	0	0	0	9¹	9	1	4	7	12.5	5.79	66	.257	.333	0	.000	-0	-2	-2	0	-0.1
Total 4	7	9	.438	71	1	0	0	4	122²	120	8	82	73	15.3	4.92	85	.258	.375	0	.000	-0	-11	-10	0	-0.8

■ **BUD DAVIS** Davis, John Wilbur "Country" b: 12/7/1896, Merry Point, Va. d: 5/26/67, Williamsburg, Va. BL/TR, 6', 207 lbs. Deb: 4/19/15

YEAR TM/L	W	L	PCT	G	GS	CG	SH	SV	IP	H	HR	BB	SO	RAT	ERA	ERA+	OAV	OOB	BH	AVG	PB	PR	/A	PD	TPI
1915 Phi-A	0	2	.000	18	2	2	0	0	66²	65	1	59	18	17.6	4.05	73	.273	.429	8	.308	2	-8	-8	-0	-0.6

■ **MARK DAVIS** Davis, Mark William b: 10/19/60, Livermore, Cal. BL/TL, 6'3", 180 lbs. Deb: 9/12/80

YEAR TM/L	W	L	PCT	G	GS	CG	SH	SV	IP	H	HR	BB	SO	RAT	ERA	ERA+	OAV	OOB	BH	AVG	PB	PR	/A	PD	TPI
1980 Phi-N	0	0	—	2	1	0	0	0	7	4	0	5	5	11.6	2.57	147	.160	.300	1	.500	0	1	1	-0	0.1
1981 Phi-N	1	4	.200	9	9	0	0	0	43	49	7	24	29	15.3	7.74	47	.299	.388	1	.091	-0	-20	-20	-1	-1.8
1983 SF-N	6	4	.600	20	20	2	2	0	111	93	14	50	83	11.8	3.49	101	.227	.315	4	.133	0	2	1	-1	0.0
1984 SF-N	5	17	.227	46	27	1	0	0	174²	201	25	54	124	13.4	5.36	65	.293	.349	6	.130	0	-34	-36	-2	-3.7
1985 SF-N	5	12	.294	77	1	0	0	7	114¹	89	13	41	131	10.5	3.54	97	.219	.295	3	.250	1	1	-1	-1	-0.1
1986 SF-N	5	7	.417	67	2	0	0	4	84¹	63	6	34	90	10.5	2.99	118	.212	.295	1	.125	0	7	5	-1	0.4
1987 SF-N	4	5	.444	20	11	1	0	0	70²	72	9	28	51	13.2	4.71	82	.273	.351	5	.217	2	-5	-7	-0	-0.5
SD-N	5	3	.625	43	0	0	0	2	62¹	51	5	31	47	12.1	3.18	124	.224	.322	2	.286	0	6	5	0	0.6
Yr	9	8	.529	63	11	1	0	2	133	123	14	59	98	12.5	3.99	98	.247	.329	0	.000	2	1	-1	-0	0.1
1988 SD-N	5	10	.333	62	0	0	0	28	98¹	70	2	42	102	10.3	2.01	169	.199	.284	2	.200	1	16	15	1	2.0
1989 SD-N	4	3	.571	70	0	0	0	**44**	92²	66	6	31	92	9.6	1.85	189	.200	.273	0	.000	-1	17	17	-1	1.6
1990 KC-A	2	7	.222	53	3	0	0	6	68²	71	9	52	73	16.6	5.11	74	.259	.385	0	—	0	-9	-10	-1	-1.0
Total 10	42	72	.368	469	74	4	2	91	927	829	96	392	827	12.1	3.86	93	.241	.323	25	.154	4	-20	-30	-6	-2.4

■ **PEACHES DAVIS** Davis, Ray Thomas b: 5/31/05, Glen Rose, Tex. BL/TR, 6'3.5", 190 lbs. Deb: 7/11/36

YEAR TM/L	W	L	PCT	G	GS	CG	SH	SV	IP	H	HR	BB	SO	RAT	ERA	ERA+	OAV	OOB	BH	AVG	PB	PR	/A	PD	TPI
1936 Cin-N	8	8	.500	26	15	5	0	5	125²	139	7	36	32	12.7	3.58	107	.280	.331	7	.163	-1	6	3	0	0.2
1937 Cin-N	11	13	.458	42	24	11	1	3	218	252	5	51	59	12.6	3.59	104	.295	.337	10	.128	-4	8	3	-2	-0.2
1938 Cin-N	7	12	.368	29	19	11	1	1	167²	193	9	40	28	12.6	3.97	92	.290	.331	15	.246	1	-3	-6	-3	-0.7
1939 Cin-N	1	0	1.000	20	0	0	0	2	30²	43	5	11	4	16.1	6.46	59	.341	.399	1	.333	0	-9	-9	0	-0.7
Total 4	27	33	.450	117	58	27	2	11	542	627	26	138	123	12.8	3.87	96	.293	.337	33	.178	-3	2	-8	-4	-1.4

■ **BOB DAVIS** Davis, Robert Edward b: 9/11/33, New York, N.Y. BR/TR, 6', 170 lbs. Deb: 7/26/58

YEAR TM/L	W	L	PCT	G	GS	CG	SH	SV	IP	H	HR	BB	SO	RAT	ERA	ERA+	OAV	OOB	BH	AVG	PB	PR	/A	PD	TPI
1958 KC-A	0	4	.000	8	4	0	0	0	31	45	5	12	22	17.1	7.84	50	.346	.410	1	.167	-0	-14	-14	0	-1.2
1960 KC-A	0	0	—	21	0	0	0	1	32	31	1	22	28	15.2	3.66	109	.263	.383	1	.250	0	1	1	1	0.2
Total 2	0	4	.000	29	4	0	0	1	63	76	6	34	50	16.1	5.71	69	.306	.396	2	.200	-0	-13	-12	1	-1.0

■ **RON DAVIS** Davis, Ronald Gene b: 8/6/55, Houston, Tex. BR/TR, 6'4", 205 lbs. Deb: 7/29/78

YEAR TM/L	W	L	PCT	G	GS	CG	SH	SV	IP	H	HR	BB	SO	RAT	ERA	ERA+	OAV	OOB	BH	AVG	PB	PR	/A	PD	TPI
1978 NY-A	0	0	—	4	0	0	0	0	2¹	3	0	3	0	23.1	11.57	31	.333	.500	0	—	0	-2	-2	0	-0.1
1979 NY-A	14	2	.875	44	0	0	0	9	85¹	84	5	28	43	11.9	2.85	143	.262	.323	0	.000	0	13	12	1	1.2
1980 *NY-A	9	3	.750	53	0	0	0	7	131	121	9	32	65	10.9	2.95	133	.246	.299	0	.000	0	16	14	0	1.5
1981 *NY-A	4	5	.444	43	0	0	0	6	73	47	6	25	83	8.9	2.71	132	.186	.259	0	—	0	8	7	-1	0.6
1982 Min-A	3	9	.250	63	0	0	0	22	106	106	16	47	89	13.1	4.42	96	.261	.339	0	—	0	-4	-2	-1	-0.2
1983 Min-A	5	8	.385	66	0	0	0	30	89	89	6	33	84	12.6	3.34	127	.266	.338	0	—	0	7	9	-2	0.7
1984 Min-A	7	11	.389	64	0	0	0	29	83	79	11	41	74	13.2	4.55	92	.253	.344	0	—	0	-5	-3	-1	-0.3
1985 Min-A	2	6	.250	57	0	0	0	25	64²	55	7	35	72	13.1	3.48	127	.230	.338	0	—	0	5	7	-1	0.6
1986 Min-A	2	6	.250	36	0	0	0	2	38²	55	7	29	30	20.5	9.08	47	.340	.451	0	—	0	-21	-21	0	-1.8
Chi-N	0	2	.000	17	0	0	0	0	20	31	3	3	10	15.3	7.65	53	.356	.378	0	.000	-0	-9	-8	-0	-0.8
1987 Chi-N	0	0	—	21	0	0	0	0	32¹	43	8	12	31	15.3	5.85	73	.328	.385	0	—	0	-6	-6	-1	-0.5
LA-N	0	0	—	4	0	0	0	0	4	7	0	6	1	31.5	6.75	59	.412	.583	0	—	0	-1	-1	0	-0.1
Yr	0	0	—	25	0	0	0	0	36¹	50	8	18	32	17.1	5.94	71	.336	.411	0	—	0	-8	-7	-0	-0.5
1988 SF-N	1	1	.500	9	0	0	0	0	17¹	15	4	6	15	11.4	4.67	70	.234	.310	0	.000	-0	-2	-3	0	-0.2
Total 11	47	53	.470	481	0	0	0	130	746²	735	82	300	597	12.7	4.05	101	.260	.336	0	.000	-0	-3	3	-5	0.7

■ **STEVE DAVIS** Davis, Steven Kennon b: 8/4/60, San Antonio, Tex. BL/TL, 6'1", 195 lbs. Deb: 8/25/85

YEAR TM/L	W	L	PCT	G	GS	CG	SH	SV	IP	H	HR	BB	SO	RAT	ERA	ERA+	OAV	OOB	BH	AVG	PB	PR	/A	PD	TPI
1985 Tor-A	2	1	.667	10	5	0	0	0	28	23	5	13	22	11.6	3.54	119	.223	.310	0	—	0	2	2	-0	0.2
1986 Tor-A	0	0	—	3	0	0	0	0	3²	8	2	5	5	31.9	17.18	25	.471	.591	0	—	0	-5	-5	0	-0.4
1989 Cle-A	1	1	.500	12	2	0	0	0	25²	34	2	14	12	16.8	8.06	49	.318	.397	0	—	0	-12	-12	-0	-1.1
Total 3	3	2	.600	25	7	0	0	0	57¹	65	9	32	39	15.2	6.44	64	.286	.375	0	—	0	-15	-15	-0	-1.3

■ **WILEY DAVIS** Davis, Wiley Anderson b: 8/1/1875, Seymour, Tenn. d: 9/22/42, Detroit, Mich. BR/TR, 5'10", 165 lbs. Deb: 4/18/1896

YEAR TM/L	W	L	PCT	G	GS	CG	SH	SV	IP	H	HR	BB	SO	RAT	ERA	ERA+	OAV	OOB	BH	AVG	PB	PR	/A	PD	TPI
1896 Cin-N	1	1	.500	2	0	0	0	0	4¹	8	0	2	1	20.8	8.31	55	.391	.446	0	.000	-0	-2	-2	1	0.0

■ **WOODY DAVIS** Davis, Woodrow Wilson "Babe" b: 4/25/13, Nicholls, Ga. BL/TR, 6'1", 200 lbs. Deb: 5/02/38

YEAR TM/L	W	L	PCT	G	GS	CG	SH	SV	IP	H	HR	BB	SO	RAT	ERA	ERA+	OAV	OOB	BH	AVG	PB	PR	/A	PD	TPI
1938 Det-A	0	0	—	2	0	0	0	0	6	3	0	4	1	10.5	1.50	333	.158	.304	0	.000	-0	2	2	-0	0.2

■ **MIKE DAVISON** Davison, Michael Lynn b: 8/4/45, Galesburg, Ill. BL/TL, 6'1", 170 lbs. Deb: 10/01/69

YEAR TM/L	W	L	PCT	G	GS	CG	SH	SV	IP	H	HR	BB	SO	RAT	ERA	ERA+	OAV	OOB	BH	AVG	PB	PR	/A	PD	TPI
1969 SF-N	0	0	—	1	0	0	0	0	2	2	0	2	2	9.0	4.50	78	.250	.250	0	—	0	-0	-0	0	0.0
1970 SF-N	3	5	.375	31	0	0	0	1	36	46	4	22	21	17.0	6.50	61	.324	.415	0	.000	0	-10	-10	1	-0.8
Total 2	3	5	.375	32	0	0	0	1	38	48	4	22	23	16.6	6.39	62	.320	.407	0	.000	0	-10	-10	1	-0.8

■ **BILL DAWLEY** Dawley, William Chester b: 2/6/58, Norwich, Conn. BR/TR, 6'5", 235 lbs. Deb: 4/15/83

YEAR TM/L	W	L	PCT	G	GS	CG	SH	SV	IP	H	HR	BB	SO	RAT	ERA	ERA+	OAV	OOB	BH	AVG	PB	PR	/A	PD	TPI
1983 Hou-N	6	6	.500	48	0	0	0	14	79²	51	9	22	60	8.4	2.82	120	.185	.247	2	.222	0	7	5	-2	0.4
1984 Hou-N	11	4	.733	60	0	0	0	5	98	82	5	35	47	10.7	1.93	172	.234	.303	3	.333	1	18	15	-1	1.7
1985 Hou-N	5	3	.625	49	0	0	0	2	81	76	7	37	48	12.6	3.56	97	.259	.341	2	.200	0	0	-1	0	0.0
1986 Chi-A	0	7	.000	46	0	0	0	2	97²	91	10	28	66	11.1	3.32	130	.247	.302	0	.000	0	9	11	-1	1.0
1987 StL-N	5	8	.385	60	0	0	0	2	96²	93	15	38	65	12.3	4.47	93	.259	.332	2	.167	0	-4	-3	1	-0.1
1988 Phi-N	0	2	.000	8	0	0	0	0	8²	16	3	4	3	20.8	13.50	26	.381	.435	0	—	0	-10	-10	0	-0.9
1989 Oak-A	0	0	—	4	0	0	0	0	9	11	0	2	3	14.0	4.00	92	.297	.350	0	—	0	-0	-0	0	0.0
Total 7	27	30	.474	275	0	0	0	25	470²	420	49	166	292	11.3	3.42	109	.243	.311	9	.214	3	21	16	-2	2.1

■ **JOE DAWSON** Dawson, Ralph Fenton b: 3/9/1897, Bow, Wash. d: 1/4/78, Longview, Tex. BR/TR, 5'11", 182 lbs. Deb: 7/04/24

YEAR TM/L	W	L	PCT	G	GS	CG	SH	SV	IP	H	HR	BB	SO	RAT	ERA	ERA+	OAV	OOB	BH	AVG	PB	PR	/A	PD	TPI
1924 Cle-A	1	2	.333	4	4	0	0	0	20¹	24	0	21	7	20.4	6.64	64	.300	.451	2	.286	-1	-5	-5	1	-0.3
1927 *Pit-N	3	7	.300	20	7	4	0	0	80²	80	2	32	17	12.5	4.46	92	.268	.338	5	.200	-1	-5	-3	-0	-0.3
1928 Pit-N	7	7	.500	31	7	1	0	3	128²	116	6	56	36	12.1	3.29	123	.242	.322	12	.279	4	10	11	-3	1.2
1929 Pit-N	0	1	.000	4	0	0	0	0	8²	13	2	3	2	16.6	8.31	57	.342	.390	1	.500	1	-3	-3	0	-0.1
Total 4	11	17	.393	59	18	5	0	3	238¹	233	10	112	62	13.1	4.15	99	.260	.343	20	.260	3	-4	-1	-2	0.5

■ **REX DAWSON** Dawson, Rexford Paul b: 2/10/1889, Skagit Co., Wash. d: 10/20/58, Indianapolis, Ind. BL/TR, 6', 185 lbs. Deb: 10/03/13

YEAR TM/L	W	L	PCT	G	GS	CG	SH	SV	IP	H	HR	BB	SO	RAT	ERA	ERA+	OAV	OOB	BH	AVG	PB	PR	/A	PD	TPI
1913 Was-A	0	0	—	1	0	0	0	0	1	1	0	1	1	9.0	0.00	—	.250	.250	0	—	0	0	0	0	0.0

■ **PEA RIDGE DAY** Day, Clyde Henry b: 8/26/1899, Pea Ridge, Ark. d: 3/21/34, Kansas City, Mo. BR/TR, 6', 190 lbs. Deb: 9/19/24

YEAR TM/L	W	L	PCT	G	GS	CG	SH	SV	IP	H	HR	BB	SO	RAT	ERA	ERA+	OAV	OOB	BH	AVG	PB	PR	/A	PD	TPI
1924 StL-N	1	1	.500	3	1	0	0	1	17²	22	0	6	3	14.3	4.58	82	.306	.359	1	.125	-1	-1	-2	-0	-0.1
1925 StL-N	2	4	.333	17	4	1	0	1	40	53	5	13	7	14.2	6.30	69	.325	.364	2	.154	-1	-9	-9	-1	-0.8
1926 Cin-N	0	0	—	4	0	0	0	0	7¹	13	1	2	2	18.4	7.36	50	.406	.441	0	.000	-0	-3	-3	-0	-0.2

YEAR TM/L	W	L	PCT	G	GS	CG	SH	SV	IP	H	HR	BB	SO	RAT	ERA	ERA+	OAV	OOB	BH	AVG	PB	PR	/A	PD	TPI
1931 Bro-N	2	2	.500	22	2	1	0	1	57¹	75	5	13	30	13.8	4.55	84	.315	.351	4	.222	0	-4	-5	-1	-0.4
Total 4	5	7	.417	46	9	3	0	2	122¹	163	11	28	48	14.3	5.30	75	.323	.362	7	.171	-2	-18	-18	-2	-1.5

■ BILL DAY
Day, William M. b: 7/28/1867, Wilmington, Del. d: 8/16/23, Wilmington, Del. TR , 5'8", 150 lbs. Deb: 8/20/1889

YEAR TM/L	W	L	PCT	G	GS	CG	SH	SV	IP	H	HR	BB	SO	RAT	ERA	ERA+	OAV	OOB	BH	AVG	PB	PR	/A	PD	TPI
1889 Phi-N	0	3	.000	4	3	2	0	0	19	16	0	23	20	18.5	5.21	84	.221	.409	0	.000	-2	-3	-2	-0	-0.2
1890 Phi-N	1	1	.500	4	2	2	0	0	23²	26	0	12	9	14.5	3.04	120	.271	.352	1	.100	-1	1	2	-1	0.0
Pit-N	0	6	.000	6	6	6	0	0	50	66	1	24	10	16.2	5.22	63	.309	.379	1	.043	-3	-9	-11	1	-0.9
Yr	1	7	.125	10	8	8	0	0	73²	92	1	36	19	15.6	4.52	75	.297	.370	0	.000	-4	-8	-9	1	-0.9
Total 2	1	10	.091	14	11	10	0	0	92²	108	1	59	39	16.2	4.66	77	.283	.379	2	.047	-6	-10	-11	1	-1.1

■ KEN DAYLEY
Dayley, Kenneth Grant b: 2/25/59, Jerome, Idaho BL/TL, 6', 171 lbs. Deb: 5/13/82

YEAR TM/L	W	L	PCT	G	GS	CG	SH	SV	IP	H	HR	BB	SO	RAT	ERA	ERA+	OAV	OOB	BH	AVG	PB	PR	/A	PD	TPI
1982 Atl-N	5	6	.455	20	11	0	0	0	71¹	79	9	25	34	13.1	4.54	82	.286	.346	5	.250	1	-7	-6	-1	-0.6
1983 Atl-N	5	8	.385	24	16	0	0	0	104²	100	12	39	70	12.1	4.30	90	.257	.328	7	.219	2	-8	-5	-2	-0.5
1984 Atl-N	0	3	.000	4	4	0	0	0	18²	28	5	6	10	16.9	5.30	73	.341	.393	2	.500	1	-4	-3	0	-0.1
StL-N	0	2	.000	3	2	0	0	0	5	16	1	5	0	37.8	18.00	19	.615	.677	0	—	0	-8	-8	-0	-0.6
Yr	0	5	.000	7	6	0	0	0	23²	44	6	11	10	20.9	7.99	47	.404	.458	2	.000	1	-12	-11	0	-0.7
1985 *StL-N	4	4	.500	57	0	0	0	11	65¹	65	2	18	62	11.4	2.76	128	.263	.313	2	.400	1	6	6	1	0.8
1986 StL-N	0	3	.000	31	0	0	0	5	38²	42	1	11	33	12.6	3.26	112	.275	.327	1	.200	0	2	2	0	0.2
1987 *StL-N	9	5	.643	53	0	0	0	4	61	52	2	33	63	12.8	2.66	156	.234	.339	0	—	0	10	10	-1	0.9
1988 StL-N	2	7	.222	54	0	0	0	5	55¹	48	2	19	38	11.1	2.77	126	.239	.308	0	.000	-0	4	4	0	0.4
1989 StL-N	4	3	.571	71	0	0	0	12	75¹	63	3	30	40	11.1	2.87	127	.228	.304	0	.000	-1	5	6	-1	0.5
1990 StL-N	4	4	.500	58	0	0	0	2	73¹	63	5	30	51	11.4	3.56	110	.233	.310	0	.000	-1	2	3	-0	0.2
Total 9	33	45	.423	375	33	0	0	39	568²	556	42	216	401	12.3	3.62	104	.260	.329	17	.210	3	2	9	-5	1.2

■ REN DEAGLE
Deagle, Lorenzo Burroughs b: 6/26/1858, New York, N.Y. d: 12/24/36, Kansas City, Mo. BR/TR, 5'9", 190 lbs. Deb: 5/17/1883

YEAR TM/L	W	L	PCT	G	GS	CG	SH	SV	IP	H	HR	BB	SO	RAT	ERA	ERA+	OAV	OOB	BH	AVG	PB	PR	/A	PD	TPI
1883 Cin-a	10	8	.556	18	18	17	1	0	148	136	0	34	48	10.3	2.31	141	.228	.270	9	.129	-5	16	16	-1	0.8
1884 Cin-a	3	1	.750	4	4	4	1	0	34	39	0	9	12	12.7	5.03	66	.273	.316	0	.000	-2	-7	-6	-0	-0.6
Lou-a	4	6	.400	12	12	8	0	0	87¹	80	0	13	23	9.6	2.58	119	.230	.258	6	.133	-3	7	5	1	0.3
Yr	7	7	.500	16	16	12	1	0	121¹	119	0	22	35	10.5	3.26	96	.243	.275	1	.017	-5	-0	-2	1	-0.3
Total 2	17	15	.531	34	34	29	2	0	269¹	255	0	56	83	10.4	2.74	117	.235	.272	15	.117	-9	16	14	-0	0.5

■ COT DEAL
Deal, Ellis Fergason b: 1/23/23, Arapaho, Okla. BB/TR, 5'10.5", 185 lbs. Deb: 9/11/47 C

YEAR TM/L	W	L	PCT	G	GS	CG	SH	SV	IP	H	HR	BB	SO	RAT	ERA	ERA+	OAV	OOB	BH	AVG	PB	PR	/A	PD	TPI
1947 Bos-A	0	1	.000	5	2	0	0	0	12²	20	0	7	6	19.2	9.24	42	.364	.435	2	.500	1	-8	-8	0	-0.6
1948 Bos-A	1	0	1.000	4	0	0	0	0	4	3	0	3	2	13.5	0.00	—	.200	.333	0	—	0	2	2	0	0.2
1950 StL-N	0	0	—	3	0	0	0	0	1	3	0	2	1	45.0	18.00	24	.500	.625	0	—	0	-2	-2	0	-0.1
1954 StL-N	2	3	.400	33	0	0	0	1	71²	85	14	36	25	15.7	6.28	65	.297	.383	2	.100	0	-18	-17	0	-1.5
Total 4	3	4	.429	45	2	0	0	1	89¹	111	14	48	34	16.4	6.55	63	.307	.394	4	.167	1	-25	-24	0	-2.0

■ CHUBBY DEAN
Dean, Alfred Lovill b: 8/24/16, Mt.Airy, N.C. d: 12/21/70, Riverside, Cal. BL/TL, 5'11", 181 lbs. Deb: 4/14/36 ♦

YEAR TM/L	W	L	PCT	G	GS	CG	SH	SV	IP	H	HR	BB	SO	RAT	ERA	ERA+	OAV	OOB	BH	AVG	PB	PR	/A	PD	TPI
1937 Phi-A	1	0	1.000	2	1	0	0	0	9	7	0	6	4	13.0	4.00	118	.219	.342	81	.262	0	1	1	0	0.1
1938 Phi-A	2	1	.667	6	1	0	0	0	23	22	3	15	3	14.5	3.52	137	.250	.359	6	.300	2	3	3	1	0.3
1939 Phi-A	5	8	.385	54	1	0	0	7	116²	132	8	80	39	16.4	5.25	90	.289	.395	27	.351	8	-8	-7	1	0.3
1940 Phi-A	6	13	.316	30	19	8	1	1	159¹	220	21	63	38	16.0	6.61	67	.324	.381	26	.289	4	-39	-38	1	-3.3
1941 Phi-A	2	4	.333	18	7	2	0	0	75²	90	9	35	22	14.9	6.19	68	.294	.367	9	.243	2	-17	-17	0	-1.2
Cle-A	1	4	.200	8	8	2	0	0	53¹	57	3	24	14	13.7	4.39	90	.282	.358	4	.160	0	-1	-3	1	-0.2
Yr	3	8	.273	26	15	4	0	0	129	147	12	59	36	14.4	5.44	75	.289	.363	7	.113	2	-19	-19	1	-1.4
1942 Cle-A	8	11	.421	27	22	8	0	1	172²	170	7	66	46	12.3	3.81	91	.261	.329	27	.267	8	-3	-7	-3	-0.6
1943 Cle-A	5	5	.500	17	9	3	0	0	76	83	1	34	29	14.0	4.50	89	.281	.358	9	.196	1	-10	-12	-1	-1.1
Total 7	30	46	.395	162	68	23	1	9	685²	781	52	323	195	14.5	5.08	79	.288	.364	287	.274	25	-75	-80	0	-5.7

■ DORY DEAN
Dean, Charles Wilson b: 11/6/1852, Cincinnati, Ohio d: 5/4/35, Nashville, Tenn. BR/TR, Deb: 6/22/1876

YEAR TM/L	W	L	PCT	G	GS	CG	SH	SV	IP	H	HR	BB	SO	RAT	ERA	ERA+	OAV	OOB	BH	AVG	PB	PR	/A	PD	TPI
1876 Cin-N	4	26	.133	30	30	26	0	0	262²	397	1	24	22	14.4	3.73	59	.326	.339	36	.261	1	-42	-45	-1	-3.7

■ HARRY DEAN
Dean, James Harry b: 5/12/15, Rockmart, Ga. d: 6/1/60, Rockmart, Ga. BR/TR, 6'4", 185 lbs. Deb: 4/16/41

YEAR TM/L	W	L	PCT	G	GS	CG	SH	SV	IP	H	HR	BB	SO	RAT	ERA	ERA+	OAV	OOB	BH	AVG	PB	PR	/A	PD	TPI
1941 Was-A	0	0	—	2	0	0	0	0	2	2	0	3	0	27.0	4.50	90	.250	.500	0	—	0	-0	-0	-0	0.0

■ DIZZY DEAN
Dean, Jay Hanna b: 1/16/11, Lucas, Ark. d: 7/17/74, Reno, Nevada BR/TR, 6'2", 182 lbs. Deb: 9/28/30 CH

YEAR TM/L	W	L	PCT	G	GS	CG	SH	SV	IP	H	HR	BB	SO	RAT	ERA	ERA+	OAV	OOB	BH	AVG	PB	PR	/A	PD	TPI
1930 StL-N	1	0	1.000	1	1	1	0	0	9	3	0	3	5	6.0	1.00	502	.103	.188	1	.333	0	4	4	1	0.5
1932 StL-N	18	15	.545	46	33	16	4	2	286	280	14	102	191	12.2	3.30	119	.260	.327	25	.258	5	18	20	-2	2.3
1933 StL-N	20	18	.526	48	34	26	3	4	293	279	11	64	199	10.7	3.04	114	.250	.293	19	.181	1	10	14	-6	1.0
1934 *StL-N	30	7	.811	50	33	24	7	7	311²	288	14	75	195	10.7	2.66	159	.241	.289	29	.246	4	49	54	-5	5.8
1935 StL-N	28	12	.700	50	36	29	3	5	324¹	326	16	82	182	11.4	3.11	132	.258	.305	30	.234	4	33	36	-5	3.5
1936 StL-N	24	13	.649	51	34	28	2	11	315	310	21	53	195	10.5	3.17	124	.253	.285	27	.223	1	30	27	-5	2.3
1937 StL-N	13	10	.565	27	25	17	4	1	197¹	200	9	33	120	10.7	2.69	148	.259	.291	15	.227	2	27	28	-4	2.8
1938 *Chi-N	7	1	.875	13	10	3	1	0	74²	63	2	8	22	8.7	1.81	212	.226	.250	5	.192	-0	16	17	-1	1.7
1939 Chi-N	6	4	.600	19	13	7	2	0	96¹	98	4	17	27	10.8	3.36	117	.261	.294	5	.147	-1	6	6	-0	0.5
1940 Chi-N	3	3	.500	10	9	3	0	0	54	68	4	20	18	14.7	5.17	73	.306	.364	4	.222	0	-8	-9	1	-0.6
1941 Chi-N	0	0	—	1	1	0	0	0	1	3	0	1	0	27.0	18.00	19	.429	.429	0	—	0	-2	-2	0	-0.1
1947 StL-A	0	0	—	1	1	0	0	0	4	3	0	1	0	9.0	0.00	—	.231	.286	1	1.000	0	2	2	-0	0.2
Total 12	150	83	.644	317	230	154	26	30	1966¹	1921	95	458	1155	11.0	3.03	130	.253	.298	161	.225	16	185	198	-24	19.9

■ PAUL DEAN
Dean, Paul Dee "Daffy" b: 8/14/13, Lucas, Ark. d: 3/17/81, Springdale, Ark. BR/TR, 6', 175 lbs. Deb: 4/18/34

YEAR TM/L	W	L	PCT	G	GS	CG	SH	SV	IP	H	HR	BB	SO	RAT	ERA	ERA+	OAV	OOB	BH	AVG	PB	PR	/A	PD	TPI
1934 *StL-N	19	11	.633	39	26	16	5	2	233¹	225	19	52	150	10.9	3.43	123	.248	.292	20	.241	1	16	21	-6	1.6
1935 StL-N	19	12	.613	46	33	19	2	5	269²	261	16	55	143	10.8	3.37	122	.249	.292	12	.133	-5	19	22	-6	1.1
1936 StL-N	5	5	.500	17	14	5	0	1	92	113	3	20	28	13.1	4.60	86	.300	.337	2	.059	-4	-6	-7	-3	-1.2
1937 StL-N	0	0	—	1	0	0	0	0	0	1	0	2	0	—	∞	—	1.000	1.000	0	—	0	-3	-3	0	-0.2
1938 StL-N	3	1	.750	5	4	2	1	0	31	37	3	5	14	12.2	2.61	151	.298	.326	2	.182	-0	4	5	-1	0.4
1939 StL-N	0	1	.000	16	2	0	0	0	43	54	4	10	16	13.6	6.07	68	.310	.351	1	.111	-1	-10	-9	-0	-0.9
1940 NY-N	4	4	.500	27	7	2	0	0	99¹	110	8	29	32	12.6	3.90	100	.281	.330	3	.115	-2	-1	-0	-1	-0.2
1941 NY-N	0	0	—	5	0	0	0	0	5²	9	0	3	3	17.5	3.18	116	.320	.393	0	—	0	0	0	-0	0.0
1943 StL-A	0	0	—	3	1	0	0	0	13¹	16	0	3	1	13.5	3.38	99	.296	.345	0	.000	-0	-0	-0	-0	0.0
Total 9	50	34	.595	159	87	44	8	8	787¹	825	53	179	387	11.7	3.75	109	.266	.309	40	.156	-11	20	28	-17	0.6

■ WAYLAND DEAN
Dean, Wayland Ogden b: 6/20/02, Richmond, W.Va. d: 4/10/30, Huntington, W.Va. BB/TR, 6'1", 178 lbs. Deb: 4/17/24

YEAR TM/L	W	L	PCT	G	GS	CG	SH	SV	IP	H	HR	BB	SO	RAT	ERA	ERA+	OAV	OOB	BH	AVG	PB	PR	/A	PD	TPI
1924 *NY-N	6	12	.333	26	20	6	0	0	125²	139	9	45	39	13.5	5.01	73	.280	.346	8	.200	1	-16	-19	3	-1.4
1925 NY-N	10	7	.588	33	14	6	1	1	151¹	169	13	50	53	13.3	4.64	87	.282	.342	12	.235	3	-6	-10	0	-0.6
1926 Phi-N	8	16	.333	33	26	15	1	0	203²	245	9	89	52	14.9	4.91	84	.307	.379	27	.265	5	-24	-17	-1	-1.1
1927 Phi-N	0	1	.000	2	0	0	0	0	3	6	0	2	1	24.0	12.00	34	.500	.571	2	.667	1	-3	-3	0	-0.0
Chi-N	0	0	—	2	0	0	0	0	2	0	0	2	2	13.5	0.00	—	.000	.429	0	—	0	1	1	0	0.1
Yr	0	1	.000	4	0	0	0	0	5	6	0	4	3	19.8	7.20	56	.375	.524	2	.400	1	-2	-2	0	0.1
Total 4	24	36	.400	96	60	27	2	1	485²	559	31	188	147	14.1	4.87	82	.293	.360	49	.250	10	-48	-47	2	-3.0

■ DENNIS DeBARR
DeBarr, Dennis Lee b: 1/16/53, Cheyenne, Wyo. BL/TL, 6'2", 190 lbs. Deb: 5/14/77

YEAR TM/L	W	L	PCT	G	GS	CG	SH	SV	IP	H	HR	BB	SO	RAT	ERA	ERA+	OAV	OOB	BH	AVG	PB	PR	/A	PD	TPI
1977 Tor-A	0	1	.000	14	0	0	0	0	21¹	29	1	8	10	15.6	5.91	71	.337	.394	0	—	0	-4	-4	0	-0.3

YEAR TM/L	W	L	PCT	G	GS	CG	SH	SV	IP	H	HR	BB	SO	RAT	ERA	ERA+	OAV	OOB	BH	AVG	PB	PR	/A	PD	TPI

■ JOE DeBERRY — DeBerry, Joseph Gaddy b: 11/29/1896, Mt.Gilead, N.C. d: 10/9/44, Southern Pines, N.C BL/TR, 6'1", 175 lbs. Deb: 8/24/20

1920 StL-A	2	4	.333	10	7	3	1	0	54²	65	2	20	12	14.3	4.94	79	.307	.372	3	.167	-1	-7	-6	0	-0.5
1921 StL-A	0	1	.000	10	1	0	0	0	12¹	15	0	10	1	18.2	6.57	68	.300	.417	0	.000	-0	-3	-3	0	-0.2
Total 2	2	5	.286	20	8	3	1	0	67	80	2	30	13	15.0	5.24	77	.305	.381	3	.150	-1	-10	-9	1	-0.7

■ DAVE DeBUSSCHERE — DeBusschere, David Albert b: 10/16/40, Detroit, Mich. BR/TR, 6'6", 225 lbs. Deb: 4/22/62

1962 Chi-A	0	0	—	12	0	0	0	0	18	5	1	23	8	14.5	2.00	195	.089	.363	0	—	0	4	4	0	0.4
1963 Chi-A	3	4	.429	24	10	1	1	0	84¹	80	9	34	53	12.6	3.09	113	.249	.329	1	.045	-2	5	4	0	0.3
Total 2	3	4	.429	36	10	1	1	0	102¹	85	10	57	61	12.9	2.90	123	.225	.335	1	.045	-2	9	8	0	0.7

■ ART DECATUR — Decatur, Arthur Rue b: 1/14/1894, Cleveland, Ohio d: 4/25/66, Talladega, Ala. BR/TR, 6'1", 190 lbs. Deb: 4/15/22

1922 Bro-N	3	4	.429	29	2	1	0	1	87²	87	3	29	31	12.0	2.77	147	.265	.327	2	.080	-2	13	13	-1	0.9
1923 Bro-N	3	3	.500	36	5	2	0	3	97¹	101	3	32	25	12.4	2.58	150	.264	.325	0	.000	-3	15	14	-1	0.9
1924 Bro-N	10	9	.526	31	10	3	0	1	126¹	156	12	27	38	13.3	4.13	91	.308	.348	5	.114	-3	-4	-5	-2	-0.9
1925 Bro-N	0	0	—	1	0	0	0	0	1	3	0	0	0	27.0	18.00	23	.600	.600	0	—	0	-2	-2	0	0.0
Phi-N	4	13	.235	25	15	4	0	2	128	170	13	35	31	14.6	5.27	91	.316	.360	2	.049	-5	-14	-7	-2	-1.1
Yr	4	13	.235	26	15	4	0	2	129	173	13	35	31	14.7	5.37	89	.319	.362	2	.049	-5	-16	-9	-2	-1.1
1926 Phi-N	0	0	—	2	1	0	0	0	3	6	0	2	0	24.0	6.00	69	.375	.444	0	.000	-0	-1	-1	-0	0.0
1927 Phi-N	3	5	.375	29	3	0	0	0	94²	130	11	20	27	14.6	7.42	56	.334	.373	6	.222	0	-37	-35	-2	-3.3
Total 6	23	34	.404	153	36	10	0	7	538¹	653	42	145	152	13.6	4.51	92	.302	.349	15	.094	-14	-29	-23	-8	-3.5

■ MARTY DECKER — Decker, Dee Martin b: 6/7/57, Upland, Cal. BR/TR, 5'10", 168 lbs. Deb: 9/20/83

| 1983 SD-N | 0 | 0 | — | 4 | 0 | 0 | 0 | 0 | 8² | 5 | 1 | 3 | 9 | 9.3 | 2.08 | 168 | .167 | .265 | 0 | — | 0 | 1 | 1 | 0 | 0.1 |

■ JOE DECKER — Decker, George Henry b: 6/16/47, Storm Lake, Ia. BR/TR, 6', 180 lbs. Deb: 9/18/69

1969 Chi-N	1	0	1.000	4	1	0	0	0	12¹	10	0	6	13	11.7	2.92	138	.222	.314	0	.000	-0	1	2	-0	0.1
1970 Chi-N	2	7	.222	24	17	1	0	0	108²	108	12	56	79	13.9	4.64	97	.263	.357	6	.176	1	-7	-2	-1	0.0
1971 Chi-N	3	2	.600	21	4	0	0	0	45²	62	2	25	37	17.1	4.73	83	.343	.422	2	.250	1	-6	-4	1	-0.2
1972 Chi-N	1	0	1.000	5	1	0	0	0	12²	9	1	4	7	9.2	2.13	179	.188	.250	0	.000	-0	2	2	-0	0.2
1973 Min-A	10	10	.500	29	24	6	3	0	170¹	167	12	88	109	13.7	4.17	95	.260	.352	0	—	0	-7	-4	0	-0.3
1974 Min-A	16	14	.533	37	37	11	1	0	248²	234	24	97	158	12.1	3.29	114	.252	.324	0	—	0	9	13	-2	1.1
1975 Min-A	1	3	.250	10	7	1	0	0	26¹	25	2	36	16	20.8	8.54	45	.260	.462	0	—	0	-14	-14	-0	-1.2
1976 Min-A	2	7	.222	13	12	0	0	0	58	60	3	51	35	17.4	5.28	68	.273	.412	0	—	0	-11	-11	1	-0.9
1979 Sea-A	0	1	.000	9	2	0	0	0	27¹	27	2	14	12	13.5	4.28	102	.255	.342	0	—	0	-0	0	1	0.1
Total 9	36	44	.450	152	105	19	4	0	710	702	58	377	458	13.8	4.17	95	.262	.355	8	.174	1	-34	-18	-1	-1.1

■ JEFF DEDMON — Dedmon, Jeffrey Linden b: 3/4/60, Torrance, Cal. BL/TR, 6'2", 200 lbs. Deb: 9/02/83

1983 Atl-N	0	0	—	5	0	0	0	0	4	10	1	0	3	22.5	13.50	29	.455	.455	0	—	0	-4	-4	0	-0.3
1984 Atl-N	4	3	.571	54	0	0	0	4	81	86	5	35	51	13.7	3.78	102	.277	.354	0	.000	-1	-2	1	2	0.2
1985 Atl-N	6	3	.667	60	0	0	0	0	86	84	5	49	41	14.0	4.08	94	.264	.364	1	.111	-0	-5	-2	3	0.1
1986 Atl-N	6	6	.500	57	0	0	0	3	99²	90	8	39	58	12.0	2.98	133	.242	.320	2	.125	-1	8	11	2	1.3
1987 Atl-N	3	4	.429	53	0	0	0	0	89²	82	8	42	40	12.5	3.91	111	.246	.332	4	.250	1	2	4	1	0.7
1988 Cle-A	1	0	1.000	21	0	0	0	1	33²	35	3	21	17	15.8	4.54	90	.276	.391	0	—	0	-2	-2	1	0.0
Total 6	20	16	.556	250	3	0	0	12	394	387	30	186	210	13.3	3.84	105	.261	.348	7	.149	-0	-3	8	9	2.0

■ DUMMY DEEGAN — Deegan, William John b: 11/16/1874, Bronx, N.Y. d: 5/17/57, Bronx, N.Y. Deb: 8/03/01

| 1901 NY-N | 0 | 1 | .000 | 2 | 1 | 1 | 0 | 0 | 17 | 27 | 0 | 6 | 8 | 17.5 | 6.35 | 52 | .357 | .404 | 0 | .000 | -1 | -6 | -6 | 0 | -0.4 |

■ JOHN DEERING — Deering, John Thomas b: 6/25/1879, Lynn, Mass. d: 2/15/43, Beverly, Mass. TR , Deb: 5/12/03

1903 Det-A	3	4	.429	10	8	5	0	0	60²	77	3	24	14	15.0	3.86	75	.308	.369	8	.333	2	-6	-6	-0	-0.3
NY-A	4	3	.571	9	7	6	1	0	60	59	0	18	14	11.6	3.75	83	.256	.310	1	.043	-3	-5	-4	-1	-0.7
Yr	7	7	.500	19	15	11	1	0	120²	136	3	42	28	13.3	3.80	79	.283	.341	0	.000	-0	-11	-11	-1	-1.0

■ MIKE DEGERICK — Degerick, Michael Arthur b: 4/1/43, New York, N.Y. BR/TR, 6'2", 178 lbs. Deb: 9/04/61

1961 Chi-A	0	0	—	1	0	0	0	0	1²	2	0	1	0	16.2	5.40	72	.400	.500	0	—	0	-0	-0	0	0.0
1962 Chi-A	0	0	—	1	0	0	0	0	1	1	0	1	0	18.0	0.00	—	.250	.400	0	—	0	0	0	0	0.1
Total 2	0	0	—	2	0	0	0	0	2²	3	0	2	0	16.9	3.38	116	.333	.455	0	—	0	0	0	0	0.1

■ PEP DEININGER — Deininger, Otto Charles b: 10/10/1877, Wasseralfingen, Germany d: 9/25/50, Boston, Mass. BL/TL, 5'8.5", 180 lbs. Deb: 4/26/02 ♦

| 1902 Bos-A | 0 | 0 | — | 2 | 1 | 0 | 0 | 0 | 12 | 19 | 3 | 9 | 2 | 21.0 | 9.75 | 37 | .358 | .451 | 2 | .333 | 1 | -8 | -8 | -0 | -0.5 |

■ JOSE DeJESUS — DeJesus, Jose Luis b: 1/6/65, Brooklyn, N.Y. BR/TR, 6'5", 175 lbs. Deb: 9/09/88

1988 KC-A	0	1	.000	2	1	0	0	0	2²	6	0	5	2	37.1	27.00	15	.429	.579	0	—	0	-7	-7	0	-0.5
1989 KC-A	0	0	—	3	1	0	0	0	8	7	1	8	2	16.9	4.50	85	.241	.405	0	—	0	-1	-1	0	0.0
1990 Phi-N	7	8	.467	22	22	3	1	0	130	97	10	73	87	11.9	3.74	102	.210	.321	3	.079	-1	1	1	-1	0.0
Total 3	7	9	.438	27	24	3	1	0	140²	110	11	86	91	12.7	4.22	91	.218	.334	3	.079	-1	-7	-6	-1	-0.5

■ TOMMY de la CRUZ — de la Cruz, Tomas (Rivero) b: 9/18/14, Marianao, Cuba d: 9/6/58, Havana, Cuba BR/TR, 6'2", 168 lbs. Deb: 4/20/44

| 1944 Cin-N | 9 | 9 | .500 | 34 | 20 | 9 | 0 | 1 | 191¹ | 170 | 9 | 45 | 65 | 10.2 | 3.25 | 108 | .238 | .284 | 9 | .155 | -0 | 8 | 5 | -1 | 0.4 |

■ JIM DELAHANTY — Delahanty, James Christopher b: 6/20/1879, Cleveland, Ohio d: 10/17/53, Cleveland, Ohio BR/TR, 5'10.5", 170 lbs. Deb: 4/19/01 ♦

1904 Bos-N	0	0	—	1	0	0	0	0	3¹	5	0	1	0	16.2	0.00	—	.357	.400	142	.285	0	1	1	0	0.1
1905 Bos-N	0	0	—	1	1	0	0	0	2	5	1	0	0	22.5	4.50	69	.500	.500	119	.258	-0	-0	-0	0	0.0
Total 2	0	0	—	2	1	0	0	0	5¹	10	1	1	0	18.6	1.69	171	.417	.440	1159	.283	1	1	1	0	0.1

■ ART DELANEY — Delaney, Arthur Dewey "Swede" (b: Arthur Dewey Helenius) b: 1/5/1895, Chicago, Ill. d: 5/2/70, Hayward, Cal. BR/TR, 5'10.5", 178 lbs. Deb: 4/16/24

1924 StL-N	1	0	1.000	8	1	1	0	0	20	19	0	6	2	11.2	1.80	210	.250	.305	2	.286	0	5	4	1	0.5
1928 Bos-N	9	17	.346	39	22	8	0	2	192¹	197	11	66	45	11.9	3.79	103	.267	.319	9	.143	-3	4	2	1	0.0
1929 Bos-N	3	5	.375	20	8	3	1	0	75	103	6	35	17	16.7	6.12	76	.336	.405	3	.143	1	-12	-12	-1	-1.0
Total 3	13	22	.371	67	31	12	1	2	287¹	319	17	97	64	13.1	4.26	96	.285	.343	14	.154	-2	-3	-5	1	-0.5

■ JOSE DeLEON — DeLeon, Jose (Chestaro) b: 12/20/60, LaVega, D.R. BR/TR, 6'3", 210 lbs. Deb: 7/23/83

1983 Pit-N	7	3	.700	15	15	3	2	0	108	75	5	47	118	10.3	2.83	131	.196	.285	2	.059	-1	10	10	-1	0.9
1984 Pit-N	7	13	.350	30	28	5	1	0	192¹	147	10	92	153	11.3	3.74	96	.214	.310	5	.085	-4	-3	-3		-0.9
1985 Pit-N	2	19	.095	31	25	1	0	0	162²	138	15	89	149	12.7	4.70	76	.231	.334	2	.056	-2	-20	-20	-2	-2.3
1986 Pit-N	1	3	.250	9	1	0	0	1	16¹	17	2	17	11	19.3	8.27	46	.266	.427	0	.000	0	-8	-8	0	-0.7
Chi-A	4	5	.444	13	13	0	0	0	79	49	7	42	68	10.8	2.96	145	.179	.297	0	—	0	11	12	0	1.2
1987 Chi-A	11	12	.478	33	31	2	0	0	206	177	24	97	153	12.4	4.02	114	.230	.324	0	—	0	13	14	0	0.9
1988 StL-N	13	10	.565	34	34	3	1	0	225¹	198	13	86	208	11.4	3.67	95	.237	.310	10	.139	-0	-6	-5	-3	-0.8
1989 StL-N	16	12	.571	36	36	5	3	0	244²	173	16	80	**201**	9.5	3.05	119	**.197**	.269	8	.096	-4	12	16	-5	0.7
1990 StL-N	7	19	.269	32	32	0	0	0	182²	168	15	86	164	12.8	4.43	88	.246	.335	6	.107	-2	-13	-10	-3	-1.4
Total 8	68	96	.415	233	215	20	7	4	1417	1142	107	636	1225	11.5	3.79	101	.221	.310	33	.097	-12	-8	3	-20	-2.4

■ LUIS DeLEON — DeLeon, Luis Antonio (Tricoche) b: 8/19/58, Ponce, P.R. BR/TR, 6'1", 153 lbs. Deb: 9/06/81

| 1981 StL-N | 0 | 1 | .000 | 10 | 0 | 0 | 0 | 0 | 15¹ | 11 | 1 | 3 | 8 | 8.2 | 2.35 | 151 | .200 | .241 | 0 | .000 | -0 | 2 | 2 | -0 | 0.2 |

YEAR TM/L	W	L	PCT	G	GS	CG	SH	SV	IP	H	HR	BB	SO	RAT	ERA	ERA+	OAV	OOB	BH	AVG	PB	PR	/A	PD	TPI
1982 SD-N	9	5	.643	61	0	0	0	15	102	77	10	16	60	8.3	2.03	169	.212	.247	1	.091	0	18	16	1	1.8
1983 SD-N	6	6	.500	63	0	0	0	13	111	89	8	27	90	9.5	2.68	130	.224	.275	2	.143	0	12	10	-2	0.8
1984 SD-N	2	2	.500	32	0	0	0	0	42²	44	12	12	44	12.7	5.48	65	.256	.319	0	.000	-0	-9	-9	-0	-0.9
1985 SD-N	0	3	.000	29	0	0	0	0	38²	39	6	10	31	12.1	4.19	84	.267	.327	1	.200	0	-3	-3	-0	-0.2
1987 Bal-A	0	2	.000	11	0	0	0	1	20²	19	1	8	13	12.6	4.79	92	.253	.341	0	—	0	-1	-1	0	0.0
1989 Sea-A	0	0	—	1	1	0	0	0	4	5	1	1	2	15.8	2.25	179	.313	.389	0	—	0	1	1	0	0.1
Total 7	17	19	.472	207	1	0	0	32	334¹	284	39	77	248	10.0	3.12	114	.232	.284	4	.114	-0	20	16	-2	1.8

■ FLAME DELHI
Delhi, Lee William b: 11/5/1892, Harqua Hala, Ariz. d: 5/9/66, San Rafael, Cal. BR/TR, 6'2.5", 198 lbs. Deb: 4/16/12

YEAR TM/L	W	L	PCT	G	GS	CG	SH	SV	IP	H	HR	BB	SO	RAT	ERA	ERA+	OAV	OOB	BH	AVG	PB	PR	/A	PD	TPI
1912 Chi-A	0	0	—	1	0	0	0	0	3	7	0	3	2	30.0	9.00	36	.412	.500			0	-2	-2	0	0.0

■ WHEEZER DELL
Dell, William George b: 6/11/1887, Tuscarora, Nev. d: 8/24/66, Independence, Cal. BR/TR, 6'4", 210 lbs. Deb: 4/22/12

YEAR TM/L	W	L	PCT	G	GS	CG	SH	SV	IP	H	HR	BB	SO	RAT	ERA	ERA+	OAV	OOB	BH	AVG	PB	PR	/A	PD	TPI
1912 StL-N				3	0	0	0	0	2¹	3	0	3	0	23.1	11.57	30	.188	.316	0	—	0	-2	-2	0	-0.1
1915 Bro-N	11	10	.524	40	24	12	4	1	215	166	5	100	94	11.5	2.34	119	.218	.315	10	.152	-1	10	10	0	1.1
1916 *Bro-N	8	9	.471	32	16	9	2	1	155	143	2	43	76	11.0	2.26	118	.256	.314	4	.091	-2	6	7	-2	0.4
1917 Bro-N	0	4	.000	17	4	0	0	1	58	55	3	25	28	12.7	3.72	75	.263	.347	1	.063	-2	-7	-6	-1	-0.8
Total 4	19	23	.452	92	44	21	6	3	430¹	367	10	171	198	11.5	2.55	108	.237	.319	15	.119	-5	7	9	-3	0.6

■ IKE DELOCK
Delock, Ivan Martin b: 11/11/29, Highland Park, Mich BR/TR, 5'11", 175 lbs. Deb: 4/17/52

YEAR TM/L	W	L	PCT	G	GS	CG	SH	SV	IP	H	HR	BB	SO	RAT	ERA	ERA+	OAV	OOB	BH	AVG	PB	PR	/A	PD	TPI
1952 Bos-A	4	9	.308	39	7	1	1	5	95	88	9	50	46	13.3	4.26	92	.245	.341	1	.045	-1	-6	-3	-0	-0.3
1953 Bos-A	3	1	.750	23	1	0	0	1	48²	60	2	20	22	15.2	4.44	95	.308	.378	1	.100	-1	-2	-1	-1	-0.2
1955 Bos-A	9	7	.563	29	18	6	0	3	143²	136	16	61	88	12.6	3.76	114	.247	.326	7	.143	-1	3	8	-1	0.7
1956 Bos-A	13	7	.650	48	8	1	0	9	128¹	122	12	80	105	14.5	4.21	110	.252	.363	3	.103	-2	-1	6	-0	0.4
1957 Bos-A	9	8	.529	49	2	0	0	11	94	80	11	45	62	12.3	3.83	104	.230	.323	1	.048	-1	-0	2	-1	0.0
1958 Bos-A	14	8	.636	31	19	9	1	2	160	155	13	56	82	11.9	3.37	119	.252	.315	3	.063	-4	7	11	-1	0.7
1959 Bos-A	11	6	.647	28	17	4	0	0	134¹	120	12	62	55	12.3	2.95	138	.236	.322	3	.064	-3	14	17	-1	1.3
1960 Bos-A	9	10	.474	24	23	3	1	0	129¹	145	21	52	49	14.0	4.73	85	.283	.354	5	.116	-3	-12	-10	-1	-1.2
1961 Bos-A	6	9	.400	28	28	3	1	0	156	185	24	52	80	13.8	4.90	85	.293	.349	5	.104	-2	-15	-13	-2	-1.4
1962 Bos-A	4	5	.444	17	13	4	2	0	86¹	89	10	24	49	11.8	3.75	110	.268	.317	2	.087	-1	2	4	-1	0.2
1963 Bos-A	1	2	.333	6	6	1	0	0	32	31	4	12	23	12.1	4.50	84	.246	.312	0	.000	-2	-3	-3	0	-0.3
Bal-A	1	3	.250	7	5	0	0	0	30¹	25	7	16	11	12.2	5.04	70	.236	.336	0	.000	-1	-5	-5	0	-0.5
Yr	2	5	.286	13	11	1	0	0	62¹	56	11	28	34	12.1	4.76	77	.240	.322	0	.000	-3	-8	-8	0	-0.8
Total 11	84	75	.528	329	147	32	6	31	1238	1236	141	530	672	13.0	4.03	102	.259	.336	31	.086	-21	-19	12	-8	-0.6

■ RAMON de los SANTOS
de los Santos, Ramon (Genero) b: 1/19/49, Santo Domingo, D.R. BL/TL, 6'1", 175 lbs. Deb: 8/21/74

YEAR TM/L	W	L	PCT	G	GS	CG	SH	SV	IP	H	HR	BB	SO	RAT	ERA	ERA+	OAV	OOB	BH	AVG	PB	PR	/A	PD	TPI
1974 Hou-N	1	1	.500	12	0	0	0	0	12¹	11	0	9	7	14.6	2.19	158	.234	.357	0	—	0	2	2	0	0.2

■ RICH DELUCIA
Delucia, Richard Anthony b: 10/7/64, Reading, Pa. BR/TR, 6', 180 lbs. Deb: 9/08/90

YEAR TM/L	W	L	PCT	G	GS	CG	SH	SV	IP	H	HR	BB	SO	RAT	ERA	ERA+	OAV	OOB	BH	AVG	PB	PR	/A	PD	TPI
1990 Sea-A	1	2	.333	5	5	1	0	0	36	30	2	9	20	9.8	2.00	198	.226	.275	0	—	0	8	8	-0	0.8

■ FRED DEMARAIS
Demarais, Frederick b: 11/1/1866, Canada d: 3/6/19, Stamford, Conn. TR Deb: 7/26/1890

YEAR TM/L	W	L	PCT	G	GS	CG	SH	SV	IP	H	HR	BB	SO	RAT	ERA	ERA+	OAV	OOB	BH	AVG	PB	PR	/A	PD	TPI
1890 Chi-N	0	0	—	1	0	0	0	0	1	1	0	1	1	9.0	0.00	—	.145	.253	0	.000	-0	1	1	0	0.1

■ AL DEMAREE
Demaree, Albert Wentworth b: 9/8/1884, Quincy, Ill. d: 4/30/62, Los Angeles, Cal. BL/TR, 6', 170 lbs. Deb: 9/26/12

YEAR TM/L	W	L	PCT	G	GS	CG	SH	SV	IP	H	HR	BB	SO	RAT	ERA	ERA+	OAV	OOB	BH	AVG	PB	PR	/A	PD	TPI
1912 NY-N	1	0	1.000	2	2	1	1	0	16	17	0	2	11	10.7	1.69	200	.270	.292	0	.000	-1	3	3	0	0.2
1913 *NY-N	13	4	.765	31	24	11	2	2	199²	176	4	38	76	9.9	2.21	141	.243	.286	7	.106	-3	22	20	-3	1.4
1914 NY-N	10	17	.370	38	30	13	2	0	224	219	3	77	89	12.2	3.09	86	.263	.331	9	.132	-2	-8	-11	-1	-1.4
1915 Phi-N	14	11	.560	32	26	13	3	1	209²	201	4	58	69	11.2	3.05	90	.260	.314	12	.176	-0	-7	-7	-4	-1.1
1916 Phi-N	19	14	.576	39	35	25	4	1	285	252	6	48	130	9.7	2.62	101	.242	.281	11	.109	-4	-0	1	-6	-1.0
1917 Chi-N	5	9	.357	24	18	6	1	1	141¹	125	5	37	43	10.4	2.55	114	.244	.297	5	.122	-2	3	5	1	0.6
NY-N	4	5	.444	15	11	1	0	0	78¹	70	1	17	23	10.1	2.64	97	.239	.283	2	.111	-1	1	-1	0	-0.1
Yr	9	14	.391	39	29	7	1	1	219²	195	6	54	66	10.2	2.58	107	.241	.290	5	.085	-2	3	5	1	0.5
1918 NY-N	8	6	.571	26	14	8	2	1	142	143	5	25	39	10.8	2.47	106	.262	.297	6	.128	-3	5	2	-0	0.0
1919 Bos-N	6	6	.500	25	13	6	0	3	128	140	8	35	34	12.9	3.80	75	.300	.348	2	.048	-5	-13	-13	-2	-2.0
Total 8	80	72	.526	232	173	84	15	9	1424	1350	34	337	514	10.9	2.77	100	.256	.304	54	.118	-20	6	0	-14	-3.4

■ LARRY DEMERY
Demery, Lawrence Calvin b: 6/4/53, Bakersfield, Cal. BR/TR, 6', 170 lbs. Deb: 6/02/74

YEAR TM/L	W	L	PCT	G	GS	CG	SH	SV	IP	H	HR	BB	SO	RAT	ERA	ERA+	OAV	OOB	BH	AVG	PB	PR	/A	PD	TPI
1974 *Pit-N	6	6	.500	19	15	2	0	0	95¹	95	12	51	51	13.8	4.25	81	.262	.354	5	.152	0	-7	-9	-1	-0.8
1975 *Pit-N	7	5	.583	45	8	1	0	4	114²	95	7	43	59	11.1	2.90	122	.230	.307	3	.125	1	9	8	-1	0.9
1976 Pit-N	10	7	.588	36	15	4	1	2	145	123	8	58	72	11.4	3.17	110	.234	.313	5	.125	-1	5	5	-0	0.4
1977 Pit-N	6	5	.545	39	8	0	0	1	90¹	100	13	47	35	14.6	5.08	78	.279	.363	3	.150	-0	-12	-11	-0	-1.0
Total 4	29	23	.558	139	46	7	1	7	445¹	413	40	199	217	12.5	3.72	97	.249	.331	16	.137	0	-4	-6	-2	-0.3

■ HARRY DeMILLER
DeMiller, Harry b: 11/12/1867, Wooster, Ohio d: 10/19/28, Santa Ana, Cal. TL Deb: 8/20/1892

YEAR TM/L	W	L	PCT	G	GS	CG	SH	SV	IP	H	HR	BB	SO	RAT	ERA	ERA+	OAV	OOB	BH	AVG	PB	PR	/A	PD	TPI
1892 Chi-N	1	1	.500	4	2	2	0	0	24	29	1	16	15	16.9	6.38	52	.307	.385	3	.300	1	-8	-8	0	-0.5

■ DON DeMOLA
DeMola, Donald John b: 7/5/52, Glen Cove, N.Y. BR/TR, 6'2", 185 lbs. Deb: 4/13/74

YEAR TM/L	W	L	PCT	G	GS	CG	SH	SV	IP	H	HR	BB	SO	RAT	ERA	ERA+	OAV	OOB	BH	AVG	PB	PR	/A	PD	TPI
1974 Mon-N	1	0	1.000	25	1	0	0	0	57²	46	7	21	47	10.5	3.12	123	.223	.295	0	.000	-1	3	5	-1	0.4
1975 Mon-N	4	7	.364	60	0	0	0	1	97²	92	8	42	63	12.7	4.15	92	.251	.335	0	.000	-1	-6	-4	-3	-0.7
Total 2	5	7	.417	85	1	0	0	1	155¹	138	15	63	110	11.9	3.77	102	.241	.321	0	.000	-2	-3	1	-3	-0.3

■ BEN DeMOTT
DeMott, Benjamin Harrison b: 4/2/1889, Green Village, N.J. d: 7/5/63, Somerville, N.J. BR/TR, 6', 192 lbs. Deb: 8/15/10

YEAR TM/L	W	L	PCT	G	GS	CG	SH	SV	IP	H	HR	BB	SO	RAT	ERA	ERA+	OAV	OOB	BH	AVG	PB	PR	/A	PD	TPI
1910 Cle-A	0	3	.000	6	4	1	0	0	28¹	45	0	8	13	17.2	5.40	48	.388	.432	3	.214	-0	-9	-9	0	-0.8
1911 Cle-A	0	1	.000	1	1	0	0	0	3²	10	0	2	2	29.5	12.27	28	.588	.632	0	.000	-0	-4	-4	0	-0.2
Total 2	0	4	.000	7	5	1	0	0	32	55	0	10	15	18.6	6.19	43	.414	.458	3	.167	-0	-13	-12	1	-1.0

■ CON DEMPSEY
Dempsey, Cornelius Francis b: 9/16/23, San Francisco, Cal BR/TR, 6'4", 190 lbs. Deb: 4/28/51

YEAR TM/L	W	L	PCT	G	GS	CG	SH	SV	IP	H	HR	BB	SO	RAT	ERA	ERA+	OAV	OOB	BH	AVG	PB	PR	/A	PD	TPI
1951 Pit-N	0	2	.000	3	2	0	0	0	7	11	2	4	3	19.3	9.00	47	.393	.469	0	.000	-0	-4	-4	0	-0.3

■ MARK DEMPSEY
Dempsey, Mark Steven b: 12/17/57, Dayton, Ohio BR/TR, 6'6", 220 lbs. Deb: 9/04/82

YEAR TM/L	W	L	PCT	G	GS	CG	SH	SV	IP	H	HR	BB	SO	RAT	ERA	ERA+	OAV	OOB	BH	AVG	PB	PR	/A	PD	TPI
1982 SF-N	0	0	—	3	1	0	0	0	5²	11	1	2	4	20.6	7.94	45	.440	.481	0	.000	-0	-3	-3	0	-0.2

■ BILL DENEHY
Denehy, William Francis b: 3/31/46, Middletown, Conn. BB/TR, 6'3", 200 lbs. Deb: 4/16/67

YEAR TM/L	W	L	PCT	G	GS	CG	SH	SV	IP	H	HR	BB	SO	RAT	ERA	ERA+	OAV	OOB	BH	AVG	PB	PR	/A	PD	TPI
1967 NY-N	1	7	.125	15	8	0	0	0	53²	51	8	29	35	13.4	4.70	72	.248	.340	0	.000	-1	-8	-8	-0	-0.8
1968 Was-A	0	0	—	2	0	0	0	0	2	4	0	4	1	36.0	9.00	34	.444	.615	0	—	0	-1	-1	0	0.0
1971 Det-A	0	3	.000	31	1	0	0	1	49	47	4	28	27	14.5	4.22	85	.250	.359	0	.000	1	-4	-3	-0	-0.2
Total 3	1	10	.091	49	9	0	0	1	104²	102	12	61	63	14.4	4.56	76	.253	.357	0	.000	0	-13	-13	-1	-1.0

■ BRIAN DENMAN
Denman, Brian John b: 2/12/56, Minneapolis, Minn. BR/TR, 6'4", 205 lbs. Deb: 8/22/82

YEAR TM/L	W	L	PCT	G	GS	CG	SH	SV	IP	H	HR	BB	SO	RAT	ERA	ERA+	OAV	OOB	BH	AVG	PB	PR	/A	PD	TPI
1982 Bos-A	3	4	.429	9	9	2	1	0	49	55	6	9	9	11.8	4.78	90	.282	.314	0	—	0	-4	-3	0	-0.2

■ DON DENNIS
Dennis, Donald Ray b: 3/3/42, Uniontown, Kan. BR/TR, 6'2", 190 lbs. Deb: 6/18/65

YEAR TM/L	W	L	PCT	G	GS	CG	SH	SV	IP	H	HR	BB	SO	RAT	ERA	ERA+	OAV	OOB	BH	AVG	PB	PR	/A	PD	TPI
1965 StL-N	2	3	.400	41	0	0	0	6	55	47	3	16	29	10.5	2.29	168	.236	.296	2	.400	1	8	9	2	1.3
1966 StL-N	4	2	.667	38	1	0	0	2	59²	73	8	17	25	13.7	4.98	72	.302	.350	1	.083	-1	-9	-9	3	-0.6
Total 2	6	5	.545	79	1	0	0	8	114²	120	11	33	54	12.2	3.69	101	.272	.326	3	.176	-0	-1	0	5	0.7

YEAR TM/L	W	L	PCT	G	GS	CG	SH	SV	IP	H	HR	BB	SO	RAT	ERA	ERA+	OAV	OOB	BH	AVG	PB	PR	/A	PD	TPI

■ JERRY DENNY　Denny, Jeremiah Dennis (b: Jeremiah Dennis Eldridge)
b: 3/16/1859, New York, N.Y.　d: 8/16/27, Houston, Tex.　BR/TR, 5'11.5", 180 lbs.　Deb: 5/02/1881　♦

| 1888 Ind-N | 0 | 0 | — | 1 | 0 | 0 | 0 | 0 | 4 | 5 | 1 | 4 | 1 | 20.3 | 9.00 | 33 | .295 | .430 | 137 | .261 | 0 | -3 | -3 | 0 | -0.1 |

■ JOHN DENNY　Denny, John Allen　b: 11/8/52, Prescott, Ariz.　BR/TR, 6'3", 185 lbs.　Deb: 9/12/74

1974 StL-N	0	0	—	2	0	0	0	0	2	3	0	0	1	13.5	0.00	—	.273	.273	0	—	0	1	1	0	0.1
1975 StL-N	10	7	.588	25	24	3	2	0	136	149	5	51	72	13.4	3.97	95	.280	.346	10	.227	1	-5	-3	2	0.0
1976 StL-N	11	9	.550	30	30	8	3	0	207	189	11	74	74	11.8	2.52	140	.246	.318	15	.224	2	23	23	2	3.1
1977 StL-N	8	8	.500	26	26	3	1	0	149²	165	9	62	60	14.0	4.51	85	.281	.355	5	.098	-3	-10	-11	3	-0.9
1978 StL-N	14	11	.560	33	33	11	2	0	234	200	13	74	103	12.8	2.96	119	.238	.304	13	.178	2	16	14	8	2.8
1979 StL-N	8	11	.421	31	31	5	2	0	206	206	24	100	99	13.5	4.85	78	.264	.350	9	.129	-1	-26	-25	2	-2.4
1980 Cle-A	8	6	.571	16	16	4	1	0	108²	116	4	47	59	13.9	4.39	93	.284	.365	0	—	0	-4	-4	1	-0.2
1981 Cle-A	10	6	.625	19	19	6	3	0	145²	139	9	66	94	12.9	3.15	115	.254	.338	0	—	0	8	8	4	1.3
1982 Cle-A	6	11	.353	21	21	5	0	0	138¹	126	11	73	94	13.3	5.01	81	.240	.340	0	—	0	-14	-14	1	-1.2
Phi-N	0	2	.000	4	4	0	0	0	22¹	18	1	10	19	11.3	4.03	91	.217	.301	1	.167	1	-1	-1	1	0.0
1983 *Phi-N	19	6	.760	36	36	7	1	0	242²	229	9	53	139	10.6	2.37	150	.250	.294	13	.169	0	34	32	2	3.8
1984 Phi-N	7	7	.500	22	22	2	0	0	154¹	122	11	29	94	9.0	2.45	148	.214	.257	9	.191	0	20	20	4	2.8
1985 Phi-N	11	14	.440	33	33	6	2	0	230²	252	15	83	123	13.2	3.82	96	.282	.345	10	.123	-2	-6	-4	1	-0.2
1986 Cin-N	11	10	.524	27	27	2	1	0	171¹	179	15	56	115	12.6	4.20	92	.272	.333	12	.222	2	-9	-6	3	-0.1
Total 13	123	108	.532	325	322	62	18	0	2148²	2093	137	778	1146	12.3	3.59	104	.258	.327	97	.170	3	25	30	33	8.9

■ EDDIE DENT　Dent, Elliott Estill　b: 12/8/1887, Baltimore, Md.　d: 11/25/74, Birmingham, Ala.　BR/TR, 6'1", 190 lbs.　Deb: 8/31/09

1909 Bro-N	2	4	.333	6	5	4	0	0	42	47	2	15	17	13.3	4.29	61	.307	.369	1	.067	-1	-8	-8	-1	-0.9
1911 Bro-N	2	1	.667	5	3	1	0	0	31²	30	0	10	3	11.9	3.69	90	.256	.326	1	.100	-0	-1	-1	1	0.0
1912 Bro-N	0	0	—	1	0	0	0	0	1	4	0	1	1	45.0	36.00	9	.571	.625	0	.000	-0	-4	-4	0	-0.2
Total 3	4	5	.444	12	8	5	0	0	74²	81	2	26	21	13.1	4.46	65	.292	.357	2	.077	-2	-13	-13	0	-1.1

■ ROGER DENZER　Denzer, Roger "Peaceful Valley"　b: 10/5/1871, Leseur, Minn.　d: 9/18/49, Leseur, Minn.　TR , 6', 180 lbs.　Deb: 4/24/1897

1897 Chi-N	2	8	.200	12	10	8	0	0	94²	125	4	34	17	15.1	5.13	87	.315	.369	6	.154	-3	-9	-7	-0	-0.8
1901 NY-N	2	6	.250	11	9	3	1	0	61²	69	2	5	22	10.8	3.36	99	.281	.295	2	.091	-1	-0	-0	-2	-0.2
Total 2	4	14	.222	23	19	11	1	0	156¹	194	6	39	39	13.4	4.43	90	.302	.342	8	.131	-4	-9	-8	-2	-1.0

■ GEORGE DERBY　Derby, George H. "Jonah"　b: 7/6/1857, Webster, Mass.　d: 7/4/25, Philadelphia, Pa.　BL/TR, 6', 175 lbs.　Deb: 5/02/1881

1881 Det-N	29	26	.527	56	55	55	9	0	494²	505	3	86	212	10.8	2.20	132	.253	.284	44	.186	-11	32	39	1	3.0
1882 Det-N	17	20	.459	40	39	38	3	0	362	386	8	81	182	11.6	3.26	90	.258	.296	29	.195	-6	-15	-13	1	-1.6
1883 Buf-N	2	10	.167	14	13	12	0	1	107²	173	3	15	34	15.7	5.85	54	.343	.362	14	.237	-1	-32	-32	1	-2.5
Total 3	48	56	.462	110	107	105	12	1	964¹	1064	14	182	428	11.6	3.01	98	.266	.298	87	.196	-18	-16	-6	3	-1.1

■ PAUL DERRINGER　Derringer, Samuel Paul "Duke"　b: 10/17/06, Springfield, Ky.　d: 11/17/87, Sarasota, Fla.　BR/TR, 6'3.5", 205 lbs.　Deb: 4/16/31

1931 *StL-N	18	8	.692	35	23	15	4	2	211²	225	9	65	134	12.5	3.36	117	.274	.330	7	.097	-6	12	14	-1	0.7
1932 StL-N	11	14	.440	39	30	14	1	0	233¹	296	6	67	78	14.1	4.05	97	.310	.356	13	.178	-0	-4	-3	-1	-0.3
1933 StL-N	0	2	.000	3	2	1	0	0	17	24	0	9	3	18.0	4.24	82	.353	.436	0	.000	-1	-2	-1	0	-0.1
Cin-N	7	25	.219	33	31	16	2	1	231	240	4	51	86	11.5	3.23	105	.271	.315	14	.184	-1	3	4	0	0.4
Yr	7	27	.206	36	33	17	2	1	248	264	4	60	89	11.9	3.30	103	.277	.323	2	.025	-2	1	3	0	0.3
1934 Cin-N	15	21	.417	47	31	18	1	4	261	297	8	59	122	12.4	3.59	114	.283	.323	18	.196	0	14	14	-2	1.3
1935 Cin-N	22	13	.629	45	33	20	3	2	276²	295	13	49	120	11.3	3.51	113	.271	.305	13	.140	-5	16	14	2	1.2
1936 Cin-N	19	19	.500	51	37	13	2	5	282¹	331	11	42	121	12.0	4.02	95	.289	.316	18	.200	-1	0	-6	-0	-0.7
1937 Cin-N	10	14	.417	43	26	12	1	1	222²	240	7	55	94	11.9	4.04	92	.271	.313	16	.200	1	-3	-8	1	-0.5
1938 Cin-N	21	14	.600	41	37	26	4	1	307	315	20	49	132	10.7	2.93	124	.262	.291	21	.176	-0	29	24	-2	2.2
1939 *Cin-N	25	7	.781	38	35	28	5	0	301	321	15	35	128	10.7	2.93	131	.272	.295	23	.209	-3	33	30	-3	2.8
1940 *Cin-N	20	12	.625	37	37	26	3	0	296²	280	17	48	115	10.0	3.06	124	.246	.276	18	.167	-2	26	24	-3	1.9
1941 Cin-N	12	14	.462	29	28	17	2	1	228¹	233	16	54	76	11.3	3.31	109	.266	.309	13	.155	-3	8	7	0	0.4
1942 Cin-N	10	11	.476	29	27	13	1	0	208²	203	4	49	68	11.0	3.06	107	.250	.296	9	.132	-2	6	5	-4	0.0
1943 Chi-N	10	14	.417	32	22	10	2	3	174	184	7	39	75	11.5	3.57	93	.264	.303	13	.224	1	-4	-4	-4	-0.7
1944 Chi-N	7	13	.350	42	16	7	0	3	180	205	13	39	69	12.2	4.15	85	.284	.321	9	.158	-2	-11	-12	-1	-1.4
1945 *Chi-N	16	11	.593	35	30	15	1	4	213²	223	8	51	80	11.6	3.45	106	.265	.308	15	.200	0	8	5	-2	0.3
Total 15	223	212	.513	579	445	251	32	29	3645	3912	158	761	1507	11.6	3.46	108	.272	.310	220	.175	-19	131	108	-18	7.5

■ JIM DERRINGTON　Derrington, Charles James "Blackie"　b: 11/29/39, Compton, Cal.　BL/TL, 6'3", 190 lbs.　Deb: 9/30/56

1956 Chi-A	0	1	.000	1	1	0	0	0	6	9	2	6	3	22.5	7.50	55	.375	.500	1	.500	0	-2	-2	-0	-0.1
1957 Chi-A	0	1	.000	20	5	0	0	0	37	29	4	29	14	14.4	4.86	77	.216	.360	0	.000	-0	-4	-5	-1	-0.5
Total 2	0	2	.000	21	6	0	0	0	43	38	6	35	17	15.5	5.23	72	.241	.381	1	.167	0	-7	-7	-1	-0.6

■ JIM DESHAIES　Deshaies, James Joseph　b: 6/23/60, Massena, N.Y.　BL/TL, 6'4", 222 lbs.　Deb: 8/07/84

1984 NY-A	0	1	.000	2	2	0	0	0	7	14	1	7	5	27.0	11.57	33	.438	.538	0	—	0	-6	-6	-0	-0.4
1985 Hou-N	0	0	—	2	0	0	0	0	3	1	0	2	3	3.0	0.00	—	.100	.100	0	—	0	1	1	0	0.1
1986 Hou-N	12	5	.706	26	26	1	1	0	144	124	16	59	128	11.6	3.25	111	.234	.313	2	.047	-1	7	6	-2	0.2
1987 Hou-N	11	6	.647	26	25	1	0	0	152	149	22	57	104	12.2	4.62	85	.257	.324	5	.094	-0	-9	-12	-1	-1.1
1988 Hou-N	11	14	.440	31	31	3	2	0	207	164	20	72	127	10.3	3.00	111	.218	.288	3	.048	-4	10	7	-2	0.1
1989 Hou-N	15	10	.600	34	34	6	3	0	225²	180	16	79	153	10.5	2.91	116	.217	.288	9	.120	-2	15	12	-1	0.9
1990 Hou-N	7	12	.368	34	34	2	0	0	209¹	186	21	84	119	12.0	3.78	99	.245	.326	4	.063	-3	0	-1	-0	-0.4
Total 7	56	48	.538	155	152	13	6	0	948	818	95	358	638	11.3	3.50	102	.234	.308	23	.077	-11	19	7	-5	-0.6

■ JIMMIE DeSHONG　DeShong, James Brooklyn　b: 11/30/09, Harrisburg, Pa.　BR/TR, 5'11", 165 lbs.　Deb: 4/12/32

1932 Phi-A	0	0	—	6	0	0	0	0	10	17	3	9	5	24.3	11.70	39	.378	.491	0	.000	-0	-8	-8	-0	-0.6
1934 NY-A	6	7	.462	31	12	6	0	0	133²	126	6	56	40	12.4	4.11	99	.243	.319	8	.190	2	6	-1	0	0.1
1935 NY-A	4	1	.800	29	3	0	0	3	69	64	6	33	30	12.9	3.26	124	.242	.331	1	.071	-1	9	6	2	0.6
1936 Was-A	18	10	.643	34	31	16	2	2	223²	255	11	96	59	14.2	4.63	103	.285	.356	15	.190	2	10	4	-1	0.3
1937 Was-A	14	15	.483	37	34	20	0	1	264¹	290	15	124	86	14.2	4.90	90	.280	.359	19	.202	2	-8	-14	1	-1.0
1938 Was-A	5	8	.385	31	14	1	0	0	131¹	160	11	83	41	16.7	6.58	69	.310	.407	12	.261	2	-26	-30	1	-2.3
1939 Was-A	0	3	.000	7	6	1	0	0	40²	56	7	31	12	19.3	8.63	50	.337	.442	3	.200	0	-18	-19	1	-1.4
Total 7	47	44	.516	175	100	44	2	9	872²	968	59	432	273	14.6	5.08	87	.281	.363	58	.198	7	-35	-63	4	-4.3

■ SHORTY DesJARDIEN　DesJardien, Paul Raymond　b: 8/24/1893, Coffeyville, Kan.　d: 3/7/56, Monrovia, Cal.　BR/TR, 6'4.5", 205 lbs.　Deb: 5/20/16

| 1916 Cle-A | 0 | 0 | — | 1 | 0 | 0 | 0 | 0 | 1 | 0 | 1 | 0 | 0 | 18.0 | 18.00 | 17 | .200 | .333 | 0 | — | 0 | -2 | -2 | -0 | -0.1 |

■ RUBE DESSAU　Dessau, Frank Rolland　b: 3/29/1883, New Galilee, Pa.　d: 5/6/52, York, Pa.　BB/TR, 5'11", 175 lbs.　Deb: 9/22/07

1907 Bos-N	0	1	.000	2	1	0	0	0	9¹	13	0	10	1	23.1	10.61	24	.394	.545	0	.000	-0	-8	-8	-0	-0.7
1910 Bro-N	2	3	.400	19	0	0	0	1	51¹	67	0	29	24	17.7	5.79	52	.328	.424	1	.067	-1	-16	-16	-1	-1.7
Total 2	2	4	.333	21	2	1	0	1	60²	80	0	39	25	18.5	6.53	45	.338	.443	1	.053	-1	-24	-24	-1	-2.4

■ TOM DETTORE　Dettore, Thomas Anthony　b: 11/17/47, Canonsburg, Pa.　BL/TR, 6'4", 200 lbs.　Deb: 6/11/73

1973 Pit-N	0	1	.000	12	1	0	0	0	22²	33	1	14	13	19.9	5.96	59	.340	.439	0	.000	-0	-6	-6	-0	-0.6
1974 Chi-N	3	5	.375	16	9	0	0	0	64²	64	4	31	43	14.1	4.18	91	.255	.351	5	.250	2	-4	-3	0	0.0
1975 Chi-N	5	4	.556	36	6	0	0	0	85¹	88	8	31	46	13.5	5.38	71	.270	.350	6	.250	1	-17	-15	1	-1.2

YEAR TM/L	W	L	PCT	G	GS	CG	SH	SV	IP	H	HR	BB	SO	RAT	ERA	ERA+	OAV	OOB	BH	AVG	PB	PR	/A	PD	TPI
1976 Chi-N	0	1	.000	4	0	0	0	0	7	11	3	2	4	16.7	10.29	38	.355	.394	0	—	0	-5	-5	0	-0.4
Total 4	8	11	.421	68	15	0	0	0	179²	196	16	78	106	14.6	5.21	73	.278	.365	11	.229	2	-32	-28	1	-2.2

■ MEL DEUTSCH
Deutsch, Melvin Elliott   b: 7/26/15, Caldwell, Tex.   BR/TR, 6'4", 215 lbs.   Deb: 4/21/46

YEAR TM/L	W	L	PCT	G	GS	CG	SH	SV	IP	H	HR	BB	SO	RAT	ERA	ERA+	OAV	OOB	BH	AVG	PB	PR	/A	PD	TPI
1946 Bos-A	0	0	—	3	0	0	0	0	6¹	7	1	3	2	14.2	5.68	64	.280	.357	0	.000	-0	-2	-1	0	-0.1

■ CHARLIE DEVENS
Devens, Charles   b: 1/1/10, Milton, Mass.   BR/TR, 6'1", 180 lbs.   Deb: 9/24/32

YEAR TM/L	W	L	PCT	G	GS	CG	SH	SV	IP	H	HR	BB	SO	RAT	ERA	ERA+	OAV	OOB	BH	AVG	PB	PR	/A	PD	TPI
1932 NY-A	1	0	1.000	1	1	1	0	0	9	6	0	7	4	13.0	2.00	204	.200	.351	0	.000	0	2	2	-0	0.2
1933 NY-A	3	3	.500	14	8	2	0	0	62	59	1	50	23	15.8	4.35	89	.250	.381	2	.095	-1	-1	-3	-1	-0.3
1934 NY-A	1	0	1.000	1	1	1	0	0	11	9	0	5	4	11.5	1.64	248	.225	.311	1	.500	1	3	3	0	0.5
Total 3	5	3	.625	16	10	4	0	0	82	74	1	62	31	14.9	3.73	105	.242	.370	3	.120	0	5	2	-0	0.4

■ ADRIAN DEVINE
Devine, Paul Adrian   b: 12/2/51, Galveston, Tex.   BR/TR, 6'4", 185 lbs.   Deb: 6/27/73

YEAR TM/L	W	L	PCT	G	GS	CG	SH	SV	IP	H	HR	BB	SO	RAT	ERA	ERA+	OAV	OOB	BH	AVG	PB	PR	/A	PD	TPI
1973 Atl-N	2	3	.400	24	1	0	0	4	32¹	45	6	12	15	16.4	6.40	61	.338	.401	1	.250	0	-10	-9	-1	-0.8
1975 Atl-N	1	0	1.000	5	2	0	0	0	16¹	19	2	7	8	14.9	4.41	86	.284	.360	0	.000	-1	-1	-1	-0	-0.1
1976 Atl-N	5	6	.455	48	1	0	0	9	73	72	3	26	48	12.2	3.21	118	.255	.320	0	.000	-2	2	5	-1	0.3
1977 Tex-A	11	6	.647	56	2	0	0	15	105²	102	8	31	67	11.7	3.58	114	.259	.319	0	—	0	6	6	2	0.8
1978 Atl-N	5	4	.556	31	6	0	0	3	65¹	84	8	25	26	15.0	5.92	68	.323	.382	1	.091	-1	-17	-14	1	-1.3
1979 Atl-N	1	2	.333	40	0	0	0	0	66²	84	8	25	22	15.0	3.24	125	.311	.374	0	.000	-1	4	6	0	0.5
1980 Tex-A	1	1	.500	13	0	0	0	0	28	49	4	9	8	19.0	4.82	81	.377	.421	0	—	0	-2	-3	-0	-0.2
Total 7	26	22	.542	217	12	0	0	31	387¹	455	34	135	194	14.0	4.21	95	.296	.357	2	.049	-4	-19	-9	1	-0.8

■ JIM DEVINE
Devine, Walter James   b: 10/5/1858, Brooklyn, N.Y.   d: 1/11/05, Syracuse, N.Y.   TL,   Deb: 5/08/1883 ♦

YEAR TM/L	W	L	PCT	G	GS	CG	SH	SV	IP	H	HR	BB	SO	RAT	ERA	ERA+	OAV	OOB	BH	AVG	PB	PR	/A	PD	TPI
1883 Bal-a	1	1	.500	2	2	1	0	0	11	15	0	1	3	13.1	7.36	47	.305	.319	2	.222	-0	-5	-5	-0	-0.3

■ HAL DEVINEY
Deviney, Harold John   b: 4/11/1893, Newton, Mass.   d: 1/4/33, Westwood, Mass.   BR/TR,   Deb: 7/30/20

YEAR TM/L	W	L	PCT	G	GS	CG	SH	SV	IP	H	HR	BB	SO	RAT	ERA	ERA+	OAV	OOB	BH	AVG	PB	PR	/A	PD	TPI
1920 Bos-A	0	0	—	1	0	0	0	0	3	7	0	2	0	27.0	15.00	24	.500	.563	2	1.000	2	-4	-4	-0	-0.1

■ JIM DEVLIN
Devlin, James Alexander   b: 1849, Philadelphia, Pa.   d: 10/10/1883, Philadelphia, Pa.   BR/TR, 5'11", 175 lbs.   Deb: 4/21/1873 ♦

YEAR TM/L	W	L	PCT	G	GS	CG	SH	SV	IP	H	HR	BB	SO	RAT	ERA	ERA+	OAV	OOB	BH	AVG	PB	PR	/A	PD	TPI
1875 Chi-n	7	16	.304	28	24	24	0	0	224	254	0	11		10.6	2.89	87	.255	.263	92	.292	7	-11	-10		-0.7
1876 Lou-N	30	35	.462	68	68	66	5	0	622	566	3	37	122	8.7	1.56	174	.226	.237	94	.315	4	51	80	1	8.7
1877 Lou-N	35	25	.583	61	61	61	4	0	559	617	4	41	141	10.6	2.25	147	.264	.277	72	.269	-1	34	65	2	7.0
Total 2	65	60	.520	129	129	127	9	0	1181	1183	7	78	263	9.6	1.89	159	.244	.256	166	.293	3	86	145	3	15.7

■ JIM DEVLIN
Devlin, James H.   b: 4/16/1866, Troy, N.Y.   d: 12/14/1900, Troy, N.Y.   TL,   Deb: 6/28/1886

YEAR TM/L	W	L	PCT	G	GS	CG	SH	SV	IP	H	HR	BB	SO	RAT	ERA	ERA+	OAV	OOB	BH	AVG	PB	PR	/A	PD	TPI
1886 NY-N	0	0	—	1	0	0	0	0	2	3	0	4	2	31.5	18.00	18	.333	.538	0	.000	-0	-3	-3	0	-0.2
1887 Phi-N	0	2	.000	2	2	2	0	0	18	20	0	10	6	15.0	6.00	70	.274	.361	2	.333	0	-4	-4	0	-0.1
1888 •StL-a	6	5	.545	11	11	10	0	0	90¹	82	3	20	45	10.2	3.19	102	.233	.275	11	.297	2	-1	1	0	0.3
1889 StL-a	5	3	.625	9	8	5	0	0	60	56	1	24	37	12.0	2.40	176	.239	.310	5	.192	-2	10	12	1	1.1
Total 4	11	10	.524	23	21	17	0	1	170¹	161	4	58	90	11.6	3.38	109	.241	.302	18	.257	1	1	6	2	1.1

■ CHARLIE DEWALD
Dewald, Charles H.   b: 1867, Newark, N.J.   d: 8/22/04, Cleveland, Ohio   TL,   Deb: 9/02/1890

YEAR TM/L	W	L	PCT	G	GS	CG	SH	SV	IP	H	HR	BB	SO	RAT	ERA	ERA+	OAV	OOB	BH	AVG	PB	PR	/A	PD	TPI
1890 Cle-P	2	0	1.000	2	2	2	0	0	14	13	0	5	6	11.6	0.64	618	.236	.299	3	.375	1	6	5	-0	0.5

■ MARK DEWEY
Dewey, Mark Alan   b: 1/3/65, Grand Rapids, Mich.   BR/TR, 6', 185 lbs.   Deb: 8/24/90

YEAR TM/L	W	L	PCT	G	GS	CG	SH	SV	IP	H	HR	BB	SO	RAT	ERA	ERA+	OAV	OOB	BH	AVG	PB	PR	/A	PD	TPI
1990 SF-N	1	1	.500	14	0	0	0	0	22²	22	1	5	11	10.7	2.78	134	.259	.300	0	.000	0	3	2	0	0.3

■ CARLOS DIAZ
Diaz, Carlos Antonio   b: 1/7/58, Kapotte, Hawaii   BR/TL, 6', 161 lbs.   Deb: 6/30/82

YEAR TM/L	W	L	PCT	G	GS	CG	SH	SV	IP	H	HR	BB	SO	RAT	ERA	ERA+	OAV	OOB	BH	AVG	PB	PR	/A	PD	TPI
1982 Atl-N	3	2	.600	19	0	0	0	1	25¹	31	3	9	16	14.2	4.62	81	.307	.364	0	.000	-0	-3	-3	0	-0.2
NY-N	0	0	—	4	0	0	0	0	3²	6	0	4	0	24.5	0.00	—	.353	.476	0	—	0	1	1	0	0.2
Yr	3	2	.600	23	0	0	0	1	29	37	3	13	16	15.5	4.03	92	.311	.379	0	.000	-0	-1	-1	0	0.0
1983 NY-N	3	1	.750	54	0	0	0	2	83¹	62	1	35	64	10.6	2.05	177	.211	.297	0	.000	-0	15	15	1	1.6
1984 LA-N	1	0	1.000	37	0	0	0	1	41	47	3	24	36	15.6	5.49	64	.285	.376	0	.000	-0	-9	-9	-1	-0.9
1985 •LA-N	6	3	.667	46	0	0	0	0	79¹	70	7	18	73	10.0	2.61	133	.230	.273	0	.000	-0	9	8	-1	0.6
1986 LA-N	0	0	—	19	0	0	0	0	25¹	33	2	7	18	14.2	4.26	81	.317	.360	0	.000	-0	-2	-2	0	-0.1
Total 5	13	6	.684	179	0	0	0	4	258	249	17	97	207	12.1	3.21	111	.253	.320	0	.000	-1	12	10	-1	1.2

■ ROB DIBBLE
Dibble, Robert Keith   b: 1/24/64, Bridgeport, Conn.   BL/TR, 6'4", 230 lbs.   Deb: 6/29/88

YEAR TM/L	W	L	PCT	G	GS	CG	SH	SV	IP	H	HR	BB	SO	RAT	ERA	ERA+	OAV	OOB	BH	AVG	PB	PR	/A	PD	TPI
1988 Cin-N	1	1	.500	37	0	0	0	0	59¹	43	2	21	59	9.9	1.82	197	.207	.283	0	.000	-0	11	12	-1	1.1
1989 Cin-N	10	5	.667	74	0	0	0	2	99	62	4	39	141	9.5	2.09	172	.176	.264	0	.000	-1	15	17	-2	1.5
1990 •Cin-N	8	3	.727	68	0	0	0	11	98	62	3	34	136	8.9	1.74	222	.183	.259	0	.000	-1	22	23	-1	2.2
Total 3	19	9	.679	179	0	0	0	13	256¹	167	9	94	336	9.3	1.90	195	.186	.267	0	.000	-2	48	51	-5	4.8

■ PEDRO DIBUT
Dibut, Pedro (Villafana)   b: 11/18/1892, Cienfuegos, Cuba   d: 12/4/79, Hialeah, Fla.   BR/TR, 5'8", 190 lbs.   Deb: 5/01/24

YEAR TM/L	W	L	PCT	G	GS	CG	SH	SV	IP	H	HR	BB	SO	RAT	ERA	ERA+	OAV	OOB	BH	AVG	PB	PR	/A	PD	TPI
1924 Cin-N	3	0	1.000	7	2	2	0	0	36²	24	1	12	15	8.8	2.21	170	.188	.257	3	.273	1	7	6	1	0.9
1925 Cin-N	0	0	—	1	0	0	0	0	0	3	0	0	0	—	∞	—	1.000	1.000	0	—	0	-2	-2	0	-0.1
Total 2	3	0	1.000	8	2	2	0	0	36²	27	1	12	15	9.6	2.70	139	.206	.273	3	.273	1	5	4	1	0.8

■ LEO DICKERMAN
Dickerman, Leo Louis   b: 10/31/1896, DeSoto, Mo.   d: 4/30/82, Atkins, Ark.   BR/TR, 6'4", 192 lbs.   Deb: 4/21/23

YEAR TM/L	W	L	PCT	G	GS	CG	SH	SV	IP	H	HR	BB	SO	RAT	ERA	ERA+	OAV	OOB	BH	AVG	PB	PR	/A	PD	TPI
1923 Bro-N	8	12	.400	35	20	7	1	0	159²	180	4	72	58	14.3	3.72	104	.283	.357	13	.250	3	5	3	2	0.7
1924 Bro-N	0	0	—	7	2	0	0	0	19²	20	0	16	9	17.4	5.49	68	.263	.404	1	.167	-0	-4	-4	0	-0.2
StL-N	7	4	.636	18	13	8	1	0	119²	108	6	51	28	12.0	2.41	157	.249	.328	9	.231	1	19	18	0	2.0
Yr	7	4	.636	25	15	8	1	0	139¹	128	6	67	37	12.6	2.84	133	.250	.337	4	.089	1	16	14	1	1.8
1925 StL-N	4	11	.267	29	20	7	2	1	130²	135	10	79	40	14.9	5.58	77	.273	.376	5	.114	-3	-19	-18	4	-1.5
Total 3	19	27	.413	89	55	22	4	1	429²	443	20	218	135	14.0	4.00	99	.270	.358	28	.199	1	2	-1	7	1.0

■ GEORGE DICKERSON
Dickerson, George Clark   b: 12/1/1892, Renner, Tex.   d: 7/9/38, Los Angeles, Cal.   BR/TR, 6'1", 170 lbs.   Deb: 8/02/17

YEAR TM/L	W	L	PCT	G	GS	CG	SH	SV	IP	H	HR	BB	SO	RAT	ERA	ERA+	OAV	OOB	BH	AVG	PB	PR	/A	PD	TPI
1917 Cle-A	0	0	—	1	0	0	0	0	1	0	0	0	0	0.0	0.00	—	.000	.000	0	—	0	0	0	0	0.0

■ EMERSON DICKMAN
Dickman, George Emerson   b: 11/12/14, Buffalo, N.Y.   d: 4/27/81, New York, N.Y.   BR/TR, 6'2", 175 lbs.   Deb: 6/27/36

YEAR TM/L	W	L	PCT	G	GS	CG	SH	SV	IP	H	HR	BB	SO	RAT	ERA	ERA+	OAV	OOB	BH	AVG	PB	PR	/A	PD	TPI
1936 Bos-A	0	0	—	1	0	0	0	0	1	2	0	1	2	27.0	9.00	59	.400	.500	0	—	0	-0	-0	0	0.0
1938 Bos-A	5	5	.500	32	11	3	1	0	104	117	9	54	22	15.1	5.28	93	.288	.377	10	.286	4	-6	-4	-0	0.0
1939 Bos-A	8	3	.727	48	1	0	0	5	113²	126	10	43	46	13.6	4.43	107	.282	.349	2	.056	-4	2	4	3	0.2
1940 Bos-A	8	6	.571	35	9	0	0	3	100	121	15	38	40	14.7	6.03	75	.291	.356	3	.107	-2	-18	-17	3	-1.5
1941 Bos-A	1	1	.500	9	3	0	0	0	31	37	4	17	16	15.7	6.39	66	.301	.386	1	.091	-1	-8	-8	-1	-0.8
Total 5	22	15	.595	125	24	6	1	8	349²	403	38	153	126	14.6	5.33	88	.288	.363	16	.145	-2	-30	-25	4	-2.1

■ JIM DICKSON
Dickson, James Edward   b: 4/20/38, Portland, Ore.   BL/TR, 6'1", 185 lbs.   Deb: 7/02/63

YEAR TM/L	W	L	PCT	G	GS	CG	SH	SV	IP	H	HR	BB	SO	RAT	ERA	ERA+	OAV	OOB	BH	AVG	PB	PR	/A	PD	TPI
1963 Hou-N	0	1	.000	13	0	0	0	2	14²	22	2	6	6	14.7	6.14	51	.344	.364	0	.000	-0	-5	-5	-0	-0.4
1964 Cin-N	1	0	1.000	4	0	0	0	0	5	8	0	5	6	23.4	7.20	50	.444	.565	0	—	0	-2	-2	0	-0.1
1965 KC-A	3	2	.600	68	0	0	0	0	85²	68	6	47	54	12.3	3.47	101	.220	.327	0	.000	-0	-0	-0	-1	0.0
1966 KC-A	1	0	1.000	24	1	0	0	1	37	37	2	19	20	14.6	5.35	68	.264	.368	1	.250	-0	-8	-8	-0	-0.7
Total 4	5	3	.625	109	1	0	0	3	142¹	135	10	77	86	13.5	4.36	79	.254	.351	1	.143	-0	-15	-15	-1	-1.2

■ LANCE DICKSON
Dickson, Lance Michael   b: 10/19/69, Fullerton, Cal.   BR/TL, 6', 185 lbs.   Deb: 8/09/90

YEAR TM/L	W	L	PCT	G	GS	CG	SH	SV	IP	H	HR	BB	SO	RAT	ERA	ERA+	OAV	OOB	BH	AVG	PB	PR	/A	PD	TPI
1990 Chi-N	0	3	.000	3	3	0	0	0	13²	20	2	4	4	15.8	7.24	57	.370	.414	0	.000	-0	-5	-5	1	-0.3

YEAR TM/L	W	L	PCT	G	GS	CG	SH	SV	IP	H	HR	BB	SO	RAT	ERA	ERA+	OAV	OOB	BH	AVG	PB	PR	/A	PD	TPI
■ **MURRY DICKSON**				Dickson, Murry Monroe			b: 8/21/16, Tracy, Mo.		d: 9/21/89, Kansas City, Kan.			BR/TR, 5'10.5", 157 lbs.			Deb: 9/30/39										
1939 StL-N	0	0	—	1	0	0	0	0	3²	1	0	1	2	4.9	0.00	—	.091	.167	0	.000	-0	2	2	0	0.2
1940 StL-N	0	0	—	1	1	0	0	0	1²	5	0	1	0	32.4	16.20	25	.500	.545	0	—	0	-2	-2	-0	-0.1
1942 StL-N	6	3	.667	36	7	2	0	2	120²	91	1	61	66	11.4	2.91	118	.216	.316	8	.190	-0	5	7	1	0.9
1943 *StL-N	8	2	.800	31	7	2	0	0	115²	114	4	49	44	12.8	3.58	94	.257	.333	9	.265	1	-3	-3	-0	-0.1
1946 *StL-N	15	6	.714	47	19	12	2	1	184¹	160	8	56	82	10.7	2.88	120	.234	.295	18	.277	5	11	12	4	2.2
1947 StL-N	13	16	.448	47	25	11	4	3	231²	211	16	88	111	11.7	3.07	135	.243	.315	17	.213	1	25	27	1	3.0
1948 StL-N	12	16	.429	42	29	11	1	1	252¹	257	39	85	113	12.2	4.14	99	.265	.325	27	.281	4	-5	-1	1	0.4
1949 Pit-N	12	14	.462	44	20	11	2	0	224¹	216	17	80	89	12.1	3.29	128	.255	.324	17	.202	1	19	23	5	2.9
1950 Pit-N	10	15	.400	51	22	8	0	3	225	227	20	83	76	12.5	3.80	115	.260	.326	21	.256	3	9	15	2	2.0
1951 Pit-N	20	16	.556	45	35	19	3	2	288²	294	32	101	112	12.5	4.02	105	.262	.327	30	.273	5	-2	7	4	1.7
1952 Pit-N	14	21	.400	43	34	21	2	2	277²	278	26	76	112	11.5	3.57	112	.261	.311	24	.224	2	5	13	4	2.1
1953 Pit-N	10	19	.345	45	26	10	1	4	200²	240	27	58	88	13.5	4.53	99	.298	.348	7	.115	-4	-5	-1	-0	-0.4
1954 Phi-N	10	20	.333	40	31	12	4	3	226¹	256	31	73	64	13.2	3.78	107	.286	.342	15	.190	0	7	7	3	0.9
1955 Phi-N	12	11	.522	36	28	12	4	0	216	190	27	82	92	11.5	3.50	113	.238	.312	18	.220	1	13	11	2	1.3
1956 Phi-N	0	3	.000	3	3	0	0	0	23	20	1	12	1	12.5	5.09	73	.241	.337	3	.333	1	-3	-3	-0	-0.1
StL-N	13	8	.619	28	27	12	3	0	196¹	175	20	57	109	10.7	3.07	123	.240	.296	19	.247	4	15	16	4	2.5
Yr	13	11	.542	31	30	12	3	0	219¹	195	21	69	110	10.9	3.28	115	.240	.301	1	.012	4	12	12	4	2.4
1957 StL-N	5	3	.625	14	13	3	1	0	74	87	8	25	29	13.7	4.14	96	.296	.353	6	.222	1	-2	-1	2	0.1
1958 KC-A	9	5	.643	27	9	3	0	1	99	99	12	31	46	12.0	3.27	119	.258	.317	9	.257	2	5	7	2	1.2
*NY-A	1	2	.333	6	2	0	0	1	20¹	18	4	12	9	13.7	5.75	61	.237	.348	2	.286	0	-4	-5	-0	-0.4
Yr	10	7	.588	33	11	3	0	2	119¹	117	16	43	55	12.1	3.70	104	.253	.318	2	.048	2	1	2	2	0.8
1959 KC-A	2	1	.667	38	0	0	0	0	71	85	9	27	36	14.2	4.94	81	.290	.350	3	.176	-1	-9	-7	-0	-0.7
Total 18	172	181	.487	625	338	149	27	23	3052¹	3024	302	1058	1281	12.1	3.66	110	.259	.323	253	.231	26	81	120	34	19.6
■ **WALT DICKSON**				Dickson, Walter R. "Hickory"			b: 12/3/1878, New Summerfield, Tex.		d: 12/9/18, Ardmore, Okla.			BR/TR, 5'11.5", 175 lbs.			Deb: 4/26/10										
1910 NY-N	1	0	1.000	12	1	0	0	0	29²	31	1	9	9	12.1	5.46	54	.272	.325	1	.250	0	-8	-8	-1	-0.8
1912 Bos-N	3	19	.136	36	20	9	1	1	189	233	2	61	47	14.1	3.86	93	.306	.360	10	.167	-2	-9	-6	2	-0.4
1913 Bos-N	6	7	.462	19	15	8	0	0	128	118	4	45	47	11.5	3.23	102	.249	.316	8	.178	-1	-0	1	-0	0.0
1914 Pit-F	9	19	.321	40	32	19	3	1	256²	262	5	74	63	11.9	3.16	101	.305	.361	7	.084	-7	1	1	1	-0.5
1915 Pit-F	7	5	.583	27	11	4	0	0	96²	115	5	33	36	14.0	4.19	72	.316	.376	4	.129	-0	-12	-13	0	-1.2
Total 5	26	50	.342	134	79	40	4	2	700	759	17	222	202	12.7	3.60	91	.295	.353	30	.135	-10	-29	-26	2	-2.9
■ **GEORGE DIEHL**				Diehl, George Krause			b: 2/25/18, Emmaus, Pa.		d: 8/24/86, Kingsport, Tenn.			BR/TR, 6'2", 196 lbs.			Deb: 4/19/42										
1942 Bos-N	0	0	—	1	0	0	0	0	3²	2	0	2	0	12.3	2.45	136	.167	.333	0	.000	-0	0	0	0	0.0
1943 Bos-N	0	0	—	1	0	0	0	0	4	4	0	3	1	15.8	4.50	76	.267	.389	0	.000	-0	-0	-0	1	0.0
Total 2	0	0	—	2	0	0	0	0	7²	6	0	5	1	14.1	3.52	96	.222	.364	0	.000	-0	-0	-0	1	0.0
■ **LARRY DIERKER**				Dierker, Lawrence Edward			b: 9/22/46, Hollywood, Cal.		BR/TR, 6'4", 215 lbs.			Deb: 9/22/64											
1964 Hou-N	0	1	.000	3	1	0	0	0	9	7	1	3	5	10.0	2.00	171	.219	.286	0	.000	-0	2	1	-0	0.1
1965 Hou-N	7	8	.467	26	19	1	0	0	146²	135	16	37	109	10.7	3.50	96	.240	.290	5	.100	-1	1	-2	-2	-0.5
1966 Hou-N	10	8	.556	29	28	8	2	0	187	173	17	45	108	10.5	3.18	108	.240	.285	10	.149	1	9	5	-0	0.5
1967 Hou-N	6	5	.545	15	15	4	0	0	99	95	4	25	68	11.0	3.36	98	.252	.300	7	.226	2	0	-1	-1	0.0
1968 Hou-N	12	15	.444	32	32	10	1	0	233²	206	14	89	161	11.7	3.31	89	.240	.317	5	.068	-3	-9	-9	-2	-1.5
1969 Hou-N	20	13	.606	39	37	20	4	0	305¹	240	18	72	232	9.2	2.33	152	.214	.262	17	.144	-1	43	41	-0	4.5
1970 Hou-N	16	12	.571	37	36	17	2	1	269²	263	31	82	191	11.7	3.87	100	.254	.313	16	.174	-0	5	0	-1	-0.1
1971 Hou-N	12	6	.667	24	23	6	2	0	159	150	8	33	91	10.5	2.72	124	.248	.289	4	.074	-3	13	11	0	0.9
1972 Hou-N	15	8	.652	31	31	12	5	0	214²	209	14	51	115	11.1	3.40	99	.256	.304	13	.167	-0	1	-1	-2	-0.2
1973 Hou-N	1	1	.500	14	3	0	0	0	27	27	3	13	18	14.0	4.33	84	.265	.359	0	.000	-0	-2	-2	-0	-0.2
1974 Hou-N	11	10	.524	33	33	7	3	0	223²	189	18	82	150	11.1	2.90	120	.232	.307	14	.197	1	18	14	-0	1.5
1975 Hou-N	14	16	.467	34	34	14	2	0	232	225	24	91	127	12.5	4.00	84	.260	.335	7	.092	-4	-10	-16	-1	-2.1
1976 Hou-N	13	14	.481	28	28	7	4	0	187²	171	9	72	112	11.9	3.69	86	.243	.319	9	.141	-0	-4	-10	-1	-1.2
1977 StL-N	2	6	.250	11	9	0	0	0	39¹	40	7	16	6	13.3	4.58	84	.267	.345	0	.000	-1	-3	-3	-0	-0.3
Total 14	139	123	.531	356	329	106	25	1	2333²	2130	184	711	1493	11.1	3.31	103	.243	.303	107	.136	-11	65	29	-11	1.4
■ **BILL DIETRICH**				Dietrich, William John "Bullfrog"			b: 3/29/10, Philadelphia, Pa.		d: 6/20/78, Philadelphia, Pa.			BR/TR, 6', 185 lbs.			Deb: 4/13/33										
1933 Phi-A	0	1	.000	8	1	0	0	0	17	13	1	19	4	16.9	5.82	74	.236	.432	1	.333	1	-3	-3	-0	-0.1
1934 Phi-A	11	12	.478	39	23	14	4	3	207²	201	12	114	88	13.8	4.68	94	.255	.351	15	.208	3	-4	-7	-2	-0.4
1935 Phi-A	7	13	.350	43	15	8	1	3	185¹	203	7	101	59	14.8	5.39	84	.276	.364	5	.083	-6	-19	-17	-0	-2.1
1936 Phi-A	4	6	.400	21	4	0	0	3	71²	91	4	40	34	16.5	6.53	78	.305	.388	3	.111	-2	-12	-11	1	-0.9
Was-A	0	1	.000	5	0	0	0	0	8¹	13	0	6	4	20.5	9.72	49	.351	.442	0	—	0	-4	-5	-0	-0.3
Chi-A	4	4	.500	14	11	6	1	0	82²	93	8	36	39	14.2	4.68	111	.284	.356	8	.267	1	3	5	-0	0.4
Yr	8	11	.421	40	15	6	1	3	162²	197	12	82	77	15.5	5.75	89	.297	.375	3	.053	-1	-13	-11	1	-0.8
1937 Chi-A	8	10	.444	29	20	7	1	1	143¹	162	15	72	62	14.7	4.90	94	.286	.366	8	.182	1	-4	-5	1	-0.2
1938 Chi-A	2	4	.333	8	7	1	0	0	48	49	7	31	11	15.0	5.44	90	.259	.364	1	.063	-1	-3	-3	-0	-0.3
1939 Chi-A	7	8	.467	25	19	2	0	0	127²	134	14	56	43	13.5	5.22	91	.272	.349	8	.216	2	-8	-7	-1	-0.4
1940 Chi-A	10	6	.625	23	17	6	1	0	149²	154	10	65	43	13.2	4.03	110	.266	.340	12	.240	3	6	7	-1	0.8
1941 Chi-A	5	8	.385	19	15	4	1	0	109¹	114	7	50	26	13.8	5.35	77	.265	.345	3	.088	0	-15	-15	-1	-1.4
1942 Chi-A	6	11	.353	26	23	6	0	0	160	173	16	70	39	13.9	4.89	74	.277	.355	5	.104	-1	-22	-23	-2	-2.3
1943 Chi-A	12	10	.545	26	26	12	2	0	186²	180	4	53	52	11.3	2.80	119	.253	.307	8	.143	0	10	11	2	1.5
1944 Chi-A	16	17	.485	36	36	15	2	0	246	269	16	68	70	12.4	3.62	95	.279	.328	9	.117	-3	-5	-1	-0	-0.8
1945 Chi-A	7	10	.412	18	16	6	3	0	122¹	136	4	36	43	12.7	4.19	79	.279	.329	6	.167	0	-11	-12	-0	-1.1
1946 Chi-A	3	3	.500	11	9	3	0	0	62	63	4	24	20	12.6	2.61	131	.267	.335	1	.053	-2	6	6	1	0.5
1947 Phi-A	5	2	.714	11	9	2	1	0	60²	48	9	40	18	13.4	3.12	122	.223	.350	2	.063	-2	4	5	-1	0.2
1948 Phi-A	1	2	.333	4	1	0	0	0	21	21	0	9	5	17.6	5.87	73	.356	.441	0	.000	-0	-3	-3	-0	-0.2
Total 16	108	128	.458	366	253	92	17	11	2003²	2117	128	890	660	13.6	4.48	92	.271	.348	94	.150	-5	-85	-84	-1	-7.1
■ **DUTCH DIETZ**				Dietz, Lloyd Arthur			b: 2/9/12, Cincinnati, Ohio		d: 10/29/72, Beaumont, Tex.			BR/TR, 5'11.5", 180 lbs.			Deb: 4/26/40										
1940 Pit-N	0	1	.000	4	2	0	0	0	15¹	22	2	4	8	15.3	5.87	65	.355	.394	1	.143	-0	-3	-4	-0	-0.3
1941 Pit-N	7	2	.778	33	6	4	1	1	100¹	88	6	33	22	11.0	2.33	155	.233	.298	4	.160	-1	15	14	0	1.5
1942 Pit-N	6	9	.400	40	13	3	0	3	134¹	139	8	57	35	13.2	3.95	86	.268	.342	7	.200	1	-10	-8	-2	-0.9
1943 Pit-N	0	3	.000	8	0	0	0	0	9	12	0	4	4	17.0	6.00	60	.324	.405	0	—	-0	-3	-3	-1	-0.1
Phi-N	1	1	.500	21	0	0	0	2	36	42	2	15	10	14.3	6.50	52	.292	.358	1	.167	0	-12	-13	-0	-1.2
Yr	1	4	.200	29	0	0	0	2	45	54	2	19	14	14.6	6.40	53	.297	.363	1	.167	0	-15	-15	1	-1.3
Total 4	14	16	.467	106	21	7	1	6	295	303	18	113	79	12.8	3.87	90	.286	.334	13	.178	-0	-14	-13	-1	-1.0
■ **REESE DIGGS**				Diggs, Reese Wilson "Diggsy"			b: 9/22/15, Mathews, Va.		d: 10/30/78, Baltimore, Md.			BR/TR, 6'2", 180 lbs.			Deb: 9/15/34										
1934 Was-A	1	2	.333	4	3	2	0	0	21¹	26	3	15	2	17.3	6.75	61	.313	.418	2	.250	-1	-5	-6	0	-0.4
■ **JACK DiLAURO**				DiLauro, Jack Edward			b: 5/3/43, Akron, Ohio		BB/TL, 6'2", 185 lbs.			Deb: 5/15/69											
1969 NY-N	1	4	.200	23	4	0	0	0	63²	50	4	18	27	9.6	2.40	152	.216	.272	0	.000	-1	8	9	0	0.8
1970 Hou-N	1	3	.250	42	0	0	0	3	33²	34	4	17	23	13.6	4.28	91	.262	.347	0	.000	-0	-1	-1	-0	-0.1
Total 2	2	7	.222	65	4	0	0	4	97¹	84	8	35	50	11.0	3.05	122	.232	.300	0	.000	-2	8	7	-0	0.7

YEAR	TM/L	W	L	PCT	G	GS	CG	SH	SV	IP	H	HR	BB	SO	RAT	ERA	ERA+	OAV	OOB	BH	AVG	PB	PR	/A	PD	TPI

■ GORDON DILLARD   Dillard, Gordon Lee   b: 5/20/64, Salinas, Cal.   BL/TL, 6'1", 190 lbs.   Deb: 8/12/88

1988	Bal-A	0	0	—	2	1	0	0	0	3	3	1	4	2	21.0	6.00	65	.273	.467	0	—	0	-1	-1	0	0.0
1989	Phi-N	0	0	—	5	0	0	0	0	4	7	0	0	2	15.8	6.75	53	.368	.368	0	—	0	-1	-1	0	0.0
Total	2	0	0	—	7	1	0	0	0	7	10	1	4	4	18.0	6.43	58	.333	.412	0	—	0	-2	-2	0	0.0

■ HARLEY DILLINGER   Dillinger, Harley Hugh "Hoke" or "Lefty"   b: 10/30/1894, Pomeroy, Ohio   d: 1/8/59, Cleveland, Ohio   BR/TL, 5'11", 175 lbs.   Deb: 8/16/14

| 1914 | Cle-A | 0 | 1 | .000 | 11 | 2 | 1 | 0 | 0 | 33² | 41 | 0 | 25 | 11 | 17.9 | 4.54 | 64 | .325 | .441 | 0 | .000 | -1 | -7 | -6 | -1 | -0.7 |

■ BILL DILLMAN   Dillman, William Howard   b: 5/25/45, Trenton, N.J.   BR/TR, 6'2", 180 lbs.   Deb: 4/14/67

1967	Bal-A	5	9	.357	32	15	2	1	3	124	115	13	33	69	11.0	4.35	72	.249	.303	5	.161	-0	-15	-17	-1	-1.8
1970	Mon-N	2	3	.400	18	0	0	0	0	30²	28	4	18	17	13.8	5.28	78	.255	.364	0	.000	-0	-4	-4	0	-0.3
Total	2	7	12	.368	50	15	2	1	3	154²	143	17	51	86	11.5	4.54	74	.250	.316	5	.152	-1	-20	-21	-0	-2.1

■ STEVE DILLON   Dillon, Stephen Edward   b: 3/20/43, Yonkers, N.Y.   BL/TL, 5'10", 160 lbs.   Deb: 9/05/63

1963	NY-N	0	0	—	1	0	0	0	0	1²	3	0	0	1	16.2	10.80	32	.429	.429	0	—	0	-1	-1	0	0.0
1964	NY-N	0	0	—	2	0	0	0	0	3	4	1	2	2	18.0	9.00	40	.333	.429	0	—	0	-2	-2	0	-0.1
Total	2	0	0	—	3	0	0	0	0	4²	7	1	2	3	17.4	9.64	37	.368	.429	0	—	0	-3	-3	0	-0.1

■ FRANK DIMICHELE   Dimichele, Frank Lawrence   b: 2/16/65, Philadelphia, Pa.   BR/TL, 6'3", 205 lbs.   Deb: 4/08/88

| 1988 | Cal-A | 0 | 0 | — | 4 | 0 | 0 | 0 | 0 | 4² | 5 | 2 | 2 | 1 | 13.5 | 9.64 | 40 | .263 | .333 | 0 | — | 0 | -3 | -3 | -0 | -0.2 |

■ BILL DINNEEN   Dinneen, William Henry "Big Bill"   b: 4/5/1876, Syracuse, N.Y.   d: 1/13/55, Syracuse, N.Y.   BR/TR, 6'1", 190 lbs.   Deb: 4/22/1898   U

1898	Was-N	9	16	.360	29	27	22	0	0	218¹	238	6	88	83	13.4	4.00	92	.275	.342	8	.100	-5	-9	-8	-0	-1.1
1899	Was-N	14	20	.412	37	35	30	0	0	291	350	6	106	91	14.1	3.93	100	.297	.355	36	.303	5	-2	-1	3	0.8
1900	Bos-N	20	14	.588	40	37	33	1	0	320²	304	11	105	107	11.5	3.12	133	.250	.309	35	.280	2	21	36	1	4.0
1901	Bos-A	15	18	.455	37	34	31	0	0	309¹	295	8	77	141	11.0	2.94	123	.250	.299	13	.211	0	13	23	-1	2.5
1902	Bos-A	21	21	.500	42	42	39	2	0	371¹	348	9	99	136	10.8	2.93	122	.248	.298	18	.128	-7	27	27	-7	1.3
1903	*Bos-A	21	13	.618	37	34	32	6	2	299	255	6	66	148	9.7	2.26	134	.230	.273	17	.160	-0	23	26	-2	2.6
1904	Bos-A	23	14	.622	37	37	37	5	0	335²	283	8	63	153	9.3	2.20	122	.230	.267	25	.208	-1	15	18	-2	1.7
1905	Bos-A	12	14	.462	31	29	23	2	1	243²	235	7	50	97	10.5	3.73	72	.255	.293	13	.148	-3	-29	-28	1	-3.1
1906	Bos-A	8	19	.296	28	27	22	1	0	218²	209	4	52	60	10.7	2.92	94	.255	.299	7	.111	-2	-6	-4	-2	-0.7
1907	Bos-A	0	4	.000	5	5	3	0	0	32²	42	5	8	8	13.8	5.23	49	.314	.352	0	.000	-1	-10	-10	-1	-1.0
	StL-A	7	10	.412	24	16	15	2	4	155¹	153	3	33	38	10.8	2.43	104	.259	.299	6	.204	1	2	1	-2	0.1
	Yr	7	14	.333	29	21	18	2	4	188	195	8	41	46	11.3	2.92	87	.269	.308	6	.102	1	-8	-8	-3	-0.9
1908	StL-A	14	7	.667	27	16	11	1	0	167	133	2	53	39	10.2	2.10	114	.231	.300	12	.203	0	5	5	-2	0.4
1909	StL-A	6	7	.462	17	13	8	3	0	112	112	3	29	26	11.4	3.46	70	.267	.316	7	.194	2	-12	-13	0	-1.1
Total	12	170	177	.490	391	352	306	23	7	3074²	2957	78	829	1127	11.1	3.01	107	.254	.304	219	.192	-7	38	70	-13	6.4

■ RON DIORIO   Diorio, Ronald Michael   b: 7/15/46, Waterbury, Conn.   BR/TR, 6'6", 212 lbs.   Deb: 8/09/73

1973	Phi-N	0	0	—	23	0	0	0	1	19¹	18	1	6	11	11.2	2.33	163	.257	.316	0	—	0	3	3	-0	0.3
1974	Phi-N	0	0	—	2	0	0	0	0	1	2	1	1	0	27.0	18.00	21	.400	.500	0	—	0	-2	-2	0	0.0
Total	2	0	0	—	25	0	0	0	1	20¹	20	2	7	11	12.0	3.10	122	.267	.329	0	—	0	1	2	0	0.3

■ FRANK DiPINO   DiPino, Frank Michael   b: 10/22/56, Syracuse, N.Y.   BL/TL, 5'10", 175 lbs.   Deb: 9/14/81

1981	Mil-A	0	0	—	2	0	0	0	0	2¹	0	0	3	3	11.6	0.00	—	.000	.300	0	—	0	1	1	0	0.1
1982	Hou-N	2	2	.500	6	6	0	0	0	28¹	32	1	11	25	13.7	6.04	55	.302	.368	0	.000	-1	-8	-9	-1	-0.9
1983	Hou-N	3	4	.429	53	0	0	0	20	71¹	52	2	20	67	9.2	2.65	128	.205	.265	1	.167	1	8	6	0	0.7
1984	Hou-N	4	9	.308	57	0	0	0	14	75¹	74	3	36	65	13.3	3.35	99	.260	.345	0	.000	-1	2	-0	0	0.0
1985	Hou-N	3	7	.300	54	0	0	0	6	76	69	7	43	49	13.5	4.03	86	.248	.353	2	.167	-0	-4	-5	-1	-0.6
1986	Hou-N	1	3	.250	31	0	0	0	3	40¹	27	5	16	27	10.0	3.57	101	.189	.280	1	.200	0	1	1	0	0.1
	Chi-N	2	4	.333	30	0	0	0	0	40	47	6	14	43	13.7	5.17	78	.297	.355	0	.000	-0	-6	-5	1	-0.3
	Yr	3	7	.300	61	0	0	0	3	80¹	74	11	30	70	11.7	4.37	87	.243	.311	0	.000	-0	-6	-5	1	-0.2
1987	Chi-N	3	3	.500	69	0	0	0	4	80	75	7	34	61	12.4	3.15	136	.252	.330	1	.500	1	8	10	1	1.1
1988	Chi-N	2	3	.400	63	0	0	0	6	90¹	102	6	32	69	13.4	4.98	72	.285	.344	1	.100	-0	-15	-14	-1	-1.5
1989	StL-N	9	0	1.000	67	0	0	0	6	88¹	73	5	20	44	9.5	2.45	148	.227	.273	1	.077	-1	10	12	0	1.2
1990	StL-N	5	2	.714	62	0	0	0	3	81	92	8	31	49	13.8	4.56	86	.294	.359	1	.250	0	-7	-6	1	-0.4
Total	10	34	37	.479	494	6	0	0	56	673¹	643	51	260	502	12.2	3.80	97	.255	.327	8	.113	-2	-10	-10	1	-0.5

■ GEORGE DISCH   Disch, George Charles   b: 3/15/1879, Lincoln, Mo.   d: 8/25/50, Rapid City, S.D.   5'11",   Deb: 8/08/05

| 1905 | Det-A | 0 | 2 | .000 | 8 | 3 | 1 | 0 | 0 | 47² | 43 | 1 | 8 | 14 | 9.6 | 2.64 | 104 | .242 | .275 | 2 | .105 | -1 | 0 | 1 | 0 | 0.0 |

■ ALEC DISTASO   Distaso, Alec John   b: 12/23/48, Los Angeles, Cal.   BR/TR, 6'2", 200 lbs.   Deb: 4/20/69

| 1969 | Chi-N | 0 | 0 | — | 2 | 0 | 0 | 0 | 0 | 4² | 6 | 0 | 1 | 1 | 13.5 | 3.86 | 104 | .316 | .350 | 0 | — | 0 | -0 | 0 | 0 | 0.0 |

■ ART DITMAR   Ditmar, Arthur John   b: 4/3/29, Winthrop, Mass.   BR/TR, 6'2", 185 lbs.   Deb: 4/19/54

1954	Phi-A	1	4	.200	14	5	0	0	0	39¹	50	4	36	14	19.9	6.41	61	.314	.444	1	.125	0	-12	-11	0	-1.0
1955	KC-A	12	12	.500	35	22	7	1	1	175¹	180	23	86	79	14.0	5.03	83	.270	.360	13	.210	-0	-21	-17	1	-1.5
1956	KC-A	12	22	.353	44	34	14	2	1	254¹	254	30	108	126	13.1	4.42	98	.262	.340	13	.143	-4	-7	-3	-1	-0.7
1957	*NY-A	8	3	.727	46	11	0	0	6	127¹	128	9	35	64	11.7	3.25	110	.261	.313	7	.200	1	8	5	-1	0.4
1958	*NY-A	9	8	.529	38	13	4	0	4	139²	124	14	38	52	10.8	3.42	103	.237	.295	11	.250	2	5	2	-2	0.2
1959	NY-A	13	9	.591	38	25	7	1	1	202	156	17	52	96	9.6	2.90	126	.211	.270	15	.197	1	22	17	-1	1.8
1960	*NY-A	15	9	.625	34	28	8	1	0	200	195	25	56	65	11.3	3.06	117	.256	.308	11	.159	0	18	12	-1	1.1
1961	NY-A	2	3	.400	12	8	1	0	0	54¹	59	9	14	24	12.4	4.64	80	.285	.336	1	.053	-2	-4	-6	1	-0.5
	KC-A	0	5	.000	20	5	0	0	1	54	60	6	23	19	14.2	5.67	73	.286	.362	2	.167	-0	-10	-9	-0	-0.8
	Yr	2	8	.200	32	13	1	0	1	108¹	119	15	37	43	13.1	5.15	76	.285	.341	3	.097	-2	-14	-15	1	-1.3
1962	KC-A	0	2	.000	6	5	0	0	0	21²	31	1	13	13	19.1	6.65	63	.323	.414	1	.167	-0	-6	-6	0	-0.5
Total	9	72	77	.483	287	156	41	5	14	1268	1237	138	461	552	12.3	3.98	97	.256	.326	75	.178	-4	-7	-17	-4	-1.5

■ SONNY DIXON   Dixon, John Craig   b: 11/5/24, Charlotte, N.C.   BB/TR, 6'2.5", 205 lbs.   Deb: 4/20/53

1953	Was-A	5	8	.385	43	6	3	0	3	120	123	13	31	40	11.7	3.75	104	.267	.316	4	.154	0	3	2	2	0.4
1954	Was-A	1	2	.333	16	0	0	0	1	29²	26	3	12	7	11.5	3.03	117	.236	.311	0	.000	-1	2	2	1	0.2
	Phi-A	5	7	.417	38	6	1	0	4	107¹	136	8	27	42	13.9	4.86	80	.308	.352	7	.250	2	-14	-11	3	-0.6
	Yr	6	9	.400	54	6	1	0	5	137	162	11	39	49	13.4	4.47	86	.293	.343	2	.059	1	-11	-10	4	-0.4
1955	KC-A	0	0	—	2	0	0	0	0	1²	6	1	0	0	32.4	16.20	26	.545	.545	0	—	0	-2	-2	0	-0.1
1956	NY-A	0	1	.000	3	0	0	0	1	4¹	4	0	5	1	20.8	2.08	186	.294	.455	0	.000	-0	1	1	0	0.1
Total	4	11	18	.379	102	12	4	0	9	263	296	25	75	90	12.9	4.17	93	.284	.335	11	.180	1	-9	-9	6	0.0

■ KEN DIXON   Dixon, Kenneth John   b: 10/17/60, Monroe, Va.   BB/TR, 5'11", 166 lbs.   Deb: 9/22/84

1984	Bal-A	0	1	.000	2	2	0	0	0	13	14	1	4	8	12.5	4.15	93	.269	.321	0	—	0	-0	-0	0	0.0
1985	Bal-A	8	4	.667	34	18	3	1	1	162	144	20	64	108	11.7	3.67	110	.237	.312	0	—	0	9	7	-1	0.5
1986	Bal-A	11	13	.458	35	33	2	0	0	202¹	194	33	83	170	12.4	4.58	90	.249	.322	0	—	0	-3	-4	0	-0.2
1987	Bal-A	7	10	.412	34	15	0	0	5	105	128	31	27	91	13.4	6.43	68	.292	.334	0	—	0	-23	-24	-0	-2.1
Total	4	26	28	.481	105	68	5	1	6	482¹	480	85	178	377	12.4	4.66	89	.256	.322	0	—	0	-24	-28	-3	-2.6

YEAR	TM/L	W	L	PCT	G	GS	CG	SH	SV	IP	H	HR	BB	SO	RAT	ERA	ERA+	OAV	OOB	BH	AVG	PB	PR	/A	PD	TPI

■ TOM DIXON
Dixon, Thomas Earl b: 4/23/55, Orlando, Fla. BR/TR, 5'11", 175 lbs. Deb: 7/30/77

YEAR	TM/L	W	L	PCT	G	GS	CG	SH	SV	IP	H	HR	BB	SO	RAT	ERA	ERA+	OAV	OOB	BH	AVG	PB	PR	/A	PD	TPI
1977	Hou-N	1	0	1.000	9	4	1	0	0	30¹	40	0	7	15	14.2	3.26	109	.320	.361	0	.000	-1	2	1	0	0.0
1978	Hou-N	7	11	.389	30	19	3	2	1	140	140	8	40	66	11.6	3.99	83	.265	.318	4	.100	-2	-6	-11	-0	-1.2
1979	Hou-N	1	2	.333	19	1	0	0	0	25²	39	2	15	9	18.9	6.66	53	.348	.425	1	1.000	0	-8	-9	1	-0.7
1983	Mon-N	0	1	.000	4	0	0	0	0	3²	6	1	1	4	19.6	9.82	37	.375	.444	0	—	0	-3	-3	0	-0.2
Total 4		9	14	.391	62	24	4	2	1	199²	225	11	63	94	13.1	4.33	78	.288	.343	5	.104	-2	-15	-21	0	-2.1

■ BILL DOAK
Doak, William Leopold "Spittin' Bill" b: 1/28/1891, Pittsburgh, Pa. d: 11/26/54, Bradenton, Fla. BR/TR, 6'0.5", 165 lbs. Deb: 9/01/12

YEAR	TM/L	W	L	PCT	G	GS	CG	SH	SV	IP	H	HR	BB	SO	RAT	ERA	ERA+	OAV	OOB	BH	AVG	PB	PR	/A	PD	TPI
1912	Cin-N	0	0	—	1	1	0	0	0	2	4	0	1	0	22.5	4.50	75	.444	.500	0	—	0	-0	-0	0	0.0
1913	StL-N	2	8	.200	15	12	5	1	1	93	79	4	39	51	11.9	3.10	104	.236	.325	1	.032	-4	1	1	1	-0.1
1914	StL-N	19	6	.760	36	33	16	7	1	256	193	2	87	118	10.1	**1.72**	**162**	.216	.290	10	.118	-3	30	31	4	3.6
1915	StL-N	16	18	.471	38	36	19	3	1	276	263	4	85	124	11.6	2.64	106	.261	.323	15	.174	1	3	5	7	1.4
1916	StL-N	12	8	.600	29	26	11	2	0	192	177	5	55	82	11.0	2.63	101	.251	.308	8	.129	-2	-0	0	2	0.1
1917	StL-N	16	20	.444	44	37	16	3	2	281¹	257	6	85	111	11.2	3.10	87	.250	.312	12	.126	-4	-12	-13	4	-1.3
1918	StL-N	9	15	.375	31	23	16	1	1	211	191	8	60	74	10.9	2.43	111	.249	.306	12	.182	1	8	7	5	1.4
1919	StL-N	13	14	.481	31	29	13	3	0	202²	182	5	55	69	10.6	3.11	90	.246	.299	7	.109	-4	-4	-7	5	-0.6
1920	StL-N	20	12	.625	39	37	20	5	1	270	256	7	80	90	11.4	2.53	118	.253	.312	10	.114	-6	18	14	0	0.8
1921	StL-N	15	6	**.714**	32	28	13	1	1	208²	224	3	37	83	11.4	2.59	142	.278	.313	10	.143	-3	28	25	2	2.4
1922	StL-N	11	13	.458	37	29	8	2	2	180¹	222	12	69	73	14.7	5.54	70	.311	.374	7	.130	-3	-29	-34	2	-3.2
1923	StL-N	8	13	.381	30	26	7	2	0	185	199	6	69	53	13.2	3.26	120	.279	.346	3	.045	-8	15	13	3	0.7
1924	StL-N	2	1	.667	11	1	0	0	3	22	25	0	14	7	16.0	3.27	116	.313	.415	1	.200	-0	1	1	1	0.2
	Bro-N	11	5	.688	21	16	8	2	0	149¹	130	8	35	32	10.1	3.07	122	.239	.289	10	.179	-0	13	11	3	1.4
	Yr	13	6	.684	32	17	8	2	3	171¹	155	8	49	39	10.9	3.10	121	.249	.307	3	.049	-1	15	12	4	1.6
1927	Bro-N	11	8	.579	27	20	6	1	0	145	153	6	40	32	12.2	3.48	114	.271	.322	6	.128	-3	7	8	2	0.7
1928	Bro-N	3	8	.273	28	12	4	1	3	99¹	104	1	35	12	13.0	3.26	122	.271	.340	3	.111	-2	8	8	3	0.7
1929	StL-N	1	2	.333	3	2	0	0	0	9	17	1	5	3	22.0	12.00	39	.415	.478	0	.000	0	-7	-7	-0	-0.5
Total 16		169	157	.518	453	368	162	34	16	2782²	2676	71	851	1014	11.6	2.98	107	.259	.319	115	.127	-41	80	64	42	7.9

■ WALT DOANE
Doane, Walter Rudolph b: 3/12/1887, Bellevue, Idaho d: 10/19/35, W.Brandywine, Pa. BL/TR, 6', 165 lbs. Deb: 9/20/09 ♦

YEAR	TM/L	W	L	PCT	G	GS	CG	SH	SV	IP	H	HR	BB	SO	RAT	ERA	ERA+	OAV	OOB	BH	AVG	PB	PR	/A	PD	TPI
1909	Cle-A	0	1	.000	1	1	0	0	0	5	10	0	1	2	19.8	5.40	47	.400	.423	1	.111	-0	-2	-2	0	-0.1
1910	Cle-A	0	0	—	6	0	0	0	0	17²	31	1	8	7	20.4	5.60	46	.413	.476	2	.286	1	-6	-6	-1	-0.5
Total 2		0	1	.000	7	1	0	0	0	22²	41	1	9	9	20.3	5.56	46	.410	.464	3	.188	1	-8	-8	-1	-0.6

■ JOHN DOBB
Dobb, John Kenneth "Lefty" b: 11/15/01, Muskegon, Mich. TL, 6'2", 180 lbs. Deb: 8/13/24

YEAR	TM/L	W	L	PCT	G	GS	CG	SH	SV	IP	H	HR	BB	SO	RAT	ERA	ERA+	OAV	OOB	BH	AVG	PB	PR	/A	PD	TPI
1924	Chi-A	0	0	—	2	0	0	0	0	2	4	0	1	2	22.5	9.00	46	.400	.455	0	—	0	-1	-1	0	0.0

■ RAY DOBENS
Dobens, Raymond Joseph "Lefty" b: 7/28/06, Nashua, N.H. d: 4/21/80, Stuart, Fla. BL/TL, 5'8", 175 lbs. Deb: 7/07/29

YEAR	TM/L	W	L	PCT	G	GS	CG	SH	SV	IP	H	HR	BB	SO	RAT	ERA	ERA+	OAV	OOB	BH	AVG	PB	PR	/A	PD	TPI
1929	Bos-A	0	0	—	11	2	0	0	0	28¹	32	0	9	4	13.3	3.81	112	.302	.362	3	.375	1	1	1	-1	0.1

■ JESS DOBERNIC
Dobernic, Andrew Joseph b: 11/20/17, Mt.Olive, Ill. BR/TR, 5'1", 170 lbs. Deb: 7/02/39

YEAR	TM/L	W	L	PCT	G	GS	CG	SH	SV	IP	H	HR	BB	SO	RAT	ERA	ERA+	OAV	OOB	BH	AVG	PB	PR	/A	PD	TPI
1939	Chi-A	0	1	.000	4	0	0	0	0	3¹	3	0	6	1	27.0	13.50	35	.231	.500	0	.000	-0	-3	-3	0	-0.2
1948	Chi-N	7	2	.778	54	0	0	0	1	85²	67	8	40	48	11.3	3.15	124	.213	.303	2	.200	-0	8	7	-2	0.5
1949	Chi-N	0	0	—	4	0	0	0	0	4	9	2	4	0	29.3	20.25	20	.450	.542	0	—	0	-7	-7	-0	-0.6
	Cin-N	0	0	—	14	0	0	0	0	19¹	28	7	16	6	20.5	9.78	43	.329	.436	0	.000	0	-12	-12	-1	-1.0
	Yr	0	0	—	18	0	0	0	0	23¹	37	9	20	6	22.0	11.57	36	.352	.456	1	.500	0	-20	-19	-0	-1.6
Total 3		7	3	.700	76	0	0	0	1	112¹	107	17	66	55	14.0	5.21	76	.247	.349	2	.154	-0	-15	-15	-2	-1.3

■ CHUCK DOBSON
Dobson, Charles Thomas b: 1/10/44, Kansas City, Mo. BR/TR, 6'4", 200 lbs. Deb: 4/19/66

YEAR	TM/L	W	L	PCT	G	GS	CG	SH	SV	IP	H	HR	BB	SO	RAT	ERA	ERA+	OAV	OOB	BH	AVG	PB	PR	/A	PD	TPI
1966	KC-A	4	6	.400	14	14	1	0	0	83²	71	7	50	61	13.2	4.09	83	.234	.346	3	.115	-1	-6	-6	1	-0.6
1967	KC-A	10	10	.500	32	29	4	1	0	197²	172	17	75	110	11.4	3.69	86	.233	.306	13	.181	0	-10	-11	0	-1.0
1968	Oak-A	12	14	.462	35	34	11	3	0	225¹	197	20	80	168	11.2	3.00	94	.234	.303	15	.200	2	-0	-4	1	-0.1
1969	Oak-A	15	13	.536	35	35	11	1	0	235¹	244	16	80	137	12.4	3.86	89	.270	.330	8	.101	-3	-6	-11	-2	-1.6
1970	Oak-A	16	15	.516	41	40	13	**5**	0	267	230	32	92	149	11.0	3.74	95	.229	.297	11	.118	-0	-1	-6	-2	-1.1
1971	Oak-A	15	5	.750	30	30	7	1	0	189	185	24	71	100	12.2	3.81	88	.259	.327	13	.197	3	-7	-10	1	-0.6
1973	Oak-A	0	1	.000	1	1	0	0	0	2¹	6	1	2	3	30.9	7.71	46	.429	.500	0	—	0	-1	-1	0	0.0
1974	Cal-A	2	3	.400	5	5	2	0	0	30	39	3	13	16	15.6	5.70	60	.315	.380	0	—	0	-7	-8	-0	-0.6
1975	Cal-A	0	2	.000	5	2	0	0	0	28	30	5	13	14	14.5	6.75	53	.275	.363	0	—	0	-9	-10	-1	-0.9
Total 9		74	69	.517	202	190	49	11	0	1258¹	1174	125	476	758	11.9	3.78	87	.247	.318	63	.153	-2	-48	-68	-0	-6.5

■ JOE DOBSON
Dobson, Joseph Gordon "Burrhead" b: 1/20/17, Durant, Okla. BR/TR, 6'2", 197 lbs. Deb: 4/26/39

YEAR	TM/L	W	L	PCT	G	GS	CG	SH	SV	IP	H	HR	BB	SO	RAT	ERA	ERA+	OAV	OOB	BH	AVG	PB	PR	/A	PD	TPI
1939	Cle-A	2	3	.400	35	3	0	0	0	78	87	3	51	27	16.0	5.88	75	.290	.395	1	.056	-2	-11	-13	1	-1.2
1940	Cle-A	3	7	.300	40	7	2	1	3	100	101	8	48	57	13.4	4.95	85	.268	.351	3	.125	-1	-6	-8	-0	-0.8
1941	Bos-A	12	5	.706	27	18	7	1	0	134¹	136	8	67	69	13.7	4.49	93	.262	.349	7	.149	-0	-5	-5	-2	-0.5
1942	Bos-A	11	9	.550	30	23	10	3	0	182²	155	9	68	72	11.1	3.30	113	.231	.303	10	.145	-1	7	9	2	1.0
1943	Bos-A	7	11	.389	25	20	9	3	0	164¹	144	4	57	63	11.0	3.12	106	.239	.305	5	.096	-3	3	4	-2	-0.1
1946	•Bos-A	13	7	.650	32	24	9	1	0	166²	148	11	68	91	11.7	3.24	113	.234	.309	5	.100	-2	5	8	2	0.8
1947	Bos-A	18	8	.692	33	31	15	1	1	228²	203	15	73	110	10.9	2.95	132	.238	**.299**	16	.208	1	19	24	-2	2.5
1948	Bos-A	16	10	.615	38	32	16	5	2	245¹	237	14	92	116	12.1	3.56	123	.253	.320	17	.202	1	20	23	-2	2.3
1949	Bos-A	14	12	.538	33	27	12	2	2	212²	219	12	97	87	13.5	3.85	113	.269	.348	10	.147	-1	8	12	-1	1.0
1950	Bos-A	15	10	.600	39	27	12	1	4	206²	217	15	81	81	13.0	4.18	117	.275	.343	15	.214	1	9	16	2	1.9
1951	Chi-A	7	6	.538	28	21	6	0	3	146²	136	17	51	67	11.5	3.62	111	.248	.312	3	.065	-6	8	7	0	0.1
1952	Chi-A	14	10	.583	29	25	11	3	1	200²	164	11	60	101	10.0	2.51	145	.222	.280	12	.190	0	26	25	-2	2.6
1953	Chi-A	5	5	.500	23	15	3	1	1	100²	96	10	37	50	11.9	3.67	110	.249	.314	2	.069	-2	4	4	-1	0.1
1954	Bos-A	0	0	—	2	0	0	0	0	2²	5	0	1	1	20.3	6.75	61	.385	.429	0	—	0	-1	-1	0	0.0
Total 14		137	103	.571	414	273	112	22	18	2170	2048	137	851	992	12.1	3.62	112	.250	.322	106	.152	-15	86	105	-5	9.7

■ PAT DOBSON
Dobson, Patrick Edward b: 2/12/42, Depew, N.Y. BR/TR, 6'3", 190 lbs. Deb: 5/31/67 C

YEAR	TM/L	W	L	PCT	G	GS	CG	SH	SV	IP	H	HR	BB	SO	RAT	ERA	ERA+	OAV	OOB	BH	AVG	PB	PR	/A	PD	TPI
1967	Det-A	1	2	.333	28	1	0	0	0	49¹	38	6	27	34	12.2	2.92	112	.216	.327	0	.000	-1	2	2	-1	0.1
1968	•Det-A	5	8	.385	47	10	2	1	7	125	89	13	48	93	10.0	2.66	113	.200	.298	4	.143	0	4	5	1	0.7
1969	Det-A	5	10	.333	49	9	1	0	9	105	100	10	39	64	12.0	3.60	104	.253	.322	2	.091	-1	0	2	0	0.4
1970	SD-N	14	15	.483	40	34	8	1	1	251	257	28	78	185	12.2	3.76	106	.265	.322	10	.141	-0	8	6	-1	0.4
1971	•Bal-A	20	8	.714	38	37	18	4	1	282¹	248	24	63	187	10.0	2.90	116	.235	.279	10	.110	-3	18	14	-1	1.0
1972	Bal-A	16	18	.471	38	36	13	3	0	268¹	220	13	66	161	9.8	2.65	116	.224	.298	12	.141	-2	12	13	-2	1.1
1973	Atl-N	3	7	.300	12	10	1	1	0	57²	73	1	19	23	14.5	4.99	79	.315	.369	1	.067	-1	-9	-7	-0	-0.7
	NY-A	9	8	.529	22	21	6	1	0	142¹	150	22	34	70	11.8	4.17	88	.266	.311	0	—	0	-6	-8	0	-0.7
1974	NY-A	19	15	.559	39	39	12	2	0	281	282	23	75	157	11.6	3.07	113	.262	.312	0	—	0	17	13	-1	1.3
1975	NY-A	11	14	.440	33	30	7	1	0	207²	205	21	83	129	12.5	4.07	89	.261	.333	0	—	0	-7	-10	-1	-1.0
1976	Cle-A	16	12	.571	35	35	6	0	0	217¹	226	13	65	117	12.1	3.48	100	.272	.327	0	—	0	1	0	-0	0.0
1977	Cle-A	3	12	.200	33	17	0	0	1	133¹	155	23	65	81	14.9	6.14	64	.299	.378	0	—	0	-31	-33	-0	-3.0
Total 11		122	129	.486	414	279	74	14	19	2120¹	2043	197	665	1301	11.9	3.54	100	.255	.314	39	.123	-8	10	-3	-3	-0.7

■ GEORGE DOCKINS
Dockins, George Woodrow "Lefty" b: 5/5/17, Clyde, Kan. BL/TL, 6', 175 lbs. Deb: 5/05/45

YEAR	TM/L	W	L	PCT	G	GS	CG	SH	SV	IP	H	HR	BB	SO	RAT	ERA	ERA+	OAV	OOB	BH	AVG	PB	PR	/A	PD	TPI
1945	StL-N	8	6	.571	31	12	5	2	0	126¹	132	4	38	33	12.1	3.21	117	.269	.321	6	.176	1	8	8	-0	0.8
1947	Bro-N	0	0	—	4	0	0	0	0	5¹	10	2	2	1	20.3	11.81	35	.400	.444	0	.000	-0	-5	-5	0	-0.3
Total 2		8	6	.571	35	12	5	2	0	131²	142	6	40	34	12.4	3.55	106	.275	.327	6	.171	1	4	3	-0	0.5

YEAR TM/L	W	L	PCT	G	GS	CG	SH	SV	IP	H	HR	BB	SO	RAT	ERA	ERA+	OAV	OOB	BH	AVG	PB	PR	/A	PD	TPI
■ **SAM DODGE**			Dodge, Samuel Edward b: 12/9/1889, Neath, Pa. d: 4/5/66, Utica, N.Y. BR/TR, 6'1", 170 lbs. Deb: 9/24/21																						
1921 Bos-A	0	0	—	1	0	0	0	0	1	1	0	1	0	18.0	9.00	47	.500	.667	0	—	0	-1	-1	0	0.0
1922 Bos-A	0	0	—	3	0	0	0	0	6	11	0	3	3	21.0	4.50	91	.379	.438	0	.000	-0	-0	-0	0	0.0
Total 2	0	0	—	4	0	0	0	0	7	12	0	4	3	20.6	5.14	80	.387	.457	0	.000	-0	-1	-1	0	0.0
■ **FRED DOE**			Doe, Alfred George "Count" b: 4/18/1864, Rockport, Mass. d: 10/4/38, Quincy, Mass. BR/TR, 5'10", 165 lbs. Deb: 8/23/1890																						
1890 Buf-P	0	1	.000	1	1	1	0	0	6	10	0	7	2	25.5	12.00	34	.356	.485	0	.000	-0	-5	-5	0	-0.3
Pit-P	0	0	—	1	0	0	0	0	4	4	0	2	2	13.5	4.50	87	.249	.332	1	.500	-0	-0	-0	-0	0.0
Yr	0	1	.000	2	1	1	0	0	10	14	0	9	4	20.7	9.00	45	.317	.433	1	.200	-0	-5	-6	0	-0.3
■ **ED DOHENY**			Doheny, Edward R. b: 11/24/1874, Northfield, Vt. d: 12/29/16, Medfield, Mass. BL/TL, 5'10.5", 165 lbs. Deb: 9/16/1895																						
1895 NY-N	0	3	.000	3	3	3	0	0	25²	37	2	19	9	19.6	6.66	70	.332	.429	1	.100	-0	-5	-6	-0	-0.4
1896 NY-N	6	7	.462	17	15	9	0	0	108¹	112	3	59	39	14.2	4.49	94	.265	.355	6	.150	-2	-1	-3	-1	-0.4
1897 NY-N	4	4	.500	10	10	10	0	0	85	69	0	45	37	12.1	2.12	196	.220	.318	7	.200	-1	21	19	3	1.9
1898 NY-N	7	19	.269	28	27	23	0	0	213	238	1	101	96	14.3	3.68	95	.280	.357	14	.163	-1	-2	-5	3	-0.2
1899 NY-N	14	17	.452	35	33	30	1	0	265¹	282	2	156	115	14.9	4.51	83	.272	.367	27	.241	0	-19	-22	5	-1.5
1900 NY-N	4	14	.222	20	18	12	0	0	133²	148	2	96	44	16.4	5.45	66	.280	.391	12	.222	-0	-26	-27	1	-2.2
1901 NY-N	2	5	.286	10	6	6	0	0	74	88	1	17	36	13.5	4.50	73	.293	.344	10	.345	3	-10	-10	0	-0.5
Pit-N	6	2	.750	11	10	6	1	0	76²	68	1	22	28	11.2	2.00	164	.236	.302	3	.115	1	11	11	-1	1.0
Yr	8	7	.533	21	16	12	1	0	150²	156	2	39	64	11.9	3.23	102	.263	.314	9	.164	4	2	1	-1	0.5
1902 Pit-N	16	4	.800	22	21	19	2	0	188¹	161	0	61	88	11.2	2.53	108	.231	.305	12	.156	-2	5	4	-1	0.2
1903 Pit-N	16	8	.667	27	25	22	2	2	222²	209	1	89	75	12.8	3.19	101	.252	.338	19	.209	-0	2	1	5	0.5
Total 9	75	83	.475	183	168	140	6	2	1392²	1412	13	665	567	13.7	3.75	94	.263	.348	111	.198	-3	-24	-37	14	-1.6
■ **JOHN DOLAN**			Dolan, John b: 9/12/1867, Newport, Ky. d: 5/8/48, Springfield, Ohio TR , 5'10", 170 lbs. Deb: 9/05/1890																						
1890 Cin-N	1	1	.500	2	2	2	0	0	18	17	3	10	9	13.5	4.50	79	.242	.337	1	.125	-1	-2	-2	-0	-0.1
1891 Col-a	12	11	.522	27	24	19	0	0	203¹	216	8	84	68	13.3	4.16	83	.263	.332	7	.090	-4	-10	-16	-2	-1.7
1893 StL-N	0	1	.000	3	1	1	0	1	17¹	26	1	7	1	17.1	4.15	114	.336	.391	1	.143	0	1	1	-0	0.1
1895 Chi-N	0	1	.000	2	2	1	0	0	11	16	0	6	1	18.0	6.55	78	.334	.408	0	.000	-0	-2	-2	0	0.0
Total 4	13	14	.481	34	29	23	0	1	249²	275	12	107	79	13.8	4.29	84	.271	.340	9	.094	-5	-13	-19	-1	-1.7
■ **COZY DOLAN**			Dolan, Patrick Henry b: 12/3/1872, Cambridge, Mass. d: 3/29/07, Louisville, Ky. BL/TL, 5'10", 160 lbs. Deb: 8/09/1892 ♦																						
1892 Was-N	2	2	.500	5	4	3	0	0	37	39	0	15	8	13.1	4.38	74	.260	.327	3	.231	0	-4	-5	-0	-0.3
1895 Bos-N	11	7	.611	25	21	18	3	0	198¹	215	11	67	47	12.8	4.27	120	.272	.329	20	.241	-1	11	18	4	1.9
1896 Bos-N	1	4	.200	6	5	3	0	0	41	55	1	27	14	18.0	4.83	94	.318	.411	2	.143	-1	-2	-1	-0	-0.2
1905 Bos-N	0	1	.000	2	0	0	0	0	4	7	2	1	1	18.0	9.00	34	.368	.400	119	.275	1	-3	-3	-0	-0.2
1906 Bos-N	0	1	.000	2	0	0	0	0	12	12	1	6	7	13.5	4.50	60	.300	.391	136	.248	0	-2	-2	-1	-0.1
Total 5	14	15	.483	40	30	24	3	1	292¹	328	15	116	77	13.7	4.43	105	.280	.280	858	.269	-1	-0	7	3	1.1
■ **TOM DOLAN**			Dolan, Thomas J. b: 1/10/1859, New York, N.Y. d: 1/16/13, St.Louis, Mo. BR/TR, Deb: 9/30/1879 ♦																						
1883 StL-a	0	0	—	1	0	0	0	0	4	4	0	0	4	9.0	4.50	78	.244	.244	63	.214	-0	-1	-0	0	0.0
■ **ART DOLL**			Doll, Arthur James "Moose" b: 5/7/13, Chicago, Ill. d: 4/28/78, Calumet City, Ill. BR/TR, 6'1", 190 lbs. Deb: 9/21/35 ♦																						
1936 Bos-N	0	1	.000	1	1	0	0	0	8	11	1	2	2	15.8	3.38	114	.355	.412	0	.000	-0	1	0	0	0.0
1938 Bos-N	0	0	—	3	0	0	0	0	4	4	0	3	1	15.8	2.25	153	.286	.412	1	1.000	0	1	1	0	0.1
Total 2	0	1	.000	4	1	0	0	0	12	15	1	5	3	15.8	3.00	123	.333	.412	2	.154	0	1	1	0	0.1
■ **RED DONAHUE**			Donahue, Francis Rostell b: 1/23/1873, Waterbury, Conn. d: 8/25/13, Philadelphia, Pa. BR/TR, Deb: 5/06/1893																						
1893 NY-N	0	0	—	2	0	0	0	1	5	8	1	3	1	19.8	9.00	52	.351	.426	0	.000	-0	-2	-2	0	-0.1
1895 StL-N	0	1	.000	1	1	1	0	0	8	9	2	3	2	13.5	6.75	72	.280	.341	0	.000	-1	-2	-2	0	-0.1
1896 StL-N	7	24	.226	32	32	28	0	0	267	376	6	98	70	16.0	5.80	75	.329	.382	17	.159	-8	-43	-43	-1	-4.0
1897 StL-N	10	35	.222	**46**	42	**38**	1	1	348	484	16	106	64	15.3	6.13	72	.326	.371	33	.213	-3	-70	-67	5	-5.2
1898 Phi-N	16	17	.485	35	35	33	1	0	284¹	327	7	80	57	12.9	3.55	97	.286	.333	16	.143	-6	2	-3	4	-0.5
1899 Phi-N	21	8	.724	35	31	27	4	0	279	292	6	63	51	11.5	3.39	109	.269	.309	20	.180	-5	15	9	3	0.6
1900 Phi-N	15	10	.600	32	24	21	2	0	240	299	6	50	41	13.1	3.60	100	.304	.338	20	.222	-1	3	-0	0	0.0
1901 Phi-N	21	13	.618	35	34	34	1	1	304¹	307	2	60	89	11.1	2.60	131	.260	.301	11	.094	-9	24	27	-1	1.7
1902 StL-A	22	11	.667	35	34	33	2	0	316¹	322	7	65	63	11.0	2.76	128	.264	.301	11	.093	-9	29	27	8	2.5
1903 StL-A	8	7	.533	16	15	14	0	0	131	145	0	22	51	11.5	2.75	124	.280	.309	8	.157	-2	3	2	1	0.2
Cle-A	7	9	.438	16	15	14	4	0	136²	142	3	12	45	10.1	2.44	117	.267	.283	8	.151	-1	8	6	2	0.7
Yr	15	16	.484	32	30	28	4	0	267²	287	3	34	96	10.8	2.59	111	.273	.296	16	.010	-3	11	9	2	0.8
1904 Cle-A	19	14	.576	35	32	30	6	0	277	281	2	49	127	10.7	2.40	106	.264	.296	17	.168	-1	6	4	2	0.5
1905 Cle-A	6	12	.333	20	18	14	1	0	137²	132	2	25	45	10.3	3.40	78	.253	.288	4	.075	-5	-11	-12	2	-1.5
1906 Det-A	13	14	.481	28	28	26	3	0	241	260	1	54	82	11.7	2.73	101	.278	.318	10	.123	-4	-1	1	0	-0.2
Total 13	165	175	.485	368	341	313	25	3	2975¹	3384	61	690	788	12.3	3.61	96	.285	.325	175	.152	-55	-40	-51	22	-5.5
■ **DEACON DONAHUE**			Donahue, John Stephen Michael b: 6/23/20, Chicago, Ill. BR/TR, 6', 180 lbs. Deb: 9/16/43																						
1943 Phi-N	0	0	—	2	0	0	0	0	4	4	0	1	1	13.5	4.50	75	.235	.316	0	—	0	-0	-1	0	0.0
1944 Phi-N	0	2	.000	6	0	0	0	0	9¹	18	0	2	2	19.3	7.71	47	.429	.455	0	.000	-0	-4	-4	0	-0.3
Total 2	0	2	.000	8	0	0	0	0	13¹	22	0	3	3	17.6	6.75	52	.373	.413	0	.000	-0	-5	-5	0	-0.3
■ **ATLEY DONALD**			Donald, Richard Atley "Swampy" b: 8/19/10, Morton, Miss. BL/TR, 6'1", 186 lbs. Deb: 4/21/38																						
1938 NY-A	0	1	.000	2	2	0	0	0	12	7	0	14	6	16.5	5.25	86	.175	.400	1	.167	-0	-1	-1	0	0.0
1939 NY-A	13	3	.813	24	20	11	2	1	153	144	12	60	55	12.0	3.71	118	.247	.317	15	.250	3	16	11	-1	1.1
1940 NY-A	8	3	.727	24	11	6	1	0	118²	113	11	59	60	13.2	3.03	133	.249	.339	6	.146	-2	18	13	-3	0.8
1941 *NY-A	9	5	.643	22	20	10	0	0	159	141	11	69	71	12.1	3.57	110	.237	.320	5	.081	-4	10	6	-0	0.2
1942 *NY-A	11	3	.786	20	19	10	1	0	147²	132	6	45	53	10.8	3.11	111	.237	.295	9	.148	-1	9	5	-2	0.2
1943 NY-A	6	4	.600	22	15	2	0	0	119¹	134	10	38	57	13.0	4.60	70	.276	.329	10	.128	-2	-17	-18	-2	-2.2
1944 NY-A	13	10	.565	30	19	9	0	0	159	173	6	59	48	13.2	3.34	104	.280	.345	10	.182	-0	2	3	-1	0.1
1945 NY-A	5	4	.556	9	9	6	2	0	63²	62	3	25	19	12.3	2.97	117	.248	.316	5	.208	0	3	4	-2	0.2
Total 8	65	33	.663	153	115	54	6	1	932¹	906	66	369	369	12.4	3.52	107	.253	.324	57	.160	-7	39	24	-9	0.4
■ **ED DONALDS**			Donalds, Edward Alexander "Erston" b: 6/22/1885, Bidwell, Ohio d: 7/3/50, Columbus, Ohio BR/TR, 5'11", 180 lbs. Deb: 9/01/12																						
1912 Cin-N	1	0	1.000	1	0	0	0	0	4	7	0	0	1	15.8	4.50	75	.412	.412	0	.000	-0	-0	-1	0	0.0
■ **MIKE DONLIN**			Donlin, Michael Joseph "Turkey Mike" b: 5/30/1878, Peoria, Ill. d: 9/24/33, Hollywood, Cal. BL/TL, 5'9", 170 lbs. Deb: 7/19/1899 ♦																						
1899 StL-N	0	1	.000	3	1	0	0	0	15¹	15	1	14	6	17.0	7.63	52	.256	.399	86	.323	1	-6	-6	1	-0.4
1902 Cin-N	0	0	—	1	0	0	0	0	1	1	0	0	0	9.00	0.00	—	.260	.260	41	.287	0	0	0	0	0.0
Total 2	0	1	.000	4	1	0	0	0	16¹	16	1	14	6	16.5	7.16	55	.256	.392	1282	.333	1	-6	-6	1	-0.4
■ **ED DONNELLY**			Donnelly, Edward "Big Ed" or "Ned" (b: Edward O'Donnell) b: 7/29/1880, Hampton, N.Y. d: 11/28/57, Rutland, Vt. BR/TR, 6'1", 205 lbs. Deb: 9/19/11																						
1911 Bos-N	3	2	.600	5	4	4	1	0	36²	33	0	9	16	10.8	2.45	156	.236	.291	1	.071	-2	4	6	0	0.4
1912 Bos-N	5	10	.333	37	18	10	0	0	184¹	225	10	72	67	14.7	4.35	82	.296	.360	19	.275	3	-19	-16	1	-1.0
Total 2	8	12	.400	42	22	14	1	0	221	258	10	81	83	14.1	4.03	90	.286	.350	20	.241	1	-15	-10	1	-0.6

YEAR	TM/L	W	L	PCT	G	GS	CG	SH	SV	IP	H	HR	BB	SO	RAT	ERA	ERA+	OAV	OOB	BH	AVG	PB	PR	/A	PD	TPI

■ ED DONNELLY   Donnelly, Edward Vincent b: 12/10/34, Allen, Mich. BR/TR, 6', 175 lbs. Deb: 8/01/59

YEAR	TM/L	W	L	PCT	G	GS	CG	SH	SV	IP	H	HR	BB	SO	RAT	ERA	ERA+	OAV	OOB	BH	AVG	PB	PR	/A	PD	TPI
1959	Chi-N	1	1	.500	9	0	0	0	0	14¹	18	1	9	6	17.0	3.14	126	.305	.397	0	—	0	1	1	0	0.1

■ FRANK DONNELLY   Donnelly, Franklin Marion b: 10/7/1869, Tamaroa, Ill. d: 2/3/53, Canton, Ill. 180 lbs. Deb: 8/15/1893

YEAR	TM/L	W	L	PCT	G	GS	CG	SH	SV	IP	H	HR	BB	SO	RAT	ERA	ERA+	OAV	OOB	BH	AVG	PB	PR	/A	PD	TPI
1893	Chi-N	3	1	.750	7	5	3	0	2	42	51	1	17	6	14.6	5.36	86	.291	.354	8	.444	4	-3	-3	0	0.0

■ BLIX DONNELLY   Donnelly, Sylvester Urban b: 1/21/14, Olivia, Minn. d: 6/20/76, Olivia, Minn. BR/TR, 5'10", 166 lbs. Deb: 5/06/44

YEAR	TM/L	W	L	PCT	G	GS	CG	SH	SV	IP	H	HR	BB	SO	RAT	ERA	ERA+	OAV	OOB	BH	AVG	PB	PR	/A	PD	TPI
1944	*StL-N	2	1	.667	27	4	2	1	2	76¹	61	2	34	45	11.4	2.12	166	.218	.307	1	.063	-1	13	12	0	1.2
1945	StL-N	8	10	.444	31	23	9	4	2	166¹	157	10	87	76	13.5	3.52	106	.250	.346	7	.130	-2	5	4	-4	-0.1
1946	StL-N	1	2	.333	13	0	0	0	0	13²	17	1	10	11	18.4	3.95	87	.347	.467	0	—	0	-1	-1	-0	0.0
	Phi-N	3	4	.429	12	8	2	0	1	76¹	64	7	24	38	10.6	2.95	116	.220	.284	7	.280	2	4	4	-1	0.5
	Yr	4	6	.400	25	8	2	0	1	90	81	8	34	49	11.7	3.10	111	.238	.310	3	.120	2	3	3	-1	0.5
1947	Phi-N	4	6	.400	38	10	5	1	5	120²	113	6	46	31	12.1	2.98	134	.265	.340	2	.063	-2	14	14	0	1.2
1948	Phi-N	5	7	.417	26	19	8	1	2	131²	125	13	49	46	11.9	3.69	107	.261	.335	10	.222	2	4	4	-2	0.3
1949	Phi-N	2	1	.667	23	10	1	0	0	78¹	84	7	40	36	14.4	5.06	78	.294	.382	4	.174	-1	-9	-10	-2	-1.1
1950	Phi-N	2	4	.333	14	1	0	0	0	21	30	5	10	10	17.1	4.29	94	.330	.396	1	.200	-0	-0	-1	0	0.0
1951	Bos-N	0	1	.000	6	0	0	0	0	7¹	8	1	6	3	18.4	7.36	50	.286	.429	0	.000	-0	-3	-3	0	-0.2
Total	8	27	36	.429	190	75	27	7	12	691²	659	52	306	296	12.8	3.49	109	.257	.340	32	.159	-1	27	24	-8	1.8

■ JIM DONOHUE   Donohue, James Thomas b: 10/31/38, St.Louis, Mo. BR/TR, 6'4", 190 lbs. Deb: 4/11/61

YEAR	TM/L	W	L	PCT	G	GS	CG	SH	SV	IP	H	HR	BB	SO	RAT	ERA	ERA+	OAV	OOB	BH	AVG	PB	PR	/A	PD	TPI
1961	Det-A	1	1	.500	14	0	0	0	1	20¹	23	2	15	20	16.8	3.54	116	.287	.400	0	.000	-0	1	1	-0	0.1
	LA-A	4	6	.400	38	7	0	0	5	100¹	93	16	50	79	12.8	4.31	105	.246	.334	4	.148	-1	-3	2	-1	0.1
	Yr	5	7	.417	52	7	0	0	6	120²	116	18	65	99	13.5	4.18	106	.253	.346	0	.000	-1	-2	4	-1	0.2
1962	LA-A	1	0	1.000	12	1	0	0	0	24¹	24	4	11	14	13.7	3.70	104	.258	.349	1	.250	0	1	0	-1	0.0
	Min-A	0	1	.000	6	1	0	0	1	10¹	12	2	6	3	15.7	6.97	59	.324	.419	0	.000	-0	-3	-3	-0	-0.2
	Yr	1	1	.500	18	2	0	0	1	34²	36	6	17	17	13.8	4.67	84	.273	.356	1	.167	0	-3	-3	-0	-0.2
Total	2	6	8	.429	70	9	0	0	7	155¹	152	24	82	116	13.7	4.29	101	.259	.351	5	.147	-1	-5	1	-1	0.0

■ PETE DONOHUE   Donohue, Peter Joseph b: 11/5/1900, Athens, Tex. d: 2/23/88, Ft.Worth, Tex. BR/TR, 6'2", 185 lbs. Deb: 7/01/21

YEAR	TM/L	W	L	PCT	G	GS	CG	SH	SV	IP	H	HR	BB	SO	RAT	ERA	ERA+	OAV	OOB	BH	AVG	PB	PR	/A	PD	TPI
1921	Cin-N	7	6	.538	21	11	7	0	1	118¹	117	5	26	44	10.9	3.35	107	.263	.304	8	.211	1	6	3	2	0.5
1922	Cin-N	18	9	.667	33	30	18	2	1	242	257	5	43	66	11.3	3.12	128	.276	.312	16	.182	-3	26	23	1	2.1
1923	Cin-N	21	15	.583	42	36	19	2	3	274¹	304	3	68	84	12.5	3.38	114	.278	.326	24	.250	3	19	15	1	1.7
1924	Cin-N	16	9	.640	35	32	16	3	0	222¹	248	9	36	72	11.9	3.60	105	.285	.321	14	.192	-0	7	4	-1	0.2
1925	Cin-N	21	14	.600	42	38	27	3	2	301	310	3	49	78	10.8	3.08	133	.268	.299	32	.294	7	40	34	-2	3.8
1926	Cin-N	20	14	.588	47	38	17	5	2	285²	298	6	39	73	10.9	3.37	109	.268	.298	33	.311	9	14	10	-3	1.6
1927	Cin-N	6	16	.273	33	24	12	1	1	190²	253	3	32	48	13.5	4.11	92	.328	.356	16	.250	1	-4	-7	1	-0.4
1928	Cin-N	7	11	.389	23	18	8	0	0	150	180	10	32	37	12.9	4.74	83	.309	.348	7	.146	-0	-13	-13	1	-1.1
1929	Cin-N	10	13	.435	32	24	7	0	0	177²	243	12	51	30	15.1	5.42	84	.331	.377	20	.333	4	-14	-17	1	-1.0
1930	Cin-N	1	3	.250	8	5	2	0	1	34¹	53	0	13	4	17.6	6.29	77	.363	.419	1	.100	-1	-5	-6	1	-0.4
	NY-N	7	6	.538	18	11	4	0	1	86²	135	6	18	26	16.1	6.13	77	.360	.392	9	.273	1	-11	-13	-1	-1.1
	Yr	8	9	.471	26	16	6	0	2	121	188	6	31	30	16.4	6.17	77	.360	.398	0	.000	0	-16	-19	-0	-1.5
1931	NY-N	0	1	.000	4	1	0	0	0	11¹	14	1	4	4	14.3	5.56	67	.311	.367	0	.000	-0	-2	-2	-0	-0.2
	Cle-A	0	0	—	2	0	0	0	0	5¹	9	1	5	4	23.6	8.44	55	.429	.538	0	.000	-0	-2	-2	-0	-0.1
1932	Bos-A	0	1	.000	4	2	0	0	0	12²	18	2	6	1	17.1	7.82	57	.340	.407	0	.000	-0	-5	-5	1	-0.3
Total	12	134	118	.532	344	270	137	16	12	2112¹	2439	68	422	571	12.4	3.87	103	.293	.330	180	.246	21	56	25	0	5.3

■ LINO DONOSO   Donoso, Lino (Galeta) b: 9/23/22, Havana, Cuba BL/TL, 5'11", 160 lbs. Deb: 6/18/55

YEAR	TM/L	W	L	PCT	G	GS	CG	SH	SV	IP	H	HR	BB	SO	RAT	ERA	ERA+	OAV	OOB	BH	AVG	PB	PR	/A	PD	TPI
1955	Pit-N	4	6	.400	25	9	3	0	1	95	106	16	35	38	13.5	5.31	78	.287	.351	5	.185	-1	-13	-13	0	-1.2
1956	Pit-N	0	0	—	3	0	0	0	0	1²	2	0	1	1	16.2	0.00	—	.250	.333	0	—	0	1	1	0	0.1
Total	2	4	6	.400	28	9	3	0	1	96²	108	16	36	39	13.5	5.21	79	.286	.350	5	.185	-1	-13	-12	1	-1.1

■ DICK DONOVAN   Donovan, Richard Edward b: 12/7/27, Boston, Mass. BL/TR, 6'3", 190 lbs. Deb: 4/24/50

YEAR	TM/L	W	L	PCT	G	GS	CG	SH	SV	IP	H	HR	BB	SO	RAT	ERA	ERA+	OAV	OOB	BH	AVG	PB	PR	/A	PD	TPI
1950	Bos-N	0	2	.000	10	3	0	0	0	29²	28	4	34	9	19.4	8.19	47	.255	.438	1	.167	1	-13	-14	0	-1.1
1951	Bos-N	0	0	—	8	2	0	0	0	13²	17	0	11	4	18.4	5.27	70	.298	.412	1	.333	1	-2	-2	0	0.0
1952	Bos-N	0	2	.000	7	2	0	0	1	13	18	1	12	6	22.2	5.54	65	.346	.485	0	.000	-0	-3	-3	1	-0.2
1954	Det-A	0	0	—	2	0	0	0	0	6	9	1	5	2	21.0	10.50	35	.360	.467	0	.000	-0	-5	-5	0	-0.3
1955	Chi-A	15	9	.625	29	24	11	5	0	187	186	17	48	88	11.4	3.32	119	.261	.311	17	.224	5	13	13	1	1.9
1956	Chi-A	12	10	.545	34	31	14	3	0	234²	212	22	59	120	10.6	3.64	113	.240	.292	20	.222	8	13	12	2	1.4
1957	Chi-A	16	6	.727	28	28	16	2	0	220²	203	17	45	88	10.4	2.77	135	.247	.293	12	.145	2	25	24	1	2.8
1958	Chi-A	15	14	.517	34	34	16	4	0	248	240	23	53	127	10.9	3.01	121	.251	.295	9	.112	-1	21	17	-1	1.5
1959	*Chi-A	9	10	.474	31	29	5	1	0	179²	171	15	58	71	11.7	3.66	103	.247	.310	8	.131	1	4	2	-1	0.1
1960	Chi-A	6	1	.857	33	8	0	0	3	78²	87	13	25	30	12.8	5.38	70	.283	.337	3	.130	-0	-13	-14	1	-1.2
1961	Was-A	10	10	.500	23	22	11	2	0	168²	138	10	35	62	9.4	2.40	167	.224	.269	10	.179	2	30	30	-0	3.4
1962	Cle-A	20	10	.667	34	34	16	5	0	250²	255	23	47	94	10.9	3.59	108	.263	.299	16	.180	6	11	8	0	1.4
1963	Cle-A	11	13	.458	30	30	7	3	0	206	211	27	28	84	10.7	4.24	85	.265	.295	9	.130	-1	-14	-14	-0	-1.4
1964	Cle-A	7	9	.438	30	23	5	0	1	158¹	181	19	29	83	12.1	4.55	79	.290	.324	7	.146	3	-16	-17	2	-1.2
1965	Cle-A	1	3	.250	12	3	0	0	0	22²	32	6	6	12	15.1	5.96	58	.333	.373	0	.000	-1	-6	-6	0	-0.6
Total	15	122	99	.552	345	273	101	25	5	2017¹	1988	198	495	880	11.3	3.67	104	.258	.306	113	.163	24	45	31	5	7.2

■ TOM DONOVAN   Donovan, Thomas Joseph b: 1/1/1873, West Troy, N.Y. d: 3/25/33, Watervliet, N.Y. BR/TR, 6'2", 168 lbs. Deb: 9/10/01 ♦

YEAR	TM/L	W	L	PCT	G	GS	CG	SH	SV	IP	H	HR	BB	SO	RAT	ERA	ERA+	OAV	OOB	BH	AVG	PB	PR	/A	PD	TPI
1901	Cle-A	0	0	—	1	1	0	0	0	7	16	0	3	0	24.4	5.14	69	.442	.485	18	.254	0	-1	-1	0	0.0

■ BILL DONOVAN   Donovan, Willard Earl b: 7/6/16, Maywood, Ill. BR/TL, 6'2", 198 lbs. Deb: 4/19/42

YEAR	TM/L	W	L	PCT	G	GS	CG	SH	SV	IP	H	HR	BB	SO	RAT	ERA	ERA+	OAV	OOB	BH	AVG	PB	PR	/A	PD	TPI
1942	Bos-N	3	6	.333	31	10	2	0	0	89¹	97	2	32	23	13.0	3.43	97	.283	.344	6	.240	1	-1	-1	2	0.3
1943	Bos-N	1	0	1.000	7	0	0	0	0	14²	17	0	9	1	16.0	1.84	185	.304	.400	1	.333	0	3	3	1	0.4
Total	2	4	6	.400	38	10	2	0	0	104	114	2	41	24	13.4	3.20	105	.286	.352	7	.250	1	1	2	4	0.7

■ BILL DONOVAN   Donovan, William Edward "Wild Bill" b: 10/13/1876, Lawrence, Mass. d: 12/9/23, Forsyth, N.Y. BR/TR, 5'11", 190 lbs. Deb: 4/22/1898 M♦

YEAR	TM/L	W	L	PCT	G	GS	CG	SH	SV	IP	H	HR	BB	SO	RAT	ERA	ERA+	OAV	OOB	BH	AVG	PB	PR	/A	PD	TPI
1898	Was-N	1	6	.143	17	7	6	0	0	88	88	0	69	36	16.1	4.30	85	.258	.383	17	.165	-1	-7	-6	-0	-0.5
1899	Bro-N	1	2	.333	5	2	2	0	1	25	35	0	13	11	17.3	4.32	91	.330	.403	3	.231	-1	-1	-1	-0	-0.1
1900	Bro-N	1	2	.333	5	4	2	0	0	31	36	0	18	13	15.7	6.68	58	.290	.380	0	.000	-2	-10	-10	1	-0.8
1901	Bro-N	25	16	.610	45	38	36	2	3	351	324	1	152	226	12.4	2.77	121	.244	.324	23	.170	-1	22	23	-2	2.0
1902	Bro-N	17	15	.531	35	33	30	4	1	297²	250	1	111	170	11.1	2.78	99	.228	.303	28	.174	-0	-0	-1	0	0.0
1903	Det-A	17	16	.515	35	34	34	4	0	307	247	3	95	187	10.0	2.29	127	.220	.281	30	.242	4	23	21	-4	2.3
1904	Det-A	17	16	.515	34	34	30	3	0	293	251	5	94	137	10.6	2.46	104	.232	.294	38	.271	5	5	3	-0	1.0
1905	Det-A	18	15	.545	34	32	27	5	0	280²	236	2	101	135	10.8	2.60	105	.224	.298	25	.192	1	4	2	-2	0.3
1906	Det-A	9	15	.375	25	25	22	0	0	211²	221	4	72	85	12.5	3.15	88	.272	.331	11	.121	-5	-11	-9	-1	-1.5
1907	*Det-A	25	4	.862	32	28	27	3	1	271	222	3	82	123	10.1	2.19	119	.225	.285	29	.266	7	11	13	-6	1.6
1908	*Det-A	18	7	.720	29	28	25	6	0	242²	210	2	53	141	10.0	2.08	117	.231	.288	13	.159	0	9	9	-7	0.2
1909	Det-A	8	7	.533	21	17	13	4	2	140¹	121	0	60	76	12.0	2.31	109	.235	.322	9	.200	1	3	3	-3	0.1
1910	Det-A	17	7	.708	26	23	20	3	0	206²	184	4	61	107	11.0	2.44	108	.243	.305	10	.145	-2	2	4	-7	-0.4
1911	Det-A	10	9	.526	20	19	15	1	0	168¹	160	4	64	89	12.1	3.31	104	.250	.321	12	.200	4	1	3	-5	0.2
1912	Det-A	1	0	1.000	2	1	1	0	0	10	5	0	2	6	7.2	0.90	362	.147	.208	1	.077	-1	3	3	0	0.2
1915	NY-A	0	3	.000	9	1	0	0	0	33²	35	1	10	17	12.3	4.81	61	.278	.336	1	.083	-1	-7	-7	-1	-0.8
1916	NY-A	0	0	—	1	0	0	0	0	1	1	0	1	0	18.0	0.00	—	.250	.400	0	—	0	0	0	0	0.0

YEAR	TM/L	W	L	PCT	G	GS	CG	SH	SV	IP	H	HR	BB	SO	RAT	ERA	ERA+	OAV	OOB	BH	AVG	PB	PR	/A	PD	TPI
1918	Det-A	1	0	1.000	2	1	0	0	0	6	5	0	1	1	9.0	1.50	177	.227	.261	1	.500	0	1	1	-0	0.1
Total	18	186	140	.571	378	327	289	35	8	2964²	2631	30	1059	1552	11.3	2.69	106	.239	.307	251	.193	9	44	54	-37	4.1

■ JOHN DOPSON
Dopson, John Robert b: 7/14/63, Baltimore, Md. BL/TR, 6'4", 205 lbs. Deb: 9/04/85

YEAR	TM/L	W	L	PCT	G	GS	CG	SH	SV	IP	H	HR	BB	SO	RAT	ERA	ERA+	OAV	OOB	BH	AVG	PB	PR	/A	PD	TPI
1985	Mon-N	0	2	.000	4	3	0	0	0	13	25	4	4	4	20.1	11.08	31	.379	.414	0	.000	0	-11	-11	0	-0.9
1988	Mon-N	3	11	.214	26	26	1	0	0	168²	150	15	58	101	11.2	3.04	118	.235	.300	3	.059	-3	8	10	-2	0.6
1989	Bos-A	12	8	.600	29	28	2	0	0	169¹	166	14	69	95	12.6	3.99	103	.257	.330	0	—	0	-2	2	3	0.5
1990	Bos-A	0	0	—	4	4	0	0	0	17²	13	2	9	9	11.2	2.04	200	.200	.297	0	—	0	4	4	1	0.5
Total	4	15	21	.417	63	61	3	0	0	368²	354	35	140	209	12.1	3.71	104	.250	.319	3	.055	-3	-2	5	1	0.7

■ JOHN DORAN
Doran, John F. b: 1869, New Jersey TL, 5'11", 175 lbs. Deb: 4/11/1891

YEAR	TM/L	W	L	PCT	G	GS	CG	SH	SV	IP	H	HR	BB	SO	RAT	ERA	ERA+	OAV	OOB	BH	AVG	PB	PR	/A	PD	TPI
1891	Lou-a	5	10	.333	15	14	12	1	0	126	160	3	75	55	16.8	5.43	67	.299	.385	10	.189	-2	-24	-25	-0	-2.1

■ MIKE DORGAN
Dorgan, Michael Cornelius b: 10/2/1853, Middletown, Conn. d: 4/26/09, Syracuse, N.Y. BR/TR, 5'9", 180 lbs. Deb: 5/08/1877 M♦

YEAR	TM/L	W	L	PCT	G	GS	CG	SH	SV	IP	H	HR	BB	SO	RAT	ERA	ERA+	OAV	OOB	BH	AVG	PB	PR	/A	PD	TPI
1879	Syr-N	0	0	—	2	0	0	0	0	12	13	0	2	8	11.3	2.25	105	.259	.287	72	.267	0	0	0	0	0.0
1880	Pro-N	0	0	—	1	0	0	0	0	8	4	0	0	2	4.5	1.13	196	.141	.141	79	.246	0	1	1	0	0.1
1883	NY-N	0	1	.000	1	1	1	0	0	7	8	0	6	3	18.0	3.86	80	.271	.394	61	.234	0	-1	-1	0	0.0
1884	NY-N	8	6	.571	14	14	12	0	0	113	98	5	51	90	11.9	3.50	85	.221	.301	94	.276	2	-7	-7	0	-0.5
Total	4	8	7	.533	18	15	13	0	0	140	123	5	59	103	11.7	3.28	88	.223	.298	802	.274	3	-6	-6	0	-0.4

■ FRITZ DORISH
Dorish, Harry b: 7/13/21, Swoyersville, Pa. BR/TR, 5'11", 204 lbs. Deb: 4/15/47 C

YEAR	TM/L	W	L	PCT	G	GS	CG	SH	SV	IP	H	HR	BB	SO	RAT	ERA	ERA+	OAV	OOB	BH	AVG	PB	PR	/A	PD	TPI
1947	Bos-A	7	8	.467	41	9	2	0	2	136	149	6	54	50	13.5	4.70	83	.283	.351	5	.143	-1	-15	-12	1	-1.2
1948	Bos-A	0	1	.000	9	0	0	0	0	14¹	18	1	6	5	15.1	5.65	78	.281	.343	1	.250	-0	-2	-2	0	-0.1
1949	Bos-A	0	0	—	5	0	0	0	0	7²	7	1	1	5	9.4	2.35	186	.241	.267	0	—	0	2	2	0	0.2
1950	StL-A	4	9	.308	29	13	4	0	0	109	162	13	36	36	17.1	6.44	77	.337	.394	5	.161	0	-23	-18	-1	-1.5
1951	Chi-A	5	6	.455	32	4	2	1	0	96²	101	6	31	29	12.3	3.54	114	.272	.328	8	.258	0	6	5	0	0.6
1952	Chi-A	8	4	.667	39	1	1	0	11	91	66	4	42	47	10.8	2.47	148	.208	.303	2	.091	-1	**12**	**12**	2	1.3
1953	Chi-A	10	6	.625	55	6	2	0	18	145²	140	9	52	69	12.2	3.40	118	.254	.325	7	.171	-2	10	10	2	1.1
1954	Chi-A	6	4	.600	37	6	2	1	6	109	88	9	29	48	9.7	2.72	137	.228	.284	3	.111	-2	12	12	-1	1.0
1955	Chi-A	2	0	1.000	13	0	0	0	1	17	16	0	9	6	13.2	1.59	249	.258	.352	1	.333	1	4	4	1	0.5
	Bal-A	3	3	.500	35	1	0	0	6	65²	58	4	28	22	11.9	3.15	121	.238	.319	0	—	-1	6	5	1	0.4
	Yr	5	3	.625	48	1	0	0	7	82²	74	4	37	28	12.2	2.83	136	.242	.326	0	.000	-1	10	9	1	0.9
1956	Bal-A	0	0	—	13	0	0	0	2	19²	22	3	4	4	11.4	4.12	95	.297	.325	0	—	0	0	-0	1	0.1
	Bos-A	0	2	.000	15	0	0	0	0	22²	23	1	10	11	13.1	3.57	129	.277	.355	0	—	0	1	3	1	0.4
	Yr	0	2	.000	28	0	0	0	2	42¹	45	4	13	15	12.3	3.83	112	.283	.337	0	—	0	2	2	2	0.5
Total	10	45	43	.511	323	40	13	2	44	834¹	850	57	301	332	12.6	3.83	106	.267	.333	32	.157	-6	14	20	7	2.8

■ GUS DORNER
Dorner, Augustus b: 8/18/1876, Chambersburg, Pa. d: 5/4/56, Chambersburg, Pa. BR/TR, 5'10", 176 lbs. Deb: 9/17/02

YEAR	TM/L	W	L	PCT	G	GS	CG	SH	SV	IP	H	HR	BB	SO	RAT	ERA	ERA+	OAV	OOB	BH	AVG	PB	PR	/A	PD	TPI
1902	Cle-A	3	1	.750	4	4	4	1	0	36	33	1	13	5	11.5	1.25	275	.244	.311	5	.385	1	9	9	0	1.2
1903	Cle-A	4	5	.444	12	8	4	2	0	73²	83	4	24	28	13.1	4.52	63	.283	.337	2	.080	-2	-13	-14	0	-1.4
1906	Cin-N	0	1	.000	2	1	1	0	0	15	16	0	4	5	12.6	1.20	230	.276	.333	0	.000	-1	2	3	-0	0.2
	Bos-N	8	25	.242	34	32	29	0	0	273¹	264	5	103	104	12.6	3.65	74	.260	.338	14	.140	-4	-31	-29	4	-3.0
	Yr	8	26	.235	36	33	30	0	0	288¹	280	5	107	109	12.6	3.53	76	.261	.337	2	.019	-5	-29	-27	4	-2.8
1907	Bos-N	12	16	.429	36	31	24	2	0	271¹	253	4	92	85	11.9	3.12	82	.255	.327	12	.130	-4	-19	-17	-3	-2.4
1908	Bos-N	8	19	.296	38	28	14	3	0	216¹	176	3	77	41	11.1	3.54	68	.224	.305	12	.179	-1	-28	-27	3	-2.8
1909	Bos-N	1	2	.333	5	2	0	0	1	24²	17	1	17	7	13.1	2.55	110	.198	.343	1	.167	-0	0	1	-0	0.0
Total	6	36	69	.343	131	106	76	8	1	910¹	842	18	330	275	12.1	3.37	78	.254	.326	46	.149	-10	-80	-74	4	-8.2

■ BERT DORR
Dorr, Charles Albert b: 2/2/1862, New York d: 6/16/14, Dickinson Town, N.Y. Deb: 8/24/1882

YEAR	TM/L	W	L	PCT	G	GS	CG	SH	SV	IP	H	HR	BB	SO	RAT	ERA	ERA+	OAV	OOB	BH	AVG	PB	PR	/A	PD	TPI
1882	StL-a	2	6	.250	8	8	8	0	0	66	53	0	1	34	7.4	2.59	108	.205	.208	4	.154	-2	1	2	0	0.0

■ CAL DORSETT
Dorsett, Calvin Leavelle "Preacher" b: 6/10/13, Lone Oak, Tex. d: 10/22/70, Elk City, Okla. BR/TR, 6', 180 lbs. Deb: 8/19/40

YEAR	TM/L	W	L	PCT	G	GS	CG	SH	SV	IP	H	HR	BB	SO	RAT	ERA	ERA+	OAV	OOB	BH	AVG	PB	PR	/A	PD	TPI
1940	Cle-A	0	0	—	1	0	0	0	0	1	1	1	0	0	9.0	9.00	47	.250	.250	0	—	0	-1	-1	0	0.0
1941	Cle-A	0	1	.000	5	2	0	0	0	11¹	21	0	10	5	24.6	10.32	38	.382	.477	0	.000	-0	-8	-8	0	-0.6
1947	Cle-A	0	0	—	2	0	0	0	0	1¹	3	1	3	1	40.5	27.00	13	.500	.667	0	—	0	-3	-3	0	-0.2
Total	3	0	1	.000	8	2	0	0	0	13²	25	2	13	6	25.0	11.85	33	.385	.487	0	.000	-0	-12	-12	0	-0.8

■ JIM DORSEY
Dorsey, James Edward b: 8/2/55, Oak Park, Ill. BR/TR, 6'7", 190 lbs. Deb: 9/02/80

YEAR	TM/L	W	L	PCT	G	GS	CG	SH	SV	IP	H	HR	BB	SO	RAT	ERA	ERA+	OAV	OOB	BH	AVG	PB	PR	/A	PD	TPI
1980	Cal-A	1	2	.333	4	4	0	0	0	15²	25	2	8	8	19.5	9.19	43	.368	.442	0	—	0	-9	-9	0	-0.7
1984	Bos-A	0	0	—	2	0	0	0	0	2²	6	0	2	4	27.0	10.13	41	.462	.533	0	—	0	-2	-2	-0	-0.1
1985	Bos-A	0	1	.000	2	1	0	0	0	5¹	12	2	10	2	37.1	20.25	21	.444	.595	0	—	0	-10	-9	-0	-0.7
Total	3	1	3	.250	8	5	0	0	0	23²	43	4	20	14	24.3	11.79	34	.398	.496	0	—	0	-20	-20	-0	-1.5

■ JERRY DORSEY
Dorsey, Michael Jeremiah b: 1854, Canada d: 11/3/38, Auburn, N.Y. Deb: 7/09/1884 ♦

YEAR	TM/L	W	L	PCT	G	GS	CG	SH	SV	IP	H	HR	BB	SO	RAT	ERA	ERA+	OAV	OOB	BH	AVG	PB	PR	/A	PD	TPI
1884	Bal-U	0	1	.000	1	1	0	0	0	7	7	1	9	3	15.8	9.00	37	.360	.360	0	.000	-1	-3	-3	0	-0.1

■ JACK DOSCHER
Doscher, John Henry Jr. b: 7/27/1880, Troy, N.Y. d: 5/27/71, Park Ridge, N.J. BL/TL, 6'1", Deb: 7/02/03

YEAR	TM/L	W	L	PCT	G	GS	CG	SH	SV	IP	H	HR	BB	SO	RAT	ERA	ERA+	OAV	OOB	BH	AVG	PB	PR	/A	PD	TPI
1903	Chi-N	0	1	.000	1	1	0	0	0	3	6	0	2	5	27.0	12.00	26	.429	.529	0	.000	-0	-3	-3	0	-0.2
	Bro-N	0	0	—	3	0	0	0	0	7	8	1	9	4	23.1	7.71	41	.296	.486	0	.000	-0	-3	-4	-0	-0.3
	Yr	0	1	.000	4	1	0	0	0	10	14	1	11	9	23.4	9.00	35	.333	.481	0	.000	-1	-6	-6	-0	-0.5
1904	Bro-N	0	0	—	2	0	0	0	0	6¹	1	0	1	2	2.8	0.00	—	.053	.100	1	.500	0	2	2	-0	0.2
1905	Bro-N	1	5	.167	12	7	6	0	0	71	60	1	30	33	11.8	3.17	91	.232	.318	2	.083	-2	-1	-2	-2	-0.5
1906	Bro-N	0	1	.000	2	1	0	0	0	14	12	0	4	10	10.3	1.29	196	.250	.308	0	.000	-1	2	2	-0	0.1
1908	Cin-N	1	3	.250	7	4	3	0	0	44¹	31	1	22	7	11.4	1.83	126	.196	.306	2	.133	0	3	2	-0	0.2
Total	5	2	10	.167	27	13	10	0	0	145²	118	3	68	61	12.0	2.84	95	.225	.323	5	.100	-3	-2	-2	-2	-0.5

■ RICHARD DOTSON
Dotson, Richard Elliott b: 1/10/59, Cincinnati, Ohio BR/TR, 6'1", 190 lbs. Deb: 9/04/79

YEAR	TM/L	W	L	PCT	G	GS	CG	SH	SV	IP	H	HR	BB	SO	RAT	ERA	ERA+	OAV	OOB	BH	AVG	PB	PR	/A	PD	TPI
1979	Chi-A	2	0	1.000	5	5	1	1	0	24¹	28	0	6	13	12.6	3.70	115	.286	.327	0	—	0	1	1	0	0.2
1980	Chi-A	12	10	.545	33	32	8	0	0	198	185	20	87	109	12.6	4.27	94	.247	.331	0	—	0	-5	-5	1	-0.4
1981	Chi-A	9	8	.529	24	24	5	4	0	141	145	13	49	73	12.6	3.77	95	.270	.336	0	—	0	-2	-3	0	-0.2
1982	Chi-A	11	15	.423	34	31	3	1	0	196²	219	19	73	109	13.6	3.84	105	.282	.348	0	—	0	5	4	-1	0.4
1983	•Chi-A	22	7	.759	35	35	8	1	0	240	209	19	106	137	12.1	3.23	130	.240	.328	0	—	0	22	26	5	3.2
1984	Chi-A	14	15	.483	32	32	14	1	0	245²	216	24	103	120	11.9	3.59	116	.238	.321	0	—	0	11	15	0	1.6
1985	Chi-A	3	4	.429	9	9	0	0	0	52¹	53	5	17	33	12.6	4.47	97	.261	.327	0	—	0	-2	-1	-0	-0.1
1986	Chi-A	10	17	.370	34	34	3	1	0	197	226	24	69	110	13.6	5.48	79	.289	.348	0	—	0	-29	-26	-1	-2.4
1987	Chi-A	11	12	.478	31	31	7	2	0	211¹	201	24	86	114	12.2	4.17	110	.249	.321	0	—	0	7	10	2	1.1
1988	NY-A	12	9	.571	32	29	4	0	0	171	178	27	72	77	13.4	5.00	79	.266	.341	0	—	0	-20	-20	-1	-2.0
1989	NY-A	2	5	.286	11	9	1	0	0	51²	69	8	17	14	15.2	5.57	69	.317	.369	0	—	0	-10	-10	-1	-0.9
	Chi-A	3	7	.300	17	17	1	0	0	99²	112	8	41	55	13.8	3.88	98	.282	.349	0	—	0	-0	-1	0	-0.0
	Yr	5	12	.294	28	26	2	0	0	151¹	181	16	58	69	14.2	4.46	86	.293	.354	0	—	0	-10	-11	-0	-0.9
1990	KC-A	0	4	.000	8	7	0	0	0	30²	37	2	18	9	17.9	8.48	45	.355	.422	0	—	0	-15	-15	0	-1.3
Total	12	111	113	.496	305	295	55	11	0	1857¹	1884	194	740	973	12.9	4.23	97	.264	.337	0	—	0	-35	-25	4	-0.7

■ GARY DOTTER
Dotter, Gary Richard b: 8/7/42, St.Louis, Mo. BL/TL, 6'1", 180 lbs. Deb: 9/10/61

YEAR	TM/L	W	L	PCT	G	GS	CG	SH	SV	IP	H	HR	BB	SO	RAT	ERA	ERA+	OAV	OOB	BH	AVG	PB	PR	/A	PD	TPI
1961	Min-A	0	0	—	2	0	0	0	0	6	6	0	4	2	15.0	9.00	47	.273	.385	0	.000	-0	-3	-3	0	-0.2
1963	Min-A	0	0	—	2	0	0	0	0	2	0	0	0	2	0.0	0.00	—	.000	.000	0	—	0	1	1	0	0.1

YEAR	TM/L	W	L	PCT	G	GS	CG	SH	SV	IP	H	HR	BB	SO	RAT	ERA	ERA+	OAV	OOB	BH	AVG	PB	PR	/A	PD	TPI
1964	Min-A	0	0	—	3	0	0	0	0	4¹	3	1	3	6	12.5	2.08	172	.188	.316	0	—	0	1	1	0	0.1
Total 3		0	0	—	7	0	0	0	0	12¹	9	1	7	10	11.7	5.11	76	.205	.314	0	.000	-0	-2	-2	0	0.0

■ BABE DOTY
Doty, Elmer L. b: 12/17/1867, Genoa, Ohio d: 11/20/29, Toledo, Ohio BL/TR, 6', 160 lbs. Deb: 8/18/1890

YEAR	TM/L	W	L	PCT	G	GS	CG	SH	SV	IP	H	HR	BB	SO	RAT	ERA	ERA+	OAV	OOB	BH	AVG	PB	PR	/A	PD	TPI
1890	Tol-a	1	0	1.000	1	1	1	0	0	9	9	0	1	4	10.0	1.00	395	.252	.273	0	.000	-0	3	3	-0	0.2

■ TOM DOUGHERTY
Dougherty, Thomas James "Sugar Boy" b: 5/30/1881, Chicago, Ill. d: 11/6/53, Milwaukee, Wis. BL/TR, Deb: 4/24/04

YEAR	TM/L	W	L	PCT	G	GS	CG	SH	SV	IP	H	HR	BB	SO	RAT	ERA	ERA+	OAV	OOB	BH	AVG	PB	PR	/A	PD	TPI
1904	Chi-A	1	0	1.000	1	0	0	0	0	9	9	0	4	1	14.0	0.00	—	.000	.000	0	.000	-0	1	1	0	0.1

■ WHAMMY DOUGLAS
Douglas, Charles William b: 2/17/35, Carrboro, N.C. BR/TR, 6'2", 185 lbs. Deb: 7/29/57

YEAR	TM/L	W	L	PCT	G	GS	CG	SH	SV	IP	H	HR	BB	SO	RAT	ERA	ERA+	OAV	OOB	BH	AVG	PB	PR	/A	PD	TPI
1957	Pit-N	3	3	.500	11	8	0	0	0	47	48	5	30	28	15.5	3.26	116	.270	.384	1	.063	-1	3	3	-0	0.1

■ LARRY DOUGLAS
Douglas, Lawrence Howard b: 6/5/1890, Jellico, Tenn. d: 11/4/49, Jellico, Tenn. 6'3", 175 lbs. Deb: 6/17/15

YEAR	TM/L	W	L	PCT	G	GS	CG	SH	SV	IP	H	HR	BB	SO	RAT	ERA	ERA+	OAV	OOB	BH	AVG	PB	PR	/A	PD	TPI
1915	Bal-F	1	0	1.000	2	0	0	0	0	3	3	0	2	1	15.0	3.00	106	.268	.379	0	—	0	0	0	0	0.0

■ PHIL DOUGLAS
Douglas, Phillip Brooks "Shufflin' Phil" b: 6/17/1890, Cedartown, Ga. d: 8/1/52, Sequatchie Valley, Tenn. BR/TR, 6'3", 190 lbs. Deb: 8/30/12

YEAR	TM/L	W	L	PCT	G	GS	CG	SH	SV	IP	H	HR	BB	SO	RAT	ERA	ERA+	OAV	OOB	BH	AVG	PB	PR	/A	PD	TPI
1912	Chi-A	0	1	.000	3	1	0	0	0	12¹	21	0	6	7	19.7	7.30	44	.382	.443	0	.000	-0	-5	-6	0	-0.4
1914	Cin-N	11	18	.379	45	25	13	0	1	239¹	186	7	92	121	10.9	2.56	115	.223	.308	10	.137	-2	6	10	-2	0.6
1915	Cin-N	1	5	.167	8	7	0	0	0	46²	53	0	23	29	14.7	5.40	53	.299	.380	2	.118	-1	-14	-13	-0	-1.3
	Bro-N	5	5	.500	20	13	5	1	0	116²	104	1	47	63	9.7	2.62	106	.241	.278	6	.154	-1	2	2	-0	0.1
	Chi-N	1	1	.500	4	4	2	1	0	25	17	0	7	18	9.0	2.16	129	.187	.253	0	.000	-1	2	2	-0	0.1
	Yr	7	11	.389	32	24	7	2	0	188¹	174	1	47	110	10.6	3.25	86	.247	.295	1	.016	-3	-10	-9	-0	-1.1
1917	Chi-N	14	20	.412	51	37	20	5	1	293¹	269	13	50	151	10.0	2.55	114	.250	.287	11	.126	-4	5	11	4	1.3
1918	*Chi-N	10	9	.526	25	19	11	2	2	156²	145	3	31	51	10.2	2.13	131	.246	.285	14	.255	1	11	11	3	1.8
1919	Chi-N	10	6	.625	25	19	8	4	0	161²	133	0	34	63	9.4	2.00	144	.230	.275	8	.157	-2	16	15	5	2.2
	NY-N	2	4	.333	8	6	4	0	0	51¹	53	0	6	21	10.5	2.10	133	.264	.288	0	.000	-2	5	4	-0	0.2
	Yr	12	10	.545	33	25	12	4	0	213	186	0	40	84	9.6	2.03	141	.238	.276	1	.015	-4	21	20	5	2.4
1920	NY-N	14	10	.583	46	21	10	3	2	226	225	6	55	71	11.2	2.71	111	.263	.309	11	.151	-4	11	7	1	0.4
1921	*NY-N	15	10	.600	40	27	13	3	2	221²	266	17	55	55	13.1	4.22	87	.308	.351	6	.198	-4	-11	-14	1	-1.1
1922	NY-N	11	4	.733	24	21	9	1	0	157²	154	6	35	33	11.0	2.63	152	.257	.302	12	.207	1	26	24	0	2.5
Total 9		94	93	.503	299	200	95	20	8	1708¹	1626	52	411	683	10.6	2.80	111	.256	.305	90	.161	-16	53	58	12	6.4

■ KIP DOWD
Dowd, James Joseph b: 2/16/1889, Holyoke, Mass. d: 12/20/60, Holyoke, Mass. BR/TR, 5'10.5", 160 lbs. Deb: 7/05/10

YEAR	TM/L	W	L	PCT	G	GS	CG	SH	SV	IP	H	HR	BB	SO	RAT	ERA	ERA+	OAV	OOB	BH	AVG	PB	PR	/A	PD	TPI
1910	Pit-N	0	0	—	1	0	0	0	0	2	4	0	2	1	31.5	0.00	—	.400	.538	0	—	0	1	1	0	0.1

■ DAVE DOWLING
Dowling, David Barclay b: 8/23/42, Baton Rouge, La. BR/TL, 6'2", 181 lbs. Deb: 10/03/64

YEAR	TM/L	W	L	PCT	G	GS	CG	SH	SV	IP	H	HR	BB	SO	RAT	ERA	ERA+	OAV	OOB	BH	AVG	PB	PR	/A	PD	TPI
1964	StL-N	0	0	—	1	0	0	0	0	1	2	0	0	0	18.0	0.00	—	.400	.400	0	—	0	0	0	0	0.0
1966	Chi-N	1	0	1.000	1	1	1	0	0	9	10	0	0	3	10.0	2.00	184	.270	.270	0	.000	-0	2	2	-0	0.1
Total 2		1	0	1.000	2	1	1	0	0	10	12	0	0	3	10.8	1.80	205	.286	.286	0	.000	-0	2	2	-0	0.1

■ PETE DOWLING
Dowling, Henry Peter b: St.Louis, Mo. d: 6/30/05, Hot Lake, Ore. TL, 5'11", Deb: 7/17/1897

YEAR	TM/L	W	L	PCT	G	GS	CG	SH	SV	IP	H	HR	BB	SO	RAT	ERA	ERA+	OAV	OOB	BH	AVG	PB	PR	/A	PD	TPI
1897	Lou-N	1	2	.333	4	4	2	0	0	26	39	0	8	3	16.3	5.88	72	.343	.386	2	.200	-0	-5	-5	0	-0.3
1898	Lou-N	13	20	.394	36	32	30	0	0	285²	284	7	120	84	12.7	4.16	86	.257	.330	21	.196	1	-17	-18	-1	-1.6
1899	Lou-N	13	17	.433	34	32	29	0	0	289²	321	4	93	88	12.9	3.11	124	.280	.334	27	.233	-1	24	24	-1	2.1
1901	Mil-A	1	4	.200	10	4	3	0	1	49²	71	1	14	25	15.4	5.62	64	.331	.372	4	.211	1	-11	-11	0	-0.8
	Cle-A	11	22	.333	33	30	28	2	0	256²	269	1	104	99	13.1	3.86	92	.267	.335	16	.162	-5	-6	-9	-0	-0.9
	Yr	12	26	.316	43	34	31	2	1	306	340	2	118	124	13.5	4.15	86	.278	.342	5	.042	-4	-16	-20	-0	-1.9
Total 4		39	65	.375	117	102	92	2	1	907¹	984	13	339	299	13.1	3.87	95	.274	.337	70	.199	-4	-14	-19	-2	-1.7

■ AL DOWNING
Downing, Alphonso Erwin b: 6/28/41, Trenton, N.J. BR/TL, 5'11", 175 lbs. Deb: 7/19/61

YEAR	TM/L	W	L	PCT	G	GS	CG	SH	SV	IP	H	HR	BB	SO	RAT	ERA	ERA+	OAV	OOB	BH	AVG	PB	PR	/A	PD	TPI
1961	NY-A	0	1	.000	5	1	0	0	0	9	7	0	12	12	20.0	8.00	46	.212	.435	0	.000	-0	-4	-4	0	-0.3
1962	NY-A	0	0	—	1	0	0	0	0	1	0	0	0	1	0.0	0.00	—	.000	.000	0	—	0	0	0	0	0.0
1963	*NY-A	13	5	.722	24	22	10	4	0	175²	114	7	80	171	9.9	2.56	137	.184	.277	6	.103	-2	21	19	-2	1.6
1964	*NY-A	13	8	.619	37	35	11	1	2	244	201	18	120	217	11.8	3.47	104	.223	.314	15	.176	1	4	4	-1	0.5
1965	NY-A	12	14	.462	35	32	8	2	0	212	185	16	105	179	12.4	3.40	100	.237	.329	8	.108	-1	1	0	-0	0.0
1966	NY-A	10	11	.476	30	30	1	0	0	200	178	23	79	152	11.6	3.56	94	.235	.309	7	.100	-2	-3	-5	-4	-1.1
1967	NY-A	14	10	.583	31	28	10	4	0	201²	158	19	61	171	10.0	2.63	119	.217	.283	8	.121	1	13	11	-1	1.1
1968	NY-A	3	3	.500	15	12	1	0	0	61¹	54	7	20	40	11.0	3.52	82	.237	.301	3	.176	-0	-4	-4	-0	-0.4
1969	NY-A	7	5	.583	30	15	5	1	0	130²	117	12	49	85	11.4	3.38	103	.240	.309	6	.136	-0	4	1	-2	0.0
1970	Oak-A	3	3	.500	10	6	1	0	0	41	39	5	22	26	13.6	3.95	90	.252	.348	2	.182	-0	-1	-2	2	0.0
	Mil-A	2	10	.167	17	16	1	0	0	94¹	79	8	59	53	13.5	3.34	113	.232	.350	2	.083	-2	4	5	0	0.4
	Yr	5	13	.278	27	22	2	0	0	135¹	118	13	81	79	13.4	3.52	105	.237	.347	0	.000	-2	3	3	2	0.4
1971	LA-N	20	9	.690	37	36	12	5	0	262¹	245	16	84	136	11.4	2.68	121	.247	.308	16	.174	2	23	16	-1	1.8
1972	LA-N	9	9	.500	31	30	7	4	0	202²	196	13	67	117	12.0	2.98	112	.254	.319	8	.121	-1	11	8	5	1.2
1973	LA-N	9	9	.500	30	28	5	2	0	193	155	19	68	124	10.4	3.31	104	.219	.289	5	.088	-1	7	3	1	0.2
1974	*LA-N	5	6	.455	21	16	1	1	0	98¹	94	7	46	63	13.0	3.66	93	.255	.341	5	.172	-0	-0	-3	1	-0.1
1975	LA-N	2	1	.667	22	6	0	0	1	74²	59	6	28	39	10.7	2.89	118	.215	.293	0	.000	-1	6	4	1	0.4
1976	LA-N	1	2	.333	17	3	0	0	0	46²	43	3	18	30	11.8	3.86	88	.250	.321	0	.000	-1	-2	-2	-0	-0.2
1977	LA-N	0	1	.000	12	1	0	0	0	20	22	4	16	23	17.1	6.75	57	.278	.400	0	.000	-0	-6	-7	-0	-0.6
Total 17		123	107	.535	405	317	73	24	3	2268¹	1946	177	933	1639	11.5	3.22	105	.232	.311	91	.127	-7	75	44	-1	4.5

■ DAVE DOWNS
Downs, David Ralph b: 6/21/52, Logan, Utah BR/TR, 6'5", 220 lbs. Deb: 9/02/72

YEAR	TM/L	W	L	PCT	G	GS	CG	SH	SV	IP	H	HR	BB	SO	RAT	ERA	ERA+	OAV	OOB	BH	AVG	PB	PR	/A	PD	TPI
1972	Phi-N	1	1	.500	4	4	1	1	0	23	25	1	3	5	11.3	2.74	131	.294	.326	2	.250	0	2	2	0	0.3

■ KELLY DOWNS
Downs, Kelly Robert b: 10/25/60, Ogden, Utah BR/TR, 6'4", 195 lbs. Deb: 7/29/86

YEAR	TM/L	W	L	PCT	G	GS	CG	SH	SV	IP	H	HR	BB	SO	RAT	ERA	ERA+	OAV	OOB	BH	AVG	PB	PR	/A	PD	TPI
1986	SF-N	4	4	.500	14	14	1	0	0	88¹	78	5	30	64	11.3	2.75	128	.236	.305	5	.172	0	9	8	0	0.7
1987	*SF-N	12	9	.571	41	28	4	3	1	186	185	14	67	137	12.4	3.63	106	.258	.324	8	.143	-0	9	4	-4	0.0
1988	SF-N	13	9	.591	27	26	6	3	0	168	140	11	47	118	10.2	3.32	98	.225	.283	4	.167	2	2	-1	-0	0.1
1989	*SF-N	4	8	.333	18	15	0	0	0	82²	82	7	26	49	11.9	4.79	70	.261	.320	2	.091	-1	-12	-13	-1	-1.4
1990	SF-N	3	2	.600	13	9	0	0	0	63	56	2	20	31	11.1	3.43	108	.233	.298	0	.000	-1	3	2	1	0.2
Total 5		36	32	.529	113	92	11	6	1	588¹	541	39	190	399	11.4	3.55	100	.243	.306	24	.138	0	12	0	-4	-0.4

■ TOM DOWSE
Dowse, Thomas Joseph b: 8/12/1866, Ireland d: 12/14/46, Riverside, Cal. BR/TR, 5'11", 175 lbs. Deb: 4/21/1890 ♦

YEAR	TM/L	W	L	PCT	G	GS	CG	SH	SV	IP	H	HR	BB	SO	RAT	ERA	ERA+	OAV	OOB	BH	AVG	PB	PR	/A	PD	TPI
1890	Cle-N	0	0	—	1	0	0	0	0	5	6	0	1	0	12.6	5.40	66	.289	.322	33	.208	-0	-1	-1	0	0.0

■ JESS DOYLE
Doyle, Jesse Herbert b: 4/14/1898, Knoxville, Tenn. d: 4/15/61, Belleville, Ill. BR/TR, 5'11", 175 lbs. Deb: 4/14/25

YEAR	TM/L	W	L	PCT	G	GS	CG	SH	SV	IP	H	HR	BB	SO	RAT	ERA	ERA+	OAV	OOB	BH	AVG	PB	PR	/A	PD	TPI
1925	Det-A	4	7	.364	45	3	0	0	8	118¹	158	6	50	31	16.2	5.93	73	.340	.410	8	.242	3	-20	-21	-0	-1.6
1926	Det-A	0	0	—	2	0	0	0	0	4¹	6	0	1	2	14.5	4.15	98	.316	.350	1	1.000	0	-0	-0	-0	0.0
1927	Det-A	0	0	—	7	0	0	0	0	12¹	16	0	5	5	15.3	8.03	52	.314	.375	1	.333	0	-5	-5	0	-0.4
1931	StL-A	0	0	—	1	0	0	0	0	1	3	0	1	0	36.0	27.00	17	.500	.571	0	.000	0	-3	-2	0	-0.1
Total 4		4	7	.364	55	3	0	0	9	136	183	6	57	38	16.2	6.22	69	.338	.406	10	.270	3	-28	-29	-0	-2.1

■ JOHN DOYLE
Doyle, John Aloysius b: 1858, Nova Scotia, Canada d: 12/24/15, Providence, R.I. Deb: 7/26/1882

YEAR	TM/L	W	L	PCT	G	GS	CG	SH	SV	IP	H	HR	BB	SO	RAT	ERA	ERA+	OAV	OOB	BH	AVG	PB	PR	/A	PD	TPI
1882	StL-a	0	3	.000	3	3	3	0	0	24	41	0	3		16.5	2.63	107	.355	.371	2	.182	-0	0	0	-0	0.0

■ SLOW JOE DOYLE
Doyle, Judd Bruce b: 9/15/1881, Clay Center, Kan. d: 11/21/47, Tannersville, N.Y. BR/TR, 5'8", 150 lbs. Deb: 8/25/06

YEAR	TM/L	W	L	PCT	G	GS	CG	SH	SV	IP	H	HR	BB	SO	RAT	ERA	ERA+	OAV	OOB	BH	AVG	PB	PR	/A	PD	TPI
1906	NY-A	2	1	.667	9	6	3	2	0	45¹	34	1	13	28	9.3	2.38	124	.211	.270	3	.214	-0	2	3	0	0.3
1907	NY-A	11	11	.500	29	23	15	1	1	193²	169	2	67	94	11.0	2.65	106	.237	.302	8	.138	-1	-2	3	-3	0.0
1908	NY-A	1	1	.500	12	4	2	1	0	48	42	1	14	20	10.9	2.63	95	.235	.297	3	.214	1	-1	-1	-1	-0.1
1909	NY-A	8	6	.571	17	15	8	3	0	125²	103	3	37	57	10.2	2.58	98	.232	.294	7	.167	0	-1	-1	-3	-0.3
1910	NY-A	0	2	.000	3	2	1	0	0	12¹	19	0	5	6	18.2	8.03	33	.365	.431	1	.250	-0	-8	-7	1	-0.6
	Cin-N	0	0	—	5	0	0	0	0	11¹	16	0	11	4	21.4	6.35	46	.327	.450	0	.000	-0	-4	-4	0	-0.4
Total 5		22	21	.512	75	50	29	7	1	436¹	383	7	147	209	11.0	2.85	95	.240	.306	22	.163	-1	-15	-7	-8	-1.1

■ PAUL DOYLE
Doyle, Paul Sinnott b: 10/2/39, Philadelphia, Pa. BL/TL, 5'11", 172 lbs. Deb: 5/28/69

YEAR	TM/L	W	L	PCT	G	GS	CG	SH	SV	IP	H	HR	BB	SO	RAT	ERA	ERA+	OAV	OOB	BH	AVG	PB	PR	/A	PD	TPI
1969	*Atl-N	2	0	1.000	36	0	0	0	4	39	31	4	16	25	10.8	2.08	174	.231	.313	0	.000	-0	7	7	1	0.7
1970	Cal-A	3	1	.750	40	0	0	0	5	42	43	7	21	34	13.9	5.14	70	.267	.355	0	.000	-0	-7	-7	1	-0.6
	SD-N	0	2	.000	9	0	0	0	2	7	9	0	6	2	19.3	6.43	62	.360	.484	0	.000	-0	-2	-2	1	0.0
1972	Cal-A	0	0	—	2	0	0	0	0	2¹	2	0	3	4	19.3	0.00	—	.250	.455	0	—	0	1	1	0	0.1
Total 3		5	3	.625	87	0	0	0	11	90¹	85	11	46	65	13.2	3.79	96	.259	.352	0	.000	-1	-1	-2	3	0.2

■ CARL DOYLE
Doyle, William Carl b: 7/30/12, Knoxville, Tenn. d: 9/4/51, Knoxville, Tenn. BR/TR, 6'1", 185 lbs. Deb: 8/05/35

YEAR	TM/L	W	L	PCT	G	GS	CG	SH	SV	IP	H	HR	BB	SO	RAT	ERA	ERA+	OAV	OOB	BH	AVG	PB	PR	/A	PD	TPI
1935	Phi-A	2	7	.222	14	9	3	0	0	79²	86	3	72	34	18.1	5.99	76	.282	.422	4	.133	-2	-14	-13	1	-1.2
1936	Phi-A	0	3	.000	8	6	1	0	0	38²	66	4	29	12	23.3	10.94	47	.369	.469	4	.267	-0	-25	-25	-1	-1.9
1939	Bro-N	1	2	.333	5	1	1	1	1	17²	8	1	7	7	7.6	1.02	395	.136	.227	1	.167	0	6	6	0	0.7
1940	Bro-N	0	0	—	3	0	0	0	1	5²	18	3	6	4	44.5	27.00	15	.545	.651	1	1.000	1	-15	-14	0	-1.0
	StL-N	3	3	.500	21	5	1	0	0	81	99	7	41	44	16.2	5.89	68	.294	.380	6	.200	2	-18	-17	-0	-1.4
	Yr	3	3	.500	24	5	1	0	1	86²	117	10	47	48	17.7	7.27	55	.313	.398	2	.065	3	-33	-32	-0	-2.4
Total 4		6	15	.286	51	21	6	1	2	222²	277	18	155	101	18.1	6.95	63	.303	.414	16	.195	1	-66	-63	-0	-4.8

■ TOM DOZIER
Dozier, Thomas Dean b: 9/5/61, San Pablo, Cal. BR/TR, 6'2", 190 lbs. Deb: 5/17/86

YEAR	TM/L	W	L	PCT	G	GS	CG	SH	SV	IP	H	HR	BB	SO	RAT	ERA	ERA+	OAV	OOB	BH	AVG	PB	PR	/A	PD	TPI
1986	Oak-A	0	0	—	4	0	0	0	0	6¹	6	1	5	4	15.6	5.68	68	.261	.393	0	—	0	-1	-1	0	0.0

■ BUZZ DOZIER
Dozier, William Joseph b: 8/31/27, Waco, Tex. BR/TR, 6'3", 185 lbs. Deb: 9/12/47

YEAR	TM/L	W	L	PCT	G	GS	CG	SH	SV	IP	H	HR	BB	SO	RAT	ERA	ERA+	OAV	OOB	BH	AVG	PB	PR	/A	PD	TPI
1947	Was-A	0	0	—	2	0	0	0	0	4²	2	0	1	2	5.8	0.00	—	.133	.188	0	.000	-0	2	2	0	0.2
1949	Was-A	0	0	—	2	0	0	0	0	6¹	12	0	6	1	25.6	11.37	37	.429	.529	0	.000	-0	-5	-5	-0	-0.4
Total 2		0	0	—	4	0	0	0	0	11	14	0	7	3	17.2	6.55	62	.326	.420	0	.000	-0	-3	-3	-0	-0.2

■ DOUG DRABEK
Drabek, Douglas Dean b: 7/25/62, Victoria, Tex. BR/TR, 6'1", 185 lbs. Deb: 5/30/86

YEAR	TM/L	W	L	PCT	G	GS	CG	SH	SV	IP	H	HR	BB	SO	RAT	ERA	ERA+	OAV	OOB	BH	AVG	PB	PR	/A	PD	TPI
1986	NY-A	7	8	.467	27	21	0	0	0	131²	126	13	50	76	12.2	4.10	100	.251	.323	0	—	0	1	-0	-1	0.0
1987	Pit-N	11	12	.478	29	28	1	1	0	176¹	165	22	46	120	10.8	3.88	106	.247	.296	7	.119	-1	4	4	0	0.4
1988	Pit-N	15	7	.682	33	32	3	1	0	219¹	194	21	50	127	10.3	3.08	111	.239	.288	13	.171	3	9	8	-1	1.1
1989	Pit-N	14	12	.538	35	34	8	5	0	244¹	215	21	69	123	10.6	2.80	120	.238	.295	8	.104	-2	19	15	0	1.4
1990	*Pit-N	**22**	6	**.786**	33	33	9	3	0	231¹	190	15	56	131	9.7	2.76	131	.225	.275	18	.214	5	26	22	2	3.1
Total 5		69	45	.605	157	148	21	10	0	1003	890	92	271	577	10.6	3.21	114	.239	.293	46	.155	6	59	49	-0	6.0

■ MOE DRABOWSKY
Drabowsky, Myron Walter b: 7/21/35, Ozanna, Poland BR/TR, 6'3", 190 lbs. Deb: 8/07/56 C

YEAR	TM/L	W	L	PCT	G	GS	CG	SH	SV	IP	H	HR	BB	SO	RAT	ERA	ERA+	OAV	OOB	BH	AVG	PB	PR	/A	PD	TPI
1956	Chi-N	2	4	.333	9	7	3	0	0	51	37	1	39	36	13.8	2.47	153	.207	.355	4	.250	0	7	7	-0	0.8
1957	Chi-N	13	15	.464	36	33	12	2	0	239²	214	22	94	170	11.9	3.53	110	.242	.321	15	.183	2	9	9	-0	1.1
1958	Chi-N	9	11	.450	22	20	4	1	0	125²	118	19	73	77	14.0	4.51	87	.245	.350	7	.156	-1	-8	-8	-0	-0.9
1959	Chi-N	5	10	.333	31	23	3	1	0	141²	138	21	75	70	13.7	4.13	96	.251	.344	5	.111	-1	-3	-3	-0	-0.3
1960	Chi-N	3	1	.750	32	7	0	0	1	50¹	71	3	23	26	17.0	6.44	59	.338	.406	0	.000	-1	-15	-15	-1	-1.5
1961	Mil-N	0	2	.000	16	0	0	0	2	25¹	26	4	18	5	16.0	4.62	81	.277	.398	1	.250	-0	-2	-2	-0	-0.1
1962	Cin-N	2	6	.250	23	10	1	0	1	83	84	13	31	56	13.1	4.99	81	.267	.344	0	.000	-2	-10	-9	-1	-1.0
	KC-A	1	1	.500	10	3	0	0	0	28	29	8	10	19	12.9	5.14	81	.266	.333	1	.167	-0	-4	-3	-0	-0.2
1963	KC-A	7	13	.350	26	22	9	2	0	174¹	135	16	64	109	10.7	3.05	126	.214	.295	10	.161	1	11	15	-2	1.6
1964	KC-A	5	13	.278	53	21	1	0	1	168¹	176	24	72	119	13.7	5.29	72	.273	.353	1	.023	-4	-31	-28	1	-3.1
1965	KC-A	1	5	.167	14	5	0	0	0	38²	44	5	18	25	15.1	4.42	79	.291	.378	1	.091	-1	-4	-4	-0	-0.4
1966	*Bal-A	6	0	1.000	44	3	0	0	7	96	62	10	29	98	8.6	2.81	118	.181	.247	8	.364	4	7	6	-1	0.9
1967	Bal-A	7	5	.583	43	0	0	0	12	95¹	66	7	25	96	8.8	1.60	196	.194	.253	7	.350	2	17	16	0	2.1
1968	Bal-A	4	4	.500	45	0	0	0	7	61¹	35	3	25	46	9.4	1.91	153	.166	.267	2	.286	0	7	7	-0	0.8
1969	Bal-A	11	9	.550	52	0	0	0	11	98	68	10	30	76	9.2	2.94	125	.190	.256	4	.235	1	7	8	1	1.0
1970	KC-A	1	2	.333	24	0	0	0	2	35²	28	3	12	38	10.6	3.28	114	.217	.294	1	.250	-0	2	2	-0	0.2
	*Bal-A	4	2	.667	21	0	0	0	1	33¹	30	7	15	21	12.4	3.78	96	.233	.317	0	.000	-1	-0	-0	-0	0.0
	Yr	5	4	.556	45	0	0	0	3	69	58	10	27	59	11.2	3.52	105	.221	.296	0	.000	-0	1	1	-0	0.2
1971	StL-N	6	1	.857	51	0	0	0	8	60¹	45	2	33	49	11.9	3.43	105	.207	.317	1	.167	-0	0	1	-1	0.0
1972	StL-N	1	1	.500	30	0	0	0	2	27²	29	4	14	22	14.3	2.60	131	.259	.346	0	.000	-0	3	2	-1	0.2
	Chi-A	0	0	—	7	0	0	0	0	7¹	6	0	2	4	9.8	2.45	127	.240	.296	0	.000	-0	0	1	-0	0.0
Total 17		88	105	.456	589	154	33	6	55	1641	1441	182	702	1162	12.1	3.71	100	.236	.321	68	.162	-0	-5	2	-6	1.2

■ DICK DRAGO
Drago, Richard Anthony b: 6/25/45, Toledo, Ohio BR/TR, 6'1", 190 lbs. Deb: 4/11/69

YEAR	TM/L	W	L	PCT	G	GS	CG	SH	SV	IP	H	HR	BB	SO	RAT	ERA	ERA+	OAV	OOB	BH	AVG	PB	PR	/A	PD	TPI
1969	KC-A	11	13	.458	41	26	10	2	1	200²	190	19	65	108	11.5	3.77	98	.248	.308	3	.058	-3	-3	-2	2	-0.2
1970	KC-A	9	15	.375	35	34	7	1	0	240	239	20	72	127	11.9	3.75	100	.266	.325	4	.053	-6	-1	-0	-0	-0.6
1971	KC-A	17	11	.607	35	34	15	4	0	241¹	251	14	46	109	11.4	2.98	115	.276	.318	10	.130	1	13	12	1	1.5
1972	KC-A	12	17	.414	34	33	11	2	0	239¹	230	22	51	135	10.8	3.01	101	.254	.298	4	.059	-2	1	1	-2	-0.4
1973	KC-A	12	14	.462	37	33	10	1	0	212²	252	16	76	98	14.2	4.23	97	.300	.363	0	—	0	-10	-3	1	-0.1
1974	Bos-A	7	10	.412	33	18	8	0	3	175²	165	17	56	90	11.6	3.48	110	.251	.315	0	—	0	3	7	-1	0.6
1975	*Bos-A	2	2	.500	40	2	0	0	15	72²	69	5	31	43	12.4	3.84	106	.247	.323	0	—	0	-1	2	0	0.2
1976	Cal-A	7	8	.467	43	0	0	0	6	79¹	80	7	31	43	13.2	4.42	75	.264	.342	0	—	0	-8	-10	-2	-1.1
1977	Cal-A	0	1	.000	13	0	0	0	2	21	22	3	3	15	10.7	3.00	130	.272	.298	0	—	0	2	2	-0	0.2
	Bal-A	6	3	.667	36	0	0	0	3	39²	49	2	15	20	14.7	3.63	104	.308	.371	0	—	0	2	1	-0	0.1
	Yr	6	4	.600	49	0	0	0	5	60²	71	5	18	35	13.4	3.41	112	.293	.345	0	—	0	4	3	-0	0.3
1978	Bos-A	4	4	.500	37	1	0	0	7	77¹	71	5	32	42	12.5	3.03	136	.246	.329	0	—	0	6	9	-1	0.9
1979	Bos-A	10	6	.625	53	1	0	0	13	89	85	6	21	67	11.0	3.03	145	.254	.304	0	—	0	12	14	-1	1.3
1980	Bos-A	7	7	.500	43	7	1	0	3	132²	127	17	44	63	11.9	4.14	102	.251	.317	0	.000	-1	-2	1	-1	0.0
1981	Sea-A	4	6	.400	39	0	0	0	0	53²	71	5	15	27	14.4	5.53	70	.324	.368	0	—	0	-11	-10	0	-0.9
Total 13		108	117	.480	519	189	62	10	58	1875	1901	157	558	987	12.1	3.62	103	.266	.324	21	.077	-10	4	23	-3	1.5

■ LOGAN DRAKE
Drake, Logan Gaffney "L.G." b: 12/26/1900, Spartanburg, S.C. d: 6/1/40, Columbia, S.C. BR/TR, 5'10.5", 165 lbs. Deb: 9/21/22

YEAR	TM/L	W	L	PCT	G	GS	CG	SH	SV	IP	H	HR	BB	SO	RAT	ERA	ERA+	OAV	OOB	BH	AVG	PB	PR	/A	PD	TPI
1922	Cle-A	0	0	—	1	0	0	0	0	3	4	0	2	1	18.0	3.00	134	.364	.462	0	.000	-0	0	0	-0	0.0
1923	Cle-A	0	0	—	4	0	0	0	0	4¹	2	0	4	2	14.5	4.15	95	.133	.350	0	—	0	-0	-0	-0	0.0
1924	Cle-A	0	1	.000	5	1	0	0	0	11¹	18	0	10	8	23.0	10.32	41	.400	.518	0	.000	-0	-8	-8	-0	-0.6
Total 3		0	1	.000	10	1	0	0	0	18²	24	0	16	11	20.3	7.71	54	.338	.472	0	.000	-0	-7	-7	-0	-0.6

■ TOM DRAKE
Drake, Thomas Kendall b: 8/7/14, Birmingham, Ala. d: 7/2/88, Birmingham, Ala. BR/TR, 6'1", 185 lbs. Deb: 4/24/39

YEAR	TM/L	W	L	PCT	G	GS	CG	SH	SV	IP	H	HR	BB	SO	RAT	ERA	ERA+	OAV	OOB	BH	AVG	PB	PR	/A	PD	TPI
1939	Cle-A	0	1	.000	8	1	0	0	0	15	23	2	19	1	26.4	9.00	49	.377	.537	0	.000	-0	-7	-8	0	-0.6
1941	Bro-N	1	1	.500	10	2	0	0	0	24²	26	2	9	12	12.8	4.38	84	.280	.343	2	.400	-0	-2	-2	-0	-0.1
Total 2		1	2	.333	18	3	0	0	0	39²	49	4	28	13	17.9	6.13	65	.318	.429	2	.286	0	-9	-10	0	-0.7

YEAR TM/L	W	L	PCT	G	GS	CG	SH	SV	IP	H	HR	BB	SO	RAT	ERA	ERA+	OAV	OOB	BH	AVG	PB	PR	/A	PD	TPI

■ DAVE DRAVECKY Dravecky, David Francis b: 2/14/56, Youngstown, Ohio BR/TL, 6'1", 195 lbs. Deb: 6/15/82

YEAR TM/L	W	L	PCT	G	GS	CG	SH	SV	IP	H	HR	BB	SO	RAT	ERA	ERA+	OAV	OOB	BH	AVG	PB	PR	/A	PD	TPI
1982 SD-N	5	3	.625	31	10	0	0	2	105	86	8	33	59	10.3	2.57	133	.225	.288	3	.130	-0	12	10	2	1.2
1983 SD-N	14	10	.583	28	28	9	1	0	183²	181	18	44	74	11.2	3.58	97	.262	.309	6	.098	-1	1	-2	1	-0.1
1984 *SD-N	9	8	.529	50	14	3	2	8	156²	125	12	51	71	10.3	2.93	122	.222	.291	4	.098	-1	11	11	-1	1.0
1985 SD-N	13	11	.542	34	31	7	2	0	214²	200	18	57	105	10.8	2.93	120	.249	.300	8	.116	-0	16	14	-1	1.4
1986 SD-N	9	11	.450	26	26	3	1	0	161¹	149	17	54	87	11.4	3.07	119	.246	.309	7	.140	0	12	10	0	1.2
1987 SD-N	3	7	.300	30	10	1	0	0	79	71	10	31	60	12.0	3.76	105	.240	.318	3	.167	0	3	2	-0	0.1
*SF-N	7	5	.583	18	18	4	3	0	112¹	115	8	33	78	12.0	3.20	120	.272	.328	5	.132	0	11	8	1	1.0
Yr	10	12	.455	48	28	5	3	0	191¹	186	18	64	138	11.9	3.43	113	.257	.319	4	.071	1	14	10	1	1.1
1988 SF-N	2	2	.500	7	7	1	0	0	37	33	4	8	19	10.0	3.16	103	.243	.285	1	.100	-0	1	0	0	0.0
1989 SF-N	2	0	1.000	2	2	0	0	0	13	8	2	4	5	9.0	3.46	97	.182	.265	1	.333	1	0	-0	0	0.1
Total 8	64	57	.529	226	146	28	9	10	1062²	968	97	315	558	11.0	3.13	115	.245	.304	38	.121	-1	67	54	2	5.9

■ CLEM DREISEWERD Dreisewerd, Clement John "Steamboat" b: 1/24/16, Old Monroe, Mo. BL/TL, 6'1.5", 195 lbs. Deb: 8/29/44

YEAR TM/L	W	L	PCT	G	GS	CG	SH	SV	IP	H	HR	BB	SO	RAT	ERA	ERA+	OAV	OOB	BH	AVG	PB	PR	/A	PD	TPI
1944 Bos-A	2	4	.333	7	7	3	0	0	48²	52	2	9	9	11.3	4.07	84	.268	.300	3	.188	0	-3	-4	-1	-0.3
1945 Bos-A	0	1	.000	2	2	0	0	0	9²	13	0	2	3	14.9	4.66	73	.325	.372	0	.000	-0	-1	-1	-0	-0.1
1946 *Bos-A	4	1	.800	20	1	0	0	0	47¹	50	3	15	19	12.4	4.18	88	.276	.332	0	.000	-1	-4	-3	1	-0.2
1948 StL-A	0	2	.000	13	0	0	0	1	22¹	28	6	8	6	14.5	5.64	81	.318	.375	0	.000	-1	-3	-3	0	-0.2
NY-N	0	0	—	4	0	0	0	1	12²	17	3	5	2	15.6	5.68	69	.321	.379	1	.250	1	-2	-2	-0	-0.1
Total 4	6	8	.429	46	10	3	0	2	140²	160	14	39	39	12.8	4.54	82	.288	.336	4	.105	-1	-14	-13	0	-0.9

■ BOB DRESSER Dresser, Robert Nicholson b: 10/4/1878, Newton, Mass. d: 7/27/24, Duxbury, Mass. TL , Deb: 8/13/02

YEAR TM/L	W	L	PCT	G	GS	CG	SH	SV	IP	H	HR	BB	SO	RAT	ERA	ERA+	OAV	OOB	BH	AVG	PB	PR	/A	PD	TPI
1902 Bos-N	0	1	.000	1	1	1	0	0	9	12	0	0	8	12.0	3.00	94	.319	.319	1	.250	0	-0	-0	-0	0.0

■ ROB DRESSLER Dressler, Robert Anthony b: 2/2/54, Portland, Ore. BR/TR, 6'3", 180 lbs. Deb: 9/07/75

YEAR TM/L	W	L	PCT	G	GS	CG	SH	SV	IP	H	HR	BB	SO	RAT	ERA	ERA+	OAV	OOB	BH	AVG	PB	PR	/A	PD	TPI
1975 SF-N	1	0	1.000	3	2	1	0	0	16¹	17	0	4	6	11.6	1.10	345	.274	.318	0	.000	-0	5	5	0	0.6
1976 SF-N	3	10	.231	25	19	0	0	0	107²	125	8	35	33	13.5	4.43	82	.291	.347	4	.129	-1	-11	-10	1	-0.9
1978 StL-N	0	1	.000	3	2	0	0	0	13	12	0	4	4	11.1	2.08	169	.267	.327	0	.000	-0	2	2	0	0.2
1979 Sea-A	3	2	.600	21	11	2	0	0	104	134	11	22	36	13.5	4.93	88	.312	.345	0	—	0	-8	-7	0	-0.5
1980 Sea-A	4	10	.286	30	14	3	0	0	149¹	161	14	33	50	11.9	3.98	104	.280	.322	0	—	0	1	3	2	0.4
Total 5	11	23	.324	82	48	6	0	0	390¹	449	33	98	129	12.7	4.17	96	.291	.335	4	.105	-2	-12	-7	3	-0.2

■ DAVE DREW Drew, David Deb: 5/14/1884 ◆

YEAR TM/L	W	L	PCT	G	GS	CG	SH	SV	IP	H	HR	BB	SO	RAT	ERA	ERA+	OAV	OOB	BH	AVG	PB	PR	/A	PD	TPI
1884 Phi-U	0	1	.000	1	0	0	0	0	7	7	0	0	2	9.0	3.86	74	.243	.243	4	.444	1	-1	-1	-0	0.0

■ KARL DREWS Drews, Karl August b: 2/22/20, Staten Island, N.Y d: 8/15/63, Dania, Fla. BR/TR, 6'4.5", 192 lbs. Deb: 9/08/46

YEAR TM/L	W	L	PCT	G	GS	CG	SH	SV	IP	H	HR	BB	SO	RAT	ERA	ERA+	OAV	OOB	BH	AVG	PB	PR	/A	PD	TPI
1946 NY-A	0	1	.000	3	1	0	0	0	6¹	6	0	6	4	18.5	8.53	40	.250	.419	0	.000	-0	-4	-4	0	-0.3
1947 *NY-A	6	6	.500	30	10	0	0	1	91²	92	6	55	45	14.9	4.91	72	.264	.373	1	.037	-2	-12	-14	1	-1.5
1948 NY-A	2	3	.400	19	2	0	0	1	38	35	3	31	11	15.6	3.79	108	.248	.384	0	.000	-1	2	1	1	0.1
StL-A	3	2	.600	20	2	0	0	2	38	43	3	38	11	19.2	8.05	57	.289	.433	0	.000	-0	-16	-15	1	-1.3
Yr	5	5	.500	39	4	0	0	3	76	78	6	69	22	17.4	5.92	73	.269	.409	4	.267	-1	-14	-14	1	-1.2
1949 StL-A	4	12	.250	31	23	3	1	0	139²	180	11	66	35	16.4	6.64	68	.317	.397	0	.000	-5	-38	-33	-1	-3.4
1951 Phi-N	1	0	1.000	5	3	1	0	0	23	29	2	7	13	15.7	6.26	61	.296	.367	2	.250	1	-6	-6	0	-0.4
1952 Phi-N	14	15	.483	33	30	15	5	0	228²	213	13	52	96	10.6	2.72	135	.252	.298	9	.110	-2	26	24	0	2.4
1953 Phi-N	9	10	.474	47	27	6	0	3	185¹	218	26	50	72	13.5	4.52	93	.293	.346	7	.119	-2	-5	-6	2	-0.6
1954 Phi-N	1	0	1.000	8	0	0	0	0	16	18	2	8	6	14.6	5.63	72	.300	.382	0	.000	-1	-3	-3	0	-0.2
Cin-N	4	4	.500	22	9	1	0	0	60	79	6	19	29	15.0	6.00	70	.326	.380	2	.167	1	-13	-12	0	-0.9
Yr	5	4	.556	30	9	1	1	0	76	97	8	27	35	14.9	5.92	70	.320	.380	4	.250	1	-16	-15	1	-1.1
Total 8	44	53	.454	218	107	26	7	7	826²	913	72	332	322	13.9	4.76	84	.284	.357	21	.083	-12	-68	-68	4	-6.1

■ DENNY DRISCOLL Driscoll, John F. b: 11/19/1855, Lowell, Mass. d: 7/11/1886, Lowell, Mass. BL/TL, 5'10.5", 160 lbs. Deb: 7/01/1880 ◆

YEAR TM/L	W	L	PCT	G	GS	CG	SH	SV	IP	H	HR	BB	SO	RAT	ERA	ERA+	OAV	OOB	BH	AVG	PB	PR	/A	PD	TPI
1880 Buf-N	1	3	.250	6	4	4	0	0	41²	48	1	9	17	12.3	3.89	63	.275	.310	10	.154	-1	-7	-7	0	-0.5
1882 Pit-a	13	9	.591	23	23	23	0	0	201	162	0	12	59	7.8	**1.21**	**216**	.206	.218	11	.138	-2	33	31	-3	2.4
1883 Pit-a	18	21	.462	41	40	35	1	0	336¹	427	3	39	79	12.5	3.99	81	.290	.309	27	.182	-4	-26	-29	6	-2.3
1884 Lou-a	6	6	.500	13	13	10	0	0	102	110	3	7	16	10.3	3.44	89	.261	.273	9	.188	-1	-2	-4	3	-0.1
Total 4	38	39	.494	83	80	72	1	0	681	747	7	67	171	10.8	3.08	96	.262	.279	60	.167	-9	-2	-8	6	-0.5

■ MICHAEL DRISCOLL Driscoll, Michael Columbus b: 10/19/1892, Rockland, Mass. d: 3/22/53, Foxboro, Mass. BR/TR, 6'1", 160 lbs. Deb: 7/06/16

YEAR TM/L	W	L	PCT	G	GS	CG	SH	SV	IP	H	HR	BB	SO	RAT	ERA	ERA+	OAV	OOB	BH	AVG	PB	PR	/A	PD	TPI
1916 Phi-A	0	1	.000	1	0	0	0	0	5	6	0	2	0	14.4	5.40	53	.273	.333	0	.000	-0	-1	-1	1	0.0

■ TOM DROHAN Drohan, Thomas F b: 8/26/1887, Fall River, Mass. d: 9/17/26, Kewanee, Ill. BR/TR, 5'10", 175 lbs. Deb: 5/01/13

YEAR TM/L	W	L	PCT	G	GS	CG	SH	SV	IP	H	HR	BB	SO	RAT	ERA	ERA+	OAV	OOB	BH	AVG	PB	PR	/A	PD	TPI
1913 Was-A	0	0	—	2	0	0	0	0	2	5	1	0	2	22.5	9.00	33	.500	.500	0	—	0	-1	-1	0	0.0

■ DICK DROTT Drott, Richard Fred "Hummer" b: 7/1/36, Cincinnati, Ohio d: 8/16/85, Glendale Heights, Ill. BR/TR, 6', 185 lbs. Deb: 4/16/57

YEAR TM/L	W	L	PCT	G	GS	CG	SH	SV	IP	H	HR	BB	SO	RAT	ERA	ERA+	OAV	OOB	BH	AVG	PB	PR	/A	PD	TPI
1957 Chi-N	15	11	.577	38	32	7	3	0	229	200	22	129	170	13.2	3.58	108	.234	.340	8	.100	-5	8	8	-1	0.1
1958 Chi-N	7	11	.389	39	31	4	0	0	167¹	156	23	99	127	14.0	5.43	72	.245	.352	15	.273	3	-28	-28	0	-2.4
1959 Chi-N	1	2	.333	8	6	1	1	0	27¹	25	5	26	15	16.8	5.93	67	.245	.398	1	.125	-0	-6	-6	-0	-0.5
1960 Chi-N	0	6	.000	23	9	0	0	0	55¹	63	7	42	32	17.6	7.16	53	.296	.419	1	.100	-1	-21	-21	-0	-2.0
1961 Chi-N	1	4	.200	35	8	0	0	0	98	75	13	51	48	11.7	4.22	99	.215	.317	6	.273	2	-2	-2	-0	0.0
1962 Hou-N	1	0	1.000	6	1	0	0	0	13	12	1	9	10	14.5	7.62	49	.240	.356	0	.000	-0	-5	-6	-0	-0.5
1963 Hou-N	2	12	.143	27	14	2	1	0	97²	95	13	49	58	13.8	4.98	63	.257	.353	3	.130	-1	-18	-20	-1	-2.1
Total 7	27	46	.370	176	101	14	5	0	687²	626	84	405	460	13.8	4.78	80	.243	.351	34	.168	-2	-72	-74	-5	-7.4

■ LOUIS DRUCKE Drucke, Louis Frank b: 12/3/1888, Waco, Tex. d: 9/22/55, Waco, Tex. TR , 6'1", 188 lbs. Deb: 9/25/09

YEAR TM/L	W	L	PCT	G	GS	CG	SH	SV	IP	H	HR	BB	SO	RAT	ERA	ERA+	OAV	OOB	BH	AVG	PB	PR	/A	PD	TPI
1909 NY-N	2	1	.667	3	3	2	0	0	24	20	0	13	8	12.4	2.25	114	.227	.327	1	.125	-0	1	1	-0	0.1
1910 NY-N	12	10	.545	34	27	15	0	0	215¹	174	3	82	151	11.2	2.47	120	.228	.312	15	.214	4	14	12	1	1.7
1911 NY-N	4	4	.500	15	10	4	0	0	75²	83	1	41	42	15.7	4.04	83	.281	.384	2	.087	-1	-5	-6	1	-0.5
1912 NY-N	0	0	—	1	0	0	0	1	2	5	0	1	0	27.0	13.50	25	.417	.462	0	—	0	-2	-2	0	-0.1
Total 4	18	15	.545	53	40	21	0	1	317	282	4	137	201	12.4	2.90	105	.243	.333	18	.178	2	7	5	1	1.1

■ CARL DRUHOT Druhot, Carl A. "Collie" b: 9/1/1882, Ohio d: 2/11/18, Portland, Ore. BL/TL, 5'7", 150 lbs. Deb: 4/18/06

YEAR TM/L	W	L	PCT	G	GS	CG	SH	SV	IP	H	HR	BB	SO	RAT	ERA	ERA+	OAV	OOB	BH	AVG	PB	PR	/A	PD	TPI
1906 Cin-N	2	2	.500	4	3	1	0	0	25	27	0	7	14	13.0	4.32	64	.270	.330	2	.222	-0	-5	-4	-1	-0.4
StL-N	6	7	.462	15	13	12	1	0	130¹	117	1	46	45	11.6	2.62	100	.238	.310	13	.232	1	0	0	1	0.2
Yr	8	9	.471	19	16	13	1	0	155¹	144	1	53	59	11.7	2.90	91	.243	.310	1	.015	1	-5	-4	-0	-0.2
1907 StL-N	0	1	.000	1	1	0	0	0	2¹	3	0	4	1	30.9	15.43	16	.600	.800	0	—	0	-3	-3	0	-0.2
Total 2	8	10	.444	20	17	13	1	0	157²	147	1	57	60	12.1	3.08	86	.247	.321	15	.231	1	-8	-8	-0	-0.4

■ TIM DRUMMOND Drummond, Timothy Darnell b: 12/24/64, LaPlata, Md. BR/TR, 6'3", 170 lbs. Deb: 9/12/87

YEAR TM/L	W	L	PCT	G	GS	CG	SH	SV	IP	H	HR	BB	SO	RAT	ERA	ERA+	OAV	OOB	BH	AVG	PB	PR	/A	PD	TPI
1987 Pit-N	0	0	—	6	0	0	0	0	6	5	0	3	5	12.0	4.50	91	.227	.320	0	.000	-0	-0	-0	0	0.0
1989 Min-A	0	0	—	8	0	0	0	1	16¹	16	0	8	9	14.3	3.86	107	.246	.347	0	—	0	0	1	-0	0.0
1990 Min-A	3	5	.375	35	4	0	0	1	91	104	8	36	49	13.9	4.35	96	.295	.362	0	—	0	-5	-2	-1	-0.2
Total 3	3	5	.375	49	4	0	0	2	113¹	125	8	47	63	13.9	4.29	97	.284	.357	0	.000	-0	-5	-1	-1	-0.2

■ DON DRYSDALE Drysdale, Donald Scott b: 7/23/36, Van Nuys, Cal. BR/TR, 6'5", 190 lbs. Deb: 4/17/56 H

YEAR TM/L	W	L	PCT	G	GS	CG	SH	SV	IP	H	HR	BB	SO	RAT	ERA	ERA+	OAV	OOB	BH	AVG	PB	PR	/A	PD	TPI
1956 *Bro-N	5	5	.500	25	12	2	0	0	99	95	9	31	55	11.7	2.64	150	.255	.317	5	.192	1	12	15	1	1.8

YEAR	TM/L	W	L	PCT	G	GS	CG	SH	SV	IP	H	HR	BB	SO	RAT	ERA	ERA+	OAV	OOB	BH	AVG	PB	PR	/A	PD	TPI
1957	Bro-N	17	9	.654	34	29	9	4	0	221	197	17	61	148	10.8	2.69	155	.236	.294	9	.123	-0	29	**36**	5	**4.6**
1958	LA-N	12	13	.480	44	29	6	1	0	211²	214	21	72	131	12.8	4.17	98	.263	.333	15	.227	9	-5	-2	3	1.1
1959	*LA-N	17	13	.567	44	36	15	**4**	2	270²	237	26	93	**242**	11.6	3.46	122	.233	.308	15	.165	4	15	23	2	3.0
1960	LA-N	15	14	.517	41	36	15	5	2	269	214	27	72	**246**	**9.9**	2.84	140	.215	**.275**	13	.157	2	27	34	4	**4.4**
1961	LA-N	13	10	.565	40	37	10	3	0	244	236	29	83	182	12.5	3.69	118	.254	.331	16	.193	5	9	18	-1	2.3
1962	LA-N	**25**	9	.735	43	41	19	2	1	**314¹**	272	21	78	**232**	10.3	2.83	128	.230	.283	22	.198	5	**39**	28	1	3.3
1963	*LA-N	19	17	.528	42	42	17	3	0	315¹	287	25	57	251	10.1	2.63	115	.242	.283	16	.167	4	23	14	3	2.2
1964	LA-N	18	16	.529	40	40	21	5	0	**321¹**	242	15	68	237	9.0	2.18	148	.207	.256	19	.173	4	**48**	**38**	2	**4.8**
1965	*LA-N	23	12	.657	44	42	20	7	1	308¹	270	30	66	210	10.2	2.77	118	.232	.280	39	.300	20	26	17	1	4.1
1966	*LA-N	13	16	.448	40	40	11	3	0	273²	279	21	45	177	11.2	3.42	96	.265	.306	20	.189	4	6	-4	-0	-0.1
1967	LA-N	13	16	.448	38	38	9	3	0	282	269	19	60	196	10.8	2.74	113	.251	.296	12	.129	-0	20	11	3	1.4
1968	LA-N	14	12	.538	31	31	12	8	0	239	201	11	56	155	10.1	2.15	129	.231	.286	14	.177	1	22	16	2	2.3
1969	LA-N	5	4	.556	12	12	1	1	0	62²	71	9	13	24	12.4	4.45	75	.291	.332	3	.136	0	-6	-8	0	-0.6
Total	14	209	166	.557	518	465	167	49	6	3432	3084	280	855	2486	10.7	2.95	121	.239	.294	218	.186	59	266	230	25	34.6

■ MONK DUBIEL

Dubiel, Walter John b: 2/12/19, Hartford, Conn. d: 10/23/69, Hartford, Conn. BR/TR, 6', 190 lbs. Deb: 4/19/44

YEAR	TM/L	W	L	PCT	G	GS	CG	SH	SV	IP	H	HR	BB	SO	RAT	ERA	ERA+	OAV	OOB	BH	AVG	PB	PR	/A	PD	TPI
1944	NY-A	13	13	.500	30	28	19	3	0	232	217	12	86	79	11.8	3.38	103	.248	.316	15	.181	-2	1	3	0	0.2
1945	NY-A	10	9	.526	26	20	9	1	0	151¹	157	9	62	45	13.0	4.64	75	.266	.335	16	.276	4	-21	-20	-1	-1.7
1948	Phi-N	8	10	.444	37	17	6	2	4	150¹	139	13	58	42	11.9	3.89	101	.248	.320	7	.167	0	1	1	-1	0.0
1949	Chi-N	6	9	.400	32	20	3	1	4	147²	142	16	54	52	12.0	4.14	97	.250	.317	10	.286	3	-2	-2	2	0.3
1950	Chi-N	6	10	.375	39	12	4	2	2	142¹	152	12	67	51	13.9	4.16	101	.270	.348	9	.200	1	-0	1	2	0.3
1951	Chi-N	2	2	.500	22	0	0	0	1	54²	46	3	22	19	11.2	2.30	178	.232	.309	0	.000	-1	10	11	0	1.0
1952	Chi-N	0	0	—	1	0	0	0	0	0²	1	0	0	1	13.5	0.00	—	.333	.333	0	—	0	0	0	0	0.0
Total	7	45	53	.459	187	97	41	9	11	879¹	854	65	349	289	12.4	3.87	98	.254	.325	57	.207	5	-11	-6	1	0.1

■ BRIAN DuBOIS

DuBois, Brian Andrew b: 4/18/67, Joliet, Ill. BL/TL, 5'10", 165 lbs. Deb: 8/17/89

YEAR	TM/L	W	L	PCT	G	GS	CG	SH	SV	IP	H	HR	BB	SO	RAT	ERA	ERA+	OAV	OOB	BH	AVG	PB	PR	/A	PD	TPI
1989	Det-A	0	4	.000	6	5	0	0	1	36	29	2	17	13	12.0	1.75	218	.218	.316	0	—	0	9	8	0	0.9
1990	Det-A	3	5	.375	12	11	0	0	0	58¹	70	9	22	34	14.3	5.09	77	.310	.373	0	—	0	-8	-8	-1	-0.8
Total	2	3	9	.250	18	16	0	0	1	94¹	99	11	39	47	13.5	3.82	102	.276	.352	0	—	0	1	1	-1	0.1

■ JEAN DUBUC

Dubuc, Jean Joseph Octave Arthur "Chauncey"
b: 9/15/1888, St.Johnsbury, Vt. d: 8/28/58, Fort Myers, Fla. BR/TR, 5'10.5", 185 lbs. Deb: 6/25/08 C♦

YEAR	TM/L	W	L	PCT	G	GS	CG	SH	SV	IP	H	HR	BB	SO	RAT	ERA	ERA+	OAV	OOB	BH	AVG	PB	PR	/A	PD	TPI
1908	Cin-N	5	6	.455	15	9	7	1	0	85¹	62	2	41	32	11.4	2.74	84	.205	.309	4	.138	-1	-4	-4	1	-0.4
1909	Cin-N	2	5	.286	19	5	2	0	1	71¹	72	0	46	19	15.4	3.66	71	.269	.384	3	.167	0	-8	-8	0	-0.8
1912	Det-A	17	10	.630	37	26	23	2	3	250	217	2	109	97	12.0	2.77	118	.235	.321	29	.269	6	15	14	4	2.5
1913	Det-A	15	14	.517	36	28	22	1	2	242²	228	1	91	73	12.1	2.89	101	.252	.325	36	.267	5	1	1	8	1.9
1914	Det-A	13	14	.481	36	27	15	2	1	224	216	3	76	70	12.0	3.46	81	.257	.324	28	.226	7	-18	-16	4	-0.4
1915	Det-A	17	12	.586	39	33	22	5	2	258	231	6	88	74	11.5	3.21	94	.245	.316	23	.205	2	-8	-5	2	-0.2
1916	Det-A	10	10	.500	36	16	8	1	1	170¹	134	1	84	40	11.8	2.96	97	.233	.336	20	.256	5	-2	-2	5	0.9
1918	*Bos-A	0	1	.000	2	1	1	0	0	10²	11	1	5	1	13.5	4.22	64	.268	.348	1	.167	0	-2	-2	0	-0.1
1919	NY-N	6	4	.600	36	5	1	0	3	132	119	4	37	32	10.8	2.66	105	.246	.303	6	.143	-1	4	2	2	0.3
Total	9	85	76	.528	256	150	101	12	13	1444¹	1290	20	577	438	11.9	3.04	96	.244	.324	150	.230	21	-22	-21	25	3.7

■ JIM DUCKWORTH

Duckworth, James Raymond b: 5/24/39, National City, Cal. BR/TR, 6'4", 194 lbs. Deb: 4/13/63

YEAR	TM/L	W	L	PCT	G	GS	CG	SH	SV	IP	H	HR	BB	SO	RAT	ERA	ERA+	OAV	OOB	BH	AVG	PB	PR	/A	PD	TPI
1963	Was-A	4	12	.250	37	15	2	0	0	120¹	131	13	67	66	15.5	6.04	61	.278	.379	0	.000	-3	-32	-31	-1	-3.4
1964	Was-A	1	6	.143	30	2	0	0	3	56	52	9	25	56	12.9	4.34	85	.244	.332	2	.222	0	-4	-4	0	-0.3
1965	Was-A	2	2	.500	17	8	0	0	0	64	45	11	36	74	11.7	3.94	88	.202	.318	0	.000	-2	-3	-3	-1	-0.6
1966	Was-A	0	3	.000	5	4	0	0	0	14¹	14	2	10	14	15.7	5.02	69	.269	.385	0	.000	-0	-3	-2	0	-0.2
	KC-A	0	2	.000	8	0	0	0	1	12	14	2	10	10	18.8	9.00	38	.292	.424	0	.000	-0	-7	-7	-0	-0.7
	Yr	0	5	.000	13	4	0	0	1	26¹	28	4	20	24	16.7	6.84	50	.269	.392	0	.000	-1	-10	-10	-1	-0.9
Total	4	7	25	.219	97	29	2	0	4	267	256	37	148	220	14.2	5.26	69	.253	.358	2	.034	-5	-50	-49	-3	-5.2

■ CLISE DUDLEY

Dudley, Elzie Clise b: 8/8/03, Graham, N.C. d: 1/12/89, Moncks Corner, S.C. BL/TR, 6'1", 195 lbs. Deb: 4/18/29

YEAR	TM/L	W	L	PCT	G	GS	CG	SH	SV	IP	H	HR	BB	SO	RAT	ERA	ERA+	OAV	OOB	BH	AVG	PB	PR	/A	PD	TPI
1929	Bro-N	6	14	.300	35	21	8	1	0	156²	202	9	64	33	15.9	5.69	81	.315	.385	5	.098	-1	-17	-19	3	-1.4
1930	Bro-N	2	4	.333	21	7	2	0	1	66²	103	3	27	18	17.8	6.35	77	.371	.430	5	.208	0	-10	-11	1	-0.8
1931	Phi-N	8	14	.364	30	24	8	0	0	179	206	10	56	50	13.5	3.52	121	.287	.343	18	.214	2	7	14	2	1.7
1932	Phi-N	1	1	.500	13	0	0	0	1	17²	23	3	8	5	15.8	7.13	62	.329	.397	4	.286	3	-6	-5	0	-0.1
1933	Pit-N	0	0	—	1	0	0	0	0	0¹	6	0	1	0	189.0	135.00	2	.857	.875	0	—	0	-5	-5	0	-0.3
Total	5	17	33	.340	100	52	18	1	2	420¹	540	25	156	106	15.3	5.03	90	.315	.378	32	.185	2	-31	-24	5	-0.9

■ HAL DUES

Dues, Hal Joseph b: 9/22/54, LaMarque, Tex. BR/TR, 6'3", 180 lbs. Deb: 9/09/77

YEAR	TM/L	W	L	PCT	G	GS	CG	SH	SV	IP	H	HR	BB	SO	RAT	ERA	ERA+	OAV	OOB	BH	AVG	PB	PR	/A	PD	TPI
1977	Mon-N	1	1	.500	6	4	0	0	0	23	26	2	9	9	13.7	4.30	88	.265	.327	0	.000	-1	-1	-1	0	-0.1
1978	Mon-N	5	6	.455	25	12	1	0	1	99	85	5	42	36	11.9	2.36	149	.240	.327	6	.194	0	13	13	-0	1.4
1980	Mon-N	0	1	.000	6	1	0	0	0	12¹	17	1	4	2	15.3	6.57	54	.333	.382	0	.000	-0	-4	-4	0	-0.3
Total	3	6	8	.429	37	17	1	0	1	134¹	128	8	55	47	12.5	3.08	116	.254	.333	6	.154	-1	8	7	1	1.0

■ LARRY DUFF

Duff, Cecil Elba b: 11/30/1897, Radersburg, Mont. d: 11/10/69, Bend, Ore. BL/TR, 6'1", 175 lbs. Deb: 9/05/22

YEAR	TM/L	W	L	PCT	G	GS	CG	SH	SV	IP	H	HR	BB	SO	RAT	ERA	ERA+	OAV	OOB	BH	AVG	PB	PR	/A	PD	TPI
1922	Chi-A	1	1	.500	3	1	0	0	0	12²	16	1	3	7	13.5	4.97	82	.340	.380	2	.400	0	-1	-1	-0	0.0

■ JIM DUFFALO

Duffalo, James Francis b: 11/25/35, Helvetia, Pa. BR/TR, 6'1", 175 lbs. Deb: 4/12/61

YEAR	TM/L	W	L	PCT	G	GS	CG	SH	SV	IP	H	HR	BB	SO	RAT	ERA	ERA+	OAV	OOB	BH	AVG	PB	PR	/A	PD	TPI
1961	SF-N	5	1	.833	24	4	1	0	1	61²	59	9	32	37	13.6	4.23	90	.257	.352	5	.294	3	-1	-3	-0	0.0
1962	SF-N	1	2	.333	24	2	0	0	0	42	42	3	23	29	13.9	3.64	104	.256	.348	0	.000	-0	1	1	-1	0.0
1963	SF-N	4	2	.667	34	5	0	0	0	75¹	56	3	37	55	11.3	2.87	112	.209	.309	2	.111	-1	4	3	1	0.3
1964	SF-N	5	1	.833	35	3	1	0	3	74	57	9	31	55	10.9	2.92	122	.209	.294	1	.071	-1	5	5	-1	0.4
1965	SF-N	0	1	.000	2	0	0	0	0	0¹	1	0	2	0	81.0	27.00	13	.500	.750	0	—	0	-1	-1	0	0.0
	Cin-N	0	1	.000	22	0	0	0	0	44¹	33	3	30	34	13.8	3.45	109	.212	.356	0	.000	-1	0	1	1	0.1
	Yr	0	2	.000	24	0	0	0	0	44²	34	3	32	34	14.3	3.63	103	.215	.364	0	.000	-1	-0	1	1	0.1
Total	5	15	8	.652	141	14	2	0	6	297²	248	27	155	210	12.5	3.39	106	.227	.329	8	.127	0	8	7	-1	0.8

■ JOHN DUFFIE

Duffie, John Brown b: 10/4/45, Greenwood, S.C. BR/TR, 6'7", 210 lbs. Deb: 9/18/67

YEAR	TM/L	W	L	PCT	G	GS	CG	SH	SV	IP	H	HR	BB	SO	RAT	ERA	ERA+	OAV	OOB	BH	AVG	PB	PR	/A	PD	TPI
1967	LA-N	0	2	.000	2	2	0	0	0	9²	11	1	4	6	14.0	2.79	111	.282	.349	0	.000	-0	1	0	0	0.0

■ BERNIE DUFFY

Duffy, Bernard Allen b: 8/18/1893, Vinson, Okla. d: 2/9/62, Abilene, Tex. BR/TR, 5'11", 180 lbs. Deb: 9/20/13

YEAR	TM/L	W	L	PCT	G	GS	CG	SH	SV	IP	H	HR	BB	SO	RAT	ERA	ERA+	OAV	OOB	BH	AVG	PB	PR	/A	PD	TPI
1913	Pit-N	0	0	—	3	2	0	0	0	11¹	18	0	3	8	16.7	5.56	54	.360	.396	1	.250	0	-3	-3	0	-0.2

■ DAN DUGAN

Dugan, Daniel Phillip b: 2/22/07, Plainfield, N.J. d: 6/25/68, Green Brook, N.J. BL/TL, 6'1.5", 187 lbs. Deb: 9/05/28

YEAR	TM/L	W	L	PCT	G	GS	CG	SH	SV	IP	H	HR	BB	SO	RAT	ERA	ERA+	OAV	OOB	BH	AVG	PB	PR	/A	PD	TPI
1928	Chi-A	0	0	—	1	0	0	0	0	0¹	0	0	0	0	0.0	0.00	—	.000	.000	0	—	0	0	0	0	0.0
1929	Chi-A	1	4	.200	19	2	0	0	1	65	77	8	19	15	13.6	6.65	64	.300	.353	3	.150	-1	-17	-17	-2	-1.7
Total	2	1	4	.200	20	2	0	0	1	65¹	77	8	19	15	13.5	6.61	65	.298	.351	3	.150	-1	-17	-17	-2	-1.7

■ ED DUGAN

Dugan, Edward J. b: 1864, Brooklyn, N.Y. Deb: 8/05/1884

YEAR	TM/L	W	L	PCT	G	GS	CG	SH	SV	IP	H	HR	BB	SO	RAT	ERA	ERA+	OAV	OOB	BH	AVG	PB	PR	/A	PD	TPI
1884	Ric-a	5	14	.263	20	20	20	0	0	166¹	196	5	15	60	11.4	4.49	74	.278	.293	8	.114	-4	-23	-22	-2	-2.3

■ BILL DUGGLEBY

Duggleby, William James "Frosty Bill" b: 3/16/1874, Utica, N.Y. d: 8/30/44, Redfield, N.Y. TR, Deb: 4/21/1898

YEAR	TM/L	W	L	PCT	G	GS	CG	SH	SV	IP	H	HR	BB	SO	RAT	ERA	ERA+	OAV	OOB	BH	AVG	PB	PR	/A	PD	TPI
1898	Phi-N	3	3	.500	9	5	4	0	0	54	70	4	18	12	14.7	5.50	62	.311	.362	5	.238	2	-11	-12	1	-0.7
1901	Phi-N	19	12	.613	34	28	25	5	0	275²	294	9	40	94	11.1	2.87	118	.271	.301	19	.171	-3	14	16	5	1.9

YEAR TM/L	W	L	PCT	G	GS	CG	SH	SV	IP	H	HR	BB	SO	RAT	ERA	ERA+	OAV	OOB	BH	AVG	PB	PR	/A	PD	TPI
1902 Phi-A	1	1	.500	2	2	2	0	0	17	19	0	4	4	12.2	3.18	116	.283	.323	0	.000	-1	1	1	1	0.1
Phi-N	11	17	.393	33	28	25	0	1	258²	282	2	57	60	12.2	3.38	83	.277	.322	17	.173	-1	-17	-16	3	-1.3
1903 Phi-N	13	16	.448	36	30	28	3	2	264¹	318	4	79	57	13.9	3.75	87	.303	.358	24	.231	2	-14	-14	2	-0.9
1904 Phi-N	12	13	.480	32	27	22	2	1	223²	265	3	53	55	13.2	3.78	71	.292	.338	14	.171	1	-26	-27	1	-2.6
1905 Phi-N	18	17	.514	38	36	27	1	0	289	270	10	83	75	11.4	2.46	119	.253	.315	11	.109	-1	17	15	-1	1.2
1906 Phi-N	13	19	.406	42	30	22	5	2	280¹	241	5	66	83	10.2	2.25	116	.227	.280	14	.141	-1	12	11	1	1.2
1907 Phi-N	0	2	.000	5	2	2	0	0	29	43	2	11	8	18.3	7.45	33	.371	.447	1	.111	0	-16	-16	1	-1.3
Pit-N	2	2	.500	9	3	1	1	0	40¹	34	0	12	4	10.7	2.68	91	.239	.308	2	.154	-0	-1	-1	2	0.0
Yr	2	4	.333	14	5	3	1	0	69¹	77	2	23	12	13.2	4.67	52	.293	.354	4	.182	-1	-17	-17	1	-1.3
Total 8	92	102	.474	240	191	158	17	6	1732	1836	39	423	452	12.1	3.19	93	.272	.322	107	.166	-3	-41	-44	15	-2.4

■ MARTIN DUKE
Duke, Martin F. "Duck" (b: Martin F. Duck) b: Columbus, Ohio d: 12/31/1898, Minneapolis, Minn. TL, Deb: 8/24/1891

YEAR TM/L	W	L	PCT	G	GS	CG	SH	SV	IP	H	HR	BB	SO	RAT	ERA	ERA+	OAV	OOB	BH	AVG	PB	PR	/A	PD	TPI
1891 Was-a	0	3	.000	4	3	2	0	0	23	36	0	19	5	21.5	7.43	50	.345	.446	1	.111	-1	-9	-9	0	-0.7

■ JAN DUKES
Dukes, Noble Jan b: 8/16/45, Cheyenne, Wyo. BL/TL, 5'11", 175 lbs. Deb: 9/06/69

YEAR TM/L	W	L	PCT	G	GS	CG	SH	SV	IP	H	HR	BB	SO	RAT	ERA	ERA+	OAV	OOB	BH	AVG	PB	PR	/A	PD	TPI
1969 Was-A	0	2	.000	8	0	0	0	1	11	8	0	4	3	9.8	2.45	141	.216	.293	0	.000	0	1	1	-0	0.1
1970 Was-A	0	0	—	5	0	0	0	0	6²	6	0	1	4	10.8	2.70	132	.240	.296	0	.000	-0	1	1	0	0.1
1972 Tex-A	0	0	—	3	0	0	0	0	2¹	1	0	5	0	23.1	3.86	78	.167	.545	0	—	0	-0	-0	0	0.0
Total 3	0	2	.000	16	0	0	0	0	20	15	0	10	7	11.7	2.70	128	.221	.329	0	.000	0	2	2	-0	0.2

■ TOM DUKES
Dukes, Thomas Earl b: 8/31/42, Knoxville, Tenn. BR/TR, 6'2", 185 lbs. Deb: 8/15/67

YEAR TM/L	W	L	PCT	G	GS	CG	SH	SV	IP	H	HR	BB	SO	RAT	ERA	ERA+	OAV	OOB	BH	AVG	PB	PR	/A	PD	TPI
1967 Hou-N	0	2	.000	17	0	0	0	1	23²	25	2	11	23	14.5	5.32	62	.275	.365	1	.500	0	-5	-5	-0	-0.5
1968 Hou-N	2	2	.500	43	0	0	0	4	52²	62	3	28	37	15.7	4.27	69	.291	.379	0	.000	-0	-8	-8	0	-0.8
1969 SD-N	1	0	1.000	13	0	0	0	1	22¹	26	2	10	15	14.5	7.25	49	.295	.367	0	.000	-0	-9	-9	0	-0.8
1970 SD-N	1	6	.143	53	0	0	0	10	69	62	7	25	56	11.6	4.04	98	.246	.319	0	.000	-1	0	-1	-1	-0.1
1971 *Bal-A	1	5	.167	28	0	0	0	4	38¹	40	4	8	30	11.5	3.52	95	.263	.304	1	.143	-0	-0	-1	-1	0.0
1972 Cal-A	0	1	.000	7	0	0	0	1	11	11	1	0	8	9.8	1.64	178	.262	.279	0	—	0	2	2	-0	0.1
Total 6	5	16	.238	161	0	0	0	21	217	226	19	82	169	13.1	4.35	79	.270	.341	2	.095	-1	-20	-22	-2	-2.1

■ BOB DULIBA
Duliba, Robert John b: 1/9/35, Glen Lyon, Pa. BR/TR, 5'10", 180 lbs. Deb: 8/11/59

YEAR TM/L	W	L	PCT	G	GS	CG	SH	SV	IP	H	HR	BB	SO	RAT	ERA	ERA+	OAV	OOB	BH	AVG	PB	PR	/A	PD	TPI
1959 StL-N	0	1	.000	11	0	0	0	1	22²	19	2	12	14	12.3	2.78	153	.237	.337	0	.000	-0	3	4	1	0.4
1960 StL-N	4	4	.500	27	0	0	0	0	40²	49	6	16	23	14.4	4.20	97	.310	.374	1	.200	-0	-2	-0	-0	0.0
1962 StL-N	2	0	1.000	28	0	0	0	2	39¹	33	3	17	22	11.4	2.06	207	.239	.323	0	.000	-0	8	10	0	0.9
1963 LA-A	1	1	.500	6	0	0	0	1	7²	3	0	6	4	10.6	1.17	292	.125	.300	0	.000	-0	2	2	0	0.2
1964 LA-A	6	4	.600	58	0	0	0	9	72²	80	5	22	33	12.8	3.59	91	.287	.341	0	.000	-1	0	-2	1	-0.1
1965 Bos-A	4	2	.667	39	0	0	0	1	64¹	60	6	22	27	11.5	3.78	99	.248	.311	0	.000	-1	-2	-0	0	0.0
1967 KC-A	0	0	—	7	0	0	0	0	9²	13	3	1	6	13.0	6.52	49	.342	.359	0	—	0	-4	-4	0	-0.3
Total 7	17	12	.586	176	0	0	0	14	257	257	25	96	129	12.4	3.47	108	.268	.335	1	.038	-2	6	8	1	1.1

■ GEORGE DUMONT
Dumont, George Henry "Pea Soup" b: 11/13/1895, Minneapolis, Minn. d: 10/13/56, Minneapolis, Minn. BR/TR, 5'11", 163 lbs. Deb: 9/14/15

YEAR TM/L	W	L	PCT	G	GS	CG	SH	SV	IP	H	HR	BB	SO	RAT	ERA	ERA+	OAV	OOB	BH	AVG	PB	PR	/A	PD	TPI
1915 Was-A	2	1	.667	6	4	3	2	0	40	23	0	12	18	8.3	2.02	145	.169	.247	2	.167	-0	4	4	-1	0.3
1916 Was-A	2	3	.400	17	5	2	0	1	53	37	0	17	21	9.3	3.06	90	.194	.263	1	.071	-0	-1	-2	-1	-0.2
1917 Was-A	5	14	.263	37	23	8	2	2	204²	171	3	76	65	11.1	2.55	103	.227	.303	2	.034	-5	3	2	-3	-0.5
1918 Was-A	1	1	.500	4	1	1	0	0	14	18	0	6	12	15.4	5.14	53	.295	.358	1	.333	1	-4	-4	0	-0.2
1919 Bos-A	0	4	.000	13	2	0	0	0	35¹	45	1	19	12	16.6	4.33	70	.326	.411	0	.000	-0	-4	-5	0	-0.4
Total 5	10	23	.303	77	35	14	4	3	347	294	4	130	128	11.3	2.85	96	.230	.306	6	.064	-5	-3	-5	-4	-1.0

■ DAN DUMOULIN
Dumoulin, Daniel Lynn b: 8/20/53, Kokomo, Ind. BR/TR, 6', 175 lbs. Deb: 9/05/77

YEAR TM/L	W	L	PCT	G	GS	CG	SH	SV	IP	H	HR	BB	SO	RAT	ERA	ERA+	OAV	OOB	BH	AVG	PB	PR	/A	PD	TPI
1977 Cin-N	0	0	—	5	0	0	0	0	5¹	12	0	3	5	25.3	13.50	29	.462	.517	0	—	0	-6	-6	0	-0.4
1978 Cin-N	1	0	1.000	3	0	0	0	0	5	7	0	3	2	19.8	1.80	197	.368	.478	0	—	0	1	1	0	0.1
Total 2	1	0	1.000	8	0	0	0	0	10¹	19	0	6	7	22.6	7.84	48	.422	.500	0	—	0	-5	-5	0	-0.3

■ NICK DUMOVICH
Dumovich, Nicholas b: 1/2/02, Sacramento, Cal. d: 12/12/78, Laguna Hills, Cal. BL/TL, 6', 170 lbs. Deb: 4/20/23

YEAR TM/L	W	L	PCT	G	GS	CG	SH	SV	IP	H	HR	BB	SO	RAT	ERA	ERA+	OAV	OOB	BH	AVG	PB	PR	/A	PD	TPI
1923 Chi-N	3	5	.375	28	8	1	0	1	94	118	4	45	23	15.9	4.60	87	.319	.397	7	.241	1	-6	-6	1	-0.3

■ ED DUNDON
Dundon, Edward Joseph "Dummy" b: 7/10/1859, Columbus, Ohio d: 8/18/1893, Columbus, Ohio TR, Deb: 6/02/1883 ♦

YEAR TM/L	W	L	PCT	G	GS	CG	SH	SV	IP	H	HR	BB	SO	RAT	ERA	ERA+	OAV	OOB	BH	AVG	PB	PR	/A	PD	TPI
1883 Col-a	3	16	.158	20	19	16	0	0	166²	213	7	38	31	13.6	4.48	69	.292	.327	15	.161	-3	-22	-26	0	-2.4
1884 Col-a	6	4	.600	11	9	7	0	0	81	85	9	15	37	11.1	3.78	80	.255	.288	12	.140	-1	-5	-7	1	-0.5
Total 2	9	20	.310	31	28	23	0	0	247²	298	16	53	68	12.8	4.25	72	.280	.315	27	.151	-4	-27	-33	2	-2.9

■ JIM DUNEGAN
Dunegan, James William b: 8/6/47, Burlington, Iowa BR/TR, 6'1", 205 lbs. Deb: 5/28/70

YEAR TM/L	W	L	PCT	G	GS	CG	SH	SV	IP	H	HR	BB	SO	RAT	ERA	ERA+	OAV	OOB	BH	AVG	PB	PR	/A	PD	TPI
1970 Chi-N	0	2	.000	7	0	0	0	0	13¹	13	2	12	3	16.9	4.73	95	.277	.424	1	.250	0	-1	-0	1	0.1

■ WILEY DUNHAM
Dunham, Henry Huston b: 1/30/1877, Piketown, Ohio d: 1/16/34, Cleveland, Ohio 6'1", 180 lbs. Deb: 5/24/02

YEAR TM/L	W	L	PCT	G	GS	CG	SH	SV	IP	H	HR	BB	SO	RAT	ERA	ERA+	OAV	OOB	BH	AVG	PB	PR	/A	PD	TPI
1902 StL-N	2	3	.400	7	5	3	0	1	38	47	1	13	15	14.9	5.68	48	.303	.368	1	.083	-1	-12	-12	-0	-1.2

■ DAVEY DUNKLE
Dunkle, Edward Perks b: 8/30/1872, Phillipsburg, Pa. d: 11/19/41, Lock Haven, Pa. BB/TR, 6'2", 220 lbs. Deb: 8/28/1897

YEAR TM/L	W	L	PCT	G	GS	CG	SH	SV	IP	H	HR	BB	SO	RAT	ERA	ERA+	OAV	OOB	BH	AVG	PB	PR	/A	PD	TPI
1897 Phi-N	5	2	.714	7	7	7	0	0	62	72	0	23	19	13.8	3.48	121	.288	.348	4	.174	-1	6	5	-0	0.3
1898 Phi-N	1	4	.200	12	7	4	0	0	68¹	83	1	38	21	15.9	6.98	49	.297	.382	6	.214	-0	-26	-27	-1	-2.3
1899 Was-N	0	2	.000	4	2	2	0	0	26	46	3	4	9	20.8	10.04	39	.383	.448	3	.273	-0	-18	-18	-0	-1.3
1903 Chi-A	4	4	.500	12	7	6	0	1	82	96	1	31	26	13.9	4.06	69	.291	.352	10	.303	2	-10	-11	-2	-1.0
Was-A	5	9	.357	14	13	10	0	0	108¹	111	4	33	51	12.0	4.24	74	.264	.318	4	.098	-4	-15	-13	-2	-1.7
Yr	9	13	.409	26	20	16	0	1	190¹	207	5	64	77	12.8	4.16	72	.276	.333	1	.014	-2	-25	-25	-4	-2.7
1904 Was-A	2	9	.182	12	11	7	0	0	74¹	95	1	23	23	14.3	4.96	54	.311	.359	4	.143	-2	-20	-19	-0	-2.0
Total 5	17	30	.362	61	47	36	0	1	421	503	10	162	139	14.2	5.02	65	.295	.356	31	.189	-4	-83	-83	-6	-8.0

■ FRED DUNLAP
Dunlap, Frederick C. "Sure Shot" b: 5/21/1859, Philadelphia, Pa. d: 12/1/02, Philadelphia, Pa. BR/TR, 5'8", 165 lbs. Deb: 5/01/1880 M♦

YEAR TM/L	W	L	PCT	G	GS	CG	SH	SV	IP	H	HR	BB	SO	RAT	ERA	ERA+	OAV	OOB	BH	AVG	PB	PR	/A	PD	TPI
1884 StL-U	0	0	—	1	1	0	0	0	0²	2	0	0	1	27.0	13.50	22	.491	.491	185	.412	1	-1	-1	0	0.0
1887 *Det-N	0	0	—	1	0	0	0	0	2	4	0	0	1	18.0	4.50	89	.404	.404	72	.265	0	-0	-0	0	0.0
Total 2	0	0	—	2	0	0	0	1	2²	6	0	0	2	20.3	6.75	56	.429	.429	1159	.292	1	-1	-1	0	0.0

■ JACK DUNLEAVY
Dunleavy, John Francis b: 9/14/1879, Harrison, N.J. d: 4/12/44, S.Norwalk, Conn. TL, 5'6", 167 lbs. Deb: 5/30/03 ♦

YEAR TM/L	W	L	PCT	G	GS	CG	SH	SV	IP	H	HR	BB	SO	RAT	ERA	ERA+	OAV	OOB	BH	AVG	PB	PR	/A	PD	TPI
1903 StL-N	6	8	.429	14	13	9	0	0	102	101	2	57	51	14.6	4.06	80	.264	.371	48	.249	2	-9	-9	-1	-0.7
1904 StL-N	1	4	.200	7	5	5	0	0	55	63	4	23	28	14.2	4.42	61	.275	.344	40	.233	2	-10	-11	0	-0.9
Total 2	7	12	.368	21	18	14	0	0	157	164	6	80	79	14.5	4.18	73	.268	.361	193	.241	3	-19	-20	1	-1.6

■ JIM DUNN
Dunn, James William "Bill" b: 2/25/31, Valdosta, Ga. BR/TR, 6'0.5", 185 lbs. Deb: 8/26/52

YEAR TM/L	W	L	PCT	G	GS	CG	SH	SV	IP	H	HR	BB	SO	RAT	ERA	ERA+	OAV	OOB	BH	AVG	PB	PR	/A	PD	TPI
1952 Pit-N	0	0	—	3	0	0	0	0	5¹	4	0	3	2	11.8	3.38	118	.190	.292	0	.000	-0	0	0	0	0.0

■ JACK DUNN
Dunn, John Joseph b: 10/6/1872, Meadville, Pa. d: 10/22/28, Towson, Md. BR/TR, 5'9", Deb: 5/06/1897 ♦

YEAR TM/L	W	L	PCT	G	GS	CG	SH	SV	IP	H	HR	BB	SO	RAT	ERA	ERA+	OAV	OOB	BH	AVG	PB	PR	/A	PD	TPI
1897 Bro-N	14	9	.609	25	21	21	0	0	216²	251	6	66	26	13.2	4.57	90	.288	.338	29	.221	-2	-6	-11	2	-1.0
1898 Bro-N	16	21	.432	41	37	31	0	0	322²	352	10	82	66	12.1	3.60	100	.276	.319	41	.246	1	0	-0	4	0.0
1899 Bro-N	23	13	.639	44	34	29	2	2	299¹	323	8	86	48	12.3	3.70	106	.275	.325	30	.246	0	5	7	4	1.0
1900 Bro-N	3	4	.429	10	7	5	0	0	63	88	1	28	6	16.6	5.57	69	.329	.393	6	.231	-0	-13	-12	1	-0.9
Phi-N	5	5	.500	10	9	9	1	0	80	87	2	29	12	13.0	4.84	75	.276	.337	10	.303	1	-10	-11	-0	-0.8
Yr	8	9	.471	20	16	14	1	0	143	175	3	57	18	14.6	5.16	72	.301	.363	1	.017	1	-23	-23	1	-1.7

YEAR	TM/L	W	L	PCT	G	GS	CG	SH	SV	IP	H	HR	BB	SO	RAT	ERA	ERA+	OAV	OOB	BH	AVG	PB	PR	/A	PD	TPI
1901	Phi-N	0	1	.000	2	2	0	0	0	4²	11	0	7	1	38.6	21.21	16	.451	.599	1	1.000	1	-9	-9	0	-0.6
	Bal-A	3	3	.500	9	6	6	0	0	59²	74	2	21	5	14.3	3.62	107	.301	.356	90	.249	0	0	2	1	0.1
1902	NY-N	0	3	.000	3	2	2	0	0	26²	28	0	12	6	13.5	3.71	76	.270	.345	72	.211	0	-3	-3	1	-0.2
1904	NY-N	0	0	—	1	0	0	0	1	4	3	1	3	1	13.5	4.50	61	.167	.286	56	.309	0	-1	-1	0	0.0
Total	7	64	59	.520	142	118	103	3	3	1076²	1217	30	334	171	13.0	4.11	92	.283	.335	397	.245	1	-36	-38	7	-2.4

■ MIKE DUNNE
Dunne, Michael Dennis b: 10/27/62, South Bend, Ind. BR/TR, 6'4", 190 lbs. Deb: 6/05/87

YEAR	TM/L	W	L	PCT	G	GS	CG	SH	SV	IP	H	HR	BB	SO	RAT	ERA	ERA+	OAV	OOB	BH	AVG	PB	PR	/A	PD	TPI
1987	Pit-N	13	6	.684	23	23	5	1	0	163¹	143	10	68	72	11.7	3.03	136	.240	.319	5	.094	-1	19	20	3	2.3
1988	Pit-N	7	11	.389	30	28	1	0	0	170	163	15	88	70	13.6	3.92	87	.255	.349	5	.109	-1	-9	-10	1	-0.9
1989	Pit-N	1	1	.500	3	3	0	0	0	14¹	21	1	9	4	19.5	7.53	45	.328	.419	1	.250	0	-6	-7	0	-0.5
	Sea-A	2	9	.182	15	15	1	0	0	85¹	104	7	37	38	15.1	5.27	76	.307	.378	0	—	-1	-13	-12	1	-1.0
1990	SD-N	0	3	.000	10	6	0	0	0	28²	28	4	17	15	14.1	5.65	68	.241	.338	0	.000	-1	-6	-6	1	-0.5
Total	4	23	30	.434	81	75	7	1	0	461²	459	37	219	199	13.4	4.07	93	.262	.346	11	.101	-1	-15	-15	4	-0.6

■ ANDY DUNNING
Dunning, Andrew Jackson b: 8/12/1871, New York, N.Y. d: 6/21/52, New York, N.Y. BR/TR, 6', 175 lbs. Deb: 5/23/1889

YEAR	TM/L	W	L	PCT	G	GS	CG	SH	SV	IP	H	HR	BB	SO	RAT	ERA	ERA+	OAV	OOB	BH	AVG	PB	PR	/A	PD	TPI
1889	Pit-N	0	2	.000	2	2	2	0	0	18	20	1	16	4	18.0	7.00	54	.272	.403	0	.000	-1	-6	-6	0	-0.5
1891	NY-N	0	1	.000	1	1	0	0	0	2	3	1	3	2	27.0	4.50	71	.334	.501	0	—	0	-0	-0	0	0.0
Total	2	0	3	.000	3	3	2	0	0	20	23	2	19	6	18.9	6.75	55	.279	.414	0	.000	-1	-6	-7	0	-0.5

■ STEVE DUNNING
Dunning, Steven John b: 5/15/49, Denver, Colo. BR/TR, 6'2", 205 lbs. Deb: 6/14/70

YEAR	TM/L	W	L	PCT	G	GS	CG	SH	SV	IP	H	HR	BB	SO	RAT	ERA	ERA+	OAV	OOB	BH	AVG	PB	PR	/A	PD	TPI
1970	Cle-A	4	9	.308	19	17	0	0	0	94¹	93	16	54	77	14.4	4.96	80	.261	.364	5	.161	-1	-13	-11	1	-0.9
1971	Cle-A	8	14	.364	31	29	3	1	1	184	173	25	109	132	14.0	4.50	85	.254	.361	10	.182	1	-21	-14	2	-0.9
1972	Cle-A	6	4	.600	16	16	1	0	0	105	98	16	43	52	12.1	3.26	99	.248	.322	9	.273	5	-2	-0	-1	0.5
1973	Cle-A	0	2	.000	4	3	0	0	0	18	17	2	13	10	15.0	6.50	60	.250	.370	0	—	0	-5	-5	0	-0.4
	Tex-A	2	6	.250	23	12	2	0	0	94¹	101	11	52	38	14.7	5.34	70	.275	.367	0	—	0	-16	-17	0	-1.6
	Yr	2	8	.200	27	15	2	0	0	112¹	118	13	65	48	14.7	5.53	68	.271	.367	0	—	0	-21	-22	0	-2.0
1974	Tex-A	0	0	—	1	0	0	0	0	2¹	3	2	3	1	23.1	19.29	18	.333	.500	0	—	0	-4	-4	0	-0.2
1976	Cal-A	0	0	—	4	0	0	0	0	6	9	2	6	4	22.5	7.50	44	.310	.429	0	—	0	-3	-3	0	-0.2
	Mon-N	2	6	.250	32	7	1	0	0	91¹	93	6	33	72	12.6	4.14	90	.274	.342	2	.133	-0	-6	-4	0	-0.3
1977	Oak-A	1	0	1.000	6	0	0	0	0	18¹	17	2	10	4	13.3	3.93	102	.254	.351	0	—	0	0	0	0	0.0
Total	7	23	41	.359	136	84	7	1	1	613²	604	82	323	390	13.8	4.56	82	.261	.355	26	.194	6	-71	-58	3	-4.0

■ FRANK DUPEE
Dupee, Frank Oliver b: 4/29/1877, Monkton, Vt. d: 8/14/56, Portland, Me. TL, 6'1", 200 lbs. Deb: 8/24/01

YEAR	TM/L	W	L	PCT	G	GS	CG	SH	SV	IP	H	HR	BB	SO	RAT	ERA	ERA+	OAV	OOB	BH	AVG	PB	PR	/A	PD	TPI
1901	Chi-A	0	1	.000	2	0	0	0	0	0	0	0	3	0	—	∞	—	—	1.000	0	—	0	-3	-3	0	-0.21

■ MIKE DUPREE
Dupree, Michael Dennis b: 5/29/53, Kansas City, Kan. BR/TR, 6'1", 185 lbs. Deb: 4/13/76

YEAR	TM/L	W	L	PCT	G	GS	CG	SH	SV	IP	H	HR	BB	SO	RAT	ERA	ERA+	OAV	OOB	BH	AVG	PB	PR	/A	PD	TPI
1976	SD-N	0	0	—	12	0	0	0	0	15²	18	4	7	5	14.4	9.19	36	.286	.357	1	1.000	0	-10	-10	0	-0.9

■ KID DURBIN
Durbin, Blaine Alphonsus b: 9/10/1886, Kansas d: 9/11/43, Kirkwood, Mo. BL/TL, 5'8", 155 lbs. Deb: 4/24/07 ◆

YEAR	TM/L	W	L	PCT	G	GS	CG	SH	SV	IP	H	HR	BB	SO	RAT	ERA	ERA+	OAV	OOB	BH	AVG	PB	PR	/A	PD	TPI
1907	Chi-N	0	1	.000	5	1	1	0	0	16²	14	0	10	5	13.5	5.40	46	.233	.352	6	.333	1	-5	-5	0	-0.5

■ RYNE DUREN
Duren, Rinold George b: 2/22/29, Cazenovia, Wis. BR/TR, 6'2", 190 lbs. Deb: 9/25/54

YEAR	TM/L	W	L	PCT	G	GS	CG	SH	SV	IP	H	HR	BB	SO	RAT	ERA	ERA+	OAV	OOB	BH	AVG	PB	PR	/A	PD	TPI
1954	Bal-A	0	0	—	1	0	0	0	0	2	3	0	1	2	18.0	9.00	40	.333	.400	0	—	0	-1	-1	0	0.0
1957	KC-A	0	3	.000	14	6	0	0	1	42²	37	4	30	37	14.6	5.27	75	.236	.365	1	.071	-1	-7	-6	0	-0.6
1958	*NY-A	6	4	.600	44	1	0	0	20	75²	40	4	43	87	10.7	2.02	175	.157	.296	1	.077	0	15	13	-0	1.3
1959	NY-A	3	6	.333	41	0	0	0	14	76²	49	6	43	96	11.2	1.88	194	.181	.301	0	.000	-1	17	15	-1	1.4
1960	*NY-A	3	4	.429	42	1	0	0	9	49	27	3	49	67	15.2	4.96	72	.160	.369	0	.000	-1	-6	-7	-0	-0.7
1961	NY-A	0	1	.000	4	0	0	0	0	5	2	2	4	7	10.8	5.40	69	.125	.300	0	—	0	-1	-1	-0	0.0
	LA-A	6	12	.333	40	14	1	1	2	99	87	13	75	108	15.0	5.18	87	.233	.366	1	.040	-2	-13	-7	-2	-1.0
	Yr	6	13	.316	44	14	1	1	2	104	89	15	79	115	14.8	5.19	86	.229	.363	3	.120	-2	-14	-8	-2	-1.0
1962	LA-A	2	9	.182	42	3	0	0	8	71¹	53	1	57	74	14.6	4.42	87	.206	.363	1	.067	-1	-4	-4	-1	-0.6
1963	Phi-N	6	2	.750	33	7	1	0	2	87¹	65	6	52	84	12.6	3.30	98	.210	.332	3	.143	1	-0	-1	-2	-0.1
1964	Phi-N	0	0	—	2	0	0	0	0	3	5	0	1	5	21.0	6.00	58	.357	.438	0	—	0	-1	-1	-0	0.0
	Cin-N	0	2	.000	26	0	0	0	1	43²	41	1	15	39	12.2	2.89	125	.248	.322	0	.000	-0	3	4	-1	0.3
	Yr	0	2	.000	28	0	0	0	1	46²	46	1	16	44	12.5	3.09	117	.256	.327	1	.200	-0	2	3	-1	0.3
1965	Phi-N	0	0	—	6	0	0	0	0	11	10	0	4	6	12.3	3.27	106	.270	.357	0	—	-0	0	0	0	0.0
	Was-A	1	1	.500	16	0	0	0	0	23	24	0	18	18	17.6	6.65	52	.286	.429	0	—	0	-8	-8	-0	-0.8
Total	10	27	44	.380	311	32	2	1	57	589¹	443	40	392	630	13.4	3.83	98	.209	.344	7	.061	-5	-5	-6	-7	-0.8

■ DON DURHAM
Durham, Donald Gary b: 3/21/49, Yosemite, Ky. BR/TR, 6', 170 lbs. Deb: 7/16/72

YEAR	TM/L	W	L	PCT	G	GS	CG	SH	SV	IP	H	HR	BB	SO	RAT	ERA	ERA+	OAV	OOB	BH	AVG	PB	PR	/A	PD	TPI
1972	StL-N	2	7	.222	10	8	1	0	0	47²	42	1	22	35	12.1	4.34	78	.240	.325	7	.500	4	-5	-5	-1	0.0
1973	Tex-A	0	4	.000	15	4	0	0	1	40¹	49	7	23	23	16.3	7.59	49	.304	.395	0	—	0	-17	-17	-0	-1.6
Total	2	2	11	.154	25	12	1	0	1	88	91	8	45	58	14.0	5.83	61	.271	.359	7	.500	4	-22	-22	-1	-1.6

■ ED DURHAM
Durham, Edward Fant "Bull" b: 8/17/08, Chester, S.C. d: 4/27/76, Chester, S.C. BL/TR, 5'11", 170 lbs. Deb: 4/19/29

YEAR	TM/L	W	L	PCT	G	GS	CG	SH	SV	IP	H	HR	BB	SO	RAT	ERA	ERA+	OAV	OOB	BH	AVG	PB	PR	/A	PD	TPI
1929	Bos-A	1	0	1.000	14	1	0	0	0	22¹	34	2	14	6	19.3	9.27	46	.374	.457	0	.000	-0	-12	-12	0	-1.1
1930	Bos-A	4	15	.211	33	12	6	1	1	140	144	9	43	28	12.2	4.69	98	.270	.326	4	.098	-4	-1	-1	-0	-0.4
1931	Bos-A	8	10	.444	38	15	7	2	0	165¹	175	9	50	53	12.5	4.25	101	.266	.322	3	.056	-6	2	1	-2	-0.6
1932	Bos-A	6	13	.316	34	22	4	0	0	175¹	187	13	49	52	12.3	3.80	118	.274	.327	7	.123	-3	13	14	1	1.1
1933	Chi-A	10	6	.625	24	21	6	0	0	138²	137	12	46	65	12.2	4.48	95	.256	.320	10	.217	0	-3	-4	-2	-0.4
Total	5	29	44	.397	143	71	23	3	1	641²	677	45	202	204	12.5	4.45	99	.271	.329	24	.119	-14	-0	-3	-3	-1.4

■ JOHN DURHAM
Durham, John Garfield b: 10/7/1881, Douglass, Kan. d: 5/7/49, Coffeyville, Kan. 6', 175 lbs. Deb: 9/15/02

YEAR	TM/L	W	L	PCT	G	GS	CG	SH	SV	IP	H	HR	BB	SO	RAT	ERA	ERA+	OAV	OOB	BH	AVG	PB	PR	/A	PD	TPI
1902	Chi-A	1	1	.500	3	3	3	0	0	20	21	0	16	3	16.6	5.85	58	.270	.395	1	.067	-1	-5	-5	0	-0.5

■ BULL DURHAM
Durham, Louis Raphael (b: Louis Raphael Staub) b: 6/27/1877, New Oxford, Pa. d: 6/28/60, Bentley, Kan. BR/TR, 5'10", Deb: 9/15/04

YEAR	TM/L	W	L	PCT	G	GS	CG	SH	SV	IP	H	HR	BB	SO	RAT	ERA	ERA+	OAV	OOB	BH	AVG	PB	PR	/A	PD	TPI
1904	Bro-N	2	0	1.000	2	2	1	0	0	11	10	0	5	1	12.3	3.27	84	.250	.333	1	.250	0	-1	-1	-0	0.0
1907	Was-A	0	0	—	2	0	0	0	0	5	10	0	4	1	25.2	12.60	19	.415	.499	0	.000	-0	-6	-6	0	-0.5
1908	NY-N	0	0	—	1	0	0	0	0	2	2	0	1	2	13.5	9.00	27	.250	.333	0	—	0	-1	-1	-0	-0.1
1909	NY-N	0	0	—	4	0	0	0	0	11	15	0	2	2	13.9	3.27	78	.326	.354	0	.000	-0	-1	-1	0	0.0
Total	4	2	0	1.000	9	2	1	0	0	29	37	0	12	6	15.2	5.28	49	.313	.377	1	.143	-0	-9	-9	-0	-0.6

■ RICH DURNING
Durning, Richard Knott b: 10/10/1892, Louisville, Ky. d: 9/23/48, Castle Point, N.Y BL/TL, 6'2", 178 lbs. Deb: 4/16/17

YEAR	TM/L	W	L	PCT	G	GS	CG	SH	SV	IP	H	HR	BB	SO	RAT	ERA	ERA+	OAV	OOB	BH	AVG	PB	PR	/A	PD	TPI
1917	Bro-N	0	0	—	1	0	0	0	0	1	0	0	0	0	0.0	0.00	—	.000	.000	0	—	0	0	0	0	0.0
1918	Bro-N	0	0	—	1	0	0	0	0	2	3	0	4	0	31.5	13.50	21	.375	.583	0	—	0	-2	-2	0	-0.1
Total	2	0	0	—	2	0	0	0	0	3	3	0	4	0	21.0	9.00	31	.273	.467	0	—	0	-2	-2	0	-0.1

■ JESSE DURYEA
Duryea, James Whitney "Cyclone Jim" b: 9/7/1862, Osage, Iowa d: 8/7/42, Algona, Iowa BR/TR, 5'10", 175 lbs. Deb: 4/20/1889

YEAR	TM/L	W	L	PCT	G	GS	CG	SH	SV	IP	H	HR	BB	SO	RAT	ERA	ERA+	OAV	OOB	BH	AVG	PB	PR	/A	PD	TPI
1889	Cin-a	32	19	.627	53	48	38	2	1	401	372	9	127	183	11.2	2.56	152	.238	.296	44	.272	6	57	60	0	6.0
1890	Cin-N	16	12	.571	33	32	29	2	0	274	270	11	60	108	10.8	2.92	121	.152	-0	19	19	15	.152	-0	19	19	0	1.9
1891	Cin-N	1	9	.100	10	10	8	0	0	77	101	4	25	23	14.7	5.38	63	.305	.354	1	.031	-4	-17	-17	-0	-1.7
	StL-a	1	1	.500	3	3	2	0	0	24	19	0	10	13	10.9	3.38	125	.210	.289	4	.364	1	1	2	0	0.3
1892	Cin-N	2	5	.286	9	7	5	0	0	68	55	3	26	21	10.7	3.57	91	.212	.284	3	.111	-1	-2	-2	1	-0.1
	Was-N	3	11	.214	18	15	13	1	2	127	102	6	45	48	10.4	2.41	135	.212	.280	6	.120	-3	12	12	4	1.2
	Yr	5	16	.238	27	22	18	1	2	195	157	9	71	69	10.5	2.82	116	.212	.280	7	.091	-4	10	10	4	1.2
1893	Was-N	4	10	.286	17	15	9	0	0	117	182	8	56	20	18.3	7.54	61	.345	.407	13	.277	2	-37	-38	1	-2.6

YEAR	TM/L	W	L	PCT	G	GS	CG	SH	SV	IP	H	HR	BB	SO	RAT	ERA	ERA+	OAV	OOB	BH	AVG	PB	PR	/A	PD	TPI
Total 5		59	67	.468	143	130	104	5	3	1088	1101	41	349	416	12.0	3.45	109	.254	.310	86	.201	0	33	36	6	5.1

■ ERV DUSAK
Dusak, Ervin Frank "Four Sack"   b: 7/29/20, Chicago, Ill.   BR/TR, 6'2", 185 lbs.   Deb: 9/18/41 ♦

YEAR	TM/L	W	L	PCT	G	GS	CG	SH	SV	IP	H	HR	BB	SO	RAT	ERA	ERA+	OAV	OOB	BH	AVG	PB	PR	/A	PD	TPI
1948	StL-N	0	0	—	1	0	0	0	0	1	0	0	1	0	9.0	0.00	—	.000	.250	65	.209	0	0	0	0	0.0
1950	StL-N	0	2	.000	14	2	0	0	1	36¹	27	2	27	16	13.6	3.72	116	.211	.353	1	.083	-0	2	2	0	0.2
1951	StL-N	0	0	—	5	0	0	0	0	10	14	0	7	8	18.9	7.20	55	.333	.429	1	.500	1	-4	-4	0	-0.1
	Pit-N	0	1	.000	3	1	0	0	0	6²	10	2	9	2	27.0	12.15	35	.357	.526	12	.308	1	-6	-6	-0	-0.4
	Yr	0	1	.000	8	1	0	0	0	16²	24	2	16	10	22.1	9.18	44	.343	.471	3	.073	2	-10	-9	0	-0.5
Total 3		0	3	.000	23	3	0	0	1	54	51	4	44	26	16.2	5.33	79	.254	.393	251	.243	2	-8	-7	0	-0.3

■ CARL DUSER
Duser, Carl Robert   b: 7/22/32, Hazleton, Pa.   BL/TL, 6'1", 175 lbs.   Deb: 9/15/56

YEAR	TM/L	W	L	PCT	G	GS	CG	SH	SV	IP	H	HR	BB	SO	RAT	ERA	ERA+	OAV	OOB	BH	AVG	PB	PR	/A	PD	TPI
1956	KC-A	1	1	.500	2	2	0	0	0	6	14	0	2	5	24.0	9.00	48	.452	.485	0	.000	-0	-3	-3	0	-0.2
1958	KC-A	0	0	—	1	0	0	0	0	2	5	0	1	0	27.0	4.50	87	.500	.545	0	—	0	-0	-0	0	0.0
Total 2		1	1	.500	3	2	0	0	0	8	19	0	3	5	24.8	7.88	54	.463	.500	0	.000	-0	-3	-3	0	-0.2

■ BOB DUSTAL
Dustal, Robert Andrew   b: 9/28/35, Sayreville, N.J.   BR/TR, 6', 172 lbs.   Deb: 4/09/63

YEAR	TM/L	W	L	PCT	G	GS	CG	SH	SV	IP	H	HR	BB	SO	RAT	ERA	ERA+	OAV	OOB	BH	AVG	PB	PR	/A	PD	TPI
1963	Det-A	0	1	.000	7	0	0	0	0	6	10	0	5	4	22.5	9.00	42	.357	.455	0		0	-4	-4	1	-0.2

■ BILL DUZEN
Duzen, William George   b: 2/21/1870, Buffalo, N.Y.   d: 3/11/44, Buffalo, N.Y.   BR/TR, 5'11", 165 lbs.   Deb: 9/21/1890

YEAR	TM/L	W	L	PCT	G	GS	CG	SH	SV	IP	H	HR	BB	SO	RAT	ERA	ERA+	OAV	OOB	BH	AVG	PB	PR	/A	PD	TPI
1890	Buf-P	0	2	.000	2	2	2	0	0	13	22	1	14	5	23.5	13.85	30	.338	.465	1	.250	1	-14	-14	-0	-0.8

■ FRANK DWYER
Dwyer, John Francis   b: 3/25/1868, Lee, Mass.   d: 2/4/43, Pittsfield, Mass.   BR/TR, 5'8", 145 lbs.   Deb: 9/20/1888   MC

YEAR	TM/L	W	L	PCT	G	GS	CG	SH	SV	IP	H	HR	BB	SO	RAT	ERA	ERA+	OAV	OOB	BH	AVG	PB	PR	/A	PD	TPI
1888	Chi-N	4	1	.800	5	5	5	1	0	42	32	1	9	17	8.8	1.07	281	.203	.247	4	.190	-0	8	9	0	1.0
1889	Chi-N	16	13	.552	32	30	27	0	1	276	307	14	72	63	12.4	3.59	116	.273	.316	27	.200	-2	13	18	-2	1.3
1890	Chi-P	3	6	.333	12	6	6	0	1	69¹	98	4	25	17	16.0	6.23	70	.319	.371	14	.264	-0	-15	-15	1	-0.9
1891	Cin-a	13	19	.406	35	31	29	1	0	289	332	12	124	101	14.2	4.52	91	.279	.347	40	.284	3	-25	-13	1	-0.4
	Mil-a	6	4	.600	10	10	10	0	0	86	92	2	21	27	11.8	2.20	206	.264	.306	9	.225	-2	15	21	0	1.6
	Yr	19	23	.452	45	41	39	1	0	375	424	12	145	128	13.7	3.98	105	.275	.338	6	.033	2	-11	8	1	1.6
1892	StL-N	2	8	.200	10	10	6	0	0	64	90	1	24	16	16.0	5.63	57	.319	.373	2	.080	-1	-17	-17	1	-1.4
	Cin-N	19	10	.655	33	27	24	3	1	259¹	251	6	49	45	10.4	2.33	141	.244	.278	21	.163	-4	28	27	-1	2.1
	Yr	21	18	.538	43	37	30	3	1	323¹	341	7	73	61	11.5	2.98	109	.260	.299	8	.052	-5	11	10	0	0.7
1893	Cin-N	18	15	.545	37	30	28	1	2	287¹	332	17	93	53	13.3	4.13	116	.281	.333	24	.200	-3	17	21	3	1.8
1894	Cin-N	19	22	.463	45	40	34	1	1	348	471	27	106	49	14.9	5.07	110	.320	.365	46	.267	1	10	19	1	1.8
1895	Cin-N	18	15	.545	37	31	23	2	0	280¹	355	10	74	46	13.8	4.24	117	.304	.345	30	.265	2	17	23	0	2.1
1896	Cin-N	24	11	.686	36	34	30	3	1	288²	321	8	60	57	11.9	3.15	146	.279	.315	29	.264	4	39	47	-2	4.5
1897	Cin-N	18	13	.581	37	31	22	0	0	247¹	315	5	56	41	13.5	3.78	120	.307	.343	25	.266	-0	15	21	-3	1.7
1898	Cin-N	16	10	.615	31	28	24	0	0	240	257	3	42	29	11.2	3.04	126	.272	.303	12	.141	-5	15	21	1	1.6
1899	Cin-N	0	5	.000	5	5	2	0	0	32²	48	1	9	2	15.7	5.51	71	.341	.380	4	.364	1	-6	-6	0	-0.3
Total 12		176	152	.537	365	318	270	12	6	2810	3301	109	764	563	13.0	3.85	115	.286	.331	287	.230	-6	113	177	-0	16.9

■ BEN DYER
Dyer, Benjamin Franklin   b: 2/13/1893, Chicago, Ill.   d: 8/7/59, Kenosha, Wis.   BR/TR, 5'10", 170 lbs.   Deb: 5/23/14 ♦

YEAR	TM/L	W	L	PCT	G	GS	CG	SH	SV	IP	H	HR	BB	SO	RAT	ERA	ERA+	OAV	OOB	BH	AVG	PB	PR	/A	PD	TPI
1918	Det-A	0	0	—	2	0	0	0	0	1²	0	0	0	0	0.0	0.00	—	.000	.000	5	.278	0	1	0	0	0.1

■ EDDIE DYER
Dyer, Edwin Hawley   b: 10/11/1900, Morgan City, La.   d: 4/20/64, Houston, Tex.   BL/TL, 5'11.5", 168 lbs.   Deb: 7/08/22   M♦

YEAR	TM/L	W	L	PCT	G	GS	CG	SH	SV	IP	H	HR	BB	SO	RAT	ERA	ERA+	OAV	OOB	BH	AVG	PB	PR	/A	PD	TPI
1922	StL-N	0	0	—	2	0	0	0	0	3²	7	0	3	3	17.2	2.45	157	.412	.412	1	.333	0	1	1	0	0.1
1923	StL-N	2	1	.667	4	3	2	1	0	22	30	0	5	7	14.7	4.09	95	.333	.375	12	.267	-0	-0	-0	-0	0.0
1924	StL-N	8	11	.421	29	15	7	1	0	136²	174	6	51	23	15.1	4.61	82	.331	.395	18	.237	1	-11	-13	2	-0.8
1925	StL-N	4	3	.571	27	5	1	0	3	82¹	93	4	24	25	13.6	4.15	104	.278	.340	3	.097	-2	1	2	0	0.0
1926	StL-N	1	0	1.000	6	0	0	0	0	9¹	7	0	14	4		11.57	34	.219	.468	1	.500	0	-8	-8	0	-0.6
1927	StL-N	0	0	—	1	0	0	0	0	2	5	1	2	1	31.5	18.00	22	.500	.583	0	—	0	-3	-3	0	-0.2
Total 6		15	15	.500	69	23	10	2	3	256	316	11	96	63	14.9	4.75	84	.313	.380	35	.223	1	-21	-22	2	-1.5

■ MIKE DYER
Dyer, Michael Lawrence   b: 9/8/66, Upland, Cal.   BR/TR, 6'3", 195 lbs.   Deb: 6/29/89

YEAR	TM/L	W	L	PCT	G	GS	CG	SH	SV	IP	H	HR	BB	SO	RAT	ERA	ERA+	OAV	OOB	BH	AVG	PB	PR	/A	PD	TPI
1989	Min-A	4	7	.364	16	12	1	0	0	71	74	2	37	37	14.3	4.82	86	.273	.365	0	—	0	-7	-5	-1	-0.5

■ JIMMY DYGERT
Dygert, James Henry "Sunny Jim"   b: 7/5/1884, Utica, N.Y.   d: 2/8/36, New Orleans, La.   TR, 5'10", 185 lbs.   Deb: 9/08/05

YEAR	TM/L	W	L	PCT	G	GS	CG	SH	SV	IP	H	HR	BB	SO	RAT	ERA	ERA+	OAV	OOB	BH	AVG	PB	PR	/A	PD	TPI
1905	Phi-A	1	4	.200	6	3	2	0	0	35¹	41	2	11	24	13.2	4.33	61	.291	.343	4	.267	0	-7	-7	2	-0.4
1906	Phi-A	11	13	.458	35	25	15	4	0	213²	175	1	91	106	11.2	2.70	101	.227	.308	13	.176	-0	-1	1	1	0.2
1907	Phi-A	21	8	.724	42	28	18	5	1	261²	200	2	85	151	9.8	2.34	112	.214	.279	12	.128	-3	6	8	-1	0.4
1908	Phi-A	11	15	.423	41	27	15	5	1	238²	184	3	97	164	11.0	2.87	89	.220	.309	6	.080	-7	-12	-8	2	-1.3
1909	Phi-A	9	4	.643	32	12	6	1	0	137¹	117	1	50	79	11.7	2.42	99	.242	.327	1	.214	1	1	-0	-2	-0.1
1910	Phi-A	4	4	.500	19	8	6	1	0	99¹	81	0	49	59	12.1	2.54	94	.231	.331	3	.083	-2	-0	-2	-0	-0.6
Total 6		57	49	.538	175	103	62	16	2	986	798	9	383	583	11.0	2.65	97	.227	.307	47	.140	-11	-12	-8	-1	-1.8

■ JIMMY DYKES
Dykes, James Joseph   b: 11/10/1896, Philadelphia, Pa.   d: 6/15/76, Philadelphia, Pa.   BR/TR, 5'9", 185 lbs.   Deb: 5/06/18   MC♦

YEAR	TM/L	W	L	PCT	G	GS	CG	SH	SV	IP	H	HR	BB	SO	RAT	ERA	ERA+	OAV	OOB	BH	AVG	PB	PR	/A	PD	TPI
1927	Phi-A	0	0	—	2	0	0	0	1	2	2	0	1	0	13.5	4.50	95	.333	.429	135	.324	1	-0	-0	0	0.0

■ ARNOLD EARLEY
Earley, Arnold Carl   b: 6/4/33, Lincoln Park, Mich.   BL/TL, 6'1", 195 lbs.   Deb: 9/27/60

YEAR	TM/L	W	L	PCT	G	GS	CG	SH	SV	IP	H	HR	BB	SO	RAT	ERA	ERA+	OAV	OOB	BH	AVG	PB	PR	/A	PD	TPI
1960	Bos-A	0	1	.000	2	0	0	0	0	4	9	1	4	5	29.3	15.75	26	.429	.520	0	.000	0	-5	-5	-0	-0.4
1961	Bos-A	2	4	.333	33	0	0	0	7	49²	42	3	34	44	13.8	3.99	105	.226	.345	0	.000	-1	0	1	-0	0.0
1962	Bos-A	4	5	.444	38	3	0	0	5	68¹	76	8	46	59	16.2	5.80	71	.281	.388	2	.200	0	-14	-13	0	-1.1
1963	Bos-A	3	7	.300	53	4	0	0	1	115²	124	13	43	97	13.6	4.75	80	.270	.343	5	.278	1	-14	-12	0	-1.1
1964	Bos-A	1	1	.500	25	3	1	0	0	50¹	51	3	18	45	12.5	2.68	144	.266	.332	1	.111	0	5	7	1	0.4
1965	Bos-A	0	1	.000	57	0	0	0	0	74¹	79	5	29	47	13.4	3.63	103	.271	.344	0	.000	-0	-1	1	0	0.0
1966	Chi-N	2	1	.667	13	0	0	0	0	17²	14	1	9	12	11.7	3.57	103	.226	.324	0	—	-0	0	0	-1	0.0
1967	Hou-N	0	0	—	2	0	0	0	0	1¹	5	1	1	1	40.5	27.00	12	.625	.667	0	—	0	-4	-4	0	-0.2
Total 8		12	20	.375	223	10	1	0	14	381¹	400	35	184	310	14.1	4.48	87	.269	.354	8	.157	0	-33	-25	0	-2.0

■ THOMAS EARLEY
Earley, Thomas Francis Aloysius   b: 2/19/17, Roxbury, Mass.   d: 4/5/88, Nantucket, Mass.   BR/TR, 6', 180 lbs.   Deb: 9/27/38

YEAR	TM/L	W	L	PCT	G	GS	CG	SH	SV	IP	H	HR	BB	SO	RAT	ERA	ERA+	OAV	OOB	BH	AVG	PB	PR	/A	PD	TPI
1938	Bos-N	1	0	1.000	2	1	1	0	0	11	8	2	1	4	8.2	3.27	105	.186	.222	0	.000	-1	1	0	0	0.0
1939	Bos-N	1	4	.200	14	2	0	0	0	40	49	1	19	9	15.7	4.72	78	.304	.385	3	.300	0	-4	-5	1	-0.3
1940	Bos-N	2	0	1.000	4	1	1	1	0	16¹	16	1	3	5	11.6	3.86	96	.267	.323	2	.400	1	-0	-0	-0	0.1
1941	Bos-N	6	8	.429	33	13	6	1	3	138²	120	9	46	54	11.0	2.53	141	.233	.300	11	.234	1	17	16	-1	1.7
1942	Bos-N	6	11	.353	27	18	6	0	1	112²	120	10	55	28	14.1	4.71	71	.276	.359	4	.118	-1	-18	-17	1	-1.7
1945	Bos-N	2	1	.667	11	2	1	0	0	41	36	4	19	4	12.1	4.61	83	.235	.320	3	.214	1	-4	-4	0	-0.2
Total 6		18	24	.429	91	37	15	2	5	359²	349	27	143	104	12.5	3.78	94	.256	.330	23	.202	2	-7	-9	0	-0.4

■ BILL EARLEY
Earley, William Albert   b: 1/30/56, Cincinnati, Ohio   BR/TL, 6'4", 200 lbs.   Deb: 9/22/86

YEAR	TM/L	W	L	PCT	G	GS	CG	SH	SV	IP	H	HR	BB	SO	RAT	ERA	ERA+	OAV	OOB	BH	AVG	PB	PR	/A	PD	TPI
1986	StL-N	0	0	—	3	0	0	0	0	3	0	0	2	2	6.0	0.00	—	.000	.182	0	—	0	1	1	0	0.1

■ GEORGE EARNSHAW
Earnshaw, George Livingston "Moose"   b: 2/15/1900, New York, N.Y.   d: 12/1/76, Little Rock, Ark.   BR/TR, 6'4", 210 lbs.   Deb: 6/03/28   C

YEAR	TM/L	W	L	PCT	G	GS	CG	SH	SV	IP	H	HR	BB	SO	RAT	ERA	ERA+	OAV	OOB	BH	AVG	PB	PR	/A	PD	TPI
1928	Phi-A	7	7	.500	26	22	7	3	1	158¹	143	7	100	117	13.9	3.81	105	.240	.351	14	.246	1	4	4	-2	0.2
1929	*Phi-A	24	8	.750	44	33	13	3	1	254²	233	8	125	149	12.8	3.29	129	.241	.331	15	.172	-2	27	27	3	2.0
1930	*Phi-A	22	13	.629	49	39	20	3	2	296	299	20	139	193	13.3	4.44	105	.266	.347	26	.228	1	7	8	-1	0.6
1931	*Phi-A	21	7	.750	43	30	23	3	6	281²	255	16	75	152	10.6	3.67	122	.236	.288	30	.263	6	22	26	-0	3.1
1932	Phi-A	19	13	.594	36	33	21	1	0	245¹	262	28	94	109	13.2	4.77	95	.270	.336	26	.286	4	-8	-7	1	-0.1

YEAR	TM/L	W	L	PCT	G	GS	CG	SH	SV	IP	H	HR	BB	SO	RAT	ERA	ERA+	OAV	OOB	BH	AVG	PB	PR	/A	PD	TPI
1933	Phi-A	5	10	.333	21	18	4	0	0	117²	153	8	58	37	16.2	5.97	72	.311	.385	8	.182	-0	-22	-22	1	-1.8
1934	Chi-A	14	11	.560	33	30	16	2	0	227	242	28	104	97	13.9	4.52	105	.270	.349	16	.203	-0	-1	5	-1	0.5
1935	Chi-A	1	2	.333	3	3	0	0	0	18	26	2	11	8	18.5	9.00	51	.342	.425	2	.286	-0	-9	-9	0	-0.6
	Bro-N	8	12	.400	25	22	6	2	0	166	175	14	53	72	12.4	4.12	96	.270	.325	13	.217	1	-2	-3	0	-0.1
1936	Bro-N	4	9	.308	19	13	4	1	1	93	113	7	30	40	14.1	5.32	78	.297	.354	8	.242	1	-13	-12	-0	-1.0
	StL-N	2	1	.667	20	6	1	0	1	57²	80	4	20	28	16.1	6.40	62	.333	.392	4	.222	-0	-15	-16	1	-1.3
	Yr	6	10	.375	39	19	5	1	2	150²	193	11	50	68	14.7	5.73	71	.310	.364	0	.000	0	-29	-28	1	-2.3
Total	9	127	93	.577	319	249	115	18	12	1915¹	1981	142	809	1002	13.2	4.38	100	.265	.339	162	.230	9	-10	0	-5	1.5

■ LOGAN EASLEY Easley, Kenneth Logan b: 11/4/61, Salt Lake City, Utah BR/TR, 6'1", 185 lbs. Deb: 4/09/87

YEAR	TM/L	W	L	PCT	G	GS	CG	SH	SV	IP	H	HR	BB	SO	RAT	ERA	ERA+	OAV	OOB	BH	AVG	PB	PR	/A	PD	TPI
1987	Pit-N	1	1	.500	17	0	0	0	1	26¹	23	5	17	21	14.0	5.47	75	.242	.363	0	.000	-0	-4	-4	1	-0.2
1989	Pit-N	1	0	1.000	10	0	0	0	1	12¹	8	1	7	6	11.7	4.38	77	.190	.320	0	.000	-0	-1	-1	0	-0.1
Total	2	2	1	.667	27	0	0	0	2	38²	31	6	24	27	13.3	5.12	75	.226	.350	0	.000	-0	-5	-5	1	-0.3

■ MAL EASON Eason, Malcolm Wayne "Kid" b: 3/13/1879, Brookville, Pa. d: 4/16/70, Douglas, Ariz. TR , Deb: 10/01/00 U

YEAR	TM/L	W	L	PCT	G	GS	CG	SH	SV	IP	H	HR	BB	SO	RAT	ERA	ERA+	OAV	OOB	BH	AVG	PB	PR	/A	PD	TPI
1900	Chi-N	1	0	1.000	1	1	1	0	0	9	9	0	3	2	12.0	1.00	361	.260	.319	0	.000	-0	3	3	-0	0.2
1901	Chi-N	8	17	.320	27	25	23	1	0	220²	246	9	60	68	13.0	3.59	90	.280	.335	12	.138	-5	-7	-9	-1	-1.3
1902	Chi-N	1	1	.500	2	2	2	0	0	18	21	0	2	4	11.5	1.00	270	.291	.310	1	.200	0	4	3	0	0.5
	Bos-N	9	11	.450	27	26	20	2	0	206¹	237	4	59	50	13.4	2.75	103	.288	.344	6	.083	-7	1	2	1	0.2
	Yr	10	12	.455	29	28	22	2	0	224¹	258	4	61	54	13.2	2.61	108	.288	.341	3	.039	-6	4	5	1	0.2
1903	Det-A	2	5	.286	7	6	6	1	0	56¹	60	1	19	21	12.6	3.36	87	.272	.330	2	.100	-2	-2	-3	2	-0.2
1905	Bro-N	5	21	.192	27	27	20	3	0	207	230	5	72	64	13.3	4.30	67	.292	.355	14	.173	-1	-30	-32	2	-3.0
1906	Bro-N	10	17	.370	34	26	18	3	1	227	212	1	74	64	11.7	3.25	78	.256	.323	8	.091	-4	-16	-18	1	-2.2
Total	6	36	72	.333	125	113	90	10	1	944¹	1015	20	289	273	12.8	3.39	85	.278	.338	43	.121	-18	-47	-54	4	-6.3

■ CARL EAST East, Carlton William b: 8/27/1894, Marietta, Ga. d: 1/15/53, Whitesburg, Ga. BL/TR, 6'2", 178 lbs. Deb: 8/24/15 ♦

YEAR	TM/L	W	L	PCT	G	GS	CG	SH	SV	IP	H	HR	BB	SO	RAT	ERA	ERA+	OAV	OOB	BH	AVG	PB	PR	/A	PD	TPI
1915	StL-A	0	0	—	1	1	0	0	0	3¹	6	0	2	1	21.6	16.20	18	.400	.471	0	.000	-0	-5	-5	-0	-0.3

■ HUGH EAST East, Gordon Hugh b: 7/7/19, Birmingham, Ala. d: 11/2/81, Charleston, S.C. BR/TR, 6'2", 185 lbs. Deb: 9/13/41

YEAR	TM/L	W	L	PCT	G	GS	CG	SH	SV	IP	H	HR	BB	SO	RAT	ERA	ERA+	OAV	OOB	BH	AVG	PB	PR	/A	PD	TPI
1941	NY-N	1	1	.500	2	2	0	0	0	15²	19	0	9	4	16.1	3.45	107	.297	.384	2	.222	0	0	0	0	0.1
1942	NY-N	0	2	.000	4	1	0	0	0	7¹	15	1	7	2	27.0	9.82	34	.429	.524	1	.500	2	-5	-5	-0	-0.2
1943	NY-N	1	3	.250	13	5	1	0	0	40¹	51	4	25	21	17.0	5.36	64	.298	.388	1	.077	-1	-9	-9	-1	-0.9
Total	3	2	6	.250	19	8	1	0	0	63¹	85	5	41	27	17.9	5.40	65	.315	.405	4	.167	1	-14	-13	-1	-1.0

■ JAMIE EASTERLY Easterly, James Morris b: 2/17/53, Houston, Tex. BL/TL, 5'9", 180 lbs. Deb: 4/06/74

YEAR	TM/L	W	L	PCT	G	GS	CG	SH	SV	IP	H	HR	BB	SO	RAT	ERA	ERA+	OAV	OOB	BH	AVG	PB	PR	/A	PD	TPI
1974	Atl-N	0	0	—	3	0	0	0	0	2²	6	0	4	0	33.8	16.88	22	.400	.526	0	—	0	-4	-4	0	-0.3
1975	Atl-N	2	9	.182	21	13	0	0	0	68²	73	5	42	34	15.3	4.98	76	.275	.379	1	.056	-2	-10	-9	-0	-1.0
1976	Atl-N	1	1	.500	4	4	0	0	0	22	23	0	13	11	14.7	4.91	77	.280	.379	1	.111	-1	-3	-3	0	-0.2
1977	Atl-N	2	4	.333	22	5	0	0	1	58²	72	5	30	37	16.1	6.14	72	.303	.387	4	.267	1	-15	-11	-1	-1.0
1978	Atl-N	3	6	.333	37	6	0	0	1	78	91	9	45	42	15.9	5.65	72	.299	.393	4	.211	1	-18	-14	0	-1.2
1979	Atl-N	0	0	—	4	0	0	0	0	2²	7	0	3	3	33.8	13.50	30	.467	.556	0	—	0	-3	-3	0	-0.2
1981	*Mil-A	3	3	.500	44	0	0	0	4	62	46	9	34	31	11.6	3.19	107	.219	.328	0	—	0	3	2	0	0.2
1982	Mil-A	0	2	.000	28	0	0	0	2	30²	39	6	15	16	15.8	4.70	81	.312	.386	0	—	0	-2	-3	1	-0.1
1983	Mil-A	0	1	.000	12	0	0	0	1	11²	14	0	10	6	20.1	3.86	97	.350	.500	0	.000	0	-0	-0	0	-0.0
	Cle-A	4	2	.667	41	0	0	0	3	57	69	4	22	39	14.7	3.63	117	.309	.377	0	—	0	3	4	0	0.4
	Yr	4	3	.571	53	0	0	0	4	68²	83	4	32	45	15.3	3.67	113	.312	.390	0	.000	0	3	4	0	0.4
1984	Cle-A	3	1	.750	26	1	0	0	2	69¹	74	3	23	42	12.7	3.38	121	.273	.332	0	—	0	5	5	0	0.6
1985	Cle-A	4	1	.800	50	7	0	0	0	98²	96	9	53	58	14.0	3.92	105	.264	.363	0	—	0	2	2	-0	0.2
1986	Cle-A	0	2	.000	13	0	0	0	0	17²	27	3	12	9	19.9	7.64	54	.365	.453	0	—	0	-7	-7	-0	-0.6
1987	Cle-A	1	1	.500	16	0	0	0	0	31²	26	4	13	22	11.4	4.55	99	.218	.301	0	—	0	-0	-0	0	-0.0
Total	13	23	33	.411	321	36	0	0	14	611¹	663	48	319	350	14.7	4.62	87	.283	.373	10	.161	-0	-49	-40	0	-3.2

■ JACK EASTON Easton, John S. b: 2/28/1867, Bridgeport, Ohio d: 11/28/03, Steubenville, Ohio Deb: 9/23/1889

YEAR	TM/L	W	L	PCT	G	GS	CG	SH	SV	IP	H	HR	BB	SO	RAT	ERA	ERA+	OAV	OOB	BH	AVG	PB	PR	/A	PD	TPI
1889	Col-a	1	0	1.000	4	1	1	0	1	18	13	0	21	7	17.0	3.50	104	.196	.389	0	.000	-1	1	0	0	0.0
1890	Col-a	15	14	.517	37	29	23	0	1	255²	213	4	125	147	11.9	3.52	102	.220	.309	19	.178	0	10	2	1	0.2
1891	Col-a	5	10	.333	18	16	13	0	0	135¹	145	3	59	52	13.6	4.52	76	.265	.336	15	.238	2	-12	-16	1	-1.1
	StL-a	3	2	.600	7	6	4	0	0	47²	48	3	23	22	13.4	5.10	83	.253	.334	5	.179	-1	-7	-5	-1	-0.5
	Col-a	0	2	.000	2	2	2	0	0	15	15	2	4	13	11.4	3.60	96	.252	.299	0	.000	-1	-0	-0	-1	-0.0
	Yr	8	14	.364	27	24	19	0	0	198	208	8	86	87	13.4	4.59	79	.261	.333	6	.059	-0	-19	-21	-1	-1.6
1892	StL-N	2	0	1.000	5	2	2	0	0	31	38	2	26	4	18.6	6.39	50	.290	.408	3	.176	-0	-11	-11	0	-0.8
1894	Pit-N	0	1	.000	3	1	1	0	0	19²	26	0	4	1	13.7	4.12	127	.315	.346	0	.000	-1	3	2	-1	0.0
Total	5	26	29	.473	76	57	46	0	2	522¹	498	14	262	246	13.1	4.12	89	.243	.329	42	.176	-3	-16	-27	-0	-2.2

■ RAWLY EASTWICK Eastwick, Rawlins Jackson b: 10/24/50, Camden, N.J. BR/TR, 6'3", 180 lbs. Deb: 9/12/74

YEAR	TM/L	W	L	PCT	G	GS	CG	SH	SV	IP	H	HR	BB	SO	RAT	ERA	ERA+	OAV	OOB	BH	AVG	PB	PR	/A	PD	TPI
1974	Cin-N	0	0	—	8	0	0	0	2	17²	12	1	5	14	8.7	2.04	171	.188	.246	0	.000	-0	3	3	-0	0.3
1975	*Cin-N	5	3	.625	58	0	0	0	22	90	77	6	25	61	10.4	2.60	138	.229	.287	1	.067	-1	10	10	-2	0.7
1976	*Cin-N	11	5	.688	71	0	0	0	26	107²	93	3	27	70	10.2	2.09	168	.232	.284	0	.000	-2	17	17	-2	1.4
1977	Cin-N	2	2	.500	23	0	0	0	7	43¹	40	3	8	17	10.0	2.91	135	.244	.279	1	.167	-0	5	5	-1	0.4
	StL-N	3	7	.300	41	1	0	0	4	53²	74	6	21	30	15.9	4.70	82	.332	.354	2	.400	1	-5	-5	-1	-0.4
	Yr	5	9	.357	64	1	0	0	11	97	114	9	29	47	13.3	3.90	100	.295	.344	2	.182	1	-0	-0	-2	0.0
1978	NY-A	2	1	.667	8	0	0	0	0	24²	22	2	4	13	9.9	3.28	110	.232	.270	0	—	0	1	1	0	0.1
	*Phi-N	2	1	.667	22	0	0	0	0	40¹	31	5	18	14	10.9	4.02	89	.209	.295	0	.000	-0	-2	-2	-1	-0.2
1979	Phi-N	3	6	.333	51	0	0	0	6	82²	90	8	25	47	12.6	4.90	78	.284	.338	0	.000	-1	-11	-10	-2	-1.2
1980	KC-A	1	0	1.000	14	0	0	0	0	22	37	2	8	5	19.2	5.32	76	.363	.420	0	—	0	-3	-3	-1	-0.1
1981	Chi-N	0	1	.000	30	0	0	0	1	43¹	43	2	15	24	12.0	2.28	162	.264	.326	0	.000	-0	6	7	0	0.7
Total	8	28	27	.509	326	1	0	0	68	525¹	519	38	156	295	11.7	3.31	112	.258	.314	4	.071	-4	22	22	-6	1.7

■ CRAIG EATON Eaton, Craig b: 9/7/54, Glendale, Ohio BR/TR, 5'11", 175 lbs. Deb: 9/05/79

YEAR	TM/L	W	L	PCT	G	GS	CG	SH	SV	IP	H	HR	BB	SO	RAT	ERA	ERA+	OAV	OOB	BH	AVG	PB	PR	/A	PD	TPI
1979	KC-A	0	0	—	5	0	0	0	0	10	8	0	3	4	9.9	2.70	158	.222	.282	0	—	0	2	2	0	0.2

■ ZEB EATON Eaton, Zebulon Vance "Red" b: 2/2/20, Cooleemee, N.C. d: 12/17/89, W.Palm Beach, Fla. BR/TR, 5'10", 185 lbs. Deb: 4/18/44

YEAR	TM/L	W	L	PCT	G	GS	CG	SH	SV	IP	H	HR	BB	SO	RAT	ERA	ERA+	OAV	OOB	BH	AVG	PB	PR	/A	PD	TPI
1944	Det-A	0	0	—	6	0	0	0	0	15²	19	2	8	4	15.5	5.74	62	.322	.403	1	.100	-1	-4	-4	-0	-0.3
1945	*Det-A	4	2	.667	17	3	0	0	0	53¹	48	0	40	15	15.4	4.05	87	.247	.384	8	.250	2	-4	-3	0	0.0
Total	2	4	2	.667	23	3	0	0	0	69	67	2	48	19	15.4	4.43	80	.265	.388	9	.214	2	-8	-7	0	-0.3

■ GARY EAVE Eave, Gary Louis b: 7/22/63, Monroe, La. BR/TR, 6'4", 200 lbs. Deb: 4/12/88

YEAR	TM/L	W	L	PCT	G	GS	CG	SH	SV	IP	H	HR	BB	SO	RAT	ERA	ERA+	OAV	OOB	BH	AVG	PB	PR	/A	PD	TPI
1988	Atl-N	0	0	—	5	0	0	0	0	5	7	0	3	0	18.0	9.00	41	.333	.417	0	—	0	-3	-3	-0	-0.2
1989	Atl-N	2	0	1.000	3	3	0	0	0	20²	15	0	12	9	12.2	1.31	279	.200	.318	0	.000	-1	5	5	-1	0.5
1990	Sea-A	0	3	.000	8	5	0	0	0	30	27	5	20	16	14.7	4.20	94	.241	.366	0	—	0	-1	-1	0	0.0
Total	3	2	3	.400	16	8	0	0	0	55²	49	5	35	25	14.1	3.56	107	.236	.354	0	.000	-1	1	2	0	0.3

■ VALLIE EAVES Eaves, Vallie Ennis "Chief" "Tom" b: 9/6/11, Allen, Okla. d: 4/19/60, Norman, Okla. BR/TR, 6'2.5", 180 lbs. Deb: 9/12/35

YEAR	TM/L	W	L	PCT	G	GS	CG	SH	SV	IP	H	HR	BB	SO	RAT	ERA	ERA+	OAV	OOB	BH	AVG	PB	PR	/A	PD	TPI
1935	Phi-A	1	2	.333	3	3	1	0	0	14	12	0	15	6	17.4	5.14	88	.240	.415	0	.000	-1	-1	-1	-0	-0.1
1939	Chi-A	0	1	.000	2	1	1	0	0	11²	11	1	8	5	15.4	4.63	102	.250	.377	2	.333	0	-0	0	0	0.0
1940	Chi-A	0	2	.000	5	3	0	0	0	18²	22	2	24	11	22.7	6.75	66	.301	.480	0	.000	-1	-5	-5	-1	-0.5

YEAR TM/L	W	L	PCT	G	GS	CG	SH	SV	IP	H	HR	BB	SO	RAT	ERA	ERA+	OAV	OOB	BH	AVG	PB	PR	/A	PD	TPI
1941 Chi-N	3	3	.500	12	7	4	0	0	58²	56	4	21	24	12.3	3.53	99	.253	.327	2	.100	-1	1	-0	-1	-0.2
1942 Chi-N	0	0	—	2	0	0	0	0	3	4	0	2	0	21.0	9.00	36	.308	.438	-2	—	0	-2	-2	-0	-0.1
Total 5	4	8	.333	24	14	6	0	0	106	105	7	70	46	15.4	4.58	86	.262	.379	4	.114	-3	-7	-8	-2	-0.9

■ EDDIE EAYRS
Eayrs, Edwin b: 11/10/1890, Blackstone, Mass. d: 11/30/69, Warwick, R.I. BL/TL, 5'7", 160 lbs. Deb: 6/30/13 ♦

YEAR TM/L	W	L	PCT	G	GS	CG	SH	SV	IP	H	HR	BB	SO	RAT	ERA	ERA+	OAV	OOB	BH	AVG	PB	PR	/A	PD	TPI
1913 Pit-N	0	0	—	2	0	0	0	0	8	8	0	6	5	15.8	2.25	134	.267	.389	1	.167	-0	1	1	0	0.1
1920 Bos-N	1	2	.333	7	3	0	0	0	26¹	36	1	12	7	17.1	5.47	56	.346	.424	80	.328	2	-7	-7	1	-0.6
1921 Bos-N	0	0	—	2	0	0	0	0	4²	9	0	9	1	34.7	17.36	21	.391	.563	1	.067	-2	-7	-7	-0	-0.5
Total 3	1	2	.333	11	3	0	0	0	39	53	1	27	13	18.9	6.23	50	.338	.441	83	.306	0	-13	-14	1	-1.0

■ HARRY ECCLES
Eccles, Harry Josiah "Bugs" b: 7/9/1893, Kennedy, N.Y. d: 6/2/55, Jamestown, N.Y. BL/TL, 6'2", 170 lbs. Deb: 9/13/15

YEAR TM/L	W	L	PCT	G	GS	CG	SH	SV	IP	H	HR	BB	SO	RAT	ERA	ERA+	OAV	OOB	BH	AVG	PB	PR	/A	PD	TPI
1915 Phi-A	0	1	.000	5	1	0	0	1	21	18	2	6	13	10.3	4.71	62	.240	.296	1	.167	-0	-4	-4	-1	-0.4

■ DENNIS ECKERSLEY
Eckersley, Dennis Lee b: 10/3/54, Oakland, Cal. BR/TR, 6'2", 190 lbs. Deb: 4/12/75

YEAR TM/L	W	L	PCT	G	GS	CG	SH	SV	IP	H	HR	BB	SO	RAT	ERA	ERA+	OAV	OOB	BH	AVG	PB	PR	/A	PD	TPI
1975 Cle-A	13	7	.650	34	24	6	2	2	186²	147	16	90	152	11.8	2.60	145	.215	.312	0	—	0	24	24	-4	2.2
1976 Cle-A	13	12	.520	36	30	9	3	1	199¹	155	13	78	200	10.7	3.43	102	.214	.295	0	—	0	2	1	-2	0.0
1977 Cle-A	14	13	.519	33	33	12	3	0	247¹	214	31	54	191	10.0	3.53	112	.231	**.278**	0	—	0	15	11	-4	0.7
1978 Bos-A	20	8	.714	35	35	16	3	0	268²	258	30	71	162	11.3	2.99	138	.251	.304	0	—	0	23	34	-2	3.4
1979 Bos-A	17	10	.630	33	33	17	2	0	246²	234	29	59	150	10.9	2.99	**148**	.250	.298	0	—	0	34	**39**	0	**4.1**
1980 Bos-A	12	14	.462	30	30	8	0	0	197²	188	25	44	121	10.7	4.28	99	.248	.291	0	—	0	-5	-1	-2	-0.2
1981 Bos-A	9	8	.529	23	23	8	2	0	154	160	9	35	79	11.6	4.27	91	.267	.310	0	—	0	-10	-7	-1	-0.7
1982 Bos-A	13	13	.500	33	33	11	3	0	224¹	228	31	43	127	11.0	3.73	115	.261	.297	0	—	0	9	14	-1	1.3
1983 Bos-A	9	13	.409	28	28	2	0	0	176¹	223	27	39	77	13.7	5.61	77	.303	.343	0	—	0	-30	-25	-0	-2.3
1984 Bos-A	4	4	.500	9	9	2	0	0	64²	71	10	13	33	11.8	5.01	83	.284	.322	0	—	0	-7	-6	-1	-0.4
*Chi-N	10	8	.556	24	24	2	0	0	160¹	152	11	36	81	10.8	3.03	129	.250	.296	6	.109	-3	10	16	1	1.6
1985 Chi-N	11	7	.611	25	25	6	2	0	169¹	145	15	19	117	8.9	3.08	129	.229	.255	7	.125	0	10	17	-0	2.0
1986 Chi-N	6	11	.353	33	32	1	0	0	201	226	21	43	137	12.2	4.57	88	.285	.324	11	.159	1	-19	-12	-0	-0.9
1987 Oak-A	6	8	.429	54	2	0	0	16	115²	99	11	17	113	9.3	3.03	136	.228	.262	0	—	0	18	14	-1	1.3
1988 *Oak-A	4	2	.667	60	0	0	0	45	72²	52	5	11	70	7.9	2.35	161	.198	.233	0	—	0	13	12	-1	1.1
1989 *Oak-A	4	0	1.000	51	0	0	0	33	57²	32	5	3	55	5.6	1.56	236	.162	.178	0	—	0	15	14	-1	1.3
1990 *Oak-A	4	2	.667	63	0	0	0	48	73¹	41	2	4	73	5.5	0.61	609	.160	.172	0	—	0	27	25	-2	2.4
Total 16	169	140	.547	604	361	100	20	145	2815¹	2625	291	659	1938	10.7	3.49	116	.245	.293	24	.133	-1	126	172	-17	16.9

■ AL ECKERT
Eckert, Albert George "Obbie" b: 5/17/06, Milwaukee, Wis. d: 4/20/74, Milwaukee, Wis. BL/TL, 5'10", 174 lbs. Deb: 4/21/30

YEAR TM/L	W	L	PCT	G	GS	CG	SH	SV	IP	H	HR	BB	SO	RAT	ERA	ERA+	OAV	OOB	BH	AVG	PB	PR	/A	PD	TPI
1930 Cin-N	0	1	.000	2	1	0	0	0	5	7	0	4	1	19.8	7.20	67	.304	.407	0	.000	-0	-1	-1	0	0.0
1931 Cin-N	0	1	.000	14	1	0	0	0	18²	26	3	9	5	16.9	9.16	41	.325	.393	1	.333	0	-11	-11	-0	-1.0
1935 StL-N	0	0	—	2	0	0	0	0	3	7	0	1	1	24.0	12.00	34	.467	.500	0	—	0	-3	-3	0	-0.2
Total 3	0	2	.000	18	2	0	0	0	26²	40	3	14	7	18.2	9.11	44	.339	.409	1	.250	0	-15	-15	0	-1.2

■ CHARLIE ECKERT
Eckert, Charles William "Buzz" b: 8/8/1897, Philadelphia, Pa. d: 8/22/86, Trevose, Pa. BR/TR, 5'10.5", 165 lbs. Deb: 9/18/19

YEAR TM/L	W	L	PCT	G	GS	CG	SH	SV	IP	H	HR	BB	SO	RAT	ERA	ERA+	OAV	OOB	BH	AVG	PB	PR	/A	PD	TPI
1919 Phi-A	0	1	.000	2	1	1	0	0	16	17	1	3	6	11.3	3.94	87	.270	.303	1	.167	-0	-1	-1	0	0.0
1920 Phi-A	0	0	—	2	0	0	0	0	5²	8	0	1	1	15.9	4.76	84	.421	.476	0	.000	-0	-1	-0	-0	0.0
1922 Phi-A	0	2	.000	21	0	0	0	0	50	61	7	23	15	15.3	4.68	91	.319	.395	1	.091	-1	-4	-2	1	-0.1
Total 3	0	3	.000	25	1	1	0	0	71²	86	8	27	22	14.4	4.52	90	.315	.381	2	.111	-2	-5	-4	1	-0.1

■ DON EDDY
Eddy, Donald Eugene b: 10/25/46, Mason City, Iowa BR/TL, 5'11", 170 lbs. Deb: 9/07/70

YEAR TM/L	W	L	PCT	G	GS	CG	SH	SV	IP	H	HR	BB	SO	RAT	ERA	ERA+	OAV	OOB	BH	AVG	PB	PR	/A	PD	TPI
1970 Chi-A	0	0	—	7	0	0	0	0	11²	10	0	6	9	12.3	2.31	168	.244	.340	0	—	0	2	2	0	0.2
1971 Chi-A	0	2	.000	22	0	0	0	0	22²	19	3	19	14	15.1	2.38	151	.232	.376	1	1.000	1	3	3	-0	0.4
Total 2	0	2	.000	29	0	0	0	0	34¹	29	3	25	23	14.2	2.36	157	.236	.365	1	1.000	1	5	5	-0	0.6

■ STEVE EDDY
Eddy, Steven Allen b: 8/21/57, Sterling, Ill. BR/TR, 6'2", 185 lbs. Deb: 6/13/79

YEAR TM/L	W	L	PCT	G	GS	CG	SH	SV	IP	H	HR	BB	SO	RAT	ERA	ERA+	OAV	OOB	BH	AVG	PB	PR	/A	PD	TPI
1979 Cal-A	1	1	.500	7	4	0	0	0	32¹	36	1	20	7	16.1	4.73	86	.290	.397	0	—	0	-2	-2	1	-0.1

■ JOE EDELEN
Edelen, Benny Joe b: 9/16/55, Durant, Okla. BR/TR, 6', 165 lbs. Deb: 4/18/81

YEAR TM/L	W	L	PCT	G	GS	CG	SH	SV	IP	H	HR	BB	SO	RAT	ERA	ERA+	OAV	OOB	BH	AVG	PB	PR	/A	PD	TPI
1981 StL-N	1	0	1.000	13	0	0	0	0	17¹	29	2	3	10	17.1	9.35	38	.367	.398	1	.333	0	-11	-11	-0	-1.0
Cin-N	1	0	1.000	5	0	0	0	0	12²	5	1	0	5	3.6	0.71	500	.128	.128	0	.000	-0	4	4	-0	0.4
Yr	2	0	1.000	18	0	0	0	0	30	34	3	3	15	11.1	5.70	62	.283	.301	1	.000	0	-7	-7	-1	-0.6
1982 Cin-N	0	0	—	9	0	0	0	0	15¹	22	2	8	11	17.6	8.80	42	.344	.417	1	.500	0	-9	-9	0	-0.7
Total 2	2	0	1.000	27	0	0	0	0	45¹	56	5	11	26	13.5	6.75	53	.308	.351	2	.286	0	-16	-16	-1	-1.3

■ ED EDELEN
Edelen, Edward Joseph "Doc" b: 3/16/12, Bryantown, Md. d: 2/1/82, LaPlata, Md. BR/TR, 6', 191 lbs. Deb: 8/20/32

YEAR TM/L	W	L	PCT	G	GS	CG	SH	SV	IP	H	HR	BB	SO	RAT	ERA	ERA+	OAV	OOB	BH	AVG	PB	PR	/A	PD	TPI
1932 Was-A	0	0	—	2	0	0	0	0	1	0	0	6	0	54.0	27.00	16	.000	.600	0	—	0	-3	-3	0	-0.1

■ JOHN EDELMAN
Edelman, John Rogers b: 7/27/35, Philadelphia, Pa. BR/TR, 6'3", 185 lbs. Deb: 6/02/55

YEAR TM/L	W	L	PCT	G	GS	CG	SH	SV	IP	H	HR	BB	SO	RAT	ERA	ERA+	OAV	OOB	BH	AVG	PB	PR	/A	PD	TPI
1955 Mil-N	0	0	—	2	0	0	0	0	5²	7	0	8	2	23.8	11.12	34	.304	.484	0	—	0	-4	-5	0	-0.3

■ CHARLIE EDEN
Eden, Charles M. b: 1/18/1855, Lexington, Ky. d: 9/17/20, Cincinnati, Ohio BR/TR, Deb: 8/17/1877 ♦

YEAR TM/L	W	L	PCT	G	GS	CG	SH	SV	IP	H	HR	BB	SO	RAT	ERA	ERA+	OAV	OOB	BH	AVG	PB	PR	/A	PD	TPI
1884 Pit-a	0	1	.000	2	1	1	0	0	12	12	1	3	3	11.3	6.00	56	.246	.290	33	.270	1	-4	-4	-0	-0.2
1885 Pit-a	1	2	.333	4	1	0	0	0	15²	22	0	3	5	14.4	5.17	62	.318	.346	103	.254	1	-3	-3	-1	-0.2
Total 2	1	3	.250	6	2	1	0	0	27²	34	1	6	8	13.0	5.53	59	.288	.323	244	.261	1	-7	-7	-1	-0.4

■ TOM EDENS
Edens, Thomas Patrick b: 6/9/61, Ontario, Ore. BR/TR, 6'3", 185 lbs. Deb: 6/02/87

YEAR TM/L	W	L	PCT	G	GS	CG	SH	SV	IP	H	HR	BB	SO	RAT	ERA	ERA+	OAV	OOB	BH	AVG	PB	PR	/A	PD	TPI
1987 NY-N	0	0	—	2	2	0	0	0	8	15	2	4	4	21.4	6.75	56	.417	.475	0	.000	-0	-2	-3	0	-0.1
1990 Mil-A	4	5	.444	35	6	0	0	2	89	89	8	33	40	12.7	4.45	85	.262	.334	0	—	0	-5	-7	-1	-0.6
Total 2	4	5	.444	37	8	0	0	2	97	104	10	37	44	13.5	4.64	82	.277	.348	0	.000	-0	-8	-9	-0	-0.7

■ BUTCH EDGE
Edge, Claude Lee b: 7/18/56, Houston, Tex. BR/TR, 6'3", 203 lbs. Deb: 8/13/79

YEAR TM/L	W	L	PCT	G	GS	CG	SH	SV	IP	H	HR	BB	SO	RAT	ERA	ERA+	OAV	OOB	BH	AVG	PB	PR	/A	PD	TPI
1979 Tor-A	3	4	.429	9	9	1	0	0	51²	60	6	24	19	14.8	5.23	83	.283	.359	0	—	0	-6	-5	-0	-0.4

■ BILL EDGERTON
Edgerton, William Albert b: 8/16/41, South Bend, Ind. BL/TL, 6'2", 185 lbs. Deb: 9/03/66

YEAR TM/L	W	L	PCT	G	GS	CG	SH	SV	IP	H	HR	BB	SO	RAT	ERA	ERA+	OAV	OOB	BH	AVG	PB	PR	/A	PD	TPI
1966 KC-A	0	1	.000	6	1	0	0	0	8¹	10	0	7	3	18.4	3.24	105	.303	.425	0	—	0	0	0	0	0.0
1967 KC-A	1	0	1.000	7	0	0	0	0	8¹	11	1	3	6	16.2	2.16	147	.324	.395	0	—	0	1	1	0	0.1
1969 Sea-A	0	1	.000	4	0	0	0	0	4	10	1	0	2	24.8	13.50	27	.455	.478	0	—	0	-4	-4	0	-0.3
Total 3	1	2	.333	17	1	0	0	0	20²	31	2	10	11	18.7	4.79	70	.348	.426	0	—	0	-3	-3	1	-0.2

■ GEORGE EDMONDSON
Edmondson, George Henderson "Big Ed" b: 5/18/1896, Waxahachie, Tex. d: 7/11/73, Waco, Tex. BR/TR, 6'1", 179 lbs. Deb: 8/15/22

YEAR TM/L	W	L	PCT	G	GS	CG	SH	SV	IP	H	HR	BB	SO	RAT	ERA	ERA+	OAV	OOB	BH	AVG	PB	PR	/A	PD	TPI
1922 Cle-A	0	0	—	2	0	0	0	0	2	4	0	0	0	18.0	9.00	45	.444	.444	0	—	0	-1	-1	0	0.0
1923 Cle-A	0	0	—	1	0	0	0	0	4	8	0	3	0	27.0	11.25	35	.444	.545	0	.000	-0	-3	-3	0	-0.2
1924 Cle-A	0	0	—	5	1	0	0	0	8	10	1	5	3	16.9	9.00	47	.294	.385	1	.333	0	-4	-4	-0	-0.3
Total 3	0	0	—	8	1	0	0	0	14	22	1	8	3	19.9	9.64	43	.361	.443	1	.250	-0	-9	-9	-0	-0.5

■ PAUL EDMONDSON
Edmondson, Paul Michael b: 2/12/43, Kansas City, Kan. d: 2/13/70, Santa Barbara, Cal. BR/TR, 6'5", 195 lbs. Deb: 6/20/69

YEAR TM/L	W	L	PCT	G	GS	CG	SH	SV	IP	H	HR	BB	SO	RAT	ERA	ERA+	OAV	OOB	BH	AVG	PB	PR	/A	PD	TPI
1969 Chi-A	1	6	.143	14	13	1	0	0	87²	72	5	39	46	11.8	3.70	104	.227	.319	5	.172	-1	-1	2	3	0.4

■ BOB EDMONDSON
Edmondson, Robert E. b: 4/30/1879, Paris, Ky. d: 8/14/31, Lawrence, Kan. BR/TR, 5'11", 185 lbs. Deb: 9/15/06 ♦

YEAR TM/L	W	L	PCT	G	GS	CG	SH	SV	IP	H	HR	BB	SO	RAT	ERA	ERA+	OAV	OOB	BH	AVG	PB	PR	/A	PD	TPI
1906 Was-A	0	1	.000	2	1	0	0	0	10	10	0	2	0	10.8	4.50	59	.263	.300	1	.333	0	-2	-2	0	-0.1

YEAR	TM/L	W	L	PCT	G	GS	CG	SH	SV	IP	H	HR	BB	SO	RAT	ERA	ERA+	OAV	OOB	BH	AVG	PB	PR	/A	PD	TPI

■ SAM EDMONSTON   Edmonston, Samuel Sherwood "Big Sam"
b: 8/30/1883, Washington, D.C.   d: 4/12/79, Corpus Christi, Tex.   BL/TL, 5′11.5″, 185 lbs.   Deb: 6/24/07

| 1907 | Was-A | 0 | 0 | — | 1 | 0 | 0 | 0 | 0 | 3 | 8 | 0 | 1 | 0 | 27.0 | 9.00 | 27 | .487 | .516 | 0 | .000 | -0 | -2 | -2 | 0 | -0.1 |

■ EDWARDS   Edwards   Deb: 9/11/1875

| 1875 | Atl-n | 0 | 1 | .000 | 1 | 1 | 0 | 0 | 0 | 2 | 6 | 0 | 0 | | 27.0 | 9.00 | 26 | .429 | .429 | 1 | .200 | -0 | -1 | -1 | | 0.0 |

■ FOSTER EDWARDS   Edwards, Foster Hamilton "Eddie"   b: 9/1/03, Holstein, Iowa   d: 1/4/80, Orleans, Mass.   BR/TR, 6′3″, 175 lbs.   Deb: 7/02/25

1925	Bos-N	0	0	—	1	0	0	0	0	2	6	0	1	1	31.5	9.00	45	.545	.583	0	—	0	-1	-1	0	0.0
1926	Bos-N	2	0	1.000	3	3	1	0	0	25	20	0	13	4	11.9	0.72	492	.230	.330	0	.000	-1	9	8	0	0.7
1927	Bos-N	2	8	.200	29	11	1	0	0	92	95	2	45	37	14.0	4.99	74	.274	.362	1	.045	-2	-11	-13	-1	-1.4
1928	Bos-N	2	1	.667	21	3	2	0	0	49¹	67	4	23	17	16.8	5.66	69	.327	.400	1	.091	-1	-9	-10	0	-0.9
1930	NY-A	0	0	—	2	0	0	0	0	1²	5	0	2	1	37.8	21.60	20	.500	.583	0	—	0	-3	-3	0	-0.2
Total	5	6	9	.400	56	17	4	0	0	170	193	4	84	60	14.9	4.76	79	.292	.377	2	.048	-4	-16	-19	-1	-1.8

■ JIM JOE EDWARDS   Edwards, James Corbette "Little Joe"   b: 12/14/1894, Banner, Miss.   d: 1/19/65, Sarepta, Miss.   BR/TL, 6′2″, 185 lbs.   Deb: 5/14/22

1922	Cle-A	3	8	.273	25	7	0	0	0	92²	113	1	40	44	15.3	4.47	90	.313	.389	2	.087	-2	-4	-5	-1	-0.6
1923	Cle-A	10	10	.500	38	21	8	1	1	179¹	200	5	75	68	14.1	3.71	107	.286	.359	7	.119	-5	5	5	0	0.0
1924	Cle-A	4	3	.571	10	7	5	1	0	57	64	3	34	15	15.5	2.84	150	.305	.402	3	.150	-1	9	9	0	0.8
1925	Cle-A	0	3	.000	13	3	1	0	0	36	60	1	23	12	21.0	8.25	54	.382	.464	1	.111	-1	-15	-15	1	-1.3
	Chi-A	1	2	.333	9	4	1	1	0	45¹	46	4	23	20	13.9	3.97	105	.263	.352	3	.176	-1	2	1	1	0.1
	Yr	1	5	.167	22	7	2	1	0	81¹	106	4	46	32	16.9	5.86	73	.318	.403	0	.000	-2	-13	-14	1	-1.2
1926	Chi-A	6	9	.400	32	16	8	3	1	142	140	4	63	41	12.9	4.18	92	.264	.343	5	.109	-3	-3	-5	-1	-0.8
1928	Cin-N	2	2	.500	18	1	0	0	2	32	43	1	20	11	17.7	7.59	52	.347	.438	3	.300	0	-13	-13	-1	-1.2
Total	6	26	37	.413	145	59	23	6	4	584¹	666	18	278	211	14.7	4.37	92	.295	.376	24	.130	-13	-19	-23	-2	-3.0

■ SHERMAN EDWARDS   Edwards, Sherman Stanley   b: 7/25/09, Mt.Ida, Ark.   BR/TR, 6′, 165 lbs.   Deb: 9/21/34

| 1934 | Cin-N | 0 | 0 | — | 1 | 0 | 0 | 0 | 0 | 3 | 4 | 0 | 1 | 1 | 15.0 | 3.00 | 136 | .333 | .385 | 0 | .000 | -0 | 0 | 0 | 0 | 0.0 |

■ WAYNE EDWARDS   Edwards, Wayne Maurice   b: 3/7/64, Burbank, Cal.   BL/TL, 6′5″, 185 lbs.   Deb: 9/11/89

1989	Chi-A	0	0	—	7	0	0	0	0	7¹	7	1	3	9	12.3	3.68	103	.269	.345	0	—	0	0	0	0	0.0
1990	Chi-A	5	3	.625	42	5	0	0	2	95	81	6	41	63	11.8	3.22	119	.234	.321	0	—	0	7	6	0	0.7
Total	2	5	3	.625	49	5	0	0	2	102¹	88	7	44	72	11.9	3.25	117	.237	.322	0	—	0	7	6	0	0.7

■ HARRY EELLS   Eells, Harry Archibald "Slippery"   b: 2/14/1881, Ida Grove, Iowa   d: 10/15/40, Los Angeles, Cal.   BR/TR, 6′1″, 195 lbs.   Deb: 4/22/06

| 1906 | Cle-A | 4 | 5 | .444 | 14 | 8 | 6 | 1 | 0 | 86¹ | 77 | 1 | 48 | 35 | 13.0 | 2.61 | 101 | .242 | .341 | 6 | .188 | 0 | 1 | 0 | 0 | 0.1 |

■ WISH EGAN   Egan, Aloysius Jerome   b: 6/16/1881, Evart, Mich.   d: 4/13/51, Detroit, Mich.   6′3″, 185 lbs.   Deb: 9/03/02

1902	Det-A	0	2	.000	3	3	2	0	0	22	23	0	6	0	11.9	2.86	127	.269	.317	2	.250	-0	2	2	1	0.3
1905	StL-N	6	15	.286	23	19	18	0	0	171	189	2	39	29	12.5	3.58	83	.285	.333	6	.102	-3	-11	-11	5	-0.8
1906	StL-N	2	9	.182	16	12	7	0	0	86¹	97	3	27	23	13.1	4.59	57	.278	.333	2	.069	-2	-19	-19	1	-1.9
Total	3	8	26	.235	42	34	27	0	0	279¹	309	5	72	52	12.6	3.83	76	.282	.332	10	.104	-5	-28	-28	7	-2.4

■ JIM EGAN   Egan, James K. "Troy Terrier"   b: 1858, Derby, Conn.   d: 9/26/1884, New Haven, Conn.   TL,   Deb: 5/15/1882 ♦

| 1882 | Tro-N | 4 | 6 | .400 | 12 | 10 | 10 | 0 | 0 | 100 | 133 | 2 | 24 | 20 | 14.1 | 4.14 | 68 | .302 | .338 | 23 | .200 | -2 | -14 | -15 | -2 | -1.2 |

■ RIP EGAN   Egan, John Joseph   b: 7/9/1871, Philadelphia, Pa.   d: 12/22/50, Cranston, R.I.   5′11″, 168 lbs.   Deb: 4/30/1894 U

| 1894 | Was-N | 0 | 0 | — | 1 | 0 | 0 | 0 | 0 | 5 | 8 | 1 | 2 | 2 | 18.0 | 10.80 | 49 | .357 | .410 | 0 | .000 | -0 | -3 | -3 | 0 | -0.1 |

■ DICK EGAN   Egan, Richard Wallis   b: 3/24/37, Berkeley, Cal.   BL/TL, 6′4″, 193 lbs.   Deb: 4/09/63 C

1963	Det-A	0	1	.000	20	0	0	0	0	21	25	4	3	16	12.0	5.14	73	.287	.311	0	—	0	-4	-3	0	-0.2
1964	Det-A	0	0	—	23	0	0	0	0	34¹	33	4	17	21	13.4	4.46	82	.246	.336	0	.000	-0	-3	-3	1	-0.2
1966	Cal-A	0	0	—	11	0	0	0	0	14¹	17	2	6	11	14.4	4.40	76	.309	.377	0	.000	-0	-2	-2	-0	-0.1
1967	LA-N	1	1	.500	20	0	0	0	0	31²	34	3	15	20	15.1	6.25	50	.272	.368	0	.000	-0	-10	-11	-0	-1.1
Total	4	1	2	.333	74	0	0	0	0	101¹	109	13	41	68	13.8	5.15	67	.272	.347	0	.000	-1	-18	-19	0	-1.6

■ HOWARD EHMKE   Ehmke, Howard Jonathan "Bob"   b: 4/24/1894, Silver Creek, N.Y.   d: 3/17/59, Philadelphia, Pa.   BR/TR, 6′3″, 190 lbs.   Deb: 4/12/15

1915	Buf-F	0	2	.000	18	2	0	0	0	53²	69	2	25	18	16.6	5.53	56	.325	.409	0	.000	-2	-15	-14	2	-1.4
1916	Det-A	3	1	.750	5	4	4	0	0	37¹	34	0	15	15	11.8	3.13	91	.252	.327	2	.143	-1	-1	-1	1	0.0
1917	Det-A	10	15	.400	35	25	13	4	2	206	174	3	88	90	11.7	2.97	89	.243	.330	17	.246	2	-7	-7	2	-0.3
1919	Det-A	17	10	.630	33	31	20	2	0	248²	255	5	107	79	13.3	3.18	100	.274	.353	23	.253	3	1	0	4	0.7
1920	Det-A	15	18	.455	38	33	23	2	3	268¹	250	8	124	98	13.0	3.25	115	.253	.344	25	.238	2	16	14	6	2.1
1921	Det-A	13	14	.481	30	22	13	1	0	196¹	220	15	81	68	14.4	4.54	94	.286	.364	21	.284	2	-6	-6	1	-0.1
1922	Det-A	17	17	.500	45	30	16	1	1	279²	299	12	101	108	13.6	4.22	92	.281	.356	16	.157	-3	-5	-10	1	-1.2
1923	Bos-A	20	17	.541	43	39	28	2	3	316²	318	12	119	121	13.0	3.78	109	.272	.349	25	.223	-2	7	12	5	1.5
1924	Bos-A	19	17	.528	45	36	26	4	4	315	324	9	81	119	11.9	3.46	126	.265	.316	28	.222	-3	27	32	1	3.1
1925	Bos-A	9	20	.310	34	31	22	0	1	260²	285	8	85	95	13.2	3.73	122	.285	.348	13	.148	-6	19	24	4	2.1
1926	Bos-A	3	10	.231	14	14	7	1	0	97¹	115	3	45	38	15.2	5.46	75	.303	.382	5	.147	-1	-16	-15	1	-1.3
	Phi-A	12	4	.750	20	18	10	1	0	147¹	125	1	50	55	10.9	2.81	148	.232	.302	7	.152	-2	20	22	0	2.2
	Yr	15	14	.517	34	32	17	2	0	244²	240	4	95	93	12.5	3.86	107	.260	.332	3	.038	-3	4	7	1	0.9
1927	Phi-A	12	10	.545	30	27	10	1	0	189²	200	13	60	68	13.0	4.22	101	.281	.349	14	.206	-1	-2	1	3	0.2
1928	Phi-A	9	8	.529	23	18	5	1	0	139¹	135	6	44	34	11.8	3.62	111	.254	.316	11	.239	1	7	6	1	0.8
1929	*Phi-A	7	2	.778	11	8	2	0	0	54²	48	2	15	20	10.5	3.29	129	.233	.288	2	.105	-2	6	6	0	0.4
1930	Phi-A	0	1	.000	3	1	0	0	0	10	22	4	2	1	24.3	11.70	40	.458	.509	1	.333	0	-8	-8	0	-0.5
Total	15	166	166	.500	427	339	199	20	14	2820²	2873	103	1042	1030	12.9	3.75	105	.271	.343	210	.208	-11	44	53	30	8.3

■ RED EHRET   Ehret, Philip Sydney   b: 8/31/1868, Louisville, Ky.   d: 7/28/40, Cincinnati, Ohio   BR/TR, 6′, 175 lbs.   Deb: 7/07/1888 ♦

1888	KC-a	3	2	.600	7	6	5	0	0	52	58	1	22	12	13.8	3.98	86	.272	.340	12	.190	-1	-5	-3	1	-0.2
1889	Lou-a	10	29	.256	45	38	35	1	0	364	441	11	115	135	13.7	4.80	80	.290	.340	65	.252	2	-38	-39	3	-2.5
1890	*Lou-a	25	14	.641	43	38	35	4	2	359	351	5	79	174	10.8	2.53	152	.248	.288	31	.212	-3	53	53	-2	4.4
1891	Lou-a	13	13	.500	26	24	23	2	0	220²	225	2	70	76	12.0	3.47	105	.255	.310	22	.242	1	6	5	0	0.5
1892	Pit-N	16	20	.444	39	36	32	0	0	316	290	7	83	101	10.6	2.65	124	.234	.282	34	.258	-3	22	23	-3	2.1
1893	Pit-N	18	18	.500	39	35	32	4	0	314¹	322	3	115	70	12.5	3.44	133	.257	.320	24	.176	-5	43	39	1	2.9
1894	Pit-N	19	21	.475	46	38	31	1	0	346²	441	12	128	102	14.8	5.14	102	.306	.363	23	.176	-10	7	4	-1	-0.6
1895	StL-N	6	19	.240	37	32	18	0	0	231²	360	11	88	55	17.4	6.02	80	.349	.400	21	.219	-2	-32	-30	-1	-2.5
1896	Cin-N	18	14	.563	34	33	29	2	0	276²	298	5	74	60	12.1	3.42	135	.273	.319	20	.196	-3	29	37	0	3.1
1897	Cin-N	8	10	.444	34	19	11	0	2	184¹	256	3	47	43	14.8	4.78	95	.326	.364	13	.197	-3	-10	-5	-1	-0.6
1898	Lou-N	3	7	.300	12	10	9	0	0	89	130	3	20	20	15.2	5.76	62	.337	.370	9	.225	1	-21	-22	-1	-1.8
Total	11	139	167	.454	362	309	260	14	4	2754¹	3172	63	841	848	13.1	4.02	105	.282	.332	274	.217	-20	55	62	-3	4.7

■ RUBE EHRHARDT   Ehrhardt, Welton Claude   b: 11/20/1894, Beecher, Ill.   d: 4/27/80, Chicago Heights, Ill.   BR/TR, 6′2″, 190 lbs.   Deb: 7/18/24

1924	Bro-N	5	3	.625	15	9	6	2	0	83²	71	5	17	13	9.6	2.26	166	.232	.275	4	.138	-2	15	14	-1	1.1
1925	Bro-N	10	14	.417	36	24	12	0	1	207²	239	10	62	47	13.2	5.03	83	.293	.345	15	.211	2	-17	-20	5	-1.1
1926	Bro-N	2	5	.286	44	1	0	0	4	97	101	5	35	25	12.6	3.90	98	.275	.338	6	.250	0	-1	-1	-0	-0.1
1927	Bro-N	3	7	.300	46	3	2	0	2	95²	90	4	37	22	12.2	3.57	111	.264	.341	6	.250	1	4	4	3	0.8
1928	Bro-N	1	3	.250	28	2	1	0	2	54	74	1	27	12	17.0	4.67	85	.352	.429	4	.286	0	-4	-4	1	-0.2

YEAR TM/L	W	L	PCT	G	GS	CG	SH	SV	IP	H	HR	BB	SO	RAT	ERA	ERA+	OAV	OOB	BH	AVG	PB	PR	/A	PD	TPI
1929 Cin-N	1	2	.333	24	1	1	1	1	49¹	58	2	22	9	14.8	4.74	96	.305	.380	2	.182	-0	-0	-1	1	0.0
Total 6	22	34	.393	193	40	22	3	10	587¹	633	26	200	128	12.9	4.15	97	.284	.345	37	.214	1	-4	-7	7	0.5

■ HACK EIBEL
Eibel, Henry Hack b: 12/6/1893, Brooklyn, N.Y. d: 10/16/45, Macon, Ga. BL/TL, 5'11", 220 lbs. Deb: 6/13/12 ♦

YEAR TM/L	W	L	PCT	G	GS	CG	SH	SV	IP	H	HR	BB	SO	RAT	ERA	ERA+	OAV	OOB	BH	AVG	PB	PR	/A	PD	TPI
1920 Bos-A	0	0		3	0	0	0	0	10¹	10	0	3	5	11.3	3.48	105	.270	.325	8	.186	-0	0	0	-0	0.0

■ JUAN EICHELBERGER
Eichelberger, Juan Tyrone b: 10/21/53, St.Louis, Mo. BR/TR, 6'2", 195 lbs. Deb: 9/07/78

YEAR TM/L	W	L	PCT	G	GS	CG	SH	SV	IP	H	HR	BB	SO	RAT	ERA	ERA+	OAV	OOB	BH	AVG	PB	PR	/A	PD	TPI
1978 SD-N	0	0	—	3	0	0	0	0	3¹	4	0	2	2	16.2	10.80	31	.267	.353	0	—	0	-3	-3	0	-0.2
1979 SD-N	1	1	.500	3	3	1	0	0	21	15	1	11	12	11.1	3.43	103	.211	.317	2	.400	1	1	0	-0	0.1
1980 SD-N	4	2	.667	15	13	0	0	0	88²	73	8	55	43	13.1	3.65	94	.233	.350	3	.111	-1	-1	-2	-1	-0.3
1981 SD-N	8	8	.500	25	24	3	1	0	141¹	136	5	74	81	13.6	3.50	93	.259	.353	4	.087	-3	-0	-4	-1	-0.5
1982 SD-N	7	14	.333	31	24	8	0	0	177²	171	23	72	74	12.4	4.20	81	.251	.325	5	.091	-2	-12	-15	-1	-1.7
1983 Cle-A	4	11	.267	28	15	2	0	0	134	132	10	59	56	13.0	4.90	86	.259	.338	0		0	-13	-10	-0	-0.9
1988 Atl-N	2	0	1.000	20	0	0	0	0	37¹	44	3	10	13	13.0	3.86	95	.297	.342	0	.000	-0	-2	-1	1	0.0
Total 7	26	36	.419	125	79	14	1	0	603¹	575	50	283	281	12.9	4.10	87	.254	.339	14	.103	-4	-29	-35	-1	-3.5

■ MARK EICHHORN
Eichhorn, Mark Anthony b: 11/21/60, San Jose, Cal. BR/TR, 6'4", 200 lbs. Deb: 8/30/82

YEAR TM/L	W	L	PCT	G	GS	CG	SH	SV	IP	H	HR	BB	SO	RAT	ERA	ERA+	OAV	OOB	BH	AVG	PB	PR	/A	PD	TPI
1982 Tor-A	0	3	.000	7	7	0	0	0	38	40	4	14	16	12.8	5.45	82	.260	.321	0		0	-6	-4	-1	-0.4
1986 Tor-A	14	6	.700	69	0	0	0	10	157	105	8	45	166	9.0	1.72	245	.191	.261	0		0	43	44	1	4.5
1987 Tor-A	10	6	.625	89	0	0	0	4	127²	110	14	52	96	11.8	3.17	142	.234	.318	0		0	18	19	2	2.0
1988 Tor-A	0	3	.000	37	0	0	0	1	66²	79	3	27	28	15.1	4.18	94	.304	.382	0		0	-2	-2	1	0.0
1989 Atl-N	5	5	.500	45	0	0	0	0	68¹	70	6	19	49	11.9	4.35	84	.275	.327	0	.000	-0	-6	-5	2	-0.3
1990 Cal-A	2	5	.286	60	0	0	0	13	84²	98	2	23	69	13.5	3.08	127	.289	.345	0		0	8	8	1	0.9
Total 6	31	28	.525	307	7	0	0	28	542¹	502	37	180	424	11.7	3.17	131	.248	.317	0	.000	-0	55	59	6	6.7

■ DAVE EILAND
Eiland, David William b: 7/5/66, Dade City, Fla. BR/TR, 6'3", 210 lbs. Deb: 8/03/88

YEAR TM/L	W	L	PCT	G	GS	CG	SH	SV	IP	H	HR	BB	SO	RAT	ERA	ERA+	OAV	OOB	BH	AVG	PB	PR	/A	PD	TPI
1988 NY-A	0	0		3	3	0	0	0	12²	15	6	4	7	14.9	6.39	62	.294	.368	0		0	-3	-3	0	-0.2
1989 NY-A	1	3	.250	6	6	0	0	0	34¹	44	5	13	11	15.5	5.77	67	.328	.396	0		0	-7	-7	-1	-0.6
1990 NY-A	2	1	.667	5	5	0	0	0	30¹	31	2	5	16	10.7	3.56	111	.254	.283	0		0	1	1	-0	0.1
Total 3	3	4	.429	14	14	0	0	0	77¹	90	13	22	34	13.5	5.00	78	.293	.348	0		0	-9	-9	-0	-0.7

■ DAVE EILERS
Eilers, David Louis b: 12/3/36, Oldenburg, Tex. BR/TR, 5'11", 188 lbs. Deb: 7/27/64

YEAR TM/L	W	L	PCT	G	GS	CG	SH	SV	IP	H	HR	BB	SO	RAT	ERA	ERA+	OAV	OOB	BH	AVG	PB	PR	/A	PD	TPI
1964 Mil-N	0	0		6	0	0	0	0	7²	11	1	1	1	15.3	4.70	75	.333	.371	0		0	-1	-1	-0	0.0
1965 Mil-N	0	0		6	0	0	0	0	3²	8	1	0	1	19.6	12.27	29	.421	.421	0		0	-4	-4	0	-0.2
NY-N	1	1	.500	11	0	0	0	2	18	20	2	4	9	13.0	4.00	88	.274	.329	1	1.000	0	-1	-1	0	0.0
Yr	1	1	.500	17	0	0	0	2	21²	28	3	4	10	14.1	5.40	65	.304	.347	0	.000	0	-4	-5	-0	-0.2
1966 NY-N	1	1	.500	23	0	0	0	0	34²	39	7	7	14	12.2	4.67	78	.287	.326	0	.000	-0	-4	-4	1	-0.3
1967 Hou-N	6	4	.600	35	0	0	0	1	59¹	68	3	17	27	13.3	3.94	84	.296	.352	0	.000	-1	-4	-4	0	-0.4
Total 4	8	6	.571	81	0	0	0	3	123¹	146	14	29	52	13.3	4.45	78	.297	.345	1	.111	-0	-13	-14	1	-0.9

■ JAKE EISENHART
Eisenhart, Jacob Henry b: 10/3/22, Perkasie, Pa. d: 12/20/87, Huntingdon, Pa. BL/TL, 6'3.5", 195 lbs. Deb: 6/10/44

YEAR TM/L	W	L	PCT	G	GS	CG	SH	SV	IP	H	HR	BB	SO	RAT	ERA	ERA+	OAV	OOB	BH	AVG	PB	PR	/A	PD	TPI
1944 Cin-N	0	0	—	1	0	0	0	0	0¹	0	0	1	0	27.0	0.00	—	.000	.500	0	—	0	0	0	0	0.0

■ HARRY EISENSTAT
Eisenstat, Harry b: 10/10/15, Brooklyn, N.Y. BL/TL, 5'11", 185 lbs. Deb: 5/19/35

YEAR TM/L	W	L	PCT	G	GS	CG	SH	SV	IP	H	HR	BB	SO	RAT	ERA	ERA+	OAV	OOB	BH	AVG	PB	PR	/A	PD	TPI
1935 Bro-N	0	1	.000	2	0	0	0	0	4²	9	0	2	2	21.2	13.50	29	.429	.478	0	.000	-0	-5	-5	1	-0.3
1936 Bro-N	1	2	.333	5	2	1	0	0	14¹	22	1	6	5	17.6	5.65	73	.344	.400	1	.333	0	-3	-2	0	-0.1
1937 Bro-N	3	3	.500	13	4	0	0	0	47²	61	2	11	12	13.8	3.97	102	.308	.348	0	.000	-1	-0	0	1	0.1
1938 Det-A	9	6	.600	32	9	5	0	4	125¹	131	4	29	37	11.6	3.73	134	.266	.308	5	.139	-1	15	18	1	1.6
1939 Det-A	2	2	.500	10	2	1	0	0	29²	32	3	9	6	14.6	6.98	70	.315	.361	3	.375	1	-8	-7	1	-0.4
Cle-A	6	7	.462	26	11	4	1	2	103²	109	8	23	38	11.5	3.30	133	.265	.304	8	.250	1	15	13	-1	1.1
Yr	8	9	.471	36	13	5	1	2	133¹	148	11	32	44	12.2	4.12	110	.277	.317	1	.025	1	7	6	0	0.7
1940 Cle-A	1	4	.200	27	3	0	0	4	71²	78	6	12	27	11.3	3.14	134	.282	.311	6	.273	1	10	9	0	0.9
1941 Cle-A	1	1	.500	21	0	0	0	0	34	43	2	16	11	16.1	4.24	93	.312	.391	2	.333	1	-0	-1	-0	0.0
1942 Cle-A	2	1	.667	29	1	0	0	2	47²	58	1	6	19	12.1	2.45	140	.304	.325	1	.250	0	6	5	-0	0.5
Total 8	25	27	.481	165	32	11	1	14	478²	550	30	114	157	12.6	3.84	114	.287	.328	26	.211	1	30	29	2	3.4

■ ED EITELJORG
Eiteljorg, Edward Henry b: 10/14/1871, Berlin, Germany d: 12/7/42, Greencastle, Ind. 6'2", 190 lbs. Deb: 5/02/1890

YEAR TM/L	W	L	PCT	G	GS	CG	SH	SV	IP	H	HR	BB	SO	RAT	ERA	ERA+	OAV	OOB	BH	AVG	PB	PR	/A	PD	TPI
1890 Chi-N	0	1	.000	1	1	0	0	0	2	5	0	1	1	27.0	22.50	16	.458	.504	0	.000	-0	-4	-4	-0	-0.2
1891 Was-a	1	5	.167	8	7	6	0	0	61¹	79	3	41	23	17.6	6.16	61	.302	.397	5	.192	-1	-17	-17	2	-1.2
Total 2	1	6	.143	9	8	6	0	0	63¹	84	3	42	24	17.9	6.68	56	.308	.401	5	.185	-1	-21	-21	1	-1.4

■ HEINIE ELDER
Elder, Henry Knox b: 8/23/1890, Seattle, Wash. d: 11/13/58, Long Beach, Cal. BL/TL, 6'2", 200 lbs. Deb: 7/07/13

YEAR TM/L	W	L	PCT	G	GS	CG	SH	SV	IP	H	HR	BB	SO	RAT	ERA	ERA+	OAV	OOB	BH	AVG	PB	PR	/A	PD	TPI
1913 Det-A	0	0	—	1	0	0	0	0	3¹	4	0	5	0	24.3	8.10	36	.286	.474	0	.000	-0	-2	-2	-0	-0.1

■ HOD ELLER
Eller, Horace Owen b: 7/5/1894, Muncie, Ind. d: 7/18/61, Indianapolis, Ind BR/TR, 5'11.5", 185 lbs. Deb: 4/16/17

YEAR TM/L	W	L	PCT	G	GS	CG	SH	SV	IP	H	HR	BB	SO	RAT	ERA	ERA+	OAV	OOB	BH	AVG	PB	PR	/A	PD	TPI
1917 Cin-N	10	5	.667	37	11	7	1	1	152¹	131	2	37	77	10.1	2.36	111	.239	.290	6	.133	-2	6	4	-2	0.0
1918 Cin-N	16	12	.571	37	22	14	0	1	217²	205	1	59	84	11.2	2.36	113	.253	.309	11	.157	-2	10	8	-5	0.1
1919 *Cin-N	19	9	.679	38	30	16	7	2	248¹	216	7	50	137	9.8	2.39	116	.238	.281	26	.280	7	14	11	-5	1.4
1920 Cin-N	13	12	.520	35	22	15	1	0	210¹	208	6	52	76	11.3	2.95	103	.266	.315	22	.253	-1	4	2	-1	0.1
1921 Cin-N	2	2	.500	13	3	0	0	1	34¹	46	3	15	7	16.0	4.98	72	.322	.386	3	.231	0	-5	-5	-1	-0.5
Total 5	60	40	.600	160	88	52	9	5	863	806	19	213	381	10.8	2.62	108	.253	.303	68	.221	4	30	19	-14	1.1

■ JOE ELLICK
Ellick, Joseph J. b: 4/3/1854, Cincinnati, Ohio d: 4/21/23, Kansas City, Kan. 5'10", 162 lbs. Deb: 5/13/1875 MU♦

YEAR TM/L	W	L	PCT	G	GS	CG	SH	SV	IP	H	HR	BB	SO	RAT	ERA	ERA+	OAV	OOB	BH	AVG	PB	PR	/A	PD	TPI
1878 Mil-N	0	1	.000	1	0	0	0	0	3	1	0	1	0	6.0	3.00	87	.099	.180	2	.154	-0	-0	-0	0	0.0

■ BRUCE ELLINGSEN
Ellingsen, Harold Bruce b: 4/26/49, Pocatello, Idaho BL/TL, 6', 180 lbs. Deb: 7/04/74

YEAR TM/L	W	L	PCT	G	GS	CG	SH	SV	IP	H	HR	BB	SO	RAT	ERA	ERA+	OAV	OOB	BH	AVG	PB	PR	/A	PD	TPI
1974 Cle-A	1	1	.500	16	2	0	0	0	42	45	5	17	16	13.3	3.21	112	.278	.346	0	—	0	2	2	0	0.2

■ CLAUDE ELLIOTT
Elliott, Claude Judson "Chaucer" or "Old Pardee"
b: 11/17/1879, Pardeeville, Wis. d: 6/21/23, Pardeeville, Wis. BR/TR, 6', 190 lbs. Deb: 4/16/04

YEAR TM/L	W	L	PCT	G	GS	CG	SH	SV	IP	H	HR	BB	SO	RAT	ERA	ERA+	OAV	OOB	BH	AVG	PB	PR	/A	PD	TPI
1904 Cin-N	3	1	.750	9	6	4	1	0	57²	53	1	23	19	12.5	2.97	99	.247	.331	5	.208	1	-1	-0	0	0.1
NY-N	0	1	.000	3	1	1	0	0	15	21	2	3	8	14.4	3.00	91	.328	.358	1	.200	0	-0	-0	-1	0.0
Yr	3	2	.600	12	7	5	1	0	72²	74	3	26	27	12.4	2.97	97	.261	.324	1	.034	1	-2	-1	-0	0.1
1905 NY-N	0	1	.000	10	2	2	0	6	38	41	3	12	20	12.8	4.03	73	.270	.327	3	.188	-0	-4	-5	0	-0.4
Total 2	3	3	.500	22	9	7	1	6	110²	115	6	38	47	12.8	3.33	87	.267	.333	9	.200	1	-6	-5	0	-0.3

■ HAL ELLIOTT
Elliott, Harold William b: 5/29/1899, Mt.Clemens, Mich. d: 4/25/63, Honolulu, Hawaii BR/TR, 6'1.5", 170 lbs. Deb: 4/19/29

YEAR TM/L	W	L	PCT	G	GS	CG	SH	SV	IP	H	HR	BB	SO	RAT	ERA	ERA+	OAV	OOB	BH	AVG	PB	PR	/A	PD	TPI
1929 Phi-N	3	7	.300	40	8	2	0	2	114¹	146	5	59	32	16.1	6.06	86	.313	.390	5	.167	-1	-17	-11	1	-0.8
1930 Phi-N	6	11	.353	48	11	2	0	0	117¹	191	7	58	37	19.2	7.67	71	.382	.447	3	.094	-3	-35	-29	1	-2.5
1931 Phi-N	0	2	.000	16	4	0	0	2	33	46	5	19	8	18.0	9.55	44	.338	.423	1	.111	-0	-21	-19	0	-1.7
1932 Phi-N	2	4	.333	16	7	0	0	0	57²	70	5	38	13	16.9	5.77	76	.297	.394	3	.167	-0	-12	-9	-1	-0.8
Total 4	11	24	.314	120	30	4	0	4	322¹	453	22	174	90	17.6	6.95	73	.338	.415	12	.135	-5	-85	-68	2	-5.8

■ GLENN ELLIOTT
Elliott, Herbert Glenn "Lefty" b: 11/11/19, Sapulpa, Okla. d: 7/27/69, Portland, Ore. BB/TL, 5'10", 170 lbs. Deb: 4/17/47

YEAR TM/L	W	L	PCT	G	GS	CG	SH	SV	IP	H	HR	BB	SO	RAT	ERA	ERA+	OAV	OOB	BH	AVG	PB	PR	/A	PD	TPI
1947 Bos-N	0	1	.000	11	0	0	0	1	19	18	4	11	8	13.7	4.74	82	.269	.372	1	.500	0	-1	-2	0	0.0
1948 Bos-N	1	0	1.000	1	1	0	0	0	3	5	0	1	2	18.0	3.00	128	.357	.400	0	.000	-0	0	0	0	0.0

YEAR	TM/L	W	L	PCT	G	GS	CG	SH	SV	IP	H	HR	BB	SO	RAT	ERA	ERA+	OAV	OOB	BH	AVG	PB	PR	/A	PD	TPI
1949	Bos-N	3	4	.429	22	6	1	0	0	68¹	70	7	27	15	12.8	3.95	96	.269	.338	1	.059	-1	1	-1	1	-0.1
Total	3	4	5	.444	34	7	1	0	1	90¹	93	11	39	25	13.2	4.08	93	.273	.347	2	.095	-1	-0	-3	1	-0.1

■ JUMBO ELLIOTT
Elliott, James Thomas   b: 10/22/1900, St.Louis, Mo.   d: 1/7/70, Terre Haute, Ind.   BR/TL, 6'3", 235 lbs.   Deb: 4/21/23

YEAR	TM/L	W	L	PCT	G	GS	CG	SH	SV	IP	H	HR	BB	SO	RAT	ERA	ERA+	OAV	OOB	BH	AVG	PB	PR	/A	PD	TPI
1923	StL-A	0	0	—	1	0	0	0	0	1	1	0	3	0	36.0	27.00	15	.333	.667	0	—	0	-3	-3	0	-0.1
1925	Bro-N	0	2	.000	3	1	0	0	0	10²	17	0	9	3	22.8	8.44	50	.362	.474	0	.000	-1	-5	-5	-0	-0.4
1927	Bro-N	6	13	.316	30	21	12	2	3	188¹	188	5	60	99	11.9	3.30	120	.269	.327	9	.141	-1	13	14	-4	0.8
1928	Bro-N	9	14	.391	41	21	7	2	1	192	194	8	64	74	12.4	3.89	102	.268	.332	12	.176	2	2	2	-3	0.1
1929	Bro-N	1	2	.333	6	3	0	0	0	19	21	2	16	7	18.0	6.63	70	.280	.413	1	.250	0	-4	-4	-0	-0.3
1930	Bro-N	10	7	.588	35	21	6	2	1	198¹	204	16	70	59	12.7	3.95	124	.271	.337	10	.147	-2	23	21	-2	1.5
1931	Phi-N	**19**	14	.576	**52**	30	12	2	5	249	288	15	83	99	13.6	4.27	100	.287	.344	11	.122	-7	-11	-1	-5	-1.0
1932	Phi-N	11	10	.524	39	22	8	0	0	166	210	14	47	62	14.0	5.42	81	.300	.346	12	.197	-1	-28	-19	-2	-1.9
1933	Phi-N	6	10	.375	35	21	6	0	2	161²	188	8	49	43	13.4	3.84	99	.295	.348	12	.231	0	-9	-0	-4	-0.2
1934	Phi-N	0	1	.000	3	1	0	0	0	5¹	8	0	4	1	21.9	10.13	47	.333	.448	0	.000	-0	-4	-3	-0	-0.2
	Bos-N	1	1	.500	7	3	0	0	0	15¹	19	2	9	6	17.0	5.87	65	.284	.377	1	.250	0	-3	-3	-0	-0.2
	Yr	1	2	.333	10	4	0	0	0	20²	27	2	13	7	17.9	6.97	58	.293	.387	1	.200	0	-7	-7	-0	-0.4
Total	10	63	74	.460	252	144	51	8	12	1206²	1338	70	414	453	13.3	4.24	100	.283	.344	68	.163	-8	-29	1	-20	-1.9

■ DOCK ELLIS
Ellis, Dock Phillip   b: 3/11/45, Los Angeles, Cal.   BB/TR, 6'3", 205 lbs.   Deb: 6/18/68

YEAR	TM/L	W	L	PCT	G	GS	CG	SH	SV	IP	H	HR	BB	SO	RAT	ERA	ERA+	OAV	OOB	BH	AVG	PB	PR	/A	PD	TPI
1968	Pit-N	6	5	.545	26	10	2	0	0	104	82	4	38	52	10.5	2.51	117	.213	.285	2	.069	-1	5	5	0	0.4
1969	Pit-N	11	17	.393	35	33	8	2	0	218²	206	14	76	173	11.8	3.58	97	.250	.316	6	.088	-3	0	-2	1	-0.4
1970	•Pit-N	13	10	.565	30	30	9	4	0	201²	194	9	87	128	13.0	3.21	121	.257	.342	7	.100	-3	19	15	2	1.5
1971	•Pit-N	19	9	.679	31	31	11	2	0	226²	207	15	63	137	10.8	3.06	111	.239	.292	16	.203	2	10	8	0	1.2
1972	•Pit-N	15	7	.682	25	25	4	1	0	163¹	156	6	33	96	10.6	2.70	123	.253	.294	9	.153	-1	14	11	-1	1.0
1973	Pit-N	12	14	.462	28	28	3	1	0	192	176	7	55	122	11.1	3.05	115	.240	.299	7	.108	-3	13	10	1	0.9
1974	Pit-N	12	9	.571	26	26	9	0	0	176²	163	13	41	91	10.7	3.16	109	.242	.292	12	.214	3	9	6	-1	0.8
1975	•Pit-N	8	9	.471	27	24	5	2	0	140	163	9	43	69	13.4	3.79	93	.292	.345	4	.111	0	-3	-4	-1	-0.4
1976	•NY-A	17	8	.680	32	32	8	1	0	211²	195	14	76	65	11.7	3.19	107	.247	.316	0	—	0	8	5	-2	0.3
1977	NY-A	1	1	.500	3	3	1	0	0	19²	18	1	8	5	11.9	1.83	215	.237	.310	0	—	0	5	5	-0	0.5
	Oak-A	1	5	.167	7	7	0	0	0	26	35	5	14	11	17.3	9.69	42	.315	.397	0	—	0	-16	-16	-0	-1.4
	Tex-A	10	6	.625	23	22	7	1	1	167¹	158	13	42	90	10.8	2.90	140	.254	.301	0	—	0	21	22	-1	2.1
	Yr	12	12	.500	33	32	8	1	1	213	211	19	64	106	11.6	3.63	112	.260	.314	0	—	0	10	10	-2	1.2
1978	Tex-A	9	7	.563	22	22	3	0	0	141¹	131	15	46	45	11.4	4.20	89	.245	.307	0	—	0	-7	-7	1	-0.6
1979	Tex-A	1	5	.167	10	9	0	0	0	46²	64	5	16	10	15.4	5.98	60	.323	.374	0	—	0	-9	-9	-0	-0.8
	NY-N	3	7	.300	17	14	1	0	0	85	110	14	9	34	41	15.4	6.04	60	.320	.383	2	.077	-1	-22	-23	0	-2.2
	Pit-N	0	0	—	3	1	0	0	0	7	9	1	2	1	14.1	2.57	151	.346	.393	0	.000	-0	1	1	0	0.1
	Yr	3	7	.300	20	15	1	0	0	92	119	10	36	42	15.2	5.77	63	.316	.375	1	.037	-2	-21	-22	0	-2.1
Total	12	138	119	.537	345	317	71	14	1	2127²	2067	140	674	1136	11.5	3.46	103	.255	.315	65	.133	-7	49	26	-1	3.0

■ JIM ELLIS
Ellis, James Russell   b: 3/25/45, Tulare, Cal.   BR/TL, 6'2", 185 lbs.   Deb: 8/11/67

YEAR	TM/L	W	L	PCT	G	GS	CG	SH	SV	IP	H	HR	BB	SO	RAT	ERA	ERA+	OAV	OOB	BH	AVG	PB	PR	/A	PD	TPI
1967	Chi-N	1	1	.500	8	1	0	0	0	16²	20	1	9	8	15.7	3.24	109	.313	.397	1	.200	0	0	1	-0	0.1
1969	StL-N	0	0	—	2	1	0	0	0	5¹	7	0	3	0	16.9	1.69	212	.318	.400	0	—	0	1	1	-0	0.1
Total	2	1	1	.500	10	2	0	0	0	22	27	1	12	8	16.0	2.86	124	.314	.398	1	.200	0	1	2	-0	0.2

■ SAMMY ELLIS
Ellis, Samuel Joseph   b: 2/11/41, Youngstown, Ohio   BL/TR, 6'1", 175 lbs.   Deb: 4/14/62   C

YEAR	TM/L	W	L	PCT	G	GS	CG	SH	SV	IP	H	HR	BB	SO	RAT	ERA	ERA+	OAV	OOB	BH	AVG	PB	PR	/A	PD	TPI
1962	Cin-N	2	2	.500	8	4	0	0	0	28	29	6	29	27	19.0	6.75	60	.269	.428	2	.200	-0	-9	-8	-0	-0.7
1964	Cin-N	10	3	.769	52	5	2	0	14	122¹	101	9	28	125	9.6	2.57	140	.223	.270	2	.083	-0	13	14	-0	1.5
1965	Cin-N	22	10	.688	44	39	15	2	2	263²	222	22	104	183	11.3	3.79	99	.226	.304	12	.125	-1	-7	-1	-3	-0.4
1966	Cin-N	12	19	.387	41	36	7	0	0	221	226	35	78	154	12.5	5.29	74	.264	.328	8	.114	-3	-41	-34	-3	-3.7
1967	Cin-N	8	11	.421	32	27	8	1	0	175²	197	18	67	80	13.7	3.84	98	.286	.353	4	.082	-2	-9	-2	-0	-0.3
1968	Cal-A	9	10	.474	42	24	3	0	2	164	150	22	56	93	11.6	3.95	74	.244	.313	1	.045	-3	-18	-19	-2	-2.5
1969	Chi-A	0	3	.000	10	5	0	0	0	29¹	42	6	16	15	18.1	5.83	66	.336	.415	1	.167	0	-7	-6	0	-0.5
Total	7	63	58	.521	229	140	35	3	18	1004	967	118	378	677	12.3	4.15	88	.253	.323	31	.104	-9	-78	-58	-8	-6.6

■ GEORGE ELLISON
Ellison, George Russell   b: 1/24/1895, California   d: 1/20/78, San Francisco, Cal   BR/TR, 6'3", 185 lbs.   Deb: 8/21/20

YEAR	TM/L	W	L	PCT	G	GS	CG	SH	SV	IP	H	HR	BB	SO	RAT	ERA	ERA+	OAV	OOB	BH	AVG	PB	PR	/A	PD	TPI
1920	Cle-A	0	0	—	1	0	0	0	0	1	0	0	2	1	18.0	0.00	—	.000	.400	0	—	0	0	0	0	0.1

■ DICK ELLSWORTH
Ellsworth, Richard Clark   b: 3/22/40, Lusk, Wyo.   BL/TL, 6'3.5", 180 lbs.   Deb: 6/22/58

YEAR	TM/L	W	L	PCT	G	GS	CG	SH	SV	IP	H	HR	BB	SO	RAT	ERA	ERA+	OAV	OOB	BH	AVG	PB	PR	/A	PD	TPI
1958	Chi-N	0	1	.000	1	1	0	0	0	2¹	4	0	3	0	30.9	15.43	25	.364	.533	0	.000	-0	-3	-3	0	-0.2
1960	Chi-N	7	13	.350	31	27	6	0	0	176²	170	12	72	94	12.4	3.72	102	.257	.332	2	.042	-3	1	1	0	-0.1
1961	Chi-N	10	11	.476	37	31	7	1	0	186²	213	23	48	91	12.7	3.86	108	.292	.338	2	.036	-5	4	7	3	0.5
1962	Chi-N	9	20	.310	37	33	6	0	1	208²	241	23	77	113	13.9	5.09	81	.291	.355	7	.113	1	-27	-22	0	-1.8
1963	Chi-N	22	10	.688	37	37	19	4	0	290²	223	14	75	185	9.3	2.11	**167**	.210	.263	9	.096	-3	38	**45**	2	**5.3**
1964	Chi-N	14	18	.438	37	36	16	1	0	256²	267	34	71	148	12.0	3.75	99	.266	.317	4	.046	-6	-1	3	2	-0.1
1965	Chi-N	14	15	.483	36	34	8	0	1	222¹	227	22	57	130	11.7	3.81	97	.265	.313	7	.096	-2	-7	-3	2	-0.2
1966	Chi-N	8	22	.267	38	37	9	0	0	269¹	321	28	51	144	12.6	3.98	92	.294	.328	14	.156	-0	-11	-9	2	-0.6
1967	Phi-N	6	7	.462	32	21	3	1	0	125¹	152	6	36	45	13.9	4.38	78	.306	.359	4	.108	-1	-14	-14	2	-1.2
1968	Bos-A	16	7	.696	31	28	10	1	0	196	196	16	37	106	11.0	3.03	104	.260	.301	4	.056	-5	-1	3	0	-0.1
1969	Bos-A	0	0	—	2	2	0	0	0	12	16	1	4	4	15.0	3.75	101	.320	.370	0	.000	-0	-0	0	0	-0.0
	Cle-A	6	9	.400	34	22	3	1	0	135	162	10	40	48	13.8	4.13	91	.301	.354	6	.133	-1	-8	-6	1	-0.5
	Yr	6	9	.400	36	24	3	1	0	147	178	11	44	52	13.9	4.10	92	.302	.356	6	.042	-1	-8	-5	1	-0.5
1970	Cle-A	3	3	.500	29	1	0	0	2	43²	49	4	14	13	13.2	4.53	87	.299	.358	0	.000	-0	-4	-3	1	-0.1
	Mil-A	0	0	—	14	0	0	0	1	15²	11	0	3	9	8.6	1.72	220	.196	.250	0	—	0	3	4	0	0.3
	Yr	3	3	.500	43	1	0	0	3	59¹	60	4	17	22	11.8	3.79	103	.269	.324	0	.000	-0	-1	1	1	0.3
1971	Mil-A	0	1	.000	11	0	0	0	0	14²	22	1	7	10	18.4	4.91	71	.361	.435	0	.000	-0	-2	-2	-0	-0.2
Total	13	115	137	.456	407	310	87	9	5	2155²	2274	194	595	1140	12.2	3.72	100	.272	.324	59	.088	-25	-37	-2	15	0.8

■ STEVE ELLSWORTH
Ellsworth, Steven Clark   b: 7/30/60, Chicago, Ill.   BR/TR, 6'8", 220 lbs.   Deb: 4/07/88

YEAR	TM/L	W	L	PCT	G	GS	CG	SH	SV	IP	H	HR	BB	SO	RAT	ERA	ERA+	OAV	OOB	BH	AVG	PB	PR	/A	PD	TPI
1988	Bos-A	1	6	.143	8	7	0	0	0	36	47	7	16	16	16.0	6.75	61	.315	.386	0	—	0	-11	-11	-0	-0.9

■ DON ELSTON
Elston, Donald Ray   b: 4/6/29, Campbellstown, Ohio   BR/TR, 6', 165 lbs.   Deb: 9/17/53

YEAR	TM/L	W	L	PCT	G	GS	CG	SH	SV	IP	H	HR	BB	SO	RAT	ERA	ERA+	OAV	OOB	BH	AVG	PB	PR	/A	PD	TPI
1953	Chi-N	0	1	.000	2	1	0	0	0	5	11	1	0	2	19.8	14.40	31	.458	.458	0	.000	-0	-6	-6	0	-0.4
1957	Bro-N	0	0	—	1	0	0	0	0	1	1	0	0	1	9.0	0.00	—	.250	.250	0	—	0	0	0	0	0.1
	Chi-N	6	7	.462	39	14	2	0	8	144	139	15	55	102	12.4	3.56	109	.259	.334	4	.108	-2	5	5	-0	0.3
	Yr	6	7	.462	40	14	2	0	8	145	140	15	55	103	12.4	3.54	109	.259	.333	1	.027	-2	5	5	0	0.4
1958	Chi-N	9	8	.529	**69**	0	0	0	10	97	75	9	39	84	10.7	2.88	136	.214	.294	5	.357	1	**12**	**11**	1	1.4
1959	Chi-N	10	8	.556	65	0	0	0	13	97²	77	11	46	82	11.6	3.32	119	.218	.313	4	.211	0	7	7	-1	0.6
1960	Chi-N	8	9	.471	60	0	0	0	11	127	109	17	55	85	11.9	3.40	111	.231	.316	3	.125	-1	5	5	-2	0.2
1961	Chi-N	6	7	.462	58	0	0	0	8	93¹	108	11	45	59	15.3	5.59	75	.297	.383	2	.182	-0	-16	-15	0	-1.3
1962	Chi-N	4	8	.333	57	0	0	0	9	66¹	57	6	32	37	12.2	2.44	170	.247	.341	0	.000	-1	11	13	1	1.3
1963	Chi-N	4	1	.800	51	0	0	0	4	70	57	6	21	41	10.3	2.83	124	.226	.291	0	.000	-0	4	5	-1	0.5
1964	Chi-N	2	5	.286	48	0	0	0	0	54¹	68	4	34	26	17.4	5.30	70	.330	.432	1	.167	-0	-11	-10	1	-0.8
Total	9	49	54	.476	450	15	2	0	63	755²	702	80	327	519	12.6	3.69	106	.251	.335	19	.153	-4	11	17	1	1.9

YEAR TM/L	W	L	PCT	G	GS	CG	SH	SV	IP	H	HR	BB	SO	RAT	ERA	ERA+	OAV	OOB	BH	AVG	PB	PR	/A	PD	TPI

■ NARCISO ELVIRA
Elvira, Narciso Delgado b: 10/29/67, Ver Cruz, Mex. BL/TL, 5'10", 160 lbs. Deb: 9/09/90

YEAR TM/L	W	L	PCT	G	GS	CG	SH	SV	IP	H	HR	BB	SO	RAT	ERA	ERA+	OAV	OOB	BH	AVG	PB	PR	/A	PD	TPI
1990 Mil-A	0	0	—	4	0	0	0	0	5	6	0	5	6	19.8	5.40	70	.300	.440	0	—	0	-1	-1	0	0.0

■ BONES ELY
Ely, William Frederick b: 6/7/1863, N.Girard, Pa. d: 1/10/52, Berkeley, Cal. BR/TR, 6'1", 155 lbs. Deb: 6/19/1884 ♦

YEAR TM/L	W	L	PCT	G	GS	CG	SH	SV	IP	H	HR	BB	SO	RAT	ERA	ERA+	OAV	OOB	BH	AVG	PB	PR	/A	PD	TPI
1884 Buf-N	0	1	.000	1	1	0	0	0	5	17	1	5	4	39.6	14.40	22	.526	.590	0	.000	-1	-6	-6	-0	-0.4
1886 Lou-a	0	4	.000	6	4	4	0	1	44	53	0	26	28	16.2	5.32	69	.285	.372	5	.156	-1	-9	-8	0	-0.7
1890 Syr-a	0	0	—	1	0	0	0	0	2	7	0	0	0	31.5	22.50	16	.542	.542	130	.262	-0	-4	-4	0	-0.2
1894 StL-N	0	0	—	1	0	0	0	0	1	0	0	3	0	27.0	0.00	—	.000	.510	156	.306	0	1	1	0	0.0
Total 4	0	5	.000	9	5	4	0	1	52	77	1	34	32	19.2	6.75	54	.329	.414	1331	.258	-2	-19	-18	0	-1.3

■ HARRY ELY
Ely, Harry Deb: 9/24/1892

YEAR TM/L	W	L	PCT	G	GS	CG	SH	SV	IP	H	HR	BB	SO	RAT	ERA	ERA+	OAV	OOB	BH	AVG	PB	PR	/A	PD	TPI
1892 Bal-N	0	1	.000	1	1	1	0	0	7	14	0	7	0	27.0	7.71	45	.400	.500	0	.000	-0	-3	-3	0	-0.2

■ RED EMBREE
Embree, Charles Willard b: 8/30/17, ElMonte, Cal. BR/TR, 6', 165 lbs. Deb: 9/10/41

YEAR TM/L	W	L	PCT	G	GS	CG	SH	SV	IP	H	HR	BB	SO	RAT	ERA	ERA+	OAV	OOB	BH	AVG	PB	PR	/A	PD	TPI
1941 Cle-A	0	1	.000	1	1	0	0	0	4	7	0	3	4	24.8	6.75	58	.438	.550	0	.000	-0	-1	-1	-0	0.0
1942 Cle-A	3	4	.429	19	6	2	0	0	63	58	0	31	44	13.0	3.86	89	.242	.333	2	.133	-0	-4	-3	-1	-0.3
1944 Cle-A	0	1	.000	3	1	0	0	0	3¹	2	0	5	4	18.9	13.50	24	.167	.412	0	—	0	-4	-4	0	-0.3
1945 Cle-A	4	4	.500	8	8	5	1	0	70	56	3	26	42	10.5	1.93	168	.215	.287	3	.143	-1	11	10	0	1.2
1946 Cle-A	8	12	.400	28	26	8	0	0	200	170	15	79	87	11.3	3.47	95	.227	.302	13	.186	1	1	-3	-1	-0.3
1947 Cle-A	8	10	.444	27	21	6	0	0	162²	137	13	67	56	11.3	3.15	110	.233	.313	9	.173	-1	10	6	1	0.5
1948 NY-A	5	3	.625	20	8	4	0	0	76²	77	6	30	25	12.7	3.76	109	.261	.331	4	.148	-1	5	3	-1	0.1
1949 StL-A	3	13	.188	35	19	4	0	1	127¹	146	13	89	24	16.8	5.37	84	.294	.405	6	.162	-1	-17	-12	-0	-1.1
Total 8	31	48	.392	141	90	29	1	1	707	653	50	330	286	12.6	3.72	98	.246	.331	37	.166	-4	4	-5	-1	-0.2

■ SLIM EMBREY
Embrey, Charles Akin b: 8/17/01, Columbia, Tenn. d: 10/10/47, Nashville, Tenn. BR/TR, 6'2", 184 lbs. Deb: 10/01/23

YEAR TM/L	W	L	PCT	G	GS	CG	SH	SV	IP	H	HR	BB	SO	RAT	ERA	ERA+	OAV	OOB	BH	AVG	PB	PR	/A	PD	TPI
1923 Chi-A	0	0	—	1	0	0	0	0	2²	7	0	2	1	30.4	10.13	39	.500	.563	0	—	0	-2	-2	0	0.0

■ CHARLIE EMIG
Emig, Charles H. b: Bellevue, Ky. Deb: 9/04/1896

YEAR TM/L	W	L	PCT	G	GS	CG	SH	SV	IP	H	HR	BB	SO	RAT	ERA	ERA+	OAV	OOB	BH	AVG	PB	PR	/A	PD	TPI
1896 Lou-N	0	1	.000	1	1	1	0	0	8	12	1	7	1	21.4	7.88	55	.343	.453	0	.000	-1	-3	-3	1	-0.1

■ SLIM EMMERICH
Emmerich, William Peter b: 9/29/19, Allentown, Pa. BR/TR, 6'1", 170 lbs. Deb: 5/14/45

YEAR TM/L	W	L	PCT	G	GS	CG	SH	SV	IP	H	HR	BB	SO	RAT	ERA	ERA+	OAV	OOB	BH	AVG	PB	PR	/A	PD	TPI
1945 NY-N	4	4	.500	31	7	1	0	0	100	111	8	33	27	13.1	4.86	80	.278	.334	3	.120	-2	-12	-11	-0	-1.1
1946 NY-N	0	0	—	2	0	0	0	0	4	6	1	0	1	13.5	4.50	76	.400	.400	0	—	0	-0	-0	0	0.0
Total 2	4	4	.500	33	7	1	0	0	104	117	9	33	28	13.1	4.85	80	.282	.336	3	.120	-2	-12	-11	0	-1.1

■ BOB EMSLIE
Emslie, Robert Daniel b: 1/27/1859, Guelph, Ont., Can. d: 4/26/43, St.Thomas, Ont., Canada BR/TR, 5'11", Deb: 7/25/1883 U

YEAR TM/L	W	L	PCT	G	GS	CG	SH	SV	IP	H	HR	BB	SO	RAT	ERA	ERA+	OAV	OOB	BH	AVG	PB	PR	/A	PD	TPI
1883 Bal-a	9	13	.409	24	23	21	1	0	201¹	188	3	41	62	10.2	3.17	110	.231	.268	16	.165	-3	3	7	2	0.5
1884 Bal-a	32	17	.653	50	50	50	4	0	455¹	419	5	88	264	10.0	2.75	126	.231	.267	37	.190	-5	25	36	0	3.1
1885 Bal-a	3	10	.231	13	13	11	0	0	107	131	0	30	27	13.5	4.29	76	.289	.333	12	.235	0	-12	-12	-1	-1.0
Phi-a	0	4	.000	4	4	3	0	0	28²	37	1	6	9	13.5	6.28	55	.300	.332	1	.083	-1	-10	-9	1	-0.7
Yr	3	14	.176	17	17	14	0	0	135²	168	1	36	36	13.5	4.71	70	.291	.333	0	.000	-1	-22	-21	-0	-1.7
Total 3	44	44	.500	91	90	85	5	0	792¹	775	9	165	362	10.7	3.19	108	.242	.279	66	.186	-9	6	22	2	1.9

■ LUIS ENCARNACION
Encarnacion, Luis Martin b: 10/20/63, Santo Domingo, D.R. BR/TR, 5'10", 178 lbs. Deb: 7/27/90

YEAR TM/L	W	L	PCT	G	GS	CG	SH	SV	IP	H	HR	BB	SO	RAT	ERA	ERA+	OAV	OOB	BH	AVG	PB	PR	/A	PD	TPI
1990 KC-A	0	0	—	4	0	0	0	0	10¹	14	1	4	8	15.7	7.84	49	.311	.367	0	—	0	-5	-5	-0	-0.4

■ JOE ENGEL
Engel, Joseph William b: 3/12/1893, Washington, D.C. d: 6/12/69, Chattanooga, Tenn BR/TL, 6'1.5", 183 lbs. Deb: 5/30/12

YEAR TM/L	W	L	PCT	G	GS	CG	SH	SV	IP	H	HR	BB	SO	RAT	ERA	ERA+	OAV	OOB	BH	AVG	PB	PR	/A	PD	TPI
1912 Was-A	2	5	.286	17	10	2	0	1	75	70	2	50	29	14.9	3.96	84	.253	.375	1	.059	-1	-5	-5	1	-0.4
1913 Was-A	8	9	.471	36	24	6	2	0	164²	124	2	85	70	12.0	3.06	96	.207	.317	3	.061	-5	-2	-2	-0	-0.7
1914 Was-A	7	5	.583	35	15	1	0	3	124¹	108	2	75	41	13.6	2.97	94	.254	.372	3	.107	1	-3	-3	1	-0.1
1915 Was-A	0	3	.000	11	3	0	0	0	33²	30	0	19	9	13.9	3.21	91	.261	.380	0	.000	-1	-1	-1	1	0.0
1917 Cin-N	0	1	.000	1	1	1	0	0	8	12	0	6	2	20.3	5.63	47	.353	.450	0	.000	-0	-3	-3	0	-0.2
1919 Cle-A	0	0	—	1	0	0	0	0	0	0	0	3	0	—	∞	—	—	1.000	0	—	0	-2	-2	0	-0.1
1920 Was-A	0	0	—	1	0	0	0	0	1²	4	0	4	0	27.0	21.60	17	.000	.556	0	.000	-0	-3	-3	0	-0.2
Total 7	17	23	.425	102	53	10	2	4	407¹	344	6	242	151	13.6	3.38	88	.237	.355	7	.067	-6	-20	-19	2	-1.7

■ STEVE ENGEL
Engel, Steven Michael b: 12/31/61, Cincinnati, Ohio BR/TL, 6'3", 216 lbs. Deb: 7/30/85

YEAR TM/L	W	L	PCT	G	GS	CG	SH	SV	IP	H	HR	BB	SO	RAT	ERA	ERA+	OAV	OOB	BH	AVG	PB	PR	/A	PD	TPI
1985 Chi-N	1	5	.167	11	8	1	0	1	51²	61	10	26	29	15.2	5.57	72	.298	.377	3	.188	2	-11	-9	0	-0.6

■ RICK ENGLE
Engle, Richard Douglas b: 4/7/57, Corbin, Ky. BR/TL, 5'11.5", 181 lbs. Deb: 9/02/81

YEAR TM/L	W	L	PCT	G	GS	CG	SH	SV	IP	H	HR	BB	SO	RAT	ERA	ERA+	OAV	OOB	BH	AVG	PB	PR	/A	PD	TPI
1981 Mon-N	0	0	—	1	0	0	0	0	2	6	0	1	2	31.5	18.00	19	.500	.538	0	—	0	-3	-3	0	-0.2

■ JACK ENRIGHT
Enright, Jackson Percy b: 11/29/1895, Fort Worth, Tex. d: 8/18/75, Pompano Beach, Fla BR/TR, 5'11", 177 lbs. Deb: 9/26/17

YEAR TM/L	W	L	PCT	G	GS	CG	SH	SV	IP	H	HR	BB	SO	RAT	ERA	ERA+	OAV	OOB	BH	AVG	PB	PR	/A	PD	TPI
1917 NY-A	0	1	.000	1	1	0	0	0	5	5	0	3	1	14.4	5.40	50	.294	.400	0	.000	-0	-2	-2	1	0.0

■ TERRY ENYART
Enyart, Terry Gene b: 10/10/50, Ironton, Ohio BR/TL, 6'2", 190 lbs. Deb: 6/17/74

YEAR TM/L	W	L	PCT	G	GS	CG	SH	SV	IP	H	HR	BB	SO	RAT	ERA	ERA+	OAV	OOB	BH	AVG	PB	PR	/A	PD	TPI
1974 Mon-N	0	0	—	2	0	0	0	0	1²	4	0	4	2	43.2	16.20	24	.444	.615	0	—	0	-2	-2	-0	-0.1

■ JOHNNY ENZMANN
Enzmann, John "Gentleman John" b: 3/4/1890, Brooklyn, N.Y. d: 3/14/84, Riverhead, N.Y. BR/TR, 5'10", 165 lbs. Deb: 7/10/14

YEAR TM/L	W	L	PCT	G	GS	CG	SH	SV	IP	H	HR	BB	SO	RAT	ERA	ERA+	OAV	OOB	BH	AVG	PB	PR	/A	PD	TPI
1914 Bro-N	1	0	1.000	7	1	0	0	0	19	21	1	8	5	15.2	4.74	80	.300	.395	0	.000	-1	-4	-4	1	-0.3
1918 Cle-A	5	7	.417	30	14	8	0	2	136²	130	2	29	38	10.8	2.37	127	.263	.310	7	.149	-3	6	10	1	0.9
1919 Cle-A	3	2	.600	14	4	2	0	0	55¹	67	0	8	13	12.5	2.28	147	.312	.342	2	.133	-0	6	7	-1	0.6
1920 Phi-N	2	3	.400	16	1	1	0	0	58²	79	1	16	35	15.3	3.84	89	.320	.373	4	.167	1	-5	-3	-0	-0.1
Total 4	11	12	.478	67	20	11	0	2	269²	297	4	61	91	12.4	2.84	111	.289	.338	13	.141	-3	3	10	-0	1.1

■ AL EPPERLY
Epperly, Albert Paul "Tub" or "Pard" b: 5/7/18, Glidden, Iowa BL/TR, 6'2", 194 lbs. Deb: 4/25/38

YEAR TM/L	W	L	PCT	G	GS	CG	SH	SV	IP	H	HR	BB	SO	RAT	ERA	ERA+	OAV	OOB	BH	AVG	PB	PR	/A	PD	TPI
1938 Chi-N	2	0	1.000	9	4	1	0	0	27	28	1	15	10	14.3	3.67	104	.264	.355	2	.250	1	0	0	0	0.2
1950 Bro-N	0	0	—	5	0	0	0	0	9	14	1	5	3	19.0	5.00	82	.378	.452	0	—	0	-1	-1	-0	0.0
Total 2	2	0	1.000	14	4	1	0	0	36	42	2	20	13	15.5	4.00	97	.294	.380	2	.250	1	-0	-0	0	0.2

■ GREG ERARDI
Erardi, Joseph Gregory b: 5/31/54, Syracuse, N.Y. BR/TR, 6'1", 190 lbs. Deb: 9/06/77

YEAR TM/L	W	L	PCT	G	GS	CG	SH	SV	IP	H	HR	BB	SO	RAT	ERA	ERA+	OAV	OOB	BH	AVG	PB	PR	/A	PD	TPI
1977 Sea-A	0	1	.000	1	1	0	0	0	5	8	1	2	6	18.0	6.00	69	.300	.391	0	—	0	-2	-2	0	-0.1

■ EDDIE ERAUTT
Erautt, Edward Lorenz Sebastian b: 9/26/24, Portland, Ore. BR/TR, 5'11.5", 185 lbs. Deb: 4/16/47

YEAR TM/L	W	L	PCT	G	GS	CG	SH	SV	IP	H	HR	BB	SO	RAT	ERA	ERA+	OAV	OOB	BH	AVG	PB	PR	/A	PD	TPI
1947 Cin-N	4	9	.308	36	10	2	0	0	119	146	5	53	43	15.2	5.07	81	.307	.379	2	.069	-1	-13	-13	1	-1.2
1948 Cin-N	0	0	—	2	0	0	0	0	3	3	0	1	0	12.0	6.00	65	.250	.308	0	—	0	-1	-1	0	0.0
1949 Cin-N	4	11	.267	39	9	1	0	1	112²	99	9	61	43	13.0	3.36	125	.247	.351	4	.174	-0	9	10	-1	1.0
1950 Cin-N	4	2	.667	33	2	1	0	1	65¹	82	9	22	35	15.2	5.65	75	.307	.373	2	.154	0	-11	-10	-0	-0.9
1951 Cin-N	0	0	—	30	0	0	0	0	39¹	50	4	23	20	17.4	5.72	71	.314	.411	0	.000	-0	-8	-7	1	-0.6
1953 Cin-N	0	0	—	4	0	0	0	0	4²	11	1	3	1	27.0	5.79	75	.500	.560	0	.000	-0	-1	-1	0	0.0
StL-N	3	1	.750	20	1	0	0	0	35²	43	6	16	15	15.4	6.31	67	.299	.377	1	.167	-0	-8	-8	1	-0.6
Yr	3	1	.750	24	1	0	0	0	40¹	54	7	19	16	16.7	6.25	68	.325	.401	0	.000	-0	-9	-9	1	-0.6
Total 6	15	23	.395	164	22	4	0	2	379²	434	34	179	157	14.9	4.86	86	.293	.376	9	.120	-2	-33	-29	1	-2.3

■ DON ERICKSON
Erickson, Don Lee b: 12/13/31, Springfield, Ill. BR/TR, 6', 175 lbs. Deb: 9/01/58

YEAR TM/L	W	L	PCT	G	GS	CG	SH	SV	IP	H	HR	BB	SO	RAT	ERA	ERA+	OAV	OOB	BH	AVG	PB	PR	/A	PD	TPI
1958 Phi-N	0	1	.000	9	0	0	0	1	11²	11	3	9	9	15.4	4.63	86	.244	.370	0	.000	-0	-1	-1	-0	0.0

YEAR TM/L	W	L	PCT	G	GS	CG	SH	SV	IP	H	HR	BB	SO	RAT	ERA	ERA+	OAV	OOB	BH	AVG	PB	PR	/A	PD	TPI

■ ERIC ERICKSON
Erickson, Eric George Adolph b: 3/13/1895, Goteborg, Sweden d: 5/19/65, Jamestown, N.Y. BR/TR, 6'2", 190 lbs. Deb: 10/06/14

YEAR TM/L	W	L	PCT	G	GS	CG	SH	SV	IP	H	HR	BB	SO	RAT	ERA	ERA+	OAV	OOB	BH	AVG	PB	PR	/A	PD	TPI
1914 NY-N	0	1	.000	1	1	0	0	0	5	8	0	3	3	19.8	0.00	—	.364	.440	0	.000	-0	2	1	-0	0.1
1916 Det-A	0	0	—	8	0	0	0	0	16	13	0	8	7	12.4	2.81	102	.220	.324	0	.000	-1	0	0	-1	0.0
1918 Det-A	4	5	.444	12	9	8	0	1	94¹	81	2	29	48	10.8	2.48	107	.240	.306	4	.121	-2	3	2	-3	-0.3
1919 Det-A	0	2	.000	3	2	0	0	0	14²	17	0	10	4	17.2	6.75	47	.293	.406	-6	.200	-0	-6	-6	0	-0.4
Was-A	6	11	.353	20	15	7	1	0	132	130	7	63	86	13.6	3.95	81	.254	.344	7	.146	-1	-11	-11	-3	-1.5
Yr	6	13	.316	23	17	7	1	0	146²	147	7	73	90	13.9	4.23	76	.258	.349	3	.057	-2	-16	-17	-3	-1.9
1920 Was-A	12	16	.429	39	27	12	0	1	239¹	231	13	128	87	13.9	3.84	97	.264	.365	23	.277	4	-1	-3	-4	-0.2
1921 Was-A	8	10	.444	32	22	9	3	0	179	181	7	65	71	12.8	3.62	114	.269	.341	9	.150	-3	13	10	-3	0.3
1922 Was-A	4	12	.250	30	17	6	2	2	141²	144	8	73	61	14.0	4.96	78	.279	.372	6	.133	-2	-14	-17	-2	-2.0
Total 7	34	57	.374	145	93	42	6	4	822	805	37	379	367	13.3	3.85	93	.264	.352	50	.179	-6	-14	-23	-16	-4.0

■ HAL ERICKSON
Erickson, Harold James b: 7/17/19, Portland, Ore. BR/TR, 6'5", 230 lbs. Deb: 4/14/53

YEAR TM/L	W	L	PCT	G	GS	CG	SH	SV	IP	H	HR	BB	SO	RAT	ERA	ERA+	OAV	OOB	BH	AVG	PB	PR	/A	PD	TPI
1953 Det-A	0	1	.000	18	0	0	0	1	32¹	43	4	10	19	15.3	4.73	86	.323	.379	0	.000	-1	-3	-2	-0	-0.2

■ PAUL ERICKSON
Erickson, Paul Walford "Li'L Abner" b: 12/14/15, Zion, Ohio BR/TR, 6'2", 200 lbs. Deb: 6/29/41

YEAR TM/L	W	L	PCT	G	GS	CG	SH	SV	IP	H	HR	BB	SO	RAT	ERA	ERA+	OAV	OOB	BH	AVG	PB	PR	/A	PD	TPI
1941 Chi-N	5	7	.417	32	15	7	1	1	141	126	2	64	85	12.3	3.70	95	.234	.318	7	.152	0	-1	-3	-2	-0.4
1942 Chi-N	1	6	.143	18	7	1	0	0	63	70	4	41	26	15.9	5.43	59	.288	.391	3	.143	-1	-15	-16	0	-1.6
1943 Chi-N	1	3	.250	15	4	0	0	0	42²	47	4	22	24	15.0	6.12	55	.280	.370	3	.200	-0	-13	-13	-1	-1.3
1944 Chi-N	5	9	.357	33	15	5	3	1	124¹	113	5	67	82	13.0	3.55	100	.243	.338	2	.056	-1	1	-0	1	0.0
1945 *Chi-N	7	4	.636	28	9	3	0	3	108¹	94	5	48	53	12.4	3.32	110	.233	.325	5	.156	0	6	4	-1	0.4
1946 Chi-N	9	7	.563	32	14	5	1	0	137	119	2	65	70	12.3	2.43	137	.232	.321	2	.050	-4	15	14	-1	0.9
1947 Chi-N	7	12	.368	40	20	6	0	1	174	179	17	93	82	14.3	4.34	91	.268	.362	15	.250	3	-6	-8	-0	-0.3
1948 Chi-N	0	0	—	3	0	0	0	0	5²	7	0	6	4	20.6	6.35	61	.292	.433	0	.000	-0	-2	-2	0	-0.1
Phi-N	2	0	1.000	4	2	0	0	0	17¹	19	2	17	5	18.7	5.19	76	.292	.439	1	.143	-0	-2	-2	0	-0.1
NY-N	0	0	—	2	0	0	0	0	1	0	0	2	1	18.0	0.00	—	.000	.400	0	—	0	0	0	0	0.0
Yr	2	0	1.000	9	2	0	0	0	24	26	2	25	10	19.1	5.25	75	.283	.436	0	.000	-0	-3	-4	0	-0.2
Total 8	37	48	.435	207	86	27	5	6	814¹	774	41	425	432	13.5	3.86	93	.250	.345	38	.147	-2	-16	-26	-2	-2.5

■ RALPH ERICKSON
Erickson, Ralph Lief b: 6/25/04, Dubois, Idaho BL/TL, 6'1", 175 lbs. Deb: 9/11/29

YEAR TM/L	W	L	PCT	G	GS	CG	SH	SV	IP	H	HR	BB	SO	RAT	ERA	ERA+	OAV	OOB	BH	AVG	PB	PR	/A	PD	TPI
1929 Pit-N	0	0	—	1	0	0	0	0	1	2	0	2	0	36.0	27.00	18	.500	.667	0	—	0	-2	-2	0	-0.1
1930 Pit-N	1	0	1.000	7	0	0	0	0	14	21	1	10	2	19.9	7.07	70	.375	.470	1	.250	-0	-3	-3	0	-0.2
Total 2	1	0	1.000	8	0	0	0	0	15	23	1	12	2	21.0	8.40	59	.383	.486	1	.250	-0	-6	-6	0	-0.3

■ ROGER ERICKSON
Erickson, Roger Farrell b: 8/30/56, Springfield, Ill. BR/TR, 6'3", 180 lbs. Deb: 4/06/78

YEAR TM/L	W	L	PCT	G	GS	CG	SH	SV	IP	H	HR	BB	SO	RAT	ERA	ERA+	OAV	OOB	BH	AVG	PB	PR	/A	PD	TPI
1978 Min-A	14	13	.519	37	37	14	0	0	265²	268	19	79	121	12.0	3.96	96	.263	.321	0	—	0	-6	-4	0	-0.3
1979 Min-A	3	10	.231	24	21	0	0	0	123	154	17	48	47	14.9	5.63	78	.310	.372	0	—	0	-19	-17	-0	-1.5
1980 Min-A	7	13	.350	32	27	7	0	0	191¹	198	13	56	97	12.1	3.25	134	.268	.322	0	—	0	17	24	0	2.5
1981 Min-A	3	8	.273	14	14	1	0	0	91¹	93	7	31	44	12.2	3.84	103	.262	.321	0	—	0	-2	1	0	-0.1
1982 Min-A	4	3	.571	7	7	2	0	0	40²	56	6	12	12	15.3	4.87	87	.326	.373	0	—	0	-4	-3	1	-0.1
NY-A	4	5	.444	16	11	0	0	1	70²	86	5	17	37	13.1	4.46	89	.301	.340	0	—	0	-3	-4	-1	-0.4
Yr	8	8	.500	23	18	2	0	1	111¹	142	11	29	49	13.8	4.61	89	.308	.349	0	—	0	-7	-7	-0	-0.5
1983 NY-A	0	1	.000	5	0	0	0	0	16²	13	1	8	7	11.3	4.32	90	.213	.304	0	—	0	-0	-1	0	0.0
Total 6	35	53	.398	135	117	24	0	1	799¹	868	68	251	365	12.8	4.13	99	.277	.334	0	—	0	-18	-4	0	0.3

■ SCOTT ERICKSON
Erickson, Scott Gavin b: 2/2/68, Long Beach, Cal. BR/TR, 6'4", 220 lbs. Deb: 6/25/90

YEAR TM/L	W	L	PCT	G	GS	CG	SH	SV	IP	H	HR	BB	SO	RAT	ERA	ERA+	OAV	OOB	BH	AVG	PB	PR	/A	PD	TPI
1990 Min-A	8	4	.667	19	17	1	0	0	113	108	9	51	53	13.1	2.87	146	.256	.343	0	—	0	13	17	0	1.8

■ DICK ERRICKSON
Errickson, Richard Merriwell "Lief" b: 3/5/14, Vineland, N.J. BL/TR, 6'1", 175 lbs. Deb: 4/27/38

YEAR TM/L	W	L	PCT	G	GS	CG	SH	SV	IP	H	HR	BB	SO	RAT	ERA	ERA+	OAV	OOB	BH	AVG	PB	PR	/A	PD	TPI
1938 Bos-N	9	7	.563	34	10	6	1	6	122¹	113	1	56	40	12.5	3.15	109	.246	.330	4	.114	-1	9	4	2	0.4
1939 Bos-N	6	9	.400	28	11	3	0	1	128¹	143	6	54	33	13.9	4.00	92	.293	.365	10	.227	1	-1	-4	2	-0.1
1940 Bos-N	12	13	.480	34	29	17	3	4	236¹	241	8	90	34	12.6	3.16	118	.270	.338	13	.157	-2	18	15	2	1.5
1941 Bos-N	6	12	.333	38	23	5	2	1	165²	192	12	62	45	14.0	4.78	75	.287	.351	8	.178	-0	-21	-22	1	-2.1
1942 Bos-N	2	5	.286	21	4	0	0	1	59¹	76	7	38	20	14.6	5.01	67	.309	.361	2	.125	-1	-11	-11	-1	-1.2
Chi-N	1	1	.500	13	0	0	0	0	24	39	1	8	9	18.0	4.13	78	.411	.462	0	.000	-1	-2	-2	1	-0.1
Yr	3	6	.333	34	4	0	0	1	83¹	115	9	28	24	15.6	4.75	69	.337	.389	0	.000	-1	-13	-13	-0	-1.3
Total 5	36	47	.434	168	77	31	6	13	736¹	804	36	290	176	13.5	3.85	93	.282	.350	37	.162	-5	-9	-21	6	-1.6

■ CARL ERSKINE
Erskine, Carl Daniel "Oisk" b: 12/13/26, Anderson, Ind. BR/TR, 5'10", 165 lbs. Deb: 7/25/48

YEAR TM/L	W	L	PCT	G	GS	CG	SH	SV	IP	H	HR	BB	SO	RAT	ERA	ERA+	OAV	OOB	BH	AVG	PB	PR	/A	PD	TPI
1948 Bro-N	6	3	.667	17	9	3	0	0	64	51	5	35	29	12.2	3.23	124	.231	.339	2	.095	-2	5	5	-1	0.4
1949 *Bro-N	8	1	.889	22	3	2	0	0	79²	68	6	51	49	13.7	4.63	89	.235	.354	3	.115	-2	-5	-5	0	-0.5
1950 Bro-N	7	6	.538	22	13	3	0	1	103	109	15	35	50	12.7	4.72	87	.273	.333	9	.243	2	-7	-7	-1	-0.5
1951 Bro-N	16	12	.571	46	19	7	0	4	189²	206	23	78	95	13.6	4.46	88	.280	.351	8	.131	-1	-11	-11	-0	-1.2
1952 *Bro-N	14	6	.700	33	26	10	4	2	206²	167	17	71	131	10.5	2.70	135	.220	.289	10	.152	-0	24	22	2	2.5
1953 *Bro-N	20	6	**.769**	39	33	16	4	3	246²	213	21	95	187	11.3	3.54	120	.230	.304	20	.215	0	20	20	-2	1.8
1954 Bro-N	18	15	.545	38	37	12	2	1	260¹	239	31	92	166	11.6	4.15	98	.243	.311	14	.159	-1	-2	-2	-1	-0.3
1955 *Bro-N	11	8	.579	31	29	7	2	1	194²	185	29	64	84	11.5	3.79	107	.253	.313	15	.203	-0	5	6	-2	0.4
1956 *Bro-N	13	11	.542	31	28	8	1	0	186¹	189	25	57	95	11.9	4.25	93	.264	.320	8	.121	-4	-10	-6	1	-0.8
1957 Bro-N	5	3	.625	15	7	1	0	0	66	62	8	20	26	11.2	3.55	118	.248	.304	2	.091	-1	2	5	-1	0.2
1958 LA-N	4	4	.500	31	9	2	1	0	98¹	115	14	35	54	13.7	5.13	80	.297	.355	1	.037	-3	-13	-11	1	-1.2
1959 LA-N	0	3	.000	10	3	0	0	1	23¹	33	5	13	15	17.7	7.71	55	.320	.397	0	.000	-1	-10	-9	-0	-0.8
Total 12	122	78	.610	335	216	71	14	13	1718²	1637	199	646	981	12.0	4.00	101	.252	.321	92	.156	-14	-0	6	-4	-0.1

■ CHICO ESCARREGA
Escarrega, Ernesto (Acosta) b: 12/27/49, Los Mochis, Mex. BR/TR, 5'11", 185 lbs. Deb: 4/26/82

YEAR TM/L	W	L	PCT	G	GS	CG	SH	SV	IP	H	HR	BB	SO	RAT	ERA	ERA+	OAV	OOB	BH	AVG	PB	PR	/A	PD	TPI
1982 Chi-A	1	3	.250	38	2	0	0	1	73²	73	3	16	33	10.9	3.67	110	.263	.303	0	—	0	3	3	-0	0.3

■ DUKE ESPER
Esper, Charles H. b: 7/28/1868, Salem, N.J. d: 8/31/10, Philadelphia, Pa. TL, 5'11.5", 185 lbs. Deb: 4/18/1890

YEAR TM/L	W	L	PCT	G	GS	CG	SH	SV	IP	H	HR	BB	SO	RAT	ERA	ERA+	OAV	OOB	BH	AVG	PB	PR	/A	PD	TPI
1890 Phi-a	8	9	.471	18	16	14	1	0	143²	176	1	67	61	15.2	4.89	78	.293	.363	18	.295	4	-16	-17	1	-0.9
Pit-N	0	2	.000	2	2	2	0	0	17	18	0	10	9	14.8	5.29	62	.264	.358	1	.143	-1	-3	-4	0	-0.2
Phi-N	5	0	1.000	5	5	4	0	0	41	40	1	16	18	12.3	3.07	119	.248	.316	3	.158	-1	2	3	0	0.2
Yr	5	2	.714	7	7	6	0	0	58	58	1	26	27	13.0	3.72	95	.253	.329	0	.000	-2	-1	-1	1	0.0
1891 Phi-N	20	15	.571	39	36	25	1	1	296	302	8	121	108	12.9	3.56	96	.254	.323	27	.220	1	-7	-5	0	-0.2
1892 Phi-N	11	6	.647	21	18	14	0	1	160¹	171	2	58	45	12.9	3.42	95	.262	.323	17	.243	2	-2	-3	-0	-0.4
Pit-N	2	0	1.000	3	3	1	0	0	18¹	18	0	12	5	14.7	5.40	61	.247	.353	0	.000	-1	-4	-4	-0	-0.4
Yr	13	6	.684	24	21	15	0	1	178²	189	2	70	50	13.0	3.63	90	.261	.326	2	.025	0	-7	-7	-0	-0.4
1893 Was-N	12	28	.300	42	36	34	0	0	334¹	442	14	156	78	16.1	4.71	98	.309	.377	41	.287	7	-1	-3	1	0.4
1894 Was-N	5	10	.333	19	15	7	0	0	122¹	191	4	40	27	17.0	7.50	70	.352	.396	16	.281	2	-30	-30	1	-2.0
*Bal-N	10	2	.833	16	9	8	0	2	102	107	1	36	25	12.6	3.88	141	.267	.327	10	.222	-1	16	18	1	1.5
Yr	15	12	.556	35	24	15	0	2	224¹	298	9	76	52	15.0	5.86	91	.316	.368	8	.078	1	-13	-13	1	-0.5
1895 *Bal-N	10	12	.455	34	25	16	1	1	218¹	248	8	79	39	13.5	3.92	122	.282	.341	16	.178	-6	21	20	-2	1.0
1896 Bal-N	14	5	.737	20	18	14	0	0	155²	168	3	39	19	12.0	3.58	119	.273	.317	13	.197	-2	13	12	-1	0.7
1897 StL-N	1	6	.143	8	8	7	0	0	61¹	95	5	12	15	15.7	5.28	83	.350	.378	8	.320	-1	-7	-6	1	-0.2
1898 StL-N	3	5	.375	8	7	6	0	0	64²	86	1	22	14	15.0	5.98	63	.317	.368	10	.370	2	-17	-16	0	-1.1
Total 9	101	100	.502	237	199	152	4	5	1735	2062	46	668	456	14.2	4.40	96	.288	.349	180	.243	6	-35	-35	2	-1.2

YEAR TM/L	W	L	PCT	G	GS	CG	SH	SV	IP	H	HR	BB	SO	RAT	ERA	ERA+	OAV	OOB	BH	AVG	PB	PR	/A	PD	TPI

■ NINO ESPINOSA Espinosa, Arnulfo Acevedo (b: Arnulfo Acevedo (Espinosa))
b: 8/15/53, Villa Altagracia, d: 12/25/87, Villa Altagracia, BR/TR, 6'1", 192 lbs. Deb: 9/13/74

YEAR TM/L	W	L	PCT	G	GS	CG	SH	SV	IP	H	HR	BB	SO	RAT	ERA	ERA+	OAV	OOB	BH	AVG	PB	PR	/A	PD	TPI
1974 NY-N	0	0	—	2	1	0	0	0	9	12	1	0	2	12.0	5.00	71	.324	.324	1	.500	0	-1	-1	0	0.0
1975 NY-N	0	1	.000	2	0	0	0	0	3¹	8	0	1	2	27.0	18.00	19	.471	.500	0	—	0	-5	-5	0	-0.4
1976 NY-N	4	4	.500	12	5	0	0	0	41²	41	3	13	30	11.7	3.67	90	.265	.321	0	.000	-1	-1	-2	-1	-0.2
1977 NY-N	10	13	.435	32	29	7	1	0	200	188	17	55	105	11.2	3.42	109	.249	.304	8	.129	-1	11	7	0	0.6
1978 NY-N	11	15	.423	32	32	6	1	0	203²	230	24	75	76	13.6	4.73	74	.292	.355	14	.209	2	-26	-28	3	-2.3
1979 Phi-N	14	12	.538	33	33	8	3	0	212	211	20	65	88	11.8	3.65	105	.262	.319	14	.194	2	2	4	1	0.6
1980 Phi-N	3	5	.375	12	12	1	0	0	76¹	73	9	19	13	11.1	3.77	100	.250	.300	3	.115	-1	-1	0	0	0.0
1981 Phi-N	2	5	.286	14	14	2	0	0	73²	98	11	24	22	15.0	6.11	59	.333	.386	4	.200	-0	-21	-20	-0	-1.9
Tor-N	0	0	—	1	0	0	0	0	1	4	0	0	0	36.0	9.00	44	.667	.667	0	—	0	-1	-1	0	0.0
Total 8	44	55	.444	140	126	24	5	0	820¹	865	85	252	338	12.4	4.17	88	.275	.331	44	.171	-1	-44	-46	3	-3.6

■ MARK ESSER Esser, Mark Gerald b: 4/1/56, Erie, Pa. BR/TL, 6'1", 190 lbs. Deb: 4/22/79

YEAR TM/L	W	L	PCT	G	GS	CG	SH	SV	IP	H	HR	BB	SO	RAT	ERA	ERA+	OAV	OOB	BH	AVG	PB	PR	/A	PD	TPI
1979 Chi-A	0	0	—	2	0	0	0	0	1²	2	0	4	1	32.4	16.20	26	.286	.545	0	—	0	-2	-2	0	-0.1

■ BILL ESSICK Essick, William Earl "Vinegar Bill" b: 12/18/1881, Grand Ridge, Ill. d: 10/12/51, Los Angeles, Cal. TR, Deb: 9/12/06

YEAR TM/L	W	L	PCT	G	GS	CG	SH	SV	IP	H	HR	BB	SO	RAT	ERA	ERA+	OAV	OOB	BH	AVG	PB	PR	/A	PD	TPI
1906 Cin-N	2	2	.500	6	4	3	0	0	39¹	39	1	16	16	13.0	2.97	93	.273	.354	1	.077	-1	-1	-1	-1	-0.2
1907 Cin-N	0	2	.000	3	2	2	0	0	21²	23	0	8	7	13.3	2.91	89	.274	.344	0	.000	-1	-1	-1	1	0.0
Total 2	2	4	.333	9	6	5	0	0	61	62	1	24	23	13.1	2.95	91	.273	.350	1	.048	-2	-3	-2	-0	-0.2

■ DICK ESTELLE Estelle, Richard Henry b: 1/18/42, Lakewood, N.J. BB/TL, 6'2", 170 lbs. Deb: 9/04/64

YEAR TM/L	W	L	PCT	G	GS	CG	SH	SV	IP	H	HR	BB	SO	RAT	ERA	ERA+	OAV	OOB	BH	AVG	PB	PR	/A	PD	TPI
1964 SF-N	1	2	.333	6	6	0	0	0	41²	39	3	23	23	13.4	3.02	118	.247	.343	1	.067	-1	2	3	-1	0.1
1965 SF-N	0	0	—	6	1	0	0	0	11¹	12	0	8	6	16.7	3.97	91	.261	.382	0	.000	0	-1	-0	0	0.0
Total 2	1	2	.333	12	7	0	0	0	53	51	3	31	29	14.1	3.23	111	.250	.352	1	.063	-0	2	2	-1	0.1

■ GEORGE ESTOCK Estock, George John b: 11/2/24, Stirling, N.J. BR/TR, 6', 185 lbs. Deb: 4/21/51

YEAR TM/L	W	L	PCT	G	GS	CG	SH	SV	IP	H	HR	BB	SO	RAT	ERA	ERA+	OAV	OOB	BH	AVG	PB	PR	/A	PD	TPI
1951 Bos-N	0	1	.000	37	1	0	0	3	60¹	56	2	37	11	13.9	4.33	85	.258	.366	2	.286	1	-2	-4	1	-0.2

■ CHUCK ESTRADA Estrada, Charles Leonard b: 2/15/38, San Luis Obispo, Cal. BR/TR, 6'1", 185 lbs. Deb: 4/21/60 C

YEAR TM/L	W	L	PCT	G	GS	CG	SH	SV	IP	H	HR	BB	SO	RAT	ERA	ERA+	OAV	OOB	BH	AVG	PB	PR	/A	PD	TPI
1960 Bal-A	**18**	11	.621	36	25	12	1	2	208²	162	18	101	144	12.0	3.58	106	**.218**	.323	9	.141	-0	7	5	-1	0.5
1961 Bal-A	15	9	.625	33	31	6	1	0	212	159	19	132	160	12.8	3.69	106	**.207**	.331	8	.114	-3	8	5	-3	0.0
1962 Bal-A	9	17	.346	34	33	6	0	0	223¹	199	24	121	165	13.3	3.83	98	.240	.343	10	.152	0	3	-2	-3	-0.5
1963 Bal-A	3	2	.600	8	7	0	0	0	31¹	26	2	19	16	13.2	4.60	77	.226	.341	1	.100	-1	-3	-4	-0	-0.4
1964 Bal-A	3	2	.600	17	6	0	0	0	54²	62	8	21	32	14.0	5.27	68	.282	.350	2	.143	-0	-10	-10	-1	-1.1
1966 Chi-N	1	1	.500	9	1	0	0	0	12¹	16	2	5	3	16.1	7.30	50	.314	.386	0	.000	-0	-5	-5	-0	-0.5
1967 NY-N	1	2	.333	9	2	0	0	0	22	28	5	17	15	18.8	9.41	36	.326	.442	0	.000	-1	-15	-15	-1	-1.4
Total 7	50	44	.532	146	105	24	2	2	764¹	652	78	416	535	13.0	4.07	93	.232	.339	30	.129	-5	-15	-25	-9	-3.4

■ OSCAR ESTRADA Estrada, Oscar b: 2/15/04, Havana, Cuba d: 1/2/78, Havana, Cuba BL/TL, 5'8", 160 lbs. Deb: 4/21/29

YEAR TM/L	W	L	PCT	G	GS	CG	SH	SV	IP	H	HR	BB	SO	RAT	ERA	ERA+	OAV	OOB	BH	AVG	PB	PR	/A	PD	TPI
1929 StL-A	0	0	—	1	0	0	0	0	1	1	0	1	0	18.0	0.00	—	.250	.400	0	—	0	0	0	0	0.1

■ JOHN EUBANK Eubank, John Franklin "Honest John" b: 9/9/1872, Servia, Ind. d: 11/3/58, Bellevue, Mich. BR/TR, 6'2", 215 lbs. Deb: 9/19/05

YEAR TM/L	W	L	PCT	G	GS	CG	SH	SV	IP	H	HR	BB	SO	RAT	ERA	ERA+	OAV	OOB	BH	AVG	PB	PR	/A	PD	TPI
1905 Det-A	1	0	1.000	3	2	0	0	0	17¹	13	0	3	1	8.3	2.08	132	.210	.246	5	.357	1	1	1	-0	0.1
1906 Det-A	4	10	.286	24	12	7	1	2	135	147	0	35	38	12.1	3.53	78	.280	.325	13	.206	-0	-13	-12	1	-1.0
1907 Det-A	3	3	.500	15	8	4	1	0	81	88	0	20	17	12.0	2.67	98	.279	.321	4	.129	-1	-1	-0	1	0.0
Total 3	8	13	.381	42	22	11	2	2	233¹	248	0	58	56	11.8	3.12	87	.275	.319	22	.204	-1	-13	-11	2	-0.9

■ UEL EUBANKS Eubanks, Uel Melvin "Poss" b: 2/14/03, Quinlan, Tex. d: 11/21/54, Dallas, Tex. BR/TR, 6'3", 175 lbs. Deb: 7/20/22

YEAR TM/L	W	L	PCT	G	GS	CG	SH	SV	IP	H	HR	BB	SO	RAT	ERA	ERA+	OAV	OOB	BH	AVG	PB	PR	/A	PD	TPI
1922 Chi-N	0	0	—	2	0	0	0	0	1²	5	0	4	1	48.6	27.00	16	.556	.692	1	1.000	1	-4	-4	0	-0.2

■ FRANK EUFEMIA Eufemia, Frank Anthony b: 12/23/59, Bronx, N.Y. BR/TR, 5'11", 185 lbs. Deb: 5/21/85

YEAR TM/L	W	L	PCT	G	GS	CG	SH	SV	IP	H	HR	BB	SO	RAT	ERA	ERA+	OAV	OOB	BH	AVG	PB	PR	/A	PD	TPI
1985 Min-A	4	2	.667	39	0	0	0	2	61²	56	7	21	30	11.2	3.79	116	.250	.314	0	—	0	2	4	1	0.5

■ CHICK EVANS Evans, Charles Franklin b: 10/15/1889, Arlington, Vt. d: 9/2/16, Schenectady, N.Y. BR/TR, Deb: 9/19/09

YEAR TM/L	W	L	PCT	G	GS	CG	SH	SV	IP	H	HR	BB	SO	RAT	ERA	ERA+	OAV	OOB	BH	AVG	PB	PR	/A	PD	TPI
1909 Bos-N	0	3	.000	4	3	1	0	0	21²	25	0	14	11	16.2	4.57	62	.305	.406	0	.000	-1	-5	-4	-0	-0.5
1910 Bos-N	1	1	.500	13	1	0	0	2	31	28	1	27	12	16.8	5.23	64	.275	.439	1	.100	-1	-8	-7	-0	-0.6
Total 2	1	4	.200	17	4	1	0	2	52²	53	1	41	23	16.6	4.96	63	.288	.425	1	.053	-2	-12	-11	-1	-1.1

■ JAKE EVANS Evans, Jacob "Bloody Jake" b: Baltimore, Md. d: 2/3/07, Baltimore, Md. TR, 5'8", 154 lbs. Deb: 5/01/1879 ♦

YEAR TM/L	W	L	PCT	G	GS	CG	SH	SV	IP	H	HR	BB	SO	RAT	ERA	ERA+	OAV	OOB	BH	AVG	PB	PR	/A	PD	TPI
1880 Tro-N	0	0	—	1	0	0	0	0	4	11	0	0	0	24.8	13.50	19	.475	.475	46	.256	0	-5	-5	-0	-0.3
1882 Wor-N	0	1	.000	1	1	1	0	0	8	13	1	0	2	14.6	5.63	55	.346	.346	71	.213	-0	-2	-2	-0	-0.1
1883 Cle-N	0	0	—	1	0	0	0	0	3	0	0	1	0	0.0	0.00	—	.000	.000	79	.238	0	1	1	1	0.1
Total 3	0	1	.000	3	1	1	0	0	15	24	1	0	2	14.4	6.60	45	.343	.343	435	.238	-0	-6	-6	1	-0.3

■ ROY EVANS Evans, Roy b: 3/19/1874, Knoxville, Tenn. d: 8/15/15, Galveston, Tex. BR/TR, 6', 180 lbs. Deb: 5/15/1897

YEAR TM/L	W	L	PCT	G	GS	CG	SH	SV	IP	H	HR	BB	SO	RAT	ERA	ERA+	OAV	OOB	BH	AVG	PB	PR	/A	PD	TPI
1897 StL-N	0	0	—	3	0	0	0	0	13	33	1	13	4	31.8	9.69	45	.469	.552	0	.000	0	-8	-8	-0	-0.5
Lou-N	5	4	.556	9	8	6	0	0	59¹	66	4	24	20	13.7	4.10	104	.279	.346	3	.130	-2	1	1	-1	-0.1
Yr	5	4	.556	12	8	6	0	0	72¹	99	5	37	24	16.9	5.10	84	.323	.396	5	.192	-1	-6	-7	-1	-0.6
1898 Was-N	3	3	.500	7	6	4	0	0	50²	50	0	25	11	13.3	3.38	108	.256	.340	1	.053	-2	1	2	-1	0.0
1899 Was-N	3	4	.429	7	7	6	0	0	54	60	1	25	27	14.2	5.67	69	.281	.356	4	.200	-1	-11	-11	-0	-0.9
1902 NY-N	8	13	.381	23	17	17	0	0	176	186	2	58	48	13.0	3.17	89	.271	.337	8	.148	-1	-8	-7	2	-0.5
Bro-N	5	6	.455	13	11	11	2	0	97¹	91	0	33	35	11.7	2.68	103	.247	.313	2	.265	2	1	1	-3	0.1
Yr	13	19	.406	36	28	28	2	0	273¹	277	2	91	83	12.2	3.00	93	.260	.320	9	.102	1	-7	-6	-1	-0.4
1903 Bro-N	5	9	.357	15	12	9	0	0	110	121	1	41	42	13.8	3.27	98	.297	.371	5	.172	-0	-0	-1	-1	-0.2
StL-A	0	4	.000	7	7	4	0	0	54	66	1	14	24	13.3	4.17	70	.300	.342	2	.105	-1	-7	-8	0	-0.7
Total 5	29	43	.403	84	68	57	2	0	614¹	673	10	233	211	13.6	3.66	88	.281	.349	32	.159	-4	-30	-30	-4	-2.8

■ RED EVANS Evans, Russell Edison b: 11/12/06, Chicago, Ill. d: 6/14/82, Lakeview, Ark. BR/TR, 5'11", 168 lbs. Deb: 4/24/36

YEAR TM/L	W	L	PCT	G	GS	CG	SH	SV	IP	H	HR	BB	SO	RAT	ERA	ERA+	OAV	OOB	BH	AVG	PB	PR	/A	PD	TPI
1936 Chi-A	0	3	.000	17	0	0	0	1	47¹	70	4	22	19	17.5	7.61	68	.338	.402	2	.133	-1	-14	-13	1	-1.0
1939 Bro-N	1	8	.111	24	6	0	0	1	64¹	74	4	26	28	14.0	5.18	78	.284	.348	4	.308	1	-9	-8	1	-0.5
Total 2	1	11	.083	41	6	0	0	2	111²	144	8	48	47	15.5	6.21	73	.308	.372	6	.214	-0	-23	-21	3	-1.5

■ ART EVANS Evans, William Arthur b: 8/3/11, Elvins, Mo. d: 1/8/52, Wichita, Kan. BB/TL, 6'1.5", 181 lbs. Deb: 6/20/32

YEAR TM/L	W	L	PCT	G	GS	CG	SH	SV	IP	H	HR	BB	SO	RAT	ERA	ERA+	OAV	OOB	BH	AVG	PB	PR	/A	PD	TPI
1932 Chi-A	0	0	—	7	0	0	0	0	18	19	1	10	6	14.5	3.00	144	.257	.345	0	.000	-0	3	3	1	0.3

■ BILL EVANS Evans, William James b: 2/10/1894, Reidsville, N.C. d: 12/21/46, Burlington, N.C. BR/TR, 6', 175 lbs. Deb: 8/13/16

YEAR TM/L	W	L	PCT	G	GS	CG	SH	SV	IP	H	HR	BB	SO	RAT	ERA	ERA+	OAV	OOB	BH	AVG	PB	PR	/A	PD	TPI
1916 Pit-N	2	5	.286	13	6	3	0	0	63	57	2	16	21	10.9	3.00	89	.249	.306	3	.150	-1	-3	-2	2	0.0
1917 Pit-N	0	4	.000	8	2	1	0	0	26²	24	0	14	5	13.2	3.38	84	.231	.328	1	.111	-0	-2	-2	0	-0.1
1919 Pit-N	0	4	.000	7	3	2	0	0	36²	41	1	18	15	14.5	5.65	54	.297	.378	0	.000	-1	-11	-11	-1	-1.1
Total 3	2	13	.133	28	11	6	0	0	126¹	122	3	48	41	12.4	3.85	73	.259	.333	4	.100	-2	-16	-14	2	-1.2

■ BILL EVANS Evans, William Lawrence b: 3/25/19, Quanah, Texas d: 11/30/83, Grand Junction, Colo. BR/TR, 6'2", 180 lbs. Deb: 4/21/49

YEAR TM/L	W	L	PCT	G	GS	CG	SH	SV	IP	H	HR	BB	SO	RAT	ERA	ERA+	OAV	OOB	BH	AVG	PB	PR	/A	PD	TPI
1949 Chi-A	0	1	.000	4	0	0	0	0	6¹	6	0	8	1	19.9	7.11	59	.261	.452	0	.000	-0	-2	-2	-0	-0.1
1951 Bos-A	0	0	—	9	0	0	0	0	15¹	15	0	8	3	13.5	4.11	109	.268	.359	0	.000	-1	0	1	0	0.0
Total 2	0	1	.000	13	0	0	0	0	21²	21	0	16	4	15.4	4.98	88	.266	.389	0	—	-1	-2	-1	-0	-0.1

YEAR TM/L	W	L	PCT	G	GS	CG	SH	SV	IP	H	HR	BB	SO	RAT	ERA	ERA+	OAV	OOB	BH	AVG	PB	PR	/A	PD	TPI

■ LEON EVERITT Everitt, Edward Leon b: 1/12/47, Marshall, Tex. BL/TR, 6'1.5", 195 lbs. Deb: 4/21/69

| 1969 SD-N | 0 | 1 | .000 | 5 | 0 | 0 | 0 | 0 | 15² | 18 | 4 | 12 | 11 | 17.8 | 8.04 | 44 | .300 | .425 | 0 | .000 | -0 | -8 | -8 | 0 | -0.6 |

■ BOB EWING Ewing, George Lemuel "Long Bob" b: 4/24/1873, New Hampshire, O. d: 6/20/47, Wapakoneta, Ohio BR/TR, 6'1.5", 170 lbs. Deb: 4/19/02

1902 Cin-N	5	6	.455	15	12	10	0	0	117²	126	1	47	61	13.5	2.98	100	.274	.345	12	.169	-1	-3	0	-1	-0.1
1903 Cin-N	14	13	.519	29	28	27	1	1	246²	254	3	64	104	12.0	2.77	128	.265	.317	24	.253	4	14	22	3	3.1
1904 Cin-N	11	13	.458	26	24	22	0	0	212	198	3	58	99	11.0	2.46	119	.253	.308	25	.258	5	7	11	-1	1.8
1905 Cin-N	20	11	.645	40	34	30	4	0	312	284	5	79	164	10.8	2.51	132	.246	.301	32	.262	4	17	28	-4	3.2
1906 Cin-N	13	14	.481	33	32	26	2	0	287²	248	4	60	145	9.7	2.38	116	.238	.281	14	.139	-3	8	12	0	1.0
1907 Cin-N	17	19	.472	41	37	32	2	0	332²	279	2	85	147	10.0	1.73	150	.231	.286	19	.154	-1	27	32	-6	3.0
1908 Cin-N	17	15	.531	37	32	23	4	3	293²	247	5	57	95	9.5	2.21	105	.241	.284	14	.149	-1	5	3	-3	-0.1
1909 Cin-N	11	12	.478	31	29	14	2	0	218¹	195	1	63	86	10.9	2.43	107	.238	.298	8	.110	-4	4	4	-4	-0.4
1910 Phi-N	16	14	.533	34	32	20	4	0	255¹	235	5	86	102	11.6	3.00	104	.251	.318	20	.222	2	1	4	-2	0.4
1911 Phi-N	0	1	.000	4	3	1	0	0	24	29	2	14	12	16.1	7.88	44	.309	.398	2	.333	0	-12	-12	-0	-0.9
1912 StL-N	0	0	—	1	1	0	0	0	1¹	2	0	1	0	20.3	0.00	—	.333	.429	0	—	0	1	1	0	0.1
Total 11	124	118	.512	291	264	205	19	4	2301¹	2097	31	614	998	10.8	2.49	116	.247	.302	170	.195	6	69	102	-18	11.1

■ JOHN EWING Ewing, John "Long Jong" b: 6/1/1863, Cincinnati, Ohio d: 4/23/1895, Denver, Colo. TR , Deb: 6/18/1883 ♦

1888 Lou-a	8	13	.381	21	21	21	2	0	191	175	3	34	87	9.8	2.83	109	.235	.268	16	.203	-1	5	5	0	0.4
1889 Lou-a	6	30	.167	40	39	37	1	0	331	407	6	147	155	15.1	4.87	79	.293	.361	23	.172	-6	-37	-38	2	-3.3
1890 NY-P	18	12	.600	35	31	27	1	2	267¹	293	6	104	145	13.4	4.24	107	.267	.330	24	.211	-2	-0	9	-1	0.6
1891 NY-N	21	8	.724	33	30	28	5	0	269¹	237	2	105	138	11.4	2.27	141	.227	.298	23	.204	-2	32	28	0	2.4
Total 4	53	63	.457	129	121	113	9	2	1058²	1112	17	390	525	12.8	3.68	101	.260	.322	87	.192	-11	-1	3	1	0.2

■ BUCK EWING Ewing, William b: 10/17/1859, Hoaglands, Ohio d: 10/20/06, Cincinnati, Ohio BR/TR, 5'10", 188 lbs. Deb: 9/09/1880 MH♦

1882 Tro-N	0	0	—	1	0	0	0	0	1	2	0	1	0	27.0	9.00	31	.395	.494	89	.271	0	-1	-1	0	0.0
1884 NY-N	0	1	.000	1	1	0	0	0	8	7	0	4	3	12.4	1.13	264	.222	.310	106	.277	0	2	2	0	0.2
1885 NY-N	1	0	1.000	1	0	0	0	0	2	4	0	3	0	31.5	4.50	59	.398	.536	104	.304	0	-0	-0	0	0.0
1888 *NY-N	0	0	—	2	0	0	0	0	7	8	1	4	6	15.4	2.57	106	.277	.365	127	.306	1	0	0	-0	0.0
1889 *NY-N	2	0	1.000	3	2	2	0	0	20	23	0	8	12	13.9	4.05	97	.279	.343	133	.327	2	-0	-0	-0	0.0
1890 NY-P	0	1	.000	1	1	0	0	0	9	11	1	3	2	14.0	4.00	114	.289	.340	119	.338	1	0	1	-0	0.0
Total 6	2	3	.400	9	4	4	0	0	47	55	2	23	23	14.9	3.45	105	.281	.356	1625	.303	4	1	1	-0	0.2

■ GEORGE EYRICH Eyrich, George Lincoln b: 3/3/25, Reading, Pa. BR/TR, 5'11", 175 lbs. Deb: 6/13/43

| 1943 Phi-N | 0 | 0 | — | 9 | 0 | 0 | 0 | 0 | 18² | 23 | 1 | 9 | 5 | 15.4 | 3.38 | 100 | .291 | .364 | 0 | .000 | -0 | 0 | -0 | -0 | 0.0 |

■ RED FABER Faber, Urban Charles b: 9/6/1888, Cascade, Iowa d: 9/25/76, Chicago, Ill. BB/TR, 6'2", 180 lbs. Deb: 4/17/14 CH

1914 Chi-A	10	9	.526	40	19	11	2	4	181¹	154	3	64	88	11.4	2.68	100	.239	.319	8	.145	1	1	0	2	0.3
1915 Chi-A	24	14	.632	50	32	21	2	2	299²	264	3	99	182	11.2	2.55	117	.240	.309	11	.131	2	13	14	-1	1.8
1916 Chi-A	17	9	.654	35	31	15	3	1	205¹	167	1	61	87	10.2	2.02	137	.228	.292	6	.095	-3	19	17	2	1.8
1917 *Chi-A	16	13	.552	41	29	16	3	3	248	224	1	85	84	11.6	1.92	138	.247	.319	4	.058	-4	20	20	2	2.1
1918 Chi-A	4	1	.800	11	9	5	1	1	80²	70	3	23	26	10.4	1.23	223	.245	.301	1	.042	-2	14	14	1	1.5
1919 Chi-A	11	9	.550	25	20	9	0	0	162¹	185	7	45	45	13.2	3.83	83	.287	.341	10	.185	-0	-11	-12	1	-1.1
1920 Chi-A	23	13	.639	40	39	28	2	1	319	332	8	88	108	12.0	2.99	126	.277	.328	11	.106	-4	29	28	-1	2.2
1921 Chi-A	25	15	.625	43	39	32	4	1	330²	293	10	87	124	10.5	2.48	171	.242	.297	16	.148	-4	66	65	1	6.2
1922 Chi-A	21	17	.553	43	38	31	4	2	352	334	10	83	148	10.8	2.81	145	.252	.299	25	.200	-2	48	49	0	4.8
1923 Chi-A	14	11	.560	32	31	15	2	0	232¹	233	6	62	91	11.7	3.41	116	.259	.311	15	.217	3	14	14	2	1.9
1924 Chi-A	9	11	.450	21	20	9	0	0	161¹	173	5	58	47	13.0	3.85	107	.282	.346	7	.148	2	7	5	-2	0.1
1925 Chi-A	12	11	.522	34	32	16	1	0	238	266	8	59	71	12.4	3.78	110	.289	.333	8	.104	-4	16	10	1	0.6
1926 Chi-A	15	9	.625	27	25	13	1	0	184²	203	3	57	65	12.8	3.56	109	.281	.335	9	.150	-0	9	6	-3	0.2
1927 Chi-A	4	7	.364	18	15	6	0	0	110²	131	2	41	39	14.4	4.55	89	.312	.380	10	.270	2	-5	-6	2	-0.1
1928 Chi-A	13	9	.591	27	27	16	2	0	201¹	223	11	68	43	13.2	3.75	108	.286	.347	8	.114	-3	6	7	2	0.4
1929 Chi-A	13	13	.500	31	31	15	1	0	234	241	10	61	68	12.0	3.88	110	.273	.327	10	.128	-3	9	10	2	0.9
1930 Chi-A	8	13	.381	29	26	10	0	1	169	188	7	49	62	12.9	4.21	110	.283	.337	2	.041	-5	8	8	2	0.5
1931 Chi-A	10	14	.417	44	19	5	1	1	184	210	11	57	49	13.2	3.82	112	.285	.339	4	.075	-1	12	9	-1	0.4
1932 Chi-A	2	11	.154	42	5	0	0	6	106	123	0	38	26	13.8	3.74	116	.290	.350	4	.222	4	9	7	-0	0.8
1933 Chi-A	3	4	.429	36	2	0	0	5	86¹	92	2	28	18	12.6	3.44	123	.275	.332	0	.000	-3	8	8	-0	0.4
Total 20	254	213	.544	669	483	273	29	28	4086²	4106	111	1213	1471	11.9	3.15	119	.266	.323	170	.134	-30	294	274	10	25.7

■ ROY FACE Face, Elroy Leon b: 2/20/28, Stephentown, N.Y. BR/TR, 5'8", 155 lbs. Deb: 4/16/53

1953 Pit-N	6	8	.429	41	13	6	0	0	119	145	19	30	56	13.4	6.58	68	.297	.340	4	.133	-2	-30	-28	-1	-2.7
1955 Pit-N	5	7	.417	42	10	4	0	5	125²	128	10	40	84	12.0	3.58	115	.268	.325	3	.115	-1	6	7	-1	0.5
1956 Pit-N	12	13	.480	68	3	0	0	6	135¹	131	16	42	96	11.6	3.52	107	.256	.314	5	.192	-0	4	4	1	0.4
1957 Pit-N	4	6	.400	59	1	0	0	10	93²	97	9	24	53	11.7	3.07	123	.270	.318	2	.125	-1	8	7	-2	0.5
1958 Pit-N	5	2	.714	57	0	0	0	20	84	77	6	22	47	10.6	2.89	134	.244	.293	0	.000	-1	10	9	1	0.9
1959 Pit-N	18	1	.947	57	0	0	0	10	93¹	91	5	25	69	11.3	2.70	143	.266	.318	3	.231	0	13	12	-1	1.2
1960 *Pit-N	10	8	.556	68	0	0	0	24	114²	93	11	29	72	9.6	2.90	129	.226	.277	7	.412	2	11	11	1	1.5
1961 Pit-N	6	12	.333	62	0	0	0	17	92	94	12	10	55	10.3	3.82	105	.267	.289	3	.273	0	2	2	2	0.4
1962 Pit-N	8	7	.533	63	0	0	0	28	91	74	7	14	45	9.2	1.88	209	.231	.274	1	.083	-1	21	21	-1	2.0
1963 Pit-N	3	9	.250	56	0	0	0	16	69²	75	6	19	41	12.5	3.23	102	.285	.340	2	.250	-1	0	1	1	0.2
1964 Pit-N	3	3	.500	55	0	0	0	4	79²	82	11	27	63	12.4	5.20	68	.269	.309	0	.000	-0	-15	-15	-0	-1.5
1965 Pit-N	5	2	.714	16	0	0	0	0	20¹	20	1	7	19	12.0	2.66	132	.263	.325	0	.000	-0	2	2	-1	0.1
1966 Pit-N	6	6	.500	54	0	0	0	18	70	68	9	24	67	12.0	2.70	132	.262	.326	0	.000	-1	7	7	0	0.6
1967 Pit-N	7	5	.583	61	0	0	0	17	74¹	62	5	22	41	10.2	2.42	139	.230	.288	0	.000	-1	8	8	-1	0.7
1968 Pit-N	2	4	.333	43	0	0	0	13	52	46	3	7	34	9.5	2.60	113	.238	.272	0	.000	-0	2	2	-0	0.4
Det-A	0	0	—	2	0	0	0	0	1	2	0	1	1	27.0	0.00	—	.500	.600	0	—	-0	0	0	0	0.0
1969 Mon-N	4	2	.667	44	0	0	0	5	11	15	1	34	11.7	3.94	93	.263	.307	1	.500	0	-2	-2	-0	-0.1
Total 16	104	95	.523	848	27	6	0	193	1375	1347	141	362	877	11.3	3.48	109	.260	.310	31	.160	-4	48	48	-1	4.8

■ TONY FAETH Faeth, Anthony Joseph b: 7/9/1893, Aberdeen, S.D. d: 12/22/82, St.Paul, Minn. BR/TR, 6', 180 lbs. Deb: 8/10/19

1919 Cle-A	0	0	—	6	0	0	0	0	18¹	13	0	10	7	11.3	0.49	682	.224	.338	0	.000	-1	6	6	-0	0.5
1920 Cle-A	0	0	—	13	0	0	0	0	25	31	0	20	14	18.7	4.32	88	.333	.456	0	.000	-1	-1	-1	-0	-0.1
Total 2	0	0	—	19	0	0	0	0	43¹	44	0	30	21	15.6	2.70	134	.291	.412	0	.000	-1	4	4	-0	0.4

■ EVERETT FAGAN Fagan, Everett Joseph b: 1/13/18, Pottersville, N.J. d: 2/16/83, Morristown, N.J. BR/TR, 6', 195 lbs. Deb: 4/24/43

1943 Phi-A	2	6	.250	18	2	0	0	3	37¹	41	4	14	9	13.7	6.27	54	.283	.354	0	.000	-0	-12	-12	0	-1.1
1946 Phi-A	0	1	.000	20	0	0	0	0	45	47	2	24	12	14.8	4.80	74	.264	.361	4	.286	1	-6	-6	-0	-0.5
Total 2	2	7	.222	38	2	0	0	3	82¹	88	6	38	21	14.3	5.47	64	.272	.358	4	.190	1	-19	-18	0	-1.6

■ BILL FAGAN Fagan, William A. "Clinkers" b: 2/15/1869, Troy, N.Y. d: 3/21/30, Troy, N.Y. 5'11", 165 lbs. Deb: 9/15/1887

1887 NY-a	1	4	.200	6	6	6	0	0	45	55	1	24	12	15.8	4.00	106	.290	.370	3	.143	-2	1	1	0	0.0
1888 KC-a	5	11	.313	17	17	15	0	0	142¹	179	4	75	49	16.1	5.69	60	.296	.374	14	.215	-1	-42	-36	1	-2.8
Total 2	6	15	.286	23	23	21	0	0	187¹	234	5	99	61	16.0	5.28	69	.295	.373	17	.198	-3	-40	-34	1	-2.8

YEAR TM/L	W	L	PCT	G	GS	CG	SH	SV	IP	H	HR	BB	SO	RAT	ERA	ERA+	OAV	OOB	BH	AVG	PB	PR	/A	PD	TPI

■ FRANK FAHEY Fahey, Francis Raymond b: 1/22/1896, Milford, Mass. d: 3/19/54, Boston, Mass. BB/TR, 6'1", 190 lbs. Deb: 4/25/18 ♦

| 1918 Phi-A | 0 | 0 | — | 3 | 0 | 0 | 0 | 0 | 9 | 5 | 0 | 14 | 1 | 20.0 | 6.00 | 49 | .200 | .500 | 3 | .176 | -0 | -3 | -3 | -0 | -0.2 |

■ JERRY FAHR Fahr, Gerald Warren b: 12/9/24, Marmaduke, Ark. BR/TR, 6'5", 185 lbs. Deb: 4/29/51

| 1951 Cle-A | 0 | 0 | — | 5 | 0 | 0 | 0 | 0 | 5² | 11 | 0 | 2 | 2 | 20.6 | 4.76 | 80 | .500 | .542 | 0 | — | 0 | -0 | -1 | 0 | 0.0 |

■ PETE FAHRER Fahrer, Clarence Willie b: 3/10/1890, Holgate, Ohio d: 6/10/67, Fremont, Mich. TR, 6', 190 lbs. Deb: 8/17/14

| 1914 Cin-N | 0 | 0 | — | 5 | 0 | 0 | 0 | 0 | 8 | 8 | 0 | 4 | 2 | 13.5 | 1.13 | 260 | .308 | .400 | 0 | .000 | -0 | 1 | 2 | 0 | 0.2 |

■ JIM FAIRBANK Fairbank, James Lee "Lee" or "Smoky" b: 3/17/1881, Deansboro, N.Y. d: 12/27/55, Utica, N.Y. 5'10", 185 lbs. Deb: 9/18/03

1903 Phi-A	1	1	.500	4	1	1	0	0	24	33	1	12	10	16.9	4.88	63	.325	.397	1	.100	-1	-5	-5	1	-0.3
1904 Phi-A	0	1	.000	3	1	1	0	0	17	19	0	13	6	16.9	6.35	42	.283	.399	0	.000	-1	-7	-7	1	-0.6
Total 2	1	2	.333	7	2	2	0	0	41	52	1	25	16	16.9	5.49	53	.309	.398	1	.063	-1	-12	-12	2	-0.9

■ RAGS FAIRCLOTH Faircloth, James Lamar b: 8/19/1892, Kenton, Tenn. d: 10/5/53, Tucson, Ariz. BR/TR, 5'11", 160 lbs. Deb: 5/06/19

| 1919 Phi-N | 0 | 0 | — | 2 | 0 | 0 | 0 | 0 | 2 | 5 | 0 | 0 | 0 | 22.5 | 9.00 | 36 | .625 | .625 | 0 | — | 0 | -1 | -1 | 0 | 0.0 |

■ PETE FALCONE Falcone, Peter Frank b: 10/1/53, Brooklyn, N.Y. BL/TL, 6'2", 185 lbs. Deb: 4/13/75

1975 SF-N	12	11	.522	34	32	3	1	0	190	171	16	111	131	13.5	4.17	91	.244	.350	4	.062	-5	-12	-8	-1	-1.2
1976 StL-N	12	16	.429	32	32	9	2	0	212	173	12	93	138	11.4	3.23	110	.222	.306	8	.129	-2	6	7	-5	0.1
1977 StL-N	4	8	.333	27	22	1	1	1	124	130	19	61	75	14.1	5.44	71	.273	.359	10	.244	2	-21	-22	-1	-1.9
1978 StL-N	2	7	.222	19	14	0	0	0	75	94	9	48	28	17.3	5.76	61	.319	.417	5	.238	1	-18	-19	-1	-1.8
1979 NY-N	6	14	.300	33	31	1	1	0	184	194	24	76	113	13.3	4.16	88	.276	.347	9	.173	0	-9	-11	-3	-1.3
1980 NY-N	7	10	.412	37	23	0	0	1	157¹	163	16	58	109	12.8	4.52	79	.269	.335	4	.146	-1	-16	-17	-3	-2.0
1981 NY-N	5	3	.625	35	9	3	1	1	95¹	84	3	36	56	11.3	2.55	137	.241	.312	4	.182	1	10	10	-2	1.0
1982 NY-N	8	10	.444	40	23	3	0	2	171	159	24	71	101	12.2	3.84	94	.252	.329	6	.113	-2	-5	-4	-3	-0.8
1983 Atl-N	9	4	.692	33	15	2	0	0	106²	102	14	60	59	13.8	3.63	107	.256	.355	3	.115	-1	-0	3	-1	-0.3
1984 Atl-N	5	7	.417	35	16	2	1	2	120	115	15	57	55	12.9	4.13	93	.252	.335	7	.212	1	-7	-4	-1	-0.3
Total 10	70	90	.438	325	217	25	7	7	1435¹	1385	152	671	865	13.0	4.07	90	.257	.341	62	.149	-6	-71	-63	-20	-8.2

■ CHET FALK Falk, Chester Emanuel "Spot" b: 5/15/05, Austin, Tex. d: 1/7/82, Austin, Tex. BL/TL, 6'2", 170 lbs. Deb: 4/20/25

1925 StL-A	0	0	—	13	0	0	0	0	25	38	2	17	7	19.8	8.28	56	.362	.451	5	.625	2	-11	-10	-0	-0.5
1926 StL-A	4	4	.500	18	8	3	0	0	74	95	1	27	7	15.6	5.35	80	.338	.408	6	.194	-1	-11	-9	-0	-0.8
1927 StL-A	1	0	1.000	9	0	0	0	0	15²	25	1	10	2	20.1	5.74	76	.352	.432	1	.200	-0	-3	-2	0	-0.1
Total 3	5	4	.556	40	8	3	0	0	114²	158	4	54	16	17.1	6.04	73	.346	.422	12	.273	1	-25	-21	1	-1.4

■ CY FALKENBERG Falkenberg, Frederick Peter b: 12/17/1880, Chicago, Ill. d: 4/14/61, San Francisco, Cal BR/TR, 6'5", 180 lbs. Deb: 4/21/03

1903 Pit-N	1	5	.167	10	6	3	0	0	56	65	0	32	24	15.9	3.86	84	.295	.390	4	.190	-0	-4	-4	1	-0.2
1905 Was-A	7	2	.778	12	10	6	2	0	75¹	71	1	35	12.2	3.82	69	.250	.324	4	.125	-2	-10	-10	-1	-1.2
1906 Was-A	14	20	.412	40	36	30	2	1	298²	277	1	108	178	11.6	2.86	92	.249	.315	18	.170	1	-6	-8	-0	-0.6
1907 Was-A	6	17	.261	32	24	17	1	1	233²	195	0	77	108	10.5	2.35	103	.229	.293	12	.140	-3	5	2	2	0.0
1908 Was-A	6	2	.750	17	8	5	1	0	82²	70	2	21	34	10.1	1.96	117	.236	.291	6	.222	0	4	3	1	0.4
Cle-A	2	4	.333	8	7	2	0	0	46¹	52	1	10	17	12.4	3.88	62	.284	.328	2	.118	-1	-8	-8	-0	-0.9
Yr	8	6	.571	25	15	7	1	0	129	122	3	31	51	10.8	2.65	88	.253	.301	0	.000	-1	-4	-5	0	-0.5
1909 Cle-A	10	9	.526	24	18	13	2	0	165	135	0	50	82	10.4	2.40	107	.231	.297	9	.173	-1	1	3	3	0.5
1910 Cle-A	14	13	.519	37	29	18	3	1	256²	246	3	75	107	11.5	2.95	88	.261	.320	15	.183	-0	-12	-10	3	-0.7
1911 Cle-A	8	5	.615	15	13	7	0	1	106²	117	0	24	46	12.2	3.29	104	.282	.326	7	.175	-1	1	1	1	0.1
1913 Cle-A	23	10	.697	39	36	23	6	0	276	238	2	88	166	10.8	2.22	137	.235	.299	10	.119	-2	22	25	-3	2.2
1914 Ind-F	25	16	.610	49	43	33	9	3	377¹	332	5	89	236	10.2	2.22	156	.236	.284	41	.168	3	41	52	1	5.8
1915 New-F	9	11	.450	25	21	14	0	1	172	175	6	47	76	12.1	3.24	88	.268	.326	3	.053	-6	-4	-8	-1	-1.2
Bro-F	3	3	.500	7	7	5	1	0	48	31	1	12	20	8.3	1.50	201	.189	.249	1	.067	-1	8	8	-0	0.8
Yr	12	14	.462	32	28	19	1	1	220	206	7	59	96	10.9	2.86	101	.250	.301	4	.028	-7	4	0	-1	-0.4
1917 Phi-A	2	6	.250	15	8	4	0	0	80²	86	1	26	35	12.5	3.35	82	.293	.350	5	.185	0	-6	-5	1	-0.3
Total 12	130	123	.514	330	266	180	27	8	2275	2090	23	690	1164	11.2	2.68	106	.248	.308	117	.152	-19	34	41	9	4.7

■ ED FALLENSTEIN Fallenstein, Edward Joseph "Jack" (b: Edward Joseph Valestin) b: 12/22/08, Newark, N.J. d: 11/24/71, Orange, N.J. BR/TR, 6'3", 180 lbs. Deb: 4/16/31

1931 Phi-N	0	0	—	24	0	0	0	0	41²	56	2	26	15	17.7	7.13	60	.333	.423	1	.200	0	-15	-13	0	-1.2
1933 Bos-N	2	1	.667	9	4	1	1	0	35	43	1	13	5	14.7	3.60	85	.305	.368	3	.375	1	-1	-2	-0	0.0
Total 2	2	1	.667	33	4	1	1	0	76²	99	3	39	20	16.3	5.52	67	.320	.398	4	.308	1	-16	-16	0	-1.2

■ BOB FALLON Fallon, Robert Joseph b: 2/18/60, Bronx, N.Y. BL/TL, 6'3", 200 lbs. Deb: 4/26/84

1984 Chi-A	0	0	—	3	3	0	0	0	14²	12	0	11	10	14.1	3.68	113	.235	.371	0	—	0	1	1	0	0.1
1985 Chi-A	0	0	—	10	0	0	0	0	16	25	5	9	17	19.1	6.19	70	.362	.436	0	—	0	-4	-3	0	-0.2
Total 2	0	0	—	13	3	0	0	0	30²	37	5	20	27	16.7	4.99	85	.308	.407	0	—	0	-3	-3	1	-0.1

■ CLIFF FANNIN Fannin, Clifford Bryson "Mule" b: 5/13/24, Louisa, Ky. d: 12/11/66, Sandusky, Ohio BL/TR, 6', 170 lbs. Deb: 9/02/45

1945 StL-A	0	0	—	5	0	0	0	0	10¹	8	0	5	5	11.3	2.61	135	.222	.317	0	.000	-0	1	1	0	0.1
1946 StL-A	5	2	.714	27	7	4	1	2	86²	76	4	42	52	12.4	3.01	124	.236	.326	5	.161	-1	5	7	-0	0.6
1947 StL-A	6	8	.429	26	18	6	2	1	145²	134	10	77	77	13.1	3.58	108	.245	.340	9	.196	-0	2	5	-0	0.5
1948 StL-A	10	14	.417	34	29	10	3	1	213²	198	14	104	102	12.8	4.17	109	.245	.332	11	.169	-0	3	9	-3	0.7
1949 StL-A	8	14	.364	30	25	5	0	1	143	177	15	93	57	17.0	6.17	73	.308	.404	9	.164	-2	-31	-26	-3	-2.7
1950 StL-A	5	9	.357	25	16	3	0	1	102	116	18	58	42	15.4	6.53	76	.280	.369	6	.176	-2	-22	-18	-0	-1.7
1951 StL-A	0	2	.000	7	1	0	0	0	15¹	20	6	5	11	14.7	6.46	68	.317	.368	1	.250	-0	-4	-4	0	-0.2
1952 StL-A	0	2	.000	10	2	0	0	0	16¹	34	5	9	6	23.7	12.67	31	.453	.512	0	.000	-0	-16	-16	0	-1.4
Total 8	34	51	.400	164	98	28	6	6	733	763	72	393	352	14.2	4.85	89	.269	.358	41	.173	-6	-63	-42	-6	-4.1

■ JACK FANNING Fanning, John Jacob b: 1863, S.Orange, N.J. d: 6/10/17, Aberdeen, Wash. 5'9", 163 lbs. Deb: 9/20/1889

1889 Ind-N	0	1	.000	1	1	0	0	0	1	3	0	2	0	45.0	18.00	23	.503	.628	0	.000	-0	-2	-2	0	-0.1
1894 Phi-N	1	3	.250	5	4	2	0	0	32¹	45	4	20	7	18.1	8.07	63	.326	.411	2	.154	-1	-10	-11	-0	-0.7
Total 2	1	4	.200	6	5	2	0	0	33¹	48	4	22	7	18.9	8.37	61	.333	.421	2	.143	-1	-11	-12	0	-0.7

■ HARRY FANOK Fanok, Harry Michael "The Flame Thrower" b: 5/11/40, Whippany, N.J. BB/TR, 6', 180 lbs. Deb: 4/16/63

1963 StL-N	2	1	.667	12	0	0	0	1	25²	24	3	21	25	16.1	5.26	67	.255	.397	2	.400	1	-6	-5	-0	-0.4
1964 StL-N	0	0	—	4	0	0	0	0	7²	5	0	3	10	9.4	5.87	65	.179	.258	0	.000	-0	-2	-2	-0	-0.1
Total 2	2	1	.667	16	0	0	0	1	33¹	29	3	24	35	14.6	5.40	67	.238	.367	2	.333	1	-8	-7	-0	-0.5

■ FRANK FANOVICH Fanovich, Frank Joseph "Lefty" b: 1/11/22, New York, N.Y. BL/TL, 5'11", 180 lbs. Deb: 4/25/49

1949 Cin-N	0	2	.000	29	1	0	0	0	43¹	44	2	28	27	15.4	5.40	77	.257	.368	0	.000	-0	-7	-6	0	-0.5
1953 Phi-A	0	3	.000	26	3	0	0	0	61²	62	5	37	37	15.3	5.55	77	.273	.389	2	.182	-0	-11	-9	-1	-0.9
Total 2	0	5	.000	55	4	0	0	0	105	106	7	65	64	15.3	5.49	77	.266	.380	2	.133	-1	-17	-14	-1	-1.4

■ STAN FANSLER Fansler, Stanley Robert b: 2/12/65, Elkins, W.V.A BR/TR, 5'11", 180 lbs. Deb: 9/06/86

| 1986 Pit-N | 0 | 3 | .000 | 5 | 5 | 0 | 0 | 0 | 24 | 20 | 2 | 15 | 13 | 13.1 | 3.75 | 102 | .247 | .365 | 1 | .167 | -0 | 0 | 0 | 0 | 0.0 |

YEAR TM/L	W	L	PCT	G	GS	CG	SH	SV	IP	H	HR	BB	SO	RAT	ERA	ERA+	OAV	OOB	BH	AVG	PB	PR	/A	PD	TPI
■ **HARRY FANWELL**				Fanwell, Harry Clayton b: 10/16/1886, Patapsco, Md. d: 7/15/65, Baltimore, Md. BB/TR, 6′, 175 lbs. Deb: 7/23/10																				
1910 Cle-A	2	9	.182	17	11	5	1	0	92	87	0	38	30	12.8	3.62	71	.260	.347	1	.033	-3	-11	-11	1	-1.2
■ **ED FARMER**				Farmer, Edward Joseph b: 10/18/49, Evergreen Park, Ill BR/TR, 6′5″, 200 lbs. Deb: 6/09/71																				
1971 Cle-A	5	4	.556	43	4	0	0	4	78²	77	9	41	48	13.8	4.35	88	.263	.359	1	.071	-1	-8	-5	0	-0.5
1972 Cle-A	2	5	.286	46	1	0	0	7	61¹	51	10	27	33	11.6	4.40	73	.231	.317	1	.143	-0	-9	-8	1	-0.8
1973 Cle-A	0	2	.000	16	0	0	0	1	17¹	25	4	5	10	15.6	4.67	84	.325	.366	0	—	0	-2	-1	-0	-0.1
Det-A	3	0	1.000	24	0	0	0	2	45	52	3	27	28	16.2	5.00	82	.292	.391	0	—	0	-6	-5	-1	-0.4
Yr	3	2	.600	40	0	0	0	3	62¹	77	7	32	38	16.0	4.91	82	.301	.383	0	—	0	-8	-6	-1	-0.5
1974 Phi-N	2	1	.667	14	3	0	0	0	31	41	5	27	20	19.7	8.42	45	.323	.442	1	.111	-1	-17	-16	-0	-1.5
1977 Bal-A	0	0	—	1	0	0	0	0	0	1	0	1	0	—	∞	—	1.000	1.000	0	—	0	-1	-1	0	0.0
1978 Mil-A	1	0	1.000	3	0	0	0	1	11	7	1	4	6	9.0	0.82	459	.175	.250	0	—	0	4	4	0	0.4
1979 Tex-A	2	0	1.000	11	2	0	0	0	33	30	2	19	25	13.9	4.36	95	.252	.364	0	—	0	-1	-1	-0	0.0
Chi-A	3	7	.300	42	3	0	0	14	81¹	66	2	34	48	11.2	2.43	175	.219	.301	0	—	0	16	16	0	1.6
Yr	5	7	.417	53	5	0	0	14	114¹	96	4	53	73	11.8	2.99	141	.226	.314	0	—	0	16	16	0	1.6
1980 Chi-A	7	9	.438	64	0	0	0	30	99²	92	6	56	54	13.5	3.34	121	.244	.343	0	—	0	8	8	1	0.8
1981 Chi-A	3	3	.500	42	0	0	0	10	52²	53	5	34	42	15.0	4.61	78	.262	.371	0	—	0	-6	-6	0	-0.5
1982 Phi-N	2	6	.250	47	4	0	0	6	76	66	2	50	58	13.7	4.86	75	.234	.349	0	.000	-1	-11	-10	-1	-1.1
1983 Phi-N	0	6	.000	12	3	0	0	0	26²	35	7	20	16	18.9	6.08	59	.307	.415	1	.167	-0	-7	-7	0	-0.6
Oak-A	0	0	—	5	1	0	0	0	10¹	15	1	0	7	13.1	3.48	111	.366	.366	0	—	0	1	0	-0	0.0
Total 11	30	43	.411	370	21	0	0	75	624	611	52	345	395	14.0	4.30	89	.257	.355	4	.085	-3	-38	-31	1	-2.7
■ **HOWARD FARMER**				Farmer, Howard Earl b: 1/18/66, Gary, Ind. BR/TR, 6′3″, 185 lbs. Deb: 7/02/90																				
1990 Mon-N	0	3	.000	6	4	0	0	0	23	26	9	10	14	14.1	7.04	53	.302	.375	2	.400	1	-8	-8	1	-0.6
■ **JIM FARR**				Farr, James Alfred b: 5/18/56, Waverly, N.Y. BR/TR, 6′1″, 195 lbs. Deb: 9/07/82																				
1982 Tex-A	0	0	—	5	0	0	0	0	18	20	1	7	6	13.5	2.50	155	.278	.342	0	—	0	3	3	-0	0.3
■ **STEVE FARR**				Farr, Steven Michael b: 12/12/56, LaPlata, Md. BR/TR, 5′10″, 198 lbs. Deb: 5/16/84																				
1984 Cle-A	3	11	.214	31	16	0	0	1	116	106	14	46	83	12.2	4.58	89	.245	.325	0	—	0	-8	-6	0	-0.5
1985 *KC-A	2	1	.667	16	3	0	0	1	37²	34	2	20	36	13.4	3.11	134	.245	.348	0	—	0	4	4	0	0.5
1986 KC-A	8	4	.667	56	0	0	0	8	109¹	90	10	39	83	10.9	3.13	136	.228	.304	0	—	0	13	14	1	1.4
1987 KC-A	4	3	.571	47	0	0	0	1	91	97	9	44	88	14.1	4.15	110	.270	.353	0	—	0	3	4	-2	0.2
1988 KC-A	5	4	.556	62	1	0	0	20	82²	74	5	30	72	11.5	2.50	159	.240	.312	0	—	0	13	14	-1	1.3
1989 KC-A	2	5	.286	51	0	0	0	18	63¹	75	5	22	56	13.9	4.12	93	.296	.355	0	—	0	-2	-2	-1	-0.2
1990 KC-A	13	7	.650	57	6	1	1	1	127	99	6	48	94	10.8	1.98	192	.220	.302	0	—	0	27	26	0	2.7
Total 7	37	35	.514	320	28	1	1	50	627	575	51	249	512	12.1	3.33	123	.246	.324	0	—	0	51	53	-2	5.4
■ **JOHN FARRELL**				Farrell, John Edward b: 8/4/62, Monmouth Beach, N.J. BR/TR, 6′4″, 210 lbs. Deb: 8/18/87																				
1987 Cle-A	5	1	.833	10	9	1	0	0	69	68	7	22	28	12.4	3.39	133	.256	.324	0	—	0	8	9	-0	0.8
1988 Cle-A	14	10	.583	31	30	4	0	0	210¹	216	15	67	92	12.5	4.24	97	.269	.332	0	—	0	-6	-3	0	-0.2
1989 Cle-A	9	14	.391	31	31	7	2	0	208	196	14	71	132	11.9	3.63	109	.244	.311	0	—	0	6	8	-2	0.6
1990 Cle-A	4	5	.444	17	17	1	0	0	96²	108	10	33	44	13.2	4.28	93	.286	.345	0	—	0	-4	-3	0	-0.2
Total 4	32	30	.516	89	87	13	2	0	584	588	46	193	296	12.4	3.93	104	.261	.326	0	—	0	4	10	-2	1.0
■ **KERBY FARRELL**				Farrell, Major Kerby b: 9/3/13, Leapwood, Tenn. d: 12/17/75, Nashville, Tenn. BL/TL, 5′11″, 172 lbs. Deb: 4/24/43 MC♦																				
1943 Bos-N	0	1	.000	5	0	0	0	0	23	24	1	9	4	12.9	4.30	79	.276	.344	75	.268	1	-2	-2	0	-0.1
■ **TURK FARRELL**				Farrell, Richard Joseph b: 4/8/34, Boston, Mass. d: 6/10/77, Great Yarmouth, England BR/TR, 6′4″, 215 lbs. Deb: 9/21/56																				
1956 Phi-N	0	1	.000	1	1	0	0	0	4¹	6	0	3	0	20.8	12.46	30	.353	.476	0	.000	-0	-4	-4	0	-0.2
1957 Phi-N	10	2	.833	52	0	0	0	10	83¹	74	2	36	54	12.1	2.38	160	.242	.326	1	.111	0	14	13	0	1.4
1958 Phi-N	8	9	.471	54	0	0	0	11	94	84	7	40	73	11.9	3.35	118	.244	.323	5	.208	0	6	6	-2	0.5
1959 Phi-N	1	6	.143	38	0	0	0	6	57	61	9	25	31	13.6	4.74	87	.288	.363	1	.167	-0	-5	-4	-0	-0.3
1960 Phi-N	10	6	.625	59	0	0	0	11	103¹	88	3	29	70	10.5	2.70	144	.239	.302	3	.200	1	12	14	-1	1.4
1961 Phi-N	2	1	.667	5	0	0	0	0	9²	10	3	6	10	15.8	6.52	63	.270	.386	1	.500	1	-3	-3	-0	-0.2
LA-N	6	6	.500	50	0	0	0	10	89	107	12	43	80	15.3	5.06	86	.296	.372	0	.000	-3	-10	-7	-2	-1.0
Yr	8	7	.533	55	0	0	0	10	98²	117	15	49	90	15.2	5.20	83	.293	.372	0	.000	-2	-13	-10	-2	-1.2
1962 Hou-N	10	20	.333	43	29	11	2	4	241²	210	21	55	203	10.1	3.02	124	.233	.280	14	.179	1	25	19	-3	1.9
1963 Hou-N	14	13	.519	34	26	12	0	1	202¹	161	12	35	141	8.8	3.02	104	.219	.256	9	.143	2	6	3	-2	0.2
1964 Hou-N	11	10	.524	32	27	7	0	0	198¹	196	21	52	117	11.4	3.27	105	.261	.311	5	.072	-3	6	3	-1	-0.1
1965 Hou-N	11	11	.500	33	29	8	3	1	208¹	202	18	35	122	10.4	3.50	96	.252	.286	10	.135	-1	1	-3	-1	-0.5
1966 Hou-N	6	10	.375	32	21	3	0	2	152²	167	23	28	101	11.5	4.60	74	.278	.310	7	.146	-0	-17	-20	-2	-2.2
1967 Hou-N	1	0	1.000	7	0	0	0	0	11²	11	0	7	10	14.7	4.63	72	.244	.358	0	.000	-0	-2	-2	0	-0.2
Phi-N	9	6	.600	50	1	0	0	12	92	76	6	15	68	9.0	2.05	166	.228	.263	2	.105	-0	14	14	-1	1.4
Yr	10	6	.625	57	1	0	0	12	103²	87	6	22	78	9.5	2.34	145	.229	.273	2	.050	-0	12	12	-1	1.3
1968 Phi-N	4	6	.400	54	0	0	0	12	83	83	7	32	57	12.7	3.47	87	.271	.344	1	.167	-0	-4	-4	-0	-0.4
1969 Phi-N	3	4	.429	46	0	0	0	3	74¹	92	8	27	40	14.5	4.00	89	.307	.366	0	.000	-1	-3	-4	-2	-0.5
Total 14	106	111	.488	590	134	41	5	83	1705	1628	152	468	1177	11.2	3.45	103	.254	.307	59	.135	-3	35	21	-17	1.3
■ **FAST**				Fast b: Milwaukee, Wis. Deb: 7/11/1887																				
1887 Ind-N	0	1	.000	4	2	1	0	1	15²	25	1	8	0	19.0	10.34	40	.351	.417	2	.182	-1	-11	-11	0	-0.8
■ **DARCY FAST**				Fast, Darcy Rae b: 3/10/47, Dallas, Ore. BL/TL, 6′3″, 195 lbs. Deb: 6/15/68																				
1968 Chi-N	0	1	.000	8	1	0	0	0	10	8	1	8	10	14.4	5.40	59	.216	.356	0	.000	-0	-3	-2	0	-0.2
■ **JACK FASZHOLZ**				Faszholz, John Edward "Preacher" b: 4/11/27, St.Louis, Mo. BR/TR, 6′3″, 205 lbs. Deb: 4/25/53																				
1953 StL-N	0	0	—	4	1	0	0	0	11²	16	3	1	7	13.9	6.94	61	.327	.353	0	.000	-0	-3	-3	-0	-0.3
■ **BILL FAUL**				Faul, William Alvan b: 4/21/40, Cincinnati, Ohio BR/TR, 5′10″, 184 lbs. Deb: 9/19/62																				
1962 Det-A	0	0	—	1	0	0	0	0	1²	4	1	3	2	43.2	32.40	13	.444	.615	0	—	0	-5	-5	0	-0.3
1963 Det-A	5	6	.455	28	10	2	0	1	97	93	14	48	64	13.5	4.64	81	.251	.343	4	.148	0	-11	-10	-2	-1.1
1964 Det-A	0	0	—	1	1	0	0	0	5	5	2	1	2	12.6	10.80	34	.250	.318	0	.000	-0	-4	-4	-0	-0.3
1965 Chi-N	6	6	.500	17	16	5	3	0	96²	83	12	18	59	9.7	3.54	104	.232	.275	3	.100	-1	0	-2	-2	0.0
1966 Chi-N	1	4	.200	17	6	1	0	0	51¹	47	12	18	32	12.1	5.08	72	.242	.319	0	.000	-2	-8	-8	-1	-1.0
1970 SF-N	0	0	—	7	0	0	0	1	9²	15	1	6	6	19.6	7.45	53	.357	.438	0	—	0	-4	-4	-0	-0.3
Total 6	12	16	.429	71	33	8	3	2	261¹	247	42	95	164	12.2	4.72	79	.249	.322	7	.097	-2	-32	-29	-5	-2.9
■ **JIM FAULKNER**				Faulkner, James Leroy "Lefty" b: 7/27/1899, Beatrice, Neb. d: 6/1/62, W.Palm Beach, Fla. BB/TL, 6′3″, 190 lbs. Deb: 9/15/27																				
1927 NY-N	1	0	1.000	3	1	0	0	0	9²	13	0	5	2	17.7	3.72	104	.317	.404	1	.500	1	0	0	-0	0.1
1928 NY-N	9	8	.529	38	8	3	0	2	117¹	131	6	41	32	13.3	3.53	111	.289	.351	9	.231	1	6	5	1	0.6
1930 Bro-N	0	0	—	2	1	0	0	0	0¹	2	1	1	0	81.0	81.00	6	.667	.750	0	—	0	-3	-3	0	-0.1
Total 3	10	8	.556	43	10	3	0	3	127¹	146	6	47	34	13.9	3.75	104	.293	.359	10	.244	2	3	2	1	0.6
■ **BUCK FAUSETT**				Fausett, Robert Shaw "Leaky" b: 4/8/08, Sheridan, Ark. BL/TR, 5′10″, 170 lbs. Deb: 4/18/44 ♦																				
1944 Cin-N	0	0	—	2	0	0	0	0	10²	13	0	7	3	18.6	5.91	59	.295	.415	3	.097	-0	-3	-3	0	-0.2

YEAR TM/L	W	L	PCT	G	GS	CG	SH	SV	IP	H	HR	BB	SO	RAT	ERA	ERA+	OAV	OOB	BH	AVG	PB	PR	/A	PD	TPI

■ CHARLIE FAUST Faust, Charles Victor "Victory" b: 10/9/1880, Marion, Kan. d: 6/18/15, Fort Steilacoom, Wash. BR/TR, 6'2", Deb: 10/07/11

| 1911 NY-N | 0 | 0 | — | 2 | 0 | 0 | 0 | 0 | 2 | 2 | 0 | 0 | 0 | 9.0 | 4.50 | 75 | .250 | .250 | 0 | — | 0 | -0 | -0 | 0 | 0.0 |

■ CLAY FAUVER Fauver, Clayton King "Cayt" b: 8/1/1872, N.Eaton, Ohio d: 3/3/42, Chatsworth, Ga. BB/TR, 5'10", Deb: 9/07/1899

| 1899 Lou-N | 1 | 0 | 1.000 | 1 | 1 | 1 | 0 | 0 | 9 | 11 | 0 | 2 | 1 | 13.0 | 0.00 | — | .301 | .337 | 0 | .000 | -1 | 4 | 4 | 0 | 0.3 |

■ VERN FEAR Fear, Luvern Carl b: 8/21/24, Everly, Iowa d: 9/6/76, Spencer, Iowa BB/TR, 6', 170 lbs. Deb: 8/03/52

| 1952 Chi-N | 0 | 0 | — | 4 | 0 | 0 | 0 | 0 | 8 | 9 | 1 | 3 | 4 | 14.6 | 7.88 | 49 | .290 | .371 | 0 | .000 | -0 | -4 | -4 | 0 | -0.3 |

■ JACK FEE Fee, John b: 1870, Carbondale, Pa. d: 3/3/13, Carbondale, Pa. Deb: 9/14/1889

| 1889 Ind-N | 2 | 2 | .500 | 7 | 3 | 2 | 0 | 0 | 40 | 39 | 2 | 31 | 10 | 15.7 | 4.27 | 98 | .247 | .371 | 3 | .143 | -2 | -1 | -0 | 1 | 0.0 |

■ HARRY FELDMAN Feldman, Harry b: 11/10/19, New York, N.Y. d: 3/16/62, Fort Smith, Ark. BR/TR, 6', 175 lbs. Deb: 9/10/41

1941 NY-N	1	1	.500	3	3	1	1	0	20¹	21	0	6	9	12.0	3.98	93	.280	.333	1	.167	0	-1	-1	-0	0.0
1942 NY-N	7	1	.875	31	6	2	1	0	114	100	5	73	49	13.7	3.16	106	.236	.350	11	.282	3	2	3	-0	0.6
1943 NY-N	4	5	.444	31	10	1	0	0	104²	114	7	58	49	15.1	4.30	80	.279	.374	4	.133	-1	-11	-10	0	-1.0
1944 NY-N	11	13	.458	40	27	8	1	2	205¹	214	18	91	70	13.5	4.16	88	.266	.342	15	.205	0	-13	-11	-2	-1.2
1945 NY-N	12	13	.480	35	30	10	3	1	217²	213	14	69	74	11.7	3.27	120	.251	.308	7	.097	-3	13	16	-2	1.1
1946 NY-N	0	2	.000	3	2	0	0	0	9	9	1	3	3	27.0	18.00	19	.474	.545	0	.000	-0	-6	-6	-0	-0.5
Total 6	35	35	.500	143	78	22	6	3	666	671	45	300	254	13.2	3.80	96	.260	.339	38	.172	-1	-16	-10	-5	-1.0

■ HARRY FELIX Felix, Harry b: 1870, Brooklyn, N.Y. d: 10/17/61, Miami, Fla. TR, 5'7.5", 160 lbs. Deb: 10/05/01

1901 NY-N	0	0	—	1	0	0	0	0	2	3	0	0	0	13.5	0.00	—	.344	.344	0	.000	-0	1	1	0	0.0
1902 Phi-N	1	3	.250	9	5	3	0	0	45	61	1	11	10	14.4	5.60	50	.323	.360	5	.135	-1	-14	-14	-0	-1.4
Total 2	1	3	.250	10	5	3	0	0	47	64	1	11	10	14.4	5.36	53	.324	.359	5	.132	-1	-13	-13	-0	-1.4

■ BOB FELLER Feller, Robert William Andrew "Rapid Robert" b: 11/3/18, Van Meter, Iowa BR/TR, 6', 185 lbs. Deb: 7/19/36 H

1936 Cle-A	5	3	.625	14	8	5	0	1	62	52	1	47	76	15.0	3.34	151	.229	.371	3	.136	-2	12	12	-1	0.8
1937 Cle-A	9	7	.563	26	19	9	0	1	148²	116	4	106	150	13.6	3.39	136	.218	.351	9	.170	-1	20	20	-1	1.8
1938 Cle-A	17	11	.607	39	36	20	2	1	277²	225	13	208	240	14.3	4.08	114	.220	.356	17	.181	2	22	17	-3	1.4
1939 Cle-A	24	9	.727	39	35	24	4	1	296²	227	13	142	246	11.3	2.85	154	.210	.303	21	.212	5	58	51	-1	5.3
1940 Cle-A	27	11	.711	43	37	31	4	4	320¹	245	13	118	261	10.3	2.61	161	.210	.285	18	.157	1	63	57	-5	5.3
1941 Cle-A	25	13	.658	44	40	28	6	2	343	284	15	194	260	12.7	3.15	125	.226	.332	18	.150	2	38	30	-3	2.9
1945 Cle-A	5	3	.625	9	9	7	1	0	72	50	1	35	59	10.9	2.50	130	.192	.293	4	.160	-0	7	6	-2	0.4
1946 Cle-A	26	15	.634	48	42	36	10	4	371¹	277	11	153	348	10.5	2.18	152	.208	.291	16	.129	-2	55	46	-3	4.5
1947 Cle-A	20	11	.645	42	37	20	5	3	299	230	17	127	196	10.9	2.68	130	.215	.300	18	.184	2	34	27	1	3.1
1948 *Cle-A	19	15	.559	44	38	18	2	3	280¹	255	20	116	164	12.0	3.56	114	.241	.317	9	.095	-8	23	15	-2	0.5
1949 Cle-A	15	14	.517	36	28	15	0	0	211	198	18	84	108	12.1	3.75	106	.248	.320	17	.236	4	10	6	-4	0.5
1950 Cle-A	16	11	.593	35	34	16	3	0	247	230	20	103	119	12.3	3.43	126	.247	.325	10	.120	-2	32	25	-4	1.8
1951 Cle-A	22	8	.733	33	32	16	4	0	249²	239	22	95	111	12.3	3.50	108	.253	.325	10	.123	-4	17	8	-3	0.0
1952 Cle-A	9	13	.409	30	30	11	0	0	191²	219	13	83	81	14.3	4.74	71	.288	.360	7	.117	-1	-23	-30	-0	-2.8
1953 Cle-A	10	7	.588	25	25	10	1	0	175²	163	16	60	60	11.6	3.59	105	.251	.317	6	.107	-2	8	3	1	0.2
1954 Cle-A	13	3	.813	19	19	9	1	0	140	127	13	39	59	10.9	3.09	119	.239	.294	9	.188	1	10	9	-2	0.9
1955 Cle-A	4	4	.500	25	11	2	1	0	83	71	7	31	25	11.2	3.47	115	.235	.308	1	.048	-2	5	5	-1	0.2
1956 Cle-A	0	4	.000	19	4	2	0	1	58	63	7	23	18	13.3	4.97	85	.280	.347	0	.000	-2	-5	-5	-0	-0.6
Total 18	266	162	.621	570	484	279	44	21	3827	3271	224	1764	2581	12.0	3.25	122	.231	.319	193	.151	-6	385	301	-32	26.2

■ TERRY FELTON Felton, Terry Lane b: 10/29/57, Texarkana, Ark. BR/TR, 6'1", 180 lbs. Deb: 9/28/79

1979 Min-A	0	0	—	1	0	0	0	0	2	0	0	1	0	0.0	—	.000	.000	0	—	0	1	1	0	0.1
1980 Min-A	0	3	.000	5	4	0	0	0	17²	20	2	9	14	15.3	7.13	61	.286	.375	0	—	0	-6	-5	-0	-0.4
1981 Min-A	0	0	—	1	0	0	0	0	1¹	4	1	2	1	40.5	40.50	10	.500	.600	0	—	0	-5	-5	-0	-0.3
1982 Min-A	0	13	.000	48	6	0	0	3	117¹	99	18	76	92	13.7	4.99	85	.230	.351	0	—	0	-12	-10	-2	-1.1
Total 4	0	16	.000	55	10	0	0	3	138¹	123	21	87	108	14.0	5.53	77	.240	.355	0	—	0	-22	-20	-3	-1.7

■ HOD FENNER Fenner, Horace Alfred b: 7/12/1897, Martin, Mich. d: 11/20/54, Detroit, Mich. BR/TR, 5'10.5", 165 lbs. Deb: 9/09/21

| 1921 Chi-A | 0 | 0 | — | 2 | 1 | 0 | 0 | 0 | 7 | 14 | 0 | 3 | 1 | 21.9 | 7.71 | 55 | .452 | .500 | 0 | .000 | -0 | -3 | -3 | -0 | -0.2 |

■ STAN FERENS Ferens, Stanley "Lefty" b: 3/5/15, Wendell, Pa. BB/TL, 5'11", 170 lbs. Deb: 6/10/42

1942 StL-A	3	4	.429	19	3	1	0	0	69	76	2	21	23	12.7	3.78	98	.279	.331	3	.143	-1	-1	-1	0	0.0
1946 StL-A	2	9	.182	34	6	1	0	0	88	100	3	38	28	14.4	4.50	83	.293	.369	4	.167	-1	-10	-8	-0	-0.8
Total 2	5	13	.278	53	9	2	0	0	157	176	5	59	51	13.6	4.18	89	.287	.353	7	.156	-1	-11	-8	-0	-0.8

■ CHARLIE FERGUSON Ferguson, Charles Augustus b: 5/10/1875, Okemos, Mich. d: 5/17/31, Sault Ste.Marie, Mich. TR, 5'11", Deb: 9/20/01

| 1901 Chi-N | 0 | 0 | — | 1 | 0 | 0 | 0 | 0 | 2 | 1 | 0 | 2 | 0 | 13.5 | 0.00 | — | .149 | .344 | 0 | .000 | -0 | 1 | 1 | 0 | 0.0 |

■ CHARLIE FERGUSON Ferguson, Charles J. b: 4/17/1863, Charlottesville, Va. d: 4/29/1888, Philadelphia, Pa. BB/TR, 6', 165 lbs. Deb: 5/01/1884

1884 Phi-N	21	25	.457	50	47	46	2	1	416²	443	13	93	194	11.6	3.54	84	.258	.296	50	.246	7	-26	-26	-2	-1.8
1885 Phi-N	26	20	.565	48	45	45	5	0	405	345	5	81	197	9.5	2.22	125	.220	.258	72	.306	17	27	25	1	4.6
1886 Phi-N	30	9	.769	48	45	43	4	2	395²	317	11	69	212	8.8	1.98	167	.211	.253	66	.253	11	58	58	5	7.8
1887 Phi-N	22	10	.688	37	33	31	2	1	297¹	297	13	47	125	10.4	3.00	140	.253	.282	89	.337	14	35	40	1	6.6
Total 4	99	64	.607	183	170	165	13	4	1514²	1402	42	290	728	10.1	2.67	121	.235	.270	277	.288	49	94	96	4	17.2

■ GEORGE FERGUSON Ferguson, George Cecil "Cecil" b: 8/19/1886, Ellsworth, Ind. d: 9/5/43, Orlando, Fla. BR/TR, 5'10", 165 lbs. Deb: 4/19/06

1906 NY-N	2	0	1.000	22	1	1	1	7	52¹	43	1	24	32	11.9	2.58	101	.229	.322	5	.333	2	0	0	1	0.3
1907 NY-N	3	2	.600	15	5	4	0	1	64	63	2	20	37	12.4	2.11	118	.266	.336	1	.056	-1	3	3	-0	0.1
1908 Bos-N	11	11	.500	37	20	13	3	0	208	168	1	84	98	11.3	2.47	98	.230	.316	11	.169	1	-2	-1	0	-0.4
1909 Bos-N	5	23	.179	36	30	19	3	0	226²	235	2	87	87	13.1	3.73	76	.282	.355	15	.205	1	-28	-23	-0	-2.2
1910 Bos-N	7	7	.500	26	14	10	1	0	123	110	3	58	40	12.8	3.80	87	.254	.351	7	.175	-1	-11	-7	0	-0.6
1911 Bos-N	1	3	.250	6	3	0	0	0	24	40	3	12	4	19.5	9.75	39	.388	.452	2	.286	1	-17	-16	0	-1.2
Total 6	29	46	.387	142	73	47	8	8	698	659	12	281	298	12.6	3.34	83	.261	.343	41	.188	3	-55	-44	-3	-4.0

■ ALEX FERGUSON Ferguson, James Alexander b: 2/16/1897, Montclair, N.J. d: 4/26/76, Sepulveda, Cal. BR/TR, 6', 180 lbs. Deb: 8/16/18

1918 NY-A	0	0	—	1	0	0	0	0	1²	2	0	1	2	21.6	0.00	—	.333	.500	0	.000	-0	1	1	0	0.0
1921 NY-A	3	1	.750	17	4	1	0	1	56¹	64	4	27	9	15.2	5.91	72	.296	.385	4	.211	-1	-10	-10	-0	-0.9
1922 Bos-A	9	16	.360	39	27	10	1	2	198¹	201	5	62	44	12.2	4.31	95	.265	.326	6	.092	-6	-6	-4	-1	-1.0
1923 Bos-A	9	13	.409	34	27	11	0	0	198¹	229	5	67	72	13.8	4.04	102	.297	.360	6	.097	-5	-1	2	-1	-0.3
1924 Bos-A	14	17	.452	41	32	15	0	2	237²	259	6	108	78	14.1	3.79	115	.286	.366	12	.140	-7	12	15	1	1.0
1925 Bos-A	0	2	.000	5	4	0	0	1	15²	22	6	5	5	16.1	10.91	42	.314	.368	0	.000	-0	-11	-11	-0	-0.9
NY-A	4	2	.667	21	5	0	0	1	54¹	83	3	42	20	21.0	7.79	55	.358	.460	1	.133	-1	-20	-21	-1	-1.8
*Was-A	5	1	.833	7	6	3	0	0	55¹	52	2	23	24	12.5	3.25	130	.256	.338	1	.050	-2	7	6	-1	0.2
Yr	9	5	.643	33	15	3	0	2	125¹	157	11	70	49	16.4	6.18	69	.309	.395	2	.051	-4	-25	-26	-1	-2.5
1926 Was-A	3	4	.429	19	4	0	1	0	47²	69	4	18	16	17.0	7.74	50	.343	.405	2	.182	-0	-20	-21	0	-1.8
1927 Phi-N	8	16	.333	31	31	16	0	0	227	280	15	65	73	13.9	4.84	85	.313	.363	7	.100	-5	-23	-18	-2	-2.0
1928 Phi-N	5	10	.333	34	19	5	1	2	131²	162	14	48	50	14.8	5.67	75	.312	.376	1	.026	-5	-25	-21	-1	-2.1
1929 Phi-N	1	2	.333	5	4	1	0	0	12²	19	2	10	3	20.6	12.08	43	.345	.446	0	.000	-1	-10	-10	-0	-0.7

YEAR	TM/L	W	L	PCT	G	GS	CG	SH	SV	IP	H	HR	BB	SO	RAT	ERA	ERA+	OAV	OOB	BH	AVG	PB	PR	/A	PD	TPI
	Bro-N	0	1	.000	3	3	0	0	0	2	7	2	1	1	36.0	22.50	20	.583	.615	1	1.000	0	-4	-4	0	-0.2
	Yr	1	3	.250	8	7	1	0	0	14²	26	4	11	4	22.7	13.50	38	.388	.474	0	.000	-0	-14	-14	1	-0.9
Total 10		61	85	.418	257	166	62	2	10	1238²	1449	68	478	396	14.3	4.90	86	.299	.367	42	.106	-34	-112	-96	1	-10.7

■ BOB FERGUSON
Ferguson, Robert Lester b: 4/18/19, Birmingham, Ala. BR/TR, 6'1.5", 180 lbs. Deb: 4/29/44

YEAR	TM/L	W	L	PCT	G	GS	CG	SH	SV	IP	H	HR	BB	SO	RAT	ERA	ERA+	OAV	OOB	BH	AVG	PB	PR	/A	PD	TPI
1944	Cin-N	0	3	.000	9	2	0	0	1	16	24	3	10	9	20.3	9.00	39	.358	.456	1	.333	0	-10	-10	0	-0.8

■ BOB FERGUSON
Ferguson, Robert V. b: 1/31/1845, Brooklyn, N.Y. d: 5/3/1894, Brooklyn, N.Y. BB/TR, 5'9.5", 149 lbs. Deb: 5/18/1871 MU♦

YEAR	TM/L	W	L	PCT	G	GS	CG	SH	SV	IP	H	HR	BB	SO	RAT	ERA	ERA+	OAV	OOB	BH	AVG	PB	PR	/A	PD	TPI
1871	Mut-n	0	0	—	1	0	0	0	0	1	8	0	0	0	72.0	27.00	14	.571	.571	1	.241	-0	-3	-3	0	-0.1
1873	Atl-n	0	1	.000	4	1	1	0	0	19²	39	2	4	2	19.7	5.03	67	.371	.394	60	.260	-0	-3	-4	0	-0.2
1874	Atl-n	0	1	.000	1	1	1	0	0	9	12	0	3	0	15.0	4.00	70	.273	.319	63	.256	0	-1	-1	0	0.0
1875	Har-n	0	0	—	1	0	0	0	0	2	9	1	0	0	40.5	13.50	19	.643	.643	88	.240	0	-2	-2	0	-0.1
1877	Har-N	1	1	.500	3	2	2	0	0	25	38	0	2	1	14.4	3.96	61	.331	.342	65	.256	0	-3	-4	0	-0.3
1883	Phi-N	0	0	—	1	0	0	0	0	1	2	0	0	0	18.0	9.00	34	.394	.394	85	.258	0	-1	-1	0	0.0
Total 4 n		0	2	.000	7	2	2	0	0	31²	68	3	7	0	21.3	5.97	53	.384	.408	294	.252	1	-9	-10	0	-0.4
Total 2		1	1	.500	4	2	2	0	0	26	40	0	2	1	14.5	4.15	59	.334	.344	625	.271	1	-4	-5	0	-0.3

■ ALEX FERNANDEZ
Fernandez, Alexander b: 8/13/69, Miami Beach, Fla. BR/TR, 6'2", 200 lbs. Deb: 8/02/90

YEAR	TM/L	W	L	PCT	G	GS	CG	SH	SV	IP	H	HR	BB	SO	RAT	ERA	ERA+	OAV	OOB	BH	AVG	PB	PR	/A	PD	TPI
1990	Chi-A	5	5	.500	13	13	3	0	0	87²	89	6	34	61	12.9	3.80	101	.265	.338	0	—	0	1	0	-0	0.0

■ SID FERNANDEZ
Fernandez, Charles Sidney b: 10/12/62, Honolulu, Hawaii BL/TL, 6'1", 220 lbs. Deb: 9/20/83

YEAR	TM/L	W	L	PCT	G	GS	CG	SH	SV	IP	H	HR	BB	SO	RAT	ERA	ERA+	OAV	OOB	BH	AVG	PB	PR	/A	PD	TPI
1983	LA-N	0	1	.000	2	1	0	0	0	6	7	0	7	9	22.5	6.00	60	.280	.455	1	1.000	0	-2	-2	0	0.0
1984	NY-N	6	6	.500	15	15	0	0	0	90	74	8	34	62	10.8	3.50	101	.226	.299	5	.179	-0	1	0	-2	-0.1
1985	NY-N	9	9	.500	26	26	3	0	0	170¹	108	14	80	180	10.0	2.80	123	**.181**	.280	11	.212	2	15	12	-1	1.3
1986	*NY-N	16	6	.727	32	31	2	1	1	204¹	161	13	91	200	11.2	3.52	100	.216	.303	11	.162	1	4	0	-3	-0.1
1987	NY-N	12	8	.600	28	27	3	1	0	156	130	16	67	134	11.8	3.81	99	.224	.313	7	.163	1	5	-1	-3	-0.2
1988	*NY-N	12	10	.545	31	31	1	1	0	187	127	15	70	189	9.8	3.03	106	**.191**	.274	14	.250	5	9	4	-4	0.6
1989	NY-N	14	5	.737	35	32	6	2	0	219¹	157	21	75	198	9.8	2.83	115	.198	.272	15	.211	4	16	11	-4	1.1
1990	NY-N	9	14	.391	30	30	2	1	0	179¹	130	18	67	181	10.1	3.46	105	**.200**	.280	11	.190	1	7	4	-2	0.2
Total 8		78	59	.569	199	193	17	6	1	1212¹	894	105	491	1153	10.5	3.26	107	.204	.288	75	.199	15	55	29	-19	2.8

■ DON FERRARESE
Ferrarese, Donald Hugh b: 6/19/29, Oakland, Cal. BR/TL, 5'9", 170 lbs. Deb: 4/11/55

YEAR	TM/L	W	L	PCT	G	GS	CG	SH	SV	IP	H	HR	BB	SO	RAT	ERA	ERA+	OAV	OOB	BH	AVG	PB	PR	/A	PD	TPI
1955	Bal-A	0	0	—	6	0	0	0	0	9	8	0	11	5	19.0	3.00	127	.276	.475	0	.000	-0	1	1	-0	0.1
1956	Bal-A	4	10	.286	36	14	3	1	2	102	86	8	64	81	13.5	5.03	78	.229	.345	1	.036	-3	-10	-13	0	-1.4
1957	Bal-A	1	1	.500	8	2	0	0	0	19	14	1	12	13	12.3	4.74	76	.200	.317	0	.000	-0	-2	-2	0	-0.2
1958	Cle-A	3	4	.429	28	10	2	0	1	94²	91	5	46	62	13.1	3.71	98	.254	.341	3	.115	-1	1	-1	-1	-0.3
1959	Cle-A	5	3	.625	15	10	4	0	0	76	58	6	51	45	13.0	3.20	115	.219	.347	7	.259	2	6	4	0	0.6
1960	Chi-N	0	1	.000	5	0	0	0	0	4	8	2	9	4	38.3	18.00	21	.400	.586	1	.500	0	-6	-6	-0	-0.5
1961	Phi-N	5	12	.294	42	14	3	1	1	138²	120	14	68	89	12.3	3.76	108	.234	.325	6	.171	-1	4	5	-3	0.1
1962	Phi-N	0	1	.000	5	0	0	0	0	6²	9	1	3	6	16.2	8.10	48	.310	.375	1	1.000	0	-3	-3	0	-0.1
	StL-N	1	4	.200	38	0	0	0	1	56²	55	2	31	45	13.8	2.70	158	.270	.369	1	.200	1	8	10	1	1.2
	Yr	1	5	.167	43	0	0	0	1	63¹	64	3	34	51	14.1	3.27	129	.274	.368	2	.000	1	5	7	1	1.1
Total 8		19	36	.345	183	50	12	2	5	506²	449	39	295	350	13.3	4.00	98	.241	.347	20	.156	-2	-2	-5	-2	-0.5

■ BILL FERRAZZI
Ferrazzi, William Joseph b: 4/19/07, W.Quincy, Mass. BR/TR, 6'2.5", 200 lbs. Deb: 9/07/35

YEAR	TM/L	W	L	PCT	G	GS	CG	SH	SV	IP	H	HR	BB	SO	RAT	ERA	ERA+	OAV	OOB	BH	AVG	PB	PR	/A	PD	TPI
1935	Phi-A	1	2	.333	3	2	0	0	0	7	7	0	5	0	15.4	5.14	88	.269	.387	0	.000	0	-1	-0	0	0.0

■ TONY FERREIRA
Ferreira, Anthony Ross b: 10/4/62, Riverside, Cal. BL/TL, 6'1", 160 lbs. Deb: 9/17/85

YEAR	TM/L	W	L	PCT	G	GS	CG	SH	SV	IP	H	HR	BB	SO	RAT	ERA	ERA+	OAV	OOB	BH	AVG	PB	PR	/A	PD	TPI
1985	KC-A	0	0	—	2	0	0	0	0	5²	6	0	2	5	12.7	7.94	52	.273	.333	0	—	0	-2	-2	0	-0.1

■ WES FERRELL
Ferrell, Wesley Cheek b: 2/2/08, Greensboro, N.C. d: 12/9/76, Sarasota, Fla. BR/TR, 6'2", 195 lbs. Deb: 9/09/27 ♦

YEAR	TM/L	W	L	PCT	G	GS	CG	SH	SV	IP	H	HR	BB	SO	RAT	ERA	ERA+	OAV	OOB	BH	AVG	PB	PR	/A	PD	TPI
1927	Cle-A	0	0	—	1	1	0	0	0	1	3	0	2	0	45.0	27.00	16	.600	.714	0	—	0	-3	-3	0	-0.1
1928	Cle-A	0	2	.000	2	2	1	0	0	16	15	0	5	4	11.3	2.25	184	.242	.299	1	.250	1	3	3	0	0.4
1929	Cle-A	21	10	.677	43	25	18	1	5	242²	256	7	109	100	13.6	3.60	124	.279	.358	22	.237	4	17	23	2	2.9
1930	Cle-A	25	13	.658	43	35	25	1	3	296¹	299	14	106	143	12.3	3.31	146	.262	.358	35	.297	9	44	50	-4	5.3
1931	Cle-A	22	12	.647	40	35	**27**	2	3	276¹	276	9	130	123	13.3	3.75	123	.255	.336	37	.319	18	19	27	5	5.0
1932	Cle-A	23	13	.639	38	34	26	3	1	287²	299	17	104	105	12.6	3.66	130	.264	.326	26	.242	5	26	35	0	4.0
1933	Cle-A	11	12	.478	28	26	16	1	0	201	225	8	70	41	13.3	4.21	106	.282	.341	38	.271	8	2	5	2	0.5
1934	Bos-A	14	5	.737	26	23	17	3	1	181	205	4	49	67	12.6	3.63	132	.282	.327	22	.282	9	17	24	-2	3.1
1935	Bos-A	**25**	14	.641	41	38	**31**	3	0	322¹	336	16	108	110	12.5	3.52	135	.267	.326	52	.347	22	34	44	2	**7.1**
1936	Bos-A	20	15	.571	39	38	**28**	3	0	301	330	11	119	106	13.6	4.19	127	.274	.343	36	.267	12	28	38	-2	4.5
1937	Bos-A	3	6	.333	12	11	5	0	0	73¹	111	14	34	31	17.9	7.61	62	.348	.412	12	.364	6	-24	-23	2	-1.2
	Was-A	11	13	.458	25	24	21	0	0	207²	214	11	88	92	13.2	3.94	112	.265	.339	27	.255	5	16	11	-1	1.0
	Yr	14	19	.424	37	35	**26**	0	0	281	325	25	122	123	14.4	4.90	92	.288	.359	16	.115	11	-9	-12	1	-0.2
1938	Was-A	13	8	.619	23	22	9	0	0	149	193	12	68	36	15.8	5.92	76	.311	.380	11	.224	6	-19	-23	1	-1.4
	NY-A	2	2	.500	5	4	1	0	0	30	52	6	18	7	21.0	8.10	56	.388	.461	2	.167	-0	-11	-12	1	-0.8
	Yr	15	10	.600	28	26	10	0	0	179	245	18	86	43	16.6	6.28	72	.324	.393	13	.262	6	-30	-35	2	-2.2
1939	NY-A	1	2	.333	3	3	1	0	0	19¹	14	2	17	6	14.4	4.66	94	.219	.383	1	.125	-0	-1	-1	0	0.0
1940	Bro-N	0	0	—	1	0	0	0	0	4	4	0	4	4	20.3	6.75	59	.250	.429	0	.000	-0	-1	-1	0	0.0
1941	Bos-N	2	1	.667	4	3	1	0	0	14	13	1	9	10	14.8	5.14	69	.241	.359	2	.500	2	-2	-2	-0	0.0
Total 15		193	128	.601	374	323	227	17	13	2623	2845	132	1040	985	13.4	4.04	117	.275	.343	329	.280	105	147	195	6	30.3

■ TOM FERRICK
Ferrick, Thomas Jerome b: 1/6/15, New York, N.Y. BR/TR, 6'2.5", 220 lbs. Deb: 4/19/41 C

YEAR	TM/L	W	L	PCT	G	GS	CG	SH	SV	IP	H	HR	BB	SO	RAT	ERA	ERA+	OAV	OOB	BH	AVG	PB	PR	/A	PD	TPI
1941	Phi-A	8	10	.444	36	4	2	1	7	119¹	130	8	33	30	12.3	3.77	111	.275	.322	9	.205	1	5	6	3	0.9
1942	Cle-A	3	2	.600	31	2	2	0	3	81¹	56	3	32	28	9.7	1.99	173	.200	.282	4	.211	0	**15**	**13**	2	1.6
1946	Cle-A	0	0	—	9	0	0	0	1	18	25	3	4	9	14.5	5.00	66	.321	.354	2	.667	0	-3	-3	0	-0.1
	StL-A	4	1	.800	25	1	0	0	5	32¹	26	1	5	13	8.6	2.78	134	.224	.256	0	.000	-1	3	3	0	0.4
	Yr	4	1	.800	34	1	0	0	6	50¹	51	4	9	22	10.7	3.58	100	.263	.296	0	.000	-0	0	0	0	0.3
1947	Was-A	1	7	.125	31	0	0	0	9	60	57	1	20	23	11.6	3.15	118	.256	.317	1	.100	-1	4	4	2	0.5
1948	Was-A	2	5	.286	37	0	0	0	10	73²	75	3	38	34	13.8	4.15	105	.261	.348	1	.067	-1	1	2	1	0.1
1949	StL-A	6	4	.600	50	0	0	0	6	104¹	102	9	41	34	12.4	3.88	117	.258	.329	3	.143	-1	4	7	2	0.8
1950	StL-A	1	3	.250	16	0	0	0	2	24	24	2	7	6	11.6	4.13	120	.267	.320	1	.250	-0	2	2	1	0.3
	*NY-A	8	4	.667	30	0	0	0	9	56²	49	5	22	20	11.3	3.65	118	.233	.306	2	.143	0	6	4	1	0.5
	Yr	9	7	.563	46	0	0	0	11	80²	73	7	29	26	11.4	3.79	118	.243	.310	2	.111	0	7	6	2	0.8
1951	NY-A	1	1	.500	9	0	0	0	1	12	21	4	7	3	21.0	7.50	51	.389	.459	1	1.000	0	-5	-5	0	-0.3
	Was-A	2	0	1.000	22	0	0	0	2	41²	36	3	7	17	9.3	2.38	172	.234	.267	2	.286	0	8	8	0	0.3
	Yr	3	1	.750	31	0	0	0	3	53²	57	7	14	20	11.9	3.52	115	.274	.320	1	.125	0	4	3	0	0.5
1952	Was-A	4	3	.571	27	0	0	0	1	50²	53	2	11	28	11.4	3.02	118	.273	.312	1	.200	1	4	3	1	0.5
Total 9		40	40	.500	323	7	4	1	56	674	654	44	227	245	11.8	3.47	117	.256	.317	27	.184	1	42	44	11	6.0

■ BOB FERRIS
Ferris, Robert Eugene b: 5/7/55, Arlington, Va. BR/TR, 6'6", 225 lbs. Deb: 9/12/79

YEAR	TM/L	W	L	PCT	G	GS	CG	SH	SV	IP	H	HR	BB	SO	RAT	ERA	ERA+	OAV	OOB	BH	AVG	PB	PR	/A	PD	TPI
1979	Cal-A	0	0	—	2	0	0	0	0	6	5	1	3	2	12.0	1.50	271	.217	.308	0	—	0	2	2	0	0.2
1980	Cal-A	0	2	.000	5	3	0	0	0	15¹	23	2	9	4	18.8	5.87	67	.354	.432	0	—	0	-3	-3	0	-0.2
Total 2		0	2	.000	7	3	0	0	0	21¹	28	3	12	6	16.9	4.64	86	.318	.400	0	—	0	-1	-2	0	0.0

YEAR	TM/L	W	L	PCT	G	GS	CG	SH	SV	IP	H	HR	BB	SO	RAT	ERA	ERA+	OAV	OOB	BH	AVG	PB	PR	/A	PD	TPI

■ **DAVE FERRISS**   Ferriss, David Meadow "Boo"   b: 12/5/21, Shaw, Miss.   BL/TR, 6'2", 208 lbs.   Deb: 4/29/45   C

YEAR	TM/L	W	L	PCT	G	GS	CG	SH	SV	IP	H	HR	BB	SO	RAT	ERA	ERA+	OAV	OOB	BH	AVG	PB	PR	/A	PD	TPI
1945	Bos-A	21	10	.677	35	31	26	5	2	264²	263	6	85	94	12.1	2.96	115	.264	.327	32	.267	11	12	13	5	3.3
1946	*Bos-A	25	6	**.806**	40	35	26	6	3	274	274	14	71	106	11.4	3.25	113	.259	.308	24	.209	2	8	13	1	1.8
1947	Bos-A	12	11	.522	33	28	14	1	0	218¹	241	14	92	64	14.0	4.04	96	.287	.362	27	.273	7	-8	-4	-0	-0.3
1948	Bos-A	7	3	.700	31	9	1	0	3	115¹	127	7	61	30	15.2	5.23	84	.286	.381	9	.243	2	-12	-11	1	-0.7
1949	Bos-A	0	0	—	4	0	0	0	0	6²	7	1	4	1	16.2	4.05	108	.292	.414	1	1.000	1	0	0	-0	0.1
1950	Bos-A	0	0	—	1	0	0	0	0	1	2	0	1	1	27.0	18.00	27	.500	.600	—	—	0	-1	-1	0	0.0
Total	6	65	30	.684	144	103	67	12	8	880	914	42	314	296	12.8	3.64	103	.272	.338	93	.250	23	-2	10	6	4.9

■ **CY FERRY**   Ferry, Alfred Joseph   b: 9/27/1878, Hudson, N.Y.   d: 9/27/38, Pittsfield, Mass.   BR/TR, 6'1", 170 lbs.   Deb: 5/12/04

YEAR	TM/L	W	L	PCT	G	GS	CG	SH	SV	IP	H	HR	BB	SO	RAT	ERA	ERA+	OAV	OOB	BH	AVG	PB	PR	/A	PD	TPI
1904	Det-A	0	1	.000	3	1	1	0	0	13	12	0	11	4	15.9	6.23	41	.246	.385	2	.333	1	-5	-5	0	-0.4
1905	Cle-A	0	0	—	1	1	0	0	0	2	3	1	0	2	13.5	13.50	20	.347	.347	0	.000	-0	-2	-2	0	-0.1
Total	2	0	1	.000	4	2	1	0	0	15	15	1	11	6	15.6	7.20	36	.261	.380	2	.286	1	-8	-8	0	-0.5

■ **JACK FERRY**   Ferry, John Francis   b: 4/7/1887, Pittsfield, Mass.   d: 8/29/54, Pittsfield, Mass.   BR/TR, 5'11", 175 lbs.   Deb: 9/04/10

YEAR	TM/L	W	L	PCT	G	GS	CG	SH	SV	IP	H	HR	BB	SO	RAT	ERA	ERA+	OAV	OOB	BH	AVG	PB	PR	/A	PD	TPI
1910	Pit-N	1	2	.333	6	3	2	0	0	31	26	0	8	12	10.2	2.32	133	.230	.287	3	.333	1	2	3	0	0.4
1911	Pit-N	6	4	.600	26	8	4	1	3	85²	83	3	27	32	11.8	3.15	109	.260	.322	9	.310	3	2	3	-1	0.4
1912	Pit-N	2	0	1.000	11	3	1	1	1	39	33	1	23	10	13.2	3.00	109	.226	.335	1	.077	-1	2	1	0	0.1
1913	Pit-N	1	0	1.000	4	0	0	0	0	5	4	0	2	2	10.8	5.40	56	.286	.375	0	—	0	-1	-1	0	0.0
Total	4	10	6	.625	47	14	7	2	4	160²	146	4	60	56	11.8	3.02	110	.247	.320	13	.255	3	5	5	-0	0.9

■ **ALEX FERSON**   Ferson, Alexander "Colonel"   b: 7/14/1866, Philadelphia, Pa.   d: 12/5/57, Boston, Mass.   BR/TR, 5'9", 165 lbs.   Deb: 5/04/1889

YEAR	TM/L	W	L	PCT	G	GS	CG	SH	SV	IP	H	HR	BB	SO	RAT	ERA	ERA+	OAV	OOB	BH	AVG	PB	PR	/A	PD	TPI
1889	Was-N	17	17	.500	36	34	28	1	0	288¹	319	9	105	85	13.2	3.90	101	.272	.331	13	.114	-5	4	2	-2	-0.4
1890	Buf-P	1	7	.125	10	10	7	0	0	71	88	5	40	13	16.2	5.45	75	.291	.374	7	.219	1	-10	-11	0	-0.7
1892	Bal-N	0	1	.000	2	1	1	0	0	9	17	1	6	8	23.0	11.00	31	.386	.460	0	.000	-1	-8	-8	-0	-0.6
Total	3	18	25	.419	48	45	36	1	0	368¹	424	15	151	106	14.0	4.37	91	.279	.344	20	.133	-5	-13	-17	-2	-1.7

■ **LOU FETTE**   Fette, Louis Henry William   b: 3/15/07, Alma, Mo.   d: 1/3/81, Warrensburg, Mo.   BR/TR, 6'1.5", 200 lbs.   Deb: 4/26/37

YEAR	TM/L	W	L	PCT	G	GS	CG	SH	SV	IP	H	HR	BB	SO	RAT	ERA	ERA+	OAV	OOB	BH	AVG	PB	PR	/A	PD	TPI
1937	Bos-N	20	10	.667	35	33	23	**5**	0	259	243	5	81	70	11.4	2.88	124	.251	.311	22	.239	3	30	20	0	2.3
1938	Bos-N	11	13	.458	33	32	17	3	1	239²	235	11	79	83	11.9	3.15	109	.258	.320	16	.188	0	17	7	2	0.8
1939	Bos-N	10	10	.500	27	26	11	**6**	0	146	123	7	61	35	11.4	2.96	125	.229	.309	3	.061	-4	16	12	3	1.1
1940	Bos-N	0	5	.000	7	5	0	0	0	32¹	38	0	18	2	15.9	5.57	67	.302	.393	3	.375	1	-6	-7	-1	-0.5
	Bro-N	0	0	—	2	0	0	0	0	3	3	0	2	0	15.0	0.00	—	.300	.417	0	—	0	1	1	0	0.1
	Yr	0	5	.000	9	5	0	0	0	35¹	41	0	20	2	15.5	5.09	73	.299	.389	1	.125	1	-5	-5	-1	-0.4
1945	Bos-N	0	2	.000	5	1	0	0	0	11	16	1	7	4	19.6	5.73	67	.356	.453	0	.000	-0	-2	-2	-1	-0.1
Total	5	41	40	.506	109	97	51	14	1	691	658	24	248	194	11.9	3.15	113	.253	.321	44	.186	-0	55	32	4	3.7

■ **MIKE FETTERS**   Fetters, Michael Lee   b: 12/19/64, Van Nuys, Cal.   BR/TR, 6'4", 200 lbs.   Deb: 9/01/89

YEAR	TM/L	W	L	PCT	G	GS	CG	SH	SV	IP	H	HR	BB	SO	RAT	ERA	ERA+	OAV	OOB	BH	AVG	PB	PR	/A	PD	TPI
1989	Cal-A	0	0	—	1	0	0	0	0	3¹	5	1	4	4	16.2	8.10	47	.333	.375	0	—	0	-2	-2	0	0.0
1990	Cal-A	1	1	.500	26	2	0	0	1	67²	77	9	20	35	13.2	4.12	95	.287	.341	0	—	0	-2	-1	1	0.0
Total	2	1	1	.500	27	2	0	0	1	71	82	10	21	39	13.3	4.31	90	.290	.343	0	—	0	-3	-3	1	0.0

■ **JOHN FICK**   Fick, John Ralph   b: 5/18/21, Baltimore, Md.   d: 6/9/58, Somers Point, N.J.   BL/TL, 5'10", 150 lbs.   Deb: 7/29/44

YEAR	TM/L	W	L	PCT	G	GS	CG	SH	SV	IP	H	HR	BB	SO	RAT	ERA	ERA+	OAV	OOB	BH	AVG	PB	PR	/A	PD	TPI
1944	Phi-N	0	0	—	4	0	0	0	0	5¹	3	0	3	2	11.8	3.38	107	.150	.292	0	—	0	0	0	0	0.0

■ **MARK FIDRYCH**   Fidrych, Mark Steven "The Bird"   b: 8/14/54, Worcester, Mass.   BR/TR, 6'3", 175 lbs.   Deb: 4/20/76

YEAR	TM/L	W	L	PCT	G	GS	CG	SH	SV	IP	H	HR	BB	SO	RAT	ERA	ERA+	OAV	OOB	BH	AVG	PB	PR	/A	PD	TPI
1976	Det-A	19	9	.679	31	29	**24**	4	0	250¹	217	12	53	97	9.8	**2.34**	159	.235	.279	0	—	0	33	**38**	5	**5.1**
1977	Det-A	6	4	.600	11	11	7	1	0	81	82	2	12	42	10.6	2.89	148	.269	.299	0	—	0	11	13	-1	1.2
1978	Det-A	2	0	1.000	3	3	2	0	0	22	17	1	5	10	9.0	2.45	157	.213	.259	0	—	0	3	3	1	0.5
1979	Det-A	0	3	.000	4	4	0	0	0	14²	23	3	9	5	20.3	10.43	41	.371	.458	0	—	0	-10	-10	0	-0.8
1980	Det-A	2	3	.400	9	9	1	0	0	44¹	58	5	20	16	16.0	5.68	72	.309	.378	0	—	0	-8	-8	1	-0.6
Total	5	29	19	.604	58	56	34	5	0	412¹	397	23	99	170	11.0	3.10	126	.255	.302	0	—	0	28	37	6	5.4

■ **CLARENCE FIEBER**   Fieber, Clarence Thomas "Lefty"   b: 9/4/13, San Francisco, Cal   d: 8/20/85, Redwood City, Cal   BL/TL, 6'4", 187 lbs.   Deb: 5/18/32

YEAR	TM/L	W	L	PCT	G	GS	CG	SH	SV	IP	H	HR	BB	SO	RAT	ERA	ERA+	OAV	OOB	BH	AVG	PB	PR	/A	PD	TPI
1932	Chi-A	1	0	1.000	3	0	0	0	0	5¹	6	0	3	1	15.2	1.69	256	.273	.360	0	—	0	2	2	0	0.2

■ **JIM FIELD**   Field, James C.   b: 4/24/1863, Philadelphia, Pa.   d: 5/13/53, Atlantic City, N.J   6'1", 170 lbs.   Deb: 6/02/1883   ♦

YEAR	TM/L	W	L	PCT	G	GS	CG	SH	SV	IP	H	HR	BB	SO	RAT	ERA	ERA+	OAV	OOB	BH	AVG	PB	PR	/A	PD	TPI
1890	Roc-a	1	0	1.000	2	1	1	0	1	9²	7	0	4	2	10.2	2.79	127	.196	.278	38	.202	0	1	1	-0	0.1

■ **JOCKO FIELDS**   Fields, John Joseph   b: 10/20/1864, Cork, Ireland   d: 10/14/50, Jersey City, N.J.   BR/TR, 5'10", 160 lbs.   Deb: 5/31/1887   ♦

YEAR	TM/L	W	L	PCT	G	GS	CG	SH	SV	IP	H	HR	BB	SO	RAT	ERA	ERA+	OAV	OOB	BH	AVG	PB	PR	/A	PD	TPI
1887	Pit-N	0	0	—	1	0	0	0	0	1	0	0	2	0	18.0	0.00	—	.000	.404	44	.268	0	0	0	0	0.0

■ **LOU FIENE**   Fiene, Louis Henry "Big Finn"   b: 12/29/1884, Ft. Dodge, Iowa   d: 12/22/64, Chicago, Ill.   BR/TR, 6', 175 lbs.   Deb: 5/07/06

YEAR	TM/L	W	L	PCT	G	GS	CG	SH	SV	IP	H	HR	BB	SO	RAT	ERA	ERA+	OAV	OOB	BH	AVG	PB	PR	/A	PD	TPI
1906	Chi-A	1	1	.500	6	2	1	0	0	31	35	0	9	12	12.8	2.90	87	.288	.337	2	.200	0	-1	-1	0	0.0
1907	Chi-A	0	1	.000	6	1	0	0	1	26	30	0	7	15	12.8	4.15	58	.291	.336	2	.182	-0	-5	-5	0	-0.5
1908	Chi-A	0	1	.000	1	1	1	0	0	9	9	0	1	3	10.0	4.00	58	.257	.278	0	.000	-0	-2	-2	0	-0.1
1909	Chi-A	2	5	.286	13	6	4	0	0	72	75	1	18	24	12.3	4.13	57	.284	.341	2	.069	-2	-13	-14	1	-1.5
Total	4	3	8	.273	26	10	7	0	1	138	149	1	35	54	12.3	3.85	62	.284	.335	6	.113	-2	-20	-22	2	-2.1

■ **DANNY FIFE**   Fife, Danny Wayne   b: 10/5/49, Harrisburg, Ill.   BR/TR, 6'3", 175 lbs.   Deb: 8/18/73

YEAR	TM/L	W	L	PCT	G	GS	CG	SH	SV	IP	H	HR	BB	SO	RAT	ERA	ERA+	OAV	OOB	BH	AVG	PB	PR	/A	PD	TPI
1973	Min-A	3	2	.600	10	7	1	0	0	51²	54	2	29	18	15.0	4.35	91	.270	.371	0	—	0	-3	-2	0	-0.1
1974	Min-A	0	0	—	4	0	0	0	0	4²	10	0	4	3	28.9	17.36	22	.417	.517	0	—	0	-7	-7	-0	-0.6
Total	2	3	2	.600	14	7	1	0	0	56¹	64	2	33	21	16.1	5.43	73	.286	.387	0	—	0	-10	-9	0	-0.7

■ **JACK FIFIELD**   Fifield, John Proctor   b: 10/5/1871, Enfield, N.H.   d: 10/12/08, Wareham, Mass.   5'11", 160 lbs.   Deb: 4/28/1897

YEAR	TM/L	W	L	PCT	G	GS	CG	SH	SV	IP	H	HR	BB	SO	RAT	ERA	ERA+	OAV	OOB	BH	AVG	PB	PR	/A	PD	TPI
1897	Phi-N	5	18	.217	27	26	21	0	0	210²	263	8	80	38	14.7	5.51	76	.303	.362	18	.234	3	-28	-31	1	-2.2
1898	Phi-N	11	9	.550	21	21	18	2	0	171¹	170	2	60	31	12.1	3.31	104	.257	.319	7	.109	-4	6	2	-2	-0.3
1899	Phi-N	3	8	.273	14	11	9	1	1	92²	110	0	36	8	14.2	4.08	90	.294	.356	9	.257	1	-2	-4	1	-0.1
	Was-N	2	4	.333	6	6	6	0	0	47	73	1	17	12	17.2	6.13	64	.353	.402	4	.200	0	-12	-12	-1	-0.9
	Yr	5	12	.294	20	17	15	1	1	139²	183	1	53	20	15.2	4.77	79	.315	.373	5	.091	0	-14	-16	0	-1.0
Total	3	21	39	.350	68	64	54	3	1	521²	616	11	193	89	14.0	4.59	83	.292	.351	38	.194	0	-36	-44	-1	-3.5

■ **FRANK FIGGEMEIER**   Figgemeier, Frank Y.   b: 4/22/1874, St.Louis, Mo.   d: 4/15/15, St.Louis, Mo.   Deb: 9/25/1894

YEAR	TM/L	W	L	PCT	G	GS	CG	SH	SV	IP	H	HR	BB	SO	RAT	ERA	ERA+	OAV	OOB	BH	AVG	PB	PR	/A	PD	TPI
1894	Phi-N	0	1	.000	1	1	1	0	0	8	12	1	4	2	18.0	11.25	45	.342	.410	1	.333	0	-5	-5	0	-0.2

■ **ED FIGUEROA**   Figueroa, Eduardo (Padilla)   b: 10/14/48, Ciales, P.R.   BR/TR, 6'1", 190 lbs.   Deb: 4/09/74

YEAR	TM/L	W	L	PCT	G	GS	CG	SH	SV	IP	H	HR	BB	SO	RAT	ERA	ERA+	OAV	OOB	BH	AVG	PB	PR	/A	PD	TPI
1974	Cal-A	2	8	.200	25	12	5	1	0	105¹	119	3	36	49	13.6	3.67	94	.294	.357	0	—	0	-1	-3	0	-0.1
1975	Cal-A	16	13	.552	33	32	16	2	0	244²	213	14	84	139	11.1	2.91	122	.233	.301	0	—	0	24	17	1	2.0
1976	*NY-A	19	10	.655	34	34	14	4	0	256²	237	13	69	119	11.7	3.02	113	.246	.315	0	—	0	14	11	-3	0.9
1977	*NY-A	16	11	.593	32	32	12	2	0	239¹	228	19	75	104	11.5	3.57	110	.252	.312	0	—	0	13	10	-1	0.9
1978	*NY-A	20	9	.690	35	35	12	4	0	253	233	22	77	92	11.1	2.99	121	.248	.307	0	—	0	22	18	0	1.9
1979	NY-A	4	6	.400	16	16	4	1	0	104²	109	6	35	42	12.4	4.13	99	.275	.333	0	—	0	1	-1	0	0.0
1980	NY-A	3	3	.500	15	9	0	0	0	58	90	3	24	16	17.8	6.98	56	.363	.421	0	—	0	-19	-20	1	-1.7
	Tex-A	0	7	.000	8	8	1	0	0	39²	62	9	12	9	16.8	5.90	66	.365	.407	0	—	0	-8	-9	1	-0.7
	Yr	3	10	.231	23	17	1	0	0	97²	152	12	36	25	17.3	6.54	60	.360	.410	0	—	0	-27	-29	2	-2.4
1981	Oak-A	0	0	—	2	1	0	0	0	8¹	8	1	6	1	15.1	5.40	64	.258	.378	0	—	0	-2	-2	0	-0.1

YEAR TM/L	W	L	PCT	G	GS	CG	SH	SV	IP	H	HR	BB	SO	RAT	ERA	ERA+	OAV	OOB	BH	AVG	PB	PR	/A	PD	TPI
Total 8	80	67	.544	200	179	63	12	1	1309²	1299	90	443	571	12.1	3.51	104	.261	.324	0	—	0	44	23	-1	3.1

■ TOM FILER   Filer, Thomas Carson   b: 12/1/56, Philadelphia, Pa.   BR/TR, 6'1", 195 lbs.   Deb: 6/08/82

YEAR TM/L	W	L	PCT	G	GS	CG	SH	SV	IP	H	HR	BB	SO	RAT	ERA	ERA+	OAV	OOB	BH	AVG	PB	PR	/A	PD	TPI
1982 Chi-N	1	2	.333	8	8	0	0	0	40²	50	5	18	15	15.0	5.53	67	.301	.370	1	.083	-1	-9	-8	2	-0.6
1985 Tor-A	7	0	1.000	11	9	0	0	0	48²	38	6	18	24	10.4	3.88	108	.222	.296	0	—	0	1	2	-0	0.1
1988 Mil-A	5	8	.385	19	16	2	1	0	101²	108	8	33	39	12.6	4.43	90	.281	.339	0	—	0	-5	-5	3	-0.1
1989 Mil-A	7	3	.700	13	13	0	0	0	72¹	74	6	23	20	12.6	3.61	106	.271	.337	0	—	0	2	1	0	0.3
1990 Mil-A	2	3	.400	7	4	0	0	0	22	26	2	9	8	14.3	6.14	62	.289	.354	0	—	0	-5	-6	-0	-0.5
Total 5	22	16	.579	58	50	2	1	0	285¹	296	27	101	106	12.7	4.42	89	.273	.338	1	.083	-1	-16	-15	5	-0.8

■ EDDIE FILES   Files, Charles Edward   b: 5/19/1883, Portland, Me.   d: 5/10/54, Cornish, Maine   BR/TR,   Deb: 10/03/08

YEAR TM/L	W	L	PCT	G	GS	CG	SH	SV	IP	H	HR	BB	SO	RAT	ERA	ERA+	OAV	OOB	BH	AVG	PB	PR	/A	PD	TPI
1908 Phi-A	0	0	—	2	0	0	0	0	9	8	0	3	6	13.0	6.00	43	.286	.394	0	.000	-0	-4	-3	-0	-0.3

■ MARC FILLEY   Filley, Marcus Lucius   b: 2/28/12, Troy, N.Y.   BR/TR, 5'11", 172 lbs.   Deb: 4/19/34

YEAR TM/L	W	L	PCT	G	GS	CG	SH	SV	IP	H	HR	BB	SO	RAT	ERA	ERA+	OAV	OOB	BH	AVG	PB	PR	/A	PD	TPI
1934 Was-A	0	0	—	1	0	0	0	0	0¹	2	0	0	0	54.0	27.00	16	.667	.667	0	—	0	-1	-1	0	0.0

■ DANA FILLINGIM   Fillingim, Dana   b: 11/6/1893, Columbus, Ga.   d: 2/3/61, Tuskegee, Ala.   BL/TR, 5'10", 175 lbs.   Deb: 8/02/15

YEAR TM/L	W	L	PCT	G	GS	CG	SH	SV	IP	H	HR	BB	SO	RAT	ERA	ERA+	OAV	OOB	BH	AVG	PB	PR	/A	PD	TPI
1915 Phi-A	0	5	.000	8	4	1	0	0	39¹	42	0	32	17	12.2	3.43	86	.313	.449	2	.167	-0	-2	-2	-0	-0.2
1918 Bos-N	7	6	.538	14	13	10	4	0	113	99	0	28	29	10.5	2.23	120	.243	.300	9	.214	-0	7	6	-0	0.7
1919 Bos-N	6	13	.316	32	19	9	0	2	186¹	185	6	39	50	10.9	3.38	85	.270	.312	16	.246	1	-10	-11	2	-0.7
1920 Bos-N	12	21	.364	37	30	22	2	0	272	292	6	79	66	12.4	3.11	98	.287	.340	16	.174	-2	1	-2	6	0.2
1921 Bos-N	15	10	.600	44	22	11	3	1	239²	249	10	56	54	11.5	3.45	106	.272	.316	21	.247	5	9	5	-1	0.8
1922 Bos-N	5	9	.357	25	12	5	1	2	117	143	6	37	25	13.9	4.54	88	.311	.363	6	.158	-2	-6	-7	-1	-0.8
1923 Bos-N	1	9	.100	35	12	1	0	0	100¹	141	6	36	27	16.0	5.20	77	.345	.399	7	.226	1	-13	-14	0	-1.1
1925 Phi-N	1	0	1.000	5	1	0	0	0	8²	19	0	6	2	26.0	10.38	46	.432	.500	0	.000	-0	-6	-5	-0	-0.4
Total 8	47	73	.392	200	113	59	10	5	1076¹	1170	32	313	270	12.5	3.56	93	.287	.340	77	.209	3	-21	-30	6	-1.5

■ PETE FILSON   Filson, William Peter   b: 9/28/58, Darby, Pa.   BB/TL, 6'2", 195 lbs.   Deb: 5/15/82

YEAR TM/L	W	L	PCT	G	GS	CG	SH	SV	IP	H	HR	BB	SO	RAT	ERA	ERA+	OAV	OOB	BH	AVG	PB	PR	/A	PD	TPI
1982 Min-A	0	2	.000	5	3	0	0	0	12¹	17	2	8	10	18.2	8.76	48	.321	.410	0	—	0	-6	-6	-0	-0.5
1983 Min-A	4	1	.800	26	8	0	0	1	90	87	9	29	49	11.7	3.40	125	.252	.312	0	—	0	7	8	-2	0.7
1984 Min-A	6	5	.545	55	7	0	0	1	118²	106	14	54	59	12.4	4.10	103	.238	.325	0	—	0	-1	-1	-1	0.0
1985 Min-A	4	5	.444	40	6	1	0	2	95²	93	13	30	42	11.6	3.67	120	.251	.307	0	—	0	5	8	-1	0.7
1986 Min-A	0	0	—	4	0	0	0	0	6¹	13	1	2	4	22.7	5.68	76	.406	.457	0	—	0	-1	-1	-0	0.0
Chi-A	0	1	.000	3	1	0	0	0	11²	14	4	5	5	14.7	6.17	70	.286	.352	0	—	0	-3	-2	-0	-0.2
Yr	0	1	.000	7	1	0	0	0	18	27	5	7	9	17.0	6.00	72	.329	.382	0	—	0	-4	-4	-0	-0.2
1987 NY-A	1	0	1.000	7	2	0	0	0	22	26	2	9	10	14.7	3.27	134	.299	.371	0	—	0	3	3	1	0.3
1990 KC-A	0	4	.000	8	7	0	0	0	35	42	6	13	9	14.7	5.91	64	.282	.348	0	—	0	-8	-8	-0	-0.7
Total 7	15	18	.455	148	34	1	0	4	391²	398	51	150	187	12.8	4.18	101	.260	.329	0	—	0	-5	3	-3	0.3

■ JOEL FINCH   Finch, Joel D   b: 8/20/56, South Bend, Ind.   BR/TR, 6'2", 175 lbs.   Deb: 9/27/79

YEAR TM/L	W	L	PCT	G	GS	CG	SH	SV	IP	H	HR	BB	SO	RAT	ERA	ERA+	OAV	OOB	BH	AVG	PB	PR	/A	PD	TPI
1979 Bos-A	0	3	.000	15	7	0	0	0	57¹	65	5	25	25	14.3	4.87	91	.289	.363	0	.000	-0	-4	-3	1	-0.1

■ BILL FINCHER   Fincher, William Allen   b: 5/26/1894, Atlanta, Ga.   d: 5/7/46, Shreveport, La.   BR/TR, 6'1", 180 lbs.   Deb: 4/23/16

YEAR TM/L	W	L	PCT	G	GS	CG	SH	SV	IP	H	HR	BB	SO	RAT	ERA	ERA+	OAV	OOB	BH	AVG	PB	PR	/A	PD	TPI
1916 StL-A	0	1	.000	12	1	0	0	0	21	22	0	7	5	12.4	2.14	128	.282	.341	1	.250	0	2	1	1	0.3

■ TOMMY FINE   Fine, Thomas Morgan   b: 10/10/14, Cleburne, Tex.   BB/TR, 6', 180 lbs.   Deb: 4/26/47

YEAR TM/L	W	L	PCT	G	GS	CG	SH	SV	IP	H	HR	BB	SO	RAT	ERA	ERA+	OAV	OOB	BH	AVG	PB	PR	/A	PD	TPI
1947 Bos-A	1	2	.333	9	1	0	0	0	36	41	0	19	10	15.3	5.50	71	.285	.372	3	.333	1	-7	-6	2	-0.3
1950 StL-A	0	1	.000	14	0	0	0	0	36²	53	6	25	6	19.1	8.10	61	.342	.433	4	.333	1	-14	-13	0	-0.9
Total 2	1	3	.250	23	7	1	0	0	72²	94	6	44	16	17.2	6.81	65	.314	.404	7	.333	2	-22	-19	2	-1.2

■ ROLLIE FINGERS   Fingers, Roland Glen   b: 8/25/46, Steubenville, Ohio   BR/TR, 6'4", 190 lbs.   Deb: 9/15/68

YEAR TM/L	W	L	PCT	G	GS	CG	SH	SV	IP	H	HR	BB	SO	RAT	ERA	ERA+	OAV	OOB	BH	AVG	PB	PR	/A	PD	TPI
1968 Oak-A	0	0	—	1	0	0	0	0	1¹	4	1	1	0	40.5	27.00	10	.571	.667	0	—	0	-4	-4	0	-0.2
1969 Oak-A	6	7	.462	60	8	1	1	12	119	116	13	41	61	12.2	3.71	93	.257	.325	5	.200	-1	-1	-4	3	0.0
1970 Oak-A	7	9	.438	45	19	1	0	2	148	137	13	48	79	11.4	3.65	97	.250	.312	4	.103	-0	1	-2	1	-0.1
1971 *Oak-A	4	6	.400	48	8	2	1	17	129¹	94	14	30	98	9.2	2.99	111	.207	.268	7	.212	1	7	5	2	0.8
1972 *Oak-A	11	9	.550	65	0	0	0	21	111¹	85	8	32	113	9.5	2.51	113	.212	.272	6	.316	2	7	4	-1	0.6
1973 *Oak-A	7	8	.467	62	2	0	0	22	126²	107	5	39	110	10.7	1.92	185	.226	.290	0	—	0	27	23	-2	2.4
1974 *Oak-A	9	5	.643	76	0	0	0	18	119	104	5	29	95	10.1	2.65	125	.240	.289	0	—	0	13	9	1	1.1
1975 *Oak-A	10	6	.625	75	0	0	0	24	126²	95	13	33	115	9.5	2.98	122	.213	.276	0	.000	0	11	9	0	1.0
1976 Oak-A	13	11	.542	70	0	0	0	20	134²	118	3	40	113	11.0	2.47	136	.243	.310	0	—	0	16	13	1	1.5
1977 SD-N	8	9	.471	78	0	0	0	35	132¹	123	12	36	113	10.9	2.99	118	.248	.300	1	.050	-2	13	8	-1	0.5
1978 SD-N	6	13	.316	67	0	0	0	37	107¹	84	4	29	72	9.6	2.52	132	.212	.267	2	.167	-0	13	10	0	1.0
1979 SD-N	9	9	.500	54	0	0	0	13	83²	91	7	37	65	13.9	4.52	78	.281	.356	1	.083	-1	-7	-9	-1	-1.0
1980 SD-N	11	9	.550	66	0	0	0	23	103	101	3	32	69	11.6	2.80	123	.263	.320	5	.278	2	9	7	-1	0.9
1981 *Mil-A	6	3	.667	47	0	0	0	28	78	55	3	13	61	8.0	1.04	330	.198	.236	0	—	0	**23**	**21**	-0	2.2
1982 Mil-A	5	6	.455	50	0	0	0	29	79²	63	5	20	71	9.5	2.60	146	.220	.273	0	—	0	13	11	0	1.0
1984 Mil-A	1	2	.333	33	0	0	0	23	46	38	5	13	40	10.2	1.96	197	.213	.267	0	—	0	10	10	1	0.9
1985 Mil-A	1	6	.143	47	0	0	0	17	55¹	59	6	19	24	12.7	5.04	83	.272	.331	0	—	0	-6	-5	1	-0.3
Total 17	114	118	.491	944	37	4	2	341	1701²	1474	123	492	1299	10.6	2.90	119	.235	.295	31	.172	3	145	105	2	11.9

■ HERMAN FINK   Fink, Herman Adam   b: 8/22/11, Concord, N.C.   d: 8/24/80, Salisbury, N.C.   BR/TR, 6'2", 198 lbs.   Deb: 9/16/35

YEAR TM/L	W	L	PCT	G	GS	CG	SH	SV	IP	H	HR	BB	SO	RAT	ERA	ERA+	OAV	OOB	BH	AVG	PB	PR	/A	PD	TPI
1935 Phi-A	0	3	.000	5	3	0	0	0	15²	18	0	10	2	16.7	9.19	49	.290	.397	1	.200	-0	-8	-8	0	-0.6
1936 Phi-A	8	16	.333	34	24	9	0	3	188²	222	18	78	53	14.3	5.39	95	.294	.360	8	.125	-4	-7	-6	-2	-0.9
1937 Phi-A	2	1	.667	28	3	1	0	1	80	82	6	35	18	13.3	4.05	116	.263	.339	5	.208	-1	5	6	0	0.5
Total 3	10	20	.333	67	30	10	0	4	284¹	322	24	123	73	14.1	5.22	95	.285	.356	14	.151	-5	-11	-8	-2	-1.0

■ PEMBROKE FINLAYSON   Finlayson, Pembroke   b: 7/31/1888, Cheraw, S.C.   d: 3/6/12, Brooklyn, N.Y.   BR/TR,   Deb: 6/06/08

YEAR TM/L	W	L	PCT	G	GS	CG	SH	SV	IP	H	HR	BB	SO	RAT	ERA	ERA+	OAV	OOB	BH	AVG	PB	PR	/A	PD	TPI
1908 Bro-N	0	0	—	1	0	0	0	0	0¹	0	0	4	0	108.0	135.00	2	.000	.800	0	—	0	-5	-5	-0	-0.3
1909 Bro-N	0	0	—	1	0	0	0	0	7	7	0	4	2	14.1	5.14	56	.212	.297	0	.000	-0	-2	-2	-0	-0.1
Total 2	0	0	—	2	0	0	0	0	7¹	7	0	8	2	18.4	11.05	23	.206	.357	0	.000	-0	-7	-7	-0	-0.4

■ CHUCK FINLEY   Finley, Charles Edward   b: 11/26/62, Monroe, La.   BL/TL, 6'6", 220 lbs.   Deb: 5/29/86

YEAR TM/L	W	L	PCT	G	GS	CG	SH	SV	IP	H	HR	BB	SO	RAT	ERA	ERA+	OAV	OOB	BH	AVG	PB	PR	/A	PD	TPI
1986 *Cal-A	3	1	.750	25	0	0	0	0	46¹	40	2	23	37	12.4	3.30	124	.235	.330	0	—	0	4	4	1	0.5
1987 Cal-A	2	7	.222	35	3	0	0	0	90²	102	7	43	63	14.7	4.67	92	.287	.369	0	—	0	-2	-4	-0	-0.3
1988 Cal-A	9	15	.375	31	31	2	0	0	194¹	191	15	82	111	12.9	4.17	93	.263	.343	0	—	0	-4	-7	-1	-0.7
1989 Cal-A	16	9	.640	29	29	9	1	0	199²	171	13	82	156	11.5	2.57	148	.233	.312	0	—	0	29	28	-4	2.6
1990 Cal-A	18	9	.667	32	32	7	2	0	236	210	17	81	177	11.2	2.40	162	.243	.309	0	—	0	39	39	-2	4.0
Total 5	48	41	.539	152	95	18	3	0	767	714	54	311	544	12.2	3.22	122	.251	.327	0	—	0	67	61	-6	6.1

■ HAPPY FINNERAN   Finneran, Joseph Ignatius "Smokey Joe"   b: 10/29/1891, E.Orange, N.J.   d: 2/3/42, Orange, N.J.   BR/TR, 5'10.5", 169 lbs.   Deb: 8/20/12

YEAR TM/L	W	L	PCT	G	GS	CG	SH	SV	IP	H	HR	BB	SO	RAT	ERA	ERA+	OAV	OOB	BH	AVG	PB	PR	/A	PD	TPI
1912 Phi-N	0	2	.000	14	4	0	0	1	46¹	50	2	10	10	11.8	2.53	144	.273	.314	2	.200	0	5	6	0	0.6
1913 Phi-N	0	0	—	3	0	0	0	0	5	12	0	2	2	25.2	7.20	46	.462	.500	2	.667	1	-2	-0	-0	-0.3
1914 Bro-F	12	11	.522	27	23	13	2	1	175¹	153	6	60	54	11.2	3.18	100	.237	.308	7	.127	-4	3	4	-0	0.2
1915 Bro-F	10	12	.455	37	24	12	1	2	215¹	197	2	87	68	12.2	2.80	108	.249	.331	11	.149	-3	6	5	-0	0.2
1918 Det-A	0	2	.000	5	2	0	0	1	13²	22	0	8	2	19.8	9.88	27	.393	.469	0	.000	-0	-11	-11	-1	-1.0
NY-A	3	6	.333	23	13	4	0	0	109¹	134	7	35	34	13.5	3.78	75	.305	.359	9	.231	1	-13	-12	-1	-1.2

YEAR TM/L	W	L	PCT	G	GS	CG	SH	SV	IP	H	HR	BB	SO	RAT	ERA	ERA+	OAV	OOB	BH	AVG	PB	PR	/A	PD	TPI
Yr	3	8	.273	28	15	4	0	1	128	156	7	43	36	14.1	4.43	63	.315	.372	3	.071	0	-23	-23	0	-2.2
Total 5	25	33	.431	109	66	29	3	5	570	568	17	202	168	12.4	3.30	93	.266	.334	31	.168	-5	-15	-14	-1	-1.7

■ STEVE FIREOVID
Fireovid, Stephen John b: 6/6/57, Bryan, Ohio BB/TR, 6'2", 195 lbs. Deb: 9/06/81

YEAR TM/L	W	L	PCT	G	GS	CG	SH	SV	IP	H	HR	BB	SO	RAT	ERA	ERA+	OAV	OOB	BH	AVG	PB	PR	/A	PD	TPI
1981 SD-N	0	1	.000	5	4	0	0	0	26¹	30	2	7	11	12.6	2.73	119	.294	.339	1	.143	-0	2	2	0	0.1
1983 SD-N	0	0	—	3	0	0	0	0	5	4	0	2	1	10.8	1.80	194	.235	.316	0	—	0	1	1	0	0.1
1984 Phi-N	0	0	—	6	0	0	0	0	5²	4	0	0	3	6.4	1.59	229	.200	.200	0	—	0	1	1	0	0.1
1985 Chi-A	0	0	—	4	0	0	0	0	7	17	0	2	2	24.4	5.14	84	.472	.500	0	—	0	-1	-1	-0	0.0
1986 Sea-A	2	0	1.000	10	1	0	0	0	21	28	1	4	10	14.1	4.29	99	.333	.371	0	—	0	-0	-0	0	0.0
Total 5	2	1	.667	28	5	0	0	0	65	83	3	15	27	13.7	3.32	112	.320	.360	1	.143	-0	3	3	0	0.4

■ TED FIRTH
Firth, John E. b: 1856, Massachusetts d: 6/23/02, Tewksbury, Mass. Deb: 8/15/1884

YEAR TM/L	W	L	PCT	G	GS	CG	SH	SV	IP	H	HR	BB	SO	RAT	ERA	ERA+	OAV	OOB	BH	AVG	PB	PR	/A	PD	TPI
1884 Ric-a	0	1	.000	1	1	1	0	0	9	14	0	5	0	19.0	8.00	41	.337	.408	1	.333	0	-5	-5	0	-0.3

■ CARL FISCHER
Fischer, Charles William b: 11/5/05, Medina, N.Y. d: 12/10/63, Medina, N.Y. BR/TL, 6', 180 lbs. Deb: 7/19/30

YEAR TM/L	W	L	PCT	G	GS	CG	SH	SV	IP	H	HR	BB	SO	RAT	ERA	ERA+	OAV	OOB	BH	AVG	PB	PR	/A	PD	TPI
1930 Was-A	1	1	.500	8	4	1	0	1	33¹	37	0	18	21	15.4	4.86	95	.285	.380	0	.000	-1	-1	-1	0	0.0
1931 Was-A	13	9	.591	46	23	7	0	3	191	207	12	80	96	13.6	4.38	98	.273	.344	8	.121	-5	-0	-2	-4	-0.9
1932 Was-A	3	2	.600	12	7	1	1	1	50²	57	4	31	23	15.6	4.97	87	.282	.378	3	.200	1	-3	-4	-2	-0.4
StL-A	3	7	.300	24	11	4	0	0	97	122	12	45	35	15.5	5.57	87	.310	.380	9	.265	1	-12	-8	-1	-0.6
Yr	6	9	.400	36	18	5	1	1	147²	179	16	76	58	15.5	5.36	87	.300	.379	3	.061	1	-15	-11	-3	-1.0
1933 Det-A	11	15	.423	35	22	9	0	3	182²	176	5	84	93	13.0	3.55	122	.251	.334	9	.145	-3	15	15	-2	0.9
1934 Det-A	6	4	.600	20	15	4	1	1	95	107	5	38	39	13.8	4.36	101	.288	.356	2	.065	-3	1	0	-2	-0.3
1935 Det-A	0	1	.000	3	1	0	0	0	12	16	2	5	7	16.5	6.00	69	.320	.393	0	.000	-0	-2	-2	-0	-0.2
Chi-A	5	5	.500	24	11	3	1	0	88²	102	7	39	31	14.5	6.19	75	.283	.356	4	.190	-1	-17	-15	-1	-1.4
Yr	5	6	.455	27	12	3	1	0	100²	118	9	44	38	14.7	6.17	74	.286	.358	2	.087	-1	-19	-18	-1	-1.6
1937 Cle-A	0	1	.000	2	0	0	0	0	0²	3	0	1	1	40.5	27.00	17	.667	.750	0	—	0	-2	-2	0	-0.1
Was-A	4	5	.444	17	11	2	0	2	72	74	6	31	30	13.1	4.38	101	.270	.344	3	.136	-1	2	0	-2	-0.1
Yr	4	6	.400	19	11	2	0	2	72²	76	6	32	31	13.4	4.58	97	.272	.350	2	.091	-1	-0	-1	-2	-0.2
Total 7	46	50	.479	191	105	31	3	11	823	900	53	372	376	14.0	4.63	96	.277	.354	38	.145	-12	-18	-18	-14	-3.1

■ HANK FISCHER
Fischer, Henry William "Bulldog" b: 1/11/40, Yonkers, N.Y. BR/TR, 6', 190 lbs. Deb: 4/16/62

YEAR TM/L	W	L	PCT	G	GS	CG	SH	SV	IP	H	HR	BB	SO	RAT	ERA	ERA+	OAV	OOB	BH	AVG	PB	PR	/A	PD	TPI
1962 Mil-N	2	3	.400	29	3	1	0	0	37¹	43	4	20	29	15.2	5.30	72	.291	.375	0	.000	-0	-6	-6	-0	-0.6
1963 Mil-N	4	3	.571	31	6	1	0	0	74¹	74	8	28	72	13.0	4.96	65	.262	.340	2	.105	-0	-14	-14	-1	-1.6
1964 Mil-N	11	10	.524	37	28	9	5	2	168¹	177	17	39	99	11.7	4.01	88	.265	.309	8	.154	1	-9	-9	-1	-0.9
1965 Mil-N	8	9	.471	31	19	2	0	0	122²	126	18	39	79	12.3	3.89	91	.270	.331	4	.108	-1	-5	-5	-2	-0.8
1966 Atl-N	2	3	.400	14	8	0	0	0	48¹	55	3	14	22	13.0	3.91	93	.296	.348	0	.000	-2	-2	-1	-1	-0.3
Cin-N	0	6	.000	11	9	0	0	0	38	53	3	15	24	16.8	6.63	59	.331	.399	1	.091	-1	-13	-12	-0	-1.1
Yr	2	9	.182	25	17	0	0	0	86¹	108	6	29	46	14.6	5.11	73	.309	.366	0	.000	-2	-14	-13	-1	-1.4
Bos-A	2	3	.400	6	5	1	0	0	31	35	4	11	26	13.6	2.90	131	.287	.351	2	.222	0	2	3	0	0.3
1967 Bos-A	1	2	.333	9	2	1	0	1	26²	24	3	8	18	11.1	2.36	148	.229	.289	1	.143	-0	3	3	0	0.3
Total 6	30	39	.435	168	77	14	5	7	546²	587	60	174	369	12.8	4.23	84	.275	.334	18	.118	-3	-43	-41	-5	-4.6

■ JEFF FISCHER
Fischer, Jeffrey Thomas b: 8/17/63, W.Palm Beach, Fla. BR/TR, 6'3", 185 lbs. Deb: 6/19/87

YEAR TM/L	W	L	PCT	G	GS	CG	SH	SV	IP	H	HR	BB	SO	RAT	ERA	ERA+	OAV	OOB	BH	AVG	PB	PR	/A	PD	TPI
1987 Mon-N	0	1	.000	4	2	0	0	0	13²	21	3	5	6	17.1	8.56	49	.362	.413	1	.200	-0	-7	-7	0	-0.5
1989 LA-N	0	0	—	2	0	0	0	0	3¹	7	1	0	2	18.9	13.50	25	.438	.438	0	—	0	-4	-4	0	-0.3
Total 2	0	1	.000	6	2	0	0	0	17	28	4	5	8	17.5	9.53	42	.378	.418	1	.200	0	-11	-10	0	-0.8

■ RUBE FISCHER
Fischer, Reuben Walter b: 9/19/16, Carlock, S.D. BR/TR, 6'4", 190 lbs. Deb: 9/12/41

YEAR TM/L	W	L	PCT	G	GS	CG	SH	SV	IP	H	HR	BB	SO	RAT	ERA	ERA+	OAV	OOB	BH	AVG	PB	PR	/A	PD	TPI
1941 NY-N	1	0	1.000	2	1	1	0	0	11	10	0	6	9	13.1	2.45	151	.238	.333	1	.333	0	1	2	-0	0.2
1943 NY-N	5	10	.333	22	17	4	0	1	130²	140	4	59	47	13.8	4.61	75	.281	.360	11	.256	3	-18	-17	-2	-1.5
1944 NY-N	6	14	.300	38	18	2	1	2	128²	128	7	87	39	15.5	5.18	71	.266	.384	5	.125	-2	-22	-22	-2	-2.4
1945 NY-N	3	8	.273	31	4	0	0	1	76²	90	6	49	27	16.4	5.63	69	.288	.387	4	.211	2	-16	-15	-1	-1.2
1946 NY-N	1	2	.333	15	1	0	0	0	35²	48	3	21	14	17.4	6.31	55	.316	.399	1	.111	-1	-11	-11	-0	-1.1
Total 5	16	34	.320	108	41	7	1	4	382²	416	20	222	136	15.2	5.10	71	.280	.377	22	.193	2	-66	-63	-4	-6.0

■ TODD FISCHER
Fischer, Todd Richard b: 9/15/60, Columbus, Ohio BR/TR, 5'10", 170 lbs. Deb: 5/29/86

YEAR TM/L	W	L	PCT	G	GS	CG	SH	SV	IP	H	HR	BB	SO	RAT	ERA	ERA+	OAV	OOB	BH	AVG	PB	PR	/A	PD	TPI
1986 Cal-A	0	0	—	9	0	0	0	0	17	18	4	8	7	13.8	4.24	97	.286	.366	0	—	0	-0	-0	0	0.0

■ BILL FISCHER
Fischer, William Charles b: 10/11/30, Wausau, Wis. BR/TR, 6', 190 lbs. Deb: 4/21/56 C

YEAR TM/L	W	L	PCT	G	GS	CG	SH	SV	IP	H	HR	BB	SO	RAT	ERA	ERA+	OAV	OOB	BH	AVG	PB	PR	/A	PD	TPI
1956 Chi-A	0	0	—	3	0	0	0	0	1²	6	0	1	2	37.8	21.60	19	.545	.583	0	—	0	-3	-3	-0	-0.2
1957 Chi-A	7	8	.467	33	11	3	1	1	124	139	1	35	48	12.8	3.48	107	.291	.344	6	.150	-2	4	3	-0	0.1
1958 Chi-A	2	3	.400	17	3	0	0	0	36¹	43	6	13	16	13.9	6.69	54	.301	.359	1	.143	-0	-12	-12	1	-1.0
Det-A	2	4	.333	22	0	0	0	0	30²	46	6	13	16	17.3	7.63	53	.362	.421	0	.000	0	-13	-12	-0	-1.1
Was-A	0	3	.000	3	3	0	0	0	21	24	1	5	10	12.9	3.86	99	.320	.370	1	.200	1	-0	-0	0	0.1
Yr	4	10	.286	42	6	0	0	0	88	113	13	31	42	14.8	6.34	60	.331	.382	2	.154	0	-25	-25	2	-2.0
1959 Was-A	9	11	.450	34	29	6	1	0	187¹	211	26	43	62	12.4	4.28	92	.281	.324	7	.130	-2	-9	-8	4	-0.4
1960 Was-A	3	5	.375	20	7	1	0	0	77	85	7	17	31	11.9	4.91	79	.281	.320	3	.158	1	-9	-9	2	-0.5
Det-A	5	3	.625	20	6	1	0	0	55	50	6	18	24	11.1	3.44	115	.244	.305	4	.364	2	3	3	0	0.6
Yr	8	8	.500	40	13	2	0	0	132	135	13	35	55	11.6	4.30	91	.265	.313	5	.167	3	-6	-6	2	-0.5
1961 Det-A	3	2	.600	26	1	0	0	3	46²	54	10	17	18	13.7	5.01	82	.292	.351	0	.000	-1	-5	-5	0	-0.5
KC-A	1	0	1.000	15	0	0	0	2	21	26	2	6	12	13.7	3.86	107	.321	.368	0	.000	0	1	1	0	0.0
Yr	4	2	.667	41	1	0	0	5	67²	80	12	23	30	13.7	4.66	88	.301	.356	0	.000	-1	-5	-4	0	-0.5
1962 KC-A	4	12	.250	34	16	5	0	2	127²	150	16	8	38	11.2	3.95	105	.293	.305	4	.105	-2	0	3	4	0.1
1963 KC-A	9	6	.600	45	2	0	0	6	95²	86	13	29	34	11.1	3.57	108	.242	.305	1	.067	0	1	3	0	0.2
1964 Min-A	0	1	.000	9	0	0	0	0	7¹	16	2	5	2	25.8	7.36	49	.471	.538	0	—	0	-3	-3	-0	-0.2
Total 9	45	58	.437	281	78	16	2	13	831¹	936	86	210	313	12.5	4.34	90	.287	.333	27	.136	-4	-46	-39	7	-2.8

■ LEO FISHEL
Fishel, Leo b: 12/13/1877, Babylon, N.Y. d: 5/19/60, Hempstead, N.Y. 6', 175 lbs. Deb: 5/03/1899

YEAR TM/L	W	L	PCT	G	GS	CG	SH	SV	IP	H	HR	BB	SO	RAT	ERA	ERA+	OAV	OOB	BH	AVG	PB	PR	/A	PD	TPI
1899 NY-N	0	1	.000	1	1	1	0	0	9	9	0	6	4	15.0	6.00	63	.260	.369	1	.250	0	-2	-2	0	-0.1

■ FISHER
Fisher b: Johnstown, Pa. Deb: 7/17/1884 ◆

YEAR TM/L	W	L	PCT	G	GS	CG	SH	SV	IP	H	HR	BB	SO	RAT	ERA	ERA+	OAV	OOB	BH	AVG	PB	PR	/A	PD	TPI
1884 Phi-U	1	7	.125	8	8	8	0	0	70²	76	0	13	42	11.3	3.57	80	.257	.288	8	.222	0	-4	-5	-1	-0.4
1885 Buf-N	0	1	.000	1	1	1	0	0	9	10	0	2	4	12.0	5.00	59	.269	.306	0	.000	-1	-2	-2	0	-0.1
Total 2	1	8	.111	9	9	9	0	0	79²	86	0	15	46	11.4	3.73	77	.258	.290	10	.145	-0	-6	-7	-1	-0.5

■ BRIAN FISHER
Fisher, Brian Kevin b: 3/18/62, Honolulu, Hawaii BR/TR, 6'4", 210 lbs. Deb: 5/07/85

YEAR TM/L	W	L	PCT	G	GS	CG	SH	SV	IP	H	HR	BB	SO	RAT	ERA	ERA+	OAV	OOB	BH	AVG	PB	PR	/A	PD	TPI
1985 NY-A	4	4	.500	55	0	0	0	14	98¹	77	4	29	85	9.7	2.38	168	.216	.275	0	—	0	19	18	-0	1.8
1986 NY-A	9	5	.643	62	0	0	0	6	96²	105	14	37	67	13.3	4.93	83	.277	.343	0	—	0	-8	-9	-2	-0.9
1987 Pit-N	11	9	.550	37	26	6	3	0	185¹	185	27	72	117	12.7	4.52	91	.262	.334	11	.190	5	-9	-8	-1	-0.5
1988 Pit-N	8	10	.444	33	22	1	1	1	146¹	157	13	57	66	13.5	4.61	74	.277	.348	2	.048	-2	-19	-20	-2	-2.3
1989 Pit-N	0	3	.000	9	3	0	0	1	17	25	2	10	8	18.5	7.94	42	.329	.407	0	—	-1	-8	-9	-0	-0.8
1990 Hou-N	0	0	—	4	0	0	0	0	5	9	1	0	1	16.2	7.20	52	.409	.409	0	—	0	-2	-2	-0	-0.1
Total 6	32	31	.508	200	51	7	4	22	548²	558	61	205	344	12.7	4.36	89	.265	.333	13	.124	0	-27	-30	-5	-2.8

■ CHAUNCEY FISHER
Fisher, Chauncey Burr "Peach" or "Whoa Bill" b: 1/8/1872, Anderson, Ind. d: 4/27/39, Los Angeles, Cal. BR/TR, 5'11", 175 lbs. Deb: 9/20/1893

YEAR TM/L	W	L	PCT	G	GS	CG	SH	SV	IP	H	HR	BB	SO	RAT	ERA	ERA+	OAV	OOB	BH	AVG	PB	PR	/A	PD	TPI
1893 Cle-N	0	2	.000	2	2	2	0	0	18	26	0	9	9	17.5	5.50	89	.328	.397	2	.250	-0	-2	-1	0	0.0

YEAR TM/L	W	L	PCT	G	GS	CG	SH	SV	IP	H	HR	BB	SO	RAT	ERA	ERA+	OAV	OOB	BH	AVG	PB	PR	/A	PD	TPI
1894 Cle-N	0	2	.000	3	2	0	0	0	11	22	0	5	0	22.1	11.45	48	.410	.460	0	.000	-1	-7	-7	1	-0.4
Cin-N	2	8	.200	11	11	10	0	0	91	134	4	44	14	17.6	7.32	76	.338	.404	10	.233	-1	-20	-18	-1	-1.3
Yr	2	10	.167	14	13	10	0	0	102	156	4	49	14	18.1	7.76	71	.347	.411	1	.021	-2	-28	-25	-0	-1.7
1896 Cin-N	10	7	.588	27	15	13	2	2	159²	199	9	36	25	13.2	4.45	104	.303	.339	14	.246	0	-2	-3	-0	0.3
1897 Bro-N	9	7	.563	20	13	11	1	1	149	184	5	43	31	13.7	4.23	97	.301	.347	12	.203	-1	1	-2	-1	-0.3
1901 NY-N	0	0	—	1	1	0	0	0	4	11	0	2	1	29.3	15.75	21	.490	.531	0	.000	-0	-6	-6	-0	-0.4
StL-N	0	0	—	1	0	0	0	0	3	7	0	1	0	24.0	15.00	21	.449	.482	0	.000	-0	-4	-4	0	-0.2
Yr	0	0	—	2	1	0	0	0	7	18	0	3	1	27.0	15.43	21	.473	.511	0	.000	-0	-9	-9	-0	-0.6
Total 5	21	26	.447	65	44	36	3	3	435²	583	18	140	80	14.9	5.37	86	.318	.366	38	.218	-3	-39	-35	-2	-2.3

■ CLARENCE FISHER
Fisher, Clarence Henry   b: 8/27/1898, Letart, W.Va.   d: 11/2/65, Point Pleasant, W.Va.   BR/TR, 6', 174 lbs.   Deb: 9/14/19

YEAR TM/L	W	L	PCT	G	GS	CG	SH	SV	IP	H	HR	BB	SO	RAT	ERA	ERA+	OAV	OOB	BH	AVG	PB	PR	/A	PD	TPI
1919 Was-A	0	0	—	2	0	0	0	0	4	8	0	3	1	24.8	13.50	24	.421	.500	0	—	-0	-5	-5	0	-0.3
1920 Was-A	0	1	.000	2	0	0	0	0	3²	5	0	5	0	24.5	9.82	38	.714	.833	0	.000	-0	-2	-2	1	-0.1
Total 2	0	1	.000	4	0	0	0	0	7²	13	0	8	1	24.7	11.74	29	.500	.618	0	.000	-0	-7	-7	1	-0.4

■ DON FISHER
Fisher, Donald Raymond   b: 2/6/16, Cleveland, Ohio   d: 7/29/73, Mayfield Heights Ohio   BR/TR, 6', 210 lbs.   Deb: 8/25/45

YEAR TM/L	W	L	PCT	G	GS	CG	SH	SV	IP	H	HR	BB	SO	RAT	ERA	ERA+	OAV	OOB	BH	AVG	PB	PR	/A	PD	TPI
1945 NY-N	1	0	1.000	2	1	1	1	0	18	12	0	7	4	10.5	2.00	196	.190	.292	1	.143	-0	4	4	0	0.4

■ EDDIE FISHER
Fisher, Eddie Gene   b: 7/16/36, Shreveport, La.   BR/TR, 6'2.5", 200 lbs.   Deb: 6/22/59

YEAR TM/L	W	L	PCT	G	GS	CG	SH	SV	IP	H	HR	BB	SO	RAT	ERA	ERA+	OAV	OOB	BH	AVG	PB	PR	/A	PD	TPI
1959 SF-N	2	6	.250	17	5	0	0	0	40	57	8	8	15	14.8	7.87	48	.339	.373	0	.000	-1	-17	-18	-0	-1.7
1960 SF-N	1	0	1.000	3	1	1	0	0	12²	11	2	2	7	9.2	3.55	98	.244	.277	3	.600	1	0	-0	0	0.1
1961 SF-N	0	2	.000	15	1	0	0	1	33²	36	7	9	16	12.0	5.35	71	.267	.313	1	.143	0	-5	-6	0	-0.5
1962 Chi-A	9	5	.643	57	12	2	1	5	182²	169	17	45	88	10.6	3.10	126	.245	.293	6	.130	-0	18	16	0	1.7
1963 Chi-A	9	8	.529	33	15	2	1	0	120²	114	14	28	67	10.7	3.95	89	.244	.290	5	.139	-1	-4	-6	1	-0.5
1964 Chi-A	6	3	.667	59	2	0	0	9	125	86	13	32	74	8.7	3.02	114	.192	.250	3	.167	-0	8	6	0	0.7
1965 Chi-A	15	7	.682	**82**	0	0	0	24	165¹	118	13	43	90	**8.9**	2.40	133	.205	.262	4	.138	0	20	15	1	1.7
1966 Chi-A	1	3	.250	23	0	0	0	6	35¹	27	1	17	18	11.5	2.29	138	.214	.313	0	.000	-0	4	3	0	0.4
Bal-A	5	3	.625	44	0	0	0	13	71²	60	4	19	39	10.2	2.64	126	.226	.282	2	.154	0	6	6	0	0.6
Yr	6	6	.500	**67**	0	0	0	19	107	87	5	36	57	10.5	2.52	130	.221	.289	0	.000	0	11	9	0	1.0
1967 Bal-A	4	3	.571	46	0	0	0	4	89²	82	7	26	53	11.2	3.61	87	.245	.307	1	.200	-0	-4	-5	-0	-0.4
1968 Cle-A	4	2	.667	54	0	0	0	4	94²	87	8	17	42	10.1	2.85	104	.248	.286	0	.000	-1	1	1	1	0.2
1969 Cal-A	3	2	.600	52	1	0	0	0	96²	100	9	28	47	12.0	3.63	96	.272	.326	0	.000	-1	-0	-2	1	-0.2
1970 Cal-A	4	4	.500	67	2	0	0	8	130¹	117	15	35	74	11.2	3.04	119	.239	.292	1	.091	-1	10	8	2	1.0
1971 Cal-A	10	8	.556	57	3	0	0	0	119	92	11	50	82	10.9	2.72	119	.211	.295	1	.063	-1	10	7	-1	0.6
1972 Cal-A	4	5	.444	43	1	0	0	4	81¹	73	6	31	32	11.5	3.76	77	.247	.319	2	.118	-1	-6	-8	-0	-0.8
Chi-A	0	1	.000	6	4	0	0	0	22¹	31	1	9	10	16.1	4.43	70	.348	.408	0	.000	-1	-3	-3	-0	-0.3
Yr	4	6	.400	49	5	0	0	4	103²	104	7	40	42	12.5	3.91	76	.267	.336	2	.000	-1	-10	-11	-0	-1.1
1973 Chi-A	6	7	.462	26	16	2	0	0	110²	135	12	38	57	14.3	4.88	81	.301	.360	0	—	0	-13	-11	1	-1.0
StL-N	2	1	.667	6	0	0	0	0	7	3	1	1	1	6.4	1.29	283	.125	.192	1	1.000	0	2	2	-0	0.2
Total 15	85	70	.548	690	63	7	2	81	1538¹	1398	149	438	812	10.9	3.41	101	.243	.299	30	.122	-4	26	5	6	1.7

■ ED FISHER
Fisher, Edward Fredrick   b: 10/31/1876, Wayne, Mich.   d: 7/24/51, Spokane, Wash.   BR/TR, 6'2", 200 lbs.   Deb: 9/05/02

YEAR TM/L	W	L	PCT	G	GS	CG	SH	SV	IP	H	HR	BB	SO	RAT	ERA	ERA+	OAV	OOB	BH	AVG	PB	PR	/A	PD	TPI
1902 Det-A	0	0	—	1	0	0	0	0	4	4	0	1	0	11.3	0.00	—	.261	.306	0	.000	-0	2	2	-0	0.1

■ FRITZ FISHER
Fisher, Frederick Brown   b: 11/28/41, Adrian, Mich.   BL/TL, 6'1", 180 lbs.   Deb: 4/19/64

YEAR TM/L	W	L	PCT	G	GS	CG	SH	SV	IP	H	HR	BB	SO	RAT	ERA	ERA+	OAV	OOB	BH	AVG	PB	PR	/A	PD	TPI
1964 Det-A	0	0	—	1	0	0	0	0	0¹	2	0	2	1	108.0	108.00	3	.667	.800	0	—	0	-4	-4	0	-0.2

■ HARRY FISHER
Fisher, Harry Devereux   b: 1/3/26, Newbury, Ont., Can.   d: 9/20/81, Waterloo, Ont., Ca   BL/TR, 6', 180 lbs.   Deb: 9/16/51 ◆

YEAR TM/L	W	L	PCT	G	GS	CG	SH	SV	IP	H	HR	BB	SO	RAT	ERA	ERA+	OAV	OOB	BH	AVG	PB	PR	/A	PD	TPI
1952 Pit-N	1	2	.333	8	3	0	0	0	18¹	17	4	13	5	15.7	6.87	58	.266	.405	5	.333	1	-6	-6	-0	-0.4

■ JACK FISHER
Fisher, John Howard "Fat Jack"   b: 3/4/39, Frostburg, Md.   BR/TR, 6'2", 215 lbs.   Deb: 4/14/59

YEAR TM/L	W	L	PCT	G	GS	CG	SH	SV	IP	H	HR	BB	SO	RAT	ERA	ERA+	OAV	OOB	BH	AVG	PB	PR	/A	PD	TPI
1959 Bal-A	1	6	.143	27	7	1	1	2	88²	76	7	38	52	11.7	3.05	124	.230	.311	3	.130	-1	8	7	-1	0.5
1960 Bal-A	12	11	.522	40	20	8	3	2	197²	174	13	78	99	11.6	3.41	111	.241	.317	11	.183	2	10	9	0	1.2
1961 Bal-A	10	13	.435	36	25	10	1	1	196	205	17	75	118	13.0	3.90	100	.270	.339	5	.089	-2	3	-0	-2	-0.4
1962 Bal-A	7	9	.438	32	25	4	0	1	152	173	23	56	81	13.7	5.09	74	.284	.346	5	.102	-1	-19	-23	-0	-2.2
1963 SF-N	6	10	.375	36	12	2	0	1	116	132	12	38	57	13.6	4.58	70	.284	.344	3	.103	1	-17	-18	-1	-1.7
1964 NY-N	10	17	.370	40	34	8	1	0	227²	256	36	56	115	12.7	4.23	85	.283	.331	12	.158	-1	-18	-16	-1	-1.6
1965 NY-N	8	24	.250	43	36	10	0	1	253²	252	22	68	116	11.5	3.94	90	.259	.310	12	.154	0	-11	-12	2	-0.9
1966 NY-N	11	14	.440	38	33	10	2	0	230	229	26	54	127	11.4	3.68	99	.260	.309	6	.090	-2	-2	-1	3	0.0
1967 NY-N	9	18	.333	39	30	7	1	0	220¹	251	21	64	117	13.0	4.70	72	.287	.339	7	.100	-2	-32	-32	2	-3.2
1968 Chi-A	8	13	.381	35	28	2	0	0	180²	176	14	48	80	11.5	2.99	101	.257	.312	6	.113	-1	-0	1	0	0.0
1969 Cin-N	4	4	.500	34	15	0	0	1	113	137	16	30	55	13.7	5.50	68	.295	.345	4	.121	-1	-24	-22	-1	-2.4
Total 11	86	139	.382	400	265	62	9	9	1975²	2061	193	605	1017	12.4	4.06	88	.269	.326	74	.125	-6	-102	-106	1	-10.7

■ MAURICE FISHER
Fisher, Maurice Wayne   b: 2/16/31, Uniondale, Ind.   BR/TR, 6'5", 210 lbs.   Deb: 4/16/55

YEAR TM/L	W	L	PCT	G	GS	CG	SH	SV	IP	H	HR	BB	SO	RAT	ERA	ERA+	OAV	OOB	BH	AVG	PB	PR	/A	PD	TPI
1955 Cin-N	0	0	—	1	0	0	0	0	2²	5	1	2	1	23.6	6.75	63	.385	.467	0	.000	-0	-1	-1	0	0.0

■ RAY FISHER
Fisher, Raymond Lyle "Chic"   b: 10/4/1887, Middlebury, Vt.   d: 11/3/82, Ann Arbor, Mich.   BR/TR, 5'11.5", 180 lbs.   Deb: 7/02/10

YEAR TM/L	W	L	PCT	G	GS	CG	SH	SV	IP	H	HR	BB	SO	RAT	ERA	ERA+	OAV	OOB	BH	AVG	PB	PR	/A	PD	TPI
1910 NY-A	5	3	.625	17	7	3	0	1	92¹	95	0	18	42	11.3	2.92	91	.274	.315	3	.103	-2	-4	-3	1	-0.3
1911 NY-A	10	11	.476	29	22	8	2	0	171²	178	3	55	99	12.5	3.25	111	.269	.330	7	.119	-3	2	7	4	0.7
1912 NY-A	2	8	.200	17	13	5	0	0	90¹	107	2	32	47	14.0	5.88	61	.312	.374	2	.065	-4	-26	-23	3	-2.1
1913 NY-A	12	16	.429	43	31	14	1	1	246¹	244	3	71	92	11.8	3.18	94	.261	.319	22	.278	-3	-7	-5	2	0.0
1914 NY-A	10	12	.455	29	26	17	2	1	209	177	2	61	86	10.4	2.28	121	.241	.303	9	.138	-2	11	11	4	1.4
1915 NY-A	18	11	.621	30	28	20	4	0	247²	219	7	62	97	10.4	2.11	139	.243	.295	9	.108	-5	23	23	0	2.0
1916 NY-A	11	8	.579	31	21	9	1	2	179	191	4	51	56	12.4	3.17	91	.285	.339	11	.177	-5	-7	-5	-0	-0.4
1917 NY-A	8	9	.471	23	18	12	3	0	144	126	3	43	64	10.7	2.19	123	.243	.304	9	.180	-0	8	8	1	1.0
1919 *Cin-N	14	5	.737	26	20	12	5	1	174¹	141	5	38	41	9.3	2.17	128	.226	.271	16	.271	3	14	12	4	2.1
1920 Cin-N	10	11	.476	33	22	10	1	1	201	189	5	50	56	11.1	2.73	111	.249	.302	17	.243	1	9	7	1	1.1
Total 10	100	94	.515	278	208	110	19	7	1755²	1667	34	481	680	11.2	2.82	105	.257	.312	105	.179	-8	23	30	21	5.5

■ TOM FISHER
Fisher, Thomas Chalmers "Red"   b: 11/1/1880, Anderson, Ind.   d: 9/3/72, Anderson, Ind.   BR/TR, 5'10.5", 185 lbs.   Deb: 4/17/04

YEAR TM/L	W	L	PCT	G	GS	CG	SH	SV	IP	H	HR	BB	SO	RAT	ERA	ERA+	OAV	OOB	BH	AVG	PB	PR	/A	PD	TPI
1904 Bos-N	6	16	.273	31	21	19	2	0	214	257	5	82	84	14.7	4.25	65	.302	.370	21	.212	3	-36	-35	-5	-3.6

■ TOM FISHER
Fisher, Thomas Gene   b: 4/4/42, Cleveland, Ohio   BR/TR, 6', 180 lbs.   Deb: 9/20/67

YEAR TM/L	W	L	PCT	G	GS	CG	SH	SV	IP	H	HR	BB	SO	RAT	ERA	ERA+	OAV	OOB	BH	AVG	PB	PR	/A	PD	TPI
1967 Bal-A	0	0	—	2	0	0	0	0	3¹	2	0	2	1	10.8	0.00	—	.182	.308	0	—	0	1	1	0	0.1

■ CHEROKEE FISHER
Fisher, William Charles   b: 12/1845, Philadelphia, Pa.   d: 9/26/12, New York, N.Y.   BR/TR, 5'9", 164 lbs.   Deb: 5/06/1871 ◆

YEAR TM/L	W	L	PCT	G	GS	CG	SH	SV	IP	H	HR	BB	SO	RAT	ERA	ERA+	OAV	OOB	BH	AVG	PB	PR	/A	PD	TPI
1871 Rok-n	4	16	.200	24	24	22	**1**	0	213	295	3	31	15	13.8	4.35	94	.281	.302	28	.228	-3	-3	-6		-0.5
1872 Bal-n	10	1	.909	19	11	9	1	**1**	110¹	89	0	11		8.2	2.53	148	**.189**	**.207**	52	.230	-1	15	15		1.1
1873 Ath-n	3	4	.429	13	5	5	0	0	85	90	1	10		10.6	3.18	119	**.228**	**.247**	64	.254	0	4	6		0.4
1874 Har-n	14	23	.378	39	35	31	0	0	317	405	1	10		11.8	3.04	104	.275	.279	54	.223	-5	-1	4		0.0
1875 Phi-n	22	19	.537	41	41	36	2	0	356²	345	6	9		8.9	1.92	131	.232	.237	41	.232	-1	21	24		2.0
1876 Cin-N	4	20	.167	28	24	23	1	0	229¹	294	6	6	29	11.9	3.02	73	.291	.295	32	.248	-1	-18	-21	-2	-2.1
1878 Pro-N	0	1	.000	1	1	1	0	0	9	14	0	0	2	14.0	4.00	55	.338	.338	0	.000	-0	-2	-2	0	-0.1
Total 5 n	53	63	.457	136	116	103	4	3	1082	1224	11	71	15	10.8	2.89	113	.251	.262	239	.234	-10	35	44		3.0

YEAR TM/L	W	L	PCT	G	GS	CG	SH	SV	IP	H	HR	BB	SO	RAT	ERA	ERA+	OAV	OOB	BH	AVG	PB	PR	/A	PD	TPI
Total 2	4	21	.160	29	25	23	0	0	238¹	308	6	6	31	11.9	3.06	72	.293	.297	32	.235	-10	-20	-23	-2	-2.2

■ MAX FISKE
Fiske, Maximilian Patrick "Ski" b: 10/12/1888, Chicago, Ill. d: 5/15/28, Chicago, Ill. BR/TR, 5'11", 185 lbs. Deb: 4/19/14

YEAR TM/L	W	L	PCT	G	GS	CG	SH	SV	IP	H	HR	BB	SO	RAT	ERA	ERA+	OAV	OOB	BH	AVG	PB	PR	/A	PD	TPI
1914 Chi-F	12	12	.500	38	22	7	0	0	198	161	7	59	87	10.3	3.14	94	.231	.298	16	.235	1	2	-4	0	-0.3

■ PAUL FITTERY
Fittery, Paul Clarence b: 10/10/1887, Lebanon, Pa. d: 1/28/74, Cartersville, Ga. BB/TL, 5'8.5", 156 lbs. Deb: 9/05/14

YEAR TM/L	W	L	PCT	G	GS	CG	SH	SV	IP	H	HR	BB	SO	RAT	ERA	ERA+	OAV	OOB	BH	AVG	PB	PR	/A	PD	TPI
1914 Cin-N	0	2	.000	8	4	2	0	0	43²	41	0	12	21	11.1	3.09	95	.246	.300	1	.059	-1	-1	-1	0	-0.1
1917 Phi-N	1	1	.500	17	2	1	0	0	55²	69	1	27	13	16.3	4.53	62	.317	.404	2	.091	-1	-11	-11	2	-0.9
Total 2	1	3	.250	25	6	3	0	0	99¹	110	1	39	34	14.0	3.90	73	.286	.360	3	.077	-2	-13	-11	2	-1.0

■ JOHN FITZGERALD
Fitzgerald, John Francis b: 9/15/33, Brooklyn, N.Y. BL/TL, 6'3", 190 lbs. Deb: 9/28/58

YEAR TM/L	W	L	PCT	G	GS	CG	SH	SV	IP	H	HR	BB	SO	RAT	ERA	ERA+	OAV	OOB	BH	AVG	PB	PR	/A	PD	TPI
1958 SF-N	0	0	—	1	1	0	0	0	3	1	1	1	3	6.0	3.00	127	.111	.200	0	.000	-0	0	0	0	0.0

■ JOHN FITZGERALD
Fitzgerald, John H. b: 5/30/1870, Natick, Mass. d: 3/31/21, Boston, Mass. Deb: 7/18/1891

YEAR TM/L	W	L	PCT	G	GS	CG	SH	SV	IP	H	HR	BB	SO	RAT	ERA	ERA+	OAV	OOB	BH	AVG	PB	PR	/A	PD	TPI
1891 Bos-a	1	1	.500	6	3	2	0	1	32	49	2	11	16	16.9	5.63	62	.340	.387	1	.071	-1	-7	-8	0	-0.6

■ JOHN FITZGERALD
Fitzgerald, John J. Deb: 4/18/1890

YEAR TM/L	W	L	PCT	G	GS	CG	SH	SV	IP	H	HR	BB	SO	RAT	ERA	ERA+	OAV	OOB	BH	AVG	PB	PR	/A	PD	TPI
1890 Roc-a	3	8	.273	11	11	8	1	0	78	77	0	45	35	14.1	4.04	88	.250	.346	6	.194	-0	-1	-4	1	-0.2

■ JOHN FITZGERALD
Fitzgerald, John T. b: Leadville, Col. Deb: 6/04/1891

YEAR TM/L	W	L	PCT	G	GS	CG	SH	SV	IP	H	HR	BB	SO	RAT	ERA	ERA+	OAV	OOB	BH	AVG	PB	PR	/A	PD	TPI
1891 Lou-a	14	18	.438	33	32	29	3	0	276	280	6	95	111	12.2	3.59	102	.254	.314	19	.170	0	4	2	-3	0.0
1892 Lou-N	1	3	.250	4	4	4	0	0	34	45	2	11	3	14.8	4.24	72	.306	.354	2	.133	-0	-4	-4	-0	-0.4
Total 2	15	21	.417	37	36	33	3	0	310	325	8	106	114	12.5	3.66	98	.260	.318	21	.165	-0	1	-2	-4	-0.4

■ PAUL FITZKE
Fitzke, Paul Frederick Herman "Bob" b: 7/30/1900, Lacrosse, Wis. d: 6/30/50, Sacramento, Cal. BR/TR, 5'11.5", 185 lbs. Deb: 9/01/24

YEAR TM/L	W	L	PCT	G	GS	CG	SH	SV	IP	H	HR	BB	SO	RAT	ERA	ERA+	OAV	OOB	BH	AVG	PB	PR	/A	PD	TPI
1924 Cle-A	0	0	—	1	0	0	0	0	4	5	0	3	1	18.0	4.50	95	.313	.421	0	.000	-0	-0	-0	-0	0.0

■ AL FITZMORRIS
Fitzmorris, Alan James b: 3/21/46, Buffalo, N.Y. BB/TR, 6'2", 190 lbs. Deb: 9/08/69

YEAR TM/L	W	L	PCT	G	GS	CG	SH	SV	IP	H	HR	BB	SO	RAT	ERA	ERA+	OAV	OOB	BH	AVG	PB	PR	/A	PD	TPI
1969 KC-A	1	1	.500	7	0	0	0	2	10²	9	1	4	3	11.0	4.22	87	.237	.310	0	.000	-0	-1	-1	0	0.0
1970 KC-A	8	5	.615	43	11	2	0	1	117²	112	14	52	47	12.5	4.44	84	.254	.333	9	.290	4	-9	-9	1	-0.3
1971 KC-A	7	5	.583	36	15	2	1	0	127¹	112	6	55	53	11.9	4.17	82	.245	.327	11	.250	2	-10	-10	2	-0.6
1972 KC-A	2	5	.286	38	2	0	0	3	101	99	10	28	51	11.4	3.74	81	.252	.303	4	.174	1	-8	-8	2	-0.5
1973 KC-A	8	3	.727	15	13	3	1	0	89	88	5	25	26	11.4	2.83	145	.259	.310	0	—	0	10	13	2	1.6
1974 KC-A	13	6	.684	34	27	9	4	1	190	189	8	63	53	11.9	2.79	137	.260	.319	0	—	0	17	22	3	2.7
1975 KC-A	16	12	.571	35	35	11	3	0	242	239	6	76	78	11.9	3.57	108	.262	.322	0	—	0	6	7	2	0.9
1976 KC-A	15	11	.577	35	33	8	2	0	220¹	227	6	56	80	11.6	3.06	114	.273	.320	0	—	0	11	11	4	1.6
1977 Cle-A	6	10	.375	29	21	1	0	0	133	164	12	53	54	14.8	5.41	73	.306	.369	0	—	0	-20	-22	0	-2.0
1978 Cle-A	0	1	.000	7	0	0	0	0	14¹	19	3	7	5	17.0	6.28	59	.333	.415	0	—	0	-4	-4	0	-0.3
Cal-A	1	0	1.000	9	2	0	0	0	31²	26	2	14	8	11.4	1.71	212	.236	.323	0	—	0	7	7	0	0.7
Yr	1	1	.500	16	2	0	0	0	46	45	5	21	13	12.9	3.13	117	.268	.349	0	—	0	3	3	0	0.4
Total 10	77	59	.566	288	159	36	11	7	1277	1284	83	433	458	12.2	3.65	101	.265	.327	24	.242	7	-1	5	16	3.8

■ FREDDIE FITZSIMMONS
Fitzsimmons, Frederick Landis "Fat Freddie" b: 7/28/01, Mishawaka, Ind. d: 11/18/79, Yucca Valley, Cal. BR/TR, 5'11", 185 lbs. Deb: 8/12/25 MC

YEAR TM/L	W	L	PCT	G	GS	CG	SH	SV	IP	H	HR	BB	SO	RAT	ERA	ERA+	OAV	OOB	BH	AVG	PB	PR	/A	PD	TPI
1925 NY-N	6	3	.667	10	8	6	1	0	74²	70	4	18	17	10.6	2.65	152	.248	.293	9	.310	2	13	12	2	1.5
1926 NY-N	14	10	.583	37	26	12	0	0	219	224	7	58	48	11.8	2.88	130	.272	.322	11	.128	-6	23	21	3	1.8
1927 NY-N	17	10	.630	42	31	14	1	3	244²	260	15	67	78	12.2	3.72	104	.275	.325	18	.207	-0	6	4	2	0.5
1928 NY-N	20	9	.690	40	32	16	1	1	261¹	264	13	65	67	11.5	3.68	106	.268	.316	18	.191	1	9	6	2	0.9
1929 NY-N	15	11	.577	37	31	14	4	1	221²	242	14	66	55	12.6	4.10	112	.285	.338	15	.183	-1	15	12	5	1.4
1930 NY-N	19	7	**.731**	41	29	17	1	1	224¹	230	26	59	76	11.6	4.25	111	.266	.314	22	.265	5	18	12	7	2.1
1931 NY-N	18	11	.621	35	33	19	4	0	253²	242	16	62	78	10.8	3.05	121	.251	.296	21	.228	8	23	18	8	**3.6**
1932 NY-N	11	11	.500	35	31	11	0	0	237²	287	18	83	65	14.1	4.43	84	.299	.356	19	.221	4	-15	-19	7	-0.8
1933 *NY-N	16	11	.593	36	35	13	1	0	251²	243	14	72	65	11.3	2.90	111	.251	.305	19	.200	3	12	9	6	1.9
1934 NY-N	18	14	.563	38	37	14	3	1	263¹	266	12	51	73	10.9	3.04	127	.261	.297	22	.232	5	30	24	5	3.4
1935 NY-N	4	8	.333	18	15	6	4	0	94	104	7	22	23	12.2	4.02	96	.281	.323	8	.258	1	-0	-2	1	0.1
1936 *NY-N	10	7	.588	28	17	7	0	2	141	147	6	39	35	11.9	3.32	117	.274	.323	7	.149	-2	11	9	1	0.8
1937 NY-N	2	2	.500	6	4	1	1	0	27¹	28	3	8	13	11.9	4.61	84	.272	.324	3	.300	2	-2	-2	-0	0.0
Bro-N	4	8	.333	13	13	4	0	0	90²	91	7	32	29	12.3	4.27	95	.263	.327	5	.167	-1	-4	-2	1	-0.1
Yr	6	10	.375	19	17	5	1	0	118	119	5	40	42	12.2	4.35	92	.265	.327	8	.050	1	-6	-5	1	-0.1
1938 Bro-N	11	8	.579	27	26	12	3	0	202²	205	6	43	38	11.1	3.02	129	.261	.302	12	.171	-1	17	20	6	2.7
1939 Bro-N	7	9	.438	27	20	5	0	3	151¹	178	6	28	44	12.4	3.87	104	.293	.327	11	.234	3	1	3	5	1.1
1940 Bro-N	16	2	**.889**	20	18	11	4	1	134¹	120	6	25	35	9.8	2.81	142	.233	.269	5	.106	-2	15	18	1	1.8
1941 *Bro-N	6	1	.857	13	12	3	1	0	82²	78	3	26	19	11.5	2.07	177	.245	.305	4	.143	-0	14	15	3	1.9
1942 Bro-N	0	0	—	1	1	0	0	0	3	6	1	1	0	21.0	15.00	22	.400	.438	1	.500	0	-4	-4	0	-0.2
1943 Bro-N	3	4	.429	9	7	1	0	0	44²	50	6	21	12	14.5	5.44	62	.281	.360	1	.071	-1	-10	-10	0	-1.0
Total 19	217	146	.598	513	426	186	29	13	3223²	3335	186	846	870	11.8	3.51	111	.268	.316	231	.200	20	174	144	66	23.4

■ PATSY FLAHERTY
Flaherty, Patrick Joseph b: 6/29/1876, Mansfield, Pa. d: 1/23/68, Alexandria, La. BL/TL, 5'8", 165 lbs. Deb: 9/08/1899 ♦

YEAR TM/L	W	L	PCT	G	GS	CG	SH	SV	IP	H	HR	BB	SO	RAT	ERA	ERA+	OAV	OOB	BH	AVG	PB	PR	/A	PD	TPI
1899 Lou-N	2	3	.400	5	4	4	0	0	39	41	0	5	5	10.6	2.31	167	.270	.293	5	.208	1	7	7	-1	0.7
1900 Pit-N	0	0	—	4	1	0	0	0	22	30	0	9	5	16.0	6.14	59	.324	.384	1	.111	-1	-6	-6	1	-0.4
1903 Chi-A	11	25	.306	40	34	29	2	1	293²	338	9	50	65	11.9	3.74	75	.288	.317	14	.137	-3	-25	-30	3	-2.9
1904 Chi-A	1	2	.333	5	5	4	0	0	43	36	1	10	14	9.6	2.09	117	.228	.274	4	.333	2	2	2	1	0.6
Pit-N	19	9	.679	29	28	24	5	0	242	210	3	59	54	10.4	2.05	134	.232	.287	22	.212	6	19	19	6	3.3
1905 Pit-N	10	10	.500	27	20	15	0	1	188	197	2	49	44	12.1	3.49	86	.272	.324	15	.197	2	-10	-10	3	-0.4
1907 Bos-N	12	15	.444	27	25	23	0	0	217	197	4	59	34	10.9	2.70	95	.248	.306	22	.191	2	-5	-3	3	0.4
1908 Bos-N	12	18	.400	31	31	21	0	0	244	221	6	81	50	11.4	3.25	74	.236	.303	12	.140	-0	-24	-23	3	-2.2
1910 Phi-N	0	0	—	1	0	0	0	0	0¹	1	0	1	0	54.0	0.00	—	.333	.500	1	.500	0	0	0	0	0.0
1911 Bos-N	0	2	.000	4	2	1	0	0	14	21	0	8	0	20.6	7.07	54	.350	.451	27	.287	1	-6	-5	-0	-0.4
Total 9	67	84	.444	173	150	125	7	2	1303	1292	25	331	271	11.5	3.10	89	.259	.309	123	.197	11	-49	-50	18	-1.1

■ MIKE FLANAGAN
Flanagan, Michael Kendall b: 12/16/51, Manchester, N.H. BL/TL, 6', 185 lbs. Deb: 9/05/75

YEAR TM/L	W	L	PCT	G	GS	CG	SH	SV	IP	H	HR	BB	SO	RAT	ERA	ERA+	OAV	OOB	BH	AVG	PB	PR	/A	PD	TPI
1975 Bal-A	0	1	.000	2	1	0	0	0	9²	9	0	6	7	14.0	2.79	126	.250	.357	0	—	0	1	1	0	0.1
1976 Bal-A	3	5	.375	20	10	4	0	0	85	83	7	33	56	12.3	4.13	79	.260	.330	0	—	0	-6	-8	0	-0.7
1977 Bal-A	15	10	.600	36	33	15	2	1	235	235	17	70	149	11.8	3.64	104	.266	.321	0	—	0	11	4	-1	0.3
1978 Bal-A	19	15	.559	40	40	17	2	0	281¹	271	24	87	167	11.5	4.03	87	.257	.315	0	—	0	-8	-17	-2	-1.8
1979 *Bal-A	**23**	9	.719	39	38	16	**5**	0	265²	245	23	70	190	10.8	3.08	130	.245	.297	0	—	0	33	27	-1	2.7
1980 Bal-A	16	13	.552	37	37	12	2	0	251¹	278	27	71	128	12.6	4.12	96	.287	.337	0	—	0	-2	-5	0	-0.3
1981 Bal-A	9	6	.600	20	20	3	2	0	116	108	11	37	72	11.4	4.19	87	.244	.305	0	—	0	-7	-7	1	-0.6
1982 Bal-A	15	11	.577	36	35	11	1	0	236	233	24	76	103	11.9	3.97	102	.259	.319	0	—	0	2	0	0	0.2
1983 *Bal-A	12	4	.750	20	20	3	1	0	125¹	135	10	31	50	12.1	3.30	120	.278	.324	0	—	0	11	9	-0	0.8
1984 Bal-A	13	13	.500	34	34	10	2	0	226²	213	24	81	115	11.7	3.53	110	.250	.316	0	—	0	11	8	-1	0.8
1985 Bal-A	4	5	.444	15	15	1	0	0	86	101	14	28	42	13.7	5.13	79	.297	.354	0	—	0	-9	-10	-0	-0.9
1986 Bal-A	7	11	.389	24	24	2	0	0	172	179	16	66	96	12.9	4.24	98	.270	.334	0	—	0	-1	-0	-0	-0.1
1987 Bal-A	3	6	.333	16	16	4	0	0	94²	102	6	36	50	13.1	4.94	89	.278	.342	0	—	0	-5	-6	-0	-0.5
Tor-A	3	2	.600	7	7	0	0	0	49¹	46	3	15	43	11.1	2.37	189	.237	.292	0	—	0	11	12	-0	1.2

YEAR TM/L	W	L	PCT	G	GS	CG	SH	SV	IP	H	HR	BB	SO	RAT	ERA	ERA+	OAV	OOB	BH	AVG	PB	PR	/A	PD	TPI
Yr	6	8	.429	23	23	4	0	0	144	148	12	51	93	12.4	4.06	109	.263	.325	0	—	0	6	6	-0	0.7
1988 Tor-A	13	13	.500	34	34	2	1	0	211	220	23	80	99	13.1	4.18	94	.271	.341	0	—	0	-5	-6	1	-0.4
1989 *Tor-A	8	10	.444	30	30	1	1	0	171²	186	10	47	47	12.5	3.93	96	.283	.335	0	—	0	-1	-3	2	0.0
1990 Tor-A	2	2	.500	5	5	0	0	0	20¹	28	3	8	5	15.9	5.31	71	.329	.387	0	—	0	-3	-3	0	-0.2
Total 16	165	136	.548	420	403	101	19	1	2637	2672	242	842	1419	12.1	3.90	100	.266	.324	0	—	0	34	-5	-2	-0.3

■ **RAY FLANIGAN**   Flanigan, Raymond Arthur b: 1/8/23, Morgantown, W.Va. BR/TR, 6', 190 lbs. Deb: 9/20/46

YEAR TM/L	W	L	PCT	G	GS	CG	SH	SV	IP	H	HR	BB	SO	RAT	ERA	ERA+	OAV	OOB	BH	AVG	PB	PR	/A	PD	TPI
1946 Cle-A	0	1	.000	3	1	0	0	0	9	11	1	8	2	19.0	11.00	30	.289	.413	1	.500	1	-7	-8	0	-0.5

■ **TOM FLANIGAN**   Flanigan, Thomas Anthony b: 9/6/34, Cincinnati, Ohio BR/TL, 6'3", 175 lbs. Deb: 4/14/54

YEAR TM/L	W	L	PCT	G	GS	CG	SH	SV	IP	H	HR	BB	SO	RAT	ERA	ERA+	OAV	OOB	BH	AVG	PB	PR	/A	PD	TPI
1954 Chi-A	0	0	—	2	0	0	0	0	1²	1	0	1	0	10.8	0.00	—	.200	.333	0	—	0	1	1	0	0.1
1958 StL-N	0	0	—	1	0	0	0	0	1	2	1	1	0	27.0	9.00	46	.500	.600	0	—	0	-1	-1	0	0.0
Total 2	0	0	—	3	0	0	0	0	2²	3	1	2	0	16.9	3.38	115	.333	.455	0	—	0	0	0	0	0.1

■ **JACK FLATER**   Flater, John William b: 9/22/1880, Sandymount, Md. d: 3/20/70, Westminster, Md. TR, 5'10", 175 lbs. Deb: 9/18/08

YEAR TM/L	W	L	PCT	G	GS	CG	SH	SV	IP	H	HR	BB	SO	RAT	ERA	ERA+	OAV	OOB	BH	AVG	PB	PR	/A	PD	TPI
1908 Phi-A	1	3	.250	5	3	3	0	0	39¹	35	0	12	8	11.2	2.06	125	.252	.320	2	.133	-0	1	2	2	0.5

■ **JOHN FLAVIN**   Flavin, John Thomas b: 5/7/42, Albany, Cal. BL/TL, 6'2", 208 lbs. Deb: 8/25/64

YEAR TM/L	W	L	PCT	G	GS	CG	SH	SV	IP	H	HR	BB	SO	RAT	ERA	ERA+	OAV	OOB	BH	AVG	PB	PR	/A	PD	TPI
1964 Chi-N	0	1	.000	5	1	0	0	0	4²	11	0	3	5	27.0	13.50	28	.500	.560	0	.000	-0	-5	-5	-0	-0.4

■ **FRANK FLEET**   Fleet, Frank H. b: 1848, New York, N.Y. d: 6/13/1900, New York, N.Y. Deb: 10/18/1871 ♦

YEAR TM/L	W	L	PCT	G	GS	CG	SH	SV	IP	H	HR	BB	SO	RAT	ERA	ERA+	OAV	OOB	BH	AVG	PB	PR	/A	PD	TPI
1871 Mut-n	0	1	.000	1	1	1	0	0	9	20	1	0	3	0	23.0	10.00	38	.370	.404	2	.333	0	-6	-6	-0.3
1873 Res-n	0	3	.000	3	3	2	0	0	24	58	1	0	21.8	7.13	52	.395	.395	22	.244	-0	-9	-9	-0.5
1875 StL-n	2	1	.667	3	3	3	0	0	27	33	0	3	12.0	2.33	95	.277	.295	1	.063	-2	0	-0	-0.1
Atl-n	0	1	.000	2	1	1	0	0	15¹	24	1	0	14.1	4.70	49	.312	.312	25	.223	-0	-4	-4	-0.2
Yr	2	2	.500	5	4	4	0	0	42¹	57	1	3	12.8	3.19	71	.291	.302	1	.008	-2	-3	-4	-0.3
Total 3 n	2	6	.250	9	8	7	0	0	75¹	135	2	6	0	16.8	5.26	43	.340	.350	85	.228	-2	-23	-25	-1.1

■ **BILL FLEMING**   Fleming, Leslie Fletchard b: 7/31/13, Rowland, Cal. BR/TR, 6', 190 lbs. Deb: 8/21/40

YEAR TM/L	W	L	PCT	G	GS	CG	SH	SV	IP	H	HR	BB	SO	RAT	ERA	ERA+	OAV	OOB	BH	AVG	PB	PR	/A	PD	TPI
1940 Bos-A	1	2	.333	10	6	1	0	0	46¹	53	4	20	24	14.6	4.86	93	.290	.366	0	.000	-2	-2	-2	-1	-0.3
1941 Bos-A	1	1	.500	16	1	0	0	1	41¹	32	4	24	20	14.2	3.92	106	.212	.320	2	.222	1	1	1	2	0.2
1942 Chi-N	5	6	.455	33	14	4	2	2	134¹	117	9	63	59	12.3	3.01	106	.230	.318	2	.051	-4	4	3	-1	-0.1
1943 Chi-N	0	1	.000	11	0	0	0	0	32¹	40	2	12	12	15.3	6.40	52	.303	.374	0	.000	-1	-11	-11	1	-1.0
1944 Chi-N	9	10	.474	39	18	9	1	0	158¹	163	6	62	42	13.3	3.13	113	.269	.337	9	.170	-1	9	7	2	0.8
1946 Chi-N	0	1	.000	14	1	0	0	0	29¹	37	2	12	10	15.3	6.14	54	.301	.368	0	—	-0	-9	-9	-0	-0.9
Total 6	16	21	.432	123	40	14	3	3	442	442	27	193	167	13.1	3.79	94	.259	.338	13	.104	-7	-8	-11	1	-1.3

■ **VAN FLETCHER**   Fletcher, Alfred Vanoide b: 8/6/24, East Bend, N.C. BR/TR, 6'2", 185 lbs. Deb: 4/12/55

YEAR TM/L	W	L	PCT	G	GS	CG	SH	SV	IP	H	HR	BB	SO	RAT	ERA	ERA+	OAV	OOB	BH	AVG	PB	PR	/A	PD	TPI
1955 Det-A	0	0	—	9	0	0	0	0	12	13	1	2	4	11.3	3.00	128	.260	.288	0	—	0	1	1	-0	0.1

■ **SAM FLETCHER**   Fletcher, Samuel S. b: Altoona, Pa. TR, 6'2", 210 lbs. Deb: 10/06/09

YEAR TM/L	W	L	PCT	G	GS	CG	SH	SV	IP	H	HR	BB	SO	RAT	ERA	ERA+	OAV	OOB	BH	AVG	PB	PR	/A	PD	TPI
1909 Bro-N	0	1	.000	1	1	1	0	0	9	13	0	2	5	15.0	8.00	32	.351	.385	0	.000	-0	-5	-5	0	-0.4
1912 Cin-N	0	0	—	2	0	0	0	0	9²	15	1	11	3	24.2	12.10	28	.357	.491	2	.500	1	-9	-9	0	-0.6
Total 2	0	1	.000	3	1	1	0	0	18²	28	1	13	8	19.8	10.13	30	.354	.446	2	.286	0	-15	-15	0	-1.0

■ **TOM FLETCHER**   Fletcher, Thomas Wayne b: 6/28/42, Elmira, N.Y. BB/TL, 6', 170 lbs. Deb: 9/12/62

YEAR TM/L	W	L	PCT	G	GS	CG	SH	SV	IP	H	HR	BB	SO	RAT	ERA	ERA+	OAV	OOB	BH	AVG	PB	PR	/A	PD	TPI
1962 Det-A	0	0	—	1	0	0	0	0	2	2	0	2	1	18.0	0.00	—	.250	.400	0	—	0	1	1	0	0.1

■ **JOHN FLINN**   Flinn, John Richard b: 9/2/54, Merced, Cal. BR/TR, 6', 175 lbs. Deb: 5/06/78

YEAR TM/L	W	L	PCT	G	GS	CG	SH	SV	IP	H	HR	BB	SO	RAT	ERA	ERA+	OAV	OOB	BH	AVG	PB	PR	/A	PD	TPI
1978 Bal-A	1	1	.500	13	0	0	0	0	15²	24	3	13	8	21.3	8.04	43	.348	.451	0	—	0	-7	-8	0	-0.7
1979 Bal-A	0	0	—	4	0	0	0	0	2²	2	0	1	0	10.1	0.00	—	.222	.300	0	—	0	1	1	0	0.1
1980 Mil-A	2	1	.667	20	1	0	0	2	37	31	3	20	15	12.4	3.89	99	.220	.317	0	—	0	1	-0	-0	0.0
1982 Bal-A	2	0	1.000	5	0	0	0	0	13²	13	1	3	13	10.5	1.32	306	.260	.302	0	—	0	4	4	0	0.4
Total 4	5	2	.714	42	1	0	0	2	69	70	7	37	36	14.0	4.17	92	.260	.350	0	—	0	-1	-3	-0	-0.2

■ **HILLY FLITCRAFT**   Flitcraft, Hildreth Milton b: 8/21/23, Woodstown, N.J. BL/TL, 6'2", 180 lbs. Deb: 8/31/42

YEAR TM/L	W	L	PCT	G	GS	CG	SH	SV	IP	H	HR	BB	SO	RAT	ERA	ERA+	OAV	OOB	BH	AVG	PB	PR	/A	PD	TPI
1942 Phi-N	0	0	—	3	0	0	0	0	3¹	6	0	2	1	21.6	8.10	41	.429	.500	0	—	0	-2	-2	0	-0.1

■ **MORT FLOHR**   Flohr, Moritz Herman "Dutch" b: 8/15/11, Canisteo, N.Y. BL/TL, 6', 173 lbs. Deb: 6/08/34

YEAR TM/L	W	L	PCT	G	GS	CG	SH	SV	IP	H	HR	BB	SO	RAT	ERA	ERA+	OAV	OOB	BH	AVG	PB	PR	/A	PD	TPI
1934 Phi-A	0	2	.000	14	3	0	0	0	30²	34	3	33	6	20.0	5.87	75	.296	.456	4	.333	1	-5	-5	1	-0.2

■ **JESSE FLORES**   Flores, Jesse Sandoval b: 11/2/14, Guadalajara, Mexico BR/TR, 5'10", 175 lbs. Deb: 4/16/42

YEAR TM/L	W	L	PCT	G	GS	CG	SH	SV	IP	H	HR	BB	SO	RAT	ERA	ERA+	OAV	OOB	BH	AVG	PB	PR	/A	PD	TPI
1942 Chi-N	0	1	.000	4	0	0	0	0	5¹	5	1	2	6	11.8	3.38	95	.227	.292	0	—	0	-0	-0	-0	0.0
1943 Phi-A	12	14	.462	31	27	13	0	0	231²	208	13	70	113	11.0	3.11	109	.240	.301	14	.175	-0	5	7	1	0.9
1944 Phi-A	9	11	.450	27	25	11	2	0	185²	172	8	49	65	10.9	3.39	103	.245	.298	11	.172	-0	1	2	-0	0.1
1945 Phi-A	7	10	.412	29	24	9	4	1	191¹	180	6	63	52	11.6	3.43	100	.250	.314	9	.148	-2	-1	-0	-3	-0.4
1946 Phi-A	9	7	.563	29	15	8	4	1	155	147	8	38	48	10.8	2.32	153	.249	.295	11	.250	3	20	21	-2	2.5
1947 Phi-A	4	13	.235	28	20	4	0	0	151¹	139	10	59	41	11.8	3.39	112	.244	.315	10	.227	1	5	7	1	0.8
1950 Cle-A	3	3	.500	28	2	1	1	4	53	53	3	25	27	13.4	3.74	116	.261	.345	0	.000	-2	5	4	-2	0.0
Total 7	44	59	.427	176	113	46	11	6	973	904	49	306	352	11.3	3.18	112	.246	.307	55	.181	-0	35	41	-6	3.9

■ **BEN FLOWERS**   Flowers, Bennett b: 6/15/27, Wilson, N.C. BR/TR, 6'4", 195 lbs. Deb: 9/29/51

YEAR TM/L	W	L	PCT	G	GS	CG	SH	SV	IP	H	HR	BB	SO	RAT	ERA	ERA+	OAV	OOB	BH	AVG	PB	PR	/A	PD	TPI
1951 Bos-A	0	0	—	1	0	0	0	0	3	2	0	1	2	9.0	0.00	—	.200	.273	0	.000	-0	1	1	0	0.1
1953 Bos-A	1	4	.200	32	6	1	1	3	79¹	87	6	24	36	12.7	3.86	109	.280	.333	3	.158	-0	1	3	1	0.3
1955 Det-A	0	0	—	4	0	0	0	0	6	5	1	2	2	10.5	6.00	64	.238	.304	0	.000	-0	-1	-1	0	0.0
StL-N	1	0	1.000	4	4	0	0	0	27¹	27	1	12	19	12.8	3.62	112	.255	.331	1	.100	-1	1	1	-0	0.0
1956 StL-N	1	1	.500	3	3	0	0	0	11²	15	1	5	5	15.4	6.94	54	.341	.408	0	.000	-0	-4	-4	0	-0.3
Phi-N	0	2	.000	32	0	0	0	0	41	54	5	10	22	14.3	5.71	65	.331	.374	0	—	-0	-9	-9	1	-0.6
Yr	1	3	.250	35	3	0	0	0	52²	69	6	15	27	14.5	5.98	62	.330	.378	1	.200	-0	-13	-13	1	-1.0
Total 4	3	7	.300	76	13	1	1	3	168¹	190	18	54	86	13.2	4.49	90	.290	.346	4	.111	-2	-10	-9	1	-0.6

■ **DICKIE FLOWERS**   Flowers, Charles Richard b: 1850, Philadelphia, Pa. d: 10/5/1892, Philadelphia, Pa. Deb: 6/03/1871 ♦

YEAR TM/L	W	L	PCT	G	GS	CG	SH	SV	IP	H	HR	BB	SO	RAT	ERA	ERA+	OAV	OOB	BH	AVG	PB	PR	/A	PD	TPI
1871 Tro-n	0	0	—	1	0	0	0	0	1	1	0	0	0	9.0	0.00	—	.333	.333	33	.314	0	0	0		0.0

■ **WES FLOWERS**   Flowers, Charles Wesley b: 8/13/13, Vanndale, Ark. d: 12/31/88, Wynne, Ark. BL/TL, 6'1.5", 190 lbs. Deb: 8/08/40

YEAR TM/L	W	L	PCT	G	GS	CG	SH	SV	IP	H	HR	BB	SO	RAT	ERA	ERA+	OAV	OOB	BH	AVG	PB	PR	/A	PD	TPI
1940 Bro-N	1	1	.500	5	2	0	0	0	21	23	2	10	8	15.4	3.43	117	.299	.400	1	.200	-0	1	1	0	0.1
1944 Bro-N	1	1	.500	9	1	0	0	0	17¹	26	3	13	3	20.8	7.79	46	.333	.435	3	.600	1	-8	-8	0	-0.5
Total 2	2	2	.500	14	3	0	0	0	38¹	49	5	23	11	17.8	5.40	70	.316	.418	4	.400	1	-7	-7	0	-0.5

■ **CARNEY FLYNN**   Flynn, Cornelius Francis Xavier b: 1/23/1875, Cincinnati, Ohio d: 2/10/47, Cincinnati, Ohio BL/TL, 5'11", 165 lbs. Deb: 7/17/1894

YEAR TM/L	W	L	PCT	G	GS	CG	SH	SV	IP	H	HR	BB	SO	RAT	ERA	ERA+	OAV	OOB	BH	AVG	PB	PR	/A	PD	TPI
1894 Cin-N	0	2	.000	2	1	0	0	0	7²	16	1	10	4	30.5	17.61	32	.420	.541	0	.000	-1	-10	-10	-0	-0.6
1896 NY-N	0	2	.000	3	2	1	0	0	10²	18	0	8	4	21.9	11.81	36	.370	.459	2	.500	2	-9	-9	-1	-0.5
Was-N	0	1	.000	4	1	1	0	0	20	43	0	10	3	23.8	8.55	52	.428	.480	2	.250	-0	-9	-9	-1	-0.7
Yr	0	3	.000	7	3	2	0	0	30²	61	0	18	7	23.2	9.68	45	.409	.473	4		1	-18	-18	-1	-1.2
Total 2	0	5	.000	9	4	2	0	0	38¹	77	1	28	11	24.7	11.27	41	.412	.488	4	.267	1	-29	-29	-1	-1.8

YEAR TM/L	W	L	PCT	G	GS	CG	SH	SV	IP	H	HR	BB	SO	RAT	ERA	ERA+	OAV	OOB	BH	AVG	PB	PR	/A	PD	TPI

■ JOCKO FLYNN   Flynn, John A. b: 6/30/1864, Lawrence, Mass. d: 12/30/07, Lawrence, Mass. 5'6.5", 143 lbs. Deb: 5/01/1886 ♦

| 1886 Chi-N | 23 | 6 | .793 | 32 | 29 | 28 | 2 | 1 | 257 | 207 | 9 | 63 | 146 | 9.5 | 2.24 | 162 | .212 | .259 | 41 | .200 | 1 | 30 | 40 | 2 | 4.7 |

■ STU FLYTHE   Flythe, Stuart Mcguire b: 12/5/11, Conway, N.C. d: 10/18/63, Durham, N.C. BR/TR, 6'2", 175 lbs. Deb: 5/31/36

| 1936 Phi-A | 0 | 0 | — | 17 | 3 | 0 | 0 | 0 | 39¹ | 49 | 4 | 61 | 14 | 25.9 | 13.04 | 39 | .302 | .500 | 4 | .267 | 0 | -35 | -35 | 0 | -2.7 |

■ GENE FODGE   Fodge, Eugene Arlan "Suds" b: 7/9/31, South Bend, Ind. BR/TR, 6', 175 lbs. Deb: 4/20/58

| 1958 Chi-N | 1 | 1 | .500 | 16 | 4 | 1 | 0 | 0 | 39² | 47 | 5 | 11 | 15 | 13.2 | 4.76 | 82 | .296 | .341 | 0 | .000 | -1 | -4 | -4 | 0 | -0.3 |

■ JIM FOGARTY   Fogarty, James G. b: 2/12/1864, San Francisco, Cal d: 5/20/1891, Philadelphia, Pa. BR, 5'10.5", 180 lbs. Deb: 5/01/1884 M♦

1884 Phi-N	0	0	—	1	0	0	0	0	1	2	0	0	1	18.0	0.00	—	.395	.395	80	.212	0	0	0	0	0.0
1886 Phi-N	0	1	.000	1	0	0	0	0	6	7	1	0	4	10.5	0.00	—	.280	.280	82	.293	0	2	2	0	0.2
1887 Phi-N	0	0	—	1	0	0	0	0	3	3	0	1	0	12.0	9.00	47	.253	.311	129	.261	0	-2	-2	0	0.0
1889 Phi-N	0	0	—	4	0	0	0	0	4	4	0	2	0	13.5	9.00	48	.252	.336	129	.259	1	-2	-2	0	-0.1
Total 4	0	1	.000	7	0	0	0	0	14	16	1	3	5	12.2	4.50	84	.277	.313	709	.246	2	-1	-1	0	0.1

■ CURRY FOLEY   Foley, Charles Joseph b: 1/14/1856, Milltown, Ireland d: 10/20/1898, Boston, Mass. TL, 180 lbs. Deb: 5/13/1879 ♦

1879 Bos-N	9	9	.500	20	16	16	1	0	161²	175	1	15	57	10.6	2.51	99	.275	.275	46	.315	5	-0	-2	0.5
1880 Bos-N	14	14	.500	36	28	21	1	0	238	264	1	40	68	11.5	3.89	58	.267	.296	97	.292	8	-40	-43	1	-3.8
1881 Buf-N	3	4	.429	10	6	2	0	0	41	70	1	5	2	16.5	5.27	53	.362	.378	96	.256	1	-11	-11	0	-0.9
1882 Buf-N	0	0	—	1	0	0	0	0	1	2	0	0	0	18.0	18.00	16	.395	.395	104	.305	0	-2	-2	0	0.0
1883 Buf-N	1	0	1.000	1	0	0	0	0	1	0	0	4	0	36.0	0.00	—	.000	.565	30	.270	0	0	0	0	0.0
Total 5	27	27	.500	68	50	39	2	0	442²	511	3	64	127	11.7	3.54	68	.274	.298	373	.286	14	-53	-56	-1	-4.2

■ JOHN FOLEY   Foley, John J b: Hannibal, Mo. TL, Deb: 9/18/1885

| 1885 Pro-N | 0 | 1 | .000 | 1 | 1 | 0 | 0 | 0 | 8 | 6 | 0 | 5 | 2 | 12.4 | 4.50 | 59 | .199 | .312 | 0 | .000 | 0 | -1 | -2 | 0 | 0.0 |

■ TOM FOLEY   Foley, Thomas Michael b: 9/9/59, Columbus, Ga. BL/TR, 6'1", 175 lbs. Deb: 4/09/83 ♦

| 1989 Mon-N | 0 | 0 | — | 1 | 0 | 0 | 0 | 0 | 0¹ | 1 | 1 | 0 | 0 | 27.0 | 27.00 | 13 | .500 | .500 | 86 | .229 | 0 | -1 | -1 | 0 | 0.0 |

■ RICH FOLKERS   Folkers, Richard Nevin b: 10/17/46, Waterloo, Iowa BL/TL, 6'2", 180 lbs. Deb: 6/10/70

1970 NY-N	0	2	.000	16	1	0	0	2	29¹	36	6	25	15	18.7	6.44	62	.313	.436	2	.333	0	-8	-8	1	-0.5
1972 StL-N	1	0	1.000	9	0	0	0	0	13¹	12	0	5	7	11.5	3.38	101	.240	.309	0	.000	-0	0	0	0	0.0
1973 StL-N	4	4	.500	34	9	1	0	3	82¹	74	10	34	44	12.1	3.61	101	.239	.321	2	.100	-1	0	-0	0	0.0
1974 StL-N	6	2	.750	55	0	0	0	2	90	65	4	38	57	10.5	3.00	119	.207	.297	1	.100	-1	6	6	-1	0.4
1975 SD-N	6	11	.353	45	15	4	0	0	142	155	8	39	87	12.4	4.18	83	.278	.327	6	.167	1	-9	-11	-0	-1.0
1976 SD-N	2	3	.400	33	3	0	0	0	59²	67	10	25	26	14.2	5.28	62	.279	.352	0	.000	-0	-12	-13	-0	-1.3
1977 Mil-A	0	1	.000	3	0	0	0	0	6¹	7	2	4	6	15.6	4.26	95	.269	.367	0	—	-0	-0	-0	0	0.0
Total 7	19	23	.452	195	28	5	0	7	423	416	40	170	242	12.6	4.11	86	.258	.332	11	.143	-1	-22	-27	-1	-2.4

■ LEW FONSECA   Fonseca, Lewis Albert b: 1/21/1899, Oakland, Cal. d: 11/26/89, Ely, Iowa BR/TR, 5'10.5", 180 lbs. Deb: 4/13/21 M♦

| 1932 Chi-A | 0 | 0 | — | 1 | 0 | 0 | 0 | 0 | 1 | 0 | 0 | 0 | 0 | 0.0 | 0.00 | — | .000 | .000 | 5 | .135 | -0 | 0 | 0 | 0 | 0.0 |

■ RAY FONTENOT   Fontenot, Silton Ray b: 8/8/57, Lake Charles, La. BL/TL, 6', 175 lbs. Deb: 6/30/83

1983 NY-A	8	2	.800	15	15	3	1	0	97¹	101	3	25	27	11.7	3.33	117	.266	.314	0	—	0	8	6	1	0.7
1984 NY-A	8	9	.471	35	24	0	0	0	169¹	189	8	58	85	13.3	3.61	105	.290	.351	0	—	0	7	3	1	0.4
1985 Chi-N	6	10	.375	38	23	0	0	0	154²	177	23	45	70	12.9	4.36	91	.294	.343	2	.049	-4	-13	-6	2	-0.7
1986 Chi-N	3	5	.375	42	0	0	0	2	56	57	5	21	24	12.5	3.86	105	.266	.332	1	.167	-0	-1	1	-0	0.1
Min-A	0	0	—	15	0	0	0	0	16¹	27	4	4	10	18.2	9.92	43	.360	.407	0	.000	-0	-10	-10	0	-0.9
Total 4	25	26	.490	145	62	3	1	2	493²	551	42	153	216	12.9	4.03	98	.287	.341	3	.063	-4	-10	-5	4	-0.4

■ JIM FOOR   Foor, James Emerson b: 1/13/49, St.Louis, Mo. BL/TL, 6'2", 170 lbs. Deb: 4/09/71

1971 Det-A	0	0	—	3	0	0	0	0	1	2	0	4	2	54.0	18.00	20	.400	.667	0	—	0	-2	-2	0	-0.1
1972 Det-A	1	0	1.000	7	0	0	0	0	3²	6	1	6	2	29.5	14.73	21	.353	.522	0	—	0	-5	-5	0	-0.4
1973 Pit-N	0	0	—	3	0	0	0	0	1¹	2	0	1	1	20.3	0.00	—	.286	.375	0	—	0	1	1	0	0.1
Total 3	1	0	1.000	13	0	0	0	0	6	10	1	11	5	31.5	12.00	28	.345	.525	0	—	0	-6	-6	0	-0.4

■ DAVY FORCE   Force, David W. "Wee Davy" or "Tom Thumb" b: 7/27/1849, New York, N.Y. d: 6/21/18, Englewood, N.J. BR/TR, 5'4", 130 lbs. Deb: 5/05/1871 ♦

1873 Bal-n	1	1	.500	3	1	1	0	0	18	26	0	0		13.0	4.00	90	.302	.302	85	.363	1	-1	-1		0.0
1874 Chi-n	0	0	—	1	0	0	0	0	7	22	4	0		28.3	12.86	24	.440	.440	93	.314	0	-8	-8		-0.4
Total 2 n	1	1	.500	4	1	1	0	0	25	48	4	0		17.3	6.48	47	.353	.353	436	.334	2	-10	-10		-0.4

■ DAVE FORD   Ford, David Alan b: 12/29/56, Cleveland, Ohio BR/TR, 6'4", 190 lbs. Deb: 9/02/78

1978 Bal-A	1	0	1.000	2	1	0	0	0	15	10	0	2	5	7.2	0.00	—	.196	.226	0	—	0	6	6	0	0.7
1979 Bal-A	2	1	.667	9	2	0	0	2	30	23	2	7	9	9.0	2.10	191	.219	.268	0	—	0	7	6	0	0.7
1980 Bal-A	1	3	.250	25	3	1	0	1	69²	66	11	13	22	10.5	4.26	93	.251	.291	0	—	0	-2	-2	-0	-0.2
1981 Bal-A	1	2	.333	15	2	0	0	0	40	61	2	10	12	16.0	6.52	56	.359	.394	0	—	0	-13	-13	-0	-1.2
Total 4	5	6	.455	51	8	1	0	3	154²	160	15	32	46	11.3	4.02	96	.272	.311	0	—	0	-1	-3	-0	-0.0

■ WHITEY FORD   Ford, Edward Charles "Chairman Of The Board" b: 10/21/28, New York, N.Y. BL/TL, 5'10", 178 lbs. Deb: 7/01/50 CH

1950 *NY-A	9	1	.900	20	12	7	2	1	112	87	7	52	59	11.3	2.81	153	.216	.309	7	.194	0	22	18	0	1.8
1953 *NY-A	18	6	.750	32	30	11	3	0	207	187	13	110	110	13.1	3.00	123	.245	.344	20	.267	6	23	16	0	2.2
1954 *NY-A	16	8	.667	34	28	11	3	1	210²	170	10	101	125	11.6	2.82	122	.227	.319	10	.161	2	21	14	0	1.7
1955 *NY-A	18	7	.720	39	33	18	5	2	253²	188	20	113	137	10.7	2.63	143	.208	.297	14	.163	2	38	31	-0	3.4
1956 *NY-A	19	6	.760	31	30	18	2	1	225²	187	13	84	141	11.0	2.47	156	.228	.303	17	.218	3	42	35	4	4.4
1957 *NY-A	11	5	.688	24	17	5	0	0	129¹	114	10	53	84	11.7	2.57	139	.237	.313	6	.143	-1	17	15	2	1.6
1958 *NY-A	14	7	.667	30	29	15	7	1	219¹	174	14	62	145	9.8	2.01	176	.217	.276	15	.205	4	43	37	1	4.4
1959 *NY-A	16	10	.615	35	29	9	2	1	204	194	13	89	114	12.5	3.04	120	.250	.328	15	.231	7	19	14	4	2.5
1960 *NY-A	12	9	.571	33	29	8	4	0	192²	168	15	65	85	10.9	3.08	116	.235	.299	8	.151	2	17	11	2	1.4
1961 *NY-A	25	4	.862	39	39	11	3	0	283	242	23	92	209	10.7	3.21	116	.229	.292	17	.177	3	26	16	-1	1.8
1962 *NY-A	17	8	.680	38	37	7	0	0	257²	243	22	69	160	11.0	2.90	129	.246	.298	10	.118	-1	31	24	4	2.9
1963 *NY-A	24	7	.774	38	37	13	3	1	269¹	240	26	56	189	10.0	2.74	128	.241	.283	13	.141	0	27	23	-1	2.4
1964 *NY-A	17	6	.739	39	36	12	8	1	244²	212	10	57	172	10.0	2.13	170	.230	.276	8	.119	1	41	40	2	4.9
1965 *NY-A	16	13	.552	37	36	9	2	1	244¹	241	22	50	162	10.8	3.24	105	.258	.297	15	.183	2	6	4	2	0.9
1966 NY-A	2	5	.286	22	9	0	0	0	73	79	8	24	43	12.7	2.47	146	.277	.333	0	.000	-2	8	7	3	0.9
1967 NY-A	2	4	.333	7	7	2	1	0	44	40	2	9	21	10.0	1.64	191	.247	.287	2	.154	-0	8	7	1	1.1
Total 16	236	106	.690	498	438	156	45	10	3170¹	2766	228	1086	1956	11.0	2.75	133	.235	.301	177	.173	25	386	315	24	38.3

■ GENE FORD   Ford, Eugene Matthew b: 6/23/12, Ft.Dodge, Iowa d: 9/7/70, Emmetsburg, Iowa BR/TR, 6'2", 195 lbs. Deb: 6/17/36

1936 Bos-N	0	0	—	2	1	0	0	0	2	2	0	3	0	22.5	13.50	28	.250	.455	0	—	0	-2	-2	0	-0.1
1938 Chi-A	0	0	—	4	0	0	0	0	14	21	1	12	2	21.2	10.29	48	.350	.458	1	.167	-0	-9	-8	0	-0.6
Total 2	0	0	—	6	1	0	0	0	16	23	1	15	2	21.4	10.69	44	.338	.458	1	.167	-0	-11	-11	0	-0.7

■ GENE FORD   Ford, Eugene Wyman b: 4/16/1881, Milton, N.S., Can. d: 8/23/73, Dunedin, Fla. BR/TR, 6', 170 lbs. Deb: 5/05/05

| 1905 Det-A | 0 | 1 | .000 | 7 | 1 | 0 | 0 | 0 | 35 | 51 | 0 | 14 | 20 | 16.7 | 5.66 | 48 | .340 | .397 | 0 | .000 | -1 | -12 | -11 | 0 | -1.1 |

YEAR TM/L	W	L	PCT	G	GS	CG	SH	SV	IP	H	HR	BB	SO	RAT	ERA	ERA+	OAV	OOB	BH	AVG	PB	PR	/A	PD	TPI
■ WENTY FORD Ford, Percival Edmund Wentworth b: 11/25/46, Nassau, Bahamas d: 7/8/80, Nassau, Bahamas BR/TR, 5'11", 165 lbs. Deb: 9/10/73																								
1973 Atl-N	1	2	.333	4	2	1	0	0	16¹	17	3	8	4	14.3	5.51	71	.279	.371	2	.400	1	-3	-3	0	-0.1
■ RUSS FORD Ford, Russell William b: 4/25/1883, Brandon, Man., Can. d: 1/24/60, Rockingham, N.C. BR/TR, 5'11", 175 lbs. Deb: 4/28/09																								
1909 NY-A	0	0	—	1	0	0	0	0	3	4	0	4	2	33.0	9.00	28	.333	.579	0	.000	-0	-2	-2	0	-0.1
1910 NY-A	26	6	.813	36	33	29	8	1	299²	194	4	70	209	8.2	1.65	161	.188	.245	20	.208	4	29	34	-5	4.0
1911 NY-A	22	11	.667	37	33	26	1	0	281¹	251	3	76	158	10.6	2.27	158	.237	.291	20	.196	-3	34	41	-1	4.0
1912 NY-A	13	21	.382	36	35	30	0	0	291²	317	10	79	112	12.4	3.55	101	.280	.329	32	.286	5	-7	1	3	1.2
1913 NY-A	12	18	.400	33	28	15	1	2	237	244	9	58	72	11.6	2.66	112	.275	.322	12	.162	0	7	9	-3	0.7
1914 Buf-F	21	6	**.778**	35	26	19	5	**6**	247¹	190	11	41	123	8.7	1.82	**181**	.214	.254	10	.128	-3	38	40	0	4.2
1915 Buf-F	5	9	.357	21	15	7	0	0	127¹	140	7	48	34	13.5	4.52	69	.285	.352	12	.279	3	-21	-20	1	-1.6
Total 7	99	71	.582	199	170	126	15	9	1487¹	1340	44	376	710	10.6	2.59	124	.243	.296	106	.209	8	77	103	-5	12.4
■ TOM FORD Ford, Thomas Walter b: 1866, Chattanooga, Tenn. 5'10.5", 155 lbs. Deb: 5/06/1890																								
1890 Col-a	0	0	—	1	0	0	0	0	2	0	0	3	0	13.5	0.00	—	.000	.336	0	.000	-0	1	1	0	0.1
Bro-a	0	6	.000	7	6	6	0	0	49	70	2	32	12	18.7	5.14	76	.325	.413	1	.033	-3	-7	-7	0	-0.8
Yr	0	6	.000	8	6	6	0	0	51	70	2	35	12	18.5	4.94	79	.317	.410	1	.032	-3	-6	-6	1	-0.7
■ HAPPY FOREMAN Foreman, August b: 7/20/1897, Memphis, Tenn. d: 2/13/53, New York, N.Y. BL/TL, 5'7", 160 lbs. Deb: 9/03/24																								
1924 Chi-A	0	0	—	3	0	0	0	0	4	7	0	4	1	24.8	2.25	183	.467	.579	0	.000	-0	1	1	-0	0.0
1926 Bos-A	0	0	—	3	0	0	0	0	7¹	3	0	5	3	9.8	3.68	111	.130	.286	0	.000	-0	0	0	1	0.1
Total 2	0	0	—	6	0	0	0	0	11¹	10	0	9	4	15.1	3.18	129	.263	.404	0	.000	-1	1	1	0	0.1
■ FRANK FOREMAN Foreman, Francis Isaiah "Monkey" b: 5/1/1863, Baltimore, Md. d: 11/19/57, Baltimore, Md. BL/TL, 6', 160 lbs. Deb: 5/15/1884 ♦																								
1884 CP-U	1	2	.333	3	3	1	0	0	18	23	0	2	10	12.5	4.00	75	.291	.309	1	.091	-2	-2	-2	0	-0.2
KC-U	0	1	.000	1	1	0	0	0	8	17	0	2	5	21.4	5.63	49	.406	.433	0	.000	-1	-2	-3	1	-0.1
Yr	1	3	.250	4	4	2	0	0	26	40	0	4	15	15.2	4.50	65	.331	.352	0	.000	-2	-4	-5	1	-0.3
1885 Bal-a	2	1	.667	3	3	2	0	0	27	33	0	9	11	14.0	6.00	54	.289	.341	4	.286	1	-8	-8	-0	-0.5
1889 Bal-a	23	21	.523	51	48	43	5	0	414	364	8	137	180	10.9	3.52	112	.229	.290	26	.144	-10	15	19	-2	0.6
1890 Cin-N	13	10	.565	25	24	20	0	0	198¹	201	6	89	57	13.2	3.95	90	.255	.331	10	.133	-1	-9	-9	-2	-0.9
1891 Was-a	18	20	.474	43	41	39	1	1	345¹	381	9	142	170	13.6	3.73	100	.271	.337	34	.222	9	-0	1	-2	0.9
1892 Was-N	2	4	.333	11	7	4	0	0	60	53	6	37	16	13.5	3.30	99	.228	.333	13	.464	7	-0	-0	-1	0.6
Bal-N	0	3	.000	4	3	2	0	0	25	40	1	11	5	18.4	6.84	50	.348	.405	4	.174	-0	-10	-9	-0	-0.6
Yr	2	7	.222	15	10	6	0	0	85	93	7	48	21	14.9	4.34	76	.267	.356	6	.118	8	-10	-10	-1	0.0
1893 NY-N	0	1	.000	2	1	0	0	0	5²	9	1	10	0	46.1	27.00	17	.531	.634	0	.000	-1	-14	-14	-0	-0.9
1895 Cin-N	11	14	.440	32	27	19	0	1	219	253	11	92	55	14.2	4.11	121	.285	.352	29	.309	4	16	21	-3	1.9
1896 Cin-N	15	6	.714	27	23	18	1	1	190²	214	2	62	38	13.0	3.68	125	.281	.335	19	.250	-1	14	20	-0	1.6
1901 Bos-A	0	1	.000	1	1	1	0	0	8	8	1	2	1	11.3	9.00	39	.257	.302	0	.000	-1	-5	-5	0	-0.3
Bal-A	12	6	.667	24	22	18	1	1	191¹	225	2	58	41	13.3	3.67	105	.290	.339	26	.325	5	-0	4	-3	0.6
Yr	12	7	.632	25	23	19	1	1	199¹	233	3	60	42	13.2	3.88	99	.288	.337	26	.036	4	-5	-1	-3	0.3
1902 Bal-A	0	2	.000	2	2	2	0	0	16¹	28	0	6	2	18.7	6.06	62	.377	.423	3	.429	1	-5	-4	1	-0.1
Total 11	97	92	.513	229	206	170	8	4	1726²	1859	47	659	591	13.1	3.94	101	.268	.331	170	.225	13	-9	10	-12	2.6
■ BROWNIE FOREMAN Foreman, John Davis b: 8/6/1875, Baltimore, Md. d: 10/10/26, Baltimore, Md. BL/TL, 5'8", 150 lbs. Deb: 7/18/1895																								
1895 Pit-N	8	6	.571	19	16	12	0	2	139²	131	0	64	54	12.6	3.22	140	**.244**	.325	3	.065	-5	24	20	2	1.4
1896 Pit-N	3	3	.500	9	9	5	0	0	61²	73	4	35	18	15.8	6.57	64	.292	.379	4	.150	0	-15	-16	1	-1.1
Cin-N	0	4	.000	4	3	2	0	0	18	39	2	16	4	27.5	16.50	28	.430	.516	1	.125	-1	-24	-24	-0	-1.6
Yr	3	7	.300	13	12	7	0	0	79²	112	6	51	22	18.4	8.81	49	.329	.416	8	.286	-0	-39	-40	1	-2.7
Total 2	11	13	.458	32	28	19	0	2	219¹	243	6	115	76	14.7	5.25	85	.277	.361	11	.095	-5	-15	-20	3	-1.3
■ BILL FORMAN Forman, William Orange b: 10/10/1886, Venango, Pa. d: 10/3/58, Uniontown, Pa. BB/TR, 5'11", 180 lbs. Deb: 9/20/09																								
1909 Was-A	0	2	.000	2	2	1	0	0	11	8	0	7	2	13.9	4.91	50	.211	.362	1	.333	-1	-3	-3	1	-0.1
1910 Was-A	0	0	—	1	0	0	0	0	0²	1	0	0	0	13.5	13.50	18	.333	.333	0	—	0	-1	-1	0	0.0
Total 2	0	2	.000	3	2	1	0	0	11²	9	0	7	2	13.9	5.40	45	.220	.360	1	.333	1	-4	-4	1	-0.1
■ MIKE FORNIELES Fornieles, Jose Miguel (Torres) b: 1/18/32, Havana, Cuba BR/TR, 5'11", 155 lbs. Deb: 9/02/52																								
1952 Was-A	2	2	.500	4	2	2	1	0	26¹	13	1	11	12	8.2	1.37	260	.143	.235	0	.000	-1	7	6	-0	0.5
1953 Chi-A	8	7	.533	39	16	5	0	3	153	160	8	61	72	13.1	3.59	112	.270	.340	4	.098	-3	7	7	2	0.6
1954 Chi-A	1	2	.333	15	6	0	0	1	42	41	4	14	18	11.8	4.29	87	.252	.311	3	.273	-3	-3	-1	1	0.0
1955 Chi-A	6	3	.667	26	9	2	0	2	86¹	84	12	29	23	12.0	3.86	102	.255	.319	3	.103	-2	1	1	1	0.0
1956 Chi-A	0	1	.000	6	0	0	0	0	15²	22	1	6	6	16.1	4.60	98	.306	.359	1	.200	-1	-1	-1	0	0.0
Bal-a	4	7	.364	30	11	1	1	1	111	109	7	25	53	10.9	3.97	99	.266	.308	5	.167	-1	2	-1	0	0.0
Yr	4	8	.333	36	11	1	1	1	126²	131	8	31	59	11.5	4.05	97	.271	.315	6	.000	-1	2	-2	0	0.0
1957 Bal-A	2	6	.250	15	4	1	1	0	57	57	4	17	43	11.7	4.26	84	.257	.310	5	.278	1	-3	-4	0	-0.2
Bos-A	8	7	.533	25	18	7	1	2	125¹	136	7	38	64	12.7	3.52	113	.271	.327	6	.136	-2	4	7	-1	0.4
Yr	10	13	.435	40	22	8	2	2	182¹	193	11	55	107	12.4	3.75	103	.267	.321	11	.032	-1	1	2	-1	0.2
1958 Bos-A	4	6	.400	37	7	1	0	1	110²	123	10	33	49	13.2	4.96	81	.284	.343	6	.207	-0	-15	-12	-0	-1.1
1959 Bos-A	5	3	.625	46	0	0	0	11	82	77	6	29	54	11.7	3.07	132	.254	.321	3	.158	-1	7	9	-0	0.8
1960 Bos-A	10	5	.667	**70**	0	0	0	**14**	109	86	6	49	64	11.6	2.64	153	.219	.315	6	.400	2	15	17	1	2.0
1961 Bos-A	9	8	.529	57	2	1	0	15	119¹	121	8	54	70	13.3	4.68	89	.265	.345	2	.156	0	-9	-7	-2	-0.4
1962 Bos-A	3	6	.333	42	1	0	0	5	82¹	96	14	37	36	15.4	5.36	77	.303	.390	3	.188	-0	-13	-11	-0	-1.0
1963 Bos-A	0	0	—	9	0	0	0	0	14	16	0	5	5	13.5	6.43	59	.286	.344	1	.333	1	-4	-4	0	-0.3
Min-A	1	1	.500	11	0	0	0	0	22²	24	0	13	7	15.5	4.76	76	.273	.379	1	.167	-1	-3	-3	-1	-0.2
Yr	1	1	.500	20	0	0	0	0	36²	40	0	18	12	14.7	5.40	68	.276	.364	0	.000	1	-7	-7	-1	-0.5
Total 12	63	64	.496	432	76	20	4	55	1156²	1165	98	421	576	12.6	3.96	100	.263	.332	52	.169	-6	-7	2	6	1.1
■ KEN FORSCH Forsch, Kenneth Roth b: 9/8/46, Sacramento, Cal. BR/TR, 6'4", 195 lbs. Deb: 9/07/70																								
1970 Hou-N	1	2	.333	4	4	1	0	0	24	28	1	5	13	12.4	5.63	69	.298	.333	0	.000	-1	-4	-5	0	-0.4
1971 Hou-N	8	8	.500	33	23	7	2	0	188¹	162	8	53	131	10.5	2.53	133	.230	.288	8	.136	-1	20	17	-2	1.5
1972 Hou-N	6	8	.429	30	24	1	0	0	156¹	163	19	62	113	13.0	3.91	86	.273	.341	6	.146	-1	-8	-10	-3	-1.3
1973 Hou-N	9	12	.429	46	26	5	0	4	201¹	197	18	74	149	12.3	4.20	86	.257	.325	4	.065	-4	-12	-13	-2	-1.8
1974 Hou-N	8	7	.533	70	0	0	0	10	103¹	98	7	37	48	12.1	2.79	124	.255	.326	0	.000	-1	10	8	-0	0.7
1975 Hou-N	4	8	.333	34	9	2	0	2	109	114	9	30	54	12.1	3.22	105	.277	.330	1	.045	-1	5	3	-0	0.1
1976 Hou-N	4	3	.571	52	0	0	0	19	92	76	5	26	49	10.2	2.15	148	.226	.286	1	.091	-0	14	11	1	1.2
1977 Hou-N	5	8	.385	42	5	0	0	8	86	80	2	28	45	11.5	2.72	131	.246	.310	1	.077	-1	11	8	1	0.8
1978 Hou-N	10	6	.625	52	6	4	2	7	133¹	136	7	37	71	11.7	2.70	123	.268	.319	5	.185	-1	13	9	1	1.0
1979 Hou-N	11	6	.647	26	24	10	2	0	177²	155	14	35	58	**9.6**	3.04	116	.236	**.275**	8	.138	0	14	9	3	1.2
1980 *Hou-N	12	13	.480	32	32	6	3	0	222¹	230	15	41	84	11.3	3.20	103	.266	.304	18	.234	3	10	2	2	0.8
1981 Cal-A	11	7	.611	20	20	10	**4**	0	153	143	7	27	55	10.2	2.88	126	.250	.289	0	—	0	13	13	1	1.5
1982 Cal-A	13	11	.542	37	35	12	4	0	228	225	25	57	73	11.6	3.87	105	.258	.311	0	—	0	5	5	-1	0.4
1983 Cal-A	11	12	.478	31	31	11	1	0	219¹	226	21	61	81	11.9	4.06	99	.266	.318	0	—	-1	-1	-1	-0	-0.1
1984 Cal-A	1	1	.500	2	2	0	0	0	16¹	14	2	6	8	11.0	3.86	101	.233	.274	-0	—	-0	3	3	1	0.5
1986 Cal-A	0	1	.000	10	0	0	0	1	17	24	4	10	13	19.1	9.53	43	.343	.439	0	—	0	-10	-10	0	-0.9
Total 16	114	113	.502	521	241	70	18	51	2127¹	2071	155	586	1047	11.4	3.37	106	.257	.311	52	.136	-5	83	48	-0	5.2

YEAR TM/L	W	L	PCT	G	GS	CG	SH	SV	IP	H	HR	BB	SO	RAT	ERA	ERA+	OAV	OOB	BH	AVG	PB	PR	/A	PD	TPI

■ BOB FORSCH   Forsch, Robert Herbert b: 1/13/50, Sacramento, Cal.   BR/TR, 6'4", 200 lbs.   Deb: 7/07/74

YEAR TM/L	W	L	PCT	G	GS	CG	SH	SV	IP	H	HR	BB	SO	RAT	ERA	ERA+	OAV	OOB	BH	AVG	PB	PR	/A	PD	TPI
1974 StL-N	7	4	.636	19	14	5	2	0	100	84	5	34	39	10.7	2.97	120	.230	.298	7	.241	1	7	7	0	0.9
1975 StL-N	15	10	.600	34	34	7	4	0	230	213	14	70	108	11.2	2.86	131	.244	.303	24	.308	10	20	23	2	3.9
1976 StL-N	8	10	.444	33	32	2	0	0	194	209	17	71	76	13.1	3.94	90	.277	.341	11	.177	1	-10	-9	1	-0.6
1977 StL-N	20	7	.741	35	35	8	2	0	217¹	210	20	69	95	11.7	3.48	111	.251	.311	12	.167	0	10	9	-1	0.8
1978 StL-N	11	17	.393	34	34	7	3	0	233²	205	15	97	114	11.8	3.70	95	.238	.318	15	.181	3	-3	-5	1	0.0
1979 StL-N	11	11	.500	33	32	7	1	0	218²	215	16	52	92	11.1	3.83	98	.262	.309	8	.110	-0	-2	-2	1	0.0
1980 StL-N	11	10	.524	31	31	8	0	0	214²	225	12	33	87	11.0	3.77	98	.273	.304	23	.295	9	-4	-2	2	1.0
1981 StL-N	10	5	.667	20	20	1	0	0	124¹	106	7	29	41	10.1	3.18	112	.232	.284	5	.122	-1	4	5	1	0.5
1982 *StL-N	15	9	.625	36	34	6	2	1	233	238	16	54	69	11.4	3.48	104	.268	.313	15	.205	3	3	4	-1	0.6
1983 StL-N	10	12	.455	34	30	6	2	0	187	190	23	54	56	11.9	4.28	85	.266	.320	13	.241	4	-14	-14	0	-0.9
1984 StL-N	2	5	.286	16	11	1	0	0	52¹	64	6	19	21	14.3	6.02	58	.303	.361	4	.250	1	-14	-15	1	-1.2
1985 *StL-N	9	6	.600	34	19	3	1	2	136	132	11	47	48	12.0	3.90	91	.258	.323	11	.244	4	-5	-6	0	-0.1
1986 StL-N	14	10	.583	33	33	3	0	0	230	211	19	68	104	11.0	3.25	112	.247	.304	13	.171	3	12	10	-0	1.4
1987 *StL-N	11	7	.611	33	30	2	1	0	179	189	15	45	89	12.0	4.32	96	.273	.321	17	.298	8	-5	-3	-1	0.4
1988 StL-N	9	4	.692	30	12	1	1	0	108²	111	8	38	40	12.4	3.73	93	.270	.333	7	.280	2	-3	-3	-2	-0.2
Hou-N	1	4	.200	6	6	0	0	0	27²	42	2	6	14	16.3	6.51	51	.359	.400	1	.143	0	-9	-10	-0	-0.9
Yr	10	8	.556	36	18	1	1	0	136¹	153	10	44	54	13.1	4.29	80	.287	.344	1	.031	2	-13	-13	-2	-1.1
1989 Hou-N	4	5	.444	37	15	0	0	0	108¹	133	10	46	40	15.0	5.32	64	.303	.370	4	.167	-0	-22	-23	-1	-2.4
Total 16	168	136	.553	498	422	67	19	3	2794²	2777	216	832	1133	11.8	3.76	97	.261	.318	190	.213	49	-35	-33	3	3.2

■ TERRY FORSTER   Forster, Terry Jay b: 1/14/52, Sioux Falls, S.D.   BL/TL, 6'3", 200 lbs.   Deb: 4/11/71

YEAR TM/L	W	L	PCT	G	GS	CG	SH	SV	IP	H	HR	BB	SO	RAT	ERA	ERA+	OAV	OOB	BH	AVG	PB	PR	/A	PD	TPI
1971 Chi-A	2	3	.400	45	3	0	0	1	49²	46	5	23	48	12.7	3.99	90	.241	.326	2	.400	-0	-3	-2	-0	-0.1
1972 Chi-A	6	5	.545	62	0	0	0	29	100	75	0	44	104	11.0	2.25	139	.208	.300	10	.526	4	9	10	1	1.7
1973 Chi-A	6	11	.353	51	12	4	0	16	172²	174	7	78	120	13.1	3.23	122	.266	.344	0	.000	-1	11	14	4	1.9
1974 Chi-A	7	8	.467	59	1	0	0	24	134¹	120	6	48	105	11.8	3.62	103	.245	.323	0	—	0	0	2	3	0.5
1975 Chi-A	3	3	.500	17	1	0	0	4	37	30	0	24	32	13.1	2.19	177	.236	.358	0	—	0	7	7	2	0.9
1976 Chi-A	2	12	.143	29	16	1	0	1	111¹	126	7	41	70	13.6	4.37	82	.288	.351	0	—	0	-10	-10	2	-0.8
1977 Pit-N	6	4	.600	33	6	0	0	1	87¹	90	7	32	58	12.8	4.43	90	.269	.337	9	.346	3	-5	-4	0	0.0
1978 *LA-N	5	4	.556	47	0	0	0	22	65¹	56	2	23	46	10.9	1.93	182	.233	.300	4	.500	2	12	11	-0	1.4
1979 LA-N	1	2	.333	17	0	0	0	2	16¹	18	0	11	8	16.0	5.51	66	.295	.403	0	—	0	-3	-3	1	-0.2
1980 LA-N	0	0	—	9	0	0	0	0	11²	10	0	4	2	10.8	3.09	113	.222	.286	0	—	0	1	1	1	0.1
1981 *LA-N	0	1	.000	21	0	0	0	0	30²	37	1	15	17	15.3	4.11	81	.308	.385	0	.000	-0	-2	-3	1	-0.1
1982 LA-N	5	6	.455	56	0	0	0	3	83	66	3	31	52	11.0	3.04	114	.221	.302	0	.000	-0	5	4	1	0.5
1983 Atl-N	3	2	.600	56	0	0	0	13	79¹	60	3	31	54	10.6	2.16	180	.217	.301	4	.500	2	13	15	1	1.9
1984 Atl-N	2	0	1.000	25	0	0	0	5	26²	30	1	7	10	12.5	2.70	143	.297	.343	2	.667	1	3	3	0	0.5
1985 Atl-N	2	3	.400	46	0	0	0	1	59¹	49	7	28	37	11.7	2.28	169	.222	.309	0	.000	-0	9	10	-1	1.0
1986 Cal-N	4	1	.800	41	0	0	0	5	41	47	2	17	28	14.7	3.51	117	.297	.376	0	—	0	3	3	1	0.4
Total 16	54	65	.454	614	39	5	0	127	1105²	1034	51	457	791	12.3	3.23	114	.251	.330	31	.397	11	48	57	15	9.6

■ GARY FORTUNE   Fortune, Garrett Reese b: 10/11/1894, High Point, N.C.   d: 9/23/55, Washington, D.C.   BB/TR, 5'11.5", 176 lbs.   Deb: 10/05/16

YEAR TM/L	W	L	PCT	G	GS	CG	SH	SV	IP	H	HR	BB	SO	RAT	ERA	ERA+	OAV	OOB	BH	AVG	PB	PR	/A	PD	TPI
1916 Phi-N	0	1	.000	1	1	0	0	0	5	2	0	4	3	10.8	3.60	74	.118	.286	0	.000	-1	-1	-1	-0	0.0
1918 Phi-N	0	2	.000	5	2	1	0	0	31	41	2	19	10	17.7	8.13	37	.333	.427	2	.200	-1	-18	-18	-0	-1.5
1920 Bos-A	0	2	.000	14	3	1	0	0	41²	46	0	23	10	14.9	5.83	63	.282	.371	2	.167	-0	-9	-10	-0	-0.9
Total 3	0	5	.000	20	6	2	0	0	77²	89	2	46	23	15.8	6.61	51	.294	.389	4	.167	-0	-28	-28	-1	-2.4

■ JERRY FOSNOW   Fosnow, Gerald Eugene b: 9/21/40, Deshler, Ohio   BR/TL, 6'4", 195 lbs.   Deb: 6/29/64

YEAR TM/L	W	L	PCT	G	GS	CG	SH	SV	IP	H	HR	BB	SO	RAT	ERA	ERA+	OAV	OOB	BH	AVG	PB	PR	/A	PD	TPI
1964 Min-A	0	1	.000	7	0	0	0	0	10²	13	3	8	9	17.7	10.97	33	.302	.412	0	—	0	-9	-9	-0	-0.8
1965 Min-A	3	3	.500	29	0	0	0	2	46²	33	7	25	35	11.4	4.44	80	.193	.299	0	.000	-1	-5	-5	0	-0.4
Total 2	3	4	.429	36	0	0	0	2	57¹	46	10	33	44	12.6	5.65	63	.215	.323	0	.000	-1	-14	-13	0	-1.2

■ LARRY FOSS   Foss, Larry Curtis b: 4/18/36, Castleton, Kan.   BR/TR, 6'2", 187 lbs.   Deb: 9/18/61

YEAR TM/L	W	L	PCT	G	GS	CG	SH	SV	IP	H	HR	BB	SO	RAT	ERA	ERA+	OAV	OOB	BH	AVG	PB	PR	/A	PD	TPI
1961 Pit-N	1	1	.500	3	3	0	0	0	15¹	15	3	11	9	16.4	5.87	68	.273	.412	1	.167	-0	-3	-3	-0	-0.2
1962 NY-N	0	1	.000	5	1	0	0	0	11²	17	2	7	3	19.3	4.63	90	.362	.455	0	.000	-0	-1	-1	0	0.0
Total 2	1	2	.333	8	4	0	0	0	27	32	5	18	12	17.7	5.33	76	.314	.431	1	.143	-0	-4	-4	-0	-0.2

■ TONY FOSSAS   Fossas, Emilio Antonio (Morejon) b: 9/23/57, Havana, Cuba   BL/TL, 6', 195 lbs.   Deb: 5/15/88

YEAR TM/L	W	L	PCT	G	GS	CG	SH	SV	IP	H	HR	BB	SO	RAT	ERA	ERA+	OAV	OOB	BH	AVG	PB	PR	/A	PD	TPI
1988 Tex-A	0	0	—	5	0	0	0	0	5²	11	0	2	0	20.6	4.76	86	.423	.464	0	—	0	-1	-0	0	0.0
1989 Mil-A	2	2	.500	51	0	0	0	1	61	57	3	22	42	11.8	3.54	108	.256	.325	0	—	0	2	2	0	0.2
1990 Mil-A	2	3	.400	32	0	0	0	0	29¹	44	5	10	24	16.6	6.44	59	.331	.378	0	—	0	-8	-9	-0	-0.8
Total 3	4	5	.444	88	0	0	0	1	96	112	8	34	66	13.8	4.50	85	.293	.353	0	—	0	-6	-7	0	-0.6

■ ALAN FOSTER   Foster, Alan Benton b: 12/8/46, Pasadena, Cal.   BR/TR, 6', 180 lbs.   Deb: 4/25/67

YEAR TM/L	W	L	PCT	G	GS	CG	SH	SV	IP	H	HR	BB	SO	RAT	ERA	ERA+	OAV	OOB	BH	AVG	PB	PR	/A	PD	TPI
1967 LA-N	0	1	.000	4	2	0	0	0	16²	10	0	3	15	7.0	2.16	143	.169	.210	0	.000	-0	2	2	0	0.2
1968 LA-N	1	1	.500	3	3	0	0	0	15²	11	1	2	10	7.5	1.72	160	.200	.228	1	.250	0	2	2	-0	0.2
1969 LA-N	3	9	.250	24	15	2	2	0	102²	119	11	29	59	13.3	4.38	76	.290	.342	2	.074	-1	-9	-12	-0	-1.2
1970 LA-N	10	13	.435	33	33	7	1	0	198²	200	22	81	83	12.8	4.26	90	.264	.337	7	.109	-1	-5	-9	-1	-1.1
1971 Cle-A	8	12	.400	36	26	3	0	0	181²	158	19	82	97	12.1	4.16	92	.232	.318	2	.039	-5	-14	-7	-4	-1.5
1972 Cal-A	0	1	.000	9	3	0	0	0	12²	12	3	6	11	14.2	4.97	59	.245	.351	0	—	0	-3	-3	-0	-0.2
1973 StL-N	13	9	.591	35	29	6	2	0	203²	195	17	63	106	11.6	3.14	116	.254	.315	13	.191	1	12	11	-2	1.1
1974 StL-N	7	10	.412	31	25	5	1	0	162¹	167	16	61	78	12.8	3.88	92	.268	.336	8	.167	-1	-5	-6	-1	-0.6
1975 SD-N	3	1	.750	17	4	1	0	0	44²	41	1	21	20	12.5	2.42	144	.242	.328	1	.091	-1	6	5	0	0.5
1976 SD-N	3	6	.333	26	11	2	0	0	86²	75	9	35	22	11.5	3.22	102	.235	.313	1	.056	-0	0	-0	0	0.0
Total 10	48	63	.432	217	148	26	6	0	1025¹	988	99	383	501	12.2	3.74	96	.254	.324	35	.119	-8	-10	-15	-7	-2.6

■ ED FOSTER   Foster, Eddy Lee "Slim" b: Birmingham, Ala.   d: 3/1/29, Montgomery, Ala.   BR/TR, 6'1",   Deb: 7/31/08

YEAR TM/L	W	L	PCT	G	GS	CG	SH	SV	IP	H	HR	BB	SO	RAT	ERA	ERA+	OAV	OOB	BH	AVG	PB	PR	/A	PD	TPI
1908 Cle-A	1	0	1.000	6	1	0	2	2	21	16	1	12	11	12.9	2.14	112	.229	.357	0	.000	-1	1	1	-1	0.0

■ RUBE FOSTER   Foster, George b: 1/5/1888, Lehigh, Okla   d: 3/1/76, Bokoshe, Okla.   BR/TR, 5'7.5", 170 lbs.   Deb: 4/10/13

YEAR TM/L	W	L	PCT	G	GS	CG	SH	SV	IP	H	HR	BB	SO	RAT	ERA	ERA+	OAV	OOB	BH	AVG	PB	PR	/A	PD	TPI
1913 Bos-A	3	4	.429	19	8	4	1	0	68¹	64	1	28	36	12.6	3.16	93	.249	.332	2	.095	-1	-2	-2	-0	-0.3
1914 Bos-A	14	8	.636	32	27	17	5	0	211²	164	2	52	89	9.5	1.70	158	.218	.274	11	.175	0	24	23	-0	2.7
1915 *Bos-A	19	8	.704	37	33	21	5	1	255¹	217	3	86	82	11.0	2.11	131	.237	.310	23	.277	7	23	19	1	3.0
1916 *Bos-A	14	7	.667	33	19	9	3	2	182¹	173	0	86	53	13.0	3.06	90	.263	.352	11	.177	0	-5	-6	2	-0.3
1917 Bos-A	8	7	.533	17	16	9	1	0	124²	108	0	53	34	11.9	2.53	102	.243	.329	11	.268	2	2	1	1	0.4
Total 5	58	34	.630	138	103	60	15	3	842¹	726	6	305	294	11.3	2.36	116	.240	.315	58	.215	9	43	35	4	5.5

■ LARRY FOSTER   Foster, Larry Lynn b: 12/24/37, Lansing, Mich.   BL/TR, 6', 185 lbs.   Deb: 9/18/63

YEAR TM/L	W	L	PCT	G	GS	CG	SH	SV	IP	H	HR	BB	SO	RAT	ERA	ERA+	OAV	OOB	BH	AVG	PB	PR	/A	PD	TPI
1963 Det-A	0	0	—	1	0	0	0	0	2	4	0	1	1	22.5	13.50	28	.364	.417	0	—	0	-2	-2	0	-0.1

■ STEVE FOUCAULT   Foucault, Steven Raymond b: 10/3/49, Duluth, Minn.   BL/TR, 6', 205 lbs.   Deb: 4/07/73

YEAR TM/L	W	L	PCT	G	GS	CG	SH	SV	IP	H	HR	BB	SO	RAT	ERA	ERA+	OAV	OOB	BH	AVG	PB	PR	/A	PD	TPI
1973 Tex-A	2	4	.333	32	0	0	0	8	52²	54	6	31	28	14.2	3.88	96	.262	.367	0	—	0	-0	-1	1	0.0
1974 Tex-A	8	9	.471	69	0	0	0	12	144¹	123	8	40	106	10.5	2.24	159	.234	.295	0	—	0	22	21	0	2.3
1975 Tex-A	8	4	.667	59	0	0	0	10	107	96	6	55	56	13.0	4.12	91	.249	.349	0	—	0	-4	-4	-0	-0.4
1976 Tex-A	8	8	.500	46	0	0	0	5	75²	68	9	25	41	11.5	3.33	108	.249	.321	0	—	0	2	2	0	0.4
1977 Det-A	7	7	.500	44	0	0	0	13	74¹	64	7	17	58	9.8	3.15	136	.226	.270	0	—	0	8	9	-1	0.9

YEAR	TM/L	W	L	PCT	G	GS	CG	SH	SV	IP	H	HR	BB	SO	RAT	ERA	ERA+	OAV	OOB	BH	AVG	PB	PR	/A	PD	TPI
1978	Det-A	2	4	.333	24	0	0	0	4	37^1	48	1	21	18	16.9	3.13	123	.324	.412	0	—	0	3	3	-1	0.2
	KC-A	0	0	—	3	0	0	0	0	2^1	5	0	1	0	23.1	3.86	99	.417	.462	0	—	0	-0	-0	0	0.0
	Yr	2	4	.333	27	0	0	0	4	39^2	53	1	22	18	17.0	3.18	122	.323	.403	0	—	0	3	3	-0	0.2
Total 6		35	36	.493	277	0	0	0	52	496^2	458	41	190	307	12.1	3.21	117	.250	.326	0	—	0	29	30	1	3.4

■ JACK FOURNIER
Fournier, Jacques Frank b: 9/29/1892, AuSable, Mich. d: 9/5/73, Tacoma, Wash. BL/TR, 6', 195 lbs. Deb: 4/13/12 ♦

YEAR	TM/L	W	L	PCT	G	GS	CG	SH	SV	IP	H	HR	BB	SO	RAT	ERA	ERA+	OAV	OOB	BH	AVG	PB	PR	/A	PD	TPI
1922	StL-N	0	0	—	1	0	0	0	0	1	1	0	0	0	0.0	0.00	—	.000	.000	119	.295	0	0	0	0	0.0

■ HENRY FOURNIER
Fournier, Julius Henry "Frenchy" b: 8/8/1865, Syracuse, N.Y. d: 12/8/45, Detroit, Mich. TL, Deb: 8/22/1894

YEAR	TM/L	W	L	PCT	G	GS	CG	SH	SV	IP	H	HR	BB	SO	RAT	ERA	ERA+	OAV	OOB	BH	AVG	PB	PR	/A	PD	TPI
1894	Cin-N	1	3	.250	6	4	4	0	0	45	71	4	20	5	18.2	5.40	103	.354	.413	2	.105	-3	-0	1	0	0.0

■ DAVE FOUTZ
Foutz, David Luther "Scissors" b: 9/7/1856, Carroll Co., Md. d: 3/5/1897, Waverly, Ind. BR/TR, 6'2", 161 lbs. Deb: 7/29/1884 M♦

YEAR	TM/L	W	L	PCT	G	GS	CG	SH	SV	IP	H	HR	BB	SO	RAT	ERA	ERA+	OAV	OOB	BH	AVG	PB	PR	/A	PD	TPI
1884	StL-a	15	6	.714	25	25	19	2	0	206^2	167	7	36	95	8.8	2.18	150	.209	.243	27	.227	1	25	25	3	2.8
1885	*StL-a	33	14	.702	47	46	46	2	0	407^2	351	8	92	147	9.8	2.63	125	.222	.265	59	.248	5	28	30	7	4.1
1886	*StL-a	41	16	**.719**	59	57	55	11	1	504	418	5	144	283	10.0	**2.11**	**163**	.215	.269	116	.280	11	75	75	2	8.9
1887	*StL-a	25	12	.676	40	38	36	1	0	339^1	369	7	90	94	12.2	3.87	117	.267	.312	151	.357	16	16	25	0	2.1
1888	Bro-a	12	7	.632	23	19	19	0	0	176	146	3	35	73	9.3	2.51	119	.218	.256	156	.277	6	11	9	3	0.9
1889	*Bro-a	3	0	1.000	12	4	3	0	0	59^2	70	2	19	21	13.4	4.37	85	.284	.335	152	.275	3	-3	-4	1	-0.3
1890	*Bro-N	2	1	.667	5	2	2	0	2	29	29	0	6	4	10.9	1.86	184	.253	.290	154	.303	2	5	5	-1	0.5
1891	Bro-N	3	2	.600	6	5	5	0	0	52	51	1	16	14	11.6	3.29	100	.247	.301	134	.257	1	0	0	0	0.0
1892	Bro-N	13	8	.619	27	20	17	0	1	203	210	3	63	56	12.1	3.41	93	.256	.310	41	.186	0	-3	-6	3	-0.4
1893	Bro-N	0	0	—	6	0	0	0	0	18	28	2	8	3	18.0	7.50	59	.345	.403	137	.246	1	-6	-6	1	-0.4
1894	Bro-N	0	0	—	2	0	0	0	0	4	0	1	0	1	22.5	13.50	37	.410	.465	90	.307	0	-2	-2	0	0.0
Total 11		147	66	.690	251	216	202	16	4	1997^1	1843	38	510	790	10.6	2.84	124	.235	.281	1253	.276	46	147	149	19	18.2

■ JESSE FOWLER
Fowler, Jesse Peter "Pete" b: 10/30/1898, Spartanburg, S.C. d: 9/23/73, Columbia, S.C. BR/TL, 5'10.5", 158 lbs. Deb: 7/29/24

YEAR	TM/L	W	L	PCT	G	GS	CG	SH	SV	IP	H	HR	BB	SO	RAT	ERA	ERA+	OAV	OOB	BH	AVG	PB	PR	/A	PD	TPI
1924	StL-N	1	1	.500	13	3	0	0	0	32^2	28	0	18	5	13.2	4.41	86	.226	.333	2	.222	0	-2	-2	-1	-0.2

■ ART FOWLER
Fowler, John Arthur b: 7/3/22, Converse, S.C. BR/TR, 5'11", 180 lbs. Deb: 4/17/54 C

YEAR	TM/L	W	L	PCT	G	GS	CG	SH	SV	IP	H	HR	BB	SO	RAT	ERA	ERA+	OAV	OOB	BH	AVG	PB	PR	/A	PD	TPI
1954	Cin-N	12	10	.545	40	29	8	1	0	227^2	256	20	85	93	13.6	3.83	109	.286	.351	6	.100	-1	6	9	-1	0.7
1955	Cin-N	11	10	.524	46	28	8	3	2	207^2	198	20	63	94	11.4	3.90	109	.250	.306	12	.200	-0	3	8	-1	0.7
1956	Cin-N	11	11	.500	45	23	8	0	1	177^2	191	15	35	86	11.4	4.05	98	.278	.313	7	.146	-0	-6	-1	1	0.0
1957	Cin-N	3	0	1.000	33	7	1	0	0	87^2	111	11	24	45	14.1	6.47	64	.310	.357	3	.176	-0	-25	-23	0	-2.1
1959	LA-N	3	4	.429	36	0	0	0	2	61	70	8	23	47	13.7	5.31	80	.294	.356	1	.083	-1	-9	-7	0	-0.7
1961	LA-A	5	8	.385	53	3	0	0	11	89	68	12	29	78	9.8	3.64	124	.209	.274	1	.077	-1	4	9	-1	0.6
1962	LA-A	4	3	.571	48	0	0	0	5	77	67	6	25	38	10.9	2.81	138	.234	.298	3	.273	1	10	9	0	1.0
1963	LA-A	5	3	.625	57	0	0	0	10	89^1	70	5	19	53	9.0	2.42	142	.219	.263	2	.222	0	12	10	-1	1.0
1964	LA-A	0	2	.000	4	0	0	0	1	7	8	2	5	5	18.0	10.29	32	.296	.424	0	.000	-0	-5	-5	0	-0.4
Total 9		54	51	.514	362	90	25	4	32	1024	1039	99	308	539	11.9	4.03	102	.265	.320	35	.152	-3	-10	7	-3	0.8

■ DICK FOWLER
Fowler, Richard John b: 3/30/21, Toronto, Ont., Can. d: 5/22/72, Oneonta, N.Y. BR/TR, 6'4.5", 215 lbs. Deb: 9/13/41

YEAR	TM/L	W	L	PCT	G	GS	CG	SH	SV	IP	H	HR	BB	SO	RAT	ERA	ERA+	OAV	OOB	BH	AVG	PB	PR	/A	PD	TPI
1941	Phi-A	1	2	.333	4	3	1	0	0	24	26	4	8	8	12.8	3.38	124	.289	.347	0	.000	-1	2	2	-0	0.1
1942	Phi-A	6	11	.353	31	17	4	0	1	140	159	13	45	38	13.1	4.95	76	.287	.341	8	.160	-1	-20	-18	-2	-2.0
1945	Phi-A	1	2	.333	7	3	2	1	0	37^1	41	1	18	21	14.2	4.82	71	.283	.362	8	.444	3	-6	-6	-1	-0.2
1946	Phi-A	9	16	.360	32	28	14	1	0	205^2	213	16	75	89	12.7	3.28	108	.263	.327	13	.183	-1	5	6	-1	0.4
1947	Phi-A	12	11	.522	36	31	16	3	0	227^1	210	12	85	75	11.8	2.81	136	.249	.316	14	.171	-3	23	25	-2	2.2
1948	Phi-A	15	8	.652	29	26	16	2	2	204^2	221	15	76	50	13.4	3.78	113	.281	.348	14	.171	-2	12	12	-1	0.8
1949	Phi-A	15	11	.577	31	28	15	4	1	213^2	210	13	115	43	13.8	3.75	110	.262	.357	18	.234	3	11	9	2	1.2
1950	Phi-A	1	5	.167	11	9	2	0	0	66^2	75	7	56	15	18.1	6.48	70	.300	.434	5	.192	-1	-14	-14	0	-1.2
1951	Phi-A	5	11	.313	22	22	4	0	0	125	141	11	72	29	15.4	5.62	76	.291	.384	8	.190	-0	-21	-19	-1	-1.7
1952	Phi-A	1	2	.333	18	3	1	0	0	58^2	71	4	28	14	15.8	6.44	61	.302	.386	0	.000	-2	-18	-16	1	-1.6
Total 10		66	79	.455	221	170	75	11	4	1303	1367	96	578	382	13.6	4.11	97	.273	.351	88	.186	-6	-27	-19	-4	-2.0

■ ALAN FOWLKES
Fowlkes, Alan Kim b: 8/8/58, Brawley, Cal. BR/TR, 6'2", 190 lbs. Deb: 4/07/82

YEAR	TM/L	W	L	PCT	G	GS	CG	SH	SV	IP	H	HR	BB	SO	RAT	ERA	ERA+	OAV	OOB	BH	AVG	PB	PR	/A	PD	TPI
1982	SF-N	4	2	.667	21	15	1	0	0	85	111	12	24	50	14.8	5.19	69	.321	.373	3	.115	-1	-15	-15	-0	-1.5
1985	Cal-A	0	0	—	2	0	0	0	0	7	8	4	4	5	15.4	9.00	46	.276	.364	0	—	0	-4	-4	0	-0.2
Total 2		4	2	.667	23	15	1	0	0	92	119	16	28	55	14.9	5.48	66	.317	.373	3	.115	-1	-19	-19	-0	-1.7

■ HENRY FOX
Fox, Henry (b: Henry Fuchs) b: 11/18/1874, Scranton, Pa. d: 6/6/27, Scranton, Pa. Deb: 9/04/02

YEAR	TM/L	W	L	PCT	G	GS	CG	SH	SV	IP	H	HR	BB	SO	RAT	ERA	ERA+	OAV	OOB	BH	AVG	PB	PR	/A	PD	TPI
1902	Phi-N	0	0	—	1	0	0	0	1	1	2	0	1	1	27.0	18.00	16	.413	.513	0	—	0	-2	-2	0	-0.1

■ HOWIE FOX
Fox, Howard Francis b: 3/1/21, Coburg, Ore. d: 10/9/55, San Antonio, Tex. BR/TR, 6'3", 210 lbs. Deb: 9/28/44

YEAR	TM/L	W	L	PCT	G	GS	CG	SH	SV	IP	H	HR	BB	SO	RAT	ERA	ERA+	OAV	OOB	BH	AVG	PB	PR	/A	PD	TPI
1944	Cin-N	0	0	—	2	0	0	0	0	2^1	2	0	0	0	7.7	0.00	—	.222	.222	0	.000	-0	1	1	0	0.1
1945	Cin-N	8	13	.381	45	15	7	0	0	164^1	169	6	77	54	13.8	4.93	76	.268	.353	13	.283	3	-21	-21	4	-1.4
1946	Cin-N	0	0	—	4	0	0	0	0	5	12	2	5	1	30.6	18.00	19	.462	.548	0	—	0	-8	-8	0	-0.7
1948	Cin-N	6	9	.400	34	24	5	0	1	171	185	11	62	63	13.1	4.53	86	.280	.343	12	.200	1	-11	-12	1	-0.8
1949	Cin-N	6	19	.240	38	30	9	0	0	215	221	13	77	60	12.6	3.98	105	.265	.330	17	.236	2	2	5	6	1.3
1950	Cin-N	11	8	.579	34	22	10	1	1	187	196	14	85	64	13.6	4.33	98	.269	.347	11	.175	-0	-4	-2	3	0.1
1951	Cin-N	9	14	.391	40	30	9	4	2	228	239	15	69	57	12.2	3.83	107	.272	.326	8	.114	-2	3	6	1	0.5
1952	Phi-N	2	7	.222	13	11	2	0	0	62	70	8	26	16	13.9	5.08	72	.287	.356	1	.048	-1	-9	-10	2	-0.9
1954	Bal-A	1	2	.333	38	0	0	0	0	73^2	80	2	34	27	14.2	3.67	98	.289	.371	4	.250	1	0	-1	2	0.2
Total 9		43	72	.374	248	132	42	5	6	1108^1	1174	71	435	342	13.2	4.33	92	.274	.343	66	.189	2	-46	-42	19	-1.6

■ JOHN FOX
Fox, John Joseph b: 2/7/1859, Roxbury, Mass. d: 4/18/1893, Boston, Mass. Deb: 6/02/1881

YEAR	TM/L	W	L	PCT	G	GS	CG	SH	SV	IP	H	HR	BB	SO	RAT	ERA	ERA+	OAV	OOB	BH	AVG	PB	PR	/A	PD	TPI
1881	Bos-N	6	8	.429	17	16	12	0	0	124^1	144	0	39	30	13.2	3.33	80	.278	.328	21	.178	-4	-8	-9	1	-1.3
1883	Bal-a	6	13	.316	20	19	18	0	0	165^1	209	2	32	49	13.1	4.03	86	.289	.320	14	.152	-4	-13	-10	-1	-1.2
1884	Pit-a	1	6	.143	7	7	7	0	0	59	76	2	16	22	14.0	5.64	60	.296	.338	6	.240	0	-16	-15	1	-1.1
1886	Was-N	0	1	.000	1	1	1	0	0	8	11	0	11	3	24.8	9.00	36	.314	.478	1	.333	0	-5	-5	0	-0.3
Total 4		13	28	.317	45	43	38	0	0	356^2	440	4	98	104	13.6	4.16	76	.287	.330	42	.176	-7	-42	-40	1	-3.9

■ TERRY FOX
Fox, Terrence Edward b: 7/31/35, Chicago, Ill. BR/TR, 6', 175 lbs. Deb: 9/04/60

YEAR	TM/L	W	L	PCT	G	GS	CG	SH	SV	IP	H	HR	BB	SO	RAT	ERA	ERA+	OAV	OOB	BH	AVG	PB	PR	/A	PD	TPI
1960	Mil-N	0	0	—	5	0	0	0	0	8^1	6	0	6	5	13.0	4.32	79	.200	.333	0	.000	-0	-1	-1	0	0.0
1961	Det-A	5	2	.714	39	0	0	0	12	57^1	42	6	16	32	9.6	1.41	290	.200	.266	2	.167	-0	17	17	1	1.8
1962	Det-A	3	1	.750	44	0	0	0	16	58	48	2	16	23	10.1	1.71	238	.227	.285	2	.250	2	15	15	1	1.8
1963	Det-A	8	6	.571	46	0	0	0	11	80^1	81	9	20	35	11.5	3.59	104	.263	.316	1	.091	-0	0	1	1	0.2
1964	Det-A	4	3	.571	32	0	0	0	5	61	77	4	16	28	13.9	3.39	108	.316	.360	3	.250	1	2	2	1	0.4
1965	Det-A	6	4	.600	42	0	0	0	10	77^2	59	7	31	34	10.8	2.78	125	.214	.300	0	.000	-1	6	6	2	0.7
1966	Det-A	0	1	.000	4	0	0	0	1	10	9	3	2	6	9.9	6.30	55	.243	.282	0	.000	-0	-3	-3	-0	-0.2
	Phi-N	3	2	.600	36	0	0	0	4	44^1	57	3	17	22	15.4	4.47	80	.322	.388	0	.000	-0	-4	-4	-0	-0.4
Total 7		29	19	.604	248	0	0	0	59	397	379	34	124	185	11.7	2.99	125	.254	.316	8	.123	1	31	33	5	4.3

■ BILL FOXEN
Foxen, William Aloysius b: 5/31/1884, Tenafly, N.J. d: 4/17/37, Brooklyn, N.Y. BL/TL, 5'11.5", 165 lbs. Deb: 5/05/08

YEAR	TM/L	W	L	PCT	G	GS	CG	SH	SV	IP	H	HR	BB	SO	RAT	ERA	ERA+	OAV	OOB	BH	AVG	PB	PR	/A	PD	TPI
1908	Phi-N	7	7	.500	22	16	10	2	0	147^1	126	2	53	52	11.4	1.95	124	.240	.319	5	.094	-3	7	8	2	0.8
1909	Phi-N	3	7	.300	18	17	5	1	0	83^1	65	0	32	37	10.9	3.35	78	.219	.303	5	.208	3	-7	-7	4	0.1
1910	Phi-N	5	5	.500	16	9	5	0	0	77^2	73	2	40	33	13.4	2.55	123	.268	.368	4	.174	-1	4	5	2	0.6
	Chi-N	0	0	—	2	0	0	0	0	5	7	0	3	2	18.0	9.00	32	.350	.435	0	.000	-0	-3	-3	0	-0.3

YEAR	TM/L	W	L	PCT	G	GS	CG	SH	SV	IP	H	HR	BB	SO	RAT	ERA	ERA+	OAV	OOB	BH	AVG	PB	PR	/A	PD	TPI
	Yr	5	5	.500	18	9	5	0	0	82²	80	2	43	35	13.4	2.94	106	.271	.364	1	.040	-1	1	2	2	0.3
1911	Chi-N	1	1	.500	3	1	0	0	0	13	12	0	12	6	16.6	2.08	160	.255	.407	1	.250	1	2	2	1	0.3
Total	4	16	20	.444	61	33	20	3	0	326¹	283	4	140	130	12.1	2.56	105	.244	.333	15	.142	0	3	4	8	1.5

■ JIMMIE FOXX
Foxx, James Emory "Beast" or "Double X" b: 10/22/07, Sudlersville, Md. d: 7/21/67, Miami, Fla. BR/TR, 6', 195 lbs. Deb: 5/01/25 H♦

YEAR	TM/L	W	L	PCT	G	GS	CG	SH	SV	IP	H	HR	BB	SO	RAT	ERA	ERA+	OAV	OOB	BH	AVG	PB	PR	/A	PD	TPI
1939	Bos-A	0	0	—	1	1	0	0	0	1	0	0	0	1	0.0	0.00	—	.000	.000	168	.360	1	1	1	0	0.0
1945	Phi-N	1	0	1.000	9	2	0	0	0	22²	13	0	14	10	11.1	1.59	241	.171	.308	60	.268	2	6	6	-1	0.6
Total	2	1	0	1.000	10	2	0	0	0	23²	13	0	14	11	10.6	1.52	254	.165	.298	2646	.325	3	6	6	-1	0.6

■ PAUL FOYTACK
Foytack, Paul Eugene b: 11/16/30, Scranton, Pa. BR/TR, 5'11", 175 lbs. Deb: 4/21/53

YEAR	TM/L	W	L	PCT	G	GS	CG	SH	SV	IP	H	HR	BB	SO	RAT	ERA	ERA+	OAV	OOB	BH	AVG	PB	PR	/A	PD	TPI
1953	Det-A	0	0	—	6	0	0	0	0	9²	15	1	9	7	23.3	11.17	36	.375	.500	0	.000	-0	-8	-8	-0	-0.6
1955	Det-A	0	1	.000	22	1	0	0	0	49²	48	4	36	38	15.2	5.26	73	.259	.380	1	.091	-1	-7	-8	-0	-0.8
1956	Det-A	15	13	.536	43	33	16	1	1	256	211	24	142	184	12.5	3.59	115	.226	.330	11	.122	-6	16	15	-1	0.8
1957	Det-A	14	11	.560	38	27	8	1	1	212	175	19	104	118	12.0	3.14	123	.226	.321	14	.222	1	15	17	-2	1.6
1958	Det-A	15	13	.536	39	33	16	2	1	230	198	23	77	135	10.9	3.44	117	.233	.299	18	.240	3	8	15	-2	1.8
1959	Det-A	14	14	.500	39	37	11	2	1	240¹	239	34	64	110	11.4	4.64	87	.259	.308	9	.111	-4	-21	-16	-1	-1.9
1960	Det-A	2	11	.154	28	13	1	0	2	96²	108	11	49	38	14.6	6.14	64	.286	.369	7	.280	2	-24	-23	-2	-2.1
1961	Det-A	11	10	.524	32	20	6	0	0	169²	152	27	56	89	11.1	3.93	104	.238	.301	12	.222	2	2	3	-3	0.2
1962	Det-A	10	7	.588	29	21	5	1	0	143²	145	18	86	63	14.5	4.39	93	.259	.359	6	.143	-1	-7	-5	1	-0.4
1963	Det-A	0	1	.000	9	0	0	0	1	17²	18	4	8	7	13.2	8.66	43	.265	.342	0	.000	-0	-10	-10	-0	-0.9
	LA-A	5	5	.500	25	8	0	0	0	70¹	68	9	29	37	12.4	3.71	92	.255	.328	4	.267	1	-1	-2	-0	-0.1
	Yr	5	6	.455	34	8	0	0	1	88	86	13	37	44	12.6	4.70	74	.256	.330	2	.105	1	-11	-12	-1	-1.0
1964	LA-A	0	0	.000	2	0	0	0	0	2¹	4	2	2	1	23.1	15.43	21	.364	.462	0	—	0	-3	-3	0	-0.2
Total	11	86	87	.497	312	193	63	7	7	1498	1381	176	662	827	12.4	4.14	97	.246	.327	82	.178	-3	-39	-24	-11	-2.6

■ KEN FRAILING
Frailing, Kenneth Douglas b: 1/19/48, Marion, Wis. BL/TL, 6', 190 lbs. Deb: 9/01/72

YEAR	TM/L	W	L	PCT	G	GS	CG	SH	SV	IP	H	HR	BB	SO	RAT	ERA	ERA+	OAV	OOB	BH	AVG	PB	PR	/A	PD	TPI
1972	Chi-A	1	0	1.000	4	0	0	0	0	3	3	1	1	1	12.0	3.00	104	.250	.308	0	—	0	0	0	0	0.0
1973	Chi-A	0	0	—	10	0	0	0	0	18¹	18	1	1	15	12.8	1.96	202	.254	.329	0	—	0	4	4	0	0.4
1974	Chi-N	6	9	.400	55	16	1	0	1	125¹	150	11	43	71	13.9	3.88	98	.296	.353	8	.258	1	-4	-4	0	0.0
1975	Chi-N	2	5	.286	41	0	0	0	0	53	61	6	26	39	15.1	5.43	71	.293	.377	1	.143	0	-11	-9	2	-0.7
1976	Chi-N	1	2	.333	6	3	0	0	0	18²	20	0	5	10	12.1	2.41	160	.274	.321	0	.000	-0	2	3	0	0.3
Total	5	10	16	.385	116	19	1	0	2	218¹	252	19	82	136	13.9	3.96	97	.290	.354	9	.220	1	-8	-3	2	0.0

■ OSSIE FRANCE
France, Osman Beverly "O. B." b: 10/4/1858, Greensburg, Ohio d: 5/2/47, Akron, Ohio BL/TL, 5'8", 155 lbs. Deb: 7/14/1890

YEAR	TM/L	W	L	PCT	G	GS	CG	SH	SV	IP	H	HR	BB	SO	RAT	ERA	ERA+	OAV	OOB	BH	AVG	PB	PR	/A	PD	TPI
1890	Chi-N	0	0	—	1	1	0	0	0	2	3	0	2	0	22.5	13.50	27	.337	.458	0	.000	-0	-2	-2	0	-0.1

■ EARL FRANCIS
Francis, Earl Coleman b: 7/14/35, Slab Fork, W.Va. BR/TR, 6'2", 210 lbs. Deb: 6/30/60

YEAR	TM/L	W	L	PCT	G	GS	CG	SH	SV	IP	H	HR	BB	SO	RAT	ERA	ERA+	OAV	OOB	BH	AVG	PB	PR	/A	PD	TPI
1960	Pit-N	1	0	1.000	7	0	0	0	0	18	14	0	4	8	9.5	2.00	188	.222	.279	0	.000	-1	4	4	0	0.3
1961	Pit-N	2	8	.200	23	15	0	0	0	102²	110	4	47	53	13.9	4.21	95	.274	.351	3	.107	-1	-2	-3	-1	-0.2
1962	Pit-N	9	8	.529	36	23	5	1	0	176	153	8	83	121	12.2	3.07	128	.235	.323	10	.164	1	17	17	1	1.9
1963	Pit-N	4	6	.400	33	13	0	0	0	97¹	107	6	43	72	14.2	4.53	73	.284	.363	8	.308	3	-13	-13	0	-1.0
1964	Pit-N	0	1	.000	2	1	0	0	0	6¹	7	2	1	6	12.8	8.53	41	.269	.321	0	.000	-0	-4	-4	-0	-0.3
1965	StL-N	0	0	—	2	0	0	0	0	5¹	7	1	3	3	16.9	5.06	76	.318	.400	0	.000	-0	-1	-1	-0	0.0
Total	6	16	23	.410	103	52	5	1	0	405²	398	21	181	263	13.0	3.77	100	.258	.340	21	.172	2	1	0	1	0.7

■ RAY FRANCIS
Francis, Ray James b: 3/8/1893, Sherman, Tex. d: 7/6/34, Atlanta, Ga. BL/TL, 6'1.5", 182 lbs. Deb: 4/18/22

YEAR	TM/L	W	L	PCT	G	GS	CG	SH	SV	IP	H	HR	BB	SO	RAT	ERA	ERA+	OAV	OOB	BH	AVG	PB	PR	/A	PD	TPI
1922	Was-A	7	18	.280	39	26	15	2	2	225	265	7	66	64	13.5	4.28	90	.303	.356	13	.167	-2	-6	-10	-0	-1.2
1923	Det-A	5	8	.385	33	6	0	0	1	79¹	95	2	28	27	14.4	4.42	87	.308	.374	3	.143	-1	-4	-5	-0	-0.6
1925	NY-A	0	0	—	4	0	0	0	0	4²	5	0	3	1	17.4	7.71	55	.278	.409	0	—	0	-2	-2	-0	-0.1
	Bos-A	0	2	.000	6	4	0	0	0	28	44	3	13	4	18.6	7.71	59	.373	.439	1	.125	-0	-10	-10	0	-0.7
	Yr	0	2	.000	10	4	0	0	0	32²	49	3	16	5	18.2	7.71	58	.358	.429	2	.250	-0	-12	-12	0	-0.8
Total	3	12	28	.300	82	36	15	2	3	337	409	12	110	96	14.2	4.65	84	.310	.368	17	.159	-4	-22	-27	-0	-2.6

■ JOHNNY FRANCO
Franco, John Anthony b: 9/17/60, Brooklyn, N.Y. BL/TL, 5'10", 170 lbs. Deb: 4/24/84

YEAR	TM/L	W	L	PCT	G	GS	CG	SH	SV	IP	H	HR	BB	SO	RAT	ERA	ERA+	OAV	OOB	BH	AVG	PB	PR	/A	PD	TPI
1984	Cin-N	6	2	.750	54	0	0	0	4	79¹	74	3	36	55	12.7	2.61	145	.256	.343	0	.000	-0	9	10	1	1.1
1985	Cin-N	12	3	.800	67	0	0	0	12	99	83	5	40	61	11.3	2.18	173	.234	.314	2	.333	1	16	18	2	2.1
1986	Cin-N	6	6	.500	74	0	0	0	29	101	90	7	44	84	12.1	2.94	132	.242	.325	0	.000	-0	9	10	1	1.2
1987	Cin-N	8	5	.615	68	0	0	0	32	82	76	6	27	61	11.3	2.52	168	.245	.306	0	.000	-0	14	16	-1	1.4
1988	Cin-N	6	6	.500	70	0	0	0	**39**	86	60	3	27	46	9.1	1.57	228	.198	.264	0	.000	-0	**18**	**19**	1	2.2
1989	Cin-N	4	8	.333	60	0	0	0	32	80²	77	3	36	60	12.6	3.12	115	.258	.337	1	.333	0	3	4	1	0.6
1990	NY-N	5	3	.625	55	0	0	0	**33**	67²	66	4	21	56	11.6	2.53	144	.252	.307	0	.000	-0	10	8	1	0.9
Total	7	47	33	.587	448	0	0	0	181	595²	526	31	231	423	11.5	2.49	152	.240	.314	3	.125	-1	78	86	5	9.5

■ TERRY FRANCONA
Francona, Terry Jon b: 4/22/59, Aberdeen, S.D. BL/TL, 6'1", 190 lbs. Deb: 8/19/81 ♦

YEAR	TM/L	W	L	PCT	G	GS	CG	SH	SV	IP	H	HR	BB	SO	RAT	ERA	ERA+	OAV	OOB	BH	AVG	PB	PR	/A	PD	TPI
1989	Mil-A	0	0	—	1	0	0	0	0	1	0	0	0	1	0.0	0.00	—	.000	.000	54	.232	1	0	0	0	0.0

■ CHARLIE FRANK
Frank, Charles b: 5/30/1870, Mobile, Ala. d: 5/24/22, Memphis, Tenn. Deb: 8/18/1893 ♦

YEAR	TM/L	W	L	PCT	G	GS	CG	SH	SV	IP	H	HR	BB	SO	RAT	ERA	ERA+	OAV	OOB	BH	AVG	PB	PR	/A	PD	TPI
1894	StL-N	0	0	—	2	0	0	0	0	3	6	1	7	1	39.0	15.00	36	.410	.601	89	.279	0	-3	-3	0	-0.1

■ FRED FRANKHOUSE
Frankhouse, Frederick Meloy b: 4/9/04, Port Royal, Pa. d: 8/17/89, Port Royal, Pa. BR/TR, 5'11", 175 lbs. Deb: 9/11/27

YEAR	TM/L	W	L	PCT	G	GS	CG	SH	SV	IP	H	HR	BB	SO	RAT	ERA	ERA+	OAV	OOB	BH	AVG	PB	PR	/A	PD	TPI
1927	StL-N	5	1	.833	6	6	5	1	0	50	41	2	16	20	10.4	2.70	146	.218	.283	5	.250	2	7	7	-1	0.7
1928	StL-N	3	2	.600	21	10	1	0	1	84	91	6	36	29	14.1	3.96	101	.277	.358	5	.185	1	0	0	1	0.2
1929	StL-N	7	2	.778	30	12	6	0	1	133¹	149	9	43	37	13.2	4.12	113	.289	.349	15	.288	4	9	8	3	1.3
1930	StL-N	2	3	.400	8	1	0	0	0	19²	31	1	11	4	19.2	7.32	69	.373	.447	0	.000	-1	-5	-5	-0	-0.4
	Bos-N	7	6	.538	27	11	3	1	0	110²	138	13	43	30	14.9	5.61	88	.313	.377	14	.359	4	-8	-8	-0	-0.6
	Yr	9	9	.500	35	12	3	1	0	130¹	169	14	54	34	15.5	5.87	84	.323	.388	4	.091	3	-13	-13	0	-0.7
1931	Bos-N	8	8	.500	26	15	6	0	1	127¹	125	4	43	50	12.1	4.03	94	.252	.315	6	.150	-0	-2	-3	1	-0.2
1932	Bos-N	4	6	.400	37	6	3	0	0	108²	113	7	45	35	13.3	3.56	106	.278	.355	3	.100	-1	4	2	3	0.4
1933	Bos-N	16	15	.516	43	30	14	2	2	244²	249	12	77	83	12.1	3.16	97	.267	.324	19	.237	4	5	-3	4	0.4
1934	Bos-N	17	9	.654	37	31	13	2	1	233²	239	10	77	78	12.3	3.20	120	.262	.322	17	.200	1	22	16	2	1.7
1935	Bos-N	11	15	.423	40	29	10	1	0	230²	278	12	81	64	14.2	4.76	80	.293	.352	20	.263	6	-19	-25	3	-1.4
1936	Bro-N	13	10	.565	41	31	9	1	2	234¹	236	18	89	84	12.6	3.65	113	.257	.325	13	.143	2	10	13	2	1.0
1937	Bro-N	10	13	.435	33	26	9	1	0	179¹	214	8	78	64	14.9	4.27	95	.297	.369	11	.190	-0	-7	-5	3	-0.1
1938	Bro-N	3	5	.375	30	8	2	1	0	93²	92	6	44	32	13.5	4.04	97	.256	.344	4	.154	-1	-3	-1	1	0.0
1939	Bro-N	0	2	.000	23	0	0	0	4	38	37	3	18	12	13.3	2.61	142	.253	.339	0	.000	-1	6	5	-1	0.3
Total	13	106	97	.522	402	216	81	10	12	1888	2033	111	701	622	13.2	3.92	100	.275	.341	132	.208	11	18	-0	18	3.6

■ JACK FRANKLIN
Franklin, James Wilford b: 10/20/19, Paris, Ill. BR/TR, 5'11.5", 170 lbs. Deb: 6/12/44

YEAR	TM/L	W	L	PCT	G	GS	CG	SH	SV	IP	H	HR	BB	SO	RAT	ERA	ERA+	OAV	OOB	BH	AVG	PB	PR	/A	PD	TPI
1944	Bro-N	0	0	—	1	0	0	0	0	2	2	1	4	0	36.0	13.50	26	.250	.571	0	—	0	-2	-2	0	-0.1

■ JAY FRANKLIN
Franklin, John William b: 3/16/53, Arlington, Va. BR/TR, 6'2", 180 lbs. Deb: 9/04/71

YEAR	TM/L	W	L	PCT	G	GS	CG	SH	SV	IP	H	HR	BB	SO	RAT	ERA	ERA+	OAV	OOB	BH	AVG	PB	PR	/A	PD	TPI
1971	SD-N	0	1	.000	3	1	0	0	0	5²	5	3	4	4	14.3	6.35	52	.250	.375	0	.000	-0	-2	-2	0	-0.1

■ CHICK FRASER
Fraser, Charles Carrolton b: 3/17/1871, Chicago, Ill. d: 5/8/40, Wendell, Idaho BR/TR, 5'10.5", 188 lbs. Deb: 4/19/1896 C

YEAR	TM/L	W	L	PCT	G	GS	CG	SH	SV	IP	H	HR	BB	SO	RAT	ERA	ERA+	OAV	OOB	BH	AVG	PB	PR	/A	PD	TPI
1896	Lou-N	12	27	.308	43	38	36	0	0	349¹	396	9	166	91	14.5	4.87	89	.283	.359	22	.151	-9	-20	-21	3	-2.2
1897	Lou-N	15	19	.441	35	34	32	0	0	286¹	332	11	133	70	14.6	4.09	104	.288	.361	18	.161	-4	7	6	6	0.6

YEAR TM/L	W	L	PCT	G	GS	CG	SH	SV	IP	H	HR	BB	SO	RAT	ERA	ERA+	OAV	OOB	BH	AVG	PB	PR	/A	PD	TPI
1898 Lou-N	7	17	.292	26	26	20	1	0	203	230	4	100	58	14.6	5.32	67	.283	.362	13	.167	-2	-39	-39	4	-3.2
Cle-N	2	3	.400	6	6	6	0	0	42	49	2	12	19	13.1	5.57	65	.289	.336	4	.250	0	-9	-9	0	-0.7
Yr	9	20	.310	32	32	26	1	0	245	279	6	112	77	14.4	5.36	67	.284	.357	6	.064	-2	-48	-48	4	-3.9
1899 Phi-N	21	12	.636	35	33	29	4	0	270²	278	1	85	68	12.1	3.36	110	.265	.320	21	.179	-2	15	10	2	0.9
1900 Phi-N	15	9	.625	29	26	22	1	0	223¹	250	7	93	58	13.8	3.14	115	.282	.350	22	.259	3	14	12	3	1.7
1901 Phi-A	22	16	.579	40	37	35	2	0	331	344	6	132	110	12.9	3.81	99	.265	.333	26	.187	-3	-5	-1	2	-0.1
1902 Phi-N	12	13	.480	27	26	24	3	0	224	238	2	74	97	13.1	3.42	82	.272	.339	15	.174	1	-16	-15	-0	-1.4
1903 Phi-N	12	17	.414	31	29	26	1	1	250	260	8	97	104	13.4	4.50	73	.267	.344	19	.204	5	-34	-34	1	-2.5
1904 Phi-N	14	24	.368	42	36	32	2	1	302	287	5	100	127	11.9	3.25	82	.246	.311	17	.155	-1	-17	-19	2	-1.8
1905 Bos-N	14	21	.400	39	38	35	2	0	334	320	8	149	130	13.0	3.29	94	.254	.340	35	.224	4	-11	-7	-1	-0.3
1906 Cin-N	10	20	.333	31	28	25	2	0	236	221	1	80	58	11.8	2.67	103	.259	.329	14	.171	-1	-1	2	2	0.4
1907 Chi-N	8	5	.615	22	15	9	2	1	138¹	112	1	46	41	10.5	2.28	110	.229	.299	3	.067	-3	3	3	1	0.1
1908 Chi-N	11	9	.550	26	17	11	2	2	162²	141	4	61	66	11.5	2.27	104	.244	.323	6	.120	-1	2	2	4	0.4
1909 Chi-N	0	0		1	0	0	0	0	3	4	0	1	1	18.0	0.00	—	.222	.462	0	.000	-0	1	1	-0	0.1
Total 14	175	212	.452	433	389	342	22	6	3355²	3460	69	1332	1098	13.1	3.68	92	.267	.338	235	.179	-14	-110	-108	29	-8.0

■ WILLIE FRASER
Fraser, William Patrick b: 5/26/64, New York, N.Y. BR/TR, 6'3", 200 lbs. Deb: 9/10/86

YEAR TM/L	W	L	PCT	G	GS	CG	SH	SV	IP	H	HR	BB	SO	RAT	ERA	ERA+	OAV	OOB	BH	AVG	PB	PR	/A	PD	TPI
1986 Cal-A	0	0		1	1	0	0	0	4¹	6	0	1	2	14.5	8.31	49	.353	.389	0	—	0	-2	-2	0	-0.1
1987 Cal-A	10	10	.500	36	23	5	1	1	176²	160	26	63	106	11.7	3.92	110	.240	.312	0	—	0	10	7	-3	0.5
1988 Cal-A	12	13	.480	34	32	2	0	0	194²	203	33	80	86	13.5	5.41	71	.267	.344	0	—	0	-31	-34	-0	-3.2
1989 Cal-A	4	7	.364	44	0	0	0	2	91²	80	6	23	46	10.6	3.24	118	.235	.293	0	—	0	7	6	0	0.6
1990 Cal-A	.5	4	.556	45	0	0	0	2	76	69	4	24	32	11.0	3.08	127	.241	.300	0	—	0	7	7	-1	0.6
Total 5	31	34	.477	160	56	7	1	5	543¹	518	69	191	272	12.1	4.26	94	.250	.320	0	—	0	-9	-15	-4	-1.6

■ VIC FRASIER
Frasier, Victor Patrick b: 8/5/04, Ruston, La. d: 1/10/77, Jacksonville, Tex. BR/TR, 6', 182 lbs. Deb: 4/18/31

YEAR TM/L	W	L	PCT	G	GS	CG	SH	SV	IP	H	HR	BB	SO	RAT	ERA	ERA+	OAV	OOB	BH	AVG	PB	PR	/A	PD	TPI
1931 Chi-A	13	15	.464	46	29	13	2	4	254	258	11	127	87	13.8	4.46	95	.259	.345	18	.209	1	-2	-6	-1	-0.5
1932 Chi-A	3	13	.188	29	21	4	0	0	146	180	14	70	33	15.7	6.23	69	.297	.374	4	.091	-3	-28	-31	2	-2.7
1933 Chi-A	1	1	.500	10	1	0	0	0	20¹	32	2	11	4	19.0	8.85	48	.368	.439	0	.000	-1	-10	-10	1	-0.8
Det-A	5	5	.500	20	14	4	0	0	104¹	129	9	59	26	16.3	6.64	65	.312	.399	7	.189	-0	-27	-27	1	-2.3
Yr	6	6	.500	30	15	4	0	0	124²	161	11	70	30	16.7	7.00	61	.321	.406	3	.073	-1	-38	-37	2	-3.1
1934 Det-A	1	3	.250	8	2	0	0	0	22²	30	0	12	11	17.1	5.96	74	.313	.394	2	.286	-0	-4	-4	2	-0.1
1937 Bos-N	0	0		3	0	0	0	0	8	12	1	1	2	14.6	5.63	64	.364	.382	0	.000	-0	-2	-2	0	-0.1
1939 Chi-A	0	1	.000	10	1	0	0	0	23²	45	1	11	7	21.3	10.27	46	.405	.459	2	.286	-0	-15	-15	0	-1.1
Total 6	23	38	.377	126	68	21	2	4	579	686	37	291	170	15.4	5.77	75	.293	.373	33	.177	-3	-88	-94	5	-7.6

■ GEORGE FRAZIER
Frazier, George Allen b: 10/13/54, Oklahoma City, Okla BR/TR, 6'5", 205 lbs. Deb: 5/25/78

YEAR TM/L	W	L	PCT	G	GS	CG	SH	SV	IP	H	HR	BB	SO	RAT	ERA	ERA+	OAV	OOB	BH	AVG	PB	PR	/A	PD	TPI
1978 StL-N	0	3	.000	14	0	0	0	0	22	22	2	6	8	11.5	4.09	86	.250	.298	1	.333	0	-1	-1	0	0.0
1979 StL-N	2	4	.333	25	0	0	0	0	32¹	35	3	12	14	13.4	4.45	84	.278	.345	0	.000	-0	-3	-2	0	-0.2
1980 StL-N	1	4	.200	22	0	0	0	3	23	24	2	7	11	12.1	2.74	135	.273	.326	0	—	0	2	2	0	0.3
1981 *NY-A	0	1	.000	16	0	0	0	3	27²	26	1	11	17	12.0	1.63	220	.245	.316	0	—	0	6	6	-0	0.6
1982 NY-A	4	4	.500	63	0	0	0	1	111²	103	7	39	69	11.8	3.47	115	.252	.325	0	—	0	8	6	0	0.6
1983 NY-A	4	4	.500	61	0	0	0	8	115¹	94	5	45	78	11.1	3.43	113	.227	.307	0	—	0	8	6	0	0.6
1984 Cle-A	3	2	.600	22	0	0	0	1	44¹	45	3	14	24	12.0	3.65	112	.259	.314	0	—	0	2	2	-1	0.1
*Chi-N	6	3	.667	37	0	0	0	3	63²	53	4	26	58	11.3	4.10	95	.221	.300	2	.286	-0	-4	-1	-1	-0.2
1985 Chi-N	7	8	.467	51	0	0	0	2	76	88	11	52	46	16.9	6.39	62	.299	.410	0	.000	-1	-24	-20	0	-2.1
1986 Chi-N	2	4	.333	35	0	0	0	0	51²	63	5	34	41	17.1	5.40	75	.310	.412	0	.000	-0	-10	-8	-1	-0.9
Min-A	1	1	.500	15	0	0	0	6	26²	23	2	16	25	13.2	4.39	98	.232	.339	0	—	0	-1	-0	0	0.0
1987 *Min-A	5	5	.500	54	0	0	0	2	81¹	77	9	51	58	14.4	4.98	93	.258	.369	0	—	0	-5	-3	0	-0.3
Total 10	35	43	.449	415	0	0	0	29	675²	653	54	313	449	13.1	4.20	96	.257	.342	3	.143	-1	-20	-14	-4	-1.4

■ BUCK FREEMAN
Freeman, Alexander Vernon b: 7/5/1893, Mart. Tex. d: 2/21/53, Fort Sam Houston, Tex. BB/TR, 5'10", 167 lbs. Deb: 4/13/21

YEAR TM/L	W	L	PCT	G	GS	CG	SH	SV	IP	H	HR	BB	SO	RAT	ERA	ERA+	OAV	OOB	BH	AVG	PB	PR	/A	PD	TPI
1921 Chi-N	9	10	.474	38	20	6	0	3	177¹	189	12	70	42	13.6	4.11	93	.281	.356	11	.208	0	-6	-6	-1	-0.5
1922 Chi-N	0	1	.000	11	1	0	0	1	25²	47	0	10	10	20.7	8.77	48	.412	.468	1	.125	-0	-13	-13	1	-1.0
Total 2	9	11	.450	49	21	6	0	4	203	236	12	80	52	14.5	4.70	82	.300	.372	12	.197	-0	-20	-19	0	-1.5

■ HARVEY FREEMAN
Freeman, Harvey Bayard "Buck" b: 12/22/1897, Nottville, Mich. d: 1/10/70, Kalamazoo, Mich. BR/TR, 5'10", 160 lbs. Deb: 7/10/21

YEAR TM/L	W	L	PCT	G	GS	CG	SH	SV	IP	H	HR	BB	SO	RAT	ERA	ERA+	OAV	OOB	BH	AVG	PB	PR	/A	PD	TPI
1921 Phi-A	1	4	.200	18	4	2	0	0	48	65	2	35	5	19.7	7.69	58	.346	.461	1	.083	-2	-18	-17	1	-1.5

■ HERSH FREEMAN
Freeman, Hershell Baskin "Buster" b: 7/1/28, Gadsden, Ala. BR/TR, 6'3", 220 lbs. Deb: 9/10/52

YEAR TM/L	W	L	PCT	G	GS	CG	SH	SV	IP	H	HR	BB	SO	RAT	ERA	ERA+	OAV	OOB	BH	AVG	PB	PR	/A	PD	TPI
1952 Bos-A	1	0	1.000	4	1	1	0	0	13²	13	1	5	5	12.5	3.29	120	.260	.339	2	.500	1	1	1	0	0.2
1953 Bos-A	1	4	.200	18	2	0	0	0	39	50	1	17	15	15.5	5.54	76	.316	.383	1	.091	-1	-7	-6	0	-0.6
1955 Bos-A	0	0		2	0	0	0	0	1²	1	0	1	1	10.8	0.00	—	.200	.333	0	—	0	1	1	0	0.1
Cin-N	7	4	.636	52	0	0	0	11	91²	94	3	30	37	12.4	2.16	196	.276	.338	3	.167	1	**19**	**21**	1	2.3
1956 Cin-N	14	5	.737	64	0	0	0	18	108²	112	6	34	50	12.2	3.40	117	.274	.331	1	.056	-1	5	7	0	0.6
1957 Cin-N	7	2	.778	52	0	0	0	8	83²	90	14	14	36	11.5	4.52	91	.277	.313	2	.200	0	-6	-4	-0	-0.3
1958 Cin-N	0	0		3	0	0	0	0	7²	4	0	5	7	10.6	3.52	118	.154	.290	0	.000	-0	0	1	0	0.1
Chi-N	0	1	.000	9	0	0	0	0	13	23	3	3	7	18.0	8.31	47	.354	.382	0	.000	-0	-6	-6	0	-0.5
Yr	0	1	.000	12	0	0	0	0	20²	27	3	8	14	15.2	6.53	61	.293	.350	0	.000	-0	-6	-6	0	-0.4
Total 6	30	16	.652	204	3	1	0	37	359	387	25	109	158	12.6	3.74	110	.281	.336	9	.143	-0	6	15	1	1.9

■ JIMMY FREEMAN
Freeman, Jimmy Lee b: 6/29/51, Carlsbad, N.Mex. BL/TL, 6'4", 180 lbs. Deb: 9/01/72

YEAR TM/L	W	L	PCT	G	GS	CG	SH	SV	IP	H	HR	BB	SO	RAT	ERA	ERA+	OAV	OOB	BH	AVG	PB	PR	/A	PD	TPI
1972 Atl-N	2	2	.500	6	6	1	0	0	36	40	5	22	18	15.5	6.00	63	.278	.373	1	.077	-0	-10	-9	-1	-0.9
1973 Atl-N	0	2	.000	13	5	0	0	1	37¹	50	7	25	20	18.1	7.71	51	.327	.421	2	.154	-0	-17	-16	-1	-1.5
Total 2	2	4	.333	19	11	1	0	1	73¹	90	12	47	38	16.8	6.87	56	.303	.398	3	.115	-1	-27	-25	-1	-2.4

■ BUCK FREEMAN
Freeman, John Frank b: 10/30/1871, Catasauqua, Pa. d: 6/25/49, Wilkes-Barre, Pa. BL/TL, 5'9", 169 lbs. Deb: 6/27/1891 ◆

YEAR TM/L	W	L	PCT	G	GS	CG	SH	SV	IP	H	HR	BB	SO	RAT	ERA	ERA+	OAV	OOB	BH	AVG	PB	PR	/A	PD	TPI
1891 Was-a	3	2	.600	5	4	4	0	0	44	35	0	33	28	13.9	3.89	96	.211	.342	4	.222	-0	-1	-1	-0	0.0
1899 Was-N	0	0	—	2	0	0	0	0	7	15	3	3	0	23.1	7.71	51	.430	.475	187	.318	1	-3	-3	0	-0.2
Total 2	3	2	.600	7	4	4	0	0	51	50	3	36	28	15.2	4.41	85	.249	.363	1235	.293	1	-4	-4	-0	-0.2

■ JULIE FREEMAN
Freeman, Julius Benjamin b: 11/7/1868, Missouri d: 6/10/21, St.Louis, Mo. Deb: 10/10/1888

YEAR TM/L	W	L	PCT	G	GS	CG	SH	SV	IP	H	HR	BB	SO	RAT	ERA	ERA+	OAV	OOB	BH	AVG	PB	PR	/A	PD	TPI
1888 StL-a	0	1	.000	1	1	0	0	0	6¹	7	0	4	1	15.6	4.26	77	.270	.368	1	.333	0	-1	-1	0	0.0

■ MARK FREEMAN
Freeman, Mark Price b: 12/7/30, Memphis, Tenn. BR/TR, 6'4", 220 lbs. Deb: 4/18/59

YEAR TM/L	W	L	PCT	G	GS	CG	SH	SV	IP	H	HR	BB	SO	RAT	ERA	ERA+	OAV	OOB	BH	AVG	PB	PR	/A	PD	TPI
1959 KC-A	0	0	—	3	0	0	0	0	3²	6	0	3	1	22.1	9.82	41	.375	.474	0	—	0	-2	-2	-0	-0.1
NY-A	0	0	—	1	1	0	0	0	7	6	0	2	4	11.6	2.57	142	.240	.321	0	.000	-0	1	1	0	0.1
Yr	0	0	—	4	1	0	0	0	10²	12	0	5	5	15.2	5.06	74	.286	.375	0	.000	-0	-1	-2	0	0.0
1960 Chi-N	3	3	.500	30	8	1	0	1	76²	70	10	33	50	12.7	5.63	67	.240	.327	3	.150	-0	-16	-16	-2	-1.7
Total 2	3	3	.500	34	9	1	0	1	87¹	82	10	38	55	13.0	5.56	68	.246	.334	3	.136	-1	-17	-17	-2	-1.7

■ MARVIN FREEMAN
Freeman, Marvin b: 4/10/63, Chicago, Ill. BR/TR, 6'7", 200 lbs. Deb: 9/16/86

YEAR TM/L	W	L	PCT	G	GS	CG	SH	SV	IP	H	HR	BB	SO	RAT	ERA	ERA+	OAV	OOB	BH	AVG	PB	PR	/A	PD	TPI
1986 Phi-N	2	0	1.000	3	3	0	0	0	16	6	0	10	8	9.0	2.25	171	.120	.267	0	.000	-1	3	3	-0	0.2
1988 Phi-N	2	3	.400	11	11	0	0	0	51²	55	4	43	37	17.2	6.10	58	.276	.407	3	.214	-0	-15	-15	0	-1.3
1989 Phi-N	0	0	—	1	1	0	0	0	3	2	0	5	0	21.0	6.00	59	.182	.438	0	.000	-0	-1	-1	0	0.0
1990 Phi-N	0	2	.000	16	3	0	0	1	32¹	34	5	14	26	14.2	5.57	69	.264	.349	0	.000	-1	-6	-6	0	-0.6

YEAR	TM/L	W	L	PCT	G	GS	CG	SH	SV	IP	H	HR	BB	SO	RAT	ERA	ERA+	OAV	OOB	BH	AVG	PB	PR	/A	PD	TPI
	Atl-N	1	0	1.000	9	0	0	0	0	15²	7	0	3	12	6.9	1.72	227	.130	.203	0	—	0	4	4	-0	0.4
	Yr	1	2	.333	25	3	0	0	1	48	41	5	17	38	11.3	4.31	89	.220	.293	0	.000	-1	-3	-2	-0	-0.2
Total	4	5	5	.500	40	18	0	0	1	118²	104	7	75	83	14.0	4.85	77	.235	.353	3	.103	-1	-16	-15	-0	-1.3

■ JAKE FREEZE   Freeze, Carl Alexander b: 4/25/1900, Huntington, Ark.   d: 4/9/83, San Angelo, Tex.   BR/TR, 5'8", 150 lbs.   Deb: 7/01/25

YEAR	TM/L	W	L	PCT	G	GS	CG	SH	SV	IP	H	HR	BB	SO	RAT	ERA	ERA+	OAV	OOB	BH	AVG	PB	PR	/A	PD	TPI
1925	Chi-A	0	0	—	2	0	0	0	0	3²	3	1	3	1	14.7	2.45	169	.200	.333	0	.000	-0	1	1	-0	0.0

■ DAVE FREISLEBEN   Freisleben, David James b: 10/31/51, Coraopolis, Pa.   BR/TR, 5'11", 195 lbs.   Deb: 4/26/74

YEAR	TM/L	W	L	PCT	G	GS	CG	SH	SV	IP	H	HR	BB	SO	RAT	ERA	ERA+	OAV	OOB	BH	AVG	PB	PR	/A	PD	TPI
1974	SD-N	9	14	.391	33	31	6	2	0	211²	194	13	112	130	13.3	3.66	97	.241	.339	11	.172	2	-1	-2	-0	0.0
1975	SD-N	5	14	.263	36	27	4	1	0	181	206	11	82	77	14.7	4.28	81	.289	.368	4	.083	-1	-13	-16	0	-1.7
1976	SD-N	10	13	.435	34	24	6	3	1	172	163	10	66	81	12.2	3.51	93	.248	.321	7	.189	1	-0	-5	2	-0.1
1977	SD-N	7	9	.438	33	23	1	0	0	138²	140	21	71	72	13.8	4.61	77	.266	.356	5	.135	0	-11	-16	-2	-1.7
1978	SD-N	0	3	.000	12	4	0	0	0	26²	41	3	15	16	18.9	6.08	55	.363	.438	0	.000	-1	-7	-8	-0	-0.8
	Cle-A	1	4	.200	12	10	0	0	0	44¹	52	4	31	19	17.3	7.11	53	.299	.411	0	—	0	-16	-17	-0	-1.5
1979	Tor-A	2	3	.400	42	2	0	0	3	91	101	5	53	35	15.4	4.95	88	.294	.391	0	—	0	-7	-6	-0	-0.5
Total	6	34	60	.362	202	121	17	6	4	865¹	897	67	430	430	14.1	4.30	83	.269	.357	27	.141	2	-56	-71	-1	-6.3

■ TONY FREITAS   Freitas, Antonio b: 5/5/08, Mill Valley, Cal.   BR/TL, 5'8", 161 lbs.   Deb: 5/31/32

YEAR	TM/L	W	L	PCT	G	GS	CG	SH	SV	IP	H	HR	BB	SO	RAT	ERA	ERA+	OAV	OOB	BH	AVG	PB	PR	/A	PD	TPI
1932	Phi-A	12	5	.706	23	18	10	1	0	150¹	150	11	48	31	12.1	3.83	118	.263	.325	8	.148	-1	11	12	2	1.2
1933	Phi-A	2	4	.333	19	9	2	0	1	64¹	90	8	24	15	16.2	7.27	59	.337	.396	1	.063	-1	-21	-21	0	-1.9
1934	Cin-N	6	12	.333	30	18	5	0	1	152²	194	6	25	37	13.1	4.01	102	.311	.341	9	.191	0	1	1	3	0.4
1935	Cin-N	5	10	.333	31	18	5	0	2	143²	174	6	38	51	13.4	4.57	87	.295	.340	6	.130	-0	-9	-9	1	-0.8
1936	Cin-N	0	2	.000	4	0	0	0	0	7	6	0	2	1	10.3	1.29	297	.240	.296	0	.000	-0	2	2	0	0.2
Total	5	25	33	.431	107	63	22	1	4	518	614	31	137	135	13.2	4.48	94	.296	.343	24	.145	-2	-16	-16	5	-0.9

■ LARRY FRENCH   French, Lawrence Herbert b: 11/1/07, Visalia, Cal.   d: 2/9/87, San Diego, Cal.   BR/TL, 6'1", 195 lbs.   Deb: 4/18/29

YEAR	TM/L	W	L	PCT	G	GS	CG	SH	SV	IP	H	HR	BB	SO	RAT	ERA	ERA+	OAV	OOB	BH	AVG	PB	PR	/A	PD	TPI
1929	Pit-N	7	5	.583	30	13	6	0	1	123	130	10	62	49	14.3	4.90	97	.276	.364	8	.190	-1	-3	-2	1	0.0
1930	Pit-N	17	18	.486	42	35	21	3	1	274²	325	20	89	90	13.8	4.36	114	.295	.351	22	.242	1	19	19	-1	1.7
1931	Pit-N	15	13	.536	39	33	20	1	1	275²	301	9	70	73	12.1	3.26	118	.278	.322	17	.179	-1	18	18	-1	1.6
1932	Pit-N	18	16	.529	47	33	19	3	4	274¹	301	17	62	72	11.9	3.02	126	.276	.316	19	.207	1	26	24	-4	2.1
1933	Pit-N	18	13	.581	47	35	21	5	1	291¹	290	9	55	88	10.8	2.72	122	.257	.294	15	.149	-2	20	19	-4	1.5
1934	Pit-N	12	18	.400	49	35	16	3	1	263²	299	8	59	103	12.3	3.58	115	.281	.321	16	.190	-0	14	16	-3	1.2
1935	*Chi-N	17	10	.630	42	30	16	4	2	246¹	279	10	44	90	11.9	2.96	133	.286	.318	12	.141	-3	29	27	2	2.5
1936	Chi-N	18	9	.667	43	28	16	4	3	252¹	262	16	54	104	11.5	3.39	118	.266	.308	18	.212	0	18	17	-3	1.4
1937	Chi-N	16	10	.615	42	28	11	4	0	208	229	7	65	100	12.8	3.98	100	.274	.327	9	.127	-4	-2	0	2	-0.1
1938	*Chi-N	10	19	.345	43	27	10	3	0	201¹	210	17	62	83	12.2	3.80	101	.271	.326	13	.210	2	-0	1	1	0.4
1939	Chi-N	15	8	.652	36	21	10	2	1	194	205	7	50	98	11.9	3.29	120	.269	.314	14	.192	1	13	14	2	1.7
1940	Chi-N	14	14	.500	40	33	18	3	2	246	240	12	64	107	11.3	3.29	114	.256	.306	14	.165	1	15	12	2	1.6
1941	Chi-N	5	14	.263	26	18	6	1	0	138	161	10	43	60	13.4	4.63	76	.285	.338	9	.191	1	-15	-17	-1	-1.7
	*Bro-N	0	0	—	6	1	0	0	0	15²	16	1	4	8	12.1	3.45	106	.267	.323	1	.250	0	0	0	0	0.1
	Yr	5	14	.263	32	19	6	1	0	153²	177	11	47	68	13.2	4.51	78	.282	.333	4	.078	1	-15	-17	-1	-1.6
1942	Bro-N	15	4	**.789**	38	14	8	4	0	147²	127	7	36	62	10.2	1.83	178	.233	.287	12	.300	4	24	24	-1	3.0
Total	14	197	171	.535	570	384	198	40	17	3152	3375	164	819	1187	12.1	3.44	114	.272	.320	199	.188	0	178	171	-7	17.0

■ BILL FRENCH   French, William b: Baltimore, Md.   Deb: 4/14/1873 ♦

YEAR	TM/L	W	L	PCT	G	GS	CG	SH	SV	IP	H	HR	BB	SO	RAT	ERA	ERA+	OAV	OOB	BH	AVG	PB	PR	/A	PD	TPI
1873	Mar-n	0	1	.000	1	1	1	0	0	9	30	1	0		30.0	11.00	33	.492	.492	4	.211	-0	-7	-7		-0.3

■ BENNY FREY   Frey, Benjamin Rudolph b: 4/6/06, Dexter, Mich.   d: 11/1/37, Jackson, Mich.   BR/TR, 5'10", 165 lbs.   Deb: 9/18/29

YEAR	TM/L	W	L	PCT	G	GS	CG	SH	SV	IP	H	HR	BB	SO	RAT	ERA	ERA+	OAV	OOB	BH	AVG	PB	PR	/A	PD	TPI
1929	Cin-N	1	2	.333	3	3	2	0	0	24	29	2	8	1	13.9	4.13	111	.302	.356	3	.375	1	2	1	1	0.3
1930	Cin-N	11	18	.379	44	28	14	2	1	245	295	15	62	43	13.2	4.70	103	.305	.349	25	.284	4	7	3	6	1.2
1931	Cin-N	8	12	.400	34	17	7	1	2	133²	166	2	36	19	13.7	4.92	76	.319	.365	14	.318	4	-16	-18	4	-0.9
1932	StL-N	0	2	.000	2	0	0	0	0	3	6	0	2	0	24.0	12.00	33	.600	.667	0	.000	-0	-3	-3	0	-0.2
	Cin-N	4	10	.286	28	15	5	0	0	131¹	159	10	30	27	13.0	4.32	89	.299	.338	9	.205	-0	-6	-7	3	-0.3
	Yr	4	12	.250	30	15	5	0	0	134¹	165	10	32	27	13.3	4.49	86	.305	.345	2	.044	-0	-9	-9	3	-0.5
1933	Cin-N	6	4	.600	37	9	1	1	0	132	144	9	21	12	11.3	3.82	89	.281	.309	11	.262	3	-7	-6	2	0.0
1934	Cin-N	11	16	.407	39	30	12	2	2	245¹	288	10	42	33	12.2	3.52	116	.289	.319	14	.171	-0	15	15	5	2.0
1935	Cin-N	6	10	.375	38	13	3	1	3	114¹	164	6	32	24	15.7	6.85	58	.335	.381	11	.344	4	-36	-36	3	-2.7
1936	Cin-N	10	8	.556	31	12	5	0	0	131¹	164	5	30	20	13.3	4.25	90	.296	.332	11	.250	2	-3	-6	1	-0.3
Total	8	57	82	.410	256	127	49	7	8	1160	1415	54	263	179	13.1	4.50	90	.303	.341	98	.255	17	-47	-55	24	-0.9

■ STEVE FREY   Frey, Steven Francis b: 7/29/63, Meadowbrook, Pa.   BR/TL, 5'9", 170 lbs.   Deb: 5/10/89

YEAR	TM/L	W	L	PCT	G	GS	CG	SH	SV	IP	H	HR	BB	SO	RAT	ERA	ERA+	OAV	OOB	BH	AVG	PB	PR	/A	PD	TPI
1989	Mon-N	3	2	.600	20	0	0	0	0	21¹	29	4	11	15	17.3	5.48	64	.326	.406	0	—	0	-5	-5	-0	-0.4
1990	Mon-N	8	2	.800	51	0	0	0	9	55²	44	4	29	29	12.0	2.10	179	.219	.320	0	.000	-0	10	10	-0	1.0
Total	2	11	4	.733	71	0	0	0	9	77	73	8	40	44	13.4	3.04	122	.252	.346	0	.000	-0	6	6	-0	0.6

■ BERNIE FRIBERG   Friberg, Bernard Albert (b: Gustaf Bernhard Friberg) b: 8/18/1899, Manchester, N.H.   d: 12/8/58, Lynn, Mass.   BR/TR, 5'11", 178 lbs.   Deb: 8/20/19 ♦

YEAR	TM/L	W	L	PCT	G	GS	CG	SH	SV	IP	H	HR	BB	SO	RAT	ERA	ERA+	OAV	OOB	BH	AVG	PB	PR	/A	PD	TPI
1925	Phi-N	0	0	—	1	0	0	0	0	4	4	0	3	1	15.8	4.50	106	.286	.412	82	.270	0	-0	-0		0.0

■ MARION FRICANO   Fricano, Marion John b: 7/15/23, Brant, N.Y.   d: 5/18/76, Tijuana, Mex.   BR/TR, 6', 170 lbs.   Deb: 9/06/52

YEAR	TM/L	W	L	PCT	G	GS	CG	SH	SV	IP	H	HR	BB	SO	RAT	ERA	ERA+	OAV	OOB	BH	AVG	PB	PR	/A	PD	TPI
1952	Phi-A	1	0	1.000	2	0	0	0	0	5	5	0	1	0	10.8	1.80	220	.238	.273	0	—	0	1	1	0	0.1
1953	Phi-A	9	12	.429	39	23	10	2	1	211	206	21	90	67	12.9	3.88	110	.257	.337	10	.145	-3	3	10	-1	0.6
1954	Phi-A	5	11	.313	37	20	4	0	1	151²	163	17	64	43	13.7	5.16	76	.275	.349	4	.098	-3	-24	-21	-1	-2.4
1955	KC-A	0	0	—	10	0	0	0	0	20	19	2	9	5	12.6	3.15	133	.253	.333	2	.667	1	2	2	0	0.4
Total	4	15	23	.395	88	43	14	0	1	387²	393	40	164	115	13.2	4.32	96	.264	.341	16	.142	-5	-19	-8	-2	-1.3

■ SKIPPER FRIDAY   Friday, Grier William b: 10/26/1897, Gastonia, N.C.   d: 8/25/62, Gastonia, N.C.   BR/TR, 5'11", 170 lbs.   Deb: 6/17/23

YEAR	TM/L	W	L	PCT	G	GS	CG	SH	SV	IP	H	HR	BB	SO	RAT	ERA	ERA+	OAV	OOB	BH	AVG	PB	PR	/A	PD	TPI
1923	Was-A	0	1	.000	7	2	1	0	0	30	35	2	22	9	17.7	6.90	55	.313	.434	2	.222	0	-10	-10	1	-0.8

■ CY FRIED   Fried, Arthur Edwin b: 7/23/1897, San Antonio, Tex.   d: 10/10/70, San Antonio, Tex.   BL/TL, 5'11.5", 150 lbs.   Deb: 9/17/20

YEAR	TM/L	W	L	PCT	G	GS	CG	SH	SV	IP	H	HR	BB	SO	RAT	ERA	ERA+	OAV	OOB	BH	AVG	PB	PR	/A	PD	TPI
1920	Det-A	0	0	—	2	0	0	0	0	1²	3	0	4	0	37.8	16.20	23	.500	.700	0	—	0	-2	-2	0	-0.1

■ BOB FRIEDRICH   Friedrich, Robert George b: 8/30/06, Cincinnati, Ohio   BR/TR, 5'11.5", 165 lbs.   Deb: 5/17/32

YEAR	TM/L	W	L	PCT	G	GS	CG	SH	SV	IP	H	HR	BB	SO	RAT	ERA	ERA+	OAV	OOB	BH	AVG	PB	PR	/A	PD	TPI
1932	Was-A	0	0	—	2	0	0	0	0	4	4	0	7	2	27.0	11.25	38	.250	.500	0	.000	-0	-3	-3	-0	-0.2

■ BILL FRIEL   Friel, William Edward b: 4/1/1876, Renovo, Pa.   d: 12/24/59, St.Louis, Mo.   BL/TR, 5'10", 215 lbs.   Deb: 5/03/01   U♦

YEAR	TM/L	W	L	PCT	G	GS	CG	SH	SV	IP	H	HR	BB	SO	RAT	ERA	ERA+	OAV	OOB	BH	AVG	PB	PR	/A	PD	TPI
1902	StL-A	0	0	—	1	0	0	0	0	4	4	0	4	0	9.0	4.50	78	.261	.261	64	.240	0	-0	-0		0.0

■ DANNY FRIEND   Friend, Daniel Sebastian b: 4/18/1873, Cincinnati, Ohio   d: 6/1/42, Chillicothe, Ohio   TL, 5'9", 175 lbs.   Deb: 9/10/1895

YEAR	TM/L	W	L	PCT	G	GS	CG	SH	SV	IP	H	HR	BB	SO	RAT	ERA	ERA+	OAV	OOB	BH	AVG	PB	PR	/A	PD	TPI
1895	Chi-N	2	2	.500	5	5	5	0	0	41	50	5	14	10	14.0	5.27	97	.296	.350	4	.235	-1	-2	-1	0	0.0
1896	Chi-N	18	14	.563	36	33	28	1	0	290²	298	11	139	86	13.5	4.74	96	.263	.344	30	.238	-1	-12	-6	-2	-0.6
1897	Chi-N	12	11	.522	24	24	23	0	0	203	244	6	86	58	14.6	4.52	99	.295	.362	25	.284	2	-5	-1	-1	0.0
1898	Chi-N	0	2	.000	2	2	2	0	0	17	20	0	10	4	15.9	5.29	68	.291	.381	2	.286	0	-3	-3	0	0.0
Total	4	32	29	.525	67	64	58	1	0	551²	612	22	249	158	14.0	4.71	96	.279	.352	61	.256	1	-22	-12	-1	-0.6

■ BOB FRIEND — Friend, Robert Bartmess "Warrior"   b: 11/24/30, Lafayette, Ind.   BR/TR, 6', 190 lbs.   Deb: 4/28/51

YEAR	TM/L	W	L	PCT	G	GS	CG	SH	SV	IP	H	HR	BB	SO	RAT	ERA	ERA+	OAV	OOB	BH	AVG	PB	PR	/A	PD	TPI
1951	Pit-N	6	10	.375	34	22	3	1	0	149²	173	12	68	41	14.5	4.27	99	.293	.366	4	.091	-2	-5	-1	1	-0.1
1952	Pit-N	7	17	.292	35	23	6	1	0	185	186	15	84	75	13.3	4.18	95	.258	.338	3	.058	-4	-9	-4	1	-0.6
1953	Pit-N	8	11	.421	32	24	8	0	0	170²	193	18	57	66	13.3	4.90	91	.286	.344	7	.135	-3	-12	-8	1	-0.8
1954	Pit-N	7	12	.368	35	20	4	2	2	170¹	204	16	58	73	13.9	5.07	83	.302	.358	14	.275	5	-19	-17	-1	-1.1
1955	Pit-N	14	9	.609	44	20	9	2	2	200¹	178	18	52	98	10.4	**2.83**	**145**	.242	.294	10	.164	-2	**27**	**29**	3	3.1
1956	Pit-N	17	17	.500	49	42	19	4	3	**314¹**	310	25	85	166	11.4	3.46	109	.258	.308	16	.165	-1	11	11	-1	0.9
1957	Pit-N	14	18	.438	40	38	17	3	0	277	273	28	68	143	11.1	3.38	112	.257	.303	18	.184	1	15	13	-2	1.3
1958	Pit-N	**22**	14	.611	38	38	16	1	0	274	299	26	61	135	12.0	3.68	105	.281	.322	10	.106	-4	8	6	-0	0.1
1959	Pit-N	8	19	.296	35	35	7	2	0	234²	267	19	52	104	12.5	4.03	96	.283	.325	12	.164	0	-2	-4	1	-0.2
1960	*Pit-N	18	12	.600	38	37	16	4	1	275²	266	18	45	183	10.2	3.00	125	.251	.281	6	.068	-5	23	23	-0	1.9
1961	Pit-N	14	19	.424	41	35	10	1	1	236	271	16	45	108	12.2	3.85	104	.289	.324	11	.139	-3	5	4	-1	0.0
1962	Pit-N	18	14	.563	39	36	13	**5**	1	261²	280	23	53	144	11.5	3.06	129	.273	.310	11	.121	-3	26	25	0	2.3
1963	Pit-N	17	16	.515	39	38	12	4	0	268²	236	13	44	144	9.5	2.34	141	.233	.269	9	.105	-3	28	28	-0	2.8
1964	Pit-N	13	18	.419	35	35	13	3	0	240¹	253	10	50	128	11.5	3.33	105	.271	.310	5	.070	-3	5	5	3	0.4
1965	Pit-N	8	12	.400	34	34	8	2	0	222	221	17	47	74	11.2	3.24	108	.260	.305	3	.042	-5	7	7	1	0.3
1966	NY-A	1	4	.200	12	8	0	0	0	44²	61	2	9	22	14.1	4.84	69	.330	.361	0	.000	-1	-7	-7	1	-0.7
	NY-N	5	8	.385	22	12	2	1	1	86	101	11	16	30	12.3	4.40	83	.289	.322	1	.034	-3	-8	-7	-1	-1.1
Total 16		197	230	.461	602	497	163	36	11	3611	3772	286	894	1734	11.5	3.58	107	.269	.315	138	.121	-36	94	100	6	8.5

■ PETE FRIES — Fries, Peter Martin   b: 10/30/1857, Scranton, Pa.   d: 7/30/37, Chicago, Ill.   BL/TL, 5'8", 160 lbs.   Deb: 8/10/1883 ♦

YEAR	TM/L	W	L	PCT	G	GS	CG	SH	SV	IP	H	HR	BB	SO	RAT	ERA	ERA+	OAV	OOB	BH	AVG	PB	PR	/A	PD	TPI
1883	Col-a	0	3	.000	3	3	3	0	0	25	34	1	14	7	17.3	6.48	48	.305	.382	3	.300	1	-9	-9	0	-0.6

■ JOHN FRILL — Frill, John Edmond   b: 4/3/1879, Reading, Pa.   d: 9/28/18, Westerly, R.I.   BR/TL, 5'10.5", 170 lbs.   Deb: 4/16/10

YEAR	TM/L	W	L	PCT	G	GS	CG	SH	SV	IP	H	HR	BB	SO	RAT	ERA	ERA+	OAV	OOB	BH	AVG	PB	PR	/A	PD	TPI
1910	NY-A	2	2	.500	10	5	3	1	1	48¹	55	1	5	27	11.4	4.47	59	.289	.311	2	.111	-1	-10	-10	0	-1.0
1912	StL-A	0	1	.000	3	3	0	0	0	4¹	16	1	1	2	37.4	20.77	16	.571	.600	1	.500	0	-8	-8	0	-0.6
	Cin-N	1	0	1.000	3	2	0	0	0	15	19	0	1	4	13.2	6.00	56	.311	.344	1	.250	0	-4	-4	0	-0.3
Total 2		3	3	.500	16	10	3	1	1	67²	90	2	7	33	13.4	5.85	49	.323	.348	4	.167	-1	-23	-22	0	-1.9

■ DANNY FRISELLA — Frisella, Daniel Vincent "Bear"   b: 3/4/46, San Francisco, Cal.   d: 1/1/77, Phoenix, Ariz.   BL/TR, 6', 185 lbs.   Deb: 7/27/67

YEAR	TM/L	W	L	PCT	G	GS	CG	SH	SV	IP	H	HR	BB	SO	RAT	ERA	ERA+	OAV	OOB	BH	AVG	PB	PR	/A	PD	TPI
1967	NY-N	1	6	.143	14	11	0	0	0	74	68	6	33	51	12.3	3.41	100	.249	.330	2	.087	-1	-0	-0	-0	0.0
1968	NY-N	2	4	.333	19	4	0	0	2	50²	53	5	17	47	12.4	3.91	77	.270	.329	1	.083	-1	-5	-5	-0	-0.5
1969	NY-N	0	0	—	3	0	0	0	0	4²	8	1	3	5	21.2	7.71	47	.381	.458	0	.000	-0	-2	-2	-0	-0.1
1970	NY-N	8	3	.727	30	1	0	0	1	65²	49	4	34	54	11.4	3.02	133	.204	.303	4	.308	-1	8	7	-0	0.8
1971	NY-N	8	5	.615	53	0	0	0	12	90²	76	6	30	93	10.8	1.99	172	.227	.296	3	.231	1	15	14	1	1.7
1972	NY-N	5	8	.385	39	0	0	0	9	67¹	63	8	20	46	11.1	3.34	101	.243	.297	2	.286	0	1	0	1	0.2
1973	Atl-N	1	2	.333	42	0	0	0	6	45	40	5	23	27	12.8	4.20	94	.241	.337	1	.500	0	-3	-1	-0	0.0
1974	Atl-N	3	4	.429	36	1	0	0	6	41²	37	4	28	27	14.0	5.18	73	.240	.357	0	.000	0	-7	-7	-0	-0.6
1975	SD-N	1	6	.143	65	0	0	0	9	97²	86	7	51	67	12.8	3.13	111	.242	.340	1	.200	0	5	4	-1	0.3
1976	StL-N	0	0	—	18	0	0	0	1	22²	19	3	13	11	12.7	3.97	89	.232	.337	0	.000	-0	-1	-1	0	0.0
	Mil-A	5	2	.714	49	1	0	0	8	49¹	39	3	34	44	11.9	2.74	128	.175	.316	0	—	4	4	-0	0.4
Total 10		34	40	.459	351	17	0	0	57	609¹	529	53	286	471	12.1	3.32	106	.235	.323	14	.179	1	14	13	-0	2.2

■ EMIL FRISK — Frisk, John Emil   b: 10/15/1874, Kalkaska, Mich.   d: 1/27/22, Seattle, Wash.   BL/TR, 6'1", 190 lbs.   Deb: 9/02/1899 ♦

YEAR	TM/L	W	L	PCT	G	GS	CG	SH	SV	IP	H	HR	BB	SO	RAT	ERA	ERA+	OAV	OOB	BH	AVG	PB	PR	/A	PD	TPI
1899	Cin-N	3	6	.333	9	9	9	0	0	68¹	81	1	17	17	12.9	3.95	99	.294	.335	7	.280	1	-1	-0	-0	0.1
1901	Det-A	5	4	.556	11	7	6	0	0	74²	94	1	26	22	14.5	4.34	89	.304	.358	15	.313	2	-6	-4	2	0.3
Total 2		8	10	.444	20	16	15	0	0	143	175	2	43	39	13.7	4.15	94	.299	.347	135	.267	3	-6	-4	2	0.4

■ CHARLIE FRITZ — Fritz, Charles Cornelius   b: 6/18/1882, Mobile, Ala.   d: 7/30/43, Mobile, Ala.   TL,   Deb: 10/05/07

YEAR	TM/L	W	L	PCT	G	GS	CG	SH	SV	IP	H	HR	BB	SO	RAT	ERA	ERA+	OAV	OOB	BH	AVG	PB	PR	/A	PD	TPI
1907	Phi-A	0	0	—	1	1	0	0	0	3	0	0	3	1	9.0	3.00	87	.000	.262	0	.000	-0	-0	-0	-0	0.0

■ BILL FROATS — Froats, William John   b: 10/20/30, New York, N.Y.   BL/TL, 6', 180 lbs.   Deb: 4/22/55

YEAR	TM/L	W	L	PCT	G	GS	CG	SH	SV	IP	H	HR	BB	SO	RAT	ERA	ERA+	OAV	OOB	BH	AVG	PB	PR	/A	PD	TPI
1955	Det-A	0	0	—	1	0	0	0	0	2	0	0	2	0	9.0	0.00	—	.000	.333	0		0	1	1	0	0.1

■ SAM FROCK — Frock, Samuel William   b: 12/23/1882, Baltimore, Md.   d: 11/3/25, Baltimore, Md.   BR/TR, 6', 168 lbs.   Deb: 9/21/07

YEAR	TM/L	W	L	PCT	G	GS	CG	SH	SV	IP	H	HR	BB	SO	RAT	ERA	ERA+	OAV	OOB	BH	AVG	PB	PR	/A	PD	TPI
1907	Bos-N	1	2	.333	5	3	3	1	0	33¹	28	1	11	12	11.1	2.97	86	.243	.320	1	.071	-1	-2	-2	-2	-0.4
1909	Pit-N	2	1	.667	8	4	3	0	1	36¹	44	0	4	11	12.6	2.48	110	.299	.331	2	.143	-1	1	1	0	0.1
1910	Pit-N	0	0	—	1	0	0	0	0	2	2	0	2	1	22.5	4.50	69	.400	.625	0	—	0	-0	-0		0.0
	Bos-N	12	19	.387	45	29	13	2	2	255¹	245	8	91	170	12.0	3.21	104	.262	.330	16	.190	-3	-5	3	-0	0.1
	Yr	12	19	.387	46	29	13	2	2	257¹	247	8	93	171	12.0	3.22	103	.263	.332	16	.012	-5	-5	3	-0	0.1
1911	Bos-N	0	1	.000	4	1	1	0	0	16	29	0	5	8	19.7	5.63	68	.426	.473	1	.200	-0	-4	-3	0	-0.2
Total 4		15	23	.395	63	37	20	3	3	343	348	9	113	202	12.4	3.23	99	.274	.339	20	.171	-5	-11	-1	-1	-0.4

■ TODD FROHWIRTH — Frohwirth, Todd Gerard   b: 9/28/62, Milwaukee, Wis.   BR/TR, 6'4", 190 lbs.   Deb: 8/10/87

YEAR	TM/L	W	L	PCT	G	GS	CG	SH	SV	IP	H	HR	BB	SO	RAT	ERA	ERA+	OAV	OOB	BH	AVG	PB	PR	/A	PD	TPI
1987	Phi-N	1	0	1.000	10	0	0	0	0	11	12	0	2	9	11.5	0.00	—	.293	.326	0	.000	-0	5	5	0	0.5
1988	Phi-N	1	2	.333	12	0	0	0	0	12	16	2	11	11	20.3	8.25	43	.327	.450	0	—	0	-6	-6	1	-0.5
1989	Phi-N	1	0	1.000	45	0	0	0	0	62²	56	4	18	39	11.1	3.59	99	.240	.303	0	.000	-0	-1	-0	0	-0.1
1990	Phi-N	0	1	.000	5	0	0	0	0	1	3	0	6	1	81.0	18.00	21	.500	.750	0	—	0	-2	-2	0	-0.1
Total 4		3	3	.500	72	0	0	0	0	86²	87	6	37	60	13.2	3.95	92	.264	.344	0	.000	-0	-4	-3	1	-0.1

■ ART FROMME — Fromme, Arthur Henry   b: 9/3/1883, Quincy, Ill.   d: 8/24/56, Los Angeles, Cal.   BR/TR, 6', 178 lbs.   Deb: 9/14/06

YEAR	TM/L	W	L	PCT	G	GS	CG	SH	SV	IP	H	HR	BB	SO	RAT	ERA	ERA+	OAV	OOB	BH	AVG	PB	PR	/A	PD	TPI
1906	StL-N	1	2	.333	3	3	3	1	0	25	19	0	10	11	10.8	1.44	182	.221	.309	2	.222	0	3	3	1	0.5
1907	StL-N	5	13	.278	23	16	13	2	0	145²	138	3	67	62	12.9	2.90	86	.256	.343	10	.182	0	-7	-6	0	-0.6
1908	StL-N	5	13	.278	20	14	9	2	0	116	102	1	50	62	11.9	2.72	87	.218	.296	5	.139	-1	-5	-5	-0	-0.6
1909	Cin-N	19	13	.594	37	34	22	4	2	279¹	195	2	101	126	9.6	1.90	137	.201	.278	18	.191	2	22	22	1	2.9
1910	Cin-N	3	4	.429	11	5	1	0	0	49¹	44	0	39	10	15.3	2.92	100	.260	.402	2	.133	-1	1	-0	0	0.0
1911	Cin-N	10	11	.476	38	26	11	1	0	208	190	8	79	107	12.3	3.46	96	.248	.331	14	.189	-1	-1	-3	0	-0.4
1912	Cin-N	16	18	.471	43	37	23	3	0	296	285	7	88	120	11.7	2.74	123	.251	.311	9	.087	-9	22	21	-0	1.1
1913	Cin-N	1	4	.200	9	7	2	0	0	56	55	1	21	24	12.7	4.18	78	.274	.351	3	.143	-0	-6	-6	-1	-0.6
	NY-N	11	6	.647	26	12	3	0	0	112¹	112	5	29	50	11.5	4.01	78	.260	.310	6	.171	-0	-10	-11	1	-0.9
	Yr	12	10	.545	35	19	5	0	0	168¹	167	6	50	74	11.7	4.06	78	.263	.319	2	.036	-1	-16	-17	1	-1.5
1914	NY-N	9	5	.643	38	12	3	1	2	138	142	7	44	57	12.6	3.20	83	.283	.349	7	.226	1	-6	-8	3	-0.3
1915	NY-N	0	1	.000	4	1	0	0	0	12¹	15	1	2	4	12.4	5.84	44	.306	.333	1	.333	1	-4	-4	0	-0.3
Total 10		80	90	.471	252	167	90	14	4	1438	1297	37	530	638	11.7	2.90	100	.244	.318	77	.162	-8	8	2	6	0.8

■ DAVE FROST — Frost, Carl David   b: 11/17/52, Long Beach, Cal.   BR/TR, 6'6", 235 lbs.   Deb: 9/11/77

YEAR	TM/L	W	L	PCT	G	GS	CG	SH	SV	IP	H	HR	BB	SO	RAT	ERA	ERA+	OAV	OOB	BH	AVG	PB	PR	/A	PD	TPI
1977	Chi-A	1	1	.500	4	3	0	0	0	23²	30	0	3	15	12.9	3.04	134	.323	.351	0	—	0	3	3	0	0.3
1978	Cal-A	5	4	.556	11	10	2	1	0	80¹	71	6	24	30	10.9	2.58	140	.240	.301	0	—	0	11	9	2	1.2
1979	*Cal-A	16	10	.615	36	33	12	2	1	239¹	226	17	77	107	11.6	3.57	114	.251	.314	0	—	0	17	13	-1	1.3
1980	Cal-A	4	8	.333	15	15	2	0	0	78¹	97	8	21	28	13.8	5.29	74	.308	.355	0	—	0	-11	-12	-1	-1.1
1981	Cal-A	1	8	.111	12	9	0	0	0	47¹	44	3	19	16	12.2	5.51	66	.250	.327	0	—	0	-10	-10	0	-0.9
1982	KC-A	6	6	.500	21	14	0	3	1	81²	103	7	30	26	15.0	5.51	74	.313	.376	0	—	0	-13	-13	-1	-1.3
Total 6		33	37	.471	99	84	16	3	1	550²	571	41	174	222	12.4	4.10	96	.271	.330	0	—	0	-3	-9	-1	-0.5

YEAR TM/L	W	L	PCT	G	GS	CG	SH	SV	IP	H	HR	BB	SO	RAT	ERA	ERA+	OAV	OOB	BH	AVG	PB	PR	/A	PD	TPI
■ JOHNSON FRY Fry, Johnson "Jay" b: 11/21/01, Huntington, W.Va. d: 4/7/59, Carmi, Ill. BR/TR, 6'1", 150 lbs. Deb: 8/24/23																									
1923 Cle-A	0	0	—	1	0	0	0	0	3²	6	0	4	0	24.5	12.27	32	.353	.476	1	1.000	1	-3	-3	0	-0.1
■ CHARLIE FRYE Frye, Charles Andrew b: 7/17/14, Hickory, N.C. d: 5/25/45, Hickory, N.C. BR/TR, 6'1", 175 lbs. Deb: 7/28/40																									
1940 Phi-N	0	6	.000	15	5	1	0	0	50¹	58	3	26	18	15.0	4.65	84	.291	.373	5	.263	1	-4	-4	-1	-0.2
■ WOODIE FRYMAN Fryman, Woodrow Thompson b: 4/15/40, Ewing, Ky. BR/TL, 6'3", 197 lbs. Deb: 4/15/66																									
1966 Pit-N	12	9	.571	36	28	9	3	1	181²	182	13	47	105	11.4	3.81	94	.261	.309	10	.159	-1	-4	-5	-2	-0.7
1967 Pit-N	3	8	.273	28	18	3	1	1	113¹	121	12	44	74	13.4	4.05	83	.276	.348	4	.118	-1	-9	-9	2	-0.7
1968 Phi-N	12	14	.462	34	32	10	5	0	213²	198	12	64	151	11.3	2.78	108	.248	.306	6	.085	-2	5	5	-2	0.2
1969 Phi-N	12	15	.444	36	35	10	1	0	228³	243	15	89	150	13.5	4.41	80	.270	.343	9	.118	-2	-21	-22	-1	-2.3
1970 Phi-N	8	6	.571	27	20	4	3	0	127²	122	11	43	97	11.7	4.09	98	.253	.315	5	.128	-2	-1	-1	-0	-0.2
1971 Phi-N	10	7	.588	37	17	3	2	2	149¹	133	7	46	104	11.0	3.38	104	.242	.304	7	.189	0	1	2	2	0.5
1972 Phi-N	4	10	.286	23	17	3	2	1	119²	131	15	39	69	12.9	4.36	82	.279	.337	5	.152	1	-12	-10	1	-0.8
*Det-A	10	3	.769	16	14	6	1	0	113²	93	6	31	72	10.4	2.06	153	.220	.285	5	.125	-2	13	14	-1	1.3
1973 Det-A	6	13	.316	34	29	1	0	0	169²	200	23	64	119	14.2	5.36	76	.294	.357	0	—	0	-29	-24	1	-2.2
1974 Det-A	6	9	.400	27	22	4	1	0	141²	120	16	67	92	12.1	4.32	88	.233	.326	0	—	0	-11	-8	-1	-0.8
1975 Mon-N	9	12	.429	38	20	7	3	3	157	141	14	68	118	12.3	3.32	115	.239	.323	10	.204	1	5	9	1	1.2
1976 Mon-N	13	13	.500	34	32	4	2	2	216¹	218	14	76	123	12.6	3.37	110	.263	.332	7	.109	-3	3	8	-0	0.6
1977 Cin-N	5	5	.500	17	12	0	0	1	75¹	83	13	45	57	15.5	5.38	73	.292	.393	7	.318	2	-12	-12	1	-0.9
1978 Chi-N	2	4	.333	13	9	0	0	0	55²	64	6	37	28	16.3	5.17	78	.309	.414	1	.063	-1	-10	-7	1	-0.6
Mon-N	5	7	.417	19	17	4	3	1	94²	93	4	37	53	12.6	3.61	98	.260	.334	2	.059	-2	-0	-1	-0	-0.3
Yr	7	11	.389	32	26	4	3	1	150¹	157	10	74	81	14.0	4.19	89	.276	.362	0	.000	-3	-10	-8	1	-0.9
1979 Mon-N	3	6	.333	44	0	0	0	10	58	52	4	22	44	11.9	2.79	131	.241	.328	0	.000	-1	6	6	1	0.6
1980 Mon-N	7	4	.636	61	0	0	0	17	80	61	1	30	59	10.5	2.25	158	.209	.287	2	.167	-0	12	12	1	1.1
1981 *Mon-N	5	3	.625	35	0	0	0	7	43	38	1	14	25	11.1	1.88	185	.247	.314	2	.667	1	8	8	0	1.0
1982 Mon-N	9	4	.692	60	0	0	0	12	69²	66	3	26	46	12.0	3.75	97	.259	.330	2	.222	1	-1	-1	1	0.1
1983 Mon-N	0	3	.000	6	0	0	0	0	3	8	1	1	1	27.0	21.00	17	.571	.600	0	—	0	-6	-6	0	-0.4
Total 18	141	155	.476	625	322	68	27	58	2411¹	2367	187	890	1587	12.4	3.77	96	.259	.329	84	.138	-12	-63	-43	3	-3.3
■ CHARLIE FUCHS Fuchs, Charles Thomas b: 11/18/13, Union City, N.J. d: 6/10/69, Weehawken, N.J. BB/TR, 5'8", 168 lbs. Deb: 4/17/42																									
1942 Det-A	3	3	.500	9	4	1	1	0	36²	43	5	19	15	15.5	6.63	60	.285	.368	1	.077	-1	-12	-11	1	-0.9
1943 Phi-N	2	7	.222	17	9	4	1	1	77²	76	4	34	12	13.1	4.29	79	.266	.350	2	.091	-2	-8	-8	-1	-1.0
StL-A	0	0	—	13	0	0	0	0	35²	42	4	11	9	13.6	4.04	82	.294	.348	0	.000	-1	-3	-3	-0	-0.3
1944 Bro-N	1	0	1.000	8	0	0	0	0	15²	25	2	9	5	20.1	5.74	62	.347	.427	0	.000	-0	-4	-4	1	-0.2
Total 3	6	10	.375	47	13	5	2	1	165²	186	15	73	41	14.4	4.89	72	.285	.363	3	.070	-4	-27	-25	1	-2.4
■ MIGUEL FUENTES Fuentes, Miguel (Pinet) b: 5/10/46, Loiza, P.R. d: 1/29/70, Loiza, P.R. BR/TR, 6', 160 lbs. Deb: 9/01/69																									
1969 Sea-A	1	3	.250	8	4	1	0	0	26	29	1	16	14	15.6	5.19	70	.284	.381	2	.333	0	-5	-5	-0	-0.4
■ OSCAR FUHR Fuhr, Oscar Lawrence b: 8/22/1893, Defiance, Mo. d: 3/27/75, Dallas, Tex. BL/TL, 6'0.5", 176 lbs. Deb: 4/19/21																									
1921 Chi-N	0	0	—	1	0	0	0	0	4	11	1	0	2	24.8	9.00	42	.500	.500	0	.000	-0	-2	-2	0	-0.1
1924 Bos-A	3	6	.333	23	10	4	1	0	80¹	100	1	39	30	16.1	5.94	74	.310	.392	4	.182	-1	-15	-14	1	-1.2
1925 Bos-A	0	6	.000	39	6	0	0	0	91¹	138	7	30	27	16.9	6.60	69	.364	.415	5	.250	0	-22	-21	1	-1.7
Total 3	3	12	.200	63	16	4	1	0	175²	249	9	69	59	16.7	6.35	70	.344	.407	9	.209	-1	-40	-37	2	-3.0
■ JOHN FULGHAM Fulgham, John Thomas b: 6/9/56, St.Louis, Mo. BR/TR, 6'2", 205 lbs. Deb: 6/19/79																									
1979 StL-N	10	6	.625	20	19	10	2	0	146	123	10	26	75	9.4	2.53	149	.227	.267	6	.143	1	20	20	-2	2.1
1980 StL-N	4	6	.400	15	14	4	1	0	85¹	66	7	32	48	10.4	3.38	109	.219	.296	0	.000	-3	2	3	-0	0.0
Total 2	14	12	.538	35	33	14	3	0	231¹	189	17	58	123	9.8	2.84	132	.224	.277	6	.087	-2	22	23	-2	2.1
■ ED FULLER Fuller, Edward Ashton b: 3/22/1868, Washington, D.C. d: 3/16/35, Hyattsville, Md. BR/TR, 6', 158 lbs. Deb: 7/11/1886																									
1886 Was-N	0	1	.000	2	1	0	0	0	13	15	0	5	3	13.8	6.92	47	.278	.339	1	.143	-0	-5	-5	0	-0.4
■ CURT FULLERTON Fullerton, Curtis Hooper b: 9/13/1898, Ellsworth, Me. d: 1/2/75, Winthrop, Mass. BL/TR, 6', 162 lbs. Deb: 4/14/21																									
1921 Bos-A	0	1	.000	4	1	1	0	0	15¹	22	3	10	4	19.4	8.80	48	.355	.452	0	.000	-0	-8	-8	-0	-0.6
1922 Bos-A	1	4	.200	31	3	0	0	0	64¹	70	4	35	19	15.4	5.46	75	.290	.391	2	.250	1	-10	-10	1	-0.6
1923 Bos-A	2	15	.118	37	15	6	0	1	143¹	167	9	71	37	15.3	5.09	81	.300	.385	11	.297	2	-18	-16	-1	-1.3
1924 Bos-A	7	12	.368	33	20	9	0	2	152	166	4	73	33	14.5	4.32	101	.283	.368	3	.071	-4	2	1	-0	-0.1
1925 Bos-A	0	3	.000	4	2	0	0	0	22²	22	1	9	3	13.1	3.18	143	.259	.344	2	.200	0	3	3	1	0.4
1933 Bos-A	0	2	.000	6	2	2	0	0	25¹	36	1	13	10	17.8	8.53	51	.364	.442	2	.222	1	-12	-12	-1	-0.9
Total 6	10	37	.213	115	43	18	0	3	423	483	19	211	104	15.2	5.11	83	.296	.384	20	.182	-1	-46	-40	-1	-3.1
■ CHICK FULMER Fulmer, Charles John b: 2/12/1851, Philadelphia, Pa. d: 2/15/40, Philadelphia, Pa. TR, 6', 158 lbs. Deb: 8/23/1871 U♦																									
1873 Phi-n	0	0	—	2	0	0	0	0	5	7	0	1		14.4	3.60	101	.292	.320	65	.274	0	-0	0		0.0
■ CHRIS FULMER Fulmer, Christopher b: 7/4/1858, Tamaqua, Pa. d: 11/9/31, Tamaqua, Pa. BR/TR, 5'8", 165 lbs. Deb: 8/04/1884 ♦																									
1886 Bal-a	0	0	—	2	0	0	0	0	2	2	0	1	0	13.5	4.50	76	.248	.331	66	.244	0	-0	0		0.0
■ BILL FULTON Fulton, William David b: 10/22/63, Pittsburgh, Pa. BR/TR, 6'3", 195 lbs. Deb: 9/12/87																									
1987 NY-A	1	0	1.000	3	0	0	0	0	4²	9	4	1	2	21.2	11.57	38	.409	.458	0		0	-4	-4	0	-0.2
■ FRANK FUNK Funk, Franklin Ray b: 8/30/35, Washington, D.C. BR/TR, 6', 175 lbs. Deb: 9/03/60 C																									
1960 Cle-A	4	2	.667	9	0	0	0	1	31²	27	3	9	18	10.2	1.99	188	.248	.305	1	.111	-0	7	6	0	0.6
1961 Cle-A	11	11	.500	56	0	0	0	11	92¹	79	9	31	64	11.1	3.31	119	.234	.306	1	.059	-1	7	6	-0	0.5
1962 Cle-A	2	1	.667	47	0	0	0	4	80²	62	11	32	49	10.9	3.24	120	.212	.298	1	.067	-1	7	6	-0	0.4
1963 Mil-N	3	3	.500	25	0	0	0	2	43²	42	3	13	19	11.5	2.68	120	.258	.316	0	.000	-0	3	3	-1	0.2
Total 4	20	17	.541	137	0	0	0	18	248¹	210	26	85	150	11.0	3.01	125	.233	.305	3	.067	-3	23	21	-1	1.7
■ TOM FUNK Funk, Thomas James b: 3/13/62, Kansas City, Mo. BL/TL, 6'2", 210 lbs. Deb: 7/24/86																									
1986 Hou-N	0	0	—	8	0	0	0	0	8¹	10	1	6	2	17.3	6.48	56	.286	.390	0	.000	-0	-3	-3	0	-0.2
■ EDDIE FUSSELBACK Fusselback, Edward L. b: 7/17/1856, Philadelphia, Pa. d: 4/14/26, Philadelphia, Pa. 5'6", 156 lbs. Deb: 5/03/1882 ♦																									
1882 StL-a	1	2	.333	4	2	2	0	1	23	34	0	2	3	14.1	4.70	60	.322	.335	31	.228	0	-5	-5	-1	-0.3
■ FRED FUSSELL Fussell, Frederick Morris "Moonlight Ace" b: 10/7/1895, Sheridan, Mo. d: 10/23/66, Syracuse, N.Y. BL/TL, 5'10", 155 lbs. Deb: 9/23/22																									
1922 Chi-N	1	1	.500	3	2	1	0	0	19	24	0	8	4	15.2	4.74	89	.333	.400	0	.000	-1	-1	-1	0	0.0
1923 Chi-N	3	5	.375	28	2	1	0	3	76¹	90	2	31	38	14.6	5.54	72	.298	.369	4	.200	-0	-13	-13	0	-1.1
1928 Pit-N	8	9	.471	28	20	9	2	1	159²	183	6	41	43	12.7	3.61	112	.295	.340	7	.121	-3	7	8	-3	-0.2
1929 Pit-N	2	2	.500	21	3	0	0	1	39²	68	8	8	18	17.5	8.62	55	.389	.418	4	.250	2	-17	-17	-0	-1.2
Total 4	14	17	.452	80	27	11	2	5	294²	365	16	88	103	14.0	4.86	85	.312	.363	15	.150	-2	-25	-23	-2	-2.1
■ FRANK GABLER Gabler, Frank Harold "The Great Gabbo" b: 11/6/11, E.Highlands, Cal. d: 11/1/67, Long Beach, Cal. BR/TR, 6'1", 175 lbs. Deb: 4/19/35																									
1935 NY-N	2	1	.667	26	1	0	0	0	60	79	6	20	24	14.9	5.70	68	.315	.365	2	.125	-1	-11	-12	0	-1.1
1936 *NY-N	9	8	.529	43	14	5	0	6	161²	170	11	34	46	11.5	3.12	125	.274	.315	10	.208	2	16	14	-1	1.5
1937 NY-N	0	0	—	6	0	0	0	0	9	20	1	2	3	22.0	10.00	39	.455	.478	0	—	0	-6	-6	0	-0.5

YEAR TM/L	W	L	PCT	G	GS	CG	SH	SV	IP	H	HR	BB	SO	RAT	ERA	ERA+	OAV	OOB	BH	AVG	PB	PR	/A	PD	TPI
Bos-N	4	7	.364	19	9	2	1	2	76	84	7	16	19	11.8	5.09	70	.283	.319	4	.182	0	-10	-13	-0	-1.1
Yr	4	7	.364	25	9	2	1	2	85	104	8	18	22	12.9	5.61	64	.305	.340	2	.091	0	-16	-19	-0	-1.6
1938 Bos-N	0	0	—	1	0	0	0	0	0^1	3	0	1	0	108.0	81.00	4	1.000	1.000	0	—	0	-3	-3	0	-0.2
Chi-A	1	7	.125	18	7	3	0	0	69^1	101	12	34	17	17.7	9.09	54	.348	.418	5	.238	0	-33	-32	-1	-2.7
Total 4	16	23	.410	113	31	10	1	8	376^1	457	37	107	109	13.6	5.26	76	.303	.351	21	.196	0	-47	-53	-2	-4.1

■ GABE GABLER
Gabler, John Richard b: 10/2/30, Kansas City, Mo. BB/TR, 6'2", 165 lbs. Deb: 9/18/59

YEAR TM/L	W	L	PCT	G	GS	CG	SH	SV	IP	H	HR	BB	SO	RAT	ERA	ERA+	OAV	OOB	BH	AVG	PB	PR	/A	PD	TPI
1959 NY-A	1	1	.500	3	1	0	0	0	19^1	21	1	10	11	14.9	2.79	130	.284	.376	0	.000	-1	2	2	0	0.1
1960 NY-A	3	3	.500	21	4	0	0	1	52	46	2	32	19	13.5	4.15	86	.242	.351	1	.091	-0	-2	-3	0	-0.3
1961 Was-A	3	8	.273	29	9	0	0	4	92^2	104	5	37	33	13.8	4.86	83	.283	.351	5	.200	1	-9	-9	1	-0.5
Total 3	7	12	.368	53	14	0	0	5	164	171	8	79	63	13.8	4.39	87	.271	.354	6	.143	0	-8	-10	2	-0.7

■ KEN GABLES
Gables, Kenneth Harlin "Coral" b: 1/31/19, Walnut Grove, Mo. d: 1/2/60, Walnut Grove, Mo. BR/TR, 5'11", 210 lbs. Deb: 4/18/45

YEAR TM/L	W	L	PCT	G	GS	CG	SH	SV	IP	H	HR	BB	SO	RAT	ERA	ERA+	OAV	OOB	BH	AVG	PB	PR	/A	PD	TPI
1945 Pit-N	11	7	.611	29	16	6	0	1	138^2	139	5	46	49	12.3	4.15	95	.256	.319	4	.103	-3	-5	-3	-2	-0.7
1946 Pit-N	2	4	.333	32	7	0	0	1	100^2	113	3	52	39	14.8	5.27	67	.281	.365	6	.250	2	-21	-20	-2	-1.9
1947 Pit-N	0	0	—	1	0	0	0	0	0^1	3	1	0	0	81.0	54.00	8	.750	.750	0	—	0	-2	-2	0	-0.1
Total 3	13	11	.542	62	23	6	0	2	239^2	255	9	98	88	13.4	4.69	80	.269	.340	10	.159	-1	-28	-25	-4	-2.7

■ JOHN GADDY
Gaddy, John Wilson "Sheriff" b: 2/5/14, Wadesboro, N.C. d: 5/3/66, Albemarle, N.C. BR/TR, 6'0.5", 182 lbs. Deb: 9/27/38

YEAR TM/L	W	L	PCT	G	GS	CG	SH	SV	IP	H	HR	BB	SO	RAT	ERA	ERA+	OAV	OOB	BH	AVG	PB	PR	/A	PD	TPI
1938 Bro-N	2	0	1.000	2	1	0	0	0	13	13	0	4	3	12.5	0.69	564	.255	.321	0	.000	-0	4	5	-0	0.4

■ BRENT GAFF
Gaff, Brent Allen b: 10/5/58, Fort Wayne, Ind. BR/TR, 6'2", 200 lbs. Deb: 7/07/82

YEAR TM/L	W	L	PCT	G	GS	CG	SH	SV	IP	H	HR	BB	SO	RAT	ERA	ERA+	OAV	OOB	BH	AVG	PB	PR	/A	PD	TPI
1982 NY-N	0	3	.000	7	5	0	0	0	31^2	41	3	10	14	14.8	4.55	80	.323	.377	0	.000	-0	-3	-3	0	-0.3
1983 NY-N	1	0	1.000	4	0	0	0	0	10^1	18	0	1	4	16.5	6.10	59	.360	.373	0	.000	-0	-3	-3	0	-0.2
1984 NY-N	3	2	.600	47	0	0	0	1	84^1	77	4	36	42	12.2	3.63	97	.247	.327	0	.000	-1	-0	-1	1	0.0
Total 3	4	5	.444	58	5	0	0	1	126^1	136	7	47	60	13.2	4.06	88	.278	.344	0	.000	-1	-7	-7	1	-0.5

■ CHARLIE GAGUS
Gagus, Charles Frederick b: 3/25/1862, San Francisco, Cal d: 1/16/17, San Francisco, Cal Deb: 8/07/1884

YEAR TM/L	W	L	PCT	G	GS	CG	SH	SV	IP	H	HR	BB	SO	RAT	ERA	ERA+	OAV	OOB	BH	AVG	PB	PR	/A	PD	TPI
1884 Was-U	10	9	.526	23	21	19	0	0	177^1	143	2	38	156	9.2	2.54	117	.206	.247	38	.247	1	9	8	1	0.9

■ NEMO GAINES
Gaines, Willard Roland b: 12/23/1897, Alexandria, Va. d: 1/26/79, Warrenton, Va. BL/TL, 6', 180 lbs. Deb: 6/26/21

YEAR TM/L	W	L	PCT	G	GS	CG	SH	SV	IP	H	HR	BB	SO	RAT	ERA	ERA+	OAV	OOB	BH	AVG	PB	PR	/A	PD	TPI
1921 Was-A	0	0	—	4	0	0	0	0	4^2	5	0	2	1	13.5	0.00	—	.294	.368	0	.000	-0	2	2	-0	0.2

■ FRED GAISER
Gaiser, Frederick Jacob b: 8/31/1885, Stuttgart, Germany d: 10/9/18, Trenton, N.J. Deb: 9/03/08

YEAR TM/L	W	L	PCT	G	GS	CG	SH	SV	IP	H	HR	BB	SO	RAT	ERA	ERA+	OAV	OOB	BH	AVG	PB	PR	/A	PD	TPI
1908 StL-N	0	0	—	1	0	0	0	0	2^1	4	0	3	2	27.0	7.71	31	.444	.583	0	.000	-0	-1	-1	0	-0.1

■ BOB GALASSO
Galasso, Robert Joseph b: 1/13/52, Connellsville, Pa. BL/TR, 6'1", 205 lbs. Deb: 7/24/77

YEAR TM/L	W	L	PCT	G	GS	CG	SH	SV	IP	H	HR	BB	SO	RAT	ERA	ERA+	OAV	OOB	BH	AVG	PB	PR	/A	PD	TPI
1977 Sea-A	0	6	.000	11	7	0	0	0	35	57	8	8	21	17.5	9.00	46	.365	.407	0	—	0	-19	-19	-0	-1.7
1979 Mil-A	3	1	.750	31	0	0	0	3	51^1	64	5	26	28	15.8	4.38	95	.299	.375	0	—	0	-1	-1	-0	-0.1
1981 Sea-A	1	1	.500	13	1	0	0	1	31^2	32	2	13	14	12.8	4.83	80	.264	.336	0	—	0	-4	-3	0	-0.3
Total 3	4	8	.333	55	8	0	0	4	118	153	15	47	63	15.5	5.87	69	.312	.375	0	—	0	-24	-24	-1	-2.1

■ MILT GALATZER
Galatzer, Milton b: 5/4/07, Chicago, Il.. d: 1/29/76, San Francisco, Cal BL/TL, 5'10", 168 lbs. Deb: 6/25/33 ♦

YEAR TM/L	W	L	PCT	G	GS	CG	SH	SV	IP	H	HR	BB	SO	RAT	ERA	ERA+	OAV	OOB	BH	AVG	PB	PR	/A	PD	TPI
1936 Cle-A	0	0	—	1	0	0	0	0	2	6	0	5	3	18.0	4.50	112	.292	.414	23	.237	0	0	0	0	0.0

■ RICH GALE
Gale, Richard Blackwell b: 1/19/54, Littleton, N.H. BR/TR, 6'7", 225 lbs. Deb: 4/30/78

YEAR TM/L	W	L	PCT	G	GS	CG	SH	SV	IP	H	HR	BB	SO	RAT	ERA	ERA+	OAV	OOB	BH	AVG	PB	PR	/A	PD	TPI
1978 KC-A	14	8	.636	31	30	9	3	0	192^1	171	10	100	88	12.8	3.09	124	.244	.340	0	—	0	14	16	-2	1.5
1979 KC-A	9	10	.474	34	31	2	1	0	181^2	197	19	99	103	14.9	5.65	75	.278	.369	0	—	0	-29	-28	-1	-2.6
1980 *KC-A	13	9	.591	32	28	6	1	1	190^2	169	16	78	97	11.8	3.92	103	.239	.316	0	—	0	2	3	-1	0.2
1981 KC-A	6	6	.500	19	15	2	0	0	101^2	107	14	38	47	13.0	5.40	67	.270	.336	0	—	0	-20	-20	-2	-2.1
1982 SF-N	7	14	.333	33	29	2	0	0	170^1	193	9	81	102	14.7	4.23	85	.294	.376	6	.125	1	-12	-12	-1	-1.0
1983 Cin-N	4	6	.400	33	7	0	0	1	89^2	103	8	43	53	14.8	5.82	65	.286	.364	3	.150	1	-22	-20	-1	-1.9
1984 Bos-A	2	3	.400	13	4	0	0	0	43^2	57	6	18	28	15.7	5.56	75	.315	.380	0	—	0	-8	-7	-0	-0.6
Total 7	55	56	.495	195	144	21	5	2	970	997	82	457	518	13.7	4.54	86	.269	.351	9	.132	2	-73	-69	-5	-6.5

■ DENNY GALEHOUSE
Galehouse, Dennis Ward b: 12/7/11, Marshallville, Ohio BR/TR, 6'1", 195 lbs. Deb: 4/30/34

YEAR TM/L	W	L	PCT	G	GS	CG	SH	SV	IP	H	HR	BB	SO	RAT	ERA	ERA+	OAV	OOB	BH	AVG	PB	PR	/A	PD	TPI
1934 Cle-A	0	0	—	1	0	0	0	0	1	2	0	1	0	27.0	18.00	25	.500	.600	0	—	0	-2	-1	0	0.0
1935 Cle-A	1	0	1.000	5	1	1	0	0	13	16	1	9	8	18.0	9.00	50	.314	.426	1	.250	-0	-7	-6	0	-0.5
1936 Cle-A	8	7	.533	36	15	5	0	1	148^1	161	5	68	71	14.0	4.85	104	.280	.358	8	.170	-0	3	3	-2	0.1
1937 Cle-A	9	14	.391	36	29	7	0	3	200^2	238	11	83	76	14.4	4.57	101	.302	.369	15	.208	-1	1	1	1	0.0
1938 Cle-A	7	8	.467	36	12	5	1	3	114	119	12	65	66	14.6	4.34	107	.275	.371	6	.154	-1	6	4	0	0.2
1939 Bos-A	9	10	.474	30	18	6	1	0	146^2	160	6	52	68	13.1	4.54	104	.276	.337	3	.064	-3	1	3	0	0.0
1940 Bos-A	6	6	.500	25	20	5	0	0	120	155	10	41	53	14.7	5.18	87	.313	.366	3	.077	-4	-11	-9	-1	-1.0
1941 StL-A	9	10	.474	30	24	11	2	0	190^1	183	10	68	61	12.1	3.64	118	.253	.320	13	.191	-0	11	14	1	1.5
1942 StL-A	12	12	.500	32	28	12	3	1	192^1	193	5	79	75	12.9	3.60	103	.262	.337	14	.194	1	1	2	1	0.4
1943 StL-A	11	11	.500	31	28	14	2	1	224	217	8	74	114	11.7	2.77	120	.255	.315	9	.125	-3	13	14	-3	0.8
1944 *StL-A	9	10	.474	24	19	6	2	0	153	162	6	44	80	12.2	3.12	115	.266	.316	4	.063	-4	5	8	-2	0.2
1946 StL-A	8	12	.400	30	24	11	2	0	180	194	9	52	90	12.3	3.65	102	.273	.322	5	.091	-4	-3	2	-3	-0.3
1947 StL-A	1	3	.250	9	4	0	0	0	32^1	42	3	16	11	16.1	6.12	63	.311	.384	0	.000	-1	-9	-8	0	-0.8
Bos-A	11	7	.611	21	21	11	3	0	149	150	7	34	38	11.1	3.32	117	.260	.301	5	.096	-4	6	9	-0	0.5
Yr	12	10	.545	30	25	11	3	0	181^1	192	10	50	49	12.0	3.82	102	.269	.317	2	.033	-5	-2	1	-0	-0.3
1948 Bos-A	8	8	.500	27	15	6	1	3	137^1	152	10	46	38	13.1	4.00	110	.282	.341	7	.167	-0	4	6	-1	0.5
1949 Bos-A	0	0	—	2	0	0	0	0	2	4	1	3	0	31.5	13.50	32	.400	.538	0	—	0	-2	-2	0	-0.1
Total 15	109	118	.480	375	258	100	17	13	2004	2148	104	735	851	13.0	3.97	105	.275	.338	92	.138	-26	20	40	-7	1.5

■ DOUG GALLAGHER
Gallagher, Douglas Eugene b: 2/21/40, Fremont, Ohio BR/TL, 6'3.5", 195 lbs. Deb: 4/09/62

YEAR TM/L	W	L	PCT	G	GS	CG	SH	SV	IP	H	HR	BB	SO	RAT	ERA	ERA+	OAV	OOB	BH	AVG	PB	PR	/A	PD	TPI
1962 Det-A	0	4	.000	9	2	0	1	0	25	31	2	15	14	16.6	4.68	87	.290	.377	2	.333	1	-2	-2	0	0.0

■ ED GALLAGHER
Gallagher, Edward Michael "Lefty" b: 11/28/10, Dorchester, Mass. d: 12/22/81, Hyannis, Mass. BB/TL, 6'2", 197 lbs. Deb: 7/08/32

YEAR TM/L	W	L	PCT	G	GS	CG	SH	SV	IP	H	HR	BB	SO	RAT	ERA	ERA+	OAV	OOB	BH	AVG	PB	PR	/A	PD	TPI
1932 Bos-A	0	3	.000	9	3	0	0	0	23^2	31	3	28	6	22.1	12.55	36	.323	.479	0	.000	-1	-21	-21	0	-1.7

■ BILL GALLAGHER
Gallagher, William John b: Philadelphia, Pa. TL, Deb: 5/02/1883 ♦

YEAR TM/L	W	L	PCT	G	GS	CG	SH	SV	IP	H	HR	BB	SO	RAT	ERA	ERA+	OAV	OOB	BH	AVG	PB	PR	/A	PD	TPI
1883 Bal-a	0	5	.000	7	5	4	0	0	51^2	79	0	6	19	14.8	5.40	64	.330	.346	10	.164	-1	-12	-11	-1	-0.8
1884 Phi-U	1	2	.333	3	3	3	0	0	25	32	3	4	12	13.0	3.24	89	.291	.316	1	.091	-1	-1	-1	0	-0.1
Total 2	1	7	.125	10	8	7	0	0	76^2	111	3	10	31	14.2	4.70	70	.318	.337	11	.138	-2	-13	-12	-1	-0.9

■ BERT GALLIA
Gallia, Melvin Allys b: 10/14/1891, Beeville, Tex. d: 3/19/76, Devine, Tex. BR/TR, 6', 165 lbs. Deb: 9/04/12

YEAR TM/L	W	L	PCT	G	GS	CG	SH	SV	IP	H	HR	BB	SO	RAT	ERA	ERA+	OAV	OOB	BH	AVG	PB	PR	/A	PD	TPI
1912 Was-A	0	0	—	2	0	0	0	0	2	0	0	3	0	13.5	0.00	—	.000	.333	0	—	0	1	1	0	0.1
1913 Was-A	1	5	.167	31	4	0	0	3	96	85	2	46	46	12.9	4.13	72	.222	.317	2	.087	-2	-13	-13	2	-1.1
1914 Was-A	0	0	—	2	0	0	0	0	6	3	0	4	4	10.5	4.50	62	.120	.241	0	—	-0	-1	-1	-0	-0.1
1915 Was-A	17	11	.607	43	29	14	3	1	259^2	220	2	64	130	10.0	2.29	128	.234	.286	14	.165	-2	19	18	-1	1.7
1916 Was-A	17	12	.586	49	31	13	1	2	283^2	278	3	99	120	12.2	2.76	100	.266	.334	18	.194	1	2	-0	-3	-0.2
1917 Was-A	9	13	.409	42	23	9	1	1	207^2	191	0	93	84	12.5	2.99	88	.258	.344	14	.209	2	-7	-8	-0	-0.7
1918 StL-A	8	6	.571	19	17	10	1	0	124	126	1	61	60	14.0	3.48	79	.268	.359	6	.130	-3	-10	-10	0	-1.3
1919 StL-A	12	14	.462	34	25	14	1	1	222^1	220	10	92	83	13.0	3.60	92	.264	.343	11	.153	-2	-9	-7	2	-0.6
1920 StL-A	0	1	.000	2	1	0	0	0	3^2	8	0	3	0	27.0	7.36	53	.400	.478	0	.000	-0	-1	-1	0	-0.1

YEAR	TM/L	W	L	PCT	G	GS	CG	SH	SV	IP	H	HR	BB	SO	RAT	ERA	ERA+	OAV	OOB	BH	AVG	PB	PR	/A	PD	TPI
	Phi-N	2	6	.250	18	5	1	0	2	72	79	2	29	35	13.9	4.50	76	.287	.362	4	.174	-1	-11	-9	-1	-1.0
Total	9	66	68	.493	242	135	61	7	10	1277	1210	21	494	550	12.3	3.14	93	.256	.331	69	.167	-7	-31	-31	-2	-3.3

■ BILL GALLIVAN
Gallivan, Philip Joseph　b: 5/29/07, Seattle, Wash.　d: 11/24/69, St.Paul, Minn.　BR/TR, 6', 170 lbs.　Deb: 4/21/31

YEAR	TM/L	W	L	PCT	G	GS	CG	SH	SV	IP	H	HR	BB	SO	RAT	ERA	ERA+	OAV	OOB	BH	AVG	PB	PR	/A	PD	TPI
1931	Bro-N	0	1	.000	6	1	0	0	0	15^1	23	2	7	1	17.6	5.28	72	.354	.417	0	.000	-0	-2	-3	1	-0.1
1932	Chi-A	1	3	.250	13	3	1	0	0	33^1	49	4	24	12	20.0	7.56	57	.338	.435	3	.375	1	-11	-12	-0	-0.9
1934	Chi-A	4	7	.364	35	7	3	0	1	126^2	155	14	64	55	15.6	5.61	84	.295	.373	9	.225	1	-16	-12	-1	-1.1
Total	3	5	11	.313	54	11	4	0	1	175^1	227	20	95	68	16.6	5.95	77	.309	.389	12	.235	1	-30	-27	-0	-2.1

■ BALVINO GALVEZ
Galvez, Balvino (Jerez)　b: 3/31/64, San Pedro De Macoris, D.R.　BR/TR, 6', 170 lbs.　Deb: 5/07/86

YEAR	TM/L	W	L	PCT	G	GS	CG	SH	SV	IP	H	HR	BB	SO	RAT	ERA	ERA+	OAV	OOB	BH	AVG	PB	PR	/A	PD	TPI
1986	LA-N	0	1	.000	10	0	0	0	0	20^2	19	3	12	11	13.5	3.92	88	.241	.341	0	.000	-0	-0	-1	0	0.0

■ JIM GALVIN
Galvin, James Francis "Pud", "Gentle Jeems" or "The Little Steam Engine"
b: 12/25/1856, St.Louis, Mo.　d: 3/7/02, Pittsburgh, Pa.　BR/TR, 5'8", 190 lbs.　Deb: 5/22/1875　MUH

YEAR	TM/L	W	L	PCT	G	GS	CG	SH	SV	IP	H	HR	BB	SO	RAT	ERA	ERA+	OAV	OOB	BH	AVG	PB	PR	/A	PD	TPI
1875	StL-n	4	2	.667	8	7	7	1	1	62	53	0	1		7.8	*2.18*	102	.209	.213	6	.128	-1	2	0		-0.1
1879	Buf-N	37	27	.578	66	66	65	6	0	593	585	3	31	136	9.3	2.28	115	.241	.251	66	.249	5	14	22	3	3.0
1880	Buf-N	20	35	.364	58	54	46	5	0	458^2	528	5	32	128	11.0	2.71	91	.274	.286	51	.212	-4	-17	-13	1	-1.3
1881	Buf-N	28	24	.538	56	53	48	5	0	474	546	4	46	136	11.2	2.37	117	.277	.293	50	.212	-1	21	21	7	2.6
1882	Buf-N	28	23	.549	52	51	48	3	0	445^1	476	8	40	162	10.4	3.17	92	.258	.274	44	.214	-5	-14	-12	1	-1.4
1883	Buf-N	46	29	.613	**76**	75	**72**	**5**	0	**656^1**	676	9	50	279	10.0	2.72	117	.251	.264	71	.220	-4	31	34	0	2.6
1884	Buf-N	46	22	.676	72	72	71	**12**	0	636^1	566	23	63	369	8.9	1.99	157	.225	.244	49	.179	-14	70	81	7	7.0
1885	Buf-N	13	19	.406	33	32	31	3	1	284	356	8	37	93	12.5	4.09	72	.293	.314	23	.189	-2	-40	-35	4	-2.8
	Pit-a	3	7	.300	11	11	9	0	0	88^1	97	2	7	27	10.6	3.67	88	.267	.281	4	.105	-3	-4	-4	-0	-0.6
1886	Pit-a	29	21	.580	50	50	49	2	0	434^2	457	3	75	72	11.0	2.67	127	.258	.288	49	.253	2	38	35	4	3.7
1887	Pit-N	28	21	.571	49	48	47	2	0	440^2	490	6	67	76	11.4	3.29	117	.274	.300	41	.212	-2	37	28	8	2.9
1888	Pit-N	23	25	.479	50	50	49	6	0	437^1	446	9	53	107	10.3	2.63	101	.255	.277	25	.143	-5	10	1	4	0.0
1889	Pit-N	23	16	.590	41	40	38	4	0	341	392	19	78	77	12.4	4.17	90	.279	.317	28	.187	-0	-6	-16	2	-1.2
1890	Pit-P	12	13	.480	26	25	23	1	0	217	275	3	49	35	13.4	4.35	90	.296	.331	20	.206	-1	-3	-11	4	-0.6
1891	Pit-N	14	14	.500	33	31	23	2	0	246^2	256	10	62	46	11.6	2.88	114	.258	.301	18	.165	-5	13	11	1	0.7
1892	Pit-N	5	6	.455	12	12	10	0	0	96	104	0	28	29	12.4	2.63	126	.265	.314	5	.122	-2	7	7	-0	0.4
	StL-N	5	6	.455	12	12	10	0	0	92	102	4	26	27	12.5	3.23	99	.270	.317	2	.051	-5	1	-0	-2	-0.5
	Yr	10	12	.455	24	24	20	0	0	188	206	4	54	56	12.4	2.92	111	.268	.316	3	.038	-7	8	7	-2	-0.1
Total	14	360	308	.539	697	682	639	56	1	5941^1	6352	122	744	1799	10.7	2.87	108	.261	.283	546	.202	-46	157	158	44	14.5

■ LOU GALVIN
Galvin, Louis J.　b: 4/1862, St.Paul, Minn.　d: 6/17/1895,　Deb: 10/01/1884

YEAR	TM/L	W	L	PCT	G	GS	CG	SH	SV	IP	H	HR	BB	SO	RAT	ERA	ERA+	OAV	OOB	BH	AVG	PB	PR	/A	PD	TPI
1884	StP-U	0	2	.000	3	3	3	0	0	25	21	0	10	17	11.2	2.88	57	.213	.285	2	.222	0	0	-3	-1	-0.3

■ BOB GAMBLE
Gamble, Robert J.　b: 2/1867, Hazelton, Pa.　5'10", 155 lbs.　Deb: 5/02/1888

YEAR	TM/L	W	L	PCT	G	GS	CG	SH	SV	IP	H	HR	BB	SO	RAT	ERA	ERA+	OAV	OOB	BH	AVG	PB	PR	/A	PD	TPI
1888	Phi-a	0	1	.000	1	1	1	0	0	9	10	0	3	2	13.0	8.00	37	.271	.326	1	.333	0	-5	-5	0	-0.3

■ GUSSIE GANNON
Gannon, James Edward　b: 11/26/1873, Erie, Pa.　d: 4/12/66, Erie, Pa.　5'11", 154 lbs.　Deb: 6/15/1895

YEAR	TM/L	W	L	PCT	G	GS	CG	SH	SV	IP	H	HR	BB	SO	RAT	ERA	ERA+	OAV	OOB	BH	AVG	PB	PR	/A	PD	TPI
1895	Pit-N	0	0	—	1	0	0	0	0	5	7	0	2	0	16.2	1.80	251	.326	.383	0	.000	-0	2	2	-0	0.1

■ BILL GANNON
Gannon, William G.　b: 1876, New Haven, Conn.　d: 4/26/27, Fort Worth, Tex.　Deb: 8/28/1898 ♦

YEAR	TM/L	W	L	PCT	G	GS	CG	SH	SV	IP	H	HR	BB	SO	RAT	ERA	ERA+	OAV	OOB	BH	AVG	PB	PR	/A	PD	TPI
1898	StL-N	0	1	.000	1	1	1	0	0	9	13	0	5	2	18.0	11.00	34	.335	.411	0	.000	-1	-7	-7	0	-0.4

■ JIM GANTNER
Gantner, James Elmer　b: 1/5/53, Fond Du Lac, Wis.　BL/TR, 6', 180 lbs.　Deb: 9/03/76 ♦

YEAR	TM/L	W	L	PCT	G	GS	CG	SH	SV	IP	H	HR	BB	SO	RAT	ERA	ERA+	OAV	OOB	BH	AVG	PB	PR	/A	PD	TPI
1979	Mil-A	0	0	—	1	0	0	0	0	2	2	0	1	0	18.0	0.00		.400	.400	59	.284	1	0	0	0	0.0

■ GENE GARBER
Garber, Henry Eugene　b: 11/13/47, Lancaster, Pa.　BR/TR, 5'10", 175 lbs.　Deb: 6/17/69

YEAR	TM/L	W	L	PCT	G	GS	CG	SH	SV	IP	H	HR	BB	SO	RAT	ERA	ERA+	OAV	OOB	BH	AVG	PB	PR	/A	PD	TPI
1969	Pit-N	0	0	—	2	0	0	0	0	5	6	3	1	3	12.6	5.40	65	.333	.368	0	.000	-0	-1	-1	-0	0.0
1970	Pit-N	0	3	.000	14	0	0	0	0	22^1	22	4	10	7	13.7	5.24	74	.275	.370	2	.667	1	-3	-3	1	0.0
1972	Pit-N	0	0	—	4	0	0	0	0	6^1	7	3	3	4	14.2	7.11	47	.269	.345	0	.000	-0	-3	-3	-0	-0.2
1973	KC-A	9	9	.500	48	8	4	0	11	152^2	164	14	49	60	12.7	4.24	97	.283	.341	0	—	0	-7	-2	1	0.0
1974	KC-A	1	2	.333	17	0	0	0	1	28	35	3	13	14	15.8	4.82	79	.313	.389	0	—	0	-4	-3	-0	-0.2
	Phi-N	4	0	1.000	34	0	0	0	4	48	39	1	31	27	13.3	2.06	183	.236	.360	0	.000	-0	8	9	0	1.0
1975	Phi-N	10	12	.455	71	0	0	0	14	104	104	13	27	69	10.9	3.60	104	.254	.304	2	.167	-0	2	0	0	1.0
1976	*Phi-N	9	3	.750	59	0	0	0	11	92^2	78	4	30	92	10.9	2.82	126	.228	.298	2	.286	1	7	8	1	1.0
1977	*Phi-N	8	6	.571	64	0	0	0	19	103^1	82	6	23	78	9.3	2.35	170	.220	.270	0	.000	-1	18	19	2	2.0
1978	Phi-N	2	1	.667	22	0	0	0	3	38^2	26	1	11	24	9.3	1.40	256	.191	.267	0	.000	-0	9	9	0	1.0
	Atl-N	4	4	.500	43	0	0	0	22	78^1	58	11	13	61	8.4	2.53	160	.204	.244	1	.091	-1	9	13	1	1.4
	Yr	6	5	.545	65	0	0	0	25	117	84	12	24	85	8.5	2.15	181	.199	.245	1	.071	-1	18	**23**	1	2.4
1979	Atl-N	6	16	.273	68	0	0	0	25	106	121	10	24	56	12.7	4.33	94	.283	.328	3	.300	1	-7	-3	1	0.0
1980	Atl-N	5	5	.500	68	0	0	0	7	82^1	95	6	24	51	13.0	3.83	98	.288	.336	1	.500	0	-2	-1	2	0.1
1981	Atl-N	4	6	.400	35	0	0	0	2	58^2	49	2	20	34	10.6	2.61	137	.214	.277	0	.000	-1	6	6	2	0.8
1982	*Atl-N	8	10	.444	69	0	0	0	30	119^1	100	4	32	68	10.1	2.34	160	.231	.288	2	.133	0	17	18	2	2.2
1983	Atl-N	4	5	.444	43	0	0	0	9	60^2	72	8	23	45	14.4	4.60	84	.300	.366	0	.000	0	-7	-5	2	-0.2
1984	Atl-N	3	6	.333	62	0	0	0	11	106	103	7	24	55	11.0	3.06	126	.254	.299	2	.143	-0	6	9	1	0.4
1985	Atl-N	6	6	.500	59	0	0	0	1	97^1	98	8	25	66	11.6	3.61	107	.263	.313	1	.200	0	-0	3	1	0.4
1986	Atl-N	5	5	.500	61	0	0	0	24	78	76	3	20	56	11.2	2.54	157	.260	.310	1	.167	0	10	12	1	1.4
1987	Atl-N	8	10	.444	49	0	0	0	10	69^2	87	7	28	48	15.1	4.41	98	.311	.375	0	.000	-0	-3	-1	2	0.1
	KC-A	0	0	—	13	0	0	0	8	14^1	13	1	1	3	9.4	2.51	181	.245	.273	0	—	0	3	3	0	0.3
1988	KC-A	0	4	.000	26	0	0	0	6	32^2	29	4	13	20	12.1	3.58	111	.238	.321	0	—	0	1	1	0	0.2
Total	19	96	113	.459	931	9	4	0	218	1510	1464	123	445	940	11.6	3.34	116	.257	.314	17	.148	-0	59	92	19	12.4

■ BOB GARBER
Garber, Robert Mitchell　b: 9/10/28, Hunker, Pa.　BR/TR, 6'1", 190 lbs.　Deb: 5/13/56

YEAR	TM/L	W	L	PCT	G	GS	CG	SH	SV	IP	H	HR	BB	SO	RAT	ERA	ERA+	OAV	OOB	BH	AVG	PB	PR	/A	PD	TPI
1956	Pit-N	0	0	—	2	0	0	0	0	4	3	1	3	3	13.5	2.25	168	.200	.333	0	—	0	1	1	-0	0.0

■ RICH GARCES
Garces, Richard Aron　b: 5/18/71, Maracay, Venez.　BR/TR, 6', 187 lbs.　Deb: 9/18/90

YEAR	TM/L	W	L	PCT	G	GS	CG	SH	SV	IP	H	HR	BB	SO	RAT	ERA	ERA+	OAV	OOB	BH	AVG	PB	PR	/A	PD	TPI
1990	Min-A	0	0	—	5	0	0	0	2	5^2	4	0	4	1	12.7	1.59	264	.200	.333	0	—	0	1	2	0	0.2

■ MIKE GARCIA
Garcia, Edward Miguel "The Big Bear"　b: 11/17/23, San Gabriel, Cal.　d: 1/13/86, Fairview Park, O.　BR/TR, 6'1", 195 lbs.　Deb: 10/03/48

YEAR	TM/L	W	L	PCT	G	GS	CG	SH	SV	IP	H	HR	BB	SO	RAT	ERA	ERA+	OAV	OOB	BH	AVG	PB	PR	/A	PD	TPI
1948	Cle-A	0	0	—	1	0	0	0	0	2	3	0	1	1	13.5	0.00		.333	.333	0	—	0	1	1	0	0.1
1949	Cle-A	14	5	.737	41	20	8	5	2	175^2	154	6	60	94	11.1	**2.36**	169	.241	.308	12	.235	3	36	32	1	3.6
1950	Cle-A	11	11	.500	33	29	11	0	0	184	191	15	74	76	13.0	3.86	112	.266	.334	13	.200	-0	15	10	2	1.0
1951	Cle-A	20	13	.606	47	30	15	1	6	254	239	10	82	118	11.5	3.15	120	.246	.307	18	.212	1	27	18	1	1.9
1952	Cle-A	22	11	.667	46	36	19	**6**	4	292^1	284	9	87	143	11.6	2.37	141	.253	.310	13	.137	-1	42	32	2	3.3
1953	Cle-A	18	9	.667	38	35	21	3	0	271^2	260	18	81	134	11.4	3.25	116	.250	.307	24	.250	4	23	15	-1	1.8
1954	*Cle-A	19	8	.704	45	34	13	**5**	5	258^2	220	6	71	129	**10.2**	2.64	139	.229	**.284**	11	.136	-2	**31**	30	0	2.9
1955	Cle-A	11	13	.458	38	31	6	2	3	210^2	230	17	56	120	12.3	4.02	99	.278	.327	15	.217	2	-1	-1	-0	0.0
1956	Cle-A	11	12	.478	35	30	8	4	0	197^2	213	16	74	119	13.3	3.78	111	.272	.339	7	.115	-3	8	9	-0	0.6
1957	Cle-A	12	8	.600	38	27	9	1	0	211^1	221	14	73	110	12.8	3.75	99	.269	.333	12	.160	-1	1	-1	-2	-0.3
1958	Cle-A	0	1	.000	6	1	0	0	0	18	22	7	9	15	25.9	9.00	41	.395	.500	0	.000	-0	-5	-5	0	-0.4
1959	Cle-A	3	6	.333	29	8	1	0	1	72	72	4	31	42	14.9	4.00	92	.265	.340	1	.071	-1	-1	-3	0	-0.3
1960	Chi-A	0	0	—	15	0	0	0	2	17^2	23	3	10	8	16.8	4.58	82	.338	.423	1	.333	0	-1	-2	0	0.0
1961	Was-A	0	1	.000	16	0	0	0	0	19	23	1	13	14	17.5	4.74	85	.287	.394	0	—	0	-2	-2	-1	-0.1

YEAR TM/L	W	L	PCT	G	GS	CG	SH	SV	IP	H	HR	BB	SO	RAT	ERA	ERA+	OAV	OOB	BH	AVG	PB	PR	/A	PD	TPI
Total 14	142	97	.594	428	281	111	27	23	2174^2	2148	122	719	1117	12.0	3.27	117	.257	.319	127	.182	1	174	134	2	14.1

■ MIGUEL GARCIA
Garcia, Miguel Angel (Silfontes) b: 4/19/66, Caracas, Venez. BL/TL, 5'11", 173 lbs. Deb: 4/30/87

YEAR TM/L	W	L	PCT	G	GS	CG	SH	SV	IP	H	HR	BB	SO	RAT	ERA	ERA+	OAV	OOB	BH	AVG	PB	PR	/A	PD	TPI
1987 Cal-A	0	0	—	1	0	0	0	0	1^2	3	0	3	0	32.4	16.20	27	.375	.545	0	—	0	-2	-2	0	-0.1
Pit-N	0	0	—	1	0	0	0	0	0^2	0	0	0	0	0.00	—	.000	.000	0	—	0	0	0	0	0.0
1988 Pit-N	0	0	—	1	0	0	0	0	2	3	1	2	2	27.0	4.50	76	.375	.545	0	—	0	-0	-0	0	0.0
1989 Pit-N	0	2	.000	11	0	0	0	0	16	25	2	7	9	18.0	8.44	40	.357	.416	1	1.000	0	-9	-9	0	-0.8
Total 3	0	2	.000	14	0	0	0	0	20^1	31	3	12	11	19.5	8.41	41	.352	.436	1	1.000	0	-11	-11	0	-0.9

■ RALPH GARCIA
Garcia, Ralph b: 12/14/48, Los Angeles, Cal. BR/TR, 6', 195 lbs. Deb: 9/26/72

YEAR TM/L	W	L	PCT	G	GS	CG	SH	SV	IP	H	HR	BB	SO	RAT	ERA	ERA+	OAV	OOB	BH	AVG	PB	PR	/A	PD	TPI
1972 SD-N	0	0	—	3	0	0	0	0	5	4	0	3	3	12.6	1.80	183	.211	.318	0	—	0	1	1	0	0.1
1974 SD-N	0	0	—	8	0	0	0	0	10^1	15	1	7	9	19.2	6.10	58	.357	.449	0	—	0	-3	-3	0	-0.2
Total 2	0	0	—	11	0	0	0	0	15^1	19	1	10	12	17.0	4.70	74	.311	.408	0	—	0	-2	-2	0	-0.1

■ RAMON GARCIA
Garcia, Ramon (Garcia) b: 3/5/24, LaEsperanza, Cuba BR/TR, 5'10", 170 lbs. Deb: 4/19/48

YEAR TM/L	W	L	PCT	G	GS	CG	SH	SV	IP	H	HR	BB	SO	RAT	ERA	ERA+	OAV	OOB	BH	AVG	PB	PR	/A	PD	TPI
1948 Was-A	0	0	—	4	0	0	0	0	3^2	11	0	4	2	39.3	17.18	25	.524	.615	1	1.000	0	-5	-5	0	-0.3

■ ART GARDINER
Gardiner, Arthur Cecil b: 12/26/1899, Brooklyn, N.Y. d: 10/21/54, Copiaque, N.Y. BR/TR, Deb: 9/25/23

YEAR TM/L	W	L	PCT	G	GS	CG	SH	SV	IP	H	HR	BB	SO	RAT	ERA	ERA+	OAV	OOB	BH	AVG	PB	PR	/A	PD	TPI
1923 Phi-N	0	0	—	1	0	0	0	0	0	1	0	1	0	—	—	—	1.000	1.000	0	—	0	0	0	0	0.0

■ MIKE GARDINER
Gardiner, Michael James b: 10/19/65, Sarnia, Ont., Can. BB/TR, 6', 185 lbs. Deb: 9/08/90

YEAR TM/L	W	L	PCT	G	GS	CG	SH	SV	IP	H	HR	BB	SO	RAT	ERA	ERA+	OAV	OOB	BH	AVG	PB	PR	/A	PD	TPI
1990 Sea-A	0	2	.000	5	3	0	0	0	12^2	22	1	5	6	20.6	10.66	37	.379	.446	0	—	0	-10	-9	0	-0.8

■ GID GARDNER
Gardner, Frank Washington b: 6/9/1859, Attleboro, Mass. d: 8/1/14, Cambridge, Mass. Deb: 8/23/1879 ♦

YEAR TM/L	W	L	PCT	G	GS	CG	SH	SV	IP	H	HR	BB	SO	RAT	ERA	ERA+	OAV	OOB	BH	AVG	PB	PR	/A	PD	TPI
1879 Tro-N	0	2	.000	2	2	2	0	0	14	27	0	3	3	17.4	5.79	43	.383	.383	1	.167	-0	-5	-5	-0	-0.4
1880 Cle-N	1	8	.111	9	9	9	0	0	77	80	2	20	21	11.7	2.57	91	.255	.299	6	.188	-0	-2	-2	0	-0.1
1883 Bal-a	1	0	1.000	2	0	0	0	0	7	9	1	1	2	12.9	5.14	68	.293	.315	44	.273	1	-1	-1	0	0.0
1884 CP-U	0	1	.000	1	1	0	0	0	6	10	0	1	4	16.5	6.00	50	.349	.371	38	.255	0	-2	-2	0	-0.1
1885 Bal-a	0	1	.000	1	1	1	0	0	9	16	2	6	3	22.0	10.00	33	.371	.448	37	.218	0	-7	-7	0	-0.4
Total 5	2	12	.143	15	13	12	0	0	113	142	5	28	33	13.5	3.90	65	.291	.330	178	.233	0	-17	-17	0	-1.0

■ FRED GARDNER
Gardner, Frederick b: Palmer, Mass. Deb: 8/09/1887

YEAR TM/L	W	L	PCT	G	GS	CG	SH	SV	IP	H	HR	BB	SO	RAT	ERA	ERA+	OAV	OOB	BH	AVG	PB	PR	/A	PD	TPI
1887 Bal-a	0	1	.000	3	2	1	0	0	13	23	0	10	3	22.8	11.08	37	.372	.459	3	.273	0	-10	-10	-0	-0.7

■ HARRY GARDNER
Gardner, Harry Ray b: 6/1/1887, Quincy, Mich. d: 8/2/61, Canby, Ore. TR, 6'2", 180 lbs. Deb: 4/17/11

YEAR TM/L	W	L	PCT	G	GS	CG	SH	SV	IP	H	HR	BB	SO	RAT	ERA	ERA+	OAV	OOB	BH	AVG	PB	PR	/A	PD	TPI
1911 Pit-N	1	1	.500	13	3	2	0	2	42	39	2	20	24	13.1	4.50	76	.244	.335	3	.214	0	-5	-5	-1	-0.5
1912 Pit-N	0	0	—	1	0	0	0	0	0^1	3	0	1	0	108.0	0.00	—	.500	.571	0	—	0	0	0	0	0.0
Total 2	1	1	.500	14	3	2	0	2	42^1	42	2	21	24	13.8	4.46	77	.253	.344	3	.214	0	-5	-5	-1	-0.5

■ JIM GARDNER
Gardner, James Anderson b: 10/4/1874, Pittsburgh, Pa. d: 4/24/05, Pittsburgh, Pa. TR, Deb: 6/20/1895

YEAR TM/L	W	L	PCT	G	GS	CG	SH	SV	IP	H	HR	BB	SO	RAT	ERA	ERA+	OAV	OOB	BH	AVG	PB	PR	/A	PD	TPI
1895 Pit-N	8	2	.800	11	10	8	0	0	85^1	99	1	27	31	13.3	2.64	171	.286	.337	9	.265	1	20	18	-1	1.5
1897 Pit-N	5	5	.500	14	11	8	0	0	95^1	115	4	32	35	13.9	5.19	81	.296	.349	12	.158	-1	-9	-11	-0	-0.9
1898 Pit-N	10	13	.435	25	22	19	1	0	185^1	179	3	48	41	11.0	3.21	111	.252	.299	14	.154	-1	8	7	-2	0.3
1899 Pit-N	1	0	1.000	6	3	0	0	0	32^1	52	1	13	2	18.1	7.52	51	.361	.414	3	.231	0	-13	-13	-1	-1.1
1902 Chi-N	1	2	.333	3	3	2	0	0	25	23	0	10	6	11.9	2.88	94	.244	.317	2	.200	0	-0	-0	0	-0.2
Total 5	25	22	.532	59	49	37	1	0	423^1	468	9	130	115	12.7	3.85	101	.278	.330	40	.179	-1	6	1	-4	-0.2

■ MARK GARDNER
Gardner, Mark Allan b: 3/1/62, Los Angeles, Cal. BR/TR, 6'1", 190 lbs. Deb: 5/16/89

YEAR TM/L	W	L	PCT	G	GS	CG	SH	SV	IP	H	HR	BB	SO	RAT	ERA	ERA+	OAV	OOB	BH	AVG	PB	PR	/A	PD	TPI
1989 Mon-N	0	3	.000	7	4	0	0	0	26^1	26	2	11	21	13.3	5.13	69	.250	.333	1	.167	-0	-5	-5	-0	-0.4
1990 Mon-N	7	9	.438	27	26	3	3	0	152^2	129	13	61	135	11.7	3.42	110	.230	.315	5	.114	-1	6	6	1	0.6
Total 2	7	12	.368	34	30	3	3	0	179	155	15	72	156	12.0	3.67	101	.233	.318	6	.120	-1	2	1	1	0.2

■ GLENN GARDNER
Gardner, Miles Glenn b: 1/25/16, Burnsville, N.C. d: 7/7/64, Rochester, N.Y. BR/TR, 5'11", 180 lbs. Deb: 7/21/45

YEAR TM/L	W	L	PCT	G	GS	CG	SH	SV	IP	H	HR	BB	SO	RAT	ERA	ERA+	OAV	OOB	BH	AVG	PB	PR	/A	PD	TPI
1945 StL-N	3	1	.750	17	4	2	1	1	54^2	50	2	27	20	12.7	3.29	114	.242	.329	7	.333	2	3	3	-0	0.4

■ ROB GARDNER
Gardner, Richard Frank b: 12/19/44, Binghamton, N.Y. BR/TL, 6'1", 176 lbs. Deb: 9/01/65

YEAR TM/L	W	L	PCT	G	GS	CG	SH	SV	IP	H	HR	BB	SO	RAT	ERA	ERA+	OAV	OOB	BH	AVG	PB	PR	/A	PD	TPI
1965 NY-N	0	2	.000	5	4	0	0	0	28	23	4	7	19	9.6	3.21	110	.217	.265	0	.000	-1	1	1	0	0.0
1966 NY-N	4	8	.333	41	17	3	0	1	133^2	147	15	64	74	14.4	5.12	71	.285	.367	7	.171	-0	-22	-22	0	-2.2
1967 Chi-N	0	2	.000	18	5	0	0	0	31^2	33	2	6	16	11.1	3.98	89	.260	.293	0	.000	-0	-2	-2	0	-0.1
1968 Cle-A	0	0	—	5	0	0	0	0	2^2	5	0	2	6	23.6	6.75	44	.417	.500	0	—	0	-1	-1	0	0.0
1970 NY-A	1	0	1.000	1	1	0	0	0	7^1	8	2	4	6	14.7	4.91	72	.276	.364	1	.333	1	-1	-1	0	0.0
1971 Oak-A	0	0	—	4	1	0	0	0	7^2	8	1	3	5	12.9	2.35	142	.267	.333	1	.500	0	1	1	0	0.2
NY-A	0	0	—	2	0	0	0	0	3	3	0	2	2	15.0	3.00	108	.273	.385	0	—	0	-0	-0	0	0.0
Yr	0	0	—	6	1	0	0	0	10^2	11	1	5	7	13.5	2.53	131	.268	.348	0	.000	0	1	1	0	0.2
1972 NY-A	8	5	.615	20	14	1	0	0	97	91	9	28	58	11.0	3.06	96	.243	.296	3	.107	-1	-0	-1	-1	-0.3
1973 Oak-A	0	0	—	3	0	0	0	0	7^1	10	2	4	2	17.2	4.91	72	.370	.452	0	—	0	-1	-1	-0	0.0
Mil-A	1	1	.500	10	0	0	0	1	12^2	17	0	13	5	22.0	9.95	38	.327	.470	0	—	0	-9	-9	0	-0.7
Yr	1	1	.500	13	0	0	0	1	20	27	2	17	7	20.2	8.10	45	.342	.464	0	—	0	-10	-10	0	-0.7
Total 8	14	18	.438	109	42	4	0	2	331	345	35	133	193	13.1	4.35	78	.269	.339	12	.138	-2	-34	-35	-0	-3.1

■ WES GARDNER
Gardner, Wesley Brian b: 4/29/61, Benton, Ark. BR/TR, 6'4", 197 lbs. Deb: 7/29/84

YEAR TM/L	W	L	PCT	G	GS	CG	SH	SV	IP	H	HR	BB	SO	RAT	ERA	ERA+	OAV	OOB	BH	AVG	PB	PR	/A	PD	TPI
1984 NY-N	1	1	.500	21	0	0	0	1	25^1	34	4	19	14	14.9	6.39	55	.321	.368	0	.000	-0	-8	-8	-0	-0.8
1985 NY-N	0	2	.000	9	0	0	0	0	12	18	1	8	11	19.5	5.25	66	.375	.464	0	—	0	-2	-2	0	-0.1
1986 Bos-A	0	0	—	1	0	0	0	0	1	1	0	0	1	9.0	9.00	46	.333	.333	0	—	0	-1	-1	0	0.0
1987 Bos-A	3	6	.333	49	1	0	0	10	89^2	98	17	42	70	14.3	5.42	84	.279	.359	0	—	0	-10	-9	-1	-0.9
1988 *Bos-A	8	6	.571	36	18	1	0	2	149	119	17	64	106	11.2	3.50	117	.220	.305	0	—	0	8	10	-0	1.0
1989 Bos-A	3	7	.300	22	16	0	0	0	86	97	10	47	81	15.2	5.97	69	.287	.376	0	—	0	-20	-18	-1	-1.7
1990 Bos-A	3	7	.300	34	9	0	0	0	77^1	77	6	35	58	13.3	4.89	83	.259	.341	0	—	0	-8	-7	-0	-0.6
Total 7	18	29	.383	172	44	1	0	13	440^1	444	51	204	346	13.4	4.84	85	.264	.346	0	.000	-0	-41	-34	-2	-3.1

■ BILL GARFIELD
Garfield, William Milton b: 10/26/1867, Sheffield, Ohio d: 12/16/41, Danville, Ill. BR/TR, 5'11.5", 160 lbs. Deb: 7/10/1889

YEAR TM/L	W	L	PCT	G	GS	CG	SH	SV	IP	H	HR	BB	SO	RAT	ERA	ERA+	OAV	OOB	BH	AVG	PB	PR	/A	PD	TPI
1889 Pit-N	0	2	.000	4	2	2	0	0	29	45	2	17	4	19.2	7.76	48	.343	.419	0	.000	-2	-12	-13	0	-1.0
1890 Cle-N	1	7	.125	9	8	7	0	0	70	91	3	35	16	16.2	4.89	73	.306	.379	4	.154	-1	-10	-10	-0	-0.9
Total 2	1	9	.100	13	10	9	0	0	99	136	5	52	20	17.1	5.73	63	.317	.391	4	.103	-3	-22	-23	0	-1.9

■ BOB GARIBALDI
Garibaldi, Robert Roy b: 3/3/42, Stockton, Cal. BL/TR, 6'4", 210 lbs. Deb: 7/15/62

YEAR TM/L	W	L	PCT	G	GS	CG	SH	SV	IP	H	HR	BB	SO	RAT	ERA	ERA+	OAV	OOB	BH	AVG	PB	PR	/A	PD	TPI
1962 SF-N	0	0	—	9	0	0	0	0	12^1	13	1	5	9	13.1	5.11	74	.265	.333	0	.000	-0	-2	-2	0	-0.1
1963 SF-N	0	1	.000	4	0	0	0	1	8	8	0	4	4	14.6	1.13	284	.276	.382	0	.000	-0	2	2	0	0.2
1966 SF-N	0	0	—	1	0	0	0	0	1	1	0	0	0	9.0	9.00	—	.250	.250	0	—	0	0	0	0	0.0
1969 SF-N	0	1	.000	1	1	0	0	0	5	6	0	2	1	14.4	1.80	194	.316	.381	0	.000	-0	1	1	0	0.1
Total 4	0	2	.000	15	1	0	0	2	26^1	28	1	11	14	13.7	3.08	116	.277	.354	0	.000	-0	2	1	0	0.2

■ LOU GARLAND
Garland, Louis Lyman b: 7/16/05, Archie, Mo. BR/TR, 6'2.5", 200 lbs. Deb: 8/31/31

YEAR TM/L	W	L	PCT	G	GS	CG	SH	SV	IP	H	HR	BB	SO	RAT	ERA	ERA+	OAV	OOB	BH	AVG	PB	PR	/A	PD	TPI
1931 Chi-A	0	2	.000	7	2	0	0	0	16^2	30	2	14	4	24.3	10.26	41	.400	.500	0	.000	-0	-11	-11	1	-0.9

■ WAYNE GARLAND
Garland, Marcus Wayne b: 10/26/50, Nashville, Tenn. BR/TR, 6', 195 lbs. Deb: 9/13/73

YEAR TM/L	W	L	PCT	G	GS	CG	SH	SV	IP	H	HR	BB	SO	RAT	ERA	ERA+	OAV	OOB	BH	AVG	PB	PR	/A	PD	TPI
1973 Bal-A	0	1	.000	4	1	0	0	0	16	14	1	7	10	11.8	3.94	95	.233	.313	0	—	0	-0	-0	0	0.0

YEAR TM/L	W	L	PCT	G	GS	CG	SH	SV	IP	H	HR	BB	SO	RAT	ERA	ERA+	OAV	OOB	BH	AVG	PB	PR	/A	PD	TPI
1974 *Bal-A	5	5	.500	20	6	0	0	1	91	68	5	26	40	9.6	2.97	116	.211	.276	0	—	0	7	5	-1	0.4
1975 Bal-A	2	5	.286	29	1	0	0	4	87¹	80	7	31	46	11.5	3.71	95	.252	.321	0	—	0	1	-2	-0	-0.1
1976 Bal-A	20	7	.741	38	25	14	4	1	232¹	224	10	64	113	11.4	2.67	122	.255	.309	0	—	0	22	15	2	1.9
1977 Cle-A	13	19	.406	38	38	21	1	0	282²	281	23	88	118	11.8	3.60	110	.261	.318	0	—	0	14	11	1	1.1
1978 Cle-A	2	3	.400	6	6	0	0	0	29²	43	6	16	13	18.2	7.89	47	.347	.426	0	—	0	-14	-14	0	-1.1
1979 Cle-A	4	10	.286	18	14	2	0	0	94²	120	11	34	40	14.9	5.23	81	.318	.379	0	—	0	-11	-10	-1	-1.0
1980 Cle-A	6	9	.400	25	20	4	1	0	150¹	163	18	48	55	13.0	4.61	88	.276	.337	0	—	0	-10	-9	-0	-0.8
1981 Cle-A	3	7	.300	12	10	2	1	0	56	89	8	14	15	16.6	5.79	63	.374	.409	0	—	0	-13	-13	-1	-1.2
Total 9	55	66	.455	190	121	43	7	6	1040	1082	89	328	450	12.4	3.89	96	.272	.330	0	—	0	-4	-18	1	-0.8

■ MIKE GARMAN
Garman, Michael Douglas b: 9/16/49, Caldwell, Idaho BR/TR, 6'3", 195 lbs. Deb: 9/22/69

YEAR TM/L	W	L	PCT	G	GS	CG	SH	SV	IP	H	HR	BB	SO	RAT	ERA	ERA+	OAV	OOB	BH	AVG	PB	PR	/A	PD	TPI
1969 Bos-A	1	0	1.000	2	2	0	0	0	12¹	13	0	10	10	16.8	4.38	87	.277	.404	2	.400	1	-1	-1	0	0.0
1971 Bos-A	1	1	.500	3	3	0	0	0	18²	15	3	9	6	12.1	3.86	96	.217	.316	2	.333	0	-1	-0	-1	0.0
1972 Bos-A	0	1	.000	3	1	0	0	0	3¹	4	1	2	1	16.2	10.80	30	.286	.375	0	—	0	-3	-3	-0	-0.2
1973 Bos-A	0	0	—	12	0	0	0	0	22	32	1	15	9	19.2	5.32	76	.352	.443	0	—	0	-4	-3	-0	-0.2
1974 StL-N	7	2	.778	64	0	0	0	6	81²	66	4	27	45	10.5	2.64	135	.227	.297	1	.100	-1	9	8	0	0.8
1975 StL-N	3	8	.273	66	0	0	0	10	79	73	3	48	48	13.9	2.39	157	.245	.352	0	.000	-0	11	12	-1	1.1
1976 Chi-N	2	4	.333	47	2	0	0	1	76¹	79	7	35	37	13.8	4.95	78	.273	.358	0	.000	-1	-12	-9	1	-0.9
1977 *LA-N	4	4	.500	49	0	0	0	12	62²	60	7	22	29	12.1	2.73	140	.254	.323	0	.000	-1	8	8	-0	0.7
1978 LA-N	0	1	.000	10	0	0	0	0	16¹	15	3	3	5	9.9	4.41	80	.259	.295	0	—	0	-2	-2	-0	-0.1
Mon-N	4	6	.400	47	0	0	0	13	61¹	54	5	31	23	12.5	4.40	80	.238	.329	0	.000	-1	-6	-6	-0	-0.6
Yr	4	7	.364	57	0	0	0	13	77²	69	8	34	28	11.9	4.40	80	.242	.323	0	.000	-1	-7	-8	-0	-0.7
Total 9	22	27	.449	303	8	0	0	42	433²	411	34	202	213	12.9	3.63	102	.254	.340	5	.119	-2	-0	4	-1	0.6

■ WILLIE GARONI
Garoni, William b: 7/28/1877, Ft.Lee, N.J. d: 9/9/14, Ft.Lee, N.J. 6'1", 165 lbs. Deb: 9/07/1899

YEAR TM/L	W	L	PCT	G	GS	CG	SH	SV	IP	H	HR	BB	SO	RAT	ERA	ERA+	OAV	OOB	BH	AVG	PB	PR	/A	PD	TPI
1899 NY-N	0	1	.000	3	1	1	0	0	10	12	0	2	2	12.6	4.50	83	.297	.330	0	.000	-1	-1	-1	0	0.0

■ SCOTT GARRELTS
Garrelts, Scott William b: 10/30/61, Urbana, Ill. BR/TR, 6'4", 195 lbs. Deb: 10/02/82

YEAR TM/L	W	L	PCT	G	GS	CG	SH	SV	IP	H	HR	BB	SO	RAT	ERA	ERA+	OAV	OOB	BH	AVG	PB	PR	/A	PD	TPI
1982 SF-N	0	0	—	1	0	0	0	0	2	3	0	2	4	22.5	13.50	27	.333	.455	0	—	0	-2	-2	0	-0.1
1983 SF-N	2	2	.500	5	5	1	1	0	35²	33	4	19	16	13.6	2.52	140	.254	.358	2	.222	0	4	4	0	0.5
1984 SF-N	2	3	.400	21	3	0	0	0	43	45	6	34	32	16.7	5.65	62	.274	.402	1	.100	-0	-10	-10	-1	-1.0
1985 SF-N	9	6	.600	74	0	0	0	13	105²	76	2	58	106	11.7	2.30	149	.198	.308	2	.222	1	15	13	1	1.6
1986 SF-N	13	9	.591	53	18	2	0	10	173²	144	11	74	125	11.4	3.11	113	.231	.314	8	.178	2	12	8	2	1.2
1987 *SF-N	11	7	.611	64	0	0	0	12	106¹	70	10	55	127	10.6	3.22	119	.192	.298	2	.200	1	10	7	-1	0.7
1988 SF-N	5	9	.357	65	0	0	0	13	98	80	3	46	86	11.8	3.58	91	.226	.318	1	.077	-1	-1	-3	-1	-0.5
1989 *SF-N	14	5	.737	30	29	2	1	0	193¹	149	11	46	119	**9.1**	**2.28**	**148**	.212	**.260**	9	.136	1	26	23	-0	2.6
1990 SF-N	12	11	.522	31	31	4	2	0	182	190	16	70	80	13.0	4.15	90	.272	.341	4	.061	-3	-7	-9	-1	-1.2
Total 9	68	52	.567	344	86	9	4	48	939²	790	69	404	695	11.6	3.23	109	.230	.314	29	.127	-1	47	31	-0	3.8

■ CLARENCE GARRETT
Garrett, Clarence Raymond "Laz" b: 3/6/1891, Reader, W.Va. d: 2/11/77, Moundsville, W.Va. BR/TR, 6'5.5", 185 lbs. Deb: 9/13/15

YEAR TM/L	W	L	PCT	G	GS	CG	SH	SV	IP	H	HR	BB	SO	RAT	ERA	ERA+	OAV	OOB	BH	AVG	PB	PR	/A	PD	TPI
1915 Cle-A	2	2	.500	4	4	2	0	0	23¹	19	1	6	5	10.0	2.31	132	.224	.283	0	.000	-0	2	2	1	0.3

■ GREG GARRETT
Garrett, Gregory b: 3/12/48, Atascadero, Cal. BB/TL, 6', 200 lbs. Deb: 4/24/70

YEAR TM/L	W	L	PCT	G	GS	CG	SH	SV	IP	H	HR	BB	SO	RAT	ERA	ERA+	OAV	OOB	BH	AVG	PB	PR	/A	PD	TPI
1970 Cal-A	5	6	.455	32	7	0	0	0	74²	48	6	44	53	11.2	2.65	136	.190	.312	1	.067	-1	9	8	-0	0.7
1971 Cin-N	0	1	.000	2	1	0	0	0	8²	7	0	10	2	17.7	1.04	323	.250	.447	1	.333	0	2	2	0	0.3
Total 2	5	7	.417	34	8	0	0	0	83¹	55	6	54	55	11.9	2.48	144	.196	.327	2	.111	-1	11	10	-0	1.0

■ CLIFF GARRISON
Garrison, Clifford William b: 8/13/05, Belmont, Okla. BR/TR, 6', 180 lbs. Deb: 4/16/28

YEAR TM/L	W	L	PCT	G	GS	CG	SH	SV	IP	H	HR	BB	SO	RAT	ERA	ERA+	OAV	OOB	BH	AVG	PB	PR	/A	PD	TPI
1928 Bos-A	0	0	—	6	0	0	0	0	16	22	2	6	0	15.8	7.88	52	.361	.418	0	.000	-0	-7	-7	1	-0.5

■ JIM GARRY
Garry, James Thomas b: 9/21/1869, Great Barrington, Mass. d: 1/15/17, Pittsfield, Mass. Deb: 5/02/1893

YEAR TM/L	W	L	PCT	G	GS	CG	SH	SV	IP	H	HR	BB	SO	RAT	ERA	ERA+	OAV	OOB	BH	AVG	PB	PR	/A	PD	TPI
1893 Bos-N	0	1	.000	1	0	0	0	0	1	5	0	4	2	81.0	63.00	8	.628	.753	0	.000	-0	-6	-6	0	-0.3

■ NED GARVER
Garver, Ned Franklin b: 12/25/25, Ney, Ohio BR/TR, 5'10.5", 180 lbs. Deb: 4/28/48

YEAR TM/L	W	L	PCT	G	GS	CG	SH	SV	IP	H	HR	BB	SO	RAT	ERA	ERA+	OAV	OOB	BH	AVG	PB	PR	/A	PD	TPI
1948 StL-A	7	11	.389	38	24	7	0	5	198	200	14	95	75	13.5	3.41	134	.268	.352	19	.288	4	19	25	1	3.1
1949 StL-A	12	17	.414	41	32	16	1	3	223²	245	14	102	70	14.1	3.98	114	.277	.354	14	.187	2	5	14	0	1.6
1950 StL-A	13	18	.419	37	31	**22**	2	0	260	264	18	108	85	13.0	3.39	**146**	.264	.338	26	.286	4	**34**	**45**	2	**5.4**
1951 StL-A	20	12	.625	33	30	**24**	1	0	246	264	17	96	84	12.4	3.73	118	.255	.328	29	.305	8	11	18	1	2.9
1952 StL-A	7	10	.412	21	21	7	2	0	148²	130	14	55	60	11.4	3.69	106	.235	.309	9	.184	-0	-0	4	0	0.5
Det-A	1	0	1.000	1	1	1	0	0	9	9	1	3	3	12.0	2.00	190	.265	.324	0	.000	0	2	2	0	0.3
Yr	8	10	.444	22	22	8	2	0	157²	139	15	58	63	11.2	3.60	100	.235	.304	5	.098	0	1	5	0	0.8
1953 Det-A	11	11	.500	30	26	13	0	1	198¹	228	16	66	69	13.4	4.45	91	.290	.347	11	.153	-1	-10	-8	2	-0.7
1954 Det-A	14	11	.560	35	32	16	3	1	246¹	216	20	62	93	10.3	2.81	131	.236	.287	13	.165	-0	25	24	2	2.7
1955 Det-A	12	16	.429	33	32	16	1	0	230²	251	21	67	83	12.6	3.98	97	.279	.333	17	.224	4	-1	-4	1	0.2
1956 Det-A	0	2	.000	6	3	1	0	0	17²	15	2	14	6	16.3	4.08	101	.234	.372	0	.000	-0	0	1	0	0.2
1957 KC-A	6	13	.316	24	23	6	1	0	145¹	120	13	55	61	11.1	3.84	103	.223	.301	8	.182	0	-1	2	-0	0.2
1958 KC-A	12	11	.522	31	28	10	3	1	201	192	24	66	72	11.6	4.03	97	.244	.304	12	.174	0	-6	-3	6	0.4
1959 KC-A	10	13	.435	32	30	9	2	1	201¹	214	22	42	61	11.6	3.71	108	.270	.309	20	.282	7	3	7	0	1.4
1960 KC-A	4	9	.308	28	15	5	2	0	122¹	110	15	35	50	10.8	3.83	104	.240	.296	2	.074	-1	1	2	-0	0.1
1961 LA-A	0	3	.000	12	2	0	0	0	29	40	2	16	9	17.4	5.59	81	.348	.427	0	.000	-1	-5	-3	1	-0.2
Total 14	129	157	.451	402	330	153	18	12	2477¹	2471	213	881	881	12.3	3.73	112	.260	.325	180	.218	26	78	122	17	17.9

■ JERRY GARVIN
Garvin, Theodore Jared b: 10/21/55, Oakland, Cal. BL/TL, 6'3", 195 lbs. Deb: 4/10/77

YEAR TM/L	W	L	PCT	G	GS	CG	SH	SV	IP	H	HR	BB	SO	RAT	ERA	ERA+	OAV	OOB	BH	AVG	PB	PR	/A	PD	TPI
1977 Tor-A	10	18	.357	34	34	12	1	0	244²	247	33	85	127	12.4	4.19	100	.264	.328	0	—	0	-4	0	5	0.2
1978 Tor-A	4	12	.250	26	22	3	0	0	144¹	189	20	48	67	15.0	5.54	71	.319	.374	0	—	0	-29	-26	2	-2.3
1979 Tor-A	0	1	.000	8	1	0	0	0	22²	15	2	10	14	10.7	2.78	156	.197	.307	0	—	0	4	4	-0	0.3
1980 Tor-A	4	7	.364	61	0	0	0	8	82²	70	6	27	52	10.6	2.29	188	.233	.296	0	—	0	16	19	0	1.9
1981 Tor-A	2	2	.333	35	4	0	0	0	53	46	3	23	25	11.7	3.40	116	.240	.321	0	—	0	2	3	0	0.3
1982 Tor-A	1	1	.500	32	4	0	0	0	58¹	81	10	26	35	16.7	7.25	62	.335	.401	0	—	0	-21	-18	2	-1.5
Total 6	20	41	.328	196	65	15	1	8	606	648	74	219	320	13.0	4.43	94	.277	.342	0	—	0	-32	-18	9	-0.8

■ NED GARVIN
Garvin, Virgil Lee b: 1/1/1874, Navasota, Tex. d: 6/16/08, Fresno, Cal. TR, 6'3.5", 160 lbs. Deb: 7/13/1896

YEAR TM/L	W	L	PCT	G	GS	CG	SH	SV	IP	H	HR	BB	SO	RAT	ERA	ERA+	OAV	OOB	BH	AVG	PB	PR	/A	PD	TPI
1896 Phi-N	0	1	.000	2	1	1	0	0	13	19	0	7	4	18.0	7.62	57	.337	.411	0	.000	-1	-5	-5	-0	-0.4
1899 Chi-N	9	13	.409	24	23	22	4	0	199	202	1	42	69	11.0	2.85	132	.263	.301	11	.155	-5	22	20	0	1.5
1900 Chi-N	10	18	.357	30	28	25	1	0	246²	225	4	63	107	10.5	2.41	150	.243	.291	14	.154	-5	**35**	33	3	3.0
1901 Mil-A	7	20	.259	37	27	22	1	2	257¹	258	4	90	122	12.2	3.46	104	.258	.319	10	.108	-9	6	4	3	-0.1
1902 Chi-N	10	10	.500	23	19	16	2	0	175¹	169	3	43	55	10.9	2.21	153	.254	.299	9	.153	-2	27	23	3	2.3
Bro-N	1	1	.500	2	2	2	1	0	18	15	0	4	7	9.5	1.00	276	.227	.271	1	.143	-0	4	4	0	0.4
1903 Bro-N	15	18	.455	38	34	30	2	2	298	277	2	84	154	11.3	3.08	104	.248	.308	8	.075	-8	6	4	7	0.2
1904 Bro-N	5	15	.250	23	22	16	2	0	181²	141	6	78	86	11.1	1.68	163	.218	.308	8	.127	-3	21	21	3	2.4
NY-A	0	1	.000	2	1	0	0	0	12	14	0	2	8	12.0	2.25	121	.292	.320	0	.000	-1	0	1	1	0.1
Total 7	57	97	.370	181	158	134	13	4	1400²	1320	20	413	612	11.3	2.72	125	.249	.306	61	.122	-34	117	104	20	9.4

■ HARRY GASPAR
Gaspar, Harry Lambert b: 4/28/1883, Kingsley, Iowa d: 5/14/40, Orange, Cal. BR/TR, 6', 180 lbs. Deb: 4/21/09

YEAR TM/L	W	L	PCT	G	GS	CG	SH	SV	IP	H	HR	BB	SO	RAT	ERA	ERA+	OAV	OOB	BH	AVG	PB	PR	/A	PD	TPI
1909 Cin-N	19	11	.633	44	29	19	4	2	260	228	0	57	65	10.2	2.01	130	.242	.291	10	.122	-3	17	17	-4	1.1

YEAR	TM/L	W	L	PCT	G	GS	CG	SH	SV	IP	H	HR	BB	SO	RAT	ERA	ERA+	OAV	OOB	BH	AVG	PB	PR	/A	PD	TPI
1910	Cin-N	15	17	.469	48	31	16	4	7	275	257	6	75	74	11.4	2.59	113	.255	.317	10	.115	-3	14	10	-1	0.5
1911	Cin-N	11	17	.393	44	32	11	2	4	253²	272	9	69	76	12.6	3.30	100	.283	.340	13	.153	-2	3	0	-1	-0.3
1912	Cin-N	1	3	.250	7	6	2	0	0	36²	38	0	16	13	13.5	4.17	81	.266	.344	3	.250	0	-3	-3	0	-0.2
Total	4	46	48	.489	143	98	48	10	13	825¹	795	15	217	228	11.5	2.69	110	.260	.318	36	.135	-8	31	25	-6	1.1

■ CHARLIE GASSAWAY
Gassaway, Charles Cason "Sheriff" b: 8/12/18, Gassaway, Tenn. BL/TL, 6'2.5", 210 lbs. Deb: 9/25/44

YEAR	TM/L	W	L	PCT	G	GS	CG	SH	SV	IP	H	HR	BB	SO	RAT	ERA	ERA+	OAV	OOB	BH	AVG	PB	PR	/A	PD	TPI
1944	Chi-N	0	1	.000	2	2	0	0	0	11²	20	3	10	7	23.1	7.71	46	.385	.484	1	.250	0	-5	-5	-0	-0.4
1945	Phi-A	4	7	.364	24	11	4	0	0	118	114	4	55	50	13.0	3.74	92	.252	.336	6	.154	-2	-5	-4	-1	-0.7
1946	Cle-A	1	1	.500	13	6	0	0	0	50²	54	2	26	23	14.9	3.91	85	.273	.368	1	.067	-1	-2	-3	0	-0.3
Total	3	5	9	.357	39	19	4	0	0	180¹	188	9	91	80	14.2	4.04	84	.268	.357	8	.138	-3	-12	-13	-2	-1.4

■ MILT GASTON
Gaston, Nathaniel Milton b: 1/27/1896, Ridgefield Park, N.J. BR/TR, 6'1", 185 lbs. Deb: 4/20/24

YEAR	TM/L	W	L	PCT	G	GS	CG	SH	SV	IP	H	HR	BB	SO	RAT	ERA	ERA+	OAV	OOB	BH	AVG	PB	PR	/A	PD	TPI
1924	NY-A	5	3	.625	29	2	0	0	1	86	92	3	44	24	14.9	4.50	92	.286	.382	6	.222	-1	-3	-3	-1	-0.4
1925	StL-A	15	14	.517	42	30	16	0	1	238²	284	8	101	84	14.7	4.41	106	.305	.376	21	.262	2	-0	7	-2	0.8
1926	StL-A	10	18	.357	32	28	14	1	0	214¹	227	13	101	39	13.9	4.33	99	.283	.366	13	.167	-2	-7	-1	-1	-0.2
1927	StL-A	13	17	.433	37	30	21	0	1	254	275	18	100	77	13.4	5.00	87	.281	.350	25	.260	6	-24	-18	1	-0.9
1928	Was-A	6	12	.333	28	22	8	3	0	148²	179	3	53	45	14.0	5.51	73	.302	.360	7	.143	-3	-24	-25	1	-2.4
1929	Bos-A	12	19	.387	39	29	20	1	2	243²	265	15	81	83	12.9	3.73	115	.289	.348	15	.192	0	14	15	-1	1.3
1930	Bos-A	13	20	.394	38	34	20	2	2	273	272	15	98	99	12.2	3.92	117	.259	.323	20	.204	-4	22	21	1	1.6
1931	Bos-A	2	13	.133	23	18	4	0	0	119	137	4	41	33	13.5	4.46	96	.291	.348	6	.158	-2	-1	-2	-0	-0.3
1932	Chi-A	7	17	.292	28	25	7	1	1	166²	183	10	73	44	13.9	4.00	108	.279	.352	14	.233	2	9	6	2	0.8
1933	Chi-A	8	12	.400	30	25	7	1	0	167	177	9	60	39	12.8	4.85	87	.272	.334	8	.154	-0	-11	-11	-1	-1.0
1934	Chi-A	6	19	.240	29	28	10	1	0	194	247	16	84	48	15.4	5.85	81	.313	.379	10	.147	-3	-29	-24	3	-2.0
Total	11	97	164	.372	355	271	127	10	8	2105	2338	114	836	615	13.7	4.55	97	.287	.355	145	.200	-4	-54	-35	1	-2.7

■ WELCOME GASTON
Gaston, Welcome Thornburg b: 12/19/1872, Guernsey Co., Ohio d: 12/13/44, Columbus, Ohio TL, Deb: 10/06/1898

YEAR	TM/L	W	L	PCT	G	GS	CG	SH	SV	IP	H	HR	BB	SO	RAT	ERA	ERA+	OAV	OOB	BH	AVG	PB	PR	/A	PD	TPI
1898	Bro-N	1	1	.500	2	2	2	0	0	16	17	0	9	0	14.6	2.81	128	.270	.362	1	.125	-0	1	1	0	0.1
1899	Bro-N	0	0	—	1	0	0	0	0	3	3	0	4	0	21.0	3.00	130	.260	.451	1	1.000	1	0	0	0	0.1
Total	2	1	1	.500	3	2	2	0	0	19	20	0	13	0	15.6	2.84	128	.269	.377	2	.222	1	2	2	0	0.2

■ HANK GASTRIGHT
Gastright, Henry Carl (b: Henry Carl Gastreich) b: 3/29/1865, Covington, Ky. d: 10/9/37, Cold Springs, Ky. BR/TR, 6'2", 190 lbs. Deb: 4/19/1889

YEAR	TM/L	W	L	PCT	G	GS	CG	SH	SV	IP	H	HR	BB	SO	RAT	ERA	ERA+	OAV	OOB	BH	AVG	PB	PR	/A	PD	TPI
1889	Col-a	10	16	.385	32	26	21	0	0	222²	255	8	104	115	14.5	4.57	79	.279	.352	17	.181	-4	-18	-23	-0	-2.2
1890	Col-a	30	14	.682	48	45	41	4	0	401¹	312	8	135	199	10.0	2.94	122	.208	.273	36	.213	3	42	29	-4	2.3
1891	Col-a	12	19	.387	35	33	28	1	0	283²	280	7	136	109	13.2	3.78	92	.249	.330	23	.197	2	-2	-10	2	-0.5
1892	Was-A	3	3	.500	11	7	6	0	0	79²	94	3	38	32	14.9	5.08	64	.282	.356	4	.138	-0	-16	-16	-1	-1.4
1893	Pit-N	3	1	.750	9	5	3	0	0	59	74	3	39	12	17.2	6.25	73	.298	.393	1	.042	-0	-10	-11	1	-1.0
	Bos-N	12	4	.750	19	18	16	0	0	156	179	9	76	27	14.7	5.13	96	.279	.356	13	.191	-3	-8	-3	-1	-0.5
	Yr	15	5	.750	28	23	19	0	0	215	253	12	115	39	15.4	5.44	89	.285	.366	8	.087	-6	-18	-14	-1	-1.5
1894	Bro-N	2	6	.250	16	8	6	1	2	93	135	1	55	20	18.4	6.39	77	.335	.415	2	.171	-2	-11	-15	-1	-1.3
1896	Cin-N	0	0	—	1	0	0	0	0	6	8	0	1	0	13.5	4.50	102	.317	.343	0	.000	-0	-0	0	0	0.0
Total	7	72	63	.533	171	142	121	6	2	1301¹	1337	39	584	514	13.3	4.20	92	.258	.333	101	.186	-7	-23	-51	-6	-4.6

■ AUBREY GATEWOOD
Gatewood, Aubrey Lee b: 11/17/38, Little Rock, Ark. BR/TR, 6'1", 170 lbs. Deb: 9/11/63

YEAR	TM/L	W	L	PCT	G	GS	CG	SH	SV	IP	H	HR	BB	SO	RAT	ERA	ERA+	OAV	OOB	BH	AVG	PB	PR	/A	PD	TPI
1963	LA-A	1	1	.500	4	3	1	0	0	24	12	0	16	13	10.5	1.50	228	.148	.289	0	.000	-1	6	5	0	0.5
1964	LA-A	3	3	.500	15	7	0	0	0	60¹	59	4	12	25	10.7	2.24	147	.258	.298	2	.100	-1	9	7	-0	0.6
1965	Cal-A	4	5	.444	46	3	0	0	0	92	91	5	37	37	12.6	3.42	99	.266	.339	3	.214	1	0	-0	-0	0.0
1970	Atl-N	0	0	—	3	0	0	0	0	2	4	0	2	0	31.5	4.50	95	.364	.500	0	—	0	-0	-0	0	0.0
Total	4	8	9	.471	68	13	1	0	0	178¹	166	9	67	75	11.9	2.78	122	.250	.322	5	.119	-1	15	12	0	1.1

■ CHIPPY GAW
Gaw, George Joseph b: 3/13/1892, W.Newton, Mass. d: 5/26/68, Boston, Mass. BR/TR, 5'11", 180 lbs. Deb: 4/20/20

YEAR	TM/L	W	L	PCT	G	GS	CG	SH	SV	IP	H	HR	BB	SO	RAT	ERA	ERA+	OAV	OOB	BH	AVG	PB	PR	/A	PD	TPI
1920	Chi-N	1	1	.500	6	1	0	0	0	13	16	1	3	4	13.8	4.85	66	.320	.370	1	.250	-0	-2	-2	-0	-0.2

■ DALE GEAR
Gear, Dale Dudley b: 2/2/1872, Lone Elm, Kan. d: 9/23/51, Topeka, Kan. 5'11", 165 lbs. Deb: 8/15/1896 ♦

YEAR	TM/L	W	L	PCT	G	GS	CG	SH	SV	IP	H	HR	BB	SO	RAT	ERA	ERA+	OAV	OOB	BH	AVG	PB	PR	/A	PD	TPI
1896	Cle-N	0	2	.000	3	2	2	0	0	23	35	1	6	6	16.0	5.48	83	.346	.383	6	.400	2	-3	-2	0	0.0
1901	Was-A	4	11	.267	24	16	14	1	1	163	199	9	22	35	12.2	4.03	91	.297	.320	47	.236	0	-7	-7	2	-0.5
Total	2	4	13	.235	27	18	16	1	1	186	234	10	28	41	12.7	4.21	90	.304	.328	57	.239	2	-9	-9	2	-0.5

■ DINTY GEARIN
Gearin, Dennis John b: 10/15/1897, Providence, R.I. d: 3/11/59, Providence, R.I. BL/TL, 5'4", 148 lbs. Deb: 8/06/23

YEAR	TM/L	W	L	PCT	G	GS	CG	SH	SV	IP	H	HR	BB	SO	RAT	ERA	ERA+	OAV	OOB	BH	AVG	PB	PR	/A	PD	TPI
1923	*NY-N	1	1	.500	6	2	1	0	0	24	23	1	10	9	12.4	3.38	113	.264	.340	2	.286	0	2	1	-0	0.1
1924	NY-N	1	2	.333	6	3	2	0	0	29	30	3	16	4	14.3	2.48	148	.275	.368	3	.333	0	4	4	-0	0.4
	Bos-N	0	1	.000	1	1	0	0	0	0	3	0	2	0	—	∞	—	1.000	1.000	0	—	0	-5	-5	-0	-0.3
	Yr	1	3	.250	7	4	2	0	0	29¹	33	3	18	4	15.8	4.03	91	.295	.392	0	.000	0	-1	-1	-0	0.2
Total	2	2	4	.333	13	6	3	0	0	53	56	4	28	13	14.3	3.74	100	.281	.370	5	.313	1	1	0	-0	0.2

■ BOB GEARY
Geary, Robert Norton "Speed" b: 5/10/1891, Cincinnati, Ohio d: 1/3/80, Cincinnati, Ohio BR/TR, 5'11", 168 lbs. Deb: 4/25/18

YEAR	TM/L	W	L	PCT	G	GS	CG	SH	SV	IP	H	HR	BB	SO	RAT	ERA	ERA+	OAV	OOB	BH	AVG	PB	PR	/A	PD	TPI
1918	Phi-A	2	5	.286	16	7	6	2	4	87	94	0	31	22	13.2	2.69	109	.289	.357	4	.148	-1	1	2	-1	0.1
1919	Phi-A	0	3	.000	9	2	1	0	0	32¹	32	1	18	9	13.9	4.73	72	.264	.360	5	.500	2	-5	-5	0	-0.2
1921	Cin-N	1	1	.500	10	1	0	0	0	29	38	1	2	10	12.4	4.34	82	.333	.345	2	.250	0	-2	-2	-0	-0.2
Total	3	3	9	.250	35	10	7	2	4	148¹	164	2	51	41	13.2	3.46	92	.293	.355	11	.244	1	-6	-5	-1	-0.3

■ BOB GEBHARD
Gebhard, Robert Henry b: 1/3/43, Lamberton, Minn. BR/TR, 6'2", 210 lbs. Deb: 8/02/71 C

YEAR	TM/L	W	L	PCT	G	GS	CG	SH	SV	IP	H	HR	BB	SO	RAT	ERA	ERA+	OAV	OOB	BH	AVG	PB	PR	/A	PD	TPI
1971	Min-A	1	2	.333	17	0	0	0	0	18	17	0	11	13	14.5	3.00	118	.243	.354	0	—	0	1	1	1	0.2
1972	Min-A	0	1	.000	13	0	0	0	1	21	36	3	13	13	21.9	8.57	37	.371	.455	0	—	0	-13	-13	1	-1.1
1974	Mon-N	0	0	—	1	0	0	0	0	2	5	1	0	0	22.5	4.50	85	.500	.500	0	—	0	-0	-0	0	0.0
Total	3	1	3	.250	31	0	0	0	1	41	58	4	24	26	18.7	5.93	57	.328	.417	0	—	0	-12	-12	1	-0.9

■ PETE GEBRIAN
Gebrian, Peter "Gabe" b: 8/10/23, Bayonne, N.J. BR/TR, 6', 170 lbs. Deb: 5/06/47

YEAR	TM/L	W	L	PCT	G	GS	CG	SH	SV	IP	H	HR	BB	SO	RAT	ERA	ERA+	OAV	OOB	BH	AVG	PB	PR	/A	PD	TPI
1947	Chi-A	2	3	.400	27	4	0	0	5	66¹	61	7	33	17	13.0	4.48	82	.247	.340	0	.000	-2	-6	-6	-1	-0.8

■ JIM GEDDES
Geddes, James Lee b: 3/23/49, Columbus, Ohio BR/TR, 6'2", 200 lbs. Deb: 4/28/72

YEAR	TM/L	W	L	PCT	G	GS	CG	SH	SV	IP	H	HR	BB	SO	RAT	ERA	ERA+	OAV	OOB	BH	AVG	PB	PR	/A	PD	TPI
1972	Chi-A	0	0	—	5	1	0	0	0	10¹	12	1	10	3	20.0	6.97	45	.293	.442	0	.000	-0	-4	-4	-0	-0.4
1973	Chi-A	0	0	—	6	1	0	0	0	15²	14	0	14	7	17.8	2.87	138	.255	.431	0	—	0	2	2	0	0.2
Total	2	0	0	—	11	2	0	0	0	26	26	1	24	10	18.7	4.50	81	.271	.435	0	.000	-0	-3	-3	-0	-0.2

■ JOE GEDEON
Gedeon, Elmer Joseph b: 12/5/1893, Sacramento, Cal. d: 5/19/41, San Francisco, Cal BR/TR, 6', 167 lbs. Deb: 5/13/13 ♦

YEAR	TM/L	W	L	PCT	G	GS	CG	SH	SV	IP	H	HR	BB	SO	RAT	ERA	ERA+	OAV	OOB	BH	AVG	PB	PR	/A	PD	TPI
1913	Was-A	0	0	—	1	0	0	0	1	0	0	0	0	0	—	—	—	.000	.000	13	.183	0	0	0	0	0.0

■ COUNT GEDNEY
Gedney, Alfred W. b: 5/10/1849, Brooklyn, N.Y. d: 3/26/22, Hackensack, N.J. 5'9", 140 lbs. Deb: 4/27/1872 ♦

YEAR	TM/L	W	L	PCT	G	GS	CG	SH	SV	IP	H	HR	BB	SO	RAT	ERA	ERA+	OAV	OOB	BH	AVG	PB	PR	/A	PD	TPI
1875	Mut-n	1	0	1.000	2	1	1	0	0	11	7	0	1	0	6.5	1.64	158	.179	.200	54	.203	-0	1	1		0.1

■ JOHNNY GEE
Gee, John Alexander "Whiz" b: 12/7/15, Syracuse, N.Y. d: 1/23/88, Cortland, N.Y. BL/TL, 6'9", 225 lbs. Deb: 9/17/39

YEAR	TM/L	W	L	PCT	G	GS	CG	SH	SV	IP	H	HR	BB	SO	RAT	ERA	ERA+	OAV	OOB	BH	AVG	PB	PR	/A	PD	TPI
1939	Pit-N	1	2	.333	3	3	1	0	0	19²	20	0	10	16	13.7	4.12	93	.253	.337	0	.000	-1	-0	-1	0	0.0
1941	Pit-N	0	2	.000	3	2	0	0	0	7¹	10	0	4	2	18.4	6.14	59	.294	.385	1	.333	0	-2	-2	0	-0.1
1943	Pit-N	4	4	.500	15	10	2	0	0	82	89	5	27	18	12.7	4.28	81	.280	.336	3	.115	-1	-8	-7	-3	-1.0
1944	Pit-N	0	0	—	4	0	0	0	0	11¹	20	0	5	3	19.9	7.15	52	.377	.431	1	.500	0	-4	-4	0	-0.3

YEAR	TM/L	W	L	PCT	G	GS	CG	SH	SV	IP	H	HR	BB	SO	RAT	ERA	ERA+	OAV	OOB	BH	AVG	PB	PR	/A	PD	TPI
	NY-N	0	0	—	4	0	0	0	0	4^2	5	0	0	3	9.6	0.00	—	.263	.263	0	—	0	2	2	0	0.2
	Yr	0	0	—	8	0	0	0	0	16	25	0	5	6	16.9	5.06	73	.347	.390	0	.000	0	-3	-2	0	-0.1
1945	NY-N	0	0	—	2	0	0	0	1	3	5	0	2	1	21.0	9.00	43	.385	.467	0	.000	-0	-2	-2	0	-0.3
1946	NY-N	2	4	.333	13	6	1	0	0	47^1	60	3	15	22	14.6	3.99	86	.308	.363	3	.231	0	-3	-3	-1	-0.3
Total	6	7	12	.368	44	21	4	0	1	175^1	209	8	64	65	14.1	4.41	80	.294	.354	8	.157	-1	-18	-17	-2	-1.6

■ BILLY GEER   Geer, William Henry Harrison (b: George Harrison Geer) b: 8/13/1849, Syracuse, N.Y. TR, 5'8", 160 lbs. Deb: 10/15/1874 ♦

YEAR	TM/L	W	L	PCT	G	GS	CG	SH	SV	IP	H	HR	BB	SO	RAT	ERA	ERA+	OAV	OOB	BH	AVG	PB	PR	/A	PD	TPI
1884	Bro-a	0	0	—	2	0	0	0	0	5	14	0	3	1	30.6	12.60	26	.478	.526	82	.210	0	-5	-5	-0	-0.3

■ HENRY GEHRING   Gehring, Henry b: 1/24/1881, St.Paul, Minn. d: 4/18/12, Kansas City, Mo. BR/TR, Deb: 7/16/07

YEAR	TM/L	W	L	PCT	G	GS	CG	SH	SV	IP	H	HR	BB	SO	RAT	ERA	ERA+	OAV	OOB	BH	AVG	PB	PR	/A	PD	TPI
1907	Was-A	3	7	.300	15	9	8	2	0	87	92	1	14	31	11.0	3.31	73	.273	.302	9	.205	3	-7	-9	-1	-0.7
1908	Was-A	0	1	.000	3	1	0	0	0	5	9	0	2	0	23.4	14.40	16	.450	.542	3	.600	2	-7	-7	0	-0.4
Total	2	3	8	.273	18	10	8	2	0	92	101	1	16	31	11.6	3.91	62	.283	.317	12	.245	5	-14	-15	-1	-1.1

■ PAUL GEHRMAN   Gehrman, Paul Arthur "Dutch" b: 5/3/12, Marquam, Ore. d: 10/23/86, Bend, Ore. BR/TR, 6', 195 lbs. Deb: 9/15/37

YEAR	TM/L	W	L	PCT	G	GS	CG	SH	SV	IP	H	HR	BB	SO	RAT	ERA	ERA+	OAV	OOB	BH	AVG	PB	PR	/A	PD	TPI
1937	Cin-N	0	1	.000	2	1	0	0	0	9^1	11	0	5	1	15.4	2.89	129	.282	.364	0	.000	-0	1	1	0	0.1

■ GARY GEIGER   Geiger, Gary Merle b: 4/4/37, Sand Ridge, Ill. BL/TR, 6', 168 lbs. Deb: 4/15/58 ♦

YEAR	TM/L	W	L	PCT	G	GS	CG	SH	SV	IP	H	HR	BB	SO	RAT	ERA	ERA+	OAV	OOB	BH	AVG	PB	PR	/A	PD	TPI
1958	Cle-A	0	0	—	1	0	0	0	0	2	2	0	1	2	13.5	9.00	41	.286	.375	45	.231	0	-1	-1	0	0.0

■ EMIL GEIS   Geis, Emil Michael b: 3/1861, Villmar, Germany TR, 5'11", 170 lbs. Deb: 7/19/1882

YEAR	TM/L	W	L	PCT	G	GS	CG	SH	SV	IP	H	HR	BB	SO	RAT	ERA	ERA+	OAV	OOB	BH	AVG	PB	PR	/A	PD	TPI
1882	Bal-a	4	9	.308	13	13	10	1	0	95^2	84	2	10	10.0		4.80	57	.220	.263	6	.146	-2	-22	-22	-2	-2.1

■ BILL GEIS   Geis, William J. (b: William J. Geiss) b: 7/15/1858, Chicago, Ill. d: 9/18/24, Chicago, Ill. 5'10", 164 lbs. Deb: 5/01/1884 ♦

YEAR	TM/L	W	L	PCT	G	GS	CG	SH	SV	IP	H	HR	BB	SO	RAT	ERA	ERA+	OAV	OOB	BH	AVG	PB	PR	/A	PD	TPI
1884	Det-N	0	0	—	1	0	0	0	0	5	14	0	2	1	28.8	14.40	20	.478	.511	50	.177	-0	-6	-6	0	-0.4

■ DAVE GEISEL   Geisel, John David b: 1/18/55, Windber, Pa. BL/TL, 6'3", 210 lbs. Deb: 6/13/78

YEAR	TM/L	W	L	PCT	G	GS	CG	SH	SV	IP	H	HR	BB	SO	RAT	ERA	ERA+	OAV	OOB	BH	AVG	PB	PR	/A	PD	TPI
1978	Chi-N	1	0	1.000	18	1	0	0	0	23^1	27	0	11	15	14.7	4.24	95	.278	.352	0	.000	-0	-2	-1	-0	0.0
1979	Chi-N	0	0	—	7	0	0	0	0	15	10	0	4	5	9.0	0.60	686	.189	.259	0	.000	-0	5	6	-0	0.6
1981	Chi-N	2	0	1.000	11	2	0	0	0	16	11	0	10	7	11.8	0.56	657	.204	.328	0	.000	-0	5	6	-0	0.6
1982	Tor-A	1	1	.500	16	2	0	0	0	31^2	32	6	17	22	14.5	3.98	113	.260	.359	0	—	0	2	2	-0	0.1
1983	Tor-A	0	3	.000	47	0	0	0	5	52^1	47	4	31	50	13.8	4.64	93	.240	.349	0	—	0	-3	-2	-1	-0.2
1984	Sea-A	1	1	.500	20	3	0	0	3	43^1	47	2	9	28	12.0	4.15	96	.273	.317	0	—	0	-1	-1	-1	-0.1
1985	Sea-A	0	0	—	12	0	0	0	0	27	35	3	15	17	16.7	6.33	67	.310	.391	0	—	0	-7	-6	-0	-0.5
Total	7	5	5	.500	131	8	0	0	8	208^2	209	15	97	144	13.5	4.01	104	.259	.343	0	.000	-1	-2	4	-3	0.5

■ VERN GEISHERT   Geishert, Vernon William b: 1/10/46, Madison, Wis. BR/TR, 6'1", 215 lbs. Deb: 8/26/69

YEAR	TM/L	W	L	PCT	G	GS	CG	SH	SV	IP	H	HR	BB	SO	RAT	ERA	ERA+	OAV	OOB	BH	AVG	PB	PR	/A	PD	TPI
1969	Cal-A	1	1	.500	11	3	0	0	1	31	32	4	7	18	11.6	4.65	75	.267	.313	0	.000	-1	-4	-4	0	-0.4

■ EMIL GEISS   Geiss, Emil August b: 3/20/1867, Chicago, Ill. d: 10/4/11, Chicago, Ill. BR, Deb: 5/18/1887 ♦

YEAR	TM/L	W	L	PCT	G	GS	CG	SH	SV	IP	H	HR	BB	SO	RAT	ERA	ERA+	OAV	OOB	BH	AVG	PB	PR	/A	PD	TPI
1887	Chi-N	0	1	.000	1	1	1	0	0	9	17	1	3	4	20.0	8.00	56	.390	.430	1	.083	-1	-4	-4	0	-0.2

■ CHARLIE GELBERT   Gelbert, Charles Magnus b: 1/26/06, Scranton, Pa. d: 1/13/67, Easton, Pa. BR/TR, 5'11", 170 lbs. Deb: 4/16/29 ♦

YEAR	TM/L	W	L	PCT	G	GS	CG	SH	SV	IP	H	HR	BB	SO	RAT	ERA	ERA+	OAV	OOB	BH	AVG	PB	PR	/A	PD	TPI
1940	Was-A	0	0	—	2	0	0	0	0	4	5	2	3	1	18.0	9.00	46	.278	.381	20	.370	1	-2	-2	0	-0.1

■ JOHN GELNAR   Gelnar, John Richard b: 6/25/43, Granite, Okla. BR/TR, 6'2", 185 lbs. Deb: 8/04/64

YEAR	TM/L	W	L	PCT	G	GS	CG	SH	SV	IP	H	HR	BB	SO	RAT	ERA	ERA+	OAV	OOB	BH	AVG	PB	PR	/A	PD	TPI
1964	Pit-N	0	0	—	7	0	0	0	0	9	11	2	1	4	12.0	5.00	70	.314	.333	0	—	0	-1	-1	-0	-0.1
1967	Pit-N	0	1	.000	10	1	0	0	0	19	30	4	11	5	20.4	8.05	42	.375	.462	1	.167	0	-10	-10	0	-0.9
1969	Sea-A	3	10	.231	39	10	0	0	3	108^2	103	7	26	69	11.1	3.31	110	.250	.302	1	.053	-2	4	4	-0	0.2
1970	Mil-A	4	3	.571	53	0	0	0	3	92^1	98	7	23	48	12.3	4.19	90	.277	.330	1	.083	-1	-5	-4	-2	-0.2
1971	Mil-A	0	0	—	2	0	0	0	0	1^1	3	0	1	0	27.0	13.50	26	.429	.500	0	—	0	-1	-1	0	0.0
Total	5	7	14	.333	111	11	0	0	7	230^1	245	20	62	126	12.5	4.18	88	.276	.332	3	.081	-2	-14	-13	2	-1.0

■ JOE GENEWICH   Genewich, Joseph Edward b: 1/15/1897, Elmira, N.Y. d: 12/21/85, Lockport, N.Y. BR/TR, 6', 174 lbs. Deb: 9/13/22

YEAR	TM/L	W	L	PCT	G	GS	CG	SH	SV	IP	H	HR	BB	SO	RAT	ERA	ERA+	OAV	OOB	BH	AVG	PB	PR	/A	PD	TPI
1922	Bos-N	0	2	.000	6	2	1	0	0	23	29	2	11	4	15.7	7.04	57	.319	.392	1	.167	-0	-8	-8	0	-0.6
1923	Bos-N	13	14	.481	43	24	12	1	1	227^1	272	15	46	54	13.9	3.72	107	.303	.341	19	.247	2	7	7	2	1.0
1924	Bos-N	10	19	.345	34	27	11	2	1	200^1	258	4	65	43	14.9	5.21	73	.329	.386	10	.167	-2	-30	-31	0	-3.0
1925	Bos-N	12	10	.545	34	21	10	0	0	169	185	4	41	34	12.4	3.99	100	.279	.327	15	.273	1	5	0	-1	0.0
1926	Bos-N	8	16	.333	37	26	12	2	2	216	232	6	63	59	12.8	3.88	92	.288	.342	11	.164	-1	-1	-8	1	-0.8
1927	Bos-N	11	8	.579	40	19	7	0	1	181	199	7	54	38	12.7	3.83	97	.279	.332	11	.193	-1	2	2	0	-0.2
1928	Bos-N	3	7	.300	13	11	4	0	0	80^2	88	14	18	15	12.2	4.13	95	.280	.325	1	.038	-3	-1	-2	1	-0.3
	NY-N	11	4	.733	26	18	10	2	3	158^1	136	10	54	37	10.9	3.18	123	.232	.298	13	.203	-1	14	13	1	1.2
	Yr	14	11	.560	39	29	14	2	3	239	224	24	72	52	11.2	3.50	112	.248	.304	2	.022	-4	13	11	2	0.9
1929	NY-N	3	7	.300	21	9	1	0	1	85	133	9	30	19	17.4	6.78	68	.359	.409	12	.375	3	-19	-21	0	-1.5
1930	NY-N	2	5	.286	18	9	3	0	3	61	71	6	20	13	13.6	5.61	84	.297	.354	3	.150	-1	-4	-6	2	-0.3
Total	9	73	92	.442	272	166	71	7	12	1401^2	1610	77	402	316	13.1	4.29	91	.293	.345	96	.207	-3	-35	-58	7	-4.5

■ GARY GENTRY   Gentry, Gary Edward b: 10/6/46, Phoenix, Ariz. BR/TR, 6', 170 lbs. Deb: 4/10/69

YEAR	TM/L	W	L	PCT	G	GS	CG	SH	SV	IP	H	HR	BB	SO	RAT	ERA	ERA+	OAV	OOB	BH	AVG	PB	PR	/A	PD	TPI
1969	*NY-N	13	12	.520	35	35	6	3	0	233^2	192	24	81	154	10.7	3.43	107	.222	.293	6	.081	-4	4	6	1	0.3
1970	NY-N	9	9	.500	32	29	5	2	1	188^1	155	19	86	134	11.9	3.68	109	.224	.318	4	.068	-2	8	7	-1	0.3
1971	NY-N	12	11	.522	32	31	8	3	0	203^1	167	16	82	155	11.3	3.23	105	.224	.305	5	.074	-5	5	4	-1	-0.1
1972	NY-N	7	10	.412	32	26	3	0	0	164	150	13	75	120	12.8	4.01	84	.250	.338	5	.104	-1	-10	-12	2	-1.1
1973	Atl-N	4	6	.400	16	14	3	0	0	86^2	74	7	35	42	11.4	3.43	115	.231	.308	7	.233	1	2	5	-1	0.5
1974	Atl-N	0	0	—	3	1	0	0	0	6^2	4	1	2	0	9.5	1.35	280	.167	.259	0	.000	-0	2	2	0	0.2
1975	Atl-N	1	1	.500	7	2	0	0	0	20	25	3	10	14	14.8	4.95	76	.313	.375	0	.000	-1	-3	-3	0	-0.2
Total	7	46	49	.484	157	138	25	8	2	902^2	770	90	369	615	11.6	3.56	103	.231	.312	27	.095	-12	8	9	-0	-0.1

■ RUFE GENTRY   Gentry, James Ruffus b: 5/18/18, Winston-Salem, N.C BR/TR, 6'1", 180 lbs. Deb: 9/10/43

YEAR	TM/L	W	L	PCT	G	GS	CG	SH	SV	IP	H	HR	BB	SO	RAT	ERA	ERA+	OAV	OOB	BH	AVG	PB	PR	/A	PD	TPI
1943	Det-A	1	3	.250	4	4	2	0	0	29^1	30	2	12	8	13.5	3.68	96	.268	.349	0	.000	-1	-1	-1	0	-0.1
1944	Det-A	12	14	.462	37	30	10	3	0	203^2	211	9	108	68	14.3	4.24	84	.273	.365	15	.197	-1	-18	-15	1	-1.4
1946	Det-A	0	0	—	2	0	0	0	0	3	6	0	7	1	33.0	15.00	24	.333	.579	0	—	0	-4	-4	0	-0.3
1947	Det-A	0	0	—	1	0	0	0	0	0^1	1	0	2	0	81.0	81.00	5	.500	.750	0	—	0	-3	-3	0	-0.2
1948	Det-A	0	0	—	4	0	0	0	0	6^2	5	0	5	1	14.9	2.70	162	.208	.367	1	1.000	0	1	1	0	0.2
Total	5	13	17	.433	48	34	12	3	0	243	251	11	134	78	14.5	4.37	82	.272	.368	16	.184	-2	-25	-21	1	-1.8

■ LEFTY GEORGE   George, Thomas Edward b: 8/13/1886, Pittsburgh, Pa. d: 5/13/55, York, Pa. BL/TR, 6', 155 lbs. Deb: 4/14/11

YEAR	TM/L	W	L	PCT	G	GS	CG	SH	SV	IP	H	HR	BB	SO	RAT	ERA	ERA+	OAV	OOB	BH	AVG	PB	PR	/A	PD	TPI
1911	StL-A	4	9	.308	27	13	6	1	0	116^1	136	4	51	23	15.2	4.18	81	.256	.332	5	.114	-3	-11	-10	-1	-1.3
1912	Cle-A	0	5	.000	11	5	2	0	0	44^1	69	1	18	18	18.1	4.87	70	.373	.434	3	.214	1	-8	-7	0	-0.5
1915	Cin-N	2	2	.500	5	3	2	1	0	28	24	1	8	11	11.9	3.86	74	.242	.330	4	.333	1	-3	-3	1	0.0
1918	Bos-N	1	5	.167	9	5	4	0	0	54^1	56	0	21	22	13.3	2.32	116	.281	.359	2	.091	-2	3	2	2	0.2
Total	4	7	21	.250	52	26	14	2	0	243	285	6	98	74	14.9	3.85	82	.281	.355	14	.152	-2	-19	-19	2	-1.6

■ BILL GEORGE   George, William M. b: 1/27/1865, Bellaire, Ohio d: 8/23/16, Wheeling, W.Va. BR/TL, 5'8", 165 lbs. Deb: 5/11/1887 ♦

YEAR	TM/L	W	L	PCT	G	GS	CG	SH	SV	IP	H	HR	BB	SO	RAT	ERA	ERA+	OAV	OOB	BH	AVG	PB	PR	/A	PD	TPI
1887	NY-N	3	9	.250	13	13	11	0	0	108	126	1	89	49	17.9	5.25	71	.283	.403	9	.170	-3	-14	-18	2	-1.5
1888	*NY-N	2	1	.667	4	3	3	1	0	33^2	18	0	11	26	7.8	1.34	204	.152	.224	9	.231	1	6	5	-0	0.5
1889	Col-a	0	0	—	2	0	0	0	0	8	11	1	3	3	15.8	7.88	46	.317	.371	4	.235	-0	-4	-4	0	-0.2

YEAR	TM/L	W	L	PCT	G	GS	CG	SH	SV	IP	H	HR	BB	SO	RAT	ERA	ERA+	OAV	OOB	BH	AVG	PB	PR	/A	PD	TPI
Total	3	5	10	.333	19	16	14	1	0	149²	155	2	103	78	15.5	4.51	78	.259	.368	26	.210	-2	-12	-17	1	-1.2

■ OSCAR GEORGY   Georgy, Oscar John   b: 11/25/16, New Orleans, La.   BR/TR, 6'3.5", 180 lbs.   Deb: 6/04/38

YEAR	TM/L	W	L	PCT	G	GS	CG	SH	SV	IP	H	HR	BB	SO	RAT	ERA	ERA+	OAV	OOB	BH	AVG	PB	PR	/A	PD	TPI
1938	NY-N	0	0	—	1	0	0	0	0	1	2	0	1	0	27.0	18.00	21	.400	.500	0	—	0	-2	-2	0	-0.1

■ DAVE GERARD   Gerard, David Frederick   b: 8/6/36, New York, N.Y.   BR/TR, 6'2", 205 lbs.   Deb: 4/10/62

YEAR	TM/L	W	L	PCT	G	GS	CG	SH	SV	IP	H	HR	BB	SO	RAT	ERA	ERA+	OAV	OOB	BH	AVG	PB	PR	/A	PD	TPI
1962	Chi-N	2	3	.400	39	0	0	0	3	58²	67	10	28	30	14.7	4.91	84	.289	.368	3	.375	1	-6	-5	-0	-0.3

■ GEORGE GERBERMAN   Gerberman, George Alois   b: 3/8/42, ElCampo, Tex.   BR/TR, 6', 180 lbs.   Deb: 9/23/62

YEAR	TM/L	W	L	PCT	G	GS	CG	SH	SV	IP	H	HR	BB	SO	RAT	ERA	ERA+	OAV	OOB	BH	AVG	PB	PR	/A	PD	TPI
1962	Chi-N	0	0	—	1	1	0	0	0	5¹	3	1	5	1	13.5	1.69	246	.158	.333	0	.000	0	1	1	0	0.2

■ RUSTY GERHARDT   Gerhardt, Allen Russell   b: 8/13/50, Baltimore, Md.   BB/TL, 5'9", 175 lbs.   Deb: 7/27/74

YEAR	TM/L	W	L	PCT	G	GS	CG	SH	SV	IP	H	HR	BB	SO	RAT	ERA	ERA+	OAV	OOB	BH	AVG	PB	PR	/A	PD	TPI
1974	SD-N	2	1	.667	23	1	0	0	1	35²	44	1	17	22	15.9	7.07	50	.308	.389	1	.167	-0	-14	-14	-0	-1.4

■ AL GERHEAUSER   Gerheauser, Albert "Lefty"   b: 6/24/17, St.Louis, Mo.   d: 5/28/72, Springfield, Mo.   BL/TL, 6'3", 190 lbs.   Deb: 4/24/43

YEAR	TM/L	W	L	PCT	G	GS	CG	SH	SV	IP	H	HR	BB	SO	RAT	ERA	ERA+	OAV	OOB	BH	AVG	PB	PR	/A	PD	TPI
1943	Phi-N	10	19	.345	38	31	11	2	0	215	222	10	70	92	12.3	3.60	94	.263	.321	8	.113	-3	-5	-5	-2	-0.9
1944	Phi-N	8	16	.333	30	29	10	2	0	182²	210	8	65	66	13.6	4.58	79	.285	.344	13	.231	3	-20	-20	-1	-1.7
1945	Pit-N	5	10	.333	32	14	5	0	1	140¹	170	5	54	55	14.4	3.91	101	.304	.366	12	.250	3	-2	1	2	0.5
1946	Pit-N	2	2	.500	35	3	1	0	0	81²	92	2	25	32	13.0	3.97	89	.286	.339	7	.333	2	-5	-4	1	0.0
1948	StL-A	0	3	.000	14	2	0	0	0	23¹	32	0	10	10	16.6	7.33	62	.317	.384	2	.333	0	-8	-7	-0	-0.6
Total	5	25	50	.333	149	79	27	4	1	643	726	25	224	255	13.4	4.13	88	.283	.342	44	.209	6	-40	-36	-1	-2.7

■ STEVE GERKIN   Gerkin, Stephen Paul "Splinter"   b: 11/19/15, Grafton, W.Va.   d: 11/9/78, Bay Pines, Fla.   BR/TR, 6'1", 162 lbs.   Deb: 5/13/45

YEAR	TM/L	W	L	PCT	G	GS	CG	SH	SV	IP	H	HR	BB	SO	RAT	ERA	ERA+	OAV	OOB	BH	AVG	PB	PR	/A	PD	TPI
1945	Phi-A	0	12	.000	21	12	3	0	0	102	112	4	27	25	12.5	3.62	95	.285	.336	2	.059	-4	-3	-2	1	-0.5

■ LES GERMAN   German, Lester Stanley   b: 6/1/1869, Baltimore, Md.   d: 6/10/34, Germantown, Md.   BR/TR, 5'8", 165 lbs.   Deb: 8/27/1890

YEAR	TM/L	W	L	PCT	G	GS	CG	SH	SV	IP	H	HR	BB	SO	RAT	ERA	ERA+	OAV	OOB	BH	AVG	PB	PR	/A	PD	TPI
1890	Bal-a	5	11	.313	17	16	15	0	0	132¹	147	2	54	37	13.7	4.83	84	.273	.339	6	.118	-2	-14	-11	-1	-1.1
1893	NY-N	8	8	.500	20	18	14	0	0	152	162	6	70	35	13.7	4.14	112	.265	.340	23	.311	3	9	9	-1	0.9
1894	NY-N	9	8	.529	23	15	10	0	0	134	178	7	66	17	16.4	5.78	91	.316	.387	17	.298	0	-7	-8	3	-0.3
1895	NY-N	7	11	.389	25	18	16	0	0	178¹	243	7	78	36	16.2	5.96	78	.320	.383	29	.261	2	-23	-26	0	-1.7
1896	NY-N	0	0	—	1	0	0	0	0	2²	9	0	1	0	33.8	13.50	31	.540	.566	0	.000	-0	-3	-3	-0	-0.1
	Was-N	2	20	.091	28	20	14	0	1	166²	240	6	74	20	17.0	6.32	70	.334	.396	16	.229	-0	-36	-35	1	-2.6
	Yr	2	20	.091	29	20	14	0	1	169¹	249	6	75	20	17.2	6.43	68	.339	.400	16	.070	-1	-39	-38	1	-2.7
1897	Was-N	3	5	.375	15	5	4	0	0	83²	117	2	33	2	16.1	5.59	78	.328	.384	15	.341	2	-12	-12	-0	-0.6
Total	6	34	63	.351	129	92	73	0	2	849²	1096	30	376	147	15.6	5.49	83	.307	.373	106	.260	5	-86	-85	2	-5.5

■ ED GERNER   Gerner, Edwin Frederick "Lefty"   b: 7/22/1897, Philadelphia, Pa.   d: 5/15/70, Philadelphia, Pa.   BL/TL, 5'8.5", 175 lbs.   Deb: 5/14/19

YEAR	TM/L	W	L	PCT	G	GS	CG	SH	SV	IP	H	HR	BB	SO	RAT	ERA	ERA+	OAV	OOB	BH	AVG	PB	PR	/A	PD	TPI
1919	Cin-N	1	0	1.000	5	1	0	0	0	17	22	0	3	2	14.3	3.18	87	.333	.380	1	.167	-0	-0	-1	1	0.0

■ LEFTY GERVAIS   Gervais, Lucien Edward   b: 7/6/1890, Grover, Wis.   d: 10/19/50, Los Angeles, Cal.   BL/TL, 5'10", 165 lbs.   Deb: 4/17/13

YEAR	TM/L	W	L	PCT	G	GS	CG	SH	SV	IP	H	HR	BB	SO	RAT	ERA	ERA+	OAV	OOB	BH	AVG	PB	PR	/A	PD	TPI
1913	Bos-N	0	1	.000	5	2	1	0	0	15²	18	0	4	1	12.6	5.74	57	.383	.431	0	.000	-0	-4	-4	-0	-0.4

■ CHARLIE GESSNER   Gessner, Charles J.   b: Philadelphia, Pa.   Deb: 7/19/1886

YEAR	TM/L	W	L	PCT	G	GS	CG	SH	SV	IP	H	HR	BB	SO	RAT	ERA	ERA+	OAV	OOB	BH	AVG	PB	PR	/A	PD	TPI
1886	Phi-a	0	1	.000	1	1	1	0	0	8	13	0	5	0	20.3	9.00	39	.349	.426	1	.250	-0	-5	-5	-0	-0.3

■ AL GETTEL   Gettel, Allen Jones   b: 9/17/17, Norfolk, Va.   BR/TR, 6'3.5", 200 lbs.   Deb: 4/20/45

YEAR	TM/L	W	L	PCT	G	GS	CG	SH	SV	IP	H	HR	BB	SO	RAT	ERA	ERA+	OAV	OOB	BH	AVG	PB	PR	/A	PD	TPI
1945	NY-A	9	8	.529	27	17	9	0	3	154²	141	11	53	67	11.7	3.90	89	.243	.314	16	.281	2	-9	-7	-1	-0.6
1946	NY-A	6	7	.462	26	11	5	2	0	103	89	6	40	54	11.4	2.97	116	.229	.305	4	.125	-2	6	5	0	0.4
1947	Cle-A	11	10	.524	31	21	8	0	0	149	122	6	62	64	11.3	3.20	109	.229	.313	15	.294	4	8	5	1	0.9
1948	Cle-A	0	1	.000	5	2	0	0	0	7²	15	2	10	4	30.5	17.61	23	.385	.520	0	.000	-0	-11	-12	-0	-1.0
	Chi-A	8	10	.444	22	19	7	0	1	148	154	7	60	49	13.3	4.01	106	.268	.342	13	.241	0	5	4	-1	0.3
	Yr	8	11	.421	27	21	7	0	1	155²	169	9	70	53	14.0	4.68	91	.275	.353	13	.000	0	-7	-7	-1	-0.7
1949	Chi-A	2	5	.286	19	7	1	1	1	63	69	12	26	22	13.9	6.43	65	.283	.357	3	.167	-0	-16	-16	-1	-1.4
	Was-A	0	2	.000	16	1	0	0	1	34²	43	4	24	7	17.4	5.45	78	.314	.416	0	.000	-1	-5	-5	-1	-0.4
	Yr	2	7	.222	35	8	1	1	2	97²	112	16	50	29	14.9	6.08	69	.292	.374	3	.115	-1	-20	-20	-1	-1.8
1951	NY-A	1	2	.333	30	1	0	0	0	57¹	52	12	25	36	12.1	4.87	80	.240	.318	1	.083	-1	-6	-6	-1	-0.5
1955	StL-N	1	0	1.000	8	0	0	0	0	17	26	6	10	7	19.1	9.00	45	.361	.439	3	.500	1	-9	-9	-1	-0.7
Total	7	38	45	.458	184	79	31	5	6	734¹	711	72	310	310	12.7	4.28	88	.255	.334	55	.228	3	-37	-40	-1	-3.0

■ CHARLIE GETTIG   Gettig, Charles Henry   b: 12/1870, Baltimore, Md.   d: 4/11/35, Baltimore, Md.   5'10", 172 lbs.   Deb: 8/05/1896 ♦

YEAR	TM/L	W	L	PCT	G	GS	CG	SH	SV	IP	H	HR	BB	SO	RAT	ERA	ERA+	OAV	OOB	BH	AVG	PB	PR	/A	PD	TPI
1896	NY-N	1	0	1.000	4	1	1	0	1	14	20	0	8	5	18.0	9.64	44	.332	.411	3	.333	1	-8	-8	0	-0.5
1897	NY-N	1	1	.500	3	2	2	0	0	19	23	0	9	7	15.2	5.21	80	.297	.370	15	.200	-0	-2	-2	0	-0.1
1898	NY-N	6	3	.667	17	8	7	0	0	115	141	4	39	14	14.1	3.83	91	.299	.353	49	.250	2	-3	-5	2	-0.3
1899	NY-N	7	8	.467	18	15	12	0	0	128	161	3	54	25	15.1	4.43	85	.307	.371	24	.247	1	-8	-10	-0	-0.6
Total	4	15	12	.556	42	26	22	0	1	276	345	4	110	51	14.8	4.50	82	.304	.366	91	.241	3	-21	-25	2	-1.5

■ TOM GETTINGER   Gettinger, Thomas L.   b: 1870, Mobile, Ala.   BL/TL, 5'10", 180 lbs.   Deb: 9/21/1889 ♦

YEAR	TM/L	W	L	PCT	G	GS	CG	SH	SV	IP	H	HR	BB	SO	RAT	ERA	ERA+	OAV	OOB	BH	AVG	PB	PR	/A	PD	TPI
1895	Lou-N	0	0	—	2	0	0	0	0	6¹	13	1	1	0	19.9	7.11	65	.415	.433	70	.269	0	-2	-2	0	0.0

■ CHARLIE GETZIEN   Getzien, Charles H. "Pretzels"   b: 2/14/1864, Germany   d: 6/19/32, Chicago, Ill.   BR/TR, 5'10", 172 lbs.   Deb: 8/13/1884

YEAR	TM/L	W	L	PCT	G	GS	CG	SH	SV	IP	H	HR	BB	SO	RAT	ERA	ERA+	OAV	OOB	BH	AVG	PB	PR	/A	PD	TPI
1884	Det-N	5	12	.294	17	17	17	1	0	147¹	118	2	25	107	8.7	1.95	148	.207	.241	6	.109	-4	17	15	-2	0.9
1885	Det-N	12	25	.324	37	37	37	1	0	330	360	8	92	110	12.3	3.03	94	.265	.312	29	.212	-1	-8	-7	-1	-0.7
1886	Det-N	30	11	.732	43	43	42	1	0	386²	388	6	85	172	11.0	3.03	109	.250	.289	29	.176	-3	12	12	-2	0.7
1887	*Det-N	29	13	**.690**	43	42	41	2	0	366²	373	24	106	135	11.8	3.73	108	.256	.307	29	.186	-2	13	12	-0	0.8
1888	Det-N	19	25	.432	46	46	45	2	0	404	411	13	54	202	10.4	3.05	90	.254	.278	41	.246	9	-10	-14	-2	-0.6
1889	Ind-N	18	22	.450	45	44	36	0	1	349	395	27	100	139	12.8	4.54	92	.276	.323	25	.180	2	-20	-14	-3	-1.1
1890	Bos-N	23	17	.575	40	40	39	4	0	350	342	5	82	140	10.9	3.19	117	.249	.291	34	.231	5	14	22	-2	2.4
1891	Bos-N	4	5	.444	11	9	7	0	0	89	112	4	23	29	13.7	3.84	95	.296	.337	7	.171	1	-5	-2	1	0.1
	Cle-N	0	1	.000	1	1	1	0	0	9	12	1	4	4	16.0	8.00	43	.308	.373	0	.000	-1	-5	-5	-0	-0.3
	Yr	4	6	.400	12	10	8	0	0	98	124	5	27	33	13.9	4.22	86	.297	.340	7	.156	1	-10	-6	1	-0.2
1892	StL-N	5	8	.385	12	10	8	0	0	108	159	5	31	32	15.8	5.67	56	.329	.370	9	.200	1	-29	-30	-1	-2.4
Total	9	145	139	.511	296	292	277	11	1	2539²	2670	95	602	1070	11.6	3.46	99	.260	.301	209	.198	8	-20	-12	-12	-0.2

■ RUBE GEYER   Geyer, Jacob Bowman   b: 3/26/1884, Allegheny, Pa.   d: 10/12/62, Ford Township, Minn.   BR/TR, 5'10", 170 lbs.   Deb: 4/24/10

YEAR	TM/L	W	L	PCT	G	GS	CG	SH	SV	IP	H	HR	BB	SO	RAT	ERA	ERA+	OAV	OOB	BH	AVG	PB	PR	/A	PD	TPI
1910	StL-N	0	1	.000	4	0	0	0	0	4	5	0	3	5	18.0	4.50	66	.294	.400	0	.000	-0	-1	-1	0	0.0
1911	StL-N	9	6	.600	29	11	7	1	0	148²	141	7	56	46	12.3	3.27	103	.259	.335	13	.228	1	2	2	-1	0.2
1912	StL-N	7	14	.333	41	18	6	0	0	181	191	4	84	61	13.9	3.28	104	.275	.356	11	.208	-0	3	3	0	0.3
1913	StL-N	1	5	.167	30	4	2	0	1	78²	83	6	38	21	14.1	5.26	61	.282	.368	2	.091	-2	-18	-18	-0	-1.9
Total	4	17	26	.395	104	33	15	1	1	412¹	420	17	181	133	13.4	3.67	92	.271	.352	26	.195	-1	-14	-14	-1	-1.4

■ TONY GHELFI   Ghelfi, Anthony Paul   b: 8/23/61, LaCrosse, Wis.   BR/TR, 6'3", 185 lbs.   Deb: 9/01/83

YEAR	TM/L	W	L	PCT	G	GS	CG	SH	SV	IP	H	HR	BB	SO	RAT	ERA	ERA+	OAV	OOB	BH	AVG	PB	PR	/A	PD	TPI
1983	Phi-N	1	1	.500	3	3	0	0	0	14¹	15	2	6	14	13.2	3.14	114	.268	.339	1	.250	0	1	1	1	0.1

■ BOB GIALLOMBARDO   Giallombardo, Robert Paul   b: 5/20/37, Brooklyn, N.Y.   BL/TL, 6', 175 lbs.   Deb: 6/21/58

YEAR	TM/L	W	L	PCT	G	GS	CG	SH	SV	IP	H	HR	BB	SO	RAT	ERA	ERA+	OAV	OOB	BH	AVG	PB	PR	/A	PD	TPI
1958	LA-N	1	1	.500	6	5	0	0	0	26¹	29	3	15	14	15.0	3.76	109	.284	.376	1	.167	-0	1	1	0	0.1

YEAR TM/L	W	L	PCT	G	GS	CG	SH	SV	IP	H	HR	BB	SO	RAT	ERA	ERA+	OAV	OOB	BH	AVG	PB	PR	/A	PD	TPI
■ JOE GIARD Giard, Joseph Oscar "Peco" b: 10/7/1898, Ware, Mass. d: 7/10/56, Worcester, Mass. BL/TL, 5'10.5", 170 lbs. Deb: 4/18/25																								
1925 StL-A	10	5	.667	30	21	9	4	0	160²	179	13	87	43	15.2	5.04	93	.295	.388	3	.057	-6	-12	-7	2	-0.9
1926 StL-A	3	10	.231	22	15	2	0	0	90	113	7	67	18	18.1	7.00	61	.318	.428	8	.276	0	-30	-27	-1	-2.4
1927 NY-A	0	0	—	16	0	0	0	0	27	38	1	19	10	19.0	8.00	48	.352	.449	2	.286	0	-12	-12	-0	-1.1
Total 3	13	15	.464	68	36	11	4	0	277²	330	21	173	71	16.5	5.96	75	.309	.408	13	.146	-6	-53	-46	1	-4.4
■ JOE GIBBON Gibbon, Joseph Charles b: 4/10/35, Hickory, Miss. BR/TL, 6'4", 200 lbs. Deb: 4/17/60																								
1960 *Pit-N	4	2	.667	27	9	0	0	0	80¹	87	5	31	60	13.2	4.03	93	.277	.342	4	.211	1	-2	-3	0	-0.1
1961 Pit-N	13	10	.565	30	29	7	3	0	195¹	185	16	57	145	11.3	3.32	120	.251	.309	8	.136	-2	16	15	-1	1.2
1962 Pit-N	3	4	.429	19	8	0	0	0	57	53	4	24	26	12.2	3.63	108	.250	.326	3	.176	-0	2	2	1	0.3
1963 Pit-N	5	12	.294	37	22	5	0	1	147¹	147	7	54	110	12.6	3.30	100	.258	.328	4	.093	-2	-0	-0	1	0.0
1964 Pit-N	10	7	.588	28	24	3	0	0	146²	145	10	54	97	12.6	3.68	95	.262	.334	12	.255	3	-2	-3	1	0.1
1965 Pit-N	4	9	.308	31	15	1	0	1	105²	85	7	34	63	10.5	4.51	78	.221	.291	3	.115	-0	-11	-12	0	-1.1
1966 SF-N	4	6	.400	37	10	1	0	1	81	86	4	16	48	11.6	3.67	100	.275	.314	3	.200	0	-1	0	1	0.2
1967 SF-N	6	2	.750	28	10	3	1	1	82	65	4	33	63	11.1	3.07	107	.220	.305	1	.042	-1	3	2	2	0.3
1968 SF-N	1	2	.333	29	0	0	0	1	40	33	3	19	22	12.1	1.57	187	.234	.333	0	.000	-0	6	6	0	0.7
1969 SF-N	1	3	.250	16	0	0	0	2	20	15	1	13	9	13.0	3.60	97	.211	.341	0	.000	-0	-0	-0	1	0.1
Pit-N	5	1	.833	35	0	0	0	9	51¹	38	5	17	35	10.0	1.93	181	.208	.282	0	.000	-1	9	9	1	1.0
Yr	6	4	.600	51	0	0	0	11	71¹	53	6	30	44	10.7	2.40	146	.208	.296	0	.000	-1	9	9	2	1.1
1970 *Pit-N	0	1	.000	41	0	0	0	5	41	44	2	24	26	15.4	4.83	81	.280	.383	0	.000	-0	-4	-4	0	-0.3
1971 Cin-N	5	6	.455	50	0	0	0	11	64¹	54	3	32	34	12.2	2.94	114	.239	.336	0	.000	-0	4	3	1	0.4
1972 Cin-N	0	0	—	2	0	0	0	0	0¹	3	1	1	1	108.0	54.00	6	.750	.800	0	—	0	-2	-2	0	-0.1
Hou-N	0	0	—	9	0	0	0	0	7¹	13	2	5	4	23.3	9.82	34	.394	.487	0	—	0	-5	-5	1	-0.4
Yr	0	0	—	11	0	0	0	0	7²	16	3	6	5	27.0	11.74	27	.429	.523	0	—	0	-7	-7	1	-0.5
Total 13	61	65	.484	419	127	20	4	32	1119²	1053	74	414	743	12.1	3.52	102	.251	.323	38	.144	-2	12	8	10	2.3
■ NORWOOD GIBSON Gibson, Norwood Ringold "Gibby" b: 3/11/1877, Peoria, Ill. d: 7/7/59, Peoria, Ill. BR/TR, 5'10", 165 lbs. Deb: 4/29/03																								
1903 Bos-A	13	9	.591	24	21	17	2	0	183¹	166	2	65	76	11.3	3.19	95	.241	.306	17	.266	5	-5	-3	0	0.2
1904 Bos-A	17	14	.548	33	32	29	1	0	273	216	8	81	112	9.8	2.21	121	.219	.278	6	.065	-6	12	14	-2	0.6
1905 Bos-A	4	7	.364	23	17	9	0	0	134	118	9	55	67	11.6	3.69	73	.238	.314	4	.095	-2	-15	-15	-2	-1.9
1906 Bos-A	0	2	.000	5	2	1	0	0	18²	25	2	7	3	15.4	5.30	52	.324	.380	1	.200	0	-5	-5	-0	-0.4
Total 4	34	32	.515	85	72	56	3	0	609	525	21	208	258	10.8	2.93	95	.233	.298	28	.138	-4	-14	-9	-4	-1.5
■ PAUL GIBSON Gibson, Paul Marshall b: 1/4/60, Southampton, N.Y. BL/TR, 6', 165 lbs. Deb: 4/08/88																								
1988 Det-A	4	2	.667	40	1	0	0	0	92	83	6	34	50	11.6	2.93	130	.240	.312	0	—	0	11	9	0	0.9
1989 Det-A	4	8	.333	45	13	0	0	0	132	129	11	57	77	13.1	4.64	82	.259	.342	0	—	0	-11	-12	-0	-1.1
1990 Det-A	5	4	.556	61	0	0	0	3	97¹	99	10	44	56	13.3	3.05	129	.269	.349	0	—	0	9	9	0	1.0
Total 3	13	14	.481	146	14	0	0	3	321¹	311	27	135	183	12.7	3.67	105	.257	.336	0	—	0	9	6	0	0.8
■ BOB GIBSON Gibson, Robert b: 11/9/35, Omaha, Neb. BR/TR, 6'1", 189 lbs. Deb: 4/15/59 CH																								
1959 StL-N	3	5	.375	13	9	2	1	0	75²	77	4	39	48	13.9	3.33	127	.273	.363	3	.115	-1	5	8	-0	0.7
1960 StL-N	3	6	.333	27	12	2	0	0	86²	97	7	48	69	15.2	5.61	73	.284	.374	5	.179	-0	-18	-15	-1	-1.3
1961 StL-N	13	12	.520	35	27	10	2	1	211¹	186	13	119	166	13.2	3.24	136	.239	.344	13	.197	-2	19	27	0	3.1
1962 StL-N	15	13	.536	32	30	15	**5**	1	233²	174	15	95	208	10.7	2.85	**150**	.204	.291	20	.263	6	28	37	-0	**4.7**
1963 StL-N	18	9	.667	36	33	14	2	0	254²	224	19	96	204	11.8	3.39	105	.233	.311	18	.207	8	-3	4	-2	1.1
1964 *StL-N	19	12	.613	40	36	17	2	1	287¹	250	25	86	245	10.8	3.01	127	.232	.294	15	.156	1	17	26	-3	3.7
1965 StL-N	20	12	.625	38	36	20	6	1	299	243	34	103	270	10.7	3.07	125	.222	.295	25	.240	9	16	26	-3	3.4
1966 StL-N	21	12	.636	35	35	20	**5**	0	280¹	210	20	78	225	9.4	2.44	147	.207	.267	20	.200	3	36	36	-2	4.1
1967 *StL-N	13	7	.650	24	24	10	2	0	175¹	151	10	40	147	10.0	2.98	130	.231	.291	8	.133	1	8	6	-0	0.7
1968 *StL-N	22	9	.710	34	34	28	**13**	0	304²	198	11	62	**268**	**7.9**	**1.12**	**258**	**.184**	**.233**	16	.170	4	**63**	**60**	-4	**7.9**
1969 *StL-N	20	13	.606	35	35	**28**	4	0	314	251	12	95	269	10.2	2.18	164	.219	.285	29	.246	8	49	49	-3	**6.2**
1970 StL-N	**23**	7	**.767**	34	34	23	3	0	294	262	13	88	274	10.8	3.12	132	.237	.296	33	.303	12	30	32	-2	4.5
1971 StL-N	16	13	.552	31	31	20	**5**	0	245²	215	14	76	185	10.9	3.04	118	.232	.296	15	.172	2	12	15	-0	2.0
1972 StL-N	19	11	.633	34	34	23	4	0	278	226	14	88	208	10.3	2.46	138	.224	.288	20	.194	7	31	29	1	4.3
1973 StL-N	12	10	.545	25	25	13	1	0	195	159	12	57	142	10.1	2.77	132	.224	.284	12	.185	2	19	19	-1	2.2
1974 StL-N	11	13	.458	33	33	9	1	0	240	236	24	104	129	12.9	3.83	93	.259	.338	17	.210	3	-6	-7	-1	-0.5
1975 StL-N	3	10	.231	22	14	1	0	2	109	120	10	62	60	15.4	5.04	75	.287	.384	5	.179	-0	-17	-16	-0	-1.4
Total 17	251	174	.591	528	482	255	56	6	3884¹	3279	257	1336	3117	10.9	2.91	127	.228	.299	274	.206	68	290	335	-20	44.7
■ BOB GIBSON Gibson, Robert Louis b: 6/19/57, Philadelphia, Pa. BR/TR, 6', 195 lbs. Deb: 4/13/83																								
1983 Mil-A	3	4	.429	27	7	0	0	2	80²	71	6	46	46	13.2	3.90	96	.237	.340	0	—	0	1	-2	-1	-0.1
1984 Mil-A	2	5	.286	18	9	1	1	0	69	61	10	47	54	14.1	4.96	78	.236	.354	0	—	0	-7	-9	0	-0.7
1985 Mil-A	6	7	.462	41	1	0	0	11	92¹	86	10	49	53	13.3	3.90	107	.260	.357	0	—	0	3	3	-0	0.3
1986 Mil-A	1	2	.333	11	1	0	0	0	26²	23	3	23	11	15.5	4.73	92	.232	.377	0	—	0	-2	-1	-0	0.0
1987 NY-N	0	0	—	1	0	0	0	0	1	0	0	1	2	9.0	0.00	—	.000	.250	0	—	0	0	0	0	0.0
Total 5	12	18	.400	98	18	1	1	13	269²	241	29	166	166	13.7	4.24	94	.243	.353	0	—	0	-5	-8	-1	-0.5
■ ROBERT GIBSON Gibson, Robert Murray b: 8/20/1869, Duncansville, Pa. d: 12/19/49, Pittsburgh, Pa. BR/TR, 6'3", 185 lbs. Deb: 6/04/1890																								
1890 Chi-N	1	0	1.000	1	1	1	0	0	9	6	0	2	1	8.0	0.00	—	.184	.231	0	.000	-0	4	4	0	0.4
Pit-N	0	3	.000	3	3	2	0	0	12	24	0	23	3	35.3	17.25	19	.404	.570	3	.231	-0	-18	-19	-1	-1.3
Yr	1	3	.250	4	4	3	0	0	21	30	0	25	4	23.6	9.86	35	.326	.470	1	.059	-1	-15	-15	-0	-0.9
■ SAM GIBSON Gibson, Samuel Braxton b: 8/5/1899, King, N.C. d: 1/31/83, High Point, N.C. BL/TR, 6'2", 198 lbs. Deb: 4/19/26																								
1926 Det-A	12	9	.571	35	24	16	2	2	196¹	199	6	75	61	12.8	3.48	117	.269	.341	18	.250	2	12	13	0	1.4
1927 Det-A	11	12	.478	33	26	11	0	0	184²	201	9	86	76	14.4	3.80	111	.285	.369	14	.212	-1	7	8	-2	0.5
1928 Det-A	5	8	.385	20	18	5	1	0	119²	155	4	53	29	16.2	5.42	76	.322	.397	12	.286	2	-18	-17	-1	-1.4
1930 NY-A	0	1	.000	2	2	0	0	0	6	14	1	6	3	30.0	15.00	29	.424	.513	1	.333	0	-7	-7	0	-0.5
1932 NY-N	4	8	.333	41	5	1	1	3	81²	107	7	30	39	15.3	4.85	77	.322	.382	5	.263	0	-9	-10	-1	-1.0
Total 5	32	38	.457	131	75	33	4	5	588¹	676	27	250	208	14.5	4.28	95	.295	.370	50	.248	3	-15	-14	-3	-1.0
■ GEORGE GICK Gick, George Edward b: 10/18/15, Dunnington, Ind. BB/TR, 6', 190 lbs. Deb: 10/03/37																								
1937 Chi-A	0	0	—	1	0	0	0	1	2	0	0	0	1	0.0	0.00	—	.000	.000	0	—	0	1	1	0	0.1
1938 Chi-A	0	0	—	1	0	0	0	0	1	0	0	0	1	9.0	0.00	—	.000	.250	0	—	0	1	1	0	0.1
Total 2	0	0	—	2	0	0	0	1	3	0	0	0	2	3.0	0.00	—	.000	.100	0	—	0	2	2	0	0.1
■ BYRON GIDEON Gideon, Byron Brett b: 8/8/63, Ozona, Tex. BR/TR, 6'2", 200 lbs. Deb: 7/05/87																								
1987 Pit-N	1	5	.167	29	0	0	0	3	36²	34	6	10	31	11.0	4.66	88	.243	.298	1	1.000	1	-2	-2	-0	-0.1
1989 Mon-N	0	0	—	4	0	0	0	0	4²	5	1	5	2	19.3	1.93	183	.294	.455	0	—	0	1	1	-0	0.1
1990 Mon-N	0	0	—	1	0	0	0	0	1	2	0	4	0	54.0	9.00	42	.500	.750	0	—	0	-1	-1	0	0.0
Total 3	1	5	.167	34	0	0	0	3	42¹	41	7	19	33	13.0	4.46	90	.255	.337	1	1.000	1	-2	-2	0	0.0
■ JIM GIDEON Gideon, James Leslie b: 9/26/53, Taylor, Tex. BR/TR, 6'3", 190 lbs. Deb: 9/14/75																								
1975 Tex-A	0	0	—	1	1	0	0	0	5²	7	1	5	2	19.1	7.94	47	.292	.414	0	—	0	-3	-3	-0	-0.2

YEAR TM/L	W	L	PCT	G	GS	CG	SH	SV	IP	H	HR	BB	SO	RAT	ERA	ERA+	OAV	OOB	BH	AVG	PB	PR	/A	PD	TPI

■ FLOYD GIEBELL
Giebell, Floyd George   b: 12/10/09, Pennsboro, W.Va.   BL/TR, 6'2.5", 172 lbs.   Deb: 4/21/39

YEAR TM/L	W	L	PCT	G	GS	CG	SH	SV	IP	H	HR	BB	SO	RAT	ERA	ERA+	OAV	OOB	BH	AVG	PB	PR	/A	PD	TPI
1939 Det-A	1	1	.500	9	0	0	0	0	15¹	19	1	12	9	18.2	2.93	167	.317	.431	0	.000	-0	3	3	-0	0.2
1940 Det-A	2	0	1.000	2	2	2	1	0	18	14	2	4	11	9.0	1.00	476	.206	.250	0	—	-1	7	8	0	0.7
1941 Det-A	0	0	—	17	2	0	0	0	34¹	45	3	26	10	18.6	6.03	75	.313	.418	2	.333	0	-7	-6	-0	-0.4
Total 3	3	1	.750	28	4	2	1	0	67²	78	6	42	30	16.0	3.99	117	.287	.382	2	.143	-1	2	5	-0	0.5

■ PAUL GIEL
Giel, Paul Robert   b: 2/29/32, Winona, Minn.   BR/TR, 5'11", 185 lbs.   Deb: 7/10/54

YEAR TM/L	W	L	PCT	G	GS	CG	SH	SV	IP	H	HR	BB	SO	RAT	ERA	ERA+	OAV	OOB	BH	AVG	PB	PR	/A	PD	TPI
1954 NY-N	0	0	—	6	0	0	0	0	4¹	8	0	2	4	20.8	8.31	49	.421	.476	0	—	0	-2	-2	-0	-0.1
1955 NY-N	4	4	.500	34	2	0	0	0	82¹	70	8	50	47	13.3	3.39	119	.233	.346	1	.053	-2	6	6	-1	0.3
1958 SF-N	4	5	.444	29	9	0	0	0	92	89	12	55	55	14.3	4.70	81	.259	.365	2	.074	-2	-8	-9	1	-0.9
1959 Pit-N	0	0	—	4	0	0	0	0	7²	17	0	6	3	27.0	14.09	27	.472	.548	0	—	0	-9	-9	0	-0.7
1960 Pit-N	2	0	1.000	16	0	0	0	0	33	35	3	15	21	13.6	5.73	65	.276	.352	0	.000	-1	-7	-7	-1	-0.8
1961 Min-A	1	0	1.000	12	0	0	0	0	19¹	24	6	17	14	19.1	9.78	43	.289	.410	1	.500	0	-12	-12	-0	-1.0
KC-A	0	0	—	1	0	0	0	0	1²	6	1	3	1	48.6	37.80	11	.600	.692	0	—	0	-6	-6	-0	-0.4
Yr	1	0	1.000	13	0	0	0	0	21	30	7	20	15	21.4	12.00	35	.319	.439	0	.000	0	-19	-18	-0	-1.4
Total 6	11	9	.550	102	11	0	0	0	240¹	249	30	148	145	15.0	5.39	73	.271	.374	4	.073	-4	-38	-39	0	-3.6

■ BOB GIGGIE
Giggie, Robert Thomas   b: 8/13/33, Dorchester, Mass.   BR/TR, 6'1", 200 lbs.   Deb: 4/18/59

YEAR TM/L	W	L	PCT	G	GS	CG	SH	SV	IP	H	HR	BB	SO	RAT	ERA	ERA+	OAV	OOB	BH	AVG	PB	PR	/A	PD	TPI
1959 Mil-N	1	0	1.000	13	0	0	0	1	20	24	2	10	15	15.3	4.05	87	.316	.395	0	.000	-0	-0	-1	1	0.0
1960 Mil-N	0	0	—	3	0	0	0	0	4¹	5	0	4	5	18.7	4.15	83	.278	.409	0	—	0	-0	-0	-0	0.0
KC-A	1	0	1.000	10	0	0	0	0	18²	24	1	15	8	18.8	5.79	69	.333	.448	0	.000	-0	-4	-4	0	-0.3
1962 KC-A	1	1	.500	4	2	0	0	0	14¹	17	5	3	4	13.2	6.28	66	.293	.339	0	.000	-1	-4	-3	-0	-0.3
Total 3	3	1	.750	30	2	0	0	1	57¹	70	8	32	32	16.2	5.18	74	.313	.401	0	.000	-1	-8	-9	1	-0.6

■ JOE GILBERT
Gilbert, Joe Dennis   b: 4/20/52, Jasper, Tex.   BR/TL, 6'1", 167 lbs.   Deb: 4/30/72

YEAR TM/L	W	L	PCT	G	GS	CG	SH	SV	IP	H	HR	BB	SO	RAT	ERA	ERA+	OAV	OOB	BH	AVG	PB	PR	/A	PD	TPI
1972 Mon-N	0	1	.000	22	0	0	0	0	33	41	3	18	25	16.1	8.45	42	.306	.388	0	.000	-0	-18	-18	-0	-1.8
1973 Mon-N	1	2	.333	21	0	0	0	1	29	30	1	19	17	15.2	4.97	77	.270	.377	0	.000	0	-4	-4	-0	-0.3
Total 2	1	3	.250	43	0	0	0	1	62	71	4	37	42	15.7	6.82	54	.290	.383	0	.000	-0	-23	-22	-0	-2.1

■ BILL GILBERT
Gilbert, Wilmer M.   b: 5/12/1870, Havre De Grace, Md   6', 180 lbs.   Deb: 9/15/1892

YEAR TM/L	W	L	PCT	G	GS	CG	SH	SV	IP	H	HR	BB	SO	RAT	ERA	ERA+	OAV	OOB	BH	AVG	PB	PR	/A	PD	TPI
1892 Bal-N	0	1	.000	2	1	1	0	0	14	14	1	17	5	19.9	5.79	60	.250	.425	2	.333	1	-4	-4	-1	-0.2

■ BILL GILBRETH
Gilbreth, William Freeman   b: 9/3/47, Abilene, Tex.   BL/TL, 6', 180 lbs.   Deb: 6/25/71

YEAR TM/L	W	L	PCT	G	GS	CG	SH	SV	IP	H	HR	BB	SO	RAT	ERA	ERA+	OAV	OOB	BH	AVG	PB	PR	/A	PD	TPI
1971 Det-A	2	1	.667	9	5	2	0	0	30	28	4	21	14	15.3	4.80	75	.264	.395	2	.182	-0	-4	-4	0	-0.3
1972 Det-A	0	0	—	2	0	0	0	0	5	10	1	4	2	25.2	16.20	19	.476	.560	0	.000	-0	-7	-7	0	-0.6
1974 Cal-A	0	0	—	3	0	0	0	0	1¹	2	0	1	0	20.3	13.50	25	.400	.500	0	—	0	-1	-1	0	-0.1
Total 3	2	1	.667	14	5	2	0	0	36¹	40	5	26	16	16.8	6.69	53	.303	.425	2	.167	-0	-13	-13	0	-1.0

■ BOB GILKS
Gilks, Robert James   b: 7/2/1864, Cincinnati, Ohio   d: 8/21/44, Brunswick, Ga.   BR/TR, 5'8", 178 lbs.   Deb: 8/25/1887 ♦

YEAR TM/L	W	L	PCT	G	GS	CG	SH	SV	IP	H	HR	BB	SO	RAT	ERA	ERA+	OAV	OOB	BH	AVG	PB	PR	/A	PD	TPI
1887 Cle-a	7	5	.583	13	13	12	1	0	108	104	1	42	28	12.2	3.08	141	.244	.312	26	.313	1	15	15	2	1.7
1888 Cle-a	0	2	.000	4	2	2	0	1	21	26	1	8	3	14.6	8.14	38	.293	.352	111	.229	-0	-12	-12	-0	-0.9
1890 Cle-N	2	2	.500	4	3	3	0	0	31²	34	0	9	5	12.2	4.26	84	.267	.315	116	.213	-0	-2	-2	-0	-0.1
Total 3	9	9	.500	21	18	17	1	1	160²	164	2	59	36	12.5	3.98	102	.255	.318	320	.231	1	0	1	2	0.7

■ ED GILL
Gill, Edward James   b: 8/7/1896, Somerville, Mass.   BL/TR, 5'10", 165 lbs.   Deb: 7/05/19

YEAR TM/L	W	L	PCT	G	GS	CG	SH	SV	IP	H	HR	BB	SO	RAT	ERA	ERA+	OAV	OOB	BH	AVG	PB	PR	/A	PD	TPI
1919 Was-A	1	1	.500	16	2	0	0	0	37¹	38	0	21	7	14.7	4.82	67	.260	.361	0	.000	-1	-7	-7	-0	-0.7

■ GEORGE GILL
Gill, George Lloyd   b: 2/13/09, Catchings, Miss.   BR/TR, 6'1", 185 lbs.   Deb: 5/04/37

YEAR TM/L	W	L	PCT	G	GS	CG	SH	SV	IP	H	HR	BB	SO	RAT	ERA	ERA+	OAV	OOB	BH	AVG	PB	PR	/A	PD	TPI
1937 Det-A	11	4	.733	31	10	4	1	1	127²	146	11	49	40	13.3	4.51	104	.285	.340	7	.140	-3	2	2	1	0.1
1938 Det-A	12	9	.571	24	23	13	1	0	164	195	15	50	30	13.6	4.12	121	.296	.348	6	.105	-4	12	16	-0	1.1
1939 Det-A	0	1	.000	3	1	0	0	0	8²	14	1	3	1	17.7	8.31	59	.368	.415	0	.000	-0	-4	-3	-0	-0.2
StL-A	1	12	.077	27	11	5	0	0	95	139	10	34	24	16.7	7.11	68	.343	.398	4	.154	-2	-26	-24	1	-2.0
Yr	1	13	.071	30	12	5	0	0	103²	153	11	37	25	16.8	7.21	68	.345	.400	4	.000	-2	-30	-27	2	-2.2
Total 3	24	26	.480	85	45	22	2	1	395¹	494	37	129	95	14.3	5.05	96	.306	.360	17	.126	-9	-16	-9	3	-1.0

■ HADDIE GILL
Gill, Harold Edward   b: 1/23/1899, Brockton, Mass.   d: 8/1/32, Brockton, Mass.   BL/TL, 5'11", 165 lbs.   Deb: 8/16/23

YEAR TM/L	W	L	PCT	G	GS	CG	SH	SV	IP	H	HR	BB	SO	RAT	ERA	ERA+	OAV	OOB	BH	AVG	PB	PR	/A	PD	TPI
1923 Cin-N	0	0	—	1	0	0	0	0	1	1	0	1	1	18.0	0.00	—	.333	.500	0	—	0	0	0	0	0.0

■ CLARAL GILLENWATER
Gillenwater, Claral Lewis   b: 5/20/1900, Sims, Ind.   d: 2/26/78, Bradenton, Fla.   BR/TR, 6', 187 lbs.   Deb: 8/20/23

YEAR TM/L	W	L	PCT	G	GS	CG	SH	SV	IP	H	HR	BB	SO	RAT	ERA	ERA+	OAV	OOB	BH	AVG	PB	PR	/A	PD	TPI
1923 Chi-A	1	3	.250	5	3	1	1	0	21¹	28	2	6	2	14.8	5.48	72	.337	.389	0	.000	-1	-4	-4	0	-0.3

■ TOM GILLES
Gilles, Thomas Bradford   b: 7/2/62, Peoria, Ill.   BR/TR, 6'1", 185 lbs.   Deb: 6/07/90

YEAR TM/L	W	L	PCT	G	GS	CG	SH	SV	IP	H	HR	BB	SO	RAT	ERA	ERA+	OAV	OOB	BH	AVG	PB	PR	/A	PD	TPI
1990 Tor-A	1	0	1.000	2	0	0	0	0	1¹	2	0	1	1	13.5	6.75	56	.333	.333	0	—	0	-0	-0	0	-0.0

■ JOHN GILLESPIE
Gillespie, John Patrick "Silent John"   b: 2/25/1900, Oakland, Cal.   d: 2/15/54, Vallejo, Cal.   BR/TR, 5'11.5", 172 lbs.   Deb: 4/12/22

YEAR TM/L	W	L	PCT	G	GS	CG	SH	SV	IP	H	HR	BB	SO	RAT	ERA	ERA+	OAV	OOB	BH	AVG	PB	PR	/A	PD	TPI
1922 Cin-N	3	3	.500	31	4	1	0	0	77²	84	9	29	21	13.6	4.52	88	.294	.367	2	.133	-1	-4	-5	1	-0.4

■ BOB GILLESPIE
Gillespie, Robert William "Bunch"   b: 10/8/18, Columbus, Ohio   BR/TR, 6'4", 187 lbs.   Deb: 5/11/44

YEAR TM/L	W	L	PCT	G	GS	CG	SH	SV	IP	H	HR	BB	SO	RAT	ERA	ERA+	OAV	OOB	BH	AVG	PB	PR	/A	PD	TPI
1944 Det-A	0	1	.000	7	0	0	0	0	11	7	0	12	4	15.5	6.55	54	.194	.396	0	.000	-0	-4	-4	0	-0.3
1947 Chi-A	5	8	.385	25	17	1	0	0	118	133	4	53	36	14.3	4.73	77	.291	.366	2	.061	-2	-13	-14	3	-1.3
1948 Chi-A	0	4	.000	25	6	1	0	0	72	81	3	33	19	14.4	5.13	83	.287	.364	0	.000	-2	-7	-7	-0	-0.8
1950 Bos-A	0	0	—	1	0	0	0	0	1¹	2	1	4	0	40.5	20.25	24	.333	.600	0	—	0	-2	-2	0	-0.1
Total 4	5	13	.278	58	23	2	0	0	202¹	223	8	102	59	14.5	5.07	76	.286	.369	2	.039	-5	-26	-27	3	-2.5

■ PAUL GILLIFORD
Gilliford, Paul Gant "Gorilla"   b: 1/12/45, Bryn Mawr, Pa.   BR/TL, 5'11", 210 lbs.   Deb: 9/20/67

YEAR TM/L	W	L	PCT	G	GS	CG	SH	SV	IP	H	HR	BB	SO	RAT	ERA	ERA+	OAV	OOB	BH	AVG	PB	PR	/A	PD	TPI
1967 Bal-A	0	0	—	2	0	0	0	0	3	6	1	1	2	21.0	12.00	26	.429	.467	0	—	0	-3	-3	0	-0.2

■ JACK GILLIGAN
Gilligan, John Patrick   b: 10/18/1884, Chicago, Ill.   d: 11/19/80, Modesto, Cal.   BB/TR, 6', 190 lbs.   Deb: 9/16/09

YEAR TM/L	W	L	PCT	G	GS	CG	SH	SV	IP	H	HR	BB	SO	RAT	ERA	ERA+	OAV	OOB	BH	AVG	PB	PR	/A	PD	TPI
1909 StL-A	1	2	.333	3	3	3	0	0	23	28	1	9	4	15.3	5.48	44	.315	.390	1	.111	-1	-8	-8	-0	-0.7
1910 StL-A	0	3	.000	9	5	2	0	0	39¹	37	0	28	10	15.1	3.66	68	.253	.377	3	.200	-0	-5	-5	0	-0.4
Total 2	1	5	.167	12	8	5	0	0	62¹	65	1	37	14	15.2	4.33	57	.277	.382	4	.167	-1	-13	-13	0	-1.1

■ GEORGE GILLPATRICK
Gillpatrick, George F.   b: 2/28/1875, Holden, Mo.   d: 12/15/41, Kansas City, Mo.   Deb: 5/22/1898

YEAR TM/L	W	L	PCT	G	GS	CG	SH	SV	IP	H	HR	BB	SO	RAT	ERA	ERA+	OAV	OOB	BH	AVG	PB	PR	/A	PD	TPI
1898 StL-N	0	2	.000	7	3	1	0	0	35	42	0	19	12	15.7	6.94	55	.295	.378	2	.125	-2	-13	-12	-1	-1.1

■ FRANK GILMORE
Gilmore, Frank T. "Shadow"   b: 4/27/1864, Webster, Mass.   d: 7/21/29, Hartford, Conn.   BR ,   Deb: 9/11/1886

YEAR TM/L	W	L	PCT	G	GS	CG	SH	SV	IP	H	HR	BB	SO	RAT	ERA	ERA+	OAV	OOB	BH	AVG	PB	PR	/A	PD	TPI
1886 Was-N	4	4	.500	9	9	9	1	0	75	57	3	22	75	9.5	2.52	130	.202	.260	0	.000	-4	7	6	-1	0.1
1887 Was-N	7	20	.259	28	27	27	1	0	234²	247	7	92	114	13.0	3.87	104	.263	.329	6	.065	-11	5	4	-3	-0.7
1888 Was-N	1	9	.100	12	11	10	0	0	95²	131	4	29	23	15.1	6.59	42	.315	.359	1	.024	-4	-40	-40	-2	-3.8
Total 3	12	33	.267	49	47	46	2	0	405¹	435	14	143	212	12.8	4.26	84	.266	.325	7	.043	-20	-29	-30	-6	-4.4

■ LEN GILMORE
Gilmore, Leonard Preston "Meow"   b: 11/3/17, Clinton, Ind.   BR/TR, 6'3", 175 lbs.   Deb: 10/01/44

YEAR TM/L	W	L	PCT	G	GS	CG	SH	SV	IP	H	HR	BB	SO	RAT	ERA	ERA+	OAV	OOB	BH	AVG	PB	PR	/A	PD	TPI
1944 Pit-N	0	1	.000	1	1	1	0	0	8	13	2	0	4	14.6	7.88	47	.361	.361	0	.000	-0	-4	-4	1	-0.2

■ JOHN GILROY
Gilroy, John M.   b: 10/26/1869, Washington, D.C.   d: 8/4/1897, Norfolk, Va.   Deb: 8/30/1895

YEAR TM/L	W	L	PCT	G	GS	CG	SH	SV	IP	H	HR	BB	SO	RAT	ERA	ERA+	OAV	OOB	BH	AVG	PB	PR	/A	PD	TPI
1895 Was-N	1	4	.200	8	4	2	0	0	41¹	63	3	24	2	18.9	6.53	73	.345	.421	7	.241	-1	-8	-8	1	-0.5
1896 Was-N	0	0	—	1	0	0	0	0	2	0	0	1	0	4.5	0.00	—	.000	.148	0	.000	-0	1	1	0	0.1

YEAR TM/L	W	L	PCT	G	GS	CG	SH	SV	IP	H	HR	BB	SO	RAT	ERA	ERA+	OAV	OOB	BH	AVG	PB	PR	/A	PD	TPI
Total 2	1	4	.200	9	4	2	0	0	43¹	63	3	25	2	18.3	6.23	77	.334	.412	7	.233	-1	-7	-7	1	-0.4

■ HAL GILSON
Gilson, Harold "Lefty" b: 2/9/42, Los Angeles, Cal. BR/TL, 6'5", 195 lbs. Deb: 4/14/68

YEAR TM/L	W	L	PCT	G	GS	CG	SH	SV	IP	H	HR	BB	SO	RAT	ERA	ERA+	OAV	OOB	BH	AVG	PB	PR	/A	PD	TPI
1968 StL-N	0	2	.000	13	0	0	0	2	21²	27	1	11	19	15.8	4.57	63	.310	.388	0	.000	-0	-4	-4	-1	-0.5
Hou-N	0	0	—	2	0	0	0	0	3²	7	0	1	1	22.1	7.36	40	.412	.474	0	—	0	-2	-2	0	-0.1
Yr	0	2	.000	15	0	0	0	2	25¹	34	1	12	20	16.7	4.97	58	.327	.402	0	.000	-0	-6	-6	-1	-0.6

■ BILLY GING
Ging, William Joseph b: 11/7/1872, Elmira, N.Y. d: 9/14/50, Elmira, N.Y. 5'10", 170 lbs. Deb: 9/25/1899

YEAR TM/L	W	L	PCT	G	GS	CG	SH	SV	IP	H	HR	BB	SO	RAT	ERA	ERA+	OAV	OOB	BH	AVG	PB	PR	/A	PD	TPI
1899 Bos-N	1	0	1.000	1	1	1	0	0	8	5	0	5	2	11.3	1.13	370	.180	.305	0	.000	-0	2	3	-0	0.2

■ JOE GINGRAS
Gingras, Joseph Elzead John b: 1/10/1894, New York, N.Y. d: 9/6/47, Jersey City, N.J. BR/TR, 6'2", 188 lbs. Deb: 6/18/15

YEAR TM/L	W	L	PCT	G	GS	CG	SH	SV	IP	H	HR	BB	SO	RAT	ERA	ERA+	OAV	OOB	BH	AVG	PB	PR	/A	PD	TPI
1915 KC-F	0	0	—	2	0	0	0	0	4	6	0	1	2	15.8	6.75	43	.354	.390	0	.000	-0	-2	-2	0	-0.1

■ CHARLIE GIRARD
Girard, Charles August b: 12/16/1884, Brooklyn, N.Y. d: 8/6/36, Brooklyn, N.Y. BR/TR, 5'10", 175 lbs. Deb: 9/14/10

YEAR TM/L	W	L	PCT	G	GS	CG	SH	SV	IP	H	HR	BB	SO	RAT	ERA	ERA+	OAV	OOB	BH	AVG	PB	PR	/A	PD	TPI
1910 Phi-N	1	2	.333	7	1	0	0	1	26²	33	2	12	11	15.9	6.41	49	.308	.388	1	.125	-0	-10	-10	-1	-1.0

■ DAVE GIUSTI
Giusti, David John b: 11/27/39, Seneca Falls, N.Y. BR/TR, 5'11", 190 lbs. Deb: 4/13/62

YEAR TM/L	W	L	PCT	G	GS	CG	SH	SV	IP	H	HR	BB	SO	RAT	ERA	ERA+	OAV	OOB	BH	AVG	PB	PR	/A	PD	TPI
1962 Hou-N	2	3	.400	22	5	0	0	0	73²	82	7	30	43	13.7	5.62	66	.280	.347	7	.292	2	-14	-15	1	-1.1
1964 Hou-N	0	0	—	8	0	0	0	0	25²	24	1	8	16	11.2	3.16	108	.253	.311	2	.286	1	1	1	1	0.3
1965 Hou-N	8	7	.533	38	13	4	1	3	131¹	132	13	46	92	12.3	4.32	78	.259	.321	6	.171	2	-11	-14	1	-1.1
1966 Hou-N	15	14	.517	34	33	9	4	0	210	215	23	54	131	11.7	4.20	81	.260	.310	17	.230	5	-14	-18	-1	-1.5
1967 Hou-N	11	15	.423	37	33	8	1	1	221²	231	23	58	157	11.9	4.18	79	.265	.313	13	.155	3	-20	-21	-2	-2.0
1968 Hou-N	11	14	.440	37	34	12	2	1	251	226	15	67	186	10.6	3.19	93	.239	.293	15	.183	-0	-6	-7	3	-0.1
1969 StL-N	3	7	.300	22	12	2	1	0	99²	96	7	37	62	12.1	3.61	99	.255	.323	5	.200	1	-0	-0	1	0.2
1970 *Pit-N	9	3	.750	66	1	0	0	26	103	98	7	39	85	12.0	3.06	128	.259	.328	3	.188	2	11	10	-0	1.1
1971 *Pit-N	5	6	.455	58	0	0	0	30	86	79	5	31	55	11.6	2.93	115	.241	.308	1	.059	-1	5	4	-1	0.2
1972 *Pit-N	7	4	.636	54	0	0	0	22	74²	59	3	20	54	9.5	1.93	172	.219	.273	0	.000	-1	13	12	0	1.2
1973 Pit-N	9	2	.818	67	0	0	0	20	98²	89	9	37	64	11.5	2.37	148	.241	.310	4	.308	1	14	13	-2	1.2
1974 *Pit-N	7	5	.583	64	2	0	0	12	105²	101	7	40	53	12.0	3.32	104	.258	.327	1	.111	-0	3	1	1	0.2
1975 *Pit-N	5	4	.556	61	0	0	0	17	91²	79	3	42	38	11.9	2.95	120	.237	.322	3	.300	1	7	6	0	0.8
1976 Pit-N	5	4	.556	40	0	0	0	6	58¹	59	7	24	33	13.3	4.32	81	.267	.347	0	.000	-0	-5	-5	-0	-0.4
1977 Oak-A	3	3	.500	40	0	0	0	6	60¹	54	4	20	28	11.0	2.98	135	.245	.308	0	—	0	7	7	0	0.7
Chi-N	0	2	.000	20	0	0	0	1	25¹	30	2	14	15	15.6	6.04	73	.297	.383	0	.000	-0	-6	-5	-0	-0.4
Total 15	100	93	.518	668	133	35	9	145	1716²	1654	126	570	1103	11.7	3.60	95	.253	.315	77	.187	17	-14	-33	3	-0.7

■ DAN GLADDEN
Gladden, Clinton Daniel b: 7/7/57, San Jose, Cal. BR/TR, 5'11", 180 lbs. Deb: 9/05/83 ♦

YEAR TM/L	W	L	PCT	G	GS	CG	SH	SV	IP	H	HR	BB	SO	RAT	ERA	ERA+	OAV	OOB	BH	AVG	PB	PR	/A	PD	TPI
1988 Min-A	0	0	—	1	0	0	0	0	1	0	0	0	0	0.0	0.00	—	.000	.000	155	.269	1	0	0	0	0.0
1989 Min-A	0	0	—	1	0	0	0	0	1	2	0	1	0	27.0	9.00	46	.400	.500	136	.295	1	-1	-1	0	0.0
Total 2	0	0	—	2	0	0	0	0	2	2	0	1	0	13.5	4.50	91	.250	.333	900	.275	2	-0	-0	0	0.0

■ FRED GLADDING
Gladding, Fred Earl b: 6/28/36, Flat Rock, Mich. BL/TR, 6'1", 220 lbs. Deb: 7/01/61 C

YEAR TM/L	W	L	PCT	G	GS	CG	SH	SV	IP	H	HR	BB	SO	RAT	ERA	ERA+	OAV	OOB	BH	AVG	PB	PR	/A	PD	TPI
1961 Det-A	1	0	1.000	8	0	0	0	0	16¹	18	1	11	11	17.1	3.31	124	.286	.408	0	.000	-0	1	1	-0	0.1
1962 Det-A	0	0	—	6	0	0	0	0	5	3	0	2	4	9.0	0.00	—	.176	.263	0	—	0	2	2	0	0.3
1963 Det-A	1	1	.500	22	0	0	0	7	27¹	19	1	14	24	10.9	1.98	189	.198	.300	0	.000	-0	5	5	0	0.6
1964 Det-A	7	4	.636	42	0	0	0	7	67¹	57	7	27	59	11.5	3.07	119	.233	.314	0	.000	-1	4	4	1	0.4
1965 Det-A	6	2	.750	46	0	0	0	5	70	63	6	29	43	12.3	2.83	123	.239	.323	0	.000	-1	5	5	-1	0.4
1966 Det-A	5	0	1.000	51	0	0	0	2	74	62	6	29	57	11.2	3.28	106	.230	.307	0	.000	-0	1	2	-1	0.1
1967 Det-A	6	4	.600	42	1	0	0	12	77	62	6	19	64	9.9	1.99	164	.227	.287	0	.000	-2	11	11	-0	1.0
1968 Hou-N	0	0	—	7	0	0	0	2	4¹	8	0	3	2	24.9	14.54	20	.421	.522	0	—	0	-6	-6	0	-0.5
1969 Hou-N	4	8	.333	57	0	0	0	29	72²	83	2	27	40	13.7	4.21	84	.289	.352	1	.100	-0	-5	-5	0	-0.5
1970 Hou-N	7	4	.636	63	0	0	0	18	71	84	4	24	46	14.1	4.06	96	.293	.354	0	.000	-1	-0	-1	1	0.0
1971 Hou-N	4	5	.444	48	0	0	0	12	51¹	51	0	22	17	14.0	2.10	160	.268	.365	0	.000	-0	8	7	-1	0.6
1972 Hou-N	5	6	.455	42	0	0	0	14	48²	38	1	12	18	9.6	2.77	121	.222	.281	0	.000	-1	4	3	-1	0.2
1973 Hou-N	2	0	1.000	16	0	0	0	1	16	18	4	9	12	12.4	4.50	81	.290	.333	0	—	0	-1	-2	0	0.0
Total 13	48	34	.585	450	1	0	0	109	601	566	38	223	394	12.2	3.13	113	.252	.327	1	.016	-6	29	28	-1	2.7

■ FRED GLADE
Glade, Frederick Monroe "Lucky" b: 1/25/1876, Dubuque, Iowa d: 11/21/34, Grand Island, Neb. BR/TR, 5'10", 175 lbs. Deb: 5/27/02

YEAR TM/L	W	L	PCT	G	GS	CG	SH	SV	IP	H	HR	BB	SO	RAT	ERA	ERA+	OAV	OOB	BH	AVG	PB	PR	/A	PD	TPI
1902 Chi-N	0	1	.000	1	1	0	0	0	8	13	0	3	3	19.1	9.00	30	.364	.428	1	.333	1	-6	-6	0	-0.3
1904 StL-A	18	15	.545	35	34	30	6	1	289	248	2	58	156	9.5	2.27	109	.233	.272	19	.186	1	10	7	0	0.8
1905 StL-A	6	25	.194	32	32	23	2	0	275	257	6	58	127	10.3	2.81	91	.249	.289	9	.092	-6	-5	-8	4	-1.1
1906 StL-A	15	14	.517	35	32	28	4	1	266²	215	4	59	96	9.2	2.36	109	.224	.269	13	.137	-4	10	7	-2	-0.6
1907 StL-A	13	9	.591	24	22	18	2	0	202	187	2	45	71	10.3	2.67	94	.248	.290	15	.205	2	-3	-3	-4	-0.6
1908 NY-A	0	4	.000	5	5	2	0	0	32	30	0	14	11	13.5	4.22	59	.275	.378	0	.000	-1	-6	-6	-1	-0.7
Total 6	52	68	.433	132	126	107	14	2	1072²	950	11	237	464	10.0	2.62	97	.240	.284	57	.150	-7	1	-10	-3	-1.9

■ JOHN GLAISER
Glaiser, John Burke "Bert" b: 7/28/1894, Yoakum, Tex. d: 3/7/59, Houston, Tex. BL/TR, 5'8", 165 lbs. Deb: 4/20/20

YEAR TM/L	W	L	PCT	G	GS	CG	SH	SV	IP	H	HR	BB	SO	RAT	ERA	ERA+	OAV	OOB	BH	AVG	PB	PR	/A	PD	TPI
1920 Det-A	0	0	—	9	1	0	0	1	17	23	1	8	3	16.9	6.35	59	.354	.432	0	.000	-0	-5	-5	1	-0.3

■ TOM GLASS
Glass, Thomas Joseph b: 4/29/1898, Greensboro, N.C. d: 12/15/81, Greensboro, N.C. BR/TR, 6'3", 170 lbs. Deb: 6/12/25

YEAR TM/L	W	L	PCT	G	GS	CG	SH	SV	IP	H	HR	BB	SO	RAT	ERA	ERA+	OAV	OOB	BH	AVG	PB	PR	/A	PD	TPI
1925 Phi-A	1	0	1.000	2	0	0	0	0	5	9	0	0	2	16.2	5.40	86	.409	.409	0	—	0	-1	-0	-0	0.0

■ JACK GLASSCOCK
Glasscock, John Wesley "Pebbly Jack" b: 7/22/1859, Wheeling, W.Va. d: 2/24/47, Wheeling, W.Va. BR/TR, 5'8", 160 lbs. Deb: 5/01/1879 M♦

YEAR TM/L	W	L	PCT	G	GS	CG	SH	SV	IP	H	HR	BB	SO	RAT	ERA	ERA+	OAV	OOB	BH	AVG	PB	PR	/A	PD	TPI
1884 Cle-N	0	0	—	2	0	0	0	0	5	8	0	2	1	18.0	5.40	58	.343	.395	70	.249	0	-1	-1	1	0.0
1887 Ind-N	0	0	—	1	0	0	0	0	1	0	0	1	0	0.0	0.00	—	.000	.000	142	.294	0	0	0	0	0.0
1888 Ind-N	0	0	—	1	0	0	0	0	0¹	1	0	2	1	81.0	54.00	5	.501	.751	119	.269	0	-2	-2	0	-0.1
1889 Ind-N	0	0	—	1	0	0	0	0	0²	3	0	3	0	81.0	0.00	—	.603	.752	205	.352	0	0	0	0	0.0
Total 4	0	0	—	5	0	0	0	0	7	12	0	7	3	24.4	6.43	53	.361	.472	2040	.290	1	-2	-2	1	-0.1

■ LUKE GLAVENICH
Glavenich, Luke Frank b: 1/17/1893, Jackson, Cal. d: 5/22/35, Stockton, Cal. 5'9.5", 189 lbs. Deb: 4/12/13

YEAR TM/L	W	L	PCT	G	GS	CG	SH	SV	IP	H	HR	BB	SO	RAT	ERA	ERA+	OAV	OOB	BH	AVG	PB	PR	/A	PD	TPI
1913 Cle-A	0	0	—	1	0	0	0	0	3	3	0	1	1	54.0	9.00	34	.500	.667	0	—	0	-1	-1	-0	0.0

■ TOM GLAVINE
Glavine, Thomas Michael b: 3/25/66, Concord, Mass. BL/TL, 6'1", 175 lbs. Deb: 8/17/87

YEAR TM/L	W	L	PCT	G	GS	CG	SH	SV	IP	H	HR	BB	SO	RAT	ERA	ERA+	OAV	OOB	BH	AVG	PB	PR	/A	PD	TPI
1987 Atl-N	2	4	.333	9	9	0	0	0	50¹	55	5	33	20	16.3	5.54	78	.279	.391	2	.125	-0	-8	-7	1	-0.5
1988 Atl-N	7	17	.292	34	34	1	0	0	195¹	201	12	63	84	12.5	4.56	81	.270	.333	11	.183	1	-24	-19	2	-1.6
1989 Atl-N	14	8	.636	29	29	6	4	0	186	172	20	40	90	10.4	3.68	99	.243	.285	10	.149	-0	-4	-4	2	0.2
1990 Atl-N	10	12	.455	33	33	1	0	0	214¹	232	18	78	129	13.1	4.28	91	.281	.343	7	.113	0	-12	-9	2	-0.5
Total 4	33	41	.446	105	105	8	4	0	646	660	55	214	323	12.4	4.29	89	.266	.328	30	.146	1	-48	-35	6	-2.5

■ RALPH GLAZE
Glaze, Daniel Ralph b: 3/13/1882, Denver, Col. d: 10/31/68, Atascadero, Cal. BR/TR, 5'9", 165 lbs. Deb: 6/01/06

YEAR TM/L	W	L	PCT	G	GS	CG	SH	SV	IP	H	HR	BB	SO	RAT	ERA	ERA+	OAV	OOB	BH	AVG	PB	PR	/A	PD	TPI
1906 Bos-A	4	6	.400	19	10	7	0	0	123	110	4	32	56	10.4	3.59	77	.242	.292	10	.182	0	-12	-11	0	-1.1
1907 Bos-A	9	13	.409	32	21	11	1	0	182¹	150	4	48	68	9.8	2.32	111	.226	.278	11	.180	0	5	5	-4	0.2
1908 Bos-A	2	2	.500	10	3	2	0	0	34²	43	1	5	13	12.5	3.38	73	.253	.274	1	.077	-1	-4	-4	-1	-0.5
Total 3	15	21	.417	61	34	20	1	0	340	303	9	85	137	10.3	2.89	91	.235	.283	22	.171	-1	-11	-10	-4	-1.4

YEAR	TM/L	W	L	PCT	G	GS	CG	SH	SV	IP	H	HR	BB	SO	RAT	ERA	ERA+	OAV	OOB	BH	AVG	PB	PR	/A	PD	TPI

■ WHITEY GLAZNER   Glazner, Charles Franklin   b: 9/17/1893, Sycamore, Ala.   d: 6/6/89, Orlando, Fla.   BR/TR, 5'9", 165 lbs.   Deb: 9/26/20

YEAR	TM/L	W	L	PCT	G	GS	CG	SH	SV	IP	H	HR	BB	SO	RAT	ERA	ERA+	OAV	OOB	BH	AVG	PB	PR	/A	PD	TPI
1920	Pit-N	0	0	—	2	0	0	0	0	8²	9	0	2	1	11.4	3.12	103	.300	.344	0	.000	-0	0	0	-0	0.0
1921	Pit-N	14	5	.737	36	25	15	0	1	234	214	5	58	88	10.9	2.77	139	.250	.306	10	.132	-3	26	28	-4	2.1
1922	Pit-N	11	12	.478	34	26	10	1	1	193	238	5	52	77	13.6	4.38	93	.309	.354	16	.246	3	-6	-7	-0	0.4
1923	Pit-N	2	1	.667	7	4	1	1	1	30	29	5	11	8	12.0	3.30	122	.250	.315	4	.333	2	2	2	0	0.2
	Phi-N	7	14	.333	28	23	12	2	1	161¹	195	11	63	51	14.7	4.69	98	.304	.371	9	.170	-0	-12	-1	-0	-0.1
	Yr	9	15	.375	35	27	13	3	2	191¹	224	16	74	59	14.3	4.47	101	.296	.363	13	.077	1	-10	1	0	0.3
1924	Phi-N	7	16	.304	35	24	8	2	0	156²	210	14	63	41	15.9	5.92	75	.339	.403	8	.157	-4	-36	-25	1	-2.5
Total 5		41	48	.461	142	102	46	6	4	783²	895	44	249	266	13.4	4.21	99	.295	.353	47	.181	-3	-25	-3	-3	-0.3

■ JOE GLEASON   Gleason, Joseph Paul   b: 7/9/1895, Phelps, N.Y.   d: 9/8/90, Phelps, N.Y.   BR/TR, 5'10.5", 175 lbs.   Deb: 9/11/20

YEAR	TM/L	W	L	PCT	G	GS	CG	SH	SV	IP	H	HR	BB	SO	RAT	ERA	ERA+	OAV	OOB	BH	AVG	PB	PR	/A	PD	TPI
1920	Was-A	0	0	—	3	0	0	0	0	8	14	2	6	2	23.6	13.50	28	.326	.420	0	.000	1	-9	-9	0	-0.6
1922	Was-A	2	2	.500	8	5	3	0	0	40²	53	3	18	12	15.9	4.65	83	.319	.389	2	.143	-0	-3	-4	-0	-0.3
Total 2		2	2	.500	11	5	3	0	0	48²	67	5	24	14	17.2	6.10	63	.321	.396	2	.125	0	-11	-12	0	-0.9

■ BILL GLEASON   Gleason, William   b: 1868, Cleveland, Ohio   d: 12/2/1893, Cleveland, Ohio   Deb: 4/24/1890

YEAR	TM/L	W	L	PCT	G	GS	CG	SH	SV	IP	H	HR	BB	SO	RAT	ERA	ERA+	OAV	OOB	BH	AVG	PB	PR	/A	PD	TPI
1890	Cle-P	0	1	.000	1	1	0	0	0	4	14	1	6	0	45.0	27.00	15	.537	.624	0	.000	-0	-10	-10	-0	-0.6

■ KID GLEASON   Gleason, William J.   b: 10/26/1866, Camden, N.J.   d: 1/2/33, Philadelphia, Pa.   BB/TR, 5'7", 158 lbs.   Deb: 4/20/1888   MC◆

YEAR	TM/L	W	L	PCT	G	GS	CG	SH	SV	IP	H	HR	BB	SO	RAT	ERA	ERA+	OAV	OOB	BH	AVG	PB	PR	/A	PD	TPI
1888	Phi-N	7	16	.304	24	23	23	0	0	199²	199	11	53	89	11.4	2.84	104	.250	.297	17	.205	-0	-0	2	-3	0.0
1889	Phi-N	9	15	.375	29	21	15	0	1	205	242	8	97	64	14.9	5.58	78	.285	.358	25	.253	3	-35	-28	1	-1.8
1890	Phi-N	38	17	.691	60	55	54	6	**2**	506	479	8	167	222	11.5	2.63	139	.243	.302	47	.210	-5	52	57	-0	4.8
1891	Phi-N	24	22	.522	53	44	40	1	1	418	431	16	165	100	12.8	3.51	97	.256	.324	53	.248	6	-8	-5	-3	0.1
1892	StL-N	20	24	.455	47	45	43	2	0	400	389	11	151	133	12.2	3.33	96	.245	.310	50	.215	8	-2	-6	5	0.8
1893	StL-N	21	22	.488	48	45	37	1	1	380¹	436	18	187	86	14.7	4.61	103	.279	.356	51	.256	3	2	5	1	1.0
1894	StL-N	2	6	.250	8	8	6	0	0	58	75	2	21	9	14.9	6.05	89	.310	.365	7	.250	-0	-5	-4	-1	-0.1
	*Bal-N	15	5	.750	21	20	19	0	0	172	224	3	44	35	14.0	4.45	123	.311	.351	30	.349	4	17	19	-1	1.8
	Yr	17	11	.607	29	28	25	0	0	230	299	5	65	44	14.2	4.85	112	.311	.355	9	.079	4	12	15	0	1.7
1895	*Bal-N	2	4	.333	9	5	3	0	0	50¹	77	4	21	6	17.5	6.97	68	.345	.402	130	.309	2	-12	-12	-0	-0.9
Total 8		138	131	.513	299	266	240	10	6	2389¹	2552	75	906	744	13.0	3.79	103	.265	.328	1944	.261	21	10	28	1	5.7

■ JERRY GLEATON   Gleaton, Jerry Don   b: 9/14/57, Brownwood, Tex.   BL/TL, 6'3", 205 lbs.   Deb: 7/11/79

YEAR	TM/L	W	L	PCT	G	GS	CG	SH	SV	IP	H	HR	BB	SO	RAT	ERA	ERA+	OAV	OOB	BH	AVG	PB	PR	/A	PD	TPI
1979	Tex-A	0	1	.000	5	2	0	0	0	9²	15	0	2	2	16.8	6.52	64	.375	.419	0		0	-2	-3	0	-0.1
1980	Tex-A	0	0	—	5	0	0	0	0	7	5	0	4	2	11.6	2.57	151	.208	.321	0		0	1	1	0	0.1
1981	Sea-A	4	7	.364	20	13	1	0	0	85¹	88	10	38	31	13.5	4.75	81	.273	.354	0		0	-10	-8	-0	-0.8
1982	Sea-A	0	0	—	3	0	0	0	0	4²	7	3	2	1	19.3	13.50	31	.333	.417	0		0	-5	-5	0	-0.3
1984	Chi-A	1	2	.333	11	1	0	0	2	18¹	20	2	6	4	13.3	3.44	121	.286	.351	0		0	1	1	-0	0.1
1985	Chi-A	1	0	1.000	31	0	0	0	1	29²	37	3	13	22	15.2	5.76	75	.316	.385	0		0	-5	-5	-0	-0.4
1987	KC-A	4	4	.500	48	0	0	0	5	50²	38	4	28	44	11.7	4.26	107	.216	.324	0		0	1	2	1	0.2
1988	KC-A	0	4	.000	42	0	0	0	3	38	33	2	17	29	12.6	3.55	112	.232	.327	0		0	2	2	-0	0.2
1989	KC-A	0	0	—	15	0	0	0	0	14¹	20	0	6	9	16.3	5.65	68	.345	.406	0		0	-3	-3	0	-0.2
1990	Det-A	1	3	.250	57	0	0	0	13	82²	62	5	25	56	9.8	2.94	134	.213	.282	0		0	9	9	0	0.9
Total 10		11	21	.344	237	16	1	0	24	340¹	325	29	141	200	12.6	4.28	95	.258	.338	0		0	-12	-9	0	-0.3

■ MARTIN GLENDON   Glendon, Martin J.   b: 2/8/1877, Milwaukee, Wis.   d: 11/6/50, Norwood Park, Ill.   5'8", 165 lbs.   Deb: 4/18/02

YEAR	TM/L	W	L	PCT	G	GS	CG	SH	SV	IP	H	HR	BB	SO	RAT	ERA	ERA+	OAV	OOB	BH	AVG	PB	PR	/A	PD	TPI
1902	Cin-N	0	1	.000	1	1	0	0	0	3	5	0	4	0	27.0	12.00	25	.370	.513	0	.000	-0	-3	-3	0	-0.2
1903	Cle-A	1	2	.333	3	3	3	0	0	27²	20	0	7	9	8.8	0.98	292	.202	.255	0	.000	-1	6	6	1	0.7
Total 2		1	3	.250	4	4	3	0	0	30²	25	0	11	9	10.6	2.05	140	.222	.292	0	.000	-1	3	3	1	0.5

■ BOB GLENN   Glenn, Burdette   b: 6/16/1894, W.Sunbury, Pa.   d: 6/3/77, Richmond, Cal.   Deb: 7/27/20

YEAR	TM/L	W	L	PCT	G	GS	CG	SH	SV	IP	H	HR	BB	SO	RAT	ERA	ERA+	OAV	OOB	BH	AVG	PB	PR	/A	PD	TPI
1920	StL-N	0	0	—	2	0	0	0	0	2	2	0	0	0	9.0	0.00	—	.222	.222	0	—	0	1	1	0	0.1

■ SAL GLIATTO   Gliatto, Salvador Michael   b: 5/7/02, Chicago, Ill.   BB/TR, 5'8.5", 150 lbs.   Deb: 4/19/30

YEAR	TM/L	W	L	PCT	G	GS	CG	SH	SV	IP	H	HR	BB	SO	RAT	ERA	ERA+	OAV	OOB	BH	AVG	PB	PR	/A	PD	TPI
1930	Cle-A	0	0	—	8	0	0	0	2	15	21	1	9	7	19.2	6.60	73	.328	.427	0	.000	-0	-3	-3	-0	-0.2

■ ED GLYNN   Glynn, Edward Paul   b: 6/3/53, Flushing, N.Y.   BR/TL, 6'2", 180 lbs.   Deb: 9/19/75

YEAR	TM/L	W	L	PCT	G	GS	CG	SH	SV	IP	H	HR	BB	SO	RAT	ERA	ERA+	OAV	OOB	BH	AVG	PB	PR	/A	PD	TPI
1975	Det-A	0	2	.000	3	1	0	0	0	14²	11	1	4	8	11.7	4.30	93	.220	.328	0	—	0	-1	-0	0	0.0
1976	Det-A	1	3	.250	5	4	1	0	0	23²	22	3	20	17	16.0	6.08	61	.265	.408	0	—	0	-7	-6	-1	-0.6
1977	Det-A	2	1	.667	8	3	0	0	0	27¹	36	3	12	13	15.8	5.27	81	.316	.381	0	—	0	-4	-3	-0	-0.2
1978	Det-A	0	0	—	10	0	0	0	0	14²	11	3	4	9	9.2	3.07	126	.208	.263	0	—	0	1	1	0	0.2
1979	NY-N	1	4	.200	46	0	0	0	7	60	57	3	40	32	14.9	3.00	121	.259	.378	0	.000	0	5	4	-1	0.3
1980	NY-N	3	3	.500	38	0	0	0	0	52¹	49	5	23	32	12.4	4.13	86	.246	.324	0	.000	-1	-3	-3	1	-0.2
1981	Cle-A	0	0	—	4	0	0	0	0	7²	5	0	4	4	10.6	1.17	309	.192	.300	0	—	0	2	2	0	0.2
1982	Cle-A	5	2	.714	47	0	0	0	4	49²	43	6	30	54	13.2	4.17	98	.232	.340	0	—	0	-1	-0	1	0.0
1983	Cle-A	2	0	1.000	11	0	0	0	0	12¹	22	2	6	13	20.4	5.84	73	.373	.431	0	—	0	-2	-2	-0	-0.1
1985	Mon-N	0	0	—	3	0	0	0	0	2¹	5	0	4	2	34.7	19.29	18	.455	.600	0	—	0	-4	-4	0	-0.2
Total 10		12	17	.414	175	8	1	0	12	264²	261	26	151	184	14.1	4.25	90	.261	.359	0	.000	-1	-13	-12	-1	-0.8

■ JOT GOAR   Goar, Joshua Mercer   b: 1/31/1870, New Lisbon, Ind.   d: 4/4/47, New Castle, Ind.   BR/TR, 5'9", 160 lbs.   Deb: 4/18/1896

YEAR	TM/L	W	L	PCT	G	GS	CG	SH	SV	IP	H	HR	BB	SO	RAT	ERA	ERA+	OAV	OOB	BH	AVG	PB	PR	/A	PD	TPI
1896	Pit-N	0	1	.000	3	0	0	0	0	13¹	36	1	8	3	29.7	16.88	25	.485	.535	1	.167	-0	-19	-19	-0	-1.3
1898	Cin-N	0	0	—	1	0	0	0	0	2	4	0	1	0	22.5	9.00	43	.411	.466	0	—	0	-1	-1	0	0.0
Total 2		0	1	.000	4	0	0	0	0	15¹	40	1	9	3	28.8	15.85	26	.476	.527	1	.167	-0	-20	-20	-0	-1.3

■ GEORGE GOETZ   Goetz, George Burt   b: Greencastle, Ind.   6'2", 180 lbs.   Deb: 6/17/1889

YEAR	TM/L	W	L	PCT	G	GS	CG	SH	SV	IP	H	HR	BB	SO	RAT	ERA	ERA+	OAV	OOB	BH	AVG	PB	PR	/A	PD	TPI
1889	Bal-a	1	0	1.000	1	1	0	0	0	9	12	0	0	2	12.0	4.00	99	.310	.310	0	.000	-1	-0	-0	0	0.0

■ JOHN GOETZ   Goetz, John Hardy   b: 10/24/37, Goetzville, Mich.   BR/TR, 6', 185 lbs.   Deb: 4/16/60

YEAR	TM/L	W	L	PCT	G	GS	CG	SH	SV	IP	H	HR	BB	SO	RAT	ERA	ERA+	OAV	OOB	BH	AVG	PB	PR	/A	PD	TPI
1960	Chi-N	0	0	—	4	0	0	0	0	6¹	10	2	4	6	19.9	12.79	30	.370	.452	0	.000	-0	-6	-6	0	-0.5

■ BILL GOGOLEWSKI   Gogolewski, William Joseph   b: 10/26/47, Oshkosh, Wis.   BL/TR, 6'4", 190 lbs.   Deb: 9/03/70

YEAR	TM/L	W	L	PCT	G	GS	CG	SH	SV	IP	H	HR	BB	SO	RAT	ERA	ERA+	OAV	OOB	BH	AVG	PB	PR	/A	PD	TPI
1970	Was-A	2	2	.500	8	5	0	0	0	33²	33	3	25	19	15.8	4.81	74	.260	.386	0	.000	-0	-4	-5	1	-0.3
1971	Was-A	6	5	.545	27	17	4	1	0	124¹	112	5	39	70	11.1	2.75	120	.241	.302	5	.156	0	10	8	-0	0.8
1972	Tex-A	4	11	.267	36	21	2	1	2	150²	136	9	58	95	11.9	4.24	71	.239	.316	5	.125	-1	-20	-21	-0	-2.3
1973	Tex-A	3	6	.333	49	2	0	0	6	123²	139	10	48	77	13.7	4.22	88	.286	.351	0	—	0	-6	-7	2	-0.4
1974	Cle-A	0	0	—	5	0	0	0	0	13²	15	1	2	3	11.9	4.61	78	.283	.321	0	—	0	-2	-1	0	-0.1
1975	Chi-A	0	0	—	19	0	0	0	0	55	61	5	28	37	14.7	5.24	74	.292	.378	0	—	0	-9	-8	1	-0.7
Total 6		15	24	.385	144	44	6	2	10	501	496	32	200	301	12.7	4.02	85	.260	.334	10	.127	-1	-30	-34	5	-2.9

■ JIM GOLDEN   Golden, James Edward   b: 3/20/36, Eldon, Mo.   BL/TR, 6', 175 lbs.   Deb: 9/30/60

YEAR	TM/L	W	L	PCT	G	GS	CG	SH	SV	IP	H	HR	BB	SO	RAT	ERA	ERA+	OAV	OOB	BH	AVG	PB	PR	/A	PD	TPI
1960	LA-N	1	0	1.000	1	1	0	0	0	7	6	1	4	4	12.9	6.43	62	.240	.345	1	.333	1	-2	-2	0	0.0
1961	LA-N	1	1	.500	28	0	0	0	0	42	52	7	20	18	15.4	5.79	75	.306	.379	0	.000	-0	-8	-7	0	-0.6
1962	Hou-N	7	11	.389	37	18	5	2	1	152²	163	13	50	88	12.6	4.07	92	.270	.326	12	.222	4	-2	-6	1	0.0
1963	Hou-N	0	1	.000	3	1	0	0	0	6¹	12	0	2	5	19.9	5.68	55	.429	.467	0	—	0	-2	-2	-0	-0.1
Total 4		9	13	.409	69	20	5	2	1	208	233	21	76	115	13.4	4.54	85	.282	.343	13	.217	4	-14	-16	1	-0.7

YEAR TM/L	W	L	PCT	G	GS	CG	SH	SV	IP	H	HR	BB	SO	RAT	ERA	ERA+	OAV	OOB	BH	AVG	PB	PR	/A	PD	TPI
■ MIKE GOLDEN Golden, Michael Henry b: 9/11/1851, Shirley, Mass. d: 1/11/29, Rockford, Ill. BR/TR, 5'8", 168 lbs. Deb: 5/05/1875 ◆																									
1875 Wes-n	1	12	.077	13	13	13	0	0	112	110	0	14		10.0	2.81	96	.225	.247	6	.130	-4	-4	-1		-0.3
Chi-n	6	7	.462	14	14	12	1	0	119	129	0	11		10.6	2.87	87	.252	.268	40	.258	1	-5	-5		-0.3
Yr	7	19	.269	27	27	25	1	0	231	239	0	25		10.3	2.84	91	.239	.258	2	.010	-4	-10	-6	0	-0.6
1878 Mil-N	3	13	.188	22	18	15	0	0	161	217	1	33	52	14.0	4.14	63	.307	.338	44	.206	-2	-33	-27	0	-2.3
■ ROY GOLDEN Golden, Roy Kramer b: 7/12/1888, Madisonville, Ill d: 10/4/61, Norwood, Ohio TR, 6'1", 195 lbs. Deb: 9/07/10																									
1910 StL-N	2	3	.400	7	6	3	0	0	42²	44	3	33	31	16.7	4.43	67	.286	.418	4	.267	1	-7	-7	1	-0.5
1911 StL-N	4	9	.308	30	25	6	0	0	148²	127	6	129	81	15.8	5.02	67	.240	.394	5	.114	-1	-27	-27	-1	-2.7
Total 2	6	12	.333	37	31	9	0	0	191¹	171	9	162	112	16.0	4.89	67	.250	.399	9	.153	-1	-33	-34	0	-3.2
■ FRED GOLDSMITH Goldsmith, Fred Ernest b: 5/15/1852, New Haven, Conn. d: 3/28/39, Berkley, Mich. BR/TR, 6'1", 195 lbs. Deb: 10/23/1875 U◆																									
1879 Tro-N	2	4	.333	8	7	7	0	0	63	61	0	1	31	8.9	1.57	159	.238	.241	9	.237	0	6	6	-0	0.6
1880 Chi-N	21	3	.875	26	24	22	4	1	210¹	189	0	18	90	8.9	1.75	138	.228	.244	37	.261	2	14	16	2	2.0
1881 Chi-N	24	13	.649	39	39	37	5	0	330	328	4	44	76	10.1	2.59	106	.248	.272	38	.241	3	7	5	6	1.3
1882 Chi-N	28	17	.622	45	45	45	4	0	405	377	7	38	109	9.2	2.42	118	.233	.250	42	.230	-1	21	20	-1	1.5
1883 Chi-N	25	19	.568	46	45	40	2	0	383¹	456	14	39	82	11.6	3.15	102	.279	.296	52	.221	-0	-0	2	2	0.4
1884 Chi-N	9	11	.450	21	21	20	1	0	188	245	11	29	34	13.1	4.26	74	.299	.323	11	.136	-3	-27	-23	-2	-2.2
Bal-a	3	1	.750	4	4	3	0	0	30	29	0	2	11	9.3	2.70	128	.240	.253	2	.143	-0	2	3	1	0.3
Total 6	112	68	.622	189	185	174	16	1	1609²	1685	38	171	433	10.4	2.73	106	.255	.274	191	.224	-1	23	28	7	3.9
■ HAL GOLDSMITH Goldsmith, Harold Eugene b: 8/18/1898, Peconic, N.Y. BR/TR, 6', 174 lbs. Deb: 6/23/26																									
1926 Bos-N	5	7	.417	19	15	5	0	0	101	135	2	28	16	14.6	4.37	81	.333	.377	8	.211	0	-6	-9	1	-0.7
1927 Bos-N	1	3	.250	22	5	1	0	1	71²	83	4	26	13	13.7	3.52	106	.289	.348	5	.238	0	3	2	0	0.2
1928 Bos-N	0	0	—	4	0	0	0	0	8¹	14	2	1	1	16.2	3.24	121	.359	.375	0	.000	-0	1	1	0	0.1
1929 StL-N	0	0	—	2	0	0	0	0	4	3	1	1	0	9.0	6.75	69	.214	.267	0	.000	-0	-1	-1	-0	0.0
Total 4	6	10	.375	47	20	6	0	1	185	235	9	56	30	14.2	4.04	90	.315	.364	13	.210	0	-3	-8	2	-0.4
■ IZZY GOLDSTEIN Goldstein, Isidore b: 6/6/08, New York, N.Y. BB/TR, 6', 160 lbs. Deb: 4/24/32																									
1932 Det-A	3	2	.600	16	6	2	0	0	56¹	63	2	41	14	17.1	4.47	105	.276	.393	5	.294	1	0	1	0	0.2
■ DAVE GOLTZ Goltz, David Allan b: 6/23/49, Pelican Rapids, Minn. BR/TR, 6'4", 200 lbs. Deb: 7/18/72																									
1972 Min-A	3	3	.500	15	11	2	0	0	91	75	5	26	38	10.0	2.67	120	.224	.280	3	.103	-1	4	5	0	0.6
1973 Min-A	6	4	.600	32	10	1	0	1	106¹	138	11	32	65	14.6	5.25	75	.318	.368	0	—	0	-17	-15	1	-1.4
1974 Min-A	10	10	.500	28	24	5	1	1	174¹	192	14	45	89	12.6	3.25	115	.282	.333	0	—	0	7	10	1	1.2
1975 Min-A	14	14	.500	32	32	15	1	0	243	235	18	72	128	11.6	3.67	105	.255	.313	0	—	0	3	5	1	0.7
1976 Min-A	14	14	.500	36	35	13	4	0	249¹	239	14	91	133	12.1	3.36	107	.254	.323	0	—	0	4	7	0	0.7
1977 Min-A	20	11	.645	39	39	19	2	0	303	284	23	91	186	11.2	3.36	119	.247	.304	0	—	0	24	21	-1	2.0
1978 Min-A	15	10	.600	29	29	13	2	0	220¹	209	12	67	116	11.3	2.49	153	.253	.309	0	—	0	31	32	0	3.6
1979 Min-A	14	13	.519	36	35	12	1	0	250²	282	22	69	132	12.6	4.16	105	.288	.336	0	—	0	1	6	-1	0.5
1980 LA-N	7	11	.389	35	27	2	2	1	171¹	198	12	59	91	13.5	4.31	81	.299	.356	6	.128	0	-13	-15	-0	-1.5
1981 *LA-N	2	7	.222	26	8	0	0	1	77	83	4	25	48	12.6	4.09	81	.288	.345	1	.059	-1	-5	-7	1	-0.6
1982 LA-N	0	1	.000	2	1	0	0	0	3²	6	0	3	3	14.7	4.91	71	.353	.353	0	.000	-0	-1	-1	0	0.0
*Cal-A	8	5	.615	28	7	1	0	3	86	82	4	32	49	12.0	4.08	99	.252	.320	0	—	0	-0	-0	-2	-0.1
1983 Cal-A	0	6	.000	15	6	0	0	0	63²	81	10	37	27	16.8	6.22	65	.315	.403	0	—	0	-15	-16	-0	-1.4
Total 12	113	109	.509	353	264	83	13	8	2039²	2104	149	646	1105	12.2	3.69	104	.269	.327	10	.106	-1	23	33	1	4.3
■ LUIS GOMEZ Gomez, Luis (Sanchez) b: 8/19/51, Guadalajara, Mex. BR/TR, 5'9", 150 lbs. Deb: 4/28/74 ◆																									
1981 Atl-N	0	0	—	1	0	0	0	0	3	2	0	2	0	45.0	27.00	13	.500	.625	7	.200	0	-3	-3	0	-0.1
■ RUBEN GOMEZ Gomez, Ruben (Colon) b: 7/13/27, Arroyo, P.R. BR/TR, 6', 170 lbs. Deb: 4/17/53																									
1953 NY-N	13	11	.542	29	26	13	3	0	204	166	17	101	113	12.0	3.40	126	.218	.313	15	.208	-0	20	20	2	2.0
1954 *NY-N	17	9	.654	37	32	10	4	0	221²	202	20	109	106	12.9	2.88	140	.244	.337	14	.173	0	29	28	2	3.0
1955 NY-N	9	10	.474	33	31	9	3	1	185¹	207	20	63	79	13.5	4.56	88	.285	.348	18	.300	4	-11	-11	3	-0.3
1956 NY-N	7	17	.292	40	31	4	2	0	196¹	191	19	77	76	12.7	4.58	83	.259	.337	11	.183	-0	-18	-17	3	-1.4
1957 NY-N	15	13	.536	38	36	16	1	0	238¹	233	28	71	92	11.7	3.78	104	.254	.311	16	.184	1	3	4	2	0.8
1958 SF-N	10	12	.455	42	30	8	1	1	207²	204	21	77	112	12.5	4.38	87	.261	.334	14	.200	1	-10	-13	2	-0.9
1959 Phi-N	3	8	.273	20	12	2	1	1	72¹	90	12	24	37	14.2	6.10	67	.300	.352	3	.176	0	-17	-16	2	-1.3
1960 Phi-N	0	3	.000	22	1	0	0	1	52¹	68	7	9	24	13.4	5.33	73	.321	.351	1	.083	-1	-9	-8	-1	-0.9
1962 Cle-A	1	2	.333	15	4	0	0	1	45¹	50	5	25	21	15.3	4.37	89	.292	.389	3	.231	0	-2	-2	1	-0.1
Min-A	1	1	.500	6	2	1	0	0	19¹	17	3	11	8	13.0	4.66	88	.254	.359	0	.000	-0	-1	-1	0	0.0
Yr	2	3	.400	21	6	1	0	1	64²	67	8	36	29	14.5	4.45	88	.276	.369	3	.056	0	-3	-4	1	-0.1
1967 Phi-N	0	0	—	7	0	0	0	0	11¹	8	2	7	9	11.9	3.97	86	.211	.333	0	—	0	-1	-1	1	0.0
Total 10	76	86	.469	289	205	63	15	5	1454	1436	154	574	677	12.7	4.09	97	.259	.334	95	.199	6	-17	-18	16	0.9
■ LEFTY GOMEZ Gomez, Vernon Louis "Goofy" b: 11/26/08, Rodeo, Cal. d: 2/17/89, Greenbrae, Cal. BL/TL, 6'2", 173 lbs. Deb: 4/29/30 H																									
1930 NY-A	2	5	.286	15	6	2	0	1	60	66	12	28	22	14.3	5.55	78	.280	.358	3	.150	-2	-6	-8	1	-0.7
1931 NY-A	21	9	.700	40	26	17	1	3	243	206	7	85	150	10.9	2.67	149	.226	.295	11	.133	-3	46	35	-1	2.9
1932 *NY-A	24	7	.774	37	31	21	1	1	265¹	266	23	105	176	12.7	4.21	97	.259	.329	18	.173	-1	8	-4	-4	-0.8
1933 NY-A	16	10	.615	35	30	14	4	2	234²	218	16	106	163	12.4	3.18	122	.240	.319	9	.112	-3	29	18	-4	1.0
1934 NY-A	26	5	.839	38	33	25	6	1	281²	223	12	96	158	10.2	2.33	174	.215	.282	13	.131	-4	68	54	-3	4.7
1935 NY-A	12	15	.444	34	30	15	2	1	246	223	18	86	138	11.4	3.18	127	.242	.309	10	.120	-6	35	24	0	1.6
1936 *NY-A	13	7	.650	31	30	10	2	0	188²	184	6	122	105	14.6	4.39	106	.254	.362	10	.145	-2	14	6	-1	0.1
1937 *NY-A	21	11	.656	34	34	25	6	0	278¹	233	10	93	194	10.6	2.33	191	.223	.287	21	.200	-1	71	65	-4	6.1
1938 *NY-A	18	12	.600	32	32	20	4	0	239	239	7	99	129	12.8	3.35	135	.260	.332	13	.151	-2	38	31	2	2.9
1939 *NY-A	12	8	.600	26	26	14	2	0	198	173	11	84	102	11.8	3.41	128	.235	.316	11	.151	-2	27	21	-1	1.7
1940 NY-A	3	3	.500	9	5	0	0	0	27¹	37	2	18	14	18.4	6.59	61	.325	.421	0	.000	-1	-7	-8	-1	-0.8
1941 NY-A	15	5	.750	23	23	8	2	0	156¹	151	10	103	76	14.7	3.74	105	.250	.360	9	.153	-1	7	3	-4	-0.1
1942 NY-A	6	4	.600	13	13	2	0	0	80	67	4	65	41	15.1	4.27	80	.237	.383	5	.152	-1	-5	-7	-2	-0.9
1943 Was-A	0	1	.000	1	1	0	0	0	4²	4	0	5	0	17.4	5.79	55	.250	.429	0	.000	-0	-1	-1	0	0.0
Total 14	189	102	.649	368	320	173	28	9	2503	2290	138	1095	1468	12.2	3.34	125	.242	.321	133	.147	-27	322	229	-19	17.7
■ JOE GONZALES Gonzales, Joe Madrid "Smokey" b: 3/19/15, San Francisco, Cal BR/TR, 5'9", 175 lbs. Deb: 8/28/37																									
1937 Bos-A	1	2	.333	8	2	2	0	0	31	37	1	11	11	13.9	4.35	109	.291	.348	0	.000	-2	1	1	0	0.0
■ JULIO GONZALES Gonzales, Julio Enrique b: 12/20/20, Havana, Cuba BR/TR, 5'11", 150 lbs. Deb: 8/09/49																									
1949 Was-A	0	0	—	13	0	0	0	0	34¹	33	3	27	5	16.0	4.72	90	.256	.389	1	.200	0	-2	-2	0	0.0
■ VINCE GONZALES Gonzales, Wenceslao O'Reilly b: 9/28/25, Quivican, Cuba d: 3/11/81, Ciudad Del Carmen Campeche, Mexico BL/TL, 6'1", 165 lbs. Deb: 4/13/55																									
1955 Was-A	0	0	—	4	0	0	0	0	4	9	0	2	3	41.5	27.00	14	.500	.600	0	—	0	-5	-5	0	-0.3
■ GERMAN GONZALEZ Gonzalez, German Jose (Caraballo) b: 3/7/62, Rio Caribe, Venez. BR/TR, 6', 170 lbs. Deb: 8/05/88																									
1988 Min-A	0	0	—	16	0	0	0	0	21¹	20	4	8	19	12.2	3.38	121	.244	.319	0	—	0	1	2	0	0.2
1989 Min-A	3	2	.600	22	0	0	0	0	29	32	2	11	25	14.6	4.66	89	.274	.356	0	—	0	-2	-2	-0	-0.1

YEAR TM/L	W	L	PCT	G	GS	CG	SH	SV	IP	H	HR	BB	SO	RAT	ERA	ERA+	OAV	OOB	BH	AVG	PB	PR	/A	PD	TPI
Total 2	3	2	.600	38	0	0	0	1	50¹	52	6	19	44	13.6	4.11	100	.261	.341	0		0	-1	-0	-0	0.1

■ RALPH GOOD
Good, Ralph Nelson "Holy" b: 4/25/1886, Monticello, Me. d: 11/24/65, Waterville, Maine BR/TR, 6', 165 lbs. Deb: 7/01/10

YEAR TM/L	W	L	PCT	G	GS	CG	SH	SV	IP	H	HR	BB	SO	RAT	ERA	ERA+	OAV	OOB	BH	AVG	PB	PR	/A	PD	TPI
1910 Bos-N	0	0	—	2	0	0	0	0	9	6	0	2	4	10.0	2.00	166	.188	.278	0	.000	-0	1	1	0	0.1

■ WILBUR GOOD
Good, Wilbur David "Lefty" b: 9/28/1885, Punxsutawney, Pa. d: 12/30/63, Brooksville, Fla. BL/TL, 5'6", 165 lbs. Deb: 8/18/05 ◆

YEAR TM/L	W	L	PCT	G	GS	CG	SH	SV	IP	H	HR	BB	SO	RAT	ERA	ERA+	OAV	OOB	BH	AVG	PB	PR	/A	PD	TPI
1905 NY-A	0	2	.000	5	2	0	0	0	19	18	1	14	13	15.2	4.74	62	.251	.374	3	.375	1	-4	-4	0	-0.2

■ HERB GOODALL
Goodall, Herbert Frank b: 3/10/1870, Mansfield, Pa. d: 1/20/38, Mansfield, Pa. BR/TR, 5'9", 180 lbs. Deb: 4/29/1890

YEAR TM/L	W	L	PCT	G	GS	CG	SH	SV	IP	H	HR	BB	SO	RAT	ERA	ERA+	OAV	OOB	BH	AVG	PB	PR	/A	PD	TPI
1890 Lou-a	8	5	.615	18	13	8	1	4	109	94	2	51	46	12.0	3.39	114	.226	.310	19	.422	5	6	6	1	1.1

■ JOHN GOODELL
Goodell, John Henry William "Lefty" b: 4/5/07, Muskogee, Okla. BR/TL, 5'10", 165 lbs. Deb: 4/19/28

YEAR TM/L	W	L	PCT	G	GS	CG	SH	SV	IP	H	HR	BB	SO	RAT	ERA	ERA+	OAV	OOB	BH	AVG	PB	PR	/A	PD	TPI
1928 Chi-A	0	0	—	2	0	0	0	0	3	6	0	2	0	27.0	18.00	23	.500	.600	0	—	0	-5	-5	0	-0.3

■ DWIGHT GOODEN
Gooden, Dwight Eugene b: 11/16/64, Tampa, Fla. BR/TR, 6'2", 190 lbs. Deb: 4/07/84

YEAR TM/L	W	L	PCT	G	GS	CG	SH	SV	IP	H	HR	BB	SO	RAT	ERA	ERA+	OAV	OOB	BH	AVG	PB	PR	/A	PD	TPI
1984 NY-N	17	9	.654	31	31	7	3	0	218	161	7	73	276	9.7	2.60	136	.202	.270	14	.200	1	24	23	-1	2.5
1985 NY-N	24	4	.857	35	35	16	8	0	276²	198	13	69	268	8.8	1.53	226	.201	.254	21	.226	6	63	59	1	7.8
1986 *NY-N	17	6	.739	33	33	12	2	0	250	197	17	80	200	10.1	2.84	124	.215	.280	7	.086	-3	24	19	2	2.0
1987 NY-N	15	7	.682	25	25	7	3	0	179²	162	11	53	148	10.9	3.21	118	.244	.301	14	.219	2	17	11	-0	1.3
1988 *NY-N	18	9	.667	34	34	10	3	0	248¹	242	8	57	175	11.1	3.19	101	.256	.303	16	.178	2	7	1	5	0.7
1989 NY-N	9	4	.692	19	17	0	0	1	118¹	93	9	47	101	10.8	2.89	113	.211	.290	8	.200	2	8	5	-0	0.7
1990 NY-N	19	7	.731	34	34	2	1	0	232²	229	10	70	223	11.8	3.83	95	.258	.317	14	.187	4	-1	-5	2	0.0
Total 7	119	46	.721	211	209	54	20	1	1523²	1282	75	449	1391	10.4	2.82	124	.227	.287	94	.183	14	143	113	8	15.1

■ ART GOODWIN
Goodwin, Arthur Ingram b: 2/27/1877, Whitley Twnshp, Pa d: 6/19/43, Franklin Township, Greene County, Pa. TR, 5'8", 195 lbs. Deb: 10/07/05

YEAR TM/L	W	L	PCT	G	GS	CG	SH	SV	IP	H	HR	BB	SO	RAT	ERA	ERA+	OAV	OOB	BH	AVG	PB	PR	/A	PD	TPI
1905 NY-A	0	0	—	1	0	0	0	0	0¹	2	0	2	0	108.0	81.00	4	.680	.809	0	—	0	-3	-3	0	-0.2

■ CLYDE GOODWIN
Goodwin, Clyde Samuel b: 11/12/1886, Shade, Ohio d: 10/12/63, Dayton, Ohio BR/TR, 5'11", 145 lbs. Deb: 9/18/06

YEAR TM/L	W	L	PCT	G	GS	CG	SH	SV	IP	H	HR	BB	SO	RAT	ERA	ERA+	OAV	OOB	BH	AVG	PB	PR	/A	PD	TPI
1906 Was-A	0	2	.000	4	3	1	0	0	22¹	20	0	13	9	13.3	4.43	59	.243	.346	1	.200	-0	-4	-4	-1	-0.4

■ JIM GOODWIN
Goodwin, James Patrick b: 8/15/26, St.Louis, Mo. BL/TL, 6'1", 170 lbs. Deb: 4/24/48

YEAR TM/L	W	L	PCT	G	GS	CG	SH	SV	IP	H	HR	BB	SO	RAT	ERA	ERA+	OAV	OOB	BH	AVG	PB	PR	/A	PD	TPI
1948 Chi-A	0	0	—	8	1	0	0	1	10¹	9	0	12	3	19.2	8.71	49	.237	.431	1	.500	0	-5	-5	-0	-0.3

■ MARV GOODWIN
Goodwin, Marvin Mardo b: 1/16/1891, Gordonsville, Va. d: 10/21/25, Houston, Tex. BR/TR, 5'11", 168 lbs. Deb: 9/07/16

YEAR TM/L	W	L	PCT	G	GS	CG	SH	SV	IP	H	HR	BB	SO	RAT	ERA	ERA+	OAV	OOB	BH	AVG	PB	PR	/A	PD	TPI
1916 Was-A	0	0	—	3	0	0	0	0	5²	5	0	3	1	12.7	3.18	87	.217	.308	0	.000	-0	-0	-0	-0	0.0
1917 StL-N	6	4	.600	14	12	6	3	0	85¹	70	1	19	38	9.4	2.21	122	.222	.266	4	.174	-0	5	5	2	0.7
1919 StL-N	11	9	.550	33	17	7	0	0	179	163	3	33	48	10.3	2.51	111	.245	.289	12	.200	1	8	6	-0	0.7
1920 StL-N	3	8	.273	32	12	3	0	1	116¹	153	1	28	23	14.4	4.95	60	.314	.357	7	.200	-0	-23	-25	-2	-2.7
1921 StL-N	1	2	.333	14	4	1	0	1	36¹	47	1	9	7	14.1	3.72	99	.315	.358	0	.000	-1	0	-0	0	0.0
1922 StL-N	0	0	—	2	0	0	0	0	4	3	0	3	0	13.5	2.25	172	.250	.400	0	—	0	1	1	0	0.1
1925 Cin-N	0	2	.000	4	3	2	0	0	20²	26	2	5	4	13.9	4.79	86	.317	.364	1	.250	0	-1	-2	1	0.0
Total 7	21	25	.457	102	48	19	3	2	447¹	467	8	100	121	11.7	3.30	90	.269	.315	24	.186	0	-11	-17	1	-1.2

■ RAY GORDINIER
Gordinier, Raymond Cornelius "Gordy" b: 4/11/1892, Rochester, N.Y. d: 11/15/60, Rochester, N.Y. BB/TR, 5'8.5", 170 lbs. Deb: 9/17/21

YEAR TM/L	W	L	PCT	G	GS	CG	SH	SV	IP	H	HR	BB	SO	RAT	ERA	ERA+	OAV	OOB	BH	AVG	PB	PR	/A	PD	TPI
1921 Bro-N	1	0	1.000	3	3	0	0	0	12	10	0	8	4	13.5	5.25	74	.227	.346	1	.250	0	-2	-2	0	0.0
1922 Bro-N	0	0	—	5	0	0	0	0	11¹	13	3	8	5	16.7	8.74	47	.289	.396	0	.000	-0	-6	-6	0	-0.5
Total 2	1	0	1.000	8	3	0	0	0	23¹	23	3	16	9	15.0	6.94	57	.258	.371	1	.167	-0	-8	-8	0	-0.5

■ DON GORDON
Gordon, Donald Thomas b: 10/10/59, New York, N.Y. BR/TR, 6'1", 175 lbs. Deb: 4/10/86

YEAR TM/L	W	L	PCT	G	GS	CG	SH	SV	IP	H	HR	BB	SO	RAT	ERA	ERA+	OAV	OOB	BH	AVG	PB	PR	/A	PD	TPI
1986 Tor-A	0	1	.000	14	0	0	0	1	21²	28	1	8	13	15.4	7.06	60	.311	.374	0	—	0	-7	-7	-0	-0.6
1987 Tor-A	0	0	—	5	0	0	0	0	11	8	2	3	3	9.0	4.09	110	.200	.256	0	—	0	0	0	-0	0.0
Cle-A	0	3	.000	21	0	0	0	0	39²	49	3	12	20	14.7	4.08	111	.295	.357	0	—	0	2	2	1	0.3
Yr	0	3	.000	26	0	0	0	0	50²	57	5	15	23	13.5	4.09	111	.277	.338	0	—	0	2	2	1	0.3
1988 Cle-A	3	4	.429	38	0	0	0	1	59¹	65	5	19	20	13.2	4.40	93	.284	.347	0	—	0	-3	-2	-1	-0.3
Total 3	3	8	.273	78	0	0	0	3	131²	150	11	42	56	13.7	4.72	91	.286	.348	0	—	0	-8	-6	1	-0.3

■ TOM GORDON
Gordon, Thomas b: 11/18/67, Sebring, Fla. BR/TR, 5'9", 160 lbs. Deb: 9/08/88

YEAR TM/L	W	L	PCT	G	GS	CG	SH	SV	IP	H	HR	BB	SO	RAT	ERA	ERA+	OAV	OOB	BH	AVG	PB	PR	/A	PD	TPI
1988 KC-A	0	2	.000	5	2	0	0	0	15²	16	1	7	18	13.2	5.17	77	.267	.343	0	—	0	-2	-2	0	-0.1
1989 KC-A	17	9	.654	49	16	1	1	1	163	122	10	86	153	11.5	3.64	106	.210	.312	0	—	0	4	4	2	0.6
1990 KC-A	12	11	.522	32	32	6	1	0	195¹	192	17	99	175	13.5	3.73	102	.257	.347	0	—	0	4	2	0	0.2
Total 3	29	22	.569	86	50	7	2	1	374	330	28	192	346	12.7	3.75	102	.238	.332	0	—	0	6	3	2	0.7

■ CHARLIE GORIN
Gorin, Charles Perry b: 2/6/28, Waco, Tex. BL/TL, 5'10", 165 lbs. Deb: 5/29/54

YEAR TM/L	W	L	PCT	G	GS	CG	SH	SV	IP	H	HR	BB	SO	RAT	ERA	ERA+	OAV	OOB	BH	AVG	PB	PR	/A	PD	TPI
1954 Mil-N	0	1	.000	5	0	0	0	0	9²	5	0	6	12	10.2	1.86	200	.152	.282	0	.000	-0	2	2	-0	-0.1
1955 Mil-N	0	0	—	2	0	0	0	0	0¹	1	0	3	0	108.0	54.00	7	.500	.800	0	—	0	-2	-2	-0	-0.1
Total 2	0	1	.000	7	0	0	0	0	10	6	0	9	12	13.5	3.60	103	.171	.341	0	.000	-0	1	0	-0	-0.1

■ JACK GORMAN
Gorman, John F. "Stooping Jack" b: 1859, St.Louis, Mo. d: 9/9/1889, St.Louis, Mo. Deb: 7/01/1883 ◆

YEAR TM/L	W	L	PCT	G	GS	CG	SH	SV	IP	H	HR	BB	SO	RAT	ERA	ERA+	OAV	OOB	BH	AVG	PB	PR	/A	PD	TPI
1884 Pit-a	1	2	.333	3	3	3	0	0	25	22	0	5	10	9.7	4.68	72	.223	.261	4	.148	-0	-4	-4	0	-0.2

■ TOM GORMAN
Gorman, Thomas Aloysius b: 1/4/25, New York, N.Y. BR/TR, 6'1", 190 lbs. Deb: 7/16/52

YEAR TM/L	W	L	PCT	G	GS	CG	SH	SV	IP	H	HR	BB	SO	RAT	ERA	ERA+	OAV	OOB	BH	AVG	PB	PR	/A	PD	TPI
1952 *NY-A	6	2	.750	12	6	1	1	1	60²	63	8	22	31	12.9	4.60	72	.272	.340	2	.087	-1	-6	-9	-0	-0.9
1953 *NY-A	4	5	.444	40	1	0	0	6	77	65	5	32	38	12.0	3.39	109	.226	.317	2	.133	-1	5	3	-0	0.2
1954 NY-A	0	0	—	23	0	0	0	2	36²	30	1	14	31	11.0	2.21	156	.222	.300	0	.000	-0	6	5	0	0.5
1955 KC-A	7	6	.538	57	0	0	0	18	109	98	11	36	46	11.4	3.55	118	.246	.314	2	.083	-2	5	8	-1	0.6
1956 KC-A	9	10	.474	52	13	1	0	3	171¹	168	23	68	56	12.5	3.83	113	.258	.330	2	.051	-4	6	9	0	0.6
1957 KC-A	5	9	.357	38	12	3	1	3	124²	125	18	33	66	11.5	3.83	103	.261	.331	4	.121	-2	-1	-2	-0	0.2
1958 KC-A	4	4	.500	50	1	0	0	8	89²	86	8	20	44	10.9	3.51	111	.258	.306	2	.118	-1	3	4	-1	0.2
1959 KC-A	1	0	1.000	17	0	0	0	1	20¹	24	3	14	9	17.3	7.08	57	.293	.402	0	—	0	-7	-7	-1	-0.7
Total 8	36	36	.500	289	33	5	2	42	689¹	659	77	239	321	12.0	3.77	105	.254	.321	14	.090	-10	11	14	-3	0.4

■ TOM GORMAN
Gorman, Thomas David "Big Tom" b: 3/16/16, New York, N.Y. d: 8/11/86, Closter, N.J. BR/TL, 6'2", 200 lbs. Deb: 9/14/39 U

YEAR TM/L	W	L	PCT	G	GS	CG	SH	SV	IP	H	HR	BB	SO	RAT	ERA	ERA+	OAV	OOB	BH	AVG	PB	PR	/A	PD	TPI
1939 NY-N	0	0	—	4	0	0	0	0	5	7	0	1	2	14.4	7.20	55	.350	.381	0	.000	-0	-2	-2	0	-0.1

■ TOM GORMAN
Gorman, Thomas Patrick b: 12/16/57, Portland, Ore. BL/TL, 6'4", 194 lbs. Deb: 9/02/81

YEAR TM/L	W	L	PCT	G	GS	CG	SH	SV	IP	H	HR	BB	SO	RAT	ERA	ERA+	OAV	OOB	BH	AVG	PB	PR	/A	PD	TPI
1981 Mon-N	0	0	—	9	0	0	0	0	15	12	0	6	13	11.4	4.20	83	.222	.311	0	—	0	-1	-1	1	0.0
1982 Mon-N	1	0	1.000	5	0	0	0	0	7	8	0	4	6	15.4	5.14	71	.286	.375	0	—	0	-1	-1	0	0.0
NY-N	0	1	.000	3	1	0	0	0	9¹	8	0	0	7	7.7	0.96	376	.235	.235	0	.000	-0	3	3	0	0.3
Yr	1	1	.500	8	1	0	0	0	16¹	16	0	4	13	11.0	2.76	132	.254	.299	0	.000	-0	2	2	0	0.3
1983 NY-N	1	4	.200	25	4	0	0	0	49¹	45	3	15	30	10.9	4.93	74	.245	.302	1	.250	-0	-7	-7	-0	-0.7
1984 NY-N	6	0	1.000	36	0	0	0	0	57²	51	6	13	40	10.1	2.97	119	.238	.285	0	—	0	4	4	0	0.4
1985 NY-N	4	4	.500	34	2	0	0	0	52²	56	8	18	32	12.6	5.13	67	.277	.336	0	.000	-1	-9	-10	1	-0.8
1986 Phi-N	0	1	.000	8	0	0	0	0	11²	21	0	5	8	20.1	7.71	50	.382	.433	0	—	0	-5	-5	-0	-0.4
1987 SD-N	0	0	—	6	0	0	0	0	11	11	1	5	8	13.1	4.09	97	.262	.340	-0	—	0	-0	-0	0	-0.0
Total 7	12	10	.545	126	7	0	0	0	213²	212	18	66	144	11.8	4.34	83	.261	.318	1	.071	-0	-17	-18	2	-1.2

YEAR TM/L	W	L	PCT	G	GS	CG	SH	SV	IP	H	HR	BB	SO	RAT	ERA	ERA+	OAV	OOB	BH	AVG	PB	PR	/A	PD	TPI

■ JOE GORMLEY Gormley, Joseph b: 12/20/1866, Summit Hill, Pa. d: 7/2/50, Summit Hill, Pa. BL/TL, Deb: 6/16/1891

| 1891 Phi-N | 0 | 1 | .000 | 1 | 1 | 1 | 0 | 0 | 8 | 10 | 0 | 5 | 2 | 16.9 | 5.63 | 61 | .295 | .385 | 0 | .000 | -1 | -2 | -2 | 0 | -0.1 |

■ HANK GORNICKI Gornicki, Henry Frank b: 1/14/11, Niagara Falls, N.Y BR/TR, 6'1", 145 lbs. Deb: 4/17/41

1941 StL-N	1	0	1.000	4	1	1	1	0	11¹	6	0	9	6	12.7	3.18	118	.158	.333	1	.250	0	1	1	-0	0.1
Chi-N	0	0	—	1	0	0	0	0	2	3	0	0	2	13.5	4.50	78	.375	.375	0	—	0	0	0	-0	0.0
Yr	1	0	1.000	5	1	1	1	0	13¹	9	0	9	8	12.2	3.38	110	.191	.321	0	.000	0	0	1	0	0.1
1942 Pit-N	5	6	.455	25	14	7	2	2	112	89	2	40	48	10.4	2.57	132	.215	.286	4	.114	-1	9	10	-1	0.9
1943 Pit-N	9	13	.409	42	19	4	1	4	147	165	10	47	63	13.1	3.98	87	.286	.342	7	.175	-1	-10	-8	-1	-1.0
1946 Pit-N	0	0	—	7	0	0	0	0	12²	12	0	11	4	16.3	3.55	99	.255	.397	0	-0	-0	-0	-0	0.0	
Total 4	15	19	.441	79	34	12	4	6	285	275	12	107	123	12.2	3.38	102	.254	.323	12	.146	-2	-0	2	-2	0.0

■ JOHNNY GORSICA Gorsica, John Joseph Perry (b: John Joseph Perry Gorczyca) b: 3/29/15, Bayonne, N.J. BR/TR, 6'2", 180 lbs. Deb: 4/22/40

1940 *Det-A	7	7	.500	29	20	5	2	0	160	170	10	57	68	13.0	4.33	110	.272	.337	12	.194	-0	1	8	6	1.4
1941 Det-A	9	11	.450	33	21	8	1	2	171	193	14	55	59	13.2	4.47	102	.281	.336	17	.298	4	-6	1	5	1.1
1942 Det-A	3	2	.600	28	0	0	0	4	53	63	2	26	19	15.6	4.75	83	.310	.397	1	.100	-0	-6	-5	4	0.0
1943 Det-A	4	5	.444	35	4	1	0	5	96¹	88	3	40	45	12.1	3.36	105	.247	.327	4	.174	0	-1	2	3	0.5
1944 Det-A	6	14	.300	34	19	8	1	4	162	192	5	32	47	12.7	4.11	87	.296	.333	7	.135	-1	-12	-10	4	-0.7
1946 Det-A	0	0	—	14	0	0	0	1	23²	28	5	11	14	14.8	4.56	80	.301	.375	2	.667	1	-3	-2	-0	-0.1
1947 Det-A	2	0	1.000	31	0	0	0	1	57²	44	5	26	20	11.2	3.75	101	.208	.300	2	.200	-0	-0	0	1	0.2
Total 7	31	39	.443	204	64	22	4	17	723²	778	44	247	272	13.0	4.18	98	.276	.338	45	.207	5	-28	-7	22	2.4

■ RICH GOSSAGE Gossage, Richard Michael "Goose" b: 7/5/51, Colorado Springs, Colo. BR/TR, 6'3", 180 lbs. Deb: 4/16/72

1972 Chi-A	7	1	.875	36	1	0	0	2	80	72	6	44	57	13.5	4.27	73	.247	.353	0	.000	-2	-11	-10	-0	-1.3
1973 Chi-A	0	4	.000	20	4	1	0	0	49²	57	9	37	33	17.6	7.43	53	.311	.435	0	—	0	-20	-19	-0	-1.8
1974 Chi-A	4	6	.400	39	3	0	0	1	89¹	92	4	47	64	14.2	4.13	90	.272	.364	0	—	0	-5	-4	0	-0.3
1975 Chi-A	9	8	.529	62	0	0	0	26	141²	99	3	70	130	11.1	1.84	210	.201	.307	0	.000	0	30	32	0	3.4
1976 Chi-A	9	17	.346	31	29	15	0	1	224	214	16	90	135	12.6	3.94	91	.254	.333	0	—	0	-10	-9	-1	-1.0
1977 Pit-N	11	9	.550	72	0	0	0	26	133	78	9	49	151	8.7	1.62	245	.170	.253	5	.217	1	34	35	-2	3.4
1978 *NY-A	10	11	.476	63	0	0	0	27	134¹	87	9	59	122	9.9	2.01	180	.187	.281	0	—	0	26	24	-2	2.3
1979 NY-A	5	3	.625	36	0	0	0	18	58¹	48	5	19	41	10.3	2.62	155	.227	.291	0	—	0	10	9	-1	0.8
1980 *NY-A	6	2	.750	64	0	0	0	33	99	74	5	37	103	10.2	2.27	173	.211	.288	0	—	0	19	18	-1	1.7
1981 *NY-A	3	2	.600	32	0	0	0	20	46²	22	2	14	48	7.1	0.77	463	.141	.216	0	—	0	15	15	-0	1.6
1982 NY-A	4	5	.444	56	0	0	0	30	93	63	5	28	102	8.8	2.23	179	.196	.261	0	—	0	19	18	-1	1.7
1983 NY-A	13	5	.722	57	0	0	0	22	87¹	82	5	25	90	11.1	2.27	172	.248	.303	0	—	0	17	16	-2	1.4
1984 *SD-N	10	6	.625	62	0	0	0	25	102¹	75	6	36	84	9.9	2.90	123	.204	.277	4	.182	0	8	8	-2	0.6
1985 SD-N	5	3	.625	50	0	0	0	26	79	64	1	17	52	9.3	1.82	194	.226	.272	0	.000	-1	16	15	-1	1.4
1986 SD-N	5	7	.417	45	0	0	0	21	64²	69	8	20	63	12.7	4.45	82	.273	.331	0	.000	-1	-5	-6	-1	-0.7
1987 SD-N	5	4	.556	40	0	0	0	11	52	47	4	19	44	11.4	3.12	127	.244	.311	0	.000	-0	6	5	-1	0.4
1988 Chi-N	4	4	.500	46	0	0	0	13	43²	50	3	15	30	14.0	4.33	83	.291	.358	0	.000	-0	-4	-4	-0	-0.3
1989 SF-N	2	1	.667	31	0	0	0	4	43²	32	2	27	24	12.2	2.68	126	.212	.331	0	.000	-0	4	3	-1	0.3
NY-A	1	0	1.000	11	0	0	0	1	14¹	14	0	3	6	11.3	3.77	103	.275	.327	0	—	0	0	0	0	0.0
Total 18	113	98	.536	853	37	16	0	307	1636	1339	98	656	1379	11.2	2.92	128	.227	.308	9	.106	-3	149	146	-17	13.6

■ JIM GOTT Gott, James William b: 8/3/59, Hollywood, Cal. BR/TR, 6'4", 215 lbs. Deb: 4/09/82

1982 Tor-A	5	10	.333	30	23	1	1	0	136	134	15	66	82	13.4	4.43	101	.255	.341	0	—	0	-5	1	-0	0.0
1983 Tor-A	9	14	.391	34	30	6	1	0	176²	195	15	68	121	13.7	4.74	91	.280	.349	0	—	0	-13	-9	-1	-0.8
1984 Tor-A	7	6	.538	35	12	1	1	2	109²	93	7	49	73	11.9	4.02	102	.233	.322	0	—	0	-0	1	-1	0.0
1985 SF-N	7	10	.412	26	26	2	0	0	148¹	144	10	51	78	11.9	3.88	89	.254	.317	10	.196	4	-5	-7	1	-0.2
1986 SF-N	0	0	—	9	2	0	0	1	13	16	0	13	9	20.1	7.62	46	.314	.453	0	.000	0	-6	-6	-0	-0.5
1987 SF-N	1	0	1.000	30	0	0	0	0	56	53	4	32	63	14.0	4.50	85	.244	.347	1	.100	1	-3	-4	-0	-0.3
Pit-N	0	2	.000	25	0	0	0	13	31	28	0	8	27	10.5	1.45	283	.233	.281	0	.000	-0	9	9	-0	0.9
Yr	1	2	.333	55	0	0	0	13	87	81	4	40	90	12.5	3.41	115	.238	.318	0	.000	-0	6	5	-1	0.6
1988 Pit-N	6	6	.500	67	0	0	0	34	77¹	68	9	22	76	10.7	3.49	97	.243	.303	0	.000	-0	-1	-1	-1	-0.1
1989 Pit-N	0	0	—	1	0	0	0	0	0²	1	0	1	1	27.0	0.00	—	.333	.500	0	—	0	0	0	0	0.0
1990 LA-N	3	5	.375	50	0	0	0	3	62	59	5	34	44	13.5	2.90	123	.257	.352	0	.000	-0	6	5	-0	0.4
Total 9	38	53	.418	307	96	10	3	53	810²	791	65	344	574	12.8	4.07	97	.256	.334	11	.164	5	-17	-12	-2	-0.6

■ TED GOULAIT Goulait, Theodore Lee b: 8/11/1889, St.Clair, Mich. d: 7/15/36, St.Clair, Mich. BR/TR, 5'9.5", 172 lbs. Deb: 9/28/12

| 1912 NY-N | 0 | 0 | — | 1 | 1 | 0 | 0 | 0 | 4 | 6 | 1 | 13 | 6 | 43.4 | 6.43 | 53 | .367 | .441 | 1 | .500 | — | -2 | -2 | 0 | -0.1 |

■ AL GOULD Gould, Albert Frank "Pudgy" b: 1/20/1893, Muscatine, Iowa d: 8/8/82, San Jose, Cal. BR/TR, 5'6.5", 160 lbs. Deb: 7/11/16

1916 Cle-A	5	7	.417	30	9	6	1	1	106²	101	0	40	41	12.2	2.53	119	.256	.329	3	.103	-2	4	6	-1	0.3
1917 Cle-A	4	4	.500	27	7	1	0	0	94	95	1	52	24	14.4	3.64	78	.281	.382	5	.208	1	-10	-8	2	-0.5
Total 2	9	11	.450	57	16	7	1	1	200²	196	1	92	65	13.2	3.05	96	.267	.354	8	.151	-1	-7	-3	1	-0.2

■ CHARLIE GOULD Gould, Charles Harvey b: 8/21/1847, Cincinnati, Ohio d: 4/10/17, Flushing, N.Y. BR/TR, 6', 172 lbs. Deb: 5/05/1871 M♦

| 1876 Cin-N | 0 | 0 | — | 2 | 0 | 0 | 0 | 0 | 4¹ | 10 | 0 | 0 | 0 | 20.8 | 0.00 | — | .425 | .425 | 65 | .252 | 0 | 1 | 1 | 0 | 0.1 |

■ LARRY GOWELL Gowell, Lawrence Clyde b: 5/2/48, Lewiston, Me. BR/TR, 6'2", 182 lbs. Deb: 9/21/72

| 1972 NY-A | 0 | 1 | .000 | 2 | 1 | 0 | 0 | 0 | 7 | 3 | 0 | 2 | 7 | 6.4 | 1.29 | 229 | .143 | .217 | 1 | 1.000 | 1 | 1 | 1 | 0 | 0.2 |

■ MAURO GOZZO Gozzo, Mauro Paul b: 3/7/66, New Britain, Conn. BR/TR, 6'2", 210 lbs. Deb: 8/08/89

1989 Tor-A	4	1	.800	9	3	0	0	0	31²	35	1	9	10	12.8	4.83	78	.289	.344	0	—	0	-3	-4	-0	-0.3
1990 Cle-A	0	0	—	2	0	0	0	0	3	2	0	2	2	12.0	0.00	—	.182	.308	0	—	0	1	1	0	0.1
Total 2	4	1	.800	11	3	0	0	0	34²	37	1	11	12	12.7	4.41	86	.280	.340	0	—	0	-2	-2	-0	-0.2

■ AL GRABOWSKI Grabowski, Alfons Francis b: 9/6/01, Syracuse, N.Y. d: 10/29/66, Memphis, N.Y. BL/TL, 5'11.5", 175 lbs. Deb: 9/11/29

1929 StL-N	3	2	.600	6	6	4	2	0	50	44	0	8	22	9.4	2.52	185	.227	.257	4	.250	2	12	12	-0	1.4
1930 StL-N	6	4	.600	33	8	1	0	1	107	122	7	49	43	14.6	4.79	105	.295	.373	12	.364	3	2	3	-0	0.4
Total 2	9	6	.600	39	14	5	2	1	157	166	7	57	65	13.0	4.07	120	.273	.338	16	.327	4	14	15	-0	1.8

■ REGGIE GRABOWSKI Grabowski, Reginald John b: 7/16/07, Syracuse, N.Y. d: 4/2/55, Syracuse, N.Y. BR/TR, 6'0.5", 185 lbs. Deb: 4/15/32

1932 Phi-N	2	2	.500	14	2	0	0	0	34¹	38	2	25	16	16.3	3.67	120	.273	.380	0	.000	-1	3	3	-0	0.2
1933 Phi-N	1	3	.250	10	5	4	1	0	48	38	4	10	9	9.2	2.44	157	.220	.266	2	.125	-1	5	7	-1	0.6
1934 Phi-N	1	3	.250	27	5	0	0	0	65¹	114	13	23	13	19.3	9.23	51	.384	.433	1	.056	-2	-38	-33	-1	-3.2
Total 3	4	8	.333	51	12	4	1	0	147²	190	19	55	37	15.3	5.73	76	.312	.375	3	.075	-4	-32	-23	-2	-2.4

■ JOHN GRAFF Graff, John F. b: Philadelphia, Pa. Deb: 7/19/1893

| 1893 Was-N | 0 | 1 | .000 | 2 | 1 | 1 | 0 | 0 | 12 | 21 | 2 | 13 | 4 | 25.5 | 11.25 | 41 | .372 | .489 | 1 | .200 | -0 | -9 | -9 | -0 | -0.6 |

■ PEACHES GRAHAM Graham, George Frederick b: 3/23/1877, Aledo, Ill. d: 7/25/39, Long Beach, Cal. BR/TR, 5'9", 180 lbs. Deb: 9/14/02 ♦

| 1903 Chi-N | 0 | 1 | .000 | 1 | 1 | 0 | 0 | 0 | 5 | 9 | 0 | 3 | 4 | 23.4 | 5.40 | 58 | .429 | .520 | 0 | .000 | -0 | -1 | -1 | 0 | -0.1 |

■ SKINNY GRAHAM Graham, Kyle b: 8/14/1899, Oak Grove, Ala. d: 12/1/73, Oak Grove, Ala. BR/TR, 6'2", 172 lbs. Deb: 9/03/24

| 1924 Bos-N | 0 | 4 | .000 | 5 | 4 | 1 | 0 | 0 | 33 | 33 | 0 | 11 | 15 | 12.0 | 3.82 | 100 | .287 | .349 | 0 | .000 | -1 | 0 | 0 | -0 | 0.0 |

YEAR	TM/L	W	L	PCT	G	GS	CG	SH	SV	IP	H	HR	BB	SO	RAT	ERA	ERA+	OAV	OOB	BH	AVG	PB	PR	/A	PD	TPI
1925	Bos-N	7	12	.368	34	23	5	0	1	157	177	6	62	32	13.9	4.41	91	.296	.365	6	.136	-2	-3	-7	-2	-1.0
1926	Bos-N	3	3	.500	15	4	1	0	0	36¹	54	3	19	7	18.6	7.93	45	.370	.449	2	.167	-1	-17	-18	0	-1.6
1929	Det-A	1	3	.250	13	6	2	0	1	51²	70	2	33	7	18.5	5.57	77	.340	.438	2	.105	-1	-8	-7	-0	-0.7
Total	4	11	22	.333	67	37	9	0	2	278	334	11	125	61	15.1	5.02	79	.314	.390	10	.122	-5	-27	-32	-2	-3.3

■ OSCAR GRAHAM
Graham, Oscar M. b: 7/20/1878, Plattsmouth, Neb. d: 10/15/31, Moline, Ill. TL, 6'0.5", Deb: 4/16/07

| 1907 | Was-A | 4 | 9 | .308 | 20 | 14 | 6 | 0 | 0 | 104 | 116 | 3 | 29 | 44 | 12.5 | 3.98 | 61 | .284 | .331 | 11 | .229 | 3 | -17 | -18 | 0 | -1.5 |

■ BILL GRAHAM
Graham, William James b: 7/22/1884, Owosso, Mich. d: 2/15/36, Holt, Mich. TL, 6', Deb: 4/18/08

1908	StL-A	6	7	.462	21	13	7	0	0	117¹	104	0	32	47	11.4	2.30	104	.240	.310	5	.119	-3	1	1	0	-0.1
1909	StL-A	8	14	.364	34	21	13	3	1	187¹	171	3	60	82	11.3	3.12	77	.256	.322	10	.159	-0	-13	-15	1	-1.5
1910	StL-A	0	8	.000	9	6	1	0	0	43	46	2	13	12	13.2	3.56	70	.297	.366	2	.154	-0	-5	-5	-2	-0.7
Total	3	14	29	.326	64	40	21	3	1	347²	321	5	105	141	11.6	2.90	83	.256	.323	17	.144	-3	-17	-19	-1	-2.3

■ BILL GRAHAM
Graham, William Albert b: 1/21/37, Flemingsburg, Ky. BR/TR, 6'3", 217 lbs. Deb: 10/02/66

1966	Det-A	0	0	—	1	0	0	0	0	2	2	0	2	2	9.0	0.00	—	.250	.250	0	—	-0	1	1	0	0.1
1967	NY-N	1	2	.333	5	3	1	0	0	27¹	20	3	11	14	10.2	2.63	129	.200	.279	1	.125	-0	2	2	-1	0.1
Total	2	1	2	.333	6	3	1	0	0	29¹	22	3	11	16	10.1	2.45	138	.204	.277	1	.125	-0	3	3	-1	0.2

■ JOE GRAHE
Grahe, Joseph Milton b: 8/14/67, W.Palm Beach, Fla. BR/TR, 6'1", 196 lbs. Deb: 8/04/90

| 1990 | Cal-A | 3 | 4 | .429 | 8 | 8 | 0 | 0 | 0 | 43¹ | 51 | 3 | 23 | 25 | 16.0 | 4.98 | 78 | .293 | .385 | 0 | — | 0 | -5 | -5 | 1 | -0.3 |

■ TOMMY GRAMLY
Gramly, Bert Thomas b: 4/19/45, Dallas, Tex. BR/TR, 6'3", 175 lbs. Deb: 4/18/68

| 1968 | Cle-A | 0 | 1 | .000 | 3 | 0 | 0 | 0 | 0 | 3¹ | 3 | 0 | 2 | 1 | 13.5 | 2.70 | 110 | .250 | .357 | 0 | — | 0 | 0 | 0 | 0 | 0.0 |

■ HANK GRAMPP
Grampp, Henry Erchardt b: 9/28/03, New York, N.Y. d: 3/24/86, New York, N.Y. BR/TR, 6'1", 185 lbs. Deb: 6/02/27

1927	Chi-N	0	0	—	2	0	0	0	0	3	4	0	1	3	15.0	9.00	43	.333	.385	0	—	0	-2	-2	0	-0.1
1929	Chi-N	0	1	.000	1	1	0	0	0	2	4	0	3	0	36.0	27.00	17	.500	.667	0	—	0	-5	-5	0	-0.3
Total	2	0	1	.000	3	1	0	0	0	5	8	0	4	3	23.4	16.20	26	.400	.520	0	—	0	-7	-7	0	-0.4

■ JACK GRANEY
Graney, John Gladstone b: 6/10/1886, St.Thomas, Ont., Can. d: 4/20/78, Louisiana, Mo. BL/TL, 5'9", 180 lbs. Deb: 4/30/08 ♦

| 1908 | Cle-A | 0 | 0 | — | 2 | 0 | 0 | 0 | 0 | 3¹ | 6 | 0 | 1 | 0 | 18.9 | 5.40 | 44 | .400 | .438 | 0 | — | 0 | -1 | -1 | -0 | 0.0 |

■ WAYNE GRANGER
Granger, Wayne Allan b: 3/15/44, Springfield, Mass. BR/TR, 6'2", 165 lbs. Deb: 6/05/68

1968	*StL-N	4	2	.667	34	0	0	0	4	44	40	2	12	27	11.0	2.25	129	.238	.297	1	.200	0	4	3	2	0.6
1969	Cin-N	9	6	.600	90	0	0	0	27	144²	143	10	40	68	11.8	2.80	134	.262	.320	2	.095	-0	13	15	2	1.8
1970	*Cin-N	6	5	.545	67	0	0	0	35	84²	79	5	27	38	11.4	2.66	152	.256	.313	1	.100	-1	13	13	2	1.5
1971	Cin-N	7	6	.538	70	0	0	0	11	100	94	8	28	51	11.1	3.33	101	.251	.304	1	.143	-1	2	0	3	0.5
1972	Min-A	4	6	.400	63	0	0	0	19	89²	83	7	28	45	11.3	3.01	107	.243	.304	2	.200	-0	0	2	-0	0.2
1973	StL-N	2	4	.333	33	0	0	0	5	46²	50	3	21	14	14.1	4.24	86	.284	.367	0	.000	-0	-3	-3	-0	-0.2
	NY-A	0	1	.000	7	0	0	0	0	15¹	19	1	3	10	13.5	1.76	208	.279	.319	0	—	0	4	3	-0	0.3
1974	Chi-A	0	0	—	5	0	0	0	0	7²	16	1	3	4	22.3	8.22	45	.432	.475	0	—	0	-4	-4	0	-0.2
1975	Hou-N	2	5	.286	55	0	0	0	5	74	76	7	23	30	12.5	3.65	92	.264	.327	0	.000	-1	-0	-2	1	-0.1
1976	Mon-N	1	0	1.000	27	0	0	0	2	32	32	3	16	16	14.1	3.66	102	.264	.360	0	.000	-0	-1	0	0	0.0
Total	9	35	35	.500	451	0	0	0	108	638²	632	47	201	303	12.0	3.14	113	.260	.322	7	.103	-1	27	28	9	4.3

■ GEORGE GRANT
Grant, George Addison b: 1/6/03, E.Tallassee, Ala. d: 3/25/86, Montgomery, Ala. BR/TR, 5'11.5", 175 lbs. Deb: 9/17/23

1923	StL-A	0	0	—	4	0	0	0	0	8²	15	3	2	2	18.7	5.19	80	.395	.439	0	.000	-0	-1	-1	0	0.0
1924	StL-A	1	2	.333	22	2	0	0	0	51¹	69	4	25	11	16.7	6.31	72	.325	.399	0	.000	-2	-12	-10	-0	-1.1
1925	StL-A	0	2	.000	12	0	0	0	0	16¹	26	2	8	7	18.7	6.06	77	.400	.466	1	.250	-0	-3	-3	0	-0.1
1927	Cle-A	4	6	.400	25	3	2	0	1	74²	85	1	40	19	15.1	4.46	94	.300	.387	2	.095	-2	-3	-2	0	-0.3
1928	Cle-A	10	8	.556	28	18	6	1	0	155¹	196	7	76	39	15.9	5.04	80	.319	.395	11	.183	-2	-17	-15	3	-1.3
1929	Cle-A	0	2	.000	12	0	0	0	0	24	41	2	23	5	24.0	10.50	42	.414	.525	0	.000	-0	-17	-16	0	-1.3
1931	Pit-N	0	0	—	11	0	0	0	0	17	28	0	7	6	19.1	7.41	52	.364	.424	0	.000	-0	-7	-7	0	-0.6
Total	7	15	20	.429	114	23	8	1	1	347¹	460	16	182	89	16.7	5.65	75	.331	.410	14	.135	-8	-59	-54	4	-4.7

■ JIM GRANT
Grant, James Ronald b: 8/4/1894, Coalville, Iowa d: 11/30/85, Des Moines, Iowa BR/TL, 5'11", 180 lbs. Deb: 4/21/23

| 1923 | Phi-N | 0 | 0 | — | 2 | 0 | 0 | 0 | 0 | 4 | 10 | 4 | 0 | 0 | 33.8 | 13.50 | 34 | .588 | .682 | 0 | .000 | -0 | -4 | -4 | 0 | -0.3 |

■ JIM GRANT
Grant, James Timothy "Mudcat" b: 8/13/35, Lacoochee, Fla. BR/TR, 6'1", 186 lbs. Deb: 4/17/58

1958	Cle-A	10	11	.476	44	28	11	1	4	204	173	20	104	111	12.3	3.84	95	.228	.321	5	.076	-4	-2	-4	-2	-0.9
1959	Cle-A	10	7	.588	38	19	6	1	3	165¹	140	23	81	85	12.1	4.14	89	.232	.325	11	.200	1	-5	-8	0	-0.7
1960	Cle-A	9	8	.529	33	19	5	0	0	159²	147	26	78	75	12.8	4.40	85	.243	.332	16	.281	3	-9	-12	-1	-0.9
1961	Cle-A	15	9	.625	35	35	11	3	0	244²	207	32	109	146	11.7	3.86	102	.227	.312	15	.170	1	4	2	0	0.3
1962	Cle-A	7	10	.412	26	23	6	1	0	149²	128	24	81	90	12.6	4.27	91	.233	.331	8	.151	-0	-5	-7	-0	-0.6
1963	Cle-A	13	14	.481	38	32	10	2	1	229¹	213	30	87	157	11.9	3.69	98	.243	.314	13	.188	3	-2	-3	-0	-0.1
1964	Cle-A	3	4	.429	13	9	1	0	0	62	82	11	25	43	15.7	5.95	60	.324	.387	6	.273	4	-16	-16	0	-1.1
	Min-A	11	9	.550	26	23	10	1	1	166	162	21	36	75	10.7	2.82	127	.248	.288	10	.167	0	15	14	1	1.6
	Yr	14	13	.519	39	32	11	1	1	228	244	32	61	118	12.0	3.67	98	.269	.315	16	.049	4	-1	-2	1	0.5
1965	*Min-A	21	7	.750	41	39	14	6	0	270¹	252	34	61	142	10.4	3.30	108	.247	.289	15	.155	2	5	8	1	1.3
1966	Min-A	13	13	.500	35	35	10	3	0	249	248	23	49	110	11.0	3.25	111	.260	.300	15	.192	5	10	3	1.7
1967	Min-A	5	6	.455	27	14	2	0	0	95¹	121	10	17	50	13.1	4.72	85	.315	.346	5	.179	0	-16	-13	-1	-1.5
1968	LA-N	6	4	.600	37	4	1	0	3	94²	77	11	19	35	9.7	2.09	132	.226	.279	4	.129	0	9	7	1	0.7
1969	Mon-N	1	6	.143	11	10	1	0	0	50²	64	7	14	20	14.0	4.80	77	.299	.345	2	.125	-1	-7	-6	1	-0.5
	StL-N	7	5	.583	30	3	1	0	7	63¹	62	9	22	35	12.2	4.12	87	.252	.319	5	.294	2	-4	-4	-1	-0.2
	Yr	8	11	.421	41	13	2	0	7	114	126	16	36	55	12.9	4.42	82	.273	.328	7	.061	1	-10	-10	-0	-0.7
1970	Oak-A	6	2	.750	72	0	0	0	24	123¹	104	8	30	54	10.0	1.82	194	.235	.288	2	.222	2	26	24	1	2.8
	Pit-N	2	1	.667	8	0	0	0	0	12	8	2	2	4	7.5	2.25	173	.190	.227	0	.000	0	1	2	0	0.0
1971	Pit-N	5	3	.625	42	0	0	0	7	75	79	8	28	22	13.0	3.60	94	.274	.341	2	.250	1	-1	-2	1	0.0
	*Oak-A	1	0	1.000	15	0	0	0	3	27¹	25	3	6	13	10.2	1.98	169	.243	.284	1	.333	0	5	4	0	0.5
Total	14	145	119	.549	571	293	89	18	53	2441²	2292	292	849	1267	11.7	3.63	100	.248	.313	135	.178	16	5	-3	2	2.9

■ MARK GRANT
Grant, Mark Andrew b: 10/24/63, Aurora, Ill. BR/TR, 6'2", 195 lbs. Deb: 4/27/84

1984	SF-N	1	4	.200	11	10	0	0	0	53²	56	6	19	32	12.7	6.37	55	.272	.336	0	.000	-1	-17	-17	-0	-1.7
1986	SF-N	0	1	.000	4	1	0	0	0	10	6	0	5	5	9.9	3.60	98	.176	.282	0	.000	-0	0	-0	0	0.0
1987	SF-N	1	2	.333	16	8	0	0	1	61	66	6	21	32	13.0	3.54	109	.282	.344	1	.083	-0	4	2	-1	0.1
	SD-N	6	7	.462	17	17	2	1	0	102	104	16	52	58	13.7	4.66	85	.263	.348	3	.094	-1	-7	-8	-0	-0.8
	Yr	7	9	.438	33	25	2	1	1	163¹	170	22	73	90	13.4	4.24	92	.269	.345	3	.068	-1	-3	-6	-1	-0.7
1988	SD-N	2	8	.200	33	11	0	0	0	97²	97	14	36	61	12.4	3.69	92	.268	.338	0	.000	-0	-3	-3	0	-0.3
1989	SD-N	8	2	.800	50	0	0	0	2	116¹	105	11	32	69	10.8	3.33	105	.248	.305	1	.050	-0	5	5	0	0.3
1990	SD-N	1	1	.500	26	0	0	0	0	39	47	5	19	29	15.2	4.85	79	.305	.382	1	.500	-0	-5	-4	1	-0.2
	Atl-N	1	2	.333	33	0	0	0	3	52¹	61	4	18	40	13.8	4.64	84	.293	.352	1	.250	1	-5	-4	-0	-0.3
	Yr	2	3	.400	59	0	0	0	3	91¹	108	9	37	69	14.4	4.73	82	.296	.362	2	.333	1	-10	-9	0	-0.5
Total	6	20	27	.426	190	48	2	1	7	532¹	542	62	202	326	12.7	4.23	87	.269	.338	7	.067	-3	-29	-33	-1	-3.0

YEAR	TM/L	W	L	PCT	G	GS	CG	SH	SV	IP	H	HR	BB	SO	RAT	ERA	ERA+	OAV	OOB	BH	AVG	PB	PR	/A	PD	TPI

■ RICK GRAPENTHIN Grapenthin, Richard Ray b: 4/16/58, Linn Grove, Iowa BR/TR, 6'2", 205 lbs. Deb: 5/03/83

1983	Mon-N	0	1	.000	1	0	0	0	0	4	4	2	1	3	11.3	9.00	40	.267	.313	0	.000	-0	-2	-2	0	-0.1
1984	Mon-N	1	2	.333	13	1	0	0	2	23	19	3	7	9	10.2	3.52	97	.235	.295	1	.200	0	0	-0	0	0.0
1985	Mon-N	0	0	—	5	0	0	0	0	7	13	0	8	4	28.3	14.14	24	.394	.524	1	1.000	0	-8	-8	-0	-0.7
Total	3	1	3	.250	19	1	0	0	2	34	36	5	16	16	14.0	6.35	54	.279	.363	2	.286	-0	-10	-11	0	-0.8

■ LOU GRASMICK Grasmick, Louis Junior b: 9/11/24, Baltimore, Md. BR/TR, 6', 195 lbs. Deb: 4/22/48

| 1948 | Phi-N | 0 | 0 | — | 2 | 0 | 0 | 0 | 0 | 5 | 3 | 1 | 8 | 2 | 19.8 | 7.20 | 55 | .176 | .440 | 1 | 1.000 | 0 | -2 | -2 | 0 | 0.0 |

■ DON GRATE Grate, Donald "Buckeye" b: 8/27/23, Greenfield, Ohio BR/TR, 6'2.5", 180 lbs. Deb: 7/06/45

1945	Phi-N	0	1	.000	4	2	0	0	0	8¹	18	0	12	6	32.4	17.28	22	.439	.566	0	.000	-0	-12	-12	-0	-1.0
1946	Phi-N	1	0	1.000	3	0	0	0	0	8	4	0	2	2	6.8	1.13	305	.160	.222	0	.000	-0	2	2	-0	0.2
Total	2	1	1	.500	7	2	0	0	0	16¹	22	0	14	8	19.8	9.37	39	.333	.450	0	.000	-0	-10	-10	-1	-0.8

■ FRANK GRAVES Graves, Frank M. b: 11/2/1860, Cincinnati, Ohio 6', 163 lbs. Deb: 5/10/1886 ◆

| 1886 | StL-N | 0 | 0 | — | 1 | 0 | 0 | 0 | 0 | 7 | 10 | 0 | 1 | 2 | 14.1 | 9.00 | 36 | .322 | .344 | 21 | .152 | -0 | -4 | -4 | 0 | -0.2 |

■ CHARLIE GRAY Gray, Charles b: 1867, Indianapolis, Ind. Deb: 4/23/1890

| 1890 | Pit-N | 1 | 4 | .200 | 5 | 4 | 3 | 0 | 0 | 31 | 48 | 0 | 24 | 10 | 20.9 | 7.55 | 44 | .344 | .440 | 3 | .200 | -0 | -14 | -15 | -1 | -1.1 |

■ DAVE GRAY Gray, David Alexander b: 1/7/43, Ogden, Utah BR/TR, 6'1", 190 lbs. Deb: 6/14/64

| 1964 | Bos-A | 0 | 0 | — | 9 | 1 | 0 | 0 | 0 | 13 | 18 | 3 | 20 | 17 | 26.3 | 9.00 | 43 | .321 | .500 | 1 | 1.000 | -0 | -8 | -7 | 0 | -0.6 |

■ CHUMMY GRAY Gray, George Edward b: 7/17/1873, Rockland, Me. d: 8/14/13, Rockland, Maine TR, 5'11.5", 163 lbs. Deb: 9/14/1899

| 1899 | Pit-N | 3 | 3 | .500 | 9 | 7 | 6 | 0 | 0 | 70² | 85 | 1 | 24 | 9 | 13.9 | 3.44 | 111 | .297 | .352 | 1 | .038 | -3 | 3 | 3 | 2 | 0.1 |

■ JEFF GRAY Gray, Jeffrey Edward b: 4/10/63, Richmond, Va. BR/TR, 6'1", 175 lbs. Deb: 6/21/88

1988	Cin-N	0	0	—	5	0	0	0	0	9¹	12	0	4	5	15.4	3.86	93	.333	.400	0	.000	-0	-0	-0	0	0.0
1990	*Bos-A	2	4	.333	41	0	0	0	9	50²	53	3	15	50	12.3	4.44	92	.268	.322	0	—	0	-3	-2	-0	-0.1
Total	2	2	4	.333	46	0	0	0	9	60	65	3	19	55	12.8	4.35	92	.278	.335	0	.000	-0	-3	-2	0	-0.1

■ JOHNNY GRAY Gray, John Leonard b: 12/11/27, W.Palm Beach, Fla. BR/TR, 6'4", 226 lbs. Deb: 7/18/54

1954	Phi-A	3	12	.200	18	16	5	0	0	105	111	10	91	51	17.3	6.51	60	.273	.406	1	.029	-4	-33	-30	-0	-3.1
1955	KC-A	0	3	.000	8	5	0	0	0	26²	28	2	24	11	17.9	6.41	65	.277	.421	1	.125	-1	-7	-7	-1	-0.6
1957	Cle-A	1	3	.250	7	3	1	1	0	20	21	1	13	3	15.3	5.85	64	.288	.395	0	.000	-1	-5	-5	-0	-0.4
1958	Phi-N	0	0	—	15	0	0	0	0	17¹	12	3	14	10	13.5	4.15	95	.222	.382	0	.000	-0	-0	-0	0	0.0
Total	4	4	18	.182	48	24	6	1	0	169	172	16	142	75	16.8	6.18	64	.271	.405	2	.043	-5	-45	-42	-1	-4.1

■ SAM GRAY Gray, Samuel David "Sad Sam" b: 10/15/1897, Van Alstyne, Tex. d: 4/16/53, McKinney, Tex. BR/TR, 5'10", 175 lbs. Deb: 4/19/24

1924	Phi-A	8	7	.533	34	19	8	2	2	151²	169	5	89	54	15.7	3.98	108	.284	.383	10	.175	-2	4	5	-1	0.2
1925	Phi-A	16	8	.667	32	28	14	4	3	203²	199	11	63	80	11.7	3.27	142	.260	.319	12	.179	-3	25	31	-3	2.6
1926	Phi-A	11	12	.478	38	18	5	0	0	150²	164	9	50	82	13.0	3.64	114	.279	.340	11	.216	1	6	9	-2	0.8
1927	Phi-A	9	6	.600	37	13	3	1	3	133¹	153	4	51	49	14.0	4.59	93	.295	.362	8	.190	-1	-7	-5	0	-0.4
1928	StL-A	20	12	.625	35	31	21	2	3	262²	236	11	86	102	11.8	3.19	132	.260	.320	19	.188	-2	25	30	3	3.1
1929	StL-A	18	15	.545	43	37	23	4	1	305	336	18	96	109	12.8	3.72	119	.285	.340	19	.184	-2	18	24	-1	2.0
1930	StL-A	4	15	.211	27	24	7	0	0	167²	215	17	52	51	14.5	6.28	78	.316	.368	11	.204	-2	-30	-26	-1	-2.3
1931	StL-A	11	24	.314	43	37	13	0	2	258	323	20	54	88	13.3	5.09	91	.297	.351	14	.177	-1	-20	-13	-1	-1.3
1932	StL-A	7	12	.368	52	18	7	3	4	206²	250	9	53	79	13.2	4.53	107	.294	.336	13	.210	-1	-1	7	-1	0.6
1933	StL-A	7	4	.636	38	6	0	0	4	112	131	7	45	36	14.2	4.10	114	.301	.368	7	.219	1	2	7	-1	0.8
Total	10	111	115	.491	379	231	101	16	22	1951¹	2196	111	639	730	13.2	4.18	108	.286	.343	124	.191	-10	23	68	-7	6.1

■ TED GRAY Gray, Ted Glenn b: 12/31/24, Detroit, Mich. BB/TL, 5'11", 175 lbs. Deb: 5/15/46

1946	Det-A	0	2	.000	3	2	0	0	1	11²	17	4	5	5	17.0	8.49	43	.340	.400	0	.000	-0	-6	-6	-0	-0.5
1948	Det-A	6	2	.750	26	11	3	1	0	85¹	73	2	72	60	15.6	4.22	104	.236	.385	7	.241	1	1	1	-1	0.1
1949	Det-A	10	10	.500	34	27	8	3	1	195	163	11	103	96	12.5	3.51	119	.227	.328	8	.127	-3	15	14	1	1.2
1950	Det-A	10	7	.588	27	21	7	0	1	149¹	139	22	72	102	12.8	4.40	107	.248	.335	7	.140	-2	3	5	-2	0.1
1951	Det-A	7	14	.333	34	28	9	1	1	197¹	194	17	95	131	13.5	4.06	103	.256	.343	9	.143	-3	1	3	-2	-0.1
1952	Det-A	12	17	.414	35	32	13	2	0	224	212	21	101	138	12.7	4.14	92	.249	.331	13	.171	-2	-12	-8	1	-0.9
1953	Det-A	10	15	.400	30	28	8	0	0	176	166	25	76	115	12.7	4.60	88	.252	.336	14	.230	2	-12	-10	-1	-0.9
1954	Det-A	3	5	.375	19	10	2	0	0	72	70	8	56	29	16.0	5.38	69	.268	.401	1	.045	-2	-13	-13	-1	-1.6
1955	Chi-A	0	0	—	2	1	0	0	0	3	9	0	2	1	33.0	18.00	22	.500	.550	0	—	-0	-5	-5	-0	-0.3
	Cle-A	0	0	—	2	0	0	0	0	2	5	1	2	1	31.5	18.00	22	.455	.538	0	—	-0	-3	-3	-0	-0.2
	NY-A	0	0	—	1	1	0	0	0	3	3	0	1	1	9.0	3.00	125	.300	.300	0	.000	-0	0	0	0	0.0
	Bal-A	1	2	.333	9	1	0	0	0	15¹	21	3	11	8	18.8	8.22	46	.344	.444	0	.000	-0	-7	-8	1	-0.6
	Yr	1	2	.333	14	3	0	0	0	23¹	38	4	15	11	20.4	9.64	40	.376	.457	0	.000	-0	-15	-15	1	-1.1
Total	9	59	74	.444	222	162	50	7	4	1134	1072	114	595	687	13.5	4.37	94	.251	.346	59	.159	-10	-38	-30	-5	-3.7

■ DOLLY GRAY Gray, William Denton b: 12/4/1878, Ishpeming, Mich. d: 4/4/56, Yuba City, Cal. BL/TL, 6'2", 160 lbs. Deb: 4/13/09

1909	Was-A	5	19	.208	36	26	19	0	0	218	210	1	77	87	12.2	3.59	68	.258	.329	13	.146	-1	-27	-28	-0	-3.2
1910	Was-A	8	19	.296	34	29	21	3	0	229	216	3	65	84	11.4	2.63	95	.249	.247	21	.247	4	-3	-4	2	0.2
1911	Was-A	2	13	.133	28	15	6	0	0	121	160	4	40	42	15.1	5.06	65	.331	.385	10	.227	1	-23	-24	1	-2.0
Total	3	15	51	.227	98	70	46	3	0	568	586	8	182	213	12.5	3.52	75	.271	.333	44	.202	3	-53	-56	3	-5.0

■ ELI GRBA Grba, Eli b: 8/9/34, Chicago, Ill. BR/TR, 6'2", 205 lbs. Deb: 7/10/59

1959	NY-A	2	5	.286	19	6	0	0	0	50¹	52	6	39	23	16.3	6.44	57	.269	.392	3	.214	1	-14	-16	0	-1.4
1960	*NY-A	6	4	.600	24	9	1	0	1	80²	65	9	46	32	12.6	3.68	97	.226	.337	5	.238	2	2	-1	-0	0.1
1961	LA-A	11	13	.458	40	30	8	0	2	211²	197	26	114	105	13.5	4.25	106	.242	.340	15	.234	5	-5	6	-0	1.2
1962	LA-A	8	9	.471	40	29	1	0	1	176¹	185	19	75	90	13.4	4.54	85	.267	.340	12	.207	3	-11	-13	1	-0.9
1963	LA-A	1	2	.333	12	1	0	0	0	17¹	14	2	10	5	13.0	4.67	73	.222	.338	0	.000	-0	-2	-2	0	-0.1
Total	5	28	33	.459	135	75	10	0	4	536¹	513	62	284	255	13.6	4.48	90	.250	.345	35	.219	10	-31	-27	1	-1.1

■ BILL GREASON Greason, William Henry "Booster" b: 9/3/24, Atlanta, Ga. BR/TR, 5'10", 170 lbs. Deb: 5/31/54

| 1954 | StL-N | 0 | 1 | .000 | 3 | 2 | 0 | 0 | 0 | 4 | 8 | 4 | 4 | 2 | 27.0 | 13.50 | 30 | .421 | .522 | 0 | .000 | -0 | -4 | -4 | 0 | -0.3 |

■ CHRIS GREEN Green, Christopher De Wayne b: 9/5/60, Los Angeles, Cal. BL/TL, 6'2", 214 lbs. Deb: 4/17/84

| 1984 | Pit-N | 0 | 0 | — | 4 | 0 | 0 | 0 | 0 | 3 | 5 | 0 | 1 | 3 | 18.0 | 6.00 | 60 | .417 | .462 | 0 | — | 0 | -1 | -1 | 0 | 0.0 |

■ ED GREEN Green, Edward M. b: 1850, Philadelphia, Pa. d: 3/22/17, Ogden, Utah Deb: 4/22/1890

| 1890 | Phi-a | 7 | 15 | .318 | 25 | 22 | 20 | 1 | 1 | 191 | 267 | 4 | 94 | 56 | 17.0 | 5.80 | 66 | .321 | .390 | 15 | .119 | -4 | -41 | -42 | 3 | -3.5 |

■ FRED GREEN Green, Fred Allen b: 9/14/33, Titusville, N.J. BR/TL, 6'4", 190 lbs. Deb: 4/15/59

1959	Pit-N	1	2	.333	17	1	0	0	0	37¹	37	2	15	20	12.5	3.13	123	.259	.329	0	.000	-1	3	3	0	0.3
1960	*Pit-N	8	4	.667	45	0	0	0	3	70	61	4	33	49	12.2	3.21	117	.243	.333	3	.375	3	4	4	-1	0.7
1961	Pit-N	0	0	—	13	0	0	0	0	20²	27	2	9	4	15.7	4.79	83	.321	.387	0	.000	-0	-2	-2	1	-0.1
1962	Was-A	0	1	.000	5	0	0	0	0	7	7	3	6	2	16.7	6.43	63	.250	.382	0	—	0	-2	-2	-0	-0.1
1964	Pit-N	0	0	—	8	0	0	0	0	7¹	10	1	0	2	12.3	1.23	286	.323	.323	0	—	0	2	2	-0	0.2

YEAR TM/L	W	L	PCT	G	GS	CG	SH	SV	IP	H	HR	BB	SO	RAT	ERA	ERA+	OAV	OOB	BH	AVG	PB	PR	/A	PD	TPI
Total 5	9	7	.563	88	1	0	0	4	142¹	142	12	63	77	13.0	3.48	110	.264	.343	3	.176	2	6	5	0	1.0

■ DALLAS GREEN   Green, George Dallas b: 8/4/34, Newport, Del.   BL/TR, 6'5", 210 lbs.   Deb: 6/18/60   M

YEAR TM/L	W	L	PCT	G	GS	CG	SH	SV	IP	H	HR	BB	SO	RAT	ERA	ERA+	OAV	OOB	BH	AVG	PB	PR	/A	PD	TPI
1960 Phi-N	3	6	.333	23	10	5	1	0	108²	100	10	44	51	12.1	4.06	96	.248	.325	7	.206	1	-4	-2	-0	-0.1
1961 Phi-N	2	4	.333	42	10	1	1	1	128	160	8	47	51	14.7	4.85	84	.315	.375	5	.152	0	-12	-11	1	-0.9
1962 Phi-N	6	6	.500	37	10	2	0	1	129¹	145	10	43	58	13.4	3.83	101	.289	.352	2	.063	-1	2	1	2	0.2
1963 Phi-N	7	5	.583	40	14	4	0	2	120	134	10	38	68	13.1	3.23	100	.286	.342	3	.086	-1	1	0	2	0.0
1964 Phi-N	2	1	.667	25	0	0	0	0	42	63	4	14	21	16.9	5.79	60	.362	.416	0	.000	-0	-10	-11	-0	-1.1
1965 Was-A	0	0	—	6	2	0	0	0	14¹	14	0	3	6	10.7	3.14	111	.241	.279	0	.000	-0	1	1	0	0.0
1966 NY-N	0	0	—	4	0	0	0	0	5	6	2	2	1	14.4	5.40	67	.333	.400	0	—	-0	-1	-1	0	0.0
1967 Phi-N	0	0	—	8	0	0	0	0	15	25	2	6	12	19.2	9.00	38	.362	.421	0	.000	-0	-9	-9	0	-0.8
Total 8	20	22	.476	185	46	12	2	4	562¹	647	46	197	268	13.7	4.26	88	.294	.356	17	.120	-3	-33	-33	5	-2.7

■ HARVEY GREEN   Green, Harvey George "Buck" b: 2/9/15, Kenosha, Wis. d: 7/24/70, Franklin, La.   BB/TR, 6'2.5", 185 lbs.   Deb: 9/12/35

YEAR TM/L	W	L	PCT	G	GS	CG	SH	SV	IP	H	HR	BB	SO	RAT	ERA	ERA+	OAV	OOB	BH	AVG	PB	PR	/A	PD	TPI
1935 Bro-N	0	0	—	2	0	0	0	0	1	2	0	3	0	54.0	9.00	44	.400	.667	0	—	0	-1	-1	0	0.0

■ TOMMY GREENE   Greene, Ira Thomas b: 4/6/67, Lumberton, N.C.   BR/TR, 6'5", 225 lbs.   Deb: 9/10/89

YEAR TM/L	W	L	PCT	G	GS	CG	SH	SV	IP	H	HR	BB	SO	RAT	ERA	ERA+	OAV	OOB	BH	AVG	PB	PR	/A	PD	TPI
1989 Atl-N	1	2	.333	4	4	1	1	0	26¹	22	5	6	17	9.6	4.10	89	.234	.280	1	.100	-1	-2	-1	-0	-0.1
1990 Atl-N	1	0	1.000	5	2	0	0	0	12¹	14	3	9	4	17.5	8.03	49	.286	.407	0	.000	-0	-6	-6	-0	-0.5
Phi-N	2	3	.400	10	7	0	0	0	39	36	5	17	17	12.2	4.15	92	.247	.325	2	.182	0	-2	-1	0	-0.5
Yr	3	3	.500	15	9	0	0	0	51¹	50	8	26	21	13.3	5.08	76	.255	.342	0	.000	-0	-7	-7	-0	-0.5
Total 2	4	5	.444	19	13	1	1	0	77²	72	13	32	38	12.2	4.75	80	.249	.326	3	.136	-0	-9	-8	-0	-0.6

■ JUNE GREENE   Greene, Julius Foust b: 6/25/1899, Ramseur, N.C. d: 3/19/74, Glendora, Cal.   BL/TR, 6'2.5", 185 lbs.   Deb: 4/20/28   ♦

YEAR TM/L	W	L	PCT	G	GS	CG	SH	SV	IP	H	HR	BB	SO	RAT	ERA	ERA+	OAV	OOB	BH	AVG	PB	PR	/A	PD	TPI
1928 Phi-N	0	0	—	1	0	0	0	0	2	5	0	0	0	22.5	9.00	47	.556	.556	3	.500	2	-1	-1	0	0.0
1929 Phi-N	0	0	—	5	0	0	0	0	13²	33	2	9	4	29.6	19.76	26	.465	.542	4	.211	0	-23	-22	0	-1.6
Total 2	0	0	—	6	0	0	0	0	15²	38	2	9	4	28.7	18.38	28	.475	.543	7	.280	2	-24	-23	1	-1.6

■ NELSON GREENE   Greene, Nelson George "Lefty" b: 9/20/1900, Philadelphia, Pa. d: 4/6/83, Lebanon, Pa.   BL/TL, 6', 185 lbs.   Deb: 4/28/24

YEAR TM/L	W	L	PCT	G	GS	CG	SH	SV	IP	H	HR	BB	SO	RAT	ERA	ERA+	OAV	OOB	BH	AVG	PB	PR	/A	PD	TPI
1924 Bro-N	0	1	.000	4	1	0	0	0	9	14	1	2	3	16.0	4.00	94	.350	.381	0	.000	-0	-0	-0	0	0.0
1925 Bro-N	2	0	1.000	11	0	0	0	1	22	45	4	7	4	21.3	10.64	39	.417	.452	2	.286	0	-16	-16	0	-1.3
Total 2	2	1	.667	15	1	0	0	1	31	59	5	9	7	19.7	8.71	47	.399	.433	2	.250	0	-16	-16	1	-1.3

■ KENT GREENFIELD   Greenfield, Kent b: 7/1/02, Guthrie, Ky. d: 3/14/78, Guthrie, Ky.   BR/TR, 6'1", 180 lbs.   Deb: 9/28/24

YEAR TM/L	W	L	PCT	G	GS	CG	SH	SV	IP	H	HR	BB	SO	RAT	ERA	ERA+	OAV	OOB	BH	AVG	PB	PR	/A	PD	TPI
1924 NY-N	0	1	.000	1	1	0	0	0	3	9	1	1	1	30.0	15.00	24	.500	.526	0	—	0	-4	-4	-0	-0.2
1925 NY-N	12	8	.600	29	21	12	0	0	171²	195	4	64	66	13.7	3.88	104	.288	.352	5	.081	-6	7	3	0	-0.2
1926 NY-N	13	12	.520	39	28	8	1	1	222²	206	17	82	74	11.8	3.96	95	.251	.322	6	.092	-5	7	4	-2	-1.1
1927 NY-N	2	2	.500	12	1	0	0	0	20	39	3	13	4	24.3	9.45	41	.411	.491	0	.000	-0	-12	-12	0	-1.1
Bos-N	11	14	.440	27	26	11	1	0	190	203	3	59	59	12.6	3.84	97	.282	.341	11	.172	-1	2	-3	-0	-0.4
Yr	13	16	.448	39	27	11	1	0	210	242	6	72	63	13.7	4.37	85	.297	.357	3	.045	-2	-11	-15	0	-1.5
1928 Bos-N	3	11	.214	32	23	5	0	0	143²	173	6	60	30	14.9	5.32	73	.307	.378	2	.053	-4	-21	-23	1	-2.3
1929 Bos-N	0	0	—	6	2	0	0	0	15²	33	1	15	7	28.7	10.91	43	.465	.568	0	.000	-1	-11	-11	0	-0.8
Bro-N	0	0	—	6	0	0	0	0	8²	13	1	3	1	16.6	8.31	56	.382	.432	0	.000	-0	-3	-4	0	-0.2
Yr	0	0	—	12	2	0	0	0	24¹	46	2	18	8	23.7	9.99	47	.430	.512	0	.000	-1	-14	-14	1	-1.0
Total 6	41	48	.461	152	102	36	2	1	775¹	871	36	297	242	13.8	4.54	85	.290	.358	24	.101	-17	-46	-58	0	-6.3

■ JOHN GREENING   Greening, John A. (b: John A. Greenig) b: Philadelphia, Pa.   Deb: 5/09/1888

YEAR TM/L	W	L	PCT	G	GS	CG	SH	SV	IP	H	HR	BB	SO	RAT	ERA	ERA+	OAV	OOB	BH	AVG	PB	PR	/A	PD	TPI
1888 Was-N	0	1	.000	1	1	1	0	0	9	17	2	4	2	21.0	11.00	25	.388	.439	0	.000	-0	-8	-8	-0	-0.5

■ BOB GREENWOOD   Greenwood, Robert Chandler "Greenie" b: 3/13/28, Cananea, Mexico   BR/TR, 6'5", 200 lbs.   Deb: 4/21/54

YEAR TM/L	W	L	PCT	G	GS	CG	SH	SV	IP	H	HR	BB	SO	RAT	ERA	ERA+	OAV	OOB	BH	AVG	PB	PR	/A	PD	TPI
1954 Phi-N	1	2	.333	11	4	0	0	0	36²	28	2	18	9	11.3	3.19	127	.209	.303	0	.000	-1	4	3	0	0.3
1955 Phi-N	0	0	—	1	0	0	0	0	2¹	7	1	0	0	27.0	15.43	26	.500	.500	0	.000	-0	-3	-3	0	-0.2
Total 2	1	2	.333	12	4	0	0	0	39	35	3	18	9	12.2	3.92	103	.236	.319	0	.000	-1	1	0	0	0.1

■ DAVE GREGG   Gregg, David Charles "Highpockets" b: 3/14/1891, Chehalis, Wash. d: 11/12/65, Clarkston, Wash.   BR/TR, 6'1", 185 lbs.   Deb: 6/15/13

YEAR TM/L	W	L	PCT	G	GS	CG	SH	SV	IP	H	HR	BB	SO	RAT	ERA	ERA+	OAV	OOB	BH	AVG	PB	PR	/A	PD	TPI
1913 Cle-A	0	0	—	1	0	0	0	0	1	2	0	0	0	27.0	18.00	17	.400	.500	0	—	0	-2	-2	0	0.0

■ HAL GREGG   Gregg, Harold Dana "Skeets" b: 7/11/21, Anaheim, Cal.   BR/TR, 6'3.5", 195 lbs.   Deb: 8/18/43

YEAR TM/L	W	L	PCT	G	GS	CG	SH	SV	IP	H	HR	BB	SO	RAT	ERA	ERA+	OAV	OOB	BH	AVG	PB	PR	/A	PD	TPI
1943 Bro-N	0	3	—	5	4	0	0	0	18²	21	2	21	7	20.3	9.64	35	.304	.467	0	.000	0	-13	-13	-0	-1.1
1944 Bro-N	9	16	.360	39	31	6	0	2	197²	201	12	137	92	15.8	5.46	65	.258	.376	14	.206	-0	-41	-42	0	-4.0
1945 Bro-N	18	13	.581	42	34	13	2	2	254¹	221	5	120	139	12.3	3.47	108	.232	.323	20	.220	3	9	8	-1	1.1
1946 *Bro-N	6	4	.600	26	16	4	1	2	117¹	103	3	44	54	11.4	2.99	113	.236	.308	4	.125	-1	5	5	-2	0.2
1947 *Bro-N	4	5	.444	37	16	2	1	1	104¹	115	6	55	59	15.0	5.87	70	.272	.361	9	.265	2	-21	-20	-0	-1.7
1948 Pit-N	2	4	.333	22	8	0	0	0	74¹	72	3	34	25	13.2	4.60	88	.255	.342	6	.273	2	-5	-4	-0	-0.2
1949 Pit-N	1	1	.500	8	1	0	0	0	18²	20	1	8	9	14.0	3.38	125	.303	.387	0	.000	-0	1	2	-0	0.1
1950 Pit-N	0	1	.000	5	1	0	0	1	5¹	10	2	7	3	30.4	13.50	32	.400	.545	0	.000	-0	-6	-5	0	-0.4
1952 NY-N	0	1	.000	16	4	1	0	1	36¹	42	7	17	13	15.1	4.71	79	.286	.367	1	.125	-0	-4	-4	-1	-0.4
Total 9	40	48	.455	200	115	27	4	9	827	805	41	443	401	13.9	4.54	82	.253	.350	54	.205	4	-73	-74	-3	-6.4

■ VEAN GREGG   Gregg, Sylveanus Augustus b: 4/13/1885, Chehalis, Wash. d: 7/29/64, Aberdeen, Was.   BR/TL, 6'1", 185 lbs.   Deb: 4/12/11

YEAR TM/L	W	L	PCT	G	GS	CG	SH	SV	IP	H	HR	BB	SO	RAT	ERA	ERA+	OAV	OOB	BH	AVG	PB	PR	/A	PD	TPI
1911 Cle-A	23	7	.767	34	26	22	5	0	244²	172	2	86	125	9.9	1.80	189	.205	.286	14	.165	-4	42	44	0	4.2
1912 Cle-A	20	13	.606	37	34	26	1	2	271¹	242	4	90	184	11.3	2.59	132	.246	.316	17	.175	-3	22	25	-3	2.0
1913 Cle-A	20	13	.606	44	34	23	3	3	285²	258	6	124	166	12.4	2.24	136	.246	.334	13	.131	-5	22	25	-3	1.9
1914 Cle-A	9	3	.750	17	12	6	1	0	96²	88	0	48	56	12.9	3.07	94	.251	.347	6	.176	1	-4	-2	-0	-0.2
Bos-A	3	4	.429	12	9	4	0	0	68¹	71	0	37	24	14.2	3.95	68	.283	.375	4	.211	0	-9	-10	-1	-0.9
Yr	12	7	.632	29	21	10	1	0	165	159	0	85	80	13.3	3.44	82	.263	.354	4	.075	1	-13	-12	-1	-1.1
1915 Bos-A	4	2	.667	18	9	3	1	3	75	71	2	32	43	13.0	3.36	83	.260	.348	7	.350	2	-4	-5	-0	-0.3
1916 Bos-A	2	5	.286	21	7	3	0	0	77²	71	0	30	41	12.1	3.01	92	.259	.339	2	.111	-1	-2	-2	-0	-0.3
1918 Phi-A	9	14	.391	30	25	17	3	2	199¹	180	4	67	63	11.4	3.12	94	.251	.320	12	.169	-3	-7	-4	-1	-0.8
1925 Was-A	2	2	.500	26	5	1	0	2	74¹	87	3	38	18	15.4	4.12	103	.318	.404	3	.214	0	2	1	-1	0.0
Total 8	92	63	.594	239	161	105	14	12	1393	1240	17	552	720	11.9	2.70	118	.248	.328	78	.171	-12	63	73	-9	5.7

■ FRANK GREGORY   Gregory, Frank Ernst b: 7/25/1888, Spring Valley Township, Wis. d: 11/5/55, Beloit, Wis.   BR/TR, 5'11", 185 lbs.   Deb: 9/05/12

YEAR TM/L	W	L	PCT	G	GS	CG	SH	SV	IP	H	HR	BB	SO	RAT	ERA	ERA+	OAV	OOB	BH	AVG	PB	PR	/A	PD	TPI
1912 Cin-N	2	0	1.000	4	2	1	0	0	15²	19	0	7	4	15.5	4.60	73	.288	.365	1	.200	0	-2	-2	-1	-0.2

■ LEE GREGORY   Gregory, Grover Leroy b: 6/2/38, Bakersfield, Cal.   BL/TL, 6'1", 180 lbs.   Deb: 4/17/64

YEAR TM/L	W	L	PCT	G	GS	CG	SH	SV	IP	H	HR	BB	SO	RAT	ERA	ERA+	OAV	OOB	BH	AVG	PB	PR	/A	PD	TPI
1964 Chi-N	0	0	—	11	0	0	0	0	18	23	3	5	8	14.0	3.50	106	.333	.378	1	.077	0	0	0	0	0.0

■ HOWIE GREGORY   Gregory, Howard Watterson b: 11/18/1886, Hannibal, Mo. d: 5/30/70, Tulsa, Okla.   BL/TR, 6', 175 lbs.   Deb: 4/16/11

YEAR TM/L	W	L	PCT	G	GS	CG	SH	SV	IP	H	HR	BB	SO	RAT	ERA	ERA+	OAV	OOB	BH	AVG	PB	PR	/A	PD	TPI
1911 StL-A	0	1	.000	3	1	0	0	0	7	11	0	4	1	19.3	5.14	66	.393	.469	0	.000	-0	-1	-1	0	-0.1

■ PAUL GREGORY   Gregory, Paul Edwin "Pop" b: 6/9/08, Tomnolen, Miss.   BR/TR, 6'2", 180 lbs.   Deb: 4/20/32

YEAR TM/L	W	L	PCT	G	GS	CG	SH	SV	IP	H	HR	BB	SO	RAT	ERA	ERA+	OAV	OOB	BH	AVG	PB	PR	/A	PD	TPI
1932 Chi-A	5	3	.625	33	9	3	0	0	117²	125	8	51	39	13.6	4.51	96	.273	.348	3	.079	-3	-0	-2	3	-0.1
1933 Chi-A	4	11	.267	23	17	5	0	0	103²	124	10	47	18	14.9	4.95	86	.296	.368	5	.143	-1	-8	-8	2	-0.7
Total 2	9	14	.391	56	26	8	0	0	221	249	18	98	57	14.2	4.72	91	.284	.358	8	.110	-4	-8	-11	4	-0.8

YEAR	TM/L	W	L	PCT	G	GS	CG	SH	SV	IP	H	HR	BB	SO	RAT	ERA	ERA+	OAV	OOB	BH	AVG	PB	PR	/A	PD	TPI
■ BILL GREIF				Greif, William Briley			b: 4/25/50, Ft.Stockton, Tex.			BR/TR, 6'4", 196 lbs.		Deb: 7/19/71													
1971	Hou-N	1	1	.500	7	3	0	0	0	16	18	1	8	14	15.8	5.06	66	.290	.389	1	.333	0	-3	-3	0	-0.2
1972	SD-N	5	16	.238	34	22	2	1	2	125¹	143	18	47	91	14.2	5.60	59	.287	.357	1	.030	-3	-30	-32	-2	-3.6
1973	SD-N	10	17	.370	36	31	9	3	1	199¹	181	20	62	120	11.2	3.21	108	.246	.309	6	.098	-2	10	6	-1	0.3
1974	SD-N	9	19	.321	43	35	7	1	1	226	244	17	95	137	14.1	4.66	76	.279	.359	4	.071	-2	-26	-28	0	-2.8
1975	SD-N	4	6	.400	59	1	0	0	9	72	74	7	38	43	14.6	3.88	90	.269	.368	0	.000	-0	-2	-3	-2	-0.4
1976	SD-N	1	3	.250	5	5	0	0	0	22¹	27	2	11	5	15.3	8.06	41	.297	.373	0	.000	-1	-11	-12	0	-1.1
	StL-N	1	5	.167	47	0	0	0	6	54²	60	5	26	32	14.5	4.12	86	.290	.374	0	.000	0	-4	-4	-1	-0.3
	Yr	2	8	.200	52	5	0	0	6	77	87	7	37	37	14.7	5.26	66	.291	.373	2	.167	-1	-15	-15	-0	-1.4
Total	6	31	67	.316	231	97	18	5	19	715²	747	70	287	442	13.5	4.41	78	.272	.349	12	.072	-6	-66	-76	-5	-8.1
■ BILL GREVELL				Grevell, William J.			b: 3/5/1898, Williamstown, N.J.			d: 6/21/23, Philadelphia, Pa.		BR/TR, 5'11", 170 lbs.		Deb: 5/14/19											
1919	Phi-A	0	0	—	5	2	0	0	0	12	15	0	18	3	25.5	14.25	24	.306	.500	0	.000	-1	-15	-14	1	-1.2
■ GREYSON				Greyson		Deb: 8/27/1873																				
1873	Was-n	1	6	.143	7	7	7	0	0	63	116	3	7		17.6	5.14	72	.366	.380	5	.185	-1	-11	-10		-0.7
■ LEE GRIFFETH				Griffeth, Leon Clifford			b: 5/20/25, Carmel, N.Y.			BB/TL, 5'11.5", 180 lbs.		Deb: 6/25/46													
1946	Phi-A	0	0	—	10	0	0	0	0	15¹	13	1	6	4	12.3	2.93	121	.232	.328	0	.000	0	1	1	-0	0.1
■ HANK GRIFFIN				Griffin, James Linton "Pepper"			b: 7/11/1886, Whitehouse, Tex.			d: 2/11/50, Terrell, Tex.		BR/TR, 6', 165 lbs.		Deb: 5/05/11											
1911	Chi-N	0	0	—	1	1	0	0	0	1	1	1	3	1	36.0	18.00	18	.250	.571	0	—	0	-2	-2	0	-0.1
	Bos-N	0	6	.000	15	6	1	0	0	82²	96	3	34	30	14.8	5.23	73	.305	.383	7	.233	-0	-17	-13	0	-1.1
	Yr	0	6	.000	16	7	1	0	0	83²	97	4	37	31	15.1	5.38	71	.304	.387	1	.033	-0	-18	-14	0	-1.2
1912	Bos-N	0	0	—	3	0	0	0	0	1²	3	0	3	0	37.8	27.00	13	.500	.700	0	—	0	-4	-4	0	-0.3
Total	2	0	6	.000	19	7	1	0	0	85¹	100	4	40	31	15.5	5.80	66	.308	.395	7	.233	-0	-23	-19	0	-1.5
■ MARTY GRIFFIN				Griffin, Martin John			b: 9/2/01, San Francisco, Cal			d: 11/19/51, Los Angeles, Cal.		BR/TR, 6'2", 200 lbs.		Deb: 7/25/28											
1928	Bos-A	0	3	.000	11	3	0	0	0	37²	42	0	17	9	14.1	5.02	82	.300	.376	4	.308	1	-4	-4	-0	-0.2
■ MIKE GRIFFIN				Griffin, Michael Leroy			b: 6/26/57, Colusa, Cal.			BR/TR, 6'4", 195 lbs.		Deb: 9/17/79												
1979	NY-A	0	0	—	3	0	0	0	1	4¹	5	0	2	5	14.5	4.15	98	.313	.389	0	—	0	0	-0	0	0.0
1980	NY-A	2	4	.333	13	9	0	0	0	54	64	6	23	25	14.7	4.83	81	.287	.356	0	—	0	-5	-5	0	-0.4
1981	NY-A	0	0	—	2	0	0	0	0	4¹	5	0	4	4	10.4	2.08	172	.278	.278	0	—	0	1	1	0	0.1
	Chi-N	2	5	.286	16	9	0	0	1	52	64	4	9	20	12.6	4.50	82	.302	.330	2	.154	-0	-6	-5	0	-0.4
1982	SD-N	0	1	.000	7	0	0	0	0	10¹	9	0	3	4	10.5	3.48	98	.237	.293	0	.000	-0	0	-0	0	0.0
1987	Bal-A	3	5	.375	23	6	1	0	1	74¹	78	9	33	42	13.8	4.36	101	.269	.350	0	—	0	1	0	-1	0.0
1989	Cin-N	0	0	—	3	0	0	0	0	4¹	10	0	3	1	27.0	12.46	29	.500	.565	1	1.000	0	-4	-4	0	-0.3
Total	6	7	15	.318	67	24	1	0	3	203²	235	19	73	101	13.8	4.60	87	.288	.349	3	.200	-0	-13	-13	0	-1.0
■ PAT GRIFFIN				Griffin, Patrick Richard			b: 5/6/1893, Niles, Ohio			d: 6/7/27, Younsgtown, Ohio		BR/TR, 6'2", 180 lbs.		Deb: 7/23/14											
1914	Cin-N	0	0	—	1	0	0	0	0	1	3	0	2	0	45.0	9.00	33	.750	.833	0	—	0	-1	-1	0	0.0
■ TOM GRIFFIN				Griffin, Thomas James			b: 2/22/48, Los Angeles, Cal.			BR/TR, 6'3", 210 lbs.		Deb: 4/10/69												
1969	Hou-N	11	10	.524	31	31	6	3	0	188¹	156	19	93	200	12.2	3.54	100	.220	.317	9	.145	2	1	0	-2	0.0
1970	Hou-N	3	13	.188	23	20	2	1	0	111¹	118	9	72	72	15.6	5.74	68	.275	.383	2	.061	4	-21	-23	-1	-2.4
1971	Hou-N	0	6	.000	10	6	0	0	0	37²	44	4	20	29	15.8	4.78	70	.288	.377	1	.111	-0	-5	-6	1	-0.5
1972	Hou-N	4	5	.556	39	5	1	1	3	94¹	92	7	38	83	12.7	3.24	104	.258	.334	7	.280	3	2	1	-1	0.4
1973	Hou-N	4	6	.400	25	12	4	0	0	99²	83	10	46	69	11.8	4.15	87	.229	.320	3	.107	0	-5	-6	0	-0.5
1974	Hou-N	14	10	.583	34	34	8	3	0	211	202	14	89	110	12.6	3.54	98	.254	.328	20	.294	8	2	-2	1	0.7
1975	Hou-N	3	8	.273	17	13	3	1	0	79¹	89	11	46	56	15.5	5.33	63	.288	.384	3	.136	0	-15	-17	1	-1.6
1976	Hou-N	5	3	.625	20	2	0	0	0	41²	44	4	37	33	17.7	6.05	53	.278	.418	0	.000	-0	-12	-13	0	-1.3
	SD-N	4	3	.571	11	11	2	0	0	70¹	56	0	42	36	12.7	2.94	111	.222	.336	2	.077	-2	4	3	-0	0.0
	Yr	9	6	.600	31	13	2	0	0	112	100	4	79	69	14.5	4.10	79	.242	.364	1	.032	-2	-7	-11	0	-1.3
1977	SD-N	6	9	.400	38	20	0	0	0	151¹	144	17	88	79	14.1	4.46	79	.254	.359	6	.133	1	-9	-16	-2	-1.5
1978	Cal-A	3	4	.429	24	4	0	0	0	56	63	8	31	35	15.3	4.02	90	.279	.368	0	—	0	-2	-3	1	-0.1
1979	SF-N	5	6	.455	59	3	0	0	2	94¹	83	9	46	82	13.6	3.91	89	.237	.333	1	.071	-1	-2	-4	1	-0.3
1980	SF-N	5	1	.833	42	4	0	0	0	107²	80	8	49	79	11.5	2.76	128	.212	.315	2	.111	0	10	9	0	1.0
1981	SF-N	8	8	.500	22	22	3	1	0	129¹	121	8	57	83	12.9	3.76	91	.249	.336	8	.195	2	-4	-5	2	0.0
1982	Pit-N	1	3	.250	6	4	0	0	0	22¹	32	5	15	8	19.3	8.87	42	.330	.425	2	.222	4	-13	-13	0	-1.1
Total	14	77	94	.450	401	191	29	10	5	1494²	1407	133	769	1054	13.4	4.07	86	.249	.345	66	.163	12	-69	-94	-1	-7.2
■ CLARK GRIFFITH				Griffith, Clark Calvin "The Old Fox"			b: 11/20/1869, Clear Creek, Mo.			d: 10/27/55, Washington, D.C.		BR/TR, 5'6.5", 156 lbs.		Deb: 4/11/1891	MH♦										
1891	StL-a	11	8	.579	27	17	12	0	0	186¹	195	8	58	68	12.2	3.33	126	.260	.313	12	.156	-4	8	18	1	1.5
	Bos-a	3	1	.750	7	4	3	0	0	40	47	3	15	20	13.9	5.62	62	.283	.357	4	.174	2	-8	-9	-1	-0.5
	Yr	14	9	.609	34	21	15	0	0	226¹	242	11	73	88	12.5	3.74	109	.264	.319	14	.140	-2	-0	9	0	1.0
1893	Chi-N	1	2	.333	4	2	2	0	0	19²	24	1	5	9	13.3	5.03	92	.292	.333	2	.182	-1	-1	-1	1	0.0
1894	Chi-N	21	14	.600	36	30	28	0	0	261¹	328	12	85	71	14.2	4.92	114	.304	.354	33	.232	-0	12	20	0	1.7
1895	Chi-N	26	14	.650	42	41	39	0	0	353	434	11	91	79	13.4	3.93	130	.298	.339	46	.319	5	34	46	2	4.6
1896	Chi-N	23	11	.676	36	35	35	0	0	317²	370	6	70	81	12.5	3.54	118	.289	.325	36	.267	8	29	35	3	3.6
1897	Chi-N	21	18	.538	41	38	**38**	1	1	343²	410	3	86	102	13.0	3.72	120	.294	.335	38	.235	3	23	28	3	3.1
1898	Chi-N	24	10	.706	38	38	36	4	0	325²	305	1	64	97	10.2	**1.88**	**191**	.246	.283	20	.164	-1	63	62	1	6.2
1899	Chi-N	22	14	.611	38	38	35	0	0	319²	329	5	65	73	11.1	2.79	134	.266	.302	31	.258	6	38	34	6	4.4
1900	Chi-N	14	13	.519	30	30	27	4	0	248	245	6	51	61	10.7	3.05	118	.258	.295	24	.253	5	18	15	-1	1.8
1901	Chi-A	24	7	**.774**	35	30	26	5	1	266²	275	4	50	67	11.0	2.67	131	.263	.297	27	.303	13	30	24	1	3.5
1902	Chi-A	15	9	.625	28	24	20	3	0	213	247	11	47	51	12.4	4.18	81	.290	.327	20	.217	2	-14	-19	-1	-1.6
1903	NY-A	14	11	.560	25	24	22	2	0	213	201	3	33	69	9.9	2.70	116	.249	.278	11	.159	2	6	10	-3	0.7
1904	NY-A	7	5	.583	16	11	8	1	0	100¹	91	3	16	36	9.6	2.87	94	.243	.274	6	.143	-1	-3	-2	-0	-0.2
1905	NY-A	9	6	.600	25	7	4	2	0	101²	82	1	15	46	8.6	1.68	175	.222	.253	7	.219	1	11	14	-2	1.6
1906	NY-A	2	2	.500	17	2	1	0	2	59²	58	0	15	16	11.0	3.02	98	.258	.304	2	.111	-2	-0	1	0	0.0
1907	NY-A	0	0	—	4	0	0	0	0	8¹	15	0	6	5	22.7	8.64	32	.390	.472	0	.000	0	-6	-5	0	-0.4
1909	Cin-N	0	1	.000	1	1	1	0	0	6	11	0	2	3	19.5	6.00	43	.379	.419	0	.000	0	-2	-2	1	-0.1
1912	Was-A	0	0	—	1	0	0	0	0	0	1	0	1	0	∞	∞	—	1.000	1.000	0	—	0	-1	-1	0	0.0
1913	Was-A	0	0	—	1	0	0	0	0	1	1	0	0	0	9.0	9.00	—	.250	.250	1	1.000	1	0	0	0	0.1
1914	Was-A	0	0	—	1	0	0	0	0	1	1	0	0	1	9.0	0.00	—	.250	.250	1	1.000	1	0	0	0	0.0
Total	20	237	146	.619	453	372	337	22	6	3385²	3670	76	774	955	11.8	3.31	121	.274	.314	321	.233	36	233	266	10	30.2
■ FRANK GRIFFITH				Griffith, Frank Wesley			b: 11/18/1872, Gilman, Ill.			d: 12/13/08,		BL ,		Deb: 8/13/1892											
1892	Chi-N	0	1	.000	1	1	0	0	0	4	3	1	6	3	20.3	11.25	29	.200	.429	0	.000	-0	-4	-4	-0	-0.2
1894	Cle-N	1	2	.333	7	6	3	0	0	42¹	64	5	37	15	21.5	9.99	55	.344	.453	8	.333	2	-22	-21	-0	-1.3
Total	2	1	3	.250	8	7	3	0	0	46¹	67	6	43	18	21.4	10.10	52	.333	.451	8	.320	2	-25	-25	-0	-1.5
■ HAL GRIGGS				Griggs, Harold Lloyd			b: 8/24/28, Shannon, Ga.			BR/TR, 6', 170 lbs.		Deb: 4/18/56												
1956	Was-A	1	6	.143	34	12	1	0	1	98²	120	14	76	48	18.0	6.02	72	.307	.421	0	.000	-1	-20	-19	1	-1.6

YEAR	TM/L	W	L	PCT	G	GS	CG	SH	SV	IP	H	HR	BB	SO	RAT	ERA	ERA+	OAV	OOB	BH	AVG	PB	PR	/A	PD	TPI
1957	Was-A	0	1	.000	2	2	0	0	0	13²	11	1	7	12	11.9	3.29	118	.229	.327	1	.250	0	1	1	0	0.1
1958	Was-A	3	11	.214	32	21	3	0	0	137	138	20	74	69	14.1	5.52	69	.262	.355	5	.122	-2	-27	-26	0	-2.7
1959	Was-A	2	8	.200	37	10	2	1	2	97²	103	8	52	43	14.4	5.25	75	.270	.359	1	.056	-2	-15	-15	-0	-1.5
Total	4	6	26	.188	105	45	6	1	3	347	372	43	209	172	15.2	5.50	73	.276	.375	7	.089	-5	-61	-58	2	-5.7

■ GUIDO GRILLI
Grilli, Guido John b: 1/9/39, Memphis, Tenn. BL/TL, 6', 188 lbs. Deb: 4/12/66

YEAR	TM/L	W	L	PCT	G	GS	CG	SH	SV	IP	H	HR	BB	SO	RAT	ERA	ERA+	OAV	OOB	BH	AVG	PB	PR	/A	PD	TPI
1966	Bos-A	0	1	.000	6	0	0	0	0	4²	5	1	9	4	27.0	7.71	49	.278	.519	1	.500	0	-2	-2	0	-0.1
	KC-A	0	1	.000	16	0	0	0	1	15²	19	0	11	8	19.0	6.89	49	.302	.429	0	—	0	-6	-6	-1	-0.6
	Yr	0	2	.000	22	0	0	0	1	20¹	24	1	20	12	20.8	7.08	49	.296	.452	1	.000	0	-8	-8	-0	-0.7

■ STEVE GRILLI
Grilli, Stephen Joseph b: 5/2/49, Brooklyn, N.Y. BR/TR, 6'2", 170 lbs. Deb: 9/19/75

YEAR	TM/L	W	L	PCT	G	GS	CG	SH	SV	IP	H	HR	BB	SO	RAT	ERA	ERA+	OAV	OOB	BH	AVG	PB	PR	/A	PD	TPI
1975	Det-A	0	0	—	3	0	0	0	0	6²	3	0	6	5	12.2	1.35	297	.136	.321	0	—	0	2	2	0	0.2
1976	Det-A	3	1	.750	36	0	0	0	3	66	63	5	41	36	14.9	4.64	80	.258	.376	0	—	0	-8	-7	2	-0.4
1977	Det-A	1	2	.333	30	2	0	0	0	72²	71	8	49	49	15.2	4.83	89	.265	.384	0	—	0	-6	-4	-1	-0.4
1979	Tor-A	0	0	—	1	0	0	0	0	2¹	1	0	0	1	3.9	0.00	—	.143	.143	0	—	0	1	1	0	0.1
Total	4	4	3	.571	70	2	0	0	3	147²	138	13	96	91	14.7	4.51	89	.255	.375	0	—	0	-12	-8	1	-0.5

■ JOHN GRIM
Grim, John Helm b: 8/9/1867, Lebanon, Ky. d: 7/28/61, Indianapolis, Ind TR, 6'2", 175 lbs. Deb: 9/29/1888 ◆

YEAR	TM/L	W	L	PCT	G	GS	CG	SH	SV	IP	H	HR	BB	SO	RAT	ERA	ERA+	OAV	OOB	BH	AVG	PB	PR	/A	PD	TPI
1890	Roc-a	0	0	—	1	0	0	0	0	3¹	3	0	4	3	18.9	0.00	—	.233	.415	51	.266	0	1	1	0	0.1

■ BOB GRIM
Grim, Robert Anton b: 3/8/30, New York, Ny. BR/TR, 6'1", 175 lbs. Deb: 4/18/54

YEAR	TM/L	W	L	PCT	G	GS	CG	SH	SV	IP	H	HR	BB	SO	RAT	ERA	ERA+	OAV	OOB	BH	AVG	PB	PR	/A	PD	TPI
1954	NY-A	20	6	.769	37	20	8	1	0	199	175	9	85	108	11.9	3.26	106	.244	.327	10	.143	-1	10	4	-1	0.1
1955	*NY-A	7	5	.583	26	11	1	1	4	92¹	81	9	42	63	12.3	4.19	89	.238	.326	3	.120	1	-2	-5	-0	-0.5
1956	NY-A	6	1	.857	26	6	1	0	5	74²	64	3	31	48	11.7	2.77	139	.235	.318	1	.063	-0	11	9	-1	0.8
1957	*NY-A	12	8	.600	46	0	0	0	19	72	60	5	36	52	12.0	2.63	137	.239	.334	1	.111	1	9	8	0	0.9
1958	NY-A	0	1	.000	11	0	0	0	0	16¹	12	3	10	11	12.7	5.51	64	.211	.338	0	.000	-0	-3	-4	-0	-0.3
	KC-A	7	6	.538	26	14	5	1	0	113²	118	7	41	54	12.8	3.56	110	.269	.336	.6	.188	-1	3	4	-1	0.3
	Yr	7	7	.500	37	14	5	1	0	130	130	10	51	65	12.7	3.81	101	.262	.335	1	.030	-1	-1	1	-1	0.0
1959	KC-A	6	10	.375	40	9	3	1	4	125¹	124	10	57	65	13.2	4.09	98	.260	.343	3	.094	-1	-3	-1	-2	-0.3
1960	Cle-A	0	1	.000	3	0	0	0	0	2¹	6	0	1	2	27.0	11.57	32	.500	.538	0	—	-0	-2	-2	0	-0.1
	Cin-N	2	2	.500	26	0	0	0	2	30¹	32.	3	10	22	12.5	4.45	86	.274	.331	0	.000	-0	-2	-2	-1	-0.2
	StL-N	1	0	1.000	15	0	0	0	0	20²	22	1	9	15	13.5	3.05	134	.272	.344	0	.000	-0	2	2	0	0.1
	Yr	3	2	.600	41	0	0	0	2	51	54	4	19	37	12.9	3.88	101	.267	.330	0	.000	-0	-1	0	-0	0.1
1962	KC-A	0	1	.000	12	0	0	0	3	13	14	0	8	3	15.2	6.23	67	.292	.393	0	.000	-0	-3	-3	1	-0.2
Total	8	61	41	.598	268	60	18	4	37	759²	708	50	330	443	12.5	3.61	104	.252	.334	24	.127	-4	19	11	-4	0.8

■ BURLEIGH GRIMES
Grimes, Burleigh Arland "Ol' Stubblebeard"
b: 8/9/1893, Emerald, Wis. d: 12/6/85, Clear Lake, Wis. BR/TR, 5'10", 175 lbs. Deb: 9/10/16 MCH

YEAR	TM/L	W	L	PCT	G	GS	CG	SH	SV	IP	H	HR	BB	SO	RAT	ERA	ERA+	OAV	OOB	BH	AVG	PB	PR	/A	PD	TPI
1916	Pit-N	2	3	.400	6	5	4	0	0	45²	40	1	10	20	9.9	2.36	114	.241	.284	3	.176	-0	1	2	1	0.2
1917	Pit-N	3	16	.158	37	17	8	1	0	194	186	5	70	72	12.2	3.53	81	.260	.331	16	.232	2	-18	-15	1	-1.2
1918	Bro-N	19	9	.679	**40**	28	19	7	1	269²	210	3	76	113	9.7	2.14	130	.216	.276	18	.200	0	19	19	3	2.7
1919	Bro-N	10	11	.476	25	21	13	1	0	181¹	179	2	60	82	12.2	3.47	86	.256	.321	17	.246	1	-11	-10	0	-0.8
1920	*Bro-N	23	11	**.676**	40	33	25	5	2	303²	271	5	67	131	10.1	2.22	144	.238	.282	34	.306	11	31	33	5	5.3
1921	Bro-N	**22**	13	.629	37	35	**30**	2	0	302¹	313	6	76	**136**	11.7	2.83	138	.274	.322	27	.237	2	32	**36**	3	**4.4**
1922	Bro-N	17	14	.548	36	34	18	1	1	259	324	17	84	99	14.4	4.76	85	.308	.363	22	.237	4	-19	-20	4	-1.0
1923	Bro-N	21	18	.538	39	38	**33**	2	0	327	356	10	100	119	12.9	3.58	108	.280	.338	20	.238	3	15	11	5	1.9
1924	Bro-N	22	13	.629	38	36	**30**	1	1	**310²**	351	15	91	135	13.0	3.82	98	.287	.339	37	.298	6	1	-3	6	0.8
1925	Bro-N	12	19	.387	33	31	19	0	0	246²	305	15	102	73	15.1	5.04	83	.309	.377	24	.250	5	-21	-23	9	-0.8
1926	Bro-N	12	13	.480	30	29	18	1	0	225¹	238	4	88	64	13.2	3.71	103	.276	.346	18	.222	1	3	3	3	0.6
1927	NY-N	19	8	.704	39	34	15	2	2	259²	274	12	87	102	12.7	3.54	109	.276	.346	18	.188	-0	11	9	4	1.3
1928	Pit-N	**25**	14	.641	**48**	37	**28**	4	3	330²	311	11	77	97	10.8	2.99	135	.248	.297	42	.321	11	36	39	6	5.8
1929	Pit-N	17	7	.708	33	29	18	2	2	232²	245	11	70	62	12.3	3.13	**152**	.269	.324	26	.286	6	**41**	42	3	**5.0**
1930	Bos-N	3	5	.375	11	9	1	0	0	49	72	4	22	15	17.8	7.35	67	.353	.424	3	.188	-0	-13	-13	0	-1.0
	*StL-N	13	6	.684	22	19	10	1	0	152¹	174	5	43	58	13.1	3.01	166	.293	.345	15	.263	2	33	34	2	3.6
	Yr	16	11	.593	33	28	11	1	0	201¹	246	9	65	73	14.1	4.07	123	.307	.362	6	.082	2	20	21	2	2.6
1931	*StL-N	17	9	.654	29	28	17	3	0	212¹	240	11	59	67	13.1	3.65	108	.286	.340	14	.184	-1	5	7	4	0.9
1932	*Chi-N	6	11	.353	30	18	5	1	1	141¹	174	8	50	36	14.3	4.78	79	.297	.354	11	.250	1	-14	-16	2	-1.2
1933	Chi-N	3	6	.333	17	7	3	1	3	69²	71	2	29	12	13.0	3.49	94	.277	.353	3	.150	-0	-1	-2	1	-0.1
	StL-N	0	1	.000	4	3	0	0	1	13²	15	1	8	4	15.8	5.27	66	.263	.364	1	.200	0	-3	-3	-1	-0.2
	Yr	3	7	.300	21	10	3	1	4	83¹	86	3	37	16	13.4	3.78	87	.274	.352	1	.040	-0	-4	-4	0	-0.3
1934	StL-N	2	1	.667	4	0	0	0	0	7²	5	1	2	1	8.2	3.52	120	.179	.233	0	—	0	1	1	0	0.1
	Pit-N	1	2	.333	8	4	0	0	0	27¹	36	0	10	9	15.5	7.24	57	.310	.370	1	.143	-0	-10	-10	1	-0.8
	Yr	3	3	.500	12	4	0	0	0	35	41	1	12	10	13.9	6.43	64	.285	.344	1	.000	-0	-9	-9	1	-0.7
	NY-A	1	2	.333	10	0	0	0	1	18	22	0	14	5	18.5	5.50	74	.319	.440	0	.000	-0	-2	-3	1	-0.1
Total	19	270	212	.560	616	495	314	35	18	4179²	4412	149	1295	1512	12.5	3.53	107	.273	.331	380	.248	52	118	121	59	25.4

■ JOHN GRIMES
Grimes, John Thomas b: 4/17/1869, Wooodstock, Md. d: 1/17/64, San Francisco, Cal BR/TR, 5'11", 160 lbs. Deb: 7/28/1897

YEAR	TM/L	W	L	PCT	G	GS	CG	SH	SV	IP	H	HR	BB	SO	RAT	ERA	ERA+	OAV	OOB	BH	AVG	PB	PR	/A	PD	TPI
1897	StL-N	0	2	.000	3	1	1	0	0	19²	24	0	8	4	14.6	5.95	74	.298	.362	2	.286	1	-4	-3	1	0.0

■ JASON GRIMSLEY
Grimsley, Jason Alan b: 8/7/67, Cleveland, Tex. BR/TR, 6'3", 180 lbs. Deb: 9/08/89

YEAR	TM/L	W	L	PCT	G	GS	CG	SH	SV	IP	H	HR	BB	SO	RAT	ERA	ERA+	OAV	OOB	BH	AVG	PB	PR	/A	PD	TPI
1989	Phi-N	1	3	.250	4	4	0	0	0	18¹	19	2	19	7	18.7	5.89	60	.268	.422	0	.000	-1	-5	-5	0	-0.4
1990	Phi-N	3	2	.600	11	11	0	0	0	57¹	47	1	43	41	14.4	3.30	116	.227	.365	3	.188	0	3	3	1	0.5
Total	2	4	5	.444	15	15	0	0	0	75²	66	3	62	48	15.5	3.93	.96	.237	.380	3	.143	-0	-2	-1	1	0.1

■ ROSS GRIMSLEY
Grimsley, Ross Albert I b: 6/4/22, Americus, Kan. BL/TL, 6', 175 lbs. Deb: 9/03/51

YEAR	TM/L	W	L	PCT	G	GS	CG	SH	SV	IP	H	HR	BB	SO	RAT	ERA	ERA+	OAV	OOB	BH	AVG	PB	PR	/A	PD	TPI
1951	Chi-A	0	0	—	7	0	0	0	0	14	12	1	10	8	14.1	3.86	105	.235	.361	0	.000	-0	0	0	-1	0.0

■ ROSS GRIMSLEY
Grimsley, Ross Albert Ii b: 1/7/50, Topeka, Kan. BL/TL, 6'3", 195 lbs. Deb: 5/16/71

YEAR	TM/L	W	L	PCT	G	GS	CG	SH	SV	IP	H	HR	BB	SO	RAT	ERA	ERA+	OAV	OOB	BH	AVG	PB	PR	/A	PD	TPI
1971	Cin-N	10	7	.588	26	26	6	3	0	161¹	151	15	43	67	10.9	3.57	94	.250	.302	6	.118	-1	-2	-4	-0	-0.5
1972	Cin-N	14	8	.636	30	28	4	1	1	197²	194	18	50	79	11.1	3.05	105	.260	.307	8	.121	-2	9	4	0	0.1
1973	Cin-N	13	10	.565	38	36	8	1	1	242¹	245	24	68	90	11.6	3.23	105	.266	.317	5	.061	-6	12	5	-1	-0.2
1974	Bal-A	18	13	.581	40	39	17	4	1	295²	267	26	76	158	10.5	3.07	112	.244	.295	0	—	0	18	12	-0	1.3
1975	Bal-A	10	13	.435	35	32	8	1	0	197	210	29	49	89	11.8	4.07	86	.276	.319	0	—	0	-6	-12	-1	-1.1
1976	Bal-A	8	7	.533	28	19	2	0	0	137¹	143	8	35	41	11.7	3.93	83	.270	.317	0	—	0	-6	-10	-1	-1.0
1977	Bal-A	14	10	.583	34	34	11	2	0	218¹	230	24	74	53	12.6	3.96	96	.277	.337	0	—	0	-2	-4	3	0.0
1978	Mon-N	20	11	.645	36	36	19	3	0	263	237	17	67	84	10.5	3.05	116	.243	.293	13	.144	-1	15	14	2	1.6
1979	Mon-N	10	9	.526	32	27	2	0	0	151¹	199	18	41	42	14.5	5.35	68	.322	.367	11	.200	1	-27	-28	2	-2.6
1980	Mon-N	2	4	.333	11	7	0	0	0	41¹	61	5	12	11	16.1	6.31	56	.351	.396	2	.222	0	-12	-13	0	-1.1
	Cle-A	1	0	1.000	3	3	0	0	0	14¹	18	2	3	5	14.4	6.28	60	.313	.358	0	—	-0	-2	-3	0	-0.2
1981	Cle-A	3	4	.429	14	11	2	0	0	74²	103	12	12	18	15.4	6.75	60	.331	.381	0	—	0	-23	-22	-0	-2.0
1982	Bal-A	1	2	.333	21	0	0	0	0	60	65	7	22	18	13.1	5.25	77	.283	.345	0	—	0	-8	-8	0	-0.7
Total	11	124	99	.556	345	295	79	15	3	2040	2105	202	559	750	11.8	3.81	92	.270	.320	45	.127	-9	-28	-67	4	-6.2

■ DAN GRINER
Griner, Donald Dexter "Rusty" b: 3/7/1888, Centerville, Tenn. d: 6/3/50, Bishopville, S.C. BL/TR, 6'1", 200 lbs. Deb: 8/17/12

YEAR	TM/L	W	L	PCT	G	GS	CG	SH	SV	IP	H	HR	BB	SO	RAT	ERA	ERA+	OAV	OOB	BH	AVG	PB	PR	/A	PD	TPI
1912	StL-N	3	4	.429	12	7	2	0	0	54	59	3	15	20	12.8	3.17	108	.273	.329	1	.077	-0	1	2	-1	0.0
1913	StL-N	10	22	.313	34	34	18	1	0	225	279	12	66	79	14.2	5.08	64	.312	.366	21	.259	5	-47	-46	2	-3.7

YEAR	TM/L	W	L	PCT	G	GS	CG	SH	SV	IP	H	HR	BB	SO	RAT	ERA	ERA+	OAV	OOB	BH	AVG	PB	PR	/A	PD	TPI
1914	StL-N	9	13	.409	37	16	11	2	2	179	163	3	57	74	11.2	2.51	111	.254	.318	14	.255	4	5	6	-1	0.9
1915	StL-N	5	11	.313	37	18	9	3	3	150¹	137	4	46	46	11.4	2.81	99	.259	.328	14	.269	4	-1	-0	-1	0.2
1916	StL-N	0	0	—	4	0	0	0	1	11	15	0	3	3	15.5	4.09	65	.341	.396	1	.250	0	-2	-2	0	-0.1
1918	Bro-N	1	5	.167	11	6	3	1	0	54¹	47	0	15	22	11.4	2.15	129	.267	.348	1	.071	-1	4	4	0	0.4
Total 6		28	55	.337	135	81	43	7	6	673²	700	22	202	244	12.5	3.49	86	.280	.342	52	.237	12	-39	-37	-2	-2.3

■ LEE GRISSOM
Grissom, Lee Theo   b: 10/23/07, Sherman, Tex.   BB/TL, 6'3", 200 lbs.   Deb: 9/02/34

YEAR	TM/L	W	L	PCT	G	GS	CG	SH	SV	IP	H	HR	BB	SO	RAT	ERA	ERA+	OAV	OOB	BH	AVG	PB	PR	/A	PD	TPI
1934	Cin-N	0	1	.000	4	1	0	0	0	7	13	0	7	4	25.7	15.43	26	.382	.488	0	.000	-0	-9	-9	0	-0.7
1935	Cin-N	1	1	.500	3	3	1	0	0	21	31	0	4	13	15.0	3.86	103	.333	.361	0	.000	-1	0	0	0	0.0
1936	Cin-N	1	1	.500	6	4	0	0	0	24¹	33	1	9	13	15.5	6.29	61	.320	.375	0	.000	-1	-6	-7	0	-0.6
1937	Cin-N	12	17	.414	50	30	14	5	6	223²	193	7	93	149	11.7	3.26	114	.232	.313	7	.109	-3	16	12	-3	0.5
1938	Cin-N	2	3	.400	14	7	0	0	0	51	60	4	22	16	14.8	5.29	69	.300	.375	3	.188	-0	-9	-9	0	-0.9
1939	*Cin-N	9	7	.563	33	21	3	0	0	153²	145	14	56	53	11.8	4.10	93	.249	.316	4	.085	-2	-3	-5	-1	-0.7
1940	NY-A	0	0	—	5	0	0	0	0	4²	4	0	2	1	11.6	0.00	—	.250	.333	0	—	0	2	2	0	0.2
	Bro-N	2	5	.286	14	10	3	1	0	73²	59	3	34	56	11.4	2.81	142	.215	.302	5	.217	-0	9	10	-1	0.9
1941	Bro-N	0	0	—	4	1	0	0	1	11¹	10	2	8	5	14.3	2.38	154	.238	.360	1	.500	0	2	2	0	0.2
	Phi-N	2	13	.133	29	18	2	0	0	131¹	120	4	70	74	13.2	3.97	93	.242	.338	6	.167	-1	-5	-4	-1	-0.5
	Yr	2	13	.133	33	19	2	0	1	142²	130	6	78	79	13.2	3.85	96	.242	.340	1	.026	-0	-3	-2	-1	-0.3
Total 8		29	48	.377	162	95	23	6	7	701²	668	35	305	384	12.6	3.89	97	.250	.329	26	.127	-8	-3	-8	-6	-1.6

■ MARV GRISSOM
Grissom, Marvin Edward   b: 3/31/18, Los Molinos, Cal.   BR/TR, 6'3", 190 lbs.   Deb: 9/10/46   C

YEAR	TM/L	W	L	PCT	G	GS	CG	SH	SV	IP	H	HR	BB	SO	RAT	ERA	ERA+	OAV	OOB	BH	AVG	PB	PR	/A	PD	TPI
1946	NY-N	0	2	.000	4	3	0	0	0	18²	17	1	13	9	14.9	4.34	79	.254	.383	1	.200	-0	-2	-2	1	0.0
1949	Det-A	2	4	.333	27	2	0	0	0	39¹	56	6	34	17	20.8	6.41	65	.335	.450	2	.222	1	-10	-10	0	-0.8
1952	Chi-A	12	10	.545	28	24	7	1	0	166	156	6	79	97	12.9	3.74	98	.250	.337	8	.151	-1	-1	-2	-2	-0.3
1953	Bos-A	2	6	.250	13	11	1	1	0	59¹	61	5	30	31	14.0	4.70	89	.266	.354	0	.000	-3	-5	-3	-1	-0.6
	NY-N	4	2	.667	21	7	3	0	0	84¹	83	6	31	46	12.3	3.95	109	.255	.321	2	.074	-2	3	3	1	0.3
1954	*NY-N	10	7	.588	56	3	1	1	19	122¹	100	13	50	64	11.6	2.35	171	.226	.314	5	.156	-1	23	23	-0	2.2
1955	NY-N	5	4	.556	55	0	0	0	8	89¹	76	6	41	49	12.4	2.92	138	.237	.334	2	.154	-1	11	11	0	1.0
1956	NY-N	1	1	.500	43	0	0	0	7	80²	71	3	16	49	9.8	1.56	242	.241	.282	1	.091	-0	**20**	**20**	-1	2.0
1957	NY-N	4	4	.500	55	0	0	0	14	82²	74	6	23	51	10.8	2.61	151	.243	.301	2	.167	0	12	12	1	1.4
1958	SF-N	7	5	.583	51	0	0	0	10	65¹	71	1	26	44	14.1	3.99	95	.287	.367	0	.000	-1	0	-1	0	-0.1
1959	StL-N	0	0	—	3	0	0	0	0	2	6	2	0	0	27.0	22.50	19	.500	.500	0	—	0	-4	-4	0	-0.3
Total 10		47	45	.511	356	52	12	3	58	810	771	65	343	459	12.7	3.41	115	.254	.335	23	.122	-7	47	47	-0	4.8

■ CONNIE GROB
Grob, Conrad George   b: 11/9/32, Cross Plains, Wis.   BL/TR, 6'0.5", 180 lbs.   Deb: 4/22/56

YEAR	TM/L	W	L	PCT	G	GS	CG	SH	SV	IP	H	HR	BB	SO	RAT	ERA	ERA+	OAV	OOB	BH	AVG	PB	PR	/A	PD	TPI
1956	Was-A	4	5	.444	37	1	0	0	1	79¹	121	14	26	27	16.8	7.83	55	.353	.400	6	.333	2	-32	-31	1	-2.5

■ JOHNNY GRODZICKI
Grodzicki, John "Grod"   b: 2/26/17, Nanticoke, Pa.   BR/TR, 6'1.5", 200 lbs.   Deb: 4/18/41   C

YEAR	TM/L	W	L	PCT	G	GS	CG	SH	SV	IP	H	HR	BB	SO	RAT	ERA	ERA+	OAV	OOB	BH	AVG	PB	PR	/A	PD	TPI
1941	StL-N	2	1	.667	5	1	0	0	0	13¹	6	0	11	10	11.5	1.35	279	.130	.298	0	.000	0	3	4	-0	0.4
1946	StL-N	0	0	—	3	0	0	0	0	4	4	1	4	2	18.0	9.00	38	.250	.400	0	—	0	-2	-2	0	-0.1
1947	StL-N	0	1	.000	16	0	0	0	0	23¹	21	5	19	8	15.4	5.40	77	.253	.392	0	.000	-0	-3	-3	0	-0.2
Total 3		2	2	.500	24	1	0	0	0	40²	31	6	34	20	14.4	4.43	89	.214	.363	0	.000	0	-3	-2	0	0.1

■ STEVE GROMEK
Gromek, Stephen Joseph   b: 1/15/20, Hamtramck, Mich.   BB/TR, 6'2", 180 lbs.   Deb: 8/18/41

YEAR	TM/L	W	L	PCT	G	GS	CG	SH	SV	IP	H	HR	BB	SO	RAT	ERA	ERA+	OAV	OOB	BH	AVG	PB	PR	/A	PD	TPI
1941	Cle-A	1	1	.500	9	2	1	0	2	23¹	25	0	11	19	13.9	4.24	93	.266	.343	1	.167	-0	-0	-1	-1	-0.1
1942	Cle-A	2	0	1.000	14	0	0	0	0	44¹	46	2	23	14	14.0	3.65	94	.267	.354	3	.333	3	0	-1	-1	0.1
1943	Cle-A	0	0	—	3	0	0	0	0	4	6	0	0	4	13.5	9.00	35	.353	.353	2	1.000	1	-3	-3	-0	-0.1
1944	Cle-A	10	9	.526	35	21	12	2	1	203²	160	5	70	115	10.3	2.56	129	**.219**	.290	19	.260	5	20	17	-3	1.9
1945	Cle-A	19	9	.679	33	30	21	3	1	251	229	6	66	101	10.7	2.55	128	.243	.295	21	.231	3	23	20	-3	2.1
1946	Cle-A	5	15	.250	29	21	5	2	4	153²	159	20	47	75	12.2	4.33	76	.264	.321	11	.196	-0	-14	-18	-0	-1.7
1947	Cle-A	3	5	.375	29	7	0	0	4	84¹	77	8	36	39	12.2	3.74	93	.240	.318	7	.318	2	-0	-2	-0	0.0
1948	*Cle-A	9	3	.750	38	9	4	1	2	130	109	10	51	50	11.5	2.84	143	.226	.307	6	.146	-1	21	18	-1	1.5
1949	Cle-A	4	4	.400	27	12	3	0	0	92	86	8	40	22	12.5	3.33	120	.250	.332	4	.167	-0	9	7	0	0.7
1950	Cle-A	10	7	.588	31	13	4	1	0	113¹	94	10	36	43	10.6	3.65	119	.226	.292	6	.158	-2	12	9	-0	0.6
1951	Cle-A	7	4	.636	27	8	4	0	1	107¹	98	6	29	40	11.0	2.77	137	.238	.295	8	.296	3	16	12	1	1.6
1952	Cle-A	7	7	.500	29	13	3	1	1	122²	109	14	28	65	10.2	3.67	91	.232	.278	3	.100	-1	0	-4	-2	-0.7
1953	Cle-A	1	1	.500	5	1	0	0	0	11	11	0	3	8	12.3	3.27	115	.268	.333	0	.000	-0	1	1	-0	0.0
	Det-A	6	8	.429	19	17	6	1	1	125²	138	17	36	59	13.0	4.51	90	.276	.335	3	.073	-4	-7	-6	-1	-1.0
	Yr	7	9	.438	24	18	6	1	1	136²	149	17	39	67	12.9	4.41	92	.275	.333	0	.000	-5	-6	-6	-1	-1.0
1954	Det-A	18	16	.529	36	32	17	4	1	252²	236	26	57	102	10.9	2.74	135	.246	.297	15	.190	1	28	27	3	2.7
1955	Det-A	13	10	.565	28	25	8	2	0	181	183	26	37	73	11.4	3.98	97	.261	.307	9	.167	-3	-0	-3	-1	0.0
1956	Det-A	8	6	.571	40	13	4	0	4	141	142	25	47	64	12.6	4.28	96	.263	.332	4	.148	2	-2	-3	-2	-0.2
1957	Det-A	0	1	.000	15	1	0	0	1	23²	32	3	13	11	17.5	6.08	63	.333	.418	0	.000	-0	-6	-6	-0	-0.6
Total 17		123	108	.532	447	225	92	17	23	2064²	1940	186	630	904	11.5	3.41	108	.247	.309	124	.197	15	96	63	-19	6.8

■ BOB GROOM
Groom, Robert   b: 9/12/1884, Belleville, Ill.   d: 2/19/48, Belleville, Ill.   BR/TR, 6'2", 175 lbs.   Deb: 4/13/09

YEAR	TM/L	W	L	PCT	G	GS	CG	SH	SV	IP	H	HR	BB	SO	RAT	ERA	ERA+	OAV	OOB	BH	AVG	PB	PR	/A	PD	TPI
1909	Was-A	7	26	.212	44	31	17	1	0	260²	218	4	105	131	11.6	2.87	85	.229	.314	8	.091	-5	-11	-13	3	-1.6
1910	Was-A	12	17	.414	34	30	22	3	0	257²	244	8	77	98	11.6	2.76	90	.260	.322	11	.120	-6	-7	-8	-1	-1.5
1911	Was-A	13	17	.433	37	32	20	2	2	254²	280	9	67	135	12.5	3.82	86	.282	.332	11	.134	-4	-13	-15	0	-1.7
1912	Was-A	24	13	.649	43	40	28	2	1	316	287	3	94	179	11.0	2.62	127	.246	.305	12	.113	-7	24	25	-2	1.7
1913	Was-A	16	16	.500	37	36	17	4	0	264¹	258	8	81	156	11.7	3.23	91	.254	.312	15	.163	1	-9	-8	-1	-0.6
1914	StL-F	13	20	.394	42	34	23	1	1	280²	281	9	75	167	11.5	3.24	104	.262	.312	15	.160	-2	-1	4	-1	0.2
1915	StL-F	11	11	.500	37	26	11	4	2	209	200	6	73	111	11.8	3.27	98	.261	.327	11	.152	-2	-6	-2	0	-0.2
1916	StL-A	13	9	.591	41	26	8	1	4	217¹	174	1	98	92	11.4	2.57	107	.226	.315	7	.111	-2	6	4	1	0.4
1917	StL-A	8	19	.296	38	28	11	4	3	232²	193	3	95	82	11.3	2.94	88	.233	.315	8	.111	-4	-7	-9	-2	-1.5
1918	Cle-A	2	2	.500	14	5	0	0	0	43¹	70	0	18	8	18.5	7.06	43	.380	.438	1	.083	-1	-21	-20	0	-2.0
Total 10		119	150	.442	367	288	157	22	13	2336¹	2205	49	783	1159	11.7	3.10	95	.254	.319	98	.128	-32	-44	-41	2	-6.8

■ DON GROSS
Gross, Donald John   b: 6/30/31, Weidman, Mich.   BL/TL, 5'11", 186 lbs.   Deb: 7/21/55

YEAR	TM/L	W	L	PCT	G	GS	CG	SH	SV	IP	H	HR	BB	SO	RAT	ERA	ERA+	OAV	OOB	BH	AVG	PB	PR	/A	PD	TPI
1955	Cin-N	4	5	.444	17	11	2	1	0	67¹	79	11	16	33	12.8	4.14	102	.298	.340	3	.158	-1	-1	1	0	0.0
1956	Cin-N	3	0	1.000	19	7	2	0	0	69¹	69	4	20	47	11.7	1.95	204	.257	.310	2	.105	-1	14	16	1	1.7
1957	Cin-N	7	9	.438	43	16	5	0	1	148¹	152	21	33	73	11.4	4.31	95	.264	.307	5	.109	-2	-7	-3	0	-0.5
1958	Pit-N	5	7	.417	40	3	0	0	7	74²	67	5	38	59	12.8	3.98	97	.241	.334	1	.056	-1	-0	-1	1	-0.1
1959	Pit-N	1	1	.500	21	0	0	0	2	33	28	3	10	15	10.6	3.55	109	.228	.291	0	.000	-0	1	1	1	0.2
1960	Pit-N	0	0	—	5	0	0	0	0	5¹	5	1	0	3	8.4	3.38	111	.238	.238	0	—	0	0	0	-0	0.0
Total 6		20	22	.476	145	37	9	1	10	398	400	45	117	230	11.8	3.73	108	.261	.316	11	.106	-5	8	14	2	1.3

■ GREG GROSS
Gross, Gregory Eugene   b: 8/1/52, York, Pa.   BL/TL, 5'10", 160 lbs.   Deb: 9/05/73   ♦

YEAR	TM/L	W	L	PCT	G	GS	CG	SH	SV	IP	H	HR	BB	SO	RAT	ERA	ERA+	OAV	OOB	BH	AVG	PB	PR	/A	PD	TPI
1986	Phi-N	0	0	—	1	0	0	0	0	0²	1	0	1	2	27.0	0.00	—	.333	.500	25	.248	0	0	0	0	0.0
1989	Hou-N	0	0	—	1	0	0	0	0	1	3	0	1	1		18.00	19	.500	.571	15	.200	0	-2	-2	0	-0.1
Total 2		0	0	—	2	0	0	0	0	1²	4	0	2	3	32.4	10.80	33	.444	.545	1073	.287	0	-1	-1	0	0.0

■ KEVIN GROSS
Gross, Kevin Frank   b: 6/8/61, Downey, Cal.   BR/TR, 6'5", 203 lbs.   Deb: 6/25/83

YEAR	TM/L	W	L	PCT	G	GS	CG	SH	SV	IP	H	HR	BB	SO	RAT	ERA	ERA+	OAV	OOB	BH	AVG	PB	PR	/A	PD	TPI
1983	Phi-N	4	6	.400	17	17	1	1	0	96	100	13	35	66	12.9	3.56	100	.265	.333	3	.091	-1	1	0	1	0.0
1984	Phi-N	8	5	.615	44	14	1	0	1	129	140	8	44	84	13.2	4.12	88	.277	.341	2	.067	-2	-8	-7	1	-0.7

YEAR TM/L	W	L	PCT	G	GS	CG	SH	SV	IP	H	HR	BB	SO	RAT	ERA	ERA+	OAV	OOB	BH	AVG	PB	PR	/A	PD	TPI
1985 Phi-N	15	13	.536	38	31	6	2	0	205²	194	11	81	151	12.3	3.41	108	.251	.328	9	.138	0	4	6	1	0.8
1986 Phi-N	12	12	.500	37	36	7	2	0	241²	240	28	94	154	12.7	4.02	96	.259	.333	15	.188	3	-8	-5	-1	-0.1
1987 Phi-N	9	16	.360	34	33	3	1	0	200²	205	26	87	110	13.5	4.35	97	.267	.350	12	.190	2	-6	-2	-2	-0.1
1988 Phi-N	12	14	.462	33	33	5	1	0	231²	209	18	89	162	12.0	3.69	96	.239	.317	13	.173	1	-6	-3	-0	-0.2
1989 Mon-N	11	12	.478	31	31	4	3	0	201¹	188	20	88	158	12.6	4.38	81	.247	.330	9	.141	1	-20	-19	-0	-1.8
1990 Mon-N	9	12	.429	31	26	2	1	0	163¹	171	9	65	111	13.2	4.57	82	.272	.344	10	.200	3	-14	-15	-2	-1.3
Total 8	80	90	.471	265	221	29	11	1	1469¹	1447	133	583	996	12.8	4.02	93	.258	.334	73	.159	7	-57	-45	-3	-3.4

■ KIP GROSS
Gross, Kip Lee b: 8/24/64, Scottsbluff, Neb. BR/TR, 6'2", 195 lbs. Deb: 4/21/90

YEAR TM/L	W	L	PCT	G	GS	CG	SH	SV	IP	H	HR	BB	SO	RAT	ERA	ERA+	OAV	OOB	BH	AVG	PB	PR	/A	PD	TPI
1990 Cin-N	0	0	—	5	0	0	0	0	6¹	6	0	2	3	11.4	4.26	91	.273	.333	0	—	0	-0	-0	-0	0.0

■ WAYNE GROSS
Gross, Wayne Dale b: 1/14/52, Riverside, Cal. BL/TR, 6'2", 210 lbs. Deb: 8/21/76 ♦

YEAR TM/L	W	L	PCT	G	GS	CG	SH	SV	IP	H	HR	BB	SO	RAT	ERA	ERA+	OAV	OOB	BH	AVG	PB	PR	/A	PD	TPI
1983 Oak-A	0	0	—	1	0	0	0	0	2¹	2	0	1	0	15.4	0.00	—	.222	.364	79	.233	1	1	1	0	0.1

■ HARLEY GROSSMAN
Grossman, Harley Joseph b: 5/5/30, Evansville, Ind. BR/TR, 6', 170 lbs. Deb: 4/22/52

YEAR TM/L	W	L	PCT	G	GS	CG	SH	SV	IP	H	HR	BB	SO	RAT	ERA	ERA+	OAV	OOB	BH	AVG	PB	PR	/A	PD	TPI
1952 Was-A	0	0	—	1	0	0	0	0	0¹	2	1	0	0	54.0	54.00	7	.667	.667	0	—	0	-2	-2	0	-0.1

■ ERNIE GROTH
Groth, Ernest John "Dango" b: 12/24/1884, Cedarsburg, Wis. d: 5/23/50, Milwaukee, Wis. BR/TR, 5'11", 175 lbs. Deb: 9/06/04

YEAR TM/L	W	L	PCT	G	GS	CG	SH	SV	IP	H	HR	BB	SO	RAT	ERA	ERA+	OAV	OOB	BH	AVG	PB	PR	/A	PD	TPI
1904 Chi-N	0	2	.000	3	2	2	0	1	16	22	1	6	9	16.3	5.63	47	.310	.372	0	.000	-1	-5	-5	-0	-0.5

■ ERNEST GROTH
Groth, Ernest William b: 5/3/22, Beaver Falls, Pa. BR/TR, 5'9", 185 lbs. Deb: 9/11/47

YEAR TM/L	W	L	PCT	G	GS	CG	SH	SV	IP	H	HR	BB	SO	RAT	ERA	ERA+	OAV	OOB	BH	AVG	PB	PR	/A	PD	TPI
1947 Cle-A	0	0	—	2	0	0	0	0	1¹	1	0	1	1	6.8	0.00	—	.000	.250	0	—	0	1	1	0	0.0
1948 Cle-A	0	0	—	1	0	0	0	0	1	1	0	2	1	27.0	9.00	45	.250	.500	0	—	0	-1	-1	0	0.0
1949 Chi-A	0	1	.000	3	0	0	0	0	5	2	2	3	1	10.8	5.40	77	.125	.300	0	—	0	-1	-1	-0	0.0
Total 3	0	1	.000	6	0	0	0	0	7¹	3	2	6	2	12.3	4.91	82	.130	.333	0	—	0	-1	-1	-0	0.1

■ ORVAL GROVE
Grove, Orval Leroy b: 8/29/19, Mineral, Kan. BR/TR, 6'3", 196 lbs. Deb: 5/28/40

YEAR TM/L	W	L	PCT	G	GS	CG	SH	SV	IP	H	HR	BB	SO	RAT	ERA	ERA+	OAV	OOB	BH	AVG	PB	PR	/A	PD	TPI
1940 Chi-A	0	0	—	3	0	0	0	0	6	4	0	4	1	12.0	3.00	147	.182	.308	0	.000	-0	1	1	-0	0.1
1941 Chi-A	0	0	—	2	0	0	0	0	7	9	2	5	5	18.0	10.29	40	.321	.424	0	.000	-0	-5	-5	0	-0.3
1942 Chi-A	4	6	.400	12	8	4	0	0	66¹	77	1	33	21	15.1	5.16	70	.283	.363	5	.227	1	-11	-11	1	-0.8
1943 Chi-A	15	9	.625	32	25	18	3	2	216¹	192	9	72	76	11.1	2.75	122	.239	.304	12	.182	2	13	14	0	1.9
1944 Chi-A	14	15	.483	34	33	11	2	0	234²	237	11	71	105	12.1	3.72	92	.263	.322	8	.104	-3	-8	-8	3	-0.7
1945 Chi-A	14	12	.538	33	30	16	4	1	217	233	12	68	54	12.7	3.44	96	.273	.330	7	.099	-4	-2	-3	2	-0.4
1946 Chi-A	8	13	.381	33	26	10	1	0	205¹	213	10	78	60	12.9	3.02	113	.272	.340	7	.108	-2	11	9	2	0.9
1947 Chi-A	6	8	.429	25	19	6	1	0	135²	158	10	70	33	15.4	4.44	82	.296	.382	7	.146	-0	-11	-12	-0	-1.2
1948 Chi-A	2	10	.167	32	11	1	0	1	87²	110	6	42	18	15.9	6.16	69	.315	.393	2	.095	-2	-18	-19	2	-1.6
1949 Chi-A	0	0	—	1	0	0	0	0	0²	4	1	1	1	81.0	54.00	8	.667	.750	0	—	0	-4	-4	0	-0.2
Total 10	63	73	.463	207	152	66	11	4	1176²	1237	62	444	374	13.1	3.78	93	.272	.340	48	.129	-9	-33	-37	11	-2.3

■ LEFTY GROVE
Grove, Robert Moses b: 3/6/1900, Lonaconing, Md. d: 5/22/75, Norwalk, Ohio BL/TL, 6'3", 190 lbs. Deb: 4/14/25 H

YEAR TM/L	W	L	PCT	G	GS	CG	SH	SV	IP	H	HR	BB	SO	RAT	ERA	ERA+	OAV	OOB	BH	AVG	PB	PR	/A	PD	TPI
1925 Phi-A	10	12	.455	45	18	5	0	1	197	207	11	131	116	15.7	4.75	98	.278	.390	8	.133	-6	-8	-2	1	-0.5
1926 Phi-A	13	13	.500	45	33	20	1	6	258	227	6	101	194	11.7	2.51	166	.244	.322	6	.099	-5	43	48	-2	4.1
1927 Phi-A	20	13	.606	51	28	14	1	9	262¹	251	6	79	174	11.4	3.19	134	.252	.309	10	.125	-3	28	31	-2	2.6
1928 Phi-A	24	8	.750	39	31	24	4	4	261²	228	10	64	183	10.1	2.58	156	.229	.277	15	.170	1	43	42	-4	3.9
1929 *Phi-A	20	6	.769	42	37	19	2	4	275¹	278	8	81	170	11.8	2.81	151	.262	.316	22	.216	1	44	43	-4	3.9
1930 *Phi-A	28	5	.848	50	32	22	2	9	291	273	8	60	209	10.5	2.54	184	.247	.288	22	.200	0	68	69	-1	6.6
1931 *Phi-A	31	4	.886	41	30	27	4	5	288²	249	10	62	175	9.7	2.06	218	.229	.271	23	.200	-2	74	78	-3	7.5
1932 Phi-A	25	10	.714	44	30	27	4	7	291²	269	13	79	188	10.8	2.84	159	.241	.292	18	.168	0	53	55	-3	5.0
1933 Phi-A	24	8	.750	45	28	21	2	6	275¹	280	12	83	114	12.0	3.20	134	.261	.316	9	.086	-7	33	33	0	2.6
1934 Bos-A	8	8	.500	22	12	5	0	0	109¹	149	5	32	43	15.0	6.50	74	.320	.365	6	.162	-0	-24	-21	-1	-1.8
1935 Bos-A	20	12	.625	35	30	23	2	1	273	269	6	65	121	11.1	2.70	176	.257	.302	7	.079	-6	53	62	1	6.0
1936 Bos-A	17	12	.586	35	30	22	6	2	253¹	237	14	65	130	10.9	2.81	189	.246	.297	11	.138	-3	63	71	0	6.6
1937 Bos-A	17	9	.654	32	32	21	3	0	262	269	9	83	153	12.1	3.02	157	.261	.317	13	.143	-3	46	50	-1	4.6
1938 Bos-A	14	4	.778	24	21	12	1	1	163²	169	8	52	99	12.2	3.08	160	.263	.319	8	.148	-1	31	34	-1	3.1
1939 Bos-A	15	4	.789	23	23	17	2	0	191	180	8	58	81	11.3	2.54	186	.249	.305	9	.134	-1	44	46	-3	4.3
1940 Bos-A	7	6	.538	22	21	9	1	0	153¹	159	20	50	62	12.3	3.99	113	.269	.328	8	.151	-1	7	9	-0	0.7
1941 Bos-A	7	7	.500	21	21	10	0	0	134	155	8	42	54	13.4	4.37	95	.287	.340	5	.111	-1	-3	-3	-2	-0.5
Total 17	300	141	.680	616	457	298	35	55	3940²	3849	162	1187	2266	11.6	3.06	148	.255	.311	202	.148	-38	595	643	-25	58.7

■ CHARLIE GROVER
Grover, Charles Burt "Bugs" (Born Charles Byrd Grover) b: 6/20/1890, Huntington Township, Ohio d: 5/24/71, Emmett, Mich. BL/TR, 6'1.5", 185 lbs. Deb: 9/09/13

YEAR TM/L	W	L	PCT	G	GS	CG	SH	SV	IP	H	HR	BB	SO	RAT	ERA	ERA+	OAV	OOB	BH	AVG	PB	PR	/A	PD	TPI
1913 Det-A	0	0	—	2	1	0	0	0	10²	9	0	7	2	13.5	3.38	86	.265	.390	0	.000	-0	-1	-1	0	0.0

■ TOM GRUBBS
Grubbs, Thomas Dillard "Judge" b: 2/22/1894, Mt.Sterling, Ky. d: 1/28/86, Mt.Sterling, Ky. BR/TR, 6'2", 165 lbs. Deb: 10/03/20

YEAR TM/L	W	L	PCT	G	GS	CG	SH	SV	IP	H	HR	BB	SO	RAT	ERA	ERA+	OAV	OOB	BH	AVG	PB	PR	/A	PD	TPI
1920 NY-N	0	1	.000	1	1	0	0	0	5	9	0	0	0	16.2	7.20	42	.409	.409	0	.000	-0	-2	-2	-0	-0.2

■ HENRY GRUBER
Gruber, Henry John b: 12/14/1863, Hamden, Conn. d: 9/26/32, New Haven, Conn. BR/TL, Deb: 7/28/1887

YEAR TM/L	W	L	PCT	G	GS	CG	SH	SV	IP	H	HR	BB	SO	RAT	ERA	ERA+	OAV	OOB	BH	AVG	PB	PR	/A	PD	TPI
1887 Det-N	4	3	.571	7	7	7	0	0	62¹	63	3	21	12	12.1	2.74	147	.255	.314	4	.167	1	9	9	-1	0.7
1888 Det-N	11	14	.440	27	25	25	3	0	240	196	8	41	71	8.9	2.29	120	.215	.249	13	.141	-1	15	12	1	1.3
1889 Cle-N	7	16	.304	25	23	23	0	1	205	198	6	94	74	12.8	3.64	111	.246	.324	7	.101	-2	9	9	-0	0.2
1890 Cle-P	22	23	.489	48	44	39	1	1	383¹	464	15	204	110	15.7	4.27	93	.287	.366	36	.221	6	-2	-13	1	-0.5
1891 Cle-N	17	22	.436	44	40	35	1	0	348²	407	10	119	79	13.6	4.13	84	.281	.335	23	.163	1	-30	-26	3	-1.8
Total 5	61	78	.439	151	139	129	5	2	1239¹	1328	42	479	346	13.1	3.67	99	.264	.328	83	.170	4	0	-7	4	0.3

■ AL GRUNWALD
Grunwald, Alfred Henry "Stretch" b: 2/13/30, Los Angeles, Cal. BL/TL, 6'4", 210 lbs. Deb: 4/18/55

YEAR TM/L	W	L	PCT	G	GS	CG	SH	SV	IP	H	HR	BB	SO	RAT	ERA	ERA+	OAV	OOB	BH	AVG	PB	PR	/A	PD	TPI
1955 Pit-N	0	0	—	3	0	0	0	0	7²	7	1	7	2	16.4	4.70	88	.241	.389	2	.500	1	-1	-0	0	0.0
1959 KC-A	0	1	.000	6	1	0	0	1	11¹	18	1	11	9	23.0	7.94	50	.360	.475	0	.000	-1	-5	-5	0	-0.4
Total 2	0	1	.000	9	1	0	0	1	19	25	2	18	11	20.4	6.63	61	.316	.443	2	.250	0	-6	-5	0	-0.4

■ JOE GRZENDA
Grzenda, Joseph Charles b: 6/8/37, Scranton, Pa. BR/TL, 6'2", 180 lbs. Deb: 4/26/61

YEAR TM/L	W	L	PCT	G	GS	CG	SH	SV	IP	H	HR	BB	SO	RAT	ERA	ERA+	OAV	OOB	BH	AVG	PB	PR	/A	PD	TPI
1961 Det-A	1	0	1.000	4	0	0	0	0	5²	9	2	2	0	17.5	7.94	52	.375	.423	1	1.000	0	-2	-2	0	-0.1
1964 KC-A	0	2	.000	20	0	0	0	0	25	34	2	13	17	17.3	5.40	71	.324	.403	0	.000	0	-5	-4	1	-0.3
1966 KC-A	0	2	.000	21	0	0	0	0	22	28	1	12	14	16.4	3.27	104	.337	.421	0	.000	-0	0	0	0	0.1
1967 NY-N	0	0	—	11	0	0	0	0	16²	14	0	8	9	12.4	2.16	157	.233	.338	0	.000	-0	2	2	-0	0.2
1969 *Min-A	4	1	.800	38	0	0	0	3	48²	52	4	17	24	12.9	3.88	94	.281	.345	0	.000	-1	-1	-1	0	0.0
1970 Was-A	3	6	.333	49	3	0	0	6	84²	86	8	34	38	13.1	5.00	71	.267	.343	0	.000	-1	-12	-14	1	-1.4
1971 Was-A	5	2	.714	46	0	0	0	5	70¹	54	2	17	56	9.2	1.92	172	.217	.270	1	.143	0	12	11	-0	1.1
1972 StL-N	1	0	1.000	30	0	0	0	0	35	46	1	17	15	17.0	5.66	60	.326	.410	0	.000	0	-9	-9	0	-0.8
Total 8	14	13	.519	219	3	0	0	14	308	323	20	120	173	13.2	4.00	88	.277	.349	2	.067	-2	-15	-17	3	-1.2

■ CECILIO GUANTE
Guante, Cecilio (Magallane) b: 2/1/60, Villa Mella, D.R. BR/TR, 6'3", 200 lbs. Deb: 5/01/82

YEAR TM/L	W	L	PCT	G	GS	CG	SH	SV	IP	H	HR	BB	SO	RAT	ERA	ERA+	OAV	OOB	BH	AVG	PB	PR	/A	PD	TPI
1982 Pit-N	0	0	—	10	0	0	0	0	27	28	1	5	26	11.7	3.33	111	.264	.310	0	.000	-1	1	1	-0	0.0
1983 Pit-N	2	6	.250	49	0	0	0	9	100¹	90	5	46	82	12.4	3.32	112	.241	.327	2	.091	-1	4	4	-1	0.3
1984 Pit-N	2	3	.400	27	0	0	0	2	41¹	32	3	16	30	10.9	2.61	138	.224	.311	0	.000	0	4	5	-1	0.4
1985 Pit-N	4	6	.400	63	0	0	0	5	109	84	5	40	92	10.7	2.72	131	.214	.295	1	.059	-1	10	10	-1	0.9
1986 Pit-N	5	2	.714	52	0	0	0	4	78	65	11	29	63	11.2	3.35	115	.225	.302	0	.000	-0	3	4	-2	0.2

YEAR TM/L	W	L	PCT	G	GS	CG	SH	SV	IP	H	HR	BB	SO	RAT	ERA	ERA+	OAV	OOB	BH	AVG	PB	PR	/A	PD	TPI
1987 NY-A	3	2	.600	23	0	0	0	1	44	42	8	20	46	12.9	5.73	77	.247	.330	0	—	0	-6	-7	-1	-0.6
1988 NY-A	5	6	.455	56	0	0	0	11	75	59	10	22	61	10.3	2.88	137	.213	.283	0	—	0	9	9	-2	0.7
Tex-A	0	0	—	7	0	0	0	1	4²	8	1	4	4	23.1	1.93	212	.400	.500	0	—	0	1	1	-0	0.1
Yr	5	6	.455	63	0	0	0	12	79²	67	11	26	65	10.5	2.82	140	.221	.283	0	—	0	10	10	-2	0.8
1989 Tex-A	6	6	.500	50	0	0	0	2	69	66	7	36	69	13.8	3.91	101	.249	.348	0	—	0	-0	0	-1	0.0
1990 Cle-A	2	3	.400	26	1	0	0	0	46²	38	10	18	30	11.4	5.01	79	.220	.304	0	—	0	-6	-5	0	-0.4
Total 9	29	34	.460	363	1	0	0	35	595	512	61	236	503	11.7	3.48	110	.232	.313	3	.061	-3	20	23	-8	1.5

■ MARK GUBICZA

Gubicza, Mark Steven b: 8/14/62, Philadelphia, Pa. BR/TR, 6'6", 215 lbs. Deb: 4/06/84

YEAR TM/L	W	L	PCT	G	GS	CG	SH	SV	IP	H	HR	BB	SO	RAT	ERA	ERA+	OAV	OOB	BH	AVG	PB	PR	/A	PD	TPI
1984 KC-A	10	14	.417	29	29	4	2	0	189	172	13	75	111	12.0	4.05	99	.243	.320	0	—	0	-1	-0	2	0.1
1985 *KC-A	14	10	.583	29	28	0	0	0	177¹	160	14	77	99	12.3	4.06	102	.238	.321	0	—	0	2	2	2	0.4
1986 KC-A	12	6	.667	35	24	3	2	0	180²	155	8	84	118	12.2	3.64	117	.233	.324	0	—	0	11	12	2	1.5
1987 KC-A	13	18	.419	35	35	10	2	0	241²	231	18	120	166	13.3	3.98	114	.259	.350	0	—	0	13	15	4	1.8
1988 KC-A	20	8	.714	35	35	8	4	0	269²	237	11	83	183	10.9	2.70	147	.234	.296	0	—	0	38	38	3	4.5
1989 KC-A	15	11	.577	36	36	8	2	0	255	252	10	63	173	11.3	3.04	127	.259	.307	0	—	0	24	23	2	2.7
1990 KC-A	4	7	.364	16	16	2	0	0	94	101	5	38	71	13.7	4.50	85	.283	.358	0	—	0	-6	-7	0	-0.6
Total 7	88	74	.543	215	203	35	12	0	1407¹	1308	79	540	921	12.0	3.57	115	.248	.322	0	—	0	80	83	15	10.4

■ MARV GUDAT

Gudat, Marvin John b: 8/27/05, Goliad, Tex. d: 3/1/54, Los Angeles, Cal. BL/TL, 5'11", 162 lbs. Deb: 5/21/29 ♦

YEAR TM/L	W	L	PCT	G	GS	CG	SH	SV	IP	H	HR	BB	SO	RAT	ERA	ERA+	OAV	OOB	BH	AVG	PB	PR	/A	PD	TPI
1929 Cin-N	1	1	.500	7	2	2	0	0	26²	29	0	4	0	11.1	3.38	135	.282	.308	2	.200	-0	4	4	-1	0.2
1932 *Chi-N	0	0	—	1	0	0	0	0	1	1	0	0	2	9.0	0.00	—	.250	.250	24	.255	-0	0	0	0	0.0
Total 2	1	1	.500	8	2	2	0	0	27²	30	0	4	2	11.1	3.25	139	.280	.306	26	.250	-0	4	4	-1	0.2

■ LEE GUETTERMAN

Guetterman, Arthur Lee b: 11/22/58, Chattanooga, Tenn. BL/TL, 6'8", 225 lbs. Deb: 9/12/84

YEAR TM/L	W	L	PCT	G	GS	CG	SH	SV	IP	H	HR	BB	SO	RAT	ERA	ERA+	OAV	OOB	BH	AVG	PB	PR	/A	PD	TPI
1984 Sea-A	0	0	—	3	0	0	0	0	4¹	9	0	2	2	22.8	4.15	96	.450	.500	0	—	0	-0	-0	0	0.0
1986 Sea-A	0	4	.000	41	4	1	0	0	76	108	7	30	38	16.8	7.34	58	.347	.412	0	—	0	-27	-26	0	-2.4
1987 Sea-A	11	4	.733	25	17	2	1	0	113¹	117	13	35	42	12.2	3.81	124	.267	.324	0	—	0	8	11	2	1.3
1988 NY-A	1	2	.333	20	2	0	0	0	40²	49	2	14	15	14.2	4.65	85	.306	.366	0	—	0	-3	-3	-0	-0.2
1989 NY-A	5	5	.500	70	0	0	0	13	103	98	6	26	51	10.8	2.45	158	.258	.305	0	—	0	16	16	2	1.9
1990 NY-A	11	7	.611	64	0	0	0	2	93	80	6	26	48	10.3	3.39	117	.236	.290	0	—	0	5	6	1	0.7
Total 6	28	22	.560	223	23	3	1	15	430¹	461	34	133	196	12.6	4.10	102	.280	.336	0	—	0	-0	4	5	1.3

■ WHITEY GUESE

Guese, Theodore b: 1/24/1872, New Bremen, Ohio d: 4/8/51, Wapakoneta, Ohio BR/TR, 6'0.5", 200 lbs. Deb: 7/13/01

YEAR TM/L	W	L	PCT	G	GS	CG	SH	SV	IP	H	HR	BB	SO	RAT	ERA	ERA+	OAV	OOB	BH	AVG	PB	PR	/A	PD	TPI
1901 Cin-N	1	4	.200	6	5	4	0	0	44¹	62	5	14	11	16.0	6.09	53	.328	.383	3	.200	1	-14	-14	-1	-1.2

■ RON GUIDRY

Guidry, Ronald Ames b: 8/28/50, Lafayette, La. BL/TL, 5'11", 161 lbs. Deb: 7/27/75

YEAR TM/L	W	L	PCT	G	GS	CG	SH	SV	IP	H	HR	BB	SO	RAT	ERA	ERA+	OAV	OOB	BH	AVG	PB	PR	/A	PD	TPI
1975 NY-A	0	1	.000	10	1	0	0	0	15²	15	0	9	15	14.4	3.45	106	.259	.368	0	—	0	1	0	-1	0.0
1976 *NY-A	0	0	—	7	0	0	0	0	16	20	1	4	12	13.5	5.63	61	.294	.333	0	—	0	-4	-4	0	-0.3
1977 *NY-A	16	7	.696	31	25	9	5	1	210²	174	12	65	176	10.2	2.82	140	.224	.284	0	—	0	29	26	-2	2.6
1978 *NY-A	25	3	.893	35	35	16	9	0	273²	187	13	72	248	8.6	1.74	208	.193	.250	0	—	0	61	57	1	6.6
1979 NY-A	18	8	.692	33	30	15	2	2	236¹	203	20	71	201	10.4	2.78	146	.236	.294	0	—	0	38	34	-2	3.3
1980 *NY-A	17	10	.630	37	29	5	3	1	219²	215	19	80	166	12.1	3.56	110	.260	.326	0	—	0	11	9	1	1.0
1981 *NY-A	11	5	.688	23	21	0	0	0	127	100	12	26	104	9.0	2.76	129	.214	.257	0	—	0	13	11	0	1.3
1982 NY-A	14	8	.636	34	33	6	1	0	222	216	22	69	162	11.6	3.81	105	.254	.311	0	—	0	6	4	-3	0.2
1983 NY-A	21	9	.700	31	31	21	3	0	250¹	232	26	60	156	10.6	3.42	114	.244	.291	0	—	0	18	13	-0	1.3
1984 NY-A	10	11	.476	29	28	5	1	0	195²	223	24	44	127	12.4	4.51	84	.287	.327	0	—	0	-11	-16	-1	-1.5
1985 NY-A	22	6	.786	34	33	11	2	0	259	243	28	42	143	9.9	3.27	122	.248	.279	0	—	0	25	21	-1	2.1
1986 NY-A	9	12	.429	30	30	5	0	0	192¹	202	28	38	140	11.3	3.98	103	.265	.301	0	—	0	4	2	-1	0.1
1987 NY-A	5	8	.385	22	17	2	0	0	117¹	111	14	38	96	11.5	3.67	119	.248	.308	0	—	0	10	9	-1	0.8
1988 NY-A	2	3	.400	12	10	0	0	0	56	57	7	15	32	11.9	4.18	94	.259	.312	0	—	0	-1	-1	-1	-0.1
Total 14	170	91	.651	368	323	95	26	4	2392	2198	226	633	1778	10.7	3.29	119	.244	.294	0	—	0	201	167	-8	17.4

■ SKIP GUINN

Guinn, Drannon Eugene b: 10/25/44, St.Charles, Mo. BR/TL, 5'10", 180 lbs. Deb: 5/07/68

YEAR TM/L	W	L	PCT	G	GS	CG	SH	SV	IP	H	HR	BB	SO	RAT	ERA	ERA+	OAV	OOB	BH	AVG	PB	PR	/A	PD	TPI
1968 Atl-N	0	0	—	3	0	0	0	0	5	3	0	3	4	10.8	3.60	83	.167	.286	0	—	0	-0	-0	-0	0.0
1969 Hou-N	1	2	.333	28	0	0	0	0	27	34	3	21	33	18.7	6.67	53	.304	.418	0	.000	-0	-9	-9	-0	-0.9
1971 Hou-N	0	0	—	4	0	0	0	1	4²	1	0	3	3	7.7	0.00	—	.067	.222	0	—	0	2	2	0	0.2
Total 3	1	2	.333	35	0	0	0	1	36²	38	3	27	40	16.2	5.40	64	.262	.382	0	.000	-0	-8	-8	-0	-0.7

■ LEFTY GUISE

Guise, Witt Orison b: 9/18/09, Driggs, Ark. d: 8/13/68, Little Rock, Ark. BL/TL, 6'2", 172 lbs. Deb: 9/13/40

YEAR TM/L	W	L	PCT	G	GS	CG	SH	SV	IP	H	HR	BB	SO	RAT	ERA	ERA+	OAV	OOB	BH	AVG	PB	PR	/A	PD	TPI
1940 Cin-N	0	0	—	2	0	0	0	0	7²	8	0	5	1	16.4	1.17	323	.296	.424	1	.333	0	2	2	0	0.3

■ DON GULLETT

Gullett, Donald Edward b: 1/6/51, Lynn, Ky. BR/TL, 6', 210 lbs. Deb: 4/10/70

YEAR TM/L	W	L	PCT	G	GS	CG	SH	SV	IP	H	HR	BB	SO	RAT	ERA	ERA+	OAV	OOB	BH	AVG	PB	PR	/A	PD	TPI
1970 *Cin-N	5	2	.714	44	2	0	0	6	77²	54	4	44	76	11.4	2.43	166	.196	.306	4	.211	1	14	14	-1	1.4
1971 Cin-N	16	6	.727	35	31	4	3	0	217²	196	14	64	107	10.8	2.65	127	.242	.299	9	.120	-2	20	17	-2	1.3
1972 *Cin-N	9	10	.474	31	16	2	0	2	134²	127	15	43	96	11.4	3.94	81	.250	.309	8	.211	2	-7	-11	-2	-1.1
1973 *Cin-N	18	8	.692	45	30	7	4	2	228¹	198	24	69	153	10.6	3.51	97	.232	.292	12	.188	3	4	-3	-1	0.0
1974 Cin-N	17	11	.607	36	35	10	3	0	243	201	22	88	183	10.8	3.04	115	.222	.292	19	.237	4	16	12	-1	1.5
1975 *Cin-N	15	4	.789	22	22	8	3	0	159²	127	11	56	98	10.4	2.42	148	.218	.289	14	.226	3	21	21	-1	2.4
1976 *Cin-N	11	3	.786	23	20	4	0	1	126	119	8	48	64	11.9	3.00	117	.253	.322	8	.182	-0	7	7	0	0.8
1977 *NY-A	14	4	.778	22	22	7	1	0	158¹	137	14	69	116	11.8	3.58	110	.232	.314	0	—	0	8	6	-2	0.4
1978 NY-A	4	2	.667	8	8	2	0	0	44²	46	3	20	28	13.5	3.63	100	.269	.349	0	—	0	1	-0	0	0.0
Total 9	109	50	.686	266	186	44	14	11	1390	1205	115	501	921	11.1	3.11	113	.233	.302	74	.194	10	83	63	-10	6.7

■ BILL GULLICKSON

Gullickson, William Lee b: 2/20/59, Marshall, Minn. BR/TR, 6'3", 200 lbs. Deb: 9/26/79

YEAR TM/L	W	L	PCT	G	GS	CG	SH	SV	IP	H	HR	BB	SO	RAT	ERA	ERA+	OAV	OOB	BH	AVG	PB	PR	/A	PD	TPI
1979 Mon-N	0	0	—	1	0	0	0	0	1	2	0	0	0	18.0	0.00	—	.500	.500	0	—	0	0	0	0	0.0
1980 Mon-N	10	5	.667	24	19	5	2	0	141	127	6	50	120	11.4	3.00	119	.238	.305	7	.175	0	9	9	-0	0.9
1981 *Mon-N	7	9	.438	22	22	3	2	0	157¹	142	3	34	115	10.3	2.80	125	.239	.284	7	.152	0	12	12	-1	1.2
1982 Mon-N	12	14	.462	34	34	6	0	0	236²	231	25	61	155	11.3	3.57	102	.254	.304	10	.122	-2	1	2	-4	-0.3
1983 Mon-N	17	12	.586	34	34	10	1	0	242¹	230	19	59	120	10.9	3.75	96	.251	.299	11	.134	1	-3	-4	-3	-1.0
1984 Mon-N	12	9	.571	32	32	3	0	0	226²	230	27	37	100	10.6	3.61	95	.265	.295	8	.110	-2	-1	-5	-3	-1.0
1985 Mon-N	14	12	.538	29	29	4	1	0	181¹	187	8	47	68	11.7	3.52	96	.271	.318	12	.188	2	1	-3	-1	-0.1
1986 Cin-N	15	12	.556	37	37	6	2	0	244²	245	24	60	121	11.3	3.38	114	.264	.310	6	.076	-4	9	13	-1	0.8
1987 Cin-N	10	11	.476	27	27	3	1	0	165	172	33	39	89	11.6	4.85	87	.267	.310	11	.208	2	-14	-11	-1	-0.9
NY-A	4	2	.667	8	8	1	0	0	48	46	7	14	28	10.9	4.88	90	.253	.299	0	—	0	-2	-3	-0	-0.2
1990 Hou-N	10	14	.417	32	32	2	1	0	193¹	221	21	61	73	13.2	3.82	98	.287	.341	0	—	0	-1	-2	-3	-0.2
Total 10	111	100	.526	280	274	43	10	0	1837¹	1833	173	459	989	11.3	3.63	101	.260	.308	81	.141	-2	12	8	-15	-0.1

■ AD GUMBERT

Gumbert, Addison Courtney b: 10/10/1868, Pittsburgh, Pa. d: 4/23/25, Pittsburgh, Pa. BR/TR, 5'10", 200 lbs. Deb: 9/15/1888

YEAR TM/L	W	L	PCT	G	GS	CG	SH	SV	IP	H	HR	BB	SO	RAT	ERA	ERA+	OAV	OOB	BH	AVG	PB	PR	/A	PD	TPI
1888 Chi-N	3	3	.500	6	6	5	0	0	48²	44	0	10	16	10.0	3.14	96	.233	.271	8	.333	2	-2	-1	-0	0.1
1889 Chi-N	16	13	.552	31	28	25	2	0	246¹	258	16	76	91	12.2	3.62	115	.261	.314	44	.288	11	11	15	-1	2.7
1890 Bos-P	23	12	.657	39	33	27	1	0	277¹	338	18	86	81	13.8	3.96	111	.288	.337	35	.241	5	8	14	2	1.9
1891 Chi-N	17	11	.607	32	31	24	1	0	256¹	282	5	90	73	13.1	3.58	93	.269	.327	32	.305	12	-7	-8	0	0.6
1892 Chi-N	22	19	.537	46	45	39	0	0	382²	399	11	107	118	11.9	3.41	97	.258	.306	42	.236	4	-5	-4	2	0.2
1893 Pit-N	11	7	.611	22	20	16	2	0	162²	207	5	78	40	15.8	5.15	89	.301	.372	21	.221	1	-9	-11	-2	-0.8
1894 Pit-N	15	14	.517	37	31	26	0	0	269	372	13	84	65	15.3	6.02	87	.324	.371	33	.292	5	-21	-23	1	-1.3

YEAR	TM/L	W	L	PCT	G	GS	CG	SH	SV	IP	H	HR	BB	SO	RAT	ERA	ERA+	OAV	OOB	BH	AVG	PB	PR	/A	PD	TPI
1895	Bro-N	11	16	.407	33	26	20	0	1	234	288	11	69	45	13.7	5.08	87	.298	.345	35	.361	10	-8	-18	-1	-0.7
1896	Bro-N	0	4	.000	5	4	2	0	0	31	34	2	11	3	13.1	3.77	109	.276	.336	2	.182	-0	2	1	1	0.2
	Phi-N	5	3	.625	11	10	7	1	0	77¹	99	0	23	14	14.2	4.54	95	.308	.355	9	.265	1	-2	-2	-1	0.0
	Yr	5	7	.417	16	14	9	1	0	108¹	133	2	34	17	13.9	4.32	99	.300	.349	1	.022	1	-1	-1	1	0.2
Total 9		123	102	.547	262	234	191	7	1	1985¹	2321	81	634	546	13.4	4.27	96	.283	.335	261	.273	51	-31	-34	3	2.9

■ HARRY GUMBERT
Gumbert, Harry Edward "Gunboat" b: 11/5/09, Elizabeth, Pa. BR/TR, 6'2", 185 lbs. Deb: 9/12/35

YEAR	TM/L	W	L	PCT	G	GS	CG	SH	SV	IP	H	HR	BB	SO	RAT	ERA	ERA+	OAV	OOB	BH	AVG	PB	PR	/A	PD	TPI
1935	NY-N	1	2	.333	6	3	1	0	0	23²	35	1	10	11	17.1	6.08	63	.330	.388	0	.000	-1	-5	-6	-0	-0.6
1936	*NY-N	11	3	.786	39	15	3	0	0	140²	157	7	54	52	13.6	3.90	100	.281	.346	11	.250	2	2	-0	3	0.5
1937	*NY-N	10	11	.476	34	24	10	1	0	200¹	194	11	62	65	11.7	3.68	106	.257	.317	13	.181	-1	5	5	8	1.2
1938	NY-N	15	13	.536	38	33	14	1	0	235²	238	13	84	84	12.6	4.01	94	.261	.328	13	.155	-3	-6	-6	8	0.0
1939	NY-N	18	11	.621	36	34	14	2	0	243²	257	21	81	81	12.5	4.32	91	.271	.329	18	.200	-0	-11	-11	6	-0.3
1940	NY-N	12	14	.462	35	30	14	2	2	237	230	17	81	77	11.9	3.76	103	.252	.316	17	.195	2	2	3	4	0.9
1941	NY-N	1	1	.500	5	5	1	0	0	32¹	34	3	18	9	14.5	4.45	83	.266	.356	2	.167	-0	-3	-3	1	-0.1
	StL-N	11	5	.688	33	17	8	3	1	144¹	139	7	30	53	10.6	2.74	137	.251	.291	17	.321	6	14	16	4	2.8
	Yr	12	6	.667	38	22	9	3	1	176²	173	10	48	62	11.3	3.06	123	.254	.304	2	.031	5	11	14	5	2.7
1942	*StL-N	9	5	.643	38	19	5	0	5	163	156	3	59	52	11.9	3.26	105	.250	.315	6	.111	-3	1	3	5	0.6
1943	StL-N	10	5	.667	21	19	7	3	0	133	115	4	32	40	9.9	2.84	118	.237	.284	7	.156	-2	2	8	2	0.9
1944	StL-N	4	2	.667	10	7	3	0	1	61¹	60	1	19	16	11.6	2.49	141	.258	.313	4	.190	-0	8	7	1	0.9
	Cin-N	10	8	.556	24	19	11	2	2	155¹	157	7	40	40	11.5	3.30	106	.262	.310	5	.096	-2	5	3	2	0.3
	Yr	14	10	.583	34	26	14	2	3	216²	217	8	59	56	11.5	3.07	114	.261	.311	4	.055	-2	13	10	4	1.2
1946	Cin-N	6	8	.429	36	10	5	0	4	119	112	8	42	44	11.7	3.25	106	.248	.314	8	.250	1	2	1	1	0.3
1947	Cin-N	10	10	.500	46	0	0	0	10	90¹	88	3	47	43	13.5	3.89	106	.260	.351	6	.273	1	2	2	0	0.3
1948	Cin-N	10	8	.556	61	0	0	0	17	106¹	123	5	34	25	13.3	3.47	113	.291	.344	1	.040	-1	6	5	4	0.8
1949	Cin-N	4	3	.571	29	0	0	0	2	40²	58	5	8	12	14.8	5.53	76	.341	.374	0	.000	-0	-7	-6	1	-0.4
	Pit-N	1	4	.200	16	0	0	0	3	27²	30	5	18	5	15.6	5.86	72	.270	.372	1	.250	0	-6	-5	1	-0.3
	Yr	5	7	.417	45	0	0	0	5	68¹	88	10	26	17	15.0	5.66	74	.312	.370	0	.000	-0	-12	-11	2	-0.7
1950	Pit-N	0	0	—	1	0	0	0	0	1²	3	0	2	0	27.0	5.40	81	.333	.455	1	1.000	-0	-0	-0	0	0.1
Total 15		143	113	.559	508	235	96	14	48	2156	2186	121	721	709	12.2	3.68	102	.263	.323	130	.184	-1	18	17	53	7.9

■ BILLY GUMBERT
Gumbert, William Skeen b: 8/8/1865, Pittsburgh, Pa. d: 4/13/46, Pittsburgh, Pa. BR/TR, 6'1.5", 200 lbs. Deb: 6/19/1890

YEAR	TM/L	W	L	PCT	G	GS	CG	SH	SV	IP	H	HR	BB	SO	RAT	ERA	ERA+	OAV	OOB	BH	AVG	PB	PR	/A	PD	TPI
1890	Pit-N	4	6	.400	10	10	8	0	0	79¹	96	0	31	18	14.4	5.22	63	.291	.351	9	.243	2	-15	-17	1	-1.1
1892	Pit-N	3	2	.600	6	3	2	0	0	39²	30	0	23	3	12.0	1.36	242	.201	.308	2	.111	-1	8	9	-1	0.7
1893	Lou-N	0	0	—	1	1	0	0	0	0²	2	0	5	0	94.5	27.00	16	.503	.780	1	1.000	1	-2	-2	0	0.0
Total 3		7	8	.467	17	14	10	0	0	119²	128	0	59	21	14.1	4.06	81	.265	.345	12	.214	2	-8	-10	0	-0.4

■ DAVE GUMPERT
Gumpert, David Lawrence b: 5/5/58, South Haven, Mich. BR/TR, 6'1", 190 lbs. Deb: 7/25/82

YEAR	TM/L	W	L	PCT	G	GS	CG	SH	SV	IP	H	HR	BB	SO	RAT	ERA	ERA+	OAV	OOB	BH	AVG	PB	PR	/A	PD	TPI
1982	Det-A	0	0	—	5	1	0	0	1	2	7	1	2	0	40.5	27.00	15	.700	.750	0	—	0	-5	-5	0	-0.4
1983	Det-A	0	2	.000	26	0	0	0	2	44¹	43	1	7	14	10.2	2.64	148	.257	.287	0	—	0	7	6	-1	0.6
1985	Chi-N	1	0	1.000	9	0	0	0	0	10¹	12	0	7	4	16.5	3.48	115	.279	.380	0	.000	-0	0	1	-0	0.0
1986	Chi-N	2	0	1.000	38	0	0	0	2	59²	60	4	28	45	13.4	4.37	92	.267	.350	0	.000	-1	-4	-2	-1	-0.3
1987	KC-A	0	0	—	8	0	0	0	0	19¹	27	3	6	13	15.4	6.05	75	.333	.379	0	—	0	-3	-3	0	-0.2
Total 5		3	2	.600	86	1	0	0	5	135²	149	9	50	76	13.3	4.31	95	.283	.347	0	.000	-1	-6	-4	-1	-0.3

■ RANDY GUMPERT
Gumpert, Randall Pennington b: 1/23/18, Monocacy, Pa. BR/TR, 6'3", 185 lbs. Deb: 6/13/36

YEAR	TM/L	W	L	PCT	G	GS	CG	SH	SV	IP	H	HR	BB	SO	RAT	ERA	ERA+	OAV	OOB	BH	AVG	PB	PR	/A	PD	TPI
1936	Phi-A	1	2	.333	22	3	2	0	2	62¹	74	2	32	9	15.3	4.76	107	.295	.375	6	.273	0	2	2	-1	0.2
1937	Phi-A	0	0	—	10	1	0	0	0	12	16	1	15	5	24.0	12.00	39	.333	.500	1	.333	0	-10	-10	0	-0.7
1938	Phi-A	0	2	.000	4	2	0	0	0	12¹	24	1	10	1	24.8	10.95	44	.393	.479	1	.250	0	-8	-8	1	-0.5
1946	NY-A	11	3	.786	33	12	4	0	1	132²	113	8	32	63	9.8	2.31	150	.229	.276	6	.128	-2	18	17	-0	1.5
1947	NY-A	4	1	.800	24	6	2	0	0	56¹	71	4	28	25	15.8	5.43	65	.311	.387	1	.071	-1	-11	-12	0	-1.2
1948	NY-A	1	0	1.000	15	0	0	0	0	25	27	0	6	12	12.2	2.88	142	.267	.315	0	—	0	4	3	0	0.3
	Chi-A	2	6	.250	16	11	6	1	0	97¹	103	6	13	31	10.9	3.79	112	.275	.303	4	.138	-2	5	5	-1	0.2
	Yr	3	6	.333	31	11	6	1	0	122¹	130	6	19	43	11.1	3.60	117	.273	.303	4	—	-2	9	8	-1	0.5
1949	Chi-A	13	16	.448	34	32	18	3	1	234	223	22	83	78	11.8	3.81	110	.253	.318	16	.190	-1	10	9	1	0.9
1950	Chi-A	5	12	.294	40	17	6	1	0	155¹	165	15	58	48	13.2	4.75	94	.275	.343	3	.071	-4	-3	-5	0	-0.7
1951	Chi-A	9	8	.529	33	16	7	1	2	141²	156	20	34	45	12.1	4.32	93	.272	.314	15	.333	-3	-3	-4	-3	-0.3
1952	Bos-A	1	0	1.000	10	1	0	0	1	19²	15	1	5	6	9.6	4.12	96	.205	.266	0	—	-1	-0	-0	0	0.0
	Was-A	4	9	.308	20	12	2	0	0	104	112	12	30	29	12.7	4.24	84	.273	.330	7	.206	0	-7	-8	-0	-0.7
	Yr	5	9	.357	30	13	2	0	1	123²	127	13	35	35	12.2	4.22	86	.262	.318	2	.051	-0	-8	-8	-0	-0.7
Total 10		51	59	.464	261	113	47	6	7	1052²	1099	92	346	352	12.5	4.17	98	.268	.328	60	.182	-8	-4	-10	-3	-1.0

■ ERIC GUNDERSON
Gunderson, Eric Andrew b: 3/29/66, Portland, Ore. BR/TL, 6', 175 lbs. Deb: 4/11/90

YEAR	TM/L	W	L	PCT	G	GS	CG	SH	SV	IP	H	HR	BB	SO	RAT	ERA	ERA+	OAV	OOB	BH	AVG	PB	PR	/A	PD	TPI
1990	SF-N	1	2	.333	7	4	0	0	0	19²	24	2	11	14	16.0	5.49	68	.293	.376	0	.000	-1	-4	-4	0	-0.3

■ RED GUNKEL
Gunkel, Woodward William b: 4/15/1894, Sheffield, Ill. d: 4/19/54, Chicago, Ill. BB/TL, 5'8", 158 lbs. Deb: 6/18/16

YEAR	TM/L	W	L	PCT	G	GS	CG	SH	SV	IP	H	HR	BB	SO	RAT	ERA	ERA+	OAV	OOB	BH	AVG	PB	PR	/A	PD	TPI
1916	Cle-A	0	0	—	1	0	0	0	0	1	0	0	1	1	18.0	0.00	—	.000	.500	0	—	0	0	0	0	0.0

■ LARRY GURA
Gura, Lawrence Cyril b: 11/26/47, Joliet, Ill. BB/TL, 6', 170 lbs. Deb: 4/30/70

YEAR	TM/L	W	L	PCT	G	GS	CG	SH	SV	IP	H	HR	BB	SO	RAT	ERA	ERA+	OAV	OOB	BH	AVG	PB	PR	/A	PD	TPI
1970	Chi-N	1	3	.250	20	3	1	0	1	38	35	6	23	21	14.0	3.79	119	.254	.364	0	.000	-1	1	3	0	0.2
1971	Chi-N	0	0	—	6	0	0	0	1	3	6	0	1	2	21.0	6.00	66	.400	.438	0	.000	-0	-1	-1	0	0.0
1972	Chi-N	0	0	—	7	0	0	0	0	12¹	11	3	6	13	10.2	3.65	104	.250	.298	0	.000	0	-0	0	0	0.0
1973	Chi-N	2	4	.333	21	7	0	0	0	64²	79	10	11	43	12.7	4.87	81	.296	.326	3	.200	-0	-9	-7	1	-0.4
1974	NY-A	5	1	.833	8	8	4	2	0	56	54	2	12	17	10.6	2.41	145	.248	.287	0	—	0	8	7	0	0.7
1975	NY-A	7	8	.467	26	20	5	0	0	151¹	173	13	41	65	12.9	3.51	104	.295	.344	0	—	0	5	2	0	0.2
1976	*KC-A	4	0	1.000	20	2	1	1	1	62²	47	4	20	22	9.8	2.30	152	.213	.281	0	—	0	9	8	1	1.0
1977	*KC-A	8	5	.615	52	6	1	1	0	106¹	108	8	28	46	11.6	3.13	129	.265	.314	0	—	0	11	11	0	1.1
1978	*KC-A	16	4	.800	35	26	8	2	0	221²	183	13	60	81	10.0	2.72	141	.229	.286	0	—	0	26	27	2	3.2
1979	KC-A	13	12	.520	39	33	7	1	0	233²	226	29	73	85	11.8	4.47	95	.253	.315	0	—	0	-7	-5	1	-0.3
1980	*KC-A	18	10	.643	36	36	16	4	0	283¹	272	20	76	113	11.2	2.95	137	.255	.307	0	—	0	34	35	1	3.7
1981	*KC-A	11	8	.579	23	23	12	2	0	172¹	139	11	35	61	9.3	2.72	133	.223	.269	0	—	0	18	17	1	1.9
1982	KC-A	18	12	.600	37	37	8	2	0	248	251	31	64	98	11.6	4.03	101	.261	.311	0	—	0	1	1	3	0.4
1983	KC-A	11	18	.379	34	31	5	0	0	200¹	220	23	76	57	13.7	4.90	83	.284	.354	0	—	0	-19	-18	3	-1.4
1984	KC-A	12	9	.571	31	25	3	0	0	168²	175	26	67	68	13.1	5.18	78	.284	.341	0	—	0	-22	-22	1	-1.9
1985	KC-A	0	0	—	3	0	0	0	1	4¹	7	1	4	2	22.8	12.46	33	.368	.478	0	—	0	-4	-4	0	-0.3
	Chi-N	0	3	.000	5	4	0	0	0	20¹	34	4	6	7	18.1	8.41	47	.370	.414	0	.000	-0	-11	-10	1	-0.8
Total 16		126	97	.565	403	261	71	16	14	2047	2020	204	600	801	11.7	3.76	105	.260	.317	3	.091	-2	39	45	14	7.3

■ CHARLIE GUTH
Guth, Charles J. b: 1856, Chicago, Ill. d: 7/5/1883, Boston, Mass. Deb: 9/30/1880

YEAR	TM/L	W	L	PCT	G	GS	CG	SH	SV	IP	H	HR	BB	SO	RAT	ERA	ERA+	OAV	OOB	BH	AVG	PB	PR	/A	PD	TPI
1880	Chi-N	1	0	1.000	1	1	0	0	0	9	12	0	1	7	13.0	5.00	48	.305	.322	1	.250	0	-3	-3	-0	-0.1

■ MARK GUTHRIE
Guthrie, Mark Andrew b: 9/22/65, Buffalo, N.Y. BB/TR, 5'11", 192 lbs. Deb: 7/25/89

YEAR	TM/L	W	L	PCT	G	GS	CG	SH	SV	IP	H	HR	BB	SO	RAT	ERA	ERA+	OAV	OOB	BH	AVG	PB	PR	/A	PD	TPI
1989	Min-A	2	4	.333	13	8	0	0	0	57¹	66	7	21	38	13.8	4.55	91	.292	.355	0	—	0	-4	-3	-0	-0.2
1990	Min-A	7	9	.438	24	21	3	1	0	144²	154	8	39	101	12.1	3.79	110	.276	.325	0	—	0	2	6	0	0.7
Total 2		9	13	.409	37	29	3	1	0	202	220	15	60	139	12.6	4.01	104	.281	.334	0	—	0	-2	4	0	0.5

YEAR	TM/L	W	L	PCT	G	GS	CG	SH	SV	IP	H	HR	BB	SO	RAT	ERA	ERA+	OAV	OOB	BH	AVG	PB	PR	/A	PD	TPI

■ JOSE GUZMAN   Guzman, Jose Alberto (Mirabal)   b: 4/9/63, Santa Isabel, P.R.   BR/TR, 6'2", 160 lbs.   Deb: 9/10/85

YEAR	TM/L	W	L	PCT	G	GS	CG	SH	SV	IP	H	HR	BB	SO	RAT	ERA	ERA+	OAV	OOB	BH	AVG	PB	PR	/A	PD	TPI
1985	Tex-A	3	2	.600	5	5	0	0	0	32²	27	3	14	24	11.3	2.76	153	.214	.293	0	—	0	5	5	0	0.6
1986	Tex-A	9	15	.375	29	29	2	0	0	172¹	199	23	60	87	13.8	4.54	95	.293	.355	0	—	0	-7	-5	1	-0.3
1987	Tex-A	14	14	.500	37	30	6	0	0	208¹	196	30	82	143	12.1	4.67	96	.251	.324	0	—	0	-5	-4	2	-0.2
1988	Tex-A	11	13	.458	30	30	6	2	0	206²	180	20	82	157	11.6	3.70	110	.231	.308	0	—	0	6	9	-1	0.8
Total	4	37	44	.457	101	94	14	2	0	620	602	76	238	411	12.4	4.21	102	.254	.326	0	—	0	-1	5	2	0.9

■ SANTIAGO GUZMAN   Guzman, Santiago Donovan (b: Santiago Donovan (Guzman))   b: 7/25/49, San Pedro De Macoris, D.R.   BR/TR, 6'2", 180 lbs.   Deb: 9/30/69

YEAR	TM/L	W	L	PCT	G	GS	CG	SH	SV	IP	H	HR	BB	SO	RAT	ERA	ERA+	OAV	OOB	BH	AVG	PB	PR	/A	PD	TPI
1969	StL-N	0	1	.000	1	1	0	0	0	7¹	9	2	3	7	14.7	4.91	73	.321	.387	1	.333	-0	-1	-1	-0	0.0
1970	StL-N	1	1	.500	8	3	1	0	0	13²	14	1	13	9	17.8	7.24	57	.275	.422	1	.200	-0	-5	-5	0	-0.4
1971	StL-N	0	0	—	2	1	0	0	0	10	6	0	2	13	7.2	0.00	—	.162	.205	0	.000	-0	4	4	-0	0.4
1972	StL-N	0	0	—	1	0	0	0	0	1	1	1	0	0	9.0	9.00	38	.250	.250	0	—	0	-1	-1	0	0.0
Total	4	1	2	.333	12	5	1	0	0	32	30	4	18	29	13.5	4.50	85	.250	.348	2	.222	0	-3	-2	-0	0.0

■ BRUNO HAAS   Haas, Bruno Philip "Boon"   b: 5/5/1891, Worcester, Mass.   d: 6/5/52, Sarasota, Fla.   BB/TL, 5'10", 180 lbs.   Deb: 6/23/15 ◆

YEAR	TM/L	W	L	PCT	G	GS	CG	SH	SV	IP	H	HR	BB	SO	RAT	ERA	ERA+	OAV	OOB	BH	AVG	PB	PR	/A	PD	TPI
1915	Phi-A	0	1	.000	6	2	1	0	0	14¹	23	0	28	7	32.0	11.93	25	.404	.600	1	.056	-1	-14	-14	0	-1.2

■ MOOSE HAAS   Haas, Bryan Edmund   b: 4/22/56, Baltimore, Md.   BR/TR, 6', 180 lbs.   Deb: 9/08/76

YEAR	TM/L	W	L	PCT	G	GS	CG	SH	SV	IP	H	HR	BB	SO	RAT	ERA	ERA+	OAV	OOB	BH	AVG	PB	PR	/A	PD	TPI
1976	Mil-A	0	1	.000	5	2	0	0	0	16	12	0	12	9	13.5	3.94	89	.207	.343	0	—	0	-1	-1	1	0.0
1977	Mil-A	10	12	.455	32	32	6	0	0	197²	195	21	84	113	12.8	4.33	94	.261	.338	0	—	0	-6	-6	-3	-0.7
1978	Mil-A	2	3	.400	7	6	2	0	1	30²	33	6	8	32	12.0	6.16	61	.273	.318	0	—	0	-8	-8	-0	-0.7
1979	Mil-A	11	11	.500	29	28	8	1	0	184²	198	26	59	95	12.5	4.78	87	.275	.330	0	—	0	-12	-13	-1	-1.2
1980	Mil-A	16	15	.516	33	33	14	3	0	252¹	246	25	56	146	10.8	3.10	125	.258	.300	0	—	0	26	21	-1	2.1
1981	*Mil-A	11	7	.611	24	22	5	0	0	137¹	146	10	40	64	12.3	4.46	77	.275	.327	0	—	0	-12	-16	-1	-1.6
1982	*Mil-A	11	8	.579	32	27	3	0	1	193²	232	15	39	104	12.8	4.47	85	.302	.339	0	—	0	-8	-15	-2	-1.5
1983	Mil-A	13	3	.813	25	25	7	3	0	179	170	12	44	75	10.7	3.27	114	.251	.296	0	—	0	16	9	-0	0.9
1984	Mil-A	9	11	.450	31	30	4	0	0	189¹	205	15	43	84	11.8	3.99	96	.279	.318	0	—	0	-0	-3	3	0.0
1985	Mil-A	8	8	.500	27	26	6	1	0	161²	165	21	25	78	10.6	3.84	108	.260	.289	0	—	0	5	6	-1	0.5
1986	Oak-A	7	2	.778	12	12	1	0	0	72¹	58	4	19	40	9.7	2.74	141	.218	.273	0	—	0	12	9	-0	0.9
1987	Oak-A	2	2	.500	9	9	0	0	0	40²	57	7	9	13	14.6	5.75	72	.335	.369	0	—	0	-6	-7	-0	-0.6
Total	12	100	83	.546	266	252	56	8	2	1655	1717	162	436	853	11.8	4.01	97	.269	.317	0	—	0	6	-23	-5	-1.9

■ BOB HABENICHT   Habenicht, Robert Julius "Hobby"   b: 2/13/26, St.Louis, Mo.   d: 12/24/80, Richmond, Va.   BR/TR, 6'2", 185 lbs.   Deb: 4/17/51

YEAR	TM/L	W	L	PCT	G	GS	CG	SH	SV	IP	H	HR	BB	SO	RAT	ERA	ERA+	OAV	OOB	BH	AVG	PB	PR	/A	PD	TPI
1951	StL-N	0	0	—	3	0	0	0	0	5	5	0	9	1	25.2	7.20	55	.278	.519	0	.000	0	-2	-2	0	0.0
1953	StL-A	0	0	—	1	0	0	0	0	1²	1	0	1	1	16.2	5.40	78	.167	.375	0	—	0	-0	-0	0	0.0
Total	2	0	0	—	4	0	0	0	0	6²	6	0	10	2	23.0	6.75	60	.250	.486	0	.000	0	-2	-2	0	0.0

■ JOHN HABYAN   Habyan, John Gabriel   b: 1/29/63, Bay Shore, N.Y.   BR/TR, 6'1", 195 lbs.   Deb: 9/09/85

YEAR	TM/L	W	L	PCT	G	GS	CG	SH	SV	IP	H	HR	BB	SO	RAT	ERA	ERA+	OAV	OOB	BH	AVG	PB	PR	/A	PD	TPI
1985	Bal-A	1	0	1.000	2	0	0	0	0	2²	3	0	0	2	10.1	0.00	—	.250	.250	0	—	0	1	1	0	0.1
1986	Bal-A	1	3	.250	6	5	0	0	0	26¹	24	3	18	14	14.4	4.44	93	.250	.368	0	—	0	-1	-1	-0	0.0
1987	Bal-A	6	7	.462	27	13	0	0	1	116¹	110	20	40	64	11.8	4.80	92	.248	.313	0	—	0	-4	-5	1	-0.3
1988	Bal-A	1	0	1.000	7	0	0	0	0	14²	22	2	4	4	16.0	4.30	91	.355	.394	0	—	0	-1	-1	0	0.0
1990	NY-A	0	0	—	6	0	0	0	0	8²	10	0	2	4	13.5	2.08	191	.294	.351	0	—	0	2	2	0	0.2
Total	5	9	10	.474	48	18	0	0	1	168²	169	25	64	88	12.6	4.48	96	.261	.331	0	—	0	-3	-4	1	-0.0

■ WARREN HACKER   Hacker, Warren Louis   b: 11/21/24, Marissa, Ill.   BR/TR, 6'1", 185 lbs.   Deb: 9/24/48

YEAR	TM/L	W	L	PCT	G	GS	CG	SH	SV	IP	H	HR	BB	SO	RAT	ERA	ERA+	OAV	OOB	BH	AVG	PB	PR	/A	PD	TPI
1948	Chi-N	0	1	.000	3	1	0	0	0	3	7	0	3	0	30.0	21.00	19	.438	.526	0	—	0	-6	-6	0	-0.4
1949	Chi-N	5	8	.385	30	12	3	0	0	125²	141	7	53	40	14.2	4.23	95	.283	.356	7	.184	-1	-3	-3	1	-0.2
1950	Chi-N	0	1	.000	5	3	1	0	1	15¹	20	3	8	5	16.4	5.28	80	.313	.389	0	.000	-1	-2	-2	1	-0.1
1951	Chi-N	0	0	—	2	0	0	0	0	1¹	3	0	0	2	27.0	13.50	30	.500	.571	0	—	0	-1	-1	0	0.0
1952	Chi-N	15	9	.625	33	20	12	5	1	185	144	17	31	84	**8.6**	2.58	149	**.212**	**.247**	7	.121	-2	24	26	-3	2.2
1953	Chi-N	12	19	.387	39	32	9	0	2	221²	225	35	54	106	11.4	4.38	101	.254	.299	17	.218	1	-2	2	-3	0.0
1954	Chi-N	6	13	.316	39	18	4	1	2	158²	157	28	37	80	11.2	4.25	99	.257	.304	13	.236	1	-3	-1	-1	0.0
1955	Chi-N	11	15	.423	35	30	13	0	3	213	202	38	43	80	10.4	4.27	96	.245	.285	18	.250	2	-5	-4	-1	-0.5
1956	Chi-N	3	13	.188	34	24	4	0	0	168	190	28	44	65	12.6	4.66	81	.285	.330	8	.148	-2	-17	-17	-2	-2.0
1957	Cin-N	3	2	.600	15	6	0	0	0	43¹	50	5	13	18	13.7	5.19	79	.294	.355	1	.125	-0	-6	-5	-0	-0.4
	Phi-N	4	4	.500	20	10	1	0	0	74	72	10	18	33	11.1	4.50	85	.257	.304	6	.261	1	-5	-6	-1	-0.4
	Yr	7	6	.538	35	16	1	0	0	117¹	122	15	31	51	11.8	4.76	82	.267	.315	2	.065	1	-11	-11	-1	-0.8
1958	Phi-N	0	1	.000	9	1	0	0	0	17	24	2	8	4	16.9	7.41	53	.329	.395	0	.000	-0	-7	-7	-0	-0.6
1961	Chi-A	3	3	.500	42	0	0	0	8	57¹	62	8	8	40	11.1	3.77	104	.272	.300	1	.111	-1	2	1	-1	0.0
Total	12	62	89	.411	306	157	47	6	17	1283¹	1297	181	320	557	11.5	4.21	96	.259	.307	78	.195	-2	-32	-22	-13	-2.4

■ JIM HACKETT   Hackett, James Joseph "Sunny Jim"   b: 10/1/1877, Jacksonville, Ill.   d: 3/28/61, Douglas, Mich.   BR/TR, 6'2", 185 lbs.   Deb: 9/14/02 ◆

YEAR	TM/L	W	L	PCT	G	GS	CG	SH	SV	IP	H	HR	BB	SO	RAT	ERA	ERA+	OAV	OOB	BH	AVG	PB	PR	/A	PD	TPI
1902	StL-N	0	3	.000	4	3	3	0	0	30¹	46	0	16	7	18.7	6.23	44	.348	.422	6	.286	1	-12	-12	0	-0.9
1903	StL-N	1	3	.250	7	6	5	0	1	48¹	47	0	18	21	12.7	3.72	88	.249	.324	80	.228	1	-2	-2	0	-0.1
Total	2	1	6	.143	11	9	8	0	1	78²	93	0	34	28	15.0	4.69	65	.290	.365	86	.231	2	-14	-14	0	-1.0

■ HARVEY HADDIX   Haddix, Harvey "The Kitten"   b: 9/18/25, Medway, Ohio   BL/TL, 5'9.5", 170 lbs.   Deb: 8/20/52 C

YEAR	TM/L	W	L	PCT	G	GS	CG	SH	SV	IP	H	HR	BB	SO	RAT	ERA	ERA+	OAV	OOB	BH	AVG	PB	PR	/A	PD	TPI
1952	StL-N	2	2	.500	7	6	3	0	0	42	31	4	10	31	9.2	2.79	133	.201	.259	3	.214	0	4	4	-1	0.5
1953	StL-N	20	9	.690	36	33	19	**6**	1	253	220	24	69	163	10.4	3.06	139	.232	.287	28	.289	10	35	34	-1	4.5
1954	StL-N	18	13	.581	43	35	13	3	4	259²	247	26	77	184	11.3	3.57	115	.249	.305	18	.194	3	14	16	-1	1.8
1955	StL-N	12	16	.429	37	30	9	2	1	208	216	27	62	150	12.2	4.46	91	.268	.325	12	.164	1	-10	-9	1	-0.7
1956	StL-N	1	0	1.000	4	4	1	1	0	23²	28	3	10	16	14.5	5.32	71	.298	.365	2	.222	1	-4	-4	-0	-0.2
	Phi-N	12	8	.600	31	26	11	2	2	206²	196	23	55	154	11.2	3.48	107	.247	.301	22	.237	4	7	5	-1	0.9
	Yr	13	8	.619	35	30	12	3	2	230¹	224	26	65	170	11.5	3.67	102	.253	.308	7	.069	5	3	1	-2	0.7
1957	Phi-N	10	13	.435	27	25	8	1	0	170²	176	18	39	136	11.4	4.06	94	.264	.306	21	.309	7	-3	-5	-3	0.0
1958	Cin-N	8	7	.533	29	26	8	1	0	184	191	28	43	110	11.8	3.52	118	.268	.315	11	.180	3	9	13	-1	1.6
1959	Pit-N	12	12	.500	31	29	14	2	0	224¹	189	26	49	149	**9.6**	3.13	124	.228	**.273**	12	.145	-0	20	18	-1	1.8
1960	*Pit-N	11	10	.524	29	28	4	0	1	172¹	189	13	38	101	11.9	3.97	94	.277	.316	17	.254	4	-4	-4	3	0.3
1961	Pit-N	10	6	.625	29	22	5	2	0	156	159	11	41	99	11.7	4.10	97	.266	.316	8	.143	0	-1	-2	-0	-0.1
1962	Pit-N	9	6	.600	28	20	4	0	0	141¹	146	17	42	101	12.1	4.20	94	.264	.319	13	.250	4	-4	-4	-1	0.0
1963	Pit-N	3	4	.429	49	1	0	0	0	70	67	7	20	70	11.7	3.34	99	.256	.318	2	.182	1	-0	-0	0	0.0
1964	Bal-A	5	5	.500	49	0	0	0	10	89²	64	7	26	81	9.3	2.31	155	.211	.268	0	.000	-0	13	13	0	1.1
1965	Bal-A	3	2	.600	24	0	0	0	1	33²	31	5	23	21	15.0	3.48	100	.248	.373	0	—	-0	-0	-0	0	0.0
Total	14	136	113	.546	453	285	99	20	21	2235	2154	240	601	1575	11.3	3.63	108	.252	.305	169	.212	35	75	74	-4	11.5

■ GEORGE HADDOCK   Haddock, George Silas "Gentleman George"   b: 12/25/1866, Portsmouth, N.H.   d: 4/18/26, Boston, Mass.   BR/TR, 5'11", 155 lbs.   Deb: 9/27/1888

YEAR	TM/L	W	L	PCT	G	GS	CG	SH	SV	IP	H	HR	BB	SO	RAT	ERA	ERA+	OAV	OOB	BH	AVG	PB	PR	/A	PD	TPI
1888	Was-N	0	2	.000	2	2	2	0	0	16	9	0	3	3	6.2	2.25	124	.159	.187	1	.200	0	1	1	1	0.2
1889	Was-N	11	19	.367	33	31	30	0	0	276¹	299	10	123	106	13.7	4.20	94	.267	.340	25	.223	7	-5	-8	0	0.0
1890	Buf-P	9	26	.257	35	34	31	0	0	290²	366	15	149	123	15.9	5.76	71	.295	.370	36	.247	7	-49	-54	3	-3.2
1891	Bos-a	34	11	.756	51	47	37	**5**	1	379²	330	8	137	169	11.1	2.49	140	.226	.293	45	.243	8	**52**	42	6	5.1
1892	Bro-N	29	13	.690	46	44	39	3	1	381¹	340	11	163	153	11.9	3.14	101	.229	.305	28	.177	-1	6	1	2	0.2
1893	Bro-N	8	9	.471	23	20	12	0	0	151	193	10	89	37	16.8	5.60	79	.302	.387	24	.282	4	-16	-20	-3	-1.4
1894	Phi-N	4	3	.571	10	7	5	0	0	56	63	0	34	7	15.6	5.79	88	.281	.376	5	.172	-1	-3	-4	1	-0.2

YEAR	TM/L	W	L	PCT	G	GS	CG	SH	SV	IP	H	HR	BB	SO	RAT	ERA	ERA+	OAV	OOB	BH	AVG	PB	PR	/A	PD	TPI
	Was-N	0	4	.000	4	4	4	0	0	29	50	2	17	1	20.8	8.69	61	.375	.445	3	.188	-0	-11	-11	0	-0.7
	Yr	4	7	.364	14	11	9	0	0	85	113	2	51	8	17.4	6.78	76	.316	.401	4	.089	-1	-14	-15	1	-0.9
Total	7	95	87	.522	204	189	160	8	2	1580	1650	56	714	599	13.5	4.07	93	.259	.334	167	.227	24	-25	-52	11	0.0

■ BUMP HADLEY
Hadley, Irving Darius b: 7/5/04, Lynn, Mass. d: 2/15/63, Lynn, Mass. BR/TR, 5'11", 190 lbs. Deb: 4/20/26

YEAR	TM/L	W	L	PCT	G	GS	CG	SH	SV	IP	H	HR	BB	SO	RAT	ERA	ERA+	OAV	OOB	BH	AVG	PB	PR	/A	PD	TPI
1926	Was-A	0	0	—	1	0	0	0	0	3	6	0	2	0	24.0	12.00	32	.429	.500	0	—	0	-3	-3	-0	-0.1
1927	Was-A	14	6	.700	30	27	13	0	0	198²	177	2	86	60	12.3	2.85	142	.244	.332	19	.271	2	28	27	0	2.9
1928	Was-A	12	13	.480	33	31	16	3	0	231²	236	4	100	80	13.4	3.54	113	.268	.348	17	.210	1	13	12	-0	1.3
1929	Was-A	6	16	.273	37	27	7	1	0	195¹	196	10	85	98	13.2	5.62	75	.263	.342	6	.097	-4	-30	-30	0	-3.0
1930	Was-A	15	11	.577	42	34	15	1	2	260¹	242	6	105	162	12.2	3.73	123	.247	.323	21	.226	1	27	25	-2	2.3
1931	Was-A	11	10	.524	55	11	2	1	8	179²	145	4	92	124	11.9	3.06	140	.218	.314	9	.167	-1	26	25	1	2.3
1932	Chi-A	1	1	.500	3	2	1	0	1	18²	17	2	8	13	12.1	3.86	112	.262	.342	1	.167	-0	1	1	0	0.1
	StL-A	13	20	.394	40	33	12	1	1	229²	244	21	163	132	16.3	5.53	88	.274	.391	22	.282	5	-27	-17	-4	-1.3
	Yr	14	21	.400	43	35	13	1	2	248¹	261	23	171	145	15.9	5.40	89	.273	.388	8	.095	-4	-25	-16	-4	-1.2
1933	StL-A	15	20	.429	45	36	19	2	3	316²	309	17	141	149	12.9	3.92	119	.256	.335	17	.156	-4	13	26	-4	1.9
1934	StL-A	10	16	.385	39	32	7	2	1	213	212	14	127	79	14.6	4.35	115	.257	.361	13	.203	-1	3	15	-0	1.4
1935	Was-A	10	15	.400	35	32	13	0	0	230¹	268	18	102	77	14.6	4.92	88	.292	.366	15	.195	1	-12	-15	1	-1.2
1936	*NY-A	14	4	.778	31	17	8	1	1	173²	194	12	89	74	14.7	4.35	107	.283	.366	16	.235	2	13	6	1	0.7
1937	*NY-A	11	8	.579	29	25	6	0	0	178¹	199	16	83	70	14.4	5.30	84	.281	.358	11	.169	-1	-13	-17	1	-1.3
1938	NY-A	9	8	.529	29	17	8	1	1	167¹	165	13	66	61	12.6	3.60	126	.254	.325	5	.093	-1	22	17	3	1.8
1939	*NY-A	12	6	.667	26	18	7	1	2	154	132	10	85	65	12.9	2.98	146	.237	.342	11	.177	-0	28	24	2	2.4
1940	NY-A	3	5	.375	25	2	0	0	2	80	88	4	52	39	15.9	5.74	70	.276	.379	3	.111	-1	-12	-15	0	-1.4
1941	NY-N	1	0	1.000	3	2	0	0	0	13	19	1	9	4	19.4	6.23	59	.345	.438	0	.000	-0	-4	-4	-0	-0.3
	Phi-A	4	6	.400	25	9	1	0	3	102¹	131	13	47	31	15.8	5.01	85	.310	.381	4	.129	-1	-10	-9	-1	-0.9
Total	16	161	165	.494	528	355	135	14	25	2945²	2980	167	1442	1318	13.7	4.24	105	.263	.350	190	.189	-1	65	69	-1	7.6

■ MICKEY HAEFNER
Haefner, Milton Arnold b: 10/9/12, Lenzburg, Ill. BL/TL, 5'8", 160 lbs. Deb: 4/22/43

YEAR	TM/L	W	L	PCT	G	GS	CG	SH	SV	IP	H	HR	BB	SO	RAT	ERA	ERA+	OAV	OOB	BH	AVG	PB	PR	/A	PD	TPI
1943	Was-A	11	5	.688	36	13	8	1	6	165¹	126	4	60	65	10.3	2.29	140	.208	.283	6	.133	0	19	17	-1	1.8
1944	Was-A	12	15	.444	31	28	18	3	1	228	221	7	71	86	11.7	3.04	107	.251	.310	11	.157	-0	10	5	1	0.5
1945	Was-A	16	14	.533	37	28	19	1	3	238¹	226	10	69	83	11.4	3.47	89	.247	.305	20	.244	4	-3	-10	1	-0.5
1946	Was-A	14	11	.560	33	27	17	2	1	227²	220	10	80	85	12.1	2.85	118	.251	.311	15	.203	4	17	13	-1	1.6
1947	Was-A	10	14	.417	31	28	14	4	1	193	195	8	85	77	13.2	3.64	102	.264	.343	8	.136	-1	1	2	-1	0.0
1948	Was-A	5	13	.278	28	20	4	0	0	147²	151	7	66	45	13.3	4.02	108	.265	.342	7	.163	-1	4	5	2	0.6
1949	Was-A	5	5	.500	19	12	4	1	0	91²	85	7	53	23	13.7	4.42	96	.249	.353	5	.200	1	-2	-2	1	0.0
	Chi-A	4	6	.400	14	12	4	1	1	80¹	84	9	41	17	14.6	4.37	95	.275	.370	6	.261	2	-2	-2	0	0.0
	Yr	9	11	.450	33	24	8	2	1	172	169	16	94	40	14.0	4.40	96	.260	.358	7	.146	2	-4	-3	2	0.0
1950	Chi-A	1	6	.143	24	9	2	0	0	70²	83	11	45	17	16.6	5.73	78	.299	.400	4	.200	0	-9	-10	-0	-0.8
	Bos-N	0	2	.000	8	2	1	0	0	24	23	3	12	10	13.1	5.63	68	.247	.333	2	.286	1	-4	-5	0	-0.3
Total	8	78	91	.462	261	179	91	13	13	1466²	1414	76	577	508	12.5	3.50	102	.252	.326	84	.188	8	31	13	3	2.9

■ BUD HAFEY
Hafey, Daniel Albert b: 8/6/12, Berkeley, Cal. d: 7/27/86, Sacramento, Cal. BR/TR, 6', 185 lbs. Deb: 4/21/35 ♦

YEAR	TM/L	W	L	PCT	G	GS	CG	SH	SV	IP	H	HR	BB	SO	RAT	ERA	ERA+	OAV	OOB	BH	AVG	PB	PR	/A	PD	TPI
1939	Phi-N	0	0	—	2	0	0	0	0	1¹	7	0	1	1	54.0	33.75	12	.700	.727	9	.176	-0	-4	-4	0	-0.3

■ LEO HAFFORD
Hafford, Leo Edgar b: 9/17/1883, Somerville, Mass. d: 10/2/11, Willimantic, Conn. TR , 6', 170 lbs. Deb: 4/15/06

YEAR	TM/L	W	L	PCT	G	GS	CG	SH	SV	IP	H	HR	BB	SO	RAT	ERA	ERA+	OAV	OOB	BH	AVG	PB	PR	/A	PD	TPI
1906	Cin-N	1	1	.500	3	1	1	0	0	19	13	0	11	5	11.8	0.95	291	.191	.313	2	.222	-0	4	4	-1	0.4

■ FRANK HAFNER
Hafner, Francis R. b: 8/14/1867, Hannibal, Mo. d: 3/2/57, Hannibal, Mo. TR , Deb: 5/05/1888

YEAR	TM/L	W	L	PCT	G	GS	CG	SH	SV	IP	H	HR	BB	SO	RAT	ERA	ERA+	OAV	OOB	BH	AVG	PB	PR	/A	PD	TPI
1888	KC-a	0	2	.000	2	2	2	0	0	18	24	2	16	5	20.0	7.00	49	.309	.427	0	.000	-1	-8	-7	-0	-0.5

■ ART HAGAN
Hagan, Arthur Charles b: 3/17/1863, Providence, R.I. d: 3/25/36, Providence, R.I. TR , Deb: 6/30/1883

YEAR	TM/L	W	L	PCT	G	GS	CG	SH	SV	IP	H	HR	BB	SO	RAT	ERA	ERA+	OAV	OOB	BH	AVG	PB	PR	/A	PD	TPI
1883	Phi-N	1	14	.067	17	16	15	0	0	137	207	2	33	39	15.8	5.45	57	.329	.363	6	.102	-5	-35	-36	-1	-3.3
	Buf-N	0	2	.000	2	2	1	0	0	15	17	0	6	7	13.8	3.60	88	.269	.333	0	.000	-1	-1	-1	0	-0.1
	Yr	1	16	.059	19	18	16	0	0	152	224	2	39	46	15.6	5.27	59	.324	.360	0	.000	-7	-36	-37	-1	-3.4
1884	Buf-N	1	2	.333	3	3	3	0	0	26	53	1	4	4	19.7	5.88	53	.400	.417	4	.308	-1	-8	-8	0	-0.6
Total	2	2	18	.100	22	21	19	0	0	178	277	3	43	50	16.2	5.36	58	.336	.369	10	.127	-6	-44	-45	-1	-4.0

■ CASEY HAGEMAN
Hageman, Kurt Moritz b: 5/12/1887, Mt.Oliver, Pa. d: 4/1/64, New Bedford, Pa. BR/TR, 5'10.5", 186 lbs. Deb: 9/18/11

YEAR	TM/L	W	L	PCT	G	GS	CG	SH	SV	IP	H	HR	BB	SO	RAT	ERA	ERA+	OAV	OOB	BH	AVG	PB	PR	/A	PD	TPI
1911	Bos-A	0	2	.000	2	2	2	0	0	17	16	2	5	8	11.6	2.12	155	.262	.328	0	.000	-0	2	2	-1	0.1
1912	Bos-A	0	0	—	2	1	0	0	0	1¹	5	0	3	1	54.0	27.00	13	.500	.615	0	—	0	-4	-3	0	-0.2
1914	StL-N	2	4	.333	12	7	2	0	0	55¹	43	0	20	21	11.1	2.44	115	.215	.302	2	.125	-1	2	2	1	0.2
	Chi-N	1	1	.500	16	1	0	0	1	46²	44	0	12	17	11.4	3.47	80	.254	.314	7	.467	3	-4	-4	-1	-0.1
	Yr	3	5	.375	28	8	2	0	1	102	87	0	32	38	10.8	2.91	96	.230	.295	1	.032	2	-1	-1	0	0.2
Total	3	3	7	.300	32	11	4	0	1	120¹	108	2	40	47	11.7	3.07	93	.243	.318	9	.257	2	-3	-3	-1	0.1

■ KEVIN HAGEN
Hagen, Kevin Eugene b: 3/8/60, Renton, Wash. BR/TR, 6'2", 185 lbs. Deb: 6/04/83

YEAR	TM/L	W	L	PCT	G	GS	CG	SH	SV	IP	H	HR	BB	SO	RAT	ERA	ERA+	OAV	OOB	BH	AVG	PB	PR	/A	PD	TPI
1983	StL-N	2	2	.500	9	4	0	0	0	22¹	34	0	7	7	16.5	4.84	75	.362	.406	0	.000	-1	-3	-3	0	-0.2
1984	StL-N	1	0	1.000	4	0	0	0	0	7¹	9	0	1	2	12.3	2.45	141	.300	.323	0	—	0	1	1	-0	0.1
Total	2	3	2	.600	13	4	0	0	0	29²	43	0	8	9	15.5	4.25	84	.347	.386	0	.000	-1	-2	-2	0	-0.1

■ RIP HAGERMAN
Hagerman, Zeriah Zequiel b: 6/20/1888, Linden, Kan. d: 1/30/30, Albuquerque, N.Mex BR/TR, 6'2", 200 lbs. Deb: 4/16/09

YEAR	TM/L	W	L	PCT	G	GS	CG	SH	SV	IP	H	HR	BB	SO	RAT	ERA	ERA+	OAV	OOB	BH	AVG	PB	PR	/A	PD	TPI
1909	Chi-N	4	4	.500	13	7	4	1	0	79	64	0	29	32	10.7	1.82	140	.225	.298	3	.130	-0	7	6	-0	0.6
1914	Cle-A	9	15	.375	37	26	12	3	0	198	189	3	118	112	14.2	3.09	93	.265	.374	1	.016	-6	-8	-4	-3	-1.3
1915	Cle-A	6	14	.300	29	22	7	0	0	151	156	4	77	69	14.2	3.52	87	.277	.370	4	.105	-3	-10	-8	-3	-1.3
1916	Cle-A	0	0	—	2	0	0	0	0	3²	5	1	2	1	22.1	12.27	25	.333	.474	0	.000	-0	-4	-4	0	-0.3
Total	4	19	33	.365	81	55	23	4	0	431²	414	8	225	214	13.6	3.09	93	.263	.360	8	.065	-9	-14	-10	-6	-2.3

■ NOODLES HAHN
Hahn, Frank George b: 4/29/1879, Nashville, Tenn. d: 2/6/60, Candler, N.C. BL/TL, 5'9", 160 lbs. Deb: 4/18/1899

YEAR	TM/L	W	L	PCT	G	GS	CG	SH	SV	IP	H	HR	BB	SO	RAT	ERA	ERA+	OAV	OOB	BH	AVG	PB	PR	/A	PD	TPI
1899	Cin-N	23	8	.742	38	34	32	4	0	309	280	3	68	145	10.1	2.68	146	.242	.284	16	.147	-4	40	43	-5	3.1
1900	Cin-N	16	19	.457	38	36	28	4	0	303¹	296	4	88	127	11.4	3.29	112	.255	.308	23	.207	0	14	13	-0	1.1
1901	Cin-N	22	19	.537	42	42	41	2	0	375¹	370	12	69	239	10.7	2.71	118	.256	.293	24	.170	-1	26	20	-2	1.7
1902	Cin-N	23	12	.657	36	36	35	6	0	321	282	2	58	142	9.7	1.77	170	.236	.275	22	.185	1	36	44	-3	4.9
1903	Cin-N	22	12	.647	34	34	33	5	0	296	297	3	47	127	10.7	2.52	141	.262	.297	18	.161	-2	25	34	-1	3.3
1904	Cin-N	16	18	.471	35	34	33	2	0	297²	258	4	35	98	9.1	2.06	143	.234	.262	17	.172	1	23	29	-0	3.4
1905	Cin-N	5	3	.625	13	8	5	1	0	77	85	0	9	17	11.2	2.81	118	.272	.297	4	.167	-1	2	5	-2	0.2
1906	NY-A	3	2	.600	6	6	3	1	0	42	38	0	6	17	9.4	3.86	77	.244	.279	4	.333	2	-5	-2	-0	-0.2
Total	8	130	93	.583	242	230	211	25	0	2021¹	1906	28	380	912	10.3	2.55	132	.249	.287	128	.176	-5	159	186	-14	17.5

■ FRED HAHN
Hahn, Frederick Aloys b: 2/16/29, Nyack, N.Y. d: 8/16/84, Valhalla, N.Y. BR/TR, 6'3", 174 lbs. Deb: 4/19/52

YEAR	TM/L	W	L	PCT	G	GS	CG	SH	SV	IP	H	HR	BB	SO	RAT	ERA	ERA+	OAV	OOB	BH	AVG	PB	PR	/A	PD	TPI
1952	StL-N	0	0	—	1	0	0	0	0	2	0	0	2	0	13.5	0.00	—	.250	.333	0	—	0	1	1	0	0.1

■ HAL HAID
Haid, Harold Augustine b: 12/21/1897, Barberton, Ohio d: 8/13/52, Los Angeles, Cal. BR/TR, 5'10.5", 150 lbs. Deb: 9/05/19

YEAR	TM/L	W	L	PCT	G	GS	CG	SH	SV	IP	H	HR	BB	SO	RAT	ERA	ERA+	OAV	OOB	BH	AVG	PB	PR	/A	PD	TPI
1919	StL-A	0	0	—	1	0	0	0	0	2	5	0	3	1	36.0	18.00	18	.556	.667	0	—	0	-3	-3	0	-0.2
1928	StL-N	2	2	.500	27	0	0	0	5	47	39	1	11	21	9.8	2.30	174	.218	.267	3	.375	-0	9	9	0	1.0
1929	StL-N	9	9	.500	38	12	8	0	4	154²	171	8	66	41	14.1	4.07	115	.284	.360	4	.082	-3	11	10	-1	0.5
1930	StL-N	3	2	.600	20	0	0	0	2	33	38	1	14	13	15.0	4.09	123	.297	.379	0	.000	-0	3	3	1	0.4
1931	Bos-N	0	2	.000	27	0	0	0	1	56	59	3	16	20	12.5	4.50	84	.263	.321	1	.125	-0	-4	-4	2	-0.2

YEAR TM/L	W	L	PCT	G	GS	CG	SH	SV	IP	H	HR	BB	SO	RAT	ERA	ERA+	OAV	OOB	BH	AVG	PB	PR	/A	PD	TPI
1933 Chi-A	0	0	—	6	0	0	0	0	14²	18	2	13	7	20.3	7.98	53	.310	.452	1	.250	0	-6	-6	0	-0.4
Total 6	14	15	.483	119	12	8	0	12	307¹	330	15	123	103	13.7	4.16	106	.275	.349	9	.125	-3	10	9	3	1.1

■ JESSE HAINES   Haines, Jesse Joseph "Pop" b: 7/22/1893, Clayton, Ohio d: 8/5/78, Dayton, Ohio BR/TR, 6', 190 lbs. Deb: 7/20/18 CH

YEAR TM/L	W	L	PCT	G	GS	CG	SH	SV	IP	H	HR	BB	SO	RAT	ERA	ERA+	OAV	OOB	BH	AVG	PB	PR	/A	PD	TPI
1918 Cin-N	0	0	—	1	0	0	0	0	5	5	0	1	0	10.8	1.80	148	.294	.333	1	1.000	0	1	0	0	0.1
1920 StL-N	13	20	.394	47	37	19	4	2	301²	303	9	80	120	11.7	2.98	100	.270	.324	19	.176	-1	5	0	-5	-0.6
1921 StL-N	18	12	.600	37	29	13	3	0	244¹	261	15	56	84	12.0	3.50	105	.286	.333	17	.181	-3	8	5	2	0.3
1922 StL-N	11	9	.550	29	26	11	2	0	183	207	10	45	62	12.6	3.84	101	.284	.329	12	.167	-2	5	1	1	0.0
1923 StL-N	20	13	.606	37	36	23	1	0	266	283	7	75	73	12.3	3.11	125	.275	.328	20	.202	-2	26	23	0	2.1
1924 StL-N	8	19	.296	35	31	16	1	0	222²	275	14	66	69	14.0	4.41	86	.309	.360	14	.189	-2	-13	-15	-1	-1.7
1925 StL-N	13	14	.481	29	25	15	0	0	207	234	11	52	63	12.5	4.57	95	.290	.334	13	.176	-2	-7	-6	-1	-0.7
1926 *StL-N	13	4	.765	33	21	14	3	1	183	186	10	48	46	11.6	3.25	120	.265	.314	13	.213	-1	12	13	-3	1.0
1927 StL-N	24	10	.706	38	36	25	6	1	300²	273	11	77	89	10.6	2.72	145	.245	.297	23	.202	-1	40	41	1	4.2
1928 *StL-N	20	8	.714	33	28	20	1	0	240¹	238	14	72	77	11.8	3.18	126	.266	.324	16	.184	-1	21	22	-3	1.7
1929 StL-N	13	10	.565	28	25	12	0	0	179²	230	21	73	59	15.3	5.71	82	.313	.376	11	.159	-2	-20	-21	-4	-2.3
1930 *StL-N	13	8	.619	29	24	14	0	1	182	215	15	54	68	13.4	4.30	117	.298	.348	16	.246	1	14	14	-3	1.2
1931 StL-N	12	3	.800	19	17	8	2	0	122¹	134	2	28	27	11.9	3.02	131	.278	.318	6	.133	-2	12	13	-1	1.0
1932 StL-N	3	5	.375	20	10	4	1	0	85¹	116	4	16	27	14.0	4.75	83	.326	.357	5	.185	0	-8	-8	0	-0.7
1933 StL-N	9	6	.600	32	10	5	0	1	115¹	113	3	37	37	11.8	2.50	139	.252	.311	2	.067	-2	11	13	-1	1.0
1934 *StL-N	4	4	.500	37	6	0	0	1	90	86	6	19	17	10.9	3.50	121	.262	.311	3	.158	-1	6	7	2	0.9
1935 StL-N	6	5	.545	30	12	3	0	2	115¹	110	4	28	24	10.8	3.59	114	.252	.299	9	.273	1	6	7	-1	0.7
1936 StL-N	7	5	.583	25	9	4	0	1	99¹	110	4	21	19	12.0	3.90	101	.284	.323	4	.167	-1	1	1	0	0.0
1937 StL-N	3	3	.500	16	6	2	0	0	65²	81	5	23	18	14.4	4.52	88	.303	.361	4	.182	-0	-4	-4	-1	-0.4
Total 19	210	158	.571	555	388	208	24	10	3208²	3460	165	871	981	12.3	3.64	108	.280	.330	209	.186	-21	114	104	-18	7.8

■ JIM HAISLIP   Haislip, James Clifton "Slim" b: 8/4/1891, Farmersville, Tex. d: 1/22/70, Dallas, Tex. BR/TR, 6'1", 186 lbs. Deb: 8/27/13

YEAR TM/L	W	L	PCT	G	GS	CG	SH	SV	IP	H	HR	BB	SO	RAT	ERA	ERA+	OAV	OOB	BH	AVG	PB	PR	/A	PD	TPI
1913 Phi-N	0	0	—	1	0	0	0	0	3	4	0	3	0	21.0	6.00	56	.400	.538	0	.000	-0	-1	-1	-0	0.0

■ ED HALBRITER   Halbriter, Edward L. b: 2/2/1860, Auburn, N.Y. d: 8/9/36, Los Angeles, Cal. Deb: 5/23/1882

YEAR TM/L	W	L	PCT	G	GS	CG	SH	SV	IP	H	HR	BB	SO	RAT	ERA	ERA+	OAV	OOB	BH	AVG	PB	PR	/A	PD	TPI
1882 Phi-a	0	1	.000	1	1	1	0	0	8	17	1	4	4	23.6	7.88	38	.406	.458	0	.000	-1	-5	-4	-0	-0.3

■ DAD HALE   Hale, Ray Luther b: 2/18/1879, Allegan, Mich. d: 2/1/46, Allegan, Mich. BR/TR, 5'10", 180 lbs. Deb: 4/21/02

YEAR TM/L	W	L	PCT	G	GS	CG	SH	SV	IP	H	HR	BB	SO	RAT	ERA	ERA+	OAV	OOB	BH	AVG	PB	PR	/A	PD	TPI
1902 Bos-N	1	4	.200	8	6	3	0	0	47	69	1	18	12	16.9	6.32	45	.341	.397	0	.000	-1	-18	-18	0	-1.7
Bal-A	0	1	.000	3	2	1	0	0	14	21	0	6	6	17.4	4.50	84	.346	.405	0	.000	-1	-1	-1	-1	-0.1

■ ED HALICKI   Halicki, Edward Louis b: 10/4/50, Newark, N.J. BR/TR, 6'7", 220 lbs. Deb: 7/08/74

YEAR TM/L	W	L	PCT	G	GS	CG	SH	SV	IP	H	HR	BB	SO	RAT	ERA	ERA+	OAV	OOB	BH	AVG	PB	PR	/A	PD	TPI
1974 SF-N	1	8	.111	16	11	2	0	0	74¹	84	6	31	40	14.2	4.24	90	.275	.345	6	.240	1	-5	-4	-1	-0.2
1975 SF-N	9	13	.409	24	23	7	2	0	159²	143	6	59	153	11.6	3.49	109	.240	.312	6	.113	-2	2	5	-1	0.3
1976 SF-N	12	14	.462	32	31	8	4	0	186¹	171	10	61	130	11.3	3.62	100	.246	.309	9	.170	1	-3	0	-1	0.1
1977 SF-N	16	12	.571	37	37	7	2	0	257²	241	27	70	168	11.1	3.32	118	.244	.298	15	.176	3	17	17	-3	1.7
1978 SF-N	9	10	.474	29	28	9	4	1	199	166	11	45	105	9.9	2.85	121	.221	**.271**	9	.136	-2	16	13	-2	1.0
1979 SF-N	5	8	.385	33	19	3	1	0	125²	134	12	47	81	13.2	4.58	76	.266	.333	7	.206	1	-12	-15	0	-1.3
1980 SF-N	0	0	—	11	2	0	0	0	25	29	5	10	14	14.0	5.40	65	.293	.358	1	.167	-0	-5	-5	0	-0.4
Cal-A	3	1	.750	10	6	0	0	0	35¹	39	5	11	16	12.7	4.84	81	.279	.331	0	—	0	-3	-4	-1	-0.3
Total 7	55	66	.455	192	157	36	13	1	1063	1007	82	334	707	11.6	3.62	102	.247	.308	53	.165	3	8	8	-8	0.9

■ DREW HALL   Hall, Andrew Clark b: 3/27/63, Louisville, Ky. BL/TL, 6'5", 200 lbs. Deb: 9/14/86

YEAR TM/L	W	L	PCT	G	GS	CG	SH	SV	IP	H	HR	BB	SO	RAT	ERA	ERA+	OAV	OOB	BH	AVG	PB	PR	/A	PD	TPI
1986 Chi-N	1	2	.333	5	4	1	0	1	23²	24	3	10	21	12.9	4.56	89	.267	.340	1	.143	0	-2	-1	-0	-0.1
1987 Chi-N	1	1	.500	21	0	0	0	0	32²	40	4	14	20	14.9	6.89	62	.308	.375	0	.000	-0	-10	-9	-0	-0.9
1988 Chi-N	1	1	.500	19	0	0	0	1	22¹	26	4	9	22	14.5	7.66	47	.295	.367	0	.000	-0	-10	-10	-0	-0.9
1989 Tex-A	2	1	.667	38	0	0	0	0	58¹	42	3	33	45	12.0	3.70	107	.207	.326	0	—	0	1	2	0	0.2
1990 Mon-N	4	7	.364	42	0	0	0	3	58¹	52	6	29	40	12.5	5.09	74	.242	.332	0	.000	-0	-8	-9	1	-0.8
Total 5	9	12	.429	125	4	1	0	5	195¹	184	20	95	148	13.0	5.21	75	.253	.343	1	.063	-1	-30	-28	-0	-2.5

■ SEA LION HALL   Hall, Charles Louis (b: Carlos Clolo) b: 7/27/1885, Ventura, Cal. d: 12/6/43, Ventura, Cal. BL/TR, 6'1", 187 lbs. Deb: 7/12/06

YEAR TM/L	W	L	PCT	G	GS	CG	SH	SV	IP	H	HR	BB	SO	RAT	ERA	ERA+	OAV	OOB	BH	AVG	PB	PR	/A	PD	TPI
1906 Cin-N	4	8	.333	14	9	9	1	0	95	86	1	50	49	13.6	3.32	83	.258	.368	6	.128	-1	-7	-6	0	-0.7
1907 Cin-N	4	2	.667	11	8	5	0	0	68	51	0	43	25	13.0	2.51	103	.226	.359	7	.269	1	-0	1	-1	0.1
1909 Bos-A	6	4	.600	11	7	3	0	0	59²	59	0	17	27	11.9	2.56	98	.271	.332	3	.158	-1	-1	0	0	0.0
1910 Bos-A	12	9	.571	35	16	13	0	2	188²	142	6	73	95	10.7	1.91	134	.207	.292	17	.207	3	13	14	0	2.0
1911 Bos-A	8	7	.533	32	10	6	0	4	146¹	149	3	72	83	13.9	3.75	87	.279	.370	9	.141	-1	-7	-8	-2	-1.0
1912 *Bos-A	15	8	.652	34	20	9	2	2	191	178	3	70	83	11.9	3.02	113	.257	.329	20	.267	5	6	8	1	1.6
1913 Bos-A	4	4	.556	35	4	2	0	2	105	97	1	46	44	12.7	3.43	86	.235	.319	9	.214	1	-6	-6	-0	-0.4
1916 StL-N	0	4	.000	10	5	2	0	1	42²	45	1	14	15	12.4	5.48	48	.280	.337	2	.143	-1	-14	-13	-1	-1.3
1918 Det-A	0	1	.000	6	1	0	0	0	13¹	14	1	6	2	13.5	6.75	39	.269	.345	0	.000	-0	-6	-6	0	-0.6
Total 9	54	47	.535	188	80	49	3	12	909²	821	16	391	427	12.4	3.09	95	.248	.334	73	.197	7	-21	-17	-2	-0.3

■ BERT HALL   Hall, Herbert Ernest b: 10/15/1888, Portland, Ore. d: 7/18/48, Seattle, Wash. BR/TR, 5'10", 178 lbs. Deb: 8/21/11

YEAR TM/L	W	L	PCT	G	GS	CG	SH	SV	IP	H	HR	BB	SO	RAT	ERA	ERA+	OAV	OOB	BH	AVG	PB	PR	/A	PD	TPI
1911 Phi-N	0	1	.000	7	1	0	0	0	18	19	0	13	8	16.5	4.00	86	.297	.423	1	.333	0	-1	-1	-1	-0.1

■ HERB HALL   Hall, Herbert Silas "Iron Duke" b: 6/5/1893, Steelville, Ill. d: 7/1/70, Fresno, Cal. BB/TR, 6'4", 220 lbs. Deb: 4/28/18

YEAR TM/L	W	L	PCT	G	GS	CG	SH	SV	IP	H	HR	BB	SO	RAT	ERA	ERA+	OAV	OOB	BH	AVG	PB	PR	/A	PD	TPI
1918 Det-A	0	0	—	3	0	0	0	0	6	12	0	7	1	31.5	15.00	18	.500	.636	0	.000	-0	-8	-8	-0	-0.7

■ JOHN HALL   Hall, John Sylvester b: 1/9/24, Muskogee, Okla. BR/TR, 6'2.5", 170 lbs. Deb: 4/21/48

YEAR TM/L	W	L	PCT	G	GS	CG	SH	SV	IP	H	HR	BB	SO	RAT	ERA	ERA+	OAV	OOB	BH	AVG	PB	PR	/A	PD	TPI
1948 Bro-N	0	0	—	3	0	0	0	0	4¹	4	1	2	2	12.5	6.23	64	.267	.353	0	—	0	-1	-1	0	0.0

■ MARC HALL   Hall, Marcus b: 8/12/1887, Joplin, Mo. d: 2/24/15, Joplin, Mo. BR/TR, 6'1.5", 190 lbs. Deb: 8/20/10

YEAR TM/L	W	L	PCT	G	GS	CG	SH	SV	IP	H	HR	BB	SO	RAT	ERA	ERA+	OAV	OOB	BH	AVG	PB	PR	/A	PD	TPI
1910 StL-A	1	7	.125	8	7	5	0	0	46¹	50	0	31	25	16.3	4.27	58	.289	.406	1	.067	-2	-9	-9	0	-0.9
1913 Det-A	10	12	.455	30	21	8	1	0	165	154	1	79	69	12.8	3.27	89	.255	.344	4	.089	-3	-6	-6	0	-0.9
1914 Det-A	4	6	.400	25	8	1	0	0	90¹	88	1	27	18	11.5	2.69	104	.267	.322	1	.043	-2	1	1	1	0.0
Total 3	15	25	.375	63	36	14	1	0	301²	292	2	137	112	12.9	3.25	87	.264	.348	6	.072	-7	-15	-15	1	-1.8

■ DICK HALL   Hall, Richard Wallace b: 9/27/30, St.Louis, Mo. BR/TR, 6'6", 200 lbs. Deb: 4/15/52 ♦

YEAR TM/L	W	L	PCT	G	GS	CG	SH	SV	IP	H	HR	BB	SO	RAT	ERA	ERA+	OAV	OOB	BH	AVG	PB	PR	/A	PD	TPI
1955 Pit-N	6	6	.500	15	13	4	0	1	94¹	92	8	28	46	11.6	3.91	105	.253	.310	7	.175	1	1	2	-2	0.2
1956 Pit-N	0	7	.000	19	9	1	0	1	62¹	64	8	21	27	12.3	4.76	79	.270	.329	10	.345	2	-7	-7	-1	-0.3
1957 Pit-N	0	0	—	8	0	0	0	0	10	17	4	5	7	20.7	10.80	35	.362	.434	0	.000	-0	-8	-8	-0	-0.7
1959 Pit-N	0	0	—	2	1	0	0	0	8²	12	1	1	3	13.5	3.12	124	.333	.351	0	.000	-0	1	1	-0	0.0
1960 KC-A	8	13	.381	29	28	9	1	0	182¹	183	28	38	79	11.1	4.05	98	.261	.301	6	.107	-3	-4	-1	-1	-0.3
1961 Bal-A	7	5	.583	29	13	4	2	4	122¹	102	10	30	92	9.7	3.09	126	.227	.275	5	.139	-2	13	11	1	1.1
1962 Bal-A	6	6	.500	43	6	1	0	6	118¹	102	9	19	71	9.2	2.28	165	.230	.262	4	.167	1	22	19	-0	2.1
1963 Bal-A	5	5	.500	47	3	0	0	12	111²	91	12	16	74	8.9	2.98	118	.224	.260	13	.464	6	8	7	1	1.4
1964 Bal-A	9	1	.900	45	0	0	0	7	87²	58	8	16	52	7.6	1.85	193	.188	.228	2	.125	-0	17	17	0	1.8
1965 Bal-A	11	8	.579	48	0	0	0	12	93²	84	8	11	79	9.1	3.07	113	.243	.266	5	.333	3	4	4	-2	0.5
1966 Bal-A	6	2	.750	32	0	0	0	7	66	59	9	4	44	9.5	3.95	84	.233	.265	2	.167	0	-4	-5	0	-0.4
1967 Phi-N	10	8	.556	48	0	0	0	8	86	83	5	12	64	10.2	2.20	155	.255	.286	1	.071	-1	11	12	1	1.3
1968 Phi-N	4	1	.800	32	0	0	0	0	46	53	6	5	31	11.5	4.89	61	.296	.319	1	.333	0	-10	-10	-0	-1.0
1969 *Bal-A	5	2	.714	39	0	0	0	6	65²	49	3	9	31	8.1	1.92	186	.213	.246	2	.286	1	12	12	-1	1.3

YEAR TM/L	W	L	PCT	G	GS	CG	SH	SV	IP	H	HR	BB	SO	RAT	ERA	ERA+	OAV	OOB	BH	AVG	PB	PR	/A	PD	TPI
1970 *Bal-A	10	5	.667	32	0	0	0	3	61¹	51	8	6	30	8.4	3.08	118	.229	.249	1	.083	-1	4	4	-1	0.2
1971 Bal-A	6	6	.500	27	0	0	0	1	43¹	52	4	11	26	13.3	4.98	67	.302	.348	2	.400	1	-7	-8	-1	-0.7
Total 16	93	75	.554	495	74	20	3	68	1259²	1152	130	236	741	10.0	3.32	111	.244	.283	150	.210	9	55	50	-5	6.5

■ BOB HALL
Hall, Robert Lewis b: 12/22/23, Swissvale, Pa. d: 3/12/83, St.Petersburg, Fla BR/TR, 6'2", 195 lbs. Deb: 4/23/49

YEAR TM/L	W	L	PCT	G	GS	CG	SH	SV	IP	H	HR	BB	SO	RAT	ERA	ERA+	OAV	OOB	BH	AVG	PB	PR	/A	PD	TPI
1949 Bos-N	6	4	.600	31	6	2	0	0	74¹	77	7	41	43	14.4	4.36	87	.272	.366	8	.364	2	-3	-5	-2	-0.4
1950 Bos-N	0	2	.000	21	4	0	0	0	50¹	58	8	33	22	16.6	6.97	55	.293	.399	1	.083	-1	-16	-17	-0	-1.6
1953 Pit-N	3	12	.200	37	17	6	1	1	152	172	17	72	68	14.5	5.39	83	.286	.364	6	.158	0	-19	-15	-1	-1.4
Total 3	9	18	.333	89	27	8	1	1	276²	307	32	146	133	14.9	5.40	77	.284	.371	15	.208	2	-37	-38	-3	-3.4

■ TOM HALL
Hall, Tom Edward b: 11/23/47, Thomasville, N.C. BL/TL, 6', 150 lbs. Deb: 6/09/68

YEAR TM/L	W	L	PCT	G	GS	CG	SH	SV	IP	H	HR	BB	SO	RAT	ERA	ERA+	OAV	OOB	BH	AVG	PB	PR	/A	PD	TPI
1968 Min-A	2	1	.667	8	4	0	0	0	29²	27	1	12	18	12.1	2.43	127	.239	.317	0	.000	-1	2	2	-0	0.1
1969 *Min-A	8	7	.533	31	18	5	2	0	140²	129	12	50	92	11.5	3.33	110	.243	.308	8	.186	1	5	5	-2	0.4
1970 *Min-A	11	6	.647	52	11	1	0	4	155¹	94	11	66	184	9.4	2.55	146	.173	.265	8	.182	-0	20	20	-3	1.7
1971 Min-A	4	7	.364	48	11	0	0	9	129²	104	13	58	137	11.2	3.33	107	.216	.300	9	.265	2	2	3	-0	0.5
1972 *Cin-N	10	1	.909	47	7	1	1	8	124¹	77	13	56	134	9.8	2.61	123	.173	.269	3	.100	-1	12	8	-3	0.5
1973 *Cin-N	8	5	.615	54	7	0	0	8	103²	74	13	48	96	10.6	3.47	98	.202	.295	1	.045	-2	2	-1	-2	-0.4
1974 Cin-N	3	1	.750	40	1	0	0	1	64	54	9	30	48	11.8	4.08	86	.232	.319	0	.000	-1	-3	-4	-0	-0.1
1975 Cin-N	0	0	—	2	0	0	0	0	2	2	0	2	3	18.0	0.00	—	.250	.400	0	—	0	1	1	0	0.1
NY-N	4	3	.571	34	4	0	0	1	60²	58	10	31	48	13.6	4.75	73	.254	.351	2	.400	1	-8	-9	-0	-0.8
Yr	4	3	.571	36	4	0	0	1	62²	60	10	33	51	13.8	4.60	75	.254	.353	2	.000	1	-7	-8	-0	-0.7
1976 NY-N	1	1	.500	5	0	0	0	0	4²	5	0	5	2	19.3	5.79	57	.250	.400	0	—	0	-1	-1	0	-0.1
*KC-A	1	1	.500	31	0	0	0	1	30¹	28	4	18	25	13.6	4.45	79	.246	.348	0	—	0	-3	-3	-0	-0.2
1977 KC-A	0	0	—	6	0	0	0	0	7²	4	2	6	10	11.7	3.52	115	.154	.313	0	—	0	0	0	0	0.1
Total 10	52	33	.612	358	63	7	3	32	852²	656	88	382	797	11.0	3.27	107	.211	.299	31	.161	-1	28	22	-11	1.6

■ BILL HALL
Hall, William Bernard "Beanie" b: 2/22/1894, Charleston, W.Va. d: 8/15/47, Newport, Ky. BR/TR, 6'2", 250 lbs. Deb: 7/04/13

YEAR TM/L	W	L	PCT	G	GS	CG	SH	SV	IP	H	HR	BB	SO	RAT	ERA	ERA+	OAV	OOB	BH	AVG	PB	PR	/A	PD	TPI
1913 Bro-N	0	0	—	3	0	0	0	0	4²	4	0	5	3	19.3	5.79	57	.267	.476	0	.000	-0	-1	-1	0	-0.1

■ JOHN HALLA
Halla, John Arthur b: 5/13/1884, St.Louis, Mo. d: 9/30/47, ElSegundo, Cal. BL/TL, 5'11", 175 lbs. Deb: 8/27/05

YEAR TM/L	W	L	PCT	G	GS	CG	SH	SV	IP	H	HR	BB	SO	RAT	ERA	ERA+	OAV	OOB	BH	AVG	PB	PR	/A	PD	TPI
1905 Cle-A	0	0	—	3	0	0	0	0	12²	12	0	0	4	8.5	2.84	93	.251	.251	1	.200	-0	-0	-0	0	0.0

■ BILL HALLAHAN
Hallahan, William Anthony "Wild Bill" b: 8/4/02, Binghamton, N.Y. d: 7/8/81, Binghamton, N.Y. BR/TL, 5'10.5", 170 lbs. Deb: 4/16/25

YEAR TM/L	W	L	PCT	G	GS	CG	SH	SV	IP	H	HR	BB	SO	RAT	ERA	ERA+	OAV	OOB	BH	AVG	PB	PR	/A	PD	TPI
1925 StL-N	1	0	1.000	6	0	0	0	0	15¹	14	0	11	8	14.7	3.52	123	.259	.385	1	.333	0	1	1	0	0.2
1926 *StL-N	1	4	.200	19	3	0	0	0	56²	45	1	32	28	12.4	3.65	107	.260	.379	4	.250	0	1	2	-1	0.1
1929 StL-N	4	4	.500	20	12	5	0	0	93²	94	6	60	52	14.8	4.42	106	.269	.376	4	.154	-1	3	3	1	0.2
1930 *StL-N	15	9	.625	35	32	13	2	2	237¹	233	15	126	177	13.6	4.66	108	.260	.351	10	.123	-6	8	9	-1	0.2
1931 *StL-N	19	9	.679	37	30	16	3	4	248²	242	10	112	159	12.8	3.29	120	.259	.339	8	.099	-4	16	18	-3	1.1
1932 StL-N	12	7	.632	25	22	13	1	1	176¹	169	10	69	108	12.1	3.11	126	.253	.323	12	.214	2	15	16	-2	1.7
1933 StL-N	16	13	.552	36	32	16	2	0	244¹	245	6	98	93	12.6	3.50	99	.260	.330	12	.150	-0	-4	-1	-3	-0.3
1934 *StL-N	8	12	.400	32	26	10	2	0	162²	195	2	66	70	14.4	4.26	99	.294	.358	10	.182	-1	-4	-1	0	-0.1
1935 StL-N	15	8	.652	40	23	8	2	1	181¹	196	5	57	73	12.6	3.42	120	.275	.329	8	.143	-2	12	14	-1	1.1
1936 StL-N	2	2	.500	9	6	1	0	0	37	58	4	17	16	18.2	6.32	62	.360	.421	5	.556	3	-9	-10	-0	-0.6
Cin-N	5	9	.357	23	19	5	2	0	135	150	3	57	32	13.9	4.33	88	.287	.359	9	.191	1	-5	-8	1	-0.5
Yr	7	11	.389	32	25	6	2	0	172	208	7	74	48	14.8	4.76	81	.305	.373	2	.036	3	-14	-17	1	-1.1
1937 Cin-N	3	9	.250	21	9	2	0	0	63	90	3	29	18	17.3	6.14	61	.345	.414	2	.095	-1	-16	-17	1	-1.6
1938 Phi-N	1	8	.111	21	10	1	0	0	89	107	4	45	22	15.6	5.46	71	.295	.376	5	.192	-0	-17	-16	0	-1.4
Total 12	102	94	.520	324	224	90	14	8	1740¹	1838	71	779	856	13.6	4.03	102	.274	.351	90	.162	-9	2	12	-7	0.4

■ JACK HALLETT
Hallett, Jack Price b: 11/13/14, Toledo, Ohio d: 6/11/82, Toledo, Ohio BR/TR, 6'4", 215 lbs. Deb: 9/13/40

YEAR TM/L	W	L	PCT	G	GS	CG	SH	SV	IP	H	HR	BB	SO	RAT	ERA	ERA+	OAV	OOB	BH	AVG	PB	PR	/A	PD	TPI
1940 Chi-A	1	1	.500	2	2	1	0	0	14	15	1	6	9	14.1	6.43	69	.273	.355	2	.400	0	-3	-3	0	-0.1
1941 Chi-A	5	5	.500	22	6	3	0	0	74²	96	7	35	25	16.2	6.03	68	.306	.381	4	.154	0	-16	-16	-1	-1.4
1942 Pit-N	0	1	.000	3	3	2	0	0	22¹	23	0	8	16	12.5	4.84	70	.274	.337	3	.375	2	-4	-4	0	-0.1
1943 Pit-N	1	2	.333	9	4	2	1	0	47²	36	0	11	11	9.1	1.70	205	.212	.264	4	.286	2	9	9	-1	1.2
1946 Pit-N	5	7	.417	35	9	3	1	0	115	107	0	39	64	11.4	3.29	107	.267	.332	6	.231	0	2	3	-0	0.3
1948 NY-N	0	0	—	2	0	0	0	0	4	3	0	4	3	15.8	4.50	87	.214	.389	0	—	-0	-0	-0	-0	-0.1
Total 6	12	16	.429	73	24	11	2	0	277²	280	8	103	128	12.6	4.05	92	.270	.339	19	.237	4	-12	-10	-1	-0.1

■ BILL HALLMAN
Hallman, William Wilson b: 3/31/1867, Pittsburgh, Pa. d: 9/11/20, Philadelphia, Pa. BR/TR, 5'8", 160 lbs. Deb: 4/23/1888 M♦

YEAR TM/L	W	L	PCT	G	GS	CG	SH	SV	IP	H	HR	BB	SO	RAT	ERA	ERA+	OAV	OOB	BH	AVG	PB	PR	/A	PD	TPI
1896 Phi-N	0	0	—	1	0	0	0	0	2	4	0	2	0	27.0	18.00	24	.411	.511	150	.320	0	-3	-3	0	-0.1

■ CHARLES HALLSTROM
Hallstrom, Charles E. b: 1/22/1864, Jonkoping, Sweden d: 5/6/49, Chicago, Ill. Deb: 9/23/1885

YEAR TM/L	W	L	PCT	G	GS	CG	SH	SV	IP	H	HR	BB	SO	RAT	ERA	ERA+	OAV	OOB	BH	AVG	PB	PR	/A	PD	TPI
1885 Pro-N	0	1	.000	1	1	1	0	0	9	18	3	6	0	24.0	11.00	24	.398	.468	0	.000	-1	-8	-8	-0	-0.5

■ DOC HAMANN
Hamann, Elmer Joseph b: 12/21/1900, New Ulm, Minn. d: 1/11/73, Milwaukee, Wis. BR/TR, 6'1", 180 lbs. Deb: 9/21/22

YEAR TM/L	W	L	PCT	G	GS	CG	SH	SV	IP	H	HR	BB	SO	RAT	ERA	ERA+	OAV	OOB	BH	AVG	PB	PR	/A	PD	TPI
1922 Cle-A	0	0	—	1	0	0	0	0	0	3	0	3	0		∞	—	1.000	1.000	0	—	0	-6	-6	0	-0.4

■ ROGER HAMBRIGHT
Hambright, Roger Dee b: 3/26/49, Sunnyside, Wash. BR/TR, 5'10", 180 lbs. Deb: 7/19/71

YEAR TM/L	W	L	PCT	G	GS	CG	SH	SV	IP	H	HR	BB	SO	RAT	ERA	ERA+	OAV	OOB	BH	AVG	PB	PR	/A	PD	TPI
1971 NY-A	3	1	.750	18	0	0	0	2	26²	22	5	10	14	10.8	4.39	74	.224	.296	1	.500	0	-3	-3	0	-0.2

■ JOHN HAMILL
Hamill, John Alexander Charles b: 12/18/1860, New York, N.Y. d: 12/6/11, Bristol, R.I. BR/TR, 5'8", 158 lbs. Deb: 5/01/1884

YEAR TM/L	W	L	PCT	G	GS	CG	SH	SV	IP	H	HR	BB	SO	RAT	ERA	ERA+	OAV	OOB	BH	AVG	PB	PR	/A	PD	TPI
1884 Was-a	2	17	.105	19	19	18	1	0	156²	197	8	43	50	13.8	4.48	68	.291	.334	7	.099	-3	-21	-25	-0	-2.4

■ DAVE HAMILTON
Hamilton, David Edward b: 12/13/47, Seattle, Wash. BL/TL, 6', 180 lbs. Deb: 5/29/72

YEAR TM/L	W	L	PCT	G	GS	CG	SH	SV	IP	H	HR	BB	SO	RAT	ERA	ERA+	OAV	OOB	BH	AVG	PB	PR	/A	PD	TPI
1972 *Oak-A	6	6	.500	25	14	1	0	0	101¹	94	7	31	55	11.2	2.93	97	.249	.307	4	.154	2	1	-1	0	0.1
1973 Oak-A	6	4	.600	16	11	1	0	0	69²	74	8	24	34	12.8	4.39	81	.274	.336	0	—	0	-4	-7	-1	-0.6
1974 Oak-A	7	4	.636	29	18	1	1	0	117	104	10	48	69	12.1	3.15	105	.241	.324	0	—	0	6	2	-0	0.2
1975 Oak-A	1	2	.333	11	4	0	0	0	35²	42	4	18	20	15.1	4.04	90	.290	.368	0	—	0	-1	-2	0	-0.1
Chi-A	6	5	.545	30	1	0	0	6	69²	63	6	29	51	11.9	2.84	136	.246	.323	0	—	0	7	8	0	0.8
Yr	7	7	.500	41	5	0	0	6	105¹	105	8	47	71	13.0	3.25	117	.261	.339	0	—	0	6	6	0	0.7
1976 Chi-A	6	6	.500	45	1	0	0	10	90¹	81	4	45	62	13.9	3.59	99	.243	.340	0	—	0	-1	-0	-1	-0.0
1977 Chi-A	4	5	.444	55	0	0	0	9	67¹	71	6	33	45	13.9	3.61	113	.270	.351	0	—	0	3	4	0	0.4
1978 StL-N	0	0	—	13	0	0	0	0	14	16	5	6	8	14.1	6.43	55	.296	.367	0	.000	-0	-4	-5	0	-0.4
Pit-N	0	2	.000	16	0	0	0	1	26¹	23	2	12	15	12.0	3.42	108	.221	.302	0	.000	-1	0	1	-0	0.0
Yr	0	2	.000	29	0	0	0	1	40¹	39	7	18	23	12.7	4.46	81	.247	.324	0	.000	-1	-4	-4	0	-0.4
1979 Oak-A	3	4	.429	40	7	1	0	5	82²	80	5	43	52	13.5	3.70	109	.261	.353	0	—	0	5	3	0	0.3
1980 Oak-A	0	3	.000	30	0	0	0	0	30	44	6	28	23	22.5	11.40	33	.344	.472	0	—	0	-25	-25	-0	-2.3
Total 9	39	41	.488	301	57	4	1	31	704	692	61	317	434	13.1	3.85	94	.259	.341	4	.121	1	-12	-22	-2	-1.6

■ EARL HAMILTON
Hamilton, Earl Andrew b: 7/19/1891, Gibson, Ill. d: 11/17/68, Anaheim, Cal. BL/TL, 5'8", 160 lbs. Deb: 4/14/11

YEAR TM/L	W	L	PCT	G	GS	CG	SH	SV	IP	H	HR	BB	SO	RAT	ERA	ERA+	OAV	OOB	BH	AVG	PB	PR	/A	PD	TPI
1911 StL-A	5	12	.294	32	17	10	1	0	177	191	4	69	55	13.4	3.97	85	.284	.354	6	.107	-1	-12	-12	1	-1.1
1912 StL-A	11	14	.440	41	26	17	1	2	249²	228	2	86	139	11.6	3.24	102	.248	.319	13	.178	-0	2	3	-3	0.0
1913 StL-A	13	12	.520	31	24	19	3	1	217¹	197	3	83	101	12.0	2.57	114	.241	.318	10	.135	-2	9	9	-2	0.6
1914 StL-A	17	18	.486	44	35	20	5	2	302¹	265	6	100	111	11.2	2.50	108	.239	.307	15	.176	4	7	4	-0	0.7
1915 StL-A	9	17	.346	35	27	13	1	0	204	203	6	69	63	12.5	2.87	100	.274	.346	7	.113	-2	2	-0	-2	-0.3
1916 StL-A	0	0	—	1	0	0	0	0	4	4	0	4	0	18.0	9.00	31	.250	.400	0	—	0	-3	-3	-0	-0.2

(continued)

YEAR TM/L	W	L	PCT	G	GS	CG	SH	SV	IP	H	HR	BB	SO	RAT	ERA	ERA+	OAV	OOB	BH	AVG	PB	PR	/A	PD	TPI
Det-A	1	2	.333	5	5	3	0	0	37^1	34	0	22	7	14.5	2.65	108	.254	.375	1	.077	-1	1	1	1	0.1
StL-A	5	7	.417	22	12	3	0	0	91^1	97	2	26	25	12.3	3.05	90	.284	.339	0	.000	-1	-2	-3	-1	-0.5
Yr	6	9	.400	28	17	6	0	0	132^2	135	2	52	32	12.8	3.12	89	.273	.344	7	.189	-2	-4	-5	0	-0.6
1917 StL-A	0	9	.000	27	8	2	0	1	83	86	1	41	19	14.0	3.14	83	.274	.361	7	.368	3	-4	-5	-1	-0.2
1918 Pit-N	6	0	1.000	6	6	6	1	0	54	47	0	13	20	10.0	0.83	345	.242	.290	6	.286	1	12	12	-0	1.7
1919 Pit-N	8	11	.421	28	19	9	1	1	160^1	167	3	49	39	12.4	3.31	91	.280	.340	7	.135	-2	-7	-5	2	-0.5
1920 Pit-N	10	13	.435	39	23	12	0	3	230^1	223	2	69	74	11.5	3.24	99	.258	.314	10	.149	-3	-3	-1	-0	-0.3
1921 Pit-N	13	15	.464	35	30	12	2	0	225	237	5	58	59	12.1	3.36	114	.272	.323	12	.160	-0	11	12	4	1.5
1922 Pit-N	11	7	.611	33	14	9	1	2	160	183	6	40	34	12.6	3.99	102	.296	.339	9	.155	-2	2	1	-0	0.0
1923 Pit-N	7	9	.438	28	15	5	0	1	141	148	6	42	42	12.2	3.77	106	.271	.324	9	.173	-2	4	4	2	0.4
1924 Phi-N	0	1	.000	3	0	0	0	0	6	9	0	2	2	18.0	10.50	42	.391	.462	0	.000	-0	-4	-4	-0	-0.3
Total 14	116	147	.441	410	261	140	16	13	2342^2	2319	43	773	790	12.1	3.16	102	.264	.329	112	.153	-9	13	15	-2	1.6

■ JACK HAMILTON
Hamilton, Jack Edwin b: 12/25/38, Burlington, Iowa BR/TR, 6', 200 lbs. Deb: 4/13/62

YEAR TM/L	W	L	PCT	G	GS	CG	SH	SV	IP	H	HR	BB	SO	RAT	ERA	ERA+	OAV	OOB	BH	AVG	PB	PR	/A	PD	TPI
1962 Phi-N	9	12	.429	41	26	4	1	2	182	185	18	107	101	14.7	5.09	76	.268	.370	3	.056	-4	-23	-25	3	-2.4
1963 Phi-N	2	1	.667	19	1	0	0	1	30	22	3	17	23	11.7	5.40	60	.200	.307	0	.000	-0	-7	-7	1	-0.6
1964 Det-A	0	1	.000	5	1	0	0	0	15	24	2	8	5	19.8	8.40	44	.364	.440	0	.000	-0	-8	-8	1	-0.6
1965 Det-A	1	1	.500	4	1	0	0	0	4^1	6	1	4	3	20.8	14.54	24	.316	.435	0	—	0	-5	-5	0	-0.4
1966 NY-N	6	13	.316	57	13	3	1	13	148^2	138	13	88	93	14.0	3.93	92	.248	.356	5	.132	-1	-5	-5	1	-0.5
1967 NY-N	2	0	1.000	17	1	0	0	1	31^1	24	2	16	22	11.8	3.73	91	.205	.306	1	.200	1	-1	-1	-0	0.0
Cal-A	9	6	.600	26	20	0	0	0	119^1	104	6	63	74	12.7	3.24	97	.239	.337	6	.158	-0	-0	-1	-0	-0.1
1968 Cal-A	3	1	.750	21	2	1	0	2	38	34	0	15	18	11.6	3.32	88	.246	.320	1	.143	-0	-1	-2	-0	-0.1
1969 Cle-A	0	2	.000	20	0	0	0	1	30^2	37	2	23	13	17.6	4.40	86	.316	.429	0	.000	-0	-3	-2	-0	-0.2
Chi-A	0	3	.000	8	0	0	0	0	12^1	23	1	7	5	21.9	11.68	33	.411	.476	0	—	-0	-11	-11	-0	-0.9
Yr	0	5	.000	28	0	0	0	1	43	60	3	30	18	18.8	6.49	58	.345	.441	0	.000	-0	-14	-13	-0	-1.1
Total 8	32	40	.444	218	65	8	2	20	611^2	597	48	348	357	14.1	4.53	78	.259	.359	16	.107	-5	-66	-67	4	-5.8

■ JEFF HAMILTON
Hamilton, Jeffrey Robert b: 3/19/64, Flint, Mich. BR/TR, 6'3", 190 lbs. Deb: 6/28/86 ♦

YEAR TM/L	W	L	PCT	G	GS	CG	SH	SV	IP	H	HR	BB	SO	RAT	ERA	ERA+	OAV	OOB	BH	AVG	PB	PR	/A	PD	TPI
1989 LA-N	0	1	.000	1	0	0	0	0	1^2	2	0	1	2	16.2	5.40	63	.286	.375	134	.245	0	-0	-0	0	0.0

■ STEVE HAMILTON
Hamilton, Steve Absher b: 11/30/35, Columbia, Ky. BL/TL, 6'6", 190 lbs. Deb: 4/23/61 C

YEAR TM/L	W	L	PCT	G	GS	CG	SH	SV	IP	H	HR	BB	SO	RAT	ERA	ERA+	OAV	OOB	BH	AVG	PB	PR	/A	PD	TPI
1961 Cle-A	0	0	—	2	0	0	0	0	3	2	0	3	4	15.0	3.00	131	.200	.385	1	1.000	0	0	0	0	0.1
1962 Was-A	3	8	.273	41	10	1	0	2	107^1	103	10	39	83	12.2	3.77	107	.248	.317	2	.077	-1	2	3	1	0.3
1963 Was-A	0	1	.000	3	0	0	0	0	2	5	0	2	1	31.5	13.50	27	.556	.636	0	—	0	-2	-2	0	-0.1
*NY-A	5	1	.833	34	0	0	0	5	62^1	49	3	24	63	10.7	2.60	135	.220	.298	4	.286	1	7	6	0	0.9
Yr	5	2	.714	37	0	0	0	5	64^1	54	3	26	64	11.3	2.94	120	.232	.312	0	.000	1	5	4	1	0.8
1964 *NY-A	7	2	.778	30	3	1	0	3	60^1	55	6	15	49	10.4	3.28	110	.246	.293	4	.200	1	2	2	0	0.3
1965 NY-A	3	1	.750	46	1	0	0	5	58^1	47	2	16	51	9.7	1.39	245	.214	.267	1	.167	-0	13	13	-2	1.3
1966 NY-A	8	3	.727	44	3	1	1	3	90	69	8	22	57	9.4	3.00	111	.218	.276	1	.053	-1	4	3	-1	0.1
1967 NY-A	2	4	.333	44	0	0	0	4	62	57	7	23	55	11.8	3.48	90	.250	.321	0	.111	-0	-2	-2	0	-0.2
1968 NY-A	2	2	.500	40	0	0	0	11	50^2	37	0	13	42	9.1	2.13	136	.211	.270	0	.000	-0	5	4	0	0.5
1969 NY-A	3	4	.429	38	0	0	0	2	57	39	7	21	39	9.5	3.32	105	.194	.270	0	.000	-1	2	1	-1	0.0
1970 NY-A	4	3	.571	35	0	0	0	3	45^1	36	3	16	33	10.5	2.78	126	.222	.296	0	.000	-1	5	4	0	0.3
Chi-A	0	0	—	3	0	0	0	0	3	4	0	1	3	15.0	6.00	65	.333	.385	0	—	0	-1	-1	0	0.0
Yr	4	3	.571	38	0	0	0	3	48^1	40	3	17	36	10.6	2.98	119	.227	.295	0	.000	-1	4	3	0	0.3
1971 *SF-N	2	2	.500	39	0	0	0	4	44^2	29	4	11	38	8.3	3.02	112	.186	.244	0	.000	-0	2	2	0	0.1
1972 Chi-N	1	0	1.000	22	0	0	0	0	17	24	1	8	13	17.5	4.76	80	.333	.407	0	.000	-0	-2	-2	-0	-0.1
Total 12	40	31	.563	421	17	3	1	42	663	556	51	214	531	10.6	3.05	114	.229	.295	14	.125	-2	36	32	-2	3.5

■ LUKE HAMLIN
Hamlin, Luke Daniel "Hot Potato" b: 7/3/04, Ferris Center, Mich. d: 2/18/78, Clare, Mich. BL/TR, 6'2", 168 lbs. Deb: 9/18/33

YEAR TM/L	W	L	PCT	G	GS	CG	SH	SV	IP	H	HR	BB	SO	RAT	ERA	ERA+	OAV	OOB	BH	AVG	PB	PR	/A	PD	TPI
1933 Det-A	1	0	1.000	3	3	0	0	0	16^2	20	3	10	10	16.2	4.86	89	.294	.385	2	.400	1	-1	-1	-1	0.0
1934 Det-A	2	3	.400	20	5	1	0	1	75^1	87	11	44	30	15.7	5.38	82	.289	.380	6	.231	-0	-7	-8	-0	-0.7
1937 Bro-N	11	13	.458	39	25	11	1	1	185^2	183	4	48	93	11.2	3.59	113	.252	.298	11	.186	-1	7	9	-3	0.6
1938 Bro-N	12	15	.444	44	30	10	3	6	237^1	243	14	65	97	11.8	3.68	106	.263	.313	11	.141	-3	3	6	-4	0.0
1939 Bro-N	20	13	.606	40	36	19	2	0	269^2	255	27	54	88	10.3	3.64	111	.248	.285	13	.126	-5	8	12	-4	0.3
1940 Bro-N	9	8	.529	33	25	9	2	0	182^1	183	17	34	91	10.8	3.06	131	.256	.292	5	.086	-5	16	19	-4	1.1
1941 Bro-N	8	8	.500	30	20	5	1	1	136	139	14	41	58	12.0	4.24	87	.261	.316	6	.146	-1	-9	-9	-1	-1.0
1942 Pit-N	4	4	.500	23	14	6	1	0	112	128	3	19	38	11.9	3.94	86	.281	.312	9	.243	1	-8	-7	-2	-0.8
1944 Phi-A	6	12	.333	29	23	9	2	0	190	204	13	38	58	11.6	3.74	93	.271	.309	13	.232	3	-7	-6	-5	-0.6
Total 9	73	76	.490	261	181	70	12	9	1405	1442	106	353	563	11.6	3.77	103	.262	.308	76	.164	-9	2	16	-24	-1.1

■ PETE HAMM
Hamm, Peter Whitfield b: 9/20/47, Buffalo, N.Y. BR/TR, 6'5", 210 lbs. Deb: 7/29/70

YEAR TM/L	W	L	PCT	G	GS	CG	SH	SV	IP	H	HR	BB	SO	RAT	ERA	ERA+	OAV	OOB	BH	AVG	PB	PR	/A	PD	TPI
1970 Min-A	0	2	.000	10	0	0	0	0	16^1	17	3	7	3	13.2	5.51	68	.262	.333	0	.000	-0	-3	-3	-0	-0.3
1971 Min-A	2	4	.333	13	8	1	0	0	44	55	7	18	16	15.1	6.75	53	.309	.376	3	.273	1	-16	-16	0	-1.4
Total 2	2	6	.250	23	8	1	0	0	60^1	72	10	25	19	14.6	6.41	56	.296	.364	3	.250	1	-19	-19	0	-1.7

■ ATLEE HAMMAKER
Hammaker, Charlton Atlee b: 1/24/58, Carmel, Cal. BB/TL, 6'3", 200 lbs. Deb: 8/13/81

YEAR TM/L	W	L	PCT	G	GS	CG	SH	SV	IP	H	HR	BB	SO	RAT	ERA	ERA+	OAV	OOB	BH	AVG	PB	PR	/A	PD	TPI
1981 KC-A	1	3	.250	10	6	0	0	0	39	44	2	12	11	12.9	5.54	65	.286	.337	0	—	0	-8	-8	-0	-0.8
1982 SF-N	12	8	.600	29	27	4	1	0	175	189	16	28	102	11.3	4.11	87	.278	.309	4	.068	-4	-10	-10	1	-1.2
1983 SF-N	10	9	.526	23	23	8	3	0	172^1	147	9	32	127	9.5	2.25	157	.228	.267	6	.102	-1	26	25	0	2.6
1984 SF-N	2	0	1.000	6	6	0	0	0	33	32	2	9	24	11.2	2.18	161	.256	.306	2	.182	1	5	5	0	0.6
1985 SF-N	5	12	.294	29	29	1	1	0	170^2	161	17	47	100	11.0	3.74	92	.247	.298	4	.085	-2	-3	-6	1	-0.7
1987 *SF-N	10	10	.500	31	27	2	0	0	168^1	159	22	57	107	11.7	3.58	107	.248	.313	7	.123	-1	9	5	1	0.3
1988 SF-N	9	9	.500	43	17	3	1	5	144^2	136	11	41	65	11.2	3.73	87	.248	.304	4	.121	-0	-5	-8	2	-0.5
1989 *SF-N	6	6	.500	28	9	0	0	0	76^2	78	5	23	30	12.0	3.76	90	.271	.327	7	.368	2	-2	-3	-1	-0.1
1990 SF-N	4	5	.444	25	6	0	0	0	67^1	69	7	21	28	12.0	4.28	87	.273	.328	1	.059	-1	-4	-4	-0	-0.5
SD-N	0	4	.000	9	1	0	0	0	19^1	16	1	6	16	10.2	4.66	83	.213	.272	1	.500	-0	-2	-2	-0	-0.1
Yr	4	9	.308	34	7	0	0	0	86^2	85	8	27	44	11.6	4.36	86	.256	.312	1	.053	-0	-5	-6	-1	-0.6
Total 9	59	66	.472	233	151	18	6	5	1066^1	1031	92	276	610	11.1	3.60	98	.254	.303	36	.118	-7	8	-7	2	-0.4

■ CHRIS HAMMOND
Hammond, Christopher Andrew b: 1/21/66, Atlanta, Ga. BL/TL, 6'1", 190 lbs. Deb: 7/16/90

YEAR TM/L	W	L	PCT	G	GS	CG	SH	SV	IP	H	HR	BB	SO	RAT	ERA	ERA+	OAV	OOB	BH	AVG	PB	PR	/A	PD	TPI
1990 Cin-N	0	2	.000	3	3	0	0	0	11^1	13	2	12	4	19.9	6.35	61	.302	.455	0	.000	-0	-3	-3	0	-0.2

■ GRANNY HAMNER
Hamner, Granville Wilbur b: 4/26/27, Richmond, Va. BR/TR, 5'10", 163 lbs. Deb: 9/14/44 ♦

YEAR TM/L	W	L	PCT	G	GS	CG	SH	SV	IP	H	HR	BB	SO	RAT	ERA	ERA+	OAV	OOB	BH	AVG	PB	PR	/A	PD	TPI
1956 Phi-N	0	1	.000	3	1	0	0	0	8^1	10	0	2	4	13.0	4.32	86	.294	.333	90	.224	1	-1	-1	0	0.0
1957 Phi-N	0	0	—	1	0	0	0	0	1	1	0		1	9.0	0.00	—	.250	.250	114	.227	0	0	0	0	0.0
1962 KC-A	0	1	.000	3	0	0	0	0	4	10	0	6	0	36.0	9.00	46	.476	.593	0	—	0	-2	-2	0	-0.1
Total 3	0	2	.000	7	1	0	0	0	13^1	21	0	8	5	19.6	5.40	71	.356	.433	1529	.262	1	-2	-2	0	-0.1

■ RALPH HAMNER
Hamner, Ralph Conant "Bruz" b: 9/12/16, Gibsland, La. BR/TR, 6'3", 165 lbs. Deb: 4/28/46

YEAR TM/L	W	L	PCT	G	GS	CG	SH	SV	IP	H	HR	BB	SO	RAT	ERA	ERA+	OAV	OOB	BH	AVG	PB	PR	/A	PD	TPI
1946 Chi-A	2	7	.222	25	7	1	0	1	71^1	80	2	39	29	15.6	4.42	77	.276	.371	3	.167	0	-7	-8	-1	-0.8
1947 Chi-N	1	2	.333	3	3	2	0	0	25	24	0	16	14	14.4	2.52	157	.267	.377	1	.125	-0	4	4	-0	0.3
1948 Chi-N	5	9	.357	27	17	5	0	0	111^1	110	12	69	53	14.9	4.69	83	.259	.369	6	.182	1	-9	-10	-2	-0.6
1949 Chi-N	0	2	.000	6	1	0	0	0	12^1	22	1	8	3	22.6	8.76	46	.407	.492	0	.000	-0	-6	-6	1	-0.4
Total 4	8	20	.286	61	28	8	0	1	220	236	15	132	99	15.5	4.58	82	.275	.378	10	.164	0	-18	-20	2	-1.5

YEAR	TM/L	W	L	PCT	G	GS	CG	SH	SV	IP	H	HR	BB	SO	RAT	ERA	ERA+	OAV	OOB	BH	AVG	PB	PR	/A	PD	TPI

■ GARRY HANCOCK Hancock, Ronald Garry b: 1/23/54, Tampa, Fla. BL/TL, 6', 175 lbs. Deb: 7/16/78 ♦

| 1984 | Oak-A | 0 | 0 | — | 1 | 0 | 0 | 0 | 0 | 1¹ | 0 | 0 | 0 | 0 | 0.0 | 0.00 | — | .000 | .000 | 13 | .217 | 0 | 1 | 1 | 0 | 0.1 |

■ RICH HAND Hand, Richard Allen b: 7/10/48, Bellevue, Wash. BR/TR, 6'1", 195 lbs. Deb: 4/09/70

1970	Cle-A	6	13	.316	35	25	3	1	3	159²	132	27	69	110	11.6	3.83	103	.228	.314	6	.146	-1	-2	2	0	0.2
1971	Cle-A	2	6	.250	15	12	0	0	0	60²	74	6	38	26	17.2	5.79	66	.311	.414	2	.125	-1	-16	-13	-1	-1.4
1972	Tex-A	10	14	.417	30	28	2	1	0	170²	139	12	103	109	12.9	3.32	91	.226	.340	8	.154	1	-5	-6	-0	-0.5
1973	Tex-A	2	3	.400	8	7	1	0	0	41²	49	2	19	14	15.1	5.40	69	.290	.368	0	—	0	-7	-8	-0	-0.7
	Cal-A	4	3	.571	16	6	0	0	0	54²	58	5	21	19	13.2	3.62	98	.274	.342	0	—	0	1	-0	1	0.0
	Yr	6	6	.500	24	13	1	0	0	96¹	107	7	40	33	13.8	4.39	82	.277	.347	0	—	0	-6	-8	1	-0.7
Total 4		24	39	.381	104	78	6	2	3	487¹	452	52	250	278	13.2	4.01	88	.249	.345	16	.147	-1	-29	-25	-0	-2.4

■ JIM HANDIBOE Handiboe, James Edward "Nick" b: 7/17/1866, Columbus, Ohio d: 11/8/42, Columbus, Ohio BR/TR, 5'11", 160 lbs. Deb: 5/28/1886

| 1886 | Pit-a | 7 | 7 | .500 | 14 | 14 | 12 | 1 | 0 | 114 | 82 | 1 | 33 | 83 | 9.1 | 3.32 | 102 | .192 | .250 | 5 | .114 | -2 | 2 | 1 | -1 | -0.1 |

■ VERN HANDRAHAN Handrahan, James Vernon b: 11/27/38, Charlottetown, P.E.I., Canada BL/TL, 6'2", 185 lbs. Deb: 4/14/64

1964	KC-A	0	1	.000	18	1	0	0	0	35²	33	9	25	18	15.1	6.06	63	.252	.380	2	.222	0	-10	-9	0	-0.8
1966	KC-A	0	1	.000	16	1	0	0	1	25¹	20	5	15	18	12.8	4.26	80	.227	.346	0	.000	-0	-2	-2	0	-0.2
Total 2		0	2	.000	34	2	0	0	1	61	53	14	40	36	14.2	5.31	69	.242	.366	2	.167	-0	-12	-11	0	-1.0

■ BILL HANDS Hands, William Alfred b: 5/6/40, Hackensack, N.J. BR/TR, 6'2", 185 lbs. Deb: 6/03/65

1965	SF-N	0	2	.000	4	2	0	0	0	6	13	0	6	5	28.5	16.50	22	.433	.528	0	.000	-0	-9	-9	0	-0.7
1966	Chi-N	8	13	.381	41	26	0	0	2	159	168	17	59	93	13.1	4.58	80	.272	.340	2	.041	-3	-17	-16	2	-1.7
1967	Chi-N	7	8	.467	49	11	3	1	6	150	134	9	48	84	11.0	2.46	144	.239	.301	4	.105	-1	15	18	0	1.9
1968	Chi-N	16	10	.615	38	34	11	4	0	258²	221	26	36	148	9.2	2.89	109	.231	.264	5	.061	-5	3	8	-0	0.4
1969	Chi-N	20	14	.588	41	41	18	3	0	300	268	21	73	181	10.4	2.49	162	.237	.287	9	.092	-5	37	51	2	5.5
1970	Chi-N	18	15	.545	39	38	12	2	1	265	278	20	76	170	12.2	3.70	122	.269	.322	10	.133	1	10	24	2	2.8
1971	Chi-N	12	18	.400	36	35	14	1	0	242¹	248	27	50	128	11.1	3.42	115	.260	.298	6	.083	-3	1	14	0	1.3
1972	Chi-N	11	8	.579	32	28	6	3	0	189	168	12	47	96	10.3	3.00	127	.237	.286	1	.018	-5	10	17	-1	1.2
1973	Min-A	7	10	.412	39	15	3	1	2	142	138	14	41	78	11.5	3.49	114	.252	.307	0	—	0	5	7	-1	0.7
1974	Min-A	4	5	.444	35	10	0	0	3	115¹	130	9	25	74	12.4	4.45	84	.284	.327	0	—	0	-11	-9	-1	-0.9
	Tex-A	2	0	1.000	2	2	1	1	0	14	11	0	3	4	9.0	1.93	185	.208	.250	0	—	0	3	3	0	0.3
	Yr	6	5	.545	37	12	1	1	3	129¹	141	9	28	78	11.8	4.18	89	.274	.311	0	—	0	-8	-6	-1	-0.6
1975	Tex-A	6	7	.462	18	18	4	1	0	109²	118	12	28	67	12.2	4.02	93	.271	.319	0	—	0	-3	-3	-0	-0.2
Total 11		111	110	.502	374	260	72	17	14	1951	1895	167	492	1128	11.2	3.35	114	.253	.302	37	.078	-21	44	104	2	10.6

■ DON HANKINS Hankins, Donald Wayne b: 2/9/02, Pendleton, Ind. d: 5/16/63, Winston-Salem, N.C BR/TR, 6'3", 183 lbs. Deb: 4/23/27

| 1927 | Det-A | 2 | 1 | .667 | 20 | 1 | 0 | 0 | 2 | 42² | 67 | 1 | 13 | 10 | 16.9 | 6.33 | 67 | .383 | .426 | 1 | .143 | -1 | -10 | -10 | 0 | -0.9 |

■ FRANK HANKINSON Hankinson, Frank Edward b: 4/29/1856, New York, N.Y. d: 4/5/11, Palisades Park, N.J BR/TR, 5'11", 168 lbs. Deb: 5/01/1878 ♦

1878	Chi-N	0	1	.000	1	1	1	0	0	9	11	0	4	4	11.0	6.00	40	.287	.287	64	.267	-0	-4	-4	-0	-0.2
1879	Chi-N	15	10	.600	26	25	25	2	0	230²	248	6	27	69	10.7	2.50	103	.257	.278	31	.181	-4	-0	2	4	0.0
1880	Cle-N	1	1	.500	4	2	2	0	1	25	20	0	3	8	8.1	1.08	218	.208	.232	55	.209	-0	4	4	1	0.4
1885	NY-a	0	0	—	1	0	0	0	0	2	2	1	1	0	13.5	4.50	66	.249	.332	81	.224	-0	-0	-0	0	0.0
Total 4		16	12	.571	32	28	28	2	1	266²	281	1	31	81	10.5	2.50	102	.254	.274	747	.228	-4	-0	1	5	0.2

■ JIM HANLEY Hanley, James Patrick b: 10/13/1885, Providence, R.I. d: 5/1/61, Elmhurst, N.J. BR/TL, 5'11", 165 lbs. Deb: 7/03/13

| 1913 | NY-A | 0 | 0 | — | 1 | 0 | 0 | 0 | 0 | 4 | 5 | 0 | 4 | 2 | 20.3 | 6.75 | 44 | .313 | .450 | 0 | .000 | -0 | -2 | -2 | 0 | -0.1 |

■ PRESTON HANNA Hanna, Preston Lee b: 9/10/54, Pensacola, Fla. BR/TR, 6'1", 195 lbs. Deb: 9/13/75

1975	Atl-N	0	0	—	4	0	0	0	0	5²	7	0	5	2	22.2	1.59	238	.304	.467	0	—	0	1	1	-0	0.1
1976	Atl-N	0	0	—	5	0	0	0	0	8	11	0	4	3	16.9	4.50	84	.333	.405	0	.000	-0	-1	-1	-0	0.0
1977	Atl-N	2	6	.250	17	9	1	0	0	60	69	6	34	37	15.8	4.95	90	.285	.378	1	.071	0	-7	-3	1	-0.1
1978	Atl-N	7	13	.350	29	28	0	0	0	140¹	132	10	93	90	14.6	5.13	79	.251	.367	9	.184	1	-24	-17	-0	-1.5
1979	Atl-N	1	1	.500	6	4	0	0	0	24¹	27	1	15	15	15.5	2.96	137	.284	.382	0	.000	0	2	3	1	0.4
1980	Atl-N	0	1	.000	32	2	0	0	0	79¹	63	3	44	35	12.5	3.18	118	.224	.335	2	.143	0	4	5	-1	0.5
1981	Atl-N	2	1	.667	20	1	0	0	0	35¹	45	2	23	22	17.3	6.37	56	.341	.439	1	.250	0	-11	-11	2	-0.8
1982	Atl-N	3	0	1.000	20	1	0	0	0	36	36	8	28	17	16.0	3.75	99	.277	.405	2	.400	1	-1	-0	-1	0.0
	Oak-A	0	4	.000	23	2	1	0	0	48¹	54	3	33	32	16.4	5.59	70	.287	.396	0	—	0	-8	-9	-1	-0.8
Total 8		17	25	.405	156	47	2	0	1	437¹	444	28	279	253	15.1	4.61	86	.269	.378	15	.161	1	-45	-31	2	-2.2

■ GERRY HANNAHS Hannahs, Gerald Ellis b: 3/6/53, Binghamton, N.Y. BL/TL, 6'3", 210 lbs. Deb: 9/08/76

1976	Mon-N	2	0	1.000	3	3	0	0	0	16	20	2	12	10	18.0	6.75	55	.323	.432	3	.375	1	-6	-5	-0	-0.4
1977	Mon-N	1	5	.167	8	7	0	0	0	37	43	7	17	21	14.6	4.86	78	.291	.364	0	.000	-0	-4	-4	-0	-0.4
1978	LA-N	0	0	—	1	0	0	0	0	2	3	0	0	5	13.5	9.00	39	.333	.333	—	—	0	-1	-1	0	0.0
1979	LA-N	0	2	.000	4	2	0	0	1	16	10	2	13	6	12.9	3.38	108	.175	.329	1	.250	0	1	0	0	0.1
Total 4		3	7	.300	16	12	0	0	1	71	76	11	42	42	15.0	5.07	74	.275	.371	4	.211	1	-10	-10	-0	-0.7

■ JIM HANNAN Hannan, James John b: 1/7/40, Jersey City, N.J. BR/TR, 6'3", 205 lbs. Deb: 4/17/62

1962	Was-A	2	4	.333	42	3	0	0	4	68	56	6	49	39	13.9	3.31	122	.230	.360	1	.091	-1	5	5	0	0.5
1963	Was-A	2	2	.500	13	2	0	0	0	27²	23	2	17	14	13.0	4.88	76	.228	.339	0	.000	-0	-4	-4	0	-0.3
1964	Was-A	4	7	.364	49	7	0	0	3	106	108	13	45	67	13.0	4.16	89	.266	.339	3	.150	-1	-6	-5	-1	-0.4
1965	Was-A	1	1	.500	4	1	1	1	0	14²	18	0	6	5	15.3	4.91	71	.340	.417	0	.000	-0	-2	-2	0	-0.2
1966	Was-A	3	9	.250	30	18	2	0	0	114	125	9	59	68	14.8	4.26	81	.288	.377	2	.067	-2	-10	-10	-0	-1.1
1967	Was-A	1	1	.500	8	2	0	0	0	21²	28	3	7	14	15.0	5.40	59	.315	.371	0	.000	-0	-5	-5	0	-0.5
1968	Was-A	10	6	.625	25	22	4	1	0	140¹	147	4	50	75	12.9	3.01	97	.272	.338	3	.064	-2	-1	-2	-0	-0.3
1969	Was-A	7	6	.538	35	28	1	1	0	158¹	138	17	91	72	13.1	3.64	95	.238	.343	6	.115	-2	-0	-3	-0	-0.5
1970	Was-A	9	11	.450	42	17	1	1	0	128	119	17	54	61	12.2	4.01	89	.250	.338	4	.129	-0	-4	-6	1	-0.5
1971	Det-A	1	0	1.000	7	0	0	0	0	11	7	1	7	6	12.3	3.27	110	.189	.333	0	.000	0	0	1	0	0.1
	Mil-A	1	1	.500	21	1	0	0	0	32¹	38	7	21	17	16.7	5.01	69	.295	.397	0	.000	-0	-6	-6	1	-0.6
	Yr	2	1	.667	28	1	0	0	0	43¹	45	8	28	23	15.4	4.57	77	.269	.378	0	.000	-1	-5	-5	1	-0.5
Total 10		41	48	.461	276	101	9	4	7	822	807	79	406	438	13.4	3.88	89	.261	.350	19	.091	-9	-34	-38	1	-4.0

■ LOY HANNING Hanning, Loy Vernon b: 10/18/17, Bunker, Mo. d: 6/24/86, Anaconda, Mo. BR/TR, 6'2", 175 lbs. Deb: 9/20/39

1939	StL-A	0	1	.000	4	1	0	0	0	10	6	1	4	8	9.0	3.60	135	.158	.238	0	—	-0	1	1	0	0.1
1942	StL-A	1	1	.500	11	0	0	0	0	17¹	26	2	12	9	20.3	7.79	48	.356	.453	1	.250	0	-8	-8	1	-0.6
Total 2		1	2	.333	15	1	0	0	0	27¹	32	3	16	17	16.1	6.26	66	.288	.383	1	.200	-0	-7	-6	1	-0.5

■ ANDY HANSEN Hansen, Andrew Viggo "Swede" b: 11/12/24, Lake Worth, Fla. BR/TR, 6'3", 185 lbs. Deb: 6/30/44

1944	NY-N	3	3	.500	23	4	0	0	1	52²	63	3	32	15	16.7	6.49	56	.301	.402	2	.167	0	-17	-17	1	-1.4
1945	NY-N	3	5	.571	23	13	4	0	3	92²	98	7	28	37	12.4	4.66	84	.273	.329	0	.000	-3	-9	-8	2	-0.8
1947	NY-N	1	5	.167	27	9	0	0	3	82¹	78	8	38	18	12.7	4.37	93	.248	.330	4	.190	-0	-3	-3	-1	-0.1
1948	NY-N	5	3	.625	36	9	3	0	1	100	96	4	36	27	11.9	2.97	133	.255	.320	1	.050	-1	11	11	-1	1.0
1949	NY-N	2	6	.250	33	2	0	0	1	66¹	58	7	28	26	11.7	4.61	86	.234	.312	0	.000	-1	-4	-5	0	-0.4
1950	NY-N	0	1	.000	31	1	0	0	0	57	64	8	26	19	14.4	5.53	74	.279	.355	0	.000	-1	-9	-9	-0	-0.9

YEAR	TM/L	W	L	PCT	G	GS	CG	SH	SV	IP	H	HR	BB	SO	RAT	ERA	ERA+	OAV	OOB	BH	AVG	PB	PR	/A	PD	TPI
1951	Phi-N	3	1	.750	24	0	0	0	0	39	34	4	7	11	9.7	2.54	152	.228	.268	1	.333	1	6	6	1	0.8
1952	Phi-N	5	6	.455	43	0	0	0	4	77¹	76	6	27	18	12.3	3.26	112	.259	.328	2	.182	1	4	3	1	0.6
1953	Phi-N	0	2	.000	30	1	0	0	3	51¹	60	6	24	17	14.9	4.03	104	.296	.373	2	.286	0	1	1	1	0.2
Total	9	23	30	.434	270	39	8	0	16	618²	627	53	246	188	12.9	4.22	93	.263	.335	12	.102	-3	-19	-20	6	-1.0

■ **SNIPE HANSEN**   Hansen, Roy Emil Frederick   b: 2/21/07, Chicago, Ill.   d: 9/11/78, Chicago, Ill.   BB/TL, 6'3", 195 lbs.   Deb: 7/05/30

YEAR	TM/L	W	L	PCT	G	GS	CG	SH	SV	IP	H	HR	BB	SO	RAT	ERA	ERA+	OAV	OOB	BH	AVG	PB	PR	/A	PD	TPI
1930	Phi-N	0	7	.000	22	9	1	0	0	84¹	123	8	38	25	17.4	6.72	81	.364	.431	3	.111	-3	-16	-12	-1	-1.2
1932	Phi-N	10	10	.500	39	23	5	0	2	191	215	13	51	56	12.8	3.72	118	.278	.328	8	.127	-4	3	15	-2	1.0
1933	Phi-N	6	14	.300	32	22	8	0	1	168¹	199	12	30	47	12.5	4.44	86	.294	.328	9	.155	-3	-21	-12	-1	-1.4
1934	Phi-N	6	12	.333	50	16	5	2	3	151	194	15	61	40	15.4	5.42	87	.307	.371	10	.233	-0	-23	-12	1	-0.8
1935	Phi-N	0	1	.000	2	1	0	0	0	4¹	8	0	5	0	27.0	12.46	36	.421	.542	0	.000	-0	-4	-4	0	-0.3
	StL-A	0	1	.000	10	0	0	0	0	26²	44	2	9	8	18.2	8.78	55	.364	.412	1	.143	-1	-13	-12	-0	-1.0
Total	5	22	45	.328	155	71	19	2	6	625²	783	50	194	176	14.3	5.01	90	.306	.358	31	.155	-10	-73	-36	-2	-3.7

■ **ROY HANSEN**   Hansen, Roy Inglof "Ing"   b: 3/6/1898, Beloit, Wis.   d: 2/9/77, Beloit, Wis.   BR/TR, 6', 165 lbs.   Deb: 5/28/18

YEAR	TM/L	W	L	PCT	G	GS	CG	SH	SV	IP	H	HR	BB	SO	RAT	ERA	ERA+	OAV	OOB	BH	AVG	PB	PR	/A	PD	TPI
1918	Was-A	1	0	1.000	5	0	0	0	0	9	10	0	3	2	14.0	3.00	91	.278	.350	0	—	0	-0	-0	0	0.0

■ **F. C. HANSFORD**   Hansford, F. C.   TL , 6', 180 lbs.   Deb: 6/09/1898

YEAR	TM/L	W	L	PCT	G	GS	CG	SH	SV	IP	H	HR	BB	SO	RAT	ERA	ERA+	OAV	OOB	BH	AVG	PB	PR	/A	PD	TPI
1898	Bro-N	0	0	—	1	0	0	0	0	7	10	0	5	0	19.3	3.86	93	.332	.428	0	.000	-1	-0	-0	-0	0.0

■ **DON HANSKI**   Hanski, Donald Thomas (b: Donald Thomas Hanyzewski)   b: 2/27/16, Laporte, Ind.   d: 9/2/57, Worth, Ill.   BL/TL, 5'11", 180 lbs.   Deb: 5/06/43   ♦

YEAR	TM/L	W	L	PCT	G	GS	CG	SH	SV	IP	H	HR	BB	SO	RAT	ERA	ERA+	OAV	OOB	BH	AVG	PB	PR	/A	PD	TPI
1943	Chi-A	0	0	—	1	0	0	0	0	1	1	0	1	0	18.0	0.00	—	.333	.500	5	.238	0	0	0	0	0.0
1944	Chi-A	0	0	—	2	0	0	0	0	3	5	0	2	0	21.0	12.00	29	.357	.438	0	.000	-0	-3	-3	0	-0.2
Total	2	0	0	—	3	0	0	0	0	4	6	0	3	0	20.3	9.00	38	.353	.450	5	.227	-0	-2	-2	0	-0.2

■ **OLLIE HANSON**   Hanson, Earl Sylvester   b: 1/19/1896, Holbrook, Mass.   d: 8/19/51, Clifton, N.J.   BR/TR, 5'11", 178 lbs.   Deb: 4/27/21

YEAR	TM/L	W	L	PCT	G	GS	CG	SH	SV	IP	H	HR	BB	SO	RAT	ERA	ERA+	OAV	OOB	BH	AVG	PB	PR	/A	PD	TPI
1921	Chi-N	0	2	.000	2	2	1	0	0	9	9	0	6	2	16.0	7.00	55	.265	.390	0	.000	-0	-3	-3	0	-0.2

■ **ERIK HANSON**   Hanson, Erik Brian   b: 5/18/65, Kinnelon, N.J.   BR/TR, 6'6", 210 lbs.   Deb: 9/05/88

YEAR	TM/L	W	L	PCT	G	GS	CG	SH	SV	IP	H	HR	BB	SO	RAT	ERA	ERA+	OAV	OOB	BH	AVG	PB	PR	/A	PD	TPI
1988	Sea-A	2	3	.400	6	6	0	0	0	41²	35	4	12	36	10.4	3.24	128	.230	.291	0	—	0	3	4	-0	0.4
1989	Sea-A	9	5	.643	17	17	1	0	0	113¹	103	7	32	75	11.1	3.18	127	.243	.304	0	—	0	9	11	0	1.1
1990	Sea-A	18	9	.667	33	33	5	1	0	236	205	15	68	211	10.5	3.24	122	.232	.289	0	—	0	17	19	-1	1.9
Total	3	29	17	.630	56	56	6	1	0	391	343	26	112	322	10.7	3.22	124	.235	.293	0	—	0	30	34	-1	3.4

■ **ED HANYZEWSKI**   Hanyzewski, Edward Michael   b: 9/18/20, Union Mills, Ind.   BR/TR, 6'1", 200 lbs.   Deb: 5/12/42

YEAR	TM/L	W	L	PCT	G	GS	CG	SH	SV	IP	H	HR	BB	SO	RAT	ERA	ERA+	OAV	OOB	BH	AVG	PB	PR	/A	PD	TPI
1942	Chi-N	1	1	.500	6	1	0	0	0	19	17	2	8	6	11.8	3.79	84	.254	.333	1	.200	-0	-1	-1	0	0.0
1943	Chi-N	8	7	.533	33	16	3	0	0	130	120	2	45	55	11.6	2.56	130	.243	.309	2	.049	-4	12	11	2	0.9
1944	Chi-N	2	5	.286	14	7	3	0	0	58¹	61	6	20	19	12.7	4.47	79	.261	.322	1	.059	-1	-6	-6	3	-0.3
1945	Chi-N	0	0	—	2	1	0	0	0	4²	7	1	1	0	15.4	5.79	63	.350	.381	0	.000	-0	-1	-1	0	0.0
1946	Chi-N	1	0	1.000	3	0	0	0	0	6	8	0	5	1	21.0	4.50	74	.348	.483	0	.000	-0	-1	-1	0	0.0
Total	5	12	13	.480	58	25	6	0	0	218	213	11	79	81	12.2	3.30	102	.254	.321	4	.062	-5	4	2	5	0.6

■ **MEL HARDER**   Harder, Melvin Leroy "Chief"   b: 10/15/09, Beemer, Neb.   BR/TR, 6'1", 195 lbs.   Deb: 4/24/28   MC

YEAR	TM/L	W	L	PCT	G	GS	CG	SH	SV	IP	H	HR	BB	SO	RAT	ERA	ERA+	OAV	OOB	BH	AVG	PB	PR	/A	PD	TPI
1928	Cle-A	0	2	.000	23	1	0	0	1	49	64	4	32	15	17.6	6.61	63	.335	.430	0	.000	-1	-14	-13	-1	-1.4
1929	Cle-A	1	0	1.000	11	0	0	0	0	17²	24	2	5	4	16.3	5.60	79	.333	.400	0	.000	-0	-3	-2	-0	-0.2
1930	Cle-A	11	10	.524	36	19	7	0	2	175¹	205	9	68	44	14.2	4.21	115	.295	.361	9	.143	-4	9	12	-1	0.7
1931	Cle-A	13	14	.481	40	24	9	0	1	194	229	8	72	63	14.2	4.36	106	.289	.352	19	.253	1	0	6	1	0.7
1932	Cle-A	15	13	.536	39	32	17	1	0	254²	277	9	68	90	12.3	3.75	127	.272	.319	17	.181	-0	21	28	3	3.0
1933	Cle-A	15	17	.469	43	31	14	2	4	253	254	10	67	81	11.5	2.95	151	.259	.309	16	.190	-1	37	42	8	5.0
1934	Cle-A	20	12	.625	44	29	17	6	4	255¹	246	6	81	91	11.8	2.61	174	.254	.316	14	.161	-1	54	55	2	5.5
1935	Cle-A	22	11	.667	42	35	17	4	2	287¹	313	6	53	95	11.5	3.29	137	.275	.307	21	.206	-1	37	39	5	4.2
1936	Cle-A	15	15	.500	36	30	13	0	1	224²	294	13	71	84	14.9	5.17	97	.313	.365	11	.138	-4	-3	-3	-0	-0.5
1937	Cle-A	15	12	.556	38	30	13	0	2	233²	269	9	86	95	13.8	4.28	108	.288	.350	15	.174	-1	9	9	2	0.8
1938	Cle-A	17	10	.630	38	29	15	2	4	240	257	16	62	102	12.2	3.83	121	.271	.319	10	.114	-5	26	22	3	1.8
1939	Cle-A	15	9	.625	29	26	12	1	1	208	213	15	64	67	12.1	3.50	126	.269	.326	10	.139	-1	26	21	-1	1.7
1940	Cle-A	12	11	.522	31	25	5	0	0	186¹	200	16	59	76	12.8	4.06	104	.278	.337	11	.177	-1	7	3	1	0.4
1941	Cle-A	5	4	.556	15	10	1	0	1	68²	76	3	27	21	15.1	5.24	75	.279	.370	2	.080	-2	-8	-10	1	-0.9
1942	Cle-A	13	14	.481	29	29	13	4	0	198²	179	8	82	74	12.0	3.44	100	.240	.317	8	.119	-3	5	0	-1	-0.1
1943	Cle-A	8	7	.533	19	18	6	1	0	135¹	126	7	61	40	12.5	3.06	102	.254	.337	10	.213	1	4	1	0	0.2
1944	Cle-A	12	10	.545	30	27	12	2	0	196¹	211	5	69	64	13.0	3.71	89	.278	.341	16	.216	1	-6	-9	-0	-0.8
1945	Cle-A	3	7	.300	11	11	2	0	0	76	93	4	23	16	13.7	3.67	88	.303	.352	2	.080	-2	-3	-4	-1	-0.4
1946	Cle-A	5	4	.556	13	12	4	1	0	92¹	85	4	31	21	11.3	3.41	97	.249	.311	3	.086	-2	1	-1	-1	-0.4
1947	Cle-A	6	4	.600	15	15	4	1	0	80	91	3	27	17	13.4	4.50	77	.289	.347	5	.179	-0	-7	-9	-1	-0.9
Total	20	223	186	.545	582	433	181	25	23	3426¹	3706	161	1118	1160	12.8	3.80	113	.276	.334	199	.165	-27	190	182	22	18.4

■ **JIM HARDIN**   Hardin, James Warren   b: 8/6/43, Morris Chapel, Tenn.   BR/TR, 6', 175 lbs.   Deb: 6/23/67

YEAR	TM/L	W	L	PCT	G	GS	CG	SH	SV	IP	H	HR	BB	SO	RAT	ERA	ERA+	OAV	OOB	BH	AVG	PB	PR	/A	PD	TPI
1967	Bal-A	8	3	.727	19	14	5	2	0	111	85	5	27	64	9.2	2.27	139	.211	.265	5	.135	-0	12	11	-1	1.1
1968	Bal-A	18	13	.581	35	35	16	2	0	244	188	20	70	160	9.9	2.51	117	.212	.277	3	.085	-3	13	11	0	0.9
1969	Bal-A	6	7	.462	30	20	3	1	1	137²	128	18	43	64	11.6	3.60	99	.248	.313	7	.156	2	0	-0	-1	0.0
1970	Bal-A	6	5	.545	36	19	3	2	1	145¹	150	13	26	78	11.0	3.53	103	.267	.301	3	.067	-1	3	2	-1	0.0
1971	Bal-A	0	0	—	6	0	0	0	0	5²	12	0	3	2	23.8	4.76	70	.480	.536	0	—	0	-1	-1	0	0.0
	NY-A	0	2	.000	12	3	0	0	0	28¹	35	3	9	14	14.3	5.08	64	.313	.369	0	—	0	-5	-6	-0	-0.6
	Yr	0	2	.000	18	3	0	0	0	34	47	3	12	17	15.9	5.03	65	.343	.400	0	.000	-0	-6	-7	-0	-0.6
1972	Atl-N	5	2	.714	26	9	1	0	2	79²	93	11	24	25	13.4	4.41	86	.287	.340	2	.095	1	-8	-5	-0	-0.4
Total	6	43	32	.573	164	100	28	7	4	751²	691	70	202	408	11.0	3.18	104	.244	.300	24	.103	-3	14	11	-3	1.0

■ **CHARLIE HARDING**   Harding, Charles Harold "Slim"   b: 1/3/1891, Nashville, Tenn.   d: 10/30/71, Bold Srpings, Tenn   BR/TR, 6'2.5", 172 lbs.   Deb: 9/18/13

YEAR	TM/L	W	L	PCT	G	GS	CG	SH	SV	IP	H	HR	BB	SO	RAT	ERA	ERA+	OAV	OOB	BH	AVG	PB	PR	/A	PD	TPI
1913	Det-A	0	0	—	1	0	0	0	0	2	3	0	1	0	18.0	4.50	65	.375	.444	0	—	0	-0	-0	0	0.0

■ **ALEX HARDY**   Hardy, David Alexander "Dooney"   b: 1877, Toronto, Ont., Canada   d: 4/22/40, Toronto, Ont., Can.   TL ,   Deb: 9/04/02

YEAR	TM/L	W	L	PCT	G	GS	CG	SH	SV	IP	H	HR	BB	SO	RAT	ERA	ERA+	OAV	OOB	BH	AVG	PB	PR	/A	PD	TPI
1902	Chi-N	2	2	.500	4	4	4	1	0	35	29	0	12	12	10.5	3.60	75	.226	.292	3	.214	0	-3	-3	-1	-0.3
1903	Chi-N	1	1	.500	3	3	1	0	0	12²	21	0	7	4	20.6	6.39	49	.375	.453	1	.167	0	-4	-5	1	-0.3
Total	2	3	3	.500	7	7	5	1	0	47²	50	0	19	16	13.2	4.34	65	.271	.342	4	.200	1	-8	-8	-0	-0.6

■ **RED HARDY**   Hardy, Francis Joseph   b: 1/6/23, Marmarth, N.Dak.   BR/TR, 5'11", 175 lbs.   Deb: 6/20/51

YEAR	TM/L	W	L	PCT	G	GS	CG	SH	SV	IP	H	HR	BB	SO	RAT	ERA	ERA+	OAV	OOB	BH	AVG	PB	PR	/A	PD	TPI
1951	NY-N	0	0	—	2	0	0	0	0	1¹	4	0	1	0	40.5	6.75	58	.571	.667	0	—	0	-0	-0	0	0.0

■ **HARRY HARDY**   Hardy, Harry   b: 11/5/1875, Steubenville, Ohio   d: 9/4/43, Steubenville, Ohio   BL/TL, 5'6", 155 lbs.   Deb: 9/26/05

YEAR	TM/L	W	L	PCT	G	GS	CG	SH	SV	IP	H	HR	BB	SO	RAT	ERA	ERA+	OAV	OOB	BH	AVG	PB	PR	/A	PD	TPI
1905	Was-A	1	1	.500	3	2	2	0	0	24	20	0	6	10	9.8	1.88	141	.228	.277	1	.111	-1	2	2	-1	0.0
1906	Was-A	0	3	.000	5	3	2	0	0	20	35	0	12	4	21.1	9.00	29	.385	.457	0	.000	-1	-14	-14	1	-1.2
Total	2	1	4	.200	8	5	4	0	0	44	55	0	18	14	14.9	5.11	52	.308	.371	1	.067	-1	-12	-12	-0	-1.2

■ **LARRY HARDY**   Hardy, Howard Lawrence   b: 1/10/48, Goose Creek, Tex.   BR/TR, 5'10", 180 lbs.   Deb: 4/28/74

YEAR	TM/L	W	L	PCT	G	GS	CG	SH	SV	IP	H	HR	BB	SO	RAT	ERA	ERA+	OAV	OOB	BH	AVG	PB	PR	/A	PD	TPI
1974	SD-N	9	4	.692	76	1	0	0	2	101²	129	9	44	57	15.3	4.69	76	.317	.384	0	.000	-1	-12	-13	1	-1.2
1975	SD-N	0	0	—	3	0	0	0	0	2²	8	3	2	3	33.8	13.50	26	.500	.556	0	—	0	-3	-3	-0	-0.2
1976	Hou-N	0	0	—	15	0	0	0	3	21²	34	2	10	10	18.3	7.06	45	.362	.423	0	.000	-0	-9	-9	0	-0.9

YEAR TM/L	W	L	PCT	G	GS	CG	SH	SV	IP	H	HR	BB	SO	RAT	ERA	ERA+	OAV	OOB	BH	AVG	PB	PR	/A	PD	TPI
Total 3	9	4	.692	94	1	0	0	5	126	171	14	56	70	16.2	5.29	66	.331	.396	0	.000	-1	-24	-25	1	-2.3

■ JACK HARDY   Hardy, John Graydon b: 10/8/59, St.Petersburg, Fla. BR/TR, 6'2", 175 lbs. Deb: 5/23/89

YEAR TM/L	W	L	PCT	G	GS	CG	SH	SV	IP	H	HR	BB	SO	RAT	ERA	ERA+	OAV	OOB	BH	AVG	PB	PR	/A	PD	TPI
1989 Chi-A	0	0	—	5	0	0	0	0	12¹	14	1	5	4	14.6	6.57	58	.286	.364	0	—	0	-4	-4	1	-0.2

■ STEVE HARGAN   Hargan, Steven Lowell b: 9/8/42, Ft.Wayne, Ind. BR/TR, 6'3", 170 lbs. Deb: 8/03/65

YEAR TM/L	W	L	PCT	G	GS	CG	SH	SV	IP	H	HR	BB	SO	RAT	ERA	ERA+	OAV	OOB	BH	AVG	PB	PR	/A	PD	TPI
1965 Cle-A	4	3	.571	17	8	1	0	2	60¹	55	2	28	37	12.5	3.43	101	.246	.332	1	.053	-1	0	0	1	0.0
1966 Cle-A	13	10	.565	38	21	7	3	0	192	173	9	45	132	10.3	2.48	138	.241	.286	7	.121	-2	20	20	1	2.1
1967 Cle-A	14	13	.519	30	29	15	6	0	223	180	9	72	141	10.3	2.62	125	.224	.290	11	.164	1	15	16	2	2.2
1968 Cle-A	8	15	.348	32	27	4	2	0	158¹	139	11	81	78	12.8	4.15	71	.241	.340	9	.176	1	-21	-21	-1	-2.3
1969 Cle-A	5	14	.263	32	23	1	1	0	143²	145	14	81	76	14.3	5.70	66	.265	.363	7	.159	-1	-33	-31	2	-2.9
1970 Cle-A	11	3	.786	23	19	8	1	0	142²	101	14	53	72	9.9	2.90	136	.201	.281	5	.111	-2	13	17	2	1.8
1971 Cle-A	1	13	.071	37	16	1	0	1	113¹	138	18	56	52	15.9	6.19	62	.304	.388	2	.063	-3	-34	-30	-1	-3.3
1972 Cle-A	0	3	.000	12	1	0	0	0	20	23	1	15	10	17.1	5.85	55	.291	.404	0	.000	-0	-6	-6	1	-0.5
1974 Tex-A	12	9	.571	37	27	8	2	0	186²	202	15	48	98	12.3	3.95	90	.275	.324	0	—	0	-7	-8	2	-0.6
1975 Tex-A	9	10	.474	33	26	8	1	0	189¹	203	17	62	93	12.9	3.80	99	.275	.336	0	—	0	-1	-1	2	0.0
1976 Tex-A	8	8	.500	35	8	2	1	1	124¹	127	8	38	63	12.2	3.62	99	.261	.318	0	—	0	-1	-0	0	0.0
1977 Tor-A	1	3	.250	6	5	1	0	0	29¹	36	2	14	11	15.3	5.22	80	.308	.382	0	—	0	-4	-3	0	-0.2
Tex-A	1	0	1.000	6	0	0	0	0	12	22	2	5	10	20.3	9.00	45	.393	.443	0	—	0	-7	-7	-0	-0.6
Yr	2	3	.400	12	5	1	0	0	41¹	58	4	19	21	16.8	6.31	66	.335	.401	0	—	0	-10	-10	-0	-0.8
1977 Atl-N	0	3	.000	16	5	0	0	0	36²	49	3	16	18	16.0	6.87	65	.325	.389	0	.000	-1	-12	-10	1	-0.8
Total 12	87	107	.448	354	215	56	17	4	1631²	1593	125	614	891	12.4	3.92	91	.257	.328	42	.129	-8	-77	-64	10	-5.0

■ ALAN HARGESHEIMER   Hargesheimer, Alan Robert b: 11/21/56, Chicago, Ill. BR/TR, 6'3", 195 lbs. Deb: 7/14/80

YEAR TM/L	W	L	PCT	G	GS	CG	SH	SV	IP	H	HR	BB	SO	RAT	ERA	ERA+	OAV	OOB	BH	AVG	PB	PR	/A	PD	TPI
1980 SF-N	4	6	.400	15	13	0	0	0	75	82	3	32	40	13.7	4.32	82	.285	.356	4	.182	1	-6	-7	-0	-0.6
1981 SF-N	1	2	.333	6	3	0	0	0	18²	20	1	9	6	14.5	4.34	79	.299	.390	1	.200	0	-2	-2	1	0.0
1983 Chi-N	0	0	—	5	0	0	0	0	4	6	0	2	5	18.0	9.00	42	.375	.444	0	—	0	-2	-2	0	-0.1
1986 KC-A	0	1	.000	5	1	0	0	0	13	18	1	7	4	18.0	6.23	68	.340	.426	0	—	0	-3	-3	-0	-0.2
Total 4	5	9	.357	31	17	0	0	0	110²	126	5	50	55	14.5	4.72	77	.297	.374	5	.185	1	-13	-14	-0	-0.9

■ MIKE HARKEY   Harkey, Michael Anthony b: 10/25/66, San Diego, Cal. BR/TR, 6'5", 220 lbs. Deb: 9/05/88

YEAR TM/L	W	L	PCT	G	GS	CG	SH	SV	IP	H	HR	BB	SO	RAT	ERA	ERA+	OAV	OOB	BH	AVG	PB	PR	/A	PD	TPI
1988 Chi-N	0	3	.000	5	5	0	0	0	34²	33	0	15	18	13.0	2.60	139	.248	.333	1	.091	-1	3	4	-1	0.3
1990 Chi-N	12	6	.667	27	27	2	1	0	173²	153	14	59	94	11.3	3.26	126	.234	.305	14	.250	4	10	17	-1	2.1
Total 2	12	9	.571	32	32	2	1	0	208¹	186	14	74	112	11.6	3.15	128	.237	.310	15	.224	3	13	21	-1	2.4

■ JOHN HARKINS   Harkins, John Joseph "Pa" b: 4/12/1859, New Brunswick, N.J d: 11/20/40, New Brunswick, N.J BR/TR, 6'1", 205 lbs. Deb: 5/02/1884

YEAR TM/L	W	L	PCT	G	GS	CG	SH	SV	IP	H	HR	BB	SO	RAT	ERA	ERA+	OAV	OOB	BH	AVG	PB	PR	/A	PD	TPI
1884 Cle-N	12	32	.273	46	45	42	3	0	391	399	7	108	192	11.7	3.68	85	.250	.298	47	.205	-5	-31	-23	-1	-2.3
1885 Bro-a	14	20	.412	34	34	33	1	0	293	303	7	56	141	11.0	3.75	88	.256	.289	42	.264	6	-16	-15	4	-0.2
1886 Bro-a	15	16	.484	34	33	33	0	0	292¹	286	6	114	118	12.3	3.60	97	.244	.311	32	.225	3	-5	-3	3	0.3
1887 Bro-a	10	14	.417	24	24	22	0	0	199	262	6	77	36	15.3	6.02	72	.306	.363	23	.235	-0	-38	-38	-1	-2.8
1888 Bal-a	0	1	.000	1	1	1	0	0	8	12	0	3	2	16.9	6.75	44	.335	.386	0	.000	-0	-3	-3	-0	-0.2
Total 5	51	83	.381	139	137	131	4	0	1183¹	1262	26	358	489	12.3	4.09	85	.261	.311	144	.228	4	-93	-82	6	-5.2

■ SPEC HARKNESS   Harkness, Frederick Harvey b: 12/13/1887, Los Angeles, Cal. d: 5/16/52, Compton, Cal. BR/TR, 5'11", 180 lbs. Deb: 6/13/10

YEAR TM/L	W	L	PCT	G	GS	CG	SH	SV	IP	H	HR	BB	SO	RAT	ERA	ERA+	OAV	OOB	BH	AVG	PB	PR	/A	PD	TPI
1910 Cle-A	10	7	.588	26	16	6	1	1	136¹	132	2	55	60	12.5	3.04	85	.268	.345	7	.140	-1	-8	-7	-1	-0.9
1911 Cle-A	2	2	.500	12	6	3	0	0	53¹	62	1	21	25	14.0	4.22	81	.310	.376	6	.316	1	-5	-5	-2	-0.4
Total 2	12	9	.571	38	22	9	1	1	189²	194	3	76	85	13.0	3.37	84	.280	.354	13	.188	-1	-13	-12	-3	-1.3

■ DICK HARLEY   Harley, Henry Risk b: 8/18/1874, Springfield, Ohio d: 5/16/61, Springfield, Ohio BR/TR, Deb: 4/15/05

YEAR TM/L	W	L	PCT	G	GS	CG	SH	SV	IP	H	HR	BB	SO	RAT	ERA	ERA+	OAV	OOB	BH	AVG	PB	PR	/A	PD	TPI
1905 Bos-N	2	5	.286	9	4	4	1	0	66	72	5	19	19	12.5	4.64	67	.286	.338	1	.045	-2	-12	-11	2	-1.1

■ LARRY HARLOW   Harlow, Larry Duane b: 11/13/51, Colorado Springs, Colo. BL/TL, 6'2", 185 lbs. Deb: 9/20/75 ♦

YEAR TM/L	W	L	PCT	G	GS	CG	SH	SV	IP	H	HR	BB	SO	RAT	ERA	ERA+	OAV	OOB	BH	AVG	PB	PR	/A	PD	TPI
1978 Bal-A	0	0	—	1	0	0	0	0	0²	2	1	4	1	81.0	67.50	5	.500	.750	112	.243	1	-5	-5	0	-0.3

■ BILL HARMAN   Harman, William Bell b: 1/2/19, Bridgewater, Va. BR/TR, 6'4", 200 lbs. Deb: 6/17/41 ♦

YEAR TM/L	W	L	PCT	G	GS	CG	SH	SV	IP	H	HR	BB	SO	RAT	ERA	ERA+	OAV	OOB	BH	AVG	PB	PR	/A	PD	TPI
1941 Phi-N	0	0	—	5	0	0	0	0	13	15	0	8	3	15.9	4.85	76	.319	.418	1	.071	-0	-2	-1	-0	-0.1

■ BOB HARMON   Harmon, Robert Green "Hickory Bob" b: 10/15/1887, Liberal, Mo. d: 11/27/61, Monroe, La. BB/TR, 6', 187 lbs. Deb: 6/23/09

YEAR TM/L	W	L	PCT	G	GS	CG	SH	SV	IP	H	HR	BB	SO	RAT	ERA	ERA+	OAV	OOB	BH	AVG	PB	PR	/A	PD	TPI
1909 StL-N	6	11	.353	21	17	10	0	0	159	155	6	65	48	12.7	3.68	69	.265	.342	13	.255	4	-19	-20	0	-1.7
1910 StL-N	13	15	.464	43	33	15	0	2	236	227	1	133	87	14.0	4.46	67	.258	.360	14	.184	2	-37	-39	2	-3.5
1911 StL-N	23	16	.590	51	41	28	2	4	348	290	10	181	144	12.4	3.13	108	.235	.336	17	.153	0	11	10	1	1.1
1912 StL-N	18	18	.500	43	34	15	3	0	268	284	4	116	73	13.5	3.93	83	.270	.344	23	.232	1	-15	-14	4	-0.9
1913 StL-N	8	21	.276	42	27	16	1	2	273¹	291	6	99	66	13.0	3.92	83	.286	.353	24	.261	5	-22	-21	2	-1.3
1914 Pit-N	13	17	.433	37	30	19	2	3	245	226	3	55	61	10.6	2.53	105	.252	.300	12	.140	-1	7	3	-1	0.1
1915 Pit-N	16	17	.485	37	32	25	5	1	269²	242	6	62	86	10.2	2.50	109	.247	.294	14	.147	1	7	7	4	1.3
1916 Pit-N	8	11	.421	31	17	10	2	0	172²	175	4	39	62	11.2	2.81	95	.267	.309	6	.109	-3	-4	-2	4	-0.1
1918 Pit-N	2	7	.222	16	9	5	0	0	82¹	76	3	12	7	9.6	2.62	110	.254	.283	4	.148	0	1	2	1	0.2
Total 9	107	133	.446	321	240	143	15	12	2054	1966	43	762	634	12.1	3.33	90	.259	.329	127	.184	7	-71	-76	17	-4.8

■ PETE HARNISCH   Harnisch, Peter Thomas b: 9/23/66, Commack, N.Y. BB/TR, 6'1", 195 lbs. Deb: 9/13/88

YEAR TM/L	W	L	PCT	G	GS	CG	SH	SV	IP	H	HR	BB	SO	RAT	ERA	ERA+	OAV	OOB	BH	AVG	PB	PR	/A	PD	TPI
1988 Bal-A	0	2	.000	2	2	0	0	0	13	13	1	9	10	15.2	5.54	70	.260	.373	0	—	0	-2	-2	-0	-0.1
1989 Bal-A	5	9	.357	18	17	2	0	0	103¹	97	10	64	70	14.5	4.62	82	.249	.362	0	—	0	-8	-9	-1	-0.9
1990 Bal-A	11	11	.500	31	31	3	0	0	188²	189	17	86	122	13.2	4.34	88	.261	.341	0	—	0	-9	-11	-2	-1.2
Total 3	16	22	.421	51	50	5	0	0	305	299	28	159	202	13.7	4.49	85	.257	.349	0	—	0	-20	-23	-3	-2.2

■ JACK HARPER   Harper, Charles William b: 4/2/1878, Galloway, Pa. d: 9/30/50, Jamestown, N.Y. BR/TR, 6', 178 lbs. Deb: 9/18/1899

YEAR TM/L	W	L	PCT	G	GS	CG	SH	SV	IP	H	HR	BB	SO	RAT	ERA	ERA+	OAV	OOB	BH	AVG	PB	PR	/A	PD	TPI
1899 Cle-N	1	4	.200	5	5	5	0	0	37	44	3	12	14	13.6	3.89	94	.295	.347	2	.182	1	-0	-1	-0	0.0
1900 StL-N	0	1	.000	1	1	0	0	0	3	4	0	2	0	18.0	12.00	30	.319	.413	0	.000	-0	-3	-3	-0	-0.1
1901 StL-N	23	13	.639	39	37	28	1	0	308²	294	7	99	128	11.8	3.62	88	.249	.315	20	.172	1	-10	-15	0	-1.3
1902 StL-A	15	11	.577	29	26	20	2	0	222¹	224	8	81	74	12.3	4.13	85	.262	.326	17	.205	0	-14	-15	1	-1.2
1903 Cin-N	8	9	.471	17	15	13	0	0	135	143	2	70	45	14.9	4.33	82	.271	.367	14	.250	2	-16	-12	2	-0.6
1904 Cin-N	23	9	.719	35	35	31	6	0	293²	262	4	85	125	10.9	2.30	128	.234	.293	18	.159	-2	14	21	-5	1.6
1905 Cin-N	9	13	.409	26	23	15	1	1	179	189	5	69	70	13.4	3.87	85	.271	.344	10	.167	1	-17	-11	-0	-0.9
1906 Cin-N	4	4	.200	5	5	3	0	0	36²	38	1	20	10	14.7	4.17	66	.286	.387	3	.273	1	-6	-6	1	-0.5
Chi-N	0	0	—	1	1	0	0	0	1	0	0	0	0	0.00	0.00	—	.000	.000	0	—	0	0	0	-0	0.0
Yr	1	4	.200	6	6	3	0	0	37²	38	1	20	10	13.9	4.06	68	.275	.367	3	.273	1	-6	-5	1	-0.5
Total 8	80	64	.556	158	148	115	10	1	1216¹	1198	25	438	466	12.4	3.55	92	.256	.326	84	.186	4	-51	-39	-3	-3.0

■ GEORGE HARPER   Harper, George B. b: 8/17/1866, Milwaukee, Wis. d: 12/11/31, Stockton, Cal. Deb: 7/11/1894

YEAR TM/L	W	L	PCT	G	GS	CG	SH	SV	IP	H	HR	BB	SO	RAT	ERA	ERA+	OAV	OOB	BH	AVG	PB	PR	/A	PD	TPI
1894 Phi-N	6	6	.500	12	9	7	0	0	86¹	128	3	49	24	18.5	5.32	96	.340	.416	6	.150	-3	-2	-1	-0	-0.4
1896 Bro-N	4	8	.333	16	11	7	0	0	86	106	4	39	22	15.2	5.55	74	.300	.370	6	.162	0	-11	-14	1	-1.0
Total 2	10	14	.417	28	20	14	0	0	172¹	234	7	88	46	16.8	5.43	85	.321	.394	12	.156	-3	-11	-16	0	-1.4

■ HARRY HARPER   Harper, Harry Clayton b: 4/24/1895, Hackensack, N.J. d: 4/23/63, New York, N.Y. BL/TL, 6'2", 165 lbs. Deb: 6/27/13

YEAR TM/L	W	L	PCT	G	GS	CG	SH	SV	IP	H	HR	BB	SO	RAT	ERA	ERA+	OAV	OOB	BH	AVG	PB	PR	/A	PD	TPI
1913 Was-A	0	0	—	4	0	0	0	0	12²	10	1	5	9	11.4	3.55	83	.204	.291	1	.250	0	-1	-1	0	0.0
1914 Was-A	2	1	.667	23	3	1	0	2	57	45	1	35	50	13.4	3.47	80	.211	.336	3	.250	0	-5	-4	1	-0.5

YEAR TM/L	W	L	PCT	G	GS	CG	SH	SV	IP	H	HR	BB	SO	RAT	ERA	ERA+	OAV	OOB	BH	AVG	PB	PR	/A	PD	TPI
1915 Was-A	4	4	.500	19	10	5	2	2	86¹	66	1	40	54	11.2	1.77	165	.222	.317	0	.000	-4	11	11	-2	0.6
1916 Was-A	14	10	.583	36	34	13	2	0	249²	209	4	101	149	11.5	2.45	112	.235	.319	18	.207	1	10	8	-5	0.5
1917 Was-A	11	12	.478	31	31	10	4	0	179¹	145	1	106	99	12.8	3.01	87	.230	.345	7	.117	-3	-7	-8	-3	-1.4
1918 Was-A	11	10	.524	35	32	14	3	1	244	182	1	104	78	10.8	2.18	125	.212	.303	11	.134	-4	16	15	-5	0.7
1919 Was-A	6	21	.222	35	31	8	0	0	208	220	3	97	87	14.1	3.72	86	.284	.370	11	.169	-2	-11	-12	-1	-1.5
1920 Bos-A	5	14	.263	27	22	11	1	0	162²	163	9	66	71	12.8	3.04	120	.275	.349	6	.120	-2	14	11	-3	0.4
1921 •NY-A	4	3	.571	8	7	4	0	0	52²	52	3	25	22	13.5	3.76	113	.263	.351	2	.125	-1	3	3	-2	0.0
1923 Bro-N	0	1	.000	1	1	0	0	0	3²	8	2	3	4	27.0	14.73	26	.421	.500	0	.000	-0	-4	-4	-0	-0.3
Total 10	57	76	.429	219	171	66	12	5	1256	1100	26	582	623	12.3	2.87	105	.243	.335	59	.147	-15	27	19	-21	-1.5

■ JACK HARPER
Harper, John Wesley b: 8/5/1893, Hendricks, W.Va. d: 6/18/27, Halstead, Kan. BR/TR, 5'11", 180 lbs. Deb: 4/17/15

YEAR TM/L	W	L	PCT	G	GS	CG	SH	SV	IP	H	HR	BB	SO	RAT	ERA	ERA+	OAV	OOB	BH	AVG	PB	PR	/A	PD	TPI
1915 Phi-A	0	0	—	3	0	0	0	0	8²	5	0	1	3	6.2	3.12	95	.161	.188	0	.000	-0	-0	-0	0	0.0

■ BILL HARPER
Harper, William Homer "Blue Sleeve" b: 6/14/1889, Bertand, Mo. d: 6/17/51, Somerville, Tenn. BB/TR, 6'1", 180 lbs. Deb: 6/10/11

YEAR TM/L	W	L	PCT	G	GS	CG	SH	SV	IP	H	HR	BB	SO	RAT	ERA	ERA+	OAV	OOB	BH	AVG	PB	PR	/A	PD	TPI
1911 StL-A	0	0	—	2	0	0	0	0	8	9	0	4	6	15.8	6.75	50	.300	.400	0	.000	-0	-3	-3	0	-0.2

■ SLIM HARRELL
Harrell, Oscar Martin b: 7/31/1890, Grandview, Tex. d: 4/30/71, Hillsboro, Tex. BR/TR, 6'3", 180 lbs. Deb: 6/21/12

YEAR TM/L	W	L	PCT	G	GS	CG	SH	SV	IP	H	HR	BB	SO	RAT	ERA	ERA+	OAV	OOB	BH	AVG	PB	PR	/A	PD	TPI
1912 Phi-A	0	0	—	1	0	0	0	0	3	4	0	0	1	12.0	0.00	—	.364	.364	0	.000	-0	1	1	-0	0.1

■ RAY HARRELL
Harrell, Raymond James "Cowboy" b: 2/16/12, Petrolia, Tex. d: 1/28/84, Alexandria, La. BR/TR, 6'1", 185 lbs. Deb: 4/16/35

YEAR TM/L	W	L	PCT	G	GS	CG	SH	SV	IP	H	HR	BB	SO	RAT	ERA	ERA+	OAV	OOB	BH	AVG	PB	PR	/A	PD	TPI
1935 StL-N	1	1	.500	11	1	0	0	0	29²	39	4	11	13	15.2	6.67	61	.320	.376	0	.000	-1	-9	-8	-0	-0.8
1937 StL-N	3	7	.300	35	15	1	1	1	96²	99	7	59	41	14.9	5.87	68	.263	.366	1	.045	-2	-21	-20	-1	-2.1
1938 StL-N	2	3	.400	32	3	1	0	2	63	78	6	29	32	15.7	4.86	81	.308	.386	0	.000	-1	-7	-6	-0	-0.6
1939 Chi-N	0	2	.000	4	2	0	0	0	17¹	29	2	6	5	18.2	8.31	47	.387	.432	0	.000	-1	-8	-8	-0	-0.7
Phi-N	3	7	.300	22	10	4	0	0	94²	101	6	56	35	15.3	5.42	74	.270	.371	3	.115	-1	-16	-15	-3	-1.7
Yr	3	9	.250	26	12	4	0	0	112	130	8	62	40	15.8	5.87	68	.290	.381	2	.065	-2	-24	-23	-3	-2.4
1940 Pit-N	0	0	—	3	0	0	0	0	3¹	5	0	2	3	18.9	8.10	47	.333	.412	0	—	0	-2	-2	0	-0.1
1945 NY-N	0	0	—	12	0	0	0	0	25¹	34	1	14	7	17.4	4.97	79	.343	.430	1	.200	1	-3	-3	0	-0.1
Total 6	9	20	.310	119	31	6	1	3	330	385	26	177	136	15.6	5.70	70	.293	.381	5	.069	-5	-66	-63	-3	-6.1

■ BILL HARRELSON
Harrelson, William Charles b: 11/17/45, Tahlequah, Okla. BB/TR, 6'5", 215 lbs. Deb: 7/31/68

YEAR TM/L	W	L	PCT	G	GS	CG	SH	SV	IP	H	HR	BB	SO	RAT	ERA	ERA+	OAV	OOB	BH	AVG	PB	PR	/A	PD	TPI
1968 Cal-A	1	6	.143	10	5	1	0	0	33²	28	4	26	22	14.7	5.08	57	.226	.364	1	.100	-0	-8	-8	-0	-0.9

■ ANDY HARRINGTON
Harrington, Andrew Francis b: 11/13/1888, Wakefield, Mass. d: 11/12/38, Malden, Mass. BR/TR, 6', 193 lbs. Deb: 9/08/13

YEAR TM/L	W	L	PCT	G	GS	CG	SH	SV	IP	H	HR	BB	SO	RAT	ERA	ERA+	OAV	OOB	BH	AVG	PB	PR	/A	PD	TPI
1913 Cin-N	0	0	—	1	0	0	0	0	4	6	0	1	1	15.8	9.00	36	.353	.389	1	.500	-0	-3	-3	-0	-0.1

■ BILL HARRINGTON
Harrington, William Womble b: 10/3/27, Sanford, N.C. BR/TR, 5'11", 160 lbs. Deb: 4/16/53

YEAR TM/L	W	L	PCT	G	GS	CG	SH	SV	IP	H	HR	BB	SO	RAT	ERA	ERA+	OAV	OOB	BH	AVG	PB	PR	/A	PD	TPI
1953 Phi-A	0	0	—	1	0	0	0	0	2	5	0	0	0	22.5	13.50	32	.500	.500	0	—	0	-2	-2	0	-0.1
1955 KC-A	3	3	.500	34	1	0	0	2	76²	69	6	41	26	13.1	4.11	102	.246	.347	2	.118	-1	-1	1	-0	-0.4
1956 KC-A	2	2	.500	23	1	0	0	1	37²	40	3	26	14	15.8	6.45	67	.274	.384	0	.000	-1	-10	-9	-0	-0.8
Total 3	5	5	.500	58	2	0	0	3	116¹	114	9	67	40	14.2	5.03	84	.261	.362	2	.083	-1	-13	-10	-0	-0.9

■ BEN HARRIS
Harris, Ben Franklin b: 12/17/1889, Donelson, Tenn. d: 4/29/27, St.Louis, Mo. BR/TR, 6', 220 lbs. Deb: 4/19/14

YEAR TM/L	W	L	PCT	G	GS	CG	SH	SV	IP	H	HR	BB	SO	RAT	ERA	ERA+	OAV	OOB	BH	AVG	PB	PR	/A	PD	TPI
1914 KC-F	7	7	.500	31	14	5	0	1	154	179	7	41	40	13.2	4.09	75	.303	.354	9	.200	1	-15	-17	2	-1.4
1915 KC-F	0	0	—	1	0	0	0	0	2	1	0	0	0	4.5	0.00	—	.155	.155	0	—	0	1	1	0	0.1
Total 2	7	7	.500	32	14	5	0	1	156	180	7	41	40	13.1	4.04	76	.301	.352	9	.200	1	-14	-17	2	-1.3

■ LUM HARRIS
Harris, Chalmer Luman b: 1/17/15, New Castle, Ala. BR/TR, 6'1", 180 lbs. Deb: 4/19/41 MC

YEAR TM/L	W	L	PCT	G	GS	CG	SH	SV	IP	H	HR	BB	SO	RAT	ERA	ERA+	OAV	OOB	BH	AVG	PB	PR	/A	PD	TPI
1941 Phi-A	4	4	.500	33	10	5	0	2	131²	134	16	51	49	12.8	4.78	88	.260	.329	11	.275	2	-9	-9	-2	-0.7
1942 Phi-A	11	15	.423	26	20	10	1	0	166	146	14	70	60	11.8	3.74	101	.234	.313	10	.161	-2	-2	1	-0	0.0
1943 Phi-A	7	21	.250	32	27	15	1	1	216¹	241	17	63	55	12.8	4.20	81	.279	.330	12	.171	-1	-22	-19	0	-1.9
1944 Phi-A	10	9	.526	23	22	12	2	0	174¹	193	8	26	33	11.3	3.30	105	.281	.308	10	.169	-1	2	3	-0	0.3
1946 Phi-A	3	14	.176	34	12	4	0	0	125¹	153	11	48	33	14.4	5.24	68	.308	.369	8	.222	1	-24	-24	3	-1.8
1947 Was-A	0	0	—	3	0	0	0	0	6¹	7	0	7	2	19.9	2.84	131	.318	.483	0	.000	-0	1	1	0	0.1
Total 6	35	63	.357	151	91	46	4	3	820	874	66	265	232	12.6	4.16	88	.273	.329	51	.190	-0	-54	-47	2	-4.0

■ BUBBA HARRIS
Harris, Charles b: 2/15/26, Sulligent, Ala. BR/TR, 6'4", 204 lbs. Deb: 4/29/48

YEAR TM/L	W	L	PCT	G	GS	CG	SH	SV	IP	H	HR	BB	SO	RAT	ERA	ERA+	OAV	OOB	BH	AVG	PB	PR	/A	PD	TPI
1948 Phi-A	5	2	.714	45	0	0	0	5	93²	89	2	35	32	12.0	4.13	104	.249	.317	3	.125	-1	2	2	-0	0.0
1949 Phi-A	1	1	.500	37	0	0	0	3	84¹	92	12	42	18	14.4	5.44	75	.286	.370	3	.125	-2	-12	-12	2	-1.0
1951 Phi-A	0	0	—	3	0	0	0	0	4	4	0	5	2	22.5	9.00	48	.250	.455	0	—	0	-2	-2	0	-0.1
Cle-A	0	0	—	2	0	0	0	0	4	5	0	4	1	20.3	4.50	84	.333	.474	0	—	0	-0	-0	0	0.0
Yr	0	0	—	5	0	0	0	0	8	9	0	9	3	20.3	6.75	60	.281	.439	0	—	0	-2	-2	0	-0.1
Total 3	6	3	.667	87	0	0	0	8	186	190	14	86	53	13.5	4.84	87	.267	.349	6	.125	-3	-12	-13	2	-1.1

■ GREG HARRIS
Harris, Greg Allen b: 11/2/55, Lynwood, Cal. BB/TR, 6', 165 lbs. Deb: 5/20/81

YEAR TM/L	W	L	PCT	G	GS	CG	SH	SV	IP	H	HR	BB	SO	RAT	ERA	ERA+	OAV	OOB	BH	AVG	PB	PR	/A	PD	TPI
1981 NY-N	3	5	.375	16	14	0	0	0	68²	65	8	28	54	12.5	4.46	78	.245	.322	4	.182	0	-7	-7	-1	-0.7
1982 Cin-N	2	6	.250	34	10	1	0	1	91¹	96	12	37	67	13.3	4.83	77	.274	.346	3	.167	-0	-12	-11	0	-1.1
1983 Cin-N	0	0	—	1	0	0	0	0	2	2	0	3	1	54.0	27.00	14	.500	.750	0	—	0	-3	-3	0	-0.1
1984 Mon-N	0	1	.000	15	0	0	0	2	17²	10	0	7	15	9.7	2.04	168	.172	.284	0	.000	-0	3	3	0	0.3
•SD-N	2	1	.667	19	1	0	0	1	36²	28	3	18	30	11.8	2.70	132	.209	.312	3	.375	1	4	4	-0	0.5
Yr	2	2	.500	34	1	0	0	3	54¹	38	3	25	45	10.8	2.48	142	.196	.294	0	.000	-0	7	6	-0	0.8
1985 Tex-A	5	4	.556	58	0	0	0	11	113	74	7	43	111	9.7	2.47	171	.186	.274	0	—	0	21	22	1	2.3
1986 Tex-A	10	8	.556	73	0	0	0	20	111¹	103	12	42	95	11.8	2.83	152	.251	.322	0	—	0	17	18	1	1.9
1987 Tex-A	5	10	.333	42	19	0	0	0	140²	157	18	56	106	13.9	4.86	92	.281	.351	0	—	0	-6	-6	-0	-0.4
1988 Phi-N	4	6	.400	66	1	0	0	1	107	80	7	52	71	11.4	2.36	151	.209	.311	3	.333	1	13	14	-0	1.7
1989 Phi-N	2	2	.500	44	0	0	0	1	75¹	64	7	43	51	13.0	3.58	99	.234	.342	1	.167	1	-1	-0	0	0.1
Bos-A	2	2	.500	15	0	0	0	0	28	21	1	15	25	11.6	2.57	159	.208	.310	0	—	0	4	5	0	0.5
1990 •Bos-A	13	9	.591	34	30	1	0	0	184¹	186	13	77	117	13.1	4.00	102	.265	.342	0	—	0	-2	2	3	0.5
Total 10	48	54	.471	417	75	2	0	38	975	886	88	421	743	12.4	3.61	110	.244	.327	14	.215	3	30	39	5	5.5

■ GREG HARRIS
Harris, Gregory Wade b: 12/1/63, Greensboro, N.C. BR/TR, 6'3", 190 lbs. Deb: 9/14/88

YEAR TM/L	W	L	PCT	G	GS	CG	SH	SV	IP	H	HR	BB	SO	RAT	ERA	ERA+	OAV	OOB	BH	AVG	PB	PR	/A	PD	TPI
1988 SD-N	2	0	1.000	3	1	0	0	0	18	13	0	3	15	8.0	1.50	226	.200	.235	0	.000	-1	4	4	-0	0.3
1989 SD-N	8	9	.471	56	8	0	0	6	135	106	8	52	106	10.7	2.60	134	.215	.293	1	.053	-1	13	13	1	1.5
1990 SD-N	8	8	.500	73	0	0	0	9	117¹	92	6	49	97	11.1	2.30	167	.220	.307	1	.083	-0	19	20	0	2.1
Total 3	18	17	.514	132	9	1	0	15	270¹	211	14	104	218	10.7	2.40	152	.216	.295	2	.053	-2	37	37	1	3.9

■ HERB HARRIS
Harris, Herbert Benjamin "Hub" or "Lefty" b: 4/24/13, Chicago, Ill. BL/TL, 6'1", 175 lbs. Deb: 7/21/36

YEAR TM/L	W	L	PCT	G	GS	CG	SH	SV	IP	H	HR	BB	SO	RAT	ERA	ERA+	OAV	OOB	BH	AVG	PB	PR	/A	PD	TPI
1936 Phi-N	0	0	—	4	0	0	0	0	7	14	0	5	0	25.7	10.29	44	.438	.526	0	.000	-0	-5	-4	0	-0.3

■ JOE HARRIS
Harris, Joseph White b: 2/1/1882, Melrose, Mass. d: 4/12/66, Melrose, Mass. TR, 6'1", 198 lbs. Deb: 9/22/05

YEAR TM/L	W	L	PCT	G	GS	CG	SH	SV	IP	H	HR	BB	SO	RAT	ERA	ERA+	OAV	OOB	BH	AVG	PB	PR	/A	PD	TPI
1905 Bos-A	1	2	.333	3	3	3	0	0	23	16	0	8	14	9.4	2.35	115	.198	.270	1	.111	-1	1	1	-0	0.0
1906 Bos-A	2	21	.087	30	24	20	1	2	235	211	5	67	99	10.6	3.52	78	.243	.297	13	.160	-2	-22	-20	6	-1.6
1907 Bos-A	0	7	.000	12	5	3	0	0	59	57	0	13	24	10.7	3.05	85	.256	.297	4	.190	-0	-3	-3	0	-0.2
Total 3	3	30	.091	45	32	26	1	2	317	284	5	88	137	10.6	3.35	81	.242	.295	18	.162	-3	-24	-22	6	-1.8

MICKEY HARRIS — Harris, Maurice Charles b: 1/30/17, New York, N.Y. d: 4/15/71, Farmington, Mich. BL/TL, 6', 195 lbs. Deb: 4/23/40

YEAR	TM/L	W	L	PCT	G	GS	CG	SH	SV	IP	H	HR	BB	SO	RAT	ERA	ERA+	OAV	OOB	BH	AVG	PB	PR	/A	PD	TPI
1940	Bos-A	4	2	.667	13	9	3	0	0	68¹	83	8	26	36	14.6	5.00	90	.292	.356	6	.273	2	-5	-4	0	0.0
1941	Bos-A	8	14	.364	35	22	11	1	1	194	189	6	86	111	12.9	3.25	128	.250	.328	6	.109	1	19	20	-1	2.1
1946	*Bos-A	17	9	.654	34	30	15	0	0	222²	236	18	76	131	12.7	3.64	101	.268	.329	18	.231	4	-3	1	-2	0.3
1947	Bos-A	5	4	.556	15	6	1	0	0	51²	42	3	23	35	11.3	2.44	159	.225	.310	5	.417	3	7	8	0	1.2
1948	Bos-A	7	10	.412	20	17	6	1	0	113²	120	10	59	44	14.3	5.30	83	.273	.360	2	.063	-1	-13	-12	-2	-1.2
1949	Bos-A	2	3	.400	7	6	2	0	0	37²	53	3	20	14	17.7	5.02	87	.323	.400	1	.083	-1	-3	-3	0	-0.2
	Was-A	2	12	.143	23	19	4	0	0	129	151	8	55	54	14.4	5.16	82	.292	.360	8	.205	1	-14	-13	-2	-1.2
	Yr	4	15	.211	30	25	6	0	0	166²	204	11	75	68	15.1	5.13	83	.299	.368	9	.176	1	-17	-16	-2	-1.4
1950	Was-A	5	9	.357	53	0	0	0	15	98	93	10	46	41	12.9	4.78	94	.247	.330	4	.235	1	-2	-3	-1	-0.3
1951	Was-A	6	8	.429	41	0	0	0	4	87¹	87	6	43	47	13.5	3.81	107	.260	.347	3	.188	1	3	3	-1	0.0
1952	Was-A	0	0	—	1	0	0	0	0	1	1	0	0	0	9.00	9.00	40	.250	.250	0	—	0	-1	-1	0	0.0
	Cle-A	3	0	1.000	29	0	0	0	1	46²	42	6	21	23	12.3	4.63	72	.249	.335	1	.200	-0	-5	-7	0	-0.6
	Yr	3	0	1.000	30	0	0	0	1	47²	43	7	21	23	12.3	4.72	71	.249	.333	0	.000	-0	-6	-7	0	-0.6
Total 9		59	71	.454	271	109	42	2	21	1050	1097	79	455	534	13.4	4.18	98	.267	.342	54	.188	11	-16	-9	-8	0.3

REGGIE HARRIS — Harris, Reginald Allen b: 8/12/68, Waynesboro, Va. BR/TR, 6'1", 180 lbs. Deb: 7/04/90

YEAR	TM/L	W	L	PCT	G	GS	CG	SH	SV	IP	H	HR	BB	SO	RAT	ERA	ERA+	OAV	OOB	BH	AVG	PB	PR	/A	PD	TPI
1990	Oak-A	1	0	1.000	16	1	0	0	0	41¹	25	5	21	31	10.5	3.48	107	.176	.291	0	—	0	2	1	-0	0.1

BOB HARRIS — Harris, Robert Arthur b: 5/1/16, Gillette, Wyo. BR/TR, 6', 185 lbs. Deb: 9/19/38

YEAR	TM/L	W	L	PCT	G	GS	CG	SH	SV	IP	H	HR	BB	SO	RAT	ERA	ERA+	OAV	OOB	BH	AVG	PB	PR	/A	PD	TPI
1938	Det-A	1	0	1.000	3	1	1	0	0	10	14	0	4	7	16.2	7.20	69	.318	.375	1	.333	0	-3	-2	0	0.0
1939	Det-A	1	1	.500	5	1	0	0	0	18	18	4	8	9	13.0	4.00	122	.269	.347	2	.400	0	1	2	0	0.2
	StL-A	3	12	.200	28	16	6	0	0	126	162	5	71	48	16.6	5.71	85	.321	.405	7	.189	-0	-15	-12	0	-0.8
	Yr	4	13	.235	33	17	6	0	0	144	180	9	79	57	16.2	5.50	89	.315	.398	9	.095	-0	-14	-10	3	-0.6
1940	StL-A	11	15	.423	35	28	8	1	1	193²	225	24	85	49	14.5	4.93	93	.290	.362	15	.250	3	-12	-7	0	-0.3
1941	StL-A	12	14	.462	34	29	9	2	1	186²	237	18	85	57	15.6	5.21	83	.312	.383	7	.115	-3	-22	-19	-1	-2.0
1942	StL-A	1	5	.167	6	6	0	0	0	33²	37	2	17	9	14.4	5.61	66	.268	.348	0	.000	-1	-7	-7	-1	-0.7
	Phi-A	1	5	.167	16	8	2	1	0	78	77	5	24	26	11.7	2.88	131	.253	.308	7	.269	1	7	8	2	1.2
	Yr	2	10	.167	22	14	2	1	0	111²	114	7	41	35	12.5	3.71	101	.258	.321	7	.028	0	-1	1	2	0.5
Total 5		30	52	.366	127	89	26	4	2	646	770	58	294	205	14.9	4.96	89	.297	.370	39	.193	1	-51	-38	3	-2.4

GENE HARRIS — Harris, Tyrone Eugene b: 12/5/64, Sebring, Fla. BR/TR, 5'11", 190 lbs. Deb: 4/05/89

YEAR	TM/L	W	L	PCT	G	GS	CG	SH	SV	IP	H	HR	BB	SO	RAT	ERA	ERA+	OAV	OOB	BH	AVG	PB	PR	/A	PD	TPI
1989	Mon-N	1	1	.500	11	0	0	0	0	20	16	1	10	11	11.7	4.95	71	.242	.342	0	.000	-0	-3	-3	2	-0.1
	Sea-A	1	4	.200	10	6	0	0	1	33¹	47	3	15	14	17.0	6.48	62	.353	.423	0	—	0	-10	-9	-0	-0.8
1990	Sea-A	1	2	.333	25	0	0	0	0	38	31	5	30	43	14.7	4.74	84	.217	.356	0	.000	-0	-4	-3	-0	-0.3
Total 2		3	7	.300	46	6	0	0	1	91¹	94	9	55	68	14.9	5.42	72	.275	.378	0	.000	-0	-16	-16	1	-1.2

BUDDY HARRIS — Harris, Walter Francis b: 12/5/48, Philadelphia, Pa. BR/TR, 6'7", 245 lbs. Deb: 9/10/70

YEAR	TM/L	W	L	PCT	G	GS	CG	SH	SV	IP	H	HR	BB	SO	RAT	ERA	ERA+	OAV	OOB	BH	AVG	PB	PR	/A	PD	TPI
1970	Hou-N	0	0	—	2	0	0	0	0	6¹	6	3	0	2	8.5	5.68	68	.240	.240	0	.000	-0	-1	-1	0	0.0
1971	Hou-N	1	1	.500	20	0	0	0	0	30²	33	3	16	21	14.4	6.46	58	.275	.360	0	.000	-0	-10	-11	-1	-1.1
Total 2		1	1	.500	22	0	0	0	0	37	39	6	16	23	13.4	6.32	55	.269	.342	0	.000	-0	-11	-12	-1	-1.1

BILL HARRIS — Harris, William Milton b: 6/23/1900, Wylie, Tex. d: 8/21/65, Indian Trail, N.C. BR/TR, 6'1", 180 lbs. Deb: 4/22/23

YEAR	TM/L	W	L	PCT	G	GS	CG	SH	SV	IP	H	HR	BB	SO	RAT	ERA	ERA+	OAV	OOB	BH	AVG	PB	PR	/A	PD	TPI
1923	Cin-N	3	2	.600	22	3	1	0	0	69²	79	3	18	18	12.9	5.17	75	.292	.342	6	.353	1	-9	-10	0	-0.7
1924	Cin-N	0	0	—	3	0	0	0	0	7	10	0	2	5	15.4	9.00	42	.323	.364	1	1.000	0	-4	-4	0	-0.2
1931	Pit-N	2	2	.500	4	4	3	1	0	31	21	0	9	10	8.7	0.87	442	.194	.256	1	.091	-1	10	10	0	1.1
1932	Pit-N	10	9	.526	37	17	4	0	2	168	178	6	38	63	11.9	3.64	105	.271	.317	10	.182	-1	4	3	-2	0.0
1933	Pit-N	4	4	.500	31	0	0	0	5	58²	68	1	14	19	12.7	3.22	103	.289	.332	0	.000	-1	1	1	-1	0.0
1934	Pit-N	0	0	—	11	0	0	0	0	19	28	2	7	8	17.1	6.63	62	.350	.409	1	.500	0	-5	-5	0	-0.4
1938	Bos-A	5	5	.500	13	11	5	1	0	80¹	83	5	21	26	11.8	4.03	122	.268	.316	6	.214	-0	7	8	0	0.7
Total 7		24	22	.522	121	37	13	2	8	433²	467	17	109	149	12.2	3.92	101	.276	.324	25	.203	-1	4	2	-2	0.5

BILL HARRIS — Harris, William Thomas b: 12/3/31, Duguayville, N.B., Canada BL/TR, 5'8", 187 lbs. Deb: 9/27/57

YEAR	TM/L	W	L	PCT	G	GS	CG	SH	SV	IP	H	HR	BB	SO	RAT	ERA	ERA+	OAV	OOB	BH	AVG	PB	PR	/A	PD	TPI
1957	Bro-N	0	1	.000	1	1	0	0	0	7	9	1	1	3	12.9	3.86	108	.321	.345	1	.500	0	0	0	0	0.1
1959	LA-N	0	0	—	1	0	0	0	0	1²	0	0	3	0	16.2	0.00	—	.000	.375	0	—	0	1	1	0	0.1
Total 2		0	1	.000	2	1	0	0	0	8²	9	1	4	3	13.5	3.12	134	.273	.351	1	.500	0	1	1	0	0.2

BOB HARRISON — Harrison, Robert Lee b: 9/22/30, St.Louis, Mo. BL/TR, 5'11", 178 lbs. Deb: 9/23/55

YEAR	TM/L	W	L	PCT	G	GS	CG	SH	SV	IP	H	HR	BB	SO	RAT	ERA	ERA+	OAV	OOB	BH	AVG	PB	PR	/A	PD	TPI
1955	Bal-A	0	0	—	1	0	0	0	0	2	3	0	4	0	31.5	9.00	42	.500	.700	0	—	0	-1	-1	0	-0.1
1956	Bal-A	0	0	—	1	1	0	0	0	1²	3	0	5	0	43.2	16.20	24	.375	.615	0	—	0	-2	-2	0	-0.1
Total 2		0	0	—	2	1	0	0	0	3²	6	0	9	0	36.8	12.27	31	.429	.652	0	—	0	-3	-3	0	-0.1

RORIC HARRISON — Harrison, Roric Edward b: 9/20/46, Los Angeles, Cal. BR/TR, 6'3", 195 lbs. Deb: 4/18/72

YEAR	TM/L	W	L	PCT	G	GS	CG	SH	SV	IP	H	HR	BB	SO	RAT	ERA	ERA+	OAV	OOB	BH	AVG	PB	PR	/A	PD	TPI
1972	Bal-A	3	4	.429	39	2	0	0	4	94	68	9	34	62	10.1	2.30	134	.209	.292	2	.118	1	8	8	-1	1.0
1973	Atl-N	11	8	.579	38	22	3	0	5	177¹	161	15	98	130	13.3	4.16	94	.242	.342	3	.056	-2	-10	-5	-2	-0.7
1974	Atl-N	6	11	.353	20	20	3	0	0	126	148	12	49	46	14.3	4.71	80	.294	.360	7	.184	3	-15	-13	-1	-1.1
1975	Atl-N	3	4	.429	15	7	2	0	1	54²	58	7	19	22	12.7	4.77	79	.266	.325	3	.200	1	-7	-6	0	-0.4
	Cle-A	7	7	.500	19	19	4	0	0	126	137	9	46	52	13.4	4.79	79	.274	.340	0	—	0	-14	-14	-1	-1.4
1978	Min-A	0	1	.000	9	0	0	0	0	12	18	0	11	7	21.8	7.50	51	.346	.460	0	—	0	-5	-5	-0	-0.4
Total 5		30	35	.462	140	70	12	0	10	590	590	45	257	319	13.1	4.24	87	.261	.340	15	.121	2	-43	-35	-5	-3.0

TOM HARRISON — Harrison, Thomas James b: 1/18/45, Trail, B.C., Canada BR/TR, 6'3", 200 lbs. Deb: 5/07/65 ♦

YEAR	TM/L	W	L	PCT	G	GS	CG	SH	SV	IP	H	HR	BB	SO	RAT	ERA	ERA+	OAV	OOB	BH	AVG	PB	PR	/A	PD	TPI
1965	KC-A	0	0	—	1	0	0	0	0	1	2	0	1	0	27.0	9.00	39	.667	.750	0	—	0	-1	-1	0	0.0

SLIM HARRISS — Harriss, William Jennings Bryan b: 12/11/1896, Brownwood, Tex. d: 9/19/63, Temple, Tex. BR/TR, 6'6", 180 lbs. Deb: 4/19/20

YEAR	TM/L	W	L	PCT	G	GS	CG	SH	SV	IP	H	HR	BB	SO	RAT	ERA	ERA+	OAV	OOB	BH	AVG	PB	PR	/A	PD	TPI
1920	Phi-A	9	14	.391	31	25	11	1	0	192	226	5	57	60	13.5	4.08	99	.305	.359	7	.106	-7	-6	-1	3	-0.4
1921	Phi-A	11	16	.407	39	28	14	0	2	227²	258	16	73	92	13.4	4.27	104	.290	.350	12	.148	-7	0	5	-1	-0.2
1922	Phi-A	9	20	.310	47	32	13	0	3	229²	262	19	94	102	14.1	5.02	85	.290	.359	13	.176	-4	-25	-19	-0	-2.1
1923	Phi-A	10	16	.385	46	28	9	0	6	209¹	221	9	95	89	13.7	4.00	103	.280	.359	4	.066	-8	-0	3	4	0.0
1924	Phi-A	6	10	.375	36	12	4	1	2	123	138	5	62	45	14.9	4.68	92	.291	.377	7	.167	-3	-6	-5	-4	-0.3
1925	Phi-A	19	12	.613	46	33	15	2	1	252²	263	8	95	95	13.0	3.49	133	.268	.336	18	.205	-3	25	33	4	3.3
1926	Phi-A	3	5	.375	12	10	2	0	0	57	66	0	22	13	13.9	4.11	102	.289	.352	1	.059	-2	-1	0	1	0.0
	Bos-A	6	10	.375	21	18	6	1	0	113	135	6	33	34	13.5	4.46	91	.311	.362	7	.206	-0	-6	-5	1	-0.3
	Yr	9	15	.375	33	28	8	1	0	170	201	6	55	47	13.7	4.34	95	.304	.359	8	.059	-2	-6	-4	1	-0.3
1927	Bos-A	14	21	.400	44	27	11	1	1	217²	253	8	66	77	13.6	4.18	101	.298	.355	8	.121	-5	-8	-7	1	-1.0
1928	Bos-A	8	11	.421	27	15	4	1	1	128¹	141	5	33	37	12.3	4.63	89	.287	.335	5	.139	-3	-8	-7	-1	-1.0
Total 9		95	135	.413	349	228	89	7	16	1750¹	1963	75	630	644	13.5	4.25	100	.290	.354	82	.145	-41	-27	3	13	-1.2

EARL HARRIST — Harrist, Earl "Irish" b: 8/20/19, Dubach, La. BR/TR, 6', 175 lbs. Deb: 8/18/45

YEAR	TM/L	W	L	PCT	G	GS	CG	SH	SV	IP	H	HR	BB	SO	RAT	ERA	ERA+	OAV	OOB	BH	AVG	PB	PR	/A	PD	TPI
1945	Cin-N	2	4	.333	14	5	1	0	0	62¹	60	2	27	15	12.0	3.61	104	.249	.327	0	.000	-2	1	1	-1	-0.1
1947	Chi-A	3	8	.273	33	4	0	0	5	93²	85	3	49	55	13.2	3.56	103	.248	.347	5	.208	-0	2	1	0	0.1
1948	Chi-A	3	3	.250	11	1	0	0	0	23	23	4	13	14	15.3	5.87	73	.267	.382	0	—	0	-4	-4	0	-0.4
	Was-A	3	3	.500	23	4	0	0	0	60²	70	1	37	21	16.3	4.60	94	.293	.394	1	.167	-1	-2	-1	0	-0.2
	Yr	4	6	.400	34	5	0	0	0	83²	93	5	50	35	15.7	4.95	87	.284	.383	0	.000	-2	-6	-6	-1	-0.5
1952	StL-A	2	8	.200	36	9	1	0	5	116²	119	7	47	49	13.6	4.01	98	.269	.352	3	.097	-3	-4	-1	1	-0.2

YEAR	TM/L	W	L	PCT	G	GS	CG	SH	SV	IP	H	HR	BB	SO	RAT	ERA	ERA+	OAV	OOB	BH	AVG	PB	PR	/A	PD	TPI
1953	Chi-A	1	0	1.000	7	0	0	0	0	8¹	9	1	5	1	15.1	7.56	53	.290	.389	0	.000	-0	-3	-3	0	-0.2
	Det-A	0	2	.000	8	1	0	0	0	18²	25	2	15	7	19.3	8.68	47	.333	.444	0	.000	-0	-10	-10	1	-0.8
	Yr	1	2	.333	15	1	0	0	0	27	34	3	20	8	18.0	8.33	49	.321	.429	1	.250	-0	-13	-13	1	-1.0
Total 5		12	28	.300	132	24	2	0	10	383¹	391	20	193	162	14.2	4.34	90	.268	.361	11	.115	-7	-21	-18	0	-1.8

■ JACK HARSHMAN
Harshman, John Elvin   b: 7/12/27, San Diego, Cal.   BL/TL, 6'2", 178 lbs.   Deb: 9/16/48 ♦

YEAR	TM/L	W	L	PCT	G	GS	CG	SH	SV	IP	H	HR	BB	SO	RAT	ERA	ERA+	OAV	OOB	BH	AVG	PB	PR	/A	PD	TPI
1952	NY-N	0	2	.000	2	2	0	0	0	6¹	12	2	6	6	25.6	14.21	26	.429	.529	0	.000	-0	-7	-7	0	-0.5
1954	Chi-A	14	8	.636	35	21	9	4	1	177	157	7	96	134	13.1	2.95	127	.238	.339	8	.143	3	15	15	-1	1.9
1955	Chi-A	11	7	.611	32	23	9	0	0	179¹	144	16	97	116	12.3	3.36	117	.224	.330	11	.183	4	12	12	-1	1.5
1956	Chi-A	15	11	.577	34	30	15	4	0	226²	183	14	102	143	11.4	3.10	132	.221	.308	12	.169	6	27	25	-3	2.9
1957	Chi-A	8	8	.500	30	26	6	0	1	151¹	142	16	82	83	13.6	4.10	91	.250	.349	10	.222	5	-5	-6	-3	-0.3
1958	Bal-A	12	15	.444	34	29	17	3	4	236¹	204	20	75	161	10.7	2.89	124	.231	.294	16	.195	7	23	18	0	3.1
1959	Bal-A	0	6	.000	14	8	0	0	0	47¹	58	6	28	24	16.7	6.85	55	.319	.415	2	.200	1	-16	-16	1	-1.2
	Bos-A	2	3	.400	8	2	0	0	0	24²	29	2	10	14	14.2	6.57	62	.284	.348	1	.143	0	-7	-7	-0	-0.6
	Cle-A	5	1	.833	13	6	5	1	1	66	46	6	13	35	8.0	2.59	142	.179	.219	7	.206	2	9	8	0	1.0
	Yr	7	10	.412	35	16	5	1	1	138	133	14	51	73	12.0	4.76	79	.244	.308	9	.176	3	-14	-15	1	-0.8
1960	Cle-A	2	4	.333	15	8	0	0	0	54¹	50	7	30	25	13.3	3.98	94	.243	.339	3	.176	-0	-1	-1	-1	-0.1
Total 8		69	65	.515	217	155	61	12	7	1169¹	1025	96	539	741	12.2	3.50	109	.235	.323	76	.179	29	50	41	-7	7.7

■ OSCAR HARSTAD
Harstad, Oscar Theander   b: 5/24/1892, Parkland, Wash.   d: 11/14/85, Corvallis, Ore.   6', 174 lbs.   Deb: 4/23/15

YEAR	TM/L	W	L	PCT	G	GS	CG	SH	SV	IP	H	HR	BB	SO	RAT	ERA	ERA+	OAV	OOB	BH	AVG	PB	PR	/A	PD	TPI
1915	Cle-A	3	5	.375	32	7	4	0	1	82	81	1	35	35	12.8	3.40	90	.270	.348	2	.125	-1	-4	-3	2	-0.1

■ BILLY HART
Hart, Joseph L.   5'8",   Deb: 7/13/1890

YEAR	TM/L	W	L	PCT	G	GS	CG	SH	SV	IP	H	HR	BB	SO	RAT	ERA	ERA+	OAV	OOB	BH	AVG	PB	PR	/A	PD	TPI
1890	StL-a	12	8	.600	26	24	20	0	0	201¹	188	6	66	95	11.4	3.67	118	.240	.299	15	.192	-1	5	15	-2	1.2

■ BILL HART
Hart, William Franklin   b: 7/19/1865, Louisville, Ky.   d: 9/19/36, Cincinnati, Ohio   TR, 5'10", 163 lbs.   Deb: 7/26/1886   U

YEAR	TM/L	W	L	PCT	G	GS	CG	SH	SV	IP	H	HR	BB	SO	RAT	ERA	ERA+	OAV	OOB	BH	AVG	PB	PR	/A	PD	TPI
1886	Phi-a	9	13	.409	22	22	22	2	0	186	183	7	66	78	12.0	3.19	110	.245	.307	10	.137	-5	5	6	1	0.3
1887	Phi-a	1	2	.333	3	3	3	0	0	26	28	1	17	4	15.6	4.50	95	.265	.367	1	.077	-2	-1	-1	0	-0.1
1892	Bro-N	9	12	.429	28	23	16	2	1	195	188	3	96	65	13.1	3.28	97	.243	.327	24	.192	2	0	-2	3	0.3
1895	Pit-N	14	17	.452	36	29	24	0	1	261²	293	4	135	85	14.7	4.75	95	.279	.361	25	.236	-2	1	-7	6	-0.2
1896	StL-N	12	29	.293	42	41	37	0	0	336	411	11	141	65	14.8	5.12	85	.299	.364	30	.186	-5	-28	-29	6	-2.2
1897	StL-N	9	27	.250	39	38	31	0	0	294²	395	10	148	67	16.6	6.26	70	.318	.391	39	.250	-1	-64	-61	3	-4.7
1898	Pit-N	5	9	.357	16	15	13	1	1	125	141	4	44	19	13.3	4.82	74	.282	.340	12	.240	-1	-17	-18	0	-1.4
1901	Cle-A	7	11	.389	20	19	16	0	0	157²	180	3	57	48	13.5	3.77	94	.283	.342	14	.219	-1	-2	-4	2	-0.2
Total 8		66	120	.355	206	190	162	5	3	1582	1819	43	704	431	14.4	4.65	86	.283	.354	155	.207	-13	-105	-114	22	-8.2

■ CHUCK HARTENSTEIN
Hartenstein, Charles Oscar "Twiggy"   b: 5/26/42, Seguin, Tex.   BR/TR, 5'11", 165 lbs.   Deb: 9/11/65   C♦

YEAR	TM/L	W	L	PCT	G	GS	CG	SH	SV	IP	H	HR	BB	SO	RAT	ERA	ERA+	OAV	OOB	BH	AVG	PB	PR	/A	PD	TPI
1966	Chi-N	0	0	—	5	0	0	0	0	9¹	8	0	3	4	11.6	1.93	191	.222	.300	0	.000	0	2	2	0	0.2
1967	Chi-N	9	5	.643	45	0	0	0	10	73	74	4	17	20	11.3	3.08	115	.278	.324	1	.063	-1	2	4	0	0.3
1968	Chi-N	2	4	.333	28	0	0	0	0	35²	41	3	11	17	13.4	4.54	70	.291	.346	0	.000	-0	-6	-5	0	-0.6
1969	Pit-N	5	4	.556	56	0	0	0	10	95²	84	9	27	44	10.8	3.95	88	.241	.303	0	.000	-0	-4	-5	2	-0.3
1970	Pit-N	1	1	.500	17	0	0	0	0	23²	25	3	8	14	12.5	4.56	85	.239	.337	0	.000	-0	-1	-2	1	0.0
	StL-N	0	0	—	6	0	0	0	0	13¹	24	1	5	9	19.6	8.78	47	.375	.420	0	.000	0	-8	-8	1	-0.5
	Yr	1	1	.500	23	0	0	0	0	37	49	4	13	23	15.1	6.08	65	.316	.369	1	.333	-0	-8	-9	1	-0.5
	Bos-A	0	3	.000	17	0	0	0	1	19	21	6	12	12	16.1	8.05	49	.288	.395	0	.000	0	-9	-9	-0	-0.8
1977	Tor-A	0	2	.000	13	0	0	0	0	27¹	40	8	6	15	15.5	6.59	64	.348	.385	0	—	0	-7	-7	-0	-0.6
Total 6		17	19	.472	187	0	0	0	23	297	317	34	89	135	12.6	4.52	80	.280	.337	2	.054	-2	-31	-29	3	-2.3

■ FRANK HARTER
Harter, Franklin Pierce "Chief"   b: 9/19/1886, Keyesport, Ill.   d: 4/14/59, Breese, Ill.   BR/TR, 5'11", 165 lbs.   Deb: 8/31/12

YEAR	TM/L	W	L	PCT	G	GS	CG	SH	SV	IP	H	HR	BB	SO	RAT	ERA	ERA+	OAV	OOB	BH	AVG	PB	PR	/A	PD	TPI
1912	Cin-N	1	2	.333	6	3	1	0	0	29¹	25	1	11	12	11.0	3.07	110	.225	.295	1	.091	-1	1	1	-1	0.0
1913	Cin-N	1	1	.500	17	2	0	0	0	46²	47	3	19	10	12.7	3.86	84	.272	.344	2	.143	-1	-3	-3	-1	-0.4
1914	Ind-F	1	2	.333	6	1	1	0	0	24²	33	0	7	8	14.6	4.01	86	.329	.373	0	.000	-1	-2	-1	-0	-0.2
Total 3		3	5	.375	29	6	2	0	0	100²	105	4	37	30	12.7	3.67	91	.273	.337	3	.091	-3	-4	-4	-1	-0.6

■ MIKE HARTLEY
Hartley, Michael Edward   b: 8/31/61, Hawthorne, Cal.   BR/TR, 6'1", 192 lbs.   Deb: 9/10/89

YEAR	TM/L	W	L	PCT	G	GS	CG	SH	SV	IP	H	HR	BB	SO	RAT	ERA	ERA+	OAV	OOB	BH	AVG	PB	PR	/A	PD	TPI
1989	LA-N	0	1	.000	5	0	0	0	0	6	2	0	0	4	3.0	1.50	228	.100	.100	0	.000	0	1	1	0	0.1
1990	LA-N	6	3	.667	32	6	1	1	1	79¹	58	7	30	76	10.2	2.95	121	.200	.280	1	.077	-1	7	5	-1	0.4
Total 2		6	4	.600	37	6	1	1	1	85¹	60	7	30	80	9.7	2.85	125	.194	.269	1	.071	-1	9	7	-1	0.5

■ CHARLIE HARTMAN
Hartman, Charles Otto   b: 8/10/1888, Los Angeles, Cal.   d: 10/22/60, Los Angeles, Cal.   Deb: 6/24/08

YEAR	TM/L	W	L	PCT	G	GS	CG	SH	SV	IP	H	HR	BB	SO	RAT	ERA	ERA+	OAV	OOB	BH	AVG	PB	PR	/A	PD	TPI
1908	Bos-A	0	0	—	1	0	0	0	0	2	1	0	2	1	13.5	4.50	55	.143	.333	0	—	0	-0	-0	0	0.0

■ BOB HARTMAN
Hartman, Robert Louis   b: 8/28/37, Kenosha, Wis.   BR/TL, 5'11", 185 lbs.   Deb: 4/26/59

YEAR	TM/L	W	L	PCT	G	GS	CG	SH	SV	IP	H	HR	BB	SO	RAT	ERA	ERA+	OAV	OOB	BH	AVG	PB	PR	/A	PD	TPI
1959	Mil-N	0	0	—	3	0	0	0	0	1²	6	0	2	1	43.2	27.00	13	.545	.615	0	—	0	-4	-4	0	-0.3
1962	Cle-A	0	1	.000	8	2	0	0	0	17¹	14	1	8	11	11.4	3.12	124	.209	.293	0	.000	-1	2	1	-0	0.1
Total 2		0	1	.000	11	2	0	0	0	19	20	1	10	12	14.2	5.21	74	.256	.341	0	.000	-1	-3	-3	-0	-0.2

■ RAY HARTRANFT
Hartranft, Raymond Joseph   b: 9/19/1890, Quakertown, Pa.   d: 2/10/55, Spring City, Pa.   BL/TL, 6'1", 195 lbs.   Deb: 6/16/13

YEAR	TM/L	W	L	PCT	G	GS	CG	SH	SV	IP	H	HR	BB	SO	RAT	ERA	ERA+	OAV	OOB	BH	AVG	PB	PR	/A	PD	TPI
1913	Phi-N	0	0	—	1	0	0	0	0	1	3	0	1	1	36.0	9.00	37	.500	.571	0	—	0	-1	-1	0	0.0

■ CLINT HARTUNG
Hartung, Clinton Clarence "Floppy" or "The Hondo Hurricane"   b: 8/10/22, Hondo, Tex.   BR/TR, 6'5", 210 lbs.   Deb: 4/15/47 ♦

YEAR	TM/L	W	L	PCT	G	GS	CG	SH	SV	IP	H	HR	BB	SO	RAT	ERA	ERA+	OAV	OOB	BH	AVG	PB	PR	/A	PD	TPI
1947	NY-N	9	7	.563	23	20	8	1	0	138	140	15	69	54	13.8	4.57	89	.263	.350	29	.309	9	-8	-8	-1	0.5
1948	NY-N	8	8	.500	36	19	6	2	1	153¹	146	15	72	42	13.1	4.75	83	.258	.347	10	.179	2	-14	-14	0	-1.1
1949	NY-N	9	11	.450	33	25	8	0	0	154²	156	16	86	48	14.3	5.00	80	.260	.357	12	.190	4	-17	-18	2	-1.1
1950	NY-N	3	3	.500	20	8	1	0	0	65¹	87	10	44	23	18.3	6.61	62	.326	.425	13	.302	4	-18	-18	3	-0.8
Total 4		29	29	.500	112	72	23	3	1	511¹	529	56	271	167	14.3	5.02	80	.269	.361	90	.238	19	-56	-57	4	-2.5

■ PAUL HARTZELL
Hartzell, Paul Franklin   b: 11/2/53, Bloomsburg, Pa.   BR/TR, 6'5", 200 lbs.   Deb: 4/10/76

YEAR	TM/L	W	L	PCT	G	GS	CG	SH	SV	IP	H	HR	BB	SO	RAT	ERA	ERA+	OAV	OOB	BH	AVG	PB	PR	/A	PD	TPI
1976	Cal-A	7	4	.636	37	15	7	2	2	166	166	6	43	51	11.9	2.77	120	.266	.323	0	—	0	14	10	2	1.3
1977	Cal-A	8	12	.400	43	23	6	0	4	189¹	208	14	38	79	11.5	3.57	110	.274	.313	0	—	0	10	7	1	0.9
1978	Cal-A	6	10	.375	54	12	5	0	0	157	168	8	41	55	12.3	3.44	105	.278	.329	0	—	0	6	3	2	0.5
1979	Min-A	6	10	.375	28	26	4	0	0	163	193	18	44	44	13.3	5.36	82	.301	.350	0	—	0	-21	-18	1	-1.4
1980	Bal-A	0	2	.000	6	0	0	0	0	17²	22	3	9	5	15.8	6.62	60	.310	.387	0	—	0	-5	-5	-0	-0.4
1984	Mil-A	0	1	.000	4	1	0	0	0	10¹	17	0	6	3	20.0	7.84	49	.370	.442	0	—	0	-4	-5	-0	-0.3
Total 6		27	39	.409	170	77	22	2	12	703¹	766	49	181	237	12.4	3.90	98	.282	.332	0	—	0	-0	-7	6	0.6

■ BRYAN HARVEY
Harvey, Bryan Stanley   b: 6/2/63, Chattanooga, Tenn.   BR/TR, 6'3", 205 lbs.   Deb: 5/16/87

YEAR	TM/L	W	L	PCT	G	GS	CG	SH	SV	IP	H	HR	BB	SO	RAT	ERA	ERA+	OAV	OOB	BH	AVG	PB	PR	/A	PD	TPI
1987	Cal-A	0	0	—	3	0	0	0	0	5	6	0	2	3	14.4	0.00	—	.300	.364	0	—	0	2	2	-0	0.2
1988	Cal-A	7	5	.583	50	0	0	0	17	76	59	4	20	67	9.5	2.13	181	.214	.269	0	—	0	15	15	-2	1.3
1989	Cal-A	3	3	.500	51	0	0	0	25	55	36	6	41	78	12.6	3.44	111	.183	.324	0	—	0	2	0	-0	0.3
1990	Cal-A	4	4	.500	54	0	0	0	25	64¹	45	4	35	82	11.2	3.22	121	.201	.309	0	—	0	5	5	-1	0.3
Total 4		14	12	.538	158	0	0	0	67	200¹	146	14	98	230	11.0	2.79	139	.204	.300	0	—	0	26	24	-3	2.1

■ ERWIN HARVEY
Harvey, Ervin King "Zaza"   b: 1/5/1879, Saratoga, Cal.   d: 6/3/54, Santa Monica, Cal.   BL, 6', 190 lbs.   Deb: 5/03/00 ♦

YEAR	TM/L	W	L	PCT	G	GS	CG	SH	SV	IP	H	HR	BB	SO	RAT	ERA	ERA+	OAV	OOB	BH	AVG	PB	PR	/A	PD	TPI
1900	Chi-N	0	0	—	1	0	0	0	0	4	3	0	1	0	9.0	0.00	—	.208	.260	0	.000	-0	2	2	0	0.2
1901	Chi-A	3	6	.333	16	9	5	0	1	92	91	2	34	27	12.2	3.62	96	.255	.320	10	.250	2	0	-1	2	0.2

YEAR TM/L	W	L	PCT	G	GS	CG	SH	SV	IP	H	HR	BB	SO	RAT	ERA	ERA+	OAV	OOB	BH	AVG	PB	PR	/A	PD	TPI
Total 2	3	6	.333	17	9	5	0	0	96	94	4	35	27	12.1	3.47	101	.253	.318	86	.332	1	2	0	2	0.4

■ HERB HASH
Hash, Herbert Howard   b: 2/13/11, Woolwine, Va.   BR/TR, 6'1", 180 lbs.   Deb: 4/19/40

YEAR TM/L	W	L	PCT	G	GS	CG	SH	SV	IP	H	HR	BB	SO	RAT	ERA	ERA+	OAV	OOB	BH	AVG	PB	PR	/A	PD	TPI
1940 Bos-A	7	7	.500	34	12	3	1	3	120	123	11	84	36	15.9	4.95	91	.266	.385	7	.175	-0	-8	-6	1	-0.4
1941 Bos-A	1	0	1.000	4	0	0	0	1	8¹	7	1	7	3	15.1	5.40	77	.226	.368	0	.000	-0	-1	-1	0	0.0
Total 2	8	7	.533	38	12	3	1	4	128¹	130	12	91	39	15.8	4.98	90	.264	.384	7	.167	-1	-9	-7	2	-0.4

■ ANDY HASSLER
Hassler, Andrew Earl   b: 10/18/51, Texas City, Tex.   BL/TL, 6'5", 220 lbs.   Deb: 5/30/71

YEAR TM/L	W	L	PCT	G	GS	CG	SH	SV	IP	H	HR	BB	SO	RAT	ERA	ERA+	OAV	OOB	BH	AVG	PB	PR	/A	PD	TPI
1971 Cal-A	0	3	.000	6	4	0	0	0	18²	25	0	15	13	19.8	3.86	84	.333	.451	0	.000	-1	-1	-1	0	-0.1
1973 Cal-A	0	4	.000	7	4	1	0	0	31²	33	0	19	19	15.6	3.69	96	.262	.372	0	—	0	0	-1	-0	0.0
1974 Cal-A	7	11	.389	23	22	10	2	1	162	132	10	79	76	12.2	2.61	132	.225	.326	0	—	0	18	15	1	1.7
1975 Cal-A	3	12	.200	30	18	6	1	0	133¹	158	12	53	82	14.6	5.94	60	.303	.373	0	—	0	-32	-35	1	-3.2
1976 Cal-A	0	6	.000	14	4	0	0	0	47¹	50	3	17	16	12.7	5.13	65	.284	.347	0	—	0	-8	-10	0	-0.9
*KC-A	5	6	.455	19	14	4	1	0	99²	89	2	39	45	11.6	2.89	121	.242	.314	0	—	0	7	7	1	0.8
Yr	5	12	.294	33	18	4	1	0	147	139	5	56	61	11.9	3.61	95	.254	.323	0	—	0	-2	-3	1	-0.1
1977 *KC-A	9	6	.600	29	27	3	1	0	156¹	166	7	75	83	14.2	4.20	96	.270	.354	0	—	0	-2	-3	0	-0.1
1978 KC-A	1	4	.200	11	9	1	0	0	58¹	76	1	24	26	15.7	4.32	88	.317	.383	0	—	0	-4	-3	-0	-0.3
Bos-A	2	1	.667	13	2	0	0	1	30	38	0	13	23	15.3	3.00	137	.302	.367	0	—	0	3	4	0	0.4
Yr	3	5	.375	24	11	1	0	1	88¹	114	1	37	49	15.4	3.87	101	.308	.371	0	—	0	-1	-0	-1	0.1
1979 Bos-A	1	2	.333	15	1	0	0	0	15¹	23	0	7	7	18.2	8.80	50	.365	.437	0	—	0	-8	-7	-0	-0.6
NY-N	4	5	.444	29	8	1	0	4	80¹	74	5	42	53	13.0	3.70	98	.252	.345	0	.000	-2	0	-1	0	-0.1
1980 Pit-N	0	0	—	6	0	0	0	0	11²	9	2	4	4	10.0	3.86	94	.243	.317	0	.000	-0	-0	-1	0	0.0
Cal-A	5	1	.833	41	0	0	0	10	83	67	8	37	75	11.4	2.49	158	.214	.299	0	—	0	14	13	-1	1.2
1981 Cal-A	4	3	.571	42	0	0	0	5	75²	72	8	33	44	12.5	3.21	114	.262	.341	0	—	0	4	4	0	0.4
1982 *Cal-A	2	1	.667	54	0	0	0	5	71¹	58	5	40	38	12.9	2.78	146	.232	.347	0	—	0	10	10	2	1.2
1983 Cal-A	0	5	.000	42	0	0	0	4	36¹	42	2	17	20	14.6	5.45	74	.302	.378	0	—	0	-6	-6	0	-0.7
1984 StL-N	1	0	1.000	3	0	0	0	0	2¹	4	2	2	1	23.1	11.57	30	.364	.462	0	—	0	-2	-2	0	-0.1
1985 StL-N	0	1	.000	10	0	0	0	0	10	9	0	4	5	11.7	1.80	196	.225	.295	0	—	0	2	2	-0	0.2
Total 14	44	71	.383	387	112	26	5	29	1123¹	1125	67	520	630	13.4	3.83	97	.264	.349	0	.000	-3	-5	-15	5	0.1

■ CHARLIE HASTINGS
Hastings, Charles Morton   b: 11/11/1870, Ironton, Ohio   d: 8/3/34, Parkersburg, W.Va.   5'11", 179 lbs.   Deb: 5/03/1893

YEAR TM/L	W	L	PCT	G	GS	CG	SH	SV	IP	H	HR	BB	SO	RAT	ERA	ERA+	OAV	OOB	BH	AVG	PB	PR	/A	PD	TPI
1893 Cle-N	4	5	.444	15	9	6	0	1	92	128	5	33	14	15.8	4.70	104	.320	.372	7	.179	-1	-0	2	-1	0.1
1896 Pit-N	5	10	.333	17	13	9	0	1	104	126	1	44	19	14.7	5.88	71	.297	.363	8	.216	-1	-18	-19	1	-1.4
1897 Pit-N	5	4	.556	16	10	9	0	0	118	138	3	47	42	14.1	4.58	91	.289	.353	10	.233	-3	-3	-5	-1	-0.2
1898 Pit-N	4	10	.286	19	13	12	0	0	137¹	142	2	52	40	12.7	3.41	105	.265	.330	10	.233	2	3	1	0	0.5
Total 4	18	29	.383	67	45	36	0	2	451¹	534	11	176	115	14.2	4.55	91	.291	.353	35	.216	5	-18	-21	-0	-1.0

■ BOB HASTY
Hasty, Robert Keller   b: 5/3/1896, Canton, Ga.   d: 5/28/72, Dallas, Ga.   BR/TR, 6'3", 210 lbs.   Deb: 9/11/19

YEAR TM/L	W	L	PCT	G	GS	CG	SH	SV	IP	H	HR	BB	SO	RAT	ERA	ERA+	OAV	OOB	BH	AVG	PB	PR	/A	PD	TPI
1919 Phi-A	0	2	.000	2	2	1	0	0	12	15	1	4	5	14.3	5.25	65	.306	.358	1	.333	0	-3	-2	-1	-0.2
1920 Phi-A	1	3	.250	19	4	1	0	0	71²	91	5	28	12	14.9	5.02	80	.323	.384	6	.250	-1	-10	-8	2	-0.5
1921 Phi-A	5	16	.238	35	22	9	0	0	179¹	238	8	40	46	14.1	4.87	92	.331	.368	20	.294	2	-12	-8	1	-0.8
1922 Phi-A	9	14	.391	28	26	14	1	0	192¹	225	20	41	33	12.6	4.26	100	.298	.336	15	.200	-2	-5	-0	-2	-0.2
1923 Phi-A	13	15	.464	44	36	10	1	1	243¹	274	11	72	56	13.1	4.44	93	.291	.347	17	.193	-3	-12	-9	-1	-1.0
1924 Phi-A	1	3	.250	18	4	0	0	0	52²	57	4	30	15	15.0	5.64	76	.282	.378	1	.077	-1	-8	-8	2	-0.6
Total 6	29	53	.354	146	94	35	2	1	751¹	900	49	215	167	13.5	4.65	91	.305	.355	60	.221	-3	-49	-35	1	-2.9

■ MICKEY HATCHER
Hatcher, Michael Vaughn   b: 3/15/55, Cleveland, Ohio   BR/TR, 6'2", 200 lbs.   Deb: 8/03/79 ◆

YEAR TM/L	W	L	PCT	G	GS	CG	SH	SV	IP	H	HR	BB	SO	RAT	ERA	ERA+	OAV	OOB	BH	AVG	PB	PR	/A	PD	TPI
1989 LA-N	0	0	—	1	0	0	0	0	1	1	0	3	0	36.0	9.00	38	.000	.667	66	.295	-0	-1	-1	0	0.0

■ GIL HATFIELD
Hatfield, Gilbert "Colonel"   b: 1/27/1855, Hoboken, N.J.   d: 5/27/21, Hoboken, N.J.   TR, 5'9.5", 168 lbs.   Deb: 9/24/1885 ◆

YEAR TM/L	W	L	PCT	G	GS	CG	SH	SV	IP	H	HR	BB	SO	RAT	ERA	ERA+	OAV	OOB	BH	AVG	PB	PR	/A	PD	TPI
1889 NY-N	2	4	.333	6	5	5	0	0	52	53	2	25	28	13.5	3.98	99	.256	.336	23	.184	-0	0	-0	0	0.0
1890 NY-P	1	1	.500	3	0	0	0	1	7²	8	1	4	3	14.1	3.52	129	.257	.342	80	.279	0	1	1	-0	0.1
1891 Was-a	0	0	—	4	0	0	0	0	18	29	1	14	3	21.5	11.00	34	.351	.445	128	.256	1	-15	-15	0	-1.0
Total 3	3	5	.375	13	5	5	0	1	77²	90	4	43	34	15.4	5.56	71	.280	.365	295	.248	1	-14	-14	0	-0.9

■ JOHN HATFIELD
Hatfield, John Van Buskirk   b: 7/20/1847, New Jersey   d: 2/20/09, Long Island City, N.Y.   5'10", 165 lbs.   Deb: 5/18/1871   M◆

YEAR TM/L	W	L	PCT	G	GS	CG	SH	SV	IP	H	HR	BB	SO	RAT	ERA	ERA+	OAV	OOB	BH	AVG	PB	PR	/A	PD	TPI
1874 Mut-n	0	1	.000	3	0	0	0	0	8	11	0	1	0	13.5	2.25	137	.324	.343	68	.235	-0	1	1	-0	0.1

■ RAY HATHAWAY
Hathaway, Ray Wilson   b: 10/13/16, Greenville, Ohio   BR/TR, 6', 165 lbs.   Deb: 4/20/45

YEAR TM/L	W	L	PCT	G	GS	CG	SH	SV	IP	H	HR	BB	SO	RAT	ERA	ERA+	OAV	OOB	BH	AVG	PB	PR	/A	PD	TPI
1945 Bro-N	0	1	.000	4	1	0	0	0	9	11	1	6	3	17.0	4.00	94	.297	.395	0	.000	-0	-0	-0	0	0.0

■ JOE HATTEN
Hatten, Joseph Hilarian   b: 11/17/16, Bancroft, Iowa   d: 12/16/88, Redding, Cal.   BR/TL, 6', 176 lbs.   Deb: 4/21/46

YEAR TM/L	W	L	PCT	G	GS	CG	SH	SV	IP	H	HR	BB	SO	RAT	ERA	ERA+	OAV	OOB	BH	AVG	PB	PR	/A	PD	TPI
1946 Bro-N	14	11	.560	42	30	13	1	2	222	207	10	110	85	13.1	2.84	119	.253	.347	6	.076	-6	14	13	-1	0.6
1947 *Bro-N	17	8	.680	42	32	11	3	0	225¹	211	9	105	76	12.8	3.63	114	.252	.339	17	.205	0	11	12	3	1.6
1948 Bro-N	13	10	.565	42	30	11	1	0	208²	228	9	94	73	14.0	3.58	112	.283	.360	13	.206	1	9	10	4	1.6
1949 *Bro-N	12	8	.600	37	29	11	2	2	187¹	194	15	69	58	12.7	4.18	98	.271	.337	12	.179	-1	-3	-2	1	-0.1
1950 Bro-N	2	2	.500	23	8	2	1	0	68²	82	10	31	29	14.8	4.59	89	.294	.365	2	.111	-1	-4	-4	-0	-0.4
1951 Bro-N	0	1	1.000	11	6	0	0	0	49¹	55	3	21	22	13.9	4.56	86	.281	.350	2	.133	-1	-3	-3	-0	-0.3
Chi-N	2	6	.250	23	6	1	0	0	75¹	82	8	37	23	14.3	5.14	80	.281	.364	4	.235	0	-10	-9	-0	-0.8
Yr	3	6	.333	34	12	1	0	0	124²	137	11	58	45	14.1	4.91	82	.281	.358	0	.000	-1	-13	-12	-1	-1.1
1952 Chi-N	4	4	.500	13	8	2	0	0	50¹	65	6	25	15	16.3	6.08	63	.314	.391	1	.067	-1	-13	-12	-1	-1.1
Total 7	65	49	.570	233	149	51	8	4	1087	1124	70	492	381	13.5	3.87	101	.271	.351	57	.160	-8	1	5	8	1.1

■ CLYDE HATTER
Hatter, Clyde Melno   b: 8/7/08, Poplar Hill, Ky.   d: 10/16/37, Yosemite, Ky.   BR/TL, 5'11", 170 lbs.   Deb: 4/23/35

YEAR TM/L	W	L	PCT	G	GS	CG	SH	SV	IP	H	HR	BB	SO	RAT	ERA	ERA+	OAV	OOB	BH	AVG	PB	PR	/A	PD	TPI
1935 Det-A	0	0	—	8	2	0	0	0	33¹	44	2	30	15	20.3	7.56	55	.319	.444	3	.300	0	-12	-13	-1	-1.1
1937 Det-A	1	0	1.000	3	0	0	0	0	9¹	17	0	11	4	28.0	11.57	40	.415	.547	0	.000	-0	-7	-7	-0	-0.5
Total 2	1	0	1.000	11	2	0	0	0	42²	61	2	41	19	21.9	8.44	51	.341	.468	3	.231	0	-19	-20	-1	-1.6

■ CHRIS HAUGHEY
Haughey, Christopher Francis "Bud"   b: 10/3/25, Astoria, N.Y.   BR/TR, 6'1", 180 lbs.   Deb: 10/03/43

YEAR TM/L	W	L	PCT	G	GS	CG	SH	SV	IP	H	HR	BB	SO	RAT	ERA	ERA+	OAV	OOB	BH	AVG	PB	PR	/A	PD	TPI
1943 Bro-N	0	1	.000	1	0	0	0	0	7	5	0	10	0	19.3	3.86	87	.238	.484	0	.000	-0	-0	-0	0	0.0

■ PHIL HAUGSTAD
Haugstad, Philip Donald   b: 2/23/24, Black River Falls Wis.   BR/TR, 6'2", 165 lbs.   Deb: 9/01/47

YEAR TM/L	W	L	PCT	G	GS	CG	SH	SV	IP	H	HR	BB	SO	RAT	ERA	ERA+	OAV	OOB	BH	AVG	PB	PR	/A	PD	TPI
1947 Bro-N	1	0	1.000	6	1	0	0	0	12¹	14	1	4	4	12.8	2.84	145	.298	.353	0	.000	-0	2	2	0	0.1
1948 Bro-N	0	0	—	1	0	0	0	0	1	1	0	0	0	9.00	—	.333	.333	0	—	0	0	0	0	0.0
1951 Bro-N	0	1	.000	21	1	0	0	0	30²	28	4	24	22	16.1	6.46	61	.233	.374	0	.000	-0	-9	-9	0	-0.7
1952 Cin-N	0	0	—	9	0	0	0	0	12	8	1	13	2	16.5	6.75	56	.190	.393	0	.000	-0	-4	-4	0	-0.3
Total 4	1	1	.500	37	2	0	0	0	56¹	51	6	41	28	15.3	5.59	70	.241	.374	0	.000	-0	-10	-10	1	-0.8

■ TOM HAUSMAN
Hausman, Thomas Matthew   b: 3/31/53, Mobridge, S.D.   BR/TR, 6'4", 190 lbs.   Deb: 4/26/75

YEAR TM/L	W	L	PCT	G	GS	CG	SH	SV	IP	H	HR	BB	SO	RAT	ERA	ERA+	OAV	OOB	BH	AVG	PB	PR	/A	PD	TPI
1975 Mil-A	3	6	.333	29	9	1	0	2	112	110	7	47	46	13.1	4.10	93	.258	.340	0	—	0	-4	-3	1	-0.2
1976 Mil-A	0	0	—	3	0	0	0	0	3¹	3	0	3	4	16.2	5.40	65	.250	.400	0	—	0	-1	-1	0	0.0
1978 NY-N	3	3	.500	10	10	0	0	0	51²	58	6	9	16	11.8	4.70	74	.287	.321	3	.176	1	-6	-7	0	-0.5
1979 NY-N	2	6	.250	19	10	1	0	0	78²	65	6	19	34	10.0	2.75	133	.226	.284	3	.115	-1	9	8	0	0.7
1980 NY-N	6	5	.545	55	4	0	0	1	122	125	2	26	50	11.4	3.98	89	.266	.308	1	.063	-1	-5	-6	2	-0.4
1981 NY-N	0	1	.000	20	0	0	0	0	33	28	2	7	13	9.5	2.18	160	.235	.278	0	.000	-0	5	5	0	0.5
1982 NY-N	1	2	.333	21	0	0	0	0	36²	44	4	6	16	12.8	4.42	82	.295	.331	0	.000	-0	-3	-3	-0	-0.3

YEAR TM/L	W	L	PCT	G	GS	CG	SH	SV	IP	H	HR	BB	SO	RAT	ERA	ERA+	OAV	OOB	BH	AVG	PB	PR	/A	PD	TPI
Atl-N	0	0	—	3	0	0	0	0	3²	6	0	4	2	24.5	4.91	76	.500	.625	0	—	0	-1	-0	0	0.0
Yr	1	2	.333	24	0	0	0	0	40¹	50	4	10	18	13.4	4.46	82	.299	.339	0	.000	-0	-4	-4	-0	-0.3
Total 7	15	23	.395	160	33	2	0	3	441	439	37	121	180	11.8	3.80	96	.262	.317	7	.111	-2	-7	-8	3	-0.3

■ CLEM HAUSMANN
Hausmann, Clemens Raymond   b: 8/17/19, Houston, Tex.   d: 8/29/72, Baytown, Tex.   BR/TR, 5'9", 165 lbs.   Deb: 4/28/44

YEAR TM/L	W	L	PCT	G	GS	CG	SH	SV	IP	H	HR	BB	SO	RAT	ERA	ERA+	OAV	OOB	BH	AVG	PB	PR	/A	PD	TPI
1944 Bos-A	4	7	.364	32	12	3	0	2	137	139	6	69	43	13.9	3.42	99	.266	.355	3	.079	-2	0	-0	0	-0.2
1945 Bos-A	5	7	.417	31	13	4	2	2	125	131	5	60	30	13.9	5.04	68	.270	.352¹	4	.103	-3	-23	-23	2	-2.3
1949 Phi-A	0	0	—	1	0	0	0	0	1	0	0	2	0	18.0	9.00	46	.000	.500	0	—	-0	-1	-1	0	0.0
Total 3	9	14	.391	64	25	7	2	4	263	270	11	131	73	13.9	4.21	81	.267	.354	7	.091	-5	-24	-23	2	-2.5

■ BRAD HAVENS
Havens, Bradley David   b: 11/17/59, Highland Park, Mich   BL/TL, 6'1", 180 lbs.   Deb: 6/05/81

YEAR TM/L	W	L	PCT	G	GS	CG	SH	SV	IP	H	HR	BB	SO	RAT	ERA	ERA+	OAV	OOB	BH	AVG	PB	PR	/A	PD	TPI
1981 Min-A	3	6	.333	14	12	1	1	0	78	76	6	24	43	11.7	3.58	110	.257	.315	0	—	0	1	3	-0	0.3
1982 Min-A	10	14	.417	33	32	4	1	0	208²	201	32	80	129	12.1	4.31	98	.250	.318	0	—	0	-6	-2	-3	-0.4
1983 Min-A	5	8	.385	16	14	1	0	0	80¹	110	11	38	40	16.6	8.18	52	.333	.402	0	—	0	-37	-35	-2	-3.2
1985 Bal-A	0	1	.000	8	1	0	0	0	14¹	20	4	10	19	18.8	8.79	46	.333	.429	0	—	0	-7	-8	-0	-0.7
1986 Bal-A	3	3	.500	46	0	0	0	1	71	64	7	29	57	11.8	4.56	91	.248	.324	0	—	0	-3	-3	1	-0.2
1987 LA-N	0	0	—	31	1	0	0	0	35¹	30	2	23	23	13.8	4.33	92	.227	.346	0	.000	-0	-1	-1	-0	-0.1
1988 LA-N	0	0	—	9	0	0	0	0	9²	15	1	4	8	17.7	4.66	72	.357	.413	0	.000	-0	-1	-1	1	0.0
Cle-A	2	3	.400	28	0	0	0	1	57¹	62	7	17	30	12.4	3.14	131	.273	.324	0	—	0	5	6	-0	0.6
1989 Cle-A	0	0	—	7	0	0	0	0	13¹	18	3	7	6	16.9	4.05	98	.353	.431	0	—	0	-0	-1	1	0.1
Det-A	1	2	.333	13	1	0	0	0	22²	28	3	14	15	17.9	5.56	69	.308	.417	0	—	0	-4	-4	0	-0.2
Yr	1	2	.333	20	1	0	0	0	36	46	6	21	21	17.5	5.00	77	.319	.417	0	—	0	-4	-5	1	-0.2
Total 8	24	37	.393	205	61	6	2	3	590²	624	76	246	370	13.3	4.81	86	.272	.344	0	.000	0	-54	-46	-4	-3.8

■ ED HAWK
Hawk, Edward   b: 5/11/1890, Neosho, Mo.   d: 3/26/36, Neosho, Mo.   BL/TR, 5'11", 175 lbs.   Deb: 9/07/11

YEAR TM/L	W	L	PCT	G	GS	CG	SH	SV	IP	H	HR	BB	SO	RAT	ERA	ERA+	OAV	OOB	BH	AVG	PB	PR	/A	PD	TPI
1911 StL-A	0	4	.000	5	4	4	0	0	37²	38	1	8	14	11.9	3.35	101	.253	.309	2	.154	-1	-0	0	0	0.0

■ BILL HAWKE
Hawke, William Victor "Dick"   b: 4/28/1870, Elsmere, Del.   d: 12/11/02, Wilmington, Del.   BR/TR, 5'8.5", 169 lbs.   Deb: 7/28/1892

YEAR TM/L	W	L	PCT	G	GS	CG	SH	SV	IP	H	HR	BB	SO	RAT	ERA	ERA+	OAV	OOB	BH	AVG	PB	PR	/A	PD	TPI
1892 StL-N	5	5	.500	14	11	10	1	0	97¹	108	2	45	55	14.1	3.70	86	.279	.344	4	.089	-4	-4	-5	-0	-0.8
1893 StL-N	0	1	.000	1	1	0	0	0	5¹	9	0	3	1	20.3	5.06	94	.363	.432	1	.333	0	-1	-0	0	0.0
Bal-N	11	16	.407	29	29	22	1	0	225	248	8	108	69	14.2	4.76	100	.271	.348	16	.172	-4	-2	0	-0	-0.2
Yr	11	17	.393	30	30	22	1	0	230¹	257	8	111	70	14.4	4.77	100	.274	.351	7	.073	-4	-2	-0	-0	-0.2
1894 *Bal-N	16	9	.640	32	25	17	0	3	205	264	9	78	68	15.0	5.84	93	.309	.367	28	.304	2	-12	-9	1	-0.3
Total 3	32	31	.508	76	66	49	2	3	532²	629	19	234	193	14.6	4.98	95	.287	.356	49	.210	-1	-19	-15	1	-1.3

■ ANDY HAWKINS
Hawkins, Melton Andrew   b: 1/21/60, Waco, Tex.   BR/TR, 6'4", 200 lbs.   Deb: 7/17/82

YEAR TM/L	W	L	PCT	G	GS	CG	SH	SV	IP	H	HR	BB	SO	RAT	ERA	ERA+	OAV	OOB	BH	AVG	PB	PR	/A	PD	TPI
1982 SD-N	2	5	.286	15	10	1	0	0	63²	66	4	27	25	13.4	4.10	84	.274	.352	0	.000	-2	-4	-5	-1	-0.6
1983 SD-N	5	7	.417	21	19	4	1	0	119²	106	8	48	59	12.0	2.93	119	.244	.326	2	.065	-1	9	7	1	0.7
1984 *SD-N	8	9	.471	36	22	2	1	0	146	143	12	72	77	13.4	4.68	76	.254	.341	8	.195	1	-18	-18	-1	-1.8
1985 SD-N	18	8	.692	33	33	5	2	0	228²	229	18	65	69	11.7	3.15	112	.267	.321	6	.078	-4	11	10	0	0.6
1986 SD-N	10	8	.556	37	35	3	1	0	209¹	218	24	75	117	12.8	4.30	85	.268	.334	10	.149	-1	-14	-15	-1	-1.6
1987 SD-N	3	10	.231	24	20	0	0	0	117²	131	16	49	51	13.9	5.05	78	.287	.358	5	.156	-0	-13	-14	-1	-1.3
1988 SD-N	14	11	.560	33	33	4	2	0	217²	196	16	76	91	11.5	3.35	101	.244	.314	7	.113	-2	2	-1	-2	-0.2
1989 NY-A	15	15	.500	34	34	5	2	0	208¹	238	23	76	98	13.8	4.80	81	.290	.355	0	—	0	-21	-21	-3	-2.3
1990 NY-A	5	12	.294	28	26	2	1	0	157²	156	20	82	74	13.7	5.37	74	.260	.351	0	—	0	-26	-24	-2	-2.4
Total 9	80	85	.485	261	232	26	10	0	1468²	1483	142	570	661	12.8	4.14	88	.265	.337	38	.117	-8	-71	-80	-8	-8.9

■ WYNN HAWKINS
Hawkins, Wynn Firth "Hawk"   b: 2/20/36, E.Palestine, Ohio   BR/TR, 6'3", 195 lbs.   Deb: 4/22/60

YEAR TM/L	W	L	PCT	G	GS	CG	SH	SV	IP	H	HR	BB	SO	RAT	ERA	ERA+	OAV	OOB	BH	AVG	PB	PR	/A	PD	TPI
1960 Cle-A	4	4	.500	15	9	1	0	0	66	68	10	39	39	14.7	4.23	88	.269	.369	2	.100	-1	-3	-4	-1	-0.3
1961 Cle-A	7	9	.438	30	21	3	1	1	133	139	16	59	51	13.5	4.06	97	.270	.347	4	.108	-2	-1	-2	-1	-0.3
1962 Cle-A	1	0	1.000	3	0	0	0	0	3²	9	1	1	0	24.5	7.36	53	.429	.455	0	—	0	-1	-1	-0	0.0
Total 3	12	13	.480	48	30	4	1	1	202²	216	27	99	90	14.1	4.17	93	.274	.357	6	.105	-2	-5	-7	-0	-0.6

■ PINK HAWLEY
Hawley, Emerson P.   b: 12/5/1872, Beaver Dam, Wis.   d: 9/19/38, Beaver Dam, Wis.   BL/TR, 5'10", 185 lbs.   Deb: 8/13/1892

YEAR TM/L	W	L	PCT	G	GS	CG	SH	SV	IP	H	HR	BB	SO	RAT	ERA	ERA+	OAV	OOB	BH	AVG	PB	PR	/A	PD	TPI
1892 StL-N	6	14	.300	20	20	18	0	0	166¹	160	4	63	63	12.1	3.19	100	.243	.309	12	.169	2	0	-2	-0	-0.3
1893 StL-N	5	17	.227	31	24	21	0	1	227	249	6	103	73	14.0	4.60	103	.270	.344	26	.286	7	-3	-3	0	0.6
1894 StL-N	19	27	.413	53	41	36	0	0	392²	481	14	149	120	14.4	4.90	110	.298	.358	43	.264	1	18	22	2	2.0
1895 Pit-N	31	22	.585	56	50	44	4	0	444¹	449	7	122	142	11.6	3.18	142	.258	.307	57	.308	13	79	66	2	6.8
1896 Pit-N	22	21	.512	49	43	37	2	0	378	382	2	157	137	12.8	3.57	118	.260	.332	39	.239	2	33	26	3	2.7
1897 Pit-N	18	18	.500	40	39	33	0	0	311¹	362	11	94	88	13.2	4.80	87	.288	.338	30	.231	-2	-17	-21	-0	-1.8
1898 Cin-N	27	11	.711	43	37	32	5	0	331	357	5	91	69	12.2	3.37	114	.273	.321	24	.185	-4	9	17	-5	0.8
1899 Cin-N	14	17	.452	34	29	25	0	1	250¹	289	7	65	46	12.7	4.24	92	.289	.332	22	.218	-1	-11	-9	-2	-0.9
1900 NY-N	18	18	.500	41	38	34	2	0	329¹	377	9	89	80	12.7	3.53	103	.287	.332	25	.203	-2	6	3	4	0.4
1901 Mil-A	7	14	.333	26	23	17	0	0	182¹	228	3	41	50	13.3	4.59	78	.302	.338	19	.260	3	-19	-20	1	-1.4
Total 10	167	179	.483	393	344	297	11	3	3012²	3334	62	974	868	12.9	3.96	107	.277	.331	297	.241	14	103	89	-0	8.9

■ SCOTT HAWLEY
Hawley, Scott   Deb: 9/22/1894

YEAR TM/L	W	L	PCT	G	GS	CG	SH	SV	IP	H	HR	BB	SO	RAT	ERA	ERA+	OAV	OOB	BH	AVG	PB	PR	/A	PD	TPI
1894 Bos-N	0	1	.000	1	1	1	0	0	7	10	0	7	1	21.9	7.71	74	.332	.458	0	.000	-1	-2	-2	0	0.0

■ HAL HAYDEL
Haydel, John Harold   b: 7/9/44, Houma, La.   BR/TR, 6', 190 lbs.   Deb: 9/07/70

YEAR TM/L	W	L	PCT	G	GS	CG	SH	SV	IP	H	HR	BB	SO	RAT	ERA	ERA+	OAV	OOB	BH	AVG	PB	PR	/A	PD	TPI
1970 Min-A	2	0	1.000	4	0	0	0	0	9	7	2	4	11	10.0	3.00	124	.226	.314	2	.667	2	1	1	0	0.3
1971 Min-A	4	2	.667	31	0	0	0	1	40	33	3	20	29	12.4	4.27	83	.243	.348	1	.333	0	-4	-3	0	-0.1
Total 2	6	2	.750	35	0	0	0	1	49	40	5	24	33	12.1	4.04	89	.240	.342	3	.500	2	-3	-2	0	0.1

■ LEFTY HAYDEN
Hayden, Eugene Franklin   b: 4/14/35, San Francisco, Cal   BL/TL, 6'2", 175 lbs.   Deb: 6/26/58

YEAR TM/L	W	L	PCT	G	GS	CG	SH	SV	IP	H	HR	BB	SO	RAT	ERA	ERA+	OAV	OOB	BH	AVG	PB	PR	/A	PD	TPI
1958 Cin-N	0	0	—	3	0	0	0	0	3²	5	0	1	3	14.7	4.91	84	.313	.353	0	—	0	-0	-0	-0	0.0

■ BEN HAYES
Hayes, Ben Joseph   b: 8/4/57, Niagara Falls, N.Y.   BR/TR, 6'1", 180 lbs.   Deb: 6/25/82

YEAR TM/L	W	L	PCT	G	GS	CG	SH	SV	IP	H	HR	BB	SO	RAT	ERA	ERA+	OAV	OOB	BH	AVG	PB	PR	/A	PD	TPI
1982 Cin-N	2	0	1.000	26	0	0	0	2	45²	37	3	22	38	11.6	1.97	188	.219	.309	0	.000	-0	8	9	-1	0.8
1983 Cin-N	4	6	.400	60	0	0	0	7	69¹	82	8	37	44	15.6	6.49	59	.301	.387	0	.000	-1	-22	-21	0	-2.1
Total 2	6	6	.500	86	0	0	0	9	115	119	11	59	82	14.0	4.70	80	.270	.357	0	.000	-1	-14	-12	-1	-1.3

■ JIM HAYES
Hayes, James Millard "Whitey"   b: 2/25/12, Montevallo, Ala.   BL/TR, 6'1", 168 lbs.   Deb: 7/13/35

YEAR TM/L	W	L	PCT	G	GS	CG	SH	SV	IP	H	HR	BB	SO	RAT	ERA	ERA+	OAV	OOB	BH	AVG	PB	PR	/A	PD	TPI
1935 Was-A	2	4	.333	7	4	1	0	0	28	38	0	23	9	19.6	8.36	52	.322	.433	2	.250	-0	-12	-13	-1	-1.1

■ JOE HAYNES
Haynes, Joseph Walton   b: 9/21/17, Lincolnton, Ga.   d: 1/6/67, Hopkins, Minn.   BR/TR, 6'2.5", 190 lbs.   Deb: 4/24/39   C

YEAR TM/L	W	L	PCT	G	GS	CG	SH	SV	IP	H	HR	BB	SO	RAT	ERA	ERA+	OAV	OOB	BH	AVG	PB	PR	/A	PD	TPI
1939 Was-A	8	12	.400	27	20	10	1	0	173	186	10	78	64	13.8	5.36	81	.276	.352	14	.209	0	-14	-19	-1	-1.8
1940 Was-A	3	6	.333	22	7	1	0	0	63¹	85	4	34	23	17.1	6.54	64	.327	.407	2	.105	-1	-15	-17	-1	-1.6
1941 Chi-A	0	0	—	8	0	0	0	0	28	30	1	11	18	13.2	3.86	106	.280	.347	3	.273	0	1	1	-0	0.1
1942 Chi-A	8	5	.615	40	1	0	0	6	103	88	6	47	35	12.1	2.62	137	.234	.324	5	.179	0	12	11	-0	1.2
1943 Chi-A	7	2	.778	35	2	1	0	3	109	114	2	32	37	12.2	2.96	113	.263	.316	9	.265	2	4	5	-1	0.6
1944 Chi-A	5	6	.455	33	12	8	0	2	154¹	148	5	43	44	11.1	2.57	134	.254	.306	10	.200	1	15	15	1	1.8
1945 Chi-A	5	5	.500	14	13	8	1	0	104	92	3	36	27	11.7	3.55	94	.237	.291	7	.175	-2	-3	-1		-0.3
1946 Chi-A	6	9	.438	32	23	9	0	0	177¹	203	6	60	43	13.6	3.76	91	.289	.349	14	.246	4	-5	-7	1	-0.2
1947 Chi-A	14	6	.700	29	22	13	3	0	182	174	6	61	50	11.7	2.42	151	.250	.312	17	.262	2	26	25	0	3.0
1948 Chi-A	9	10	.474	27	22	6	0	0	149²	167	13	52	40	13.3	3.97	107	.284	.344	8	.160	-1	5	5	-2	0.2

YEAR TM/L	W	L	PCT	G	GS	CG	SH	SV	IP	H	HR	BB	SO	RAT	ERA	ERA+	OAV	OOB	BH	AVG	PB	PR	/A	PD	TPI
1949 Was-A	2	9	.182	37	10	0	0	2	96¹	106	6	55	19	15.3	6.26	68	.283	.380	6	.240	1	-22	-21	1	-1.7
1950 Was-A	7	5	.583	27	10	1	1	0	101²	124	14	46	15	15.5	5.84	77	.305	.382	7	.200	1	-14	-15	1	-1.1
1951 Was-A	1	4	.200	26	3	1	0	2	73	85	9	37	18	15.2	4.56	90	.290	.372	7	.333	2	-4	-4	-1	-0.1
1952 Was-A	0	3	.000	22	0	0	0	3	66	70	2	35	18	14.5	4.50	79	.275	.364	2	.105	-1	-6	-7	-0	-0.7
Total 14	76	82	.481	379	147	53	5	21	1581	1672	95	620	475	13.2	4.01	96	.272	.342	111	.213	7	-20	-31	-0	-0.6

■ RAY HAYWARD
Hayward, Raymond Alton b: 4/27/61, Enid, Okla. BL/TL, 6'1", 190 lbs. Deb: 9/20/86

YEAR TM/L	W	L	PCT	G	GS	CG	SH	SV	IP	H	HR	BB	SO	RAT	ERA	ERA+	OAV	OOB	BH	AVG	PB	PR	/A	PD	TPI
1986 SD-N	0	2	.000	3	3	0	0	0	10	16	1	4	6	18.0	9.00	41	.340	.392	0	.000	-0	-6	-6	-0	-0.5
1987 SD-N	0	0	—	4	0	0	0	0	6	12	3	3	2	22.5	16.50	24	.444	.500	0	.000	-0	-8	-8	1	-0.6
1988 Tex-A	4	6	.400	12	12	1	1	0	62²	63	6	35	37	14.1	5.46	75	.276	.373	0	—	0	-10	-10	1	-0.7
Total 3	4	8	.333	19	15	1	1	0	78²	91	10	42	45	15.2	6.75	60	.301	.387	0	.000	-1	-25	-24	1	-1.8

■ BILL HAYWOOD
Haywood, William Kiernan b: 4/21/37, Colon, Panama BR/TR, 6'3", 205 lbs. Deb: 7/28/68

YEAR TM/L	W	L	PCT	G	GS	CG	SH	SV	IP	H	HR	BB	SO	RAT	ERA	ERA+	OAV	OOB	BH	AVG	PB	PR	/A	PD	TPI
1968 Was-A	0	0	—	14	0	0	0	0	23	27	1	12	10	16.0	4.70	62	.314	.410	0	—	0	-4	-5	0	-0.4

■ ED HEAD
Head, Edward Marvin b: 1/25/18, Selma, La. d: 1/31/80, Bastrop, La. BR/TR, 6'1", 175 lbs. Deb: 7/27/40

YEAR TM/L	W	L	PCT	G	GS	CG	SH	SV	IP	H	HR	BB	SO	RAT	ERA	ERA+	OAV	OOB	BH	AVG	PB	PR	/A	PD	TPI
1940 Bro-N	1	2	.333	13	5	2	0	0	39¹	40	0	18	13	13.3	4.12	97	.260	.337	2	.182	-0	-1	-1	-1	-0.1
1942 Bro-N	10	6	.625	36	15	5	1	4	136²	118	11	47	78	11.1	3.56	97	.231	.300	13	.333	4	-4	-4	0	0.0
1943 Bro-N	9	10	.474	47	18	7	3	6	169²	166	8	66	83	12.3	3.66	92	.250	.318	7	.152	-2	-5	-6	1	-0.6
1944 Bro-N	4	3	.571	9	8	5	1	0	63¹	54	2	19	17	10.4	2.70	132	.232	.290	5	.263	1	6	6	-1	0.6
1946 Bro-N	3	2	.600	13	7	3	1	1	56	56	3	24	17	12.9	3.21	105	.267	.342	5	.313	1	1	1	-0	0.2
Total 5	27	23	.540	118	53	22	6	11	465	434	24	174	208	11.8	3.48	98	.245	.314	32	.244	5	-2	-4	-1	0.1

■ RALPH HEAD
Head, Ralph b: 8/30/1893, Tallapoosa, Ga. d: 10/8/62, Muscadine, Ala. BR/TR, 5'10", 175 lbs. Deb: 4/18/23

YEAR TM/L	W	L	PCT	G	GS	CG	SH	SV	IP	H	HR	BB	SO	RAT	ERA	ERA+	OAV	OOB	BH	AVG	PB	PR	/A	PD	TPI
1923 Phi-N	2	9	.182	35	13	5	0	2	132¹	185	13	57	24	16.5	6.66	69	.341	.404	3	.071	-5	-39	-30	-0	-3.1

■ TOM HEALEY
Healey, Thomas F. b: 1853, Cranston, R.I. d: 2/6/1891, Lewiston, Maine Deb: 6/13/1878

YEAR TM/L	W	L	PCT	G	GS	CG	SH	SV	IP	H	HR	BB	SO	RAT	ERA	ERA+	OAV	OOB	BH	AVG	PB	PR	/A	PD	TPI
1878 Pro-N	0	3	.000	3	3	3	0	0	24	27	1	7	2	12.8	3.00	73	.270	.318	2	.222	0	-2	-2	0	-0.1
Ind-N	6	4	.600	11	10	9	0	1	89	98	1	13	18	11.2	2.22	91	.266	.291	8	.178	-1	1	-2	0	-0.2
Yr	6	7	.462	14	13	12	0	1	113	125	2	20	20	11.5	2.39	86	.267	.297	0	.000	-1	-1	-4	0	-0.3

■ JOHN HEALY
Healy, John J. "Egyptian" or "Long John" b: 10/27/1866, Cairo, Ill. d: 3/16/1899, St.Louis, Mo. BR/TR, 6'2", 158 lbs. Deb: 9/11/1885

YEAR TM/L	W	L	PCT	G	GS	CG	SH	SV	IP	H	HR	BB	SO	RAT	ERA	ERA+	OAV	OOB	BH	AVG	PB	PR	/A	PD	TPI
1885 StL-N	1	7	.125	8	8	8	0	0	66	54	0	20	32	10.1	3.00	91	.213	.270	-3	.042	-3	-1	-2	0	-0.3
1886 StL-N	17	23	.425	43	41	39	3	0	353²	315	5	118	213	11.0	2.88	112	.229	.290	14	.097	-11	17	14	-2	0.0
1887 Ind-N	12	29	.293	41	41	40	3	0	341	415	24	108	75	13.8	5.17	80	.292	.342	24	.174	-4	-43	-40	-3	-3.7
1888 Ind-N	12	24	.333	37	37	36	1	0	321¹	347	13	87	124	12.2	3.89	76	.266	.312	30	.229	4	-38	-34	1	-2.6
1889 Was-N	1	11	.083	13	12	10	1	0	101	139	2	38	49	15.8	6.24	63	.317	.371	10	.222	1	-25	-26	1	-1.8
Chi-N	1	4	.200	5	5	5	0	0	46	48	4	18	22	12.9	4.50	93	.260	.326	2	.100	-2	-2	-2	-0	-0.2
Yr	2	15	.118	18	17	15	1	0	147	187	6	56	71	14.9	5.69	71	.300	.358	0	.000	-1	-27	-27	1	-2.0
1890 Tol-a	22	21	.512	46	46	44	2	0	389	326	6	127	225	10.5	2.89	137	.221	.282	34	.218	5	42	46	-2	4.7
1891 Bal-a	8	10	.444	23	22	19	0	0	170¹	179	6	57	54	12.5	3.75	100	.261	.318	9	.141	-2	-1	-0	-5	-0.5
1892 Bal-N	3	6	.333	9	8	5	0	0	68¹	82	4	21	24	13.6	4.74	73	.286	.334	6	.222	1	-11	-10	-0	-0.7
Lou-N	1	1	.500	2	2	2	0	0	18¹	15	0	5	4	9.8	1.96	156	.214	.267	-2	.286	1	3	2	-0	0.3
Yr	4	7	.364	11	10	7	0	0	86²	97	4	26	28	12.8	4.15	81	.272	.321	3	.088	1	-8	-8	-0	-0.4
Total 8	78	136	.364	227	222	208	9	0	1875	1920	63	599	822	12.1	3.84	94	.256	.311	132	.174	-12	-59	-52	-11	-4.8

■ CHARLIE HEARD
Heard, Charles b: 1/30/1872, Philadelphia, Pa. d: 2/20/45, Philadelphia, Pa. BR/TR, 6'2", 190 lbs. Deb: 7/14/1890 ♦

YEAR TM/L	W	L	PCT	G	GS	CG	SH	SV	IP	H	HR	BB	SO	RAT	ERA	ERA+	OAV	OOB	BH	AVG	PB	PR	/A	PD	TPI
1890 Pit-N	0	6	.000	6	6	5	0	0	44	75	5	32	13	21.9	8.39	39	.366	.452	8	.186	-1	-24	-25	-1	-1.8

■ JAY HEARD
Heard, Jehosie b: 1/17/20, Atlanta, Ga. BL/TL, 5'7", 155 lbs. Deb: 4/24/54

YEAR TM/L	W	L	PCT	G	GS	CG	SH	SV	IP	H	HR	BB	SO	RAT	ERA	ERA+	OAV	OOB	BH	AVG	PB	PR	/A	PD	TPI
1954 Bal-A	0	0	—	2	0	0	0	0	3¹	6	1	3	2	24.3	13.50	27	.375	.474	0	—	0	-4	-4	0	-0.2

■ BUNNY HEARN
Hearn, Bunn b: 5/21/1891, Chapel Hill, N.C. d: 10/10/59, Wilson, N.C. BL/TL, 5'11", 190 lbs. Deb: 9/17/10

YEAR TM/L	W	L	PCT	G	GS	CG	SH	SV	IP	H	HR	BB	SO	RAT	ERA	ERA+	OAV	OOB	BH	AVG	PB	PR	/A	PD	TPI
1910 StL-N	1	3	.250	5	5	4	0	0	39	49	2	16	14	15.2	5.08	59	.322	.391	2	.133	-0	-9	-9	-1	-0.8
1911 StL-N	0	0	—	2	0	0	0	0	2²	7	1	0	1	23.6	13.50	25	.538	.538	0	.000	-0	-3	-3	-0	-0.2
1913 NY-N	1	1	.500	2	2	1	0	0	13	13	0	7	3	13.8	2.77	113	.277	.370	2	.400	1	1	1	-0	0.1
1915 Pit-F	6	11	.353	29	17	8	1	0	175²	187	6	37	49	11.6	3.38	89	.285	.326	10	.189	0	-7	-7	-0	-0.7
1918 Bos-N	5	6	.455	17	12	9	1	0	126¹	119	2	29	30	10.5	2.49	108	.256	.300	8	.178	-1	3	3	1	0.3
1920 Bos-N	0	3	.000	11	4	2	0	0	43	54	3	11	9	13.8	5.65	54	.329	.375	2	.143	-1	-12	-12	0	-1.2
Total 6	13	24	.351	66	40	24	2	0	399²	429	14	100	111	12.0	3.56	82	.287	.333	24	.180	-1	-26	-29	0	-2.5

■ BUNNY HEARN
Hearn, Elmer Lafayette b: 1/13/04, Brooklyn, N.Y. d: 3/31/74, Venice, Fla. BL/TL, 5'8", 160 lbs. Deb: 4/13/26

YEAR TM/L	W	L	PCT	G	GS	CG	SH	SV	IP	H	HR	BB	SO	RAT	ERA	ERA+	OAV	OOB	BH	AVG	PB	PR	/A	PD	TPI
1926 Bos-N	4	9	.308	34	12	3	0	2	117¹	121	2	56	40	13.6	4.22	84	.276	.358	3	.100	-2	-5	-9	2	-0.8
1927 Bos-N	0	2	.000	8	0	0	0	0	12²	16	0	9	5	17.8	4.26	87	.327	.431	2	.400	1	-0	-1	0	0.0
1928 Bos-N	1	0	1.000	7	0	0	0	0	10	6	0	8	8	13.5	6.30	62	.167	.333	0	.000	-0	-3	-3	-0	-0.0
1929 Bos-N	2	0	1.000	10	1	0	0	0	18¹	18	2	9	12	13.3	4.42	106	.277	.365	0	.000	0	1	-1	0	0.1
Total 4	7	11	.389	59	13	3	0	2	158¹	161	4	82	65	13.9	4.38	85	.273	.363	5	.132	-2	-8	-12	2	-0.9

■ JIM HEARN
Hearn, James Tolbert b: 4/11/21, Atlanta, Ga. BR/TR, 6'3", 205 lbs. Deb: 4/17/47

YEAR TM/L	W	L	PCT	G	GS	CG	SH	SV	IP	H	HR	BB	SO	RAT	ERA	ERA+	OAV	OOB	BH	AVG	PB	PR	/A	PD	TPI
1947 StL-N	12	7	.632	37	21	4	1	1	162	151	9	63	57	11.9	3.22	128	.248	.319	8	.145	-1	15	16	-1	1.4
1948 StL-N	8	6	.571	34	13	5	0	1	89²	92	9	35	27	12.9	4.22	97	.271	.342	5	.200	-0	-3	-1	-2	-0.2
1949 StL-N	1	3	.250	17	4	0	0	1	42	48	3	23	18	15.6	5.14	81	.294	.388	1	.100	-0	-5	-5	-0	-0.4
1950 StL-N	0	1	.000	6	0	0	0	0	9	12	1	6	4	18.0	10.00	43	.333	.429	1	1.000	0	-6	-6	0	-0.4
NY-N	11	3	.786	16	16	11	5	0	125	72	8	38	54	7.9	1.94	211	.169	.237	6	.136	-0	31	30	3	3.2
Yr	11	4	.733	22	16	11	5	0	134	84	9	44	58	8.6	2.49	165	.182	.253	5	.111	0	25	24	2	2.8
1951 *NY-N	17	9	.654	34	34	11	0	0	211¹	204	21	82	66	12.3	3.62	108	.251	.321	12	.162	-0	8	7	6	1.3
1952 NY-N	14	7	.667	34	34	11	1	1	223²	208	16	97	89	12.5	3.78	98	.245	.326	14	.182	4	-1	-2	4	0.6
1953 NY-N	9	12	.429	36	32	6	0	0	196²	206	22	84	77	13.4	4.53	95	.266	.341	9	.136	0	-5	-5	-2	-0.2
1954 NY-N	8	8	.500	29	18	3	2	1	130	137	10	46	45	14.2	4.15	97	.272	.359	5	.111	-1	-1	-2	2	0.0
1955 NY-N	14	16	.467	39	33	11	1	0	226²	225	27	64	86	11.7	3.73	108	.260	.314	12	.156	1	9	8	3	1.1
1956 NY-N	5	11	.313	30	19	2	0	0	129¹	124	17	44	66	11.9	3.97	95	.254	.319	4	.098	-3	-3	-3	-0	-0.5
1957 Phi-N	5	1	.833	36	4	1	0	3	74	79	6	18	46	12.0	3.65	104	.274	.321	0	.000	-2	2	1	1	0.0
1958 Phi-N	5	3	.625	39	1	0	0	0	73¹	88	6	27	33	14.1	4.17	95	.292	.351	0	.000	-1	-2	-2	-0	-0.3
1959 Phi-N	0	2	.000	11	1	0	0	0	11	11	1	7	6	17.2	5.73	72	.333	.412	0	.000	1	-2	-2	0	-0.1
Total 13	109	89	.551	396	229	63	10	8	1703²	1661	157	655	669	12.4	3.81	105	.255	.326	77	.141	-3	35	35	14	5.6

■ SPENCER HEATH
Heath, Spencer Paul b: 11/5/1894, Chicago, Ill. d: 1/25/30, Chicago, Ill. BB/TR, 6', 170 lbs. Deb: 5/04/20

YEAR TM/L	W	L	PCT	G	GS	CG	SH	SV	IP	H	HR	BB	SO	RAT	ERA	ERA+	OAV	OOB	BH	AVG	PB	PR	/A	PD	TPI
1920 Chi-A	0	0	—	4	0	0	0	0	7	19	1	2	0	27.0	15.43	27	.475	.500	0	.000	-1	-9	-9	0	-0.7

■ JEFF HEATHCOCK
Heathcock, Ronald Jeffrey b: 11/18/60, Covina, Cal. BR/TR, 6'4", 205 lbs. Deb: 9/03/83

YEAR TM/L	W	L	PCT	G	GS	CG	SH	SV	IP	H	HR	BB	SO	RAT	ERA	ERA+	OAV	OOB	BH	AVG	PB	PR	/A	PD	TPI
1983 Hou-N	2	1	.667	6	3	0	0	0	28	19	1	4	12	7.7	3.21	106	.181	.218	0	.000	-1	1	1	0	0.0
1985 Hou-N	3	1	.750	14	7	1	0	1	56¹	50	9	13	25	10.2	3.36	103	.239	.287	1	.063	0	1	1	0	0.1
1987 Hou-N	4	2	.667	19	2	0	0	0	42²	44	4	9	15	11.4	3.16	124	.267	.320	0	.000	0	1	0	0	0.3
1988 Hou-N	0	5	.000	17	1	0	0	0	31	32	2	16	12	14.5	5.81	57	.270	.365	0	.000	-0	-8	-9	1	-0.8
Total 4	9	9	.500	56	13	1	0	3	158	146	16	42	64	10.9	3.76	94	.246	.300	1	.029	-2	-1	-4	1	-0.4

YEAR	TM/L	W	L	PCT	G	GS	CG	SH	SV	IP	H	HR	BB	SO	RAT	ERA	ERA+	OAV	OOB	BH	AVG	PB	PR	/A	PD	TPI

■ NEAL HEATON Heaton, Neal b: 3/3/60, Holtsville, N.Y. BL/TL, 6'1", 197 lbs. Deb: 9/03/82

YEAR	TM/L	W	L	PCT	G	GS	CG	SH	SV	IP	H	HR	BB	SO	RAT	ERA	ERA+	OAV	OOB	BH	AVG	PB	PR	/A	PD	TPI
1982	Cle-A	0	2	.000	8	4	0	0	0	31	32	1	16	14	13.9	5.23	78	.260	.345	0	—	0	-4	-4	-0	-0.3
1983	Cle-A	11	7	.611	39	16	4	3	7	149¹	157	11	44	75	12.2	4.16	102	.269	.321	0	—	0	-2	1	-1	0.0
1984	Cle-A	12	15	.444	38	34	4	1	0	198²	231	21	75	75	13.9	5.21	78	.293	.354	0	—	0	-27	-25	-2	-2.5
1985	Cle-A	9	17	.346	36	33	5	1	0	207²	244	19	80	82	14.3	4.90	84	.298	.365	0	—	0	-17	-18	-2	-1.8
1986	Cle-A	3	6	.333	12	12	2	0	0	74¹	73	8	34	24	13.1	4.24	98	.254	.335	0	—	0	-1	-1	-0	0.0
	Min-A	4	9	.308	21	17	3	0	1	124¹	128	18	47	66	12.7	3.98	108	.273	.340	0	—	0	3	4	-0	0.4
	Yr	7	15	.318	33	29	5	0	1	198²	201	26	81	90	12.8	4.08	104	.266	.337	0	—	0	2	4	-0	0.4
1987	Mon-N	13	10	.565	32	32	3	1	0	193¹	207	25	37	105	11.5	4.52	93	.273	.310	14	.209	2	-9	-7	-1	-0.4
1988	Mon-N	3	10	.231	32	11	0	0	2	97¹	98	14	43	43	13.3	4.99	72	.271	.354	3	.143	-0	-17	-15	0	-1.5
1989	Pit-N	6	7	.462	42	18	1	0	0	147¹	127	12	55	67	11.5	3.05	110	.233	.311	9	.214	1	7	5	1	0.6
1990	Pit-N	12	9	.571	30	24	0	0	0	146	143	17	38	68	11.3	3.45	105	.263	.314	2	.047	+2	-6	-6	-0	-0.6
Total	9	73	92	.442	290	201	22	6	10	1369¹	1440	146	469	619	12.7	4.35	92	.273	.335	28	.162	0	-61	-56	-6	-5.4

■ DAVE HEAVERLO Heaverlo, David Wallace b: 8/25/50, Ellensburg, Wash. BR/TR, 6'2", 200 lbs. Deb: 4/14/75

YEAR	TM/L	W	L	PCT	G	GS	CG	SH	SV	IP	H	HR	BB	SO	RAT	ERA	ERA+	OAV	OOB	BH	AVG	PB	PR	/A	PD	TPI
1975	SF-N	3	1	.750	42	0	0	0	1	64	62	2	31	35	13.2	2.39	159	.262	.349	2	.500	1	9	10	1	1.2
1976	SF-N	4	4	.500	61	0	0	0	1	75	85	2	15	40	12.2	4.44	82	.289	.328	1	.333	0	-8	-7	1	-0.5
1977	SF-N	5	1	.833	56	0	0	0	1	98²	92	10	21	58	10.6	2.55	153	.251	.297	0	.000	-0	15	15	2	1.7
1978	Oak-A	3	6	.333	69	0	0	0	10	130	141	11	41	71	12.8	3.25	112	.281	.339	0	—	0	7	6	3	0.9
1979	Oak-A	4	11	.267	62	0	0	0	9	85²	97	7	42	40	15.0	4.20	96	.294	.380	0	.000	0	-2	0	-0	0.0
1980	Sea-A	6	3	.667	60	0	0	0	4	78²	75	9	35	42	13.2	3.89	106	.253	.342	0	—	0	1	2	-1	0.1
1981	Oak-A	1	0	1.000	6	0	0	0	0	5²	7	0	3	2	15.9	1.59	219	.292	.370	0	—	0	1	1	-0	0.1
Total	7	26	26	.500	356	0	0	0	26	537²	559	41	188	288	12.8	3.41	113	.273	.339	3	.231	1	26	26	5	3.5

■ WALLY HEBERT Hebert, Wallace Andrew "Preacher" b: 8/21/07, Lake Charles, La. BL/TL, 6'1", 195 lbs. Deb: 5/01/31

YEAR	TM/L	W	L	PCT	G	GS	CG	SH	SV	IP	H	HR	BB	SO	RAT	ERA	ERA+	OAV	OOB	BH	AVG	PB	PR	/A	PD	TPI
1931	StL-A	6	7	.462	23	13	5	0	1	103	128	11	43	26	15.2	5.07	91	.306	.375	9	.209	-2	-8	-5	-2	-0.6
1932	StL-A	1	12	.077	35	15	2	0	1	108¹	145	6	45	29	16.0	6.48	75	.322	.386	12	.353	2	-24	-20	0	-1.4
1933	StL-A	4	6	.400	33	10	3	0	0	88¹	114	4	35	19	15.3	5.30	88	.308	.369	9	.391	3	-10	-6	1	-0.2
1943	Pit-N	10	11	.476	34	23	12	1	0	184	197	3	45	41	11.9	2.98	117	.272	.316	13	.220	1	8	10	1	1.4
Total	4	21	36	.368	125	61	22	1	3	483²	584	24	168	115	14.1	4.63	91	.298	.355	43	.270	5	-34	-21	-1	-0.8

■ GUY HECKER Hecker, Guy Jackson b: 4/3/1856, Youngville, Pa. d: 12/3/38, Wooster, Ohio BR/TR, 6', 190 lbs. Deb: 5/02/1882 MU♦

YEAR	TM/L	W	L	PCT	G	GS	CG	SH	SV	IP	H	HR	BB	SO	RAT	ERA	ERA+	OAV	OOB	BH	AVG	PB	PR	/A	PD	TPI
1882	Lou-a	6	6	.500	13	11	10	0	0	104	75	0	5	33	**6.9**	1.30	190	**.188**	**.198**	94	.276	4	16	13	3	1.3
1883	Lou-a	26	23	.531	51	50	49	3	0	451	509	4	72	153	11.6	3.33	89	.267	.293	88	.273	11	-1	-18	3	-2.3
1884	Lou-a	52	20	.722	**75**	73	**72**	6	0	**670²**	526	4	56	**385**	**7.8**	1.80	171	.204	**.221**	94	.297	26	108	**95**	6	**12.5**
1885	Lou-a	30	23	.566	53	53	51	2	0	480	454	6	54	209	9.5	2.18	148	.239	.260	81	.273	9	57	56	5	**7.0**
1886	Lou-a	26	23	.531	49	48	45	2	0	420²	390	6	118	133	10.9	2.87	127	.234	.285	117	.341	19	27	36	2	7.1
1887	Lou-a	18	12	.600	34	32	32	2	1	285¹	325	9	50	58	11.8	4.16	105	.276	.306	118	.319	10	4	7	6	0.6
1888	Lou-a	8	17	.320	26	25	25	0	0	223¹	251	5	43	63	11.8	3.39	91	.274	.306	48	.227	2	-8	-8	2	-0.6
1889	Lou-a	5	13	.278	19	16	15	0	0	151¹	215	7	47	33	15.6	5.59	69	.324	.369	93	.284	4	-29	-29	1	-2.3
1890	Pit-N	2	9	.182	14	12	11	0	0	119²	160	9	42	32	15.3	5.11	64	.312	.366	77	.226	1	-21	-24	-1	-1.9
Total	9	173	146	.542	334	320	310	15	1	2906	2905	50	489	1099	10.5	2.92	113	.248	.278	810	.283	87	154	127	27	23.5

■ HARRY HEDGPETH Hedgpeth, Harry Malcolm b: 9/4/1888, Fayetteville, N.C. d: 7/30/66, Richmond, Va. BL/TL, 6'1.5", 194 lbs. Deb: 10/03/13

YEAR	TM/L	W	L	PCT	G	GS	CG	SH	SV	IP	H	HR	BB	SO	RAT	ERA	ERA+	OAV	OOB	BH	AVG	PB	PR	/A	PD	TPI
1913	Was-A	0	0	—	1	0	0	0	1	1	1	0	0	0	9.0	0.00	—	.250	.250	0	—	0	0	0	-0	0.1

■ MIKE HEDLUND Hedlund, Michael David "Red" b: 8/11/46, Dallas, Tex. BR/TR, 6'1", 182 lbs. Deb: 9/08/65

YEAR	TM/L	W	L	PCT	G	GS	CG	SH	SV	IP	H	HR	BB	SO	RAT	ERA	ERA+	OAV	OOB	BH	AVG	PB	PR	/A	PD	TPI
1965	Cle-A	0	0	—	6	0	0	0	0	5¹	6	0	5	4	18.6	5.06	59	.286	.423	0	.000	-0	-1	-1	-0	0.0
1968	Cle-A	0	0	—	3	0	0	0	0	1²	6	0	2	0	48.6	10.80	27	.545	.643	0	—	0	-6	-6	-0	-0.6
1969	KC-A	3	6	.333	34	16	1	0	2	125	123	8	40	74	11.8	3.24	114	.259	.318	5	.152	-1	5	6	1	0.8
1970	KC-A	2	3	.400	9	0	0	0	0	15	18	4	7	5	15.0	7.20	52	.300	.373	0	.000	-0	-6	-6	-0	-0.6
1971	KC-A	15	8	.652	32	30	7	1	0	205²	168	15	72	76	10.5	2.71	126	.227	.296	6	.088	-0	17	16	4	1.8
1972	KC-A	5	7	.417	29	16	1	0	0	113	119	10	41	52	13.1	4.78	63	.275	.343	6	.188	-0	-22	-22	1	-2.2
Total	6	25	24	.510	113	62	9	1	2	465²	440	39	167	211	11.9	3.56	96	.253	.321	17	.123	-5	-7	-8	6	-0.2

■ DANNY HEEP Heep, Daniel William b: 7/3/57, San Antonio, Tex. BL/TL, 5'11", 185 lbs. Deb: 8/31/79 ♦

YEAR	TM/L	W	L	PCT	G	GS	CG	SH	SV	IP	H	HR	BB	SO	RAT	ERA	ERA+	OAV	OOB	BH	AVG	PB	PR	/A	PD	TPI
1988	*LA-N	0	0	—	1	0	0	0	0	2	2	1	0	0	9.00	37	.222	.222	36	.242	0	-1	-1	0	0.0
1990	*Bos-A	0	0	—	1	0	0	0	0	1	4	0	0	0	36.00	9.00	45	.667	.667	12	.174	0	-1	-1	-0	0.0
Total	2	0	0	—	2	0	0	0	0	3	6	1	0	0	18.00	9.00	40	.400	.400	498	.256	1	-2	-2	0	0.0

■ BOB HEFFNER Heffner, Robert Frederic b: 9/13/38, Allentown, Pa. BR/TR, 6'4", 200 lbs. Deb: 6/19/63

YEAR	TM/L	W	L	PCT	G	GS	CG	SH	SV	IP	H	HR	BB	SO	RAT	ERA	ERA+	OAV	OOB	BH	AVG	PB	PR	/A	PD	TPI
1963	Bos-A	4	9	.308	20	19	3	1	0	124²	131	15	36	77	12.2	4.26	89	.267	.319	5	.116	-1	-9	-7	0	-0.7
1964	Bos-A	7	9	.438	55	10	1	1	6	158²	152	20	44	112	11.3	4.08	94	.251	.305	7	.159	0	-8	-4	-1	-0.3
1965	Bos-A	0	2	.000	27	1	0	0	0	49	59	9	18	42	14.3	7.16	52	.304	.366	0	.000	-1	-20	-19	-1	-2.0
1966	Cle-A	0	1	.000	5	1	0	0	0	13	12	1	3	7	10.4	3.46	99	.240	.283	0	.000	-0	-0	-0	-0	0.0
1968	Cal-A	0	0	—	7	0	0	0	0	8	6	0	6	3	13.5	2.25	129	.240	.387	0	—	0	1	1	0	0.1
Total	5	11	21	.344	114	31	4	2	6	353¹	360	45	107	241	12.0	4.51	84	.264	.320	12	.128	-1	-36	-29	-2	-2.9

■ RANDY HEFLIN Heflin, Randolph Rutherford b: 9/11/18, Fredericksburg, Va. BL/TL, 6', 185 lbs. Deb: 6/09/45

YEAR	TM/L	W	L	PCT	G	GS	CG	SH	SV	IP	H	HR	BB	SO	RAT	ERA	ERA+	OAV	OOB	BH	AVG	PB	PR	/A	PD	TPI
1945	Bos-A	4	10	.286	20	14	6	1	0	102	102	3	61	39	14.7	4.06	84	.272	.380	3	.086	-3	-8	-7	1	-0.9
1946	Bos-A	0	1	.000	5	1	0	0	0	14²	16	0	12	6	17.8	2.45	149	.296	.433	2	.667	1	2	2	1	0.4
Total	2	4	11	.267	25	15	6	2	0	116²	118	3	73	45	15.1	3.86	89	.275	.387	5	.132	-2	-6	-5	2	-0.5

■ JAKE HEHL Hehl, Herman Jacob b: 12/8/1899, Brooklyn, N.Y. d: 7/4/61, Brooklyn, N.Y. BR/TR, 5'11", 180 lbs. Deb: 6/20/18

YEAR	TM/L	W	L	PCT	G	GS	CG	SH	SV	IP	H	HR	BB	SO	RAT	ERA	ERA+	OAV	OOB	BH	AVG	PB	PR	/A	PD	TPI
1918	Bro-N	0	0	—	1	0	0	0	0	1	0	0	0	0	9.0	0.00	—	.000	.250	0	—	0	0	0	0	0.1

■ EMMETT HEIDRICK Heidrick, John Emmett "Snags" b: 7/9/1876, Queenstown, Pa. d: 1/20/16, Clarion, Pa. BL/TR, 6', 185 lbs. Deb: 9/14/1898 ♦

YEAR	TM/L	W	L	PCT	G	GS	CG	SH	SV	IP	H	HR	BB	SO	RAT	ERA	ERA+	OAV	OOB	BH	AVG	PB	PR	/A	PD	TPI
1902	StL-A	0	0	—	1	0	0	0	0	1	0	0	0	0	0.0	0.00	—	.000	.000	129	.289	0	0	0	0	0.0

■ FRANK HEIFER Heifer, Franklin "Heck" b: 1/18/1854, Reading, Pa. d: 8/29/1893, Reading, Pa. 5'10.5", 175 lbs. Deb: 6/04/1875 ♦

YEAR	TM/L	W	L	PCT	G	GS	CG	SH	SV	IP	H	HR	BB	SO	RAT	ERA	ERA+	OAV	OOB	BH	AVG	PB	PR	/A	PD	TPI
1875	Bos-n	0	0	—	2	0	0	0	1	2¹	7	0	0	0	27.0	7.71	31	.500	.500	14	.275	1	-1	-1	-0	0.0

■ FRED HEIMACH Heimach, Frederick Amos "Lefty" b: 1/27/01, Camden, N.J. d: 6/1/73, Ft.Myers, Fla. BL/TL, 6', 175 lbs. Deb: 10/01/20

YEAR	TM/L	W	L	PCT	G	GS	CG	SH	SV	IP	H	HR	BB	SO	RAT	ERA	ERA+	OAV	OOB	BH	AVG	PB	PR	/A	PD	TPI
1920	Phi-A	0	1	.000	1	1	0	0	0	5	13	0	1	0	25.2	14.40	28	.542	.560	0	.000	-0	-6	-6	1	-0.3
1921	Phi-A	1	0	1.000	1	1	1	0	0	9	7	0	1	0	8.0	2.00	—	.226	.250	1	.250	-0	4	4	1	0.6
1922	Phi-A	7	11	.389	37	19	7	0	1	171²	220	18	63	47	15.0	5.03	85	.316	.375	15	.250	2	-19	-15	1	-1.0
1923	Phi-A	6	12	.333	40	19	10	0	0	208¹	238	14	69	63	13.5	4.32	95	.292	.352	30	.254	2	-8	-5	0	-0.0
1924	Phi-A	14	12	.538	40	26	10	0	0	198	243	6	60	60	14.0	4.73	90	.306	.357	29	.322	6	-11	-10	2	-0.0
1925	Phi-A	0	1	.000	10	0	0	0	0	20¹	24	7	2	9	15.0	3.98	117	.312	.391	1	.167	-0	0	2	0	0.1
1926	Phi-A	1	0	1.000	13	1	0	0	0	31²	28	1	5	8	9.4	2.84	147	.239	.270	1	.100	-1	5	7	2	0.6
	Bos-A	2	9	.182	20	13	6	0	0	102	119	5	42	17	14.2	5.65	72	.303	.370	13	.295	2	-18	-18	3	-1.0
	Yr	3	9	.250	33	14	6	0	0	133²	147	6	47	25	13.1	4.98	82	.288	.348	3	.056	2	-14	-13	5	-0.4
1928	NY-A	3	4	.400	18	9	5	0	0	68	66	5	16	25	11.0	3.31	114	.250	.295	5	.167	-1	6	3	0	0.2
1929	NY-A	11	6	.647	35	10	3	3	4	134²	141	4	29	26	11.6	4.01	96	.272	.314	9	.184	1	4	-2	2	0.0
1930	Bro-N	0	2	.000	9	0	0	0	0	7¹	14	0	3	1	20.9	4.91	100	.424	.472	1	.250	-0	0	/0	0	0.0

YEAR	TM/L	W	L	PCT	G	GS	CG	SH	SV	IP	H	HR	BB	SO	RAT	ERA	ERA+	OAV	OOB	BH	AVG	PB	PR	/A	PD	TPI
1931	Bro-N	9	7	.563	31	10	7	1	1	135¹	145	6	23	43	11.2	3.46	110	.274	.306	12	.197	1	6	5	4	1.0
1932	Bro-N	9	4	.692	36	15	7	0	0	167²	203	7	28	30	12.7	3.97	96	.299	.333	9	.164	1	-2	-3	2	0.0
1933	Bro-N	0	1	.000	10	3	0	0	0	29²	49	2	11	7	18.8	10.01	32	.374	.431	2	.200	-0	-22	-22	0	-2.0
Total	13	62	69	.473	296	127	56	5	7	1288²	1510	64	360	334	13.2	4.46	90	.296	.346	128	.236	12	-61	-61	18	-1.8

■ GORMAN HEIMUELLER
Heimueller, Gorman John b: 9/24/55, Los Angeles, Cal. BL/TL, 6'4", 195 lbs. Deb: 7/12/83

YEAR	TM/L	W	L	PCT	G	GS	CG	SH	SV	IP	H	HR	BB	SO	RAT	ERA	ERA+	OAV	OOB	BH	AVG	PB	PR	/A	PD	TPI
1983	Oak-A	3	5	.375	16	14	2	1	0	83²	93	8	29	31	13.2	4.41	87	.286	.346	0	—	0	-3	-5	3	-0.2
1984	Oak-A	0	1	.000	6	0	0	0	0	14²	21	2	7	3	17.2	6.14	61	.344	.412	0	—	0	-3	-4	0	-0.3
Total	2	3	6	.333	22	14	2	1	0	98¹	114	10	36	34	13.8	4.67	82	.295	.357	0	—	0	-7	-9	3	-0.5

■ DON HEINKEL
Heinkel, Donald Elliott b: 10/20/59, Racine, Wis. BL/TR, 6', 185 lbs. Deb: 4/07/88

YEAR	TM/L	W	L	PCT	G	GS	CG	SH	SV	IP	H	HR	BB	SO	RAT	ERA	ERA+	OAV	OOB	BH	AVG	PB	PR	/A	PD	TPI
1988	Det-A	0	0	—	21	0	0	0	1	36¹	30	4	12	30	10.7	3.96	96	.219	.287	0	—	0	-1	-0	0	0.0
1989	StL-N	1	1	.500	7	5	0	0	0	26¹	40	2	7	16	16.1	5.81	62	.348	.385	0	.000	-0	-6	-6	0	-0.5
Total	2	1	1	.500	28	5	0	0	1	62²	70	6	19	46	12.9	4.74	79	.278	.331	0	.000	-0	-7	-7	0	-0.5

■ KEN HEINTZELMAN
Heintzelman, Kenneth Alphonse b: 10/14/15, Peruque, Mo. BR/TL, 5'11.5", 185 lbs. Deb: 10/03/37

YEAR	TM/L	W	L	PCT	G	GS	CG	SH	SV	IP	H	HR	BB	SO	RAT	ERA	ERA+	OAV	OOB	BH	AVG	PB	PR	/A	PD	TPI
1937	Pit-N	1	0	1.000	1	1	1	0	0	9	6	0	3	4	10.0	2.00	193	.207	.303	0	.000	-1	2	2	-0	0.1
1938	Pit-N	0	0	—	1	0	0	0	0	2	1	0	3	1	18.0	9.00	42	.167	.444	0	—	0	-1	-1	0	0.0
1939	Pit-N	1	1	.500	17	2	1	0	0	35²	35	2	18	18	13.4	5.05	76	.250	.335	2	.222	-0	-4	-5	-0	-0.4
1940	Pit-N	8	8	.500	39	16	5	2	3	165	193	7	65	71	14.3	4.47	85	.292	.359	8	.167	-1	-11	-12	2	-1.0
1941	Pit-N	11	11	.500	35	24	13	2	0	196	206	8	83	81	13.3	3.44	105	.272	.345	8	.127	-2	4	4	1	0.2
1942	Pit-N	8	11	.421	27	18	5	3	0	130	143	9	63	39	14.3	4.57	74	.281	.361	3	.086	-2	-18	-17	-2	-2.0
1946	Pit-N	8	12	.400	32	24	6	2	1	157²	165	7	86	57	14.3	3.77	94	.271	.362	6	.136	-1	-6	-4	2	-0.3
1947	Pit-N	0	0	—	2	1	0	0	0	4	9	2	6	2	33.8	20.25	21	.409	.536	0	—	0	-7	-7	-0	-0.5
	Phi-N	7	10	.412	24	19	8	0	1	136	144	12	46	55	12.7	4.04	99	.277	.338	5	.116	-2	0	-0	-3	-0.4
	Yr	7	10	.412	26	20	8	0	1	140	153	14	52	57	13.3	4.50	89	.282	.347	5	.047	-2	-7	-8	-3	-0.9
1948	Phi-N	6	11	.353	27	16	5	2	2	130	117	10	45	57	11.3	4.29	92	.241	.307	5	.135	-1	-5	-5	-1	-0.6
1949	Phi-N	17	10	.630	33	32	15	**5**	0	250	239	19	93	65	12.0	3.02	130	.255	.323	13	.155	-1	28	26	-2	2.3
1950	*Phi-N	3	9	.250	23	17	4	1	0	125¹	122	6	54	39	12.6	4.09	99	.250	.325	2	.053	-3	1	-1	-2	-0.5
1951	Phi-N	6	12	.333	35	12	3	0	2	118¹	119	13	53	55	13.4	4.18	92	.267	.350	3	.107	-1	-3	-4	-1	-0.6
1952	Phi-N	1	3	.250	23	1	0	0	1	42²	41	1	12	20	11.2	3.16	115	.266	.319	0	.000	-0	3	2	-1	0.1
Total	13	77	98	.440	319	183	66	18	10	1501²	1540	100	630	564	13.1	3.93	96	.267	.341	56	.127	-15	-18	-23	-6	-3.6

■ CLARENCE HEISE
Heise, Clarence Edward "Lefty" b: 8/7/07, Topeka, Kan. BL/TL, 5'10", 172 lbs. Deb: 4/22/34

YEAR	TM/L	W	L	PCT	G	GS	CG	SH	SV	IP	H	HR	BB	SO	RAT	ERA	ERA+	OAV	OOB	BH	AVG	PB	PR	/A	PD	TPI
1934	StL-N	0	0	—	1	0	0	0	0	2	3	1	0	1	13.5	4.50	94	.300	.300	0	—	0	-0	-0	0	0.0

■ JIM HEISE
Heise, James Edward b: 10/2/32, Scottdale, Pa. BR/TR, 6'1", 185 lbs. Deb: 6/29/57

YEAR	TM/L	W	L	PCT	G	GS	CG	SH	SV	IP	H	HR	BB	SO	RAT	ERA	ERA+	OAV	OOB	BH	AVG	PB	PR	/A	PD	TPI
1957	Was-A	0	3	.000	8	2	0	0	0	19	25	2	16	8	19.4	8.05	48	.329	.446	0	.000	-0	-9	-9	0	-0.8

■ ROY HEISER
Heiser, Le Roy Barton b: 6/22/42, Baltimore, Md. BR/TR, 6'4", 190 lbs. Deb: 9/02/61

YEAR	TM/L	W	L	PCT	G	GS	CG	SH	SV	IP	H	HR	BB	SO	RAT	ERA	ERA+	OAV	OOB	BH	AVG	PB	PR	/A	PD	TPI
1961	Was-A	0	0	—	3	0	0	0	0	5²	6	1	9	1	25.4	6.35	63	.261	.485	0	.000	-0	-1	-1	-0	-0.1

■ CRESE HEISMANN
Heismann, Christian Ernest b: 4/16/1880, Cincinnati, Ohio d: 11/19/51, Cincinnati, Ohio BR/TL, 6'2", 175 lbs. Deb: 9/25/01

YEAR	TM/L	W	L	PCT	G	GS	CG	SH	SV	IP	H	HR	BB	SO	RAT	ERA	ERA+	OAV	OOB	BH	AVG	PB	PR	/A	PD	TPI
1901	Cin-N	0	1	.000	3	2	1	0	0	13²	16	1	6	6	16.5	5.93	54	.290	.390	2	.400	1	-4	-4	-0	-0.2
1902	Cin-N	2	1	.667	5	3	2	0	0	33	33	1	10	15	13.1	2.45	122	.260	.338	3	.214	0	1	2	0	0.3
	Bal-A	0	3	.000	3	3	2	0	0	16	20	1	12	2	18.0	8.44	45	.306	.414	1	.143	-1	-9	-8	-0	-0.7
Total	2	2	5	.286	11	8	5	0	0	62²	69	3	28	23	15.1	4.74	69	.279	.371	6	.231	0	-11	-10	-1	-0.6

■ HARRY HEITMANN
Heitmann, Henry Anton b: 10/6/1896, Albany, N.Y. d: 12/15/58, Brooklyn, N.Y. BR/TR, 6', 175 lbs. Deb: 7/27/18

YEAR	TM/L	W	L	PCT	G	GS	CG	SH	SV	IP	H	HR	BB	SO	RAT	ERA	ERA+	OAV	OOB	BH	AVG	PB	PR	/A	PD	TPI
1918	Bro-N	0	1	.000	1	1	0	0	0	0¹	4	0	0	0	108.0	108.00	3	1.000	1.000	0	—	0	-4	-4	0	-0.3

■ MEL HELD
Held, Melvin Nicholas "Country" b: 4/12/29, Edon, Ohio BR/TR, 6'1", 178 lbs. Deb: 4/27/56

YEAR	TM/L	W	L	PCT	G	GS	CG	SH	SV	IP	H	HR	BB	SO	RAT	ERA	ERA+	OAV	OOB	BH	AVG	PB	PR	/A	PD	TPI
1956	Bal-A	0	0	—	4	0	0	0	0	7	7	1	4	4	12.9	5.14	76	.318	.400	0	—	0	-1	-1	0	0.0

■ HORACE HELMBOLD
Helmbold, Horace b: Philadelphia, Pa. Deb: 10/11/1890

YEAR	TM/L	W	L	PCT	G	GS	CG	SH	SV	IP	H	HR	BB	SO	RAT	ERA	ERA+	OAV	OOB	BH	AVG	PB	PR	/A	PD	TPI
1890	Phi-a	0	1	.000	1	1	1	0	0	7	17	0	6	3	29.6	14.14	27	.451	.526	0	.000	-0	-8	-8	0	-0.5

■ RUSS HEMAN
Heman, Russell Fredrick b: 2/10/33, Olive, Cal. BR/TR, 6'4", 200 lbs. Deb: 4/20/61

YEAR	TM/L	W	L	PCT	G	GS	CG	SH	SV	IP	H	HR	BB	SO	RAT	ERA	ERA+	OAV	OOB	BH	AVG	PB	PR	/A	PD	TPI
1961	Cle-A	0	0	—	6	0	0	0	1	10	8	0	8	4	15.3	3.60	109	.216	.370	0	.000	-0	0	0	0	0.0
	LA-A	0	0	—	6	0	0	0	0	10	4	1	2	6	6.3	1.80	251	.125	.200	0	.000	-0	2	3	0	0.3
	Yr	0	0	—	12	0	0	0	1	20	12	1	10	10	10.3	2.70	156	.171	.284	0	.000	-0	3	3	0	0.3

■ GEORGE HEMMING
Hemming, George Earl "Old Wax Figger" b: 12/15/1868, Carrollton, Ohio d: 6/3/30, Springfield, Mass. BR/TR, 5'11", 170 lbs. Deb: 4/21/1890

YEAR	TM/L	W	L	PCT	G	GS	CG	SH	SV	IP	H	HR	BB	SO	RAT	ERA	ERA+	OAV	OOB	BH	AVG	PB	PR	/A	PD	TPI
1890	Cle-P	0	1	.000	3	1	1	0	0	21	25	1	19	3	18.9	6.86	58	.283	.410	2	.182	-1	-6	-7	1	-0.4
	Bro-P	8	4	.667	19	11	11	0	3	123	117	3	59	32	12.9	3.80	117	.240	.322	9	.158	-4	6	9	0	0.4
	Yr	8	5	.615	22	12	12	0	3	144	142	4	78	35	13.8	4.25	103	.247	.336	11	.015	-5	-0	2	1	0.0
1891	Bro-N	8	15	.348	27	22	19	1	1	199²	231	11	84	83	14.2	4.96	67	.279	.345	13	.159	-1	-36	-37	0	-3.0
1892	Cin-N	0	1	.000	1	0	0	0	0	6	10	1	2	0	18.0	7.50	44	.357	.400	1	.333	0	-3	-3	-0	-0.1
	Lou-N	2	2	.500	4	4	4	0	0	35	36	1	17	12	13.6	4.63	66	.255	.335	1	.077	-1	-5	-6	-0	-0.5
	Yr	2	3	.400	5	4	4	0	0	41	46	2	19	12	14.3	5.05	61	.272	.346	2	.125	-1	-8	-9	-0	-0.6
1893	Lou-N	18	17	.514	41	33	33	1	1	332	373	7	176	79	14.9	5.18	85	.275	.358	2	.203	-2	-19	-29	2	-2.3
1894	Lou-N	13	19	.406	35	32	32	1	0	294¹	358	7	133	66	15.0	4.37	117	.297	.367	33	.252	-2	31	24	-1	1.8
	*Bal-N	4	0	1.000	6	6	4	0	0	45¹	48	0	26	4	14.7	3.57	153	.269	.362	6	.286	1	9	9	0	0.9
	Yr	17	19	.472	41	38	36	1	0	339²	406	7	159	70	15.0	4.27	121	.293	.366	6	.039	3	40	33	-1	2.7
1895	Bal-N	20	13	.606	34	31	26	1	0	262¹	288	10	96	43	13.2	4.05	118	.275	.336	33	.282	3	21	21	-3	1.7
1896	Bal-N	15	6	.714	25	21	20	3	0	202	233	6	54	33	12.8	4.19	102	.287	.331	25	.258	4	4	2	-3	0.3
1897	Lou-N	3	4	.429	9	8	7	0	0	67	80	1	25	7	14.1	5.10	83	.294	.353	5	.179	-1	-6	-6	-1	-0.5
Total	8	91	82	.526	204	169	157	7	6	1587²	1799	55	691	362	14.1	4.55	97	.279	.349	160	.223	1	-3	-22	-1	-1.7

■ BERNIE HENDERSON
Henderson, Bernard "Barnyard" b: 4/12/1899, Douglasville, Tex. d: 6/6/66, Linden, Tex. BR/TR, 5'9", 175 lbs. Deb: 9/05/21

YEAR	TM/L	W	L	PCT	G	GS	CG	SH	SV	IP	H	HR	BB	SO	RAT	ERA	ERA+	OAV	OOB	BH	AVG	PB	PR	/A	PD	TPI
1921	Cle-A	0	1	.000	2	1	0	0	0	3	5	0	0	1	15.0	9.00	47	.333	.333	0	.000	0	-2	-2	-0	0.0

■ ED HENDERSON
Henderson, Edward J. (b: Eugene J. Ball) b: 12/25/1884, Newark, N.J. d: 1/15/64, New York, N.Y. BL/TL, 5'9", 168 lbs. Deb: 5/15/14

YEAR	TM/L	W	L	PCT	G	GS	CG	SH	SV	IP	H	HR	BB	SO	RAT	ERA	ERA+	OAV	OOB	BH	AVG	PB	PR	/A	PD	TPI
1914	Pit-F	0	1	.000	6	1	1	0	0	16	14	2	8	4	12.4	3.94	81	.243	.335	0	.000	-0	-1	-1	-0	-0.1
	Ind-F	1	0	1.000	2	1	1	0	0	10	8	0	4	1	13.5	4.50	77	.227	.355	1	—	-1	-1	-1	-0	-0.1
	Yr	1	1	.500	8	2	2	0	0	26	22	2	12	5	12.8	4.15	79	.237	.343	1	.143	-1	-3	-2	-0	-0.2

■ HARDIE HENDERSON
Henderson, James Harding b: 10/31/1862, Philadelphia, Pa. d: 2/6/03, Philadelphia, Pa. BR/TR, Deb: 5/02/1883 U

YEAR	TM/L	W	L	PCT	G	GS	CG	SH	SV	IP	H	HR	BB	SO	RAT	ERA	ERA+	OAV	OOB	BH	AVG	PB	PR	/A	PD	TPI
1883	Phi-N	0	1	.000	1	1	1	0	0	9	26	1	2	2	28.0	19.00	16	.484	.503	2	.250	0	-16	-16	0	-0.8
	Bal-a	10	32	.238	45	42	38	0	0	358¹	383	4	87	145	11.8	4.02	87	.256	.297	31	.162	-7	-28	-21	-2	-2.5
1884	Bal-a	27	23	.540	52	52	50	4	0	439¹	382	9	116	346	10.2	2.62	132	.221	.270	46	.227	3	31	41	0	4.4
1885	Bal-a	25	35	.417	61	61	59	0	0	539¹	539	7	117	263	10.9	3.19	102	.249	.288	51	.223	3	4	4	-1	0.4
1886	Bal-a	3	15	.167	19	19	19	0	0	171¹	188	6	88	133	13.3	4.62	74	.266	.329	16	.235	2	-22	-23	3	-1.4
	Bro-a	10	4	.714	14	14	14	0	0	124	112	2	51	49	11.8	2.90	120	.230	.303	9	.180	-1	8	8	0	0.6
	Yr	13	19	.406	33	33	33	0	0	295¹	300	2	117	137	12.7	3.90	89	.251	.318	11	.093	1	-15	-15	3	-0.8

YEAR TM/L	W	L	PCT	G	GS	CG	SH	SV	IP	H	HR	BB	SO	RAT	ERA	ERA+	OAV	OOB	BH	AVG	PB	PR	/A	PD	TPI
1887 Bro-a	5	8	.385	13	12	12	0	0	111²	127	3	63	28	15.3	3.95	109	.276	.363	5	.122	-3	4	4	1	0.2
1888 Pit-N	1	3	.250	5	5	4	0	0	35¹	43	0	20	9	16.0	5.35	50	.290	.374	5	.278	1	-10	-11	0	-0.8
Total 6	81	121	.401	210	206	197	4	0	1788¹	1800	25	522	930	11.7	3.50	98	.249	.299	165	.204	-2	-30	-13	1	0.3

■ JOE HENDERSON
Henderson, Joseph Lee b: 7/4/46, Lake Cormorant, Miss. BL/TR, 6'2", 195 lbs. Deb: 6/07/74

YEAR TM/L	W	L	PCT	G	GS	CG	SH	SV	IP	H	HR	BB	SO	RAT	ERA	ERA+	OAV	OOB	BH	AVG	PB	PR	/A	PD	TPI
1974 Chi-A	1	0	1.000	5	3	0	0	0	15	21	2	11	12	19.2	8.40	44	.328	.427	0	.000	0	-8	-8	0	-0.7
1976 Cin-N	2	0	1.000	4	0	0	0	0	11	9	0	8	7	13.9	0.00	—	.225	.354	0	—	0	4	4	0	0.5
1977 Cin-N	0	2	.000	7	0	0	0	0	9	17	2	6	8	23.0	12.00	33	.386	.460	0	.000	-0	-8	-8	-0	-0.7
Total 3	3	2	.600	16	3	0	0	0	35	47	4	25	27	18.5	6.69	55	.318	.416	0	.000	-0	-12	-12	-0	-0.9

■ BILL HENDERSON
Henderson, William Maxwell b: 11/4/01, Pensacola, Fla. d: 10/6/66, Pensacola, Fla. BR/TR, 6', 190 lbs. Deb: 6/20/30

YEAR TM/L	W	L	PCT	G	GS	CG	SH	SV	IP	H	HR	BB	SO	RAT	ERA	ERA+	OAV	OOB	BH	AVG	PB	PR	/A	PD	TPI
1930 NY-A	0	0	—	3	0	0	0	0	8	7	1	4	2	12.4	4.50	96	.250	.344	1	.500	0	0	-0	0	0.0

■ BOB HENDLEY
Hendley, Charles Robert b: 4/30/39, Macon, Ga. BR/TL, 6'2", 190 lbs. Deb: 6/23/61

YEAR TM/L	W	L	PCT	G	GS	CG	SH	SV	IP	H	HR	BB	SO	RAT	ERA	ERA+	OAV	OOB	BH	AVG	PB	PR	/A	PD	TPI
1961 Mil-N	5	7	.417	19	13	3	0	0	97	96	8	39	44	12.5	3.90	96	.262	.333	1	.032	-3	1	-2	1	-0.2
1962 Mil-N	11	13	.458	35	29	7	2	1	200	188	17	59	112	11.1	3.60	105	.247	.301	7	.119	1	8	4	1	0.5
1963 Mil-N	9	9	.500	41	24	7	3	3	169¹	153	16	64	105	11.6	3.93	82	.244	.315	5	.106	-1	-12	-13	-1	-1.3
1964 SF-N	10	11	.476	30	29	4	1	0	163¹	161	18	59	104	12.2	3.64	98	.258	.325	5	.106	-1	-2	-1	-2	-0.3
1965 SF-N	0	0	—	8	2	0	0	0	15	27	6	13	13	24.6	12.60	29	.397	.500	0	.000	-0	-15	-15	0	-1.3
Chi-N	4	4	.500	18	10	2	0	0	62	59	9	25	38	12.3	4.35	85	.244	.317	0	.000	-2	-6	-5	0	-0.5
Yr	4	4	.500	26	12	2	0	0	77	86	15	38	46	14.6	5.96	62	.277	.357	0	.000	-2	-21	-20	1	-1.8
1966 Chi-N	4	5	.444	43	6	0	0	7	89²	98	10	39	65	13.8	3.91	94	.285	.358	3	.167	1	-3	-2	1	0.0
1967 Chi-N	2	0	1.000	7	0	0	0	1	12¹	17	4	3	10	14.6	6.57	54	.315	.351	0	.000	-1	-4	-4	-0	-0.4
NY-N	3	3	.500	15	13	2	0	0	70²	65	11	28	36	12.0	3.44	99	.241	.314	2	.111	-0	-1	-0	-2	-0.1
Yr	5	3	.625	22	13	2	0	1	83	82	15	31	46	12.4	3.90	87	.253	.320	2	.083	-1	-5	-5	-2	-0.5
Total 7	48	52	.480	216	126	25	6	12	879¹	864	99	329	522	12.3	3.97	90	.257	.325	23	.095	-6	-34	-38	0	-3.6

■ ED HENDRICKS
Hendricks, Edward "Big Ed" b: 6/20/1886, Zeeland, Mich. d: 11/28/30, Jackson, Mich. 6'3", 200 lbs. Deb: 9/15/10

YEAR TM/L	W	L	PCT	G	GS	CG	SH	SV	IP	H	HR	BB	SO	RAT	ERA	ERA+	OAV	OOB	BH	AVG	PB	PR	/A	PD	TPI
1910 NY-N	0	1	.000	4	1	1	0	1	12	12	0	4	2	12.0	3.75	79	.261	.320	0	.000	-1	-1	-1	-0	-0.1

■ ELLIE HENDRICKS
Hendricks, Elrod Jerome b: 12/22/40, Charlotte Amalie, V.I. BL/TR, 6'1", 175 lbs. Deb: 4/13/68 C◆

YEAR TM/L	W	L	PCT	G	GS	CG	SH	SV	IP	H	HR	BB	SO	RAT	ERA	ERA+	OAV	OOB	BH	AVG	PB	PR	/A	PD	TPI
1978 Bal-A	0	0	—	1	0	0	0	0	2¹	1	0	1	0	7.7	0.00	—	.125	.222	6	.333	1	1	1	0	0.1

■ DON HENDRICKSON
Hendrickson, Donald William b: 7/14/15, Kewanna, Ind. d: 1/19/77, Norfolk, Va. BR/TR, 6'2", 204 lbs. Deb: 7/04/45

YEAR TM/L	W	L	PCT	G	GS	CG	SH	SV	IP	H	HR	BB	SO	RAT	ERA	ERA+	OAV	OOB	BH	AVG	PB	PR	/A	PD	TPI
1945 Bos-N	4	8	.333	37	2	1	0	5	73¹	74	8	39	14	14.0	4.91	78	.260	.353	3	.167	-0	-9	-9	-0	-0.8
1946 Bos-N	0	1	.000	2	0	0	0	0	2	4	0	2	2	27.0	4.50	76	.364	.462	0	.000	-0	-0	-0	-0	0.0
Total 2	4	9	.308	39	2	1	0	5	75¹	78	8	41	16	14.3	4.90	78	.265	.357	3	.158	-0	-9	-9	-0	-0.8

■ CLAUDE HENDRIX
Hendrix, Claude Raymond b: 4/13/1889, Olathe, Kan. d: 3/22/44, Allentown, Pa. BR/TR, 6', 195 lbs. Deb: 6/07/11

YEAR TM/L	W	L	PCT	G	GS	CG	SH	SV	IP	H	HR	BB	SO	RAT	ERA	ERA+	OAV	OOB	BH	AVG	PB	PR	/A	PD	TPI
1911 Pit-N	4	6	.400	22	12	6	1	1	118²	85	1	53	57	10.5	2.73	126	.204	.295	4	.098	-1	9	9	4	1.2
1912 Pit-N	24	9	.727	39	32	25	4	1	288²	256	6	105	176	11.5	2.59	126	.239	.313	39	.322	15	26	22	4	4.1
1913 Pit-N	14	15	.483	42	25	17	2	3	241	216	3	89	138	11.6	2.84	106	.248	.321	27	.273	9	10	5	1	1.5
1914 Chi-F	29	10	.744	49	37	34	6	5	362	262	6	77	189	8.6	1.69	175	.203	.251	30	.231	6	61	51	6	6.9
1915 Chi-F	16	15	.516	40	31	26	5	4	285	256	7	84	107	10.8	3.00	93	.241	.298	30	.265	12	1	-7	-4	0.1
1916 Chi-N	8	16	.333	36	24	15	3	2	218	193	4	67	117	11.0	2.68	108	.242	.306	16	.200	2	-2	5	2	1.2
1917 Chi-N	10	12	.455	40	21	13	1	1	215	202	6	72	81	11.6	2.60	112	.257	.322	22	.256	4	3	7	-2	1.2
1918 *Chi-N	20	7	.741	32	27	21	3	0	233	229	2	54	86	11.1	2.78	100	.259	.305	24	.264	9	-0	0	1	1.1
1919 Chi-N	10	14	.417	33	25	15	2	0	206¹	208	3	42	69	11.3	2.62	110	.266	.311	15	.192	-0	7	6	2	0.8
1920 Chi-N	9	12	.429	27	23	12	0	0	203²	216	6	54	72	12.1	3.58	90	.273	.322	15	.181	-5	-10	-8	-0	-1.0
Total 10	144	116	.554	360	257	184	27	17	2371¹	2123	41	697	1092	10.9	2.65	113	.243	.302	222	.241	53	105	93	13	17.1

■ LAFAYETTE HENION
Henion, Lafayette Marion b: 6/7/1899, Eureka, Cal. d: 7/22/55, San Luis Obispo, Cal. BR/TR, 5'11", 154 lbs. Deb: 9/10/19

YEAR TM/L	W	L	PCT	G	GS	CG	SH	SV	IP	H	HR	BB	SO	RAT	ERA	ERA+	OAV	OOB	BH	AVG	PB	PR	/A	PD	TPI
1919 Bro-N	0	0	—	1	0	0	0	0	3	2	0	2	2	12.0	6.00	50	.200	.333	0	.000	-0	-1	-1	0	0.0

■ TOM HENKE
Henke, Thomas Anthony b: 12/21/57, Kansas City, Mo. BR/TR, 6'5", 215 lbs. Deb: 9/10/82

YEAR TM/L	W	L	PCT	G	GS	CG	SH	SV	IP	H	HR	BB	SO	RAT	ERA	ERA+	OAV	OOB	BH	AVG	PB	PR	/A	PD	TPI
1982 Tex-A	1	0	1.000	8	0	0	0	0	15²	14	0	8	9	13.2	1.15	337	.246	.348	0	—	0	5	5	0	0.5
1983 Tex-A	1	0	1.000	8	0	0	0	1	16	16	1	4	17	11.3	3.38	119	.262	.308	0	—	0	1	1	0	0.1
1984 Tex-A	1	1	.500	25	0	0	0	2	28¹	36	0	20	25	18.1	6.35	65	.313	.419	0	—	0	-7	-7	-0	-0.6
1985 *Tor-A	3	3	.500	28	0	0	0	13	40	29	4	8	42	8.3	2.02	208	.206	.248	0	—	0	9	10	-0	0.9
1986 Tor-A	9	5	.643	63	0	0	0	27	91¹	63	6	32	118	9.5	3.35	126	.191	.265	0	—	0	8	9	-2	0.6
1987 Tor-A	0	6	.000	72	0	0	0	34	94	62	10	25	128	8.3	2.49	180	.188	.245	0	—	0	21	21	0	2.1
1988 Tor-A	4	4	.500	52	0	0	0	25	68	60	6	24	66	11.4	2.91	135	.237	.308	0	—	0	8	8	-0	0.8
1989 *Tor-A	8	3	.727	64	0	0	0	20	89	66	5	25	116	9.4	1.92	196	.205	.266	0	—	0	19	18	-1	1.8
1990 Tor-A	2	4	.333	61	0	0	0	32	74²	58	8	19	75	9.4	2.17	175	.213	.267	0	—	0	14	13	-1	1.3
Total 9	29	26	.527	381	0	0	0	154	517	404	40	165	596	10.0	2.72	150	.215	.281	0	—	0	79	78	-4	7.5

■ WELDON HENLEY
Henley, Weldon b: 10/25/1880, Jasper, Ga. d: 11/16/60, Palatka, Fla. BR/TR, 6', 175 lbs. Deb: 4/23/03

YEAR TM/L	W	L	PCT	G	GS	CG	SH	SV	IP	H	HR	BB	SO	RAT	ERA	ERA+	OAV	OOB	BH	AVG	PB	PR	/A	PD	TPI
1903 Phi-A	12	10	.545	29	21	13	1	0	186¹	186	3	67	86	12.2	3.91	78	.259	.323	9	.132	-3	-20	-18	0	-2.0
1904 Phi-A	15	17	.469	36	34	31	5	0	295²	245	3	76	130	9.8	2.53	106	.227	.277	24	.222	2	2	5	6	1.5
1905 Phi-A	4	11	.267	25	19	13	1	0	183²	155	4	67	82	10.9	2.60	102	.230	.300	11	.169	-1	1	1	5	0.5
1907 Bro-N	1	5	.167	7	7	5	0	0	56	54	2	21	11	12.2	3.05	77	.273	.345	4	.200	1	-4	-2	-1	-0.1
Total 4	32	43	.427	97	81	62	7	0	721²	640	12	231	309	10.9	2.94	93	.240	.300	48	.184	-2	-20	-16	12	-0.1

■ MIKE HENNEMAN
Henneman, Michael Alan b: 12/11/61, St.Charles, Mo. BR/TR, 6'4", 205 lbs. Deb: 5/11/87

YEAR TM/L	W	L	PCT	G	GS	CG	SH	SV	IP	H	HR	BB	SO	RAT	ERA	ERA+	OAV	OOB	BH	AVG	PB	PR	/A	PD	TPI
1987 *Det-A	11	3	.786	55	0	0	0	7	96²	86	8	30	75	11.1	2.98	142	.238	.301	0	.000	0	16	13	0	1.3
1988 Det-A	9	6	.600	65	0	0	0	22	91¹	72	7	24	58	9.7	1.87	204	.218	.275	0	—	0	21	20	-1	1.9
1989 Det-A	11	4	.733	60	0	0	0	8	90	84	4	51	69	14.0	3.70	103	.251	.358	0	—	0	2	1	0	0.1
1990 Det-A	8	6	.571	69	0	0	0	22	94¹	90	4	33	50	12.0	3.05	129	.253	.321	0	—	0	9	9	1	1.0
Total 4	39	19	.672	249	0	0	0	59	372¹	332	23	138	252	11.7	2.90	136	.240	.315	0	.000	0	48	44	-0	4.3

■ GEORGE HENNESSEY
Hennessey, George "Three Star" b: 10/28/07, Slatington, Pa. d: 1/15/88, Princeton, N.J. BR/TR, 5'10", 168 lbs. Deb: 9/02/37

YEAR TM/L	W	L	PCT	G	GS	CG	SH	SV	IP	H	HR	BB	SO	RAT	ERA	ERA+	OAV	OOB	BH	AVG	PB	PR	/A	PD	TPI
1937 StL-A	0	1	.000	5	0	0	0	0	7	15	2	6	4	27.0	10.29	47	.500	.583	0	.000	0	-4	-4	0	-0.3
1942 Phi-N	1	1	.500	5	1	0	0	0	17	11	1	10	2	11.1	2.65	125	.180	.296	0	.000	-1	1	1	-0	0.0
1945 Chi-N	0	0	—	2	0	0	0	0	3²	7	0	1	2	19.6	7.36	50	.438	.471	0	.000	-0	-2	-2	0	0.0
Total 3	1	2	.333	12	1	0	0	0	27²	33	3	17	8	16.3	5.20	72	.308	.403	0	.000	-1	-5	-5	0	-0.3

■ PHIL HENNIGAN
Hennigan, Phillip Winston b: 4/10/46, Jasper, Tex. BR/TR, 5'11.5", 185 lbs. Deb: 9/02/69

YEAR TM/L	W	L	PCT	G	GS	CG	SH	SV	IP	H	HR	BB	SO	RAT	ERA	ERA+	OAV	OOB	BH	AVG	PB	PR	/A	PD	TPI
1969 Cle-A	2	1	.667	9	0	0	0	0	16¹	14	0	4	10	10.5	3.31	114	.241	.302	0	.000	-0	1	1	-1	0.0
1970 Cle-A	6	3	.667	42	1	0	0	3	71²	69	7	44	43	14.7	4.02	99	.263	.377	1	.143	1	-2	-0	1	0.2
1971 Cle-A	4	3	.571	57	0	0	0	14	82	80	13	51	69	14.7	4.94	77	.261	.371	0	.000	-0	-13	-10	-1	-1.1
1972 Cle-A	5	3	.625	38	1	0	0	5	67¹	54	8	18	44	9.9	2.67	120	.226	.286	1	.083	-0	3	4	-1	0.3
1973 NY-N	0	4	.000	30	0	0	0	3	43¹	50	6	16	22	13.9	6.23	58	.289	.353	1	.333	0	-12	-13	-0	-1.2
Total 5	17	14	.548	176	2	0	0	25	280²	267	34	133	188	13.2	4.26	86	.257	.347	3	.100	-0	-25	-18	-2	-1.8

■ PETE HENNING
Henning, Ernest Herman b: 12/28/1887, Crown Point, Ind. d: 11/4/39, Dyer, Ind. BR/TR, 5'11", 185 lbs. Deb: 4/17/14

YEAR TM/L	W	L	PCT	G	GS	CG	SH	SV	IP	H	HR	BB	SO	RAT	ERA	ERA+	OAV	OOB	BH	AVG	PB	PR	/A	PD	TPI
1914 KC-F	5	10	.333	28	14	7	0	2	138	153	5	58	45	14.2	4.83	64	.291	.369	8	.182	1	-25	-27	0	-2.4

YEAR TM/L	W	L	PCT	G	GS	CG	SH	SV	IP	H	HR	BB	SO	RAT	ERA	ERA+	OAV	OOB	BH	AVG	PB	PR	/A	PD	TPI
1915 KC-F	9	15	.375	40	20	15	1	2	207	181	5	76	73	11.3	3.17	92	.235	.307	14	.206	-0	-3	-6	4	-0.2
Total 2	14	25	.359	68	34	22	1	4	345	334	10	134	118	12.5	3.83	78	.258	.332	22	.196	1	-28	-32	4	-2.6

■ RICK HENNINGER Henninger, Richard Lee b: 1/11/48, Hastings, Neb. BR/TR, 6'6", 225 lbs. Deb: 9/03/73

YEAR TM/L	W	L	PCT	G	GS	CG	SH	SV	IP	H	HR	BB	SO	RAT	ERA	ERA+	OAV	OOB	BH	AVG	PB	PR	/A	PD	TPI
1973 Tex-A	1	0	1.000	6	2	0	0	0	23	23	1	11	6	13.3	2.74	136	.261	.343	0	—	0	3	3	-0	0.2

■ RANDY HENNIS Hennis, Randall Philip b: 12/16/65, Clearlake, Cal. BR/TR, 6'6", 220 lbs. Deb: 9/17/90

YEAR TM/L	W	L	PCT	G	GS	CG	SH	SV	IP	H	HR	BB	SO	RAT	ERA	ERA+	OAV	OOB	BH	AVG	PB	PR	/A	PD	TPI
1990 Hou-N	0	0	—	3	1	0	0	0	9²	1	0	3	4	4.7	0.00	—	.033	.147	0	.000	-0	4	4	0	0.4

■ DWAYNE HENRY Henry, Dwayne Allen b: 2/16/62, Elkton, Md. BR/TR, 6'3", 205 lbs. Deb: 9/07/84

YEAR TM/L	W	L	PCT	G	GS	CG	SH	SV	IP	H	HR	BB	SO	RAT	ERA	ERA+	OAV	OOB	BH	AVG	PB	PR	/A	PD	TPI
1984 Tex-A	0	1	.000	3	0	0	0	0	4¹	5	0	7	2	24.9	8.31	50	.294	.500	0	—	0	-2	-2	0	-0.1
1985 Tex-A	2	2	.500	16	0	0	0	3	21	16	0	7	20	9.9	2.57	164	.211	.277	0	—	0	4	4	-0	0.4
1986 Tex-A	1	0	1.000	19	0	0	0	0	19¹	14	1	22	17	17.2	4.66	92	.209	.411	0	—	0	-1	-1	0	0.0
1987 Tex-A	0	0	—	5	0	0	0	0	10	12	2	9	7	18.9	9.00	50	.293	.420	0	—	0	-5	-5	0	-0.3
1988 Tex-A	0	1	.000	11	0	0	0	1	10¹	15	1	9	10	23.5	8.71	47	.326	.466	0	—	0	-5	-5	-0	-0.4
1989 Atl-N	0	2	.000	12	0	0	0	1	12²	12	2	16	12	12.1	4.26	86	.250	.321	0	—	0	-1	-1	-0	0.0
1990 Atl-N	2	2	.500	34	0	0	0	0	38¹	41	3	25	34	15.5	5.63	69	.273	.377	0	—	0	-8	-7	-1	-0.7
Total 7	5	8	.385	100	0	0	0	5	116	115	9	84	106	15.7	5.43	75	.258	.381	0	—	0	-19	-17	-1	-1.1

■ EARL HENRY Henry, Earl Clifford "Hook" b: 6/10/17, Roseville, Ohio BL/TL, 5'11", 172 lbs. Deb: 9/23/44

YEAR TM/L	W	L	PCT	G	GS	CG	SH	SV	IP	H	HR	BB	SO	RAT	ERA	ERA+	OAV	OOB	BH	AVG	PB	PR	/A	PD	TPI
1944 Cle-A	1	1	.500	2	2	1	0	0	17²	18	0	3	5	10.7	4.58	72	.269	.300	0	.000	-0	-2	-3	0	-0.1
1945 Cle-A	0	3	.000	15	1	0	0	0	21²	20	0	20	10	17.0	5.40	60	.253	.410	2	.500	1	-5	-5	1	-0.3
Total 2	1	4	.200	17	3	1	0	0	39¹	38	0	23	15	14.2	5.03	65	.260	.365	2	.222	0	-7	-8	1	-0.4

■ DUTCH HENRY Henry, Frank John b: 5/12/02, Cleveland, Ohio d: 8/23/68, Cleveland, Ohio BL/TL, 6'1", 175 lbs. Deb: 9/16/21

YEAR TM/L	W	L	PCT	G	GS	CG	SH	SV	IP	H	HR	BB	SO	RAT	ERA	ERA+	OAV	OOB	BH	AVG	PB	PR	/A	PD	TPI
1921 StL-A	0	0	—	1	0	0	0	0	2	2	0	1		9.0	4.50	100	.250	.250	1	1.000	0	-0	-0	0	0.0
1922 StL-A	0	0	—	4	0	0	0	0	5	7	0	5	3	21.6	5.40	77	.280	.400	0	—	0	-1	-1	0	0.0
1923 Bro-N	4	6	.400	17	9	5	2	0	94¹	105	9	28	28	12.9	3.91	99	.281	.334	8	.229	1	1	0	0	0.0
1924 Bro-N	1	2	.333	16	4	0	0	0	46	69	0	15	11	16.4	5.67	66	.352	.398	5	.250	1	-9	-10	0	-0.3
1927 NY-N	11	6	.647	45	15	7	1	4	163²	184	6	31	40	11.8	4.23	91	.278	.311	13	.236	1	-6	-7	-1	-0.6
1928 NY-N	3	6	.333	17	8	4	0	1	64	82	4	25	23	15.2	3.80	103	.325	.388	3	.158	-1	1	1	1	0.1
1929 NY-N	5	6	.455	27	9	4	0	1	101¹	129	10	31	27	14.3	3.82	120	.316	.366	7	.250	2	10	9	-0	0.9
Chi-A	1	0	1.000	2	1	1	0	0	15	20	1	7	2	16.2	6.00	71	.308	.375	3	.143	-1	-3	-3	-0	-0.2
1930 Chi-A	2	17	.105	35	16	4	0	0	155	211	12	48	34	15.3	4.88	95	.331	.381	12	.235	1	-4	-4	3	-0.6
Total 8	27	43	.386	164	62	25	3	6	646¹	809	42	190	169	14.0	4.39	95	.308	.356	50	.231	5	-10	-16	2	-0.6

■ JIM HENRY Henry, James Francis b: 6/26/10, Danville, Pa. d: 8/15/76, Memphis, Tenn. BR/TR, 6'2", 175 lbs. Deb: 4/23/36

YEAR TM/L	W	L	PCT	G	GS	CG	SH	SV	IP	H	HR	BB	SO	RAT	ERA	ERA+	OAV	OOB	BH	AVG	PB	PR	/A	PD	TPI
1936 Bos-A	5	1	.833	21	8	2	0	0	76¹	75	10	40	36	13.8	4.60	116	.255	.348	3	.115	-1	4	6	0	0.5
1937 Bos-A	1	0	1.000	3	2	1	0	0	15¹	15	2	11	8	15.3	5.28	90	.263	.382	0	.000	-1	-1	-0	0	0.0
1939 Phi-N	0	1	.000	9	1	0	0	1	23	24	3	8	7	12.9	5.09	79	.276	.344	0	.000	-1	-3	-3	-0	-0.3
Total 3	6	2	.750	33	11	3	0	1	114²	114	15	59	51	13.8	4.79	104	.260	.352	3	.083	-2	-0	2	-0	0.2

■ JOHN HENRY Henry, John Michael b: 9/2/1863, Springfield, Mass. d: 6/11/39, Hartford, Conn. Deb: 8/13/1884 ◆

YEAR TM/L	W	L	PCT	G	GS	CG	SH	SV	IP	H	HR	BB	SO	RAT	ERA	ERA+	OAV	OOB	BH	AVG	PB	PR	/A	PD	TPI
1884 Cle-N	1	4	.200	5	5	5	1	0	42	46	2	26	23	15.4	3.64	86	.264	.359	4	.154	-1	-3	-2	1	-0.2
1885 Bal-a	2	7	.222	9	9	9	0	0	71	71	0	13	31	10.6	4.31	76	.249	.282	9	.265	1	-8	-8	2	-0.3
1886 Was-N	1	3	.250	4	4	4	0	0	27²	35	1	15	19	16.3	4.23	78	.296	.376	5	.357	1	-3	-3	-0	-0.1
Total 3	4	14	.222	18	18	18	1	0	140²	152	3	54	73	13.2	4.09	79	.263	.326	18	.243	1	-14	-13	2	-0.6

■ BILL HENRY Henry, William Francis b: 2/15/42, Long Beach, Cal. BL/TL, 6'3", 195 lbs. Deb: 9/13/66

YEAR TM/L	W	L	PCT	G	GS	CG	SH	SV	IP	H	HR	BB	SO	RAT	ERA	ERA+	OAV	OOB	BH	AVG	PB	PR	/A	PD	TPI
1966 NY-A	0	0	—	2	0	0	0	0	3	0	0	2	3	6.0	0.00	—	.000	.200	0	—	0	1	1	0	0.2

■ BILL HENRY Henry, William Rodman b: 10/15/27, Alice, Tex. BL/TL, 6'2", 180 lbs. Deb: 4/17/52

YEAR TM/L	W	L	PCT	G	GS	CG	SH	SV	IP	H	HR	BB	SO	RAT	ERA	ERA+	OAV	OOB	BH	AVG	PB	PR	/A	PD	TPI
1952 Bos-A	5	4	.556	13	10	5	0	0	76²	75	7	36	23	13.3	3.87	102	.254	.339	8	.258	2	-2	1	-1	0.2
1953 Bos-A	5	5	.500	21	12	4	1	1	85²	86	4	33	56	12.9	3.26	129	.260	.334	6	.188	-0	7	9	-1	0.8
1954 Bos-A	3	7	.300	24	13	3	1	0	95²	104	9	49	38	14.5	4.52	91	.270	.354	4	.118	-2	-8	-4	-1	-0.5
1955 Bos-A	2	4	.333	17	7	0	0	0	59²	56	7	21	23	11.6	3.32	129	.247	.310	2	.105	-1	4	6	0	0.6
1958 Chi-N	5	4	.556	44	0	0	0	6	81¹	63	8	17	58	9.0	2.88	136	.214	.259	4	.235	-1	10	9	-1	1.0
1959 Chi-N	9	8	.529	65	0	0	0	12	134¹	111	19	26	115	9.2	2.68	147	.227	.267	6	.194	0	19	19	-1	1.8
1960 Cin-N	1	5	.167	51	0	0	0	17	67²	62	8	20	58	11.4	3.19	120	.247	.313	0	.000	-1	4	5	0	0.4
1961 *Cin-N	2	1	.667	47	0	0	0	16	53¹	50	8	15	53	11.0	2.19	185	.244	.295	0	.000	-1	11	11	-0	1.0
1962 Cin-N	4	2	.667	40	0	0	0	11	37¹	40	5	20	35	14.7	4.58	88	.280	.372	1	.333	0	-3	-2	-1	-0.2
1963 Cin-N	1	3	.250	47	0	0	0	14	52	55	4	11	45	11.6	4.15	81	.279	.321	1	.167	0	-5	-5	-0	-0.5
1964 Cin-N	2	2	.500	37	0	0	0	6	52	31	2	12	28	8.0	0.87	418	.170	.234	3	.500	1	15	16	1	1.8
1965 Cin-N	2	0	1.000	3	0	0	0	0	5	3	0	1	5	7.2	0.00	—	.176	.222	0	—	0	2	2	0	0.2
SF-N	2	2	.500	35	0	0	0	0	42	40	2	8	35	10.5	3.64	99	.248	.288	1	.200	0	-0	-0	-0	0.0
Yr	4	2	.667	38	0	0	0	0	47	43	2	9	40	10.1	3.26	111	.242	.282	1	.200	0	1	2	-0	0.2
1966 SF-N	1	1	.500	35	0	0	0	1	22	15	3	10	15	10.6	2.45	149	.190	.289	0	.000	0	3	3	0	0.3
1967 SF-N	2	0	1.000	28	0	0	0	2	21²	16	1	9	23	11.2	2.08	158	.198	.293	0	—	-0	3	3	-0	0.3
1968 SF-N	0	2	.000	7	0	0	0	0	5	4	0	3	4	14.4	5.40	55	.250	.400	0	—	0	-1	-1	0	0.0
Pit-N	0	0	—	10	0	0	0	0	16²	29	2	3	9	18.4	8.10	36	.382	.420	0	.000	0	-9	-10	-1	-1.0
Yr	0	2	.000	17	1	0	0	0	21²	33	2	6	13	17.0	7.48	39	.355	.406	0	.000	0	-11	-11	-0	-1.0
1969 Hou-N	0	0	—	3	0	0	0	0	5	2	0	2	2	7.2	0.00	—	.111	.200	0	—	0	2	2	-0	0.2
Total 16	46	50	.479	527	44	12	2	90	913	842	89	296	621	11.5	3.26	119	.244	.308	36	.177	-0	51	63	-6	6.5

■ ROY HENSHAW Henshaw, Roy Knikelbine b: 7/29/11, Chicago, Ill. BR/TL, 5'8", 155 lbs. Deb: 4/15/33

YEAR TM/L	W	L	PCT	G	GS	CG	SH	SV	IP	H	HR	BB	SO	RAT	ERA	ERA+	OAV	OOB	BH	AVG	PB	PR	/A	PD	TPI
1933 Chi-N	2	1	.667	21	1	0	0	0	38²	32	1	20	16	12.6	4.19	78	.230	.335	2	.200	-0	-4	-4	-1	-0.4
1935 *Chi-N	13	5	.722	31	18	7	3	1	142²	135	6	68	53	13.1	3.28	120	.249	.337	13	.255	2	12	10	-3	0.8
1936 Chi-N	6	5	.545	39	14	6	2	1	129¹	152	8	56	69	14.8	3.97	100	.296	.370	6	.136	-2	1	0	-2	-0.3
1937 Bro-N	5	12	.294	42	16	4	2	0	156¹	176	14	69	98	14.3	5.07	80	.278	.352	8	.167	-2	-20	-18	-1	-1.8
1938 StL-N	5	11	.313	27	15	4	0	0	130	132	7	48	34	12.5	4.02	99	.266	.332	9	.220	-0	-3	-1	-1	-0.1
1942 Det-A	2	4	.333	23	2	0	0	1	61²	63	3	27	24	13.3	4.09	97	.269	.347	1	.083	-1	-3	-1	-1	-0.1
1943 Det-A	0	2	.000	26	3	0	0	2	71¹	75	2	33	33	14.0	3.79	93	.276	.360	2	.111	-1	-4	-2	-0	-0.2
1944 Det-A	0	0	—	7	1	0	0	0	12¹	17	0	6	10	16.8	8.76	41	.315	.383	0	.000	-1	-7	-7	-0	-0.7
Total 8	33	40	.452	216	69	22	5	7	742¹	782	40	327	337	13.7	4.16	94	.271	.349	41	.179	-5	-29	-22	-8	-2.8

■ PHIL HENSIEK Hensiek, Philip Frank "Sid" b: 10/13/01, St.Louis, Mo. d: 2/21/72, St.Louis, Mo. BR/TR, 6', 160 lbs. Deb: 8/15/35

YEAR TM/L	W	L	PCT	G	GS	CG	SH	SV	IP	H	HR	BB	SO	RAT	ERA	ERA+	OAV	OOB	BH	AVG	PB	PR	/A	PD	TPI
1935 Was-A	0	3	.000	6	1	0	0	1	13	21	2	9	6	20.8	9.69	45	.356	.441	2	.667	1	-8	-8	-0	-0.5

■ CHUCK HENSLEY Hensley, Charles Floyd b: 3/11/59, Tulare, Cal. BL/TL, 6'3", 190 lbs. Deb: 5/10/86

YEAR TM/L	W	L	PCT	G	GS	CG	SH	SV	IP	H	HR	BB	SO	RAT	ERA	ERA+	OAV	OOB	BH	AVG	PB	PR	/A	PD	TPI
1986 SF-N	0	0	—	11	0	0	0	1	7¹	5	2	2	6	8.6	2.45	143	.179	.233	0	—	0	1	1	0	0.1

■ BILL HEPLER Hepler, William Lewis b: 9/25/45, Covington, Va. BL/TL, 6', 160 lbs. Deb: 4/23/66

YEAR TM/L	W	L	PCT	G	GS	CG	SH	SV	IP	H	HR	BB	SO	RAT	ERA	ERA+	OAV	OOB	BH	AVG	PB	PR	/A	PD	TPI
1966 NY-N	3	3	.500	37	3	0	0	0	69	71	3	51	25	16.3	3.52	103	.274	.399	3	.214	-0	1	-0	-0	0.1

■ RON HERBEL Herbel, Ronald Samuel b: 1/16/38, Denver, Colo. BR/TR, 6'1", 195 lbs. Deb: 9/10/63

YEAR TM/L	W	L	PCT	G	GS	CG	SH	SV	IP	H	HR	BB	SO	RAT	ERA	ERA+	OAV	OOB	BH	AVG	PB	PR	/A	PD	TPI
1963 SF-N	0	0	—	2	0	0	0	0	1¹	1	0	1	1	13.5	6.75	47	.200	.333	0	—	0	-1	-1	0	0.0

YEAR TM/L	W	L	PCT	G	GS	CG	SH	SV	IP	H	HR	BB	SO	RAT	ERA	ERA+	OAV	OOB	BH	AVG	PB	PR	/A	PD	TPI
1964 SF-N	9	9	.500	40	22	7	2	1	161	162	7	61	98	12.6	3.07	116	.259	.328	0	.000	-4	8	9	2	0.7
1965 SF-N	12	9	.571	47	21	1	0	1	170²	172	16	47	106	11.7	3.85	94	.261	.313	1	.020	-4	-6	-5	2	-0.6
1966 SF-N	4	5	.444	32	18	0	0	1	129²	149	15	39	55	13.2	4.16	88	.291	.344	1	.026	-4	-8	-7	-0	-1.0
1967 SF-N	4	5	.444	42	11	1	1	1	125²	125	10	35	52	11.6	3.08	107	.268	.322	3	.107	-4	4	3	4	0.7
1968 SF-N	0	0	—	28	2	0	0	0	42²	55	5	15	18	15.0	3.38	87	.309	.366	0	.000	-0	-2	-2	1	-0.1
1969 SF-N	4	1	.800	39	4	2	0	1	87¹	92	7	23	34	12.0	4.02	87	.275	.323	0	.000	-1	-4	-5	1	-0.5
1970 SD-N	7	5	.583	64	1	0	0	9	111	114	14	39	53	12.7	4.95	80	.266	.333	0	.000	-1	-11	-12	0	-1.2
NY-N	2	2	.500	12	0	0	0	1	13	14	1	2	8	11.1	1.38	291	.275	.302	0	—	0	4	4	-0	0.4
Yr	9	7	.563	76	1	0	0	10	124	128	15	41	61	12.3	4.57	87	.262	.319	1	.077	-1	-7	-8	-0	-0.8
1971 Atl-N	0	1	.000	25	0	0	0	1	51²	61	6	23	22	15.3	5.23	71	.300	.383	1	.091	-1	-10	-9	-0	-0.9
Total 9	42	37	.532	331	79	11	3	16	894	945	81	285	447	12.6	3.83	94	.273	.332	6	.029	-16	-25	-25	10	-2.5

■ ERNIE HERBERT

Herbert, Ernie Albert "Tex" b: 1/30/1887, Hale, Mo. d: 1/13/68, Dallas, Tex. BR/TR, 5'10", 165 lbs. Deb: 7/27/13

YEAR TM/L	W	L	PCT	G	GS	CG	SH	SV	IP	H	HR	BB	SO	RAT	ERA	ERA+	OAV	OOB	BH	AVG	PB	PR	/A	PD	TPI
1913 Cin-N	0	0	—	6	0	0	0	0	17¹	12	0	5	5	9.3	2.08	156	.179	.247	1	.250	0	2	2	-1	0.2
1914 StL-F	1	1	.500	18	2	0	0	1	50¹	56	2	27	24	15.6	3.75	90	.293	.392	7	.538	3	-3	-2	-2	-0.1
1915 StL-F	1	0	1.000	11	1	1	0	0	48	48	1	18	23	12.9	3.38	95	.253	.327	5	.278	1	-2	-1	-1	0.0
Total 3	2	1	.667	35	3	1	0	1	115²	116	3	50	52	13.5	3.35	98	.259	.344	13	.371	4	-3	-1	-3	0.1

■ FRED HERBERT

Herbert, Frederick (b: Herbert Frederick Kemman) b: 3/4/1887, Lagrange, Ill. d: 5/29/63, Tice, Fla. BR/TR, 6', 185 lbs. Deb: 9/25/15

YEAR TM/L	W	L	PCT	G	GS	CG	SH	SV	IP	H	HR	BB	SO	RAT	ERA	ERA+	OAV	OOB	BH	AVG	PB	PR	/A	PD	TPI
1915 NY-N	1	1	.500	2	2	1	0	0	17	12	0	4	6	8.5	1.06	242	.197	.246	1	.167	-0	3	3	0	0.3

■ RAY HERBERT

Herbert, Raymond Ernest b: 12/15/29, Detroit, Mich. BR/TR, 5'11", 185 lbs. Deb: 8/27/50

YEAR TM/L	W	L	PCT	G	GS	CG	SH	SV	IP	H	HR	BB	SO	RAT	ERA	ERA+	OAV	OOB	BH	AVG	PB	PR	/A	PD	TPI
1950 Det-A	1	2	.333	8	3	1	0	1	22¹	20	1	12	5	12.9	3.63	129	.244	.340	2	.286	0	2	3	1	0.3
1951 Det-A	4	0	1.000	5	0	0	0	0	12²	8	0	9	9	12.1	1.42	294	.190	.333	0	.000	0	4	4	-0	0.3
1953 Det-A	4	6	.400	43	3	0	0	6	87²	109	5	46	37	15.9	5.24	78	.308	.387	3	.158	-0	-12	-11	3	-0.7
1954 Det-A	3	6	.333	42	4	0	0	0	84¹	114	6	50	44	17.7	5.87	63	.334	.422	3	.176	2	-20	-20	2	-1.6
1955 KC-A	1	8	.111	23	11	2	0	0	87²	99	10	40	30	14.4	6.26	67	.292	.368	4	.190	0	-22	-20	2	-1.6
1958 KC-A	8	8	.500	42	16	5	0	3	175	161	20	55	108	11.3	3.50	112	.248	.311	10	.192	1	5	8	2	1.2
1959 KC-A	11	11	.500	37	26	10	2	1	183²	196	24	62	99	12.7	4.85	83	.275	.334	12	.211	2	-20	-17	-1	-1.5
1960 KC-A	14	15	.483	37	33	14	0	1	252²	256	17	72	122	11.9	3.28	121	.267	.323	13	.171	1	17	20	3	2.5
1961 KC-A	3	6	.333	13	12	1	0	0	83²	103	10	30	34	14.5	5.38	77	.303	.363	3	.107	-1	-13	-12	0	-1.1
Chi-A	9	6	.600	21	20	4	0	0	137²	142	15	36	50	11.6	4.05	97	.265	.311	12	.226	4	-0	-2	1	0.3
Yr	12	12	.500	34	32	5	0	0	221¹	245	25	66	84	12.6	4.55	88	.278	.328	5	.062	3	-13	-14	1	-0.8
1962 Chi-A	20	9	.690	35	35	12	2	0	236²	228	13	74	115	11.5	3.27	119	.255	.312	16	.195	5	18	17	4	2.6
1963 Chi-A	13	10	.565	33	33	14	7	0	224²	230	12	35	105	10.7	3.24	108	.265	.295	14	.222	6	10	7	3	1.6
1964 Chi-A	6	7	.462	20	19	1	1	0	111²	117	14	17	40	11.0	3.47	100	.275	.306	5	.139	-1	2	-0	0	0.0
1965 Phi-N	5	8	.385	25	19	4	1	1	130²	162	13	19	51	12.5	3.86	90	.304	.334	11	.268	3	-5	-6	1	-0.1
1966 Phi-N	2	5	.286	23	2	0	0	2	50¹	55	7	14	15	12.5	4.29	84	.293	.345	1	.077	-1	-4	-4	0	-0.0
Total 14	104	107	.493	407	236	68	13	15	1881¹	2000	167	571	864	12.4	4.01	96	.276	.331	109	.192	20	-38	-36	21	1.8

■ UBALDO HEREDIA

Heredia, Ubaldo Jose (Martinez) b: 5/4/56, Ciudad Bolivar, Ven. BR/TR, 6'2", 180 lbs. Deb: 5/12/87

YEAR TM/L	W	L	PCT	G	GS	CG	SH	SV	IP	H	HR	BB	SO	RAT	ERA	ERA+	OAV	OOB	BH	AVG	PB	PR	/A	PD	TPI
1987 Mon-N	0	1	.000	2	2	0	0	0	10	12	2	3	6	12.6	5.40	78	.263	.333	0	.000	-0	-1	-1	0	0.0

■ ART HERMAN

Herman, Arthur b: 5/11/1871, Louisville, Ky. d: 9/20/55, Los Angeles, Cal. Deb: 6/29/1896

YEAR TM/L	W	L	PCT	G	GS	CG	SH	SV	IP	H	HR	BB	SO	RAT	ERA	ERA+	OAV	OOB	BH	AVG	PB	PR	/A	PD	TPI
1896 Lou-N	4	6	.400	14	12	9	0	0	94¹	122	4	36	13	15.1	5.63	77	.311	.368	5	.139	-4	-13	-14	-1	-1.4
1897 Lou-N	0	1	.000	3	2	1	0	0	18	23	1	5	4	14.0	4.00	107	.308	.351	2	.333	1	1	1	0	0.2
Total 2	4	7	.364	17	14	10	0	0	112¹	145	5	41	17	14.9	5.37	80	.310	.366	7	.167	-2	-13	-13	-1	-1.2

■ JESUS HERNAIZ

Hernaiz, Jesus Rafael (Rodriguez) b: 1/8/48, Santurce, P.R. BR/TR, 6'2", 175 lbs. Deb: 6/14/74

YEAR TM/L	W	L	PCT	G	GS	CG	SH	SV	IP	H	HR	BB	SO	RAT	ERA	ERA+	OAV	OOB	BH	AVG	PB	PR	/A	PD	TPI
1974 Phi-N	2	3	.400	27	0	0	0	1	41¹	53	6	25	16	17.0	5.88	64	.323	.413	0	.000	0	-10	-10	0	-0.9

■ XAVIER HERNANDEZ

Hernandez, Francis Xavier b: 8/16/65, Port Arthur, Tex. BL/TR, 6'2", 185 lbs. Deb: 6/04/89

YEAR TM/L	W	L	PCT	G	GS	CG	SH	SV	IP	H	HR	BB	SO	RAT	ERA	ERA+	OAV	OOB	BH	AVG	PB	PR	/A	PD	TPI
1989 Tor-A	1	0	1.000	7	0	0	0	0	22²	25	2	8	7	13.5	4.76	79	.278	.343	0	—	0	-2	-3	-0	-0.2
1990 Hou-N	2	1	.667	34	1	0	0	0	62¹	60	8	24	24	12.7	4.62	81	.256	.336	1	.333	0	-6	-6	-1	-0.6
Total 2	3	1	.750	41	1	0	0	0	85	85	10	32	31	12.9	4.66	80	.262	.338	1	.333	0	-8	-9	-1	-0.8

■ EVELIO HERNANDEZ

Hernandez, Gregorio Evelio (Lopez) b: 12/24/30, Guanabacoa, Havana, Cuba BR/TR, 6'1", 195 lbs. Deb: 9/12/56

YEAR TM/L	W	L	PCT	G	GS	CG	SH	SV	IP	H	HR	BB	SO	RAT	ERA	ERA+	OAV	OOB	BH	AVG	PB	PR	/A	PD	TPI
1956 Was-A	1	1	.500	4	4	1	0	0	22²	24	2	8	9	12.7	4.76	91	.276	.337	2	.182	-0	-2	-1	-0	-0.1
1957 Was-A	0	0	—	14	2	0	0	0	36	38	2	20	15	14.5	4.25	92	.268	.358	0	.000	-1	-1	-1	-0	-0.2
Total 2	1	1	.500	18	6	1	0	0	58²	62	4	28	24	13.8	4.45	91	.271	.350	2	.118	-1	-3	-3	-1	-0.3

■ WILLIE HERNANDEZ

Hernandez, Guillermo (Villanueva) b: 11/14/54, Aguada, P.R. BL/TL, 6'3", 180 lbs. Deb: 4/09/77

YEAR TM/L	W	L	PCT	G	GS	CG	SH	SV	IP	H	HR	BB	SO	RAT	ERA	ERA+	OAV	OOB	BH	AVG	PB	PR	/A	PD	TPI
1977 Chi-N	8	7	.533	67	1	0	0	4	110	94	11	28	78	10.1	3.03	145	.234	.285	1	.063	-2	11	17	3	1.8
1978 Chi-N	8	2	.800	54	0	0	0	3	59²	57	6	35	38	14.0	3.77	107	.263	.368	0	.000	-0	-1	2	0	0.2
1979 Chi-N	4	4	.500	51	2	0	0	0	79	85	8	39	53	14.6	5.01	82	.281	.370	2	.250	0	-11	-8	0	-0.7
1980 Chi-N	1	9	.100	53	7	0	0	0	108¹	115	8	45	75	13.5	4.40	89	.276	.349	4	.211	0	-10	-6	2	-0.3
1981 Chi-N	0	0	—	12	0	0	0	2	13²	14	0	8	13	14.5	3.95	94	.280	.379	0	—	0	-1	-0	0	0.0
1982 Chi-N	4	6	.400	75	0	0	0	10	75	74	3	24	54	11.9	3.00	124	.268	.329	0	.000	-0	5	6	2	0.9
1983 Chi-N	1	0	1.000	11	0	0	0	1	19²	16	0	6	18	10.1	3.20	118	.222	.282	1	.500	0	1	1	0	0.2
*Phi-N	8	4	.667	63	0	0	0	7	95²	93	9	26	75	11.3	3.29	108	.254	.305	5	.385	2	4	3	-0	0.5
Yr	9	4	.692	74	0	0	0	8	115¹	109	9	32	93	11.1	3.28	110	.249	.301	6	.400	2	4	4	0	0.7
1984 *Det-A	9	3	.750	80	0	0	0	32	140¹	96	6	36	112	8.7	1.92	204	.194	.254	0	—	0	32	31	-1	3.1
1985 Det-A	8	10	.444	74	0	0	0	31	106²	82	13	14	76	8.2	2.70	151	.210	.239	0	.000	0	17	16	-2	1.5
1986 Det-A	8	7	.533	64	0	0	0	24	88²	87	13	21	77	11.5	3.55	116	.251	.304	0	—	0	6	6	0	0.6
1987 *Det-A	3	4	.429	45	0	0	0	8	49	53	8	20	30	13.4	3.67	115	.276	.344	0	—	0	3	3	-1	0.2
1988 Det-A	6	5	.545	63	0	0	0	10	67²	50	8	31	59	11.3	3.06	125	.208	.309	0	—	0	7	6	1	0.7
1989 Det-A	2	2	.500	32	0	0	0	15	31¹	36	4	16	30	15.2	5.74	66	.293	.379	0	—	0	-6	-7	0	-0.6
Total 13	70	63	.526	744	11	0	0	147	1044²	952	97	349	788	11.4	3.38	118	.245	.311	13	.206	1	57	70	5	8.1

■ MANNY HERNANDEZ

Hernandez, Manuel Antonio (Montas) b: 5/7/61, LaRomana, D.R. BR/TR, 6', 150 lbs. Deb: 6/05/86

YEAR TM/L	W	L	PCT	G	GS	CG	SH	SV	IP	H	HR	BB	SO	RAT	ERA	ERA+	OAV	OOB	BH	AVG	PB	PR	/A	PD	TPI
1986 Hou-N	2	3	.400	9	4	0	0	0	27²	33	2	12	9	14.6	3.90	92	.306	.375	0	.000	-1	-1	-1	0	-0.0
1987 Hou-N	0	4	.000	6	3	0	0	0	21²	25	1	5	12	12.9	5.40	73	.301	.348	0	.000	-0	-3	-4	0	-0.3
1989 NY-N	0	0	—	1	0	0	0	0	1	0	0	0	1	0.0	0.00	—	.000	.000	0	—	0	0	0	0	0.0
Total 3	2	7	.222	16	7	0	0	0	50¹	58	3	17	22	13.6	4.47	83	.299	.358	0	.000	-1	-3	-4	0	-0.3

■ RAMON HERNANDEZ

Hernandez, Ramon (Gonzalez) b: 8/31/40, Carolina, P.R. BB/TL, 5'11", 165 lbs. Deb: 4/11/67

YEAR TM/L	W	L	PCT	G	GS	CG	SH	SV	IP	H	HR	BB	SO	RAT	ERA	ERA+	OAV	OOB	BH	AVG	PB	PR	/A	PD	TPI
1967 Atl-N	0	2	.000	46	0	0	0	5	51²	60	5	14	28	13.2	4.18	79	.296	.347	0	.000	-0	-5	-4	1	-0.4
1968 Chi-N	0	0	—	8	0	0	0	0	9	14	1	0	3	15.0	9.00	35	.350	.366	0	—	0	-6	-6	0	-0.5
1971 Pit-N	0	1	.000	10	0	0	0	4	12¹	5	0	2	7	5.1	0.73	463	.122	.163	1	.500	0	4	4	0	0.5
1972 *Pit-N	5	0	1.000	53	0	0	0	14	70	50	3	22	47	9.6	1.67	199	.194	.265	2	.167	0	14	13	0	1.4
1973 Pit-N	4	5	.444	59	0	0	0	11	69²	71	5	25	64	10.0	2.41	146	.218	.282	1	.125	0	12	11	0	1.0
1974 *Pit-N	5	2	.714	58	0	0	0	9	68²	68	3	18	33	11.5	2.75	125	.258	.310	1	.250	-1	7	5	-1	0.6
1975 *Pit-N	7	2	.778	46	0	0	0	5	64	62	6	28	40	12.7	2.95	120	.252	.328	0	.000	0	5	4	0	0.5
1976 Pit-N	2	2	.500	37	0	0	0	3	43	42	3	16	17	12.3	3.56	98	.262	.333	0	.000	-0	-0	-0	0	0.0
Chi-N	0	0	—	2	0	0	0	0	1²	2	0	0	1	10.8	0.00	—	.333	.333	0	—	0	1	1	0	0.1

YEAR TM/L	W	L	PCT	G	GS	CG	SH	SV	IP	H	HR	BB	SO	RAT	ERA	ERA+	OAV	OOB	BH	AVG	PB	PR	/A	PD	TPI
Yr	2	2	.500	39	0	0	0	3	44²	44	3	16	18	12.1	3.43	102	.257	.321	0	.000	-0	0	0	-0	0.1
1977 Chi-N	0	0	—	6	0	0	0	1	7²	11	1	3	4	16.4	8.22	53	.306	.359	0	.000	-0	-4	-3	0	-0.2
Bos-A	0	1	.000	12	0	0	0	1	12²	14	2	7	8	15.6	5.68	79	.280	.379	0	—	0	-2	-2	0	-0.1
Total 9	23	15	.605	337	0	0	0	46	430¹	399	23	135	255	11.5	3.03	115	.245	.308	5	.125	1	25	22	1	3.1

■ RUDY HERNANDEZ
Hernandez, Rudolph Albert (Fuentes) b: 12/10/31, Santiago, D.R.   BR/TR, 6'3", 185 lbs.   Deb: 7/03/60

YEAR TM/L	W	L	PCT	G	GS	CG	SH	SV	IP	H	HR	BB	SO	RAT	ERA	ERA+	OAV	OOB	BH	AVG	PB	PR	/A	PD	TPI
1960 Was-A	4	1	.800	21	0	0	0	0	34²	34	2	21	22	14.5	4.41	88	.262	.368	1	.167	-0	-2	-2	-0	-0.2
1961 Was-A	0	1	.000	7	0	0	0	0	9	8	0	3	4	11.0	3.00	134	.250	.314	0	—	0	1	1	0	0.1
Total 2	4	2	.667	28	0	0	0	0	43²	42	2	24	26	13.8	4.12	95	.259	.358	1	.167	-0	-1	-1	0	-0.1

■ WALT HERRELL
Herrell, Walter William "Reds" b: 2/19/1889, Rockville, Md. d: 1/23/49, Front Royal, Va.   Deb: 6/10/11

YEAR TM/L	W	L	PCT	G	GS	CG	SH	SV	IP	H	HR	BB	SO	RAT	ERA	ERA+	OAV	OOB	BH	AVG	PB	PR	/A	PD	TPI
1911 Was-A	0	0	—	1	0	0	0	0	2	5	0	2	0	31.5	18.00	18	.556	.636	0	.000	-0	-3	-3	0	-0.2

■ BOBBY HERRERA
Herrera, Procopio Rodriguez "Tito" (b: Procopio Rodriguez (Herrera)) b: 7/26/26, Nuevo Laredo, Mex BR/TR, 6', 184 lbs.   Deb: 4/19/51

YEAR TM/L	W	L	PCT	G	GS	CG	SH	SV	IP	H	HR	BB	SO	RAT	ERA	ERA+	OAV	OOB	BH	AVG	PB	PR	/A	PD	TPI
1951 StL-A	0	0	—	3	0	0	0	0	2¹	6	2	4	1	42.4	27.00	16	.462	.611	0	—	0	-6	-6	0	-0.4

■ TROY HERRIAGE
Herriage, William Troy "Dutch" b: 12/20/30, Tipton, Okla.   BR/TR, 6'1", 170 lbs.   Deb: 4/25/56

YEAR TM/L	W	L	PCT	G	GS	CG	SH	SV	IP	H	HR	BB	SO	RAT	ERA	ERA+	OAV	OOB	BH	AVG	PB	PR	/A	PD	TPI
1956 KC-A	1	13	.071	31	16	1	0	0	103	135	16	64	59	17.9	6.64	65	.321	.418	3	.120	-1	-28	-26	-2	-2.7

■ TOM HERRIN
Herrin, Thomas Edward b: 9/12/29, Shreveport, La.   BR/TR, 6'3", 190 lbs.   Deb: 4/13/54

YEAR TM/L	W	L	PCT	G	GS	CG	SH	SV	IP	H	HR	BB	SO	RAT	ERA	ERA+	OAV	OOB	BH	AVG	PB	PR	/A	PD	TPI
1954 Bos-A	1	2	.333	14	1	0	0	0	28¹	34	3	22	8	17.8	7.31	56	.315	.431	1	.125	-1	-11	-10	1	-0.8

■ ART HERRING
Herring, Arthur L "Red" or "Sandy" b: 3/10/07, Altus, Okla.   BR/TR, 5'7", 168 lbs.   Deb: 9/12/29

YEAR TM/L	W	L	PCT	G	GS	CG	SH	SV	IP	H	HR	BB	SO	RAT	ERA	ERA+	OAV	OOB	BH	AVG	PB	PR	/A	PD	TPI
1929 Det-A	2	1	.667	4	4	2	0	0	32	38	0	19	15	16.3	4.78	90	.302	.397	3	.214	1	-2	-2	0	0.0
1930 Det-A	3	3	.500	23	6	1	0	0	77²	97	2	36	16	15.8	5.33	90	.315	.392	3	.130	-2	-6	-5	0	-0.5
1931 Det-A	7	13	.350	35	16	9	0	1	165	186	8	67	64	14.2	4.31	106	.281	.355	11	.200	-1	1	5	2	0.6
1932 Det-A	1	2	.333	12	0	0	0	2	22¹	25	2	15	12	16.5	5.24	90	.284	.394	0	.000	-0	-2	-1	0	0.0
1933 Det-A	1	2	.333	24	3	1	0	0	61	61	6	20	20	12.1	3.84	112	.264	.325	1	.077	-1	3	3	-0	0.2
1934 Bro-N	2	4	.333	14	4	2	0	0	49¹	63	2	29	15	16.8	6.20	63	.307	.393	2	.143	1	-12	-13	-0	-1.1
1939 Chi-A	0	0	—	7	0	0	0	0	14¹	13	2	5	8	11.9	5.65	84	.250	.328	0	.000	-0	-2	-1	0	-0.1
1944 Bro-N	3	4	.429	12	6	3	1	1	55¹	59	3	17	19	12.5	3.42	104	.277	.333	3	.200	0	1	1	0	0.2
1945 Bro-N	7	4	.636	22	15	7	2	2	124	103	11	43	34	10.8	3.48	108	.222	.292	4	.095	-2	4	4	1	0.3
1946 Bro-N	7	2	.778	35	2	0	0	5	86	91	2	29	34	12.7	3.35	101	.277	.338	4	.182	0	1	0	2	0.3
1947 Pit-N	1	3	.250	11	0	0	0	2	10²	18	3	4	6	18.6	8.44	50	.360	.407	0	.000	-0	-5	-5	-0	-0.4
Total 11	34	38	.472	199	56	25	3	13	697²	754	41	284	243	13.6	4.32	96	.276	.349	31	.149	-5	-18	-14	5	-0.5

■ HERB HERRING
Herring, Herbert Lee b: 7/22/1891, Danville, Ark. d: 4/22/64, Tucson, Ariz.   BR/TR, 5'11", 178 lbs.   Deb: 9/04/12

YEAR TM/L	W	L	PCT	G	GS	CG	SH	SV	IP	H	HR	BB	SO	RAT	ERA	ERA+	OAV	OOB	BH	AVG	PB	PR	/A	PD	TPI
1912 Was-A	0	0	—	1	0	0	0	0	1	1	0	1	0	18.0	0.00	—	.250	.400	0	—	0	0	0	0	0.0

■ LEFTY HERRING
Herring, Silas Clarke b: 3/4/1880, Philadelphia, Pa. d: 2/11/65, Massapequa, N.Y.   BL/TL, 5'11", 160 lbs.   Deb: 5/16/1899 ◆

YEAR TM/L	W	L	PCT	G	GS	CG	SH	SV	IP	H	HR	BB	SO	RAT	ERA	ERA+	OAV	OOB	BH	AVG	PB	PR	/A	PD	TPI
1899 Was-N	0	0	—	2	0	0	0	0	2	0	0	2	0	9.0	0.00	—	.000	.260	1	1.000	1	1	1	0	0.2

■ BILL HERRING
Herring, William Francis "Smoke" b: 10/31/1893, New York, N.Y. d: 9/10/62, Honesdale, Pa.   6'3", 185 lbs.   Deb: 6/26/15

YEAR TM/L	W	L	PCT	G	GS	CG	SH	SV	IP	H	HR	BB	SO	RAT	ERA	ERA+	OAV	OOB	BH	AVG	PB	PR	/A	PD	TPI
1915 Bro-F	0	0	—	3	0	0	0	0	3	5	1	2	3	24.0	15.00	20	.379	.494	0	—	0	-4	-4	-0	-0.3

■ LEROY HERRMANN
Herrmann, Leroy George b: 2/27/06, Steward, Ill. d: 7/3/72, Livermore, Cal.   BR/TR, 5'10", 185 lbs.   Deb: 7/30/32

YEAR TM/L	W	L	PCT	G	GS	CG	SH	SV	IP	H	HR	BB	SO	RAT	ERA	ERA+	OAV	OOB	BH	AVG	PB	PR	/A	PD	TPI
1932 Chi-N	2	1	.667	7	0	0	0	0	12²	18	0	9	5	19.2	6.39	59	.346	.443	1	.500	0	-4	-4	0	-0.2
1933 Chi-N	0	1	.000	9	1	0	0	1	21	26	3	8	4	16.3	5.57	59	.299	.384	1	.167	-0	-5	-5	-1	-0.5
1935 Cin-N	3	5	.375	29	8	2	0	0	108	124	9	31	30	13.6	3.58	111	.297	.357	8	.267	1	5	5	0	0.6
Total 3	5	7	.417	45	9	2	0	1	141²	168	12	48	39	14.5	4.13	93	.302	.370	10	.263	1	-4	-4	-1	-0.1

■ MARTY HERRMANN
Herrmann, Martin John "Lefty" b: 1/10/1893, Oldenburg, Ind. d: 9/11/56, Cincinnati, Ohio   BL/TL, 5'10", 150 lbs.   Deb: 7/10/18

YEAR TM/L	W	L	PCT	G	GS	CG	SH	SV	IP	H	HR	BB	SO	RAT	ERA	ERA+	OAV	OOB	BH	AVG	PB	PR	/A	PD	TPI
1918 Bro-N	0	0	—	1	0	0	0	0	1	0	0	1	0	9.0	0.00	—	.000	.250	0	—	0	0	0	0	0.0

■ FRANK HERSHEY
Hershey, Frank b: 12/13/1877, Gorham, N.Y. d: 12/15/49, Canadaigua, N.Y.   TR , 175 lbs.   Deb: 4/20/05

YEAR TM/L	W	L	PCT	G	GS	CG	SH	SV	IP	H	HR	BB	SO	RAT	ERA	ERA+	OAV	OOB	BH	AVG	PB	PR	/A	PD	TPI
1905 Bos-N	0	1	.000	1	1	0	0	0	4	9	2	2	1	15.8	6.75	46	.313	.389	0	.000	-0	-2	-2	-0	-0.1

■ OREL HERSHISER
Hershiser, Orel Leonard b: 9/16/58, Buffalo, N.Y.   BR/TR, 6'3", 190 lbs.   Deb: 9/01/83

YEAR TM/L	W	L	PCT	G	GS	CG	SH	SV	IP	H	HR	BB	SO	RAT	ERA	ERA+	OAV	OOB	BH	AVG	PB	PR	/A	PD	TPI
1983 LA-N	0	0	—	8	0	0	0	1	8	7	1	6	5	14.6	3.38	106	.233	.361	0	—	0	0	0	0	0.0
1984 LA-N	11	8	.579	45	20	8	4	2	189²	160	9	50	150	10.2	2.66	133	.225	.279	10	.200	2	20	18	0	2.2
1985 *LA-N	19	3	.864	36	34	9	5	0	239²	179	8	68	157	9.5	2.03	171	.206	.268	15	.197	3	42	39	2	4.9
1986 LA-N	14	14	.500	35	35	8	1	0	231¹	213	13	86	153	11.8	3.85	90	.243	.314	17	.239	4	-3	-10	2	-0.3
1987 LA-N	16	16	.500	37	35	10	1	1	264²	247	17	74	190	11.2	3.06	130	.247	.305	19	.211	4	30	27	1	3.3
1988 *LA-N	23	8	.742	35	34	15	8	1	267	208	18	73	178	9.6	2.26	147	.213	.271	11	.129	-0	35	32	6	4.3
1989 LA-N	15	15	.500	35	33	8	4	0	256²	226	9	77	178	10.7	2.31	148	.240	.299	14	.182	3	34	31	4	4.4
1990 LA-N	1	1	.500	4	4	0	0	0	25¹	26	1	4	16	11.0	4.26	84	.260	.295	0	.000	-1	-1	-2	0	-0.2
Total 8	99	65	.604	235	195	58	23	5	1482¹	1266	76	438	1027	10.5	2.71	130	.230	.290	86	.189	15	156	135	15	18.4

■ JOE HESKETH
Hesketh, Joseph Thomas b: 2/15/59, Lackawanna, N.Y.   BR/TL, 6'2", 170 lbs.   Deb: 8/07/84

YEAR TM/L	W	L	PCT	G	GS	CG	SH	SV	IP	H	HR	BB	SO	RAT	ERA	ERA+	OAV	OOB	BH	AVG	PB	PR	/A	PD	TPI
1984 Mon-N	2	2	.500	11	5	1	1	1	45	38	2	15	32	10.6	1.80	190	.233	.298	1	.100	0	9	8	-0	0.9
1985 Mon-N	10	5	.667	25	25	2	1	0	155¹	125	10	45	113	9.8	2.49	136	.222	.280	4	.091	-1	19	16	-1	1.5
1986 Mon-N	6	5	.545	15	15	0	0	0	82²	92	11	31	67	13.6	5.01	74	.283	.349	0	.000	-2	-12	-12	-1	-1.4
1987 Mon-N	0	0	—	18	0	0	0	0	28²	23	2	15	31	12.6	3.14	134	.211	.317	0	.000	-0	3	3	-1	0.2
1988 Mon-N	4	3	.571	60	0	0	0	9	72²	63	1	35	64	12.1	2.85	126	.242	.332	0	.000	0	5	6	1	0.8
1989 Mon-N	6	4	.600	43	0	0	0	3	48¹	54	5	26	44	14.9	5.77	61	.292	.379	1	.500	0	-12	-12	1	-1.1
1990 Mon-N	1	0	1.000	2	0	0	0	0	3	2	0	2	3	12.0	0.00	—	.200	.333	0	—	0	1	1	0	0.1
Atl-N	0	2	.000	31	0	0	0	0	31	30	5	12	21	12.5	5.81	67	.248	.321	0	.000	-0	-7	-7	-0	-0.6
Yr	1	2	.333	33	0	0	0	0	34	32	5	14	24	12.4	5.29	74	.244	.322	0	.000	-0	-6	-5	-0	-0.5
Bos-A	0	4	.000	12	2	0	0	0	25²	37	2	11	26	16.8	3.51	116	.333	.393	0	—	0	1	2	-0	0.1
Total 7	29	25	.537	217	47	3	2	19	492¹	464	38	192	401	12.1	3.51	103	.251	.323	6	.070	-2	7	5	-2	0.5

■ OTTO HESS
Hess, Otto C. b: 10/10/1878, Berne, Switzerland d: 2/25/26, Tucson, Ariz.   BL/TL, 6'1", 170 lbs.   Deb: 8/03/02 ◆

YEAR TM/L	W	L	PCT	G	GS	CG	SH	SV	IP	H	HR	BB	SO	RAT	ERA	ERA+	OAV	OOB	BH	AVG	PB	PR	/A	PD	TPI
1902 Cle-A	2	4	.333	7	4	4	0	0	43²	67	0	23	13	18.5	5.98	58	.351	.421	1	.071	-1	-12	-12	1	-1.0
1904 Cle-A	8	7	.533	21	16	15	4	0	151¹	134	2	31	64	9.8	1.67	152	.238	.278	12	.120	-3	16	15	-0	1.1
1905 Cle-A	10	15	.400	26	25	22	4	0	213²	179	1	72	109	10.6	3.16	83	.229	.294	44	.254	5	-12	-12	-1	-1.3
1906 Cle-A	20	17	.541	43	36	33	7	3	333²	274	4	85	167	9.7	1.83	143	.227	.278	31	.201	1	32	29	-3	3.1
1907 Cle-A	6	6	.500	17	14	7	0	1	93¹	84	1	37	36	11.7	2.89	87	.242	.315	4	.133	-0	-4	-4	-1	-0.5
1908 Cle-A	0	0	—	4	0	0	0	0	7	11	0	1	2	15.4	5.14	47	.407	.429	0	.000	-1	-2	-2	-0	-0.1
1912 Bos-N	12	17	.414	33	31	21	0	0	254	270	3	90	80	13.3	3.76	95	.274	.344	23	.245	3	-10	-5	-3	-0.4
1913 Bos-N	7	17	.292	29	27	19	2	0	218¹	231	12	70	80	12.7	3.83	86	.279	.340	26	.313	9	-15	-13	1	-0.3
1914 Bos-N	5	6	.455	14	11	7	1	0	89	89	2	33	24	12.8	3.03	91	.271	.347	11	.234	1	-2	-3	-0	-0.2
1915 Bos-N	0	1	.000	4	1	1	0	0	14	16	0	6	5	15.4	3.86	67	.286	.375	2	.400	1	-2	-2	0	0.0
Total 10	70	90	.438	198	165	129	18	5	1418	1355	25	448	580	11.6	2.98	98	.255	.316	154	.216	14	-11	-11	-2	0.4

■ GEORGE HESSELBACHER
Hesselbacher, George Edward b: 1/18/1895, Philadelphia, Pa. d: 2/18/80, Rydal, Pa.   BR/TR, 6'2", 175 lbs.   Deb: 6/29/16

YEAR TM/L	W	L	PCT	G	GS	CG	SH	SV	IP	H	HR	BB	SO	RAT	ERA	ERA+	OAV	OOB	BH	AVG	PB	PR	/A	PD	TPI
1916 Phi-A	0	4	.000	6	4	2	0	0	26	37	3	22	6	20.4	7.27	40	.349	.461	1	.125	-1	-13	-13	1	-1.1

YEAR TM/L	W	L	PCT	G	GS	CG	SH	SV	IP	H	HR	BB	SO	RAT	ERA	ERA+	OAV	OOB	BH	AVG	PB	PR	/A	PD	TPI

■ LARRY HESTERFER
Hesterfer, Lawrence b: 6/9/1878, Newark, N.J. d: 9/22/43, Cedar Grove, N.J. BR/TL, 5'8", 145 lbs. Deb: 9/05/01

YEAR TM/L	W	L	PCT	G	GS	CG	SH	SV	IP	H	HR	BB	SO	RAT	ERA	ERA+	OAV	OOB	BH	AVG	PB	PR	/A	PD	TPI
1901 NY-N	0	1	.000	1	1	1	0	0	6	15	0	3	2	27.0	7.50	44	.466	.511	0	.000	0	-3	-3	0	-0.1

■ JOHNNY HETKI
Hetki, John Edward b: 5/12/22, Leavenworth, Kan. BR/TR, 6'1", 202 lbs. Deb: 9/14/45

YEAR TM/L	W	L	PCT	G	GS	CG	SH	SV	IP	H	HR	BB	SO	RAT	ERA	ERA+	OAV	OOB	BH	AVG	PB	PR	/A	PD	TPI
1945 Cin-N	1	2	.333	5	2	2	0	0	32²	28	1	11	9	10.7	3.58	105	.235	.300	1	.091	-1	1	1	1	0.0
1946 Cin-N	6	6	.500	32	11	4	0	1	126¹	121	3	31	41	10.9	2.99	112	.253	.300	11	.333	3	6	5	-0	0.8
1947 Cin-N	3	4	.429	37	5	2	0	0	96	110	7	48	33	14.9	5.81	71	.287	.368	6	.222	1	-19	-18	0	-1.6
1948 Cin-N	0	1	.000	3	0	0	0	0	6²	8	0	3	3	14.9	9.45	41	.286	.355	0	.000	0	-4	-4	-0	-0.3
1950 Cin-N	1	2	.333	22	1	0	0	0	53	53	9	27	21	14.1	5.09	83	.265	.361	2	.222	0	-6	-5	-0	-0.4
1952 StL-A	0	1	.000	3	1	0	0	0	9¹	15	2	2	4	16.4	3.86	101	.357	.386	0	.000	0	-0	0	0	0.0
1953 Pit-N	3	6	.333	54	2	1	0	3	118¹	120	9	33	37	11.7	3.95	113	.266	.318	5	.208	1	4	7	0	0.8
1954 Pit-N	4	4	.500	58	1	0	0	9	83	102	11	30	27	14.3	4.99	84	.297	.353	2	.222	-0	-8	-7	-1	-0.7
Total 8	18	26	.409	214	23	8	0	13	525¹	557	42	185	175	12.8	4.39	91	.272	.335	27	.235	5	-26	-23	-1	-1.4

■ ERIC HETZEL
Hetzel, Eric Paul b: 9/25/63, Crowley, La. BR/TR, 6'3", 175 lbs. Deb: 7/01/89

YEAR TM/L	W	L	PCT	G	GS	CG	SH	SV	IP	H	HR	BB	SO	RAT	ERA	ERA+	OAV	OOB	BH	AVG	PB	PR	/A	PD	TPI
1989 Bos-A	2	3	.400	12	11	0	0	0	50¹	61	7	28	33	16.3	6.26	66	.296	.386	0	—	0	-13	-12	-1	-1.2
1990 Bos-A	1	4	.200	9	8	0	0	0	35	39	3	21	20	15.7	5.91	69	.281	.379	0	—	0	-8	-7	-0	-0.6
Total 2	3	7	.300	21	19	0	0	0	85¹	100	10	49	53	16.0	6.12	67	.290	.383	0	—	0	-21	-19	-1	-1.8

■ ED HEUSSER
Heusser, Edward Burlton "The Wild Elk Of The Wasatch" b: 5/7/09, Mill Creek, Utah d: 3/1/56, Aurora, Cal. BB/TR, 6'0.5", 187 lbs. Deb: 4/25/35

YEAR TM/L	W	L	PCT	G	GS	CG	SH	SV	IP	H	HR	BB	SO	RAT	ERA	ERA+	OAV	OOB	BH	AVG	PB	PR	/A	PD	TPI
1935 StL-N	5	5	.500	33	11	2	0	0	123¹	125	5	27	39	11.2	2.92	140	.263	.305	4	.118	-1	15	16	-1	1.4
1936 StL-N	7	3	.700	42	3	0	0	3	104¹	130	6	38	26	14.8	5.43	73	.310	.373	7	.269	3	-16	-17	0	-1.3
1938 Phi-N	0	0	—	1	0	0	0	0	1	2	1	1	0	27.0	27.00	14	.400	.500	0	—	0	-3	-3	0	-0.1
1940 Phi-A	6	13	.316	41	6	2	0	5	110	144	11	42	39	15.4	4.99	89	.308	.368	5	.167	1	-7	-7	1	-0.4
1943 Cin-N	4	3	.571	26	10	2	1	0	91	97	4	23	28	11.9	3.46	96	.275	.319	5	.185	-1	-1	-1	-1	-0.2
1944 Cin-N	13	11	.542	30	23	17	4	2	192²	165	9	42	42	9.7	**2.38**	**146**	.231	.275	15	.217	1	26	24	-1	2.5
1945 Cin-N	11	16	.407	31	30	18	4	1	223	248	10	60	56	12.6	3.71	101	.280	.328	19	.247	1	2	1	0	0.5
1946 Cin-N	7	14	.333	29	21	9	1	2	167²	167	11	39	47	11.1	3.22	104	.260	.304	11	.208	1	4	2	-2	0.2
1948 Phi-N	3	2	.600	33	0	0	0	3	74	89	9	28	22	14.2	4.99	79	.299	.359	3	.158	-1	-8	-9	0	-0.8
Total 9	56	67	.455	266	104	50	10	18	1087	1167	66	300	299	12.3	3.69	101	.274	.324	69	.206	8	11	6	-3	1.8

■ JOE HEVING
Heving, Joseph William b: 9/2/1900, Covington, Ky. d: 4/11/70, Covington, Ky. BR/TR, 6'1", 185 lbs. Deb: 4/29/30

YEAR TM/L	W	L	PCT	G	GS	CG	SH	SV	IP	H	HR	BB	SO	RAT	ERA	ERA+	OAV	OOB	BH	AVG	PB	PR	/A	PD	TPI
1930 NY-N	7	5	.583	41	2	0	0	6	89²	109	7	27	37	13.8	5.22	91	.309	.360	5	.227	-0	-2	-5	4	0.0
1931 NY-N	1	6	.143	22	0	0	0	3	42¹	48	4	11	26	13.0	4.89	76	.277	.328	1	.125	-0	-5	-6	1	-0.4
1933 Chi-A	7	5	.583	40	6	3	1	6	118	113	6	27	47	10.8	2.67	159	.249	.295	8	.211	0	21	21	0	2.0
1934 Chi-A	1	7	.125	33	2	0	0	4	88	133	12	48	40	18.8	7.26	65	.343	.419	5	.185	1	-27	-25	1	-2.0
1937 Cle-A	8	4	.667	40	0	0	0	5	72²	92	6	30	35	15.4	4.83	95	.311	.378	5	.263	0	-2	-2	1	0.0
1938 Cle-A	1	1	.500	3	0	0	0	0	6	10	1	0	5	22.5	9.00	52	.370	.469	0	.000	-0	-3	-3	-0	-0.2
Bos-A	8	1	.889	16	11	7	1	2	82	94	5	22	34	12.8	3.73	132	.283	.330	4	.133	-2	10	11	2	1.1
Yr	9	2	.818	19	11	7	1	2	88	104	5	27	34	13.5	4.09	120	.290	.341	4	.032	-2	7	8	2	0.9
1939 Bos-A	11	3	.786	46	5	1	0	7	107	124	8	34	43	13.5	3.70	128	.295	.350	6	.188	-1	**11**	**12**	0	1.1
1940 Bos-A	12	7	.632	39	7	0	0	3	119	129	7	42	55	13.2	4.01	112	.272	.335	8	.200	0	5	6	0	0.7
1941 Cle-A	5	2	.714	27	3	2	1	5	70²	63	2	31	18	12.1	2.29	172	.240	.323	0	.000	-1	15	13	2	1.4
1942 Cle-A	5	3	.625	27	2	0	0	3	46¹	55	4	25	13	15.9	4.86	71	.294	.383	0	.000	-1	-6	-7	-0	-0.7
1943 Cle-A	1	1	.500	30	1	0	0	9	72	58	1	34	34	11.8	2.75	113	.230	.326	1	.071	-0	4	3	2	0.4
1944 Cle-A	8	3	.727	**63**	1	0	0	10	119²	106	2	41	46	11.2	1.96	169	.239	.307	4	.182	-1	**20**	18	1	1.9
1945 Bos-N	1	0	1.000	3	0	0	0	0	3	3	0	3	1	15.2	3.38	114	.294	.429	0	.000	0	0	0	1	0.1
Total 13	76	48	.613	430	40	17	3	63	1038²	1139	64	380	429	13.4	3.90	108	.279	.344	47	.170	-4	40	36	14	5.4

■ JAKE HEWITT
Howitt, Charles Jacob b: 6/6/1870, Maidsville, W.Va. d: 5/18/50, Morgantown, W.Va. DL/TL, 5'7", 150 lbs. Deb: 8/00/1895

YEAR TM/L	W	L	PCT	G	GS	CG	SH	SV	IP	H	HR	BB	SO	RAT	ERA	ERA+	OAV	OOB	BH	AVG	PB	PR	/A	PD	TPI
1895 Pit-N	1	0	1.000	4	2	1	0	0	13	13	0	2	4	10.4	4.15	109	.256	.285	1	.167	-1	1	1	-0	0.0

■ GREG HEYDEMAN
Heydeman, Gregory George b: 1/2/52, Carmel, Cal. BR/TR, 6', 180 lbs. Deb: 9/02/73

YEAR TM/L	W	L	PCT	G	GS	CG	SH	SV	IP	H	HR	BB	SO	RAT	ERA	ERA+	OAV	OOB	BH	AVG	PB	PR	/A	PD	TPI
1973 LA-N	0	0	—	1	0	0	0	0	2	2	0	1	1	18.0	4.50	76	.222	.364	0	—	0	-0	0	0	0.0

■ JOHN HEYNER
Heyner, John b: Hyde Park, Ill. Deb: 8/19/1890

YEAR TM/L	W	L	PCT	G	GS	CG	SH	SV	IP	H	HR	BB	SO	RAT	ERA	ERA+	OAV	OOB	BH	AVG	PB	PR	/A	PD	TPI
1890 Pit-N	0	0	—	1	0	0	0	0	4	7	2	5	1	27.0	13.50	24	.372	.504	0	.000	-0	-4	-5	0	-0.3

■ GREG HIBBARD
Hibbard, James Gregory b: 9/13/64, New Orleans, La. BL/TL, 6', 180 lbs. Deb: 5/31/89

YEAR TM/L	W	L	PCT	G	GS	CG	SH	SV	IP	H	HR	BB	SO	RAT	ERA	ERA+	OAV	OOB	BH	AVG	PB	PR	/A	PD	TPI
1989 Chi-A	6	7	.462	23	23	2	0	0	137¹	142	5	41	55	12.1	3.21	118	.268	.323	0	—	0	10	9	2	1.1
1990 Chi-A	14	9	.609	33	33	3	1	0	211	202	11	55	92	11.2	3.16	121	.255	.308	0	—	0	18	16	-0	1.6
Total 2	20	16	.556	56	56	5	1	0	348¹	344	16	96	147	11.6	3.18	120	.260	.314	0	—	0	28	25	1	2.7

■ JOHN HIBBARD
Hibbard, John Denison b: 12/2/1864, Chicago, Ill. d: 11/17/37, Hollywood, Cal. TL, Deb: 7/31/1884

YEAR TM/L	W	L	PCT	G	GS	CG	SH	SV	IP	H	HR	BB	SO	RAT	ERA	ERA+	OAV	OOB	BH	AVG	PB	PR	/A	PD	TPI
1884 Chi-N	1	1	.500	2	2	2	1	0	17	18	1	9	4	14.3	2.65	119	.257	.342	0	.000	-1	1	1	0	0.0

■ JIM HICKEY
Hickey, James Robert "Sid" b: 10/22/20, N.Abington, Mass. BR/TR, 6'1", 204 lbs. Deb: 4/25/42

YEAR TM/L	W	L	PCT	G	GS	CG	SH	SV	IP	H	HR	BB	SO	RAT	ERA	ERA+	OAV	OOB	BH	AVG	PB	PR	/A	PD	TPI
1942 Bos-N	0	1	.000	1	1	0	0	0	1¹	4	1	2	0	40.5	20.25	16	.500	.600	0	.000	-0	-3	-3	0	-0.1
1944 Bos-N	0	0	—	8	0	0	0	0	9¹	15	0	5	3	20.3	4.82	79	.366	.447	0	.000	-0	-1	-1	0	0.0
Total 2	0	1	.000	9	1	0	0	0	10²	19	1	7	3	22.8	6.75	56	.388	.474	0	.000	-0	-4	-4	0	-0.1

■ JOHN HICKEY
Hickey, John William b: 11/3/1881, Minneapolis, Minn. d: 12/28/41, Seattle, Wash. BR/TL, Deb: 4/16/04

YEAR TM/L	W	L	PCT	G	GS	CG	SH	SV	IP	H	HR	BB	SO	RAT	ERA	ERA+	OAV	OOB	BH	AVG	PB	PR	/A	PD	TPI
1904 Cle-A	0	1	.000	2	2	1	0	0	12¹	14	0	11	5	18.2	7.30	35	.286	.417	0	.000	-1	-6	-7	0	-0.5

■ KEVIN HICKEY
Hickey, Kevin John b: 2/25/57, Chicago, Ill. BL/TL, 6'1", 170 lbs. Deb: 4/14/81

YEAR TM/L	W	L	PCT	G	GS	CG	SH	SV	IP	H	HR	BB	SO	RAT	ERA	ERA+	OAV	OOB	BH	AVG	PB	PR	/A	PD	TPI
1981 Chi-A	0	2	.000	41	0	0	0	3	44¹	38	3	18	17	11.6	3.65	98	.232	.311	0	—	0	0	-0	1	0.1
1982 Chi-A	4	4	.500	60	0	0	0	6	78	73	4	30	38	12.1	3.00	134	.256	.331	0	—	0	9	9	2	1.1
1983 Chi-A	1	2	.333	23	0	0	0	5	20²	23	5	11	8	14.8	5.23	80	.264	.347	0	—	0	-3	-2	0	-0.1
1989 Bal-A	2	3	.400	51	0	0	0	0	49¹	38	3	23	28	11.3	2.92	130	.220	.315	0	—	0	5	5	-0	0.4
1990 Bal-A	1	3	.250	37	0	0	0	0	26¹	26	3	13	17	13.3	5.13	75	.265	.351	0	—	0	-4	-4	0	-0.3
Total 5	8	14	.364	212	0	0	0	17	218²	198	18	95	108	12.2	3.58	108	.245	.328	0	—	0	8	7	3	1.2

■ CHARLIE HICKMAN
Hickman, Charles Taylor "Cheerful Charlie" or "Piano Legs"
b: 3/4/1876, Taylortown, Dunkard Township, Pa. d: 4/19/34, Morgantown, W.Va. BR/TR, 5'11.5", 215 lbs. Deb: 9/08/1897 ♦

YEAR TM/L	W	L	PCT	G	GS	CG	SH	SV	IP	H	HR	BB	SO	RAT	ERA	ERA+	OAV	OOB	BH	AVG	PB	PR	/A	PD	TPI
1897 *Bos-N	0	0	—	2	0	0	0	1	7²	10	0	5	0	17.6	5.87	76	.312	.405	2	.667	2	-1	-1	0	0.0
1898 Bos-N	1	2	.333	6	3	3	1	2	33	22	0	13	9	9.5	2.18	169	.189	.270	15	.259	0	5	6	-1	0.5
1899 Bos-N	6	0	1.000	11	9	5	2	1	66¹	52	3	40	14	12.5	4.48	93	.216	.328	25	.397	6	-5	-2	-1	0.0
1901 NY-N	3	5	.375	9	9	6	0	0	65	76	1	26	11	14.5	4.57	72	.290	.360	113	.278	2	-9	-9	1	-0.8
1902 Cle-A	0	1	.000	1	1	0	0	0	8	11	0	5	1	18.0	7.88	44	.327	.414	161	.378	1	-4	-4	-0	-0.2
1907 Was-A	0	0	—	1	0	0	0	0	5	4	0	5	2	16.2	3.60	67	.221	.390	55	.278	1	-1	-1	0	0.0
Total 6	10	8	.556	30	22	15	3	4	185	175	4	94	37	13.2	4.28	86	.249	.340	1176	.295	11	-14	-12	-0	0.3

■ ERNIE HICKMAN
Hickman, Ernest P. b: 1856, E.St.Louis, Ill. d: 11/19/1891, E.St.Louis, Ill Deb: 6/07/1884

YEAR TM/L	W	L	PCT	G	GS	CG	SH	SV	IP	H	HR	BB	SO	RAT	ERA	ERA+	OAV	OOB	BH	AVG	PB	PR	/A	PD	TPI
1884 KC-U	4	13	.235	17	17	15	0	0	137¹	172	5	36	68	13.6	4.52	61	.287	.327	12	.167	-3	-23	-27	-1	-2.5

YEAR TM/L	W	L	PCT	G	GS	CG	SH	SV	IP	H	HR	BB	SO	RAT	ERA	ERA+	OAV	OOB	BH	AVG	PB	PR	/A	PD	TPI
■ JIM HICKMAN Hickman, James Lucius b: 5/10/37, Henning, Tenn. BR/TR, 6'3", 192 lbs. Deb: 4/14/62 ♦																									
1967 LA-N	0	0	—	1	0	0	0	0	2	2	1	0	0	9.0	4.50	69	.286	.286	16	.163	0	-0	-0	0	0.0
■ JESSE HICKMAN Hickman, Jesse Owens b: 2/18/39, Lecompte, La. BR/TR, 6'2", 186 lbs. Deb: 6/05/65																									
1965 KC-A	0	1	.000	12	0	0	0	0	15¹	9	3	8	16	10.0	5.87	59	.184	.298	0	—	0	-4	-4	-0	-0.3
1966 KC-A	0	0	—	1	0	0	0	0	1	0	0	1	0	9.0	0.00	—	.000	.333	0	—	0	0	0	0	0.0
Total 2	0	1	.000	13	0	0	0	0	16¹	9	3	9	16	9.9	5.51	63	.176	.300	0	—	0	-4	-4	-0	-0.3
■ KIRBY HIGBE Higbe, Walter Kirby b: 4/8/15, Columbia, S.C. d: 5/6/85, Columbia, S.C. BR/TR, 5'11", 190 lbs. Deb: 10/03/37																									
1937 Chi-N	1	0	1.000	1	0	0	0	0	5	4	1	1	2	9.0	5.40	74	.182	.217	0	.000	-0	-1	-1	-0	0.0
1938 Chi-N	0	0	—	2	2	0	0	0	10	10	1	6	4	14.4	5.40	71	.263	.364	0	.000	-0	-2	-2	1	-0.1
1939 Chi-N	2	1	.667	9	2	0	0	0	22²	12	0	22	16	13.5	3.18	124	.158	.347	2	.286	1	2	2	-0	0.2
Phi-N	10	14	.417	34	26	14	1	2	187¹	208	10	101	79	15.3	4.85	83	.283	.378	11	.167	-2	-19	-18	-4	-2.2
Yr	12	15	.444	43	28	14	1	2	210	220	10	123	95	15.1	4.67	86	.272	.374	0	-.000	-2	-18	-16	-4	-2.0
1940 Phi-N	14	19	.424	41	36	20	1	1	283	242	12	121	**137**	11.6	3.72	105	.232	.313	17	.165	-2	4	6	-2	0.3
1941 *Bro-N	**22**	9	.710	**48**	39	19	2	3	298	244	17	132	121	11.5	3.14	117	.220	.306	21	.188	1	16	17	-4	1.4
1942 Bro-N	16	11	.593	38	32	13	2	0	221²	180	17	106	115	11.7	3.25	100	.223	.315	8	.104	-4	2	0	-2	-0.5
1943 Bro-N	13	10	.565	35	27	8	1	0	185	189	4	95	108	14.1	3.70	91	.264	.354	9	.138	-2	-6	-7	-2	-0.7
1946 Bro-N	17	8	.680	42	29	11	3	1	210²	178	6	107	134	12.2	3.03	111	.229	.323	10	.130	-4	9	8	0	0.5
1947 Bro-N	2	0	1.000	4	3	0	0	0	15²	18	0	12	10	17.8	5.17	80	.295	.419	1	.200	-0	-2	-2	0	0.0
Pit-N	11	17	.393	46	30	10	1	5	225	204	22	110	99	12.7	3.72	113	.240	.329	10	.139	-2	8	13	-4	0.7
Yr	13	17	.433	50	33	10	1	5	240²	222	22	122	109	13.0	3.81	111	.243	.334	2	.026	-1	7	11	-4	0.7
1948 Pit-N	8	7	.533	56	8	3	0	10	158	140	11	83	86	12.9	3.36	121	.240	.337	10	.208	1	10	12	-2	1.2
1949 Pit-N	0	2	.000	7	1	0	0	0	15¹	25	2	12	5	21.7	13.50	31	.379	.474	0	.000	-0	-16	-16	-0	-1.3
NY-N	2	0	1.000	37	2	0	0	2	80¹	72	12	41	38	12.8	3.47	115	.242	.335	1	.067	-0	5	5	-1	0.3
Yr	2	2	.500	44	3	0	0	2	95²	97	14	53	43	14.2	5.08	79	.266	.361	3	.167	-1	-11	-11	-1	-1.0
1950 NY-N	0	3	.000	18	1	0	0	0	34²	37	2	30	17	17.4	4.93	83	.285	.419	1	.250	1	-3	-3	1	-0.1
Total 12	118	101	.539	418	238	98	11	24	1952¹	1763	117	979	971	12.8	3.69	102	.241	.333	101	.153	-14	7	14	-18	-0.6
■ IRV HIGGINBOTHAM Higginbotham, Irving Clinton b: 4/26/1882, Homer, Neb. d: 6/12/59, Seattle, Wash. TR, 6'1", 196 lbs. Deb: 8/11/06																									
1906 StL-N	1	4	.200	7	6	4	0	0	47¹	50	1	11	14	11.8	3.23	81	.266	.310	4	.222	-1	-3	-3	1	-0.1
1908 StL-N	3	8	.273	19	11	7	1	0	107	113	0	33	38	12.5	3.20	74	.270	.328	5	.132	-2	-10	-10	-1	-1.3
1909 StL-N	1	0	1.000	3	1	0	0	0	11¹	5	0	2	2	5.6	1.59	159	.143	.189	0	.000	-0	1	1	-0	0.0
Chi-N	5	2	.714	19	6	4	0	1	78	64	0	20	32	10.0	2.19	116	.213	.269	6	.231	1	4	3	-1	0.3
Yr	6	2	.750	22	7	5	0	1	89¹	69	0	22	34	9.5	2.12	120	.205	.260	6	.034	0	5	4	-1	0.3
Total 3	10	14	.417	48	24	16	1	1	243²	232	1	66	86	11.3	2.81	88	.246	.300	15	.176	-1	-8	-9	-1	-1.1
■ DENNIS HIGGINS Higgins, Dennis Dean b: 8/4/39, Jefferson City, Mo. BR/TR, 6'3", 180 lbs. Deb: 4/12/66																									
1966 Chi-A	1	0	1.000	42	1	0	0	5	93	66	9	33	86	10.1	2.52	126	.202	.286	3	.176	0	9	7	0	0.8
1967 Chi-A	1	2	.333	9	0	0	0	0	12¹	13	0	10	8	19.0	5.84	53	.271	.426	0	.000	-0	-4	-4	-0	-0.3
1968 Was-A	4	4	.500	59	0	0	0	13	99²	81	8	46	66	11.7	3.25	90	.226	.319	2	.133	-0	-3	-4	-1	-0.5
1969 Was-A	10	9	.526	55	0	0	0	16	85¹	79	7	56	71	14.6	3.48	100	.252	.371	1	.091	-1	1	-0	-1	-0.1
1970 Cle-A	4	6	.400	58	0	0	0	11	90¹	82	8	54	82	13.7	3.99	99	.248	.358	3	.250	1	-3	-0	0	0.1
1971 StL-N	1	0	1.000	3	0	0	0	0	7	6	0	2	6	10.3	3.86	93	.240	.296	0	.000	-0	-0	-0	0	0.0
1972 StL-N	1	2	.333	15	1	0	0	1	22²	19	0	22	20	16.3	3.97	86	.226	.387	0	.000	-0	-1	-1	-0	-0.1
Total 7	22	23	.489	241	2	0	0	46	410¹	346	32	223	339	12.8	3.42	98	.233	.340	9	.155	0	-0	-3	-2	-0.1
■ EDDIE HIGGINS Higgins, Thomas Edward "Doc" or "Irish" b: 3/18/1888, Nevada, Ill. d: 2/14/59, Elgin, Ill. BR/TR, 6'0.5", 174 lbs. Deb: 5/14/09																									
1909 StL-N	3	3	.500	16	5	5	0	0	66	68	4	17	15	11.7	4.50	56	.273	.322	4	.190	-0	-14	-14	1	-1.4
1910 StL-N	0	1	.000	2	0	0	0	0	10¹	15	0	7	1	19.2	4.35	68	.349	.440	2	.400	1	-2	-2	1	0.0
Total 2	3	4	.429	18	5	5	0	0	76¹	83	4	24	16	12.7	4.48	58	.284	.341	6	.231	1	-15	-16	1	-1.4
■ ED HIGH High, Edward T. "Lefty" b: 12/26/1876, Baltimore, Md. d: 2/10/26, Baltimore, Md. TL , Deb: 7/04/01																									
1901 Det-A	1	0	1.000	4	1	1	0	0	18	21	0	6	4	13.5	3.50	110	.288	.342	0	.000	-1	0	1	-0	0.0
■ TEDDY HIGUERA Higuera, Teodoro Valenzuela (Valenzuela) b: 11/9/58, Los Mochis, Mexico BB/TL, 5'10", 178 lbs. Deb: 4/23/85																									
1985 Mil-A	15	8	.652	32	30	7	2	0	212¹	186	22	63	127	10.7	3.90	107	.235	.293	0	—	0	6	6	-3	0.3
1986 Mil-A	20	11	.645	34	34	15	4	0	248¹	226	26	74	207	11.0	2.79	155	.241	.299	0	—	0	38	42	-2	4.3
1987 Mil-A	18	10	.643	35	35	14	3	0	261²	236	24	87	240	11.2	3.85	119	.241	.304	0	—	0	18	21	-3	1.7
1988 Mil-A	16	9	.640	31	31	8	1	0	227¹	168	15	59	192	**9.2**	2.45	162	.207	**.265**	0	—	0	**38**	38	0	4.2
1989 Mil-A	9	6	.600	22	22	2	1	0	135¹	125	9	48	91	11.6	3.46	101	.248	.318	0	—	0	6	6	-2	0.3
1990 Mil-A	11	10	.524	27	27	4	1	0	170	167	16	50	129	11.6	3.76	101	.256	.312	0	—	0	3	0	-1	0.0
Total 6	89	54	.622	181	179	50	12	0	1255	1108	112	381	986	10.8	3.34	124	.237	.297	0	—	0	109	114	-11	10.8
■ WHITEY HILCHER Hilcher, Walter Frank b: 2/28/09, Chicago, Ill. d: 11/21/62, Minneapolis, Minn. BR/TR, 6', 174 lbs. Deb: 9/17/31																									
1931 Cin-N	0	1	.000	2	1	0	0	0	12	16	0	4	5	15.8	3.00	125	.320	.382	0	.000	-1	1	1	-0	0.0
1932 Cin-N	0	3	.000	11	2	1	0	0	18²	24	3	10	4	16.4	7.71	50	.316	.395	1	.333	0	-8	-8	0	-0.6
1935 Cin-N	2	0	1.000	4	2	1	1	0	19¹	19	0	5	9	11.2	2.79	142	.264	.312	0	.167	-0	3	3	1	0.3
1936 Cin-N	1	2	.333	14	1	0	0	0	35	44	3	14	10	15.2	6.17	62	.299	.364	0	.000	-0	-8	-9	-1	-0.9
Total 4	3	6	.333	31	6	1	1	0	85	103	6	33	28	14.6	5.29	73	.299	.363	2	.095	-1	-13	-14	0	-1.2
■ ORAL HILDEBRAND Hildebrand, Oral Clyde b: 4/7/07, Indianapolis, Ind. d: 9/8/77, Southport, Ind. BR/TR, 6'3", 175 lbs. Deb: 9/08/31																									
1931 Cle-A	2	1	.667	5	2	2	0	0	26²	25	0	13	6	13.8	4.39	105	.243	.345	2	.182	-1	-0	1	-0	0.0
1932 Cle-A	8	6	.571	27	15	7	0	0	129¹	124	7	62	49	12.9	3.69	129	.249	.333	7	.146	-3	11	15	-2	1.0
1933 Cle-A	16	11	.593	36	31	15	**6**	0	220¹	205	8	88	90	12.0	3.76	118	.245	.318	16	.190	-1	13	17	-0	1.5
1934 Cle-A	11	9	.550	33	28	10	1	1	198	225	14	99	72	14.9	4.50	101	.282	.364	13	.171	-1	-0	1	1	0.1
1935 Cle-A	9	8	.529	34	20	8	0	5	171¹	171	12	63	49	12.4	3.94	114	.263	.331	9	.164	-2	10	11	0	0.8
1936 Cle-A	10	11	.476	36	21	9	0	4	174²	197	18	83	65	14.6	4.90	103	.283	.362	12	.190	0	3	3	-1	0.2
1937 StL-A	8	17	.320	30	27	12	1	1	201¹	228	18	87	75	14.2	5.14	94	.284	.356	14	.200	-1	-12	-7	-1	-0.7
1938 StL-A	8	10	.444	23	23	10	0	0	163	194	18	73	66	14.9	5.69	87	.297	.370	15	.254	1	-16	-13	-3	-1.2
1939 *NY-A	10	4	.714	21	15	7	1	2	126²	102	11	41	50	10.2	3.06	143	.219	.284	8	.182	-1	22	18	-1	1.6
1940 NY-A	1	1	.500	13	0	0	0	0	19¹	19	1	14	11	15.8	1.86	217	.268	.395	0	.000	-0	5	5	-0	0.4
Total 10	83	78	.516	258	182	80	9	13	1430²	1490	99	623	527	13.4	4.35	107	.267	.343	96	.187	-9	36	50	-7	3.7
■ TOM HILGENDORF Hilgendorf, Thomas Eugene b: 3/10/42, Clinton, Iowa BB/TL, 6'1.5", 187 lbs. Deb: 8/15/69																									
1969 StL-N	0	0	—	6	0	0	0	2	6¹	3	0	2	2	7.1	1.42	251	.150	.227	1	1.000	1	2	2	0	0.2
1970 StL-N	0	4	.000	23	0	0	0	3	20²	22	0	13	13	15.2	3.92	105	.272	.372	0	.000	-0	0	0	0	0.1
1972 Cle-A	3	1	.750	19	5	1	0	0	47	51	4	21	25	14.2	2.68	120	.283	.365	1	.077	-1	2	3	0	0.3
1973 Cle-A	5	3	.625	48	1	1	0	6	94²	87	9	36	58	12.0	3.14	125	.242	.316	0	—	0	9	8	1	0.4
1974 Cle-A	4	3	.571	35	0	0	0	3	48¹	58	6	17	23	14.2	4.84	75	.302	.362	0	—	0	-7	-7	0	-0.6
1975 Phi-N	7	3	.700	53	0	0	0	0	96²	81	6	38	52	11.2	2.14	174	.230	.307	3	.250	1	16	17	1	2.0
Total 6	19	14	.576	184	6	2	0	14	313²	302	25	127	173	12.5	3.04	122	.255	.331	5	.185	-1	20	24	1	3.0
■ CARMEN HILL Hill, Carmen Proctor "Specs" or "Bunker" b: 10/1/1895, Royalton, Minn. d: 1/1/90, Indianapolis, Ind. BR/TR, 6'1", 180 lbs. Deb: 8/24/15																									
1915 Pit-N	2	1	.667	8	3	2	1	0	47	42	0	13	24	10.9	1.15	238	.255	.317	2	.154	0	8	8	1	1.1

YEAR TM/L	W	L	PCT	G	GS	CG	SH	SV	IP	H	HR	BB	SO	RAT	ERA	ERA+	OAV	OOB	BH	AVG	PB	PR	/A	PD	TPI
1916 Pit-N	0	0	—	2	0	0	0	0	6¹	11	0	5	5	24.2	8.53	31	.611	.708	0	—	0	-4	-4	-0	-0.3
1918 Pit-N	2	3	.400	6	4	3	0	0	43²	24	0	17	15	8.5	1.24	232	.160	.246	2	.167	0	7	8	0	1.0
1919 Pit-N	0	0	—	4	0	0	0	0	5	12	0	1	1	23.4	9.00	34	.480	.500	0	—	0	-3	-3	0	-0.2
1922 NY-N	2	1	.667	8	4	0	0	0	28¹	33	0	5	6	12.1	4.76	84	.295	.325	2	.182	-0	-2	-2	1	-0.1
1926 Pit-N	3	3	.500	6	6	4	1	0	39²	42	2	9	8	12.0	3.40	116	.288	.338	3	.176	-1	2	2	1	0.3
1927 *Pit-N	22	11	.667	43	31	22	2	3	277²	260	12	80	95	11.2	3.24	127	.249	.305	22	.212	2	21	27	0	3.0
1928 Pit-N	16	10	.615	36	31	16	1	2	237	229	16	81	73	11.9	3.53	115	.259	.324	20	.233	2	12	14	-3	1.3
1929 Pit-N	2	3	.400	27	3	0	0	3	79	94	4	35	28	14.7	3.99	120	.297	.366	1	.036	-3	6	7	0	0.3
StL-N	0	0	—	3	1	0	0	0	8²	10	2	8	1	19.7	8.31	56	.303	.452	0	.000	-0	-3	-4	0	-0.2
Yr	2	3	.400	30	4	0	0	3	87²	104	6	43	29	15.2	4.41	108	.297	.376	1	.032	-4	3	3	0	0.1
1930 StL-N	0	1	.000	4	2	0	0	0	14²	12	2	13	8	15.3	7.36	68	.240	.397	1	.333	0	-4	-4	-0	-0.2
Total 10	49	33	.598	147	85	47	5	8	787	769	38	267	264	12.0	3.44	116	.261	.326	53	.191	-0	40	49	1	6.0

■ RED HILL
Hill, Clifford Joseph b: 1/20/1893, Marshall, Tex. d: 8/11/38, ElPaso, Tex. BB/TL Deb: 4/21/17

YEAR TM/L	W	L	PCT	G	GS	CG	SH	SV	IP	H	HR	BB	SO	RAT	ERA	ERA+	OAV	OOB	BH	AVG	PB	PR	/A	PD	TPI
1917 Phi-A	0	0	—	1	0	0	0	0	2²	5	0	1	0	20.3	6.75	41	.385	.429	0	—	0	-1	-1	0	0.0

■ DAVE HILL
Hill, David Burnham b: 11/11/37, New Orleans, La. BR/TL, 6'2", 170 lbs. Deb: 8/22/57

YEAR TM/L	W	L	PCT	G	GS	CG	SH	SV	IP	H	HR	BB	SO	RAT	ERA	ERA+	OAV	OOB	BH	AVG	PB	PR	/A	PD	TPI
1957 KC-A	0	0	—	2	0	0	0	0	2¹	6	3	3	1	34.7	27.00	15	.462	.563	0	—	0	-6	-6	0	-0.4

■ DON HILL
Hill, Donald Earl b: 11/12/60, Pomona, Cal. BB/TR, 5'10", 160 lbs. Deb: 7/25/83 ◆

YEAR TM/L	W	L	PCT	G	GS	CG	SH	SV	IP	H	HR	BB	SO	RAT	ERA	ERA+	OAV	OOB	BH	AVG	PB	PR	/A	PD	TPI
1990 Cal-A	0	0	—	1	0	0	0	0	1	0	0	1	1	9.0	0.00	—	.000	.250	93	.264	1	0	0	0	0.0

■ GARRY HILL
Hill, Garry Alton b: 11/3/46, Rutherfordton, N.C. BR/TR, 6'2", 195 lbs. Deb: 6/12/69

YEAR TM/L	W	L	PCT	G	GS	CG	SH	SV	IP	H	HR	BB	SO	RAT	ERA	ERA+	OAV	OOB	BH	AVG	PB	PR	/A	PD	TPI
1969 Atl-N	0	1	.000	1	1	0	0	0	2¹	6	1	1	2	27.0	15.43	23	.462	.500	0	—	0	-3	-3	0	-0.2

■ HERBERT HILL
Hill, Herbert Lee b: 8/19/1891, Hutchins, Tex. d: 9/2/70, Farmers Branch, Tex. 5'11.5", 175 lbs. Deb: 7/17/15

YEAR TM/L	W	L	PCT	G	GS	CG	SH	SV	IP	H	HR	BB	SO	RAT	ERA	ERA+	OAV	OOB	BH	AVG	PB	PR	/A	PD	TPI
1915 Cle-A	0	0	—	1	0	0	0	0	2	1	0	2	0	13.5	0.00	—	.250	.500	0	—	0	1	1	0	0.1

■ KEN HILL
Hill, Kenneth Wade b: 12/14/65, Lynn, Mass. BR/TR, 6'4", 200 lbs. Deb: 9/03/88

YEAR TM/L	W	L	PCT	G	GS	CG	SH	SV	IP	H	HR	BB	SO	RAT	ERA	ERA+	OAV	OOB	BH	AVG	PB	PR	/A	PD	TPI
1988 StL-N	0	1	.000	4	1	0	0	0	14	16	0	6	6	14.1	5.14	68	.286	.355	0	.000	-0	-3	-3	0	-0.2
1989 StL-N	7	15	.318	33	33	2	1	0	196²	186	9	99	112	13.3	3.80	96	.252	.344	9	.153	-0	-7	-4	0	-0.3
1990 StL-N	5	6	.455	17	14	1	0	0	78²	79	7	33	58	12.9	5.49	71	.264	.339	4	.211	1	-15	-14	0	-1.2
Total 3	12	22	.353	54	48	3	1	0	289¹	281	16	138	176	13.2	4.32	86	.257	.343	13	.160	0	-24	-20	1	-1.7

■ BILL HILL
Hill, William Cicero "Still Bill" b: 8/2/1874, Chattanooga, Tenn. d: 1/28/38, Cincinnati, Ohio BL/TL, 6'1", 201 lbs. Deb: 4/18/1896

YEAR TM/L	W	L	PCT	G	GS	CG	SH	SV	IP	H	HR	BB	SO	RAT	ERA	ERA+	OAV	OOB	BH	AVG	PB	PR	/A	PD	TPI
1896 Lou-N	9	28	.243	43	39	32	0	2	319²	353	14	155	104	14.3	4.34	100	.278	.356	24	.207	-5	1	-0	3	-0.1
1897 Lou-N	7	17	.292	27	26	20	1	0	199	209	6	69	55	12.6	3.62	118	.268	.327	7	.095	-8	15	14	1	0.7
1898 Cin-N	13	14	.481	33	32	26	2	0	262	261	3	119	75	13.1	3.98	96	.258	.336	13	.133	-7	-11	-4	1	-0.8
1899 Cle-N	3	6	.333	11	10	7	0	0	72¹	96	0	39	26	16.8	6.97	53	.318	.396	4	.129	-2	-25	-26	0	-2.3
Bal-N	3	4	.429	8	7	6	0	0	61	64	1	18	17	12.1	3.25	122	.269	.321	7	.292	1	4	5	1	0.6
Bro-N	1	0	1.000	2	1	1	0	1	11	11	0	6	3	13.9	0.82	478	.260	.352	3	.600	2	4	4	0	0.6
Yr	7	10	.412	21	18	14	0	1	144¹	171	1	63	46	14.6	4.93	78	.294	.363	3	.050	0	-17	-18	1	-1.1
Total 4	36	69	.343	124	115	92	3	3	925	994	24	406	280	13.6	4.17	98	.273	.346	58	.167	-20	-12	-7	6	-1.3

■ HOMER HILLEBRAND
Hillebrand, Homer Hiller Henry "Doc" b: 10/10/1879, Freeport, Ill. d: 1/20/74, Elsinore, Cal. 5'8", 165 lbs. Deb: 4/24/05 ◆

YEAR TM/L	W	L	PCT	G	GS	CG	SH	SV	IP	H	HR	BB	SO	RAT	ERA	ERA+	OAV	OOB	BH	AVG	PB	PR	/A	PD	TPI
1905 Pit-N	5	2	.714	10	6	4	0	1	60²	43	0	19	37	9.5	2.82	107	.198	.269	26	.236	1	1	1	-1	0.1
1906 Pit-N	3	2	.600	7	5	4	1	0	53	42	1	21	32	10.9	2.21	121	.220	.300	5	.238	1	3	3	1	0.6
1908 Pit-N	0	0	—	1	0	0	0	0	1	1	0	1	1	9.0	0.00	—	.333	.333	0	—	0	0	0	0	0.0
Total 3	8	4	.667	18	11	8	1	1	114²	86	1	40	70	10.1	2.51	113	.209	.284	31	.237	2	4	4	0	0.7

■ SHAWN HILLEGAS
Hillegas, Shawn Patrick b: 8/21/64, Dos Palos, Cal. BR/TR, 6'3", 205 lbs. Deb: 8/09/87

YEAR TM/L	W	L	PCT	G	GS	CG	SH	SV	IP	H	HR	BB	SO	RAT	ERA	ERA+	OAV	OOB	BH	AVG	PB	PR	/A	PD	TPI
1987 LA-N	4	3	.571	12	10	0	0	0	58	52	5	31	51	12.9	3.57	111	.241	.336	0	.000	-1	3	3	-1	0.0
1988 LA-N	3	4	.429	11	10	0	0	0	56²	54	5	17	30	11.8	4.13	81	.250	.314	2	.133	0	-4	-5	-1	-0.5
Chi-A	3	2	.600	6	6	0	0	0	40	30	4	18	26	11.0	3.15	126	.207	.299	0	—	0	4	4	-0	0.4
1989 Chi-A	7	11	.389	50	13	0	0	3	119²	132	12	51	76	14.0	4.74	80	.279	.353	0	—	0	-11	-12	-1	-1.3
1990 Chi-A	0	0	—	7	0	0	0	0	11¹	4	0	5	5	7.1	0.79	481	.111	.220	0	—	0	4	4	0	0.4
Total 4	17	20	.459	86	39	0	0	3	285²	272	26	122	188	12.6	4.00	94	.250	.330	2	.069	-1	-5	-7	-3	-1.0

■ FRANK HILLER
Hiller, Frank Walter "Dutch" b: 7/13/20, Newark, N.J. d: 1/8/87, West Chester, Pa. BR/TR, 6', 200 lbs. Deb: 5/25/46

YEAR TM/L	W	L	PCT	G	GS	CG	SH	SV	IP	H	HR	BB	SO	RAT	ERA	ERA+	OAV	OOB	BH	AVG	PB	PR	/A	PD	TPI
1946 NY-A	0	2	.000	3	1	0	0	0	11¹	13	2	6	4	15.1	4.76	72	.295	.380	1	.250	0	-2	-2	0	-0.1
1948 NY-A	5	2	.714	22	5	1	0	0	62¹	59	8	30	25	13.0	4.04	101	.244	.330	6	.375	2	2	0	0	0.0
1949 NY-A	0	2	.000	4	0	0	0	1	7²	9	0	7	3	18.8	5.87	69	.290	.421	1	.500	0	-1	-2	0	0.0
1950 Chi-N	12	5	.706	38	17	9	2	1	153	153	16	32	55	11.1	3.53	119	.258	.300	5	.114	-3	10	11	1	0.9
1951 Chi-N	6	12	.333	24	21	6	2	1	141¹	147	17	31	50	11.9	4.84	85	.268	.317	6	.125	-2	-14	-12	-1	-1.1
1952 Cin-N	5	8	.385	28	15	6	1	1	124¹	129	7	37	50	12.5	4.63	81	.271	.331	5	.167	1	-12	-12	1	-1.0
1953 NY-N	2	1	.667	19	1	0	0	1	33²	43	6	15	10	16.6	6.15	70	.303	.385	2	.500	1	-7	-7	1	-0.4
Total 7	30	32	.484	138	60	22	5	4	533²	553	56	158	197	12.4	4.42	92	.266	.325	26	.176	-1	-24	-22	4	-1.5

■ JOHN HILLER
Hiller, John Frederick b: 4/8/43, Toronto, Ont., Canada BR/TL, 6'1", 185 lbs. Deb: 9/06/65

YEAR TM/L	W	L	PCT	G	GS	CG	SH	SV	IP	H	HR	BB	SO	RAT	ERA	ERA+	OAV	OOB	BH	AVG	PB	PR	/A	PD	TPI
1965 Det-A	0	0	—	5	0	0	0	1	6	5	0	1	4	9.0	0.00	—	.227	.261	0	—	0	2	2	-0	0.2
1966 Det-A	0	0	—	1	0	0	0	0	2	2	0	2	1	18.0	9.00	39	.286	.444	0	—	0	-1	-1	0	0.0
1967 Det-A	4	3	.571	23	6	2	2	3	65	57	4	9	49	9.1	2.63	124	.233	.260	2	.133	-0	4	5	-0	0.5
1968 *Det-A	9	6	.600	39	12	4	1	2	128	92	9	51	78	10.1	2.39	126	.200	.280	3	.081	-2	8	9	-0	0.8
1969 Det-A	4	4	.500	40	8	1	1	4	99¹	97	13	44	74	12.9	3.99	94	.257	.336	6	.286	2	-4	-3	-1	-0.1
1970 Det-A	6	6	.500	47	5	1	1	3	104	82	12	46	89	11.3	3.03	123	.219	.307	0	.000	-2	8	8	-1	0.5
1972 *Det-A	1	2	.333	24	3	1	0	3	44¹	39	4	13	26	11.2	2.03	155	.232	.299	0	.000	-0	5	5	1	0.7
1973 Det-A	10	5	.667	65	0	0	0	38	125¹	89	7	39	124	9.2	1.44	285	.198	.262	0	—	0	33	37	3	3.9
1974 Det-A	17	14	.548	59	0	0	0	13	150	127	16	62	134	11.5	2.64	144	.231	.312	0	—	0	16	19	-3	1.8
1975 Det-A	2	3	.400	36	0	0	0	14	70²	52	6	36	87	11.2	2.17	185	.205	.303	0	—	0	13	15	-1	1.4
1976 Det-A	12	8	.600	56	1	1	1	13	121	97	7	67	117	12.0	2.38	156	.219	.329	0	.000	-0	15	18	-2	1.8
1977 Det-A	8	14	.364	45	8	3	0	7	124	120	15	61	115	13.2	3.56	121	.258	.345	0	—	0	7	10	-2	0.8
1978 Det-A	9	4	.692	51	0	0	0	15	92¹	64	6	35	74	9.6	2.34	165	.202	.281	0	—	0	15	16	-2	1.5
1979 Det-A	4	7	.364	43	0	0	0	9	79¹	83	14	55	46	15.7	5.22	83	.274	.385	0	—	0	-9	-8	-0	-0.7
1980 Det-A	1	0	1.000	11	0	0	0	0	30²	38	3	14	18	15.3	4.40	93	.309	.380	0	—	0	-1	-1	0	0.0
Total 15	87	76	.534	545	43	13	6	125	1242	1040	110	535	1036	11.5	2.83	133	.229	.312	11	.109	-3	112	130	-11	13.1

■ DAVE HILLMAN
Hillman, Darius Dutton b: 9/14/27, Dungannon, Va. BR/TR, 5'11", 168 lbs. Deb: 4/30/55

YEAR TM/L	W	L	PCT	G	GS	CG	SH	SV	IP	H	HR	BB	SO	RAT	ERA	ERA+	OAV	OOB	BH	AVG	PB	PR	/A	PD	TPI
1955 Chi-N	0	0	—	25	3	0	0	0	57²	63	10	25	23	13.9	5.31	77	.283	.357	1	.100	0	-8	-8	0	-0.6
1956 Chi-N	0	2	.000	2	2	0	0	0	12¹	11	0	5	6	11.7	2.19	172	.216	.286	0	.000	-1	2	2	0	0.2
1957 Chi-N	6	11	.353	32	14	1	0	1	103¹	115	13	37	53	13.2	4.35	89	.280	.340	0	.000	-2	-5	-6	-0	-0.7
1958 Chi-N	4	8	.333	31	16	3	0	1	125²	132	12	31	65	11.7	3.15	124	.265	.308	6	.146	-1	11	11	0	1.0
1959 Chi-N	8	11	.421	39	24	4	1	0	191	178	17	43	88	10.5	3.53	112	.248	.292	9	.150	1	9	9	1	1.1
1960 Bos-A	0	3	.000	16	3	0	0	0	36²	41	6	12	14	13.0	5.65	72	.281	.335	0	.000	-0	-7	-7	1	-0.5
1961 Bos-A	3	2	.600	28	1	0	0	0	78	70	8	23	39	10.7	2.77	151	.242	.298	0	.000	-2	11	12	0	1.1
1962 Cin-N	0	0	—	2	0	0	0	0	3²	8	0	1	0	22.1	9.82	41	.421	.450	0	—	0	-2	-2	-0	-0.1
NY-N	0	0	—	13	1	0	0	1	15²	21	5	8	8	17.2	6.32	66	.333	.417	0	.000	-0	-4	-4	0	-0.3

YEAR TM/L	W	L	PCT	G	GS	CG	SH	SV	IP	H	HR	BB	SO	RAT	ERA	ERA+	OAV	OOB	BH	AVG	PB	PR	/A	PD	TPI
Yr	0	0	—	15	1	0	0	1	19¹	29	5	9	8	18.2	6.98	59	.354	.424	0	.000	-0	-7	-6	0	-0.4
Total 8	21	37	.362	188	64	8	1	3	624	639	71	185	296	11.9	3.87	103	.264	.317	16	.098	-5	6	8	2	1.2

■ CHARLIE HILSEY   Hilsey, Charles T. b: 3/23/1864, Philadelphia, Pa. d: 10/31/18, Philadelphia, Pa. 5'7", 180 lbs. Deb: 9/27/1883 ♦

YEAR TM/L	W	L	PCT	G	GS	CG	SH	SV	IP	H	HR	BB	SO	RAT	ERA	ERA+	OAV	OOB	BH	AVG	PB	PR	/A	PD	TPI
1883 Phi-N	0	3	.000	3	3	3	0	0	26	36	1	4	8	13.8	5.54	56	.310	.333	1	.100	-1	-7	-7	-0	-0.6
1884 Phi-a	2	1	.667	3	3	3	0	0	27	29	0	5	10	11.3	4.67	73	.260	.292	5	.208	0	-4	-4	1	-0.2
Total 2	2	4	.333	6	6	6	0	0	53	65	1	9	18	12.6	5.09	64	.286	.313	6	.176	-1	-11	-11	0	-0.8

■ HOWARD HILTON   Hilton, Howard James b: 1/3/64, Oxnard, Cal. BR/TR, 6'3", 230 lbs. Deb: 4/09/90

YEAR TM/L	W	L	PCT	G	GS	CG	SH	SV	IP	H	HR	BB	SO	RAT	ERA	ERA+	OAV	OOB	BH	AVG	PB	PR	/A	PD	TPI
1990 StL-N	0	0	—	2	0	0	0	0	3	2	0	3	2	15.0	0.00	—	.182	.357	0	—	0	1	1	0	0.1

■ SAM HINDS   Hinds, Samuel Russell b: 7/11/53, Frederick, Md. BR/TR, 6'6", 215 lbs. Deb: 5/21/77

YEAR TM/L	W	L	PCT	G	GS	CG	SH	SV	IP	H	HR	BB	SO	RAT	ERA	ERA+	OAV	OOB	BH	AVG	PB	PR	/A	PD	TPI
1977 Mil-A	0	3	.000	29	1	0	0	2	72¹	72	5	40	46	14.2	4.73	86	.266	.364	0	—	0	-5	-5	-1	-0.5

■ PAUL HINES   Hines, Paul A. b: 3/1/1852, Washington, D.C. d: 7/10/35, Hyattsville, Md. BR/TR, 5'9.5", 173 lbs. Deb: 4/20/1872 ♦

YEAR TM/L	W	L	PCT	G	GS	CG	SH	SV	IP	H	HR	BB	SO	RAT	ERA	ERA+	OAV	OOB	BH	AVG	PB	PR	/A	PD	TPI
1884 *Pro-N	0	0	—	1	0	0	0	0	1	3	0	0	0	27.0	0.00	—	.495	.495	148	.302	0	0	0	0	0.0

■ PAUL HINRICHS   Hinrichs, Paul Edwin "Herky" b: 8/31/25, Marengo, Iowa BR/TR, 6', 180 lbs. Deb: 5/16/51

YEAR TM/L	W	L	PCT	G	GS	CG	SH	SV	IP	H	HR	BB	SO	RAT	ERA	ERA+	OAV	OOB	BH	AVG	PB	PR	/A	PD	TPI
1951 Bos-A	0	0	—	4	0	0	0	0	3¹	7	1	4	1	29.7	21.60	21	.412	.524	0	—	0	-6	-6	0	-0.5

■ DUTCH HINRICHS   Hinrichs, William Louis b: 4/27/1889, Orange, Cal. d: 8/18/72, Kingsburg, Cal. BR/TR, 6'3", 195 lbs. Deb: 6/25/10

YEAR TM/L	W	L	PCT	G	GS	CG	SH	SV	IP	H	HR	BB	SO	RAT	ERA	ERA+	OAV	OOB	BH	AVG	PB	PR	/A	PD	TPI
1910 Was-A	0	1	.000	3	0	0	0	1	7	10	0	3	5	16.7	2.57	97	.357	.419	0	—	-1	-0	-0	-0	0.0

■ JERRY HINSLEY   Hinsley, Jerry Dean b: 4/9/44, Hugo, Okla. BR/TR, 5'11", 165 lbs. Deb: 4/18/64

YEAR TM/L	W	L	PCT	G	GS	CG	SH	SV	IP	H	HR	BB	SO	RAT	ERA	ERA+	OAV	OOB	BH	AVG	PB	PR	/A	PD	TPI
1964 NY-N	0	2	.000	9	2	0	0	0	15¹	21	0	7	11	16.4	8.22	44	.313	.378	0	.000	-0	-8	-8	-1	-0.8
1967 NY-N	0	0	—	2	0	0	0	0	5	6	0	4	3	18.0	3.60	94	.316	.435	0	—	0	-0	-0	0	0.0
Total 2	0	2	.000	11	2	0	0	0	20¹	27	0	11	14	16.8	7.08	50	.314	.392	0	.000	-0	-8	-8	-1	-0.8

■ RICH HINTON   Hinton, Richard Michael b: 5/22/47, Tucson, Ariz. BL/TL, 6'2", 185 lbs. Deb: 7/17/71

YEAR TM/L	W	L	PCT	G	GS	CG	SH	SV	IP	H	HR	BB	SO	RAT	ERA	ERA+	OAV	OOB	BH	AVG	PB	PR	/A	PD	TPI
1971 Chi-A	3	4	.429	18	2	0	0	0	24¹	27	1	6	15	12.6	4.44	81	.310	.362	0	.000	-0	-3	-2	1	-0.1
1972 NY-A	1	0	1.000	7	3	0	0	0	16²	20	2	8	13	15.1	4.86	61	.299	.373	0	.000	-0	-3	-4	-0	-0.4
Tex-A	0	1	.000	5	0	0	0	0	11¹	7	1	10	4	13.5	2.38	126	.171	.333	1	.500	1	1	1	0	0.2
Yr	1	1	.500	12	3	0	0	0	28	27	3	18	17	14.5	3.86	77	.245	.352	1	.000	1	-2	-3	-0	-0.2
1975 Chi-A	1	0	1.000	15	0	0	0	0	37¹	41	3	15	30	13.5	4.82	80	.270	.335	0	—	0	-4	-4	1	-0.2
1976 Cin-N	1	2	.333	12	1	0	0	0	17²	30	4	11	8	20.9	7.64	46	.380	.456	0	.000	-0	-8	-8	-0	-0.8
1978 Chi-A	2	6	.250	29	4	2	0	1	80²	78	5	28	48	12.0	4.02	95	.261	.328	0	—	0	-2	-2	-1	-0.2
1979 Chi-A	1	2	.333	16	2	0	0	2	41²	57	4	8	27	14.5	6.05	70	.331	.368	0	—	0	-8	-8	0	-0.7
Sea-A	0	2	.000	14	1	0	0	0	20	23	4	5	7	13.5	5.40	81	.284	.341	0	—	0	-3	-2	0	-0.1
Yr	1	4	.200	30	3	0	0	2	61²	80	8	13	34	13.9	5.84	73	.310	.348	0	—	0	-11	-11	0	-0.8
Total 6	9	17	.346	116	13	2	0	3	249²	283	24	91	152	13.7	4.87	78	.289	.354	1	.143	0	-31	-30	1	-2.3

■ HERB HIPPAUF   Hippauf, Herbert August b: 5/9/40, New York, N.Y. BR/TL, 6', 180 lbs. Deb: 4/27/66

YEAR TM/L	W	L	PCT	G	GS	CG	SH	SV	IP	H	HR	BB	SO	RAT	ERA	ERA+	OAV	OOB	BH	AVG	PB	PR	/A	PD	TPI
1966 Atl-N	0	1	.000	3	0	0	0	0	2²	6	0	1	1	23.6	13.50	27	.462	.500	0	—	0	-3	-3	-0	-0.2

■ HARLEY HISNER   Hisner, Harley Parnell b: 11/6/26, Naples, Ind. BR/TR, 6'1", 185 lbs. Deb: 9/30/51

YEAR TM/L	W	L	PCT	G	GS	CG	SH	SV	IP	H	HR	BB	SO	RAT	ERA	ERA+	OAV	OOB	BH	AVG	PB	PR	/A	PD	TPI
1951 Bos-A	0	1	.000	1	1	0	0	0	6	7	0	4	3	16.5	4.50	99	.292	.393	1	.500	0	-0	-0	0	0.0

■ BRUCE HITT   Hitt, Bruce Smith b: 3/14/1897, Comanche, Tex. d: 11/10/73, Portland, Ore. BR/TR, 6'1", 190 lbs. Deb: 9/23/17

YEAR TM/L	W	L	PCT	G	GS	CG	SH	SV	IP	H	HR	BB	SO	RAT	ERA	ERA+	OAV	OOB	BH	AVG	PB	PR	/A	PD	TPI
1917 StL-N	0	0	—	2	0	0	0	0	4	7	1	1	1	18.0	9.00	30	.368	.400	0	.000	-0	-3	-3	0	-0.2

■ ROY HITT   Hitt, Roy Wesley "Rhino" b: 6/22/1887, Carleton, Neb. d: 2/8/56, Pomona, Cal. TL, 5'10", 200 lbs. Deb: 4/27/07

YEAR TM/L	W	L	PCT	G	GS	CG	SH	SV	IP	H	HR	BB	SO	RAT	ERA	ERA+	OAV	OOB	BH	AVG	PB	PR	/A	PD	TPI
1907 Cin-N	6	10	.375	21	18	14	2	0	153¹	143	2	56	63	12.4	3.40	76	.258	.339	10	.179	0	-16	-14	-1	-1.5

■ LLOYD HITTLE   Hittle, Lloyd Eldon "Red" b: 2/21/24, Lodi, Cal. BR/TL, 5'10.5", 164 lbs. Deb: 6/12/49

YEAR TM/L	W	L	PCT	G	GS	CG	SH	SV	IP	H	HR	BB	SO	RAT	ERA	ERA+	OAV	OOB	BH	AVG	PB	PR	/A	PD	TPI
1949 Was-A	5	7	.417	36	9	3	2	0	109	123	2	57	32	14.9	4.21	101	.285	.369	4	.143	-2	-0	1	-1	-0.1
1950 Was-A	2	4	.333	11	4	1	0	0	43¹	60	1	17	9	16.0	4.98	90	.326	.383	1	.077	-1	-2	-2	1	-0.1
Total 2	7	11	.389	47	13	4	2	0	152¹	183	3	74	41	15.2	4.43	98	.298	.373	5	.122	-3	-2	-2	1	-0.2

■ MYRIL HOAG   Hoag, Myril Oliver b: 3/9/08, Davis, Cal. d: 7/28/71, High Springs, Fla BR/TR, 5'11", 180 lbs. Deb: 4/15/31 ♦

YEAR TM/L	W	L	PCT	G	GS	CG	SH	SV	IP	H	HR	BB	SO	RAT	ERA	ERA+	OAV	OOB	BH	AVG	PB	PR	/A	PD	TPI
1939 StL-A	0	0	—	1	0	0	0	0	1	0	0	0	0	0.0	0.00	—	.000	.000	142	.295	0	1	1	0	0.1
1945 Cle-A	0	0	—	2	0	0	0	0	3	3	0	1	0	12.0	0.00	—	.300	.364	27	.211	0	1	1	0	0.1
Total 2	0	0	—	3	0	0	0	0	4	3	0	1	0	9.0	0.00	—	.214	.267	854	.271	1	2	2	0	0.2

■ ED HOBAUGH   Hobaugh, Edward Russell b: 6/27/34, Kittanning, Pa. BR/TR, 6', 176 lbs. Deb: 4/19/61

YEAR TM/L	W	L	PCT	G	GS	CG	SH	SV	IP	H	HR	BB	SO	RAT	ERA	ERA+	OAV	OOB	BH	AVG	PB	PR	/A	PD	TPI
1961 Was-A	7	9	.438	26	18	3	0	0	126¹	142	12	64	67	14.7	4.42	91	.281	.363	4	.098	-2	-6	-6	0	-0.6
1962 Was-A	2	1	.667	26	2	0	0	1	69¹	66	9	25	37	11.8	3.76	107	.258	.324	2	.167	0	2	2	-1	0.2
1963 Was-A	0	0	—	9	1	0	0	0	16	20	3	6	11	15.8	6.19	60	.308	.384	1	.500	2	-5	-4	0	-0.2
Total 3	9	10	.474	61	21	3	0	1	211²	228	24	95	115	13.9	4.34	92	.276	.352	7	.127	-1	-8	-8	-0	-0.6

■ GLEN HOBBIE   Hobbie, Glen Frederick b: 4/24/36, Witt, Ill. BR/TR, 6'2", 195 lbs. Deb: 9/20/57

YEAR TM/L	W	L	PCT	G	GS	CG	SH	SV	IP	H	HR	BB	SO	RAT	ERA	ERA+	OAV	OOB	BH	AVG	PB	PR	/A	PD	TPI
1957 Chi-N	0	0	—	2	1	0	0	0	4¹	6	0	5	3	22.8	10.38	37	.333	.478	0	.000	-0	-3	-3	0	-0.2
1958 Chi-N	10	6	.625	55	16	2	1	2	168¹	163	13	93	91	14.1	3.74	105	.252	.353	7	.146	-2	4	3	4	0.5
1959 Chi-N	16	13	.552	46	33	10	3	0	234	204	15	106	138	12.2	3.69	107	.236	.324	9	.114	-3	7	7	1	0.4
1960 Chi-N	16	20	.444	46	36	16	4	1	258²	253	27	101	134	12.6	3.97	95	.256	.330	13	.151	1	-6	-5	5	0.4
1961 Chi-N	7	13	.350	36	29	7	2	2	198²	207	26	54	103	12.1	4.26	98	.268	.321	11	.167	2	-5	-2	4	0.4
1962 Chi-N	5	14	.263	42	23	5	0	0	162	198	19	62	87	14.6	5.22	79	.304	.367	6	.122	-2	-23	-19	1	-1.9
1963 Chi-N	7	10	.412	36	24	4	1	0	165¹	172	17	49	94	13.4	3.92	90	.270	.328	4	.080	-2	-12	-8	-1	-1.1
1964 Chi-N	0	3	.000	8	4	0	0	0	27¹	39	4	10	14	16.5	7.90	47	.325	.382	0	.000	0	-13	-13	0	-1.1
StL-N	1	2	.333	13	5	1	0	1	44¹	41	4	15	18	11.6	4.26	89	.241	.306	2	.154	1	-4	-2	1	0.0
Yr	1	5	.167	21	9	1	0	1	71²	80	8	25	32	13.3	5.65	67	.275	.334	2	.111	1	-17	-15	1	-1.1
Total 8	62	81	.434	284	170	45	11	6	1263	1283	125	495	682	12.9	4.20	93	.264	.337	52	.131	-5	-55	-42	14	-3.0

■ JOHN HOBBS   Hobbs, John Douglas b: 11/11/56, Philadelphia, Pa. BR/TL, 6'3", 190 lbs. Deb: 8/31/81

YEAR TM/L	W	L	PCT	G	GS	CG	SH	SV	IP	H	HR	BB	SO	RAT	ERA	ERA+	OAV	OOB	BH	AVG	PB	PR	/A	PD	TPI
1981 Min-A	0	0	—	4	0	0	0	0	5²	5	0	6	1	20.6	3.18	124	.238	.448	0	—	0	0	0	0	0.0

■ HARRY HOCH   Hoch, Harry Keller b: 1/9/1887, Woodside, Del. d: 10/26/81, Lewes, Del. BR/TR, 5'10.5", 165 lbs. Deb: 4/16/08

YEAR TM/L	W	L	PCT	G	GS	CG	SH	SV	IP	H	HR	BB	SO	RAT	ERA	ERA+	OAV	OOB	BH	AVG	PB	PR	/A	PD	TPI
1908 Phi-N	2	1	.667	3	3	2	0	0	26	20	0	13	4	12.1	2.77	88	.211	.318	1	.200	1	-1	-1	1	0.0
1914 StL-A	0	2	.000	15	2	1	0	0	54	55	1	27	13	14.0	3.00	90	.284	.377	1	.056	-2	-2	-2	2	-0.1
1915 StL-A	0	4	.000	12	3	1	0	0	40	52	2	26	9	18.2	7.20	40	.311	.413	2	.200	0	-19	-19	0	-1.8
Total 3	2	7	.222	30	8	4	0	0	120	127	3	66	26	15.0	4.35	62	.279	.378	4	.121	-1	-22	-22	2	-1.9

■ CHUCK HOCKENBERY   Hockenbery, Charles Marion b: 12/15/50, Lacrosse, Wis. BB/TR, 6'1", 195 lbs. Deb: 7/04/75

YEAR TM/L	W	L	PCT	G	GS	CG	SH	SV	IP	H	HR	BB	SO	RAT	ERA	ERA+	OAV	OOB	BH	AVG	PB	PR	/A	PD	TPI
1975 Cal-A	0	5	.000	16	4	0	0	1	41	48	3	19	15	15.4	5.27	67	.296	.380	0	—	0	-7	-8	0	-0.7

■ GEORGE HOCKETTE   Hockette, George Edward "Lefty" b: 4/7/08, Perth, Miss. d: 1/20/74, Plantation, Fla. BL/TL, 6', 174 lbs. Deb: 9/17/34

YEAR TM/L	W	L	PCT	G	GS	CG	SH	SV	IP	H	HR	BB	SO	RAT	ERA	ERA+	OAV	OOB	BH	AVG	PB	PR	/A	PD	TPI
1934 Bos-A	2	1	.667	3	3	3	2	0	27¹	22	3	6	14	9.2	1.65	292	.218	.262	3	.273	0	9	10	-0	1.1
1935 Bos-A	2	3	.400	23	4	0	0	0	61	83	6	12	11	14.2	5.16	92	.329	.362	2	.143	-1	-5	-3	3	0.0

YEAR TM/L	W	L	PCT	G	GS	CG	SH	SV	IP	H	HR	BB	SO	RAT	ERA	ERA+	OAV	OOB	BH	AVG	PB	PR	/A	PD	TPI
Total 2	4	4	.500	26	7	3	2	0	88¹	105	9	18	25	12.6	4.08	117	.297	.333	5	.200	-0	4	7	3	1.1

■ SHOVEL HODGE
Hodge, Clarence Clemet b: 7/6/1893, Mount Andrew, Ala. d: 12/31/67, Ft.Walton Beach, Fla. BL/TR, 6'4", 190 lbs. Deb: 9/06/20

YEAR TM/L	W	L	PCT	G	GS	CG	SH	SV	IP	H	HR	BB	SO	RAT	ERA	ERA+	OAV	OOB	BH	AVG	PB	PR	/A	PD	TPI
1920 Chi-A	1	1	.500	4	2	1	0	0	19²	15	0	12	5	12.4	2.29	165	.224	.342	0	.000	-1	3	3	-0	0.2
1921 Chi-A	6	8	.429	36	10	5	0	2	142²	191	7	54	25	15.8	6.56	65	.335	.397	17	.327	3	-36	-37	3	-2.6
1922 Chi-A	7	6	.538	35	8	2	0	1	139	154	3	65	37	14.3	4.14	98	.300	.381	12	.207	-1	-2	-1	2	0.0
Total 3	14	15	.483	75	20	8	0	3	301¹	360	10	131	67	14.9	5.17	80	.313	.387	29	.250	1	-34	-35	5	-2.4

■ ED HODGE
Hodge, Ed Oliver b: 4/19/58, Bellflower, Cal. BL/TL, 6'2", 192 lbs. Deb: 5/01/84

YEAR TM/L	W	L	PCT	G	GS	CG	SH	SV	IP	H	HR	BB	SO	RAT	ERA	ERA+	OAV	OOB	BH	AVG	PB	PR	/A	PD	TPI
1984 Min-A	4	3	.571	25	15	0	0	0	100	116	13	29	59	13.1	4.77	88	.291	.340	0	—	0	-9	-6	-2	-0.7

■ ELI HODKEY
Hodkey, Aloysius Joseph b: 11/3/17, Lorain, Ohio BL/TL, 6'4", 185 lbs. Deb: 9/12/46

YEAR TM/L	W	L	PCT	G	GS	CG	SH	SV	IP	H	HR	BB	SO	RAT	ERA	ERA+	OAV	OOB	BH	AVG	PB	PR	/A	PD	TPI
1946 Phi-N	0	1	.000	2	1	0	0	0	4¹	9	0	5	0	29.1	12.46	28	.391	.500	0	.000	-0	-4	-4	-0	-0.3

■ CHARLIE HODNETT
Hodnett, Charles b: 1861, Iowa Deb: 5/03/1883

YEAR TM/L	W	L	PCT	G	GS	CG	SH	SV	IP	H	HR	BB	SO	RAT	ERA	ERA+	OAV	OOB	BH	AVG	PB	PR	/A	PD	TPI
1883 StL-a	2	2	.500	4	4	3	0	0	32	28	1	7	6	9.8	1.41	249	.220	.261	2	.182	-0	7	7	0	0.7
1884 StL-U	12	2	.857	14	14	12	1	0	121	121	0	16	41	10.2	2.01	147	.243	.267	12	.207	1	14	13	-1	1.1
Total 2	14	4	.778	18	18	15	1	0	153	149	1	23	47	10.1	1.88	163	.238	.266	14	.203	1	20	20	-1	1.8

■ GEORGE HODSON
Hodson, George S. b: 1876, Hartford, Conn. Deb: 8/09/1894

YEAR TM/L	W	L	PCT	G	GS	CG	SH	SV	IP	H	HR	BB	SO	RAT	ERA	ERA+	OAV	OOB	BH	AVG	PB	PR	/A	PD	TPI
1894 Bos-N	4	4	.500	12	11	8	0	0	74	103	4	35	12	16.8	5.84	97	.326	.393	3	.100	-4	-4	-1	-1	-0.4
1895 Phi-N	1	2	.333	4	2	1	0	0	17	27	4	9	6	19.1	9.53	50	.354	.422	0	.000	-1	-9	-9	-0	-0.7
Total 2	5	6	.455	16	13	9	0	0	91	130	8	44	18	17.2	6.53	84	.331	.399	3	.086	-5	-13	-10	-2	-1.1

■ BILLY HOEFT
Hoeft, William Frederick b: 5/17/32, Oshkosh, Wis. BL/TL, 6'3", 180 lbs. Deb: 4/18/52

YEAR TM/L	W	L	PCT	G	GS	CG	SH	SV	IP	H	HR	BB	SO	RAT	ERA	ERA+	OAV	OOB	BH	AVG	PB	PR	/A	PD	TPI
1952 Det-A	2	7	.222	34	10	1	0	4	125	123	14	63	67	13.8	4.32	88	.260	.353	6	.150	-1	-9	-7	1	-0.6
1953 Det-A	9	14	.391	29	27	9	0	2	197²	223	24	58	90	13.0	4.83	84	.283	.335	11	.172	0	-18	-17	-1	-1.6
1954 Det-A	7	15	.318	34	25	10	4	1	175	180	22	59	114	12.5	4.58	81	.266	.328	10	.192	4	-17	-17	-3	-1.5
1955 Det-A	16	7	.696	32	29	17	**7**	0	220	187	17	75	133	11.0	2.99	129	.229	.298	17	.207	3	24	21	-3	2.1
1956 Det-A	20	14	.588	38	34	18	4	0	248	276	22	104	172	14.0	4.06	101	.287	.360	20	.250	6	3	1	-3	0.4
1957 Det-A	9	11	.450	34	28	10	1	1	207	188	15	69	111	11.4	3.48	111	.244	.310	10	.149	2	7	9	-2	0.9
1958 Det-A	10	9	.526	36	21	6	0	3	143	148	15	49	94	12.5	4.15	97	.268	.328	12	.273	3	-6	-2	-2	0.0
1959 Det-A	1	1	.500	2	2	0	0	0	9	6	0	4	2	11.0	5.00	81	.188	.297	1	.333	0	-1	-1	0	0.0
Bos-A	0	3	.000	5	3	0	0	0	17²	22	1	8	8	15.8	5.60	72	.319	.397	0	.000	-0	-3	-3	-0	-0.2
Bal-A	1	1	.500	16	3	0	0	0	41	50	6	19	30	15.1	5.71	66	.307	.379	3	.250	1	-8	-9	-0	-0.7
Yr	2	5	.286	23	8	0	0	0	67²	78	7	31	40	14.5	5.59	70	.290	.363	0	.000	-0	-13	-13	-0	-0.9
1960 Bal-A	2	1	.667	19	0	0	0	0	18²	18	2	14	14	15.4	4.34	88	.240	.360	0	.000	-0	-1	-1	0	0.0
1961 Bal-A	7	4	.636	35	12	3	1	3	138	106	7	55	100	10.6	2.02	193	.216	.296	7	.179	1	31	29	1	3.2
1962 Bal-A	4	8	.333	57	4	0	0	7	113²	103	7	43	73	11.6	4.59	82	.243	.315	3	.158	2	-8	-11	0	-0.7
1963 SF-N	2	0	1.000	23	0	0	0	4	24¹	26	5	10	8	13.3	4.44	72	.271	.340	1	1.000	0	-3	-3	-0	-0.1
1964 Mil-N	4	0	1.000	42	0	0	0	4	73¹	76	9	18	47	11.7	3.80	93	.271	.318	2	.222	1	-2	-2	0	0.0
1965 Chi-N	2	2	.500	29	2	1	0	1	51¹	41	3	20	44	10.7	2.81	131	.215	.289	3	.273	1	4	5	-1	0.5
1966 Chi-N	1	2	.333	36	0	0	0	3	41	43	4	14	30	12.7	4.61	80	.264	.326	1	.250	1	-5	-4	1	-0.3
SF-N	0	2	.000	4	0	0	0	0	3²	4	0	3	3	17.2	7.36	50	.250	.368	0	—	0	-2	-2	-0	-0.1
Yr	1	4	.200	40	0	0	0	3	44²	47	4	17	33	12.9	4.84	76	.261	.325	0	.000	0	-6	-6	1	-0.4
Total 15	97	101	.490	505	200	75	17	33	1847¹	1820	173	685	1140	12.4	3.94	98	.259	.327	107	.202	24	-15	-13	-12	1.2

■ ART HOELSKOETTER
Hoelskoetter, Arthur "Holley" or "Hoss" (a.k.a. Arthur H. Hostetter) b: 9/30/1882, St.Louis, Mo. d: 8/3/54, St.Louis, Mo. BR/TR, 6'2", Deb: 9/10/05 ♦

YEAR TM/L	W	L	PCT	G	GS	CG	SH	SV	IP	H	HR	BB	SO	RAT	ERA	ERA+	OAV	OOB	BH	AVG	PB	PR	/A	PD	TPI
1905 StL-N	0	1	.000	1	1	1	0	0	6	6	1	5	4	16.5	1.50	199	.273	.407	20	.241	0	1	1	0	0.1
1906 StL-N	1	4	.200	12	3	2	0	0	58¹	53	1	34	20	13.6	4.63	57	.240	.344	71	.224	1	-13	-13	-0	-1.3
1907 StL-N	0	0	—	2	0	0	0	0	11	9	0	10	8	17.2	5.73	44	.209	.382	98	.247	0	-4	-4	-1	-0.3
Total 3	1	5	.167	15	4	3	0	0	75¹	68	2	49	32	14.3	4.54	58	.238	.355	225	.236	1	-16	-16	-1	-1.5

■ JOE HOERNER
Hoerner, Joseph Walter b: 11/12/36, Dubuque, Iowa BR/TL, 6'1", 200 lbs. Deb: 9/27/63

YEAR TM/L	W	L	PCT	G	GS	CG	SH	SV	IP	H	HR	BB	SO	RAT	ERA	ERA+	OAV	OOB	BH	AVG	PB	PR	/A	PD	TPI
1963 Hou-N	0	0	—	1	0	0	0	0	3	2	0	0	2	6.0	0.00	—	.182	.182	0	.000	-0	1	1	0	0.1
1964 Hou-N	0	0	—	7	0	0	0	0	11	13	3	6	4	15.5	4.91	70	.310	.396	0	.000	-0	-2	-2	0	-0.1
1966 StL-N	5	1	.833	57	0	0	0	13	76	57	5	21	63	9.7	1.54	233	.212	.279	1	.125	1	17	17	-1	1.8
1967 *StL-N	4	4	.500	57	0	0	0	15	66	52	5	20	50	10.0	2.59	127	.225	.290	2	.182	0	6	5	-0	0.5
1968 *StL-N	8	2	.800	47	0	0	0	17	48²	34	2	12	42	8.5	1.48	196	.192	.243	0	.000	-1	8	8	-1	0.7
1969 StL-N	2	3	.400	45	0	0	0	15	53¹	44	5	9	35	9.1	2.87	125	.230	.269	0	.000	-1	4	4	0	0.4
1970 Phi-N	9	5	.643	44	0	0	0	9	57²	53	5	20	39	11.5	2.65	150	.247	.314	2	.200	1	9	9	-2	0.8
1971 Phi-N	4	5	.444	49	0	0	0	9	73	57	6	21	57	9.7	1.97	179	.215	.275	1	.100	-1	12	13	-1	1.2
1972 Phi-N	0	2	.000	15	0	0	0	3	21²	21	2	5	12	11.2	2.08	173	.259	.310	0	.000	-0	3	4	-0	0.3
Atl-N	1	3	.250	25	0	0	0	2	23¹	34	4	8	19	16.6	6.56	58	.351	.406	0	.000	-0	-8	-7	-0	-0.8
Yr	1	5	.167	40	0	0	0	5	45	55	6	13	31	13.8	4.40	84	.301	.350	0	.000	-1	-5	-4	-1	-0.5
1973 Atl-N	2	2	.500	20	0	0	0	2	12²	17	1	4	10	14.9	6.39	61	.333	.382	0	—	0	-4	-3	-0	-0.3
KC-A	2	0	1.000	30	0	0	0	4	19¹	28	0	13	15	19.1	5.12	80	.329	.418	0	—	0	-3	-2	-0	-0.2
1974 KC-A	2	3	.400	30	0	0	0	2	35¹	32	3	12	24	12.2	3.82	100	.244	.327	0	—	0	-1	-0	-1	0.0
1975 Phi-N	0	0	—	25	0	0	0	0	21	25	3	8	15	14.6	2.57	145	.298	.366	0	.000	-0	2	3	1	0.2
1976 Tex-A	4	0	1.000	41	0	0	0	8	35	41	3	19	15	15.4	5.14	70	.315	.403	0	—	0	-6	-6	-0	-0.6
1977 Cin-N	0	0	—	8	0	0	0	0	5²	9	3	4	5	23.8	12.71	31	.375	.500	0	—	0	-6	-6	-0	-0.5
Total 14	39	34	.534	493	0	0	0	99	562²	519	50	181	412	11.5	2.99	119	.249	.314	6	.102	-1	35	36	-7	3.5

■ LEFTY HOERST
Hoerst, Frank Joseph b: 8/11/17, Philadelphia, Pa. BL/TL, 6'3", 192 lbs. Deb: 4/26/40

YEAR TM/L	W	L	PCT	G	GS	CG	SH	SV	IP	H	HR	BB	SO	RAT	ERA	ERA+	OAV	OOB	BH	AVG	PB	PR	/A	PD	TPI
1940 Phi-N	1	0	1.000	6	0	0	0	0	12	12	1	8	3	15.0	5.25	74	.250	.357	0	.000	-0	-2	-2	1	0.0
1941 Phi-N	3	10	.231	37	11	1	0	0	105²	111	7	50	33	13.8	5.20	71	.275	.357	4	.182	0	-18	-18	2	-1.5
1942 Phi-N	4	16	.200	33	22	5	0	1	150²	162	11	78	52	14.4	5.20	64	.271	.357	7	.152	-0	-32	-32	2	-3.0
1946 Phi-N	1	6	.143	18	7	2	0	0	68¹	77	4	36	17	15.0	4.61	74	.288	.375	1	.059	-1	-9	-9	-1	-1.0
1947 Phi-N	1	1	.500	4	1	0	0	0	11¹	19	1	3	0	17.5	7.94	50	.358	.393	2	.500	1	-5	-5	0	-0.3
Total 5	10	33	.233	98	41	8	0	1	348	381	24	175	105	14.5	5.17	68	.279	.362	14	.154	-1	-66	-65	4	-5.8

■ RED HOFF
Hoff, Chester Cornelius b: 5/8/1891, Ossining, N.Y. BL/TL, 5'9", 162 lbs. Deb: 9/06/11

YEAR TM/L	W	L	PCT	G	GS	CG	SH	SV	IP	H	HR	BB	SO	RAT	ERA	ERA+	OAV	OOB	BH	AVG	PB	PR	/A	PD	TPI
1911 NY-A	0	1	.000	5	1	0	0	0	20²	21	0	7	10	12.2	2.18	165	.262	.322	2	.286	-0	3	3	1	0.4
1912 NY-A	0	1	.000	5	1	0	0	0	15²	20	0	6	14	14.9	6.89	52	.303	.361	1	.200	-0	-6	-6	-0	-0.5
1913 NY-A	0	0	—	2	0	0	0	0	3	0	0	1	2	3.0	0.00	—	.000	.111	0	.000	-0	1	1	-0	0.1
1915 StL-A	2	2	.500	11	3	2	0	0	43²	26	0	24	23	10.5	1.24	232	.169	.285	3	.176	-1	8	8	1	0.9
Total 4	2	4	.333	23	5	2	0	0	83	67	0	38	49	11.5	2.49	128	.218	.305	6	.200	-1	6	6	1	0.9

■ BILL HOFFER
Hoffer, William Leopold "Chick" or "Wizard" b: 11/8/1870, Cedar Rapids, Iowa d: 7/21/59, Cedar Rapids, Ia. BR/TR, 5'9", 155 lbs. Deb: 4/26/1895

YEAR TM/L	W	L	PCT	G	GS	CG	SH	SV	IP	H	HR	BB	SO	RAT	ERA	ERA+	OAV	OOB	BH	AVG	PB	PR	/A	PD	TPI
1895 *Bal-N	31	6	**.838**	41	38	32	**4**	0	314	296	9	124	80	12.0	3.21	148	.245	.316	27	.214	-4	55	54	-2	4.1
1896 *Bal-N	25	7	**.781**	35	35	32	3	0	309	317	1	95	93	12.0	3.38	127	.281	.317	38	.304	10	34	31	2	3.8
1897 *Bal-N	22	11	.667	38	33	29	1	0	303¹	350	5	104	62	13.5	4.30	97	.287	.343	33	.237	1	0	-4	1	-0.1
1898 Bal-N	0	4	.000	4	4	4	0	0	34¹	62	0	16	5	20.4	7.34	49	.386	.442	5	.208	0	-14	-14	-0	-1.1
Pit-N	3	0	1.000	4	3	3	0	0	31	26	0	15	11	11.9	1.74	204	.226	.316	1	.091	-1	6	6	-0	0.5

YEAR	TM/L	W	L	PCT	G	GS	CG	SH	SV	IP	H	HR	BB	SO	RAT	ERA	ERA+	OAV	OOB	BH	AVG	PB	PR	/A	PD	TPI
	Yr	3	4	.429	8	7	7	0	0	65¹	88	0	31	16	16.4	4.68	76	.320	.388	4	.114	-0	-8	-8	-0	-0.6
1899	Pit-N	8	10	.444	23	19	15	2	0	163²	169	5	64	44	12.8	3.63	105	.266	.334	18	.198	-2	4	3	0	0.1
1901	Cle-A	3	8	.273	16	10	10	0	**3**	99	113	2	35	19	13.5	4.55	78	.283	.341	6	.136	-1	-10	-11	1	-0.9
Total	6	92	46	.667	161	142	125	10	3	1254¹	1333	22	453	314	12.8	3.75	112	.270	.331	128	.229	3	76	65	0	6.4

■ DANNY HOFFMAN
Hoffman, Daniel John b: 3/2/1880, Canaan, Conn. d: 3/14/22, Manchester, Conn. BL/TL, 5'9", 175 lbs. Deb: 4/20/03 ♦

YEAR	TM/L	W	L	PCT	G	GS	CG	SH	SV	IP	H	HR	BB	SO	RAT	ERA	ERA+	OAV	OOB	BH	AVG	PB	PR	/A	PD	TPI
1903	Phi-A	0	0	—	1	0	0	0	0	3	2	0	2	0	12.0	3.00	102	.189	.319	61	.246	0	-0	-0	-0	0.0

■ FRANK HOFFMAN
Hoffman, Frank J. "The Texas Wonder" b: Houston, Tex. Deb: 8/13/1888

YEAR	TM/L	W	L	PCT	G	GS	CG	SH	SV	IP	H	HR	BB	SO	RAT	ERA	ERA+	OAV	OOB	BH	AVG	PB	PR	/A	PD	TPI
1888	KC-a	3	9	.250	12	12	12	0	0	104	102	3	42	38	12.5	2.77	124	.247	.317	6	.154	-2	3	8	0	0.7

■ GUY HOFFMAN
Hoffman, Guy Alan b: 7/9/56, Ottawa, Ill. BL/TL, 5'9", 175 lbs. Deb: 7/04/79

YEAR	TM/L	W	L	PCT	G	GS	CG	SH	SV	IP	H	HR	BB	SO	RAT	ERA	ERA+	OAV	OOB	BH	AVG	PB	PR	/A	PD	TPI
1979	Chi-A	0	5	.000	24	0	0	0	2	30¹	30	0	23	18	16.0	5.34	80	.261	.388	0	—	0	-4	-4	0	-0.2
1980	Chi-A	1	0	1.000	23	1	0	0	0	37²	38	1	17	24	13.1	2.63	153	.268	.346	0	—	0	6	6	-1	0.5
1983	Chi-A	1	0	1.000	11	0	0	0	0	6	14	1	2	2	24.0	7.50	56	.483	.516	0	—	0	-2	-2	0	-0.1
1986	Chi-N	6	2	.750	32	8	1	0	0	84	92	6	29	47	13.2	3.86	105	.288	.351	1	.067	-1	-1	2	-1	0.0
1987	Cin-N	9	10	.474	36	22	0	0	0	158²	160	20	49	87	12.1	4.37	97	.265	.325	5	.111	-2	-5	-2	-1	-0.4
1988	Tex-A	0	0	—	11	0	0	0	0	22¹	22	5	8	9	12.5	5.24	78	.247	.316	0	—	0	-3	-3	0	-0.2
Total	6	17	17	.500	137	31	1	0	3	339	356	33	128	187	13.1	4.25	98	.274	.343	6	.100	-2	-10	-3	-3	-0.4

■ BILL HOFFMAN
Hoffman, William Joseph b: 3/3/18, Philadelphia, Pa. BL/TL, 5'9", 170 lbs. Deb: 8/13/39

YEAR	TM/L	W	L	PCT	G	GS	CG	SH	SV	IP	H	HR	BB	SO	RAT	ERA	ERA+	OAV	OOB	BH	AVG	PB	PR	/A	PD	TPI
1939	Phi-N	0	0	—	3	0	0	0	0	6	8	2	7	1	27.0	13.50	30	.333	.529	0	.000	-0	-6	-6	0	-0.5

■ JOHN HOFFORD
Hofford, John William b: 5/25/1863, Philadelphia, Pa. d: 12/16/15, Philadelphia, Pa. Deb: 9/26/1885

YEAR	TM/L	W	L	PCT	G	GS	CG	SH	SV	IP	H	HR	BB	SO	RAT	ERA	ERA+	OAV	OOB	BH	AVG	PB	PR	/A	PD	TPI
1885	Pit-a	0	3	.000	3	3	3	0	0	25	28	1	9	21	13.3	3.60	89	.271	.330	1	.125	-1	-1	-1	0	0.0
1886	Pit-a	3	6	.333	9	9	9	0	0	81	88	1	40	25	14.2	4.33	78	.264	.343	10	.294	3	-8	-8	1	-0.3
Total	2	3	9	.250	12	12	12	0	0	106	116	2	49	46	14.0	4.16	81	.266	.340	11	.262	2	-9	-10	1	-0.3

■ GEORGE HOGAN
Hogan, George A. b: 9/25/1885, Marion, Ohio d: 2/22/22, Bartlesville, Okla. BR/TR, 6', 160 lbs. Deb: 4/18/14

YEAR	TM/L	W	L	PCT	G	GS	CG	SH	SV	IP	H	HR	BB	SO	RAT	ERA	ERA+	OAV	OOB	BH	AVG	PB	PR	/A	PD	TPI
1914	KC-F	0	1	.000	4	1	0	0	0	13	12	1	7	7	13.8	4.15	74	.253	.361	0	.000	-1	-1	-2	0	-0.1

■ EDDIE HOGAN
Hogan, Robert Edward b: 4/1860, St.Louis, Mo. BR, 5'7", 153 lbs. Deb: 7/05/1882 ♦

YEAR	TM/L	W	L	PCT	G	GS	CG	SH	SV	IP	H	HR	BB	SO	RAT	ERA	ERA+	OAV	OOB	BH	AVG	PB	PR	/A	PD	TPI
1882	StL-a	0	1	.000	1	1	1	0	0	8	10	0	0	4	11.3	1.13	249	.287	.287	1	.333	0	1	1	-0	0.1

■ BRAD HOGG
Hogg, Carter Bradley b: 3/26/1888, Buena Vista, Ga. d: 4/2/35, Buena Vista, Ga. BR/TR, 6', 185 lbs. Deb: 9/01/11

YEAR	TM/L	W	L	PCT	G	GS	CG	SH	SV	IP	H	HR	BB	SO	RAT	ERA	ERA+	OAV	OOB	BH	AVG	PB	PR	/A	PD	TPI
1911	Bos-N	0	3	.000	8	3	2	0	1	25²	33	0	14	8	16.8	6.66	57	.337	.425	4	.444	1	-9	-8	0	-0.5
1912	Bos-N	1	1	.500	10	1	0	0	1	31	37	2	16	12	16.0	6.97	51	.289	.377	1	.091	-1	-12	-12	-0	-1.1
1915	Chi-N	1	0	1.000	2	2	1	1	0	13	12	1	6	0	13.2	2.08	134	.245	.339	0	.000	-0	1	1	1	0.1
1918	Phi-N	13	13	.500	29	25	17	3	1	228	201	3	61	81	10.6	2.53	119	.245	.302	18	.228	3	6	12	2	2.0
1919	Phi-N	5	12	.294	22	19	13	0	0	150¹	163	7	55	48	13.4	4.43	73	.292	.360	17	.283	3	-25	-20	-2	-1.9
Total	5	20	29	.408	71	50	33	4	3	448	446	13	152	149	12.3	3.70	85	.270	.337	40	.247	6	-40	-27	-0	-1.4

■ BILL HOGG
Hogg, William "Buffalo Bill" b: 1880, Port Huron, Mich. d: 12/8/09, New Orleans, La. BR/TR, 6', Deb: 4/25/05

YEAR	TM/L	W	L	PCT	G	GS	CG	SH	SV	IP	H	HR	BB	SO	RAT	ERA	ERA+	OAV	OOB	BH	AVG	PB	PR	/A	PD	TPI
1905	NY-A	9	13	.409	39	22	9	3	1	205	178	1	101	125	12.2	3.20	92	.235	.325	4	.060	-6	-12	-6	-6	-1.7
1906	NY-A	14	13	.519	28	25	15	3	0	206	171	5	72	107	10.6	2.93	101	.229	.297	9	.125	-5	-5	1	-5	-0.8
1907	NY-A	10	8	.556	25	21	13	0	0	166²	173	3	83	64	13.8	3.08	91	.269	.353	11	.183	-0	-10	-5	-1	-0.5
1908	NY-A	4	16	.200	24	21	6	0	0	152¹	155	4	63	72	13.1	3.01	82	.262	.337	4	.093	-3	-10	-9	-1	-1.4
Total	4	37	50	.425	116	89	43	6	1	730	677	13	319	368	12.3	3.06	92	.247	.327	28	.116	-14	-38	-20	-13	-4.4

■ CHIEF HOGSETT
Hogsett, Elon Chester b: 11/2/03, Brownell, Kan. BL/TL, 6', 190 lbs. Deb: 9/18/29

YEAR	TM/L	W	L	PCT	G	GS	CG	SH	SV	IP	H	HR	BB	SO	RAT	ERA	ERA+	OAV	OOB	BH	AVG	PB	PR	/A	PD	TPI
1929	Det-A	1	2	.333	4	4	2	1	0	28²	34	0	9	9	13.8	2.83	152	.312	.370	2	.200	-0	5	5	0	0.5
1930	Det-A	9	8	.529	33	17	4	0	1	146	174	9	63	54	15.2	5.42	88	.300	.377	17	.293	3	-13	-10	2	-0.4
1931	Det-A	3	9	.250	22	12	5	0	2	112¹	150	8	33	47	15.1	5.93	77	.324	.375	11	.234	0	-19	-17	0	-1.4
1932	Det-A	11	9	.550	47	15	7	0	7	178	201	8	66	56	13.8	3.54	133	.286	.351	14	.246	3	19	23	2	2.7
1933	Det-A	6	10	.375	45	2	0	0	9	116	137	7	56	39	15.3	4.50	96	.296	.377	8	.211	-0	-3	-2	1	0.0
1934	*Det-A	3	2	.600	26	0	0	0	3	50¹	61	4	19	23	14.4	4.29	102	.303	.367	3	.231	-0	1	1	1	0.1
1935	*Det-A	6	6	.500	40	0	0	0	5	96²	109	1	49	39	15.2	3.54	118	.288	.377	6	.261	2	10	7	3	1.1
1936	Det-A	0	1	.000	3	0	0	0	0	4	8	1	1	1	20.3	9.00	55	.400	.429	0	—	0	-2	-2	0	0.0
	StL-A	13	15	.464	39	29	10	0	1	215¹	278	15	90	67	16.0	5.52	97	.310	.383	10	.143	-2	-11	-3	1	-0.3
	Yr	13	16	.448	42	29	10	0	1	219¹	286	16	91	68	16.1	5.58	96	.312	.384	10	.114	-2	-13	-5	1	-0.3
1937	StL-A	6	19	.240	37	26	8	1	2	177¹	245	19	75	75	16.5	6.29	77	.328	.393	13	.210	-0	-33	-29	-1	-2.5
1938	Was-A	5	6	.455	31	9	1	0	3	91	107	12	36	33	14.9	6.03	75	.292	.368	7	.304	3	-13	-15	0	-1.0
1944	Det-A	0	0	—	3	0	0	0	0	6¹	7	1	4	5	18.5	0.00	—	.250	.382	0	.000	-0	2	3	-0	0.2
Total	11	63	87	.420	330	114	37	2	33	1222	1511	85	501	441	15.3	5.02	94	.305	.376	91	.226	8	-57	-42	10	-1.0

■ CAL HOGUE
Hogue, Calvin Grey b: 10/24/27, Dayton, Ohio BR/TR, 6', 185 lbs. Deb: 7/15/52

YEAR	TM/L	W	L	PCT	G	GS	CG	SH	SV	IP	H	HR	BB	SO	RAT	ERA	ERA+	OAV	OOB	BH	AVG	PB	PR	/A	PD	TPI
1952	Pit-N	1	8	.111	19	12	3	0	0	83²	79	7	68	34	16.2	4.84	82	.258	.399	6	.250	1	-10	-8	-1	-0.7
1953	Pit-N	1	1	.500	3	2	2	0	0	19	19	4	16	10	17.1	5.21	86	.250	.387	0	.000	-1	-2	-2	0	-0.1
1954	Pit-N	0	1	.000	3	2	0	0	0	11	11	1	12	7	18.8	4.91	85	.282	.451	0	.000	-0	-1	-1	0	0.0
Total	3	2	10	.167	25	16	5	0	0	113²	109	12	96	51	16.6	4.91	83	.259	.402	6	.188	0	-13	-10	-1	-0.8

■ BOBBY HOGUE
Hogue, Robert Clinton b: 4/5/21, Miami, Fla. d: 12/22/87, Miami, Fla. BR/TR, 5'10", 195 lbs. Deb: 4/24/48

YEAR	TM/L	W	L	PCT	G	GS	CG	SH	SV	IP	H	HR	BB	SO	RAT	ERA	ERA+	OAV	OOB	BH	AVG	PB	PR	/A	PD	TPI
1948	Bos-N	8	2	.800	40	1	0	0	2	86¹	88	4	19	43	11.4	3.23	119	.265	.309	2	.095	-1	7	6	-1	0.4
1949	Bos-N	2	2	.500	33	0	0	0	3	72	78	4	25	23	13.1	3.13	121	.280	.343	6	.286	1	7	5	2	0.8
1950	Bos-N	3	5	.375	36	1	0	0	7	62²	69	8	31	15	14.9	5.03	77	.280	.370	3	.231	1	-6	-8	1	-0.6
1951	Bos-N	0	0	—	3	0	0	0	0	5	4	1	3	0	12.6	5.40	68	.235	.350	1	.500	1	-1	-1	-0	0.0
	StL-A	1	1	.500	18	0	0	0	1	29²	31	1	23	11	16.4	5.16	85	.279	.403	2	.667	1	-3	-3	1	0.2
	*NY-A	1	0	1.000	7	0	0	0	0	7¹	4	0	3	2	8.6	0.00	—	.174	.269	0	—	0	3	3	0	0.3
	Yr	2	1	.667	25	0	0	0	1	37	35	1	26	13	14.8	4.14	104	.261	.381	2	.667	1	-0	1	1	0.3
1952	NY-A	3	5	.375	27	0	0	0	4	47¹	52	6	25	12	14.8	5.32	62	.294	.384	0	.273	0	-9	-11	-1	-1.0
	StL-A	0	1	.000	8	1	0	0	0	16¹	10	1	13	2	12.7	2.76	142	.179	.333	0	.000	-0	2	2	0	0.2
	Yr	3	6	.333	35	1	0	0	4	63²	62	7	38	14	14.1	4.66	74	.265	.368	0	.000	0	-7	-8	-1	-0.8
Total	5	18	16	.529	172	3	0	0	17	326²	336	25	142	108	13.4	3.97	96	.271	.356	17	.233	3	-0	-6	2	0.1

■ WALLY HOLBOROW
Holborow, Walter Albert b: 11/30/13, New York, N.Y. d: 7/14/86, Ft.Lauderdale, Fla. BR/TR, 5'11", 187 lbs. Deb: 9/27/44

YEAR	TM/L	W	L	PCT	G	GS	CG	SH	SV	IP	H	HR	BB	SO	RAT	ERA	ERA+	OAV	OOB	BH	AVG	PB	PR	/A	PD	TPI
1944	Was-A	0	0	—	1	0	0	0	0	3	0	0	2	1	6.0	0.00	—	.000	.182	0	—	0	1	1	0	0.1
1945	Was-A	1	1	.500	15	1	1	1	0	31¹	20	0	16	14	10.3	2.30	135	.189	.295	0	.000	-0	4	3	-1	0.2
1948	Phi-A	1	2	.333	5	1	0	0	0	17¹	32	1	7	3	20.3	5.71	75	.421	.470	2	.500	1	-3	-3	1	0.0
Total	3	2	3	.400	21	2	2	1	0	51²	52	1	25	18	13.4	3.31	106	.272	.356	2	.333	1	2	1	0	0.3

■ KEN HOLCOMBE
Holcombe, Kenneth Edward b: 8/23/18, Burnsville, N.C. BR/TR, 5'11.5", 169 lbs. Deb: 4/27/45

YEAR	TM/L	W	L	PCT	G	GS	CG	SH	SV	IP	H	HR	BB	SO	RAT	ERA	ERA+	OAV	OOB	BH	AVG	PB	PR	/A	PD	TPI
1945	NY-A	3	3	.500	23	2	0	0	1	55¹	45	3	27	20	11.4	1.79	194	.226	.323	2	.133	-1	10	10	-0	1.0
1948	Cin-N	0	0	—	2	0	0	0	0	2¹	3	0	2	2	11.6	7.71	51	.300	.300	0	—	0	-1	-1	0	0.0
1950	Chi-A	3	10	.231	24	15	5	0	1	96	122	6	45	37	15.7	4.59	98	.307	.378	5	.156	-2	-0	-1	0	-0.2
1951	Chi-A	11	12	.478	28	23	12	2	0	159¹	142	9	68	39	11.9	3.78	107	.241	.321	11	.250	1	6	4	3	0.8
1952	Chi-A	0	5	.000	7	7	1	0	0	35	38	3	18	12	14.9	6.17	59	.286	.379	0	.000	-1	-10	-10	1	-0.9

YEAR	TM/L	W	L	PCT	G	GS	CG	SH	SV	IP	H	HR	BB	SO	RAT	ERA	ERA+	OAV	OOB	BH	AVG	PB	PR	/A	PD	TPI
	StL-A	0	2	.000	12	1	0	0	0	21	20	1	9	7	12.4	3.86	101	.263	.341	1	.333	0	-0	0	0	0.1
	Yr	0	7	.000	19	8	1	0	0	56	58	4	27	19	13.7	5.30	71	.275	.357	0	.000	-1	-10	-10	1	-0.8
1953	Bos-A	1	0	1.000	3	0	0	0	1	6	9	0	3	1	18.0	6.00	70	.333	.400	0	.000	-0	-1	-1	0	0.0
Total	6	18	32	.360	99	48	18	2	2	375	377	25	170	118	13.2	3.98	101	.265	.345	19	.179	-3	3	2	3	0.8

■ FRED HOLDSWORTH
Holdsworth, Fredrick William b: 5/29/52, Detroit, Mich. BR/TR, 6'1", 190 lbs. Deb: 7/27/72

YEAR	TM/L	W	L	PCT	G	GS	CG	SH	SV	IP	H	HR	BB	SO	RAT	ERA	ERA+	OAV	OOB	BH	AVG	PB	PR	/A	PD	TPI
1972	Det-A	0	1	.000	2	2	0	0	0	7	13	0	2	5	19.3	12.86	24	.419	.455	1	.333	0	-8	-8	0	-0.6
1973	Det-A	0	1	.000	5	2	0	0	0	14²	13	3	6	9	11.7	6.75	61	.236	.311	0	—	0	-5	-4	-0	-0.4
1974	Det-A	0	3	.000	8	5	0	0	0	35²	40	4	14	16	13.9	4.29	89	.286	.355	0	—	0	-3	-2	-1	-0.2
1976	Bal-A	4	1	.800	16	0	0	0	2	39²	24	0	13	24	8.4	2.04	160	.179	.252	0	—	0	7	5	-0	0.5
1977	Bal-A	0	1	.000	12	0	0	0	0	14¹	17	0	16	4	21.3	6.28	60	.333	.500	0	—	0	-4	-4	-0	-0.3
	Mon-N	3	3	.500	14	6	0	0	0	42¹	35	6	18	21	11.3	3.19	119	.230	.312	0	.000	-1	3	3	0	0.2
1978	Mon-N	0	0	—	6	0	0	0	0	8²	16	3	8	1	24.9	7.27	48	.381	.480	0	—	0	-4	-4	0	-0.3
1980	Mil-A	0	0	—	9	0	0	0	0	19²	24	2	9	12	15.1	4.58	85	.286	.355	0	—	0	-1	-2	0	0.0
Total	7	7	10	.412	72	15	0	0	2	182	182	18	86	94	13.4	4.40	84	.264	.347	1	.077	-1	-13	-15	-1	-1.1

■ WALTER HOLKE
Holke, Walter Henry "Union Man" b: 12/25/1892, St.Louis, Mo. d: 10/12/54, St.Louis, Mo. BB/TL, 6'1.5", 185 lbs. Deb: 10/06/14 C◆

YEAR	TM/L	W	L	PCT	G	GS	CG	SH	SV	IP	H	HR	BB	SO	RAT	ERA	ERA+	OAV	OOB	BH	AVG	PB	PR	/A	PD	TPI
1923	Phi-N	0	0	—	1	0	0	0	0	0¹	1	0	0	0	27.0	0.00	—	.500	.500	175	.311	0	0	0	0	0.0

■ AL HOLLAND
Holland, Alfred Willis b: 8/16/52, Roanoke, Va. BR/TL, 5'11", 207 lbs. Deb: 9/05/77

YEAR	TM/L	W	L	PCT	G	GS	CG	SH	SV	IP	H	HR	BB	SO	RAT	ERA	ERA+	OAV	OOB	BH	AVG	PB	PR	/A	PD	TPI
1977	Pit-N	0	0	—	2	0	0	0	0	2¹	4	0	0	1	15.4	7.71	52	.400	.400	0	—	0	-1	-1	0	0.0
1979	SF-N	0	0	—	3	0	0	0	0	7	3	0	5	7	10.3	0.00	—	.125	.276	0	—	0	3	3	-0	0.3
1980	SF-N	5	3	.625	54	0	0	0	7	82¹	71	2	34	65	11.6	1.75	202	.233	.312	1	.200	1	17	16	0	1.9
1981	SF-N	7	5	.583	47	3	0	0	7	100²	87	4	44	78	11.9	2.41	142	.233	.317	1	.063	-1	12	11	-1	1.0
1982	SF-N	7	3	.700	58	7	0	0	5	129²	115	12	40	97	10.8	3.33	108	.231	.289	2	.059	-3	4	4	-0	0.1
1983	*Phi-N	8	4	.667	68	0	0	0	25	91²	63	8	30	100	9.1	2.26	158	.188	.255	0	.000	-1	14	13	-2	1.1
1984	Phi-N	5	10	.333	68	0	0	0	29	98¹	82	14	30	61	10.3	3.39	107	.225	.286	0	.000	-1	2	3	-2	0.0
1985	Phi-N	0	1	.000	3	0	0	0	1	4	5	0	4	1	20.3	4.50	82	.333	.474	0	—	0	-0	-0	0	0.0
	Pit-N	1	3	.250	38	0	0	0	4	58²	48	5	17	47	10.0	3.38	106	.227	.285	2	.400	2	1	1	-1	0.2
	Yr	1	4	.200	41	0	0	0	5	62²	53	5	21	48	10.6	3.45	104	.233	.298	1	.200	2	1	1	-0	0.2
	Cal-A	0	1	.000	15	0	0	0	0	24¹	17	4	10	14	10.0	1.48	278	.193	.276	0	—	0	7	7	-0	0.7
1986	NY-A	1	0	1.000	25	1	0	0	0	40²	44	5	9	37	11.7	5.09	80	.268	.306	0	—	0	-4	-5	-1	-0.5
1987	NY-A	0	0	—	3	0	0	0	0	6¹	9	1	9	5	25.6	14.21	31	.321	.486	0	—	0	-7	-7	-0	-0.5
Total	10	34	30	.531	384	11	0	0	78	646	548	55	232	513	10.9	2.98	121	.227	.296	6	.083	-2	48	46	-7	4.3

■ MUL HOLLAND
Holland, Howard Arthur b: 1/6/03, Franklin, Va. d: 2/16/69, Winchester, Va. BR/TL, 6'4", 185 lbs. Deb: 5/25/26

YEAR	TM/L	W	L	PCT	G	GS	CG	SH	SV	IP	H	HR	BB	SO	RAT	ERA	ERA+	OAV	OOB	BH	AVG	PB	PR	/A	PD	TPI
1926	Cin-N	0	0	—	3	0	0	0	0	6²	3	0	5	0	10.8	1.35	273	.136	.296	1	.500	0	2	2	1	0.3
1927	NY-N	1	0	1.000	2	0	0	0	0	2	0	0	3	0	13.5	0.00	—	.000	.333	0	—	0	1	1	0	0.1
1929	StL-N	0	1	.000	8	0	0	0	0	14¹	13	3	7	5	13.2	9.42	50	.232	.328	1	.250	0	-7	-8	-0	-0.5
Total	3	1	1	.500	13	0	0	0	0	23	16	3	15	5	12.5	6.26	69	.190	.320	2	.333	1	-5	-5	1	-0.1

■ BILL HOLLAND
Holland, William David "Dutch" b: 6/4/15, Varina, N.C. BL/TL, 6'1", 190 lbs. Deb: 9/17/39

YEAR	TM/L	W	L	PCT	G	GS	CG	SH	SV	IP	H	HR	BB	SO	RAT	ERA	ERA+	OAV	OOB	BH	AVG	PB	PR	/A	PD	TPI
1939	Was-A	0	1	.000	3	0	0	0	0	4	6	1	5	2	24.8	11.25	39	.400	.550	0	—	0	-3	-3	0	-0.2

■ ED HOLLEY
Holley, Edward Edgar b: 7/23/1899, Benton, Ky. d: 10/26/86, Paducah, Ky. BR/TR, 6'1.5", 195 lbs. Deb: 5/24/28

YEAR	TM/L	W	L	PCT	G	GS	CG	SH	SV	IP	H	HR	BB	SO	RAT	ERA	ERA+	OAV	OOB	BH	AVG	PB	PR	/A	PD	TPI
1928	Chi-N	0	0	—	13	1	0	0	0	31	31	1	16	10	14.2	3.77	102	.265	.363	0	.000	-0	1	0	-0	0.0
1932	Phi-N	11	14	.440	34	30	16	2	0	228	247	15	55	87	12.2	3.95	112	.273	.319	12	.132	-6	-2	12	-2	0.5
1933	Phi-N	13	15	.464	30	28	12	3	0	206²	219	18	62	56	12.8	3.53	108	.273	.335	12	.162	-2	-4	7	-3	0.3
1934	Phi-N	1	8	.111	15	13	2	0	0	72²	85	10	31	14	14.9	7.18	66	.294	.370	5	.208	-1	-25	-20	-1	-1.9
	Pit-N	0	3	.000	5	4	0	0	0	9¹	20	1	6	2	27.0	15.43	27	.426	.509	2	1.000	2	-12	-12	-0	-0.8
	Yr	1	11	.083	20	17	2	0	0	82	105	11	37	16	15.8	8.12	57	.309	.380	0	.000	1	-37	-32	-1	-2.7
Total	4	25	40	.385	97	76	30	5	0	547²	602	45	170	169	13.1	4.40	95	.279	.339	31	.158	-8	-42	-13	-6	-1.9

■ BUG HOLLIDAY
Holliday, James Wear b: 2/8/1867, St.Louis, Mo. d: 2/15/10, Cincinnati, Ohio BR/TR, 5'11", 151 lbs. Deb: 4/17/1889 U◆

YEAR	TM/L	W	L	PCT	G	GS	CG	SH	SV	IP	H	HR	BB	SO	RAT	ERA	ERA+	OAV	OOB	BH	AVG	PB	PR	/A	PD	TPI
1892	Cin-N	0	0	—	1	0	0	0	0	4	13	0	1	0	31.5	11.25	29	.520	.539	176	.292	0	-4	-4	0	-0.2
1896	Cin-N	0	0	—	1	0	0	0	0	1	4	0	2	0	54.0	0.00	—	.582	.676	27	.321	0	0	1	0	0.0
Total	2	0	0	—	2	0	0	0	0	5	17	0	3	0	36.0	9.00	39	.533	.574	1134	.311	1	-3	-3	0	-0.2

■ CARL HOLLING
Holling, Carl b: 7/9/1896, Dana, Cal. d: 7/18/62, Santa Rosa, Cal. BR/TR, 6'1", 172 lbs. Deb: 4/19/21

YEAR	TM/L	W	L	PCT	G	GS	CG	SH	SV	IP	H	HR	BB	SO	RAT	ERA	ERA+	OAV	OOB	BH	AVG	PB	PR	/A	PD	TPI
1921	Det-A	3	7	.300	35	11	4	0	4	136	162	8	58	38	14.8	4.30	99	.305	.378	13	.271	1	-0	-0	2	0.2
1922	Det-A	1	1	.500	5	1	0	0	0	9¹	21	1	5	2	27.0	15.43	25	.525	.596	0	.000	-0	-12	-12	0	-1.0
Total	2	4	8	.333	40	12	4	0	4	145¹	183	9	63	40	15.6	5.02	85	.320	.394	13	.260	1	-12	-12	2	-0.8

■ AL HOLLINGSWORTH
Hollingsworth, Albert Wayne "Boots" b: 2/25/08, St.Louis, Mo. BL/TL, 6', 174 lbs. Deb: 4/16/35 C

YEAR	TM/L	W	L	PCT	G	GS	CG	SH	SV	IP	H	HR	BB	SO	RAT	ERA	ERA+	OAV	OOB	BH	AVG	PB	PR	/A	PD	TPI
1935	Cin-N	6	13	.316	38	22	8	0	0	173¹	165	5	76	89	12.6	3.89	102	.243	.321	8	.148	-2	2	2	0	0.0
1936	Cin-N	9	10	.474	29	25	9	0	0	184	204	4	66	76	13.5	4.16	92	.281	.345	23	.315	7	-3	-7	-2	-0.2
1937	Cin-N	9	15	.375	43	24	11	1	5	202¹	224	8	73	74	13.3	3.91	95	.278	.339	19	.250	3	0	-4	1	0.0
1938	Cin-N	2	2	.500	9	4	1	0	0	34	43	2	12	13	14.6	7.15	51	.307	.362	3	.250	1	-13	-13	0	-1.1
	Phi-N	5	16	.238	24	21	11	1	0	174¹	177	4	77	80	13.1	3.82	102	.264	.340	15	.224	-0	-1	1	-3	-0.1
	Yr	7	18	.280	33	25	12	1	0	208¹	220	6	89	93	13.3	4.36	88	.272	.344	0	.000	1	-13	-12	-2	-1.1
1939	Phi-N	1	9	.100	15	10	3	0	0	60	78	2	27	24	15.8	5.85	69	.317	.385	2	.100	-1	-13	-12	-0	-1.2
	Bro-N	1	2	.333	8	5	1	0	0	27¹	33	1	11	11	14.8	5.27	76	.311	.381	1	.125	-1	-4	-4	1	-0.2
	Yr	2	11	.154	23	15	4	0	0	87¹	111	3	38	35	15.5	5.67	71	.315	.384	1	.036	-2	-17	-16	1	-1.4
1940	Was-A	1	0	1.000	3	2	0	0	0	18	18	0	11	7	14.5	5.50	76	.261	.363	1	.167	0	-2	-3	1	-0.1
1942	StL-A	10	6	.625	33	18	7	1	4	161	173	4	52	60	12.7	2.96	125	.272	.329	10	.179	0	12	13	0	1.4
1943	StL-A	6	13	.316	35	20	9	1	3	154	169	7	51	63	13.0	4.21	79	.281	.339	7	.140	-1	-16	-15	-1	-1.7
1944	*StL-A	5	7	.417	26	10	3	2	1	92²	108	5	37	22	14.2	4.47	81	.291	.357	2	.071	-2	-11	-9	-1	-1.0
1945	StL-A	12	9	.571	26	22	15	1	1	173¹	164	4	68	64	12.0	2.70	130	.251	.322	12	.197	1	13	16	2	2.1
1946	StL-A	0	0	—	5	0	0	0	0	11	23	1	4	3	22.1	6.55	57	.411	.450	0	.000	-0	-4	-3	-0	-0.3
	Chi-A	3	2	.600	21	2	0	0	1	55	63	4	22	22	13.9	4.58	74	.288	.353	0	.000	-1	-7	-7	-0	-0.8
	Yr	3	2	.600	26	2	0	0	1	66	86	3	26	25	15.3	4.91	71	.313	.372	1	.071	-1	-10	-11	-1	-1.1
Total	11	70	104	.402	315	185	78	7	15	1520¹	1642	47	587	608	13.3	3.99	93	.275	.341	103	.196	3	-44	-44	-1	-3.1

■ BONNIE HOLLINGSWORTH
Hollingsworth, John Burnette b: 12/26/1895, Jacksboro, Tenn. d: 1/4/90, Knoxville, Tenn. BR/TR, 5'10", 170 lbs. Deb: 5/30/22

YEAR	TM/L	W	L	PCT	G	GS	CG	SH	SV	IP	H	HR	BB	SO	RAT	ERA	ERA+	OAV	OOB	BH	AVG	PB	PR	/A	PD	TPI
1922	Pit-N	0	0	—	9	0	0	0	0	13²	17	0	8	7	17.1	7.90	52	.315	.413	0	—	0	-6	-6	-0	-0.5
1923	Was-A	3	7	.300	17	8	1	0	0	72²	72	3	50	26	15.5	4.09	92	.272	.393	2	.091	-1	-3	-3	-1	-0.4
1924	Bro-N	1	0	1.000	3	1	0	0	0	8²	8	0	10	7	18.7	6.23	60	.267	.450	0	.000	-0	-2	-2	0	-0.2
1928	Bos-N	0	2	.000	7	2	1	0	0	22¹	30	2	13	10	17.3	5.24	75	.341	.426	1	.167	-0	-3	-3	0	-0.2
Total	4	4	9	.308	36	11	2	0	0	117¹	127	5	81	50	16.3	4.91	78	.291	.406	3	.097	-2	-12	-14	-1	-1.3

■ JOHN HOLLISON
Hollison, John Henry "Swede" b: 5/3/1870, Chicago, Ill. d: 8/19/69, Chicago, Ill. BR/TL, 5'8", 162 lbs. Deb: 8/13/1892

YEAR	TM/L	W	L	PCT	G	GS	CG	SH	SV	IP	H	HR	BB	SO	RAT	ERA	ERA+	OAV	OOB	BH	AVG	PB	PR	/A	PD	TPI
1892	Chi-N	0	0	—	1	0	0	0	0	4	1	0	2	0	2.3	2.25	147	.077	.077	0	.000	-0	0	0	0	0.0

■ BOBO HOLLOMAN
Holloman, Alva Lee b: 3/7/25, Thomaston, Ga. d: 5/1/87, Athens, Ga. BR/TR, 6'2", 207 lbs. Deb: 4/18/53

YEAR	TM/L	W	L	PCT	G	GS	CG	SH	SV	IP	H	HR	BB	SO	RAT	ERA	ERA+	OAV	OOB	BH	AVG	PB	PR	/A	PD	TPI
1953	StL-A	3	7	.300	22	10	1	1	0	65¹	69	2	50	25	16.5	5.23	80	.275	.397	2	.105	-2	-9	-8	0	-0.8

JIM HOLLOWAY
Holloway, James Madison b: 9/22/08, Plaquemine, La. BR/TR, 6'1", 165 lbs. Deb: 5/17/29

YEAR TM/L	W	L	PCT	G	GS	CG	SH	SV	IP	H	HR	BB	SO	RAT	ERA	ERA+	OAV	OOB	BH	AVG	PB	PR	/A	PD	TPI
1929 Phi-N	0	0	—	3	0	0	0	0	4²	10	2	5	1	28.9	13.50	38	.455	.556	1	1.000	0	-5	-4	0	-0.2

KEN HOLLOWAY
Holloway, Kenneth Eugene (b: Kenneth Eugene Holloway) b: 8/8/1897, Thomas County, Ga. d: 9/25/68, Thomasville, Ga. BR/TR, 6', 185 lbs. Deb: 8/27/22

YEAR TM/L	W	L	PCT	G	GS	CG	SH	SV	IP	H	HR	BB	SO	RAT	ERA	ERA+	OAV	OOB	BH	AVG	PB	PR	/A	PD	TPI
1922 Det-A	0	0	—	1	0	0	0	0	1	1	0	1	0	9.0	0.00	—	.250	.250	0	—	0	0	0	0	0.0
1923 Det-A	11	10	.524	42	24	7	1	1	194	232	12	75	55	14.7	4.45	87	.302	.372	8	.123	-5	-10	-13	2	-1.4
1924 Det-A	14	6	.700	49	14	5	0	3	181¹	209	6	61	46	13.7	4.07	101	.299	.361	11	.190	-1	3	1	3	0.2
1925 Det-A	13	4	.765	38	14	6	0	2	157²	170	8	67	29	13.6	4.62	93	.282	.356	11	.229	-0	-4	-6	-1	-0.6
1926 Det-A	4	6	.400	36	12	3	0	2	139	192	2	42	43	15.7	5.12	79	.343	.397	11	.239	-0	-17	-16	0	-1.4
1927 Det-A	11	12	.478	36	23	11	1	6	183¹	210	10	61	36	13.5	4.07	103	.299	.359	8	.129	-5	1	3	2	0.0
1928 Det-A	4	8	.333	30	11	5	0	2	120¹	137	2	32	32	13.0	4.34	95	.291	.343	4	.121	-2	-4	-3	2	-0.3
1929 Cle-A	6	5	.545	25	11	6	2	0	119	118	2	37	32	11.9	3.03	147	.264	.323	7	.171	-2	16	19	-1	1.5
1930 Cle-A	1	1	.500	12	2	0	0	2	30	49	5	14	8	18.9	8.40	57	.374	.434	0	.000	-2	-13	-12	1	-1.0
NY-A	0	0	—	16	0	0	0	0	34¹	52	3	8	11	15.7	5.24	82	.374	.408	3	.231	-0	-2	-4	0	-0.3
Yr	1	1	.500	28	2	0	0	2	64¹	101	8	22	19	17.2	6.72	68	.374	.421	0	.000	-3	-15	-16	1	-1.3
Total 9	64	52	.552	285	111	43	4	18	1160	1370	50	397	293	14.0	4.40	95	.303	.364	63	.167	-18	-29	-30	6	-3.3

JEFF HOLLY
Holly, Jeffrey Owen b: 3/1/53, San Pedro, Cal. BL/TL, 6'5", 210 lbs. Deb: 5/01/77

YEAR TM/L	W	L	PCT	G	GS	CG	SH	SV	IP	H	HR	BB	SO	RAT	ERA	ERA+	OAV	OOB	BH	AVG	PB	PR	/A	PD	TPI
1977 Min-A	2	3	.400	18	5	0	0	0	48¹	57	8	12	32	13.0	6.89	58	.300	.345	0	—	0	-15	-16	-1	-1.4
1978 Min-A	1	1	.500	15	1	0	0	0	35¹	28	1	18	12	11.7	3.57	107	.222	.319	0	—	0	1	1	0	0.1
1979 Min-A	0	0	—	6	0	0	0	0	6¹	10	0	3	5	18.5	7.11	62	.385	.448	0	—	0	-2	-2	0	-0.1
Total 3	3	4	.429	39	6	0	0	0	90	95	9	33	49	12.9	5.60	70	.278	.343	0	—	0	-16	-17	-0	-1.4

BRIAN HOLMAN
Holman, Brian Scott b: 1/25/65, Denver, Colo. BR/TR, 6'4", 185 lbs. Deb: 6/25/88

YEAR TM/L	W	L	PCT	G	GS	CG	SH	SV	IP	H	HR	BB	SO	RAT	ERA	ERA+	OAV	OOB	BH	AVG	PB	PR	/A	PD	TPI
1988 Mon-N	4	8	.333	18	16	1	1	0	100¹	101	3	34	58	12.1	3.23	111	.264	.324	3	.107	-1	2	4	-1	0.2
1989 Mon-N	1	2	.333	10	3	0	0	0	31²	34	2	15	23	14.2	4.83	73	.270	.352	1	.125	-0	-5	-5	-0	-0.4
Sea-A	8	10	.444	23	22	6	2	0	159²	160	9	62	82	12.9	3.44	117	.261	.335	0	—	0	8	10	1	1.2
1990 Sea-A	11	11	.500	28	28	3	0	0	189²	188	17	66	121	12.3	4.03	98	.260	.327	0	.000	-1	-3	-2	-1	-0.2
Total 3	24	31	.436	79	69	10	3	0	481¹	483	31	177	284	12.6	3.72	104	.262	.331	4	.108	-1	3	8	-1	0.8

SCOTT HOLMAN
Holman, Randy Scott b: 9/18/58, Santa Paula, Cal. BR/TR, 6'1", 190 lbs. Deb: 9/20/80

YEAR TM/L	W	L	PCT	G	GS	CG	SH	SV	IP	H	HR	BB	SO	RAT	ERA	ERA+	OAV	OOB	BH	AVG	PB	PR	/A	PD	TPI
1980 NY-N	0	0	—	4	0	0	0	0	7	6	0	1	3	9.0	1.29	276	.250	.280	0	—	0	2	2	-0	0.2
1982 NY-N	2	1	.667	4	4	1	0	0	26²	23	2	7	11	10.1	2.36	154	.232	.283	2	.222	0	4	4	1	0.5
1983 NY-N	1	7	.125	35	10	0	0	0	101	90	7	52	44	12.7	3.74	97	.242	.336	5	.217	-1	-1	-1	2	0.1
Total 3	3	8	.273	43	14	1	0	0	134²	119	9	60	58	12.0	3.34	108	.240	.324	7	.219	1	4	4	3	0.8

SHAWN HOLMAN
Holman, Shawn Leroy b: 11/10/64, Sewickley, Pa. BR/TR, 6'2", 185 lbs. Deb: 9/05/89

YEAR TM/L	W	L	PCT	G	GS	CG	SH	SV	IP	H	HR	BB	SO	RAT	ERA	ERA+	OAV	OOB	BH	AVG	PB	PR	/A	PD	TPI
1989 Det-A	0	0	—	5	0	0	0	0	10	8	0	11	9	17.1	1.80	212	.211	.388	0	—	0	2	2	-0	0.2

DARREN HOLMES
Holmes, Darren Lee b: 4/25/66, Asheville, N.C. BR/TR, 6', 199 lbs. Deb: 9/01/90

YEAR TM/L	W	L	PCT	G	GS	CG	SH	SV	IP	H	HR	BB	SO	RAT	ERA	ERA+	OAV	OOB	BH	AVG	PB	PR	/A	PD	TPI
1990 LA-N	0	1	.000	14	0	0	0	0	17¹	15	1	11	19	13.5	5.19	69	.238	.351	0	—	0	-3	-3	-0	-0.2

CHICK HOLMES
Holmes, Elwood Marter b: 3/22/1896, Beverly, N.J. d: 4/15/54, Camden, N, J. TR, Deb: 6/27/18

YEAR TM/L	W	L	PCT	G	GS	CG	SH	SV	IP	H	HR	BB	SO	RAT	ERA	ERA+	OAV	OOB	BH	AVG	PB	PR	/A	PD	TPI
1918 Phi-A	0	0	—	2	0	0	0	0	2	4	0	2	1	27.0	13.50	22	.400	.500	0	—	0	-2	-2	0	-0.2

JIM HOLMES
Holmes, James Scott b: 8/2/1882, Lawrenceburg, Ky. d: 3/10/60, Jacksonville, Fla. Deb: 9/08/06

YEAR TM/L	W	L	PCT	G	GS	CG	SH	SV	IP	H	HR	BB	SO	RAT	ERA	ERA+	OAV	OOB	BH	AVG	PB	PR	/A	PD	TPI
1906 Phi-A	0	1	.000	3	1	1	0	0	9	10	0	8	1	18.0	4.00	68	.284	.417	3	.600	1	-1	-1	0	0.0
1908 Bro-N	1	4	.200	13	1	1	0	0	40	37	0	20	10	13.5	3.37	69	.270	.375	1	.077	-1	-4	-5	-2	-0.7
Total 2	1	5	.167	16	2	1	0	0	49	47	0	28	11	14.3	3.49	69	.273	.384	4	.222	0	-6	-6	-2	-0.7

DUCKY HOLMES
Holmes, James William b: 1/28/1869, Des Moines, Iowa d: 8/6/32, Truro, Iowa BL/TR, 5'6", 170 lbs. Deb: 8/08/1895 ♦

YEAR TM/L	W	L	PCT	G	GS	CG	SH	SV	IP	H	HR	BB	SO	RAT	ERA	ERA+	OAV	OOB	BH	AVG	PB	PR	/A	PD	TPI
1895 Lou-N	1	0	1.000	2	1	1	0	0	14	16	1	4	0	12.9	5.79	80	.283	.330	60	.373	1	-2	-2	0	0.0
1896 Lou-N	0	1	.000	2	1	0	0	0	12	26	0	8	3	25.5	7.50	58	.430	.497	38	.270	-0	-4	-4	0	-0.2
Total 2	1	1	.500	4	2	1	0	0	26	42	1	12	3	18.7	6.58	68	.359	.418	1014	.282	1	-6	-6	0	-0.2

HERM HOLSHOUSER
Holshouser, Herman Alexander b: 1/20/07, Rockwell, N.C. BR/TR, 6', 170 lbs. Deb: 4/15/30

YEAR TM/L	W	L	PCT	G	GS	CG	SH	SV	IP	H	HR	BB	SO	RAT	ERA	ERA+	OAV	OOB	BH	AVG	PB	PR	/A	PD	TPI
1930 StL-A	0	1	.000	25	1	0	0	1	62¹	103	8	28	37	19.3	7.80	63	.376	.439	2	.125	-1	-22	-20	-1	-1.7

VERN HOLTGRAVE
Holtgrave, Lavern George "Woody" b: 10/18/42, Aviston, Ill. BR/TR, 6'1", 183 lbs. Deb: 9/26/65

YEAR TM/L	W	L	PCT	G	GS	CG	SH	SV	IP	H	HR	BB	SO	RAT	ERA	ERA+	OAV	OOB	BH	AVG	PB	PR	/A	PD	TPI
1965 Det-A	0	0	—	1	0	0	0	0	3	4	0	2	2	18.0	6.00	58	.308	.400	0	—	0	-1	-1	0	0.0

BRIAN HOLTON
Holton, Brian John b: 11/29/59, McKeesport, Pa. BR/TR, 6'2", 190 lbs. Deb: 9/09/85

YEAR TM/L	W	L	PCT	G	GS	CG	SH	SV	IP	H	HR	BB	SO	RAT	ERA	ERA+	OAV	OOB	BH	AVG	PB	PR	/A	PD	TPI
1985 LA-N	1	1	.500	3	0	0	0	0	4	9	0	1	1	22.5	9.00	39	.450	.476	0	—	0	-2	-2	0	-0.1
1986 LA-N	2	3	.400	12	3	0	0	0	24¹	28	1	6	24	12.9	4.44	78	.292	.340	0	.000	-0	-2	-3	-0	-0.2
1987 LA-N	3	2	.600	53	1	0	0	2	83¹	87	11	32	58	12.9	3.89	102	.269	.335	1	.200	0	2	1	1	0.2
1988 *LA-N	7	3	.700	45	0	0	0	1	84²	69	1	26	49	10.2	1.70	196	.228	.292	0	.000	-1	16	15	0	1.6
1989 Bal-A	5	7	.417	39	12	0	0	0	116¹	140	11	39	51	13.9	4.02	94	.300	.355	0	—	0	-2	-3	-0	-0.2
1990 Bal-A	2	3	.400	33	0	0	0	0	58	68	7	21	27	13.8	4.50	85	.292	.350	0	—	0	-4	-4	1	-0.3
Total 6	20	19	.513	185	16	0	0	3	370²	401	31	125	210	12.8	3.62	102	.278	.337	1	.050	-1	8	4	2	1.0

KEN HOLTZMAN
Holtzman, Kenneth Dale b: 11/3/45, St.Louis, Mo. BR/TL, 6'2", 175 lbs. Deb: 9/04/65

YEAR TM/L	W	L	PCT	G	GS	CG	SH	SV	IP	H	HR	BB	SO	RAT	ERA	ERA+	OAV	OOB	BH	AVG	PB	PR	/A	PD	TPI
1965 Chi-N	0	0	—	3	0	0	0	0	4	2	1	3	3	11.3	2.25	164	.143	.294	0	—	0	1	1	0	0.1
1966 Chi-N	11	16	.407	34	33	9	0	0	220²	194	27	68	171	10.8	3.79	97	.235	.296	9	.123	-3	-5	-3	-3	-0.7
1967 Chi-N	9	0	1.000	12	12	3	0	0	92²	76	11	44	62	11.6	2.53	140	.222	.314	7	.200	1	9	10	0	1.3
1968 Chi-N	11	14	.440	34	32	6	3	1	215	201	17	76	151	11.8	3.35	94	.248	.317	10	.125	-2	-9	-4	1	-0.5
1969 Chi-N	17	13	.567	39	39	12	6	0	261¹	248	18	93	176	11.9	3.58	112	.247	.314	15	.150	-1	0	13	-1	1.3
1970 Chi-N	17	11	.607	39	38	15	1	0	287²	271	30	94	202	11.5	3.38	133	.248	.309	21	.200	2	21	36	0	4.1
1971 Chi-N	9	15	.375	30	29	9	3	0	195	213	18	64	143	12.9	4.48	88	.276	.333	9	.130	-0	-22	-12	-1	-1.2
1972 *Oak-A	19	11	.633	39	37	16	4	0	265¹	232	23	52	134	9.8	2.51	113	.236	.278	16	.178	1	16	10	-1	1.3
1973 *Oak-A	21	13	.618	40	40	16	4	0	297¹	275	22	66	157	10.4	2.97	120	.243	.287	0	—	0	28	19	-1	1.9
1974 *Oak-A	19	17	.528	39	38	9	3	0	255¹	273	14	51	117	11.5	3.07	108	.272	.309	0	—	0	16	7	0	0.8
1975 *Oak-A	18	14	.563	39	38	13	2	0	266¹	217	16	108	122	11.2	3.14	115	.222	.303	0	.000	0	19	14	4	1.8
1976 Bal-A	5	4	.556	13	13	6	1	0	97²	100	4	35	25	12.5	2.86	115	.271	.336	0	—	0	7	5	0	0.6
NY-A	9	7	.563	21	21	10	2	0	149	165	14	35	41	12.1	4.17	82	.283	.323	0	—	0	-11	-12	0	-1.2
Yr	14	11	.560	34	34	16	3	0	246²	265	18	70	66	12.2	3.65	92	.277	.326	0	—	0	-4	-8	1	-0.6
1977 NY-A	2	3	.400	18	11	0	0	0	71²	105	7	24	14	16.3	5.78	68	.362	.413	0	—	0	-14	-15	2	-1.1
1978 NY-A	1	0	1.000	5	3	0	0	0	17²	21	2	9	3	15.3	4.08	89	.313	.395	0	—	0	-1	-1	1	0.0
Chi-N	0	3	.000	23	6	0	0	2	53	61	10	35	36	16.5	6.11	68	.286	.390	2	.200	1	-15	-12	-1	-1.2
1979 Chi-N	6	9	.400	23	20	3	2	0	117²	133	15	53	44	14.7	4.59	90	.287	.368	10	.233	2	-11	-6	-2	-0.4
Total 15	174	150	.537	451	410	127	31	3	2867²	2787	249	910	1601	11.8	3.49	104	.255	.315	99	.163	-0	31	48	3	6.9

RICK HONEYCUTT
Honeycutt, Frederick Wayne b: 6/29/52, Chattanooga, Tenn. BL/TL, 6'1", 185 lbs. Deb: 8/24/77

YEAR TM/L	W	L	PCT	G	GS	CG	SH	SV	IP	H	HR	BB	SO	RAT	ERA	ERA+	OAV	OOB	BH	AVG	PB	PR	/A	PD	TPI
1977 Sea-A	0	1	.000	10	3	0	0	0	29	26	7	11	17	12.4	4.34	95	.239	.325	0	—	0	-1	-1	-1	0.0
1978 Sea-A	5	11	.313	26	24	4	1	0	134¹	150	12	49	50	13.5	4.89	78	.285	.349	0	—	0	-17	-16	2	-1.4
1979 Sea-A	11	12	.478	33	28	8	1	0	194	201	22	67	83	12.7	4.04	108	.268	.333	0	—	0	4	7	-1	0.6

YEAR	TM/L	W	L	PCT	G	GS	CG	SH	SV	IP	H	HR	BB	SO	RAT	ERA	ERA+	OAV	OOB	BH	AVG	PB	PR	/A	PD	TPI
1980	Sea-A	10	17	.370	30	30	9	1	0	203^1	221	22	60	79	12.6	3.94	105	.280	.333	0	—	0	2	4	0	0.4
1981	Tex-A	11	6	.647	20	20	8	2	0	127^2	120	12	17	40	9.7	3.31	105	.246	.272	0	—	0	5	2	1	0.4
1982	Tex-A	5	17	.227	30	26	4	1	0	164	201	20	54	64	14.2	5.27	73	.305	.360	0	—	0	-22	-25	2	-2.2
1983	Tex-A	14	8	.636	25	25	5	2	0	174^2	168	9	37	56	10.9	2.42	165	.262	.308	0	—	0	32	31	3	3.7
	*LA-N	2	3	.400	9	7	1	0	0	39	46	6	13	18	14.1	5.77	62	.297	.359	1	.083	-1	-9	-9	2	-0.7
1984	LA-N	10	9	.526	29	28	6	2	0	183^2	180	11	51	75	11.4	2.84	124	.258	.310	8	.143	-0	15	14	3	1.8
1985	*LA-N	8	12	.400	31	25	1	0	1	142	141	9	49	67	12.1	3.42	102	.261	.323	5	.132	0	3	1	3	0.4
1986	LA-N	11	9	.550	32	28	0	0	0	171	164	9	45	100	11.2	3.32	104	.249	.300	3	.070	0	8	3	2	0.5
1987	LA-N	2	12	.143	27	20	1	1	0	115^2	133	10	45	92	14.0	4.59	86	.278	.343	7	.233	2	-7	-8	-0	-0.6
	Oak-A	1	4	.200	7	4	0	0	0	23^2	25	3	9	10	13.7	5.32	77	.275	.353	0	—	0	-2	-3	0	-0.2
1988	*Oak-A	3	2	.600	55	0	0	0	7	79^2	74	6	25	47	11.5	3.50	108	.253	.318	0	—	0	4	2	1	1.3
1989	*Oak-A	2	2	.500	64	0	0	0	12	76^2	56	5	26	52	9.7	2.35	157	.207	.279	0	—	0	13	11	1	1.3
1990	*Oak-A	2	2	.500	63	0	0	0	7	63^1	46	2	22	38	9.8	2.70	138	.204	.278	0	.000	0	8	7	1	0.8
Total	14	97	127	.433	491	268	47	11	27	1921^2	1952	165	580	888	12.1	3.73	102	.265	.322	24	.133	2	36	19	19	5.2

■ DON HOOD
Hood, Donald Harris b: 10/16/49, Florence, S.C. BL/TL, 6'2", 180 lbs. Deb: 7/16/73

YEAR	TM/L	W	L	PCT	G	GS	CG	SH	SV	IP	H	HR	BB	SO	RAT	ERA	ERA+	OAV	OOB	BH	AVG	PB	PR	/A	PD	TPI
1973	Bal-A	3	2	.600	8	4	1	1	1	32^1	31	1	6	18	10.6	3.90	96	.256	.297	0	—	0	-0	-1	-1	0.0
1974	Bal-A	1	1	.500	20	2	0	0	1	57^1	47	1	20	26	10.5	3.45	100	.223	.290	0	—	0	1	-0	-0	0.0
1975	Cle-A	6	10	.375	29	19	2	0	0	135^1	136	16	57	51	12.8	4.39	86	.268	.342	0	—	0	-9	-9	-1	-1.0
1976	Cle-A	3	5	.375	33	6	0	0	1	77^2	89	14	41	32	15.5	4.87	72	.296	.387	0	—	0	-12	-12	1	-1.1
1977	Cle-A	2	1	.667	41	5	1	0	0	105	87	8	49	62	12.0	3.00	131	.224	.317	0	—	0	12	11	-1	1.0
1978	Cle-A	5	6	.455	36	19	1	0	0	154^2	166	13	77	73	14.2	4.48	83	.278	.361	0	—	0	-12	-13	1	-1.1
1979	Cle-A	1	0	1.000	13	0	0	0	1	22	13	1	14	7	11.5	3.68	116	.169	.304	0	—	0	1	1	0	0.2
	NY-A	3	1	.750	27	6	0	0	1	67^1	62	3	30	22	12.6	3.07	132	.252	.338	0	—	0	9	7	1	0.8
	Yr	4	1	.800	40	6	0	0	1	89^1	75	4	44	29	12.2	3.22	128	.231	.327	0	—	0	10	9	1	1.0
1980	StL-N	4	6	.400	33	8	1	0	0	82^1	90	2	34	35	13.8	3.39	109	.288	.362	4	.200	-0	2	3	1	0.4
1982	KC-A	4	0	1.000	30	3	0	0	0	66^2	71	7	22	31	12.8	3.51	116	.276	.338	0	—	0	4	4	0	0.5
1983	KC-A	2	3	.400	27	0	0	0	0	47^2	48	5	14	17	12.1	2.27	180	.273	.333	0	—	0	10	10	1	1.1
Total	10	34	35	.493	297	72	6	1	6	848^1	840	57	364	374	13.0	3.79	101	.263	.342	4	.200	-0	5	2	1	0.8

■ WALLY HOOD
Hood, Wallace James Jr. b: 9/24/25, Los Angeles, Cal. BR/TR, 6'1", 190 lbs. Deb: 9/23/49

YEAR	TM/L	W	L	PCT	G	GS	CG	SH	SV	IP	H	HR	BB	SO	RAT	ERA	ERA+	OAV	OOB	BH	AVG	PB	PR	/A	PD	TPI
1949	NY-A	0	0	—	2	0	0	0	0	2^1	0	0	1	2	3.9	0.00	—	.000	.143	0	—	0	1	1	0	0.1

■ JAY HOOK
Hook, James Wesley b: 11/18/36, Waukegan, Ill. BL/TR, 6'2", 182 lbs. Deb: 9/03/57

YEAR	TM/L	W	L	PCT	G	GS	CG	SH	SV	IP	H	HR	BB	SO	RAT	ERA	ERA+	OAV	OOB	BH	AVG	PB	PR	/A	PD	TPI
1957	Cin-N	0	1	.000	3	2	0	0	0	10	6	0	8	6	12.6	4.50	91	.176	.333	0	.000	-0	-1	-0	0	0.0
1958	Cin-N	0	1	.000	1	1	0	0	0	3	3	2	2	5	15.0	12.00	35	.250	.357	0	.000	-0	-3	-3	0	-0.2
1959	Cin-N	5	5	.500	17	15	4	0	0	79	79	11	39	37	13.8	5.13	79	.266	.357	3	.125	-1	-10	-9	-1	-0.9
1960	Cin-N	11	18	.379	36	33	10	2	0	222	222	31	73	103	12.2	4.50	85	.263	.325	6	.083	-3	-18	-17	-1	-2.0
1961	Cin-N	1	3	.250	22	5	0	0	0	62^2	83	14	22	36	15.8	7.76	52	.322	.386	2	.133	-1	-26	-26	-1	-2.4
1962	NY-N	8	19	.296	37	34	13	0	0	213^2	230	31	71	113	13.0	4.84	86	.273	.335	14	.203	-2	-21	-16	-0	-1.2
1963	NY-N	4	14	.222	41	20	3	0	1	152^2	168	21	53	89	13.6	5.48	64	.281	.348	9	.237	-3	-37	-34	-1	-3.3
1964	NY-N	0	1	.000	3	2	0	0	0	9^2	17	2	7	5	22.3	9.31	38	.395	.480	0	.000	-0	-6	-6	0	-0.5
Total	8	29	62	.319	160	112	30	2	1	752^2	808	112	275	394	13.3	5.23	75	.276	.344	34	.151	-1	-123	-110	-3	-10.5

■ BUCK HOOKER
Hooker, William Edward b: 8/28/1880, Richmond, Va. d: 7/2/29, Richmond, Va. TR , 5'6", Deb: 9/05/02

YEAR	TM/L	W	L	PCT	G	GS	CG	SH	SV	IP	H	HR	BB	SO	RAT	ERA	ERA+	OAV	OOB	BH	AVG	PB	PR	/A	PD	TPI
1902	Cin-N	0	1	.000	1	1	1	0	0	8	11	1	0	0	12.4	4.50	67	.326	.326	0	.000	-0	-2	-1	-0	-0.1
1903	Cin-N	0	0	—	1	0	0	0	0	2^1	2	0	2	0	15.4	0.00	—	.250	.400	0	.000	-0	1	1	0	0.1
Total	2	0	1	.000	2	1	1	0	0	10^1	13	1	2	0	13.1	3.48	90	.311	.343	0	.000	-1	-1	-0	-0	0.0

■ HARRY HOOPER
Hooper, Harry Bartholomew b: 8/24/1887, Bell Station, Cal. d: 12/18/74, Santa Cruz, Cal. BL/TR, 5'10", 168 lbs. Deb: 4/16/09 H♦

YEAR	TM/L	W	L	PCT	G	GS	CG	SH	SV	IP	H	HR	BB	SO	RAT	ERA	ERA+	OAV	OOB	BH	AVG	PB	PR	/A	PD	TPI
1913	Bos-A	0	0	—	1	0	0	0	0	2	2	0	1	0	13.5	0.00	—	.333	.429	169	.288	0	1	1	0	0.1

■ BOB HOOPER
Hooper, Robert Nelson b: 5/30/22, Leamington, Ont., Canada d: 3/17/80, New Brunswick, N.J BR/TR, 5'11", 195 lbs. Deb: 4/19/50

YEAR	TM/L	W	L	PCT	G	GS	CG	SH	SV	IP	H	HR	BB	SO	RAT	ERA	ERA+	OAV	OOB	BH	AVG	PB	PR	/A	PD	TPI
1950	Phi-A	15	10	.600	45	20	3	0	5	170^1	181	15	91	58	14.4	5.02	91	.272	.361	7	.125	-2	-8	-9	3	-0.6
1951	Phi-A	12	10	.545	38	23	9	0	5	189	192	13	61	64	12.2	4.38	98	.267	.327	15	.208	-1	-5	-2	1	0.0
1952	Phi-A	8	15	.348	43	14	4	0	6	144^1	158	13	68	40	14.3	5.18	76	.279	.361	8	.195	1	-24	-20	3	-1.4
1953	Cle-A	5	4	.556	43	0	0	0	7	69^1	50	4	38	16	11.7	4.02	93	.206	.318	1	.083	-0	-0	-2	1	-0.1
1954	Cle-A	0	0	—	17	0	0	0	2	34^2	39	4	16	12	14.5	4.93	74	.289	.368	0	.000	-1	-5	-5	0	-0.5
1955	Cin-N	0	2	.000	8	0	0	0	0	13	20	2	6	8	18.0	7.62	56	.357	.419	0	.000	-0	-5	-5	0	-0.4
Total	6	40	41	.494	194	57	16	0	25	620^2	640	50	280	196	13.6	4.80	87	.268	.348	31	.166	-3	-48	-42	9	-3.0

■ LEON HOOTEN
Hooten, Michael Leon b: 4/4/48, Downey, Cal. BR/TR, 5'11", 180 lbs. Deb: 4/13/74

YEAR	TM/L	W	L	PCT	G	GS	CG	SH	SV	IP	H	HR	BB	SO	RAT	ERA	ERA+	OAV	OOB	BH	AVG	PB	PR	/A	PD	TPI
1974	Oak-A	0	0	—	6	0	0	0	0	8^1	6	1	4	1	11.9	3.24	102	.207	.324	0	—	0	0	0	0	0.0

■ BURT HOOTON
Hooton, Burt Carlton b: 2/17/50, Greenville, Tex. BR/TR, 6'1", 210 lbs. Deb: 6/17/71

YEAR	TM/L	W	L	PCT	G	GS	CG	SH	SV	IP	H	HR	BB	SO	RAT	ERA	ERA+	OAV	OOB	BH	AVG	PB	PR	/A	PD	TPI
1971	Chi-N	2	0	1.000	3	3	2	1	0	21^1	8	2	10	22	7.6	2.11	186	.111	.220	0	.000	-1	3	4	-0	0.4
1972	Chi-N	11	14	.440	33	31	9	3	0	218^1	201	13	81	132	11.7	2.80	136	.246	.315	9	.125	-1	16	24	1	2.8
1973	Chi-N	14	17	.452	42	34	9	2	0	239^2	248	12	73	134	12.2	3.68	107	.270	.327	9	.129	-0	-1	7	-0	0.7
1974	Chi-N	7	11	.389	48	21	3	1	1	176^1	214	16	51	94	13.7	4.80	79	.299	.348	3	.060	-4	-23	-19	3	-1.9
1975	Chi-N	0	2	.000	3	3	0	0	0	11	18	2	4	5	18.0	8.18	47	.383	.431	0	.000	-0	-6	-5	1	-0.4
	LA-N	18	7	.720	31	30	12	4	0	223^2	172	16	64	148	9.5	2.82	131	.210	.267	9	.129	1	20	14	-2	1.4
	Yr	18	9	.667	34	33	12	4	0	234^2	190	18	68	153	9.9	3.07	111	.219	.276	4	.055	0	14	9	-1	1.0
1976	LA-N	11	15	.423	33	33	8	4	0	226^2	203	16	60	116	10.5	3.26	104	.241	.292	6	.097	-2	6	3	-1	0.0
1977	*LA-N	12	7	.632	32	31	6	2	1	223^1	184	14	60	153	10.0	2.62	146	.225	.281	11	.164	-0	32	30	-0	3.1
1978	*LA-N	19	10	.655	32	32	10	3	0	236	196	17	61	104	9.8	2.71	130	.226	.277	10	.149	1	23	21	-0	2.3
1979	LA-N	11	10	.524	29	29	12	1	0	212	191	11	63	129	10.9	2.97	122	.244	.302	11	.147	0	18	16	-1	1.5
1980	LA-N	14	8	.636	34	33	4	2	1	206^2	194	22	64	118	11.2	3.66	96	.249	.306	4	.063	-3	-1	-4	-0	-0.7
1981	*LA-N	11	6	.647	23	23	5	4	0	142^1	124	3	33	74	10.1	2.28	146	.237	.285	8	.190	2	19	16	-1	2.0
1982	LA-N	4	7	.364	21	21	2	0	0	120^2	130	5	33	51	12.3	4.03	86	.275	.325	3	.086	-1	-6	-8	1	-0.7
1983	LA-N	9	8	.529	33	27	2	0	0	160	156	11	59	87	12.2	4.22	85	.254	.321	8	.160	1	-11	-11	0	-1.0
1984	LA-N	3	6	.333	54	6	0	0	4	110	109	5	43	62	12.4	3.44	103	.263	.333	1	.071	-1	2	1	0	0.0
1985	Tex-A	5	8	.385	29	20	2	0	0	149	148	4	42	62	11.8	5.23	81	.297	.349	0	—	0	-15	-14	-1	-1.3
Total	15	151	136	.526	480	377	86	29	7	2652	2497	193	799	1491	11.3	3.38	108	.250	.306	92	.123	-9	77	77	-1	8.2

■ JOHN HOOVER
Hoover, John Nicklaus b: 11/22/62, Fresno.Cal. BR/TR, 6'2", 190 lbs. Deb: 5/23/90

YEAR	TM/L	W	L	PCT	G	GS	CG	SH	SV	IP	H	HR	BB	SO	RAT	ERA	ERA+	OAV	OOB	BH	AVG	PB	PR	/A	PD	TPI
1990	Tex-A	0	0	—	2	0	0	0	0	4^2	8	0	3	0	21.2	11.57	34	.364	.440	0	—	0	-4	-4	-0	-0.3

■ DICK HOOVER
Hoover, Richard Lloyd b: 12/11/25, Columbus, Ohio d: 4/12/81, Lake Placid, Fla. BL/TL, 6', 170 lbs. Deb: 4/16/52

YEAR	TM/L	W	L	PCT	G	GS	CG	SH	SV	IP	H	HR	BB	SO	RAT	ERA	ERA+	OAV	OOB	BH	AVG	PB	PR	/A	PD	TPI
1952	Bos-N	0	0	—	2	0	0	0	0	4^2	8	1	3	0	21.2	7.71	47	.348	.423	0	—	0	-2	-2	0	-0.1

■ SAM HOPE
Hope, Samuel b: 12/4/1878, Brooklyn, N.Y. d: 6/30/46, Greenport, N.Y. BR/TR, 5'10", Deb: 8/05/07

YEAR	TM/L	W	L	PCT	G	GS	CG	SH	SV	IP	H	HR	BB	SO	RAT	ERA	ERA+	OAV	OOB	BH	AVG	PB	PR	/A	PD	TPI
1907	Phi-A	0	0	—	1	0	0	0	0	0^1	3	0	0	0	81.0	0.00	—	.762	.762	0	—	0	0	0	0	0.0

■ PAUL HOPKINS
Hopkins, Paul Henry b: 9/25/04, Chester, Conn. BR/TR, 6', 175 lbs. Deb: 9/29/27

YEAR	TM/L	W	L	PCT	G	GS	CG	SH	SV	IP	H	HR	BB	SO	RAT	ERA	ERA+	OAV	OOB	BH	AVG	PB	PR	/A	PD	TPI
1927	Was-A	1	0	1.000	2	1	0	0	0	9	13	1	4	5	17.0	5.00	81	.361	.425	2	.667	1	-1	-1	0	0.0
1929	Was-A	0	1	.000	7	0	0	0	0	16^1	15	1	9	5	13.2	2.20	192	.250	.348	0	.000	-1	4	4	-0	0.3

YEAR TM/L	W	L	PCT	G	GS	CG	SH	SV	IP	H	HR	BB	SO	RAT	ERA	ERA+	OAV	OOB	BH	AVG	PB	PR	/A	PD	TPI
StL-A	0	0	—	2	0	0	0	0	2	0	0	2	1	9.0	0.00	—	.000	.286	0	—	0	1	1	0	0.1
Yr	0	1	.000	9	0	0	0	0	18¹	15	1	11	6	12.8	1.96	217	.231	.342	0	.000	-1	5	5	-0	0.4
Total 2	1	1	.500	11	1	0	0	0	27¹	28	2	15	11	14.2	2.96	142	.277	.371	2	.333	1	4	4	0	0.4

■ LEFTY HOPPER
Hopper, C. F.   b: Ridgewood, N.J.   TL ,   Deb: 10/10/1898

YEAR TM/L	W	L	PCT	G	GS	CG	SH	SV	IP	H	HR	BB	SO	RAT	ERA	ERA+	OAV	OOB	BH	AVG	PB	PR	/A	PD	TPI
1898 Bro-N	0	2	.000	2	2	2	0	0	11	14	0	5	5	15.5	4.91	73	.307	.376	0	.000	-1	-2	-2	1	-0.1

■ JIM HOPPER
Hopper, James McDaniel   b: 9/1/19, Charlotte, N.C.   d: 1/23/82, Charlotte, N.C.   BR/TR, 6'1", 175 lbs.   Deb: 4/21/46

YEAR TM/L	W	L	PCT	G	GS	CG	SH	SV	IP	H	HR	BB	SO	RAT	ERA	ERA+	OAV	OOB	BH	AVG	PB	PR	/A	PD	TPI
1946 Pit-N	0	1	.000	2	1	0	0	0	4	6	1	3	1	20.3	11.25	31	.316	.409	0	—	0	-3	-3	0	-0.2

■ BILL HOPPER
Hopper, William Booth "Bird Dog"   b: 10/26/1890, Jackson, Tenn.   d: 1/14/65, Allen Park, Mich.   BR/TR, 6', 175 lbs.   Deb: 9/11/13

YEAR TM/L	W	L	PCT	G	GS	CG	SH	SV	IP	H	HR	BB	SO	RAT	ERA	ERA+	OAV	OOB	BH	AVG	PB	PR	/A	PD	TPI
1913 StL-N	0	3	.000	3	3	2	0	0	24	20	2	8	3	11.6	3.75	86	.230	.316	3	.375	1	-1	-1	0	0.0
1914 StL-N	0	0	—	3	0	0	0	0	5	6	0	5	1	19.8	3.60	78	.286	.423	0	—	0	-0	-0	0	0.0
1915 Was-A	0	1	.000	13	0	0	0	1	31¹	39	0	16	8	16.1	4.60	64	.348	.434	1	.200	0	-6	-6	1	-0.4
Total 3	0	4	.000	19	3	2	0	1	60¹	65	2	29	12	14.6	4.18	73	.295	.387	4	.308	1	-8	-8	1	-0.4

■ JOHN HORAN
Horan, John J.   b: 1863, Ireland   d: 12/21/05, Chicago, Ill.   Deb: 5/17/1884

YEAR TM/L	W	L	PCT	G	GS	CG	SH	SV	IP	H	HR	BB	SO	RAT	ERA	ERA+	OAV	OOB	BH	AVG	PB	PR	/A	PD	TPI
1884 CP-U	3	6	.333	13	10	9	0	0	98	94	0	24	55	10.8	3.49	86	.236	.279	6	.088	-5	-5	-5	-0	-1.0

■ JOE HORLEN
Horlen, Joel Edward   b: 8/14/37, San Antonio, Tex.   BR/TR, 6', 170 lbs.   Deb: 9/04/61

YEAR TM/L	W	L	PCT	G	GS	CG	SH	SV	IP	H	HR	BB	SO	RAT	ERA	ERA+	OAV	OOB	BH	AVG	PB	PR	/A	PD	TPI
1961 Chi-A	1	3	.250	5	4	0	0	0	17²	25	3	13	11	19.4	6.62	59	.338	.437	0	.000	-1	-5	-5	0	-0.4
1962 Chi-A	7	6	.538	20	19	5	1	0	108²	108	10	43	63	12.7	4.89	80	.262	.335	2	.053	-3	-11	-12	2	-1.1
1963 Chi-A	11	7	.611	33	21	3	0	0	124	122	10	55	61	13.0	3.27	107	.261	.341	9	.225	1	5	3	2	0.6
1964 Chi-A	13	9	.591	32	28	9	2	0	210²	142	11	55	138	**8.6**	1.88	184	**.190**	**.250**	11	.159	-1	41	37	3	4.4
1965 Chi-A	13	13	.500	34	34	7	4	0	219	203	16	39	125	10.1	2.88	111	.245	.281	9	.132	0	14	8	0	0.8
1966 Chi-A	10	13	.435	37	29	4	2	1	211	185	14	53	124	10.4	2.43	130	.233	.286	4	.067	-3	24	17	6	2.2
1967 Chi-A	19	7	**.731**	35	35	13	**6**	0	258	188	13	58	103	**8.7**	2.06	151	.203	**.253**	14	.169	1	**34**	**30**	4	**3.9**
1968 Chi-A	12	14	.462	35	35	4	1	0	223²	197	16	70	102	11.3	2.37	127	.238	.308	7	.104	-1	15	16	2	2.1
1969 Chi-A	13	16	.448	36	35	7	2	0	235²	237	20	77	121	12.2	3.78	102	.261	.323	14	.182	-1	-4	2	-1	0.1
1970 Chi-A	6	16	.273	28	26	4	0	0	172¹	198	18	41	77	12.7	4.86	80	.287	.331	6	.115	-2	-22	-18	4	-1.5
1971 Chi-A	8	9	.471	34	18	3	0	2	137¹	150	12	30	82	12.1	4.26	84	.284	.329	4	.100	-2	-12	-10	1	-1.1
1972 *Oak-A	3	4	.429	32	6	0	0	1	84	74	3	20	58	10.5	3.00	95	.236	.291	3	.176	-0	1	-1	0	0.0
Total 12	116	117	.498	361	290	59	18	4	2002	1829	145	554	1065	11.0	3.11	109	.243	.300	83	.134	-12	78	66	24	10.0

■ TRADER HORNE
Horne, Berlyn Dale "Sonny"   b: 4/12/1899, Bachman, Ohio   d: 2/3/83, Franklin, Ohio   BB/TL, 5'9", 155 lbs.   Deb: 4/24/29

YEAR TM/L	W	L	PCT	G	GS	CG	SH	SV	IP	H	HR	BB	SO	RAT	ERA	ERA+	OAV	OOB	BH	AVG	PB	PR	/A	PD	TPI
1929 Chi-N	1	1	.500	11	1	0	0	0	23	24	3	21	6	17.6	5.09	91	.273	.413	2	.400	1	-1	-1	0	0.0

■ JACK HORNER
Horner, William Frank   b: 9/21/1863, Baltimore, Md.   d: 7/14/10, New Orleans, La.   Deb: 5/07/1894

YEAR TM/L	W	L	PCT	G	GS	CG	SH	SV	IP	H	HR	BB	SO	RAT	ERA	ERA+	OAV	OOB	BH	AVG	PB	PR	/A	PD	TPI
1894 Bal-N	0	1	.000	2	1	1	0	1	11	15	0	7	2	18.0	9.00	61	.321	.410	1	.167	-0	-4	-4	0	-0.2

■ JOE HORNUNG
Hornung, Michael Joseph "Ubbo Ubbo"   b: 6/12/1857, Carthage, N.Y.   d: 10/30/31, Howard Beach, N.Y.   BR/TR, 5'8.5", 164 lbs.   Deb: 5/01/1879   U♦

YEAR TM/L	W	L	PCT	G	GS	CG	SH	SV	IP	H	HR	BB	SO	RAT	ERA	ERA+	OAV	OOB	BH	AVG	PB	PR	/A	PD	TPI
1880 Buf-N	0	0	—	1	0	0	0	0	3	2	0	1	0	9.0	6.00	41	.180	.247	91	.266	0	-1	-1	0	0.0

■ HANSON HORSEY
Horsey, Hanson   b: 11/26/1889, Galena, Md.   d: 12/1/49, Millington, Md.   BR/TR, 5'11", 165 lbs.   Deb: 4/27/12

YEAR TM/L	W	L	PCT	G	GS	CG	SH	SV	IP	H	HR	BB	SO	RAT	ERA	ERA+	OAV	OOB	BH	AVG	PB	PR	/A	PD	TPI
1912 Cin-N	0	0	—	1	0	0	0	0	4	14	0	3	0	38.3	22.50	15	.583	.630	0	.000	-0	-8	-9	-0	-0.5

■ OSCAR HORSTMANN
Horstmann, Oscar Theodore   b: 6/2/1891, Alma, Mo.   d: 5/11/77, Salina, Kan.   BR/TR, 5'11", 165 lbs.   Deb: 4/18/17

YEAR TM/L	W	L	PCT	G	GS	CG	SH	SV	IP	H	HR	BB	SO	RAT	ERA	ERA+	OAV	OOB	BH	AVG	PB	PR	/A	PD	TPI
1917 StL-N	9	4	.692	35	11	4	1	1	138²	111	5	54	50	11.0	3.44	78	.225	.307	9	.196	0	-11	-12	-0	-1.2
1918 StL-N	0	2	.000	9	2	0	0	0	23	29	0	14	6	16.8	5.48	49	.349	.443	0	.000	-0	-7	-7	1	-0.6
1919 StL-N	0	1	.000	6	2	0	0	0	15	14	0	12	5	15.6	3.00	93	.264	.400	1	.500	0	-0	-0	0	0.0
Total 3	9	7	.563	50	15	4	1	1	176²	154	5	80	61	12.1	3.67	74	.245	.334	10	.192	1	-18	-19	1	-1.8

■ ELMER HORTON
Horton, Elmer E. "Herky Jerky"   b: 9/4/1869, Hamilton, Ohio   d: 8/12/20, Vienna, N.Y.   Deb: 9/24/1896

YEAR TM/L	W	L	PCT	G	GS	CG	SH	SV	IP	H	HR	BB	SO	RAT	ERA	ERA+	OAV	OOB	BH	AVG	PB	PR	/A	PD	TPI
1896 Pit-N	0	2	.000	2	2	2	0	0	15	22	0	9	3	18.6	9.60	44	.338	.419	0	.000	-1	-9	-9	-1	-0.7
1898 Bro-N	0	1	.000	1	1	1	0	0	9	16	0	6	0	22.0	10.00	36	.383	.460	1	.250	-0	-6	-6	0	-0.4
Total 2	0	3	.000	3	3	3	0	0	24	38	0	15	3	19.9	9.75	41	.356	.435	1	.091	-1	-15	-15	-1	-1.1

■ RICKY HORTON
Horton, Ricky Neal   b: 7/30/59, Poughkeepsie, N.Y.   BL/TL, 6'2", 195 lbs.   Deb: 4/07/84

YEAR TM/L	W	L	PCT	G	GS	CG	SH	SV	IP	H	HR	BB	SO	RAT	ERA	ERA+	OAV	OOB	BH	AVG	PB	PR	/A	PD	TPI
1984 StL-N	9	4	.692	37	18	1	1	1	125²	140	14	39	76	12.9	3.44	101	.285	.339	2	.065	-2	2	0	3	0.2
1985 *StL-N	3	2	.600	49	3	0	0	1	89²	84	5	34	59	12.1	2.91	121	.251	.326	1	.063	-0	7	6	2	0.8
1986 StL-N	4	3	.571	42	9	1	0	3	100¹	77	7	26	49	9.3	2.24	162	.218	.273	1	.056	0	16	16	2	1.8
1987 *StL-N	8	3	.727	67	6	0	0	7	125	127	15	42	55	12.2	3.82	109	.263	.323	5	.172	-1	4	5	3	0.8
1988 Chi-A	6	10	.375	52	9	1	0	2	109¹	120	6	36	28	13.3	4.86	82	.291	.355	0	—	0	-11	-11	-2	-0.8
*LA-N	1	1	.500	12	0	0	0	0	9	11	2	2	8	13.0	5.00	67	.306	.342	0	—	0	-2	-2	1	0.0
1989 LA-N	0	0	—	23	0	0	0	0	26²	35	1	11	12	15.9	5.06	67	.343	.412	0	.000	0	-5	-5	0	-0.4
StL-N	0	3	.000	11	8	0	0	0	45²	50	2	10	14	12.4	4.73	77	.282	.332	3	.273	1	-6	-6	1	-0.3
Yr	0	3	.000	34	8	0	0	0	72¹	85	3	21	26	13.6	4.85	73	.301	.356	3	.000	1	-11	-10	1	-0.7
1990 StL-N	1	1	.500	32	0	0	0	1	42	52	3	22	18	16.1	4.93	79	.315	.399	0	.000	-0	-5	-5	2	-0.2
Total 7	32	27	.542	325	53	3	1	15	673¹	696	55	222	319	12.5	3.76	100	.273	.334	12	.109	-1	0	-1	13	1.9

■ DAVE HOSKINS
Hoskins, David Taylor   b: 8/3/25, Greenwood, Miss.   d: 4/2/70, Flint, Mich.   BL/TR, 6'1", 180 lbs.   Deb: 4/18/53

YEAR TM/L	W	L	PCT	G	GS	CG	SH	SV	IP	H	HR	BB	SO	RAT	ERA	ERA+	OAV	OOB	BH	AVG	PB	PR	/A	PD	TPI
1953 Cle-A	9	3	.750	26	7	3	0	1	112²	102	9	38	55	11.5	3.99	94	.243	.312	15	.259	4	0	-3	0	0.1
1954 Cle-A	0	1	.000	14	1	0	0	0	26²	29	3	10	9	13.2	3.04	121	.284	.348	0	.000	-1	2	2	0	0.1
Total 2	9	4	.692	40	8	3	0	1	139¹	131	12	48	64	11.8	3.81	98	.251	.319	15	.227	3	2	-1	0	0.2

■ GENE HOST
Host, Eugene Earl "Twinkles" or "Slick"   b: 1/1/33, Leeper, Pa.   BB/TL, 5'11", 190 lbs.   Deb: 9/16/56

YEAR TM/L	W	L	PCT	G	GS	CG	SH	SV	IP	H	HR	BB	SO	RAT	ERA	ERA+	OAV	OOB	BH	AVG	PB	PR	/A	PD	TPI
1956 Det-A	0	0	—	1	1	0	0	0	4²	9	2	2	5	21.2	7.71	53	.409	.458	0	.000	-0	-2	-2	-0	-0.1
1957 KC-A	0	2	.000	11	2	0	0	0	23²	29	5	14	9	16.4	7.23	55	.315	.406	0	.000	-1	-9	-9	0	-0.8
Total 2	0	2	.000	12	3	0	0	0	28¹	38	7	16	14	17.2	7.31	55	.333	.415	0	.000	-1	-11	-10	0	-0.9

■ BYRON HOUCK
Houck, Byron Simon "Duke"   b: 8/28/1891, Prosper, Minn.   d: 6/17/69, Santa Cruz, Cal.   BR/TR, 6', 175 lbs.   Deb: 5/15/12

YEAR TM/L	W	L	PCT	G	GS	CG	SH	SV	IP	H	HR	BB	SO	RAT	ERA	ERA+	OAV	OOB	BH	AVG	PB	PR	/A	PD	TPI
1912 Phi-A	8	8	.500	30	17	10	0	1	180²	148	9	74	75	11.7	2.94	105	.234	.326	4	.065	-6	8	3	-0	-0.3
1913 Phi-A	14	6	.700	41	19	4	1	0	176	147	3	122	71	14.1	4.14	67	.214	.337	5	.083	-4	-24	-27	-1	-3.2
1914 Phi-A	0	0	—	3	3	0	0	0	11	14	0	6	4	16.4	3.27	80	.318	.400	1	.333	0	-1	-1	0	0.0
Bro-F	2	6	.250	17	9	3	0	0	92	95	4	43	45	13.3	3.13	102	.272	.355	7	.233	2	1	1	-3	0.0
1918 StL-A	2	4	.333	27	2	0	0	2	71²	58	0	29	29	10.9	2.39	115	.225	.303	3	.150	-1	3	3	-1	0.2
Total 4	26	24	.520	118	50	17	1	3	531¹	462	8	274	224	12.8	3.30	89	.234	.334	20	.114	-8	-13	-21	-5	-3.3

■ CHARLIE HOUGH
Hough, Charles Oliver   b: 1/5/48, Honolulu, Hawaii   BR/TR, 6'2", 190 lbs.   Deb: 8/12/70

YEAR TM/L	W	L	PCT	G	GS	CG	SH	SV	IP	H	HR	BB	SO	RAT	ERA	ERA+	OAV	OOB	BH	AVG	PB	PR	/A	PD	TPI
1970 LA-N	0	0	—	8	0	0	0	2	17	18	7	11	8	15.4	5.29	72	.265	.367	1	.333	0	-2	-3	0	-0.1
1971 LA-N	0	0	—	4	0	0	0	0	4¹	3	1	3	4	12.5	4.15	78	.200	.333	0	—	0	-0	-0	0	0.0
1972 LA-N	0	0	—	2	0	0	0	0	2²	2	0	2	4	16.9	3.38	99	.200	.385	0	—	0	-0	-0	0	0.0
1973 LA-N	4	2	.667	37	0	0	0	5	71²	52	3	45	70	12.9	2.76	124	.207	.341	3	.214	0	7	5	0	0.6
1974 *LA-N	9	4	.692	49	0	0	0	6	96	65	9	40	63	10.2	3.75	91	.196	.296	1	.000	0	-4	-0	0	-0.4
1975 LA-N	3	7	.300	38	0	0	0	4	61	43	3	34	34	11.5	2.95	115	.195	.323	2	.333	0	5	3	0	0.3
1976 LA-N	12	8	.600	77	0	0	0	18	142²	102	6	77	81	11.8	2.21	153	.200	.314	6	.286	2	**20**	**19**	-1	2.1

YEAR	TM/L	W	L	PCT	G	GS	CG	SH	SV	IP	H	HR	BB	SO	RAT	ERA	ERA+	OAV	OOB	BH	AVG	PB	PR	/A	PD	TPI
1977	*LA-N	6	12	.333	70	1	0	0	22	127¹	98	10	70	105	12.4	3.32	115	.213	.326	4	.182	1	8	7	-1	0.7
1978	*LA-N	5	5	.500	55	0	0	0	7	93¹	69	6	48	66	11.8	3.28	107	.205	.313	4	.333	1	3	2	-0	0.3
1979	LA-N	7	5	.583	42	14	0	0	0	151¹	152	16	66	76	13.4	4.76	76	.264	.348	6	.158	-0	-17	-19	0	-1.8
1980	LA-N	1	3	.250	19	1	0	0	1	32¹	37	4	21	25	16.7	5.57	63	.291	.400	1	.500	0	-7	-7	-1	-0.7
	Tex-A	2	2	.500	16	2	2	1	0	61¹	54	2	37	47	13.8	3.96	98	.240	.355	0	—	-1	0	-0	-1	0.0
1981	Tex-A	4	1	.800	21	5	2	0	1	82	61	4	31	69	10.4	2.96	117	.207	.290	0	—	0	6	5	0	0.4
1982	Tex-A	16	13	.552	34	34	12	2	0	228	217	21	72	128	11.7	3.95	98	.251	.314	0	—	0	3	-2	1	0.0
1983	Tex-A	15	13	.536	34	33	11	3	0	252	219	22	95	152	11.3	3.18	126	.238	.311	0	—	0	25	23	4	2.8
1984	Tex-A	16	14	.533	36	36	17	1	0	266	260	26	94	164	12.3	3.76	110	.255	.324	0	—	0	7	12	3	1.5
1985	Tex-A	14	16	.467	34	34	14	1	0	250¹	198	23	83	141	10.4	3.31	128	.215	.285	0	—	0	23	26	1	2.7
1986	Tex-A	17	10	.630	33	33	7	2	0	230¹	188	32	89	146	11.2	3.79	113	.221	.302	0	—	0	10	13	1	1.4
1987	Tex-A	18	13	.581	40	40	13	0	0	285¹	238	36	124	223	12.0	3.79	118	.223	.314	0	—	0	21	22	3	2.5
1988	Tex-A	15	16	.484	34	34	10	0	0	252	202	20	126	174	12.1	3.32	123	.221	.324	0	—	0	18	21	4	2.6
1989	Tex-A	10	13	.435	30	30	5	1	0	182	168	28	95	94	13.3	4.35	91	.245	.342	0	—	0	-9	-8	-1	-0.8
1990	Tex-A	12	12	.500	32	32	5	0	0	218²	190	24	119	114	13.2	4.07	98	.235	.342	0	—	0	-4	-2	0	-0.1
Total	21	186	169	.524	745	329	98	11	61	3107²	2636	306	1382	1988	12.0	3.63	109	.230	.320	27	.208	4	116	111	12	14.0

■ PAT HOUSE

House, Patrick Lory b: 9/1/40, Boise, Idaho BL/TL, 6'3", 185 lbs. Deb: 9/06/67

YEAR	TM/L	W	L	PCT	G	GS	CG	SH	SV	IP	H	HR	BB	SO	RAT	ERA	ERA+	OAV	OOB	BH	AVG	PB	PR	/A	PD	TPI
1967	Hou-N	1	0	1.000	6	0	0	0	1	4	3	0	0	2	9.0	4.50	74	.214	.267	0	—	0	-1	-1	0	0.0
1968	Hou-N	1	1	.500	18	0	0	0	0	16¹	21	0	6	6	16.0	7.71	38	.323	.397	0	—	0	-9	-9	0	-0.9
Total	2	2	1	.667	24	0	0	0	1	20¹	24	0	6	8	14.6	7.08	43	.304	.375	0	—	0	-9	-9	0	-0.9

■ TOM HOUSE

House, Thomas Ross b: 4/29/47, Seattle, Wash. BL/TL, 5'11", 190 lbs. Deb: 6/23/71 C

YEAR	TM/L	W	L	PCT	G	GS	CG	SH	SV	IP	H	HR	BB	SO	RAT	ERA	ERA+	OAV	OOB	BH	AVG	PB	PR	/A	PD	TPI
1971	Atl-N	1	0	1.000	11	0	0	0	0	20²	20	2	3	11	10.5	3.05	122	.263	.300	2	.400	1	1	2	0	0.2
1972	Atl-N	0	0	—	8	0	0	0	2	9¹	7	1	6	7	13.5	2.89	131	.226	.368	0	.000	-0	1	1	0	0.1
1973	Atl-N	4	2	.667	52	0	0	0	4	67¹	58	13	31	42	12.2	4.68	84	.243	.335	2	.200	0	-8	-6	-0	-0.5
1974	Atl-N	6	2	.750	56	0	0	0	11	102²	74	5	27	64	9.1	1.93	196	.203	.264	4	.400	1	19	21	1	2.5
1975	Atl-N	7	7	.500	58	0	0	0	11	79¹	79	4	36	36	13.3	3.18	119	.262	.344	1	.111	-0	4	5	1	0.6
1976	Bos-A	1	3	.250	36	0	0	0	4	43²	39	4	19	27	12.4	4.33	90	.241	.328	0	—	0	-4	-2	1	0.0
1977	Bos-A	1	0	1.000	8	0	0	0	0	7²	15	0	6	6	24.7	12.91	35	.405	.488	0	—	0	-8	-7	-0	-0.6
	Sea-A	4	5	.444	26	11	1	0	1	89¹	94	12	19	39	11.8	3.93	105	.268	.313	0	—	0	1	2	-1	0.1
	Yr	5	5	.500	34	11	1	0	1	97	109	12	25	45	12.8	4.64	89	.281	.331	0	—	0	-6	-5	-1	-0.5
1978	Sea-A	5	4	.556	34	9	3	0	0	116	130	10	35	29	13.2	4.66	82	.289	.347	0	—	0	-12	-11	0	-1.0
Total	8	29	23	.558	289	31	4	0	33	536	516	49	182	261	12.1	3.79	102	.256	.324	9	.257	2	-5	1	1	1.4

■ FRED HOUSE

House, Willard Edwin b: 10/3/1890, Cabool, Mo. d: 11/16/23, Kansas City, Mo. BR/TR, 6'3", 190 lbs. Deb: 4/22/13

YEAR	TM/L	W	L	PCT	G	GS	CG	SH	SV	IP	H	HR	BB	SO	RAT	ERA	ERA+	OAV	OOB	BH	AVG	PB	PR	/A	PD	TPI
1913	Det-A	1	2	.333	19	2	0	0	0	53²	64	1	17	16	13.9	5.20	56	.325	.384	0	.000	-1	-14	-14	1	-1.3

■ CHARLIE HOUSEHOLDER

Householder, Charles F. b: 1856, Harrisburg, Pa. 5'7", 150 lbs. Deb: 4/20/1884 ♦

YEAR	TM/L	W	L	PCT	G	GS	CG	SH	SV	IP	H	HR	BB	SO	RAT	ERA	ERA+	OAV	OOB	BH	AVG	PB	PR	/A	PD	TPI
1884	CP-U	0	0	—	2	0	0	0	0	3	4	0	0	3	12.0	3.00	101	.300	.300	74	.239	0	0	0	0	0.0

■ FRANK HOUSEMAN

Houseman, Frank b: Holland Deb: 9/02/1886

YEAR	TM/L	W	L	PCT	G	GS	CG	SH	SV	IP	H	HR	BB	SO	RAT	ERA	ERA+	OAV	OOB	BH	AVG	PB	PR	/A	PD	TPI
1886	Bal-a	0	1	.000	1	1	1	0	0	8	6	0	1	5	7.9	3.38	101	.199	.224	1	.250	-0	0	0	0	0.0

■ JOE HOUSER

Houser, Joseph William b: 7/3/1891, Steubenville, Ohio d: 1/3/53, Orlando, Fla. BL/TL, 5'9.5", 160 lbs. Deb: 4/24/14

YEAR	TM/L	W	L	PCT	G	GS	CG	SH	SV	IP	H	HR	BB	SO	RAT	ERA	ERA+	OAV	OOB	BH	AVG	PB	PR	/A	PD	TPI
1914	Buf-F	0	1	.000	7	2	0	0	0	23	21	1	20	6	16.0	5.48	60	.251	.395	1	.143	-0	-6	-6	1	-0.4

■ ART HOUTTEMAN

Houtteman, Arthur Joseph b: 8/7/27, Detroit, Mich. BR/TR, 6'2", 188 lbs. Deb: 4/29/45

YEAR	TM/L	W	L	PCT	G	GS	CG	SH	SV	IP	H	HR	BB	SO	RAT	ERA	ERA+	OAV	OOB	BH	AVG	PB	PR	/A	PD	TPI
1945	Det-A	0	2	.000	13	0	0	0	0	25¹	27	1	11	9	13.9	5.33	66	.270	.348	0	.000	-1	-6	-5	1	-0.4
1946	Det-A	0	1	.000	1	1	0	0	0	8	15	1	0	2	16.9	9.00	41	.385	.385	1	.500	0	-5	-5	0	-0.3
1947	Det-A	7	2	.778	23	9	7	2	0	110²	106	6	36	58	11.6	3.42	110	.247	.306	12	.300	2	4	4	-0	0.6
1948	Det-A	2	16	.111	43	20	4	0	10	164¹	186	11	52	74	13.1	4.66	94	.287	.342	11	.196	-2	-7	-5	-4	-0.2
1949	Det-A	15	10	.600	34	25	13	2	0	203²	227	19	59	85	12.9	3.71	112	.282	.335	19	.244	1	11	10	5	1.6
1950	Det-A	19	12	.613	41	34	21	4	4	274²	257	29	99	88	11.9	3.54	132	.251	.322	14	.151	-3	32	35	3	3.5
1952	Det-A	8	20	.286	35	28	10	2	1	221	218	19	65	109	11.7	4.36	87	.253	.309	7	.101	-5	-17	-14	1	-1.2
1953	Det-A	2	6	.250	16	9	3	1	1	68²	87	11	29	28	15.7	5.90	69	.309	.381	3	.158	-0	-15	-14	-0	-1.2
	Cle-A	7	7	.500	22	13	6	1	3	109	113	4	25	40	11.8	3.80	99	.269	.318	5	.147	-1	2	-1	0	-0.1
	Yr	9	13	.409	38	22	9	2	4	177²	200	15	54	68	13.1	4.61	84	.283	.339	1	.019	-1	-12	-15	0	-1.3
1954	*Cle-A	15	7	.682	32	25	11	1	0	188	198	14	59	68	12.4	3.35	110	.273	.330	18	.277	5	8	7	2	1.4
1955	Cle-A	10	6	.625	35	12	3	1	0	124¹	126	15	44	53	12.5	3.98	100	.265	.330	6	.158	-1	-0	0	3	0.0
1956	Cle-A	2	2	.500	22	4	0	0	1	46²	60	5	31	19	18.3	6.56	64	.317	.424	2	.167	-1	-12	-12	0	-1.0
1957	Cle-A	0	0	—	3	0	0	0	0	4	6	1	3	3	20.3	6.75	55	.353	.450	0	—	0	-1	-1	-0	-0.1
	Bal-A	0	0	—	5	1	0	0	0	6²	20	0	3	3	31.1	17.55	20	.513	.548	1	.500	0	-10	-10	0	-0.8
	Yr	0	0	—	8	1	0	0	0	10²	26	1	6	6	27.0	13.50	27	.464	.516	0	.000	0	-12	-12	0	-0.9
Total	12	87	91	.489	325	181	78	14	20	1555	1646	136	516	639	12.7	4.14	99	.272	.333	99	.193	-4	-16	-11	19	1.6

■ ED HOVLIK

Hovlik, Edward Charles b: 8/20/1891, Cleveland, Ohio d: 3/19/55, Painesville, Ohio BR/TR, 6', 180 lbs. Deb: 7/14/18

YEAR	TM/L	W	L	PCT	G	GS	CG	SH	SV	IP	H	HR	BB	SO	RAT	ERA	ERA+	OAV	OOB	BH	AVG	PB	PR	/A	PD	TPI
1918	Was-A	2	1	.667	8	1	1	0	0	28	25	0	10	10	11.3	1.29	212	.272	.343	1	.125	-1	5	4	-0	0.4
1919	Was-A	0	0	—	3	0	0	0	0	5²	12	0	9	3	33.4	12.71	25	.480	.618	0	.000	-0	-6	-6	0	-0.5
Total	2	2	1	.667	11	2	1	0	0	33²	37	0	19	13	15.0	3.21	88	.316	.412	1	.100	-1	-1	-1	0	-0.1

■ JOE HOVLIK

Hovlik, Joseph b: 8/16/1884, Czechoslovakia d: 11/3/51, Oxford Junction, Ia BR/TR, 5'10.5", 194 lbs. Deb: 7/10/09

YEAR	TM/L	W	L	PCT	G	GS	CG	SH	SV	IP	H	HR	BB	SO	RAT	ERA	ERA+	OAV	OOB	BH	AVG	PB	PR	/A	PD	TPI
1909	Was-A	0	0	—	3	0	0	0	0	6	13	0	3	1	25.5	4.50	54	.419	.486	0	.000	0	-1	-1	0	0.0
1910	Was-A	0	0	—	1	0	0	0	0	1²	6	0	0	2	37.8	16.20	15	.500	.538	0	—	0	-3	-3	0	-0.1
1911	Chi-A	2	0	1.000	12	3	1	1	0	47	47	1	20	24	12.8	3.06	105	.257	.330	1	.077	-0	1	1	0	0.1
Total	3	2	0	1.000	16	3	1	1	0	54²	66	1	23	25	15.0	3.62	86	.292	.363	1	.067	-0	-2	-3	1	0.1

■ BRUCE HOWARD

Howard, Bruce Ernest b: 3/23/43, Salisbury, Md. BB/TR, 6'2", 180 lbs. Deb: 9/04/63

YEAR	TM/L	W	L	PCT	G	GS	CG	SH	SV	IP	H	HR	BB	SO	RAT	ERA	ERA+	OAV	OOB	BH	AVG	PB	PR	/A	PD	TPI
1963	Chi-A	2	1	.667	7	0	0	0	0	17	12	0	14	9	13.8	2.65	132	.207	.361	1	.250	0	2	2	-0	0.1
1964	Chi-A	2	1	.667	3	3	1	1	0	22¹	10	0	8	17	7.7	0.81	429	.139	.235	0	.000	-1	7	7	0	0.7
1965	Chi-A	9	8	.529	30	22	1	1	0	148	123	13	72	120	11.9	3.47	92	.224	.316	6	.146	2	-0	-4	-1	-0.3
1966	Chi-A	9	5	.643	27	21	4	2	0	149	110	14	44	85	9.4	2.30	138	.202	.263	3	.070	-0	19	14	0	1.5
1967	Chi-A	3	10	.231	30	17	1	0	0	112²	102	9	52	76	12.5	3.43	90	.240	.327	5	.179	1	-3	-4	1	-0.2
1968	Bal-A	2	0	1.000	10	5	0	0	0	31	30	2	26	19	16.8	3.77	78	.268	.414	2	.286	2	-3	-3	0	0.0
	Was-A	1	6	.143	13	7	0	0	0	48²	62	7	23	23	15.7	5.36	54	.330	.403	0	.000	-2	-13	-13	1	-1.4
	Yr	1	6	.143	23	12	0	0	0	79²	92	9	49	42	15.9	4.74	62	.302	.398	1	.043	-0	-16	-16	1	-1.4
Total	6	26	31	.456	120	75	7	4	1	528²	449	45	239	349	11.8	3.18	99	.231	.317	17	.116	2	9	-2	1	0.4

■ EARL HOWARD

Howard, Earl Nycum b: 6/25/1893, Everett, Pa. d: 4/4/37, Everett, Pa. TR, 6'1", 160 lbs. Deb: 4/18/18

YEAR	TM/L	W	L	PCT	G	GS	CG	SH	SV	IP	H	HR	BB	SO	RAT	ERA	ERA+	OAV	OOB	BH	AVG	PB	PR	/A	PD	TPI
1918	StL-N	0	0	—	1	0	0	0	0	2	0	0	2	0	9.0	0.00	—	.000	.286	0	—	0	1	1	1	0.1

■ FRED HOWARD

Howard, Fred Irving b: 9/2/56, Portland, Maine BR/TR, 6'3", 190 lbs. Deb: 5/26/79

YEAR	TM/L	W	L	PCT	G	GS	CG	SH	SV	IP	H	HR	BB	SO	RAT	ERA	ERA+	OAV	OOB	BH	AVG	PB	PR	/A	PD	TPI
1979	Chi-A	1	5	.167	28	6	0	0	0	68	73	5	32	36	14.0	3.57	119	.283	.364	0	—	0	5	5	-1	0.4

■ DEL HOWARD

Howard, George Elmer b: 12/24/1877, Kenney, Ill. d: 12/24/56, Seattle, Wash. BL/TR, 6', 180 lbs. Deb: 4/15/05 ♦

YEAR	TM/L	W	L	PCT	G	GS	CG	SH	SV	IP	H	HR	BB	SO	RAT	ERA	ERA+	OAV	OOB	BH	AVG	PB	PR	/A	PD	TPI
1905	Pit-N	0	0	—	1	0	0	0	0	6	4	0	1	0	9.0	0.00	—	.200	.273	127	.292	0	2	2	0	0.2

YEAR TM/L	W	L	PCT	G	GS	CG	SH	SV	IP	H	HR	BB	SO	RAT	ERA	ERA+	OAV	OOB	BH	AVG	PB	PR	/A	PD	TPI

■ LEE HOWARD   Howard, Lee Vincent b: 11/11/23, Staten Island, N.Y BL/TL, 6'2", 175 lbs. Deb: 9/22/46

1946 Pit-N	0	1	.000	3	2	1	0	0	13¹	14	0	9	6	15.5	2.03	174	.286	.397	0	.000	-1	2	2	-0	0.1
1947 Pit-N	0	0	—	2	0	0	0	0	2²	4	1	0	2	13.5	3.38	125	.333	.333	0	—	0	0	0	0	0.0
Total 2	0	1	.000	5	2	1	0	0	16	18	1	9	8	15.2	2.25	162	.295	.386	0	.000	-1	2	2	-0	0.1

■ CAL HOWE   Howe, Calvin Earl b: 11/27/24, Rock Falls, Ill. BL/TL, 6'3", 205 lbs. Deb: 9/26/52

| 1952 Chi-N | 0 | 0 | — | 1 | 0 | 0 | 0 | 0 | 2 | 0 | 0 | 1 | 2 | 4.5 | 0.00 | — | .000 | .143 | 0 | — | 0 | 1 | 1 | 0 | 0.1 |

■ LES HOWE   Howe, Lester Curtis "Lucky" b: 8/24/1895, Brooklyn, N.Y. d: 7/16/76, Woodmere, N.Y. BR/TR, 5'11.5", 170 lbs. Deb: 8/18/23

1923 Bos-A	1	0	1.000	12	2	0	0	0	30	23	0	7	7	9.3	2.40	171	.211	.265	0	.000	-1	5	6	0	0.5
1924 Bos-A	1	0	1.000	4	0	0	0	0	7¹	11	1	2	3	17.2	7.36	59	.423	.483	1	.500	-1	-3	-2	0	-0.1
Total 2	2	0	1.000	16	2	0	0	0	37¹	34	1	9	10	10.8	3.38	123	.252	.308	1	.125	-1	3	3	0	0.4

■ STEVE HOWE   Howe, Steven Roy b: 3/10/58, Pontiac, Mich. BL/TL, 6'1", 180 lbs. Deb: 4/11/80

1980 LA-N	7	9	.438	59	0	0	0	17	84²	83	1	22	39	11.4	2.66	132	.256	.307	1	.091	-1	9	8	1	0.9
1981 *LA-N	5	3	.625	41	0	0	0	8	54	51	2	18	32	11.5	2.50	133	.254	.315	0	.000	0	6	5	-1	0.5
1982 LA-N	7	5	.583	66	0	0	0	13	99¹	87	3	17	49	9.4	2.08	166	.240	.274	0	.000	-1	17	15	-0	1.5
1983 LA-N	4	7	.364	46	0	0	0	18	68²	55	2	12	52	8.9	1.44	249	.217	.256	1	.125	0	17	16	1	1.9
1985 LA-N	1	1	.500	19	0	0	0	3	22	30	2	5	11	14.7	4.91	71	.319	.360	0	—	0	-3	-4	0	-0.2
Min-A	2	3	.400	13	0	0	0	0	19	28	1	7	10	16.6	6.16	72	.333	.385	0	—	0	-4	-4	-0	-0.3
1987 Tex-A	3	3	.500	24	0	0	0	1	31¹	33	2	8	19	12.6	4.31	104	.280	.341	0	—	0	1	1	0	0.1
Total 6	29	31	.483	268	0	0	0	60	379	367	13	89	212	11.0	2.71	133	.255	.302	2	.074	-1	41	38	2	4.4

■ HARRY HOWELL   Howell, Henry Harry b: 11/14/1876, New Jersey d: 5/22/56, Spokane, Wash. BR/TR, 5'9", Deb: 10/10/1898 U♦

1898 Bro-N	2	0	1.000	2	2	2	0	0	18	15	0	11	2	13.0	5.00	72	.225	.335	2	.250	0	-3	-3	-0	-0.1
1899 Bal-N	13	8	.619	28	25	21	0	1	209¹	248	1	69	58	13.6	3.91	101	.294	.347	12	.146	-4	-1	1	1	0.0
1900 *Bro-N	6	5	.545	21	10	7	2	0	110¹	131	4	36	26	13.6	3.75	102	.294	.347	12	.286	-4	-1	1	1	0.6
1901 Bal-A	14	22	.389	37	34	32	1	0	294²	333	5	79	93	12.6	3.67	106	.281	.326	41	.218	1	0	7	-2	0.8
1902 Bal-A	9	15	.375	26	23	19	1	0	199	243	5	48	33	13.2	4.12	92	.301	.340	93	.268	6	-12	-8	5	-0.6
1903 NY-A	9	6	.600	25	15	13	0	0	155²	140	4	44	62	10.6	3.53	89	.240	.293	23	.217	-2	-10	-7	3	0.0
1904 StL-A	13	21	.382	34	33	32	2	0	299²	254	1	60	122	9.4	2.19	113	.231	.270	25	.221	5	14	10	9	2.7
1905 StL-A	15	22	.405	38	37	**35**	4	0	323	252	2	101	198	9.8	1.98	129	.216	.279	26	.193	2	25	20	16	4.6
1906 StL-A	15	14	.517	35	33	30	6	1	276²	233	1	61	140	9.6	2.11	122	.231	.275	13	.126	-3	18	14	7	2.0
1907 StL-A	16	15	.516	42	35	26	2	3	316¹	258	0	88	118	9.4	1.93	130	.225	.280	27	.237	6	22	21	8	3.9
1908 StL-A	18	18	.500	41	32	27	2	1	324¹	279	1	70	117	10.2	1.89	127	.240	.293	22	.183	2	18	18	1	2.4
1909 StL-A	1	1	.500	10	3	0	0	0	37¹	42	0	16	12	12.8	3.13	77	.294	.344	6	.176	0	-3	-3	-0	-0.2
1910 StL-A	0	0	—	1	0	0	0	0	3¹	7	0	2	1	24.3	10.80	23	.467	.529	0	.000	-0	-3	-3	-0	-0.2
Total 13	131	147	.471	340	282	244	20	6	2567²	2435	27	677	986	11.0	2.74	108	.252	.302	302	.217	20	64	64	49	15.9

■ JAY HOWELL   Howell, Jay Canfield b: 11/26/55, Miami, Fla. BR/TR, 6'3", 200 lbs. Deb: 8/10/80

1980 Cin-N	0	0	—	5	0	0	0	0	3¹	8	0	1	4	24.3	13.50	26	.471	.500	0	—	0	-4	-4	-0	-0.3
1981 Chi-N	2	0	1.000	10	2	0	0	0	22¹	23	3	10	10	14.1	4.84	76	.277	.368	0	.000	0	-3	-3	1	-0.1
1982 NY-A	2	3	.400	6	6	0	0	0	28	42	1	13	21	17.7	7.71	52	.341	.404	0	—	0	-11	-12	-0	-1.0
1983 NY-A	1	5	.167	19	12	2	0	0	82	89	7	35	61	13.9	5.38	72	.275	.351	0	—	0	-12	-14	0	-1.2
1984 NY-A	9	4	.692	61	1	0	0	7	103²	86	5	34	109	10.4	2.69	141	.223	.286	0	—	0	15	13	1	1.4
1985 Oak-A	9	8	.529	63	0	0	0	29	98	98	5	31	68	11.9	2.85	135	.261	.319	0	—	0	14	11	-0	1.1
1986 Oak-A	3	6	.333	38	0	0	0	16	53¹	53	3	23	42	13.0	3.38	115	.262	.341	0	—	0	5	3	-0	0.3
1987 Oak-A	3	4	.429	36	0	0	0	16	44¹	48	6	21	35	14.2	5.89	70	.277	.359	0	—	0	-7	-9	-0	-0.8
1988 *LA-N	5	3	.625	50	0	0	0	21	65	44	1	21	70	9.1	2.08	160	.188	.258	0	.000	-0	10	9	0	1.0
1989 LA-N	5	3	.625	56	0	0	0	28	79²	60	3	22	55	9.3	1.58	216	.211	.268	0	.000	-0	17	16	0	1.7
1990 LA-N	5	5	.500	45	0	0	0	16	66	59	5	20	59	11.6	2.18	163	.242	.315	0	.000	-0	12	10	-0	1.0
Total 11	44	41	.518	389	21	2	0	133	645²	610	39	230	531	11.9	3.43	109	.249	.318	0	.000	-1	35	22	1	3.0

■ KEN HOWELL   Howell, Kenneth b: 11/28/60, Detroit, Mich. BR/TR, 6'3", 200 lbs. Deb: 6/25/84

1984 LA-N	5	5	.500	32	1	0	0	6	51¹	51	1	9	54	10.7	3.33	106	.267	.303	0	.000	-1	1	1	0	0.1
1985 *LA-N	4	7	.364	56	0	0	0	12	86	66	8	35	85	10.6	3.77	92	.208	.287	0	.000	-0	-2	-3	-0	-0.3
1986 LA-N	6	12	.333	62	0	0	0	12	97²	86	7	63	104	14.0	3.87	89	.239	.357	0	.000	-0	-2	-5	-2	-0.6
1987 LA-N	3	4	.429	40	2	0	0	1	55	54	7	29	60	13.6	4.91	81	.265	.356	1	.250	-0	-5	-6	-0	-0.5
1988 LA-N	0	1	.000	4	1	0	0	0	12²	16	0	4	12	14.2	6.39	52	.320	.370	0	.000	-0	-4	-4	-0	-0.4
1989 Phi-N	12	12	.500	33	32	1	1	0	204	155	11	86	164	10.7	3.44	103	.215	.300	6	.092	-1	2	-2	0	0.0
1990 Phi-N	8	7	.533	18	18	2	0	0	106²	106	12	49	70	13.3	4.64	82	.260	.343	1	.067	-1	-10	-10	-1	-1.1
Total 7	38	48	.442	245	54	3	1	31	613¹	534	46	275	549	12.0	3.95	91	.237	.323	9	.079	-5	-20	-24	-5	-2.2

■ DIXIE HOWELL   Howell, Millard b: 1/7/20, Bowman, Ky. d: 3/18/60, Hollywood, Fla. BL/TR, 6'2", 210 lbs. Deb: 9/14/40

1940 Cle-A	0	0	—	3	0	0	0	0	5	2	0	4	2	10.8	1.80	234	.143	.333	0	—	0	1	1	0	0.1
1949 Cin-N	0	1	.000	5	1	0	0	0	13¹	21	3	8	7	19.6	8.10	52	.362	.439	1	.111	-0	-6	-6	0	-0.5
1955 Chi-A	8	3	.727	35	0	0	0	9	73²	70	1	25	25	11.6	2.93	135	.250	.311	8	.381	2	8	8	2	1.2
1956 Chi-A	5	6	.455	34	1	0	0	4	64¹	79	4	36	28	16.4	4.62	89	.309	.398	4	.235	2	-3	-4	0	0.0
1957 Chi-A	6	5	.545	37	0	0	0	6	68¹	64	6	30	37	12.4	3.29	113	.255	.335	5	.185	4	4	3	1	0.9
1958 Chi-A	0	0	—	1	0	0	0	0	1²	0	0	0	0	0.0	0.00	—	.000	.000	0	—	-0	1	1	0	0.0
Total 6	19	15	.559	115	2	0	0	19	226¹	236	13	103	99	13.6	3.78	104	.273	.352	18	.243	8	5	4	3	1.7

■ ROLAND HOWELL   Howell, Roland Boatner "Billiken" b: 1/3/1892, Napoleonville, La. d: 3/31/73, Baton Rouge, La. 6'4", 210 lbs. Deb: 6/14/12

| 1912 StL-N | 0 | 0 | — | 3 | 0 | 0 | 0 | 0 | 1² | 5 | 0 | 5 | 0 | 54.0 | 27.00 | 13 | .556 | .714 | 0 | — | 0 | -4 | -4 | 0 | -0.3 |

■ TEX HOYLE   Hoyle, Roland Edison b: 7/17/21, Carbondale, Pa. BR/TR, 6'4", 170 lbs. Deb: 4/18/52

| 1952 Phi-A | 0 | 0 | — | 3 | 0 | 0 | 0 | 0 | 2¹ | 9 | 2 | 1 | 1 | 38.6 | 27.00 | 15 | .563 | .588 | 0 | — | 0 | -6 | -6 | 0 | -0.4 |

■ LA MARR HOYT   Hoyt, Dewey La Marr b: 1/1/55, Columbia, S.C. BR/TR, 6'3", 195 lbs. Deb: 9/14/79

1979 Chi-A	0	0	—	2	0	0	0	0	3	2	0	0	6	6.0	0.00	—	.200	.200	0	—	0	1	1	0	0.1
1980 Chi-A	9	3	.750	24	13	3	1	0	112¹	123	8	41	55	13.3	4.57	88	.281	.345	0	—	0	-7	-7	-1	-0.7
1981 Chi-A	9	3	.750	43	1	0	0	10	90²	80	10	28	60	11.0	3.57	100	.240	.305	0	—	0	1	0	-0	0.0
1982 Chi-A	**19**	15	.559	39	32	14	2	0	239²	248	17	48	124	11.2	3.53	114	.266	.303	0	—	0	14	13	-1	1.3
1983 *Chi-A	24	10	.706	36	36	11	1	0	260²	236	27	31	148	**9.3**	3.66	114	.238	**.262**	0	—	0	12	15	5	2.1
1984 Chi-A	13	18	.419	34	34	11	1	0	235²	244	31	43	126	11.2	4.47	93	.266	.302	0	—	0	-13	-8	1	-0.6
1985 SD-N	16	8	.667	31	31	8	3	0	210¹	210	20	20	83	9.9	3.47	102	.261	.281	4	.063	-4	2	2	0	0.0
1986 SD-N	8	11	.421	35	25	1	0	0	159	170	27	68	85	13.6	5.15	71	.276	.351	6	.130	-1	-25	-26	-2	-2.3
Total 8	98	68	.590	244	172	48	8	10	1311¹	1313	140	279	681	11.0	3.99	98	.260	.302	10	.091	-5	-13	-10	2	-0.6

■ WAITE HOYT   Hoyt, Waite Charles "Schoolboy" b: 9/9/1899, Brooklyn, N.Y. d: 8/25/84, Cincinnati, Ohio BR/TR, 6', 180 lbs. Deb: 7/24/18 H

1918 NY-N	0	0	—	1	0	0	0	0	1	0	0	0	2	0.0	0.00	—	.000	.000	0	.000	-0	0	0	0	0.0
1919 Bos-A	4	6	.400	13	11	6	2	0	105¹	99	1	22	28	10.3	3.25	93	.262	.303	5	.132	-2	0	-3	1	-0.4
1920 Bos-A	6	6	.500	22	11	6	2	1	121¹	123	2	47	45	12.7	4.38	83	.270	.339	5	.116	-3	-8	-10	1	-1.1
1921 *NY-A	19	13	.594	43	32	21	1	3	282¹	301	3	81	102	12.3	3.09	137	.276	.329	22	.222	-2	37	36	-1	3.2
1922 *NY-A	19	12	.613	37	31	17	3	0	265	271	13	76	95	12.1	3.43	117	.269	.326	20	.217	1	18	17	-2	1.6

YEAR TM/L	W	L	PCT	G	GS	CG	SH	SV	IP	H	HR	BB	SO	RAT	ERA	ERA+	OAV	OOB	BH	AVG	PB	PR	/A	PD	TPI
1923 *NY-A	17	9	.654	37	28	19	1	1	238²	227	9	66	60	11.2	3.02	131	.253	.307	16	.190	-2	26	24	-0	2.2
1924 NY-A	18	13	.581	46	32	14	2	4	247	295	8	76	71	13.6	3.79	110	.300	.352	10	.133	-5	12	10	-0	0.5
1925 NY-A	11	14	.440	46	30	17	1	6	243	283	14	78	86	13.4	4.00	107	.292	.346	24	.304	5	11	7	3	1.3
1926 *NY-A	16	12	.571	40	28	12	1	4	217²	224	4	62	79	11.9	3.85	100	.284	.316	16	.211	-0	4	0	-3	-0.2
1927 *NY-A	22	7	.759	36	32	23	3	1	256¹	242	10	54	86	10.5	2.63	146	.251	.294	22	.222	0	43	35	-0	3.3
1928 *NY-A	23	7	.767	42	31	19	3	8	273	279	16	60	67	11.2	3.36	112	.272	.313	28	.257	2	21	12	-1	1.2
1929 NY-A	10	9	.526	30	25	12	0	1	201²	219	9	69	57	13.0	4.24	91	.279	.339	17	.224	1	0	-9	-1	-0.8
1930 NY-A	2	2	.500	8	7	2	0	0	47²	64	7	9	10	13.8	4.53	95	.317	.346	1	.063	-2	1	-1	-0	-0.2
Det-A	9	8	.529	26	20	8	1	4	135²	176	7	47	25	14.9	4.78	100	.313	.368	9	.196	-2	-2	-0	-2	-0.3
Yr	11	10	.524	34	27	10	1	4	183¹	240	14	56	35	14.6	4.71	99	.314	.363	2	.032	-4	-1	-1	-2	-0.5
1931 Det-A	3	8	.273	16	12	5	0	0	92	124	2	32	10	15.5	5.87	78	.319	.374	4	.133	-2	-15	-13	0	-1.3
*Phi-A	10	5	.667	16	14	9	2	0	111	130	9	37	30	13.5	4.22	107	.298	.353	13	.302	3	2	3	1	0.7
Yr	13	13	.500	32	26	14	2	0	203	254	11	69	40	14.3	4.97	91	.307	.360	2	.027	0	-13	-10	1	-0.6
1932 Bro-N	1	3	.250	8	4	0	0	1	26²	38	3	12	7	16.9	7.76	49	.342	.407	0	.000	-1	-12	-12	1	-0.9
NY-N	5	7	.417	18	12	3	0	0	97¹	103	6	25	29	12.3	3.42	109	.275	.328	3	.097	-2	5	3	1	0.2
Yr	6	10	.375	26	16	3	0	1	124	141	9	37	36	13.0	4.35	86	.290	.347	0	.000	-3	-7	-9	2	-0.7
1933 Pit-N	5	7	.417	36	8	4	1	4	117	118	3	19	44	10.6	2.92	114	.262	.293	5	.156	-1	5	5	1	0.5
1934 Pit-N	15	6	.714	48	15	8	3	5	190²	184	6	43	105	10.8	2.93	141	.252	.296	10	.179	-1	24	25	-1	2.4
1935 Pit-N	7	11	.389	39	11	5	0	6	164	187	8	27	63	11.8	3.40	121	.285	.315	14	.259	2	11	13	0	1.3
1936 Pit-N	7	5	.583	22	9	6	0	1	116²	115	5	20	37	10.6	2.70	150	.255	.291	6	.154	-1	17	18	1	1.8
1937 Pit-N	1	2	.333	11	0	0	0	2	28	31	3	6	21	11.9	4.50	86	.270	.306	1	.083	-1	-2	-2	-1	-0.3
Bro-N	7	7	.500	27	19	10	1	0	167	180	5	30	44	11.3	3.23	125	.270	.301	4	.083	-2	13	15	-0	1.3
Yr	8	9	.471	38	19	10	1	2	195	211	8	36	65	11.4	3.42	117	.270	.302	6	.100	-3	11	13	-1	1.0
1938 Bro-N	0	3	.000	6	1	0	0	0	16¹	24	1	5	3	16.0	4.96	79	.333	.377	0	.000	-0	-2	-2	-0	-0.1
Total 21	237	182	.566	674	423	226	26	52	3762¹	4037	154	1003	1206	12.2	3.59	112	.276	.325	255	.198	-16	210	173	-3	16.1

■ AL HRABOSKY
Hrabosky, Alan Thomas　b: 7/21/49, Oakland, Cal.　BR/TL, 5'11", 185 lbs.　Deb: 6/16/70

YEAR TM/L	W	L	PCT	G	GS	CG	SH	SV	IP	H	HR	BB	SO	RAT	ERA	ERA+	OAV	OOB	BH	AVG	PB	PR	/A	PD	TPI
1970 StL-N	2	1	.667	16	1	0	0	0	19	22	2	7	12	13.7	4.74	87	.286	.345	0	.000	-0	-1	-1	-1	-0.1
1971 StL-N	0	0	—	1	0	0	0	0	2	2	0	0	2	9.0	0.00	—	.250	.250	0	—	0	1	1	0	0.1
1972 StL-N	1	0	1.000	5	0	0	0	0	7	2	0	3	9	6.4	0.00	—	.087	.192	0	.000	-0	3	3	-0	0.3
1973 StL-N	2	4	.333	44	0	0	0	5	56	45	2	21	57	10.9	2.09	174	.220	.298	0	.000	-0	10	10	-1	0.9
1974 StL-N	8	1	.889	65	0	0	0	9	88¹	71	3	38	82	11.2	2.95	121	.221	.306	4	.308	1	7	6	-2	0.6
1975 StL-N	13	3	.813	65	0	0	0	22	97¹	72	3	33	82	9.8	1.66	226	.205	.275	3	.200	-1	21	23	-2	2.2
1976 StL-N	8	6	.571	68	0	0	0	13	95¹	89	5	39	73	12.5	3.30	107	.252	.333	0	.000	-0	2	2	-1	0.2
1977 StL-N	6	5	.545	65	0	0	0	10	86¹	82	12	41	68	13.1	4.38	88	.256	.346	0	.000	-1	-5	-5	-1	-0.6
1978 *KC-A	8	7	.533	58	0	0	0	20	75	52	6	35	60	10.6	2.88	133	.200	.297	0	—	0	7	8	-0	0.8
1979 KC-A	9	4	.692	58	0	0	0	11	65	67	3	41	39	15.1	3.74	114	.272	.378	0	—	0	3	4	-2	0.2
1980 Atl-N	4	2	.667	45	0	0	0	3	59²	50	8	31	31	12.2	3.62	103	.223	.318	0	.000	-0	0	1	-1	0.0
1981 Atl-N	1	1	.500	24	0	0	0	1	33²	24	1	9	13	8.8	1.07	335	.207	.264	0	.000	-0	9	9	-1	0.9
1982 Atl-N	2	1	.667	31	0	0	0	3	37¹	41	5	17	20	14.0	5.54	67	.285	.360	1	.333	0	-8	-8	-1	-0.7
Total 13	64	35	.646	545	1	0	0	97	722	619	50	315	548	11.8	3.10	121	.234	.318	8	.143	0	49	52	-12	4.8

■ CARL HUBBELL
Hubbell, Carl Owen "King Carl" or "The Mealticket"
b: 6/22/03, Carthage, Mo.　d: 11/21/88, Scottsdale, Ariz.　BR/TL, 6', 170 lbs.　Deb: 7/26/28　H

YEAR TM/L	W	L	PCT	G	GS	CG	SH	SV	IP	H	HR	BB	SO	RAT	ERA	ERA+	OAV	OOB	BH	AVG	PB	PR	/A	PD	TPI
1928 NY-N	10	6	.625	20	14	8	1	1	124	117	7	21	37	10.2	2.83	138	.248	.284	5	.106	-3	16	15	2	1.4
1929 NY-N	18	11	.621	39	35	19	1	1	268	273	17	67	106	11.6	3.69	124	.265	.313	12	.129	-6	30	27	4	2.3
1930 NY-N	17	12	.586	37	32	17	3	2	241²	263	11	58	117	12.4	3.87	122	.278	.327	13	.151	-5	29	23	-2	1.5
1931 NY-N	14	12	.538	36	30	21	4	3	248	211	14	67	155	10.2	2.65	140	.227	.282	20	.241	4	34	29	-3	3.1
1932 NY-N	18	11	.621	40	32	22	0	2	284	260	20	40	137	9.6	2.50	148	.238	.268	26	.241	4	43	38	6	5.0
1933 *NY-N	23	12	.657	45	33	22	10	5	308²	256	6	47	156	8.9	1.66	193	.227	.260	20	.183	1	58	53	7	7.0
1934 NY-N	21	12	.636	49	34	25	5	8	313	286	17	37	118	9.3	2.30	168	.239	.263	23	.197	-1	61	54	4	5.9
1935 NY-N	23	12	.657	42	35	24	1	0	302²	314	27	49	150	10.9	3.27	118	.263	.294	26	.239	4	25	20	4	2.7
1936 *NY-N	26	6	.813	42	34	25	3	3	304	265	7	57	123	9.7	2.31	169	.236	.276	25	.227	1	58	54	1	5.7
1937 *NY-N	22	8	.733	39	32	18	4	4	261²	261	18	55	159	11.0	3.20	122	.257	.298	21	.216	1	21	20	-2	1.9
1938 NY-N	13	10	.565	24	22	13	1	1	179	171	16	33	104	10.4	3.07	123	.249	.285	9	.155	-2	14	14	-2	1.0
1939 NY-N	11	9	.550	29	18	10	0	2	154	150	11	24	62	10.3	2.75	143	.249	.280	8	.151	-1	20	20	1	2.1
1940 NY-N	11	12	.478	31	27	11	2	0	214¹	220	22	59	86	11.8	3.65	106	.259	.309	15	.185	-0	5	5	2	0.7
1941 NY-N	11	9	.550	26	22	11	1	1	164	169	10	53	75	12.3	3.57	104	.266	.325	8	.140	-2	1	2	-3	-0.1
1942 NY-N	11	8	.579	24	20	11	0	0	157¹	158	17	34	61	11.0	3.95	85	.259	.299	11	.183	-0	-11	-10	-1	-1.1
1943 NY-N	4	4	.500	12	11	3	0	0	66	87	7	24	31	15.1	4.91	70	.322	.378	4	.200	-0	-11	-11	-1	-1.1
Total 16	253	154	.622	535	431	260	36	33	3590¹	3461	227	725	1677	10.6	2.98	130	.251	.291	246	.191	-5	393	355	17	38.0

■ BILL HUBBELL
Hubbell, Wilbert William　b: 6/17/1897, San Francisco, Cal.　d: 8/3/80, Lakewood, Colo.　BR/TR, 6'1.5", 195 lbs.　Deb: 9/24/19

YEAR TM/L	W	L	PCT	G	GS	CG	SH	SV	IP	H	HR	BB	SO	RAT	ERA	ERA+	OAV	OOB	BH	AVG	PB	PR	/A	PD	TPI
1919 NY-N	1	1	.500	2	2	2	0	0	18¹	19	0	2	3	11.3	1.96	143	.260	.299	1	.125	-1	2	2	-0	0.1
1920 NY-N	0	1	.000	14	0	0	0	2	30	26	2	15	8	12.6	2.10	143	.239	.336	1	.200	-0	3	3	1	0.4
Phi-N	9	9	.500	24	20	9	1	2	150	176	3	42	26	13.3	3.84	89	.301	.352	7	.132	-4	-12	-7	-2	-1.1
Yr	9	10	.474	38	20	9	1	4	180	202	5	57	34	13.1	3.55	94	.291	.348	3	.052	-4	-8	-4	-0	-0.7
1921 Phi-N	9	16	.360	36	30	15	1	2	220¹	269	18	38	43	12.7	4.33	98	.306	.337	12	.160	-2	-13	-2	-0	-0.2
1922 Phi-N	7	15	.318	35	24	11	1	1	189	257	14	41	33	14.4	5.00	93	.317	.353	12	.171	-2	-19	-7	-1	-0.6
1923 Phi-N	1	6	.143	22	5	1	0	0	55	102	13	17	8	19.8	8.35	55	.394	.435	4	.235	0	-27	-23	0	-1.9
1924 Phi-N	10	9	.526	36	22	9	2	2	179	233	9	45	30	14.1	4.83	92	.324	.365	13	.220	-1	-19	-7	-1	-0.5
1925 Phi-N	0	0	—	2	0	0	0	0	2²	5	0	1	0	20.3	0.00	—	.385	.429	0	.000	-0	-1	-0	-1	-0.1
Bro-N	3	6	.333	33	5	3	0	1	86²	120	8	24	16	15.2	5.30	79	.337	.382	3	.150	-0	-10	-10	1	-0.8
Yr	3	6	.333	35	5	3	0	1	89¹	125	8	25	16	15.3	5.14	82	.339	.384	4	.190	0	-9	-9	2	-0.6
Total 7	40	63	.388	204	108	50	5	10	931	1207	67	225	167	14.0	4.68	89	.317	.359	53	.172	-8	-93	-52	3	-4.4

■ EARL HUCKLEBERRY
Huckleberry, Earl Eugene　b: 5/23/10, Konawa, Okla.　BR/TR, 5'11", 165 lbs.　Deb: 9/13/35

YEAR TM/L	W	L	PCT	G	GS	CG	SH	SV	IP	H	HR	BB	SO	RAT	ERA	ERA+	OAV	OOB	BH	AVG	PB	PR	/A	PD	TPI
1935 Phi-A	1	0	1.000	1	1	0	0	0	8	8	1	4	2	16.2	9.45	48	.296	.387	0	.000	-0	-4	-4	0	-0.2

■ WILLIS HUDLIN
Hudlin, George Willis "Ace"　b: 5/23/06, Wagoner, Okla.　BR/TR, 6', 190 lbs.　Deb: 8/15/26　C

YEAR TM/L	W	L	PCT	G	GS	CG	SH	SV	IP	H	HR	BB	SO	RAT	ERA	ERA+	OAV	OOB	BH	AVG	PB	PR	/A	PD	TPI
1926 Cle-A	1	3	.250	8	2	1	0	0	32¹	25	1	13	6	11.1	2.78	146	.227	.320	1	.125	0	4	5	2	0.6
1927 Cle-A	18	12	.600	43	30	18	1	0	264²	291	3	83	65	13.1	4.01	105	.283	.343	24	.250	2	4	6	3	1.1
1928 Cle-A	14	14	.500	42	26	10	0	7	220¹	231	7	90	62	13.4	4.04	103	.279	.355	14	.194	-0	0	2	2	0.4
1929 Cle-A	17	15	.531	40	33	22	2	1	280¹	299	7	73	60	12.0	3.34	133	.272	.318	19	.196	-3	28	34	7	3.9
1930 Cle-A	13	16	.448	37	33	13	1	1	216²	255	12	76	60	13.8	4.57	106	.293	.351	16	.219	-1	2	6	5	0.9
1931 Cle-A	15	14	.517	44	34	15	1	4	254¹	313	14	88	83	14.2	4.60	100	.301	.356	20	.200	1	-6	1	4	0.6
1932 Cle-A	12	8	.600	33	21	12	0	2	181²	204	10	59	65	13.1	4.71	101	.278	.332	13	.203	1	-5	1	1	0.3
1933 Cle-A	5	13	.278	34	17	6	0	1	147¹	161	7	61	44	13.7	3.97	112	.275	.346	6	.146	-1	5	8	4	1.0
1934 Cle-A	15	10	.600	36	26	15	1	4	195	210	8	65	58	12.9	4.75	96	.277	.338	14	.206	3	-6	-4	6	0.4
1935 Cle-A	15	11	.577	36	29	14	3	5	231²	252	8	61	45	12.3	3.69	122	.277	.324	24	.279	6	20	21	1	2.7
1936 Cle-A	1	5	.167	27	7	1	0	0	64	112	1	31	20	20.4	9.00	56	.397	.460	2	.111	-1	-28	-28	1	-2.3
1937 Cle-A	12	11	.522	35	23	10	2	2	175²	213	16	43	31	13.2	4.10	112	.295	.337	10	.169	-1	10	10	4	1.2
1938 Cle-A	8	8	.500	29	15	8	0	1	127	158	13	45	27	14.5	4.89	95	.303	.361	5	.116	-2	-1	-4	2	-0.3
1939 Cle-A	9	10	.474	27	20	7	0	3	143	175	6	42	28	13.7	4.91	90	.303	.352	9	.188	1	-5	-8	5	-0.1

YEAR	TM/L	W	L	PCT	G	GS	CG	SH	SV	IP	H	HR	BB	SO	RAT	ERA	ERA+	OAV	OOB	BH	AVG	PB	PR	/A	PD	TPI
1940	Cle-A	2	1	.667	4	4	2	0	0	23²	31	3	2	8	12.5	4.94	85	.316	.330	1	.125	-0	-1	-2	0	-0.1
	Was-A	1	2	.333	8	6	1	0	0	37¹	50	9	5	9	13.7	6.51	64	.314	.343	1	.100	-1	-9	-10	0	-0.8
	StL-A	0	1	.000	6	1	0	0	0	11¹	19	0	8	4	21.4	11.12	41	.358	.443	1	.500	0	-8	-8	0	-0.6
	Yr	3	4	.429	18	11	3	0	0	72¹	100	12	15	21	14.3	6.72	63	.321	.352	1	.050	-0	-19	-20	0	-1.5
	NY-N	0	1	.000	1	1	0	0	0	5	9	1	1	1	18.0	10.80	36	.409	.435	0	.000	-0	-4	-4	0	-0.2
1944	StL-A	0	1	.000	1	0	0	0	0	2	3	0	0	1	13.5	4.50	80	.300	.300	0	—	0	-0	-0	0	-0.0
Total	16	158	156	.503	491	328	155	11	31	2613¹	3011	118	846	677	13.4	4.41	102	.289	.345	180	.201	4	-0	26	46	8.7

■ CHARLIE HUDSON
Hudson, Charles   b: 8/18/49, Ada, Okla.   BL/TL, 6'3", 185 lbs.   Deb: 5/21/72

YEAR	TM/L	W	L	PCT	G	GS	CG	SH	SV	IP	H	HR	BB	SO	RAT	ERA	ERA+	OAV	OOB	BH	AVG	PB	PR	/A	PD	TPI
1972	StL-N	1	0	1.000	12	0	0	0	0	12¹	10	0	7	4	13.1	5.11	67	.233	.353	0	—	0	-2	-2	0	-0.1
1973	Tex-A	4	2	.667	25	4	1	1	1	62¹	59	3	31	34	13.0	4.62	81	.254	.342	0	—	0	-6	-6	0	-0.5
1975	Cal-A	0	1	.000	3	1	0	0	0	5²	7	0	4	0	17.5	9.53	37	.304	.407	0	—	0	-4	-4	0	-0.3
Total	3	5	3	.625	40	5	1	1	1	80¹	76	3	42	38	13.3	5.04	73	.255	.349	0	—	0	-11	-12	0	-0.9

■ CHARLES HUDSON
Hudson, Charles Lynn   b: 3/16/59, Ennis, Tex.   BB/TR, 6'3", 185 lbs.   Deb: 5/31/83

YEAR	TM/L	W	L	PCT	G	GS	CG	SH	SV	IP	H	HR	BB	SO	RAT	ERA	ERA+	OAV	OOB	BH	AVG	PB	PR	/A	PD	TPI
1983	*Phi-N	8	8	.500	26	26	3	0	0	169¹	158	13	53	101	11.2	3.35	106	.248	.305	5	.093	-2	5	4	-0	0.2
1984	Phi-N	9	11	.450	30	30	1	1	0	173²	181	12	52	94	12.2	4.04	90	.265	.319	5	.089	-2	-9	-8	-2	-1.1
1985	Phi-N	8	13	.381	38	26	3	0	0	193	188	23	74	122	12.3	3.78	97	.252	.320	8	.140	-1	-4	-2	-2	-0.4
1986	Phi-N	7	10	.412	33	23	0	0	0	144	165	20	58	82	13.9	4.94	78	.291	.357	2	.047	-3	-20	-17	-0	-2.0
1987	NY-A	11	7	.611	35	16	6	2	0	154²	137	19	57	100	11.5	3.61	122	.239	.311	0	—	0	15	13	-1	1.1
1988	NY-A	6	6	.500	28	12	1	0	2	106¹	93	9	36	58	11.3	4.49	88	.235	.306	0	—	0	-6	-6	-0	-0.6
1989	Det-A	1	5	.167	18	7	0	0	0	66²	75	14	31	23	14.6	6.35	60	.288	.369	0	—	0	-18	-19	-1	-1.8
Total	7	50	60	.455	208	140	14	3	2	1007¹	997	110	361	580	12.2	4.14	92	.258	.324	20	.095	-8	-37	-35	-6	-4.6

■ HAL HUDSON
Hudson, Hal Campbell "Bud" or "Lefty"   b: 5/4/27, Grosse Point, Mich.   BL/TL, 5'10", 175 lbs.   Deb: 4/20/52

YEAR	TM/L	W	L	PCT	G	GS	CG	SH	SV	IP	H	HR	BB	SO	RAT	ERA	ERA+	OAV	OOB	BH	AVG	PB	PR	/A	PD	TPI
1952	StL-A	0	0	—	3	0	0	0	0	5²	9	0	6	0	23.8	12.71	31	.360	.484	0	.000	-0	-6	-6	-0	-0.5
	Chi-A	0	0	—	2	0	0	0	0	4	7	0	1	4	18.0	2.25	162	.389	.421	0	—	0	1	1	-0	0.0
	Yr	0	0	—	5	0	0	0	0	9²	16	0	7	4	21.4	8.38	45	.372	.460	0	.000	-0	-5	-5	-0	-0.5
1953	Chi-A	0	0	—	1	0	0	0	0	0²	0	0	0	0	0.0	0.00	—	.000	.000	0	0	0	0	0	0	0.0
Total	2	0	0	—	6	0	0	0	0	10¹	16	0	7	4	20.0	7.84	49	.364	.451	0	.000	-0	-5	-5	-0	-0.5

■ JESSE HUDSON
Hudson, Jesse James   b: 7/22/48, Mansfield, La.   BL/TL, 6'2", 165 lbs.   Deb: 9/19/69

YEAR	TM/L	W	L	PCT	G	GS	CG	SH	SV	IP	H	HR	BB	SO	RAT	ERA	ERA+	OAV	OOB	BH	AVG	PB	PR	/A	PD	TPI
1969	NY-N	0	0	—	1	0	0	0	0	2	2	0	3	3	18.0	4.50	81	.250	.400	0	—	0	-0	-0	0	0.0

■ NAT HUDSON
Hudson, Nathaniel P.   b: 1/12/1859, Chicago, Ill.   d: 3/14/28, Chicago, Ill.   TR ,   Deb: 4/18/1886

YEAR	TM/L	W	L	PCT	G	GS	CG	SH	SV	IP	H	HR	BB	SO	RAT	ERA	ERA+	OAV	OOB	BH	AVG	PB	PR	/A	PD	TPI
1886	*StL-a	16	10	.615	29	27	25	0	1	234¹	224	3	62	100	11.0	3.03	113	.240	.287	35	.233	1	11	11	-1	1.0
1887	StL-a	4	4	.500	9	9	7	0	0	67	91	2	20	15	14.9	4.97	91	.313	.357	12	.250	0	-5	-3	-2	-0.2
1888	StL-a	25	10	.714	39	37	36	5	0	333	283	8	59	130	9.2	2.54	128	.222	.256	50	.255	5	19	27	-1	3.5
1889	StL-a	3	2	.600	9	5	4	0	0	60	71	2	15	13	12.9	4.20	101	.285	.326	13	.250	0	-2	-0	0	0.1
Total	4	48	26	.649	86	78	72	5	1	694¹	669	15	156	258	10.7	3.08	114	.243	.284	110	.247	7	23	34	-3	4.4

■ REX HUDSON
Hudson, Rex Haughton   b: 8/11/53, Tulsa, Okla.   BB/TR, 5'11", 165 lbs.   Deb: 7/27/74

YEAR	TM/L	W	L	PCT	G	GS	CG	SH	SV	IP	H	HR	BB	SO	RAT	ERA	ERA+	OAV	OOB	BH	AVG	PB	PR	/A	PD	TPI
1974	LA-N	0	0	—	1	0	0	0	0	2	6	2	0	0	27.0	22.50	15	.500	.500	0	—	0	-4	-4	-0	-0.3

■ SID HUDSON
Hudson, Sidney Charles   b: 1/3/17, Coalfield, Tenn.   BR/TR, 6'4", 180 lbs.   Deb: 4/18/40   C

YEAR	TM/L	W	L	PCT	G	GS	CG	SH	SV	IP	H	HR	BB	SO	RAT	ERA	ERA+	OAV	OOB	BH	AVG	PB	PR	/A	PD	TPI
1940	Was-A	17	16	.515	38	31	19	3	1	252	272	20	81	96	12.7	4.57	91	.274	.330	22	.237	2	-5	-11	1	-0.7
1941	Was-A	13	14	.481	33	33	17	3	0	249²	242	12	97	108	12.3	3.46	117	.253	.322	16	.186	-0	19	16	2	1.8
1942	Was-A	10	17	.370	35	31	19	1	2	239¹	266	9	70	72	12.8	4.36	84	.276	.328	18	.213	1	-19	-19	4	-1.3
1946	Was-A	8	11	.421	31	15	6	1	1	142¹	160	9	37	35	12.7	3.60	93	.280	.328	12	.279	3	-2	-4	2	0.0
1947	Was-A	6	9	.400	20	17	5	1	0	106	113	8	58	37	14.6	5.60	66	.272	.363	12	.308	2	-22	-22	1	-1.8
1948	Was-A	4	16	.200	39	29	4	0	1	182	217	11	107	53	16.3	5.88	74	.299	.394	14	.237	2	-32	-31	3	-2.3
1949	Was-A	8	17	.320	40	27	11	2	1	209	234	11	91	54	14.2	4.22	101	.283	.357	16	.239	-2	-1	-1	4	0.6
1950	Was-A	14	14	.500	30	30	17	0	0	237²	261	17	98	75	13.8	4.09	110	.284	.356	20	.215	-1	13	11	3	1.2
1951	Was-A	5	12	.294	23	19	8	0	0	138²	168	8	52	43	14.5	5.13	80	.302	.365	12	.273	2	-15	-16	3	-1.0
1952	Was-A	3	4	.429	7	7	6	0	0	62²	59	4	29	24	12.6	2.73	130	.257	.340	4	.167	-0	7	6	2	0.8
	Bos-A	7	9	.438	21	18	7	0	0	134¹	145	9	36	50	12.6	3.62	109	.276	.330	-1	.174	-1	1	5	4	0.9
	Yr	10	13	.435	28	25	13	0	0	197	204	13	65	74	12.6	3.34	114	.270	.333	3	.043	-1	7	11	6	1.7
1953	Bos-A	6	9	.400	30	17	4	0	0	156	164	13	49	60	12.5	3.52	120	.269	.327	7	.140	-2	8	12	1	1.0
1954	Bos-A	3	4	.429	33	5	0	0	5	65¹	86	7	35	30	14.5	4.42	93	.296	.369	2	.154	-1	-5	-2	1	-0.1
Total	12	104	152	.406	380	279	123	11	13	2181	2384	136	835	734	13.5	4.28	95	.278	.345	164	.220	9	-54	-55	29	-0.9

■ AL HUENKE
Huenke, Albert A.   b: 6/26/1891, New Bremen, Ohio   d: 9/20/74, St.Mary's, Ohio   BR/TR, 6', 175 lbs.   Deb: 10/06/14

YEAR	TM/L	W	L	PCT	G	GS	CG	SH	SV	IP	H	HR	BB	SO	RAT	ERA	ERA+	OAV	OOB	BH	AVG	PB	PR	/A	PD	TPI
1914	NY-N	0	0	—	1	0	0	0	0	2	2	0	2	0	9.0	4.50	59	.250	.250	0	.000	-0	-0	-0	0	0.0

■ PHIL HUFFMAN
Huffman, Phillip Lee   b: 6/20/58, Freeport, Tex.   BR/TR, 6'2", 180 lbs.   Deb: 4/10/79

YEAR	TM/L	W	L	PCT	G	GS	CG	SH	SV	IP	H	HR	BB	SO	RAT	ERA	ERA+	OAV	OOB	BH	AVG	PB	PR	/A	PD	TPI
1979	Tor-A	6	18	.250	31	31	2	1	0	173	220	25	68	56	15.0	5.77	75	.304	.364	0	—	0	-30	-28	0	-2.4
1985	Bal-A	0	0	—	2	1	0	0	0	4²	7	1	5	2	23.1	15.43	26	.350	.480	0	—	0	-6	-6	0	-0.4
Total	2	6	18	.250	33	32	2	1	0	177²	227	26	73	58	15.2	6.03	72	.305	.367	0	—	0	-36	-33	0	-2.8

■ ED HUGHES
Hughes, Edward J.   b: 10/5/1880, Chicago, Ill.   d: 10/11/27, McHenry, Ill.   6'1", 180 lbs.   Deb: 8/29/02   ♦

YEAR	TM/L	W	L	PCT	G	GS	CG	SH	SV	IP	H	HR	BB	SO	RAT	ERA	ERA+	OAV	OOB	BH	AVG	PB	PR	/A	PD	TPI
1905	Bos-A	3	2	.600	6	4	2	0	0	33¹	38	0	9	8	12.7	4.59	59	.288	.333	3	.214	-0	-7	-7	-2	-0.8
1906	Bos-A	0	0	—	2	0	0	0	0	10	15	0	3	3	16.2	5.40	51	.349	.392	0	.000	-0	-3	-3	0	-0.2
Total	2	3	2	.600	8	4	2	0	0	43¹	53	0	12	11	13.5	4.78	57	.303	.347	4	.190	-1	-10	-10	-2	-1.0

■ JIM HUGHES
Hughes, James Jay "Jay"   b: 1/22/1874, Sacramento, Cal.   d: 6/2/24, Sacramento, Cal.   BR/TR,   Deb: 4/18/1898

YEAR	TM/L	W	L	PCT	G	GS	CG	SH	SV	IP	H	HR	BB	SO	RAT	ERA	ERA+	OAV	OOB	BH	AVG	PB	PR	/A	PD	TPI
1898	Bal-N	23	12	.657	38	35	31	5	0	300²	268	4	100	81	11.0	3.20	112	.237	.299	37	.226	4	14	13	3	2.1
1899	Bro-N	28	6	.824	35	35	30	3	0	291²	250	6	119	99	11.4	2.68	146	.232	.308	38	.252	5	38	40	2	4.5
1901	Bro-N	17	12	.586	31	29	24	0	0	250²	265	3	102	96	13.6	3.27	103	.269	.346	16	.176	-1	2	2	3	0.5
1902	Bro-N	15	11	.577	31	30	28	0	0	254	228	3	55	94	10.3	2.87	96	.240	.288	20	.213	4	-3	-3	3	0.5
Total	4	83	41	.669	135	129	113	8	0	1097	1011	16	376	370	11.6	3.00	114	.244	.310	100	.219	13	51	52	9	7.4

■ JIM HUGHES
Hughes, James Michael   b: 7/2/51, Los Angeles, Cal.   BR/TR, 6'3", 190 lbs.   Deb: 9/14/74

YEAR	TM/L	W	L	PCT	G	GS	CG	SH	SV	IP	H	HR	BB	SO	RAT	ERA	ERA+	OAV	OOB	BH	AVG	PB	PR	/A	PD	TPI
1974	Min-A	0	2	.000	2	2	1	0	0	10¹	8	2	4	8	10.5	5.23	72	.216	.293	0	—	0	-2	-2	-0	-0.1
1975	Min-A	16	14	.533	37	34	12	2	0	249²	241	17	127	130	13.7	3.82	101	.255	.351	0	—	0	-1	1	1	0.2
1976	Min-A	9	14	.391	37	26	3	0	0	177	190	17	73	87	13.8	4.98	72	.281	.358	0	—	0	-29	-27	-1	-2.8
1977	Min-A	0	0	—	2	0	0	0	0	4¹	4	0	1	1	10.4	2.08	192	.250	.294	0	—	0	1	1	-0	0.1
Total	4	25	30	.455	78	62	16	2	0	441¹	443	36	205	226	13.6	4.30	82	.265	.352	0	—	0	-31	-27	-0	-2.6

■ JIM HUGHES
Hughes, James Robert   b: 3/21/23, Chicago, Ill.   BR/TR, 6'1", 200 lbs.   Deb: 9/13/52

YEAR	TM/L	W	L	PCT	G	GS	CG	SH	SV	IP	H	HR	BB	SO	RAT	ERA	ERA+	OAV	OOB	BH	AVG	PB	PR	/A	PD	TPI
1952	Bro-N	2	1	.667	6	0	0	0	0	18²	16	0	11	8	13.0	1.45	252	.235	.342	0	.000	-0	5	5	-1	0.4
1953	*Bro-N	4	3	.571	48	0	0	0	9	85²	80	6	41	49	12.8	3.47	123	.245	.332	4	.286	1	8	8	-1	0.7
1954	Bro-N	8	4	.667	60	0	0	0	24	86²	76	7	44	58	12.5	3.22	127	.239	.331	3	.188	-0	8	8	-1	0.7
1955	Bro-N	0	2	.000	24	0	0	0	6	42²	46	4	25	29	14.5	4.22	96	.256	.335	0	.000	-0	-2	-2	-0	-0.1
1956	Bro-N	0	0	—	5	0	0	0	0	12	10	0	4	8	10.5	5.25	76	.233	.298	0	.000	0	-2	-2	-0	-0.1
	Chi-N	1	3	.250	25	1	0	0	0	45¹	43	4	30	20	15.3	5.16	73	.259	.385	2	.286	1	-7	-7	-0	-0.6
	Yr	1	3	.250	30	1	0	0	0	57¹	53	7	34	28	14.3	5.18	74	.254	.368	0	.000	0	-9	-9	-1	-0.7

YEAR TM/L	W	L	PCT	G	GS	CG	SH	SV	IP	H	HR	BB	SO	RAT	ERA	ERA+	OAV	OOB	BH	AVG	PB	PR	/A	PD	TPI
1957 Chi-A	0	0	—	4	0	0	0	0	5	12	0	3	2	27.0	10.80	35	.462	.517	0	—	0	-4	-4	-0	-0.3
Total 6	15	13	.536	172	1	0	0	39	296	278	30	152	165	13.2	3.83	106	.251	.344	9	.170	-1	7	7	-2	0.7

■ MICKEY HUGHES
Hughes, Michael J.   b: 10/25/1866, New York, N.Y.   d: 4/10/31, Jersey City, N.J.   TR , 5'6", 165 lbs.   Deb: 4/22/1888

YEAR TM/L	W	L	PCT	G	GS	CG	SH	SV	IP	H	HR	BB	SO	RAT	ERA	ERA+	OAV	OOB	BH	AVG	PB	PR	/A	PD	TPI
1888 Bro-a	25	13	.658	40	40	40	2	0	363	281	5	98	159	9.4	2.13	140	.206	.259	19	.137	-6	38	34	-0	2.6
1889 •Bro-a	9	8	.529	20	17	13	0	0	153	172	6	86	54	15.2	4.35	86	.275	.363	12	.176	-3	-9	-11	0	-1.1
1890 Bro-N	4	4	.500	9	8	6	0	0	66¹	77	1	30	22	14.5	5.16	67	.282	.353	4	.038	-1	-12	-13	0	-1.2
Phi-a	1	3	.250	6	5	4	0	0	41¹	64	0	21	15	18.5	5.44	70	.343	.410	1	.125	-1	-7	-7	-1	-0.6
Total 3	39	28	.582	75	70	63	2	0	623²	594	12	235	250	12.0	3.22	102	.243	.309	34	.137	-13	10	4	-1	-0.3

■ DICK HUGHES
Hughes, Richard Henry   b: 2/13/38, Stephens, Ark.   BR/TR, 6'3", 195 lbs.   Deb: 9/11/66

YEAR TM/L	W	L	PCT	G	GS	CG	SH	SV	IP	H	HR	BB	SO	RAT	ERA	ERA+	OAV	OOB	BH	AVG	PB	PR	/A	PD	TPI
1966 StL-N	2	1	.667	6	2	1	1	1	21	12	0	7	20	9.0	1.71	209	.162	.253	2	.400	1	4	4	0	0.6
1967 •StL-N	16	6	.727	37	27	12	3	3	222¹	164	22	48	161	8.8	2.67	123	.203	.252	10	.128	-1	17	15	-2	1.3
1968 •StL-N	2	2	.500	25	5	0	0	4	64	45	7	21	49	9.3	3.52	82	.202	.270	0	.000	-1	-4	-4	-1	-0.5
Total 3	20	9	.690	68	34	13	4	8	307¹	221	29	76	230	8.9	2.78	116	.200	.256	12	.122	-2	18	15	-1	1.4

■ TOM HUGHES
Hughes, Thomas Edward   b: 9/13/34, Ancon, C.Z., Pan.   BL/TR, 6'2", 180 lbs.   Deb: 9/13/59

YEAR TM/L	W	L	PCT	G	GS	CG	SH	SV	IP	H	HR	BB	SO	RAT	ERA	ERA+	OAV	OOB	BH	AVG	PB	PR	/A	PD	TPI
1959 StL-N	0	2	.000	2	2	0	0	0	4	9	2	6	2	24.8	15.75	27	.409	.458	0	.000	-0	-5	-5	-0	-0.4

■ TOM HUGHES
Hughes, Thomas James "Long Tom"   b: 11/29/1878, Chicago, Ill.   d: 2/8/56, Chicago, Ill.   BR/TR, 6'1",   Deb: 9/07/00

YEAR TM/L	W	L	PCT	G	GS	CG	SH	SV	IP	H	HR	BB	SO	RAT	ERA	ERA+	OAV	OOB	BH	AVG	PB	PR	/A	PD	TPI
1900 Chi-N	1	1	.500	3	3	3	0	0	21	31	0	7	12	16.3	5.14	70	.341	.389	0	.000	-0	-3	-4	0	-0.2
1901 Chi-N	10	23	.303	37	35	32	1	0	308¹	309	4	115	225	12.8	3.24	100	.259	.331	14	.119	-7	3	-0	-4	-1.0
1902 Bal-A	7	5	.583	13	13	12	1	0	108¹	120	2	32	45	12.6	3.90	97	.281	.331	6	.140	-2	-4	-2	1	-0.2
Bos-A	3	3	.500	9	8	4	0	0	49¹	51	0	24	15	13.7	3.28	109	.267	.349	11	.367	2	2	2	0	0.4
Yr	10	8	.556	22	21	16	1	0	157²	171	2	56	60	13.0	3.71	100	.277	.337	3	.041	-0	-2	0	0	0.2
1903 •Bos-A	20	7	.741	33	31	25	5	0	244²	232	4	60	110	10.7	2.57	118	.250	.295	26	.280	7	11	13	-4	1.6
1904 NY-A	7	11	.389	19	18	12	1	0	136¹	141	3	48	75	12.5	3.70	73	.268	.329	13	.241	-1	-17	-15	-1	-1.6
Was-A	2	13	.133	16	14	14	0	1	124¹	133	4	34	48	12.1	3.47	77	.274	.322	13	.228	3	-12	-11	-1	-0.8
Yr	9	24	.273	35	32	26	1	1	260²	274	7	82	123	12.3	3.59	75	.271	.326	3	.027	4	-29	-26	-3	-2.4
1905 Was-A	17	20	.459	39	35	26	6	0	291¹	239	3	79	149	9.8	2.35	113	.225	.279	22	.212	4	10	10	-5	1.0
1906 Was-A	7	17	.292	30	24	18	1	0	204	230	5	81	90	13.7	3.62	73	.287	.353	14	.212	3	-21	-22	-4	-2.4
1907 Was-A	7	14	.333	34	23	18	2	4	211	206	1	47	102	10.8	3.11	78	.258	.299	19	.237	3	-13	-16	-1	-1.4
1908 Was-A	18	15	.545	43	31	24	3	4	276¹	224	3	77	165	10.0	2.21	103	.227	.287	17	.195	2	6	2	0	0.4
1909 Was-A	4	7	.364	22	13	7	2	1	120¹	113	1	33	77	11.3	2.69	90	.246	.303	3	.083	-2	-3	-3	-1	-0.6
1911 Was-A	11	17	.393	34	27	17	2	0	223	251	3	77	86	13.4	3.47	95	.288	.348	15	.185	-1	-3	-5	-2	-0.7
1912 Was-A	13	10	.565	31	26	11	1	0	196	201	8	78	108	13.1	2.94	113	.270	.344	13	.194	1	8	9	0	1.0
1913 Was-A	4	12	.250	36	12	4	0	6	129²	129	6	61	59	14.2	4.30	69	.253	.350	4	.111	-1	-20	-19	1	-1.9
Total 13	131	175	.428	399	313	227	25	16	2644	2610	51	853	1368	12.0	3.09	93	.259	.320	190	.198	13	-57	-64	-21	-6.4

■ TOM HUGHES
Hughes, Thomas L. "Salida Tom"   b: 1/28/1884, Coal Creek, Colo.   d: 11/1/61, Los Angeles, Cal.   BR/TR, 6'2", 175 lbs.   Deb: 9/18/06

YEAR TM/L	W	L	PCT	G	GS	CG	SH	SV	IP	H	HR	BB	SO	RAT	ERA	ERA+	OAV	OOB	BH	AVG	PB	PR	/A	PD	TPI
1906 NY-A	1	0	1.000	3	1	1	0	0	15	11	2	1	5	7.2	4.20	71	.208	.222	1	.200	-1	-3	-2	-1	-0.1
1907 NY-A	2	0	1.000	4	3	2	0	0	27	16	0	11	10	9.0	2.67	105	.174	.262	1	.143	-0	-0	-1	0	0.0
1909 NY-A	7	8	.467	24	16	9	2	1	118²	109	3	37	69	11.4	2.65	95	.249	.313	5	.128	1	-2	-1	-0	-0.1
1910 NY-A	7	9	.438	23	15	11	0	1	151²	153	2	37	64	11.5	3.50	76	.271	.320	9	.164	-1	-17	-14	-1	-1.3
1914 Bos-N	2	0	1.000	2	2	1	0	0	17	14	0	4	11	9.5	2.65	104	.226	.273	0	.000	-1	0	1	0	0.0
1915 Bos-N	16	14	.533	50	25	17	4	9	280¹	208	4	58	171	8.9	2.12	122	.213	.265	9	.100	-3	20	15	-3	0.9
1916 Bos-N	16	3	.842	40	14	7	1	5	161	121	5	51	97	10.1	2.35	106	.215	.290	10	.192	2	5	2	-2	0.2
1917 Bos-N	5	3	.625	11	8	6	2	0	74	54	1	30	40	10.6	1.95	131	.216	.307	0	.000	-2	6	5	-1	0.2
1918 Bos-N	0	2	.000	3	3	1	0	0	18¹	17	0	6	9	11.3	3.44	78	.250	.311	2	.333	1	-1	-2	0	0.0
Total 9	56	39	.589	160	87	55	9	16	863	703	14	235	476	10.1	2.56	102	.229	.291	37	.130	-4	8	4	-6	-0.2

■ TOMMY HUGHES
Hughes, Thomas Owen   b: 10/7/19, Wilkes-Barre, Pa.   BR/TR, 6'1", 190 lbs.   Deb: 4/19/41

YEAR TM/L	W	L	PCT	G	GS	CG	SH	SV	IP	H	HR	BB	SO	RAT	ERA	ERA+	OAV	OOB	BH	AVG	PB	PR	/A	PD	TPI
1941 Phi-N	9	14	.391	34	24	5	2	0	170	187	12	82	59	14.5	4.45	83	.280	.362	11	.200	0	-15	-14	-1	-1.2
1942 Phi-N	12	18	.400	40	31	19	0	1	253	224	8	99	77	11.5	3.06	108	.238	.310	8	.100	-5	7	7	3	0.5
1946 Phi-N	6	9	.400	29	13	3	2	1	111	123	5	44	34	13.6	4.38	78	.281	.349	3	.097	-1	-12	-12	-1	-1.4
1947 Phi-N	4	11	.267	29	15	4	1	1	127	121	5	59	44	12.8	3.47	115	.265	.350	2	.050	-4	8	8	0	0.4
1948 Cin-N	0	4	.000	12	4	0	0	0	27	43	3	24	7	22.3	9.00	43	.364	.472	1	.143	-0	-15	-15	0	-1.4
Total 5	31	56	.356	144	87	31	5	3	688	698	33	308	221	13.2	3.92	91	.266	.344	25	.117	-10	-27	-26	3	-3.1

■ VERN HUGHES
Hughes, Vernon Alexander "Lefty"   b: 4/15/1893, Etna, Pa.   d: 9/26/61, Sewickley, Pa.   BL/TL, 5'10", 155 lbs.   Deb: 7/06/14

YEAR TM/L	W	L	PCT	G	GS	CG	SH	SV	IP	H	HR	BB	SO	RAT	ERA	ERA+	OAV	OOB	BH	AVG	PB	PR	/A	PD	TPI
1914 Bal-F	0	0	—	3	0	0	0	0	5²	5	0	3	0	12.7	3.18	106	.244	.341	0	.000	-0	0	0	0	0.0

■ BILL HUGHES
Hughes, William Nesbert   b: 11/18/1896, Philadelphia, Pa.   d: 2/25/63, Birmingham, Ala.   BR/TR, 5'10.5", 155 lbs.   Deb: 9/15/21

YEAR TM/L	W	L	PCT	G	GS	CG	SH	SV	IP	H	HR	BB	SO	RAT	ERA	ERA+	OAV	OOB	BH	AVG	PB	PR	/A	PD	TPI
1921 Pit-N	0	0	—	1	0	0	0	0	2	3	0	1	2	22.5	4.50	85	.375	.500	0	—	0	-0	0	0	0.0

■ BILL HUGHES
Hughes, William R.   b: 11/25/1866, Bladensville, Ill.   d: 8/25/43, Santa Ana, Cal.   BL/TL,   Deb: 9/28/1884   ♦

YEAR TM/L	W	L	PCT	G	GS	CG	SH	SV	IP	H	HR	BB	SO	RAT	ERA	ERA+	OAV	OOB	BH	AVG	PB	PR	/A	PD	TPI
1885 Phi-a	0	2	.000	2	2	2	0	0	16²	18	0	10	4	15.1	4.86	71	.264	.358	3	.188	0	-3	-3	0	-0.1

■ JIM HUGHEY
Hughey, James Ulysses "Coldwater Jim"   b: 3/8/1869, Wakashma, Mich.   d: 3/29/45, Coldwater, Mich.   TR , 6',   Deb: 9/29/1891

YEAR TM/L	W	L	PCT	G	GS	CG	SH	SV	IP	H	HR	BB	SO	RAT	ERA	ERA+	OAV	OOB	BH	AVG	PB	PR	/A	PD	TPI
1891 Mil-a	1	0	1.000	2	1	1	0	0	15	18	1	3	9	12.6	3.00	146	.287	.320	1	.143	-1	1	2	0	0.2
1893 Chi-N	0	1	.000	2	1	1	0	0	9	14	0	3	4	17.0	11.00	42	.345	.390	0	.000	-0	-6	-6	-0	-0.4
1896 Pit-N	6	8	.429	25	14	11	0	0	155	171	3	67	48	13.8	4.99	84	.278	.349	14	.215	-1	-11	-14	-3	-1.4
1897 Pit-N	6	10	.375	25	17	13	0	1	149¹	193	3	45	38	14.3	5.06	83	.310	.357	8	.127	-5	-12	-15	-2	-1.7
1898 StL-N	7	24	.226	35	33	31	0	0	283²	325	2	71	74	12.6	3.93	96	.285	.327	11	.113	-6	-10	-5	-1	-0.9
1899 Cle-N	4	30	.118	36	34	32	0	0	283	403	9	88	54	15.6	5.41	68	.334	.379	18	.162	-5	-49	-54	-4	-5.3
1900 StL-N	5	7	.417	20	12	11	0	0	112²	147	2	40	23	14.9	5.19	70	.314	.368	7	.171	-5	-19	-19	-1	-1.7
Total 7	29	80	.266	145	113	100	0	1	1007²	1271	20	317	250	14.2	4.87	80	.306	.355	59	.153	-17	-106	-110	-11	-11.2

■ TEX HUGHSON
Hughson, Cecil Carlton   b: 2/9/16, Kyle, Tex.   BR/TR, 6'3", 198 lbs.   Deb: 4/16/41

YEAR TM/L	W	L	PCT	G	GS	CG	SH	SV	IP	H	HR	BB	SO	RAT	ERA	ERA+	OAV	OOB	BH	AVG	PB	PR	/A	PD	TPI
1941 Bos-A	5	3	.625	12	8	4	0	0	61	70	3	13	22	12.4	4.13	101	.289	.328	1	.059	-1	0	0	0	0.0
1942 Bos-A	22	6	.786	38	30	22	4	4	281	258	10	75	113	10.7	2.59	144	.245	.296	18	.176	1	33	35	1	4.1
1943 Bos-A	12	15	.444	35	32	20	4	2	266	242	23	73	114	10.7	2.64	126	.247	.300	9	.105	-4	19	20	1	1.9
1944 Bos-A	18	5	.783	28	23	19	2	5	203¹	172	4	41	112	9.5	2.26	151	.225	.267	10	.152	-1	26	26	-1	2.7
1946 •Bos-A	20	11	.645	39	35	21	6	3	278	252	15	51	172	9.9	2.75	133	.238	.274	12	.132	-2	23	28	-2	2.6
1947 Bos-A	12	11	.522	29	26	13	3	0	189¹	173	17	71	119	11.7	3.33	117	.244	.314	2	.033	-6	8	12	-1	0.6
1948 Bos-A	3	1	.750	15	0	0	0	0	19¹	21	0	7	6	13.0	5.12	86	.276	.337	0	.000	-0	-2	-1	-1	-0.1
1949 Bos-A	4	2	.667	29	2	0	0	3	77²	82	5	41	35	14.4	5.33	82	.268	.356	1	.045	-3	-10	-8	-2	-1.1
Total 8	96	54	.640	225	156	99	19	17	1375²	1270	77	372	693	10.8	2.94	125	.245	.297	53	.119	-16	99	111	-4	10.7

■ MARK HUISMANN
Huismann, Mark Lawrence   b: 5/11/58, Littleton, Colo.   BR/TR, 6'3", 195 lbs.   Deb: 8/16/83

YEAR TM/L	W	L	PCT	G	GS	CG	SH	SV	IP	H	HR	BB	SO	RAT	ERA	ERA+	OAV	OOB	BH	AVG	PB	PR	/A	PD	TPI
1983 KC-A	2	1	.667	13	0	0	0	0	30²	29	1	17	20	13.5	5.58	73	.250	.346	0	—	0	-5	-5	-1	-0.5
1984 •KC-A	3	3	.500	38	0	0	0	3	75	84	7	21	54	12.7	4.20	96	.286	.335	0	—	0	-2	-1	0	-0.1
1985 KC-A	1	0	1.000	9	0	0	0	0	18²	14	1	9	8	12.2	1.93	216	.219	.254	0	—	0	5	5	0	0.5
1986 KC-A	0	0	—	11	0	0	0	1	17¹	18	1	6	13	13.0	4.15	102	.269	.329	0	—	0	0	1	0	0.1
Sea-A	3	3	.500	36	1	0	0	4	80	80	18	19	59	11.2	3.71	114	.256	.301	0	—	0	4	4	0	0.5
Yr	3	4	.429	46	1	0	0	5	97¹	98	19	25	72	11.5	3.79	112	.258	.305	0	—	0	4	5	0	0.6

YEAR	TM/L	W	L	PCT	G	GS	CG	SH	SV	IP	H	HR	BB	SO	RAT	ERA	ERA+	OAV	OOB	BH	AVG	PB	PR	/A	PD	TPI
1987	Sea-A	0	0	—	6	0	0	0	0	14²	10	1	4	15	9.8	4.91	96	.196	.281	0	—	0	-1	-0	0	0.0
	Cle-A	2	3	.400	20	0	0	0	2	35¹	38	6	8	23	11.7	5.09	89	.271	.311	0	—	0	-3	-2	-0	-0.1
	Yr	2	3	.400	26	0	0	0	2	50	48	7	12	38	10.8	5.04	91	.247	.291	0	—	0	-3	-3	0	-0.1
1988	Det-A	1	0	1.000	5	0	0	0	0	5¹	6	0	2	6	13.5	5.06	75	.286	.348	0	—	0	-1	-1	0	0.0
1989	Bal-A	0	0	—	8	0	0	0	1	11¹	13	0	0	13	10.3	6.35	60	.277	.277	0	—	0	-3	-3	1	-0.2
1990	Pit-N	1	0	1.000	2	0	0	0	0	3	6	1	2	2	24.0	9.00	40	.462	.533	0	—	0	-2	-2	0	-0.1
Total 8		13	11	.542	147	1	0	0	11	291¹	298	37	81	214	11.9	4.36	96	.265	.317	0	—	0	-7	-5	1	0.1

■ HARRY HULIHAN
Hulihan, Harry Joseph b: 4/18/1899, Rutland, Vt. d: 9/11/80, Rutland, Vt. BR/TL, 5'11", 170 lbs. Deb: 8/16/22

YEAR	TM/L	W	L	PCT	G	GS	CG	SH	SV	IP	H	HR	BB	SO	RAT	ERA	ERA+	OAV	OOB	BH	AVG	PB	PR	/A	PD	TPI
1922	Bos-N	2	3	.400	7	6	2	0	0	40	40	0	26	16	15.7	3.15	127	.274	.398	2	.154	-0	4	4	-1	0.2

■ HANK HULVEY
Hulvey, James Hensel b: 7/18/1897, Mt.Sidney, Va. d: 4/9/82, Mount Sidney, Va. BB/TR, 6', 180 lbs. Deb: 9/05/23

YEAR	TM/L	W	L	PCT	G	GS	CG	SH	SV	IP	H	HR	BB	SO	RAT	ERA	ERA+	OAV	OOB	BH	AVG	PB	PR	/A	PD	TPI
1923	Phi-A	0	1	.000	1	1	0	0	0	7	10	1	2	2	15.4	7.71	53	.357	.400	1	.500	0	-3	-3	0	-0.1

■ TOM HUME
Hume, Thomas Hubert b: 3/29/53, Cincinnati, Ohio BR/TR, 6'1", 185 lbs. Deb: 5/25/77

YEAR	TM/L	W	L	PCT	G	GS	CG	SH	SV	IP	H	HR	BB	SO	RAT	ERA	ERA+	OAV	OOB	BH	AVG	PB	PR	/A	PD	TPI
1977	Cin-N	3	3	.500	14	5	0	0	0	43	54	5	17	22	14.9	7.12	55	.305	.366	2	.200	1	-15	-15	-0	-1.3
1978	Cin-N	8	11	.421	42	23	3	0	1	174	198	12	50	90	13.0	4.14	86	.289	.341	3	.067	-3	-11	-11	1	-1.3
1979	*Cin-N	10	9	.526	57	12	2	0	17	163	162	12	33	80	10.8	2.76	**135**	.262	.300	8	.174	0	18	18	-0	1.9
1980	Cin-N	9	10	.474	78	0	0	0	25	137	121	6	38	68	10.6	2.56	140	.240	.297	3	.188	0	16	15	3	2.0
1981	Cin-N	9	4	.692	51	0	0	0	13	67²	63	7	31	27	12.6	3.46	103	.259	.345	0	.000	-0	1	1	1	0.4
1982	Cin-N	2	6	.250	46	0	0	0	17	63²	72	5	21	22	11.2	3.11	119	.245	.310	0	.000	-1	3	4	-0	0.4
1983	Cin-N	3	5	.375	48	0	0	0	9	66	66	8	41	34	15.0	4.77	80	.264	.374	0	.000	-1	-8	-7	1	-0.6
1984	Cin-N	4	13	.235	54	8	0	0	3	113¹	142	14	41	59	14.6	5.64	67	.309	.367	3	.136	-0	-26	-23	1	-2.2
1985	Cin-N	3	5	.375	56	0	0	0	3	80	65	7	35	50	11.6	3.26	116	.234	.314	0	.000	-1	3	5	-0	0.4
1986	Phi-N	4	1	.800	48	1	0	0	4	94¹	89	5	34	51	12.0	2.77	139	.252	.323	0	.000	-1	10	11	1	1.2
1987	Phi-N	1	4	.200	38	6	0	0	0	70²	75	10	41	29	15.3	5.60	76	.277	.380	3	.200	0	-12	-11	1	-0.8
	Cin-N	1	0	1.000	11	0	0	0	0	13¹	14	0	2	4	11.5	4.05	105	.292	.333	0	—	0	-0	-0	0	-0.0
	Yr	2	4	.333	49	6	0	0	0	84	89	10	43	33	14.3	5.36	79	.274	.360	3	.000	0	-12	-10	1	-0.8
Total 11		57	71	.445	543	55	5	0	92	1086	1106	88	384	536	12.5	3.85	97	.268	.334	22	.120	-5	-22	-14	7	-0.3

■ BILL HUMPHREY
Humphrey, Byron William b: 6/17/11, Vienna, Mo. BR/TR, 6', 180 lbs. Deb: 4/24/38

YEAR	TM/L	W	L	PCT	G	GS	CG	SH	SV	IP	H	HR	BB	SO	RAT	ERA	ERA+	OAV	OOB	BH	AVG	PB	PR	/A	PD	TPI
1938	Bos-A	0	0	—	2	0	0	0	0	2	5	0	1	0	27.0	9.00	55	.500	.545	0	—	0	-1	-1	0	0.0

■ BOB HUMPHREYS
Humphreys, Robert William b: 8/18/35, Covington, Va. BR/TR, 5'11", 165 lbs. Deb: 9/08/62

YEAR	TM/L	W	L	PCT	G	GS	CG	SH	SV	IP	H	HR	BB	SO	RAT	ERA	ERA+	OAV	OOB	BH	AVG	PB	PR	/A	PD	TPI
1962	Det-A	0	1	.000	4	0	0	0	1	5	8	3	2	3	18.0	7.20	57	.381	.435	0	—	0	-2	-2	0	-0.1
1963	StL-N	0	1	.000	9	0	0	0	0	10²	11	4	7	7	16.0	5.06	70	.282	.404	0	—	0	-2	-2	0	-0.1
1964	*StL-N	2	0	1.000	28	0	0	0	2	42²	32	3	15	36	10.1	2.53	150	.213	.289	1	.250	1	5	6	-0	0.7
1965	Chi-N	2	0	1.000	41	0	0	0	0	65²	59	6	27	38	12.1	3.15	117	.244	.325	0	.000	-0	3	4	-1	0.3
1966	Was-A	7	3	.700	58	1	0	0	3	111²	91	6	28	88	9.9	2.82	123	.229	.287	2	.167	1	8	8	-1	0.9
1967	Was-A	6	2	.750	48	2	0	0	4	105²	93	13	41	54	11.7	4.17	76	.238	.316	2	.133	1	-11	-12	-1	-1.3
1968	Was-A	5	7	.417	56	0	0	0	2	92²	78	13	30	56	10.5	3.69	79	.233	.296	2	.400	1	-7	-8	1	-0.6
1969	Was-A	3	3	.500	47	0	0	0	5	79²	69	3	38	43	12.2	3.05	114	.233	.322	1	.077	-1	5	4	1	0.4
1970	Was-A	0	0	—	5	0	0	0	0	6²	4	1	9	4	17.6	1.35	263	.200	.448	0	—	0	2	2	0	0.2
	Mil-A	2	4	.333	23	1	0	0	3	45²	37	3	22	32	12.0	3.15	120	.222	.319	0	.000	-0	3	3	0	0.3
	Yr	2	4	.333	28	1	0	0	3	52¹	41	4	31	38	12.7	2.92	129	.219	.336	1	.111	0	5	5	0	0.5
Total 9		27	21	.563	319	4	0	0	20	566	482	55	219	364	11.4	3.36	101	.234	.312	8	.131	-1	3	3	-2	0.7

■ BERT HUMPHRIES
Humphries, Albert b: 9/26/1880, California, Pa. d: 9/21/45, Orlando, Fla. 5'11.5", 182 lbs. Deb: 4/16/10

YEAR	TM/L	W	L	PCT	G	GS	CG	SH	SV	IP	H	HR	BB	SO	RAT	ERA	ERA+	OAV	OOB	BH	AVG	PB	PR	/A	PD	TPI
1910	Phi-N	0	0	—	5	0	0	0	2	9²	13	0	3	3	15.8	4.66	67	.317	.378	0	—	0	-2	-2	0	0.0
1911	Phi-N	3	1	.750	11	5	2	0	1	41	56	1	10	13	15.8	4.17	83	.339	.398	5	.333	3	-4	-3	-0	0.0
	Cin-N	4	3	.571	14	7	3	0	0	65	62	3	18	16	11.9	2.35	141	.266	.335	1	.063	-1	8	7	1	0.7
	Yr	7	4	.636	25	12	5	0	1	106	118	4	28	29	12.9	3.06	110	.292	.347	6	.097	2	4	4	0	0.7
1912	Cin-N	9	11	.450	30	15	9	2	2	158²	162	6	36	58	11.7	3.23	104	.259	.308	7	.137	-2	3	2	-1	0.0
1913	Chi-N	16	4	**.800**	28	20	13	2	1	181	169	10	24	61	9.7	2.69	118	.250	.277	12	.194	1	10	10	-2	1.0
1914	Chi-N	10	11	.476	34	22	8	1	0	171	162	5	37	62	10.6	2.68	104	.250	.293	13	.236	3	8	7	0	0.7
1915	Chi-N	8	13	.381	31	22	10	4	3	171²	183	6	23	45	11.1	2.31	120	.249	.309	8	.174	0	8	9	-1	0.8
Total 6		50	43	.538	153	91	45	10	9	798	807	31	151	258	11.1	2.79	110	.265	.307	46	.186	5	26	25	-1	3.2

■ JOHNNY HUMPHRIES
Humphries, John William b: 6/23/15, Clifton Forge, Va. d: 6/24/65, New Orleans, La. BR/TR, 6'1", 185 lbs. Deb: 5/08/38

YEAR	TM/L	W	L	PCT	G	GS	CG	SH	SV	IP	H	HR	BB	SO	RAT	ERA	ERA+	OAV	OOB	BH	AVG	PB	PR	/A	PD	TPI
1938	Cle-A	9	8	.529	**45**	6	1	0	6	103¹	105	6	63	56	14.7	5.23	89	.264	.367	3	.103	-1	-5	-7	-1	-0.7
1939	Cle-A	2	4	.333	15	1	0	0	2	28¹	30	4	32	12	20.0	8.26	53	.294	.467	0	.000	-1	-11	-12	-0	-1.1
1940	Cle-A	0	2	.000	19	1	1	0	1	33²	35	5	29	17	17.6	8.29	51	.269	.410	0	.000	-1	-15	-15	-1	-1.4
1941	Chi-A	4	2	.667	14	6	4	4	1	73¹	63	2	22	25	10.6	1.84	223	.230	.290	2	.087	1	19	18	-1	1.6
1942	Chi-A	12	12	.500	28	28	17	2	0	228¹	227	9	59	71	11.5	2.68	134	.257	.309	18	.225	4	25	23	-1	2.8
1943	Chi-A	11	11	.500	28	27	8	2	0	188¹	198	7	54	51	12.3	3.30	101	.268	.322	20	.290	4	-0	-1	-0	-0.6
1944	Chi-A	8	10	.444	30	20	8	0	1	169	170	9	57	42	12.3	3.67	93	.267	.331	10	.189	0	-5	-5	-3	-0.7
1945	Chi-A	6	14	.300	22	21	10	1	1	153	172	11	48	33	13.1	4.24	78	.282	.337	8	.148	-3	-15	-16	-3	-2.1
1946	Phi-N	0	0	—	10	1	0	0	0	24²	24	1	9	10	12.4	4.01	85	.258	.330	2	.250	1	-2	-2	-1	-0.2
Total 9		52	63	.452	211	111	49	9	12	1002	1024	50	373	317	12.8	3.78	97	.265	.334	63	.191	4	-9	-13	-12	-1.2

■ BEN HUNT
Hunt, Benjamin Franklin "High Pockets" b: 1888, Eufaula, Okla. BL/TL, 6'5", 190 lbs. Deb: 8/24/10

YEAR	TM/L	W	L	PCT	G	GS	CG	SH	SV	IP	H	HR	BB	SO	RAT	ERA	ERA+	OAV	OOB	BH	AVG	PB	PR	/A	PD	TPI
1910	Bos-A	2	3	.400	7	4	3	0	0	46²	45	4	20	19	12.5	4.05	63	.266	.344	1	.056	-2	-8	-8	-0	-0.9
1913	StL-N	0	1	.000	2	1	0	0	0	8	6	0	9	6	18.0	3.38	96	.240	.457	0	—	-0	-0	-0	1	0.0
Total 2		2	4	.333	9	8	3	0	0	54²	51	4	29	25	13.3	3.95	67	.263	.362	1	.050	-2	-8	-8	0	-0.9

■ KEN HUNT
Hunt, Kenneth Raymond b: 12/14/38, Ogden, Utah BR/TR, 6'4", 200 lbs. Deb: 4/16/61

YEAR	TM/L	W	L	PCT	G	GS	CG	SH	SV	IP	H	HR	BB	SO	RAT	ERA	ERA+	OAV	OOB	BH	AVG	PB	PR	/A	PD	TPI
1961	*Cin-N	9	10	.474	29	22	4	0	0	136¹	130	13	66	75	13.3	3.96	103	.257	.349	7	.179	0	1	2	-1	0.1

■ GEORGE HUNTER
Hunter, George Henry b: 7/8/1887, Buffalo, N.Y. d: 1/11/68, Harrisburg, Pa. BB, 5'8.5", 165 lbs. Deb: 5/04/09 ◆

YEAR	TM/L	W	L	PCT	G	GS	CG	SH	SV	IP	H	HR	BB	SO	RAT	ERA	ERA+	OAV	OOB	BH	AVG	PB	PR	/A	PD	TPI
1909	Bro-N	4	10	.286	16	13	10	0	0	113¹	104	0	38	43	11.5	2.46	105	.254	.322	28	.228	2	2	2	0	0.2

■ JIM HUNTER
Hunter, James Augustus "Catfish" b: 4/8/46, Hertford, N.C. BR/TR, 6', 190 lbs. Deb: 5/13/65 H

YEAR	TM/L	W	L	PCT	G	GS	CG	SH	SV	IP	H	HR	BB	SO	RAT	ERA	ERA+	OAV	OOB	BH	AVG	PB	PR	/A	PD	TPI
1965	KC-A	8	8	.500	32	20	3	2	0	133	124	21	46	82	11.6	4.26	82	.246	.311	6	.150	-1	-12	-11	-2	-1.3
1966	KC-A	9	11	.450	30	25	4	0	0	176²	158	17	64	103	11.4	4.02	84	.239	.308	9	.153	1	-12	-12	-3	-1.4
1967	KC-A	13	17	.433	35	35	13	5	0	259²	209	16	84	196	10.2	2.81	113	.219	.284	18	.196	4	12	11	-5	1.1
1968	Oak-A	13	13	.500	36	34	11	2	1	234	210	29	69	172	10.9	3.35	84	.238	.296	19	.232	5	-10	-14	-3	-1.3
1969	Oak-A	12	15	.444	38	35	10	3	0	247	210	34	85	150	10.9	3.35	103	.234	.304	19	.224	4	7	2	-1	-0.5
1970	Oak-A	18	14	.563	40	40	9	4	0	262¹	253	32	74	178	11.5	3.81	93	.260	.307	18	.230	4	-3	-8	-3	-0.6
1971	*Oak-A	21	11	.656	37	37	16	4	0	273²	225	27	80	181	10.2	2.96	113	.223	.282	36	.350	12	15	11	-3	2.2
1972	*Oak-A	21	7	**.750**	38	37	16	5	0	295¹	200	21	70	191	8.3	2.04	139	.189	.242	23	.219	-2	33	26	-3	3.0
1973	*Oak-A	21	5	**.808**	36	36	11	3	0	256¹	222	39	69	124	10.3	3.34	106	.232	.284	1	1.000	0	14	6	-3	0.3
1974	*Oak-A	25	12	.676	41	41	23	6	0	318¹	268	25	46	143	**9.0**	2.49	133	.229	**.260**	0	.000	-0	**40**	29	-3	2.8
1975	NY-A	23	14	.622	39	39	**30**	7	0	328	248	29	83	177	**9.2**	2.58	141	**.208**	**.263**	0	—	0	44	39	-4	3.7
1976	*NY-A	17	15	.531	36	36	21	2	0	298²	268	30	68	173	10.2	3.53	97	.241	.286	0	.000	0	-0	-4	-3	-0.6
1977	*NY-A	9	9	.500	22	22	8	0	0	143¹	137	29	47	52	11.7	4.71	84	.250	.313	0	—	0	-10	-12	-3	-1.3

YEAR TM/L	W	L	PCT	G	GS	CG	SH	SV	IP	H	HR	BB	SO	RAT	ERA	ERA+	OAV	OOB	BH	AVG	PB	PR	/A	PD	TPI
1978 *NY-A	12	6	.667	21	20	5	1	0	118	98	16	35	56	10.2	3.58	101	.226	.286	0	—	0	2	0	-0	0.0
1979 NY-A	2	9	.182	19	19	1	0	0	105	128	15	34	34	14.0	5.31	77	.312	.366	0	—	0	-13	-14	-1	-1.3
Total 15	224	166	.574	500	476	181	42	1	3449¹	2958	374	954	2012	10.3	3.26	104	.231	.287	149	.226	32	109	50	-38	5.8

■ LEM HUNTER
Hunter, Robert Lemuel b: 1/16/1863, Warren, Ohio d: 11/9/56, W.Lafayette, Ohio   Deb: 9/01/1883 ♦

YEAR TM/L	W	L	PCT	G	GS	CG	SH	SV	IP	H	HR	BB	SO	RAT	ERA	ERA+	OAV	OOB	BH	AVG	PB	PR	/A	PD	TPI
1883 Cle-N	0	0	—	1	0	0	0	0	6¹	10	0	2	4	17.1	1.42	222	.339	.381	1	.250	-0	1	1	0	0.1

■ WILLARD HUNTER
Hunter, Willard Mitchell b: 3/8/34, Newark, N.J. BR/TL, 6'2", 180 lbs. Deb: 4/16/62

YEAR TM/L	W	L	PCT	G	GS	CG	SH	SV	IP	H	HR	BB	SO	RAT	ERA	ERA+	OAV	OOB	BH	AVG	PB	PR	/A	PD	TPI
1962 LA-N	0	0	—	1	0	0	0	0	2	6	1	4	1	45.0	40.50	9	.545	.667	0	—	0	-8	-8	0	-0.5
NY-N	1	6	.143	27	6	1	0	0	63	67	9	34	40	14.6	5.57	75	.270	.360	3	.231	0	-11	-10	-1	-0.9
Yr	1	6	.143	28	6	1	0	0	65	73	10	38	41	15.5	6.65	63	.281	.375	3	.000	0	-20	-18	-1	-1.4
1964 NY-N	3	3	.500	41	0	0	0	5	49	54	4	9	22	11.9	4.41	81	.284	.323	1	1.000	0	-5	-5	-0	-0.3
Total 2	4	9	.308	69	6	1	0	5	114	127	14	47	63	14.0	5.68	69	.283	.355	4	.286	1	-24	-22	-1	-1.7

■ WALT HUNTZINGER
Huntzinger, Walter Henry "Shakes" b: 2/6/1899, Pottsville, Pa. d: 8/11/81, Upper Darby, Pa. BR/TR, 6', 150 lbs. Deb: 9/29/23

YEAR TM/L	W	L	PCT	G	GS	CG	SH	SV	IP	H	HR	BB	SO	RAT	ERA	ERA+	OAV	OOB	BH	AVG	PB	PR	/A	PD	TPI
1923 NY-N	0	1	.000	2	1	0	0	0	8	9	0	1	2	11.3	7.88	49	.290	.313	0	.000	-0	-3	-4	-0	-0.3
1924 NY-N	1	1	.500	12	2	0	0	1	32¹	41	3	9	6	13.9	4.45	82	.318	.362	4	.500	1	-2	-3	-0	-0.1
1925 NY-N	5	1	.833	26	1	0	0	0	64¹	68	3	17	19	11.9	3.50	115	.281	.328	1	.091	-1	6	4	-1	0.2
1926 StL-N	0	4	.000	9	4	2	0	0	34	35	4	9	13	13.0	4.24	92	.267	.338	0	.000	-1	-2	-1	1	0.0
Chi-N	1	1	.500	11	0	0	0	2	28²	26	0	8	4	11.6	0.94	408	.260	.333	1	.143	0	9	9	0	0.9
Yr	1	5	.167	20	4	2	0	2	62²	61	4	22	13	12.4	2.73	142	.264	.336	1	.067	-2	8	8	1	0.9
Total 4	7	8	.467	60	8	2	0	3	167¹	179	10	49	40	12.4	3.60	108	.283	.337	6	.167	-1	8	6	-0	0.7

■ TOM HURD
Hurd, Thomas Carr "Whitey" b: 5/27/24, Danville, Va. d: 9/5/82, Waterloo, Iowa BR/TR, 5'9", 155 lbs. Deb: 7/30/54

YEAR TM/L	W	L	PCT	G	GS	CG	SH	SV	IP	H	HR	BB	SO	RAT	ERA	ERA+	OAV	OOB	BH	AVG	PB	PR	/A	PD	TPI
1954 Bos-A	2	0	1.000	16	0	0	0	1	29²	21	2	12	14	10.0	3.03	135	.198	.280	1	.333	0	2	4	0	0.5
1955 Bos-A	8	6	.571	43	0	0	0	5	80²	72	7	38	48	12.4	3.01	142	.242	.330	1	.071	-1	8	11	-0	1.0
1956 Bos-A	3	4	.429	40	0	0	0	5	76	84	5	47	34	15.9	5.33	87	.289	.393	6	.500	2	-10	-6	-1	-0.4
Total 3	13	10	.565	99	0	0	0	11	186¹	177	14	97	96	13.4	3.96	111	.255	.350	8	.276	1	1	9	-1	1.1

■ BRUCE HURST
Hurst, Bruce Vee b: 3/24/58, St.George, Utah BL/TL, 6'4", 200 lbs. Deb: 4/12/80

YEAR TM/L	W	L	PCT	G	GS	CG	SH	SV	IP	H	HR	BB	SO	RAT	ERA	ERA+	OAV	OOB	BH	AVG	PB	PR	/A	PD	TPI
1980 Bos-A	2	2	.500	12	7	0	0	0	30²	39	4	16	16	16.7	9.10	46	.307	.393	0	—	0	-17	-17	-0	-1.5
1981 Bos-A	2	0	1.000	5	5	0	0	0	23	23	1	12	11	14.1	4.30	90	.258	.353	0	—	0	-2	-1	-0	-0.1
1982 Bos-A	3	7	.300	28	19	0	0	0	117	161	16	40	53	15.7	5.77	75	.333	.388	0	—	0	-22	-19	1	-1.6
1983 Bos-A	12	12	.500	33	32	6	2	0	211¹	241	22	62	115	13.0	4.09	106	.290	.342	0	—	0	-1	6	1	0.7
1984 Bos-A	12	12	.500	33	33	9	2	0	218	232	25	88	136	13.5	3.92	106	.271	.343	0	—	0	2	6	0	0.6
1985 Bos-A	11	13	.458	35	31	6	1	0	229¹	243	31	70	189	12.4	4.51	95	.273	.328	0	—	0	-9	-6	-0	-0.5
1986 *Bos-A	13	8	.619	25	25	11	4	0	174¹	169	18	50	167	11.5	2.99	139	.256	.311	0	—	0	23	23	-1	2.2
1987 Bos-A	15	13	.536	33	33	15	3	0	238²	239	35	76	190	11.9	4.41	103	.262	.320	0	—	0	1	3	0	0.3
1988 *Bos-A	18	6	.750	33	32	7	1	0	216²	222	21	65	166	12.0	3.66	113	.264	.318	0	—	0	7	11	0	1.2
1989 SD-N	15	11	.577	33	33	10	0	0	244²	214	16	66	179	10.3	2.69	130	.237	.289	5	.071	-2	22	22	1	2.3
1990 SD-N	11	9	.550	33	33	9	4	0	223²	188	21	63	162	10.1	3.14	123	.228	.284	6	.090	-2	16	18	0	1.6
Total 11	114	93	.551	303	283	73	19	0	1927¹	1971	210	608	1384	12.2	3.91	105	.266	.324	11	.080	-4	20	46	2	5.2

■ BILL HUSTED
Husted, William J. b: 10/11/1866, Gloucester, N.J. d: 5/17/41, Gloucester, N.J. Deb: 4/29/1890

YEAR TM/L	W	L	PCT	G	GS	CG	SH	SV	IP	H	HR	BB	SO	RAT	ERA	ERA+	OAV	OOB	BH	AVG	PB	PR	/A	PD	TPI
1890 Phi-P	5	10	.333	18	17	12	0	0	129	148	2	67	33	15.0	4.88	88	.276	.356	6	.107	-6	-9	-9	-2	-1.2

■ BERT HUSTING
Husting, Berthold Juneau "Pete" b: 3/6/1878, Fond Du Lac, Wis. d: 9/3/48, Milwaukee, Wis. BR/TR, Deb: 8/16/00

YEAR TM/L	W	L	PCT	G	GS	CG	SH	SV	IP	H	HR	BB	SO	RAT	ERA	ERA+	OAV	OOB	BH	AVG	PB	PR	/A	PD	TPI
1900 Pit-N	0	0	—	2	0	0	0	0	8	10	2	5	7	16.9	5.63	65	.305	.397	0	.000	-0	-2	-2	1	-0.1
1901 Mil-A	10	15	.400	34	26	19	0	1	217¹	234	5	95	67	13.6	4.27	84	.272	.344	19	.202	-1	-14	-16	5	-1.0
1902 Bos-A	0	1	.000	1	1	1	0	0	8	15	0	4	4	25.9	9.00	40	.398	.504	1	.250	1	-5	-5	-0	-0.2
Phi-A	14	5	.737	32	27	17	1	0	204	240	7	91	44	14.6	3.79	97	.293	.364	13	.159	-3	-5	-3	3	-0.2
Yr	14	6	.700	33	28	18	1	0	212	255	7	99	48	15.0	3.99	92	.298	.371	0	.000	-3	-10	-8	3	-0.4
Total 3	24	21	.533	69	54	37	1	1	437¹	499	14	199	122	14.4	4.16	87	.285	.358	33	.180	-4	-26	-26	9	-1.5

■ JOHNNY HUTCHINGS
Hutchings, John Richard Joseph b: 4/14/16, Chicago, Ill. d: 4/27/63, Indianapolis, Ind. BB/TR, 6'2", 250 lbs. Deb: 4/26/40

YEAR TM/L	W	L	PCT	G	GS	CG	SH	SV	IP	H	HR	BB	SO	RAT	ERA	ERA+	OAV	OOB	BH	AVG	PB	PR	/A	PD	TPI
1940 *Cin-N	2	1	.667	19	4	0	0	0	54	53	3	18	18	12.0	3.50	108	.260	.323	2	.154	0	2	-1	0	0.1
1941 Cin-N	0	0	—	8	0	0	0	0	11	9	4	5	13.1	4.09	88	.279	.340	0	—	0	-1	-1	0	0.0
Bos-N	1	6	.143	36	7	1	1	2	95²	110	6	22	36	12.8	4.14	86	.287	.333	4	.148	0	-5	-6	-0	-0.5
Yr	1	6	.143	44	7	1	1	2	106²	122	6	26	41	12.8	4.13	86	.286	.333	4	.074	0	-6	-7	0	-0.5
1942 Bos-N	1	0	1.000	20	3	0	0	0	65²	66	2	34	27	14.0	4.39	76	.260	.352	1	.050	-2	-8	-8	-1	-1.0
1944 Bos-N	1	4	.200	14	1	0	0	1	56²	55	3	26	26	13.0	3.97	96	.252	.335	1	.067	-1	-2	-1	-1	-0.1
1945 Bos-N	7	6	.538	57	12	3	2	3	185	173	21	75	99	12.3	3.75	102	.244	.330	13	.241	2	1	2	-1	0.3
1946 Bos-N	0	1	.000	1	0	0	0	0	3	5	1	1	1	18.0	9.00	38	.357	.400	0	.000	-0	-2	-2	-0	-0.1
Total 6	12	18	.400	155	34	5	3	6	471	474	36	180	212	12.7	3.96	93	.260	.330	21	.162	-1	-15	-14	-3	-1.3

■ FRED HUTCHINSON
Hutchinson, Frederick Charles b: 8/12/19, Seattle, Wash. d: 11/12/64, Bradenton, Fla. BL/TR, 6'2", 190 lbs. Deb: 5/02/39 M♦

YEAR TM/L	W	L	PCT	G	GS	CG	SH	SV	IP	H	HR	BB	SO	RAT	ERA	ERA+	OAV	OOB	BH	AVG	PB	PR	/A	PD	TPI
1939 Det-A	3	6	.333	13	12	3	0	0	84²	95	9	51	22	15.5	5.21	94	.287	.382	13	.382	3	-6	-3	0	0.1
1940 *Det-A	3	7	.300	17	10	1	0	0	76	85	6	26	32	13.4	5.68	84	.281	.342	8	.267	0	-11	-8	-0	-0.5
1946 Det-A	14	11	.560	28	26	16	3	2	207	184	14	66	138	10.9	3.09	118	.236	.295	28	.315	8	10	13	3	2.7
1947 Det-A	18	10	.643	33	25	18	3	2	219²	211	14	61	113	11.2	3.03	124	.251	.304	32	.302	11	16	18	2	3.4
1948 Det-A	13	11	.542	33	28	15	0	0	221	223	32	48	90	11.1	4.32	101	.258	.297	5	.205	5	-1	-1	3	0.1
1949 Det-A	15	7	.682	33	21	9	4	1	188²	167	19	18	52	54	10.5	2.96	141	.237	.290	18	.247	4	26	25	2	3.3
1950 Det-A	17	8	.680	39	26	10	1	0	231²	269	18	48	71	12.5	3.96	118	.290	.329	31	.326	10	16	19	3	3.1
1951 Det-A	10	10	.500	31	20	9	2	2	188¹	204	11	27	53	11.1	3.68	113	.275	.302	16	.188	-2	9	10	3	1.1
1952 Det-A	2	1	.667	12	1	0	0	0	37¹	40	4	9	12	12.1	3.38	113	.276	.323	1	.056	-1	1	2	2	0.3
1953 Det-A	0	0	—	3	0	0	0	0	9²	9	0	0	4	8.4	2.79	146	.243	.243	1	1	0	1	1	-0	0.2
Total 10	95	71	.572	242	169	81	13	7	1464	1487	126	388	591	11.6	3.73	113	.262	.311	171	.263	40	62	79	17	13.8

■ IRA HUTCHINSON
Hutchinson, Ira Kendall b: 8/31/10, Chicago, Ill. d: 8/21/73, Chicago, Ill. BR/TR, 5'10.5", 180 lbs. Deb: 9/24/33

YEAR TM/L	W	L	PCT	G	GS	CG	SH	SV	IP	H	HR	BB	SO	RAT	ERA	ERA+	OAV	OOB	BH	AVG	PB	PR	/A	PD	TPI
1933 Chi-A	0	0	—	1	1	0	0	0	4	7	1	3	2	22.5	13.50	31	.368	.455	1	.500	0	-4	-4	-0	-0.2
1937 Bos-N	4	6	.400	31	8	1	0	0	91²	99	4	35	29	13.3	3.73	96	.286	.353	1	.115	-1	2	-1	1	-0.1
1938 Bos-N	9	8	.529	36	12	4	1	4	151	150	3	61	38	12.8	2.74	125	.258	.332	9	.173	-1	18	12	1	1.2
1939 Bro-N	5	2	.714	41	1	0	0	1	105²	103	9	51	46	13.2	4.34	93	.265	.352	1	.037	-3	-5	-4	1	-0.5
1940 StL-N	4	2	.667	20	2	1	0	1	63¹	68	9	19	22	12.4	3.13	128	.271	.322	4	.222	0	5	6	0	0.7
1941 StL-N	1	5	.167	29	0	0	0	5	46²	32	3	19	19	10.2	3.86	98	.196	.288	2	.250	0	-1	-0	0	0.0
1944 Bos-N	9	7	.563	40	8	1	1	1	119²	136	8	53	22	14.4	4.21	91	.296	.373	4	.138	-1	-8	-5	-1	-0.4
1945 Bos-N	2	3	.400	11	0	0	0	1	28²	33	2	8	4	13.2	5.02	76	.277	.328	0	.000	-1	-4	-4	1	-0.3
Total 8	34	33	.507	209	32	7	2	13	610²	628	33	249	179	13.1	3.76	100	.270	.344	24	.140	-7	2	-1	5	0.4

■ BILL HUTCHINSON
Hutchinson, William Forrest "Wild Bill" b: 12/17/1859, New Haven, Conn. d: 3/19/26, Kansas City, Mo. TR Deb: 6/10/1884

YEAR TM/L	W	L	PCT	G	GS	CG	SH	SV	IP	H	HR	BB	SO	RAT	ERA	ERA+	OAV	OOB	BH	AVG	PB	PR	/A	PD	TPI
1884 KC-U	1	1	.500	2	2	2	0	0	17	14	0	1	5	7.9	2.65	104	.209	.221	2	.250	-0	1	0	2	0.2
1889 Chi-N	16	17	.485	37	36	33	3	0	318	306	11	117	136	12.0	3.54	118	.245	.310	21	.158	-5	17	22	4	2.0
1890 Chi-N	42	25	.627	71	66	65	5	2	603	505	20	199	289	10.5	2.70	135	.221	.283	53	.203	-4	58	64	4	6.0
1891 Chi-N	44	19	.698	66	58	56	4	1	561	508	26	178	261	11.0	2.81	118	.232	.290	45	.185	-0	34	32	-3	2.5
1892 Chi-N	37	36	.507	75	71	67	5	0	627	572	11	187	316	10.9	2.74	121	.233	.288	57	.217	4	38	40	3	4.5

YEAR	TM/L	W	L	PCT	G	GS	CG	SH	SV	IP	H	HR	BB	SO	RAT	ERA	ERA+	OAV	OOB	BH	AVG	PB	PR	/A	PD	TPI
1893	Chi-N	16	24	.400	44	40	38	2	0	348¹	420	9	156	80	14.9	4.75	97	.289	.358	41	.253	2	-3	-5	-3	-0.5
1894	Chi-N	14	16	.467	36	34	28	0	0	277²	373	9	140	59	16.6	6.06	93	.318	.391	42	.309	6	-23	-14	-1	-0.5
1895	Chi-N	13	21	.382	38	35	30	2	0	291	371	13	129	85	15.5	4.73	108	.305	.372	25	.198	-7	2	12	-0	0.4
1897	StL-N	1	4	.200	6	5	2	0	0	40	55	5	22	5	17.3	6.07	73	.324	.401	5	.278	1	-8	-7	-1	-0.5
Total	9	184	163	.530	375	347	321	21	3	3083	3124	104	1129	1236	12.4	3.58	111	.255	.318	291	.216	-4	115	139	5	14.1

■ HERB HUTSON
Hutson, George Herbert b: 7/17/49, Savannah, Ga. BR/TR, 6'2", 205 lbs. Deb: 4/10/74

YEAR	TM/L	W	L	PCT	G	GS	CG	SH	SV	IP	H	HR	BB	SO	RAT	ERA	ERA+	OAV	OOB	BH	AVG	PB	PR	/A	PD	TPI
1974	Chi-N	0	2	.000	20	2	0	0	0	28²	24	3	15	22	12.6	3.45	110	.233	.336	0	.000	0	1	1	-0	0.0

■ TOM HUTTON
Hutton, Thomas George b: 4/20/46, Los Angeles, Cal. BL/TL, 5'11", 180 lbs. Deb: 9/16/66 ♦

YEAR	TM/L	W	L	PCT	G	GS	CG	SH	SV	IP	H	HR	BB	SO	RAT	ERA	ERA+	OAV	OOB	BH	AVG	PB	PR	/A	PD	TPI
1980	Mon-N	0	0	—	1	0	0	0	0	1	3	1	1	1	36.0	27.00	13	.500	.571	12	.218	0	-3	-3	0	-0.1

■ DICK HYDE
Hyde, Richard Elde b: 8/3/28, Hindsboro, Ill. BR/TR, 5'11", 170 lbs. Deb: 4/23/55

YEAR	TM/L	W	L	PCT	G	GS	CG	SH	SV	IP	H	HR	BB	SO	RAT	ERA	ERA+	OAV	OOB	BH	AVG	PB	PR	/A	PD	TPI
1955	Was-A	0	0	—	3	0	0	0	0	2	2	0	1	1	13.5	4.50	85	.286	.375	0	—	0	-0	-0	0	0.0
1957	Was-A	4	3	.571	52	2	0	0	1	109¹	104	4	56	46	13.7	4.12	95	.261	.361	3	.167	-0	-4	-3	1	-0.1
1958	Was-A	10	3	.769	53	0	0	0	18	103	82	1	35	49	10.4	1.75	218	.220	.291	0	.000	-2	23	24	2	2.5
1959	Was-A	2	5	.286	37	0	0	0	4	54¹	56	5	27	29	14.1	4.97	79	.269	.359	0	.000	-1	-7	-6	2	-0.4
1960	Was-A	0	1	.000	9	0	0	0	0	8²	11	5	2	4	17.7	4.15	94	.355	.459	0	—	0	-4	-4	0	-0.1
1961	Bal-A	1	2	.333	15	0	0	0	0	21	18	1	13	15	13.7	5.57	70	.228	.344	1	1.000	0	-4	-4	1	-0.1
Total	6	17	14	.548	169	2	0	0	23	298¹	273	16	137	144	12.8	3.56	109	.249	.339	4	.093	-3	8	10	6	1.9

■ JIM HYNDMAN
Hyndman, James William b: 1864, Kingston, Pa. Deb: 7/23/1886 ♦

YEAR	TM/L	W	L	PCT	G	GS	CG	SH	SV	IP	H	HR	BB	SO	RAT	ERA	ERA+	OAV	OOB	BH	AVG	PB	PR	/A	PD	TPI
1886	Phi-a	0	1	.000	1	1	0	0	0	2	5	1	5	1	45.0	27.00	13	.452	.623	0	.000	-1	-5	-5	0	-0.3

■ PAT HYNES
Hynes, Patrick J. b: 3/12/1884, St.Louis, Mo. d: 3/12/07, St.Louis, Mo. TL , Deb: 9/27/03 ♦

YEAR	TM/L	W	L	PCT	G	GS	CG	SH	SV	IP	H	HR	BB	SO	RAT	ERA	ERA+	OAV	OOB	BH	AVG	PB	PR	/A	PD	TPI
1903	StL-N	0	1	.000	1	1	1	0	0	9	10	0	6	1	16.0	4.00	82	.294	.400	0	.000	-0	-1	-1	-0	-0.1
1904	StL-A	1	0	1.000	5	2	1	0	0	26	35	1	7	6	14.5	6.23	40	.322	.363	60	.236	0	-10	-11	-1	-1.0
Total	2	1	1	.500	6	3	2	0	0	35	45	1	13	7	14.9	5.66	47	.316	.373	60	.233	0	-11	-12	-1	-1.1

■ HAM IBURG
Iburg, Herman Edward b: 10/29/1877, San Francisco, Cal d: 2/11/45, San Francisco, Cal BR/TR, 5'11", 165 lbs. Deb: 4/17/02

YEAR	TM/L	W	L	PCT	G	GS	CG	SH	SV	IP	H	HR	BB	SO	RAT	ERA	ERA+	OAV	OOB	BH	AVG	PB	PR	/A	PD	TPI
1902	Phi-N	11	18	.379	30	30	20	1	0	236	286	1	62	106	13.7	3.89	72	.299	.348	12	.138	-4	-29	-28	0	-3.1

■ GARY IGNASIAK
Ignasiak, Gary Raymond b: 9/1/49, Mt.Clemens, Mich. BR/TL, 5'11", 185 lbs. Deb: 9/20/73

YEAR	TM/L	W	L	PCT	G	GS	CG	SH	SV	IP	H	HR	BB	SO	RAT	ERA	ERA+	OAV	OOB	BH	AVG	PB	PR	/A	PD	TPI
1973	Det-A	0	0	—	3	0	0	0	0	4²	5	0	3	4	15.4	3.86	106	.278	.381	0	—	0	-0	-0	0	0.0

■ DOC IMLAY
Imlay, Harry Miller b: 1/12/1889, Allentown, N.J. d: 10/7/48, Bordentown, N.J. BR/TR, 5'11", 168 lbs. Deb: 7/07/13

YEAR	TM/L	W	L	PCT	G	GS	CG	SH	SV	IP	H	HR	BB	SO	RAT	ERA	ERA+	OAV	OOB	BH	AVG	PB	PR	/A	PD	TPI
1913	Phi-N	0	0	—	9	0	0	0	0	13²	19	1	7	7	17.1	7.24	46	.358	.433	0	.000	-0	-6	-6	0	-0.5

■ BOB INGERSOLL
Ingersoll, Robert Randolph b: 1/8/1883, Rapid City, S.D. d: 1/13/27, Minneapolis, Minn. BR/TR, 5'11.5", 175 lbs. Deb: 4/23/14

YEAR	TM/L	W	L	PCT	G	GS	CG	SH	SV	IP	H	HR	BB	SO	RAT	ERA	ERA+	OAV	OOB	BH	AVG	PB	PR	/A	PD	TPI
1914	Cin-N	0	0	—	4	0	0	0	0	6	5	0	5	2	16.5	3.00	98	.250	.423	1	1.000	0	-0	-0	0	0.0

■ BERT INKS
Inks, Albert Preston (b: Albert Preston Inkstein) b: 1/27/1871, Ligonier, Ind. d: 10/3/41, Ligonier, Ind. BL/TL, 6'3", 175 lbs. Deb: 9/02/1891

YEAR	TM/L	W	L	PCT	G	GS	CG	SH	SV	IP	H	HR	BB	SO	RAT	ERA	ERA+	OAV	OOB	BH	AVG	PB	PR	/A	PD	TPI
1891	Bro-N	3	10	.231	13	13	11	1	0	96¹	99	2	43	47	13.3	4.02	82	.256	.330	10	.286	2	-7	-8	-1	-0.5
1892	Bro-N	4	2	.667	9	8	4	1	0	58	48	0	33	25	12.6	3.88	82	.216	.318	10	.400	3	-4	-5	-0	0.0
	Was-N	1	2	.333	3	3	3	0	0	21	29	0	10	11	16.7	5.14	63	.315	.382	3	.300	1	-4	-4	-0	-0.3
	Yr	5	4	.556	12	11	7	1	0	79	77	0	43	36	13.7	4.22	76	.245	.336	2	.057	4	-8	-9	-0	-0.3
1894	Bal-N	9	4	.692	22	14	10	0	1	133	181	4	54	30	15.9	5.55	98	.321	.380	18	.316	2	-3	-1	-0	0.0
	Lou-N	2	6	.250	8	8	8	0	0	59²	87	2	34	8	18.3	6.49	79	.336	.413	12	.444	3	-8	-9	-0	-0.4
	Yr	11	10	.524	30	22	18	0	1	192²	268	6	88	38	16.6	5.84	92	.326	.391	6	.071	4	-11	-11	-1	-0.4
1895	Lou-N	7	20	.259	28	27	21	0	0	205¹	294	3	78	42	16.3	6.40	72	.331	.385	21	.250	-0	-37	-40	1	-3.0
1896	Phi-N	0	1	.000	3	1	0	0	0	10¹	21	1	5	2	22.6	7.84	55	.415	.467	1	.200	-1	-4	-4	-0	-0.3
	Cin-N	1	1	.500	3	3	2	0	0	20	21	0	9	2	13.5	4.50	102	.268	.343	0	.000	-1	-0	-0	-0	0.0
	Yr	1	2	.333	6	4	2	0	0	30¹	42	1	14	4	16.6	5.64	80	.325	.391	1	.083	-1	-4	-4	-0	-0.3
Total	5	27	46	.370	89	77	59	2	1	603²	780	12	266	167	15.6	5.52	81	.307	.372	75	.300	9	-68	-72	-1	-4.5

■ JEFF INNIS
Innis, Jeffrey David b: 7/5/62, Decatur, Ill. BR/TR, 6'1", 170 lbs. Deb: 5/16/87

YEAR	TM/L	W	L	PCT	G	GS	CG	SH	SV	IP	H	HR	BB	SO	RAT	ERA	ERA+	OAV	OOB	BH	AVG	PB	PR	/A	PD	TPI
1987	NY-N	0	1	.000	17	1	0	0	0	25²	29	5	4	28	11.9	3.16	120	.279	.312	0	.000	-0	3	2	0	0.1
1988	NY-N	1	1	.500	12	0	0	0	0	19	22	2	14	14	9.9	1.89	170	.250	.269	0	—	0	3	3	1	0.2
1989	NY-N	0	1	.000	29	0	0	0	0	39²	38	2	16	16	10.7	3.18	103	.255	.297	0	.000	-0	1	1	0	0.1
1990	NY-N	1	3	.250	18	0	0	0	1	26¹	19	4	10	12	10.3	2.39	152	.209	.294	0	—	0	4	4	0	0.4
Total	4	2	6	.250	76	1	0	0	1	110²	105	11	24	70	10.7	2.77	125	.250	.295	0	.000	-0	11	9	0	0.8

■ DANE IORG
Iorg, Dane Charles b: 5/11/50, Eureka, Cal. BL/TR, 6', 180 lbs. Deb: 4/09/77 ♦

YEAR	TM/L	W	L	PCT	G	GS	CG	SH	SV	IP	H	HR	BB	SO	RAT	ERA	ERA+	OAV	OOB	BH	AVG	PB	PR	/A	PD	TPI
1986	SD-N	0	0	—	2	0	0	0	0	3	5	2	1	2	18.0	12.00	30	.357	.400	24	.226	0	-3	-3	0	-0.2

■ HOOKS IOTT
Iott, Clarence Eugene b: 12/3/19, Mountain Grove, Mo. d: 8/17/80, St.Petersburg, Fla BB/TL, 6'2", 200 lbs. Deb: 9/06/41

YEAR	TM/L	W	L	PCT	G	GS	CG	SH	SV	IP	H	HR	BB	SO	RAT	ERA	ERA+	OAV	OOB	BH	AVG	PB	PR	/A	PD	TPI
1941	StL-A	0	0	—	2	0	0	0	0	2	2	0	1	1	13.5	9.00	48	.250	.333	0	—	0	-1	-1	0	0.0
1947	StL-A	0	1	.000	4	0	0	0	0	8¹	15	4	14	6	31.3	16.20	24	.375	.537	0	.000	-0	-12	-11	0	-0.9
	NY-N	3	8	.273	20	9	2	1	0	71¹	67	3	52	46	15.1	5.93	69	.251	.375	3	.143	1	-15	-15	-1	-1.3
Total	2	3	9	.250	26	9	2	1	0	81²	84	7	67	53	16.8	7.05	58	.267	.397	3	.130	1	-27	-27	-1	-2.2

■ DARYL IRVINE
Irvine, Daryl Keith b: 11/15/64, Harrisonburg, Va. BR/TR, 6'3", 195 lbs. Deb: 4/28/90

YEAR	TM/L	W	L	PCT	G	GS	CG	SH	SV	IP	H	HR	BB	SO	RAT	ERA	ERA+	OAV	OOB	BH	AVG	PB	PR	/A	PD	TPI
1990	Bos-A	1	1	.500	11	0	0	0	0	17¹	15	0	10	9	13.0	4.67	87	.246	.352	0	—	0	-1	-1	0	0.0

■ ARTHUR IRWIN
Irwin, Arthur Albert "Doc" or "Sandy" b: 2/14/1858, Toronto, Ont., Can. d: 7/16/21, Atlantic Ocean BL/TR, 5'8.5", 158 lbs. Deb: 5/01/1880 MU♦

YEAR	TM/L	W	L	PCT	G	GS	CG	SH	SV	IP	H	HR	BB	SO	RAT	ERA	ERA+	OAV	OOB	BH	AVG	PB	PR	/A	PD	TPI
1884	*Pro-N	0	0	—	1	0	0	0	0	3	5	0	1	0	18.0	3.00	94	.353	.395	97	.240	-0	-0	-0	0	0.0
1889	Was-N	0	0	—	1	0	0	0	0	1	1	0	0	0	9.0	0.00	—	.252	.252	73	.233	0	0	0	0	0.0
Total	2	0	0	—	2	0	0	0	0	4	6	0	1	0	15.8	2.25	138	.331	.366	934	.241	0	0	0	0	0.0

■ BILL IRWIN
Irwin, William Franklin "Phil" b: 9/16/1859, Neville, Ohio d: 8/7/33, Ft.Thomas, Ky. BR/TR, 6', 195 lbs. Deb: 8/30/1886

YEAR	TM/L	W	L	PCT	G	GS	CG	SH	SV	IP	H	HR	BB	SO	RAT	ERA	ERA+	OAV	OOB	BH	AVG	PB	PR	/A	PD	TPI
1886	Cin-a	0	2	.000	2	2	2	0	0	17	18	2	8	6	13.8	5.82	60	.259	.336	0	.000	-1	-4	-4	1	-0.3

■ FRANK ISBELL
Isbell, William Frank "Bald Eagle" b: 8/21/1875, Delevan, N.Y. d: 7/15/41, Wichita, Kan. BL/TR, 5'11", 190 lbs. Deb: 5/01/1898 ♦

YEAR	TM/L	W	L	PCT	G	GS	CG	SH	SV	IP	H	HR	BB	SO	RAT	ERA	ERA+	OAV	OOB	BH	AVG	PB	PR	/A	PD	TPI
1898	Chi-N	4	7	.364	13	9	7	0	0	81	86	0	42	16	14.2	3.56	101	.270	.355	37	.233	-0	0	0	0	0.0
1901	Chi-A	0	0	—	1	0	0	0	0	1	2	0	0	0	18.0	9.00	39	.409	.409	143	.257	0	-1	-1	0	0.0
1902	Chi-A	0	0	—	1	1	0	0	0	1	3	0	1	1	36.0	9.00	38	.514	.585	130	.252	0	-1	-1	0	0.0
1906	*Chi-A	0	0	—	1	0	0	0	0	1	0	0	0	2	4.5	0.00	—	.152	.152	153	.279	0	1	1	0	0.1
1907	Chi-A	0	0	—	1	0	0	0	1	0¹	1	0	0	0	27.0	0.00	—	.000	.000	118	.243	0	0	0	0	0.0
Total	5	4	7	.364	17	10	7	0	1	85¹	92	0	43	19	14.2	3.59	99	.273	.356	1056	.250	0	-0	-0	1	0.1

■ AL JACKSON
Jackson, Alvin Neil b: 12/25/35, Waco, Tex. BL/TL, 5'10", 169 lbs. Deb: 6/01/59 C

YEAR	TM/L	W	L	PCT	G	GS	CG	SH	SV	IP	H	HR	BB	SO	RAT	ERA	ERA+	OAV	OOB	BH	AVG	PB	PR	/A	PD	TPI
1959	Pit-N	0	0	—	8	3	0	0	0	18	30	1	8	13	19.0	6.50	60	.405	.463	1	.200	0	-5	-5	0	-0.4
1961	Pit-N	1	0	1.000	3	2	1	0	0	23²	20	2	4	15	9.1	3.42	117	.233	.267	0	.000	0	2	1	1	0.1
1962	NY-N	8	20	.286	36	33	12	4	0	231¹	244	16	78	118	12.7	4.40	95	.273	.335	5	.068	-3	-4	-5	-4	-0.4
1963	NY-N	13	17	.433	37	34	11	0	1	227	237	16	84	142	13.2	3.96	94	.267	.338	16	.203	2	-17	-12	2	-0.8
1964	NY-N	11	16	.407	40	31	11	3	1	213¹	229	14	60	112	12.4	4.26	84	.272	.323	11	.153	2	-17	-16	0	-1.3
1965	NY-N	8	20	.286	37	31	7	3	1	205¹	217	17	61	120	12.5	4.34	81	.271	.329	7	.117	-1	-18	-18	2	-1.7

YEAR	TM/L	W	L	PCT	G	GS	CG	SH	SV	IP	H	HR	BB	SO	RAT	ERA	ERA+	OAV	OOB	BH	AVG	PB	PR	/A	PD	TPI
1966	StL-N	13	15	.464	36	30	11	3	0	232²	222	18	45	90	10.4	2.51	143	.250	.288	13	.176	2	28	28	5	4.0
1967	StL-N	9	4	.692	38	11	1	1	1	107	117	7	29	43	12.4	3.95	83	.279	.327	8	.258	2	-7	-8	3	-0.2
1968	NY-N	3	7	.300	25	9	0	0	3	92²	88	5	17	59	10.4	3.69	82	.249	.287	7	.250	1	-7	-7	1	-0.4
1969	NY-N	0	0	—	9	0	0	0	0	11	18	1	4	10	18.8	10.64	34	.353	.411	0	.000	-0	-9	-9	-0	-0.7
	Cin-N	1	0	1.000	33	0	0	0	3	27¹	27	5	17	16	15.5	5.27	71	.260	.379	1	.250	0	-5	-5	-0	-0.4
	Yr	1	0	1.000	42	0	0	0	3	38¹	45	6	21	26	16.2	6.81	55	.285	.379	0	.000	0	-14	-13	-0	-1.1
Total	10	67	99	.404	302	184	54	14	10	1389¹	1449	115	407	738	12.3	3.98	91	.268	.324	69	.159	3	-67	-56	17	-2.2

■ CHARLIE JACKSON
Jackson, Charles Bernard b: 8/4/1876, Versailles, Ohio d: 11/23/57, Scottsbluff, Neb.   Deb: 8/11/05

YEAR	TM/L	W	L	PCT	G	GS	CG	SH	SV	IP	H	HR	BB	SO	RAT	ERA	ERA+	OAV	OOB	BH	AVG	PB	PR	/A	PD	TPI
1905	Det-A	0	2	.000	2	2	1	0	0	11	14	1	7	3	17.2	5.73	48	.311	.403	1	.250	0	-4	-4	-0	-0.3

■ DANNY JACKSON
Jackson, Danny Lynn b: 1/5/62, San Antonio, Tex. BR/TL, 6', 205 lbs. Deb: 9/11/83

YEAR	TM/L	W	L	PCT	G	GS	CG	SH	SV	IP	H	HR	BB	SO	RAT	ERA	ERA+	OAV	OOB	BH	AVG	PB	PR	/A	PD	TPI
1983	KC-A	1	1	.500	4	3	0	0	0	19	26	1	6	9	15.2	5.21	78	.325	.372	0	—	0	-2	-2	0	-0.1
1984	KC-A	2	6	.250	15	11	0	0	0	76	84	4	35	40	14.7	4.26	94	.285	.370	0	—	0	-2	-2	-0	-0.1
1985	*KC-A	14	12	.538	32	32	4	3	0	208	209	7	76	114	12.6	3.42	122	.261	.329	0	—	0	17	17	-1	1.6
1986	KC-A	11	12	.478	32	27	4	1	1	185²	177	13	79	115	12.6	3.20	133	.256	.335	0	—	0	20	22	-1	2.1
1987	KC-A	9	18	.333	36	34	11	2	0	224	219	11	109	152	13.5	4.02	113	.258	.347	0	—	0	11	13	-2	1.1
1988	Cin-N	23	8	.742	35	35	15	6	0	260²	206	13	71	161	9.6	2.73	131	.218	.275	13	.144	-0	21	25	3	3.0
1989	Cin-N	6	11	.353	20	20	1	0	0	115²	122	10	57	70	14.0	5.60	64	.271	.354	8	.222	1	-27	-26	-0	-2.4
1990	*Cin-N	6	6	.500	22	21	0	0	0	117¹	119	11	40	76	12.3	3.61	107	.266	.329	2	.054	-2	2	3	-1	0.1
Total	8	72	74	.493	196	183	36	12	1	1206¹	1162	70	473	737	12.4	3.66	110	.255	.328	23	.141	-1	39	51	-3	5.3

■ DARRELL JACKSON
Jackson, Darrell Preston b: 4/3/56, Los Angeles, Cal. BB/TL, 5'10", 150 lbs. Deb: 6/16/78

YEAR	TM/L	W	L	PCT	G	GS	CG	SH	SV	IP	H	HR	BB	SO	RAT	ERA	ERA+	OAV	OOB	BH	AVG	PB	PR	/A	PD	TPI
1978	Min-A	4	6	.400	19	15	1	1	0	92¹	89	9	48	54	13.5	4.48	85	.256	.350	0	—	0	-7	-7	-1	-0.7
1979	Min-A	4	4	.500	24	8	1	0	0	69¹	89	5	26	43	15.1	4.28	102	.319	.379	0	—	0	-1	1	1	0.1
1980	Min-A	9	9	.500	32	25	1	0	1	172	161	15	69	90	12.1	3.87	113	.250	.325	0	—	0	3	9	-0	0.9
1981	Min-A	3	3	.500	14	5	0	0	0	32²	35	1	19	26	15.2	4.41	90	.282	.382	0	—	0	-3	-2	-1	-0.2
1982	Min-A	0	5	.000	13	7	0	0	0	44²	51	6	24	16	15.3	6.25	68	.297	.386	0	—	0	-11	-10	-0	-0.9
Total	5	20	27	.426	102	60	3	1	1	411	425	36	186	229	13.5	4.38	96	.272	.352	0	—	0	-18	-8	-1	-0.8

■ GRANT JACKSON
Jackson, Grant Dwight "Buck" b: 9/28/42, Fostoria, Ohio BB/TL, 6', 180 lbs. Deb: 9/03/65 C

YEAR	TM/L	W	L	PCT	G	GS	CG	SH	SV	IP	H	HR	BB	SO	RAT	ERA	ERA+	OAV	OOB	BH	AVG	PB	PR	/A	PD	TPI
1965	Phi-N	1	1	.500	6	2	0	0	0	13²	17	4	5	15	14.5	7.24	48	.304	.361	0	.000	-0	-6	-6	0	-0.5
1966	Phi-N	0	0	—	2	0	0	0	0	1²	1	0	3	0	27.0	5.40	67	.333	.556	0	—	-0	-0	-0	0	0.0
1967	Phi-N	2	3	.400	43	4	0	0	1	84¹	86	3	43	83	14.0	3.84	89	.267	.357	2	.133	-0	-4	-4	-2	-0.6
1968	Phi-N	1	6	.143	33	6	1	0	1	61	59	4	20	49	11.7	2.95	102	.248	.306	3	.300	1	0	1	0	0.1
1969	Phi-N	14	18	.438	38	35	13	4	1	253	237	16	92	180	11.9	3.34	106	.249	.318	12	.140	-0	7	6	-2	0.3
1970	Phi-N	5	15	.250	32	23	1	0	0	149²	170	17	61	104	14.0	5.29	75	.288	.356	4	.091	-2	-21	-22	-0	-2.2
1971	*Bal-A	4	3	.571	29	9	0	0	0	77²	72	7	20	51	10.9	3.13	107	.249	.302	2	.091	-0	3	2	0	0.2
1972	Bal-A	1	1	.500	32	0	0	0	8	41	33	1	9	34	9.2	2.63	117	.217	.261	0	.000	-0	2	2	0	0.2
1973	*Bal-A	8	0	1.000	45	0	0	0	9	80¹	54	5	24	47	8.7	1.90	196	.198	.263	0	—	0	17	16	-0	1.7
1974	*Bal-A	6	4	.600	49	0	0	0	12	66²	48	7	22	56	9.6	2.57	135	.198	.268	0	—	0	8	7	-2	0.5
1975	Bal-A	4	3	.571	41	0	0	0	7	48¹	42	3	21	39	11.9	3.35	105	.241	.327	0	—	0	2	1	-0	0.0
1976	Bal-A	1	1	.500	13	0	0	0	3	19¹	19	1	9	14	14.0	5.12	64	.268	.366	0	—	0	-3	-4	-0	-0.3
	*NY-A	6	0	1.000	21	2	1	1	1	58²	38	1	16	25	8.4	1.69	202	.186	.249	0	—	0	12	11	-1	1.1
	Yr	7	1	.875	34	2	1	1	4	78	57	2	25	39	9.6	2.54	133	.205	.273	0	—	0	8	7	-1	0.8
1977	Pit-N	5	3	.625	49	2	0	0	4	91	81	11	39	41	12.0	3.86	103	.240	.321	6	.333	2	1	1	-1	0.2
1978	*Pit-N	7	5	.583	60	0	0	0	5	77¹	89	5	32	45	14.2	3.26	114	.298	.367	3	.250	1	3	4	0	0.5
1979	*Pit-N	8	5	.615	72	0	0	0	14	82	67	9	35	39	11.4	2.96	131	.230	.317	0	.000	-1	7	8	-1	0.7
1980	Pit-N	8	4	.667	61	0	0	0	9	71	71	4	20	31	11.5	2.92	125	.275	.327	0	.000	-1	5	6	0	0.5
1981	Pit-N	1	2	.333	35	0	0	0	0	32¹	30	1	10	17	11.1	2.51	143	.248	.305	0	.000	-0	4	4	-1	0.3
	Mon-N	1	0	1.000	10	0	0	0	0	10²	14	2	9	4	19.4	7.59	46	.333	.451	0	—	0	-5	-5	-0	-0.4
	Yr	2	2	.500	45	0	0	0	0	43	44	3	19	21	13.2	3.77	95	.267	.342	0	.000	-0	-1	-1	-1	-0.1
1982	KC-A	3	1	.750	20	0	0	0	0	38¹	42	7	21	15	15.3	5.17	79	.271	.365	0	—	0	-5	-5	-0	-0.4
	Pit-N	0	0	—	1	0	0	0	0	1	0	0	0	0	0	13.5		.333	.333	0	—	0	-1	-1	-0	0.0
Total	18	86	75	.534	692	83	16	5	79	1358²	1272	109	511	889	11.9	3.46	104	.251	.322	32	.136	-2	26	22	-9	1.9

■ JOHN JACKSON
Jackson, John Lewis b: 7/15/09, Wynnefield, Pa. d: 10/24/56, Somers Point, N.J. BR/TR, 6'2", 180 lbs. Deb: 6/20/33

YEAR	TM/L	W	L	PCT	G	GS	CG	SH	SV	IP	H	HR	BB	SO	RAT	ERA	ERA+	OAV	OOB	BH	AVG	PB	PR	/A	PD	TPI
1933	Phi-N	2	2	.500	10	7	1	0	0	54	74	3	35	11	19.0	6.00	64	.329	.430	3	.143	-1	-16	-13	-2	-1.4

■ LARRY JACKSON
Jackson, Lawrence Curtis b: 6/2/31, Nampa, Idaho d: 8/28/90, Boise, Idaho BR/TR, 6'1.5", 175 lbs. Deb: 4/17/55

YEAR	TM/L	W	L	PCT	G	GS	CG	SH	SV	IP	H	HR	BB	SO	RAT	ERA	ERA+	OAV	OOB	BH	AVG	PB	PR	/A	PD	TPI
1955	StL-N	9	14	.391	37	25	4	1	2	177¹	189	25	72	88	13.7	4.31	94	.277	.353	3	.053	-6	-5	-5	0	-0.9
1956	StL-N	2	2	.500	51	1	0	0	9	85¹	75	5	45	50	12.8	4.11	92	.240	.337	1	.091	-0	-3	-3	2	-0.1
1957	StL-N	15	9	.625	41	22	6	2	1	210¹	196	21	57	96	11.0	3.47	114	.248	.302	13	.181	0	10	12	4	1.7
1958	StL-N	13	13	.500	49	23	11	4	8	198	211	21	51	124	12.4	3.68	112	.272	.325	9	.150	-2	6	10	2	0.6
1959	StL-N	14	13	.519	40	37	12	3	0	256	271	13	64	145	11.9	3.30	128	.270	.316	9	.112	-4	18	27	0	2.5
1960	StL-N	18	13	.581	43	38	14	3	0	282	277	22	70	171	11.2	3.48	118	.257	.304	20	.211	2	9	19	-1	2.2
1961	StL-N	14	11	.560	33	28	12	3	0	211	203	20	56	114	11.2	3.75	117	.252	.303	11	.176	0	7	15	2	1.8
1962	StL-N	16	11	.593	36	35	11	4	0	252¹	267	25	64	112	12.0	3.75	114	.269	.318	15	.169	2	6	15	2	2.0
1963	Chi-N	14	18	.438	37	37	13	4	0	275	256	11	54	153	10.3	2.55	137	.245	.286	17	.195	3	22	29	2	4.0
1964	Chi-N	24	11	.686	40	38	19	3	0	297²	265	17	58	148	9.8	3.14	118	.235	.273	20	.175	1	13	19	7	2.9
1965	Chi-N	14	21	.400	39	39	12	4	0	257¹	268	28	57	131	11.5	3.85	96	.267	.310	11	.128	1	-9	-5	3	0.0
1966	Chi-N	0	2	.000	3	2	0	0	0	8	14	3	4	5	20.3	13.50	27	.368	.429	0	.000	-0	-9	-9	0	-0.7
	Phi-N	15	13	.536	35	33	12	5	0	247	243	22	58	107	11.1	2.99	120	.259	.306	13	.146	-0	17	17	2	2.1
	Yr	15	15	.500	38	35	12	5	0	255	257	25	62	112	11.4	3.32	108	.264	.311	13	.033	-1	8	8	2	1.4
1967	Phi-N	13	15	.464	40	37	11	4	0	261²	242	17	54	139	10.4	3.10	110	.241	.284	14	.161	-0	8	9	5	1.6
1968	Phi-N	13	17	.433	34	34	12	2	0	243²	229	9	60	127	10.8	2.77	109	.248	.297	12	.141	-0	6	6	2	0.9
Total	14	194	183	.515	558	429	149	37	20	3262¹	3206	259	824	1709	11.3	3.40	113	.256	.306	170	.156	-5	95	155	29	20.6

■ MIKE JACKSON
Jackson, Michael Ray b: 12/22/64, Houston, Tex. BR/TR, 6'1", 185 lbs. Deb: 8/11/86

YEAR	TM/L	W	L	PCT	G	GS	CG	SH	SV	IP	H	HR	BB	SO	RAT	ERA	ERA+	OAV	OOB	BH	AVG	PB	PR	/A	PD	TPI
1986	Phi-N	0	0	—	9	0	0	0	0	13¹	12	2	4	3	12.2	3.38	114	.250	.333	0	—	0	1	1	-0	0.0
1987	Phi-N	3	10	.231	55	7	0	0	1	109¹	88	16	56	93	12.1	4.20	101	.219	.319	2	.118	-0	-1	-1	-0	0.0
1988	Sea-A	6	5	.545	62	0	0	0	4	99¹	74	10	43	76	10.8	2.63	158	.209	.298	0	—	0	15	17	-0	1.7
1989	Sea-A	4	6	.400	65	0	0	0	7	99¹	81	8	54	94	12.8	3.17	127	.223	.333	0	—	0	8	9	-1	0.9
1990	Sea-A	5	7	.417	63	0	0	0	3	77¹	64	8	44	69	12.8	4.54	87	.229	.338	0	—	0	-5	-5	-1	-0.3
Total	5	18	28	.391	254	7	0	0	15	398²	319	44	201	335	12.1	3.59	114	.221	.322	2	.118	-0	16	23	-2	2.3

■ MIKE JACKSON
Jackson, Michael Warren b: 3/27/46, Paterson, N.J. BL/TL, 6'3", 190 lbs. Deb: 5/10/70

YEAR	TM/L	W	L	PCT	G	GS	CG	SH	SV	IP	H	HR	BB	SO	RAT	ERA	ERA+	OAV	OOB	BH	AVG	PB	PR	/A	PD	TPI
1970	Phi-N	1	1	.500	5	0	0	0	0	6¹	6	0	4	4	14.2	1.42	281	.286	.400	1	1.000	0	2	2	0	0.2
1971	StL-N	0	0	—	1	0	0	0	0	0²	1	0	1	0	27.0	0.00	—	.333	.500	0	.000	-0	0	0	0	0.0
1972	KC-A	1	2	.333	7	3	0	0	0	19²	24	0	14	15	17.4	6.41	47	.320	.427	0	.000	-1	-7	-7	1	-0.7
1973	KC-A	0	0	—	9	0	0	0	0	21²	25	3	20	13	19.1	7.06	58	.301	.442	0	—	0	-8	-7	0	-0.6
	Cle-A	0	0	—	1	0	0	0	0	0²	1	0	0	1	13.5	0.00	—	.333	.333	0	—	0	0	0	0	0.0
	Yr	0	0	—	10	0	0	0	0	22¹	26	3	20	14	18.5	6.85	60	.295	.426	0	—	0	-8	-7	0	-0.6
Total	4	2	3	.400	23	3	0	0	0	49	57	3	39	33	17.8	5.88	62	.308	.431	1	.143	-0	-13	-12	1	-1.1

YEAR TM/L	W	L	PCT	G	GS	CG	SH	SV	IP	H	HR	BB	SO	RAT	ERA	ERA+	OAV	OOB	BH	AVG	PB	PR	/A	PD	TPI

■ ROY LEE JACKSON   Jackson, Roy Lee b: 5/1/54, Opelika, Ala.   BR/TR, 6'2", 190 lbs.   Deb: 9/13/77

1977 NY-N	0	2	.000	4	4	0	0	0	24	25	2	15	13	16.1	6.00	62	.263	.381	0	.000	-1	-6	-6	-1	-0.6
1978 NY-N	0	0	—	4	2	0	0	0	12²	21	2	6	6	20.6	9.24	38	.429	.509	2	.667	1	-8	-8	-0	-0.6
1979 NY-N	1	0	1.000	8	0	0	0	0	16¹	11	1	5	10	9.4	2.20	165	.200	.279	1	1.000	0	3	3	0	0.3
1980 NY-N	1	7	.125	24	8	1	0	1	70²	78	4	20	58	12.5	4.20	84	.287	.336	3	.188	-1	-5	-5	-1	-0.5
1981 Tor-A	1	2	.333	39	0	0	0	7	61²	65	5	25	27	13.3	2.63	150	.275	.347	0	—	0	7	9	0	1.0
1982 Tor-A	8	8	.500	48	2	0	0	6	97	77	7	31	71	10.2	3.06	146	.218	.284	0	—	0	11	15	-0	1.5
1983 Tor-A	8	3	.727	49	0	0	0	7	92	92	6	41	48	13.3	4.50	96	.267	.351	0	—	0	-4	-2	1	-0.1
1984 Tor-A	7	8	.467	54	0	0	0	10	86	73	12	31	58	11.0	3.56	115	.230	.301	0	—	0	4	5	0	0.5
1985 SD-N	2	3	.400	22	0	0	0	2	40	32	4	13	28	10.3	2.70	131	.224	.293	0	.000	-1	4	4	0	0.3
1986 Min-A	0	1	.000	28	0	0	0	1	58¹	57	7	16	32	11.7	3.86	112	.256	.314	0	—	0	2	3	0	0.2
Total 10	28	34	.452	280	18	1	0	34	558²	531	50	203	351	12.1	3.77	107	.254	.325	6	.194	1	8	17	-1	2.0

■ TONY JACOBS   Jacobs, Anthony Robert b: 8/5/25, Dixmoor, Ill.   d: 12/21/80, Nashville, Tenn.   BB/TR, 5'9", 150 lbs.   Deb: 9/19/48

1948 Chi-N	0	0	—	1	0	0	0	0	2	3	1	0	2	13.5	4.50	87	.333	.333	0	—	0	-0	-0	0	-0.0
1955 StL-N	0	0	—	1	0	0	0	0	2	6	1	1	1	31.5	18.00	23	.500	.538	0	.000	-0	-3	-3	0	-0.2
Total 2	0	0	—	2	0	0	0	0	4	9	2	1	3	22.5	11.25	35	.429	.455	0	.000	-0	-3	-3	0	-0.2

■ ART JACOBS   Jacobs, Arthur Edward b: 8/28/02, Luckey, Ohio   d: 6/8/67, Inglewood, Cal.   BL/TL, 5'10", 170 lbs.   Deb: 6/18/39

| 1939 Cin-N | 0 | 0 | — | 1 | 0 | 0 | 0 | 1 | 1 | 2 | 0 | 1 | 0 | 27.0 | 9.00 | 43 | .400 | .500 | 0 | — | 0 | -1 | -1 | 0 | 0.0 |

■ BUCKY JACOBS   Jacobs, Newton Smith b: 3/21/13, Altavista, Va.   d: 6/15/90, Richmond, Va.   BR/TR, 5'11", 155 lbs.   Deb: 6/27/37

1937 Was-A	1	1	.500	11	1	0	0	0	22¹	26	0	11	8	14.9	4.84	92	.295	.374	0	.000	-1	-1	-1	0	0.0
1939 Was-A	0	0	—	2	0	0	0	0	3	1	0	0	1	3.0	0.00	—	.100	.100	0	—	0	2	1	0	0.1
1940 Was-A	0	1	.000	9	0	0	0	0	15	16	1	9	6	16.2	6.00	69	.271	.386	0	.000	-0	-3	-3	1	-0.1
Total 3	1	2	.333	22	1	0	0	0	40¹	43	1	20	15	14.5	4.91	88	.274	.363	0	.000	-1	-2	-3	2	0.0

■ ELMER JACOBS   Jacobs, William Elmer b: 8/10/1892, Salem, Mo.   d: 2/10/58, Salem, Mo.   BR/TR, 6', 165 lbs.   Deb: 4/23/14

1914 Phi-N	1	3	.250	14	7	1	0	0	50²	65	2	20	17	15.6	4.80	61	.342	.413	0	.000	-2	-11	-10	1	-1.1
1916 Pit-N	6	10	.375	34	17	8	0	0	153	151	2	38	46	11.4	2.94	91	.258	.308	3	.075	-2	-5	-4	-1	-0.7
1917 Pit-N	6	19	.240	38	25	10	1	2	227¹	214	7	76	58	11.7	2.81	101	.262	.329	12	.179	-1	-2	1	2	0.2
1918 Pit-N	0	1	.000	8	4	0	0	0	23¹	31	0	14	2	17.4	5.79	50	.344	.433	2	.286	-0	-8	-8	1	-0.6
Phi-N	9	5	.643	18	14	12	4	1	123	96	3	42	33	10.4	2.41	124	.221	.296	6	.158	-1	5	8	-2	0.6
Yr	9	6	.600	26	18	12	4	1	146¹	127	3	56	35	11.5	2.95	101	.242	.320	8	.178	-1	-3	-0	-1	0.0
1919 Phi-N	6	10	.375	17	15	13	0	0	128²	150	5	44	37	14.0	3.85	84	.304	.368	8	.178	-1	-13	-9	1	-0.8
StL-N	3	6	.333	17	8	4	1	1	85¹	81	2	25	31	11.7	2.53	110	.264	.329	8	.348	3	4	2	-0	0.6
Yr	9	16	.360	34	23	17	1	1	214	231	7	69	68	12.8	3.32	92	.287	.347	2	.029	2	-10	-6	1	-0.2
1920 StL-N	4	8	.333	23	9	1	0	1	77²	91	2	33	21	14.9	5.21	57	.296	.374	5	.192	-0	-18	-19	1	-1.8
1924 Chi-N	11	12	.478	38	22	13	1	1	190¹	181	9	72	50	12.1	3.74	104	.258	.329	6	.111	-3	-2	4	2	0.1
1925 Chi-N	2	3	.400	18	4	1	1	0	55²	63	9	22	19	13.9	5.17	84	.274	.340	3	.231	-0	-6	-5	0	-0.4
1927 Chi-A	2	4	.333	25	8	2	1	0	74¹	105	3	37	22	17.7	4.60	88	.354	.432	3	.150	-1	-4	-5	0	-0.2
Total 9	50	81	.382	250	133	65	9	7	1189¹	1228	40	423	336	12.8	3.55	91	.276	.344	56	.161	-9	-57	-44	7	-4.2

■ BEANY JACOBSON   Jacobson, Albert L. (b: Albin L. Jacobson) b: 6/5/1881, Port Washington, Wis.   d: 1/31/33, Decatur, Ill.   BL/TL, 6', 170 lbs.   Deb: 4/30/04

1904 Was-A	6	23	.207	33	30	23	1	0	253²	276	6	57	75	11.8	3.55	75	.278	.317	8	.091	-6	-27	-25	2	-2.9
1905 Was-A	7	8	.467	22	17	12	0	0	144¹	139	1	35	50	10.8	3.30	80	.254	.299	7	.159	1	-10	-10	-2	-1.1
1906 StL-A	9	9	.500	24	15	12	0	0	155	146	3	27	53	10.0	2.50	103	.252	.285	5	.091	-4	3	1	1	-0.1
1907 StL-A	1	6	.143	7	7	6	0	0	57¹	55	1	26	16	12.7	2.98	84	.254	.334	4	.222	-1	-3	-3	-0	-0.3
Bos-A	0	0	—	2	1	0	0	0	2	2	0	3	1	22.5	9.00	29	.262	.470	0	—	0	-1	-1	0	-0.1
Yr	1	6	.143	9	8	6	0	0	59¹	57	1	29	17	13.0	3.19	79	.255	.340	0	.000	-0	-4	-4	-0	-0.3
Total 4	23	46	.333	88	70	53	1	0	612¹	618	11	148	195	11.3	3.19	82	.264	.307	24	.117	-9	-38	-38	1	-4.4

■ LARRY JACOBUS   Jacobus, Stuart Louis b: 12/18/1893, Cincinnati, Ohio   d: 8/19/65, N.College Hill, O.   BB/TR, 6'2", 186 lbs.   Deb: 7/15/18

| 1918 Cin-N | 0 | 1 | .000 | 5 | 0 | 0 | 0 | 0 | 17¹ | 25 | 0 | 14 | 13 | 21.3 | 5.71 | 47 | .368 | .377 | 0 | .000 | -1 | -6 | -6 | -0 | -0.6 |

■ PAT JACQUEZ   Jacquez, Patrick Thomas b: 4/23/47, Stockton, Cal.   BR/TR, 6', 200 lbs.   Deb: 4/18/71

| 1971 Chi-A | 0 | 0 | — | 2 | 0 | 0 | 0 | 0 | 2 | 4 | 0 | 2 | 1 | 27.0 | 4.50 | 80 | .444 | .545 | 0 | .000 | -0 | -0 | -0 | -0 | -0.0 |

■ JAKE JAECKEL   Jaeckel, Paul Henry b: 4/1/42, E.Los Angeles, Cal.   BR/TR, 5'10", 170 lbs.   Deb: 9/19/64

| 1964 Chi-N | 1 | 0 | 1.000 | 4 | 0 | 0 | 0 | 1 | 8 | 4 | 0 | 3 | 2 | 7.9 | 0.00 | — | .160 | .250 | 0 | .000 | -0 | 3 | 3 | 0 | 0.4 |

■ CHARLIE JAEGER   Jaeger, Charles Thomas b: 4/17/1875, Ottawa, Ill.   d: 9/27/42, Ottawa, Ill.   BR/TR, Deb: 9/09/04

| 1904 Det-A | 3 | 3 | .500 | 8 | 6 | 5 | 0 | 0 | 49 | 49 | 0 | 15 | 13 | 11.8 | 2.57 | 99 | .261 | .316 | 1 | .059 | -0 | 0 | -0 | -0 | -0.1 |

■ JOE JAEGER   Jaeger, Joseph Peter "Zip" b: 3/3/1895, St.Cloud, Minn.   d: 12/13/63, Hampton, Iowa   BR/TR, 6'1", 190 lbs.   Deb: 7/28/20

| 1920 Chi-N | 0 | 0 | — | 2 | 0 | 0 | 0 | 0 | 3 | 6 | 0 | 4 | 0 | 30.0 | 12.00 | 27 | .500 | .625 | 0 | — | 0 | -3 | -3 | -0 | -0.2 |

■ SIG JAKUCKI   Jakucki, Sigmund "Jack" b: 8/20/09, Camden, N.J.   d: 5/28/79, Galveston, Tex.   BR/TR, 6'2.5", 198 lbs.   Deb: 8/30/36

1936 StL-A	0	3	.000	7	2	0	0	0	20²	32	2	12	9	19.6	8.71	48	.348	.429	0	.000	-1	-8	-8	0	-0.6
1944 *StL-A	13	9	.591	35	24	12	4	3	198	211	17	54	67	12.2	3.55	101	.268	.318	11	.151	-2	-3	1	1	0.1
1945 StL-A	12	10	.545	30	24	15	1	2	192¹	188	9	65	55	11.9	3.51	100	.267	.318	13	.186	0	-3	-1	0	0.2
Total 3	25	22	.532	72	50	27	5	5	411	431	28	131	131	12.4	3.79	96	.268	.325	24	.161	-2	-14	-6	2	-0.3

■ LEFTY JAMERSON   Jamerson, Charles Dewey "Charlie" b: 1/26/1900, Enfield, Ill.   d: 8/4/80, Mockville, N.C.   BL/TL, 6'1", 195 lbs.   Deb: 8/16/24

| 1924 Bos-A | 0 | 0 | — | 1 | 0 | 0 | 0 | 0 | 1 | 0 | 3 | 0 | 36.0 | 18.00 | 24 | .250 | .571 | 0 | — | 0 | -2 | -2 | 0 | 0.0 |

■ JEFF JAMES   James, Jeffrey Lynn "Jesse" b: 9/29/41, Indianapolis, Ind.   BR/TR, 6'3", 195 lbs.   Deb: 4/13/68

1968 Phi-N	4	4	.500	29	13	4	1	0	116	112	8	46	83	12.6	4.27	70	.256	.332	4	.121	-1	-17	-16	0	-1.8
1969 Phi-N	2	2	.500	6	5	1	0	0	31²	36	5	14	21	14.2	5.40	66	.288	.360	2	.182	-0	-6	-7	-0	-0.6
Total 2	6	6	.500	35	18	2	1	0	147²	148	13	60	104	12.9	4.51	69	.263	.338	6	.136	-1	-23	-23	-0	-2.4

■ JOHNNY JAMES   James, John Phillip b: 7/23/33, Bonner's Ferry, Idaho   BL/TR, 5'10", 160 lbs.   Deb: 9/06/58

1958 NY-A	0	0	—	1	0	0	0	0	3	2	0	4	1	18.0	0.00	—	.250	.500	0	.000	-0	1	1	0	0.1
1960 NY-A	5	1	.833	28	0	0	0	0	43¹	38	3	26	29	13.9	4.36	82	.248	.368	0	.000	-0	-2	-4	0	-0.3
1961 NY-A	0	0	—	1	0	0	0	0	1¹	1	0	0	2	6.8	0.00	—	.250	.250	0	—	0	1	1	0	0.1
LA-A	0	2	.000	36	3	0	0	0	71¹	66	12	54	41	15.4	5.30	85	.246	.377	0	.000	-2	-10	-6	0	-0.6
Yr	0	2	.000	37	3	0	0	0	72²	67	12	54	43	15.2	5.20	86	.246	.375	1	.077	-2	-10	-6	0	-0.5
Total 3	5	3	.625	66	3	0	0	0	119	107	15	84	73	14.8	4.76	82	.247	.375	1	.000	-2	-11	-8	0	-0.7

■ RICK JAMES   James, Richard Lee b: 10/11/47, Sheffield, Ala.   BR/TR, 6'2.5", 205 lbs.   Deb: 9/20/67

| 1967 Chi-N | 0 | 1 | .000 | 3 | 1 | 0 | 0 | 0 | 4² | 9 | 1 | 2 | 2 | 21.2 | 13.50 | 26 | .529 | .579 | 0 | .000 | -0 | -5 | -5 | -0 | -0.4 |

■ BOB JAMES   James, Robert Harvey b: 8/15/58, Glendale, Cal.   BR/TR, 6'4", 215 lbs.   Deb: 9/07/78

1978 Mon-N	0	1	.000	4	1	0	0	0	4	4	1	4	3	18.0	9.00	39	.267	.421	0	—	0	-2	-2	0	-0.1
1979 Mon-N	0	0	—	2	0	0	0	0	2	2	0	3	1	22.5	13.50	27	.250	.455	0	—	0	-2	-2	0	-0.1
1982 Mon-N	0	0	—	7	0	0	0	0	9	10	0	8	11	18.0	6.00	61	.294	.429	0	—	0	-2	-2	0	-0.2

YEAR TM/L	W	L	PCT	G	GS	CG	SH	SV	IP	H	HR	BB	SO	RAT	ERA	ERA+	OAV	OOB	BH	AVG	PB	PR	/A	PD	TPI
Det-A	0	2	.000	12	1	0	0	0	19²	22	4	8	20	13.7	5.03	81	.278	.345	0	—	0	-2	-2	-0	-0.1
1983 Det-A	0	0	—	4	0	0	0	0	4	5	2	3	4	18.0	11.25	35	.313	.421	0	—	0	-3	-3	-0	-0.2
Mon-N	1	0	1.000	27	0	0	0	7	50	37	3	23	56	11.3	2.88	125	.210	.312	2	.286	0	4	4	1	0.6
1984 Mon-N	6	6	.500	62	0	0	0	10	96	92	6	45	91	13.2	3.66	94	.251	.339	2	.143	-0	-1	-2	-2	-0.4
1985 Chi-A	8	7	.533	69	0	0	0	32	110	90	5	23	88	9.4	2.13	203	.226	.271	0	—	0	25	27	-1	2.6
1986 Chi-A	5	4	.556	49	0	0	0	14	58¹	61	8	23	32	13.6	5.25	82	.268	.345	0	—	0	-7	-6	-0	-0.5
1987 Chi-A	4	6	.400	43	0	0	0	10	54	54	10	17	34	12.5	4.67	86	.256	.323	0	—	0	-1	-1	0	0.0
Total 8	24	26	.480	279	2	0	0	73	407	377	39	157	340	12.2	3.80	105	.246	.323	4	.190	0	8	9	-2	1.6

■ LEFTY JAMES
James, William A. b: 7/1/1889, Glenroy, Ohio d: 5/3/33, Portsmouth, Ohio BL/TL, 5'11.5", 175 lbs. Deb: 4/13/12

YEAR TM/L	W	L	PCT	G	GS	CG	SH	SV	IP	H	HR	BB	SO	RAT	ERA	ERA+	OAV	OOB	BH	AVG	PB	PR	/A	PD	TPI
1912 Cle-A	0	1	.000	3	1	0	0	1	6	8	0	4	2	21.0	7.50	45	.348	.483	0	.000	-1	-3	-3	-0	-0.2
1913 Cle-A	2	2	.500	11	4	3	0	0	39	42	0	9	18	13.5	3.00	101	.273	.325	3	.231	-0	-0	0	-1	0.0
1914 Cle-A	0	3	.000	17	6	1	0	0	50²	44	0	32	16	13.9	3.20	90	.251	.373	0	.000	-1	-3	-2	2	0.0
Total 3	2	6	.250	31	11	4	0	1	95²	94	0	45	36	13.7	3.39	88	.267	.361	3	.107	-1	-6	-4	1	-0.2

■ BILL JAMES
James, William Henry "Big Bill" b: 1/20/1887, Detroit, Mich. d: 5/24/42, Venice, Cal. BB/TR, 6'4", 195 lbs. Deb: 6/12/11

YEAR TM/L	W	L	PCT	G	GS	CG	SH	SV	IP	H	HR	BB	SO	RAT	ERA	ERA+	OAV	OOB	BH	AVG	PB	PR	/A	PD	TPI
1911 Cle-A	2	4	.333	8	6	4	0	0	51²	58	1	32	21	16.0	4.88	70	.284	.387	1	.059	-2	-9	-8	-0	-0.9
1912 Cle-A	0	0	—	3	0	0	0	0	13²	15	0	9	5	15.8	4.61	74	.288	.393	0	.000	-0	-2	-2	-0	-0.1
1914 StL-A	15	14	.517	44	35	20	3	1	284	269	4	109	109	12.2	2.85	95	.257	.330	10	.112	-3	-3	-5	5	-0.3
1915 StL-A	7	10	.412	34	23	8	0	1	170¹	155	2	92	58	13.4	3.59	80	.255	.359	8	.190	-1	-12	-14	2	-1.1
Det-A	7	3	.700	11	9	3	1	0	67	57	1	33	24	12.1	2.42	125	.243	.336	6	.286	2	4	5	1	0.9
Yr	14	13	.519	45	32	11	1	1	237¹	212	3	125	82	12.8	3.26	89	.249	.345	8	.127	3	-9	-9	3	-0.2
1916 Det-A	8	12	.400	30	20	8	0	1	151²	141	1	79	61	13.7	3.68	78	.255	.360	3	.068	-3	-14	-14	-0	-1.8
1917 Det-A	13	10	.565	34	23	10	2	1	198	163	2	96	62	12.3	2.09	127	.229	.330	12	.211	2	13	12	0	1.6
1918 Det-A	6	11	.353	19	18	8	1	0	122	127	3	68	42	14.8	3.76	71	.279	.379	5	.109	-3	-13	-15	2	-1.6
1919 Det-A	1	0	1.000	2	1	0	0	0	9¹	12	0	7	3	18.3	5.79	55	.324	.432	1	.250	0	-3	-3	-0	-0.2
Bos-A	3	5	.375	13	7	4	0	0	72²	74	2	39	12	14.4	4.09	74	.280	.373	1	.143	-1	-7	-9	1	-0.8
*Chi-A	3	2	.600	5	5	3	2	0	39¹	39	0	14	11	12.6	2.52	126	.281	.355	2	.143	-1	3	3	-1	0.1
Yr	7	7	.500	20	13	7	2	0	121¹	125	2	60	26	13.9	3.71	83	.282	.370	2	.051	-1	-6	-8	0	-0.9
Total 8	65	71	.478	203	147	68	9	4	1179²	1110	16	578	408	13.2	3.20	88	.258	.352	51	.142	-8	-44	-49	10	-4.2

■ BILL JAMES
James, William Lawrence "Seattle Bill" b: 3/12/1892, Iowa Hill, Cal. d: 3/10/71, Oroville, Cal. BR/TR, 6'3", 196 lbs. Deb: 4/17/13

YEAR TM/L	W	L	PCT	G	GS	CG	SH	SV	IP	H	HR	BB	SO	RAT	ERA	ERA+	OAV	OOB	BH	AVG	PB	PR	/A	PD	TPI
1913 Bos-N	6	10	.375	24	14	10	1	0	135²	134	4	57	73	13.1	2.79	118	.264	.347	12	.255	1	6	8	0	1.0
1914 *Bos-N	26	7	**.788**	46	37	30	4	2	332¹	261	7	118	156	10.6	1.90	145	.225	.304	33	.256	4	**33**	**32**	-1	**3.9**
1915 Bos-N	5	4	.556	13	10	4	0	0	68¹	68	2	25	23	12.1	3.03	86	.269	.332	1	.048	-1	-2	-3	1	-0.3
1919 Bos-N	0	0	—	1	0	0	0	0	5¹	6	0	2	1	13.5	3.38	85	.273	.333	0	.000	-0	-0	-0	0	0.0
Total 4	37	21	.638	84	61	44	5	2	541²	469	14	199	253	11.5	2.28	126	.242	.319	46	.231	4	37	35	1	4.6

■ CHARLIE JAMIESON
Jamieson, Charles Devine "Cuckoo" b: 2/7/1893, Paterson, N.J. d: 10/27/69, Paterson, N.J. BL/TL, 5'8.5", 165 lbs. Deb: 9/20/15 ♦

YEAR TM/L	W	L	PCT	G	GS	CG	SH	SV	IP	H	HR	BB	SO	RAT	ERA	ERA+	OAV	OOB	BH	AVG	PB	PR	/A	PD	TPI
1916 Was-A	0	0	—	1	0	0	0	0	4	2	0	3	2	11.3	4.50	61	.143	.294	0	.000	-1	-1	-1	0	0.0
1917 Was-A	0	0	—	1	0	0	0	0	2¹	10	0	2	1	46.3	38.57	7	.625	.667	6	.171	0	-9	-9	-0	-0.6
1918 Phi-A	2	1	.667	5	2	1	0	0	23	24	0	13	2	15.3	4.30	68	.261	.364	84	.202	0	-4	-4	-0	-0.3
1919 Cle-A	0	0	—	4	1	0	0	0	13	12	0	8	0	13.8	5.54	60	.250	.357	6	.353	0	-2	-2	-0	-0.2
1922 Cle-A	0	0	—	2	0	0	0	0	5²	7	0	4	2	17.5	3.18	126	.318	.423	183	.323	0	-1	-1	-0	0.1
Total 5	2	1	.667	13	3	1	0	0	48	55	0	30	7	16.3	6.19	51	.286	.388	1990	.303	2	-17	-16	-0	-1.0

■ JERRY JANESKI
Janeski, Gerard Joseph b: 4/18/46, Pasadena, Cal. BR/TR, 6'4", 205 lbs. Deb: 4/10/70

YEAR TM/L	W	L	PCT	G	GS	CG	SH	SV	IP	H	HR	BB	SO	RAT	ERA	ERA+	OAV	OOB	BH	AVG	PB	PR	/A	PD	TPI
1970 Chi-A	10	17	.370	35	35	4	1	0	205²	247	22	63	79	13.8	4.77	82	.300	.353	5	.076	-4	-24	-20	2	-2.1
1971 Was-A	1	5	.167	23	10	0	0	1	61²	72	5	34	19	15.9	4.96	67	.304	.398	3	.214	1	-10	-11	1	-0.9
1972 Tex-A	0	1	.000	4	1	0	0	0	12²	11	0	7	7	12.8	2.84	106	.229	.327	0	.000	0	0	0	0	0.0
Total 3	11	23	.324	62	46	4	1	1	280	330	27	104	105	14.2	4.72	79	.298	.362	8	.098	-4	-34	-31	3	-3.0

■ LARRY JANSEN
Jansen, Lawrence Joseph b: 7/16/20, Verboort, Ore. BR/TR, 6'2", 190 lbs. Deb: 4/17/47 C

YEAR TM/L	W	L	PCT	G	GS	CG	SH	SV	IP	H	HR	BB	SO	RAT	ERA	ERA+	OAV	OOB	BH	AVG	PB	PR	/A	PD	TPI
1947 NY-N	21	5	**.808**	42	30	20	1	1	248	241	23	57	104	10.9	3.16	129	.262	.306	16	.186	-0	25	25	0	2.6
1948 NY-N	18	12	.600	42	36	15	4	2	277	283	25	54	126	11.0	3.61	109	.265	.303	13	.137	-2	11	10	2	1.0
1949 NY-N	15	16	.484	37	35	17	3	0	259²	271	36	62	113	11.6	3.85	104	.263	.306	16	.165	-0	6	4	2	0.6
1950 NY-N	19	13	.594	40	35	21	**5**	3	275	238	31	55	161	**9.6**	3.01	136	.232	**.271**	16	.167	-0	35	33	1	3.4
1951 *NY-N	**23**	11	.676	39	34	18	3	0	278²	254	26	56	145	10.1	3.04	129	.239	.279	9	.094	-5	29	27	2	2.6
1952 NY-N	11	11	.500	34	27	8	1	2	167¹	183	16	47	74	12.7	4.09	91	.281	.335	8	.178	3	-7	-7	2	-0.1
1953 NY-N	11	16	.407	36	26	6	0	1	184²	185	24	55	88	11.8	4.14	104	.256	.311	8	.133	-1	3	3	-1	0.1
1954 NY-N	2	2	.500	13	7	0	0	0	40²	57	5	15	15	16.2	5.98	68	.337	.395	4	.286	1	-9	-9	1	-0.5
1956 Cin-N	2	3	.400	8	7	2	0	1	34²	39	5	9	16	12.7	5.19	77	.281	.329	0	.000	-1	-5	-5	-0	-0.5
Total 9	122	89	.578	291	237	107	17	10	1765²	1751	191	410	842	11.1	3.58	112	.258	.302	90	.150	-6	87	82	10	9.2

■ RAY JARVIS
Jarvis, Raymond Arnold b: 5/10/46, Providence, R.I. BR/TR, 6'2", 198 lbs. Deb: 4/15/69

YEAR TM/L	W	L	PCT	G	GS	CG	SH	SV	IP	H	HR	BB	SO	RAT	ERA	ERA+	OAV	OOB	BH	AVG	PB	PR	/A	PD	TPI
1969 Bos-A	5	6	.455	29	12	2	0	1	100¹	105	9	43	36	13.5	4.75	80	.274	.352	2	.069	-2	-13	-11	1	-1.1
1970 Bos-A	0	1	.000	15	0	0	0	0	16	17	1	14	8	18.6	3.94	101	.274	.423	0	—	0	-0	0	0	0.0
Total 2	5	7	.417	44	12	2	0	1	116¹	122	9	57	44	14.2	4.64	82	.274	.363	2	.069	-2	-13	-11	1	-1.1

■ PAT JARVIS
Jarvis, Robert Patrick b: 3/18/41, Carlyle, Ill. BR/TR, 5'10.5", 180 lbs. Deb: 8/04/66

YEAR TM/L	W	L	PCT	G	GS	CG	SH	SV	IP	H	HR	BB	SO	RAT	ERA	ERA+	OAV	OOB	BH	AVG	PB	PR	/A	PD	TPI
1966 Atl-N	6	2	.750	10	9	3	1	0	62¹	46	1	12	41	8.5	2.31	157	.206	.250	0	.000	-2	9	9	-1	0.7
1967 Atl-N	15	10	.600	32	30	7	1	0	194	195	15	62	118	12.1	3.66	91	.260	.320	6	.085	-3	-6	-7	-2	-1.2
1968 Atl-N	16	12	.571	34	34	14	1	0	256	202	15	50	157	8.9	2.60	115	.214	.255	12	.141	-2	11	11	-2	1.0
1969 *Atl-N	13	11	.542	37	33	9	1	0	217¹	204	25	73	123	11.5	4.43	81	.246	.308	8	.113	-3	-20	-20	0	-2.2
1970 Atl-N	16	16	.500	36	34	11	1	0	254	240	21	72	173	11.1	3.61	119	.247	.299	15	.183	-0	12	19	2	2.2
1971 Atl-N	6	14	.300	35	23	3	3	1	162¹	162	16	51	68	12.0	4.10	90	.261	.320	5	.106	-2	-12	-7	1	-0.7
1972 Atl-N	11	7	.611	37	6	0	0	2	98²	94	7	44	56	12.6	4.10	92	.260	.341	3	.125	-1	-7	-3	1	-0.2
1973 Mon-N	2	1	.667	28	0	0	0	0	39¹	37	6	16	19	12.4	3.20	119	.250	.327	0	.000	-0	2	3	-0	0.2
Total 8	85	73	.538	249	169	42	8	3	1284	1180	106	380	755	11.0	3.58	101	.243	.300	49	.121	-10	-11	3	-2	-0.2

■ HI JASPER
Jasper, Henry W. b: 11/15/1880, St.Louis, Mo. d: 5/22/37, St.Louis, Mo. BR/TR, 5'11", 180 lbs. Deb: 4/19/14

YEAR TM/L	W	L	PCT	G	GS	CG	SH	SV	IP	H	HR	BB	SO	RAT	ERA	ERA+	OAV	OOB	BH	AVG	PB	PR	/A	PD	TPI
1914 Chi-A	1	0	1.000	16	0	0	0	0	32¹	22	0	20	19	12.0	3.34	80	.210	.341	0	.000	-1	-2	-2	1	-0.1
1915 Chi-A	0	1	.000	3	2	1	0	0	15²	8	2	9	15	9.8	4.60	65	.157	.283	2	.286	-0	-3	-3	1	-0.2
1916 StL-N	5	6	.455	21	11	2	0	1	107	97	0	42	37	12.3	3.28	81	.254	.339	7	.212	1	-8	-8	2	-0.5
1919 Cle-A	4	5	.444	12	10	5	0	0	82²	83	1	28	25	12.1	3.59	93	.269	.330	3	.103	-2	-3	-2	1	-0.3
Total 4	10	12	.455	52	23	8	0	1	237²	210	3	99	96	12.0	3.48	84	.248	.333	12	.162	-2	-16	-15	5	-1.0

■ LARRY JASTER
Jaster, Larry Edward b: 1/13/44, Midland, Mich. BL/TL, 6'3", 190 lbs. Deb: 9/17/65

YEAR TM/L	W	L	PCT	G	GS	CG	SH	SV	IP	H	HR	BB	SO	RAT	ERA	ERA+	OAV	OOB	BH	AVG	PB	PR	/A	PD	TPI
1965 StL-N	3	0	1.000	4	3	3	0	0	28	21	1	7	10	9.0	1.61	239	.206	.257	2	.200	0	6	7	-0	0.8
1966 StL-N	11	5	.688	26	21	6	**5**	0	151²	124	17	45	92	10.3	3.26	110	.227	.291	8	.178	1	6	5	-1	0.6
1967 *StL-N	9	7	.563	34	23	2	1	3	152¹	141	12	44	87	11.0	3.01	109	.244	.300	5	.100	-1	6	5	-2	0.2
1968 *StL-N	9	13	.409	31	21	3	1	0	154¹	153	13	38	70	11.5	3.50	83	.262	.313	6	.140	0	-9	-10	-1	-1.2
1969 Mon-N	1	6	.143	24	11	1	0	0	77	95	17	29	39	14.6	5.49	67	.302	.362	8	.421	3	-16	-16	-1	-1.3
1970 Atl-N	1	1	.500	14	0	0	0	0	22¹	33	5	8	9	16.5	6.85	63	.359	.410	0	.000	-0	-7	-6	-0	-0.5
1972 Atl-N	1	1	.500	5	1	0	0	0	12¹	12	4	8	6	14.6	5.11	74	.267	.377	0	.000	-0	-2	-2	0	-0.1

YEAR	TM/L	W	L	PCT	G	GS	CG	SH	SV	IP	H	HR	BB	SO	RAT	ERA	ERA+	OAV	OOB	BH	AVG	PB	PR	/A	PD	TPI
Total	7	35	33	.515	138	80	15	7	5	598	579	69	178	313	11.6	3.64	93	.256	.314	29	.170	4	-16	-17	-5	-1.5

■ AL JAVERY
Javery, Alva William "Beartracks"   b: 6/5/18, Worcester, Mass.   d: 9/13/77, Woodstock, Conn.   BR/TR, 6'3", 183 lbs.   Deb: 4/23/40

YEAR	TM/L	W	L	PCT	G	GS	CG	SH	SV	IP	H	HR	BB	SO	RAT	ERA	ERA+	OAV	OOB	BH	AVG	PB	PR	/A	PD	TPI
1940	Bos-N	2	4	.333	29	4	1	0	1	83¹	99	2	36	42	14.8	5.51	68	.293	.364	2	.087	-1	-15	-17	-2	-1.8
1941	Bos-N	10	11	.476	34	23	9	1	1	160²	181	5	65	54	14.1	4.31	83	.283	.355	6	.103	-4	-12	-13	1	-1.5
1942	Bos-N	12	16	.429	42	37	19	5	0	261	251	8	78	85	11.4	3.03	110	.251	.307	9	.105	-5	8	9	2	0.7
1943	Bos-N	17	16	.515	41	35	19	5	0	303	288	13	99	134	11.6	3.21	106	.248	.309	17	.163	-3	6	7	1	0.6
1944	Bos-N	10	19	.345	40	33	11	3	3	254	248	12	118	137	13.0	3.54	108	.262	.345	12	.152	-3	2	8	-3	0.2
1945	Bos-N	2	7	.222	17	14	2	1	0	77¹	92	4	51	18	16.6	6.28	61	.295	.394	6	.207	-0	-21	-21	1	-1.8
1946	Bos-N	0	1	.000	2	1	0	0	0	3¹	5	0	5	0	27.0	13.50	25	.417	.588	0	.000	-0	-4	-4	-0	-0.3
Total	7	53	74	.417	205	147	61	15	5	1142²	1164	44	452	470	12.9	3.80	94	.264	.335	52	.137	-16	-37	-31	-0	-3.9

■ JOEY JAY
Jay, Joseph Richard   b: 8/15/35, Middletown, Conn.   BB/TR, 6'4", 228 lbs.   Deb: 7/21/53

YEAR	TM/L	W	L	PCT	G	GS	CG	SH	SV	IP	H	HR	BB	SO	RAT	ERA	ERA+	OAV	OOB	BH	AVG	PB	PR	/A	PD	TPI
1953	Mil-N	1	0	1.000	3	1	1	1	0	10	6	0	5	4	9.9	0.00	—	.188	.297	0	.000	-0	5	4	-0	0.4
1954	Mil-N	1	0	1.000	15	1	0	0	0	18	21	2	16	13	19.0	6.50	57	.304	.442	0	—	0	-5	-6	0	-0.5
1955	Mil-N	0	0	—	12	1	0	0	0	19	23	2	13	3	17.1	4.74	79	.324	.429	2	.667	1	-1	-2	-0	-0.1
1957	Mil-N	0	0	—	1	0	0	0	0	0²	1	0	0	0	0.0	0.00	—	.000	.000	0	—	0	0	0	0	0.0
1958	Mil-N	7	5	.583	18	12	6	3	0	96²	60	8	43	74	9.7	2.14	164	.177	.272	3	.094	-1	19	15	-0	1.4
1959	Mil-N	6	11	.353	34	19	4	1	0	136¹	130	11	64	88	13.1	4.09	87	.248	.336	3	.086	-1	-2	-8	2	-0.7
1960	Mil-N	9	8	.529	32	11	3	0	1	133¹	128	10	59	90	13.0	3.24	106	.254	.339	7	.156	-0	8	3	-0	0.2
1961	*Cin-N	21	10	.677	34	34	14	4	0	247¹	217	25	92	157	11.4	3.53	115	.236	.309	8	.090	-6	14	15	-1	0.8
1962	Cin-N	21	14	.600	39	37	16	4	0	273	269	26	100	155	12.3	3.76	107	.260	.327	15	.167	3	6	8	-1	1.0
1963	Cin-N	7	18	.280	30	22	4	1	1	170	172	19	73	116	13.1	4.29	78	.266	.343	8	.160	0	-19	-18	-0	-1.7
1964	Cin-N	11	11	.500	34	23	10	0	2	183	167	17	36	134	10.1	3.39	107	.245	.285	3	.057	-3	3	5	-2	0.0
1965	Cin-N	9	8	.529	37	24	1	1	1	155²	150	21	63	102	12.5	4.22	89	.252	.328	2	.041	-3	-12	-8	-0	-1.0
1966	Cin-N	6	2	.750	12	10	1	1	0	73²	78	8	23	44	12.7	3.91	100	.275	.335	3	.115	-1	-2	-0	-1	-0.2
	Atl	0	4	.000	9	8	0	0	1	29²	39	4	20	19	18.2	7.89	46	.315	.414	1	.125	-0	-14	-14	-0	-1.3
	Yr	6	6	.500	21	18	1	1	1	103¹	117	12	43	63	14.0	5.05	76	.285	.354	2	.059	-1	-17	-14	-1	-1.6
Total	13	99	91	.521	310	203	63	16	7	1546¹	1460	153	607	999	12.2	3.77	99	.251	.325	55	.114	-10	-1	-5	-5	-1.6

■ TEX JEANES
Jeanes, Ernest Lee   b: 12/19/1900, Maypearl, Tex.   d: 4/5/73, Longview, Tex.   BR/TR, 6', 176 lbs.   Deb: 4/20/21 ♦

YEAR	TM/L	W	L	PCT	G	GS	CG	SH	SV	IP	H	HR	BB	SO	RAT	ERA	ERA+	OAV	OOB	BH	AVG	PB	PR	/A	PD	TPI
1922	Cle-A	0	0	—	1	0	0	0	0	0	0	0	1	0	—	—	—	—	1.000	0	.000	0	0	0	0	0.0
1927	NY-N	0	0	—	1	0	0	0	0	1	2	0	2	0	36.0	9.00	43	.400	.571	6	.300	-1	-1	0	0	0.0
Total	2	0	0	—	2	0	0	0	0	1	2	0	3	0	45.0	9.00	43	.400	.625	20	.274	-0	-1	-1	0	0.0

■ GEORGE JEFFCOAT
Jeffcoat, George Edward   b: 12/24/13, New Brookland, S.C.   d: 10/13/78, Leesville, S.C.   BR/TR, 5'11.5", 175 lbs.   Deb: 4/20/36

YEAR	TM/L	W	L	PCT	G	GS	CG	SH	SV	IP	H	HR	BB	SO	RAT	ERA	ERA+	OAV	OOB	BH	AVG	PB	PR	/A	PD	TPI
1936	Bro-N	5	6	.455	40	5	3	0	3	95²	84	7	63	46	14.6	4.52	92	.239	.366	3	.130	-1	-5	-4	-1	-0.5
1937	Bro-N	1	3	.250	21	3	1	1	0	54¹	58	4	27	29	14.2	5.13	79	.274	.358	0	.000	-2	-7	-7	-0	-0.8
1939	Bro-N	0	0	—	1	0	0	0	0	2	2	0	0	1	9.0	0.00	—	.286	.286	0	—	0	1	1	0	0.1
1943	Bos-N	1	2	.333	8	1	0	0	0	17²	15	1	10	10	12.7	3.06	112	.217	.316	2	.500	1	1	1	0	0.2
Total	4	7	11	.389	70	9	4	1	3	169²	159	12	100	86	14.2	4.51	89	.248	.358	5	.128	-2	-11	-9	-1	-1.0

■ HAL JEFFCOAT
Jeffcoat, Harold Bentley   b: 9/6/24, W.Columbia, S.C.   BR/TR, 5'10.5", 185 lbs.   Deb: 4/20/48 ♦

YEAR	TM/L	W	L	PCT	G	GS	CG	SH	SV	IP	H	HR	BB	SO	RAT	ERA	ERA+	OAV	OOB	BH	AVG	PB	PR	/A	PD	TPI
1954	Chi-N	5	6	.455	43	3	1	0	7	104	110	12	58	35	14.9	5.19	81	.276	.373	8	.258	2	-13	-11	1	-0.6
1955	Chi-N	8	6	.571	50	1	0	0	6	100²	107	5	53	32	14.7	2.95	139	.276	.369	4	.174	1	12	13	1	1.4
1956	Chi-N	8	2	.800	38	16	2	0	2	171	189	12	55	55	13.1	3.84	104	.281	.340	8	.148	-1	-3	4	0	0.5
1957	Cin-N	12	13	.480	37	31	10	1	0	207	236	29	46	63	12.6	4.52	91	.294	.338	14	.203	6	-15	-9	-0	-0.2
1958	Cin-N	6	8	.429	49	0	0	0	9	75	76	8	26	35	12.5	3.72	111	.268	.333	5	.556	2	2	4	2	0.8
1959	Cin-N	0	1	.000	17	0	0	0	1	21²	21	3	10	12	12.9	3.32	122	.253	.333	1	1.000	1	2	2	0	0.3
	StL-N	0	1	.000	11	0	0	0	0	17²	33	4	9	7	21.4	9.17	46	.402	.462	0	.000	-0	-10	-10	0	-0.9
	Yr	0	2	.000	28	0	0	0	1	39¹	54	7	19	19	16.7	5.95	70	.327	.397	0	.000	0	-9	-8	0	-0.9
Total	6	39	37	.513	245	51	13	1	25	697	772	73	257	239	13.6	4.22	97	.285	.352	487	.248	11	-24	-10	7	1.3

■ MIKE JEFFCOAT
Jeffcoat, James Michael   b: 8/3/59, Pine Bluff, Ark.   BL/TL, 6'2", 187 lbs.   Deb: 8/21/83

YEAR	TM/L	W	L	PCT	G	GS	CG	SH	SV	IP	H	HR	BB	SO	RAT	ERA	ERA+	OAV	OOB	BH	AVG	PB	PR	/A	PD	TPI
1983	Cle-A	1	3	.250	11	2	0	0	0	32²	32	1	13	9	12.7	3.31	128	.256	.331	0	—	0	3	3	0	0.3
1984	Cle-A	5	2	.714	63	1	0	0	0	75¹	82	7	24	41	12.8	2.99	137	.281	.338	0	—	0	8	9	1	1.0
1985	Cle-A	0	0	—	9	0	0	0	0	9²	8	1	6	4	13.0	2.79	148	.235	.350	0	—	0	1	1	1	0.2
	SF-N	0	2	.000	19	1	0	0	0	22	27	4	6	10	14.3	5.32	65	.307	.365	0	.000	0	-4	-7	-0	-0.3
1987	Tex-A	0	1	.000	2	2	0	0	0	7	11	4	4	1	19.3	12.86	35	.355	.429	0	—	0	-7	-7	-0	-0.5
1988	Tex-A	0	2	.000	5	2	0	0	0	10	19	1	5	5	23.4	11.70	35	.432	.510	0	—	0	-9	-8	-0	-0.7
1989	Tex-A	9	6	.600	22	22	2	2	0	130²	139	7	33	64	12.1	3.58	111	.270	.319	0	—	0	4	6	1	0.6
1990	Tex-A	5	6	.455	44	12	1	0	5	110²	122	12	28	58	12.4	4.47	89	.283	.330	0	—	0	-7	-6	-1	-0.6
Total	7	20	22	.476	175	42	3	2	5	398	440	37	119	192	12.9	4.14	97	.282	.338	0	.000	0	-9	-6	2	0.0

■ JESSE JEFFERSON
Jefferson, Jesse Harrison   b: 3/3/49, Midlothian, Va.   BR/TR, 6'3", 188 lbs.   Deb: 6/23/73

YEAR	TM/L	W	L	PCT	G	GS	CG	SH	SV	IP	H	HR	BB	SO	RAT	ERA	ERA+	OAV	OOB	BH	AVG	PB	PR	/A	PD	TPI
1973	Bal-A	6	5	.545	18	15	3	0	0	100²	104	15	46	52	13.4	4.11	91	.267	.345	0	—	0	-3	-4	1	-0.3
1974	Bal-A	1	0	1.000	20	2	0	0	0	57¹	55	2	38	31	14.6	4.40	79	.261	.373	0	—	0	-5	-6	0	-0.5
1975	Bal-A	0	2	.000	4	0	0	0	0	7²	5	0	8	4	15.3	2.35	149	.227	.433	0	—	0	1	1	0	0.1
	Chi-A	5	9	.357	22	21	1	0	0	107²	100	10	94	67	16.4	5.10	76	.249	.394	0	—	0	-16	-15	-0	-1.3
	Yr	5	11	.313	26	21	1	0	0	115¹	105	10	102	71	16.3	4.92	78	.248	.397	0	—	0	-15	-14	-0	-1.2
1976	Chi-A	2	5	.286	19	9	0	0	0	62¹	86	3	42	30	18.8	8.52	50	.339	.436	0	—	0	-35	-34	1	-3.1
1977	Tor-A	9	17	.346	33	33	8	0	0	217	224	23	83	114	12.8	4.31	97	.269	.336	0	—	0	-6	-3	-0	-0.2
1978	Tor-A	7	16	.304	31	30	9	2	0	211²	214	28	86	97	12.9	4.38	90	.267	.340	0	—	0	-15	-11	-0	-1.0
1979	Tor-A	2	10	.167	34	10	2	0	0	116	150	19	45	43	15.3	5.51	79	.328	.390	0	—	0	-17	-15	1	-1.3
1980	Tor-A	4	13	.235	29	18	2	0	0	121²	130	12	52	53	13.6	5.47	79	.281	.357	0	—	0	-19	-15	1	-1.4
	Pit-N	1	0	1.000	1	0	0	0	0	6²	3	0	2	4	6.8	1.35	270	.143	.217	0	.000	-0	2	2	0	0.0
1981	Cal-A	2	4	.333	26	5	0	0	0	77	80	4	24	27	12.4	3.62	101	.269	.328	0	—	0	0	0	-1	0.0
Total	9	39	81	.325	237	144	25	4	1	1085²	1151	116	520	522	14.0	4.81	83	.277	.360	0	.000	-0	-112	-101	4	-8.8

■ FERGIE JENKINS
Jenkins, Ferguson Arthur   b: 12/13/43, Chatham, Ont., Can.   BR/TR, 6'5", 205 lbs.   Deb: 9/10/65

YEAR	TM/L	W	L	PCT	G	GS	CG	SH	SV	IP	H	HR	BB	SO	RAT	ERA	ERA+	OAV	OOB	BH	AVG	PB	PR	/A	PD	TPI
1965	Phi-N	2	1	.667	7	0	0	0	1	12¹	7	2	2	10	6.6	2.19	158	.159	.196	0	.000	-0	2	2	-0	0.1
1966	Phi-N	0	0	—	1	0	0	0	0	2¹	3	0	1	2	15.4	3.86	93	.273	.333	0	—	0	-0	-0	0	0.0
	Chi-N	6	8	.429	60	12	2	1	5	182	147	24	51	148	9.9	3.31	111	.219	.277	7	.137	1	6	7	-2	0.6
	Yr	6	8	.429	61	12	2	1	5	184¹	150	24	52	150	10.0	3.32	111	.220	.278	3	.059	1	6	7	-2	0.6
1967	Chi-N	20	13	.606	38	38	20	3	0	289¹	230	30	83	236	9.9	2.80	127	.217	.277	14	.151	1	19	24	1	3.0
1968	Chi-N	20	15	.571	40	40	20	3	0	308	255	26	65	260	9.4	2.63	120	.222	.266	16	.160	3	12	18	-2	2.3
1969	Chi-N	21	15	.583	43	42	23	7	1	311¹	284	27	71	273	10.5	3.21	125	.242	.290	15	.139	-1	13	28	-1	3.1
1970	Chi-N	22	16	.579	40	39	24	3	0	313	265	30	60	274	9.5	3.39	133	.224	.265	14	.124	-3	23	39	-2	3.7
1971	Chi-N	24	13	.649	39	39	30	3	0	325	304	29	37	263	9.6	2.77	142	.246	.271	28	.243	12	25	42	1	6.7
1972	Chi-N	20	12	.625	36	36	23	5	0	289¹	253	32	62	184	10.0	3.20	119	.234	.280	20	.183	2	8	19	3	2.8
1973	Chi-N	14	16	.467	38	38	7	2	0	271	267	35	57	170	10.9	3.89	101	.259	.301	10	.119	-2	-7	2	3	0.5
1974	Tex-A	25	12	.676	41	41	29	6	0	328¹	286	27	45	225	9.3	2.82	126	.232	.264	1	.500	-1	29	27	-0	2.9
1975	Tex-A	17	18	.486	37	37	22	4	0	270	261	37	56	157	10.9	3.93	95	.257	.295	0	—	0	-5	-0		-0.4
1976	Bos-A	12	11	.522	30	29	12	3	0	209	201	20	43	142	10.7	3.27	119	.253	.296	0	—	0	6	15	-1	1.5
1977	Bos-A	10	10	.500	28	28	11	1	0	193	190	30	36	105	10.5	3.68	122	.257	.291	0	—	0	8	17	1	1.9

YEAR TM/L	W	L	PCT	G	GS	CG	SH	SV	IP	H	HR	BB	SO	RAT	ERA	ERA+	OAV	OOB	BH	AVG	PB	PR	/A	PD	TPI
1978 Tex-A	18	8	.692	34	30	16	4	0	249	228	21	41	157	9.8	3.04	123	.245	.279	0	—	0	20	20	2	2.3
1979 Tex-A	16	14	.533	37	37	10	3	0	259	252	40	81	164	11.7	4.07	102	.256	.314	0	—	0	4	2	4	0.6
1980 Tex-A	12	12	.500	29	29	12	0	0	198	190	22	52	129	11.2	3.77	103	.250	.301	0	—	0	6	3	0	0.3
1981 Tex-A	5	8	.385	19	16	1	0	0	106	122	14	40	63	13.8	4.50	77	.290	.351	0	—	0	-10	-12	2	-1.0
1982 Chi-N	14	15	.483	34	34	4	1	0	217¹	221	19	68	134	12.2	3.15	119	.264	.323	10	.149	-1	11	14	-1	1.3
1983 Chi-N	6	9	.400	33	29	1	1	0	167¹	176	19	46	96	12.3	4.30	88	.275	.329	13	.245	3	-13	-10	-2	-0.6
Total 19	284	226	.557	664	594	267	49	7	4500²	4142	484	997	3192	10.4	3.34	115	.243	.289	148	.165	15	157	254	7	31.6

■ JACK JENKINS
Jenkins, Warren Washington b: 12/22/42, Covington, Va. BR/TR, 6'2", 195 lbs. Deb: 9/13/62

YEAR TM/L	W	L	PCT	G	GS	CG	SH	SV	IP	H	HR	BB	SO	RAT	ERA	ERA+	OAV	OOB	BH	AVG	PB	PR	/A	PD	TPI
1962 Was-A	0	1	.000	3	1	1	0	0	13¹	12	4	7	10	12.8	4.05	100	.245	.339	0	.000	-0	-0	-0	-0	-0.2
1963 Was-A	0	2	.000	4	2	0	0	0	12¹	16	2	12	5	20.4	5.84	64	.340	.475	1	.333	0	-3	-3	0	-0.2
1969 LA-N	0	0	—	1	0	0	0	0	1	0	0	0	1	0.0	0.00	—	.000	.000	0	—	0	0	0	0	0.0
Total 3	0	3	.000	8	3	1	0	0	26²	28	6	19	16	15.9	4.73	82	.283	.398	1	.143	-0	-3	-3	0	-0.2

■ WILLIE JENSEN
Jensen, William Christian b: 11/17/1889, Philadelphia, Pa. d: 3/27/17, Philadelphia, Pa. BL/TR, 5'11.5", 170 lbs. Deb: 9/10/12

YEAR TM/L	W	L	PCT	G	GS	CG	SH	SV	IP	H	HR	BB	SO	RAT	ERA	ERA+	OAV	OOB	BH	AVG	PB	PR	/A	PD	TPI
1912 Det-A	1	2	.333	5	4	1	0	0	33	43	1	18	8	17.2	4.91	66	.339	.429	0	.000	-2	-6	-6	-0	-0.6
1914 Phi-A	0	1	.000	1	1	1	0	0	9	7	1	2	1	9.0	2.00	132	.226	.273	0	.000	0	1	1	0	0.1
Total 2	1	3	.250	6	5	2	0	0	42	50	2	20	9	15.4	4.29	73	.316	.400	0	.000	-2	-5	-5	-0	-0.5

■ VIRGIL JESTER
Jester, Virgil Milton b: 7/23/27, Denver, Colo. BR/TR, 5'11", 188 lbs. Deb: 6/18/52

YEAR TM/L	W	L	PCT	G	GS	CG	SH	SV	IP	H	HR	BB	SO	RAT	ERA	ERA+	OAV	OOB	BH	AVG	PB	PR	/A	PD	TPI
1952 Bos-N	3	5	.375	19	8	4	1	0	73	80	5	23	25	12.8	3.33	108	.283	.339	4	.211	1	3	2	-1	0.3
1953 Mil-N	0	0	—	2	0	0	0	0	2	4	1	4	0	36.0	22.50	17	.400	.571	0	—	0	-4	-4	0	-0.3
Total 2	3	5	.375	21	8	4	1	0	75	84	6	27	25	13.4	3.84	94	.287	.349	4	.211	1	-1	-2	-1	0.0

■ GERMAN JIMENEZ
Jimenez, German (Camarena) b: 12/5/62, Santiago, Mex. BL/TL, 5'11", 200 lbs. Deb: 6/28/88

YEAR TM/L	W	L	PCT	G	GS	CG	SH	SV	IP	H	HR	BB	SO	RAT	ERA	ERA+	OAV	OOB	BH	AVG	PB	PR	/A	PD	TPI
1988 Atl-N	1	6	.143	15	9	0	0	0	55²	65	4	12	26	12.6	5.01	73	.294	.333	1	.059	-1	-10	-8	-1	-1.0

■ JUAN JIMENEZ
Jimenez, Juan Antonio (Martes) b: 3/8/49, LaTorre, La Vega, D.R. BR/TR, 6'1", 165 lbs. Deb: 9/09/74

YEAR TM/L	W	L	PCT	G	GS	CG	SH	SV	IP	H	HR	BB	SO	RAT	ERA	ERA+	OAV	OOB	BH	AVG	PB	PR	/A	PD	TPI
1974 Pit-N	0	0	—	4	0	0	0	0	4	6	0	2	2	18.0	6.75	51	.353	.421	0	—	0	-1	-1	-0	-0.1

■ TOMMY JOHN
John, Thomas Edward b: 5/22/43, Terre Haute, Ind. BR/TL, 6'3", 180 lbs. Deb: 9/06/63

YEAR TM/L	W	L	PCT	G	GS	CG	SH	SV	IP	H	HR	BB	SO	RAT	ERA	ERA+	OAV	OOB	BH	AVG	PB	PR	/A	PD	TPI
1963 Cle-A	0	2	.000	6	3	0	0	0	20¹	23	1	6	9	12.8	2.21	164	.284	.333	0	.000	-1	3	3	0	0.3
1964 Cle-A	2	9	.182	25	14	2	1	0	94¹	97	10	35	65	12.4	3.91	92	.262	.326	5	.208	0	-3	-3	1	-0.2
1965 Chi-A	14	7	.667	39	27	6	1	3	183²	162	12	58	126	10.9	3.09	103	.237	.298	10	.169	1	8	2	3	0.7
1966 Chi-A	14	11	.560	34	33	10	5	0	223	195	13	57	138	10.5	2.62	121	.235	.290	10	.145	2	20	14	1	1.8
1967 Chi-A	10	13	.435	31	29	9	6	0	178¹	143	12	47	110	9.8	2.47	126	.219	.277	8	.157	-0	15	13	6	2.1
1968 Chi-A	10	5	.667	25	25	5	1	0	177¹	135	10	49	117	9.9	1.98	153	.212	.280	12	.194	2	20	21	6	3.5
1969 Chi-A	9	11	.450	33	33	6	2	0	232¹	230	16	90	128	12.4	3.25	119	.261	.330	9	.114	-2	9	16	7	2.3
1970 Chi-A	12	17	.414	37	37	10	3	0	269¹	253	19	101	138	12.1	3.27	119	.251	.321	17	.202	1	13	19	4	2.6
1971 Chi-A	13	16	.448	38	35	10	3	0	229¹	244	17	58	131	12.0	3.61	99	.274	.321	10	.145	-1	-4	-1	-1	-0.2
1972 LA-N	11	5	.688	29	29	4	1	0	186²	172	14	40	117	10.4	2.89	115	.244	.287	10	.159	-1	12	9	4	1.3
1973 LA-N	16	7	.696	36	31	4	2	0	218	202	16	50	116	10.6	3.10	111	.246	.293	15	.203	2	14	8	7	1.8
1974 LA-N	13	3	.813	22	22	5	3	0	153	133	4	42	78	10.4	2.59	131	.235	.289	6	.118	-1	18	14	2	1.6
1976 LA-N	10	10	.500	31	31	6	2	0	207	207	7	61	91	11.7	3.09	110	.261	.314	7	.109	-2	10	7	-1	0.4
1977 *LA-N	20	7	.741	31	31	11	3	0	220¹	225	12	50	123	11.4	2.78	138	.267	.311	14	.177	1	28	26	3	3.1
1978 *LA-N	17	10	.630	33	30	7	0	1	213	230	11	53	124	12.2	3.30	106	.271	.318	8	.121	-1	7	5	2	0.6
1979 NY-A	21	9	.700	37	36	17	3	0	276¹	268	9	65	111	11.0	2.96	137	.260	.306	0	—	0	38	34	2	3.7
1980 *NY-A	22	9	.710	36	36	16	6	0	265¹	270	13	56	78	11.3	3.43	114	.268	.311	0	—	0	18	15	2	1.7
1981 *NY-A	9	8	.529	20	20	7	0	0	140¹	135	10	39	50	11.4	2.63	136	.256	.311	0	—	0	16	15	2	1.8
1982 NY-A	10	10	.500	30	26	9	2	0	186²	190	11	34	54	10.9	3.66	109	.266	.302	0	—	0	8	7	3	0.9
*Cal-A	4	2	.667	7	7	1	0	0	35	49	4	5	14	13.9	3.06	105	.336	.358	0	—	0	1	1	0	0.1
Yr	14	12	.538	37	33	10	2	0	221²	239	15	39	68	11.3	3.69	108	.274	.305	0	—	0	9	7	3	-1.0
1983 Cal-A	11	13	.458	34	34	9	0	0	234²	287	20	49	65	13.0	4.33	93	.304	.340	0	—	0	-7	-8	2	-0.6
1984 Cal-A	7	13	.350	32	29	4	1	0	181¹	223	15	56	47	14.0	4.52	88	.306	.359	0	—	0	-11	-7	1	-0.9
1985 Cal-A	2	4	.333	12	6	0	0	0	38¹	51	3	15	17	15.7	4.70	87	.329	.392	0	—	0	-3	-3	1	0.0
Oak-A	2	6	.250	11	11	0	0	0	48	66	6	13	8	15.2	6.19	62	.332	.376	0	—	0	-11	-12	-1	-0.9
Yr	4	10	.286	23	17	0	0	0	86¹	117	9	28	25	15.2	5.53	72	.328	.378	0	—	0	-13	-15	2	-0.9
1986 NY-A	5	3	.625	13	10	1	0	0	70²	73	9	15	28	11.5	2.93	140	.275	.319	0	—	0	10	9	1	1.0
1987 NY-A	13	6	.684	33	33	3	1	0	187²	212	12	47	63	12.7	4.03	109	.288	.336	0	—	0	9	7	-0	0.7
1988 NY-A	9	8	.529	35	32	0	0	0	176¹	221	11	46	81	13.9	4.49	88	.308	.355	0	—	0	-10	-11	-2	-0.7
1989 NY-A	2	7	.222	10	10	0	0	0	63²	87	6	22	18	15.8	5.80	67	.336	.394	0	—	0	-14	-14	2	-1.0
Total 26	288	231	.555	760	700	162	46	4	4710¹	4783	302	1259	2245	11.7	3.34	110	.265	.316	141	.157	1	214	179	63	27.5

■ AUGIE JOHNS
Johns, Augustus Francis "Lefty" b: 9/10/1899, St.Louis, Mo. d: 9/12/75, San Antonio, Tex. BL/TL, 5'8.5", 170 lbs. Deb: 4/16/26

YEAR TM/L	W	L	PCT	G	GS	CG	SH	SV	IP	H	HR	BB	SO	RAT	ERA	ERA+	OAV	OOB	BH	AVG	PB	PR	/A	PD	TPI
1926 Det-A	6	4	.600	35	14	3	1	1	112²	117	6	69	40	15.3	5.35	76	.271	.377	4	.143	-1	-17	-16	-2	-1.7
1927 Det-A	0	0	—	1	0	0	0	0	1	1	0	1	1	18.0	9.00	47	.333	.500	0	—	0	-1	-0	0	0.0
Total 2	6	4	.600	36	14	3	1	1	113²	118	6	70	41	15.3	5.38	75	.271	.378	4	.143	-1	-17	-17	-2	-1.7

■ OLLIE JOHNS
Johns, Oliver Tracy b: 8/21/1879, Trenton, Ohio. d: 6/17/61, Hamilton, Ohio BL/TL. Deb: 9/24/05

YEAR TM/L	W	L	PCT	G	GS	CG	SH	SV	IP	H	HR	BB	SO	RAT	ERA	ERA+	OAV	OOB	BH	AVG	PB	PR	/A	PD	TPI
1905 Cin-N	1	0	1.000	4	1	1	0	0	18	31	1	4	8	17.5	3.50	94	.369	.398	1	.200	-0	-1	-0	-0	0.0

■ ABE JOHNSON
Johnson, Abraham b: London, Ont., Can. Deb: 7/16/1893

YEAR TM/L	W	L	PCT	G	GS	CG	SH	SV	IP	H	HR	BB	SO	RAT	ERA	ERA+	OAV	OOB	BH	AVG	PB	PR	/A	PD	TPI
1893 Chi-N	0	0	—	1	0	0	0	1	1	2	0	2	0	36.0	36.00	13	.403	.575	0	—	0	-3	-3	0	-0.2

■ RANKIN JOHNSON
Johnson, Adam Rankin Jr. b: 3/1/17, Hayden, Ariz. BR/TR, 6'3", 177 lbs. Deb: 4/17/41

YEAR TM/L	W	L	PCT	G	GS	CG	SH	SV	IP	H	HR	BB	SO	RAT	ERA	ERA+	OAV	OOB	BH	AVG	PB	PR	/A	PD	TPI
1941 Phi-A	1	0	1.000	7	0	0	0	0	10	14	0	3	0	15.3	3.60	116	.326	.370	0	.000	-0	1	1	0	0.1

■ RANKIN JOHNSON
Johnson, Adam Rankin Sr. "Tex" b: 2/4/1888, Burnet, Tex. d: 7/2/72, Williamsport, Pa. BR/TR, 6'1.5", 185 lbs. Deb: 4/20/14

YEAR TM/L	W	L	PCT	G	GS	CG	SH	SV	IP	H	HR	BB	SO	RAT	ERA	ERA+	OAV	OOB	BH	AVG	PB	PR	/A	PD	TPI
1914 Bos-A	4	9	.308	16	13	4	2	0	99¹	92	2	34	24	11.7	3.08	87	.265	.336	4	.133	-1	-4	-4	-1	-0.6
Chi-F	9	5	.643	16	14	12	2	0	120	88	5	29	60	9.1	1.58	187	.209	.267	4	.108	-2	22	18	-2	1.5
1915 Chi-F	2	4	.333	11	6	3	0	1	57	58	2	23	19	12.9	4.42	63	.270	.343	1	.045	-2	-9	-10	-2	-1.4
Bal-F	7	11	.389	23	19	12	2	1	150²	143	3	58	62	12.1	3.35	95	.255	.326	8	.157	-1	-5	-3	-3	-0.6
Yr	9	15	.375	34	25	15	2	2	207²	201	5	81	81	12.3	3.64	85	.259	.330	4	.055	-3	-14	-13	-5	-2.0
1918 StL-N	1	1	.500	6	1	0	0	0	23	20	0	7	4	10.6	2.74	99	.263	.325	1	.250	0	0	-0	1	0.1
Total 3	23	30	.434	72	53	31	6	2	450	401	12	151	169	11.2	2.92	101	.248	.315	18	.125	-6	4	1	-6	-0.2

■ ART JOHNSON
Johnson, Arthur Gilbert b: 2/15/1897, Warren, Pa. d: 6/7/82, Sarasota, Fla. BB/TL, 6'1", 167 lbs. Deb: 9/18/27

YEAR TM/L	W	L	PCT	G	GS	CG	SH	SV	IP	H	HR	BB	SO	RAT	ERA	ERA+	OAV	OOB	BH	AVG	PB	PR	/A	PD	TPI
1927 NY-N	0	0	—	1	0	0	0	0	3	1	0	1	0	6.0	0.00	—	.125	.222	0	—	0	1	1	0	0.1

■ ART JOHNSON
Johnson, Arthur Henry "Lefty" b: 7/16/16, Winchester, Mass. BL/TL, 6'2", 185 lbs. Deb: 9/22/40

YEAR TM/L	W	L	PCT	G	GS	CG	SH	SV	IP	H	HR	BB	SO	RAT	ERA	ERA+	OAV	OOB	BH	AVG	PB	PR	/A	PD	TPI
1940 Bos-N	0	1	.000	2	1	0	0	0	6	10	3	4	1	21.0	10.50	35	.345	.424	0	.000	-0	-4	-5	0	-0.3
1941 Bos-N	7	15	.318	43	18	6	0	1	183¹	189	7	71	70	13.0	3.53	101	.270	.342	8	.145	-2	2	1	0	0.0
1942 Bos-N	0	0	—	4	0	0	0	0	6¹	4	0	4	0	14.2	1.42	235	.190	.370	0	.000	-0	1	1	0	0.1
Total 3	7	16	.304	49	19	6	0	1	195²	203	7	79	71	13.3	3.68	97	.271	.346	8	.140	-2	-1	-2	1	-0.2

■ BEN JOHNSON
Johnson, Benjamin Franklin b: 5/16/31, Greenwood, S.C. BR/TR, 6'2", 190 lbs. Deb: 9/06/59

YEAR TM/L	W	L	PCT	G	GS	CG	SH	SV	IP	H	HR	BB	SO	RAT	ERA	ERA+	OAV	OOB	BH	AVG	PB	PR	/A	PD	TPI
1959 Chi-N	0	0	—	4	2	0	0	0	16^2	17	1	4	6	11.3	2.16	183	.262	.304	0	.000	-0	3	3	-0	0.3
1960 Chi-N	2	1	.667	17	0	0	0	1	29^1	39	3	11	9	15.6	4.91	77	.355	.418	0	.000	-0	-4	-4	1	-0.2
Total 2	2	1	.667	21	2	0	0	1	46	56	4	15	15	14.1	3.91	98	.320	.377	0	.000	-1	-0	-0	1	0.1

■ CHET JOHNSON
Johnson, Chester Lillis "Chesty Chet" b: 8/1/17, Redmond, Wash. d: 4/10/83, Seattle, Wash. BL/TL, 6', 175 lbs. Deb: 9/12/46

YEAR TM/L	W	L	PCT	G	GS	CG	SH	SV	IP	H	HR	BB	SO	RAT	ERA	ERA+	OAV	OOB	BH	AVG	PB	PR	/A	PD	TPI
1946 StL-A	0	0	—	5	3	0	0	0	18	20	0	13	8	16.5	5.00	75	.286	.398	0	.000	-1	-3	-3	-1	-0.3

■ BART JOHNSON
Johnson, Clair Barth b: 1/3/50, Torrance, Cal. BR/TR, 6'5", 190 lbs. Deb: 9/08/69

YEAR TM/L	W	L	PCT	G	GS	CG	SH	SV	IP	H	HR	BB	SO	RAT	ERA	ERA+	OAV	OOB	BH	AVG	PB	PR	/A	PD	TPI
1969 Chi-A	1	3	.250	4	3	0	0	0	22^1	22	2	6	18	11.3	3.22	120	.259	.308	1	.167	0	1	2	-0	0.2
1970 Chi-A	4	7	.364	18	15	2	1	0	89^2	92	11	46	71	14.1	4.82	81	.268	.358	8	.276	2	-11	-9	-0	-0.6
1971 Chi-A	12	10	.545	53	16	4	0	14	178	148	9	111	153	13.4	2.93	122	.227	.345	11	.193	0	10	13	-2	1.3
1972 Chi-A	0	3	.000	9	0	0	0	1	13^2	18	2	13	9	21.1	9.22	34	.327	.464	0	.000	-0	-9	-9	0	-0.9
1973 Chi-A	3	3	.500	22	9	0	0	0	80^2	76	6	40	56	13.2	4.13	96	.252	.343	0	—	0	-3	-2	-0	-0.1
1974 Chi-A	10	4	.714	18	18	8	2	0	121^2	105	6	32	76	10.2	2.74	136	.229	.281	0	—	0	12	13	-2	1.2
1976 Chi-A	9	16	.360	32	32	8	3	0	211^1	231	20	62	91	12.5	4.73	75	.282	.334	0	—	0	-28	-27	1	-2.6
1977 Chi-A	4	5	.444	29	4	0	0	2	92	114	5	38	46	15.1	4.01	102	.302	.369	0	—	0	0	1	0	0.1
Total 8	43	51	.457	185	97	22	6	17	809^1	806	61	348	520	13.0	3.94	95	.261	.339	20	.215	3	-28	-19	-4	-1.4

■ CONNIE JOHNSON
Johnson, Clifford b: 12/27/22, Stone Mountain, Ga BR/TR, 6'4", 200 lbs. Deb: 4/17/53

YEAR TM/L	W	L	PCT	G	GS	CG	SH	SV	IP	H	HR	BB	SO	RAT	ERA	ERA+	OAV	OOB	BH	AVG	PB	PR	/A	PD	TPI
1953 Chi-A	4	4	.500	14	10	2	1	0	60^2	55	4	38	44	14.1	3.56	113	.238	.351	1	.050	-2	3	3	-1	0.0
1955 Chi-A	7	4	.636	17	16	5	2	0	99	95	5	52	72	13.5	3.45	114	.251	.343	5	.152	-1	6	5	-2	0.3
1956 Chi-A	0	1	.000	5	2	0	0	0	12^1	11	1	7	6	13.1	3.65	112	.234	.333	0	.000	-0	1	1	0	0.0
Bal-A	9	10	.474	26	25	9	2	0	183^2	165	12	62	130	11.2	3.43	114	.239	.303	15	.259	3	15	10	-3	1.0
Yr	9	11	.450	31	27	9	2	0	196	176	13	69	136	11.3	3.44	114	.239	.305	6	.200	3	16	11	-3	1.0
1957 Bal-A	14	11	.560	35	30	14	3	0	242	212	17	66	177	10.5	3.20	112	.235	.289	12	.135	-4	16	11	-4	0.2
1958 Bal-A	6	9	.400	26	17	4	0	1	118^1	116	13	32	68	11.3	3.88	93	.260	.310	7	.206	1	-1	-4	-2	-0.4
Total 5	40	39	.506	123	100	34	8	1	716	654	52	257	497	11.5	3.44	109	.243	.310	40	.169	-3	38	26	-11	1.1

■ DAVE JOHNSON
Johnson, David Charles b: 10/4/48, Abilene, Tex. BR/TR, 6'1", 183 lbs. Deb: 7/02/74

YEAR TM/L	W	L	PCT	G	GS	CG	SH	SV	IP	H	HR	BB	SO	RAT	ERA	ERA+	OAV	OOB	BH	AVG	PB	PR	/A	PD	TPI
1974 Bal-A	2	2	.500	11	0	0	0	2	15^1	17	1	5	6	12.9	2.93	118	.274	.328	0	—	0	1	1	-0	0.1
1975 Bal-A	0	1	.000	6	0	0	0	0	8^2	8	0	7	4	15.6	4.15	84	.250	.385	0	—	0	-0	-1	0	0.0
1977 Min-A	2	5	.286	30	6	0	0	0	72^2	86	7	23	33	14.1	4.58	87	.299	.361	0	—	0	-4	-5	0	-0.4
1978 Min-A	0	2	.000	6	1	0	0	0	12	15	1	9	7	18.0	7.50	51	.313	.421	0	—	0	-5	-5	0	-0.4
Total 4	4	10	.286	53	7	0	0	2	108^2	126	9	44	50	14.5	4.64	83	.293	.365	0	—	0	-8	-10	0	-0.7

■ DAVE JOHNSON
Johnson, David Wayne b: 10/24/59, Baltimore, Md. BR/TR, 5'10", 180 lbs. Deb: 5/29/87

YEAR TM/L	W	L	PCT	G	GS	CG	SH	SV	IP	H	HR	BB	SO	RAT	ERA	ERA+	OAV	OOB	BH	AVG	PB	PR	/A	PD	TPI
1987 Pit-N	0	0	—	5	0	0	0	0	6^1	13	1	2	4	21.3	9.95	41	.448	.484	0	—	0	-4	-4	0	-0.3
1989 Bal-A	4	7	.364	14	14	4	0	0	89^1	90	11	28	26	12.3	4.23	90	.265	.328	0	—	0	-3	-4	-2	-0.5
1990 Bal-A	13	9	.591	30	29	3	0	0	180	196	30	43	68	12.1	4.10	93	.280	.324	0	—	0	-4	-6	-3	-0.7
Total 3	17	16	.515	49	43	7	0	0	275^2	299	42	73	98	12.4	4.28	89	.280	.330	0	—	0	-11	-14	-4	-1.5

■ DON JOHNSON
Johnson, Donald Roy b: 11/12/26, Portland, Ore. BR/TR, 6'3", 200 lbs. Deb: 4/20/47

YEAR TM/L	W	L	PCT	G	GS	CG	SH	SV	IP	H	HR	BB	SO	RAT	ERA	ERA+	OAV	OOB	BH	AVG	PB	PR	/A	PD	TPI
1947 NY-A	4	3	.571	15	8	2	0	0	54^1	57	2	23	16	13.4	3.64	97	.270	.345	0	.000	-1	0	-1	-0	-0.2
1950 NY-A	1	0	1.000	8	0	0	0	0	18	35	2	12	9	23.5	10.00	43	.398	.470	0	.000	-0	-11	-11	-0	-1.0
StL-A	5	6	.455	25	12	4	1	1	96	126	14	55	31	17.1	6.09	81	.325	.410	2	.069	-3	-16	-12	-1	-1.3
Yr	6	6	.500	33	12	4	1	1	114	161	16	67	40	18.1	6.71	72	.338	.421	1	.031	-4	-27	-24	-1	-2.3
1951 StL-A	0	1	.000	6	3	0	0	0	15	27	4	18	8	27.6	12.60	35	.391	.523	1	.333	0	-14	-14	0	-1.1
Was-A	7	11	.389	21	20	8	1	0	143^2	138	9	58	52	12.4	3.95	104	.255	.329	4	.085	-5	3	2	-0	-0.2
Yr	7	12	.368	27	23	8	1	0	158^2	165	13	76	60	13.8	4.76	87	.270	.352	5	.101	-5	-11	-11	-0	-1.3
1952 Was-A	0	5	.000	29	6	0	0	2	69	80	4	33	37	15.3	4.43	80	.287	.370	1	.077	-1	-6	-7	-0	-0.8
1954 Chi-A	8	7	.533	46	16	3	3	7	144	129	14	43	68	10.8	3.13	119	.243	.300	1	.029	-3	10	10	0	0.7
1955 Bal-A	2	4	.333	31	5	0	0	1	68	89	4	35	27	16.4	5.82	65	.333	.411	0	.000	-1	-14	-15	-1	-1.5
1958 SF-N	0	1	.000	17	0	0	0	1	23	31	2	8	14	16.0	6.26	61	.323	.387	0	.000	-0	-6	-6	-0	-0.6
Total 7	27	38	.415	198	70	17	5	12	631	712	55	285	262	14.4	4.78	84	.288	.364	9	.058	-16	-54	-55	-1	-6.0

■ EARL JOHNSON
Johnson, Earl Douglas "Lefty" b: 4/2/19, Redmond, Was. BL/TL, 6'3", 190 lbs. Deb: 7/20/40

YEAR TM/L	W	L	PCT	G	GS	CG	SH	SV	IP	H	HR	BB	SO	RAT	ERA	ERA+	OAV	OOB	BH	AVG	PB	PR	/A	PD	TPI
1940 Bos-A	6	2	.750	17	10	2	0	0	70^1	69	0	39	26	14.1	4.09	110	.260	.359	2	.074	-3	2	3	1	0.2
1941 Bos-A	4	5	.444	17	12	4	0	0	93^2	90	4	51	46	13.8	4.52	92	.247	.344	10	.294	2	-4	-4	2	0.1
1946 *Bos-A	5	4	.556	29	5	0	0	3	80	78	5	39	40	13.4	3.71	99	.250	.337	5	.227	2	-2	-0	-0	0.1
1947 Bos-A	12	11	.522	45	17	6	3	8	142^1	129	7	62	65	12.2	2.97	131	.246	.328	12	.273	1	12	14	2	1.9
1948 Bos-A	10	4	.714	35	3	1	0	5	91^1	98	7	42	45	13.8	4.53	97	.276	.353	3	.097	-3	-2	-1	2	-0.1
1949 Bos-A	3	6	.333	19	3	0	0	0	49^1	65	1	29	20	17.9	7.48	58	.327	.422	0	.000	-1	-18	-17	-1	-1.7
1950 Bos-A	0	0	—	11	0	0	0	0	13^2	18	0	8	6	17.8	7.24	68	.333	.429	0	.000	-0	-4	-4	-1	-0.2
1951 Det-A	0	0	—	6	0	0	0	1	5^2	9	0	2	2	17.5	6.35	66	.375	.423	0	—	0	-1	-1	0	0.0
Total 8	40	32	.556	179	50	13	3	17	546^1	556	24	272	250	13.9	4.30	96	.265	.353	32	.187	-2	-18	-10	7	0.3

■ WALT JOHNSON
Johnson, Ellis Walter b: 12/8/1892, Minneapolis, Minn. d: 1/4/65, Minneapolis, Minn. BR/TR, 6'0.5", 180 lbs. Deb: 7/06/12

YEAR TM/L	W	L	PCT	G	GS	CG	SH	SV	IP	H	HR	BB	SO	RAT	ERA	ERA+	OAV	OOB	BH	AVG	PB	PR	/A	PD	TPI
1912 Chi-A	0	0	—	3	0	0	0	0	11^2	11	0	7	7	14.7	3.86	83	.262	.308	0	.000	-0	-1	-1	-0	0.0
1915 Chi-A	0	0	—	1	0	0	0	0	2	3	0	0	3	13.5	9.00	33	.333	.333	0	—	0	-1	-1	0	0.0
1917 Phi-A	0	2	.000	4	2	0	0	0	13^2	15	0	5	8	13.2	7.24	38	.294	.357	0	.000	0	-7	-7	0	-0.5
Total 3	0	2	.000	8	2	0	0	0	27^1	29	0	12	18	13.8	5.93	50	.284	.365	0	.000	0	-9	-9	0	-0.5

■ ERNIE JOHNSON
Johnson, Ernest Thorwald b: 6/16/24, Brattleboro, Vt. BR/TR, 6'3.5", 190 lbs. Deb: 4/28/50

YEAR TM/L	W	L	PCT	G	GS	CG	SH	SV	IP	H	HR	BB	SO	RAT	ERA	ERA+	OAV	OOB	BH	AVG	PB	PR	/A	PD	TPI
1950 Bos-N	2	0	1.000	16	1	0	0	0	20^2	37	1	13	15	21.8	6.97	55	.394	.467	1	.500	0	-6	-7	1	-0.4
1952 Bos-N	6	3	.667	29	10	2	1	1	92	100	7	31	45	13.0	4.11	88	.270	.329	2	.091	-0	-4	-5	1	-0.3
1953 Mil-N	4	3	.571	36	1	0	0	0	81	79	4	22	36	11.6	2.67	147	.263	.320	1	.071	-1	15	11	0	1.0
1954 Mil-N	5	2	.714	40	4	1	0	0	99^1	77	11	34	68	10.1	2.81	133	.219	.290	3	.231	0	14	10	1	1.1
1955 Mil-N	5	7	.417	40	2	0	0	4	92	81	5	55	43	13.5	3.42	110	.240	.349	2	.100	-1	6	3	-0	0.2
1956 Mil-N	4	3	.571	36	0	0	0	6	51	54	9	21	26	13.4	3.71	93	.270	.342	1	.250	0	-1	-0	0	0.0
1957 *Mil-N	7	3	.700	30	0	0	0	4	65	67	9	26	44	13.0	3.88	90	.265	.336	6	.353	3	0	-3	1	0.1
1958 Mil-N	3	1	.750	15	0	0	0	1	23^1	35	4	10	13	17.7	8.10	43	.357	.422	0	—	0	-11	-12	0	-1.0
1959 Bal-A	4	1	.800	31	1	0	0	1	50^1	57	6	19	29	14.1	4.11	92	.286	.357	2	.333	0	-1	-2	0	0.0
Total 9	40	23	.635	273	19	3	1	19	574^2	587	56	231	319	13.0	3.77	98	.266	.340	18	.180	2	13	-5	4	0.7

■ FRED JOHNSON
Johnson, Frederick Edward "Deacon" or "Cactus" b: 3/10/1894, Tolar, Tex. d: 6/14/73, Kerrville, Tex. BR/TR, 6', 185 lbs. Deb: 9/27/22

YEAR TM/L	W	L	PCT	G	GS	CG	SH	SV	IP	H	HR	BB	SO	RAT	ERA	ERA+	OAV	OOB	BH	AVG	PB	PR	/A	PD	TPI
1922 NY-N	0	2	.000	2	2	1	0	0	18	20	3	1	8	10.5	4.00	100	.294	.304	0	.000	-1	0	0	-0	0.0
1923 NY-N	2	0	1.000	3	2	1	0	0	17	11	2	7	5	9.5	4.24	90	.177	.261	0	.000	-1	-0	-1	1	0.0
1938 StL-A	3	7	.300	17	6	3	0	3	69	91	7	27	24	15.5	5.61	89	.316	.377	6	.240	-0	-6	-5	-1	-0.5
1939 StL-A	0	1	.000	5	2	1	0	0	14	23	0	9	2	20.6	6.43	76	.383	.464	0	.000	-1	-3	-2	1	-0.1
Total 4	5	10	.333	27	12	6	0	3	118	145	12	44	39	14.5	5.26	88	.303	.363	6	.154	-2	-9	-8	0	-0.6

■ CHIEF JOHNSON
Johnson, George Howard "Murphy" or "Big Murph" b: 3/30/1886, Winnebago, Neb. d: 6/11/22, Des Moines, Iowa BR/TR, 5'11.5", 190 lbs. Deb: 4/16/13

YEAR TM/L	W	L	PCT	G	GS	CG	SH	SV	IP	H	HR	BB	SO	RAT	ERA	ERA+	OAV	OOB	BH	AVG	PB	PR	/A	PD	TPI
1913 Cin-N	14	16	.467	44	31	13	3	0	269	251	8	86	107	11.5	3.01	108	.256	.320	10	.114	-3	6	7	0	0.5

YEAR	TM/L	W	L	PCT	G	GS	CG	SH	SV	IP	H	HR	BB	SO	RAT	ERA	ERA+	OAV	OOB	BH	AVG	PB	PR	/A	PD	TPI
1914	Cin-N	0	0	—	1	1	0	0	0	4	6	0	2	1	18.0	6.75	43	.333	.400	0	—	0	-2	-2	-0	-0.1
	KC-F	9	10	.474	20	19	12	2	0	134	157	2	33	78	13.0	3.16	98	.298	.345	6	.122	-1	1	-1	-3	-0.5
1915	KC-F	17	17	.500	46	34	19	4	2	281¹	253	5	71	118	10.6	2.75	106	.242	.295	11	.126	-2	9	5	1	0.5
Total	3	40	43	.482	111	85	44	9	2	688¹	667	15	192	304	11.5	2.95	104	.259	.315	27	.121	-6	14	10	-2	0.4

■ **HANK JOHNSON**   Johnson, Henry Ward b: 5/21/06, Bradenton, Fla. d: 8/20/82, Bradenton, Fla. BR/TL, 5'11.5", 175 lbs. Deb: 4/17/25

YEAR	TM/L	W	L	PCT	G	GS	CG	SH	SV	IP	H	HR	BB	SO	RAT	ERA	ERA+	OAV	OOB	BH	AVG	PB	PR	/A	PD	TPI
1925	NY-A	1	3	.250	24	4	2	1	0	67	88	3	37	25	17.9	6.85	62	.319	.414	1	.059	-1	-18	-19	1	-1.7
1926	NY-A	0	0	—	1	0	0	0	1	1	2	0	2	0	36.0	18.00	21	.400	.571	0	—	0	-2	-2	0	-0.0
1928	NY-A	14	9	.609	31	22	10	1	0	199	188	16	104	110	13.7	4.30	88	.250	.351	19	.241	1	-6	-12	-0	-1.0
1929	NY-A	3	3	.500	12	8	2	0	0	42²	37	5	39	24	16.0	5.06	76	.237	.390	1	.071	-1	-4	-6	-1	-0.6
1930	NY-A	14	11	.560	44	15	7	1	2	175¹	177	12	104	115	14.5	4.67	92	.265	.366	17	.266	5	-0	-7	1	-0.1
1931	NY-A	13	8	.619	40	23	8	0	4	196¹	176	13	102	106	12.8	4.72	84	.234	.326	15	.195	2	-7	-16	-3	-1.6
1932	NY-A	2	2	.500	5	4	2	0	0	31¹	34	7	15	27	14.1	4.88	83	.266	.343	3	.231	-0	-1	-3	-0	-0.2
1933	Bos-A	8	6	.571	25	21	7	0	1	155¹	156	13	74	65	13.5	4.06	108	.263	.347	12	.231	3	4	-6	-2	0.7
1934	Bos-A	6	8	.429	31	14	7	1	1	124¹	162	12	53	66	15.9	5.36	90	.316	.385	10	.233	1	-12	-8	-0	-0.6
1935	Bos-A	2	1	.667	13	2	0	0	1	31	41	3	14	14	16.0	5.52	86	.331	.399	0	.000	-1	-4	-3	-1	-0.4
1936	Phi-A	0	0	—	3	3	0	0	0	11²	16	4	10	6	20.8	7.71	66	.296	.415	1	.250	-0	-3	-3	-0	-0.2
1939	Cin-N	0	3	.000	20	0	0	0	1	31¹	30	1	13	10	12.4	2.01	191	.268	.344	2	.400	1	7	6	-1	0.6
Total	12	63	56	.529	249	116	45	4	11	1066¹	1107	89	567	568	14.4	4.75	88	.268	.361	81	.215	9	-47	-67	-8	-5.1

■ **JIM JOHNSON**   Johnson, James Brian b: 11/3/45, Muskegon, Mich. BL/TL, 5'11", 175 lbs. Deb: 4/13/70

YEAR	TM/L	W	L	PCT	G	GS	CG	SH	SV	IP	H	HR	BB	SO	RAT	ERA	ERA+	OAV	OOB	BH	AVG	PB	PR	/A	PD	TPI
1970	SF-N	1	0	1.000	3	0	0	0	0	6²	8	0	5	2	17.6	8.10	49	.320	.433	0	.000	0	-3	-3	0	-0.2

■ **JERRY JOHNSON**   Johnson, Jerry Michael b: 12/3/43, Miami, Fla. BR/TR, 6'3", 200 lbs. Deb: 7/17/68

YEAR	TM/L	W	L	PCT	G	GS	CG	SH	SV	IP	H	HR	BB	SO	RAT	ERA	ERA+	OAV	OOB	BH	AVG	PB	PR	/A	PD	TPI
1968	Phi-N	4	4	.500	16	11	2	0	0	80²	82	5	29	40	12.6	3.24	93	.264	.330	2	.080	-0	-2	-2	1	-0.1
1969	Phi-N	6	13	.316	33	21	4	2	1	147¹	151	18	57	82	12.9	4.28	83	.268	.338	9	.209	2	-11	-12	-0	-1.0
1970	StL-N	2	0	1.000	7	0	0	0	1	11¹	6	1	3	5	7.1	3.18	130	.146	.205	0	.000	0	1	1	-0	0.1
	SF-N	3	4	.429	33	1	0	0	3	65¹	67	5	38	44	14.6	4.27	93	.266	.364	1	.067	-1	-2	-2	-0	-0.3
	Yr	5	4	.556	40	1	0	0	4	76²	73	6	41	49	13.5	4.11	97	.249	.343	1	.063	-1	-1	-1	-1	-0.2
1971	*SF-N	12	9	.571	67	0	0	0	18	109	93	9	48	85	11.7	2.97	114	.230	.313	2	.154	-0	6	5	-0	0.5
1972	SF-N	8	6	.571	48	0	0	0	8	73¹	73	4	40	57	13.9	4.42	79	.261	.353	0	.000	-1	-8	-8	0	-0.8
1973	Cle-A	5	6	.455	39	1	0	0	5	59²	70	7	39	45	16.4	6.18	63	.299	.399	0	—	0	-16	-15	0	-1.4
1974	Hou-N	2	1	.667	34	0	0	0	0	45	47	2	24	32	14.2	4.80	72	.276	.366	0	.000	-0	-6	-7	-0	-0.6
1975	SD-N	3	1	.750	21	0	0	0	0	54	60	3	31	18	15.2	5.17	67	.282	.373	1	.083	-0	-9	-10	-0	-1.0
1976	SD-N	1	3	.250	24	1	0	0	0	39	39	0	26	27	15.0	5.31	62	.260	.369	0	.000	-0	-8	-9	-0	-0.8
1977	Tor-A	2	4	.333	43	0	0	0	5	86	91	9	54	54	15.2	4.60	91	.279	.382	0	—	0	-5	-4	-0	-0.3
Total	10	48	51	.485	365	39	6	2	41	770²	779	63	389	489	13.7	4.31	83	.265	.352	15	.123	-2	-60	-62	-1	-5.8

■ **JOHNNY JOHNSON**   Johnson, John Clifford "Swede" b: 9/29/14, Belmore, Ohio BL/TL, 6', 182 lbs. Deb: 4/19/44

YEAR	TM/L	W	L	PCT	G	GS	CG	SH	SV	IP	H	HR	BB	SO	RAT	ERA	ERA+	OAV	OOB	BH	AVG	PB	PR	/A	PD	TPI
1944	NY-A	0	2	.000	22	1	0	0	3	26²	25	0	24	11	16.9	4.05	86	.243	.391	3	.500	1	-2	-2	-1	-0.0
1945	Chi-A	3	0	1.000	29	0	0	0	4	69²	85	2	35	38	15.6	4.26	78	.306	.385	4	.286	2	-7	-7	-1	-0.6
Total	2	3	2	.600	51	1	0	0	7	96¹	110	2	59	49	16.0	4.20	80	.289	.387	7	.350	3	-9	-9	-2	-0.6

■ **YOUNGY JOHNSON**   Johnson, John Godfred b: 7/22/1877, San Francisco, Cal. D/Aug.28, 1936 Berkeley, Cal. TR , Deb: 4/29/1897

YEAR	TM/L	W	L	PCT	G	GS	CG	SH	SV	IP	H	HR	BB	SO	RAT	ERA	ERA+	OAV	OOB	BH	AVG	PB	PR	/A	PD	TPI
1897	Phi-N	1	2	.333	5	2	1	0	0	29	39	0	12	7	15.8	4.66	90	.319	.380	1	.077	-2	-1	-1	-0	-0.2
1899	NY-N	0	0	—	1	0	0	0	0	2	0	0	2	1	9.0	0.00	—	.000	.260	0	.000	-0	1	1	0	0.1
Total	2	1	2	.333	6	2	1	0	0	31	39	0	14	8	15.4	4.35	96	.305	.373	1	.071	-2	-0	-1	-0	-0.1

■ **JOHN HENRY JOHNSON**   Johnson, John Henry b: 8/21/56, Houston, Tex. BL/TL, 6'2", 190 lbs. Deb: 4/10/78

YEAR	TM/L	W	L	PCT	G	GS	CG	SH	SV	IP	H	HR	BB	SO	RAT	ERA	ERA+	OAV	OOB	BH	AVG	PB	PR	/A	PD	TPI
1978	Oak-A	11	10	.524	33	30	7	2	0	186	164	18	82	91	11.9	3.39	107	.238	.319	0	—	0	8	5	-2	0.3
1979	Oak-A	2	8	.200	14	13	1	0	0	84²	89	13	36	50	13.4	4.36	93	.269	.342	0	—	0	-1	-3	-1	-0.3
	Tex-A	2	6	.250	17	12	1	0	0	82¹	79	12	36	46	12.7	4.92	84	.255	.334	0	—	0	-6	-7	-0	-0.6
	Yr	4	14	.222	31	25	2	0	0	167	168	25	72	96	13.0	4.63	88	.261	.336	0	—	0	-8	-10	-1	-0.9
1980	Tex-A	2	2	.500	33	0	0	0	4	38²	27	2	15	44	10.0	2.33	167	.199	.283	0	—	0	7	7	-0	0.6
1981	Tex-A	3	1	.750	24	0	0	0	2	23²	19	2	6	8	9.9	2.66	130	.232	.292	0	—	0	3	2	1	0.3
1983	Bos-A	3	2	.600	34	1	0	0	1	53¹	58	3	20	51	13.3	3.71	117	.283	.350	0	—	0	2	4	-1	0.3
1984	Bos-A	1	2	.333	30	3	0	0	1	63²	64	7	27	57	12.9	3.53	118	.260	.333	0	—	0	3	4	-0	0.4
1986	Mil-A	2	1	.667	19	0	0	0	1	44	43	2	10	42	10.8	2.66	163	.251	.293	0	—	0	7	7	-0	0.5
1987	Mil-A	0	1	.000	10	2	0	0	0	20	25	2	11	18	20.5	9.57	48	.365	.451	0	—	0	-15	-15	-0	-1.2
Total	8	26	33	.441	214	61	9	2	9	602²	585	60	250	407	12.5	3.90	102	.256	.331	0	—	0	8	6	-5	0.5

■ **JOHN JOHNSON**   Johnson, John Louis (b: John Louis Mercer) b: 11/18/1869, Pekin, Ill. d: 1/28/41, Kansas City, Mo. TL , 165 lbs. Deb: 9/11/1894

YEAR	TM/L	W	L	PCT	G	GS	CG	SH	SV	IP	H	HR	BB	SO	RAT	ERA	ERA+	OAV	OOB	BH	AVG	PB	PR	/A	PD	TPI
1894	Phi-N	1	1	.500	4	3	2	0	0	32²	44	3	15	10	16.3	6.06	84	.319	.385	3	.188	-1	-3	-3	0	-0.2

■ **JOE JOHNSON**   Johnson, Joseph Richard b: 10/30/61, Brookline, Mass. BR/TR, 6'2", 195 lbs. Deb: 7/25/85

YEAR	TM/L	W	L	PCT	G	GS	CG	SH	SV	IP	H	HR	BB	SO	RAT	ERA	ERA+	OAV	OOB	BH	AVG	PB	PR	/A	PD	TPI
1985	Atl-N	4	4	.500	15	14	1	0	0	85²	95	9	24	34	12.8	4.10	94	.285	.339	1	.043	-1	-5	-2	-1	-0.4
1986	Atl-N	6	7	.462	17	15	2	0	0	87	101	8	35	49	14.3	4.97	80	.289	.358	3	.115	-1	-12	-10	2	-0.8
	Tor-A	7	2	.778	16	15	0	0	0	88	94	3	22	39	12.2	3.89	109	.281	.331	0	—	0	3	3	-1	0.2
1987	Tor-A	3	5	.375	14	14	0	0	0	66²	77	10	18	27	13.1	5.13	88	.289	.342	0	—	0	-5	-5	-0	-0.3
Total	3	20	18	.526	62	58	3	0	0	327¹	367	30	99	149	13.1	4.48	92	.286	.342	4	.082	-2	-19	-13	-0	-1.3

■ **KEN JOHNSON**   Johnson, Kenneth Travis b: 6/16/33, W.Palm Beach, Fla. BR/TR, 6'4", 210 lbs. Deb: 9/13/58

YEAR	TM/L	W	L	PCT	G	GS	CG	SH	SV	IP	H	HR	BB	SO	RAT	ERA	ERA+	OAV	OOB	BH	AVG	PB	PR	/A	PD	TPI
1958	KC-A	0	0	—	2	0	0	0	0	2¹	6	1	3	1	34.7	27.00	14	.429	.529	0	—	0	-6	-6	0	-0.4
1959	KC-A	1	1	.500	2	2	0	0	0	11	11	2	5	8	13.1	4.09	98	.268	.348	0	.000	-0	-0	-0	0	0.0
1960	KC-A	5	10	.333	42	6	2	0	3	120¹	120	16	45	83	12.9	4.26	93	.263	.338	5	.167	-1	-5	-4	1	-0.2
1961	KC-A	0	4	.000	6	1	0	0	0	9¹	11	2	7	4	17.4	10.61	39	.297	.409	0	.000	-0	-7	-7	1	-0.5
	*Cin-N	6	2	.750	15	11	3	1	1	83	71	11	22	42	10.3	3.25	125	.229	.284	6	.240	1	7	7	1	1.0
1962	Hou-N	7	16	.304	33	31	5	1	0	197	195	18	46	109	11.3	3.84	97	.257	.305	4	.077	-3	2	-2	1	-0.4
1963	Hou-N	11	17	.393	37	32	6	1	1	224	204	12	50	148	10.5	2.65	119	.242	.291	5	.068	-4	16	12	2	1.2
1964	Hou-N	11	16	.407	35	35	7	1	0	218	209	15	44	117	10.7	3.63	94	.250	.293	6	.079	-2	-2	-5	2	-0.5
1965	Hou-N	3	2	.600	8	8	1	0	0	51²	52	4	11	28	11.7	4.18	80	.267	.319	2	.111	-0	-4	-5	1	-0.3
	Mil-N	13	8	.619	29	26	8	1	2	179²	165	15	37	123	10.3	3.21	110	.240	.282	7	—	-2	7	6	-3	0.1
	Yr	16	10	.615	37	34	9	1	2	231¹	217	19	48	151	10.4	3.42	102	.244	.285	0	.000	-2	3	2	-2	-0.2
1966	Atl-N	14	8	.636	32	31	11	2	0	215²	213	24	46	105	10.8	3.30	110	.262	.301	10	.143	0	7	8	0	0.9
1967	Atl-N	13	9	.591	29	29	6	0	0	210¹	191	19	38	85	10.1	2.74	121	.244	.285	9	.127	-0	15	14	1	1.4
1968	Atl-N	5	8	.385	31	16	0	0	0	135	145	10	25	57	11.9	3.47	86	.279	.324	7	.175	-0	-7	-7	-1	-0.8
1969	Atl-N	0	1	.000	9	2	0	0	1	29	32	4	9	20	12.7	4.97	73	.283	.336	0	.000	-0	-4	-4	0	-0.4
	NY-A	1	2	.333	12	0	0	0	0	26	19	1	11	21	10.4	3.46	100	.202	.286	0	.000	-0	0	0	1	0.1
	Chi-N	1	2	.333	9	1	0	0	1	19	17	2	13	18	14.2	2.84	142	.230	.345	0	.000	-0	2	2	-0	0.2
1970	Mon-N	0	0	—	3	0	0	0	0	6	9	1	1	4	18.0	7.50	55	.321	.387	0	—	0	-2	-2	0	-0.1
Total	13	91	106	.462	334	231	50	7	9	1737¹	1670	157	413	1042	11.1	3.46	101	.253	.302	61	.114	-12	18	8	6	1.3

■ **KEN JOHNSON**   Johnson, Kenneth Wandersee "Hook" b: 1/14/23, Topeka, Kan. BL/TL, 6'1", 185 lbs. Deb: 9/18/47

YEAR	TM/L	W	L	PCT	G	GS	CG	SH	SV	IP	H	HR	BB	SO	RAT	ERA	ERA+	OAV	OOB	BH	AVG	PB	PR	/A	PD	TPI
1947	StL-N	1	0	1.000	2	1	1	0	0	10	2	0	5	8	7.2	0.00	—	.063	.211	2	.500	1	5	5	0	0.6
1948	StL-N	2	4	.333	13	4	0	0	0	45¹	43	1	30	20	14.7	4.76	86	.262	.379	6	.300	2	-4	-3	-0	-0.1

YEAR	TM/L	W	L	PCT	G	GS	CG	SH	SV	IP	H	HR	BB	SO	RAT	ERA	ERA+	OAV	OOB	BH	AVG	PB	PR	/A	PD	TPI
1949	StL-N	0	1	.000	14	2	0	0	0	33^2	29	1	35	18	17.9	6.42	65	.250	.435	2	.250	0	-9	-8	1	-0.6
1950	StL-N	0	0	—	2	0	0	0	0	2	1	0	3	1	18.0	0.00	—	.167	.444	0	—	0	1	1	0	0.0
	*Phi-N	4	1	.800	14	8	3	1	0	60^2	61	3	43	32	15.6	4.01	101	.260	.376	3	.158	-0	1	0	0	0.0
	Yr	4	1	.800	16	8	3	1	0	62^2	62	3	46	33	15.7	3.88	105	.257	.378	1	.053	-0	2	1	0	0.1
1951	Phi-N	5	8	.385	20	18	4	3	0	106^1	103	8	68	58	14.7	4.57	84	.259	.371	5	.143	-1	-7	-9	-1	-0.9
1952	Det-A	0	0	—	9	1	0	0	0	11^1	12	1	11	10	18.3	6.35	60	.273	.418	1	.333	0	-3	-3	0	-0.2
Total 6		12	14	.462	74	34	8	4	0	269^1	251	14	195	147	15.2	4.58	87	.252	.379	19	.213	1	-17	-18	1	-1.1

■ **LLOYD JOHNSON**
Johnson, Lloyd William "Eppa" b: 12/24/10, Santa Rosa, Cal. d: 10/8/80, Stockton, Cal. BL/TL, 6'4", 204 lbs. Deb: 4/21/34

YEAR	TM/L	W	L	PCT	G	GS	CG	SH	SV	IP	H	HR	BB	SO	RAT	ERA	ERA+	OAV	OOB	BH	AVG	PB	PR	/A	PD	TPI
1934	Pit-N	0	0	—	1	0	0	0	0	1	1	0	0	0	9.0	0.00	—	.333	.333	0	—	0	0	0	0	0.0

■ **MIKE JOHNSON**
Johnson, Michael Norton b: 3/2/51, Slayton, Minn. BR/TR, 6'1", 185 lbs. Deb: 7/25/74

YEAR	TM/L	W	L	PCT	G	GS	CG	SH	SV	IP	H	HR	BB	SO	RAT	ERA	ERA+	OAV	OOB	BH	AVG	PB	PR	/A	PD	TPI
1974	SD-N	0	2	.000	18	0	0	0	0	21^1	29	1	15	15	19.0	4.64	77	.326	.429	0	—	0	-2	-3	-0	-0.2

■ **RANDY JOHNSON**
Johnson, Randall David b: 9/10/63, Walnut Creek, Cal. BR/TL, 6'10", 225 lbs. Deb: 9/15/88

YEAR	TM/L	W	L	PCT	G	GS	CG	SH	SV	IP	H	HR	BB	SO	RAT	ERA	ERA+	OAV	OOB	BH	AVG	PB	PR	/A	PD	TPI
1988	Mon-N	3	0	1.000	4	4	1	0	0	26	23	3	7	25	10.4	2.42	148	.225	.275	1	.111	-0	3	3	-1	0.2
1989	Mon-N	0	4	.000	7	6	0	0	0	29^2	29	2	26	26	16.7	6.67	53	.264	.404	1	.143	-0	-10	-10	0	-0.9
	Sea-A	7	9	.438	22	22	2	0	0	131	118	11	70	104	13.1	4.40	92	.244	.344	0	—	0	-7	-5	0	-0.4
1990	Sea-A	14	11	.560	33	33	5	2	0	219^2	174	26	120	194	12.3	3.65	109	.216	.321	0	—	0	6	8	-2	0.6
Total 3		24	24	.500	66	65	8	2	0	406^1	344	42	223	349	12.7	4.03	97	.229	.332	2	.125	-1	-9	-5	-3	-0.5

■ **BOB JOHNSON**
Johnson, Robert Dale b: 4/25/43, Aurora, Ill. BL/TR, 6'4", 220 lbs. Deb: 9/19/69

YEAR	TM/L	W	L	PCT	G	GS	CG	SH	SV	IP	H	HR	BB	SO	RAT	ERA	ERA+	OAV	OOB	BH	AVG	PB	PR	/A	PD	TPI
1969	NY-N	0	0	—	2	0	0	0	1	1^2	1	0	1	1	10.8	0.00	—	.167	.286	0	—	0	1	1	0	0.1
1970	KC-A	8	13	.381	40	26	10	1	4	214	178	18	82	206	11.4	3.07	122	.228	.310	6	.105	-1	15	16	-2	1.3
1971	*Pit-N	9	10	.474	31	27	7	1	0	174^2	170	19	55	101	12.0	3.45	98	.259	.323	3	.063	-1	0	-1	-1	-0.3
1972	*Pit-N	4	4	.500	31	11	1	0	3	115^2	98	14	46	79	11.5	2.96	112	.231	.312	5	.143	-0	6	5	-2	0.2
1973	Pit-N	4	2	.667	50	2	0	0	4	92	98	12	34	68	13.4	3.62	97	.276	.348	0	.000	-1	0	-1	-2	-0.4
1974	Cle-A	3	4	.429	14	10	0	0	0	72	75	12	37	36	14.4	4.38	83	.273	.365	0	—	0	-6	-6	-0	-0.5
1977	Atl-N	0	1	.000	15	0	0	0	0	22^1	24	7	14	16	16.1	7.25	61	.270	.381	1	.333	0	-8	-7	-1	-0.6
Total 7		28	34	.452	183	76	18	2	12	692^1	644	82	269	507	12.3	3.48	102	.249	.327	15	.096	-3	9	6	-8	-0.2

■ **ROY JOHNSON**
Johnson, Roy J "Hardrock" b: 10/1/1895, Madill, Okla. d: 1/10/86, Scottsdale, Ariz. BR/TR, 6', 185 lbs. Deb: 8/07/18 MC

YEAR	TM/L	W	L	PCT	G	GS	CG	SH	SV	IP	H	HR	BB	SO	RAT	ERA	ERA+	OAV	OOB	BH	AVG	PB	PR	/A	PD	TPI
1918	Phi-A	1	5	.167	10	8	3	0	0	50	47	0	34	12	14.9	3.42	86	.254	.376	1	.067		-4	-3	0	-0.4

■ **JING JOHNSON**
Johnson, Russell Conwell b: 10/9/1894, Parker Ford, Pa. d: 12/6/50, Pottstown, Pa. BR/TR, 5'9", 172 lbs. Deb: 6/27/16

YEAR	TM/L	W	L	PCT	G	GS	CG	SH	SV	IP	H	HR	BB	SO	RAT	ERA	ERA+	OAV	OOB	BH	AVG	PB	PR	/A	PD	TPI
1916	Phi-A	2	8	.200	12	12	8	0	0	84^1	90	3	39	25	13.8	3.74	77	.288	.368	2	.074	-1	-8	-8	3	-0.5
1917	Phi-A	9	12	.429	34	23	13	0	0	191	184	3	56	55	11.5	2.78	99	.260	.319	12	.203	2	-2	-1	2	0.4
1919	Phi-A	9	15	.375	34	25	12	0	0	202	222	8	62	67	12.8	3.61	95	.291	.346	14	.194	0	-9	-4	5	0.1
1927	Phi-A	4	2	.667	17	3	2	0	0	51^2	42	2	16	16	10.8	3.48	122	.235	.312	2	.167	-1	4	4	1	0.5
1928	Phi-A	0	0	—	3	0	0	0	0	10^2	13	1	5	3	15.2	5.06	79	.310	.383	2	.500	1	-1	-1	0	0.0
Total 5		24	37	.393	100	63	35	0	0	539^2	551	17	178	166	12.4	3.35	95	.275	.338	32	.184	2	-17	-9	11	0.5

■ **SI JOHNSON**
Johnson, Silas Kenneth b: 10/5/06, Marseilles, Ill. BR/TR, 5'11.5", 185 lbs. Deb: 5/02/28

YEAR	TM/L	W	L	PCT	G	GS	CG	SH	SV	IP	H	HR	BB	SO	RAT	ERA	ERA+	OAV	OOB	BH	AVG	PB	PR	/A	PD	TPI
1928	Cin-N	0	0	—	3	0	0	0	0	10^1	9	0	5	1	12.2	4.35	91	.250	.341	1	.250	0	-0	-0	0	0.0
1929	Cin-N	0	0	—	1	0	0	0	0	2	2	0	1	0	13.5	4.50	101	.250	.333	0	—	0	0	0	0	0.0
1930	Cin-N	3	1	.750	35	3	0	0	0	78^1	86	5	31	47	13.9	4.94	98	.286	.360	4	.235	-0	0	-1	-1	-0.1
1931	Cin-N	11	19	.367	42	33	14	0	0	262^1	273	5	74	95	12.1	3.77	99	.269	.323	13	.149	-3	3	-1	-5	-0.9
1932	Cin-N	13	15	.464	42	27	14	2	2	245	246	8	57	94	11.2	3.27	118	.259	.302	10	.125	-4	17	16	-1	1.1
1933	Cin-N	7	18	.280	34	28	14	4	1	211^1	212	7	54	51	11.5	3.49	97	.263	.312	3	.042	-7	-4	-2	-1	-0.4
1934	Cin-N	7	22	.241	46	31	9	0	3	215^2	264	15	84	89	14.8	5.22	78	.297	.362	10	.139	-3	-28	-27	-3	-3.0
1935	Cin-N	5	11	.313	30	20	4	1	0	130	155	14	59	40	15.0	6.23	64	.293	.367	1	.024	-4	-32	-33	-1	-3.3
1936	Cin-N	0	0	—	2	0	0	0	0	4	7	1	0	2	15.8	13.50	28	.368	.368	0	—	0	-4	-4	-0	-0.3
	StL-N	5	3	.625	12	9	3	1	0	61^2	82	4	11	21	13.7	4.38	90	.314	.344	4	.190	-2	-3	-3	-1	-0.6
	Yr	5	3	.625	14	9	3	1	0	65^2	89	5	11	23	13.8	4.93	80	.318	.346	0	.000	-0	-7	-7	-1	-0.6
1937	StL-N	12	12	.500	38	21	12	1	1	192^1	222	14	43	64	12.4	3.32	120	.292	.330	9	.138	-3	13	14	-1	1.0
1938	StL-N	3	0	.000	6	3	0	0	0	15^2	27	0	6	4	19.0	7.47	53	.380	.429	0	.000	-0	-6	-6	0	-0.5
1940	Phi-N	5	14	.263	37	14	5	0	1	138^1	145	8	42	58	12.3	4.88	80	.268	.323	6	.140	-2	-16	-15	-2	-1.8
1941	Phi-N	5	12	.294	39	21	6	1	2	163^1	207	8	54	80	14.4	4.52	82	.309	.362	7	.149	-2	-16	-15	-1	-1.7
1942	Phi-N	8	19	.296	39	26	10	1	0	195^1	198	6	72	78	12.5	3.69	90	.266	.332	6	.103	-4	-8	-3	-1	-1.5
1943	Phi-N	8	3	.727	21	14	9	1	0	113	110	4	25	46	10.8	3.27	103	.252	.292	6	.182	0	1	1	-1	0.1
1946	Phi-N	0	0	—	1	0	0	0	0	3	7	1	0	2	21.0	3.00	114	.538	.538	1	1.000	0	0	0	0	0.1
	Bos-N	6	5	.545	28	12	5	1	1	127	134	8	35	41	12.3	2.76	124	.272	.325	5	.135	-2	9	9	-1	0.8
	Yr	6	5	.545	29	12	5	1	1	130	141	9	35	43	12.5	2.77	124	.279	.330	1	.026	-1	9	10	-1	0.9
1947	Bos-N	6	8	.429	36	10	3	0	2	112^2	124	7	34	27	12.7	4.23	92	.275	.327	1	.033	-3	-2	-4	3	-0.3
Total 17		101	165	.380	492	272	108	13	15	2281^1	2510	120	687	840	12.8	4.09	92	.279	.333	87	.123	-37	-76	-79	-17	-11.6

■ **SYL JOHNSON**
Johnson, Sylvester W b: 12/31/1900, Portland, Ore. d: 2/20/85, Portland, Ore. BR/TR, 5'11", 180 lbs. Deb: 4/24/22 C

YEAR	TM/L	W	L	PCT	G	GS	CG	SH	SV	IP	H	HR	BB	SO	RAT	ERA	ERA+	OAV	OOB	BH	AVG	PB	PR	/A	PD	TPI
1922	Det-A	7	3	.700	29	8	3	0	1	97	99	7	30	29	12.3	3.71	105	.273	.336	8	.222	0	4	2	-2	0.0
1923	Det-A	12	7	.632	37	18	7	0	0	176^1	181	12	47	93	11.8	3.98	97	.274	.325	10	.161	-1	0	-2	-6	-0.8
1924	Det-A	5	4	.556	29	9	2	0	3	104	117	8	42	55	14.2	4.93	83	.287	.360	7	.206	-0	-8	-9	-2	-1.0
1925	Det-A	0	2	.000	6	0	0	0	0	13	11	1	10	5	14.5	3.46	124	.250	.389	0	.000	-1	1	1	0	0.1
1926	StL-N	0	3	.000	19	6	1	0	1	49	54	3	15	10	13.0	4.22	92	.297	.357	0	.000	-2	-2	-2	-1	-0.3
1927	StL-N	0	0	—	2	0	0	0	0	3	3	1	0	2	9.0	6.00	66	.250	.250	0	—	0	-1	-1	0	0.0
1928	*StL-N	8	4	.667	34	6	2	0	3	120	117	6	33	66	11.6	3.90	102	.259	.315	6	.158	-0	1	1	-2	0.0
1929	StL-N	13	7	.650	42	19	12	3	3	182^1	186	11	56	80	12.3	3.60	129	.265	.325	7	.117	-2	23	21	-4	1.3
1930	*StL-N	12	10	.545	32	24	9	2	2	187^2	215	13	38	92	12.3	4.65	108	.293	.332	15	.214	-0	7	8	-3	0.4
1931	*StL-N	11	9	.550	32	24	12	2	2	186	186	9	29	82	10.5	3.00	131	.255	.286	14	.233	2	18	19	-3	1.9
1932	StL-N	5	14	.263	32	22	7	0	2	164^2	199	14	35	70	13.0	4.92	80	.299	.338	10	.196	-1	-19	-18	-1	-1.8
1933	StL-N	3	3	.500	35	1	0	0	3	84	89	7	16	28	11.6	4.29	81	.271	.311	5	.238	0	-9	-8	-1	-0.8
1934	Cin-N	0	0	—	2	0	0	0	0	6^2	9	2	0	0	12.2	2.70	151	.310	.310	1	.500	1	1	1	-0	0.2
	Phi-N	5	9	.357	42	10	4	0	3	133^2	122	14	24	54	9.9	3.50	135	.242	.277	8	.195	-1	8	18	-4	1.5
	Yr	5	9	.357	44	10	4	0	3	140^1	131	16	24	54	10.0	3.46	136	.245	.279	3	.070	1	9	19	-4	1.7
1935	Phi-N	10	8	.556	37	18	8	1	6	174^1	182	15	31	89	11.1	3.56	128	.265	.299	14	.241	2	9	19	-4	1.8
1936	Phi-N	5	7	.417	39	8	1	0	7	111	129	10	29	48	13.1	4.30	106	.288	.335	9	.250	-0	-3	3	-2	0.1
1937	Phi-N	4	10	.286	32	15	4	0	3	138	155	20	22	46	11.7	5.02	86	.288	.318	7	.146	-3	-17	-11	-1	-1.2
1938	Phi-N	2	7	.222	26	6	2	0	2	83	87	4	11	21	10.6	4.23	97	.267	.291	1	.034	-3	-4	-3	-2	-0.7
1939	Phi-N	8	8	.500	22	14	6	0	2	111	112	10	15	37	10.4	3.81	105	.264	.291	5	.152	-1	1	2	-1	0.0
1940	Phi-N	2	2	.500	17	2	2	0	2	40^2	37	6	5	13	9.3	4.20	93	.236	.259	0	.000	-1	-2	-1	-0	-0.2
Total 19		112	117	.489	542	210	82	11	43	2165^2	2290	173	488	920	11.7	4.06	104	.273	.316	127	.181	-10	8	43	-36	0.5

■ **TOM JOHNSON**
Johnson, Thomas Raymond b: 4/2/51, St.Paul, Minn. BR/TR, 6'1", 185 lbs. Deb: 9/10/74

YEAR	TM/L	W	L	PCT	G	GS	CG	SH	SV	IP	H	HR	BB	SO	RAT	ERA	ERA+	OAV	OOB	BH	AVG	PB	PR	/A	PD	TPI
1974	Min-A	2	0	1.000	4	0	0	0	1	5	4	0	4	5	10.0	0.00	—	.167	.167	0	—	0	3	3	0	0.3
1975	Min-A	1	2	.333	18	0	0	0	3	38^2	40	4	21	17	14.7	4.19	92	.263	.360	0	—	0	-2	-1	0	0.0
1976	Min-A	3	1	.750	18	1	0	0	0	48^1	44	2	8	37	9.7	2.61	138	.243	.275	0	—	0	5	5	-0	0.6
1977	Min-A	16	7	.696	71	0	0	0	15	146^2	152	11	47	87	12.5	3.13	127	.272	.334	0	—	0	15	14	1	1.4

YEAR TM/L	W	L	PCT	G	GS	CG	SH	SV	IP	H	HR	BB	SO	RAT	ERA	ERA+	OAV	OOB	BH	AVG	PB	PR	/A	PD	TPI
1978 Min-A	1	4	.200	18	0	0	0	3	32²	42	2	17	21	16.8	5.51	69	.318	.404	0	—	0	-6	-6	0	-0.5
Total 5	23	14	.622	129	1	0	0	22	273¹	282	19	93	166	12.6	3.39	114	.269	.334	0	—	0	15	15	1	1.8

■ VIC JOHNSON Johnson, Victor Oscar b: 8/3/20, Eau Claire, Wis. BR/TL, 6′, 160 lbs. Deb: 5/03/44

YEAR TM/L	W	L	PCT	G	GS	CG	SH	SV	IP	H	HR	BB	SO	RAT	ERA	ERA+	OAV	OOB	BH	AVG	PB	PR	/A	PD	TPI
1944 Bos-A	0	3	.000	7	5	0	0	0	27¹	42	0	15	7	18.8	6.26	54	.362	.435	0	.000	-1	-9	-9	1	-0.8
1945 Bos-A	6	4	.600	26	9	4	1	2	85¹	90	4	46	21	14.6	4.01	85	.276	.369	5	.167	-1	-6	-6	1	-0.5
1946 Cle-A	0	1	.000	9	1	0	0	0	13²	20	1	8	3	18.4	9.22	36	.357	.438	0	—	-0	-9	-9	1	-0.8
Total 3	6	8	.429	42	15	4	1	2	126¹	152	5	69	31	15.9	5.06	67	.305	.392	5	.119	-3	-23	-23	3	-2.1

■ WALTER JOHNSON Johnson, Walter Perry "Barney" or "The Big Train" b: 11/6/1887, Humboldt, Kan. d: 12/10/46, Washington, D.C. BR/TR, 6′1″, 200 lbs. Deb: 8/02/07 MH♦

YEAR TM/L	W	L	PCT	G	GS	CG	SH	SV	IP	H	HR	BB	SO	RAT	ERA	ERA+	OAV	OOB	BH	AVG	PB	PR	/A	PD	TPI
1907 Was-A	5	9	.357	14	12	11	2	0	110¹	100	1	20	71	9.8	1.88	129	.244	.279	4	.111	-2	8	7	-3	0.2
1908 Was-A	14	14	.500	36	29	23	6	1	257¹	194	0	53	160	9.0	1.64	139	.211	.262	13	.165	-2	22	18	-5	1.7
1909 Was-A	13	25	.342	40	36	27	4	1	297	247	1	84	164	10.5	2.21	110	.221	.284	13	.129	-2	9	7	-3	0.2
1910 Was-A	25	17	.595	45	42	38	8	1	374	269	1	76	313	8.6	1.35	185	.210	.262	24	.175	1	49	48	-4	5.2
1911 Was-A	25	13	.658	40	37	36	6	1	323¹	292	8	70	207	10.3	1.89	174	.238	.283	30	.234	3	52	50	3	5.9
1912 Was-A	33	12	.733	50	37	34	7	2	368	259	2	76	303	8.6	1.39	239	.196	.248	38	.264	9	79	79	-1	9.8
1913 Was-A	36	7	.837	48	36	29	11	2	346	232	9	38	243	7.3	1.14	258	.187	.217	35	.261	10	69	69	-1	9.5
1914 Was-A	28	18	.609	51	40	33	9	1	371²	287	3	74	225	9.0	1.72	162	.217	.265	30	.221	8	42	44	2	6.4
1915 Was-A	27	13	.675	47	39	35	7	4	336²	258	1	56	203	8.9	1.55	189	.214	.260	34	.231	6	52	52	1	6.8
1916 Was-A	25	20	.556	48	38	36	3	1	371	290	0	82	228	9.2	1.89	146	.220	.270	32	.225	8	39	36	-6	4.3
1917 Was-A	23	16	.590	47	34	30	8	3	328	259	3	67	188	9.3	2.30	114	.220	.270	33	.254	10	13	12	-1	2.2
1918 Was-A	23	13	.639	39	29	29	8	3	325	241	2	70	162	8.8	1.27	214	.210	.260	40	.267	6	54	53	-3	7.4
1919 Was-A	20	14	.588	39	29	27	7	2	290¹	235	0	51	147	9.1	1.49	216	.219	.259	24	.192	2	56	56	-0	6.6
1920 Was-A	8	10	.444	21	15	12	4	3	143²	135	5	27	78	10.5	3.13	119	.245	.286	17	.266	4	11	10	-2	1.1
1921 Was-A	17	14	.548	35	32	25	1	1	264	265	7	92	143	12.2	3.51	117	.263	.326	30	.270	4	23	18	-4	1.6
1922 Was-A	15	16	.484	41	31	23	4	4	280	283	8	99	105	12.5	2.99	129	.267	.334	22	.204	-1	33	27	0	2.6
1923 Was-A	17	12	.586	42	34	18	3	4	261¹	265	9	73	130	12.3	3.48	108	.271	.335	18	.194	1	15	8	-2	0.6
1924 *Was-A	23	7	.767	38	38	20	6	0	277²	233	10	77	158	10.4	2.72	148	.224	.284	32	.283	6	47	41	-2	4.4
1925 *Was-A	20	7	.741	30	29	16	3	0	229	211	7	78	108	11.6	3.07	138	.243	.311	42	.433	16	34	30	-4	4.0
1926 Was-A	15	16	.484	33	33	22	2	0	261²	259	13	73	125	11.6	3.61	107	.263	.317	20	.194	1	12	7	-5	0.2
1927 Was-A	5	6	.455	18	15	7	1	0	107¹	113	7	26	48	12.2	5.10	80	.278	.332	16	.348	6	-11	-12	0	-0.5
Total 21	417	279	.599	802	665	531	110	34	5923²	4927	97	1362	3509	9.9	2.17	146	.227	.280	547	.235	98	705	662	-41	80.2

■ BILL JOHNSON Johnson, William C. b: 10/6/60, Wilmington, Del. BR/TR, 6′5″, 205 lbs. Deb: 9/06/83

YEAR TM/L	W	L	PCT	G	GS	CG	SH	SV	IP	H	HR	BB	SO	RAT	ERA	ERA+	OAV	OOB	BH	AVG	PB	PR	/A	PD	TPI
1983 Chi-N	1	0	1.000	10	0	0	0	0	12¹	17	0	3	4	14.6	4.38	87	.347	.385	0	—	0	-1	-1	1	0.0
1984 Chi-N	0	0	—	4	0	0	0	0	5¹	4	0	1	3	8.4	1.69	232	.235	.278	0	—	0	1	1	0	0.2
Total 2	1	0	1.000	14	0	0	0	0	17²	21	0	4	7	12.7	3.57	107	.318	.357	0	—	0	0	1	1	0.2

■ ROY JOINER Joiner, Roy Merrill "Pop" b: 10/30/06, Red Bluff, Cal. d: 12/26/89, Red Bluff, Cal. BL/TL, 6′, 170 lbs. Deb: 4/30/34

YEAR TM/L	W	L	PCT	G	GS	CG	SH	SV	IP	H	HR	BB	SO	RAT	ERA	ERA+	OAV	OOB	BH	AVG	PB	PR	/A	PD	TPI
1934 Chi-N	0	1	.000	20	2	0	0	0	34	61	3	8	9	18.3	8.21	47	.391	.421	2	.200	-0	-16	-16	0	-1.5
1935 Chi-N	0	0	—	2	0	0	0	0	3¹	6	0	2	0	21.6	5.40	73	.429	.500	0	.000	-0	-1	-1	1	0.0
1940 NY-N	3	2	.600	30	2	0	0	1	53	66	8	17	25	14.9	3.40	114	.308	.373	3	.273	1	3	3	0	0.4
Total 3	3	3	.500	52	4	0	0	1	90¹	133	11	27	34	16.4	5.28	74	.346	.397	5	.227	1	-13	-14	1	-1.1

■ DAVE JOLLY Jolly, David "Gabby" b: 10/14/24, Stony Point, N.C. d: 5/27/63, Durham, N.C. BR/TR, 6′, 160 lbs. Deb: 5/09/53

YEAR TM/L	W	L	PCT	G	GS	CG	SH	SV	IP	H	HR	BB	SO	RAT	ERA	ERA+	OAV	OOB	BH	AVG	PB	PR	/A	PD	TPI
1953 Mil-N	0	1	.000	24	0	0	0	0	38¹	34	4	27	23	14.6	3.52	111	.239	.365	1	.500	1	3	2	0	0.2
1954 Mil-N	11	6	.647	47	1	0	0	10	111¹	87	6	64	62	12.4	2.43	154	.215	.326	9	.290	3	20	16	0	2.0
1955 Mil-N	2	3	.400	36	0	0	0	1	58¹	58	6	51	23	17.0	5.71	66	.258	.397	1	.167	-1	-11	-13	1	-1.0
1956 Mil-N	2	3	.400	29	0	0	0	7	45²	39	7	35	20	14.6	3.74	92	.228	.359	0	.000	-0	-1	-1	-1	-0.2
1957 Mil-N	1	1	.500	23	0	0	0	1	37²	37	4	21	27	14.6	5.02	70	.264	.372	3	.600	1	-5	-6	0	-0.4
Total 5	16	14	.533	159	1	0	0	19	291¹	255	27	198	155	14.2	3.77	98	.236	.357	14	.292	5	8	-3	0	0.6

■ COWBOY JONES Jones, Albert Edward "Bronco" b: 8/23/1874, Golden, Colo. d: 2/9/58, Inglewood, Cal. BL/TL, 5′11″, 160 lbs. Deb: 6/24/1898

YEAR TM/L	W	L	PCT	G	GS	CG	SH	SV	IP	H	HR	BB	SO	RAT	ERA	ERA+	OAV	OOB	BH	AVG	PB	PR	/A	PD	TPI
1898 Cle-N	4	4	.500	9	9	7	0	0	72	76	0	29	26	13.1	3.00	121	.269	.337	2	.071	-3	5	5	-2	0.0
1899 StL-N	6	5	.545	12	12	9	0	0	85¹	111	1	22	28	14.0	3.59	111	.314	.354	5	.172	0	3	4	2	0.5
1900 StL-N	13	19	.406	39	36	29	3	0	292²	334	7	82	68	12.8	3.57	102	.286	.333	21	.179	-3	4	2	5	0.4
1901 StL-N	2	6	.250	10	9	7	0	0	76¹	97	4	22	25	14.4	4.48	71	.307	.358	4	.148	0	-10	-11	2	-0.8
Total 4	25	34	.424	70	66	52	3	0	526¹	618	12	155	147	13.3	3.63	100	.292	.341	32	.159	-5	2	-0	7	0.1

■ ALEX JONES Jones, Alexander b: 12/25/1869, Pittsburgh, Pa. d: 4/4/41, Woodville, Pa. BL/TL, 5′6″, 135 lbs. Deb: 9/25/1889

YEAR TM/L	W	L	PCT	G	GS	CG	SH	SV	IP	H	HR	BB	SO	RAT	ERA	ERA+	OAV	OOB	BH	AVG	PB	PR	/A	PD	TPI
1889 Pit-N	1	0	1.000	1	1	1	0	0	9	7	0	1	0	10.0	3.00	125	.208	.231	1	.200	0	1	1	0	0.1
1892 Lou-N	5	11	.313	18	16	13	1	0	146²	130	3	56	44	11.4	3.31	93	.228	.297	8	.145	-1	-0	-4	2	-0.2
Was-N	0	3	.000	4	4	3	0	0	27	33	0	14	7	15.7	4.00	81	.290	.367	3	.273	0	-2	-2	-1	-0.1
Yr	5	14	.263	22	20	16	1	0	173²	163	3	70	51	12.1	3.42	91	.238	.309	8	.121	-1	-3	-6	1	-0.3
1894 Phi-N	1	0	1.000	1	1	1	0	0	9	10	0	4	2	10.0	2.00	255	.278	.278	1	.250	-0	3	3	0	0.2
1903 Det-A	0	1	.000	2	2	0	0	0	8²	19	0	6	2	26.0	12.46	23	.435	.503	0	.000	-1	-9	-9	0	-0.7
Total 4	7	15	.318	26	24	18	1	0	200¹	199	3	77	65	12.4	3.73	86	.250	.316	13	.165	-1	-7	-12	2	-0.7

■ AL JONES Jones, Alfornia b: 2/10/59, Charleston, Miss. BR/TR, 6′4″, 210 lbs. Deb: 8/06/83

YEAR TM/L	W	L	PCT	G	GS	CG	SH	SV	IP	H	HR	BB	SO	RAT	ERA	ERA+	OAV	OOB	BH	AVG	PB	PR	/A	PD	TPI
1983 Chi-A	0	0	—	2	0	0	0	0	2¹	3	0	2	2	19.3	3.86	109	.375	.500	0	—	0	0	0	0	0.0
1984 Chi-A	1	1	.500	20	0	0	0	5	20¹	23	3	11	15	15.5	4.43	94	.299	.393	0	—	0	-1	-1	0	0.0
1985 Chi-A	1	0	1.000	5	0	0	0	0	6	3	0	3	2	9.0	1.50	288	.167	.286	0	—	0	2	2	0	0.2
Total 3	2	1	.667	27	0	0	0	5	28²	29	3	16	19	14.4	3.77	111	.282	.383	0	—	0	1	1	0	0.2

■ ART JONES Jones, Arthur Lennox b: 2/7/06, Kershaw, S.C. d: 11/25/80, Columbia, S.C. BR/TR, 6′, 165 lbs. Deb: 4/23/32

YEAR TM/L	W	L	PCT	G	GS	CG	SH	SV	IP	H	HR	BB	SO	RAT	ERA	ERA+	OAV	OOB	BH	AVG	PB	PR	/A	PD	TPI
1932 Bro-N	0	0	—	1	0	0	0	0	1	2	0	1	0	27.0	18.00	21	.667	.750	0	—	0	-2	-2	0	0.0

■ BARRY JONES Jones, Barry Louis b: 2/15/63, Centerville, Ind. BR/TR, 6′2″, 215 lbs. Deb: 7/18/86

YEAR TM/L	W	L	PCT	G	GS	CG	SH	SV	IP	H	HR	BB	SO	RAT	ERA	ERA+	OAV	OOB	BH	AVG	PB	PR	/A	PD	TPI
1986 Pit-N	3	4	.429	26	0	0	0	3	37¹	29	3	21	29	12.1	2.89	132	.215	.321	1	.200	0	3	4	0	0.5
1987 Pit-N	2	4	.333	32	0	0	0	0	43¹	55	6	23	28	16.2	5.61	73	.314	.394	0	.000	-0	-7	-7	0	-0.6
1988 Pit-N	1	1	.500	42	0	0	0	2	56¹	57	3	21	31	12.6	3.04	112	.271	.341	0	.000	-0	3	2	0	0.2
Chi-A	2	2	.500	17	0	0	0	1	26	15	3	17	17	11.1	2.42	164	.170	.305	0	—	0	4	4	0	0.5
1989 Chi-A	3	2	.600	22	0	0	0	1	30¹	22	2	16	21	11.2	2.37	160	.208	.270	0	—	0	5	5	1	0.6
1990 Chi-A	11	4	.733	65	0	0	0	1	74	62	9	33	45	11.7	2.31	165	.235	.322	0	—	0	13	12	2	1.5
Total 5	22	17	.564	204	0	0	0	9	267¹	240	19	123	167	12.3	3.10	122	.245	.332	1	.077	-0	21	21	3	2.7

■ DEACON JONES Jones, Carroll Elmer b: 12/20/1892, Arcadia, Kan. d: 12/28/52, Pittsburg, Kan. BR/TR, 6′1″, 174 lbs. Deb: 9/23/16

YEAR TM/L	W	L	PCT	G	GS	CG	SH	SV	IP	H	HR	BB	SO	RAT	ERA	ERA+	OAV	OOB	BH	AVG	PB	PR	/A	PD	TPI
1916 Det-A	0	0	—	1	0	0	0	0	7	7	0	5	2	15.4	2.57	111	.269	.387	0	.000	-0	0	0	0	0.0
1917 Det-A	4	4	.500	24	6	2	0	0	77	69	0	26	28	11.8	2.92	91	.256	.334	0	.000	-0	-2	-2	1	-0.1
1918 Det-A	3	1	.750	21	4	1	0	0	67	60	0	38	15	13.3	3.09	86	.244	.347	5	.185	-1	-2	-3	1	-0.2
Total 3	7	5	.583	46	10	3	0	0	151	136	0	69	45	12.6	2.98	89	.251	.343	5	.114	-2	-4	-5	3	-0.3

■ BUMPUS JONES Jones, Charles Leander b: 1/1/1870, Cedarville, Ohio d: 6/25/38, Xenia, Ohio BR/TR, Deb: 10/15/1892

YEAR TM/L	W	L	PCT	G	GS	CG	SH	SV	IP	H	HR	BB	SO	RAT	ERA	ERA+	OAV	OOB	BH	AVG	PB	PR	/A	PD	TPI
1892 Cin-N	1	0	1.000	1	1	1	0	0	9	0	0	4	3	4.0	0.00	—	.000	.129	0	.000	-0	3	3	-0	0.3
1893 Cin-N	1	3	.250	6	5	2	0	0	28²	37	1	23	6	18.8	10.05	48	.304	.414	4	.250	1	-17	-17	-1	-1.2

YEAR	TM/L	W	L	PCT	G	GS	CG	SH	SV	IP	H	HR	BB	SO	RAT	ERA	ERA+	OAV	OOB	BH	AVG	PB	PR	/A	PD	TPI
	NY-N	0	1	.000	1	1	0	0	0	4	5	0	10	1	33.8	11.25	41	.297	.559	0	—	0	-3	-3	1	-0.1
	Yr	1	4	.200	7	6	2	0	0	32²	42	1	33	7	20.7	10.19	47	.303	.437	2	.125	1	-20	-20	-0	-1.3
Total 2		2	4	.333	8	7	3	0	0	41²	42	1	37	10	17.1	7.99	56	.254	.390	4	.222	1	-17	-16	-1	-1.0

■ CHARLEY JONES
Jones, Charles Wesley "Baby" (b: Benjamin Wesley Rippay)   b: 4/30/1850, Alamance Co., N.C.   BR/TR, 5'11.5", 202 lbs.   Deb: 5/04/1875   U♦

YEAR	TM/L	W	L	PCT	G	GS	CG	SH	SV	IP	H	HR	BB	SO	RAT	ERA	ERA+	OAV	OOB	BH	AVG	PB	PR	/A	PD	TPI
1887	NY-a	0	0	—	2	0	0	0	0	3	2	0	4	0	18.0	3.00	142	.183	.401	63	.255	0	0	0	-0	0.0

■ DALE JONES
Jones, Dale Eldon "Nubs"   b: 12/17/18, Marquette, Neb.   d: 11/8/80, Orlando, Fla.   BR/TR, 6'1", 172 lbs.   Deb: 9/07/41

YEAR	TM/L	W	L	PCT	G	GS	CG	SH	SV	IP	H	HR	BB	SO	RAT	ERA	ERA+	OAV	OOB	BH	AVG	PB	PR	/A	PD	TPI
1941	Phi-N	0	1	.000	2	1	0	0	0	8¹	13	0	6	2	20.5	7.56	49	.342	.432	1	.333	1	-4	-4	-0	-0.2

■ JACK JONES
Jones, Daniel Albion "Jumping Jack"   b: 10/23/1860, Litchfield, Conn.   d: 10/19/36, Wallingford, Conn.   TR,   Deb: 7/09/1883

YEAR	TM/L	W	L	PCT	G	GS	CG	SH	SV	IP	H	HR	BB	SO	RAT	ERA	ERA+	OAV	OOB	BH	AVG	PB	PR	/A	PD	TPI
1883	Det-N	6	5	.545	12	12	9	1	0	92²	103	0	19	33	11.8	3.50	89	.265	.300	8	.190	-2	-4	-4	-2	-0.5
	Phi-a	5	2	.714	7	7	7	0	0	65	58	1	6	28	8.9	2.63	133	.223	.241	6	.240	0	5	6	-0	0.6

■ DICK JONES
Jones, Decatur Poindexter   b: 5/22/02, Meadville, Miss.   BL/TR, 6', 184 lbs.   Deb: 9/11/26

YEAR	TM/L	W	L	PCT	G	GS	CG	SH	SV	IP	H	HR	BB	SO	RAT	ERA	ERA+	OAV	OOB	BH	AVG	PB	PR	/A	PD	TPI
1926	Was-A	2	1	.667	4	3	1	0	0	21	20	0	11	3	13.3	4.29	90	.263	.356	2	.200	-0	-1	-1	0	0.0
1927	Was-A	0	0	—	2	0	0	0	0	3¹	8	0	5	1	35.1	21.60	19	.444	.565	0	—	0	-6	-6	0	-0.4
Total 2		2	1	.667	6	3	1	0	0	24¹	28	0	16	4	16.3	6.66	58	.298	.400	2	.200	-0	-7	-7	0	-0.4

■ DOUG JONES
Jones, Douglas Reid   b: 6/24/57, Lebanon, Ind.   BR/TR, 6'3", 195 lbs.   Deb: 4/09/82

YEAR	TM/L	W	L	PCT	G	GS	CG	SH	SV	IP	H	HR	BB	SO	RAT	ERA	ERA+	OAV	OOB	BH	AVG	PB	PR	/A	PD	TPI
1982	Mil-A	0	0	—	4	0	0	0	0	2²	5	1	1	1	20.3	10.13	37	.385	.429	0	—	0	-2	-2	0	-0.1
1986	Cle-A	1	0	1.000	11	0	0	0	1	18	18	0	6	12	12.5	2.50	166	.257	.325	0	—	0	3	3	0	0.4
1987	Cle-A	6	5	.545	49	0	0	0	8	91¹	101	4	24	87	12.9	3.15	143	.281	.336	0	—	0	13	14	0	1.4
1988	Cle-A	3	4	.429	51	0	0	0	37	83¹	69	1	16	72	9.4	2.27	181	.218	.260	0	—	0	16	17	0	1.8
1989	Cle-A	7	10	.412	59	0	0	0	32	80²	76	4	13	65	10.0	2.34	169	.251	.284	0	—	0	14	14	0	1.5
1990	Cle-A	5	5	.500	66	0	0	0	43	84¹	66	5	22	55	9.6	2.56	155	.218	.275	0	—	0	13	13	-1	1.3
Total 6		22	24	.478	240	0	0	0	121	360¹	335	15	82	292	10.7	2.65	157	.245	.294	0	—	0	57	60	-0	6.3

■ EARL JONES
Jones, Earl Leslie "Lefty"   b: 6/11/19, Fresno, Cal.   d: 1/24/89, Fresno, Cal.   BL/TL, 5'10.5", 190 lbs.   Deb: 7/06/45

YEAR	TM/L	W	L	PCT	G	GS	CG	SH	SV	IP	H	HR	BB	SO	RAT	ERA	ERA+	OAV	OOB	BH	AVG	PB	PR	/A	PD	TPI
1945	StL-A	0	0	—	10	0	0	0	0	28¹	18	0	18	13	11.4	2.54	139	.184	.310	2	.200	1	3	3	-0	0.4

■ ELIJAH JONES
Jones, Elijah Albert "Bumpus"   b: 1/27/1882, Oxford, Mich.   d: 4/29/43, Pontiac, Mich.   BR/TR,   Deb: 4/13/07

YEAR	TM/L	W	L	PCT	G	GS	CG	SH	SV	IP	H	HR	BB	SO	RAT	ERA	ERA+	OAV	OOB	BH	AVG	PB	PR	/A	PD	TPI
1907	Det-A	0	1	.000	4	1	1	0	1	16	23	0	4	9	15.2	5.06	52	.338	.375	0	.000	-1	-4	-4	-0	-0.4
1909	Det-A	1	1	.500	2	2	0	0	0	10	10	0	0	2	9.0	2.70	93	.278	.278	1	.250	0	-0	-0	-0	0.0
Total 2		1	2	.333	6	3	1	0	1	26	33	0	4	11	12.8	4.15	62	.317	.343	1	.125	-1	-5	-5	-1	-0.4

■ GARY JONES
Jones, Gareth Howell   b: 6/12/45, Huntington Park, Cal.   BL/TL, 6', 191 lbs.   Deb: 9/25/70

YEAR	TM/L	W	L	PCT	G	GS	CG	SH	SV	IP	H	HR	BB	SO	RAT	ERA	ERA+	OAV	OOB	BH	AVG	PB	PR	/A	PD	TPI
1970	NY-A	0	0	—	2	0	0	0	0	2	3	0	1	2	18.0	0.00	—	.375	.444	0	—	0	1	1	0	0.1
1971	NY-A	0	0	—	12	0	0	0	0	14	19	1	7	10	16.7	9.00	36	.317	.388	0	.000	-0	-9	-9	-0	-0.9
Total 2		0	0	—	14	0	0	0	0	16	22	1	8	12	16.9	7.88	41	.324	.395	0	.000	-0	-8	-8	-0	-0.8

■ GORDON JONES
Jones, Gordon Bassett   b: 4/2/30, Portland, Ore.   BR/TR, 6', 185 lbs.   Deb: 8/06/54   C

YEAR	TM/L	W	L	PCT	G	GS	CG	SH	SV	IP	H	HR	BB	SO	RAT	ERA	ERA+	OAV	OOB	BH	AVG	PB	PR	/A	PD	TPI
1954	StL-N	4	4	.500	11	10	4	2	0	81	78	3	19	48	10.9	2.00	206	.248	.293	3	.125	-1	19	19	-0	1.9
1955	StL-N	1	4	.200	15	9	0	0	0	57	66	10	28	46	15.0	5.84	70	.286	.365	1	.071	-1	-11	-11	-1	-1.2
1956	StL-N	0	2	.000	5	1	0	0	0	11¹	14	2	5	6	15.1	5.56	68	.311	.380	0	.000	-0	-2	-2	0	-0.2
1957	NY-N	0	1	.000	10	0	0	0	0	11²	16	1	3	5	15.4	6.17	64	.320	.370	1	.500	0	-3	-3	-0	-0.2
1958	SF-N	3	1	.750	11	1	0	0	1	30¹	33	2	5	8	11.6	2.37	161	.284	.320	0	.000	-1	5	5	1	0.5
1959	SF-N	3	2	.600	31	0	0	0	2	43²	45	6	19	29	13.4	4.33	88	.280	.359	0	.000	-0	-2	-3	-0	-0.2
1960	Bal-A	1	1	.500	29	0	0	0	2	55	59	9	13	30	11.9	4.42	86	.281	.326	2	.400	1	-3	-4	-0	-0.2
1961	Bal-A	0	0	—	3	0	0	0	1	5	5	3	0	4	9.0	5.40	72	.250	.250	0	—	0	-1	-1	0	0.0
1962	KC-A	3	2	.600	21	0	0	0	6	32²	31	10	14	28	12.4	6.34	66	.252	.328	0	.000	-1	-9	-8	-1	-0.8
1964	Hou-N	0	1	.000	34	0	0	0	0	50	58	3	14	28	13.0	4.14	83	.290	.336	1	.250	0	-3	-4	-0	-0.3
1965	Hou-N	0	0	—	1	0	0	0	0	1	0	0	0	0	0.0	0.00	—	.000	.000	0	—	0	0	0	0	0.0
Total 11		15	18	.455	171	21	4	2	12	378²	405	49	120	232	12.6	4.16	94	.275	.332	8	.119	-3	-10	-11	-2	-0.7

■ HENRY JONES
Jones, Henry M. "Baldy"   b: Cadillac, Mich.   Deb: 8/20/1884   ♦

YEAR	TM/L	W	L	PCT	G	GS	CG	SH	SV	IP	H	HR	BB	SO	RAT	ERA	ERA+	OAV	OOB	BH	AVG	PB	PR	/A	PD	TPI
1890	Pit-N	2	1	.667	5	4	2	0	0	31	35	1	14	13	14.2	3.48	94	.277	.349	2	.222	-0	0	-1	-1	0.0

■ JIMMY JONES
Jones, James Condia   b: 4/20/64, Dallas, Tex.   BR/TR, 6'2", 175 lbs.   Deb: 9/21/86

YEAR	TM/L	W	L	PCT	G	GS	CG	SH	SV	IP	H	HR	BB	SO	RAT	ERA	ERA+	OAV	OOB	BH	AVG	PB	PR	/A	PD	TPI
1986	SD-N	2	0	1.000	3	3	1	1	0	18	10	1	3	15	6.5	2.50	146	.164	.203	1	.167	-0	2	2	-0	0.2
1987	SD-N	9	7	.563	30	22	2	1	0	145²	154	14	54	51	13.2	4.14	96	.270	.339	8	.163	1	-1	-3	2	0.0
1988	SD-N	9	14	.391	29	29	3	0	0	179	192	14	44	82	12.0	4.12	82	.277	.323	9	.164	2	-13	-14	2	-1.0
1989	NY-A	2	1	.667	11	6	0	0	0	48	56	7	16	25	13.9	5.25	74	.293	.354	0	—	0	-7	-7	1	-0.5
1990	NY-A	1	2	.333	17	7	0	0	0	50	72	8	23	25	17.3	6.30	63	.344	.412	0	—	0	-13	-13	-0	-1.2
Total 5		23	24	.489	90	67	6	2	0	440²	484	44	140	198	13.0	4.43	84	.281	.339	18	.164	3	-33	-35	5	-2.5

■ JIM JONES
Jones, James Tilford "Sheriff"   b: 12/25/1876, London, Ky.   d: 5/6/53, London, Ky.   TR, 5'10", 162 lbs.   Deb: 6/29/1897   ♦

YEAR	TM/L	W	L	PCT	G	GS	CG	SH	SV	IP	H	HR	BB	SO	RAT	ERA	ERA+	OAV	OOB	BH	AVG	PB	PR	/A	PD	TPI
1897	Lou-N	0	0	—	1	0	0	0	0	6²	19	1	5	0	32.4	18.90	23	.498	.556	1	.250	1	-11	-11	-0	-0.6
1901	NY-N	0	1	.000	1	1	1	0	0	5	6	0	2	3	14.4	10.80	31	.295	.358	19	.209	0	-4	-4	0	-0.2
Total 2		0	1	.000	2	1	1	0	0	11²	25	1	7	3	24.7	15.43	25	.428	.489	79	.230	1	-15	-15	-0	-0.8

■ JEFF JONES
Jones, Jeffrey Allen   b: 7/29/56, Detroit, Mich.   BR/TR, 6'3", 210 lbs.   Deb: 4/10/80

YEAR	TM/L	W	L	PCT	G	GS	CG	SH	SV	IP	H	HR	BB	SO	RAT	ERA	ERA+	OAV	OOB	BH	AVG	PB	PR	/A	PD	TPI
1980	Oak-A	1	3	.250	35	0	0	0	5	44¹	32	2	26	34	12.0	2.84	133	.204	.321	0	—	0	6	5	1	0.6
1981	*Oak-A	4	1	.800	33	0	0	0	3	61	51	7	40	43	13.9	3.39	102	.233	.359	0	—	0	2	1	-1	0.0
1982	Oak-A	3	1	.750	18	2	0	0	0	37	44	6	26	18	17.3	5.11	76	.306	.415	0	—	0	-4	-5	-0	-0.4
1983	Oak-A	1	1	.500	13	1	0	0	0	29²	43	7	8	14	16.1	5.76	67	.339	.387	0	—	0	-6	-6	0	-0.5
1984	Oak-A	0	3	.000	13	0	0	0	0	33	31	4	12	19	11.7	3.55	106	.258	.326	0	—	0	2	1	0	0.1
Total 5		9	9	.500	112	3	0	0	8	205	201	26	112	128	14.0	3.95	94	.262	.361	0	—	0	-1	-5	-0	-0.2

■ BROADWAY JONES
Jones, Jesse Frank   b: 11/15/1898, Millsboro, Del.   d: 9/7/77, Lewes, Del.   BR/TR, 5'9", 154 lbs.   Deb: 7/04/23

YEAR	TM/L	W	L	PCT	G	GS	CG	SH	SV	IP	H	HR	BB	SO	RAT	ERA	ERA+	OAV	OOB	BH	AVG	PB	PR	/A	PD	TPI
1923	Phi-N	0	0	—	3	0	0	0	0	8	5	0	7	1	13.5	9.00	51	.185	.353	1	.500	0	-4	-4	-0	-0.2

■ JOHNNY JONES
Jones, John Paul "Admiral"   b: 8/25/1892, Arcadia, La.   d: 6/5/80, Ruston, La.   BR/TR, 6'1", 151 lbs.   Deb: 4/24/19

YEAR	TM/L	W	L	PCT	G	GS	CG	SH	SV	IP	H	HR	BB	SO	RAT	ERA	ERA+	OAV	OOB	BH	AVG	PB	PR	/A	PD	TPI
1919	NY-N	0	0	—	2	0	0	0	1	6²	9	0	3	3	17.6	5.40	52	.310	.394	0	.000	-0	-2	-2	0	-0.1
1920	Bos-N	1	0	1.000	3	1	0	0	0	9²	16	1	5	6	19.6	6.52	47	.372	.438	1	.250	1	-4	-4	0	-0.2
Total 2		1	0	1.000	5	1	0	0	1	16¹	25	1	8	9	18.7	6.06	49	.347	.420	1	.143	0	-5	-6	0	-0.3

■ KEN JONES
Jones, Kenneth Frederick "Broadway"   b: 4/13/04, Dover, N.J.   BR/TR, 6'3", 193 lbs.   Deb: 5/19/24

YEAR	TM/L	W	L	PCT	G	GS	CG	SH	SV	IP	H	HR	BB	SO	RAT	ERA	ERA+	OAV	OOB	BH	AVG	PB	PR	/A	PD	TPI
1924	Det-A	0	0	—	1	1	0	0	0	2	1	0	1	0	9.0	0.00	—	.143	.250	0	—	0	1	1	0	0.1
1930	Bos-N	0	1	.000	8	1	0	0	1	19²	28	1	4	4	14.6	5.95	83	.359	.390	1	.200	-0	-2	-2	-0	-0.1
Total 2		0	1	.000	9	1	0	0	1	21²	29	1	5	4	14.1	5.40	90	.341	.378	1	.200	-0	-1	-1	0	0.0

■ MIKE JONES
Jones, Michael   b: Hamilton, Ont., Canada   d: 3/24/1894, Hamilton, Ont., Can   BL,   Deb: 8/12/1890

YEAR	TM/L	W	L	PCT	G	GS	CG	SH	SV	IP	H	HR	BB	SO	RAT	ERA	ERA+	OAV	OOB	BH	AVG	PB	PR	/A	PD	TPI
1890	Lou-a	2	0	1.000	3	3	2	0	0	22	21	2	9	6	12.3	3.27	118	.244	.315	4	.444	2	1	1	0	0.3

■ MIKE JONES
Jones, Michael Carl   b: 7/30/59, Penfield, N.Y.   BL/TL, 6'6", 215 lbs.   Deb: 9/06/80

YEAR	TM/L	W	L	PCT	G	GS	CG	SH	SV	IP	H	HR	BB	SO	RAT	ERA	ERA+	OAV	OOB	BH	AVG	PB	PR	/A	PD	TPI
1980	KC-A	0	1	.000	3	1	0	0	0	4²	6	0	5	2	21.2	11.57	35	.333	.478	0	—	0	-4	-4	-0	-0.3

YEAR TM/L	W	L	PCT	G	GS	CG	SH	SV	IP	H	HR	BB	SO	RAT	ERA	ERA+	OAV	OOB	BH	AVG	PB	PR	/A	PD	TPI
1981 *KC-A	6	3	.667	12	11	0	0	0	75²	74	7	28	29	12.4	3.21	112	.256	.326	0	—	0	4	3	0	0.4
1984 *KC-A	2	3	.400	23	12	0	0	0	81	86	10	36	43	13.7	4.89	82	.270	.346	0	—	0	-8	-8	-1	-0.8
1985 KC-A	3	3	.500	33	1	0	0	0	64	62	6	39	32	14.2	4.78	87	.257	.361	0	—	0	-5	-4	0	-0.3
Total 4	11	10	.524	71	25	0	0	0	225¹	228	23	108	106	13.5	4.43	88	.263	.347	0	—	0	-13	-13	-1	-1.0

■ ODELL JONES   Jones, Odell b: 1/13/53, Tulare, Cal.   BR/TR, 6'3", 175 lbs.   Deb: 9/11/75

YEAR TM/L	W	L	PCT	G	GS	CG	SH	SV	IP	H	HR	BB	SO	RAT	ERA	ERA+	OAV	OOB	BH	AVG	PB	PR	/A	PD	TPI
1975 Pit-N	0	0	—	2	0	0	0	0	3	1	0	0	2	3.0	0.00	—	.100	.100	0	—	0	1	1	0	0.1
1977 Pit-N	3	7	.300	34	15	1	0	0	108	118	14	31	66	12.7	5.08	78	.278	.332	4	.143	-1	-14	-13	-2	-1.5
1978 Pit-N	2	0	1.000	3	1	0	0	0	9	7	0	4	10	11.0	2.00	185	.206	.289	0	.000	-0	2	2	0	0.2
1979 Sea-A	3	11	.214	25	19	3	0	0	118²	151	16	58	72	16.1	6.07	72	.317	.395	0	—	-0	-24	-23	-2	-2.2
1981 Pit-N	4	5	.444	13	8	0	0	0	54¹	51	3	23	30	12.3	3.31	108	.250	.326	2	.200	-0	1	2	0	0.2
1983 Tex-A	3	6	.333	42	0	0	0	10	67	56	4	22	50	10.7	3.09	130	.223	.291	0	—	0	7	7	-1	0.6
1984 Tex-A	2	4	.333	33	0	0	0	2	59¹	62	7	23	28	13.2	3.64	114	.281	.354	0	—	0	2	3	1	0.4
1986 Bal-A	2	2	.500	21	0	0	0	0	49¹	58	4	23	32	14.8	3.83	108	.305	.380	0	—	0	2	2	-0	0.1
1988 Mil-A	5	0	1.000	28	2	0	0	1	80²	75	8	29	48	11.7	4.35	91	.251	.319	0	—	0	-3	-3	-1	-0.3
Total 9	24	35	.407	201	45	4	0	13	549¹	579	56	213	338	13.2	4.42	92	.275	.344	6	.154	-1	-27	-23	-5	-2.4

■ OSCAR JONES   Jones, Oscar Winfield "Flip Flap" b: 1/21/1879, London Grove, Pa.   d: 10/8/46, Perkasie, Pa.   BR/TR, 5'7", 163 lbs.   Deb: 4/20/03

YEAR TM/L	W	L	PCT	G	GS	CG	SH	SV	IP	H	HR	BB	SO	RAT	ERA	ERA+	OAV	OOB	BH	AVG	PB	PR	/A	PD	TPI
1903 Bro-N	19	14	.576	38	36	31	4	0	324¹	320	4	77	95	11.5	2.94	109	.260	.313	32	.256	3	12	9	-3	0.8
1904 Bro-N	17	25	.405	46	41	38	0	0	377	387	7	92	96	11.8	2.75	100	.270	.321	24	.175	-1	-0	0	-6	-0.7
1905 Bro-N	8	15	.348	29	20	14	0	1	174	197	6	56	66	13.6	4.66	62	.285	.347	13	.200	1	-32	-34	-3	-3.6
Total 3	44	54	.449	113	97	83	4	1	875¹	904	17	225	257	12.1	3.20	92	.269	.324	69	.211	2	-20	-25	-12	-3.5

■ PERCY JONES   Jones, Percy Lee b: 10/28/1899, Harwood, Tex.   d: 3/18/79, Dallas, Tex.   BR/TL, 5'11.5", 175 lbs.   Deb: 8/06/20

YEAR TM/L	W	L	PCT	G	GS	CG	SH	SV	IP	H	HR	BB	SO	RAT	ERA	ERA+	OAV	OOB	BH	AVG	PB	PR	/A	PD	TPI
1920 Chi-N	0	0	—	4	0	0	0	0	7	15	1	3	0	24.4	11.57	28	.455	.514	0	.000	-0	-7	-7	0	-0.6
1921 Chi-N	3	5	.375	32	5	1	0	0	98²	116	2	39	46	14.5	4.56	84	.295	.365	6	.222	-0	-9	-8	-2	-0.9
1922 Chi-N	8	9	.471	44	26	7	2	1	162	197	10	68	45	15.0	4.78	88	.310	.381	4	.085	-4	-12	-10	-1	-1.2
1925 Chi-N	6	6	.500	28	13	6	1	0	124	123	12	71	60	14.4	4.65	93	.263	.366	6	.154	-3	-5	-4	2	-0.4
1926 Chi-N	12	7	.632	30	20	10	2	2	160¹	151	3	90	80	13.8	3.09	125	.256	.359	13	.260	3	13	13	-2	1.5
1927 Chi-N	7	8	.467	30	11	5	1	0	112²	123	4	72	37	16.1	4.07	95	.285	.394	14	.350	3	-2	-3	2	0.2
1928 Chi-N	10	6	.625	39	18	9	1	3	154	167	4	56	41	13.4	4.03	95	.288	.358	11	.196	-0	-1	-3	0	-0.3
1929 Bos-N	7	15	.318	35	22	11	1	0	188¹	219	15	84	69	14.7	4.64	101	.298	.373	9	.148	-3	2	1	1	0.0
1930 Pit-N	0	1	.000	9	2	0	0	0	19	26	3	11	3	18.9	6.63	75	.329	.430	0	.000	-0	-4	-3	-0	-0.3
Total 9	53	57	.482	251	117	49	8	6	1026	1137	53	494	381	14.7	4.34	95	.288	.373	63	.194	-5	-24	-24	0	-2.0

■ RANDY JONES   Jones, Randall Leo b: 1/12/50, Fullerton, Cal.   BR/TL, 6', 178 lbs.   Deb: 6/16/73

YEAR TM/L	W	L	PCT	G	GS	CG	SH	SV	IP	H	HR	BB	SO	RAT	ERA	ERA+	OAV	OOB	BH	AVG	PB	PR	/A	PD	TPI
1973 SD-N	7	6	.538	20	19	6	1	0	139²	129	13	37	77	10.8	3.16	110	.241	.291	8	.167	0	8	5	0	0.5
1974 SD-N	8	22	.267	40	34	4	1	2	208¹	217	16	78	124	13.0	4.45	80	.270	.339	10	.154	-1	-19	-21	2	-1.9
1975 SD-N	20	12	.625	37	36	18	6	0	285	242	17	56	103	9.4	2.24	155	.232	.271	11	.133	-1	44	39	5	4.8
1976 SD-N	22	14	.611	40	40	25	5	0	315¹	274	15	50	93	9.4	2.74	119	.234	.267	6	.058	-6	27	19	9	2.3
1977 SD-N	6	12	.333	27	25	1	0	0	147¹	173	12	36	44	12.8	4.58	77	.291	.332	5	.116	-1	-11	-17	5	-1.3
1978 SD-N	13	14	.481	37	36	7	2	0	253	263	6	64	71	11.6	2.88	115	.272	.317	15	.183	1	20	12	3	1.7
1979 SD-N	11	12	.478	39	39	6	0	0	263	257	17	64	112	11.1	3.63	97	.259	.306	15	.174	0	3	-3	4	0.1
1980 SD-N	5	13	.278	24	24	4	3	0	154¹	165	14	29	53	11.3	3.91	88	.276	.310	3	.067	-3	-5	-8	3	-0.7
1981 NY-N	1	8	.111	13	12	0	0	0	59¹	65	8	38	14	15.8	4.85	72	.274	.377	2	.118	-1	-9	-9	2	-0.7
1982 NY-N	7	10	.412	28	20	2	1	0	107²	130	11	51	44	15.5	4.60	79	.304	.384	4	.148	-1	-12	-13	3	-0.8
Total 10	100	123	.448	305	285	73	19	2	1933	1915	129	503	735	11.3	3.42	101	.260	.309	79	.132	-11	44	6	36	4.0

■ SAM JONES   Jones, Samuel "Toothpick Sam" b: 12/14/25, Stewartsville, Ohio   d: 11/5/71, Morgantown, W.Va.   BR/TR, 6'4", 192 lbs.   Deb: 9/22/51

YEAR TM/L	W	L	PCT	G	GS	CG	SH	SV	IP	H	HR	BB	SO	RAT	ERA	ERA+	OAV	OOB	BH	AVG	PB	PR	/A	PD	TPI
1951 Cle-A	0	1	.000	2	1	0	0	0	8²	4	0	5	4	9.3	2.08	182	.143	.273	0	.000	-0	2	2	0	0.1
1952 Cle-A	2	3	.400	14	4	0	0	1	36	38	6	37	28	19.8	7.25	46	.270	.434	1	.100	-1	-14	-16	-1	-1.6
1955 Chi-N	14	20	.412	36	34	12	4	0	241²	175	22	185	198	13.9	4.10	100	.206	.357	14	.182	-2	-2	-0	-1	-0.2
1956 Chi-N	9	14	.391	33	28	8	2	0	188²	155	21	115	176	13.3	3.91	96	.221	.338	10	.175	-0	-3	-3	-2	-0.5
1957 StL-N	12	9	.571	28	27	10	2	0	182²	164	17	71	154	11.9	3.60	110	.239	.316	10	.159	-1	6	7	-1	0.6
1958 StL-N	14	13	.519	35	35	14	2	0	250	204	23	107	225	11.4	2.88	143	.223	.309	9	.100	-6	30	35	-2	2.9
1959 SF-N	21	15	.583	50	35	16	4	4	270²	232	18	109	209	11.6	2.83	135	.228	.307	11	.129	-2	34	30	-2	2.6
1960 SF-N	18	14	.563	39	35	13	3	0	234	200	18	91	190	11.3	3.19	109	.230	.306	16	.200	1	15	7	-2	0.6
1961 SF-N	8	8	.500	37	17	2	0	1	128¹	134	12	57	105	14.0	4.49	85	.264	.348	5	.139	-1	-7	-10	-2	-1.1
1962 Det-A	2	4	.333	30	6	1	0	1	81¹	77	13	35	73	12.6	3.65	111	.254	.335	2	.095	-1	3	4	-0	0.3
1963 StL-N	2	0	1.000	11	0	0	0	2	11	15	0	5	6	16.4	9.00	39	.319	.385	0	.000	-0	-7	-7	-0	-0.6
1964 Bal-A	0	0	—	7	0	0	0	0	10¹	5	1	5	6	8.7	2.61	137	.152	.263	0	—	0	1	1	0	0.1
Total 12	102	101	.502	322	222	76	17	9	1643¹	1403	151	822	1376	12.5	3.59	108	.230	.328	78	.149	-11	58	50	-13	3.2

■ SAM JONES   Jones, Samuel Pond "Sad Sam" b: 7/26/1892, Woodsfield, Ohio   d: 7/6/66, Barnesville, Ohio   BR/TR, 6', 170 lbs.   Deb: 6/13/14

YEAR TM/L	W	L	PCT	G	GS	CG	SH	SV	IP	H	HR	BB	SO	RAT	ERA	ERA+	OAV	OOB	BH	AVG	PB	PR	/A	PD	TPI
1914 Cle-A	0	0	—	1	0	0	0	0	3¹	2	0	2	0	10.8	2.70	107	.200	.333	1	.500	0	0	0	0	0.1
1915 Cle-A	4	9	.308	48	9	2	0	4	145²	131	6	63	42	12.0	3.65	84	.252	.334	5	.156	-0	-11	-10	1	-0.8
1916 Bos-A	0	1	.000	12	0	0	0	0	27	25	0	10	7	11.7	3.67	76	.272	.343	2	.333	-0	-3	-3	-0	-0.2
1917 Bos-A	0	1	.000	9	1	0	0	1	16¹	15	1	6	5	11.6	4.41	59	.259	.328	0	.000	-1	-3	-3	1	-0.3
1918 *Bos-A	16	5	.762	24	21	16	5	0	184	151	1	70	44	11.2	2.25	119	.230	.312	10	.175	-2	11	9	-1	1.1
1919 Bos-A	12	20	.375	35	31	21	5	1	245	258	6	95	67	13.2	3.75	81	.278	.350	11	.136	-0	-14	-20	3	-1.7
1920 Bos-A	13	16	.448	37	33	21	3	0	274	302	9	79	86	12.6	3.94	93	.288	.340	20	.217	1	-4	-9	-1	-0.8
1921 Bos-A	23	16	.590	40	38	25	5	1	298²	318	11	78	98	12.1	3.22	131	.279	.329	24	.240	5	35	33	-3	3.3
1922 *NY-A	13	13	.500	45	28	20	0	8	260	270	16	76	81	12.1	3.67	109	.275	.329	8	.264	8	11	10	-1	1.6
1923 *NY-A	21	8	.724	39	27	18	3	4	243	239	11	69	68	11.6	3.63	109	.257	.312	19	.224	2	10	8	1	1.1
1924 NY-A	9	6	.600	36	21	8	3	3	178²	187	6	76	53	13.3	3.63	115	.276	.350	9	.176	-0	12	11	-1	0.9
1925 NY-A	15	21	.417	43	31	14	1	2	246²	267	14	104	92	13.6	4.63	92	.281	.354	13	.162	-3	-7	-10	-1	-1.1
1926 *NY-A	9	8	.529	39	23	6	1	5	161	186	6	80	69	15.1	4.98	77	.298	.381	10	.204	1	-17	-20	-2	-1.9
1927 StL-A	8	14	.364	30	26	11	0	0	189²	211	13	102	72	15.0	4.32	101	.282	.371	6	.109	-2	-4	1	-2	-0.2
1928 Was-A	17	7	.708	30	27	19	4	0	224²	209	5	78	63	11.6	2.84	141	.252	.319	20	.253	6	30	29	1	3.7
1929 Was-A	9	9	.500	24	24	8	1	0	153²	156	9	49	36	12.2	3.92	108	.264	.324	8	.157	0	5	5	-1	0.5
1930 Was-A	15	7	.682	25	25	14	1	0	183¹	195	4	61	60	12.7	4.07	113	.277	.337	9	.148	-1	12	11	-1	0.7
1931 Was-A	9	10	.474	25	24	8	1	1	148	185	10	47	58	14.4	4.32	99	.304	.358	15	.313	4	1	-0	0	0.3
1932 Chi-A	10	15	.400	30	28	10	0	0	200¹	217	9	75	64	13.3	4.22	102	.270	.335	11	.193	2	6	2	2	0.6
1933 Chi-A	10	12	.455	27	25	11	2	0	176²	181	13	65	60	12.7	3.36	126	.265	.333	9	.155	-0	18	17	-1	1.5
1934 Chi-A	8	12	.400	27	26	11	1	0	183¹	217	16	60	60	13.7	5.11	93	.289	.343	12	.200	-1	-12	-8	-1	-0.6
1935 Chi-A	8	7	.533	21	19	7	0	0	140	162	3	38	33	13.8	4.05	114	.284	.343	8	.167	0	6	9	0	0.9
Total 22	229	217	.513	647	487	250	36	31	3883	4084	152	1396	1223	12.9	3.84	104	.274	.339	245	.197	25	81	61	-5	8.7

■ SHELDON JONES   Jones, Sheldon Leslie "Available" b: 2/2/22, Tecumseh, Neb.   BR/TR, 6', 180 lbs.   Deb: 9/09/46

YEAR TM/L	W	L	PCT	G	GS	CG	SH	SV	IP	H	HR	BB	SO	RAT	ERA	ERA+	OAV	OOB	BH	AVG	PB	PR	/A	PD	TPI
1946 NY-N	1	2	.333	6	4	1	0	0	28	21	4	17	24	12.5	3.21	107	.208	.328	2	.250	0	1	1	-0	0.1
1947 NY-N	2	2	.500	15	6	0	0	0	55²	51	2	29	24	13.4	3.88	105	.250	.352	2	.125	-1	1	1	-1	0.0
1948 NY-N	16	8	.667	55	21	8	1	5	201¹	204	16	90	82	13.4	3.35	117	.263	.344	13	.203	1	14	13	0	1.5
1949 NY-N	15	12	.556	42	27	11	1	0	207¹	198	19	88	79	12.8	3.34	119	.248	.331	8	.121	-3	16	15	-0	1.1
1950 NY-N	13	16	.448	40	28	11	2	2	199	188	26	90	97	12.9	4.61	89	.249	.335	6	.105	-2	-10	-11	-2	-1.5

YEAR TM/L	W	L	PCT	G	GS	CG	SH	SV	IP	H	HR	BB	SO	RAT	ERA	ERA+	OAV	OOB	BH	AVG	PB	PR	/A	PD	TPI
1951 *NY-N	6	11	.353	41	12	2	0	4	120¹	119	12	52	58	13.1	4.26	92	.260	.340	3	.097	-1	-4	-5	0	-0.4
1952 Bos-N	1	4	.200	39	1	0	0	1	70	81	8	31	40	14.5	4.76	76	.286	.359	1	.125	-0	-8	-9	0	-0.8
1953 Chi-N	0	2	.000	22	2	0	0	0	38¹	47	3	16	9	16.0	5.40	82	.299	.382	0	.000	-1	-5	-4	0	-0.4
Total 8	54	57	.486	260	101	33	4	12	920	909	90	413	413	13.3	3.96	100	.258	.342	35	.136	-7	4	1	-3	-0.4

■ **SHERMAN JONES**   Jones, Sherman Jarvis "Roadblock" b: 2/10/35, Winton, N.C. BL/TR, 6'4", 205 lbs. Deb: 8/02/60

YEAR TM/L	W	L	PCT	G	GS	CG	SH	SV	IP	H	HR	BB	SO	RAT	ERA	ERA+	OAV	OOB	BH	AVG	PB	PR	/A	PD	TPI
1960 SF-N	1	1	.500	16	0	0	0	1	32	37	3	11	10	13.8	3.09	112	.291	.353	2	.286	0	2	1	-1	0.1
1961 *Cin-N	1	1	.500	24	2	0	0	2	55	51	6	27	32	13.1	4.42	92	.256	.351	2	.182	0	-2	-2	-0	-0.1
1962 NY-N	0	4	.000	8	3	0	0	0	23¹	31	3	8	11	15.8	7.71	54	.326	.390	3	.429	1	-10	-9	0	-0.6
Total 3	2	6	.250	48	5	0	0	3	110¹	119	12	46	53	13.9	4.73	83	.283	.360	7	.280	1	-10	-10	-0	-0.6

■ **STEVE JONES**   Jones, Steven Howell b: 4/22/41, Huntington Park, Cal. BL/TR, 5'10", 175 lbs. Deb: 8/15/67

YEAR TM/L	W	L	PCT	G	GS	CG	SH	SV	IP	H	HR	BB	SO	RAT	ERA	ERA+	OAV	OOB	BH	AVG	PB	PR	/A	PD	TPI
1967 Chi-A	2	2	.500	11	3	0	0	0	25²	21	1	12	17	11.6	4.21	74	.223	.311	1	.250	0	-3	-3	-0	-0.2
1968 Was-A	1	2	.333	7	0	0	0	0	10²	8	3	7	11	12.7	5.91	49	.205	.326	0	.000	-0	-3	-4	-0	-0.4
1969 KC-A	2	3	.400	20	4	0	0	0	44²	45	3	24	31	14.5	4.23	87	.260	.360	1	.125	1	-3	-3	-0	-0.1
Total 3	5	7	.417	38	7	0	0	0	81	74	7	43	59	13.3	4.44	76	.242	.341	2	.154	1	-9	-9	-0	-0.7

■ **RICK JONES**   Jones, Thomas Fredrick b: 4/16/55, Jacksonville, Fla. BL/TL, 6'5", 190 lbs. Deb: 4/18/76

YEAR TM/L	W	L	PCT	G	GS	CG	SH	SV	IP	H	HR	BB	SO	RAT	ERA	ERA+	OAV	OOB	BH	AVG	PB	PR	/A	PD	TPI
1976 Bos-A	5	3	.625	24	14	1	0	0	104¹	133	6	26	45	13.8	3.36	116	.311	.352	0	—	0	2	6	-0	0.7
1977 Sea-A	1	4	.200	10	10	0	0	0	42¹	47	10	37	16	17.9	5.10	81	.283	.414	0	—	0	-5	-5	-0	-0.3
1978 Sea-A	0	2	.000	3	2	0	0	0	12¹	17	1	7	11	17.5	5.84	65	.315	.393	0	—	0	-3	-3	-0	-0.2
Total 3	6	9	.400	37	26	1	0	0	159	197	17	70	72	15.2	4.02	99	.304	.373	0	—	0	-6	-1	0	0.2

■ **TIM JONES**   Jones, Timmothy Byron b: 1/24/54, Sacramento, Cal. BB/TR, 6'5", 220 lbs. Deb: 9/04/77

YEAR TM/L	W	L	PCT	G	GS	CG	SH	SV	IP	H	HR	BB	SO	RAT	ERA	ERA+	OAV	OOB	BH	AVG	PB	PR	/A	PD	TPI
1977 Pit-N	1	0	1.000	3	1	0	0	0	10	4	0	3	5	6.3	0.00	—	.118	.189	0	.000	-0	4	4	-0	0.4

■ **TIM JONES**   Jones, William Timothy b: 12/1/62, Sumter, S.C. BL/TR, 5'10", 172 lbs. Deb: 7/26/88 ♦

YEAR TM/L	W	L	PCT	G	GS	CG	SH	SV	IP	H	HR	BB	SO	RAT	ERA	ERA+	OAV	OOB	BH	AVG	PB	PR	/A	PD	TPI
1990 StL-N	0	0	—	1	0	0	0	0	1¹	1	0	2	0	20.3	6.75	58	.167	.375	28	.219	0	-0	-0	0	0.0

■ **CLAUDE JONNARD**   Jonnard, Claude Alfred b: 11/23/1897, Nashville, Tenn. d: 8/27/59, Nashville, Tenn. BR/TR, 6'1", 165 lbs. Deb: 10/01/21

YEAR TM/L	W	L	PCT	G	GS	CG	SH	SV	IP	H	HR	BB	SO	RAT	ERA	ERA+	OAV	OOB	BH	AVG	PB	PR	/A	PD	TPI
1921 NY-N	0	0	—	1	0	0	0	1	4	4	0	0	7	9.0	0.00	—	.267	.267	0	.000	-0	2	2	-0	0.1
1922 NY-N	6	1	.857	33	0	0	0	5	96	96	7	28	44	11.9	3.84	104	.272	.331	1	.042	-3	3	2	-2	-0.2
1923 *NY-N	4	3	.571	45	1	1	0	5	96	105	6	35	45	13.1	3.28	116	.279	.340	1	.038	-3	8	6	-1	0.2
1924 *NY-N	4	5	.444	34	3	1	0	5	89²	80	2	24	40	10.6	2.41	152	.229	.282	1	.045	-3	15	13	-0	0.9
1926 StL-A	0	2	.000	13	3	0	0	1	36	46	1	24	13	17.5	6.00	71	.313	.409	0	.000	-1	-8	-7	1	-0.5
1929 Chi-N	0	1	.000	12	2	0	0	0	27²	41	4	11	11	17.2	7.48	62	.320	.379	2	.200	1	-9	-9	-0	-0.6
Total 6	14	12	.538	137	9	2	0	17	349¹	372	20	122	160	12.9	3.79	104	.272	.334	5	.056	-8	10	6	-2	-0.1

■ **CHARLIE JORDAN**   Jordan, Charles T. "Kid" b: 10/4/1871, Baltimore, Md. d: 6/1/28, Hazleton, Pa. Deb: 7/31/1896

YEAR TM/L	W	L	PCT	G	GS	CG	SH	SV	IP	H	HR	BB	SO	RAT	ERA	ERA+	OAV	OOB	BH	AVG	PB	PR	/A	PD	TPI
1896 Phi-N	0	0	—	2	0	0	0	0	4²	9	0	2	3	21.2	7.71	56	.402	.451	1	.500	0	-2	-2	0	0.0

■ **HARRY JORDAN**   Jordan, Harry J. b: 2/14/1873, Pittsburgh, Pa. d: 3/1/20, Pittsburgh, Pa. Deb: 9/25/1894

YEAR TM/L	W	L	PCT	G	GS	CG	SH	SV	IP	H	HR	BB	SO	RAT	ERA	ERA+	OAV	OOB	BH	AVG	PB	PR	/A	PD	TPI
1894 Pit-N	1	0	1.000	1	1	1	0	0	9	10	0	2	1	12.0	4.00	131	.278	.316	0	.000	-0	1	1	-0	0.1
1895 Pit-N	0	2	.000	2	2	2	0	0	17	24	0	4	4	15.9	4.24	107	.327	.378	2	.286	-0	1	1	-0	0.0
Total 2	1	2	.333	3	3	3	0	0	26	34	0	6	5	14.5	4.15	115	.311	.358	2	.200	-0	2	2	-0	0.1

■ **MILT JORDAN**   Jordan, Milton Mignot b: 5/24/27, Mineral Springs, Pa. BR/TR, 6'2.5", 207 lbs. Deb: 4/16/53

YEAR TM/L	W	L	PCT	G	GS	CG	SH	SV	IP	H	HR	BB	SO	RAT	ERA	ERA+	OAV	OOB	BH	AVG	PB	PR	/A	PD	TPI
1953 Det-A	0	1	.000	8	1	0	0	0	17	26	3	5	4	16.4	5.82	70	.366	.408	1	.500	-0	-3	-3	0	-0.2

■ **NILES JORDAN**   Jordan, Niles Chapman b: 12/1/25, Lyman, Wash. BL/TL, 5'11", 180 lbs. Deb: 8/26/51

YEAR TM/L	W	L	PCT	G	GS	CG	SH	SV	IP	H	HR	BB	SO	RAT	ERA	ERA+	OAV	OOB	BH	AVG	PB	PR	/A	PD	TPI
1951 Phi-N	2	3	.400	5	5	2	1	0	36²	35	4	8	11	10.6	3.19	121	.250	.291	1	.077	-1	3	3	-0	0.1
1952 Cin-N	0	1	.000	3	1	0	0	0	6¹	14	1	3	2	24.2	9.95	38	.452	.500	0	.000	-0	-4	-4	0	-0.3
Total 2	2	4	.333	8	6	2	1	0	43	49	5	11	13	12.6	4.19	92	.287	.330	1	.071	-1	-1	-2	-0	-0.2

■ **RIP JORDAN**   Jordan, Raymond Willis "Lanky" b: 9/28/1889, Portland, Me. d: 6/5/60, Meriden, Conn. BL/TR, 6', 172 lbs. Deb: 6/25/12

YEAR TM/L	W	L	PCT	G	GS	CG	SH	SV	IP	H	HR	BB	SO	RAT	ERA	ERA+	OAV	OOB	BH	AVG	PB	PR	/A	PD	TPI
1912 Chi-A	0	0	—	4	0	0	0	0	12¹	13	2	3	1	12.4	5.11	63	.289	.347	0	.000	-1	-2	-3	-0	-0.2
1919 Was-A	0	0	—	1	1	0	0	0	4	6	1	2	2	18.0	11.25	29	.353	.421	0	.000	-0	-4	-4	-0	-0.2
Total 2	0	0	—	5	1	0	0	0	16¹	19	3	5	3	13.8	6.61	48	.306	.368	0	.000	-1	-6	-6	-0	-0.4

■ **ORVILLE JORGENS**   Jorgens, Orville Edward b: 6/4/08, Rockford, Ill. BR/TR, 6'1", 180 lbs. Deb: 4/19/35

YEAR TM/L	W	L	PCT	G	GS	CG	SH	SV	IP	H	HR	BB	SO	RAT	ERA	ERA+	OAV	OOB	BH	AVG	PB	PR	/A	PD	TPI
1935 Phi-N	10	15	.400	53	24	6	0	2	188¹	216	12	96	95	15.3	4.83	94	.283	.370	6	.097	-5	-17	-6	3	-0.6
1936 Phi-N	8	8	.500	39	21	4	0	0	167¹	196	16	69	58	14.6	4.79	95	.290	.361	12	.200	-1	-14	-5	1	-0.3
1937 Phi-N	3	4	.429	52	11	1	0	3	140²	159	12	68	34	14.8	4.41	98	.298	.383	5	.143	-1	-8	-1	2	0.0
Total 3	21	27	.438	144	56	11	0	5	496¹	571	40	233	149	14.9	4.70	95	.290	.370	23	.146	-8	-39	-12	6	-0.9

■ **ADDIE JOSS**   Joss, Adrian b: 4/12/1880, Woodland, Wis. d: 4/14/11, Toledo, Ohio BR/TR, 6'3", 185 lbs. Deb: 4/26/02 H

YEAR TM/L	W	L	PCT	G	GS	CG	SH	SV	IP	H	HR	BB	SO	RAT	ERA	ERA+	OAV	OOB	BH	AVG	PB	PR	/A	PD	TPI
1902 Cle-A	17	13	.567	32	29	28	5	0	269¹	225	2	75	106	10.0	2.77	124	.228	.282	12	.117	-5	24	20	6	2.0
1903 Cle-A	18	13	.581	32	31	31	3	0	283²	232	3	37	120	8.5	2.19	130	.223	.250	22	.193	0	24	21	4	2.7
1904 Cle-A	14	10	.583	25	24	20	5	0	192¹	160	0	30	83	8.9	1.59	160	.227	.259	10	.132	-3	22	20	0	1.9
1905 Cle-A	20	12	.625	33	32	31	3	0	286	246	4	46	132	9.2	2.01	131	.233	.266	13	.134	-0	21	20	5	2.7
1906 Cle-A	21	9	.700	34	31	28	9	1	282	220	3	43	106	8.4	1.72	152	.218	.250	21	.210	2	30	28	2	3.8
1907 Cle-A	27	11	.711	42	38	34	6	2	338²	279	2	54	127	8.8	1.83	137	.226	.259	13	.114	-5	27	26	9	3.3
1908 Cle-A	24	11	.686	42	35	29	9	2	325	232	2	30	130	7.3	1.16	206	.197	.218	15	.155	2	45	44	2	6.1
1909 Cle-A	14	13	.519	33	28	24	4	0	242²	198	0	31	67	8.6	1.71	150	.226	.255	8	.100	-3	21	23	1	2.5
1910 Cle-A	5	5	.500	13	12	9	1	0	107¹	96	2	18	49	9.7	2.26	114	.245	.282	4	.111	-1	3	4	2	0.5
Total 9	160	97	.623	286	260	234	45	5	2327	1888	19	364	920	8.7	1.89	142	.223	.255	118	.144	-13	216	207	30	25.5

■ **MIKE JOYCE**   Joyce, Michael Lewis b: 2/12/41, Detroit, Mich. BR/TR, 6'2", 193 lbs. Deb: 7/02/62

YEAR TM/L	W	L	PCT	G	GS	CG	SH	SV	IP	H	HR	BB	SO	RAT	ERA	ERA+	OAV	OOB	BH	AVG	PB	PR	/A	PD	TPI
1962 Chi-A	2	1	.667	25	1	0	0	2	43¹	40	2	14	9	11.2	3.32	118	.247	.307	3	.429	1	3	3	-0	0.4
1963 Chi-A	0	0	—	6	0	0	0	0	10²	13	1	8	7	17.7	8.44	42	.289	.396	0	—	0	-6	-6	-0	-0.5
Total 2	2	1	.667	31	1	0	0	2	54	53	3	22	16	12.5	4.33	88	.256	.328	3	.429	1	-3	-3	-0	-0.1

■ **DICK JOYCE**   Joyce, Richard Edward b: 11/18/43, Portland, Me. BL/TL, 6'5", 225 lbs. Deb: 9/03/65

YEAR TM/L	W	L	PCT	G	GS	CG	SH	SV	IP	H	HR	BB	SO	RAT	ERA	ERA+	OAV	OOB	BH	AVG	PB	PR	/A	PD	TPI
1965 KC-A	0	1	.000	5	3	0	0	0	13	12	0	4	7	11.1	2.77	126	.240	.296	0	.000	-0	1	1	0	0.1

■ **BOB JOYCE**   Joyce, Robert Emmett b: 1/14/15, Stockton, Cal. d: 12/10/81, San Francisco, Cal BR/TR, 6'1", 180 lbs. Deb: 5/04/39

YEAR TM/L	W	L	PCT	G	GS	CG	SH	SV	IP	H	HR	BB	SO	RAT	ERA	ERA+	OAV	OOB	BH	AVG	PB	PR	/A	PD	TPI
1939 Phi-A	3	5	.375	30	6	1	0	0	107²	156	13	37	25	16.2	6.69	70	.337	.387	3	.086	-3	-25	-24	1	-2.2
1946 NY-N	3	4	.429	14	7	2	0	0	60²	79	3	20	24	14.7	5.34	64	.315	.365	3	.158	0	-13	-13	1	-1.1
Total 2	6	9	.400	44	13	3	0	0	168¹	235	16	57	49	15.7	6.20	69	.329	.380	6	.111	-3	-38	-37	2	-3.3

■ **RALPH JUDD**   Judd, Ralph Wesley b: 12/7/01, Perrysburg, Ohio d: 5/6/57, Lapeer, Mich. BL/TR, 5'10", 170 lbs. Deb: 10/02/27

YEAR TM/L	W	L	PCT	G	GS	CG	SH	SV	IP	H	HR	BB	SO	RAT	ERA	ERA+	OAV	OOB	BH	AVG	PB	PR	/A	PD	TPI
1927 Was-A	0	0	—	1	0	0	0	0	4	8	0	2	2	22.5	6.75	60	.400	.455	0	.000	-0	-1	-1	-0	0.0
1929 NY-N	3	0	1.000	18	0	0	0	0	50²	49	4	11	21	10.7	2.66	172	.261	.302	0	.000	-2	12	11	0	0.8
1930 NY-N	0	0	—	2	0	0	0	0	7²	13	0	3	0	18.8	5.87	81	.390	.441	0	.000	-1	-1	-0	0	0.0
Total 3	3	0	1.000	21	0	0	0	0	62¹	70	4	16	23	12.4	3.32	138	.290	.334	0	.000	-3	10	9	0	0.8

YEAR TM/L	W	L	PCT	G	GS	CG	SH	SV	IP	H	HR	BB	SO	RAT	ERA	ERA+	OAV	OOB	BH	AVG	PB	PR	/A	PD	TPI

■ OSCAR JUDD
Judd, Thomas William Oscar "Ossie" b: 2/14/08, London, Ont., Can.   BL/TL, 6'0.5", 180 lbs.   Deb: 4/16/41

YEAR TM/L	W	L	PCT	G	GS	CG	SH	SV	IP	H	HR	BB	SO	RAT	ERA	ERA+	OAV	OOB	BH	AVG	PB	PR	/A	PD	TPI
1941 Bos-A	0	0	—	7	0	0	0	1	12¹	15	1	10	5	18.2	8.76	48	.300	.417	2	.500	2	-6	-6	0	-0.3
1942 Bos-A	8	10	.444	31	19	11	0	2	150¹	135	3	90	70	13.6	3.89	96	.239	.346	18	.269	6	-4	-3	-0	0.3
1943 Bos-A	11	6	.647	23	20	8	1	0	155¹	131	2	69	53	11.8	2.90	114	.230	.317	14	.259	4	7	7	2	1.4
1944 Bos-A	1	1	.500	9	6	1	0	0	30	30	1	15	9	13.5	3.60	94	.261	.346	2	.182	1	-1	-1	-0	0.0
1945 Bos-A	0	1	.000	2	1	0	0	0	6¹	10	1	3	5	18.5	8.53	40	.333	.394	1	.500	0	-4	-4	-0	-0.2
Phi-N	5	4	.556	23	9	3	1	2	82²	80	3	40	36	13.2	3.81	101	.254	.340	8	.267	3	-0	0	1	0.4
1946 Phi-N	11	12	.478	30	24	12	1	2	173¹	169	6	90	65	13.5	3.53	97	.260	.350	25	.316	8	-2	-2	4	1.0
1947 Phi-N	4	15	.211	32	19	8	1	0	146²	155	6	69	54	13.9	4.60	87	.279	.361	12	.188	2	-9	-10	-1	-0.5
1948 Phi-N	0	2	.000	4	1	0	0	0	14¹	19	1	11	7	18.8	6.91	57	.317	.423	1	.167	0	-5	-5	-0	-0.3
Total 8	40	51	.440	161	99	43	4	7	771¹	744	24	397	304	13.4	3.90	93	.256	.347	83	.262	26	-23	-22	7	1.8

■ HOWIE JUDSON
Judson, Howard Kolls b: 2/16/26, Hebron, Ill.   BR/TR, 6'1", 195 lbs.   Deb: 4/22/48

YEAR TM/L	W	L	PCT	G	GS	CG	SH	SV	IP	H	HR	BB	SO	RAT	ERA	ERA+	OAV	OOB	BH	AVG	PB	PR	/A	PD	TPI
1948 Chi-A	4	5	.444	40	5	1	0	8	107¹	102	7	56	38	13.5	4.78	89	.255	.351	3	.103	-2	-6	-6	0	-0.7
1949 Chi-A	1	14	.067	26	12	3	0	1	108	114	13	70	36	15.4	4.58	91	.274	.380	2	.065	-3	-5	-5	0	-0.6
1950 Chi-A	2	3	.400	46	3	1	0	0	112	105	10	63	34	13.7	3.94	114	.252	.353	2	.100	-1	8	7	-1	0.5
1951 Chi-A	5	6	.455	27	14	3	0	1	121²	124	9	55	43	13.4	3.77	107	.264	.343	4	.121	-2	5	4	0	0.1
1952 Chi-A	0	1	.000	21	0	0	0	1	34	30	4	22	15	13.8	4.24	86	.244	.359	0	.000	-0	-2	-2	-0	-0.2
1953 Cin-N	0	1	.000	10	6	0	0	0	38²	58	8	11	11	16.1	5.59	78	.341	.381	1	.111	1	-6	-5	-0	-0.3
1954 Cin-N	5	7	.417	37	8	0	0	3	93¹	86	9	42	27	12.6	3.95	106	.251	.338	2	.083	-2	1	2	-1	0.0
Total 7	17	37	.315	207	48	8	0	14	615	619	60	319	204	13.9	4.29	98	.265	.356	14	.093	-9	-4	-6	-2	-1.2

■ KEN JUNGELS
Jungels, Kenneth Peter "Curly" b: 6/23/16, Aurora, Ill.   d: 9/9/75, West Bend, Wis.   BR/TR, 6'1", 180 lbs.   Deb: 9/15/37

YEAR TM/L	W	L	PCT	G	GS	CG	SH	SV	IP	H	HR	BB	SO	RAT	ERA	ERA+	OAV	OOB	BH	AVG	PB	PR	/A	PD	TPI
1937 Cle-A	0	0	—	2	0	0	0	0	3	3	0	1	0	12.0	0.00	—	.273	.333	0	—	0	2	2	0	0.1
1938 Cle-A	1	0	1.000	9	0	0	0	0	15¹	21	1	18	7	24.1	8.80	53	.339	.500	0	.000	-1	-7	-7	0	-0.6
1940 Cle-A	0	0	—	2	0	0	0	0	3¹	3	0	1	1	10.8	2.70	156	.273	.333	0	.000	-0	1	1	0	0.0
1941 Cle-A	0	0	—	6	0	0	0	0	13²	17	4	8	6	17.1	7.24	54	.293	.388	0	.000	-0	-5	-5	-0	-0.4
1942 Pit-N	0	0	—	6	0	0	0	0	13²	12	0	4	7	10.5	6.59	51	.235	.291	1	.500	-0	-5	-5	-0	-0.4
Total 5	1	0	1.000	25	0	0	0	0	49	56	5	32	21	16.7	6.80	60	.290	.399	1	.100	-1	-14	-15	-0	-1.3

■ MIKE JUREWICZ
Jurewicz, Michael Allen b: 9/20/45, Buffalo, N.Y.   BB/TL, 6'3", 205 lbs.   Deb: 9/07/65

YEAR TM/L	W	L	PCT	G	GS	CG	SH	SV	IP	H	HR	BB	SO	RAT	ERA	ERA+	OAV	OOB	BH	AVG	PB	PR	/A	PD	TPI
1965 NY-A	0	0	—	2	0	0	0	0	2¹	5	0	1	2	23.1	7.71	44	.417	.462	0	—	0	-1	-1	0	0.0

■ AL JURISICH
Jurisich, Alvin Joseph b: 8/25/21, New Orleans, La.   d: 11/3/81, New Orleans, La.   BR/TR, 6'2", 193 lbs.   Deb: 4/26/44

YEAR TM/L	W	L	PCT	G	GS	CG	SH	SV	IP	H	HR	BB	SO	RAT	ERA	ERA+	OAV	OOB	BH	AVG	PB	PR	/A	PD	TPI
1944 *StL-N	7	9	.438	30	14	5	2	1	130	102	7	65	53	11.9	3.39	104	.221	.323	8	.178	-1	3	2	-1	0.0
1945 StL-N	3	3	.500	27	6	1	0	0	71²	61	7	41	42	12.9	5.15	73	.232	.338	2	.087	-2	-11	-11	-1	-1.3
1946 Phi-N	4	3	.571	13	10	2	1	1	68¹	71	9	31	34	13.6	3.69	93	.263	.341	3	.130	-0	-2	-2	-1	-0.3
1947 Phi-N	1	7	.125	34	12	5	0	3	118¹	110	15	52	48	12.4	4.94	81	.258	.340	1	.032	-3	-12	-12	-1	-1.5
Total 4	15	22	.405	104	42	13	3	5	388¹	344	38	189	177	12.5	4.24	87	.242	.334	14	.115	-6	-21	-24	-5	-3.1

■ WALT JUSTIS
Justis, Walter Newton "Smoke" b: 8/17/1883, Moores Hill, Ind.   d: 10/4/41, Lawrenceburg, Ind.   5'11.5", 195 lbs.   Deb: 8/01/05

YEAR TM/L	W	L	PCT	G	GS	CG	SH	SV	IP	H	HR	BB	SO	RAT	ERA	ERA+	OAV	OOB	BH	AVG	PB	PR	/A	PD	TPI
1905 Det-A	0	0	—	2	0	0	0	0	3¹	4	0	6	0	27.0	8.10	34	.298	.515	0	—	0	-2	-2	-0	-0.1

■ HEROLD JUUL
Juul, Earl Herold b: 5/21/1893, Chicago, Ill.   d: 1/4/42, Chicago, Ill.   BR/TR, 5'9.5", 150 lbs.   Deb: 4/24/14

YEAR TM/L	W	L	PCT	G	GS	CG	SH	SV	IP	H	HR	BB	SO	RAT	ERA	ERA+	OAV	OOB	BH	AVG	PB	PR	/A	PD	TPI
1914 Bro-F	0	3	.000	9	3	0	0	0	29	26	0	31	16	18.0	6.21	51	.247	.423	2	.222	-0	-10	-10	-0	-0.9

■ HERB JUUL
Juul, Herbert Victor b: 2/2/1886, Chicago, Ill.   d: 11/14/28, Chicago, Ill.   BL/TL, 5'11", 150 lbs.   Deb: 7/11/11 ♦

YEAR TM/L	W	L	PCT	G	GS	CG	SH	SV	IP	H	HR	BB	SO	RAT	ERA	ERA+	OAV	OOB	BH	AVG	PB	PR	/A	PD	TPI
1911 Cin-N	0	0	—	1	0	0	0	0	4	3	0	4	2	15.8	4.50	74	.231	.412	0	.000	-0	-0	-1	-0	0.0

■ JIM KAAT
Kaat, James Lee b: 11/7/38, Zeeland, Mich.   BL/TL, 6'4.5", 205 lbs.   Deb: 8/02/59 C♦

YEAR TM/L	W	L	PCT	G	GS	CG	SH	SV	IP	H	HR	BB	SO	RAT	ERA	ERA+	OAV	OOB	BH	AVG	PB	PR	/A	PD	TPI
1959 Was-A	0	2	.000	3	2	0	0	0	5	7	1	4	2	23.4	12.60	31	.350	.500	0	.000	-0	-5	-5	0	-0.4
1960 Was-A	1	5	.167	13	9	0	0	0	50	48	8	31	25	15.1	5.58	70	.255	.375	2	.143	-1	-9	-9	0	-0.8
1961 Min-A	9	17	.346	36	29	8	1	0	200²	188	12	82	122	12.6	3.90	109	.248	.331	15	.238	4	3	8	3	1.5
1962 Min-A	18	14	.563	39	35	16	5	1	269	243	23	75	173	11.2	3.14	130	.243	.307	18	.180	3	25	28	6	**4.0**
1963 Min-A	10	10	.500	31	27	7	1	1	178¹	195	24	38	105	12.2	4.19	87	.274	.319	8	.131	-0	-11	-11	4	-0.6
1964 Min-A	17	11	.607	36	34	13	0	1	243	231	23	60	171	11.1	3.22	111	.251	.304	14	.169	5	11	10	3	1.9
1965 *Min-A	18	11	.621	45	42	7	2	2	264¹	267	25	63	154	11.4	2.83	126	.258	.304	23	.247	6	19	21	4	3.6
1966 Min-A	**25**	13	.658	41	41	**19**	3	0	304²	271	29	55	205	9.7	2.75	131	.235	.271	23	.195	4	23	**29**	0	3.8
1967 Min-A	16	13	.552	42	38	13	2	0	263¹	269	21	42	211	10.9	3.04	114	.260	.295	17	.172	3	6	12	1	1.9
1968 Min-A	14	12	.538	30	29	9	2	0	208	192	16	40	130	10.2	2.94	105	.243	.282	12	.156	0	1	3	0	0.4
1969 Min-A	14	13	.519	40	32	10	0	1	242¹	252	23	75	139	12.5	3.49	105	.265	.325	18	.207	6	3	4	-3	0.9
1970 *Min-A	14	10	.583	45	34	4	1	0	230¹	244	26	58	120	11.9	3.56	105	.273	.319	15	.197	4	4	7	2	1.0
1971 Min-A	13	14	.481	39	38	15	4	0	260¹	275	16	47	137	11.3	3.32	107	.268	.304	15	.161	-0	4	7	0	0.8
1972 Min-A	10	2	.833	15	15	5	0	0	113¹	94	6	20	64	9.1	2.06	155	.227	.263	13	.289	5	13	14	0	2.4
1973 Min-A	11	12	.478	29	28	7	2	0	181²	206	26	39	93	12.3	4.41	90	.282	.322	0	—	0	-12	-9	-1	-0.9
Chi-A	4	1	.800	7	7	3	1	0	42²	44	4	4	16	10.1	4.22	94	.260	.277	0	—	0	-2	-1	-1	-0.1
Yr	15	13	.536	36	35	10	3	0	224¹	250	30	43	109	11.8	4.37	90	.276	.309	0	—	0	-14	-10	-1	-1.0
1974 Chi-A	21	13	.618	42	39	15	3	0	277¹	263	18	63	142	10.8	2.92	128	.250	.296	0	.000	—	0	21	25	-1	2.5
1975 Chi-A	20	14	.588	43	41	12	1	0	303²	321	20	77	142	12.1	3.11	124	.274	.324	0	—	0	22	26	-1	2.6
1976 *Phi-N	12	14	.462	38	35	7	1	0	227²	241	21	32	83	10.8	3.48	102	.274	.300	14	.177	2	1	2	-2	0.2
1977 Phi-N	6	11	.353	35	27	2	0	0	160¹	211	20	40	55	14.2	5.39	74	.320	.361	10	.189	1	-26	-25	-1	-2.4
1978 Phi-N	8	5	.615	26	24	2	1	0	140¹	150	9	32	48	12.0	4.10	87	.280	.326	7	.146	-1	-8	-8	-1	-1.0
1979 Phi-N	1	0	1.000	3	1	0	0	0	8¹	9	1	5	2	15.1	4.32	89	.281	.378	0	.000	-0	-1	-0	0	0.0
NY-A	2	3	.400	40	1	0	0	2	58¹	64	4	14	23	12.3	3.86	106	.287	.335	0	—	0	2	1	-1	0.1
1980 NY-A	0	1	.000	4	0	0	0	0	5	8	0	4	1	21.6	7.20	54	.381	.480	0	—	0	-2	-2	1	0.0
StL-N	8	7	.533	49	14	6	1	4	129²	140	6	33	36	12.0	3.82	97	.281	.325	5	.143	-1	-3	-1	1	-0.1
1981 StL-N	6	6	.500	41	1	0	0	4	53	60	2	17	8	13.1	3.40	105	.299	.353	3	.375	1	1	1	0	0.3
1982 *StL-N	5	3	.625	62	2	0	0	2	75	79	6	23	35	12.5	4.08	89	.276	.334	0	.000	-1	-4	-4	1	-0.4
1983 StL-N	0	0	—	24	0	0	0	0	34²	48	5	11	9	15.1	3.89	93	.327	.369	0	.000	-0	-1	-1	0	-0.1
Total 25	283	237	.544	898	625	180	31	18	4530¹	4620	395	1083	2461	11.6	3.45	107	.264	.311	232	.185	43	74	119	12	21.1

■ GEORGE KAHLER
Kahler, George Runnells "Krum" b: 9/6/1889, Athens, Ohio   d: 2/7/24, Battle Creek, Va.   BR/TR, 6', 183 lbs.   Deb: 8/13/10

YEAR TM/L	W	L	PCT	G	GS	CG	SH	SV	IP	H	HR	BB	SO	RAT	ERA	ERA+	OAV	OOB	BH	AVG	PB	PR	/A	PD	TPI
1910 Cle-A	6	4	.600	12	12	8	2	0	95¹	80	0	46	38	12.3	1.60	161	.237	.335	5	.143	-2	10	10	-1	0.9
1911 Cle-A	9	8	.529	30	17	10	0	1	154¹	153	1	66	97	13.5	3.27	105	.270	.360	9	.167	-2	1	3	-1	0.0
1912 Cle-A	12	19	.387	41	32	17	3	1	246¹	263	1	121	104	14.4	3.69	92	.291	.382	9	.112	-6	-10	-8	-4	-1.5
1913 Cle-A	5	11	.313	24	15	5	0	0	117²	118	1	32	43	11.8	3.14	97	.266	.322	2	.061	-3	-3	-1	-3	-0.7
1914 Cle-A	0	1	.000	2	1	1	0	0	14	17	0	7	3	15.4	3.86	75	.309	.387	0	—	0	-2	-2	-0	-0.1
Total 5	32	43	.427	109	77	41	5	2	627²	631	3	272	285	13.4	3.17	101	.274	.358	25	.121	-14	-4	3	-9	-1.4

■ DON KAINER
Kainer, Donald Wayne b: 9/3/55, Houston, Tex.   BR/TR, 6'3", 205 lbs.   Deb: 9/06/80

YEAR TM/L	W	L	PCT	G	GS	CG	SH	SV	IP	H	HR	BB	SO	RAT	ERA	ERA+	OAV	OOB	BH	AVG	PB	PR	/A	PD	TPI
1980 Tex-A	0	0	—	4	3	0	0	0	20	22	0	9	10	15.3	1.80	216	.289	.386	0	—	0	5	5	1	0.7

■ DON KAISER
Kaiser, Clyde Donald "Tiger" b: 2/3/35, Byng, Okla.   BR/TR, 6'5", 195 lbs.   Deb: 7/20/55

YEAR TM/L	W	L	PCT	G	GS	CG	SH	SV	IP	H	HR	BB	SO	RAT	ERA	ERA+	OAV	OOB	BH	AVG	PB	PR	/A	PD	TPI
1955 Chi-N	0	0	—	11	0	0	0	0	18¹	20	2	5	11	12.8	5.40	76	.274	.329	0	.000	-0	-3	-3	-0	-0.2
1956 Chi-N	4	9	.308	27	22	5	1	0	150¹	144	15	52	74	11.8	3.59	105	.247	.310	2	.043	-5	3	3	0	-0.1

YEAR	TM/L	W	L	PCT	G	GS	CG	SH	SV	IP	H	HR	BB	SO	RAT	ERA	ERA+	OAV	OOB	BH	AVG	PB	PR	/A	PD	TPI
1957	Chi-N	2	6	.250	20	13	1	0	0	72	91	4	28	23	14.9	5.00	77	.316	.377	2	.105	-1	-9	-9	2	-0.7
Total	3	6	15	.286	58	35	6	1	0	240²	255	21	85	108	12.8	4.15	92	.270	.332	4	.059	-6	-9	-9	2	-1.0

■ JEFF KAISER
Kaiser, Jeffrey Patrick b: 7/24/60, Wyandotte, Mich. BR/TL, 6'3", 195 lbs. Deb: 4/11/85

YEAR	TM/L	W	L	PCT	G	GS	CG	SH	SV	IP	H	HR	BB	SO	RAT	ERA	ERA+	OAV	OOB	BH	AVG	PB	PR	/A	PD	TPI
1985	Oak-A	0	0	—	15	0	0	0	0	16²	25	6	20	10	24.8	14.58	26	.342	.489	0	—	0	-19	-20	1	-1.7
1987	Cle-A	0	0	—	2	0	0	0	0	3¹	4	1	3	2	21.6	16.20	28	.286	.444	0	—	0	-4	-4	0	-0.3
1988	Cle-A	0	0	—	3	0	0	0	0	2²	2	0	1	0	10.1	0.00	—	.286	.375	0	—	0	1	1	0	0.2
1989	Cle-A	0	1	.000	6	0	0	0	0	3²	5	1	5	4	24.5	7.36	54	.313	.476	0	—	0	-1	-1	0	-0.1
1990	Cle-A	0	0	—	5	0	0	0	0	12²	16	2	7	9	16.3	3.55	112	.308	.390	0	—	0	0	1	0	0.1
Total	5	0	1	.000	31	0	0	0	0	39	52	10	36	25	20.8	9.46	42	.321	.450	0	—	0	-23	-24	1	-1.8

■ BOB KAISER
Kaiser, Robert Thomas b: 4/29/50, Cincinnati, Ohio BB/TL, 5'10", 175 lbs. Deb: 9/03/71

YEAR	TM/L	W	L	PCT	G	GS	CG	SH	SV	IP	H	HR	BB	SO	RAT	ERA	ERA+	OAV	OOB	BH	AVG	PB	PR	/A	PD	TPI
1971	Cle-A	0	0	—	5	0	0	0	0	6	8	2	3	4	19.5	4.50	85	.333	.448	0	—	0	-1	-0	0	0.0

■ GEORGE KAISERLING
Kaiserling, George b: 5/12/1893, Steubenville, Ohio d: 3/2/18, Steubenville, Ohio BR/TR, 6', 175 lbs. Deb: 4/20/14

YEAR	TM/L	W	L	PCT	G	GS	CG	SH	SV	IP	H	HR	BB	SO	RAT	ERA	ERA+	OAV	OOB	BH	AVG	PB	PR	/A	PD	TPI
1914	Ind-F	17	10	.630	37	33	20	1	0	275¹	288	8	72	75	12.3	3.11	112	.274	.330	11	.112	-6	3	11	-2	0.5
1915	New-F	15	15	.500	41	29	16	5	2	261¹	246	1	73	75	11.3	2.24	127	.257	.316	12	.152	-2	23	18	-0	1.6
Total	2	32	25	.561	78	62	36	6	2	536²	534	9	145	150	11.8	2.68	118	.266	.323	23	.130	-7	26	28	-2	2.1

■ BILL KALFASS
Kalfass, William Philip "Lefty" b: 3/3/16, New York, N.Y. d: 9/8/68, Brooklyn, N.Y. BR/TL, 6'3.5", 190 lbs. Deb: 9/15/37

YEAR	TM/L	W	L	PCT	G	GS	CG	SH	SV	IP	H	HR	BB	SO	RAT	ERA	ERA+	OAV	OOB	BH	AVG	PB	PR	/A	PD	TPI
1937	Phi-A	1	0	1.000	3	1	1	0	0	12	10	0	10	9	15.0	3.00	157	.233	.377	0	.000	-1	2	2	-0	0.1

■ RUDY KALLIO
Kallio, Rudolph b: 12/14/1892, Portland, Ore. d: 4/6/79, Newport, Ore. BR/TR, 5'10", 160 lbs. Deb: 4/25/18

YEAR	TM/L	W	L	PCT	G	GS	CG	SH	SV	IP	H	HR	BB	SO	RAT	ERA	ERA+	OAV	OOB	BH	AVG	PB	PR	/A	PD	TPI
1918	Det-A	8	14	.364	30	22	10	2	0	181¹	178	0	76	70	12.7	3.62	73	.261	.336	9	.161	-1	-17	-19	-1	-2.2
1919	Det-A	0	0	—	12	1	0	0	1	22¹	28	0	8	3	14.9	5.64	57	.326	.389	0	.000	-1	-6	-6	-0	-0.6
1925	Bos-A	1	4	.200	7	4	0	0	0	18²	28	0	9	2	18.3	7.71	59	.364	.437	2	.333	0	-7	-7	0	-0.5
Total	3	9	18	.333	49	27	10	2	1	222¹	234	0	93	75	13.4	4.17	69	.277	.351	11	.167	-1	-30	-32	-1	-3.3

■ BOB KAMMEYER
Kammeyer, Robert Lynn b: 12/2/50, Kansas City, Kan. BR/TR, 6'4", 210 lbs. Deb: 7/03/78

YEAR	TM/L	W	L	PCT	G	GS	CG	SH	SV	IP	H	HR	BB	SO	RAT	ERA	ERA+	OAV	OOB	BH	AVG	PB	PR	/A	PD	TPI
1978	NY-A	0	0	—	7	0	0	0	0	21²	24	1	6	11	13.3	5.82	62	.276	.337	0	—	0	-5	-5	1	-0.4
1979	NY-A	0	0	—	1	0	0	0	0	0	7	2	0	0	—	∞	—	1.000	1.000	0	—	0	-8	-8	0	-0.5
Total	2	0	0	—	8	0	0	0	0	21²	31	3	6	11	16.6	9.14	40	.330	.388	0	—	0	-13	-13	1	-0.9

■ IKE KAMP
Kamp, Alphonse Francis b: 9/5/1900, Roxbury, Mass. d: 2/25/55, Boston, Mass. BB/TL, 6', 170 lbs. Deb: 9/16/24

YEAR	TM/L	W	L	PCT	G	GS	CG	SH	SV	IP	H	HR	BB	SO	RAT	ERA	ERA+	OAV	OOB	BH	AVG	PB	PR	/A	PD	TPI
1924	Bos-N	0	1	.000	1	1	0	0	0	7	9	0	5	4	18.0	5.14	74	.360	.467	0	.000	-0	-1	-1	0	0.0
1925	Bos-N	2	4	.333	24	4	1	0	0	58¹	68	0	35	20	15.9	5.09	79	.301	.395	2	.167	-0	-5	-7	0	-0.6
Total	2	2	5	.286	25	5	1	0	0	65¹	77	0	40	24	16.1	5.10	78	.307	.402	2	.154	-0	-6	-8	0	-0.6

■ HARRY KANE
Kane, Harry "Klondike" (b: Harry Cohen) b: 7/27/1883, Hamburg, Ark. d: 9/15/32, Portland, Ore. BL/TL, Deb: 8/08/02

YEAR	TM/L	W	L	PCT	G	GS	CG	SH	SV	IP	H	HR	BB	SO	RAT	ERA	ERA+	OAV	OOB	BH	AVG	PB	PR	/A	PD	TPI
1902	StL-A	0	1	.000	4	1	1	0	0	23	34	2	16	7	19.6	5.48	64	.343	.434	1	.111	-1	-5	-5	0	-0.4
1903	Det-A	0	2	.000	3	3	2	0	0	18	26	0	8	10	17.0	8.50	34	.336	.398	1	.143	-0	-11	-11	-1	-0.9
1905	Phi-N	1	1	.500	2	2	2	1	0	17	12	0	8	12	10.6	1.59	184	.203	.299	1	.167	-0	3	3	0	0.2
1906	Phi-N	1	3	.250	6	3	2	0	0	28	28	0	18	14	15.8	3.86	68	.255	.374	0	.000	-1	-4	-4	0	-0.4
Total	4	2	7	.222	15	9	7	1	0	86	100	2	50	43	16.0	4.81	62	.289	.384	3	.100	-2	-17	-17	-1	-1.5

■ ERV KANTLEHNER
Kantlehner, Erving Leslie "Peanuts" b: 7/31/1892, San Jose, Cal. d: 2/3/90, Santa Barbara, Cal. BL/TL, 6', 190 lbs. Deb: 4/17/14

YEAR	TM/L	W	L	PCT	G	GS	CG	SH	SV	IP	H	HR	BB	SO	RAT	ERA	ERA+	OAV	OOB	BH	AVG	PB	PR	/A	PD	TPI
1914	Pit-N	3	2	.600	21	5	3	2	0	67	51	0	39	26	12.5	3.09	86	.218	.337	1	.067	-0	-2	-3	-0	-0.3
1915	Pit-N	5	12	.294	29	18	10	1	3	163	135	1	58	64	10.9	2.26	121	.230	.304	15	.288	3	9	8	1	1.4
1916	Pit-N	5	15	.250	34	21	7	2	2	165	151	1	57	49	11.6	3.16	85	.249	.317	8	.174	-0	-10	-9	2	-0.7
	Phi-N	0	0	—	3	0	0	0	0	4	7	0	3	2	22.5	9.00	29	.500	.588	0	—	0	-3	-3	0	-0.2
	Yr	5	15	.250	37	21	7	2	2	169	158	1	60	51	11.6	3.30	81	.253	.318	2	.043	-0	-13	-12	2	-0.9
Total	3	13	29	.310	87	44	20	5	5	399	344	2	157	141	11.5	2.84	95	.239	.318	24	.212	2	-6	-6	3	0.2

■ PAUL KARDOW
Kardow, Paul Otto "Tex" b: 9/19/15, Humble, Tex. d: 4/27/68, San Antonio, Tex. BR/TR, 6'6", 210 lbs. Deb: 7/01/36

YEAR	TM/L	W	L	PCT	G	GS	CG	SH	SV	IP	H	HR	BB	SO	RAT	ERA	ERA+	OAV	OOB	BH	AVG	PB	PR	/A	PD	TPI
1936	Cle-A	0	0	—	2	0	0	0	0	2	1	0	2	0	13.5	4.50	112	.167	.375	0	—	0	0	0	0	0.0

■ ED KARGER
Karger, Edwin "Loose" b: 5/6/1883, San Angelo, Tex. d: 9/9/57, Delta, Colo. BR/TL, 5'11", 185 lbs. Deb: 4/15/06

YEAR	TM/L	W	L	PCT	G	GS	CG	SH	SV	IP	H	HR	BB	SO	RAT	ERA	ERA+	OAV	OOB	BH	AVG	PB	PR	/A	PD	TPI
1906	Pit-N	2	3	.400	6	2	0	0	0	28	21	0	9	8	10.3	1.93	139	.204	.281	1	.091	-1	2	2	1	0.3
	StL-N	5	16	.238	25	20	17	0	1	191²	193	0	43	73	11.4	2.72	96	.271	.319	17	.233	4	-2	-2	4	0.5
	Yr	7	19	.269	31	22	17	0	1	219²	214	0	52	81	11.2	2.62	100	.262	.312	1	.012	3	0	0	5	0.8
1907	StL-N	15	19	.441	38	31	28	6	1	310	251	2	64	132	9.4	2.03	123	.218	.265	20	.179	1	15	16	4	2.5
1908	StL-N	4	9	.308	22	15	9	1	0	141¹	148	5	50	34	12.7	3.06	77	.260	.322	13	.241	2	-11	-11	-0	-1.0
1909	Cin-N	1	3	.250	9	5	1	0	0	34¹	26	0	30	8	15.2	4.46	58	.217	.382	3	.273	2	-7	-7	0	-0.5
	Bos-A	5	2	.714	12	6	3	0	0	68	71	0	22	17	12.7	3.18	79	.273	.337	1	.125	-0	-5	-5	0	-0.5
1910	Bos-A	11	7	.611	27	25	16	1	1	183¹	162	5	53	81	10.8	3.19	80	.230	.289	20	.294	6	-14	-13	-2	-0.9
1911	Bos-A	5	8	.385	25	18	6	1	0	131	134	4	42	57	12.4	3.37	97	.272	.334	11	.234	3	-0	-1	0	0.2
Total	6	48	67	.417	164	122	80	9	3	1087²	1006	12	313	410	11.2	2.79	94	.245	.304	88	.220	17	-22	-21	7	0.6

■ ANDY KARL
Karl, Anton Andrew b: 4/8/14, Mt.Vernon, N.Y. d: 4/8/89, San Diego, Cal. BR/TR, 6'1.5", 175 lbs. Deb: 4/24/43

YEAR	TM/L	W	L	PCT	G	GS	CG	SH	SV	IP	H	HR	BB	SO	RAT	ERA	ERA+	OAV	OOB	BH	AVG	PB	PR	/A	PD	TPI
1943	Bos-A	1	1	.500	11	0	0	0	1	26	31	0	13	6	15.2	3.46	96	.310	.389	2	.286	0	-0	-0	1	0.1
	Phi-N	1	2	.333	9	2	0	0	0	26²	44	0	11	4	18.6	7.09	48	.383	.437	2	.250	1	-11	-11	0	-0.9
1944	Phi-N	3	2	.600	38	0	0	0	2	89	76	1	21	26	9.9	2.33	155	.237	.287	3	.200	1	**13**	13	1	1.5
1945	Phi-N	8	8	.500	67	2	1	0	15	180²	175	7	50	51	11.4	2.99	128	.253	.306	7	.143	-2	**16**	17	1	1.6
1946	Phi-N	3	7	.300	39	0	0	0	6	65¹	84	6	22	15	14.7	4.96	69	.321	.375	1	.100	-0	-11	-11	1	-1.0
1947	Bos-N	2	3	.400	27	0	0	0	3	35	41	2	13	5	13.9	3.86	101	.318	.380	1	.167	-0	1	0	2	0.2
Total	5	18	23	.439	191	4	1	0	26	422²	451	16	130	107	12.5	3.51	104	.279	.334	16	.168	-0	7	7	6	1.5

■ BILL KARNS
Karns, William Arthur b: Chicago, Ill. TL, Deb: 8/14/01

YEAR	TM/L	W	L	PCT	G	GS	CG	SH	SV	IP	H	HR	BB	SO	RAT	ERA	ERA+	OAV	OOB	BH	AVG	PB	PR	/A	PD	TPI
1901	Bal-A	1	0	1.000	3	1	1	0	0	17	30	0	9	5	20.6	6.35	61	.379	.443	1	.143	-1	-5	-5	-0	-0.4

■ HERB KARPEL
Karpel, Herbert "Lefty" b: 12/27/17, Brooklyn, N.Y. BL/TL, 5'9.5", 180 lbs. Deb: 4/19/46

YEAR	TM/L	W	L	PCT	G	GS	CG	SH	SV	IP	H	HR	BB	SO	RAT	ERA	ERA+	OAV	OOB	BH	AVG	PB	PR	/A	PD	TPI
1946	NY-A	0	0	—	2	0	0	0	0	1²	4	0	0	0	21.6	10.80	32	.500	.500	0	—	0	-1	-1	0	0.0

■ BENN KARR
Karr, Benjamin Joyce "Baldy" b: 11/28/1893, Mt.Pleasant, Miss. d: 12/8/68, Memphis, Tenn. BL/TR, 6', 175 lbs. Deb: 4/20/20

YEAR	TM/L	W	L	PCT	G	GS	CG	SH	SV	IP	H	HR	BB	SO	RAT	ERA	ERA+	OAV	OOB	BH	AVG	PB	PR	/A	PD	TPI
1920	Bos-A	3	8	.273	26	2	0	0	1	91²	109	3	24	21	13.2	4.81	76	.304	.349	5	.280	5	-10	-12	-1	-1.0
1921	Bos-A	8	7	.533	26	7	5	0	0	117²	123	8	38	37	12.4	3.67	115	.283	.342	16	.258	-0	8	7	-0	0.7
1922	Bos-A	5	12	.294	41	13	7	0	1	183¹	212	10	45	41	12.9	4.47	92	.302	.348	21	.214	-1	-9	-7	-0	-0.7
1925	Cle-A	11	12	.478	32	24	12	1	0	197²	248	8	80	41	15.2	4.78	92	.317	.385	24	.261	4	-8	-8	2	-0.1
1926	Cle-A	5	6	.455	30	7	4	0	1	113¹	137	9	41	23	14.6	5.00	81	.291	.355	10	.222	2	-12	-12	1	-0.8
1927	Cle-A	3	3	.500	22	5	1	0	2	76²	92	5	32	17	14.7	5.05	83	.315	.385	20	.200	1	-8	-7	2	-0.3
Total	6	35	48	.422	177	58	29	1	5	780¹	921	43	260	180	13.9	4.60	90	.303	.362	96	.245	12	-40	-39	3	-2.2

■ JACK KATOLL
Katoll, John "Big Jack" b: 6/24/1872, Germany d: 6/18/55, Hartland, Ill. BR/TR, 5'11", 195 lbs. Deb: 9/09/1898

YEAR	TM/L	W	L	PCT	G	GS	CG	SH	SV	IP	H	HR	BB	SO	RAT	ERA	ERA+	OAV	OOB	BH	AVG	PB	PR	/A	PD	TPI
1898	Chi-N	0	1	.000	2	1	1	0	0	11	8	0	1	1	7.4	0.82	438	.202	.222	0	.000	-1	3	3	-0	0.3
1899	Chi-N	1	1	.500	2	2	2	0	0	18	17	0	4	1	10.5	6.00	62	.249	.291	0	.000	-0	-4	-5	-0	-0.3
1901	Chi-A	11	10	.524	27	25	19	0	0	208	231	3	53	59	12.3	2.81	124	.278	.321	10	.125	-4	20	15	2	1.2

YEAR TM/L	W	L	PCT	G	GS	CG	SH	SV	IP	H	HR	BB	SO	RAT	ERA	ERA+	OAV	OOB	BH	AVG	PB	PR	/A	PD	TPI
1902 Chi-A	0	0	—	1	0	0	0	0	1	1	0	0	2	9.0	0.00	—	.261	.261	0	.000	-0	0	0	0	0.0
Bal-A	5	10	.333	15	13	13	0	0	123	175	5	32	25	15.1	4.02	94	.334	.373	10	.175	-0	-6	-3	4	0.1
Yr	5	10	.333	16	13	13	0	0	124	176	5	32	27	15.1	3.99	94	.334	.372	8	.138	-0	-6	-3	4	0.1
Total 4	17	22	.436	47	41	35	0	0	361	432	8	90	90	13.0	3.32	109	.295	.335	20	.134	-6	13	11	6	1.3

■ BOB KATZ
Katz, Robert Clyde   b: 1/30/11, Lancaster, Pa.   d: 12/14/62, St.Joseph, Mich.   BR/TR, 5'11.5", 190 lbs.   Deb: 5/12/44

YEAR TM/L	W	L	PCT	G	GS	CG	SH	SV	IP	H	HR	BB	SO	RAT	ERA	ERA+	OAV	OOB	BH	AVG	PB	PR	/A	PD	TPI
1944 Cin-N	0	1	.000	6	2	0	0	0	18^1	17	0	7	4	11.8	3.93	89	.254	.324	0	.000	-1	-1	-1	1	0.0

■ CURT KAUFMAN
Kaufman, Curt Gerrard   b: 7/19/57, Omaha, Neb.   BR/TR, 6'2", 175 lbs.   Deb: 9/10/82

YEAR TM/L	W	L	PCT	G	GS	CG	SH	SV	IP	H	HR	BB	SO	RAT	ERA	ERA+	OAV	OOB	BH	AVG	PB	PR	/A	PD	TPI
1982 NY-A	1	0	1.000	7	0	0	0	0	8^2	9	2	6	1	15.6	5.19	77	.265	.375	0	—	0	-1	-1	-0	0.1
1983 NY-A	0	0	—	4	0	0	0	0	8^2	10	0	4	8	14.5	3.12	125	.303	.378	0	—	0	1	1	0	0.1
1984 Cal-A	2	3	.400	29	1	0	0	1	69	68	13	20	41	11.5	4.57	87	.254	.306	0	—	0	-4	-5	0	-0.3
Total 3	3	3	.500	40	1	0	0	1	86^1	87	15	30	50	12.2	4.48	88	.260	.321	0	—	0	-5	-5	0	-0.2

■ TONY KAUFMANN
Kaufmann, Anthony Charles   b: 12/16/1900, Chicago, Ill.   d: 6/4/82, Elgin, Ill.   BR/TR, 5'11", 165 lbs.   Deb: 9/23/21   C♦

YEAR TM/L	W	L	PCT	G	GS	CG	SH	SV	IP	H	HR	BB	SO	RAT	ERA	ERA+	OAV	OOB	BH	AVG	PB	PR	/A	PD	TPI
1921 Chi-N	1	0	1.000	2	1	1	0	0	13	12	0	3	6	10.4	4.15	92	.240	.283	2	.400	1	-1	-0	-0	0.0
1922 Chi-N	7	13	.350	37	9	4	1	3	153	161	15	57	45	13.1	4.06	103	.273	.343	9	.200	1	1	2	-1	0.3
1923 Chi-N	14	10	.583	33	24	18	2	3	206^1	209	14	67	72	12.5	3.10	129	.264	.330	16	.216	3	21	21	-1	2.2
1924 Chi-N	16	11	.593	34	26	16	3	0	208^1	218	21	66	79	12.4	4.02	97	.272	.330	24	.316	6	-3	-3	-2	0.1
1925 Chi-N	13	13	.500	31	23	14	2	2	196	221	9	77	49	14.0	4.50	96	.292	.363	15	.192	1	-5	-4	0	-0.1
1926 Chi-N	9	7	.563	26	21	14	1	2	169^2	169	6	44	52	11.6	3.02	127	.262	.316	15	.250	2	15	15	-1	1.6
1927 Chi-N	3	3	.500	9	6	3	0	0	53^1	75	8	19	21	16.5	6.41	64	.338	.400	5	.313	3	-15	-15	2	-0.9
Phi-N	0	3	.000	5	5	1	0	0	18^2	37	2	8	4	21.7	10.61	39	.425	.474	1	.143	0	-14	-13	-0	-1.1
StL-N	0	0	—	1	0	0	0	0	0^1	4	0	1	0	135.0	81.00	5	1.000	1.000	0	—	0	-3	-3	0	-0.1
Yr	3	6	.333	15	11	4	0	0	72^1	116	10	28	25	17.9	7.84	50	.366	.417	4	.174	3	-32	-31	1	-2.1
1928 StL-N	0	0	—	4	1	0	0	0	4^2	8	1	4	2	25.1	9.64	41	.444	.565	0	—	0	-3	-3	0	-0.2
1930 StL-N	0	1	.000	2	1	0	0	0	10^1	15	2	4	2	16.5	7.84	64	.357	.413	1	.333	0	-3	-3	-0	-0.2
1931 StL-N	1	1	.500	15	1	0	0	1	49	65	3	17	13	15.2	6.06	65	.319	.374	2	.111	-1	-12	-12	0	-1.1
1935 StL-N	0	0	—	3	0	0	0	0	3^2	4	0	1	0	12.3	2.45	167	.286	.333	0	—	0	1	1	0	0.1
Total 11	64	62	.508	202	118	71	9	12	1086^1	1198	81	368	345	13.3	4.18	97	.284	.347	91	.220	17	-22	-17	-3	0.6

■ STEVE KEALEY
Kealey, Steven William   b: 5/13/47, Torrance, Cal.   BR/TR, 6', 185 lbs.   Deb: 9/09/68

YEAR TM/L	W	L	PCT	G	GS	CG	SH	SV	IP	H	HR	BB	SO	RAT	ERA	ERA+	OAV	OOB	BH	AVG	PB	PR	/A	PD	TPI
1968 Cal-A	0	1	.000	6	0	0	0	0	10	10	0	5	4	13.5	2.70	108	.256	.341	0	—	0	0	0	-0	0.0
1969 Cal-A	2	0	1.000	15	3	1	1	0	36^2	48	4	13	17	15.2	3.93	89	.322	.380	0	.000	-1	-1	-2	-1	-0.3
1970 Cal-A	1	0	1.000	17	0	0	0	1	21^2	19	2	6	14	10.4	4.15	87	.260	.316	1	.250	-0	-1	-1	-1	-0.1
1971 Chi-A	2	2	.500	54	1	0	0	6	77^1	69	10	26	50	11.1	3.84	93	.239	.302	2	.200	1	-3	-2	-0	-0.1
1972 Chi-A	3	2	.600	40	0	0	0	4	57^1	50	4	12	37	9.7	3.30	95	.234	.274	0	—	-0	-2	-1	-1	-0.1
1973 Chi-A	0	0	—	7	0	0	0	0	11^1	23	2	7	4	23.8	15.09	26	.418	.484	0	—	0	-14	-14	-0	-1.2
Total 6	8	5	.615	139	4	1	1	11	214^1	219	22	69	126	12.1	4.28	80	.267	.325	3	.115	-0	-21	-20	-3	-1.8

■ ED KEAS
Keas, Edward James   b: 2/2/1863, Dubuque, Iowa   d: 1/12/40, Dubuque, Iowa   Deb: 8/25/1888

YEAR TM/L	W	L	PCT	G	GS	CG	SH	SV	IP	H	HR	BB	SO	RAT	ERA	ERA+	OAV	OOB	BH	AVG	PB	PR	/A	PD	TPI
1888 Cle-a	3	3	.500	6	6	6	0	0	51	53	1	12	18	11.5	2.29	136	.258	.299	2	.087	-2	4	5	1	0.3

■ RAY KEATING
Keating, Raymond Herbert   b: 7/21/1891, Bridgeport, Conn.   d: 12/28/63, Sacramento, Cal.   BR/TR, 5'11", 185 lbs.   Deb: 9/12/12

YEAR TM/L	W	L	PCT	G	GS	CG	SH	SV	IP	H	HR	BB	SO	RAT	ERA	ERA+	OAV	OOB	BH	AVG	PB	PR	/A	PD	TPI
1912 NY-A	0	3	.000	6	5	3	0	0	35^2	36	0	18	21	13.9	5.80	62	.265	.355	6	.375	2	-10	-9	0	-0.5
1913 NY-A	6	12	.333	28	21	9	2	0	151^1	147	3	51	83	11.9	3.21	93	.253	.316	3	.070	-3	-5	-4	-2	-0.8
1914 NY-A	7	11	.389	34	25	14	0	1	210	198	1	67	109	11.6	2.96	93	.253	.316	12	.169	-0	-5	-5	2	-0.2
1915 NY-A	3	6	.333	11	10	8	1	0	79^1	66	3	45	37	12.9	3.63	81	.228	.337	4	.154	-1	-6	-6	1	-0.5
1916 NY-A	5	6	.455	34	14	6	0	0	91	91	4	37	35	12.9	3.07	94	.272	.349	7	.241	1	-2	-2	0	0.1
1918 NY-A	2	2	.500	15	6	1	0	0	48^1	39	0	30	16	13.2	3.91	72	.238	.362	6	.188	-0	-6	-6	0	-0.1
1919 Bos-N	7	11	.389	22	13	9	1	0	136	129	2	45	48	11.6	2.98	96	.261	.325	7	.152	-1	-1	-2	1	-0.1
Total 7	30	51	.370	130	92	50	4	1	751^2	706	13	293	349	12.2	3.29	88	.254	.329	42	.170	-2	-35	-33	4	-2.5

■ BOB KEATING
Keating, Robert M.   b: 9/22/1862, Springfield, Mass.   d: 1/19/22, Springfield, Mass.   BL/TL, 6'4",   Deb: 8/27/1887

YEAR TM/L	W	L	PCT	G	GS	CG	SH	SV	IP	H	HR	BB	SO	RAT	ERA	ERA+	OAV	OOB	BH	AVG	PB	PR	/A	PD	TPI
1887 Bal-a	0	1	.000	1	1	1	0	0	9	16	0	6	0	22.0	11.00	37	.373	.450	1	.250	-0	-7	-7	0	-0.3

■ CACTUS KECK
Keck, Frank Joseph   b: 1/13/1899, St.Louis, Mo.   d: 2/6/81, Kirkwood, Mo.   BR/TR, 5'11", 170 lbs.   Deb: 5/26/22

YEAR TM/L	W	L	PCT	G	GS	CG	SH	SV	IP	H	HR	BB	SO	RAT	ERA	ERA+	OAV	OOB	BH	AVG	PB	PR	/A	PD	TPI
1922 Cin-N	7	6	.538	27	15	5	1	1	131	138	4	29	27	11.8	3.37	119	.276	.322	7	.159	-1	11	9	-3	0.4
1923 Cin-N	3	6	.333	35	6	1	0	2	87	84	5	32	16	12.3	3.72	104	.254	.325	1	.059	-1	3	1	1	0.1
Total 2	10	12	.455	62	21	6	1	3	218	222	9	61	43	12.0	3.51	112	.267	.323	8	.131	-2	13	10	-2	0.5

■ DAVE KEEFE
Keefe, David Edwin   b: 1/9/1897, Williston, Vt.   d: 2/4/78, Kansas City, Mo.   BL/TR, 5'9", 165 lbs.   Deb: 4/21/17   C

YEAR TM/L	W	L	PCT	G	GS	CG	SH	SV	IP	H	HR	BB	SO	RAT	ERA	ERA+	OAV	OOB	BH	AVG	PB	PR	/A	PD	TPI
1917 Phi-A	1	0	1.000	3	0	0	0	0	5	5	0	4	1	16.2	1.80	153	.278	.409	0	.000	-0	0	1	0	0.1
1919 Phi-A	0	1	.000	1	1	0	0	0	9	8	0	3	5	11.0	4.00	86	.242	.306	0	.000	-0	-1	-1	0	0.0
1920 Phi-A	6	7	.462	31	13	7	1	0	130^1	129	2	30	41	11.4	2.97	136	.262	.313	10	.250	-0	12	15	1	1.6
1921 Phi-A	2	9	.182	44	12	4	0	1	173	214	19	64	68	14.7	4.68	95	.311	.374	10	.175	-3	-8	-4	-2	-0.8
1922 Cle-A	0	0	—	18	1	0	0	0	36^1	47	2	12	11	14.6	6.19	65	.333	.386	2	.333	1	-9	-9	0	-0.7
Total 5	9	17	.346	97	27	12	1	1	353^2	403	23	113	126	13.4	4.15	101	.294	.352	22	.206	-3	-5	2	-1	0.2

■ GEORGE KEEFE
Keefe, George W.   b: 1/7/1867, Washington, D.C.   d: 8/24/35, Washington, D.C.   BL/TL, 5'9", 168 lbs.   Deb: 7/30/1886

YEAR TM/L	W	L	PCT	G	GS	CG	SH	SV	IP	H	HR	BB	SO	RAT	ERA	ERA+	OAV	OOB	BH	AVG	PB	PR	/A	PD	TPI
1886 Was-N	0	3	.000	4	4	4	0	0	31^1	28	0	15	5	12.4	5.17	63	.229	.314	0	.000	-2	-6	-7	-1	-0.7
1887 Was-N	0	1	.000	1	1	1	0	0	8	16	1	4	0	22.5	9.00	45	.404	.459	0	.000	-1	-4	-4	-0	-0.3
1888 Was-N	6	7	.462	13	13	13	1	0	114	87	2	43	52	10.3	2.84	98	.204	.277	9	.214	1	-0	-1	1	0.1
1889 Was-N	4	18	.308	30	27	24	0	0	230	266	6	143	90	16.0	5.13	77	.280	.375	16	.163	-2	-28	-30	-3	-2.8
1890 Buf-P	6	16	.273	25	22	22	0	0	196	280	11	138	55	19.2	6.52	63	.322	.414	16	.203	1	-50	-53	-3	-3.9
1891 Was-a	0	3	.000	5	4	4	0	0	37	44	0	17	11	14.8	2.68	140	.286	.357	2	.143	-0	4	4	1	0.4
Total 6	20	48	.294	78	71	68	1	1	616^1	721	20	360	213	15.8	5.05	74	.281	.370	43	.172	-3	-85	-90	-3	-7.2

■ JOHN KEEFE
Keefe, John Thomas   b: 5/5/1867, Fitchburg, Mass.   d: 8/9/37, Fitchburg, Mass.   TL,   Deb: 4/28/1890

YEAR TM/L	W	L	PCT	G	GS	CG	SH	SV	IP	H	HR	BB	SO	RAT	ERA	ERA+	OAV	OOB	BH	AVG	PB	PR	/A	PD	TPI
1890 Syr-a	17	24	.415	43	41	36	2	0	352^1	355	9	148	120	12.8	4.32	82	.254	.325	30	.191	-4	-17	-30	1	-2.8

■ BOBBY KEEFE
Keefe, Robert Francis   b: 6/16/1882, Folsom, Cal.   d: 12/7/64, Sacramento, Cal.   BR/TR, 5'11", 155 lbs.   Deb: 4/15/07

YEAR TM/L	W	L	PCT	G	GS	CG	SH	SV	IP	H	HR	BB	SO	RAT	ERA	ERA+	OAV	OOB	BH	AVG	PB	PR	/A	PD	TPI
1907 NY-A	3	5	.375	19	3	0	0	3	57^2	60	1	20	20	12.5	2.50	112	.270	.330	1	.053	-2	0	2	0	0.1
1911 Cin-N	12	13	.480	39	26	15	0	3	234^1	196	9	76	105	10.6	2.69	123	.229	.294	6	.086	-2	19	16	-6	0.8
1912 Cin-N	1	3	.250	17	6	0	0	2	68^2	78	0	33	29	15.1	5.24	64	.283	.367	3	.167	-1	-14	-14	0	-1.3
Total 3	16	21	.432	75	35	15	0	8	360^2	334	8	129	154	11.7	3.14	103	.246	.315	10	.093	-5	5	4	-6	-0.4

■ TIM KEEFE
Keefe, Timothy John "Smiling Tim" or "Sir Timothy"
b: 1/1/1857, Cambridge, Mass.   d: 4/23/33, Cambridge, Mass.   BR/TR, 5'10.5", 185 lbs.   Deb: 8/06/1880   UH

YEAR TM/L	W	L	PCT	G	GS	CG	SH	SV	IP	H	HR	BB	SO	RAT	ERA	ERA+	OAV	OOB	BH	AVG	PB	PR	/A	PD	TPI
1880 Tro-N	6	6	.500	12	12	12	0	0	105	71	0	17	43	7.5	0.86	294	.182	.216	10	.233	-0	18	19	1	2.2
1881 Tro-N	18	27	.400	45	45	45	4	0	402	442	4	81	103	11.7	3.25	91	.267	.302	35	.230	4	-21	-13	-0	-0.6
1882 Tro-N	17	26	.395	43	42	41	1	0	375	368	4	81	116	10.8	2.50	113	.242	.281	43	.228	5	16	13	4	2.1
1883 NY-a	41	27	.603	68	68	68	5	0	619	486	6	98	361	8.5	2.41	138	.202	.233	57	.220	4	61	63	6	6.7
1884 *NY-a	37	17	.685	58	58	57	4	0	491^2	388	6	75	323	8.5	2.29	136	.205	.235	50	.235	11	52	45	-0	5.3
1885 NY-N	32	13	.711	46	46	45	7	0	398	297	6	103	230	9.0	1.58	168	.198	.249	27	.163	-0	55	48	0	4.6
1886 NY-N	42	20	.677	64	64	62	2	0	540	478	9	100	291	9.6	2.53	127	.228	.263	35	.171	1	46	40	1	3.8

YEAR TM/L	W	L	PCT	G	GS	CG	SH	SV	IP	H	HR	BB	SO	RAT	ERA	ERA+	OAV	OOB	BH	AVG	PB	PR	/A	PD	TPI
1887 NY-N	35	19	.648	56	56	54	2	0	478²	447	11	108	186	10.4	3.10	121	.240	.282	42	.220	8	50	34	3	3.7
1888 *NY-N	35	12	.745	51	51	48	8	0	434¹	316	5	91	333	8.4	1.74	156	.196	.239	23	.127	-6	53	47	0	4.2
1889 *NY-N	28	13	.683	47	45	38	3	1	364	310	9	151	209	11.4	3.31	119	.223	.299	23	.154	-4	29	26	2	2.0
1890 NY-P	17	11	.607	30	30	23	1	0	229	228	6	88	122	12.3	3.38	134	.248	.312	10	.109	-6	22	30	1	2.2
1891 NY-N	2	5	.286	8	7	4	0	0	55	71	1	27	29	16.0	5.24	61	.302	.373	2	.095	-1	-12	-12	0	-1.0
Phi-N	3	6	.333	11	10	9	0	1	78¹	84	2	28	35	12.9	3.91	87	.264	.323	5	.172	0	-5	-4	-0	-0.3
Yr	5	11	.313	19	17	13	0	1	133¹	155	5	55	64	14.2	4.45	75	.280	.345	7	.140	-1	-16	-17	0	-1.3
1892 Phi-N	19	16	.543	39	38	31	2	0	313¹	264	4	100	127	10.5	2.36	138	.219	.279	10	.085	-7	32	31	-1	2.2
1893 Phi-N	10	7	.588	22	22	17	0	0	178	202	3	79	53	14.2	4.40	104	.277	.348	18	.228	1	5	4	-2	0.1
Total 14	342	225	.603	600	594	554	39	2	5061¹	4452	75	1224	2527	10.1	2.62	125	.226	.271	390	.187	11	402	371	13	37.2

■ ED KEEGAN Keegan, Edward Charles b: 7/8/39, Camden, N.J. BR/TR, 6'3", 165 lbs. Deb: 8/24/59

YEAR TM/L	W	L	PCT	G	GS	CG	SH	SV	IP	H	HR	BB	SO	RAT	ERA	ERA+	OAV	OOB	BH	AVG	PB	PR	/A	PD	TPI
1959 Phi-N	0	3	.000	3	3	0	0	0	9	19	2	13	3	33.0	18.00	23	.432	.569	0	.000	-0	-14	-14	0	-1.1
1961 KC-A	0	0	—	6	0	0	0	1	6	6	0	5	3	16.5	4.50	91	.261	.393	0	—	0	-0	-0	0	0.0
1962 Phi-N	0	0	—	4	0	0	0	0	8	6	1	5	5	13.5	2.25	172	.214	.353	0	—	0	2	1	-0	0.1
Total 3	0	3	.000	13	3	0	0	1	23	31	3	23	11	21.9	9.00	45	.326	.467	0	.000	-0	-13	-13	-0	-1.0

■ BOB KEEGAN Keegan, Robert Charles "Smiley" b: 8/4/20, Rochester, N.Y. BR/TR, 6'2.5", 207 lbs. Deb: 5/24/53

YEAR TM/L	W	L	PCT	G	GS	CG	SH	SV	IP	H	HR	BB	SO	RAT	ERA	ERA+	OAV	OOB	BH	AVG	PB	PR	/A	PD	TPI
1953 Chi-A	7	5	.583	22	11	4	2	1	98²	80	4	33	32	10.5	2.74	147	.223	.293	9	.321	2	14	14	1	1.8
1954 Chi-A	16	9	.640	31	27	14	2	2	209²	211	16	82	61	12.6	3.09	121	.266	.336	9	.120	-2	15	15	-0	1.4
1955 Chi-A	2	5	.286	18	11	1	0	0	58²	83	4	28	29	17.2	5.83	68	.336	.406	6	.333	2	-12	-12	0	-0.9
1956 Chi-A	5	7	.417	20	16	4	0	0	105¹	119	15	35	32	13.3	3.93	104	.286	.344	4	.125	-1	3	2	0	0.1
1957 Chi-A	10	8	.556	30	20	6	2	2	142²	131	22	37	36	10.7	3.53	106	.243	.294	4	.103	-1	4	3	-1	0.1
1958 Chi-A	0	2	.000	14	2	0	0	0	29²	44	9	18	8	18.8	6.07	60	.358	.440	0	.000	-1	-8	-8	1	-0.7
Total 6	40	36	.526	135	87	29	6	5	644²	668	70	233	198	12.7	3.66	105	.270	.335	32	.163	-2	16	14	1	1.8

■ BURT KEELEY Keeley, Burton Elwood "Speed" b: 11/2/1879, Wilmington, Ill. d: 5/3/52, Ely, Minn. BR/TR, 5'9", 170 lbs. Deb: 4/18/08

YEAR TM/L	W	L	PCT	G	GS	CG	SH	SV	IP	H	HR	BB	SO	RAT	ERA	ERA+	OAV	OOB	BH	AVG	PB	PR	/A	PD	TPI
1908 Was-A	6	11	.353	28	16	12	1	1	169²	173	3	48	68	11.9	2.97	77	.259	.313	5	.102	-3	-11	-13	2	-1.5
1909 Was-A	0	0	—	2	0	0	0	0	7	12	0	1	0	18.0	11.57	21	.364	.400	1	.500	0	-7	-7	1	-0.5
Total 2	6	11	.353	30	16	12	1	1	176²	185	3	49	68	12.2	3.31	69	.264	.317	6	.118	-2	-18	-20	3	-2.0

■ VIC KEEN Keen, Howard Victor b: 3/16/1899, Belair, Md. d: 12/10/76, Salisbury, Md. BR/TR, 5'9", 165 lbs. Deb: 8/13/18

YEAR TM/L	W	L	PCT	G	GS	CG	SH	SV	IP	H	HR	BB	SO	RAT	ERA	ERA+	OAV	OOB	BH	AVG	PB	PR	/A	PD	TPI
1918 Phi-A	0	1	.000	1	1	0	0	0	8	9	1	1	1	11.3	3.38	87	.300	.323	0	.000	-0	-1	-0	-0	0.0
1921 Chi-N	0	3	.000	5	4	1	0	0	25	29	0	9	9	14.0	4.68	82	.319	.386	0	.000	-0	-2	-2	0	-0.2
1922 Chi-N	1	2	.333	7	3	2	0	1	34²	36	4	10	11	12.2	3.89	108	.275	.331	4	.333	1	1	1	-0	0.2
1923 Chi-N	12	8	.600	35	17	10	0	1	177	169	8	57	46	11.7	3.00	133	.255	.319	8	.151	-3	20	20	-1	1.5
1924 Chi-N	15	14	.517	40	28	15	0	3	234²	242	17	80	75	12.5	3.80	103	.272	.335	12	.156	-4	2	3	-3	-0.4
1925 Chi-N	2	6	.250	30	8	1	0	0	83¹	125	8	41	19	17.9	6.26	69	.359	.427	6	.240	0	-18	-18	1	-1.4
1926 *StL-N	10	9	.526	26	21	12	1	0	152	179	15	42	29	13.1	4.56	86	.295	.342	3	.057	-6	-12	-11	-2	-1.7
1927 StL-N	2	1	.667	21	0	0	0	0	33²	39	3	8	12	13.1	4.81	82	.293	.343	1	.250	0	-3	-3	0	-0.2
Total 8	42	44	.488	165	82	41	1	6	748²	828	56	248	202	13.1	4.11	97	.287	.346	34	.148	-13	-15	-11	-5	-2.2

■ KID KEENAN Keenan, Harry Leon b: 1875, Louisville, Ky. d: 6/11/03, Covington, Ky. TR, .095 lbs. Deb: 8/11/1891

YEAR TM/L	W	L	PCT	G	GS	CG	SH	SV	IP	H	HR	BB	SO	RAT	ERA	ERA+	OAV	OOB	BH	AVG	PB	PR	/A	PD	TPI
1891 Cin-a	0	1	.000	1	1	1	0	0	8	6	0	4	5	11.3	0.00	—	.201	.296	2	.500	1	3	4	-0	0.4

■ JIM KEENAN Keenan, James W. b: 2/10/1858, New Haven, Conn. d: 9/21/26, Cincinnati, Ohio BR/TR, 5'10", 186 lbs. Deb: 5/17/1875 ♦

YEAR TM/L	W	L	PCT	G	GS	CG	SH	SV	IP	H	HR	BB	SO	RAT	ERA	ERA+	OAV	OOB	BH	AVG	PB	PR	/A	PD	TPI
1884 Ind-a	0	0	—	1	0	0	0	0	3	2	0	0	0	6.0	3.00	109	.179	.179	73	.293	0	0	0	0	0.0
1885 Cin-a	0	0	—	1	0	0	0	0	8	7	0	1	0	9.0	1.13	290	.225	.249	35	.265	0	2	2	0	0.2
1886 Cin-a	0	1	.000	2	0	0	0	0	8	8	0	3	2	12.4	3.38	104	.248	.312	40	.270	0	0	0	0	0.0
Total 3	0	1	.000	4	0	0	0	0	19	17	0	4	2	9.9	2.37	142	.228	.268	452	.241	1	2	2	0	0.2

■ JIMMIE KEENAN Keenan, James William "Sparkplug" b: 5/25/1898, Avon, N.Y. d: 6/5/80, Seminole, Fla. BL/TL, 5'7", 155 lbs. Deb: 9/09/20

YEAR TM/L	W	L	PCT	G	GS	CG	SH	SV	IP	H	HR	BB	SO	RAT	ERA	ERA+	OAV	OOB	BH	AVG	PB	PR	/A	PD	TPI
1920 Phi-N	0	0	—	1	0	0	0	0	3	3	0	1	2	12.0	3.00	114	.333	.400	0	.000	-0	0	0	0	0.0
1921 Phi-N	1	2	.333	15	2	0	0	0	32¹	48	3	15	7	17.8	6.68	63	.364	.432	0	.000	-2	-10	-9	-1	-0.9
Total 2	1	2	.333	16	2	0	0	0	35¹	51	3	16	9	17.3	6.37	65	.362	.430	0	.000	-2	-10	-9	-1	-0.9

■ JEFF KEENER Keener, Jeffrey Bruce b: 1/14/59, Pana, Ill. BL/TR, 6', 170 lbs. Deb: 6/08/82

YEAR TM/L	W	L	PCT	G	GS	CG	SH	SV	IP	H	HR	BB	SO	RAT	ERA	ERA+	OAV	OOB	BH	AVG	PB	PR	/A	PD	TPI
1982 StL-N	1	1	.500	19	0	0	0	0	22¹	19	1	19	25	15.3	1.61	224	.235	.380	0	—	0	5	5	0	0.5
1983 StL-N	0	0	—	4	0	0	0	0	4¹	6	1	1	4	16.6	8.31	44	.333	.400	0	—	0	-2	-2	0	-0.1
Total 2	1	1	.500	23	0	0	0	0	26²	25	1	20	29	15.5	2.70	134	.253	.383	0	—	0	3	3	0	0.4

■ JOE KEENER Keener, Joseph Donald b: 4/21/53, San Pedro, Cal. BR/TR, 6'4", 200 lbs. Deb: 9/18/76

YEAR TM/L	W	L	PCT	G	GS	CG	SH	SV	IP	H	HR	BB	SO	RAT	ERA	ERA+	OAV	OOB	BH	AVG	PB	PR	/A	PD	TPI
1976 Mon-N	0	1	.000	2	2	0	0	0	4¹	7	0	8	1	33.2	10.38	36	.389	.593	0	.000	-0	-3	-3	0	-0.2

■ HARRY KEENER Keener, Joshua Harry "Beans" b: 9/1869, Easton, Pa. d: 3/5/12, Easton, Pa. Deb: 6/27/1896

YEAR TM/L	W	L	PCT	G	GS	CG	SH	SV	IP	H	HR	BB	SO	RAT	ERA	ERA+	OAV	OOB	BH	AVG	PB	PR	/A	PD	TPI
1896 Phi-N	3	11	.214	16	13	11	0	0	113¹	144	5	39	28	14.5	5.88	73	.307	.360	16	.314	2	-19	-20	0	-1.3

■ RICKEY KEETON Keeton, Rickey b: 3/18/57, Cincinnati, Ohio BR/TR, 6'2", 190 lbs. Deb: 5/27/80

YEAR TM/L	W	L	PCT	G	GS	CG	SH	SV	IP	H	HR	BB	SO	RAT	ERA	ERA+	OAV	OOB	BH	AVG	PB	PR	/A	PD	TPI
1980 Mil-A	2	2	.500	5	5	0	0	0	28¹	35	4	9	8	14.0	4.76	81	.307	.358	0	—	0	-2	-3	0	-0.2
1981 Mil-A	1	0	1.000	17	0	0	0	0	35¹	47	4	11	9	14.8	5.09	67	.329	.377	0	—	0	-6	-7	0	-0.5
Total 2	3	2	.600	22	5	0	0	0	63²	82	8	20	17	14.4	4.95	73	.319	.368	0	—	0	-8	-9	0	-0.7

■ FRANK KEFFER Keffer, C. Frank b: Philadelphia, Pa. d: 10/1/32, Chicago, Ill. Deb: 4/19/1890

YEAR TM/L	W	L	PCT	G	GS	CG	SH	SV	IP	H	HR	BB	SO	RAT	ERA	ERA+	OAV	OOB	BH	AVG	PB	PR	/A	PD	TPI
1890 Syr-a	1	1	.500	2	1	1	0	0	16	15	0	9	4	13.5	5.63	63	.240	.336	1	.143	-0	-3	-4	0	-0.2

■ CHET KEHN Kehn, Chester Lawrence b: 10/30/21, San Diego, Cal. d: 4/5/84, San Diego, Cal. BR/TR, 5'11", 168 lbs. Deb: 4/30/42

YEAR TM/L	W	L	PCT	G	GS	CG	SH	SV	IP	H	HR	BB	SO	RAT	ERA	ERA+	OAV	OOB	BH	AVG	PB	PR	/A	PD	TPI
1942 Bro-N	0	0	—	3	1	0	0	0	7²	8	2	4	3	14.1	7.04	46	.267	.353	2	1.000	1	-3	-3	0	-0.1

■ KATSY KEIFER Keifer, Sherman Carl b: 9/3/1891, California, Pa. d: 2/19/27, Outwood, Ken. BB/TL, Deb: 10/08/14

YEAR TM/L	W	L	PCT	G	GS	CG	SH	SV	IP	H	HR	BB	SO	RAT	ERA	ERA+	OAV	OOB	BH	AVG	PB	PR	/A	PD	TPI
1914 Ind-F	1	0	1.000	1	1	1	0	0	9	6	0	2	2	8.0	2.00	173	.196	.246	1	.333	0	1	1	0	0.2

■ MIKE KEKICH Kekich, Michael Dennis b: 4/2/45, San Diego, Cal. BR/TL, 6'1", 196 lbs. Deb: 6/09/65

YEAR TM/L	W	L	PCT	G	GS	CG	SH	SV	IP	H	HR	BB	SO	RAT	ERA	ERA+	OAV	OOB	BH	AVG	PB	PR	/A	PD	TPI
1965 LA-N	0	1	.000	5	1	0	0	0	10¹	10	2	13	9	20.0	9.58	34	.263	.451	0	.000	-0	-7	-7	-0	-0.7
1968 LA-N	2	10	.167	25	20	1	1	0	115	116	9	46	84	12.8	3.91	71	.267	.339	3	.081	-1	-12	-15	-1	-1.8
1969 NY-A	4	6	.400	28	13	1	0	1	105	91	11	49	66	12.2	4.54	77	.236	.325	3	.111	-1	-11	-12	-1	-1.4
1970 NY-A	6	3	.667	26	14	1	0	0	98²	103	12	55	63	14.5	4.83	73	.267	.360	3	.094	-1	-12	-14	-1	-1.6
1971 NY-A	10	9	.526	37	24	3	0	0	170¹	167	13	82	93	13.4	4.07	79	.257	.344	8	.154	-0	-11	-16	1	-1.5
1972 NY-A	10	13	.435	29	28	2	0	0	175¹	172	13	76	78	12.9	3.70	80	.263	.344	8	.136	-1	-12	-15	-1	-1.7
1973 NY-A	1	1	.500	5	4	0	0	0	14²	20	1	14	4	22.1	9.20	40	.351	.493	0	—	0	-9	-9	0	-0.7
Cle-A	1	4	.200	16	6	0	0	0	50	73	6	35	26	19.4	7.02	56	.349	.443	0	—	0	-18	-17	-1	-1.7
Yr	2	5	.286	21	10	0	0	0	64²	93	7	49	30	19.8	7.52	51	.346	.447	0	—	0	-27	-26	-1	-2.4
1975 Tex-A	0	0	—	23	0	0	0	0	31¹	33	2	21	19	15.5	3.73	101	.282	.391	0	—	0	0	0	1	0.4
1977 Sea-A	5	4	.556	41	2	0	0	3	90	90	11	51	55	14.4	5.60	73	.265	.365	0	—	0	-15	-15	-0	-1.4
Total 9	39	51	.433	235	112	8	1	6	860²	875	80	442	497	13.9	4.59	72	.268	.358	25	.120	-5	-108	-121	-4	-12.4

YEAR TM/L	W	L	PCT	G	GS	CG	SH	SV	IP	H	HR	BB	SO	RAT	ERA	ERA+	OAV	OOB	BH	AVG	PB	PR	/A	PD	TPI

■ **GEORGE KELB** — Kelb, George Francis "Pugger" or "Lefty" b: 7/17/1870, Toledo, Ohio d: 10/20/36, Toledo, Ohio TL , Deb: 4/17/1898

| 1898 Cle-N | 0 | 1 | .000 | 3 | 1 | 1 | 0 | 0 | 16¹ | 23 | 0 | 1 | 8 | 13.2 | 4.41 | 82 | .329 | .339 | 1 | .200 | -0 | -1 | -1 | 0 | -0.1 |

■ **HAL KELLEHER** — Kelleher, Harold Joseph b: 6/24/13, Philadelphia, Pa. d: 8/27/89, Cape May Court House, N.J. BR/TR, 6', 165 lbs. Deb: 9/17/35

1935 Phi-N	2	0	1.000	3	3	2	1	0	25	26	0	12	12	14.0	1.80	252	.260	.345	3	.375	1	6	8	0	1.0
1936 Phi-N	0	5	.000	14	4	1	0	0	44	60	2	29	13	18.8	5.32	85	.331	.432	2	.167	-0	-6	-4	0	-0.3
1937 Phi-N	2	4	.333	27	2	1	0	0	58¹	72	3	31	20	17.0	6.63	65	.308	.404	3	.176	-0	-18	-15	-0	-1.3
1938 Phi-N	0	0	—	6	0	0	0	0	7¹	16	0	9	4	30.7	18.41	21	.432	.543	1	.500	0	-12	-12	0	-0.9
Total 4	4	9	.308	50	9	4	1	0	134²	174	5	81	49	17.8	5.95	74	.315	.413	9	.231	1	-30	-23	1	-1.5

■ **RON KELLER** — Keller, Ronald Lee b: 6/3/43, Indianapolis, Ind. BR/TR, 6'2", 200 lbs. Deb: 7/09/66

1966 Min-A	0	0	—	2	0	0	0	0	5¹	7	1	1	1	13.5	5.06	71	.318	.348	0	.000	-0	-1	-1	0	0.0
1968 Min-A	0	1	.000	7	1	0	0	0	16	18	2	4	11	12.9	2.81	110	.305	.359	0	.000	-0	0	0	0	0.0
Total 2	0	1	.000	9	1	0	0	0	21¹	25	3	5	12	13.1	3.38	95	.309	.356	0	.000	-0	-1	-0	0	0.0

■ **AL KELLETT** — Kellett, Alfred Henry b: 10/30/01, Red Bank, N.J. d: 7/14/60, New York, N.Y. 6'3", 200 lbs. Deb: 7/01/23

1923 Phi-A	0	1	.000	5	0	0	0	0	10	11	0	8	1	17.1	6.30	65	.282	.404	1	.333	0	-3	-2	1	0.0
1924 Bos-A	0	0	—	1	0	0	0	0	0	0	0	2	0	—	∞	—	—	1.000	0	—	0	-2	-2	0	-0.1
Total 2	0	1	.000	6	0	0	0	0	10	11	0	10	1	18.9	8.10	51	.282	.429	1	.333	0	-5	-4	1	-0.1

■ **HARRY KELLEY** — Kelley, Harry Leroy b: 2/13/06, Parkin, Ark. d: 3/23/58, Parkin, Ark. BR/TR, 5'9.5", 170 lbs. Deb: 4/16/25

1925 Was-A	1	1	.500	6	1	0	0	0	16	30	0	12	7	23.6	9.00	47	.405	.488	0	.000	-1	-8	-8	0	-0.7
1926 Was-A	0	0	—	7	1	0	0	0	10	17	0	8	6	23.4	8.10	48	.405	.510	0	.000	-0	-5	-5	-0	-0.4
1936 Phi-A	15	12	.556	35	27	20	1	3	235¹	250	21	75	82	12.5	3.86	132	.275	.332	18	.198	-1	31	32	-2	2.7
1937 Phi-A	13	21	.382	41	29	14	0	0	205	267	16	79	68	15.3	5.36	88	.306	.365	16	.225	1	-17	-15	-1	-1.2
1938 Phi-A	0	2	.000	4	3	0	0	0	8	17	0	10	3	30.4	16.88	29	.436	.551	0	.000	-0	-11	-11	-0	-0.8
Was-A	9	8	.529	38	14	7	2	1	148¹	162	12	46	44	12.7	4.49	100	.276	.330	12	.250	1	5	0	1	0.1
Yr	9	10	.474	42	17	7	2	1	156¹	179	12	56	47	13.6	5.12	88	.286	.346	1	.020	1	-6	-10	1	-0.7
1939 Was-A	4	3	.571	15	3	2	0	1	53²	69	2	14	20	14.4	4.70	93	.314	.363	4	.267	1	-0	-2	-0	-0.1
Total 6	42	47	.472	146	78	43	3	5	676¹	812	51	244	230	14.2	4.86	98	.296	.356	50	.216	0	-5	-8	-2	-0.4

■ **DICK KELLEY** — Kelley, Richard Anthony b: 1/8/40, Boston, Mass BR/TL, 5'11.5", 174 lbs. Deb: 4/15/64

1964 Mil-N	0	0	—	2	0	0	0	0	2	2	0	3	2	22.5	18.00	20	.250	.455	0	—	0	-3	-3	-0	-0.2
1965 Mil-N	1	1	.500	21	4	0	0	0	45	37	5	20	31	11.4	3.00	117	.226	.310	0	.000	-1	3	3	-0	0.2
1966 Atl-N	7	5	.583	20	13	2	2	0	81	75	6	21	50	11.0	3.22	113	.247	.302	1	.036	-3	3	4	-2	0.0
1967 Atl-N	2	9	.182	39	9	1	1	2	98	88	8	42	75	12.0	3.77	88	.247	.328	4	.250	1	-4	-5	1	-0.2
1968 Atl-N	2	4	.333	31	11	1	1	1	98	86	4	45	73	12.1	2.76	109	.238	.324	1	.043	-1	3	3	1	0.3
1969 SD-N	4	8	.333	27	23	1	1	0	136	113	11	61	96	11.8	3.57	99	.230	.321	5	.106	-2	0	-1	1	0.0
1971 SD-N	2	3	.400	48	1	0	0	2	59²	52	5	23	42	11.9	3.47	95	.232	.315	1	.333	0	-0	-1	0	0.0
Total 7	18	30	.375	188	61	5	5	5	519²	453	39	215	369	11.8	3.39	100	.237	.319	12	.096	-5	1	-1	1	0.1

■ **TOM KELLEY** — Kelley, Thomas Henry b: 1/5/44, Manchester, Conn. BR/TR, 6', 185 lbs. Deb: 5/05/64

1964 Cle-A	0	0	—	6	0	0	0	0	9²	9	1	9	7	17.7	5.59	64	.237	.396	0	—	0	-2	-2	0	-0.1
1965 Cle-A	2	1	.667	4	4	1	0	0	30	19	3	13	31	9.6	2.40	145	.186	.278	2	.222	0	4	4	-0	0.4
1966 Cle-A	4	8	.333	31	7	1	0	0	95¹	97	14	42	64	13.1	4.34	79	.264	.340	4	.143	-1	-10	-10	-1	-1.1
1967 Cle-A	0	0	—	1	0	0	0	0	1	0	0	2	0	18.0	0.00	—	.000	.500	0	—	0	0	0	0	0.1
1971 Atl-N	9	5	.643	28	20	5	0	0	143	140	8	69	68	13.2	2.96	125	.262	.347	2	.047	-4	8	12	-0	0.8
1972 Atl-N	5	7	.417	27	14	2	1	0	116¹	122	12	65	59	14.5	4.56	83	.272	.364	3	.088	-2	-14	-10	-2	-1.4
1973 Atl-N	0	1	.000	7	0	0	0	0	12²	13	0	7	5	14.2	2.84	138	.289	.385	0	.000	-0	1	2	-0	0.1
Total 7	20	22	.476	104	45	9	1	0	408	400	38	207	234	13.2	3.75	97	.260	.349	11	.095	-7	-13	-4	-4	-1.2

■ **ALEX KELLNER** — Kellner, Alexander Raymond b: 8/26/24, Tucson, Ariz. BR/TL, 6', 200 lbs. Deb: 4/29/48

1948 Phi-A	0	0	—	13	1	0	0	0	23	21	0	16	14	15.3	7.83	55	.239	.368	0	.000	-1	-9	-9	-0	-0.9
1949 Phi-A	20	12	.625	38	27	19	0	1	245	243	18	129	94	13.7	3.75	110	.261	.352	20	.217	1	12	10	-0	1.1
1950 Phi-A	8	20	.286	36	29	15	0	2	225¹	253	28	112	85	14.7	5.47	83	.282	.363	16	.200	-1	-22	-23	-2	-2.3
1951 Phi-A	11	14	.440	33	29	11	1	2	209²	218	20	93	94	13.5	4.46	96	.272	.350	18	.228	-1	-8	-4	-1	-0.5
1952 Phi-A	12	14	.462	34	33	14	2	0	231¹	223	21	86	105	12.2	4.36	91	.252	.321	17	.207	0	-18	-10	-2	-1.0
1953 Phi-A	11	12	.478	25	25	14	2	0	201²	210	8	51	81	11.8	3.93	109	.269	.317	15	.217	1	2	8	-2	0.8
1954 Phi-A	6	17	.261	27	27	8	1	0	173²	204	16	88	69	15.4	5.39	72	.301	.387	10	.182	-0	-32	-29	0	-2.7
1955 KC-A	11	8	.579	30	24	6	3	0	162²	164	18	60	75	12.7	4.20	99	.265	.335	12	.214	2	-4	-1	-0	0.2
1956 KC-A	7	4	.636	20	17	5	0	0	91²	103	15	33	44	13.5	4.32	100	.289	.353	6	.200	-0	-2	0	0	0.0
1957 KC-A	6	5	.545	28	21	3	0	0	132²	141	18	41	72	12.5	4.27	93	.278	.335	11	.234	4	-7	-5	0	0.0
1958 KC-A	0	2	.000	7	6	0	0	0	33²	40	5	8	22	12.8	5.88	66	.315	.356	1	.091	-0	-8	-7	0	-0.6
Cin-N	7	3	.700	18	7	4	0	0	82	74	8	20	42	10.6	2.30	180	.243	.296	10	.357	3	15	17	-2	1.9
1959 StL-N	2	1	.667	12	4	0	0	0	37	31	9	10	19	10.2	3.16	134	.220	.276	2	.222	0	3	4	-0	0.4
Total 12	101	112	.474	321	250	99	9	5	1849¹	1925	184	747	816	13.2	4.41	95	.270	.343	138	.215	8	-78	-47	-9	-3.6

■ **WALT KELLNER** — Kellner, Walter Joseph b: 4/26/29, Tucson, Ariz. BR/TR, 6', 200 lbs. Deb: 9/06/52

1952 Phi-A	0	0	—	1	0	0	0	1	4	4	0	3	2	15.8	6.75	59	.250	.368	0	.000	-0	-1	-1	0	0.0
1953 Phi-A	0	0	—	2	0	0	0	0	3	1	0	4	4	18.0	6.00	71	.111	.429	0	—	0	-1	-1	-0	0.0
Total 2	0	0	—	3	0	0	0	1	7	5	0	7	6	16.7	6.43	64	.200	.394	0	.000	-0	-2	-2	0	0.0

■ **AL KELLOGG** — Kellogg, Albert C. b: 9/9/1886, Providence, R.I. d: 7/21/53, Portland, Ore. Deb: 9/25/08

| 1908 Phi-A | 0 | 2 | .000 | 3 | 3 | 2 | 0 | 0 | 17 | 20 | 1 | 9 | 8 | 15.9 | 5.82 | 44 | .294 | .385 | 1 | .125 | -1 | -6 | -6 | 0 | -0.5 |

■ **WIN KELLUM** — Kellum, Winford Ansley b: 4/11/1876, Waterford, Ont., Canada d: 8/10/51, Big Rapids, Mich. BB/TL, 5'10", 190 lbs. Deb: 4/26/01

1901 Bos-A	2	3	.400	6	6	5	0	0	48	61	3	7	8	12.8	6.38	55	.306	.329	3	.167	-1	-14	-15	1	-1.1
1904 Cin-N	15	10	.600	31	24	22	1	2	224²	206	1	46	70	10.5	2.60	113	.244	.291	13	.159	1	3	8	1	1.2
1905 StL-N	3	3	.500	11	7	5	1	0	74	70	1	10	19	9.9	2.92	102	.255	.283	5	.200	1	1	0	1	0.2
Total 3	20	16	.556	48	37	32	2	2	346²	337	5	63	97	10.7	3.19	95	.256	.295	21	.168	1	-10	-6	3	0.3

■ **BRYAN KELLY** — Kelly, Bryan Keith b: 2/24/59, Silver Spring, Md. BR/TR, 6'2", 195 lbs. Deb: 9/02/86

1986 Det-A	1	2	.333	6	4	0	0	0	20	21	4	10	18	13.9	4.50	92	.269	.352	0	—	0	-1	-1	0	0.0
1987 Det-A	0	1	.000	5	0	0	0	0	10²	12	2	7	10	16.0	5.06	83	.286	.388	0	—	0	-1	-1	-0	0.0
Total 2	1	3	.250	11	4	0	0	0	30²	33	6	17	28	14.7	4.70	89	.275	.365	0	—	0	-1	-2	-0	0.0

■ **ED KELLY** — Kelly, Edward Leo b: 12/10/1888, Pawtucket, R.I. d: 11/4/28, Red Lodge, Mont. BR/TR, 5'11.5", 173 lbs. Deb: 4/14/14

| 1914 Bos-A | 0 | 0 | — | 3 | 0 | 0 | 0 | 0 | 2¹ | 1 | 0 | 1 | 4 | 7.7 | 0.00 | — | .100 | .182 | 0 | .000 | -0 | 1 | 1 | 0 | 0.1 |

■ **GEORGE KELLY** — Kelly, George Lange "Highpockets" b: 9/10/1895, San Francisco, Cal. d: 10/13/84, Burlingame, Cal. BR/TR, 6'4", 190 lbs. Deb: 8/18/15 CH◆

| 1917 NY-N | 1 | 0 | 1.000 | 4 | 0 | 0 | 0 | 0 | 5 | 4 | 0 | 1 | 2 | 9.0 | — | — | .211 | .250 | -0 | — | -0 | 2 | -1 | -0 | 0.2 |

■ **HERB KELLY** — Kelly, Herbert Barrett "Moke" b: 6/4/1892, Mobile, Ala. d: 5/18/73, Torrance, Cal. BL/TL, 5'9", 160 lbs. Deb: 9/25/14

1914 Pit-N	0	2	.000	5	2	2	0	0	25²	24	1	7	6	10.9	2.45	108	.253	.304	2	.222	0	1	1	0	0.1
1915 Pit-N	1	1	.500	5	1	0	0	0	11	10	0	4	6	12.3	4.09	67	.250	.333	1	.500	1	-2	-2	1	0.0
Total 2	1	3	.250	10	3	2	0	0	36²	34	1	11	12	11.3	2.95	91	.252	.313	3	.273	1	-1	-1	1	0.1

YEAR	TM/L	W	L	PCT	G	GS	CG	SH	SV	IP	H	HR	BB	SO	RAT	ERA	ERA+	OAV	OOB	BH	AVG	PB	PR	/A	PD	TPI

■ MIKE KELLY
Kelly, Michael J.   b: 11/9/02, St.Louis, Mo.   BR/TR, 6'1", 178 lbs.   Deb: 9/03/26

| 1926 | Phi-N | 0 | 0 | — | 4 | 0 | 0 | 0 | 0 | 6² | 9 | 0 | 4 | 2 | 18.9 | 9.45 | 44 | .346 | .452 | 0 | .000 | -1 | -4 | -4 | -0 | -0.3 |

■ KING KELLY
Kelly, Michael Joseph   b: 12/31/1857, Troy, N.Y.   d: 11/8/1894, Boston, Mass.   BR/TR, 5'10", 170 lbs.   Deb: 5/01/1878   MH♦

1880	Chi-N	0	0	—	1	0	0	0	0	3	3	0	1	1	12.0	0.00	—	.247	.305	100	.291	0	1	1	0	0.1
1883	Chi-N	0	0	—	1	0	0	0	0	1	1	0	0	0	9.0	0.00	—	.245	.245	109	.255	0	0	0	0	0.0
1884	Chi-N	0	1	.000	2	0	0	0	0	5¹	12	2	2	1	23.6	8.44	37	.424	.462	160	.354	1	-3	-3	-0	-0.2
1887	Bos-N	1	0	1.000	3	0	0	0	0	13	17	1	14	0	21.5	3.46	116	.307	.447	156	.322	1	1	1	0	0.1
1890	Bos-P	1	0	1.000	1	0	0	0	0	2	1	0	2	2	13.5	4.50	98	.142	.332	111	.326	0	-0	-0	0	0.0
1891	Cin-a	0	1	.000	3	0	0	0	0	15¹	21	2	7	0	16.4	5.28	78	.315	.380	84	.297	1	-3	-2	0	-0.1
1892	*Bos-N	0	0	—	1	0	0	0	0	6	8	0	4	0	18.0	1.50	234	.308	.400	53	.189	0	1	1	-0	0.1
Total	7	2	2	.500	12	0	0	0	0	45²	63	5	30	4	18.3	4.14	91	.316	.405	1813	.308	4	-3	-2	0	-0.1

■ REN KELLY
Kelly, Reynolds Joseph   b: 11/18/1899, San Francisco, Cal   d: 8/24/63, Millbrae, Cal.   BR/TR, 6', 183 lbs.   Deb: 9/18/23

| 1923 | Phi-A | 0 | 0 | — | 1 | 0 | 0 | 0 | 0 | 7 | 7 | 0 | 4 | 1 | 14.1 | 2.57 | 160 | .259 | .355 | 0 | .000 | -1 | 1 | 1 | -0 | 0.0 |

■ BOB KELLY
Kelly, Robert Edward   b: 10/4/27, Cleveland, Ohio   BR/TR, 6', 180 lbs.   Deb: 5/04/51

1951	Chi-N	7	4	.636	35	11	4	0	0	123²	130	8	55	48	13.5	4.66	88	.275	.352	5	.161	-1	-10	-8	0	-0.7
1952	Chi-N	4	9	.308	31	15	3	2	0	125¹	114	7	46	50	11.7	3.59	107	.236	.306	8	.216	0	2	4	1	0.5
1953	Chi-N	0	1	.000	14	0	0	0	0	17	27	2	9	6	19.6	9.53	47	.375	.451	0	.000	-0	-10	-10	0	-0.8
	Cin-N	1	2	.333	28	5	0	0	2	66¹	71	7	26	29	13.2	4.34	100	.276	.343	2	.118	-1	-0	-0	0	0.0
	Yr	1	3	.250	42	5	0	0	2	83¹	98	9	35	35	14.4	5.40	81	.297	.364	0	.000	-1	-10	-9	1	-0.8
1958	Cin-N	0	0	—	2	1	0	0	0	2	3	0	3	1	27.0	4.50	92	.500	.667	0	—	0	-0	-0	0	0.0
	Cle-A	0	2	.000	13	3	0	0	0	27²	29	4	13	12	14.0	5.20	70	.282	.368	1	.250	-1	-4	-5	0	-0.3
Total	4	12	18	.400	123	35	7	2	2	362	374	28	152	146	13.2	4.50	90	.268	.343	16	.178	-1	-22	-18	2	-1.3

■ BILL KELSO
Kelso, William Eugene   b: 2/19/40, Kansas City, Mo.   BR/TR, 6'4", 215 lbs.   Deb: 7/31/64

1964	LA-A	2	0	1.000	10	1	1	1	0	23²	19	3	9	21	11.0	2.28	144	.218	.299	0	.000	-0	4	3	0	0.3
1966	Cal-A	1	1	.500	5	0	0	0	0	11¹	11	1	6	11	14.3	2.38	141	.244	.346	0	.000	-0	1	1	0	0.1
1967	Cal-A	5	3	.625	69	1	0	0	11	112	85	6	63	91	12.2	2.97	106	.219	.333	2	.105	-1	3	2	0	0.2
1968	Cin-N	4	1	.800	35	0	0	0	1	54	56	6	15	39	12.3	4.00	79	.277	.336	0	.000	-1	-6	-5	-1	-0.7
Total	4	12	5	.706	119	2	1	1	12	201	171	16	93	162	12.2	3.13	102	.237	.331	2	.059	-2	2	1	-0	-0.1

■ RUSS KEMMERER
Kemmerer, Russell Paul "Rusty" or "Dutch"   b: 11/1/31, Pittsburgh, Pa.   BR/TR, 6'2", 198 lbs.   Deb: 6/27/54

1954	Bos-A	5	3	.625	19	9	2	1	0	75¹	71	4	41	37	13.6	3.82	108	.257	.357	3	.143	-0	-1	2	0	0.3
1955	Bos-A	1	1	.500	7	2	0	0	0	17¹	18	3	15	13	17.1	7.27	59	.269	.402	0	.000	-0	-6	-6	-0	-0.5
1957	Bos-A	0	0	—	1	0	0	0	0	4	5	0	2	1	15.8	4.50	89	.333	.412	0	.000	-0	-0	-0	-0	0.0
	Was-A	7	11	.389	39	26	6	0	0	172¹	214	20	71	81	15.0	4.96	79	.309	.375	3	.067	-1	-22	-20	-2	-2.3
	Yr	7	11	.389	40	26	6	0	0	176¹	219	20	73	82	15.0	4.95	79	.309	.375	4	.087	-1	-23	-21	-3	-2.3
1958	Was-A	6	15	.286	40	30	6	0	0	224¹	234	25	74	111	12.5	4.61	83	.276	.330	11	.159	-2	-21	-20	0	-2.1
1959	Was-A	8	17	.320	37	28	8	0	0	206	221	20	71	89	12.9	4.50	87	.276	.338	8	.133	-1	-15	-13	1	-1.3
1960	Was-A	0	2	.000	3	3	0	0	0	17¹	18	2	10	10	15.1	7.79	50	.269	.372	0	.000	0	-8	-8	0	-0.5
	Chi-A	6	3	.667	36	7	2	1	2	120²	111	5	45	76	11.7	2.98	127	.248	.318	0	.000	-3	12	11	-0	0.8
	Yr	6	5	.545	39	10	2	1	2	138	129	7	55	86	12.1	3.59	106	.250	.323	4	.121	-3	4	3	0	0.3
1961	Chi-A	3	3	.500	47	2	0	0	2	96²	102	10	26	35	11.9	4.38	89	.278	.326	3	.200	1	-4	-5	1	-0.2
1962	Chi-A	2	1	.667	20	0	0	0	0	28	30	3	11	17	13.2	3.86	101	.270	.336	1	.500	1	0	0	1	0.2
	Hou-N	5	3	.625	36	2	0	0	3	68	72	10	15	23	11.9	4.10	91	.272	.318	3	.333	1	-1	-3	1	0.0
1963	Hou-N	0	0	—	17	0	0	0	1	36²	48	1	8	12	13.7	5.65	56	.320	.354	2	.286	1	-10	-10	1	-0.8
Total	9	43	59	.422	302	109	24	2	8	1066²	1144	103	389	505	13.1	4.46	86	.277	.342	34	.128	-5	-76	-72	2	-6.4

■ DUTCH KEMNER
Kemner, Herman John   b: 3/4/1899, Quincy, Ill.   d: 1/16/88, Quincy, Ill.   BR/TR, 5'10.5", 175 lbs.   Deb: 4/19/29

| 1929 | Cin-N | 0 | 0 | — | 9 | 0 | 0 | 0 | 1 | 15¹ | 19 | 0 | 8 | 10 | 15.8 | 7.63 | 60 | .328 | .409 | 1 | .250 | 0 | -5 | -5 | 0 | -0.4 |

■ ED KENNA
Kenna, Edward Benninghaus "The Pitching Poet"   b: 10/17/1877, Charleston, W.Va.   d: 3/22/12, Grant, Fla.   TR, 6', 180 lbs.   Deb: 5/05/02

| 1902 | Phi-A | 1 | 1 | .500 | 2 | 1 | 1 | 0 | 0 | 17 | 19 | 1 | 11 | 5 | 15.9 | 5.29 | 69 | .283 | .384 | 1 | .125 | -0 | -3 | -3 | 0 | -0.2 |

■ VERN KENNEDY
Kennedy, Lloyd Vernon   b: 3/20/07, Kansas City, Mo.   BL/TR, 6', 175 lbs.   Deb: 9/18/34

1934	Chi-A	0	2	.000	3	3	1	0	0	19¹	21	1	9	7	14.0	3.72	127	.300	.380	2	.286	0	2	2	1	0.3
1935	Chi-A	11	11	.500	31	25	16	2	1	211²	211	17	95	65	13.2	3.91	118	.262	.343	18	.247	1	13	17	3	1.9
1936	Chi-A	21	9	.700	35	34	20	1	0	274¹	282	13	147	99	14.2	4.63	112	.268	.360	32	.283	5	13	17	0	2.1
1937	Chi-A	14	13	.519	32	30	15	1	0	221	238	16	124	114	14.9	5.09	90	.273	.366	20	.230	2	-12	-12	-0	-0.8
1938	Det-A	12	9	.571	33	26	11	0	2	190¹	215	13	113	53	15.6	5.06	99	.287	.382	23	.291	3	-6	-1	2	0.4
1939	Det-A	3	0	.000	4	4	1	0	0	21	25	4	9	9	15.0	6.43	76	.301	.376	2	.286	0	-4	-4	1	-0.2
	StL-A	9	17	.346	33	27	12	1	0	191²	229	18	115	55	16.2	5.73	85	.297	.389	10	.149	-3	-24	-18	-0	-1.8
	Yr	9	20	.310	37	31	13	1	0	212²	254	22	124	64	16.0	5.80	84	.297	.387	3	.041	-2	-28	-22	0	-2.0
1940	StL-A	12	17	.414	34	32	18	0	0	222¹	263	18	122	70	15.7	5.59	82	.298	.385	25	.298	7	-30	-25	2	-1.3
1941	StL-A	2	4	.333	6	6	2	0	0	45	44	5	27	6	14.2	4.40	98	.259	.360	6	.400	2	-1	-1	0	0.2
	Was-A	1	7	.125	17	7	2	0	0	66¹	77	5	39	22	16.0	5.70	71	.297	.393	3	.143	-1	-11	-12	0	-1.1
	Yr	3	11	.214	23	13	4	0	0	111¹	121	10	66	28	15.3	5.17	80	.282	.380	9	.205	1	-13	-13	0	-0.9
1942	Cle-A	4	8	.333	28	12	4	0	1	108	99	1	50	37	12.5	4.08	84	.244	.328	6	.200	1	-5	-8	0	-0.2
1943	Cle-A	10	7	.588	28	17	8	1	0	146²	130	4	59	63	11.7	2.45	127	.242	.319	12	.231	1	14	11	1	1.4
1944	Cle-A	2	5	.286	12	10	2	0	0	59	66	0	37	17	15.7	5.03	66	.289	.389	2	.087	-2	-11	-11	1	-1.1
	Phi-N	1	5	.167	12	7	3	0	0	55¹	60	3	20	23	13.0	4.23	85	.269	.329	6	.286	1	-4	-4	0	-0.2
1945	Phi-N	0	3	.000	12	3	0	0	0	36	43	2	14	13	14.3	5.50	70	.297	.358	2	.182	0	-7	-7	1	-0.4
	Cin-N	5	12	.294	24	20	11	1	1	157²	170	10	69	38	13.8	4.00	94	.280	.356	12	.226	2	-3	-4	1	0.0
	Yr	5	15	.250	36	23	11	1	1	193²	213	12	83	51	13.9	4.28	88	.283	.356	2	.031	2	-10	-11	2	-0.4
Total	12	104	132	.441	344	263	126	7	5	2025²	2173	130	1049	691	14.4	4.67	94	.277	.363	181	.244	19	-77	-63	13	-1.2

■ MONTE KENNEDY
Kennedy, Montia Calvin   b: 5/11/22, Amelia, Va.   BR/TL, 6'2", 185 lbs.   Deb: 4/18/46

1946	NY-N	9	10	.474	38	27	10	1	1	186²	153	14	116	71	13.2	3.42	101	.224	.340	15	.234	2	-0	0	0	0.3
1947	NY-N	9	12	.429	34	24	9	0	0	148¹	158	8	88	60	15.2	4.85	84	.272	.372	8	.167	-1	-13	-13	-0	-1.2
1948	NY-N	3	9	.250	25	16	7	1	0	114¹	118	10	57	63	14.0	4.01	98	.264	.351	4	.129	-1	-1	-1	-0	-0.2
1949	NY-N	12	14	.462	38	32	14	4	1	223¹	208	13	100	95	12.5	3.43	116	.250	.323	12	.145	-1	15	14	-3	1.0
1950	NY-N	5	4	.556	36	17	5	0	2	114¹	120	14	53	41	13.9	4.72	87	.269	.351	2	.056	-3	-7	-8	-0	-1.0
1951	*NY-N	1	2	.333	29	5	1	0	0	68	68	6	31	22	13.1	2.25	174	.270	.350	3	.200	0	13	13	0	1.3
1952	NY-N	3	4	.429	31	6	2	1	0	83¹	73	6	41	48	11.4	3.02	122	.230	.303	2	.091	-1	7	6	0	0.6
1953	NY-N	0	0	—	18	0	0	0	0	22²	30	2	19	11	19.9	7.15	60	.337	.459	0	.000	-0	-7	-7	0	-0.6
Total	8	42	55	.433	249	127	48	7	4	961	928	67	495	411	13.5	3.84	101	.253	.344	46	.153	-5	6	4	-3	0.2

■ TED KENNEDY
Kennedy, Theodore A.   b: 2/1865, Henry, Ill.   d: 10/31/07, St.Louis, Mo.   BL,   Deb: 6/12/1885

1885	Chi-N	7	2	.778	9	9	8	0	0	78²	91	5	28	36	13.6	3.43	88	.277	.333	3	.083	-4	-5	-3	-0	-0.6
1886	Phi-a	5	15	.250	20	19	19	0	0	172²	196	4	65	68	13.6	4.53	77	.273	.333	3	.041	-9	-21	-20	1	-2.2
	Lou-a	0	4	.000	4	4	4	0	0	32	53	1	16	14	19.4	5.34	68	.354	.416	1	.077	-1	-7	-6	-0	-0.5
	Yr	5	19	.208	24	23	23	0	0	204²	249	5	81	82	14.5	4.66	76	.287	.348	4	.049	-11	-27	-26	0	-2.7
Total	2	12	21	.364	33	32	31	0	0	283¹	340	10	109	118	14.3	4.32	79	.284	.344	7	.060	-15	-33	-29	0	-3.3

YEAR	TM/L	W	L	PCT	G	GS	CG	SH	SV	IP	H	HR	BB	SO	RAT	ERA	ERA+	OAV	OOB	BH	AVG	PB	PR	/A	PD	TPI

■ BILL KENNEDY
Kennedy, William Aulton "Lefty" b: 3/14/21, Carnesville, Ga. d: 4/9/83, Seattle, Wash. BL/TL, 6'2", 195 lbs. Deb: 4/26/48

YEAR	TM/L	W	L	PCT	G	GS	CG	SH	SV	IP	H	HR	BB	SO	RAT	ERA	ERA+	OAV	OOB	BH	AVG	PB	PR	/A	PD	TPI
1948	Cle-A	1	0	1.000	6	3	0	0	0	11¹	16	0	13	12	23.0	11.12	37	.333	.475	2	.667	1	-9	-9	0	-0.6
	StL-A	7	8	.467	26	20	3	0	0	132	132	10	104	77	16.4	4.70	97	.259	.389	11	.250	1	-6	-2	-1	-0.1
	Yr	8	8	.500	32	23	3	0	0	143¹	148	10	117	89	17.0	5.21	87	.265	.397	4	.085	2	-15	-11	-1	-0.7
1949	StL-A	4	11	.267	48	16	2	0	1	153²	172	12	73	69	14.5	4.69	97	.285	.365	6	.150	-2	-8	-3	-0	-0.5
1950	StL-A	0	0	—	1	0	0	0	0	2	1	0	2	1	13.5	0.00	—	.143	.333	0	—	0	1	1	-0	0.1
1951	StL-A	1	5	.167	19	5	1	0	0	56	76	4	37	29	18.3	5.79	76	.332	.427	2	.125	-2	-10	-9	1	-0.8
1952	Chi-A	2	2	.500	47	1	0	0	5	70²	54	4	38	46	11.8	2.80	130	.213	.318	3	.231	0	7	7	-1	0.6
1953	Bos-A	0	0	—	16	0	0	0	2	24¹	24	2	17	14	15.5	3.70	114	.255	.375	1	.500	1	1	1	-0	0.1
1956	Cin-N	0	0	—	1	0	0	0	0	2	6	1	0	0	27.0	18.00	22	.667	.667	0	—	0	-3	-3	0	-0.2
1957	Cin-N	0	2	.000	8	0	0	0	3	12²	16	1	5	8	15.6	6.39	64	.314	.386	0	.000	0	-4	-3	0	-0.2
Total	8	15	28	.349	172	45	6	0	11	464²	497	34	289	256	15.5	4.73	92	.275	.379	25	.208	-1	-31	-20	-3	-1.6

■ BILL KENNEDY
Kennedy, William Gorman b: 12/22/18, Alexandria, Va. BL/TL, 6'1", 175 lbs. Deb: 5/01/42

YEAR	TM/L	W	L	PCT	G	GS	CG	SH	SV	IP	H	HR	BB	SO	RAT	ERA	ERA+	OAV	OOB	BH	AVG	PB	PR	/A	PD	TPI
1942	Was-A	0	1	.000	8	2	1	0	2	18	21	1	10	4	15.5	8.00	46	.296	.383	0	.000	-1	-9	-9	1	-0.7
1946	Was-A	1	2	.333	21	2	0	0	3	39	40	1	29	18	15.9	6.00	56	.270	.390	1	.125	-0	-11	-11	-0	-1.1
1947	Was-A	0	0	—	2	0	0	0	0	6²	10	1	5	1	20.3	8.10	46	.370	.469	0	.000	-0	-3	-3	0	-0.2
Total	3	1	3	.250	31	4	1	0	5	63²	71	3	44	23	16.3	6.79	51	.289	.397	1	.071	-1	-23	-23	1	-2.0

■ BRICKYARD KENNEDY
Kennedy, William P. b: 10/7/1867, Bellaire, Ohio d: 9/23/15, Bellaire, Ohio BR/TR, 5'11", 160 lbs. Deb: 4/26/1892

YEAR	TM/L	W	L	PCT	G	GS	CG	SH	SV	IP	H	HR	BB	SO	RAT	ERA	ERA+	OAV	OOB	BH	AVG	PB	PR	/A	PD	TPI
1892	Bro-N	13	8	.619	26	21	18	0	1	191	189	3	95	108	13.4	3.86	82	.248	.331	14	.165	-1	-12	-15	-1	-1.4
1893	Bro-N	25	20	.556	46	44	40	2	1	382²	376	15	168	107	12.8	3.72	119	.249	.325	39	.248	2	41	30	5	3.0
1894	Bro-N	24	20	.545	48	41	34	0	2	360²	445	15	149	107	14.8	4.92	101	.300	.364	49	.304	4	16	1	2	0.4
1895	Bro-N	19	12	.613	39	33	26	2	1	279²	335	13	93	39	13.8	5.12	86	.292	.345	30	.307	4	-10	-22	-0	-1.6
1896	Bro-N	17	20	.459	42	38	28	1	1	305²	334	12	130	76	13.7	4.42	93	.276	.346	23	.189	-6	-2	-10	2	-1.2
1897	Bro-N	18	20	.474	44	40	36	2	1	343¹	370	6	149	81	13.6	3.91	105	.273	.345	40	.272	4	16	8	2	1.1
1898	Bro-N	16	22	.421	40	39	38	0	0	339¹	360	12	123	73	12.8	3.37	107	.270	.332	34	.252	3	9	8	6	1.6
1899	Bro-N	22	9	.710	40	33	27	2	2	277¹	297	11	86	55	12.4	2.79	140	.274	.327	27	.248	4	33	35	0	3.7
1900	Bro-N	20	13	.606	42	35	26	2	0	292	316	5	111	75	13.2	3.91	98	.275	.339	37	.301	8	-7	-2	1	0.6
1901	Bro-N	3	5	.375	14	8	6	0	0	85¹	80	1	24	28	11.1	3.06	110	.246	.300	6	.167	-1	3	3	-0	0.1
1902	NY-N	1	4	.200	6	6	4	1	0	38²	44	0	16	9	14.0	3.96	71	.286	.353	4	.267	1	-5	-5	-0	-0.4
1903	*Pit-N	9	6	.600	18	15	10	1	0	125¹	130	5	57	39	13.6	3.45	94	.277	.357	21	.362	8	-2	-3	-1	0.4
Total	12	187	159	.540	405	353	293	13	9	3021	3276	93	1201	797	13.3	3.96	103	.273	.340	333	.261	29	78	33	16	6.3

■ ART KENNEY
Kenney, Arthur Joseph b: 4/29/16, Milford, Mass. BL/TL, 6', 175 lbs. Deb: 7/01/38

YEAR	TM/L	W	L	PCT	G	GS	CG	SH	SV	IP	H	HR	BB	SO	RAT	ERA	ERA+	OAV	OOB	BH	AVG	PB	PR	/A	PD	TPI
1938	Bos-N	0	0	—	2	0	0	0	0	2¹	3	0	8	2	42.4	15.43	22	.300	.611	0	—	0	-3	-3	0	-0.2

■ ED KENT
Kent, Edward C. b: 1859, New York TL, 5'6.5", 152 lbs. Deb: 8/14/1884

YEAR	TM/L	W	L	PCT	G	GS	CG	SH	SV	IP	H	HR	BB	SO	RAT	ERA	ERA+	OAV	OOB	BH	AVG	PB	PR	/A	PD	TPI
1884	Tol-a	0	1	.000	1	1	1	0	0	9	14	0	3	4	17.0	6.00	57	.337	.382	0	.000	-1	-3	-3	-0	-0.1

■ MAURY KENT
Kent, Maurice Allen b: 9/17/1885, Marshalltown, Ia. d: 4/19/66, Iowa City, Iowa BR/TR, 6', 168 lbs. Deb: 4/15/12

YEAR	TM/L	W	L	PCT	G	GS	CG	SH	SV	IP	H	HR	BB	SO	RAT	ERA	ERA+	OAV	OOB	BH	AVG	PB	PR	/A	PD	TPI
1912	Bro-N	5	5	.500	20	9	2	1	0	93	107	3	46	24	14.9	4.84	69	.284	.363	8	.229	1	-15	-15	1	-1.2
1913	Bro-N	0	0	—	3	0	0	0	0	7¹	5	0	3	1	9.8	2.45	134	.192	.276	0	.000	-0	1	1	-0	0.0
Total	2	5	5	.500	23	9	2	1	0	100¹	112	3	49	25	14.5	4.66	72	.278	.358	8	.211	0	-14	-15	1	-1.2

■ MATT KEOUGH
Keough, Matthew Lon b: 7/3/55, Pomona, Cal. BR/TR, 6'3", 190 lbs. Deb: 9/03/77

YEAR	TM/L	W	L	PCT	G	GS	CG	SH	SV	IP	H	HR	BB	SO	RAT	ERA	ERA+	OAV	OOB	BH	AVG	PB	PR	/A	PD	TPI
1977	Oak-A	1	3	.250	7	6	0	0	0	42²	39	4	22	23	13.1	4.85	83	.247	.343	0	—	0	-4	-4	-1	-0.3
1978	Oak-A	8	15	.348	32	32	6	0	0	197¹	178	9	85	108	12.2	3.24	112	.241	.323	0	—	0	11	9	2	1.1
1979	Oak-A	2	17	.105	30	28	7	1	0	176²	220	18	78	95	15.5	5.04	80	.315	.389	0	—	0	-16	-20	2	-1.6
1980	Oak-A	16	13	.552	34	32	20	2	0	250	218	24	94	121	11.4	2.92	129	.236	.310	0	—	0	31	24	-1	2.3
1981	*Oak-A	10	6	.625	19	19	10	2	0	140¹	125	11	45	60	10.9	3.40	102	.239	.299	0	—	0	4	1	-2	0.0
1982	Oak-A	11	18	.379	34	34	10	2	0	209¹	233	38	101	75	14.6	5.72	68	.284	.366	0	—	0	-38	-42	-2	-4.1
1983	Oak-A	2	3	.400	14	4	0	0	0	44	50	7	31	28	16.6	5.52	70	.284	.391	0	—	0	-7	-8	-1	-0.8
	NY-A	3	4	.429	12	12	0	0	0	55²	59	12	20	26	13.1	5.17	75	.266	.332	0	—	0	-7	-8	-0	-0.7
	Yr	5	7	.417	26	16	0	0	0	99²	109	19	51	54	14.6	5.33	73	.273	.358	0	—	0	-14	-16	-1	-1.5
1985	StL-N	0	1	.000	4	1	0	0	0	10	10	0	4	10	13.5	4.50	79	.278	.366	0	.000	-0	-1	-1	0	0.0
1986	Chi-N	2	2	.500	19	2	0	0	0	29	36	4	12	19	15.2	4.97	81	.316	.386	2	.400	1	-4	-3	-0	-0.1
	Hou-N	3	2	.600	10	5	0	0	0	35	22	5	18	25	10.5	3.09	117	.180	.291	4	.364	1	2	2	-1	0.3
	Yr	5	4	.556	29	7	0	0	0	64	58	9	30	44	12.5	3.94	96	.245	.332	6	.333	2	-2	-1	-1	0.2
Total	9	58	84	.408	215	175	53	7	0	1190	1190	132	510	590	13.1	4.17	91	.262	.341	6	.333	2	-28	-50	-3	-3.9

■ KURT KEPSHIRE
Kepshire, Kurt David b: 7/3/59, Bridgeport, Conn. BL/TR, 6'1", 180 lbs. Deb: 7/04/84

YEAR	TM/L	W	L	PCT	G	GS	CG	SH	SV	IP	H	HR	BB	SO	RAT	ERA	ERA+	OAV	OOB	BH	AVG	PB	PR	/A	PD	TPI
1984	StL-N	6	5	.545	17	16	2	2	0	109	100	7	44	71	11.9	3.30	105	.249	.323	2	.056	-2	3	2	-2	-0.1
1985	StL-N	10	9	.526	32	29	2	0	0	153¹	155	16	71	67	13.3	4.75	74	.264	.343	6	.118	-1	-20	-21	-1	-2.2
1986	StL-N	0	1	.000	2	1	0	0	0	8	8	2	4	6	13.5	4.50	81	.258	.343	0	.000	-0	-1	-1	0	0.0
Total	3	16	15	.516	51	46	2	2	0	270¹	263	25	119	144	12.7	4.16	84	.258	.335	8	.091	-3	-17	-20	-3	-2.3

■ CHARLIE KERFELD
Kerfeld, Charles Patrick b: 9/28/63, Knob Knoster, Mo. BR/TR, 6'6", 225 lbs. Deb: 7/27/85

YEAR	TM/L	W	L	PCT	G	GS	CG	SH	SV	IP	H	HR	BB	SO	RAT	ERA	ERA+	OAV	OOB	BH	AVG	PB	PR	/A	PD	TPI
1985	Hou-N	4	2	.667	11	6	0	0	0	44¹	44	2	25	30	14.0	4.06	85	.268	.365	0	.000	-1	-2	-3	-1	-0.4
1986	*Hou-N	11	2	.846	61	0	0	0	7	93²	71	5	42	77	11.0	2.69	134	.213	.305	1	.111	-0	11	9	-1	0.9
1987	Hou-N	0	2	.000	21	0	0	0	0	29²	34	3	21	17	17.0	6.67	59	.309	.424	0	.000	-0	-9	-9	0	-0.8
1990	Hou-N	0	0	—	5	0	0	0	0	3¹	9	0	6	4	40.5	16.20	23	.529	.652	0	—	0	-5	-5	-0	-0.4
	Atl-N	3	1	.750	25	0	0	0	2	30²	31	2	23	27	15.8	5.58	70	.270	.391	0	—	0	-6	-6	-1	-0.5
	Yr	3	3	.500	30	0	0	0	2	34	40	2	29	31	18.3	6.62	59	.303	.429	0	—	0	-11	-10	-1	-0.9
Total	4	18	9	.667	123	6	0	0	9	201²	189	12	117	155	13.8	4.24	86	.256	.360	1	.038	-2	-11	-13	-2	-1.2

■ GUS KERIAZAKOS
Keriazakos, Constantine Nicholas b: 7/28/31, W.Orange, N.J. BR/TR, 6'3", 187 lbs. Deb: 10/01/50

YEAR	TM/L	W	L	PCT	G	GS	CG	SH	SV	IP	H	HR	BB	SO	RAT	ERA	ERA+	OAV	OOB	BH	AVG	PB	PR	/A	PD	TPI
1950	Chi-A	0	1	.000	1	1	0	0	0	2¹	7	0	5	1	46.3	19.29	23	.500	.632	1	1.000	0	-4	-4	0	-0.2
1954	Was-A	2	3	.400	22	3	2	0	0	59²	59	4	30	33	13.4	3.77	94	.262	.349	1	.067	-1	-0	-1	-0	-0.2
1955	KC-A	0	1	.000	5	1	0	0	0	11²	15	4	7	8	17.0	12.34	34	.333	.423	0	.000	-0	-11	-11	-0	-0.9
Total	3	2	5	.286	28	5	2	0	0	73²	81	8	42	42	15.0	5.62	65	.285	.377	2	.105	-1	-15	-16	-0	-1.3

■ BILL KERKSIECK
Kerksieck, Wayman William b: 12/6/13, Ulm, Ark. d: 3/11/70, Stuttgart, Ark. BR/TR, 6'1", 183 lbs. Deb: 6/21/39

YEAR	TM/L	W	L	PCT	G	GS	CG	SH	SV	IP	H	HR	BB	SO	RAT	ERA	ERA+	OAV	OOB	BH	AVG	PB	PR	/A	PD	TPI
1939	Phi-N	0	2	.000	23	2	1	0	0	62²	81	13	32	13	16.2	7.18	56	.328	.405	1	.083	-0	-23	-22	-0	-2.1

■ JIM KERN
Kern, James Lester b: 3/15/49, Gladwin, Mich. BR/TR, 6'5", 185 lbs. Deb: 9/06/74

YEAR	TM/L	W	L	PCT	G	GS	CG	SH	SV	IP	H	HR	BB	SO	RAT	ERA	ERA+	OAV	OOB	BH	AVG	PB	PR	/A	PD	TPI
1974	Cle-A	0	1	.000	4	3	1	0	0	15¹	16	1	14	11	17.6	4.70	77	.262	.400	0	—	0	-2	-2	-0	-0.1
1975	Cle-A	1	2	.333	13	7	0	0	0	71²	60	5	45	55	13.8	3.77	100	.233	.357	0	—	0	0	0	-0	0.0
1976	Cle-A	10	7	.588	50	2	0	0	15	117²	91	4	60	111	11.2	2.37	147	.222	.314	0	—	0	15	15	-1	1.5
1977	Cle-A	8	10	.444	60	0	0	0	18	92	85	3	47	91	13.5	3.42	115	.260	.363	0	—	0	6	5	-0	0.5
1978	Cle-A	10	10	.500	58	0	0	0	13	99¹	77	4	58	95	12.5	3.08	121	.224	.342	0	.000	0	8	7	0	0.8
1979	Tex-A	13	5	.722	71	0	0	0	29	143	99	5	62	136	10.3	1.57	264	.199	.290	0	—	0	42	41	-1	4.0
1980	Tex-A	3	11	.214	38	1	0	0	2	63¹	64	5	45	40	15.9	4.83	81	.279	.400	0	—	0	-6	-7	0	-0.5
1981	Tex-A	1	2	.333	23	0	0	0	6	30	21	0	22	20	13.2	2.70	128	.204	.349	0	—	0	3	3	-0	0.2
1982	Cin-N	3	5	.375	50	0	0	0	2	76	61	3	48	43	13.1	2.84	130	.222	.342	0	.000	-1	6	7	1	0.8

YEAR	TM/L	W	L	PCT	G	GS	CG	SH	SV	IP	H	HR	BB	SO	RAT	ERA	ERA+	OAV	OOB	BH	AVG	PB	PR	/A	PD	TPI
	Chi-A	2	1	.667	13	1	0	0	3	28	20	3	12	23	10.3	5.14	78	.204	.291	0	—	0	-3	-3	0	-0.2
1983	Chi-A	0	0	—	1	0	0	0	0	0²	1	0	0	0	13.5	0.00	—	.333	.333	0	—	0	0	0	0	0.0
1984	Phi-N	0	1	.000	8	0	0	0	0	13¹	20	3	10	8	20.3	10.13	36	.339	.435	0	.000	-0	-10	-10	0	-0.9
	Mil-A	1	0	1.000	6	0	0	0	0	4²	6	0	3	4	17.4	0.00	—	.300	.391	0	—	0	2	2	0	0.2
1985	Mil-A	0	1	.000	5	0	0	0	0	11	14	1	5	3	15.5	6.55	64	.318	.388	0	—	0	-3	-3	1	-0.1
1986	Cle-A	1	1	.500	16	0	0	0	0	27¹	34	1	23	11	19.8	7.90	52	.298	.429	0	—	0	-11	-11	1	-0.9
Total	13	53	57	.482	416	14	1	0	88	793¹	670	35	444	651	13.0	3.32	115	.235	.344	0	.000	-0	48	45	-0	5.3

■ DICKIE KERR
Kerr, Richard Henry b: 7/3/1893, St.Louis, Mo. d: 5/4/63, Houston, Tex. BL/TL, 5'7", 155 lbs. Deb: 4/25/19

YEAR	TM/L	W	L	PCT	G	GS	CG	SH	SV	IP	H	HR	BB	SO	RAT	ERA	ERA+	OAV	OOB	BH	AVG	PB	PR	/A	PD	TPI
1919	*Chi-A	13	7	.650	39	17	10	1	0	212¹	208	2	64	79	11.6	2.88	110	.259	.316	17	.250	5	8	7	1	1.4
1920	Chi-A	21	9	.700	45	28	19	3	5	253²	266	7	72	72	12.1	3.37	112	.278	.331	14	.156	-4	12	11	3	1.0
1921	Chi-A	19	17	.528	44	37	25	3	1	308²	357	12	96	80	13.5	4.72	90	.295	.352	25	.238	5	-15	-17	0	-1.0
1925	Chi-A	0	1	.000	12	2	0	0	0	36²	45	3	18	4	15.7	5.15	81	.304	.383	4	.333	1	-3	-4	1	-0.2
Total	4	53	34	.609	140	84	54	7	6	811¹	876	24	250	235	12.7	3.84	99	.281	.338	60	.218	7	2	-2	5	1.2

■ JOE KERRIGAN
Kerrigan, Joseph Thomas b: 11/30/54, Philadelphia, Pa. BR/TR, 6'5", 205 lbs. Deb: 7/09/76 C

YEAR	TM/L	W	L	PCT	G	GS	CG	SH	SV	IP	H	HR	BB	SO	RAT	ERA	ERA+	OAV	OOB	BH	AVG	PB	PR	/A	PD	TPI
1976	Mon-N	2	6	.250	38	0	0	0	1	56²	63	3	23	22	14.0	3.81	98	.289	.362	0	.000	-0	-2	-1	1	0.0
1977	Mon-N	3	5	.375	66	0	0	0	11	89¹	80	4	33	43	11.7	3.22	118	.241	.315	0	.000	-1	7	6	1	0.6
1978	Bal-A	3	1	.750	26	2	0	0	3	71²	75	10	36	41	14.2	4.77	73	.273	.361	0	—	0	-8	-10	2	-0.8
1980	Bal-A	0	0	—	1	0	0	0	0	2¹	3	0	0	1	11.6	3.86	103	.273	.273	0	—	0	0	0	0	0.0
Total	4	8	12	.400	131	2	0	0	15	220	221	17	92	107	13.1	3.89	95	.264	.342	0	.000	-1	-3	-5	3	-0.2

■ RICK KESTER
Kester, Richard Lee b: 7/7/46, Iola, Kan. BR/TR, 6', 190 lbs. Deb: 8/18/68

YEAR	TM/L	W	L	PCT	G	GS	CG	SH	SV	IP	H	HR	BB	SO	RAT	ERA	ERA+	OAV	OOB	BH	AVG	PB	PR	/A	PD	TPI
1968	Atl-N	0	0	—	5	0	0	0	0	6¹	8	0	3	9	15.6	5.68	53	.308	.379	0	—	0	-2	-2	-0	-0.1
1969	Atl-N	0	0	—	1	0	0	0	0	2	5	1	0	2	22.5	13.50	27	.455	.455	0	—	0	-2	-2	0	-0.1
1970	Atl-N	0	0	—	15	0	0	0	0	32¹	36	3	19	20	15.3	5.57	77	.283	.377	0	.000	-1	-5	-5	-1	-0.5
Total	3	0	0	—	21	0	0	0	0	40²	49	4	22	31	15.7	5.98	68	.299	.382	0	.000	-1	-10	-9	-1	-0.7

■ GUS KETCHUM
Ketchum, Augustus Franklin b: 3/21/1897, Royce City, Tex. d: 9/6/80, Oklahoma City, Okla. BR/TR, 5'9.5", 170 lbs. Deb: 8/07/22

YEAR	TM/L	W	L	PCT	G	GS	CG	SH	SV	IP	H	HR	BB	SO	RAT	ERA	ERA+	OAV	OOB	BH	AVG	PB	PR	/A	PD	TPI
1922	Phi-A	0	1	.000	6	0	0	0	0	16	19	2	8	4	15.8	5.63	76	.302	.389	0	.000	-1	-3	-2	-1	-0.3

■ HENRY KEUPPER
Keupper, Henry J. b: 6/24/1887, Staunton, Ill. d: 8/14/60, Marion, Ill. BL/TL, 6'1", 185 lbs. Deb: 4/19/14

YEAR	TM/L	W	L	PCT	G	GS	CG	SH	SV	IP	H	HR	BB	SO	RAT	ERA	ERA+	OAV	OOB	BH	AVG	PB	PR	/A	PD	TPI
1914	StL-F	8	20	.286	42	25	12	1	0	213	256	3	49	70	13.1	4.27	89	.291	.332	17	.250	2	-25	-21	3	-1.5

■ JIMMY KEY
Key, James Edward b: 4/22/61, Huntsville, Ala. BR/TL, 6'1", 185 lbs. Deb: 4/06/84

YEAR	TM/L	W	L	PCT	G	GS	CG	SH	SV	IP	H	HR	BB	SO	RAT	ERA	ERA+	OAV	OOB	BH	AVG	PB	PR	/A	PD	TPI
1984	Tor-A	4	5	.444	63	0	0	0	0	62	70	8	32	44	15.0	4.65	88	.286	.371	0	—	0	-5	-4	1	-0.2
1985	*Tor-A	14	6	.700	35	32	3	0	0	212²	188	22	50	85	10.2	3.00	140	.237	.284	0	—	0	27	28	5	3.4
1986	Tor-A	14	11	.560	36	35	4	2	0	232	222	24	74	141	11.6	3.57	118	.256	.317	0	—	0	16	17	3	2.0
1987	Tor-A	17	8	.680	36	36	8	1	0	261	210	24	66	161	9.6	2.76	163	.221	.273	0	—	0	49	50	2	5.4
1988	Tor-A	12	5	.706	21	21	2	2	0	131¹	127	13	30	65	11.1	3.29	119	.250	.298	0	—	0	10	9	0	1.0
1989	*Tor-A	13	14	.481	33	33	5	1	0	216	226	18	27	118	10.7	3.88	97	.270	.295	0	—	0	0	-3	2	0.0
1990	Tor-A	13	7	.650	27	27	0	0	0	154²	169	20	22	88	11.2	4.25	89	.281	.307	0	—	0	-6	-8	0	-0.7
Total	7	87	56	.608	251	184	22	6	10	1269²	1212	129	301	702	10.8	3.47	118	.252	.299	0	—	0	91	90	13	10.9

■ DANA KIECKER
Kiecker, Dana Ervin b: 2/25/61, Sleepy Eye, Minn. BR/TR, 6'3", 180 lbs. Deb: 4/12/90

YEAR	TM/L	W	L	PCT	G	GS	CG	SH	SV	IP	H	HR	BB	SO	RAT	ERA	ERA+	OAV	OOB	BH	AVG	PB	PR	/A	PD	TPI
1990	*Bos-A	8	9	.471	32	25	0	0	0	152	145	7	54	93	12.3	3.97	103	.253	.328	0	—	0	-1	2	2	0.4

■ JOE KIEFER
Kiefer, Joseph William "Harlem Joe" or "Smoke" b: 7/19/1899, W.Leyden, N.Y. d: 7/5/75, Utica, N.Y. BR/TR, 5'11", 190 lbs. Deb: 10/01/20

YEAR	TM/L	W	L	PCT	G	GS	CG	SH	SV	IP	H	HR	BB	SO	RAT	ERA	ERA+	OAV	OOB	BH	AVG	PB	PR	/A	PD	TPI
1920	Chi-A	0	1	.000	2	1	0	0	0	5	7	0	5	1	23.4	14.40	26	.333	.481	0	.000	-0	-6	-6	-0	-0.5
1925	Bos-A	0	2	.000	2	2	0	0	0	15	20	0	9	4	18.0	6.00	76	.351	.448	0	.000	-1	-3	-2	1	-0.1
1926	Bos-A	0	2	.000	11	1	0	0	0	30	29	2	16	4	14.1	4.80	85	.266	.370	1	.143	-0	-3	-2	0	-0.1
Total	3	0	5	.000	15	4	0	0	0	50	56	2	30	9	16.2	6.12	68	.299	.407	1	.077	-1	-11	-11	1	-0.7

■ LEO KIELY
Kiely, Leo Patrick "Kiki" b: 11/30/29, Hoboken, N.J. d: 1/18/84, Montclair, N.J. BL/TL, 6'2", 180 lbs. Deb: 6/27/51

YEAR	TM/L	W	L	PCT	G	GS	CG	SH	SV	IP	H	HR	BB	SO	RAT	ERA	ERA+	OAV	OOB	BH	AVG	PB	PR	/A	PD	TPI
1951	Bos-A	7	7	.500	17	16	4	0	0	113¹	106	9	39	46	11.7	3.34	134	.251	.317	5	.143	-1	10	14	2	1.5
1954	Bos-A	5	8	.385	28	19	4	1	0	131	153	12	58	59	14.6	3.50	117	.295	.367	9	.180	0	3	9	-1	0.9
1955	Bos-A	3	3	.500	33	4	0	0	6	90	91	5	37	36	12.8	2.80	153	.269	.331	5	.192	-0	12	15	1	1.7
1956	Bos-A	2	2	.500	23	0	0	0	3	31¹	47	1	14	9	18.1	5.17	89	.362	.432	1	.167	-0	-4	-2	0	-0.1
1958	Bos-A	5	2	.714	47	0	0	0	12	81	77	3	18	26	10.8	3.00	134	.254	.300	0	.000	-2	7	9	1	0.0
1959	Bos-A	3	3	.500	41	0	0	0	7	55²	67	8	18	30	13.9	4.20	97	.299	.354	0	.000	-1	-2	-1	1	0.0
1960	KC-A	1	2	.333	20	0	0	0	1	20²	21	1	5	6	11.8	1.74	229	.266	.318	0	.000	0	5	5	1	0.7
Total	7	26	27	.491	209	39	8	1	29	523	562	39	189	212	13.1	3.37	125	.279	.343	20	.144	-4	31	49	6	5.6

■ JOHN KILEY
Kiley, John Frederick b: 7/1/1859, S.Dedham, Mass. d: 12/18/40, Norwood, Mass. BL/TL, Deb: 5/01/1884 ♦

YEAR	TM/L	W	L	PCT	G	GS	CG	SH	SV	IP	H	HR	BB	SO	RAT	ERA	ERA+	OAV	OOB	BH	AVG	PB	PR	/A	PD	TPI
1891	Bos-N	0	1	.000	1	1	1	0	0	8	13	3	5	1	20.3	6.75	54	.352	.429	0	.000	-0	-3	-3	0	-0.1

■ PAUL KILGUS
Kilgus, Paul Nelson b: 2/2/62, Bowling Green, Ky. BL/TL, 6'1", 175 lbs. Deb: 6/07/87

YEAR	TM/L	W	L	PCT	G	GS	CG	SH	SV	IP	H	HR	BB	SO	RAT	ERA	ERA+	OAV	OOB	BH	AVG	PB	PR	/A	PD	TPI
1987	Tex-A	2	7	.222	25	12	0	0	0	89¹	95	14	31	42	12.9	4.13	108	.271	.334	0	—	0	3	3	-1	0.3
1988	Tex-A	12	15	.444	32	32	5	3	0	203¹	190	18	71	88	12.0	4.16	98	.243	.314	0	—	0	-4	-2	2	0.0
1989	*Chi-N	6	10	.375	35	23	0	0	2	145²	164	9	49	61	13.5	4.39	86	.283	.344	3	.073	-3	-14	-10	1	-1.1
1990	Tor-A	0	0	—	11	0	0	0	0	16¹	19	2	7	7	14.9	6.06	63	.306	.386	0	—	0	-4	-4	0	-0.3
Total	4	20	32	.385	103	67	5	3	2	454²	468	43	158	198	12.7	4.30	94	.264	.330	3	.073	-3	-20	-12	2	-1.1

■ MIKE KILKENNY
Kilkenny, Michael David b: 4/11/45, Bradford, Ont., Can. BR/TL, 6'3.5", 175 lbs. Deb: 4/11/69

YEAR	TM/L	W	L	PCT	G	GS	CG	SH	SV	IP	H	HR	BB	SO	RAT	ERA	ERA+	OAV	OOB	BH	AVG	PB	PR	/A	PD	TPI
1969	Det-A	8	6	.571	39	15	6	4	2	128¹	99	13	63	97	11.6	3.37	111	.211	.310	2	.054	-3	4	5	-0	0.3
1970	Det-A	7	6	.538	36	21	3	0	0	129	141	10	70	105	14.9	5.16	72	.279	.369	3	.077	-3	-21	-21	0	-2.2
1971	Det-A	4	5	.444	30	11	2	0	1	86¹	83	8	44	47	13.4	5.00	72	.247	.338	2	.083	-2	-15	-14	-0	-1.5
1972	Det-A	0	0	—	1	0	0	0	0	1	1	1	0	0	9.0	9.00	35	.250	.250	0	—	0	-1	-1	0	0.0
	Oak-A	0	0	—	1	0	0	0	0	1	0	0	0	0	0.0	0.00	—	.000	.000	0	—	0	0	0	0	0.0
	Yr	0	0	—	2	0	0	0	0	2	1	1	0	0	4.5	4.50	67	.143	.143	0	—	0	-0	-0	0	0.0
	SD-N	0	0	—	5	0	0	0	0	4¹	7	1	3	5	20.8	8.31	40	.350	.435	0	—	0	-2	-2	0	-0.1
	Cle-A	4	1	.800	22	7	1	0	1	58	51	5	39	44	14.0	3.41	94	.237	.354	1	.071	-1	-2	-1	1	-0.1
1973	Cle-A	0	0	—	5	0	0	0	0	2	5	1	5	3	49.5	22.50	17	.455	.647	0	—	0	-4	-4	0	-0.3
Total	5	23	18	.561	139	54	12	4	4	410	387	39	224	301	13.6	4.43	82	.248	.345	8	.070	-8	-41	-37	1	-3.9

■ EVANS KILLEEN
Killeen, Evans Henry b: 2/27/36, Brooklyn, N.Y. BR/TR, 6', 190 lbs. Deb: 9/07/59

YEAR	TM/L	W	L	PCT	G	GS	CG	SH	SV	IP	H	HR	BB	SO	RAT	ERA	ERA+	OAV	OOB	BH	AVG	PB	PR	/A	PD	TPI
1959	KC-A	0	0	—	4	0	0	0	0	5²	4	0	4	1	12.7	4.76	84	.211	.348	0	—	0	-1	-0	-0	0.0

■ HENRY KILLEEN
Killeen, Henry b: 1871, Troy, N.Y. Deb: 9/11/1891

YEAR	TM/L	W	L	PCT	G	GS	CG	SH	SV	IP	H	HR	BB	SO	RAT	ERA	ERA+	OAV	OOB	BH	AVG	PB	PR	/A	PD	TPI
1891	Cle-N	0	1	.000	1	1	1	0	0	8²	11	1	8	3	19.7	6.23	56	.298	.423	0	.000	-0	-3	-3	0	-0.1

■ FRANK KILLEN
Killen, Frank Bissell "Lefty" b: 11/30/1870, Pittsburgh, Pa. d: 12/3/39, Pittsburgh, Pa. BL/TL, 6'1", 200 lbs. Deb: 8/27/1891

YEAR	TM/L	W	L	PCT	G	GS	CG	SH	SV	IP	H	HR	BB	SO	RAT	ERA	ERA+	OAV	OOB	BH	AVG	PB	PR	/A	PD	TPI
1891	Mil-a	7	4	.636	11	11	11	2	0	96²	73	1	51	38	11.5	1.68	262	.202	.301	8	.229	1	22	29	0	3.1
1892	Was-N	29	26	.527	60	52	46	2	0	459²	448	15	182	147	12.3	3.31	98	.245	.314	37	.199	9	-1	-3	3	1.0
1893	Pit-N	36	14	.720	55	48	38	2	0	415	401	12	140	99	11.7	3.64	125	.246	.306	47	.275	14	47	42	1	4.8
1894	Pit-N	14	11	.560	28	28	20	1	0	204	261	3	86	62	15.3	4.50	116	.308	.371	21	.262	-0	19	17	1	1.4

YEAR TM/L	W	L	PCT	G	GS	CG	SH	SV	IP	H	HR	BB	SO	RAT	ERA	ERA+	OAV	OOB	BH	AVG	PB	PR	/A	PD	TPI
1895 Pit-N	5	5	.500	13	11	6	0	0	95	113	2	57	25	16.1	5.49	82	.291	.382	13	.342	4	-8	-10	1	-0.4
1896 Pit-N	**30**	18	.625	**52**	50	**44**	5	0	432¹	476	7	119	134	12.4	3.41	123	.277	.324	40	.231	8	46	38	2	4.1
1897 Pit-N	17	23	.425	42	41	**38**	1	0	337¹	417	4	76	99	13.2	4.46	94	.301	.337	32	.248	4	-5	-10	-0	-0.5
1898 Pit-N	10	11	.476	23	23	17	0	0	177²	201	3	41	48	12.3	3.75	95	.283	.322	17	.262	2	-3	-4	-0	-0.1
Was-N	6	9	.400	17	16	15	0	0	128¹	149	4	29	43	12.5	3.58	102	.288	.326	15	.273	4	0	1	-0	0.5
Yr	16	20	.444	40	39	32	0	0	306	350	7	70	91	12.4	3.68	98	.285	.324	18	.150	6	-2	-2	-1	0.4
1899 Was-N	0	2	.000	2	2	1	0	0	12	18	0	4	3	16.5	6.00	65	.345	.392	1	.200	-0	-3	-3	-1	-0.2
Bos-N	7	5	.583	12	12	11	0	0	99¹	108	3	26	23	12.1	4.26	98	.277	.322	7	.171	-2	-4	-1	0	-0.2
Yr	7	7	.500	14	14	12	0	0	111¹	126	3	30	26	12.6	4.45	93	.285	.330	1	.022	-3	-7	-4	-1	-0.4
1900 Chi-N	3	3	.500	6	6	6	0	0	54	65	1	11	4	12.7	4.67	77	.297	.331	3	.150	-1	-6	-6	0	-0.5
Total 10	164	131	.556	321	300	253	13	0	2511¹	2730	55	822	725	12.7	3.78	109	.272	.327	241	.241	42	104	92	6	13.0

■ ED KILLIAN
Killian, Edwin Henry "Twilight Ed" b: 11/12/1876, Racine, Wis. d: 7/18/28, Detroit, Mich. BL/TL, 5'11", 170 lbs. Deb: 8/25/03

YEAR TM/L	W	L	PCT	G	GS	CG	SH	SV	IP	H	HR	BB	SO	RAT	ERA	ERA+	OAV	OOB	BH	AVG	PB	PR	/A	PD	TPI
1903 Cle-A	3	4	.429	9	8	7	3	0	61²	61	1	13	18	10.8	2.48	115	.258	.296	5	.179	-0	3	3	0	0.2
1904 Det-A	14	20	.412	40	34	32	4	1	331²	293	0	93	124	10.5	2.44	104	.238	.291	18	.143	-3	6	4	-5	-0.3
1905 Det-A	23	14	.622	39	37	33	**8**	0	313¹	263	0	102	110	10.5	2.27	121	.229	.292	32	.271	7	14	16	-3	2.2
1906 Det-A	10	6	.625	21	16	14	0	2	149²	165	0	54	47	13.2	3.43	81	.283	.343	9	.170	-1	-12	-11	-2	-1.4
1907 *Det-A	25	13	.658	41	34	29	3	1	314	286	1	91	96	10.8	1.78	147	.245	.299	39	.320	10	27	29	-1	4.6
1908 *Det-A	12	9	.571	27	23	15	0	1	180²	170	3	53	47	11.5	2.99	81	.252	.314	10	.137	-3	-12	-11	3	-1.1
1909 Det-A	11	9	.550	25	19	14	3	1	173¹	150	1	49	54	10.6	1.71	147	.236	.297	10	.161	-1	15	15	-1	1.6
1910 Det-A	4	3	.571	11	9	5	1	0	74	75	2	27	20	13.1	3.04	87	.268	.345	4	.148	-1	-4	-3	-1	-0.5
Total 8	102	78	.567	213	180	149	22	6	1598¹	1463	8	482	516	11.1	2.38	110	.245	.304	127	.209	7	36	42	-9	5.3

■ JACK KILLILAY
Killilay, John William b: 5/24/1887, Leavenworth, Kan. d: 10/21/68, Tulsa, Okla. BR/TR, 5'11", 165 lbs. Deb: 5/13/11

YEAR TM/L	W	L	PCT	G	GS	CG	SH	SV	IP	H	HR	BB	SO	RAT	ERA	ERA+	OAV	OOB	BH	AVG	PB	PR	/A	PD	TPI
1911 Bos-A	4	2	.667	14	7	1	0	0	61	65	1	36	28	16.4	3.54	93	.302	.425	1	.042	-2	-1	-2	0	-0.3

■ MATT KILROY
Kilroy, Matthew Aloysius "Matches" b: 6/21/1866, Philadelphia, Pa. d: 3/2/40, Philadelphia, Pa. TL, 5'9", 175 lbs. Deb: 4/17/1886

YEAR TM/L	W	L	PCT	G	GS	CG	SH	SV	IP	H	HR	BB	SO	RAT	ERA	ERA+	OAV	OOB	BH	AVG	PB	PR	/A	PD	TPI
1886 Bal-a	29	34	.460	**68**	68	**66**	5	0	583	476	10	182	**513**	10.2	3.37	102	.212	.272	38	.174	-6	6	4	4	0.2
1887 Bal-a	**46**	19	.708	**69**	69	**66**	6	0	589¹	585	9	157	217	11.3	3.07	134	.249	.297	59	.247	9	**80**	67	10	**7.2**
1888 Bal-a	17	21	.447	40	40	35	2	0	321	347	5	79	135	11.9	4.04	74	.266	.308	26	.179	-0	-35	-38	-1	-3.4
1889 Bal-a	29	25	.537	59	56	**55**	5	0	480²	476	8	142	217	11.6	2.85	139	.250	.303	57	.274	10	54	59	8	**7.1**
1890 Bos-P	9	15	.375	30	27	18	0	0	217²	268	14	87	48	14.7	4.26	103	.290	.351	20	.215	-0	-1	3	1	0.4
1891 Cin-a	1	4	.200	7	6	4	0	0	45¹	51	1	19	6	13.9	2.98	138	.274	.342	3	.150	-1	4	6	1	0.5
1892 Was-N	1	1	.500	4	3	2	0	0	26¹	20	0	15	1	12.0	2.39	136	.202	.307	2	.200	-0	3	3	2	0.4
1893 Lou-N	3	2	.600	5	5	5	1	0	35	57	2	23	4	20.6	9.00	49	.355	.436	7	.438	3	-17	-18	1	-1.0
1894 Lou-N	0	5	.000	8	7	3	0	0	37	46	2	20	11	16.1	3.89	131	.302	.383	2	.118	-2	6	5	1	0.3
1898 Chi-N	6	7	.462	13	11	10	0	0	99	119	2	30	18	13.4	4.31	83	.293	.341	22	.229	2	-8	-8	1	-0.6
Total 10	141	133	.515	303	292	264	19	0	2435²	2445	53	754	1170	11.8	3.47	109	.252	.305	236	.222	15	92	83	28	11.1

■ MIKE KILROY
Kilroy, Michael Joseph b: 11/4/1872, Philadelphia, Pa. d: 10/2/60, Philadelphia, Pa. TR , Deb: 9/01/1888

YEAR TM/L	W	L	PCT	G	GS	CG	SH	SV	IP	H	HR	BB	SO	RAT	ERA	ERA+	OAV	OOB	BH	AVG	PB	PR	/A	PD	TPI
1888 Bal-a	0	1	.000	1	1	1	0	0	9	12	1	5	1	17.0	8.00	37	.309	.388	0	.000	-1	-5	-5	0	-0.3
1891 Phi-N	0	2	.000	3	1	0	0	0	10	15	1	4	3	17.1	9.90	34	.334	.388	2	.400	1	-7	-7	-0	-0.4
Total 2	0	3	.000	4	2	1	0	0	19	27	2	9	4	17.1	9.00	36	.322	.388	2	.222	0	-12	-12	-0	-0.7

■ NEWT KIMBALL
Kimball, Newell W. b: 3/27/15, Logan, Utah BR/TR, 6'2.5", 190 lbs. Deb: 5/07/37

YEAR TM/L	W	L	PCT	G	GS	CG	SH	SV	IP	H	HR	BB	SO	RAT	ERA	ERA+	OAV	OOB	BH	AVG	PB	PR	/A	PD	TPI
1937 Chi-N	0	0	—	2	0	0	0	0	5	12	1	1	0	23.4	10.80	37	.444	.464	0	.000	-0	-4	-4	0	-0.2
1938 Chi-N	0	0	—	1	0	0	0	0	1	3	0	0	1	27.0	9.00	43	.500	.500	0	—	0	-1	-1	0	0.0
1940 Bro-N	3	1	.750	21	0	0	0	1	33²	29	2	15	21	11.8	3.21	125	.238	.321	0	.000	-1	2	3	-0	0.2
StL-N	1	0	1.000	2	1	1	0	0	14	11	1	6	6	10.9	2.57	155	.208	.288	2	.333	1	2	2	-0	0.3
Yr	4	1	.800	23	1	1	0	1	47²	40	3	21	27	11.5	3.02	132	.229	.311	2	.000	0	4	5	-1	0.5
1941 Bro-N	3	1	.750	15	5	1	0	1	52	43	0	29	17	12.5	3.63	101	.225	.327	3	.214	0	-0	0	0	0.0
1942 Bro-N	2	0	1.000	14	1	0	0	1	29¹	27	0	19	8	14.4	3.68	89	.265	.385	1	.200	0	-1	-1	-1	-0.2
1943 Bro-N	1	1	.500	5	0	0	0	1	11	9	0	5	2	11.5	1.64	205	.214	.298	0	.000	-0	2	2	-0	0.2
Phi-N	1	6	.143	34	6	2	0	2	89²	85	4	42	33	12.8	4.12	82	.253	.338	3	.188	1	-7	-7	-2	-0.8
Yr	2	7	.222	39	6	2	0	3	100²	94	4	47	35	12.7	3.84	88	.249	.333	5	.263	1	-5	-5	-2	-0.5
Total 6	11	9	.550	94	13	4	0	5	235²	219	8	117	88	12.9	3.78	94	.249	.339	9	.180	1	-6	-6	-4	-0.5

■ SAM KIMBER
Kimber, Samuel Jackson b: 10/29/1852, Philadelphia, Pa. d: 11/7/25, Philadelphia, Pa. BR/TR, 5'10.5", 165 lbs. Deb: 5/01/1884

YEAR TM/L	W	L	PCT	G	GS	CG	SH	SV	IP	H	HR	BB	SO	RAT	ERA	ERA+	OAV	OOB	BH	AVG	PB	PR	/A	PD	TPI
1884 Bro-a	18	20	.474	41	41	41	4	0	361¹	364	6	72	122	10.9	3.81	87	.248	.283	21	.148	-5	-23	-20	-0	-2.1
1885 Pro-N	0	1	.000	1	1	1	0	0	8	15	1	5	4	22.5	11.25	24	.383	.452	0	.000	-0	-7	-8	0	-0.5
Total 2	18	21	.462	42	42	42	4	0	369¹	379	7	77	126	11.1	3.97	83	.251	.288	21	.145	-6	-30	-27	0	-2.6

■ HARRY KIMBERLIN
Kimberlin, Harry Lydle "Murphy" or "Mule Trader" b: 3/13/09, Sullivan, Mo. BR/TR, 6'3", 175 lbs. Deb: 7/11/36

YEAR TM/L	W	L	PCT	G	GS	CG	SH	SV	IP	H	HR	BB	SO	RAT	ERA	ERA+	OAV	OOB	BH	AVG	PB	PR	/A	PD	TPI
1936 StL-A	0	0	—	13	0	0	0	0	20	24	3	16	4	18.0	5.40	100	.296	.412	0	.000	-0	-1	-0	-0	0.0
1937 StL-A	0	2	.000	3	2	1	0	0	15¹	16	2	9	5	14.7	2.35	206	.254	.347	1	.200	-0	4	4	-0	0.4
1938 StL-A	0	0	—	1	1	1	0	0	8	8	1	3	1	12.4	3.38	147	.286	.355	0	.000	-0	1	1	-0	0.1
1939 StL-A	1	2	.333	17	3	0	0	0	41	59	6	19	11	17.6	5.49	89	.326	.396	3	.333	0	-4	-3	0	-0.1
Total 4	1	4	.200	34	6	2	0	0	84¹	107	12	47	21	16.6	4.70	106	.303	.388	4	.250	0	0	3	-0	0.4

■ HAL KIME
Kime, Harold Lee "Lefty" b: 3/15/1899, W.Salem, Ohio d: 5/16/39, Columbus, Ohio BL/TL, 5'9", 160 lbs. Deb: 6/19/20

YEAR TM/L	W	L	PCT	G	GS	CG	SH	SV	IP	H	HR	BB	SO	RAT	ERA	ERA+	OAV	OOB	BH	AVG	PB	PR	/A	PD	TPI
1920 StL-N	0	0	—	4	0	0	0	0	7	9	0	2	1	15.4	2.57	116	.333	.400	0	.000	-0	0	0	0	0.0

■ CHAD KIMSEY
Kimsey, Clyde Elias b: 8/6/06, Copperhill, Tenn. d: 12/3/42, Pryor, Okla. BL/TR, 6'2", 200 lbs. Deb: 4/21/29

YEAR TM/L	W	L	PCT	G	GS	CG	SH	SV	IP	H	HR	BB	SO	RAT	ERA	ERA+	OAV	OOB	BH	AVG	PB	PR	/A	PD	TPI
1929 StL-A	3	6	.333	24	3	1	0	1	64¹	83	2	19	19	14.3	5.04	88	.340	.388	8	.267	3	-6	-4	3	0.1
1930 StL-A	6	10	.375	42	4	1	0	1	113¹	139	8	45	32	14.8	6.35	77	.312	.377	24	.343	8	-21	-19	1	-0.7
1931 StL-A	4	6	.400	42	1	0	0	7	94¹	121	1	27	27	14.3	4.39	106	.312	.360	10	.270	5	-0	**3**	2	1.0
1932 StL-A	4	2	.667	33	0	0	0	3	78¹	85	3	33	13	13.6	4.02	121	.281	.352	6	.333	1	4	7	1	0.9
Chi-A	1	1	.500	7	0	0	0	2	11	8	0	5	6	11.5	2.45	176	.211	.308	-0	.000	-0	2	2	1	0.3
Yr	5	3	.625	40	0	0	0	5	89¹	93	3	38	19	13.3	3.83	125	.274	.348	1	.050	1	6	**10**	2	1.2
1933 Chi-A	4	1	.800	28	2	0	0	0	96	124	7	36	19	15.4	5.53	77	.318	.381	5	.152	-2	-13	-14	1	-1.2
1936 Det-A	2	3	.400	22	0	0	0	3	52	58	2	29	11	15.2	4.85	102	.284	.376	5	.313	2	1	1	2	0.4
Total 6	24	29	.453	198	10	2	0	17	509¹	618	23	194	121	14.5	5.07	92	.307	.371	58	.282	16	-33	-24	12	0.8

■ ELLIS KINDER
Kinder, Ellis Raymond "Old Folks" b: 7/26/14, Atkins, Ark. d: 10/16/68, Jackson, Tenn. BR/TR, 6', 195 lbs. Deb: 4/30/46

YEAR TM/L	W	L	PCT	G	GS	CG	SH	SV	IP	H	HR	BB	SO	RAT	ERA	ERA+	OAV	OOB	BH	AVG	PB	PR	/A	PD	TPI
1946 StL-A	3	3	.500	33	7	1	0	1	86²	78	8	36	59	11.8	3.32	112	.241	.318	1	.053	-1	2	4	-1	0.2
1947 StL-A	8	15	.348	34	26	10	2	1	194¹	201	11	82	110	13.1	4.49	86	.264	.336	8	.129	-4	-17	-13	-3	-1.9
1948 Bos-A	10	7	.588	28	22	10	1	0	178	183	10	63	53	12.5	3.74	117	.266	.330	6	.097	-4	11	13	0	0.6
1949 Bos-A	23	6	**.793**	43	30	19	**6**	4	252	251	20	99	138	12.6	3.36	130	.260	.330	12	.130	-4	24	28	-4	1.9
1950 Bos-A	14	12	.538	48	23	11	1	9	207	212	23	78	95	12.7	4.26	115	.265	.328	13	.183	-1	7	15	-2	1.2
1951 Bos-A	11	2	.846	**63**	2	1	0	**14**	127	108	9	46	84	10.9	2.55	175	.230	.298	4	.118	-3	**22**	27	-2	2.2
1952 Bos-A	5	6	.455	23	10	4	0	4	97¹	85	11	28	50	10.5	2.58	153	.234	.309	0	.000	-5	12	15	-1	1.1
1953 Bos-A	10	6	.625	**69**	0	0	0	**27**	107	84	8	38	39	10.4	1.85	227	.215	.288	11	.379	3	**26**	28	1	3.2
1954 Bos-A	8	8	.500	48	2	0	0	15	107	106	7	36	67	11.9	3.62	114	.260	.321	5	.185	0	1	6	-2	0.5
1955 Bos-A	5	5	.500	43	0	0	0	18	66²	57	5	15	31	9.9	2.84	151	.229	.275	3	.250	0	8	11	-1	1.1
1956 StL-N	2	0	1.000	22	0	0	0	6	25²	23	3	9	4	11.2	3.51	108	.245	.311	0	.000	-0	1	1	-1	0.0

YEAR	TM/L	W	L	PCT	G	GS	CG	SH	SV	IP	H	HR	BB	SO	RAT	ERA	ERA+	OAV	OOB	BH	AVG	PB	PR	/A	PD	TPI
	Chi-A	3	1	.750	29	0	0	0	3	29²	33	2	8	19	12.4	2.73	150	.277	.323	0	.000	-0	5	5	-0	0.4
1957	Chi-A	0	0	—	1	0	0	0	0	1	0	0	1	0	9.0	0.00	—	.000	.250	0	—	0	0	0	0	0.0
Total	12	102	71	.590	484	122	56	10	102	1479²	1421	118	539	749	12.0	3.43	125	.252	.318	63	.142	-20	101	139	-17	10.5

■ SILVER KING
King, Charles Frederick (b: Charles Frederick Koenig) b: 1/11/1868, St.Louis, Mo. d: 5/21/38, St.Louis, Mo. BR/TR, 6', 170 lbs. Deb: 9/02/1886

YEAR	TM/L	W	L	PCT	G	GS	CG	SH	SV	IP	H	HR	BB	SO	RAT	ERA	ERA+	OAV	OOB	BH	AVG	PB	PR	/A	PD	TPI
1886	KC-N	1	3	.250	5	5	5	0	0	39	43	1	9	23	12.0	4.85	78	.269	.308	1	.045	-2	-7	-5	1	-0.4
1887	*StL-a	32	12	.727	46	44	43	2	1	390	401	4	109	128	11.8	3.78	120	.256	.305	46	.207	-4	22	33	-4	2.1
1888	*StL-a	45	21	.682	66	65	64	6	0	585²	437	6	76	258	7.9	1.64	198	.200	.227	43	.208	10	92	105	-1	11.8
1889	StL-a	35	16	.686	56	53	47	2	1	458	462	15	125	188	11.5	3.14	134	.254	.302	43	.228	1	36	55	-3	5.0
1890	Chi-P	30	22	.577	56	56	48	4	0	461	420	5	163	185	11.4	2.69	161	.232	.296	31	.168	-6	79	84	6	7.1
1891	Pit-N	14	29	.326	48	44	40	3	1	384¹	382	7	144	160	12.3	3.11	105	.249	.314	25	.169	-1	10	7	-2	0.4
1892	NY-N	23	24	.489	52	47	46	1	0	419¹	397	15	174	177	12.3	3.24	99	.240	.312	35	.210	6	2	-1	-1	0.4
1893	NY-N	3	4	.429	7	7	4	0	0	49	69	4	26	13	17.4	8.63	54	.322	.396	3	.176	1	-22	-22	0	-1.5
	Cin-N	5	6	.455	17	15	8	1	1	105	119	2	56	30	15.0	4.89	98	.277	.360	6	.162	-0	-3	-1	-0	0.0
	Yr	8	10	.444	24	22	12	1	1	154	188	6	82	43	15.8	6.08	78	.292	.372	15	.278	1	-24	-23	-1	-1.5
1896	Was-N	10	7	.588	22	16	12	0	1	145¹	179	3	43	35	13.7	4.09	108	.300	.347	16	.276	4	4	5	-3	0.5
1897	Was-N	6	9	.400	23	19	12	0	1	154	196	7	45	32	14.1	4.79	91	.307	.353	11	.193	0	-8	-8	1	-0.4
Total	10	204	153	.571	398	371	329	19	6	3190²	3105	69	970	1229	11.5	3.18	122	.246	.300	260	.199	10	207	253	-5	25.0

■ CLYDE KING
King, Clyde Edward b: 5/23/25, Goldsboro, N.C. BB/TR, 6'1", 175 lbs. Deb: 6/21/44 MC

YEAR	TM/L	W	L	PCT	G	GS	CG	SH	SV	IP	H	HR	BB	SO	RAT	ERA	ERA+	OAV	OOB	BH	AVG	PB	PR	/A	PD	TPI
1944	Bro-N	2	1	.667	14	3	1	0	0	43²	42	1	12	14	11.3	3.09	115	.256	.311	2	.200	-0	3	2	-1	0.1
1945	Bro-N	5	5	.500	42	2	0	0	3	112¹	131	8	48	29	14.3	4.09	92	.295	.364	4	.125	-2	-4	-4	1	-0.4
1947	Bro-N	6	5	.545	29	9	2	0	0	87²	85	11	29	31	11.7	2.77	149	.252	.311	3	.115	-1	13	13	-1	1.1
1948	Bro-N	0	1	.000	9	0	0	0	0	12¹	14	3	6	5	15.3	8.03	50	.286	.375	0	.000	-0	-6	-6	0	-0.4
1951	Bro-N	14	7	.667	48	3	1	0	6	121¹	118	15	50	33	12.7	4.15	94	.263	.341	4	.138	-0	-3	-3	1	-0.1
1952	Bro-N	2	0	1.000	23	0	0	0	0	42²	56	5	12	17	14.6	5.06	72	.318	.365	0	.000	-1	-6	-7	1	-0.7
1953	Cin-N	3	6	.333	35	4	0	0	2	76	78	15	32	21	13.3	5.21	84	.271	.348	0	.000	-1	-8	-7	0	-0.7
Total	7	32	25	.561	200	21	4	0	11	496	524	58	189	150	13.1	4.14	95	.275	.343	13	.114	-4	-11	-11	1	-0.9

■ ERIC KING
King, Eric Steven b: 4/10/64, Oxnard, Cal. BR/TR, 6'2", 180 lbs. Deb: 5/15/86

YEAR	TM/L	W	L	PCT	G	GS	CG	SH	SV	IP	H	HR	BB	SO	RAT	ERA	ERA+	OAV	OOB	BH	AVG	PB	PR	/A	PD	TPI
1986	Det-A	11	4	.733	33	16	3	1	3	138¹	108	11	63	79	11.6	3.51	117	.216	.313	0	—	0	10	9	0	1.0
1987	*Det-A	6	9	.400	55	4	0	0	9	116	111	15	60	89	13.6	4.89	86	.251	.345	0	—	0	-6	-9	2	-0.5
1988	Det-A	4	1	.800	23	5	0	0	3	68²	60	5	34	45	13.0	3.41	112	.233	.334	0	—	0	4	3	-0	0.3
1989	Chi-A	9	10	.474	25	25	1	1	0	159¹	144	13	64	72	12.0	3.39	112	.244	.322	0	—	0	9	7	-0	0.7
1990	Chi-A	12	4	.750	25	25	2	2	0	151	135	10	40	70	10.8	3.28	117	.237	.294	0	—	0	11	9	-1	0.8
Total	5	42	28	.600	161	75	6	4	15	633¹	558	54	261	355	12.0	3.67	108	.236	.319	0	—	0	28	20	1	2.3

■ NELLIE KING
King, Nelson Joseph b: 3/15/28, Shenandoah, Pa. BR/TR, 6'6", 185 lbs. Deb: 4/15/54

YEAR	TM/L	W	L	PCT	G	GS	CG	SH	SV	IP	H	HR	BB	SO	RAT	ERA	ERA+	OAV	OOB	BH	AVG	PB	PR	/A	PD	TPI
1954	Pit-N	0	0	—	4	0	0	0	0	7	10	0	1	3	14.1	5.14	81	.400	.423	0	—	0	-1	-1	0	0.0
1955	Pit-N	1	3	.250	17	4	0	0	0	54¹	60	2	14	21	12.6	2.98	138	.286	.336	0	.000	-2	6	7	0	0.5
1956	Pit-N	4	1	.800	38	0	0	0	5	60	54	8	19	25	11.1	3.15	120	.241	.303	0	.000	-1	4	4	-1	0.3
1957	Pit-N	2	1	.667	36	0	0	0	1	52	69	7	16	23	15.1	4.50	84	.337	.390	0	.000	-1	-4	-4	-0	-0.4
Total	4	7	5	.583	95	4	0	0	6	173¹	193	17	50	72	12.9	3.58	109	.291	.345	0	.000	-3	6	6	-1	0.4

■ BRIAN KINGMAN
Kingman, Brian Paul b: 7/27/54, Los Angeles, Cal. BR/TR, 6'2", 200 lbs. Deb: 6/28/79

YEAR	TM/L	W	L	PCT	G	GS	CG	SH	SV	IP	H	HR	BB	SO	RAT	ERA	ERA+	OAV	OOB	BH	AVG	PB	PR	/A	PD	TPI
1979	Oak-A	8	7	.533	18	17	5	1	0	112²	128	10	33	58	11.9	4.31	94	.258	.314	0	—	0	-1	-3	-2	-0.4
1980	Oak-A	8	20	.286	32	30	10	1	0	211¹	209	21	82	116	12.6	3.83	98	.256	.326	0	—	0	5	-2	-2	-0.3
1981	*Oak-A	3	6	.333	18	15	3	1	0	100¹	112	10	32	52	13.3	3.95	88	.286	.347	0	—	0	-3	-5	-2	-0.6
1982	Oak-A	4	12	.250	23	20	3	0	1	122²	131	11	57	46	14.3	4.48	87	.279	.365	0	—	0	-5	-8	-2	-0.9
1983	SF-N	0	0	—	3	0	0	0	0	4²	10	0	1	1	21.2	7.71	46	.417	.440	0	—	0	-2	-2	-0	-0.1
Total	5	23	45	.338	94	82	21	3	1	551²	575	52	205	273	13.0	4.13	92	.269	.338	0	—	0	-7	-20	-8	-2.3

■ DAVE KINGMAN
Kingman, David Arthur b: 12/21/48, Pendleton, Ore. BR/TR, 6'6", 210 lbs. Deb: 7/30/71 ♦

YEAR	TM/L	W	L	PCT	G	GS	CG	SH	SV	IP	H	HR	BB	SO	RAT	ERA	ERA+	OAV	OOB	BH	AVG	PB	PR	/A	PD	TPI
1973	SF-N	0	0	—	2	0	0	0	0	4	3	0	6	4	20.3	9.00	42	.200	.429	62	.203	1	-2	-2	-0	-0.1

■ DENNIS KINNEY
Kinney, Dennis Paul b: 2/26/52, Toledo, Ohio BL/TL, 6'1", 175 lbs. Deb: 4/09/78

YEAR	TM/L	W	L	PCT	G	GS	CG	SH	SV	IP	H	HR	BB	SO	RAT	ERA	ERA+	OAV	OOB	BH	AVG	PB	PR	/A	PD	TPI
1978	Cle-A	0	2	.000	18	0	0	0	5	38²	37	3	14	19	12.1	4.42	84	.259	.329	0	—	0	-3	-3	-0	-0.2
	SD-N	0	1	.000	7	0	0	0	0	7	6	3	4	2	12.9	6.43	52	.222	.323	0	.000	-0	-2	-2	-0	-0.2
1979	SD-N	0	0	—	13	0	0	0	0	18	17	2	8	11	13.0	3.50	101	.250	.338	0	.000	-0	0	0	-0	0.0
1980	SD-N	4	6	.400	50	0	0	0	1	82²	79	3	37	40	12.7	4.25	81	.252	.333	1	.083	-0	-6	-7	-0	-0.8
1981	Det-A	0	0	—	6	0	0	0	0	3²	5	0	4	3	22.1	9.82	38	.313	.450	0	—	0	-3	-2	0	-0.2
1982	Oak-A	0	0	—	3	0	0	0	0	4¹	9	1	4	0	27.0	8.31	47	.474	.565	0	—	0	-2	-2	-0	-0.1
Total	5	4	9	.308	97	0	0	0	6	154¹	153	12	71	75	13.2	4.55	78	.261	.344	1	.071	-1	-15	-17	-1	-1.5

■ WALT KINNEY
Kinney, Walter William b: 9/9/1893, Denison, Tex. d: 7/1/71, Escondido, Cal. BL/TL, 6'2", 186 lbs. Deb: 7/26/18

YEAR	TM/L	W	L	PCT	G	GS	CG	SH	SV	IP	H	HR	BB	SO	RAT	ERA	ERA+	OAV	OOB	BH	AVG	PB	PR	/A	PD	TPI
1918	Bos-A	0	0	—	5	0	0	0	0	15	5	0	8	9	9.0	1.80	149	.106	.263	0	.000	-1	2	1	0	0.1
1919	Phi-A	9	15	.375	43	21	13	0	2	202²	199	7	91	97	13.2	3.64	94	.262	.347	25	.284	5	-9	-5	2	0.5
1920	Phi-A	2	4	.333	10	8	5	1	0	61	59	3	28	19	13.0	3.10	130	.261	.345	9	.346	1	5	6	0	0.9
1923	Phi-A	0	1	.000	5	1	0	0	0	12	11	0	9	4	15.0	7.50	55	.229	.351	1	.167	1	-5	-5	-0	-0.3
Total	4	11	20	.355	63	30	18	1	2	290²	274	10	136	129	13.0	3.59	99	.254	.343	35	.280	7	-8	-2	2	1.2

■ MIKE KINNUNEN
Kinnunen, Michael John b: 4/1/58, Seattle, Wash. BL/TL, 6'1", 185 lbs. Deb: 6/12/80

YEAR	TM/L	W	L	PCT	G	GS	CG	SH	SV	IP	H	HR	BB	SO	RAT	ERA	ERA+	OAV	OOB	BH	AVG	PB	PR	/A	PD	TPI
1980	Min-A	0	0	—	21	0	0	0	0	24²	29	1	9	8	14.2	5.11	85	.290	.355	0	—	0	-3	-2	0	-0.1
1986	Bal-A	0	0	—	9	0	0	0	0	7	8	1	5	1	16.7	6.43	64	.308	.419	0	—	0	-2	-2	0	0.0
1987	Bal-A	0	0	—	18	0	0	0	0	20	27	3	16	14	19.3	4.95	89	.338	.448	0	—	0	-1	-1	0	-0.0
Total	3	0	0	—	48	0	0	0	0	51²	64	5	30	23	16.5	5.23	83	.311	.401	0	—	0	-6	-5	0	-0.1

■ ED KINSELLA
Kinsella, Edward William "Rube" b: 1/15/1882, Lexington, Ill. d: 1/17/76, Bloomington, Ill. BR/TR, 6'1.5", 175 lbs. Deb: 9/16/05

YEAR	TM/L	W	L	PCT	G	GS	CG	SH	SV	IP	H	HR	BB	SO	RAT	ERA	ERA+	OAV	OOB	BH	AVG	PB	PR	/A	PD	TPI
1905	Pit-N	0	1	.000	3	2	2	0	0	17	19	0	3	11	12.2	2.65	113	.292	.333	0	.000	-0	1	1	-1	0.0
1910	StL-A	1	3	.250	10	5	2	0	0	50	62	0	16	10	14.4	3.78	65	.321	.379	3	.250	2	-7	-7	1	-0.4
Total	2	1	4	.200	13	7	4	0	0	67	81	0	19	21	13.8	3.49	75	.314	.368	3	.200	2	-6	-7	0	-0.4

■ MATT KINZER
Kinzer, Matthew Roy b: 6/17/63, Indianapolis, Ind. BR/TR, 6'2", 210 lbs. Deb: 5/18/89

YEAR	TM/L	W	L	PCT	G	GS	CG	SH	SV	IP	H	HR	BB	SO	RAT	ERA	ERA+	OAV	OOB	BH	AVG	PB	PR	/A	PD	TPI
1989	StL-N	0	2	.000	8	1	0	0	0	13¹	25	3	4	8	19.6	12.83	28	.403	.439	0	.000	-0	-14	-14	-0	-1.3
1990	Det-A	0	0	—	1	0	0	0	0	1²	3	0	3	1	32.4	16.20	24	.375	.545	0	—	0	-2	-2	-0	-0.1
Total	2	0	2	.000	9	1	0	0	0	15	28	3	7	9	21.0	13.20	28	.400	.455	0	.000	-0	-16	-16	-0	-1.4

■ HARRY KINZY
Kinzy, Henry Hershel "Slim" b: 7/19/10, Hallsville, Tex. BR/TR, 6'4", 185 lbs. Deb: 6/08/34

YEAR	TM/L	W	L	PCT	G	GS	CG	SH	SV	IP	H	HR	BB	SO	RAT	ERA	ERA+	OAV	OOB	BH	AVG	PB	PR	/A	PD	TPI
1934	Chi-A	0	1	.000	13	2	1	0	0	34¹	38	1	31	12	19.1	4.98	95	.290	.440	3	.300	1	-2	-1	-0	0.0

■ FRED KIPP
Kipp, Fred Leo b: 10/1/31, Piqua, Kan. BL/TL, 6'4", 200 lbs. Deb: 9/10/57

YEAR	TM/L	W	L	PCT	G	GS	CG	SH	SV	IP	H	HR	BB	SO	RAT	ERA	ERA+	OAV	OOB	BH	AVG	PB	PR	/A	PD	TPI
1957	Bro-N	0	0	—	1	0	0	0	0	4	6	2	0	3	13.5	9.00	46	.333	.333	0	.000	-0	-2	-2	-0	-0.1
1958	LA-N	6	6	.500	40	9	0	0	0	102¹	107	16	45	58	13.5	5.01	82	.273	.349	9	.250	1	-12	-10	1	-0.7
1959	LA-N	0	0	—	2	0	0	0	0	2²	2	0	3	1	16.9	0.00	—	.222	.417	0	.000	-0	1	1	0	0.2
1960	NY-A	0	1	.000	4	0	0	0	0	4¹	4	0	0	2	8.3	6.23	57	.250	.250	0	—	0	-1	-1	0	0.0
Total	4	6	7	.462	47	9	0	0	0	113¹	119	18	48	64	13.3	5.08	80	.274	.347	9	.243	1	-14	-13	1	-0.6

YEAR TM/L	W	L	PCT	G	GS	CG	SH	SV	IP	H	HR	BB	SO	RAT	ERA	ERA+	OAV	OOB	BH	AVG	PB	PR	/A	PD	TPI

■ BOB KIPPER
Kipper, Robert Wayne   b: 7/8/64, Aurora, Ill.   BR/TL, 6'2", 200 lbs.   Deb: 4/12/85

YEAR TM/L	W	L	PCT	G	GS	CG	SH	SV	IP	H	HR	BB	SO	RAT	ERA	ERA+	OAV	OOB	BH	AVG	PB	PR	/A	PD	TPI
1985 Cal-A	0	1	.000	2	1	0	0	0	3¹	7	1	3	0	27.0	21.60	19	.467	.556	0	—	0	-6	-6	0	-0.5
Pit-N	1	2	.333	5	4	0	0	0	24²	21	4	7	13	10.2	5.11	70	.221	.275	2	.250	0	-4	-4	0	-0.3
1986 Pit-N	6	8	.429	20	19	0	0	0	114	123	17	34	81	12.6	4.03	95	.271	.324	1	.030	-3	-4	-2	-1	-0.5
1987 Pit-N	5	9	.357	24	20	1	1	0	110²	117	25	52	83	13.9	5.94	69	.271	.352	8	.242	2	-23	-22	-0	-1.9
1988 Pit-N	2	6	.250	50	0	0	0	0	65	54	7	26	39	11.4	3.74	91	.234	.317	0	.000	-0	-2	-2	1	0.0
1989 Pit-N	3	4	.429	52	0	0	0	4	83	55	5	33	58	9.5	2.93	115	.188	.270	1	.111	-0	5	4	-1	0.3
1990 Pit-N	5	2	.714	41	1	0	0	3	62²	44	7	26	35	10.5	3.02	120	.195	.286	1	.143	-0	5	4	0	0.4
Total 6	22	32	.407	194	45	1	1	7	463¹	421	66	181	309	11.9	4.29	86	.241	.316	13	.138	-1	-29	-30	-1	-2.5

■ THORNTON KIPPER
Kipper, Thornton John   b: 9/27/28, Bagley, Wis.   BR/TR, 6'3", 190 lbs.   Deb: 6/07/53

YEAR TM/L	W	L	PCT	G	GS	CG	SH	SV	IP	H	HR	BB	SO	RAT	ERA	ERA+	OAV	OOB	BH	AVG	PB	PR	/A	PD	TPI
1953 Phi-N	3	3	.500	20	3	0	0	0	45²	59	8	12	15	14.0	4.73	89	.319	.360	1	.091	-1	-2	-3	0	-0.3
1954 Phi-N	0	0	—	11	0	0	0	1	13²	22	0	12	5	23.0	7.90	51	.379	.493	0	.000	-0	-6	-6	0	-0.5
1955 Phi-N	0	1	.000	24	0	0	0	1	39²	47	4	22	15	15.9	4.99	80	.301	.391	1	.333	0	-4	-5	-0	-0.4
Total 3	3	4	.429	55	3	0	0	1	99	128	12	46	35	16.0	5.27	78	.321	.394	2	.125	-1	-12	-13	-0	-1.2

■ CLAY KIRBY
Kirby, Clayton Laws   b: 6/25/48, Washington, D.C.   BR/TR, 6'3", 175 lbs.   Deb: 4/11/69

YEAR TM/L	W	L	PCT	G	GS	CG	SH	SV	IP	H	HR	BB	SO	RAT	ERA	ERA+	OAV	OOB	BH	AVG	PB	PR	/A	PD	TPI
1969 SD-N	7	20	.259	35	35	2	0	0	215²	204	18	100	113	12.9	3.80	93	.252	.339	4	.061	-2	-5	-6	-2	-1.0
1970 SD-N	10	16	.385	36	34	6	1	0	214²	198	29	120	154	13.7	4.53	88	.248	.352	11	.149	-0	-11	-13	-2	-1.5
1971 SD-N	15	13	.536	38	36	13	2	0	267¹	213	20	103	231	10.7	2.83	117	.216	.292	8	.093	-3	19	14	-1	1.0
1972 SD-N	12	14	.462	34	34	9	2	0	238²	197	21	116	175	11.9	3.13	105	.226	.318	5	.068	-4	9	4	-1	0.0
1973 SD-N	8	18	.308	34	31	4	2	0	191²	214	30	66	129	13.2	4.79	72	.282	.341	5	.093	-2	-24	-28	-2	-3.2
1974 Cin-N	12	9	.571	36	35	7	1	0	230²	210	15	91	160	11.8	3.28	106	.242	.316	7	.095	-3	9	5	-2	0.0
1975 Cin-N	10	6	.625	26	19	1	0	0	110²	113	13	54	48	14.0	4.72	76	.263	.352	6	.188	1	-13	-14	-2	-1.4
1976 Mon-N	1	8	.111	22	15	0	0	0	78²	81	10	63	51	16.7	5.72	65	.273	.403	1	.056	-1	-19	-18	-1	-1.8
Total 8	75	104	.419	261	239	42	8	0	1548	1430	156	713	1061	12.6	3.84	92	.246	.331	47	.098	-15	-37	-56	-14	-7.9

■ JOHN KIRBY
Kirby, John F.   b: 1/13/1865, St.Louis, Mo.   d: 10/6/31, St.Louis, Mo.   TR, 5'8", 172 lbs.   Deb: 8/01/1884

YEAR TM/L	W	L	PCT	G	GS	CG	SH	SV	IP	H	HR	BB	SO	RAT	ERA	ERA+	OAV	OOB	BH	AVG	PB	PR	/A	PD	TPI
1884 KC-U	0	1	.000	2	2	1	0	0	11	13	0	2	1	12.3	4.09	68	.275	.305	1	.143	-1	-1	-2	1	0.0
1885 StL-N	5	8	.385	14	14	14	0	0	129¹	118	0	44	46	11.3	3.55	77	.232	.293	3	.060	-5	-11	-12	-2	-1.6
1886 StL-N	11	26	.297	41	41	38	1	0	325	329	9	134	129	12.8	3.30	98	.252	.322	15	.110	-9	0	-3	-0	-1.0
1887 Ind-N	1	6	.143	8	8	5	0	0	62	70	3	43	7	16.4	6.10	68	.277	.382	4	.138	-2	-14	-14	-0	-1.2
Cle-a	0	5	.000	5	5	5	0	0	41	62	1	28	6	19.8	9.00	48	.336	.424	3	.167	-1	-21	-21	0	-1.5
1888 KC-a	1	4	.200	5	5	5	0	0	43	48	0	7	11	11.5	4.19	82	.272	.300	1	.063	-0	-5	-4	-0	-0.4
Total 5	18	50	.265	75	75	68	1	0	611¹	640	13	258	200	13.2	4.09	80	.259	.329	27	.105	-21	-52	-55	-2	-5.7

■ LA RUE KIRBY
Kirby, La Rue   b: 12/30/1889, Eureka, Mich.   d: 6/10/61, Lansing, Mich.   BB/TR, 6', 185 lbs.   Deb: 8/07/12 ◆

YEAR TM/L	W	L	PCT	G	GS	CG	SH	SV	IP	H	HR	BB	SO	RAT	ERA	ERA+	OAV	OOB	BH	AVG	PB	PR	/A	PD	TPI
1912 NY-N	1	0	1.000	3	1	1	0	0	11	13	1	6	2	16.4	5.73	59	.289	.385	1	.200	0	-3	-3	0	-0.1
1915 StL-F	0	0	—	1	0	0	0	0	7	7	1	2	7	11.6	5.14	62	.268	.320	38	.213	0	-2	-2	-0	0.0
Total 2	1	0	1.000	4	1	1	0	0	18	20	2	8	9	14.5	5.50	60	.281	.362	87	.230	0	-4	-4	-0	-0.1

■ MIKE KIRCHER
Kircher, Michael Andrew (b: Wolfgang Andrew Kerscher)   b: 9/30/1897, Rochester, N.Y.   d: 6/26/72, Rochester.N.Y.   BB/TR, 6', 180 lbs.   Deb: 8/08/19

YEAR TM/L	W	L	PCT	G	GS	CG	SH	SV	IP	H	HR	BB	SO	RAT	ERA	ERA+	OAV	OOB	BH	AVG	PB	PR	/A	PD	TPI
1919 Phi-A	0	0	—	2	0	0	0	0	8	15	0	3	2	20.3	7.88	44	.429	.474	0	.000	-0	-4	-4	-0	-0.3
1920 StL-N	2	1	.667	9	3	0	0	0	36²	50	0	5	5	14.0	5.40	55	.333	.363	3	.273	0	-9	-10	-1	-1.0
1921 StL-N	0	1	.000	3	0	0	0	0	3¹	4	0	1	2	16.2	8.10	45	.364	.462	0	—	0	-2	-2	0	0.0
Total 3	2	2	.500	14	3	1	0	0	48	69	0	9	9	15.2	6.00	52	.352	.389	3	.214	-0	-15	-15	-1	-1.3

■ BILL KIRK
Kirk, William Partlemore   b: 7/19/35, Coatesville, Pa.   BL/TL, 6', 165 lbs.   Deb: 9/23/61

YEAR TM/L	W	L	PCT	G	GS	CG	SH	SV	IP	H	HR	BB	SO	RAT	ERA	ERA+	OAV	OOB	BH	AVG	PB	PR	/A	PD	TPI
1961 KC-A	0	0	—	1	1	0	0	0	3	6	2	1	3	21.0	12.00	34	.375	.412	0	—	0	-3	-3	0	-0.1

■ DON KIRKWOOD
Kirkwood, Donald Paul   b: 9/24/49, Pontiac, Mich.   BR/TR, 6'3", 175 lbs.   Deb: 9/13/74

YEAR TM/L	W	L	PCT	G	GS	CG	SH	SV	IP	H	HR	BB	SO	RAT	ERA	ERA+	OAV	OOB	BH	AVG	PB	PR	/A	PD	TPI
1974 Cal-A	0	0	—	3	0	0	0	0	7¹	12	0	6	4	22.1	8.59	40	.375	.474	0	—	0	-4	-4	-0	-0.3
1975 Cal-A	6	5	.545	44	2	0	0	7	84	85	6	28	49	12.1	3.11	114	.270	.329	0	—	0	6	4	-0	0.4
1976 Cal-A	6	12	.333	28	26	4	0	0	157²	167	12	57	78	12.8	4.62	72	.278	.341	0	—	0	-19	-23	2	-2.1
1977 Cal-A	1	0	1.000	13	0	0	0	1	17²	20	3	9	10	14.8	5.09	77	.290	.372	0	—	0	-2	-2	1	0.0
Chi-A	1	1	.500	16	0	0	0	0	40	49	3	10	24	13.5	5.17	79	.310	.355	0	—	0	-5	-5	-0	-0.4
Yr	2	1	.667	29	0	0	0	1	57²	69	6	19	34	13.9	5.15	78	.304	.360	0	—	0	-7	-7	1	-0.4
1978 Tor-A	4	5	.444	16	9	3	0	0	68	76	6	25	29	13.4	4.24	93	.289	.351	0	—	0	-4	-2	0	-0.1
Total 5	18	23	.439	120	37	7	0	8	374²	409	30	135	194	13.1	4.37	82	.284	.347	0	—	0	-28	-33	3	-2.5

■ HARRY KIRSCH
Kirsch, Harry Louis "Casey"   b: 10/17/1887, Pittsburgh, Pa.   d: 12/25/25, Overbrook, Pa.   TR, 5'11", 170 lbs.   Deb: 4/16/10

YEAR TM/L	W	L	PCT	G	GS	CG	SH	SV	IP	H	HR	BB	SO	RAT	ERA	ERA+	OAV	OOB	BH	AVG	PB	PR	/A	PD	TPI
1910 Cle-A	0	0	—	2	0	0	0	0	3	5	0	1	0	18.0	6.00	43	.385	.429	0	—	0	-1	-1	-0	0.0

■ RUBE KISINGER
Kisinger, Charles Samuel   b: 12/13/1876, Adrian, Mich.   d: 7/14/41, Huron, Ohio   BR/TR, 6', 190 lbs.   Deb: 9/10/02

YEAR TM/L	W	L	PCT	G	GS	CG	SH	SV	IP	H	HR	BB	SO	RAT	ERA	ERA+	OAV	OOB	BH	AVG	PB	PR	/A	PD	TPI
1902 Det-A	2	3	.400	5	5	5	0	0	43¹	48	0	14	7	12.9	3.12	117	.281	.335	3	.158	-1	2	3	-0	0.2
1903 Det-A	7	9	.438	16	14	13	2	0	118²	118	0	27	33	11.0	2.96	98	.259	.300	6	.128	-3	0	-1	1	-0.1
Total 2	9	12	.429	21	19	18	2	0	162	166	0	41	40	11.5	3.00	103	.265	.310	9	.136	-3	2	2	1	0.1

■ BRUCE KISON
Kison, Bruce Eugene   b: 2/18/50, Pasco, Wash.   BR/TR, 6'4", 178 lbs.   Deb: 7/04/71

YEAR TM/L	W	L	PCT	G	GS	CG	SH	SV	IP	H	HR	BB	SO	RAT	ERA	ERA+	OAV	OOB	BH	AVG	PB	PR	/A	PD	TPI
1971 •Pit-N	6	5	.545	18	13	2	1	0	95¹	93	6	36	60	12.7	3.40	100	.259	.337	2	.065	-1	1	-0	1	0.0
1972 •Pit-N	9	7	.563	32	18	6	1	3	152	123	11	69	102	11.9	3.26	102	.220	.316	10	.189	2	3	1	-1	0.2
1973 Pit-N	3	0	1.000	7	7	0	0	0	43²	36	4	24	26	12.6	3.09	114	.232	.339	1	.083	0	3	2	0	0.2
1974 •Pit-N	9	8	.529	40	16	1	0	2	129	123	8	57	71	13.3	3.49	99	.247	.338	4	.108	-0	2	-1	1	0.0
1975 •Pit-N	12	11	.522	33	29	6	0	0	192	160	10	92	89	12.0	3.23	109	.227	.320	7	.119	-2	8	7	3	0.8
1976 Pit-N	14	9	.609	31	29	6	1	1	193	180	10	52	98	11.0	3.08	113	.247	.299	12	.203	4	9	9	1	1.4
1977 Pit-N	9	10	.474	33	32	3	1	0	193	209	25	55	122	12.6	4.90	81	.278	.333	18	.261	5	-21	-20	1	-1.4
1978 Pit-N	6	6	.500	28	11	0	0	0	96	81	3	39	62	11.7	3.19	116	.229	.314	4	.138	1	4	5	1	0.7
1979 •Pit-N	13	7	.650	33	25	3	1	0	172¹	157	13	45	105	10.8	3.19	122	.246	.300	8	.145	0	10	13	1	1.6
1980 Cal-A	3	6	.333	13	13	2	1	0	73¹	73	6	32	28	13.3	4.91	80	.264	.346	0	—	0	-7	-8	-0	-0.7
1981 Cal-A	1	1	.500	11	4	0	0	0	44	40	8	14	19	11.0	3.48	105	.241	.300	0	—	0	1	1	1	0.1
1982 •Cal-A	10	5	.667	33	16	3	1	1	142	120	15	44	86	10.7	3.17	128	.226	.292	0	—	0	14	14	2	1.6
1983 Cal-A	11	5	.688	26	17	4	1	2	126²	128	13	43	83	12.4	4.05	99	.264	.330	0	—	0	0	-1	1	0.0
1984 Cal-A	4	5	.444	20	7	0	0	2	65¹	72	10	28	66	14.6	5.37	74	.280	.364	0	—	0	-10	-10	-1	-1.0
1985 Bos-A	5	3	.625	22	9	0	0	0	79	98	9	32	56	14.8	4.11	104	.274	.335	0	—	0	2	2	0	0.4
Total 15	115	88	.567	380	246	36	8	12	1809²	1693	150	662	1073	12.1	3.66	102	.248	.321	66	.163	8	18	14	10	3.9

■ BILL KISSINGER
Kissinger, William Francis "Shang"   b: 8/15/1871, Dayton, Ky.   d: 4/20/29, Cincinnati, Ohio   BR/TR, 185 lbs.   Deb: 5/30/1895 ◆

YEAR TM/L	W	L	PCT	G	GS	CG	SH	SV	IP	H	HR	BB	SO	RAT	ERA	ERA+	OAV	OOB	BH	AVG	PB	PR	/A	PD	TPI
1895 Bal-N	1	0	1.000	2	2	1	0	0	11¹	18	0	2	3	15.9	3.97	120	.354	.378	1	.200	-0	1	1	0	0.0
StL-N	4	12	.250	24	14	9	0	0	140²	222	8	51	31	17.5	6.72	72	.352	.401	24	.247	-2	-30	-29	0	-2.3
Yr	5	12	.294	26	16	10	0	0	152	240	8	53	34	17.3	6.51	74	.353	.399	0	.000	-2	-29	-28	0	-2.3
1896 StL-N	2	9	.182	20	12	11	0	1	136	209	5	55	22	17.5	6.49	67	.349	.403	22	.301	1	-32	-32	2	-2.2
1897 StL-N	0	4	.000	7	4	2	0	0	31¹	51	2	15	5	19.0	11.49	38	.362	.423	13	.333	2	-25	-25	0	-1.8
Total 3	7	25	.219	53	32	23	0	1	319¹	500	15	123	61	17.6	6.99	66	.352	.403	60	.280	2	-86	-85	3	-6.3

YEAR TM/L	W	L	PCT	G	GS	CG	SH	SV	IP	H	HR	BB	SO	RAT	ERA	ERA+	OAV	OOB	BH	AVG	PB	PR	/A	PD	TPI

■ FRANK KITSON Kitson, Frank L. b: 4/11/1872, Hopkins, Mich. d: 4/14/30, Allegan, Mich. BL/TR, 5'11", 165 lbs. Deb: 5/19/1898

YEAR TM/L	W	L	PCT	G	GS	CG	SH	SV	IP	H	HR	BB	SO	RAT	ERA	ERA+	OAV	OOB	BH	AVG	PB	PR	/A	PD	TPI
1898 Bal-N	8	5	.615	17	13	13	1	0	119¹	123	0	35	32	11.9	3.24	111	.264	.316	27	.314	4	5	5	0	1.1
1899 Bal-N	22	16	.579	40	37	35	3	0	329²	329	6	66	75	10.8	2.76	144	.260	.296	27	.201	-2	40	44	-2	3.9
1900 *Bro-N	15	13	.536	40	30	21	2	4	253¹	283	12	56	55	12.0	4.19	92	.282	.320	32	.294	5	-14	-10	-5	-0.7
1901 Bro-N	19	11	.633	38	32	26	5	2	280²	312	9	67	127	12.5	2.98	112	.279	.326	35	.263	5	11	12	-2	1.6
1902 Bro-N	19	12	.613	31	30	28	3	0	259²	251	4	48	107	10.6	2.84	97	.254	.294	31	.274	8	-2	-2	1	0.7
1903 Det-N	15	16	.484	31	28	28	2	0	257²	277	8	38	102	11.0	2.58	113	.274	.300	21	.181	-1	11	9	-1	0.6
1904 Det-A	8	13	.381	26	24	19	0	1	199²	211	7	38	69	11.2	3.07	83	.272	.306	15	.208	0	-10	-11	0	-1.1
1905 Det-A	12	14	.462	33	27	21	3	1	225²	230	3	57	78	11.4	3.47	79	.265	.310	16	.184	-1	-20	-18	-2	-2.1
1906 Was-A	6	14	.300	30	21	15	1	0	197	196	2	57	59	11.6	3.65	72	.262	.315	22	.244	8	-21	-22	0	-1.4
1907 Was-A	0	3	.000	5	3	2	0	0	32	41	1	9	11	14.1	3.94	62	.313	.357	1	.100	-0	-5	-5	-0	-0.6
NY-A	4	0	1.000	12	4	3	0	0	61	75	0	17	14	13.6	3.10	90	.304	.349	7	.280	1	-4	-2	-1	-0.2
Yr	4	3	.571	17	7	5	0	0	93	116	1	26	25	13.7	3.39	79	.307	.352	1	.029	-0	-9	-7	-2	-0.8
Total 10	128	117	.522	303	249	211	20	8	2215²	2328	52	488	729	11.5	3.17	100	.270	.310	234	.240	26	-9	-3	-12	1.8

■ MALACHI KITTRIDGE Kittridge, Malachi Jedediah "Jedediah" b: 10/12/1869, Clinton, Mass. d: 6/23/28, Gary, Ind. BR/TR, 5'7", 170 lbs. Deb: 4/19/1890 M♦

YEAR TM/L	W	L	PCT	G	GS	CG	SH	SV	IP	H	HR	BB	SO	RAT	ERA	ERA+	OAV	OOB	BH	AVG	PB	PR	/A	PD	TPI
1896 Chi-N	0	0	—	1	0	0	0	0	1²	2	0	1	0	16.2	5.40	84	.295	.385	48	.223	-0	-0	-0	0	0.0

■ HUGO KLAERNER Klaerner, Hugo Emil "Dutch" b: 10/15/08, Fredericksburg, Tex. d: 2/3/82, Fredericksburg, Tex. BR/TR, 5'11", 190 lbs. Deb: 9/10/34

YEAR TM/L	W	L	PCT	G	GS	CG	SH	SV	IP	H	HR	BB	SO	RAT	ERA	ERA+	OAV	OOB	BH	AVG	PB	PR	/A	PD	TPI
1934 Chi-N	0	2	.000	3	3	1	0	0	17¹	24	4	16	9	20.8	10.90	43	.329	.449	2	.333	1	-12	-12	-1	-0.7

■ FRED KLAGES Klages, Frederick Albert Antony b: 10/31/43, Ambridge, Pa. BR/TR, 6'2", 185 lbs. Deb: 9/11/66

YEAR TM/L	W	L	PCT	G	GS	CG	SH	SV	IP	H	HR	BB	SO	RAT	ERA	ERA+	OAV	OOB	BH	AVG	PB	PR	/A	PD	TPI
1966 Chi-A	1	0	1.000	3	3	0	0	0	15²	9	0	7	6	9.2	1.72	184	.167	.262	3	.500	1	3	3	0	0.4
1967 Chi-A	4	4	.500	11	9	0	0	0	44²	43	6	16	17	12.1	3.83	81	.256	.324	0	.000	-1	-3	-4	-1	-0.5
Total 2	5	4	.556	14	12	0	0	0	60¹	52	6	23	23	11.3	3.28	95	.234	.309	3	.167	-0	0	-1	-1	-0.1

■ AL KLAWITTER Klawitter, Albert "Dutch" b: 4/12/1888, Wilkes-Barre, Pa. d: 5/2/50, Milwaukee, Wis. BR/TR, 5'11.5", 187 lbs. Deb: 9/20/09

YEAR TM/L	W	L	PCT	G	GS	CG	SH	SV	IP	H	HR	BB	SO	RAT	ERA	ERA+	OAV	OOB	BH	AVG	PB	PR	/A	PD	TPI
1909 NY-N	1	1	.500	6	3	2	0	1	27	24	1	13	6	12.3	2.00	128	.247	.336	3	.333	1	2	2	1	0.5
1910 NY-N	0	0	—	1	0	0	0	0	1	2	0	2	0	36.0	9.00	33	.400	.571	0	—	0	-1	-1	-0	0.0
1913 Det-A	1	2	.333	8	3	1	0	0	32	39	0	15	10	15.2	5.91	49	.305	.378	0	.000	-2	-11	-11	0	-1.1
Total 3	2	3	.400	15	6	3	0	1	60	65	1	30	16	14.3	4.20	66	.283	.365	3	.150	-0	-9	-10	1	-0.6

■ TOM KLAWITTER Klawitter, Thomas Carl b: 6/24/58, LaCrosse, Wis. BR/TL, 6'2", 190 lbs. Deb: 4/14/85

YEAR TM/L	W	L	PCT	G	GS	CG	SH	SV	IP	H	HR	BB	SO	RAT	ERA	ERA+	OAV	OOB	BH	AVG	PB	PR	/A	PD	TPI
1985 Min-A	0	0	—	7	2	0	0	0	9¹	7	2	13	5	19.3	6.75	65	.226	.455	0	—	0	-3	-2	0	-0.1

■ HAL KLEINE Kleine, Harold John b: 6/8/23, St.Louis, Mo. d: 12/10/57, St.Louis, Mo. BL/TL, 6'2", 193 lbs. Deb: 4/26/44

YEAR TM/L	W	L	PCT	G	GS	CG	SH	SV	IP	H	HR	BB	SO	RAT	ERA	ERA+	OAV	OOB	BH	AVG	PB	PR	/A	PD	TPI
1944 Cle-A	1	2	.333	11	6	1	0	0	40²	38	0	36	13	16.4	5.75	57	.248	.392	2	.143	-1	-11	-11	-1	-1.1
1945 Cle-A	0	0	—	3	0	0	0	0	7	8	0	7	5	19.3	3.86	84	.286	.429	1	.333	0	-0	-0	0	0.0
Total 2	1	2	.333	14	6	1	0	0	47²	46	0	43	18	16.8	5.48	60	.254	.397	3	.176	-0	-11	-12	-1	-1.1

■ TED KLEINHANS Kleinhans, Theodore Otto b: 4/8/1899, Deer Park, Wis. d: 7/24/85, Redington Beach, Fla. BR/TL, 6', 170 lbs. Deb: 4/20/34

YEAR TM/L	W	L	PCT	G	GS	CG	SH	SV	IP	H	HR	BB	SO	RAT	ERA	ERA+	OAV	OOB	BH	AVG	PB	PR	/A	PD	TPI
1934 Phi-N	0	0	—	5	0	0	0	0	6	11	1	3	2	21.0	9.00	52	.379	.438	0	.000	-0	-3	-3	0	-0.2
Cin-N	2	6	.250	24	9	0	0	0	80	107	2	38	23	16.4	5.74	71	.321	.392	3	.130	-1	-15	-15	2	-1.3
Yr	2	6	.250	29	9	0	0	0	86	118	3	41	25	16.7	5.97	69	.326	.396	1	.042	-1	-18	-18	2	-1.5
1936 NY-A	1	1	.500	19	0	0	0	1	29¹	36	0	23	10	18.1	5.83	80	.300	.413	1	.167	-0	-3	-4	-0	-0.3
1937 Cin-N	1	2	.333	7	3	1	0	0	27¹	29	1	12	13	13.8	2.30	162	.271	.350	2	.250	0	5	4	-1	0.4
1938 Cin-N	0	0	—	1	0	0	0	0	1	2	0	0	0	18.0	9.00	41	.400	.400	0	—	0	-1	-1	0	0.0
Total 4	4	9	.308	56	12	1	0	1	143²	185	4	76	48	16.5	5.26	79	.311	.391	6	.158	-1	-16	-17	1	-1.4

■ NUB KLEINKE Kleinke, Norbert Georbe b: 5/19/11, Fond Du Lac, Wis. d: 3/16/50, Off Marin Coast, Cal. BR/TR, 6'1", 170 lbs. Deb: 4/25/35

YEAR TM/L	W	L	PCT	G	GS	CG	SH	SV	IP	H	HR	BB	SO	RAT	ERA	ERA+	OAV	OOB	BH	AVG	PB	PR	/A	PD	TPI
1935 StL-N	0	0	—	4	2	0	0	0	12²	19	1	3	5	15.6	4.97	82	.358	.393	0	.000	-0	-1	-1	0	-0.1
1937 StL-N	1	1	.500	5	2	1	0	0	20²	25	0	7	9	13.9	4.79	83	.321	.376	0	.000	-1	-2	-2	0	-0.2
Total 2	1	1	.500	9	4	1	0	0	33¹	44	1	10	14	14.6	4.86	83	.336	.383	0	.000	-1	-3	-3	0	-0.3

■ ED KLEPFER Klepfer, Edward Lloyd "Big Ed" b: 3/17/1888, Summerville, Pa. d: 8/9/50, Tulsa, Okla. BR/TR, 6', 185 lbs. Deb: 7/04/11

YEAR TM/L	W	L	PCT	G	GS	CG	SH	SV	IP	H	HR	BB	SO	RAT	ERA	ERA+	OAV	OOB	BH	AVG	PB	PR	/A	PD	TPI
1911 NY-A	0	0	—	2	0	0	0	0	4	5	0	4	2	15.8	6.75	53	.250	.318	0	.000	-0	-2	-1	0	0.0
1913 NY-A	0	1	.000	8	1	0	0	0	24²	38	2	12	10	19.0	7.66	39	.373	.448	1	.167	0	-13	-13	0	-1.1
1915 Chi-A	1	0	1.000	3	2	1	0	0	12²	11	0	5	3	11.4	2.84	105	.234	.308	0	.000	-0	0	0	-0	0.0
Cle-A	1	6	.143	8	7	2	0	0	43	47	0	11	13	12.1	2.09	146	.283	.328	2	.167	-0	4	5	1	0.5
Yr	2	6	.250	11	9	3	0	0	55²	58	0	16	16	12.0	2.26	134	.272	.323	2	.133	-0	4	5	1	0.5
1916 Cle-A	6	6	.500	31	13	4	1	2	143	136	0	46	62	11.7	2.52	119	.262	.327	1	.025	-4	5	8	-0	0.4
1917 Cle-A	14	4	.778	41	27	9	0	1	213	208	0	55	66	11.1	2.37	120	.264	.312	2	.032	-7	7	11	-1	0.4
1919 Cle-A	0	0	—	5	0	0	0	0	7¹	12	1	6	7	22.1	7.36	45	.375	.474	0	.000	-0	-3	-3	0	-0.2
Total 6	22	17	.564	98	50	16	1	3	447²	457	3	137	165	12.1	2.81	104	.273	.330	6	.048	-11	-2	6	-1	-0.0

■ ED KLIEMAN Klieman, Edward Frederick "Specs" or "Babe" b: 3/21/18, Norwood, Ohio d: 11/15/79, Homosassa, Fla. BR/TR, 6'1", 190 lbs. Deb: 9/24/43

YEAR TM/L	W	L	PCT	G	GS	CG	SH	SV	IP	H	HR	BB	SO	RAT	ERA	ERA+	OAV	OOB	BH	AVG	PB	PR	/A	PD	TPI
1943 Cle-A	0	1	.000	1	1	1	0	0	9	8	0	5	2	13.0	1.00	311	.286	.394	0	.000	-0	2	2	0	0.2
1944 Cle-A	11	13	.458	47	19	5	1	5	178¹	185	4	70	44	13.2	3.38	98	.274	.348	6	.105	-3	1	-2	1	-0.3
1945 Cle-A	5	8	.385	38	12	4	1	4	126¹	123	3	49	33	12.5	3.85	84	.261	.336	8	.200	1	-7	-8	3	-0.4
1946 Cle-A	0	0	—	9	0	0	0	0	15	18	0	10	2	16.8	6.60	50	.290	.389	0	.000	-0	-5	-5	-1	-0.5
1947 Cle-A	5	4	.556	**58**	0	0	0	17	92	78	5	39	21	11.6	3.03	115	.231	.315	2	.105	-1	7	5	2	0.6
1948 *Cle-A	3	2	.600	44	0	0	0	4	79²	62	3	46	18	12.4	2.60	156	.229	.345	2	.143	-0	**15**	**13**	2	1.4
1949 Was-A	0	0	—	2	0	0	0	0	3	8	0	3	1	33.0	18.00	24	.500	.579	1	1.000	0	-5	-5	0	-0.3
Chi-A	2	0	1.000	18	0	0	0	3	33	33	2	15	9	13.1	3.00	139	.273	.353	2	.250	1	4	4	1	0.5
Yr	2	0	1.000	20	0	0	0	3	36	41	2	18	10	14.8	4.25	98	.299	.381	0	.000	1	-0	-0	1	0.2
1950 Phi-A	0	0	—	5	0	0	0	0	5²	10	0	2	0	22.2	9.53	48	.357	.438	0	.000	-0	-3	-3	-0	-0.2
Total 8	26	28	.481	222	32	10	2	33	542	525	17	239	130	13.0	3.49	100	.261	.345	21	.146	-3	10	1	8	1.0

■ RON KLIMKOWSKI Klimkowski, Ronald Bernard b: 3/1/44, Jersey City, N.J. BR/TR, 6'2", 190 lbs. Deb: 9/15/69

YEAR TM/L	W	L	PCT	G	GS	CG	SH	SV	IP	H	HR	BB	SO	RAT	ERA	ERA+	OAV	OOB	BH	AVG	PB	PR	/A	PD	TPI
1969 NY-A	0	0	—	3	1	0	0	0	14	6	0	5	3	7.1	0.64	541	.130	.216	0	.000	-0	5	4	-0	0.4
1970 NY-A	6	7	.462	45	3	1	1	1	98¹	80	7	33	40	10.6	2.65	132	.223	.294	1	.053	-1	12	9	0	0.9
1971 Oak-A	2	2	.500	26	0	0	0	2	45¹	37	3	23	25	12.1	3.38	99	.220	.318	2	.400	1	0	-0	1	0.2
1972 NY-A	0	3	.000	16	2	0	0	1	31¹	32	3	15	11	13.8	4.02	73	.271	.358	0	.000	-0	-3	-4	0	-0.4
Total 4	8	12	.400	90	6	1	1	4	189	155	13	76	79	11.2	2.90	116	.224	.306	3	.091	-2	13	10	1	1.0

■ BOBBY KLINE Kline, John Robert b: 1/27/29, St.Petersburg, Fla BR/TR, 6', 179 lbs. Deb: 4/11/55 ♦

YEAR TM/L	W	L	PCT	G	GS	CG	SH	SV	IP	H	HR	BB	SO	RAT	ERA	ERA+	OAV	OOB	BH	AVG	PB	PR	/A	PD	TPI
1955 Was-A	0	0	—	1	0	0	0	0	1	4	1	1	0	45.0	27.00	14	.667	.714	31	.221	0	-3	-3	0	-0.1

■ BOB KLINE Kline, Robert George "Junior" b: 12/9/09, Enterprise, Ohio d: 3/16/87, Westerville, Ohio BR/TR, 6'3", 200 lbs. Deb: 9/17/30

YEAR TM/L	W	L	PCT	G	GS	CG	SH	SV	IP	H	HR	BB	SO	RAT	ERA	ERA+	OAV	OOB	BH	AVG	PB	PR	/A	PD	TPI
1930 Bos-A	0	0	—	1	0	0	0	0	1	1	0	0	0	9.0	0.00	—	.333	.333	0	—	0	1	1	0	0.0
1931 Bos-A	5	5	.500	28	10	3	0	0	98	110	3	35	25	13.6	4.41	98	.298	.364	9	.333	2	-0	-1	2	0.3
1932 Bos-A	11	13	.458	47	19	4	1	2	172	203	10	76	31	14.7	5.28	85	.294	.365	7	.130	-3	-15	-15	3	-1.3
1933 Bos-A	7	8	.467	46	8	1	0	4	127	127	5	67	16	14.2	4.54	97	.265	.362	6	.176	-1	-4	-2	4	0.0
1934 Phi-A	6	2	.750	20	0	0	0	1	39²	50	6	13	14	14.3	6.35	69	.314	.366	3	.333	1	-8	-9	1	-0.5
Was-A	1	0	1.000	6	0	0	0	0	4	10	0	4	1	33.8	15.75	27	.500	.600	0	—	0	-5	-5	0	-0.3

YEAR TM/L	W	L	PCT	G	GS	CG	SH	SV	IP	H	HR	BB	SO	RAT	ERA	ERA+	OAV	OOB	BH	AVG	PB	PR	/A	PD	TPI
Yr	7	2	.778	26	0	0	0	1	43²	60	6	17	15	16.1	7.21	61	.335	.396	0	.000	1	-13	-14	2	-0.8
Total 5	30	28	.517	148	37	8	1	7	441²	501	24	195	87	14.4	5.05	87	.291	.367	25	.202	-1	-32	-32	10	-1.8

■ RON KLINE
Kline, Ronald Lee b: 3/9/32, Callery, Pa. BR/TR, 6'3", 205 lbs. Deb: 4/21/52

YEAR TM/L	W	L	PCT	G	GS	CG	SH	SV	IP	H	HR	BB	SO	RAT	ERA	ERA+	OAV	OOB	BH	AVG	PB	PR	/A	PD	TPI
1952 Pit-N	0	7	.000	27	11	0	0	0	78²	74	4	66	27	16.7	5.49	73	.253	.401	0	.000	-2	-15	-13	-1	-1.6
1955 Pit-N	6	13	.316	36	19	2	1	2	136²	161	13	53	48	14.4	4.15	99	.298	.366	5	.132	-2	-2	-1	3	0.0
1956 Pit-N	14	18	.438	44	39	9	2	2	264	263	26	81	125	11.9	3.38	112	.263	.321	10	.127	-3	12	12	-0	0.9
1957 Pit-N	9	16	.360	40	31	11	2	0	205	214	26	61	88	12.1	4.04	94	.268	.321	4	.061	-5	-4	-6	-1	-1.1
1958 Pit-N	13	16	.448	32	32	11	2	0	237¹	220	25	92	109	11.8	3.53	110	.252	.323	2	.027	-6	11	9	1	0.3
1959 Pit-N	11	13	.458	33	29	7	0	0	186	186	23	70	91	12.5	4.26	91	.263	.331	8	.136	-2	-6	-8	-0	-0.9
1960 StL-N	4	9	.308	34	17	1	0	1	117²	133	21	43	54	13.5	6.04	68	.284	.347	5	.143	-2	-30	-25	1	-2.4
1961 LA-N	3	6	.333	26	12	0	0	1	104²	119	16	44	70	14.1	4.90	92	.288	.358	3	.097	-2	-10	-5	1	-0.4
Det-A	5	3	.625	10	8	3	1	0	56¹	53	3	17	27	11.2	2.72	151	.245	.300	3	.167	0	8	9	-0	0.9
Yr	8	9	.471	36	20	3	1	1	161	172	19	61	97	13.0	4.14	106	.272	.336	2	.041	-2	-2	4	0	0.5
1962 Det-A	3	6	.333	36	4	0	0	2	77¹	88	9	28	47	13.7	4.31	94	.284	.347	2	.125	-1	-3	-2	1	-0.1
1963 Was-A	3	8	.273	62	1	0	0	17	93²	85	3	30	49	11.3	2.79	133	.249	.316	1	.091	-0	9	10	0	1.0
1964 Was-A	10	7	.588	61	0	0	0	14	81¹	81	4	21	40	11.5	2.32	159	.262	.313	1	.167	-0	12	12	-0	1.3
1965 Was-A	7	6	.538	74	0	0	0	29	99¹	106	7	32	52	12.7	2.63	132	.275	.333	0	.000	-1	9	9	-1	0.8
1966 Was-A	6	4	.600	63	0	0	0	23	90¹	79	12	17	46	9.6	2.39	145	.237	.274	1	.167	-0	10	11	-1	1.0
1967 Min-A	7	1	.875	54	0	0	0	5	71²	71	10	15	36	10.9	3.77	92	.261	.302	0	.000	-1	-4	-2	-0	-0.2
1968 Pit-N	12	5	.706	56	0	0	0	7	112²	94	3	31	48	10.1	1.68	174	.234	.293	0	.000	-1	16	16	-1	1.5
1969 Pit-N	1	3	.250	20	0	0	0	3	31	37	3	5	15	12.5	5.81	60	.296	.328	0	.000	-1	-8	-8	0	-0.8
SF-N	0	2	.000	7	0	0	0	0	11	16	1	6	7	18.0	4.09	86	.364	.440	0	—	0	-1	-1	0	0.0
Yr	1	5	.167	27	0	0	0	3	42	53	4	11	22	13.7	5.36	65	.310	.352	0	.000	-1	-8	-9	0	-0.8
Bos-A	0	1	.000	16	0	0	0	1	17	24	4	17	7	21.7	4.76	80	.329	.456	0	—	0	-2	-2	0	0.0
1970 Atl-N	0	0	—	5	0	0	0	1	6¹	9	4	2	3	15.6	7.11	60	.321	.367	0	—	0	-2	-2	-0	-0.1
Total 17	114	144	.442	736	203	44	8	108	2078	2113	218	731	989	12.5	3.75	101	.266	.331	45	.092	-28	1	13	-1	0.1

■ STEVE KLINE
Kline, Steven Jack b: 10/6/47, Wenatchee, Wash. BR/TR, 6'3", 200 lbs. Deb: 7/10/70

YEAR TM/L	W	L	PCT	G	GS	CG	SH	SV	IP	H	HR	BB	SO	RAT	ERA	ERA+	OAV	OOB	BH	AVG	PB	PR	/A	PD	TPI
1970 NY-A	6	6	.500	16	15	5	0	0	100¹	99	8	24	49	11.0	3.41	103	.254	.298	5	.179	1	3	1	1	0.3
1971 NY-A	12	13	.480	31	30	15	1	0	222¹	206	21	37	81	9.8	2.96	109	.244	.276	9	.136	-0	13	7	3	1.0
1972 NY-A	16	9	.640	32	32	11	4	0	236¹	210	11	44	58	10.1	2.40	123	.237	.281	7	.092	-3	17	14	3	1.7
1973 NY-A	4	7	.364	14	13	2	1	0	74	76	5	31	19	13.1	4.01	91	.270	.344	0	-2	-3	-0	-0.2
1974 NY-A	2	2	.500	4	4	0	0	0	26	26	3	5	6	11.1	3.46	101	.263	.305	0	0	0	0	0.0
Cle-A	3	8	.273	16	11	1	0	0	71	70	9	31	17	13.3	5.07	71	.266	.352	0	—	0	-11	-11	1	-1.0
Yr	5	10	.333	20	15	1	0	0	97	96	12	36	23	12.6	4.64	77	.264	.337	0	—	0	-11	-11	1	-1.0
1977 Atl-N	0	0	—	16	0	0	0	1	20¹	21	4	12	10	14.6	6.64	67	.259	.355	0	—	0	-6	-5	-0	-0.4
Total 6	43	45	.489	129	105	34	6	1	750¹	708	61	184	240	10.9	3.26	101	.249	.298	21	.124	-1	14	3	7	1.4

■ BILL KLING
Kling, William b: 1/14/1867, Kansas City, Mo. d: 8/26/34, Kansas City, Mo. BL/TR, 6', 190 lbs. Deb: 8/13/1891

YEAR TM/L	W	L	PCT	G	GS	CG	SH	SV	IP	H	HR	BB	SO	RAT	ERA	ERA+	OAV	OOB	BH	AVG	PB	PR	/A	PD	TPI
1891 Phi-N	4	2	.667	12	7	4	0	0	75	90	2	32	26	14.6	4.32	79	.286	.352	6	.194	1	-8	-8	-1	-0.6
1892 Bal-N	0	2	.000	2	2	0	0	0	11	17	1	7	7	19.6	11.45	30	.340	.421	1	.250	1	-10	-10	0	-0.6
1895 Lou-N	0	0	—	1	0	0	0	0	1	0	0	1	0	9.0	0.00	—	.000	.256	0	.000	-0	1	1	0	0.0
Total 3	4	4	.500	15	9	4	0	0	87	107	3	40	33	15.2	5.17	66	.291	.361	7	.194	2	-18	-17	-1	-1.2

■ BOB KLINGER
Klinger, Robert Harold b: 6/4/08, Allenton, Mo. d: 8/19/77, Villa Ridge, Mo. BR/TR, 6', 180 lbs. Deb: 4/19/38

YEAR TM/L	W	L	PCT	G	GS	CG	SH	SV	IP	H	HR	BB	SO	RAT	ERA	ERA+	OAV	OOB	BH	AVG	PB	PR	/A	PD	TPI
1938 Pit-N	12	5	.706	28	21	10	1	1	159¹	152	7	42	58	11.3	2.99	127	.253	.308	10	.167	-2	14	14	0	1.3
1939 Pit-N	14	17	.452	37	33	10	2	0	225	251	11	81	64	13.4	4.36	88	.284	.346	17	.202	0	-11	-13	3	-0.9
1940 Pit-N	8	13	.381	39	22	3	0	3	142	196	5	53	48	16.1	5.39	71	.329	.388	6	.143	-2	-24	-25	1	-2.4
1941 Pit-N	9	4	.692	35	9	3	0	4	116²	127	5	30	36	12.2	3.93	92	.276	.322	8	.250	2	-4	-4	0	-0.1
1942 Pit-N	8	11	.421	37	19	8	1	1	152²	151	6	45	58	11.7	3.24	104	.252	.307	8	.200	1	1	2	1	0.5
1943 Pit-N	11	8	.579	33	25	14	3	0	195	185	6	58	65	11.2	2.72	128	.252	.307	16	.246	3	14	16	3	2.1
1946 *Bos-A	3	2	.600	28	1	0	0	9	57	49	1	25	16	11.8	2.37	155	.238	.323	5	.313	1	7	8	0	1.0
1947 Bos-A	1	1	.500	28	0	0	0	5	42	42	5	24	12	14.4	3.86	101	.253	.351	1	.111	-1	-1	0	-0	0.0
Total 8	66	61	.520	265	130	48	7	23	1089²	1153	46	358	357	12.6	3.68	100	.271	.331	71	.204	3	-3	-0	5	1.5

■ JOE KLINK
Klink, Joseph Charles b: 2/3/62, Johnstown, Pa. BL/TL, 5'11", 170 lbs. Deb: 4/09/87

YEAR TM/L	W	L	PCT	G	GS	CG	SH	SV	IP	H	HR	BB	SO	RAT	ERA	ERA+	OAV	OOB	BH	AVG	PB	PR	/A	PD	TPI
1987 Min-A	0	1	.000	12	0	0	0	0	23	37	4	11	17	18.8	6.65	69	.359	.421	0	—	0	-6	-5	-0	-0.4
1990 *Oak-A	0	0	—	40	0	0	0	1	39²	34	1	18	19	11.8	2.04	183	.233	.317	0	—	0	8	7	-1	0.7
Total 2	0	1	.000	52	0	0	0	1	62²	71	5	29	36	14.4	3.73	108	.285	.360	0	—	0	3	2	-1	0.3

■ JOHNNY KLIPPSTEIN
Klippstein, John Calvin b: 10/17/27, Washington, D.C. BR/TR, 6'1", 173 lbs. Deb: 5/03/50

YEAR TM/L	W	L	PCT	G	GS	CG	SH	SV	IP	H	HR	BB	SO	RAT	ERA	ERA+	OAV	OOB	BH	AVG	PB	PR	/A	PD	TPI
1950 Chi-N	2	9	.182	33	11	3	0	1	104²	112	9	64	51	15.5	5.25	80	.279	.383	11	.333	4	-13	-12	-1	-0.7
1951 Chi-N	6	6	.500	35	11	1	1	2	123²	125	10	53	56	13.4	4.29	95	.263	.344	4	.108	-2	-5	-3	0	-0.3
1952 Chi-N	9	14	.391	41	25	7	2	3	202²	208	17	89	110	13.5	4.44	87	.265	.344	11	.175	1	-16	-13	1	-1.0
1953 Chi-N	10	11	.476	48	19	5	0	6	167²	169	15	107	113	15.2	4.83	92	.258	.369	9	.155	-1	-10	-7	-2	-0.8
1954 Chi-N	4	11	.267	36	21	4	0	1	148	155	16	96	65	15.5	5.29	79	.272	.381	6	.133	-2	-20	-18	1	-1.7
1955 Cin-N	9	10	.474	39	14	3	2	0	138	120	13	60	68	12.0	3.39	125	.233	.318	2	.065	-2	10	13	-0	1.1
1956 Cin-N	12	11	.522	37	29	11	0	1	211	219	26	82	86	13.3	4.09	97	.275	.350	7	.099	-4	-8	-3	1	-0.5
1957 Cin-N	8	11	.421	46	18	3	1	3	146	146	16	68	99	13.4	5.05	81	.261	.344	3	.073	-3	-19	-15	-1	-1.9
1958 Cin-N	3	2	.600	12	4	0	0	1	33	37	5	14	22	14.2	4.91	84	.285	.359	1	.125	-0	-4	-3	-1	-0.3
LA-N	3	5	.375	45	0	0	0	9	90	81	12	44	73	12.7	3.80	108	.248	.341	1	.050	-2	2	3	-1	0.0
Yr	6	7	.462	57	4	0	0	10	123	118	17	58	95	13.0	4.10	100	.258	.344	0	.000	-3	-2	0	-1	-0.3
1959 *LA-N	4	0	1.000	28	0	0	0	2	45²	47	8	30	30	16.4	5.91	72	.276	.397	1	.143	-0	-10	-9	-0	-0.8
1960 Cle-A	5	5	.500	49	0	0	0	14	74¹	53	8	35	46	10.8	2.91	129	.205	.303	2	.143	-0	8	7	0	0.7
1961 Was-A	2	5	.500	42	1	0	0	0	71²	83	13	43	41	16.3	6.78	59	.297	.399	1	.143	-0	-22	-22	0	-2.0
1962 Cin-N	7	6	.538	40	7	0	0	4	108²	113	13	64	67	15.0	4.47	90	.278	.381	3	.125	0	-6	-5	1	-0.3
1963 Phi-N	5	6	.455	49	1	0	0	8	112	80	3	46	86	10.4	1.93	168	.204	.293	1	.038	-2	17	16	-1	1.5
1964 Phi-N	2	1	.667	11	0	0	0	0	22¹	22	6	8	13	12.9	4.03	86	.250	.327	0	—	0	-1	-1	0	0.0
Min-A	0	4	.000	33	0	0	0	2	45²	44	4	20	39	12.8	1.97	181	.260	.342	0	.000	0	8	8	1	1.0
1965 *Min-A	9	3	.750	56	0	0	0	5	76¹	59	8	31	59	11.0	2.24	159	.217	.304	0	.000	-1	10	11	-1	1.0
1966 Min-A	1	1	.500	26	0	0	0	3	39²	35	2	20	26	12.9	3.40	106	.238	.337	0	.000	-0	0	1	-0	0.0
1967 Det-A	0	0	—	5	0	0	0	0	6²	6	1	1	4	9.5	5.40	60	.250	.280	0	—	0	-2	-2	-0	-0.1
Total 18	101	118	.461	711	161	37	6	66	1967²	1915	203	978	1158	13.6	4.24	94	.258	.350	63	.125	-15	-80	-54	-1	-5.1

■ FRED KLOBEDANZ
Klobedanz, Frederick Augustus "Duke" b: 6/13/1871, Waterbury, Conn. d: 4/12/40, Waterbury, Conn. BL/TL, 5'11", 190 lbs. Deb: 8/20/1896

YEAR TM/L	W	L	PCT	G	GS	CG	SH	SV	IP	H	HR	BB	SO	RAT	ERA	ERA+	OAV	OOB	BH	AVG	PB	PR	/A	PD	TPI
1896 Bos-N	6	4	.600	10	9	9	0	0	80²	69	5	31	26	11.2	3.01	151	.230	.302	13	.317	3	12	14	-1	1.4
1897 *Bos-N	26	7	.788	38	37	30	2	0	309¹	344	13	125	92	13.6	4.60	97	.279	.346	48	.324	8	-10	-4	-5	0.3
1898 Bos-N	19	10	.655	35	33	25	0	0	270²	281	13	99	51	12.6	3.89	95	.266	.329	27	.213	-0	-8	-6	0	-0.4
1899 Bos-N	1	4	.200	5	5	4	0	0	33¹	39	2	9	8	13.0	4.86	86	.291	.336	2	.182	1	-4	-3	1	0.0
1902 Bos-N	1	0	1.000	1	1	1	0	0	8	9	0	2	4	13.5	1.13	251	.265	.345	1	.500	1	1	1	0	0.3
Total 5	53	25	.679	89	85	69	2	0	702	742	33	266	181	12.9	4.12	101	.269	.334	91	.277	12	-8	-2	-5	1.6

■ STAN KLOPP
Klopp, Stanley Harold "Betz" b: 12/22/10, Womelsdorf, Pa. d: 3/11/80, Robesonia, Pa. BR/TR, 6'1.5", 180 lbs. Deb: 4/30/44

YEAR TM/L	W	L	PCT	G	GS	CG	SH	SV	IP	H	HR	BB	SO	RAT	ERA	ERA+	OAV	OOB	BH	AVG	PB	PR	/A	PD	TPI
1944 Bos-N	1	2	.333	24	0	0	0	0	46¹	47	1	33	17	15.5	4.27	89	.272	.388	2	.286	0	-3	-2	-1	-0.2

YEAR	TM/L	W	L	PCT	G	GS	CG	SH	SV	IP	H	HR	BB	SO	RAT	ERA	ERA+	OAV	OOB	BH	AVG	PB	PR	/A	PD	TPI
■ **BRENT KNACKERT**						Knackert, Brent Bradley				b: 8/1/69, Los Angeles, Cal.			BR/TR, 6'3", 185 lbs.		Deb: 4/10/90										
1990	Sea-A	1	1	.500	24	2	0	0	0	37^1	50	5	21	28	17.6	6.51	61	.313	.399	0	—	0	-11	-11	0	-1.0
■ **CHRIS KNAPP**						Knapp, Robert Christian				b: 9/16/53, Cherry Point, N.C.			BR/TR, 6'5", 195 lbs.		Deb: 9/04/75										
1975	Chi-A	0	0	—	2	0	0	0	0	2	2	0	4	3	27.0	4.50	86	.250	.500	0	—	0	-0	-0	0	0.0
1976	Chi-A	3	1	.750	11	6	1	0	0	52^1	54	5	32	41	15.0	4.82	74	.273	.377	0	—	0	-8	-7	-1	-0.7
1977	Chi-A	12	7	.632	27	26	4	0	0	146^1	66	16	61	103	8.2	4.80	85	.112	.205	0	—	0	-12	-12	-1	-1.1
1978	Cal-A	14	8	.636	30	29	6	0	0	188^1	178	25	67	126	11.8	4.21	86	.250	.317	0	—	0	-9	-13	-2	-1.4
1979	*Cal-A	5	5	.500	20	18	3	0	0	98	109	8	35	36	13.4	5.51	74	.275	.337	0	—	0	-14	-16	0	-1.4
1980	Cal-A	2	11	.154	32	20	1	0	1	117^1	133	18	51	46	14.7	6.14	64	.289	.369	0	—	0	-27	-29	-1	-2.7
Total	6	36	32	.529	122	99	15	0	1	604^1	542	72	250	355	12.1	4.99	77	.230	.309	0	—	0	-70	-76	-4	-7.3
■ **FRANK KNAUSS**						Knauss, Frank H.				b: 1868, Cleveland, Ohio			BL/TL, 170 lbs.		Deb: 6/25/1890										
1890	Col-a	17	12	.586	37	34	28	3	2	275^2	206	3	106	148	10.2	2.81	128	**.201**	.276	24	.226	5	33	24	-1	2.4
1891	Cle-N	0	3	.000	3	3	1	0	0	15	23	2	8	6	18.6	7.20	48	.339	.409	1	.167	-0	-6	-6	0	-0.4
1892	Cin-N	0	0	—	1	0	0	0	0	8	13	0	5	2	20.3	3.38	97	.351	.429	1	.333	0	-0	-0	0	0.0
1894	Cle-N	0	1	.000	2	2	1	0	0	11	7	0	14	2	17.2	5.73	95	.181	.399	0	.000	-1	-0	-0	1	0.0
1895	NY-N	0	0	—	1	1	0	0	0	3^2	9	0	2	1	27.0	17.18	27	.458	.509	0	.000	-0	-5	-5	-0	-0.3
Total	5	17	16	.515	44	40	30	3	2	313^1	258	5	135	159	11.3	3.30	110	.218	.298	26	.217	4	20	12	-0	1.7
■ **RUDY KNEISCH**						Kneisch, Rudolph Frank				b: 4/10/1899, Baltimore, Md.		d: 4/6/65, Baltimore, Md.		BR/TL, 5'10.5", 175 lbs.		Deb: 9/21/26										
1926	Det-A	0	1	.000	2	1	0	0	0	17	18	2	6	4	13.8	2.65	153	.273	.351	0	.000	-1	3	3	0	0.2
■ **PHIL KNELL**						Knell, Philip Louis				b: 3/12/1865, San Francisco, Cal		d: 6/5/44, Santa Monica, Cal.		BR/TL, 5'7.5", 154 lbs.		Deb: 7/06/1888										
1888	Pit-N	1	2	.333	3	3	3	0	0	26^1	20	1	18	15	13.0	3.76	71	.203	.326	1	.091	-1	-3	-3	-0	-0.3
1890	Phi-P	22	11	.667	35	31	30	2	0	286^2	287	10	166	99	14.2	3.83	112	.249	.344	29	.220	-1	13	14	-0	1.1
1891	Col-a	28	27	.509	58	52	47	**5**	0	462	363	4	226	228	11.5	2.92	118	**.209**	.300	34	.158	-8	41	28	4	1.8
1892	Was-N	9	13	.409	22	21	17	1	0	170	156	4	76	74	12.3	3.65	89	.234	.313	8	.113	-4	-7	-8	-0	-1.0
	Phi-N	5	5	.500	11	9	7	0	0	80	87	0	35	43	13.7	4.05	80	.266	.337	3	.088	-3	-7	-7	-2	-0.9
	Yr	14	18	.438	33	30	24	1	0	250	243	4	111	117	12.7	3.78	86	.245	.321	6	.059	-7	-14	-15	-2	-1.9
1894	Pit-N	0	0	—	1	0	0	0	0	7	11	0	6	0	21.9	11.57	45	.353	.458	0	.000	-1	-5	-5	1	-0.2
	Lou-N	7	21	.250	32	28	25	0	0	247	330	9	104	67	15.8	5.32	96	.317	.379	31	.274	1	0	-6	-2	-0.6
	Yr	7	21	.250	33	28	25	0	0	254	341	9	110	67	15.5	5.49	93	.318	.381	0	.000	-0	-5	-11	-2	-0.8
1895	Lou-N	0	6	.000	10	6	3	0	0	56^2	75	3	21	19	15.2	6.51	71	.313	.369	6	.231	0	-11	-12	1	-0.8
	Cle-N	7	5	.583	20	13	9	0	0	116^2	149	7	53	30	15.6	5.40	92	.306	.374	11	.200	-3	-8	-5	0	-0.5
	Yr	7	11	.389	30	19	12	0	0	173^1	224	10	74	49	15.5	5.76	85	.308	.372	2	.025	-3	-19	-17	1	-1.3
Total	6	79	90	.467	192	163	141	8	0	1452^1	1478	38	705	575	13.5	4.05	99	.256	.337	123	.187	-20	14	-5	1	-1.4
■ **CHARLIE KNEPPER**						Knepper, Charles				b: 2/18/1871, Anderson, Ind.		d: 2/6/46, Muncie, Ind.		BR/TR, 6'4", 190 lbs.		Deb: 5/26/1899										
1899	Cle-N	4	22	.154	27	26	26	0	0	219^2	307	11	77	43	15.7	5.78	64	.329	.381	12	.135	-5	-47	-51	-1	-4.6
■ **BOB KNEPPER**						Knepper, Robert Wesley				b: 5/25/54, Akron, Ohio			BL/TL, 6'3", 195 lbs.		Deb: 9/10/76										
1976	SF-N	1	2	.333	4	4	0	0	0	25	26	0	7	11	11.9	3.24	112	.277	.327	1	.111	-0	1	1	0	0.1
1977	SF-N	11	9	.550	27	27	6	2	0	166	151	14	72	100	12.3	3.36	116	.242	.273	10	.182	1	10	10	-1	1.1
1978	SF-N	17	11	.607	36	35	16	**6**	0	260	218	10	85	147	10.6	2.63	131	.229	.295	5	.063	-3	**27**	24	-2	2.0
1979	SF-N	9	12	.429	34	34	6	2	0	207^1	241	30	77	123	13.9	4.64	75	.289	.352	12	.182	3	-21	-27	-1	-2.4
1980	SF-N	9	16	.360	35	33	8	1	0	215^1	242	15	61	103	13.0	4.10	86	.281	.335	10	.152	-0	-12	-13	2	-1.1
1981	*Hou-N	9	5	.643	22	22	6	5	0	156^2	128	5	38	75	9.8	2.18	151	.226	.280	7	.149	1	23	19	0	2.3
1982	Hou-N	5	15	.250	33	29	4	0	1	180	193	14	60	108	12.8	4.45	75	.278	.338	3	.058	-2	-17	-23	1	-2.4
1983	Hou-N	6	13	.316	35	29	4	3	0	203	202	12	71	125	12.3	3.19	107	.261	.326	12	.182	3	10	5	1	0.9
1984	Hou-N	15	10	.600	35	34	11	3	0	233^2	223	26	55	140	10.7	3.20	104	.251	.296	13	.171	4	10	3	-1	0.6
1985	Hou-N	15	13	.536	37	37	4	0	0	241	253	21	54	131	11.6	3.55	98	.271	.313	11	.141	0	1	-2	-2	-0.4
1986	*Hou-N	17	12	.586	40	38	8	**5**	0	258	232	19	62	143	10.4	3.14	115	.242	.290	9	.099	-3	17	13	3	1.4
1987	Hou-N	8	17	.320	33	31	1	0	0	177^2	226	26	54	76	14.4	5.27	74	.313	.364	5	.098	-1	-23	-27	3	-2.4
1988	Hou-N	14	5	.737	27	27	3	2	0	175	156	13	67	103	11.6	3.14	106	.243	.316	6	.125	-0	6	4	2	0.6
1989	Hou-N	4	10	.286	22	20	0	0	0	113	135	12	60	45	15.7	5.89	57	.303	.388	7	.226	5	-30	-31	1	-2.4
	SF-N	3	2	.600	13	6	1	1	0	52	55	4	15	19	12.3	3.46	97	.270	.323	1	.083	-1	0	-1	-1	0.0
	Yr	7	12	.368	35	26	1	1	0	165	190	16	75	64	14.5	5.13	66	.292	.364	9	.209	5	-30	-32	1	-2.4
1990	SF-N	3	3	.500	12	7	0	0	0	44^1	56	7	19	24	15.4	5.68	65	.311	.380	3	.231	1	-9	-10	0	-0.8
Total	15	146	155	.485	445	413	78	30	1	2708	2737	228	857	1473	12.1	3.68	95	.264	.323	115	.137	7	-8	-55	5	-2.9
■ **LOU KNERR**						Knerr, Wallace Luther				b: 8/21/21, Strasburg, Pa.		d: 3/23/80, Denver, Pa.		BR/TR, 6'1", 210 lbs.		Deb: 4/17/45										
1945	Phi-A	5	11	.313	27	17	5	0	0	130	142	6	74	41	15.0	4.22	81	.283	.376	9	.191	-1	-12	-11	0	-1.2
1946	Phi-A	3	16	.158	30	22	6	0	0	148^1	171	13	67	58	14.5	5.40	66	.288	.361	9	.180	-0	-31	-31	-0	-2.9
1947	Was-A	0	0	—	6	0	0	0	0	9	17	1	8	5	25.0	11.00	34	.405	.500	1	1.000	0	-7	-7	0	-0.5
Total	3	8	27	.229	63	39	11	0	0	287^1	330	20	149	104	15.1	5.04	69	.290	.373	19	.194	-1	-51	-49	0	-4.6
■ **ELMER KNETZER**						Knetzer, Elmer Ellsworth "Baron"				b: 7/22/1885, Carrick, Pa.		d: 10/3/75, Pittsburgh, Pa.		BR/TR, 5'10", 180 lbs.		Deb: 9/11/09										
1909	Bro-N	1	3	.250	5	4	3	0	0	35^2	33	2	22	7	13.9	3.03	86	.252	.359	0	.000	-2	-2	-2	1	-0.2
1910	Bro-N	7	5	.583	20	15	10	3	0	132^2	122	1	60	56	12.4	3.19	95	.255	.339	2	.053	-3	-2	-2	-2	-0.6
1911	Bro-N	11	12	.478	35	20	11	3	0	204	202	1	93	66	13.1	3.49	96	.277	.359	6	.097	-3	-2	-3	-1	-0.7
1912	Bro-N	7	9	.438	33	16	4	1	0	140^1	135	6	70	61	13.4	4.55	74	.250	.340	5	.135	-1	-18	-19	-1	-1.8
1914	Pit-F	20	12	.625	37	30	20	3	1	272	257	9	88	146	11.5	2.88	111	.254	.315	9	.099	-7	10	9	0	0.2
1915	Pit-F	18	14	.563	41	33	22	3	3	279	256	5	89	120	11.2	2.58	117	.251	.311	12	.132	-5	14	13	-1	0.8
1916	Bos-N	0	2	.000	2	0	0	0	0	5	11	0	2	2	23.4	7.20	35	.524	.565	0	—	0	-3	-3	1	-0.1
	Cin-N	5	12	.294	36	16	12	0	1	171^1	161	6	48	70	11.1	2.89	90	.252	.307	8	.154	-1	-5	-6	3	-0.4
	Yr	5	14	.263	38	16	12	0	1	176^1	172	6	50	72	11.5	3.01	86	.261	.316	1	.019	-0	-8	-8	3	-0.5
1917	Cin-N	0	0	—	11	0	0	0	1	27^1	29	0	12	7	14.2	2.96	88	.282	.368	0	—	0	-1	-1	0	0.0
Total	8	69	69	.500	220	134	82	13	6	1267^1	1206	30	484	535	12.1	3.15	97	.258	.329	42	.109	-22	-8	-13	1	-2.8
■ **LON KNIGHT**						Knight, Alonzo P.				b: 6/16/1853, Philadelphia, Pa.		d: 4/23/32, Philadelphia, Pa.		BR/TR, 5'11.5", 165 lbs.		Deb: 9/04/1875 MU♦										
1875	Ath-n	6	5	.545	13	13	12	0	0	107	114	0	12		10.6	2.44	108	.259	.279	6	.128	-4	0	2		0.0
1876	Phi-N	10	22	.313	34	32	27	0	0	282	383	0	34	12	13.3	2.62	93	.303	.322	60	.250	-1	-10	-6	-1	-0.5
1884	Phi-a	0	1	.000	2	1	1	0	0	14	24	0	4	2	18.0	9.00	38	.353	.395	131	.271	-0	-9	-9	0	-0.6
1885	Phi-a	0	0	—	1	0	0	0	0	5	4	0	2	1	10.8	1.80	191	.210	.285	25	.210	-0	1	1	0	0.1
	Pro-N	0	0	—	1	0	0	0	0	4	4	1	4	1	18.0	6.75	39	.248	.398	13	.160	-0	-2	-2	-0	-0.1
Total	3	10	23	.303	38	33	28	0	0	305	415	1	44	16	13.5	2.95	84	.304	.326	549	.245	-1	-20	-16	-1	-1.1
■ **JACK KNIGHT**						Knight, Elma Russell				b: 1/12/1895, Pittsboro, Miss.		d: 7/30/76, San Antonio, Tex.		BL/TR, 6', 175 lbs.		Deb: 9/20/22										
1922	StL-N	0	0	—	1	1	0	0	0	9	9	0	3	1	27.0	9.00	43	.474	.545	1	.500	0	-2	-2	0	-0.1
1925	Phi-N	7	6	.538	33	11	4	0	3	105^1	161	14	36	19	16.9	6.84	70	.354	.402	9	.205	-1	-30	-24	-1	-2.2
1926	Phi-N	3	12	.200	35	15	5	0	2	142^2	206	14	48	29	16.0	6.62	63	.347	.396	12	.214	1	-44	-39	5	-3.0
1927	Bos-N	0	0	—	3	0	0	0	0	3	6	0	2	0	24.0	15.00	25	.429	.500	0	—	0	-4	-4	1	-0.2
Total	4	10	18	.357	72	27	9	0	5	255	382	28	89	49	16.7	6.85	64	.353	.403	22	.216	0	-80	-70	5	-5.5

YEAR TM/L	W	L	PCT	G	GS	CG	SH	SV	IP	H	HR	BB	SO	RAT	ERA	ERA+	OAV	OOB	BH	AVG	PB	PR	/A	PD	TPI

■ GEORGE KNIGHT
Knight, George Henry b: 11/24/1855, Lakeville, Conn. d: 10/4/12, Lakeville, Conn. Deb: 9/28/1875

YEAR TM/L	W	L	PCT	G	GS	CG	SH	SV	IP	H	HR	BB	SO	RAT	ERA	ERA+	OAV	OOB	BH	AVG	PB	PR	/A	PD	TPI
1875 NH-n	1	0	1.000	1	1	1	0	0	9	12	0	0		12.0	2.00	113	.293	.293	0	.000	-1	0	0		0.0

■ JOE KNIGHT
Knight, Jonas William "Quiet Joe" b: 9/28/1859, Point Stanley, Ont., Canada d: 10/18/38, St.Thomas, Ont., Can. BL/TL, 5'11", 185 lbs. Deb: 5/16/1884 ♦

YEAR TM/L	W	L	PCT	G	GS	CG	SH	SV	IP	H	HR	BB	SO	RAT	ERA	ERA+	OAV	OOB	BH	AVG	PB	PR	/A	PD	TPI
1884 Phi-N	2	4	.333	6	6	6	0	0	51	66	2	21	8	15.4	5.47	55	.297	.358	6	.250	1	-14	-14	0	-1.0

■ HUB KNOLLS
Knolls, Oscar Edward b: 12/18/1883, Valparaiso, Ind. d: 7/1/46, Chicago, Ill. TR, 6'2", 190 lbs. Deb: 5/01/06

YEAR TM/L	W	L	PCT	G	GS	CG	SH	SV	IP	H	HR	BB	SO	RAT	ERA	ERA+	OAV	OOB	BH	AVG	PB	PR	/A	PD	TPI
1906 Bro-N	0	0	—	2	0	0	0	0	6²	13	0	2	3	20.3	4.05	62	.382	.417	1	1.000	1	-1	-1	-0	0.0

■ JACK KNOTT
Knott, John Henry b: 3/2/07, Dallas, Tex. d: 10/13/81, Brownwood, Tex. BR/TR, 6'2.5", 200 lbs. Deb: 4/13/33

YEAR TM/L	W	L	PCT	G	GS	CG	SH	SV	IP	H	HR	BB	SO	RAT	ERA	ERA+	OAV	OOB	BH	AVG	PB	PR	/A	PD	TPI
1933 StL-A	1	8	.111	20	9	0	0	0	82²	88	11	33	19	13.4	5.01	93	.269	.340	7	.304	1	-7	-3	-1	-0.2
1934 StL-A	10	3	.769	45	10	2	0	4	138	149	17	67	56	14.2	4.96	101	.278	.359	4	.133	-1	-7	1	1	0.0
1935 StL-A	11	8	.579	48	19	7	2	7	187²	219	8	78	45	13.3	4.60	104	.287	.353	7	.115	-6	-3	4	1	0.0
1936 StL-A	9	17	.346	47	23	9	0	6	192²	272	15	93	60	17.2	7.29	74	.330	.401	4	.070	-6	-48	-41	-1	-3.9
1937 StL-A	8	18	.308	38	22	8	0	2	191¹	220	25	91	74	14.9	4.89	99	.291	.370	8	.140	-4	-6	-1	-2	-0.6
1938 StL-A	1	2	.333	7	4	0	0	0	30	35	3	15	8	15.0	4.80	104	.285	.362	1	.100	-1	-0	1	-0	0.0
Chi-A	5	10	.333	20	18	9	0	0	131	135	8	54	35	13.0	4.05	121	.271	.342	5	.125	-2	11	12	1	1.0
Yr	6	12	.333	27	22	9	0	0	161	170	11	69	43	13.4	4.19	117	.273	.346	2	.040	-3	11	13	1	1.0
1939 Chi-A	11	6	.647	25	23	8	0	0	149²	157	13	41	56	12.0	4.15	114	.269	.318	8	.151	-3	8	10	-1	0.6
1940 Chi-A	11	9	.550	25	23	4	2	0	158	166	12	52	44	12.5	4.56	97	.265	.324	5	.088	-4	-3	-2	-0	-0.5
1941 Phi-A	13	11	.542	27	26	11	0	0	194¹	212	20	81	54	13.7	4.40	95	.279	.350	5	.077	-3	-5	-5	-2	-0.9
1942 Phi-A	2	10	.167	20	14	4	0	0	95¹	127	7	36	31	15.5	5.57	68	.310	.367	4	.138	-1	-20	-19	1	-1.7
1946 Phi-A	0	1	.000	3	1	0	0	0	6¹	7	1	1	2	12.8	5.68	62	.280	.333	0		0	-2	-2	-0	-0.1
Total 11	82	103	.443	325	192	62	4	19	1557	1787	140	642	484	14.2	4.97	95	.287	.355	58	.120	-30	-83	-46	-3	-6.3

■ ED KNOUFF
Knouff, Edward "Fred" b: 1867, Philadelphia, Pa. d: 9/14/1900, Philadelphia, Pa. BR/TR, 210 lbs. Deb: 7/01/1885 ♦

YEAR TM/L	W	L	PCT	G	GS	CG	SH	SV	IP	H	HR	BB	SO	RAT	ERA	ERA+	OAV	OOB	BH	AVG	PB	PR	/A	PD	TPI
1885 Phi-a	7	6	.538	14	13	12	0	0	106	103	0	44	43	12.5	3.65	94	.244	.315	9	.188	-2	-5	-2	1	-0.1
1886 Bal-a	0	1	.000	1	1	1	0	0	9	2	0	5	8	7.0	2.00	171	.068	.204	0	.000	-1	1	1	1	0.2
1887 Bal-a	2	6	.250	9	9	6	0	0	63	79	0	41	27	17.1	7.57	54	.296	.389	9	.290	0	-23	-24	0	-1.7
StL-a	4	2	.667	6	6	6	1	0	50	40	0	36	18	13.7	4.50	101	.211	.337	10	.179	-1	-1	-0	-0	-0.0
Yr	6	8	.429	15	15	12	1	0	113	119	0	77	45	15.6	6.21	69	.261	.367	2	.023	-1	-24	-24	-0	-1.7
1888 StL-a	5	4	.556	9	9	9	0	0	81	66	0	37	25	11.4	2.67	122	.214	.299	3	.097	-2	4	5	-1	0.2
Cle-a	0	1	.000	2	2	1	0	0	9	8	0	3	2	11.0	1.00	311	.230	.291	1	.167	0	2	2	1	0.3
Yr	5	5	.500	11	11	10	0	0	90	74	0	40	27	11.4	2.50	130	.216	.298	4	.108	-2	6	7	-1	0.5
1889 Phi-a	2	0	1.000	3	3	2	0	0	25	37	2	9	5	16.6	3.96	95	.333	.383	3	.250	0	-0	-1	-0	-0.1
Total 5	20	20	.500	44	43	37	1	0	343	335	2	175	128	13.4	4.17	89	.246	.332	35	.187	-5	-22	-18	1	-1.1

■ DAROLD KNOWLES
Knowles, Darold Duane b: 12/9/41, Brunswick, Mo. BL/TL, 6', 180 lbs. Deb: 4/18/65 C

YEAR TM/L	W	L	PCT	G	GS	CG	SH	SV	IP	H	HR	BB	SO	RAT	ERA	ERA+	OAV	OOB	BH	AVG	PB	PR	/A	PD	TPI
1965 Bal-A	0	1	.000	5	1	0	0	0	14²	14	2	10	12	16.6	9.20	38	.250	.391	0	.000	-0	-9	-9	0	-0.8
1966 Phi-N	6	5	.545	69	0	0	0	13	100¹	98	4	46	88	13.5	3.05	118	.260	.351	4	.250	0	6	6	2	0.9
1967 Was-A	6	8	.429	61	1	0	0	14	113¹	91	5	52	85	11.7	2.70	117	.228	.322	1	.063	-1	7	6	2	0.7
1968 Was-A	1	1	.500	32	0	0	0	4	41¹	38	0	12	37	11.1	2.18	134	.241	.298	1	.250	1	4	3	0	0.5
1969 Was-A	9	2	.818	53	0	0	0	13	84¹	73	8	31	59	11.5	2.24	155	.236	.314	1	.077	0	13	11	0	1.2
1970 Was-A	2	14	.125	71	0	0	0	27	119¹	100	4	58	71	12.2	2.04	175	.231	.328	1	.050	-1	22	20	2	2.1
1971 Was-A	2	2	.500	12	0	0	0	2	15¹	17	2	6	16	13.5	3.52	94	.266	.329	0	.000	-0	-0	-0	-0	0.0
*Oak-A	5	2	.714	43	0	0	0	7	52²	40	3	16	40	10.1	3.59	93	.221	.295	1	.125	-0	-1	-1	1	0.0
Yr	7	4	.636	55	0	0	0	9	68	57	5	22	56	10.9	3.57	93	.233	.304	0	.000	-1	-1	-2	1	0.0
1972 Oak-A	5	1	.833	54	0	0	0	11	65²	49	1	37	36	11.8	1.37	207	.212	.321	3	.250	1	12	11	3	1.7
1973 *Oak-A	6	8	.429	52	5	1	1	9	99	87	7	49	46	12.6	3.09	115	.246	.343	0	—	0	8	5	2	0.7
1974 Oak-A	3	3	.500	45	1	0	0	3	53¹	61	6	35	18	16.5	4.22	79	.296	.403	0	—	0	-4	-5	1	-0.4
1975 Chi-N	6	9	.400	58	0	0	0	15	88¹	107	6	36	63	14.9	5.81	66	.298	.367	1	.067	-1	-21	-19	3	-1.7
1976 Chi-N	5	7	.417	58	0	0	0	9	71²	61	6	22	39	10.7	2.89	134	.242	.308	1	.143	1	5	8	2	1.2
1977 Tex-A	5	2	.714	42	0	0	0	4	50¹	50	3	23	14	13.4	3.22	127	.272	.359	0	—	0	5	5	1	0.6
1978 Mon-N	3	3	.500	60	0	0	0	6	72	63	5	30	34	11.6	2.38	148	.250	.330	1	.167	-0	10	9	2	1.1
1979 StL-N	2	5	.286	48	0	0	0	6	48²	54	5	17	22	13.1	4.07	92	.277	.335	0	.000	-0	-2	-2	-0	-0.2
1980 StL-N	0	1	.000	2	0	0	0	0	1²	3	1	0	1	16.2	10.80	34	.375	.375	0	—	0	-1	-1	0	0.0
Total 16	66	74	.471	765	8	1	1	143	1092	1006	65	480	681	12.6	3.12	112	.250	.336	15	.120	-1	53	45	19	7.6

■ TOM KNOWLSON
Knowlson, Thomas Herbert "Doc" b: 4/23/1895, Pittsburgh, Pa. d: 4/11/43, Miami Shores, Fla. BB/TR, 5'11", 178 lbs. Deb: 7/03/15

YEAR TM/L	W	L	PCT	G	GS	CG	SH	SV	IP	H	HR	BB	SO	RAT	ERA	ERA+	OAV	OOB	BH	AVG	PB	PR	/A	PD	TPI
1915 Phi-A	4	6	.400	18	9	8	0	0	100²	99	1	60	24	14.8	3.49	84	.273	.386	3	.083	-3	-6	-6	0	-0.8

■ BILL KNOWLTON
Knowlton, William Young b: 8/18/1892, Philadelphia, Pa. d: 2/25/44, Philadelphia, Pa. BR/TR, Deb: 9/03/20

YEAR TM/L	W	L	PCT	G	GS	CG	SH	SV	IP	H	HR	BB	SO	RAT	ERA	ERA+	OAV	OOB	BH	AVG	PB	PR	/A	PD	TPI
1920 Phi-A	0	1	.000	1	1	0	0	0	5²	9	0	3	5	23.8	4.76	84	.346	.469	0	.000	-0	-1	-0	0	0.0

■ MARK KNUDSON
Knudson, Mark Richard b: 10/28/60, Denver, Colo. BR/TR, 6'5", 215 lbs. Deb: 7/08/85

YEAR TM/L	W	L	PCT	G	GS	CG	SH	SV	IP	H	HR	BB	SO	RAT	ERA	ERA+	OAV	OOB	BH	AVG	PB	PR	/A	PD	TPI
1985 Hou-N	0	2	.000	2	2	0	0	0	11	21	0	3	4	19.6	9.00	38	.429	.462	0	.000	0	-7	-7	0	-0.5
1986 Hou-N	1	5	.167	9	7	0	0	0	42²	48	5	15	20	13.5	4.22	85	.279	.340	0	.000	-1	-2	-3	-1	-0.3
Mil-A	0	1	.000	4	1	0	0	0	17²	22	7	5	9	13.8	7.64	57	.286	.329	0	—	0	-7	-7	0	-0.5
1987 Mil-A	4	4	.500	15	8	1	0	0	62	68	7	14	26	14.8	5.37	85	.331	.364	0	—	0	-6	-6	-1	-0.5
1988 Mil-A	0	0	—	5	0	0	0	0	16	17	1	2	7	10.7	1.13	354	.279	.302	0	—	0	5	5	0	0.6
1989 Mil-A	8	5	.615	40	7	1	0	0	123²	110	15	29	47	10.3	3.35	115	.237	.286	0	—	0	7	7	0	0.6
1990 Mil-A	10	9	.526	30	27	4	2	0	168¹	187	14	40	56	12.3	4.12	92	.282	.325	0	—	0	-4	-6	-1	-0.6
Total 6	23	26	.469	105	52	6	2	0	441¹	493	49	108	169	12.4	4.24	92	.281	.325	0	.000	0	-14	-16	-3	-1.2

■ KEVIN KOBEL
Kobel, Kevin Richard b: 10/2/53, Buffalo, N.Y. BR/TL, 6', 180 lbs. Deb: 9/08/73

YEAR TM/L	W	L	PCT	G	GS	CG	SH	SV	IP	H	HR	BB	SO	RAT	ERA	ERA+	OAV	OOB	BH	AVG	PB	PR	/A	PD	TPI
1973 Mil-A	0	1	.000	2	1	0	0	0	8¹	9	2	8	4	18.4	8.64	44	.273	.415	0	—	0	-4	-5	0	-0.3
1974 Mil-A	6	14	.300	34	24	3	2	0	169¹	166	16	54	74	11.8	3.99	91	.258	.317	0	—	0	-7	-7	1	-0.5
1976 Mil-A	0	1	.000	3	0	0	0	0	4	6	3	3	1	22.5	11.25	31	.375	.500	0	—	0	-3	-3	0	-0.2
1978 NY-N	5	6	.455	32	11	1	0	0	108¹	95	9	30	51	10.6	2.91	120	.239	.295	4	.160	1	8	7	-0	0.7
1979 NY-N	6	8	.429	30	27	1	1	0	161²	169	14	46	67	12.1	3.51	104	.274	.328	9	.196	1	4	2	1	0.4
1980 NY-N	1	4	.200	14	1	0	0	0	24¹	36	5	11	8	17.4	7.03	51	.353	.416	0	.000	-0	-9	-9	0	-0.9
Total 6	18	34	.346	115	64	5	3	0	476	481	49	152	205	12.1	3.88	93	.266	.326	13	.178	1	-12	-15	1	-0.8

■ ALAN KOCH
Koch, Alan Goodman b: 3/25/38, Decatur, Ala. BR/TR, 6'4", 195 lbs. Deb: 7/26/63

YEAR TM/L	W	L	PCT	G	GS	CG	SH	SV	IP	H	HR	BB	SO	RAT	ERA	ERA+	OAV	OOB	BH	AVG	PB	PR	/A	PD	TPI
1963 Det-A	1	1	.500	7	1	0	0	0	10	21	3	9	5	27.0	10.80	35	.467	.564	2	.667	1	-8	-8	0	-0.6
1964 Det-A	0	0	—	3	0	0	0	0	4	6	1	3	1	20.3	6.75	54	.375	.474	0	—	0	-1	-1	-0	-0.1
Was-A	3	10	.231	32	14	1	0	0	114	110	18	43	67	12.3	4.89	76	.253	.325	8	.250	2	-16	-15	-2	-1.5
Yr	3	10	.231	35	14	1	0	0	118	116	19	46	68	12.6	4.96	75	.257	.331	0	.000	2	-17	-17	-2	-1.6
Total 2	4	11	.267	42	15	1	0	0	128	137	22	55	73	13.8	5.41	68	.277	.354	10	.286	3	-25	-24	-2	-2.2

■ DICK KOECHER
Koecher, Richard Finlay "Highpockets" b: 3/30/26, Philadelphia, Pa. BL/TL, 6'5", 196 lbs. Deb: 9/29/46

YEAR TM/L	W	L	PCT	G	GS	CG	SH	SV	IP	H	HR	BB	SO	RAT	ERA	ERA+	OAV	OOB	BH	AVG	PB	PR	/A	PD	TPI
1946 Phi-N	0	1	.000	1	1	0	0	0	2²	7	0	1	2	27.0	10.13	34	.467	.500	0	.000	-0	-2	-2	0	-0.1
1947 Phi-N	0	2	.000	3	2	1	0	0	17	20	1	10	4	16.4	4.76	84	.299	.397	0	.000	-1	-1	-1	0	-0.1
1948 Phi-N	0	1	.000	3	0	0	0	0	6	4	0	3	2	10.5	3.00	132	.235	.350	0	—	0	1	1	0	0.1

YEAR TM/L	W	L	PCT	G	GS	CG	SH	SV	IP	H	HR	BB	SO	RAT	ERA	ERA+	OAV	OOB	BH	AVG	PB	PR	/A	PD	TPI
Total 3	0	4	.000	7	3	1	0	0	25²	31	1	14	8	16.1	4.91	80	.313	.404	0	.000	-1	-3	-3	0	-0.1

■ MARK KOENIG   Koenig, Mark Anthony b: 7/19/02, San Francisco, Cal BB/TR, 6', 180 lbs. Deb: 9/08/25 ♦

YEAR TM/L	W	L	PCT	G	GS	CG	SH	SV	IP	H	HR	BB	SO	RAT	ERA	ERA+	OAV	OOB	BH	AVG	PB	PR	/A	PD	TPI
1930 Det-A	0	1	.000	2	1	0	0	0	9	11	0	8	6	20.0	10.00	48	.314	.455	64	.240	0	-5	-5	-0	-0.3
1931 Det-A	0	0	—	3	0	0	0	0	7	7	0	11	3	23.1	6.43	71	.280	.500	92	.253	0	-2	-1	0	0.0
Total 2	0	1	.000	5	1	0	0	0	16	18	0	19	9	21.4	8.44	56	.300	.475	1190	.279	0	-7	-7	0	-0.3

■ WILL KOENIGSMARK   Koenigsmark, William Thomas b: 2/27/1896, Waterloo, Ill. d: 7/1/72, Waterloo, Ill. BR/TR, 6'4", 180 lbs. Deb: 9/10/19

YEAR TM/L	W	L	PCT	G	GS	CG	SH	SV	IP	H	HR	BB	SO	RAT	ERA	ERA+	OAV	OOB	BH	AVG	PB	PR	/A	PD	TPI
1919 StL-N	0	0	—	1	0	0	0	0	0	2	0	1	0	∞	∞	—	1.000	1.000	0	—	-0	-2	-2	0	-0.1

■ ELMER KOESTNER   Koestner, Elmer Joseph "Bob" b: 11/30/1885, Piper City, Ill. d: 10/27/59, Fairbury, Ill. BR/TR, 6'1.5", 175 lbs. Deb: 4/23/10

YEAR TM/L	W	L	PCT	G	GS	CG	SH	SV	IP	H	HR	BB	SO	RAT	ERA	ERA+	OAV	OOB	BH	AVG	PB	PR	/A	PD	TPI
1910 Cle-A	5	10	.333	27	13	8	1	2	145	145	0	63	44	13.3	3.04	85	.282	.367	15	.313	3	-8	-7	-1	-0.5
1914 Chi-N	0	0	—	4	0	0	0	0	6¹	6	0	4	6	14.2	2.84	98	.261	.370	0	.000	-0	-0	-0	0	0.0
Cin-N	0	0	—	5	1	0	0	0	18¹	18	0	9	6	13.3	4.42	66	.265	.351	2	.400	1	-3	-3	0	-0.1
Yr	0	0	—	9	1	0	0	0	24²	24	0	13	12	13.5	4.01	72	.264	.356	0	.000	1	-3	-3	0	-0.1
Total 2	5	10	.333	36	14	8	1	2	169²	169	0	76	56	13.3	3.18	83	.279	.365	17	.315	3	-12	-10	-1	-0.6

■ JOE KOHLMAN   Kohlman, Joseph James "Blackie" b: 1/28/13, Philadelphia, Pa. d: 3/16/74, Philadelphia, Pa. BR/TR, 6', 160 lbs. Deb: 9/26/37

YEAR TM/L	W	L	PCT	G	GS	CG	SH	SV	IP	H	HR	BB	SO	RAT	ERA	ERA+	OAV	OOB	BH	AVG	PB	PR	/A	PD	TPI
1937 Was-A	1	0	1.000	2	2	1	0	0	13	15	0	3	3	12.5	4.15	107	.283	.321	1	.200	-0	1	0	-0	0.0
1938 Was-A	0	0	—	7	0	0	0	0	14¹	12	1	11	5	14.4	6.28	72	.240	.377	0	.000	-0	-2	-3	0	-0.2
Total 2	1	0	1.000	9	2	1	0	0	27¹	27	1	14	8	13.5	5.27	85	.262	.350	1	.125	-1	-2	-2	0	-0.2

■ EDDIE KOLB   Kolb, Edward William b: 7/20/1880, Cincinnati, Ohio BR/TR, Deb: 10/15/1899

YEAR TM/L	W	L	PCT	G	GS	CG	SH	SV	IP	H	HR	BB	SO	RAT	ERA	ERA+	OAV	OOB	BH	AVG	PB	PR	/A	PD	TPI
1899 Cle-N	0	1	.000	1	1	1	0	0	8	18	0	5	1	25.9	10.13	36	.442	.503	1	.250	-0	-6	-6	-0	-0.4

■ RAY KOLP   Kolp, Raymond Carl "Jockey" b: 10/1/1894, New Berlin, Ohio d: 7/29/67, New Orleans, La. BR/TR, 5'10.5", 187 lbs. Deb: 4/16/21

YEAR TM/L	W	L	PCT	G	GS	CG	SH	SV	IP	H	HR	BB	SO	RAT	ERA	ERA+	OAV	OOB	BH	AVG	PB	PR	/A	PD	TPI
1921 StL-A	8	7	.533	37	18	5	1	0	166²	208	12	51	43	14.0	4.97	90	.314	.363	7	.127	-6	-13	-9	1	-1.1
1922 StL-A	14	4	.778	32	18	9	1	0	169²	199	10	36	54	12.7	3.93	106	.292	.332	17	.298	5	2	4	-4	0.5
1923 StL-A	5	12	.294	34	17	11	1	1	171¹	178	11	54	44	12.5	3.89	107	.273	.335	6	.111	-4	2	5	-1	0.0
1924 StL-A	5	7	.417	25	12	5	1	0	96²	131	4	25	29	14.9	5.68	79	.329	.375	6	.200	-0	-16	-13	0	-1.1
1927 Cin-N	3	3	.500	24	5	2	1	3	82¹	86	5	29	28	12.7	3.06	124	.278	.342	6	.200	-0	8	7	0	0.7
1928 Cin-N	13	10	.565	44	24	12	1	3	209	219	9	55	61	12.0	3.19	124	.280	.330	15	.214	3	19	18	1	2.1
1929 Cin-N	8	10	.444	30	16	4	1	0	145¹	151	8	39	27	11.8	4.03	113	.278	.328	8	.163	-1	11	9	1	0.7
1930 Cin-N	7	12	.368	37	19	5	2	3	168¹	180	10	34	40	11.4	4.22	114	.278	.314	12	.245	1	14	11	-1	1.0
1931 Cin-N	4	9	.308	30	10	2	0	1	107	144	8	39	24	15.7	4.96	75	.332	.392	4	.125	-1	-13	-15	-1	-1.6
1932 Cin-N	6	10	.375	32	19	7	2	1	159²	176	13	27	42	11.6	3.89	99	.280	.313	9	.184	-1	-0	-1	-2	-0.3
1933 Cin-N	6	9	.400	30	14	4	0	3	150¹	168	7	23	28	11.5	3.53	96	.290	.318	7	.156	-1	-3	-2	1	-0.1
1934 Cin-N	0	2	.000	28	2	0	0	3	61²	78	1	12	19	13.4	4.52	90	.312	.348	1	.083	-1	-3	-3	2	-0.1
Total 12	79	95	.454	383	174	66	11	18	1688	1918	98	424	439	12.7	4.08	102	.292	.338	98	.184	-7	8	13	-4	0.7

■ HAL KOLSTAD   Kolstad, Harold Everette b: 6/1/35, Rice Lake, Wis. BR/TR, 5'9", 190 lbs. Deb: 4/22/62

YEAR TM/L	W	L	PCT	G	GS	CG	SH	SV	IP	H	HR	BB	SO	RAT	ERA	ERA+	OAV	OOB	BH	AVG	PB	PR	/A	PD	TPI
1962 Bos-A	0	2	.000	27	2	0	0	2	61¹	65	11	35	36	15.0	5.43	76	.269	.366	1	.056	-2	-10	-9	0	-0.9
1963 Bos-A	0	2	.000	7	0	0	0	0	11	16	4	6	6	19.6	13.09	29	.340	.436	0	.000	-0	-12	-11	0	-1.0
Total 2	0	4	.000	34	2	0	0	2	72¹	81	15	41	42	15.7	6.59	62	.280	.377	1	.053	-2	-22	-20	0	-1.9

■ ED KONETCHY   Konetchy, Edward Joseph "Big Ed" b: 9/3/1885, Lacrosse, Wis. d: 5/27/47, Ft.Worth, Tex. BR/TR, 6'2.5", 195 lbs. Deb: 6/29/07 ♦

YEAR TM/L	W	L	PCT	G	GS	CG	SH	SV	IP	H	HR	BB	SO	RAT	ERA	ERA+	OAV	OOB	BH	AVG	PB	PR	/A	PD	TPI
1910 StL-N	0	0	—	1	0	0	0	0	4	4	0	1	0	11.3	4.50	66	.267	.313	157	.302	0	-1	-1	-0	0.0
1913 StL-N	1	0	1.000	1	0	0	0	0	4²	1	0	4	3	9.6	0.00	—	.071	.278	139	.276	0	2	2	-0	0.2
1918 Bos-N	0	1	.000	1	1	1	0	0	8	14	1	2	3	18.0	6.75	40	.378	.410	103	.236	0	-4	-4	-0	-0.2
Total 3	1	1	.500	3	1	1	0	0	16²	19	1	7	6	14.0	4.32	67	.288	.356	2150	.281	1	-3	-3	-1	-0.2

■ DOUG KONIECZNY   Konieczny, Douglas James b: 9/27/51, Detroit, Mich. BR/TR, 6'4", 220 lbs. Deb: 9/11/73

YEAR TM/L	W	L	PCT	G	GS	CG	SH	SV	IP	H	HR	BB	SO	RAT	ERA	ERA+	OAV	OOB	BH	AVG	PB	PR	/A	PD	TPI
1973 Hou-N	0	1	.000	2	2	0	0	0	13	12	0	4	6	11.1	5.54	66	.279	.340	0	.000	-0	-3	-3	-0	-0.2
1974 Hou-N	0	3	.000	6	3	0	0	0	16	18	0	12	8	18.0	7.88	44	.290	.421	0	.000	-0	-8	-8	-0	-0.7
1975 Hou-N	6	13	.316	32	34	4	1	0	171	184	15	87	89	14.3	4.47	75	.280	.365	8	.160	1	-16	-21	-1	-2.1
1977 Hou-N	1	1	.500	4	4	0	0	0	21	26	1	8	7	15.0	6.00	59	.302	.368	1	.143	-0	-5	-6	0	-0.4
Total 4	7	18	.280	44	38	4	1	0	221	240	16	111	110	14.5	4.93	69	.283	.368	9	.138	-1	-31	-37	-1	-3.4

■ ALEX KONIKOWSKI   Konikowski, Alexander James "Whitey" b: 6/8/28, Throop, Pa. BR/TR, 6'1", 187 lbs. Deb: 6/16/48

YEAR TM/L	W	L	PCT	G	GS	CG	SH	SV	IP	H	HR	BB	SO	RAT	ERA	ERA+	OAV	OOB	BH	AVG	PB	PR	/A	PD	TPI
1948 NY-N	2	3	.400	22	1	0	0	1	33¹	46	7	17	9	17.0	7.56	52	.346	.420	0	.000	0	-13	-13	1	-1.1
1951 •NY-N	0	0	—	3	0	0	0	0	4	2	0	5	4	4.5	0.00	—	.154	.154	0	—	0	2	2	0	0.2
1954 NY-N	0	0	—	10	0	0	0	0	12	10	1	12	6	16.5	7.50	54	.244	.415	0	—	0	-5	-5	-0	-0.4
Total 3	2	3	.400	35	1	0	0	1	49¹	58	8	29	20	15.9	6.93	57	.310	.403	0	.000	0	-16	-16	0	-1.3

■ JIM KONSTANTY   Konstanty, Casimir James b: 3/2/17, Strykersville, N.Y. d: 6/11/76, Oneonta, N.Y. BR/TR, 6'1.5", 202 lbs. Deb: 6/18/44

YEAR TM/L	W	L	PCT	G	GS	CG	SH	SV	IP	H	HR	BB	SO	RAT	ERA	ERA+	OAV	OOB	BH	AVG	PB	PR	/A	PD	TPI
1944 Cin-N	6	4	.600	20	12	5	1	0	112²	113	11	33	19	11.7	2.80	125	.266	.320	10	.294	2	10	9	1	1.2
1946 Bos-N	0	1	.000	10	1	0	0	0	15¹	17	2	7	9	14.1	5.28	65	.283	.358	0	.000	-0	-3	-3	1	-0.2
1948 Phi-N	1	0	1.000	6	0	0	0	2	9²	7	0	2	7	8.4	0.93	424	.233	.281	0	.000	-0	3	3	0	0.3
1949 Phi-N	9	5	.643	53	0	0	0	7	97	98	9	29	43	11.9	3.25	121	.280	.337	3	.176	-0	9	8	1	0.8
1950 •Phi-N	16	7	.696	74	0	0	0	22	152	108	11	50	56	9.4	2.66	152	.205	.274	4	.108	-2	25	23	-1	2.0
1951 Phi-N	4	11	.267	58	1	0	0	9	115²	127	9	31	27	12.3	4.05	95	.282	.328	3	.158	-0	-1	-3	2	0.0
1952 Phi-N	5	3	.625	42	2	2	1	6	80	87	9	21	16	12.1	3.94	93	.274	.319	1	.071	-0	-2	-3	0	-0.2
1953 Phi-N	14	10	.583	48	19	7	0	5	170²	198	18	42	45	12.8	4.43	95	.290	.334	11	.220	-0	-3	-4	1	-0.2
1954 Phi-N	2	3	.400	33	1	0	0	3	50¹	62	7	12	11	13.2	3.75	108	.316	.356	0	.000	-2	2	2	0	0.0
NY-A	1	1	.500	9	0	0	0	2	18¹	11	0	6	3	8.3	0.98	350	.183	.258	0	.000	-0	6	5	0	0.5
1955 NY-A	7	2	.778	45	0	0	0	11	73²	68	5	24	19	11.2	2.32	161	.247	.308	1	.125	0	13	12	0	1.2
1956 NY-A	0	0	—	8	0	0	0	2	11	15	3	6	6	17.2	4.91	79	.319	.396	0	.000	-0	-1	-1	-0	-0.1
StL-N	1	1	.500	27	0	0	0	5	39¹	46	4	9	7	13.5	4.58	83	.301	.327	-0	—	0	-4	-3	-0	-0.3
Total 11	66	48	.579	433	36	14	2	74	945²	957	88	269	268	11.7	3.46	112	.268	.320	33	.163	-4	54	44	5	5.0

■ ERNIE KOOB   Koob, Ernest Gerald b: 9/11/1893, Keeler, Mich. d: 11/12/41, Lemay, Mo. BL/TL, 5'10", 160 lbs. Deb: 6/23/15

YEAR TM/L	W	L	PCT	G	GS	CG	SH	SV	IP	H	HR	BB	SO	RAT	ERA	ERA+	OAV	OOB	BH	AVG	PB	PR	/A	PD	TPI
1915 StL-A	4	5	.444	28	13	6	0	1	133²	119	2	50	37	12.1	2.36	122	.254	.339	5	.135	-1	9	8	-1	0.6
1916 StL-A	11	8	.579	33	20	10	2	2	166²	153	1	56	26	11.6	2.54	108	.252	.321	0	.000	-1	5	4	-3	0.0
1917 StL-A	6	14	.300	39	18	3	1	1	133²	139	1	57	47	13.6	3.91	67	.280	.361	4	.114	-1	-18	-19	0	-2.1
1919 StL-A	2	3	.400	25	4	0	0	0	66	77	3	23	11	13.9	4.64	72	.296	.358	0	.000	-2	-10	-10	1	-1.1
Total 4	23	30	.434	125	55	19	3	4	500	488	7	186	121	12.6	3.13	90	.266	.342	9	.070	-5	-15	-18	-3	-2.6

■ CAL KOONCE   Koonce, Calvin Lee b: 11/18/40, Fayetteville, N.C. BR/TR, 6'1", 185 lbs. Deb: 4/14/62

YEAR TM/L	W	L	PCT	G	GS	CG	SH	SV	IP	H	HR	BB	SO	RAT	ERA	ERA+	OAV	OOB	BH	AVG	PB	PR	/A	PD	TPI
1962 Chi-N	10	10	.500	35	30	3	1	0	190²	200	17	86	84	13.8	3.97	105	.271	.353	6	.094	-4	-0	4	-0	0.0
1963 Chi-N	2	6	.250	21	13	0	0	0	72²	75	9	32	44	13.5	4.58	77	.273	.353	2	.105	-0	-10	-9	1	-0.7
1964 Chi-N	3	0	1.000	6	2	0	0	0	31	30	1	7	17	10.7	2.03	183	.254	.296	0	.000	-0	5	6	2	0.7
1965 Chi-N	7	9	.438	38	23	3	1	0	173	181	17	52	88	12.4	3.69	100	.271	.329	5	.102	-0	-3	-0	0	0.0
1966 Chi-N	5	5	.500	45	5	0	0	0	108²	113	13	35	65	12.3	3.81	97	.268	.325	3	.130	0	-2	-2	0	-0.2
1967 Chi-N	2	2	.500	34	0	0	0	0	51	52	2	21	28	13.1	4.59	77	.268	.343	0	.000	-1	-7	-6	1	-0.5
NY-N	3	3	.500	11	6	2	1	0	45	45	2	7	24	10.4	2.80	121	.259	.287	2	.154	-0	3	3	1	0.2
Yr	5	5	.500	45	6	2	1	2	96	97	4	28	52	11.7	3.75	93	.262	.314	0	.000	-1	-4	-3	2	-0.1

YEAR TM/L	W	L	PCT	G	GS	CG	SH	SV	IP	H	HR	BB	SO	RAT	ERA	ERA+	OAV	OOB	BH	AVG	PB	PR	/A	PD	TPI
1968 NY-N	6	4	.600	55	2	0	0	11	97	80	4	32	50	10.5	2.41	125	.235	.303	0	.000	-1	6	7	-0	0.6
1969 NY-N	6	3	.667	40	0	0	0	7	83	85	8	42	48	14.1	4.99	73	.269	.360	4	.235	-0	-13	-12	1	-1.0
1970 NY-N	0	2	.000	13	0	0	0	0	22	25	2	14	10	16.4	3.27	123	.301	.408	0	.000	-0	2	2	0	0.2
Bos-A	3	4	.429	23	8	1	0	2	76¹	64	7	29	37	11.3	3.54	112	.231	.311	2	.095	-0	2	4	2	0.6
1971 Bos-A	0	1	.000	13	1	0	0	0	21	22	3	11	9	14.1	5.57	66	.278	.367	0	.000	0	-5	-4	1	-0.3
Total 10	47	49	.490	334	90	9	3	24	971¹	972	85	368	504	12.6	3.78	98	.264	.335	24	.100	-6	-23	-9	11	0.0

■ **JERRY KOOSMAN** Koosman, Jerome Martin b: 12/23/42, Appleton, Minn. BR/TL, 6'2", 205 lbs. Deb: 4/14/67

YEAR TM/L	W	L	PCT	G	GS	CG	SH	SV	IP	H	HR	BB	SO	RAT	ERA	ERA+	OAV	OOB	BH	AVG	PB	PR	/A	PD	TPI
1967 NY-N	0	2	.000	9	3	0	0	0	22¹	22	3	19	11	16.5	6.04	56	.259	.394	0	.000	0	-7	-7	0	-0.5
1968 NY-N	19	12	.613	35	34	17	7	0	263²	221	16	69	178	10.2	2.08	145	.228	.285	7	.077	-3	26	27	-1	2.8
1969 *NY-N	17	9	.654	32	32	16	6	0	241	187	14	68	180	9.7	2.28	160	.216	.277	4	.048	-7	35	37	-1	3.3
1970 NY-N	12	7	.632	30	29	5	1	0	212	189	22	71	118	11.1	3.14	128	.237	.300	6	.086	-2	21	21	-2	1.7
1971 NY-N	6	11	.353	26	24	4	0	0	165²	160	12	51	96	11.5	3.04	112	.256	.313	8	.160	0	8	7	-0	0.7
1972 NY-N	11	12	.478	34	24	4	1	1	163	155	14	52	147	11.8	4.14	81	.250	.314	4	.085	-3	-12	-14	-1	-1.7
1973 *NY-N	14	15	.483	35	35	12	3	0	263	234	18	76	156	10.7	2.84	127	.242	.300	8	.103	-3	24	23	-0	2.0
1974 NY-N	15	11	.577	35	35	13	0	0	265	258	16	85	188	11.0	3.36	106	.257	.320	16	.186	2	8	6	-1	0.2
1975 NY-N	14	13	.519	36	34	11	4	2	239²	234	19	98	173	12.6	3.42	101	.261	.337	14	.179	1	5	1	-1	0.2
1976 NY-N	21	10	.677	34	32	17	3	0	247¹	205	19	66	200	9.9	2.69	122	.226	.279	17	.215	3	22	17	0	2.1
1977 NY-N	8	20	.286	32	32	6	1	0	226²	195	17	81	192	11.1	3.49	107	.232	.302	8	.111	-3	10	6	-3	0.0
1978 NY-N	3	15	.167	38	32	3	0	2	235¹	221	18	84	160	12.0	3.75	93	.255	.327	6	.086	-3	-4	-7	1	-0.9
1979 Min-A	20	13	.606	37	36	10	2	0	263²	268	19	83	157	12.1	3.38	130	.268	.326	0	—	0	24	29	3	3.2
1980 Min-A	16	13	.552	38	34	8	0	2	243¹	252	24	69	149	12.1	4.03	108	.272	.326	0	—	0	0	0	0	-0.2
1981 Min-A	3	9	.250	19	13	2	1	5	94¹	98	8	34	55	12.6	4.20	94	.272	.335	0	—	0	-6	-3	-0	-0.2
Chi-A	1	4	.200	8	3	1	0	0	27	27	2	7	21	11.3	3.33	107	.260	.306	0	—	0	1	1	0	0.0
Yr	4	13	.235	27	16	3	1	5	121¹	125	10	41	76	12.3	4.01	96	.267	.325	0	—	0	-5	-2	-0	-0.2
1982 Chi-A	11	7	.611	42	19	3	1	3	173¹	194	9	38	88	12.1	3.84	105	.287	.327	0	—	0	4	4	0	0.4
1983 *Chi-A	11	7	.611	37	24	2	1	2	169²	176	19	53	90	12.5	4.77	88	.266	.326	0	—	0	-13	-11	0	-1.0
1984 Phi-N	14	15	.483	36	34	3	1	0	224	232	16	60	137	11.9	3.25	112	.267	.317	8	.108	-3	8	9	-1	0.6
1985 Phi-N	6	4	.600	19	9	1	0	0	99¹	107	14	34	60	13.0	4.62	80	.276	.340	3	.088	-2	-11	-10	-0	-1.1
Total 19	222	209	.515	612	527	140	33	17	3839¹	3635	290	1198	2556	11.5	3.36	110	.252	.313	109	.119	-22	145	143	-6	13.3

■ **HOWIE KOPLITZ** Koplitz, Howard Dean b: 5/4/38, Oshkosh, Wis. BR/TR, 5'10.5", 190 lbs. Deb: 9/08/61

YEAR TM/L	W	L	PCT	G	GS	CG	SH	SV	IP	H	HR	BB	SO	RAT	ERA	ERA+	OAV	OOB	BH	AVG	PB	PR	/A	PD	TPI
1961 Det-A	2	0	1.000	4	1	1	0	0	12	16	0	8	9	18.0	2.25	182	.327	.421	0	.000	-1	2	2	-0	0.2
1962 Det-A	3	0	1.000	10	6	1	0	0	37²	54	5	10	10	15.3	5.26	77	.342	.381	3	.231	1	-5	-5	-0	-0.3
1964 Was-A	0	0	—	6	1	0	0	0	17	20	3	13	9	17.5	4.76	78	.290	.402	0	.000	-0	-2	-2	0	-0.1
1965 Was-A	4	7	.364	33	11	0	0	0	106²	97	11	48	59	12.5	4.05	86	.249	.336	3	.100	-1	-7	-7	1	-0.6
1966 Was-A	0	0	—	1	0	0	0	0	2	0	0	1	0	4.5	0.00	—	.000	.200	0	—	0	1	1	0	0.1
Total 5	9	7	.563	54	19	2	0	1	175¹	187	19	80	87	13.9	4.21	87	.280	.359	6	.118	-1	-11	-11	0	-0.7

■ **GEORGE KORINCE** Korince, George Eugene "Moose" b: 1/10/46, Ottawa, Ont., Canada BR/TR, 6'3", 210 lbs. Deb: 9/10/66

YEAR TM/L	W	L	PCT	G	GS	CG	SH	SV	IP	H	HR	BB	SO	RAT	ERA	ERA+	OAV	OOB	BH	AVG	PB	PR	/A	PD	TPI
1966 Det-A	0	0	—	2	0	0	0	0	3	1	0	3	2	15.0	0.00	—	.091	.333	0	—	0	1	1	0	0.1
1967 Det-A	1	0	1.000	9	0	0	0	0	14	10	1	11	11	13.5	5.14	63	.204	.350	0	.000	-0	-3	-3	0	-0.2
Total 2	1	0	1.000	11	0	0	0	0	17	11	1	14	13	13.8	4.24	78	.183	.347	0	.000	-0	-2	-2	0	-0.1

■ **JIM KORWAN** Korwan, James "Long Jim" b: 3/4/1874, Brooklyn, N.Y. d: 8/1899, Brooklyn, N.Y. BR/TR, 6'1", 181 lbs. Deb: 4/24/1894

YEAR TM/L	W	L	PCT	G	GS	CG	SH	SV	IP	H	HR	BB	SO	RAT	ERA	ERA+	OAV	OOB	BH	AVG	PB	PR	/A	PD	TPI
1894 Bro-N	0	0	—	1	0	0	0	0	5	9	1	5	2	25.2	14.40	34	.385	.493	0	.000	-0	-5	-5	0	-0.3
1897 Chi-N	1	2	.333	5	4	3	0	0	34	47	1	28	12	19.9	5.82	77	.325	.435	0	.000	-2	-6	-5	2	-0.4
Total 2	1	2	.333	6	4	3	0	0	39	56	2	33	14	20.5	6.92	66	.333	.443	0	.000	-3	-11	-10	2	-0.7

■ **BILL KOSKI** Koski, William John "T-Bone" b: 2/6/32, Madera, Cal. BR/TR, 6'4", 185 lbs. Deb: 4/28/51

YEAR TM/L	W	L	PCT	G	GS	CG	SH	SV	IP	H	HR	BB	SO	RAT	ERA	ERA+	OAV	OOB	BH	AVG	PB	PR	/A	PD	TPI
1951 Pit-N	0	1	.000	12	0	0	0	0	27	26	2	28	6	18.0	6.67	63	.257	.419	0	.000	-1	-8	-7	-1	-0.7

■ **DAVE KOSLO** Koslo, George Bernard (b: George Bernard Koslowski) b: 3/31/20, Menasha, Wis. d: 12/1/75, Menasha, Wis. BL/TL, 5'11", 180 lbs. Deb: 9/12/41

YEAR TM/L	W	L	PCT	G	GS	CG	SH	SV	IP	H	HR	BB	SO	RAT	ERA	ERA+	OAV	OOB	BH	AVG	PB	PR	/A	PD	TPI
1941 NY-N	1	2	.333	4	3	2	0	0	23²	17	0	10	12	10.3	1.90	194	.202	.287	1	.111	-1	5	5	0	0.4
1942 NY-N	3	6	.333	19	11	3	1	0	78	79	7	32	42	12.9	5.08	66	.261	.333	3	.120	-0	-15	-15	-1	-1.5
1946 NY-N	14	19	.424	40	35	17	3	1	265¹	251	15	101	121	12.1	3.63	95	.249	.320	11	.125	-3	-6	-6	2	-0.7
1947 NY-N	15	10	.600	39	31	10	3	0	217¹	223	23	82	86	12.8	4.39	93	.259	.326	10	.128	-1	-8	-8	-0	-0.8
1948 NY-N	8	10	.444	35	18	5	3	3	149	168	7	62	58	14.0	3.87	102	.290	.359	5	.114	-1	2	1	1	0.0
1949 NY-N	11	14	.440	38	23	15	0	4	212	193	13	43	64	**10.0**	**2.50**	**159**	.239	**.278**	10	.145	1	**36**	35	0	**3.8**
1950 NY-N	13	15	.464	40	22	7	1	3	186²	190	18	66	56	12.7	3.91	105	.268	.337	8	.123	-1	5	4	0	0.3
1951 *NY-N	10	9	.526	39	16	5	2	3	149²	153	18	45	54	12.0	3.31	118	.258	.313	5	.100	-1	11	10	2	1.1
1952 NY-N	10	7	.588	41	17	8	2	5	166¹	154	10	47	67	11.0	3.19	116	.242	.296	2	.037	-4	10	9	2	0.7
1953 NY-N	6	12	.333	37	12	2	0	2	111²	135	8	36	36	13.9	4.76	90	.296	.349	1	.033	-3	-6	-6	1	-0.7
1954 Bal-A	0	1	.000	3	1	0	0	0	14¹	20	1	3	3	14.4	3.14	114	.333	.365	0	.000	-0	1	1	-0	0.0
Mil-N	1	1	.500	12	0	0	0	1	17¹	13	0	9	7	11.4	3.12	120	.228	.333	0	—	0	2	1	-1	0.0
1955 Mil-N	0	1	.000	1	0	0	0	0	0	1	1	0	0	—	∞	—	1.000	1.000	0	—	0	-1	-1	0	0.0
Total 12	92	107	.462	348	189	74	15	22	1591¹	1597	121	538	606	12.2	3.68	105	.260	.321	56	.109	-15	34	32	4	2.6

■ **JOE KOSTAL** Kostal, Joseph William "Cudgey" b: 3/17/1876, Chicago, Ill. d: 10/17/33, Guelph, Ont., Can. BR/TR, 5'6", 130 lbs. Deb: 7/14/1896

YEAR TM/L	W	L	PCT	G	GS	CG	SH	SV	IP	H	HR	BB	SO	RAT	ERA	ERA+	OAV	OOB	BH	AVG	PB	PR	/A	PD	TPI
1896 Lou-N	0	0	—	2	0	0	0	0	2	4	0	0	0	18.0	0.00	—	.411	.411	0	—	0	1	1	-0	0.1

■ **SANDY KOUFAX** Koufax, Sanford b: 12/30/35, Brooklyn, N.Y. BR/TL, 6'2", 210 lbs. Deb: 6/24/55 H

YEAR TM/L	W	L	PCT	G	GS	CG	SH	SV	IP	H	HR	BB	SO	RAT	ERA	ERA+	OAV	OOB	BH	AVG	PB	PR	/A	PD	TPI
1955 Bro-N	2	2	.500	12	5	2	2	0	41²	33	2	28	30	13.4	3.02	134	.216	.341	0	.000	-2	5	5	-0	0.3
1956 Bro-N	2	4	.333	16	10	0	0	0	58²	66	10	29	30	14.6	4.91	81	.286	.365	2	.118	-0	-7	-6	-1	-0.7
1957 Bro-N	5	4	.556	34	13	2	0	0	104¹	83	14	51	122	11.7	3.88	107	.216	.311	0	.000	-3	-0	3	-3	-0.2
1958 LA-N	11	11	.500	40	26	5	0	1	158²	132	19	105	131	13.5	4.48	91	**.220**	.337	6	.122	-2	-9	-7	-1	-0.9
1959 *LA-N	8	6	.571	35	23	6	1	2	153¹	136	23	92	173	13.4	4.05	104	.235	.340	6	.111	-2	-2	3	-2	0.0
1960 LA-N	8	13	.381	37	26	7	2	1	175	133	20	100	197	12.0	3.91	102	**.207**	.315	7	.123	-2	-3	1	-2	-0.2
1961 LA-N	18	13	.581	42	35	15	2	1	255²	212	27	96	**269**	10.9	3.52	123	.222	.295	5	.065	-5	15	23	-4	1.5
1962 LA-N	14	7	.667	28	26	11	2	1	184¹	134	13	57	216	**9.4**	**2.54**	143	**.197**	**.261**	6	.087	-2	29	22	-4	1.6
1963 *LA-N	25	5	.833	40	40	20	**11**	0	311	214	18	58	**306**	**8.0**	**1.88**	161	**.189**	**.230**	7	.064	-3	49	39	-5	3.5
1964 LA-N	19	5	**.792**	29	28	15	**7**	1	223	154	13	53	223	**8.4**	**1.74**	**187**	**.191**	**.241**	7	.095	-1	45	37	-5	3.4
1965 *LA-N	26	8	.765	**43**	41	**27**	8	2	**335²**	216	26	71	**382**	**7.8**	2.04	160	**.179**	**.228**	20	.177	5	**56**	46	-5	5.0
1966 *LA-N	**27**	9	.750	41	41	**27**	5	0	**323**	241	19	77	**317**	8.9	**1.73**	**191**	.205	.253	9	.076	-5	**67**	56	-5	5.1
Total 12	165	87	.655	397	314	137	40	9	2324¹	1754	204	817	2396	10.0	2.76	131	.205	.276	75	.097	-24	243	221	-35	18.4

■ **JOE KOUKALIK** Koukalik, Joseph b: 3/3/1880, Chicago, Ill. d: 12/27/45, Chicago, Ill. 5'8", 160 lbs. Deb: 9/01/04

YEAR TM/L	W	L	PCT	G	GS	CG	SH	SV	IP	H	HR	BB	SO	RAT	ERA	ERA+	OAV	OOB	BH	AVG	PB	PR	/A	PD	TPI
1904 Bro-N	0	1	.000	1	1	1	0	0	8	10	0	4	1	15.8	1.13	244	.333	.412	0	.000	-0	1	1	-0	0.1

■ **LOU KOUPAL** Koupal, Louis Laddie b: 12/19/1898, Tabor, S.D. d: 12/8/61, San Gabriel, Cal. BR/TR, 5'11", 175 lbs. Deb: 4/17/25

YEAR TM/L	W	L	PCT	G	GS	CG	SH	SV	IP	H	HR	BB	SO	RAT	ERA	ERA+	OAV	OOB	BH	AVG	PB	PR	/A	PD	TPI
1925 Pit-N	0	0	—	6	0	0	0	0	9	14	1	7	0	21.0	9.00	50	.378	.477	0	.000	-0	-5	-5	0	-0.3
1926 Pit-N	0	2	.000	6	2	1	0	0	19²	22	2	8	7	14.2	3.20	123	.289	.365	1	.250	0	1	2	-0	0.2
1928 Bro-N	1	0	.500	17	1	1	0	1	37¹	43	1	15	10	14.2	2.41	165	.303	.373	1	.111	-1	7	6	1	0.7
1929 Bro-N	0	1	.000	18	3	0	0	4	40¹	49	3	25	17	16.5	5.36	86	.308	.402	1	.071	-2	-3	-3	-0	-0.4
Phi-N	5	5	.500	15	12	3	0	2	86²	106	5	29	18	14.2	4.78	109	.305	.362	4	.125	-2	-1	4	-1	0.1

YEAR	TM/L	W	L	PCT	G	GS	CG	SH	SV	IP	H	HR	BB	SO	RAT	ERA	ERA+	OAV	OOB	BH	AVG	PB	PR	/A	PD	TPI
	Yr	5	6	.455	33	15	3	0	6	127	155	8	54	35	15.0	4.96	101	.306	.375	0	.000	-4	-3	1	-1	-0.3
1930	Phi-N	0	4	.000	13	4	1	0	0	36²	52	4	17	11	17.2	8.59	64	.344	.414	1	.083	-2	-15	-13	-1	-1.2
1937	StL-A	4	9	.308	26	13	6	0	0	105²	150	10	55	24	17.5	6.56	74	.339	.412	3	.094	-3	-23	-20	-0	-2.0
Total	6	10	21	.323	101	35	12	0	7	335¹	436	23	156	87	16.0	5.58	86	.322	.394	11	.106	-9	-38	-29	-1	-2.9

■ FABIAN KOWALIK
Kowalik, Fabian Lorenz b: 4/22/08, Falls City, Tex. d: 8/14/54, Karnes City, Tex. BR/TR, 5'11", 185 lbs. Deb: 9/04/32

YEAR	TM/L	W	L	PCT	G	GS	CG	SH	SV	IP	H	HR	BB	SO	RAT	ERA	ERA+	OAV	OOB	BH	AVG	PB	PR	/A	PD	TPI
1932	Chi-A	0	1	.000	2	1	0	0	0	10¹	16	2	4	2	18.3	6.97	62	.340	.404	5	.385	1	-3	-3	0	-0.2
1935	*Chi-N	2	2	.500	20	2	1	0	1	55	60	2	19	20	12.9	4.42	89	.280	.339	3	.200	-0	-2	-3	1	-0.2
1936	Chi-N	0	2	.000	6	0	0	0	1	16	24	1	7	1	17.4	6.75	59	.358	.419	0	.000	-1	-5	-5	0	-0.4
	Phi-N	1	5	.167	22	8	2	0	0	77	100	5	31	19	15.5	5.38	84	.308	.372	13	.228	-0	-12	-7	-1	-0.7
	Bos-N	0	1	.000	1	1	1	0	0	9	18	0	2	0	20.0	8.00	48	.419	.444	2	.400	1	-4	-4	0	-0.2
	Yr	1	8	.111	29	9	3	0	1	102	142	6	40	20	16.1	5.82	75	.325	.382	15	.030	-0	-20	-16	-1	-1.3
Total	3	3	11	.214	51	12	4	0	2	167¹	218	10	63	42	15.3	5.43	78	.313	.373	23	.242	-0	-26	-22	-0	-1.7

■ JOE KRAEMER
Kraemer, Joseph Wayne b: 9/10/64, Olympia, Wash. BL/TL, 6'2", 185 lbs. Deb: 8/22/89

YEAR	TM/L	W	L	PCT	G	GS	CG	SH	SV	IP	H	HR	BB	SO	RAT	ERA	ERA+	OAV	OOB	BH	AVG	PB	PR	/A	PD	TPI
1989	Chi-N	0	1	.000	1	1	0	0	0	3²	7	0	2	5	22.1	4.91	77	.368	.429	0	.000	-0	-1	-0	0	0.0
1990	Chi-N	0	0	—	18	0	0	0	0	25	31	2	14	16	16.9	7.20	57	.310	.409	0	—	0	-9	-9	0	-0.7
Total	2	0	1	.000	19	1	0	0	0	28²	38	2	16	21	17.6	6.91	59	.319	.409	0	.000	-0	-10	-9	0	-0.7

■ JOE KRAKAUSKAS
Krakauskas, Joseph Victor Lawrence b: 3/28/15, Montreal, Que., Can d: 7/8/60, Hamilton, Ont., Can BL/TL, 6'1", 203 lbs. Deb: 9/09/37

YEAR	TM/L	W	L	PCT	G	GS	CG	SH	SV	IP	H	HR	BB	SO	RAT	ERA	ERA+	OAV	OOB	BH	AVG	PB	PR	/A	PD	TPI
1937	Was-A	4	1	.800	5	4	3	0	0	40	33	0	22	18	12.4	2.70	164	.226	.327	2	.125	-0	9	8	-1	0.6
1938	Was-A	7	5	.583	29	10	5	1	0	121¹	99	4	88	104	14.1	3.12	145	.220	.352	6	.182	1	23	19	-2	1.6
1939	Was-A	11	17	.393	39	29	12	0	1	217¹	230	13	114	110	14.3	4.60	95	.276	.364	16	.208	3	1	-6	-2	-0.5
1940	Was-A	1	6	.143	32	10	2	0	2	109	137	7	73	68	17.3	6.44	65	.309	.406	8	.250	1	-25	-28	1	-2.3
1941	Cle-A	1	2	.333	12	5	0	0	0	41²	39	3	29	25	14.7	4.10	96	.245	.362	1	.077	-1	-0	-1	1	0.0
1942	Cle-A	0	0	—	3	0	0	0	0	7	7	1	4	2	14.1	3.86	89	.259	.355	0	.000	-0	-0	-0	1	0.0
1946	Cle-A	2	5	.286	29	5	0	0	1	47¹	60	2	25	20	16.2	5.51	60	.314	.394	0	.000	-1	-11	-12	1	-1.1
Total	7	26	36	.419	149	63	22	1	4	583²	605	30	355	347	14.9	4.53	93	.269	.369	33	.180	2	-4	-20	-2	-1.7

■ JACK KRALICK
Kralick, John Francis b: 6/1/35, Youngstown, Ohio BL/TL, 6'2", 180 lbs. Deb: 4/15/59

YEAR	TM/L	W	L	PCT	G	GS	CG	SH	SV	IP	H	HR	BB	SO	RAT	ERA	ERA+	OAV	OOB	BH	AVG	PB	PR	/A	PD	TPI
1959	Was-A	0	0	—	6	0	0	0	0	12¹	13	5	6	7	13.9	6.57	60	.289	.373	0	.000	-0	-4	-4	1	-0.2
1960	Was-A	8	6	.571	35	18	7	2	1	151	139	12	45	71	11.2	3.04	128	.245	.305	5	.122	-1	14	14	-0	1.3
1961	Min-A	13	11	.542	33	33	11	2	0	242	257	21	64	137	12.0	3.61	118	.274	.323	13	.151	-2	11	17	2	1.8
1962	Min-A	12	11	.522	39	37	7	1	0	242²	239	30	61	139	11.2	3.86	106	.258	.305	18	.202	3	3	6	1	1.1
1963	Min-A	1	4	.200	5	5	1	1	0	25²	28	2	8	13	13.0	3.86	94	.280	.339	1	.167	1	-1	-1	0	0.1
	Cle-A	13	9	.591	28	27	10	3	0	197¹	187	19	41	116	10.4	2.92	124	.249	.288	11	.183	1	16	15	-1	1.7
	Yr	14	13	.519	33	32	11	4	0	223	215	21	49	129	10.7	3.03	120	.252	.293	4	.061	2	15	15	-1	1.8
1964	Cle-A	12	7	.632	30	29	8	3	0	190²	196	17	51	119	12.1	3.21	112	.267	.322	10	.156	-1	9	8	1	0.9
1965	Cle-A	5	11	.313	30	16	1	0	0	86	106	9	21	34	13.5	4.92	71	.298	.340	3	.143	-1	-14	-14	-0	-1.4
1966	Cle-A	3	4	.429	27	4	0	0	0	68¹	69	9	20	31	11.9	3.82	90	.268	.324	1	.077	-1	-3	-3	1	-0.2
1967	Cle-A	0	2	.000	2	0	0	0	0	2	4	0	1	1	22.5	9.00	36	.444	.500	0	—	0	-1	-1	1	0.0
Total	9	67	65	.508	235	169	45	12	1	1218	1238	124	318	668	11.7	3.56	108	.264	.314	62	.162	0	30	38	6	5.1

■ STEVE KRALY
Kraly, Steve Charles "Lefty" b: 4/18/29, Whiting, Ind. BL/TL, 5'10", 152 lbs. Deb: 8/09/53

YEAR	TM/L	W	L	PCT	G	GS	CG	SH	SV	IP	H	HR	BB	SO	RAT	ERA	ERA+	OAV	OOB	BH	AVG	PB	PR	/A	PD	TPI
1953	NY-A	0	2	.000	5	3	0	0	1	25	19	2	16	8	13.3	3.24	114	.209	.339	0	.000	-1	2	1	0	0.1

■ JACK KRAMER
Kramer, John Henry b: 1/5/18, New Orleans, La. BR/TR, 6'2", 190 lbs. Deb: 4/25/39

YEAR	TM/L	W	L	PCT	G	GS	CG	SH	SV	IP	H	HR	BB	SO	RAT	ERA	ERA+	OAV	OOB	BH	AVG	PB	PR	/A	PD	TPI
1939	StL-A	9	16	.360	40	31	10	2	0	211²	269	18	127	68	17.0	5.83	84	.318	.409	9	.136	-1	-28	-23	-0	-2.1
1940	StL-A	3	7	.300	16	9	1	0	0	64²	86	4	26	12	15.6	6.26	73	.327	.388	1	.050	-1	-14	-12	1	-1.0
1941	StL-A	4	3	.571	29	3	0	0	2	59¹	69	5	40	20	16.5	5.16	83	.289	.391	0	.000	1	-7	-6	0	-0.3
1943	StL-A	0	0	—	3	0	0	0	0	9	11	0	8	4	20.0	8.00	42	.297	.435	1	.500	1	-5	-5	0	-0.3
1944	*StL-A	17	13	.567	33	31	18	1	0	257	233	3	75	124	10.8	2.49	145	.241	.297	14	.165	1	27	32	3	4.1
1945	StL-A	10	15	.400	29	25	15	3	2	193	190	13	73	99	12.3	3.36	105	.254	.320	9	.148	-0	0	4	1	0.5
1946	StL-A	13	11	.542	31	28	13	3	0	194²	190	6	68	69	11.9	3.19	117	.257	.319	8	.136	-1	7	12	0	1.1
1947	StL-A	11	16	.407	33	28	9	1	1	199¹	206	16	89	77	13.4	4.97	78	.270	.348	7	.113	-2	-28	-24	1	-2.4
1948	Bos-A	18	5	.783	29	29	14	2	0	205	233	12	64	72	13.0	4.35	101	.284	.284	11	.151	-1	-1	-3	-3	-0.1
1949	Bos-A	6	8	.429	21	18	7	2	1	111²	126	8	49	24	14.2	5.16	85	.286	.358	9	.257	3	-12	-10	-0	-0.6
1950	NY-N	3	6	.333	35	9	1	0	1	86²	91	6	39	27	13.7	3.53	116	.268	.346	2	.100	1	6	5	0	0.7
1951	NY-N	0	0	—	4	1	0	0	0	4²	11	0	3	2	27.0	15.43	25	.524	.583	0	—	0	-6	-6	-0	-0.4
	NY-A	1	3	.250	19	3	0	0	0	40	46	1	21	15	14.8	4.65	82	.280	.362	1	.100	-2	-4	-1	-0	-0.4
Total	12	95	103	.480	322	215	88	14	7	1637¹	1761	92	682	613	13.5	4.24	96	.276	.347	72	.144	0	-63	-35	2	-1.2

■ RANDY KRAMER
Kramer, Randall John b: 9/20/60, Palo Alto, Cal. BR/TR, 6'2", 170 lbs. Deb: 9/11/88

YEAR	TM/L	W	L	PCT	G	GS	CG	SH	SV	IP	H	HR	BB	SO	RAT	ERA	ERA+	OAV	OOB	BH	AVG	PB	PR	/A	PD	TPI
1988	Pit-N	1	2	.333	5	1	0	0	0	10	12	1	1	7	12.6	5.40	63	.316	.350	0	.000	-0	-2	-2	-0	-0.2
1989	Pit-N	5	9	.357	35	15	1	1	2	111¹	90	10	61	52	12.8	3.96	85	.224	.337	5	.152	-0	-6	-7	-1	-0.8
1990	Pit-N	0	1	.000	12	2	0	0	0	25²	27	3	9	15	13.3	4.91	74	.273	.345	0	.000	-0	-3	-4	1	-0.3
	Chi-N	0	2	.000	10	2	0	0	0	20¹	20	3	12	12	14.6	3.98	104	.253	.359	0	.000	-0	-0	0	0	-0.0
	Yr	0	3	.000	22	4	0	0	0	46	47	6	21	27	13.5	4.50	85	.261	.342	0	.000	-1	-4	-3	1	-0.3
Total	3	6	14	.300	62	20	1	1	2	167¹	149	17	83	86	13.1	4.20	83	.241	.342	5	.122	-1	-12	-13	-1	-1.3

■ GENE KRAPP
Krapp, Eugene Hamley "Rubber Arm" b: 5/12/1887, Rochester, N.Y. d: 4/13/23, Detroit, Mich. BR/TR, 5'5", 165 lbs. Deb: 4/14/11

YEAR	TM/L	W	L	PCT	G	GS	CG	SH	SV	IP	H	HR	BB	SO	RAT	ERA	ERA+	OAV	OOB	BH	AVG	PB	PR	/A	PD	TPI
1911	Cle-A	13	9	.591	35	26	14	1	1	222	188	1	138	132	13.7	3.41	100	.232	.353	17	.230	4	-1	0	4	0.8
1912	Cle-A	2	5	.286	9	7	4	0	0	58²	57	0	42	22	15.8	4.60	74	.273	.404	7	.318	1	-8	-8	3	0.0
1914	Buf-F	16	14	.533	36	29	18	1	0	252²	198	4	115	106	11.6	2.49	132	.210	.304	11	.143	-1	20	22	6	3.0
1915	Buf-F	9	19	.321	38	30	14	1	0	231	188	6	123	93	12.3	3.51	89	.230	.333	9	.129	-2	-12	-10	7	-0.4
Total	4	40	47	.460	118	92	50	3	1	764¹	631	11	418	353	12.7	3.23	102	.227	.335	44	.181	2	-2	5	19	3.1

■ JACK KRAUS
Kraus, John William "Tex" or "Texas Jack" b: 4/26/18, San Antonio, Tex. d: 1/2/76, San Antonio, Tex. BR/TL, 6'4", 190 lbs. Deb: 4/25/43

YEAR	TM/L	W	L	PCT	G	GS	CG	SH	SV	IP	H	HR	BB	SO	RAT	ERA	ERA+	OAV	OOB	BH	AVG	PB	PR	/A	PD	TPI
1943	Phi-N	9	15	.375	34	25	10	1	2	199²	197	7	78	48	12.4	3.16	107	.259	.328	4	.067	-5	5	5	1	0.2
1945	Phi-N	4	9	.308	19	13	0	0	0	81²	96	3	40	28	15.4	5.40	71	.293	.376	3	.120	-1	-15	-14	0	-1.3
1946	NY-N	2	1	.667	17	1	0	0	0	25	25	4	15	7	14.8	6.12	56	.260	.366	0	.000	-0	-8	-7	1	-0.6
Total	3	15	25	.375	70	39	10	1	2	306¹	318	14	133	83	13.4	4.00	88	.268	.345	7	.080	-6	-17	-17	2	-1.7

■ HARRY KRAUSE
Krause, Harry William "Hal" b: 7/12/1887, San Francisco, Cal. d: 10/23/40, San Francisco, Cal BB/TL, 5'10", 165 lbs. Deb: 4/20/08

YEAR	TM/L	W	L	PCT	G	GS	CG	SH	SV	IP	H	HR	BB	SO	RAT	ERA	ERA+	OAV	OOB	BH	AVG	PB	PR	/A	PD	TPI
1908	Phi-A	1	1	.500	4	2	2	0	0	21	20	0	4	10	11.6	2.57	100	.247	.307	0	.000	-0	-1	-0	-1	-0.1
1909	Phi-A	18	8	.692	32	21	16	7	0	213	151	2	49	139	9.0	1.39	173	.204	.266	12	.156	-1	26	24	-3	2.3
1910	Phi-A	6	6	.500	16	11	9	2	0	112¹	99	4	42	60	11.9	2.88	82	.254	.339	8	.211	1	-5	-6	-2	-0.8
1911	Phi-A	11	8	.579	27	19	12	1	2	169	155	2	47	85	11.2	3.04	104	.251	.313	15	.254	-2	6	6	-3	0.1
1912	Phi-A	0	2	.000	4	2	0	0	0	5¹	10	0	2	3	20.2	13.50	23	.435	.500	1	.250	0	-6	-5	-0	-0.5
	Cle-A	0	1	.000	2	2	0	0	0	4²	11	0	2	1	25.1	11.57	29	.500	.542	0	—	0	-4	-4	-0	-0.3
	Yr	0	3	.000	6	4	0	0	0	10	21	0	4	4	22.5	12.60	26	.457	.500	1	.000	0	-10	-10	-0	-0.8
Total	5	36	26	.581	85	57	39	10	2	525¹	446	8	146	298	10.7	2.50	107	.238	.305	36	.195	1	16	10	-9	0.7

■ LEW KRAUSSE
Krausse, Lewis Bernard Jr. b: 4/25/43, Media, Pa. BR/TR, 6', 175 lbs. Deb: 6/16/61

YEAR	TM/L	W	L	PCT	G	GS	CG	SH	SV	IP	H	HR	BB	SO	RAT	ERA	ERA+	OAV	OOB	BH	AVG	PB	PR	/A	PD	TPI
1961	KC-A	2	5	.286	12	8	2	1	0	55²	49	3	46	32	15.5	4.85	85	.243	.386	2	.118	-1	-5	-5	-1	-0.5

YEAR	TM/L	W	L	PCT	G	GS	CG	SH	SV	IP	H	HR	BB	SO	RAT	ERA	ERA+	OAV	OOB	BH	AVG	PB	PR	/A	PD	TPI
1964	KC-A	0	2	.000	5	4	0	0	0	14²	22	1	9	9	20.3	7.36	52	.349	.446	0	.000	0	-6	-6	-0	-0.5
1965	KC-A	2	4	.333	7	5	0	0	0	25	29	1	8	22	13.3	5.04	69	.284	.336	0	.000	-1	-4	-4	-1	-0.5
1966	KC-A	14	9	.609	36	22	4	1	3	177²	144	8	63	87	10.8	2.99	114	.222	.297	8	.154	0	9	8	-3	0.6
1967	KC-A	7	17	.292	48	19	0	0	6	160	140	17	67	96	11.9	4.27	75	.236	.317	6	.146	1	-19	-19	-0	-1.9
1968	Oak-A	10	11	.476	36	25	2	0	4	185	147	16	62	105	10.3	3.11	91	.217	.286	9	.161	3	-3	-6	-1	-0.4
1969	Oak-A	7	7	.500	43	16	4	2	7	140	134	23	48	85	12.0	4.44	77	.256	.325	8	.167	4	-13	-16	-1	-1.2
1970	Mil-A	13	18	.419	37	35	8	1	0	216	235	33	67	130	12.8	4.75	80	.275	.330	9	.138	1	-25	-23	0	-2.2
1971	Mil-A	8	12	.400	43	22	1	0	0	180¹	164	23	62	92	11.5	2.94	118	.239	.307	1	.023	-3	10	11	-1	0.7
1972	Bos-A	1	3	.250	24	7	0	0	1	60²	74	7	28	35	15.6	6.38	50	.308	.387	2	.125	-0	-22	-21	-1	-2.2
1973	StL-N	0	0	—	1	0	0	0	0	2	2	0	1	1	13.5	0.00	—	.250	.333	0	—	0	1	1	0	0.1
1974	Atl-N	4	3	.571	29	4	0	0	0	66²	65	3	32	27	13.4	4.18	90	.258	.346	2	.333	2	-4	-3	-0	0.0
Total	12	68	91	.428	321	167	34	5	21	1283²	1205	137	493	721	12.2	4.00	85	.248	.322	47	.133	6	-81	-84	-7	-8.0

■ LEW KRAUSSE
Krausse, Lewis Bernard Sr. b: 6/8/12, Media, Pa. d: 9/6/88, Sarasota, Fla. BR/TR, 6'0.5", 167 lbs. Deb: 6/11/31

YEAR	TM/L	W	L	PCT	G	GS	CG	SH	SV	IP	H	HR	BB	SO	RAT	ERA	ERA+	OAV	OOB	BH	AVG	PB	PR	/A	PD	TPI
1931	Phi-A	1	0	1.000	3	1	1	0	0	11	6	2	6	1	9.8	4.09	110	.150	.261	0	.000	0	0	0	0	0.1
1932	Phi-A	4	1	.800	20	3	2	1	0	57	64	3	24	16	13.9	4.58	99	.281	.349	2	.133	-0	-1	-0	1	0.1
Total	2	5	1	.833	23	4	3	1	0	68	70	5	30	17	13.2	4.50	100	.261	.336	2	.118	0	-0	0	2	0.2

■ KEN KRAVEC
Kravec, Kenneth Peter b: 7/29/51, Cleveland, Ohio BL/TL, 6'2", 185 lbs. Deb: 9/04/75

YEAR	TM/L	W	L	PCT	G	GS	CG	SH	SV	IP	H	HR	BB	SO	RAT	ERA	ERA+	OAV	OOB	BH	AVG	PB	PR	/A	PD	TPI
1975	Chi-A	0	1	.000	2	1	0	0	0	4¹	1	0	8	1	18.7	6.23	62	.071	.409	0	—	0	-1	-1	1	0.0
1976	Chi-A	1	5	.167	9	8	1	0	0	49²	49	3	32	38	14.9	4.89	73	.257	.366	0	—	0	-8	-7	-0	-0.7
1977	Chi-A	11	8	.579	26	25	6	1	0	166²	161	12	57	125	12.1	4.10	99	.250	.317	0	—	0	-1	-0	0	-0.0
1978	Chi-A	11	16	.407	30	30	7	2	0	203	188	22	95	154	13.0	4.08	93	.245	.336	0	—	0	-7	-6	-2	-0.7
1979	Chi-A	15	13	.536	36	35	10	3	1	250	208	20	111	132	12.0	3.74	113	.233	.327	0	—	0	13	14	-1	1.3
1980	Chi-A	3	6	.333	20	15	0	0	0	81²	100	13	44	37	16.4	6.94	58	.298	.387	0	—	0	-26	-26	-0	-2.3
1981	Chi-N	1	6	.143	24	12	0	0	0	78¹	80	5	39	50	14.1	5.06	73	.268	.361	0	.000	-1	-14	-12	1	-1.2
1982	Chi-N	1	1	.500	13	2	0	0	0	25	27	3	18	20	16.2	6.12	61	.267	.378	0	.000	-0	-7	-7	-0	-0.6
Total	8	43	56	.434	160	128	24	6	1	858²	814	78	404	557	13.2	4.47	89	.251	.341	0	.000	-1	-51	-46	-1	-4.2

■ RAY KRAWCZYK
Krawczyk, Raymond Allen b: 10/9/59, Pittsburgh, Pa. BR/TR, 6'1", 184 lbs. Deb: 6/29/84

YEAR	TM/L	W	L	PCT	G	GS	CG	SH	SV	IP	H	HR	BB	SO	RAT	ERA	ERA+	OAV	OOB	BH	AVG	PB	PR	/A	PD	TPI
1984	Pit-N	0	0	—	4	0	0	0	0	5¹	7	0	4	3	18.6	3.38	107	.350	.458	0	—	0	0	0	-0	0.0
1985	Pit-N	0	2	.000	8	0	0	0	0	8¹	20	1	6	9	29.2	14.04	25	.455	.529	0	—	0	-10	-10	0	-0.8
1986	Pit-N	0	1	.000	12	0	0	0	0	12¹	17	3	10	7	19.7	7.30	53	.321	.429	0	—	0	-5	-5	-0	-0.4
1988	Cal-A	0	1	.000	14	1	0	0	1	24¹	29	2	8	17	14.4	4.81	80	.299	.364	0	—	0	-2	-3	1	-0.1
1989	Mil-A	0	0	—	1	0	0	0	0	2	4	0	1	6	22.5	13.50	28	.400	.455	0	—	0	-2	-2	-0	-0.1
Total	5	0	4	.000	39	1	0	0	1	52¹	77	6	29	42	18.7	7.05	54	.344	.426	0	—	0	-19	-19	0	-1.4

■ RAY KREMER
Kremer, Remy Peter "Wiz" b: 3/23/1893, Oakland, Cal. d: 2/8/65, Pinole, Cal. BR/TR, 6'1", 190 lbs. Deb: 4/18/24

YEAR	TM/L	W	L	PCT	G	GS	CG	SH	SV	IP	H	HR	BB	SO	RAT	ERA	ERA+	OAV	OOB	BH	AVG	PB	PR	/A	PD	TPI
1924	Pit-N	18	10	.643	**41**	30	17	**4**	1	259¹	262	7	51	64	11.0	3.19	120	.265	.304	13	.151	-4	19	19	-2	1.3
1925	*Pit-N	17	8	.680	40	27	14	0	2	214²	232	19	47	62	12.1	3.69	121	.278	.323	14	.197	1	14	18	-3	1.6
1926	Pit-N	**20**	6	**.769**	37	26	18	3	5	231¹	221	9	51	74	10.7	**2.61**	**151**	.252	.296	21	.253	3	**31**	**34**	-3	**3.6**
1927	*Pit-N	19	8	.704	35	28	18	3	2	226	205	9	53	63	10.3	**2.47**	**166**	.244	.289	14	.169	-2	36	41	-3	3.9
1928	Pit-N	15	13	.536	34	31	17	1	0	219	253	15	68	61	13.4	4.64	87	.297	.352	14	.179	0	-16	-14	-4	-1.6
1929	Pit-N	18	10	.643	34	27	14	0	0	221²	226	21	60	66	11.7	4.26	112	.271	.320	11	.128	-2	11	13	-3	0.7
1930	Pit-N	**20**	12	.625	39	38	18	1	0	276	366	29	63	58	14.0	5.02	99	.322	.359	16	.157	-4	-2	-1	-5	-0.7
1931	Pit-N	11	15	.423	30	30	15	1	0	230	246	6	65	58	12.4	3.33	116	.271	.323	17	.227	4	14	13	-5	1.2
1932	Pit-N	4	3	.571	11	10	3	1	0	56²	65	5	16	6	12.4	4.29	89	.270	.321	2	.105	-1	-3	-3	-1	-0.5
1933	Pit-N	1	0	1.000	7	0	0	0	0	20	36	2	9	4	20.2	10.35	32	.387	.441	0	.000	-1	-16	-16	1	-1.4
Total	10	143	85	.627	308	247	134	14	10	1954²	2108	122	483	516	12.1	3.76	113	.278	.323	122	.178	-6	90	104	-26	8.1

■ JIM KREMMEL
Kremmel, James Louis b: 2/28/48, Belleville, Ill. BL/TL, 6', 175 lbs. Deb: 7/04/73

YEAR	TM/L	W	L	PCT	G	GS	CG	SH	SV	IP	H	HR	BB	SO	RAT	ERA	ERA+	OAV	OOB	BH	AVG	PB	PR	/A	PD	TPI
1973	Tex-A	0	2	.000	4	2	0	0	0	9	15	1	6	6	23.0	9.00	41	.366	.469	0	—	0	-5	-5	0	-0.4
1974	Chi-N	0	2	.000	23	2	0	0	0	31	37	3	18	22	16.3	5.23	73	.303	.397	0	.000	-0	-6	-5	-0	-0.4
Total	2	0	4	.000	27	4	0	0	0	40	52	4	24	28	17.8	6.07	62	.319	.416	0	.000	-0	-11	-10	-0	-0.8

■ RED KRESS
Kress, Ralph b: 1/2/07, Columbia, Cal. d: 11/29/62, Los Angeles, Cal. BR/TR, 5'11.5", 165 lbs. Deb: 9/24/27 C♦

YEAR	TM/L	W	L	PCT	G	GS	CG	SH	SV	IP	H	HR	BB	SO	RAT	ERA	ERA+	OAV	OOB	BH	AVG	PB	PR	/A	PD	TPI
1935	Was-A	0	0	—	3	0	0	0	0	5²	8	0	5	5	20.6	12.71	34	.333	.440	75	.298	1	-5	-5	0	-0.4
1946	NY-N	0	0	—	1	0	0	0	0	3²	5	1	1	1	17.2	12.27	28	.333	.412	0	.000	0	-4	-4	1	-0.1
Total	2	0	0	—	4	0	0	0	0	9¹	13	1	6	6	19.3	12.54	32	.333	.435	1454	.286	1	-9	-9	1	-0.5

■ LOU KRETLOW
Kretlow, Louis Henry "Lena" b: 6/27/21, Apache, Okla. BR/TR, 6'2", 185 lbs. Deb: 9/26/46

YEAR	TM/L	W	L	PCT	G	GS	CG	SH	SV	IP	H	HR	BB	SO	RAT	ERA	ERA+	OAV	OOB	BH	AVG	PB	PR	/A	PD	TPI
1946	Det-A	1	0	1.000	1	1	1	0	0	9	7	2	2	4	9.0	3.00	122	.206	.250	2	.500	1	1	1	0	0.2
1948	Det-A	2	1	.667	5	2	1	0	0	23¹	21	1	11	9	12.3	4.63	94	.233	.317	4	.500	1	-1	-1	0	-0.1
1949	Det-A	3	2	.600	25	10	1	0	0	76	85	5	69	40	18.4	6.16	68	.290	.427	0	.000	-4	-17	-17	2	-1.7
1950	StL-A	0	2	.000	9	2	0	0	0	14¹	25	2	18	10	28.3	11.93	41	.403	.549	0	.000	-1	-12	-11	-0	-0.9
	Chi-A	0	0	—	11	1	0	0	0	21¹	17	1	27	14	18.6	3.80	118	.221	.423	0	.000	-1	2	2	-1	0.0
	Yr	0	2	.000	20	3	0	0	0	35²	42	3	45	24	22.0	7.07	66	.298	.468	0	.000	-1	-10	-9	-1	-0.9
1951	Chi-A	6	9	.400	26	18	7	1	0	137	129	7	74	89	13.5	4.20	96	.250	.347	4	.083	-5	-1	-3	-1	-0.7
1952	Chi-A	4	4	.500	19	11	4	2	1	79	52	5	56	63	12.4	2.96	123	.186	.323	1	.050	-1	6	6	-1	0.4
1953	Chi-A	0	0	—	9	3	0	0	0	20²	12	2	30	15	18.7	3.48	116	.171	.426	0	.000	-0	1	1	1	0.2
	StL-A	1	5	.167	22	11	0	0	0	81	93	5	52	37	16.1	5.11	82	.286	.385	5	.200	-1	-10	-8	-2	-0.9
	Yr	1	5	.167	31	14	0	0	0	101²	105	7	82	52	16.6	4.78	87	.265	.391	5	.200	-1	-9	-7	-1	-0.7
1954	Bal-A	6	11	.353	32	20	5	0	0	166²	169	12	82	92	13.6	4.37	82	.269	.354	8	.157	-0	-12	-15	0	-1.4
1955	Bal-A	0	4	.000	15	5	0	0	0	38¹	50	3	27	26	18.3	8.22	46	.316	.419	1	.091	-1	-18	-19	1	-1.7
1956	KC-A	4	9	.308	25	20	3	0	0	118²	121	17	74	61	14.8	5.31	82	.262	.364	2	.061	-3	-15	-13	-1	-1.5
Total	10	27	47	.365	199	104	22	3	1	785¹	781	62	522	450	15.0	4.87	82	.261	.372	27	.114	-13	-76	-77	-2	-7.9

■ RICK KREUGER
Kreuger, Richard Allen b: 11/3/48, Grand Rapids, Mich. BR/TL, 6'2", 185 lbs. Deb: 9/06/75

YEAR	TM/L	W	L	PCT	G	GS	CG	SH	SV	IP	H	HR	BB	SO	RAT	ERA	ERA+	OAV	OOB	BH	AVG	PB	PR	/A	PD	TPI
1975	Bos-A	0	0	—	2	0	0	0	0	4	3	0	1	1	9.0	4.50	90	.200	.250	0	—	0	-0	-0	0	0.0
1976	Bos-A	2	1	.667	8	4	1	0	0	31	31	3	16	12	13.6	4.06	96	.272	.362	0	—	0	-2	-1	1	0.0
1977	Bos-A	0	1	.000	1	0	0	0	0	0¹	2	0	0	0	—	∞	—	1.000	1.000	0	—	0	-2	-2	0	-0.1
1978	Cle-A	0	0	—	6	0	0	0	0	9¹	6	1	3	7	8.7	3.86	97	.194	.265	0	—	0	-0	-0	0	0.0
Total	4	2	2	.500	17	4	1	0	0	44¹	42	4	20	20	12.6	4.47	87	.259	.341	0	—	0	-4	-3	1	-0.1

■ FRANK KREUTZER
Kreutzer, Franklin James b: 2/7/39, Buffalo, N.Y. BR/TL, 6'1", 175 lbs. Deb: 9/20/62

YEAR	TM/L	W	L	PCT	G	GS	CG	SH	SV	IP	H	HR	BB	SO	RAT	ERA	ERA+	OAV	OOB	BH	AVG	PB	PR	/A	PD	TPI
1962	Chi-A	0	0	—	1	0	0	0	0	1¹	1	0	1	1	6.8	0.00	—	.000	.200	0	—	0	1	1	0	0.1
1963	Chi-A	1	0	1.000	1	1	0	0	0	5	3	1	1	0	7.2	1.80	195	.188	.235	0	.000	-0	1	1	0	0.1
1964	Chi-A	3	1	.750	17	2	0	0	1	40¹	37	1	18	32	12.3	3.35	103	.239	.318	1	.125	-0	1	0	1	0.1
	Was-A	2	6	.250	13	9	0	0	0	45¹	48	6	23	27	14.3	4.76	78	.267	.353	0	.000	-1	-6	-5	0	-0.6
	Yr	5	7	.417	30	11	0	0	1	85²	85	7	41	59	13.3	4.10	87	.253	.336	1	.000	-1	-5	-5	1	-0.5
1965	Was-A	2	6	.250	33	14	2	1	0	85¹	73	7	54	65	13.6	4.32	80	.232	.348	1	.045	-1	-8	-8	-2	-1.0
1966	Was-A	0	5	.000	9	6	0	0	0	31¹	30	9	10	24	11.8	6.03	57	.236	.297	2	.250	-0	-9	-9	0	-0.8
1969	Was-A	0	0	—	2	0	0	0	0	2	3	0	2	2	22.5	4.50	77	.333	.455	0	—	0	-0	-0	0	0.0
Total	6	8	18	.308	78	32	2	1	1	210²	194	24	109	151	13.1	4.40	80	.241	.334	4	.078	-2	-20	-21	-1	-2.1

YEAR TM/L	W	L	PCT	G	GS	CG	SH	SV	IP	H	HR	BB	SO	RAT	ERA	ERA+	OAV	OOB	BH	AVG	PB	PR	/A	PD	TPI
■ **KRIEGER** Krieger Deb: 7/28/1884 ◆																									
1884 KC-U	0	1	.000	1	1	0	0	0	7	9	0	5	3	18.0	0.00	—	.292	.391	0	.000	-0	2	2	0	0.1
■ **KURT KRIEGER** Krieger, Kurt Ferdinand "Dutch" b: 9/16/26, Traisen, Austria d: 8/16/70, St.Louis, Mo. BR/TR, 6'3", 212 lbs. Deb: 4/21/49																									
1949 StL-N	0	0	—	1	0	0	0	0	1	0	0	1	0	9.0	0.00	—	.000	.250	0	—	0	0	0	0	0.0
1951 StL-N	0	0	—	2	0	0	0	0	4	6	1	5	3	24.8	15.75	25	.353	.500	0	—	0	-5	-5	0	-0.4
Total 2	0	0	—	3	0	0	0	0	5	6	1	6	3	21.6	12.60	32	.300	.462	0	—	0	-5	-5	0	-0.4
■ **HOWIE KRIST** Krist, Howard Wilbur "Spud" b: 2/28/16, W.Henrietta, N.Y. d: 4/23/89, Buffalo, N.Y. BL/TR, 6'1", 175 lbs. Deb: 9/12/37																									
1937 StL-N	3	1	.750	6	4	1	0	0	27²	34	0	10	6	14.3	4.23	94	.304	.361	0	.000	-1	-1	-1	-0	-0.1
1938 StL-N	0	0	—	2	0	0	0	0	1¹	1	0	0	1	6.8	0.00	—	.250	.250	0	—	0	1	1	0	0.1
1941 StL-N	10	0	1.000	37	8	2	0	2	114	107	10	35	36	11.3	4.03	93	.246	.304	9	.237	1	-5	-3	-1	-0.2
1942 StL-N	13	3	.813	34	8	3	0	1	118¹	103	2	43	47	11.3	2.51	136	.233	.304	6	.143	-1	11	12	-2	1.0
1943 *StL-N	11	5	.688	34	17	9	2	3	164¹	141	5	62	57	11.3	2.90	116	.233	.309	10	.167	-2	9	8	-5	0.2
1946 StL-N	0	2	.000	15	0	0	0	0	18²	22	3	8	3	14.9	6.75	51	.306	.383	0	—	0	-7	-7	0	-0.6
Total 6	37	11	.771	128	37	15	2	6	444¹	408	20	158	150	11.6	3.32	106	.244	.313	25	.168	-3	7	10	-8	0.4
■ **GUS KROCK** Krock, August H. b: 5/9/1866, Milwaukee, Wis. d: 3/22/05, Pasadena, Cal. TL , 6', 196 lbs. Deb: 4/24/1888																									
1888 Chi-N	25	14	.641	39	39	39	4	0	339²	295	20	45	161	9.0	2.44	123	.225	.251	22	.164	-3	15	22	-3	1.7
1889 Chi-N	3	3	.500	7	7	5	0	0	60²	86	10	14	16	14.8	4.90	85	.323	.357	4	.167	-1	-6	-5	0	-0.4
Ind-N	2	2	.500	4	4	3	0	0	32	48	2	14	10	17.4	7.31	57	.363	.395	5	.357	1	-12	-11	-1	-0.7
Was-N	2	4	.333	6	6	6	0	0	48	65	1	22	17	16.3	5.25	75	.313	.379	2	.087	-2	-7	-7	-0	-0.7
Yr	7	9	.438	17	17	14	0	0	140²	199	13	50	43	15.9	5.57	74	.323	.374	2	.033	-2	-24	-23	-1	-1.8
1890 Buf-P	0	0	—	4	3	3	0	0	25	43	1	15	5	20.9	6.12	67	.363	.435	1	.083	-1	-5	-6	1	-0.4
Total 3	32	26	.552	60	59	56	4	0	505¹	537	34	110	209	11.5	3.49	97	.263	.300	34	.164	-7	-14	-6	-3	-0.5
■ **RUBE KROH** Kroh, Floyd Myron b: 8/25/1886, Friendship, N.Y. d: 3/17/44, New Orleans, La. BL/TL, 6'2", 186 lbs. Deb: 9/30/06																									
1906 Bos-A	1	0	1.000	1	1	1	1	0	9	2	0	4	5	6.0	0.00	—	.074	.192	0	.000	-0	3	3	0	0.3
1907 Bos-A	1	4	.200	7	5	1	0	0	34¹	33	0	8	8	10.7	2.62	99	.255	.298	3	.273	0	-0	-0	0	0.0
1908 Chi-N	0	0	—	2	1	0	0	0	12	9	0	4	11	9.8	1.50	157	.200	.265	0	.000	-0	1	1	0	0.1
1909 Chi-N	9	4	.692	17	13	10	2	0	120¹	97	2	30	51	9.6	1.65	155	.224	.276	6	.150	-0	13	12	1	1.5
1910 Chi-N	3	1	.750	6	4	1	0	0	34¹	33	1	15	16	13.1	4.46	65	.254	.340	3	.250	0	-5	-6	1	-0.4
1912 Bos-N	0	0	—	3	1	0	0	0	6¹	8	0	6	1	19.9	5.68	63	.364	.500	1	.500	0	-2	-1	1	0.0
Total 6	14	9	.609	36	25	13	3	0	216¹	182	3	67	92	10.5	2.29	115	.231	.294	13	.181	-0	9	8	3	1.5
■ **GARY KROLL** Kroll, Gary Melvin b: 7/8/41, Culver City, Cal. BR/TR, 6'6", 220 lbs. Deb: 7/26/64																									
1964 Phi-N	0	0	—	2	0	0	0	0	3	3	0	2	2	15.0	3.00	116	.250	.357	0	—	0	0	0	0	0.0
NY-N	0	1	.000	8	2	0	0	0	21²	19	1	15	24	14.5	4.15	86	.241	.368	1	.333	0	-1	-1	1	0.0
Yr	0	1	.000	10	2	0	0	0	24²	22	1	17	26	14.6	4.01	89	.242	.367	0	.000	0	-1	-1	1	0.0
1965 NY-N	6	6	.500	32	11	1	0	1	87	83	12	41	62	13.4	4.45	79	.249	.342	3	.115	-1	-9	-9	-0	-0.9
1966 Hou-N	0	0	—	10	0	0	0	0	23²	26	2	11	22	14.1	3.80	90	.280	.356	0	.000	-0	-1	-1	0	0.0
1969 Cle-A	0	0	—	19	0	0	0	0	24	16	3	22	28	14.3	4.13	91	.188	.355	0	—	0	-1	-1	-0	0.0
Total 4	6	7	.462	71	13	1	0	1	159¹	147	18	91	138	13.8	4.24	84	.244	.350	4	.125	-1	-12	-12	0	-0.9
■ **BILL KRUEGER** Krueger, William Culp b: 4/24/58, Waukegan, Ill. BL/TL, 6'5", 205 lbs. Deb: 4/10/83																									
1983 Oak-A	7	6	.538	17	16	2	0	0	109²	104	7	53	58	13.0	3.61	107	.252	.340	0	—	0	5	3	-2	0.1
1984 Oak-A	10	10	.500	26	24	1	0	0	142	156	9	85	61	15.4	4.75	79	.285	.383	0	—	0	-12	-16	-2	-1.6
1985 Oak-A	9	10	.474	32	23	2	0	0	151³	165	13	69	56	14.0	4.52	85	.276	.353	0	—	0	-6	-11	-1	-1.0
1986 Oak-A	1	2	.333	11	3	0	0	1	34¹	40	4	13	10	13.9	6.03	64	.301	.363	0	—	0	-7	-8	1	-0.6
1987 Oak-A	0	3	.000	9	0	0	0	0	5²	9	0	8	2	27.0	9.53	43	.360	.515	0	—	0	-3	-3	-0	-0.2
LA-N	0	0	—	2	0	0	0	0	2¹	3	0	1	2	15.4	0.00	—	.250	.308	0	—	0	1	1	0	0.1
1988 LA-N	0	0	—	1	1	0	0	0	2¹	4	0	2	1	27.0	11.57	29	.364	.500	0	—	0	-2	-2	0	-0.1
1989 Mil-A	3	2	.600	34	5	0	0	3	93²	96	9	33	72	12.4	3.84	100	.264	.325	0	—	0	0	-0	-1	0.0
1990 Mil-A	6	8	.429	30	17	0	0	0	129	137	10	54	64	13.5	3.98	95	.276	.351	0	—	0	-1	-3	-1	-0.2
Total 8	36	41	.468	162	89	5	0	4	670¹	714	52	318	326	14.0	4.35	88	.275	.356	0	—	0	-25	-40	-4	-3.5
■ **ABE KRUGER** Kruger, Abraham b: 2/14/1885, Morris Run, Pa. d: 7/4/62, Elmira, N.Y. BR/TR, 6'2", 190 lbs. Deb: 10/06/08																									
1908 Bro-N	0	1	.000	2	1	0	0	0	6¹	5	0	3	2	15.6	4.26	55	.238	.407	0	.000	-0	-1	-1	1	0.0
■ **MIKE KRUKOW** Krukow, Michael Edward b: 1/21/52, Long Beach, Cal. BR/TR, 6'5", 205 lbs. Deb: 9/06/76																									
1976 Chi-N	0	0	—	2	0	0	0	0	4¹	6	0	2	1	16.6	8.31	46	.333	.400	0	.000	-0	-2	-2	0	-0.1
1977 Chi-N	8	14	.364	34	33	1	1	0	172	195	16	61	106	13.6	4.40	100	.281	.341	11	.200	-0	-9	-0	1	0.1
1978 Chi-N	9	3	.750	27	20	3	1	0	138	125	11	53	81	11.9	3.91	103	.243	.320	11	.244	3	-5	-2	-0	0.5
1979 Chi-N	9	9	.500	28	28	0	0	0	164²	172	13	81	119	14.0	4.21	98	.275	.361	16	.314	5	-9	-2	-2	0.2
1980 Chi-N	10	15	.400	34	34	3	0	0	205	200	13	80	130	12.6	4.39	89	.258	.334	16	.246	3	-18	-11	-3	-1.0
1981 Chi-N	9	9	.500	25	25	2	1	0	144¹	146	11	55	101	12.7	3.68	100	.264	.333	9	.180	-1	0	0	1	0.1
1982 Phi-N	13	11	.542	33	33	7	2	0	208	211	8	82	138	12.8	3.12	118	.268	.339	13	.181	-0	11	13	2	1.5
1983 SF-N	11	11	.500	31	31	2	1	0	184¹	189	17	76	136	13.1	3.95	89	.261	.333	16	.254	5	-7	-9	-2	-0.6
1984 SF-N	11	12	.478	35	33	3	1	1	199¹	234	22	78	141	14.3	4.56	77	.290	.356	10	.139	-1	-22	-23	-2	-2.6
1985 SF-N	8	11	.421	28	28	6	1	0	194²	176	19	49	150	10.5	3.38	102	.238	.288	12	.218	4	5	1	-1	0.5
1986 SF-N	20	9	.690	34	34	10	2	0	245	204	24	55	178	9.7	2.94	120	.223	.271	12	.146	-1	21	16	-1	1.6
1987 *SF-N	5	6	.455	30	28	3	0	0	163	182	24	46	104	12.7	4.80	80	.288	.338	9	.167	1	-13	-17	2	-1.4
1988 SF-N	7	4	.636	20	20	1	0	0	124²	111	13	31	75	10.6	3.54	92	.236	.291	3	.073	-0	-1	-4	-0	-0.4
1989 SF-N	4	3	.571	8	8	0	0	0	43	37	5	18	18	11.7	3.98	85	.236	.318	1	.063	-1	-2	-3	-0	-0.3
Total 14	124	117	.515	369	355	41	10	1	2190¹	2188	196	767	1478	12.3	3.89	96	.260	.325	139	.193	18	-54	-39	-6	-1.9
■ **AL KRUMM** Krumm, Albert b: Columbus, Ohio TR , Deb: 5/17/1889																									
1889 Pit-N	0	1	.000	1	1	1	0	0	9	8	0	10	4	18.0	10.00	38	.231	.403	0	.000	-1	-6	-6	-0	-0.4
■ **JOHNNY KUCAB** Kucab, John Albert b: 12/17/19, Olyphant, Pa. d: 5/26/77, Youngstown, Ohio BR/TR, 6'2", 185 lbs. Deb: 9/14/50																									
1950 Phi-A	1	1	.500	4	2	2	0	0	26	29	4	8	8	12.8	3.46	131	.282	.333	1	.111	-0	3	3	-0	0.2
1951 Phi-A	4	3	.571	30	1	0	0	4	74²	76	9	23	23	12.1	4.22	101	.265	.322	0	.000	-0	-1	0	-2	-0.2
1952 Phi-A	0	1	.000	25	0	0	0	2	51¹	64	5	20	17	14.9	5.26	75	.312	.376	2	.200	-0	-9	-7	0	-0.7
Total 3	5	5	.500	59	3	2	0	6	152	169	18	51	48	13.1	4.44	95	.284	.343	3	.086	-2	-7	-4	-2	-0.7
■ **JACK KUCEK** Kucek, John Andrew Charles b: 6/8/53, Warren, Ohio BR/TR, 6'2", 200 lbs. Deb: 8/08/74																									
1974 Chi-A	1	4	.200	9	7	0	0	0	37²	48	3	21	25	16.7	5.26	71	.320	.407	0	—	0	-7	-6	1	-0.5
1975 Chi-A	0	0	—	2	0	0	0	0	3²	9	0	4	2	31.9	4.91	79	.500	.591	0	—	0	-0	-0	0	0.0
1976 Chi-A	0	0	—	2	0	0	0	0	4²	9	0	4	3	25.1	9.64	37	.429	.520	0	—	0	-3	-3	-0	-0.2
1977 Chi-A	0	1	.000	8	3	0	0	0	34²	35	4	10	25	12.2	3.63	112	.267	.329	0	—	0	2	2	1	0.3
1978 Chi-A	2	3	.400	10	5	3	0	1	52	42	5	27	30	11.9	3.29	116	.220	.317	0	—	0	3	3	-0	0.3
1979 Chi-A	0	0	—	2	0	0	0	0	0²		0	1	0	40.5	10.00	—	.000	.500	0	—	0	-0	-0	0	0.0
Phi-N	1	0	1.000	4	0	0	0	0	4¹	6	2	1	2	14.5	8.31	46	.333	.368	0	—	0	-2	-2	0	-0.1
1980 Tor-A	3	8	.273	23	12	0	0	1	68	83	9	41	35	16.5	6.75	64	.300	.392	0	—	0	-21	-19	-1	-1.7
Total 7	7	16	.304	59	27	3	0	2	205²	232	25	111	121	15.2	5.12	78	.287	.376	0	—	0	-29	-26	1	-1.9

YEAR TM/L	W	L	PCT	G	GS	CG	SH	SV	IP	H	HR	BB	SO	RAT	ERA	ERA+	OAV	OOB	BH	AVG	PB	PR	/A	PD	TPI
■ **JOHNNY KUCKS**				Kucks, John Charles		b: 7/27/33, Hoboken, N.J.			BR/TR, 6'3", 170 lbs.			Deb: 4/17/55													
1955 *NY-A	8	7	.533	29	13	3	1	0	126²	122	8	44	49	11.9	3.41	110	.252	.317	2	.050	-4	8	5	0	0.1
1956 *NY-A	18	9	.667	34	31	12	3	0	224¹	223	19	72	67	12.2	3.85	100	.261	.326	11	.143	-1	8	0	1	0.0
1957 *NY-A	8	10	.444	37	23	4	1	2	179¹	169	13	59	78	11.8	3.56	101	.251	.319	6	.109	-2	4	0	4	0.2
1958 *NY-A	8	8	.500	34	15	4	1	4	126	132	14	39	46	12.6	3.93	90	.269	.331	5	.125	-1	-2	-6	1	-0.5
1959 NY-A	0	1	.000	9	1	0	0	0	16²	21	5	9	9	16.2	8.64	42	.323	.405	0	.000	-0	-9	-9	0	-0.8
KC-A	8	11	.421	33	23	6	1	1	151¹	163	10	42	51	12.9	3.87	104	.278	.339	4	.085	-3	-0	2	2	0.1
Yr	8	12	.400	42	24	6	1	1	168	184	15	51	60	13.2	4.34	91	.282	.345	3	.061	-3	-9	-7	2	-0.7
1960 KC-A	4	10	.286	31	17	1	0	0	114	140	22	43	38	14.5	6.00	66	.306	.367	4	.133	-1	-27	-26	0	-2.5
Total 6	54	56	.491	207	123	30	7	7	938¹	970	91	308	338	12.6	4.10	92	.269	.333	32	.110	-12	-18	-32	8	-3.4
■ **BERT KUCZYNSKI**				Kuczynski, Bernard Carl		b: 1/8/20, Philadelphia, Pa.			BR/TR, 6', 195 lbs.			Deb: 6/02/43													
1943 Phi-A	0	1	.000	6	1	0	0	0	24²	36	2	9	8	17.1	4.01	85	.336	.398	0	.000	-0	-2	-2	-0	-0.1
■ **FRED KUHAULUA**				Kuhaulua, Fred Mahele		b: 2/23/53, Honolulu, Hawaii			BL/TL, 5'11", 175 lbs.			Deb: 8/02/77													
1977 Cal-A	0	0	—	3	1	0	0	0	6¹	15	1	7	3	31.3	15.63	25	.455	.550	0	—	0	-8	-8	0	-0.6
1981 SD-N	1	0	1.000	5	4	0	0	0	29¹	28	1	9	16	11.4	2.45	133	.257	.314	1	.111	-0	3	3	-1	0.1
Total 2	1	0	1.000	8	5	0	0	0	35²	43	2	16	19	14.9	4.79	70	.303	.373	1	.111	-0	-5	-6	-1	-0.5
■ **BUB KUHN**				Kuhn, Bernard Daniel		b: 10/12/1899, Vicksburg, Mich.			d: 11/20/56, Detroit, Mich.			BL/TR, 6'1.5", 182 lbs.			Deb: 9/01/24									
1924 Cle-A	0	1	.000	1	0	0	0	0	1	4	1	0	0	36.0	27.00	16	.667	.667	0	—	-0	-3	-3	-0	-0.1
■ **JOHN KULL**				Kull, John A.		b: 6/24/1882, Shenandoah, Pa.			d: 3/30/36, Schuylkill, Pa.			BL/TL, 6'2", 190 lbs.			Deb: 10/02/09									
1909 Phi-A	1	0	1.000	1	0	0	0	0	3	3	0	5	4	27.0	3.00	80	.250	.500	1	1.000	-0	-0	-0	0	0.0
■ **MIKE KUME**				Kume, John Michael		b: 5/19/26, Premier, W.Va.			BR/TR, 6'1", 195 lbs.			Deb: 8/26/55												
1955 KC-A	0	2	.000	6	4	0	0	0	23²	35	1	15	7	20.2	7.99	52	.354	.453	1	.125	-1	-11	-10	0	-0.9
■ **JEFF KUNKEL**				Kunkel, Jeffrey William		b: 3/25/62, W.Palm Beach, Fla.			BR/TR, 6'2", 180 lbs.			Deb: 7/23/84 ♦										
1988 Tex-A	0	0	—	1	0	0	0	0	1	0	0	0	1	0.0	0.00	—	.000	.000	35	.227	1	0	0	0	0.0
1989 Tex-A	0	0	—	1	0	0	0	0	1²	4	1	3	0	37.8	21.60	18	.444	.583	79	.270	1	-3	-3	0	-0.2
Total 2	0	0	—	2	0	0	0	0	2²	4	1	3	1	23.6	13.50	30	.333	.467	188	.224	2	-3	-3	0	-0.2
■ **BILL KUNKEL**				Kunkel, William Gustave James		b: 7/7/36, Hoboken, N.J.			d: 5/4/85, Red Bank, N.J.			BR/TR, 6'1", 187 lbs.			Deb: 4/15/61 U							
1961 KC-A	3	4	.429	58	2	0	0	4	88²	103	11	32	46	13.7	5.18	80	.289	.348	1	.125	-0	-11	-10	-0	-0.9
1962 KC-A	0	0	—	9	0	0	0	0	7²	8	3	4	6	14.1	3.52	118	.258	.343	0	—	0	1	0	0	0.0
1963 NY-A	3	2	.600	22	0	0	0	0	46¹	42	3	13	31	10.7	2.72	129	.239	.291	2	.333	1	5	4	-1	0.4
Total 3	6	6	.500	89	2	0	0	4	142²	153	17	49	83	12.7	4.29	91	.272	.330	3	.214	1	-6	-6	-1	-0.5
■ **EARL KUNZ**				Kunz, Earl Dewey "Pinches"		b: 12/25/1899, Sacramento, Cal.			d: 4/14/63, Sacramento, Cal.			BR/TR, 5'10", 170 lbs.			Deb: 4/19/23							
1923 Pit-N	1	2	.333	21	2	1	0	1	45²	48	2	24	12	14.2	5.52	73	.293	.383	1	.083	-1	-8	-8	-1	-0.8
■ **RYAN KUROSAKI**				Kurosaki, Ryan Yoshitomo		b: 7/3/52, Honolulu, Hawaii			BR/TR, 5'10", 160 lbs.			Deb: 5/20/75										
1975 StL-N	0	0	—	7	0	0	0	0	13	15	3	7	6	15.2	7.62	49	.283	.367	0	.000	-0	-6	-6	-0	-0.5
■ **HAL KURTZ**				Kurtz, Harold James "Bud"		b: 8/20/43, Washington, D.C.			BR/TR, 6'3", 205 lbs.			Deb: 4/18/68										
1968 Cle-A	1	0	1.000	28	0	0	0	1	38	37	2	15	16	13.5	5.21	57	.255	.345	0	.000	-0	-9	-10	-0	-1.0
■ **ED KUSEL**				Kusel, Edward D.		b: 2/15/1886, Cleveland, Ohio			d: 10/20/48, Cleveland, Ohio			TR , 6', 165 lbs.			Deb: 9/18/09							
1909 StL-A	0	3	.000	3	3	3	0	0	24	43	1	1	2	16.5	7.13	34	.384	.389	3	.300	1	-12	-13	-0	-1.0
■ **EMIL KUSH**				Kush, Emil Benedict		b: 11/4/16, Chicago, Ill.			d: 11/26/69, River Grove, Ill.			BR/TR, 5'11", 185 lbs.			Deb: 9/21/41							
1941 Chi-N	0	0	—	2	0	0	0	0	4	2	0	0	2	4.5	2.25	156	.143	.143	0	.000	-0	1	1	-0	0.0
1942 Chi-N	0	0	—	1	0	0	0	0	2	1	0	1	1	9.0	0.00	—	.167	.286	0	.000	-0	1	1	0	0.1
1946 Chi-N	9	2	.818	40	6	1	1	2	129²	120	4	43	50	11.5	3.05	109	.253	.319	8	.211	0	5	4	3	0.7
1947 Chi-N	8	3	.727	47	1	1	0	5	91	80	7	53	44	13.5	3.36	117	.247	.358	5	.250	1	7	6	1	0.8
1948 Chi-N	1	4	.200	34	1	0	0	3	72	70	5	37	31	13.6	4.38	89	.253	.345	2	.154	0	-3	-4	1	-0.2
1949 Chi-N	3	3	.500	26	0	0	0	2	47²	51	7	24	22	14.5	3.78	107	.283	.374	3	.333	1	1	1	1	0.3
Total 6	21	12	.636	150	8	2	1	12	346¹	324	24	158	150	12.8	3.48	106	.254	.341	18	.220	2	12	9	5	1.7
■ **CRAIG KUSICK**				Kusick, Craig Robert		b: 9/30/48, Milwaukee, Wis.			BR/TR, 6'3", 210 lbs.			Deb: 9/08/73 ♦									
1979 Tor-A	0	0	—	1	0	0	0	0	3²	3	1	0	0	7.4	4.91	88	.214	.214	11	.204	1	-0	-0	-0	0.0
■ **MARTY KUTYNA**				Kutyna, Marion John		b: 11/14/32, Philadelphia, Pa.			BR/TR, 6', 190 lbs.			Deb: 9/19/59									
1959 KC-A	0	0	—	4	0	0	0	1	7¹	7	0	1	1	9.8	0.00	—	.250	.276	0	—	0	3	3	0	0.4
1960 KC-A	3	2	.600	51	0	0	0	4	61²	64	7	32	20	14.0	3.94	101	.274	.361	1	.200	-0	-0	-0	0	0.1
1961 Was-A	6	8	.429	50	6	0	0	3	143	147	12	48	64	12.4	3.97	101	.271	.332	7	.206	-0	1	1	3	0.4
1962 Was-A	5	6	.455	54	0	0	0	0	78	83	9	27	25	12.7	4.04	100	.275	.334	1	.125	-0	-1	-0	1	0.1
Total 4	14	16	.467	159	6	0	0	8	290	301	28	108	110	12.8	3.88	103	.272	.338	9	.191	-0	3	4	5	1.0
■ **JERRY KUTZLER**				Kutzler, Jerry Scott		b: 3/25/65, Waukegan, Ill.			BL/TR, 6'1", 175 lbs.			Deb: 4/28/90									
1990 Chi-A	2	1	.667	7	7	0	0	0	31¹	38	2	14	21	14.9	6.03	63	.304	.374	0	—	0	-7	-8	-0	-0.7
■ **BOB KUZAVA**				Kuzava, Robert Leroy "Sarge"		b: 5/28/23, Wyandotte, Mich.			BB/TL, 6'2", 202 lbs.			Deb: 9/21/46								
1946 Cle-A	1	0	1.000	2	2	0	0	0	12	9	0	11	4	15.8	3.00	110	.191	.356	1	.200	-0	1	0	0	0.1
1947 Cle-A	1	1	.500	4	4	1	1	0	21²	22	1	9	9	13.3	4.15	84	.265	.344	1	.111	-1	-1	-2	1	-0.1
1949 Chi-A	10	6	.625	29	18	9	1	0	156²	139	6	91	83	13.3	4.02	104	.240	.344	2	.036	-6	3	3	-3	-0.5
1950 Chi-A	1	3	.250	10	7	1	0	0	44¹	43	5	27	21	14.2	5.68	79	.257	.361	1	.083	-0	-5	-6	0	-0.5
Was-A	8	7	.533	22	22	8	1	0	155	156	8	75	84	13.5	3.95	114	.263	.346	5	.100	-2	11	9	-1	0.6
Yr	9	10	.474	32	29	9	1	0	199¹	199	13	102	105	13.6	4.33	98	.261	.350	9	.145	-2	5	3	-1	0.1
1951 Was-A	3	3	.500	8	8	3	0	0	52¹	57	3	28	22	15.0	5.50	74	.284	.377	3	.176	-0	-8	-8	0	-0.7
*NY-A	8	4	.667	23	8	4	1	5	82¹	76	5	27	50	11.4	2.40	159	.241	.303	3	.136	-0	16	13	-1	1.2
Yr	11	7	.611	31	16	7	1	5	134²	133	10	55	72	12.6	3.61	109	.257	.329	8	.205	-0	8	5	-1	0.5
1952 *NY-A	8	8	.500	28	12	6	1	3	133	115	7	63	67	12.1	3.45	96	.240	.329	4	.093	-1	3	-2	-2	-0.4
1953 *NY-A	6	5	.545	33	6	2	2	4	92¹	92	9	34	48	12.3	3.31	111	.264	.330	1	.048	-1	7	4	-2	0.1
1954 NY-A	1	3	.250	20	3	0	0	1	39²	46	3	18	22	14.5	5.45	63	.297	.370	0	.000	-0	-8	-9	-1	-0.9
Bal-A	1	3	.250	4	4	0	0	0	23²	30	4	11	15	15.6	4.18	86	.323	.394	0	.000	-1	-1	-2	-0	-0.2
Yr	2	6	.250	24	7	0	0	1	63¹	76	7	29	37	14.9	4.97	70	.306	.379	1	.077	-1	-9	-10	-1	-1.1
1955 Bal-A	1	0	1.000	6	1	0	0	0	12¹	10	0	4	5	10.2	3.65	105	.222	.286	0	—	-0	-0	-0	0	0.0
Phi-N	1	0	1.000	17	4	0	0	0	32¹	47	5	12	13	16.4	7.24	55	.333	.386	1	.143	-0	-11	-12	0	-1.0
1957 Pit-N	0	0	—	4	0	0	0	0	2	3	0	3	1	27.0	9.00	42	.333	.500	0	—	0	-1	-1	0	0.0
StL-N	0	0	—	3	0	0	0	0	2¹	4	0	2	2	23.1	3.86	103	.364	.462	0	—	0	0	0	0	0.0
Yr	0	0	—	7	0	0	0	0	4¹	7	0	5	3	24.9	6.23	62	.350	.480	0	—	0	-1	-1	0	0.0
Total 10	49	44	.527	213	99	34	7	13	862	849	46	415	446	13.3	4.05	97	.260	.345	22	.086	-13	5	-12	-8	-2.3

YEAR	TM/L	W	L	PCT	G	GS	CG	SH	SV	IP	H	HR	BB	SO	RAT	ERA	ERA+	OAV	OOB	BH	AVG	PB	PR	/A	PD	TPI

■ CLEM LABINE   Labine, Clement Walter   b: 8/6/26, Lincoln, R.I.   BR/TR, 6′, 180 lbs.   Deb: 4/18/50

YEAR	TM/L	W	L	PCT	G	GS	CG	SH	SV	IP	H	HR	BB	SO	RAT	ERA	ERA+	OAV	OOB	BH	AVG	PB	PR	/A	PD	TPI
1950	Bro-N	0	0	—	1	0	0	0	0	2	2	0	1	0	13.5	4.50	91	.286	.375	0	—	0	-0	-0	0	0.0
1951	Bro-N	5	1	.833	14	6	5	2	0	65¹	52	4	20	39	9.9	2.20	178	.223	.285	3	.143	-1	13	12	-1	1.2
1952	Bro-N	8	4	.667	25	9	0	0	0	77	76	3	47	43	14.5	5.14	71	.259	.364	1	.045	-2	-12	-13	1	-1.3
1953	*Bro-N	11	6	.647	37	7	0	0	7	110¹	92	9	30	44	10.0	2.77	154	.225	.278	2	.071	-1	19	18	1	1.7
1954	Bro-N	7	6	.538	47	2	0	0	5	108¹	101	7	56	43	13.1	4.15	98	.247	.339	1	.033	-2	-1	-1	1	-0.1
1955	*Bro-N	13	5	.722	**60**	8	1	0	11	144¹	121	12	55	67	11.0	3.24	125	.229	.301	3	.097	1	13	13	3	1.7
1956	*Bro-N	10	6	.625	62	3	1	0	**19**	115²	111	11	39	75	11.9	3.35	119	.253	.318	2	.087	-1	5	8	0	0.7
1957	Bro-N	5	7	.417	58	0	0	0	**17**	104²	104	8	27	67	11.4	3.44	121	.259	.307	2	.100	-1	5	8	2	1.0
1958	LA-N	6	6	.500	52	2	0	0	14	104	112	8	33	43	12.6	4.15	99	.283	.340	1	.056	-1	-2	-1	1	0.0
1959	*LA-N	5	10	.333	56	0	0	0	9	84²	91	11	25	37	12.4	3.93	108	.282	.335	0	.000	-2	0	3	2	0.3
1960	LA-N	0	1	.000	13	0	0	0	1	17	26	1	8	15	18.0	5.82	68	.356	.420	1	.500	1	-4	-4	0	-0.2
	Det-A	0	3	.000	14	0	0	0	2	19¹	19	2	12	6	14.4	5.12	77	.257	.360	0	.000	-0	-3	-2	0	-0.2
	*Pit-N	3	0	1.000	15	0	0	0	3	30¹	29	0	11	21	12.2	1.48	253	.254	.325	0	.000	-0	8	8	0	0.8
1961	Pit-N	4	1	.800	56	1	0	0	8	92²	102	4	31	49	13.1	3.69	108	.284	.344	1	.100	-1	4	3	-0	0.2
1962	NY-N	0	0	—	3	0	0	0	0	4	5	1	1	2	13.5	11.25	37	.278	.316	0	—	0	-3	-3	0	-0.2
Total	13	77	56	.579	513	38	7	2	96	1079²	1043	81	396	551	12.1	3.63	112	.256	.323	17	.075	-11	41	50	10	5.6

■ BOB LACEY   Lacey, Robert Joseph   b: 8/25/53, Fredericksburg, Va.   BR/TL, 6′5″, 210 lbs.   Deb: 5/13/77

YEAR	TM/L	W	L	PCT	G	GS	CG	SH	SV	IP	H	HR	BB	SO	RAT	ERA	ERA+	OAV	OOB	BH	AVG	PB	PR	/A	PD	TPI
1977	Oak-A	6	8	.429	64	0	0	0	7	121²	100	13	43	69	10.6	3.03	133	.234	.304	0	—	0	14	13	3	1.7
1978	Oak-A	8	9	.471	**74**	0	0	0	5	119²	126	10	35	60	12.2	3.01	121	.270	.323	0	—	0	10	8	2	1.1
1979	Oak-A	1	5	.167	42	0	0	0	4	47²	66	7	24	33	17.2	5.85	69	.327	.401	0	—	0	-9	-10	0	-0.8
1980	Oak-A	3	2	.600	47	1	1	1	6	79²	68	7	21	45	10.2	2.94	128	.234	.288	0	—	0	10	7	0	0.7
1981	Cle-A	0	0	—	14	0	0	0	0	21¹	36	5	3	11	16.5	7.59	48	.371	.390	0	—	0	-9	-9	0	-0.9
	Tex-A	0	0	—	1	0	0	0	0	1	1	1	0	0	9.0	9.00	39	.250	.250	0	—	0	-1	-1	0	0.0
	Yr	0	0	—	15	0	0	0	0	22¹	37	6	3	11	16.1	7.66	47	.356	.374	0	—	0	-10	-10	0	-0.9
1983	Cal-A	1	2	.333	8	0	0	0	0	8²	12	1	0	7	12.5	5.19	77	.343	.343	0	—	0	-1	-1	0	0.0
1984	SF-N	1	3	.250	34	1	0	0	0	51	55	5	13	26	12.1	3.88	90	.276	.321	2	.333	1	-2	-2	0	0.0
Total	7	20	29	.408	284	2	1	1	22	450²	464	49	139	251	12.1	3.67	103	.269	.325	2	.333	1	12	6	6	1.8

■ MARCEL LACHEMANN   Lachemann, Marcel Ernest   b: 6/13/41, Los Angeles, Cal.   BR/TR, 6′, 185 lbs.   Deb: 6/04/69   C

YEAR	TM/L	W	L	PCT	G	GS	CG	SH	SV	IP	H	HR	BB	SO	RAT	ERA	ERA+	OAV	OOB	BH	AVG	PB	PR	/A	PD	TPI
1969	Oak-A	4	1	.800	28	0	0	0	2	43¹	43	1	19	16	13.3	3.95	87	.261	.344	0	.000	-0	-2	-2	1	-0.1
1970	Oak-A	3	3	.500	41	0	0	0	3	58¹	58	6	18	39	12.0	2.78	127	.266	.328	0	.000	-1	6	5	1	0.6
1971	Oak-A	0	0	—	1	0	0	0	0	0¹	2	0	1	0	81.0	54.00	6	1.000	1.000	0	—	0	-2	-2	0	-0.1
Total	3	7	4	.636	70	0	0	0	5	102	103	7	38	55	12.8	3.44	102	.268	.340	0	.000	-1	3	1	2	0.4

■ AL LACHOWICZ   Lachowicz, Allen Richard   b: 9/6/60, Pittsburgh, Pa.   BR/TR, 6′3″, 198 lbs.   Deb: 9/13/83

YEAR	TM/L	W	L	PCT	G	GS	CG	SH	SV	IP	H	HR	BB	SO	RAT	ERA	ERA+	OAV	OOB	BH	AVG	PB	PR	/A	PD	TPI
1983	Tex-A	0	1	.000	2	1	0	0	0	8	9	0	2	8	12.4	2.25	178	.281	.324	0	—	0	2	2	0	0.2

■ GEORGE LaCLAIRE   LaClaire, George Lewis "Frenchy"   b: 10/18/1886, Milton, Vt.   d: 10/10/18, Farnham, Que., Can.   TR, 5′9″, 170 lbs.   Deb: 6/05/14

YEAR	TM/L	W	L	PCT	G	GS	CG	SH	SV	IP	H	HR	BB	SO	RAT	ERA	ERA+	OAV	OOB	BH	AVG	PB	PR	/A	PD	TPI
1914	Pit-F	5	2	.714	22	7	5	1	0	103¹	99	1	25	49	10.9	4.01	79	.262	.309	5	.147	-1	-9	-9	-0	-1.0
1915	Pit-F	1	2	.333	14	3	1	0	1	45²	43	1	13	10	11.0	3.35	90	.253	.306	2	.154	-1	-2	-2	1	-0.1
	Buf-F	0	0	—	1	0	0	0	0	3	4	0	1	2	15.0	6.00	52	.333	.385	0	—	0	-1	-1	-0	0.0
	Bal-F	1	8	.111	18	9	6	1	1	84	76	2	22	30	10.5	2.46	129	.246	.296	2	.083	-2	5	7	1	0.6
	Yr	2	10	.167	33	12	7	1	2	132²	123	3	36	42	10.8	2.85	110	.251	.302	1	.027	-3	3	4	1	0.5
Total	2	7	12	.368	55	19	12	2	2	236	222	4	61	91	10.8	3.36	94	.255	.305	9	.127	-4	-6	-5	1	-0.5

■ FRANK LaCORTE   LaCorte, Frank Joseph   b: 10/13/51, San Jose, Cal.   BR/TR, 6′1″, 180 lbs.   Deb: 9/08/75

YEAR	TM/L	W	L	PCT	G	GS	CG	SH	SV	IP	H	HR	BB	SO	RAT	ERA	ERA+	OAV	OOB	BH	AVG	PB	PR	/A	PD	TPI
1975	Atl-N	0	3	.000	3	2	0	0	0	13²	13	1	6	10	12.5	5.27	72	.245	.322	0	.000	-1	-3	-2	0	-0.2
1976	Atl-N	3	12	.200	19	17	1	0	0	105¹	97	6	53	79	13.3	4.70	81	.249	.348	3	.091	-2	-14	-11	-1	-1.3
1977	Atl-N	1	8	.111	14	7	0	0	0	37	67	10	29	28	23.8	11.68	38	.394	.488	2	.200	-2	-32	-30	0	-2.6
1978	Atl-N	0	1	.000	2	2	0	0	0	14²	9	0	4	7	8.0	3.68	110	.180	.241	0	.000	-1	-0	1	-0	0.0
1979	Atl-N	0	0	—	6	0	0	0	0	8¹	9	2	5	6	15.1	7.56	54	.273	.368	0	.000	-0	-4	-3	-0	-0.3
	Hou-N	1	2	.333	12	3	0	0	0	27	21	3	10	24	10.3	5.00	70	.208	.279	0	.000	-0	-4	-4	-1	-0.5
	Yr	1	2	.333	18	3	0	0	0	35¹	30	5	15	30	11.5	5.60	65	.224	.302	0	.000	-0	-7	-8	-1	-0.8
1980	*Hou-N	8	5	.615	55	0	0	0	11	83	61	4	43	66	11.3	2.82	117	.210	.311	1	.167	0	7	4	-2	0.2
1981	*Hou-N	4	2	.667	37	0	0	0	5	42	41	1	21	40	13.3	3.64	90	.258	.344	1	.333	1	-1	-2	-0	-0.1
1982	Hou-N	1	5	.167	55	0	0	0	7	76¹	71	5	46	51	13.8	4.48	74	.247	.350	0	.000	-1	-7	-10	-2	-1.2
1983	Hou-N	4	4	.500	37	0	0	0	3	53¹	35	8	28	48	11.0	5.06	67	.190	.304	1	.200	0	-9	-10	-1	-0.9
1984	Cal-A	1	2	.333	13	1	0	0	0	29¹	33	9	13	13	14.1	7.06	56	.282	.354	0	—	0	-10	-10	-0	-0.9
Total	10	23	44	.343	253	32	1	0	26	490	457	49	258	372	13.3	5.01	72	.249	.345	8	.104	-4	-75	-77	-7	-7.8

■ MIKE LaCOSS   LaCoss, Michael James   b: 5/30/56, Glendale, Cal.   BR/TR, 6′5″, 185 lbs.   Deb: 7/18/78

YEAR	TM/L	W	L	PCT	G	GS	CG	SH	SV	IP	H	HR	BB	SO	RAT	ERA	ERA+	OAV	OOB	BH	AVG	PB	PR	/A	PD	TPI
1978	Cin-N	4	8	.333	16	15	2	1	0	96	104	5	46	31	14.2	4.50	79	.288	.370	2	.067	-2	-10	-10	0	-1.1
1979	*Cin-N	14	8	.636	35	32	6	1	0	205²	202	13	79	73	12.4	3.50	107	.263	.333	9	.129	-1	5	5	1	0.5
1980	Cin-N	10	12	.455	34	29	4	2	0	169¹	207	9	68	59	14.7	4.62	77	.303	.367	5	.091	-3	-19	-20	2	-2.0
1981	Cin-N	4	7	.364	20	13	1	1	1	78	102	7	30	22	15.3	6.12	58	.325	.386	0	.000	-2	-23	-22	1	-2.3
1982	Hou-N	6	6	.500	41	8	0	0	1	115	107	3	54	51	12.9	2.90	115	.252	.342	6	.250	-2	9	5	-0	0.7
1983	Hou-N	5	7	.417	38	17	2	0	1	138	142	6	56	53	13.0	4.43	77	.273	.346	3	.086	-2	-12	-16	1	-1.6
1984	Hou-N	7	5	.583	39	18	2	1	3	132	132	3	55	86	12.8	4.02	83	.261	.334	4	.129	-0	-6	-10	0	-1.0
1985	KC-A	1	1	.500	21	0	0	0	0	40²	49	2	29	26	17.3	5.09	82	.304	.411	0	—	0	-4	-4	0	-0.3
1986	SF-N	10	13	.435	37	31	4	1	0	204¹	179	14	70	86	11.2	3.57	99	.240	.310	14	.230	5	3	-1	1	0.6
1987	*SF-N	13	10	.565	39	26	2	1	0	171	184	16	63	79	13.1	3.68	104	.283	.348	3	.060	-2	8	3	4	0.5
1988	SF-N	7	7	.500	19	19	1	1	0	114¹	99	5	47	70	11.6	3.62	90	.234	.312	8	.242	-2	-2	-5	3	0.1
1989	*SF-N	10	10	.500	45	18	1	0	6	150¹	143	3	65	78	12.9	3.17	106	.255	.340	3	.073	-1	5	3	-0	0.2
1990	SF-N	6	4	.600	13	12	1	0	0	77²	75	5	39	39	13.2	3.94	94	.259	.347	1	.043	-1	-1	-2	-1	-0.3
Total	13	97	98	.497	397	238	26	9	12	1692¹	1725	95	701	753	13.0	3.93	90	.269	.344	58	.123	-5	-48	-73	13	-6.0

■ PETER LADD   Ladd, Peter Linwood   b: 7/17/56, Portland, Maine   BR/TR, 6′3″, 228 lbs.   Deb: 8/17/79

YEAR	TM/L	W	L	PCT	G	GS	CG	SH	SV	IP	H	HR	BB	SO	RAT	ERA	ERA+	OAV	OOB	BH	AVG	PB	PR	/A	PD	TPI
1979	Hou-N	1	1	.500	10	0	0	0	0	12¹	8	1	8	6	13.1	2.92	120	.178	.327	0	.000	-0	1	1	0	0.1
1982	*Mil-A	1	3	.250	16	0	0	0	3	18	16	5	6	12	11.0	4.00	95	.239	.301	0	—	0	0	-0	-0	0.0
1983	Mil-A	3	4	.429	44	0	0	0	25	49¹	30	3	16	41	8.6	2.55	146	.172	.246	0	—	0	8	6	-1	0.6
1984	Mil-A	4	9	.308	54	1	0	0	3	91	91	6	38	75	13.2	5.24	73	.266	.339	0	—	0	-13	-14	-2	-1.5
1985	Mil-A	0	0	—	29	0	0	0	2	45²	58	6	10	22	13.8	4.53	92	.315	.357	0	—	0	-2	-2	-0	-0.1
1986	Sea-A	8	6	.571	52	0	0	0	6	70²	69	10	18	53	11.5	3.82	111	.258	.313	0	—	0	3	3	-1	0.2
Total	6	17	23	.425	205	1	0	0	39	287	275	40	96	209	11.9	4.14	96	.252	.318	0	.000	-0	-2	-6	-4	-0.7

■ DOYLE LADE   Lade, Doyle Marion "Porky"   b: 2/17/21, Fairbury, Neb.   BR/TR, 5′10″, 183 lbs.   Deb: 9/18/46

YEAR	TM/L	W	L	PCT	G	GS	CG	SH	SV	IP	H	HR	BB	SO	RAT	ERA	ERA+	OAV	OOB	BH	AVG	PB	PR	/A	PD	TPI
1946	Chi-N	0	2	.000	3	2	0	0	0	15¹	15	0	3	8	11.2	4.11	81	.238	.284	1	.200	-0	-1	-1	0	0.0
1947	Chi-N	11	10	.524	34	25	7	1	0	187¹	202	10	79	62	13.5	3.94	100	.276	.347	13	.217	2	2	0	3	0.5
1948	Chi-N	5	6	.455	19	12	6	0	0	87¹	99	4	31	29	13.5	4.02	97	.283	.343	5	.156	-1	-1	-2	2	0.0
1949	Chi-N	4	5	.444	36	13	5	1	1	129²	141	6	58	43	14.0	5.00	81	.274	.350	7	.219	4	-14	-14	0	-1.1
1950	Chi-N	5	6	.455	34	12	2	0	2	117²	126	14	50	36	13.6	4.74	89	.275	.349	10	.286	3	-8	-7	3	0.0
Total	5	25	29	.463	126	64	20	2	3	537¹	583	47	221	178	13.6	4.39	91	.275	.346	36	.220	6	-21	-23	8	-0.6

YEAR TM/L	W	L	PCT	G	GS	CG	SH	SV	IP	H	HR	BB	SO	RAT	ERA	ERA+	OAV	OOB	BH	AVG	PB	PR	/A	PD	TPI
■ STEVE LADEW Ladew, Stephen b: St.Louis, Mo. Deb: 9/27/1889 ♦																									
1889 KC-a	0	0	—	1	0	0	0	0	2	1	0	3	0	18.0	4.50	93	.144	.403	0	.000	-0	-0	-0	0	0.0
■ FLIP LAFFERTY Lafferty, Frank Bernard b: 5/4/1854, Scranton, Pa. d: 2/8/10, Wilmington, Del. TR , Deb: 9/15/1876 ♦																									
1876 Phi-N	0	1	.000	1	1	0	0	0	9	5	0	0	0	5.0	0.00	—	.151	.151	0	.000	-1	2	2	0	0.2
■ ED LAFITTE Lafitte, Edward Francis "Doc" b: 4/7/1886, New Orleans, La. d: 4/12/71, Jenkintown, Pa. BR/TR, 6'2", 188 lbs. Deb: 4/16/09																									
1909 Det-A	0	1	.000	3	1	1	0	1	14	22	2	2	11	16.1	3.86	65	.344	.373	1	.250	0	-2	-2	0	-0.1
1911 Det-A	11	8	.579	29	20	15	0	1	172¹	205	2	52	63	13.7	3.92	88	.302	.356	11	.157	-3	-11	-9	-2	-1.1
1912 Det-A	0	0	—	1	0	0	0	0	1²	2	0	2	0	21.6	16.20	20	.333	.500	0	—	-0	-2	-2	0	-0.1
1914 Bro-F	18	15	.545	42	33	23	0	2	290²	260	7	127	137	12.5	2.63	121	.248	.338	26	.257	4	19	18	3	2.8
1915 Bro-F	6	9	.400	17	16	7	0	0	117²	126	7	57	34	14.1	3.98	76	.288	.371	14	.264	3	-12	-13	-2	-1.1
Buf-F	2	2	.500	14	5	1	1	1	50¹	53	0	22	17	13.8	3.40	92	.286	.368	2	.118	-1	-2	-2	0	-0.1
Yr	8	11	.421	31	21	8	1	1	168	179	7	79	51	13.9	3.80	80	.287	.369	2	.029	2	-14	-14	-2	-1.2
Total 5	37	35	.514	106	75	47	1	5	646²	668	18	262	262	13.3	3.34	96	.276	.353	54	.220	4	-11	-9	0	0.3
■ ED LAGGER Lagger, Edwin Joseph b: 7/14/12, Joliet, Ill. d: 11/10/81, Joliet, Ill. BR/TR, 6'3", 200 lbs. Deb: 6/15/34																									
1934 Phi-A	0	0	—	8	0	0	0	0	18	27	1	14	2	21.0	11.00	40	.342	.447	0	.000	-1	-13	-13	1	-1.0
■ LERRIN LaGROW LaGrow, Lerrin Harris b: 7/8/48, Phoenix, Ariz. BR/TR, 6'5", 220 lbs. Deb: 7/28/70																									
1970 Det-A	0	1	.000	10	0	0	0	0	12¹	16	2	6	7	16.1	7.30	51	.308	.379	0	.000	-0	-5	-5	0	-0.4
1972 *Det-A	0	1	.000	16	0	0	0	2	27¹	22	0	6	9	9.2	1.32	239	.222	.267	0	—	0	5	6	0	0.7
1973 Det-A	1	5	.167	21	3	0	0	3	54	54	8	23	33	13.0	4.33	94	.263	.341	0	—	0	-3	-1	1	0.0
1974 Det-A	8	19	.296	37	34	11	0	0	216¹	245	21	80	85	13.6	4.66	82	.287	.350	0	—	0	-25	-21	3	-1.7
1975 Det-A	7	14	.333	32	26	7	2	0	164¹	183	15	66	75	13.7	4.38	92	.280	.348	0	—	0	-11	-7	-2	-0.7
1976 StL-N	0	1	.000	8	2	1	0	0	24¹	21	0	7	10	10.7	1.48	239	.241	.305	0	.000	-1	5	6	0	0.6
1977 Chi-A	7	3	.700	66	0	0	0	25	98²	81	10	35	63	10.7	2.46	166	.230	.302	0	—	0	17	18	0	1.8
1978 Chi-A	6	5	.545	52	0	0	0	16	88	85	9	38	41	12.9	4.40	86	.260	.342	0	—	0	-6	-6	2	-0.3
1979 Chi-A	0	3	.000	11	2	0	0	1	17²	27	2	16	9	22.4	9.17	46	.346	.463	0	—	0	-10	-10	-0	-0.8
LA-N	5	1	.833	31	0	0	0	4	37	38	2	18	22	13.6	3.41	107	.270	.352	1	.333	1	1	1	-0	0.1
1980 Phi-N	0	2	.000	25	0	0	0	3	39	42	5	17	21	13.6	4.15	91	.276	.349	1	.250	0	-2	-2	0	-0.1
Total 10	34	55	.382	309	67	19	2	54	779	814	74	312	375	13.1	4.11	94	.271	.342	2	.154	-0	-33	-21	4	-0.8
■ JEFF LAHTI Lahti, Jeffrey Allen b: 10/8/56, Oregon City, Ore. BR/TR, 6', 180 lbs. Deb: 6/27/82																									
1982 *StL-N	5	4	.556	33	1	0	0	0	56²	53	3	21	22	12.1	3.81	95	.245	.318	1	.077	-1	-1	-1	2	0.0
1983 StL-N	3	3	.500	53	0	0	0	0	74	64	2	29	26	11.4	3.16	114	.240	.316	0	.000	-1	4	4	1	0.4
1984 StL-N	4	2	.667	63	0	0	0	1	84²	69	6	34	45	11.2	3.72	93	.225	.306	1	.167	-0	-1	-2	0	-0.1
1985 *StL-N	5	2	.714	52	0	0	0	19	68¹	63	3	26	41	11.7	1.84	192	.251	.321	0	.000	-1	13	13	-0	1.2
1986 StL-N	0	0	—	4	0	0	0	0	2¹	3	0	1	3	15.4	0.00	—	.333	.400	0	—	0	1	1	0	0.1
Total 5	17	11	.607	205	1	0	0	20	286	252	14	111	137	11.6	3.12	114	.240	.316	2	.053	-3	15	14	3	1.6
■ EDDIE LAKE Lake, Edward Erving "Sparky" b: 3/18/16, Antioch, Cal. BR/TR, 5'7", 159 lbs. Deb: 9/26/39 ♦																									
1944 Bos-A	0	0	—	6	0	0	0	0	19¹	20	2	11	7	15.8	4.19	81	.278	.395	26	.206	1	-2	-2	0	-0.1
■ JOE LAKE Lake, Joseph Henry b: 1/6/1881, Brooklyn, N.Y. d: 6/30/50, Brooklyn, N.Y. BR/TR, 6', 185 lbs. Deb: 4/21/08																									
1908 NY-A	9	22	.290	38	27	19	2	0	269¹	252	6	77	118	11.2	3.17	78	.242	.298	21	.188	0	-23	-21	-4	-2.6
1909 NY-A	14	11	.560	31	26	17	3	1	215¹	180	2	59	117	10.2	1.88	135	.225	.283	14	.173	1	14	16	5	2.5
1910 StL-A	11	17	.393	35	29	24	1	2	261¹	243	3	77	141	11.1	2.20	112	.248	.304	21	.231	2	9	8	-0	1.0
1911 StL-A	10	15	.400	30	25	14	2	0	215¹	245	3	40	69	12.1	3.30	102	.282	.352	21	.262	2	1	2	5	0.9
1912 StL-A	1	7	.125	11	6	4	0	0	57	70	0	16	28	13.7	4.42	75	.314	.363	3	.150	-1	-7	-7	-2	-0.5
Det-A	9	11	.450	26	14	11	0	1	162²	190	3	39	86	12.8	3.10	105	.296	.340	9	.145	-3	4	3	-1	0.0
Yr	10	18	.357	37	20	15	0	1	219²	260	3	55	114	13.0	3.44	95	.301	.345	12	.012	-4	-3	-4	1	-0.5
1913 Det-A	8	7	.533	28	12	6	0	1	137	149	3	24	35	11.4	3.28	89	.278	.345	12	.267	4	-5	-6	3	0.2
Total 6	62	90	.408	199	139	95	8	5	1318	1329	20	332	594	11.5	2.85	99	.261	.309	101	.206	4	-7	-5	10	1.5
■ AL LAKEMAN Lakeman, Albert Wesley "Moose" b: 12/31/18, Cincinnati, Ohio d: 5/25/76, Spartanburg, S.C. BR/TR, 6'2", 195 lbs. Deb: 4/19/42 C♦																									
1948 Phi-N	0	0	—	1	0	0	0	0	0²	1	1	0	0	13.5	13.50	29	.333	.333	11	.162	-0	-1	-1	0	0.0
■ JACK LAMABE Lamabe, John Alexander b: 10/3/36, Farmingdale, N.Y. BR/TR, 6'1", 198 lbs. Deb: 4/17/62																									
1962 Pit-N	3	1	.750	46	0	0	0	0	78	70	4	40	56	12.7	2.88	136	.238	.329	0	.000	-1	9	9	1	0.9
1963 Bos-A	7	4	.636	65	2	0	0	6	151¹	139	8	46	93	11.2	3.15	120	.247	.308	3	.094	-1	8	11	1	1.1
1964 Bos-A	9	13	.409	39	25	3	0	1	177¹	235	25	57	109	14.9	5.89	65	.318	.369	6	.115	-1	-45	-40	0	-3.9
1965 Bos-A	0	3	.000	14	0	0	0	0	25¹	34	5	14	17	18.1	8.17	46	.340	.436	0	.000	-0	-13	-13	0	-1.2
Hou-N	0	2	.000	3	2	0	0	0	12²	17	3	3	6	14.2	4.26	79	.315	.351	1	.250	0	-1	-1	0	0.0
1966 Chi-A	7	9	.438	34	17	3	2	0	121¹	116	9	35	67	11.3	3.93	81	.251	.305	2	.057	-2	-7	-10	-0	-1.3
1967 Chi-A	1	0	1.000	3	0	0	0	0	5	7	0	1	3	14.4	1.80	172	.318	.348	0	—	0	1	1	0	0.1
NY-N	0	3	.000	16	2	0	0	1	31²	24	4	8	23	9.1	3.98	85	.200	.250	0	.000	-0	-2	-2	0	-0.2
*StL-N	3	4	.429	23	1	1	1	4	47²	43	2	10	30	10.0	2.83	116	.244	.285	2	.200	1	3	2	-0	0.3
Yr	3	7	.300	39	3	1	1	5	79¹	67	6	18	53	9.6	3.29	101	.226	.270	2	.067	-0	1	0	-0	0.1
1968 Chi-N	3	2	.600	42	0	0	0	1	61¹	68	7	24	30	13.6	4.26	74	.289	.358	1	.200	0	-9	-7	-0	-0.7
Total 7	33	41	.446	285	49	7	3	15	711²	753	67	238	434	12.7	4.24	85	.272	.333	15	.096	-6	-55	-51	1	-4.9
■ AL LaMACCHIA LaMacchia, Alfred Anthony b: 7/22/21, St.Louis, Mo. BR/TR, 5'10.5", 190 lbs. Deb: 9/27/43																									
1943 StL-A	0	1	.000	1	1	0	0	0	4	9	0	2	2	24.8	11.25	30	.450	.500	0	.000	-0	-4	-4	-0	-0.2
1945 StL-A	2	0	1.000	5	0	0	0	0	9	6	0	3	2	9.0	2.00	176	.207	.281	0	.000	-0	1	2	0	0.2
1946 StL-A	0	0	—	8	0	0	0	0	15	17	2	7	3	14.4	6.00	62	.279	.353	0	.000	-0	-4	-4	-0	-0.3
Was-A	0	1	.000	2	0	0	0	0	2²	6	1	2	0	27.0	16.88	20	.462	.533	0	—	0	-4	-4	-0	-0.3
Yr	0	1	.000	10	0	0	0	0	17²	23	3	9	3	16.3	7.64	48	.311	.386	1	.333	-0	-8	-8	-0	-0.6
Total 3	2	2	.500	16	1	0	0	0	30²	38	3	14	7	15.3	6.46	55	.309	.380	1	—	-0	-10	-10	-0	-0.6
■ HANK LAMANNA Lamanna, Frank b: 8/22/19, Watertown, Pa. d: 9/1/80, Syracuse, N.Y. BR/TR, 6'2.5", 195 lbs. Deb: 4/16/40																									
1940 Bos-N	1	0	1.000	5	1	0	0	0	13¹	13	1	8	3	14.2	4.73	79	.271	.375	1	.200	0	-1	-1	0	0.0
1941 Bos-N	5	4	.556	35	4	0	0	1	72²	77	5	56	23	16.6	5.33	67	.285	.410	9	.281	1	-14	-14	1	-1.1
1942 Bos-N	0	1	.000	5	0	0	0	0	6²	5	1	3	2	10.8	5.40	62	.208	.296	0	.000	-0	-2	-2	0	-0.1
Total 3	6	5	.545	45	5	1	0	1	92²	95	7	67	28	15.8	5.24	68	.278	.398	10	.256	1	-17	-17	1	-1.2
■ FRANK LAMANSKE Lamanske, Frank James "Lefty" b: 9/30/06, Oglesby, Ill. d: 8/4/71, Olney, Ill. BL/TL, 5'11", 170 lbs. Deb: 4/27/35																									
1935 Bro-N	0	0	—	2	0	0	0	0	1	1	0	2	0	14.7	7.36	54	.313	.353	0	.000	-0	-1	-1	0	0.0
■ WAYNE LaMASTER LaMaster, Wayne Lee b: 2/13/07, Speed, Ind. BL/TL, 5'8", 170 lbs. Deb: 4/19/37																									
1937 Phi-N	15	19	.441	50	30	10	1	4	220¹	255	24	82	135	13.8	5.31	80	.290	.352	15	.190	-2	-34	-24	-5	-2.8
1938 Phi-N	4	7	.364	18	12	1	1	0	63²	80	8	31	35	16.1	7.77	50	.301	.380	9	.409	4	-28	-27	1	-2.1
Bro-N	0	1	.000	3	0	0	0	0	11¹	17	0	3	3	15.9	4.76	82	.340	.377	1	.167	-0	-1	-1	0	0.0
Yr	4	8	.333	21	12	1	1	0	75	97	8	34	38	15.7	7.32	53	.304	.371	2	.071	4	-29	-29	1	-2.1
Total 2	19	27	.413	71	42	11	2	4	295¹	352	32	116	173	14.4	5.82	72	.295	.360	25	.234	1	-64	-53	-5	-4.9

YEAR	TM/L	W	L	PCT	G	GS	CG	SH	SV	IP	H	HR	BB	SO	RAT	ERA	ERA+	OAV	OOB	BH	AVG	PB	PR	/A	PD	TPI

■ JOHN LAMB   Lamb, John Andrew   b: 7/20/46, Sharon, Conn.   BR/TR, 6'3", 180 lbs.   Deb: 8/12/70

1970	Pit-N	0	1	.000	23	0	0	0	3	32¹	23	2	13	24	10.6	2.78	140	.209	.304	0	.000	-0	5	4	-1	0.3
1971	Pit-N	0	0	—	2	0	0	0	0	4¹	3	0	1	1	8.3	0.00	—	.188	.235	0	.000	-0	2	2	0	0.2
1973	Pit-N	0	1	.000	22	0	0	0	2	29²	37	3	10	11	14.3	6.07	58	.308	.362	0	.000	-0	-8	-8	0	-0.8
Total	3	0	2	.000	47	0	0	0	5	66¹	63	5	24	36	12.1	4.07	91	.256	.327	0	.000	-1	-2	-3	-0	-0.3

■ RAY LAMB   Lamb, Raymond Richard   b: 12/28/44, Glendale, Cal.   BR/TR, 6'1", 170 lbs.   Deb: 8/01/69

1969	LA-N	0	1	.000	10	0	0	0	1	15	12	2	7	11	11.4	1.80	185	.235	.328	0	.000	-0	3	3	0	0.3
1970	LA-N	6	1	.857	35	0	0	0	0	57	59	4	27	32	14.2	3.79	101	.277	.369	0	.000	-0	2	0	-1	0.0
1971	Cle-A	6	12	.333	43	21	3	1	1	158¹	147	11	69	91	12.3	3.35	114	.247	.326	4	.093	-2	2	8	-2	0.5
1972	Cle-A	5	6	.455	34	9	0	0	0	107²	101	5	29	64	11.0	3.09	104	.248	.299	0	.000	-1	-0	1	-1	0.0
1973	Cle-A	3	3	.500	32	1	0	0	2	86	98	7	42	60	14.9	4.60	85	.291	.373	0	—	-0	-8	-7	-1	-0.6
Total	5	20	23	.465	154	31	3	1	4	424	417	29	174	258	12.7	3.54	104	.260	.335	4	.058	-4	-1	7	-4	0.2

■ CLAYTON LAMBERT   Lambert, Clayton Patrick   b: 3/26/17, Summitt, Ill.   d: 4/3/81, Ogden, Utah   BR/TR, 6'2", 185 lbs.   Deb: 4/22/46

1946	Cin-N	2	2	.500	23	4	2	0	1	52²	48	3	20	20	11.8	4.27	78	.251	.325	2	.154	-1	-5	-5	-1	-0.6
1947	Cin-N	0	0	—	3	0	0	0	0	5²	12	3	6	1	28.6	15.88	26	.444	.545	0	.000	-0	-7	-7	0	-0.5
Total	2	2	2	.500	26	4	2	0	1	58¹	60	6	26	21	13.4	5.40	63	.275	.355	2	.143	-1	-12	-13	-1	-1.1

■ GENE LAMBERT   Lambert, Eugene Marion   b: 4/26/21, Crenshaw, Miss.   BR/TR, 5'11", 175 lbs.   Deb: 9/14/41

1941	Phi-N	0	1	.000	2	1	0	0	0	9	11	0	2	3	13.0	2.00	185	.297	.333	0	.000	-0	2	2	-0	0.1
1942	Phi-N	0	0	—	1	0	0	0	0	1	3	0	0	1	27.0	9.00	37	.500	.500	0	—	0	-1	-1	0	0.0
Total	2	0	1	.000	3	1	0	0	0	10	14	0	2	4	14.4	2.70	136	.326	.356	0	.000	-0	1	1	0	0.1

■ OTIS LAMBETH   Lambeth, Otis Samuel   b: 5/13/1890, Berlin, Kan.   d: 6/5/76, Moran, Kan.   BR/TR, 6', 175 lbs.   Deb: 7/16/16

1916	Cle-A	4	3	.571	15	9	3	0	1	74	69	1	38	28	13.4	2.92	103	.256	.354	3	.111	-1	-1	1	-2	-0.2
1917	Cle-A	7	6	.538	26	10	2	0	2	97¹	97	2	30	27	12.8	3.14	90	.274	.349	6	.188	-0	-5	-3	-1	-0.4
1918	Cle-A	0	0	—	2	0	0	0	0	7	10	0	6	3	20.6	6.43	47	.370	.485	1	1.000	-0	-3	-3	-0	-0.1
Total	3	11	9	.550	43	19	5	0	3	178¹	176	3	74	58	13.3	3.18	92	.270	.357	10	.167	-1	-9	-5	-3	-0.7

■ FRED LAMLINE   Lamline, Frederick Arthur "Dutch" (b: Frederick Arthur Lamlein)   b: 8/14/1887, Port Huron, Mich.   d: 9/20/70, Port Huron, Mich.   BR/TR, 5'11", 171 lbs.   Deb: 9/18/12

1912	Chi-A	0	0	—	1	0	0	0	0	2	7	0	2	1	40.5	31.50	10	.583	.643	0	—	0	-6	-6	0	-0.4
1915	StL-N	0	0	—	4	0	0	0	0	19	21	0	3	11	12.3	1.42	196	.300	.347	1	.125	-0	3	3	0	0.3
Total	2	0	0	—	5	0	0	0	0	21	28	0	5	12	15.0	4.29	66	.341	.393	1	.125	-0	-3	-3	0	-0.1

■ DENNIS LAMP   Lamp, Dennis Patrick   b: 9/23/52, Los Angeles, Cal.   BR/TR, 6'4", 200 lbs.   Deb: 8/21/77

1977	Chi-N	0	2	.000	11	3	0	0	0	30	43	3	8	12	15.9	6.30	70	.344	.393	3	.375	1	-8	-6	1	-0.4
1978	Chi-N	7	15	.318	37	36	6	3	0	223²	221	16	56	73	11.3	3.30	122	.258	.307	15	.205	-1	7	18	4	2.5
1979	Chi-N	11	10	.524	38	32	6	1	0	200¹	223	14	46	86	12.3	3.50	117	.287	.331	9	.155	-1	5	14	4	1.8
1980	Chi-N	10	14	.417	41	37	2	1	0	202²	259	16	82	83	15.2	5.20	75	.317	.380	6	.098	-3	-36	-29	3	-2.8
1981	Chi-A	7	6	.538	27	10	3	0	0	127	103	4	43	71	10.4	2.41	148	.222	.289	0	—	0	18	16	1	1.9
1982	Chi-A	11	8	.579	44	27	3	2	5	189²	206	9	59	78	12.9	3.99	101	.279	.337	0	—	0	2	1	2	0.3
1983	*Chi-A	7	7	.500	49	5	1	0	15	116¹	123	6	29	44	12.1	3.71	113	.275	.325	0	—	0	5	6	1	0.7
1984	Tor-A	8	8	.500	56	4	0	0	9	85	97	9	38	45	14.4	4.55	90	.285	.359	0	—	0	-5	-4	1	-0.2
1985	*Tor-A	11	0	1.000	53	1	0	0	2	105²	96	7	27	68	10.5	3.32	127	.247	.296	0	—	0	10	10	2	1.2
1986	Tor-A	2	6	.250	40	2	0	0	2	73	93	5	23	30	14.3	5.05	83	.309	.358	0	—	0	-7	-7	0	-0.5
1987	Oak-A	1	3	.250	36	5	0	0	0	56²	76	5	22	36	15.7	5.08	81	.326	.387	0	—	0	-4	-6	0	-0.5
1988	Bos-A	7	6	.538	46	0	0	0	0	82²	92	3	19	49	12.3	3.48	118	.284	.328	0	—	0	4	6	2	0.7
1989	Bos-A	4	2	.667	42	0	0	0	2	112¹	96	4	27	61	9.9	2.32	176	.235	.283	0	—	0	19	22	2	2.5
1990	*Bos-A	3	5	.375	47	1	0	0	0	105²	114	10	30	49	12.5	4.68	87	.279	.333	0	—	0	-9	-7	1	-0.6
Total	14	89	92	.492	567	163	21	7	35	1710²	1842	111	509	785	12.5	3.87	105	.278	.332	33	.165	-3	0	36	22	6.6

■ HENRY LAMPE   Lampe, Henry Joseph   b: 9/19/1872, Boston, Mass.   d: 9/16/36, Dorchester, Mass.   BR/TL, 5'11.5", 175 lbs.   Deb: 5/14/1894

1894	Bos-N	0	1	.000	2	1	0	0	0	5¹	17	5	7	1	40.5	11.81	48	.525	.610	0	.000	-0	-4	-4	0	-0.2
1895	Phi-N	0	2	.000	7	3	2	0	0	44	68	3	33	18	20.7	7.57	63	.348	.442	2	.125	-1	-14	-14	-0	-1.0
Total	2	0	3	.000	9	4	2	0	0	49¹	85	8	40	19	22.8	8.03	61	.373	.467	2	.111	-1	-17	-17	0	-1.2

■ DICK LANAHAN   Lanahan, Richard Anthony   b: 9/27/11, Washington, D.C.   d: 3/12/75, Rochester, Minn.   BL/TL, 6', 186 lbs.   Deb: 9/15/35

1935	Was-A	0	3	.000	3	3	0	0	0	20²	27	2	17	10	20.0	5.66	76	.314	.438	1	.167	-0	-3	-3	0	-0.2
1937	Was-A	0	1	.000	6	2	0	0	0	11¹	16	2	13	2	23.8	12.71	35	.320	.469	0	.000	0	-10	-10	0	-0.7
1940	Pit-N	6	8	.429	40	8	4	0	2	108	121	8	42	45	13.7	4.25	90	.279	.345	4	.118	-2	-5	-5	0	-0.6
1941	Pit-N	0	1	.000	7	0	0	0	0	12	13	1	3	5	13.5	5.25	69	.283	.353	0	.000	-0	-2	-2	0	-0.1
Total	4	6	13	.316	56	13	4	0	2	152	177	13	75	62	15.3	5.15	76	.288	.371	5	.119	-2	-20	-21	0	-1.6

■ LESTER LANCASTER   Lancaster, Lester Wayne   b: 4/21/62, Dallas, Tex.   BR/TR, 6'2", 205 lbs.   Deb: 4/07/87

1987	Chi-N	8	3	.727	27	18	0	0	0	132¹	138	14	51	78	12.9	4.90	87	.268	.335	4	.082	-2	-12	-9	-1	-1.1
1988	Chi-N	4	6	.400	44	3	1	0	5	85²	89	4	34	36	13.0	3.78	95	.273	.343	1	.050	-1	-3	-2	1	-0.1
1989	*Chi-N	4	2	.667	42	0	0	0	8	72²	60	7	15	56	9.3	1.36	276	.226	.267	2	.182	-1	17	19	-1	2.1
1990	Chi-N	9	5	.643	55	6	1	1	6	109	121	11	40	65	13.4	4.62	89	.283	.346	1	.050	-1	-10	-6	1	-0.5
Total	4	25	16	.610	168	27	2	1	19	399²	408	31	140	235	12.4	3.94	101	.266	.329	8	.080	-5	-8	3	1	0.4

■ GARY LANCE   Lance, Gary Dean   b: 9/21/48, Greenville, S.C.   BB/TR, 6'3", 195 lbs.   Deb: 9/28/77

| 1977 | KC-A | 0 | 1 | .000 | 1 | 0 | 0 | 0 | 0 | 2 | 2 | 0 | 2 | 0 | 18.0 | 4.50 | 90 | .286 | .444 | 0 | — | 0 | -0 | -0 | 0 | 0.0 |

■ DOC LANDIS   Landis, Samuel H.   b: 8/16/1854, Philadelphia, Pa.   5'11", 172 lbs.   Deb: 5/02/1882

1882	Phi-a	1	1	.500	2	2	2	0	0	17	16	1	1	13	9.0	3.18	94	.232	.243	2	.167	-0	-1	-0	-0	0.0
	Bal-a	11	27	.289	42	39	35	0	0	341	409	6	46	62	12.0	3.33	83	.278	.300	29	.166	-6	-24	-22	-2	-2.7
	Yr	12	28	.300	44	41	37	0	0	358	425	7	47	75	11.9	3.32	83	.276	.298	3	.016	-7	-25	-22	-3	-2.7

■ BILL LANDIS   Landis, William Henry   b: 10/8/42, Hanford, Cal.   BL/TL, 6'2", 178 lbs.   Deb: 9/28/63

1963	KC-A	0	0	—	1	0	0	0	0	1²	0	0	1	3	5.4	0.00	—	.000	.167	0	—	0	1	1	0	0.1
1967	Bos-A	1	0	1.000	18	1	0	0	0	25²	24	6	11	23	12.3	5.26	66	.253	.330	0	.000	-0	-6	-5	-1	-0.6
1968	Bos-A	3	3	.500	38	1	0	0	3	60	48	4	30	59	12.0	3.15	100	.223	.324	0	—	0	-1	-0	-1	-0.1
1969	Bos-A	5	5	.500	45	5	0	0	1	82¹	82	7	49	50	14.6	5.25	72	.269	.375	0	—	0	-15	-13	-1	-1.2
Total	4	9	8	.529	102	7	0	0	4	169²	154	17	91	135	13.3	4.46	79	.248	.349	0	.000	-1	-21	-17	-2	-1.8

■ LARRY LANDRETH   Landreth, Larry Robert   b: 3/11/55, Stratford, Ont., Can   BR/TR, 6'1", 175 lbs.   Deb: 9/16/76

1976	Mon-N	1	2	.333	3	3	0	0	0	11	13	1	10	7	18.8	4.09	91	.310	.442	0	.000	-0	-1	-0	-0	0.0
1977	Mon-N	0	2	.000	4	1	0	0	0	9¹	16	0	8	5	23.1	9.64	39	.381	.480	0	.000	-0	-6	-6	-0	-0.5
Total	2	1	4	.200	7	4	0	0	0	20¹	29	1	18	12	20.8	6.64	57	.345	.461	0	.000	-1	-7	-6	-0	-0.7

■ JOE LANDRUM   Landrum, Joseph Butler   b: 12/13/28, Columbia, S.C.   BR/TR, 5'11", 180 lbs.   Deb: 7/13/50

1950	Bro-N	0	0	—	7	0	0	0	1	6²	12	1	5	5	18.9	8.10	51	.414	.452	0	—	0	-3	-3	0	-0.1
1952	Bro-N	1	3	.250	9	5	2	0	0	38	46	3	10	17	13.5	5.21	70	.301	.348	1	.125	-0	-6	-7	-0	-0.6
Total	2	1	3	.250	16	5	2	0	1	44²	58	5	11	22	14.3	5.64	66	.319	.364	1	.125	-0	-9	-10	0	-0.7

YEAR	TM/L	W	L	PCT	G	GS	CG	SH	SV	IP	H	HR	BB	SO	RAT	ERA	ERA+	OAV	OOB	BH	AVG	PB	PR	/A	PD	TPI

■ BILL LANDRUM
Landrum, Thomas William b: 8/17/57, Columbia, S.C. BR/TR, 6'2", 185 lbs. Deb: 8/31/86

1986	Cin-N	0	0	—	10	0	0	0	0	13¹	23	0	4	14	18.2	6.75	57	.390	.429	0	.000	-0	-4	-4	-0	-0.4
1987	Cin-N	3	2	.600	44	2	0	0	2	65	68	3	34	42	14.1	4.71	90	.292	.382	1	.200	0	-5	-3	1	-0.2
1988	Chi-N	1	0	1.000	7	0	0	0	0	12¹	19	1	3	6	16.1	5.84	62	.365	.400	0	.000	-0	-3	-3	-0	-0.3
1989	Pit-N	2	3	.400	56	0	0	0	26	81	60	2	28	51	9.8	1.67	201	.205	.275	0	—	0	16	15	0	1.6
1990	*Pit-N	7	3	.700	54	0	0	0	13	71²	69	4	21	39	11.3	2.13	169	.262	.317	1	.111	0	13	12	-0	1.2
Total	5	13	8	.619	171	2	0	0	41	243¹	239	10	90	152	12.2	3.11	119	.266	.333	2	.095	-1	17	16	0	1.9

■ JERRY LANE
Lane, Jerald Hal b: 2/7/26, Ashland, N.Y. d: 7/24/88, Chattanooga, Tenn BR/TR, 6'0.5", 205 lbs. Deb: 7/07/53

1953	Was-A	1	4	.200	20	2	0	0	0	56²	64	3	16	26	12.9	4.92	79	.288	.339	1	.111	0	-6	-6	-0	-0.6
1954	Cin-N	1	0	1.000	3	0	0	0	0	10²	9	0	3	2	10.1	1.69	248	.237	.293	0	.000	0	3	3	-0	0.2
1955	Cin-N	0	2	.000	8	0	0	0	1	11	11	2	6	5	13.9	4.91	86	.289	.386	0	—	0	-1	-1	0	0.0
Total	3	2	6	.250	31	2	0	0	1	78¹	84	5	25	33	12.6	4.48	89	.282	.340	1	.077	0	-4	-4	-0	-0.4

■ SAM LANFORD
Lanford, Lewis Grover b: 1/8/1886, Woodruff, S.C. d: 9/14/70, Woodruff, S.C. BR/TR, 5'9", 155 lbs. Deb: 8/19/07

| 1907 | Was-A | 0 | 1 | .000 | 2 | 1 | 0 | 0 | 0 | 7 | 10 | 0 | 5 | 2 | 19.3 | 5.14 | 47 | .337 | .432 | 1 | .333 | 0 | -2 | -2 | -0 | -0.1 |

■ WALT LANFRANCONI
Lanfranconi, Walter Oswald b: 11/9/16, Barre, Vt. d: 8/18/86, Barre, Vt. BR/TR, 5'7.5", 155 lbs. Deb: 9/12/41

1941	Chi-N	0	1	.000	2	1	0	0	0	6	7	0	2	1	13.5	3.00	117	.280	.333	0	.000	-0	0	0	0	0.0
1947	Bos-N	4	4	.500	36	4	1	0	1	64	65	2	27	18	12.9	2.95	132	.272	.346	0	.000	-1	8	7	1	0.7
Total	2	4	5	.444	38	5	1	0	1	70	72	2	29	19	13.0	2.96	131	.273	.345	0	.000	-1	8	7	1	0.7

■ MARTY LANG
Lang, Martin John b: 9/27/05, Hooper, Neb. d: 1/13/68, Lakewood, Colo. BR/TL, 5'11", 160 lbs. Deb: 7/04/30

| 1930 | Pit-N | 0 | 0 | — | 2 | 0 | 0 | 0 | 0 | 1² | 9 | 2 | 3 | 2 | 64.8 | 54.00 | 9 | .692 | .750 | 0 | — | 0 | -9 | -9 | 0 | -0.6 |

■ CHIP LANG
Lang, Robert David b: 8/21/52, Pittsburgh, Pa. BR/TR, 6'4", 205 lbs. Deb: 9/08/75

1975	Mon-N	0	0	—	1	1	0	0	0	1²	2	0	3	2	27.0	10.80	35	.333	.556	0	—	0	-1	-1	0	0.0
1976	Mon-N	1	3	.250	29	2	0	0	0	62¹	56	3	34	30	13.4	4.19	89	.242	.347	1	.167	-0	-5	-3	0	-0.2
Total	2	1	3	.250	30	3	0	0	0	64	58	3	37	32	13.8	4.36	85	.245	.354	1	.167	-0	-6	-5	0	-0.2

■ FRANK LANGE
Lange, Frank Herman "Seagan" b: 10/28/1883, Columbia, Wis. d: 12/26/45, Madison, Wis. BR/TR, 5'11", 180 lbs. Deb: 5/16/10

1910	Chi-A	9	4	.692	23	15	6	1	0	130²	93	2	54	98	10.7	1.65	145	.204	.301	13	.255	3	13	11	-3	1.2
1911	Chi-A	8	8	.500	29	22	8	1	0	161²	151	3	77	104	12.9	3.23	100	.251	.339	22	.289	8	2	-0	-1	0.6
1912	Chi-A	10	10	.500	31	20	11	2	3	165¹	165	4	68	96	12.9	3.27	98	.270	.347	14	.215	2	1	-1	-1	0.0
1913	Chi-A	1	3	.250	12	3	0	0	0	40²	46	0	20	20	14.8	4.87	60	.295	.379	3	.167	1	-9	-9	1	-0.6
Total	4	28	25	.528	95	60	25	4	3	498¹	455	9	219	318	12.5	2.96	100	.249	.335	52	.248	13	7	1	-3	1.2

■ ERV LANGE
Lange, Erwin Henry b: 8/12/1887, Forest Park, Ill. d: 4/24/71, Maywood, Ill. BR/TR, 5'10", 170 lbs. Deb: 4/19/14

| 1914 | Chi-F | 12 | 11 | .522 | 36 | 22 | 10 | 2 | 2 | 190 | 162 | 3 | 55 | 87 | 10.4 | 2.23 | 133 | .224 | .282 | 9 | .176 | 2 | 21 | 15 | -3 | 1.5 |

■ DICK LANGE
Lange, Richard Otto b: 9/1/48, Harbor Beach, Mich. BR/TR, 5'10", 185 lbs. Deb: 9/09/72

1972	Cal-A	0	0	—	2	1	0	0	0	7²	7	0	2	8	10.6	4.70	62	.233	.281	0	.000	-0	-1	-2	0	-0.1
1973	Cal-A	2	1	.667	17	4	1	0	0	52²	61	9	21	27	14.2	4.44	80	.292	.359	0	—	0	-4	-5	0	-0.4
1974	Cal-A	3	8	.273	21	18	1	0	0	113²	111	10	47	57	12.8	3.80	90	.248	.325	0	—	0	-2	-5	-1	-0.5
1975	Cal-A	4	6	.400	30	8	1	0	1	102	119	12	53	45	15.3	5.21	68	.292	.374	0	—	0	-16	-19	0	-1.8
Total	4	9	15	.375	70	31	3	0	1	276	298	31	123	137	13.9	4.47	78	.272	.349	0	.000	-0	-24	-30	-1	-2.8

■ RICK LANGFORD
Langford, James Rick b: 3/20/52, Farmville, Va. BR/TR, 6', 180 lbs. Deb: 6/13/76

1976	Pit-N	0	1	.000	12	1	0	0	0	23	27	2	14	17	16.0	6.26	56	.307	.402	1	.200	0	-7	-7	0	-0.6
1977	Oak-A	8	19	.296	37	31	6	1	0	208¹	223	18	73	141	12.9	4.02	100	.273	.334	0	—	0	1	0	1	0.1
1978	Oak-A	7	13	.350	37	24	4	2	0	175²	169	15	56	92	11.7	3.43	106	.253	.314	0	—	0	6	4	2	0.6
1979	Oak-A	12	16	.429	34	29	14	1	0	218²	233	22	57	101	12.1	4.28	94	.273	.322	0	—	0	-2	-6	-2	-0.2
1980	Oak-A	19	12	.613	35	33	**28**	2	0	290	276	29	64	102	10.6	3.26	116	.255	.297	0	—	0	25	16	2	1.8
1981	*Oak-A	12	10	.545	24	24	**18**	2	0	195¹	190	14	58	84	11.6	2.99	116	.255	.311	0	—	0	14	10	-1	1.0
1982	Oak-A	11	16	.407	32	31	15	2	0	237¹	265	33	49	79	12.0	4.21	93	.281	.318	0	.000	0	-4	-8	-1	-0.6
1983	Oak-A	0	4	.000	7	7	0	0	0	20	43	4	10	2	24.7	12.15	32	.448	.509	0	—	0	-18	-18	-0	-1.5
1984	Oak-A	0	0	—	3	2	0	0	0	8²	15	2	2	2	17.7	8.31	45	.366	.395	0	—	0	-4	-4	-0	-0.3
1985	Oak-A	3	5	.375	23	3	0	0	0	59	60	8	15	21	11.4	3.51	110	.261	.306	0	—	0	4	2	0	0.2
1986	Oak-A	1	10	.091	16	11	0	0	0	55	69	13	18	30	14.4	7.36	53	.300	.353	0	—	0	-19	-21	-1	-2.0
Total	11	73	106	.408	260	196	85	10	0	1491	1570	160	416	671	12.1	4.01	95	.271	.322	1	.167	0	-3	-32	5	-1.5

■ MARK LANGSTON
Langston, Mark Edward b: 8/20/60, San Diego, Cal. BR/TL, 6'2", 177 lbs. Deb: 4/07/84

1984	Sea-A	17	10	.630	35	33	5	2	0	225	188	16	118	**204**	12.6	3.40	117	.230	.332	0	—	0	15	15	0	1.6
1985	Sea-A	7	14	.333	24	24	2	0	0	126²	122	22	91	72	15.3	5.47	77	.255	.376	0	—	0	-19	-18	2	-1.4
1986	Sea-A	12	14	.462	37	36	9	0	0	239¹	234	30	123	**245**	14.0	4.85	87	.255	.346	0	—	0	-18	-16	-2	-1.4
1987	Sea-A	19	13	.594	35	35	14	3	0	272	242	30	114	**262**	11.9	3.84	123	.238	.318	0	—	0	19	27	2	2.6
1988	Sea-A	15	11	.577	35	35	9	3	0	261¹	222	32	110	235	11.5	3.34	125	.233	.314	0	—	0	18	24	2	2.7
1989	Sea-A	4	5	.444	10	10	2	1	0	73¹	60	3	19	60	10.2	3.56	113	.221	.282	0	—	0	3	4	-0	0.3
	Mon-N	12	9	.571	24	24	6	4	0	176²	138	13	93	175	11.8	2.39	147	.218	.318	11	.172	0	22	22	-1	2.4
1990	Cal-A	10	17	.370	33	33	5	1	0	223	215	13	104	195	13.1	4.40	89	.259	.345	0	—	0	-12	-12	2	-1.0
Total	7	96	93	.508	233	230	52	14	0	1597¹	1421	159	772	1448	12.5	3.88	106	.240	.331	11	.172	0	27	44	3	5.6

■ MAX LANIER
Lanier, Hubert Max b: 8/18/15, Denton, N.C. BR/TL, 5'11", 180 lbs. Deb: 4/20/38

1938	StL-N	0	3	.000	18	3	1	0	0	45	57	1	28	14	17.4	4.20	94	.317	.414	1	.100	-1	-2	-1	0	-0.1
1939	StL-N	2	1	.667	7	6	2	0	0	37²	29	0	13	14	10.3	2.39	172	.220	.295	4	.286	1	6	7	-0	0.8
1940	StL-N	9	6	.600	35	11	4	2	3	105	113	1	38	49	13.0	3.34	119	.276	.339	6	.200	-0	6	8	1	0.9
1941	StL-N	10	8	.556	35	18	8	2	3	153	126	4	59	93	10.9	2.82	133	.225	.300	10	.192	-1	14	16	2	1.8
1942	*StL-N	13	8	.619	34	20	8	2	2	161	137	4	60	93	11.1	2.96	116	.234	.308	12	.255	3	6	8	1	1.3
1943	*StL-N	15	7	.682	32	25	14	2	3	213¹	195	4	75	123	11.5	**1.90**	177	.246	.312	12	.164	-2	35	35	0	3.7
1944	*StL-N	17	12	.586	33	30	16	5	0	224¹	192	5	71	141	10.7	2.65	133	.234	.297	14	.182	-0	24	22	-1	2.2
1945	StL-N	2	2	.500	4	3	3	0	0	26	22	0	8	16	10.4	1.73	216	.222	.280	2	.182	-0	6	6	-0	0.6
1946	StL-N	6	0	1.000	6	6	6	2	0	56	45	1	19	36	10.4	1.93	179	.228	.300	5	.200	-0	9	9	-0	1.1
1949	StL-N	5	4	.556	15	15	4	1	0	92	92	6	35	37	12.4	3.82	109	.261	.328	2	.074	-2	2	4	-1	0.1
1950	StL-N	11	9	.550	27	27	10	2	0	181¹	173	6	68	79	12.0	3.13	137	.249	.317	11	.162	-1	20	24	0	2.4
1951	StL-N	11	9	.550	31	23	9	2	1	160	149	14	50	59	11.2	3.26	122	.248	.306	8	.151	-2	12	12	0	1.1
1952	NY-N	7	12	.368	37	16	4	1	5	137	124	11	65	47	12.6	3.94	94	.244	.333	11	.268	3	-3	-4	3	0.2
1953	NY-N	0	0	—	3	0	0	0	0	5¹	8	1	3	2	18.6	6.75	64	.381	.458	0	.000	-0	-1	-1	0	0.0
	StL-A	0	1	.000	10	1	0	0	0	21	28	2	9	8	18.6	7.25	58	.322	.443	1	.167	-0	-8	-8	0	-0.7
Total	14	108	82	.568	327	204	91	21	17	1619¹	1490	65	611	821	11.8	3.01	125	.247	.318	99	.185	-3	127	136	4	15.4

■ JOHNNY LANNING
Lanning, John Young "Tobacco Chewin' Johnny" b: 9/6/10, Asheville, N.C. BR/TR, 6'1", 185 lbs. Deb: 4/17/36

1936	Bos-N	7	11	.389	28	20	3	1	0	153	154	9	55	33	12.3	3.65	105	.263	.326	7	.135	-2	6	3	-1	0.0
1937	Bos-N	5	7	.417	32	11	4	1	2	116²	107	10	40	37	11.4	3.93	91	.236	.300	4	.121	-1	-0	-5	-0	-0.5
1938	Bos-N	8	7	.533	32	18	4	1	0	138	146	5	52	39	13.0	3.72	92	.267	.332	9	.188	-1	1	-4	-1	-0.5
1939	Bos-N	5	6	.455	37	6	3	0	4	129	120	6	53	45	12.2	3.42	108	.252	.329	6	.143	-1	7	4	0	0.3

YEAR	TM/L	W	L	PCT	G	GS	CG	SH	SV	IP	H	HR	BB	SO	RAT	ERA	ERA+	OAV	OOB	BH	AVG	PB	PR	/A	PD	TPI
1940	Pit-N	8	4	.667	38	7	2	0	2	115²	119	8	39	42	12.3	4.05	94	.268	.327	7	.200	1	-3	-3	0	-0.1
1941	Pit-N	11	11	.500	34	23	9	0	1	175²	175	6	47	41	11.4	3.13	116	.256	.304	6	.107	-2	10	9	1	1.0
1942	Pit-N	6	8	.429	34	8	2	1	1	119¹	125	7	26	31	11.5	3.32	102	.274	.314	4	.138	-0	-0	1	-0	0.1
1943	Pit-N	4	1	.800	12	2	0	0	2	27	23	0	9	11	10.7	2.33	149	.223	.286	1	.167	-0	3	3	-1	0.3
1945	Pit-N	0	0	—	1	0	0	0	0	2	8	1	0	0	36.0	36.00	11	.571	.571	0	—	0	-7	-7	0	-0.4
1946	Pit-N	4	5	.444	27	9	3	0	1	91	97	3	31	16	12.8	3.07	115	.269	.329	3	.143	-0	3	5	1	0.5
1947	Bos-N	0	0	—	3	0	0	0	0	3²	4	0	6	0	24.5	9.82	40	.400	.625	0	—	0	-2	-2	0	-0.1
Total	11	58	60	.492	278	104	30	4	13	1071	1078	55	358	295	12.1	3.58	101	.261	.321	47	.146	-6	19	5	0	0.6

■ RED LANNING
Lanning, Lester Alfred b: 5/13/1895, Harvard, Ill. d: 6/13/62, Bristol, Conn. BL/TL, 5′9″, 165 lbs. Deb: 6/20/16 ♦

YEAR	TM/L	W	L	PCT	G	GS	CG	SH	SV	IP	H	HR	BB	SO	RAT	ERA	ERA+	OAV	OOB	BH	AVG	PB	PR	/A	PD	TPI
1916	Phi-A	0	3	.000	6	3	1	0	0	24¹	38	1	17	9	21.1	8.14	35	.362	.460	6	.182	1	-14	-14	0	-1.3

■ TOM LANNING
Lanning, Thomas Newton b: 4/22/07, Asheville, N.C. d: 11/4/67, Marietta, Ga. BL/TL, 6′1″, 165 lbs. Deb: 9/14/38

YEAR	TM/L	W	L	PCT	G	GS	CG	SH	SV	IP	H	HR	BB	SO	RAT	ERA	ERA+	OAV	OOB	BH	AVG	PB	PR	/A	PD	TPI
1938	Phi-N	0	1	.000	3	1	0	0	0	7	9	0	2	2	14.1	6.43	60	.300	.344	1	1.000	0	-2	-2	-0	-0.1

■ GENE LANSING
Lansing, Eugene Hewitt "Jigger" b: 1/11/1898, Albany, N.Y. d: 1/18/45, Rensselaer, N.Y. BR/TR, 6′1″, 185 lbs. Deb: 4/27/22

YEAR	TM/L	W	L	PCT	G	GS	CG	SH	SV	IP	H	HR	BB	SO	RAT	ERA	ERA+	OAV	OOB	BH	AVG	PB	PR	/A	PD	TPI
1922	Bos-N	0	1	.000	15	1	0	0	0	40²	46	1	22	14	15.0	5.98	67	.301	.389	0	.000	-1	-8	-9	-0	-0.9

■ PAUL LaPALME
LaPalme, Paul Edmore "Lefty" b: 12/14/23, Springfield, Mass. BL/TL, 5′10″, 175 lbs. Deb: 5/28/51

YEAR	TM/L	W	L	PCT	G	GS	CG	SH	SV	IP	H	HR	BB	SO	RAT	ERA	ERA+	OAV	OOB	BH	AVG	PB	PR	/A	PD	TPI
1951	Pit-N	1	5	.167	22	8	1	1	0	54¹	79	6	31	24	18.4	6.29	67	.333	.413	1	.100	-0	-14	-12	-1	-1.2
1952	Pit-N	1	2	.333	31	4	0	0	0	59²	56	6	37	25	14.2	3.92	102	.253	.363	1	.100	-0	-1	0	1	0.1
1953	Pit-N	8	16	.333	35	24	7	1	2	176¹	191	20	64	86	13.0	4.59	97	.272	.333	5	.085	-5	-6	-2	-2	-0.8
1954	Pit-N	4	10	.286	33	15	2	0	0	120¹	147	15	54	57	15.0	5.52	76	.302	.372	5	.143	-0	-19	-18	-0	-1.7
1955	StL-N	4	3	.571	56	0	0	0	3	91²	76	10	34	39	10.9	2.75	148	.228	.301	4	.211	0	13	13	1	1.5
1956	StL-N	0	0	—	1	0	0	0	0	0²	4	0	2	0	81.0	81.00	5	.667	.750	0	—	0	-6	-6	0	-0.4
	Cin-N	2	4	.333	11	2	0	0	0	27	26	7	4	4	10.0	4.67	85	.257	.286	2	.500	1	-3	-2	0	0.0
	Yr	2	4	.333	12	2	0	0	0	27²	30	7	6	4	11.7	6.51	61	.280	.319	0	.000	1	-8	-8	-0	-0.4
	Chi-A	3	1	.750	29	0	0	0	2	45²	31	2	27	23	11.4	2.36	173	.195	.312	0	.000	-1	9	9	1	0.8
1957	Chi-A	1	4	.200	35	0	0	0	7	40¹	35	5	19	19	12.3	3.35	112	.235	.325	2	.500	1	2	2	1	0.4
Total	7	24	45	.348	253	51	10	2	14	616¹	645	71	272	277	13.4	4.42	95	.269	.345	20	.136	-4	-25	-16	0	-1.3

■ ANDY LAPIHUSKA
Lapihuska, Andrew "Apples" b: 11/1/22, Delmont, N.J. BL/TR, 5′10.5″, 175 lbs. Deb: 9/12/42

YEAR	TM/L	W	L	PCT	G	GS	CG	SH	SV	IP	H	HR	BB	SO	RAT	ERA	ERA+	OAV	OOB	BH	AVG	PB	PR	/A	PD	TPI
1942	Phi-N	0	2	.000	3	2	0	0	0	20²	17	0	13	8	13.9	5.23	63	.221	.348	2	.286	0	-4	-4	0	-0.3
1943	Phi-N	0	0	—	1	0	0	0	0	2¹	5	1	3	0	30.9	23.14	15	.417	.533	0	.000	-0	-5	-5	0	-0.4
Total	2	0	2	.000	4	2	0	0	0	23	22	1	16	8	15.7	7.04	47	.247	.374	2	.222	0	-10	-10	0	-0.7

■ DAVE LaPOINT
LaPoint, David Jeffrey b: 7/29/59, Glens Falls, N.Y. BL/TL, 6′3″, 205 lbs. Deb: 9/10/80

YEAR	TM/L	W	L	PCT	G	GS	CG	SH	SV	IP	H	HR	BB	SO	RAT	ERA	ERA+	OAV	OOB	BH	AVG	PB	PR	/A	PD	TPI
1980	Mil-A	1	0	1.000	5	3	0	0	1	15	17	2	13	5	18.0	6.00	64	.293	.423	0	—	0	-3	-4	-1	-0.3
1981	StL-N	1	0	1.000	3	2	0	0	0	10²	12	1	2	4	12.7	4.22	84	.293	.341	0	.000	-1	-1	-1	0	0.0
1982	*StL-N	9	3	.750	42	21	0	0	0	152²	170	8	52	81	13.3	3.42	106	.290	.350	2	.053	-3	3	3	-3	-0.2
1983	StL-N	12	9	.571	37	29	1	0	0	191¹	191	12	84	113	13.1	3.95	92	.267	.347	9	.153	1	-7	-7	-1	-0.7
1984	StL-N	12	10	.545	33	33	2	1	0	193	205	9	77	130	13.2	3.96	88	.278	.347	4	.068	-3	-8	-11	-2	-1.5
1985	SF-N	7	17	.292	31	31	2	1	0	206²	215	18	74	122	12.6	3.57	96	.269	.331	10	.167	2	0	-3	-2	-0.3
1986	Det-A	3	6	.333	16	8	0	0	0	67²	85	11	32	36	15.6	5.72	72	.307	.379	0	—	0	-12	-12	-0	-1.1
	SD-N	1	4	.200	24	4	0	0	0	61¹	67	8	24	41	13.5	4.26	86	.276	.343	0	.000	-1	-4	-4	-0	-0.4
1987	StL-N	1	1	.500	6	2	0	0	0	16	26	4	5	8	17.4	6.75	62	.351	.392	0	.000	-0	-5	-5	-0	-0.4
	Chi-A	6	3	.667	14	12	2	1	0	82²	69	7	31	43	11.0	2.94	156	.224	.297	0	—	0	14	15	2	1.7
1988	Chi-A	10	11	.476	25	25	1	1	0	161¹	151	10	47	79	11.2	3.40	117	.245	.300	0	—	0	10	10	-2	0.8
	Pit-N	4	2	.667	8	8	1	0	0	52	54	4	10	19	11.1	2.77	123	.271	.306	1	.063	-1	4	4	0	0.3
1989	NY-A	6	9	.400	20	20	0	0	0	113²	146	12	45	51	15.3	5.62	69	.310	.373	0	—	0	-22	-22	-2	-2.2
1990	NY-A	7	10	.412	28	27	2	0	0	157²	180	11	57	67	13.6	4.11	97	.292	.353	0	—	0	-4	-2	-0	-0.1
Total	11	80	85	.485	292	225	11	4	1	1481²	1588	117	553	799	13.1	3.98	94	.276	.342	26	.104	-6	-33	-39	-10	-4.4

■ TERRY LARKIN
Larkin, Frank S. d: 9/16/1894, Brooklyn, N.Y. BR/TR, Deb: 5/20/1876 ♦

YEAR	TM/L	W	L	PCT	G	GS	CG	SH	SV	IP	H	HR	BB	SO	RAT	ERA	ERA+	OAV	OOB	BH	AVG	PB	PR	/A	PD	TPI
1876	NY-N	0	1	.000	1	1	1	0	0	9	9	0	0	0	9.0	3.00	71	.243	.243	0	.000	-1	-1	-1	0	0.0
1877	Har-N	29	25	.537	56	56	55	4	0	501	510	2	53	96	10.1	2.14	114	.249	.268	52	.228	6	37	16	-1	1.5
1878	Chi-N	29	26	.527	56	56	56	1	0	506	511	4	31	163	9.6	2.24	108	.249	.261	65	.288	14	4	10	-4	2.1
1879	Chi-N	31	23	.574	58	58	57	4	0	513¹	514	5	30	142	9.5	2.44	105	.244	.255	50	.219	2	3	7	-7	0.3
1880	Tro-N	0	5	.000	5	5	3	0	0	38	83	1	10	5	22.0	8.76	29	.418	.446	3	.150	-0	-27	-26	0	-1.9
Total	5	89	80	.527	176	176	172	9	0	1567¹	1627	12	124	406	10.1	2.43	102	.253	.267	215	.235	20	17	9	-11	2.0

■ PAT LARKIN
Larkin, Patrick Clibborn b: 6/14/60, Arcadia, Cal. BL/TL, 6′, 180 lbs. Deb: 7/16/83

YEAR	TM/L	W	L	PCT	G	GS	CG	SH	SV	IP	H	HR	BB	SO	RAT	ERA	ERA+	OAV	OOB	BH	AVG	PB	PR	/A	PD	TPI
1983	SF-N	0	0	—	5	0	0	0	0	10¹	13	1	3	6	15.7	4.35	81	.317	.391	0	.000	-0	-1	-1	0	-0.4

■ STEVE LARKIN
Larkin, Stephen Patrick b: 12/9/10, Cincinnati, Ohio d: 5/2/69, Norristown, Pa. BR/TR, 6′1″, 195 lbs. Deb: 5/06/34

YEAR	TM/L	W	L	PCT	G	GS	CG	SH	SV	IP	H	HR	BB	SO	RAT	ERA	ERA+	OAV	OOB	BH	AVG	PB	PR	/A	PD	TPI
1934	Det-A	0	0	—	2	1	0	0	0	6	8	0	5	8	19.5	1.50	293	.296	.406	1	.333	0	2	2	0	0.3

■ DAVE LaROCHE
LaRoche, David Eugene b: 5/14/48, Colorado Springs, Colo. BL/TL, 6′2″, 200 lbs. Deb: 5/11/70 C

YEAR	TM/L	W	L	PCT	G	GS	CG	SH	SV	IP	H	HR	BB	SO	RAT	ERA	ERA+	OAV	OOB	BH	AVG	PB	PR	/A	PD	TPI
1970	Cal-A	4	1	.800	38	0	0	0	4	49²	41	6	21	44	12.0	3.44	105	.224	.317	2	.250	1	1	1	0	0.2
1971	Cal-A	5	1	.833	56	0	0	0	9	72	55	3	27	63	10.4	2.50	129	.212	.289	1	.091	-0	8	6	-1	0.5
1972	Min-A	5	7	.417	62	0	0	0	10	95¹	72	9	39	79	11.0	2.83	113	.209	.300	1	.091	-0	4	4	-0	0.5
1973	Chi-N	4	1	.800	45	0	0	0	4	54¹	55	7	29	34	14.1	5.80	68	.274	.368	2	.500	1	-13	-11	1	-0.8
1974	Chi-N	5	6	.455	49	4	0	0	5	92	103	9	47	49	15.0	4.79	80	.286	.373	9	.333	3	-12	-10	1	-0.7
1975	Cle-A	5	3	.625	61	0	0	0	17	82¹	61	5	57	94	13.1	2.19	173	.210	.344	0	—	0	15	15	0	1.6
1976	Cle-A	1	4	.200	61	0	0	0	21	96¹	72	2	49	104	10.0	2.24	156	.175	.285	0	—	0	14	13	-1	1.3
1977	Cle-A	2	2	.500	13	0	0	0	4	18²	15	3	7	18	10.6	5.30	74	.234	.310	0	—	0	-3	-3	-0	-0.2
	Cal-A	6	5	.545	46	0	0	0	13	81¹	64	8	37	61	11.4	3.10	126	.218	.310	0	—	0	9	7	-0	0.7
	Yr	8	7	.533	59	0	0	0	17	100	79	11	44	79	11.3	3.51	112	.220	.309	0	—	0	6	5	-0	0.5
1978	Cal-A	10	9	.526	59	0	0	0	25	95²	73	7	48	70	11.6	2.82	128	.215	.316	0	—	0	10	8	0	0.8
1979	*Cal-A	7	11	.389	53	1	0	0	10	85²	107	13	32	59	14.8	5.57	73	.314	.376	0	—	0	-13	-14	1	-1.2
1980	Cal-A	3	5	.375	52	9	1	0	4	128	122	14	39	89	11.5	4.08	96	.256	.317	0	—	0	-1	-2	-0	-0.2
1981	*NY-A	4	1	.800	26	1	0	0	0	47	38	3	16	24	10.5	2.49	144	.229	.301	0	—	0	6	6	-0	0.6
1982	NY-A	4	2	.667	25	0	0	0	0	50	54	4	11	31	11.9	3.42	117	.273	.314	0	—	0	4	3	-1	0.2
1983	NY-A	0	0	—	1	0	0	0	0	1	2	1	0	0	18.0	18.00	22	.400	.400	0	—	0	-2	-2	0	0.0
Total	14	65	58	.528	647	15	1	0	126	1049¹	919	94	459	819	12.1	3.53	105	.239	.325	15	.246	5	26	22	-3	3.3

■ JOHN LaROSE
LaRose, Henry John b: 10/25/51, Pawtucket, R.I. BL/TL, 6′1″, 185 lbs. Deb: 9/20/78

YEAR	TM/L	W	L	PCT	G	GS	CG	SH	SV	IP	H	HR	BB	SO	RAT	ERA	ERA+	OAV	OOB	BH	AVG	PB	PR	/A	PD	TPI
1978	Bos-A	0	0	—	1	0	0	0	0	2	3	1	3	0	27.0	22.50	18	.375	.545	0	—	0	-4	-4	0	-0.2

■ DON LARSEN
Larsen, Don James b: 8/7/29, Michigan City, Ind. BR/TR, 6′4″, 215 lbs. Deb: 4/18/53

YEAR	TM/L	W	L	PCT	G	GS	CG	SH	SV	IP	H	HR	BB	SO	RAT	ERA	ERA+	OAV	OOB	BH	AVG	PB	PR	/A	PD	TPI
1953	StL-A	7	12	.368	38	22	7	2	2	192²	201	11	64	96	12.6	4.16	101	.267	.328	23	.284	6	-3	1	-1	0.8
1954	Bal-A	3	21	.125	29	28	12	1	0	201²	213	18	89	80	13.5	4.37	82	.274	.349	22	.250	8	-15	-18	1	-0.9
1955	*NY-A	9	2	.818	19	13	5	1	2	97	81	8	51	44	12.4	3.06	122	.229	.329	6	.146	0	10	7	-0	0.9
1956	*NY-A	11	5	.688	38	20	6	1	1	179²	133	19	96	107	11.8	3.26	119	.204	.313	19	.241	6	18	12	-1	1.6
1957	*NY-A	10	4	.714	27	20	4	1	0	139²	113	12	87	81	12.9	3.74	96	.220	.333	14	.250	5	1	-2	-0	0.1
1958	*NY-A	9	6	.600	19	19	5	3	0	114¹	100	4	52	55	12.3	3.07	115	.233	.322	15	.306	8	9	6	-1	1.3

YEAR	TM/L	W	L	PCT	G	GS	CG	SH	SV	IP	H	HR	BB	SO	RAT	ERA	ERA+	OAV	OOB	BH	AVG	PB	PR	/A	PD	TPI
1959	NY-A	6	7	.462	25	18	3	1	3	124²	122	14	76	69	14.4	4.33	84	.260	.365	12	.255	4	-7	-10	0	-0.5
1960	KC-A	1	10	.091	22	15	0	0	0	83²	97	11	42	43	15.0	5.38	74	.293	.373	6	.207	0	-14	-13	-1	-1.3
1961	KC-A	1	0	1.000	8	1	0	0	0	15	21	2	11	13	19.8	4.20	98	.344	.452	6	.300	1	-0	-0	0	0.0
	Chi-A	7	2	.778	25	3	0	0	2	74¹	64	5	29	53	11.4	4.12	95	.231	.306	8	.320	3	-1	-2	0	0.1
	Yr	8	2	.800	33	4	0	0	2	89¹	85	7	40	66	12.7	4.13	96	.251	.332	1	.022	4	-1	-2	0	0.1
1962	*SF-N	5	4	.556	49	0	0	0	11	86¹	83	9	47	58	13.8	4.38	87	.256	.354	5	.200	1	-4	-6	0	-0.4
1963	SF-N	7	7	.500	46	0	0	0	3	62	46	8	30	44	11.0	3.05	105	.203	.296	2	.182	0	2	1	0	0.2
1964	SF-N	0	1	.000	6	0	0	0	0	10¹	10	0	6	6	13.9	4.35	82	.256	.356	0	.000	-0	-1	-1	-0	0.0
	Hou-N	4	8	.333	30	10	2	1	1	103¹	92	4	20	58	9.8	2.26	151	.233	.272	3	.097	0	15	13	0	1.5
	Yr	4	9	.308	36	10	2	1	1	113²	102	4	26	64	10.2	2.45	140	.235	.280	4	.125	0	14	12	0	1.5
1965	Hou-N	0	0	—	1	1	0	0	0	5¹	8	3	3	1	18.6	5.06	66	.348	.423	0	.000	-0	-1	-1	1	0.0
	Bal-A	1	2	.333	27	1	0	0	1	54	53	4	20	40	12.3	2.67	130	.255	.323	3	.273	1	5	5	1	0.7
1967	Chi-N	0	0	—	3	0	0	0	0	4	5	1	2	1	15.8	9.00	39	.333	.412	0	—	0	-3	-2	0	-0.1
Total	14	81	91	.471	412	171	44	11	26	1548	1442	130	725	849	12.8	3.78	99	.247	.332	144	.242	44	10	-9	-1	4.0

■ DAN LARSON   Larson, Daniel James b: 7/4/54, Los Angeles, Cal. BR/TR, 6', 175 lbs. Deb: 7/18/76

YEAR	TM/L	W	L	PCT	G	GS	CG	SH	SV	IP	H	HR	BB	SO	RAT	ERA	ERA+	OAV	OOB	BH	AVG	PB	PR	/A	PD	TPI
1976	Hou-N	5	8	.385	13	13	5	0	0	92¹	81	3	28	42	10.7	3.02	106	.236	.296	9	.290	3	5	2	0	0.5
1977	Hou-N	1	7	.125	32	10	1	0	1	97²	108	13	45	44	14.3	5.81	61	.280	.358	6	.214	1	-21	-24	0	-2.2
1978	Phi-N	0	0	—	1	0	0	0	0	1	1	1	1	2	18.0	9.00	40	.250	.400	0	—	0	-1	-1	0	0.0
1979	Phi-N	1	1	.500	3	3	0	0	0	19	17	1	9	9	12.8	4.26	90	.250	.346	0	.000	-1	-1	-1	0	0.0
1980	Phi-N	0	5	.000	12	7	0	0	0	45²	46	4	24	17	13.8	3.15	120	.271	.361	2	.154	0	2	3	-0	0.3
1981	Phi-N	3	0	1.000	5	4	1	0	0	28	27	4	15	15	13.5	4.18	87	.260	.353	1	.111	0	-2	-2	-0	-0.1
1982	Chi-N	0	4	.000	12	6	0	0	0	39²	51	4	18	22	16.1	5.67	66	.327	.403	3	.273	0	-9	-9	1	-0.6
Total	7	10	25	.286	78	43	7	0	1	323¹	331	30	140	151	13.3	4.40	80	.269	.346	21	.216	4	-26	-31	1	-2.1

■ AL LARY   Lary, Alfred Allen b: 9/26/29, Northport, Ala. BR/TR, 6'3", 185 lbs. Deb: 9/06/54 ♦

YEAR	TM/L	W	L	PCT	G	GS	CG	SH	SV	IP	H	HR	BB	SO	RAT	ERA	ERA+	OAV	OOB	BH	AVG	PB	PR	/A	PD	TPI
1954	Chi-N	0	0	—	1	1	0	0	0	6	3	0	7	4	15.0	3.00	140	.150	.370	1	.500	0	1	1	0	0.1
1962	Chi-N	0	1	.000	15	3	0	0	0	34	42	5	15	18	15.1	7.15	58	.311	.380	1	.167	0	-12	-11	-0	-1.0
Total	2	0	1	.000	16	4	0	0	0	40	45	5	22	22	15.1	6.52	64	.290	.379	2	.250	1	-11	-11	-0	-0.9

■ FRANK LARY   Lary, Frank Strong "Mule" or "The Yankee Killer" b: 4/10/30, Northport, Ala. BR/TR, 5'11", 175 lbs. Deb: 9/14/54

YEAR	TM/L	W	L	PCT	G	GS	CG	SH	SV	IP	H	HR	BB	SO	RAT	ERA	ERA+	OAV	OOB	BH	AVG	PB	PR	/A	PD	TPI
1954	Det-A	0	0	—	3	0	0	0	0	3²	4	0	3	5	17.2	2.45	150	.286	.412	0	—	0	1	1	-0	0.0
1955	Det-A	14	15	.483	36	31	16	2	1	235	232	10	89	98	12.5	3.10	124	.262	.334	16	.195	1	22	19	2	2.2
1956	Det-A	21	13	.618	41	38	20	3	1	294	289	20	116	165	12.8	3.15	131	.257	.333	19	.184	0	33	31	0	3.2
1957	Det-A	11	16	.407	40	35	12	2	3	237²	250	23	72	107	12.6	3.98	97	.276	.337	9	.123	-3	-5	-3	1	-0.5
1958	Det-A	16	15	.516	39	34	**19**	3	1	260¹	249	20	68	131	11.4	2.90	139	.251	.307	15	.170	-1	25	33	0	3.4
1959	Det-A	17	10	.630	32	32	11	3	0	223	225	23	46	137	11.4	3.55	114	.261	.307	10	.125	-2	8	13	-0	1.1
1960	Det-A	15	15	.500	38	36	**15**	2	1	274¹	262	25	62	149	11.3	3.51	113	.249	.302	17	.183	4	11	14	-2	1.7
1961	Det-A	23	9	.719	36	36	**22**	4	0	275¹	252	24	66	146	10.6	3.24	127	.243	.293	25	.231	4	24	26	4	**3.6**
1962	Det-A	2	6	.250	17	14	2	1	0	80	98	17	21	41	13.8	5.74	71	.297	.346	4	.167	1	-16	-15	-1	-1.4
1963	Det-A	4	9	.308	16	14	6	0	0	107¹	99	15	26	46	10.1	3.27	114	.226	.281	8	.229	1	4	6	2	0.9
1964	Det-A	0	2	.000	6	4	0	0	0	18	24	3	10	6	18.5	7.00	52	.316	.416	0	.000	-1	-7	-7	-0	-0.6
	NY-N	2	3	.400	13	8	3	1	1	57¹	62	7	14	27	12.6	4.55	79	.279	.333	2	.118	1	-6	-6	-0	-0.5
	Mil-N	1	0	1.000	5	2	0	0	0	12¹	15	4	0	4	10.9	4.38	80	.306	.306	0	.000	-0	-1	-1	1	0.0
	Yr	3	3	.500	18	10	3	1	1	69²	77	11	14	31	11.8	4.52	79	.279	.314	4	.200	1	-8	-7	1	-0.5
1965	NY-N	1	3	.250	14	7	0	0	0	57¹	48	2	16	23	10.2	2.98	118	.233	.291	4	.211	0	4	3	1	0.5
	Chi-A	1	0	1.000	14	1	0	0	2	26²	23	4	7	14	10.8	4.05	79	.230	.294	1	.500	0	-2	-3	0	-0.1
Total	12	128	116	.525	350	292	126	21	11	2162¹	2123	197	616	1099	11.8	3.49	113	.257	.316	130	.177	5	95	112	5	13.5

■ FRED LASHER   Lasher, Frederick Walter b: 8/19/41, Poughkeepsie, N.Y. BR/TR, 6'3", 190 lbs. Deb: 4/12/63

YEAR	TM/L	W	L	PCT	G	GS	CG	SH	SV	IP	H	HR	BB	SO	RAT	ERA	ERA+	OAV	OOB	BH	AVG	PB	PR	/A	PD	TPI
1963	Min-A	0	0	—	11	0	0	0	0	11¹	12	1	11	10	18.3	4.76	76	.286	.434	0	.000	-0	-1	-1	0	0.0
1967	Det-A	2	1	.667	17	0	0	0	0	30	25	1	11	28	11.1	3.90	84	.221	.296	1	.111	-0	-2	-2	-0	-0.2
1968	*Det-A	5	1	.833	34	0	0	0	5	48²	37	5	22	32	10.9	3.33	90	.215	.304	1	.111	-0	-2	-2	1	-0.1
1969	Det-A	2	1	.667	32	0	0	0	0	44	34	5	22	26	11.9	3.07	122	.224	.330	0	.000	-0	3	3	0	0.3
1970	Det-A	1	3	.250	12	0	0	0	3	9	10	0	12	8	23.0	5.00	75	.278	.469	0	.000	-0	-1	-1	0	0.0
	Cle-A	1	7	.125	43	1	0	0	5	57²	57	6	30	44	14.0	4.06	98	.264	.361	0	.000	-1	-2	-1	-1	-0.2
	Yr	2	10	.167	55	1	0	0	8	66²	67	6	42	52	15.1	4.18	94	.264	.375	0	.000	-1	-3	-2	-1	-0.2
1971	Cal-A	0	0	—	2	0	0	0	0	1¹	4	0	2	2	40.5	27.00	14	.667	.750	0	—	0	-3	-4	0	-0.2
Total	6	11	13	.458	151	1	0	0	22	202	179	18	110	148	13.2	3.88	91	.243	.347	2	.063	-2	-10	-8	0	-0.4

■ BILL LASKEY   Laskey, William Alan b: 12/20/57, Toledo, Ohio BR/TR, 6'5", 190 lbs. Deb: 4/23/82

YEAR	TM/L	W	L	PCT	G	GS	CG	SH	SV	IP	H	HR	BB	SO	RAT	ERA	ERA+	OAV	OOB	BH	AVG	PB	PR	/A	PD	TPI
1982	SF-N	13	12	.520	32	31	7	1	0	189¹	186	14	43	88	11.0	3.14	115	.261	.304	8	.129	-2	10	10	1	0.8
1983	SF-N	13	10	.565	25	25	1	0	0	148¹	151	18	45	81	12.1	4.19	84	.266	.323	5	.106	0	-9	-11	-1	-1.1
1984	SF-N	9	14	.391	35	34	2	0	0	207²	222	20	50	71	12.0	4.33	81	.273	.320	4	.063	-3	-17	-19	-2	-2.3
1985	SF-N	5	11	.313	19	19	0	0	0	114	110	10	39	42	11.8	3.55	97	.255	.317	4	.133	1	0	-1	1	0.0
	Mon-N	0	5	.000	11	7	0	0	0	34¹	55	9	14	18	18.6	9.44	36	.362	.423	1	.143	-0	-22	-23	1	-2.0
	Yr	5	16	.238	30	26	0	0	0	148¹	165	19	53	60	13.3	4.91	70	.281	.343	4	.108	1	-22	-25	1	-2.0
1986	SF-N	1	1	.500	20	0	0	0	1	27¹	28	5	13	8	13.5	4.28	82	.275	.357	0	.000	-0	-2	-2	1	-0.1
1988	Cle-A	1	0	1.000	17	0	0	0	1	24¹	32	0	6	17	14.1	5.18	79	.320	.358	0	—	0	-3	-3	0	-0.2
Total	6	42	53	.442	159	116	10	1	2	745¹	784	76	210	325	12.2	4.14	85	.272	.325	22	.105	-4	-44	-50	-0	-4.9

■ BILL LASLEY   Lasley, Willard Almond b: 7/13/02, Gallipolis, Ohio d: 8/21/90, Seattle, Wash. BB/TR, 6', 175 lbs. Deb: 9/19/24

YEAR	TM/L	W	L	PCT	G	GS	CG	SH	SV	IP	H	HR	BB	SO	RAT	ERA	ERA+	OAV	OOB	BH	AVG	PB	PR	/A	PD	TPI
1924	StL-A	0	0	—	2	0	0	0	0	4	7	0	2	0	20.3	6.75	67	.412	.474	0	.000	-0	-1	-1	-0	0.0

■ TOM LASORDA   Lasorda, Thomas Charles b: 9/22/27, Norristown, Pa. BL/TL, 5'10", 175 lbs. Deb: 8/05/54 MC

YEAR	TM/L	W	L	PCT	G	GS	CG	SH	SV	IP	H	HR	BB	SO	RAT	ERA	ERA+	OAV	OOB	BH	AVG	PB	PR	/A	PD	TPI
1954	Bro-N	0	0	—	4	0	0	0	0	9	8	2	5	5	13.0	5.00	82	.242	.342	0	.000	-0	-1	-1	-0	0.0
1955	Bro-N	0	0	—	4	1	0	0	0	4	5	1	6	4	27.0	13.50	30	.313	.522	0	—	0	-4	-4	-0	-0.3
1956	KC-A	0	4	.000	18	5	0	0	1	45¹	40	6	45	28	17.5	6.15	70	.240	.409	1	.077	-1	-10	-9	0	-0.9
Total	3	0	4	.000	26	6	0	0	1	58¹	53	9	56	37	17.4	6.48	66	.245	.409	1	.071	-2	-15	-14	0	-1.2

■ BILL LATHAM   Latham, William Carol b: 8/29/60, Birmingham, Ala. BL/TL, 6'2", 190 lbs. Deb: 4/15/85

YEAR	TM/L	W	L	PCT	G	GS	CG	SH	SV	IP	H	HR	BB	SO	RAT	ERA	ERA+	OAV	OOB	BH	AVG	PB	PR	/A	PD	TPI
1985	NY-N	1	3	.250	7	3	0	0	0	22²	21	1	7	10	11.1	3.97	87	.250	.308	1	.333	1	-1	-1	1	0.0
1986	Min-A	0	1	.000	7	2	0	0	0	16	24	1	6	8	17.4	7.31	59	.358	.419	0	—	0	-6	-5	-0	-0.4
Total	2	1	4	.200	14	5	0	0	0	38²	45	2	13	18	13.7	5.35	71	.298	.358	1	.333	1	-7	-7	0	-0.4

■ BILL LATHROP   Lathrop, William George b: 8/12/1891, Hanover, Wis. d: 11/20/58, Janesville, Wis. BR/TR, 6'2.5", 184 lbs. Deb: 7/29/13

YEAR	TM/L	W	L	PCT	G	GS	CG	SH	SV	IP	H	HR	BB	SO	RAT	ERA	ERA+	OAV	OOB	BH	AVG	PB	PR	/A	PD	TPI
1913	Chi-A	0	1	.000	6	0	0	0	0	17	16	0	12	9	15.4	4.24	69	.262	.392	0	.000	-1	-2	-2	0	-0.2
1914	Chi-A	1	2	.333	19	1	0	0	0	47²	41	0	19	7	11.7	2.64	102	.241	.325	0	.000	-1	1	0	1	0.0
Total	2	1	3	.250	25	1	0	0	0	64²	57	0	31	16	12.7	3.06	90	.247	.343	0	.000	-2	-2	-2	1	-0.2

■ BARRY LATMAN   Latman, Arnold Barry b: 5/21/36, Los Angeles, Cal. BR/TR, 6'3", 210 lbs. Deb: 9/10/57

YEAR	TM/L	W	L	PCT	G	GS	CG	SH	SV	IP	H	HR	BB	SO	RAT	ERA	ERA+	OAV	OOB	BH	AVG	PB	PR	/A	PD	TPI
1957	Chi-A	1	2	.333	7	2	0	0	1	12¹	14	2	13	9	19.0	8.03	47	.267	.441	0	.000	-0	-6	-6	0	-0.5
1958	Chi-A	3	0	1.000	13	3	1	1	0	47²	27	1	17	29	8.5	0.76	481	.162	.243	1	.083	-0	16	15	-1	1.6
1959	Chi-A	8	5	.615	37	21	5	2	0	156	138	15	72	97	12.3	3.75	100	.235	.323	6	.128	-1	2	0	-3	-0.3
1960	Cle-A	7	7	.500	31	20	4	0	0	147¹	146	19	72	94	13.7	4.03	93	.258	.348	9	.220	1	-3	-5	-1	-0.4

YEAR	TM/L	W	L	PCT	G	GS	CG	SH	SV	IP	H	HR	BB	SO	RAT	ERA	ERA+	OAV	OOB	BH	AVG	PB	PR	/A	PD	TPI
1961	Cle-A	13	5	.722	45	18	4	2	5	176²	163	23	54	108	11.3	4.02	98	.244	.306	4	.073	-3	-0	-2	-3	-0.7
1962	Cle-A	8	13	.381	45	21	7	1	5	179¹	179	23	72	117	12.8	4.17	93	.261	.336	10	.189	2	-4	-6	-1	-0.4
1963	Cle-A	7	12	.368	38	21	4	2	2	149¹	146	23	52	133	12.3	4.94	73	.257	.325	8	.182	2	-22	-22	2	-1.7
1964	LA-A	6	10	.375	40	18	2	1	2	138	128	15	52	81	12.2	3.85	85	.244	.321	5	.125	-1	-3	-9	-1	-1.0
1965	Cal-A	1	1	.500	18	0	0	0	0	31²	30	3	16	18	13.1	2.84	120	.254	.343	0	.000	-0	2	2	1	0.1
1966	Hou-N	2	7	.222	31	9	1	1	1	103	88	5	35	74	11.4	2.71	126	.233	.310	4	.154	0	10	8	-0	0.8
1967	Hou-N	3	6	.333	39	1	0	0	0	77²	73	13	34	70	13.1	4.52	73	.252	.342	1	.091	-1	-10	-10	0	-1.1
Total	11	59	68	.465	344	134	28	10	16	1219	1130	142	489	829	12.3	3.91	94	.246	.325	48	.145	-1	-17	-34	-9	-3.6

■ **BILL LATTIMORE**   Lattimore, William Hershel "Slothful Bill" b: 5/25/1884, Roxton, Tex. d: 10/30/19, Colorado Springs, Colo. BL/TL, 5'9", 165 lbs. Deb: 4/17/08

| 1908 | Cle-A | 1 | 2 | .333 | 4 | 4 | 1 | 1 | 0 | 24 | 24 | 0 | 7 | 5 | 11.6 | 4.50 | 53 | .247 | .298 | 4 | .444 | 1 | -6 | -6 | -1 | -0.4 |

■ **CHUCK LAUER**   Lauer, John Charles b: 1865, Pittsburgh, Pa. TR , Deb: 7/17/1884 ♦

| 1884 | Pit-a | 0 | 2 | .000 | 3 | 3 | 2 | 0 | 0 | 19 | 23 | 0 | 9 | 8 | 15.2 | 7.58 | 44 | .284 | .355 | 5 | .114 | -1 | -9 | -9 | -1 | -0.6 |

■ **GEORGE LAUZERIQUE**   Lauzerique, George Albert b: 7/22/47, Havana, Cuba BR/TR, 6'1", 180 lbs. Deb: 9/17/67

1967	KC-A	0	2	.000	3	2	0	0	0	16	11	2	6	10	10.1	2.25	142	.193	.281	0	.000	-0	2	2	0	0.2
1968	Oak-A	0	0	—	1	0	0	0	0	1	0	0	1	0	9.0	0.00	—	.000	.333	0	—	0	0	0	0	0.1
1969	Oak-A	3	4	.429	19	8	1	0	0	61¹	58	14	27	39	12.8	4.70	73	.250	.333	2	.100	-1	-7	-9	1	-0.8
1970	Mil-A	1	2	.333	11	4	1	0	0	35	41	7	14	24	14.4	6.94	55	.295	.364	2	.200	1	-13	-12	-0	-1.0
Total	4	4	8	.333	34	14	2	0	0	113¹	110	23	48	73	12.9	5.00	70	.256	.336	4	.121	-0	-18	-19	1	-1.5

■ **GARY LAVELLE**   Lavelle, Gary Robert b: 1/3/49, Scranton, Pa. BB/TL, 6'2", 190 lbs. Deb: 9/10/74

1974	SF-N	0	3	.000	10	0	0	0	0	16²	14	1	10	12	13.0	2.16	176	.222	.329	0	.000	-0	3	3	-0	0.3
1975	SF-N	6	3	.667	65	0	0	0	8	82¹	80	3	48	51	14.3	2.95	129	.260	.365	1	.111	-0	6	8	0	0.8
1976	SF-N	10	6	.625	65	0	0	0	12	110¹	102	6	52	71	12.7	2.69	135	.246	.333	1	.077	-1	10	11	-2	1.0
1977	SF-N	7	7	.500	73	0	0	0	20	118¹	106	4	37	93	10.9	2.05	190	.239	.298	0	.000	-2	24	24	0	2.4
1978	SF-N	13	10	.565	67	0	0	0	14	97²	96	3	44	63	13.1	3.32	140	.263	.345	1	.067	-1	3	1	0	0.1
1979	SF-N	7	9	.438	70	0	0	0	20	96²	86	5	42	80	12.1	2.51	139	.247	.332	1	.250	1	13	11	-0	1.1
1980	SF-N	6	8	.429	62	0	0	0	9	100	106	4	36	66	12.8	3.42	103	.275	.336	0	.000	-1	2	1	0	0.0
1981	SF-N	2	6	.250	34	0	0	0	4	65²	58	3	23	45	11.4	3.84	89	.244	.316	3	.273	1	-3	-3	1	0.0
1982	SF-N	10	7	.588	68	0	0	0	8	104²	97	6	29	76	10.9	2.67	135	.247	.300	2	.154	0	11	11	2	1.3
1983	SF-N	7	4	.636	56	0	0	0	20	87	73	4	19	68	9.5	2.59	137	.229	.272	0	.000	-1	10	9	2	1.0
1984	SF-N	5	4	.556	77	0	0	0	12	101	92	5	42	71	12.0	2.76	127	.246	.324	0	.000	-0	9	8	-1	0.8
1985	*Tor-A	5	7	.417	69	0	0	0	8	72²	54	5	36	50	11.1	3.10	136	.214	.313	0	—	0	8	9	-0	0.9
1987	Tor-A	2	3	.400	23	0	0	0	1	27²	36	2	19	17	17.9	5.53	81	.313	.410	0	—	0	-3	-3	1	-0.2
	Oak-A	0	0	—	6	0	0	0	0	4¹	4	0	3	6	14.5	8.31	50	.267	.389	0	—	0	-2	-2	0	-0.1
	Yr	2	3	.400	29	0	0	0	1	32	40	2	22	23	17.4	5.91	75	.305	.405	0	—	0	-5	-5	1	-0.3
Total	13	80	77	.510	745	3	0	0	136	1085	1004	51	440	769	12.1	2.93	125	.249	.325	9	.081	-6	92	89	3	9.4

■ **JIMMY LAVENDER**   Lavender, James Sanford b: 3/25/1884, Barnesville, Ga. d: 1/12/60, Cartersville, Ga. BR/TR, 5'11", 165 lbs. Deb: 4/23/12

1912	Chi-N	16	13	.552	42	31	15	3	3	251²	240	8	89	109	12.1	3.04	110	.251	.321	13	.149	-3	10	8	1	0.5
1913	Chi-N	10	14	.417	40	20	10	0	2	204	206	6	98	91	14.0	3.66	87	.267	.359	8	.118	-4	-10	-11	-2	-1.7
1914	Chi-N	11	11	.500	37	28	11	2	0	214¹	191	11	87	87	12.1	3.07	91	.247	.331	11	.175	2	-7	-7	3	-0.1
1915	Chi-N	10	16	.385	41	24	13	1	4	220	178	5	67	117	10.4	2.58	118	.228	.298	9	.134	-2	4	5	3	0.6
1916	Chi-N	10	14	.417	36	25	9	4	2	188	163	3	62	91	11.2	2.82	103	.240	.312	8	.151	-2	-4	2	-1	0.0
1917	Phi-N	6	8	.429	28	14	7	0	1	129¹	119	5	44	52	11.6	3.55	79	.250	.317	5	.139	-1	-12	-11	-2	-1.4
Total	6	63	76	.453	224	142	65	10	12	1207¹	1097	38	447	547	11.9	3.09	97	.247	.324	54	.144	-9	-19	-12	2	-2.1

■ **RON LAW**   Law, Ronald David b: 3/14/46, Hamilton, Ont., Can. BR/TR, 6'2", 165 lbs. Deb: 6/29/69

| 1969 | Cle-A | 3 | 4 | .429 | 35 | 1 | 0 | 0 | 1 | 52¹ | 68 | 2 | 34 | 29 | 17.9 | 4.99 | 76 | .325 | .424 | 1 | .143 | -0 | -8 | -7 | 0 | -0.6 |

■ **VANCE LAW**   Law, Vance Aaron b: 10/1/56, Boise, Idaho BR/TR, 6'2", 185 lbs. Deb: 6/01/80 ♦

1986	Mon-N	0	0	—	3	0	0	0	0	4	3	0	2	0	11.3	2.25	164	.214	.313	81	.225	1	1	1	0	0.1
1987	Mon-N	0	0	—	3	0	0	0	0	3¹	5	0	0	2	13.5	5.40	78	.333	.333	119	.273	1	-0	-0	0	0.0
Total	2	0	0	—	6	0	0	0	0	7¹	8	0	2	2	12.3	3.68	106	.276	.323	944	.257	2	0	0	0	0.1

■ **VERN LAW**   Law, Vernon Sanders "Deacon" b: 3/12/30, Meridian, Idaho BR/TR, 6'2", 195 lbs. Deb: 6/11/50 C

1950	Pit-N	7	9	.438	27	17	5	1	0	128	137	11	49	57	13.4	4.92	89	.272	.341	3	.073	-2	-11	-8	-2	-1.0
1951	Pit-N	6	9	.400	28	14	2	1	2	114	109	9	51	41	13.1	4.50	94	.253	.341	11	.344	-3	-7	-3	-1	0.1
1954	Pit-N	9	13	.409	39	18	7	0	3	161²	201	20	56	57	14.5	5.51	76	.311	.368	12	.231	4	-26	-24	-1	-1.8
1955	Pit-N	10	10	.500	43	24	8	1	1	200²	221	19	61	82	12.7	3.81	108	.280	.333	16	.254	3	5	7	1	1.1
1956	Pit-N	8	16	.333	39	32	6	0	2	195²	218	24	49	60	12.6	4.32	87	.281	.329	10	.175	1	-12	-12	0	-1.0
1957	Pit-N	10	8	.556	31	25	9	3	1	172²	172	18	32	55	10.7	2.87	132	.256	.291	12	.190	1	19	18	-1	1.8
1958	Pit-N	14	12	.538	35	29	6	1	3	202¹	235	16	39	56	12.2	3.96	98	.297	.331	12	.194	6	-0	-2	0	0.4
1959	Pit-N	18	9	.667	34	33	20	2	1	266	245	25	53	110	10.2	2.98	130	.243	.282	16	.167	1	29	26	1	3.0
1960	*Pit-N	20	9	.690	35	35	**18**	3	0	271²	266	25	40	120	10.3	3.08	122	.257	.287	17	.181	3	21	20	2	2.7
1961	Pit-N	3	4	.429	11	10	1	0	0	59¹	72	10	18	20	13.8	4.70	85	.305	.357	5	.263	1	-4	-5	-1	-0.1
1962	Pit-N	10	7	.588	23	20	7	2	0	139¹	156	21	27	78	11.9	3.94	100	.276	.310	14	.311	5	0	-0	1	0.6
1963	Pit-N	4	5	.444	18	12	1	1	0	76²	91	11	13	31	12.2	4.93	67	.296	.325	5	.217	1	-14	-14	2	-1.1
1964	Pit-N	12	13	.480	35	29	7	5	0	192	203	18	32	93	11.1	3.61	97	.270	.300	19	.311	8	-2	-2	1	0.7
1965	Pit-N	17	9	.654	29	28	13	4	0	217¹	182	17	35	101	9.1	2.15	163	.229	.264	20	.244	4	33	33	1	4.4
1966	Pit-N	12	8	.600	31	28	8	4	0	177²	203	19	24	88	11.7	4.05	88	.292	.320	16	.242	5	-9	-9	2	-0.2
1967	Pit-N	2	6	.250	25	10	1	0	0	97	122	5	18	43	13.1	4.18	81	.308	.340	3	.111	-0	-9	-9	-0	-0.9
Total	16	162	147	.524	483	364	119	28	13	2672	2833	268	597	1092	11.7	3.77	101	.272	.314	191	.216	45	14	15	7	8.7

■ **BROOKS LAWRENCE**   Lawrence, Brooks Ulysses "Bull" b: 1/30/25, Springfield, Ohio BR/TR, 6', 205 lbs. Deb: 6/24/54

1954	StL-N	15	6	.714	35	18	8	0	1	158²	141	17	72	72	12.5	3.74	110	.243	.335	10	.189	0	6	6	0	0.7
1955	StL-N	3	8	.273	46	10	2	1	1	96	102	11	58	52	15.7	6.56	62	.278	.387	2	.095	-2	-27	-27	1	-2.5
1956	Cin-N	19	10	.655	49	30	11	1	0	218²	210	26	71	96	11.6	3.99	100	.256	.317	11	.157	-1	-5	-0	3	0.3
1957	Cin-N	16	13	.552	49	32	12	1	4	250¹	234	26	76	121	11.4	3.52	117	.247	.309	14	.171	-0	10	16	-0	1.7
1958	Cin-N	8	13	.381	46	23	6	2	5	181	194	12	55	74	12.6	4.13	100	.275	.331	6	.113	-2	-4	-0	-0	0.0
1959	Cin-N	7	12	.368	43	14	3	0	10	128¹	144	17	45	64	13.5	4.77	85	.281	.344	6	.150	-1	-12	-10	0	-1.0
1960	Cin-N	1	0	1.000	7	0	0	0	1	7	9	1	8	2	20.0	10.57	36	.310	.459	0	—	0	-6	-6	0	-0.4
Total	7	69	62	.527	275	127	42	5	22	1040²	1034	110	385	481	12.6	4.25	96	.261	.332	49	.154	-5	-38	-20	5	-1.2

■ **BOB LAWRENCE**   Lawrence, Robert Andrew "Larry" b: 12/14/1899, Brooklyn, N.Y. d: 11/6/83, Jamaica, N.Y. BR/TR, 5'11", 180 lbs. Deb: 7/19/24

| 1924 | Chi-A | 0 | 0 | — | 1 | 0 | 0 | 0 | 0 | 1 | 1 | 0 | 1 | 1 | 18.0 | 9.00 | 46 | .250 | .400 | 0 | — | 0 | -1 | -1 | 0 | 0.0 |

■ **AL LAWSON**   Lawson, Alfred William b: 3/24/1869, London, England d: 11/29/54, San Antonio, Tex. BR/TR, 5'11", 161 lbs. Deb: 5/13/1890

1890	Bos-N	0	1	.000	1	1	1	0	0	9	12	1	4	0	16.0	4.00	94	.311	.376	0	.000	-0	-0	-0	0	0.0
	Pit-N	0	2	.000	2	2	1	0	0	10	15	0	10	2	22.5	9.00	37	.337	.458	0	.000	-1	-6	-6	0	-0.4
	Yr	0	3	.000	3	3	2	0	0	19	27	0	14	3	19.4	6.63	53	.325	.422	1	.167	-1	-6	-7	0	-0.4

YEAR	TM/L	W	L	PCT	G	GS	CG	SH	SV	IP	H	HR	BB	SO	RAT	ERA	ERA+	OAV	OOB	BH	AVG	PB	PR	/A	PD	TPI

■ ROXIE LAWSON Lawson, Alfred Voyle b: 4/13/06, Donnellson, Iowa d: 4/9/77, Stockport, Iowa BR/TR, 6', 170 lbs. Deb: 8/03/30

1930	Cle-A	1	2	.333	7	4	2	0	0	33²	46	1	23	10	18.4	6.15	79	.324	.418	1	.091	-1	-6	-5	0	-0.4
1931	Cle-A	0	2	.000	17	3	0	0	0	55²	72	5	36	20	17.5	7.60	61	.304	.396	2	.143	-0	-20	-18	-1	-1.6
1933	Det-A	0	1	.000	4	2	0	0	0	16	17	2	17	6	19.1	7.31	59	.270	.425	0	.000	-1	-5	-5	0	-0.3
1935	Det-A	3	1	.750	7	4	4	2	2	40	34	3	24	16	13.0	1.57	265	.233	.341	4	.308	1	13	12	-1	1.2
1936	Det-A	8	6	.571	41	8	3	0	3	128	139	13	71	34	15.0	5.48	90	.281	.376	10	.222	1	-6	-8	1	-0.4
1937	Det-A	18	7	.720	37	29	15	0	1	217¹	236	17	115	68	14.6	5.26	89	.271	.357	21	.259	3	-15	-14	-1	-1.0
1938	Det-A	8	9	.471	27	16	5	0	1	127	154	13	82	39	16.7	5.46	92	.299	.395	2	.044	-5	-9	-6	1	-0.9
1939	Det-A	1	1	.500	2	1	0	0	0	11¹	7	1	7	4	11.1	4.76	103	.167	.286	0	.000	-1	-0	0	0	0.0
	StL-A	3	7	.300	36	14	5	0	0	150²	181	10	83	43	15.9	5.32	92	.307	.394	8	.186	-1	-12	-8	-0	-0.7
	Yr	4	8	.333	38	15	5	0	0	162	188	11	90	47	15.6	5.28	92	.297	.387	0	.000	-2	-12	-7	0	-0.7
1940	StL-A	5	3	.625	30	2	0	0	4	72	77	5	54	18	16.4	5.13	89	.278	.396	1	.045	-3	-6	-4	0	-0.6
Total	9	47	39	.547	208	83	34	2	11	851²	963	70	512	258	15.7	5.37	89	.285	.380	49	.173	-7	-67	-57	-0	-4.8

■ BOB LAWSON Lawson, Robert Baker b: 8/23/1876, Brookneal, Va. d: 10/28/52, Chapel Hill, N.C. BR/TR, 5'10", 170 lbs. Deb: 5/07/01

1901	Bos-N	2	2	.500	6	4	4	0	0	46	45	1	28	12	14.7	3.33	109	.254	.363	4	.148	-0	-0	1	1	0.2
1902	Bal-A	0	2	.000	3	2	1	0	0	13	21	0	3	5	16.6	4.85	78	.363	.394	1	.167	-0	-2	-2	1	0.0
Total	2	2	4	.333	9	6	5	0	0	59	66	0	31	17	15.1	3.66	100	.281	.370	5	.152	-1	-2	-0	1	0.2

■ STEVE LAWSON Lawson, Steven George b: 12/28/50, Oakland, Cal. BR/TL, 6'1", 175 lbs. Deb: 8/03/72

| 1972 | Tex-A | 0 | 0 | — | 13 | 0 | 0 | 0 | 1 | 16 | 13 | 1 | 10 | 13 | 12.9 | 2.81 | 107 | .213 | .324 | 1 | 1.000 | 0 | 0 | 0 | -0 | 0.1 |

■ BILL LAXTON Laxton, William Harry b: 1/5/48, Camden, N.J. BL/TL, 6'1", 190 lbs. Deb: 9/15/70

1970	Phi-N	0	0	—	2	0	0	0	0	2	2	2	2	2	22.5	13.50	30	.250	.455	0	—	0	-2	-2	0	-0.1
1971	SD-N	0	2	.000	18	0	0	0	0	27²	32	4	26	23	19.2	6.83	48	.305	.447	0	—	0	-10	-11	0	-1.0
1974	SD-N	0	1	.000	30	1	0	0	0	44²	37	5	38	40	15.7	4.03	88	.226	.380	1	.200	0	-2	-2	-1	-0.2
1976	Det-A	0	5	.000	26	3	0	0	2	94²	77	13	51	74	12.7	4.09	91	.221	.331	0	—	0	-6	-4	-2	-0.5
1977	Sea-A	3	2	.600	43	0	0	0	3	72²	62	10	39	49	13.0	4.95	83	.233	.340	0	—	0	-7	-7	-1	-0.7
	Cle-A	0	0	—	2	0	0	0	0	1²	2	0	2	1	21.6	5.40	73	.286	.444	0	—	0	-0	-0	0	-0.0
	Yr	3	2	.600	45	0	0	0	3	74¹	64	10	41	50	12.7	4.96	83	.228	.326	0	—	0	-7	-7	-1	-0.7
Total	5	3	10	.231	121	4	0	0	5	243¹	212	34	158	189	14.2	4.73	79	.236	.359	1	.200	0	-28	-26	-4	-2.5

■ TIM LAYANA Layana, Timothy Joseph b: 3/2/64, Inglewood, Cal. BR/TR, 6'2", 195 lbs. Deb: 4/09/90

| 1990 | Cin-N | 5 | 3 | .625 | 55 | 0 | 0 | 0 | 2 | 80 | 71 | 7 | 44 | 53 | 13.2 | 3.49 | 111 | .244 | .347 | 0 | .000 | -1 | 3 | 3 | 0 | 0.3 |

■ DANNY LAZAR Lazar, John Dan b: 11/14/43, East Chicago, Ind. BL/TL, 6'1", 190 lbs. Deb: 6/21/68

1968	Chi-A	0	1	.000	8	1	0	0	0	13¹	14	1	4	11	12.2	4.05	75	.269	.321	0	.000	0	-2	-2	0	-0.1
1969	Chi-A	0	0	—	9	3	0	0	0	20²	21	5	11	9	14.4	6.53	59	.280	.379	0	.000	-0	-7	-6	-0	-0.6
Total	2	0	1	.000	17	4	0	0	0	34	35	6	15	20	13.5	5.56	63	.276	.357	0	.000	-0	-8	-8	-0	-0.7

■ JACK LAZORKO Lazorko, Jack Thomas b: 3/30/56, Hoboken, N.J. BR/TR, 5'11", 200 lbs. Deb: 6/04/84

1984	Mil-A	0	1	.000	15	1	0	0	1	39²	37	7	22	24	13.6	4.31	89	.245	.345	0	—	0	-1	-2	0	-0.1
1985	Sea-A	0	0	—	15	0	0	0	1	20¹	23	1	8	7	15.0	3.54	119	.291	.378	0	—	0	1	2	1	0.2
1986	Det-A	0	0	—	3	0	0	0	0	6²	8	0	4	3	16.2	4.05	102	.296	.387	0	—	0	0	0	0	0.0
1987	Cal-A	5	6	.455	26	11	2	0	0	117²	108	20	44	55	11.8	4.59	94	.248	.320	0	—	0	-2	-4	2	-0.1
1988	Cal-A	0	1	.000	10	3	0	0	0	37²	37	5	16	19	12.9	3.35	115	.255	.333	0	—	0	3	2	0	0.3
Total	5	5	8	.385	69	15	2	0	2	222	213	33	94	108	12.7	4.22	98	.254	.334	0	—	0	1	-2	3	0.3

■ CHARLIE LEA Lea, Charles William b: 12/25/56, Orleans, France BR/TR, 6'4", 194 lbs. Deb: 6/12/80

1980	Mon-N	7	5	.583	21	19	0	0	0	104	103	5	55	56	13.8	3.72	96	.262	.356	3	.081	-2	-1	-2	-1	-0.4
1981	Mon-N	5	4	.556	16	11	2	2	0	64¹	63	4	26	31	12.6	4.62	76	.268	.344	2	.133	-0	-8	-8	0	-0.8
1982	Mon-N	12	10	.545	27	27	4	2	0	177²	145	16	56	115	10.2	3.24	112	.222	.283	8	.123	-1	7	8	-1	0.6
1983	Mon-N	16	11	.593	33	33	8	4	0	222	195	15	84	137	11.4	3.12	115	.238	.309	8	.114	-2	12	11	-1	0.9
1984	Mon-N	15	10	.600	30	30	8	0	0	224¹	198	19	68	123	10.8	2.89	119	.239	.299	8	.111	-3	17	13	1	1.2
1987	Mon-N	0	1	.000	1	1	0	0	0	1	4	1	2	1	54.0	36.00	12	.571	.667	0	—	0	-4	-4	0	-0.2
1988	Min-A	7	7	.500	24	23	0	0	0	130	156	19	50	72	14.6	4.85	84	.301	.368	0	—	0	-13	-11	-0	-1.1
Total	7	62	48	.564	152	144	22	8	0	923¹	864	79	341	535	11.9	3.54	102	.250	.320	29	.112	-7	11	8	-3	0.2

■ RICK LEACH Leach, Richard Max b: 5/4/57, Ann Arbor, Mich. BL/TL, 6'1", 180 lbs. Deb: 4/30/81 ♦

| 1984 | Tor-A | 0 | 0 | — | 1 | 0 | 0 | 0 | 0 | 1 | 2 | 1 | 2 | 0 | 36.0 | 27.00 | 15 | .400 | .571 | 23 | .261 | 0 | -3 | -3 | 0 | -0.1 |

■ TERRY LEACH Leach, Terry Hester b: 3/13/54, Selma, Ala. BR/TR, 6', 215 lbs. Deb: 8/12/81

1981	NY-N	1	1	.500	21	1	0	0	0	35¹	26	2	12	16	9.7	2.55	137	.205	.273	0	.000	1	4	4	1	0.5
1982	NY-N	2	1	.667	21	1	1	1	3	45¹	46	2	18	30	12.7	4.17	87	.271	.340	1	.125	-0	-3	-3	-0	-0.2
1985	NY-N	3	4	.429	22	4	1	1	1	55²	48	3	14	30	10.2	2.91	119	.235	.288	2	.167	1	4	3	1	0.6
1986	NY-N	0	0	—	6	0	0	0	0	6²	6	0	3	4	12.2	2.70	131	.222	.300	0	—	0	1	1	0	0.1
1987	NY-N	11	1	.917	44	12	1	1	0	131¹	132	14	29	61	11.1	3.22	117	.262	.304	2	.061	-1	13	8	2	0.8
1988	*NY-N	7	2	.778	52	0	0	0	3	92	95	5	24	51	11.9	2.54	127	.268	.320	2	.143	0	9	7	2	1.0
1989	NY-N	0	0	—	10	0	0	0	0	21¹	19	1	4	2	10.1	4.22	77	.244	.289	0	.000	-0	-2	-2	1	-0.1
	KC-A	5	6	.455	30	3	0	0	0	73²	78	4	36	34	14.0	4.15	93	.278	.362	0	—	0	-2	-3	1	0.0
1990	Min-A	2	5	.286	55	0	0	0	2	81²	84	2	21	46	11.7	3.20	131	.268	.316	0	—	0	6	9	1	1.0
Total	8	31	20	.608	261	21	3	3	9	543	534	33	161	274	11.7	3.27	112	.260	.316	7	.097	-1	30	24	8	3.7

■ LUIS LEAL Leal, Luis Enrique (b: Luis Enrique Albarado (Leal)) b: 3/21/57, Barquisimeto, Venz. BR/TR, 6'3", 205 lbs. Deb: 5/25/80

1980	Tor-A	3	4	.429	13	10	1	0	0	59²	72	6	31	26	15.7	4.53	95	.314	.398	0	—	0	-3	-1	-1	-0.1
1981	Tor-A	7	13	.350	29	19	3	0	0	129²	127	8	44	71	12.2	3.68	107	.254	.321	0	—	0	-0	4	-1	0.3
1982	Tor-A	12	15	.444	38	38	10	0	0	249²	250	24	79	111	12.0	3.93	114	.262	.320	0	—	0	4	15	-0	1.5
1983	Tor-A	13	12	.520	35	35	7	1	0	217¹	216	23	65	116	11.9	4.31	100	.257	.315	0	—	0	-6	-0	0	0.0
1984	Tor-A	13	8	.619	35	35	6	2	0	222¹	221	27	77	134	12.2	3.89	105	.258	.323	0	—	0	3	5	0	0.5
1985	Tor-A	3	6	.333	15	14	0	0	0	67¹	82	13	24	33	14.6	5.75	73	.303	.366	0	—	0	-12	-12	0	-1.0
Total	6	51	58	.468	165	151	27	3	1	946	968	101	320	491	12.5	4.14	103	.265	.328	0	—	0	-15	11	-1	1.2

■ KING LEAR Lear, Charles Bernard b: 1/23/1891, Greencastle, Pa. d: 10/31/76, Greencastle, Pa. BR/TR, 6', 175 lbs. Deb: 5/02/14

1914	Cin-N	1	2	.333	17	4	3	1	1	55²	55	3	19	20	12.3	3.07	95	.271	.339	3	.188	1	-2	-1	-0	0.0
1915	Cin-N	6	10	.375	40	15	9	0	0	167²	169	7	45	46	11.8	3.01	95	.270	.324	8	.170	-1	-5	-3	-0	-0.7
Total	2	7	12	.368	57	19	12	1	1	223¹	224	10	64	66	11.9	3.02	95	.270	.328	11	.175	-0	-6	-4	-0	-0.7

■ FRANK LEARY Leary, Francis Patrick b: 2/26/1881, Wayland, Mass. d: 10/4/07, Natick, Mass. Deb: 4/30/07

| 1907 | Cin-N | 0 | 1 | .000 | 2 | 1 | 0 | 0 | 0 | 8 | 7 | 0 | 6 | 4 | 14.6 | 1.13 | 231 | .269 | .406 | 0 | .000 | -0 | 1 | 1 | 0 | 0.2 |

■ JACK LEARY Leary, John J. b: 1858, New Haven, Conn. TL, 5'11", 186 lbs. Deb: 8/21/1880 ♦

1880	Bos-N	0	1	.000	1	1	0	0	0	3	8	0	0	1	24.0	15.00	15	.467	.467	0	.000	-0	-4	-4	0	-0.3
1881	Det-N	0	2	.000	2	2	1	0	0	13	13	0	2	2	10.4	4.15	70	.249	.277	3	.273	1	-2	-2	-0	0.0
1882	Pit-a	1	0	1.000	3	2	1	0	0	18²	28	0	3	5	14.9	6.27	42	.325	.348	75	.292	1	-7	-8	-0	-0.5
	Bal-a	2	1	.667	3	3	3	0	0	26	29	1	8	2	12.8	1.38	199	.264	.314	4	.222	0	4	4	0	0.4

YEAR TM/L	W	L	PCT	G	GS	CG	SH	SV	IP	H	HR	BB	SO	RAT	ERA	ERA+	OAV	OOB	BH	AVG	PB	PR	/A	PD	TPI
Yr	3	1	.750	6	5	4	0	0	44²	57	1	11	7	13.7	3.43	79	.291	.329	5	.018	1	-4	-4	0	-0.1
1884 Alt-U	0	3	.000	3	3	2	0	0	24	31	0	2	7	12.4	5.25	63	.293	.306	3	.091	-2	-6	-5	0	-0.3
CP-U	0	2	.000	2	1	1	0	0	10	14	0	5	6	17.1	5.40	56	.310	.379	7	.175	-0	-3	-3	0	-0.1
Yr	0	5	.000	5	4	3	0	0	34	45	0	7	13	13.8	5.29	61	.298	.330	1	.014	-2	-9	-8	0	-0.4
Total 4	3	9	.250	14	12	8	0	0	94²	123	1	20	23	13.6	4.56	63	.296	.328	125	.232	-1	-18	-18	0	-0.8

■ TIM LEARY
Leary, Timothy James b: 12/23/58, Santa Monica, Cal. BR/TR, 6'3", 205 lbs. Deb: 4/12/81

YEAR TM/L	W	L	PCT	G	GS	CG	SH	SV	IP	H	HR	BB	SO	RAT	ERA	ERA+	OAV	OOB	BH	AVG	PB	PR	/A	PD	TPI
1981 NY-N	0	0	—	1	1	0	0	0	2	0	0	1	3	4.5	0.00	—	.000	.143	0	.000	-0	1	1	0	0.1
1983 NY-N	1	1	.500	2	2	1	0	0	10²	15	0	4	9	16.0	3.38	107	.319	.373	1	.333	0	0	0	0	0.1
1984 NY-N	3	3	.500	20	7	0	0	0	53²	61	2	18	29	13.6	4.02	88	.285	.346	3	.300	2	-3	-3	-1	-0.1
1985 Mil-A	1	4	.200	5	5	0	0	0	33¹	40	5	8	29	13.2	4.05	103	.296	.340	0	—	0	0	0	0	0.1
1986 Mil-A	12	12	.500	33	30	3	2	0	188¹	216	20	53	110	13.2	4.21	103	.289	.342	0	—	0	-1	3	1	0.4
1987 LA-N	3	11	.214	39	12	0	0	1	107²	121	15	36	61	13.3	4.76	83	.285	.344	7	.304	2	-8	-10	1	-0.6
1988 *LA-N	17	11	.607	35	34	9	6	0	228²	201	13	56	180	10.4	2.91	114	.234	.285	18	.269	5	14	11	1	1.8
1989 LA-N	6	7	.462	19	17	2	0	0	117¹	107	9	37	59	11.2	3.38	101	.247	.309	2	.061	-2	2	1	1	0.0
Cin-N	2	7	.222	14	14	0	0	0	89²	98	8	31	64	13.2	3.71	97	.278	.342	5	.192	2	-2	-1	0	0.1
Yr	8	14	.364	33	31	2	0	0	207	205	17	68	123	12.0	3.52	99	.259	.320	4	.068	-0	-1	-1	1	0.1
1990 NY-A	9	19	.321	31	31	6	1	0	208	202	18	78	138	12.4	4.11	97	.257	.330	0	—	0	-5	-3	2	0.0
Total 9	54	75	.419	199	153	21	9	1	1039¹	1061	90	322	682	12.2	3.79	99	.265	.324	36	.221	9	-2	-2	7	1.9

■ RAZOR LEDBETTER
Ledbetter, Ralph Overton b: 12/8/1894, Rutherford College N.C. d: 2/1/69, W.Palm Beach, Fla. BR/TR, 6'3", 190 lbs. Deb: 4/16/15

YEAR TM/L	W	L	PCT	G	GS	CG	SH	SV	IP	H	HR	BB	SO	RAT	ERA	ERA+	OAV	OOB	BH	AVG	PB	PR	/A	PD	TPI
1915 Det-A	0	0	—	1	0	0	0	0	1	1	0	0	0	9.0	0.00	—	.333	.333	0	—	0	0	0	0	0.1

■ DON LEE
Lee, Donald Edward b: 2/26/34, Globe, Ariz. BR/TR, 6'4", 205 lbs. Deb: 4/23/57

YEAR TM/L	W	L	PCT	G	GS	CG	SH	SV	IP	H	HR	BB	SO	RAT	ERA	ERA+	OAV	OOB	BH	AVG	PB	PR	/A	PD	TPI
1957 Det-A	1	3	.250	11	6	0	0	0	38²	48	6	18	19	15.6	4.66	83	.308	.383	2	.167	-0	-4	-3	-0	-0.3
1958 Det-A	0	0	—	1	0	0	0	0	2	1	1	1	0	13.5	9.00	45	.143	.333	0	—	0	-1	-1	0	0.0
1960 Was-A	8	7	.533	44	20	1	0	3	165	160	16	64	88	12.4	3.44	113	.258	.330	5	.116	-0	8	8	1	0.9
1961 Min-A	3	6	.333	37	10	4	0	3	115	93	12	35	65	10.3	3.52	120	.221	.288	2	.067	-3	6	9	2	0.9
1962 Min-A	3	3	.500	9	9	1	0	0	52	51	8	24	28	14.2	4.50	91	.256	.357	4	.211	0	-3	-2	0	-0.1
LA-A	8	8	.500	27	22	4	2	2	153¹	153	12	39	74	11.4	3.11	124	.256	.305	9	.184	-0	15	13	-1	1.1
Yr	11	11	.500	36	31	5	2	2	205¹	204	20	63	102	11.8	3.46	113	.254	.310	13	.015	0	12	10	-1	1.0
1963 LA-A	8	11	.421	40	22	3	2	1	154	148	12	51	89	12.2	3.68	93	.251	.320	7	.156	-1	-1	-4	-1	-0.5
1964 LA-A	5	4	.556	33	8	0	0	2	89¹	99	6	25	73	12.6	2.72	121	.279	.328	6	.261	2	9	6	-1	0.7
1965 Cal-A	1	0	1.000	10	0	0	0	0	14	21	4	5	12	17.4	6.43	53	.350	.409	1	.333	-1	-5	-5	-0	-0.3
Hou-N	0	0	—	7	0	0	0	0	8	8	0	3	3	13.5	3.38	99	.267	.353	0	.000	-0	0	0	0	0.0
1966 Hou-N	2	0	1.000	9	0	0	0	0	18	17	1	4	9	10.5	2.50	137	.250	.292	1	1.000	0	2	2	1	0.3
Chi-N	2	1	.667	16	0	0	0	0	19	28	3	12	7	18.9	7.11	52	.346	.430	0	—	0	-7	-7	0	-0.6
Yr	4	1	.800	25	0	0	0	0	37	45	4	16	16	14.8	4.86	73	.302	.370	0	.000	-0	-5	-5	1	-0.3
Total 9	40	44	.476	244	97	13	4	11	828¹	827	81	281	467	12.4	3.61	104	.260	.326	37	.164	-1	20	14	2	2.1

■ MARK LEE
Lee, Mark Linden b: 6/14/53, Inglewood, Cal. BR/TR, 6'4", 225 lbs. Deb: 4/23/78

YEAR TM/L	W	L	PCT	G	GS	CG	SH	SV	IP	H	HR	BB	SO	RAT	ERA	ERA+	OAV	OOB	BH	AVG	PB	PR	/A	PD	TPI
1978 SD-N	5	1	.833	56	0	0	0	2	85	74	2	36	31	11.9	3.28	101	.240	.324	0	.000	-1	3	0	2	0.2
1979 SD-N	2	4	.333	46	1	0	0	5	65	88	3	25	25	15.9	4.29	82	.332	.394	2	.333	1	-4	-6	1	-0.3
1980 Pit-N	0	1	.000	4	0	0	0	0	5²	7	0	3	2	12.7	4.76	76	.227	.320	0	—	0	-1	-1	0	0.0
1981 Pit-N	0	2	.000	12	0	0	0	2	19²	17	1	5	5	10.1	2.75	131	.233	.282	1	.500	0	2	2	1	0.4
Total 4	7	8	.467	118	1	0	0	9	175¹	184	6	69	63	13.2	3.64	94	.275	.347	3	.231	1	-0	-4	4	0.3

■ MARK LEE
Lee, Mark Owen b: 7/20/64, Williston, N.Dak. BL/TL, 6'3", 198 lbs. Deb: 9/08/88

YEAR TM/L	W	L	PCT	G	GS	CG	SH	SV	IP	H	HR	BB	SO	RAT	ERA	ERA+	OAV	OOB	BH	AVG	PB	PR	/A	PD	TPI
1988 KC-A	0	0	—	4	0	0	0	0	5	6	0	1	0	12.6	3.60	111	.300	.333	0	—	0	0	0	0	0.0
1990 Mil-A	1	0	1.000	11	0	0	0	0	21¹	20	1	4	14	10.1	2.11	179	.256	.293	0	—	0	4	4	-0	0.4
Total 2	1	0	1.000	15	0	0	0	0	26¹	26	1	5	14	10.6	2.39	160	.265	.301	0	—	0	4	4	-0	0.4

■ MIKE LEE
Lee, Michael Randall b: 5/19/41, Bell, Cal. BL/TL, 6'5", 220 lbs. Deb: 5/06/60

YEAR TM/L	W	L	PCT	G	GS	CG	SH	SV	IP	H	HR	BB	SO	RAT	ERA	ERA+	OAV	OOB	BH	AVG	PB	PR	/A	PD	TPI
1960 Cle-A	0	0	—	7	0	0	0	0	9	6	1	11	6	18.0	2.00	187	.207	.439	0	—	0	2	2	-0	0.1
1963 LA-A	1	1	.500	6	4	0	0	0	26	30	3	14	11	15.6	3.81	90	.300	.391	0	.000	-1	-1	-1	1	0.0
Total 2	1	1	.500	13	4	0	0	0	35	36	4	25	17	16.2	3.34	105	.279	.404	0	.000	-1	1	1	1	0.1

■ BOB LEE
Lee, Robert Dean "Moose" or "Horse" b: 11/26/37, Ottumwa, Iowa BR/TR, 6'3", 225 lbs. Deb: 4/15/64

YEAR TM/L	W	L	PCT	G	GS	CG	SH	SV	IP	H	HR	BB	SO	RAT	ERA	ERA+	OAV	OOB	BH	AVG	PB	PR	/A	PD	TPI
1964 LA-A	6	5	.545	64	5	0	0	19	137	87	6	58	111	9.6	1.51	217	.182	.272	0	.000	-2	**32**	27	-2	2.4
1965 Cal-A	9	7	.563	69	0	0	0	23	131¹	95	11	42	89	9.5	1.92	177	.205	.272	3	.143	1	22	22	-1	2.3
1966 Cal-A	5	4	.556	61	0	0	0	16	101²	90	8	31	46	10.8	2.74	122	.237	.297	0	.000	-0	8	7	-1	0.7
1967 LA-N	0	0	—	4	0	0	0	0	6²	6	2	3	2	13.5	5.40	57	.222	.323	0	—	0	-2	-2	0	-0.1
Cin-N	3	3	.500	27	1	0	0	2	50²	51	0	25	33	13.5	4.44	84	.262	.345	3	.375	1	-6	-4	-1	-0.3
Yr	3	3	.500	31	1	0	0	2	57¹	57	2	28	35	13.3	4.55	81	.254	.337	3	.000	1	-8	-6	-1	-0.4
1968 Cin-N	2	4	.333	44	1	0	0	3	65¹	73	4	37	34	15.3	5.10	62	.302	.396	1	.200	0	-15	-14	-1	-1.6
Total 5	25	23	.521	269	7	0	0	63	492²	402	31	196	315	11.0	2.70	125	.225	.304	7	.104	-1	40	36	-5	3.4

■ ROY LEE
Lee, Roy Edwin b: 9/28/17, Elmira, N.Y. d: 11/11/85, St.Louis, Mo. BL/TL, 5'11.5", 175 lbs. Deb: 9/23/45

YEAR TM/L	W	L	PCT	G	GS	CG	SH	SV	IP	H	HR	BB	SO	RAT	ERA	ERA+	OAV	OOB	BH	AVG	PB	PR	/A	PD	TPI
1945 NY-N	0	2	.000	3	1	0	0	0	7	8	3	3	0	14.1	11.57	34	.267	.333	0	.000	-0	-6	-6	-0	-0.5

■ TOM LEE
Lee, Thomas Frank b: 6/8/1862, Philadelphia, Pa. d: 3/4/1886, Milwaukee, Wis. Deb: 6/14/1884

YEAR TM/L	W	L	PCT	G	GS	CG	SH	SV	IP	H	HR	BB	SO	RAT	ERA	ERA+	OAV	OOB	BH	AVG	PB	PR	/A	PD	TPI
1884 Chi-N	1	4	.200	5	5	5	0	0	45¹	55	12	15	14	13.9	3.77	83	.284	.335	3	.125	-2	-4	-3	0	-0.3
Bal-U	5	8	.385	15	14	12	0	0	122	121	1	29	81	11.1	3.39	98	.242	.283	23	.280	1	-5	-1	0	0.1

■ THORNTON LEE
Lee, Thornton Starr "Lefty" b: 9/13/06, Sonoma, Cal. BL/TL, 6'3", 205 lbs. Deb: 9/19/33

YEAR TM/L	W	L	PCT	G	GS	CG	SH	SV	IP	H	HR	BB	SO	RAT	ERA	ERA+	OAV	OOB	BH	AVG	PB	PR	/A	PD	TPI
1933 Cle-A	1	1	.500	3	2	1	0	0	17¹	13	1	11	7	12.5	4.15	107	.203	.320	3	.375	1	0	1	-0	0.2
1934 Cle-A	1	1	.500	24	6	0	0	0	85²	105	8	44	41	16.0	5.04	90	.308	.392	2	.095	-1	-5	-5	0	-0.4
1935 Cle-A	7	10	.412	32	20	8	1	1	180²	179	6	71	81	12.7	4.04	112	.259	.331	12	.197	-1	8	9	2	1.0
1936 Cle-A	3	5	.375	43	8	2	0	3	127	138	7	67	49	14.7	4.89	103	.271	.358	5	.122	-2	**2**	2	0	0.2
1937 Chi-A	12	10	.545	30	25	13	2	0	204²	209	17	60	80	11.9	3.52	131	.260	.312	15	.211	1	25	25	-1	2.3
1938 Chi-A	13	12	.520	33	30	18	1	1	245¹	252	12	94	77	12.8	3.49	140	.263	.331	25	.258	6	36	**38**	-1	**4.2**
1939 Chi-A	15	11	.577	33	29	15	2	3	235	260	14	70	81	12.8	4.21	112	.285	.338	11	.165	-3	11	14	1	1.1
1940 Chi-A	12	13	.480	28	27	24	1	0	228	223	13	56	87	11.1	3.47	127	.254	.300	23	.274	4	23	24	-3	2.5
1941 Chi-A	22	11	.667	35	34	**30**	3	1	300¹	258	18	92	130	**10.6**	**2.37**	**173**	.232	**.293**	29	.254	5	**59**	**58**	-2	**6.5**
1942 Chi-A	2	6	.250	11	8	6	1	0	76	82	4	31	25	13.6	3.32	109	.278	.351	6	.200	0	3	2	-2	0.1
1943 Chi-A	5	9	.357	19	19	7	1	0	127	129	8	50	35	13.0	4.18	80	.266	.340	4	.071	-4	-12	-12	-2	-1.8
1944 Chi-A	3	9	.250	15	14	6	0	0	113¹	105	3	25	39	10.4	3.02	114	.246	.290	4	.095	-3	5	5	2	0.4
1945 Chi-A	15	12	.556	29	28	19	1	0	228¹	208	6	76	108	11.6	2.44	136	.245	.314	14	.179	-1	23	22	-2	2.1
1946 Chi-A	4	4	.333	7	7	2	0	0	43¹	39	1	23	13	13.1	3.53	97	.244	.342	4	.267	-1	-0	-1	-0	0.0
1947 Chi-A	3	7	.300	21	11	2	1	1	86²	86	5	56	57	15.0	4.47	82	.261	.372	6	.207	0	-7	-8	2	-0.7
1948 NY-N	1	3	.250	11	4	1	0	0	32²	41	3	12	17	14.9	4.41	89	.304	.365	1	.091	-1	-2	-2	0	-0.1
Total 16	117	124	.485	374	272	155	14	10	2331¹	2327	121	838	937	12.4	3.56	119	.260	.326	167	.200	1	169	172	-6	17.6

■ BILL LEE
Lee, William Crutcher "Big Bill" b: 10/21/09, Plaquemine, La. d: 6/15/77, Plaquemine, La. BR/TR, 6'3", 195 lbs. Deb: 4/29/34

YEAR TM/L	W	L	PCT	G	GS	CG	SH	SV	IP	H	HR	BB	SO	RAT	ERA	ERA+	OAV	OOB	BH	AVG	PB	PR	/A	PD	TPI
1934 *Chi-N	13	14	.481	35	29	16	4	1	214¹	218	9	74	104	12.3	3.40	114	.263	.325	10	.132	-2	16	11	1	1.0

YEAR TM/L	W	L	PCT	G	GS	CG	SH	SV	IP	H	HR	BB	SO	RAT	ERA	ERA+	OAV	OOB	BH	AVG	PB	PR	/A	PD	TPI
1935 *Chi-N	20	6	**.769**	39	32	18	3	1	252	241	11	84	100	11.8	2.96	133	.251	.314	24	.235	2	30	27	-0	2.9
1936 Chi-N	18	11	.621	43	33	20	4	1	258²	238	14	93	102	11.6	3.31	121	.246	.314	12	.138	-3	21	19	1	1.7
1937 Chi-N	14	15	.483	42	33	17	2	3	272¹	289	14	73	108	12.0	3.54	113	.273	.320	15	.172	-1	11	13	3	1.6
1938 *Chi-N	**22**	9	**.710**	44	37	19	**9**	2	291	281	18	74	121	11.0	**2.66**	**144**	.252	.299	20	.198	1	**37**	**38**	1	**4.2**
1939 Chi-N	19	15	.559	37	36	20	1	0	282¹	295	18	85	105	12.1	3.44	114	.272	.325	13	.126	-4	15	16	5	1.6
1940 Chi-N	9	17	.346	37	30	9	1	0	211¹	246	12	70	70	13.5	5.03	75	.294	.350	10	.132	-2	-28	-30	-0	-3.1
1941 Chi-N	8	14	.364	28	22	12	0	1	167¹	179	6	43	62	12.0	3.76	93	.270	.316	11	.186	1	-2	-5	1	-0.2
1942 Chi-N	13	13	.500	32	30	18	1	0	219²	221	4	67	75	11.8	3.85	83	.258	.312	11	.159	1	-13	-16	1	-1.4
1943 Chi-N	3	7	.300	13	12	4	0	0	78¹	83	4	27	18	12.6	3.56	94	.273	.332	7	.269	1	-2	-2	-1	-0.1
Phi-N	1	5	.167	13	7	2	0	3	60²	70	4	21	17	13.6	4.60	73	.298	.358	1	.059	-2	-8	-8	-1	-1.0
Yr	4	12	.250	26	19	6	0	3	139	153	8	48	35	13.1	4.01	84	.284	.344	2	.047	-0	-10	-10	-1	-1.1
1944 Phi-N	10	11	.476	31	28	11	3	1	208¹	199	9	57	50	11.2	3.15	115	.248	.300	14	.194	-0	11	11	2	1.3
1945 Phi-N	3	6	.333	13	13	2	0	0	77¹	107	0	30	13	15.9	4.66	82	.318	.374	4	.167	-1	-7	-7	1	-0.6
Bos-N	6	3	.667	16	13	6	1	0	106¹	112	6	36	12	12.5	2.79	137	.279	.338	4	.129	-1	12	12	1	1.3
Yr	9	9	.500	29	26	8	1	0	183²	219	6	66	25	14.0	3.58	107	.297	.354	5	.091	-1	5	5	2	0.7
1946 Bos-N	10	9	.526	25	21	8	0	0	140	148	7	45	32	12.5	4.18	82	.273	.330	8	.170	-1	-12	-12	2	-1.0
1947 Chi-N	0	2	.000	14	2	0	0	0	24	26	2	14	9	15.4	4.50	88	.268	.366	1	.333	0	-1	-1	0	0.0
Total 14	169	157	.518	462	378	182	29	13	2864	2953	138	893	998	12.2	3.54	106	.266	.322	165	.168	-10	78	66	17	8.2

■ BILL LEE

Lee, William Francis b: 12/28/46, Burbank, Cal. BL/TL, 6'3", 205 lbs. Deb: 6/25/69

YEAR TM/L	W	L	PCT	G	GS	CG	SH	SV	IP	H	HR	BB	SO	RAT	ERA	ERA+	OAV	OOB	BH	AVG	PB	PR	/A	PD	TPI
1969 Bos-A	1	3	.250	20	1	0	0	0	52	56	9	28	45	14.9	4.50	84	.281	.376	0	.000	-1	-5	-4	-1	-0.5
1970 Bos-A	2	2	.500	11	5	0	0	1	37	48	3	14	19	15.1	4.62	86	.320	.378	0	.000	-1	-4	-3	1	-0.2
1971 Bos-A	9	2	.818	47	3	0	0	2	102	102	7	46	74	13.1	2.74	135	.256	.335	5	.217	0	8	11	0	1.3
1972 Bos-A	7	4	.636	47	0	0	0	5	84¹	75	5	32	43	11.5	3.20	100	.248	.322	3	.188	1	-1	0	3	0.5
1973 Bos-A	17	11	.607	38	33	18	1	1	284²	275	20	76	120	11.3	2.75	146	.257	.309	0	—	0	34	40	2	4.6
1974 Bos-A	17	15	.531	38	37	16	1	0	282¹	320	25	67	95	12.5	3.51	110	.290	.333	0	—	0	3	11	4	1.6
1975 *Bos-A	17	9	.654	41	34	17	4	0	260	274	20	69	78	12.0	3.95	103	.273	.322	0	—	0	-5	4	2	0.6
1976 Bos-A	5	7	.417	24	14	1	0	3	96	124	13	28	29	14.5	5.63	70	.307	.356	0	—	0	-22	-18	1	-1.7
1977 Bos-A	9	5	.643	27	16	4	0	1	128	155	14	29	31	12.9	4.43	101	.306	.344	0	—	0	-5	1	2	0.3
1978 Bos-A	10	10	.500	28	24	8	1	0	177	198	20	59	44	13.2	3.46	119	.285	.343	0	—	0	6	13	1	1.4
1979 Mon-N	16	10	.615	33	33	6	3	0	222	230	20	46	59	11.2	3.04	121	.265	.303	16	.216	2	17	15	2	2.0
1980 Mon-N	4	6	.400	24	18	2	0	0	118	156	13	22	34	13.8	4.96	72	.319	.352	9	.220	1	-18	-18	0	-1.6
1981 *Mon-N	5	6	.455	31	7	0	0	6	88²	90	6	14	34	10.8	2.94	119	.265	.298	8	.364	3	5	5	3	1.3
1982 Mon-N	0	0	—	7	0	0	0	0	12¹	19	1	1	8	14.6	4.38	83	.352	.364	0	—	0	-1	-1	0	0.0
Total 14	119	90	.569	416	225	72	10	19	1944¹	2122	176	531	713	12.4	3.62	107	.280	.329	41	.208	5	12	55	21	9.6

■ WATTY LEE

Lee, Wyatt Arnold b: 8/12/1879, Lynch's Station, Va. d: 3/6/36, Washington, D.C. TL, 5'10.5", 171 lbs. Deb: 4/30/01 ♦

YEAR TM/L	W	L	PCT	G	GS	CG	SH	SV	IP	H	HR	BB	SO	RAT	ERA	ERA+	OAV	OOB	BH	AVG	PB	PR	/A	PD	TPI
1901 Was-A	16	16	.500	36	33	25	2	0	262	328	14	45	63	12.8	4.40	83	.303	.330	33	.256	4	-21	-21	2	-1.2
1902 Was-A	5	7	.417	13	10	10	0	0	98	118	5	20	24	12.7	5.05	73	.298	.332	100	.256	3	-16	-15	1	-1.2
1903 Was-A	8	12	.400	22	20	15	2	0	166²	169	5	40	70	11.3	3.08	102	.262	.305	48	.208	2	-2	1	2	0.1
1904 Pit-N	1	2	.333	5	3	1	0	0	22²	34	0	9	5	18.3	8.74	31	.337	.407	4	.333	1	-15	-15	0	-1.1
Total 4	30	37	.448	76	66	51	4	0	549¹	649	24	114	162	12.5	4.29	81	.292	.327	185	.242	10	-55	-50	5	-3.4

■ SAM LEEVER

Leever, Samuel "Deacon" or "The Goshen Schoolmaster"
b: 12/23/1871, Goshen, Ohio d: 5/19/53, Goshen, Ohio BR/TR, 5'10.5", 175 lbs. Deb: 5/26/1898

YEAR TM/L	W	L	PCT	G	GS	CG	SH	SV	IP	H	HR	BB	SO	RAT	ERA	ERA+	OAV	OOB	BH	AVG	PB	PR	/A	PD	TPI
1898 Pit-N	1	0	1.000	5	3	2	0	0	33	26	0	5	15	8.5	2.45	145	.215	.247	3	.250	0	4	4	-0	0.4
1899 Pit-N	21	23	.477	51	39	35	4	3	379	353	7	122	121	11.3	3.18	120	.247	.306	33	.226	3	28	27	1	2.9
1900 *Pit-N	15	13	.536	30	29	25	3	0	232²	236	2	48	84	11.0	2.71	134	.263	.300	18	.205	0	26	24	-1	2.2
1901 Pit-N	14	5	.737	21	20	18	2	0	176	182	2	39	82	11.6	2.86	114	.265	.310	13	.183	-1	9	8	1	0.9
1902 Pit-N	15	7	.682	28	26	23	4	2	222	203	2	31	86	9.7	2.39	114	.243	.276	16	.178	-0	10	9	-3	0.5
1903 *Pit-N	25	7	**.781**	36	34	30	7	1	284¹	255	2	60	90	10.1	**2.06**	**157**	.238	.282	19	.165	-3	38	37	-0	3.4
1904 Pit-N	18	11	.621	34	32	26	1	0	253¹	224	2	54	63	10.1	2.17	127	.237	.282	26	.263	6	16	16	-0	2.4
1905 Pit-N	20	5	**.800**	33	29	20	3	1	230	199	3	54	81	10.4	2.70	111	.231	.286	9	.102	-3	8	8	0	0.4
1906 Pit-N	22	7	.759	36	31	25	6	0	260¹	232	3	47	76	9.9	2.32	115	.243	.284	20	.211	2	9	10	-5	0.9
1907 Pit-N	14	9	.609	31	24	17	5	0	216²	182	3	46	65	9.8	1.66	146	.229	.278	11	.151	-1	20	19	-5	1.5
1908 Pit-N	15	7	.682	38	20	14	4	2	192²	179	1	41	28	10.6	2.10	109	.249	.295	9	.148	-3	6	4	-3	0.1
1909 Pit-N	8	1	.889	19	4	2	0	2	70	74	0	14	23	11.8	2.83	96	.276	.322	4	.167	0	-2	-1	0	0.0
1910 Pit-N	6	5	.545	26	8	4	0	2	111	104	2	25	33	10.9	2.76	112	.259	.313	2	.065	-3	3	4	1	0.3
Total 13	194	100	.660	388	299	241	39	13	2661	2449	29	587	847	10.5	2.47	123	.245	.292	183	.184	1	175	169	-12	15.9

■ BILL LeFEBVRE

LeFebvre, Wilfrid Henry "Lefty" b: 11/11/15, Natick, R.I. BL/TL, 5'11.5", 180 lbs. Deb: 6/10/38 ♦

YEAR TM/L	W	L	PCT	G	GS	CG	SH	SV	IP	H	HR	BB	SO	RAT	ERA	ERA+	OAV	OOB	BH	AVG	PB	PR	/A	PD	TPI
1938 Bos-A	0	0	—	1	0	0	0	0	4	8	2	0	0	20.3	13.50	37	.400	.429	1	1.000	1	-4	-4	-0	-0.1
1939 Bos-A	1	1	.500	5	3	0	0	0	26¹	35	2	14	8	16.7	5.81	81	.333	.412	3	.300	1	-3	-3	-0	-0.1
1943 Was-A	2	0	1.000	6	3	1	0	0	32¹	33	3	16	10	13.6	4.45	72	.268	.353	4	.286	2	-4	-4	-0	-0.2
1944 Was-A	2	4	.333	24	4	2	0	0	69²	86	3	21	18	14.0	4.52	72	.305	.355	16	.258	3	-8	-10	-0	-0.9
Total 4	5	5	.500	36	10	3	0	0	132¹	162	10	51	36	14.6	5.03	71	.306	.369	24	.276	7	-20	-21	-1	-1.3

■ CRAIG LEFFERTS

Lefferts, Craig Lindsey b: 9/29/57, Munich, W.Germany BL/TL, 6'1", 180 lbs. Deb: 4/07/83

YEAR TM/L	W	L	PCT	G	GS	CG	SH	SV	IP	H	HR	BB	SO	RAT	ERA	ERA+	OAV	OOB	BH	AVG	PB	PR	/A	PD	TPI
1983 Chi-N	3	4	.429	56	5	0	0	1	89	80	13	29	60	11.2	3.13	121	.243	.308	2	.111	-1	5	6	0	0.6
1984 *SD-N	3	4	.429	62	0	0	0	10	105²	88	4	24	56	9.6	2.13	167	.229	.276	5	.294	1	17	17	-1	1.8
1985 SD-N	7	6	.538	60	0	0	0	2	83¹	75	7	30	48	11.3	3.35	106	.244	.312	1	.250	0	2	2	0	0.1
1986 SD-N	9	8	.529	**83**	0	0	0	4	107²	98	7	44	72	12.0	3.09	118	.253	.331	1	.125	1	7	7	2	0.9
1987 SD-N	2	2	.500	33	0	0	0	2	51¹	56	9	15	39	12.8	4.38	90	.272	.327	1	.333	0	-2	-2	-1	-0.2
*SF-N	3	3	.500	44	0	0	0	4	47¹	36	4	18	18	10.3	3.23	119	.216	.292	1	.250	0	4	3	-0	0.3
Yr	5	5	.500	77	0	0	0	6	98²	92	13	33	57	11.4	3.83	102	.245	.306	0	.000	1	3	1	-1	0.1
1988 SF-N	3	8	.273	64	0	0	0	11	92¹	74	7	23	58	9.6	2.92	112	.225	.278	0	.000	-1	5	3	-1	0.2
1989 *SF-N	2	4	.333	70	0	0	0	20	107	93	11	22	71	9.8	2.69	125	.233	.275	0	.000	-1	10	8	-1	0.6
1990 SD-N	7	5	.583	56	0	0	0	23	78²	68	10	22	60	10.4	2.52	153	.228	.283	1	.250	0	11	12	0	1.2
Total 8	39	44	.470	528	5	0	0	77	762¹	668	72	227	482	10.7	2.95	122	.238	.297	12	.162	1	60	56	-3	5.5

■ REGIS LEHENY

Leheny, Regis Francis b: 1/5/08, Pittsburgh, Pa. d: 11/2/76, Pittsburgh, Pa. BL/TL, 6'0.5", 180 lbs. Deb: 5/21/32

YEAR TM/L	W	L	PCT	G	GS	CG	SH	SV	IP	H	HR	BB	SO	RAT	ERA	ERA+	OAV	OOB	BH	AVG	PB	PR	/A	PD	TPI
1932 Bos-A	0	0	—	2	0	0	0	0	2²	5	0	3	1	27.0	16.88	27	.417	.533	0	.000	-0	-4	-4	0	-0.2

■ JIM LEHEW

Lehew, James Anthony b: 8/19/37, Baltimore, Md. BR/TR, 6', 185 lbs. Deb: 9/13/61

YEAR TM/L	W	L	PCT	G	GS	CG	SH	SV	IP	H	HR	BB	SO	RAT	ERA	ERA+	OAV	OOB	BH	AVG	PB	PR	/A	PD	TPI
1961 Bal-A	0	0	—	2	0	0	0	0	2	1	0	0	0	4.5	0.00	—	.167	.167	0	—	0	1	1	0	0.1
1962 Bal-A	0	0	—	6	0	0	0	0	9²	10	0	3	2	12.1	1.86	202	.303	.361	0	.000	-0	2	2	0	0.2
Total 2	0	0	—	8	0	0	0	0	11²	11	0	3	2	10.8	1.54	245	.282	.333	0	.000	-0	3	3	1	0.3

■ KEN LEHMAN

Lehman, Kenneth Karl b: 6/10/28, Seattle, Wash. BL/TL, 6', 170 lbs. Deb: 9/05/52

YEAR TM/L	W	L	PCT	G	GS	CG	SH	SV	IP	H	HR	BB	SO	RAT	ERA	ERA+	OAV	OOB	BH	AVG	PB	PR	/A	PD	TPI
1952 *Bro-N	1	2	.333	4	3	0	0	0	15¹	19	1	6	7	14.7	5.28	69	.297	.357	0	.000	0	-3	-3	0	-0.1
1956 Bro-N	2	3	.400	25	4	0	0	0	49¹	65	11	23	29	16.1	5.66	70	.325	.395	3	.300	1	-10	-9	1	-0.7
1957 Bro-N	0	0	—	3	0	0	0	0	7	7	0	1	1	10.3	0.00	—	.259	.286	1	.500	0	3	3	0	0.4
Bal-A	8	3	.727	30	3	1	0	6	68	57	1	22	32	10.5	2.78	129	.232	.289	4	.200	1	8	6	-0	0.7
1958 Bal-A	2	1	.667	31	1	1	0	0	62	64	5	18	36	12.2	3.48	103	.276	.333	1	.071	-1	2	1	0	0.0
1961 Phi-N	1	1	.500	41	2	0	0	1	63¹	61	6	25	27	12.4	4.26	96	.260	.333	0	.000	-1	-2	-1	1	0.0

YEAR TM/L	W	L	PCT	G	GS	CG	SH	SV	IP	H	HR	BB	SO	RAT	ERA	ERA+	OAV	OOB	BH	AVG	PB	PR	/A	PD	TPI
Total 5	14	10	.583	134	13	2	0	7	265	273	24	95	134	12.6	3.91	97	.272	.337	9	.161	1	-2	-3	2	0.3

■ NORM LEHR Lehr, Norman Carl Michael "King" b: 5/28/01, Rochester, N.Y. d: 7/17/68, Livonia, N.Y. BR/TR, 6', 168 lbs. Deb: 5/20/26

YEAR TM/L	W	L	PCT	G	GS	CG	SH	SV	IP	H	HR	BB	SO	RAT	ERA	ERA+	OAV	OOB	BH	AVG	PB	PR	/A	PD	TPI
1926 Cle-A	0	0	—	4	0	0	0	0	14^2	11	0	4	4	9.2	3.07	132	.216	.273	0	.000	-1	2	2	1	0.2

■ HANK LEIBER Leiber, Henry Edward b: 1/17/11, Phoenix, Ariz. BR/TR, 6'1.5", 205 lbs. Deb: 4/16/33 ♦

YEAR TM/L	W	L	PCT	G	GS	CG	SH	SV	IP	H	HR	BB	SO	RAT	ERA	ERA+	OAV	OOB	BH	AVG	PB	PR	/A	PD	TPI
1942 NY-N	0	1	.000	1	1	1	0	0	9	9	0	5	5	15.0	6.00	56	.290	.405	32	.218	0	-3	-3	0	-0.1

■ CHARLIE LEIBRANDT Leibrandt, Charles Louis b: 10/4/56, Chicago, Ill. BR/TL, 6'3", 195 lbs. Deb: 9/17/79

YEAR TM/L	W	L	PCT	G	GS	CG	SH	SV	IP	H	HR	BB	SO	RAT	ERA	ERA+	OAV	OOB	BH	AVG	PB	PR	/A	PD	TPI
1979 *Cin-N	0	0	—	3	0	0	0	0	4^1	2	0	2	1	8.3	0.00	—	.154	.267	0	—	0	2	2	0	0.2
1980 Cin-N	10	9	.526	36	27	5	2	0	173^2	200	15	54	62	13.3	4.25	84	.292	.346	11	.196	1	-13	-13	2	-0.9
1981 Cin-N	1	1	.500	7	4	1	1	0	30	28	0	15	9	12.9	3.60	99	.262	.352	0	.000	-0	-0	-0	0	0.0
1982 Cin-N	5	7	.417	36	11	0	0	2	107^2	130	4	48	34	15.0	5.10	73	.308	.381	2	.080	-1	-18	-17	0	-1.7
1984 *KC-A	11	7	.611	23	23	0	0	0	143^1	158	11	38	53	12.5	3.63	111	.277	.326	0	—	0	6	6	-1	0.5
1985 *KC-A	17	9	.654	33	33	8	3	0	237^2	223	17	68	108	11.1	2.69	155	.248	.302	0	—	0	38	39	4	4.6
1986 KC-A	14	11	.560	35	34	8	1	0	231^1	238	18	63	108	11.9	4.09	104	.268	.319	0	—	0	2	4	3	0.7
1987 KC-A	16	11	.593	35	35	8	3	0	240^1	235	23	74	151	11.6	3.41	134	.253	.308	0	—	0	28	31	4	3.5
1988 KC-A	13	12	.520	35	35	7	2	0	243	244	20	62	125	11.5	3.19	125	.264	.313	0	—	0	21	22	3	2.5
1989 KC-A	5	11	.313	33	27	3	1	0	161	196	13	54	73	14.1	5.14	75	.304	.360	0	—	0	-23	-23	0	-2.2
1990 Atl-N	9	11	.450	24	24	5	2	0	162^1	164	9	35	76	11.3	3.16	124	.261	.304	9	.180	1	11	14	2	1.7
Total 11	101	89	.532	300	253	45	15	2	1735	1818	130	513	800	12.2	3.71	109	.271	.325	22	.158	0	55	64	17	8.9

■ LEFTY LEIFIELD Leifield, Albert Peter b: 9/5/1883, Trenton, Ill. d: 10/10/70, Alexandria, Va. BL/TL, 6'1", 165 lbs. Deb: 9/03/05 C

YEAR TM/L	W	L	PCT	G	GS	CG	SH	SV	IP	H	HR	BB	SO	RAT	ERA	ERA+	OAV	OOB	BH	AVG	PB	PR	/A	PD	TPI
1905 Pit-N	5	2	.714	8	7	6	1	0	56	52	0	14	10	11.3	2.89	104	.248	.307	7	.350	3	1	1	1	0.5
1906 Pit-N	18	13	.581	37	31	24	8	1	255^2	214	3	68	111	10.4	1.87	143	.231	.294	11	.125	-3	22	23	1	2.4
1907 Pit-N	20	16	.556	40	33	24	6	1	286	270	1	100	112	12.0	2.33	104	.256	.328	15	.147	0	5	3	4	0.8
1908 Pit-N	15	14	.517	34	26	18	5	2	218^2	168	1	86	87	10.9	2.10	110	.212	.299	17	.227	3	6	5	-1	0.8
1909 *Pit-N	19	8	.704	32	27	13	3	0	201^2	172	4	54	43	10.4	2.37	115	.229	.286	14	.192	2	5	8	-1	1.0
1910 Pit-N	15	13	.536	40	30	13	3	2	218^1	197	6	67	64	11.3	2.64	117	.253	.320	11	.183	1	10	11	3	1.6
1911 Pit-N	16	16	.500	42	37	26	2	1	318	301	7	82	111	11.3	2.63	130	.260	.318	24	.235	6	27	28	-0	3.6
1912 Pit-N	1	2	.333	6	1	1	1	0	23^2	29	0	10	8	15.6	4.18	78	.290	.366	1	.143	-0	-2	-2	1	0.0
Chi-N	7	2	.778	13	9	4	1	0	70^2	68	0	21	23	11.7	2.42	138	.250	.311	3	.115	-1	8	7	1	0.7
Yr	8	4	.667	19	10	5	2	0	94^1	97	0	31	31	12.5	2.86	116	.259	.321	3	.091	-1	6	5	2	0.7
1913 Chi-N	0	1	.000	6	1	0	0	0	21^1	28	0	5	4	13.9	5.48	58	.329	.367	0	—	-0	-5	-5	-1	-0.5
1918 StL-A	2	6	.250	15	6	3	1	0	67	61	1	19	22	11.0	2.55	107	.252	.312	1	.053	-2	2	1	1	0.1
1919 StL-A	6	4	.600	19	9	6	2	0	92	96	4	25	18	12.2	2.93	113	.270	.325	3	.100	-3	3	4	1	0.2
1920 StL-A	0	0	—	4	0	0	0	0	9	17	0	3	2	20.0	7.00	56	.405	.444	0	.000	-0	-3	-3	-0	-0.2
Total 12	124	97	.561	296	217	138	33	7	1838	1673	27	554	616	11.3	2.47	116	.247	.312	107	.175	6	77	80	12	11.0

■ DAVE LEIPER Leiper, David Paul b: 6/18/62, Whittier, Cal. BL/TL, 6'1", 160 lbs. Deb: 9/02/84

YEAR TM/L	W	L	PCT	G	GS	CG	SH	SV	IP	H	HR	BB	SO	RAT	ERA	ERA+	OAV	OOB	BH	AVG	PB	PR	/A	PD	TPI
1984 Oak-A	1	0	1.000	8	0	0	0	0	7	12	5	2	5	21.9	9.00	42	.353	.436	0	—	0	-4	-4	0	-0.3
1986 Oak-A	2	2	.500	33	0	0	0	1	31^2	28	3	18	15	13.6	4.83	80	.252	.366	0	—	0	-2	-3	0	-0.2
1987 Oak-A	2	1	.667	45	0	0	0	1	52^1	49	6	18	33	11.7	3.78	109	.246	.312	0	—	0	4	2	1	0.3
SD-N	1	0	1.000	12	0	0	0	1	16	16	2	5	10	11.8	4.50	88	.267	.323	0	—	0	-1	-1	-0	0.0
1988 SD-N	3	0	1.000	35	0	0	0	1	54	45	1	14	33	9.8	2.17	157	.231	.282	1	.500	0	8	7	0	0.9
1989 SD-N	0	1	.000	22	0	0	0	0	28^2	40	2	20	7	19.5	5.02	70	.333	.437	0	.000	-0	-5	-5	1	-0.4
Total 5	9	4	.692	155	0	0	0	4	189^2	190	16	80	101	13.0	3.94	96	.264	.342	1	.333	0	-0	-4	2	0.3

■ JACK LEIPER Leiper, John Henry Thomas b: 12/23/1867, Chester, Pa. d: 8/23/60, West Goshen, Pa. BL/TL, 5'11", Deb: 9/04/1891

YEAR TM/L	W	L	PCT	G	GS	CG	SH	SV	IP	H	HR	BB	SO	RAT	ERA	ERA+	OAV	OOB	BH	AVG	PB	PR	/A	PD	TPI
1891 Col-a	2	2	.500	6	5	4	0	0	45	41	3	39	19	16.0	5.40	64	.234	.374	3	.143	-2	-8	-10	-0	-0.9

■ JOHN LEISTER Leister, John William b: 1/3/61, San Antonio, Tex. BR/TR, 6'2", 200 lbs. Deb: 5/28/87

YEAR TM/L	W	L	PCT	G	GS	CG	SH	SV	IP	H	HR	BB	SO	RAT	ERA	ERA+	OAV	OOB	BH	AVG	PB	PR	/A	PD	TPI
1987 Bos-A	0	2	.000	8	6	0	0	0	30^1	49	9	12	16	18.1	9.20	49	.368	.421	0	—	0	-16	-16	-0	-1.3
1990 Bos-A	0	0	—	2	1	0	0	0	5^2	7	0	4	3	17.5	4.76	86	.304	.407	0	—	0	-1	-0	-0	0.0
Total 2	0	2	.000	10	7	0	0	0	36	56	9	16	19	18.0	8.50	53	.359	.419	0	—	0	-17	-16	-0	-1.3

■ AL LEITER Leiter, Alois Terry b: 10/23/65, Toms River, N.J. BL/TL, 6'2", 200 lbs. Deb: 9/15/87

YEAR TM/L	W	L	PCT	G	GS	CG	SH	SV	IP	H	HR	BB	SO	RAT	ERA	ERA+	OAV	OOB	BH	AVG	PB	PR	/A	PD	TPI
1987 NY-A	2	2	.500	4	4	0	0	0	22^2	24	2	15	28	15.5	6.35	69	.273	.379	0	—	0	-5	-5	-0	-0.4
1988 NY-A	4	4	.500	14	14	0	0	0	57^1	49	7	33	60	13.7	3.92	100	.231	.348	0	—	0	0	0	0	0.0
1989 NY-A	1	2	.333	4	4	0	0	0	26^2	23	1	21	22	15.5	6.08	64	.235	.380	0	—	0	-6	-7	-0	-0.5
Tor-A	0	0	—	1	1	0	0	0	6^2	9	1	2	4	14.9	4.05	93	.310	.355	0	—	0	-0	-0	-0	0.0
Yr	1	2	.333	5	5	0	0	0	33^1	32	2	23	26	14.9	5.67	68	.246	.359	0	—	0	-7	-7	-1	-0.5
1990 Tor-A	0	0	—	4	0	0	0	0	6^1	1	0	2	5	4.3	0.00	—	.050	.136	0	—	0	3	3	0	0.3
Total 4	7	8	.467	27	23	0	0	0	119^2	106	11	73	119	14.0	4.66	86	.237	.353	0	—	0	-8	-9	-1	-0.6

■ MARK LEITER Leiter, Mark Edward b: 4/13/63, Joliet, Ill. BR/TR, 6'3", 200 lbs. Deb: 7/24/90

YEAR TM/L	W	L	PCT	G	GS	CG	SH	SV	IP	H	HR	BB	SO	RAT	ERA	ERA+	OAV	OOB	BH	AVG	PB	PR	/A	PD	TPI
1990 NY-A	1	1	.500	8	3	0	0	0	26^1	33	5	9	21	15.0	6.84	58	.314	.379	0	—	0	-9	-8	1	-0.6

■ BILL LEITH Leith, William "Shady Bill" b: 5/31/1873, Matteawan, N.Y. d: 7/16/40, Beacon, N.Y. Deb: 9/25/1899

YEAR TM/L	W	L	PCT	G	GS	CG	SH	SV	IP	H	HR	BB	SO	RAT	ERA	ERA+	OAV	OOB	BH	AVG	PB	PR	/A	PD	TPI
1899 Was-N	0	0	—	1	0	0	0	0	2	4	0	2	1	27.0	18.00	22	.413	.513	0	.000	-0	-3	-3	-0	-0.2

■ DOC LEITNER Leitner, George Aloysius b: 9/14/1865, Piermont, N.Y. d: 5/18/37, New York, N.Y. BR/TR, 5'11.5", 185 lbs. Deb: 8/10/1887

YEAR TM/L	W	L	PCT	G	GS	CG	SH	SV	IP	H	HR	BB	SO	RAT	ERA	ERA+	OAV	OOB	BH	AVG	PB	PR	/A	PD	TPI
1887 Ind-N	2	6	.250	8	8	8	0	0	65	69	6	41	27	15.2	5.68	73	.265	.365	4	.148	-3	-12	-11	-2	-1.1

■ DUMMY LEITNER Leitner, George Michael b: 6/19/1871, Parkton, Md. d: 2/20/60, Baltimore, Md. 5'7", 120 lbs. Deb: 6/29/01

YEAR TM/L	W	L	PCT	G	GS	CG	SH	SV	IP	H	HR	BB	SO	RAT	ERA	ERA+	OAV	OOB	BH	AVG	PB	PR	/A	PD	TPI
1901 Phi-A	0	0	—	1	0	0	0	0	2	1	0	1	1	9.0	0.00	—	.148	.257	0	.000	-0	1	1	0	0.1
NY-N	0	2	.000	2	2	2	0	0	18	27	0	4	3	16.0	4.50	73	.344	.383	1	.143	-0	-2	-2	-0	-0.2
1902 Cle-A	0	0	—	1	1	0	0	0	8	11	0	1	0	13.5	4.50	77	.327	.346	1	.250	-0	-1	-1	0	0.0
Chi-A	0	0	—	1	0	0	0	0	4	9	0	2	0	24.8	13.50	25	.443	.492	0	.000	-0	-4	-4	0	-0.3
Yr	0	0	—	2	1	0	0	0	12	20	0	3	0	17.3	7.50	46	.370	.403	1	.143	-0	-5	-5	1	-0.3
Total 2	0	2	.000	5	3	2	0	0	32	48	0	8	4	16.0	5.34	63	.344	.384	2	.133	-1	-7	-7	0	-0.4

■ BILL LELIVELT Lelivelt, William John b: 10/21/1884, Chicago, Ill. d: 2/14/68, Chicago, Ill. BR/TR, 6', 195 lbs. Deb: 7/19/09

YEAR TM/L	W	L	PCT	G	GS	CG	SH	SV	IP	H	HR	BB	SO	RAT	ERA	ERA+	OAV	OOB	BH	AVG	PB	PR	/A	PD	TPI
1909 Det-A	0	1	.000	4	2	1	0	1	20	27	0	2	4	13.0	4.50	56	.325	.341	2	.333	1	-4	-4	0	-0.2
1910 Det-A	0	1	.000	1	1	1	0	0	9	6	0	3	2	9.0	1.00	263	.207	.281	1	.500	1	2	2	0	0.3
Total 2	0	2	.000	5	3	2	0	1	29	33	0	5	6	11.8	3.41	75	.295	.325	3	.375	2	-3	-3	0	0.1

■ DAVE LEMANCZYK Lemanczyk, David Lawrence b: 8/17/50, Syracuse, N.Y. BR/TR, 6'4", 235 lbs. Deb: 4/15/73

YEAR TM/L	W	L	PCT	G	GS	CG	SH	SV	IP	H	HR	BB	SO	RAT	ERA	ERA+	OAV	OOB	BH	AVG	PB	PR	/A	PD	TPI
1973 Det-A	0	0	—	1	0	0	0	0	2^1	4	0	0	0	15.4	11.57	35	.364	.364	0	—	0	-2	-2	0	-0.1
1974 Det-A	2	1	.667	22	3	0	0	0	78^2	79	12	44	52	14.3	4.00	95	.261	.358	0	—	0	-3	-2	0	-0.4
1975 Det-A	2	7	.222	26	6	4	0	0	109	120	8	46	67	14.0	4.46	90	.281	.355	0	—	0	-8	-5	0	-0.4
1976 Det-A	4	6	.400	20	10	1	0	0	81^1	86	7	34	51	13.3	5.09	73	.271	.342	0	—	0	-14	-12	1	-1.1
1977 Tor-A	13	16	.448	34	34	11	0	0	252	278	20	87	105	13.2	4.25	99	.282	.343	0	—	0	-5	-1	1	0.0
1978 Tor-A	4	14	.222	29	20	3	0	0	136^2	176	16	65	60	15.8	6.26	63	.313	.389	0	—	0	-38	-35	-0	-3.3
1979 Tor-A	8	10	.444	22	20	11	3	0	143	137	12	45	63	11.8	3.71	117	.258	.324	0	—	0	8	10	0	0.3
1980 Tor-A	2	5	.286	10	8	0	0	0	43^1	57	4	15	10	15.0	5.40	80	.322	.375	0	—	0	-7	-5	1	-0.3

YEAR	TM/L	W	L	PCT	G	GS	CG	SH	SV	IP	H	HR	BB	SO	RAT	ERA	ERA+	OAV	OOB	BH	AVG	PB	PR	/A	PD	TPI
	Cal-A	2	4	.333	21	2	0	0	0	66²	81	8	27	19	14.9	4.32	91	.301	.369	0	—	0	-2	-3	-1	-0.3
	Yr	4	9	.308	31	10	0	0	0	110	138	12	42	29	14.9	4.75	86	.308	.370	0	—	0	-9	-8	-0	-0.6
Total 8		37	63	.370	185	103	30	3	0	913	1012	87	363	429	13.8	4.62	88	.284	.354	0	—	0	-72	-56	1	-4.5

■ DENNY LEMASTER
Lemaster, Denver Clayton b: 2/25/39, Corona, Cal. BR/TL, 6'1", 182 lbs. Deb: 7/15/62

YEAR	TM/L	W	L	PCT	G	GS	CG	SH	SV	IP	H	HR	BB	SO	RAT	ERA	ERA+	OAV	OOB	BH	AVG	PB	PR	/A	PD	TPI
1962	Mil-N	3	4	.429	17	12	4	1	0	86²	75	11	32	69	11.4	3.01	126	.233	.308	4	.121	-1	9	8	-2	0.4
1963	Mil-N	11	14	.440	46	31	10	1	1	237	199	30	85	190	10.8	3.04	106	.227	.296	14	.189	3	7	5	-3	0.5
1964	Mil-N	17	11	.607	39	35	9	3	1	221	176	27	75	185	12.0	4.15	85	.252	.315	9	.134	0	-15	-15	-1	-1.5
1965	Mil-N	7	13	.350	32	23	4	1	0	146¹	140	12	58	111	12.4	4.43	80	.251	.325	4	.089	-1	-14	-15	-0	-1.6
1966	Atl-N	11	8	.579	27	27	10	3	0	171	170	25	41	139	11.2	3.74	97	.258	.303	7	.119	-1	-2	-2	-2	-0.4
1967	Atl-N	9	9	.500	31	31	8	2	0	215¹	184	20	72	148	10.8	3.34	99	.229	.295	7	.104	-2	1	-1	-1	-0.2
1968	Hou-N	10	15	.400	33	32	7	2	0	224	231	11	72	146	12.3	2.81	105	.262	.321	2	.031	-3	4	4	-3	-0.2
1969	Hou-N	13	17	.433	38	37	11	1	1	244²	232	20	72	173	11.2	3.16	112	.246	.300	15	.170	3	12	10	-0	1.3
1970	Hou-N	7	12	.368	39	21	3	0	3	162	169	22	65	103	13.1	4.56	85	.268	.338	8	.178	2	-9	-12	-1	-1.1
1971	Hou-N	0	2	.000	42	0	0	0	2	60	59	4	22	28	12.3	3.45	98	.262	.331	1	.167	0	-1	0	0	0.0
1972	Mon-N	2	0	1.000	13	0	0	0	0	19²	28	2	6	13	16.0	7.78	46	.329	.380	1	.333	1	-9	-9	-0	-0.8
Total 11		90	105	.462	357	249	66	14	8	1787²	1703	184	600	1305	11.7	3.58	96	.249	.312	72	.130	0	-18	-28	-14	-3.6

■ DICK LeMAY
LeMay, Richard Paul b: 8/28/38, Cincinnati, Ohio BL/TL, 6'3", 190 lbs. Deb: 6/13/61

YEAR	TM/L	W	L	PCT	G	GS	CG	SH	SV	IP	H	HR	BB	SO	RAT	ERA	ERA+	OAV	OOB	BH	AVG	PB	PR	/A	PD	TPI
1961	SF-N	3	6	.333	27	5	1	0	3	83¹	65	11	36	54	11.3	3.56	107	.217	.309	2	.077	-1	4	2	-0	0.0
1962	SF-N	0	1	.000	9	0	0	0	1	9¹	9	2	9	5	11.4	7.71	49	.265	.419	0	—	0	-4	-4	0	-0.3
1963	Chi-N	0	1	.000	9	1	0	0	0	15¹	26	1	4	10	17.6	5.28	66	.394	.429	0	.000	-0	-3	-3	0	-0.3
Total 3		3	8	.273	45	6	1	0	4	108	100	14	49	69	12.8	4.17	91	.250	.338	2	.071	-1	-3	-5	0	-0.6

■ BOB LEMON
Lemon, Robert Granville b: 9/22/20, San Bernardino, Cal. BL/TR, 6', 180 lbs. Deb: 9/09/41 MCH♦

YEAR	TM/L	W	L	PCT	G	GS	CG	SH	SV	IP	H	HR	BB	SO	RAT	ERA	ERA+	OAV	OOB	BH	AVG	PB	PR	/A	PD	TPI
1946	Cle-A	4	5	.444	32	5	1	0	1	94	77	1	68	39	13.9	2.49	133	.229	.359	16	.180	2	11	9	4	1.5
1947	Cle-A	11	5	.688	37	15	6	1	3	167¹	150	7	97	65	13.5	3.44	101	.242	.348	18	.321	8	5	1	5	1.6
1948	*Cle-A	20	14	.588	43	37	**20**	**10**	2	293²	231	12	129	147	11.1	2.82	144	.216	.302	34	.286	13	**48**	40	8	**6.4**
1949	Cle-A	22	10	.688	37	33	22	2	1	279²	211	19	137	138	11.4	2.99	133	.211	.309	29	.269	15	37	31	6	5.4
1950	Cle-A	**23**	11	.676	44	37	**22**	3	3	288	281	28	146	**170**	13.4	3.84	113	.257	.345	37	.272	16	23	16	4	3.4
1951	Cle-A	17	14	.548	42	34	17	1	2	263¹	244	19	124	132	12.6	3.52	108	.244	.328	21	.206	4	18	8	4	1.5
1952	Cle-A	22	11	.667	42	36	**28**	5	4	309²	236	15	105	131	10.1	2.50	134	**.208**	.279	28	.226	6	40	29	7	4.5
1953	Cle-A	21	15	.583	41	36	23	5	1	286²	283	16	110	98	12.7	3.36	112	.262	.336	26	.232	8	20	13	8	3.0
1954	*Cle-A	**23**	7	.767	36	33	**21**	2	0	258¹	228	12	92	110	11.3	2.72	135	.237	.307	21	.214	5	29	27	4	**4.0**
1955	Cle-A	**18**	10	.643	35	31	5	0	2	211¹	218	17	74	100	12.6	3.88	103	.266	.330	19	.244	6	2	3	1	2.3
1956	Cle-A	20	14	.588	39	35	21	2	3	255¹	230	23	89	94	11.5	3.03	139	.239	.307	18	.194	5	32	33	5	4.5
1957	Cle-A	6	11	.353	21	17	2	0	0	117¹	129	9	64	45	15.3	4.60	81	.287	.385	3	.065	-3	-11	-12	3	-1.0
1958	Cle-A	0	1	.000	11	1	0	0	0	25¹	41	3	16	8	20.6	5.33	68	.376	.460	3	.231	0	-4	-5	1	-0.3
Total 13		207	128	.618	460	350	188	31	22	2850	2559	181	1251	1277	12.2	3.23	119	.241	.324	274	.232	86	251	193	62	35.7

■ DAVE LEMONDS
Lemonds, David Lee b: 7/5/48, Charlotte, N.C. BL/TL, 6'1.5", 180 lbs. Deb: 6/30/69

YEAR	TM/L	W	L	PCT	G	GS	CG	SH	SV	IP	H	HR	BB	SO	RAT	ERA	ERA+	OAV	OOB	BH	AVG	PB	PR	/A	PD	TPI
1969	Chi-N	0	1	.000	2	1	0	0	0	4²	5	0	5	0	19.3	3.86	104	.313	.476	0	.000	-0	-0	0	0	0.0
1972	Chi-A	4	7	.364	31	18	0	0	0	94²	87	6	38	69	12.0	2.95	106	.247	.322	3	.120	-1	1	2	-0	0.1
Total 2		4	8	.333	33	19	0	0	0	99¹	92	6	43	69	12.3	2.99	106	.250	.330	3	.115	-1	1	2	-0	0.1

■ MARK LEMONGELLO
Lemongello, Mark b: 7/21/55, Jersey City, N.J. BR/TR, 6'1", 180 lbs. Deb: 9/14/76

YEAR	TM/L	W	L	PCT	G	GS	CG	SH	SV	IP	H	HR	BB	SO	RAT	ERA	ERA+	OAV	OOB	BH	AVG	PB	PR	/A	PD	TPI
1976	Hou-N	3	1	.750	4	4	1	0	0	29	26	2	7	9	10.2	2.79	114	.236	.282	0	.000	-1	2	1	1	0.2
1977	Hou-N	9	14	.391	34	30	9	1	0	214²	237	20	52	83	12.2	3.48	102	.281	.325	6	.087	-3	10	2	0	-0.1
1978	Hou-N	9	14	.391	33	30	9	1	1	210¹	204	20	66	77	11.9	3.94	84	.259	.323	11	.172	1	-8	-15	1	-1.3
1979	Tor-A	1	9	.100	18	10	2	0	0	83	97	14	34	40	14.5	6.29	69	.299	.371	0	—	0	-19	-18	1	-1.5
Total 4		22	38	.367	89	74	17	1	1	537	564	56	159	209	12.4	4.06	88	.273	.329	17	.121	-3	-15	-30	3	-2.7

■ ED LENNON
Lennon, Edward Francis b: 8/17/1897, Philadelphia, Pa. d: 9/13/47, Philadelphia, Pa. BR/TR, 5'11", 170 lbs. Deb: 6/30/28

YEAR	TM/L	W	L	PCT	G	GS	CG	SH	SV	IP	H	HR	BB	SO	RAT	ERA	ERA+	OAV	OOB	BH	AVG	PB	PR	/A	PD	TPI
1928	Phi-N	0	0	—	5	0	0	0	0	12¹	19	0	10	6	21.2	8.76	49	.373	.475	0	.000	-1	-7	-6	-0	-0.6

■ IZZY LEON
Leon, Isidoro (Becerra) b: 1/4/11, Cruces, Las Villas, Cuba BR/TR, 5'10", 160 lbs. Deb: 6/21/45

YEAR	TM/L	W	L	PCT	G	GS	CG	SH	SV	IP	H	HR	BB	SO	RAT	ERA	ERA+	OAV	OOB	BH	AVG	PB	PR	/A	PD	TPI
1945	Phi-N	0	4	.000	14	4	0	0	0	38²	49	3	19	11	15.8	5.35	72	.312	.386	1	.111	-0	-7	-7	0	-0.6

■ MAX LEON
Leon, Maximino (Molino) b: 2/4/50, Pozo Hondo, Aculo, Mexico BR/TR, 5'10", 145 lbs. Deb: 7/18/73

YEAR	TM/L	W	L	PCT	G	GS	CG	SH	SV	IP	H	HR	BB	SO	RAT	ERA	ERA+	OAV	OOB	BH	AVG	PB	PR	/A	PD	TPI
1973	Atl-N	2	2	.500	12	1	1	0	0	27	30	6	9	18	14.0	5.33	74	.278	.350	2	.286	0	-5	-4	-0	-0.3
1974	Atl-N	4	7	.364	34	2	1	1	3	75	68	5	14	38	10.0	2.64	143	.242	.280	2	.133	-1	8	9	1	1.0
1975	Atl-N	2	1	.667	50	1	0	0	6	85	90	5	33	53	13.8	4.13	91	.274	.352	3	.333	1	-5	-3	1	-0.1
1976	Atl-N	2	4	.333	30	0	0	0	3	36	32	2	15	16	12.3	2.75	138	.234	.318	0	.000	-0	3	4	-1	0.4
1977	Atl-N	4	4	.500	31	9	0	0	1	81²	89	9	25	44	13.6	3.97	112	.280	.349	6	.316	1	-1	4	0	0.6
1978	Atl-N	0	0	—	5	0	0	0	0	5²	6	1	4	1	17.5	6.35	64	.273	.407	0	—	0	-2	-1	0	-0.1
Total 6		14	18	.438	162	13	2	1	13	310¹	315	28	100	170	12.7	3.71	107	.264	.332	13	.250	1	-1	9	1	1.5

■ DENNIS LEONARD
Leonard, Dennis Patrick b: 5/8/51, Brooklyn, N.Y. BR/TR, 6'1", 190 lbs. Deb: 9/04/74

YEAR	TM/L	W	L	PCT	G	GS	CG	SH	SV	IP	H	HR	BB	SO	RAT	ERA	ERA+	OAV	OOB	BH	AVG	PB	PR	/A	PD	TPI
1974	KC-A	0	4	.000	5	4	0	0	0	22	28	0	12	8	17.6	5.32	72	.329	.430	0	—	0	-4	-4	1	-0.2
1975	KC-A	15	7	.682	32	30	8	0	0	212¹	212	18	90	146	13.2	3.77	102	.263	.344	0	—	0	0	2	-0	0.2
1976	*KC-A	17	10	.630	35	34	16	2	0	259	247	16	70	150	11.4	3.51	100	.255	.313	0	—	0	0	-0	-4	-0.4
1977	*KC-A	**20**	12	.625	38	37	21	5	1	292²	246	18	79	244	10.2	3.04	133	.227	.285	0	—	0	33	32	-3	3.0
1978	*KC-A	21	17	.553	40	40	20	4	0	294²	283	27	78	183	11.3	3.33	115	.254	.308	0	—	0	14	16	-0	1.7
1979	KC-A	14	12	.538	32	32	12	**5**	0	236	226	33	56	126	10.8	4.08	104	.253	.299	0	—	0	4	5	-0	0.4
1980	KC-A	20	11	.645	38	38	9	3	0	280¹	271	30	80	155	11.3	3.79	107	.263	.306	0	—	0	8	8	-1	0.7
1981	*KC-A	13	11	.542	26	26	9	2	0	**201²**	202	15	41	107	11.0	2.99	121	.258	.298	0	—	0	15	14	0	1.5
1982	KC-A	10	6	.625	21	21	2	0	0	130²	145	20	46	58	13.3	5.10	80	.279	.340	0	—	0	-15	-15	1	-1.3
1983	KC-A	6	3	.667	10	10	1	0	0	63	69	3	19	31	12.6	3.71	110	.277	.328	0	—	0	2	3	0	0.3
1985	KC-A	0	0	—	2	0	0	0	0	2	1	0	1	4	4.5	0.00	—	.143	.143	0	—	0	1	1	0	0.1
1986	KC-A	8	13	.381	33	30	5	2	0	192²	207	22	51	114	12.2	4.44	96	.275	.324	0	—	0	-6	-4	1	-0.2
Total 12		144	106	.576	312	302	103	23	1	2187	2137	202	622	1323	11.6	3.70	106	.257	.312	0	—	0	52	58	-6	5.8

■ ELMER LEONARD
Leonard, Elmer Ellsworth "Tiny" b: 11/12/1888, Napa, Cal. d: 5/27/81, Napa, Cal. BR/TR, 6'3.5", 210 lbs. Deb: 6/22/11

YEAR	TM/L	W	L	PCT	G	GS	CG	SH	SV	IP	H	HR	BB	SO	RAT	ERA	ERA+	OAV	OOB	BH	AVG	PB	PR	/A	PD	TPI
1911	Phi-A	2	2	.500	5	1	1	0	0	19	26	0	10	10	18.0	2.84	111	.329	.418	2	.286	1	1	1	-0	0.1

■ DUTCH LEONARD
Leonard, Emil John b: 3/25/09, Auburn, Ill. d: 4/17/83, Springfield, Ill. BR/TR, 6', 175 lbs. Deb: 8/31/33 C

YEAR	TM/L	W	L	PCT	G	GS	CG	SH	SV	IP	H	HR	BB	SO	RAT	ERA	ERA+	OAV	OOB	BH	AVG	PB	PR	/A	PD	TPI
1933	Bro-N	2	3	.400	10	3	2	0	0	40	42	0	10	6	11.7	2.93	110	.261	.304	0	.000	-1	2	1	0	0.0
1934	Bro-N	14	11	.560	44	20	11	2	5	183²	210	12	33	58	12.1	3.28	119	.286	.320	12	.179	-1	16	13	2	1.3
1935	Bro-N	2	9	.182	43	11	4	0	**8**	137²	152	11	29	41	11.9	3.92	101	.280	.318	1	.026	-4	-1	1	-1	-0.3
1936	Bro-N	0	0	—	16	0	0	0	1	32	34	2	5	8	11.0	3.66	113	.262	.289	2	.400	0	1	2	1	0.3
1938	Was-A	12	15	.444	33	31	15	3	0	223¹	221	11	53	68	**11.3**	3.43	116	.256	**.305**	19	.232	3	34	27	1	2.8
1939	Was-A	20	8	.714	34	34	21	2	0	269¹	273	16	59	88	11.3	3.54	123	.262	.305	21	.221	0	32	24	2	2.5
1940	Was-A	14	19	.424	35	35	23	2	0	289	328	16	78	124	12.7	3.49	120	.286	.332	16	.158	-4	29	22	5	2.1
1941	Was-A	18	13	.581	34	33	19	4	0	256	271	6	54	91	11.5	3.45	117	.270	.309	9	.102	-5	20	17	-1	1.0
1942	Was-A	2	2	.500	6	5	1	0	0	35	28	1	5	15	8.5	4.11	89	.214	.243	1	.100	-0	-2	-2	0	-0.1

YEAR	TM/L	W	L	PCT	G	GS	CG	SH	SV	IP	H	HR	BB	SO	RAT	ERA	ERA+	OAV	OOB	BH	AVG	PB	PR	/A	PD	TPI
1943	Was-A	11	13	.458	31	30	15	2	1	219²	218	9	46	51	11.0	3.28	98	.257	.298	7	.104	-4	0	-2	2	-0.3
1944	Was-A	14	14	.500	32	31	17	3	0	229¹	222	8	37	62	10.3	3.06	106	.252	.284	18	.228	2	9	5	2	0.8
1945	Was-A	17	7	.708	31	29	12	4	1	216	208	5	35	96	10.2	2.13	146	.248	.279	18	.231	1	30	23	-0	2.6
1946	Phi-A	10	10	.500	26	23	7	2	0	161²	182	9	36	62	12.4	3.56	94	.281	.323	9	.170	-1	-1	-4	3	-0.1
1947	Phi-N	17	12	.586	32	29	19	3	0	235	224	14	57	103	10.8	2.68	149	.258	.306	14	.175	-1	36	35	2	3.8
1948	Phi-N	12	17	.414	34	31	16	1	0	225²	226	9	54	92	11.3	2.51	157	.265	.312	12	.145	-3	36	36	4	3.9
1949	Chi-N	7	16	.304	33	28	10	1	0	180	198	4	43	83	12.4	4.15	97	.272	.319	12	.203	0	-2	-2	1	0.0
1950	Chi-N	5	1	.833	35	1	0	0	6	74	70	7	27	28	12.0	3.77	111	.248	.318	1	.063	-2	3	4	1	0.2
1951	Chi-N	10	6	.625	41	1	0	0	3	81²	69	3	28	30	10.9	2.64	155	.234	.305	0	.000	-3	12	13	2	1.2
1952	Chi-N	2	2	.500	45	0	0	0	11	66²	56	3	24	37	11.2	2.16	178	.235	.313	2	.200	-0	12	13	2	1.5
1953	Chi-N	2	3	.400	45	0	0	0	8	62²	72	9	24	27	13.9	4.60	97	.289	.354	3	.300	1	-2	-1	0	0.0
Total	20	191	181	.513	640	375	192	30	44	3218¹	3304	158	737	1170	11.5	3.25	119	.265	.309	177	.168	-21	267	224	26	23.2

■ DUTCH LEONARD
Leonard, Hubert Benjamin b: 4/16/1892, Birmingham, Ohio d: 7/11/52, Fresno, Cal. BL/TL, 5'10.5", 185 lbs. Deb: 4/12/13

YEAR	TM/L	W	L	PCT	G	GS	CG	SH	SV	IP	H	HR	BB	SO	RAT	ERA	ERA+	OAV	OOB	BH	AVG	PB	PR	/A	PD	TPI
1913	Bos-A	14	16	.467	42	28	14	3	1	259¹	245	0	94	144	11.9	2.39	123	.253	.321	15	.181	1	16	16	-2	1.6
1914	Bos-A	19	5	.792	36	25	17	7	3	224²	139	3	60	176	**8.3**	**0.96**	**280**	**.180**	**.246**	10	.147	-1	**44**	43	-5	4.4
1915	*Bos-A	15	7	.682	32	21	10	2	0	183¹	130	3	67	116	10.4	2.36	118	**.208**	.299	14	.264	5	12	9	-5	0.9
1916	*Bos-A	18	12	.600	48	34	17	6	6	274	244	6	66	144	10.4	2.36	117	.247	.300	17	.200	2	14	12	-6	0.8
1917	Bos-A	16	17	.485	37	36	26	4	1	294¹	257	4	72	144	10.2	2.17	119	.236	.286	9	.087	-6	16	14	-6	0.1
1918	Bos-A	8	6	.571	16	16	12	3	0	125²	119	0	53	47	12.5	2.72	99	.254	.332	8	.186	0	1	-1	-2	-0.1
1919	Det-A	14	13	.519	29	28	18	4	0	217¹	212	7	65	102	11.8	2.77	115	.254	.313	11	.155	-3	11	10	-4	0.3
1920	Det-A	10	17	.370	28	27	10	3	0	191¹	192	8	63	76	12.4	4.33	86	.271	.338	12	.211	2	-11	-13	-2	-1.2
1921	Det-A	11	13	.458	36	32	16	1	1	245	273	15	63	120	12.7	3.75	114	.286	.336	14	.171	-4	15	14	-3	0.6
1924	Det-A	3	2	.600	9	7	3	0	1	51¹	68	1	18	26	15.3	4.56	90	.327	.383	4	.211	-0	-2	-3	-0	-0.2
1925	Det-A	11	4	.733	18	18	9	0	0	125¹	143	7	43	65	13.4	4.51	95	.289	.347	10	.200	-1	-2	-3	-3	-0.5
Total	11	139	112	.554	331	272	152	33	13	2192	2022	54	664	1160	11.3	2.76	115	.249	.311	124	.173	-5	114	98	-38	6.7

■ DAVE LEONHARD
Leonhard, David Paul b: 1/22/42, Arlington, Va. BR/TR, 5'11", 165 lbs. Deb: 9/21/67

YEAR	TM/L	W	L	PCT	G	GS	CG	SH	SV	IP	H	HR	BB	SO	RAT	ERA	ERA+	OAV	OOB	BH	AVG	PB	PR	/A	PD	TPI
1967	Bal-A	0	0	—	3	2	0	0	1	14¹	11	1	6	9	11.3	3.14	100	.200	.290	0	.000	-1	0	0	0	0.0
1968	Bal-A	7	7	.500	28	18	5	2	1	126¹	95	10	57	61	11.0	3.13	93	.216	.309	4	.129	-1	-2	-3	2	-0.1
1969	*Bal-A	7	4	.636	37	3	1	1	1	94	78	8	38	37	11.1	2.49	143	.228	.305	2	.095	-0	12	11	-0	1.1
1970	Bal-A	0	0	—	23	0	0	0	1	28¹	32	5	18	14	15.9	5.08	72	.294	.394	0	.000	-0	-4	-5	1	-0.3
1971	*Bal-A	2	3	.400	12	6	1	1	1	54	51	5	19	18	11.8	2.83	118	.252	.320	5	.278	1	4	3	1	0.5
1972	Bal-A	0	0	—	14	0	0	0	0	20	20	3	12	7	14.4	4.50	68	.260	.360	1	1.000	1	-3	-3	0	-0.1
Total	6	16	14	.533	117	29	7	4	5	337	287	32	150	146	11.8	3.15	103	.234	.320	12	.156	1	6	4	4	1.1

■ RUDY LEOPOLD
Leopold, Rudolph Matas b: 7/27/05, Grand Cane, La. d: 9/3/65, Baton Rouge, La. BL/TL, 6', 160 lbs. Deb: 7/04/28

YEAR	TM/L	W	L	PCT	G	GS	CG	SH	SV	IP	H	HR	BB	SO	RAT	ERA	ERA+	OAV	OOB	BH	AVG	PB	PR	/A	PD	TPI
1928	Chi-A	0	0	—	2	0	0	0	0	2¹	3	0	0	0	11.6	3.86	105	.273	.273	0	.000	-0	0	0	-0	0.0

■ RANDY LERCH
Lerch, Randy Louis b: 10/9/54, Sacramento, Cal. BL/TL, 6'5", 190 lbs. Deb: 9/14/75

YEAR	TM/L	W	L	PCT	G	GS	CG	SH	SV	IP	H	HR	BB	SO	RAT	ERA	ERA+	OAV	OOB	BH	AVG	PB	PR	/A	PD	TPI
1975	Phi-N	0	0	—	3	0	0	0	0	7	6	1	1	8	9.0	6.43	58	.231	.259	0	—	0	-2	-2	-0	-0.1
1976	Phi-N	0	0	—	1	0	0	0	1	3	3	0	0	0	9.0	3.00	118	.250	.250	1	1.000	1	0	0	0	0.1
1977	Phi-N	10	6	.625	32	28	3	0	0	168²	207	20	75	81	15.1	5.07	79	.312	.383	9	.167	-0	-22	-20	2	-1.6
1978	*Phi-N	11	8	.579	33	28	5	0	0	184	183	15	70	96	12.4	3.96	90	.263	.332	15	.250	7	-8	-8	1	0.0
1979	Phi-N	10	13	.435	37	35	6	1	0	214	228	20	60	92	12.2	3.74	102	.281	.333	11	.153	-1	-0	2	2	0.5
1980	Phi-N	4	14	.222	30	22	2	0	0	150	178	15	55	57	14.0	5.16	73	.302	.362	12	.267	4	-26	-23	1	-1.7
1981	*Mil-A	7	9	.438	23	18	1	0	0	110²	134	8	43	53	14.4	4.31	79	.303	.365	0	—	0	-8	-11	0	-1.0
1982	Mil-A	8	7	.533	21	20	1	1	0	108¹	123	12	51	33	14.7	4.97	76	.286	.366	0	—	0	-11	-14	-1	-1.4
	Mon-N	2	0	1.000	6	4	0	0	0	23²	26	0	8	4	12.9	3.42	106	.289	.347	2	.250	0	0	1	0	0.1
1983	Mon-N	1	3	.250	19	5	0	0	0	38²	45	6	18	24	14.9	6.75	53	.292	.370	2	.222	1	-13	-14	-0	-1.2
	SF-N	1	0	1.000	7	0	0	0	0	10²	9	1	8	6	14.3	3.38	105	.231	.362	0	—	0	0	0	0	0.0
	Yr	2	3	.400	26	5	0	0	0	49¹	54	7	26	30	14.6	6.02	59	.277	.362	1	.111	1	-13	-13	-0	-1.2
1984	SF-N	5	3	.625	37	4	0	0	2	72¹	80	3	36	48	14.6	4.23	83	.287	.370	2	.133	1	-5	-6	0	-0.4
1986	Phi-N	1	1	.500	4	0	0	0	0	8	10	0	7	5	19.1	7.88	49	.286	.405	1	.333	1	-4	-4	0	-0.2
Total	11	60	64	.484	253	164	18	2	3	1099¹	1232	101	432	507	13.7	4.53	82	.289	.356	55	.206	15	-98	-98	6	-6.9

■ LOUIS LeROY
LeRoy, Louis Paul "Chief" b: 2/18/1879, Omro Village, Wis. d: 10/10/44, Shawano, Wis. BR/TR, 5'10", 180 lbs. Deb: 9/22/05

YEAR	TM/L	W	L	PCT	G	GS	CG	SH	SV	IP	H	HR	BB	SO	RAT	ERA	ERA+	OAV	OOB	BH	AVG	PB	PR	/A	PD	TPI
1905	NY-A	1	1	.500	3	3	2	0	0	24	26	2	1	8	10.1	3.75	78	.277	.285	1	.125	-0	-3	-2	-0	-0.2
1906	NY-A	2	0	1.000	11	2	1	0	1	44²	33	0	12	28	9.1	2.22	134	.209	.265	2	.143	-1	2	4	1	0.4
1910	Bos-A	0	0	—	1	0	0	0	0	4	7	1	2	3	20.3	11.25	23	.389	.450	0	.000	-0	-4	-4	0	-0.3
Total	3	3	1	.750	15	5	3	0	1	72²	66	3	15	39	10.0	3.22	91	.245	.285	3	.130	-1	-4	-2	1	-0.1

■ BARRY LERSCH
Lersch, Barry Lee b: 9/7/44, Denver, Colo. BB/TR, 6', 175 lbs. Deb: 4/08/69

YEAR	TM/L	W	L	PCT	G	GS	CG	SH	SV	IP	H	HR	BB	SO	RAT	ERA	ERA+	OAV	OOB	BH	AVG	PB	PR	/A	PD	TPI
1969	Phi-N	0	3	.000	10	0	0	0	2	17²	20	6	10	13	15.8	7.13	50	.286	.383	0	.000	-0	-7	-7	1	-0.6
1970	Phi-N	6	3	.667	42	11	3	0	3	138	119	17	47	92	10.9	3.26	122	.232	.297	2	.065	-2	12	11	-0	0.9
1971	Phi-N	5	14	.263	38	30	3	0	0	214¹	203	28	50	113	10.7	3.78	93	.252	.298	10	.169	2	-7	-6	-0	-0.4
1972	Phi-N	4	6	.400	36	8	3	1	0	100²	86	8	33	48	10.9	3.04	118	.231	.299	0	.000	-2	5	6	0	0.4
1973	Phi-N	3	6	.333	42	4	0	0	1	98¹	105	10	27	51	12.3	4.39	86	.279	.330	3	.176	-0	-8	-7	-0	-0.6
1974	StL-N	0	0	—	1	0	0	0	0	1¹	3	1	5	0	54.0	40.50	9	.429	.667	0	—	0	-5	-5	-0	-0.3
Total	6	18	32	.360	169	53	9	1	6	570¹	536	70	172	317	11.3	3.82	97	.250	.308	15	.113	-3	-11	-8	-0	-0.6

■ DON LESHNOCK
Leshnock, Donald Lee b: 11/25/46, Youngstown, Ohio BR/TL, 6'3", 195 lbs. Deb: 6/07/72

YEAR	TM/L	W	L	PCT	G	GS	CG	SH	SV	IP	H	HR	BB	SO	RAT	ERA	ERA+	OAV	OOB	BH	AVG	PB	PR	/A	PD	TPI
1972	Det-A	0	0	—	1	0	0	0	0	1	2	0	0	2	18.0	0.00	—	.400	.400	0	—	0	0	0	0	0.0

■ BRAD LESLEY
Lesley, Bradley Jay b: 9/11/58, Turlock, Cal. BR/TR, 6'6", 230 lbs. Deb: 7/31/82

YEAR	TM/L	W	L	PCT	G	GS	CG	SH	SV	IP	H	HR	BB	SO	RAT	ERA	ERA+	OAV	OOB	BH	AVG	PB	PR	/A	PD	TPI
1982	Cin-N	0	2	.000	28	0	0	0	4	38¹	27	1	13	29	9.4	2.58	143	.197	.267	0	.000	-0	4	5	-0	0.5
1983	Cin-N	0	0	—	5	0	0	0	0	8¹	9	1	0	5	9.7	2.16	176	.290	.290	0	—	0	1	2	0	0.2
1984	Cin-N	0	1	.000	16	0	0	0	2	19¹	17	3	14	7	14.4	5.12	74	.246	.373	1	.500	0	-3	-3	0	-0.1
1985	Mil-A	1	0	1.000	5	0	0	0	0	6¹	8	2	2	5	14.2	9.95	42	.296	.345	0	—	0	-4	-4	0	-0.3
Total	4	1	3	.250	54	0	0	0	6	72¹	61	7	29	46	11.2	3.86	98	.231	.307	1	.333	-1	-2	-0	0	0.3

■ WALT LEVERENZ
Leverenz, Walter Fred "Tiny" b: 7/21/1887, Chicago, Ill. d: 3/19/73, Atascadero, Cal. BL/TL, 5'10", 175 lbs. Deb: 4/18/13

YEAR	TM/L	W	L	PCT	G	GS	CG	SH	SV	IP	H	HR	BB	SO	RAT	ERA	ERA+	OAV	OOB	BH	AVG	PB	PR	/A	PD	TPI
1913	StL-A	6	17	.261	30	27	13	2	1	202²	159	3	89	87	11.5	2.58	114	.222	.318	12	.176	-1	8	8	-2	0.6
1914	StL-A	1	12	.077	27	16	5	0	1	111¹	107	5	63	41	14.1	3.80	71	.264	.368	6	.182	-0	-13	-14	-1	-1.5
1915	StL-A	0	2	.000	5	1	0	0	1	9	11	0	8	3	20.0	8.00	36	.333	.476	0	.000	-0	-5	-5	0	-0.4
Total	3	7	31	.184	62	44	18	2	2	323	277	8	160	131	12.7	3.15	91	.240	.341	18	.176	-1	-10	-11	-3	-1.3

■ DIXIE LEVERETT
Leverett, Gorham Vance b: 3/29/1894, Georgetown, Tex. d: 2/20/57, Beaverton, Ore. BR/TR, 5'11", 190 lbs. Deb: 5/06/22

YEAR	TM/L	W	L	PCT	G	GS	CG	SH	SV	IP	H	HR	BB	SO	RAT	ERA	ERA+	OAV	OOB	BH	AVG	PB	PR	/A	PD	TPI
1922	Chi-A	13	10	.565	33	27	16	4	2	223²	224	11	79	60	12.3	3.34	122	.264	.329	21	.253	5	18	18	-0	2.1
1923	Chi-A	10	13	.435	38	24	9	0	3	192²	212	6	64	64	13.2	4.06	97	.280	.341	16	.267	4	-2	-2	0	0.1
1924	Chi-A	2	3	.400	21	11	4	0	0	99	123	2	41	29	15.2	5.82	71	.314	.383	6	.188	-1	-17	-19	0	-1.6
1926	Chi-A	1	1	.500	6	3	1	0	0	24	31	1	7	12	14.3	6.00	64	.316	.362	1	.143	-0	-5	-6	0	-0.4
1929	Bos-N	3	7	.300	24	12	3	0	1	97²	135	5	30	28	15.7	6.36	74	.339	.393	6	.188	-0	-18	-18	-0	-1.6
Total	5	29	34	.460	122	77	33	4	6	637	725	25	221	193	13.6	4.51	92	.295	.353	50	.234	6	-25	-27	-1	-1.4

YEAR	TM/L	W	L	PCT	G	GS	CG	SH	SV	IP	H	HR	BB	SO	RAT	ERA	ERA+	OAV	OOB	BH	AVG	PB	PR	/A	PD	TPI

■ HOD LEVERETTE Leverette, Horace Wilbur "Levy" b: 2/4/1889, Shreveport, La. d: 4/10/58, St.Petersburg, Fla BR/TR, 6', 180 lbs. Deb: 4/22/20

| 1920 | StL-A | 0 | 2 | .000 | 3 | 2 | 0 | 0 | 0 | 10¹ | 9 | 1 | 12 | 0 | 18.3 | 5.23 | 75 | .250 | .438 | 0 | .000 | -1 | -2 | -1 | 1 | 0.0 |

■ DUTCH LEVSEN Levsen, Emil Henry b: 4/29/1898, Wyoming, Iowa d: 3/12/72, St.Louis Park, Minn. BR/TR, 6', 180 lbs. Deb: 9/28/23

1923	Cle-A	0	0	—	3	0	0	0	0	4¹	4	0	0	1	8.3	0.00	—	.267	.267	0	.000	-0	2	2	1	0.3
1924	Cle-A	1	1	.500	4	1	0	0	0	16¹	22	0	4	3	14.3	4.41	97	.333	.371	0	.000	-1	-0	-0	0	0.0
1925	Cle-A	1	2	.333	4	3	2	0	0	24¹	30	1	16	9	17.4	5.55	80	.313	.416	2	.250	0	-3	-3	-1	-0.2
1926	Cle-A	16	13	.552	33	31	18	2	0	237¹	235	11	85	53	12.4	3.41	119	.261	.330	17	.205	-0	16	17	-0	1.6
1927	Cle-A	3	7	.300	25	13	2	1	0	80¹	96	1	37	15	15.1	5.49	77	.303	.379	5	.200	-1	-12	-11	1	-0.9
1928	Cle-A	0	3	.000	11	3	0	0	0	41¹	39	4	31	7	15.7	5.44	76	.258	.391	0	.000	-2	-6	-6	-0	-0.6
Total	6	21	26	.447	80	51	23	3	0	404	426	17	173	88	13.6	4.17	99	.276	.354	24	.178	-4	-4	-2	2	0.2

■ DENNIS LEWALLYN Lewallyn, Dennis Dale b: 8/11/53, Pensacola, Fla. BR/TR, 6'4", 200 lbs. Deb: 9/21/75

1975	LA-N	0	0	—	2	0	0	0	0	3	1	0	0	0	3.0	0.00	—	.100	.100	0	—	0	1	1	0	0.1
1976	LA-N	1	1	.500	4	2	0	0	0	16²	12	1	6	4	9.7	2.16	157	.207	.281	0	.000	-1	2	2	0	0.2
1977	LA-N	3	1	.750	5	1	0	0	1	17	22	1	4	8	13.8	4.24	90	.306	.342	0	—	-1	-1	-1	-0	-0.1
1978	LA-N	0	0	—	1	0	0	0	0	2	2	0	0	0	9.0	0.00	—	.250	.250	0	—	0	1	1	0	0.1
1979	LA-N	0	1	.000	7	0	0	0	0	12¹	19	1	0	5	1	18.2	5.11	71	.358	.424	1	.500	0	-2	-2	1	0.0
1980	Tex-A	0	0	—	4	0	0	0	0	5²	7	0	4	1	17.5	7.94	49	.304	.407	0	—	0	-2	-3	-0	-0.1
1981	Cle-A	0	0	—	7	0	0	0	0	13¹	16	1	2	11	12.2	5.40	67	.296	.321	0	—	0	-3	-3	-0	-0.2
1982	Cle-A	0	1	.000	4	0	0	0	0	10¹	13	3	1	3	12.2	6.97	59	.310	.326	0	—	0	-3	-3	-0	-0.2
Total	8	4	4	.500	34	3	0	0	1	80¹	92	6	22	28	12.9	4.48	82	.287	.335	1	.077	-1	-6	-7	1	-0.2

■ DAN LEWANDOWSKI Lewandowski, Daniel William b: 1/6/28, Buffalo, N.Y. BR/TR, 6', 180 lbs. Deb: 9/22/51

| 1951 | StL-N | 0 | 1 | .000 | 2 | 0 | 0 | 0 | 0 | 1 | 3 | 0 | 1 | 1 | 36.0 | 9.00 | 44 | .500 | .571 | 0 | — | -0 | -1 | -1 | 0 | 0.0 |

■ LEWIS Lewis b: Brooklyn, N.Y. Deb: 7/12/1890 ♦

| 1890 | Buf-P | 0 | 1 | .000 | 1 | 1 | 0 | 0 | 0 | 3 | 13 | 3 | 7 | 1 | 60.0 | 60.00 | 7 | .590 | .689 | 1 | .200 | -0 | -19 | -19 | 1 | -0.9 |

■ TED LEWIS Lewis, Edward Morgan "Parson" b: 12/25/1872, Machynlleth, Wales d: 5/24/36, Durham, N.H. 5'10.5", 158 lbs. Deb: 7/06/1896

1896	Bos-N	1	4	.200	6	5	4	0	0	41²	37	2	27	12	13.8	3.24	140	.236	.349	2	.111	-2	5	6	1	0.4
1897	*Bos-N	21	12	.636	38	34	30	2	1	290	316	11	125	65	13.7	3.85	116	.275	.346	28	.248	-2	15	20	-4	1.3
1898	Bos-N	26	8	.765	41	33	29	1	2	313¹	267	9	109	72	10.8	2.90	127	.229	.295	37	.282	4	25	28	-0	3.1
1899	Bos-N	17	11	.607	29	25	23	2	0	234²	245	11	73	60	12.2	3.49	119	.269	.323	25	.260	1	10	17	-4	1.4
1900	Bos-N	13	12	.520	30	22	19	1	0	209	215	11	86	66	13.0	4.13	100	.265	.336	10	.137	-4	-10	-0	-3	-0.4
1901	Bos-A	16	17	.485	39	34	31	1	1	316¹	299	14	91	103	11.1	3.53	100	.247	.299	21	.174	-2	5	0	-1	-0.3
Total	6	94	64	.595	183	153	136	7	4	1405	1379	57	511	378	12.1	3.53	113	.255	.319	123	.223	-4	49	71	-12	5.5

■ DUFFY LEWIS Lewis, George Edward b: 4/18/1888, San Francisco, Cal d: 6/17/79, Salem, N.H. BL/TL, 5'10.5", 165 lbs. Deb: 4/16/10 C♦

| 1913 | Bos-A | 0 | 0 | — | 1 | 0 | 0 | 0 | 0 | 1 | 3 | 0 | 0 | 1 | 27.0 | 18.00 | 16 | .500 | .500 | 164 | .298 | 0 | -2 | -2 | 0 | -0.1 |

■ JIM LEWIS Lewis, James Martin b: 10/12/55, Miami, Fla. BR/TR, 6'3", 190 lbs. Deb: 9/12/79

1979	Sea-A	0	0	—	2	0	0	0	0	2¹	10	1	1	0	42.4	15.43	28	.625	.647	0	—	0	-3	-3	-0	-0.2
1982	NY-A	0	0	—	1	0	0	0	0	0²	3	0	3	0	81.0	54.00	7	.500	.667	0	—	0	-4	-4	-0	-0.2
1983	Min-A	0	0	—	6	0	0	0	0	18	24	5	7	8	16.0	6.50	65	.324	.390	0	—	0	-5	-5	-0	-0.3
1985	Sea-A	0	1	.000	2	1	0	0	0	4²	8	1	1	1	21.2	7.71	55	.421	.500	0	—	0	-2	-2	-0	-0.1
Total	4	0	1	.000	11	1	0	0	0	25²	45	7	12	9	21.0	8.77	48	.391	.462	0	—	0	-13	-13	-0	-0.8

■ SCOTT LEWIS Lewis, Scott Allen b: 12/5/65, Grants Pass, Ore. BR/TR, 6'3", 190 lbs. Deb: 9/25/90

| 1990 | Cal-A | 1 | 1 | .500 | 2 | 2 | 1 | 0 | 0 | 16¹ | 10 | 2 | 2 | 9 | 6.6 | 2.20 | 177 | .172 | .200 | 0 | — | 0 | 3 | 3 | -0 | 0.3 |

■ BERT LEWIS Lewis, William Burton b: 10/3/1895, Tonawanda, N.Y. d: 3/24/50, Tonawanda, N.Y. BR/TR, 6'2", 176 lbs. Deb: 4/19/24

| 1924 | Phi-N | 0 | 0 | — | 12 | 0 | 0 | 0 | 0 | 18 | 23 | 1 | 7 | 3 | 15.5 | 6.00 | 74 | .315 | .383 | 0 | .000 | -1 | -4 | -3 | 0 | -0.3 |

■ TERRY LEY Ley, Terrence Richard b: 2/21/47, Portland, Ore. BL/TL, 6', 190 lbs. Deb: 8/20/71

| 1971 | NY-A | 0 | 0 | — | 6 | 0 | 0 | 0 | 0 | 9 | 9 | 1 | 9 | 7 | 20.0 | 5.00 | 65 | .257 | .435 | 0 | — | 0 | -2 | -2 | 0 | -0.1 |

■ AL LIBKE Libke, Albert Walter b: 9/12/18, Tacoma, Wash. BL/TR, 6'4", 215 lbs. Deb: 4/19/45 ♦

1945	Cin-N	0	0	—	4	0	0	0	0	4¹	3	0	2	2	12.5	0.00	—	.200	.333	127	.283	1	2	2	0	0.2
1946	Cin-N	0	0	—	1	1	0	0	0	5	4	0	3	2	12.6	3.60	93	.235	.350	109	.253	0	-0	-0	-0	0.0
Total	2	0	0	—	5	1	0	0	0	9¹	7	0	6	4	12.5	1.93	183	.219	.342	236	.268	2	2	2	0	0.2

■ DON LIDDLE Liddle, Donald Eugene b: 5/25/25, Mt.Carmel, Ill. BL/TL, 5'10", 165 lbs. Deb: 4/17/53

1953	Mil-N	7	6	.538	31	15	4	0	2	128²	119	6	55	63	12.3	3.08	127	.248	.328	3	.088	-2	17	12	-0	0.9
1954	*NY-N	9	4	.692	28	19	4	3	0	126²	100	5	44	44	11.2	3.06	132	.223	.312	7	.189	2	14	14	-1	1.5
1955	NY-N	10	4	.714	33	13	4	0	1	106¹	97	18	61	56	13.7	4.23	95	.246	.353	5	.185	1	-2	-2	-1	-0.1
1956	NY-N	1	2	.333	11	5	1	0	1	41¹	45	5	14	21	13.1	3.92	97	.278	.339	2	.167	-0	-1	-1	0	0.0
	StL-N	1	2	.333	14	2	0	0	0	24²	36	8	18	14	19.7	8.39	45	.353	.450	0	.000	-0	-13	-13	-0	-1.2
	Yr	2	4	.333	25	7	1	0	1	66	81	13	32	35	15.4	5.59	68	.302	.377	1	.071	-0	-13	-13	-1	-1.2
Total	4	28	18	.609	117	54	13	3	4	427²	397	42	203	198	12.8	3.75	106	.250	.339	17	.152	1	16	10	-1	1.1

■ DUTCH LIEBER Lieber, Charles Edwin b: 2/1/10, Alameda, Cal. d: 12/31/61, Sawtelle, Cal. BR/TR, 6'0.5", 180 lbs. Deb: 4/18/35

1935	Phi-A	1	1	.500	18	1	0	0	2	46²	45	1	19	14	12.5	3.09	147	.263	.340	2	.143	-1	7	8	0	0.6
1936	Phi-A	0	1	.000	3	0	0	0	0	11²	17	0	6	1	17.7	7.71	66	.362	.434	0	.000	-0	-3	-3	1	-0.2
Total	2	1	2	.333	21	1	0	0	2	58¹	62	1	25	15	13.6	4.01	116	.284	.361	2	.118	-2	4	4	1	0.4

■ GLENN LIEBHARDT Liebhardt, Glenn Ignatius "Sandy" b: 7/31/10, Cleveland, Ohio BR/TR, 5'10.5", 170 lbs. Deb: 4/22/30

1930	Phi-A	0	1	.000	5	0	0	0	0	9	14	2	8	2	22.0	11.00	42	.359	.468	0	.000	-0	-6	-6	-0	-0.5
1936	StL-A	0	0	—	24	0	0	0	0	55¹	98	4	27	20	20.7	8.78	61	.375	.438	0	.000	-2	-23	-21	-1	-1.9
1938	StL-A	0	0	—	2	0	0	0	0	3	4	1	0	1	12.0	6.00	83	.308	.308	0	—	-0	-0	-0	0	0.0
Total	3	0	1	.000	31	0	0	0	0	67¹	116	7	35	23	20.5	8.96	59	.371	.437	0	.000	-2	-30	-28	-2	-2.4

■ GLENN LIEBHARDT Liebhardt, Glenn John b: 3/10/1883, Milton, Ind. d: 7/13/56, Cleveland, Ohio 5'10", 175 lbs. Deb: 10/02/06

1906	Cle-A	2	0	1.000	2	2	2	0	0	18	9	0	9	7	9.0	1.50	175	.205	.218	0	.000	-1	2	2	0	0.2
1907	Cle-A	18	14	.563	38	34	27	4	1	280¹	254	1	85	110	10.9	2.05	122	.244	.301	14	.161	-1	15	14	1	1.5
1908	Cle-A	15	16	.484	38	26	19	3	0	262	222	1	81	146	10.5	2.20	109	.235	.297	14	.175	0	6	6	-0	0.6
1909	Cle-A	1	5	.167	12	4	1	0	0	52¹	54	0	16	15	12.2	2.92	87	.314	.376	0	.000	-2	-3	-2	-1	-0.5
Total	4	36	35	.507	90	66	49	7	2	612²	543	3	183	280	10.7	2.17	114	.244	.303	28	.147	-3	21	20	-1	1.8

■ GENE LILLARD Lillard, Robert Eugene b: 11/12/13, Santa Barbara, Cal BR/TR, 5'10.5", 178 lbs. Deb: 5/08/36 ♦

1939	Chi-N	3	5	.375	20	7	2	0	0	55	68	2	36	31	17.5	6.55	60	.309	.413	1	.100	1	-16	-16	0	-1.3
1940	StL-N	0	1	.000	2	1	0	0	0	4²	8	1	4	2	25.1	13.50	30	.364	.481	0	—	0	-5	-5	0	-0.3
Total	2	3	6	.333	22	8	2	0	0	59²	76	3	40	33	18.1	7.09	56	.314	.420	8	.182	1	-21	-21	0	-1.6

■ JIM LILLIE Lillie, James J. "Grasshopper" b: 1862, New Haven, Conn. d: 11/9/1890, Kansas City, Mo. Deb: 5/17/1883 ♦

| 1883 | Buf-N | 0 | 1 | .000 | 3 | 0 | 0 | 0 | 0 | 12 | 16 | 0 | 2 | 4 | 13.5 | 3.00 | 106 | .302 | .328 | 47 | .234 | 0 | 0 | 0 | 0 | 0.0 |

YEAR	TM/L	W	L	PCT	G	GS	CG	SH	SV	IP	H	HR	BB	SO	RAT	ERA	ERA+	OAV	OOB	BH	AVG	PB	PR	/A	PD	TPI
1884	Buf-N	0	1	.000	2	1	0	0	0	13	22	0	5	4	18.7	6.23	50	.356	.404	105	.223	-0	-5	-4	0	-0.3
1886	KC-N	0	0	—	1	0	0	0	0	6	8	0	1	0	13.5	4.50	84	.308	.333	73	.175	-0	-1	-0	0	0.0
Total	3	0	2	.000	6	1	0	0	0	31	46	0	8	8	15.7	4.65	70	.327	.363	332	.219	-0	-5	-5	1	-0.3

■ DEREK LILLIQUIST
Lilliquist, Derek Jansen   b: 2/20/66, Winter Park, Fla.   BL/TL, 6', 200 lbs.   Deb: 4/13/89

YEAR	TM/L	W	L	PCT	G	GS	CG	SH	SV	IP	H	HR	BB	SO	RAT	ERA	ERA+	OAV	OOB	BH	AVG	PB	PR	/A	PD	TPI
1989	Atl-N	8	10	.444	32	30	0	0	0	165²	202	16	34	79	12.9	3.97	92	.301	.337	12	.190	0	-9	-6	-1	-0.6
1990	Atl-N	2	8	.200	12	11	0	0	0	61²	75	10	19	34	13.9	6.28	62	.301	.353	8	.348	4	-17	-16	-1	-1.2
	SD-N	3	3	.500	16	7	1	1	0	60¹	61	6	23	29	12.8	4.33	89	.266	.339	3	.150	0	-4	-3	-1	-0.4
	Yr	5	11	.313	28	18	1	1	0	122	136	16	42	63	13.3	5.31	73	.282	.342	1	.023	4	-21	-19	-2	-1.6
Total	2	13	21	.382	60	48	1	1	0	287²	338	32	76	142	13.1	4.54	83	.294	.341	23	.217	4	-29	-25	-3	-2.2

■ EZRA LINCOLN
Lincoln, Ezra Perry   b: 11/17/1868, Raynham, Mass.   d: 5/7/51, Taunton, Mass.   TL, 5'11", 160 lbs.   Deb: 5/02/1890

YEAR	TM/L	W	L	PCT	G	GS	CG	SH	SV	IP	H	HR	BB	SO	RAT	ERA	ERA+	OAV	OOB	BH	AVG	PB	PR	/A	PD	TPI
1890	Cle-N	3	11	.214	15	15	13	0	0	118	157	1	53	22	16.0	4.42	81	.311	.376	8	.157	-3	-11	-11	1	-1.1
	Syr-a	0	3	.000	3	3	2	0	0	20	33	1	4	6	16.6	10.35	34	.358	.384	0	.000	-1	-14	-15	0	-1.1

■ VIVE LINDAMAN
Lindaman, Vivan Alexander   b: 10/28/1877, Charles City, Iowa   d: 2/13/27, Charles City, Iowa   BR/TR, 6'1", 200 lbs.   Deb: 4/14/06

YEAR	TM/L	W	L	PCT	G	GS	CG	SH	SV	IP	H	HR	BB	SO	RAT	ERA	ERA+	OAV	OOB	BH	AVG	PB	PR	/A	PD	TPI
1906	Bos-N	12	23	.343	39	37	32	2	0	307¹	303	4	90	115	11.8	2.43	111	.264	.324	14	.132	-1	7	9	-1	0.7
1907	Bos-N	11	15	.423	34	28	24	2	1	260	252	10	108	90	13.0	3.63	70	.265	.349	11	.122	-2	-34	-31	-2	-3.7
1908	Bos-N	12	16	.429	43	30	21	2	1	270²	246	7	70	68	10.8	2.36	102	.249	.306	15	.176	0	0	2	-2	0.0
1909	Bos-N	1	6	.143	15	6	6	1	0	66	75	1	28	13	14.2	4.64	61	.299	.371	6	.273	1	-15	-13	-1	-1.3
Total	4	36	60	.375	131	101	83	7	2	904	876	22	296	286	12.0	2.92	88	.263	.329	46	.152	-2	-41	-34	-6	-4.3

■ PAUL LINDBLAD
Lindblad, Paul Aaron   b: 8/9/41, Chanute, Kan.   BL/TL, 6'1", 185 lbs.   Deb: 9/15/65

YEAR	TM/L	W	L	PCT	G	GS	CG	SH	SV	IP	H	HR	BB	SO	RAT	ERA	ERA+	OAV	OOB	BH	AVG	PB	PR	/A	PD	TPI
1965	KC-A	0	1	.000	4	0	0	0	0	7¹	12	3	0	12	16.0	11.05	32	.353	.371	0	.000	-0	-6	-6	0	-0.5
1966	KC-A	5	10	.333	38	14	0	0	1	121	138	14	37	69	13.2	4.17	82	.292	.348	5	.147	0	-10	-10	0	-1.0
1967	KC-A	5	8	.385	46	10	1	1	6	115²	106	15	35	83	11.4	3.58	89	.241	.306	7	.206	2	-4	-5	-0	-0.3
1968	Oak-A	4	3	.571	47	1	0	0	2	56¹	51	6	14	42	10.4	2.40	118	.237	.284	3	.375	1	4	3	0	0.5
1969	Oak-A	9	6	.600	60	0	0	0	9	78¹	72	8	33	64	12.3	4.14	83	.240	.319	4	.333	1	-4	-6	-0	-0.4
1970	Oak-A	8	2	.800	62	0	0	0	3	63¹	52	7	28	42	11.4	2.70	131	.222	.305	0	.000	-1	7	6	0	0.5
1971	Oak-A	1	0	1.000	8	0	0	0	0	16	18	1	2	4	11.8	3.94	85	.295	.328	1	.333	0	-1	-1	0	0.0
	Was-A	6	4	.600	43	0	0	0	8	83²	58	6	29	50	9.6	2.58	128	.196	.272	3	.158	0	8	7	1	0.8
	Yr	7	4	.636	51	0	0	0	8	99²	76	7	31	54	9.8	2.80	118	.212	.279	0	.000	1	7	6	1	0.8
1972	Tex-A	5	8	.385	66	0	0	0	9	99²	95	7	29	51	11.2	2.62	115	.257	.311	3	.200	0	5	4	-0	0.4
1973	*Oak-A	1	5	.167	36	3	0	0	2	78	89	6	28	33	13.8	3.69	96	.292	.357	0	—	0	1	-1	-0	-0.1
1974	Oak-A	4	4	.500	45	2	0	0	6	100²	85	4	30	46	10.5	2.06	161	.231	.292	0	—	0	17	14	0	1.5
1975	*Oak-A	9	1	.900	68	0	0	0	7	122¹	105	6	43	53	10.9	2.72	133	.237	.305	0	.000	0	14	12	1	1.4
1976	Oak-A	6	5	.545	65	0	0	0	5	114²	111	5	24	37	10.8	3.06	110	.253	.296	0	—	0	6	4	1	0.5
1977	Tex-A	4	5	.444	42	1	0	0	4	98²	103	16	29	46	12.1	4.20	97	.270	.324	0	—	0	-2	-1	-0	0.0
1978	Tex-A	1	1	.500	18	0	0	0	2	39²	41	2	15	25	13.2	3.63	103	.279	.354	0	—	0	1	0	-0	0.0
	*NY-A	0	0	—	7	1	0	0	0	18¹	21	4	8	9	14.2	4.42	82	.284	.354	0	—	0	-1	-2	0	0.0
	Yr	1	1	.500	25	1	0	0	2	58	62	6	23	34	13.2	3.88	95	.276	.343	0	—	0	-1	-1	-0	0.0
Total	14	68	63	.519	655	32	1	1	64	1213²	1157	112	384	671	11.6	3.29	104	.253	.314	26	.195	4	35	17	4	3.3

■ LYMAN LINDE
Linde, Lyman Gilbert   b: 9/20/20, Beaver Dam, Wis.   BR/TR, 5'11", 185 lbs.   Deb: 9/11/47

YEAR	TM/L	W	L	PCT	G	GS	CG	SH	SV	IP	H	HR	BB	SO	RAT	ERA	ERA+	OAV	OOB	BH	AVG	PB	PR	/A	PD	TPI
1947	Cle-A	0	0	—	1	0	0	0	0	0²	3	0	1	0	54.0	27.00	13	.600	.667	0	—	0	-2	-2	0	-0.1
1948	Cle-A	0	0	—	3	0	0	0	0	10	9	1	4	0	11.7	5.40	75	.243	.317	0	.000	-0	-1	-1	-0	-0.1
Total	2	0	0	—	4	0	0	0	0	10²	12	1	5	0	14.3	6.75	60	.286	.362	0	.000	-0	-3	-3	-0	-0.2

■ JOHNNY LINDELL
Lindell, John Harlan   b: 8/30/16, Greeley, Colo.   d: 8/27/85, Newport Beach, Cal.   BR/TR, 6'4.5", 217 lbs.   Deb: 4/18/41 ♦

YEAR	TM/L	W	L	PCT	G	GS	CG	SH	SV	IP	H	HR	BB	SO	RAT	ERA	ERA+	OAV	OOB	BH	AVG	PB	PR	/A	PD	TPI
1942	NY-A	2	1	.667	23	2	0	0	1	52²	52	3	22	28	12.8	3.76	92	.254	.329	6	.250	1	-1	-2	-0	0.0
1953	Pit-N	5	16	.238	27	23	13	1	0	175²	173	17	116	102	15.1	4.71	95	.262	.377	26	.286	7	-8	-5	2	-0.3
	Phi-N	1	1	.500	5	3	2	0	0	23¹	22	0	23	16	17.4	4.24	99	.259	.417	7	.389	2	0	-0	-0	0.0
	Yr	6	17	.261	32	26	15	1	0	199	195	17	139	118	15.1	4.66	95	.259	.375	24	.220	9	-8	-5	2	-0.3
Total	2	8	18	.308	55	28	15	1	1	251²	247	20	161	146	14.8	4.47	95	.260	.371	762	.273	10	-9	-7	2	-0.3

■ ERNIE LINDEMANN
Lindemann, Ernest   b: 6/10/1883, New York, N.Y.   d: 12/27/51, Brooklyn, N.Y.   BR/TR,   Deb: 6/28/07

YEAR	TM/L	W	L	PCT	G	GS	CG	SH	SV	IP	H	HR	BB	SO	RAT	ERA	ERA+	OAV	OOB	BH	AVG	PB	PR	/A	PD	TPI
1907	Bos-N	0	0	—	1	1	0	0	0	6¹	6	0	4	3	14.2	5.68	45	.286	.400	1	.500	0	-2	-2	0	-0.1

■ CARL LINDQUIST
Lindquist, Carl Emil   b: 5/9/19, Morris Run, Pa.   BR/TR, 6'2", 185 lbs.   Deb: 9/27/43

YEAR	TM/L	W	L	PCT	G	GS	CG	SH	SV	IP	H	HR	BB	SO	RAT	ERA	ERA+	OAV	OOB	BH	AVG	PB	PR	/A	PD	TPI
1943	Bos-N	0	2	.000	2	2	0	0	0	13	17	3	4	1	14.5	6.23	55	.315	.362	0	.000	-1	-4	-4	0	-0.3
1944	Bos-N	0	0	—	5	0	0	0	0	8²	8	1	2	4	10.4	3.12	123	.222	.263	0	.000	-0	0	1	-0	0.0
Total	2	0	2	.000	7	2	0	0	0	21²	25	4	6	5	12.9	4.98	72	.278	.323	0	.000	-1	-4	-3	-0	-0.3

■ JIM LINDSEY
Lindsey, James Kendrick   b: 1/24/1898, Greensburg, La.   d: 10/25/63, Jackson, La.   BR/TR, 6'1", 175 lbs.   Deb: 5/01/22

YEAR	TM/L	W	L	PCT	G	GS	CG	SH	SV	IP	H	HR	BB	SO	RAT	ERA	ERA+	OAV	OOB	BH	AVG	PB	PR	/A	PD	TPI
1922	Cle-A	4	5	.444	29	5	0	0	1	83²	105	4	24	29	14.2	6.02	67	.324	.376	4	.167	-1	-18	-19	-1	-1.8
1924	Cle-A	0	0	—	3	0	0	0	0	3	8	0	3	0	33.0	21.00	20	.500	.579	0	.000	-1	-6	-6	-0	-0.4
1929	StL-N	1	1	.500	2	2	1	0	0	16¹	20	1	2	8	12.7	5.51	85	.290	.319	1	.200	-0	-1	-2	-0	-0.1
1930	*StL-N	7	5	.583	39	6	3	0	5	105²	131	6	46	50	15.4	4.43	113	.312	.385	8	.286	1	6	7	-3	0.4
1931	*StL-N	6	4	.600	35	2	1	0	7	74²	77	2	45	32	14.7	2.77	142	.270	.370	1	.111	0	**9**	**10**	0	0.9
1932	StL-N	3	3	.500	33	5	0	0	3	89¹	96	6	38	31	13.7	4.94	80	.279	.354	3	.143	-1	-10	-10	-1	-1.0
1933	StL-N	0	0	—	1	0	0	0	0	2	2	0	1	1	13.5	4.50	77	.286	.375	0	—	-0	-0	-0	-0	0.0
1934	Cin-N	0	0	—	4	0	0	0	0	4	4	0	2	2	15.8	4.50	91	.286	.412	0	—	-0	-0	-0	-0	0.0
	StL-N	0	1	.000	11	0	0	0	0	14	21	2	3	7	15.4	6.43	66	.328	.358	0	.000	-0	-4	-3	-0	-0.3
	Yr	0	1	.000	15	0	0	0	0	18	25	2	5	9	15.0	6.00	70	.316	.357	0	.000	-0	-4	-4	-0	-0.3
1937	Bro-N	0	1	.000	20	0	0	0	2	38¹	43	4	12	15	13.1	3.52	115	.295	.352	1	.167	-0	2	2	-0	0.1
Total	9	21	20	.512	177	20	5	1	19	431	507	25	176	175	14.5	4.70	91	.300	.370	18	.186	-3	-23	-21	-5	-2.2

■ AXEL LINDSTROM
Lindstrom, Axel Olaf   b: 8/26/1895, Gustavsberg, Sweden   d: 6/24/40, Asheville, N.C.   BR/TR, 5'10", 180 lbs.   Deb: 10/03/16

YEAR	TM/L	W	L	PCT	G	GS	CG	SH	SV	IP	H	HR	BB	SO	RAT	ERA	ERA+	OAV	OOB	BH	AVG	PB	PR	/A	PD	TPI
1916	Phi-A	0	0	—	1	0	0	0	1	4	2	0	0	1	6.8	4.50	64	.182	.250	1	.500	0	-1	-1	0	0.0

■ DICK LINES
Lines, Richard George   b: 8/17/38, Montreal, Que., Can.   BR/TL, 6'1", 175 lbs.   Deb: 4/16/66

YEAR	TM/L	W	L	PCT	G	GS	CG	SH	SV	IP	H	HR	BB	SO	RAT	ERA	ERA+	OAV	OOB	BH	AVG	PB	PR	/A	PD	TPI
1966	Was-A	5	2	.714	53	0	0	0	2	83	63	4	24	49	9.5	2.28	152	.213	.274	0	.000	-1	11	11	2	1.3
1967	Was-A	2	5	.286	54	0	0	0	4	85²	83	6	24	54	11.2	3.36	94	.245	.295	1	.111	1	-1	-2	0	0.0
Total	2	7	7	.500	107	0	0	0	6	168²	146	10	48	103	10.4	2.83	117	.230	.285	1	.053	-1	9	9	2	1.3

■ FRED LINK
Link, Edward Theodore "Laddie"   b: 3/11/1886, Columbus, Ohio   d: 5/22/39, Houston, Tex.   BL/TL, 6'1", 700 lbs.   Deb: 4/15/1910

YEAR	TM/L	W	L	PCT	G	GS	CG	SH	SV	IP	H	HR	BB	SO	RAT	ERA	ERA+	OAV	OOB	BH	AVG	PB	PR	/A	PD	TPI
1910	Cle-A	5	6	.455	22	13	6	1	1	127²	121	0	50	55	12.5	3.17	82	.259	.340	7	.167	-1	-9	-8	-1	-1.1
	StL-A	0	1	.000	3	3	0	0	0	17	24	0	13	5	20.1	4.24	58	.375	.487	1	.167	-0	-3	-3	-0	-0.3
	Yr	5	7	.417	25	16	6	1	1	144²	145	0	63	60	13.0	3.30	78	.270	.347	2	.042	-1	-12	-12	-2	-1.4

■ ED LINKE
Linke, Edward Karl "Babe"   b: 11/9/11, Chicago, Ill.   d: 6/21/88, Chicago, Ill.   BR/TR, 5'11", 180 lbs.   Deb: 4/27/33

YEAR	TM/L	W	L	PCT	G	GS	CG	SH	SV	IP	H	HR	BB	SO	RAT	ERA	ERA+	OAV	OOB	BH	AVG	PB	PR	/A	PD	TPI
1933	Was-A	1	0	1.000	3	2	0	0	0	16	15	0	11	6	14.6	5.06	83	.250	.366	1	.167	0	-1	-2	0	0.0
1934	Was-A	2	2	.500	7	4	2	0	0	34²	39	2	16	9	12.2	4.15	104	.277	.322	2	.182	0	1	0	0	0.1
1935	Was-A	11	7	.611	40	22	10	1	3	178	211	6	80	51	14.8	5.01	86	.296	.367	20	.294	6	-11	-14	-1	-0.8
1936	Was-A	1	5	.167	13	6	1	0	0	52	73	4	14	11	15.1	7.10	67	.330	.370	6	.400	4	-12	-13	1	-0.6
1937	Was-A	6	1	.857	36	7	0	0	3	128²	158	11	59	61	15.5	5.60	79	.304	.379	10	.217	1	-14	-17	-1	-1.4

YEAR TM/L	W	L	PCT	G	GS	CG	SH	SV	IP	H	HR	BB	SO	RAT	ERA	ERA+	OAV	OOB	BH	AVG	PB	PR	/A	PD	TPI
1938 StL-A	1	7	.125	21	2	0	0	0	39²	60	6	33	18	21.1	7.94	63	.357	.463	2	.200	0	-14	-13	1	-1.0
Total 6	22	22	.500	120	43	13	1	6	449	555	28	206	156	15.4	5.61	79	.305	.377	41	.263	12	-51	-58	0	-3.7

■ **ROYCE LINT**   Lint, Royce James b: 1/1/21, Birmingham, Ala. BL/TL, 6'1", 165 lbs. Deb: 4/13/54

YEAR TM/L	W	L	PCT	G	GS	CG	SH	SV	IP	H	HR	BB	SO	RAT	ERA	ERA+	OAV	OOB	BH	AVG	PB	PR	/A	PD	TPI
1954 StL-N	2	3	.400	30	4	1	1	0	70¹	75	9	30	36	13.4	4.86	85	.273	.344	1	.100	1	-6	-6	1	-0.3

■ **FRANK LINZY**   Linzy, Frank Alfred b: 9/15/40, Ft.Gibson, Okla. BR/TR, 6'1", 190 lbs. Deb: 8/14/63

YEAR TM/L	W	L	PCT	G	GS	CG	SH	SV	IP	H	HR	BB	SO	RAT	ERA	ERA+	OAV	OOB	BH	AVG	PB	PR	/A	PD	TPI
1963 SF-N	0	0	—	8	1	0	0	0	16²	22	0	10	14	17.8	4.86	66	.324	.418	0	.000	-0	-3	-3	0	-0.2
1965 SF-N	9	3	.750	57	0	0	0	21	81²	76	2	23	35	11.2	1.43	251	.250	.309	4	.222	1	**19**	**20**	6	2.9
1966 SF-N	7	11	.389	51	0	0	0	16	100¹	107	4	34	57	12.8	2.96	124	.273	.334	3	.150	0	7	8	1	0.9
1967 SF-N	7	7	.500	57	0	0	0	17	95²	67	4	34	38	9.5	1.51	218	.203	.277	0	.000	-2	20	19	4	2.3
1968 SF-N	9	8	.529	57	0	0	0	12	94²	76	1	27	36	9.9	2.09	141	.218	.277	0	.000	-1	9	9	4	1.4
1969 SF-N	14	9	.609	58	0	0	0	11	116¹	129	5	38	62	13.2	3.64	96	.283	.342	8	.267	3	-1	-2	3	0.4
1970 SF-N	2	1	.667	20	0	0	0	1	25²	33	2	11	16	15.8	7.01	57	.327	.398	0	.000	-0	-8	-9	0	-0.8
StL-N	3	5	.375	47	0	0	0	2	61¹	66	3	23	19	13.1	3.67	112	.282	.346	0	.000	-1	3	3	1	0.3
Yr	5	6	.455	67	0	0	0	3	87	99	5	34	35	13.8	4.66	88	.293	.358	0	.000	-1	-6	-6	1	-0.5
1971 StL-N	4	3	.571	50	0	0	0	6	59¹	49	2	27	24	11.5	2.12	170	.226	.311	2	.500	1	9	10	1	1.3
1972 Mil-A	2	2	.500	47	0	0	0	12	77¹	70	4	27	24	11.5	3.03	100	.248	.318	1	.111	-0	0	0	1	0.1
1973 Mil-A	2	6	.250	42	1	0	0	13	63	68	7	21	21	12.9	3.57	105	.282	.342	0	—	0	2	1	0	0.2
1974 Phi-N	3	2	.600	22	0	0	0	1	24²	27	1	7	12	12.4	3.28	115	.284	.333	0	—	0	1	1	1	0.2
Total 11	62	57	.521	516	2	0	0	111	816²	790	35	282	358	12.0	2.85	122	.257	.323	18	.149	0	58	57	22	9.0

■ **ANGELO LiPETRI**   LiPetri, Michael Angelo b: 7/6/30, Brooklyn, N.Y. BR/TR, 6'1.5", 180 lbs. Deb: 4/25/56

YEAR TM/L	W	L	PCT	G	GS	CG	SH	SV	IP	H	HR	BB	SO	RAT	ERA	ERA+	OAV	OOB	BH	AVG	PB	PR	/A	PD	TPI
1956 Phi-N	0	0	—	6	0	0	0	0	11	7	2	3	8	9.0	3.27	114	.175	.250	0	.000	-0	1	1	0	0.1
1958 Phi-N	0	0	—	4	0	0	0	0	4	6	1	0	1	15.8	11.25	35	.353	.389	0	—	0	-3	-3	0	-0.2
Total 2	0	0	—	10	0	0	0	0	15	13	3	3	9	10.8	5.40	70	.228	.290	0	.000	-0	-3	-3	0	-0.1

■ **TOM LIPP**   Lipp, Thomas C. (b: Thomas C. Lieb) b: 6/4/1870, Baltimore, Md. d: 5/30/32, Baltimore, Md. 5'11.5", 170 lbs. Deb: 9/18/1897

YEAR TM/L	W	L	PCT	G	GS	CG	SH	SV	IP	H	HR	BB	SO	RAT	ERA	ERA+	OAV	OOB	BH	AVG	PB	PR	/A	PD	TPI
1897 Phi-N	0	1	.000	1	1	0	0	0	3	8	0	2	1	30.0	15.00	28	.482	.537	1	1.000	0	-4	-4	-0	-0.1

■ **NIG LIPSCOMB**   Lipscomb, Gerard b: 2/24/11, Rutherfordton, N.C. d: 2/27/78, Huntersville, N.C. BR/TR, 6', 175 lbs. Deb: 4/23/37 ♦

YEAR TM/L	W	L	PCT	G	GS	CG	SH	SV	IP	H	HR	BB	SO	RAT	ERA	ERA+	OAV	OOB	BH	AVG	PB	PR	/A	PD	TPI
1937 StL-A	0	0	—	3	0	0	0	0	9²	13	3	5	1	16.8	6.52	74	.333	.409	31	.323	1	-2	-2	-0	-0.1

■ **HOD LISENBEE**   Lisenbee, Horace Milton b: 9/23/1898, Clarksville, Tenn d: 11/14/87, Clarksville, Tenn. BR/TR, 5'11", 170 lbs. Deb: 4/23/27

YEAR TM/L	W	L	PCT	G	GS	CG	SH	SV	IP	H	HR	BB	SO	RAT	ERA	ERA+	OAV	OOB	BH	AVG	PB	PR	/A	PD	TPI
1927 Was-A	18	9	.667	39	34	17	**4**	0	242	221	6	78	105	13.1	3.57	114	.245	.307	11	.133	-4	15	13	-3	0.6
1928 Was-A	2	6	.250	16	9	3	0	0	77	102	4	32	13	16.2	6.08	66	.326	.397	4	.174	-1	-17	-18	-1	-1.6
1929 Bos-A	0	0	—	5	0	0	0	0	8²	10	1	4	2	14.5	5.19	82	.294	.368	0	.000	-0	-1	-1	0	0.0
1930 Bos-A	10	17	.370	37	31	15	0	0	237¹	254	20	86	47	13.1	4.40	105	.280	.346	7	.267	1	7	6	-3	0.3
1931 Bos-A	5	12	.294	41	17	6	0	0	164²	190	13	49	42	13.2	5.19	83	.281	.332	12	.226	0	-15	-16	-1	-1.5
1932 Bos-A	0	4	.000	19	6	3	0	0	73¹	87	9	25	13	13.9	5.65	80	.296	.353	1	.048	-2	-10	-9	-1	-1.0
1936 Phi-A	1	7	.125	19	7	4	0	0	85²	115	9	24	17	14.6	6.20	82	.322	.365	3	.120	-1	-11	-10	-0	-0.9
1945 Cin-N	1	3	.250	31	3	0	0	1	80¹	97	12	16	14	12.9	5.49	68	.294	.330	0	.000	-3	-15	-15	-1	-1.8
Total 8	37	58	.389	207	107	48	4	1	969	1076	74	314	253	13.1	4.81	90	.282	.340	51	.169	-10	-47	-51	-10	-5.9

■ **AD LISKA**   Liska, Adolph James b: 7/10/06, Dwight, Neb. BR/TR, 5'11.5", 160 lbs. Deb: 4/17/29

YEAR TM/L	W	L	PCT	G	GS	CG	SH	SV	IP	H	HR	BB	SO	RAT	ERA	ERA+	OAV	OOB	BH	AVG	PB	PR	/A	PD	TPI
1929 Was-A	3	9	.250	24	10	4	0	0	94¹	87	1	42	33	12.6	4.77	89	.249	.335	5	.172	-1	-6	-6	3	-0.2
1930 Was-A	9	7	.563	32	16	7	1	1	150²	140	6	71	40	12.9	3.29	140	.250	.340	5	.096	-4	23	22	6	2.3
1931 Was-A	0	1	.000	2	1	0	0	0	4	9	0	1	2	22.5	6.75	64	.450	.476	0	.000	-0	-1	-1	0	0.0
1932 Phi-N	2	0	1.000	8	0	0	0	1	26²	22	0	10	6	11.1	1.69	261	.239	.320	0	.000	-1	6	8	1	0.9
1933 Phi-N	3	1	.750	45	1	0	0	1	75²	96	5	26	23	14.5	4.52	84	.310	.363	1	.071	-1	-10	-6	4	-0.3
Total 5	17	18	.486	111	28	11	1	3	351¹	354	12	150	104	13.1	3.87	112	.266	.344	11	.107	-7	13	19	15	2.7

■ **MARK LITTELL**   Littell, Mark Alan b: 1/17/53, Cape Girardeau, Mo. BL/TR, 6'3", 210 lbs. Deb: 6/14/73

YEAR TM/L	W	L	PCT	G	GS	CG	SH	SV	IP	H	HR	BB	SO	RAT	ERA	ERA+	OAV	OOB	BH	AVG	PB	PR	/A	PD	TPI
1973 KC-A	1	3	.250	8	7	1	0	0	38	44	5	23	16	15.9	5.68	72	.288	.381	0	—	0	-8	-7	-0	-0.6
1975 KC-A	1	2	.333	7	3	1	0	0	24¹	19	1	15	19	12.6	3.70	104	.229	.347	0	—	0	0	0	1	0.1
1976 *KC-A	8	4	.667	60	1	0	0	16	104	68	1	60	92	11.1	2.08	169	.188	.304	0	.000	0	**17**	16	-2	1.6
1977 *KC-A	8	4	.667	48	5	0	0	12	104²	73	6	55	106	11.1	3.61	112	.198	.304	0	.000	-0	5	5	-2	0.3
1978 StL-N	4	8	.333	72	2	0	0	11	106¹	80	8	59	130	12.1	2.79	126	.213	.326	0	.000	-0	9	9	-1	0.7
1979 StL-N	9	4	.692	63	0	0	0	13	82¹	60	2	39	67	10.8	2.19	172	.203	.296	0	.000	-1	14	14	-1	1.3
1980 StL-N	0	2	.000	14	0	0	0	2	10²	14	2	7	7	17.7	9.28	40	.318	.412	0	.000	-0	-7	-7	-0	-0.6
1981 StL-N	1	3	.250	28	1	0	0	2	41	36	2	31	22	14.7	4.39	81	.237	.366	2	.250	-0	-4	-4	-1	-0.3
1982 StL-N	0	1	.000	16	0	0	0	0	20²	22	1	15	7	16.1	5.23	69	.272	.385	0	.000	-0	-4	-4	-0	-0.4
Total 9	32	31	.508	316	19	2	0	56	532	416	28	304	466	12.3	3.32	112	.217	.326	2	.059	-2	23	24	-6	2.1

■ **JEFF LITTLE**   Little, Donald Jeffrey b: 12/25/54, Fremont, Ohio BR/TL, 6'6", 220 lbs. Deb: 9/06/80

YEAR TM/L	W	L	PCT	G	GS	CG	SH	SV	IP	H	HR	BB	SO	RAT	ERA	ERA+	OAV	OOB	BH	AVG	PB	PR	/A	PD	TPI
1980 StL-N	1	1	.500	7	2	0	0	0	18²	18	0	9	17	13.0	3.86	96	.250	.333	1	.167	-0	-1	-0	-0	0.0
1982 Min-A	2	0	1.000	33	0	0	0	0	36¹	33	6	27	26	14.9	4.21	101	.244	.370	0	—	0	-1	0	-1	0.0
Total 2	3	1	.750	40	2	0	0	0	55	51	6	36	43	14.2	4.09	99	.246	.358	1	.167	-0	-1	-0	-1	0.0

■ **JOHN LITTLEFIELD**   Littlefield, John Andrew b: 1/5/54, Covina, Cal. BR/TR, 6'2", 200 lbs. Deb: 6/08/80

YEAR TM/L	W	L	PCT	G	GS	CG	SH	SV	IP	H	HR	BB	SO	RAT	ERA	ERA+	OAV	OOB	BH	AVG	PB	PR	/A	PD	TPI
1980 StL-N	5	5	.500	52	0	0	0	9	66	71	2	20	22	12.5	3.14	118	.282	.337	0	.000	-1	3	4	0	0.3
1981 SD-N	2	3	.400	42	0	0	0	2	64	53	5	28	21	11.5	3.66	89	.235	.322	0	.000	-0	-1	-3	0	-0.2
Total 2	7	8	.467	94	0	0	0	11	130	124	7	48	43	12.0	3.39	102	.259	.330	0	.000	-1	2	1	0	0.1

■ **DICK LITTLEFIELD**   Littlefield, Richard Bernard b: 3/18/26, Detroit, Mich. BL/TL, 6', 180 lbs. Deb: 7/07/50

YEAR TM/L	W	L	PCT	G	GS	CG	SH	SV	IP	H	HR	BB	SO	RAT	ERA	ERA+	OAV	OOB	BH	AVG	PB	PR	/A	PD	TPI
1950 Bos-A	2	2	.500	15	2	0	0	1	23¹	27	6	24	13	20.1	9.26	53	.297	.448	0	.000	-1	-12	-11	1	-0.9
1951 Chi-A	1	1	.500	4	2	0	0	0	9²	7	1	17	7	24.2	8.38	48	.243	.481	0	.000	0	-5	-5	0	-0.3
1952 Det-A	0	3	.000	28	1	0	0	1	47²	46	4	25	32	13.4	4.34	88	.257	.348	1	.143	-0	-4	-3	-1	-0.3
StL-A	2	3	.400	7	5	3	0	0	46¹	35	4	17	34	10.1	2.72	144	.205	.277	1	.063	-2	5	6	-1	0.3
Yr	2	6	.250	35	6	3	0	1	94	81	8	42	66	11.8	3.54	109	.231	.314	2	.100	-2	1	3	-2	0.0
1953 StL-A	7	12	.368	36	22	2	0	0	152¹	153	17	84	104	14.2	5.08	83	.264	.361	8	.190	-1	-18	-15	-1	-1.5
1954 Bal-A	0	0	—	3	0	0	0	0	6	8	0	6	5	22.5	10.50	34	.333	.484	0	.000	-0	-5	-5	-0	-0.4
Pit-N	10	11	.476	23	21	7	1	0	155	140	10	85	92	13.2	3.60	116	.239	.337	8	.163	0	8	10	-3	0.7
1955 Pit-N	5	12	.294	35	17	4	1	0	130	148	16	50	76	15.1	5.12	80	.290	.375	6	.176	0	-16	-15	-2	-1.5
1956 Pit-N	0	0	—	6	2	0	0	0	12²	14	2	6	10	14.2	4.26	88	.286	.364	0	.000	-0	-1	-1	-0	0.0
StL-N	0	2	.000	3	2	0	0	0	9²	9	2	4	5	12.1	7.45	51	.237	.310	0	.000	-0	-4	-4	-0	-0.3
NY-N	4	4	.500	31	7	0	0	2	97	78	16	39	65	10.9	4.08	93	.231	.319	1	.036	-2	-3	-3	-0	-0.4
Yr	4	6	.400	40	11	0	0	2	119¹	101	20	49	80	11.3	4.37	86	.238	.316	1	.036	-2	-8	-8	-0	-0.7
1957 Chi-N	2	3	.400	48	2	0	0	4	65²	76	12	37	51	15.6	5.35	72	.295	.385	2	.182	0	-11	-11	-1	-1.1
1958 Mil-N	0	1	.000	4	0	0	0	0	6¹	7	2	6	3	17.1	4.26	83	.280	.333	0	—	0	-0	-1	-0	0.0
Total 9	33	54	.379	243	83	16	2	9	761²	750	91	413	495	13.9	4.71	86	.260	.355	28	.145	-5	-65	-56	-10	-5.7

■ **CARLISLE LITTLEJOHN**   Littlejohn, Charles Carlisle b: 10/6/01, Irene, Tex. d: 10/27/77, Kansas City, Mo. BR/TR, 5'10", 175 lbs. Deb: 5/11/27

YEAR TM/L	W	L	PCT	G	GS	CG	SH	SV	IP	H	HR	BB	SO	RAT	ERA	ERA+	OAV	OOB	BH	AVG	PB	PR	/A	PD	TPI
1927 StL-N	3	1	.750	14	2	1	0	0	42	47	4	14	16	13.1	4.50	88	.292	.349	5	.417	2	-3	-3	-1	-0.1
1928 StL-N	2	1	.667	12	2	1	0	0	32	36	2	14	6	14.1	3.66	109	.286	.357	0	.000	-2	1	1	-0	0.0
Total 2	5	2	.714	26	4	2	0	0	74	83	6	28	22	13.5	4.14	96	.289	.352	5	.217	-0	-2	-1	-1	-0.1

YEAR TM/L	W	L	PCT	G	GS	CG	SH	SV	IP	H	HR	BB	SO	RAT	ERA	ERA+	OAV	OOB	BH	AVG	PB	PR	/A	PD	TPI

■ BUDDY LIVELY   Lively, Everett Adrian "Red" b: 2/14/25, Birmingham, Ala. BR/TR, 6'0.5", 200 lbs. Deb: 4/17/47

1947 Cin-N	4	7	.364	38	17	3	1	0	123	126	16	63	52	13.8	4.68	88	.265	.351	6	.188	2	-9	-8	-0	-0.5
1948 Cin-N	0	0	—	10	0	0	0	0	22²	13	0	11	12	9.9	2.38	164	.165	.275	0	.000	-0	4	4	-0	0.3
1949 Cin-N	4	6	.400	31	10	3	1	1	103¹	91	11	53	30	12.5	3.92	107	.245	.339	4	.154	0	1	3	-1	0.2
Total 3	8	13	.381	79	27	6	2	1	249	230	27	127	94	12.9	4.16	99	.248	.339	10	.167	1	-3	-1	-1	0.0

■ JACK LIVELY   Lively, Henry Everett b: 5/29/1885, Joppa, Ala. d: 12/5/67, Arab, Ala. BR , 5'9", 185 lbs. Deb: 4/16/11

| 1911 Det-A | 7 | 5 | .583 | 18 | 14 | 10 | 0 | 0 | 113² | 143 | 1 | 34 | 45 | 14.6 | 4.59 | 75 | .313 | .369 | 11 | .256 | 3 | -16 | -14 | -1 | -1.1 |

■ WES LIVENGOOD   Livengood, Wesley Amos b: 7/18/10, Salisbury, N.C. BR/TR, 6'2", 172 lbs. Deb: 5/30/39

| 1939 Cin-N | 0 | 0 | — | 5 | 0 | 0 | 0 | 0 | 5² | 9 | 3 | 3 | 4 | 19.1 | 9.53 | 40 | .360 | .429 | 0 | — | 0 | -4 | -4 | 0 | -0.3 |

■ JAKE LIVINGSTON   Livingston, Jacob M. (b: Jacob M. Livingstone) b: 1/1/1880, Petrograd, Russia d: 3/22/49, Wassaic, N.Y. Deb: 9/06/01

| 1901 NY-N | 0 | 0 | — | 2 | 0 | 0 | 0 | 0 | 12 | 26 | 0 | 7 | 6 | 27.0 | 9.00 | 37 | .430 | .511 | 1 | .167 | 0 | -8 | -8 | -0 | -0.6 |

■ CLEM LLEWELLYN   Llewellyn, Clement Manley "Lew" b: 8/1/1895, Dobson, N.C. d: 11/26/69, Concord, N.C. BL/TR, 6'2", 195 lbs. Deb: 6/18/22

| 1922 NY-A | 0 | 0 | — | 1 | 0 | 0 | 0 | 0 | 1 | 1 | 0 | 0 | 0 | 9.0 | 0.00 | — | .250 | .250 | 0 | — | 0 | 0 | 0 | 0 | 0.0 |

■ HARRY LOCHHEAD   Lochhead, Robert Henry b: 3/29/1876, Stockton, Cal. d: 8/22/09, Stockton, Cal. TR , Deb: 4/16/1899 ♦

| 1899 Cle-N | 0 | 0 | — | 1 | 0 | 0 | 0 | 0 | 3² | 4 | 0 | 2 | 0 | 14.7 | 0.00 | — | .277 | .365 | 129 | .238 | 0 | 2 | 1 | -0 | 0.1 |

■ CHUCK LOCKE   Locke, Charles Edward b: 5/5/32, Malden, Mo. BR/TR, 5'11", 185 lbs. Deb: 9/16/55

| 1955 Bal-A | 0 | 0 | — | 2 | 0 | 0 | 0 | 0 | 3 | 0 | 0 | 1 | 1 | 3.0 | 0.00 | — | .000 | .100 | 0 | — | 0 | 1 | 1 | 0 | 0.1 |

■ BOBBY LOCKE   Locke, Lawrence Donald b: 3/3/34, Rowes Run, Pa. BR/TR, 5'11", 185 lbs. Deb: 6/18/59

1959 Cle-A	3	2	.600	24	7	0	0	2	77²	66	6	41	40	12.7	3.13	118	.233	.336	8	.333	3	6	5	0	0.8
1960 Cle-A	3	5	.375	32	11	2	2	2	123	121	10	37	53	11.7	3.37	111	.255	.311	9	.237	3	7	5	2	1.0
1961 Cle-A	4	4	.500	37	4	0	0	2	95¹	112	12	40	37	14.5	4.53	87	.300	.371	4	.211	0	-5	-6	1	-0.4
1962 StL-N	0	0	—	1	0	0	0	0	2	1	0	2	1	13.5	0.00	—	.143	.333	0	0	1	1	1	0	0.1
Phi-N	1	0	1.000	5	0	0	0	0	15²	16	4	10	9	14.9	5.74	67	.262	.366	2	.286	0	-3	-3	1	-0.1
Yr	1	0	1.000	6	0	0	0	0	17²	17	4	12	10	14.8	5.09	77	.250	.363	0	.000	0	-2	-2	1	0.0
1963 Phi-N	0	0	—	9	0	0	0	0	10²	10	0	5	7	12.7	5.91	66	.244	.326	0	.000	-0	-3	-3	-0	-0.3
1964 Phi-N	0	0	—	8	0	0	0	0	19¹	21	2	6	11	12.6	2.79	124	.276	.329	0	.000	-0	2	1	0	0.1
1965 Cin-N	0	1	.000	11	0	0	0	0	17¹	20	2	8	8	14.5	5.71	66	.299	.373	0	.000	0	-4	-4	1	-0.2
1967 Cal-A	3	0	1.000	9	1	0	0	2	19¹	14	1	3	7	8.4	2.33	135	.203	.247	2	.667	1	2	2	0	0.3
1968 Cal-A	2	3	.400	29	0	0	0	2	36¹	51	3	13	21	16.1	6.44	45	.331	.387	0	.000	-0	-14	-14	-0	-1.6
Total 9	16	15	.516	165	23	2	2	10	416²	432	40	165	194	13.1	4.02	91	.269	.340	25	.255	7	-12	-17	5	-0.3

■ RON LOCKE   Locke, Ronald Thomas b: 4/4/42, Wakefield, R.I. BR/TL, 5'11", 168 lbs. Deb: 4/23/64

| 1964 NY-N | 1 | 2 | .333 | 25 | 3 | 0 | 0 | 0 | 41¹ | 46 | 3 | 22 | 17 | 15.0 | 3.48 | 103 | .289 | .379 | 0 | .000 | -1 | 0 | 0 | 0 | 0.0 |

■ BOB LOCKER   Locker, Robert Awtry b: 3/15/38, George, Iowa BB/TR, 6'3", 200 lbs. Deb: 4/14/65

1965 Chi-A	5	2	.714	51	0	0	0	2	91¹	71	6	30	69	10.1	3.15	101	.216	.285	0	.000	-1	3	0	3	0.2
1966 Chi-A	9	8	.529	56	0	0	0	12	95	73	2	23	70	9.6	2.46	129	.206	.264	4	.250	1	10	7	2	1.2
1967 Chi-A	7	5	.583	77	0	0	0	20	124²	102	5	23	80	9.7	2.09	148	.222	.274	0	.000	-1	16	14	5	2.0
1968 Chi-A	5	4	.556	70	0	0	0	10	90¹	78	4	27	62	10.6	2.29	132	.234	.293	0	.000	-1	7	7	1	1.1
1969 Chi-A	2	3	.400	17	0	0	0	4	22	26	6	6	15	13.1	6.55	59	.292	.337	0	.000	-0	-7	-7	0	-0.6
Sea-A	3	3	.500	51	0	0	0	6	78¹	69	3	26	46	11.3	2.18	166	.234	.302	1	.083	-0	13	13	2	1.5
Yr	5	6	.455	68	0	0	0	10	100¹	95	9	32	61	11.7	3.14	117	.247	.310	1	.077	-1	5	6	2	0.9
1970 Mil-A	0	1	.000	28	0	0	0	3	31²	37	1	10	19	14.8	3.41	111	.306	.382	0	.000	-0	1	1	-0	0.1
Oak-A	3	3	.500	38	0	0	0	4	56¹	49	1	19	33	11.0	2.88	123	.232	.299	1	.167	-0	5	4	1	0.5
Yr	3	4	.429	66	0	0	0	7	88	86	2	29	52	11.9	3.07	118	.254	.315	0	.000	-0	6	5	0	0.6
1971 *Oak-A	7	2	.778	47	0	0	0	6	72¹	68	3	19	46	10.9	2.86	116	.249	.300	0	.000	-0	5	4	1	0.5
1972 *Oak-A	6	1	.857	56	0	0	0	10	78	69	1	16	47	10.0	2.65	107	.235	.280	0	.000	0	4	2	-1	0.1
1973 Chi-N	10	6	.625	63	0	0	0	18	106¹	96	6	42	76	12.0	2.54	155	.244	.323	1	.067	-1	13	17	1	1.8
1975 Chi-N	0	1	.000	22	0	0	0	0	32²	38	3	16	14	15.4	4.96	77	.306	.394	0	—	-1	-5	-4	1	-0.3
Total 10	57	39	.594	576	0	0	0	95	879	776	41	257	577	10.9	2.75	122	.237	.300	7	.074	-4	64	58	18	8.1

■ SKIP LOCKWOOD   Lockwood, Claude Edward b: 8/17/46, Boston, Mass. BR/TR, 6'1", 175 lbs. Deb: 4/23/65 ♦

1969 Sea-A	0	1	.000	6	3	0	0	0	23	24	3	6	10	11.7	3.52	103	.279	.326	0	.000	-1	0	0	1	0.0
1970 Mil-A	5	12	.294	27	26	3	1	0	173²	173	22	79	93	13.4	4.30	88	.266	.351	12	.226	2	-11	-10	-1	-0.8
1971 Mil-A	10	15	.400	33	32	5	1	0	208	191	13	91	115	12.4	3.33	104	.246	.329	5	.081	-1	3	3	-3	0.0
1972 Mil-A	8	15	.348	29	27	5	3	0	170	148	11	71	106	11.8	3.60	84	.232	.313	7	.132	-1	-10	-11	-3	-1.5
1973 Mil-A	5	12	.294	37	15	3	0	0	154²	164	10	59	87	13.3	3.90	96	.280	.352	0	—	0	-1	-2	-0	-0.2
1974 Cal-A	2	5	.286	37	2	0	0	1	81¹	81	8	32	39	13.1	4.32	80	.264	.343	0	—	0	-6	-8	-0	-0.7
1975 NY-N	1	3	.250	24	0	0	0	2	48¹	28	3	25	61	10.1	1.49	232	.174	.289	1	.167	-0	11	11	-1	1.0
1976 NY-N	10	7	.588	56	0	0	0	19	94¹	62	6	34	108	9.3	2.67	123	.186	.266	6	.333	3	9	7	-1	0.8
1977 NY-N	4	8	.333	63	0	0	0	20	104	87	5	31	84	10.6	3.38	111	.227	.297	3	.200	0	6	4	-2	0.2
1978 NY-N	7	13	.350	57	0	0	0	15	90²	78	10	31	73	10.8	3.57	98	.236	.302	2	.182	1	-1	-2	-1	-0.1
1979 NY-N	2	5	.286	27	0	0	0	9	42¹	33	3	14	42	10.0	1.49	245	.224	.292	0	.000	-0	11	10	-1	1.0
1980 Bos-A	3	1	.750	24	1	0	0	2	22	15	4	17	11	15.4	5.32	79	.321	.377	0	—	-0	-7	-6	-1	-0.5
Total 12	57	97	.370	420	106	16	5	68	1236	1130	98	490	829	12.0	3.55	99	.246	.323	40	.154	-4	4	-3	-13	-0.8

■ MILO LOCKWOOD   Lockwood, Milo Hathaway b: 4/7/1858, Solon, Ohio d: 10/9/1897, Economy, Pa. 5'10", 160 lbs. Deb: 4/17/1884 ♦

| 1884 Was-U | 1 | 9 | .100 | 11 | 10 | 6 | 0 | 0 | 67² | 99 | 4 | 15 | 48 | 15.2 | 7.45 | 40 | .320 | .351 | 14 | .209 | 0 | -33 | -34 | 1 | -2.5 |

■ BILLY LOES   Loes, William b: 12/13/29, Long Island City, N.Y. BR/TR, 6'1", 165 lbs. Deb: 5/18/50

1950 Bro-N	0	0	—	10	0	0	0	0	12²	16	5	5	2	14.9	7.82	52	.314	.375	0	.000	0	-5	-5	-0	-0.4
1952 *Bro-N	13	8	.619	39	21	8	4	1	187¹	154	12	71	115	11.0	2.69	135	.224	.299	5	.093	-3	22	20	-1	1.7
1953 *Bro-N	14	8	.636	32	25	9	1	0	162¹	165	21	53	75	12.2	4.54	94	.261	.322	7	.125	-2	-5	-5	3	-0.3
1954 Bro-N	13	5	.722	28	21	6	0	0	147²	154	14	60	97	13.1	4.14	99	.269	.339	6	.118	-2	-1	-1	-3	-0.4
1955 *Bro-N	10	4	.714	22	19	6	0	0	128	116	16	46	85	11.5	3.59	113	.240	.308	4	.091	-3	6	7	-0	0.3
1956 Bro-N	0	1	.000	1	1	0	0	0	1¹	5	1	1	2	40.5	40.50	10	.556	.600	0	—	0	-5	-5	0	-0.3
Bal-A	4	7	.222	21	6	1	0	3	56²	64	4	23	62	14.3	4.76	82	.291	.363	3	.176	-1	-4	-5	1	-0.4
1957 Bal-A	12	7	.632	31	18	8	3	4	155¹	142	8	37	86	10.6	3.24	111	.245	.295	4	.080	-3	9	6	1	0.5
1958 Bal-A	3	9	.250	32	10	1	0	5	114	106	10	44	44	12.5	3.63	99	.252	.334	2	.067	-2	2	-0	0	-0.2
1959 Bal-A	4	7	.364	37	0	0	0	14	64¹	58	5	25	34	12.0	4.06	93	.239	.317	1	.125	-0	-1	-2	1	0.0
1960 SF-N	3	2	.600	37	0	0	0	5	45²	40	9	17	28	12.0	4.93	71	.247	.333	1	.250	0	-6	-7	1	-0.4
1961 SF-N	6	5	.545	26	18	3	1	0	114²	114	13	39	55	12.4	4.24	99	.258	.325	5	.156	1	-3	-5	1	-0.5
Total 11	80	63	.559	316	139	42	9	32	1190¹	1135	118	421	645	12.0	3.89	99	.252	.321	38	.110	-17	9	-5	7	-0.4

■ FRANK LOFTUS   Loftus, Francis Patrick b: 3/10/1898, Scranton, Pa. d: 10/27/80, Belchertown, Mass. BR/TR, 5'9", 190 lbs. Deb: 9/26/26

| 1926 Was-A | 0 | 0 | — | 1 | 0 | 0 | 0 | 0 | 1 | 3 | 0 | 2 | 0 | 45.0 | 9.00 | 43 | .600 | .714 | 0 | — | 0 | -1 | -1 | 0 | 0.0 |

■ BOB LOGAN   Logan, Robert Dean "Lefty" b: 2/10/10, Thompson, Neb. d: 5/20/78, Indianapolis, Ind. BR/TL, 5'10", 170 lbs. Deb: 4/18/35

| 1935 Bro-N | 0 | 1 | .000 | 2 | 0 | 0 | 0 | 0 | 2² | 2 | 0 | 1 | 1 | 10.1 | 3.38 | 118 | .182 | .250 | 0 | — | 0 | 0 | 0 | 0 | 0.0 |

YEAR TM/L	W	L	PCT	G	GS	CG	SH	SV	IP	H	HR	BB	SO	RAT	ERA	ERA+	OAV	OOB	BH	AVG	PB	PR	/A	PD	TPI
1937 Det-A	0	0	—	1	0	0	0	0	0^2	1	0	1	1	27.0	0.00		.333	.500	0	—	0	0	0	0	0.0
Chi-N	0	0	—	4	0	0	0	1	6^1	6	0	4	2	14.2	1.42	280	.261	.370	0	.000	-0	2	2	-0	0.1
1938 Chi-N	0	2	.000	14	0	0	0	2	22^2	18	0	17	10	14.3	2.78	138	.222	.364	0	.000	-0	3	3	-0	0.2
1941 Cin-N	0	1	.000	2	0	0	0	0	3^1	5	0	5	0	27.0	8.10	44	.333	.500	0	—	0	-2	-2	0	0.0
1945 Bos-N	7	11	.389	34	25	5	1	1	187	213	9	53	53	12.9	3.18	121	.283	.331	13	.213	1	13	14	0	1.5
Total 5	7	15	.318	57	25	5	1	4	222^2	245	9	81	67	13.3	3.15	122	.277	.339	13	.200	1	16	17	1	1.8

■ BILL LOHRMAN
Lohrman, William Le Roy b: 5/22/13, Brooklyn, N.Y. BR/TR, 6'1", 185 lbs. Deb: 6/19/34

YEAR TM/L	W	L	PCT	G	GS	CG	SH	SV	IP	H	HR	BB	SO	RAT	ERA	ERA+	OAV	OOB	BH	AVG	PB	PR	/A	PD	TPI
1934 Phi-N	0	1	.000	4	0	0	0	1	6	5	0	1	2	9.0	4.50	105	.217	.250	1	.500	0	-0	0	0	0.1
1937 NY-N	1	0	1.000	2	1	1	0	1	10	5	0	2	3	6.3	0.90	432	.152	.200	0	.000	-0	3	3	0	0.4
1938 NY-N	9	6	.600	31	14	3	0	0	152	152	9	33	52	11.1	3.32	114	.253	.294	4	.082	-4	8	8	2	0.6
1939 NY-N	12	13	.480	38	24	9	1	1	185^2	200	15	45	70	12.0	4.07	96	.282	.327	14	.233	4	-3	-3	0	0.1
1940 NY-N	10	15	.400	31	28	11	4	1	195	200	19	43	73	11.4	3.78	103	.264	.306	8	.123	-3	1	2	3	0.2
1941 NY-N	9	10	.474	33	20	6	2	3	159	184	7	40	61	12.7	4.02	92	.286	.327	11	.229	4	-7	-6	1	-0.1
1942 StL-N	1	1	.500	5	0	0	0	0	12^2	11	0	2	6	9.2	1.42	241	.244	.277	2	.667	1	3	3	0	0.4
NY-N	13	4	.765	26	19	12	2	0	158	143	11	33	41	10.1	2.56	131	.240	.282	7	.121	-3	13	14	-1	1.2
Yr	14	5	.737	31	19	12	2	0	170^2	154	11	35	47	10.1	2.48	136	.240	.281	2	.033	-2	16	17	-1	1.6
1943 NY-N	5	6	.455	17	12	3	0	1	80^1	110	7	25	16	15.3	5.15	67	.324	.374	1	.037	-3	-16	-15	-1	-1.8
Bro-N	0	2	.000	6	2	2	0	0	27^2	29	2	10	5	13.0	3.58	94	.274	.342	1	.143	0	-1	-1	0	0.0
Yr	5	8	.385	23	14	5	0	1	108	139	9	35	21	14.6	4.75	72	.311	.362	2	.059	-3	-16	-16	-1	-1.8
1944 Bro-N	0	0	—	3	0	0	0	0	2^2	4	0	4	1	27.0	0.00	—	.500	.667	0	—	0	1	1	0	0.1
Cin-N	0	1	.000	2	1	0	0	0	1^2	5	0	2	0	37.8	27.00	13	.500	.583	0	—	0	-4	-4	0	-0.3
Yr	0	1	.000	5	1	0	0	0	4^1	9	0	6	1	31.2	10.38	34	.500	.625	0	—	0	-3	-3	0	-0.2
Total 9	60	59	.504	198	121	47	9	8	990^2	1048	70	240	330	11.8	3.69	101	.271	.315	49	.153	-3	-1	2	4	0.9

■ MICKEY LOLICH
Lolich, Michael Stephen b: 9/12/40, Portland, Ore. BB/TL, 6'1", 170 lbs. Deb: 5/12/63

YEAR TM/L	W	L	PCT	G	GS	CG	SH	SV	IP	H	HR	BB	SO	RAT	ERA	ERA+	OAV	OOB	BH	AVG	PB	PR	/A	PD	TPI
1963 Det-A	5	9	.357	33	18	4	0	0	144^1	145	13	56	103	12.8	3.55	105	.265	.338	2	.056	-1	1	3	-1	0.2
1964 Det-A	18	9	.667	44	33	12	6	2	232	196	26	64	192	10.3	3.26	112	.225	.282	7	.109	1	9	10	-2	0.9
1965 Det-A	15	9	.625	43	37	7	3	3	243^2	216	23	72	226	11.1	3.44	101	.236	.301	5	.058	-6	1	1	-3	-0.7
1966 Det-A	14	14	.500	40	33	5	1	3	203^2	204	24	83	173	12.9	4.77	73	.257	.331	9	.141	1	-30	-29	-3	-3.1
1967 Det-A	14	13	.519	31	30	11	6	1	204	165	14	56	174	10.1	3.04	107	.221	.282	12	.197	3	4	5	-2	0.6
1968 *Det-A	17	9	.654	39	32	8	4	1	220	178	23	65	197	10.4	3.19	94	.219	.286	8	.114	0	-5	-4	-2	-0.7
1969 Det-A	19	11	.633	37	36	15	1	1	280^2	214	22	122	271	11.2	3.14	119	.210	.304	8	.088	-3	15	18	-1	1.6
1970 Det-A	14	19	.424	40	39	13	3	0	272^2	272	27	109	230	12.7	3.80	98	.260	.333	11	.134	1	-2	-2	1	0.0
1971 Det-A	25	14	.641	45	45	29	4	0	376	336	36	92	308	10.4	2.92	123	.237	.287	15	.130	1	23	28	-5	2.8
1972 *Det-A	22	14	.611	41	41	23	4	0	327^1	282	29	74	250	10.1	2.50	126	.234	.284	6	.067	-0	20	23	-4	2.2
1973 Det-A	16	15	.516	42	42	17	3	0	308^2	315	35	79	214	11.6	3.82	107	.266	.315	0	—	0	-0	9	-1	0.8
1974 Det-A	16	21	.432	41	41	27	3	0	308	310	38	78	202	11.4	4.15	92	.268	.316	0	—	0	-18	-12	-4	-1.5
1975 Det-A	12	18	.400	32	32	19	1	0	240^2	260	19	64	139	12.1	3.78	106	.279	.325	0	—	0	-0	6	-2	-0.5
1976 NY-N	8	13	.381	31	30	5	2	0	192^2	184	14	52	120	11.0	3.22	102	.252	.302	7	.130	0	6	2	-1	0.1
1978 SD-N	2	1	.667	20	2	0	0	1	34^2	30	0	11	13	10.9	1.56	214	.240	.307	0	.000	-0	8	7	0	0.7
1979 SD-N	0	2	.000	27	5	0	0	0	49^1	59	4	22	20	14.8	4.74	74	.304	.375	0	.000	-0	-6	-7	0	-0.6
Total 16	217	191	.532	586	496	195	41	11	3638^1	3366	347	1099	2832	11.3	3.44	104	.246	.306	90	.110	-4	25	58	-30	3.8

■ TIM LOLLAR
Lollar, William Timothy b: 3/17/56, Poplar Bluff, Mo. BL/TL, 6'3", 200 lbs. Deb: 6/28/80

YEAR TM/L	W	L	PCT	G	GS	CG	SH	SV	IP	H	HR	BB	SO	RAT	ERA	ERA+	OAV	OOB	BH	AVG	PB	PR	/A	PD	TPI
1980 NY-A	1	0	1.000	14	1	0	0	2	32^1	33	3	20	13	14.8	3.34	117	.280	.384	0	—	0	2	2	0	0.2
1981 SD-N	2	8	.200	24	11	0	0	1	76^2	87	4	51	38	16.6	6.10	53	.293	.402	3	.167	1	-22	-24	2	-2.1
1982 SD-N	16	9	.640	34	34	4	2	0	232^2	192	20	87	150	10.9	3.13	109	.224	.298	21	.247	8	12	8	-0	1.6
1983 SD-N	7	12	.368	30	30	1	0	0	175^2	170	22	85	135	13.3	4.61	76	.258	.347	14	.241	5	-19	-22	-2	-1.8
1984 *SD-N	11	13	.458	31	31	3	2	0	195^2	168	18	105	131	12.6	3.91	91	.234	.333	15	.221	7	-7	-7	-3	-0.2
1985 Chi-A	3	5	.375	18	13	0	0	0	83	83	10	58	61	15.4	4.66	93	.266	.383	0	—	0	-5	-3	0	-0.3
Bos-A	5	5	.500	16	10	1	0	1	67	57	9	40	44	13.2	4.57	94	.230	.339	0	.000	0	-3	-2	-1	-0.2
Yr	8	10	.444	34	23	1	0	1	150	140	19	98	105	14.3	4.62	93	.248	.360	0	.000	0	-8	-5	-1	-0.5
1986 Bos-A	2	0	1.000	32	1	0	0	0	43	51	7	34	28	18.4	6.91	60	.304	.429	1	1.000	0	-13	-13	1	-1.1
Total 7	47	52	.475	199	131	9	4	4	906	841	93	480	600	13.3	4.27	85	.249	.345	54	.234	23	-55	-63	-3	-3.9

■ VIC LOMBARDI
Lombardi, Victor Alvin b: 9/20/22, Reedley, Cal. BL/TL, 5'7", 158 lbs. Deb: 4/18/45

YEAR TM/L	W	L	PCT	G	GS	CG	SH	SV	IP	H	HR	BB	SO	RAT	ERA	ERA+	OAV	OOB	BH	AVG	PB	PR	/A	PD	TPI
1945 Bro-N	10	11	.476	38	24	9	0	4	203^2	195	11	86	64	12.6	3.31	113	.252	.331	13	.183	-1	11	10	-0	0.9
1946 Bro-N	13	10	.565	41	25	13	2	3	193	170	10	84	60	11.9	2.89	117	.235	.316	14	.230	2	11	10	1	1.4
1947 *Bro-N	12	11	.522	33	20	7	3	3	174^2	156	12	65	72	11.5	2.99	138	.241	.312	16	.242	2	21	22	1	2.6
1948 Pit-N	10	9	.526	38	17	9	0	4	163	156	9	67	54	12.4	3.70	110	.255	.330	10	.208	1	5	7	1	0.9
1949 Pit-N	5	5	.500	34	12	4	0	1	134	149	14	68	64	14.8	4.57	92	.286	.372	17	.347	5	-8	-5	1	0.1
1950 Pit-N	0	5	.000	39	2	0	0	1	76^1	93	14	48	26	16.9	6.60	66	.310	.409	4	.250	1	-21	-19	1	-1.6
Total 6	50	51	.495	223	100	42	5	16	944^2	919	70	418	340	12.9	3.68	106	.257	.337	74	.238	10	19	25	4	4.3

■ LOU LOMBARDO
Lombardo, Louis b: 11/18/28, Carlstadt, N.J. BL/TL, 6'2", 210 lbs. Deb: 9/22/48

YEAR TM/L	W	L	PCT	G	GS	CG	SH	SV	IP	H	HR	BB	SO	RAT	ERA	ERA+	OAV	OOB	BH	AVG	PB	PR	/A	PD	TPI
1948 NY-N	0	0	—	2	0	0	0	0	5^1	5	1	5	0	18.6	6.75	58	.250	.423	0	.000	-0	-2	-2	0	-0.1

■ JIM LONBORG
Lonborg, James Reynold b: 4/16/42, Santa Maria, Cal. BR/TR, 6'5", 200 lbs. Deb: 4/23/65

YEAR TM/L	W	L	PCT	G	GS	CG	SH	SV	IP	H	HR	BB	SO	RAT	ERA	ERA+	OAV	OOB	BH	AVG	PB	PR	/A	PD	TPI
1965 Bos-A	9	17	.346	32	31	7	1	0	185^1	193	20	65	113	12.7	4.47	83	.262	.324	8	.136	0	-21	-15	-2	-1.6
1966 Bos-A	10	10	.500	45	23	3	1	2	181^2	173	18	55	131	11.6	3.86	98	.249	.310	5	.093	-2	-9	-1	-1	-0.3
1967 *Bos-A	22	9	.710	39	39	15	2	0	273^1	228	23	83	246	10.9	3.16	110	.225	.296	14	.141	-1	2	10	-3	0.7
1968 Bos-A	6	10	.375	23	17	4	1	0	113^1	89	11	59	73	12.6	4.29	74	.216	.330	11	.282	4	-16	-14	-2	-1.3
1969 Bos-A	7	11	.389	29	23	4	0	0	143^2	148	15	65	100	13.8	4.51	84	.270	.355	4	.098	-1	-14	-11	-0	-1.1
1970 Bos-A	4	1	.800	9	4	0	0	0	34	33	3	9	21	11.1	3.18	125	.260	.309	4	.444	2	2	3	0	0.6
1971 Bos-A	10	7	.588	27	26	5	1	0	167^2	167	15	67	100	13.3	4.13	89	.259	.342	4	.170	0	-13	-8	1	-0.6
1972 Mil-A	14	12	.538	33	30	11	2	1	223	197	17	76	143	11.5	2.83	107	.238	.311	10	.145	-1	6	5	-2	0.2
1973 Phi-N	13	16	.448	38	30	6	0	0	199^1	218	25	80	106	13.9	4.88	78	.279	.353	8	.136	0	-27	-24	-1	-2.4
1974 Phi-N	17	13	.567	39	39	16	3	0	283	280	22	70	121	11.3	3.21	118	.261	.310	9	.096	-4	13	18	-3	1.2
1975 Phi-N	8	6	.571	27	26	6	2	0	159^1	161	12	45	72	11.9	4.12	90	.257	.312	1	.023		-9	-7	0	-0.8
1976 *Phi-N	18	10	.643	33	32	8	1	1	222	210	18	50	118	10.7	3.08	115	.249	.294	11	.164	1	10	11	-2	1.1
1977 *Phi-N	11	4	.733	25	25	4	1	0	157^2	157	15	50	76	12.1	4.11	97	.261	.323	5	.104	-2	-4	-2	-1	-0.4
1978 Phi-N	8	10	.444	22	22	1	0	0	113^2	132	16	44	68	14.2	5.23	68	.293	.359	6	.176	1	-21	-17	0	-1.9
1979 Phi-N	0	1	.000	7	6	1	0	0	7^1	14	3	4	7	23.3	11.05	35	.389	.463	0	.000	-0	-6	-6	0	-0.5
Total 15	157	137	.534	425	368	90	15	4	2464^1	2400	233	823	1475	12.2	3.86	94	.255	.322	105	.136	-5	-106	-63	-16	-7.1

■ LEP LONG
Long, Lester b: 7/12/1888, Summit, N.J. d: 10/21/58, Birmingham, Ala. BR/TR, 5'10", 153 lbs. Deb: 6/29/11

YEAR TM/L	W	L	PCT	G	GS	CG	SH	SV	IP	H	HR	BB	SO	RAT	ERA	ERA+	OAV	OOB	BH	AVG	PB	PR	/A	PD	TPI
1911 Phi-A	0	0	—	4	0	0	0	0	8	15	0	5	4	22.5	4.50	70	.405	.476	0	.000	-0	-1	-1	0	-0.1

■ RED LONG
Long, Nelson b: 9/28/1876, Burlington, Ont., Canada d: 8/11/29, Hamilton, Ont., Can BR/TR, 6'1", 190 lbs. Deb: 9/11/02

YEAR TM/L	W	L	PCT	G	GS	CG	SH	SV	IP	H	HR	BB	SO	RAT	ERA	ERA+	OAV	OOB	BH	AVG	PB	PR	/A	PD	TPI
1902 Bos-N	0	0	—	1	1	1	0	0	8	4	0	3	5	9.0	1.13	251	.150	.260	0	.000	-0	1	2	-0	0.1

■ BOB LONG
Long, Robert Earl b: 11/11/54, Jasper, Tenn. BR/TR, 6'3", 178 lbs. Deb: 9/02/81

YEAR TM/L	W	L	PCT	G	GS	CG	SH	SV	IP	H	HR	BB	SO	RAT	ERA	ERA+	OAV	OOB	BH	AVG	PB	PR	/A	PD	TPI
1981 Pit-N	1	2	.333	5	3	0	0	0	19^2	23	2	10	8	15.1	5.95	60	.299	.379	0	.000	-0	-5	-5	-0	-0.5
1985 Sea-A	0	0	—	28	0	0	0	0	38^1	30	7	17	29	11.5	3.76	112	.210	.302	0	—	0	2	2	-0	0.2

YEAR TM/L	W	L	PCT	G	GS	CG	SH	SV	IP	H	HR	BB	SO	RAT	ERA	ERA+	OAV	OOB	BH	AVG	PB	PR	/A	PD	TPI
Total 2	1	2	.333	33	3	0	0	0	58	53	9	27	37	12.7	4.50	89	.241	.329	0	.000	-0	-4	-3	-1	-0.3

■ **TOM LONG**   Long, Thomas Francis "Little Hawk"   b: 4/22/1898, Memphis, Tenn.   d: 9/16/73, Louisville, Ky.   BL/TL, 5'9", 154 lbs.   Deb: 4/26/24

YEAR TM/L	W	L	PCT	G	GS	CG	SH	SV	IP	H	HR	BB	SO	RAT	ERA	ERA+	OAV	OOB	BH	AVG	PB	PR	/A	PD	TPI
1924 Bro-N	0	0	—	1	0	0	0	0	2	2	0	2	0	18.0	9.00	42	.333	.500	0	—	0	-1	-1	0	0.0

■ **BILL LONG**   Long, William Douglas   b: 2/29/60, Cincinnati, Ohio   BR/TR, 6', 185 lbs.   Deb: 7/21/85

YEAR TM/L	W	L	PCT	G	GS	CG	SH	SV	IP	H	HR	BB	SO	RAT	ERA	ERA+	OAV	OOB	BH	AVG	PB	PR	/A	PD	TPI
1985 Chi-A	0	1	.000	4	3	0	0	0	14	25	4	5	13	19.3	10.29	42	.391	.435	0	—	0	-10	-9	0	-0.7
1987 Chi-A	8	8	.500	29	23	5	2	1	169	179	20	28	72	11.2	4.37	105	.272	.304	0	—	0	2	4	0	0.4
1988 Chi-A	8	11	.421	47	18	3	0	2	174	187	21	43	77	12.1	4.03	98	.280	.327	0	—	0	-1	-1	-0	0.0
1989 Chi-A	5	5	.500	30	8	0	0	1	98²	101	8	37	51	13.0	3.92	97	.265	.336	0	—	0	-0	-1	0	0.0
1990 Chi-A	0	1	.000	4	0	0	0	0	5²	6	2	2	2	12.7	6.35	60	.261	.320	0	—	0	-2	-2	0	0.0
Chi-N	6	1	.857	42	0	0	0	5	55²	66	8	21	32	14.2	4.37	95	.301	.365	0	.000	-0	-4	-1	0	0.0
Total 5	27	27	.500	156	52	8	2	9	517	564	63	136	247	12.4	4.35	96	.280	.329	0	.000	-0	-15	-11	2	-0.3

■ **PETE LOOS**   Loos, Ivan   b: 3/23/1878, Philadelphia, Pa.   d: 2/23/56, Darby, Pa.   TR,   Deb: 5/02/01

YEAR TM/L	W	L	PCT	G	GS	CG	SH	SV	IP	H	HR	BB	SO	RAT	ERA	ERA+	OAV	OOB	BH	AVG	PB	PR	/A	PD	TPI
1901 Phi-A	0	1	.000	1	1	0	0	0	1	2	0	4	0	54.0	27.00	14	.409	.675	0	—	0	-3	-3	0	-0.1

■ **EDDIE LOPAT**   Lopat, Edmund Walter (b: Edmund Walter Lopatynski)   b: 6/21/18, New York, N.Y.   BL/TL, 5'10", 185 lbs.   Deb: 4/30/44   MC

YEAR TM/L	W	L	PCT	G	GS	CG	SH	SV	IP	H	HR	BB	SO	RAT	ERA	ERA+	OAV	OOB	BH	AVG	PB	PR	/A	PD	TPI
1944 Chi-A	11	10	.524	27	25	13	1	0	210	217	12	59	59	11.9	3.26	105	.265	.316	25	.309	6	4	4	1	1.2
1945 Chi-A	10	13	.435	26	24	17	1	1	199¹	226	8	56	74	13.0	4.11	81	.285	.336	24	.293	5	-16	-17	-1	-1.3
1946 Chi-A	13	13	.500	29	29	20	2	0	231	216	18	48	89	10.3	2.73	125	.248	.288	22	.253	6	20	18	1	2.7
1947 Chi-A	16	13	.552	31	31	22	3	0	252²	241	17	73	109	11.3	2.81	130	.253	.307	19	.198	0	25	24	-1	2.4
1948 NY-A	17	11	.607	33	31	13	3	0	226²	246	16	66	83	12.5	3.65	112	.284	.336	14	.173	-1	16	11	2	1.1
1949 *NY-A	15	10	.600	31	30	14	4	1	215¹	222	19	69	70	12.4	3.26	124	.269	.330	20	.263	7	22	19	1	2.7
1950 *NY-A	18	8	.692	35	32	15	3	1	236¹	244	19	65	72	11.9	3.47	124	.266	.317	19	.232	7	29	22	2	2.9
1951 *NY-A	21	9	.700	31	31	20	4	0	234²	209	12	71	93	10.9	2.91	131	.234	.298	15	.179	1	31	24	2	2.6
1952 *NY-A	10	5	.667	20	19	10	2	0	149¹	127	11	53	56	11.1	2.53	131	.234	.307	4	.173	1	19	13	1	1.5
1953 *NY-A	16	4	.800	25	24	9	3	0	178¹	169	13	32	50	10.3	2.42	152	.250	.288	12	.190	1	31	25	2	2.9
1954 NY-A	12	4	.750	26	23	7	0	0	170	184	14	33	54	12.1	3.55	97	.288	.328	1	.018	-5	3	-2	-1	-0.7
1955 NY-A	4	8	.333	16	12	3	1	0	86²	101	12	16	24	12.3	3.74	100	.294	.328	4	.138	-1	2	0	-1	-0.1
Bal-A	3	4	.429	10	7	1	0	0	49	57	8	9	10	12.7	4.22	90	.294	.335	3	.176	0	-1	-2	1	-0.1
Yr	7	12	.368	26	19	4	1	0	135²	158	20	25	34	12.3	3.91	96	.293	.328	2	.043	-1	1	-2	0	-0.1
Total 12	166	112	.597	340	318	164	27	3	2439¹	2464	179	650	859	11.6	3.21	116	.264	.315	187	.211	28	186	138	8	17.9

■ **ART LOPATKA**   Lopatka, Arthur Joseph   b: 5/28/19, Chicago, Ill.   BB/TL, 5'10", 170 lbs.   Deb: 9/12/45

YEAR TM/L	W	L	PCT	G	GS	CG	SH	SV	IP	H	HR	BB	SO	RAT	ERA	ERA+	OAV	OOB	BH	AVG	PB	PR	/A	PD	TPI
1945 StL-N	1	0	1.000	4	1	1	0	0	11²	7	0	3	5	8.5	1.54	243	.159	.229	1	.250	0	3	3	-0	0.3
1946 Phi-N	0	1	.000	4	1	0	0	0	5¹	13	1	4	4	28.7	16.88	20	.448	.515	0	—	0	-8	-8	0	-0.7
Total 2	1	1	.500	8	2	1	0	0	17	20	1	7	9	14.8	6.35	57	.274	.346	1	.250	0	-5	-5	-0	-0.4

■ **AURELIO LOPEZ**   Lopez, Aurelio Alejandro (Rios)   b: 9/21/48, Tecamachalco Puebla, Mexico   BR/TR, 6', 185 lbs.   Deb: 9/01/74

YEAR TM/L	W	L	PCT	G	GS	CG	SH	SV	IP	H	HR	BB	SO	RAT	ERA	ERA+	OAV	OOB	BH	AVG	PB	PR	/A	PD	TPI
1974 KC-A	0	0	—	8	1	0	0	0	16	21	0	10	5	17.4	5.63	68	.344	.437	0	—	0	-4	-3	0	-0.2
1978 StL-N	4	2	.667	25	4	0	0	0	65	52	4	32	46	11.8	4.29	82	.218	.313	3	.214	0	-5	-6	-1	-0.6
1979 Det-A	10	5	.667	61	0	0	0	21	127	95	12	51	106	10.6	2.41	179	.210	.294	0	—	0	25	27	-1	2.6
1980 Det-A	13	6	.684	67	1	0	0	21	124	125	15	45	97	12.6	3.77	109	.263	.330	0	—	0	4	5	-2	0.3
1981 Det-A	5	2	.714	29	3	0	0	3	81²	70	8	31	53	11.4	3.64	104	.233	.309	0	—	0	1	1	-0	0.1
1982 Det-A	3	1	.750	19	0	0	0	3	41	41	8	19	26	13.2	5.27	77	.268	.349	0	—	0	-5	-5	0	-0.5
1983 Det-A	9	8	.529	57	0	0	0	18	115¹	87	12	49	90	10.7	2.81	139	.210	.295	0	—	0	16	14	-1	1.3
1984 *Det-A	10	1	.909	71	0	0	0	14	137²	109	16	52	94	10.7	2.94	133	.221	.298	0	—	0	16	15	-2	1.3
1985 Det-A	3	7	.300	51	0	0	0	5	86¹	82	15	41	53	12.9	4.80	85	.250	.335	0	—	0	-6	-7	-0	-0.6
1986 *Hou-N	3	3	.500	45	0	0	0	7	78	64	6	25	44	10.3	3.46	104	.221	.283	0	.000	-1	2	1	-1	0.0
1987 Hou-N	2	1	.667	26	0	0	0	1	38	39	6	12	21	12.6	4.50	87	.273	.338	0	.000	-0	-2	-2	0	-0.2
Total 11	62	36	.633	459	9	0	0	93	910	785	102	367	635	11.5	3.56	111	.234	.313	3	.125	-1	41	39	-8	3.5

■ **RAMON LOPEZ**   Lopez, Jose Ramon (Hevia)   b: 5/26/33, Las Villas, Cuba   d: 9/4/82, Miami, Fla.   BR/TR, 6', 175 lbs.   Deb: 8/21/66

YEAR TM/L	W	L	PCT	G	GS	CG	SH	SV	IP	H	HR	BB	SO	RAT	ERA	ERA+	OAV	OOB	BH	AVG	PB	PR	/A	PD	TPI
1966 Cal-A	0	1	.000	4	1	0	0	0	7	4	1	4	2	10.3	5.14	65	.154	.267	0	—	0	-1	-1	-0	-0.1

■ **MARCELINO LOPEZ**   Lopez, Marcelino Pons   b: 9/23/43, Havana, Cuba   BR/TL, 6'3", 195 lbs.   Deb: 4/14/63

YEAR TM/L	W	L	PCT	G	GS	CG	SH	SV	IP	H	HR	BB	SO	RAT	ERA	ERA+	OAV	OOB	BH	AVG	PB	PR	/A	PD	TPI
1963 Phi-N	1	0	1.000	4	2	0	0	0	6	8	0	7	2	22.5	6.00	54	.333	.484	0	.000	-0	-2	-2	0	-0.1
1965 Cal-A	14	13	.519	35	32	8	1	1	215¹	185	12	82	122	11.3	2.93	134	.230	.305	14	.203	3	13	11	4	2.1
1966 Cal-A	7	14	.333	37	32	6	2	1	199	188	20	68	132	12.0	3.93	85	.251	.321	11	.190	2	-11	-13	2	-1.0
1967 Cal-A	0	2	.000	4	3	0	0	0	9	11	1	9	6	20.0	9.00	35	.324	.465	1	.500	0	-6	-6	-0	-0.5
Bal-A	1	0	1.000	4	4	0	0	0	17²	15	1	10	15	12.7	2.55	124	.227	.329	0	.000	-0	1	1	-1	0.0
Yr	1	2	.333	8	7	0	0	0	26²	26	2	19	21	15.2	4.73	67	.257	.375	1	.143	-0	-4	-5	-1	-0.5
1969 *Bal-A	5	3	.625	27	4	0	0	0	69¹	65	3	34	57	13.1	4.41	81	.252	.344	3	.214	1	-6	-7	-1	-0.6
1970 *Bal-A	1	1	.500	25	3	0	0	0	60²	47	2	37	49	12.5	2.08	176	.217	.331	1	.077	0	11	11	-1	1.0
1971 Mil-A	2	7	.222	31	11	0	0	0	67²	64	5	60	42	16.5	4.66	75	.251	.394	1	.059	-1	-9	-9	1	-0.9
1972 Cle-A	0	0	—	4	2	0	0	0	8¹	8	0	10	1	19.4	5.40	60	.276	.462	0	.000	-0	-2	-2	0	-0.1
Total 8	31	40	.437	171	93	14	3	2	653	591	44	317	426	12.7	3.62	94	.243	.334	31	.171	4	-11	-15	4	-0.1

■ **BRIS LORD**   Lord, Bristol Robotham "The Human Eyeball"   b: 9/21/1883, Upland, Pa.   d: 11/13/64, Annapolis, Md.   BR/TR, 5'9", 185 lbs.   Deb: 4/21/05   ♦

YEAR TM/L	W	L	PCT	G	GS	CG	SH	SV	IP	H	HR	BB	SO	RAT	ERA	ERA+	OAV	OOB	BH	AVG	PB	PR	/A	PD	TPI
1907 Phi-A	0	0	—	1	0	0	0	0	1	3	0	0	0	27.0	9.00	29	.516	.516	31	.182	0	-1	-1	0	0.0

■ **LEFTY LORENZEN**   Lorenzen, Adolph Andreas   b: 1/12/1893, Davenport, Iowa   d: 3/5/63, Davenport, Iowa   BL/TL, 5'10", 164 lbs.   Deb: 9/12/13

YEAR TM/L	W	L	PCT	G	GS	CG	SH	SV	IP	H	HR	BB	SO	RAT	ERA	ERA+	OAV	OOB	BH	AVG	PB	PR	/A	PD	TPI
1913 Det-A	0	0	—	1	0	0	0	0	2	4	0	3	0	31.5	18.00	16	.667	.778	1	.500	0	-3	-3	1	-0.1

■ **JOE LOTZ**   Lotz, Joseph Peter "Smokey"   b: 1/2/1891, Remsen, Iowa   d: 1/1/71, Castro Valley, Cal.   BR/TR, 5'8.5", 175 lbs.   Deb: 7/15/16

YEAR TM/L	W	L	PCT	G	GS	CG	SH	SV	IP	H	HR	BB	SO	RAT	ERA	ERA+	OAV	OOB	BH	AVG	PB	PR	/A	PD	TPI
1916 StL-N	0	3	.000	12	3	1	0	0	40	31	1	17	18	11.0	4.27	62	.225	.314	4	.333	1	-7	-7	-0	-0.6

■ **ART LOUDELL**   Loudell, Arthur (b: Arthur Laudel)   b: 4/10/1882, Latham, Mo.   d: 2/19/61, Kansas City, Mo.   BR/TR, 5'11", 173 lbs.   Deb: 8/13/10

YEAR TM/L	W	L	PCT	G	GS	CG	SH	SV	IP	H	HR	BB	SO	RAT	ERA	ERA+	OAV	OOB	BH	AVG	PB	PR	/A	PD	TPI
1910 Det-A	1	1	.500	5	2	1	0	0	21¹	23	0	14	12	15.6	3.38	78	.284	.389	1	.143	-0	-2	-2	-1	-0.2

■ **LARRY LOUGHLIN**   Loughlin, Larry John   b: 8/16/41, Tacoma, Wash.   BL/TL, 6'1", 190 lbs.   Deb: 5/27/67

YEAR TM/L	W	L	PCT	G	GS	CG	SH	SV	IP	H	HR	BB	SO	RAT	ERA	ERA+	OAV	OOB	BH	AVG	PB	PR	/A	PD	TPI
1967 Phi-N	0	0	—	3	0	0	0	0	5¹	9	1	4	5	21.9	15.19	22	.375	.464	1	1.000	1	-7	-7	-0	-0.5

■ **DON LOUN**   Loun, Donald Nelson   b: 11/9/40, Frederick, Md.   BR/TL, 6'2", 185 lbs.   Deb: 9/23/64

YEAR TM/L	W	L	PCT	G	GS	CG	SH	SV	IP	H	HR	BB	SO	RAT	ERA	ERA+	OAV	OOB	BH	AVG	PB	PR	/A	PD	TPI
1964 Was-A	1	1	.500	2	2	1	0	0	13	13	0	3	3	11.1	2.08	178	.250	.291	0	.000	-0	2	2	1	0.3

■ **SLIM LOVE**   Love, Edward Haughton   b: 8/1/1890, Love, Miss.   d: 11/30/42, Memphis, Tenn.   BL/TL, 6'7", 195 lbs.   Deb: 9/08/13

YEAR TM/L	W	L	PCT	G	GS	CG	SH	SV	IP	H	HR	BB	SO	RAT	ERA	ERA+	OAV	OOB	BH	AVG	PB	PR	/A	PD	TPI
1913 Was-A	1	0	1.000	5	1	0	0	0	16²	14	0	6	5	10.8	1.62	182	.226	.294	1	.200	0	2	2	-1	0.2
1916 NY-A	2	0	1.000	20	1	0	0	1	47²	46	2	23	21	13.0	4.91	59	.274	.361	0	.000	-2	-11	-11	-0	-1.2
1917 NY-A	6	5	.545	33	9	2	0	1	130¹	115	0	57	82	11.9	2.35	115	.251	.335	6	.167	-1	5	5	-2	0.1
1918 NY-A	13	12	.520	38	29	13	1	1	228²	207	1	116	95	13.1	3.07	92	.263	.353	17	.233	2	-7	-6	-5	-0.9
1919 Det-A	6	4	.600	22	8	4	0	1	89²	92	3	40	46	13.9	3.01	106	.275	.363	6	.222	0	2	2	-2	0.0
1920 Det-A	0	0	—	1	0	0	0	0	4¹	6	0	4	2	20.8	8.31	45	.375	.500	0	—	0	-2	-2	0	-0.1
Total 6	28	21	.571	119	48	19	1	4	517¹	480	8	246	251	12.9	3.04	94	.259	.351	30	.192	-0	-11	-10	-10	-1.9

YEAR TM/L	W	L	PCT	G	GS	CG	SH	SV	IP	H	HR	BB	SO	RAT	ERA	ERA+	OAV	OOB	BH	AVG	PB	PR	/A	PD	TPI

■ VANCE LOVELACE
Lovelace, Vance Odell   b: 8/9/63, Tampa, Fla.   BL/TL, 6'5", 205 lbs.   Deb: 9/10/88

YEAR TM/L	W	L	PCT	G	GS	CG	SH	SV	IP	H	HR	BB	SO	RAT	ERA	ERA+	OAV	OOB	BH	AVG	PB	PR	/A	PD	TPI
1988 Cal-A	0	0	—	3	0	0	0	0	1¹	2	1	3	0	33.8	13.50	29	.400	.625	0	—	0	-1	-1	0	0.0
1989 Cal-A	0	0	—	1	0	0	0	0	1	0	0	1	1	9.0	0.00	—	.000	.250	0	—	0	0	0	0	0.0
1990 Sea-A	0	0	—	5	0	0	0	0	2¹	3	0	6	1	38.6	3.86	103	.300	.588	0	—	0	0	0	0	0.0
Total 3	0	0	—	9	0	0	0	0	4²	5	1	10	2	30.9	5.79	67	.278	.552	0	—	0	-1	-1	0	0.0

■ LYNN LOVENGUTH
Lovenguth, Lynn Richard   b: 11/29/22, Camden, N.Y.   BL/TR, 5'10.5", 170 lbs.   Deb: 4/18/55

YEAR TM/L	W	L	PCT	G	GS	CG	SH	SV	IP	H	HR	BB	SO	RAT	ERA	ERA+	OAV	OOB	BH	AVG	PB	PR	/A	PD	TPI
1955 Phi-N	0	1	.000	14	0	0	0	0	18	17	1	10	14	14.5	4.50	88	.258	.372	0	.000	-0	-1	-1	-0	-0.1
1957 StL-N	0	1	.000	2	1	0	0	0	9	6	0	6	6	12.0	2.00	198	.182	.308	0	.000	-0	2	2	-0	0.1
Total 2	0	2	.000	16	1	0	0	0	27	23	1	16	20	13.7	3.67	108	.232	.350	0	.000	-1	1	1	-1	0.0

■ JOHN LOVETT
Lovett, John   b: 5/6/1877, Monday, Ohio   d: 12/5/37, Murray City, Ohio   Deb: 5/22/03

YEAR TM/L	W	L	PCT	G	GS	CG	SH	SV	IP	H	HR	BB	SO	RAT	ERA	ERA+	OAV	OOB	BH	AVG	PB	PR	/A	PD	TPI
1903 StL-N	0	0	—	3	1	0	0	0	5	6	0	5	3	21.6	5.40	60	.300	.462	1	.333	0	-1	-1	0	0.0

■ LEN LOVETT
Lovett, Leonard Walker   b: 7/17/1852, Lancaster Co., Pa   d: 11/18/22, Newark, Del.   BR/TR,   Deb: 08/04/1873 ♦

YEAR TM/L	W	L	PCT	G	GS	CG	SH	SV	IP	H	HR	BB	SO	RAT	ERA	ERA+	OAV	OOB	BH	AVG	PB	PR	/A	PD	TPI
1873 Res-n	0	1	.000	1	1	1	0	0	9	21	0	1		22.0	6.00	62	.382	.393	2	.400	0	-2	-2		0.0

■ TOM LOVETT
Lovett, Thomas Joseph   b: 12/7/1863, Providence, R.I.   d: 3/20/28, Providence, R.I.   BR, 5'8", 162 lbs.   Deb: 6/04/1885

YEAR TM/L	W	L	PCT	G	GS	CG	SH	SV	IP	H	HR	BB	SO	RAT	ERA	ERA+	OAV	OOB	BH	AVG	PB	PR	/A	PD	TPI
1885 Phi-a	7	8	.467	16	16	15	1	0	138²	130	3	38	56	10.9	3.70	93	.237	.287	13	.224	0	-7	-4	-1	-0.3
1889 *Bro-a	17	10	.630	29	28	23	1	0	229	234	3	65	92	11.8	4.32	86	.256	.306	19	.190	-1	-12	-15	-1	-1.3
1890 *Bro-N	30	11	.732	44	41	39	4	0	372	327	14	141	124	11.3	2.78	123	.229	.299	33	.201	-1	32	27	0	2.4
1891 Bro-N	23	19	.548	44	43	39	3	0	365²	361	14	129	129	12.1	3.69	90	.248	.309	25	.163	-5	-14	-16	-2	-1.9
1893 Bro-N	3	5	.375	14	8	6	0	1	96	134	2	35	15	15.8	6.56	68	.321	.373	9	.180	-2	-20	-23	-1	-1.9
1894 Bos-N	8	6	.571	15	13	10	0	0	104	155	12	36	23	16.5	5.97	95	.341	.389	7	.143	-5	-7	-3	-1	-0.6
Total 6	88	59	.599	162	149	132	9	1	1305¹	1341	48	444	439	12.3	3.94	94	.257	.316	106	.185	-13	-28	-35	-5	-3.6

■ PETE LOVRICH
Lovrich, Peter   b: 10/16/42, Blue Island, Ill.   BR/TR, 6'4", 200 lbs.   Deb: 4/26/63

YEAR TM/L	W	L	PCT	G	GS	CG	SH	SV	IP	H	HR	BB	SO	RAT	ERA	ERA+	OAV	OOB	BH	AVG	PB	PR	/A	PD	TPI
1963 KC-A	1	1	.500	20	1	0	0	0	20²	25	5	10	16	15.7	7.84	49	.291	.371	0	—	0	-10	-9	-1	-0.9

■ GROVER LOWDERMILK
Lowdermilk, Grover Cleveland "Slim"   b: 1/15/1885, Sandborn, Ind.   d: 3/31/68, Odin, Ill.   BR/TR, 6'4", 190 lbs.   Deb: 7/03/09

YEAR TM/L	W	L	PCT	G	GS	CG	SH	SV	IP	H	HR	BB	SO	RAT	ERA	ERA+	OAV	OOB	BH	AVG	PB	PR	/A	PD	TPI
1909 StL-N	0	2	.000	7	3	1	0	0	29	28	0	30	14	18.9	6.21	41	.292	.473	1	.100	-1	-12	-12	-0	-1.2
1911 StL-N	0	1	.000	11	2	1	1	0	33¹	37	1	33	15	19.4	7.29	46	.301	.456	1	.111	-1	-14	-14	-0	-1.3
1912 Chi-N	0	1	.000	2	1	1	0	0	13	17	1	14	8	21.5	9.69	34	.293	.431	0	.000	-1	-9	-9	-0	-0.7
1915 StL-A	9	17	.346	38	29	14	1	0	222¹	183	1	133	130	13.4	3.12	92	.234	.357	9	.125	-2	-4	-6	-1	-0.9
Det-A	4	1	.800	7	5	0	0	0	28	17	0	24	18	13.5	4.18	73	.185	.359	1	.125	-0	-4	-4	0	-0.3
Yr	13	18	.419	45	34	14	1	0	250¹	200	1	157	148	12.9	3.24	89	.225	.342	7	.087	-3	-8	-10	-1	-1.2
1916 Det-A	0	0	—	1	0	0	0	0	0¹	0	0	3	0	81.0	0.00	—	.000	.750	0	—	0	0	0	0	0.0
Cle-A	1	5	.167	10	9	2	0	0	51¹	52	0	45	28	17.5	3.16	95	.277	.424	3	.167	-0	-2	-1	-0	0.0
Yr	1	5	.167	11	9	2	0	0	51²	52	0	48	28	17.9	3.14	96	.275	.429	0	.000	-0	-2	-1	0	0.0
1917 StL-A	2	1	.667	3	2	2	1	0	19	16	0	4	9	9.5	1.42	183	.225	.267	0	.000	-1	3	2	0	0.2
1918 StL-A	2	6	.250	13	11	4	0	0	80	74	1	38	25	12.9	3.15	87	.255	.347	7	.250	1	-3	-4	2	0.0
1919 StL-A	0	0	—	7	0	0	0	0	12	6	0	4	6	11.3	0.75	442	.176	.349	0	.000	-0	3	3	0	0.3
*Chi-A	5	5	.500	20	11	5	0	0	96²	95	0	43	43	13.2	2.79	114	.268	.353	3	.088	-3	5	4	1	0.2
Yr	5	5	.500	27	11	5	0	0	108²	101	0	47	49	12.6	2.57	125	.256	.342	0	.000	-3	8	8	1	0.5
1920 Chi-A	0	0	—	3	0	0	0	0	5¹	9	0	5	0	23.6	6.75	56	.409	.519	0	—	0	-2	-2	1	0.0
Total 9	23	39	.371	122	73	30	3	0	590¹	534	4	376	296	14.4	3.58	82	.253	.375	25	.131	-8	-40	-41	4	-3.7

■ LOU LOWDERMILK
Lowdermilk, Louis Bailey   b: 2/23/1887, Sandborn, Ind.   d: 12/27/75, Centralia, Ill.   BR/TL, 6'1", 180 lbs.   Deb: 4/20/11

YEAR TM/L	W	L	PCT	G	GS	CG	SH	SV	IP	H	HR	BB	SO	RAT	ERA	ERA+	OAV	OOB	BH	AVG	PB	PR	/A	PD	TPI
1911 StL-N	3	4	.429	16	3	3	0	0	65	72	0	29	20	14.7	3.46	98	.304	.391	2	.111	-1	-0	-1	-2	-0.2
1912 StL-N	1	1	.500	4	1	1	0	1	15	14	0	9	2	13.8	3.00	114	.233	.333	1	.250	-0	1	1	0	0.1
Total 2	4	5	.444	20	4	4	0	1	80	86	0	38	22	14.5	3.37	100	.290	.379	3	.136	-1	0	0	-1	-0.1

■ GEORGE LOWE
Lowe, George Wesley "Doc"   b: 4/25/1895, Ridgefield Park, N.J.   d: 9/2/81, Somers Point, N.J.   6'2", 180 lbs.   Deb: 7/28/20

YEAR TM/L	W	L	PCT	G	GS	CG	SH	SV	IP	H	HR	BB	SO	RAT	ERA	ERA+	OAV	OOB	BH	AVG	PB	PR	/A	PD	TPI
1920 Cin-N	0	0	—	1	0	0	0	0	2	1	0	1	0	9.0	0.00	—	.167	.286	0	—	0	1	1	0	0.1

■ BOBBY LOWE
Lowe, Robert Lincoln "Link"   b: 7/10/1868, Pittsburgh, Pa.   d: 12/8/51, Detroit, Mich.   BR/TR, 5'10", 150 lbs.   Deb: 4/19/1890   M♦

YEAR TM/L	W	L	PCT	G	GS	CG	SH	SV	IP	H	HR	BB	SO	RAT	ERA	ERA+	OAV	OOB	BH	AVG	PB	PR	/A	PD	TPI
1891 Bos-N	0	0	—	1	0	0	0	0	1	3	0	1	0	36.0	9.00	41	.501	.572	129	.260	0	-1	-1	0	0.0

■ TURK LOWN
Lown, Omar Joseph   b: 5/30/24, Brooklyn, N.Y.   BR/TR, 6', 180 lbs.   Deb: 4/24/51

YEAR TM/L	W	L	PCT	G	GS	CG	SH	SV	IP	H	HR	BB	SO	RAT	ERA	ERA+	OAV	OOB	BH	AVG	PB	PR	/A	PD	TPI
1951 Chi-N	4	9	.308	31	18	3	1	0	127	125	14	90	39	15.3	5.46	75	.260	.378	8	.205	1	-21	-19	0	-1.6
1952 Chi-N	4	11	.267	33	19	5	0	0	156²	154	13	93	73	14.4	4.37	88	.257	.359	7	.140	-0	-11	-9	1	-0.7
1953 Chi-N	8	7	.533	49	12	2	0	3	148¹	166	20	84	76	15.3	5.16	86	.282	.373	6	.125	-2	-14	-12	2	-1.0
1954 Chi-N	0	2	.000	15	0	0	0	0	22	23	1	15	16	15.5	6.14	68	.261	.369	0	—	0	-5	-5	0	-0.3
1956 Chi-N	9	8	.529	61	0	0	0	13	110²	95	10	78	74	14.2	3.58	105	.240	.366	5	.217	2	2	2	-1	0.4
1957 Chi-N	5	7	.417	67	0	0	0	12	93	74	10	51	51	12.1	3.77	103	.221	.324	2	.200	-1	1	1	2	0.3
1958 Chi-N	0	0	—	4	0	0	0	0	4	2	0	3	4	11.3	4.50	87	.154	.313	0	—	0	-0	-0	-0	0.0
Cin-N	0	2	.000	11	0	0	0	0	11²	12	2	12	9	18.5	5.40	77	.273	.429	0	.000	-0	-2	-2	-0	-0.1
Yr	0	2	.000	15	0	0	0	0	15²	14	2	15	13	16.7	5.17	79	.246	.403	0	.000	-0	-2	-2	-0	-0.1
Chi-A	3	3	.500	27	0	0	0	8	40²	49	1	28	40	17.0	3.98	91	.308	.412	3	.333	1	-1	-2	0	0.0
1959 *Chi-A	9	2	.818	60	0	0	0	15	93¹	73	12	42	63	11.3	2.89	130	.215	.305	3	.250	1	10	9	1	1.0
1960 Chi-A	2	3	.400	45	0	0	0	5	67¹	60	6	34	39	12.6	3.88	98	.239	.330	1	.200	1	-0	-1	0	0.0
1961 Chi-A	7	5	.583	59	0	0	0	11	101	87	13	35	50	10.9	2.76	142	.238	.304	0	.000	-2	14	13	-0	1.1
1962 Chi-A	4	2	.667	42	0	0	0	6	56¹	58	3	25	40	13.4	3.04	129	.269	.347	0	.000	-0	6	5	1	0.6
Total 11	55	61	.474	504	49	10	1	73	1032	978	105	590	574	13.8	4.12	96	.252	.352	35	.164	1	-21	-18	6	-0.3

■ SAM LOWRY
Lowry, Samuel Joseph   b: 3/25/20, Philadelphia, Pa.   BR/TR, 5'11", 170 lbs.   Deb: 9/19/42

YEAR TM/L	W	L	PCT	G	GS	CG	SH	SV	IP	H	HR	BB	SO	RAT	ERA	ERA+	OAV	OOB	BH	AVG	PB	PR	/A	PD	TPI
1942 Phi-A	0	0	—	1	0	0	0	0	3	3	0	1	0	12.0	6.00	63	.250	.308	0	.000	-0	-1	-1	0	0.0
1943 Phi-A	0	0	—	5	0	0	0	0	18	18	1	9	3	13.5	5.00	68	.269	.355	1	.167	-0	-3	-3	-0	-0.2
Total 2	0	0	—	6	0	0	0	0	21	21	1	10	3	13.3	5.14	67	.266	.348	1	.143	-0	-4	-4	0	-0.2

■ MIKE LOYND
Loynd, Michael Wallace   b: 3/26/64, St.Louis, Mo.   BR/TR, 6'4", 210 lbs.   Deb: 7/24/86

YEAR TM/L	W	L	PCT	G	GS	CG	SH	SV	IP	H	HR	BB	SO	RAT	ERA	ERA+	OAV	OOB	BH	AVG	PB	PR	/A	PD	TPI
1986 Tex-A	2	2	.500	9	8	0	0	0	42	49	4	19	33	15.0	5.36	80	.290	.368	0	—	0	-6	-5	0	-0.4
1987 Tex-A	1	5	.167	26	8	0	0	1	69¹	82	14	38	48	15.7	6.10	73	.287	.372	0	—	0	-13	-13	-1	-1.1
Total 2	3	7	.300	35	16	0	0	2	111¹	131	18	57	81	15.4	5.82	76	.288	.371	0	—	0	-18	-17	-1	-1.5

■ PAT LUBY
Luby, John Perkins   b: 1868, Charleston, S.C.   d: 4/24/1899, Charleston, S.C.   TR, 6', 185 lbs.   Deb: 6/16/1890

YEAR TM/L	W	L	PCT	G	GS	CG	SH	SV	IP	H	HR	BB	SO	RAT	ERA	ERA+	OAV	OOB	BH	AVG	PB	PR	/A	PD	TPI
1890 Chi-N	20	9	.690	34	31	26	0	1	267²	226	6	95	85	10.8	3.19	114	.222	.289	31	.267	8	11	14	-1	1.9
1891 Chi-N	8	11	.421	30	24	18	0	1	206	221	11	94	52	13.8	4.76	70	.264	.338	24	.245	7	-32	-33	0	-2.1
1892 Chi-N	10	16	.385	31	26	24	1	1	247¹	247	10	106	64	12.8	3.13	106	.250	.322	31	.190	1	4	5	1	0.7
1895 Lou-N	1	5	.167	11	6	5	0	0	71¹	115	5	19	12	16.9	6.81	68	.357	.393	15	.283	2	-16	-17	1	-0.9
Total 4	39	41	.488	106	87	73	1	3	792¹	809	32	314	213	12.8	3.91	91	.256	.323	101	.235	17	-33	-31	1	-0.4

■ RED LUCAS
Lucas, Charles Frederick "The Nashville Narcissus"   b: 4/28/02, Columbia, Tenn.   d: 7/9/86, Nashville, Tenn.   BL/TR, 5'9.5", 170 lbs.   Deb: 4/19/23 ♦

YEAR TM/L	W	L	PCT	G	GS	CG	SH	SV	IP	H	HR	BB	SO	RAT	ERA	ERA+	OAV	OOB	BH	AVG	PB	PR	/A	PD	TPI
1923 NY-N	0	0	—	3	0	0	0	0	5¹	9	0	4	3	21.9	0.00	—	.346	.433	0	.000	-0	2	2	0	0.2
1924 Bos-N	1	4	.200	27	4	1	0	0	83²	112	5	18	30	14.6	5.16	74	.332	.377	11	.333	2	-12	-12	1	-0.9
1926 Cin-N	8	5	.615	39	11	7	1	2	154	161	6	30	34	11.3	3.68	100	.277	.314	23	.303	6	2	0	-0	0.9

YEAR	TM/L	W	L	PCT	G	GS	CG	SH	SV	IP	H	HR	BB	SO	RAT	ERA	ERA+	OAV	OOB	BH	AVG	PB	PR	/A	PD	TPI
1927	Cin-N	18	11	.621	37	23	19	4	2	239²	231	6	39	51	10.1	3.38	112	.256	.287	47	.313	6	14	11	-0	1.1
1928	Cin-N	13	9	.591	27	19	13	**4**	1	167¹	164	9	42	35	11.1	3.39	117	.258	.304	23	.315	6	11	10	0	1.7
1929	Cin-N	19	12	.613	32	32	**28**	2	0	270	267	14	58	72	**10.9**	3.60	127	**.257**	**.297**	41	.293	10	33	29	0	2.7
1930	Cin-N	14	16	.467	33	28	18	1	1	210²	270	15	44	53	13.5	5.38	90	.315	.349	38	.336	14	-10	-13	-2	-1.0
1931	Cin-N	14	13	.519	29	29	**24**	3	0	238	261	10	39	56	11.3	3.59	104	.280	.309	43	.281	10	7	4	1	0.4
1932	Cin-N	13	17	.433	31	31	**28**	0	0	269¹	261	10	35	63	9.9	2.94	131	.249	.274	43	.287	13	28	27	0	2.8
1933	Cin-N	10	16	.385	29	29	21	3	0	219²	248	13	18	40	11.0	3.40	100	.289	.305	35	.287	12	-2	-0	0	0.0
1934	Pit-N	10	9	.526	29	21	12	1	0	172²	198	14	40	44	12.5	4.38	94	.283	.324	23	.219	3	-6	-5	-2	-0.4
1935	Pit-N	8	6	.571	20	19	8	2	0	125²	136	10	23	29	11.5	3.44	119	.272	.307	21	.318	8	8	9	-0	0.9
1936	Pit-N	15	4	.789	27	22	12	0	0	175²	178	7	26	53	10.6	3.18	128	.257	.287	26	.241	4	16	17	-0	1.7
1937	Pit-N	8	10	.444	20	20	9	1	0	126¹	150	12	23	20	12.4	4.27	90	.290	.322	5	.268	5	-5	-6	-1	-0.5
1938	Pit-N	6	3	.667	13	13	4	0	0	84	90	5	16	19	11.5	3.54	107	.283	.319	5	.109	-2	2	2	-1	0.2
Total	15	157	135	.538	396	301	204	22	7	2542	2736	136	455	602	11.4	3.72	107	.275	.308	404	.281	97	92	77	-5	9.8

■ GARY LUCAS
Lucas, Gary Paul b: 11/8/54, Riverside, Cal. BL/TL, 6'5", 200 lbs. Deb: 4/16/80

YEAR	TM/L	W	L	PCT	G	GS	CG	SH	SV	IP	H	HR	BB	SO	RAT	ERA	ERA+	OAV	OOB	BH	AVG	PB	PR	/A	PD	TPI
1980	SD-N	5	8	.385	46	18	0	0	3	150	138	8	43	85	10.9	3.24	106	.250	.306	6	.171	-0	6	3	0	0.3
1981	SD-N	7	7	.500	**57**	0	0	0	13	90	78	1	36	53	11.7	2.00	163	.247	.330	1	.100	-0	**15**	13	0	1.3
1982	SD-N	1	10	.091	65	0	0	0	16	97¹	89	6	29	64	11.0	3.24	106	.245	.302	0	.000	-1	4	2	1	0.2
1983	SD-N	5	8	.385	62	0	0	0	17	91	85	9	34	60	11.8	2.87	122	.245	.312	0	.000	-1	8	6	-1	0.4
1984	Mon-N	0	3	.000	55	0	0	0	8	53	54	4	20	42	12.6	2.72	126	.267	.333	0	.000	-0	5	4	1	0.5
1985	Mon-N	6	2	.750	49	0	0	0	1	67²	63	6	24	31	11.6	3.19	106	.251	.316	0	.000	-1	3	1	0	0.1
1986	•Cal-A	4	1	.800	27	0	0	0	2	45²	45	1	6	31	10.1	3.15	130	.253	.277	0	—	0	5	5	1	0.6
1987	Cal-A	1	5	.167	48	0	0	0	3	74¹	66	7	35	44	12.5	3.63	118	.241	.331	0	—	0	7	6	1	0.6
Total	8	29	44	.397	409	18	0	0	63	669	618	42	227	410	11.5	3.01	118	.249	.314	7	.087	-4	53	40	3	4.0

■ RAY LUCAS
Lucas, Ray Wesley "Luke" b: 10/2/08, Springfield, Ohio d: 10/9/69, Harrison, Mich. BR/TR, 6'2", 175 lbs. Deb: 9/28/29

YEAR	TM/L	W	L	PCT	G	GS	CG	SH	SV	IP	H	HR	BB	SO	RAT	ERA	ERA+	OAV	OOB	BH	AVG	PB	PR	/A	PD	TPI
1929	NY-N	0	0	—	3	0	0	0	1	8	3	0	3	1	6.8	0.00	—	.111	.200	1	.500	0	4	4	0	0.5
1930	NY-N	0	0	—	6	0	0	0	0	10¹	9	2	10	1	17.4	6.97	68	.265	.444	0	.000	-0	-2	-3	1	-0.1
1931	NY-N	0	0	—	1	0	0	0	0	2	1	1	1	0	9.0	4.50	82	.143	.250	0	—	0	-0	-0	0	0.0
1933	Bro-N	0	0	—	2	0	0	0	0	5	6	0	4	0	19.8	7.20	45	.316	.458	0	—	0	-2	-2	0	-0.1
1934	Bro-N	1	1	.500	10	2	0	0	0	30²	39	2	14	3	16.4	6.75	58	.328	.412	2	.333	1	-9	-10	1	-0.6
Total	5	1	1	.500	22	2	0	0	1	56	58	5	32	5	15.3	5.79	71	.282	.391	3	.333	1	-10	-11	2	-0.3

■ JOE LUCEY
Lucey, Joseph Earl "Scootch" b: 3/27/1897, Holyoke, Mass. d: 7/30/80, Holyoke, Mass. BR/TR, 6', 168 lbs. Deb: 7/06/20 ♦

YEAR	TM/L	W	L	PCT	G	GS	CG	SH	SV	IP	H	HR	BB	SO	RAT	ERA	ERA+	OAV	OOB	BH	AVG	PB	PR	/A	PD	TPI
1925	Bos-A	0	1	.000	7	0	0	0	0	11	18	0	14	2	26.2	9.00	50	.360	.500	1	.133	-1	-6	-5	1	-0.4

■ CON LUCID
Lucid, Cornelius Cecil b: 2/24/1874, Dublin, Ireland d: 6/25/31, Houston, Tex. Deb: 5/01/1893

YEAR	TM/L	W	L	PCT	G	GS	CG	SH	SV	IP	H	HR	BB	SO	RAT	ERA	ERA+	OAV	OOB	BH	AVG	PB	PR	/A	PD	TPI
1893	Lou-N	0	1	.000	2	1	0	0	0	6	10	0	10	0	30.0	15.00	29	.360	.530	1	.333	0	-7	-7	-0	-0.4
1894	Bro-N	5	3	.625	10	9	7	0	0	71¹	87	6	44	15	16.5	6.56	75	.298	.389	7	.212	-2	-10	-13	-2	-1.2
1895	Bro-N	10	7	.588	21	19	12	2	0	137	164	4	72	24	15.5	5.52	80	.292	.373	3	.245	-2	-11	-17	-1	-1.2
	Phi-N	6	3	.667	10	10	7	1	0	69²	80	3	35	19	14.9	5.94	81	.284	.363	10	.345	3	-9	-9	-2	-0.4
	Yr	16	10	.615	31	29	19	3	0	206²	244	7	107	43	15.3	5.66	80	.289	.369	10	.122	5	-20	-26	-2	-1.6
1896	Phi-N	1	4	.200	5	5	5	0	0	42	75	2	17	3	19.7	8.36	52	.384	.433	2	.125	-2	-19	-19	-1	-1.5
1897	StL-N	1	5	.167	6	6	5	0	0	49	66	0	26	4	16.9	3.67	120	.319	.395	3	.176	-0	3	4	1	0.4
Total	5	23	23	.500	54	50	36	3	0	375	482	15	204	65	16.5	6.02	76	.308	.388	36	.238	2	-52	-60	-5	-4.3

■ LOU LUCIER
Lucier, Louis Joseph b: 3/23/18, Northbridge, Mass. BR/TR, 5'8", 160 lbs. Deb: 4/23/43

YEAR	TM/L	W	L	PCT	G	GS	CG	SH	SV	IP	H	HR	BB	SO	RAT	ERA	ERA+	OAV	OOB	BH	AVG	PB	PR	/A	PD	TPI
1943	Bos-A	3	4	.429	16	9	3	0	0	74	94	1	33	23	15.7	3.89	85	.322	.394	4	.200	-0	-5	-5	3	-0.1
1944	Bos-A	0	0	—	3	0	0	0	0	5¹	7	0	7	2	23.6	5.06	67	.292	.452	0	.000	-0	-1	-1	-0	0.0
	Phi-N	0	0	—	1	0	0	0	0	2	3	0	2	1	22.5	13.50	27	.333	.455	0	—	0	-2	-2	0	-0.1
1945	Phi-N	0	1	.000	13	0	0	0	1	20¹	14	1	5	5	8.4	2.21	173	.194	.247	1	.250	0	4	4	1	0.5
Total	3	3	5	.375	33	9	3	0	1	101²	118	2	47	31	14.8	3.81	90	.297	.374	5	.200	-0	-4	-4	4	0.3

■ HOWARD LUCKEY
Luckey, Howard J. b: Philadelphia, Pa. Deb: 10/02/1890

YEAR	TM/L	W	L	PCT	G	GS	CG	SH	SV	IP	H	HR	BB	SO	RAT	ERA	ERA+	OAV	OOB	BH	AVG	PB	PR	/A	PD	TPI
1890	Phi-a	0	0	—	1	0	0	0	0	2	1	0	3	1	18.0	9.00	42	.144	.403	0	.000	-0	-1	-1	0	0.0

■ WILLIE LUDOLPH
Ludolph, William Francis "Wee Willie" b: 1/21/1900, San Francisco, Cal d: 4/8/52, Oakland, Cal. BR/TR, 6'1.5", 170 lbs. Deb: 5/28/24

YEAR	TM/L	W	L	PCT	G	GS	CG	SH	SV	IP	H	HR	BB	SO	RAT	ERA	ERA+	OAV	OOB	BH	AVG	PB	PR	/A	PD	TPI
1924	Det-A	0	0	—	3	0	0	0	0	5²	5	0	2	1	12.7	4.76	86	.250	.348	0	.000	-0	-0	-0	0	0.0

■ STEVE LUEBBER
Luebber, Stephen Lee b: 7/9/49, Clinton, Mo. BR/TR, 6'3", 185 lbs. Deb: 6/27/71

YEAR	TM/L	W	L	PCT	G	GS	CG	SH	SV	IP	H	HR	BB	SO	RAT	ERA	ERA+	OAV	OOB	BH	AVG	PB	PR	/A	PD	TPI
1971	Min-A	2	5	.286	18	12	0	0	1	68	73	7	37	35	15.1	5.03	71	.278	.375	1	.053	-2	-12	-11	0	-1.2
1972	Min-A	0	0	—	2	0	0	0	0	2¹	3	0	2	1	19.3	0.00	—	.333	.455	0	—	0	1	1	0	0.1
1976	Min-A	4	5	.444	38	12	2	1	2	119¹	109	9	62	45	13.0	4.00	90	.248	.342	0	—	0	-6	-5	-1	-0.5
1979	Tor-A	0	0	—	1	0	0	0	0	0	2	0	1	0	—	∞	—	1.000	1.000	0	—	0	-1	-1	0	0.0
1981	Bal-A	0	0	—	7	0	0	0	0	16²	26	3	4	12	16.7	7.56	48	.366	.408	0	—	0	-7	-7	0	-0.6
Total	5	6	10	.375	66	24	2	1	3	206¹	213	19	106	93	14.2	4.62	77	.271	.362	1	.053	-2	-26	-24	-0	-2.2

■ DICK LUEBKE
Luebke, Richard Raymond b: 4/8/35, Chicago, Ill. d: 12/4/74, San Diego, Cal. BR/TL, 6'4", 200 lbs. Deb: 8/11/62

YEAR	TM/L	W	L	PCT	G	GS	CG	SH	SV	IP	H	HR	BB	SO	RAT	ERA	ERA+	OAV	OOB	BH	AVG	PB	PR	/A	PD	TPI
1962	Bal-A	0	1	.000	10	0	0	0	0	13¹	12	0	6	7	12.2	2.70	139	.250	.333	0	—	0	2	2	-0	0.1

■ RICK LUECKEN
Luecken, Richard Fred b: 11/15/60, McAllen, Tex. BR/TR, 6'6", 210 lbs. Deb: 6/06/89

YEAR	TM/L	W	L	PCT	G	GS	CG	SH	SV	IP	H	HR	BB	SO	RAT	ERA	ERA+	OAV	OOB	BH	AVG	PB	PR	/A	PD	TPI
1989	KC-A	2	1	.667	19	0	0	0	1	23²	23	3	13	16	13.7	3.42	112	.258	.353	0	—	0	1	1	-0	0.1
1990	Atl-N	1	4	.200	36	0	0	0	1	53	73	5	30	35	18.0	5.77	68	.336	.424	1	.333	1	-12	-11	0	-1.0
	Tor-A	0	0	—	1	0	0	0	0	1	2	1	1	0	27.0	9.00	42	.500	.600	0	—	0	-1	-1	0	0.0
Total	2	3	5	.375	56	0	0	0	2	77²	98	9	44	51	16.8	5.10	76	.316	.406	1	.333	1	-11	-10	-0	-0.9

■ HENRY LUFF
Luff, Henry T. b: 9/14/1856, Philadelphia, Pa. d: 10/11/16, Philadelphia, Pa. 5'11", 175 lbs. Deb: 4/21/1875 ♦

YEAR	TM/L	W	L	PCT	G	GS	CG	SH	SV	IP	H	HR	BB	SO	RAT	ERA	ERA+	OAV	OOB	BH	AVG	PB	PR	/A	PD	TPI
1875	NH-n	1	6	.143	10	7	5	0	0	69²	100	2	3		13.3	4.78	47	.297	.303	46	.279	3	-18	-20		-1.5

■ RAFAEL LUGO
Lugo, Rafael Urbano (Colina) b: 8/12/62, Punto Fijo, Venez. BR/TR, 6', 185 lbs. Deb: 4/28/85

YEAR	TM/L	W	L	PCT	G	GS	CG	SH	SV	IP	H	HR	BB	SO	RAT	ERA	ERA+	OAV	OOB	BH	AVG	PB	PR	/A	PD	TPI
1985	Cal-A	3	4	.429	20	10	1	0	0	83	86	10	29	42	12.9	3.69	111	.274	.343	0	—	0	4	4	0	0.4
1986	Cal-A	1	1	.500	6	3	0	0	0	21¹	21	4	6	9	11.4	3.80	108	.266	.318	0	—	0	1	1	0	0.1
1987	Cal-A	0	2	.000	7	5	0	0	0	28	42	8	18	24	19.3	9.32	46	.339	.423	0	—	0	-15	-16	-0	-1.3
1988	Cal-A	0	0	—	1	0	0	0	0	2	2	1	1	1	13.5	9.00	43	.250	.333	0	—	0	-1	-1	0	0.0
1989	Mon-N	0	0	—	3	0	0	0	0	4	4	1	0	3	9.0	6.75	52	.250	.250	0	—	0	-1	-1	0	-0.1
1990	Det-A	2	0	1.000	13	1	0	0	0	24¹	30	9	13	12	17.0	7.03	56	.313	.411	0	—	0	-8	-8	1	-0.7
Total	6	6	7	.462	50	19	1	0	0	162²	185	33	67	91	14.3	5.31	77	.290	.364	0	—	0	-21	-22	0	-1.6

■ WILD BILL LUHRSEN
Luhrsen, William Ferdinand b: 4/14/1884, Buckley, Ill. d: 8/15/73, Little Rock, Ark. BR/TR, 5'9", 165 lbs. Deb: 8/23/13

YEAR	TM/L	W	L	PCT	G	GS	CG	SH	SV	IP	H	HR	BB	SO	RAT	ERA	ERA+	OAV	OOB	BH	AVG	PB	PR	/A	PD	TPI
1913	Pit-N	3	1	.750	5	3	2	0	0	29	25	3	16	11	13.3	2.48	121	.248	.361	0	.000	-1	2	2	1	0.1

■ AL LUKENS
Lukens, Albert P. b: 11/1868, Pennsylvania Deb: 6/23/1894

YEAR	TM/L	W	L	PCT	G	GS	CG	SH	SV	IP	H	HR	BB	SO	RAT	ERA	ERA+	OAV	OOB	BH	AVG	PB	PR	/A	PD	TPI
1894	Phi-N	0	1	.000	3	2	1	0	0	15	26	0	10	0	21.6	10.20	50	.376	.455	0	.000	-2	-8	-8	-0	-0.6

■ RALPH LUMENTI
Lumenti, Raphael Anthony b: 12/21/36, Milford, Mass. BL/TL, 6'3", 185 lbs. Deb: 9/07/57

YEAR	TM/L	W	L	PCT	G	GS	CG	SH	SV	IP	H	HR	BB	SO	RAT	ERA	ERA+	OAV	OOB	BH	AVG	PB	PR	/A	PD	TPI
1957	Was-A	0	1	.000	3	2	0	0	0	9¹	9	1	5	8	14.5	6.75	58	.250	.357	0	.000	-0	-3	-3	0	-0.2

YEAR TM/L	W	L	PCT	G	GS	CG	SH	SV	IP	H	HR	BB	SO	RAT	ERA	ERA+	OAV	OOB	BH	AVG	PB	PR	/A	PD	TPI
1958 Was-A	1	2	.333	8	4	0	0	0	21	21	2	36	20	24.9	8.57	44	.266	.500	2	.250	0	-11	-11	0	-1.0
1959 Was-A	0	0	—	2	0	0	0	0	3	2	0	1	2	9.0	0.00	—	.200	.273	0	—	0	1	1	0	0.1
Total 3	1	3	.250	13	6	0	0	0	33^1	32	3	42	30	20.5	7.29	53	.256	.450	2	.200	-0	-13	-13	0	-1.1

■ MEMO LUNA
Luna, Guillermo Romero   b: 6/25/30, Tacubaya, Mexico   BL/TL, 6', 168 lbs.   Deb: 4/20/54

YEAR TM/L	W	L	PCT	G	GS	CG	SH	SV	IP	H	HR	BB	SO	RAT	ERA	ERA+	OAV	OOB	BH	AVG	PB	PR	/A	PD	TPI
1954 StL-N	0	1	.000	1	1	0	0	0	0^2	2	0	2	0	54.0	27.00	15	.667	.800	0	—	0	-2	-2	0	-0.1

■ JACK LUNDBOM
Lundbom, John Frederick   b: 3/10/1877, Manistee, Mich.   d: 10/31/49, Manistee, Mich.   BR/TR, 6'2", 187 lbs.   Deb: 5/09/02

YEAR TM/L	W	L	PCT	G	GS	CG	SH	SV	IP	H	HR	BB	SO	RAT	ERA	ERA+	OAV	OOB	BH	AVG	PB	PR	/A	PD	TPI
1902 Cle-A	1	1	.500	8	3	1	0	0	34	48	1	16	7	16.9	6.62	52	.332	.399	4	.267	1	-11	-12	-0	-1.0

■ CARL LUNDGREN
Lundgren, Carl Leonard   b: 2/16/1880, Marengo, Ill.   d: 8/21/34, Marengo, Ill.   BR/TR, 5'11", 175 lbs.   Deb: 6/19/02

YEAR TM/L	W	L	PCT	G	GS	CG	SH	SV	IP	H	HR	BB	SO	RAT	ERA	ERA+	OAV	OOB	BH	AVG	PB	PR	/A	PD	TPI
1902 Chi-N	9	9	.500	18	18	17	1	0	160	158	2	45	68	11.8	1.97	137	.258	.315	7	.106	-4	14	13	-3	0.6
1903 Chi-N	11	9	.550	27	20	16	0	3	193	191	1	60	67	12.0	2.94	107	.262	.323	7	.115	-1	7	4	-2	0.4
1904 Chi-N	17	9	.654	31	27	25	2	1	242	203	2	77	106	10.6	2.60	102	.226	.290	20	.222	4	4	2	-1	0.4
1905 Chi-N	13	5	.722	23	19	16	3	0	169	132	3	53	69	10.3	2.24	133	.220	.293	11	.180	1	14	14	1	1.7
1906 Chi-N	17	6	.739	27	24	21	5	2	207^2	160	3	89	103	11.1	2.21	120	.221	.313	12	.179	2	10	10	-1	1.3
1907 Chi-N	18	7	.720	28	25	21	7	0	207	130	0	92	84	9.7	1.17	213	.185	.282	7	.106	-3	30	30	-0	3.3
1908 Chi-N	6	9	.400	23	15	9	1	0	138^2	149	5	56	38	13.3	4.22	56	.284	.353	7	.149	-1	-29	-29	-1	-3.2
1909 Chi-N	0	1	.000	2	1	0	0	0	4^1	6	0	4	0	20.8	4.15	61	.353	.476	1	.500	0	-1	-1	-0	0.0
Total 8	91	55	.623	179	149	125	19	6	1321^2	1129	16	476	535	11.2	2.42	113	.235	.308	72	.157	-1	50	44	-7	4.1

■ DEL LUNDGREN
Lundgren, Ebin Delmar   b: 9/21/1899, Lindsborg, Kan.   d: 10/19/84, Lindsborg, Kan.   BR/TR, 5'8", 160 lbs.   Deb: 4/27/24

YEAR TM/L	W	L	PCT	G	GS	CG	SH	SV	IP	H	HR	BB	SO	RAT	ERA	ERA+	OAV	OOB	BH	AVG	PB	PR	/A	PD	TPI
1924 Pit-N	0	1	.000	8	1	0	0	0	16^2	25	0	3	4	15.7	6.48	59	.403	.439	0	.000	-1	-5	-5	0	-0.4
1926 Bos-A	0	2	.000	18	1	0	0	0	31	35	2	28	11	19.2	7.55	54	.307	.455	0	.000	-0	-12	-12	0	-1.0
1927 Bos-A	5	12	.294	30	17	5	2	0	136^1	160	7	87	39	16.6	6.27	67	.302	.405	7	.159	-2	-32	-31	-2	-3.1
Total 3	5	15	.250	56	19	5	2	0	184	220	9	118	54	16.9	6.51	64	.312	.416	7	.137	-3	-49	-48	-2	-4.5

■ DOLF LUQUE
Luque, Adolfo "The Pride Of Havana"   b: 8/4/1890, Havana, Cuba   d: 7/3/57, Havana, Cuba   BR/TR, 5'7", 160 lbs.   Deb: 5/20/14   C

YEAR TM/L	W	L	PCT	G	GS	CG	SH	SV	IP	H	HR	BB	SO	RAT	ERA	ERA+	OAV	OOB	BH	AVG	PB	PR	/A	PD	TPI
1914 Bos-N	0	1	.000	2	1	1	0	0	8^2	5	0	4	1	9.3	4.15	66	.167	.265	0	.000	-0	-1	-1	-0	-0.1
1915 Bos-N	0	0	—	2	1	0	0	0	5	6	0	4	3	18.0	3.60	72	.286	.400	0	.000	-0	-0	-1	0	0.0
1918 Cin-N	6	3	.667	12	10	9	1	0	83	84	1	32	26	12.7	3.80	70	.277	.348	9	.321	4	-10	-10	-0	-0.6
1919 *Cin-N	10	3	.769	30	9	6	2	3	106	89	2	36	40	10.8	2.63	105	.237	.308	4	.125	-0	3	2	1	0.2
1920 Cin-N	13	9	.591	37	23	10	1	1	207^2	168	5	60	72	10.1	2.51	121	.225	.286	17	.266	4	14	12	-2	1.5
1921 Cin-N	17	19	.472	41	36	25	3	3	304	318	13	64	102	11.3	3.38	106	.273	.312	30	.270	6	14	7	0	1.2
1922 Cin-N	13	23	.361	39	32	18	0	0	261	266	7	72	79	11.7	3.31	121	.268	.318	18	.209	1	23	20	0	2.0
1923 Cin-N	27	8	.771	41	37	28	6	2	322	279	2	88	151	10.4	1.93	200	.235	.291	21	.202	2	74	69	0	7.3
1924 Cin-N	10	15	.400	31	28	13	2	0	219^1	229	5	53	86	11.7	3.16	119	.271	.316	13	.178	-1	17	15	1	1.5
1925 Cin-N	16	18	.471	36	36	22	4	0	291	263	7	78	140	10.6	2.63	156	.239	.291	26	.255	5	53	48	3	5.6
1926 Cin-N	13	16	.448	34	30	16	1	0	233^2	231	7	77	83	11.9	3.43	108	.260	.321	27	.346	8	10	7	2	1.6
1927 Cin-N	13	12	.520	29	27	17	2	0	230^2	225	10	56	76	11.0	3.20	118	.260	.305	18	.217	2	18	15	3	2.1
1928 Cin-N	11	10	.524	33	29	11	1	1	234^1	254	12	84	72	13.1	3.57	111	.284	.347	8	.119	-1	11	10	-2	0.6
1929 Cin-N	5	16	.238	32	22	8	1	0	176	213	7	56	43	13.9	4.50	101	.310	.364	15	.278	4	1	0	0	0.5
1930 Bro-N	14	8	.636	31	24	16	2	2	199	221	18	58	62	12.6	4.30	114	.287	.337	18	.240	1	15	13	2	1.5
1931 Bro-N	7	6	.538	19	15	5	0	0	102^2	122	6	27	25	13.1	4.56	84	.297	.342	4	.133	0	-8	-9	-0	-0.8
1932 NY-N	6	7	.462	38	5	1	0	5	110	128	4	32	32	13.1	4.01	93	.290	.338	1	.040	-2	-2	-4	2	-0.3
1933 *NY-N	8	2	.800	35	0	0	0	4	81	75	4	19	23	10.5	2.69	119	.251	.296	5	.263	1	6	5	0	0.3
1934 NY-N	4	3	.571	26	0	0	0	7	42^1	54	3	17	12	15.3	3.83	101	.316	.381	2	.286	1	1	0	1	0.2
1935 NY-N	1	0	1.000	2	0	0	0	0	3^2	1	0	1	2	4.9	0.00	—	.077	.143	1	1.000	0	2	2	-0	0.2
Total 20	194	179	.520	550	365	206	26	28	3220^1	3231	113	918	1130	11.7	3.24	117	.265	.318	237	.227	35	245	200	11	24.8

■ JOHNNY LUSH
Lush, John Charles   b: 10/8/1885, Williamsport, Pa.   d: 11/18/46, Beverly Hills, Cal   BL/TL, 5'9.5", 165 lbs.   Deb: 4/22/04   ◆

YEAR TM/L	W	L	PCT	G	GS	CG	SH	SV	IP	H	HR	BB	SO	RAT	ERA	ERA+	OAV	OOB	BH	AVG	PB	PR	/A	PD	TPI
1904 Phi-N	0	6	.000	7	6	3	0	0	42^2	52	0	27	27	18.1	3.59	75	.301	.415	102	.276	2	-4	-4	0	-0.7
1905 Phi-N	2	0	1.000	2	2	1	0	0	17	12	0	8	8	11.1	1.59	184	.194	.296	5	.313	0	3	3	0	0.3
1906 Phi-N	18	15	.545	37	35	24	5	0	281	254	2	119	151	12.5	2.37	110	.236	.321	56	.264	7	8	8	2	0.8
1907 Phi-N	3	5	.375	8	8	5	2	0	57^1	48	0	21	20	11.3	2.98	81	.227	.306	8	.200	1	-3	-4	1	-0.3
StL-N	7	10	.412	20	19	15	3	0	144	132	2	42	71	11.4	2.50	100	.246	.311	23	.280	6	-0	0	-1	0.5
Yr	10	15	.400	28	27	20	5	0	201^1	180	2	63	91	11.2	2.64	94	.240	.306	6	.049	6	-4	-4	0	0.5
1908 StL-N	11	18	.379	38	32	23	3	1	250^2	221	6	57	93	10.4	2.12	111	.231	.283	15	.169	1	7	7	1	0.9
1909 StL-N	11	18	.379	34	28	21	2	0	221^1	215	1	69	66	12.0	3.13	81	.260	.324	22	.239	-4	-15	-15	-1	-1.0
1910 StL-N	14	13	.519	36	24	13	1	1	225^1	235	6	70	54	12.5	3.20	93	.276	.336	21	.226	4	-4	-5	-1	-0.2
Total 7	66	85	.437	182	154	105	16	2	1239^1	1169	17	413	490	11.9	2.68	97	.249	.318	252	.254	24	-7	-11	1	1.0

■ SPARKY LYLE
Lyle, Albert Walter   b: 7/22/44, DuBois, Pa.   BL/TL, 6'1", 182 lbs.   Deb: 7/04/67

YEAR TM/L	W	L	PCT	G	GS	CG	SH	SV	IP	H	HR	BB	SO	RAT	ERA	ERA+	OAV	OOB	BH	AVG	PB	PR	/A	PD	TPI
1967 Bos-A	1	2	.333	27	0	0	0	5	43^1	33	3	14	42	10.2	2.28	153	.213	.287	2	.250	1	5	6	-0	0.7
1968 Bos-A	6	1	.857	49	0	0	0	11	65^2	67	6	14	52	11.1	2.74	115	.261	.299	1	.125	-0	2	3	-1	0.2
1969 Bos-A	8	3	.727	71	0	0	0	17	102^2	91	8	48	93	12.3	2.54	150	.240	.327	2	.118	-1	12	14	0	1.5
1970 Bos-A	1	7	.125	63	0	0	0	20	67^1	62	5	34	51	13.0	3.88	102	.244	.336	0	.000	-1	-1	1	-1	0.0
1971 Bos-A	6	4	.600	50	0	0	0	16	52^1	41	5	23	37	11.0	2.75	134	.228	.315	3	1.000	1	4	5	0	0.8
1972 NY-A	9	5	.643	59	0	0	0	35	107^2	84	3	29	75	9.4	1.92	153	.216	.271	4	.190	1	14	12	-1	1.3
1973 NY-A	5	9	.357	51	0	0	0	27	82^1	66	4	18	63	9.2	2.51	146	.216	.259	0	—	0	12	11	-0	1.1
1974 NY-A	9	3	.750	66	0	0	0	15	114	93	4	43	89	10.8	1.66	210	.226	.300	0	.000	0	25	23	-1	2.3
1975 NY-A	5	7	.417	49	0	0	0	6	89^1	94	1	36	65	13.3	3.12	117	.275	.347	0	—	0	6	5	0	0.5
1976 *NY-A	7	8	.467	64	0	0	0	23	103^2	82	5	42	61	10.8	2.26	151	.225	.305	0	—	0	15	13	-1	1.3
1977 *NY-A	13	5	.722	72	0	0	0	26	137	131	7	33	68	10.9	2.17	182	.257	.305	0	—	0	29	27	-1	2.7
1978 *NY-A	9	3	.750	59	0	0	0	9	111^2	116	6	33	33	12.3	3.47	104	.278	.337	0	—	0	4	2	1	0.3
1979 Tex-A	5	8	.385	67	0	0	0	13	95	78	9	28	48	10.0	3.13	133	.226	.284	0	—	0	11	11	-1	0.9
1980 Tex-A	3	2	.600	49	0	0	0	8	80^2	97	9	28	43	13.9	4.69	83	.306	.362	0	—	0	-6	-7	-0	-0.6
Phi-N	0	0	—	10	0	0	0	2	14	11	0	6	10	10.9	1.93	196	.220	.304	0	—	0	3	3	0	0.3
1981 *Phi-N	9	6	.600	48	0	0	0	2	75	85	4	33	29	14.3	4.44	82	.301	.377	2	.400	1	-8	-7	1	-0.4
1982 Phi-N	3	3	.500	34	0	0	0	2	36^2	50	3	12	12	15.2	5.15	71	.327	.376	1	.500	1	-6	-6	1	-0.4
Chi-A	0	0	—	11	0	0	0	1	12	11	0	7	6	13.5	3.00	134	.262	.367	0	—	0	1	1	0	0.1
Total 16	99	76	.566	899	0	0	0	238	1390^1	1292	84	481	873	11.6	2.88	127	.251	.316	15	.192	2	121	119	-5	12.6

■ JIM LYLE
Lyle, James Charles   b: 7/24/1900, Lake, Miss.   d: 10/10/77, Williamsport, Pa.   BR/TR, 6'1", 180 lbs.   Deb: 10/02/25

YEAR TM/L	W	L	PCT	G	GS	CG	SH	SV	IP	H	HR	BB	SO	RAT	ERA	ERA+	OAV	OOB	BH	AVG	PB	PR	/A	PD	TPI
1925 Was-A	0	0	—	1	0	0	0	0	3	5	0	1	3	18.0	6.00	70	.333	.375	0	—	0	-1	-1	-0	0.0

■ ADRIAN LYNCH
Lynch, Adrian Ryan   b: 2/9/1897, Laurens, Iowa   d: 3/16/34, Davenport, Iowa   BB/TR, 6'1.5", 185 lbs.   Deb: 8/04/20

YEAR TM/L	W	L	PCT	G	GS	CG	SH	SV	IP	H	HR	BB	SO	RAT	ERA	ERA+	OAV	OOB	BH	AVG	PB	PR	/A	PD	TPI
1920 StL-A	2	0	1.000	5	3	1	0	0	22^1	23	1	17	8	16.5	5.24	75	.277	.406	2	.222	0	-4	-3	-0	-0.2

■ ED LYNCH
Lynch, Edward Francis   b: 2/25/56, Brooklyn, N.Y.   BR/TR, 6'6", 230 lbs.   Deb: 8/31/80

YEAR TM/L	W	L	PCT	G	GS	CG	SH	SV	IP	H	HR	BB	SO	RAT	ERA	ERA+	OAV	OOB	BH	AVG	PB	PR	/A	PD	TPI
1980 NY-N	1	1	.500	5	4	0	0	0	19^1	24	0	5	9	14.0	5.12	69	.304	.353	2	.333	0	-3	-3	-0	-0.2
1981 NY-N	4	4	.444	17	13	0	0	0	80^1	79	6	21	27	11.3	2.91	120	.254	.303	3	.143	1	5	5	-1	0.6
1982 NY-N	4	8	.333	43	12	0	0	2	139^1	145	6	40	51	12.0	3.55	102	.273	.325	0	.000	-3	1	1	-1	-0.2
1983 NY-N	10	10	.500	30	27	1	0	0	174^2	208	17	41	44	13.0	4.28	85	.302	.344	8	.154	-1	-13	-13	-1	-1.3
1984 NY-N	9	8	.529	40	13	0	0	2	124	169	14	24	62	14.3	4.50	79	.324	.359	6	.222	1	-13	-13	-1	-1.3

YEAR	TM/L	W	L	PCT	G	GS	CG	SH	SV	IP	H	HR	BB	SO	RAT	ERA	ERA+	OAV	OOB	BH	AVG	PB	PR	/A	PD	TPI
1985	NY-N	10	8	.556	31	29	6	1	0	191	188	19	27	65	10.2	3.44	100	.256	.283	4	.077	-2	3	0	-2	-0.4
1986	NY-N	0	0	—	1	0	0	0	0	1^2	2	0	0	1	10.8	0.00	—	.286	.286	0	—	0	1	1	0	0.1
	Chi-N	7	5	.583	23	13	1	1	0	99^2	105	10	23	57	11.6	3.79	107	.279	.322	1	.033	-2	-1	3	-0	0.0
	Yr	7	5	.583	24	13	1	1	0	101^1	107	10	23	58	11.6	3.73	108	.279	.321	2	.067	-2	-0	3	-0	0.1
1987	Chi-N	2	9	.182	58	8	0	0	4	110^1	130	17	48	80	14.7	5.38	79	.295	.367	3	.188	-0	-16	-14	1	-1.2
Total 8		47	54	.465	248	119	8	2	8	940^1	1050	89	229	396	12.4	4.00	92	.284	.329	27	.114	-6	-35	-33	-5	-3.9

■ JACK LYNCH Lynch, John H. b: 2/5/1857, New York, N.Y. d: 4/20/23, Bronx, N.Y. BR/TR, 5'8", 185 lbs. Deb: 5/02/1881

YEAR	TM/L	W	L	PCT	G	GS	CG	SH	SV	IP	H	HR	BB	SO	RAT	ERA	ERA+	OAV	OOB	BH	AVG	PB	PR	/A	PD	TPI
1881	Buf-N	10	9	.526	20	19	17	0	0	165^2	203	2	29	32	12.6	3.59	77	.289	.317	13	.167	-3	-15	-15	1	-1.4
1883	NY-a	13	15	.464	29	29	29	1	0	255	263	6	25	119	10.2	4.09	81	.249	.267	20	.187	-3	-22	-22	-0	-2.0
1884	NY-a	37	15	.712	54	53	53	5	0	487	410	10	42	286	8.4	2.64	118	.216	.233	30	.154	-6	33	25	-5	-2.7
1885	NY-a	23	21	.523	44	43	43	1	0	379	410	17	42	177	10.7	3.61	82	.264	.284	30	.196	2	-15	-27	-5	-2.7
1886	NY-a	20	30	.400	51	50	50	1	0	432^2	485	10	116	193	12.5	3.95	86	.270	.315	27	.160	-6	-24	-26	-3	-2.9
1887	NY-a	7	14	.333	21	21	21	0	0	187	245	8	36	45	13.5	5.10	83	.305	.335	14	.169	-4	-17	-18	2	-1.4
1890	Bro-a	0	1	.000	1	1	1	0	0	9	22	1	5	1	27.0	12.00	32	.452	.503	3	.750	2	-8	-8	1	-0.3
Total 7		110	105	.512	220	216	214	8	0	1915^1	2038	54	295	853	11.0	3.69	88	.259	.286	137	.174	-16	-69	-91	-9	-9.5

■ MIKE LYNCH Lynch, Michael Joseph b: 6/28/1880, Holyoke, Mass. d: 4/2/27, Garrison, N.Y. BR/TR, 5'10", 155 lbs. Deb: 6/21/04

YEAR	TM/L	W	L	PCT	G	GS	CG	SH	SV	IP	H	HR	BB	SO	RAT	ERA	ERA+	OAV	OOB	BH	AVG	PB	PR	/A	PD	TPI
1904	Pit-N	15	11	.577	27	24	24	1	0	222^2	200	1	91	95	12.4	2.71	101	.243	.330	20	.230	4	1	1	-3	0.2
1905	Pit-N	17	8	.680	33	22	13	0	2	206	191	3	107	106	13.2	3.80	79	.254	.254	11	.136	-1	-18	-18	-0	-1.9
1906	Pit-N	6	5	.545	18	12	7	0	0	119	101	2	31	48	10.6	2.42	110	.232	.295	8	.205	0	3	3	-0	0.3
1907	Pit-N	2	2	.500	7	4	2	0	0	36	37	0	22	9	15.0	2.25	108	.282	.390	3	.250	1	1	1	2	0.3
	NY-N	3	6	.333	12	10	7	0	1	72	68	3	30	34	12.3	3.38	73	.249	.323	8	.296	2	-7	-7	0	-0.4
	Yr	5	8	.385	19	14	9	0	1	108	105	3	52	43	13.1	3.00	82	.259	.344	2	.051	3	-6	-6	2	-0.1
Total 4		43	32	.573	97	72	53	1	3	655^2	597	9	281	292	12.4	3.05	91	.248	.333	50	.203	6	-21	-20	-1	-1.5

■ DUMMY LYNCH Lynch, Thomas S. b: 1863, Peru, Ill. d: 5/13/03, Peru, Ill. 5'11", 175 lbs. Deb: 8/05/1884

YEAR	TM/L	W	L	PCT	G	GS	CG	SH	SV	IP	H	HR	BB	SO	RAT	ERA	ERA+	OAV	OOB	BH	AVG	PB	PR	/A	PD	TPI
1884	Chi-N	0	0	—	1	1	0	0	0	7	7	1	3	2	12.9	2.57	122	.246	.318	0	.000	-1	0	0	0	0.0

■ RED LYNN Lynn, Japhet Monroe b: 12/27/13, Kenney, Tex. d: 10/27/77, Bellville, Tex. BR/TR, 6', 162 lbs. Deb: 4/25/39

YEAR	TM/L	W	L	PCT	G	GS	CG	SH	SV	IP	H	HR	BB	SO	RAT	ERA	ERA+	OAV	OOB	BH	AVG	PB	PR	/A	PD	TPI
1939	Det-A	0	1	.000	4	0	0	0	0	8^1	11	2	3	3	16.2	8.64	57	.324	.395	0	.000	-0	-4	-3	0	-0.2
	NY-N	1	0	1.000	26	0	0	0	1	49^2	44	3	21	22	12.1	3.08	127	.240	.325	0	.000	-1	5	5	-1	0.3
1940	NY-N	4	3	.571	33	0	0	0	0	42^1	40	3	24	25	13.8	3.83	101	.247	.348	0	.000	-1	0	0	-1	0.0
1944	Chi-N	5	4	.556	22	7	4	1	1	84^1	80	4	37	35	12.6	4.06	87	.251	.331	6	.207	-1	-4	-5	1	-0.2
Total 3		10	8	.556	85	7	4	1	5	184^2	175	12	85	85	12.9	3.95	96	.251	.336	6	.146	-1	-3	-4	-1	-0.1

■ AL LYONS Lyons, Albert Harold b: 7/18/18, St.Joseph, Mo. d: 12/20/65, Inglewood, Cal. BR/TR, 6'2", 195 lbs. Deb: 4/19/44

YEAR	TM/L	W	L	PCT	G	GS	CG	SH	SV	IP	H	HR	BB	SO	RAT	ERA	ERA+	OAV	OOB	BH	AVG	PB	PR	/A	PD	TPI
1944	NY-A	0	0	—	11	0	0	0	0	39^2	43	2	24	15	15.7	4.54	77	.291	.397	9	.346	2	-5	-5	-1	-0.2
1946	NY-A	0	1	.000	2	1	0	0	0	8^1	11	0	6	4	19.4	5.40	64	.314	.429	0	.000	-1	-2	-2	0	-0.1
1947	NY-A	1	0	1.000	6	0	0	0	0	11	18	2	9	7	22.1	9.00	39	.367	.466	4	.667	1	-6	-7	0	-0.3
	Pit-N	1	2	.333	13	0	0	0	0	28^1	36	4	12	16	15.6	7.31	58	.300	.368	2	.200	1	-10	-10	1	-0.6
1948	Bos-N	1	0	1.000	7	0	0	0	0	12^2	17	1	8	5	17.8	7.82	49	.309	.397	2	.167	0	-5	-6	1	-0.4
Total 4		3	3	.500	39	1	0	0	0	100	125	9	59	47	16.9	6.30	59	.307	.400	17	.293	5	-29	-28	2	-1.6

■ GEORGE LYONS Lyons, George Tony "Smooth" b: 1/25/1891, Bible Grove, Ill. d: 8/12/81, Nevada, Mo. BR/TR, 5'11", 180 lbs. Deb: 9/06/20

YEAR	TM/L	W	L	PCT	G	GS	CG	SH	SV	IP	H	HR	BB	SO	RAT	ERA	ERA+	OAV	OOB	BH	AVG	PB	PR	/A	PD	TPI
1920	StL-N	2	1	.667	7	2	1	0	0	23^1	21	2	9	5	12.0	3.09	97	.262	.344	1	.143	-0	0	-0	1	0.0
1924	StL-A	3	2	.600	26	6	2	0	0	77^2	97	2	45	25	17.0	5.21	83	.323	.420	5	.250	-0	-8	-6	1	-0.3
Total 2		5	3	.625	33	8	3	0	0	101	118	4	54	30	15.9	4.72	88	.311	.405	6	.222	-0	-8	-7	2	-0.3

■ HARRY LYONS Lyons, Harry P. b: 3/25/1866, Chester, Pa. d: 6/30/12, Mauricetown, N.J. BR/TR, 5'10.5", 157 lbs. Deb: 8/29/1887 ♦

YEAR	TM/L	W	L	PCT	G	GS	CG	SH	SV	IP	H	HR	BB	SO	RAT	ERA	ERA+	OAV	OOB	BH	AVG	PB	PR	/A	PD	TPI
1890	Roc-a	0	0	—	1	0	0	0	0	3^2	8	0	1	2	22.1	12.27	29	.424	.453	152	.260	0	-3	-4	0	-0.2

■ HERSH LYONS Lyons, Herschel Englebert b: 7/23/15, Fresno, Cal. BR/TR, 5'11", 195 lbs. Deb: 4/17/41

YEAR	TM/L	W	L	PCT	G	GS	CG	SH	SV	IP	H	HR	BB	SO	RAT	ERA	ERA+	OAV	OOB	BH	AVG	PB	PR	/A	PD	TPI
1941	StL-N	0	0	—	1	0	0	0	0	1^1	1	0	3	1	27.0	0.00	—	.200	.500	0	—	0	1	1	0	0.1

■ STEVE LYONS Lyons, Stephen John b: 6/3/60, Tacoma, Wash. BL/TR, 6'3", 190 lbs. Deb: 4/15/85 ♦

YEAR	TM/L	W	L	PCT	G	GS	CG	SH	SV	IP	H	HR	BB	SO	RAT	ERA	ERA+	OAV	OOB	BH	AVG	PB	PR	/A	PD	TPI
1990	Chi-A	0	0	—	1	0	0	0	0	2	2	0	4	1	27.0	4.50	85	.250	.500	28	.192	0	-0	-0	0	0.0

■ TED LYONS Lyons, Theodore Amar b: 12/28/1900, Lake Charles, La. d: 7/25/86, Sulphur, La. BB/TR, 5'11", 200 lbs. Deb: 7/02/23 MCH♦

YEAR	TM/L	W	L	PCT	G	GS	CG	SH	SV	IP	H	HR	BB	SO	RAT	ERA	ERA+	OAV	OOB	BH	AVG	PB	PR	/A	PD	TPI
1923	Chi-A	2	1	.667	9	1	0	0	0	22^2	30	2	15	6	18.3	6.35	62	.333	.422	1	.200	-0	-6	-6	1	-0.4
1924	Chi-A	12	11	.522	41	22	12	0	3	216^1	279	10	72	52	14.7	4.87	85	.322	.375	17	.221	0	-15	-18	-2	-1.8
1925	Chi-A	**21**	11	.656	43	32	19	**5**	3	262^1	274	7	83	45	12.3	3.26	128	.278	.335	18	.186	-3	33	26	2	2.4
1926	Chi-A	18	16	.529	39	31	24	3	2	283^2	268	6	106	51	11.9	3.01	128	.252	.320	22	.212	-0	32	27	4	3.0
1927	Chi-A	**22**	14	.611	39	34	**30**	2	2	307^2	291	7	67	71	10.5	2.84	143	.251	.292	28	.255	5	**45**	**41**	1	**4.7**
1928	Chi-A	15	14	.517	39	27	21	0	6	240	276	11	68	60	13.0	3.98	102	.295	.344	23	.253	1	2	2	0	0.4
1929	Chi-A	14	20	.412	37	31	21	1	2	259^1	276	11	76	57	12.3	4.10	105	.278	.331	20	.220	1	4	5	3	0.9
1930	Chi-A	22	15	.595	42	36	**29**	1	1	**297^2**	331	12	57	69	11.8	3.78	122	.285	.319	38	.311	8	29	28	4	3.7
1931	Chi-A	4	6	.400	22	12	7	0	0	101	117	6	33	16	13.4	4.01	106	.296	.350	5	.152	-1	4	3	-0	0.1
1932	Chi-A	10	15	.400	33	26	19	1	2	230^2	243	10	71	58	12.4	3.28	132	.272	.327	19	.260	5	31	27	-1	2.9
1933	Chi-A	10	21	.323	36	27	14	2	1	228	260	10	74	74	13.2	4.38	97	.280	.333	26	.286	6	-3	-4	0	0.2
1934	Chi-A	11	13	.458	30	24	21	0	1	205^1	249	15	66	53	13.9	4.87	97	.293	.345	20	.260	1	-8	-3	2	0.1
1935	Chi-A	15	8	.652	23	22	19	3	0	190^2	194	15	56	54	11.9	3.02	153	.262	.317	18	.220	-0	30	34	-1	3.3
1936	Chi-A	10	13	.435	26	24	15	1	0	182	227	21	45	48	13.6	5.14	101	.305	.347	11	.157	-3	-2	1	2	0.0
1937	Chi-A	12	7	.632	22	22	11	0	0	169^1	184	12	45	45	12.1	4.15	111	.287	.326	12	.211	1	9	9	1	0.2
1938	Chi-A	9	11	.450	23	23	17	1	0	194^2	238	13	52	54	13.4	3.70	132	.299	.342	14	.194	-1	24	26	2	2.6
1939	Chi-A	14	6	.700	22	21	16	0	0	172^2	162	7	26	65	**9.9**	2.76	171	.247	**.276**	18	.295	4	36	38	-1	4.1
1940	Chi-A	12	8	.600	22	22	17	4	0	186^1	188	17	37	72	10.9	3.24	137	.252	.287	18	.240	2	24	25	-2	2.5
1941	Chi-A	12	10	.545	22	22	19	2	0	187^1	199	9	37	63	11.5	3.70	111	.269	.308	20	.270	4	9	8	1	1.3
1942	Chi-A	14	6	.700	20	20	20	1	0	180^1	167	11	26	50	9.7	**2.10**	**172**	.245	.275	16	.239	4	31	30	4	4.0
1946	Chi-A	1	4	.200	5	5	5	0	0	42^2	38	2	9	10	9.9	2.32	147	.235	.275	0	.000	-1	6	5	0	0.5
Total 21		260	230	.531	594	484	356	27	23	4161	4489	223	1121	1073	12.2	3.67	118	.276	.324	364	.233	32	313	302	17	35.5

■ TOBY LYONS Lyons, Thomas A. b: 3/27/1869, Cambridge, Mass. d: 8/27/20, Boston, Mass. Deb: 4/18/1890

YEAR	TM/L	W	L	PCT	G	GS	CG	SH	SV	IP	H	HR	BB	SO	RAT	ERA	ERA+	OAV	OOB	BH	AVG	PB	PR	/A	PD	TPI
1890	Syr-a	0	2	.000	3	3	2	0	0	22^1	40	1	21	6	24.6	10.48	34	.377	.480	4	.333	1	-16	-17	0	-1.1

■ RICK LYSANDER Lysander, Richard Eugene b: 2/21/53, Huntington Park, Cal. BR/TR, 6'2", 190 lbs. Deb: 4/12/80

YEAR	TM/L	W	L	PCT	G	GS	CG	SH	SV	IP	H	HR	BB	SO	RAT	ERA	ERA+	OAV	OOB	BH	AVG	PB	PR	/A	PD	TPI
1980	Oak-A	0	0	—	5	0	0	0	0	13^2	24	1	4	5	18.4	7.90	48	.381	.418	0	—	0	-6	-6	0	-0.5
1983	Min-A	5	12	.294	61	4	1	1	3	125	132	8	43	58	12.7	3.38	126	.275	.337	0	—	0	9	12	1	1.3
1984	Min-A	4	3	.571	36	0	0	0	5	56^2	62	2	27	22	14.1	3.49	120	.283	.362	0	—	0	3	4	0	0.5
1985	Min-A	0	2	.000	35	1	0	0	3	36	45	5	22	26	13.9	6.05	73	.305	.364	0	—	0	-13	-11	0	-1.0
Total 4		9	17	.346	137	5	1	1	11	256^1	290	16	96	111	13.6	4.28	99	.291	.354	0	—	0	-6	-1	0	0.3

■ BILL LYSTON Lyston, William Edward b: 1863, Near Baltimore, Md. d: 8/4/44, Baltimore, Md. TR, Deb: 8/29/1891

YEAR	TM/L	W	L	PCT	G	GS	CG	SH	SV	IP	H	HR	BB	SO	RAT	ERA	ERA+	OAV	OOB	BH	AVG	PB	PR	/A	PD	TPI
1891	Col-a	0	1	.000	1	1	1	0	0	6	10	1	6	0	24.0	10.50	33	.359	.473	0	.000	-0	-5	-5	-0	-0.3
1894	Cle-N	0	0	—	1	1	0	0	0	3^2	5	1	4	0	22.1	9.82	56	.321	.460	0	.000	-0	-2	-2	-0	-0.1
Total 2		0	1	.000	2	2	1	0	0	9^2	15	1	10	1	23.3	10.24	41	.346	.468	0	.000	-0	-6	-7	-0	-0.4

DUKE MAAS
Maas, Duane Fredrick b: 1/31/29, Utica, Mich. d: 12/7/76, Mt.Clemens, Mich. BR/TR, 5'10", 170 lbs. Deb: 4/21/55

YEAR TM/L	W	L	PCT	G	GS	CG	SH	SV	IP	H	HR	BB	SO	RAT	ERA	ERA+	OAV	OOB	BH	AVG	PB	PR	/A	PD	TPI
1955 Det-A	5	6	.455	18	16	5	2	0	86²	91	7	50	42	14.8	4.88	79	.271	.369	5	.167	0	-9	-10	0	-0.9
1956 Det-A	0	7	.000	26	7	0	0	0	63¹	81	9	32	34	16.9	6.54	63	.313	.401	3	.188	0	-17	-17	-0	-1.6
1957 Det-A	10	14	.417	45	26	8	2	6	219¹	210	23	65	116	11.4	3.28	118	.252	.309	6	.085	-4	12	14	0	1.1
1958 KC-A	4	5	.444	10	7	3	1	1	55¹	49	3	13	19	10.2	3.90	100	.241	.290	3	.176	0	-1	0	0	0.1
*NY-A	7	3	.700	22	13	2	1	0	101¹	93	9	36	50	11.6	3.82	92	.242	.310	3	.088	-2	-1	-3	-1	-0.5
Yr	11	8	.579	32	20	5	2	1	156²	142	12	49	69	11.1	3.85	95	.241	.302	4	.078	-1	-1	-3	-1	-0.4
1959 NY-A	14	8	.636	38	21	3	1	4	138	149	14	53	67	13.3	4.43	82	.278	.345	5	.125	-1	-9	-12	1	-1.2
1960 *NY-A	5	1	.833	35	1	0	0	4	70¹	70	6	35	28	13.6	4.09	87	.265	.353	0	.000	-1	-2	-4	1	-0.3
1961 NY-A	0	0	—	1	0	0	0	0	0¹	2	0	0	0	54.0	54.00	7	1.000	1.000	0	—	0	-2	-2	0	-0.1
Total 7	45	44	.506	195	91	21	7	15	734²	745	71	284	356	12.8	4.19	90	.264	.336	25	.117	-7	-27	-34	1	-3.4

BOB MABE
Mabe, Robert Lee b: 10/8/29, Danville, Va. BR/TR, 5'11", 165 lbs. Deb: 4/18/58

YEAR TM/L	W	L	PCT	G	GS	CG	SH	SV	IP	H	HR	BB	SO	RAT	ERA	ERA+	OAV	OOB	BH	AVG	PB	PR	/A	PD	TPI
1958 StL-N	3	9	.250	31	13	4	0	0	111²	113	11	41	74	12.7	4.51	91	.260	.330	1	.042	-2	-7	-5	0	-0.6
1959 Cin-N	4	2	.667	18	1	0	0	3	29²	29	6	19	8	14.6	5.46	74	.254	.361	0	.000	-1	-5	-5	-0	-0.5
1960 Bal-A	0	0	—	2	0	0	0	0	0²	4	0	1	0	67.5	27.00	14	.571	.625	0	—	0	-2	-2	0	-0.1
Total 3	7	11	.389	51	14	4	0	3	142	146	17	61	82	13.4	4.82	85	.263	.340	1	.032	-3	-14	-11	0	-1.2

MAC MacARTHUR
MacArthur, Malcolm b: 1/19/1862, Glasgow, Scotland d: 10/18/32, Detroit, Mich. TR, Deb: 5/02/1884

YEAR TM/L	W	L	PCT	G	GS	CG	SH	SV	IP	H	HR	BB	SO	RAT	ERA	ERA+	OAV	OOB	BH	AVG	PB	PR	/A	PD	TPI
1884 Ind-a	1	5	.167	6	6	6	0	0	52	57	1	21	19	13.5	5.02	65	.264	.329	2	.095	-2	-10	-10	0	-0.9

FRANK MacCORMACK
MacCormack, Frank Louis b: 9/21/54, Jersey City, N.J. BR/TR, 6'4", 210 lbs. Deb: 6/14/76

YEAR TM/L	W	L	PCT	G	GS	CG	SH	SV	IP	H	HR	BB	SO	RAT	ERA	ERA+	OAV	OOB	BH	AVG	PB	PR	/A	PD	TPI
1976 Det-A	0	5	.000	9	8	0	0	0	32²	35	1	34	14	19.3	5.79	64	.294	.455	0	.000	0	-8	-8	-0	-0.7
1977 Sea-A	0	0	—	3	3	0	0	0	7	4	0	12	4	24.4	3.86	107	.174	.500	0	—	0	0	0	0	0.0
Total 2	0	5	.000	12	11	0	0	0	39²	39	1	46	18	20.2	5.45	69	.275	.464	0	.000	0	-8	-7	0	-0.7

ROB MacDONALD
MacDonald, Robert Joseph b: 4/27/65, East Orange, N.J. BL/TL, 6'3", 200 lbs. Deb: 8/14/90

YEAR TM/L	W	L	PCT	G	GS	CG	SH	SV	IP	H	HR	BB	SO	RAT	ERA	ERA+	OAV	OOB	BH	AVG	PB	PR	/A	PD	TPI
1990 Tor-A	0	0	—	4	0	0	0	0	2¹	0	0	2	0	7.7	0.00	—	.000	.250	0	—	0	1	1	0	0.1

BILL MACDONALD
Macdonald, William Paul b: 3/28/29, Alameda, Cal. BR/TR, 5'10", 170 lbs. Deb: 5/06/50

YEAR TM/L	W	L	PCT	G	GS	CG	SH	SV	IP	H	HR	BB	SO	RAT	ERA	ERA+	OAV	OOB	BH	AVG	PB	PR	/A	PD	TPI
1950 Pit-N	8	10	.444	32	20	6	2	1	153	138	17	88	60	13.4	4.29	102	.243	.346	6	.122	-2	-3	2	-3	-0.2
1953 Pit-N	0	1	.000	4	1	0	0	0	7¹	12	0	8	4	25.8	12.27	36	.400	.538	0	—	0	-7	-6	0	-0.5
Total 2	8	11	.421	36	21	6	2	1	160¹	150	17	96	64	13.9	4.66	94	.251	.356	6	.122	-2	-9	-5	-3	-0.7

JIMMY MACE
Mace, Harry L. b: Washington, D.C. 5'11", 185 lbs. Deb: 5/05/1891

YEAR TM/L	W	L	PCT	G	GS	CG	SH	SV	IP	H	HR	BB	SO	RAT	ERA	ERA+	OAV	OOB	BH	AVG	PB	PR	/A	PD	TPI
1891 Was-a	0	1	.000	3	1	0	0	0	16	18	0	8	3	14.6	7.31	51	.274	.353	0	.000	-1	-6	-6	0	-0.5

DANNY MacFAYDEN
MacFayden, Daniel Knowles "Deacon Danny" b: 6/10/05, N.Truro, Mass. d: 8/26/72, Brunswick, Me. BR/TR, 5'11", 170 lbs. Deb: 8/25/26

YEAR TM/L	W	L	PCT	G	GS	CG	SH	SV	IP	H	HR	BB	SO	RAT	ERA	ERA+	OAV	OOB	BH	AVG	PB	PR	/A	PD	TPI
1926 Bos-A	0	1	.000	3	1	1	0	0	13	10	0	7	1	11.8	4.85	84	.217	.321	1	.333	0	-1	-1	1	0.0
1927 Bos-A	5	8	.385	34	16	6	1	2	160¹	176	9	59	42	13.5	4.27	99	.294	.363	13	.283	4	-2	-1	-1	0.1
1928 Bos-A	9	15	.375	33	28	9	0	0	195	215	12	78	61	13.8	4.75	87	.289	.361	9	.143	-1	-15	-14	-1	-1.4
1929 Bos-A	10	18	.357	32	26	14	4	0	221	225	8	81	61	12.7	3.62	118	.271	.340	13	.176	-3	15	16	2	1.5
1930 Bos-A	11	14	.440	36	33	18	1	0	269¹	293	9	93	76	13.1	4.21	109	.281	.343	13	.141	-4	13	12	2	0.8
1931 Bos-A	16	12	.571	35	32	17	2	0	230²	263	4	79	74	13.6	4.02	107	.281	.341	10	.123	-5	9	7	2	0.4
1932 Bos-A	1	10	.091	12	11	6	0	0	77²	91	3	33	29	14.5	5.10	88	.289	.358	3	.120	-2	-5	-5	0	-0.5
NY-A	7	5	.583	17	15	9	0	1	121¹	137	11	37	33	13.1	3.93	104	.281	.334	5	.102	-2	7	2	-1	-0.1
Yr	8	15	.348	29	26	15	0	1	199	228	14	70	62	13.6	4.39	97	.284	.342	2	.027	-4	2	-3	-1	-0.6
1933 NY-A	3	2	.600	25	6	2	0	0	90¹	120	8	37	28	15.8	5.88	66	.319	.383	1	.029	-4	-16	-20	0	-2.1
1934 NY-A	4	3	.571	22	11	4	0	0	96	110	5	31	41	13.4	4.50	90	.288	.345	4	.103	-2	-5	-5	-1	-0.6
1935 Cin-N	1	2	.333	7	4	1	0	0	36	39	1	13	13	13.0	4.75	84	.281	.342	1	.091	-1	-3	-3	1	-0.2
Bos-N	5	13	.278	28	20	7	1	0	151²	200	3	34	46	14.2	5.10	74	.314	.354	8	.157	-1	-18	-22	2	-1.9
Yr	6	15	.286	35	24	8	1	0	187²	239	4	47	59	14.0	5.04	76	.308	.352	0	.000	-2	-21	-25	3	-2.1
1936 Bos-N	17	13	.567	37	31	21	2	0	266²	268	5	66	86	11.4	2.87	134	.259	.307	8	.096	-5	34	29	3	2.7
1937 Bos-N	14	14	.500	32	32	16	2	0	246	250	5	60	70	11.4	2.93	123	.268	.313	13	.157	-2	27	18	1	1.7
1938 Bos-N	14	9	.609	29	29	19	5	0	219²	208	4	64	58	11.3	2.95	116	.247	.304	9	.179	-1	20	12	-1	0.6
1939 Bos-N	8	14	.364	33	28	8	0	2	191²	221	11	59	46	13.3	3.90	95	.291	.345	12	.179	-1	0	-4	1	-0.3
1940 Pit-N	5	4	.556	35	8	0	0	2	91¹	112	5	27	24	14.1	3.55	107	.302	.356	5	.179	-0	3	3	1	0.3
1941 Was-A	0	1	.000	5	0	0	0	0	7	12	1	5	3	21.9	10.29	39	.375	.459	0	—	0	-5	-5	0	-0.3
1943 Bos-N	2	1	.667	10	1	0	0	0	9	9	1	9	5	17.3	5.91	58	.344	.410	1	.250	0	-6	-6	0	-0.5
Total 17	132	159	.454	465	332	158	18	9	2706	2931	112	872	797	13.0	3.96	101	.281	.340	129	.142	-32	58	11	12	0.2

JULIO MACHADO
Machado, Julio Segundo (Rondon) b: 12/1/65, Zulia, Venezuela BR/TR, 6', 175 lbs. Deb: 9/07/89

YEAR TM/L	W	L	PCT	G	GS	CG	SH	SV	IP	H	HR	BB	SO	RAT	ERA	ERA+	OAV	OOB	BH	AVG	PB	PR	/A	PD	TPI
1989 NY-N	0	1	.000	10	0	0	0	0	11	9	0	3	14	9.8	3.27	100	.214	.267	0	—	0	0	-0	-0	0.0
1990 NY-N	4	1	.800	27	0	0	0	0	34¹	32	4	17	27	13.4	3.15	116	.248	.345	0	—	0	2	2	-0	0.2
Mil-A	0	0	—	10	0	0	0	3	13	9	0	8	12	11.8	0.69	546	.191	.309	0	—	0	5	4	0	0.5
Total 2	4	2	.667	47	0	0	0	3	58¹	50	4	28	53	12.3	2.62	137	.229	.323	0	—	0	7	6	-0	0.7

CHUCK MACHEMEHL
Machemehl, Charles Walter b: 4/20/47, Brenham, Tex. BR/TR, 6'4", 200 lbs. Deb: 4/06/71

YEAR TM/L	W	L	PCT	G	GS	CG	SH	SV	IP	H	HR	BB	SO	RAT	ERA	ERA+	OAV	OOB	BH	AVG	PB	PR	/A	PD	TPI
1971 Cle-A	0	2	.000	14	0	0	0	3	18¹	16	2	15	9	15.2	6.38	60	.246	.387	1	.500	0	-6	-5	0	-0.4

DENNY MACK
Mack, Dennis Joseph (b: Dennis Joseph McGee) b: 1851, Easton, Pa. d: 4/10/1888, Wilkes-Barre, Pa. BR/TR, 5'7", 164 lbs. Deb: 5/06/1871 MU♦

YEAR TM/L	W	L	PCT	G	GS	CG	SH	SV	IP	H	HR	BB	SO	RAT	ERA	ERA+	OAV	OOB	BH	AVG	PB	PR	/A	PD	TPI
1871 Rok-n	0	1	.000	3	1	0	0	0	13	20	0	3	1	15.9	3.46	118	.299	.329	30	.246	-0	1	1		0.1

FRANK MACK
Mack, Frank George "Stubby" b: 2/2/1900, Okahoma City, Okla. d: 7/2/71, Clearwater, Fla. BR/TR, 6'1.5", 180 lbs. Deb: 8/16/22

YEAR TM/L	W	L	PCT	G	GS	CG	SH	SV	IP	H	HR	BB	SO	RAT	ERA	ERA+	OAV	OOB	BH	AVG	PB	PR	/A	PD	TPI
1922 Chi-A	2	2	.500	8	4	1	1	0	34¹	36	2	16	11	13.6	3.67	111	.281	.361	3	.250	1	1	2	-1	0.1
1923 Chi-A	0	1	.000	11	0	0	0	0	23¹	23	0	11	6	13.1	4.24	93	.284	.370	0	.000	-1	-1	-1	0	0.0
1925 Chi-A	0	0	—	8	0	0	0	0	13¹	24	1	13	6	25.0	9.45	44	.444	.552	1	.333	0	-7	-8	-0	-0.6
Total 3	2	3	.400	27	4	1	1	0	71	83	3	40	23	15.6	4.94	82	.316	.406	4	.190	0	-7	-7	-1	-0.5

TONY MACK
Mack, Tony Lynn b: 4/30/61, Lexington, Ky. BR/TR, 5'10", 177 lbs. Deb: 7/27/85

YEAR TM/L	W	L	PCT	G	GS	CG	SH	SV	IP	H	HR	BB	SO	RAT	ERA	ERA+	OAV	OOB	BH	AVG	PB	PR	/A	PD	TPI
1985 Cal-A	0	1	.000	1	1	0	0	0	2¹	8	1	1	0	30.9	15.43	27	.571	.571	0	—	0	-3	-3	0	-0.2

BILL MACK
Mack, William Francis b: 2/12/1885, Elmira, N.Y. d: 9/30/71, Elmira, N.Y. 6'1", 155 lbs. Deb: 7/14/08

YEAR TM/L	W	L	PCT	G	GS	CG	SH	SV	IP	H	HR	BB	SO	RAT	ERA	ERA+	OAV	OOB	BH	AVG	PB	PR	/A	PD	TPI
1908 Chi-N	0	0	—	2	0	0	0	0	6	5	1	1	2	10.5	3.00	79	.263	.333	2	.667	1	-0	-0	0	0.1

KEN MacKENZIE
MacKenzie, Kenneth Purvis b: 3/10/34, Gore Bay, Ont., Can. BR/TL, 6', 185 lbs. Deb: 5/02/60

YEAR TM/L	W	L	PCT	G	GS	CG	SH	SV	IP	H	HR	BB	SO	RAT	ERA	ERA+	OAV	OOB	BH	AVG	PB	PR	/A	PD	TPI
1960 Mil-N	0	1	.000	9	0	0	0	0	8¹	9	2	3	9	13.0	6.48	53	.281	.343	0	.000	-0	-3	-3	-0	-0.2
1961 Mil-N	0	1	.000	5	0	0	0	0	7	8	1	2	5	14.1	5.14	73	.296	.367	0	.000	-0	-1	-1	0	0.0
1962 NY-N	5	4	.556	42	1	0	0	1	80	87	10	34	51	13.9	4.95	84	.280	.356	1	.083	-1	-9	-7	0	-0.6
1963 NY-N	3	1	.750	34	0	0	0	3	58	63	11	12	41	11.9	4.97	70	.267	.308	0	—	0	-11	-10	-1	-1.1
StL-N	0	0	—	8	0	0	0	0	9	9	1	3	7	12.0	4.00	89	.250	.308	0	—	0	-1	-0	0	0.0
Yr	3	1	.750	42	0	0	0	3	67	72	12	15	48	11.7	4.84	72	.262	.300	0	.000	-1	-12	-10	-1	-1.1
1964 SF-N	0	0	—	10	0	0	0	0	9	9	1	3	3	12.0	5.00	71	.306	.324	0	—	0	-1	-0	0	0.0
1965 Hou-N	0	3	.000	21	0	0	0	0	37	46	7	6	26	12.6	3.89	86	.299	.325	3	.273	1	-1	-2	-0	-0.1
Total 6	8	10	.444	129	1	0	0	5	208¹	231	33	63	142	13.0	4.80	78	.278	.334	4	.111	-2	-27	-24	-1	-2.0

YEAR TM/L	W	L	PCT	G	GS	CG	SH	SV	IP	H	HR	BB	SO	RAT	ERA	ERA+	OAV	OOB	BH	AVG	PB	PR	/A	PD	TPI

■ JOHN MACKINSON Mackinson, John Joseph b: 10/29/23, Orange, N.J. d: 10/17/89, Reseda, Cal. BR/TR, 5'10.5", 160 lbs. Deb: 4/16/53

1953 Phi-A	0	0	—	1	0	0	0	0	1¹	1	0	2	0	20.3	0.00	—	.200	.429	0	—	0	1	1	0	0.1
1955 StL-N	0	1	.000	8	1	0	0	0	20²	24	3	10	8	15.2	7.84	52	.296	.380	0	.000	-0	-9	-9	0	-0.7
Total 2	0	1	.000	9	1	0	0	0	22	25	3	12	8	15.5	7.36	55	.291	.384	0	.000	-0	-8	-8	0	-0.6

■ BILLY MacLEOD MacLeod, William Daniel b: 5/13/42, Gloucester, Mass. BL/TL, 6'2", 190 lbs. Deb: 9/13/62

| 1962 Bos-A | 0 | 1 | .000 | 2 | 0 | 0 | 0 | 0 | 1² | 4 | 0 | 1 | 2 | 27.0 | 5.40 | 76 | .444 | .500 | 0 | — | 0 | -0 | -0 | 0 | 0.0 |

■ MAX MACON Macon, Max Cullen b: 10/14/15, Pensacola, Fla. d: 8/5/89, Jupiter, Fla. BL/TL, 6'3", 175 lbs. Deb: 4/21/38 ♦

1938 StL-N	4	11	.267	38	12	5	1	2	129¹	133	9	61	39	13.8	4.11	96	.268	.352	11	.306	2	-5	-2	1	0.1
1940 Bro-N	1	0	1.000	2	0	0	0	0	2	5	2	0	1	22.5	22.50	18	.455	.455	1	1.000	0	-4	-4	0	-0.2
1942 Bro-N	5	3	.625	14	8	4	1	1	84	67	3	33	27	10.9	1.93	169	.220	.300	12	.279	4	13	12	-0	1.8
1943 Bro-N	7	5	.583	25	9	0	0	0	77	89	4	32	21	14.6	5.96	56	.284	.358	9	.164	-1	-22	-22	1	-2.3
1944 Bos-N	0	0	—	1	0	0	0	0	3	10	2	1	1	33.0	21.00	18	.556	.579	100	.273	0	-6	-6	0	-0.4
1947 Bos-N	0	0	—	1	0	0	0	0	2	1	0	1	1	9.0	0.00	—	.167	.286	0	.000	-0	1	1	0	0.1
Total 6	17	19	.472	81	29	9	2	3	297¹	305	20	128	90	13.4	4.24	85	.265	.344	133	.265	5	-23	-21	2	-0.9

■ HARRY MacPHERSON MacPherson, Harry William b: 7/10/26, N.Andover, Mass. BR/TR, 5'10", 150 lbs. Deb: 8/14/44

| 1944 Bos-N | 0 | 0 | — | 1 | 0 | 0 | 0 | 0 | 1 | 0 | 0 | 1 | 1 | 9.0 | — | — | .000 | .250 | 0 | — | 0 | 0 | 0 | 0 | 0.0 |

■ JIMMY MACULLAR Macullar, James F. "Little Mac" b: 1/16/1855, Boston, Mass. d: 4/8/24, Baltimore, Md. BR/TL, Deb: 5/05/1879 MU♦

| 1886 Bal-a | 0 | 0 | — | 1 | 0 | 0 | 0 | 0 | 2 | 4 | 0 | 0 | 1 | 18.0 | 9.00 | 38 | .398 | .398 | 55 | .205 | 0 | -1 | -1 | 0 | 0.0 |

■ KEITH MacWHORTER MacWhorter, Keith b: 12/30/55, Worcester, Mass. BR/TR, 6'4", 190 lbs. Deb: 5/10/80

| 1980 Bos-A | 0 | 3 | .000 | 14 | 2 | 0 | 0 | 0 | 42¹ | 46 | 3 | 18 | 21 | 14.0 | 5.53 | 76 | .280 | .359 | 0 | — | 0 | -7 | -6 | 0 | -0.5 |

■ LEN MADDEN Madden, Leonard Joseph "Lefty" b: 7/2/1890, Toledo, Ohio d: 9/9/49, Toledo, Ohio BL/TL, 6'2", 165 lbs. Deb: 8/31/12

| 1912 Chi-N | 0 | 1 | .000 | 6 | 2 | 0 | 0 | 0 | 12¹ | 16 | 1 | 9 | 5 | 19.0 | 2.92 | 114 | .291 | .400 | 1 | .250 | 0 | 1 | 1 | -0 | 0.0 |

■ MIKE MADDEN Madden, Michael Anthony b: 1/13/58, Denver, Colo. BL/TL, 6'1", 190 lbs. Deb: 4/05/83

1983 Hou-N	9	5	.643	28	13	0	0	0	94²	76	4	45	44	11.6	3.14	108	.231	.325	1	.045	-1	5	3	1	0.2
1984 Hou-N	2	3	.400	17	7	0	0	0	40²	46	1	35	29	17.9	5.53	60	.297	.426	2	.333	1	-9	-10	-1	-0.9
1985 Hou-N	0	0	—	13	0	0	0	0	19	29	1	11	16	18.9	4.26	81	.363	.440	0	—	0	-1	-2	-0	-0.1
1986 Hou-N	1	2	.333	13	6	0	0	0	39²	47	3	22	30	15.7	4.08	88	.297	.383	0	.000	-1	-2	-2	-0	-0.2
Total 4	12	10	.545	71	26	0	0	0	194	198	9	113	119	14.5	3.94	87	.274	.373	3	.081	-1	-7	-11	-1	-1.0

■ KID MADDEN Madden, Michael Joseph b: 10/22/1866, Portland, Me. d: 3/16/1896, Portland, Maine TL, 5'7.5", 130 lbs. Deb: 5/06/1887

1887 Bos-N	21	14	.600	37	37	36	3	0	321	317	20	122	81	12.3	3.79	106	.251	.317	32	.242	3	9	9	-1	1.0
1888 Bos-N	7	11	.389	20	18	17	1	0	165	142	6	24	53	9.1	2.95	96	.224	.252	11	.164	-2	-2	-1	1	-0.2
1889 Bos-N	10	10	.500	22	19	18	1	1	178	194	7	71	64	13.4	4.40	95	.269	.334	25	.291	3	-7	-4	0	-0.2
1890 Bos-P	3	2	.600	10	7	5	1	0	62	85	2	25	24	16.0	4.79	92	.313	.371	7	.184	-1	-4	-3	0	-0.2
1891 Bos-a	0	1	.000	1	1	1	0	0	8	10	2	6	6	18.0	6.75	52	.296	.402	2	.667	1	-3	-3	0	0.0
Bal-a	13	12	.520	32	27	20	1	1	224	239	4	88	56	13.1	4.10	91	.264	.329	29	.271	5	-9	-9	4	0.1
Yr	13	13	.500	33	28	21	1	1	232	249	6	94	62	13.3	4.19	89	.265	.332	9	.082	5	-12	-12	4	0.1
Total 5	54	50	.519	122	109	97	7	2	958	987	41	336	284	12.4	3.92	97	.258	.317	106	.245	8	-16	-13	4	0.7

■ MORRIS MADDEN Madden, Morris De Wayne b: 8/31/60, Laurens, S.C. BL/TL, 6' ", 155 lbs. Deb: 6/11/87

1987 Det-A	0	0	—	2	0	0	0	0	1²	4	0	3	1	37.8	16.20	26	.444	.583	0	—	0	-2	-2	-0	-0.1
1988 Pit-N	0	0	—	5	0	0	0	0	5²	5	0	7	3	19.1	0.00	—	.294	.500	0	—	0	2	2	0	0.3
1989 Pit-N	2	2	.500	9	3	0	0	0	14	17	0	13	6	19.3	7.07	47	.327	.462	0	.000	-0	-6	-6	-1	-0.6
Total 3	2	2	.500	16	3	0	0	0	21¹	26	0	23	9	20.7	5.91	58	.333	.485	0	.000	-0	-6	-6	-0	-0.4

■ NICK MADDOX Maddox, Nicholas b: 11/9/1886, Gavanstown, Md. d: 11/27/54, Pittsburgh, Pa. TR, 6', 175 lbs. Deb: 9/13/07

1907 Pit-N	5	1	.833	6	6	6	1	0	54	32	0	13	38	8.2	0.83	292	.178	.249	5	.250	2	10	10	-1	1.4
1908 Pit-N	23	8	.742	36	32	22	4	1	260²	209	5	90	70	10.7	2.28	101	.223	.298	25	.266	8	2	1	0	0.9
1909 *Pit-N	13	8	.619	31	27	17	4	0	203¹	173	2	39	56	10.0	2.21	123	.232	.283	15	.224	4	9	12	-1	1.7
1910 Pit-N	2	3	.400	20	7	2	0	0	87¹	73	0	28	29	10.9	3.40	91	.246	.321	6	.214	1	-4	-3	-0	-0.1
Total 4	43	20	.683	93	72	47	9	1	605¹	487	7	170	193	10.3	2.29	112	.225	.292	51	.244	15	17	19	-1	3.9

■ GREG MADDUX Maddux, Gregory Alan b: 4/14/66, San Angelo, Tex. BR/TR, 6', 150 lbs. Deb: 9/03/86

1986 Chi-N	2	4	.333	6	5	1	0	0	31	44	3	11	20	16.3	5.52	73	.336	.392	4	.333	1	-6	-5	0	-0.3
1987 Chi-N	6	14	.300	30	27	1	1	0	155²	181	17	74	101	15.0	5.61	76	.294	.374	5	.119	-2	-26	-23	6	-1.7
1988 Chi-N	18	8	.692	34	34	9	3	0	249	230	13	81	140	11.6	3.18	113	.244	.309	19	.198	2	7	12	3	1.9
1989 *Chi-N	19	12	.613	35	35	7	1	0	238¹	222	13	82	135	11.7	2.95	128	.249	.317	17	.210	2	15	21	4	3.1
1990 Chi-N	15	15	.500	35	35	8	2	0	237	242	11	71	144	12.5	3.46	119	.265	.321	12	.145	-2	9	18	8	2.6
Total 5	60	53	.531	140	136	26	7	0	911	919	57	319	540	12.5	3.68	106	.263	.329	57	.182	1	-2	23	20	5.6

■ MIKE MADDUX Maddux, Michael Ausley b: 8/27/61, Dayton, Ohio BL/TR, 6'2", 180 lbs. Deb: 6/03/86

1986 Phi-N	3	7	.300	16	16	0	0	0	78	88	6	34	44	14.4	5.42	71	.286	.362	1	.045	-2	-15	-14	-1	-1.4
1987 Phi-N	2	0	1.000	7	2	0	0	0	17	17	0	5	15	11.6	2.65	160	.254	.306	0	.000	-0	3	3	-0	0.2
1988 Phi-N	4	3	.571	25	11	0	0	0	88²	91	6	34	59	13.2	3.76	95	.275	.351	3	.130	-0	-3	-2	1	0.0
1989 Phi-N	1	3	.250	16	4	2	1	0	43²	52	3	14	26	14.0	5.15	69	.304	.364	0	.000	-1	-8	-8	2	-0.6
1990 LA-N	0	1	.000	11	2	0	0	0	20²	24	3	4	11	12.6	6.53	55	.293	.333	0	.000	-0	-6	-7	-0	-0.6
Total 5	10	14	.417	75	35	2	1	1	248	272	18	91	155	13.6	4.68	79	.284	.352	4	.067	-3	-29	-27	2	-2.4

■ TONY MADIGAN Madigan, William "Tice" b: 1868, Washington, D.C. d: 12/4/54, Washington, D.C. TR, 5'5.5", 126 lbs. Deb: 7/10/1886

| 1886 Was-N | 1 | 13 | .071 | 14 | 14 | 13 | 0 | 0 | 115² | 159 | 3 | 44 | 29 | 15.8 | 5.06 | 65 | .314 | .369 | 4 | .083 | -4 | -23 | -23 | 1 | -2.1 |

■ DAVE MADISON Madison, David Pledger b: 2/1/21, Boroksville, Miss. d: 12/8/85, Macon, Miss. BR/TR, 6'3", 190 lbs. Deb: 9/26/50

1950 NY-A	0	0	—	1	0	0	0	0	3	3	1	1	1	12.0	6.00	72	.273	.333	•0	—	0	-0	-1	0	0.0
1952 StL-A	4	2	.667	31	4	0	0	0	78	78	7	48	35	15.0	4.38	89	.264	.374	2	.118	-1	-6	-4	0	-0.4
Det-A	1	1	.500	10	1	0	0	0	15	16	1	10	7	16.2	7.80	49	.291	.409	0	.000	0	-7	-7	-0	-0.6
Yr	5	3	.625	41	5	0	0	0	93	94	8	58	42	14.8	4.94	79	.270	.385	1	.053	-1	-13	-11	-0	-1.0
1953 Det-A	3	4	.429	32	1	0	0	0	62	76	7	44	27	17.9	6.82	60	.303	.413	1	.091	-1	-19	-19	0	-1.8
Total 3	8	7	.533	74	6	0	0	0	158	173	16	103	70	16.2	5.70	70	.282	.392	3	.100	-2	-33	-30	0	-2.8

■ ALEX MADRID Madrid, Alexander b: 4/18/63, Springerville, Ariz BR/TR, 6'3", 200 lbs. Deb: 7/20/87

1987 Mil-A	0	0	—	3	0	0	0	0	5¹	11	1	1	1	20.3	15.19	30	.440	.462	0	—	0	-6	-6	-0	-0.5
1988 Phi-N	1	1	.500	5	2	1	0	0	16¹	15	0	6	2	11.6	2.76	129	.246	.313	0	.000	-0	1	1	-0	0.1
1989 Phi-N	1	2	.333	6	3	0	0	0	24²	32	3	14	13	17.1	5.47	65	.314	.402	0	.000	-0	-5	-5	-0	-0.5
Total 3	2	3	.400	14	5	1	0	0	46¹	58	4	21	16	15.5	5.63	65	.309	.381	0	.000	-1	-11	-10	-0	-0.9

■ HECTOR MAESTRI Maestri, Hector Anibal (Garcia) b: 4/19/35, Havana, Cuba BR/TR, 5'10", 158 lbs. Deb: 9/24/60

1960 Was-A	0	0	—	1	1	0	0	0	2	1	0	1	1	9.0	0.00	—	.167	.286	0	—	0	1	1	0	0.1
1961 Was-A	0	1	.000	1	1	0	0	0	6	6	1	2	2	12.0	1.50	268	.250	.308	0	.000	-0	2	2	0	0.2
Total 2	0	1	.000	2	1	0	0	0	8	7	1	3	3	11.3	1.13	354	.233	.303	0	.000	-0	3	3	0	0.3

YEAR TM/L	W	L	PCT	G	GS	CG	SH	SV	IP	H	HR	BB	SO	RAT	ERA	ERA+	OAV	OOB	BH	AVG	PB	PR	/A	PD	TPI

■ BILL MAGEE
Magee, William J. b: 1875, Canada   5'10", 154 lbs.   Deb: 5/18/1897

YEAR TM/L	W	L	PCT	G	GS	CG	SH	SV	IP	H	HR	BB	SO	RAT	ERA	ERA+	OAV	OOB	BH	AVG	PB	PR	/A	PD	TPI
1897 Lou-N	4	12	.250	22	16	13	1	0	155¹	186	6	99	44	16.5	5.39	79	.294	.390	13	.210	-2	-19	-19	1	-1.6
1898 Lou-N	16	15	.516	38	33	29	3	0	295¹	294	8	129	55	12.9	4.05	88	.258	.333	14	.126	-9	-15	-16	-1	-2.3
1899 Lou-N	3	7	.300	12	10	6	1	0	71	91	1	28	13	15.1	5.20	74	.311	.371	3	.111	-2	-11	-11	1	-0.9
Phi-N	3	5	.375	9	9	7	0	0	70	82	0	32	4	14.7	5.66	65	.292	.364	5	.161	-2	-14	-15	-1	-1.4
Was-N	1	4	.200	8	7	4	0	0	42	54	3	28	11	17.6	8.57	46	.311	.407	5	.333	1	-22	-22	1	-1.5
Yr	7	16	.304	29	26	17	1	0	183	227	4	88	28	15.5	6.15	62	.304	.377	2	.027	-2	-47	-48	1	-3.8
1901 StL-N	0	0	—	1	1	0	0	0	8	8	0	4	3	13.5	4.50	71	.259	.344	2	.500	1	-1	-1	-0	0.0
NY-N	0	4	.000	6	5	4	0	0	42¹	56	4	11	14	14.7	5.95	56	.316	.362	-1	.143	-1	-12	-12	-0	-1.0
Yr	0	4	.000	7	6	4	0	0	50¹	64	4	15	17	14.5	5.72	57	.307	.360	1	.056	1	-13	-14	-0	-1.0
1902 NY-N	0	0	—	2	1	0	0	0	5	5	0	1	2	10.8	3.60	78	.260	.297	0	.000	-0	-0	-0	0	0.0
Phi-N	2	4	.333	8	6	6	0	0	53²	61	1	18	15	13.8	3.69	76	.286	.350	4	.211	-0	-5	-5	0	-0.5
Yr	2	4	.333	10	7	6	0	0	58²	66	1	19	17	13.5	3.68	76	.284	.345	0	.000	-1	-6	-6	0	-0.5
Total 5	29	51	.363	106	88	69	5	0	742²	837	23	350	161	14.4	4.93	75	.283	.359	48	.169	-13	-99	-102	0	-9.2

■ SAL MAGLIE
Maglie, Salvatore Anthony "The Barber" b: 4/26/17, Niagara Falls, N.Y   BR/TR, 6'2", 180 lbs.   Deb: 8/09/45   C

YEAR TM/L	W	L	PCT	G	GS	CG	SH	SV	IP	H	HR	BB	SO	RAT	ERA	ERA+	OAV	OOB	BH	AVG	PB	PR	/A	PD	TPI
1945 NY-N	5	4	.556	13	10	7	3	0	84¹	72	2	22	32	10.2	2.35	167	.231	.286	5	.167	-1	14	15	0	1.5
1950 NY-N	18	4	.818	47	16	12	5	1	206	169	14	86	96	11.6	2.71	151	.226	.314	8	.121	-1	33	32	3	3.4
1951 *NY-N	23	6	.793	42	37	22	3	4	298	254	27	86	146	10.4	2.93	134	.230	.289	17	.152	-3	34	33	1	3.3
1952 NY-N	18	8	.692	35	31	12	5	1	216	199	16	75	112	11.7	2.92	127	.244	.312	5	.072	-3	20	19	1	1.7
1953 NY-N	8	9	.471	27	24	9	3	0	145¹	158	19	47	80	12.8	4.15	103	.278	.334	13	.271	2	2	2	-2	0.2
1954 *NY-N	14	6	.700	34	32	9	1	2	218¹	222	21	70	117	12.2	3.26	124	.262	.320	8	.127	-2	20	19	0	1.7
1955 NY-N	9	5	.643	23	21	6	0	0	129²	142	18	48	71	13.4	3.75	107	.278	.344	5	.125	-2	4	4	-2	0.0
Cle-A	0	2	.000	10	2	0	0	2	25²	26	0	7	11	11.9	3.86	103	.252	.306	0	.000	-0	0	0	-1	0.0
1956 Cle-A	0	0	—	2	0	0	0	0	5	6	1	2	2	14.4	3.60	117	.300	.364	0	—	0	0	0	-0	0.0
*Bro-N	13	5	.722	28	26	9	3	0	191	154	21	52	108	9.9	2.87	138	.222	.281	9	.129	-4	19	23	-2	1.9
1957 Bro-N	6	6	.500	19	17	4	1	1	101¹	94	12	26	50	11.0	2.93	142	.245	.300	1	.034	-3	11	14	-0	1.1
NY-A	2	0	1.000	6	3	1	1	3	26	22	1	7	9	10.4	1.73	207	.227	.286	2	.250	0	6	5	0	0.6
1958 NY-A	1	1	.500	7	3	0	0	0	23¹	27	3	9	7	13.9	4.63	76	.300	.364	1	.143	1	-2	-3	-0	-0.1
StL-N	2	6	.250	10	10	2	0	0	53	46	14	25	21	12.4	4.75	87	.232	.324	2	.125	-1	-5	-4	-1	-0.4
Total 10	119	62	.657	303	232	93	25	14	1723	1591	169	562	862	11.5	3.15	127	.245	.309	76	.135	-17	156	160	-2	14.9

■ JIM MAGNUSON
Magnuson, James Robert b: 8/18/46, Marinette, Wis.   BR/TL, 6'2", 190 lbs.   Deb: 6/28/70

YEAR TM/L	W	L	PCT	G	GS	CG	SH	SV	IP	H	HR	BB	SO	RAT	ERA	ERA+	OAV	OOB	BH	AVG	PB	PR	/A	PD	TPI
1970 Chi-A	1	5	.167	13	6	0	0	0	44²	45	7	16	20	12.5	4.84	81	.263	.330	0	.000	-1	-6	-5	0	-0.5
1971 Chi-A	1	1	.500	15	4	0	0	0	30	30	0	16	11	14.4	4.50	80	.265	.366	0	.000	-0	-3	-3	0	-0.3
1973 NY-A	0	1	.000	8	0	0	0	0	27¹	38	2	9	9	15.5	4.28	86	.342	.392	0	—	0	-1	-2	0	0.0
Total 3	2	7	.222	36	10	0	0	0	102	113	9	41	40	13.9	4.59	82	.286	.358	0	.000	-2	-10	-10	0	-0.8

■ JOE MAGRANE
Magrane, Joseph David b: 7/2/64, Des Moines, Iowa   BR/TL, 6'6", 225 lbs.   Deb: 4/25/87

YEAR TM/L	W	L	PCT	G	GS	CG	SH	SV	IP	H	HR	BB	SO	RAT	ERA	ERA+	OAV	OOB	BH	AVG	PB	PR	/A	PD	TPI
1987 *StL-N	9	7	.563	27	26	4	2	0	170¹	157	9	60	101	12.0	3.54	117	.245	.320	7	.135	1	10	12	-0	1.3
1988 StL-N	5	9	.357	24	24	4	3	0	165¹	133	6	51	100	10.1	2.18	160	.217	.280	8	.167	1	23	24	2	3.2
1989 StL-N	18	9	.667	34	33	9	3	0	234²	219	10	72	127	11.4	2.91	124	.251	.313	11	.138	1	15	19	-1	2.0
1990 StL-N	10	17	.370	31	31	3	2	0	203¹	204	10	59	100	12.0	3.59	109	.264	.322	7	.127	-0	5	7	2	0.9
Total 4	42	42	.500	116	114	20	10	0	773²	713	30	242	428	11.4	3.07	123	.246	.310	33	.140	3	53	62	3	7.4

■ PETE MAGRINI
Magrini, Peter Alexander b: 6/8/42, San Francisco, Cal.   BR/TR, 6', 195 lbs.   Deb: 4/13/66

YEAR TM/L	W	L	PCT	G	GS	CG	SH	SV	IP	H	HR	BB	SO	RAT	ERA	ERA+	OAV	OOB	BH	AVG	PB	PR	/A	PD	TPI
1966 Bos-A	0	1	.000	3	1	0	0	0	7¹	8	0	8	3	20.9	9.82	39	.308	.486	0	.000	-0	-5	-5	-0	-0.4

■ ART MAHAFFEY
Mahaffey, Arthur b: 6/4/38, Cincinnati, Ohio   BR/TR, 6'1", 185 lbs.   Deb: 7/30/60

YEAR TM/L	W	L	PCT	G	GS	CG	SH	SV	IP	H	HR	BB	SO	RAT	ERA	ERA+	OAV	OOB	BH	AVG	PB	PR	/A	PD	TPI
1960 Phi-N	7	3	.700	14	12	5	1	0	93¹	78	9	34	56	10.9	2.31	168	.229	.301	3	.100	-2	15	16	-1	1.5
1961 Phi-N	11	19	.367	36	32	12	3	0	219¹	205	27	70	158	11.6	4.10	99	.249	.314	8	.127	-2	-2	-1	-2	-0.4
1962 Phi-N	19	14	.576	41	39	20	2	0	274	253	36	81	177	11.4	3.94	98	.246	.309	13	.141	1	0	-2	-4	-0.5
1963 Phi-N	7	10	.412	26	22	6	1	0	149	143	18	48	97	11.8	3.99	81	.255	.319	10	.200	2	-12	-12	-0	-1.0
1964 Phi-N	12	9	.571	34	29	2	2	0	157¹	161	17	82	80	14.2	4.52	77	.269	.362	6	.120	0	-17	-18	-2	-1.9
1965 Phi-N	2	5	.286	22	9	1	0	0	71	82	11	32	52	15.3	6.21	56	.294	.381	2	.095	-1	-21	-22	-1	-2.3
1966 StL-N	1	4	.200	12	5	0	0	1	35	37	7	21	19	15.2	6.43	56	.276	.378	0	.000	-1	-11	-11	-0	-1.1
Total 7	59	64	.480	185	148	46	9	1	999	959	125	368	639	12.3	4.17	89	.255	.328	42	.134	-2	-47	-50	-11	-5.7

■ ROY MAHAFFEY
Mahaffey, Lee Roy "Popeye" b: 2/9/03, Belton, S.C.   d: 7/23/69, Anderson, S.C.   BR/TR, 6', 180 lbs.   Deb: 8/31/26

YEAR TM/L	W	L	PCT	G	GS	CG	SH	SV	IP	H	HR	BB	SO	RAT	ERA	ERA+	OAV	OOB	BH	AVG	PB	PR	/A	PD	TPI
1926 Pit-N	0	0	—	4	0	0	0	0	4²	5	0	1	3	13.5	0.00	—	.294	.368	0	—	-0	2	2	-0	0.1
1927 Pit-N	1	0	1.000	2	1	0	0	0	9¹	9	0	9	4	20.3	7.71	53	.300	.500	2	.400	0	-4	-4	-0	-0.2
1930 Phi-A	9	5	.643	33	16	6	0	0	152²	186	16	53	38	14.3	5.01	93	.298	.357	7	.119	-5	-6	-6	-1	-0.9
1931 *Phi-A	15	4	.789	30	20	8	0	2	162¹	161	9	82	59	13.6	4.21	107	.258	.347	12	.190	1	3	5	-3	0.3
1932 Phi-A	13	13	.500	37	28	13	0	0	222²	245	27	96	106	14.0	5.09	89	.274	.348	15	.172	-2	-15	-14	-2	-1.5
1933 Phi-A	13	10	.565	33	23	9	0	0	179¹	198	5	74	66	13.9	5.17	83	.275	.346	14	.215	-0	-18	-18	-2	-1.7
1934 Phi-A	6	7	.462	37	14	3	0	2	129	142	10	55	37	13.8	5.37	82	.276	.347	13	.271	2	-13	-14	-1	-1.1
1935 Phi-A	8	4	.667	27	17	5	0	0	136	153	11	42	39	13.2	3.90	116	.283	.341	9	.176	-2	8	10	-1	0.6
1936 StL-A	2	6	.250	21	9	1	0	1	60	82	6	40	13	18.5	8.10	66	.315	.409	1	.063	-1	-20	-18	-2	-1.7
Total 9	67	49	.578	224	128	45	0	5	1056	1181	84	452	365	14.1	5.01	90	.280	.353	73	.184	-7	-63	-57	-12	-6.1

■ LOU MAHAFFEY
Mahaffey, Louis Wood b: 1/3/1874, Kentucky   d: 10/26/49, Torrance, Cal.   5'9", 170 lbs.   Deb: 4/26/1898

YEAR TM/L	W	L	PCT	G	GS	CG	SH	SV	IP	H	HR	BB	SO	RAT	ERA	ERA+	OAV	OOB	BH	AVG	PB	PR	/A	PD	TPI
1898 Lou-N	0	1	.000	1	1	1	0	0	9	10	0	5	1	15.0	3.00	119	.279	.367	0	.000	-0	1	1	-0	0.0

■ ART MAHAN
Mahan, Arthur Leo b: 6/8/13, Somerville, Mass.   BL/TL, 5'11", 178 lbs.   Deb: 4/30/40   ♦

YEAR TM/L	W	L	PCT	G	GS	CG	SH	SV	IP	H	HR	BB	SO	RAT	ERA	ERA+	OAV	OOB	BH	AVG	PB	PR	/A	PD	TPI
1940 Phi-N	0	0	—	1	0	0	0	0	1	1	0	0	0	9.0	0.00	—	.333	.333	133	.244	0	0	0	0	0.0

■ MICKEY MAHLER
Mahler, Michael James b: 7/30/52, Montgomery, Ala.   BB/TL, 6'3", 189 lbs.   Deb: 9/13/77

YEAR TM/L	W	L	PCT	G	GS	CG	SH	SV	IP	H	HR	BB	SO	RAT	ERA	ERA+	OAV	OOB	BH	AVG	PB	PR	/A	PD	TPI
1977 Atl-N	1	2	.333	5	5	0	0	0	23	31	4	9	14	16.0	6.26	71	.326	.390	3	.500	2	-6	-5	-0	-0.2
1978 Atl-N	4	11	.267	34	21	1	0	0	134²	130	16	66	92	13.6	4.68	87	.255	.349	4	.098	-3	-16	-9	-1	-1.2
1979 Atl-N	5	11	.313	26	18	1	0	0	100	123	11	47	71	15.6	5.85	69	.304	.381	3	.111	-1	-24	-20	-2	-2.0
1980 Pit-N	0	0	—	2	0	0	0	0	1	4	1	3	1	63.0	63.00	6	.571	.700	0	—	0	-7	-7	0	-0.5
1981 Cal-A	0	0	—	6	0	0	0	0	6¹	1	0	2	5	4.3	0.00	—	.056	.150	0	—	0	3	3	0	0.3
1982 Cal-A	2	0	1.000	6	0	0	0	0	9	6	0	6	5	16.9	1.13	360	.300	.417	0	—	0	3	3	0	0.3
1985 Mon-N	1	4	.200	9	7	1	1	1	48¹	40	3	24	32	12.1	3.54	96	.229	.325	3	.188	1	0	-1	-1	0.0
Det-A	1	2	.333	3	2	0	0	0	20²	19	2	4	14	10.0	1.74	234	.241	.277	0	—	0	6	5	-0	0.6
1986 Tex-A	0	2	.000	29	5	0	0	3	63	71	3	29	28	14.7	4.14	104	.295	.377	0	—	0	1	1	0	0.1
Tor-A	0	0	—	2	0	0	0	0	1	1	0	0	0	18.0	0.00	—	.200	.333	0	—	0	0	0	0	0.1
Yr	0	2	.000	31	5	0	0	3	64	72	3	29	28	14.3	4.08	105	.285	.360	0	—	0	1	2	0	0.2
Total 8	14	32	.304	122	58	3	1	4	406	429	40	190	262	14.1	4.68	86	.274	.359	13	.144	-1	-41	-29	-2	-2.5

■ RICK MAHLER
Mahler, Richard Keith b: 8/5/53, Austin, Tex.   BR/TR, 6'1", 195 lbs.   Deb: 4/20/79

YEAR TM/L	W	L	PCT	G	GS	CG	SH	SV	IP	H	HR	BB	SO	RAT	ERA	ERA+	OAV	OOB	BH	AVG	PB	PR	/A	PD	TPI
1979 Atl-N	0	0	—	15	0	0	0	0	22	28	4	11	12	16.0	6.14	66	.311	.386	1	.500	0	-6	-5	0	-0.4
1980 Atl-N	0	0	—	2	0	0	0	0	3²	2	0	1	4	4.9	2.45	152	.154	.154	0	—	0	0	1	0	0.1
1981 Atl-N	8	6	.571	34	14	1	0	2	112¹	109	5	43	54	12.3	2.80	128	.258	.328	4	.148	-1	9	10	1	1.0
1982 *Atl-N	9	10	.474	39	33	5	2	0	205¹	213	18	62	105	12.1	4.21	89	.272	.327	11	.190	2	-14	-11	2	-0.6

YEAR TM/L	W	L	PCT	G	GS	CG	SH	SV	IP	H	HR	BB	SO	RAT	ERA	ERA+	OAV	OOB	BH	AVG	PB	PR	/A	PD	TPI
1983 Atl-N	0	0	—	10	0	0	0	0	14¹	16	0	9	7	15.7	5.02	77	.296	.397	0	.000	-0	-2	-2	-0	-0.1
1984 Atl-N	13	10	.565	38	29	9	1	0	222	209	13	62	106	11.1	3.12	123	.251	.305	21	.296	5	12	18	3	2.9
1985 Atl-N	17	15	.531	39	39	6	1	0	266²	272	24	79	107	11.9	3.48	111	.268	.322	14	.156	-1	3	11	2	1.3
1986 Atl-N	14	18	.438	39	39	7	1	0	237²	283	25	95	137	14.4	4.88	81	.301	.367	16	.193	2	-31	-24	2	-1.9
1987 Atl-N	8	13	.381	39	28	3	1	0	197	212	24	85	95	13.7	4.98	87	.283	.357	11	.169	1	-20	-14	3	-0.9
1988 Atl-N	9	16	.360	39	34	5	0	0	249	279	17	42	131	11.9	3.69	100	.282	.317	9	.125	-2	-7	-0	1	0.0
1989 Cin-N	9	13	.409	40	31	5	2	0	220²	242	15	51	102	12.4	3.83	94	.282	.329	11	.177	2	-8	-6	0	-0.3
1990 *Cin-N	7	6	.538	35	16	2	1	4	134²	134	16	39	68	11.8	4.28	91	.261	.317	4	.114	-1	-7	-6	0	-0.6
Total 12	94	107	.468	369	263	43	9	6	1885¹	1999	161	578	925	12.5	3.98	97	.275	.332	102	.180	8	-71	-29	13	0.5

■ AL MAHON   Mahon, Alfred Gwinn "Lefty" b: 9/23/09, Albion, Neb. d: 12/26/77, New Haven, Conn. BL/TL, 5'11", 160 lbs. Deb: 4/22/30

YEAR TM/L	W	L	PCT	G	GS	CG	SH	SV	IP	H	HR	BB	SO	RAT	ERA	ERA+	OAV	OOB	BH	AVG	PB	PR	/A	PD	TPI
1930 Phi-A	0	0	—	3	0	0	0	0	4¹	11	0	7	0	37.4	22.85	20	.579	.692	0	.000	0	-9	-9	0	-0.6

■ CHRIS MAHONEY   Mahoney, Christopher John b: 6/11/1885, Milton, Mass. d: 7/15/54, Visalia, Cal. BR/TR, 5'9", 160 lbs. Deb: 7/12/10

YEAR TM/L	W	L	PCT	G	GS	CG	SH	SV	IP	H	HR	BB	SO	RAT	ERA	ERA+	OAV	OOB	BH	AVG	PB	PR	/A	PD	TPI
1910 Bos-A	0	1	.000	2	1	0	0	1	11	16	1	5	6	17.2	3.27	78	.327	.389	1	.143	-0	-1	-1	1	0.0

■ MIKE MAHONEY   Mahoney, George W. "Big Mike" b: 12/5/1873, Boston, Mass. d: 1/3/40, Boston, Mass. BR, 6'4", 220 lbs. Deb: 5/18/1897 ♦

YEAR TM/L	W	L	PCT	G	GS	CG	SH	SV	IP	H	HR	BB	SO	RAT	ERA	ERA+	OAV	OOB	BH	AVG	PB	PR	/A	PD	TPI
1897 Bos-N	0	0	—	1	0	0	0	0	1	3	0	1	1	36.0	18.00	25	.511	.582	1	.500	0	-2	-2	0	0.0

■ BOB MAHONEY   Mahoney, Robert Paul b: 6/20/28, LeRoy, Minn. BR/TR, 6'1", 185 lbs. Deb: 5/03/51

YEAR TM/L	W	L	PCT	G	GS	CG	SH	SV	IP	H	HR	BB	SO	RAT	ERA	ERA+	OAV	OOB	BH	AVG	PB	PR	/A	PD	TPI
1951 Chi-A	0	0	—	3	0	0	0	0	6²	5	1	5	3	13.5	5.40	75	.208	.345	0	—	0	-1	-1	-0	0.0
StL-A	2	5	.286	30	4	0	0	0	81	86	7	41	30	14.1	4.44	99	.274	.358	4	.222	-0	-3	-0	-0	0.0
Yr	2	5	.286	33	4	0	0	0	87²	91	8	46	33	14.1	4.52	97	.269	.357	2	.111	-0	-4	-1	-1	0.0
1952 StL-A	0	0	—	3	0	0	0	0	3	8	0	4	1	36.0	18.00	22	.500	.600	0	—	0	-5	-5	0	-0.4
Total 2	2	5	.286	36	4	0	0	0	90²	99	8	50	34	14.8	4.96	88	.280	.369	4	.222	-0	-9	-6	-1	-0.4

■ WALTER MAILS   Mails, John Walter "Duster" or "The Great" b: 10/1/1895, San Quentin, Cal. d: 7/5/74, San Francisco, Cal BL/TL, 6', 195 lbs. Deb: 9/28/15

YEAR TM/L	W	L	PCT	G	GS	CG	SH	SV	IP	H	HR	BB	SO	RAT	ERA	ERA+	OAV	OOB	BH	AVG	PB	PR	/A	PD	TPI
1915 Bro-N	0	1	.000	2	0	0	0	0	5	6	2	5	3	19.8	3.60	77	.333	.478	0	.000	-0	-0	-0	0	0.0
1916 Bro-N	0	1	.000	11	0	0	0	0	17¹	15	1	9	13	12.5	3.63	74	.242	.338	1	.250	0	-2	-2	-1	-0.2
1920 *Cle-A	7	0	1.000	9	8	6	2	0	63¹	54	1	18	25	10.2	1.85	206	.230	.285	4	.200	0	14	14	-1	1.3
1921 Cle-A	14	8	.636	34	24	10	2	2	194¹	210	4	89	87	13.9	3.94	108	.283	.361	6	.094	-4	8	7	-3	0.0
1922 Cle-A	4	7	.364	26	13	4	1	0	104	122	8	40	54	14.4	5.28	76	.291	.359	5	.161	-0	-14	-15	0	-1.3
1925 StL-N	7	7	.500	21	14	9	0	0	131	145	11	58	49	14.4	4.60	94	.279	.360	6	.133	-0	-5	-4	-1	-0.6
1926 StL-N	0	1	.000	1	0	0	0	0	1	2	0	1	1	27.0	0.00	—	.400	.500	0	—	0	0	0	0	0.0
Total 7	32	25	.561	104	59	29	5	2	516	554	27	220	232	13.7	4.10	100	.277	.352	22	.133	-7	0	0	-6	-0.8

■ WOODY MAIN   Main, Forrest Harry b: 2/12/22, Delano, Cal. BR/TR, 6'3.5", 195 lbs. Deb: 4/21/48

YEAR TM/L	W	L	PCT	G	GS	CG	SH	SV	IP	H	HR	BB	SO	RAT	ERA	ERA+	OAV	OOB	BH	AVG	PB	PR	/A	PD	TPI
1948 Pit-N	1	1	.500	17	0	0	0	0	27	35	4	19	12	18.0	8.33	49	.324	.425	0	.000	-0	-13	-13	0	-1.1
1950 Pit-N	1	0	1.000	12	0	0	0	1	20¹	21	2	11	12	14.6	4.87	90	.256	.351	2	.400	1	-2	-1	0	0.0
1952 Pit-N	2	12	.143	48	11	2	0	0	153¹	149	14	52	79	11.8	4.46	90	.253	.314	2	.054	-3	-12	-8	-3	-1.3
1953 Pit-N	0	0	—	2	0	0	0	0	4	5	1	2	4	15.8	11.25	40	.294	.368	0	—	0	-3	-3	-0	-0.2
Total 4	4	13	.235	79	11	2	0	3	204²	210	21	84	107	13.0	5.14	79	.264	.335	4	.091	-3	-30	-25	-3	-2.6

■ ALEX MAIN   Main, Miles Grant b: 5/13/1884, Montrose, Mich. d: 12/29/65, Royal Oak, Mich. BL/TR, 6'5", 195 lbs. Deb: 4/18/14

YEAR TM/L	W	L	PCT	G	GS	CG	SH	SV	IP	H	HR	BB	SO	RAT	ERA	ERA+	OAV	OOB	BH	AVG	PB	PR	/A	PD	TPI
1914 Det-A	6	6	.500	32	12	5	1	3	138¹	131	2	59	55	12.6	2.67	105	.259	.340	4	.100	-2	1	2	4	0.5
1915 KC-F	13	14	.481	35	28	18	2	3	230	181	4	75	91	10.2	2.54	115	.222	.291	15	.197	1	13	10	3	1.5
1918 Phi-N	2	2	.500	8	4	1	1	0	35	30	1	16	14	13.1	4.63	65	.240	.349	1	.091	-1	-7	-6	0	-0.6
Total 3	21	22	.488	75	44	24	4	6	403¹	342	7	150	160	11.3	2.77	105	.236	.313	20	.157	-1	6	6	7	1.4

■ JIM MAINS   Mains, James Royal b: 6/12/22, Bridgton, Maine d: 3/17/69, Bridgton, Maine BR/TR, 6'2", 190 lbs. Deb: 8/22/43

YEAR TM/L	W	L	PCT	G	GS	CG	SH	SV	IP	H	HR	BB	SO	RAT	ERA	ERA+	OAV	OOB	BH	AVG	PB	PR	/A	PD	TPI
1943 Phi-A	0	1	.000	1	1	1	0	0	8	9	0	3	4	13.5	5.63	60	.281	.343	0	.000	0	-2	-2	-0	-0.1

■ WILLARD MAINS   Mains, Willard Eben "Grasshopper" b: 7/7/1868, N.Windham, Maine d: 5/23/23, Bridgton, Maine TR, 6'2", 190 lbs. Deb: 8/03/1888

YEAR TM/L	W	L	PCT	G	GS	CG	SH	SV	IP	H	HR	BB	SO	RAT	ERA	ERA+	OAV	OOB	BH	AVG	PB	PR	/A	PD	TPI
1888 Chi-N	1	1	.500	2	2	1	0	0	11	8	0	6	5	11.5	4.91	61	.196	.299	1	.143	-0	-3	-2	0	-0.1
1891 Cin-a	12	12	.500	30	23	19	0	0	204	196	3	107	76	13.4	2.69	153	.244	.333	22	.244	1	23	32	3	3.5
Mil-a	0	2	.000	2	2	1	0	0	10	14	1	10	2	21.6	10.80	41	.320	.447	3	.600	-0	-8	-7	0	-0.4
Yr	12	14	.462	32	25	20	0	0	214	210	4	117	78	13.8	3.07	134	.248	.339	5	.053	-0	16	25	3	3.1
1896 Bos-N	3	2	.600	8	5	3	0	1	42²	43	1	31	13	15.6	5.48	83	.260	.377	6	.273	-0	-5	-4	0	-0.3
Total 3	16	17	.485	42	32	24	0	1	267²	261	5	154	96	14.0	3.53	118	.248	.344	32	.258	2	8	18	3	2.7

■ FRANK MAKOSKY   Makosky, Frank b: 1/20/10, Boonton, N.J. d: 1/10/87, Stroudsburg, Pa. BR/TR, 6'1", 185 lbs. Deb: 4/30/37

YEAR TM/L	W	L	PCT	G	GS	CG	SH	SV	IP	H	HR	BB	SO	RAT	ERA	ERA+	OAV	OOB	BH	AVG	PB	PR	/A	PD	TPI
1937 NY-A	5	2	.714	26	1	1	0	3	58	64	6	24	27	13.7	4.97	90	.277	.345	5	.313	1	-2	-3	2	0.0

■ TOM MAKOWSKI   Makowski, Thomas Anthony b: 12/22/50, Buffalo, N.Y. BR/TL, 5'11", 185 lbs. Deb: 5/01/75

YEAR TM/L	W	L	PCT	G	GS	CG	SH	SV	IP	H	HR	BB	SO	RAT	ERA	ERA+	OAV	OOB	BH	AVG	PB	PR	/A	PD	TPI
1975 Det-A	0	0	—	3	0	0	0	0	9¹	10	2	9	3	18.3	4.82	83	.278	.422	0	—	0	-1	-1	0	0.0

■ JOHN MALARKEY   Malarkey, John S. "Liz" b: 5/4/1872, Springfield, Ohio d: 10/29/49, Cincinnati, Ohio TR, 5'11", 155 lbs. Deb: 9/21/1894

YEAR TM/L	W	L	PCT	G	GS	CG	SH	SV	IP	H	HR	BB	SO	RAT	ERA	ERA+	OAV	OOB	BH	AVG	PB	PR	/A	PD	TPI
1894 Was-N	2	1	.667	3	3	3	0	0	26	42	1	5	3	16.3	4.15	127	.359	.386	1	.071	-2	3	3	-1	0.0
1895 Was-N	0	8	.000	22	8	5	0	2	100²	135	3	60	32	17.4	5.99	80	.316	.401	5	.135	-4	-14	-13	-1	-1.4
1896 Was-N	0	1	.000	1	1	0	0	0	7	9	1	3	0	15.4	1.29	343	.309	.374	1	.500	0	2	2	0	0.3
1899 Chi-N	0	1	.000	1	1	1	0	0	9	19	0	5	7	24.0	13.00	29	.426	.484	1	.200	-0	-9	-9	-0	-0.5
1902 Bos-N	8	10	.444	21	19	17	1	1	170¹	158	0	58	39	11.4	2.59	109	.246	.308	13	.210	2	4	4	3	1.1
1903 Bos-N	11	16	.407	32	27	25	2	0	253	266	6	96	98	13.3	3.09	104	.272	.344	14	.161	0	5	3	2	0.5
Total 6	21	37	.362	80	59	51	3	3	566	629	10	227	179	13.8	3.64	96	.281	.350	35	.169	-3	-8	-9	3	0.0

■ BILL MALARKEY   Malarkey, William John b: 11/26/1878, Port Byron, Ill. d: 12/12/56, Phoenix, Ariz. BR/TR, 5'10", 185 lbs. Deb: 4/16/08

YEAR TM/L	W	L	PCT	G	GS	CG	SH	SV	IP	H	HR	BB	SO	RAT	ERA	ERA+	OAV	OOB	BH	AVG	PB	PR	/A	PD	TPI
1908 NY-N	0	2	.000	15	0	0	0	2	35	31	1	10	12	10.8	2.57	94	.242	.302	0	.000	-1	-1	-1	-0	-0.1

■ CARLOS MALDONADO   Maldonado, Carlos Cesar b: 10/18/66, Chepo, Panama BB/TR, 6'2", 175 lbs. Deb: 9/16/90

YEAR TM/L	W	L	PCT	G	GS	CG	SH	SV	IP	H	HR	BB	SO	RAT	ERA	ERA+	OAV	OOB	BH	AVG	PB	PR	/A	PD	TPI
1990 KC-A	0	0	—	4	0	0	0	0	6	9	0	4	4	19.5	9.00	42	.346	.433	0	—	0	-3	-3	-0	-0.3

■ CY MALIS   Malis, Cyrus Sol b: 2/26/07, Philadelphia, Pa. d: 1/12/71, N.Hollywood, Cal. BR/TR, 5'11", 175 lbs. Deb: 8/17/34

YEAR TM/L	W	L	PCT	G	GS	CG	SH	SV	IP	H	HR	BB	SO	RAT	ERA	ERA+	OAV	OOB	BH	AVG	PB	PR	/A	PD	TPI
1934 Phi-N	0	0	—	1	0	0	0	0	3²	4	0	2	1	14.7	4.91	96	.267	.353	0	—	0	-0	-0	0	0.0

■ MAL MALLETTE   Mallette, Malcolm Francis b: 1/30/22, Syracuse, N.Y. BL/TL, 6'2", 200 lbs. Deb: 9/25/50

YEAR TM/L	W	L	PCT	G	GS	CG	SH	SV	IP	H	HR	BB	SO	RAT	ERA	ERA+	OAV	OOB	BH	AVG	PB	PR	/A	PD	TPI
1950 Bro-N	0	0	—	2	0	0	0	0	1¹	2	0	1	2	20.3	0.00	—	.333	.429	0	—	0	1	1	0	0.1

■ ROB MALLICOAT   Mallicoat, Robbin Dale b: 11/16/64, St.Helens, Ore. BL/TL, 6'3", 180 lbs. Deb: 9/11/87

YEAR TM/L	W	L	PCT	G	GS	CG	SH	SV	IP	H	HR	BB	SO	RAT	ERA	ERA+	OAV	OOB	BH	AVG	PB	PR	/A	PD	TPI
1987 Hou-N	0	0	—	4	1	0	0	0	6²	8	0	6	4	18.9	6.75	58	.320	.452	0	—	0	-2	-2	0	-0.1

■ ALEX MALLOY   Malloy, Archibald Alexander "Lick" b: 10/31/1886, Laurinburg, N.C. d: 3/1/61, Ferris, Tex. BR/TR, 6'2", 180 lbs. Deb: 9/10/10

YEAR TM/L	W	L	PCT	G	GS	CG	SH	SV	IP	H	HR	BB	SO	RAT	ERA	ERA+	OAV	OOB	BH	AVG	PB	PR	/A	PD	TPI
1910 StL-A	0	6	.000	7	6	4	0	0	52²	47	0	17	27	11.3	2.56	97	.261	.332	1	.063	-1	-0	-1	0	-0.1

■ HERM MALLOY   Malloy, Herman "Tug" b: 6/1/1885, Massillon, Ohio d: 5/9/42, Nimishillen, Ohio BR/TR, 6', Deb: 10/06/07

YEAR TM/L	W	L	PCT	G	GS	CG	SH	SV	IP	H	HR	BB	SO	RAT	ERA	ERA+	OAV	OOB	BH	AVG	PB	PR	/A	PD	TPI
1907 Det-A	0	1	.000	1	1	1	0	0	8	13	1	5	6	20.3	5.63	46	.366	.444	1	.250	0	-3	-3	0	-0.1
1908 Det-A	0	2	.000	3	2	2	0	0	17	20	1	4	8	13.8	3.71	65	.278	.333	3	.333	1	-2	-2	1	0.0
Total 2	0	3	.000	4	3	3	0	0	25	33	2	9	14	15.8	4.32	57	.307	.371	4	.308	1	-5	-5	1	-0.1

YEAR TM/L	W	L	PCT	G	GS	CG	SH	SV	IP	H	HR	BB	SO	RAT	ERA	ERA+	OAV	OOB	BH	AVG	PB	PR	/A	PD	TPI

■ BOB MALLOY
Malloy, Robert Paul b: 5/28/18, Canonsburg, Pa. BR/TR, 5'11", 185 lbs. Deb: 5/04/43

YEAR TM/L	W	L	PCT	G	GS	CG	SH	SV	IP	H	HR	BB	SO	RAT	ERA	ERA+	OAV	OOB	BH	AVG	PB	PR	/A	PD	TPI
1943 Cin-N	0	0	—	6	0	0	0	0	10	14	1	8	4	19.8	6.30	53	.778	.846	2	.667	1	-3	-3	-0	-0.2
1944 Cin-N	1	1	.500	9	0	0	0	0	23¹	22	0	11	4	12.7	3.09	113	.265	.351	0	.000	-1	1	1	0	0.0
1946 Cin-N	2	5	.286	27	3	1	0	2	72	71	2	26	24	12.4	2.75	122	.265	.334	5	.278	1	5	5	-1	0.5
1947 Cin-N	0	0	—	1	0	0	0	0	1	3	1	0	1	27.0	18.00	23	.600	.600	0	—	0	-2	-2	0	0.0
1949 StL-A	1	1	.500	5	0	0	0	0	9²	6	0	7	2	12.1	2.79	162	.200	.351	0	.000	-0	2	2	0	0.1
Total 5	4	7	.364	48	3	1	0	2	116	116	4	52	35	13.2	3.26	106	.287	.371	7	.226	1	3	3	-1	0.4

■ BOB MALLOY
Malloy, Robert William b: 11/24/64, Arlington, Va. BR/TR, 6'5", 200 lbs. Deb: 5/26/87

YEAR TM/L	W	L	PCT	G	GS	CG	SH	SV	IP	H	HR	BB	SO	RAT	ERA	ERA+	OAV	OOB	BH	AVG	PB	PR	/A	PD	TPI
1987 Tex-A	0	0	—	2	2	0	0	0	11	13	6	3	8	13.1	6.55	68	.271	.314	0	—	0	-3	-3	-0	-0.1
1990 Mon-N	0	0	—	1	0	0	0	0	2	1	0	1	1	9.0	0.00	—	.143	.250	0	—	0	1	1	0	0.1
Total 2	0	0	—	3	2	0	0	0	13	14	6	4	9	12.5	5.54	79	.255	.305	0	—	0	-2	-2	-0	0.0

■ MALONE
Malone Deb: 6/20/1872

YEAR TM/L	W	L	PCT	G	GS	CG	SH	SV	IP	H	HR	BB	SO	RAT	ERA	ERA+	OAV	OOB	BH	AVG	PB	PR	/A	PD	TPI
1872 Eck-n	0	3	.000	3	3	3	0	0	27	98	1	0		32.7	11.33	31	.516	.516	5	.313	0	-23	-24		-1.2

■ CHUCK MALONE
Malone, Charles Ray b: 7/8/65, Harrisburg, Ark. BR/TR, 6'7", 250 lbs. Deb: 9/06/90

YEAR TM/L	W	L	PCT	G	GS	CG	SH	SV	IP	H	HR	BB	SO	RAT	ERA	ERA+	OAV	OOB	BH	AVG	PB	PR	/A	PD	TPI
1990 Phi-N	1	0	1.000	7	0	0	0	0	7¹	3	1	11	7	17.2	3.68	104	.130	.412	0	—	0	0	0	-0	0.0

■ PAT MALONE
Malone, Perce Leigh b: 9/25/02, Altoona, Pa. d: 5/13/43, Altoona, Pa. BL/TR, 6', 200 lbs. Deb: 4/12/28

YEAR TM/L	W	L	PCT	G	GS	CG	SH	SV	IP	H	HR	BB	SO	RAT	ERA	ERA+	OAV	OOB	BH	AVG	PB	PR	/A	PD	TPI
1928 Chi-N	18	13	.581	42	25	16	2	2	250²	218	15	99	155	11.6	2.84	136	.236	.314	18	.189	1	32	28	-1	2.8
1929 *Chi-N	22	10	.688	40	30	19	5	2	267	283	12	102	166	13.2	3.57	129	.276	.345	22	.210	2	34	31	-4	2.6
1930 Chi-N	20	9	.690	45	35	22	1	4	271²	290	14	96	142	13.0	3.94	124	.271	.334	26	.248	5	31	28	-2	2.8
1931 Chi-N	16	9	.640	36	30	12	2	0	228¹	229	8	88	112	12.7	3.90	99	.258	.328	17	.215	2	-1	-1	-0	0.0
1932 *Chi-N	15	17	.469	37	33	17	2	0	237	222	13	78	120	11.6	3.38	111	.244	.308	14	.179	0	13	10	-4	0.6
1933 Chi-N	10	14	.417	31	26	13	2	0	186¹	186	10	59	72	12.1	3.91	84	.258	.318	10	.159	-2	-12	-13	-1	-1.6
1934 Chi-N	14	7	.667	34	21	8	1	0	191	200	14	55	111	12.2	3.53	110	.270	.322	11	.172	-2	11	7	-2	0.4
1935 NY-A	3	5	.375	29	2	0	0	3	56¹	53	7	33	25	13.9	5.43	75	.252	.357	0	.000	-2	-6	-9	-0	-1.0
1936 *NY-A	12	4	.750	35	9	5	0	9	134²	144	4	60	72	13.9	3.81	122	.273	.352	10	.196	-0	18	13	-2	0.9
1937 NY-A	4	4	.500	28	9	3	0	6	92	109	5	35	49	14.5	5.48	81	.291	.357	1	.030	-4	-9	-11	-2	-1.5
Total 10	134	92	.593	357	220	115	15	26	1915	1934	103	705	1024	12.6	3.74	111	.262	.330	129	.188	-2	112	85	-17	6.0

■ CHARLIE MALONEY
Maloney, Charles Michael b: 5/22/1886, Cambridge, Mass. d: 1/17/67, Arlington, Mass. BR/TR, 5'8", 155 lbs. Deb: 8/10/08

YEAR TM/L	W	L	PCT	G	GS	CG	SH	SV	IP	H	HR	BB	SO	RAT	ERA	ERA+	OAV	OOB	BH	AVG	PB	PR	/A	PD	TPI
1908 Bos-N	0	0	—	1	0	0	0	0	2	3	0	1	0	18.0	4.50	54	.429	.500	0	—	0	-0	-0	0	0.0

■ JIM MALONEY
Maloney, James William b: 6/2/40, Fresno, Cal. BL/TR, 6'2", 190 lbs. Deb: 7/27/60

YEAR TM/L	W	L	PCT	G	GS	CG	SH	SV	IP	H	HR	BB	SO	RAT	ERA	ERA+	OAV	OOB	BH	AVG	PB	PR	/A	PD	TPI
1960 Cin-N	2	6	.250	11	10	2	1	0	63²	61	5	37	48	14.1	4.66	82	.255	.360	2	.111	-0	-6	-6	-0	-0.6
1961 *Cin-N	6	7	.462	27	11	1	0	2	94²	86	16	59	57	13.9	4.37	93	.242	.352	11	.379	4	-4	-3	-1	0.0
1962 Cin-N	9	7	.563	22	17	3	0	1	115¹	90	11	66	105	12.3	3.51	115	.214	.323	8	.186	0	6	7	-2	0.5
1963 Cin-N	23	7	.767	33	33	13	6	0	250¹	183	17	88	265	10.0	2.77	121	.202	.276	15	.169	1	14	16	-3	1.6
1964 Cin-N	15	10	.600	31	31	11	2	0	216	175	16	83	214	10.8	2.71	133	.222	.297	11	.151	1	20	22	-3	2.3
1965 Cin-N	20	9	.690	33	33	14	5	0	255¹	189	13	110	244	10.7	2.54	148	.206	.295	20	.225	7	28	34	-1	4.6
1966 Cin-N	16	8	.667	32	32	10	5	0	224²	174	18	90	216	11.0	2.80	139	.214	.300	18	.222	3	20	27	-1	3.4
1967 Cin-N	15	11	.577	30	29	6	3	0	196¹	181	9	72	153	11.7	3.25	115	.247	.317	11	.159	-0	3	11	-1	1.2
1968 Cin-N	16	10	.615	33	32	8	5	0	207	183	17	80	181	11.5	3.61	88	.239	.313	18	.243	6	-14	-10	-2	-0.6
1969 Cin-N	12	5	.706	30	27	6	3	0	178²	135	11	86	102	11.2	2.77	136	.208	.302	11	.200	6	16	20	-1	2.8
1970 Cin-N	0	1	.000	7	3	0	0	1	16²	26	3	15	7	23.2	11.34	36	.366	.489	0	.000	-0	-14	-14	-0	-1.1
1971 Cal-N	0	3	.000	13	4	0	0	0	30¹	35	3	24	13	17.8	5.04	64	.294	.417	1	.200	0	-5	-6	0	-0.5
Total 12	134	84	.615	302	262	74	30	4	1849	1518	138	810	1605	11.5	3.19	115	.224	.310	126	.201	28	64	98	-14	13.6

■ PAUL MALOY
Maloy, Paul Augustus "Biff" b: 6/4/1892, Bascom, Ohio d: 3/18/76, Sandusky, Ohio BR/TR, 5'11", 185 lbs. Deb: 7/11/13

YEAR TM/L	W	L	PCT	G	GS	CG	SH	SV	IP	H	HR	BB	SO	RAT	ERA	ERA+	OAV	OOB	BH	AVG	PB	PR	/A	PD	TPI
1913 Bos-A	0	0	—	2	0	0	0	0	2	2	0	1	0	22.5	9.00	33	.286	.500	0	—	0	-1	-1	-0	-0.1

■ GORDON MALTZBERGER
Maltzberger, Gordon Ralph "Maltzy" b: 9/4/12, Utopia, Tex. d: 12/11/74, Rialto, Cal. BR/TR, 6', 170 lbs. Deb: 4/27/43 C

YEAR TM/L	W	L	PCT	G	GS	CG	SH	SV	IP	H	HR	BB	SO	RAT	ERA	ERA+	OAV	OOB	BH	AVG	PB	PR	/A	PD	TPI
1943 Chi-A	7	4	.636	37	0	0	0	14	98²	86	8	24	48	10.2	2.46	136	.236	.287	3	.120	0	9	10	0	1.1
1944 Chi-A	10	5	.667	46	0	0	0	12	91¹	81	2	19	49	10.0	2.96	116	.235	.277	3	.136	-1	5	5	1	0.4
1946 Chi-A	2	0	1.000	19	0	0	0	2	39²	30	3	6	17	8.4	1.59	215	.205	.242	0	.000	-0	8	8	-1	0.8
1947 Chi-A	1	4	.200	33	0	0	0	5	63²	61	4	25	22	12.3	3.39	108	.257	.331	1	.143	1	2	2	1	0.3
Total 4	20	13	.606	135	0	0	0	33	293¹	258	17	74	136	10.3	2.70	128	.236	.288	7	.117	0	25	24	-0	2.6

■ AL MAMAUX
Mamaux, Albert Leon b: 5/30/1894, Pittsburgh, Pa. d: 1/2/63, Santa Monica, Cal. BR/TR, 6'0.5", 168 lbs. Deb: 9/23/13

YEAR TM/L	W	L	PCT	G	GS	CG	SH	SV	IP	H	HR	BB	SO	RAT	ERA	ERA+	OAV	OOB	BH	AVG	PB	PR	/A	PD	TPI
1913 Pit-N	0	0	—	1	0	0	0	0	3	2	0	2	2	12.0	3.00	100	.167	.286	0	—	-0	0	0	0	0.0
1914 Pit-N	5	2	.714	13	6	4	2	0	63	41	1	24	30	9.6	1.71	155	.186	.272	5	.250	1	8	7	1	1.0
1915 Pit-N	21	8	.724	38	31	17	8	0	251²	182	3	96	152	10.3	2.04	134	.208	.293	15	.163	-2	20	19	-4	1.3
1916 Pit-N	21	15	.583	45	38	26	1	2	310	264	3	136	163	11.9	2.53	106	.239	.327	21	.191	1	3	5	-0	0.7
1917 Pit-N	2	11	.154	16	13	5	0	0	85²	92	1	50	22	15.2	5.25	54	.278	.378	7	.226	0	-24	-23	-1	-2.3
1918 Bro-N	0	1	.000	2	1	0	0	0	8	14	0	2	2	18.0	6.75	41	.438	.471	0	.000	-0	-4	-4	1	-0.2
1919 Bro-N	10	12	.455	30	22	16	2	0	199¹	174	2	66	80	11.0	2.66	112	.245	.312	11	.175	-0	6	7	-1	0.7
1920 *Bro-N	12	8	.600	41	18	9	2	4	190²	172	2	63	101	11.3	2.69	119	.255	.322	10	.167	-0	9	11	-1	1.0
1921 Bro-N	3	3	.500	12	1	0	0	1	43	36	1	13	21	10.5	3.14	124	.240	.305	2	.182	-0	3	4	1	0.4
1922 Bro-N	1	4	.200	37	7	1	0	3	87²	97	7	33	35	13.6	3.70	110	.290	.358	4	.235	3	4	4	0	0.7
1923 Bro-N	0	2	.000	5	0	0	0	0	13	20	0	6	5	18.0	8.31	47	.385	.448	1	.500	0	-6	-6	-0	-0.4
1924 NY-A	1	1	.500	14	2	0	0	0	38	44	2	20	12	15.4	5.68	73	.308	.396	1	.077	-1	-6	-6	-1	-0.7
Total 12	76	67	.531	254	140	78	15	10	1293	1138	22	511	625	11.7	2.90	104	.245	.325	77	.182	2	13	17	-5	2.2

■ HAL MANDERS
Manders, Harold Carl b: 6/14/17, Waukee, Iowa BR/TR, 6', 187 lbs. Deb: 8/12/41

YEAR TM/L	W	L	PCT	G	GS	CG	SH	SV	IP	H	HR	BB	SO	RAT	ERA	ERA+	OAV	OOB	BH	AVG	PB	PR	/A	PD	TPI
1941 Det-A	1	0	1.000	8	0	0	0	0	15¹	13	0	8	7	12.9	2.35	194	.236	.344	0	.000	-1	3	4	-0	0.3
1942 Det-A	2	0	1.000	18	0	0	0	0	33	39	4	15	14	15.0	4.09	97	.307	.385	1	.250	0	-2	-1	0	0.0
1946 Det-A	0	0	—	2	0	0	0	0	6	8	1	2	3	16.5	10.50	35	.364	.440	1	.500	0	-5	-5	-0	-0.3
Chi-N	0	1	.000	2	1	0	0	0	6	11	1	3	4	22.5	9.00	37	.423	.500	0	.000	-0	-4	-4	-0	-0.3
Total 3	3	1	.750	30	1	0	0	0	60¹	71	6	28	28	15.4	4.77	84	.309	.393	2	.167	-0	-7	-5	-0	-0.3

■ LEO MANGUM
Mangum, Leo Allan "Blackie" b: 5/24/1896, Durham, N.C. d: 7/9/74, Lima, Ohio BR/TR, 6'1", 187 lbs. Deb: 7/11/24

YEAR TM/L	W	L	PCT	G	GS	CG	SH	SV	IP	H	HR	BB	SO	RAT	ERA	ERA+	OAV	OOB	BH	AVG	PB	PR	/A	PD	TPI
1924 Chi-A	1	4	.200	13	7	1	0	0	47	69	4	25	12	18.2	7.09	58	.359	.436	1	.071	-1	-15	-15	0	-1.4
1925 Chi-A	1	0	1.000	7	0	0	0	0	15	25	0	6	6	18.6	7.80	53	.373	.425	2	.500	1	-6	-6	-0	-0.4
1928 NY-N	0	0	—	1	1	0	0	0	3	6	0	5	1	33.0	15.00	26	.500	.647	1	1.000	0	-4	-4	1	-0.1
1932 Bos-N	0	0	—	7	0	0	0	0	10¹	17	1	0	3	14.8	5.23	72	.333	.333	0	.000	-0	-2	-2	1	0.0
1933 Bos-N	4	3	.571	25	5	2	1	0	84	93	2	11	28	11.1	3.32	92	.280	.303	2	.091	-2	0	-2	2	-0.2
1934 Bos-N	5	3	.625	29	3	1	0	1	94¹	127	6	23	28	14.3	5.72	67	.315	.352	9	.281	2	-17	-20	1	-1.5
1935 Bos-N	0	0	—	3	0	0	0	0	4²	6	0	2	0	15.4	3.86	98	.300	.364	0	—	0	-0	-0	0	0.0
Total 7	11	10	.524	85	16	4	1	1	258	343	15	72	78	14.5	5.37	68	.318	.362	15	.200	0	-43	-49	4	-3.6

■ ERNIE MANNING
Manning, Ernest Devon "Ed" b: 10/9/1890, Florala, Ala. d: 4/28/73, Pensacola, Fla. BL/TR, 6', 175 lbs. Deb: 5/03/14

YEAR TM/L	W	L	PCT	G	GS	CG	SH	SV	IP	H	HR	BB	SO	RAT	ERA	ERA+	OAV	OOB	BH	AVG	PB	PR	/A	PD	TPI
1914 StL-A	0	0	—	4	0	0	0	0	10	11	0	3	3	12.6	3.60	75	.297	.350	0	.000	-0	-1	-1	0	-0.1

YEAR TM/L	W	L	PCT	G	GS	CG	SH	SV	IP	H	HR	BB	SO	RAT	ERA	ERA+	OAV	OOB	BH	AVG	PB	PR	/A	PD	TPI
JIM MANNING			Manning, James Benjamin		b: 7/21/43, L'Anse, Mich.				BR/TR, 6'1", 185 lbs.			Deb: 4/15/62													
1962 Min-A	0	0	—	5	1	0	0	0	7	14	0	1	3	20.6	5.14	79	.389	.421	0	.000	-0	-1	-1	0	0.0
JACK MANNING			Manning, John E.		b: 12/20/1853, Braintree, Mass.				d: 8/15/29, Boston, Mass.			BR/TR, 5'8.5", 158 lbs.			Deb: 4/23/1873	M♦									
1874 Bal-n	4	16	.200	22	20	18	0	0	179²	231	3	10		12.1	3.41	89	.272	.281	59	.351	7	-8	-7		0.5
1875 Bos-n	15	2	.882	27	17	8	1	7	139²	153	1	14		10.8	2.19	108	.258	.275	94	.274	4	4	3		0.2
1876 Bos-N	18	5	.783	34	20	13	0	5	197¹	213	1	32	24	11.2	2.14	105	.257	.285	76	.264	3	4	2	0	0.2
1877 Cin-N	0	4	.000	10	4	2	0	1	44	83	1	7	6	18.4	6.95	38	.380	.400	80	.317	4	-20	-21	0	-1.6
1878 Bos-N	1	0	1.000	3	1	1	0	0	11¹	24	1	5	2	23.0	14.29	17	.411	.457	63	.254	0	-15	-15	0	-1.1
Total 2 n	19	18	.514	49	37	26	1	7	319¹	384	4	24		11.5	2.87	95	.266	.278	196	.291	11	-4	-5		0.7
Total 3	19	9	.679	47	25	16	0	6	252²	320	3	44	32	13.0	3.53	66	.290	.317	725	.257	11	-32	-34	1	-2.5
RUBE MANNING			Manning, Walter S.		b: 4/29/1883, Chambersburg, Pa.				d: 4/23/30, Williamsport, Pa.			BR/TR, 6', 180 lbs.			Deb: 9/25/07											
1907 NY-A	0	1	.000	1	1	1	0	0	9	8	0	3	3	11.0	3.00	93	.240	.303	0	.000	-0	-0	-0	-0	0.0
1908 NY-A	13	16	.448	41	26	19	2	1	245	228	4	86	113	12.2	2.94	84	.256	.334	17	.187	1	-15	-12	-1	-1.4
1909 NY-A	7	11	.389	26	21	11	2	1	173	167	2	48	71	11.7	3.17	80	.265	.326	11	.183	-0	-13	-12	-0	-1.3
1910 NY-A	2	4	.333	16	9	4	0	0	75	80	4	25	25	13.1	3.72	71	.283	.349	5	.192	0	-10	-9	-0	-0.9
Total 4	22	32	.407	84	57	35	4	2	502	483	10	162	212	12.1	3.14	81	.263	.333	33	.183	0	-39	-34	-2	-3.6
RAMON MANON			Manon, Ramon (Reyes)		b: 1/20/68, Santo Domingo, D.R.				BR/TR, 6', 150 lbs.			Deb: 4/19/90													
1990 Tex-A	0	0	—	1	0	0	0	0	2	3	0	3	0	27.0	13.50	30	.333	.500	0	—	-0	-2	-2	0	-0.1
TOM MANSELL			Mansell, Thomas E. "Brick"		b: 1/1/1855, Auburn, N.Y.				d: 10/6/34, Auburn, N.Y.			BL/TL, 5'8", 160 lbs.			Deb: 5/01/1879	♦									
1883 Det-N	0	0	—	1	0	0	0	0	6²	8	2	5	3	35.1	18.90	16	.506	.559	29	.221	0	-12	-12	-0	-0.6
LOU MANSKE			Manske, Louis Hugo		b: 7/4/1884, Milwaukee, Wis.				d: 4/27/63, Milwaukee, Wis.			BL/TL, 6',			Deb: 8/31/06											
1906 Pit-N	0	0	—	2	1	0	0	0	8	12	0	5	6	19.1	5.63	48	.387	.472	0	.000	-1	-3	-3	0	-0.3
MOXIE MANUEL			Manuel, Mark Garfield		b: 10/16/1881, Metropolis, Ill.				d: 4/26/24, Memphis, Tenn.			BR/TB, 5'11", 170 lbs.			Deb: 9/25/05										
1905 Was-A	0	0	—	3	1	1	0	0	10	9	0	3	3	10.8	5.40	49	.242	.298	1	.250	0	-3	-3	0	-0.2
1908 Chi-A	3	4	.429	18	6	3	0	1	60¹	52	0	25	25	11.8	3.28	71	.251	.338	1	.063	-1	-6	-6	0	-0.7
Total 2	3	4	.429	21	7	4	0	1	70¹	61	0	28	28	11.6	3.58	66	.250	.332	2	.100	-1	-9	-10	0	-0.9
DICK MANVILLE			Manville, Richard Wesley		b: 12/25/26, Des Moines, Iowa				BR/TR, 6'4", 192 lbs.			Deb: 4/30/50													
1950 Bos-N	0	0	—	1	0	0	0	0	2	0	0	3	2	13.5	0.00	—	.000	.300	0	—	-0	1	1	0	0.1
1952 Chi-N	0	0	—	11	0	0	0	0	17	25	2	12	6	19.6	7.94	48	.362	.457	1	.500	0	-8	-8	-0	-0.6
Total 2	0	0	—	12	0	0	0	0	19	25	2	15	8	18.9	7.11	54	.329	.440	1	.500	0	-7	-7	-0	-0.5
RAVELO MANZANILLO			Manzanillo, Ravelo (Adams)		b: 10/17/63, San Pedro De Macoris, D.R.				BL/TL, 6', 210 lbs.			Deb: 9/25/88												
1988 Chi-A	0	1	.000	2	2	0	0	0	9¹	7	1	12	10	19.3	5.79	69	.212	.435	0	—	0	-2	-2	0	-0.1
ROLLA MAPEL			Mapel, Rolla Hamilton "Lefty"		b: 3/9/1890, Lee's Summitt, Mo.				d: 4/6/66, San Diego, Cal.			BL/TL, 5'11.5", 165 lbs.			Deb: 8/31/19									
1919 StL-A	0	3	.000	4	3	2	0	0	20	17	0	17	2	16.6	4.50	74	.262	.435	1	.167	-0	-3	-3	1	-0.1
PAUL MARAK			Marak, Paul Patrick		b: 8/2/65, Lakenheath, England				BR/TR, 6'2", 175 lbs.			Deb: 9/01/90													
1990 Atl-N	1	2	.333	7	7	1	0	0	39	39	2	19	15	14.1	3.69	106	.267	.363	1	.091	-0	0	1	1	0.2
GEORGES MARANDA			Maranda, Georges Henri		b: 1/15/32, Levis, Que., Can.				BR/TR, 6'2", 195 lbs.			Deb: 4/26/60												
1960 SF-N	1	4	.200	17	4	0	0	0	50²	50	6	30	28	14.2	4.62	75	.254	.352	2	.167	-0	-5	-6	2	-0.4
1962 Min-A	1	3	.250	32	4	0	0	0	72²	69	11	35	36	13.4	4.46	92	.252	.345	4	.250	1	-4	-3	1	0.0
Total 2	2	7	.222	49	8	0	0	0	123¹	119	17	65	64	13.7	4.52	85	.253	.348	6	.214	1	-9	-10	3	-0.4
FIRPO MARBERRY			Marberry, Fredrick		b: 11/30/1898, Streetman, Tex.				d: 6/30/76, Mexia, Tex.			BR/TR, 6'1", 190 lbs.			Deb: 8/11/23	U									
1923 Was-A	4	0	1.000	11	4	2	0	0	44²	42	1	17	18	12.5	2.82	133	.258	.339	2	.143	-1	6	5	-0	0.3
1924 *Was-A	11	12	.478	50	15	6	0	15	195¹	190	3	70	68	12.4	3.09	131	.262	.335	8	.136	-4	25	21	-1	1.5
1925 *Was-A	9	5	.643	55	0	0	0	15	93¹	84	4	45	53	12.8	3.47	122	.246	.341	5	.263	1	10	8	1	0.9
1926 Was-A	12	7	.632	64	5	3	0	22	138	120	4	66	43	12.3	3.00	129	.243	.336	6	.176	-1	16	13	-1	1.1
1927 Was-A	10	7	.588	56	10	2	0	9	155¹	177	4	68	74	14.4	4.64	88	.296	.371	5	.122	-9	-10	-2	-1.3
1928 Was-A	13	13	.500	48	11	7	1	3	161¹	160	4	42	76	11.4	3.85	104	.268	.319	5	.109	-4	3	3	-2	-0.1
1929 Was-A	19	12	.613	49	26	16	0	11	250¹	233	6	69	121	11.1	3.06	139	.252	**.308**	19	.235	2	33	33	-3	3.0
1930 Was-A	15	5	.750	33	22	9	1	7	185	190	15	53	56	11.8	4.09	113	.270	.321	24	.329	5	12	11	-1	1.3
1931 Was-A	16	4	.800	45	25	11	1	7	219	211	13	63	88	11.4	3.45	124	.252	.307	19	.232	0	20	20	-2	1.9
1932 Was-A	8	4	.667	54	15	8	1	13	197²	202	13	72	66	12.6	4.01	108	.268	.333	11	.167	-2	10	7	1	0.6
1933 Det-A	16	11	.593	37	32	15	1	2	238¹	232	13	61	84	11.1	3.29	131	.254	**.302**	11	.122	-5	26	27	-3	1.9
1934 *Det-A	15	5	.750	38	19	6	1	3	155²	174	12	48	64	12.0	4.57	96	.276	.327	12	.218	-2	-1	-3	-1	-0.1
1935 Det-A	0	1	.000	5	2	1	0	0	19	22	4	9	7	14.7	4.26	98	.289	.365	1	.200	0	0	-0	-0	-0.1
1936 NY-N	0	0	—	1	0	0	0	0	0¹	1	0	0	0	27.0	0.00	—	.500	.500	0	—	-0	0	0	0	0.0
Was-A	0	2	.000	5	1	0	0	0	14	11	2	3	4	9.6	3.86	124	.208	.263	0	.000	-0	2	1	0	0.1
Total 14	148	88	.627	551	187	86	7	101	2067¹	2049	96	686	822	12.1	3.63	116	.262	.325	128	.192	-8	156	136	-12	11.1
WALT MARBET			Marbet, Walter William		b: 9/13/1890, Plymouth Co., Ia.				d: 9/24/56, Hohenwald, Tenn.			6'1", 175 lbs.			Deb: 6/17/13									
1913 StL-N	0	1	.000	3	1	0	0	0	3¹	9	0	4	1	35.1	16.20	20	.500	.591	0	—	0	-5	-5	-0	-0.4
PHIL MARCHILDON			Marchildon, Philip Joseph "Babe"		b: 10/25/13, Penetanguishene, Ont., Canada				BR/TR, 5'10.5", 170 lbs.			Deb: 9/22/40									
1940 Phi-A	0	2	.000	2	2	1	0	0	10	12	1	8	4	18.0	7.20	62	.286	.400	0	.000	-0	-3	-3	0	-0.2
1941 Phi-A	10	15	.400	30	27	14	1	0	204¹	188	15	118	74	13.6	3.57	117	.245	.348	11	.167	1	13	14	-3	1.1
1942 Phi-A	17	14	.548	38	31	18	1	0	244	215	14	140	110	13.2	4.20	90	.235	.339	20	.238	3	-15	-12	-3	-1.1
1945 Phi-A	0	1	.000	3	2	0	0	0	9	5	0	11	2	16.0	4.00	86	.179	.410	1	.500	-1	-1	-1	0	0.0
1946 Phi-A	13	16	.448	36	29	16	1	1	226²	197	14	114	81	12.5	3.49	101	.237	.332	5	.067	-6	0	1	-2	-0.5
1947 Phi-A	19	9	.679	35	35	21	2	0	276²	228	15	141	128	12.2	3.22	118	.224	.323	15	.153	-2	15	18	-3	1.4
1948 Phi-A	9	15	.375	33	30	12	1	0	226¹	214	19	131	66	13.9	4.53	95	.251	.353	5	.069	-5	-6	-6	-1	-1.1
1949 Phi-A	0	3	.000	7	6	0	0	0	16	24	3	19	2	24.8	11.81	35	.358	.506	1	.167	-0	-14	-14	0	-1.1
1950 Bos-A	0	0	—	1	1	0	0	0	1¹	2	0	2	0	20.3	6.75	73	.200	.429	0	—	0	-0	-0	0	0.0
Total 9	68	75	.476	185	162	82	6	2	1214¹	1084	81	684	481	13.3	3.93	100	.240	.342	58	.143	-9	-10	-1	-11	-1.5
JOHNNY MARCUM			Marcum, John Alfred "Footsie"		b: 9/9/09, Campbellsburg, Ky.				d: 9/10/84, Louisville, Ky.			BL/TR, 5'11", 197 lbs.			Deb: 9/07/33	♦								
1933 Phi-A	3	2	.600	5	5	4	2	0	37	38	0	20	14	11.7	1.95	220	.200	.300	2	.167	0	10	10	0	1.1
1934 Phi-A	14	11	.560	37	31	17	2	0	232	257	13	88	92	13.5	4.50	97	.280	.346	30	.268	6	-0	-3	-0	0.1
1935 Phi-A	17	12	.586	39	27	19	2	3	242²	256	9	83	99	12.6	4.08	111	.268	.328	37	.311	9	10	13	-3	1.8
1936 Bos-A	8	13	.381	31	23	9	1	0	174	194	14	52	57	12.7	4.81	100	.281	.332	18	.205	1	4	10	0	1.2
1937 Bos-A	13	11	.542	37	23	9	1	3	183²	230	17	47	59	13.7	4.85	98	.306	.348	23	.267	5	-5	-2	2	0.5
1938 Bos-A	5	6	.455	15	11	7	0	0	92¹	113	11	25	25	13.5	4.09	120	.298	.342	5	.135	-1	7	9	1	0.7
1939 StL-A	2	5	.286	12	6	2	0	0	47²	63	10	12	21	15.3	7.74	63	.332	.382	11	.275	5	-17	-15	-0	-1.0
Chi-A	3	3	.500	19	6	2	0	0	90	125	16	15	19	14.4	6.00	79	.326	.357	16	.281	-1	-14	-13	-1	-1.0
Yr	5	8	.385	31	12	4	0	0	137²	191	27	29	46	14.4	6.60	72	.327	.359	6	.076	6	-30	-28	-1	-2.0
Total 7	65	63	.508	195	132	69	8	7	1099¹	1269	91	344	392	13.3	4.66	101	.287	.340	141	.265	26	-4	7	-2	3.2

YEAR TM/L	W	L	PCT	G	GS	CG	SH	SV	IP	H	HR	BB	SO	RAT	ERA	ERA+	OAV	OOB	BH	AVG	PB	PR	/A	PD	TPI

■ LEO MARENTETTE
Marentette, Leo John b: 2/18/41, Detroit, Mich. BR/TR, 6'2", 200 lbs. Deb: 9/26/65

YEAR TM/L	W	L	PCT	G	GS	CG	SH	SV	IP	H	HR	BB	SO	RAT	ERA	ERA+	OAV	OOB	BH	AVG	PB	PR	/A	PD	TPI
1965 Det-A	0	0	—	2	0	0	0	0	3	1	0	1	3	6.0	0.00	—	.111	.200	0	—	0	1	1	0	0.1
1969 Mon-N	0	0	—	3	0	0	0	0	5¹	9	1	1	4	16.9	6.75	54	.391	.417	0	.000	-0	-2	-2	0	-0.1
Total 2	0	0	—	5	0	0	0	0	8¹	10	1	2	7	13.0	4.32	83	.313	.353	0	.000	-0	-1	-1	0	0.0

■ JOE MARGONERI
Margoneri, Joseph Emanuel b: 1/13/30, Somerset, Pa. BL/TL, 6', 185 lbs. Deb: 4/25/56

YEAR TM/L	W	L	PCT	G	GS	CG	SH	SV	IP	H	HR	BB	SO	RAT	ERA	ERA+	OAV	OOB	BH	AVG	PB	PR	/A	PD	TPI
1956 NY-N	6	6	.500	23	13	2	0	0	91²	88	12	49	49	13.5	3.93	96	.254	.346	3	.103	-1	-2	-1	-0	-0.2
1957 NY-N	1	1	.500	13	2	1	0	0	34¹	44	1	21	18	17.3	5.24	75	.314	.407	0	.000	-1	-5	-5	-0	-0.5
Total 2	7	7	.500	36	15	3	0	0	126	132	13	70	67	14.5	4.29	89	.271	.364	3	.081	-2	-7	-6	-0	-0.7

■ JUAN MARICHAL
Marichal, Juan Antonio (Sanchez) "Manito" b: 10/20/37, Laguna Verde, D.R. BR/TR, 6', 185 lbs. Deb: 7/19/60 H

YEAR TM/L	W	L	PCT	G	GS	CG	SH	SV	IP	H	HR	BB	SO	RAT	ERA	ERA+	OAV	OOB	BH	AVG	PB	PR	/A	PD	TPI
1960 SF-N	6	2	.750	11	11	6	1	0	81¹	59	5	28	58	9.6	2.66	131	.200	.269	4	.129	0	10	7	0	0.7
1961 SF-N	13	10	.565	29	27	9	3	0	185	183	24	48	124	11.3	3.89	98	.257	.306	7	.119	-2	3	-2	-1	-0.4
1962 *SF-N	18	11	.621	37	36	18	3	1	262²	233	34	90	153	11.2	3.36	113	.234	.300	21	.236	4	17	13	-1	1.6
1963 SF-N	25	8	.758	41	40	18	5	0	321¹	259	27	61	248	9.0	2.41	133	.216	.256	20	.179	3	31	28	-3	3.0
1964 SF-N	21	8	.724	33	33	22	4	0	269	241	18	52	206	9.8	2.48	144	.236	.273	14	.144	-1	17	13	0	3.5
1965 SF-N	22	13	.629	39	37	24	**10**	1	295¹	224	27	46	240	8.3	2.13	**169**	.205	.240	17	.173	1	46	48	-1	**5.6**
1966 SF-N	25	6	**.806**	37	36	25	4	0	307¹	228	32	36	222	**7.9**	2.23	165	**.202**	**.230**	28	.250	6	47	49	-0	**6.4**
1967 SF-N	14	10	.583	26	26	18	2	0	202¹	195	20	42	166	10.6	2.76	119	.249	.288	14	.177	3	14	12	-2	1.4
1968 SF-N	**26**	9	.743	38	38	30	5	0	**326**	295	21	46	218	9.6	2.43	121	.238	.269	20	.163	1	20	19	3	2.8
1969 SF-N	21	11	.656	37	36	27	**8**	0	299²	244	15	54	205	**9.1**	**2.10**	**167**	.222	.265	15	.138	-1	**50**	47	3	5.6
1970 SF-N	12	10	.545	34	33	14	1	0	242²	269	28	48	123	11.8	4.12	97	.277	.312	5	.059	-6	-2	-4	3	-0.7
1971 *SF-N	18	11	.621	37	37	18	4	0	279	244	27	56	159	9.8	2.94	116	.233	.274	14	.133	0	16	14	3	1.9
1972 SF-N	6	16	.273	25	24	6	0	0	165	176	15	46	72	12.3	3.71	94	.277	.329	13	.196	1	-5	-4	-0	-0.2
1973 SF-N	11	15	.423	34	32	9	2	0	207¹	231	22	37	87	11.7	3.82	100	.277	.309	13	.188	1	-4	-0	4	0.6
1974 Bos-A	5	1	.833	11	9	0	0	0	57¹	61	3	14	21	12.1	4.87	79	.270	.318	0	—	0	-8	-7	0	-0.6
1975 LA-N	0	1	.000	2	2	0	0	0	6	11	2	5	1	24.0	13.50	25	.407	.500	0	.000	-0	-7	-7	0	-0.5
Total 16	243	142	.631	471	457	244	52	2	3507¹	3153	320	709	2303	10.0	2.89	122	.237	.278	202	.165	11	262	247	9	30.7

■ DAN MARION
Marion, Donald G. "Rube" b: 7/31/1890, Cleveland, Ohio d: 1/18/33, Milwaukee, Wis. BR/TR, 6'1", 187 lbs. Deb: 4/23/14

YEAR TM/L	W	L	PCT	G	GS	CG	SH	SV	IP	H	HR	BB	SO	RAT	ERA	ERA+	OAV	OOB	BH	AVG	PB	PR	/A	PD	TPI
1914 Bro-F	3	2	.600	17	9	4	0	0	89¹	97	1	38	41	14.2	3.93	81	.281	.362	7	.194	-1	-7	-7	-1	-0.9
1915 Bro-F	12	9	.571	35	25	15	2	0	208¹	193	1	64	46	11.2	3.20	94	.248	.308	13	.176	-0	-4	-4	0	-0.4
Total 2	15	11	.577	52	34	19	2	0	297²	290	2	102	87	12.1	3.42	90	.258	.325	20	.182	-1	-11	-11	-1	-1.3

■ DUKE MARKELL
Markell, Harry Duquesne (b: Harry Duquesne Makowsky)
b: 8/17/23, Paris, France d: 6/14/84, Ft.Lauderdale, Fla. BR/TR, 6'1.5", 209 lbs. Deb: 9/06/51

YEAR TM/L	W	L	PCT	G	GS	CG	SH	SV	IP	H	HR	BB	SO	RAT	ERA	ERA+	OAV	OOB	BH	AVG	PB	PR	/A	PD	TPI
1951 StL-A	1	1	.500	5	2	1	0	0	21¹	25	3	20	10	19.0	6.33	69	.298	.433	1	.167	-0	-5	-5	-1	-0.4

■ CLIFF MARKLE
Markle, Clifford Monroe b: 5/3/1894, Dravosburg, Pa. d: 5/24/74, Temple City, Cal. BR/TR, 5'9", 163 lbs. Deb: 9/18/15

YEAR TM/L	W	L	PCT	G	GS	CG	SH	SV	IP	H	HR	BB	SO	RAT	ERA	ERA+	OAV	OOB	BH	AVG	PB	PR	/A	PD	TPI
1915 NY-A	2	0	1.000	3	2	2	0	0	23	15	1	6	12	8.2	0.39	749	.185	.241	0	.000	0	7	6	-1	0.7
1916 NY-A	4	3	.571	11	7	3	1	0	45²	41	0	31	14	15.0	4.53	64	.256	.390	0	.000	-2	-9	-8	-0	-1.0
1921 Cin-N	2	6	.250	10	6	5	0	0	67	75	0	20	23	12.8	3.76	95	.291	.342	3	.125	-1	0	-1	-1	-0.3
1922 Cin-N	4	5	.444	25	3	2	1	0	75²	75	3	33	34	12.8	3.81	105	.268	.345	3	.150	-1	2	2	-0	0.1
1924 NY-A	0	3	.000	7	3	0	0	0	23¹	29	5	20	7	18.9	8.87	47	.333	.458	0	.000	-1	-12	-12	-0	-1.1
Total 5	12	17	.414	56	21	12	2	0	234²	235	9	110	90	13.4	4.10	87	.271	.356	6	.087	-4	-12	-14	-2	-1.6

■ DICK MARLOWE
Marlowe, Richard Burton b: 6/27/29, Hickory, N.C. d: 12/30/68, Toledo, Ohio BR/TR, 6'2", 165 lbs. Deb: 9/19/51

YEAR TM/L	W	L	PCT	G	GS	CG	SH	SV	IP	H	HR	BB	SO	RAT	ERA	ERA+	OAV	OOB	BH	AVG	PB	PR	/A	PD	TPI
1951 Det-A	0	1	.000	2	1	0	0	0	1²	5	0	2	1	37.8	32.40	13	.500	.583	0	—	0	-5	-5	0	-0.4
1952 Det-A	0	2	.000	4	1	0	0	0	11	21	1	3	3	19.6	7.36	52	.420	.453	0	.000	-0	-5	-4	-0	-0.4
1953 Det-A	6	7	.462	42	11	2	0	0	119²	152	13	42	52	14.7	5.26	77	.319	.377	7	.219	-0	-17	-16	-1	-1.5
1954 Det-A	5	4	.556	38	2	0	0	2	84	76	11	40	39	12.4	4.18	88	.244	.330	3	.167	0	-4	-5	-1	-0.4
1955 Det-A	1	0	1.000	4	1	1	0	1	15	12	1	4	9	9.6	1.80	213	.218	.271	0	.000	-0	4	3	-0	0.3
1956 Det-A	1	1	.500	7	1	0	0	0	11	12	1	9	4	17.2	5.73	72	.279	.404	0	.000	-0	-2	-2	-0	-0.1
Chi-A	0	0	—	1	0	0	0	0	1	2	1	1	0	27.0	9.00	46	.500	.600	0	—	0	-1	-1	0	0.0
Yr	1	1	.500	8	1	0	0	0	12	14	2	10	4	18.0	6.00	69	.298	.421	0	.000	-0	-2	-3	-0	-0.1
Total 6	13	15	.464	98	17	3	0	3	243¹	280	28	101	108	14.2	4.99	78	.295	.364	10	.175	-1	-30	-29	-2	-2.5

■ LOU MARONE
Marone, Louis Stephen b: 12/3/45, San Diego, Cal. BR/TL, 5'11", 185 lbs. Deb: 5/30/69

YEAR TM/L	W	L	PCT	G	GS	CG	SH	SV	IP	H	HR	BB	SO	RAT	ERA	ERA+	OAV	OOB	BH	AVG	PB	PR	/A	PD	TPI
1969 Pit-N	1	1	.500	29	0	0	0	0	35¹	24	2	13	25	9.9	2.55	137	.195	.283	0	—	0	4	4	-0	0.3
1970 Pit-N	0	0	—	1	0	0	0	0	2¹	2	1	0	0	7.7	3.86	101	.222	.222	0	—	0	0	0	0	0.0
Total 2	1	1	.500	30	0	0	0	0	37²	26	3	13	25	9.8	2.63	134	.197	.279	0	—	0	4	4	-0	0.3

■ RUBE MARQUARD
Marquard, Richard William b: 10/9/1889, Cleveland, Ohio d: 6/1/80, Baltimore, Md. BB/TL, 6'3", 180 lbs. Deb: 9/25/08 H

YEAR TM/L	W	L	PCT	G	GS	CG	SH	SV	IP	H	HR	BB	SO	RAT	ERA	ERA+	OAV	OOB	BH	AVG	PB	PR	/A	PD	TPI
1908 NY-N	0	1	.000	1	1	0	0	0	5	6	0	2	2	16.2	3.60	67	.316	.409	0	.000	-0	-1	-1	0	0.0
1909 NY-N	5	13	.278	29	21	8	0	1	173	155	2	73	109	12.3	2.60	98	.248	.335	8	.148	-1	-0	-1	-1	-0.3
1910 NY-N	4	4	.500	13	8	2	0	0	70²	65	2	40	52	13.9	4.46	67	.254	.363	3	.111	-1	-11	-12	-1	-1.3
1911 *NY-N	24	7	**.774**	45	33	22	5	3	277²	221	9	106	**237**	10.7	2.50	135	.219	.296	17	.163	-1	28	27	-5	2.1
1912 *NY-N	**26**	11	.703	43	38	22	1	1	294²	286	9	80	175	11.3	2.57	132	.249	.300	21	.219	2	28	27	-3	2.5
1913 *NY-N	23	10	.697	42	33	20	4	3	288	248	10	49	151	9.4	2.50	125	.237	.273	23	.219	2	23	20	-6	1.6
1914 NY-N	12	22	.353	39	33	15	4	2	268	261	9	47	92	10.4	3.06	87	.262	.297	15	.179	-1	-8	-12	1	-1.2
1915 NY-N	9	8	.529	27	20	10	2	2	169	178	8	33	79	11.3	3.73	69	.272	.308	6	.109	-2	-18	-22	0	-2.5
Bro-N	2	2	.500	6	3	0	0	1	24²	29	0	5	13	12.4	6.20	45	.276	.309	1	.125	-0	-9	-9	-0	-0.9
Yr	11	10	.524	33	23	10	2	3	193²	207	8	38	92	11.4	4.04	64	.272	.307	7	.032	-3	-28	-31	0	-3.4
1916 *Bro-N	13	6	.684	36	20	15	2	5	205	169	2	38	107	9.1	1.58	170	.229	.267	9	.143	-1	24	25	-4	2.4
1917 Bro-N	19	12	.613	37	29	14	2	0	232²	200	5	60	117	10.1	2.55	110	.232	.282	15	.200	0	6	6	-4	0.3
1918 Bro-N	9	18	.333	34	29	19	4	0	239	231	7	59	89	11.0	2.64	106	.260	.307	13	.171	-2	3	4	-2	0.0
1919 Bro-N	3	3	.500	8	7	3	0	0	59	54	1	10	29	9.8	2.29	130	.244	.277	6	.261	1	4	4	1	0.5
1920 *Bro-N	10	7	.588	28	26	10	1	0	189²	181	4	35	89	10.3	3.23	99	.251	.287	10	.169	-1	-2	-0	-4	-0.6
1921 Cin-N	17	14	.548	39	35	18	2	0	265²	291	8	50	88	11.8	3.39	106	.285	.323	14	.222	-1	12	6	-3	0.1
1922 Bos-N	11	15	.423	39	24	7	0	1	198	255	12	66	57	14.6	5.09	69	.322	.374	12	.140	-6	7	7	-0	0.0
1923 Bos-N	11	14	.440	38	29	11	3	0	239	265	10	65	78	12.5	3.73	107	.288	.337	12	.140	-6	7	7	-0	0.0
1924 Bos-N	1	2	.333	6	6	1	0	0	36	33	3	13	10	11.8	3.00	127	.254	.326	3	.273	0	3	3	0	0.4
1925 Bos-N	2	8	.200	26	8	0	0	0	72	105	5	29	19	16.5	5.75	70	.341	.394	3	.136	-1	-12	-14	-2	-1.5
Total 18	201	177	.532	536	403	197	30	19	3306²	3233	107	858	1593	11.2	3.08	103	.260	.309	198	.179	-16	53	36	-36	-0.5

■ JIM MARQUIS
Marquis, James Milburn b: 11/18/1900, Yoakum, Tex. BR/TR, 5'11", 174 lbs. Deb: 8/08/25

YEAR TM/L	W	L	PCT	G	GS	CG	SH	SV	IP	H	HR	BB	SO	RAT	ERA	ERA+	OAV	OOB	BH	AVG	PB	PR	/A	PD	TPI
1925 NY-A	0	0	—	2	0	0	0	0	7¹	12	1	6	0	22.1	9.82	43	.414	.514	0	.000	-0	-4	-5	0	-0.3

■ CONNIE MARRERO
Marrero, Conrado Eugenio (Ramos) b: 4/25/11, Las Villas, Cuba BR/TR, 5'7", 158 lbs. Deb: 4/21/50

YEAR TM/L	W	L	PCT	G	GS	CG	SH	SV	IP	H	HR	BB	SO	RAT	ERA	ERA+	OAV	OOB	BH	AVG	PB	PR	/A	PD	TPI
1950 Was-A	6	10	.375	27	19	8	1	1	152	159	17	55	63	12.9	4.50	100	.269	.335	6	.122	-1	1	-0	-3	-0.3
1951 Was-A	11	9	.550	25	25	16	2	0	187	198	8	71	66	13.1	3.90	105	.268	.335	10	.164	-2	5	4	-2	0.1
1952 Was-A	11	8	.579	22	22	16	2	0	184¹	175	9	53	77	11.3	2.88	123	.249	.305	5	.079	-5	16	14	-3	0.6
1953 Was-A	8	7	.533	22	20	10	2	2	145²	130	14	48	65	11.3	3.03	129	.241	.309	6	.125	-2	16	14	-1	1.1
1954 Was-A	3	6	.333	22	8	1	0	0	66¹	74	12	22	26	13.0	4.75	75	.287	.343	0	.000	-1	-8	-9	-1	-1.0
Total 5	39	40	.494	118	94	51	7	3	735¹	736	60	249	297	12.3	3.67	108	.260	.323	27	.114	-11	30	23	-9	0.5

YEAR	TM/L	W	L	PCT	G	GS	CG	SH	SV	IP	H	HR	BB	SO	RAT	ERA	ERA+	OAV	OOB	BH	AVG	PB	PR	/A	PD	TPI

■ BUCK MARROW
Marrow, Charles Kennon b: 8/29/09, Tarboro, N.C. d: 11/21/82, Newport News, Va. BR/TR, 6'4", 200 lbs. Deb: 7/03/32

YEAR	TM/L	W	L	PCT	G	GS	CG	SH	SV	IP	H	HR	BB	SO	RAT	ERA	ERA+	OAV	OOB	BH	AVG	PB	PR	/A	PD	TPI
1932	Det-A	2	5	.286	18	7	2	0	1	63²	70	6	29	31	14.8	4.81	98	.278	.366	3	.158	-0	-2	-1	0	0.0
1937	Bro-N	1	2	.333	6	3	1	0	0	16¹	19	2	9	2	15.4	6.61	61	.284	.368	0	.000	-1	-5	-5	0	-0.4
1938	Bro-N	0	1	.000	15	0	0	0	0	19²	23	1	11	6	16.9	4.58	85	.291	.398	0	.000	-0	-2	-1	0	0.0
Total	3	3	8	.273	39	10	3	0	1	99²	112	9	49	39	15.4	5.06	88	.281	.373	3	.120	-1	-9	-7	1	-0.4

■ ED MARS
Mars, Edward M. b: 12/4/1866, Chicago, Ill. d: 12/9/41, Chicago, Ill. 5'9", 166 lbs. Deb: 8/12/1890

YEAR	TM/L	W	L	PCT	G	GS	CG	SH	SV	IP	H	HR	BB	SO	RAT	ERA	ERA+	OAV	OOB	BH	AVG	PB	PR	/A	PD	TPI
1890	Syr-a	9	5	.643	16	14	14	0	0	121¹	132	2	49	59	13.4	4.67	76	.269	.335	14	.275	4	-11	-15	1	-0.9

■ CUDDLES MARSHALL
Marshall, Clarence Westly b: 4/28/25, Bellingham, Wash. BR/TR, 6'3", 200 lbs. Deb: 4/24/46

YEAR	TM/L	W	L	PCT	G	GS	CG	SH	SV	IP	H	HR	BB	SO	RAT	ERA	ERA+	OAV	OOB	BH	AVG	PB	PR	/A	PD	TPI
1946	NY-A	3	4	.429	23	11	1	0	0	81	96	4	56	32	16.9	5.33	65	.308	.413	4	.143	-1	-16	-17	1	-1.6
1948	NY-A	0	0	—	1	0	0	0	0	1	0	0	3	0	27.0	0.00	—	.000	.500	0	—	0	0	0	0	0.0
1949	NY-A	3	0	1.000	21	2	0	0	3	49¹	48	3	48	13	17.9	5.11	79	.259	.417	1	.111	-0	-5	-6	1	-0.4
1950	StL-A	1	3	.250	28	2	0	0	1	53²	72	1	51	24	20.8	7.88	63	.321	.449	4	.333	0	-20	-17	-1	-1.6
Total	4	7	7	.500	73	15	1	0	4	185	216	8	158	69	18.3	5.98	67	.298	.426	9	.184	-0	-41	-40	0	-3.6

■ MIKE MARSHALL
Marshall, Michael Grant b: 1/15/43, Adrian, Mich. BR/TR, 5'10", 180 lbs. Deb: 5/31/67 ♦

YEAR	TM/L	W	L	PCT	G	GS	CG	SH	SV	IP	H	HR	BB	SO	RAT	ERA	ERA+	OAV	OOB	BH	AVG	PB	PR	/A	PD	TPI
1967	Det-A	1	3	.250	37	0	0	0	10	59	51	6	20	41	11.1	1.98	165	.233	.303	2	.222	0	8	8	1	1.0
1969	Sea-A	3	10	.231	20	14	3	1	0	87²	99	8	35	47	14.0	5.13	71	.281	.350	7	.259	3	-15	-15	3	-0.8
1970	Hou-N	0	1	.000	4	0	0	0	0	5¹	8	0	4	5	21.9	8.44	46	.400	.520	0	—	0	-3	-3	1	-0.1
	Mon-N	3	7	.300	24	5	0	0	3	64²	56	4	29	38	11.8	3.48	118	.225	.306	1	.091	0	4	5	2	0.6
	Yr	3	8	.273	28	5	0	0	3	70	64	4	33	43	12.5	3.86	106	.237	.320	3	.273	0	1	2	2	0.5
1971	Mon-N	5	8	.385	66	0	0	0	23	111¹	100	9	50	85	12.4	4.28	82	.247	.336	3	.188	0	-10	-9	3	-0.6
1972	Mon-N	14	8	.636	65	0	0	0	18	116	82	3	47	95	10.2	1.78	199	.202	.289	3	.136	0	22	23	0	2.5
1973	Mon-N	14	11	.560	92	0	0	0	31	179	163	10	75	124	12.2	2.66	143	.252	.333	8	.242	0	20	23	3	2.8
1974	*LA-N	15	12	.556	106	0	0	0	21	208¹	191	9	56	143	10.7	2.42	141	.247	.299	8	.235	1	28	23	1	2.5
1975	LA-N	9	14	.391	57	0	0	0	13	109¹	98	8	39	64	11.6	3.29	103	.242	.315	1	.067	-1	4	1	2	0.2
1976	LA-N	4	3	.571	30	0	0	0	6	62²	64	2	25	39	12.9	4.45	78	.270	.342	0	.000	0	-7	-7	2	-0.5
	Atl-N	2	1	.667	24	0	0	0	6	36²	35	4	14	17	12.3	3.19	119	.259	.333	1	.167	0	1	2	1	0.3
	Yr	6	4	.600	54	0	0	0	14	99¹	99	6	39	56	12.6	3.99	89	.264	.335	4	.364	1	-5	-5	2	-0.2
1977	Atl-N	1	0	1.000	4	0	0	0	0	6	12	1	2	6	21.0	9.00	49	.400	.438	1	1.000	0	-3	-3	-0	-0.2
	Tex-A	2	2	.500	12	4	0	0	1	35²	42	0	13	18	14.4	4.04	101	.304	.373	0	—	0	0	0	0	0.0
1978	Min-A	10	12	.455	54	0	0	0	21	99	80	3	37	56	10.7	2.45	156	.225	.300	0	—	0	14	15	1	1.7
1979	Min-A	10	15	.400	90	1	0	0	32	142²	132	8	48	81	11.6	2.65	165	.254	.322	0	—	0	25	27	2	3.0
1980	Min-A	1	3	.250	18	0	0	0	1	32¹	42	2	12	13	15.6	6.12	71	.323	.389	0	—	0	-8	-6	1	-0.5
1981	NY-N	3	2	.600	20	0	0	0	0	31	26	2	8	8	9.9	2.61	133	.224	.274	0	—	0	3	3	0	0.4
Total	14	97	112	.464	723	24	3	1	188	1386²	1281	79	514	880	11.9	3.14	118	.249	.321	35	.196	6	84	87	19	12.3

■ RUBE MARSHALL
Marshall, Roy De Verne "Cy" b: 1/19/1890, Salineville, Ohio d: 6/11/80, Dover, Ohio BR/TR, 5'11", 170 lbs. Deb: 9/28/12

YEAR	TM/L	W	L	PCT	G	GS	CG	SH	SV	IP	H	HR	BB	SO	RAT	ERA	ERA+	OAV	OOB	BH	AVG	PB	PR	/A	PD	TPI
1912	Phi-N	0	1	.000	2	1	0	0	0	3	12	0	1	2	39.0	21.00	17	.545	.565	0	—	0	-6	-6	0	-0.4
1913	Phi-N	0	1	.000	14	3	0	0	1	45¹	54	2	22	18	15.3	4.57	73	.297	.376	1	.091	-1	-7	-6	0	-0.6
1914	Phi-N	6	7	.462	27	19	7	0	1	134¹	144	2	50	49	13.3	3.75	78	.278	.349	6	.140	-2	-14	-12	1	-1.3
1915	Buf-F	2	1	.667	21	4	2	0	0	59¹	62	1	33	21	14.7	3.94	79	.281	.379	5	.294	1	-6	-5	-1	-0.4
Total	4	8	10	.444	64	27	9	0	2	242	272	5	106	90	14.4	4.17	74	.289	.366	12	.169	-2	-33	-30	1	-2.7

■ PHONNEY MARTIN
Martin, Alphonse Case b: 8/4/1845, New York, N.Y. d: 5/24/33, Hollis, N.Y. 5'7", 148 lbs. Deb: 4/26/1872 ♦

YEAR	TM/L	W	L	PCT	G	GS	CG	SH	SV	IP	H	HR	BB	SO	RAT	ERA	ERA+	OAV	OOB	BH	AVG	PB	PR	/A	PD	TPI
1872	Tro-n	1	2	.333	8	3	0	0	0	37¹	73	0	2		18.1	5.79	64	.365	.371	34	.283	0	-9	-9		-0.5
	Eck-n	2	7	.222	10	9	9	0	0	85	142	1	4		15.5	4.45	78	.318	.324	14	.177	-2	-7	-9		-0.9
	Yr	3	9	.250	18	12	9	0	0	122¹	215	1	6		16.3	4.86	73	.332	.338	1	.005	-2	-15	-18		-1.4
1873	Mut-n	0	1	.000	6	1	1	0	0	34¹	49	0	7		14.7	3.67	95	.297	.326	30	.221	-0	-0	-1		0.0
Total	2 n	3	10	.231	24	13	10	0	0	156²	264	1	13		15.9	4.60	76	.325	.336	78	.233	-2	-17	-19		-1.4

■ BARNEY MARTIN
Martin, Barnes Robertson b: 3/3/23, Columbia, S.C. BR/TR, 5'11", 170 lbs. Deb: 4/22/53

YEAR	TM/L	W	L	PCT	G	GS	CG	SH	SV	IP	H	HR	BB	SO	RAT	ERA	ERA+	OAV	OOB	BH	AVG	PB	PR	/A	PD	TPI
1953	Cin-N	0	0	—	1	0	0	0	0	3	3	0	1	1	18.0	9.00	48	.333	.400	0	—	0	-1	-1	0	0.0

■ RENIE MARTIN
Martin, Donald Renie b: 8/30/55, Dover, Del. BR/TR, 6'4", 190 lbs. Deb: 5/09/79

YEAR	TM/L	W	L	PCT	G	GS	CG	SH	SV	IP	H	HR	BB	SO	RAT	ERA	ERA+	OAV	OOB	BH	AVG	PB	PR	/A	PD	TPI
1979	KC-A	0	3	.000	25	0	0	0	5	34²	32	1	14	25	12.2	5.19	82	.248	.326	0	—	0	-4	-4	1	-0.2
1980	*KC-A	10	10	.500	32	20	2	0	2	137¹	133	18	70	68	13.4	4.39	92	.255	.345	0	—	0	-5	-5	-0	-0.4
1981	*KC-A	4	5	.444	29	0	0	0	4	61²	55	2	29	25	12.3	2.77	130	.244	.331	0	—	0	6	6	1	0.7
1982	SF-N	7	10	.412	29	25	1	0	0	141¹	148	14	64	63	13.5	4.65	77	.274	.350	13	.265	3	-16	-17	1	-1.2
1983	SF-N	2	4	.333	37	6	0	0	1	94¹	95	11	51	43	14.2	4.20	84	.268	.365	9	.346	4	-6	-7	1	0.0
1984	SF-N	1	1	.500	12	0	0	0	0	23¹	29	2	16	8	17.4	3.86	91	.305	.405	3	.500	1	-1	-1	1	0.1
	Phi-N	0	2	.000	9	0	0	0	0	15²	17	2	12	5	16.7	4.60	79	.274	.392	0	.000	-0	-2	-2	1	0.0
	Yr	1	3	.250	21	0	0	0	0	39	46	4	28	13	17.1	4.15	86	.293	.400	3	.273	1	-2	-3	2	0.1
Total	6	24	35	.407	173	51	3	0	12	508¹	509	50	256	237	13.6	4.27	88	.264	.352	25	.301	8	-28	-29	5	-1.0

■ SPEED MARTIN
Martin, Elwood Good b: 9/15/1893, Wawawai, Wash. d: 6/14/83, Lemon Grove, Cal. BR/TR, 6', 165 lbs. Deb: 7/05/17

YEAR	TM/L	W	L	PCT	G	GS	CG	SH	SV	IP	H	HR	BB	SO	RAT	ERA	ERA+	OAV	OOB	BH	AVG	PB	PR	/A	PD	TPI
1917	StL-A	0	2	.000	9	2	0	0	0	15²	20	0	5	5	14.4	5.74	45	.339	.391	0	.000	-0	-5	-5	1	-0.4
1918	Chi-N	5	2	.714	9	5	4	1	1	53²	47	0	14	16	10.4	1.84	151	.246	.301	3	.188	-0	5	6	3	0.7
1919	Chi-N	8	8	.500	35	14	7	2	2	163²	158	9	52	54	11.8	2.47	116	.259	.321	8	.182	-1	8	7	2	0.9
1920	Chi-N	4	15	.211	35	13	6	0	2	136	165	2	50	44	14.3	4.83	66	.305	.365	7	.159	-4	-26	-25	1	-2.3
1921	Chi-N	11	15	.423	37	28	13	1	1	217¹	245	12	68	86	13.0	4.35	88	.298	.353	17	.233	1	-14	-13	2	-0.8
1922	Chi-N	1	0	1.000	1	1	0	0	0	6	10	0	2	2	18.0	7.50	56	.385	.429	0	.000	0	-2	-2	-0	-0.1
Total	6	29	42	.408	126	63	30	4	6	592¹	645	16	191	207	12.8	3.78	87	.287	.344	35	.194	-0	-33	-32	7	-2.0

■ FRED MARTIN
Martin, Fred Turner b: 6/27/15, Williams, Okla. d: 6/11/79, Chicago, Ill. BR/TR, 6'1", 185 lbs. Deb: 4/21/46 C

YEAR	TM/L	W	L	PCT	G	GS	CG	SH	SV	IP	H	HR	BB	SO	RAT	ERA	ERA+	OAV	OOB	BH	AVG	PB	PR	/A	PD	TPI
1946	StL-N	2	1	.667	6	3	2	0	0	28²	29	4	8	19	11.6	4.08	85	.254	.303	3	.273	0	-2	-2	0	0.0
1949	StL-N	6	0	1.000	21	5	3	0	0	70	65	3	20	30	10.9	2.44	170	.243	.295	6	.300	1	12	13	0	1.5
1950	StL-N	4	2	.667	30	2	0	0	0	63¹	87	4	30	19	16.8	5.12	84	.331	.401	4	.267	1	-7	-6	1	-0.3
Total	3	12	3	.800	57	10	5	0	0	162	181	7	58	68	13.3	3.78	108	.281	.341	13	.283	2	3	6	1	1.2

■ DOC MARTIN
Martin, Harold Winthrop b: 9/23/1887, Roxbury, Mass. d: 4/14/35, Milton, Mass. BR/TR, 5'11", 165 lbs. Deb: 10/07/08

YEAR	TM/L	W	L	PCT	G	GS	CG	SH	SV	IP	H	HR	BB	SO	RAT	ERA	ERA+	OAV	OOB	BH	AVG	PB	PR	/A	PD	TPI
1908	Phi-A	0	1	.000	1	1	0	0	0	2	2	0	3	2	27.0	13.50	19	.286	.545	0	.000	-0	-2	-2	0	-0.2
1911	Phi-A	1	1	.500	11	3	1	0	0	38	40	1	17	21	14.7	4.50	70	.272	.367	3	.214	0	-5	-6	0	-0.4
1912	Phi-A	0	0	—	2	0	0	0	0	4¹	5	0	5	4	22.8	10.38	30	.333	.524	0	.000	-0	-3	-4	0	-0.2
Total	3	1	2	.333	14	4	1	0	0	44¹	47	1	25	27	16.0	5.48	57	.278	.393	3	.167	-0	-11	-12	1	-0.8

■ PEPPER MARTIN
Martin, John Leonard Roosevelt "The Wild Horse Of The Osage"
b: 2/29/04, Temple, Okla. d: 3/5/65, McAlester, Okla. BR/TR, 5'8", 170 lbs. Deb: 4/16/28 C♦

YEAR	TM/L	W	L	PCT	G	GS	CG	SH	SV	IP	H	HR	BB	SO	RAT	ERA	ERA+	OAV	OOB	BH	AVG	PB	PR	/A	PD	TPI
1934	*StL-N	0	0	—	1	0	0	0	0	2	1	0	0	0	4.5	4.50	94	.167	.167	131	.289	0	-0	-0	0	0.0
1936	StL-N	0	0	—	1	0	0	0	0	2	1	0	2	0	13.5	0.00	—	.200	.429	177	.309	0	1	1	0	0.1
Total	2	0	0	—	2	0	0	0	0	4	2	0	2	0	9.0	2.25	181	.182	.308	1227	.298	0	1	1	0	0.1

■ JOHN MARTIN
Martin, John Robert b: 4/11/56, Wyandotte, Mich. BB/TL, 6', 190 lbs. Deb: 8/27/80

YEAR	TM/L	W	L	PCT	G	GS	CG	SH	SV	IP	H	HR	BB	SO	RAT	ERA	ERA+	OAV	OOB	BH	AVG	PB	PR	/A	PD	TPI
1980	StL-N	2	3	.400	9	5	1	0	0	42	39	1	9	23	10.3	4.29	86	.247	.287	3	.273	1	-3	-3	-1	-0.2

YEAR TM/L	W	L	PCT	G	GS	CG	SH	SV	IP	H	HR	BB	SO	RAT	ERA	ERA+	OAV	OOB	BH	AVG	PB	PR	/A	PD	TPI
1981 StL-N	8	5	.615	17	15	4	0	0	102²	85	10	26	36	9.9	3.42	104	.228	.283	7	.212	2	1	2	0	0.4
1982 StL-N	4	5	.444	24	7	0	0	0	66	56	6	30	21	11.7	4.23	86	.230	.314	1	.091	-0	-5	-4	-1	-0.5
1983 StL-N	3	1	.750	26	5	0	0	0	66¹	60	6	26	29	11.9	3.53	103	.242	.319	4	.222	1	1	1	1	0.2
Det-A	0	0	—	15	0	0	0	1	13¹	15	2	4	11	12.8	7.43	53	.294	.345	0	—	0	-5	-5	0	-0.4
Total 4	17	14	.548	91	32	5	1	0	290²	255	25	95	120	11.0	3.94	92	.238	.302	15	.205	3	-11	-10	-1	-0.5

■ MORRIE MARTIN
Martin, Morris Webster "Lefty" b: 9/3/22, Dixon, Mo. BL/TL, 6', 173 lbs. Deb: 4/25/49

YEAR TM/L	W	L	PCT	G	GS	CG	SH	SV	IP	H	HR	BB	SO	RAT	ERA	ERA+	OAV	OOB	BH	AVG	PB	PR	/A	PD	TPI
1949 Bro-N	1	3	.250	10	4	0	0	0	30²	39	5	15	15	16.4	7.04	58	.320	.403	2	.200	-0	-10	-10	0	-0.8
1951 Phi-A	11	4	.733	35	13	3	1	0	138	139	13	63	35	13.5	3.78	113	.259	.343	11	.220	-1	5	8	2	0.9
1952 Phi-A	0	2	.000	5	5	0	0	0	25¹	32	1	15	13	17.4	6.39	62	.302	.398	1	.111	-1	-8	-7	-0	-0.7
1953 Phi-A	10	12	.455	58	11	2	0	7	156¹	158	12	59	64	13.0	4.43	97	.262	.336	4	.095	-4	-8	-3	-0	-0.5
1954 Phi-A	2	4	.333	13	6	2	0	0	52²	57	9	19	24	13.3	5.47	71	.278	.345	4	.235	-0	-10	-9	-0	-0.8
Chi-A	5	4	.556	35	2	1	0	5	70	52	5	24	31	9.9	2.06	182	.210	.282	2	.133	-0	13	13	-0	1.3
Yr	7	8	.467	48	8	3	0	5	122²	109	14	43	55	11.2	3.52	108	.240	.307	6	.000	-0	3	4	-0	0.5
1955 Chi-A	2	3	.400	37	0	0	0	2	52	50	4	20	22	12.5	3.63	109	.259	.335	3	.300	-1	2	2	1	0.4
1956 Chi-A	1	0	1.000	10	0	0	0	0	18¹	21	1	7	9	13.7	4.91	84	.292	.354	1	.200	-0	-2	-2	0	0.0
Bal-A	1	1	.500	9	0	0	0	0	5	10	1	2	3	23.4	10.80	36	.400	.464	0	—	0	-4	-4	0	-0.3
Yr	2	1	.667	19	0	0	0	0	23¹	31	2	9	12	15.8	6.17	66	.316	.380	1	.200	-0	-5	-5	0	-0.3
1957 StL-N	0	0	—	4	1	0	0	0	10²	5	0	4	7	8.4	2.53	157	.143	.250	0	.000	-0	2	2	0	0.2
1958 StL-N	3	1	.750	17	0	0	0	0	24²	19	3	12	16	12.0	4.74	87	.211	.317	0	.000	-1	-2	-2	-0	-0.2
Cle-A	2	0	1.000	14	0	0	0	1	18²	20	0	8	5	13.5	2.41	151	.294	.368	0	—	0	3	3	0	0.3
1959 Chi-N	0	0	—	3	0	0	0	0	2¹	5	2	1	1	27.0	19.29	20	.455	.538	0	—	0	-4	-4	0	-0.3
Total 10	38	34	.528	250	42	8	1	15	604²	607	56	249	245	13.1	4.29	95	.262	.341	28	.170	-6	-23	-13	3	-0.5

■ PAT MARTIN
Martin, Patrick Francis b: 4/13/1892, Brooklyn, N.Y. d: 2/4/49, Brooklyn, N.Y. BL/TL, 5'11.5", 170 lbs. Deb: 9/20/19

YEAR TM/L	W	L	PCT	G	GS	CG	SH	SV	IP	H	HR	BB	SO	RAT	ERA	ERA+	OAV	OOB	BH	AVG	PB	PR	/A	PD	TPI
1919 Phi-A	0	2	.000	2	2	1	0	0	11	11	0	8	6	15.5	4.09	84	.256	.373	0	.000	-0	-1	-1	-0	-0.1
1920 Phi-A	1	4	.200	8	5	2	0	0	32¹	48	2	25	14	21.4	6.12	66	.364	.478	4	.400	1	-8	-8	-1	-0.6
Total 2	1	6	.143	10	7	3	0	0	43¹	59	2	33	20	19.9	5.61	69	.337	.453	4	.308	1	-9	-8	-1	-0.7

■ PAUL MARTIN
Martin, Paul Charles b: 3/10/32, Brownstone, Pa. BR/TR, 6'6", 235 lbs. Deb: 7/02/55

YEAR TM/L	W	L	PCT	G	GS	CG	SH	SV	IP	H	HR	BB	SO	RAT	ERA	ERA+	OAV	OOB	BH	AVG	PB	PR	/A	PD	TPI
1955 Pit-N	0	1	.000	7	1	0	0	0	7	13	0	17	3	39.9	14.14	29	.464	.674	0	—	0	-8	-8	0	-0.6

■ RAY MARTIN
Martin, Raymond Joseph b: 3/13/25, Norwood, Mass. BR/TR, 6'2", 177 lbs. Deb: 8/15/43

YEAR TM/L	W	L	PCT	G	GS	CG	SH	SV	IP	H	HR	BB	SO	RAT	ERA	ERA+	OAV	OOB	BH	AVG	PB	PR	/A	PD	TPI
1943 Bos-N	0	0	—	2	0	0	0	0	3¹	3	0	1	1	10.8	8.10	42	.231	.286	0	.000	-0	-2	-2	0	-0.1
1947 Bos-N	1	0	1.000	1	1	1	0	0	9	7	0	4	2	11.0	1.00	389	.212	.297	0	.000	-0	3	3	0	0.4
1948 Bos-N	0	0	—	2	0	0	0	0	2¹	0	0	1	0	3.9	0.00	—	.000	.125	0	—	0	1	1	0	0.1
Total 3	1	0	1.000	5	1	1	0	0	14²	10	0	6	3	9.8	2.45	154	.189	.271	0	.000	-0	2	2	1	0.4

■ JOE MARTINA
Martina, Joseph John "Oyster Joe" b: 7/8/1889, New Orleans, La. d: 3/22/62, New Orleans, La. BR/TR, 6', 183 lbs. Deb: 4/19/24

YEAR TM/L	W	L	PCT	G	GS	CG	SH	SV	IP	H	HR	BB	SO	RAT	ERA	ERA+	OAV	OOB	BH	AVG	PB	PR	/A	PD	TPI
1924 *Was-A	6	8	.429	24	13	8	0	0	125¹	129	7	56	57	13.7	4.67	86	.271	.355	14	.326	3	-6	-9	-2	-0.7

■ ALFREDO MARTINEZ
Martinez, Alfredo b: 3/15/57, Los Angeles, Cal. BR/TR, 6'3", 185 lbs. Deb: 4/20/80

YEAR TM/L	W	L	PCT	G	GS	CG	SH	SV	IP	H	HR	BB	SO	RAT	ERA	ERA+	OAV	OOB	BH	AVG	PB	PR	/A	PD	TPI
1980 Cal-A	7	9	.438	30	23	4	1	0	149¹	150	14	59	57	12.7	4.52	87	.259	.328	0	—	0	-8	-10	-2	-1.0
1981 Cal-A	0	0	—	2	0	0	0	0	6	5	1	3	4	12.0	3.00	122	.227	.320	0	—	0	0	0	0	0.1
Total 2	7	9	.438	32	23	4	1	0	155¹	155	15	62	61	12.6	4.46	88	.257	.328	0	—	0	-8	-9	-1	-0.9

■ DAVE MARTINEZ
Martinez, David b: 9/26/64, New York, N.Y. BL/TL, 5'10", 150 lbs. Deb: 6/15/86 ♦

YEAR TM/L	W	L	PCT	G	GS	CG	SH	SV	IP	H	HR	BB	SO	RAT	ERA	ERA+	OAV	OOB	BH	AVG	PB	PR	/A	PD	TPI
1990 Mon-N	0	0	—	1	0	0	0	0	0¹	2	0	2	0	108.0	54.00	7	.667	.800	109	.279	0	-2	-2	0	-0.1

■ TIPPY MARTINEZ
Martinez, Felix Anthony b: 5/31/50, LaJunta, Colo. BL/TL, 5'10", 180 lbs. Deb: 8/09/74

YEAR TM/L	W	L	PCT	G	GS	CG	SH	SV	IP	H	HR	BB	SO	RAT	ERA	ERA+	OAV	OOB	BH	AVG	PB	PR	/A	PD	TPI
1974 NY-A	0	0	—	10	0	0	0	0	12²	14	0	9	10	17.1	4.26	82	.286	.407	0	—	0	-1	-1	0	0.0
1975 NY-A	1	2	.333	23	2	0	0	8	37	27	2	32	20	14.6	2.68	136	.208	.368	0	—	0	5	4	-1	0.3
1976 NY-A	2	0	1.000	11	0	0	0	2	28	18	1	14	14	10.3	1.93	177	.191	.296	0	—	0	5	5	1	0.6
Bal-A	3	1	.750	28	0	0	0	8	41²	32	0	28	31	13.2	2.59	126	.222	.353	0	—	0	4	3	1	0.4
Yr	5	1	.833	39	0	0	0	10	69²	50	1	42	45	12.0	2.33	143	.210	.331	0	—	0	9	8	2	1.0
1977 Bal-A	5	1	.833	41	0	0	0	9	50	47	2	27	29	13.3	2.70	140	.266	.363	0	—	0	8	6	1	0.7
1978 Bal-A	3	3	.500	42	0	0	0	5	69	77	4	40	57	15.4	4.83	72	.281	.375	0	—	0	-8	-10	1	-0.8
1979 *Bal-A	10	3	.769	39	0	0	0	3	78	59	0	31	68	10.5	2.88	139	.210	.291	0	—	0	12	10	1	1.0
1980 Bal-A	4	4	.500	53	0	0	0	10	80²	69	5	34	68	11.6	3.01	131	.240	.322	0	—	0	9	8	1	1.0
1981 Bal-A	3	3	.500	37	0	0	0	11	59	48	4	32	50	12.2	2.90	125	.231	.333	0	—	0	5	5	0	0.5
1982 Bal-A	8	8	.500	76	0	0	0	16	95	81	6	37	78	11.3	3.41	118	.240	.317	0	—	0	7	7	-1	0.6
1983 *Bal-A	9	3	.750	65	0	0	0	21	103¹	76	10	37	81	9.8	2.35	168	.211	.284	0	—	0	20	18	2	2.0
1984 Bal-A	4	9	.308	55	0	0	0	17	89²	88	9	51	72	14.0	3.91	99	.260	.356	0	—	0	1	-0	0	0.0
1985 Bal-A	3	3	.500	49	0	0	0	4	70	70	8	37	47	13.8	5.40	75	.261	.351	0	—	0	-10	-11	1	-0.9
1986 Bal-A	0	2	.000	14	0	0	0	1	16	18	1	12	11	16.9	5.63	73	.295	.411	0	—	0	-3	-3	0	-0.2
1988 Min-A	0	0	—	3	0	0	0	0	4	8	1	4	3	29.3	18.00	23	.471	.591	0	—	0	-6	-6	0	-0.5
Total 14	55	42	.567	546	2	0	0	115	834	732	53	425	632	12.6	3.45	111	.242	.337	0	—	0	47	34	7	4.7

■ BUCK MARTINEZ
Martinez, John Albert b: 11/7/48, Redding, Cal. BR/TR, 5'10", 190 lbs. Deb: 6/18/69 ♦

YEAR TM/L	W	L	PCT	G	GS	CG	SH	SV	IP	H	HR	BB	SO	RAT	ERA	ERA+	OAV	OOB	BH	AVG	PB	PR	/A	PD	TPI
1979 Mil-A	0	0	—	1	0	0	0	0	1	1	0	1	0	18.0	9.00	46	.250	.400	53	.270	1	-1	-1	0	0.0

■ DENNIS MARTINEZ
Martinez, Jose Dennis (Emilia) b: 5/14/55, Granada, Nicaragua BR/TR, 6'1", 160 lbs. Deb: 9/14/76

YEAR TM/L	W	L	PCT	G	GS	CG	SH	SV	IP	H	HR	BB	SO	RAT	ERA	ERA+	OAV	OOB	BH	AVG	PB	PR	/A	PD	TPI
1976 Bal-A	1	2	.333	4	2	1	0	0	27²	23	1	8	18	10.1	2.60	126	.237	.295	0	—	0	3	2	0	0.2
1977 Bal-A	14	7	.667	42	13	5	0	4	166²	157	10	64	107	12.4	4.10	92	.253	.330	0	—	0	-1	-6	0	-0.5
1978 Bal-A	16	11	.593	40	38	15	0	0	276¹	257	20	93	142	11.5	3.52	99	.250	.314	0	—	0	8	-1	4	0.3
1979 *Bal-A	15	16	.484	40	39	18	3	0	292¹	279	28	78	132	11.0	3.66	109	.253	.303	0	—	0	18	11	4	1.5
1980 Bal-A	6	4	.600	25	12	2	0	1	99²	103	12	44	42	13.5	3.97	100	.272	.351	0	—	0	1	-0	0	0.0
1981 Bal-A	14	5	.737	25	24	9	2	0	178²	173	10	62	88	11.9	3.32	109	.254	.318	0	—	0	7	6	1	1.1
1982 Bal-A	16	12	.571	40	39	10	2	0	252	262	30	87	111	12.7	4.21	96	.267	.331	0	—	0	-4	-5	0	-0.4
1983 Bal-A	7	16	.304	32	25	4	0	0	153	209	21	71	71	15.1	5.53	71	.330	.376	0	—	0	-25	-27	6	-2.0
1984 Bal-A	6	9	.400	34	20	2	0	0	141²	145	26	37	77	11.9	5.02	77	.263	.315	0	—	0	-16	-18	1	-1.6
1985 Bal-A	13	11	.542	33	31	3	1	0	180	203	29	63	68	13.8	5.15	78	.288	.353	0	—	0	-20	-22	1	-2.0
1986 Bal-A	0	0	—	4	0	0	0	0	6²	11	1	2	2	17.6	6.75	61	.367	.406	0	—	0	-2	-2	0	-0.1
Mon-N	3	6	.333	19	15	1	1	0	98	103	11	28	63	12.3	4.59	80	.274	.329	3	.100	-0	-10	-10	1	-0.8
1987 Mon-N	11	4	.733	22	22	2	1	0	144²	133	9	40	84	11.1	3.30	127	.244	.302	3	.065	-2	13	15	1	1.3
1988 Mon-N	15	13	.536	34	34	9	2	0	235¹	215	21	55	120	10.6	2.72	132	.239	.287	15	.192	2	19	23	1	2.9
1989 Mon-N	16	7	.696	34	33	5	2	0	232	227	21	49	142	11.0	3.18	111	.257	.301	9	.125	-1	8	9	4	1.3
1990 Mon-N	10	11	.476	32	32	7	2	0	226	191	16	49	156	9.8	2.95	127	.228	.275	7	.103	-2	21	20	1	2.1
Total 15	163	134	.549	460	379	93	18	5	2710²	2691	265	804	1423	11.8	3.82	100	.260	.317	37	.126	-4	19	-4	27	3.3

■ MARTY MARTINEZ
Martinez, Orlando (Oliva) b: 8/23/41, Havana, Cuba BB/TR, 6', 170 lbs. Deb: 5/02/62 MC♦

YEAR TM/L	W	L	PCT	G	GS	CG	SH	SV	IP	H	HR	BB	SO	RAT	ERA	ERA+	OAV	OOB	BH	AVG	PB	PR	/A	PD	TPI
1969 Hou-N	0	0	—	1	0	0	0	0	1	1	0	1	0	13.5	13.50	26	.333	.333	61	.308	0	-1	-1	0	0.0

■ RAMON MARTINEZ
Martinez, Ramon Jaime (b: Ramon Jaime (Martinez)) b: 3/22/68, Santo Domingo, D.R. BR/TR, 6'4¹6", 508 lbs. Deb: /13/1988

YEAR TM/L	W	L	PCT	G	GS	CG	SH	SV	IP	H	HR	BB	SO	RAT	ERA	ERA+	OAV	OOB	BH	AVG	PB	PR	/A	PD	TPI
1988 LA-N	1	3	.250	9	6	0	0	0	35²	27	0	22	23	12.4	3.79	88	.216	.333	0	.000	-1	-1	-2	-0	-0.2
1989 LA-N	6	4	.600	15	15	2	2	0	98²	79	11	41	89	11.4	3.19	107	.219	.308	6	.162	0	3	2	1	0.3

YEAR	TM/L	W	L	PCT	G	GS	CG	SH	SV	IP	H	HR	BB	SO	RAT	ERA	ERA+	OAV	OOB	BH	AVG	PB	PR	/A	PD	TPI
1990	LA-N	20	6	.769	33	33	**12**	3	0	234¹	191	22	67	223	10.1	2.92	122	.220	.279	10	.125	-1	23	17	-1	1.5
Total	3	27	13	.675	57	54	14	5	0	368²	297	33	130	335	10.6	3.08	114	.220	.292	16	.129	-2	25	18	-0	1.6

■ ROGELIO MARTINEZ
Martinez, Rogelio (Ulloa) "Limonar" b: 11/5/18, Cidra, Cuba BR/TR, 6', 180 lbs. Deb: 7/13/50

YEAR	TM/L	W	L	PCT	G	GS	CG	SH	SV	IP	H	HR	BB	SO	RAT	ERA	ERA+	OAV	OOB	BH	AVG	PB	PR	/A	PD	TPI
1950	Was-A	0	1	.000	2	1	0	0	0	1¹	4	0	2	0	40.5	27.00	17	.500	.600	0	—	0	-3	-3	0	-0.2

■ SILVIO MARTINEZ
Martinez, Silvio Ramon (Cabrera) b: 8/19/55, Santiago, D.R. BR/TR, 5'10", 170 lbs. Deb: 4/09/77

YEAR	TM/L	W	L	PCT	G	GS	CG	SH	SV	IP	H	HR	BB	SO	RAT	ERA	ERA+	OAV	OOB	BH	AVG	PB	PR	/A	PD	TPI
1977	Chi-A	0	1	.000	10	0	0	0	0	21	28	4	12	10	17.1	5.57	73	.337	.421	0	—	0	-4	-3	0	-0.2
1978	StL-N	9	8	.529	22	22	5	2	0	137²	114	11	71	45	12.2	3.66	96	.228	.326	8	.170	0	-1	-2	-1	-0.2
1979	StL-N	15	8	.652	32	29	7	2	0	206²	204	14	67	102	11.8	3.27	115	.259	.317	8	.129	-2	11	11	-3	0.7
1980	StL-N	5	10	.333	25	20	2	0	0	119²	127	8	48	39	13.3	4.81	77	.273	.343	3	.086	-2	-16	-15	-2	-1.8
1981	StL-N	2	5	.286	18	16	0	0	0	97	95	4	39	34	12.5	3.99	89	.260	.333	7	.200	1	-5	-5	-1	-0.4
Total	5	31	32	.492	107	87	14	4	1	582	568	41	237	230	12.5	3.88	94	.258	.331	26	.145	-3	-16	-14	-5	-1.9

■ WEDO MARTINI
Martini, Guido Joe "Southern" b: 7/1/13, Birmingham, Ala. d: 10/28/70, Philadelphia, Pa. BR/TR, 5'10", 165 lbs. Deb: 7/28/35

YEAR	TM/L	W	L	PCT	G	GS	CG	SH	SV	IP	H	HR	BB	SO	RAT	ERA	ERA+	OAV	OOB	BH	AVG	PB	PR	/A	PD	TPI
1935	Phi-A	0	2	.000	3	2	0	0	0	6¹	8	0	11	1	27.0	17.05	27	.333	.543	0	.000	-0	-9	-9	1	-0.6

■ JOE MARTY
Marty, Joseph Anton b: 9/1/13, Sacramento, Cal. d: 10/4/84, Sacramento, Cal. BR/TR, 6', 182 lbs. Deb: 4/22/37 ♦

YEAR	TM/L	W	L	PCT	G	GS	CG	SH	SV	IP	H	HR	BB	SO	RAT	ERA	ERA+	OAV	OOB	BH	AVG	PB	PR	/A	PD	TPI
1939	Phi-N	0	0	—	1	0	0	0	0	4	2	0	3	1	11.3	4.50	89	.154	.313	76	.254	0	-0	-0	-0	0.0

■ RANDY MARTZ
Martz, Randy Carl b: 5/28/56, Harrisburg, Pa. BL/TR, 6'4", 210 lbs. Deb: 9/06/80

YEAR	TM/L	W	L	PCT	G	GS	CG	SH	SV	IP	H	HR	BB	SO	RAT	ERA	ERA+	OAV	OOB	BH	AVG	PB	PR	/A	PD	TPI
1980	Chi-N	1	2	.333	6	6	0	0	0	30¹	28	1	11	5	11.6	2.08	188	.241	.307	1	.111	-1	5	6	1	0.7
1981	Chi-N	5	7	.417	33	14	1	0	6	107²	103	6	49	32	12.8	3.68	100	.256	.338	6	.214	-1	-2	0	0	0.2
1982	Chi-N	11	10	.524	28	24	1	0	1	147²	157	17	36	40	11.9	4.21	89	.272	.318	6	.143	1	-10	-8	1	-0.4
1983	Chi-A	0	0	—	1	1	0	0	0	5	4	0	4	1	14.4	3.60	116	.211	.348	0	—	0	0	0	0	0.0
Total	4	17	19	.472	68	45	2	0	7	290²	292	24	100	78	12.3	3.78	99	.262	.325	13	.165	2	-7	-1	3	0.5

■ DEL MASON
Mason, Adelbert William b: 10/29/1883, Newfane, N.Y. d: 12/31/62, Winter Park, Fla. BR/TR, 6', 160 lbs. Deb: 4/23/04

YEAR	TM/L	W	L	PCT	G	GS	CG	SH	SV	IP	H	HR	BB	SO	RAT	ERA	ERA+	OAV	OOB	BH	AVG	PB	PR	/A	PD	TPI
1904	Was-A	0	3	.000	5	3	2	0	0	33	45	1	13	16	15.8	6.00	44	.325	.383	0	.000	-2	-12	-12	-1	-1.3
1906	Cin-N	0	1	.000	2	1	1	0	0	12	10	1	6	4	14.8	4.50	61	.250	.362	0	.000	-1	-2	-2	-0	-0.2
1907	Cin-N	5	12	.294	25	17	13	1	0	146	144	2	55	45	12.6	3.14	83	.277	.353	8	.182	-0	-11	-9	1	-0.8
Total	3	5	16	.238	32	21	16	1	0	191	199	4	74	65	13.2	3.72	70	.285	.360	8	.125	-3	-26	-23	0	-2.3

■ CHARLIE MASON
Mason, Charles E. b: 6/25/1853, New Orleans, La. d: 10/21/36, Philadelphia, Pa. TR , Deb: 4/26/1875 M♦

YEAR	TM/L	W	L	PCT	G	GS	CG	SH	SV	IP	H	HR	BB	SO	RAT	ERA	ERA+	OAV	OOB	BH	AVG	PB	PR	/A	PD	TPI
1875	Was-n	0	0	—	1	0	0	0	0	2	3	0	1	0	18.0	4.50	58	.300	.364	3	.088	-0	-0	-0		0.0

■ ERNIE MASON
Mason, Ernest b: New Orleans, La. d: 7/30/04, Covington, La. Deb: 7/17/1894

YEAR	TM/L	W	L	PCT	G	GS	CG	SH	SV	IP	H	HR	BB	SO	RAT	ERA	ERA+	OAV	OOB	BH	AVG	PB	PR	/A	PD	TPI
1894	StL-N	0	3	.000	4	2	2	0	0	22²	34	1	10	3	17.5	7.15	76	.342	.403	3	.250	-0	-5	-4	-0	-0.3

■ HANK MASON
Mason, Henry b: 6/19/31, Marshall, Mo. BR/TR, 6', 185 lbs. Deb: 9/12/58

YEAR	TM/L	W	L	PCT	G	GS	CG	SH	SV	IP	H	HR	BB	SO	RAT	ERA	ERA+	OAV	OOB	BH	AVG	PB	PR	/A	PD	TPI
1958	Phi-N	0	0	—	1	0	0	0	0	5	7	0	2	3	18.0	10.80	37	.368	.455	0	.000	-0	-4	-4	-0	-0.3
1960	Phi-N	0	0	—	3	0	0	0	0	5²	9	1	5	3	22.2	9.53	41	.375	.483	0	.000	-0	-4	-4	-0	-0.3
Total	2	0	0	—	4	0	0	0	0	10²	16	1	7	6	20.3	10.13	39	.372	.471	0	.000	-0	-7	-7	-0	-0.6

■ MIKE MASON
Mason, Michael Paul b: 11/21/58, Faribault, Minn. BL/TL, 6'2", 205 lbs. Deb: 9/13/82

YEAR	TM/L	W	L	PCT	G	GS	CG	SH	SV	IP	H	HR	BB	SO	RAT	ERA	ERA+	OAV	OOB	BH	AVG	PB	PR	/A	PD	TPI
1982	Tex-A	1	2	.333	4	4	0	0	0	23	21	3	9	8	11.7	5.09	76	.244	.316	0	—	0	-3	-3	0	-0.2
1983	Tex-A	0	2	.000	5	0	0	0	0	10²	10	0	6	9	14.3	5.91	68	.244	.354	0	—	0	-2	-2	0	-0.1
1984	Tex-A	9	13	.409	36	24	4	0	0	184¹	159	18	51	113	10.4	3.61	115	.233	.288	0	—	0	8	11	-1	1.0
1985	Tex-A	8	15	.348	38	30	1	1	0	179	212	22	73	92	14.5	4.83	88	.299	.366	0	—	0	-14	-12	0	-1.0
1986	Tex-A	7	3	.700	27	22	2	1	0	135	135	11	56	85	12.7	4.33	99	.257	.329	0	—	0	-2	-0	1	0.0
1987	Tex-A	0	2	.000	8	6	0	0	0	29	37	6	22	21	19.6	5.59	80	.322	.447	0	—	0	-4	-4	0	-0.2
	Chi-N	4	1	.800	17	4	0	0	0	38	43	4	23	28	15.9	5.68	75	.303	.404	2	.222	0	-7	-6	0	-0.4
1988	Min-A	0	1	.000	5	0	0	0	0	6²	8	1	9	7	23.0	10.80	38	.286	.459	0	—	0	-5	-5	-0	-0.4
Total	7	29	39	.426	140	90	7	2	0	605²	625	65	249	363	13.2	4.53	93	.268	.342	2	.222	0	-28	-21	-0	-1.3

■ ROGER MASON
Mason, Roger Le Roy b: 9/18/58, Bellaire, Mich. BR/TR, 6'6", 215 lbs. Deb: 9/04/84

YEAR	TM/L	W	L	PCT	G	GS	CG	SH	SV	IP	H	HR	BB	SO	RAT	ERA	ERA+	OAV	OOB	BH	AVG	PB	PR	/A	PD	TPI
1984	Det-A	1	1	.500	5	2	0	0	1	22	23	1	10	15	13.5	4.50	87	.271	.347	0	—	0	-1	-1	0	0.0
1985	SF-N	1	3	.250	5	5	1	1	0	29²	28	1	11	26	11.8	2.12	162	.243	.310	1	.091	-0	5	4	-0	0.4
1986	SF-N	3	4	.429	11	11	1	0	0	60	56	5	30	43	13.4	4.80	73	.250	.346	1	.048	-2	-7	-9	-1	-1.0
1987	SF-N	1	1	.500	5	5	0	0	0	26	30	4	10	18	13.8	4.50	85	.303	.367	1	.125	0	-1	-2	0	-0.1
1989	Hou-N	0	0	—	2	0	0	0	0	1¹	2	0	2	3	27.0	20.25	17	.333	.500	0	—	0	-2	-2	0	-0.1
Total	5	6	9	.400	28	23	2	1	1	139	139	11	63	105	13.3	4.27	85	.263	.345	3	.075	-2	-7	-10	-1	-0.8

■ WALT MASTERS
Masters, Walter Thomas b: 3/28/07, Pen Argyl, Pa. BR/TR, 5'10.5", 180 lbs. Deb: 7/09/31

YEAR	TM/L	W	L	PCT	G	GS	CG	SH	SV	IP	H	HR	BB	SO	RAT	ERA	ERA+	OAV	OOB	BH	AVG	PB	PR	/A	PD	TPI
1931	Was-A	0	0	—	3	0	0	0	1	9	7	0	4	1	11.0	2.00	215	.226	.314	0	.000	-0	2	2	1	0.2
1937	Phi-N	0	0	—	1	0	0	0	0	1	5	0	1	0	54.0	36.00	12	.714	.750	0	—	0	-4	-4	0	-0.2
1939	Phi-A	0	0	—	4	0	0	0	0	11	15	0	8	2	18.8	6.55	72	.300	.404	0	.000	-0	-2	-2	0	-0.1
Total	3	0	0	—	8	0	0	0	1	21	27	0	13	3	17.1	6.00	75	.310	.400	0	.000	-1	-4	-3	1	-0.1

■ PAUL MASTERSON
Masterson, Paul Nickalis "Lefty" b: 10/16/15, Chicago, Ill. BL/TL, 5'11", 165 lbs. Deb: 9/15/40

YEAR	TM/L	W	L	PCT	G	GS	CG	SH	SV	IP	H	HR	BB	SO	RAT	ERA	ERA+	OAV	OOB	BH	AVG	PB	PR	/A	PD	TPI
1940	Phi-N	0	0	—	2	0	0	0	0	5	5	0	2	3	12.6	7.20	54	.263	.333	0	.000	-0	-2	-2	0	-0.1
1941	Phi-N	1	0	1.000	2	1	1	0	0	11¹	11	0	6	8	13.5	4.76	78	.250	.340	0	.000	-1	-1	-1	0	-0.1
1942	Phi-N	0	0	—	4	0	0	0	0	8¹	10	1	5	3	16.2	6.48	51	.303	.395	0	—	0	-3	-3	0	-0.2
Total	3	1	0	1.000	8	1	1	0	0	24²	26	1	13	14	14.2	5.84	62	.277	.358	0	.000	-1	-6	-6	0	-0.4

■ WALT MASTERSON
Masterson, Walter Edward b: 6/22/20, Philadelphia, Pa. BR/TR, 6'2", 189 lbs. Deb: 5/08/39

YEAR	TM/L	W	L	PCT	G	GS	CG	SH	SV	IP	H	HR	BB	SO	RAT	ERA	ERA+	OAV	OOB	BH	AVG	PB	PR	/A	PD	TPI
1939	Was-A	2	2	.500	24	5	1	0	0	58¹	66	2	48	12	17.9	5.55	78	.293	.422	2	.154	-0	-6	-8	-0	-0.7
1940	Was-A	3	13	.188	31	19	3	0	2	130¹	128	6	88	68	15.1	4.90	85	.257	.371	7	.184	0	-8	-11	-1	-1.0
1941	Was-A	4	3	.571	34	6	1	0	3	78¹	101	3	53	40	17.8	5.97	68	.321	.420	2	.105	-1	-16	-17	1	-1.6
1942	Was-A	5	9	.357	25	15	8	4	2	142²	138	6	54	63	12.2	3.34	109	.281	.321	7	.156	-0	5	5	-2	0.3
1945	Was-A	1	2	.333	4	2	1	1	0	25	21	1	10	14	11.2	1.08	287	.228	.304	1	.111	-1	6	6	0	0.4
1946	Was-A	5	6	.455	29	9	2	0	1	91¹	105	8	67	61	17.2	6.01	56	.295	.411	2	.080	-1	-25	-27	-0	-2.7
1947	Was-A	12	16	.429	35	31	14	4	1	253	215	11	97	135	11.2	3.13	119	.234	.309	11	.133	-3	16	17	2	1.7
1948	Was-A	8	15	.348	33	27	9	2	2	188	171	12	122	72	14.2	3.83	113	.247	.363	11	.193	-0	10	11	-2	0.8
1949	Was-A	3	2	.600	10	7	3	0	0	53	42	4	21	17	11.2	3.23	132	.216	.303	1	.056	-2	6	6	1	0.5
	Bos-A	3	4	.429	18	5	1	0	4	55	58	2	35	19	15.2	4.25	102	.283	.387	2	.118	-0	-0	1	-1	0.0
	Yr	6	6	.500	28	12	4	0	4	108	100	6	56	36	13.0	3.75	115	.249	.341	5	.143	-2	5	7	0	0.5
1950	Bos-A	8	6	.571	33	15	6	0	1	129¹	145	15	82	60	15.9	5.64	87	.287	.387	6	.136	-3	-15	-11	1	-1.0
1951	Bos-A	3	0	1.000	30	1	0	0	2	59¹	53	1	32	39	12.9	3.34	134	.228	.322	2	.182	-1	5	7	0	0.7
1952	Bos-A	1	1	.500	5	1	0	0	0	8¹	11	1	11	3	28.0	11.57	34	.400	.518	0	.000	-0	-8	-8	0	-0.7
	Was-A	9	8	.529	24	21	11	0	2	160²	153	11	72	89	12.8	3.70	96	.253	.336	6	.120	-1	6	7	0	0.4
	Yr	10	9	.526	29	22	11	0	2	170	171	12	83	92	13.6	4.13	87	.263	.350	5	.096	-1	-9	-10	1	-1.0
1953	Was-A	10	12	.455	29	20	10	4	0	166¹	145	16	62	95	11.4	3.63	107	.232	.304	7	.137	-1	7	5	-0	0.4
1956	Det-A	1	1	.500	35	0	0	0	0	49²	54	2	32	28	15.8	4.17	99	.289	.395	1	.250	-0	-0	-0	0	-0.0
Total	14	78	100	.438	399	184	70	15	20	1649²	1613	101	886	815	13.8	4.15	96	.258	.353	68	.140	-14	-24	-27	-1	-2.9

YEAR TM/L	W	L	PCT	G	GS	CG	SH	SV	IP	H	HR	BB	SO	RAT	ERA	ERA+	OAV	OOB	BH	AVG	PB	PR	/A	PD	TPI

■ LEN MATARAZZO   Matarazzo, Leonard   b: 9/12/28, New Castle, Pa.   BR/TR, 6'4", 195 lbs.   Deb: 9/06/52

| 1952 Phi-A | 0 | 0 | — | 1 | 0 | 0 | 0 | 0 | 1 | 1 | 0 | 1 | 0 | 18.0 | 0.00 | — | .250 | .400 | 0 | — | 0 | 0 | 0 | 0 | 0.0 |

■ GREG MATHEWS   Mathews, Gregory Inman   b: 5/17/62, Harbor City, Cal.   BR/TL, 6'2", 180 lbs.   Deb: 6/03/86

1986 StL-N	11	8	.579	23	22	1	0	0	145¹	139	15	44	67	11.5	3.65	100	.259	.317	2	.047	-3	1	-0	-2	-0.4
1987 *StL-N	11	11	.500	32	32	2	1	0	197²	184	17	71	108	11.6	3.73	111	.249	.314	13	.191	1	8	9	-1	1.0
1988 StL-N	4	6	.400	13	13	1	0	0	68	61	4	33	31	12.7	4.24	82	.247	.340	4	.174	0	-6	-6	0	-0.5
1990 StL-N	0	5	.000	11	10	0	0	0	50²	53	2	30	18	15.1	5.33	74	.277	.381	3	.214	1	-9	-8	2	-0.4
Total 4	26	30	.464	79	77	4	1	0	461²	437	38	178	224	12.1	3.96	98	.255	.327	22	.149	0	-6	-5	-1	-0.3

■ BOBBY MATHEWS   Mathews, Robert T.   b: 11/21/1851, Baltimore, Md.   d: 4/17/1898, Baltimore, Md.   BR/TR, 5'5.5", 140 lbs.   Deb: 5/04/1871   U♦

1871 Kek-n	6	11	.353	19	19	19	1	0	169	261	5	21	17	15.0	5.17	88	.305	.322	24	.270	-3	-18	-11		-0.7
1872 Bal-n	25	18	.581	49	47	39	0	0	405¹	477	3	55		11.8	3.15	119	.257	.278	50	.226	-7	25	27		1.4
1873 Mut-n	29	23	.558	52	52	47	2	0	442²	486	5	62		11.1	2.85	123	.250	.273	43	.193	-3	37	32		2.0
1874 Mut-n	42	22	.656	65	65	62	4	0	578	647	3	39		10.7	2.30	134	.258	.270	70	.236	-3	44	50		3.8
1875 Mut-n	29	38	.433	70	70	69	2	0	626²	709	3	23		10.5	2.41	107	.259	.265	47	.175	-13	3	13		0.2
1876 NY-N	21	34	.382	56	56	55	2	0	516	693	8	24	37	12.5	2.86	75	.301	.308	40	.183	-9	-32	-41	-3	-4.6
1877 Cin-N	3	12	.200	15	15	13	0	0	129¹	208	0	17	19	15.7	4.04	66	.343	.361	10	.169	-3	-18	-20	-1	-2.0
1879 Pro-N	12	6	.667	27	25	15	1	1	189	194	4	26	90	10.5	2.29	103	.249	.273	35	.202	-0	4	1	0	0.0
1881 Pro-N	4	8	.333	14	14	10	1	0	102¹	121	2	21	28	12.5	3.17	84	.282	.315	11	.193	-2	-4	-6	-1	-0.6
Bos-N	1	0	1.000	5	1	1	0	2	23	22	0	11	5	12.9	2.35	113	.241	.323	12	.169	-1	1	1	-0	0.1
Yr	5	8	.385	19	15	11	1	2	125¹	143	2	32	33	12.6	3.02	88	.275	.317	23	.225	-3	-3	-5	-1	-0.5
1882 Bos-N	19	15	.559	34	32	31	0	0	285	278	5	22	153	9.5	2.87	99	.241	.255	38	.225	-2	0	-1	-4	-0.6
1883 Phi-a	30	13	.698	44	44	41	1	0	381	396	11	31	203	10.1	2.46	142	.251	.265	31	.186	-8	36	44	-1	3.3
1884 Phi-a	30	18	.625	49	49	48	3	0	430²	401	10	49	286	9.4	3.32	102	.233	.255	34	.185	-5	-4	4	-3	-0.2
1885 Phi-a	30	17	.638	48	48	46	2	0	422¹	394	3	57	286	9.6	2.43	137	.237	.262	30	.168	-7	38	47	-1	3.8
1886 Phi-a	13	9	.591	24	24	22	0	0	197²	226	3	53	93	12.7	3.96	88	.274	.318	21	.239	-0	-11	-10	0	-0.8
1887 Phi-a	3	4	.429	7	7	7	0	0	58	75	4	25	9	15.5	6.67	64	.302	.366	5	.200	-0	-15	-15	1	-1.0
Total 5 n	131	112	.539	255	253	236	9	0	2221²	2580	19	200	17	11.3	2.82	116	.261	.275	234	.213	-28	92	112		6.7
Total 10	166	136	.550	323	315	289	10	3	2734¹	3008	50	336	1199	11.0	3.00	100	.264	.285	267	.192	-28	-4	-2	-13	-2.6

■ CHRISTY MATHEWSON   Mathewson, Christopher "Matty" or "Big Six"   b: 8/12/1880, Factoryville, Pa.   d: 10/7/25, Saranac Lake, N.Y.   BR/TR, 6'1.5", 195 lbs.   Deb: 7/17/00   MCH

1900 NY-N	0	3	.000	6	1	1	0	0	33²	37	1	20	15	15.2	5.08	71	.278	.373	2	.182	0	-5	-5	0	-0.3
1901 NY-N	20	17	.541	40	38	36	5	0	336	288	3	97	221	10.6	2.41	137	.230	.291	28	.215	-1	34	33	6	4.0
1902 NY-N	14	17	.452	34	32	29	8	0	276²	241	3	73	159	10.5	2.11	133	.235	.291	26	.205	1	20	21	3	2.9
1903 NY-N	30	13	.698	45	42	37	3	2	366¹	321	4	100	267	10.6	2.26	148	.231	.287	28	.226	3	41	44	0	4.8
1904 NY-N	33	12	.733	48	46	33	4	1	367²	306	7	78	212	9.5	2.03	134	.226	.270	30	.226	6	29	28	5	4.4
1905 *NY-N	31	9	.775	43	37	32	8	0	339	252	4	64	206	8.4	1.27	230	.205	.245	30	.236	9	65	62	6	8.9
1906 NY-N	22	12	.647	38	35	22	6	1	266²	262	3	77	128	11.5	2.97	88	.259	.313	24	.264	7	-10	-11	4	0.0
1907 NY-N	24	12	.667	41	36	31	8	2	315	250	6	53	178	8.7	2.00	124	.212	.247	20	.187	2	17	17	1	2.2
1908 NY-N	37	11	.771	56	44	34	11	5	390²	285	5	42	259	7.6	1.43	169	.200	.225	20	.155	1	41	43	8	6.4
1909 NY-N	25	6	.806	37	33	26	8	2	275¹	192	2	36	149	7.5	1.14	224	.200	.228	25	.263	7	45	43	5	6.9
1910 NY-N	27	9	.750	38	35	27	2	0	318¹	292	5	60	184	10.0	1.89	157	.248	.286	25	.234	7	40	38	6	5.8
1911 *NY-N	26	13	.667	45	37	29	5	3	307	303	5	38	141	10.0	1.99	169	.259	.283	22	.196	0	48	47	8	5.9
1912 *NY-N	23	12	.657	43	34	27	0	4	310	311	6	34	134	10.1	2.12	159	.253	.275	29	.264	5	44	43	1	5.1
1913 *NY-N	25	11	.694	40	35	25	4	2	306	291	8	21	93	9.2	2.06	152	.252	.266	19	.184	-0	39	36	5	4.4
1914 NY-N	24	13	.649	41	35	29	5	2	312	314	16	23	80	9.8	3.00	88	.263	.278	23	.219	6	-7	-12	3	-0.4
1915 NY-N	8	14	.364	27	24	11	1	0	186	199	9	20	57	10.6	3.58	72	.277	.298	8	.157	2	-17	-21	2	-1.8
1916 NY-N	3	4	.429	12	6	4	1	2	65²	59	3	7	16	9.0	2.33	104	.243	.264	0	.000	-1	2	1	2	0.2
Cin-N	1	0	1.000	1	1	1	0	0	9	15	1	1	3	16.0	8.00	32	.366	.381	0	—	0	-5	-5	0	-0.2
Yr	4	4	.500	13	7	5	1	2	74²	74	4	8	19	9.9	3.01	81	.261	.281	4	.182	1	-3	-5	2	0.0
Total 17	373	188	.665	635	551	434	79	28	4781	4218	91	844	2502	9.6	2.13	136	.236	.272	362	.215	57	420	403	63	59.2

■ HENRY MATHEWSON   Mathewson, Henry   b: 12/24/1886, Factoryville, Pa.   d: 7/1/17, Factoryville, Pa.   6'3", 175 lbs.   Deb: 9/28/06

1906 NY-N	0	1	.000	2	1	1	0	1	10	7	0	14	2	19.8	5.40	48	.194	.431	0	.000	-0	-3	-3	0	-0.2
1907 NY-N	0	0	—	1	0	0	0	1	1	1	0	0	0	9.0	0.00	—	.250	.250	0	—	0	0	0	0	0.0
Total 2	0	1	.000	3	1	1	0	2	11	8	0	14	2	18.8	4.91	53	.200	.418	0	.000	-0	-3	-3	0	-0.2

■ CARL MATHIAS   Mathias, Carl Lynwood "Stubby"   b: 6/13/36, Bechtelsville, Pa   BB/TL, 5'11", 195 lbs.   Deb: 7/31/60

1960 Cle-A	0	1	.000	7	0	0	0	0	15¹	14	2	8	13	12.9	3.52	106	.233	.324	0	.000	-0	1	0	0	0.0
1961 Was-A	0	1	.000	4	3	0	0	0	13²	22	3	4	7	17.8	11.20	36	.361	.409	1	.200	-0	-11	-11	0	-0.9
Total 2	0	2	.000	11	3	0	0	0	29	36	5	12	20	15.2	7.14	54	.298	.366	1	.167	-0	-10	-11	0	-0.9

■ RON MATHIS   Mathis, Ronald Vance   b: 9/25/58, Kansas City, Mo.   BR/TR, 6', 175 lbs.   Deb: 4/13/85

1985 Hou-N	3	5	.375	23	8	0	0	1	70	83	7	27	34	14.3	6.04	57	.293	.357	1	.071	-1	-19	-20	0	-2.0
1987 Hou-N	0	1	.000	8	0	0	0	0	12	10	2	11	8	15.8	5.25	75	.233	.389	0	.000	-0	-2	-2	0	-0.1
Total 2	3	6	.333	31	8	0	0	1	82	93	9	38	42	14.5	5.93	60	.285	.362	1	.063	-1	-21	-22	0	-2.1

■ JON MATLACK   Matlack, Jonathan Trumpbour   b: 1/19/50, West Chester, Pa.   BL/TL, 6'3", 205 lbs.   Deb: 7/11/71

1971 NY-N	0	3	.000	7	6	0	0	0	37	31	2	15	24	11.2	4.14	82	.228	.305	3	.273	1	-3	-3	-1	-0.2
1972 NY-N	15	10	.600	34	32	8	4	0	244	215	14	71	169	10.6	2.32	145	.234	.291	10	.128	1	31	28	-0	3.2
1973 *NY-N	14	16	.467	34	34	14	3	0	242	210	16	99	205	11.6	3.20	113	.236	.314	9	.138	2	12	11	0	1.4
1974 NY-N	13	15	.464	34	34	14	7	0	265¹	221	8	76	195	10.2	2.41	148	.226	.285	8	.101	-4	36	34	-1	3.2
1975 NY-N	16	12	.571	33	32	8	3	0	228²	224	15	58	154	11.1	3.38	102	.254	.300	7	.100	0	6	2	-2	0.0
1976 NY-N	17	10	.630	35	35	16	6	0	262	236	18	57	153	10.2	2.95	112	.242	.286	17	.193	4	16	10	-1	1.3
1977 NY-N	7	15	.318	26	26	5	3	0	169	175	19	43	123	11.7	4.21	89	.273	.321	3	.060	-2	-9	-9	0	-1.0
1978 Tex-A	15	13	.536	35	33	18	2	1	270	252	14	51	157	10.2	2.27	165	.245	.284	0	—	0	45	44	5	5.0
1979 Tex-A	5	4	.556	13	13	2	0	0	85	98	9	15	35	12.1	4.13	100	.293	.325	0	—	0	1	0	0	0.1
1980 Tex-A	10	10	.500	35	34	8	1	1	234²	265	17	48	142	12.0	3.68	106	.287	.323	0	—	0	9	6	-3	0.3
1981 Tex-A	4	7	.364	17	16	1	1	0	104¹	101	8	41	63	12.3	4.14	84	.258	.330	0	—	0	-6	-8	0	-0.7
1982 Tex-A	7	7	.500	33	14	1	0	1	147²	158	14	37	78	12.0	3.53	109	.275	.321	0	—	0	9	6	0	0.6
1983 Tex-A	2	4	.333	25	14	2	0	0	73¹	90	7	27	38	14.7	4.66	86	.307	.372	0	—	0	-5	-5	1	-0.4
Total 13	125	126	.498	361	318	97	30	3	2363	2276	161	638	1516	11.2	3.18	114	.254	.305	57	.129	2	145	115	-5	12.8

■ AL MATTERN   Mattern, Alonzo Albert   b: 6/16/1883, W.Rush, N.Y.   d: 11/6/58, West Rush, N.Y.   BL/TR, 5'10", 165 lbs.   Deb: 9/16/08

1908 Bos-N	1	2	.333	5	3	1	0	0	30¹	30	0	6	8	10.7	2.08	116	.265	.303	1	.125	-0	1	1	-0	0.1
1909 Bos-N	15	21	.417	47	32	24	2	3	316¹	322	4	108	98	12.3	2.85	99	.268	.330	17	.168	-1	-9	-1	3	0.1
1910 Bos-N	16	19	.457	51	37	17	6	1	305	288	5	121	94	12.2	2.98	112	.257	.332	16	.163	-5	2	12	1	1.0
1911 Bos-N	4	15	.211	33	21	11	0	0	186¹	228	13	63	51	14.4	4.97	77	.320	.376	11	.175	-2	-33	-24	2	-2.1
1912 Bos-N	0	1	.000	2	1	0	0	0	6¹	10	0	1	3	15.6	7.11	50	.294	.314	0	.000	-0	-3	-2	0	-0.1
Total 5	36	58	.383	138	94	53	9	4	844¹	878	22	299	254	12.7	3.37	95	.276	.340	45	.165	-9	-41	-15	6	-1.0

■ C. V. MATTERSON   Matterson, C. V.   b: Ohio   Deb: 6/13/1884   ♦

| 1884 StL-U | 1 | 0 | 1.000 | 1 | 1 | 0 | 0 | 0 | 6 | 9 | 1 | 3 | 3 | 18.0 | 9.00 | 33 | .325 | .391 | 0 | .000 | -1 | -4 | -4 | -0 | -0.3 |

YEAR	TM/L	W	L	PCT	G	GS	CG	SH	SV	IP	H	HR	BB	SO	RAT	ERA	ERA+	OAV	OOB	BH	AVG	PB	PR	/A	PD	TPI

■ EDDIE MATTESON   Matteson, Henry Edson "Matty"   b: 9/7/1884, Guys Mills, Pa.   d: 9/1/43, Westfield, N.Y.   BR/TR, 5'10.5", 160 lbs.   Deb: 5/30/14

1914	Phi-N	3	2	.600	15	3	2	0	0	58	58	1	23	28	12.7	3.10	95	.278	.352	4	.182	-0	-2	-1	-2	-0.2
1918	Was-A	5	3	.625	14	6	2	0	0	67²	57	2	15	17	9.7	1.73	158	.238	.286	2	.105	-2	8	8	-1	0.6
Total	2	8	5	.615	29	9	4	0	0	125²	115	3	38	45	11.1	2.36	120	.257	.318	6	.146	-2	6	6	-2	0.4

■ JOE MATTHEWS   Matthews, John Joseph "Lefty"   b: 9/29/1898, Baltimore, Md.   d: 2/8/68, Hagerstown, Md.   BB/TL, 6', 170 lbs.   Deb: 9/18/22

| 1922 | Bos-N | 0 | 1 | .000 | 3 | 1 | 0 | 0 | 0 | 10 | 5 | 1 | 6 | 0 | 10.8 | 3.60 | 111 | .143 | .286 | 0 | .000 | -0 | 1 | 0 | -0 | 0.0 |

■ WILLIAM MATTHEWS   Matthews, William Calvin   b: 1/12/1878, Mahanoy City, Pa.   d: 1/23/46, Mahanoy City, Pa.   TR ,   Deb: 8/28/09

| 1909 | Bos-A | 0 | 0 | — | 5 | 1 | 0 | 0 | 0 | 16² | 16 | 1 | 10 | 6 | 14.0 | 3.24 | 77 | .271 | .377 | 0 | .000 | -1 | -1 | -1 | -0 | -0.2 |

■ DALE MATTHEWSON   Matthewson, Dale Wesley   b: 5/15/23, Catasaqua, Pa.   d: 2/20/84, Blairsville, Ga.   BR/TR, 5'11.5", 145 lbs.   Deb: 7/03/43

1943	Phi-N	0	3	.000	11	1	0	0	0	26	26	1	8	8	11.8	4.85	70	.271	.327	0	.000	-0	-4	-4	-0	-0.4
1944	Phi-N	0	0	—	17	1	0	0	0	32	27	1	16	8	12.1	3.94	92	.237	.331	1	.333	0	-1	-1	-0	0.0
Total	2	0	3	.000	28	2	0	0	0	58	53	2	24	16	11.9	4.34	81	.252	.329	1	.200	-0	-5	-5	-0	-0.4

■ MIKE MATTIMORE   Mattimore, Michael Joseph   b: 1859, Renovo, Pa.   d: 4/28/31, Butte, Mont.   BL/TL, 5'8.5", 160 lbs.   Deb: 5/03/1887 ♦

1887	NY-N	3	3	.500	7	7	6	1	0	57¹	47	2	28	12	11.8	2.35	159	.217	.307	8	.250	-0	11	9	-1	0.7
1888	Phi-a	15	10	.600	26	24	24	4	0	221	221	6	65	80	11.6	3.38	88	.251	.302	38	.268	7	-8	-10	4	0.4
1889	Phi-a	2	1	.667	5	1	1	0	1	31	43	0	13	6	16.3	5.81	65	.319	.379	17	.233	1	-7	-7	-0	-0.5
	KC-a	0	0	—	1	0	0	0	0	3	3	1	2	1	15.0	3.00	139	.250	.360	12	.160	-0	0	0	0	0.0
	Yr	2	1	.667	6	1	1	0	1	34	46	1	15	7	16.1	5.56	69	.313	.377	12	.081	-0	-6	-7	-0	-0.5
1890	Bro-a	6	13	.316	19	19	19	0	0	178¹	201	3	76	33	14.0	4.54	86	.276	.344	17	.132	-3	-13	-13	0	-1.3
Total	4	26	27	.491	58	51	50	5	1	490²	515	12	184	132	12.8	3.83	90	.261	.324	92	.204	4	-17	-20	3	-0.7

■ EARL MATTINGLY   Mattingly, Laurence Earl   b: 11/4/04, Newport, Md.   BR/TR, 5'10.5", 164 lbs.   Deb: 4/15/31

| 1931 | Bro-N | 0 | 1 | .000 | 8 | 0 | 0 | 0 | 0 | 14¹ | 15 | 0 | 10 | 6 | 17.0 | 2.51 | 152 | .268 | .397 | 0 | .000 | -0 | 2 | 2 | 1 | 0.2 |

■ RICK MATULA   Matula, Richard Carlton   b: 11/22/53, Wharton, Tex.   BR/TR, 6', 190 lbs.   Deb: 4/08/79

1979	Atl-N	8	10	.444	28	28	1	0	0	171¹	193	14	64	67	13.7	4.15	98	.286	.350	5	.094	-3	-8	-2	1	-0.3
1980	Atl-N	11	13	.458	33	30	3	1	0	176²	195	17	60	62	13.0	4.58	82	.286	.343	6	.105	-3	-19	-17	2	-1.7
1981	Atl-N	0	0	—	5	0	0	0	0	7	8	1	2	0	12.9	6.43	56	.286	.333	0	.000	-0	-2	-2	0	-0.1
Total	3	19	23	.452	66	58	4	1	0	355	396	32	126	129	13.3	4.41	88	.286	.347	11	.099	-6	-30	-21	2	-2.1

■ HARRY MATUZAK   Matuzak, Harry George "Matty"   b: 1/27/10, Omer, Mich.   d: 11/16/78, Fair Hope, Ala.   BR/TR, 5'11.5", 185 lbs.   Deb: 4/19/34

1934	Phi-A	0	3	.000	11	0	0	0	0	24	28	2	10	9	14.6	4.88	90	.292	.364	1	.167	0	-1	-1	0	0.0
1936	Phi-A	0	1	.000	6	1	0	0	0	15	21	0	4	8	15.0	7.20	71	.318	.357	0	.000	-0	-4	-3	0	-0.2
Total	2	0	4	.000	17	1	0	0	0	39	49	2	14	17	14.8	5.77	81	.302	.362	1	.111	-0	-5	-5	0	-0.2

■ HAL MAUCK   Mauck, Alfred Maris   b: 3/6/1869, Princeton, Ind.   d: 4/27/21, Princeton, Ind.   BR/TR, 5'11", 185 lbs.   Deb: 4/29/1893

| 1893 | Chi-N | 8 | 10 | .444 | 23 | 18 | 12 | 1 | 0 | 143 | 168 | 2 | 60 | 23 | 14.3 | 4.41 | 105 | .284 | .350 | 9 | .148 | -5 | 4 | 3 | -0 | -0.1 |

■ AL MAUL   Maul, Albert Joseph "Smiling Al"   b: 10/9/1865, Philadelphia, Pa.   d: 5/3/58, Philadelphia, Pa.   BR/TR, 6', 175 lbs.   Deb: 6/20/1884 ♦

1884	Phi-U	0	1	.000	1	1	1	0	0	8	10	0	1	7	12.4	4.50	64	.287	.306	0	.000	-1	-1	-1	-0	-0.1
1887	Phi-N	4	2	.667	7	5	4	0	0	50¹	72	2	15	18	15.6	5.54	76	.327	.369	17	.304	3	-8	-7	0	-0.5
1888	Pit-N	0	2	.000	3	1	1	0	0	17	26	0	5	12	16.4	6.35	42	.339	.379	54	.208	0	-7	-7	-0	-0.5
1889	Pit-N	1	4	.200	6	4	4	0	0	42	64	3	28	11	19.7	9.86	38	.339	.425	71	.276	2	-27	-28	1	-2.0
1890	Pit-P	16	12	.571	30	28	26	2	0	246²	258	13	104	81	13.2	3.79	103	.258	.327	42	.259	6	12	3	4	1.2
1891	Pit-N	1	2	.333	8	3	3	0	1	39	44	0	16	13	13.8	2.31	142	.304	.340	28	.188	1	5	4	0	0.4
1893	Was-N	12	21	.364	37	33	29	1	0	297	355	17	144	72	15.1	5.30	87	.288	.362	34	.254	10	-21	-22	0	-0.8
1894	Was-N	11	15	.423	28	26	21	0	0	201²	272	12	73	34	15.4	5.98	88	.319	.373	30	.242	1	-15	-16	2	-0.7
1895	Was-N	10	5	.667	16	16	14	0	0	135²	136	5	37	34	11.5	2.45	196	.257	.305	18	.250	1	35	35	1	3.4
1896	Was-N	5	2	.714	8	8	7	0	0	62	75	0	20	18	13.8	3.63	121	.296	.348	8	.286	2	5	5	-1	0.5
1897	Was-N	0	1	.000	1	1	0	0	0	2	4	0	1	0	22.5	9.00	48	.411	.465	0	.000	-0	-1	-1	0	-0.1
	Bal-N	0	0	—	2	2	0	0	0	7²	9	0	8	2	20.0	7.04	59	.290	.436	1	.333	0	-2	-2	-0	-0.1
	Yr	0	1	.000	3	3	0	0	0	9²	13	0	9	2	20.5	7.45	56	.319	.442	0	.000	-0	-3	-3	-0	-0.1
1898	Bal-N	20	7	.741	28	28	26	1	0	239²	207	3	49	31	9.6	2.10	170	.231	.271	19	.204	3	40	39	-4	4.0
1899	Bro-N	2	0	1.000	4	4	2	0	0	26	35	1	6	2	14.2	4.50	87	.321	.357	3	.273	0	-2	-2	0	0.0
1900	Phi-N	2	3	.400	5	4	3	0	0	38	53	2	3	6	13.3	6.16	59	.329	.341	3	.200	0	-10	-11	0	-0.8
1901	NY-N	0	3	.000	3	3	2	0	0	19	39	1	8	5	22.7	11.37	29	.417	.468	3	.375	1	-17	-17	1	-1.1
Total	15	84	80	.512	187	167	143	4	1	1431²	1659	59	518	346	13.7	4.43	96	.284	.342	331	.241	30	-15	-28	6	2.9

■ ERNIE MAUN   Maun, Ernest Gerald   b: 2/3/01, Clearwater, Kan.   d: 1/1/87, Corpus Christi, Tex.   BR/TR, 6', 165 lbs.   Deb: 5/16/24

1924	NY-N	1	1	.500	22	0	0	0	1	35	46	2	10	5	14.7	5.91	62	.326	.375	2	.667	1	-8	-9	-0	-0.7
1926	Phi-N	1	4	.200	14	5	0	0	0	37²	57	4	18	9	18.2	6.45	64	.339	.406	3	.250	-0	-11	-10	0	-0.8
Total	2	2	5	.286	36	5	0	0	1	72²	103	6	28	14	16.5	6.19	63	.333	.392	5	.333	1	-19	-18	-0	-1.5

■ DICK MAUNEY   Mauney, Richard   b: 1/26/20, Concord, N.C.   d: 2/6/70, Albemarle, N.C.   BR/TR, 5'11.5", 164 lbs.   Deb: 6/13/45

1945	Phi-N	6	10	.375	20	16	6	2	1	122²	127	7	27	35	11.4	3.08	124	.268	.310	6	.146	-0	10	10	1	1.1
1946	Phi-N	6	4	.600	24	7	3	1	2	90	98	4	18	31	11.9	2.70	127	.279	.320	4	.167	-1	7	7	0	0.8
1947	Phi-N	0	0	—	9	1	0	0	1	16¹	15	1	7	6	12.7	3.86	104	.288	.383	0	.000	-0	0	0	1	0.1
Total	3	12	14	.462	53	24	9	3	4	229	240	12	52	72	11.7	2.99	123	.274	.319	10	.149	-1	17	18	2	2.0

■ HARRY MAUPIN   Maupin, Henry Carr   b: 7/11/1872, Wellesville, Mo.   d: 8/23/52,   Deb: 10/05/1898

1898	StL-N	0	2	.000	2	2	2	0	0	18	22	0	3	3	12.5	5.50	69	.299	.326	3	.429	1	-4	-3	-1	-0.2
1899	Cle-N	0	3	.000	5	3	2	0	0	25	55	0	7	3	22.3	12.60	29	.436	.466	0	.000	-2	-24	-25	-1	-1.9
Total	2	0	5	.000	7	5	4	0	0	43	77	0	10	6	18.2	9.63	39	.385	.415	3	.176	-1	-28	-28	-1	-2.1

■ RALPH MAURIELLO   Mauriello, Ralph "Tami"   b: 8/25/34, Brooklyn, N.Y.   BR/TR, 6'3", 195 lbs.   Deb: 9/13/58

| 1958 | LA-N | 1 | 1 | .500 | 3 | 2 | 0 | 0 | 0 | 11² | 10 | 1 | 8 | 11 | 13.9 | 4.63 | 89 | .238 | .360 | 0 | .000 | -1 | -1 | -1 | -0 | 0.0 |

■ LARRY MAXIE   Maxie, Larry Hans   b: 10/10/40, Upland, Cal.   BR/TR, 6'4", 220 lbs.   Deb: 8/30/69

| 1969 | Atl-N | 0 | 0 | — | 2 | 0 | 0 | 0 | 0 | 3 | 1 | 0 | 1 | 1 | 9.0 | 3.00 | 120 | .111 | .273 | 0 | — | 0 | 0 | 0 | 0 | 0.1 |

■ BERT MAXWELL   Maxwell, James Albert   b: 10/17/1886, Texarkana, Ark.   d: 12/10/61, Brady, Tex.   BB/TR, 6', 180 lbs.   Deb: 9/12/06

1906	Pit-N	0	1	.000	1	1	0	0	0	8	8	0	2	1	11.3	5.63	48	.286	.333	0	.000	-0	-3	-3	0	-0.2
1908	Phi-A	0	0	—	4	0	0	0	0	13	23	0	9	7	23.5	11.08	33	.348	.442	0	.000	-1	-13	-12	0	-1.1
1911	NY-N	1	2	.333	4	3	3	0	0	31	37	0	7	8	13.4	2.90	116	.311	.359	1	.111	-0	2	2	1	0.2
1914	Bro-F	3	4	.429	12	8	6	1	1	71¹	76	0	24	19	12.7	3.28	97	.276	.337	2	.087	-2	-1	-1	1	-0.1
Total	4	4	7	.364	21	12	9	1	1	123¹	144	0	42	35	13.9	4.16	76	.295	.357	3	.075	-3	-14	-14	2	-1.2

■ JAKIE MAY   May, Frank Spruiell   b: 11/25/1895, Youngville, N.C.   d: 6/3/70, Wendell, N.C.   BR/TL, 5'8", 178 lbs.   Deb: 6/26/17

1917	StL-N	0	0	—	15	1	0	0	0	29¹	29	0	11	18	13.2	3.38	80	.302	.391	0	.000	-1	-2	-2	1	-0.1
1918	StL-N	5	6	.455	29	16	6	0	0	152²	149	2	69	61	13.6	3.83	71	.264	.358	3	.067	-1	-18	-19	-3	-2.3
1919	StL-N	3	12	.200	28	19	8	1	0	125²	99	1	87	58	14.3	3.22	87	.230	.377	6	.162	-1	-4	-6	-1	-0.9
1920	StL-N	1	4	.200	16	5	3	0	0	70²	65	0	37	33	13.9	3.06	98	.251	.360	5	.227	1	1	-1	-2	-0.1

YEAR TM/L	W	L	PCT	G	GS	CG	SH	SV	IP	H	HR	BB	SO	RAT	ERA	ERA+	OAV	OOB	BH	AVG	PB	PR	/A	PD	TPI
1921 StL-N	1	3	.250	5	5	1	0	0	21	29	0	12	5	17.6	4.71	78	.333	.414	2	.333	1	-2	-2	-1	-0.1
1924 Cin-N	3	3	.500	38	4	2	0	6	99	104	2	29	59	12.6	3.00	126	.276	.337	3	.111	-2	10	8	-1	0.6
1925 Cin-N	8	9	.471	36	12	7	1	2	137²	146	3	45	74	13.0	3.87	106	.272	.337	8	.186	0	6	4	-0	0.3
1926 Cin-N	13	9	.591	45	15	9	1	3	167²	175	4	44	103	12.1	3.22	115	.276	.329	7	.146	-1	11	9	-2	0.5
1927 Cin-N	15	12	.556	44	28	17	2	1	235²	242	4	70	121	12.4	3.51	108	.274	.337	14	.184	0	11	7	-0	0.7
1928 Cin-N	3	5	.375	21	11	1	1	1	79¹	99	1	35	39	15.3	4.42	89	.315	.386	8	.296	1	-4	-4	-1	-0.3
1929 Cin-N	10	14	.417	41	24	10	0	3	199	219	7	75	92	13.5	4.61	99	.285	.352	13	.203	-1	2	-1	-1	-0.2
1930 Cin-N	3	11	.214	26	18	5	1	0	112¹	147	6	41	44	15.5	5.77	84	.320	.383	5	.128	-1	-10	-12	0	-1.0
1931 Chi-N	5	5	.500	31	4	1	0	2	79	81	2	43	38	14.5	3.87	100	.275	.372	5	.227	1	-0	-0	0	0.1
1932 *Chi-N	2	2	.500	35	0	0	0	1	53²	61	3	19	20	13.8	4.36	86	.281	.345	1	.125	-0	-3	-4	-0	-0.3
Total 14	72	95	.431	410	162	70	7	19	1562¹	1645	35	617	765	13.5	3.88	97	.278	.355	80	.171	-4	-3	-23	-10	-3.1

■ RUDY MAY   May, Rudolph b: 7/18/44, Coffeyville, Kan.   BL/TL, 6'2", 205 lbs.   Deb: 4/18/65

YEAR TM/L	W	L	PCT	G	GS	CG	SH	SV	IP	H	HR	BB	SO	RAT	ERA	ERA+	OAV	OOB	BH	AVG	PB	PR	/A	PD	TPI
1965 Cal-A	4	9	.308	30	19	2	1	0	124	111	7	78	76	14.0	3.92	87	.245	.361	6	.200	3	-6	-7	-2	-0.5
1969 Cal-A	10	13	.435	43	25	4	0	2	180¹	142	20	66	133	10.5	3.44	101	.220	.296	4	.082	-2	4	1	-1	-0.1
1970 Cal-A	7	13	.350	38	34	2	2	0	208²	190	20	81	164	11.8	4.01	90	.245	.319	6	.087	-2	-7	-9	-0	-1.1
1971 Cal-A	11	12	.478	32	31	7	2	0	208¹	160	12	87	156	10.8	3.02	107	.213	.297	10	.147	0	10	5	-1	0.4
1972 Cal-A	12	11	.522	35	30	10	3	1	205¹	162	15	82	169	10.7	2.94	99	.215	.293	7	.113	-1	3	-1	-2	-0.2
1973 Cal-A	7	17	.292	34	28	10	4	0	185	177	20	80	134	12.6	4.38	81	.254	.333	0	—	0	-12	-17	2	-1.4
1974 Cal-A	0	1	.000	18	3	0	0	2	27	29	2	10	12	13.3	7.00	49	.274	.342	0	—	0	-10	-11	1	-0.8
NY-A	8	4	.667	17	15	8	2	0	114¹	75	5	48	90	10.0	2.28	153	.188	.282	0	—	0	17	15	-2	1.5
Yr	8	5	.615	35	18	8	2	2	141¹	104	7	58	102	10.6	3.18	109	.204	.291	0	—	0	7	5	-1	0.7
1975 NY-A	14	12	.538	32	31	13	1	0	212	179	9	99	145	11.9	3.06	119	.231	.320	0	—	0	17	14	-2	1.3
1976 NY-A	4	3	.571	11	11	2	1	0	68	49	5	28	38	10.3	3.57	96	.206	.292	0	—	0	-0	-1	0	0.0
Bal-A	11	7	.611	24	21	5	1	0	152¹	156	11	42	71	11.7	3.78	87	.267	.316	0	—	0	-4	-9	-1	-0.9
Yr	15	10	.600	35	32	7	2	0	220¹	205	16	70	109	11.2	3.72	89	.249	.308	0	—	0	-5	-10	-1	-0.9
1977 Bal-A	18	14	.563	37	37	11	4	0	251²	243	25	78	105	11.7	3.61	105	.255	.315	0	—	0	13	5	-3	0.2
1978 Mon-N	8	10	.444	27	23	4	1	0	144	141	15	42	87	11.8	3.88	91	.255	.315	6	.143	0	-5	-6	-2	-0.7
1979 Mon-N	10	3	.769	33	7	2	1	0	93²	88	4	31	67	11.8	2.31	159	.255	.324	3	.143	-0	15	14	0	1.5
1980 *NY-A	15	5	.750	41	17	3	1	3	175¹	144	14	39	133	**9.4**	**2.46**	**159**	.224	**.268**	0	—	0	31	28	-0	2.9
1981 *NY-A	6	11	.353	27	22	4	0	1	147²	137	10	41	79	11.0	4.14	86	.246	.300	0	—	0	-8	-9	1	-0.7
1982 NY-A	6	6	.500	41	6	0	0	3	106	109	4	14	85	10.5	2.89	138	.267	.292	0	—	0	14	13	1	1.4
1983 NY-A	1	5	.167	15	0	0	0	0	18¹	22	1	12	16	17.2	6.87	57	.293	.398	0	—	0	-6	-6	0	-0.5
Total 16	152	156	.494	535	360	87	24	12	2622	2314	199	958	1760	11.4	3.46	102	.238	.310	42	.123	-2	64	20	-10	2.1

■ SCOTT MAY   May, Scott Francis b: 11/11/61, West Bend, Wis.   BR/TR, 6'1", 185 lbs.   Deb: 9/02/88

YEAR TM/L	W	L	PCT	G	GS	CG	SH	SV	IP	H	HR	BB	SO	RAT	ERA	ERA+	OAV	OOB	BH	AVG	PB	PR	/A	PD	TPI
1988 Tex-A	0	0	—	3	1	0	0	0	7¹	8	3	4	4	14.7	8.59	48	.296	.387	0	—	0	-4	-4	0	-0.3

■ BUCKSHOT MAY   May, William Herbert b: 12/13/1899, Bakersfield, Cal.   d: 3/15/84, Bakersfield, Cal.   BR/TR, 6'2", 169 lbs.   Deb: 5/09/24

YEAR TM/L	W	L	PCT	G	GS	CG	SH	SV	IP	H	HR	BB	SO	RAT	ERA	ERA+	OAV	OOB	BH	AVG	PB	PR	/A	PD	TPI
1924 Pit-N	0	0	—	1	0	0	0	0	1	2	0	0	1	18.0	0.00	—	.500	.500	0	—	0	0	0	0	0.0

■ ED MAYER   Mayer, Edwin David b: 11/30/31, San Francisco, Cal   BL/TL, 6'2", 185 lbs.   Deb: 9/15/57

YEAR TM/L	W	L	PCT	G	GS	CG	SH	SV	IP	H	HR	BB	SO	RAT	ERA	ERA+	OAV	OOB	BH	AVG	PB	PR	/A	PD	TPI
1957 Chi-N	0	0	—	3	1	0	0	0	7²	8	2	2	3	12.9	5.87	66	.258	.324	1	.500	0	-2	-2	0	0.0
1958 Chi-N	2	2	.500	19	0	0	0	1	23²	15	0	16	14	12.9	3.80	103	.190	.347	1	.200	-0	0	0	-0	0.0
Total 2	2	2	.500	22	1	0	0	1	31¹	23	2	18	17	12.9	4.31	91	.209	.341	2	.286	0	-1	-1	0	0.0

■ ERSKINE MAYER   Mayer, Erskine John (b: James Erskine) b: 1/16/1889, Atlanta, Ga.   d: 3/10/57, Los Angeles, Cal.   BR/TR, 6', 168 lbs.   Deb: 9/04/12

YEAR TM/L	W	L	PCT	G	GS	CG	SH	SV	IP	H	HR	BB	SO	RAT	ERA	ERA+	OAV	OOB	BH	AVG	PB	PR	/A	PD	TPI
1912 Phi-N	0	1	.000	7	1	0	0	0	21¹	27	1	7	5	14.8	6.33	57	.310	.368	0	.000	-0	-7	-6	0	-0.5
1913 Phi-N	9	9	.500	39	20	7	2	1	170²	172	6	46	51	12.0	3.11	107	.272	.330	6	.120	-2	2	4	1	0.3
1914 Phi-N	21	19	.525	48	39	24	4	2	321	308	8	91	114	11.6	2.58	114	.256	.315	21	.194	2	8	13	5	2.3
1915 *Phi-N	21	15	.583	43	33	20	2	2	274²	240	9	59	114	10.3	2.36	116	.243	.295	21	.239	5	12	12	1	2.0
1916 Phi-N	7	7	.500	28	16	7	2	0	140	148	7	33	62	11.9	3.15	84	.281	.328	5	.132	-1	-8	-8	3	-0.5
1917 Phi-N	11	6	.647	28	18	11	1	0	160	160	6	33	64	11.1	2.76	102	.268	.310	0	.196	-0	-1	1	-0	0.1
1918 Phi-N	7	4	.636	13	13	7	0	0	104	108	2	26	16	11.9	3.12	96	.276	.328	8	.216	1	-4	-1	0	0.0
Pit-N	9	3	.750	15	14	11	1	0	123¹	122	1	27	25	11.2	2.26	127	.268	.314	7	.167	2	7	8	-2	1.0
Yr	16	7	.696	28	27	18	1	0	227¹	230	3	53	41	11.4	2.65	110	.270	.316	6	.076	2	3	7	-1	1.0
1919 Pit-N	5	3	.625	18	10	6	0	1	88¹	100	2	12	20	11.6	4.48	67	.292	.294	2	.207	-0	-15	-14	-1	-1.3
*Chi-A	1	3	.250	6	2	0	0	0	23²	30	1	11	9	15.6	8.37	38	.316	.387	0	.000	-1	-14	-14	-0	-1.3
Total 8	91	70	.565	245	166	93	12	6	1427	1415	43	345	482	11.4	2.96	99	.264	.315	84	.185	6	-21	-5	8	1.9

■ SAM MAYER   Mayer, Samuel Frankel (b: Samuel Frankel Erskine) b: 2/28/1893, Atlanta, Ga.   d: 7/1/62, Atlanta, Ga.   BR/TL, 5'10", 164 lbs.   Deb: 9/14/15 ♦

YEAR TM/L	W	L	PCT	G	GS	CG	SH	SV	IP	H	HR	BB	SO	RAT	ERA	ERA+	OAV	OOB	BH	AVG	PB	PR	/A	PD	TPI
1915 Was-A	0	0	—	1	0	0	0	0	0	0	0	2	0	—	—	—	—	1.000	7	.241	0	0	0	0	0.0

■ AL MAYS   Mays, Albert C. b: 5/17/1865, Canal Dover, Ohio   d: 5/7/05, Parkersburg, W.Va.   BR ,   Deb: 5/10/1885

YEAR TM/L	W	L	PCT	G	GS	CG	SH	SV	IP	H	HR	BB	SO	RAT	ERA	ERA+	OAV	OOB	BH	AVG	PB	PR	/A	PD	TPI
1885 Lou-a	6	11	.353	17	17	17	0	0	150	129	3	43	61	10.3	2.76	117	.222	.276	13	.213	0	8	8	0	0.7
1886 NY-a	11	28	.282	41	41	39	1	0	350	330	7	140	163	12.1	3.39	101	.238	.307	16	.119	-10	2	1	-0	-0.7
1887 NY-a	17	34	.333	52	52	50	0	0	441¹	551	11	136	124	14.0	4.73	90	.295	.343	45	.204	-1	-21	-24	6	-1.4
1888 Bro-a	9	9	.500	18	18	17	1	0	160¹	150	1	32	67	10.2	2.80	107	.238	.275	5	.079	-4	5	3	2	0.1
1889 Col-a	10	7	.588	21	19	13	1	0	140	167	4	56	52	14.3	4.82	75	.287	.350	7	.130	-1	-15	-19	1	-1.5
1890 Col-a	0	1	.000	1	1	1	0	0	9	14	0	8	2	22.0	8.00	45	.344	.452	0	.000	-0	-4	-4	0	-0.3
Total 6	53	90	.371	150	148	137	3	0	1251	1341	26	415	469	12.6	3.91	94	.263	.319	86	.160	-16	-25	-35	8	-3.1

■ CARL MAYS   Mays, Carl William "Sub" b: 11/12/1891, Liberty, Ky.   d: 4/4/71, ElCajon, Cal.   BL/TR, 5'11.5", 195 lbs.   Deb: 4/15/15

YEAR TM/L	W	L	PCT	G	GS	CG	SH	SV	IP	H	HR	BB	SO	RAT	ERA	ERA+	OAV	OOB	BH	AVG	PB	PR	/A	PD	TPI
1915 Bos-A	6	5	.545	38	6	2	0	7	131²	119	0	21	65	9.9	2.60	107	.244	.282	9	.237	2	5	3	1	0.6
1916 *Bos-A	18	13	.581	44	24	14	2	3	245	208	3	74	76	10.7	2.39	116	.234	.299	18	.234	7	12	10	10	3.1
1917 Bos-A	22	9	.710	35	33	27	2	0	289	230	1	74	91	9.9	1.74	148	.221	.282	27	.252	6	30	27	8	5.0
1918 *Bos-A	21	13	.618	35	33	**30**	**8**	0	293¹	230	2	81	114	9.9	2.21	121	.221	.284	30	.288	9	19	15	9	4.0
1919 Bos-A	5	11	.313	21	16	14	2	2	146	131	3	40	53	10.8	2.47	123	.247	.306	8	.151	-2	12	9	3	1.0
NY-A	9	3	.750	13	13	12	1	0	120	96	2	37	54	10.4	1.65	193	.216	.283	14	.311	3	21	21	1	2.9
Yr	14	14	.500	34	29	26	3	2	266	227	5	77	107	10.5	2.10	148	.231	.291	4	.041	1	33	30	4	3.9
1920 NY-A	26	11	.703	45	37	26	**6**	2	312	310	13	84	92	11.6	3.06	125	.263	.316	26	.239	2	26	26	7	3.5
1921 *NY-A	**27**	9	**.750**	**49**	38	30	1	7	**336²**	332	11	76	70	11.1	3.05	139	.257	.303	49	.343	12	46	44	5	5.9
1922 *NY-A	12	14	.462	34	29	21	1	2	240	257	12	50	41	11.8	3.60	111	.285	.327	23	.250	1	12	11	7	1.8
1923 NY-A	5	2	.714	23	7	2	0	0	81¹	119	8	32	16	17.2	6.20	64	.357	.420	4	.148	1	-20	-20	3	-1.5
1924 Cin-N	20	9	.690	37	27	15	2	0	226	238	3	36	63	11.1	3.15	120	.270	.302	24	.289	7	18	16	8	3.2
1925 Cin-N	3	5	.375	12	5	3	0	2	51²	60	0	13	10	13.1	3.31	124	.294	.342	4	.250	1	6	5	1	0.6
1926 Cin-N	19	12	.613	39	33	**24**	3	1	281	286	3	53	58	11.0	3.14	118	.269	.306	22	.224	2	21	17	11	3.1
1927 Cin-N	3	7	.300	14	9	6	0	0	82	89	1	10	17	11.0	3.51	108	.276	.300	13	.406	5	4	2	4	1.2
1928 Cin-N	4	1	.800	14	7	4	1	0	62²	67	3	22	10	12.8	3.88	102	.275	.335	8	.296	1	1	0	0	0.2
1929 NY-N	7	2	.778	37	8	1	0	4	123	140	8	31	32	12.7	4.32	106	.287	.333	12	.353	4	5	4	2	0.9
Total 15	207	126	.622	490	325	231	29	31	3021¹	2912	73	734	862	11.1	2.92	119	.257	.307	291	.268	62	217	189	78	35.5

■ JACK McADAMS   McAdams, George D. b: 12/17/1886, Benton, Ark.   d: 5/21/37, San Francisco, Cal   BR/TR, 6'1.5", 170 lbs.   Deb: 7/22/11

YEAR TM/L	W	L	PCT	G	GS	CG	SH	SV	IP	H	HR	BB	SO	RAT	ERA	ERA+	OAV	OOB	BH	AVG	PB	PR	/A	PD	TPI
1911 StL-N	0	0	—	6	0	0	0	0	9²	7	0	5	4	13.0	3.72	91	.226	.368	0	.000	-0	-0	-0	0	0.0

YEAR	TM/L	W	L	PCT	G	GS	CG	SH	SV	IP	H	HR	BB	SO	RAT	ERA	ERA+	OAV	OOB	BH	AVG	PB	PR	/A	PD	TPI

■ BILL McAFEE
McAfee, William Fort b: 9/7/07, Smithville, Ga. d: 7/8/58, Culpepper, Va. BR/TR, 6'2", 186 lbs. Deb: 5/12/30

YEAR	TM/L	W	L	PCT	G	GS	CG	SH	SV	IP	H	HR	BB	SO	RAT	ERA	ERA+	OAV	OOB	BH	AVG	PB	PR	/A	PD	TPI
1930	Chi-N	0	0	—	2	0	0	0	0	1	3	0	2	0	45.0	0.00	—	.375	.500	1	1	0	1	1	0	0.0
1931	Bos-N	0	1	.000	18	1	0	0	0	29²	39	2	10	9	14.9	6.37	59	.333	.386	0	.000	-0	-8	-9	0	-0.7
1932	Was-A	6	1	.857	8	5	2	0	0	41¹	47	3	22	10	15.0	3.92	110	.287	.371	2	.111	-1	3	2	1	0.1
1933	Was-A	3	2	.600	27	1	0	0	5	53	64	3	21	14	14.6	6.62	63	.296	.361	4	.267	2	-14	-14	0	-1.0
1934	StL-A	1	0	1.000	28	0	0	0	0	61²	84	4	26	11	16.5	5.84	86	.332	.401	3	.188	-0	-9	-6	-1	-0.5
Total	5	10	4	.714	83	7	2	0	5	186²	237	12	81	44	15.5	5.69	78	.313	.382	9	.173	-0	-28	-26	-1	-2.1

■ JIMMY McALEER
McAleer, James Robert "Loafer" b: 7/10/1864, Youngstown, Ohio d: 4/29/31, Youngstown, Ohio BR/TR, 6', 175 lbs. Deb: 4/24/1889 M♦

YEAR	TM/L	W	L	PCT	G	GS	CG	SH	SV	IP	H	HR	BB	SO	RAT	ERA	ERA+	OAV	OOB	BH	AVG	PB	PR	/A	PD	TPI
1901	Cle-A	0	0	—	1	0	0	0	0	0¹	2	0	3	0	135.0	0.00	—	.675	.839	1	.143	-0	0	0	0	0.0

■ JACK McALEESE
McAleese, John James b: 1877, Sharon, Pa. d: 11/15/50, New York, N.Y. TR , 5'8", Deb: 8/10/01 ♦

YEAR	TM/L	W	L	PCT	G	GS	CG	SH	SV	IP	H	HR	BB	SO	RAT	ERA	ERA+	OAV	OOB	BH	AVG	PB	PR	/A	PD	TPI
1901	Chi-A	0	0	—	1	0	0	0	0	3	7	0	1	1	24.0	9.00	39	.447	.480	0	.000	-0	-2	-2	0	-0.1

■ SPORT McALLISTER
McAllister, Lewis William b: 7/23/1874, Austin, Miss. d: 7/17/62, Wyandotte, Mich. BB/TR, 5'11", 180 lbs. Deb: 8/07/1896 ♦

YEAR	TM/L	W	L	PCT	G	GS	CG	SH	SV	IP	H	HR	BB	SO	RAT	ERA	ERA+	OAV	OOB	BH	AVG	PB	PR	/A	PD	TPI
1896	Cle-N	0	0	—	1	0	0	0	0	4	9	0	2	0	24.8	6.75	67	.439	.489	6	.222	-0	-1	-1	0	0.0
1897	Cle-N	1	2	.333	4	3	3	0	0	28	29	3	9	10	12.2	4.50	100	.265	.321	30	.219	-0	-1	-0	1	0.0
1898	Cle-N	3	4	.429	9	7	6	0	0	65¹	73	2	23	9	13.2	4.55	80	.280	.339	13	.228	1	-7	-7	-0	-0.4
1899	Cle-N	0	1	.000	3	1	1	0	0	16	29	0	10	2	21.9	9.56	38	.389	.461	99	.237	0	-10	-10	-0	-0.7
Total	4	4	7	.364	17	11	10	0	0	113¹	140	5	44	21	14.6	5.32	73	.301	.362	358	.247	1	-19	-18	1	-1.1

■ ERNIE McANALLY
McAnally, Ernest Lee b: 8/15/46, Pittsburg, Tex. BR/TR, 6'1", 190 lbs. Deb: 4/11/71

YEAR	TM/L	W	L	PCT	G	GS	CG	SH	SV	IP	H	HR	BB	SO	RAT	ERA	ERA+	OAV	OOB	BH	AVG	PB	PR	/A	PD	TPI
1971	Mon-N	11	12	.478	31	25	8	2	0	177²	150	9	87	98	12.4	3.90	90	.228	.326	7	.117	-2	-9	-7	0	-0.8
1972	Mon-N	6	15	.286	29	27	4	2	0	170	165	13	71	102	12.7	3.81	93	.259	.337	6	.113	-2	-7	-5	3	-0.3
1973	Mon-N	7	9	.438	27	24	4	0	0	147	158	13	54	72	13.2	4.04	94	.274	.340	9	.184	-1	-6	-4	0	-0.4
1974	Mon-N	6	13	.316	25	21	5	2	0	128²	126	10	56	79	13.0	4.48	86	.256	.336	5	.119	-2	-12	-9	1	-1.0
Total	4	30	49	.380	112	97	21	6	0	623¹	599	45	268	351	12.8	4.03	91	.253	.334	27	.132	-6	-34	-25	4	-2.5

■ JIM McANDREW
McAndrew, James Clement b: 1/11/44, Lost Nation, Iowa BR/TR, 6'2", 185 lbs. Deb: 7/21/68

YEAR	TM/L	W	L	PCT	G	GS	CG	SH	SV	IP	H	HR	BB	SO	RAT	ERA	ERA+	OAV	OOB	BH	AVG	PB	PR	/A	PD	TPI
1968	NY-N	4	7	.364	12	12	2	1	0	79	66	5	17	46	9.9	2.28	133	.230	.282	1	.045	-1	6	7	-0	0.6
1969	NY-N	6	7	.462	27	21	4	2	0	135	112	12	44	90	10.5	3.47	105	.225	.291	5	.135	0	2	3	-1	0.1
1970	NY-N	10	14	.417	32	27	9	3	2	184¹	166	18	38	111	10.1	3.56	113	.239	.281	8	.148	1	10	9	-1	0.9
1971	NY-N	2	5	.286	24	10	0	0	0	90¹	78	10	32	42	11.1	4.38	78	.227	.294	1	.043	-1	-9	-10	1	-1.0
1972	NY-N	11	8	.579	28	23	4	0	1	160²	133	12	38	81	9.9	2.80	120	.225	.278	2	.047	-2	12	10	-0	0.8
1973	NY-N	3	8	.273	23	12	0	0	1	80¹	109	9	31	38	16.0	5.38	67	.330	.393	2	.133	2	-15	-16	-1	-1.4
1974	SD-N	1	4	.200	15	5	1	0	0	41²	48	7	13	16	13.2	5.62	63	.284	.335	1	.143	0	-9	-10	-0	-0.9
Total	7	37	53	.411	161	110	20	6	4	771¹	712	73	213	424	11.0	3.65	98	.245	.300	20	.100	-2	-4	-6	-3	-0.9

■ DIXIE McARTHUR
McArthur, Oland Alexander b: 2/1/1892, Vernon, Ala. d: 5/31/86, West Point, Miss. BR/TR, 6'1", 185 lbs. Deb: 7/10/14

YEAR	TM/L	W	L	PCT	G	GS	CG	SH	SV	IP	H	HR	BB	SO	RAT	ERA	ERA+	OAV	OOB	BH	AVG	PB	PR	/A	PD	TPI
1914	Pit-N	0	0	—	1	0	0	0	0	1	1	0	0	1	9.0	0.00	—	.250	.250	0	—	0	0	0	0	0.0

■ WICKEY McAVOY
McAvoy, James Eugene b: 10/22/1894, Rochester, N.Y. d: 7/5/73, Rochester, N.Y. BR/TR, 5'11", 172 lbs. Deb: 9/29/13 ♦

YEAR	TM/L	W	L	PCT	G	GS	CG	SH	SV	IP	H	HR	BB	SO	RAT	ERA	ERA+	OAV	OOB	BH	AVG	PB	PR	/A	PD	TPI
1918	Phi-A	0	0	—	1	0	0	0	0	0-1	1	1	0	0	—	∞	—	.500	.500	66	.244	0	-1	-1	0	0.0

■ TOM McAVOY
McAvoy, Thomas John b: 8/12/36, Brooklyn, N.Y. BL/TL, 6'3", 200 lbs. Deb: 9/27/59

YEAR	TM/L	W	L	PCT	G	GS	CG	SH	SV	IP	H	HR	BB	SO	RAT	ERA	ERA+	OAV	OOB	BH	AVG	PB	PR	/A	PD	TPI
1959	Was-A	0	0	—	1	0	0	0	0	2²	1	0	2	0	10.1	0.00	—	.125	.300	0	.000	-0	1	1	0	0.1

■ AL McBEAN
McBean, Alvin O'Neal b: 5/15/38, Charlotte Amalie, V.I. BR/TR, 5'11.5", 165 lbs. Deb: 7/02/61

YEAR	TM/L	W	L	PCT	G	GS	CG	SH	SV	IP	H	HR	BB	SO	RAT	ERA	ERA+	OAV	OOB	BH	AVG	PB	PR	/A	PD	TPI
1961	Pit-N	3	2	.600	27	2	0	0	0	74¹	72	4	42	49	14.3	3.75	106	.263	.369	4	.267	1	2	2	2	0.5
1962	Pit-N	15	10	.600	33	29	6	2	0	189²	212	11	65	119	13.5	3.70	106	.285	.348	14	.209	2	5	5	0	0.7
1963	Pit-N	13	3	.813	55	7	2	1	11	122¹	100	5	39	74	10.4	2.57	128	.222	.287	6	.194	2	10	10	2	1.4
1964	Pit-N	8	3	.727	58	0	0	0	22	89²	76	4	17	41	9.7	1.91	184	.234	.280	1	.083	-1	16	16	4	2.1
1965	Pit-N	6	6	.500	62	1	0	0	18	114	111	5	42	54	12.3	2.29	153	.260	.331	6	.222	1	16	15	1	1.9
1966	Pit-N	4	3	.571	47	0	0	0	3	86²	95	9	24	54	12.6	3.22	111	.280	.332	1	.100	-1	4	3	1	0.4
1967	Pit-N	7	4	.636	51	8	5	0	4	131	118	6	43	54	11.1	2.54	132	.248	.312	6	.207	2	12	12	1	1.7
1968	Pit-N	9	12	.429	36	28	9	2	0	198¹	204	10	63	100	12.3	3.58	82	.269	.330	13	.194	2	-13	-15	5	-0.8
1969	SD-N	0	1	.000	1	1	0	0	0	7	10	1	2	1	15.4	5.14	69	.345	.387	1	.500	0	-1	-1	0	0.0
	LA-N	2	6	.250	31	0	0	0	4	48¹	46	6	21	26	12.8	3.91	85	.258	.343	0	.000	0	-2	-3	-1	-0.3
	Yr	2	7	.222	32	1	0	0	4	55¹	56	7	23	27	13.2	4.07	82	.271	.349	1	.200	0	-3	-4	-1	-0.3
1970	LA-N	0	0	—	1	0	0	0	0	1	1	0	0	0	9.0	0.00	—	.333	.333	0	—	0	0	0	0	0.0
	Pit-N	0	0	—	7	0	0	0	1	10	13	2	7	3	18.0	8.10	48	.317	.417	0	.000	-0	-5	-5	0	-0.3
	Yr	0	0	—	8	0	0	0	1	11	14	2	7	3	17.2	7.36	53	.318	.412	0	.000	-0	-4	-4	0	-0.3
Total	10	67	50	.573	409	76	22	5	63	1072¹	1058	63	365	575	12.2	3.13	111	.262	.327	52	.197	9	45	40	15	7.3

■ PRYOR McBEE
McBee, Pryor Edward "Lefty" b: 6/20/01, Blanco, Okla. d: 4/19/63, Roseville, Cal. BR/TL, 6'1", 190 lbs. Deb: 5/22/26

YEAR	TM/L	W	L	PCT	G	GS	CG	SH	SV	IP	H	HR	BB	SO	RAT	ERA	ERA+	OAV	OOB	BH	AVG	PB	PR	/A	PD	TPI
1926	Chi-A	0	0	—	1	0	0	0	0	1¹	1	0	3	1	27.0	6.75	57	.250	.571	0	—	0	-0	-0	0	0.0

■ DICK McBRIDE
McBride, James Dickson b: 1845, Philadelphia, Pa. d: 10/10/16, Philadelphia, Pa. TR , 5'9", 150 lbs. Deb: 5/20/1871 M

YEAR	TM/L	W	L	PCT	G	GS	CG	SH	SV	IP	H	HR	BB	SO	RAT	ERA	ERA+	OAV	OOB	BH	AVG	PB	PR	/A	PD	TPI
1871	Ath-n	18	5	.783	25	25	25	0	0	222	285	3	40	15	13.2	4.58	88	.280	.307	31	.235	-4	-9	-14		-1.1
1872	Ath-n	30	14	.682	47	47	47	1	0	419	513	3	26		11.6	3.01	121	.268	.278	73	.281	3	33	29		2.1
1873	Ath-n	24	19	.558	46	46	38	3	0	382	459	2	46		11.9	3.06	123	.266	.285	70	.277	2	23	30		2.5
1874	Ath-n	33	22	.600	55	55	55	0	0	487	514	5	29		10.0	2.55	124	.241	.251	57	.216	-8	24	33		2.2
1875	Ath-n	44	14	.759	60	60	59	6	0	538	603	4	25		10.5	1.97	134	.266	.274	73	.271	4	29	40		4.2
1876	Bos-N	0	4	.000	4	4	3	0	0	33	53	1	5	2	15.8	2.73	83	.340	.360	3	.188	-1	-2	-2	-0	-0.2
Total	5 n	149	74	.668	233	233	224	10	0	2048	2374	17	166	15	11.2	2.81	119	.262	.275	304	.258	-3	100	124		9.9

■ KEN McBRIDE
McBride, Kenneth Faye b: 8/12/35, Huntsville, Ala. BR/TR, 6'1", 190 lbs. Deb: 8/04/59 C

YEAR	TM/L	W	L	PCT	G	GS	CG	SH	SV	IP	H	HR	BB	SO	RAT	ERA	ERA+	OAV	OOB	BH	AVG	PB	PR	/A	PD	TPI
1959	Chi-A	0	1	.000	11	2	0	0	1	22²	20	1	17	12	14.7	3.18	118	.230	.356	1	.167	-0	2	1	1	0.2
1960	Chi-A	0	1	.000	5	0	0	0	0	4²	6	0	3	4	19.3	3.86	98	.333	.455	0	—	0	0	-0	0	0.0
1961	LA-A	12	15	.444	38	36	11	1	1	241²	229	28	102	180	12.6	3.65	124	.252	.332	7	.084	-6	10	23	4	2.3
1962	LA-A	11	5	.688	24	23	6	4	0	149¹	136	9	70	83	13.0	3.50	110	.249	.344	9	.164	0	8	5	1	1.1
1963	LA-A	13	12	.520	36	36	11	2	0	251	198	22	82	147	10.5	3.26	105	.218	.293	15	.172	2	10	5	3	0.9
1964	LA-A	4	13	.235	29	21	0	0	1	116¹	104	14	66	145	15.1	5.26	62	.239	.370	6	.214	3	-21	-26	3	-1.9
1965	Cal-A	0	3	.000	8	4	0	0	0	22	24	1	14	11	16.4	6.14	55	.270	.381	0	.000	-0	-7	-7	-0	-0.6
Total	7	40	50	.444	151	122	28	7	3	807²	717	75	363	503	12.6	3.79	101	.240	.332	38	.144	-1	2	2	16	2.0

■ PETE McBRIDE
McBride, Peter William b: 7/9/1875, Adams, Mass. d: 7/3/44, N.Adams, Mass. 5'10", 170 lbs. Deb: 9/20/1898

YEAR	TM/L	W	L	PCT	G	GS	CG	SH	SV	IP	H	HR	BB	SO	RAT	ERA	ERA+	OAV	OOB	BH	AVG	PB	PR	/A	PD	TPI
1898	Cle-N	0	1	.000	1	1	1	0	0	7	9	0	4	6	16.7	6.43	56	.309	.393	2	1.000	1	-2	-2	-0	0.0
1899	StL-N	2	4	.333	11	6	4	0	0	64	65	4	40	26	14.8	4.08	98	.263	.366	5	.185	0	-2	-1	-1	0.0
Total	2	2	5	.286	12	7	5	0	0	71	74	4	44	32	15.0	4.31	91	.268	.369	7	.241	2	-4	-3	-1	0.0

■ RALPH McCABE
McCabe, Ralph Herbert "Mack" b: 10/21/18, Napanee, Ont., Can. d: 5/3/74, Windsor, Ont., Can. BR/TR, 6'4", 195 lbs. Deb: 9/18/46

YEAR	TM/L	W	L	PCT	G	GS	CG	SH	SV	IP	H	HR	BB	SO	RAT	ERA	ERA+	OAV	OOB	BH	AVG	PB	PR	/A	PD	TPI
1946	Cle-A	0	1	.000	1	1	0	0	0	4	5	3	2	3	18.0	11.25	29	.313	.421	0	.000	-0	-3	-4	0	-0.2

YEAR TM/L	W	L	PCT	G	GS	CG	SH	SV	IP	H	HR	BB	SO	RAT	ERA	ERA+	OAV	OOB	BH	AVG	PB	PR	/A	PD	TPI
■ **DICK McCABE** McCabe, Richard James b: 2/21/1896, Mamaroneck, N.Y. d: 4/11/50, Buffalo, N.Y. BR/TR, 5'10.5", 159 lbs. Deb: 5/30/18																								
1918 Bos-A	0	1	.000	3	1	0	0	0	9²	13	0	2	3	14.0	2.79	96	.351	.385	0	.000	-0	-0	-0	0	0.0
1922 Chi-A	1	0	1.000	3	0	0	0	0	3¹	4	0	0	1	10.8	5.40	75	.308	.308	0	—	0	-1	-0	-0	0.0
Total 2	1	1	.500	6	1	0	0	0	13	17	0	2	4	13.2	3.46	88	.340	.365	0	.000	-0	-1	-1	0	0.0
■ **TIM McCABE** McCabe, Timothy J. b: 10/19/1894, Ironton, Mo. d: 4/12/77, Ironton, Mo. BR/TR, 6', 190 lbs. Deb: 8/16/15																								
1915 StL-A	3	1	.750	7	4	4	1	0	41²	25	1	9	17	7.6	1.30	221	.177	.232	1	.067	-1	8	7	-1	0.7
1916 StL-A	2	0	1.000	13	0	0	0	0	25²	29	0	7	7	13.3	3.16	87	.282	.339	0	.000	-0	-1	-1	1	0.0
1917 StL-A	0	0	—	1	0	0	0	0	2¹	4	1	4	2	30.9	23.14	11	.400	.571	0	—	0	-5	-5	0	-0.3
1918 StL-A	0	0	—	1	0	0	0	0	1¹	2	0	1	0	20.3	13.50	20	.333	.429	0	—	0	-2	-2	0	-0.1
Total 4	5	1	.833	22	4	4	1	0	71	60	2	21	26	10.6	2.92	96	.231	.296	1	.053	-1	-0	-1	1	0.3
■ **HARRY McCAFFERY** McCaffery, Harry Charles b: 11/25/1858, St.Louis, Mo. d: 4/19/28, St.Louis, Mo. BR/TR, 5'10.5", 185 lbs. Deb: 6/15/1882 U♦																								
1885 Cin-a	1	0	1.000	1	1	1	0	0	9	13	1	2	2	15.0	6.00	54	.324	.356	0	.000	-1	-3	-3	-0	-0.2
■ **BILL McCAHAN** McCahan, William Glenn b: 6/7/21, Philadelphia, Pa. d: 7/3/86, Fort Worth, Tex. BR/TR, 5'11", 200 lbs. Deb: 9/15/46																								
1946 Phi-A	1	1	.500	4	2	2	1	0	18	16	0	9	6	12.5	1.00	355	.246	.338	2	.400	1	5	5	0	0.7
1947 Phi-A	10	5	.667	29	19	10	1	0	165¹	160	7	62	47	12.1	3.32	115	.252	.318	9	.164	-1	7	9	1	1.0
1948 Phi-A	4	7	.364	17	15	5	0	0	86²	98	8	65	20	16.9	5.71	75	.284	.398	8	.258	1	-14	-14	-1	-1.2
1949 Phi-A	1	1	.500	7	4	0	0	0	20²	23	0	9	3	13.9	2.61	157	.291	.364	1	.200	-0	4	3	-0	0.3
Total 4	16	14	.533	57	40	17	2	0	290²	297	15	145	76	13.7	3.84	103	.264	.348	20	.208	1	2	4	0	0.8
■ **WINDY McCALL** McCall, John William b: 7/18/25, San Francisco, Cal BL/TL, 6', 180 lbs. Deb: 4/25/48																								
1948 Bos-A	0	1	.000	1	1	0	0	0	1¹	6	1	1	0	47.3	20.25	22	.600	.636	0	—	0	-2	-2	0	-0.1
1949 Bos-A	0	0	—	5	0	0	0	0	9¹	13	2	10	8	22.2	11.57	38	.333	.469	2	.667	1	-8	-7	-0	-0.5
1950 Pit-N	0	0	—	2	0	0	0	0	6²	12	2	4	5	21.6	9.45	46	.387	.457	0	.000	0	-4	-4	0	-0.2
1954 NY-N	2	5	.286	33	4	0	0	2	61	50	5	29	38	12.1	3.25	124	.219	.315	0	.000	-1	6	5	-1	0.3
1955 NY-N	6	5	.545	42	6	4	0	0	95	86	8	37	50	12.2	3.69	109	.244	.326	2	.118	-1	4	3	1	0.0
1956 NY-N	3	4	.429	46	0	0	0	7	77¹	74	7	20	41	11.1	3.61	105	.252	.302	3	.200	-0	1	1	-1	0.0
1957 NY-N	0	0	—	5	0	0	0	0	3	8	1	2	2	33.0	15.00	26	.533	.611	0	—	0	-4	-4	0	-0.3
Total 7	11	15	.423	134	15	4	0	12	253²	249	26	103	144	12.9	4.22	94	.257	.335	7	.146	-1	-7	-7	-2	-0.5
■ **LARRY McCALL** McCall, Larry Stephen b: 9/8/52, Asheville, N.C. BL/TR, 6'2", 195 lbs. Deb: 9/10/77																								
1977 NY-A	0	1	.000	2	0	0	0	0	6	12	1	1	0	19.5	7.50	53	.375	.394	0	—	0	-2	-2	-0	-0.1
1978 NY-A	1	1	.500	5	1	0	0	0	16	20	2	6	7	15.2	5.63	64	.323	.391	0	—	0	-3	-4	0	-0.2
1979 Tex-A	1	0	1.000	2	1	0	0	0	8¹	7	0	3	3	10.8	2.16	192	.226	.294	0	—	0	2	2	0	0.2
Total 3	2	2	.500	9	2	0	0	0	30¹	39	3	10	10	14.8	5.04	76	.312	.368	0	—	0	-4	-4	0	-0.1
■ **DUTCH McCALL** McCall, Robert Leonard b: 12/27/20, Columbia, Tenn. BL/TL, 6'1", 184 lbs. Deb: 4/27/48																								
1948 Chi-N	4	13	.235	30	20	5	0	0	151¹	158	14	85	89	14.5	4.82	81	.268	.361	9	.170	1	-14	-15	1	-1.3
■ **RANDY McCAMENT** McCament, Larry Randall b: 7/29/62, Albuquerque, N.Mex BR/TR, 6'3", 195 lbs. Deb: 6/28/89																								
1989 SF-N	1	1	.500	25	0	0	0	0	36²	32	4	23	12	13.7	3.93	86	.241	.357	1	.333	0	-2	-2	1	-0.2
1990 SF-N	0	0	—	3	0	0	0	0	6	8	0	5	5	19.5	3.00	124	.333	.448	0	.000	-0	1	0	0	0.0
Total 2	1	1	.500	28	0	0	0	0	42²	40	4	28	17	14.6	3.80	90	.255	.371	1	.250	0	-1	-2	1	-0.1
■ **GENE McCANN** McCann, Henry Eugene "Mike" b: 6/13/1876, Baltimore, Md. d: 4/26/43, New York, N.Y. TR, 5'10", Deb: 4/19/01																								
1901 Bro-N	2	3	.400	6	5	3	0	0	34	34	1	16	9	14.3	3.44	97	.259	.357	0	.000	-1	-0	-0	0	0.0
1902 Bro-N	1	2	.333	3	3	3	0	0	30	32	0	12	9	13.2	2.40	115	.273	.340	1	.083	-1	1	1	0	0.1
Total 2	3	5	.375	9	8	6	0	0	64	66	1	28	18	13.8	2.95	104	.265	.349	1	.045	-2	1	1	1	0.1
■ **ARCH McCARTHY** McCarthy, Archibald Joseph b: Ypsilanti, Mich. Deb: 8/14/02																								
1902 Det-A	2	7	.222	10	8	8	0	0	72	90	2	31	10	15.1	6.13	60	.306	.372	2	.071	-3	-20	-20	-2	-2.0
■ **JOHNNY McCARTHY** McCarthy, John Joseph b: 1/7/10, Chicago, Ill. d: 9/13/73, Mundelein, Ill. BL/TL, 6'1.5", 185 lbs. Deb: 9/02/34 ♦																								
1939 NY-N	0	0	—	1	0	0	0	0	5	8	1	2	0	18.0	7.20	55	.364	.417	21	.262	0	-2	-2	0	-0.1
■ **TOMMY McCARTHY** McCarthy, Thomas Francis Michael b: 7/24/1863, Boston, Mass. d: 8/5/22, Boston, Mass. BR/TR, 5'7", 170 lbs. Deb: 7/10/1884 MH♦																								
1884 Bos-U	0	7	.000	7	6	5	0	0	56	73	2	14	18	14.0	4.82	61	.295	.333	45	.215	-0	-11	-12	2	-0.9
1886 Phi-N	0	0	—	1	0	0	0	0	1	0	0	1	1	9.0	0.00	—	.000	.250	5	.185	0	0	0	0	0.0
1888 •StL-a	0	0	—	2	0	0	0	0	4¹	3	1	2	1	10.4	4.15	79	.188	.279	140	.274	0	-1	-0	-0	0.0
1889 StL-a	0	0	—	1	0	0	0	0	5	4	0	6	1	18.0	7.20	59	.213	.403	176	.291	0	-2	-2	0	-0.1
1891 StL-a	0	0	—	1	0	0	0	0	1	2	0	0	0	18.0	9.00	47	.402	.402	179	.310	0	-1	-1	0	0.0
1894 Bos-N	0	0	—	1	0	0	0	0	2	1	0	3	0	18.0	4.50	126	.148	.410	188	.349	0	0	0	0	0.0
Total 6	0	7	.000	13	6	5	0	0	69¹	83	3	26	21	14.1	4.93	64	.280	.338	1496	.292	1	-14	-14	1	-0.9
■ **TOM McCARTHY** McCarthy, Thomas Michael b: 6/18/61, Lundstahl, W.Ger. BR/TR, 6', 180 lbs. Deb: 7/05/85																								
1985 Bos-A	0	0	—	3	0	0	0	0	5	7	1	4	2	19.8	10.80	40	.350	.458	0	—	0	-4	-4	0	-0.2
1988 Chi-A	2	0	1.000	6	0	0	0	1	13	9	0	2	5	9.0	1.38	287	.191	.255	0	—	0	4	4	0	0.4
1989 Chi-A	1	2	.333	31	0	0	0	0	66²	72	8	20	27	12.7	3.51	108	.280	.337	0	—	0	3	2	1	0.3
Total 3	3	2	.600	40	0	0	0	1	84²	88	9	26	34	12.5	3.61	107	.272	.333	0	—	0	3	2	1	0.5
■ **TOM McCARTHY** McCarthy, Thomas Patrick b: 5/22/1884, Ft.Wayne, Ind. d: 3/28/33, Mishawaka, Ind. TR, 5'7", 170 lbs. Deb: 5/10/08																								
1908 Cin-N	0	1	.000	1	1	0	0	0	3²	6	0	3	3	22.1	9.82	23	.300	.391	0	.000	-0	-3	-3	0	-0.2
Pit-N	0	0	—	2	1	0	0	0	6	3	0	6	1	13.5	0.00	—	.176	.391	0	.000	-0	2	2	1	0.2
Bos-N	7	3	.700	14	11	7	2	0	94	77	0	28	27	10.1	1.63	148	.235	.298	6	.171	-0	8	8	0	1.0
Yr	7	4	.636	17	13	7	2	0	103²	86	0	37	31	10.8	1.82	132	.236	.308	6	.024	-1	6	7	1	1.0
1909 Bos-N	0	5	.000	8	7	3	0	0	46¹	47	3	28	11	15.0	3.50	81	.272	.379	2	.125	-0	-5	-3	-0	-0.3
Total 2	7	9	.438	25	20	10	2	0	150	133	3	65	42	12.1	2.34	108	.248	.332	8	.140	-1	2	3	1	0.7
■ **BILL McCARTHY** McCarthy, William Thomas b: 4/11/1882, Ashland, Mass. d: 5/29/39, Boston, Mass. BR/TR, 5'11", 180 lbs. Deb: 4/21/06																								
1906 Bos-N	0	0	—	1	0	0	0	0	2	2	0	3	0	22.5	9.00	30	.182	.357	0	.000	-0	-1	-1	0	-0.1
■ **JOHN McCARTY** McCarty, John A. b: St.Louis, Mo. TR , Deb: 4/18/1889																								
1889 KC-a	8	6	.571	15	14	13	0	0	119²	147	4	61	36	15.6	3.91	107	.293	.370	18	.228	-2	-1	4	-0	0.2
■ **KIRK McCASKILL** McCaskill, Kirk Edward b: 4/9/61, Kapuskasing, Ont.Can BR/TR, 6'1", 185 lbs. Deb: 5/01/85																								
1985 Cal-A	12	12	.500	30	29	6	1	0	189²	189	23	64	102	12.2	4.70	87	.258	.321	0	—	0	-12	-12	-0	-1.1
1986 •Cal-A	17	10	.630	34	33	10	2	0	246¹	207	19	92	202	11.1	3.36	122	.229	.303	0	—	0	22	20	-1	2.0
1987 Cal-A	4	6	.400	14	13	1	1	0	74²	84	14	34	56	14.5	5.67	76	.286	.364	0	—	0	-10	-11	1	-0.9
1988 Cal-A	8	6	.571	23	23	4	2	0	146¹	155	9	61	98	13.3	4.31	90	.274	.346	0	—	0	-6	-7	-0	-0.6
1989 Cal-A	15	10	.600	32	32	6	4	0	212	202	16	59	107	11.2	2.93	130	.254	.308	0	—	0	22	21	3	2.5
1990 Cal-A	12	11	.522	29	29	2	1	0	174¹	161	9	72	78	12.1	3.25	120	.244	.320	0	—	0	13	13	4	1.5
Total 6	68	55	.553	162	159	29	11	0	1043¹	998	90	382	643	12.1	3.80	105	.253	.321	0	—	0	30	23	4	3.4

YEAR	TM/L	W	L	PCT	G	GS	CG	SH	SV	IP	H	HR	BB	SO	RAT	ERA	ERA+	OAV	OOB	BH	AVG	PB	PR	/A	PD	TPI

■ STEVE McCATTY   McCatty, Steven Earl   b: 3/20/54, Detroit, Mich.   BR/TR, 6'3", 195 lbs.   Deb: 9/17/77

1977	Oak-A	0	0	—	4	2	0	0	0	14¹	16	1	7	9	15.1	5.02	80	.276	.364	0	—	0	-2	-2	-0	-0.1
1978	Oak-A	0	0	—	9	0	0	0	0	20	26	1	9	10	15.7	4.50	81	.310	.376	0	—	0	-2	-2	-0	-0.1
1979	Oak-A	11	12	.478	31	23	8	0	0	185²	207	17	80	87	14.4	4.22	96	.284	.363	0	—	0	-0	-4	-1	-0.4
1980	Oak-A	14	14	.500	33	31	11	1	0	221²	202	27	99	114	12.5	3.86	98	.240	.325	0	—	0	4	-2	-1	-0.2
1981	*Oak-A	**14**	7	.667	22	22	16	**4**	0	185²	140	12	61	91	9.8	2.33	149	**.211**	.279	0	—	0	27	24	-1	**2.6**
1982	Oak-A	6	3	.667	21	20	2	0	0	128²	124	16	70	66	13.8	3.99	98	.255	.354	0	—	0	1	-1	-1	-0.1
1983	Oak-A	6	9	.400	38	24	3	2	5	167	156	16	82	65	12.9	3.99	97	.247	.334	0	—	0	1	-2	-2	-0.3
1984	Oak-A	8	14	.364	33	30	4	0	0	179²	206	24	71	63	13.9	4.76	79	.289	.355	0	—	0	-15	-20	-1	-2.0
1985	Oak-A	4	4	.500	30	9	1	0	0	85²	95	10	41	36	14.7	5.57	69	.286	.371	0	—	0	-14	-16	-0	-1.4
Total	9	63	63	.500	221	161	45	7	5	1188¹	1172	124	520	541	13.0	3.99	95	.258	.339	0	—	0	2	-26	-7	-2.0

■ AL McCAULEY   McCauley, Allen A.   b: 3/4/1863, Indianapolis, Ind.   d: 8/24/17, Wayne Twnshp., Ind   BL/TL, 6', 180 lbs.   Deb: 6/21/1884 ♦

| 1884 | Ind-a | 2 | 7 | .222 | 10 | 9 | 9 | 0 | 0 | 76 | 87 | 2 | 25 | 34 | 13.3 | 5.09 | 64 | .272 | .325 | 10 | .189 | 1 | -16 | -15 | 2 | -0.8 |

■ JOE McCLAIN   McClain, Joseph Fred   b: 5/5/33, Johnson City, Tenn.   BR/TR, 6', 183 lbs.   Deb: 4/14/61

1961	Was-A	8	18	.308	33	29	7	2	1	212	221	22	48	76	11.6	3.86	104	.270	.313	14	.206	1	4	4	-2	0.3
1962	Was-A	0	4	.000	10	4	0	0	0	24	33	8	11	6	17.3	9.38	43	.327	.404	1	.143	-0	-14	-14	0	-1.2
Total	2	8	22	.267	43	33	7	2	1	236	254	30	59	82	12.2	4.42	91	.276	.324	15	.200	1	-11	-11	-2	-0.9

■ PAUL McCLELLAN   McClellan, Paul William   b: 2/8/66, San Mateo, Cal.   BR/TR, 6'2", 180 lbs.   Deb: 9/02/90

| 1990 | SF-N | 0 | 1 | .000 | 4 | 1 | 0 | 0 | 0 | 7² | 14 | 3 | 6 | 2 | 24.7 | 11.74 | 32 | .389 | .488 | 1 | .500 | 0 | -7 | -7 | 0 | -0.5 |

■ JIM McCLOSKEY   McCloskey, James Ellwood "Irish"   b: 5/26/10, Danville, Pa.   d: 8/17/71, Jersey City, N.J.   BL/TL, 5'9.5", 180 lbs.   Deb: 4/21/36

| 1936 | Bos-N | 0 | 0 | — | 4 | 1 | 0 | 0 | 0 | 8 | 14 | 1 | 3 | 2 | 20.3 | 11.25 | 34 | .378 | .439 | 0 | .000 | -0 | -6 | -7 | 0 | -0.5 |

■ JOHN McCLOSKEY   McCloskey, James John   b: 8/20/1882, Wyoming, Pa.   d: 6/5/19, Wilkes-Barre, Pa.   Deb: 5/03/06

1906	Phi-N	3	2	.600	9	4	3	0	0	41	46	2	9	6	12.3	2.85	92	.280	.322	3	.200	0	-1	-1	-0	-0.1
1907	Phi-N	0	0	—	3	0	0	0	0	9	15	0	6	3	22.0	7.00	35	.417	.512	0	.000	-0	-5	-5	-0	-0.4
Total	2	3	2	.600	12	4	3	0	0	50	61	2	15	9	14.0	3.60	72	.305	.359	3	.158	0	-6	-6	-0	-0.5

■ BOB McCLURE   McClure, Robert Craig   b: 4/29/52, Oakland, Cal.   BR/TL, 5'11", 170 lbs.   Deb: 8/13/75

1975	KC-A	1	0	1.000	12	0	0	0	1	15¹	9	0	14	15	10.6	0.00	—	.077	.273	0	—	0	6	7	-0	0.6
1976	KC-A	0	0	—	8	0	0	0	0	4	3	0	8	3	24.8	9.00	39	.214	.500	0	—	0	-2	-2	-0	-0.2
1977	Mil-A	2	1	.667	68	0	0	0	6	71¹	64	2	34	57	12.5	2.52	161	.249	.339	0	—	0	12	12	1	1.4
1978	Mil-A	2	6	.250	44	0	0	0	9	65	53	6	30	47	12.3	3.74	101	.223	.325	0	—	0	0	0	-1	0.0
1979	Mil-A	5	2	.714	36	0	0	0	6	51	53	6	24	37	14.1	3.88	107	.269	.357	0	—	0	2	2	-1	0.1
1980	Mil-A	5	8	.385	52	5	2	1	10	90²	83	6	37	47	12.1	3.08	126	.241	.318	0	—	0	10	8	-1	0.7
1981	*Mil-A	0	0	—	4	0	0	0	0	7²	7	1	4	6	12.9	3.52	97	.233	.324	0	—	0	0	-0	-0	0.0
1982	*Mil-A	12	7	.632	34	26	5	0	0	172²	160	21	74	99	12.4	4.22	90	.248	.329	0	—	0	-3	-8	-1	-0.8
1983	Mil-A	9	9	.500	24	23	4	0	0	142	152	11	68	68	14.3	4.50	83	.277	.362	0	—	0	-7	-12	-1	-1.1
1984	Mil-A	4	8	.333	39	18	1	0	1	139²	154	9	52	68	13.4	4.38	88	.282	.347	0	—	0	-6	-8	-0	-0.7
1985	Mil-A	4	1	.800	38	1	0	0	3	85²	91	10	30	57	13.0	4.31	97	.274	.340	0	—	0	-2	-1	-0	-0.1
1986	Mil-A	2	1	.667	13	0	0	0	0	16¹	18	2	10	11	15.4	3.86	112	.286	.384	0	—	0	1	1	-0	0.1
	Mon-N	2	5	.286	52	0	0	0	6	62²	53	2	23	42	11.1	3.02	122	.232	.306	1	.250	0	5	5	0	0.5
1987	Mon-N	6	1	.857	52	0	0	0	5	52¹	47	8	20	33	11.5	3.44	122	.241	.312	0	.000	-0	4	4	0	0.4
1988	Mon-N	1	3	.250	19	0	0	0	2	19	23	3	6	12	14.2	6.16	58	.307	.366	0	.000	-0	-6	-5	-0	-0.5
	NY-N	1	0	1.000	14	0	0	0	1	11	12	1	2	7	12.3	4.09	79	.279	.326	0	—	0	-1	-1	-0	0.0
	Yr	2	3	.400	33	0	0	0	3	30	35	4	8	19	13.2	5.40	64	.289	.338	0	.000	0	-7	-6	-0	-0.5
1989	Cal-A	6	1	.857	48	0	0	0	3	52¹	39	2	15	36	9.5	1.55	246	.212	.275	0	—	0	14	13	-1	1.3
1990	Cal-A	2	0	1.000	11	0	0	0	0	7	7	0	3	6	12.9	6.43	61	.269	.345	0	—	0	-2	-2	-0	-0.1
Total	16	64	53	.547	568	73	12	1	52	1065²	1023	92	454	651	12.7	3.78	102	.255	.335	1	.125	-0	25	11	-4	1.6

■ HARRY McCLUSKEY   McCluskey, Harry Robert   b: 3/29/1892, Clay Center, Ohio   d: 6/7/62, Toledo, Ohio   BL/TL, 5'11.5", 173 lbs.   Deb: 7/29/15

| 1915 | Cin-N | 0 | 0 | — | 3 | 0 | 0 | 0 | 0 | 5 | 4 | 0 | 2 | 7.2 | | 5.40 | 53 | .182 | .182 | 0 | .000 | -0 | -1 | -1 | -0 | -0.1 |

■ ALEX McCOLL   McColl, Alexander Boyd "Red"   b: 3/29/1894, Eagleville, Ohio   BB/TR, 6'1", 178 lbs.   Deb: 8/27/33

1933	*Was-A	1	0	1.000	4	1	1	0	0	17	13	0	7	5	10.6	2.65	158	.210	.290	2	.333	1	3	3	0	0.3
1934	Was-A	3	4	.429	42	2	1	0	1	112	129	6	36	29	13.3	3.86	112	.291	.345	3	.097	-2	8	6	2	0.6
Total	2	4	4	.500	46	3	2	0	1	129	142	6	43	34	13.0	3.70	116	.281	.338	5	.135	-1	11	9	2	0.9

■ RALPH McCONNAUGHEY   McConnaughey, Ralph James   b: 8/5/1889, Pennsylvania   d: 6/4/66, Detroit, Mich.   BR/TR, 5'8.5", 166 lbs.   Deb: 7/08/14

| 1914 | Ind-F | 0 | 2 | .000 | 7 | 2 | 1 | 0 | 0 | 26 | 23 | 3 | 16 | 7 | 13.8 | 4.85 | 72 | .245 | .361 | 1 | .125 | -0 | -5 | -4 | 0 | -0.3 |

■ GEORGE McCONNELL   McConnell, George Neely "Slats"   b: 9/16/1877, Shelbyville, Tenn   d: 5/10/64, Chattanooga, Tenn.   BR/TR, 6'3", 190 lbs.   Deb: 4/13/09 ♦

1909	NY-A	0	1	.000	2	1	0	0	0	4	5	0	3	4	13.5	2.25	112	.231	.375	0	.209	0	0	0	0	0.0
1912	NY-A	8	12	.400	23	20	19	0	0	176²	172	3	52	91	11.6	2.75	131	.269	.328	27	.297	3	11	17	6	3.1
1913	NY-A	4	15	.211	35	20	8	0	0	180	162	2	60	72	11.4	3.20	93	.245	.314	12	.179	-1	-5	-4	5	0.0
1914	Chi-N	0	1	.000	1	1	0	0	0	7	3	0	3	3	7.7	1.29	216	.125	.222	0	.000	-0	1	1	0	0.1
1915	Chi-F	**25**	10	**.714**	44	35	23	4	1	303	262	8	89	151	10.7	2.20	127	.232	.292	31	.248	6	28	20	2	3.1
1916	Chi-N	4	12	.250	28	20	8	1	0	171¹	137	8	35	82	9.3	2.57	113	.223	.271	9	.158	-2	1	6	1	0.8
Total	6	41	51	.446	133	97	58	5	4	842	739	21	242	403	10.7	2.60	117	.240	.300	88	.229	6	36	40	14	7.1

■ BILLY McCOOL   McCool, William John   b: 7/14/44, Batesville, Ind.   BR/TL, 6'2", 195 lbs.   Deb: 4/24/64

1964	Cin-N	6	5	.545	40	3	0	0	7	89¹	66	3	29	87	9.7	2.42	150	.206	.274	0	.000	-2	11	12	-2	0.9
1965	Cin-N	9	10	.474	62	2	0	0	21	105¹	93	9	47	120	12.3	4.27	88	.237	.324	1	.037	-2	-9	-6	-1	-0.8
1966	Cin-N	8	8	.500	57	0	0	0	18	105¹	76	5	41	104	10.3	2.48	157	.205	.290	3	.167	-0	13	17	2	2.0
1967	Cin-N	3	7	.300	31	11	0	0	2	97¹	92	8	56	83	14.1	3.42	110	.246	.352	2	.077	-1	-1	4	-1	0.2
1968	Cin-N	3	4	.429	30	4	0	0	2	50²	59	4	41	30	17.8	4.97	64	.294	.383	1	.125	-0	-11	-10	-1	-1.1
1969	SD-N	3	5	.375	54	0	0	0	7	58²	59	2	42	35	16.4	4.30	82	.266	.396	0	.000	-0	-5	-5	-0	-0.4
1970	StL-N	0	3	.000	18	0	0	0	1	21²	20	0	16	12	15.0	6.23	66	.250	.375	0	.000	-0	-5	-5	-0	-0.4
Total	7	32	42	.432	292	20	0	0	58	528¹	465	31	272	471	12.9	3.59	103	.237	.336	7	.069	-6	-6	6	-2	0.3

■ JIM McCORMICK   McCormick, James   b: 1856, Glasgow, Scotland   d: 3/10/18, Paterson, N.J.   BR/TR, 5'10.5", 215 lbs.   Deb: 5/20/1878 M

1878	Ind-N	5	8	.385	14	14	12	1	0	117	128	6	15	36	11.0	1.69	120	.265	.287	8	.143	-2	8	4	2	0.3
1879	Cle-N	20	40	.333	62	60	59	3	0	546¹	582	4	74	197	10.8	2.42	103	.256	.279	62	.220	-1	5	5	4	0.7
1880	Cle-N	**45**	28	.616	**74**	74	**72**	7	0	**657³**	585	2	75	260	9.0	1.85	127	.226	.248	71	.246	1	38	**37**	1	**3.9**
1881	Cle-N	26	30	.464	59	58	**57**	2	0	526	484	4	84	178	9.7	2.45	107	**.234**	.264	79	.256	6	19	10	-3	1.1
1882	Cle-N	**36**	30	.545	**68**	67	65	4	0	595²	550	14	103	200	9.9	2.37	121	.231	.263	57	.218	-4	34	28	-2	1.8
1883	Cle-N	28	12	**.700**	43	41	36	1	1	342	316	1	65	145	10.0	**1.84**	**171**	.231	.266	37	.236	-1	49	50	7	5.2
1884	Cle-N	19	22	.463	42	41	39	3	0	359	357	17	75	182	10.8	2.86	110	.245	.282	50	.263	2	5	12	0	1.4
	Cin-U	21	3	**.875**	24	24	24	**7**	0	210	151	3	14	161	**7.1**	**1.54**	**205**	.188	**.202**	27	.245	-1	34	38	1	3.6
1885	Pro-N	1	3	.250	4	4	4	0	0	37	34	1	20	8	13.1	2.43	109	.233	.282	2	.214	0	2	1	3	0.4
	*Chi-N	20	4	.833	24	24	24	3	0	215	187	8	40	88	9.5	2.43	125	.223	.259	23	.223	0	9	14	3	1.8
	Yr	21	7	.750	28	28	28	3	0	252	221	9	60	96	10.0	2.43	123	.225	.269	2	.017	1	11	15	5	2.2

YEAR TM/L	W	L	PCT	G	GS	CG	SH	SV	IP	H	HR	BB	SO	RAT	ERA	ERA+	OAV	OOB	BH	AVG	PB	PR	/A	PD	TPI
1886 *Chi-N	31	11	.738	42	42	38	2	0	347²	341	18	100	172	11.4	2.82	129	.246	.297	41	.236	2	19	32	2	3.7
1887 Pit-N	13	23	.361	36	36	36	0	0	322¹	377	12	84	77	12.9	4.30	90	.284	.326	33	.243	-0	-9	-16	5	-0.9
Total 10	265	214	.553	492	485	466	33	1	4275²	4092	84	749	1704	10.2	2.43	118	.239	.271	491	.236	2	213	213	22	23.0

■ JERRY McCORMICK
McCormick, John b: Philadelphia, Pa. d: 9/19/05, Philadelphia, Pa. Deb: 5/01/1883 ♦

YEAR TM/L	W	L	PCT	G	GS	CG	SH	SV	IP	H	HR	BB	SO	RAT	ERA	ERA+	OAV	OOB	BH	AVG	PB	PR	/A	PD	TPI
1884 Phi-U	0	0	—	1	0	0	0	0	2	5	1	0	3	22.5	9.00	32	.446	.446	84	.285	0	-1	-1	0	0.0

■ MIKE McCORMICK
McCormick, Michael Francis b: 9/29/38, Pasadena, Cal. BL/TL, 6'2", 195 lbs. Deb: 9/03/56

YEAR TM/L	W	L	PCT	G	GS	CG	SH	SV	IP	H	HR	BB	SO	RAT	ERA	ERA+	OAV	OOB	BH	AVG	PB	PR	/A	PD	TPI
1956 NY-N	0	1	.000	3	2	0	0	0	6²	7	1	10	4	23.0	9.45	40	.269	.472	0	.000	-0	-4	-4	0	-0.3
1957 NY-N	3	1	.750	24	5	1	0	0	74²	79	7	32	50	13.7	4.10	96	.280	.360	6	.273	1	-2	-1	-1	0.0
1958 SF-N	11	8	.579	42	28	8	2	1	178¹	192	19	60	82	12.9	4.59	83	.276	.336	12	.222	1	-13	-15	2	-1.1
1959 SF-N	12	16	.429	47	31	7	3	4	225²	213	24	86	151	12.0	3.99	96	.248	.317	7	.106	-2	-1	-4	1	-0.5
1960 SF-N	15	12	.556	40	34	15	4	3	253	228	15	65	154	10.5	**2.70**	129	.241	.291	16	.182	1	**30**	22	3	2.7
1961 SF-N	13	16	.448	40	35	13	3	0	250	235	33	75	163	11.2	3.20	119	.249	.306	15	.188	1	23	17	-1	1.6
1962 SF-N	5	5	.500	28	15	1	0	0	98²	112	18	45	42	14.4	5.38	71	.286	.361	3	.107	1	-16	-17	-0	-1.6
1963 Bal-A	6	8	.429	25	21	2	0	0	136	132	18	66	75	13.1	4.30	82	.256	.340	8	.174	1	-10	-12	-0	-1.1
1964 Bal-A	0	2	.000	4	2	0	0	0	17¹	21	1	8	13	15.1	5.19	69	.288	.358	1	.167	-0	-3	-3	0	-0.2
1965 Was-A	8	8	.500	44	21	3	1	1	158	158	17	36	88	11.1	3.36	103	.261	.301	3	.073	-1	2	2	-1	0.0
1966 Was-A	11	14	.440	41	32	8	3	0	216	193	23	51	101	10.3	3.46	100	.236	.282	14	.212	4	-1	0	-1	0.3
1967 SF-N	**22**	10	.688	40	35	14	5	0	262¹	220	25	81	150	10.5	2.85	115	.226	.289	10	.119	0	15	13	-2	1.2
1968 SF-N	12	14	.462	38	28	9	2	1	198¹	196	17	49	121	11.2	3.58	82	.254	.300	6	.103	1	-13	-14	-2	-1.6
1969 SF-N	11	9	.550	32	28	9	0	0	196²	175	20	77	76	11.6	3.34	105	.237	.310	9	.136	1	6	3	-0	0.4
1970 SF-N	3	4	.429	23	11	1	0	2	78¹	80	15	36	37	13.7	6.20	64	.262	.346	4	.160	0	-19	-19	1	-1.7
NY-A	2	0	1.000	9	4	0	0	0	20²	26	2	13	12	17.0	6.10	58	.295	.386	1	.200	0	-5	-6	-0	-0.5
1971 KC-A	0	0	—	4	1	0	0	0	9²	14	0	5	2	17.7	9.31	37	.350	.422	0	.000	-0	-6	-6	1	-0.4
Total 16	134	128	.511	484	333	91	23	12	2380¹	2281	255	795	1321	11.7	3.73	95	.251	.313	115	.156	9	-18	-45	-1	-2.8

■ HARRY McCORMICK
McCormick, Patrick Henry b: 10/25/1855, Syracuse, N.Y. d: 8/8/1889, Syracuse, N.Y. TR , 5'9", 155 lbs. Deb: 5/01/1879

YEAR TM/L	W	L	PCT	G	GS	CG	SH	SV	IP	H	HR	BB	SO	RAT	ERA	ERA+	OAV	OOB	BH	AVG	PB	PR	/A	PD	TPI
1879 Syr-N	18	33	.353	54	54	49	5	0	457¹	517	3	31	96	10.8	2.99	79	.267	.279	51	.222	-0	-25	-32	-7	-3.5
1881 Wor-N	1	8	.111	9	9	9	1	0	78¹	89	1	15	7	11.9	3.56	85	.274	.306	6	.133	-2	-7	-5	-1	-0.6
1882 Cin-a	14	11	.560	25	25	24	3	0	219²	177	3	42	33	9.0	1.52	175	.206	.243	12	.129	-5	29	28	1	2.2
1883 Cin-a	8	6	.571	15	15	14	1	0	128²	139	1	27	21	11.6	2.87	114	.258	.294	17	.309	4	6	6	1	0.9
Total 4	41	58	.414	103	103	96	10	0	884	922	8	115	157	10.6	2.66	99	.252	.275	86	.203	-4	3	-3	-6	-1.0

■ BILL McCORRY
McCorry, William Charles b: 7/9/1887, Saranac Lake, N.Y. d: 3/22/73, Augusta, Ga. BL/TR, 5'9", 157 lbs. Deb: 9/17/09

YEAR TM/L	W	L	PCT	G	GS	CG	SH	SV	IP	H	HR	BB	SO	RAT	ERA	ERA+	OAV	OOB	BH	AVG	PB	PR	/A	PD	TPI
1909 StL-A	0	2	.000	2	2	2	0	0	15	29	1	6	10	21.0	9.00	27	.397	.443	0	.000	-0	-11	-11	-1	-0.9

■ LES McCRABB
McCrabb, Lester William "Buster" b: 11/4/14, Wakefield, Pa. BR/TR, 5'11", 175 lbs. Deb: 9/07/39 C

YEAR TM/L	W	L	PCT	G	GS	CG	SH	SV	IP	H	HR	BB	SO	RAT	ERA	ERA+	OAV	OOB	BH	AVG	PB	PR	/A	PD	TPI
1939 Phi-A	1	2	.333	5	4	2	0	0	35²	42	4	10	11	13.4	4.04	117	.290	.340	0	.000	-2	2	3	0	0.0
1940 Phi-A	0	0	—	4	0	0	0	0	11²	19	2	2	4	17.0	6.94	64	.365	.400	1	.250	0	-3	-3	0	-0.2
1941 Phi-A	9	13	.409	26	23	11	1	2	157¹	188	16	49	40	13.7	5.49	76	.293	.346	8	.143	-2	-24	-23	-1	-2.3
1942 Phi-A	0	0	—	1	0	0	0	0	4	14	2	2	0	38.3	31.50	12	.560	.607	0	.000	-0	-12	-12	0	-0.7
1950 Phi-A	0	0	—	2	0	0	0	0	1¹	7	0	0	2	47.3	27.00	17	.636	.636	0	—	0	-3	-3	0	-0.2
Total 5	10	15	.400	38	27	13	1	2	210	270	24	63	57	14.5	5.96	72	.309	.359	9	.122	-4	-40	-39	-1	-3.4

■ ED McCREERY
McCreery, Esley Porterfield "Big Ed" b: 12/24/1889, Cripple Creek, Colo. d: 10/19/60, Sacramento, Cal. BR/TR, 6', 190 lbs. Deb: 8/16/14

YEAR TM/L	W	L	PCT	G	GS	CG	SH	SV	IP	H	HR	BB	SO	RAT	ERA	ERA+	OAV	OOB	BH	AVG	PB	PR	/A	PD	TPI
1914 Det-A	1	0	1.000	3	1	0	0	0	4	6	0	3	4	20.3	11.25	25	.316	.409	0	.000	-0	-4	-4	0	-0.3

■ TOM McCREERY
McCreery, Thomas Livingston b: 10/19/1874, Beaver, Pa. d: 7/3/41, Beaver, Pa. BB , 5'11", 180 lbs. Deb: 6/08/1895 ♦

YEAR TM/L	W	L	PCT	G	GS	CG	SH	SV	IP	H	HR	BB	SO	RAT	ERA	ERA+	OAV	OOB	BH	AVG	PB	PR	/A	PD	TPI
1895 Lou-N	3	1	.750	8	4	3	1	1	48²	51	0	38	14	16.5	5.36	86	.265	.387	35	.324	1	-3	-4	1	-0.2
1896 Lou-N	0	1	.000	1	1	0	0	0	1	4	1	5	0	81.0	36.00	12	.582	.758	155	.351	0	-4	-4	0	-0.2
1900 Pit-N	0	0	—	1	0	0	0	0	3	3	2	1	0	12.0	12.00	30	.260	.319	29	.220	0	-3	-3	0	-0.1
Total 3	3	2	.600	10	5	3	1	1	52²	58	3	44	14	17.4	6.32	72	.276	.401	855	.290	2	-9	-10	2	-0.5

■ LANCE McCULLERS
McCullers, Lance Graye b: 3/8/64, Tampa, Fla. BB/TR, 6'1", 185 lbs. Deb: 8/12/85

YEAR TM/L	W	L	PCT	G	GS	CG	SH	SV	IP	H	HR	BB	SO	RAT	ERA	ERA+	OAV	OOB	BH	AVG	PB	PR	/A	PD	TPI
1985 SD-N	0	2	.000	21	0	0	0	5	35	23	3	16	27	10.3	2.31	153	.195	.296	0	.000	-0	5	5	0	0.4
1986 SD-N	10	10	.500	70	7	0	0	5	136	103	12	58	92	10.9	2.78	131	.216	.306	2	.091	0	14	13	-1	1.3
1987 SD-N	8	10	.444	78	0	0	0	16	123¹	115	11	59	126	12.8	3.72	106	.244	.331	1	.071	-1	5	3	-0	0.2
1988 SD-N	3	6	.333	60	0	0	0	10	97²	70	8	55	81	11.5	2.49	136	.205	.315	2	.250	1	10	10	-0	1.1
1989 NY-A	4	3	.571	52	1	0	0	3	84²	83	9	37	82	13.1	4.57	85	.255	.337	0	—	0	-6	-7	-1	-0.6
1990 NY-A	1	0	1.000	11	0	0	0	0	15	14	2	6	11	12.0	3.60	110	.241	.313	0	—	0	1	1	0	0.1
Det-A	1	0	1.000	9	0	0	0	0	29²	18	2	13	20	9.4	2.73	144	.170	.261	0	—	0	4	4	-1	0.3
Yr	2	0	1.000	20	1	0	0	0	44²	32	4	19	31	10.3	3.02	130	.194	.277	0	—	0	4	5	-1	0.4
Total 6	27	31	.466	301	9	0	0	39	521¹	426	47	244	439	11.7	3.23	115	.225	.316	5	.104	0	32	29	-3	2.8

■ CHARLIE McCULLOUGH
McCullough, Charles F. b: 1867, Dublin, Ireland Deb: 4/23/1890

YEAR TM/L	W	L	PCT	G	GS	CG	SH	SV	IP	H	HR	BB	SO	RAT	ERA	ERA+	OAV	OOB	BH	AVG	PB	PR	/A	PD	TPI
1890 Bro-a	4	21	.160	26	25	24	0	0	215²	247	5	102	61	14.6	4.59	85	.279	.353	2	.023	-12	-17	-17	-2	-2.5
Syr-a	1	2	.333	3	3	3	0	0	26	29	1	14	8	14.9	7.27	49	.274	.358	1	.111	0	-10	-11	-0	-0.7
Yr	5	23	.179	29	28	27	0	0	241²	276	6	116	69	14.6	4.88	79	.278	.354	6	.063	-12	-27	-27	-2	-3.2

■ PAUL McCULLOUGH
McCullough, Paul Willard b: 7/28/1898, New Castle, Pa. d: 11/7/70, New Castle, Pa. BR/TR, 5'9.5", 190 lbs. Deb: 7/02/29

YEAR TM/L	W	L	PCT	G	GS	CG	SH	SV	IP	H	HR	BB	SO	RAT	ERA	ERA+	OAV	OOB	BH	AVG	PB	PR	/A	PD	TPI
1929 Was-A	0	0	—	3	0	0	0	0	7¹	7	1	2	3	11.0	8.59	49	.250	.300	0	.000	-0	-4	-4	-0	-0.3

■ PHIL McCULLOUGH
McCullough, Pinson Lamar b: 7/22/17, Stockbridge, Ga. BR/TR, 6'4", 204 lbs. Deb: 4/22/42

YEAR TM/L	W	L	PCT	G	GS	CG	SH	SV	IP	H	HR	BB	SO	RAT	ERA	ERA+	OAV	OOB	BH	AVG	PB	PR	/A	PD	TPI
1942 Was-A	0	0	—	1	0	0	0	0	3	5	0	2	2	21.0	6.00	61	.333	.412	0	.000	-0	-1	-1	0	0.0

■ LINDY McDANIEL
McDaniel, Lyndall Dale b: 12/13/35, Hollis, Okla. BR/TR, 6'3", 195 lbs. Deb: 9/02/55

YEAR TM/L	W	L	PCT	G	GS	CG	SH	SV	IP	H	HR	BB	SO	RAT	ERA	ERA+	OAV	OOB	BH	AVG	PB	PR	/A	PD	TPI
1955 StL-N	0	0	—	4	2	0	0	0	19	22	4	7	7	13.7	4.74	86	.293	.354	1	.200	-0	-1	-1	0	0.0
1956 StL-N	7	6	.538	39	7	1	0	0	116¹	121	7	42	59	12.6	3.40	111	.273	.335	7	.219	2	5	5	1	0.8
1957 StL-N	15	9	.625	30	26	10	1	0	191	196	13	53	75	11.9	3.49	114	.266	.317	19	.257	4	8	10	1	1.6
1958 StL-N	5	7	.417	26	17	2	1	0	108²	139	17	31	47	14.2	5.80	71	.305	.362	2	.067	-3	-22	-20	2	-1.9
1959 StL-N	14	12	.538	62	7	1	0	**15**	132	144	11	41	86	12.7	3.82	111	.283	.338	1	.034	-2	2	6	2	0.0
1960 StL-N	12	4	.750	65	2	1	0	**26**	116¹	85	8	24	105	8.5	2.09	196	.207	.253	6	.231	1	**22**	**26**	0	2.9
1961 StL-N	10	6	.625	55	0	0	0	9	94¹	117	11	31	65	14.3	4.87	90	.305	.351	4	.235	-0	-9	-5	1	-0.3
1962 StL-N	3	10	.231	55	2	0	0	14	107	96	12	29	79	10.6	4.12	104	.239	.292	2	.095	-1	-2	2	2	0.3
1963 Chi-N	13	7	.650	57	0	0	0	**22**	88	82	7	27	75	11.1	2.86	123	.251	.308	2	.091	-0	4	6	-0	0.6
1964 Chi-N	1	7	.125	63	0	0	0	15	95	104	4	23	71	12.1	3.88	96	.276	.319	2	.125	-1	-4	-2	-0	-0.2
1965 Chi-N	5	6	.455	71	0	0	0	2	128²	115	12	47	92	11.3	2.59	142	.241	.309	2	.091	-1	14	16	1	1.8
1966 SF-N	10	5	.667	64	0	0	0	6	121²	103	5	35	93	10.3	2.66	138	.228	.284	2	.091	-1	13	14	1	1.4
1967 SF-N	2	6	.250	41	3	0	0	3	72²	69	5	24	48	11.8	3.72	88	.248	.313	1	.091	-1	-3	-3	2	-0.2
1968 SF-N	0	0	—	12	0	0	0	0	19¹	30	2	5	9	16.3	7.45	40	.357	.393	0	.000	-0	-10	-10	0	-0.9
NY-A	4	1	.800	24	0	0	0	10	51¹	30	5	12	43	7.5	1.75	165	.166	.222	0	.000	-1	7	7	2	0.8
1969 NY-A	5	6	.455	51	0	0	0	5	83²	84	4	23	60	11.5	3.55	98	.261	.310	0	.000	-1	1	-1	1	0.0
1970 NY-A	9	5	.643	62	0	0	0	29	111²	88	7	23	81	8.9	2.01	174	.217	.259	4	.167	-0	21	19	0	2.0
1971 NY-A	5	10	.333	44	0	0	0	4	69²	82	12	24	39	13.7	5.04	64	.294	.352	1	.111	-0	-12	-14	0	-1.4
1972 NY-A	3	1	.750	37	0	0	0	7	68	54	4	25	47	10.5	2.25	131	.217	.288	2	.286	1	6	5	1	0.9

YEAR TM/L	W	L	PCT	G	GS	CG	SH	SV	IP	H	HR	BB	SO	RAT	ERA	ERA+	OAV	OOB	BH	AVG	PB	PR	/A	PD	TPI
1973 NY-A	12	6	.667	47	3	1	0	10	160¹	148	11	49	93	11.1	2.86	128	.250	.309	0	.000	0	17	14	3	1.8
1974 KC-A	1	4	.200	38	5	2	0	1	106²	109	6	24	47	11.2	3.46	110	.265	.306	0	—	0	2	4	1	0.6
1975 KC-A	5	1	.833	40	0	0	0	1	78	81	3	24	40	12.1	4.15	93	.273	.327	0	—	0	-3	-3	-0	-0.2
Total 21	141	119	.542	987	74	18	2	172	2139¹	2099	172	623	1361	11.5	3.45	109	.258	.312	56	.148	-3	55	74	20	11.0

■ **VON McDANIEL** McDaniel, Max Von b: 4/18/39, Hollis, Okla. BR/TR, 6'2.5", 180 lbs. Deb: 6/13/57

YEAR TM/L	W	L	PCT	G	GS	CG	SH	SV	IP	H	HR	BB	SO	RAT	ERA	ERA+	OAV	OOB	BH	AVG	PB	PR	/A	PD	TPI
1957 StL-N	7	5	.583	17	13	4	2	0	86²	71	7	31	45	10.7	3.22	123	.225	.296	0	.000	-3	6	7	-1	0.3
1958 StL-N	0	0	—	2	1	0	0	0	2	5	0	5	0	45.0	13.50	31	.500	.667	0	—	0	-2	-2	0	-0.1
Total 2	7	5	.583	19	14	4	2	0	88²	76	7	36	45	11.5	3.45	115	.233	.311	0	.000	-3	4	5	-1	0.2

■ **JOE McDERMOTT** McDermott, Joseph Deb: 5/04/1871 ♦

YEAR TM/L	W	L	PCT	G	GS	CG	SH	SV	IP	H	HR	BB	SO	RAT	ERA	ERA+	OAV	OOB	BH	AVG	PB	PR	/A	PD	TPI
1872 Eck-n	0	7	.000	7	7	7	0	0	63	142	3	12		22.0	8.29	42	.374	.393	9	.273	1	-32	-34		-1.9

■ **MICKEY McDERMOTT** McDermott, Maurice Joseph "Maury" b: 8/29/28, Poughkeepsie, N.Y. BL/TL, 6'2", 170 lbs. Deb: 4/24/48 C♦

YEAR TM/L	W	L	PCT	G	GS	CG	SH	SV	IP	H	HR	BB	SO	RAT	ERA	ERA+	OAV	OOB	BH	AVG	PB	PR	/A	PD	TPI
1948 Bos-A	0	0	—	7	0	0	0	0	23¹	16	2	35	17	20.1	6.17	71	.208	.460	3	.375	1	-5	-5	1	-0.2
1949 Bos-A	5	4	.556	12	12	6	2	0	80	63	5	52	50	13.3	4.05	108	.220	.345	7	.212	1	1	3	-0	0.4
1950 Bos-A	7	3	.700	38	15	4	0	5	130	119	8	124	96	17.0	5.19	94	.249	.406	16	.364	7	-9	-4	0	0.3
1951 Bos-A	8	8	.500	34	19	9	1	3	172	141	10	92	127	12.5	3.35	133	.226	.330	18	.273	3	15	21	1	2.5
1952 Bos-A	10	9	.526	30	21	7	2	0	162	139	14	92	117	13.0	3.72	106	.234	.340	14	.226	3	-1	4	-1	0.7
1953 Bos-A	18	10	.643	32	30	8	4	0	206¹	169	9	109	92	12.2	3.01	140	.224	.323	28	.301	7	23	27	1	**3.8**
1954 Was-A	7	15	.318	30	26	11	1	1	196¹	172	8	110	95	13.1	3.44	103	.239	.342	19	.200	3	6	3	0	0.5
1955 Was-A	10	10	.500	31	20	8	1	1	156	140	9	100	78	14.4	3.75	102	.243	.364	25	.263	7	4	1	0	0.1
1956 *NY-A	2	6	.250	23	9	1	0	0	87	85	10	47	38	13.7	4.24	91	.261	.354	11	.212	3	-1	-4	-0	-0.3
1957 KC-A	1	4	.200	29	4	0	0	0	69	68	9	50	29	15.4	5.48	72	.266	.386	12	.245	4	-13	-12	1	-1.1
1958 Det-A	0	0	—	2	0	0	0	0	2	6	0	2	0	36.0	9.00	45	.500	.571	1	.333	0	-1	-1	0	0.0
1961 StL-N	1	0	1.000	19	0	0	0	4	27	29	3	15	15	14.7	3.67	120	.271	.361	1	.071	-1	1	2	-0	0.1
KC-A	0	0	—	4	0	0	0	0	5²	10	1	10	3	38.1	14.29	29	.452	.585	1	.200	1	-6	-6	-0	-0.5
Total 12	69	69	.500	291	156	54	11	14	1316¹	1161	87	838	757	13.9	3.91	105	.240	.355	156	.252	37	14	29	3	6.3

■ **MIKE McDERMOTT** McDermott, Michael Joseph b: 9/7/1862, St.Louis, Mo. d: 6/30/43, St.Louis, Mo. TR, 5'8", 145 lbs. Deb: 9/02/1889

YEAR TM/L	W	L	PCT	G	GS	CG	SH	SV	IP	H	HR	BB	SO	RAT	ERA	ERA+	OAV	OOB	BH	AVG	PB	PR	/A	PD	TPI
1889 Lou-a	1	8	.111	9	9	9	0	0	84¹	108	4	34	22	15.2	4.16	92	.302	.362	6	.182	-1	-3	-3	0	-0.2
1895 Lou-N	4	19	.174	33	26	18	0	0	207¹	258	8	103	42	15.7	5.99	77	.300	.375	13	.159	-2	-28	-31	1	-2.4
1896 Lou-N	2	7	.222	12	10	4	1	0	65	87	4	44	12	18.1	7.34	59	.318	.412	8	.296	1	-21	-22	1	-1.5
1897 Cle-N	4	5	.444	9	7	4	0	0	62	75	2	25	12	14.5	4.50	100	.296	.360	8	.320	1	-1	-0	1	0.2
StL-N	1	2	.333	4	4	1	0	0	21¹	23	2	19	3	17.7	9.28	47	.273	.407	2	.222	-0	-12	-12	-0	-0.7
Yr	5	7	.417	13	11	5	0	0	83¹	98	4	44	15	15.3	5.72	78	.291	.372	0	.000	1	-13	-12	2	-0.5
Total 4	12	41	.226	67	56	36	1	0	440	551	20	225	91	15.9	5.79	76	.301	.378	37	.210	-0	-65	-67	4	-4.6

■ **DANNY McDEVITT** McDevitt, Daniel Eugene b: 11/18/32, New York, N.Y BL/TL, 5'10", 175 lbs. Deb: 6/17/57

YEAR TM/L	W	L	PCT	G	GS	CG	SH	SV	IP	H	HR	BB	SO	RAT	ERA	ERA+	OAV	OOB	BH	AVG	PB	PR	/A	PD	TPI
1957 Bro-N	7	4	.636	22	17	5	2	0	119	105	5	72	90	13.8	3.25	128	.238	.353	6	.154	-0	8	12	2	1.4
1958 LA-N	2	6	.250	13	10	2	0	0	48¹	71	6	31	26	19.0	7.45	55	.355	.442	2	.133	-0	-19	-18	-0	-1.7
1959 LA-N	10	8	.556	39	22	6	2	4	145	149	16	51	106	13.3	3.97	106	.263	.339	5	.109	-2	-0	4	0	0.3
1960 LA-N	0	4	.000	24	7	0	0	0	53	51	7	42	30	16.8	4.25	93	.260	.406	2	.200	0	-3	-2	0	0.0
1961 NY-A	1	2	.333	8	2	0	0	1	13	18	2	8	8	18.7	7.62	49	.353	.450	0	.000	-0	-5	-6	0	-0.4
Min-A	1	0	1.000	16	1	0	0	0	26²	20	1	19	15	14.5	2.36	179	.213	.368	0	.000	-0	5	6	1	0.6
Yr	2	2	.500	24	3	0	0	1	39²	38	3	27	23	15.7	4.08	100	.259	.388	1	.250	-0	-0	-0	1	0.2
1962 KC-A	0	3	.000	33	1	0	0	2	51	47	5	41	28	15.7	5.82	71	.250	.388	2	.222	0	-11	-9	1	-0.7
Total 6	21	27	.438	155	60	13	4	7	456	461	42	264	303	14.9	4.40	94	.265	.372	17	.138	-3	-25	-13	3	-0.5

■ **HANK McDONALD** McDonald, Henry Monroe b: 1/16/11, Santa Monica, Cal. d: 10/17/82, Hemet, Cal. BR/TR, 6'3", 200 lbs. Deb: 4/16/31

YEAR TM/L	W	L	PCT	G	GS	CG	SH	SV	IP	H	HR	BB	SO	RAT	ERA	ERA+	OAV	OOB	BH	AVG	PB	PR	/A	PD	TPI
1931 Phi-A	2	4	.333	19	10	1	1	0	70¹	62	3	41	23	13.3	3.71	121	.239	.346	2	.095	-1	5	6	-1	0.4
1933 Phi-A	1	1	.500	4	1	0	0	0	12¹	14	0	4	1	13.1	5.11	84	.264	.316	0	.000	-0	-1	-1	0	0.0
StL-A	0	4	.000	25	5	0	0	0	58¹	83	6	34	22	18.5	8.64	54	.332	.418	2	.143	-1	-28	-26	-0	-2.3
Yr	1	5	.167	29	6	0	0	0	70²	97	6	38	23	17.6	8.02	57	.320	.401	2	.143	-1	-29	-27	-0	-2.3
Total 2	3	9	.250	48	16	1	1	0	141	159	9	79	46	15.4	5.87	77	.283	.375	4	.103	-2	-24	-21	-1	-1.9

■ **JIM McDONALD** McDonald, Jimmie Le Roy "Hot Rod" b: 5/17/27, Grants Pass, Ore. BR/TR, 5'10.5", 185 lbs. Deb: 7/27/50

YEAR TM/L	W	L	PCT	G	GS	CG	SH	SV	IP	H	HR	BB	SO	RAT	ERA	ERA+	OAV	OOB	BH	AVG	PB	PR	/A	PD	TPI
1950 Bos-A	1	0	1.000	9	0	0	0	0	19	23	1	10	5	16.1	3.79	129	.329	.420	1	.333	1	2	2	1	0.4
1951 StL-A	4	7	.364	16	11	5	0	0	84	84	5	46	28	14.1	4.07	108	.260	.356	6	.207	-0	0	3	1	0.4
1952 NY-A	3	4	.429	26	5	1	0	0	69¹	71	1	40	20	14.7	3.50	95	.268	.368	6	.316	3	-1	-3	3	0.5
1953 *NY-A	9	7	.563	27	18	6	2	0	129²	128	4	39	43	11.7	3.82	97	.260	.316	4	.098	-3	3	-2	2	-0.1
1954 NY-A	4	1	.800	16	10	3	1	0	71	54	3	45	20	12.7	3.17	108	.213	.334	4	.211	2	4	2	1	0.5
1955 Bal-A	3	5	.375	21	8	0	0	0	51²	76	5	30	20	18.5	7.14	53	.345	.424	2	.182	1	-18	-19	1	-1.5
1956 Chi-A	0	2	.000	8	3	0	0	0	18²	29	2	7	10	17.8	8.68	47	.377	.435	0	.000	-0	-9	-9	-0	-0.8
1957 Chi-A	0	1	.000	10	0	0	0	0	22¹	18	2	10	12	11.3	2.01	185	.234	.322	0	.000	-0	4	4	0	0.5
1958 Chi-A	0	0	—	3	0	0	0	0	2¹	6	1	4	0	38.6	19.29	19	.429	.556	0	—	0	-4	-4	-0	-0.3
Total 9	24	27	.471	136	55	15	3	1	468	489	24	231	158	14.0	4.27	89	.273	.359	23	.180	4	-17	-25	9	-0.4

■ **JOHN McDONALD** McDonald, John Joseph (b: John Joseph McDonnell) b: 1/27/1883, Throop, Pa. d: 4/9/50, Roselle, N.J. BR/TR, 6'1", 170 lbs. Deb: 9/13/07

YEAR TM/L	W	L	PCT	G	GS	CG	SH	SV	IP	H	HR	BB	SO	RAT	ERA	ERA+	OAV	OOB	BH	AVG	PB	PR	/A	PD	TPI
1907 Was-A	0	0	—	1	0	0	0	0	6	12	0	2	3	21.0	9.00	27	.415	.453	1	.333	1	-4	-4	0	-0.3

■ **BEN McDONALD** McDonald, Larry Benard b: 11/14/67, Baton Rouge, La. BR/TR, 6'7", 212 lbs. Deb: 9/06/89

YEAR TM/L	W	L	PCT	G	GS	CG	SH	SV	IP	H	HR	BB	SO	RAT	ERA	ERA+	OAV	OOB	BH	AVG	PB	PR	/A	PD	TPI
1989 Bal-A	1	0	1.000	6	0	0	0	0	7¹	8	2	4	3	14.7	8.59	44	.286	.375	0	—	0	-4	-4	0	-0.3
1990 Bal-A	8	5	.615	21	15	3	2	0	118²	88	9	35	65	9.3	2.43	158	.205	.265	0	—	0	20	18	0	2.0
Total 2	9	5	.643	27	15	3	2	0	126	96	11	39	68	9.6	2.79	137	.210	.272	0	—	0	16	15	0	1.7

■ **MC DOOLAN** McDoolan Deb: 4/14/1873

YEAR TM/L	W	L	PCT	G	GS	CG	SH	SV	IP	H	HR	BB	SO	RAT	ERA	ERA+	OAV	OOB	BH	AVG	PB	PR	/A	PD	TPI
1873 Mar-n	0	1	.000	1	1	1	0	0	9	18	0	0		18.0	10.00	36	.305	.305	0	.000	-1	-6	-6		-0.3

■ **SANDY McDOUGAL** McDougal, John Auchanbolt b: 5/21/1874, Buffalo, N.Y. d: 10/2/10, Buffalo, N.Y. BR/TR, 5'10", 155 lbs. Deb: 6/12/1895

YEAR TM/L	W	L	PCT	G	GS	CG	SH	SV	IP	H	HR	BB	SO	RAT	ERA	ERA+	OAV	OOB	BH	AVG	PB	PR	/A	PD	TPI
1895 Bro-N	0	0	—	1	0	0	0	1	3	3	0	5	2	24.0	12.00	37	.256	.479	0	—	-0	-2	-3	-0	-0.1
1905 StL-N	1	4	.200	5	5	5	0	0	44²	50	0	12	10	12.5	3.43	87	.301	.348	2	.133	-1	-2	-2	3	-0.1
Total 2	1	4	.200	6	5	5	0	1	47²	53	0	17	12	13.2	3.97	78	.298	.360	2	.125	-1	-5	-5	3	-0.1

■ **DEWEY McDOUGAL** McDougal, John H. b: 9/19/1871, Aledo, Ill. d: 4/28/36, Galesburg, Ill. 170 lbs. Deb: 4/24/1895

YEAR TM/L	W	L	PCT	G	GS	CG	SH	SV	IP	H	HR	BB	SO	RAT	ERA	ERA+	OAV	OOB	BH	AVG	PB	PR	/A	PD	TPI
1895 StL-N	3	10	.231	18	14	10	0	0	114²	187	11	46	23	18.3	8.32	58	.360	.412	6	.146	-2	-45	-44	-1	-3.4
1896 StL-N	0	1	.000	3	1	0	0	0	10	13	2	4	0	15.3	8.10	54	.312	.372	0	.000	-1	-4	-4	1	-0.2
Total 2	3	11	.214	21	15	10	0	0	124²	200	13	50	23	18.0	8.30	58	.356	.409	6	.136	-3	-49	-49	-0	-3.6

■ **JACK McDOWELL** McDowell, Jack Burns b: 1/16/66, Van Nuys, Cal. BR/TR, 6'5", 180 lbs. Deb: 9/15/87

YEAR TM/L	W	L	PCT	G	GS	CG	SH	SV	IP	H	HR	BB	SO	RAT	ERA	ERA+	OAV	OOB	BH	AVG	PB	PR	/A	PD	TPI
1987 Chi-A	3	0	1.000	4	4	0	0	0	28	16	1	6	15	7.7	1.93	237	.168	.233	0	—	0	8	8	0	0.9
1988 Chi-A	5	10	.333	26	26	1	0	0	158²	147	12	68	84	12.6	3.97	100	.245	.329	0	—	0	-0	-0	-1	0.0
1990 Chi-A	14	9	.609	33	33	4	0	0	205	189	20	77	165	12.0	3.82	100	.244	.317	0	—	0	2	0	-1	0.0
Total 3	22	19	.537	63	63	5	0	0	391²	352	33	151	264	11.9	3.75	105	.239	.317	0	—	0	10	8	-2	0.9

YEAR TM/L	W	L	PCT	G	GS	CG	SH	SV	IP	H	HR	BB	SO	RAT	ERA	ERA+	OAV	OOB	BH	AVG	PB	PR	/A	PD	TPI
■ ROGER McDOWELL				McDowell, Roger Alan b: 12/21/60, Cincinnati, Ohio BR/TR, 6'1", 175 lbs. Deb: 4/11/85																				
1985 NY-N	6	5	.545	62	2	0	0	17	127¹	108	9	37	70	10.3	2.83	122	.230	.287	3	.158	0	11	9	2	1.2
1986 *NY-N	14	9	.609	75	0	0	0	22	128	107	4	42	65	10.7	3.02	117	.228	.296	5	.278	1	10	7	3	1.2
1987 NY-N	7	5	.583	56	0	0	0	25	88²	95	7	28	32	12.7	4.16	91	.276	.334	3	.231	1	-1	-4	1	0.0
1988 *NY-N	5	5	.500	62	0	0	0	16	89	80	1	31	46	11.5	2.63	122	.238	.308	3	.333	2	8	6	2	1.0
1989 NY-N	1	5	.167	25	0	0	0	4	35¹	34	1	16	15	13.2	3.31	99	.254	.342	1	.500	1	-1	-0	2	0.3
Phi-N	3	3	.500	44	0	0	0	19	56²	45	2	22	32	10.8	1.11	319	.220	.298	0	.000	-0	15	15	1	1.8
Yr	4	8	.333	69	0	0	0	23	92	79	3	38	47	11.5	1.96	176	.231	.310	0	.000	0	16	15	4	2.1
1990 Phi-N	6	8	.429	72	0	0	0	22	86¹	92	2	35	39	13.4	3.86	99	.286	.359	0	.000	-0	-1	-0	2	0.1
Total 6	42	40	.512	396	2	0	0	125	611¹	561	26	211	299	11.6	3.05	116	.246	.314	15	.234	5	43	33	14	5.6
■ SAM McDOWELL				McDowell, Samuel Edward Thomas "Sudden Sam" b: 9/21/42, Pittsburgh, Pa. BL/TL, 6'5", 190 lbs. Deb: 9/15/61																				
1961 Cle-A	0	0	—	1	1	0	0	0	6¹	3	0	5	5	11.4	0.00	—	.136	.296	0	.000	-0	3	3	0	0.3
1962 Cle-A	3	7	.300	25	13	0	0	1	87²	81	9	70	70	15.9	6.06	64	.243	.381	4	.154	-1	-20	-21	-0	-2.1
1963 Cle-A	3	5	.375	14	12	3	1	0	65	63	6	44	63	14.8	4.85	75	.256	.369	4	.211	0	-9	-9	-1	-0.8
1964 Cle-A	11	6	.647	31	24	6	2	1	173¹	148	8	100	177	13.0	2.70	133	.229	.336	8	.143	0	18	17	-1	1.7
1965 Cle-A	17	11	.607	42	35	14	3	4	273	178	9	132	325	10.4	2.18	160	.185	.287	12	.126	-3	39	40	-1	4.1
1966 Cle-A	9	8	.529	35	28	8	5	3	194¹	130	12	102	225	11.0	2.87	120	.188	.298	12	.200	1	12	12	0	1.5
1967 Cle-A	13	15	.464	37	37	10	1	0	236¹	201	21	123	236	12.6	3.85	85	.233	.333	15	.183	1	-16	-15	-2	-1.9
1968 Cle-A	15	14	.517	38	37	11	3	0	269	181	13	110	283	10.1	1.81	164	.189	.279	13	.153	0	35	34	-2	4.0
1969 Cle-A	18	14	.563	39	38	18	4	1	285	222	13	102	279	10.5	2.94	128	.213	.288	16	.174	-1	22	26	-1	2.6
1970 Cle-A	20	12	.625	39	39	19	1	0	305	236	25	131	304	11.0	2.92	136	.213	.300	13	.124	-4	27	35	-3	3.2
1971 Cle-A	13	17	.433	35	31	8	2	1	214²	160	22	153	192	13.2	3.40	113	.207	.340	13	.178	-1	2	10	-3	0.8
1972 SF-N	10	8	.556	28	25	4	0	0	164¹	155	12	86	122	13.5	4.33	81	.253	.350	7	.119	-1	-16	-15	-1	-1.7
1973 SF-N	1	2	.333	18	3	0	0	3	40	45	4	29	35	16.6	4.50	85	.285	.396	2	.167	-0	-4	-3	-0	-0.3
NY-A	5	8	.385	16	15	2	1	0	95²	73	9	64	75	12.9	3.95	93	.212	.335	0	—	0	-1	-3	0	-0.7
1974 NY-A	1	6	.143	13	7	0	0	0	48	42	6	41	33	15.6	4.69	74	.236	.379	0	—	0	-6	-6	-1	-0.7
1975 Pit-N	2	1	.667	14	1	0	0	0	34²	30	7	20	29	13.0	2.86	124	.242	.347	0	.000	-1	3	3	0	0.2
Total 15	141	134	.513	425	346	103	23	14	2492¹	1948	164	1312	2453	12.0	3.17	112	.215	.318	119	.154	-8	88	107	-15	11.0
■ CHUCK McELROY				McElroy, Charles Dwayne b: 10/1/67, Galveston, Tex. BL/TL, 6', 160 lbs. Deb: 9/04/89																				
1989 Phi-N	0	0	—	11	0	0	0	0	10¹	12	1	4	8	13.9	1.74	203	.286	.348	0	—	0	2	2	-0	0.2
1990 Phi-N	0	1	.000	16	0	0	0	0	14	24	0	10	16	21.9	7.71	49	.369	.453	0	—	0	-6	-6	-0	-0.6
Total 2	0	1	.000	27	0	0	0	0	24¹	36	1	14	24	18.5	5.18	72	.336	.413	0	—	0	-4	-4	-1	-0.4
■ JIM McELROY				McElroy, James D. b: 1863, San Francisco, Cal. d: 7/24/1889, Needles, Cal. 5'10", 170 lbs. Deb: 5/26/1884																				
1884 Phi-N	1	12	.077	13	13	13	0	0	111	115	1	54	45	13.7	4.86	61	.253	.332	7	.146	-3	-23	-23	0	-2.1
Wil-U	0	1	.000	1	1	0	0	0	5	10	0	0	3	18.0	10.80	30	.391	.391	0	.000	-0	-4	-4	0	-0.2
■ WILL McENANEY				McEnaney, William Henry b: 2/14/52, Springfield, Ohio BL/TL, 6', 180 lbs. Deb: 7/03/74																				
1974 Cin-N	2	1	.667	24	0	0	0	2	27	24	4	9	13	11.0	4.33	80	.250	.314	0	—	0	-2	-3	-1	-0.2
1975 *Cin-N	5	2	.714	70	0	0	0	15	91	92	6	23	48	11.6	2.47	145	.264	.314	0	.000	-2	12	11	-1	0.9
1976 Cin-N	2	6	.250	55	0	0	0	7	72¹	97	3	23	28	15.1	4.85	72	.323	.373	1	.167	1	-11	-11	0	-1.0
1977 Mon-N	3	5	.375	69	0	0	0	3	86²	92	6	22	38	12.0	3.95	96	.271	.319	0	.000	-1	-0	-1	-0	-0.1
1978 Pit-N	0	0	—	6	0	0	0	0	8²	15	3	2	6	18.7	10.38	36	.395	.439	0	—	0	-7	-6	0	-0.5
1979 StL-N	0	3	.000	45	0	0	0	2	64	60	3	16	15	11.0	2.95	127	.251	.304	0	.000	-0	6	6	2	0.8
Total 6	12	17	.414	269	0	0	0	29	349²	380	25	95	148	12.4	3.76	97	.279	.330	1	.032	-2	-3	-4	0	-0.1
■ LOU McEVOY				McEvoy, Louis Anthony b: 5/30/02, Williamsburg, Kan. d: 12/17/53, Webster Groves, Mo BR/TR, 6'2.5", 203 lbs. Deb: 4/28/30																				
1930 NY-A	1	3	.250	28	1	0	0	3	52¹	64	4	29	14	16.3	6.71	64	.288	.375	2	.125	-1	-12	-14	-1	-1.3
1931 NY-A	0	0	—	6	0	0	0	1	12¹	19	1	12	3	23.4	12.41	32	.358	.485	0	.000	-1	-11	-12	0	-0.9
Total 2	1	3	.250	34	1	0	0	4	64²	83	5	41	17	17.7	7.79	54	.302	.398	2	.100	-1	-23	-26	-0	-2.2
■ BARNEY McFADDEN				McFadden, Bernard Joseph b: 2/22/1874, Eckley, Pa. d: 4/28/24, Mauch Chunk, Pa. BR/TR, 6'1", 195 lbs. Deb: 4/24/01																				
1901 Cin-N	3	4	.429	8	5	4	0	0	46	54	2	40	11	19.6	6.07	53	.291	.431	3	.150	-1	-14	-15	1	-1.2
1902 Phi-N	0	1	.000	1	1	1	0	0	9	14	1	7	3	21.0	8.00	35	.354	.451	0	.000	-0	-5	-5	0	-0.4
Total 2	3	5	.375	9	6	5	0	0	55	68	3	47	14	19.8	6.38	49	.302	.435	3	.130	-1	-19	-20	1	-1.6
■ DAN McFARLAN				McFarlan, Anderson Daniel b: 11/1/1873, Gainesville, Tex. d: 9/23/24, Louisville, Ky. Deb: 9/02/1895																				
1895 Lou-N	0	7	.000	7	7	6	0	0	46	80	4	15	10	18.6	6.65	70	.375	.416	5	.238	-1	-10	-10	1	-0.7
1899 Bro-N	0	0	—	1	0	0	0	0	6	6	1	3	0	13.5	1.50	261	.260	.345	0	.000	-0	2	2	0	0.2
Was-N	8	18	.308	32	28	22	1	0	211²	268	5	64	41	14.1	4.76	82	.308	.355	16	.186	-1	-21	-20	-0	-1.7
Yr	8	18	.308	33	28	22	1	0	217²	274	6	67	41	14.1	4.67	84	.307	.355	5	.057	-1	-20	-18	0	-1.5
Total 2	8	25	.242	40	35	28	1	0	263²	354	10	82	51	14.9	5.02	81	.320	.367	21	.193	-2	-29	-29	1	-2.2
■ CHAPPIE McFARLAND				McFarland, Charles A. b: 3/13/1875, White Hill, Ill. d: 12/14/24, Houston, Tex. TR, 6'1", Deb: 9/15/02																				
1902 StL-N	0	1	.000	2	1	1	0	0	11	11	1	3	3	11.5	5.73	48	.260	.309	0	.000	-1	-4	-4	0	-0.3
1903 StL-N	9	19	.321	28	26	25	1	0	229	253	2	48	76	12.1	3.07	106	.284	.325	8	.108	-3	5	5	3	0.4
1904 StL-N	14	18	.438	32	31	28	1	0	269¹	266	7	56	111	10.9	3.21	84	.248	.288	13	.131	-3	-14	-15	6	-1.2
1905 StL-N	8	18	.308	31	28	22	3	1	250	281	3	65	85	12.7	3.82	78	.284	.332	14	.165	1	-23	-23	1	-2.1
1906 StL-N	2	1	.667	6	4	2	0	1	37¹	33	1	8	16	9.9	1.93	136	.219	.258	2	.133	-1	3	3	1	0.3
Pit-N	1	3	.250	6	5	2	1	0	35¹	39	0	7	11	12.2	2.55	105	.298	.343	5	.385	1	0	0	0	0.2
Bro-N	0	1	.000	1	1	1	0	0	9	10	1	5	5	15.0	8.00	32	.286	.375	0	.000	-0	-5	-5	-0	-0.4
Yr	3	5	.375	13	10	5	1	1	81²	82	2	20	32	11.2	2.87	92	.257	.301	0	.000	0	-2	-2	1	0.1
Total 5	34	61	.358	106	96	81	6	2	841	893	15	192	307	11.8	3.35	87	.270	.313	42	.143	-6	-37	-39	11	-3.1
■ CHRIS McFARLAND				McFarland, Christopher b: 8/17/1861, Fall River, Mass. d: 5/24/18, New Bedford, Mass. 5'9", 170 lbs. Deb: 4/19/1884 ◆																				
1884 Bal-U	0	1	.000	1	1	0	0	0	3	9	1	1	3	30.0	15.00	22	.491	.517	3	.214	-0	-4	-4	0	-0.2
■ MONTE McFARLAND				McFarland, La Mont A. b: 1873, Illinois d: 11/15/13, Peoria, Ill. Deb: 9/14/1895																				
1895 Chi-N	2	0	1.000	2	2	2	0	0	14	21	0	5	5	16.7	5.14	99	.341	.390	1	.143	-1	-1	-0	0	0.0
1896 Chi-N	0	4	.000	4	3	2	0	0	25	32	0	21	3	19.1	7.20	63	.308	.425	0	.000	-2	-8	-7	1	-0.6
Total 2	2	4	.333	6	5	4	0	0	39	53	0	26	8	18.2	6.46	73	.321	.413	1	.053	-3	-8	-7	1	-0.6
■ JACK McFETRIDGE				McFetridge, John Reed b: 8/25/1869, Philadelphia, Pa. d: 1/10/17, Philadelphia, Pa. 6', 175 lbs. Deb: 6/07/1890																				
1890 Phi-N	1	0	1.000	1	1	1	0	0	9	5	0	2	4	7.0	1.00	365	.158	.208	3	.750	1	3	3	-0	0.4
1903 Phi-N	1	11	.083	14	13	11	0	0	103	120	2	49	31	15.0	4.89	67	.299	.379	6	.176	1	-19	-19	-1	-1.6
Total 2	2	11	.154	15	14	12	0	0	112	125	2	51	35	14.4	4.58	72	.288	.367	9	.237	2	-16	-16	-1	-1.2
■ ANDY McGAFFIGAN				McGaffigan, Andrew Joseph b: 10/25/56, W.Palm Beach, Fla. BR/TR, 6'3", 185 lbs. Deb: 9/22/81																				
1981 NY-A	0	0	—	2	0	0	0	0	7	5	1	3	2	10.3	2.57	139	.200	.286	0	—	0	1	1	-0	0.1
1982 SF-N	0	1	.000	4	0	0	0	0	8	5	0	1	4	7.9	0.00	—	.179	.233	0	.000	-0	3	3	-0	0.3
1983 SF-N	3	9	.250	43	16	0	0	2	134¹	131	17	39	93	11.5	4.29	82	.255	.309	2	.067	-1	-10	-11	-3	-1.6
1984 Mon-N	3	4	.429	21	3	0	0	1	46	37	2	15	39	10.2	2.54	135	.220	.284	0	.000	-1	5	4	-0	0.4
Cin-N	0	2	.000	9	3	0	0	0	23	23	2	8	18	12.1	5.48	69	.261	.323	0	.000	-0	-5	-4	-1	-0.4

YEAR	TM/L	W	L	PCT	G	GS	CG	SH	SV	IP	H	HR	BB	SO	RAT	ERA	ERA+	OAV	OOB	BH	AVG	PB	PR	/A	PD	TPI
	Yr	3	6	.333	30	6	0	0	1	69	60	4	23	57	10.8	3.52	101	.233	.296	0	.000	-1	1	0	-1	0.0
1985	Cin-N	3	3	.500	15	15	2	0	0	94¹	88	4	30	83	11.4	3.72	102	.247	.309	1	.034	-2	-1	1	0	0.0
1986	Mon-N	10	5	.667	48	14	1	1	2	142²	114	9	55	104	10.8	2.65	139	.223	.301	2	.061	-2	17	17	-2	1.4
1987	Mon-N	5	2	.714	69	0	0	0	12	120¹	105	5	42	100	11.2	2.39	176	.235	.305	0	.000	-1	23	24	-1	2.3
1988	Mon-N	6	0	1.000	63	0	0	0	4	91¹	81	4	37	71	11.8	2.76	130	.233	.311	0	.000	-0	7	8	-1	0.8
1989	Mon-N	3	5	.375	57	0	0	0	2	75	85	3	30	40	14.2	4.68	75	.293	.365	1	1.000	0	-10	-10	-1	-1.0
1990	SF-N	0	0	—	4	0	0	0	0	4²	10	2	4	4	27.0	17.36	21	.455	.538	0	—	0	-7	-7	-0	-0.6
	KC-A	4	3	.571	24	11	0	0	1	78²	75	6	28	49	12.0	3.09	123	.248	.315	0	—	0	7	6	-1	0.6
Total	10	38	33	.535	359	62	3	1	24	825¹	759	55	292	607	11.6	3.37	110	.245	.313	6	.048	-7	30	32	-9	2.3

■ JACK McGEACHEY
McGeachey, John Charles b: 5/23/1864, Clinton, Mass. d: 4/5/30, Cambridge, Mass. BR , 5'8", 165 lbs. Deb: 6/17/1886 ♦

YEAR	TM/L	W	L	PCT	G	GS	CG	SH	SV	IP	H	HR	BB	SO	RAT	ERA	ERA+	OAV	OOB	BH	AVG	PB	PR	/A	PD	TPI
1887	Ind-N	0	1	.000	1	0	0	0	0	6¹	13	2	4	3	24.2	11.37	36	.410	.476	109	.269	0	-5	-5	0	-0.3
1888	Ind-N	0	0	—	1	0	0	0	0	5	5	1	3	0	14.4	7.20	41	.251	.349	99	.219	0	-2	-2	0	-0.1
1889	Ind-N	0	0	—	3	0	0	0	0	4²	7	2	6	3	25.1	11.57	36	.336	.484	142	.267	0	-4	-4	-0	-0.2
Total	3	0	1	.000	5	0	0	0	0	16	25	5	13	6	21.4	10.13	37	.345	.445	604	.245	0	-11	-11	-0	-0.6

■ BILL McGEE
McGee, William Henry "Fiddler Bill" b: 11/16/09, Batchtown, Ill. d: 2/11/87, St.Louis, Mo. BR/TR, 6'1", 215 lbs. Deb: 9/29/35

YEAR	TM/L	W	L	PCT	G	GS	CG	SH	SV	IP	H	HR	BB	SO	RAT	ERA	ERA+	OAV	OOB	BH	AVG	PB	PR	/A	PD	TPI
1935	StL-N	1	0	1.000	1	1	0	0	0	9	3	0	1	2	4.0	1.00	410	.103	.133	1	.333	0	3	3	-0	0.3
1936	StL-N	1	1	.500	7	2	0	0	0	16	23	3	4	8	15.2	7.88	50	.359	.397	1	.250	0	-7	-7	0	-0.5
1937	StL-N	1	0	1.000	4	1	1	0	0	14	13	1	4	9	11.6	2.57	155	.255	.321	1	.200	-0	2	2	0	0.2
1938	StL-N	7	12	.368	47	25	10	1	5	216	216	4	78	104	12.3	3.21	123	.257	.321	14	.209	1	14	18	-1	1.9
1939	StL-N	12	5	.706	43	17	5	4	0	156	155	14	59	56	12.3	3.81	108	.261	.328	8	.145	-3	2	5	0	0.3
1940	StL-N	16	10	.615	38	31	11	3	0	218	222	13	96	78	13.2	3.80	105	.263	.340	13	.178	-1	1	5	-2	0.2
1941	StL-N	0	1	.000	4	3	0	0	0	14	17	1	13	2	19.9	5.14	73	.298	.437	0	.000	-1	-2	-2	0	-0.2
	NY-N	2	9	.182	22	14	1	0	0	106	117	9	54	41	14.5	4.92	75	.285	.368	5	.161	-1	-15	-14	-2	-1.6
	Yr	2	10	.167	26	17	1	0	0	120	134	10	67	43	15.1	4.95	75	.286	.375	0	.000	-2	-18	-17	-2	-1.8
1942	NY-N	6	3	.667	31	8	2	1	1	104	95	8	46	40	12.3	2.94	114	.244	.326	3	.103	-2	4	5	-1	0.2
Total	8	46	41	.529	197	102	31	9	6	853	861	53	355	340	12.9	3.74	104	.263	.336	46	.170	-6	2	14	-5	0.8

■ CONNY McGEEHAN
McGeehan, Cornelius Bernard b: 8/25/1882, Drifton, Pa. d: 7/4/07, Hazleton, Pa. Deb: 7/15/03

YEAR	TM/L	W	L	PCT	G	GS	CG	SH	SV	IP	H	HR	BB	SO	RAT	ERA	ERA+	OAV	OOB	BH	AVG	PB	PR	/A	PD	TPI
1903	Phi-A	1	0	1.000	3	0	0	0	0	10	9	0	1	4	9.0	4.50	68	.240	.260	0	.000	-1	-2	-2	0	-0.1

■ PAT McGEHEE
McGehee, Patrick Henry b: 7/2/1888, Meadville, Miss. d: 12/30/46, Paducah, Ky. BL/TR, 6'2.5", 180 lbs. Deb: 8/23/12

YEAR	TM/L	W	L	PCT	G	GS	CG	SH	SV	IP	H	HR	BB	SO	RAT	ERA	ERA+	OAV	OOB	BH	AVG	PB	PR	/A	PD	TPI
1912	Det-A	0	0	—	1	1	0	0	0	0	1	0	1	0	—	—	—	1.000	1.000	0	—	0	0	0	0	0.0

■ RANDY McGILBERRY
McGilberry, Randall Kent b: 10/29/53, Mobile, Ala. BB/TR, 6'1", 195 lbs. Deb: 9/06/77

YEAR	TM/L	W	L	PCT	G	GS	CG	SH	SV	IP	H	HR	BB	SO	RAT	ERA	ERA+	OAV	OOB	BH	AVG	PB	PR	/A	PD	TPI
1977	KC-A	0	1	.000	3	0	0	0	0	7	7	1	1	1	10.3	5.14	78	.280	.308	0	—	0	-1	-1	0	0.0
1978	KC-A	0	1	.000	18	0	0	0	0	25²	27	2	18	12	15.8	4.21	91	.276	.388	0	—	0	-1	-1	0	0.0
Total	2	0	2	.000	21	0	0	0	0	32²	34	3	19	13	14.6	4.41	88	.276	.373	0	—	0	-2	-2	0	0.0

■ BILL McGILL
McGill, William John "Parson" b: 6/29/1880, Galva, Kan. d: 8/7/59, Alva, Okla. BR/TR, 6'2", Deb: 9/16/07

YEAR	TM/L	W	L	PCT	G	GS	CG	SH	SV	IP	H	HR	BB	SO	RAT	ERA	ERA+	OAV	OOB	BH	AVG	PB	PR	/A	PD	TPI
1907	StL-A	1	0	1.000	2	2	1	0	0	18¹	22	0	2	8	11.8	3.44	73	.299	.318	0	.000	-1	-2	-2	0	-0.2

■ WILLIE McGILL
McGill, William Vaness "Kid" b: 11/10/1873, Atlanta, Ga. d: 8/29/44, Indianapolis, Ind. TL , 5'6.5", 170 lbs. Deb: 5/08/1890

YEAR	TM/L	W	L	PCT	G	GS	CG	SH	SV	IP	H	HR	BB	SO	RAT	ERA	ERA+	OAV	OOB	BH	AVG	PB	PR	/A	PD	TPI
1890	Cle-P	11	9	.550	24	20	19	0	0	183²	222	5	96	82	15.6	4.12	97	.286	.365	10	.147	2	2	-3	1	0.0
1891	Cin-a	2	5	.286	8	8	6	0	0	65	69	1	37	19	14.7	4.98	83	.263	.354	2	.100	0	-9	-6	-1	-0.4
	StL-a	19	10	.655	35	31	22	1	1	249	225	10	131	154	12.9	2.93	144	.233	.325	14	.161	1	22	35	-5	3.1
	Yr	21	15	.583	43	39	28	1	1	314	294	11	168	173	13.2	3.35	125	.239	.331	37	.346	1	13	29	-5	2.7
1892	Cin-N	1	1	.500	3	3	1	0	0	17	18	0	5	7	12.2	5.29	62	.261	.311	2	.286	0	-4	-4	0	-0.2
1893	Chi-N	17	18	.486	39	34	26	1	0	302²	311	6	181	91	14.6	4.61	100	.258	.355	29	.234	2	2	0	-5	-0.1
1894	Chi-N	7	19	.269	27	23	22	0	0	208	272	2	117	58	16.8	5.84	96	.312	.394	20	.244	0	-12	-5	-2	-0.4
1895	Phi-N	10	8	.556	20	20	13	0	0	146	177	2	81	70	15.9	5.55	86	.295	.379	14	.222	-0	-12	-12	-0	-0.9
1896	Phi-N	5	4	.556	12	11	7	0	0	79²	87	0	53	29	15.8	5.31	81	.276	.380	6	.207	-0	-8	-9	0	-0.7
Total	7	72	74	.493	168	150	116	2	1	1251	1381	26	701	510	15.0	4.59	100	.273	.361	97	.202	6	-19	-2	-12	0.4

■ JOHN McGILLEN
McGillen, John Joseph b: 8/6/17, Eddystone, Pa. d: 8/11/87, Upland, Pa. BL/TL, 6'1", 175 lbs. Deb: 4/20/44

YEAR	TM/L	W	L	PCT	G	GS	CG	SH	SV	IP	H	HR	BB	SO	RAT	ERA	ERA+	OAV	OOB	BH	AVG	PB	PR	/A	PD	TPI
1944	Phi-A	0	0	—	2	0	0	0	0	1	1	0	2	0	27.0	18.00	19	.333	.600	0	—	0	-2	-2	0	-0.1

■ JIM McGINLEY
McGinley, James William b: 10/2/1878, Groveland, Mass. d: 9/20/61, Haverhill, Mass. 5'9.5", 165 lbs. Deb: 9/22/04

YEAR	TM/L	W	L	PCT	G	GS	CG	SH	SV	IP	H	HR	BB	SO	RAT	ERA	ERA+	OAV	OOB	BH	AVG	PB	PR	/A	PD	TPI
1904	StL-N	2	1	.667	3	3	3	0	0	27	28	0	6	6	12.3	2.00	135	.267	.325	1	.091	-1	2	2	-1	0.0
1905	StL-N	0	1	.000	1	1	0	0	0	3	5	1	2	0	21.0	15.00	20	.333	.412	1	1.000	0	-4	-4	-0	-0.2
Total	2	2	2	.500	4	4	3	0	0	30	33	1	8	6	13.2	3.30	83	.275	.336	2	.167	-0	-2	-2	-1	-0.2

■ DAN McGINN
McGinn, Daniel Michael b: 11/29/43, Omaha, Neb. BL/TL, 6', 185 lbs. Deb: 9/03/68

YEAR	TM/L	W	L	PCT	G	GS	CG	SH	SV	IP	H	HR	BB	SO	RAT	ERA	ERA+	OAV	OOB	BH	AVG	PB	PR	/A	PD	TPI
1968	Cin-N	0	1	.000	14	0	0	0	0	12	13	1	11	16	18.8	5.25	60	.271	.417	0	.000	-0	-3	-3	0	-0.2
1969	Mon-N	7	10	.412	74	1	0	0	6	132¹	123	8	65	112	13.1	3.94	93	.245	.337	5	.172	1	-5	-4	1	-0.2
1970	Mon-N	7	10	.412	52	19	3	2	0	130²	154	13	78	83	16.5	5.44	76	.296	.395	4	.114	-2	-20	-19	2	-1.8
1971	Mon-N	1	4	.200	28	6	1	0	0	71	74	7	42	40	14.8	5.96	59	.274	.374	4	.235	0	-20	-19	1	-1.7
1972	Chi-N	0	5	.000	42	2	0	0	4	62²	78	5	29	42	15.9	5.89	65	.301	.380	2	.250	1	-17	-14	-1	-1.4
Total	5	15	30	.333	210	28	4	2	10	408²	442	34	225	293	15.1	5.11	74	.276	.372	15	.165	-0	-65	-59	3	-5.3

■ GUS McGINNIS
McGinnis, August b: 1870, Painesville, Ohio 5'11", 168 lbs. Deb: 4/27/1893

YEAR	TM/L	W	L	PCT	G	GS	CG	SH	SV	IP	H	HR	BB	SO	RAT	ERA	ERA+	OAV	OOB	BH	AVG	PB	PR	/A	PD	TPI
1893	Chi-N	2	5	.286	13	5	3	0	0	67¹	85	2	31	13	15.5	5.35	86	.299	.368	6	.240	2	-5	-5	1	-0.2
	Phi-N	1	3	.250	5	4	4	1	0	37¹	39	0	17	12	13.5	4.34	106	.261	.336	3	.200	-1	1	1	0	0.1
	Yr	3	8	.273	18	9	7	1	0	104²	124	2	48	25	14.8	4.99	92	.286	.357	9	.225	1	-4	-4	1	-0.1

■ JUMBO McGINNIS
McGinnis, George Washington b: 2/22/1864, Alton, Mo. d: 5/18/34, St.Louis, Mo. 5'10", 197 lbs. Deb: 5/02/1882

YEAR	TM/L	W	L	PCT	G	GS	CG	SH	SV	IP	H	HR	BB	SO	RAT	ERA	ERA+	OAV	OOB	BH	AVG	PB	PR	/A	PD	TPI
1882	StL-a	25	17	.595	44	44	42	3	0	379¹	376	2	52	134	10.2	2.47	114	.242	.266	44	.217	1	9	14	-5	1.1
1883	StL-a	28	16	.636	45	45	41	6	0	382²	325	3	69	128	9.3	2.33	150	.215	.249	36	.200	-6	41	50	1	4.2
1884	StL-a	24	16	.600	40	40	39	5	0	354¹	331	4	35	141	9.3	2.84	115	.234	.252	34	.233	3	16	17	-0	1.8
1885	StL-a	6	6	.500	13	13	12	3	0	112	98	1	19	41	9.4	3.38	97	.225	.258	11	.220	1	-2	-1	-1	-0.2
1886	StL-a	5	5	.500	10	10	10	1	0	87²	107	2	27	30	13.8	3.80	91	.287	.336	7	.189	-0	-3	-3	0	-0.1
	Bal-a	11	13	.458	26	25	24	0	0	209¹	235	6	48	70	12.2	3.48	98	.271	.309	16	.188	-1	-1	-1	1	-0.1
	Yr	16	18	.471	36	35	34	1	0	297	342	8	75	100	12.6	3.58	96	.276	.317	23	.189	-1	-4	-5	1	-0.3
1887	Cin-a	3	5	.375	8	8	8	0	0	69¹	85	3	43	18	16.6	5.45	79	.291	.382	6	.194	-1	-9	-9	0	-0.6
Total	6	102	78	.567	186	185	176	18	0	1594²	1557	21	293	562	10.4	2.92	113	.241	.274	154	.210	-5	52	67	-5	6.1

■ JOE McGINNITY
McGinnity, Joseph Jerome "Iron Man" b: 3/19/1871, Rock Island, Ill. d: 11/14/29, Brooklyn, N.Y. BR/TR, 5'11", 206 lbs. Deb: 4/18/1899 CH

YEAR	TM/L	W	L	PCT	G	GS	CG	SH	SV	IP	H	HR	BB	SO	RAT	ERA	ERA+	OAV	OOB	BH	AVG	PB	PR	/A	PD	TPI
1899	Bal-N	28	16	.636	48	41	38	4	2	366¹	358	3	93	74	11.1	2.68	148	.256	.302	28	.193	-6	48	52	1	4.6
1900	*Bro-N	28	8	.778	44	37	32	1	0	343	350	5	113	93	12.1	2.94	131	.264	.322	28	.193	-8	29	34	-2	2.6
1901	Bal-A	26	20	.565	48	43	39	1	1	382	412	6	96	75	12.0	3.56	109	.272	.315	31	.209	-4	5	13	-1	0.8
1902	Bal-A	13	10	.565	25	23	19	0	0	198²	219	3	46	39	12.0	3.44	110	.280	.320	25	.287	5	3	7	-2	1.1
	NY-N	8	8	.500	19	16	16	1	0	153	122	1	32	67	9.5	2.06	136	.219	.271	8	.121	-4	12	13	1	1.0
1903	NY-N	31	20	.608	55	48	44	3	2	434	391	4	109	171	10.8	2.43	130	.236	.291	34	.206	-2	41	44	-3	3.9
1904	NY-N	35	8	.814	51	44	38	9	5	408	307	8	86	144	9.0	1.61	169	.206	.256	25	.176	-1	51	51	4	6.0
1905	*NY-N	21	15	.583	46	38	26	2	3	320	289	6	71	125	10.5	2.87	102	.240	.290	28	.233	6	5	2	3	1.1

YEAR	TM/L	W	L	PCT	G	GS	CG	SH	SV	IP	H	HR	BB	SO	RAT	ERA	ERA+	OAV	OOB	BH	AVG	PB	PR	/A	PD	TPI
1906	NY-N	27	12	.692	45	37	32	3	2	339²	316	1	71	105	10.4	2.25	116	.246	.289	15	.130	-4	14	13	2	1.3
1907	NY-N	18	18	.500	47	34	23	3	4	310¹	320	6	58	120	11.4	3.16	78	.266	.308	18	.175	-0	-24	-24	3	-2.3
1908	NY-N	11	7	.611	37	20	7	5	5	186	192	8	37	55	11.4	2.27	106	.267	.310	11	.180	-0	2	3	0	0.3
Total	10	246	142	.634	465	381	314	32	24	3441	3276	52	812	1068	10.9	2.66	120	.249	.297	251	.194	-16	186	207	7	20.4

■ LYNN McGLOTHEN
McGlothen, Lynn Everatt　b: 3/27/50, Monroe, La.　d: 8/14/84, Dubach, La.　BL/TR, 6'2", 185 lbs.　Deb: 6/25/72

YEAR	TM/L	W	L	PCT	G	GS	CG	SH	SV	IP	H	HR	BB	SO	RAT	ERA	ERA+	OAV	OOB	BH	AVG	PB	PR	/A	PD	TPI
1972	Bos-A	8	7	.533	22	22	4	1	0	145	135	9	59	112	12.5	3.41	94	.247	.328	10	.189	1	-6	-3	3	0.1
1973	Bos-A	1	2	.333	6	3	0	0	0	23	39	6	8	16	18.8	8.22	49	.386	.436	0	—	0	-11	-11	0	-0.9
1974	StL-N	16	12	.571	31	31	8	3	0	237¹	212	12	89	142	11.5	2.69	133	.241	.312	15	.181	-1	24	23	1	2.5
1975	StL-N	15	13	.536	35	34	9	2	0	239	231	21	97	146	12.5	3.92	96	.254	.329	7	.087	-5	-8	-4	-2	-1.1
1976	StL-N	13	15	.464	33	32	10	4	0	205	209	10	68	106	12.3	3.91	90	.268	.330	15	.211	2	-9	-8	-1	-0.7
1977	SF-N	2	9	.182	21	15	2	0	0	80	94	9	52	42	16.5	5.62	69	.299	.401	2	.105	-1	-15	-15	-2	-1.6
1978	SF-N	0	0	—	5	1	0	0	0	12²	15	0	4	9	13.5	4.97	69	.313	.365	0	.000	-0	-2	-2	0	-0.2
	Chi-N	5	3	.625	49	1	0	0	0	80	77	7	39	60	13.0	3.04	137	.257	.342	3	.231	1	5	9	-2	0.8
	Yr	5	3	.625	54	2	0	0	0	92²	92	7	43	69	13.1	3.30	120	.264	.344	1	.063	0	3	7	-2	0.6
1979	Chi-N	13	14	.481	42	29	6	1	2	212	236	27	55	147	12.5	4.12	100	.283	.330	16	.225	2	-9	-0	-2	0.0
1980	Chi-N	12	14	.462	39	27	2	2	0	182¹	211	24	64	119	13.6	4.79	82	.293	.352	10	.196	2	-24	-18	-2	-1.7
1981	Chi-N	1	4	.200	20	6	0	0	0	54²	71	1	28	26	16.5	4.77	77	.317	.395	1	.083	-1	-8	-7	1	-0.6
	Chi-A	0	0	—	11	0	0	0	0	21²	14	0	7	12	9.1	4.15	86	.189	.268	0	—	0	-1	-1	-0	-0.1
1982	NY-A	0	0	—	4	0	0	0	0	5	9	1	2	2	19.8	10.80	37	.375	.423	0	—	0	-4	-4	0	-0.2
Total	11	86	93	.480	318	201	41	13	2	1497²	1553	127	572	939	12.9	3.98	94	.270	.339	79	.173	-0	-68	-42	-7	-3.7

■ PAT McGLOTHIN
McGlothin, Ezra Mac　b: 10/20/20, Coalfield, Tenn.　BL/TR, 6'3.5", 180 lbs.　Deb: 4/25/49

YEAR	TM/L	W	L	PCT	G	GS	CG	SH	SV	IP	H	HR	BB	SO	RAT	ERA	ERA+	OAV	OOB	BH	AVG	PB	PR	/A	PD	TPI
1949	Bro-N	1	1	.500	7	0	0	0	0	15²	13	2	5	11	10.3	4.60	89	.224	.286	0	.000	-0	-1	-1	1	0.0
1950	Bro-N	0	0	—	1	0	0	0	0	2	5	0	1	2	27.0	13.50	30	.455	.500	0	—	0	-2	-2	0	-0.1
Total	2	1	1	.500	8	0	0	0	0	17²	18	2	6	13	12.2	5.60	73	.261	.320	0	.000	-0	-3	-3	1	-0.1

■ JIM McGLOTHLIN
McGlothlin, James Milton "Red"　b: 10/6/43, Los Angeles, Cal.　d: 12/23/75, Union, Ky.　BR/TR, 6'1", 185 lbs.　Deb: 9/20/65

YEAR	TM/L	W	L	PCT	G	GS	CG	SH	SV	IP	H	HR	BB	SO	RAT	ERA	ERA+	OAV	OOB	BH	AVG	PB	PR	/A	PD	TPI
1965	Cal-A	0	3	.000	3	3	1	0	0	18	18	1	7	9	12.5	3.50	97	.261	.329	0	.000	-1	-0	-0	-0	0.0
1966	Cal-A	3	1	.750	19	11	0	0	0	67²	79	9	19	41	13.2	4.52	74	.292	.340	1	.059	-0	-8	-9	-0	-0.9
1967	Cal-A	12	8	.600	32	29	9	6	0	197¹	163	13	56	137	10.2	2.96	106	.226	.286	8	.140	-0	6	4	1	0.5
1968	Cal-A	10	15	.400	40	32	8	0	3	208¹	187	19	60	135	11.0	3.54	82	.244	.305	7	.111	-1	-13	-15	2	-1.5
1969	Cal-A	8	16	.333	37	35	4	1	0	201	188	19	58	96	11.2	3.18	110	.249	.307	7	.121	-1	10	7	2	0.8
1970	*Cin-N	14	10	.583	35	34	5	3	0	210²	192	19	86	97	12.0	3.59	112	.245	.322	8	.121	1	11	10	6	1.7
1971	Cin-N	8	12	.400	30	26	6	0	0	170²	151	15	47	93	10.7	3.22	104	.243	.301	7	.137	1	5	3	1	0.5
1972	*Cin-N	9	8	.529	31	21	3	1	0	145	165	15	49	69	13.3	3.91	82	.287	.343	8	.174	3	-7	-11	0	-0.8
1973	Cin-N	3	3	.500	24	9	0	0	0	63¹	91	13	23	18	16.2	6.68	51	.340	.392	2	.125	0	-21	-23	1	-2.0
	Chi-A	0	1	.000	5	0	0	0	0	18¹	13	2	13	14	12.8	3.93	101	.203	.338	0	—	0	-0	-0	0	0.0
Total	9	67	77	.465	256	201	36	11	3	1300¹	1247	125	418	709	11.7	3.61	93	.255	.317	48	.126	2	-19	-34	13	-1.7

■ STONEY McGLYNN
McGlynn, Ulysses Simpson Grant　b: 5/26/1872, Lancaster, Pa.　d: 8/26/41, Manitowoc, Wis.　BR/TR, 5'11", 185 lbs.　Deb: 9/20/06

YEAR	TM/L	W	L	PCT	G	GS	CG	SH	SV	IP	H	HR	BB	SO	RAT	ERA	ERA+	OAV	OOB	BH	AVG	PB	PR	/A	PD	TPI
1906	StL-N	2	2	.500	6	6	6	0	0	48	43	0	15	25	11.1	2.44	108	.249	.312	1	.059	-1	1	1	2	0.2
1907	StL-N	14	25	.359	45	39	33	3	1	352¹	329	6	112	109	11.4	2.91	86	.251	.312	25	.200	3	-17	-16	-0	-1.4
1908	StL-N	1	6	.143	16	6	4	0	1	75²	76	0	17	23	11.3	3.45	68	.256	.301	2	.077	-1	-9	-9	1	-0.9
Total	3	17	33	.340	67	51	43	3	2	476	448	6	144	157	11.3	2.95	85	.252	.310	28	.167	1	-25	-24	3	-2.1

■ MICKEY McGOWAN
McGowan, Tullis Earl　b: 11/26/21, Dothan, Ala.　BL/TL, 6'2", 200 lbs.　Deb: 4/22/48

YEAR	TM/L	W	L	PCT	G	GS	CG	SH	SV	IP	H	HR	BB	SO	RAT	ERA	ERA+	OAV	OOB	BH	AVG	PB	PR	/A	PD	TPI
1948	NY-N	0	0	—	3	0	0	0	0	3²	3	1	4	2	17.2	7.36	53	.231	.412	0	.000	-0	-1	-1	0	0.0

■ HOWARD McGRANER
McGraner, Howard "Muck"　b: 9/11/1889, Hanley Run, Ohio　d: 10/22/52, Zaleski, Ohio　BL/TL, 5'7", 155 lbs.　Deb: 9/12/12

YEAR	TM/L	W	L	PCT	G	GS	CG	SH	SV	IP	H	HR	BB	SO	RAT	ERA	ERA+	OAV	OOB	BH	AVG	PB	PR	/A	PD	TPI
1912	Cin-N	1	0	1.000	4	0	0	0	0	19	22	2	7	5	14.2	7.11	47	.286	.353	2	.250	1	-8	-8	1	-0.5

■ TUG McGRAW
McGraw, Frank Edwin　b: 8/30/44, Martinez, Cal.　BR/TL, 6', 170 lbs.　Deb: 4/18/65

YEAR	TM/L	W	L	PCT	G	GS	CG	SH	SV	IP	H	HR	BB	SO	RAT	ERA	ERA+	OAV	OOB	BH	AVG	PB	PR	/A	PD	TPI
1965	NY-N	2	7	.222	37	9	2	0	1	97²	88	8	48	57	12.8	3.32	106	.249	.344	3	.130	-1	2	2	-1	0.1
1966	NY-N	2	9	.182	15	12	1	0	0	62¹	72	11	25	34	14.0	5.34	68	.294	.359	4	.235	1	-12	-12	-0	-1.0
1967	NY-N	0	3	.000	4	4	0	0	0	17¹	13	3	13	18	13.5	7.79	44	.206	.342	1	.250	0	-9	-8	0	-0.7
1969	*NY-N	9	3	.750	42	4	1	0	12	100¹	89	6	47	92	12.2	2.24	163	.243	.329	4	.167	0	15	16	0	1.8
1970	NY-N	4	6	.400	57	0	0	0	10	90²	77	6	49	81	12.6	3.28	123	.231	.332	4	.308	1	8	8	1	1.0
1971	NY-N	11	4	.733	51	1	0	0	8	111	73	4	41	109	9.5	1.70	200	.189	.271	4	.222	2	22	21	-1	2.4
1972	NY-N	8	6	.571	54	0	0	0	27	106	71	3	40	92	9.7	1.70	198	.197	.282	2	.100	-0	21	20	0	2.1
1973	*NY-N	5	6	.455	60	2	0	0	25	118²	106	11	55	81	12.4	3.87	93	.243	.331	4	.167	1	-3	-3	1	-0.1
1974	NY-N	6	11	.353	41	4	1	1	3	88²	96	12	32	54	13.0	4.16	86	.279	.340	1	.071	-0	-5	-6	-1	-0.6
1975	Phi-N	9	6	.600	56	0	0	0	14	102²	84	9	36	55	10.8	2.98	125	.226	.299	2	.154	-0	7	9	0	0.9
1976	*Phi-N	7	6	.538	58	0	0	0	11	97¹	81	4	42	76	11.4	2.50	142	.226	.307	1	.143	0	11	11	-1	1.1
1977	*Phi-N	7	3	.700	45	0	0	0	9	79	62	6	24	58	9.9	2.62	153	.221	.284	4	.400	2	11	12	0	1.4
1978	*Phi-N	8	7	.533	55	1	0	0	9	89²	82	6	23	63	10.5	3.21	111	.245	.293	0	.000	-0	4	3	0	0.4
1979	Phi-N	4	3	.571	65	1	0	0	16	83²	83	9	29	57	12.3	5.16	74	.259	.324	1	.167	-0	-13	-12	-1	-1.3
1980	*Phi-N	5	4	.556	57	0	0	0	20	92¹	62	3	23	75	8.5	1.46	259	.194	.253	2	.250	0	22	24	0	2.6
1981	*Phi-N	2	4	.333	34	0	0	0	10	44	35	2	14	26	10.0	2.66	136	.219	.282	0	.000	-0	4	5	0	0.4
1982	Phi-N	3	3	.500	34	0	0	0	5	39²	50	3	12	25	14.3	4.31	85	.305	.356	0	.000	-0	-3	-3	1	-0.2
1983	Phi-N	2	1	.667	34	1	0	0	0	55²	58	4	19	30	12.4	3.56	100	.271	.330	1	.333	0	0	0	1	0.1
1984	Phi-N	2	0	1.000	25	0	0	0	0	38	36	1	10	26	10.9	3.79	96	.245	.293	1	.333	0	-1	-1	0	0.0
Total	19	96	92	.511	824	39	5	1	180	1514²	1318	108	582	1109	11.4	3.14	116	.237	.312	39	.182	5	81	85	-2	10.3

■ JOHN McGRAW
McGraw, John　b: 1890　d: 11/14/18, Cleveland, Ohio　190 lbs.　Deb: 7/29/14

YEAR	TM/L	W	L	PCT	G	GS	CG	SH	SV	IP	H	HR	BB	SO	RAT	ERA	ERA+	OAV	OOB	BH	AVG	PB	PR	/A	PD	TPI
1914	Bro-F	0	0	—	1	0	0	0	0	2	0	0	1	0	4.5	0.00	—	.000	.155	0	—	0	1	1	0	0.1

■ BOB McGRAW
McGraw, Robert Emmett　b: 4/10/1895, LaVeta, Colo.　d: 6/2/78, Boise, Idaho　BR/TR, 6'2", 160 lbs.　Deb: 9/25/17

YEAR	TM/L	W	L	PCT	G	GS	CG	SH	SV	IP	H	HR	BB	SO	RAT	ERA	ERA+	OAV	OOB	BH	AVG	PB	PR	/A	PD	TPI
1917	NY-A	0	1	.000	2	1	1	0	0	11	9	0	3	3	9.8	0.82	329	.257	.316	0	.000	-0	2	2	-0	0.2
1918	NY-A	0	1	.000	1	1	0	0	0	0	0	0	4	0	—	∞	—	—	1.000	0	—	0	-4	-4	0	-0.3
1919	NY-A	1	0	1.000	6	0	0	0	0	16¹	11	1	10	3	12.1	3.31	97	.216	.355	0	.000	-0	-0	-0	0	-0.0
	Bos-A	0	2	.000	10	1	0	0	0	26²	33	0	17	6	17.9	6.75	45	.347	.461	1	.100	-1	-10	-11	-1	-1.1
	Yr	1	2	.333	16	1	0	0	0	43	44	1	27	9	15.5	5.44	57	.299	.418	1	.077	-1	-11	-11	-1	-1.1
1920	NY-A	0	0	—	15	0	0	0	0	27	24	1	20	11	15.0	4.67	82	.240	.372	0	.000	-0	-3	-3	-1	-0.3
1925	Bro-N	0	2	.000	2	2	0	0	0	19²	14	0	13	3	12.4	3.20	130	.202	.355	1	.167	-0	2	2	-1	0.1
1926	Bro-N	9	13	.409	33	21	10	0	1	174¹	197	12	67	49	13.7	4.59	83	.292	.358	8	.145	-2	-15	-15	-1	-1.6
1927	Bro-N	0	1	.000	1	1	0	0	0	4	5	1	2	2	15.8	9.00	44	.313	.389	0	.000	-0	-2	-2	0	-0.1
	StL-N	4	5	.444	18	12	4	1	0	94	121	3	30	37	14.5	5.07	78	.323	.373	6	.182	1	-12	-12	1	-0.9
	Yr	4	6	.400	19	13	4	1	0	98	126	4	32	39	14.5	5.23	75	.322	.374	0	.000	1	-14	-14	1	-1.0
1928	Phi-N	7	8	.467	39	3	0	0	0	132	150	7	56	28	14.1	4.64	92	.326	.400	4	.111	-2	-10	-5	0	-0.7
1929	Phi-N	5	5	.500	41	4	0	0	4	86¹	113	6	43	22	16.5	5.73	91	.324	.401	4	.200	0	-10	-5	1	-0.2
Total	9	26	38	.406	168	47	17	1	6	591¹	677	31	265	164	14.5	4.89	83	.305	.382	24	.138	-6	-61	-54	-1	-4.9

■ SCOTT McGREGOR
McGregor, Scott Houston　b: 1/18/54, Inglewood, Cal.　BB/TL, 6'1", 190 lbs.　Deb: 9/19/76

YEAR	TM/L	W	L	PCT	G	GS	CG	SH	SV	IP	H	HR	BB	SO	RAT	ERA	ERA+	OAV	OOB	BH	AVG	PB	PR	/A	PD	TPI
1976	Bal-A	0	1	.000	3	2	0	0	0	14²	17	0	5	6	13.5	3.68	89	.293	.349	0	—	0	-0	-1	0	0.0

YEAR	TM/L	W	L	PCT	G	GS	CG	SH	SV	IP	H	HR	BB	SO	RAT	ERA	ERA+	OAV	OOB	BH	AVG	PB	PR	/A	PD	TPI
1977	Bal-A	3	5	.375	29	5	1	0	4	114	119	8	30	55	12.3	4.42	86	.275	.333	0	—	0	-5	-8	-1	-0.8
1978	Bal-A	15	13	.536	35	32	13	4	1	233	217	19	47	94	10.2	3.32	105	.248	.287	0	—	0	11	4	1	0.6
1979	*Bal-A	13	6	.684	27	23	7	2	0	174²	165	19	23	81	**9.8**	3.35	120	.248	**.275**	0	—	0	17	13	-1	1.2
1980	Bal-A	20	8	.714	36	36	12	4	0	252	254	16	58	119	11.2	3.32	119	.265	.308	0	—	0	20	18	-2	1.6
1981	Bal-A	13	5	.722	24	22	8	3	0	160	167	13	40	82	11.6	3.26	111	.273	.318	0	—	0	7	6	1	0.8
1982	Bal-A	14	12	.538	37	37	7	1	0	226¹	238	31	52	84	11.6	4.61	87	.267	.308	0	—	0	-14	-15	-1	-1.4
1983	*Bal-A	18	7	.720	36	36	12	2	0	260	271	24	45	86	11.0	3.18	124	.269	.301	0	—	0	25	22	0	2.3
1984	Bal-A	15	12	.556	30	30	10	3	0	196¹	216	18	54	67	12.6	3.94	98	.280	.331	0	—	0	1	-2	2	0.0
1985	Bal-A	14	14	.500	35	34	8	1	0	204	226	34	65	86	12.9	4.81	84	.283	.337	0	—	0	-15	-18	-0	-1.6
1986	Bal-A	11	15	.423	34	33	4	2	0	203	216	35	57	95	12.2	4.52	91	.270	.321	0	—	0	-8	-9	0	-0.7
1987	Bal-A	2	7	.222	26	15	1	1	0	85¹	112	15	35	39	15.8	6.64	66	.326	.393	0	—	0	-21	-21	3	-1.6
1988	Bal-A	0	3	.000	4	4	0	0	0	17¹	27	3	7	10	17.7	8.83	44	.370	.425	0	—	0	-9	-9	1	-0.7
Total 13		138	108	.561	356	309	83	23	5	2140²	2245	235	518	904	11.7	3.99	98	.271	.316	0	—	0	10	-19	2	-0.3

■ SLIM McGREW
McGrew, Walter Howard b: 8/5/1899, Yoakum, Tex. d: 8/21/67, Houston, Tex. BR/TR, 6'7.5", 235 lbs. Deb: 4/18/22

YEAR	TM/L	W	L	PCT	G	GS	CG	SH	SV	IP	H	HR	BB	SO	RAT	ERA	ERA+	OAV	OOB	BH	AVG	PB	PR	/A	PD	TPI
1922	Was-A	0	0	—	1	0	0	0	0	1²	4	0	2	1	32.4	10.80	36	.500	.600	0	.000	-0	-1	-1	0	0.0
1923	Was-A	0	0	—	3	0	0	0	0	5	11	0	3	1	25.2	12.60	30	.440	.500	0	.000	-0	-5	-5	0	-0.3
1924	Was-A	0	1	.000	6	2	0	0	0	23¹	25	1	12	8	14.3	5.01	80	.281	.366	0	.000	-1	-2	-3	-1	-0.3
Total 3		0	1	.000	10	2	0	0	0	30	40	1	17	10	17.1	6.60	60	.328	.410	0	.000	-2	-8	-9	-0	-0.6

■ McGUIRE
McGuire Deb: 6/16/1894

YEAR	TM/L	W	L	PCT	G	GS	CG	SH	SV	IP	H	HR	BB	SO	RAT	ERA	ERA+	OAV	OOB	BH	AVG	PB	PR	/A	PD	TPI
1894	Cin-N	0	0	—	1	0	0	0	0	6	15	0	5	1	30.0	10.50	53	.465	.537	1	.250	-0	-3	-3	0	-0.1

■ DEACON McGUIRE
McGuire, James Thomas b: 11/18/1863, Youngstown, Ohio d: 10/31/36, Albion, Mich. BR/TR, 6'1", 185 lbs. Deb: 6/21/1884 MC♦

YEAR	TM/L	W	L	PCT	G	GS	CG	SH	SV	IP	H	HR	BB	SO	RAT	ERA	ERA+	OAV	OOB	BH	AVG	PB	PR	/A	PD	TPI
1890	Roc-a	0	0	—	1	0	0	0	0	4	10	0	1	1	24.8	6.75	53	.458	.481	99	.299	0	-1	-1	0	0.0

■ TOM McGUIRE
McGuire, Thomas Patrick "Elmer" b: 2/1/1892, Chicago, Ill. d: 12/7/59, Phoenix, Ariz. BR/TR, 6', 175 lbs. Deb: 4/18/14

YEAR	TM/L	W	L	PCT	G	GS	CG	SH	SV	IP	H	HR	BB	SO	RAT	ERA	ERA+	OAV	OOB	BH	AVG	PB	PR	/A	PD	TPI
1914	Chi-F	5	6	.455	24	12	7	0	0	131¹	143	7	57	37	14.0	3.70	80	.288	.366	19	.271	4	-7	-11	1	-0.3
1919	Chi-A	0	0	—	1	0	0	0	0	3	5	0	3	0	24.0	9.00	35	.500	.615	0	.000	-0	-2	-2	0	-0.1
Total 2		5	6	.455	25	12	7	0	0	134¹	148	7	60	37	14.2	3.82	77	.292	.371	19	.268	4	-9	-13	1	-0.4

■ BILL McGUNNIGLE
McGunnigle, William Henry "Gunner" b: 1/1/1855, Boston, Mass. d: 3/9/1899, Brockton, Mass. BR/TR, 5'9", 155 lbs. Deb: 5/02/1879 M♦

YEAR	TM/L	W	L	PCT	G	GS	CG	SH	SV	IP	H	HR	BB	SO	RAT	ERA	ERA+	OAV	OOB	BH	AVG	PB	PR	/A	PD	TPI
1879	Buf-N	9	5	.643	14	13	13	2	0	120	113	0	16	62	9.7	2.63	100	**.233**	.257	30	.175	-2	-2	-0	1	0.0
1880	Buf-N	2	3	.400	5	5	4	1	0	37	43	0	8	3	12.4	3.41	72	.276	.312	4	.182	-1	-4	-4	-1	-0.4
Total 2		11	8	.579	19	18	17	3	0	157	156	0	24	65	10.3	2.81	92	.243	.271	35	.173	-3	-6	-4	0	-0.4

■ MARTY McHALE
McHale, Martin Joseph b: 10/30/1888, Stoneham, Mass. d: 5/7/79, Hempstead, N.Y. BR/TR, 5'11.5", 174 lbs. Deb: 9/28/10

YEAR	TM/L	W	L	PCT	G	GS	CG	SH	SV	IP	H	HR	BB	SO	RAT	ERA	ERA+	OAV	OOB	BH	AVG	PB	PR	/A	PD	TPI
1910	Bos-A	0	2	.000	2	2	1	0	0	13²	15	0	6	14	14.5	4.61	55	.259	.338	0	.000	-1	-3	-3	-0	-0.3
1911	Bos-A	0	0	—	4	1	0	0	0	9¹	19	1	3	3	22.2	9.64	34	.475	.523	0	.000	-0	-7	-7	-0	-0.5
1913	NY-A	2	4	.333	7	6	4	1	0	48²	49	1	10	11	11.1	2.96	101	.266	.308	0	.000	-1	-0	0	-1	-0.1
1914	NY-A	7	16	.304	31	23	12	0	1	191	195	3	33	75	10.9	2.97	93	.268	.303	12	.200	2	-5	-4	-3	-0.5
1915	NY-A	3	7	.300	13	11	6	0	0	78¹	86	1	19	25	12.1	4.25	69	.277	.318	3	.143	1	-11	-11	0	-1.0
1916	Bos-A	0	1	.000	2	1	0	0	0	6	7	0	4	1	18.0	3.00	92	.280	.400	0	—	0	-0	-0	0	0.1
	Cle-A	0	0	—	5	0	0	0	0	11¹	10	1	6	2	12.7	5.56	54	.270	.372	0	.000	-0	-3	-3	-0	-0.3
	Yr	0	1	.000	7	1	0	0	0	17¹	17	1	10	3	14.0	4.67	63	.270	.370	1	.500	0	-4	-3	0	-0.2
Total 6		12	30	.286	64	44	23	1	1	358¹	381	7	81	131	11.8	3.57	80	.275	.319	15	.140	-0	-30	-29	-3	-2.6

■ VANCE McILREE
McIlree, Vance Elmer b: 10/14/1897, Riverside, Iowa d: 5/6/59, Kansas City, Mo. BR/TR, 6', 160 lbs. Deb: 9/13/21

YEAR	TM/L	W	L	PCT	G	GS	CG	SH	SV	IP	H	HR	BB	SO	RAT	ERA	ERA+	OAV	OOB	BH	AVG	PB	PR	/A	PD	TPI
1921	Was-A	0	0	—	1	0	0	0	0	1	1	0	0	0	9.0	9.00	46	.200	.200	0	—	0	-1	-1	0	0.0

■ IRISH McILVEEN
McIlveen, Henry Cooke b: 7/27/1880, Belfast, Ireland d: 10/18/60, Lorain, Ohio TL, 5'11.5", 180 lbs. Deb: 7/10/06 ♦

YEAR	TM/L	W	L	PCT	G	GS	CG	SH	SV	IP	H	HR	BB	SO	RAT	ERA	ERA+	OAV	OOB	BH	AVG	PB	PR	/A	PD	TPI
1906	Pit-N	0	1	.000	2	1	0	0	0	7	10	1	2	3	15.4	7.71	35	.357	.400	2	.400	1	-4	-4	0	-0.3

■ STOVER McILWAIN
McIlwain, Stover William "Smokey" b: 9/22/39, Savannah, Ga. d: 1/15/66, Buffalo, N.Y. BR/TR, 6'2", 195 lbs. Deb: 9/25/57

YEAR	TM/L	W	L	PCT	G	GS	CG	SH	SV	IP	H	HR	BB	SO	RAT	ERA	ERA+	OAV	OOB	BH	AVG	PB	PR	/A	PD	TPI
1957	Chi-A	0	0	—	1	0	0	0	0	1	2	0	1	0	27.0	0.00	—	.500	.600	0	—	0	0	0	0	0.0
1958	Chi-A	0	0	—	1	1	0	0	0	4	4	1	0	4	9.0	2.25	162	.250	.250	0	.000	-0	1	1	0	0.0
Total 2		0	0	—	2	1	0	0	0	5	6	1	1	4	12.6	1.80	203	.300	.333	0	.000	-0	1	1	0	0.0

■ HARRY McINTIRE
McIntire, John Reid b: 1/11/1879, Dayton, Ohio d: 1/9/49, Daytona Beach, Fla. BR/TR, 5'11", 180 lbs. Deb: 4/14/05

YEAR	TM/L	W	L	PCT	G	GS	CG	SH	SV	IP	H	HR	BB	SO	RAT	ERA	ERA+	OAV	OOB	BH	AVG	PB	PR	/A	PD	TPI
1905	Bro-N	8	25	.242	40	35	29	1	1	309	340	6	101	135	13.4	3.70	78	.285	.351	34	.246	6	-24	-28	-3	-2.4
1906	Bro-N	13	21	.382	39	31	25	4	3	276	254	2	89	121	11.6	2.97	85	.247	.316	18	.175	1	-10	-14	-1	-1.5
1907	Bro-N	7	15	.318	28	22	19	3	0	199²	178	2	79	49	11.9	2.39	98	.248	.329	15	.217	5	-2	-1	-0	0.3
1908	Bro-N	11	20	.355	40	35	26	4	2	288	259	5	90	108	11.5	2.69	87	.252	.324	20	.200	2	-10	-11	-2	-1.2
1909	Bro-N	7	17	.292	32	26	20	2	1	228	200	5	91	82	12.3	3.63	71	.246	.337	13	.171	1	-26	-26	0	-2.6
1910	*Chi-N	13	9	.591	28	19	10	2	0	176	152	5	50	65	10.8	3.07	94	.240	.305	17	.258	3	-1	-4	-0	0.0
1911	Chi-N	11	7	.611	25	17	9	1	0	149	147	5	33	56	11.1	4.11	81	.257	.302	14	.264	4	-12	-13	-1	-0.8
1912	Chi-N	1	2	.333	4	3	2	0	0	23²	22	0	6	8	10.6	3.80	88	.247	.295	3	.300	1	-1	-1	0	0.0
1913	Cin-N	0	1	.000	1	0	0	0	0	1	3	0	0	0	27.0	27.00	12	.600	.600	0	—	0	-3	-3	0	-0.1
Total 9		71	117	.378	237	188	140	17	7	1650¹	1555	34	539	626	11.9	3.22	83	.256	.326	134	.218	23	-85	-100	-6	-8.3

■ JOE McINTOSH
McIntosh, Joseph Anthony b: 8/4/51, Billings, Mont. BB/TR, 6'2", 185 lbs. Deb: 4/05/74

YEAR	TM/L	W	L	PCT	G	GS	CG	SH	SV	IP	H	HR	BB	SO	RAT	ERA	ERA+	OAV	OOB	BH	AVG	PB	PR	/A	PD	TPI
1974	SD-N	0	4	.000	10	5	0	0	0	37¹	36	3	17	22	13.0	3.62	98	.250	.333	0	.000	-1	0	-0	-0	-0.1
1975	SD-N	8	15	.348	37	28	4	1	0	183	195	14	60	71	12.6	3.69	94	.273	.332	9	.188	2	-1	-4	-0	-0.2
Total 2		8	19	.296	47	33	4	1	0	220¹	231	17	77	93	12.7	3.68	95	.270	.332	9	.155	1	-1	-5	-0	-0.3

■ FRANK McINTYRE
McIntyre, Frank W. b: Detroit d: 7/8/1887, Detroit, Mich. Deb: 5/16/1883

YEAR	TM/L	W	L	PCT	G	GS	CG	SH	SV	IP	H	HR	BB	SO	RAT	ERA	ERA+	OAV	OOB	BH	AVG	PB	PR	/A	PD	TPI
1883	Det-N	1	0	1.000	1	1	1	0	0	11	11	0	1	0	9.8	0.82	380	.245	.262	0	.000	-0	3	3	0	0.3
	Col-a	1	1	.500	2	2	2	0	0	19	20	0	7	6	12.8	5.21	59	.253	.314	0	.000	-0	-4	-5	-1	-0.4

■ DOC McJAMES
McJames, James McCutchen (b: James Mc Cutchen James) b: 8/27/1873, Williamsburg, S.C. d: 9/23/01, Charleston, S.C. TR, Deb: 9/24/1895

YEAR	TM/L	W	L	PCT	G	GS	CG	SH	SV	IP	H	HR	BB	SO	RAT	ERA	ERA+	OAV	OOB	BH	AVG	PB	PR	/A	PD	TPI
1895	Was-N	1	1	.500	2	2	2	0	0	17	17	0	16	9	17.5	1.59	302	.256	.401	1	.143	-1	6	6	0	0.5
1896	Was-N	12	20	.375	37	33	29	0	1	280¹	310	2	135	103	14.3	4.27	103	.278	.356	18	.162	-9	3	4	-1	-0.3
1897	Was-N	15	23	.395	44	39	33	3	2	323²	361	7	137	**156**	13.8	3.61	120	.280	.349	21	.169	-7	25	26	-1	1.6
1898	Bal-N	27	15	.643	45	42	40	2	0	374	327	6	113	178	10.6	2.36	152	.234	.349	27	.181	-4	52	51	-4	4.2
1899	Bro-N	19	15	.559	37	34	27	1	1	275¹	295	4	122	105	13.6	3.50	112	.274	.347	19	.170	-5	11	13	2	0.9
1901	Bro-N	5	6	.455	13	12	6	0	0	91	104	1	40	42	14.9	4.75	71	.285	.367	1	.029	-4	-14	-14	-2	-1.7
Total 6		79	80	.497	178	162	137	6	4	1361¹	1414	19	563	593	13.1	3.43	117	.266	.337	87	.162	-29	83	86	-4	5.2

■ ARCHIE McKAIN
McKain, Archie Richard "Happy" b: 5/12/11, Delphos, Kan. d: 5/21/85, Salina, Kan. BB/TL, 5'10", 175 lbs. Deb: 4/25/37

YEAR	TM/L	W	L	PCT	G	GS	CG	SH	SV	IP	H	HR	BB	SO	RAT	ERA	ERA+	OAV	OOB	BH	AVG	PB	PR	/A	PD	TPI
1937	Bos-A	8	8	.500	36	18	3	0	2	137	152	7	64	66	14.2	4.66	102	.275	.351	13	.265	3	-1	1	0	0.4
1938	Bos-A	5	4	.556	37	5	1	0	6	99²	119	6	44	27	14.9	4.52	109	.297	.369	2	.065	-2	3	**5**	2	0.4
1939	Det-A	5	6	.455	32	11	4	1	4	129²	120	6	54	49	12.1	3.68	133	.247	.322	9	.220	4	14	17	-2	1.9
1940	*Det-A	5	0	1.000	27	0	0	0	3	51	48	2	25	24	12.9	2.82	168	.247	.330	3	.143	-0	9	11	1	1.2
1941	Det-A	2	1	.667	15	0	0	0	1	43	58	3	11	14	14.4	5.02	90	.330	.369	0	.000	-1	-4	-2	3	0.0
	StL-A	0	1	.000	8	0	0	0	0	10	16	2	4	2	18.9	8.10	53	.364	.429	0	.000	-0	-4	-4	1	-0.3
	Yr	2	2	.500	23	0	0	0	1	53	74	5	15	16	15.3	5.60	80	.336	.381	1	.077	-2	-9	-7	3	-0.3

YEAR TM/L	W	L	PCT	G	GS	CG	SH	SV	IP	H	HR	BB	SO	RAT	ERA	ERA+	OAV	OOB	BH	AVG	PB	PR	/A	PD	TPI
1943 StL-A	1	1	.500	10	0	0	0	0	16	16	0	6	6	12.4	3.94	84	.242	.306	0	.000	-0	-1	-1	0	0.0
Total 6	26	21	.553	165	34	8	1	16	486¹	529	26	208	188	13.7	4.26	112	.276	.348	25	.176	3	15	27	5	3.6

■ HAL McKAIN   McKain, Harold Le Roy   b: 7/10/06, Logan, Iowa   d: 1/24/70, Sacramento, Cal.   BL/TR, 5'11", 185 lbs.   Deb: 9/22/27

YEAR TM/L	W	L	PCT	G	GS	CG	SH	SV	IP	H	HR	BB	SO	RAT	ERA	ERA+	OAV	OOB	BH	AVG	PB	PR	/A	PD	TPI
1927 Cle-A	0	1	.000	2	1	0	0	0	11	18	0	4	5	18.0	4.09	103	.391	.440	0	.000	-1	0	0	0	0.0
1929 Chi-A	6	9	.400	34	10	4	1	1	158	158	10	85	33	14.4	3.65	117	.275	.378	10	.227	2	11	11	4	1.7
1930 Chi-A	6	4	.600	32	5	0	0	5	89	108	0	42	52	15.5	5.56	83	.299	.377	13	.419	7	-9	-9	1	-0.1
1931 Chi-A	6	9	.400	27	8	3	0	0	112	134	10	57	39	15.6	5.71	75	.295	.377	5	.119	-1	-16	-18	1	-1.5
1932 Chi-A	0	0	—	8	0	0	0	0	11¹	17	1	5	7	17.5	11.12	39	.340	.400	0	.000	-0	-8	-9	0	-0.6
Total 5	18	23	.439	103	24	7	1	6	381¹	435	21	193	136	15.2	4.93	88	.293	.380	28	.230	8	-23	-24	7	-0.5

■ REEVE McKAY   McKay, Reeve Stewart "Rip"   b: 11/16/1881, Morgan, Tex.   d: 1/18/46, Dallas, Tex.   TR, 6'1.5", 168 lbs.   Deb: 10/02/15

YEAR TM/L	W	L	PCT	G	GS	CG	SH	SV	IP	H	HR	BB	SO	RAT	ERA	ERA+	OAV	OOB	BH	AVG	PB	PR	/A	PD	TPI
1915 StL-A	0	0	—	1	0	0	0	0	1	1	0	0	0	9.0	9.00	32	.500	.500	0	—	0	-1	-1	0	0.0

■ JIM McKEE   McKee, James Marion   b: 2/1/47, Columbus, Ohio   BR/TR, 6'7", 215 lbs.   Deb: 9/15/72

YEAR TM/L	W	L	PCT	G	GS	CG	SH	SV	IP	H	HR	BB	SO	RAT	ERA	ERA+	OAV	OOB	BH	AVG	PB	PR	/A	PD	TPI
1972 Pit-N	1	0	1.000	2	0	0	0	0	5	2	0	1	4	5.4	0.00	—	.125	.176	0	—	0	2	2	-0	0.2
1973 Pit-N	0	1	.000	15	1	0	0	0	27	31	2	17	13	16.3	5.67	62	.287	.389	0	.000	-0	-6	-6	-0	-0.6
Total 2	1	1	.500	17	1	0	0	0	32	33	2	18	17	14.6	4.78	73	.266	.364	0	.000	-0	-4	-5	-0	-0.4

■ ROGERS McKEE   McKee, Rogers Hornsby   b: 9/16/26, Shelby, N.C.   BL/TL, 6'1", 160 lbs.   Deb: 8/18/43

YEAR TM/L	W	L	PCT	G	GS	CG	SH	SV	IP	H	HR	BB	SO	RAT	ERA	ERA+	OAV	OOB	BH	AVG	PB	PR	/A	PD	TPI
1943 Phi-N	1	0	1.000	4	1	1	0	0	13¹	12	0	5	1	11.5	6.08	56	.226	.293	1	.200	0	-4	-4	0	-0.3
1944 Phi-N	0	0	—	1	0	0	0	0	2	2	1	1	0	13.5	4.50	80	.250	.333	0	—	-0	-0	-0	0	0.0
Total 2	1	0	1.000	5	1	1	0	0	15¹	14	1	6	1	11.7	5.87	58	.230	.299	1	.200	0	-4	-4	0	-0.3

■ TIM McKEITHAN   McKeithan, Emmett James   b: 11/2/06, Lawndale, N.C.   d: 8/20/69, Forest City, N.C.   BR/TR, 6'2", 182 lbs.   Deb: 7/21/32

YEAR TM/L	W	L	PCT	G	GS	CG	SH	SV	IP	H	HR	BB	SO	RAT	ERA	ERA+	OAV	OOB	BH	AVG	PB	PR	/A	PD	TPI
1932 Phi-A	0	1	.000	4	2	0	0	0	12²	18	0	5	0	16.3	7.11	64	.340	.397	0	.000	0	-4	-4	0	-0.2
1933 Phi-A	1	0	1.000	3	1	0	0	0	9	10	0	4	3	14.0	4.00	107	.278	.350	1	.333	0	0	0	0	0.1
1934 Phi-A	0	0	—	3	0	0	0	0	4	7	2	5	0	27.0	15.75	28	.389	.522	0	.000	-0	-5	-5	-0	-0.4
Total 3	1	1	.500	10	3	0	0	0	25²	35	2	14	3	17.2	7.36	60	.327	.405	1	.143	0	-8	-8	0	-0.5

■ RUSS McKELVY   McKelvy, Russell Errett   b: 9/8/1856, Meadville, Pa.   d: 10/19/15, Omaha, Neb.   BR/TR,   Deb: 5/01/1878 ♦

YEAR TM/L	W	L	PCT	G	GS	CG	SH	SV	IP	H	HR	BB	SO	RAT	ERA	ERA+	OAV	OOB	BH	AVG	PB	PR	/A	PD	TPI
1878 Ind-N	0	2	.000	4	1	1	0	0	25	38	1	3	3	14.8	2.16	94	.333	.350	57	.225	0	0	-0	1	0.0

■ KIT McKENNA   McKenna, James William   b: 2/10/1873, Lynchburg, Va.   d: 3/31/41, Lynchburg, Va.   Deb: 7/07/1898

YEAR TM/L	W	L	PCT	G	GS	CG	SH	SV	IP	H	HR	BB	SO	RAT	ERA	ERA+	OAV	OOB	BH	AVG	PB	PR	/A	PD	TPI
1898 Bro-N	2	6	.250	14	9	7	0	0	100²	118	4	57	27	15.6	5.63	64	.290	.377	9	.225	1	-23	-23	2	-1.7
1899 Bal-N	2	3	.400	8	4	4	0	1	45	66	1	19	7	17.0	4.60	86	.340	.399	1	.059	-1	-4	-3	-0	-0.3
Total 2	4	9	.308	22	13	11	0	1	145²	184	5	76	34	16.1	5.31	70	.306	.384	10	.175	-0	-26	-26	2	-2.0

■ LIMB McKENRY   McKenry, Frank Gordon "Big Pete"   b: 8/13/1888, Piney Flats, Tenn.   d: 11/1/56, Fresno, Cal.   BR/TR, 6'4", 205 lbs.   Deb: 8/27/15

YEAR TM/L	W	L	PCT	G	GS	CG	SH	SV	IP	H	HR	BB	SO	RAT	ERA	ERA+	OAV	OOB	BH	AVG	PB	PR	/A	PD	TPI
1915 Cin-N	5	5	.500	21	11	5	0	0	110¹	94	2	39	37	11.1	2.94	97	.238	.311	5	.152	0	-2	-1	1	0.1
1916 Cin-N	1	1	.500	6	1	0	0	0	14²	14	0	8	2	14.7	4.30	60	.259	.375	2	.400	2	-3	-3	0	0.0
Total 2	6	6	.500	27	12	5	0	0	125	108	2	47	39	11.5	3.10	91	.241	.319	7	.184	2	-5	-4	1	0.1

■ JOEL McKEON   McKeon, Joel Jacob   b: 2/25/63, Covington, Ky.   BL/TL, 6', 185 lbs.   Deb: 5/06/86

YEAR TM/L	W	L	PCT	G	GS	CG	SH	SV	IP	H	HR	BB	SO	RAT	ERA	ERA+	OAV	OOB	BH	AVG	PB	PR	/A	PD	TPI
1986 Chi-A	3	1	.750	30	0	0	0	1	33	18	2	17	18	9.5	2.45	176	.165	.278	0	—	0	6	7	-0	0.6
1987 Chi-A	1	2	.333	13	0	0	0	0	21	27	8	15	14	18.0	9.43	49	.318	.420	0	—	0	-12	-11	-0	-1.0
Total 2	4	3	.571	43	0	0	0	1	54	45	10	32	32	12.8	5.17	85	.232	.341	0	—	0	-5	-5	-1	-0.4

■ LARRY McKEON   McKeon, Lawrence G.   b: 3/25/1866, New York   d: 7/18/15, Indianapolis, Ind   5'10", 168 lbs.   Deb: 5/01/1884

YEAR TM/L	W	L	PCT	G	GS	CG	SH	SV	IP	H	HR	BB	SO	RAT	ERA	ERA+	OAV	OOB	BH	AVG	PB	PR	/A	PD	TPI
1884 Ind-a	18	41	.305	61	60	59	2	0	512	488	20	94	308	10.2	3.50	93	.238	.271	53	.212	-3	-14	-13	7	-0.8
1885 Cin-a	20	13	.606	33	33	32	2	0	290	273	5	50	117	10.0	2.86	114	.238	.270	20	.165	-5	13	13	1	0.7
1886 Cin-a	8	8	.500	19	19	16	0	0	156	174	6	54	46	13.2	5.08	69	.269	.326	19	.253	1	-28	-27	1	-2.0
KC-N	0	2	.000	3	3	3	0	0	21	44	0	8	3	22.3	10.71	35	.411	.452	0	.000	-2	-17	-16	0	-1.2
Total 3	46	64	.418	116	115	110	4	0	979	979	31	206	474	10.9	3.71	89	.248	.285	92	.202	-8	-47	-44	8	-3.3

■ DENNY McLAIN   McLain, Dennis Dale   b: 3/29/44, Chicago, Ill.   BR/TR, 6'1", 185 lbs.   Deb: 9/21/63

YEAR TM/L	W	L	PCT	G	GS	CG	SH	SV	IP	H	HR	BB	SO	RAT	ERA	ERA+	OAV	OOB	BH	AVG	PB	PR	/A	PD	TPI
1963 Det-A	2	1	.667	3	3	2	0	0	21	20	2	16	22	15.4	4.29	87	.253	.379	1	.200	1	-2	-1	0	0.0
1964 Det-A	4	5	.444	19	16	3	0	0	100	84	16	37	70	11.0	4.05	90	.225	.297	5	.135	-1	-5	-4	-2	-0.7
1965 Det-A	16	6	.727	33	29	13	4	1	220¹	174	25	62	192	9.7	2.61	133	.216	.273	4	.054	-4	21	21	-1	1.8
1966 Det-A	20	14	.588	38	38	14	4	0	264¹	205	42	104	192	10.6	3.92	89	.214	.294	10	.183	2	-14	-13	-1	-1.2
1967 Det-A	17	16	.515	37	37	10	3	0	235	209	35	73	161	10.9	3.79	86	.237	.297	10	.118	-3	-15	-14	-2	-1.9
1968 *Det-A	**31**	6	**.838**	41	41	**28**	6	0	**336**	241	31	63	280	8.3	1.96	154	.200	.243	18	.162	0	38	**39**	0	**4.9**
1969 Det-A	**24**	9	.727	42	41	23	**9**	0	**325**	288	25	67	181	9.9	2.80	133	.237	.279	17	.160	-1	30	34	-4	3.2
1970 Det-A	3	5	.375	14	14	1	0	0	91¹	100	19	28	52	12.9	4.63	80	.273	.300	2	.065	-1	-9	-9	1	-1.0
1971 Was-A	10	22	.313	33	32	9	3	0	216²	233	31	72	103	12.8	4.28	77	.281	.341	6	.103	-1	-20	-23	-2	-2.4
1972 Oak-A	1	2	.333	5	5	0	0	0	22¹	32	4	8	8	16.1	6.04	47	.323	.374	0	.000	-0	-7	-8	0	-0.7
Atl-N	3	5	.375	15	8	2	0	1	54	60	12	18	21	13.2	6.50	58	.279	.338	2	.167	0	-18	-16	-1	-1.6
Total 10	131	91	.590	280	264	105	29	2	1886	1646	242	548	1282	10.6	3.39	101	.234	.292	82	.133	-9	-1	5	-9	0.4

■ BARNEY McLAUGHLIN   McLaughlin, Bernard   b: 1857, Ireland   d: 2/13/21, Lowell, Mass.   BR/TR,   Deb: 8/02/1884 ♦

YEAR TM/L	W	L	PCT	G	GS	CG	SH	SV	IP	H	HR	BB	SO	RAT	ERA	ERA+	OAV	OOB	BH	AVG	PB	PR	/A	PD	TPI
1884 KC-U	1	3	.250	7	4	4	0	0	48²	62	2	15	14	14.2	5.36	51	.291	.337	37	.228	1	-13	-14	0	-1.0

■ BYRON McLAUGHLIN   McLaughlin, Byron Scott   b: 9/29/55, Van Nuys, Cal.   BR/TR, 6'1", 175 lbs.   Deb: 9/18/77

YEAR TM/L	W	L	PCT	G	GS	CG	SH	SV	IP	H	HR	BB	SO	RAT	ERA	ERA+	OAV	OOB	BH	AVG	PB	PR	/A	PD	TPI
1977 Sea-A	0	0	—	1	0	0	0	0	1¹	5	1	0	1	33.8	27.00	15	.625	.625	0	—	0	-3	-3	0	-0.2
1978 Sea-A	4	8	.333	20	17	4	0	0	107	97	15	39	87	11.9	4.37	87	.238	.314	0	—	0	-7	-7	-2	-0.8
1979 Sea-A	7	7	.500	47	7	1	0	14	123²	114	13	60	74	12.8	4.22	103	.251	.340	0	—	0	-0	2	-2	0.0
1980 Sea-A	3	6	.333	45	4	0	0	2	90²	124	15	50	41	17.5	6.85	60	.331	.412	0	—	0	-28	-27	-1	-2.7
1983 Cal-A	2	4	.333	16	7	0	0	0	55²	63	3	22	45	14.1	5.17	78	.286	.357	0	—	0	-7	-7	-0	-0.6
Total 5	16	25	.390	129	35	5	0	16	378¹	403	47	171	248	13.9	5.11	80	.275	.356	0	—	0	-46	-43	-5	-4.3

■ FRANK McLAUGHLIN   McLaughlin, Francis Edward   b: 6/19/1856, Lowell, Mass.   d: 4/5/17, Lowell, Mass.   BR/TR, 5'9", 160 lbs.   Deb: 8/09/1882 ♦

YEAR TM/L	W	L	PCT	G	GS	CG	SH	SV	IP	H	HR	BB	SO	RAT	ERA	ERA+	OAV	OOB	BH	AVG	PB	PR	/A	PD	TPI
1883 Pit-a	0	0	—	2	0	0	0	0	9	14	0	3	1	17.0	13.00	25	.334	.378	25	.219	0	-10	-10	-0	-0.6
1884 KC-U	0	0	—	2	1	0	0	0	10	15	0	2	3	15.3	5.40	51	.325	.353	24	.228	0	-3	-3	-0	-0.1
Total 2	0	0	—	4	1	0	0	0	19	29	0	5	4	16.1	9.00	33	.329	.365	97	.228	0	-12	-13	-1	-0.7

■ JIM McLAUGHLIN   McLaughlin, James C.   b: 1860, Cleveland, Ohio   d: 11/16/1895, Cleveland, Ohio   TL,   Deb: 5/03/1884 ♦

YEAR TM/L	W	L	PCT	G	GS	CG	SH	SV	IP	H	HR	BB	SO	RAT	ERA	ERA+	OAV	OOB	BH	AVG	PB	PR	/A	PD	TPI
1884 Bal-a	1	2	.333	3	2	2	0	0	22	27	2	11	8	15.5	3.68	94	.286	.361	5	.227	0	-1	-1	0	0.0

■ JOEY McLAUGHLIN   McLaughlin, Joey Richard   b: 7/11/56, Tulsa, Okla.   BR/TR, 6'2", 205 lbs.   Deb: 6/11/77

YEAR TM/L	W	L	PCT	G	GS	CG	SH	SV	IP	H	HR	BB	SO	RAT	ERA	ERA+	OAV	OOB	BH	AVG	PB	PR	/A	PD	TPI
1977 Atl-N	0	0	—	3	2	0	0	0	6	10	3	3	3	19.5	15.00	30	.385	.448	0	.000	-0	-7	-7	0	-0.5
1979 Atl-N	5	3	.625	37	0	0	0	5	69	54	3	34	40	11.6	2.48	163	.224	.322	2	.182	0	10	12	-0	1.2
1980 Tor-A	6	9	.400	55	10	0	0	4	135²	159	16	53	79	14.3	4.51	95	.302	.370	0	—	0	-7	-3	-0	-0.3
1981 Tor-A	1	5	.167	40	0	0	0	10	60	55	2	21	38	11.4	2.85	138	.249	.314	0	—	0	5	7	-0	0.7
1982 Tor-A	8	6	.571	44	0	0	0	8	70	54	7	30	49	10.9	3.21	139	.212	.297	0	—	0	7	10	1	1.0
1983 Tor-A	7	4	.636	50	0	0	0	9	64²	63	11	37	47	13.9	4.45	97	.259	.357	0	—	0	-3	-1	-0	0.0
1984 Tor-A	0	0	—	6	0	0	0	0	10²	12	0	7	3	16.0	2.53	162	.286	.388	0	—	0	2	2	0	0.2

YEAR TM/L	W	L	PCT	G	GS	CG	SH	SV	IP	H	HR	BB	SO	RAT	ERA	ERA+	OAV	OOB	BH	AVG	PB	PR	/A	PD	TPI
Tex-A	2	1	.667	15	0	0	0	0	32²	33	4	13	21	12.7	4.41	94	.260	.329	0	—	0	-2	-1	-0	0.0
Yr	2	1	.667	21	0	0	0	0	43¹	45	4	20	24	13.5	3.95	105	.265	.342	0	—	0	0	1	-0	0.2
Total 7	29	28	.509	250	12	0	0	36	448²	440	46	198	268	12.9	3.85	110	.262	.341	2	.167	-0	5	19	-0	2.3

■ JUD McLAUGHLIN

McLaughlin, Justin Theodore b: 3/24/12, Brighton, Mass. d: 9/27/64, Cambridge, Mass. BL/TL, 5'11", 155 lbs. Deb: 6/23/31

YEAR TM/L	W	L	PCT	G	GS	CG	SH	SV	IP	H	HR	BB	SO	RAT	ERA	ERA+	OAV	OOB	BH	AVG	PB	PR	/A	PD	TPI
1931 Bos-A	0	0	—	9	0	0	0	0	12	23	1	8	3	23.3	12.00	36	.397	.470	0	—	0	-10	-10	0	-0.8
1932 Bos-A	0	0	—	1	0	0	0	0	3	5	0	4	0	27.0	15.00	30	.385	.529	0	.000	-0	-4	-4	0	-0.2
1933 Bos-A	0	0	—	6	0	0	0	0	8²	14	1	5	1	19.7	6.23	70	.359	.432	0	—	0	-2	-2	-0	-0.1
Total 3	0	0	—	16	0	0	0	0	23²	42	2	17	4	22.4	10.27	42	.382	.465	0	.000	-0	-16	-16	0	-1.1

■ BO McLAUGHLIN

McLaughlin, Michael Duane b: 10/23/53, Oakland, Cal. BR/TR, 6'5", 210 lbs. Deb: 7/20/76

YEAR TM/L	W	L	PCT	G	GS	CG	SH	SV	IP	H	HR	BB	SO	RAT	ERA	ERA+	OAV	OOB	BH	AVG	PB	PR	/A	PD	TPI
1976 Hou-N	4	5	.444	17	11	4	2	1	79	71	6	17	32	10.3	2.85	112	.244	.290	0	.000	-1	6	3	0	0.2
1977 Hou-N	4	7	.364	46	6	0	0	5	84²	81	6	34	59	12.9	4.25	84	.260	.344	0	.000	-1	-3	-6	1	-0.6
1978 Hou-N	0	1	.000	12	1	0	0	2	23¹	30	2	16	10	18.5	5.01	66	.313	.421	0	.000	-0	-4	-4	0	-0.4
1979 Hou-N	1	2	.333	12	0	0	0	0	16¹	22	2	4	12	14.3	5.51	64	.314	.351	0	.000	-0	-3	-4	0	-0.3
Atl-N	1	1	.500	37	1	0	0	0	49²	63	2	16	45	14.7	4.89	83	.303	.358	0	.000	-1	-6	-5	-2	-0.6
Yr	2	3	.400	49	1	0	0	0	66	85	4	20	57	14.6	5.05	78	.305	.355	0	.000	-1	-10	-8	-2	-0.9
1981 Oak-A	0	0	—	11	0	0	0	1	11²	17	1	9	3	20.8	11.57	30	.333	.443	0	—	0	-10	-10	-0	-0.9
1982 Oak-A	0	4	.000	21	2	1	0	0	48¹	51	3	27	27	14.7	4.84	81	.267	.361	0	—	0	-4	-5	0	-0.4
Total 6	10	20	.333	156	21	5	2	9	313	335	22	123	188	13.6	4.49	80	.275	.348	0	.000	-3	-25	-32	-0	-3.0

■ PAT McLAUGHLIN

McLaughlin, Patrick Elmer b: 8/17/10, Taylor, Tex. BR/TR, 6'2", 175 lbs. Deb: 4/25/37

YEAR TM/L	W	L	PCT	G	GS	CG	SH	SV	IP	H	HR	BB	SO	RAT	ERA	ERA+	OAV	OOB	BH	AVG	PB	PR	/A	PD	TPI
1937 Det-A	0	2	.000	10	3	0	0	0	32²	39	3	16	8	15.2	6.34	74	.291	.367	1	.100	-1	-6	-6	-1	-0.6
1940 Phi-A	0	0	—	1	0	0	0	0	1²	4	1	1	0	27.0	16.20	27	.444	.500	0	—	0	-2	-2	0	-0.1
1945 Det-A	0	0	—	1	0	0	0	0	1	2	0	0	0	18.0	9.00	39	.400	.400	0	—	0	-1	-1	0	-0.0
Total 3	0	2	.000	12	3	0	0	0	35¹	45	4	17	8	15.8	6.88	67	.304	.376	1	.100	-1	-9	-9	-1	-0.7

■ WARREN McLAUGHLIN

McLaughlin, Warren A. b: 1/22/1876, N.Plainfield, N.J. d: 10/22/23, Plainfield, N.J. TL, Deb: 7/07/00

YEAR TM/L	W	L	PCT	G	GS	CG	SH	SV	IP	H	HR	BB	SO	RAT	ERA	ERA+	OAV	OOB	BH	AVG	PB	PR	/A	PD	TPI
1900 Phi-N	0	0	—	1	0	0	0	0	6	4	0	6	1	15.0	4.50	80	.190	.369	1	.500	1	-1	-1	0	0.0
1902 Pit-N	3	0	1.000	3	3	3	0	0	26	27	0	9	13	12.8	2.77	99	.268	.334	4	.364	1	0	-0	-1	0.0
1903 Phi-N	0	3	.000	3	2	2	0	0	23	38	0	11	3	19.6	7.04	46	.376	.442	2	.200	0	-10	-10	-0	-0.7
Total 3	3	3	.500	7	5	5	0	0	55	69	0	26	17	15.9	4.75	64	.309	.386	7	.304	2	-10	-10	-1	-0.7

■ AL McLEAN

McLean, Albert Eldon "Elrod" b: 9/20/12, Chicago, Ill. BR/TR, 6', 175 lbs. Deb: 7/16/35

YEAR TM/L	W	L	PCT	G	GS	CG	SH	SV	IP	H	HR	BB	SO	RAT	ERA	ERA+	OAV	OOB	BH	AVG	PB	PR	/A	PD	TPI
1935 Was-A	0	0	—	4	0	0	0	0	8²	12	0	5	3	17.7	7.27	59	.324	.405	0	.000	-0	-3	-3	-0	-0.2

■ WAYNE McLELAND

McLeland, Wayne Gaffney "Nubbin" b: 8/29/24, Milton, Iowa BR/TR, 6', 180 lbs. Deb: 4/20/51

YEAR TM/L	W	L	PCT	G	GS	CG	SH	SV	IP	H	HR	BB	SO	RAT	ERA	ERA+	OAV	OOB	BH	AVG	PB	PR	/A	PD	TPI
1951 Det-A	0	1	.000	6	1	0	0	0	11	20	1	4	0	20.5	8.18	51	.400	.455	0	.000	-0	-5	-5	0	-0.4
1952 Det-A	0	0	—	4	0	0	0	0	2²	4	0	6	0	33.8	10.13	38	.444	.667	0	—	0	-2	-2	0	-0.1
Total 2	0	1	.000	10	1	0	0	0	13²	24	1	10	0		8.56	48	.407	.500	0	—	-0	-7	-7	0	-0.5

■ CAL McLISH

McLish, Calvin Coolidge Julius Caesar Tuskahoma "Buster" b: 12/1/25, Anadarko, Okla. BB/TR, 6', 179 lbs. Deb: 5/13/44 C

YEAR TM/L	W	L	PCT	G	GS	CG	SH	SV	IP	H	HR	BB	SO	RAT	ERA	ERA+	OAV	OOB	BH	AVG	PB	PR	/A	PD	TPI
1944 Bro-N	3	10	.231	23	13	3	0	0	84	110	10	48	24	17.0	7.82	45	.321	.406	7	.219	0	-39	-40	-1	-3.7
1946 Bro-N	0	0	—	1	0	0	0	0	0	1	0	0	0	—	∞	—	1.000	1.000	0	—	0	-2	-2	0	-0.1
1947 Pit-N	0	0	—	1	0	0	0	0	1	2	0	0	0	27.0	18.00	23	.400	.500	0	—	0	-2	-2	0	0.0
1948 Pit-N	0	0	—	2	1	0	0	0	5	8	0	2	1	18.0	9.00	45	.400	.455	0	.000	-0	-3	-3	0	-0.1
1949 Chi-N	1	1	.500	8	2	0	0	0	23	31	5	12	6	16.8	5.87	69	.341	.417	3	.333	2	-5	-5	1	-0.2
1951 Chi-N	4	10	.286	30	17	5	1	0	145²	159	16	52	46	13.2	4.45	92	.283	.347	5	.119	-1	-8	-6	0	-0.5
1956 Cle-A	2	4	.333	37	2	0	0	1	61²	67	5	32	27	14.4	4.96	85	.282	.367	1	.111	-1	-6	-5	1	-0.2
1957 Cle-A	9	7	.563	42	7	2	0	1	144¹	118	11	67	88	11.7	2.74	135	.220	.309	8	.186	3	17	16	1	2.0
1958 Cle-A	16	8	.667	39	30	13	0	1	225²	214	25	70	97	11.4	2.99	122	.251	.309	6	.094	-1	19	16	1	1.7
1959 Cle-A	19	8	.704	35	32	13	0	1	235¹	253	26	72	113	12.6	3.63	101	.270	.326	14	.189	1	6	1	3	0.6
1960 Cin-N	4	14	.222	37	21	2	1	0	151¹	170	16	48	56	13.4	4.16	92	.287	.348	2	.049	-4	-7	-6	2	-0.7
1961 Chi-A	10	13	.435	31	27	4	0	1	162¹	178	21	47	80	12.5	4.38	89	.280	.330	9	.167	-1	-6	-8	2	-0.6
1962 Phi-N	11	5	.688	32	24	5	1	1	154²	184	15	45	71	13.4	4.25	91	.293	.343	4	.078	-2	-5	-6	-0	-0.7
1963 Phi-N	13	11	.542	32	32	10	2	0	209²	184	14	56	98	10.5	3.26	99	.239	.294	14	.203	4	1	-1	3	0.6
1964 Phi-N	0	1	.000	2	1	0	0	0	5¹	6	0	1	6	11.8	3.38	103	.261	.292	0	.000	-0	0	0	0	0.0
Total 15	92	92	.500	352	209	57	5	6	1609	1685	164	552	713	12.7	4.01	93	.270	.332	73	.149	4	-39	-50	12	-1.9

■ SAM McMACKIN

McMackin, Samuel b: 1872, Cleveland, Ohio d: 2/11/03, Columbus, Ohio TL, Deb: 9/04/02

YEAR TM/L	W	L	PCT	G	GS	CG	SH	SV	IP	H	HR	BB	SO	RAT	ERA	ERA+	OAV	OOB	BH	AVG	PB	PR	/A	PD	TPI
1902 Chi-A	0	0	—	1	0	0	0	0	3	1	0	0	2	3.0	0.00	—	.105	.105	0	.000	-0	1	1	0	0.1
Det-A	0	1	.000	1	1	1	0	0	8¹	9	0	4	2	14.0	3.24	113	.276	.355	2	.500	1	0	0	0	0.1
Yr	0	1	.000	2	1	1	0	0	11¹	10	0	4	4	11.1	2.38	150	.237	.304	0	.000	0	2	2	1	0.2

■ JACK McMAHAN

McMahan, Jack Wally b: 7/22/32, Hot Springs, Ark. BR/TL, 6', 175 lbs. Deb: 4/18/56

YEAR TM/L	W	L	PCT	G	GS	CG	SH	SV	IP	H	HR	BB	SO	RAT	ERA	ERA+	OAV	OOB	BH	AVG	PB	PR	/A	PD	TPI
1956 Pit-N	0	0	—	11	0	0	0	0	13¹	18	1	9	9	18.2	6.08	62	.340	.435	0	.000	-0	-3	-3	0	-0.2
KC-A	0	5	.000	23	9	0	0	0	61²	69	7	31	13	14.9	4.82	90	.290	.376	0	.000	-2	-5	-3	0	-0.4

■ DON McMAHON

McMahon, Donald John b: 1/4/30, Brooklyn, N.Y. d: 7/22/87, Los Angeles, Cal. BR/TR, 6'2", 215 lbs. Deb: 6/30/57 C

YEAR TM/L	W	L	PCT	G	GS	CG	SH	SV	IP	H	HR	BB	SO	RAT	ERA	ERA+	OAV	OOB	BH	AVG	PB	PR	/A	PD	TPI
1957 *Mil-N	2	3	.400	32	0	0	0	9	46²	33	0	29	46	12.0	1.54	227	.196	.315	2	.250	1	12	10	-1	1.1
1958 *Mil-N	7	2	.778	38	0	0	0	8	58²	50	4	29	37	12.4	3.68	96	.235	.332	1	.111	0	2	-1	-0	0.0
1959 Mil-N	5	3	.625	60	0	0	0	15	80²	81	5	37	55	13.3	2.57	138	.259	.339	2	.222	1	12	9	-1	0.8
1960 Mil-N	3	6	.333	48	0	0	0	10	63²	66	9	32	50	14.1	5.94	58	.263	.351	0	.000	-1	-15	-18	0	-1.8
1961 Mil-N	6	4	.600	53	0	0	0	8	92	84	4	51	55	13.4	2.84	132	.249	.351	3	.188	0	12	9	1	1.0
1962 Mil-N	0	1	.000	2	0	0	0	0	3	3	1	0	3	9.0	6.00	63	.250	.250	0	.000	0	-1	-0	0	0.0
Hou-N	5	5	.500	51	0	0	0	8	76²	53	4	33	69	10.2	1.53	245	.201	.292	1	.083	-1	21	19	-0	1.8
Yr	5	6	.455	53	0	0	0	8	79²	56	5	33	72	10.2	1.69	221	.203	.290	0	.000	-1	20	18	-0	1.8
1963 Hou-N	1	5	.167	49	2	0	0	5	80	83	10	26	51	12.3	4.05	78	.270	.327	1	.083	0	-7	-8	-0	-0.7
1964 Cle-A	6	4	.600	70	0	0	0	16	101	67	7	52	90	10.8	2.41	150	.189	.297	2	.143	-0	14	13	1	1.3
1965 Cle-A	3	3	.500	58	0	0	0	11	85	79	8	37	60	12.4	3.28	106	.248	.329	2	.222	0	2	2	1	0.3
1966 Cle-A	1	1	.500	12	0	0	0	1	12¹	8	1	6	5	10.2	2.92	118	.190	.292	0	.000	0	1	1	0	0.1
Bos-A	8	7	.533	49	0	0	0	9	78	65	7	38	57	12.2	2.65	143	.232	.330	1	.091	-0	7	10	-0	1.0
Yr	9	8	.529	61	0	0	0	10	90¹	73	8	44	62	12.0	2.69	140	.226	.324	1	.077	-0	7	11	-0	1.0
1967 Bos-A	1	2	.333	11	0	0	0	2	17²	14	4	13	10	13.8	3.57	98	.215	.346	0	.000	-0	-1	-0	0	0.0
Chi-A	5	0	1.000	52	0	0	0	3	91¹	54	5	27	74	8.5	1.67	186	.173	.252	2	.182	-0	16	15	-0	1.6
Yr	6	2	.750	63	0	0	0	5	109¹	68	9	40	84	9.4	1.98	160	.180	.270	2	.182	-0	15	14	-0	1.6
1968 Chi-A	2	1	.667	25	0	0	0	2	46	31	2	20	32	10.6	1.96	155	.190	.290	1	.333	0	5	5	-1	0.4
*Det-A	3	1	.750	20	0	0	0	1	35²	22	2	10	33	8.1	2.02	149	.180	.242	0	.000	-0	4	4	-0	0.4
Yr	5	2	.714	45	0	0	0	1	81²	53	4	30	65	9.1	1.98	152	.186	.259	0	.000	-0	9	9	-1	1.0
1969 Det-A	3	5	.375	34	0	0	0	11	37	25	2	18	38	10.7	3.89	96	.192	.295	1	.000	-1	-1	-0	0	-0.0
SF-N	3	1	.750	13	0	0	0	2	23²	13	1	9	21	8.4	3.04	115	.157	.239	1	.333	0	1	1	0	0.2
1970 SF-N	9	5	.643	61	0	0	0	19	94¹	70	9	45	74	11.2	2.96	134	.202	.297	2	.143	0	11	11	-1	1.0
1971 *SF-N	10	6	.625	61	0	0	0	4	82	73	9	37	71	12.8	4.06	84	.243	.338	0	.000	-1	-5	-6	1	-0.6
1972 SF-N	3	3	.500	44	0	0	0	5	63	46	8	21	45	9.7	3.71	94	.206	.278	1	.250	0	-2	-2	-0	-0.1
1973 SF-N	4	0	1.000	22	0	0	0	6	30¹	21	1	7	20	8.3	1.48	257	.189	.237	1	1.000	0	7	8	0	0.9

YEAR TM/L	W	L	PCT	G	GS	CG	SH	SV	IP	H	HR	BB	SO	RAT	ERA	ERA+	OAV	OOB	BH	AVG	PB	PR	/A	PD	TPI
1974 SF-N	0	0	—	9	0	0	0	0	11²	13	2	2	5	11.6	3.09	123	.283	.313	0	—	0	1	1	0	0.1
Total 18	90	68	.570	874	2	0	0	153	1310²	1054	105	579	1003	11.4	2.96	119	.221	.310	23	.137	-1	96	83	-2	8.9

■ DOC McMAHON
McMahon, Henry John b: 12/19/1886, Woburn, Mass. d: 12/11/29, Woburn, Mass. Deb: 10/06/08

YEAR TM/L	W	L	PCT	G	GS	CG	SH	SV	IP	H	HR	BB	SO	RAT	ERA	ERA+	OAV	OOB	BH	AVG	PB	PR	/A	PD	TPI
1908 Bos-A	1	0	1.000	1	1	1	0	0	9	14	0	3	3	14.0	3.00	82	.350	.350	2	.400	1	-1	-1	-0	0.0

■ SADIE McMAHON
McMahon, John Joseph b: 9/19/1867, Wilmington, Del. d: 2/20/54, Delaware City, Del BR/TR, 5'9.5", 165 lbs. Deb: 7/05/1889

YEAR TM/L	W	L	PCT	G	GS	CG	SH	SV	IP	H	HR	BB	SO	RAT	ERA	ERA+	OAV	OOB	BH	AVG	PB	PR	/A	PD	TPI
1889 Phi-a	14	12	.538	28	27	27	2	0	242	230	5	102	117	12.3	3.53	107	.243	.316	16	.154	-5	8	7	4	0.4
1890 Phi-a	29	18	.617	48	46	44	0	1	410	414	5	133	225	12.0	3.34	115	.254	.311	40	.229	3	24	22	8	3.0
Bal-a	7	3	.700	12	11	11	1	0	99	84	1	33	66	10.6	3.00	135	.223	.285	4	.103	-4	10	12	1	0.9
Yr	36	21	.632	60	57	55	1	1	509	498	6	166	291	11.7	3.27	118	.248	.306	8	.037	-1	34	34	9	3.9
1891 Bal-a	35	24	.593	61	58	53	5	1	503	493	13	149	219	11.5	2.81	133	.248	.300	43	.205	-3	51	52	4	4.7
1892 Bal-N	19	25	.432	48	46	44	2	1	397	430	9	145	118	13.0	3.24	106	.265	.326	25	.141	-10	2	9	0	0.1
1893 Bal-N	23	18	.561	43	40	35	0	1	346¹	378	6	156	79	13.9	4.37	109	.269	.343	36	.243	-4	12	16	-1	1.0
1894 Bal-N	25	8	.758	35	33	26	0	0	275²	317	7	111	60	14.0	4.21	130	.285	.350	36	.286	-4	34	38	3	3.3
1895 *Bal-N	10	4	.714	15	15	15	4	0	122¹	110	1	32	37	10.4	2.94	162	.237	.286	16	.314	1	25	25	-1	2.2
1896 Bal-N	11	9	.550	22	22	19	0	0	175²	195	4	55	33	12.8	3.48	123	.279	.331	9	.123	-7	17	16	0	0.8
1897 Bro-N	0	6	.000	9	7	5	0	0	63	75	1	29	13	14.9	5.86	70	.293	.365	5	.200	-1	-11	-12	0	-1.0
Total 9	173	127	.577	321	305	279	14	4	2634	2726	52	945	967	12.5	3.51	118	.260	.321	230	.204	-29	173	184	19	15.4

■ JOHN McMAKIN
McMakin, John Weaver "Spartanburg John" b: 3/6/1878, Spartanburg, S.C. d: 9/25/56, Lyman, S.C. BR/TL, 5'11", 165 lbs. Deb: 4/19/02

YEAR TM/L	W	L	PCT	G	GS	CG	SH	SV	IP	H	HR	BB	SO	RAT	ERA	ERA+	OAV	OOB	BH	AVG	PB	PR	/A	PD	TPI
1902 Bro-N	2	2	.500	4	4	4	0	0	32	34	0	11	6	13.5	3.09	89	.272	.345	2	.182	0	-1	-1	0	0.0

■ JOE McMANUS
McManus, Joab Logan b: 9/7/1887, Palmyra, Ill. d: 12/23/55, Beckley, W.Va. BR/TR, 5'11", 180 lbs. Deb: 4/12/13

YEAR TM/L	W	L	PCT	G	GS	CG	SH	SV	IP	H	HR	BB	SO	RAT	ERA	ERA+	OAV	OOB	BH	AVG	PB	PR	/A	PD	TPI
1913 Cin-N	0	0	—	1	0	0	0	0	2	3	0	4	1	31.5	18.00	18	.375	.583	0	—	0	-3	-3	0	-0.2

■ PAT McMANUS
McManus, Patrick b: Ireland d: 10/6/17, Brooklyn, N.Y. Deb: 5/22/1879

YEAR TM/L	W	L	PCT	G	GS	CG	SH	SV	IP	H	HR	BB	SO	RAT	ERA	ERA+	OAV	OOB	BH	AVG	PB	PR	/A	PD	TPI
1879 Tro-N	0	2	.000	2	2	2	0	0	21	24	1	1	6	10.7	3.00	83	.269	.277	1	.125	-1	-1	-1	0	0.0

■ GEORGE McMULLEN
McMullen, George b: California Deb: 7/02/1887

YEAR TM/L	W	L	PCT	G	GS	CG	SH	SV	IP	H	HR	BB	SO	RAT	ERA	ERA+	OAV	OOB	BH	AVG	PB	PR	/A	PD	TPI
1887 NY-a	2	1	.667	3	3	2	0	0	21	25	2	19	2	18.9	7.71	55	.285	.412	1	.083	-2	-8	-8	0	-0.6

■ JOHN McMULLIN
McMullin, John F. "Lefty" b: 1848, Philadelphia, Pa. d: 4/11/1881, Philadelphia, Pa. BL/TL, 5'9", 160 lbs. Deb: 5/09/1871 ◆

YEAR TM/L	W	L	PCT	G	GS	CG	SH	SV	IP	H	HR	BB	SO	RAT	ERA	ERA+	OAV	OOB	BH	AVG	PB	PR	/A	PD	TPI
1871 Tro-n	12	15	.444	29	29	28	0	0	249	430	4	75	12	18.3	5.53	76	.342	.379	38	.279	1	-36	-36		-2.1
1872 Mut-n	1	0	1.000	3	1	1	0	0	15	18	0	2		12.0	3.60	96	.247	.267	60	.253	0	0	-0		0.0
1873 Ath-n	1	0	1.000	1	1	1	0	0	8	10	0	1		12.4	2.25	168	.303	.324	60	.270	0	1	1		0.1
1875 Phi-n	0	0	—	4	0	0	0	0	12²	31	0	1		22.7	6.39	39	.425	.432	56	.251	1	-6	-5		-0.3
Total 4 n	14	15	.483	37	31	30	0	0	284²	489	4	79	12	18.0	5.37	47	.340	.374	303	.281	2	-92	-90		-2.3

■ CRAIG McMURTRY
McMurtry, Joe Craig b: 11/5/59, Troy, Tex. BR/TR, 6'5", 195 lbs. Deb: 4/10/83

YEAR TM/L	W	L	PCT	G	GS	CG	SH	SV	IP	H	HR	BB	SO	RAT	ERA	ERA+	OAV	OOB	BH	AVG	PB	PR	/A	PD	TPI
1983 Atl-N	15	9	.625	36	35	6	3	0	224²	204	13	88	105	11.7	3.08	126	.243	.315	6	.086	-4	14	20	4	2.2
1984 Atl-N	9	17	.346	37	30	0	0	0	183¹	184	16	102	99	14.1	4.32	89	.268	.363	6	.115	-1	-15	-10	4	-0.5
1985 Atl-N	0	3	.000	17	6	0	0	0	45	56	6	27	28	16.8	6.60	58	.306	.398	1	.071	-1	-15	-14	1	-1.3
1986 Atl-N	1	6	.143	37	5	0	0	0	79²	82	6	43	50	14.3	4.74	84	.265	.359	2	.125	-0	-9	-7	0	-0.6
1988 Tex-A	3	3	.500	32	0	0	0	3	60	37	5	24	35	9.3	2.25	181	.180	.270	0	—	0	11	12	1	1.4
1989 Tex-A	0	0	—	19	0	0	0	0	23	29	3	13	14	17.2	7.43	53	.312	.407	0	—	0	-9	-9	0	-0.8
1990 Tex-A	0	3	.000	23	3	0	0	0	41²	43	4	30	14	16.0	4.32	92	.281	.402	0	—	0	-2	-2	1	0.0
Total 7	28	41	.406	201	79	6	3	4	657¹	635	54	327	345	13.3	4.03	97	.257	.346	15	.099	-6	-25	-8	11	0.4

■ EDGAR McNABB
McNabb, Edgar J. "Texas" b: 10/24/1865, Mt.Vernon, Ohio d: 2/28/1894, Pittsburgh, Pa. TL, 5'11.5", 170 lbs. Deb: 5/12/1893

YEAR TM/L	W	L	PCT	G	GS	CG	SH	SV	IP	H	HR	BB	SO	RAT	ERA	ERA+	OAV	OOB	BH	AVG	PB	PR	/A	PD	TPI
1893 Bal-N	8	7	.533	21	14	12	0	0	142	167	3	53	18	13.9	4.12	116	.284	.344	13	.194	-3	9	10	0	0.7

■ DAVE McNALLY
McNally, David Arthur b: 10/31/42, Billings, Mont. BR/TL, 5'11", 185 lbs. Deb: 9/26/62

YEAR TM/L	W	L	PCT	G	GS	CG	SH	SV	IP	H	HR	BB	SO	RAT	ERA	ERA+	OAV	OOB	BH	AVG	PB	PR	/A	PD	TPI
1962 Bal-A	1	0	1.000	1	1	1	1	0	9	2	0	3	4	5.0	0.00	—	.071	.161	0	.000	-0	4	4	0	0.4
1963 Bal-A	7	8	.467	29	20	2	0	1	125²	133	9	55	78	13.8	4.58	77	.276	.356	2	.053	-2	-13	-15	-1	-1.7
1964 Bal-A	9	11	.450	30	23	5	3	0	159¹	157	15	51	88	12.3	3.67	97	.260	.327	7	.137	0	-1	-2	0	-0.1
1965 Bal-A	11	6	.647	35	29	6	2	0	198²	163	15	73	116	11.0	2.85	122	.230	.298	6	.092	-3	13	14	0	1.2
1966 *Bal-A	13	6	.684	34	33	5	1	0	213	212	22	64	158	11.8	3.17	105	.256	.313	15	.195	3	6	4	0	0.7
1967 Bal-A	7	7	.500	24	22	3	1	0	119	134	13	39	70	13.2	4.54	69	.295	.354	6	.158	0	-17	-18	-2	-2.0
1968 Bal-A	22	10	.688	35	35	18	5	0	273	175	24	55	202	7.9	1.95	150	.182	.234	11	.128	4	31	30	-3	3.7
1969 Bal-A	20	7	.741	41	40	11	4	0	268²	232	21	84	166	10.8	3.22	111	.234	.297	8	.085	-2	12	10	-3	0.5
1970 *Bal-A	24	9	.727	40	40	16	1	0	296	277	29	78	185	11.0	3.22	113	.250	.304	14	.133	4	16	14	-2	1.7
1971 *Bal-A	21	5	.808	30	30	11	1	0	224¹	188	24	58	91	10.1	2.89	116	.229	.284	12	.162	3	14	12	0	1.6
1972 Bal-A	13	17	.433	36	36	12	6	0	241	220	15	68	120	10.8	2.95	104	.247	.302	12	.152	2	3	3	1	0.7
1973 *Bal-A	17	17	.500	38	38	17	4	0	266	247	16	81	87	11.3	3.21	116	.251	.312	0	—	0	18	15	2	1.8
1974 *Bal-A	16	10	.615	39	37	13	4	1	259	260	19	81	111	12.1	3.58	96	.270	.331	0	—	0	1	-4	2	-0.1
1975 Mon-N	3	6	.333	12	12	0	0	0	77¹	88	8	36	36	14.9	5.24	73	.280	.362	4	.190	2	-14	-12	-0	-0.9
Total 14	184	119	.607	424	396	120	33	2	2730	2488	230	826	1512	11.2	3.24	106	.245	.306	97	.133	9	74	55	-5	7.5

■ TIM McNAMARA
McNamara, Timothy Augustine b: 11/20/1898, Millville, Mass. BR/TR, 5'11", 170 lbs. Deb: 4/27/22

YEAR TM/L	W	L	PCT	G	GS	CG	SH	SV	IP	H	HR	BB	SO	RAT	ERA	ERA+	OAV	OOB	BH	AVG	PB	PR	/A	PD	TPI
1922 Bos-N	3	4	.429	24	5	4	2	0	70²	55	2	26	16	10.4	2.42	165	.225	.303	2	.118	-1	13	12	-0	1.1
1923 Bos-N	3	13	.188	32	16	3	0	0	139¹	185	8	29	32	14.1	4.91	81	.320	.357	7	.179	-1	-14	-14	-2	-1.4
1924 Bos-N	8	12	.400	35	21	6	2	0	179	242	9	31	35	13.9	5.18	74	.334	.364	6	.140	-1	-26	-27	1	-2.5
1925 Bos-N	0	0	—	1	0	0	0	0	0²	6	0	2	1	108.0	81.00	5	.857	.889	0	—	0	-6	-6	0	-0.3
1926 NY-N	0	0	—	6	0	0	0	0	6	7	0	4	4	16.5	9.00	42	.304	.407	0	—	0	-3	-3	0	-0.2
Total 5	14	29	.326	98	42	13	4	0	395²	495	19	92	88	13.6	4.78	82	.314	.355	15	.152	-1	-36	-38	-1	-3.3

■ GORDON McNAUGHTON
McNaughton, Gordon Joseph b: 7/31/10, Chicago, Ill. d: 8/6/42, Chicago, Ill. BR/TR, 6'1", 190 lbs. Deb: 8/13/32

YEAR TM/L	W	L	PCT	G	GS	CG	SH	SV	IP	H	HR	BB	SO	RAT	ERA	ERA+	OAV	OOB	BH	AVG	PB	PR	/A	PD	TPI
1932 Bos-A	0	1	.000	6	2	0	0	0	21	21	1	22	6	19.7	6.43	70	.259	.434	2	.250	0	-5	-5	1	-0.2

■ HARRY McNEAL
McNeal, John Harley b: 8/11/1877, Iberia, Ohio d: 1/11/45, Cleveland, Ohio BR/TR, 6'3", 175 lbs. Deb: 8/05/01

YEAR TM/L	W	L	PCT	G	GS	CG	SH	SV	IP	H	HR	BB	SO	RAT	ERA	ERA+	OAV	OOB	BH	AVG	PB	PR	/A	PD	TPI
1901 Cle-A	5	5	.500	12	10	9	0	0	85¹	120	4	30	15	15.8	4.43	80	.328	.379	6	.162	-2	-7	-8	-2	-0.9

■ ED McNICHOL
McNichol, Edwin Briggs b: 1/10/1879, Martins Ferry, O. d: 11/1/52, Salineville, O. BR/TR, 5'5", 170 lbs. Deb: 7/09/04

YEAR TM/L	W	L	PCT	G	GS	CG	SH	SV	IP	H	HR	BB	SO	RAT	ERA	ERA+	OAV	OOB	BH	AVG	PB	PR	/A	PD	TPI
1904 Bos-N	2	12	.143	17	15	12	1	0	122	120	3	74	39	14.7	4.28	64	.262	.371	4	.093	-3	-21	-21	-1	-2.4

■ FRANK McPARTLIN
McPartlin, Frank b: 2/16/1872, Hoosick Falls, N.Y. d: 11/13/43, New York, N.Y. TR, 6', 180 lbs. Deb: 8/22/1899

YEAR TM/L	W	L	PCT	G	GS	CG	SH	SV	IP	H	HR	BB	SO	RAT	ERA	ERA+	OAV	OOB	BH	AVG	PB	PR	/A	PD	TPI
1899 NY-N	0	0	—	1	0	0	0	0	4	4	0	3	2	15.8	4.50	83	.260	.381	0	.000	-0	-0	-0	0	0.0

■ JOHN McPHERSON
McPherson, John Jacob b: 3/9/1869, Easton, Pa. d: 9/30/41, Easton, Pa. Deb: 7/12/01

YEAR TM/L	W	L	PCT	G	GS	CG	SH	SV	IP	H	HR	BB	SO	RAT	ERA	ERA+	OAV	OOB	BH	AVG	PB	PR	/A	PD	TPI
1901 Phi-A	0	1	.000	1	1	0	0	0	4	7	0	4	0	24.8	11.25	34	.377	.488	0	.000	-0	-3	-3	0	-0.1
1904 Phi-N	1	12	.077	15	12	11	1	0	128	130	1	46	32	12.8	3.66	73	.264	.334	3	.064	-4	-13	-14	1	-1.6
Total 2	1	13	.071	16	13	11	1	0	132	137	1	50	32	13.2	3.89	70	.268	.340	3	.063	-4	-16	-17	1	-1.7

■ HERB McQUAID
McQuaid, Herbert George b: 3/29/1899, San Francisco, Cal d: 4/4/66, Richmond, Cal. BR/TR, 6'2", 185 lbs. Deb: 6/22/23

YEAR TM/L	W	L	PCT	G	GS	CG	SH	SV	IP	H	HR	BB	SO	RAT	ERA	ERA+	OAV	OOB	BH	AVG	PB	PR	/A	PD	TPI
1923 Cin-N	1	0	1.000	12	1	0	0	0	34¹	31	0	10	9	11.5	2.36	164	.238	.308	0	.000	-1	6	6	1	0.5
1926 NY-A	1	0	1.000	17	1	0	0	0	38¹	48	5	13	6	14.8	6.10	63	.329	.391	0	.000	-1	-9	-10	1	-0.8

YEAR TM/L	W	L	PCT	G	GS	CG	SH	SV	IP	H	HR	BB	SO	RAT	ERA	ERA+	OAV	OOB	BH	AVG	PB	PR	/A	PD	TPI
Total 2	2	0	1.000	29	2	0	0	0	72²	79	4	23	15	13.3	4.33	89	.286	.352	0	.000	-2	-3	-4	2	-0.3

■ MIKE McQUEEN McQueen, Michael Robert b: 8/30/50, Oklahoma City, Okla BL/TL, 6', 188 lbs. Deb: 10/02/69

YEAR TM/L	W	L	PCT	G	GS	CG	SH	SV	IP	H	HR	BB	SO	RAT	ERA	ERA+	OAV	OOB	BH	AVG	PB	PR	/A	PD	TPI
1969 Atl-N	0	0	—	1	1	0	0	0	3	2	0	3	3	15.0	3.00	120	.182	.357	0	—	0	0	0	0	0.0
1970 Atl-N	1	5	.167	22	8	1	0	0	66	67	10	31	54	13.5	5.59	77	.266	.349	6	.300	2	-11	-10	-1	-0.7
1971 Atl-N	4	1	.800	17	3	0	0	1	56	47	7	23	38	11.6	3.54	105	.228	.312	4	.211	0	-0	1	-1	0.1
1972 Atl-N	0	5	.000	23	7	1	0	1	78¹	79	11	44	40	14.2	4.60	82	.260	.355	2	.087	-2	-10	-7	-1	-0.9
1974 Cin-N	0	0	—	10	0	0	0	0	15	17	4	11	5	16.8	5.40	65	.288	.400	1	1.000	0	-3	-3	-0	-0.2
Total 5	5	11	.313	73	19	2	0	3	218¹	212	32	112	140	13.5	4.66	84	.255	.346	13	.206	1	-24	-18	-3	-1.7

■ GEORGE McQUILLAN McQuillan, George Watt b: 5/1/1885, Brooklyn, N.Y. d: 3/30/40, Columbus, Ohio BR/TR, 5'11.5", 175 lbs. Deb: 5/08/07

YEAR TM/L	W	L	PCT	G	GS	CG	SH	SV	IP	H	HR	BB	SO	RAT	ERA	ERA+	OAV	OOB	BH	AVG	PB	PR	/A	PD	TPI
1907 Phi-N	4	0	1.000	6	5	5	3	0	41	21	0	11	28	7.2	0.66	368	.158	.228	4	.364	3	8	8	-2	1.2
1908 Phi-N	23	17	.575	48	42	32	7	2	359²	263	1	91	114	9.0	1.53	159	.207	.263	18	.151	-1	33	36	-2	3.9
1909 Phi-N	13	16	.448	41	28	16	4	2	247²	202	5	54	96	9.3	2.14	121	.226	.271	9	.118	-3	13	13	-2	0.8
1910 Phi-N	9	6	.600	24	17	13	3	1	152¹	109	2	50	71	9.6	1.60	196	.204	.276	7	.149	-1	24	26	-0	2.8
1911 Cin-N	2	6	.250	19	5	2	0	0	77	92	2	31	28	14.8	4.68	71	.308	.380	2	.091	-1	-11	-12	-1	-1.3
1913 Pit-N	8	6	.571	25	16	7	0	1	141²	144	1	35	59	11.4	3.43	88	.273	.319	4	.103	-1	-4	-7	-1	-0.8
1914 Pit-N	13	17	.433	45	28	15	0	4	259¹	248	8	60	96	11.0	2.98	89	.261	.310	5	.068	-4	-6	-10	-1	-1.4
1915 Pit-N	8	10	.444	30	20	9	0	1	149	160	1	39	56	12.1	2.84	96	.284	.332	4	.091	-3	-1	-2	0	-0.4
Phi-N	4	3	.571	9	8	5	0	0	63²	60	1	11	13	10.2	2.12	129	.247	.282	1	.043	-2	4	4	-0	0.2
Yr	12	13	.480	39	28	14	0	1	212²	220	2	50	69	11.5	2.62	104	.272	.315	5	.045	-5	3	3	0	-0.2
1916 Phi-N	1	7	.125	21	3	1	0	2	62	58	2	15	22	11.0	2.76	96	.251	.305	1	.091	-1	-1	-1	-0	-0.1
1918 Cle-A	0	1	.000	5	1	0	0	1	23	25	0	4	7	11.3	2.35	128	.284	.315	0	.000	-0	1	2	0	0.2
Total 10	85	89	.489	273	173	105	17	14	1576¹	1382	23	401	590	10.4	2.38	114	.241	.294	55	.117	-15	62	59	-7	5.1

■ HUGH McQUILLAN McQuillan, Hugh A. "Handsome Hugh" b: 9/15/1897, New York, N.Y. d: 8/26/47, New York, N.Y. BR/TR, 6', 170 lbs. Deb: 7/26/18

YEAR TM/L	W	L	PCT	G	GS	CG	SH	SV	IP	H	HR	BB	SO	RAT	ERA	ERA+	OAV	OOB	BH	AVG	PB	PR	/A	PD	TPI
1918 Bos-N	1	0	1.000	1	1	1	0	0	9	7	0	5	1	12.0	3.00	90	.219	.324	1	.250	0	-0	-0	0	0.0
1919 Bos-N	2	3	.400	16	7	2	0	1	60	66	3	14	13	12.2	3.45	83	.288	.332	4	.222	0	-4	-4	-1	-0.4
1920 Bos-N	11	15	.423	38	27	17	1	5	225²	230	3	70	53	12.0	3.55	86	.273	.330	19	.257	6	-10	-13	2	-0.5
1921 Bos-N	13	17	.433	45	31	13	2	5	250	284	9	90	94	13.5	4.00	91	.291	.352	18	.205	1	-6	-10	-0	-0.8
1922 Bos-N	5	10	.333	28	17	7	0	0	136	154	3	56	33	14.0	4.24	94	.299	.369	7	.167	-1	-2	-4	-1	-0.3
*NY-N	6	5	.545	15	13	5	0	1	94¹	111	7	34	24	13.8	3.82	105	.301	.360	7	.189	-1	3	2	-1	0.0
Yr	11	15	.423	43	30	12	0	1	230¹	265	10	90	57	13.9	4.06	98	.299	.364	1	.013	-2	1	-2	-0	-0.3
1923 *NY-N	15	14	.517	38	32	15	5	0	229²	224	12	66	75	11.6	3.41	112	.259	.315	14	.171	-2	15	11	-1	0.7
1924 *NY-N	14	8	.636	27	23	14	1	3	184	179	8	43	49	11.0	2.69	136	.259	.304	14	.209	-1	24	20	-2	1.7
1925 NY-N	2	3	.400	14	11	2	0	1	70	95	9	23	23	15.3	6.04	67	.343	.395	3	.143	-1	-14	-16	1	-1.3
1926 NY-N	11	10	.524	33	22	12	1	0	167	171	7	42	47	11.5	3.72	101	.271	.318	7	.132	-3	2	1	2	0.0
1927 NY-N	5	4	.556	11	9	5	0	0	58	73	4	22	17	14.9	4.50	86	.309	.371	4	.211	-1	-4	-4	0	-0.2
Bos-N	3	5	.375	13	11	2	0	0	78	109	2	24	17	15.6	5.54	67	.332	.381	5	.227	0	-14	-16	0	-1.3
Yr	8	9	.471	24	20	7	0	0	136	182	6	46	34	15.2	5.10	74	.322	.375	3	.073	1	-18	-20	1	-1.5
Total 10	88	94	.484	279	204	95	10	16	1561²	1703	67	489	446	12.7	3.83	95	.284	.340	103	.195	-10	-10	-32	2	-2.4

■ NORM McRAE McRae, Norman b: 9/26/47, Elizabeth, N.J. BR/TR, 6'1", 195 lbs. Deb: 9/13/69

YEAR TM/L	W	L	PCT	G	GS	CG	SH	SV	IP	H	HR	BB	SO	RAT	ERA	ERA+	OAV	OOB	BH	AVG	PB	PR	/A	PD	TPI
1969 Det-A	0	0	—	3	0	0	0	0	3	2	0	1	3	9.0	6.00	62	.200	.273	0	—	0	-1	-1	0	0.0
1970 Det-A	0	0	—	19	0	0	0	0	31¹	26	1	25	16	14.9	2.87	130	.226	.369	0	.000	-0	3	3	1	0.4
Total 2	0	0	—	22	0	0	0	0	34¹	28	1	26	19	14.4	3.15	118	.224	.362	0	.000	-0	2	2	1	0.4

■ TRICK McSORLEY McSorley, John Bernard b: 12/6/1858, St.Louis, Mo. d: 2/9/36, St.Louis, Mo. TR, 5'4", 142 lbs. Deb: 5/06/1875 ♦

YEAR TM/L	W	L	PCT	G	GS	CG	SH	SV	IP	H	HR	BB	SO	RAT	ERA	ERA+	OAV	OOB	BH	AVG	PB	PR	/A	PD	TPI
1884 Tol-a	0	0	—	1	0	0	0	0	2	5	0	0	1	22.5	4.50	76	.450	.450	17	.250	0	-0	-0	0	0.0

■ BILL McTIGUE McTigue, William Patrick "Rebel" b: 1/3/1891, Nashville, Tenn. d: 5/8/20, Nashville, Tenn. BL/TL, 6'1.5", 175 lbs. Deb: 5/02/11 ♦

YEAR TM/L	W	L	PCT	G	GS	CG	SH	SV	IP	H	HR	BB	SO	RAT	ERA	ERA+	OAV	OOB	BH	AVG	PB	PR	/A	PD	TPI
1911 Bos-N	0	5	.000	14	8	0	0	0	37	34	3	49	23	21.4	7.05	54	.280	.481	1	.083	-1	-15	-13	-1	-1.3
1912 Bos-N	2	0	1.000	10	1	1	0	0	34²	39	0	18	17	14.8	5.45	66	.285	.368	1	.077	-1	-8	-7	0	-0.6
1916 Det-A	0	0	—	3	0	0	0	0	5¹	5	0	5	1	16.9	5.06	57	.278	.435	0	.000	-0	-1	-1	0	0.0
Total 3	2	5	.286	27	9	1	0	0	77	81	3	72	41	18.1	6.19	59	.282	.429	2	.077	-2	-24	-22	0	-1.9

■ CAL McVEY McVey, Calvin Alexander b: 8/30/1850, Montrose, Iowa d: 8/20/26, San Francisco, Cal BR/TR, 5'9", 170 lbs. Deb: 5/05/1871 M♦

YEAR TM/L	W	L	PCT	G	GS	CG	SH	SV	IP	H	HR	BB	SO	RAT	ERA	ERA+	OAV	OOB	BH	AVG	PB	PR	/A	PD	TPI
1875 Bos-n	1	0	1.000	3	2	0	0	1	11	15	0	1		13.1	3.27	72	.294	.308	137	.352	2	-1	-1		0.0
1876 Chi-N	5	2	.714	11	6	5	0	2	59¹	57	0	2	9	8.9	1.52	161	.235	.242	107	.347	3	5	6	0	0.6
1877 Chi-N	4	8	.333	17	10	6	0	2	92	129	2	11	20	13.7	4.50	66	.313	.331	98	.368	7	-17	-16	-1	-1.2
1879 Cin-N	0	2	.000	3	1	1	0	0	14	34	1	2	7	23.1	8.36	28	.439	.453	105	.297	1	-9	-9	0	-0.7
Total 3	9	12	.429	31	17	12	0	4	165¹	220	3	15	36	12.8	3.76	73	.301	.315	393	.328	11	-21	-19	-0	-1.3

■ DOUG McWEENY McWeeny, Douglas Lawrence "Buzz" b: 8/17/1896, Chicago, Ill. d: 1/1/53, Melrose Park, Ill. BR/TR, 6'2", 190 lbs. Deb: 4/24/21

YEAR TM/L	W	L	PCT	G	GS	CG	SH	SV	IP	H	HR	BB	SO	RAT	ERA	ERA+	OAV	OOB	BH	AVG	PB	PR	/A	PD	TPI
1921 Chi-A	3	6	.333	27	8	3	0	2	97²	127	7	45	46	15.8	6.08	70	.325	.394	1	.032	-4	-20	-20	-1	-2.1
1922 Chi-A	0	1	.000	4	1	0	0	0	10²	13	0	7	5	16.9	5.91	69	.325	.426	0	.000	0	-2	-2	-0	-0.1
1924 Chi-A	1	3	.250	13	5	2	0	0	43¹	47	2	17	18	13.7	4.57	90	.294	.369	0	.000	-0	-2	-3	3	0.0
1926 Bro-N	11	13	.458	42	24	10	1	1	216²	213	6	84	96	12.7	3.04	126	.258	.333	7	.109	-4	19	19	-1	1.3
1927 Bro-N	4	8	.333	34	22	6	0	1	164¹	167	3	70	73	13.4	3.56	111	.266	.347	2	.043	-4	7	7	1	0.4
1928 Bro-N	14	14	.500	42	32	12	4	1	244	218	11	114	79	12.4	3.17	125	.235	.322	14	.173	-1	22	22	3	2.4
1929 Bro-N	4	10	.286	36	24	4	0	1	146	167	17	93	59	16.2	6.10	76	.288	.390	5	.104	-2	-22	-24	-2	-2.4
1930 Cin-N	0	2	.000	8	2	0	0	0	25²	28	2	20	10	16.8	7.36	66	.283	.403	1	.143	0	-7	-7	0	-0.5
Total 8	37	57	.394	206	118	37	5	6	948	980	56	450	386	13.8	4.17	98	.269	.353	30	.104	-16	-5	-8	2	-1.0

■ LARRY McWILLIAMS McWilliams, Larry Dean b: 2/10/54, Wichita, Kan. BL/TL, 6'5", 180 lbs. Deb: 7/17/78

YEAR TM/L	W	L	PCT	G	GS	CG	SH	SV	IP	H	HR	BB	SO	RAT	ERA	ERA+	OAV	OOB	BH	AVG	PB	PR	/A	PD	TPI
1978 Atl-N	9	3	.750	15	15	3	1	0	99¹	84	11	35	42	11.0	2.81	144	.224	.294	2	.063	-2	8	14	1	1.5
1979 Atl-N	3	2	.600	13	13	1	0	0	66¹	69	4	22	32	12.9	5.56	73	.272	.339	5	.208	1	-13	-11	2	-0.8
1980 Atl-N	9	14	.391	30	30	4	1	0	163²	188	27	39	77	12.9	4.95	76	.285	.332	8	.157	-0	-25	-22	-0	-2.1
1981 Atl-N	2	1	.667	6	5	2	0	0	37²	31	2	8	23	9.3	3.11	115	.230	.273	1	.100	-0	2	2	1	0.3
1982 Atl-N	2	3	.400	27	2	0	0	0	37²	52	3	20	24	17.7	6.21	60	.327	.409	1	.167	0	-11	-10	2	-0.8
Pit-N	6	5	.545	19	18	2	2	1	121²	106	9	24	94	9.9	3.11	119	.232	.276	6	.188	-0	7	8	1	1.0
Yr	8	8	.500	46	20	2	2	1	159¹	158	12	44	118	11.6	3.84	89	.255	.309	7	.026	-0	-4	-2	3	0.2
1983 Pit-N	15	8	.652	35	35	8	4	0	238	205	19	87	199	11.2	3.25	114	.230	.300	9	.114	-3	10	12	1	1.0
1984 Pit-N	12	11	.522	34	32	7	2	1	227¹	226	18	78	149	12.1	2.93	123	.263	.326	9	.122	-3	17	17	1	1.5
1985 Pit-N	7	9	.438	30	19	2	0	0	126¹	139	9	62	52	14.8	4.70	76	.283	.371	5	.125	-1	-16	-16	-1	-1.6
1986 Pit-N	3	11	.214	49	15	0	0	0	122¹	129	16	49	80	13.6	5.15	74	.268	.345	4	.138	-0	-19	-18	-0	-1.7
1987 Atl-N	0	1	.000	9	2	0	0	0	20¹	25	2	7	13	15.0	5.75	76	.301	.370	1	.200	0	-4	-3	0	-0.2
1988 StL-N	6	9	.400	42	17	2	1	1	136	130	14	45	70	11.8	3.90	89	.253	.319	6	.162	1	-7	-6	-0	-0.5
1989 Phi-N	2	11	.154	40	16	2	1	0	120²	123	3	49	56	11.6	4.10	86	.265	.340	3	.111	-1	-8	-7	1	-0.0
KC-A	2	2	.500	8	5	1	0	0	32²	31	2	8	24	11.6	4.13	93	.254	.316	0	—	-1	-1	-1	0	0.0
1990 KC-A	0	0	—	13	0	0	0	0	8¹	10	2	9	7	21.6	9.72	39	.313	.476	0	—	0	-5	-5	0	-0.4
Total 13	78	90	.464	370	224	34	13	3	1558¹	1548	137	542	940	12.4	3.99	93	.259	.326	60	.135	-8	-66	-48	9	-3.5

■ JOHNNY MEADOR Meador, John Davis b: 12/4/1892, Madison, N.C. d: 4/11/70, Winston-Salem, N.C BR/TR, 5'10.5", 165 lbs. Deb: 4/24/20

YEAR TM/L	W	L	PCT	G	GS	CG	SH	SV	IP	H	HR	BB	SO	RAT	ERA	ERA+	OAV	OOB	BH	AVG	PB	PR	/A	PD	TPI
1920 Pit-N	0	2	.000	12	2	0	0	0	36¹	48	1	7	5	13.6	4.21	76	.340	.372	1	.167	-0	-4	-4	1	-0.3

YEAR	TM/L	W	L	PCT	G	GS	CG	SH	SV	IP	H	HR	BB	SO	RAT	ERA	ERA+	OAV	OOB	BH	AVG	PB	PR	/A	PD	TPI

■ LEE MEADOWS — Meadows, Henry Lee "Specs" b: 7/12/1894, Oxford, N.C. d: 1/29/63, Daytona Beach, Fla BL/TR, 5'9", 190 lbs. Deb: 4/19/15

YEAR	TM/L	W	L	PCT	G	GS	CG	SH	SV	IP	H	HR	BB	SO	RAT	ERA	ERA+	OAV	OOB	BH	AVG	PB	PR	/A	PD	TPI
1915	StL-N	13	11	.542	39	26	14	1	0	244	232	5	88	104	12.0	2.99	93	.259	.329	8	.096	-4	-6	-5	-3	-1.2
1916	StL-N	12	23	.343	51	36	11	1	2	289	261	3	119	120	12.3	2.58	102	.247	.332	15	.158	-1	1	2	1	0.2
1917	StL-N	15	9	.625	43	37	18	4	2	265²	253	5	90	100	11.8	3.08	87	.262	.328	9	.101	-6	-11	-12	-3	-2.2
1918	StL-N	8	14	.364	30	21	12	0	1	165¹	176	1	56	49	13.2	3.59	75	.280	.348	7	.127	-2	-15	-16	-1	-2.0
1919	StL-N	4	10	.286	22	12	3	1	0	92	100	3	30	28	12.9	3.03	92	.292	.352	3	.103	-2	-1	-2	-3	-0.1
	Phi-N	8	10	.444	18	17	15	3	0	158¹	128	2	49	88	10.5	2.33	138	.229	.300	6	.118	-4	10	16	-2	1.2
	Yr	12	20	.375	40	29	18	4	0	250¹	228	5	79	116	11.3	2.59	118	.252	.317	3	.038	-5	9	13	1	1.1
1920	Phi-N	16	14	.533	35	33	19	3	0	247	249	5	90	95	12.6	2.84	120	.270	.341	14	.171	-3	8	16	0	1.4
1921	Phi-N	11	16	.407	28	27	15	2	0	194¹	226	10	62	52	13.5	4.31	98	.288	.343	13	.210	2	-11	-2	4	0.5
1922	Phi-N	12	18	.400	33	33	19	2	0	237	264	8	71	62	13.1	4.03	116	.288	.346	27	.314	4	2	17	3	2.5
1923	Phi-N	1	3	.250	8	5	0	0	1	19²	40	1	15	10	25.2	13.27	35	.430	.509	4	.400	2	-20	-19	0	-1.4
	Pit-N	16	10	.615	31	25	17	1	0	227	250	3	44	66	11.7	3.01	133	.284	.319	22	.250	3	25	25	2	3.0
	Yr	17	13	.567	39	30	17	1	1	246²	290	3	59	76	12.8	3.83	106	.298	.339	2	.020	5	5	6	2	1.6
1924	Pit-N	13	12	.520	36	30	15	3	0	229¹	240	7	51	61	11.6	3.26	118	.278	.322	16	.195	-1	16	15	-1	1.2
1925	*Pit-N	19	10	.655	35	31	20	1	1	255¹	272	11	67	87	12.2	3.67	122	.273	.323	17	.175	-1	17	23	1	2.2
1926	Pit-N	**20**	9	.690	36	31	15	1	0	226²	254	10	52	54	12.3	3.97	99	.287	.329	20	.227	-1	-4	-1	3	0.2
1927	*Pit-N	19	10	.655	40	38	**25**	2	0	299¹	315	11	66	84	11.7	3.40	121	.273	.317	18	.157	-5	17	24	-1	1.9
1928	Pit-N	1	1	.500	4	2	1	0	0	10	18	0	5	3	20.7	8.10	50	.383	.442	2	.500	1	-5	-4	0	-0.3
1929	Pit-N	0	0	—	1	0	0	0	0	0²	2	0	1	0	40.5	13.50	35	.500	.600	0	.000	-0	-1	-1	0	0.0
Total 15		188	180	.511	490	404	219	25	7	3160²	3280	84	956	1063	12.3	3.37	106	.274	.332	201	.180	-19	22	71	5	7.1

■ RUFUS MEADOWS — Meadows, Rufus Rivers b: 8/25/07, Chase City, Va. d: 5/10/70, Wichita, Kan. BL/TL, 5'11", 175 lbs. Deb: 4/23/26

YEAR	TM/L	W	L	PCT	G	GS	CG	SH	SV	IP	H	HR	BB	SO	RAT	ERA	ERA+	OAV	OOB	BH	AVG	PB	PR	/A	PD	TPI
1926	Cin-N	0	0	—	1	0	0	0	0	0¹	0	0	0	0	0.0	0.00	—	.000	.000	0	.000	-0	0	0	0	0.0

■ DAVE MEADS — Meads, David Donald b: 1/7/64, Montclair, N.J. BL/TL, 6', 175 lbs. Deb: 4/13/87

YEAR	TM/L	W	L	PCT	G	GS	CG	SH	SV	IP	H	HR	BB	SO	RAT	ERA	ERA+	OAV	OOB	BH	AVG	PB	PR	/A	PD	TPI
1987	Hou-N	5	3	.625	45	0	0	0	0	48²	60	8	16	32	14.2	5.55	71	.321	.377	1	.333	1	-8	-9	-1	-0.8
1988	Hou-N	3	1	.750	22	2	0	0	0	39²	37	4	14	27	11.6	3.18	105	.240	.304	1	.250	1	1	1	0	0.1
Total 2		8	4	.667	67	2	0	0	0	88¹	97	12	30	59	13.0	4.48	81	.284	.344	2	.286	1	-7	-8	-1	-0.7

■ GEORGE MEAKIM — Meakim, George Clinton b: 7/11/1865, Brooklyn, N.Y. d: 2/17/23, Queens, N.Y. 5'7.5", 154 lbs. Deb: 5/02/1890

YEAR	TM/L	W	L	PCT	G	GS	CG	SH	SV	IP	H	HR	BB	SO	RAT	ERA	ERA+	OAV	OOB	BH	AVG	PB	PR	/A	PD	TPI
1890	*Lou-a	12	7	.632	28	21	16	3	1	192	173	4	63	123	11.1	2.91	132	.233	.293	11	.153	-2	21	20	-2	1.5
1891	Phi-a	1	4	.200	6	6	4	0	0	35	51	1	22	13	18.8	6.94	55	.329	.412	3	.200	0	-13	-12	2	-0.7
1892	Chi-N	0	1	.000	1	1	1	0	0	9	18	0	2	0	20.0	11.00	30	.400	.426	2	.400	0	-8	-8	-0	-0.4
	Cin-N	1	1	.500	3	3	1	0	0	13²	19	1	9	4	18.4	8.56	38	.317	.406	0	.000	-1	-8	-8	0	-0.4
	Yr	1	2	.333	4	4	2	0	0	22²	37	1	11	4	19.1	9.53	34	.352	.414	0	.000	-0	-16	-16	-0	-1.0
1895	Lou-N	1	0	1.000	1	1	1	0	0	7	7	0	4	2	14.1	2.57	180	.256	.352	1	.333	0	2	2	0	0.1
Total 4		15	13	.536	39	32	23	3	1	256²	268	6	100	142	12.9	4.03	95	.260	.326	17	.170	-2	-6	-6	1	-0.1

■ DOC MEDICH — Medich, George Francis b: 12/9/48, Aliquippa, Pa. BR/TR, 6'5", 225 lbs. Deb: 9/05/72

YEAR	TM/L	W	L	PCT	G	GS	CG	SH	SV	IP	H	HR	BB	SO	RAT	ERA	ERA+	OAV	OOB	BH	AVG	PB	PR	/A	PD	TPI
1972	NY-A	0	0	—	1	1	0	0	0	0	0	2	0	2	0	∞	—	1.000	1.000	0	—	0	-2	-2	0	-0.1
1973	NY-A	14	9	.609	34	32	11	3	0	235	217	20	74	145	11.3	2.95	124	.241	.300	0	—	0	23	19	-3	1.7
1974	NY-A	19	15	.559	38	38	17	4	0	279²	275	24	91	154	12.0	3.60	97	.259	.323	0	—	0	0	-4	-1	-0.4
1975	NY-A	16	16	.500	38	37	15	2	0	272¹	271	25	72	132	11.4	3.50	104	.264	.313	0	—	0	8	4	-2	0.2
1976	Pit-N	8	11	.421	29	26	3	0	0	179	193	10	48	86	12.2	3.52	99	.281	.330	5	.096	-2	-0	-1	1	0.0
1977	Oak-A	10	6	.625	26	25	1	0	0	147²	155	19	49	74	12.6	4.69	86	.265	.325	0	—	0	-10	-11	-1	-1.1
	Sea-A	2	0	1.000	3	3	1	0	0	22¹	26	1	4	3	12.9	3.63	113	.286	.330	0	—	0	1	1	-1	0.1
	Yr	12	6	.667	29	28	2	0	0	170	181	20	53	77	12.5	4.55	89	.265	.319	0	—	0	-9	-10	-2	-1.0
	NY-N	0	1	.000	1	1	0	0	0	7	6	0	1	3	9.0	3.86	97	.261	.292	0	.000	-0	-0	-0	0	0.0
1978	Tex-A	9	8	.529	28	22	6	2	2	171	166	10	52	71	11.6	3.74	100	.255	.313	0	—	0	0	0	1	0.2
1979	Tex-A	10	7	.588	29	19	4	1	0	149	156	9	49	58	12.6	4.17	100	.269	.330	0	—	0	1	-0	2	0.1
1980	Tex-A	14	11	.560	34	32	6	0	0	204¹	230	13	56	91	12.7	3.92	99	.285	.334	0	—	0	3	-1	-1	0.0
1981	Tex-A	10	6	.625	20	20	4	**4**	0	143¹	136	8	33	65	10.7	3.08	113	.252	.297	0	—	0	9	6	1	0.8
1982	Tex-A	7	11	.389	21	21	2	0	0	122²	146	8	61	37	15.4	5.06	76	.307	.390	0	—	0	-13	-16	1	-1.4
	*Mil-A	5	4	.556	10	10	1	0	0	63	57	4	32	36	12.9	5.00	76	.242	.335	0	—	0	-6	-9	-0	-0.8
	Yr	12	15	.444	31	31	3	0	0	185²	203	12	93	73	14.4	5.04	76	.281	.364	0	—	0	-20	-25	-0	-2.2
Total 11		124	105	.541	312	287	71	16	2	1996¹	2036	151	624	955	12.1	3.78	98	.266	.324	5	.093	-2	13	-13	-2	-0.7

■ IRV MEDLINGER — Medlinger, Irving John b: 6/18/27, Chicago, Ill. d: 9/3/75, Wheeling, Ill. BL/TL, 5'11", 185 lbs. Deb: 4/20/49

YEAR	TM/L	W	L	PCT	G	GS	CG	SH	SV	IP	H	HR	BB	SO	RAT	ERA	ERA+	OAV	OOB	BH	AVG	PB	PR	/A	PD	TPI
1949	StL-A	0	0	—	3	0	0	0	0	4	11	1	3	4	31.5	27.00	17	.478	.538	0	—	0	-10	-10	-0	-0.7
1951	StL-A	0	0	—	6	0	0	0	0	9²	10	1	12	5	20.5	8.38	52	.270	.449	0	—	0	-5	-4	-0	-0.3
Total 2		0	0	—	9	0	0	0	0	13²	21	2	15	9	23.7	13.83	32	.350	.480	0	—	0	-15	-14	-0	-1.0

■ SCOTT MEDVIN — Medvin, Scott Howard b: 9/16/61, North Olmstead, O. BR/TR, 6'1", 195 lbs. Deb: 5/11/88

YEAR	TM/L	W	L	PCT	G	GS	CG	SH	SV	IP	H	HR	BB	SO	RAT	ERA	ERA+	OAV	OOB	BH	AVG	PB	PR	/A	PD	TPI
1988	Pit-N	3	0	1.000	17	0	0	0	0	27²	23	1	9	16	10.7	4.88	70	.230	.300	0	.000	-0	-4	-5	0	-0.4
1989	Pit-N	0	1	.000	6	0	0	0	0	6¹	6	0	5	4	15.6	5.68	59	.240	.367	0	—	0	-2	-2	0	0.0
1990	Sea-A	0	1	.000	5	0	0	0	0	4¹	7	0	2	1	20.8	6.23	64	.368	.455	0	—	0	-1	-1	0	0.0
Total 3		3	2	.600	28	0	0	0	0	38¹	36	1	16	21	12.7	5.17	67	.250	.333	0	.000	-0	-7	-7	1	-0.4

■ PETE MEEGAN — Meegan, Peter J. "Steady Pete" b: 11/13/1863, San Francisco, Cal d: 3/15/05, San Francisco, Cal Deb: 8/12/1884

YEAR	TM/L	W	L	PCT	G	GS	CG	SH	SV	IP	H	HR	BB	SO	RAT	ERA	ERA+	OAV	OOB	BH	AVG	PB	PR	/A	PD	TPI
1884	Ric-a	7	12	.368	22	22	22	1	0	179	177	7	29	106	10.4	4.32	77	.244	.273	12	.160	-2	-21	-20	1	-1.7
1885	Pit-a	7	8	.467	18	16	14	1	0	146	146	1	38	58	11.3	3.39	95	.249	.295	13	.194	-1	-2	-3	-1	-0.3
Total 2		14	20	.412	40	38	36	2	0	325	323	8	67	164	10.8	3.90	84	.247	.283	25	.176	-3	-24	-23	1	-2.0

■ BILL MEEHAN — Meehan, William Thomas b: 9/4/1889, Osceola Mills, Pa. d: 10/8/82, Douglas, Wyo. BR/TR, 5'9", 155 lbs. Deb: 9/17/15

YEAR	TM/L	W	L	PCT	G	GS	CG	SH	SV	IP	H	HR	BB	SO	RAT	ERA	ERA+	OAV	OOB	BH	AVG	PB	PR	/A	PD	TPI
1915	Phi-A	0	1	.000	1	1	0	0	0	4	7	0	3	4	22.5	11.25	26	.389	.476	1	1.000	0	-4	-4	0	-0.2

■ ROY MEEKER — Meeker, Charles Roy b: 9/15/1900, Lead Mines, Mo. d: 3/25/29, Orlando, Fla. BL/TL, 5'9", 175 lbs. Deb: 9/22/23

YEAR	TM/L	W	L	PCT	G	GS	CG	SH	SV	IP	H	HR	BB	SO	RAT	ERA	ERA+	OAV	OOB	BH	AVG	PB	PR	/A	PD	TPI
1923	Phi-A	3	0	1.000	5	2	2	0	0	25	24	0	13	12	13.3	3.60	114	.253	.343	1	.111	-1	1	1	-0	0.0
1924	Phi-A	5	12	.294	30	14	5	1	0	146	166	7	81	37	15.5	4.68	91	.288	.381	11	.229	-0	-7	-6	-1	-0.6
1926	Cin-N	0	2	.000	7	1	1	0	0	21	24	1	9	5	14.1	6.43	57	.324	.398	0	.000	-1	-6	-6	0	-0.6
Total 3		8	14	.364	42	17	8	1	0	192	214	8	103	54	15.1	4.73	89	.287	.377	12	.190	-2	-12	-11	-1	-1.2

■ JOUETT MEEKIN — Meekin, Jouett b: 2/21/1867, New Albany, Ind. d: 12/14/44, New Albany, Ind. 6'1", 180 lbs. Deb: 6/13/1891

YEAR	TM/L	W	L	PCT	G	GS	CG	SH	SV	IP	H	HR	BB	SO	RAT	ERA	ERA+	OAV	OOB	BH	AVG	PB	PR	/A	PD	TPI
1891	Lou-a	10	16	.385	29	26	25	2	0	228	227	2	113	144	13.4	4.30	85	.251	.334	21	.216	4	-15	-16	-2	-1.2
1892	Lou-N	7	10	.412	19	18	17	0	0	156¹	168	3	78	67	14.2	4.03	76	.264	.344	5	.078	-4	-13	-17	-0	-1.8
	Was-N	3	10	.231	14	14	13	1	0	112	112	2	48	58	12.9	3.46	94	.250	.323	6	.133	-1	-2	-3	-0	-0.2
	Yr	10	20	.333	33	32	30	1	0	268¹	280	5	126	125	13.6	3.79	83	.258	.335	9	.083	-5	-15	-19	-0	-2.0
1893	Was-N	10	15	.400	31	28	24	1	0	245	289	6	140	91	15.8	4.96	93	.285	.372	29	.257	3	-8	-9	-0	-0.4
1894	*NY-N	33	9	**.786**	52	48	40	1	2	409	404	13	171	133	**12.7**	3.70	142	.255	**.328**	48	.282	7	74	70	-3	5.9
1895	NY-N	16	11	.593	29	29	24	1	0	225²	296	10	73	76	14.7	5.30	88	.311	.361	28	.292	4	-13	-17	-1	-1.0
1896	NY-N	26	14	.650	42	41	34	0	0	334¹	378	8	127	110	13.6	3.82	110	.283	.345	43	.299	12	20	14	-3	1.9
1897	NY-N	20	11	.645	37	34	30	2	0	303²	328	9	99	83	12.7	3.76	110	.273	.329	41	.299	5	19	13	-2	1.4
1898	NY-N	16	18	.471	38	37	34	1	0	320	329	9	108	82	12.3	3.77	92	.264	.323	27	.209	1	-6	-10	-4	-0.2
1899	NY-N	5	11	.313	18	18	16	1	0	148¹	169	4	70	30	14.5	4.37	86	.286	.362	12	.207	1	-8	-10	-3	-1.0

YEAR TM/L	W	L	PCT	G	GS	CG	SH	SV	IP	H	HR	BB	SO	RAT	ERA	ERA+	OAV	OOB	BH	AVG	PB	PR	/A	PD	TPI
Bos-N	7	6	.538	13	13	12	0	0	108	111	0	23	23	11.2	2.83	147	.265	.304	7	.171	-1	12	16	-2	1.2
Yr	12	17	.414	31	31	28	0	0	256¹	280	4	93	53	13.1	3.72	105	.277	.338	5	.051	-0	4	6	-5	0.2
1900 Pit-N	0	2	.000	2	2	1	0	0	13	20	1	8	3	19.4	6.92	52	.351	.431	0	.000	-1	-5	-5	-1	-0.4
Total 10	153	133	.535	324	308	270	9	2	2603¹	2831	67	1058	900	13.4	4.07	102	.273	.340	267	.243	30	55	27	-21	3.2

■ PHIL MEELER
Meeler, Charles Phillip b: 7/3/48, South Boston, Va. BR/TR, 6'5", 215 lbs. Deb: 5/10/72

YEAR TM/L	W	L	PCT	G	GS	CG	SH	SV	IP	H	HR	BB	SO	RAT	ERA	ERA+	OAV	OOB	BH	AVG	PB	PR	/A	PD	TPI
1972 Det-A	0	1	.000	7	0	0	0	0	8¹	10	0	7	5	18.4	4.32	73	.303	.425	0	.000	-0	-1	-1	0	0.0

■ RUSS MEERS
Meers, Russell Harlan "Babe" b: 11/28/18, Tilton, Ill. BL/TL, 5'10", 170 lbs. Deb: 9/28/41

YEAR TM/L	W	L	PCT	G	GS	CG	SH	SV	IP	H	HR	BB	SO	RAT	ERA	ERA+	OAV	OOB	BH	AVG	PB	PR	/A	PD	TPI
1941 Chi-N	0	1	.000	1	1	0	0	0	8	5	0	0	5	6.8	1.13	312	.172	.200	0	.000	-0	2	2	-0	0.2
1946 Chi-N	1	2	.333	7	2	0	0	0	11¹	10	0	10	2	15.9	3.18	104	.238	.385	1	1.000	0	0	0	0	0.1
1947 Chi-N	2	0	1.000	35	1	0	0	0	64¹	61	5	38	28	14.1	4.48	88	.263	.371	2	.143	-1	-3	-4	-0	-0.3
Total 3	3	3	.500	43	4	0	0	0	83²	76	5	48	35	13.7	3.98	96	.251	.359	3	.176	-0	-0	-1	-0	0.0

■ HEINIE MEINE
Meine, Henry William "The Count Of Luxemburg" b: 5/1/1896, St.Louis, Mo. d: 3/18/68, St.Louis, Mo. BR/TR, 5'11", 180 lbs. Deb: 8/16/22

YEAR TM/L	W	L	PCT	G	GS	CG	SH	SV	IP	H	HR	BB	SO	RAT	ERA	ERA+	OAV	OOB	BH	AVG	PB	PR	/A	PD	TPI
1922 StL-A	0	0	—	1	0	0	0	0	4	5	1	2	0	15.8	4.50	92	.313	.389	0	.000	-0	-0	0	0	0.0
1929 Pit-N	7	6	.538	22	13	7	1	1	108	120	4	34	19	13.4	4.50	106	.291	.355	4	.103	-2	3	3	-1	0.0
1930 Pit-N	6	8	.429	20	16	4	0	1	117¹	168	6	44	18	16.6	6.14	81	.346	.406	5	.122	-3	-15	-15	3	-1.2
1931 Pit-N	**19**	13	.594	36	35	22	3	0	**284**	278	8	87	58	11.8	2.98	129	.254	.313	14	.146	-2	28	27	0	2.6
1932 Pit-N	12	9	.571	28	25	13	1	1	172¹	193	6	45	32	12.6	3.86	99	.278	.324	10	.164	-2	0	-1	-0	-0.3
1933 Pit-N	15	8	.652	32	29	12	2	0	207¹	227	10	50	50	12.1	3.65	91	.278	.321	13	.173	-1	-7	-8	-3	-1.1
1934 Pit-N	7	6	.538	26	14	2	0	0	106¹	134	12	25	22	13.5	4.32	95	.306	.345	3	.107	-1	-3	-2	-1	-0.3
Total 7	66	50	.569	165	132	60	7	3	999¹	1125	47	287	199	12.9	3.95	101	.284	.337	49	.144	-12	5	4	-2	-0.3

■ FRANK MEINKE
Meinke, Frank Louis b: 10/18/1863, Chicago, Ill. d: 11/8/31, Chicago, Ill. 5'10.5", 172 lbs. Deb: 5/01/1884 ♦

YEAR TM/L	W	L	PCT	G	GS	CG	SH	SV	IP	H	HR	BB	SO	RAT	ERA	ERA+	OAV	OOB	BH	AVG	PB	PR	/A	PD	TPI
1884 Det-N	8	23	.258	35	31	31	1	0	289	341	10	63	124	12.6	3.18	91	.278	.314	56	.164	-3	-6	-9	-1	-0.7
1885 Det-N	0	1	.000	1	1	0	0	0	5	13	0	4	0	30.6	3.60	79	.462	.529	0	.000	-0	-0	-0	0	0.0
Total 2	8	24	.250	36	32	31	1	0	294	354	10	67	124	12.9	3.18	91	.282	.319	56	.163	-3	-7	-9	-1	-0.7

■ SAM MEJIAS
Mejias, Samuel Elias b: 5/9/52, Santiago, D.R. BR/TR, 6', 170 lbs. Deb: 9/06/76 ♦

YEAR TM/L	W	L	PCT	G	GS	CG	SH	SV	IP	H	HR	BB	SO	RAT	ERA	ERA+	OAV	OOB	BH	AVG	PB	PR	/A	PD	TPI
1978 Mon-N	0	0	—	1	0	0	0	0	1	0	0	0	0	9.0	0.00	—	.000	.250	13	.232	0	0	0	0	0.0

■ JOSE MELENDEZ
Melendez, Jose Luis (Garcia) b: 9/2/65, Naguabo, P.R. BR/TR, 6'2", 175 lbs. Deb: 9/11/90

YEAR TM/L	W	L	PCT	G	GS	CG	SH	SV	IP	H	HR	BB	SO	RAT	ERA	ERA+	OAV	OOB	BH	AVG	PB	PR	/A	PD	TPI
1990 Sea-A	0	0	—	3	0	0	0	0	5¹	8	2	3	7	20.3	11.81	34	.333	.429	0	—	0	-5	-5	-0	-0.3

■ STEVE MELTER
Melter, Stephen Blazius b: 1/2/1886, Cherokee, Iowa d: 1/28/62, Mishawaka, Ind. BR/TR, 6'2", 180 lbs. Deb: 6/27/09

YEAR TM/L	W	L	PCT	G	GS	CG	SH	SV	IP	H	HR	BB	SO	RAT	ERA	ERA+	OAV	OOB	BH	AVG	PB	PR	/A	PD	TPI
1909 StL-N	0	1	.000	23	1	0	0	3	64¹	79	1	20	24	14.1	3.50	72	.322	.378	2	.133	-0	-6	-7	1	-0.6

■ CLIFF MELTON
Melton, Clifford George "Mickey Mouse" or "Mountain Music" b: 1/3/12, Brevard, N.C. d: 7/28/86, Baltimore, Md. BL/TL, 6'5.5", 203 lbs. Deb: 4/25/37

YEAR TM/L	W	L	PCT	G	GS	CG	SH	SV	IP	H	HR	BB	SO	RAT	ERA	ERA+	OAV	OOB	BH	AVG	PB	PR	/A	PD	TPI
1937 *NY-N	20	9	.690	46	27	14	2	7	248	216	9	55	142	10.1	2.61	149	.233	.280	10	.122	-5	36	**35**	3	3.4
1938 NY-N	14	14	.500	36	31	10	1	0	243	266	19	61	101	12.1	3.89	97	.276	.319	14	.175	-1	-3	-3	2	-0.2
1939 NY-N	12	15	.444	41	23	9	2	5	207¹	214	7	65	95	12.3	3.56	110	.269	.327	12	.182	-1	8	8	1	0.8
1940 NY-N	10	11	.476	37	21	4	1	2	166²	185	9	68	91	13.8	4.91	79	.285	.355	12	.222	2	-20	-19	1	-1.5
1941 NY-N	8	11	.421	42	22	9	3	1	194¹	181	14	61	100	11.3	3.01	123	.246	.305	7	.115	-3	13	15	3	1.5
1942 NY-N	11	5	.688	23	17	12	2	1	143²	122	9	33	61	9.8	2.63	128	.229	.276	11	.234	2	11	12	3	1.8
1943 NY-N	9	13	.409	34	28	6	2	0	186¹	184	7	69	55	12.4	3.19	108	.257	.325	8	.148	0	4	5	4	1.0
1944 NY-N	2	2	.500	13	10	1	0	0	64¹	78	5	19	15	13.7	4.06	90	.294	.344	3	.120	-2	-3	-3	1	-0.2
Total 8	86	80	.518	272	179	65	13	16	1453²	1446	79	431	660	11.8	3.42	109	.259	.314	77	.164	-9	47	50	18	6.6

■ RUBE MELTON
Melton, Reuben Franklin b: 2/27/17, Cramerton, N.C. d: 9/11/71, Greer, S.C. BR/TR, 6'5", 205 lbs. Deb: 4/17/41

YEAR TM/L	W	L	PCT	G	GS	CG	SH	SV	IP	H	HR	BB	SO	RAT	ERA	ERA+	OAV	OOB	BH	AVG	PB	PR	/A	PD	TPI
1941 Phi-N	1	5	.167	25	5	2	0	0	83²	81	7	47	57	13.8	4.73	78	.258	.355	2	.105	-1	-10	-10	-2	-1.2
1942 Phi-N	9	20	.310	42	29	10	1	4	209¹	180	7	114	107	12.8	3.70	89	.234	.335	8	.123	-1	-9	-9	-2	-1.2
1943 Bro-N	5	8	.385	30	17	4	2	0	119¹	102	3	79	63	14.0	3.92	86	.233	.357	4	.105	-2	-7	-7	-1	-1.1
1944 Bro-N	9	13	.409	37	23	6	1	0	187¹	178	1	96	91	13.3	3.46	103	.254	.345	7	.123	-3	3	2	-0	0.0
1946 Bro-N	6	3	.667	24	12	3	2	1	99²	72	3	52	44	11.5	1.99	170	.206	.314	3	.107	-2	16	15	-0	1.5
1947 Bro-N	0	1	.000	4	1	0	0	0	4²	7	1	7	1	27.0	13.50	31	.350	.519	1	1.000	0	-5	-5	-0	-0.3
Total 6	30	50	.375	162	87	25	6	5	704	620	22	395	363	13.1	3.62	95	.239	.343	25	.120	-9	-12	-14	-6	-2.3

■ MARIO MENDOZA
Mendoza, Mario (Aizpuru) b: 12/26/50, Chihuahua, Mex. BR/TR, 5'11", 170 lbs. Deb: 4/26/74 C♦

YEAR TM/L	W	L	PCT	G	GS	CG	SH	SV	IP	H	HR	BB	SO	RAT	ERA	ERA+	OAV	OOB	BH	AVG	PB	PR	/A	PD	TPI
1977 Pit-N	0	0	—	1	0	0	0	0	2	3	1	2	0	22.5	13.50	30	.375	.500	16	.198	0	-2	-2	0	-0.1

■ MIKE MENDOZA
Mendoza, Michael Joseph b: 11/26/55, Inglewood, Cal. BR/TR, 6'5", 215 lbs. Deb: 9/07/79 ♦

YEAR TM/L	W	L	PCT	G	GS	CG	SH	SV	IP	H	HR	BB	SO	RAT	ERA	ERA+	OAV	OOB	BH	AVG	PB	PR	/A	PD	TPI
1979 Hou-N	0	0	—	1	0	0	0	0	1	0	0	0	0	0.0	0.00	—	.000	.000	0	—	0	0	0	0	0.0

■ JOCK MENEFEE
Menefee, John b: 1/15/1868, West Virginia d: 3/11/53, Belle Vernon, Pa. BR/TR, 6', Deb: 8/17/1892 ♦

YEAR TM/L	W	L	PCT	G	GS	CG	SH	SV	IP	H	HR	BB	SO	RAT	ERA	ERA+	OAV	OOB	BH	AVG	PB	PR	/A	PD	TPI
1892 Pit-N	0	0	—	1	0	0	0	0	4	10	0	2	0	27.0	11.25	29	.455	.500	0	.000	-0	-4	-4	0	-0.2
1893 Lou-N	8	7	.533	15	15	14	1	0	129¹	150	3	40	30	13.2	4.24	104	.282	.332	20	.274	3	6	2	2	0.7
1894 Lou-N	8	17	.320	28	24	20	1	0	211²	258	3	50	43	13.1	4.29	119	.297	.336	13	.165	-5	24	19	2	1.1
Pit-N	5	8	.385	13	13	13	0	0	111²	159	4	39	33	16.0	5.40	97	.331	.381	12	.255	-0	-1	-2	2	0.0
Yr	13	25	.342	41	37	33	1	0	323¹	417	7	89	76	14.1	4.68	110	.309	.352	11	.087	-5	23	17	4	1.1
1895 Pit-N	0	1	.000	2	1	0	0	0	1²	2	0	7	0	48.6	16.20	28	.293	.651	0	—	-0	-2	-2	0	-0.1
1898 NY-N	0	1	.000	1	1	0	0	0	9¹	11	0	2	3	12.5	4.82	72	.291	.327	0	.000	-0	-1	-1	0	-0.1
1900 Chi-N	9	4	.692	16	13	11	0	0	117	140	1	35	30	13.5	3.85	94	.296	.344	5	.109	-4	-2	-3	-2	-0.6
1901 Chi-N	8	12	.400	21	20	19	0	0	182¹	201	4	34	55	11.9	3.80	85	.278	.316	39	.257	3	-10	-11	0	-1.0
1902 Chi-N	12	10	.545	22	21	20	4	0	197¹	202	2	26	60	10.7	2.42	112	.265	.294	50	.231	2	8	6	-1	0.7
1903 Chi-N	8	10	.444	20	17	13	1	0	147	157	3	38	39	12.3	3.00	105	.275	.327	13	.203	1	4	2	3	0.6
Total 9	58	70	.453	139	125	111	7	0	1111¹	1290	20	273	293	12.8	3.81	101	.288	.331	152	.222	-1	23	6	7	1.1

■ MIKE MEOLA
Meola, Emile Michael b: 10/19/05, New York, N.Y. d: 9/1/76, Fair Lawn, N.J. BR/TR, 5'11", 175 lbs. Deb: 4/24/33

YEAR TM/L	W	L	PCT	G	GS	CG	SH	SV	IP	H	HR	BB	SO	RAT	ERA	ERA+	OAV	OOB	BH	AVG	PB	PR	/A	PD	TPI
1933 Bos-A	0	0	—	3	0	0	0	0	2¹	5	0	2	1	27.0	23.14	19	.417	.500	0	—	0	-5	-5	0	-0.3
1936 StL-A	0	1	.000	9	0	0	0	0	19¹	29	0	13	6	20.0	9.31	58	.358	.453	1	.500	1	-9	-8	0	-0.5
Bos-A	0	2	.000	6	3	1	0	1	21¹	29	0	10	8	16.9	5.48	97	.326	.400	1	.143	-1	-1	-0	1	0.0
Yr	0	3	.000	15	3	1	0	1	40²	58	0	23	14	18.1	7.30	73	.339	.421	0	.000	-0	-10	-9	1	-0.5
Total 2	0	3	.000	18	3	1	0	1	43	63	0	25	15	18.8	8.16	65	.346	.431	2	.222	-0	-15	-14	1	-0.8

■ WIN MERCER
Mercer, George Barclay b: 6/20/1874, Chester, W.Va. d: 1/12/03, San Francisco, Cal TR, 5'7", 140 lbs. Deb: 4/21/1894 ♦

YEAR TM/L	W	L	PCT	G	GS	CG	SH	SV	IP	H	HR	BB	SO	RAT	ERA	ERA+	OAV	OOB	BH	AVG	PB	PR	/A	PD	TPI
1894 Was-N	17	23	.425	49	38	30	0	3	333	431	9	125	69	15.0	3.76	140	.310	.367	46	.284	3	58	56	2	4.7
1895 Was-N	13	23	.361	43	38	32	0	2	311	414	17	96	84	15.2	4.46	108	.323	.368	50	.255	0	11	12	-1	0.9
1896 Was-N	25	18	.581	46	45	38	2	0	366¹	456	10	117	94	14.1	4.13	107	.302	.353	58	.244	-1	10	11	1	1.1
1897 Was-N	20	20	.500	45	42	34	**3**	2	332	395	5	102	88	13.5	3.25	134	.293	.343	43	.319	8	39	40	-1	4.3
1898 Was-N	12	18	.400	33	30	24	0	0	233²	309	3	71	52	14.6	4.81	76	.316	.362	61	.321	8	-31	-30	-1	-2.6
1899 Was-N	7	14	.333	23	21	21	0	0	186	234	2	53	28	13.9	4.60	85	.307	.352	112	.299	5	-15	-14	3	-1.2
1900 NY-N	13	17	.433	33	29	26	1	0	242²	303	6	58	57	13.4	3.86	94	.305	.343	73	.294	7	-4	-7	2	-0.5
1901 Was-A	9	13	.409	24	22	19	1	1	179²	217	8	50	31	13.4	4.56	80	.295	.340	42	.300	6	-18	-18	-1	-1.5
1902 Det-A	15	18	.455	35	33	28	4	1	281²	282	5	80	40	11.6	3.04	120	.261	.312	18	.180	-2	17	19	4	2.1

YEAR TM/L	W	L	PCT	G	GS	CG	SH	SV	IP	H	HR	BB	SO	RAT	ERA	ERA+	OAV	OOB	BH	AVG	PB	PR	/A	PD	TPI
Total 9	131	164	.444	331	298	252	11	9	2466	3057	64	752	525	13.9	3.98	106	.302	.350	502	.285	33	66	71	10	7.3

■ JACK MERCER
Mercer, Harry Vernon b: 3/10/1889, Zanesville, Ohio d: 6/25/45, Dayton Ohio Deb: 8/02/10

YEAR TM/L	W	L	PCT	G	GS	CG	SH	SV	IP	H	HR	BB	SO	RAT	ERA	ERA+	OAV	OOB	BH	AVG	PB	PR	/A	PD	TPI
1910 Pit-N	0	0	—	1	0	0	0	0	1	0	0	2	1	18.0	0.00	—	.000	.500	0	—	0	0	0	0	0.0

■ MARK MERCER
Mercer, Mark Kenneth b: 5/22/54, Fort Bragg, N.C. BL/TL, 6'5", 220 lbs. Deb: 9/01/81

YEAR TM/L	W	L	PCT	G	GS	CG	SH	SV	IP	H	HR	BB	SO	RAT	ERA	ERA+	OAV	OOB	BH	AVG	PB	PR	/A	PD	TPI
1981 Tex-A	0	1	.000	7	0	0	0	2	7²	7	1	7	8	16.4	4.70	74	.241	.389	0	—	0	-1	-1	0	0.0

■ KENT MERCKER
Mercker, Kent Franklin b: 2/1/68, Indianapolis, Ind. BL/TL, 6'1", 175 lbs. Deb: 9/22/89

YEAR TM/L	W	L	PCT	G	GS	CG	SH	SV	IP	H	HR	BB	SO	RAT	ERA	ERA+	OAV	OOB	BH	AVG	PB	PR	/A	PD	TPI
1989 Atl-N	0	0	—	2	1	0	0	0	4¹	8	0	6	4	29.1	12.46	29	.400	.538	0	.000	-0	-4	-4	0	-0.3
1990 Atl-N	4	7	.364	36	0	0	0	7	48¹	43	6	24	39	12.8	3.17	124	.236	.332	0	.000	-0	3	4	-1	0.3
Total 2	4	7	.364	38	1	0	0	7	52²	51	6	30	43	14.2	3.93	99	.252	.355	0	.000	-0	-1	-0	-1	0.0

■ SPIKE MERENA
Merena, John Joseph b: 11/18/09, Paterson, N.J. d: 3/9/77, Bridgeport, Conn. BL/TL, 6', 185 lbs. Deb: 9/16/34

YEAR TM/L	W	L	PCT	G	GS	CG	SH	SV	IP	H	HR	BB	SO	RAT	ERA	ERA+	OAV	OOB	BH	AVG	PB	PR	/A	PD	TPI
1934 Bos-A	1	2	.333	4	3	2	1	0	24²	20	2	16	7	13.5	2.92	165	.222	.346	1	.143	-0	4	5	-1	0.4

■ RON MERIDITH
Meridith, Ronald Knox b: 11/26/56, San Pedro, Cal. BL/TL, 6', 175 lbs. Deb: 9/16/84

YEAR TM/L	W	L	PCT	G	GS	CG	SH	SV	IP	H	HR	BB	SO	RAT	ERA	ERA+	OAV	OOB	BH	AVG	PB	PR	/A	PD	TPI
1984 Chi-N	0	0	—	3	0	0	0	0	5¹	6	1	2	4	13.5	3.38	116	.273	.333	0	—	0	0	0	0	0.0
1985 Chi-N	3	2	.600	32	0	0	0	1	46¹	53	3	24	23	15.2	4.47	89	.301	.388	1	.250	0	-5	-2	0	-0.1
1986 Tex-A	1	0	1.000	5	0	0	0	0	3	2	0	1	2	9.0	3.00	143	.286	.375	0	—	0	0	0	0	0.1
1987 Tex-A	1	0	1.000	11	0	0	0	0	20²	25	7	12	17	16.1	6.10	73	.298	.385	0	—	0	-4	-4	0	-0.2
Total 4	5	2	.714	51	0	0	0	1	75¹	86	11	39	46	15.1	4.78	87	.298	.383	1	.250	0	-8	-5	1	-0.2

■ GEORGE MERRITT
Merritt, George Washington b: 4/14/1880, Paterson, N.J. d: 2/21/38, Memphis, Tenn. TR, 6', 160 lbs. Deb: 9/06/01 ♦

YEAR TM/L	W	L	PCT	G	GS	CG	SH	SV	IP	H	HR	BB	SO	RAT	ERA	ERA+	OAV	OOB	BH	AVG	PB	PR	/A	PD	TPI
1901 Pit-N	3	0	1.000	3	3	3	0	0	24	28	0	5	5	13.1	4.88	67	.289	.337	3	.273	1	-4	-4	-0	-0.2
1903 Pit-N	0	0	—	1	0	0	0	0	4	4	0	1	2	11.3	2.25	144	.267	.313	4	.148	-0	0	0	0	0.0
Total 2	3	0	1.000	4	3	3	0	0	28	32	0	6	7	12.9	4.50	73	.286	.334	10	.213	1	-4	-4	-0	-0.2

■ JIM MERRITT
Merritt, James Joseph b: 12/9/43, Altadena, Cal. BL/TL, 6'3", 175 lbs. Deb: 8/02/65

YEAR TM/L	W	L	PCT	G	GS	CG	SH	SV	IP	H	HR	BB	SO	RAT	ERA	ERA+	OAV	OOB	BH	AVG	PB	PR	/A	PD	TPI
1965 *Min-A	5	4	.556	16	9	1	0	2	76²	68	11	20	61	10.3	3.17	112	.239	.289	3	.136	0	2	3	-0	0.4
1966 Min-A	7	14	.333	31	18	5	1	3	144	112	17	33	124	9.1	3.38	107	.212	.258	4	.103	-1	1	4	-1	0.3
1967 Min-A	13	7	.650	37	28	11	4	0	227²	196	21	30	161	9.2	2.53	137	.230	.262	10	.135	0	18	24	-2	2.6
1968 Min-A	12	16	.429	38	34	11	1	1	238¹	207	21	52	181	10.0	3.25	95	.232	.279	10	.141	0	-7	-4	0	-0.3
1969 Cin-N	17	9	.654	42	36	8	1	0	251	269	33	61	144	12.0	4.37	86	.273	.318	11	.143	0	-22	-17	-3	-1.8
1970 *Cin-N	20	12	.625	35	35	12	1	0	234	248	21	53	136	11.6	4.08	99	.270	.311	14	.169	3	-1	-1	-2	0.0
1971 Cin-N	1	11	.083	28	11	0	0	0	107	115	14	31	38	12.5	4.37	77	.279	.334	4	.138	0	-11	-12	-1	-1.3
1972 Cin-N	1	0	1.000	4	1	0	0	0	8	13	1	2	4	16.9	4.50	71	.361	.395	0	.000	-0	-1	-1	0	-0.1
1973 Tex-A	5	13	.278	35	19	8	1	1	160	191	18	34	65	12.7	4.05	92	.296	.332	0	—	0	-4	-6	-1	-0.6
1974 Tex-A	0	0	—	26	1	0	0	0	32²	46	3	6	18	14.3	4.13	86	.329	.356	0	—	0	-2	-2	-0	-0.2
1975 Tex-A	0	0	—	5	0	0	0	0	3²	3	0	0	0	9.8	0.00	—	.214	.267	0	—	0	2	2	0	0.1
Total 11	81	86	.485	297	192	56	9	7	1483	1468	160	322	932	11.0	3.65	98	.257	.300	56	.141	3	-25	-11	-9	-0.9

■ LLOYD MERRITT
Merritt, Lloyd Wesley b: 4/8/33, St.Louis, Mo. BR/TR, 6', 189 lbs. Deb: 4/22/57

YEAR TM/L	W	L	PCT	G	GS	CG	SH	SV	IP	H	HR	BB	SO	RAT	ERA	ERA+	OAV	OOB	BH	AVG	PB	PR	/A	PD	TPI
1957 StL-N	1	2	.333	44	0	0	0	7	65¹	60	7	28	35	12.7	3.31	120	.251	.339	0	.000	-0	4	5	0	0.5

■ SAM MERTES
Mertes, Samuel Blair "Sandow" b: 8/6/1872, San Francisco, Cal. d: 3/11/45, San Francisco, Cal BR/TR, 5'10", 185 lbs. Deb: 6/30/1896 ♦

YEAR TM/L	W	L	PCT	G	GS	CG	SH	SV	IP	H	HR	BB	SO	RAT	ERA	ERA+	OAV	OOB	BH	AVG	PB	PR	/A	PD	TPI
1902 Chi-A	1	0	1.000	1	0	0	0	0	8	6	0	0	0	6.8	1.13	301	.209	.209	140	.282	0	2	2	-0	0.2

■ JIM MERTZ
Mertz, James Verlin b: 8/10/16, Lima, Ohio BR/TR, 5'10.5", 170 lbs. Deb: 5/01/43

YEAR TM/L	W	L	PCT	G	GS	CG	SH	SV	IP	H	HR	BB	SO	RAT	ERA	ERA+	OAV	OOB	BH	AVG	PB	PR	/A	PD	TPI
1943 Was-A	5	7	.417	33	10	2	0	3	116²	109	7	58	53	12.9	4.63	69	.251	.339	7	.184	0	-17	-18	0	-1.8

■ JOSE MESA
Mesa, Jose Ramon b: 5/22/66, Pueblo Viejo, D.R. BR/TR, 6'3", 170 lbs. Deb: 9/10/87

YEAR TM/L	W	L	PCT	G	GS	CG	SH	SV	IP	H	HR	BB	SO	RAT	ERA	ERA+	OAV	OOB	BH	AVG	PB	PR	/A	PD	TPI
1987 Bal-A	1	3	.250	6	5	0	0	0	31¹	38	7	15	17	15.2	6.03	73	.297	.371	0	—	0	-5	-6	-1	-0.5
1990 Bal-A	3	2	.600	7	7	0	0	0	46²	37	2	27	24	12.5	3.86	99	.218	.328	0	—	0	0	-0	-0	0.0
Total 2	4	5	.444	13	12	0	0	0	78	75	9	42	41	13.6	4.73	86	.252	.346	0	—	0	-5	-6	-1	-0.5

■ BUD MESSENGER
Messenger, Andrew Warren b: 2/1/1898, Grand Blanc, Mich. d: 11/4/71, Lansing, Mich. BR/TR, 6', 175 lbs. Deb: 7/31/24

YEAR TM/L	W	L	PCT	G	GS	CG	SH	SV	IP	H	HR	BB	SO	RAT	ERA	ERA+	OAV	OOB	BH	AVG	PB	PR	/A	PD	TPI
1924 Cle-A	2	0	1.000	5	2	1	0	0	25	28	4	14	4	15.1	4.32	99	.283	.372	1	.125	-0	-0	-0	0	0.0

■ ANDY MESSERSMITH
Messersmith, John Alexander b: 8/6/45, Toms River, N.J. BR/TR, 6'1", 200 lbs. Deb: 7/04/68

YEAR TM/L	W	L	PCT	G	GS	CG	SH	SV	IP	H	HR	BB	SO	RAT	ERA	ERA+	OAV	OOB	BH	AVG	PB	PR	/A	PD	TPI
1968 Cal-A	4	2	.667	28	5	2	1	4	81¹	44	3	35	74	8.9	2.21	132	.157	.253	2	.100	-1	7	6	0	0.7
1969 Cal-A	16	11	.593	40	33	10	2	2	250	159	17	100	211	9.9	2.52	138	.190	.276	12	.156	2	31	27	-2	2.9
1970 Cal-A	11	10	.524	37	26	6	1	5	194²	144	21	78	162	10.5	3.01	120	.205	.290	11	.157	0	15	13	-1	1.3
1971 Cal-A	20	13	.606	38	38	14	4	0	276²	224	16	121	179	11.5	2.99	108	.218	.304	16	.172	4	14	8	1	1.2
1972 Cal-A	8	11	.421	25	21	10	3	2	169²	125	5	68	142	10.3	2.81	104	.207	.290	10	.189	2	5	2	0	0.4
1973 LA-N	14	10	.583	33	33	10	3	0	249²	196	24	77	177	10.1	2.70	127	.214	.279	15	.169	2	27	20	-1	2.2
1974 *LA-N	20	6	.769	39	39	13	3	0	292¹	227	24	94	221	10.0	2.59	132	.212	.278	23	.240	9	34	26	-0	3.8
1975 LA-N	19	14	.576	42	40	19	7	1	321²	244	22	96	213	9.7	2.29	148	.213	.276	17	.157	2	47	40	-2	4.3
1976 Atl-N	11	11	.500	29	28	12	3	1	207¹	166	14	74	135	10.5	3.04	125	.219	.290	12	.179	0	11	17	1	2.1
1977 Atl-N	5	4	.556	16	16	1	0	0	102¹	101	12	39	69	12.5	4.40	101	.256	.326	4	.118	0	-6	1	0	0.1
1978 NY-A	0	3	.000	6	5	0	0	0	22¹	24	7	15	16	16.1	5.64	64	.267	.377	0	—	0	-5	-5	-0	-0.4
1979 LA-N	2	4	.333	11	11	1	0	0	62¹	55	9	34	26	12.9	4.91	74	.244	.344	2	.091	-1	-8	-9	-0	-0.8
Total 12	130	99	.568	344	295	98	27	15	2230¹	1719	174	831	1625	10.5	2.86	121	.212	.289	124	.170	19	172	145	-4	17.8

■ TOM METCALF
Metcalf, Thomas John b: 7/16/40, Amherst, Wis. BR/TR, 6'2.5", 174 lbs. Deb: 8/04/63

YEAR TM/L	W	L	PCT	G	GS	CG	SH	SV	IP	H	HR	BB	SO	RAT	ERA	ERA+	OAV	OOB	BH	AVG	PB	PR	/A	PD	TPI
1963 NY-A	1	0	1.000	8	0	0	0	0	13	12	2	3	3	10.4	2.77	127	.250	.294	0	—	0	1	1	0	0.1

■ DEWEY METIVIER
Metivier, George Dewey b: 5/6/1898, Cambridge, Mass. d: 3/2/47, Cambridge, Mass. BL/TR, 5'11", 175 lbs. Deb: 9/15/22

YEAR TM/L	W	L	PCT	G	GS	CG	SH	SV	IP	H	HR	BB	SO	RAT	ERA	ERA+	OAV	OOB	BH	AVG	PB	PR	/A	PD	TPI
1922 Cle-A	2	0	1.000	2	2	2	0	0	18	18	1	3	1	11.0	4.50	89	.265	.306	1	.167	-0	-1	-1	-0	0.0
1923 Cle-A	4	2	.667	26	5	1	0	1	73¹	111	1	38	9	19.0	6.50	61	.368	.448	3	.150	-0	-21	-21	1	-1.8
1924 Cle-A	1	5	.167	26	6	1	0	3	76¹	110	3	34	14	17.0	5.31	81	.358	.422	3	.125	-2	-9	-9	-0	-0.9
Total 3	7	7	.500	54	13	4	0	4	167²	239	5	75	24	17.2	5.74	72	.353	.423	7	.140	-3	-31	-30	-0	-2.7

■ BUTCH METZGER
Metzger, Clarence Edward b: 5/23/52, Lafayette, Ind. BR/TR, 6'1", 185 lbs. Deb: 9/08/74

YEAR TM/L	W	L	PCT	G	GS	CG	SH	SV	IP	H	HR	BB	SO	RAT	ERA	ERA+	OAV	OOB	BH	AVG	PB	PR	/A	PD	TPI
1974 SF-N	1	0	1.000	10	0	0	0	0	12²	11	0	12	5	16.3	3.55	107	.239	.397	0	—	0	0	-0	-0	0.0
1975 SD-N	1	0	1.000	4	0	0	0	0	4²	6	1	4	6	19.3	7.71	45	.316	.435	0	—	0	-2	-2	0	-0.1
1976 SD-N	11	4	.733	77	0	0	0	16	123¹	119	5	52	89	12.7	2.92	112	.258	.337	0	.000	-0	8	5	-1	0.4
1977 SD-N	0	0	—	17	1	0	0	0	22²	27	5	12	6	15.9	5.56	64	.307	.396	0	.000	-0	-4	-5	-0	-0.5
StL-N	4	2	.667	58	0	0	0	7	92²	78	8	38	48	11.4	3.11	124	.228	.307	0	.000	-0	8	8	-1	0.6
Yr	4	2	.667	75	1	0	0	7	115¹	105	13	50	54	12.2	3.59	105	.242	.322	0	.000	-1	4	3	-1	0.1
1978 NY-N	1	3	.250	25	0	0	0	0	37¹	48	4	22	21	17.1	6.51	54	.324	.415	0	—	0	-12	-13	-0	-1.2
Total 5	18	9	.667	191	1	0	0	23	293¹	289	23	140	175	13.3	3.74	94	.262	.348	0	.000	-1	-2	-7	-2	-0.8

■ BRIAN MEYER
Meyer, Brian Scott b: 1/29/63, Camden, N.J. BR/TR, 6', 190 lbs. Deb: 9/03/88

YEAR TM/L	W	L	PCT	G	GS	CG	SH	SV	IP	H	HR	BB	SO	RAT	ERA	ERA+	OAV	OOB	BH	AVG	PB	PR	/A	PD	TPI
1988 Hou-N	0	0	—	8	0	0	0	0	12¹	9	2	4	10	9.5	1.46	227	.225	.295	0	—	0	3	3	1	0.3
1989 Hou-N	0	1	.000	12	0	0	0	1	18	16	0	13	13	15.0	4.50	75	.239	.370	0	—	0	-2	-2	0	-0.1
1990 Hou-N	0	4	.000	14	0	0	0	1	20¹	16	3	6	6	9.7	2.21	169	.211	.268	0	.000	-0	4	3	1	0.4

YEAR	TM/L	W	L	PCT	G	GS	CG	SH	SV	IP	H	HR	BB	SO	RAT	ERA	ERA+	OAV	OOB	BH	AVG	PB	PR	/A	PD	TPI
Total	3	0	5	.000	34	0	0	0	2	50²	41	5	23	29	11.5	2.84	124	.224	.314	0	.000	-0	4	4	2	0.6

■ JACK MEYER
Meyer, John Robert   b: 3/23/32, Philadelphia, Pa.   d: 3/9/67, Philadelphia, Pa.   BR/TR, 6'1", 175 lbs.   Deb: 4/16/55

YEAR	TM/L	W	L	PCT	G	GS	CG	SH	SV	IP	H	HR	BB	SO	RAT	ERA	ERA+	OAV	OOB	BH	AVG	PB	PR	/A	PD	TPI
1955	Phi-N	6	11	.353	50	5	0	0	**16**	110¹	75	14	66	97	11.7	3.43	116	.190	.310	2	.100	0	8	7	-1	0.6
1956	Phi-N	7	11	.389	41	7	2	0	0	96	86	8	51	66	13.2	4.41	84	.242	.343	4	.200	1	-7	-7	0	-0.5
1957	Phi-N	0	2	.000	19	2	0	0	0	37²	44	7	28	34	17.4	5.73	66	.297	.412	1	.167	0	-8	-8	0	-0.6
1958	Phi-N	3	6	.333	37	5	1	0	2	90¹	77	8	33	87	11.1	3.59	110	.232	.303	5	.278	1	4	4	-2	0.3
1959	Phi-N	5	3	.625	47	1	1	0	1	93²	76	9	53	71	12.5	3.36	122	.222	.328	1	.071	-1	6	8	-0	0.7
1960	Phi-N	3	1	.750	7	4	0	0	0	25	25	2	11	18	13.0	4.32	90	.272	.350	1	.125	-0	-2	-1	0	0.0
1961	Phi-N	0	0	—	1	0	0	0	0	2	2	1	2	2	18.0	9.00	45	.286	.444	0	—	0	-1	-1	0	0.0
Total	7	24	34	.414	202	24	4	0	21	455	385	49	244	375	12.6	3.92	100	.230	.332	14	.163	1	0	0	-2	0.5

■ BOB MEYER
Meyer, Robert Bernard   b: 8/4/39, Toledo, Ohio   BR/TL, 6'2", 185 lbs.   Deb: 4/20/64

YEAR	TM/L	W	L	PCT	G	GS	CG	SH	SV	IP	H	HR	BB	SO	RAT	ERA	ERA+	OAV	OOB	BH	AVG	PB	PR	/A	PD	TPI
1964	NY-A	0	3	.000	7	1	0	0	0	18¹	16	1	12	12	13.7	4.91	74	.235	.350	0	.000	-0	-3	-3	1	-0.2
	LA-A	1	1	.500	6	5	0	0	0	18	25	1	13	13	19.5	5.00	66	.333	.438	0	.000	-1	-3	-3	0	-0.3
	KC-A	1	4	.200	9	7	2	0	0	42	37	2	33	30	15.0	3.86	99	.248	.385	0	.000	-1	-1	-0	-1	-0.1
	Yr	2	8	.200	22	13	2	0	0	78¹	78	5	58	55	15.6	4.37	84	.266	.387	1	.048	-2	-6	-6	-0	-0.6
1969	Sea-A	0	3	.000	6	5	1	0	0	32²	30	4	10	17	11.6	3.31	110	.252	.321	1	.091	-1	1	1	-1	0.0
1970	Mil-A	0	1	.000	10	0	0	0	0	18¹	24	3	12	20	17.7	6.38	59	.329	.424	1	.333	1	-5	-5	0	-0.4
Total	3	2	12	.143	38	18	3	0	0	129¹	132	12	80	92	15.0	4.38	84	.273	.379	2	.057	-3	-11	-10	-1	-1.0

■ RUSS MEYER
Meyer, Russell Charles "Rowdy" or "The Mad Monk"   b: 10/25/23, Peru, Ill.   BB/TR, 6'1", 175 lbs.   Deb: 9/13/46

YEAR	TM/L	W	L	PCT	G	GS	CG	SH	SV	IP	H	HR	BB	SO	RAT	ERA	ERA+	OAV	OOB	BH	AVG	PB	PR	/A	PD	TPI
1946	Chi-N	0	0	—	4	1	0	0	1	17	21	2	10	10	16.4	3.18	104	.309	.397	1	.200	1	0	0	0	0.1
1947	Chi-N	3	2	.600	23	2	1	0	0	45	43	4	14	22	11.6	3.40	116	.257	.319	3	.250	0	3	3	-0	0.3
1948	Chi-N	10	10	.500	29	26	8	3	0	164²	157	8	77	89	12.8	3.66	107	.254	.338	6	.107	-3	5	4	-0	0.1
1949	Phi-N	17	8	.680	37	28	14	2	1	213	199	14	70	78	11.4	3.08	128	.250	.311	10	.143	-1	23	20	-2	1.7
1950	•Phi-N	9	11	.450	32	25	3	0	1	159²	193	21	67	74	14.8	5.30	76	.304	.373	7	.140	-1	-21	-22	1	-2.0
1951	Phi-N	8	9	.471	28	24	7	2	0	168	172	13	55	65	12.3	3.48	111	.263	.322	5	.104	-2	9	7	-2	0.2
1952	Phi-N	13	14	.481	37	32	14	1	1	232¹	235	10	65	92	11.7	3.14	116	.260	.311	7	.089	-2	15	13	-2	1.0
1953	•Bro-N	15	5	.750	34	32	10	2	0	191¹	201	25	63	106	12.5	4.56	93	.269	.327	11	.147	-2	-6	-6	-0	-0.7
1954	Bro-N	11	6	.647	36	28	6	2	0	180¹	193	17	49	70	12.2	3.99	102	.275	.324	2	.043	-3	2	2	-1	0.2
1955	•Bro-N	6	2	.750	18	11	2	1	0	73	86	8	31	26	14.4	5.42	75	.300	.368	1	.037	-3	-11	-11	2	-1.1
1956	Chi-N	1	6	.143	20	9	0	0	0	57	71	11	26	28	15.6	6.32	60	.313	.388	1	.083	-1	-16	-16	2	-1.4
	Cin-N	0	0	—	1	0	0	0	0	1	1	0	0	1	9.0	0.00	—	.250	.250	0	—	0	0	0	0	0.1
	Yr	1	6	.143	21	9	0	0	0	58	72	11	26	29	15.2	6.21	61	.305	.374	1	.083	-1	-16	-16	2	-1.3
1957	Bos-A	0	0	—	2	1	0	0	0	5	10	1	3	1	23.4	5.40	74	.417	.481	1	1.000	0	-1	-1	1	0.0
1959	KC-A	1	0	1.000	18	0	0	0	0	34	33	1	11	10	13.5	4.50	89	.261	.346	0	—	-0	-2	-1	-0	-0.1
Total	13	94	73	.563	319	219	65	13	5	1531¹	1606	136	541	672	12.7	3.99	99	.271	.334	55	.114	-18	2	-8	-3	-2.0

■ LEVI MEYERLE
Meyerle, Levi Samuel "Long Levi"   b: 7/1845, Philadelphia, Pa.   d: 11/4/21, Philadelphia, Pa.   BR/TR, 6'1", 177 lbs.   Deb: 5/20/1871   ♦

YEAR	TM/L	W	L	PCT	G	GS	CG	SH	SV	IP	H	HR	BB	SO	RAT	ERA	ERA+	OAV	OOB	BH	AVG	PB	PR	/A	PD	TPI
1871	Ath-n	0	0	—	1	0	0	0	0	1	1	0	2	0	27.0	9.00	45	.250	.500	64	.492	1	-1	-1		0.0
1876	Phi-N	0	2	.000	2	2	2	0	0	18	28	0	1	0	14.5	5.00	48	.333	.341	87	.340	1	-5	-5	-0	-0.3

■ GENE MICHAEL
Michael, Eugene Richard "Stick"   b: 6/2/38, Kent, Ohio   BB/TR, 6'2", 183 lbs.   Deb: 7/15/66   MC♦

YEAR	TM/L	W	L	PCT	G	GS	CG	SH	SV	IP	H	HR	BB	SO	RAT	ERA	ERA+	OAV	OOB	BH	AVG	PB	PR	/A	PD	TPI
1968	NY-A	0	0	—	1	0	0	0	0	3	5	0	0	3	18.0	0.00	—	.357	.400	23	.198	0	1	1	0	0.1

■ JOHN MICHAELS
Michaels, John Joseph   b: 7/10/07, Bridgeport, Conn.   BL/TL, 5'10.5", 154 lbs.   Deb: 4/16/32

YEAR	TM/L	W	L	PCT	G	GS	CG	SH	SV	IP	H	HR	BB	SO	RAT	ERA	ERA+	OAV	OOB	BH	AVG	PB	PR	/A	PD	TPI
1932	Bos-A	1	6	.143	28	8	2	0	0	80²	101	4	27	16	14.6	5.13	88	.304	.362	3	.143	-1	-6	-6	1	-0.4

■ JOHN MICHAELSON
Michaelson, John August "Mike"   b: 8/12/1893, Tivalkoski, Finland   d: 4/16/68, Woodruff, Wis.   BR/TR, 5'9", 165 lbs.   Deb: 8/28/21

YEAR	TM/L	W	L	PCT	G	GS	CG	SH	SV	IP	H	HR	BB	SO	RAT	ERA	ERA+	OAV	OOB	BH	AVG	PB	PR	/A	PD	TPI
1921	Chi-A	0	0	—	2	0	0	0	0	2²	4	0	1	1	16.9	10.13	42	.400	.455	0	—	0	-2	-2	-0	-0.1

■ GLENN MICKENS
Mickens, Glenn Roger   b: 7/26/30, Wilmar, Cal.   BR/TR, 6', 175 lbs.   Deb: 7/19/53

YEAR	TM/L	W	L	PCT	G	GS	CG	SH	SV	IP	H	HR	BB	SO	RAT	ERA	ERA+	OAV	OOB	BH	AVG	PB	PR	/A	PD	TPI
1953	Bro-N	0	1	.000	4	2	0	0	0	6¹	11	2	4	5	21.3	11.37	37	.393	.469	0	.000	-0	-5	-5	-0	-0.4

■ JIM MIDDLETON
Middleton, James Blaine "Rifle Jim"   b: 5/28/1889, Argos, Ind.   d: 1/12/74, Argos, Ind.   BR/TR, 5'11.5", 165 lbs.   Deb: 4/18/17

YEAR	TM/L	W	L	PCT	G	GS	CG	SH	SV	IP	H	HR	BB	SO	RAT	ERA	ERA+	OAV	OOB	BH	AVG	PB	PR	/A	PD	TPI
1917	NY-N	1	1	.500	13	0	0	0	1	36	35	1	8	9	11.0	2.75	93	.255	.301	0	.000	-1	-0	-1	1	0.0
1921	Det-A	6	11	.353	38	10	2	0	7	121²	149	5	44	31	14.4	5.03	85	.302	.361	5	.147	-2	-10	-10	2	-0.9
Total	2	7	12	.368	51	10	2	0	8	157²	184	6	52	40	13.6	4.51	86	.292	.348	5	.119	-3	-10	-11	2	-0.9

■ JOHN MIDDLETON
Middleton, John Wayne "Lefty"   b: 4/11/1900, Mt.Calm, Tex.   d: 11/3/86, Amarillo, Tex.   BL/TL, 6'1", 185 lbs.   Deb: 9/06/22

YEAR	TM/L	W	L	PCT	G	GS	CG	SH	SV	IP	H	HR	BB	SO	RAT	ERA	ERA+	OAV	OOB	BH	AVG	PB	PR	/A	PD	TPI
1922	Cle-A	0	1	.000	2	1	0	0	0	7¹	8	1	6	2	17.2	7.36	54	.286	.412	1	.333	0	-3	-3	0	-0.1

■ DICK MIDKIFF
Midkiff, Richard   b: 9/28/14, Gonzales, Tex.   d: 10/30/56, Temple, Tex.   BR/TR, 6'2", 185 lbs.   Deb: 4/24/38

YEAR	TM/L	W	L	PCT	G	GS	CG	SH	SV	IP	H	HR	BB	SO	RAT	ERA	ERA+	OAV	OOB	BH	AVG	PB	PR	/A	PD	TPI
1938	Bos-A	1	1	.500	13	2	0	0	0	35¹	43	5	21	10	16.3	5.09	97	.305	.395	2	.200	0	-1	-1	0	0.0

■ GARY MIELKE
Mielke, Gary Roger   b: 1/28/63, St.James, Minn.   BR/TR, 6'3", 185 lbs.   Deb: 8/19/87

YEAR	TM/L	W	L	PCT	G	GS	CG	SH	SV	IP	H	HR	BB	SO	RAT	ERA	ERA+	OAV	OOB	BH	AVG	PB	PR	/A	PD	TPI
1987	Tex-A	0	0	—	3	0	0	0	0	3	3	2	1	3	12.0	6.00	75	.250	.308	0	—	0	-1	-1	0	0.0
1989	Tex-A	1	0	1.000	43	0	0	0	1	49²	52	4	25	26	14.3	3.26	122	.280	.371	0	—	0	3	4	-0	0.4
1990	Tex-A	0	3	.000	33	0	0	0	0	41	42	4	15	13	13.0	3.73	107	.271	.343	0	—	0	1	1	0	0.1
Total	3	1	3	.250	79	0	0	0	1	93²	97	10	41	42	13.6	3.56	112	.275	.357	0	—	0	4	5	0	0.5

■ PETE MIKKELSEN
Mikkelsen, Peter James   b: 10/25/39, Staten Island, N.Y.   BR/TR, 6'2", 210 lbs.   Deb: 4/17/64

YEAR	TM/L	W	L	PCT	G	GS	CG	SH	SV	IP	H	HR	BB	SO	RAT	ERA	ERA+	OAV	OOB	BH	AVG	PB	PR	/A	PD	TPI
1964	•NY-A	7	4	.636	50	0	0	0	12	86	79	3	41	63	13.0	3.56	102	.247	.340	1	.063	-1	1	1	1	0.0
1965	NY-A	4	9	.308	41	3	0	0	1	82¹	78	10	36	69	12.8	3.28	104	.249	.332	1	.100	-0	2	1	1	0.2
1966	Pit-N	9	8	.529	71	0	0	0	14	126	106	8	51	76	11.6	3.07	116	.234	.318	3	.150	0	7	7	-0	0.7
1967	Pit-N	1	2	.333	32	0	0	0	2	56¹	50	7	19	30	11.5	4.31	78	.237	.309	0	.000	0	-6	-6	-1	-0.7
	Chi-N	0	0	—	7	0	0	0	0	7	9	1	5	0	19.3	6.43	55	.333	.455	0	—	0	-2	-2	0	-0.1
	Yr	1	2	.333	39	0	0	0	2	63¹	59	8	24	30	11.9	4.55	74	.244	.315	1	.250	0	-8	-8	-1	-0.8
1968	Chi-N	0	0	—	3	0	0	0	0	4²	7	3	1	5	15.4	7.71	41	.350	.381	1	1.000	0	-2	-2	-0	-0.1
	StL-N	0	0	—	5	0	0	0	0	16	10	0	7	8	9.6	1.13	257	.179	.270	0	.000	0	3	3	-0	0.3
	Yr	0	0	—	8	0	0	0	0	20²	17	3	8	13	10.9	2.61	113	.224	.298	1	.000	0	1	1	-0	0.2
1969	LA-N	7	5	.583	48	0	0	0	4	81¹	57	9	30	51	10.1	2.77	120	.193	.277	1	.167	-0	7	5	1	0.6
1970	LA-N	4	2	.667	33	0	0	0	6	62	48	5	20	47	10.5	2.76	139	.211	.287	2	.333	1	9	7	0	0.8
1971	LA-N	8	5	.615	41	0	0	0	5	74	67	6	17	46	10.3	3.65	89	.242	.288	2	.200	1	-2	-3	1	-0.2
1972	LA-N	5	5	.500	33	0	0	0	5	57²	65	5	23	41	14.5	4.06	82	.283	.360	0	.000	0	-4	-5	-0	-0.5
Total	9	45	40	.529	364	3	0	0	49	653¹	576	59	250	436	11.8	3.38	102	.237	.316	11	.133	-2	13	6	2	1.0

■ HANK MIKLOS
Miklos, John Joseph   b: 11/27/10, Chicago, Ill.   BL/TL, 5'11", 175 lbs.   Deb: 4/23/44

YEAR	TM/L	W	L	PCT	G	GS	CG	SH	SV	IP	H	HR	BB	SO	RAT	ERA	ERA+	OAV	OOB	BH	AVG	PB	PR	/A	PD	TPI
1944	Chi-N	0	0	—	2	0	0	0	0	2	4	0	1	0	22.5	7.71	46	.333	.400	1	.000	-0	-3	-3	1	-0.2

■ BOB MILACKI
Milacki, Robert   b: 7/28/64, Trenton, N.J.   BR/TR, 6'4", 220 lbs.   Deb: 9/18/88

YEAR	TM/L	W	L	PCT	G	GS	CG	SH	SV	IP	H	HR	BB	SO	RAT	ERA	ERA+	OAV	OOB	BH	AVG	PB	PR	/A	PD	TPI
1988	Bal-A	2	0	1.000	3	3	1	0	0	25	9	1	9	18	6.5	0.72	542	.110	.198	0	—	0	9	9	0	1.1
1989	Bal-A	14	12	.538	37	36	3	2	0	243	233	21	88	113	12.0	3.74	101	.254	.320	0	—	0	4	1	-0	0.1
1990	Bal-A	5	8	.385	27	24	1	1	0	135¹	143	18	61	60	13.6	4.46	86	.273	.349	0	—	0	-8	-9	1	-0.8
Total	3	21	20	.512	67	63	5	4	0	403¹	385	40	158	191	12.2	3.79	100	.253	.324	0	—	0	5	1	1	0.4

■ CARL MILES
Miles, Carl Thomas b: 3/22/18, Trenton, Mo. BB/TL, 5'11", 178 lbs. Deb: 6/08/40

YEAR TM/L	W	L	PCT	G	GS	CG	SH	SV	IP	H	HR	BB	SO	RAT	ERA	ERA+	OAV	OOB	BH	AVG	PB	PR	/A	PD	TPI
1940 Phi-A	0	0	—	2	0	0	0	0	8	9	2	8	6	19.1	13.50	33	.281	.425	3	.750	2	-8	-8	0	-0.4

■ JIM MILES
Miles, James Charlie b: 8/8/43, Grenada, Miss. BR/TR, 6'2", 210 lbs. Deb: 9/07/68

YEAR TM/L	W	L	PCT	G	GS	CG	SH	SV	IP	H	HR	BB	SO	RAT	ERA	ERA+	OAV	OOB	BH	AVG	PB	PR	/A	PD	TPI
1968 Was-A	0	0	—	3	0	0	0	0	4¹	8	0	2	5	20.8	12.46	23	.421	.476	0	—	0	-5	-5	-0	-0.4
1969 Was-A	0	1	.000	10	1	0	0	0	20¹	19	2	15	15	16.8	6.20	56	.257	.409	1	.333	0	-6	-6	1	-0.4
Total 2	0	1	.000	13	1	0	0	0	24²	27	2	17	20	17.5	7.30	46	.290	.421	1	.333	0	-10	-11	1	-0.8

■ JOHNNY MILJUS
Miljus, John Kenneth "Jovo" or "Big Serb" b: 6/30/1895, Pittsburgh, Pa. d: 2/11/76, Poulson, Montana BR/TR, 6'1", 178 lbs. Deb: 10/02/15

YEAR TM/L	W	L	PCT	G	GS	CG	SH	SV	IP	H	HR	BB	SO	RAT	ERA	ERA+	OAV	OOB	BH	AVG	PB	PR	/A	PD	TPI
1915 Pit-F	0	0	—	1	0	0	0	0	1	1	0	0	0	9.0	0.00	—	.268	.268	0	—	0	0	0	0	0.1
1917 Bro-N	0	1	.000	4	1	1	0	0	15	14	0	8	9	15.0	0.60	466	.250	.373	0	.000	-1	4	4	0	0.2
1920 Bro-N	1	0	1.000	9	0	0	0	0	23¹	24	2	4	9	10.8	3.09	104	.267	.298	2	.333	1	0	0	1	0.2
1921 Bro-N	6	3	.667	28	9	3	0	1	93²	115	1	27	37	13.8	4.23	92	.312	.362	5	.167	-2	-5	-4	2	-0.3
1927 *Pit-N	8	3	.727	19	6	3	2	0	75²	62	0	17	24	9.4	1.90	216	.228	.273	5	.179	-1	17	19	2	2.0
1928 Pit-N	5	7	.417	21	10	3	0	1	69²	90	2	33	26	16.3	5.30	77	.313	.389	8	.308	1	-10	-10	-0	-0.8
Cle-A	1	4	.200	11	4	1	0	1	50¹	46	1	20	19	11.7	2.66	156	.243	.316	3	.200	-0	8	8	0	0.8
1929 Cle-A	8	8	.500	34	15	4	0	2	128¹	174	10	64	42	16.9	5.19	86	.331	.406	11	.256	1	-13	-11	0	-0.8
Total 7	29	26	.527	127	45	15	2	5	457¹	526	16	173	166	14.0	3.92	104	.293	.359	34	.222	0	0	7	4	1.6

■ BURT MILLER
Miller, Burt b: Kalamazoo, Mich. Deb: 7/15/1897

YEAR TM/L	W	L	PCT	G	GS	CG	SH	SV	IP	H	HR	BB	SO	RAT	ERA	ERA+	OAV	OOB	BH	AVG	PB	PR	/A	PD	TPI
1897 Lou-N	0	1	.000	4	1	1	0	0	17	32	0	3	3	18.5	7.94	54	.396	.418	1	.167	-0	-7	-7	0	-0.5

■ DYAR MILLER
Miller, Dyar K b: 5/29/46, Batesville, Ind. BR/TR, 6'1", 195 lbs. Deb: 6/09/75 C

YEAR TM/L	W	L	PCT	G	GS	CG	SH	SV	IP	H	HR	BB	SO	RAT	ERA	ERA+	OAV	OOB	BH	AVG	PB	PR	/A	PD	TPI
1975 Bal-A	6	3	.667	30	0	0	0	8	46¹	32	3	16	33	9.3	2.72	129	.199	.271	0	—	0	5	4	0	0.4
1976 Bal-A	2	4	.333	49	0	0	0	0	88²	79	5	36	37	11.8	2.94	111	.246	.324	0	—	0	6	3	-1	0.2
1977 Bal-A	2	2	.500	12	0	0	0	1	22¹	25	6	10	9	14.1	5.64	67	.278	.350	0	—	0	-4	-5	0	-0.4
Cal-A	4	4	.500	41	0	0	0	4	92¹	81	10	30	49	10.8	3.02	129	.242	.304	0	—	0	11	9	-1	0.8
Yr	6	6	.500	53	0	0	0	5	114²	106	16	40	58	11.5	3.53	110	.249	.314	0	—	0	7	5	-1	0.4
1978 Cal-A	6	2	.750	41	0	0	0	1	84²	85	3	41	34	13.9	2.66	136	.264	.356	0	—	0	10	9	-2	0.8
1979 Cal-A	1	0	1.000	14	1	0	0	0	35¹	44	2	13	16	15.0	3.31	123	.319	.386	0	—	0	4	3	-1	0.2
Tor-A	0	0	—	10	0	0	0	0	15¹	27	3	5	7	18.8	10.57	41	.391	.432	0	—	0	-11	-11	-0	-0.9
Yr	1	0	1.000	24	1	0	0	0	50²	71	5	18	23	15.8	5.51	75	.333	.385	0	—	0	-7	-8	-1	-0.7
1980 NY-N	1	2	.333	31	0	0	0	1	42	37	1	11	28	10.3	1.93	184	.242	.293	0	.000	-0	8	8	-1	0.7
1981 NY-N	1	0	1.000	23	0	0	0	0	38¹	49	2	15	22	15.3	3.29	106	.327	.392	1	.333	1	1	1	-0	0.0
Total 7	23	17	.575	251	1	0	0	22	465¹	459	35	177	235	12.5	3.23	113	.264	.335	1	.250	0	30	22	-5	1.8

■ ELMER MILLER
Miller, Elmer Joseph "Lefty" b: 4/17/03, Detroit, Mich. d: 1/8/87, Corona, Cal. BL/TL, 5'11", 189 lbs. Deb: 6/21/29 ♦

YEAR TM/L	W	L	PCT	G	GS	CG	SH	SV	IP	H	HR	BB	SO	RAT	ERA	ERA+	OAV	OOB	BH	AVG	PB	PR	/A	PD	TPI
1929 Phi-N	0	1	.000	8	2	0	0	0	11¹	12	1	21	5	28.6	11.12	47	.279	.537	9	.237	0	-8	-7	0	-0.6

■ FRANK MILLER
Miller, Frank Lee "Bullet" b: 5/13/1886, Allegan, Mich. d: 2/19/74, Allegan, Mich. BR/TR, 6', 188 lbs. Deb: 7/12/13

YEAR TM/L	W	L	PCT	G	GS	CG	SH	SV	IP	H	HR	BB	SO	RAT	ERA	ERA+	OAV	OOB	BH	AVG	PB	PR	/A	PD	TPI
1913 Chi-A	0	1	.000	1	1	0	0	0	1²	4	0	3	2	37.8	27.00	11	.571	.700	0	—	0	-4	-4	0	-0.3
1916 Pit-N	7	10	.412	30	20	10	2	1	173	135	4	49	88	9.9	2.29	117	.226	.292	7	.137	-1	6	8	-1	0.7
1917 Pit-N	10	19	.345	38	28	14	5	1	224	216	1	60	92	11.3	3.13	91	.251	.304	9	.118	-5	-11	-7	1	-1.2
1918 Pit-N	11	8	.579	23	23	14	2	0	170¹	152	0	37	47	10.4	2.38	121	.250	.301	6	.105	-4	7	9	0	0.7
1919 Pit-N	13	12	.520	32	26	16	3	0	201²	170	6	34	59	9.3	3.03	100	.234	.272	7	.106	-5	-3	-0	1	-0.3
1922 Bos-N	11	13	.458	31	23	14	2	1	200	213	7	60	65	12.4	3.51	114	.279	.333	8	.118	-5	13	11	1	0.6
1923 Bos-N	0	3	.000	8	6	0	0	1	39¹	54	2	11	6	15.6	4.58	87	.335	.389	1	.143	-0	-3	-3	-1	-0.2
Total 7	52	66	.441	163	127	68	14	4	1010	944	21	254	359	10.9	3.01	104	.253	.306	38	.117	-19	7	15	1	-0.0

■ FRED MILLER
Miller, Frederick Holman "Speedy" b: 6/28/1886, Fairfield, Ind. d: 5/2/53, Brookville, Ind. BL/TL, 6'2", 190 lbs. Deb: 7/08/10

YEAR TM/L	W	L	PCT	G	GS	CG	SH	SV	IP	H	HR	BB	SO	RAT	ERA	ERA+	OAV	OOB	BH	AVG	PB	PR	/A	PD	TPI
1910 Bro-N	1	1	.500	6	2	0	0	0	21	25	1	13	2	17.6	4.71	64	.309	.423	2	.250		-4	-4	1	-0.2

■ JAKE MILLER
Miller, Jacob Walter b: 2/28/1898, Wagram, Ohio d: 8/20/75, Venice, Fla. BL/TL, 6'2", 170 lbs. Deb: 9/11/24

YEAR TM/L	W	L	PCT	G	GS	CG	SH	SV	IP	H	HR	BB	SO	RAT	ERA	ERA+	OAV	OOB	BH	AVG	PB	PR	/A	PD	TPI
1924 Cle-A	0	1	.000	2	2	1	0	0	12	13	0	5	4	13.5	3.00	142	.265	.333	0	.000	-1	2	2	0	0.1
1925 Cle-A	10	13	.435	32	22	13	0	2	190¹	207	4	62	51	13.1	3.31	133	.279	.340	13	.183	-4	23	23	0	1.9
1926 Cle-A	7	4	.636	18	11	5	3	1	82²	99	1	18	24	13.0	3.27	124	.307	.348	2	.083	-2	7	7	-1	0.4
1927 Cle-A	10	8	.556	34	23	11	0	0	185¹	189	4	48	53	11.8	3.21	131	.271	.324	8	.138	-4	19	21	1	1.7
1928 Cle-A	8	9	.471	25	24	8	0	0	158	203	6	43	37	14.3	4.44	93	.332	.381	7	.135	-4	-7	-5	1	-0.7
1929 Cle-A	14	12	.538	29	29	14	2	0	206	227	7	60	58	12.8	3.58	124	.279	.334	15	.200	-3	15	20	1	1.8
1930 Cle-A	4	4	.500	24	9	1	0	0	88¹	147	6	38	31	19.3	7.13	68	.373	.433	10	.303	1	-24	-23	2	-1.6
1931 Cle-A	2	1	.667	10	5	1	1	0	41¹	45	2	19	17	13.9	4.35	106	.273	.348	1	.077	-2	0	1	1	0.1
1933 Chi-A	5	6	.455	26	14	4	2	0	105²	130	3	47	30	15.6	5.62	75	.297	.373	7	.189	-1	-16	-16	1	-1.4
Total 9	60	58	.508	200	139	58	8	3	1069²	1260	33	340	305	13.8	4.09	106	.298	.355	63	.171	-19	19	30	6	2.3

■ OX MILLER
Miller, John Anthony b: 5/4/15, Gause, Tex. BR/TR, 6'1", 190 lbs. Deb: 8/07/43

YEAR TM/L	W	L	PCT	G	GS	CG	SH	SV	IP	H	HR	BB	SO	RAT	ERA	ERA+	OAV	OOB	BH	AVG	PB	PR	/A	PD	TPI
1943 Was-A	0	0	—	3	0	0	0	0	6	10	1	5	1	22.5	10.50	31	.370	.469	0	.000	-0	-5	-5	1	-0.3
StL-A	0	0	—	2	0	0	0	0	6	7	2	3	3	18.0	12.00	28	.304	.429	0	.000	-0	-6	-6	1	-0.4
Yr	0	0	—	5	0	0	0	0	12	17	3	8	4	20.3	11.25	29	.340	.450	0	.000	-0	-11	-11	1	-0.7
1945 StL-A	2	1	.667	4	3	3	0	0	28¹	23	2	5	4	8.9	1.59	222	.219	.255	2	.182	-0	6	6	-1	0.5
1946 StL-A	1	3	.250	11	3	0	1	0	35¹	52	5	15	12	17.1	6.88	54	.338	.396	2	.286	1	-13	-12	1	-1.0
1947 Chi-N	1	2	.333	4	4	1	0	0	16	31	2	5	7	20.3	10.13	39	.397	.434	3	.429	2	-11	-11	-0	-0.7
Total 4	4	6	.400	24	10	4	1	0	91²	123	12	33	27	15.5	6.38	57	.318	.374	7	.259	2	-29	-28	1	-1.9

■ JOHN MILLER
Miller, John Ernest b: 5/30/41, Baltimore, Md. BR/TR, 6'2", 210 lbs. Deb: 9/22/62

YEAR TM/L	W	L	PCT	G	GS	CG	SH	SV	IP	H	HR	BB	SO	RAT	ERA	ERA+	OAV	OOB	BH	AVG	PB	PR	/A	PD	TPI
1962 Bal-A	1	1	.500	2	1	0	0	0	10	2	0	5	4	6.3	0.90	418	.065	.194	0	.000	-0	3	3	0	0.3
1963 Bal-A	1	1	.500	3	2	0	0	0	17	12	0	14	16	13.8	3.18	111	.194	.342	0	.000	-1	1	1	-0	0.0
1965 Bal-A	6	4	.600	16	16	1	0	0	93¹	75	4	58	71	12.9	3.18	109	.223	.338	3	.100	-1	3	3	0	0.3
1966 Bal-A	4	8	.333	23	16	0	0	0	100²	92	15	58	81	13.4	4.74	70	.241	.342	4	.118	-1	-15	-16	0	-1.6
1967 Bal-A	0	0	—	2	0	0	0	0	6	7	1	3	4	18.0	7.50	42	.304	.429	0	—	0	-3	-3	0	-0.2
Total 5	12	14	.462	46	35	1	0	0	227	188	20	138	178	13.0	3.89	88	.225	.337	7	.096	-3	-10	-12	1	-1.2

■ CYCLONE MILLER
Miller, Joseph H. b: 9/24/1859, Springfield, Mass d: 10/13/16, New London, Conn. TL, 5'9.5", 165 lbs. Deb: 7/11/1884

YEAR TM/L	W	L	PCT	G	GS	CG	SH	SV	IP	H	HR	BB	SO	RAT	ERA	ERA+	OAV	OOB	BH	AVG	PB	PR	/A	PD	TPI
1884 CP-U	1	0	1.000	1	1	1	0	0	9	4	0	0	13	4.0	1.00	302	.125	.125	1	.250	-0	2	2	1	0.3
Pro-N	3	2	.600	6	5	2	0	0	34²	36	0	11	12	12.2	2.08	136	.253	.307	1	.043	-3	3	3	-0	0.0
Phi-N	0	1	.000	1	1	1	0	0	9	17	5	6	1	23.0	10.00	30	.382	.455	0	.000	-1	-7	-7	0	-0.4
Yr	3	3	.500	7	6	3	0	0	43²	53	5	17	13	14.4	3.71	77	.284	.344	1	.037	-3	-4	-4	0	-0.4
1886 Phi-a	10	8	.556	19	19	19	1	0	169²	158	6	59	99	11.5	2.97	118	.235	.297	9	.136	-1	9	10	1	0.9
Total 2	14	11	.560	27	26	23	1	0	222¹	215	6	76	125	11.8	3.04	110	.242	.301	11	.113	-5	8	8	1	0.8

■ WHITEY MILLER
Miller, Kenneth Albert b: 5/2/15, St.Louis, Mo. BR/TR, 6'1", 195 lbs. Deb: 9/15/44

YEAR TM/L	W	L	PCT	G	GS	CG	SH	SV	IP	H	HR	BB	SO	RAT	ERA	ERA+	OAV	OOB	BH	AVG	PB	PR	/A	PD	TPI
1944 NY-N	0	1	.000	4	0	0	0	0	5	1	0	4	2	9.0	0.00	—	.059	.238	0	.000	-0	2	2	0	0.2

■ LARRY MILLER
Miller, Larry Don b: 6/19/37, Topeka, Kan. BL/TL, 6', 195 lbs. Deb: 6/21/64

YEAR TM/L	W	L	PCT	G	GS	CG	SH	SV	IP	H	HR	BB	SO	RAT	ERA	ERA+	OAV	OOB	BH	AVG	PB	PR	/A	PD	TPI
1964 LA-N	4	8	.333	16	14	1	0	0	79²	87	1	28	50	13.2	4.18	78	.275	.338	7	.269	2	-6	-8	-0	-0.7
1965 NY-N	1	4	.200	28	5	0	0	0	57¹	66	6	25	36	14.4	5.02	70	.289	.362	2	.182	0	-9	-10	-0	-0.9

YEAR TM/L	W	L	PCT	G	GS	CG	SH	SV	IP	H	HR	BB	SO	RAT	ERA	ERA+	OAV	OOB	BH	AVG	PB	PR	/A	PD	TPI
1966 NY-N	0	2	.000	4	1	0	0	0	8^1	9	3	4	7	14.0	7.56	48	.273	.351	1	.500	0	-4	-4	-0	-0.3
Total 3	5	14	.263	48	20	1	0	0	145^1	162	10	57	93	13.7	4.71	72	.281	.349	10	.256	2	-19	-21	-1	-1.9

■ **RED MILLER** Miller, Leo Alphonso b: 2/11/1897, Philadelphia, Pa. d: 10/20/73, Orlando, Fla. BR/TR, 5'11", 195 lbs. Deb: 4/13/23

YEAR TM/L	W	L	PCT	G	GS	CG	SH	SV	IP	H	HR	BB	SO	RAT	ERA	ERA+	OAV	OOB	BH	AVG	PB	PR	/A	PD	TPI
1923 Phi-N	0	0	—	1	0	0	0	0	1^2	6	0	1	0	37.8	32.40	14	.545	.583	0	.000	-0	-5	-5	0	-0.3

■ **RALPH MILLER** Miller, Ralph Darwin b: 3/15/1873, Cincinnati, Ohio d: 5/8/73, Cincinnati, Ohio BR/TR, 5'11", 170 lbs. Deb: 5/04/1898

YEAR TM/L	W	L	PCT	G	GS	CG	SH	SV	IP	H	HR	BB	SO	RAT	ERA	ERA+	OAV	OOB	BH	AVG	PB	PR	/A	PD	TPI
1898 Bro-N	4	14	.222	23	21	16	0	0	151^2	161	4	86	43	14.7	5.34	67	.270	.362	12	.194	-1	-29	-30	2	-2.4
1899 Bal-N	1	3	.250	5	4	3	0	0	34	42	0	13	3	14.6	4.76	83	.303	.363	2	.182	1	-3	-3	-0	-0.1
Total 2	5	17	.227	28	25	19	0	0	185^2	203	4	99	46	14.6	5.24	70	.276	.362	14	.192	-0	-33	-33	2	-2.5

■ **RALPH MILLER** Miller, Ralph Henry "Moose" or "Lefty" b: 1/14/1899, Vinton, Iowa d: 2/18/67, White Bear Lake, Minn. BR/TL, 6'1.5", 190 lbs. Deb: 9/16/21

YEAR TM/L	W	L	PCT	G	GS	CG	SH	SV	IP	H	HR	BB	SO	RAT	ERA	ERA+	OAV	OOB	BH	AVG	PB	PR	/A	PD	TPI
1921 Was-A	0	0	—	1	0	0	0	0	1	0	0	0	0	0.0	0.00	—	.000	.000	0	—	0	0	0	0	0.0

■ **RANDY MILLER** Miller, Randall Scott b: 3/18/53, Oxnard, Cal. BR/TR, 6'1", 180 lbs. Deb: 9/07/77

YEAR TM/L	W	L	PCT	G	GS	CG	SH	SV	IP	H	HR	BB	SO	RAT	ERA	ERA+	OAV	OOB	BH	AVG	PB	PR	/A	PD	TPI
1977 Bal-A	0	0	—	1	0	0	0	0	0^2	4	0	0	0	54.0	40.50	9	.800	.800	0	—	0	-3	-3	0	-0.1
1978 Mon-N	0	1	.000	5	0	0	0	0	7	11	1	3	6	18.0	10.29	34	.393	.452	0	.000	-0	-5	-5	0	-0.4
Total 2	0	1	.000	6	0	0	0	0	7^2	15	1	3	6	21.1	12.91	27	.455	.500	0	.000	-0	-8	-8	0	-0.5

■ **BOB MILLER** Miller, Robert Gerald b: 7/15/35, Berwyn, Ill. BR/TL, 6'1", 185 lbs. Deb: 6/25/53

YEAR TM/L	W	L	PCT	G	GS	CG	SH	SV	IP	H	HR	BB	SO	RAT	ERA	ERA+	OAV	OOB	BH	AVG	PB	PR	/A	PD	TPI
1953 Det-A	1	2	.333	13	1	0	0	0	36^1	43	2	21	9	16.1	5.94	68	.289	.380	1	.125	-1	-8	-8	1	-0.6
1954 Det-A	1	1	.500	32	1	0	0	1	69^2	62	1	26	27	11.4	2.45	150	.244	.314	2	.133	-0	10	10	-1	0.9
1955 Det-A	2	1	.667	7	3	1	0	0	25^1	26	4	12	11	13.5	2.49	154	.263	.342	2	.222	0	4	4	-0	0.4
1956 Det-A	0	2	.000	11	3	0	0	0	31^2	37	5	22	16	16.8	5.68	72	.308	.415	1	.143	0	-5	-6	-0	-0.5
1962 Cin-N	0	0	—	6	0	0	0	0	5^1	14	1	3	4	32.1	21.94	18	.538	.613	0	.000	-0	-11	-11	0	-0.9
NY-N	2	2	.500	17	0	0	0	1	20^1	24	2	8	8	14.6	7.08	59	.312	.384	0	.000	-0	-7	-7	0	-0.5
Yr	2	2	.500	23	0	0	0	1	25^2	38	3	11	12	17.5	10.17	41	.355	.420	0	.000	-0	-18	-17	0	-1.4
Total 5	6	8	.429	86	8	1	0	2	188^2	206	15	92	75	14.4	4.72	83	.284	.368	6	.146	-1	-17	-17	-1	-1.2

■ **BOB MILLER** Miller, Robert John b: 6/16/26, Detroit, Mich. BR/TR, 6'3", 190 lbs. Deb: 9/16/49

YEAR TM/L	W	L	PCT	G	GS	CG	SH	SV	IP	H	HR	BB	SO	RAT	ERA	ERA+	OAV	OOB	BH	AVG	PB	PR	/A	PD	TPI
1949 Phi-N	0	0	—	3	0	0	0	0	2^2	2	0	2	0	13.5	0.00	—	.200	.333	0	—	0	1	1	0	0.1
1950 *Phi-N	11	6	.647	35	22	7	2	1	174	190	9	57	44	13.0	3.57	113	.277	.337	11	.180	-1	11	9	2	1.1
1951 Phi-N	2	1	.667	17	3	0	0	0	34^1	47	1	18	10	17.3	6.82	56	.331	.410	3	.429	1	-11	-11	-1	-1.0
1952 Phi-N	0	1	.000	3	1	0	0	0	9	13	2	1	2	14.0	6.00	61	.351	.368	0	.000	-0	-2	-2	0	-0.1
1953 Phi-N	8	9	.471	35	20	8	3	2	157^1	169	14	62	63	12.2	4.00	105	.271	.319	10	.182	-1	5	4	-0	0.2
1954 Phi-N	7	9	.438	30	16	5	0	0	150	176	14	39	42	13.1	4.56	89	.300	.347	8	.160	-0	-8	-9	2	-0.6
1955 Phi-N	8	4	.667	40	0	0	0	1	89^2	80	6	28	28	10.9	2.41	165	.242	.304	5	.278	1	16	16	0	1.7
1956 Phi-N	3	6	.333	49	6	3	1	5	122^1	115	14	34	53	11.2	3.24	115	.248	.303	2	.091	-1	7	7	0	0.6
1957 Phi-N	2	5	.286	32	1	0	0	6	60^1	61	4	17	12	11.8	2.69	142	.265	.319	2	.250	2	8	8	-0	0.9
1958 Phi-N	1	1	.500	17	0	0	0	0	22^1	36	7	9	9	18.1	11.69	34	.360	.413	0	.000	-0	-19	-19	-0	-1.7
Total 10	42	42	.500	261	69	23	6	15	822	889	72	247	263	12.6	3.96	101	.277	.332	41	.184	1	8	2	3	1.2

■ **BOB MILLER** Miller, Robert Lane b: 2/18/39, St.Louis, Mo. BR/TR, 6'1", 180 lbs. Deb: 6/26/57 C

YEAR TM/L	W	L	PCT	G	GS	CG	SH	SV	IP	H	HR	BB	SO	RAT	ERA	ERA+	OAV	OOB	BH	AVG	PB	PR	/A	PD	TPI
1957 StL-N	0	0	—	5	0	0	0	0	9	13	2	5	7	18.0	7.00	57	.325	.400	0	—	0	-3	-3	0	-0.2
1959 StL-N	4	3	.571	11	10	3	0	0	70^2	66	2	21	43	11.2	3.31	128	.248	.306	5	.208	1	5	7	1	1.0
1960 StL-N	4	3	.571	15	7	0	0	0	52^2	53	2	17	33	12.1	3.42	120	.262	.323	2	.143	-1	2	4	0	0.4
1961 StL-N	1	3	.250	34	5	0	0	3	74^1	82	6	46	39	15.5	4.24	104	.290	.389	5	.357	2	-2	1	1	0.4
1962 NY-N	1	12	.077	33	21	1	0	0	143^2	146	20	62	91	13.4	4.89	86	.259	.339	5	.122	-1	-15	-11	2	-0.9
1963 LA-N	10	8	.556	42	23	2	0	1	187	171	7	65	125	11.6	2.89	105	.244	.311	4	.070	-2	8	3	5	0.6
1964 LA-N	7	7	.500	**74**	2	0	0	9	137^2	115	7	63	94	11.8	2.62	124	.226	.314	3	.158	-1	14	10	3	1.3
1965 *LA-N	6	7	.462	61	1	0	0	9	103	82	9	26	77	9.7	2.97	110	.225	.282	0	.000	-1	7	3	2	0.4
1966 *LA-N	4	2	.667	46	0	0	0	5	84^1	70	5	29	58	10.7	2.77	119	.230	.299	1	.077	-1	8	5	-1	0.3
1967 LA-N	2	9	.182	52	4	0	0	0	85^2	88	7	27	32	12.4	4.31	72	.273	.335	1	.125	-0	-9	-12	-1	-1.0
1968 Min-A	0	3	.000	45	0	0	0	2	72^1	65	1	24	41	11.7	2.74	113	.239	.312	1	.143	-0	2	3	1	0.4
1969 *Min-A	5	5	.500	48	11	1	0	3	119^1	118	9	32	57	11.3	3.02	121	.264	.313	0	.000	-3	8	8	2	0.7
1970 Cle-A	2	2	.500	15	2	0	0	1	28	35	1	15	15	16.1	4.18	95	.310	.391	1	.200	0	-1	-1	1	0.0
Chi-A	4	6	.400	15	12	0	0	0	70	88	11	33	36	16.1	5.01	78	.315	.396	4	.174	-1	-10	-9	2	-0.5
Yr	6	8	.429	30	14	0	0	1	98	123	12	48	51	16.1	4.78	82	.313	.393	4	.143	1	-12	-9	-0	-0.5
Chi-N	0	0	—	7	1	0	0	2	9	6	3	6	4	12.0	5.00	90	.194	.324	0	—	0	-1	-0	0	0.0
1971 Chi-N	0	0	—	2	0	0	0	0	7	10	1	0	1	14.1	5.14	76	.357	.379	0	.000	-0	-1	-1	0	0.0
SD-N	7	3	.700	38	0	0	0	7	63^2	53	0	26	36	11.3	1.41	233	.227	.308	0	.000	-1	15	13	1	1.4
*Pit-N	1	2	.333	16	0	0	0	3	28	20	1	13	13	10.6	1.29	263	.200	.292	0	.000	0	7	7	0	0.8
Yr	8	5	.615	56	0	0	0	10	98^2	83	1	40	51	11.2	1.64	205	.229	.305	1	.083	-1	20	19	2	2.2
1972 *Pit-N	5	2	.714	36	0	0	0	3	54^1	54	3	24	18	13.1	2.65	125	.263	.343	0	.000	-0	5	4	0	0.4
1973 SD-N	0	0	—	18	0	0	0	0	30^2	29	4	12	15	12.0	4.11	84	.244	.313	0	.000	-0	-2	-2	-1	-0.2
NY-N	0	0	—	1	0	0	0	0	1	0	0	0	1	0.0	0.00	—	.000	.000	0	—	0	0	0	0	0.0
Yr	0	0	—	19	0	0	0	0	31^2	29	4	12	16	11.7	3.98	87	.236	.304	0	.000	-0	-1	-2	-1	-0.2
Det-A	4	2	.667	22	0	0	0	1	42	34	3	22	23	12.0	3.43	119	.230	.329	0	—	0	2	3	0	0.3
1974 NY-N	2	2	.500	58	0	0	0	1	78	89	2	39	35	14.9	3.58	100	.296	.378	1	.111	-0	-0	-0	0	0.0
Total 17	69	81	.460	694	99	7	0	51	1551^1	1487	101	608	895	12.3	3.37	105	.255	.328	33	.110	-8	38	31	20	5.6

■ **BOB MILLER** Miller, Robert W. b: 1862, Deb: 8/30/1890

YEAR TM/L	W	L	PCT	G	GS	CG	SH	SV	IP	H	HR	BB	SO	RAT	ERA	ERA+	OAV	OOB	BH	AVG	PB	PR	/A	PD	TPI
1890 Roc-a	3	7	.300	13	12	11	0	0	92^1	89	2	26	20	11.2	4.29	83	.246	.296	6	.150	-1	-4	-7	0	-0.6
1891 Was-a	2	5	.286	7	7	3	0	0	42	53	3	24	13	16.5	4.29	87	.298	.381	2	.111	-2	-3	-3	1	-0.2
Total 2	5	12	.294	20	19	14	0	1	134^1	142	5	50	33	12.9	4.29	84	.263	.325	8	.138	-3	-7	-10	1	-0.8

■ **ROGER MILLER** Miller, Roger Wesley b: 8/1/54, Connellsville, Pa. BR/TR, 6'3", 200 lbs. Deb: 9/08/74

YEAR TM/L	W	L	PCT	G	GS	CG	SH	SV	IP	H	HR	BB	SO	RAT	ERA	ERA+	OAV	OOB	BH	AVG	PB	PR	/A	PD	TPI
1974 Mil-A	0	0	—	2	0	0	0	0	2^1	3	1	0	2	15.4	11.57	31	.300	.364	0	—	0	-2	-2	0	-0.1

■ **RONNIE MILLER** Miller, Roland Arthur b: 8/28/18, Mason City, Iowa BB/TR, 5'11", 167 lbs. Deb: 9/10/41

YEAR TM/L	W	L	PCT	G	GS	CG	SH	SV	IP	H	HR	BB	SO	RAT	ERA	ERA+	OAV	OOB	BH	AVG	PB	PR	/A	PD	TPI
1941 Was-A	0	0	—	1	0	0	0	0	2	2	0	1	0	13.5	4.50	90	.333	.429	0	—	0	-0	-0	0	0.0

■ **ROSCOE MILLER** Miller, Roscoe Clyde "Roxy" or "Rubberlegs" b: 12/2/1876, Greenville, Ind. d: 4/18/13, Corydon, Ind. 6'2", 190 lbs. Deb: 4/25/01

YEAR TM/L	W	L	PCT	G	GS	CG	SH	SV	IP	H	HR	BB	SO	RAT	ERA	ERA+	OAV	OOB	BH	AVG	PB	PR	/A	PD	TPI
1901 Det-A	23	13	.639	38	36	35	3	1	332	339	1	98	79	11.8	2.95	130	.261	.313	27	.208	1	26	33	4	3.7
1902 Det-A	6	12	.333	20	18	15	1	1	148^2	158	3	57	39	13.0	3.69	99	.273	.338	11	.183	-2	-2	-1	1	0.0
NY-N	1	8	.111	10	9	7	0	0	72^2	77	1	11	15	11.5	4.58	61	.272	.310	1	.048	-3	-15	-14	-1	-1.6
1903 NY-N	2	5	.286	15	8	6	0	3	85	101	1	24	30	13.3	4.13	81	.302	.351	5	.161	-1	-8	-7	-0	-0.7
1904 Pit-N	7	7	.500	19	17	11	2	0	134^1	133	4	39	35	11.8	3.35	82	.256	.313	2	.043	-4	-9	-9	-1	-1.3
Total 4	39	45	.464	102	88	74	6	5	772^2	808	10	229	198	12.2	3.45	100	.268	.322	46	.160	-8	-7	1	3	0.1

■ **RUSS MILLER** Miller, Russell Lewis b: 3/25/1900, Etna, Ohio d: 4/30/62, Bucyrus, Ohio BR/TR, 5'11", 165 lbs. Deb: 9/24/27

YEAR TM/L	W	L	PCT	G	GS	CG	SH	SV	IP	H	HR	BB	SO	RAT	ERA	ERA+	OAV	OOB	BH	AVG	PB	PR	/A	PD	TPI
1927 Phi-N	1	1	.500	2	2	1	0	0	15^1	21	2	3	4	14.7	5.28	78	.339	.379	1	.333	0	-2	-2	0	-0.1
1928 Phi-N	0	12	.000	33	12	1	0	1	108	137	14	34	19	14.3	5.42	79	.315	.365	4	.148	-1	-17	-14	1	-1.3
Total 2	1	13	.071	35	14	2	0	1	123^1	158	16	37	23	14.3	5.40	79	.318	.366	5	.167	-1	-19	-16	1	-1.4

YEAR TM/L	W	L	PCT	G	GS	CG	SH	SV	IP	H	HR	BB	SO	RAT	ERA	ERA+	OAV	OOB	BH	AVG	PB	PR	/A	PD	TPI

■ STU MILLER   Miller, Stuart Leonard   b: 12/26/27, Northampton, Mass.   BR/TR, 5'11.5", 165 lbs.   Deb: 8/12/52

YEAR TM/L	W	L	PCT	G	GS	CG	SH	SV	IP	H	HR	BB	SO	RAT	ERA	ERA+	OAV	OOB	BH	AVG	PB	PR	/A	PD	TPI
1952 StL-N	6	3	.667	12	11	6	2	0	88	63	3	26	64	9.3	2.05	182	.197	.262	3	.120	-1	16	16	3	2.0
1953 StL-N	7	8	.467	40	18	8	2	4	137²	161	19	47	79	13.7	5.56	77	.293	.351	8	.186	1	-19	-20	5	-1.3
1954 StL-N	2	3	.400	19	4	0	0	2	46²	55	5	29	22	16.8	5.79	71	.307	.412	4	.308	1	-9	-9	2	-0.4
1956 StL-N	0	1	.000	3	0	0	0	1	7¹	12	3	5	5	20.9	4.91	77	.387	.472	0	.000	-0	-1	-1	0	0.0
Phi-N	5	8	.385	24	15	2	0	0	106²	109	16	51	55	13.8	4.47	83	.263	.349	4	.160	2	-8	-9	0	-0.6
Yr	5	9	.357	27	15	2	0	1	114	121	19	56	60	14.3	4.50	83	.271	.357	8	.308	2	-9	-10	0	-0.6
1957 NY-N	7	9	.438	38	13	0	0	1	124	110	15	45	60	11.5	3.63	108	.242	.315	2	.057	-3	3	4	2	0.3
1958 SF-N	6	9	.400	41	20	4	1	0	182	160	16	49	119	10.4	**2.47**	**154**	.233	**.286**	6	.120	-0	30	27	1	2.9
1959 SF-N	8	7	.533	59	9	2	0	8	167²	164	15	57	95	12.1	2.84	134	.260	.326	2	.044	-3	**21**	18	3	1.9
1960 SF-N	7	6	.538	47	3	2	0	2	101²	100	9	31	65	11.9	3.90	89	.256	.315	5	.200	1	-2	-5	2	-0.2
1961 SF-N	14	5	.737	63	0	0	0	**17**	122	95	4	37	89	9.8	2.66	143	.215	.277	4	.200	1	**19**	16	2	1.9
1962 *SF-N	5	8	.385	59	0	0	0	19	107	107	8	42	78	12.7	4.12	92	.268	.341	2	.125	-0	-2	-4	0	-0.3
1963 Bal-A	5	8	.385	**71**	0	0	0	**27**	112¹	93	5	53	114	11.9	2.24	157	.232	.326	5	.313	2	17	16	1	2.0
1964 Bal-A	7	7	.500	66	0	0	0	23	97	77	7	34	87	10.6	3.06	117	.222	.297	1	.111	-0	6	5	0	0.6
1965 Bal-A	14	7	.667	67	0	0	0	24	119¹	87	5	32	104	9.1	1.89	184	.207	.265	1	.063	-1	21	21	0	2.3
1966 Bal-A	9	4	.692	51	0	0	0	18	92	65	5	22	67	8.9	2.25	148	.201	.260	2	.105	-1	12	11	-1	1.0
1967 Bal-A	3	10	.231	42	0	0	0	8	81¹	63	5	36	60	11.1	2.55	124	.220	.309	0	.000	-1	6	5	-0	0.4
1968 Atl-N	0	0	—	2	0	0	0	0	1¹	1	0	4	1	33.8	27.00	11	.500	.833	0	—	0	-4	-4	0	-0.2
Total 16	105	103	.505	704	93	24	5	154	1694	1522	140	600	1164	11.5	3.24	115	.242	.312	49	.133	-2	107	90	20	12.3

■ WALT MILLER   Miller, Walter W.   b: 10/19/1884, Gas City, Ind.   d: 3/1/56, Marion, Ind.   BR/TR, 5'11.5", 180 lbs.   Deb: 9/20/11

YEAR TM/L	W	L	PCT	G	GS	CG	SH	SV	IP	H	HR	BB	SO	RAT	ERA	ERA+	OAV	OOB	BH	AVG	PB	PR	/A	PD	TPI
1911 Bro-N	0	1	.000	3	2	0	0	0	11	16	0	6	0	18.8	6.55	51	.356	.442	0	.000	-1	-4	-4	0	-0.3

■ BILL MILLER   Miller, William Francis "Wild Bill"   b: 4/12/10, Hannibal, Mo.   d: 2/26/82, Hannibal, Mo.   BR/TR, 6', 180 lbs.   Deb: 10/02/37

YEAR TM/L	W	L	PCT	G	GS	CG	SH	SV	IP	H	HR	BB	SO	RAT	ERA	ERA+	OAV	OOB	BH	AVG	PB	PR	/A	PD	TPI
1937 StL-A	0	1	.000	1	1	0	0	0	4	7	1	4	1	27.0	13.50	36	.389	.522	0	.000	-0	-4	-4	0	-0.2

■ BILL MILLER   Miller, William Paul "Lefty" or "Hooks"   b: 7/26/27, Minersville, Pa.   BL/TL, 6', 175 lbs.   Deb: 4/20/52

YEAR TM/L	W	L	PCT	G	GS	CG	SH	SV	IP	H	HR	BB	SO	RAT	ERA	ERA+	OAV	OOB	BH	AVG	PB	PR	/A	PD	TPI
1952 NY-A	4	6	.400	21	13	5	2	0	88	78	4	49	45	13.2	3.48	96	.241	.345	6	.214	1	2	-2	-0	-0.1
1953 NY-A	2	1	.667	13	3	0	0	1	34	46	3	19	17	17.5	4.76	77	.324	.407	2	.200	0	-3	-4	1	-0.2
1954 NY-A	0	1	.000	2	1	0	0	0	5²	9	0	1	6	15.9	6.35	54	.375	.400	0	.000	-0	-2	-2	-0	-0.1
1955 Bal-A	0	1	.000	5	1	0	0	0	4	3	0	10	4	29.3	13.50	28	.200	.520	1	1.000	0	-4	-4	0	-0.3
Total 4	6	9	.400	41	18	5	2	1	131²	136	7	79	72	14.9	4.24	81	.270	.372	9	.225	1	-7	-12	0	-0.7

■ JOHN MILLIGAN   Milligan, John Alexander   b: 1/22/04, Schuylersville, N.Y.   d: 5/15/72, Fort Pierce, Fla.   BR/TL, 5'10", 172 lbs.   Deb: 8/11/28

YEAR TM/L	W	L	PCT	G	GS	CG	SH	SV	IP	H	HR	BB	SO	RAT	ERA	ERA+	OAV	OOB	BH	AVG	PB	PR	/A	PD	TPI
1928 Phi-N	2	5	.286	13	7	3	0	0	68	69	2	32	22	13.5	4.37	98	.274	.358	1	.050	-2	-3	-1	1	-0.1
1929 Phi-N	0	1	.000	8	3	0	0	0	9²	29	0	10	2	38.2	16.76	31	.527	.612	1	.333	0	-13	-12	0	-0.9
1930 Phi-N	1	2	.333	9	2	1	0	0	28¹	26	0	21	7	15.6	3.18	172	.255	.392	1	.111	-1	6	7	1	0.7
1931 Phi-N	0	0	—	3	0	0	0	0	8	11	0	4	5	18.0	3.38	126	.324	.410	0	.000	-0	0	1	-0	0.0
1934 Was-A	0	0	—	2	0	0	0	0	2²	6	0	0	1	20.3	10.13	43	.500	.500	0	—	0	-2	-2	0	0.0
Total 5	3	8	.273	35	12	4	0	0	116²	141	2	67	37	16.5	5.17	90	.310	.405	3	.088	-4	-11	-7	2	-0.3

■ BILLY MILLIGAN   Milligan, William Joseph   b: 8/19/1878, Buffalo, N.Y.   d: 10/14/28, Buffalo, N.Y.   TL, 5'7",   Deb: 4/30/01

YEAR TM/L	W	L	PCT	G	GS	CG	SH	SV	IP	H	HR	BB	SO	RAT	ERA	ERA+	OAV	OOB	BH	AVG	PB	PR	/A	PD	TPI
1901 Phi-A	0	3	.000	6	3	2	0	0	33	43	1	14	5	15.5	4.36	86	.311	.374	5	.333	2	-3	-2	-0	0.0
1904 NY-N	0	1	.000	5	1	1	0	2	25	36	2	4	6	14.8	5.40	51	.310	.339	1	.111	0	-7	-7	0	-0.6
Total 2	0	4	.000	11	4	3	0	2	58	79	3	18	11	15.2	4.81	69	.311	.359	6	.250	2	-10	-10	-0	-0.6

■ BOB MILLIKEN   Milliken, Robert Fogle "Bobo"   b: 8/25/26, Majorsville, W.Va.   BR/TR, 6', 195 lbs.   Deb: 4/22/53   C

YEAR TM/L	W	L	PCT	G	GS	CG	SH	SV	IP	H	HR	BB	SO	RAT	ERA	ERA+	OAV	OOB	BH	AVG	PB	PR	/A	PD	TPI
1953 *Bro-N	8	4	.667	37	10	3	0	2	117²	94	13	42	65	10.4	3.37	127	.214	.283	4	.118	-1	12	12	-2	0.8
1954 Bro-N	5	2	.714	24	3	0	0	2	62²	58	12	18	25	11.0	4.02	102	.246	.305	3	.176	-0	0	0	-1	0.0
Total 2	13	6	.684	61	13	3	0	4	180¹	152	25	60	90	10.7	3.59	117	.225	.290	7	.137	-2	12	12	-3	0.8

■ ALAN MILLS   Mills, Alan Bernard   b: 10/18/66, Lakeland, Fla.   BR/TR, 6'1", 190 lbs.   Deb: 4/14/90

YEAR TM/L	W	L	PCT	G	GS	CG	SH	SV	IP	H	HR	BB	SO	RAT	ERA	ERA+	OAV	OOB	BH	AVG	PB	PR	/A	PD	TPI
1990 NY-A	1	5	.167	36	0	0	0	0	41²	48	4	33	24	17.7	4.10	97	.298	.421	0	—	0	-1	-1	1	0.0

■ ART MILLS   Mills, Arthur Grant   b: 3/2/03, Utica, N.Y.   d: 7/23/75, Utica, N.Y.   BR/TR, 5'10", 155 lbs.   Deb: 4/16/27   C

YEAR TM/L	W	L	PCT	G	GS	CG	SH	SV	IP	H	HR	BB	SO	RAT	ERA	ERA+	OAV	OOB	BH	AVG	PB	PR	/A	PD	TPI
1927 Bos-N	0	1	.000	15	1	0	0	0	37²	41	1	18	7	14.8	3.82	97	.287	.378	0	.000	-1	0	-0	1	0.0
1928 Bos-N	0	0	—	4	0	0	0	0	7²	17	3	8	0	31.7	12.91	30	.472	.587	0	.000	-0	-8	-8	0	-0.6
Total 2	0	1	.000	19	1	0	0	0	45¹	58	4	26	7	17.7	5.36	70	.324	.424	0	.000	-1	-7	-8	1	-0.6

■ LEFTY MILLS   Mills, Howard Robinson   b: 5/12/10, Dedham, Mass.   d: 9/23/82, Riverside, Cal.   BL/TL, 6'1", 187 lbs.   Deb: 6/10/34

YEAR TM/L	W	L	PCT	G	GS	CG	SH	SV	IP	H	HR	BB	SO	RAT	ERA	ERA+	OAV	OOB	BH	AVG	PB	PR	/A	PD	TPI
1934 StL-A	0	0	—	4	0	0	0	0	8²	10	0	11	2	21.8	4.15	120	.303	.477	1	.333	0	0	1	-0	0.1
1937 StL-A	1	1	.500	2	2	1	0	0	12²	16	1	10	10	18.5	6.39	75	.286	.394	0	.000	-1	-2	-2	0	-0.2
1938 StL-A	10	12	.455	30	27	15	1	0	210¹	216	16	116	134	14.5	5.31	94	.262	.358	6	.091	-3	-12	-8	-3	-1.0
1939 StL-A	4	11	.267	34	14	4	0	2	144¹	147	16	113	103	16.1	6.55	74	.264	.395	11	.234	1	-31	-27	-1	-2.1
1940 StL-A	0	6	.000	26	5	1	0	0	59	64	7	52	18	18.2	7.78	59	.275	.413	2	.154	-0	-22	-21	0	-1.8
Total 5	15	30	.333	96	48	21	1	2	435	453	40	302	267	16.0	6.06	81	.266	.382	20	.149	-3	-67	-57	-4	-5.0

■ DICK MILLS   Mills, Richard Alan   b: 1/29/45, Boston, Mass.   BR/TR, 6'3", 195 lbs.   Deb: 9/07/70

YEAR TM/L	W	L	PCT	G	GS	CG	SH	SV	IP	H	HR	BB	SO	RAT	ERA	ERA+	OAV	OOB	BH	AVG	PB	PR	/A	PD	TPI
1970 Bos-A	0	0	—	2	0	0	0	0	3²	6	0	3	3	24.5	2.45	161	.353	.476	0	—	0	1	1	0	0.1

■ WILLIE MILLS   Mills, William Grant "Wee Willie"   b: 8/15/1877, Schenevus, N.Y.   d: 7/5/14, Norwood, N.Y.   5'7", 150 lbs.   Deb: 7/13/01

YEAR TM/L	W	L	PCT	G	GS	CG	SH	SV	IP	H	HR	BB	SO	RAT	ERA	ERA+	OAV	OOB	BH	AVG	PB	PR	/A	PD	TPI
1901 NY-N	0	2	.000	2	2	2	0	0	16	21	2	4	3	14.6	8.44	39	.314	.362	1	.167	0	-9	-9	-0	-0.7

■ AL MILNAR   Milnar, Albert Joseph "Happy"   b: 12/26/13, Cleveland, Ohio   BL/TL, 6'2", 195 lbs.   Deb: 4/30/36

YEAR TM/L	W	L	PCT	G	GS	CG	SH	SV	IP	H	HR	BB	SO	RAT	ERA	ERA+	OAV	OOB	BH	AVG	PB	PR	/A	PD	TPI
1936 Cle-A	1	2	.333	4	3	1	0	0	22	26	0	18	9	18.0	7.36	68	.286	.404	3	.300	0	-6	-6	0	-0.3
1938 Cle-A	3	1	.750	23	5	2	0	1	68¹	90	5	26	29	15.3	5.00	93	.320	.378	4	.154	-0	-2	-3	0	-0.2
1939 Cle-A	14	12	.538	37	26	12	2	3	209	212	11	99	76	13.4	3.79	116	.264	.345	20	.253	3	19	14	0	1.7
1940 Cle-A	18	10	.643	37	33	15	4	3	242¹	242	14	99	99	12.7	3.27	129	.257	.328	17	.181	-1	30	26	-4	1.9
1941 Cle-A	12	19	.387	35	30	9	1	0	229¹	236	9	116	82	13.9	4.36	90	.266	.352	14	.171	2	-5	-11	-2	-1.0
1942 Cle-A	6	8	.429	28	19	8	2	0	157	146	3	85	35	13.5	4.13	84	.251	.350	12	.171	2	-8	-12	1	-0.8
1943 Cle-A	1	3	.250	16	6	0	0	0	39	51	0	35	12	20.1	8.08	38	.329	.455	4	.211	0	-21	-22	0	-2.0
StL-A	1	2	.333	3	2	1	0	0	14²	23	0	9	7	19.6	5.52	60	.354	.432	2	.333	1	-4	-4	0	-0.1
Yr	2	5	.286	19	8	1	0	0	53²	74	0	44	19	19.8	7.38	43	.335	.445	0	.000	1	-24	-25	1	-2.1
1946 StL-A	1	1	.500	4	2	1	1	0	14²	15	1	6	1	12.9	2.45	152	.278	.350	3	.750	1	2	2	0	0.4
Phi-N	0	0	—	1	1	0	0	0	0	2	0	2	0	—	∞	—	1.000	1.000	0	—	0	-4	-4	0	-0.2
Total 8	57	58	.496	188	127	49	10	7	996¹	1043	43	495	350	14.0	4.22	96	.270	.354	79	.203	9	2	-18	-4	-0.6

■ GEORGE MILSTEAD   Milstead, George Earl "Cowboy"   b: 6/26/03, Cleburne, Tex.   d: 8/9/77, Cleburne, Tex.   BL/TL, 5'10", 144 lbs.   Deb: 6/27/24

YEAR TM/L	W	L	PCT	G	GS	CG	SH	SV	IP	H	HR	BB	SO	RAT	ERA	ERA+	OAV	OOB	BH	AVG	PB	PR	/A	PD	TPI
1924 Chi-N	1	1	.500	13	2	1	0	0	29²	41	3	13	6	16.7	6.07	64	.328	.396	1	.167	0	-7	-7	0	-0.5
1925 Chi-N	1	1	.500	5	3	1	0	0	21	26	0	8	7	14.6	3.00	144	.310	.370	0	.000	0	3	3	0	0.2
1926 Chi-N	1	5	.167	18	4	0	0	2	55¹	63	0	24	14	14.3	3.58	107	.309	.384	1	.053	-2	2	2	3	0.2
Total 3	3	7	.300	36	9	2	0	2	106	130	3	45	27	15.0	4.16	95	.315	.385	2	.063	-3	-3	-2	3	-0.1

■ LARRY MILTON   Milton, Samuel Lawrence "Tug"   b: 5/4/1879, Owensboro, Ky.   d: 5/16/42, Hannibal, Mo.   TR,   Deb: 5/07/03

YEAR TM/L	W	L	PCT	G	GS	CG	SH	SV	IP	H	HR	BB	SO	RAT	ERA	ERA+	OAV	OOB	BH	AVG	PB	PR	/A	PD	TPI
1903 StL-N	0	0	—	1	0	0	0	0	4	3	0	1	0	9.0	2.25	145	.200	.250	1	.500	0	0	0	0	0.1

YEAR TM/L	W	L	PCT	G	GS	CG	SH	SV	IP	H	HR	BB	SO	RAT	ERA	ERA+	OAV	OOB	BH	AVG	PB	PR	/A	PD	TPI
■ COTTON MINAHAN								Minahan, Edmund Joseph			b: 12/10/1882, Springfield, Ohio		d: 5/20/58, E.Orange, N.J.	BR/TR, 6′, 190 lbs.	Deb: 4/21/07										
1907 Cin-N	0	2	.000	2	2	1	0	0	14	12	0	13	4	16.7	1.29	202	.261	.433	0	.000	-1	2	2	-0	0.1
■ RUDY MINARCIN								Minarcin, Rudy Anthony "Buster"			b: 3/25/30, N.Vandergrift, Pa.			BR/TR, 6′, 195 lbs.	Deb: 4/11/55										
1955 Cin-N	5	9	.357	41	12	3	1	1	115²	116	17	51	45	13.2	4.90	86	.261	.341	5	.179	-1	-11	-9	2	-0.6
1956 Bos-A	1	0	1.000	3	1	0	0	0	9²	9	2	8	5	16.8	2.79	165	.250	.400	1	.500	1	1	2	0	0.3
1957 Bos-A	0	0	—	26	0	0	0	2	44²	44	5	30	20	15.1	4.43	90	.267	.383	0	.000	0	-3	-2	0	-0.1
Total 3	6	9	.400	70	13	3	1	3	170	169	24	89	70	13.9	4.66	90	.262	.356	6	.188	0	-13	-9	2	-0.4
■ RAY MINER								Miner, Raymond Theadore "Lefty"			b: 4/4/1897, Glens Falls, N.Y.		d: 9/15/63, Glenridge, N.Y.	BR/TL, 5′11″, 160 lbs.	Deb: 9/15/21										
1921 Phi-A	0	0	—	1	0	0	0	0	1	2	0	3	0	45.0	36.00	12	.400	.625	0	—	0	-4	-4	0	-0.2
■ CRAIG MINETTO								Minetto, Craig Stephen			b: 4/25/54, Stockton, Cal.			BL/TL, 6′, 185 lbs.	Deb: 7/04/78										
1978 Oak-A	0	0	—	4	1	0	0	0	12	13	1	7	3	16.5	3.75	97	.283	.400	0	—	0	0	-0	0	0.0
1979 Oak-A	1	5	.167	36	13	0	0	0	118¹	131	16	58	64	14.6	5.55	73	.282	.365	0	—	0	-18	-20	-2	-1.9
1980 Oak-A	0	2	.000	7	1	0	0	1	8	11	2	3	5	15.8	7.88	48	.324	.378	0	—	0	-3	-4	-0	-0.3
1981 Oak-A	0	0	—	8	0	0	0	0	7	7	0	4	4	15.4	2.57	135	.280	.400	0	—	0	1	1	-0	0.0
Total 4	1	7	.125	55	15	0	0	1	145¹	162	19	72	76	14.9	5.39	74	.284	.370	0	—	0	-20	-23	-2	-2.2
■ STEVE MINGORI								Mingori, Stephen Bernard			b: 2/29/44, Kansas City, Mo.			BL/TL, 5′10″, 165 lbs.	Deb: 8/05/70										
1970 Cle-A	1	0	1.000	21	0	0	0	1	20¹	17	2	12	16	13.3	2.66	149	.227	.341	0	.000	-0	2	3	0	0.3
1971 Cle-A	1	2	.333	54	0	0	0	4	56²	31	2	24	45	8.9	1.43	268	.166	.264	1	.500	0	13	15	1	1.8
1972 Cle-A	0	6	.000	41	0	0	0	10	57	67	4	36	47	16.6	3.95	81	.293	.393	1	.125	-0	-6	-5	0	-0.4
1973 Cle-A	0	0	—	5	0	0	0	0	11²	10	3	10	4	15.4	6.17	64	.233	.377	0	—	0	-3	-3	1	-0.1
KC-A	3	3	.500	19	1	0	0	1	56¹	59	6	23	46	13.6	3.04	135	.267	.344	0	—	0	5	7	-0	0.6
Yr	3	3	.500	24	1	0	0	1	68	69	9	33	50	13.9	3.57	114	.261	.350	0	—	0	2	4	0	0.5
1974 KC-A	2	3	.400	36	0	0	0	2	67¹	53	4	23	43	10.4	2.81	136	.212	.284	0	—	0	6	8	2	1.0
1975 KC-A	0	3	.000	36	0	0	0	2	50¹	42	2	20	25	11.3	2.50	154	.226	.304	0	.000	0	7	8	0	0.8
1976 *KC-A	5	5	.500	55	0	0	0	10	85¹	73	3	25	38	10.7	2.32	151	.238	.301	0	—	0	11	11	3	1.5
1977 *KC-A	2	4	.333	43	0	0	0	4	64	59	4	19	19	11.1	3.09	130	.254	.313	0	—	0	7	7	1	0.7
1978 *KC-A	1	4	.200	45	0	0	0	7	69	64	5	16	28	10.8	2.74	140	.242	.292	0	—	0	8	8	0	0.9
1979 KC-A	3	3	.500	30	1	0	0	1	46²	69	10	17	18	16.8	5.79	74	.348	.403	0	—	0	-8	-8	-0	-0.7
Total 10	18	33	.353	385	2	0	0	42	584²	544	45	225	329	12.1	3.03	126	.248	.323	2	.167	0	43	51	7	6.4
■ PAUL MINNER								Minner, Paul Edison "Lefty"			b: 7/30/23, New Wilmington, Pa.			BL/TL, 6′5″, 200 lbs.	Deb: 9/12/46										
1946 Bro-N	0	1	.000	3	0	0	0	0	4	6	1	3	3	20.3	6.75	50	.333	.429	0	—	0	-1	-1	-0	-0.1
1948 Bro-N	4	3	.571	28	2	0	0	1	62²	61	5	26	23	12.5	2.44	164	.257	.331	4	.190	1	11	11	1	1.2
1949 *Bro-N	3	1	.750	27	1	0	0	2	47¹	49	7	18	17	12.9	3.80	108	.272	.342	3	.214	-0	1	2	1	0.2
1950 Chi-N	8	13	.381	39	24	9	1	4	190¹	217	18	72	99	13.7	4.11	102	.287	.350	14	.215	3	1	2	2	0.7
1951 Chi-N	6	17	.261	33	28	14	3	1	201²	219	20	64	68	12.6	3.79	108	.277	.331	18	.254	5	4	7	4	1.6
1952 Chi-N	14	9	.609	28	27	12	2	0	180²	180	13	54	61	11.7	3.74	103	.258	.312	15	.234	6	-0	1	1	1.1
1953 Chi-N	12	15	.444	31	27	9	2	1	201	227	15	40	64	12.1	4.21	106	.283	.320	15	.221	2	2	5	4	1.2
1954 Chi-N	11	11	.500	32	29	12	0	1	218	236	19	50	79	11.8	3.96	106	.280	.321	13	.171	3	3	6	2	1.1
1955 Chi-N	9	9	.500	22	22	7	1	0	157²	173	15	47	53	12.6	3.48	117	.283	.335	13	.232	2	10	11	2	1.5
1956 Chi-N	2	5	.286	10	9	1	0	0	47	60	9	19	14	15.5	6.89	55	.324	.393	3	.250	2	-16	-16	1	-1.3
Total 10	69	84	.451	253	169	64	9	10	1310¹	1428	122	393	481	12.6	3.94	105	.279	.332	98	.219	23	12	27	17	7.3
■ DON MINNICK								Minnick, Donald Athey			b: 4/14/31, Lynchburg, Va.			BR/TR, 6′3″, 195 lbs.	Deb: 9/23/57										
1957 Was-A	0	1	.000	2	1	0	0	0	9¹	14	1	2	7	15.4	4.82	81	.341	.372	0	.000	-0	-1	-1	-0	0.0
■ JIM MINSHALL								Minshall, James Edward			b: 7/4/47, Covington, Ky.			BR/TR, 6′6″, 215 lbs.	Deb: 9/14/74										
1974 Pit-N	0	1	.000	5	0	0	0	0	4¹	1	0	2	3	6.2	0.00	—	.083	.214	0	—	0	2	2	-0	0.2
1975 Pit-N	0	0	—	1	0	0	0	0	1	0	0	2	2	18.0	0.00	—	.000	.400	0	—	0	0	0	0	0.0
Total 2	0	1	.000	6	0	0	0	0	5¹	1	0	4	5	8.4	0.00	—	.067	.263	0	—	0	2	2	-0	0.2
■ GREG MINTON								Minton, Gregory Brian			b: 7/29/51, Lubbock, Tex.			BB/TR, 6′2″, 180 lbs.	Deb: 9/07/75										
1975 SF-N	1	1	.500	4	2	0	0	0	17	19	1	11	6	16.4	6.88	55	.288	.397	0	.000	-1	-6	-6	1	-0.5
1976 SF-N	0	3	.000	10	2	0	0	0	25²	32	0	12	7	15.8	4.91	74	.317	.395	1	.200	-0	-4	-4	0	-0.3
1977 SF-N	1	1	.500	2	2	0	0	0	14	14	0	4	5	11.6	4.50	87	.264	.351	1	.333	1	-1	-1	1	0.0
1978 SF-N	0	1	.000	11	0	0	0	0	15²	22	3	8	6	17.8	8.04	43	.338	.419	0	.000	-0	-8	-8	0	-0.7
1979 SF-N	4	3	.571	46	0	0	0	4	79²	59	0	27	33	9.9	1.81	193	.215	.289	0	.000	-0	17	15	2	1.8
1980 SF-N	4	6	.400	68	0	0	0	19	91¹	81	0	34	42	11.3	2.46	144	.243	.313	1	.125	-0	12	11	2	1.3
1981 SF-N	4	5	.444	55	0	0	0	21	84¹	84	0	36	29	12.8	2.88	119	.267	.342	0	.000	-1	6	5	3	0.7
1982 SF-N	10	4	.714	78	0	0	0	30	123	108	5	42	58	11.1	1.83	196	.244	.313	3	.176	0	24	24	1	2.7
1983 SF-N	7	11	.389	73	0	0	0	22	106²	117	6	47	38	13.8	3.54	100	.283	.356	6	.545	4	1	-0	0	0.4
1984 SF-N	4	9	.308	74	1	0	0	19	124¹	130	6	57	48	13.5	3.76	93	.267	.344	1	.048	-1	-2	-4	2	-0.2
1985 SF-N	5	4	.556	68	0	0	0	4	96²	98	6	54	37	14.2	3.54	97	.272	.367	0	.000	-1	1	-1	3	0.1
1986 SF-N	4	4	.500	48	0	0	0	5	68²	63	4	34	34	12.8	3.93	90	.251	.343	2	.400	2	-2	-3	2	0.0
1987 SF-N	1	0	1.000	15	0	0	0	1	23¹	30	2	10	9	15.8	3.47	111	.323	.394	0	.000	-0	2	1	0	0.1
Cal-A	5	4	.556	41	0	0	0	10	76	71	4	29	35	12.0	3.08	140	.257	.330	0	—	0	12	10	2	1.2
1988 Cal-A	4	5	.444	44	0	0	0	7	79	67	1	34	46	11.8	2.85	135	.233	.320	0	—	0	10	9	2	1.1
1989 Cal-A	4	3	.571	62	0	0	0	8	90	76	4	37	42	11.5	2.20	173	.230	.311	0	—	0	17	16	2	1.8
1990 Cal-A	1	1	.500	11	0	0	0	0	15¹	11	1	7	4	11.2	2.35	166	.212	.317	0	—	0	3	3	0	0.3
Total 16	59	65	.476	710	7	0	0	150	1130²	1082	43	483	479	12.6	3.10	117	.257	.336	15	.146	2	80	68	22	9.8
■ GINO MINUTELLI								Minutelli, Gino Michael			b: 5/23/64, Wilmington, Del.			BL/TL, 6′, 180 lbs.	Deb: 9/18/90										
1990 Cin-N	0	0	—	2	0	0	0	0	1	0	0	2	2	27.0	9.00	43	.000	.500	0	—	0	-1	-1	0	0.0
■ PAUL MIRABELLA								Mirabella, Paul Thomas			b: 3/20/54, Belleville, N.J.			BL/TL, 6′1″, 190 lbs.	Deb: 7/28/78										
1978 Tex-A	3	2	.600	10	4	0	0	1	28	30	2	17	23	15.1	5.79	65	.286	.385	0	—	0	-6	-6	-0	-0.6
1979 NY-A	0	4	.000	10	1	0	0	0	14¹	16	3	10	4	17.0	8.79	46	.276	.391	0	—	0	-7	-8	0	-0.6
1980 Tor-A	5	12	.294	33	22	3	1	0	130²	151	16	66	63	15.2	4.34	99	.294	.378	0	—	0	-4	-1	0	-0.3
1981 Tor-A	0	0	—	8	1	0	0	0	14²	20	2	7	9	17.2	7.36	53	.313	.389	0	—	0	-6	-6	-0	-0.5
1982 Tex-A	1	1	.500	40	0	0	0	3	50²	46	4	22	29	12.4	4.80	81	.241	.326	0	—	0	-4	-5	-0	-0.4
1983 Bal-A	0	0	—	3	2	0	0	0	9²	9	1	7	4	14.9	5.59	71	.243	.364	0	—	0	-2	-2	-0	-0.1
1984 Sea-A	2	5	.286	52	1	0	0	3	68	74	6	32	41	14.2	4.37	91	.282	.363	0	—	0	-3	-3	1	-0.3
1985 Sea-A	0	0	—	10	0	0	0	0	13²	9	0	4	8	9.9	1.32	320	.188	.278	0	—	0	4	4	0	0.4
1986 Sea-A	0	0	—	8	0	0	0	0	6¹	13	1	3	6	22.7	8.53	50	.419	.471	0	—	0	-3	-3	0	-0.2
1987 Mil-A	2	1	.667	29	0	0	0	2	29¹	30	1	16	14	14.1	4.91	93	.268	.359	0	—	0	-1	-1	1	-0.1
1988 Mil-A	2	2	.500	38	0	0	0	4	60	44	3	21	33	9.8	1.65	241	.204	.274	0	—	0	15	16	1	1.7
1989 Mil-A	0	0	—	13	0	0	0	0	15¹	18	1	7	6	15.3	7.63	50	.290	.371	0	—	0	-6	-6	1	-0.5
1990 Mil-A	4	2	.667	59	0	0	0	0	59	66	9	27	28	14.5	3.97	95	.281	.360	0	—	0	-0	-1	-0	0.0
Total 13	19	29	.396	298	33	3	1	13	499²	526	43	239	258	14.0	4.45	91	.272	.356	0	—	0	-24	-22	1	-0.9

YEAR TM/L	W	L	PCT	G	GS	CG	SH	SV	IP	H	HR	BB	SO	RAT	ERA	ERA+	OAV	OOB	BH	AVG	PB	PR	/A	PD	TPI

■ **ROY MITCHELL**   Mitchell, Albert Roy b: 4/19/1885, Belton, Tex. d: 9/8/59, Temple, Tex. BR/TR, 5'9.5", 170 lbs. Deb: 9/10/10

YEAR TM/L	W	L	PCT	G	GS	CG	SH	SV	IP	H	HR	BB	SO	RAT	ERA	ERA+	OAV	OOB	BH	AVG	PB	PR	/A	PD	TPI
1910 StL-A	4	2	.667	6	6	6	0	0	52	43	0	12	23	9.9	2.60	95	.244	.300	4	.211	0	-0	-1	1	0.0
1911 StL-A	4	8	.333	28	12	8	1	0	133¹	134	4	45	40	12.5	3.85	88	.273	.341	11	.224	2	-7	-7	-0	-0.5
1912 StL-A	3	4	.429	13	7	5	0	0	62	81	2	17	22	14.8	4.65	71	.323	.375	6	.316	3	-9	-9	-1	-0.6
1913 StL-A	13	16	.448	33	27	21	4	1	245¹	265	6	47	59	11.6	3.01	98	.280	.318	13	.148	0	-2	-2	-0	-0.3
1914 StL-A	4	5	.444	28	9	4	0	4	103¹	134	1	38	38	15.5	4.35	62	.320	.384	7	.206	1	-19	-19	0	-1.8
1918 Chi-A	0	1	.000	2	0	0	0	0	12	18	1	4	3	16.5	7.50	36	.346	.393	0	.000	-0	-6	-6	0	-0.5
Cin-N	4	0	1.000	5	3	3	2	0	36¹	27	0	5	9	7.9	0.74	359	.208	.237	3	.214	0	8	8	-0	1.0
1919 Cin-N	0	1	.000	7	1	0	0	0	31	32	0	9	10	11.9	2.32	119	.276	.328	0	.000	-1	2	2	1	0.1
Total 7	32	37	.464	122	67	47	7	5	675¹	734	14	177	204	12.4	3.42	86	.284	.336	44	.187	3	-34	-35	1	-2.6

■ **CHARLIE MITCHELL**   Mitchell, Charles Ross b: 6/24/62, Dickson, Tenn. BR/TR, 6'3", 170 lbs. Deb: 8/09/84

YEAR TM/L	W	L	PCT	G	GS	CG	SH	SV	IP	H	HR	BB	SO	RAT	ERA	ERA+	OAV	OOB	BH	AVG	PB	PR	/A	PD	TPI
1984 Bos-A	0	0	—	10	0	0	0	0	16¹	14	1	6	7	12.1	2.76	151	.226	.314	0	—	0	2	3	0	0.3
1985 Bos-A	0	0	—	2	0	0	0	0	1²	5	1	0	2	27.0	16.20	26	.500	.500	0	—	0	-2	-2	0	-0.1
Total 2	0	0	—	12	0	0	0	0	18	19	2	6	9	13.5	4.00	104	.264	.338	0	—	0	0	0	0	0.2

■ **CLARENCE MITCHELL**   Mitchell, Clarence Elmer b: 2/22/1891, Franklin, Neb. d: 11/6/63, Grand Island, Neb. BL/TL, 5'11.5", 190 lbs. Deb: 6/02/11 C◆

YEAR TM/L	W	L	PCT	G	GS	CG	SH	SV	IP	H	HR	BB	SO	RAT	ERA	ERA+	OAV	OOB	BH	AVG	PB	PR	/A	PD	TPI
1911 Det-A	1	0	1.000	5	1	0	0	0	14¹	20	1	7	4	17.0	8.16	42	.351	.422	2	.500	1	-8	-7	-0	-0.5
1916 Cin-N	11	10	.524	29	24	17	1	0	194²	211	4	45	52	12.3	3.14	83	.285	.334	28	.239	2	-11	-12	1	-0.6
1917 Cin-N	9	15	.375	32	20	10	2	1	159¹	166	4	34	37	11.4	3.22	81	.268	.308	25	.278	4	-9	-11	1	-0.4
1918 Bro-N	0	1	.000	1	1	0	0	0	0¹	4	0	0	0	108.0	108.00	3	1.000	1.000	6	.250	0	-4	-4	0	-0.3
1919 Bro-N	7	5	.583	23	11	9	0	0	108²	123	0	23	43	12.1	3.06	97	.297	.334	18	.367	6	-2	-1	1	0.7
1920 *Bro-N	5	2	.714	19	7	3	1	1	78²	85	1	23	18	12.4	3.09	104	.288	.340	25	.234	1	0	1	2	0.1
1921 Bro-N	11	9	.550	37	18	13	**3**	2	190	206	7	46	39	12.2	2.89	135	.280	.327	24	.264	3	19	21	3	3.0
1922 Bro-N	0	3	.000	5	3	0	0	0	12²	28	0	7	1	25.6	14.21	29	.467	.529	45	.290	2	-14	-14	1	-1.1
1923 Phi-N	9	10	.474	29	19	8	1	0	139¹	170	8	46	41	14.2	4.72	98	.299	.355	21	.269	4	-11	-2	-3	0.0
1924 Phi-N	6	13	.316	30	26	9	1	1	165	223	10	58	36	15.7	5.62	79	.321	.379	26	.255	-1	-32	-21	3	-1.9
1925 Phi-N	10	17	.370	32	26	12	1	1	199¹	245	15	46	43	13.6	5.28	90	.302	.347	18	.196	-2	-22	-11	5	-0.6
1926 Phi-N	9	14	.391	28	25	12	0	1	178²	232	7	55	52	14.7	4.58	90	.318	.369	19	.244	1	-15	-9	4	-0.2
1927 Phi-N	6	3	.667	13	12	8	1	0	94²	99	7	28	17	12.3	4.09	101	.271	.327	10	.238	2	-2	0	1	0.3
1928 Phi-N	0	0	—	3	0	0	0	0	5²	13	0	2	0	23.8	9.53	45	.542	.577	1	.250	0	-3	-3	0	-0.2
*StL-N	8	9	.471	19	18	9	1	0	150	149	8	38	31	11.4	3.30	121	.265	.315	7	.125	-3	11	12	3	1.1
Yr	8	9	.471	22	18	9	1	0	155²	162	8	40	31	11.9	3.53	114	.276	.326	0	.000	-3	8	8	3	0.9
1929 StL-N	8	11	.421	25	22	16	0	0	173	221	13	60	39	14.9	4.27	109	.320	.379	18	.273	4	9	8	-1	1.0
1930 StL-N	1	0	1.000	1	1	0	0	0	3	5	0	2	1	21.0	6.00	84	.357	.438	1	.500	0	-0	-0	0	-0.0
NY-N	10	3	.769	24	16	5	0	0	129	151	10	36	40	13.1	3.98	119	.298	.346	12	.255	0	14	11	2	1.2
Yr	11	3	.786	25	17	5	0	0	132	156	10	38	41	13.3	4.02	118	.300	.349	1	.020	1	14	11	2	1.2
1931 NY-N	13	11	.542	27	25	13	0	0	190¹	221	12	52	39	13.1	4.07	91	.285	.332	16	.219	2	-4	-8	-1	-0.6
1932 NY-N	1	3	.250	8	3	1	0	2	30¹	41	1	11	7	15.7	4.15	89	.325	.384	2	.200	0	-1	-1	-1	-0.1
Total 18	125	139	.473	390	278	145	12	9	2217	2613	116	624	543	13.4	4.12	95	.297	.347	324	.252	27	-86	-54	21	0.9

■ **CRAIG MITCHELL**   Mitchell, Craig Seton b: 4/14/54, Santa Rosa, Cal. BR/TR, 6'3", 180 lbs. Deb: 9/25/75

YEAR TM/L	W	L	PCT	G	GS	CG	SH	SV	IP	H	HR	BB	SO	RAT	ERA	ERA+	OAV	OOB	BH	AVG	PB	PR	/A	PD	TPI
1975 Oak-A	0	1	.000	1	1	0	0	0	3²	6	0	2	2	19.6	12.27	30	.375	.444	0	—	0	-3	-4	0	-0.2
1976 Oak-A	0	0	—	1	0	0	0	0	3¹	3	0	0	0	8.1	2.70	124	.231	.231	0	—	0	0	0	0	0.0
1977 Oak-A	0	1	.000	3	1	0	0	0	5²	9	1	2	1	17.5	7.94	51	.346	.393	0	—	0	-2	-2	0	-0.1
Total 3	0	2	.000	5	2	0	0	0	12²	18	1	4	3	15.6	7.82	48	.327	.373	0	—	0	-6	-6	0	-0.3

■ **FRED MITCHELL**   Mitchell, Frederick Francis (b: Frederick Francis Yapp) b: 6/5/1878, Cambridge, Mass. d: 10/13/70, Newton, Mass. BR/TR, 5'9.5", 185 lbs. Deb: 4/27/01 M◆

YEAR TM/L	W	L	PCT	G	GS	CG	SH	SV	IP	H	HR	BB	SO	RAT	ERA	ERA+	OAV	OOB	BH	AVG	PB	PR	/A	PD	TPI
1901 Bos-A	6	6	.500	17	13	10	0	0	108²	115	2	51	34	13.7	3.81	93	.268	.346	7	.159	-1	-2	-3	0	-0.3
1902 Bos-A	0	1	.000	1	0	0	0	0	4	8	1	5	2	29.3	11.25	32	.414	.534	0	.000	-0	-3	-3	0	-0.2
Phi-A	5	7	.417	18	14	9	0	1	107²	120	4	59	22	15.0	3.59	102	.282	.370	9	.188	-1	-0	1	3	0.3
Yr	5	8	.385	19	14	9	0	1	111²	128	5	64	24	15.5	3.87	95	.288	.378	1	.020	-1	-4	-3	3	0.1
1903 Phi-N	11	16	.407	28	28	24	1	0	227	250	4	102	69	14.7	4.48	73	.284	.370	19	.200	-1	-31	-30	-3	-3.0
1904 Phi-N	4	7	.364	13	13	11	0	0	108²	133	3	25	29	13.7	3.40	79	.306	.353	17	.207	1	-8	-9	3	-0.3
Bro-N	2	5	.286	8	8	8	1	0	66	73	0	23	16	13.5	3.82	72	.291	.357	7	.292	2	-8	-8	1	-0.4
Yr	6	12	.333	21	21	19	1	0	174²	206	3	48	45	13.2	3.56	76	.297	.354	6	.057	3	-16	-17	5	-0.7
1905 Bro-N	3	7	.300	12	10	9	0	0	96	107	2	38	44	14.1	4.78	60	.285	.358	15	.190	0	-19	-20	1	-1.8
Total 5	31	49	.387	97	86	71	2	1	718	806	16	303	216	14.3	4.10	78	.286	.362	120	.210	1	-71	-73	6	-5.7

■ **JOHN MITCHELL**   Mitchell, John Kyle b: 8/11/65, Dickson, Tenn. BR/TR, 6'2", 165 lbs. Deb: 9/08/86

YEAR TM/L	W	L	PCT	G	GS	CG	SH	SV	IP	H	HR	BB	SO	RAT	ERA	ERA+	OAV	OOB	BH	AVG	PB	PR	/A	PD	TPI
1986 NY-N	0	1	.000	4	1	0	0	0	10	10	1	4	2	12.6	3.60	98	.278	.350	0	.000	-0	0	-0	0	0.0
1987 NY-N	3	6	.333	20	19	1	0	0	111²	124	6	36	57	13.1	4.11	92	.279	.336	4	.114	-1	-0	-4	2	-0.3
1988 NY-N	0	0	—	1	0	0	0	0	1	2	0	1	1	27.0	0.00	—	.500	.600	0	.000	-0	0	0	0	0.0
1989 NY-N	0	1	.000	2	0	0	0	0	3	3	0	4	4	21.0	6.00	54	.231	.412	0	—	0	-1	-1	0	0.0
1990 Bal-A	6	6	.500	24	17	0	0	0	114¹	133	7	48	43	14.5	4.64	82	.300	.372	0	—	0	-9	-10	1	-0.9
Total 5	9	14	.391	51	37	1	0	0	240	272	14	93	107	13.9	4.35	87	.289	.356	4	.105	-1	-10	-15	2	-1.2

■ **MONROE MITCHELL**   Mitchell, Monroe Barr b: 9/11/01, Starkville, Miss. d: 9/4/76, Valdosta, Ga. BR/TL, 6'1.5", 170 lbs. Deb: 7/11/23

YEAR TM/L	W	L	PCT	G	GS	CG	SH	SV	IP	H	HR	BB	SO	RAT	ERA	ERA+	OAV	OOB	BH	AVG	PB	PR	/A	PD	TPI
1923 Was-A	2	4	.333	10	6	3	1	2	41²	57	0	22	8	17.3	6.48	58	.350	.430	3	.250	1	-12	-13	-0	-1.0

■ **PAUL MITCHELL**   Mitchell, Paul Michael b: 8/19/49, Worcester, Mass. BR/TR, 6'1", 195 lbs. Deb: 7/01/75

YEAR TM/L	W	L	PCT	G	GS	CG	SH	SV	IP	H	HR	BB	SO	RAT	ERA	ERA+	OAV	OOB	BH	AVG	PB	PR	/A	PD	TPI
1975 Bal-A	3	0	1.000	11	4	1	0	0	57	41	8	19	31	9.5	3.63	97	.204	.273	0	—	0	1	-1	-1	-0.1
1976 Oak-A	9	7	.563	26	26	4	1	0	142	169	15	30	67	12.7	4.25	79	.294	.331	0	—	0	-11	-14	-1	-1.5
1977 Oak-A	0	3	.000	5	3	0	0	0	13²	21	3	7	5	18.4	10.54	38	.339	.406	0	—	0	-10	-10	0	-0.8
Sea-A	3	3	.500	9	9	0	0	0	39²	50	7	16	20	15.2	4.99	82	.311	.376	0	—	0	-4	-4	0	-0.2
Yr	3	6	.333	14	12	0	0	0	53¹	71	10	23	25	16.0	6.41	64	.318	.385	0	—	0	-14	-14	1	-0.7
1978 Sea-A	8	14	.364	29	29	4	2	0	168	173	21	79	75	13.6	4.18	91	.270	.352	0	—	0	-8	-7	-1	-0.7
1979 Sea-A	1	4	.200	10	6	1	0	0	36²	46	4	15	14	15.0	4.42	99	.309	.372	0	—	0	-1	-0	0	0.0
Mil-A	3	3	.500	18	8	0	0	0	75	81	11	10	32	11.3	5.76	72	.276	.307	0	—	0	-13	-13	-1	-1.2
Yr	4	7	.364	28	14	1	0	0	111²	127	15	25	50	12.5	5.32	79	.287	.329	0	—	0	-14	-14	-1	-1.2
1980 Mil-A	5	5	.500	17	11	1	1	1	89¹	92	7	15	29	10.9	3.53	110	.267	.300	0	—	0	5	3	1	0.4
Total 6	32	39	.451	125	96	11	4	1	621¹	673	76	191	277	12.6	4.45	85	.278	.332	0	—	0	-41	-46	-2	-4.1

■ **BOBBY MITCHELL**   Mitchell, Robert McKasha b: 2/6/1856, Cincinnati, Ohio d: 5/1/33, Springfield, Ohio BL/TL, 5'5", 135 lbs. Deb: 9/06/1877 ◆

YEAR TM/L	W	L	PCT	G	GS	CG	SH	SV	IP	H	HR	BB	SO	RAT	ERA	ERA+	OAV	OOB	BH	AVG	PB	PR	/A	PD	TPI
1877 Cin-N	6	5	.545	12	12	11	1	0	100	123	0	11	41	12.1	3.51	75	.286	.304	10	.204	-0	-8	-10	-0	-0.8
1878 Cin-N	7	2	.778	9	9	9	1	0	80	69	1	18	51	9.8	2.14	99	**.221**	.263	12	.245	1	1	-0	-0	0.0
1879 Cle-N	7	15	.318	23	22	20	0	0	194²	236	0	42	90	12.9	3.28	76	.281	.315	16	.147	-4	-17	-17	-4	-2.2
1882 StL-a	0	1	.000	1	1	0	0	0	7	12	0	2	2	18.0	7.71	36	.355	.391	0	.000	-1	-4	-4	0	-0.3
Total 4	20	23	.465	45	44	40	2	0	381²	440	1	73	184	12.1	3.18	78	.272	.304	38	.180	-5	-27	-30	-4	-3.3

■ **WILLIE MITCHELL**   Mitchell, William b: 12/1/1889, Pleasant Grove, Miss. d: 11/23/73, Sardis, Miss. BR/TL, 6', 176 lbs. Deb: 9/22/09

YEAR TM/L	W	L	PCT	G	GS	CG	SH	SV	IP	H	HR	BB	SO	RAT	ERA	ERA+	OAV	OOB	BH	AVG	PB	PR	/A	PD	TPI
1909 Cle-A	1	2	.333	3	3	3	0	0	23	18	0	10	8	12.5	1.57	163	.225	.340	2	.286	1	2	3	0	0.4
1910 Cle-A	12	8	.600	35	18	11	1	0	183²	155	0	55	102	11.0	2.60	100	.236	.310	10	.159	-3	-2	-0	-3	-0.5
1911 Cle-A	7	14	.333	30	22	9	0	0	177¹	190	1	60	78	13.3	3.76	91	.284	.354	7	.109	-5	-8	-7	-0	-1.1

YEAR	TM/L	W	L	PCT	G	GS	CG	SH	SV	IP	H	HR	BB	SO	RAT	ERA	ERA+	OAV	OOB	BH	AVG	PB	PR	/A	PD	TPI
1912	Cle-A	5	8	.385	29	15	8	0	1	163²	149	0	56	94	11.7	2.80	122	.240	.309	6	.113	-4	9	11	-3	0.4
1913	Cle-A	14	8	.636	35	22	14	4	0	217	153	1	88	141	10.3	1.91	159	.199	.288	10	.143	-2	25	27	-3	2.4
1914	Cle-A	12	17	.414	39	32	16	3	1	257	228	3	124	179	12.6	3.19	91	.238	.330	7	.086	-4	-13	-9	-6	-1.9
1915	Cle-A	11	14	.440	36	30	12	1	1	236	210	1	84	149	11.3	2.82	108	.241	.309	10	.127	-5	3	6	-5	-0.3
1916	Cle-A	2	5	.286	12	6	1	0	1	43²	55	2	19	24	15.3	5.15	58	.309	.376	0	.000	-1	-11	-10	-1	-1.2
	Det-A	7	5	.583	23	17	7	2	0	127²	119	0	48	60	12.1	3.31	86	.253	.329	4	.250	2	-7	-6	-3	-0.7
	Yr	9	10	.474	35	23	8	2	1	171¹	174	2	67	84	12.9	3.78	77	.269	.342	7	.149	1	-18	-17	-4	-1.9
1917	Det-A	12	8	.600	30	22	12	5	0	185¹	172	2	46	80	11.2	2.19	121	.250	.309	7	.119	-3	10	10	-3	0.4
1918	Det-A	0	1	.000	1	1	0	0	0	4	3	0	5	2	18.0	9.00	30	.200	.400	0	.000	-0	-3	-3	0	-0.2
1919	Det-A	1	2	.333	3	2	0	0	0	13²	12	2	10	4	15.1	5.27	61	.255	.397	1	.200	0	-3	-3	0	-0.2
Total	11	84	92	.477	276	190	93	16	4	1632	1464	14	605	921	11.8	2.88	103	.243	.320	69	.130	-24	3	18	-27	-2.5

■ VINEGAR BEND MIZELL
Mizell, Wilmer David b: 8/13/30, Leakesville, Miss. BR/TL, 6'3.5", 205 lbs. Deb: 4/22/52

YEAR	TM/L	W	L	PCT	G	GS	CG	SH	SV	IP	H	HR	BB	SO	RAT	ERA	ERA+	OAV	OOB	BH	AVG	PB	PR	/A	PD	TPI
1952	StL-N	10	8	.556	30	30	7	2	0	190	171	12	103	146	13.0	3.65	102	.237	.333	3	.044	-5	2	1	-2	-0.5
1953	StL-N	13	11	.542	33	33	10	1	0	224¹	193	12	114	173	12.5	3.49	122	.227	.321	7	.084	-4	20	19	-1	1.4
1956	StL-N	14	14	.500	33	33	11	3	0	208²	172	20	92	153	11.7	3.62	104	.222	.310	8	.107	-3	3	4	-0	0.1
1957	StL-N	8	10	.444	33	21	7	2	0	149¹	136	18	51	87	11.3	3.74	106	.241	.305	4	.089	-2	2	4	1	0.3
1958	StL-N	10	14	.417	30	29	8	2	0	189²	178	17	91	80	12.9	3.42	121	.252	.339	7	.115	-3	11	15	-0	1.2
1959	StL-N	13	10	.565	31	30	8	1	0	201¹	196	21	89	108	13.1	4.20	101	.252	.334	14	.187	1	-6	1	-2	0.0
1960	StL-N	1	3	.250	9	9	0	0	0	55¹	64	7	28	42	15.0	4.55	90	.291	.371	2	.111	-1	-5	-3	0	-0.2
	*Pit-N	13	5	.722	23	23	8	3	0	155²	141	7	46	71	11.0	3.12	120	.247	.306	7	.137	-1	11	11	-2	0.8
	Yr	14	8	.636	32	32	8	3	0	211	205	14	74	113	12.0	3.50	110	.259	.325	5	.072	-1	6	8	-2	0.6
1961	Pit-N	7	10	.412	25	17	2	1	0	100	120	16	31	37	13.6	5.04	79	.299	.350	3	.130	-1	-11	-12	-2	-1.3
1962	Pit-N	1	1	.500	4	3	0	0	0	16¹	15	3	10	6	14.3	4.96	79	.254	.371	0	.000	-0	-2	-2	1	-0.1
	NY-N	0	2	.000	17	2	0	0	0	38	48	10	25	15	17.5	7.34	57	.324	.425	2	.250	0	-14	-13	-1	-1.2
	Yr	1	3	.250	21	5	0	0	0	54¹	63	13	35	21	16.4	6.63	62	.301	.404	1	.071	-0	-16	-15	0	-1.3
Total	9	90	88	.506	268	230	61	15	0	1528²	1434	143	680	918	12.6	3.85	104	.247	.329	57	.111	-19	12	25	-9	0.5

■ KEVIN MMAHAT
Mmahat, Kevin Paul b: 11/9/64, Memphis, Tenn. BL/TL, 6'5", 220 lbs. Deb: 9/09/89

| 1989 | NY-A | 0 | 2 | .000 | 4 | 2 | 0 | 0 | 0 | 7² | 13 | 2 | 8 | 3 | 25.8 | 12.91 | 30 | .406 | .537 | 0 | — | 0 | -8 | -8 | -0 | -0.6 |

■ MIKE MODAK
Modak, Michael Joseph Aloysius b: 5/18/22, Campbell, Ohio BR/TR, 5'10.5", 195 lbs. Deb: 7/04/45

| 1945 | Cin-N | 1 | 2 | .333 | 20 | 3 | 1 | 1 | 1 | 42¹ | 52 | 0 | 23 | 7 | 15.9 | 5.74 | 65 | .308 | .391 | 1 | .100 | -1 | -9 | -9 | -1 | -1.0 |

■ JOE MOELLER
Moeller, Joseph Douglas b: 2/15/43, Blue Island, Ill. BR/TR, 6'5", 192 lbs. Deb: 4/12/62

1962	LA-N	6	5	.545	19	15	1	0	1	85²	87	10	58	46	15.2	5.25	69	.266	.377	7	.212	1	-12	-15	1	-1.2
1964	LA-N	7	13	.350	27	24	1	0	0	145¹	153	14	31	97	11.6	4.21	77	.265	.307	3	.067	-2	-11	-16	-0	-1.8
1966	*LA-N	2	4	.333	29	8	0	0	0	78²	73	4	14	31	10.3	2.52	131	.244	.285	2	.167	1	10	7	2	1.0
1967	LA-N	0	0	—	6	0	0	0	0	5	9	1	3	2	21.6	9.00	34	.409	.480	0	—	0	-3	-3	0	-0.2
1968	LA-N	1	1	.500	3	3	0	0	0	16	17	1	2	11	11.3	5.06	55	.270	.303	0	.000	-1	-4	-4	0	-0.4
1969	LA-N	1	0	1.000	23	4	0	0	1	51¹	54	4	13	25	11.7	3.33	100	.278	.324	2	.200	1	1	-0	1	0.1
1970	LA-N	7	9	.438	31	19	2	1	4	135¹	131	16	43	63	11.6	3.92	98	.248	.306	6	.154	0	-2	-1	-1	-0.3
1971	LA-N	2	4	.333	28	1	0	0	1	66¹	72	5	12	32	11.4	3.80	85	.279	.311	0	.000	-0	-2	-4	1	-0.3
Total	8	26	36	.419	166	74	4	1	7	583²	596	55	176	307	12.0	4.01	86	.263	.318	20	.129	-2	-20	-37	4	-3.0

■ RON MOELLER
Moeller, Ronald Ralph "The Kid" b: 10/13/38, Cincinnati, Ohio BL/TL, 6', 180 lbs. Deb: 9/08/56

1956	Bal-A	0	1	.000	4	1	0	0	0	8²	10	0	3	2	13.5	4.15	94	.286	.342	0	.000	-0	-0	-0	0	0.0
1958	Bal-A	0	0	—	4	0	0	0	0	4¹	6	0	3	3	18.7	4.15	87	.333	.429	0	—	0	-0	-0	0	0.0
1961	LA-A	4	8	.333	33	18	1	1	0	112²	122	15	83	87	16.5	5.83	77	.275	.392	6	.207	2	-23	-17	0	-1.2
1963	LA-A	0	0	—	3	0	0	0	0	2²	5	1	1	2	20.3	6.75	51	.385	.429	0	—	0	-1	-1	0	0.0
	Was-A	2	0	1.000	8	3	0	0	0	24¹	31	4	10	10	15.5	6.29	59	.316	.385	2	.222	0	-7	-7	-1	-0.7
	Yr	2	0	1.000	11	3	0	0	0	27	36	5	11	12	16.0	6.33	58	.324	.390	0	.000	0	-8	-8	0	-0.7
Total	4	6	9	.400	52	22	1	1	0	152²	174	20	100	104	16.3	5.78	74	.287	.390	8	.205	2	-31	-25	0	-1.9

■ SAM MOFFETT
Moffett, Samuel R. b: 3/14/1857, Wheeling, W.Va. d: 5/5/07, Butte, Mont. TR , 6', 175 lbs. Deb: 5/15/1884 ♦

1884	Cle-N	3	19	.136	24	22	21	0	0	197²	236	9	58	84	13.4	3.87	81	.281	.327	47	.184	-3	-20	-16	2	-1.3
1887	Ind-N	1	5	.167	6	6	6	0	0	50	47	1	23	3	12.6	3.78	109	.242	.322	5	.122	-2	1	2	-0	-0.1
1888	Ind-N	2	5	.286	7	7	6	1	0	56	62	3	17	7	12.7	4.66	63	.271	.321	4	.114	-1	-11	-11	-1	-1.1
Total	3	6	29	.171	37	35	33	1	0	303²	345	13	98	94	13.1	4.00	82	.273	.325	56	.169	-6	-29	-24	1	-2.5

■ RANDY MOFFITT
Moffitt, Randall James b: 10/13/48, Long Beach, Cal. BR/TR, 6'3", 190 lbs. Deb: 6/11/72

1972	SF-N	1	5	.167	40	0	0	0	4	70²	72	5	30	37	13.2	3.69	94	.266	.343	0	.000	-1	-2	-2	0	-0.1
1973	SF-N	4	4	.500	60	0	0	0	14	100¹	86	9	31	65	10.6	2.42	158	.225	.285	1	.059	-1	14	16	-1	1.4
1974	SF-N	5	7	.417	61	1	0	0	15	102	99	9	29	49	11.5	4.50	84	.256	.311	5	.313	2	-10	-8	1	-0.4
1975	SF-N	4	5	.444	55	0	0	0	11	74	73	6	32	39	13.1	3.89	98	.257	.339	3	.214	1	-2	-1	-0	-0.0
1976	SF-N	6	6	.500	58	0	0	0	14	103	92	6	35	50	11.2	2.27	160	.238	.303	2	.143	-0	14	16	-0	1.6
1977	SF-N	4	9	.308	64	0	0	0	11	87²	91	4	39	68	13.7	3.59	109	.271	.355	0	.000	-0	3	3	1	0.3
1978	SF-N	8	4	.667	70	0	0	0	12	81²	79	5	33	52	12.7	3.31	104	.258	.336	1	.143	-1	2	1	-1	0.0
1979	SF-N	2	5	.286	28	0	0	0	2	35	53	5	14	16	17.7	7.71	45	.356	.418	0	.000	-1	-15	-16	0	-1.6
1980	SF-N	1	1	.500	13	0	0	0	0	16²	18	2	4	10	12.4	4.86	73	.281	.333	0	.000	-0	-2	-2	-0	-0.2
1981	SF-N	0	0	—	10	0	0	0	0	11¹	15	2	2	11	13.5	7.94	43	.313	.340	0	—	0	-6	-6	-0	-0.5
1982	Hou-N	2	4	.333	30	0	0	0	3	41²	36	3	13	20	11.7	3.02	110	.228	.307	0	.000	-0	3	1	-1	0.0
1983	Tor-A	6	2	.750	45	0	0	0	10	57¹	52	5	24	38	12.1	3.77	114	.243	.322	0	—	0	2	3	0	0.3
Total	12	43	52	.453	534	1	0	0	96	781¹	766	61	286	455	12.4	3.65	102	.257	.327	12	.140	-1	0	5	-2	0.8

■ HERB MOFORD
Moford, Herbert b: 8/6/28, Brooksville, Ky. BR/TR, 6'1", 175 lbs. Deb: 4/12/55

1955	StL-N	1	1	.500	14	1	0	0	2	24	29	5	15	8	16.9	7.88	52	.299	.398	0	.000	-0	-10	-10	-1	-0.8
1958	Det-A	4	9	.308	25	11	6	0	1	109²	83	10	42	58	11.0	3.61	112	.214	.305	1	.027	-4	2	5	1	0.3
1959	Bos-A	0	2	.000	4	2	0	0	0	8²	10	3	6	7	16.6	11.42	36	.286	.390	0	.000	-0	-7	-7	0	-0.6
1962	NY-N	0	1	.000	7	0	0	0	0	15	21	3	1	5	13.2	7.20	58	.318	.328	1	.250	0	-5	-5	-0	-0.4
Total	4	5	13	.278	50	14	6	0	3	157¹	143	21	64	78	12.4	5.03	81	.244	.329	2	.045	-5	-21	-17	2	-1.5

■ GEORGE MOGRIDGE
Mogridge, George Anthony b: 2/18/1889, Rochester, N.Y. d: 3/4/62, Rochester, N.Y. BL/TL, 6'2", 165 lbs. Deb: 8/17/11

1911	Chi-A	0	2	.000	4	1	0	0	0	12²	12	1	1	5	9.2	4.97	65	.255	.271	2	.400	0	-2	-2	0	-0.1
1912	Chi-A	3	4	.429	17	8	2	0	3	64²	69	2	15	31	11.8	4.04	79	.264	.307	2	.125	-0	-5	-6	-1	-0.6
1915	NY-A	2	3	.400	6	5	3	1	0	41	33	0	11	11	10.3	1.76	167	.219	.295	1	.083	-1	5	5	-0	0.5
1916	NY-A	6	12	.333	30	21	10	2	0	194²	174	3	45	66	10.4	2.31	125	.252	.305	14	.212	1	11	13	2	1.7
1917	NY-A	9	11	.450	29	25	15	1	0	196¹	185	5	39	46	10.7	2.98	90	.255	.301	11	.159	-1	-7	-6	2	-0.5
1918	NY-A	16	13	.552	45	19	13	1	7	239¹	232	6	43	62	10.6	2.18	130	.263	.304	15	.190	-0	16	17	3	2.3
1919	NY-A	10	7	.588	35	18	13	0	1	169	159	6	46	58	11.2	2.77	115	.250	.307	6	.135	-1	9	8	1	0.9
1920	NY-A	5	9	.357	26	15	7	0	1	125¹	146	4	36	35	13.3	4.31	89	.287	.338	7	.167	-1	-7	-7	1	-0.5
1921	Was-A	18	14	.563	38	36	21	4	0	288	301	12	66	101	11.7	3.00	137	.269	.313	15	.153	-5	41	36	2	3.0
1922	Was-A	18	13	.581	34	32	18	3	0	251²	300	13	72	66	13.7	3.58	108	.304	.358	21	.244	4	13	8	-0	1.1
1923	Was-A	13	13	.500	33	30	17	3	1	211	228	10	56	62	12.2	3.11	121	.285	.334	17	.227	1	20	15	2	1.8
1924	*Was-A	16	11	.593	30	30	13	2	0	213	217	2	61	48	12.0	3.76	107	.270	.327	13	.176	-2	11	7	1	0.4

YEAR	TM/L	W	L	PCT	G	GS	CG	SH	SV	IP	H	HR	BB	SO	RAT	ERA	ERA+	OAV	OOB	BH	AVG	PB	PR	/A	PD	TPI
1925	Was-A	3	4	.429	10	8	3	0	0	53	58	2	18	12	13.6	4.08	104	.291	.362	2	.105	-2	2	1	0	0.0
	StL-A	1	1	.500	2	2	1	0	0	15¹	17	2	5	8	13.5	5.87	80	.279	.343	0	.000	-0	-3	-2	0	-0.1
	Yr	4	5	.444	12	10	4	0	0	68¹	75	4	23	20	13.0	4.48	97	.284	.344	2	.087	-2	-1	-1	0	-0.1
1926	Bos-N	6	10	.375	39	10	2	0	3	142	173	6	36	46	13.4	4.50	79	.311	.356	8	.174	-1	-11	-15	2	-1.3
1927	Bos-N	6	4	.600	20	1	0	0	5	48²	48	4	15	26	12.0	3.70	100	.257	.319	3	.200	0	1	0	0	0.0
Total	15	132	131	.502	398	261	138	20	20	2265²	2352	77	565	678	11.9	3.23	109	.273	.323	137	.182	-8	95	75	14	8.6

■ GEORGE MOHART
Mohart, George Benjamin   b: 3/6/1892, Buffalo, N.Y.   d: 10/2/70, Silver Creek, N.Y.   BR/TR, 5'9", 165 lbs.   Deb: 4/15/20

YEAR	TM/L	W	L	PCT	G	GS	CG	SH	SV	IP	H	HR	BB	SO	RAT	ERA	ERA+	OAV	OOB	BH	AVG	PB	PR	/A	PD	TPI
1920	Bro-N	0	1	.000	13	1	0	0	0	35²	33	0	7	13	10.9	1.77	181	.250	.303	1	.125	-0	5	6	1	0.7
1921	Bro-N	0	0	—	2	0	0	0	0	7	8	0	1	1	12.9	3.86	101	.296	.345	1	.500	0	-0	0	-0	0.0
Total	2	0	1	.000	15	1	0	0	0	42²	41	0	8	14	11.2	2.11	157	.258	.310	2	.200	0	5	6	1	0.7

■ DALE MOHORCIC
Mohorcic, Dale Robert   b: 1/25/56, Cleveland, Ohio   BL/TL, 6'3", 220 lbs.   Deb: 5/31/86

YEAR	TM/L	W	L	PCT	G	GS	CG	SH	SV	IP	H	HR	BB	SO	RAT	ERA	ERA+	OAV	OOB	BH	AVG	PB	PR	/A	PD	TPI
1986	Tex-A	2	4	.333	58	0	0	0	7	79	86	5	15	29	11.6	2.51	172	.279	.315	0	—	0	15	16	1	1.6
1987	Tex-A	7	6	.538	74	0	0	0	16	99¹	88	11	19	48	9.9	2.99	150	.244	.286	0	—	0	16	16	2	1.8
1988	Tex-A	2	6	.250	43	0	0	0	5	52	62	6	20	25	15.1	4.85	84	.295	.370	0	—	0	-5	-4	1	-0.3
	NY-A	2	2	.500	13	0	0	0	1	22²	21	1	9	19	13.1	2.78	142	.239	.330	0	—	0	3	3	-1	0.2
	Yr	4	8	.333	56	0	0	0	6	74²	83	7	29	44	13.9	4.22	96	.269	.338	0	—	0	-2	-2	0	-0.1
1989	NY-A	2	1	.667	32	0	0	0	2	57²	65	8	18	24	13.9	4.99	77	.286	.355	0	—	0	-7	-7	1	-0.6
1990	Mon-N	1	2	.333	34	0	0	0	2	53	56	6	18	29	13.2	3.23	116	.286	.358	1	.125	-0	3	3	0	0.3
Total	5	16	21	.432	254	0	0	0	33	363²	378	37	99	174	12.3	3.49	119	.272	.330	1	.125	-0	25	26	4	3.0

■ BILL MOISAN
Moisan, William Joseph   b: 7/30/25, Bradford, Mass.   BL/TR, 6'1", 170 lbs.   Deb: 9/17/53

YEAR	TM/L	W	L	PCT	G	GS	CG	SH	SV	IP	H	HR	BB	SO	RAT	ERA	ERA+	OAV	OOB	BH	AVG	PB	PR	/A	PD	TPI
1953	Chi-N	0	0	—	3	0	0	0	0	5	5	0	2	1	14.4	5.40	82	.278	.381	0	—	0	-1	-1	0	0.0

■ CARLTON MOLESWORTH
Molesworth, Carlton   b: 2/15/1876, Frederick, Md.   d: 7/25/61, Frederick, Md.   TL, 5'6", 200 lbs.   Deb: 9/14/1895

YEAR	TM/L	W	L	PCT	G	GS	CG	SH	SV	IP	H	HR	BB	SO	RAT	ERA	ERA+	OAV	OOB	BH	AVG	PB	PR	/A	PD	TPI
1895	Was-N	0	2	.000	4	3	1	0	0	16	33	1	15	7	27.0	14.63	33	.416	.509	1	.143	-1	-17	-17	-0	-1.2

■ RICHIE MOLONEY
Moloney, Richard Henry   b: 6/7/50, Brookline, Mass.   BR/TR, 6'3", 185 lbs.   Deb: 9/20/70

YEAR	TM/L	W	L	PCT	G	GS	CG	SH	SV	IP	H	HR	BB	SO	RAT	ERA	ERA+	OAV	OOB	BH	AVG	PB	PR	/A	PD	TPI
1970	Chi-A	0	0	—	1	0	0	0	0	1	2	0	1	0	18.0	10.00	—	.400	.400	0	—	0	0	0	0	0.0

■ VINCE MOLYNEAUX
Molyneaux, Vincent Leo   b: 8/17/1888, Lewiston, N.Y.   d: 5/4/50, Stamford, Conn.   BR/TR, 6', 180 lbs.   Deb: 7/05/17

YEAR	TM/L	W	L	PCT	G	GS	CG	SH	SV	IP	H	HR	BB	SO	RAT	ERA	ERA+	OAV	OOB	BH	AVG	PB	PR	/A	PD	TPI
1917	StL-A	0	0	—	7	0	0	0	0	22	18	0	20	4	15.5	4.91	53	.237	.396	0	.000	-1	-5	-6	0	-0.5
1918	Bos-A	1	0	1.000	6	0	0	0	0	10²	3	0	8	1	9.3	3.38	80	.086	.256	0	.000	-0	-1	-1	0	0.0
Total	2	1	0	1.000	13	0	0	0	0	32²	21	0	28	5	13.5	4.41	60	.189	.353	0	.000	-1	-6	-6	1	-0.5

■ RINTY MONAHAN
Monahan, Edward Francis   b: 4/28/28, Brooklyn, N.Y.   BR/TR, 6'1.5", 195 lbs.   Deb: 8/09/53

YEAR	TM/L	W	L	PCT	G	GS	CG	SH	SV	IP	H	HR	BB	SO	RAT	ERA	ERA+	OAV	OOB	BH	AVG	PB	PR	/A	PD	TPI
1953	Phi-A	0	0	—	4	0	0	0	0	10²	11	0	7	2	15.2	4.22	102	.275	.383	0	.000	-0	-0	0	-0	0.0

■ BILL MONBOUQUETTE
Monbouquette, William Charles   b: 8/11/36, Medford, Mass.   BR/TR, 5'11", 190 lbs.   Deb: 7/18/58   C

YEAR	TM/L	W	L	PCT	G	GS	CG	SH	SV	IP	H	HR	BB	SO	RAT	ERA	ERA+	OAV	OOB	BH	AVG	PB	PR	/A	PD	TPI
1958	Bos-A	3	4	.429	10	8	3	0	0	54¹	52	4	20	30	11.9	3.31	121	.251	.317	3	.176	-1	3	4	-1	0.3
1959	Bos-A	7	7	.500	34	17	4	0	0	151²	165	15	33	87	11.9	4.15	98	.285	.327	3	.065	-4	-5	-2	-0	-0.5
1960	Bos-A	14	11	.560	35	30	12	3	0	215	217	18	68	134	12.0	3.64	111	.263	.320	6	.092	-3	6	10	-0	0.7
1961	Bos-A	14	14	.500	32	32	12	1	0	236¹	233	24	100	161	12.7	3.39	123	.254	.327	9	.130	-1	17	20	-2	1.9
1962	Bos-A	15	13	.536	35	35	11	4	0	235¹	227	22	65	153	11.3	3.33	124	.251	.303	7	.096	-3	17	21	-4	1.5
1963	Bos-A	20	10	.667	37	36	13	1	0	266²	258	31	42	174	10.1	3.81	99	.250	.280	10	.114	-4	-5	-1	-1	-0.2
1964	Bos-A	13	14	.481	36	35	7	5	1	234	258	34	40	120	11.5	4.04	95	.277	.308	6	.083	-2	-11	-5	1	-0.4
1965	Bos-A	10	18	.357	35	35	10	2	0	228²	239	32	40	110	11.0	3.70	101	.269	.301	4	.059	-3	6	1	1	0.0
1966	Det-A	7	8	.467	30	14	2	1	0	102²	120	14	22	61	12.7	4.73	74	.293	.333	4	.154	-0	-15	-14	-1	-1.5
1967	Det-A	0	0	—	2	0	0	0	0	2	1	0	0	2	4.5	0.00	—	.143	.143	0	—	0	1	1	0	0.1
	NY-A	6	5	.545	33	10	2	1	1	133¹	122	6	17	53	9.7	2.36	132	.246	.277	5	.156	-0	13	11	-0	1.2
	Yr	6	5	.545	35	10	2	1	1	135¹	123	6	17	55	9.6	2.33	134	.245	.275	1	.031	-0	14	12	-0	1.3
1968	NY-A	5	7	.417	17	11	2	0	0	89¹	92	7	13	32	10.9	4.43	65	.264	.296	3	.115	-0	-14	-15	1	-1.4
	SF-N	0	1	.000	7	0	0	0	1	12¹	11	4	2	5	9.5	3.65	81	.239	.271	0	—	0	-1	-1	0	0.0
Total	11	114	112	.504	343	263	78	18	3	1961²	1995	211	462	1122	11.4	3.68	104	.263	.307	60	.103	-21	-2	29	-3	1.7

■ SID MONGE
Monge, Isidro Pedroza   b: 4/11/51, Agua Preita, Mexico   BB/TL, 6'2", 185 lbs.   Deb: 9/12/75

YEAR	TM/L	W	L	PCT	G	GS	CG	SH	SV	IP	H	HR	BB	SO	RAT	ERA	ERA+	OAV	OOB	BH	AVG	PB	PR	/A	PD	TPI
1975	Cal-A	0	2	.000	4	2	2	0	0	23²	22	3	10	17	12.5	4.18	85	.242	.324	0	—	0	-1	-2	-0	-0.1
1976	Cal-A	6	7	.462	32	13	2	0	0	117²	108	10	49	53	12.1	3.37	99	.248	.326	0	—	0	2	-1	-0	0.0
1977	Cal-A	0	1	.000	4	0	0	0	1	12¹	14	2	6	4	14.6	2.92	134	.304	.385	0	—	0	2	1	0	0.2
	Cle-A	1	2	.333	33	0	0	0	3	39	47	6	27	25	17.1	6.23	63	.309	.413	0	—	0	-9	-10	-1	-0.9
	Yr	1	3	.250	37	0	0	0	4	51¹	61	8	33	29	16.5	5.44	72	.307	.405	0	—	0	-8	-9	-0	-0.7
1978	Cle-A	4	3	.571	48	2	0	0	6	84²	71	4	51	54	13.0	2.76	135	.225	.332	0	—	0	9	9	-0	0.9
1979	Cle-A	12	10	.545	76	0	0	0	19	131	96	9	64	108	11.1	2.40	177	.209	.307	0	—	0	26	27	-1	2.6
1980	Cle-A	3	5	.375	67	0	0	0	14	94¹	80	12	40	61	11.7	3.53	115	.227	.311	0	—	0	5	6	-2	0.4
1981	Cle-A	3	5	.375	31	0	0	0	4	58	58	9	21	41	12.3	4.34	83	.266	.331	0	—	0	-4	-5	-1	-0.5
1982	Phi-N	7	1	.875	47	0	0	0	2	72	70	8	22	43	11.8	3.75	98	.256	.316	1	.111	-0	-1	-1	1	0.0
1983	Phi-N	3	0	1.000	14	0	0	0	0	11²	20	4	6	7	20.1	6.94	51	.377	.441	0	.000	-0	-4	-4	-0	-0.4
	SD-N	7	3	.700	47	0	0	0	7	68²	65	4	31	32	12.7	3.15	111	.257	.340	1	.100	-0	4	3	-0	0.2
	Yr	10	3	.769	61	0	0	0	7	80¹	85	8	37	39	13.8	3.70	95	.277	.357	1	.000	-1	-1	-2	-0	-0.2
1984	SD-N	2	1	.667	13	0	0	0	0	15	17	3	17	7	20.4	4.80	74	.293	.453	0	.000	-0	-2	-2	-0	-0.2
	Det-A	1	0	1.000	19	0	0	0	0	36	40	5	12	19	13.5	4.25	92	.282	.346	0	—	0	-1	-1	-0	-0.1
Total	10	49	40	.551	435	17	4	0	56	764	708	79	356	471	12.7	3.53	107	.248	.334	2	.095	-1	25	20	-5	2.1

■ ED MONROE
Monroe, Edward Oliver "Peck"   b: 2/22/1895, Louisville, Ky.   d: 4/29/69, Louisville, Ky.   BR/TR, 6'5", 187 lbs.   Deb: 5/29/17

YEAR	TM/L	W	L	PCT	G	GS	CG	SH	SV	IP	H	HR	BB	SO	RAT	ERA	ERA+	OAV	OOB	BH	AVG	PB	PR	/A	PD	TPI
1917	NY-A	1	0	1.000	9	1	1	0	1	28²	35	1	6	12	13.5	3.45	78	.310	.355	2	.167	-0	-3	-2	0	-0.2
1918	NY-A	0	0	—	1	0	0	0	0	2	1	0	2	1	13.5	4.50	63	.143	.333	0	—	0	-0	-0	0	0.0
Total	2	1	0	1.000	10	1	1	0	1	30²	36	1	8	13	13.5	3.52	77	.300	.354	2	.167	-0	-3	-3	0	-0.2

■ LARRY MONROE
Monroe, Lawrence James   b: 6/20/56, Detroit, Mich.   BR/TR, 6'4", 200 lbs.   Deb: 8/23/76

YEAR	TM/L	W	L	PCT	G	GS	CG	SH	SV	IP	H	HR	BB	SO	RAT	ERA	ERA+	OAV	OOB	BH	AVG	PB	PR	/A	PD	TPI
1976	Chi-A	0	1	.000	8	2	0	0	0	21²	23	0	13	9	15.0	4.15	86	.284	.383	0	—	0	-2	-1	0	-0.1

■ ZACH MONROE
Monroe, Zachary Charles   b: 7/8/31, Peoria, Ill.   BR/TR, 6', 198 lbs.   Deb: 6/27/58

YEAR	TM/L	W	L	PCT	G	GS	CG	SH	SV	IP	H	HR	BB	SO	RAT	ERA	ERA+	OAV	OOB	BH	AVG	PB	PR	/A	PD	TPI
1958	*NY-A	4	2	.667	21	6	1	0	1	58	57	8	27	18	13.0	3.26	108	.263	.344	2	.118	-1	3	2	1	0.0
1959	NY-A	0	0	—	3	0	0	0	0	3¹	3	2	2	1	13.5	5.40	67	.231	.333	0	—	0	-1	-1	0	0.0
Total	2	4	2	.667	24	6	1	0	1	61¹	60	10	29	19	13.1	3.38	105	.261	.344	2	.118	-1	3	1	1	0.2

■ JOHN MONTAGUE
Montague, John Evans   b: 9/12/47, Newport News, Va.   BR/TR, 6'2", 213 lbs.   Deb: 9/09/73

YEAR	TM/L	W	L	PCT	G	GS	CG	SH	SV	IP	H	HR	BB	SO	RAT	ERA	ERA+	OAV	OOB	BH	AVG	PB	PR	/A	PD	TPI
1973	Mon-N	0	0	—	4	0	0	0	0	7²	8	0	2	7	12.9	3.52	108	.286	.355	0	.000	-0	0	0	-0	0.0
1974	Mon-N	3	4	.429	46	1	0	0	3	82²	73	5	38	43	12.5	3.16	122	.241	.333	1	.100	-0	4	6	-1	0.5
1975	Mon-N	0	1	.000	12	0	0	0	0	17²	23	4	6	9	15.8	5.60	68	.324	.392	0	—	0	-4	-3	0	-0.3
	Phi-N	0	0	—	3	0	0	0	0	5	8	1	4	1	21.6	9.00	41	.400	.500	0	—	0	-3	-3	0	-0.2
	Yr	0	1	.000	15	0	0	0	0	22²	31	5	10	10	16.3	6.35	60	.336	.408	0	.000	-0	-7	-6	0	-0.5
1977	Sea-A	8	12	.400	47	15	2	0	4	182¹	193	20	75	98	13.4	4.29	96	.272	.345	0	—	0	-5	-4	1	-0.2
1978	Sea-A	1	3	.250	19	0	0	0	0	43²	52	7	24	14	15.7	6.18	62	.308	.394	0	—	0	-12	-12	-0	-1.1
1979	Sea-A	6	4	.600	41	1	0	0	1	116¹	125	14	47	60	13.5	5.57	78	.284	.356	0	—	0	-18	-16	0	-1.4

YEAR TM/L	W	L	PCT	G	GS	CG	SH	SV	IP	H	HR	BB	SO	RAT	ERA	ERA+	OAV	OOB	BH	AVG	PB	PR	/A	PD	TPI
*Cal-A	2	0	1.000	14	0	0	0	6	17²	16	3	9	6	12.7	5.09	80	.242	.333	0	—	0	-2	-2	-1	-0.2
Yr	8	4	.667	55	1	0	0	7	134	141	17	56	66	13.2	5.51	78	.273	.344	0	—	0	-19	-18	-0	-1.6
1980 Cal-A	4	2	.667	37	0	0	0	3	73²	97	8	21	22	14.5	5.13	77	.324	.371	0	—	0	-9	-10	1	-0.8
Total 7	24	26	.480	223	17	2	0	21	546²	595	57	226	260	13.7	4.76	85	.283	.356	1	.083	-0	-47	-42	-0	-3.7

■ RAFAEL MONTALVO
Montalvo, Rafael Edgardo (Torres)   b: 3/31/64, Rio Piedras, P.R.   BR/TR, 6', 185 lbs.   Deb: 4/13/86

YEAR TM/L	W	L	PCT	G	GS	CG	SH	SV	IP	H	HR	BB	SO	RAT	ERA	ERA+	OAV	OOB	BH	AVG	PB	PR	/A	PD	TPI
1986 Hou-N	0	0	—	1	0	0	0	0	1	1	0	2	0	27.0	9.00	40	.250	.500	0	—	0	-1	-1	0	0.0

■ AURELIO MONTEAGUDO
Monteagudo, Aurelio Faustino (Cintra)   b: 11/19/43, Caibarien, Cuba   BR/TR, 5'11", 180 lbs.   Deb: 9/01/63

YEAR TM/L	W	L	PCT	G	GS	CG	SH	SV	IP	H	HR	BB	SO	RAT	ERA	ERA+	OAV	OOB	BH	AVG	PB	PR	/A	PD	TPI
1963 KC-A	0	0	—	4	0	0	0	0	7	4	0	3	3	9.0	2.57	149	.182	.280	0	—	0	1	1	0	0.1
1964 KC-A	0	4	.000	11	6	0	0	0	31¹	40	11	10	14	14.6	8.90	43	.317	.372	2	.286	1	-18	-18	-0	-1.5
1965 KC-A	0	0	—	4	0	0	0	0	7	5	1	4	5	11.6	3.86	90	.185	.290	0	—	0	-0	-0	-0	0.0
1966 KC-A	0	0	—	6	0	0	0	0	12²	12	0	7	3	13.5	2.84	120	.261	.358	0	—	0	1	1	0	0.1
Hou-N	0	0	—	10	0	0	0	1	15¹	14	1	11	7	14.7	4.70	73	.241	.362	0	.000	-0	-2	-2	0	-0.1
1967 Chi-A	0	1	.000	1	1	0	0	0	1¹	4	1	2	0	40.5	20.25	15	.500	.600	0	—	0	-3	-3	0	-0.1
1970 KC-A	1	1	.500	21	0	0	0	0	27¹	20	2	9	18	9.9	2.96	126	.200	.273	0	.000	-0	2	2	-1	0.2
1973 Cal-A	2	1	.667	15	0	0	0	3	30	23	2	16	8	12.9	4.20	84	.215	.339	0	—	0	-1	-2	0	-0.1
Total 7	3	7	.300	72	7	0	0	4	132	122	18	62	58	13.0	5.05	72	.247	.338	2	.200	1	-20	-21	-0	-1.4

■ RENE MONTEAGUDO
Monteagudo, Rene (Miranda)   b: 3/12/16, Havana, Cuba   d: 9/14/73, Hialeah, Fla.   BL/TL, 5'7", 165 lbs.   Deb: 9/06/38 ♦

YEAR TM/L	W	L	PCT	G	GS	CG	SH	SV	IP	H	HR	BB	SO	RAT	ERA	ERA+	OAV	OOB	BH	AVG	PB	PR	/A	PD	TPI
1938 Was-A	1	1	.500	5	3	2	0	0	22	26	3	15	13	16.8	5.73	79	.286	.387	3	.500	1	-2	-3	-1	-0.1
1940 Was-A	2	6	.250	27	8	3	0	2	100²	128	7	52	64	16.4	6.08	69	.316	.398	6	.182	0	-19	-21	-1	-2.0
1945 Phi-N	0	0	—	14	0	0	0	0	45²	67	1	28	16	19.1	7.49	51	.347	.435	58	.301	2	-19	-19	-1	-1.6
Total 3	3	7	.300	46	11	5	0	2	168¹	221	11	95	93	17.2	6.42	64	.321	.407	78	.289	4	-40	-43	-3	-3.7

■ JOHN MONTEFUSCO
Montefusco, John Joseph "Count"   b: 5/25/50, Long Branch, N.J.   BR/TR, 6'1", 180 lbs.   Deb: 9/03/74

YEAR TM/L	W	L	PCT	G	GS	CG	SH	SV	IP	H	HR	BB	SO	RAT	ERA	ERA+	OAV	OOB	BH	AVG	PB	PR	/A	PD	TPI
1974 SF-N	3	2	.600	7	5	1	1	0	39¹	41	3	19	34	13.7	4.81	79	.256	.335	4	.286	3	-5	-4	-1	-0.1
1975 SF-N	15	9	.625	35	34	10	4	0	243²	210	11	86	215	11.2	2.88	132	.233	.305	7	.087	-3	20	25	-2	2.2
1976 SF-N	16	14	.533	37	36	11	**6**	0	253¹	224	11	74	172	10.7	2.84	128	.238	.296	8	.103	-2	19	22	-4	1.8
1977 SF-N	7	12	.368	26	25	4	0	0	157	170	10	46	110	12.6	3.50	112	.273	.326	6	.122	-1	7	7	-2	0.4
1978 SF-N	11	9	.550	36	36	3	0	0	238²	233	25	68	177	11.5	3.81	91	.255	.310	4	.057	-3	-6	-10	-2	-1.4
1979 SF-N	3	8	.273	22	22	0	0	0	137	145	15	51	76	13.0	3.94	89	.279	.346	7	.167	1	-3	-7	0	-0.5
1980 SF-N	4	8	.333	22	17	1	0	0	113¹	120	15	39	85	12.8	4.37	81	.265	.327	1	.033	-2	-10	-10	-2	-1.4
1981 Atl-N	2	3	.400	26	9	0	0	1	77¹	75	9	27	34	11.9	3.49	103	.260	.324	1	.067	-1	0	1	0	0.0
1982 SD-N	10	11	.476	32	32	1	0	0	184¹	177	17	41	83	10.8	4.00	86	.251	.295	5	.086	-2	-8	-12	-0	-1.4
1983 SD-N	9	4	.692	31	10	1	0	4	95¹	94	6	32	52	12.0	3.30	105	.265	.327	1	.053	-1	3	2	-1	0.0
NY-A	5	0	1.000	6	6	0	0	0	38	39	3	10	15	11.8	3.32	117	.271	.323	0	—	0	3	2	-0	0.2
1984 NY-A	5	3	.625	11	11	0	0	0	55¹	55	5	13	23	11.2	3.58	106	.253	.299	0	—	0	3	1	-0	0.1
1985 NY-A	0	0	—	3	1	0	0	0	7	12	3	2	2	18.0	10.29	39	.387	.424	0	—	0	-5	-5	0	-0.3
1986 NY-A	0	0	—	4	0	0	0	0	12¹	9	2	5	3	10.2	2.19	187	.200	.280	0	—	0	3	3	1	0.3
Total 13	90	83	.520	298	244	32	11	5	1652	1604	135	513	1081	11.7	3.54	102	.255	.314	44	.097	-10	20	15	-13	-0.1

■ MANNY MONTEJO
Montejo, Manuel (Bofill)   b: 10/16/35, Caibarien, Cuba   BR/TR, 5'11", 150 lbs.   Deb: 7/25/61

YEAR TM/L	W	L	PCT	G	GS	CG	SH	SV	IP	H	HR	BB	SO	RAT	ERA	ERA+	OAV	OOB	BH	AVG	PB	PR	/A	PD	TPI
1961 Det-A	0	0	—	12	0	0	0	0	16	13	2	6	15	11.6	3.86	106	.217	.309	0	—	0	0	0	-1	0.0

■ RICH MONTELEONE
Monteleone, Richard   b: 3/22/63, Tampa, Fla.   BR/TR, 6'2", 205 lbs.   Deb: 4/15/87

YEAR TM/L	W	L	PCT	G	GS	CG	SH	SV	IP	H	HR	BB	SO	RAT	ERA	ERA+	OAV	OOB	BH	AVG	PB	PR	/A	PD	TPI
1987 Sea-A	0	0	—	3	0	0	0	0	7	10	2	4	2	19.3	6.43	73	.345	.441	0	—	0	-2	-1	0	0.0
1988 Cal-A	0	0	—	3	0	0	0	0	4¹	4	0	1	3	12.5	0.00	—	.222	.300	0	—	0	2	2	0	0.2
1989 Cal-A	2	2	.500	24	0	0	0	0	39²	39	3	13	27	12.0	3.18	120	.255	.317	0	—	0	3	3	1	0.3
1990 NY-A	0	1	.000	5	0	0	0	0	7¹	8	0	2	8	12.3	6.14	65	.276	.323	0	—	0	-2	-2	0	-0.1
Total 4	2	3	.400	35	0	0	0	0	58¹	61	5	20	40	13.0	3.70	106	.266	.333	0	—	0	2	2	1	0.4

■ JEFF MONTGOMERY
Montgomery, Jeffrey Thomas   b: 1/7/62, Wellston, Ohio   BR/TR, 5'11", 170 lbs.   Deb: 8/01/87

YEAR TM/L	W	L	PCT	G	GS	CG	SH	SV	IP	H	HR	BB	SO	RAT	ERA	ERA+	OAV	OOB	BH	AVG	PB	PR	/A	PD	TPI
1987 Cin-N	2	2	.500	14	1	0	0	0	19¹	25	2	9	13	15.8	6.52	65	.313	.382	0	.000	-0	-5	-5	0	-0.4
1988 KC-A	7	2	.778	45	0	0	0	1	62²	54	6	30	47	12.4	3.45	116	.231	.323	0	—	0	4	4	0	0.4
1989 KC-A	7	3	.700	63	0	0	0	18	92	66	3	25	94	9.1	1.37	281	.198	.258	0	—	0	**26**	**25**	-1	2.5
1990 KC-A	6	5	.545	73	0	0	0	24	94¹	81	6	34	94	11.4	2.39	160	.227	.303	0	—	0	16	15	0	1.5
Total 4	22	12	.647	195	1	0	0	43	268¹	226	17	98	248	11.2	2.58	151	.225	.299	0	.000	-0	40	39	0	4.0

■ MONTY MONTGOMERY
Montgomery, Monty Bryson   b: 9/1/46, Albemarle, N.C.   BR/TR, 6'3", 200 lbs.   Deb: 9/14/71

YEAR TM/L	W	L	PCT	G	GS	CG	SH	SV	IP	H	HR	BB	SO	RAT	ERA	ERA+	OAV	OOB	BH	AVG	PB	PR	/A	PD	TPI
1971 KC-A	3	0	1.000	3	2	0	0	0	21¹	16	0	3	12	8.0	2.11	163	.205	.235	0	.000	-0	3	3	0	0.3
1972 KC-A	3	3	.500	9	8	1	1	0	56¹	55	2	17	24	11.5	3.04	100	.263	.319	3	.176	0	0	-0	-0	0.0
Total 2	6	3	.667	12	10	1	1	0	77²	71	2	20	36	10.5	2.78	113	.247	.296	3	.125	0	3	3	-0	0.3

■ RAMON MONZANT
Monzant, Ramon Segundo (Espina)   b: 1/4/33, Maracaibo, Venez.   BR/TR, 6', 160 lbs.   Deb: 7/02/54

YEAR TM/L	W	L	PCT	G	GS	CG	SH	SV	IP	H	HR	BB	SO	RAT	ERA	ERA+	OAV	OOB	BH	AVG	PB	PR	/A	PD	TPI
1954 NY-N	0	0	—	6	1	0	0	0	7²	8	0	11	5	22.3	4.70	86	.276	.475	0	.000	-0	-1	-1	-0	0.0
1955 NY-N	4	8	.333	28	12	3	0	0	94²	98	11	43	54	13.7	3.99	101	.278	.361	3	.125	-1	0	0	-1	-0.1
1956 NY-N	1	0	1.000	4	1	1	0	0	13	8	4	7	11	10.4	4.15	91	.170	.278	0	.000	-1	-1	-1	0	0.0
1957 NY-N	2	3	.600	24	2	0	0	0	49²	55	6	16	37	13.2	3.99	99	.286	.348	3	.300	1	-1	-0	-0	0.0
1958 SF-N	8	11	.421	43	16	4	1	1	150²	160	21	57	93	13.3	4.72	81	.273	.344	8	.163	-1	-13	-15	1	-1.4
1960 SF-N	0	0	—	1	0	0	0	0	1	1	0	1	1	9.0	9.00	39	.250	.250	0	—	0	-1	-1	0	0.0
Total 6	16	21	.432	106	32	8	1	1	316²	330	43	134	201	13.5	4.38	89	.273	.350	14	.157	-2	-15	-17	-1	-1.5

■ LEO MOON
Moon, Leo "Lefty"   b: 6/22/1899, Belmont, N.C.   d: 8/25/70, New Orleans, La.   BR/TL, 5'11", 165 lbs.   Deb: 7/09/32

YEAR TM/L	W	L	PCT	G	GS	CG	SH	SV	IP	H	HR	BB	SO	RAT	ERA	ERA+	OAV	OOB	BH	AVG	PB	PR	/A	PD	TPI
1932 Cle-A	0	0	—	1	0	0	0	0	5²	11	0	7	1	28.6	11.12	43	.379	.500	1	.500	0	-4	-4	0	-0.2

■ JIM MOONEY
Mooney, Jim Irving   b: 9/4/06, Mooresburg, Tenn.   d: 4/27/79, Johnson City, Tenn   BR/TL, 5'11", 168 lbs.   Deb: 8/14/31

YEAR TM/L	W	L	PCT	G	GS	CG	SH	SV	IP	H	HR	BB	SO	RAT	ERA	ERA+	OAV	OOB	BH	AVG	PB	PR	/A	PD	TPI
1931 NY-N	7	1	.875	10	8	6	2	0	71²	71	1	16	38	11.1	2.01	184	.262	.306	4	.160	-1	15	13	-1	1.2
1932 NY-N	6	10	.375	29	18	4	1	0	124²	154	18	42	37	14.1	5.05	73	.299	.352	5	.122	-2	-16	-19	-1	-2.0
1933 StL-N	2	5	.286	21	8	2	0	1	77¹	87	1	26	14	13.2	3.72	93	.296	.353	1	.050	-2	-3	-2	1	-0.2
1934 *StL-N	2	4	.333	32	7	1	0	1	82¹	114	3	49	27	18.3	5.47	77	.326	.414	1	.053	-2	-13	-11	-1	-1.3
Total 4	17	20	.459	92	41	13	3	2	356	426	23	133	116	14.3	4.25	89	.298	.360	11	.105	-7	-18	-18	-2	-2.3

■ BILL MOONEYHAM
Mooneyham, William Craig   b: 8/16/60, Livermore, Cal.   BR/TR, 6', 175 lbs.   Deb: 4/19/86

YEAR TM/L	W	L	PCT	G	GS	CG	SH	SV	IP	H	HR	BB	SO	RAT	ERA	ERA+	OAV	OOB	BH	AVG	PB	PR	/A	PD	TPI
1986 Oak-A	4	5	.444	45	6	0	0	2	99²	103	4	67	75	15.6	4.52	86	.270	.384	0	—	0	-4	-7	1	-0.5

■ BALOR MOORE
Moore, Balor Lilbon   b: 1/25/51, Smithville, Tex.   BL/TL, 6'2", 178 lbs.   Deb: 5/21/70

YEAR TM/L	W	L	PCT	G	GS	CG	SH	SV	IP	H	HR	BB	SO	RAT	ERA	ERA+	OAV	OOB	BH	AVG	PB	PR	/A	PD	TPI
1970 Mon-N	0	2	.000	6	2	0	0	0	9²	14	0	8	6	20.5	7.45	55	.368	.478	1	.333	0	-4	-4	0	-0.2
1972 Mon-N	9	9	.500	22	22	6	3	0	147²	122	15	59	161	11.3	3.47	102	.226	.307	8	.145	-0	-0	1	-1	0.0
1973 Mon-N	7	16	.304	35	32	3	1	0	176¹	151	18	109	151	13.4	4.49	85	.233	.346	3	.057	-3	-16	-13	-2	-1.7
1974 Mon-N	0	2	.000	8	2	0	0	0	13²	13	1	15	16	18.4	3.95	97	.245	.412	0	.000	-0	-1	-0	-0	0.0
1977 Cal-A	0	2	.000	7	3	0	0	0	22²	28	7	10	14	16.3	3.97	99	.298	.383	0	—	0	0	-0	-0	0.0
1978 Tor-A	6	9	.400	37	18	2	0	0	144¹	165	16	54	75	14.1	4.93	80	.294	.363	0	—	0	-19	-16	1	-1.4
1979 Tor-A	5	7	.417	34	16	5	0	0	139¹	135	17	79	51	14.3	5.09	80	.262	.369	0	—	0	-10	-8	-1	-0.7
1980 Tor-A	1	1	.500	31	3	0	0	0	64²	76	6	31	22	15.4	5.29	81	.309	.395	0	—	0	-9	-7	-0	-0.6
Total 8	28	48	.368	180	98	16	4	1	718¹	704	80	365	496	13.8	4.52	87	.261	.355	12	.106	-4	-58	-47	-2	-4.6

YEAR TM/L	W	L	PCT	G	GS	CG	SH	SV	IP	H	HR	BB	SO	RAT	ERA	ERA+	OAV	OOB	BH	AVG	PB	PR	/A	PD	TPI

■ **BRAD MOORE** Moore, Bradley Alan b: 6/21/64, Loveland, Colo. BR/TR, 6'1", 185 lbs. Deb: 6/14/88

1988 Phi-N	0	0	—	5	0	0	0	0	5²	4	0	4	2	12.7	0.00	—	.267	.421	0	—	0	2	2	0	0.3
1990 Phi-N	0	0	—	3	0	0	0	0	2²	4	0	2	1	20.3	3.38	113	.400	.500	0	—	0	0	0	0	0.0
Total 2	0	0	—	8	0	0	0	0	8¹	8	0	6	3	15.1	1.08	338	.320	.452	0	—	0	2	2	0	0.3

■ **CARLOS MOORE** Moore, Carlos Whitman b: 8/13/06, Clinton, Tenn. d: 7/2/58, New Orleans, La. BR/TR, 6'1.5", 180 lbs. Deb: 5/04/30

| 1930 Was-A | 0 | 0 | — | 4 | 0 | 0 | 0 | 0 | 11² | 9 | 0 | 4 | 2 | 10.0 | 2.31 | 199 | .225 | .295 | 0 | .000 | -1 | 3 | 3 | 0 | 0.2 |

■ **DEE MOORE** Moore, D C b: 4/6/14, Hedley, Tex. BR/TR, 5'11", 190 lbs. Deb: 9/12/36 ♦

| 1936 Cin-N | 0 | 0 | — | 2 | 1 | 0 | 0 | 0 | 7 | 3 | 0 | 2 | 3 | 6.4 | 0.00 | — | .120 | .185 | 4 | .400 | 1 | 3 | 3 | 0 | 0.3 |

■ **DONNIE MOORE** Moore, Donnie Ray b: 2/13/54, Lubbock, Tex. d: 7/18/89, Anaheim, Cal. BL/TR, 6', 185 lbs. Deb: 9/14/75

1975 Chi-N	0	0	—	4	1	0	0	0	8²	12	1	4	8	16.6	4.15	92	.316	.381	0	.000	-0	-1	-0	0	0.0
1977 Chi-N	4	2	.667	27	1	0	0	0	48²	51	1	18	34	12.8	4.07	108	.285	.350	3	.300	1	-1	2	1	0.4
1978 Chi-N	9	7	.563	71	1	0	0	4	103	117	7	31	50	13.1	4.11	98	.287	.340	4	.267	1	-6	-1	0	0.1
1979 Chi-N	1	4	.200	39	1	0	0	1	73	95	8	25	43	15.0	5.18	79	.321	.378	2	.154	0	-12	-9	1	-0.6
1980 StL-N	1	1	.500	11	0	0	0	0	21²	25	1	5	10	12.9	6.23	59	.298	.344	3	.750	2	-6	-6	-1	-0.4
1981 Mil-A	0	0	—	3	0	0	0	0	4	4	0	2	2	18.0	6.75	51	.286	.444	0	—	0	-1	-1	0	0.0
1982 *Atl-N	3	1	.750	16	0	0	0	1	27²	32	1	7	17	13.3	4.23	88	.294	.347	0	.000	-0	-2	-2	0	0.0
1983 Atl-N	2	3	.400	43	0	0	0	6	68²	72	6	10	41	10.7	3.67	106	.279	.306	4	.500	1	-0	2	-1	0.3
1984 Atl-N	4	5	.444	47	0	0	0	16	64¹	63	3	18	47	11.5	2.94	131	.258	.312	0	.000	-0	5	7	0	0.7
1985 Cal-A	8	8	.500	65	0	0	0	31	103	91	9	21	72	9.8	1.92	214	.237	.277	0	—	0	25	25	-1	2.4
1986 *Cal-A	4	5	.444	49	0	0	0	21	72²	60	10	22	53	10.2	2.97	138	.228	.288	0	—	0	10	9	-1	0.8
1987 Cal-A	2	2	.500	14	0	0	0	5	26²	28	2	13	17	13.8	2.70	159	.259	.339	0	—	0	5	5	-0	0.4
1988 Cal-A	5	2	.714	27	0	0	0	0	33	48	4	8	22	15.3	4.91	79	.343	.378	0	—	0	-3	-4	0	-0.3
Total 13	43	40	.518	416	4	0	0	89	655	698	53	186	416	12.3	3.67	110	.276	.328	16	.281	5	12	27	-1	3.8

■ **EARL MOORE** Moore, Earl Alonzo "Big Ebbie" or "Crossfire" b: 7/29/1879, Pickerington, O. d: 11/28/61, Columbus, Ohio BR/TR, 6', 195 lbs. Deb: 4/25/01

1901 Cle-A	16	14	.533	31	30	28	4	0	251²	234	4	107	99	12.2	2.90	122	.244	.320	16	.162	-4	21	18	-5	0.7
1902 Cle-A	17	17	.500	36	34	29	4	1	293	304	8	101	84	12.4	2.95	117	.268	.328	24	.212	-0	20	16	-1	1.4
1903 Cle-A	19	9	.679	29	27	27	3	1	247²	196	0	62	148	9.4	1.74	164	.217	.268	8	.092	-5	34	31	-4	2.3
1904 Cle-A	12	11	.522	26	24	22	1	0	227²	186	2	61	139	9.8	2.25	113	.224	.277	12	.140	-2	9	7	-8	-0.2
1905 Cle-A	15	15	.500	31	30	28	3	0	269	232	6	92	131	10.8	2.64	100	.234	.299	10	.104	-4	1	-0	-3	-0.7
1906 Cle-A	1	1	.500	5	4	2	0	0	29²	27	1	18	8	13.7	3.94	66	.246	.352	0	.000	-1	-4	-4	-1	-0.6
1907 Cle-A	1	1	.500	3	2	1	0	0	19¹	18	0	8	7	12.1	4.66	54	.249	.323	0	.000	-1	-5	-5	-0	-0.4
NY-A	2	6	.250	12	9	3	0	1	64	72	1	30	28	14.3	3.94	71	.286	.362	6	.273	1	-10	-8	-0	-0.7
Yr	3	7	.300	15	11	4	0	1	83¹	90	1	38	35	13.8	4.10	67	.277	.353	6	.034	0	-14	-13	-1	-1.1
1908 Phi-N	2	1	.667	3	3	3	1	0	26	20	0	8	16	10.4	0.00	—	.217	.294	2	.222	1	7	7	-1	0.9
1909 Phi-N	18	12	.600	38	34	24	4	0	299²	238	7	108	173	10.7	2.10	124	.210	.283	9	.094	-4	17	17	-6	0.7
1910 Phi-N	22	15	.595	46	35	18	6	0	283	228	5	121	185	11.4	2.58	121	.228	.318	20	.230	2	14	17	-5	1.6
1911 Phi-N	15	19	.441	42	36	21	5	1	308¹	265	11	164	174	12.9	2.63	131	.240	.345	11	.109	-6	27	28	-3	1.9
1912 Phi-N	9	14	.391	31	24	10	1	0	182¹	186	3	77	79	13.3	3.31	110	.268	.347	6	.107	-4	2	7	-2	0.0
1913 Phi-N	1	3	.250	12	4	0	0	0	52	50	3	40	24	15.8	5.02	66	.254	.382	0	.000	-2	-10	-10	1	-1.0
Chi-N	1	1	.500	7	2	0	0	0	28¹	34	3	12	12	14.6	4.45	72	.321	.390	1	.125	-0	-4	-4	1	-0.3
Yr	2	4	.333	19	6	0	0	1	80¹	84	6	52	36	15.2	4.82	68	.276	.382	1	.042	-3	-14	-14	2	-1.3
1914 Buf-F	11	15	.423	36	27	14	2	2	194²	184	3	99	96	13.5	4.30	77	.263	.362	9	.161	-1	-24	-22	-2	-2.4
Total 14	162	154	.513	388	325	230	34	7	2776	2474	57	1108	1403	11.8	2.78	111	.241	.318	134	.141	-32	95	95	-37	3.2

■ **EUEL MOORE** Moore, Euel Walton "Chief" b: 5/27/08, Reagan, Okla. d: 2/12/89, Tishomingo, Okla. BR/TR, 6'2", 185 lbs. Deb: 7/08/34

1934 Phi-N	5	7	.417	20	16	3	0	1	122¹	145	9	41	38	13.7	4.05	117	.288	.342	5	.109	-5	0	9	-1	0.4
1935 Phi-N	1	6	.143	15	8	1	0	0	40¹	63	5	20	15	19.0	7.81	58	.354	.425	6	.400	1	-17	-15	0	-1.1
NY-N	1	0	1.000	6	0	0	0	0	8	9	0	4	3	14.6	5.63	69	.281	.361	0	.000	-0	-1	-2	0	-0.1
Yr	2	6	.250	21	8	1	0	0	48¹	72	5	24	18	17.9	7.45	59	.340	.407	0	.000	1	-18	-16	0	-1.2
1936 Phi-N	2	3	.400	20	5	1	0	1	54¹	76	4	12	19	14.7	6.96	65	.306	.360	4	.222	-0	-18	-15	-1	-1.4
Total 3	9	16	.360	61	29	5	0	3	225	293	18	77	75	14.9	5.48	84	.306	.360	15	.185	-4	-36	-22	-2	-2.2

■ **GENE MOORE** Moore, Eugene Sr. "Blue Goose" b: 11/9/1885, Lancaster, Tex. d: 8/31/38, Dallas, Tex. BL/TL, 6'2", 185 lbs. Deb: 9/28/09

1909 Pit-N	0	0	—	1	0	0	0	0	2	4	0	3	2	31.5	18.00	15	.364	.500	0	.000	-0	-3	-3	0	-0.2
1910 Pit-N	2	1	.667	4	1	0	0	0	17¹	19	1	7	9	13.5	3.12	99	.268	.333	0	.000	-1	-0	-0	0	0.0
1912 Cin-N	0	1	.000	5	2	0	0	1	14²	17	0	11	6	18.4	4.91	68	.298	.429	0	.000	-1	-2	-3	-0	-0.2
Total 3	2	2	.500	10	3	0	0	1	34	40	1	21	17	16.7	4.76	67	.288	.389	0	.000	-2	-6	-6	0	-0.4

■ **GEORGE MOORE** Moore, George Raymond b: 11/25/1872, Cambridge, Mass. d: 11/17/48, Barnstable, Mass. BB/TR, 5'10", 165 lbs. Deb: 6/14/05

| 1905 Pit-N | 0 | 0 | — | 1 | 0 | 0 | 0 | 0 | 3 | 2 | 0 | 1 | 0 | 6.0 | 0.00 | — | .200 | .200 | 0 | .000 | -0 | 1 | 1 | -0 | 0.1 |

■ **JIM MOORE** Moore, James Stanford b: 12/14/03, Prescott, Ark. d: 5/19/73, Seattle, Wash. BR/TR, 6', 165 lbs. Deb: 9/21/28

1928 Cle-A	0	1	.000	1	1	1	0	0	9	5	0	5	1	10.0	2.00	207	.161	.278	0	.000	-0	2	2	-0	0.1
1929 Cle-A	0	0	—	2	0	0	0	0	5²	6	1	4	0	15.9	9.53	47	.273	.385	0	.000	-0	-3	-3	-0	-0.2
1930 Chi-A	2	1	.667	9	5	2	0	1	40	42	6	12	11	12.1	3.60	128	.268	.320	3	.231	-0	5	5	0	0.4
1931 Chi-A	0	2	.000	33	4	0	0	0	83²	93	3	27	15	13.0	4.95	86	.282	.338	1	.063	-1	-5	-6	1	-0.5
1932 Chi-A	0	0	—	1	0	0	0	0	1	1	0	1	2	18.0	0.00	—	.250	.400	0	.000	-0	0	0	0	0.0
Total 5	2	4	.333	46	10	3	0	1	139¹	147	4	49	29	12.7	4.52	97	.270	.332	4	.114	-2	-1	-2	1	-0.2

■ **WHITEY MOORE** Moore, Lloyd Albert b: 6/10/12, Tuscarawas, Ohio d: 12/10/87, Ulrichsville, O. BR/TR, 6'1", 195 lbs. Deb: 9/27/36

1936 Cin-N	1	0	1.000	1	0	0	0	0	5	3	0	3	4	10.8	5.40	71	.167	.286	0	.000	-0	-1	-1	-0	0.0
1937 Cin-N	0	3	.000	13	6	0	0	0	38²	32	1	39	27	17.5	4.89	76	.239	.424	0	.000	-1	-4	-5	-0	-0.5
1938 Cin-N	6	4	.600	19	11	3	1	0	90¹	66	4	42	38	11.1	3.49	105	.205	.302	2	.077	-2	3	2	-1	-0.1
1939 *Cin-N	13	12	.520	42	24	9	2	3	187²	177	10	95	81	13.3	3.45	111	.254	.348	6	.098	-4	10	8	-1	0.3
1940 *Cin-N	8	8	.500	25	15	5	1	1	116²	100	8	56	60	12.6	3.63	104	.231	.349	5	.128	-1	3	2	-3	-0.2
1941 Cin-N	2	1	.667	23	4	1	0	0	61²	62	4	45	17	16.1	4.38	82	.256	.379	3	.167	-1	-5	-5	-0	-0.6
1942 Cin-N	0	0	—	1	0	0	0	0	1	0	0	1	0	9.0	0.00	—	.000	.250	0	—	0	0	0	0	0.0
StL-N	0	1	.000	9	0	0	0	0	12¹	10	0	11	1	16.1	4.38	78	.217	.379	0	.000	-0	-1	-1	-0	-0.1
Yr	0	1	.000	10	0	0	0	0	13¹	10	0	12	1	15.5	4.05	84	.204	.371	0	.000	-0	-1	-1	-0	-0.1
Total 7	30	29	.508	133	60	18	4	4	513¹	450	25	292	228	13.4	3.75	100	.237	.346	16	.103	-10	4	-0	-6	-1.2

■ **MIKE MOORE** Moore, Michael Wayne b: 11/26/59, Eakly, Okla. BR/TR, 6'4", 205 lbs. Deb: 4/11/82

1982 Sea-A	7	14	.333	28	27	1	1	0	144¹	159	21	79	73	15.0	5.36	79	.285	.376	0	—	0	-21	-18	2	-1.5
1983 Sea-A	6	8	.429	22	21	3	2	0	128	130	10	60	108	13.6	4.71	90	.267	.352	0	—	0	-9	-6	1	-0.4
1984 Sea-A	7	17	.292	34	33	6	0	0	212	236	16	85	158	13.6	4.97	80	.282	.352	0	—	0	-23	-23	3	-1.9
1985 Sea-A	17	10	.630	35	34	14	2	0	247	230	18	70	155	11.1	3.46	124	.247	.302	0	—	0	19	21	2	2.4
1986 Sea-A	11	13	.458	38	37	11	1	1	266	279	28	94	146	13.0	4.30	99	.273	.341	0	—	0	-4	-2	0	-0.1
1987 Sea-A	9	19	.321	33	33	12	0	0	231	268	29	84	115	13.7	4.71	100	.292	.351	0	.000	-0	-7	0	1	0.1
1988 Sea-A	9	15	.375	37	32	9	3	0	228²	196	24	63	182	10.3	3.78	110	.232	.289	0	—	0	5	10	1	1.1
1989 *Oak-A	19	11	.633	35	35	6	3	0	241²	193	14	83	172	10.4	2.61	141	.219	.288	0	—	0	34	29	2	3.3
1990 *Oak-A	13	15	.464	33	33	3	0	0	199¹	204	14	84	73	13.1	4.65	80	.267	.342	0	—	0	-16	-20	2	-1.7

YEAR TM/L	W	L	PCT	G	GS	CG	SH	SV	IP	H	HR	BB	SO	RAT	ERA	ERA+	OAV	OOB	BH	AVG	PB	PR	/A	PD	TPI
Total 9	98	122	.445	295	285	65	12	2	1898	1895	174	702	1182	12.5	4.18	99	.262	.330	0	.000	0	-22	-11	14	1.3

■ RAY MOORE Moore, Raymond Leroy "Farmer" b: 6/1/26, Meadows, Md. BR/TR, 6', 195 lbs. Deb: 8/01/52

YEAR TM/L	W	L	PCT	G	GS	CG	SH	SV	IP	H	HR	BB	SO	RAT	ERA	ERA+	OAV	OOB	BH	AVG	PB	PR	/A	PD	TPI
1952 Bro-N	1	2	.333	14	2	0	0	0	28¹	29	3	26	11	18.1	4.76	76	.274	.425	0	.000	-0	-3	-4	0	-0.3
1953 Bro-N	0	1	.000	1	1	1	0	0	8	6	1	4	4	11.3	3.38	126	.214	.313	0	.000	-0	1	1	-0	0.0
1955 Bal-A	10	10	.500	46	14	3	1	6	151²	128	14	80	80	12.6	3.92	97	.229	.329	6	.136	-2	1	-2	-2	-0.4
1956 Bal-A	12	7	.632	32	27	9	1	0	185	161	12	99	105	12.7	4.18	94	.238	.336	19	.271	5	-1	-5	-2	-0.1
1957 Bal-A	11	13	.458	34	32	7	1	0	227¹	196	17	112	117	12.3	3.72	97	.236	.328	18	.214	3	2	-3	-2	-0.2
1958 Chi-A	9	7	.563	32	20	4	2	2	136²	107	10	70	73	11.7	3.82	95	.220	.318	9	.205	2	-1	-3	-1	-0.1
1959 *Chi-A	3	6	.333	29	8	0	0	0	89²	86	10	46	49	13.3	4.12	91	.261	.354	2	.087	-1	-3	-4	-1	-0.5
1960 Chi-A	1	1	.500	14	0	0	0	0	20²	19	5	11	3	13.1	5.66	67	.253	.349	0	.000	-0	-4	-4	-0	-0.4
Was-A	3	2	.600	37	0	0	0	13	65²	49	5	27	29	10.6	2.88	135	.213	.298	1	.071	-1	7	7	-1	0.5
Yr	4	3	.571	51	0	0	0	13	86¹	68	10	38	32	11.2	3.54	109	.222	.310	0	.000	-1	3	3	-1	0.1
1961 Min-A	4	4	.500	46	0	0	0	14	56¹	49	8	38	45	14.1	3.67	115	.233	.353	0	.000	-1	2	4	-0	0.3
1962 Min-A	8	3	.727	49	0	0	0	9	64²	55	8	30	58	12.1	4.73	86	.231	.322	0	.000	-1	-5	-5	-1	-0.5
1963 Min-A	1	3	.250	31	1	0	0	2	38²	50	8	17	38	15.8	6.98	52	.309	.378	1	.333	0	-14	-14	-0	-1.4
Total 11	63	59	.516	365	105	24	5	46	1072²	935	101	560	612	12.7	4.06	93	.238	.335	56	.187	5	-18	-32	-10	-3.1

■ BARRY MOORE Moore, Robert Barry b: 4/3/43, Statesville, N.C. BL/TL, 6'1", 190 lbs. Deb: 5/29/65

YEAR TM/L	W	L	PCT	G	GS	CG	SH	SV	IP	H	HR	BB	SO	RAT	ERA	ERA+	OAV	OOB	BH	AVG	PB	PR	/A	PD	TPI
1965 Was-A	0	0	—	1	0	0	0	0	1	1	0	1	0	18.0	0.00	—	.333	.500	0	—	0	0	0	0	0.0
1966 Was-A	3	3	.500	12	11	1	0	0	62¹	55	3	39	28	13.7	3.75	92	.240	.353	2	.105	-1	-2	-2	0	-0.2
1967 Was-A	7	11	.389	27	26	3	1	0	143²	127	15	71	74	12.6	3.76	84	.240	.333	6	.130	-0	-8	-10	1	-0.8
1968 Was-A	4	6	.400	32	18	0	0	3	117²	116	8	42	56	12.2	3.37	87	.261	.327	3	.097	-1	-5	-6	1	-0.6
1969 Was-A	9	8	.529	31	25	4	0	0	134	123	12	67	51	12.9	4.30	81	.246	.338	9	.209	1	-10	-12	-2	-1.2
1970 Cle-A	3	5	.375	13	12	0	0	0	70¹	70	8	46	35	15.0	4.22	94	.262	.373	2	.095	-1	-4	-2	1	-0.1
Chi-A	0	4	.000	24	7	0	0	0	70²	85	12	34	34	16.2	6.37	61	.302	.393	5	.263	1	-21	-19	1	-1.7
Yr	3	9	.250	37	19	0	0	0	141	155	20	80	69	15.5	5.30	74	.281	.380	1	.025	-0	-25	-21	2	-1.8
Total 6	26	37	.413	140	99	8	1	3	599²	577	58	300	278	13.4	4.16	82	.256	.348	27	.151	-1	-50	-51	3	-4.6

■ BOBBY MOORE Moore, Robert Devell b: 11/8/58, Sweetwater, La. BR/TR, 6'4", 200 lbs. Deb: 9/11/85

YEAR TM/L	W	L	PCT	G	GS	CG	SH	SV	IP	H	HR	BB	SO	RAT	ERA	ERA+	OAV	OOB	BH	AVG	PB	PR	/A	PD	TPI
1985 SF-N	0	0	—	11	0	0	0	0	16²	18	1	10	10	15.1	3.24	106	.269	.364	0	.000	-0	1	0	-0	0.0

■ ROY MOORE Moore, Roy Daniel b: 10/26/1898, Austin, Tex. d: 4/5/51, Seattle, Wash. BB/TL, 6', 185 lbs. Deb: 4/15/20

YEAR TM/L	W	L	PCT	G	GS	CG	SH	SV	IP	H	HR	BB	SO	RAT	ERA	ERA+	OAV	OOB	BH	AVG	PB	PR	/A	PD	TPI
1920 Phi-A	1	13	.071	24	14	5	0	0	132²	161	6	64	45	15.5	4.68	86	.314	.393	10	.200	-1	-13	-10	1	-0.8
1921 Phi-A	10	10	.500	29	26	12	0	0	191²	206	4	122	64	15.6	4.51	99	.280	.385	19	.257	3	-5	-1	2	0.5
1922 Phi-A	0	3	.000	15	6	0	0	0	50²	65	1	32	29	17.8	7.64	56	.319	.418	5	.263	1	-20	-19	-1	-1.6
Det-A	0	0	—	9	0	0	0	2	19²	29	0	10	9	20.1	5.95	65	.367	.468	3	.429	1	-4	-5	-0	-0.3
Yr	0	3	.000	24	6	0	0	2	70¹	94	1	42	38	18.0	7.17	58	.329	.423	3	.115	2	-24	-24	-1	-1.9
1923 Det-A	0	0	—	3	0	0	0	1	12	15	0	11	7	19.5	3.00	129	.288	.413	0	.000	-0	1	1	1	0.1
Total 4	11	26	.297	80	46	17	0	3	406²	476	11	239	154	16.2	4.98	85	.300	.397	37	.239	4	-41	-33	4	-2.1

■ TERRY MOORE Moore, Terry Bluford b: 5/27/12, Vernon, Ala. BR/TR, 5'11", 195 lbs. Deb: 4/16/35 MC♦

YEAR TM/L	W	L	PCT	G	GS	CG	SH	SV	IP	H	HR	BB	SO	RAT	ERA	ERA+	OAV	OOB	BH	AVG	PB	PR	/A	PD	TPI
1939 StL-N	0	0	—	1	0	0	0	0	1	0	0	0	1	0.0	0.00	—	.000	.000	123	.295	0	0	0	0	0.0

■ TOMMY MOORE Moore, Tommy Joe b: 7/7/48, Lynwood, Cal. BR/TR, 5'11", 175 lbs. Deb: 9/15/72

YEAR TM/L	W	L	PCT	G	GS	CG	SH	SV	IP	H	HR	BB	SO	RAT	ERA	ERA+	OAV	OOB	BH	AVG	PB	PR	/A	PD	TPI
1972 NY-N	0	0	—	3	1	0	0	0	12¹	12	1	1	5	9.5	2.92	115	.273	.289	1	.333	0	1	1	0	0.1
1973 NY-N	0	1	.000	3	1	0	0	0	3¹	6	1	3	1	24.3	10.80	33	.400	.500	0	—	0	-3	-3	0	-0.2
1975 StL-N	0	0	—	10	0	0	0	0	18²	15	2	12	6	13.0	3.86	97	.203	.314	1	.500	0	-0	-0	0	0.1
Tex-A	0	2	.000	12	0	0	0	0	21	31	1	12	15	18.9	8.14	46	.352	.436	0	—	0	-10	-10	0	-0.9
1977 Sea-A	2	1	.667	14	1	0	0	0	33	36	1	21	13	16.4	4.91	84	.281	.395	0	—	0	-3	-3	-1	-0.2
Total 4	2	4	.333	42	3	0	0	0	88¹	100	6	49	40	15.6	5.40	71	.287	.381	2	.400	1	-16	-15	0	-1.1

■ CY MOORE Moore, William Austin b: 2/7/05, Elberton, Ga. d: 3/28/72, Augusta, Ga. BR/TR, 6'1", 178 lbs. Deb: 6/07/29

YEAR TM/L	W	L	PCT	G	GS	CG	SH	SV	IP	H	HR	BB	SO	RAT	ERA	ERA+	OAV	OOB	BH	AVG	PB	PR	/A	PD	TPI
1929 Bro-N	3	3	.500	32	4	0	0	0	68	87	3	31	17	15.6	5.56	83	.320	.389	3	.188	-0	-6	-7	-1	-0.6
1930 Bro-N	0	0	—	1	0	0	0	0	0	2	0	0	0	—	—	—	1.000	1.000	0	—	0	0	0	0	0.0
1931 Bro-N	1	2	.333	23	1	1	0	0	61²	62	5	13	35	11.5	3.79	100	.262	.311	2	.154	-1	0	-0	-0	0.0
1932 Bro-N	0	3	.000	20	2	0	0	0	48²	56	3	17	21	13.7	4.81	79	.293	.354	3	.214	0	-5	-5	0	-0.4
1933 Phi-N	8	9	.471	36	18	9	3	1	161¹	177	7	42	53	12.4	3.74	102	.279	.326	3	.063	-5	-7	1	-0	-0.2
1934 Phi-N	4	9	.308	35	15	3	0	0	126²	163	11	65	55	16.3	6.47	73	.309	.387	6	.143	-3	-34	-25	-1	-2.6
Total 6	16	26	.381	147	40	13	3	3	466¹	547	29	168	181	14.0	4.86	86	.293	.355	17	.128	-9	-52	-34	-2	-3.8

■ BILL MOORE Moore, William Christopher b: 9/3/02, Corning, N.Y. d: 1/24/84, Corning, N.Y. BR/TR, 6'3", 195 lbs. Deb: 4/15/25

YEAR TM/L	W	L	PCT	G	GS	CG	SH	SV	IP	H	HR	BB	SO	RAT	ERA	ERA+	OAV	OOB	BH	AVG	PB	PR	/A	PD	TPI
1925 Det-A	0	0	—	1	0	0	0	0	0	0	0	3	0	—	∞	—	—	1.000	0	—	0	-2	-2	0	-0.1

■ WILCY MOORE Moore, William Wilcy "Cy" b: 5/20/1897, Bonita, Tex. d: 3/29/63, Hollis, Okla. BR/TR, 6', 195 lbs. Deb: 4/14/27

YEAR TM/L	W	L	PCT	G	GS	CG	SH	SV	IP	H	HR	BB	SO	RAT	ERA	ERA+	OAV	OOB	BH	AVG	PB	PR	/A	PD	TPI
1927 *NY-A	19	7	.731	50	12	6	1	**13**	213	185	2	59	75	**10.4**	**2.28**	**169**	**.234**	**.289**	6	.080	-6	44	37	8	3.8
1928 NY-A	4	4	.500	35	2	0	0	2	60¹	71	4	31	18	15.2	4.18	90	.286	.366	2	.143	-1	-1	-3	1	-0.1
1929 NY-A	6	4	.600	41	0	0	0	8	61	64	4	19	21	12.2	4.13	93	.268	.322	1	.067	-2	1	-2	2	-0.1
1931 Bos-A	11	13	.458	53	15	8	1	**10**	185¹	195	7	55	37	12.2	3.88	111	.269	.322	9	.161	-3	10	9	6	1.1
1932 Bos-A	4	10	.286	37	2	0	0	4	84¹	98	5	42	28	15.0	5.23	86	.284	.363	1	.045	-3	-7	-7	3	-0.5
*NY-A	2	0	1.000	10	1	0	0	4	25	27	1	6	8	11.9	2.52	162	.273	.314	0	.000	-1	5	4	0	0.3
Yr	6	10	.375	47	3	0	0	8	109¹	125	6	48	36	14.2	4.61	95	.281	.351	1	.033	-4	-2	-3	3	-0.2
1933 NY-A	5	6	.455	35	0	0	0	8	62	92	1	20	17	16.3	5.52	70	.333	.378	2	.133	-1	-9	-11	0	-1.0
Total 6	51	44	.537	261	32	14	2	49	691	732	24	232	204	12.6	3.70	110	.269	.327	21	.102	-16	44	27	21	3.5

■ BOB MOORHEAD Moorhead, Charles Robert b: 1/23/38, Chambersburg, Pa. d: 12/3/86, Lemoyne, Pa. BR/TR, 6'1", 208 lbs. Deb: 4/11/62

YEAR TM/L	W	L	PCT	G	GS	CG	SH	SV	IP	H	HR	BB	SO	RAT	ERA	ERA+	OAV	OOB	BH	AVG	PB	PR	/A	PD	TPI
1962 NY-N	0	2	.000	38	7	0	0	0	105¹	118	13	42	63	14.0	4.53	92	.289	.361	1	.045	-1	-7	-4	2	-0.1
1965 NY-N	0	1	.000	9	0	0	0	0	14¹	16	0	5	5	13.2	4.40	80	.271	.328	0	—	0	-1	-1	0	0.0
Total 2	0	3	.000	47	7	0	0	0	119²	134	13	47	68	13.9	4.51	91	.287	.357	1	.045	-1	-8	-5	2	-0.1

■ BOB MOOSE Moose, Robert Ralph b: 10/9/47, Export, Pa. d: 10/9/76, Martins Ferry, Ohio BR/TR, 6', 200 lbs. Deb: 9/19/67

YEAR TM/L	W	L	PCT	G	GS	CG	SH	SV	IP	H	HR	BB	SO	RAT	ERA	ERA+	OAV	OOB	BH	AVG	PB	PR	/A	PD	TPI
1967 Pit-N	1	0	1.000	2	2	1	0	0	14²	14	1	4	7	11.7	3.68	91	.259	.322	2	.333	1	-1	-1	0	0.1
1968 Pit-N	8	12	.400	38	22	3	3	3	171¹	136	5	41	126	9.5	2.73	107	.218	.269	5	.093	-2	5	4	2	0.4
1969 Pit-N	14	3	.824	44	19	6	1	4	170	149	9	62	165	11.4	2.91	120	.231	.303	4	.075	-1	13	11	0	1.0
1970 *Pit-N	11	10	.524	28	27	9	2	0	189²	186	14	64	119	12.0	3.99	98	.262	.326	12	.182	3	1	-2	-1	0.0
1971 *Pit-N	11	7	.611	30	18	3	1	1	140	169	12	35	68	13.2	4.11	82	.301	.344	4	.103	-1	-10	-11	1	-1.1
1972 *Pit-N	13	10	.565	31	30	6	3	1	226	213	11	47	144	10.5	2.91	114	.248	.290	12	.169	2	14	10	1	1.5
1973 Pit-N	12	13	.480	33	29	6	3	0	201¹	219	11	70	111	13.1	3.53	100	.280	.342	9	.134	-3	-0	-2	1	0.0
1974 Pit-N	1	5	.167	7	6	0	0	0	35²	59	4	7	15	17.2	7.57	45	.386	.420	2	.182	0	-16	-16	2	-1.2
1975 Pit-N	2	2	.500	23	5	1	0	0	67²	63	4	25	34	12.0	3.72	95	.246	.318	3	.167	0	-1	-1	2	0.0
1976 Pit-N	3	9	.250	53	2	0	0	10	90	100	4	32	38	13.9	3.68	95	.294	.362	3	.250	2	-2	-2	-0	0.0
Total 10	76	71	.517	289	160	35	13	19	1304¹	1308	75	387	827	11.9	3.50	98	.262	.319	56	.141	4	7	-9	8	0.8

■ JAKE MOOTY Mooty, J T b: 4/13/13, Bennett, Tex. d: 4/20/70, Fort Worth, Tex. BR/TR, 5'10.5", 170 lbs. Deb: 9/09/36

YEAR TM/L	W	L	PCT	G	GS	CG	SH	SV	IP	H	HR	BB	SO	RAT	ERA	ERA+	OAV	OOB	BH	AVG	PB	PR	/A	PD	TPI
1936 Cin-N	0	0	—	8	0	0	0	1	13²	10	0	4	11	9.2	3.95	97	.204	.264	0	.000	-0	0	-0	-0	0.0
1937 Cin-N	0	3	.000	14	2	0	0	1	39	54	2	22	11	17.5	8.31	45	.327	.406	0	.000	-1	-19	-20	0	-1.8

YEAR TM/L	W	L	PCT	G	GS	CG	SH	SV	IP	H	HR	BB	SO	RAT	ERA	ERA+	OAV	OOB	BH	AVG	PB	PR	/A	PD	TPI
1940 Chi-N	6	6	.500	20	12	6	0	1	114	101	11	49	42	11.9	2.92	128	.243	.325	10	.263	1	12	10	-1	1.1
1941 Chi-N	8	9	.471	33	14	7	1	4	153¹	143	9	56	45	11.8	3.35	105	.251	.320	10	.200	1	5	3	1	0.5
1942 Chi-N	2	5	.286	19	10	1	0	1	84¹	89	11	44	28	14.2	4.70	68	.265	.350	6	.214	0	-13	-14	0	-1.3
1943 Chi-N	0	0	—	2	0	0	0	0	1	2	0	1	1	27.0	0.00	—	.400	.500	0		0	0	0	0	0.0
1944 Det-A	0	0	—	15	0	0	0	0	28¹	35	0	18	7	17.2	4.45	80	.310	.409	1	.143	-0	-3	-3	-0	-0.2
Total 7	16	23	.410	111	38	14	1	8	433²	434	33	194	145	13.1	4.03	88	.263	.341	27	.205	1	-18	-23	0	-1.7

■ HIKER MORAN
Moran, Albert Thomas b: 1/1/12, Rochester, N.Y. BR/TR, 6'4.5", 185 lbs. Deb: 9/29/38

YEAR TM/L	W	L	PCT	G	GS	CG	SH	SV	IP	H	HR	BB	SO	RAT	ERA	ERA+	OAV	OOB	BH	AVG	PB	PR	/A	PD	TPI
1938 Bos-N	0	0	—	1	0	0	0	0	3	1	0	1	0	6.0	0.00	—	.111	.200	0	.000	-0	1	1	0	0.1
1939 Bos-N	1	1	.500	6	2	1	0	0	20	21	3	11	4	14.4	4.50	82	.276	.368	1	.200	1	-1	-2	-0	-0.1
Total 2	1	1	.500	7	2	1	0	0	23	22	3	12	4	13.3	3.91	94	.259	.351	1	.167	0	-0	-1	-0	0.0

■ BILL MORAN
Moran, Carl William "Bugs" b: 9/26/50, Portsmouth, Va. BR/TR, 6'4", 210 lbs. Deb: 4/12/74

YEAR TM/L	W	L	PCT	G	GS	CG	SH	SV	IP	H	HR	BB	SO	RAT	ERA	ERA+	OAV	OOB	BH	AVG	PB	PR	/A	PD	TPI
1974 Chi-A	1	3	.250	15	5	0	0	0	46¹	57	5	23	17	16.7	4.66	80	.302	.394	0	—	0	-5	-5	-1	-0.5

■ CHARLIE MORAN
Moran, Charles Barthell "Uncle Charlie" b: 2/22/1878, Nashville, Tenn. d: 6/14/49, Horse Cave, Ky. BR/TR, 5'8", 180 lbs. Deb: 9/09/03 U♦

YEAR TM/L	W	L	PCT	G	GS	CG	SH	SV	IP	H	HR	BB	SO	RAT	ERA	ERA+	OAV	OOB	BH	AVG	PB	PR	/A	PD	TPI
1903 StL-N	0	1	.000	3	2	2	0	0	24	30	0	19	7	18.8	5.25	62	.297	.413	6	.429	1	-5	-5	-1	-0.3

■ HARRY MORAN
Moran, Harry Edwin b: 4/2/1889, Slater, W.Va. d: 11/28/62, Beckley, W.Va. BL/TL, 6'1", 165 lbs. Deb: 6/23/12

YEAR TM/L	W	L	PCT	G	GS	CG	SH	SV	IP	H	HR	BB	SO	RAT	ERA	ERA+	OAV	OOB	BH	AVG	PB	PR	/A	PD	TPI
1912 Det-A	0	1	.000	5	2	1	0	0	14²	19	1	12	3	20.3	4.91	66	.339	.471	1	.200	-0	-3	-3	0	-0.2
1914 Buf-F	10	7	.588	34	16	7	2	2	154	159	7	53	73	13.0	4.27	77	.276	.348	10	.196	1	-18	-17	-1	-1.6
1915 New-F	13	9	.591	34	23	13	2	0	205²	193	2	66	87	12.1	2.54	112	.262	.337	11	.180	1	11	7	1	1.0
Total 3	23	17	.575	73	41	21	4	2	374¹	371	10	131	163	12.8	3.34	91	.271	.348	22	.188	1	-9	-13	0	-0.8

■ SAM MORAN
Moran, Samuel b: 9/16/1870, Rochester, N.Y. d: 8/29/1897, Rochester, N.Y. TL, 160 lbs. Deb: 8/28/1895

YEAR TM/L	W	L	PCT	G	GS	CG	SH	SV	IP	H	HR	BB	SO	RAT	ERA	ERA+	OAV	OOB	BH	AVG	PB	PR	/A	PD	TPI
1895 Pit-N	2	4	.333	10	6	6	0	0	62²	78	2	51	19	18.5	7.47	61	.300	.415	4	.154	-1	-19	-21	0	-1.5

■ FORREST MORE
More, Forrest b: 9/30/1883, Hayden, Ind. d: 8/17/68, Columbus, Ind. 6', 180 lbs. Deb: 4/15/09

YEAR TM/L	W	L	PCT	G	GS	CG	SH	SV	IP	H	HR	BB	SO	RAT	ERA	ERA+	OAV	OOB	BH	AVG	PB	PR	/A	PD	TPI
1909 StL-N	1	5	.167	15	3	1	0	0	50	48	0	20	17	12.8	5.04	50	.258	.340	2	.154	1	-14	-14	1	-1.3
Bos-N	1	5	.167	10	4	3	0	0	48²	47	0	20	10	13.1	4.44	64	.270	.359	1	.067	-1	-10	-9	0	-0.9
Yr	2	10	.167	25	7	4	0	0	98²	95	0	40	27	12.7	4.74	56	.262	.342	3	.107	-1	-23	-23	1	-2.2

■ DAVE MOREHEAD
Morehead, David Michael "Moe" b: 9/5/42, San Diego, Cal. BR/TR, 6'1", 185 lbs. Deb: 4/13/63

YEAR TM/L	W	L	PCT	G	GS	CG	SH	SV	IP	H	HR	BB	SO	RAT	ERA	ERA+	OAV	OOB	BH	AVG	PB	PR	/A	PD	TPI
1963 Bos-A	10	13	.435	29	29	6	1	0	174²	137	20	99	136	12.2	3.81	99	.211	.316	6	.105	-3	-4	-1	-0	-0.2
1964 Bos-A	8	15	.348	32	30	3	1	0	166²	156	14	112	139	14.7	4.97	78	.248	.365	5	.093	-2	-25	-21	-1	-2.3
1965 Bos-A	10	18	.357	34	33	5	2	0	192²	157	18	113	163	12.8	4.06	92	.217	.326	8	.131	-0	-13	-7	-2	-0.8
1966 Bos-A	1	2	.333	12	5	0	0	0	28	31	7	7	20	12.2	5.46	70	.274	.317	3	.500	1	-6	-5	-0	-0.4
1967 *Bos-A	5	4	.556	10	9	1	1	0	47²	48	0	22	40	13.6	4.34	80	.264	.350	2	.083	-0	-6	-5	-1	-0.5
1968 Bos-A	1	4	.200	11	9	3	1	0	55	52	3	20	28	12.1	2.45	129	.249	.320	2	.125	-0	3	4	-1	0.3
1969 KC-A	2	3	.400	21	2	0	0	0	33	28	7	28	32	15.3	5.73	64	.239	.386	0	.000	0	-8	-7	-0	-0.7
1970 KC-A	3	5	.375	28	17	1	0	1	121²	121	9	62	69	13.6	3.62	103	.261	.349	6	.167	-0	1	2	-2	0.0
Total 8	40	64	.385	177	134	19	6	1	819¹	730	78	463	627	13.2	4.15	90	.237	.338	31	.127	-5	-57	-39	-7	-4.6

■ SETH MOREHEAD
Morehead, Seth Marvin "Moe" b: 8/15/34, Houston, Tex. BL/TL, 6'0.5", 195 lbs. Deb: 4/27/57

YEAR TM/L	W	L	PCT	G	GS	CG	SH	SV	IP	H	HR	BB	SO	RAT	ERA	ERA+	OAV	OOB	BH	AVG	PB	PR	/A	PD	TPI
1957 Phi-N	1	1	.500	34	1	1	0	1	58²	57	1	20	36	12.1	3.68	103	.254	.321	0	.000	-1	1	1	-1	0.0
1958 Phi-N	1	6	.143	27	11	0	0	0	92¹	121	8	26	54	14.4	5.85	68	.319	.365	4	.182	0	-19	-19	-2	-1.9
1959 Phi-N	0	2	.000	3	3	0	0	0	10	15	3	3	8	17.1	9.90	41	.333	.388	0	.000	-0	-7	-6	0	-0.5
Chi-N	0	1	.000	11	2	0	0	0	18²	25	1	8	9	15.9	4.82	82	.313	.375	1	.500	1	-2	-2	-1	-0.1
Yr	0	3	.000	14	5	0	0	0	28²	40	4	11	17	16.0	6.59	61	.317	.372	1	.500	0	-8	-8	-1	-0.6
1960 Chi-N	2	9	.182	45	7	2	0	4	123¹	123	17	46	64	12.5	3.94	96	.258	.326	4	.138	-1	-2	-2	-0	-0.2
1961 Mil-N	1	0	1.000	12	0	0	0	0	15¹	16	4	7	13	14.1	6.46	58	.271	.358	0	—	0	-4	-5	-0	-0.4
Total 5	5	19	.208	132	24	3	0	5	318¹	357	34	110	184	13.4	4.81	80	.282	.343	9	.145	-1	-33	-34	-3	-3.1

■ LEW MOREN
Moren, Lewis Howard "Hicks" b: 8/4/1883, Pittsburgh, Pa. d: 11/2/66, Pittsburgh, Pa. TR, 5'11", 150 lbs. Deb: 9/21/03

YEAR TM/L	W	L	PCT	G	GS	CG	SH	SV	IP	H	HR	BB	SO	RAT	ERA	ERA+	OAV	OOB	BH	AVG	PB	PR	/A	PD	TPI
1903 Pit-N	0	1	.000	1	1	1	0	0	6	9	0	2	2	18.0	9.00	36	.346	.414	0	.000	-0	-4	-4	0	-0.2
1904 Pit-N	0	0	—	1	0	0	0	0	4	7	1	4	0	27.0	9.00	30	.412	.545	0	.000	-0	-3	-3	0	-0.1
1907 Phi-N	11	18	.379	37	31	21	3	1	255	202	3	101	98	11.0	2.54	95	.226	.311	6	.081	-2	-2	-3	-0	-0.6
1908 Phi-N	8	9	.471	28	16	9	4	0	154	146	1	49	72	11.5	2.92	83	.258	.320	12	.245	2	-10	-8	-0	-0.7
1909 Phi-N	16	15	.516	40	31	19	2	1	257²	226	6	93	110	11.3	2.65	98	.239	.309	10	.111	-3	-2	-2	-5	-0.9
1910 Phi-N	13	14	.481	34	26	12	1	1	205¹	207	6	82	74	13.1	3.55	88	.269	.347	11	.149	-1	-12	-10	-1	-1.0
Total 6	48	57	.457	141	105	62	10	3	882	797	17	331	356	11.8	2.95	90	.248	.323	39	.134	-5	-31	-30	-4	-3.5

■ ANGEL MORENO
Moreno, Angel (Veneroso) b: 6/6/55, LaMendosa Soledad Mex. BL/TL, 5'9", 165 lbs. Deb: 8/15/81

YEAR TM/L	W	L	PCT	G	GS	CG	SH	SV	IP	H	HR	BB	SO	RAT	ERA	ERA+	OAV	OOB	BH	AVG	PB	PR	/A	PD	TPI
1981 Cal-A	1	3	.250	8	4	1	0	0	31¹	27	2	14	12	11.8	2.87	127	.233	.315	0	—	0	3	3	-0	0.3
1982 Cal-A	3	7	.300	13	8	2	0	1	49¹	55	7	23	22	14.4	4.74	85	.288	.367	0	—	0	-4	-4	0	-0.3
Total 2	4	10	.286	21	12	3	0	1	80²	82	9	37	34	13.4	4.02	97	.267	.348	0	—	0	-1	-1	-0	0.0

■ JULIO MORENO
Moreno, Julio (Gonzalez) b: 1/28/21, Guines, Cuba d: 1/2/87, Miami, Fla. BR/TR, 5'8", 165 lbs. Deb: 9/08/50

YEAR TM/L	W	L	PCT	G	GS	CG	SH	SV	IP	H	HR	BB	SO	RAT	ERA	ERA+	OAV	OOB	BH	AVG	PB	PR	/A	PD	TPI
1950 Was-A	1	1	.500	4	3	1	0	0	21¹	22	1	12	7	14.8	4.64	97	.268	.368	1	.125	-1	-0	-0	0	0.0
1951 Was-A	5	11	.313	31	18	5	0	2	132²	132	18	80	37	14.4	4.88	84	.256	.357	7	.175	-1	-11	-12	-0	-1.1
1952 Was-A	9	9	.500	26	22	7	0	0	147¹	154	10	52	62	12.9	3.97	90	.270	.337	6	.122	-2	-5	-7	-1	-1.0
1953 Was-A	3	1	.750	12	2	1	0	0	35¹	41	2	13	13	13.8	2.80	139	.291	.351	0	.000	-1	5	4	-0	0.3
Total 4	18	22	.450	73	45	14	0	2	336²	349	31	157	119	13.7	4.25	91	.267	.349	14	.132	-5	-12	-15	-1	-1.8

■ ROGELIO MORET
Moret, Rogelio (Torres) b: 9/16/49, Guayama, P.R. BB/TL, 6'4", 170 lbs. Deb: 9/13/70

YEAR TM/L	W	L	PCT	G	GS	CG	SH	SV	IP	H	HR	BB	SO	RAT	ERA	ERA+	OAV	OOB	BH	AVG	PB	PR	/A	PD	TPI
1970 Bos-A	1	0	1.000	3	1	0	0	0	8¹	7	0	4	2	11.9	3.24	122	.226	.314	0	.000	-0	0	1	0	0.0
1971 Bos-A	4	3	.571	13	7	4	1	0	71	50	5	40	47	11.7	2.92	127	.205	.322	2	.087	-1	4	6	-0	0.6
1972 Bos-A	0	0	—	3	0	0	0	0	5	5	0	6	4	19.8	3.60	89	.263	.440	0	.000	-0	-0	-0	-0	0.0
1973 Bos-A	13	2	.867	30	15	5	2	3	156¹	138	19	67	90	12.0	3.17	127	.238	.320	0	—	0	11	15	-0	1.5
1974 Bos-A	9	10	.474	31	21	10	1	2	173¹	158	15	79	111	12.4	3.74	103	.243	.327	0	—	0	-2	-2	0	0.0
1975 *Bos-A	14	3	.824	36	16	4	1	1	145	132	8	76	80	13.0	3.60	113	.248	.344	0	—	0	3	8	-1	0.6
1976 Atl-N	3	5	.375	27	12	1	0	1	77¹	84	7	27	30	13.0	5.00	76	.280	.341	3	.130	-1	-13	-10	0	-1.1
1977 Tex-A	3	3	.500	18	8	0	0	4	72¹	59	6	38	39	12.1	3.73	109	.220	.317	0	—	0	3	3	-1	0.2
1978 Tex-A	0	1	.000	7	2	0	0	1	14²	23	1	2	5	16.0	4.91	76	.390	.419	0	—	0	-2	-2	-0	-0.1
Total 9	47	27	.635	168	82	24	5	12	723¹	656	61	339	408	12.5	3.66	107	.245	.332	5	.100	-3	4	22	-5	1.7

■ DAVE MOREY
Morey, David Beale b: 2/25/1889, Malden, Mass. d: 1/4/86, Oak Bluff, Mass. BL/TR, 6', 185 lbs. Deb: 7/04/13

YEAR TM/L	W	L	PCT	G	GS	CG	SH	SV	IP	H	HR	BB	SO	RAT	ERA	ERA+	OAV	OOB	BH	AVG	PB	PR	/A	PD	TPI
1913 Phi-A	0	0	—	2	0	0	0	0	4	2	0	2	1	11.3	4.50	61	.182	.357	0	.000	-0	-1	-1	0	0.0

■ CY MORGAN
Morgan, Cyril Arlon b: 12/11/1896, Lakeville, Mass. d: 9/11/46, Lakeville, Mass. BR/TR, 6', 170 lbs. Deb: 6/08/21

YEAR TM/L	W	L	PCT	G	GS	CG	SH	SV	IP	H	HR	BB	SO	RAT	ERA	ERA+	OAV	OOB	BH	AVG	PB	PR	/A	PD	TPI
1921 Bos-N	1	1	.500	17	0	0	0	0	30¹	37	0	17	8	16.3	6.53	56	.314	.404	0	.000	-1	-9	-10	1	-0.8
1922 Bos-N	0	0	—	2	0	0	0	0	1¹	8	0	2	0	67.5	27.00	15	.667	.714	0	—	0	-3	-3	0	-0.2
Total 2	1	1	.500	19	0	0	0	0	31²	45	0	19	8	18.5	7.39	50	.346	.433	0	.000	-1	-13	-13	1	-1.0

■ CY MORGAN
Morgan, Harry Richard b: 11/10/1878, Pomeroy, Ohio d: 6/28/62, Wheeling, W.Va. BR/TR, 6', 175 lbs. Deb: 9/18/03

YEAR TM/L	W	L	PCT	G	GS	CG	SH	SV	IP	H	HR	BB	SO	RAT	ERA	ERA+	OAV	OOB	BH	AVG	PB	PR	/A	PD	TPI
1903 StL-A	0	2	.000	2	1	1	0	0	13	12	0	6	6	12.5	4.15	70	.245	.327	1	.250	0	-2	-2	-0	-0.1

YEAR	TM/L	W	L	PCT	G	GS	CG	SH	SV	IP	H	HR	BB	SO	RAT	ERA	ERA+	OAV	OOB	BH	AVG	PB	PR	/A	PD	TPI
1904	StL-A	0	2	.000	8	3	2	0	0	51	51	3	10	24	10.8	3.71	67	.261	.297	1	.056	-2	-6	-7	1	-0.7
1905	StL-A	2	5	.286	13	8	5	1	0	77¹	82	1	37	44	13.8	3.61	71	.273	.353	8	.258	2	-8	-9	2	-0.5
1907	StL-A	2	5	.286	10	6	4	0	0	55	77	3	17	14	15.4	6.05	42	.332	.378	2	.100	-1	-21	-22	2	-2.0
	Bos-A	6	6	.500	16	13	9	2	0	114¹	77	1	34	50	8.7	1.97	131	.193	.257	2	.057	-4	7	8	-1	0.3
	Yr	8	11	.421	26	19	13	2	0	169¹	154	4	51	64	10.9	3.30	78	.244	.301	1	.018	-5	-14	-14	1	-1.7
1908	Bos-A	14	13	.519	30	26	17	2	1	205	166	7	90	99	11.7	2.46	100	.226	.319	8	.127	-3	-1	0	1	0.2
1909	Bos-A	2	6	.250	12	10	5	0	1	64²	52	0	31	30	12.4	2.37	106	.240	.350	1	.050	-2	1	1	2	0.2
	Phi-A	16	11	.593	28	26	21	5	0	228²	152	3	71	81	9.4	1.65	146	.191	.271	8	.108	-3	21	19	-1	1.8
	Yr	18	17	.514	40	36	26	5	1	293¹	204	3	102	111	9.9	1.81	134	**.200**	.283	2	.021	-4	22	20	2	2.0
1910	Phi-A	18	12	.600	36	34	23	3	0	290²	214	0	117	134	10.8	1.55	153	.216	.310	14	.141	-3	31	27	1	2.8
1911	Phi-A	15	7	.682	38	30	15	2	1	249²	217	0	113	136	12.7	2.70	117	.243	.341	15	.160	-5	18	12	3	1.0
1912	Phi-A	3	8	.273	16	14	5	0	0	93²	75	0	51	47	12.6	3.75	82	.226	.338	1	.033	-3	-4	-7	2	-0.7
1913	Cin-N	0	1	.000	1	1	0	0	0	2¹	5	0	1	2	27.0	15.43	21	.500	.583	0	.000	-0	-3	-3	0	-0.2
Total 10		78	78	.500	210	172	107	15	3	1445¹	1180	18	578	667	11.4	2.51	105	.229	.316	61	.125	-24	32	19	13	1.7

■ BILL MORGAN
Morgan, Henry William b: 10/1857, Washington, D.C. Deb: 5/04/1875 ♦

YEAR	TM/L	W	L	PCT	G	GS	CG	SH	SV	IP	H	HR	BB	SO	RAT	ERA	ERA+	OAV	OOB	BH	AVG	PB	PR	/A	PD	TPI
1875	RS-n	1	3	.250	7	4	4	1	0	42	38	0	1		8.4	3.43	71	.200	.204	18	.261	1	-5	-5		-0.3

■ MIKE MORGAN
Morgan, Michael Thomas b: 10/8/59, Tulare, Cal. BR/TR, 6'3", 195 lbs. Deb: 6/11/78

YEAR	TM/L	W	L	PCT	G	GS	CG	SH	SV	IP	H	HR	BB	SO	RAT	ERA	ERA+	OAV	OOB	BH	AVG	PB	PR	/A	PD	TPI
1978	Oak-A	0	3	.000	3	3	1	0	0	12¹	19	1	8	0	19.7	7.30	50	.373	.458	0	—	0	-5	-5	1	-0.3
1979	Oak-A	2	10	.167	13	13	2	0	0	77¹	102	7	50	17	18.0	5.94	68	.332	.431	0	—	0	-15	-16	1	-1.3
1982	NY-A	7	11	.389	30	23	2	0	0	150¹	167	15	67	71	14.1	4.37	91	.285	.360	0	—	0	-5	-6	1	-0.4
1983	Tor-A	0	3	.000	16	4	0	0	0	45¹	48	6	21	22	13.7	5.16	83	.273	.350	0	—	0	-6	-4	1	-0.3
1985	Sea-A	1	1	.500	2	2	0	0	0	6	11	2	5	2	24.0	12.00	35	.393	.485	0	—	0	-5	-5	0	-0.4
1986	Sea-A	11	17	.393	37	33	9	1	1	216¹	243	24	86	116	13.9	4.53	94	.286	.354	0	—	0	-9	-7	0	-0.6
1987	Sea-A	12	17	.414	34	31	8	2	0	207	245	25	53	85	13.2	4.65	101	.296	.342	0	—	0	-5	2	2	0.3
1988	Bal-A	1	6	.143	22	10	2	0	1	71¹	70	6	23	29	11.9	5.43	72	.255	.315	0	—	0	-12	-12	0	-1.0
1989	LA-N	8	11	.421	40	19	0	0	0	152²	130	6	33	72	9.7	2.53	135	.234	.280	3	.083	-2	16	15	5	2.0
1990	LA-N	11	15	.423	33	33	6	**4**	0	211	216	19	60	106	12.0	3.75	95	.266	.321	8	.113	-2	1	-4	4	-0.2
Total 10		53	94	.361	230	171	30	7	2	1149²	1251	111	406	520	13.1	4.37	92	.280	.343	11	.103	-3	-43	-45	15	-2.2

■ TOM MORGAN
Morgan, Tom Stephen "Plowboy" b: 5/20/30, ElMonte, Cal. d: 1/13/87, Anaheim, Cal. BR/TR, 6'1", 180 lbs. Deb: 4/20/51 C

YEAR	TM/L	W	L	PCT	G	GS	CG	SH	SV	IP	H	HR	BB	SO	RAT	ERA	ERA+	OAV	OOB	BH	AVG	PB	PR	/A	PD	TPI
1951	*NY-A	9	3	.750	27	16	4	2	2	124²	119	11	36	57	11.4	3.68	104	.253	.310	12	.273	2	6	2	2	0.5
1952	NY-A	5	4	.556	16	12	2	1	2	93²	86	8	33	35	11.8	3.07	108	.252	.325	6	.182	1	6	3	3	0.7
1954	NY-A	11	5	.688	32	17	7	4	1	143	149	8	40	34	12.2	3.34	103	.274	.330	7	.143	0	6	2	3	0.7
1955	*NY-A	7	3	.700	40	1	0	0	10	72	72	3	24	17	12.6	3.25	115	.267	.338	4	.222	0	6	4	3	0.7
1956	*NY-A	6	7	.462	41	0	0	0	11	71¹	74	2	27	20	13.1	4.16	93	.284	.357	2	.154	-0	-2	1		0.0
1957	KC-A	9	7	.563	46	13	5	0	7	143¹	160	19	61	32	14.0	4.64	85	.299	.373	3	.091	-2	-14	-11	4	-0.8
1958	Det-A	2	5	.286	39	1	0	0	1	62²	70	7	4	32	10.8	3.16	128	.286	.300	2	.200	-0	4	6	-0	0.6
1959	Det-A	1	4	.200	46	1	0	0	9	92²	94	11	18	39	11.5	3.98	102	.265	.311	9	.391	4	-1	1	0	0.5
1960	Det-A	3	2	.600	22	0	0	0	1	29	33	6	10	12	13.3	4.66	85	.295	.352	0	—	0	-3	-2	1	-0.1
	Was-A	1	3	.250	14	0	0	0	0	24	36	6	5	11	15.8	3.75	104	.343	.378	0	.000	-1	0	0	0	0.0
	Yr	4	5	.444	36	0	0	0	1	53	69	12	15	23	14.4	4.25	92	.315	.362	0	.000	-1	-2	-2	1	-0.1
1961	LA-A	8	2	.800	59	0	0	0	10	91²	74	7	17	39	9.4	2.36	191	.224	.272	1	.083	-1	17	**22**	1	2.3
1962	LA-A	5	2	.714	48	0	0	0	9	58²	53	6	19	29	11.2	2.91	132	.247	.311	0	.000	-1	7	6	-1	0.5
1963	LA-A	0	0	—	13	0	0	0	1	16¹	20	1	6	7	16.0	5.51	62	.313	.397	0	.000	-0	-3	-4	-0	-0.3
Total 12		67	47	.588	443	61	18	7	64	1023¹	1040	95	300	364	12.1	3.61	106	.270	.329	46	.186	2	32	26	17	5.1

■ GENE MORIARITY
Moriarity, Eugene John b: Holyoke, Mass. BL/TL, 5'8", 130 lbs. Deb: 6/18/1884 ♦

YEAR	TM/L	W	L	PCT	G	GS	CG	SH	SV	IP	H	HR	BB	SO	RAT	ERA	ERA+	OAV	OOB	BH	AVG	PB	PR	/A	PD	TPI
1884	Ind-a	0	2	.000	2	2	2	0	0	13²	16	0	7	4	15.1	5.27	62	.277	.355	8	.216	0	-3	-3	1	-0.2
1885	Det-N	0	0	—	1	0	0	0	0	2	3	0	1	1	18.0	9.00	32	.331	.398	1	.026	-0	-1	-1	-0	0.0
Total 2		0	2	.000	3	2	2	0	0	15²	19	0	8	5	15.5	5.74	56	.284	.361	41	.152	-0	-4	-4	0	-0.2

■ JOHN MORLAN
Morlan, John Glen b: 11/22/47, Columbus, Ohio BR/TR, 6', 178 lbs. Deb: 7/20/73

YEAR	TM/L	W	L	PCT	G	GS	CG	SH	SV	IP	H	HR	BB	SO	RAT	ERA	ERA+	OAV	OOB	BH	AVG	PB	PR	/A	PD	TPI
1973	Pit-N	2	2	.500	10	7	1	0	0	41	42	4	23	23	14.3	3.95	89	.276	.371	2	.182	1	-1	-2	-1	-0.1
1974	Pit-N	0	3	.000	39	0	0	0	0	65	54	2	48	38	14.5	4.29	80	.227	.363	0	.000	-1	-5	-6	-1	-0.7
Total 2		2	5	.286	49	7	1	0	0	106	96	6	71	61	14.4	4.16	83	.246	.366	2	.111	0	-6	-8	-1	-0.8

■ DAN MOROGIELLO
Morogiello, Daniel Joseph b: 3/26/55, Brooklyn, N.Y. BL/TL, 6'1", 200 lbs. Deb: 5/20/83

YEAR	TM/L	W	L	PCT	G	GS	CG	SH	SV	IP	H	HR	BB	SO	RAT	ERA	ERA+	OAV	OOB	BH	AVG	PB	PR	/A	PD	TPI
1983	Bal-A	0	1	.000	22	0	0	0	1	37²	39	1	10	15	11.9	2.39	165	.265	.316	0	—	0	7	7	-1	0.6

■ JIM MORONEY
Moroney, James Francis b: 12/4/1885, Boston, Mass. d: 2/26/29, Philadelphia, Pa. BL/TL, 6'1", 175 lbs. Deb: 4/24/06

YEAR	TM/L	W	L	PCT	G	GS	CG	SH	SV	IP	H	HR	BB	SO	RAT	ERA	ERA+	OAV	OOB	BH	AVG	PB	PR	/A	PD	TPI
1906	Bos-N	0	3	.000	3	3	3	0	0	27	28	1	12	11	15.3	5.33	50	.259	.365	1	.100	-1	-8	-8	0	-0.7
1910	Phi-N	1	2	.333	12	2	1	0	1	42	43	1	11	13	12.4	2.14	146	.295	.360	0	.000	-1	4	5	-0	0.3
1912	Chi-N	1	1	.500	10	3	1	0	1	23²	25	0	17	5	17.5	4.56	73	.294	.434	3	.500	1	-3	-3	0	-0.1
Total 3		2	6	.250	25	8	5	0	2	92²	96	2	40	29	14.6	3.69	83	.283	.382	4	.154	-1	-7	-7	-0	-0.5

■ BILL MORRELL
Morrell, Willard Blackmer b: 4/9/1900, Boston, Mass. d: 8/5/75, Brimingham, Ala. BR/TR, 6', 172 lbs. Deb: 4/20/26

YEAR	TM/L	W	L	PCT	G	GS	CG	SH	SV	IP	H	HR	BB	SO	RAT	ERA	ERA+	OAV	OOB	BH	AVG	PB	PR	/A	PD	TPI
1926	Was-A	3	3	.500	26	2	1	0	1	69²	83	5	29	16	14.7	5.30	73	.311	.383	4	.235	1	-10	-11	-1	-1.0
1930	NY-N	0	0	—	2	0	0	0	0	8	6	0	1	3	7.9	1.13	421	.214	.241	0	.000	-0	3	3	0	0.3
1931	NY-N	5	3	.625	20	7	2	0	1	66	66	4	27	16	15.0	4.36	85	.306	.369	2	.111	-0	-4	-5	-0	-0.4
Total 3		8	6	.571	48	9	3	0	2	143²	172	9	57	35	14.5	4.64	83	.304	.370	6	.162	0	-10	-13	-1	-1.1

■ JOHN MORRILL
Morrill, John Francis "Honest John" b: 2/19/1855, Boston, Mass. d: 4/2/32, Boston, Mass. BR/TR, 5'10.5", 155 lbs. Deb: 4/24/1876 M♦

YEAR	TM/L	W	L	PCT	G	GS	CG	SH	SV	IP	H	HR	BB	SO	RAT	ERA	ERA+	OAV	OOB	BH	AVG	PB	PR	/A	PD	TPI
1880	Bos-N	0	0	—	3	0	0	0	0	10²	9	0	1	0	8.4	0.84	269	.217	.236	81	.237	0	2	2	0	0.2
1881	Bos-N	0	1	.000	3	0	0	0	1	5²	9	0	1	0	15.9	7.94	33	.345	.369	90	.289	1	-3	-3	-0	-0.2
1882	Bos-N	0	0	—	1	0	0	0	0	2	3	0	0	2	13.5	0.00	—	.328	.328	101	.289	0	1	1	0	0.1
1883	Bos-N	1	0	1.000	2	1	1	0	0	13	15	0	4	5	13.2	2.77	112	.273	.322	129	.319	1	1	0	-0	0.0
1884	Bos-N	0	1	.000	7	1	1	0	2	23	34	0	6	13	15.7	7.43	39	.326	.362	114	.260	1	-11	-12	0	-0.9
1886	Bos-N	0	0	—	1	0	0	0	0	4	5	0	0	2	11.3	0.00	—	.294	.294	106	.247	0	1	1	0	0.1
1889	Was-N	0	0	—	1	0	0	0	0	0¹	1	0	0	0	0.0	0.00	—	.000	.000	27	.185	0	0	0	0	0.0
Total 7		1	2	.333	18	2	2	0	3	58²	75	0	12	22	13.3	4.45	63	.295	.327	1275	.260	4	-10	-11	0	-0.7

■ DANNY MORRIS
Morris, Danny Walker b: 6/11/46, Greenville, Ky. BR/TR, 6'1", 200 lbs. Deb: 9/10/68

YEAR	TM/L	W	L	PCT	G	GS	CG	SH	SV	IP	H	HR	BB	SO	RAT	ERA	ERA+	OAV	OOB	BH	AVG	PB	PR	/A	PD	TPI
1968	Min-A	0	1	.000	3	2	0	0	0	10²	11	0	4	6	12.7	1.69	183	.262	.326	0	.000	-0	2	2	0	0.2
1969	Min-A	0	1	.000	3	1	0	0	0	5¹	5	1	4	1	15.2	5.06	72	.238	.360	0	—	0	-1	-1	0	0.0
Total 2		0	2	.000	6	3	0	0	0	16	16	1	8	7	13.5	2.81	117	.254	.338	0	.000	-0	1	1	0	0.2

■ E. MORRIS
Morris, E. b: Trenton, N.J. Deb: 9/11/1884 ♦

YEAR	TM/L	W	L	PCT	G	GS	CG	SH	SV	IP	H	HR	BB	SO	RAT	ERA	ERA+	OAV	OOB	BH	AVG	PB	PR	/A	PD	TPI
1884	Bal-U	0	0	—	1	0	0	0	0	1	2	0	2	0	36.0	9.00	37	.391	.562	0	.000	-1	-1	-1	-0	0.0

■ ED MORRIS
Morris, Edward "Cannonball" b: 9/29/1862, Brooklyn, N.Y. d: 4/12/37, Pittsburgh, Pa. BR/TL, 165 lbs. Deb: 5/01/1884

YEAR	TM/L	W	L	PCT	G	GS	CG	SH	SV	IP	H	HR	BB	SO	RAT	ERA	ERA+	OAV	OOB	BH	AVG	PB	PR	/A	PD	TPI
1884	Col-a	34	13	**.723**	52	52	47	3	0	429²	335	3	51	302	8.1	2.18	139	**.203**	.227	37	.186	1	51	41	1	3.9
1885	Pit-a	39	24	.619	**63**	**63**	**63**	**7**	0	581	459	5	101	**298**	**8.7**	2.35	137	**.208**	**.242**	44	.186	-5	58	56	-1	4.6
1886	Pit-a	41	20	.672	64	63	63	**12**	**1**	555¹	455	5	118	326	**9.3**	2.45	139	.213	**.254**	38	.167	-7	62	58	-2	4.4
1887	Pit-N	14	22	.389	38	38	37	1	0	317²	375	13	71	91	12.6	4.31	90	.286	.322	25	.198	-4	-9	-16	-2	-1.8

YEAR	TM/L	W	L	PCT	G	GS	CG	SH	SV	IP	H	HR	BB	SO	RAT	ERA	ERA+	OAV	OOB	BH	AVG	PB	PR	/A	PD	TPI
1888	Pit-N	29	23	.558	**55**	55	**54**	5	0	480	470	7	74	135	10.2	2.31	115	.247	.275	19	.101	-10	28	18	1	0.7
1889	Pit-N	6	13	.316	21	21	18	0	0	170	196	4	48	40	12.9	4.13	91	.280	.326	7	.097	-5	-2	-7	-2	-1.1
1890	Pit-P	8	7	.533	18	15	15	1	0	144¹	178	5	35	25	13.3	4.86	80	.290	.329	9	.143	-3	-10	-15	-2	-1.6
Total 7		171	122	.584	311	307	297	29	1	2678	2468	42	498	1217	10.0	2.82	116	.235	.269	179	.161	-33	178	135	-7	9.1

■ JACK MORRIS
Morris, John Scott b: 5/16/55, St.Paul, Minn.   BR/TR, 6'3", 195 lbs.   Deb: 7/26/77

YEAR	TM/L	W	L	PCT	G	GS	CG	SH	SV	IP	H	HR	BB	SO	RAT	ERA	ERA+	OAV	OOB	BH	AVG	PB	PR	/A	PD	TPI
1977	Det-A	1	1	.500	7	6	1	0	0	45²	38	4	23	28	12.0	3.74	114	.235	.330	0	—	0	2	3	0	0.3
1978	Det-A	3	5	.375	28	7	0	0	0	106	107	8	49	48	13.5	4.33	89	.268	.352	0	—	0	-7	-5	-0	-0.5
1979	Det-A	17	7	.708	27	27	9	1	0	197²	179	19	59	113	11.0	3.28	132	.244	.304	0	—	0	21	23	-1	2.3
1980	Det-A	16	15	.516	36	36	11	2	0	250	252	20	87	112	12.3	4.18	98	.262	.326	0	—	0	-4	-2	3	0.1
1981	Det-A	**14**	7	.667	25	25	15	1	0	198	153	14	78	97	10.6	3.05	124	.218	.298	0	—	0	13	16	-0	1.7
1982	Det-A	17	16	.515	37	37	17	3	0	266¹	247	37	96	135	11.6	4.06	100	.247	.312	0	—	0	1	0	-0	0.0
1983	Det-A	20	13	.606	37	37	20	1	0	**293²**	257	30	83	**232**	10.5	3.34	117	.233	.289	0	—	0	24	19	-1	1.7
1984	*Det-A	19	11	.633	35	35	9	1	0	240¹	221	20	87	148	11.6	3.60	109	.241	.308	0	—	0	11	9	2	1.0
1985	Det-A	16	11	.593	35	35	13	4	0	257	212	21	110	191	11.5	3.33	122	.225	.309	0	—	0	23	21	-1	2.0
1986	Det-A	21	8	.724	35	35	15	**6**	0	267	229	40	82	223	10.5	3.27	126	.229	.287	0	—	0	27	25	-1	2.5
1987	*Det-A	18	11	.621	34	34	13	0	0	266	227	39	93	208	10.9	3.38	125	.228	.294	0	.000	0	32	25	-2	2.2
1988	Det-A	15	13	.536	34	34	10	2	0	235	225	20	83	168	11.9	3.94	97	.251	.318	0	—	0	1	-3	-0	-1.8
1989	Det-A	6	14	.300	24	24	10	0	0	170¹	189	23	59	115	13.2	4.86	79	.283	.342	0	—	0	-19	-20	0	-1.8
1990	Det-A	15	18	.455	36	36	**11**	3	0	249²	231	26	97	162	12.0	4.51	87	.242	.316	0	—	0	-17	-16	-1	-1.6
Total 14		198	150	.569	430	408	154	24	0	3042²	2767	321	1086	1980	11.5	3.73	107	.242	.310	0	.000	0	107	95	-4	9.6

■ JOHN MORRIS
Morris, John Wallace b: 8/23/41, Lewes, Del.   BR/TL, 6'2", 195 lbs.   Deb: 7/19/66

YEAR	TM/L	W	L	PCT	G	GS	CG	SH	SV	IP	H	HR	BB	SO	RAT	ERA	ERA+	OAV	OOB	BH	AVG	PB	PR	/A	PD	TPI
1966	Phi-N	1	1	.500	13	0	0	0	0	13²	15	2	3	8	12.5	5.27	68	.278	.328	0	—	0	-3	-3	0	-0.1
1968	Bal-A	2	0	1.000	19	0	0	0	0	31²	19	4	17	22	11.4	2.56	114	.173	.305	0	.000	-1	1	1	0	0.1
1969	Sea-A	0	0	—	6	0	0	0	0	12²	16	2	8	8	17.1	6.39	57	.308	.400	1	1.000	1	-4	-4	1	-0.1
1970	Mil-A	4	3	.571	20	9	2	0	0	73¹	70	4	22	40	11.5	3.93	96	.253	.312	3	.176	0	-2	-1	1	0.0
1971	Mil-A	2	2	.500	43	1	0	0	1	67²	69	4	27	42	12.6	3.72	93	.270	.342	1	.200	0	-2	-2	1	0.0
1972	SF-N	0	0	—	7	0	0	0	0	6¹	9	2	2	5	15.6	4.26	82	.310	.355	0	—	0	-1	-1	0	0.0
1973	SF-N	1	0	1.000	7	0	0	0	0	6¹	12	0	3	3	21.3	8.53	45	.429	.484	0	.000	-0	-3	-3	0	-0.2
1974	SF-N	1	1	.500	17	0	0	1	0	20¹	17	1	4	9	9.1	3.05	125	.215	.253	1	1.000	1	1	2	-1	0.2
Total 8		11	7	.611	132	10	2	0	2	232¹	227	19	86	137	12.4	3.95	90	.256	.328	6	.194	1	-11	-10	3	-0.1

■ BUGS MORRIS
Morris, Joseph Harley (a.k.a. Joseph Harley Bennett In 1918)
b: 4/19/1892, Kansas City, Mo.   d: 11/21/57, Noel, Mo.   BR/TR, 5'9.5", 163 lbs.   Deb: 7/20/18

YEAR	TM/L	W	L	PCT	G	GS	CG	SH	SV	IP	H	HR	BB	SO	RAT	ERA	ERA+	OAV	OOB	BH	AVG	PB	PR	/A	PD	TPI
1918	StL-A	0	2	.000	4	2	0	0	0	10¹	12	1	7	0	16.5	3.48	79	.308	.413	1	.250	0	-1	-1	0	0.0
1921	Chi-A	0	3	.000	3	2	1	0	0	17²	19	1	16	2	17.8	6.11	69	.297	.438	2	.333	0	-4	-4	1	-0.2
	StL-A	0	0	—	3	1	0	0	0	5²	11	1	6	3	30.2	14.29	31	.407	.543	1	1.000	0	-6	-6	-0	-0.4
	Yr	0	3	.000	6	3	1	0	0	23¹	30	2	22	5	20.8	8.10	53	.330	.470	0	.000	1	-10	-10	0	-0.6
Total 2		0	5	.000	10	5	1	0	0	33²	42	3	29	5	19.5	6.68	57	.323	.453	4	.364	1	-11	-11	1	-0.6

■ ED MORRIS
Morris, Walter Edward "Big Ed" b: 12/7/1899, Foshee, Ala.   d: 3/3/32, Century, Fla.   BR/TR, 6'2", 185 lbs.   Deb: 8/05/22

YEAR	TM/L	W	L	PCT	G	GS	CG	SH	SV	IP	H	HR	BB	SO	RAT	ERA	ERA+	OAV	OOB	BH	AVG	PB	PR	/A	PD	TPI
1922	Chi-N	0	0	—	5	0	0	0	0	12	22	1	6	5	21.0	8.25	51	.386	.444	1	.250	-0	-6	-5	-0	-0.4
1928	Bos-A	19	15	.559	47	29	20	0	5	257²	255	7	80	104	11.9	3.53	117	.264	.323	14	.154	-4	15	17	-2	1.1
1929	Bos-A	14	14	.500	33	26	17	2	1	208¹	227	7	95	73	14.0	4.45	96	.282	.360	16	.232	2	-5	-4	-2	-0.3
1930	Bos-A	4	9	.308	18	9	3	0	0	65¹	67	1	38	28	14.5	4.13	112	.260	.355	6	.316	2	4	3	-1	0.4
1931	Bos-A	5	7	.417	37	14	3	0	0	130²	131	4	74	46	14.5	4.75	91	.260	.361	6	.158	-2	-5	-6	0	-0.6
Total 5		42	45	.483	140	78	43	2	6	674	702	20	293	256	13.4	4.19	101	.271	.348	43	.195	-1	3	4	-4	0.2

■ BILL MORRISETTE
Morrisette, William Lee b: 1/17/1893, Baltimore, Md.   d: 3/25/66, Virginia Beach, Va   BR/TR, 6', 176 lbs.   Deb: 9/19/15

YEAR	TM/L	W	L	PCT	G	GS	CG	SH	SV	IP	H	HR	BB	SO	RAT	ERA	ERA+	OAV	OOB	BH	AVG	PB	PR	/A	PD	TPI
1915	Phi-A	2	0	1.000	4	1	0	0	0	20	15	0	5	11	9.0	1.35	218	.195	.244	2	.286	0	4	4	0	0.4
1916	Phi-A	0	0	—	1	0	0	0	0	4	6	0	5	2	24.8	6.75	43	.429	.579	0	.000	0	-2	-2	1	0.0
1920	Det-A	1	1	.500	8	3	1	0	0	27	25	0	19	15	15.7	4.33	86	.245	.379	0	.000	-1	-2	-2	-0	-0.2
Total 3		3	1	.750	13	4	2	0	0	51	46	0	29	28	13.8	3.35	100	.238	.347	2	.125	-1	0	0	0	0.2

■ JIM MORRISON
Morrison, James Forrest b: 9/23/52, Pensacola, Fla.   BR/TR, 5'11", 175 lbs.   Deb: 9/18/77 ♦

YEAR	TM/L	W	L	PCT	G	GS	CG	SH	SV	IP	H	HR	BB	SO	RAT	ERA	ERA+	OAV	OOB	BH	AVG	PB	PR	/A	PD	TPI
1988	Atl-N	0	0	—	3	0	0	0	0	3²	3	0	2	1	12.3	0.00	—	.214	.313	14	.152	0	1	1	-0	0.2

■ JOHNNY MORRISON
Morrison, John Dewey "Jughandle Johnny" b: 10/22/1895, Pellville, Ky.   d: 3/20/66, Louisville, Ky.   BR/TR, 5'11", 188 lbs.   Deb: 9/28/20

YEAR	TM/L	W	L	PCT	G	GS	CG	SH	SV	IP	H	HR	BB	SO	RAT	ERA	ERA+	OAV	OOB	BH	AVG	PB	PR	/A	PD	TPI
1920	Pit-N	1	0	1.000	2	1	1	0	0	7	4	0	1	3	6.4	0.00	—	.167	.200	0	.000	-0	2	3	0	0.2
1921	Pit-N	9	7	.563	21	17	11	**3**	0	144	131	3	33	52	10.3	2.88	133	.258	.305	5	.119	-1	15	15	0	1.4
1922	Pit-N	17	11	.607	45	33	20	**5**	1	286¹	315	10	87	104	12.8	3.43	119	.286	.341	20	.198	-2	21	21	0	1.7
1923	Pit-N	25	13	.658	42	37	27	2	2	301²	287	6	110	114	12.0	3.49	115	.253	.307	21	.183	-3	17	17	-1	1.3
1924	Pit-N	11	16	.407	**41**	25	10	0	2	237²	213	7	73	85	11.0	3.75	102	.245	.307	13	.169	-2	3	2	-3	-0.2
1925	*Pit-N	17	14	.548	**44**	26	10	0	**4**	211	245	12	60	60	13.3	3.88	115	.291	.343	13	.178	-2	9	14	-2	0.9
1926	Pit-N	6	8	.429	26	13	6	2	2	122¹	119	2	44	39	12.1	3.38	116	.267	.335	3	.077	-4	6	7	-2	0.2
1927	Pit-N	3	2	.600	21	2	1	0	3	53²	63	2	21	21	14.1	4.19	98	.304	.368	2	.154	-0	-2	-0	-1	-0.1
1929	Bro-N	13	7	.650	39	10	4	0	**8**	136²	150	11	61	57	14.1	4.48	103	.279	.355	7	.163	-2	4	2	-3	-0.2
1930	Bro-N	1	2	.333	16	0	0	0	0	34²	47	4	16	11	16.4	5.45	90	.346	.414	0	.000	-0	-2	-2	-0	-0.2
Total 10		103	80	.563	297	164	90	13	23	1535	1574	57	506	546	12.4	3.65	113	.271	.332	84	.164	-19	74	79	-11	5.0

■ MIKE MORRISON
Morrison, Michael b: 2/6/1867, Erie, Pa.   d: 6/16/55, Erie, Pa.   BR/TR, 5'8.5", 156 lbs.   Deb: 4/19/1887

YEAR	TM/L	W	L	PCT	G	GS	CG	SH	SV	IP	H	HR	BB	SO	RAT	ERA	ERA+	OAV	OOB	BH	AVG	PB	PR	/A	PD	TPI
1887	Cle-a	12	25	.324	40	40	35	0	0	316²	385	13	205	158	16.8	4.92	89	.289	.384	27	.191	-4	-22	-20	9	-1.1
1888	Cle-a	1	3	.250	4	4	4	0	0	35	40	3	19	14	15.2	5.40	58	.277	.361	4	.235	-0	-9	-9	0	-0.7
1890	Syr-a	6	9	.400	17	14	13	1	0	127	131	4	81	69	15.0	5.88	61	.258	.360	29	.242	3	-28	-33	2	-2.6
	Bal-a	1	2	.333	4	4	3	0	0	26	15	0	20	13	12.1	3.81	107	.163	.312	1	.111	-1	0	1	1	0.1
	Yr	7	11	.389	21	18	16	1	0	153	146	4	101	82	14.5	5.53	66	.244	.353	6	.047	2	-28	-32	2	-2.5
Total 3		20	39	.339	65	62	55	1	0	504²	571	20	325	254	16.0	5.14	79	.275	.373	61	.213	-2	-59	-61	11	-4.3

■ PHIL MORRISON
Morrison, Philip Melvin b: 10/18/1894, Rockport, Ind.   d: 1/18/55, Lexington, Ky.   BB/TR, 6'2", 190 lbs.   Deb: 9/30/21

YEAR	TM/L	W	L	PCT	G	GS	CG	SH	SV	IP	H	HR	BB	SO	RAT	ERA	ERA+	OAV	OOB	BH	AVG	PB	PR	/A	PD	TPI
1921	Pit-N	0	0	—	1	0	0	0	0	0²	1	0	0	1	13.5	0.00	—	.333	.333	0	—	0	0	0	0	0.0

■ HANK MORRISON
Morrison, Stephen Henry b: 5/22/1866, Olneyville, R.I.   d: 9/30/27, Attleboro, Mass.   BR/TR, 5'10", 180 lbs.   Deb: 5/28/1887

YEAR	TM/L	W	L	PCT	G	GS	CG	SH	SV	IP	H	HR	BB	SO	RAT	ERA	ERA+	OAV	OOB	BH	AVG	PB	PR	/A	PD	TPI
1887	Ind-N	3	4	.429	7	7	5	0	0	57	79	2	27	13	16.7	7.58	54	.320	.387	3	.115	-2	-22	-22	-1	-1.8

■ GUY MORRISON
Morrison, Walter Guy b: 8/29/1895, Hinton, W.Va.   d: 8/14/34, Grand Rapids, Mich   BR/TR, 5'11", 185 lbs.   Deb: 8/31/27

YEAR	TM/L	W	L	PCT	G	GS	CG	SH	SV	IP	H	HR	BB	SO	RAT	ERA	ERA+	OAV	OOB	BH	AVG	PB	PR	/A	PD	TPI
1927	Bos-N	1	2	.333	11	3	1	0	0	34¹	40	1	15	6	14.4	4.46	83	.296	.367	1	.125	1	-2	-3	1	0.0
1928	Bos-N	0	0	—	1	0	0	0	0	3	4	1	3	0	21.0	12.00	33	.308	.438	0	—	0	-3	-3	0	-0.1
Total 2		1	2	.333	12	3	1	0	0	37¹	44	2	18	6	14.9	5.06	74	.297	.373	1	.125	1	-5	-6	1	-0.1

■ FRANK MORRISSEY
Morrissey, Michael Joseph "Deacon" b: 5/5/1876, Baltimore, Md.   d: 2/22/39, Baltimore, Md.   TR, 5'4", 140 lbs.   Deb: 7/13/01

YEAR	TM/L	W	L	PCT	G	GS	CG	SH	SV	IP	H	HR	BB	SO	RAT	ERA	ERA+	OAV	OOB	BH	AVG	PB	PR	/A	PD	TPI
1901	Bos-A	0	0	—	1	0	0	0	0	4¹	5	0	2	1	14.5	2.08	170	.286	.359	0	.000	-1	1	1	0	0.0
1902	Chi-N	1	3	.250	5	5	5	0	0	40	40	0	8	13	10.8	2.25	120	.260	.297	2	.091	-1	2	2	0	0.1
Total 2		1	3	.250	6	5	5	0	0	44¹	45	0	10	14	11.2	2.23	125	.263	.304	2	.080	-1	3	3	0	0.1

■ CARL MORTON　Morton, Carl Wendle　b: 1/18/44, Kansas City, Mo.　d: 4/12/83, Tulsa, Okla.　BR/TR, 6', 200 lbs.　Deb: 4/11/69

YEAR TM/L	W	L	PCT	G	GS	CG	SH	SV	IP	H	HR	BB	SO	RAT	ERA	ERA+	OAV	OOB	BH	AVG	PB	PR	/A	PD	TPI
1969 Mon-N	0	3	.000	8	5	0	0	0	29¹	29	2	18	16	15.0	4.60	80	.264	.377	0	.000	-0	-3	-3	1	-0.2
1970 Mon-N	18	11	.621	43	37	10	4	0	284²	281	27	125	154	13.0	3.60	114	.262	.341	15	.161	2	14	16	1	2.0
1971 Mon-N	10	18	.357	36	35	9	0	1	213²	252	22	83	84	14.3	4.80	73	.295	.360	14	.182	2	-32	-30	3	-2.5
1972 Mon-N	7	13	.350	27	27	3	1	0	172	170	16	53	51	11.8	3.92	90	.258	.316	7	.135	1	-9	-7	2	-0.4
1973 Atl-N	15	10	.600	38	37	10	4	0	256¹	254	18	70	112	11.5	3.41	115	.259	.311	17	.181	4	7	15	0	2.2
1974 Atl-N	16	12	.571	38	38	7	1	0	274²	293	10	89	113	12.6	3.15	120	.277	.334	10	.112	-4	14	19	-0	1.7
1975 Atl-N	17	16	.515	39	39	11	2	0	277²	302	19	82	78	12.5	3.50	108	.278	.330	15	.160	-1	4	8	1	1.0
1976 Atl-N	4	9	.308	26	24	1	1	0	140¹	172	6	45	42	14.2	4.17	91	.306	.362	8	.178	-0	-10	-6	2	-0.2
Total 8	87	92	.486	255	242	51	13	1	1648²	1753	120	565	650	12.8	3.73	102	.275	.336	86	.156	4	-15	13	10	3.6

■ CHARLIE MORTON　Morton, Charles Hazen　b: 10/12/1854, Kingsville, Ohio　d: 12/9/21, Massillon, Ohio　TR,　Deb: 5/02/1882　MU♦

YEAR TM/L	W	L	PCT	G	GS	CG	SH	SV	IP	H	HR	BB	SO	RAT	ERA	ERA+	OAV	OOB	BH	AVG	PB	PR	/A	PD	TPI
1884 Tol-a	0	1	.000	3	1	1	0	0	23¹	18	0	5	7	8.9	3.09	111	.201	.244	18	.162	-0	0	1	-1	0.1

■ GUY MORTON　Morton, Guy Sr. "The Alabama Blossom"　b: 6/1/1893, Vernon, Ala.　d: 10/18/34, Sheffield, Ala.　BR/TR, 6'1", 175 lbs.　Deb: 6/20/14

YEAR TM/L	W	L	PCT	G	GS	CG	SH	SV	IP	H	HR	BB	SO	RAT	ERA	ERA+	OAV	OOB	BH	AVG	PB	PR	/A	PD	TPI
1914 Cle-A	1	13	.071	25	13	5	0	1	128	116	1	55	80	12.2	3.02	95	.257	.341	1	.029	-4	-4	-2	-2	-0.7
1915 Cle-A	16	15	.516	34	27	15	6	1	240	189	5	60	134	9.4	2.14	143	.216	.268	12	.146	-4	21	24	-1	2.0
1916 Cle-A	12	8	.600	27	18	9	0	0	149²	139	1	42	88	11.1	2.89	104	.246	.302	12	.211	-1	-1	2	-1	0.0
1917 Cle-A	10	10	.500	35	18	6	1	2	161	158	3	59	62	12.2	2.74	104	.266	.335	4	.085	-5	-1	2	-2	-0.4
1918 Cle-A	14	8	.636	30	28	13	1	0	214²	189	1	77	123	11.3	2.64	114	.240	.310	12	.156	-2	3	9	-2	0.6
1919 Cle-A	9	9	.500	26	20	9	3	0	147¹	128	3	47	64	10.7	2.81	119	.233	.293	9	.161	-2	7	9	-1	0.6
1920 Cle-A	8	6	.571	29	17	6	1	1	137	140	2	57	72	13.0	4.47	85	.270	.344	10	.217	-1	-10	-10	-3	-1.2
1921 Cle-A	8	3	.727	30	7	3	2	0	107²	98	1	32	45	11.0	2.76	155	.244	.303	6	.171	-2	18	18	-2	1.4
1922 Cle-A	14	9	.609	38	23	13	3	0	202²	218	7	85	102	13.6	4.00	100	.277	.351	13	.191	-2	1	0	3	0.1
1923 Cle-A	6	6	.500	33	14	3	2	1	129¹	133	3	56	54	13.3	4.24	93	.276	.354	7	.159	-2	-4	-4	-1	-0.6
1924 Cle-A	0	1	.000	10	0	0	0	0	12¹	12	0	13	6	18.2	6.57	65	.250	.410	0	.000	-0	-3	-3	-0	-0.2
Total 11	98	88	.527	317	185	82	19	6	1629²	1520	27	583	830	11.7	3.13	108	.251	.319	86	.157	-24	27	48	-11	1.6

■ SPARROW MORTON　Morton, William P.　TL,　Deb: 7/15/1884

YEAR TM/L	W	L	PCT	G	GS	CG	SH	SV	IP	H	HR	BB	SO	RAT	ERA	ERA+	OAV	OOB	BH	AVG	PB	PR	/A	PD	TPI
1884 Phi-N	0	2	.000	2	2	2	0	0	17	16	0	11	5	14.3	5.29	56	.235	.342	3	.375	1	-4	-4	-0	-0.2

■ EARL MOSELEY　Moseley, Earl Victor "Vic"　b: 9/7/1884, Middleburg, Ohio　d: 7/1/63, Alliance, Ohio　BR/TR, 5'9.5", 168 lbs.　Deb: 6/17/13

YEAR TM/L	W	L	PCT	G	GS	CG	SH	SV	IP	H	HR	BB	SO	RAT	ERA	ERA+	OAV	OOB	BH	AVG	PB	PR	/A	PD	TPI
1913 Bos-A	8	5	.615	24	15	7	3	0	120²	105	1	49	62	11.5	3.13	94	.245	.322	3	.081	-2	-3	-3	1	-0.3
1914 Ind-F	19	18	.514	43	38	29	4	1	316²	303	5	123	205	12.2	3.47	100	.258	.302	12	.110	-7	-9	-0	-1	-0.7
1915 New-F	15	15	.500	38	32	22	5	1	268	222	2	99	142	10.8	**1.91**	149	.229	.302	13	.148	-2	33	28	-4	2.3
1916 Cin-N	7	10	.412	31	15	7	0	1	150¹	145	5	69	60	12.8	3.89	67	.257	.338	4	.087	-2	-21	-22	-2	-2.7
Total 4	49	48	.505	136	100	65	12	3	855²	775	13	340	469	11.8	3.01	101	.247	.322	32	.114	-13	0	3	-6	-1.4

■ WALTER MOSER　Moser, Walter Fredrick　b: 2/27/1881, Concord, N.C.　d: 12/10/46, Philadelphia, Pa.　BR/TR, 5'9", 170 lbs.　Deb: 9/03/06

YEAR TM/L	W	L	PCT	G	GS	CG	SH	SV	IP	H	HR	BB	SO	RAT	ERA	ERA+	OAV	OOB	BH	AVG	PB	PR	/A	PD	TPI
1906 Phi-N	0	4	.000	6	4	4	0	0	42²	49	0	15	17	13.7	3.59	73	.295	.357	0	.000	-2	-5	-5	-1	-0.6
1911 Bos-A	0	1	.000	6	3	1	0	0	24²	37	0	11	11	17.9	4.01	82	.366	.434	0	.000	-1	-2	-2	0	-0.2
StL-A	0	2	.000	2	2	0	0	0	3¹	11	0	4	2	40.5	21.60	16	.478	.556	1	1.000	0	-7	-7	0	-0.4
Yr	0	3	.000	8	5	1	0	0	28	48	0	15	13	20.3	6.11	54	.384	.450	0	.000	-1	-9	-9	0	-0.6
Total 2	0	7	.000	14	9	5	0	0	70²	97	0	30	30	16.4	4.58	63	.334	.401	1	.045	-2	-13	-13	-1	-1.2

■ JOHN MOSES　Moses, John William　b: 8/9/57, Los Angeles, Cal.　BB/TL, 5'10", 165 lbs.　Deb: 8/23/82　♦

YEAR TM/L	W	L	PCT	G	GS	CG	SH	SV	IP	H	HR	BB	SO	RAT	ERA	ERA+	OAV	OOB	BH	AVG	PB	PR	/A	PD	TPI
1989 Min-A	0	0	—	1	0	0	0	0	1	0	0	1	0	9.0	0.00	—	.000	.333	68	.281	1	0	0	0	0.0
1990 Min-A	0	0	—	2	0	0	0	0	2	5	0	2	0	31.5	13.50	31	.455	.538	38	.221	1	-2	-2	0	-0.1
Total 2	0	0	—	3	0	0	0	0	3	5	0	3	0	24.0	9.00	46	.385	.500	434	.258	1	-2	-2	0	-0.1

■ PAUL MOSKAU　Moskau, Paul Richard　b: 12/20/53, St.Joseph, Mo.　BR/TR, 6'2", 200 lbs.　Deb: 6/21/77

YEAR TM/L	W	L	PCT	G	GS	CG	SH	SV	IP	H	HR	BB	SO	RAT	ERA	ERA+	OAV	OOB	BH	AVG	PB	PR	/A	PD	TPI
1977 Cin-N	6	6	.500	20	19	2	2	0	108	116	10	40	71	13.1	4.00	98	.278	.342	7	.184	2	-1	-1	1	0.2
1978 Cin-N	6	4	.600	26	25	2	1	1	145	139	17	57	88	12.4	3.97	89	.255	.329	10	.204	3	-6	-7	-2	-0.5
1979 Cin-N	5	4	.556	21	15	1	0	0	106¹	107	9	51	58	13.4	3.89	96	.263	.345	3	.081	-2	-2	-2	1	-0.2
1980 Cin-N	9	7	.563	33	19	2	1	2	152²	147	13	41	94	11.1	4.01	89	.257	.308	7	.159	-0	-7	-7	0	-0.7
1981 Cin-N	2	1	.667	27	1	0	0	2	54²	54	4	32	32	14.3	4.94	72	.258	.360	0	.000	-0	-9	-8	1	-0.8
1982 Pit-N	1	3	.250	13	5	0	0	0	35	43	7	8	15	13.1	4.37	85	.303	.340	1	.091	-1	-3	-3	-0	-0.3
1983 Chi-N	3	2	.600	8	8	0	0	0	32	44	7	14	16	16.3	6.75	56	.331	.395	2	.182	0	-11	-11	0	-0.9
Total 7	32	27	.542	148	92	7	4	5	633²	650	67	243	374	12.8	4.22	87	.268	.336	30	.153	2	-39	-39	-0	-3.2

■ JIM MOSOLF　Mosolf, James Frederick　b: 8/21/05, Puyallup, Wash.　d: 12/28/79, Dallasyore.　BL/TR, 5'10", 186 lbs.　Deb: 9/09/29　♦

YEAR TM/L	W	L	PCT	G	GS	CG	SH	SV	IP	H	HR	BB	SO	RAT	ERA	ERA+	OAV	OOB	BH	AVG	PB	PR	/A	PD	TPI
1930 Pit-N	0	0	—	1	0	0	0	0	0¹	1	0	0	1	27.0	27.00	18	.500	.500	17	.333	0	-1	-1	0	0.0

■ MAL MOSS　Moss, Charles Malcolm　b: 4/18/05, Sullivan, Ind.　d: 2/5/83, Savannah, Ga.　BR/TL, 6', 175 lbs.　Deb: 4/29/30

YEAR TM/L	W	L	PCT	G	GS	CG	SH	SV	IP	H	HR	BB	SO	RAT	ERA	ERA+	OAV	OOB	BH	AVG	PB	PR	/A	PD	TPI
1930 Chi-N	0	0	—	12	1	0	0	1	18²	18	0	14	4	15.4	6.27	78	.254	.376	3	.273	0	-3	-3	0	-0.1

■ RAY MOSS　Moss, Raymond Earl　b: 12/5/01, Chattanooga, Tenn.　BR/TR, 6'1", 185 lbs.　Deb: 4/17/26

YEAR TM/L	W	L	PCT	G	GS	CG	SH	SV	IP	H	HR	BB	SO	RAT	ERA	ERA+	OAV	OOB	BH	AVG	PB	PR	/A	PD	TPI
1926 Bro-N	0	0	—	1	0	0	0	0	1	3	0	0	0	27.0	9.00	42	.600	.600	0	.000	-0	-1	-1	0	0.0
1927 Bro-N	1	0	1.000	1	1	0	0	0	8¹	11	0	1	1	13.0	3.24	122	.333	.353	1	.333	1	1	1	-0	0.1
1928 Bro-N	0	3	.000	22	5	1	1	1	60¹	62	5	35	5	14.5	4.92	81	.279	.377	8	.320	2	-6	-6	0	-0.3
1929 Bro-N	11	6	.647	39	20	7	2	0	182	214	6	81	59	14.9	5.04	91	.296	.373	5	.076	-5	-7	-9	-2	-1.3
1930 Bro-N	9	6	.600	36	11	5	0	1	118¹	127	13	55	30	14.1	5.10	96	.270	.362	6	.154	-2	-2	-2	-1	-0.4
1931 Bro-N	0	0	—	1	0	0	0	0	1	1	0	1	0	18.0	0.00	—	.333	.500	0	—	0	0	0	0	0.1
Bos-N	1	3	.250	12	5	0	0	0	45	56	2	16	14	14.4	4.60	82	.306	.362	2	.133	-1	-4	-4	-0	-0.4
Yr	1	3	.250	13	5	0	0	0	46	57	2	17	14	14.5	4.50	84	.306	.365	1	.067	-1	-3	-4	0	-0.3
Total 6	22	18	.550	112	42	13	3	2	416	474	29	189	109	14.6	4.95	89	.289	.367	22	.148	-5	-18	-21	-3	-2.2

■ DON MOSSI　Mossi, Donald Louis "The Sphinx"　b: 1/11/29, St.Helena, Cal.　BL/TL, 6'1", 195 lbs.　Deb: 4/17/54

YEAR TM/L	W	L	PCT	G	GS	CG	SH	SV	IP	H	HR	BB	SO	RAT	ERA	ERA+	OAV	OOB	BH	AVG	PB	PR	/A	PD	TPI
1954 *Cle-A	6	1	.857	40	5	2	0	7	93	56	5	39	55	9.3	1.94	190	.176	.268	3	.158	0	**18**	**18**	-1	1.8
1955 Cle-A	4	3	.571	57	1	0	0	9	81²	81	4	18	69	11.0	2.42	164	.253	.295	1	.111	0	14	14	2	1.6
1956 Cle-A	6	5	.545	48	3	0	0	11	87²	79	6	33	59	11.6	3.59	117	.240	.311	3	.150	0	6	6	0	0.6
1957 Cle-A	11	10	.524	36	22	6	1	2	159	165	16	57	97	12.7	4.13	90	.265	.329	12	.218	2	-6	-7	-1	-0.6
1958 Cle-A	7	8	.467	43	5	0	0	3	101²	106	14	30	55	12.4	3.90	94	.269	.327	3	.115	-2	-1	-3	0	-0.3
1959 Det-A	17	9	.654	34	30	15	3	0	228	210	21	49	125	10.3	3.36	121	.243	.286	13	.169	0	13	18	1	2.0
1960 Det-A	9	8	.529	23	22	9	2	0	158¹	158	32	32	69	10.9	3.47	114	.258	.296	5	.116	-0	7	9	-0	0.9
1961 Det-A	15	7	.682	35	34	12	1	1	240¹	237	29	47	137	10.6	2.96	139	.258	.294	13	.165	1	28	**30**	3	3.3
1962 Det-A	11	13	.458	35	27	8	1	1	180¹	195	24	36	121	11.6	4.19	97	.270	.305	9	.164	1	-4	-2	-2	-0.2
1963 Det-A	7	7	.500	24	16	3	0	2	122²	110	20	17	68	9.6	3.74	100	.236	.269	8	.205	2	-2	0	0	0.3
1964 Chi-A	3	1	.750	34	0	0	0	7	40	37	9	7	36	10.1	2.93	118	.240	.278	1	.167	-0	3	2	0	0.2
1965 KC-A	5	8	.385	51	0	0	0	7	55¹	59	6	20	41	12.8	3.74	93	.278	.341	0	.000	-1	-2	-2	-0	-0.2
Total 12	101	80	.558	460	165	55	8	50	1548	1493	156	385	932	11.0	3.43	114	.252	.299	71	.163	4	74	83	-1	9.4

■ EARL MOSSOR　Mossor, Earl Dalton　b: 7/21/25, Forbes, Tenn.　BL/TR, 6'1", 175 lbs.　Deb: 4/30/51

YEAR TM/L	W	L	PCT	G	GS	CG	SH	SV	IP	H	HR	BB	SO	RAT	ERA	ERA+	OAV	OOB	BH	AVG	PB	PR	/A	PD	TPI
1951 Bro-N	0	0	—	3	0	0	0	0	1²	2	1	7	1	48.6	32.40	12	.333	.692	1	1.000	0	-5	-5	0	-0.4

YEAR TM/L	W	L	PCT	G	GS	CG	SH	SV	IP	H	HR	BB	SO	RAT	ERA	ERA+	OAV	OOB	BH	AVG	PB	PR	/A	PD	TPI
■ GLEN MOULDER									Moulder, Glen Hubert b: 9/28/17, Cleveland, Okla. BR/TR, 6', 180 lbs. Deb: 4/28/46															
1946 Bro-N	0	0	—	1	0	0	0	0	2	2	1	1	1	13.5	4.50	75	.286	.375	0	—	-0	-0	-0	0	0.0
1947 StL-A	4	2	.667	32	2	0	0	2	73	78	4	43	13	14.9	3.82	101	.283	.379	4	.235	-0	-1	0	1	0.1
1948 Chi-A	3	6	.333	33	9	0	0	2	85²	108	8	54	26	17.1	6.41	66	.316	.411	6	.300	2	-20	-20	0	-1.7
Total 3	7	8	.467	66	11	0	0	4	160²	188	13	98	50	16.1	5.21	78	.301	.396	10	.270	1	-21	-20	1	-1.6
■ FRANK MOUNTAIN									Mountain, Frank Henry b: 5/17/1860, Ft.Edward, N.Y. d: 11/19/39, Schenectady, N.Y. TR , 5'11", 185 lbs. Deb: 7/19/1880 ♦															
1880 Tro-N	1	1	.500	2	2	2	0	0	17	23	0	6	2	15.4	5.29	48	.308	.359	2	.222	-0	-6	-5	0	-0.4
1881 Det-N	3	4	.429	7	7	7	0	0	60	80	2	18	13	14.7	5.25	56	.307	.352	4	.160	-0	-17	-16	-1	-1.3
1882 Wor-N	0	5	.000	5	5	3	0	0	42	54	4	10	8	13.7	3.00	103	.295	.332	1	.063	-3	-1	0	-0	-0.1
Phi-a	2	6	.250	8	8	8	0	0	69	72	1	11	15	10.8	3.91	76	.251	.279	12	.333	3	-9	-7	2	-0.1
Wor-N	2	11	.154	13	13	13	0	0	102	131	0	25	21	13.8	3.97	78	.295	.333	19	.271	2	-12	-10	-1	-0.5
1883 Col-a	26	33	.441	59	59	57	4	0	503	546	8	123	159	12.0	3.60	86	.259	.300	60	.217	7	-16	-29	1	-1.9
1884 Col-a	23	17	.575	42	41	40	5	1	360²	289	7	78	156	9.2	2.45	124	.208	.250	50	.238	8	32	23	4	3.5
1885 Pit-a	1	4	.200	5	5	5	0	0	46	56	1	24	7	15.7	4.30	75	.288	.366	2	.100	-1	-5	-6	0	-0.4
1886 Pit-a	0	2	.000	2	2	2	0	0	16	22	0	14	2	20.3	7.88	43	.312	.426	8	.145	0	-8	-8	0	-0.5
Total 7	58	83	.411	143	142	137	9	1	1215²	1273	23	309	383	11.7	3.47	88	.254	.297	158	.220	15	-42	-55	5	-1.7
■ BILL MOUNTJOY									Mountjoy, William R. "Medicine Bill" b: 1857, Port Huron, Mich. d: 5/19/34, London, Ont., Can. Deb: 9/29/1883															
1883 Cin-a	0	1	.000	1	1	1	0	0	8	9	0	2	3	12.4	2.25	145	.266	.307	0	.000	-0	1	1	0	0.0
1884 Cin-a	19	12	.613	33	33	32	3	0	289	274	5	43	96	9.9	2.93	114	.237	.264	18	.151	-4	10	13	-0	0.9
1885 Cin-a	10	7	.588	17	17	17	1	0	153²	149	5	52	50	11.8	3.16	103	.244	.303	10	.167	-1	1	2	-1	0.1
Bal-a	2	4	.333	6	6	6	1	0	53	72	1	13	15	14.4	5.43	60	.311	.348	1	.056	-0	-13	-13	1	-0.9
Yr	12	11	.522	23	23	23	2	0	206²	221	6	65	65	12.5	3.75	87	.262	.315	15	.192	-1	-11	-11	0	-0.8
Total 3	31	24	.564	57	57	56	5	0	503²	504	11	110	164	11.0	3.25	102	.248	.286	29	.145	-5	-0	3	-0	0.1
■ ED MOYER									Moyer, Charles Edward b: 8/15/1885, Andover, Ohio d: 11/18/62, Jacksonville, Fla. Deb: 7/20/10															
1910 Was-A	0	3	.000	6	3	2	0	0	25	22	1	13	3	13.7	3.24	77	.253	.369	1	.125	-1	-2	-2	2	0.0
■ JAMIE MOYER									Moyer, Jamie b: 11/18/62, Sellersville, Pa. BL/TL, 6', 170 lbs. Deb: 6/16/86															
1986 Chi-N	7	4	.636	16	16	1	1	0	87¹	107	10	42	45	15.7	5.05	80	.311	.391	2	.091	-0	-13	-10	1	-0.7
1987 Chi-N	12	15	.444	35	33	1	1	0	201	210	28	97	147	14.0	5.10	84	.271	.355	14	.230	3	-23	-19	2	-1.2
1988 Chi-N	9	15	.375	34	30	3	1	0	202	212	20	55	121	12.1	3.48	104	.272	.324	5	.083	-2	-1	3	3	0.4
1989 Tex-A	4	9	.308	15	15	1	0	0	76	84	10	33	44	14.1	4.86	82	.283	.358	0	—	0	-8	-8	1	-0.5
1990 Tex-A	2	6	.250	33	10	1	0	0	102¹	115	6	39	58	13.9	4.66	85	.290	.360	0	—	0	-9	-8	0	-0.6
Total 5	34	49	.410	133	104	7	2	0	668²	728	74	266	415	13.6	4.51	88	.281	.352	21	.147	1	-53	-41	7	-2.6
■ RON MROZINSKI									Mrozinski, Ronald Frank b: 9/16/30, White Haven, Pa. BR/TL, 5'11", 160 lbs. Deb: 6/20/54															
1954 Phi-N	1	1	.500	15	4	1	0	0	48	49	10	25	26	13.9	4.50	90	.261	.347	1	.083	-1	-2	-2	-1	-0.3
1955 Phi-N	0	2	.000	22	1	0	0	1	34¹	38	2	19	18	16.0	6.55	61	.299	.407	0	.000	-1	-10	-10	-0	-0.9
Total 2	1	3	.250	37	5	1	0	1	82¹	87	12	44	44	14.8	5.36	75	.276	.372	1	.063	-2	-12	-12	-1	-1.2
■ PHIL MUDROCK									Mudrock, Philip Ray b: 6/12/37, Louisville, Colo. BR/TR, 6'1", 190 lbs. Deb: 4/19/63															
1963 Chi-N	0	0	—	1	0	0	0	0	1	2	0	0	0	18.0	9.00	39	.400	.400	0	—	0	-1	-1	0	0.0
■ GORDIE MUELLER									Mueller, Joseph Gordon b: 12/10/22, Baltimore, Md. BR/TR, 6'4", 200 lbs. Deb: 4/19/50															
1950 Bos-A	0	0	—	8	0	0	0	0	7	11	1	13	1	30.9	10.29	48	.344	.533	0	.000	-0	-4	-4	0	-0.3
■ LES MUELLER									Mueller, Leslie Clyde b: 3/4/19, Belleville, Ill. BR/TR, 6'3", 190 lbs. Deb: 8/15/41															
1941 Det-A	0	0	—	4	0	0	0	0	13	9	1	10	8	13.2	4.85	94	.205	.352	0	.000	-0	-1	-0	0	0.0
1945 *Det-A	6	8	.429	26	18	6	2	1	134²	117	8	58	42	11.8	3.68	96	.234	.316	8	.182	1	-5	-2	-2	-0.2
Total 2	6	8	.429	30	18	6	2	1	147²	126	9	68	50	11.9	3.78	95	.231	.319	8	.170	0	-6	-3	-1	-0.2
■ WILLIE MUELLER									Mueller, Willard Lawrence b: 8/30/56, West Bend, Wis. BR/TR, 6'4", 220 lbs. Deb: 8/12/78															
1978 Mil-A	1	0	1.000	5	0	0	0	0	12²	16	1	6	6	15.6	6.39	59	.291	.361	0	—	0	-4	-4	0	-0.3
1981 Mil-A	0	0	—	1	0	0	0	0	2	4	0	1	1	18.0	4.50	76	.400	.400	0	—	0	-0	-0	0	0.0
Total 2	1	0	1.000	6	0	0	0	0	14²	20	1	7	7	16.0	6.14	60	.308	.366	0	—	0	-4	-4	0	-0.3
■ BILLY MUFFETT									Muffett, Billy Arnold "Muff" b: 9/21/30, Hammond, Ind. BR/TR, 6'1", 198 lbs. Deb: 8/03/57 C															
1957 StL-N	3	2	.600	23	0	0	0	8	44	35	1	13	21	9.8	2.25	176	.222	.281	0	.000	-1	8	8	-1	0.7
1958 StL-N	4	6	.400	35	6	1	0	5	84	107	11	42	41	16.5	4.93	84	.316	.399	4	.200	-0	-9	-7	-0	-0.6
1959 SF-N	0	0	—	5	0	0	0	0	6²	11	2	3	3	18.9	5.40	71	.407	.467	0	—	0	-1	-1	0	-0.1
1960 Bos-A	6	4	.600	23	14	4	1	0	125	116	6	36	75	11.3	3.24	125	.242	.301	11	.268	2	9	11	0	1.4
1961 Bos-A	3	11	.214	38	11	2	0	2	112²	130	18	36	47	13.4	5.67	73	.291	.346	5	.217	2	-21	-19	0	-1.5
1962 Bos-A	0	0	—	1	1	0	0	0	4	8	0	2	1	22.5	9.00	46	.471	.526	0	.000	-0	-2	-2	-0	-0.1
Total 6	16	23	.410	125	32	7	1	15	376¹	407	38	132	188	13.2	4.33	94	.277	.342	20	.217	4	-16	-10	-1	-0.1
■ JOE MUICH									Muich, Ignatius Andrew b: 11/23/03, St.Louis, Mo. BR/TR, 6'2", 175 lbs. Deb: 9/04/24															
1924 Bos-N	0	0	—	2	0	0	0	0	9	19	1	5	1	24.0	11.00	35	.432	.490	0	.000	-0	-7	-7	0	-0.6
■ JOE MUIR									Muir, Joseph Allen b: 11/26/22, Oriole, Md. d: 6/25/80, Baltimore, Md. BL/TL, 6'1", 172 lbs. Deb: 4/21/51															
1951 Pit-N	0	2	.000	9	1	0	0	0	16¹	11	2	7	5	9.9	2.76	153	.180	.265	0	.000	-0	2	3	1	0.3
1952 Pit-N	2	3	.400	12	5	1	0	0	35²	42	3	18	17	15.1	6.31	63	.288	.366	1	.111	-0	-10	-9	-0	-0.8
Total 2	2	5	.286	21	6	1	0	0	52	53	5	25	22	13.5	5.19	78	.256	.336	1	.100	-0	-8	-7	1	-0.5
■ HUGH MULCAHY									Mulcahy, Hugh Noyes "Losing Pitcher" b: 9/9/13, Brighton, Mass. BR/TR, 6'2", 190 lbs. Deb: 7/24/35 C															
1935 Phi-N	1	5	.167	18	5	0	0	1	52²	62	2	25	11	15.7	4.78	95	.295	.383	0	.000	-3	-4	-1	1	-0.2
1936 Phi-N	1	1	.500	3	2	2	0	0	22²	20	0	12	3	13.5	3.18	143	.238	.347	2	.250	0	2	3	0	0.4
1937 Phi-N	8	18	.308	56	25	9	1	3	215²	256	17	97	54	15.0	5.13	84	.296	.372	11	.151	-3	-29	-19	4	-1.6
1938 Phi-N	10	20	.333	46	34	15	0	1	267¹	294	14	120	90	14.1	4.61	80	.278	.354	16	.170	-2	-24	-22	1	-2.2
1939 Phi-N	9	16	.360	38	31	14	1	4	225²	246	19	93	59	14.0	4.99	80	.282	.359	12	.158	-3	-27	-25	0	-2.5
1940 Phi-N	13	22	.371	36	36	21	3	0	280	283	12	91	82	12.1	3.60	108	.261	.320	19	.202	1	8	9	3	1.4
1945 Phi-N	1	3	.250	5	4	1	0	0	28¹	33	1	9	2	13.3	3.81	101	.295	.347	0	.000	-1	-0	0	1	0.1
1946 Phi-N	2	4	.333	16	5	1	0	0	62²	69	3	33	12	15.4	4.45	77	.285	.393	1	.188	-1	-7	-7	1	-0.4
1947 Pit-N	0	0	—	2	1	0	0	0	6²	8	1	7	2	20.3	4.05	104	.333	.484	1	.333	0	0	0	1	0.1
Total 9	45	89	.336	220	143	63	5	9	1161²	1271	69	487	314	13.9	4.49	89	.280	.355	64	.165	-9	-82	-61	12	-4.9
■ TERRY MULHOLLAND									Mulholland, Terence John b: 3/9/63, Uniontown, Pa. BR/TL, 6'3", 200 lbs. Deb: 6/08/86															
1986 SF-N	1	7	.125	15	10	0	0	0	54²	51	3	35	27	14.3	4.94	71	.251	.364	1	.053	-1	-7	-9	-0	-0.9
1988 SF-N	2	1	.667	9	6	2	1	0	46	50	3	7	18	11.3	3.72	88	.281	.312	0	.000	-1	-1	-2	0	-0.2
1989 SF-N	0	0	—	5	1	0	0	0	6	10	0	4	6	15.5	4.09	82	.319	.373	0	—	-0	-1	-1	0	0.0
Phi-N	4	7	.364	20	17	2	1	0	104¹	122	8	32	60	13.6	5.00	71	.292	.348	2	.059	-2	-17	-17	1	-1.8
Yr	4	7	.364	25	18	2	1	0	115¹	137	8	36	66	13.8	4.92	72	.295	.350	2	.000	-2	-18	-18	1	-1.8
1990 Phi-N	9	10	.474	33	26	6	1	0	180²	172	15	42	75	10.8	3.34	114	.252	.297	6	.097	-2	9	10	-2	0.5
Total 4	16	25	.390	82	60	10	3	0	396²	410	29	120	186	12.2	4.06	89	.268	.325	9	.069	-7	-18	-19	-1	-2.4

YEAR TM/L	W	L	PCT	G	GS	CG	SH	SV	IP	H	HR	BB	SO	RAT	ERA	ERA+	OAV	OOB	BH	AVG	PB	PR	/A	PD	TPI

■ TONY MULLANE

Mullane, Anthony John "Count" or "The Apollo Of The Box" b: 1/20/1859, Cork, Ireland d: 4/25/44, Chicago, Ill. BB/TB, 5'10.5", 165 lbs. Deb: 8/27/1881 ♦

YEAR TM/L	W	L	PCT	G	GS	CG	SH	SV	IP	H	HR	BB	SO	RAT	ERA	ERA+	OAV	OOB	BH	AVG	PB	PR	/A	PD	TPI
1881 Det-N	1	4	.200	5	5	5	0	0	44	55	2	17	7	14.7	4.91	59	.293	.352	5	.263	-0	-10	-10	0	-0.7
1882 Lou-a	30	24	.556	55	55	51	5	0	460¹	418	4	78	170	9.7	1.88	131	.226	.257	78	.257	11	41	30	11	5.0
1883 StL-a	35	15	.700	53	49	49	3	1	460²	372	3	74	191	8.7	2.19	160	.226	.258	69	.225	1	57	67	1	6.7
1884 Tol-a	36	26	.581	67	65	64	7	0	567	485	5	89	325	9.1	2.52	135	.219	.249	97	.276	16	46	56	9	8.9
1886 Cin-a	33	27	.550	63	56	55	1	0	529²	501	11	166	250	11.3	3.70	95	.238	.294	73	.225	2	-15	-12	2	-0.4
1887 Cin-a	31	17	.646	48	48	47	6	0	416¹	414	11	121	97	11.6	3.24	133	.250	.301	44	.221	1	49	50	-0	4.4
1888 Cin-a	26	16	.619	44	42	41	4	1	380¹	341	9	75	186	9.8	2.84	111	.231	.268	44	.251	5	9	13	-0	1.9
1889 Cin-a	11	9	.550	33	24	17	0	5	220	218	4	89	112	12.6	2.99	131	.251	.320	58	.296	9	21	22	-1	3.5
1890 Cin-N	12	10	.545	25	21	21	0	1	209	175	7	96	91	11.7	2.24	159	.221	.305	79	.276	6	31	30	0	2.9
1891 Cin-N	23	26	.469	51	47	42	1	0	426¹	390	15	187	124	12.2	3.23	104	.234	.312	31	.148	-5	6	7	2	0.3
1892 Cin-N	21	13	.618	37	34	30	3	1	295	222	11	127	109	10.6	2.59	126	.201	.283	20	.169	-2	23	22	5	2.5
1893 Cin-N	6	6	.500	15	13	11	0	1	122¹	130	4	65	24	14.3	4.41	108	.264	.350	15	.288	2	3	5	0	0.7
Bal-N	12	16	.429	34	26	23	0	1	244²	277	4	124	71	14.8	4.45	107	.277	.356	26	.228	-3	6	9	3	0.7
Yr	18	22	.450	49	39	34	0	2	367	407	8	189	95	14.6	4.44	108	.273	.354	10	.060	-1	9	14	3	1.4
1894 Bal-N	6	9	.400	21	15	9	0	4	122²	155	4	90	43	18.0	6.31	87	.305	.410	21	.396	5	-13	-12	-1	-0.4
Cle-N	1	2	.333	4	4	3	0	0	33	46	3	10	3	15.3	7.64	72	.326	.371	1	.077	-1	-8	-8	2	-0.4
Yr	7	11	.389	25	19	12	0	4	155²	201	7	100	46	17.4	6.59	83	.310	.402	10	.152	4	-22	-20	1	-0.8
Total 13	284	220	.563	555	504	468	30	15	4531¹	4199	97	1408	1803	11.1	3.05	117	.235	.291	661	.243	48	245	267	31	35.6

■ JOE MULLIGAN

Mulligan, Joseph Ignatius b: 7/31/13, E.Weymouth, Mass. d: 6/5/86, W.Roxbury, Mass. BR/TR, 6'4", 210 lbs. Deb: 6/28/34

YEAR TM/L	W	L	PCT	G	GS	CG	SH	SV	IP	H	HR	BB	SO	RAT	ERA	ERA+	OAV	OOB	BH	AVG	PB	PR	/A	PD	TPI
1934 Bos-A	1	0	1.000	14	2	1	0	0	44²	46	1	27	13	15.1	3.63	132	.279	.387	0	.000	-2	4	6	0	0.5

■ DICK MULLIGAN

Mulligan, Richard Charles b: 3/18/18, Wilkes-Barre, Pa. BL/TL, 6', 167 lbs. Deb: 9/24/41

YEAR TM/L	W	L	PCT	G	GS	CG	SH	SV	IP	H	HR	BB	SO	RAT	ERA	ERA+	OAV	OOB	BH	AVG	PB	PR	/A	PD	TPI
1941 Was-A	0	1	.000	1	1	1	0	0	9	11	0	2	2	13.0	5.00	81	.306	.342	0	.000	-0	-1	-1	0	0.0
1946 Phi-N	2	2	.500	19	5	1	0	1	54²	61	0	27	16	15.1	4.77	72	.289	.380	0	.000	-1	-8	-8	0	-0.8
Bos-N	1	0	1.000	4	0	0	0	0	15¹	6	1	9	4	8.8	2.35	146	.122	.259	0	—	0	2	2	-0	0.2
Yr	3	2	.600	23	5	1	0	1	70	67	1	36	20	13.2	4.24	81	.254	.343	4	.267	-1	-6	-6	-0	-0.6
1947 Bos-N	0	0	—	1	0	0	0	0	2	4	0	1	1	22.5	9.00	43	.400	.455	0	—	0	-1	-1	0	0.0
Total 3	3	3	.500	25	6	2	0	1	81	82	1	39	23	13.9	4.44	79	.268	.358	0	.000	-1	-8	-8	-0	-0.6

■ GEORGE MULLIN

Mullin, George Joseph "Wabash George" b: 7/4/1880, Toledo, Ohio d: 1/7/44, Wabash, Ind. BR/TR, 5'11", 188 lbs. Deb: 5/04/02 ♦

YEAR TM/L	W	L	PCT	G	GS	CG	SH	SV	IP	H	HR	BB	SO	RAT	ERA	ERA+	OAV	OOB	BH	AVG	PB	PR	/A	PD	TPI
1902 Det-A	13	16	.448	35	30	25	0	0	260	282	4	95	78	13.1	3.67	99	.277	.338	39	.335	10	-3	-1	2	1.2
1903 Det-A	19	15	.559	41	36	31	6	2	320²	284	4	106	170	10.9	2.25	130	.237	.299	35	.278	8	26	24	5	4.0
1904 Det-A	17	23	.425	45	44	42	7	0	382¹	345	1	131	161	11.2	2.40	106	.242	.306	45	.290	11	8	6	8	3.1
1905 Det-A	21	21	.500	44	41	35	1	0	347¹	303	4	138	168	11.4	2.51	109	.236	.310	35	.259	7	6	9	7	2.6
1906 Det-A	21	18	.538	40	40	35	2	0	330	315	3	108	123	11.5	2.78	99	.254	.314	32	.225	4	-3	-1	3	0.8
1907 *Det-A	20	20	.500	46	42	35	5	3	357¹	346	1	106	146	11.4	2.59	101	.256	.310	34	.217	3	-2	1	4	1.1
1908 *Det-A	17	13	.567	39	30	26	1	0	290²	301	1	71	121	11.7	3.10	78	.271	.319	32	.256	7	-23	-22	3	-1.2
1909 *Det-A	29	8	.784	40	35	29	3	1	303²	258	1	78	124	10.2	2.22	113	.234	.289	27	.214	5	9	10	2	2.0
1910 Det-A	21	12	.636	38	32	27	5	0	289	260	7	102	98	11.7	2.87	92	.254	.330	33	.256	6	-11	-8	1	0.2
1911 Det-A	18	10	.643	30	29	25	2	0	234¹	245	7	61	87	12.2	3.07	113	.276	.331	28	.286	8	7	10	-2	1.6
1912 Det-A	12	17	.414	30	29	22	2	0	226	214	3	92	88	12.5	3.54	92	.255	.335	25	.278	9	-6	-7	0	0.2
1913 Det-A	1	6	.143	7	7	4	0	0	52¹	53	1	18	16	12.6	2.75	106	.268	.335	7	.350	3	1	1	0	0.5
Was-A	3	5	.375	11	9	3	0	0	57¹	69	1	25	14	15.5	5.02	59	.283	.361	4	.190	0	-13	-13	1	-1.1
Yr	4	11	.267	18	16	7	0	0	109²	122	2	43	30	14.0	3.94	75	.275	.346	7	.171	3	-12	-12	2	-0.6
1914 Ind-F	14	10	.583	36	20	11	1	2	203	202	4	91	74	13.4	2.70	128	.261	.331	24	.312	9	11	17	-3	2.7
1915 New-F	2	2	.500	5	4	3	0	0	32¹	41	0	16	14	15.9	5.85	49	.317	.392	1	.100	-0	-10	-11	-1	-1.0
Total 14	228	196	.538	487	428	353	35	8	3686²	3518	42	1238	1482	11.8	2.82	101	.254	.319	401	.262	90	-3	16	27	16.7

■ DOMINIC MULRENAN

Mulrenan, Dominic Joseph b: 12/18/1893, Woburn, Mass. d: 7/27/64, Melrose, Mass. TR, 5'11", 170 lbs. Deb: 4/24/21

YEAR TM/L	W	L	PCT	G	GS	CG	SH	SV	IP	H	HR	BB	SO	RAT	ERA	ERA+	OAV	OOB	BH	AVG	PB	PR	/A	PD	TPI
1921 Chi-A	2	8	.200	12	10	3	0	0	56	84	2	36	10	19.6	7.23	59	.359	.449	3	.150	-1	-18	-19	1	-1.6

■ FRANK MULRONEY

Mulroney, Francis Joseph b: 4/8/03, Mallard, Iowa d: 11/11/85, Aberdeen, Wash. BR/TR, 6', 170 lbs. Deb: 4/15/30

YEAR TM/L	W	L	PCT	G	GS	CG	SH	SV	IP	H	HR	BB	SO	RAT	ERA	ERA+	OAV	OOB	BH	AVG	PB	PR	/A	PD	TPI
1930 Bos-A	0	1	.000	2	0	0	0	0	3	3	0	0	2	9.0	3.00	154	.273	.273	0	—	0	1	1	0	0.1

■ BOB MUNCRIEF

Muncrief, Robert Cleveland b: 1/28/16, Madill, Okla. BR/TR, 6'2", 190 lbs. Deb: 9/30/37

YEAR TM/L	W	L	PCT	G	GS	CG	SH	SV	IP	H	HR	BB	SO	RAT	ERA	ERA+	OAV	OOB	BH	AVG	PB	PR	/A	PD	TPI
1937 StL-A	0	0	—	1	1	0	0	0	2	3	1	2	0	22.5	4.50	107	.300	.417	0	—	0	0	0	0	0.0
1939 StL-A	0	0	—	2	0	0	0	0	3	7	1	3	1	30.0	15.00	30	.500	.588	0	—	0	-3	-3	0	-0.2
1941 StL-A	13	9	.591	36	24	12	2	1	214¹	221	18	53	67	11.7	3.65	118	.266	.314	18	.237	2	12	15	-1	1.7
1942 StL-A	6	8	.429	24	18	7	1	0	134¹	149	11	31	39	12.1	3.89	95	.280	.319	5	.111	-1	-3	-3	-0	-0.3
1943 StL-A	13	12	.520	35	27	12	3	1	205	211	13	48	80	11.5	2.81	118	.264	.307	10	.152	-2	11	12	-3	0.8
1944 *StL-A	13	8	.619	33	27	14	3	1	219¹	216	11	50	88	11.0	3.08	117	.258	.302	18	.231	1	9	13	-1	1.5
1945 StL-A	13	4	.765	27	15	10	0	1	145²	132	8	44	54	11.0	2.72	130	.239	.297	3	.067	-4	10	13	-1	0.9
1946 StL-A	3	12	.200	29	14	4	1	0	115¹	149	6	31	49	14.0	4.99	75	.314	.356	1	.031	-3	-19	-16	-1	-2.0
1947 StL-A	8	14	.364	31	23	7	0	0	176¹	210	14	51	74	13.4	4.90	79	.299	.348	6	.105	-4	-23	-20	-0	-2.2
1948 *Cle-A	5	4	.556	21	9	1	1	0	72¹	76	8	31	24	13.3	3.98	102	.279	.353	2	.111	-1	2	1	-0	0.0
1949 Pit-N	1	5	.167	13	4	1	0	0	35²	44	8	13	11	14.4	6.31	67	.310	.368	1	.143	-0	-9	-8	1	-0.6
Chi-N	5	6	.455	34	3	1	0	2	75	80	9	31	36	13.4	4.56	88	.276	.348	6	.286	1	-4	-4	-0	-0.2
Yr	6	11	.353	47	7	2	0	2	110²	124	17	44	47	13.7	5.12	80	.287	.354	1	.048	1	-13	-13	1	-0.8
1951 NY-A	0	0	—	2	0	0	0	0	3	5	0	4	2	27.0	9.00	43	.417	.563	0	—	0	-2	-2	0	-0.1
Total 12	80	82	.494	288	165	67	11	9	1401¹	1503	108	392	525	12.3	3.80	100	.275	.325	68	.155	-10	-20	-3	-5	-0.6

■ RED MUNGER

Munger, George David b: 10/4/18, Houston, Tex. BR/TR, 6'2", 200 lbs. Deb: 5/01/43

YEAR TM/L	W	L	PCT	G	GS	CG	SH	SV	IP	H	HR	BB	SO	RAT	ERA	ERA+	OAV	OOB	BH	AVG	PB	PR	/A	PD	TPI
1943 StL-N	9	5	.643	32	9	5	0	2	93¹	101	2	42	45	13.8	3.95	85	.281	.357	6	.214	1	-6	-6	1	-0.4
1944 StL-N	11	3	.786	21	12	7	2	2	121	92	2	41	55	10.0	1.34	263	.212	.284	5	.114	-3	31	29	3	3.3
1946 *StL-N	2	2	.500	10	7	2	0	1	48²	47	0	12	28	10.9	3.33	104	.255	.301	4	.250	1	0	1	0	0.3
1947 StL-N	16	5	.762	40	31	13	6	3	224¹	218	12	76	123	11.9	3.37	123	.255	.318	15	.185	1	17	19	2	2.2
1948 StL-N	10	11	.476	39	25	7	2	0	166	179	13	74	72	13.8	4.50	91	.277	.347	8	.160	0	-10	-8	2	-0.4
1949 StL-N	15	8	.652	35	28	12	2	2	188¹	179	13	87	82	12.8	3.87	108	.255	.339	17	.258	4	4	6	1	1.1
1950 StL-N	7	8	.467	32	20	5	1	0	154²	158	15	70	61	13.4	3.90	110	.262	.342	7	.137	-2	4	7	1	0.6
1951 StL-N	4	6	.400	23	11	3	0	0	94²	106	13	46	44	14.5	5.32	74	.286	.365	5	.172	1	-14	-14	2	-1.1
1952 StL-N	0	1	.000	1	1	0	0	0	4¹	7	2	1	1	18.7	12.46	30	.389	.450	0	.000	-0	-4	-4	0	-0.2
Pit-N	0	3	.000	5	4	0	0	0	26¹	30	6	10	8	13.7	7.18	56	.283	.345	0	.000	-1	-10	-9	1	-0.7
Yr	0	4	.000	6	5	0	0	0	30²	37	8	11	9	14.1	7.92	50	.296	.353	0	.000	-1	-14	-14	2	-0.9
1956 Pit-N	3	4	.429	35	13	0	0	2	107	126	8	41	45	14.0	4.04	93	.299	.361	3	.107	1	-3	-3	-1	-0.3
Total 10	77	56	.579	273	161	54	13	12	1228²	1243	86	500	564	12.8	3.83	103	.264	.336	70	.174	1	8	17	13	4.4

■ VAN MUNGO

Mungo, Van Lingle b: 6/8/11, Pageland, S.C. d: 2/12/85, Pageland, S.C. BR/TR, 6'2", 185 lbs. Deb: 9/07/31

YEAR TM/L	W	L	PCT	G	GS	CG	SH	SV	IP	H	HR	BB	SO	RAT	ERA	ERA+	OAV	OOB	BH	AVG	PB	PR	/A	PD	TPI
1931 Bro-N	3	1	.750	5	4	2	1	0	31	27	0	13	12	11.9	2.32	164	.241	.325	3	.250	1	5	5	-0	0.6
1932 Bro-N	13	11	.542	39	33	11	1	2	223¹	224	9	115	107	13.9	4.43	86	.260	.351	16	.203	0	-14	-15	1	-1.3
1933 Bro-N	16	15	.516	41	28	18	3	0	248	223	7	84	110	11.1	2.72	118	.236	.298	15	.179	-0	17	14	0	1.5
1934 Bro-N	18	16	.529	45	38	22	3	3	315¹	300	15	104	184	11.6	3.37	116	.249	.310	30	.248	4	24	19	1	2.3

YEAR	TM/L	W	L	PCT	G	GS	CG	SH	SV	IP	H	HR	BB	SO	RAT	ERA	ERA+	OAV	OOB	BH	AVG	PB	PR	/A	PD	TPI
1935	Bro-N	16	10	.615	37	26	18	**4**	2	214¹	205	13	90	143	12.5	3.65	109	.252	.328	26	.289	5	9	8	0	1.2
1936	Bro-N	18	19	.486	45	37	22	2	3	311²	275	8	118	**238**	11.4	3.35	123	**.234**	.305	22	.179	-4	23	27	0	2.3
1937	Bro-N	9	11	.450	25	21	14	0	3	161	136	3	56	122	10.9	2.91	139	**.229**	.298	16	.250	2	18	20	2	2.6
1938	Bro-N	4	11	.267	24	18	6	2	0	133¹	133	11	72	72	14.0	3.92	100	.259	.353	9	.191	1	-2	-0	1	0.2
1939	Bro-N	4	5	.444	14	10	1	0	0	77¹	70	7	33	34	12.3	3.26	124	.239	.322	10	.345	2	6	7	-1	0.7
1940	Bro-N	1	0	1.000	7	0	0	0	1	22	24	1	10	9	13.9	2.45	163	.282	.358	0	.000	-1	3	4	-0	0.3
1941	Bro-N	0	0	—	2	0	0	0	0	2	1	0	2	0	13.5	4.50	81	.143	.333	0	—	0	-0	-0	0	0.0
1942	NY-N	1	2	.333	9	5	0	0	0	36¹	38	4	21	27	14.6	5.94	57	.273	.369	3	.214	-0	-11	-10	0	-1.0
1943	NY-N	3	7	.300	45	13	2	2	2	154¹	140	7	79	83	13.1	3.91	88	.243	.341	7	.159	-1	-9	-8	1	-0.8
1945	NY-N	14	7	.667	26	26	7	2	0	183	161	4	71	101	11.6	3.20	122	.238	.314	17	.233	4	12	15	-1	1.8
Total	14	120	115	.511	364	259	123	20	16	2113	1957	89	868	1242	12.2	3.47	110	.245	.321	174	.221	13	83	83	3	10.4

■ MANNY MUNIZ   Muniz, Manuel (Rodriguez) b: 12/31/47, Caguas, P.R.   BR/TR, 5'11", 190 lbs.   Deb: 9/03/71

YEAR	TM/L	W	L	PCT	G	GS	CG	SH	SV	IP	H	HR	BB	SO	RAT	ERA	ERA+	OAV	OOB	BH	AVG	PB	PR	/A	PD	TPI
1971	Phi-N	0	1	.000	5	0	0	0	0	10¹	9	2	8	6	14.8	6.97	51	.225	.354	0	.000	-0	-4	-4	-0	-0.3

■ SCOTT MUNNINGHOFF   Munninghoff, Scott Andrew b: 12/5/58, Cincinnati, Ohio BR/TR, 6', 175 lbs.   Deb: 4/13/80

YEAR	TM/L	W	L	PCT	G	GS	CG	SH	SV	IP	H	HR	BB	SO	RAT	ERA	ERA+	OAV	OOB	BH	AVG	PB	PR	/A	PD	TPI
1980	Phi-N	0	0	—	4	0	0	0	0	6	8	0	5	2	19.5	4.50	84	.320	.433	1	1.000	1	-1	-0	0	0.1

■ LES MUNNS   Munns, Leslie Ernest "Big Ed" or "Nemo" b: 12/1/08, Fort Bragg, Cal.   BR/TR, 6'5", 212 lbs.   Deb: 4/22/34

YEAR	TM/L	W	L	PCT	G	GS	CG	SH	SV	IP	H	HR	BB	SO	RAT	ERA	ERA+	OAV	OOB	BH	AVG	PB	PR	/A	PD	TPI
1934	Bro-N	3	7	.300	33	9	4	0	0	99¹	106	7	60	41	15.0	4.71	83	.280	.378	7	.241	2	-7	-9	2	-0.4
1935	Bro-N	1	3	.250	21	5	0	0	1	58¹	74	5	33	13	17.1	5.55	72	.319	.413	3	.188	-0	-10	-10	-1	-1.0
1936	StL-N	0	3	.000	7	1	0	0	1	24	23	2	12	4	13.1	3.00	131	.240	.324	1	.111	-1	3	3	1	0.3
Total	3	4	13	.235	61	15	4	0	2	181²	203	14	105	58	15.5	4.76	83	.287	.382	11	.204	1	-14	-17	2	-1.1

■ MIKE MUNOZ   Munoz, Michael Anthony b: 7/12/65, Baldwin Park, Cal.   BL/TL, 6'2", 190 lbs.   Deb: 9/06/89

YEAR	TM/L	W	L	PCT	G	GS	CG	SH	SV	IP	H	HR	BB	SO	RAT	ERA	ERA+	OAV	OOB	BH	AVG	PB	PR	/A	PD	TPI
1989	LA-N	0	0	—	3	0	0	0	0	2²	5	1	2	3	23.6	16.88	20	.417	.500	0	—	0	-4	-4	0	-0.3
1990	LA-N	0	1	.000	8	0	0	0	0	5²	6	0	3	2	14.3	3.18	112	.300	.391	0	.000	-0	0	0	-0	0.0
Total	2	0	1	.000	11	0	0	0	0	8¹	11	1	5	5	17.3	7.56	47	.344	.432	0	.000	-0	-4	-4	0	-0.3

■ STEVE MURA   Mura, Stephen Andrew b: 2/12/55, New Orleans, La.   BR/TR, 6'2", 188 lbs.   Deb: 9/05/78

YEAR	TM/L	W	L	PCT	G	GS	CG	SH	SV	IP	H	HR	BB	SO	RAT	ERA	ERA+	OAV	OOB	BH	AVG	PB	PR	/A	PD	TPI
1978	SD-N	0	2	.000	5	2	0	0	0	7²	15	1	5	5	23.5	11.74	28	.441	.513	0	.000	-0	-7	-7	-0	-0.6
1979	SD-N	4	4	.500	38	5	0	0	2	73	57	6	37	59	11.7	3.08	114	.217	.316	0	.000	-1	5	4	-1	0.2
1980	SD-N	8	7	.533	37	23	3	1	2	168²	149	9	86	109	12.7	3.68	93	.246	.343	7	.137	-0	-2	-5	0	-0.4
1981	SD-N	5	14	.263	23	22	2	0	0	138²	156	10	50	70	13.4	4.28	76	.285	.344	6	.136	-0	-12	-16	1	-1.5
1982	StL-N	12	11	.522	35	30	7	1	0	184¹	196	16	80	84	13.5	4.05	89	.278	.352	3	.057	-4	-9	-9	-1	-1.3
1983	Chi-A	0	0	—	6	0	0	0	0	12¹	13	1	6	4	13.9	4.38	96	.260	.339	0	—	0	-0	-0	-0	-0.0
1985	Oak-A	1	1	.500	23	1	0	0	1	48	41	3	25	29	12.4	4.13	93	.225	.319	0	—	0	0	-1	-0	-0.1
Total	7	30	39	.435	167	83	12	2	5	632²	627	46	289	360	13.1	4.00	88	.263	.343	16	.101	-5	-25	-35	-1	-3.7

■ MASANORI MURAKAMI   Murakami, Masanori b: 5/6/44, Otsuki, Japan   BL/TL, 6', 180 lbs.   Deb: 9/01/64

YEAR	TM/L	W	L	PCT	G	GS	CG	SH	SV	IP	H	HR	BB	SO	RAT	ERA	ERA+	OAV	OOB	BH	AVG	PB	PR	/A	PD	TPI
1964	SF-N	1	0	1.000	9	0	0	0	1	15	8	1	1	15	5.4	1.80	198	.163	.180	0	.000	-0	3	3	-1	0.2
1965	SF-N	4	1	.800	45	1	0	0	8	74¹	57	9	22	85	9.9	3.75	96	.205	.271	2	.154	-0	-2	-1	-2	-0.3
Total	2	5	1	.833	54	1	0	0	9	89¹	65	10	23	100	9.2	3.43	105	.199	.258	2	.125	-1	1	2	-3	-0.1

■ TIM MURCHISON   Murchison, Thomas Malcolm b: 10/8/1896, Liberty, N.C. d: 10/20/62, Liberty, N.C.   BR/TL, 6', 185 lbs.   Deb: 6/21/17

YEAR	TM/L	W	L	PCT	G	GS	CG	SH	SV	IP	H	HR	BB	SO	RAT	ERA	ERA+	OAV	OOB	BH	AVG	PB	PR	/A	PD	TPI
1917	StL-N	0	0	—	1	0	0	0	0	1	0	0	2	2	18.0	0.00	—	.000	.400	0	—	0	0	0	0	0.0
1920	Cle-A	0	0	—	2	0	0	0	0	5	3	0	4	0	12.6	0.00	—	.200	.368	0	.000	-0	2	2	1	0.3
Total	2	0	0	—	3	0	0	0	0	6	3	0	6	2	13.5	0.00	—	.167	.375	0	.000	-0	2	2	1	0.3

■ RED MURFF   Murff, John Robert b: 4/1/21, Burlington, Tex.   BR/TR, 6'3", 195 lbs.   Deb: 4/21/56

YEAR	TM/L	W	L	PCT	G	GS	CG	SH	SV	IP	H	HR	BB	SO	RAT	ERA	ERA+	OAV	OOB	BH	AVG	PB	PR	/A	PD	TPI
1956	Mil-N	0	0	—	14	1	0	0	1	24¹	25	3	7	18	11.8	4.44	78	.272	.323	1	.200	0	-2	-3	0	-0.2
1957	Mil-N	2	2	.500	12	1	0	0	2	26	31	3	11	13	14.5	4.85	72	.301	.368	0	.000	-1	-3	-4	0	-0.3
Total	2	2	2	.500	26	2	0	0	3	50¹	56	6	18	31	13.2	4.65	75	.287	.347	1	.091	-1	-5	-7	1	-0.5

■ CON MURPHY   Murphy, Cornelius B. "Monk" or "Razzle Dazzle" b: 10/15/1863, Worcester, Mass. d: 8/1/14, Worcester, Mass.   5'9", 130 lbs.   Deb: 9/11/1884

YEAR	TM/L	W	L	PCT	G	GS	CG	SH	SV	IP	H	HR	BB	SO	RAT	ERA	ERA+	OAV	OOB	BH	AVG	PB	PR	/A	PD	TPI
1884	Phi-N	0	3	.000	3	3	3	0	0	26	37	1	6	10	14.9	6.58	45	.317	.351	0	.000	-1	-10	-10	1	-0.8
1890	Bro-P	4	9	.308	18	13	11	0	1	131	157	8	78	27	16.1	4.67	95	.284	.373	15	.227	-1	-6	-3	-0	-0.2
	Bro-a	3	9	.250	12	12	10	0	0	96	121	6	46	26	15.7	5.72	68	.299	.370	9	.180	-0	-20	-19	2	-1.3
	Bro-P	0	1	.000	2	1	0	0	1	8	11	0	4	2	16.9	6.75	66	.313	.384	0	.000	-0	-2	-2	0	-0.1
Total	2	7	22	.241	35	29	24	0	2	261	326	9	134	65	15.9	5.31	77	.294	.370	24	.186	-3	-39	-35	3	-2.4

■ DANNY MURPHY   Murphy, Daniel Francis b: 8/23/42, Beverly, Mass.   BL/TR, 5'11", 185 lbs.   Deb: 6/18/60 ◆

YEAR	TM/L	W	L	PCT	G	GS	CG	SH	SV	IP	H	HR	BB	SO	RAT	ERA	ERA+	OAV	OOB	BH	AVG	PB	PR	/A	PD	TPI
1969	Chi-A	2	1	.667	17	0	0	0	4	31¹	28	2	10	16	11.5	2.01	192	.252	.325	0	.000	0	6	6	-0	0.7
1970	Chi-A	2	3	.400	51	0	0	0	5	80²	82	11	49	42	15.1	5.69	68	.273	.382	2	.333	2	-18	-16	-0	-1.4
Total	2	4	4	.500	68	0	0	0	9	112	110	13	59	58	14.1	4.66	83	.268	.368	23	.177	2	-12	-10	-1	-0.7

■ DAN MURPHY   Murphy, Daniel Lee b: 9/18/64, Artesia, Cal.   BR/TR, 6'2", 195 lbs.   Deb: 8/10/89

YEAR	TM/L	W	L	PCT	G	GS	CG	SH	SV	IP	H	HR	BB	SO	RAT	ERA	ERA+	OAV	OOB	BH	AVG	PB	PR	/A	PD	TPI
1989	SD-N	0	0	—	7	0	0	0	0	6¹	6	1	4	1	14.2	5.68	61	.231	.333	0	—	0	-2	-2	0	-0.1

■ ED MURPHY   Murphy, Edward J. b: 1/22/1877, Auburn, N.Y. d: 1/29/35, Weedsport, N.Y.   TR , 6'1", 186 lbs.   Deb: 4/23/1898

YEAR	TM/L	W	L	PCT	G	GS	CG	SH	SV	IP	H	HR	BB	SO	RAT	ERA	ERA+	OAV	OOB	BH	AVG	PB	PR	/A	PD	TPI
1898	Phi-N	1	2	.333	7	3	2	0	0	30	41	3	10	8	15.3	5.10	67	.323	.372	5	.357	1	-5	-6	1	-0.2
1901	StL-N	10	9	.526	23	21	16	0	0	165	201	5	32	42	12.8	4.20	76	.298	.331	16	.250	3	-16	-19	2	-1.2
1902	StL-N	10	6	.625	23	17	12	1	1	164	187	7	31	37	12.1	3.02	91	.286	.321	16	.262	1	-4	-5	2	-0.1
1903	StL-N	4	8	.333	15	12	9	0	0	106	108	2	38	16	12.9	3.31	99	.262	.333	13	.203	-0	-1	-1	1	0.0
Total	4	25	25	.500	68	53	39	1	1	465	537	17	111	103	12.7	3.64	84	.288	.331	50	.246	5	-26	-30	6	-1.5

■ JOHN MURPHY   Murphy, John H. b: 3/8/1867, Philadelphia, Pa.   Deb: 4/17/1884

YEAR	TM/L	W	L	PCT	G	GS	CG	SH	SV	IP	H	HR	BB	SO	RAT	ERA	ERA+	OAV	OOB	BH	AVG	PB	PR	/A	PD	TPI
1884	Wil-U	0	6	.000	7	6	5	0	0	48	52	3	2	27	10.1	3.00	110	.258	.266	2	.065	-3	0	2	-0	-0.1
	Alt-U	5	6	.455	14	10	10	0	0	111²	141	3	9	46	12.1	3.87	85	.289	.302	14	.149	-5	-11	-7	1	-0.9
	Yr	5	12	.294	21	16	15	0	0	159²	193	6	11	73	11.5	3.61	91	.280	.291	7	.056	-7	-10	-6	1	-1.0

■ JOHNNY MURPHY   Murphy, John Joseph "Grandma" "Fireman" Or "Fordham Johnny"
b: 7/14/08, New York, N.Y. d: 1/14/70, New York, N.Y.   BR/TR, 6'2", 190 lbs.   Deb: 5/19/32

YEAR	TM/L	W	L	PCT	G	GS	CG	SH	SV	IP	H	HR	BB	SO	RAT	ERA	ERA+	OAV	OOB	BH	AVG	PB	PR	/A	PD	TPI
1932	NY-A	0	0	—	2	0	0	0	0	3¹	7	0	3	2	27.0	16.20	25	.438	.526	1	1.000	0	-4	-4	0	-0.2
1934	NY-A	14	10	.583	40	20	10	0	4	207²	193	11	76	70	11.7	3.12	130	.250	.317	7	.099	-3	32	22	1	1.9
1935	NY-A	10	5	.667	40	8	4	0	5	117	110	7	55	28	12.7	4.08	99	.243	.325	5	.156	2	5	-0	-0	0.1
1936	*NY-A	9	3	.750	27	5	2	0	5	88	90	5	36	34	13.0	3.38	138	.262	.334	13	.361	4	16	13	1	1.5
1937	*NY-A	13	4	.765	39	4	0	0	10	110	121	7	50	36	14.1	4.17	107	.277	.352	8	.229	2	5	3	4	0.8
1938	*NY-A	8	2	.800	32	2	1	0	**11**	91¹	90	5	41	43	13.0	4.24	107	.256	.336	2	.063	-3	6	3	1	0.1
1939	*NY-A	3	6	.333	38	0	0	0	**19**	61¹	57	2	28	30	12.5	4.40	99	.252	.335	2	.182	1	-1	-0	0	0.1
1940	NY-A	8	4	.667	35	1	0	0	9	63¹	58	5	15	23	10.4	3.69	109	.247	.292	1	.077	1	5	2	1	0.3
1941	*NY-A	8	3	.727	35	0	0	0	**15**	77¹	68	1	40	29	12.6	1.98	199	.240	.335	1	.056	-1	**19**	**17**	-1	1.4
1942	NY-A	4	2	.667	31	0	0	0	**11**	58	66	2	23	24	14.1	3.41	101	.293	.364	2	.154	2	0	0	0	0.1
1943	*NY-A	12	4	.750	37	0	0	0	8	68	44	2	30	31	9.8	2.51	128	.183	.273	1	.053	-2	6	5	-0	0.3
1946	NY-A	4	2	.667	27	0	0	0	7	45	40	4	19	19	11.8	3.40	102	.240	.317	0	.000	-0	1	0	1	0.1
1947	Bos-A	0	0	—	32	0	0	0	3	54²	41	1	28	9	11.4	2.80	139	.206	.304	3	.273	1	6	7	0	0.8

YEAR TM/L	W	L	PCT	G	GS	CG	SH	SV	IP	H	HR	BB	SO	RAT	ERA	ERA+	OAV	OOB	BH	AVG	PB	PR	/A	PD	TPI
Total 13	93	53	.637	415	40	17	0	107	1045	985	52	444	378	12.4	3.50	117	.249	.326	46	.154	0	98	68	10	7.3

■ JOE MURPHY
Murphy, Joseph Akin   b: 9/7/1866, St.Louis, Mo.   d: 3/28/51, Coral Gables, Fla.   5'11", 160 lbs.   Deb: 4/28/1886

YEAR TM/L	W	L	PCT	G	GS	CG	SH	SV	IP	H	HR	BB	SO	RAT	ERA	ERA+	OAV	OOB	BH	AVG	PB	PR	/A	PD	TPI
1886 Cin-a	2	3	.400	5	5	5	0	0	46	50	0	21	11	13.9	4.89	72	.264	.338	0	.000	-3	-7	-7	-1	-0.8
StL-N	0	4	.000	4	4	3	0	0	33	45	3	16	11	16.6	8.18	39	.312	.381	3	.214	-0	-18	-18	-0	-1.3
StL-a	1	0	1.000	1	1	1	0	0	7	5	0	3	3	10.3	3.86	89	.191	.274	0	.000	-1	-0	-0	-0	0.0
1887 StL-a	1	0	1.000	1	1	1	0	0	9	13	0	4	5	17.0	5.00	91	.326	.387	1	.167	-1	-1	-0	0	0.0
Total 2	4	7	.364	11	11	10	0	0	95	113	3	44	30	14.9	5.97	59	.283	.354	4	.098	-4	-26	-26	-1	-2.1

■ ROB MURPHY
Murphy, Robert Albert   b: 5/26/60, Miami, Fla.   BL/TL, 6'2", 200 lbs.   Deb: 9/13/85

YEAR TM/L	W	L	PCT	G	GS	CG	SH	SV	IP	H	HR	BB	SO	RAT	ERA	ERA+	OAV	OOB	BH	AVG	PB	PR	/A	PD	TPI
1985 Cin-N	0	0	—	2	0	0	0	0	3	2	1	2	1	12.0	6.00	63	.200	.333	0	—	0	-1	-1	0	0.0
1986 Cin-N	6	0	1.000	34	0	0	0	1	50¹	26	0	21	36	8.4	0.72	541	.155	.249	0	.000	-0	17	18	0	1.9
1987 Cin-N	8	5	.615	87	0	0	0	3	100²	91	7	32	99	11.0	3.04	140	.239	.299	1	.200	0	12	13	-0	1.3
1988 Cin-N	0	6	.000	76	0	0	0	3	84²	69	3	38	74	11.5	3.08	116	.229	.318	0	—	0	3	5	0	0.5
1989 Bos-A	5	7	.417	74	0	0	0	9	105	97	7	41	107	11.9	2.74	149	.251	.325	0	—	0	13	16	0	1.7
1990 *Bos-A	0	6	.000	68	0	0	0	7	57	85	10	32	54	18.6	6.32	65	.348	.426	0	—	0	-15	-14	0	-1.3
Total 6	19	24	.442	341	0	0	0	23	400²	370	28	166	371	12.1	3.17	126	.248	.325	1	.125	-0	29	37	1	4.1

■ BOB MURPHY
Murphy, Robert J.   b: 12/26/1866, Dutchess Co., N.Y.   Deb: 4/24/1890

YEAR TM/L	W	L	PCT	G	GS	CG	SH	SV	IP	H	HR	BB	SO	RAT	ERA	ERA+	OAV	OOB	BH	AVG	PB	PR	/A	PD	TPI
1890 NY-N	1	0	1.000	3	2	1	0	0	18	23	0	10	8	16.5	5.50	64	.302	.383	1	.111	-1	-4	-4	-0	-0.3

■ TOM MURPHY
Murphy, Thomas Andrew   b: 12/30/45, Cleveland, Ohio   BR/TR, 6'3", 185 lbs.   Deb: 6/13/68

YEAR TM/L	W	L	PCT	G	GS	CG	SH	SV	IP	H	HR	BB	SO	RAT	ERA	ERA+	OAV	OOB	BH	AVG	PB	PR	/A	PD	TPI
1968 Cal-A	5	6	.455	15	15	3	0	0	99¹	67	5	28	56	9.1	2.17	134	.191	.261	0	.000	-2	9	8	-1	0.5
1969 Cal-A	10	16	.385	36	35	4	0	0	215²	213	12	69	100	12.6	4.21	83	.260	.333	10	.141	-0	-14	-18	2	-1.6
1970 Cal-A	16	13	.552	39	38	5	2	0	227	223	32	81	99	12.3	4.24	85	.261	.330	14	.184	2	-13	-16	-0	-1.3
1971 Cal-A	6	17	.261	37	36	7	0	0	243¹	228	24	82	89	11.8	3.77	86	.256	.325	13	.173	1	-8	-14	2	-1.1
1972 Cal-A	0	0	—	6	0	0	0	0	10	13	0	8	2	18.9	5.40	54	.342	.457	0	.000	-0	-3	-3	1	-0.1
KC-A	4	4	.500	18	9	1	1	1	70¹	77	3	16	34	12.7	3.07	99	.287	.341	0	.000	-1	-0	-0	1	0.0
Yr	4	4	.500	24	9	1	1	1	80¹	90	3	24	36	13.4	3.36	90	.293	.356	1	.071	-1	-3	-3	1	-0.1
1973 StL-N	3	7	.300	19	13	2	0	0	88²	89	5	22	42	11.6	3.76	97	.269	.320	4	.174	-1	-1	-1	1	0.0
1974 Mil-A	10	10	.500	70	0	0	0	20	123	97	6	51	47	11.0	1.90	190	.224	.309	1	.500	1	23	23	2	2.8
1975 Mil-A	1	9	.100	52	0	0	0	20	72¹	85	5	27	32	14.6	4.60	83	.295	.366	0	—	0	-7	-6	0	-0.5
1976 Mil-A	0	1	.000	15	0	0	0	1	18¹	25	2	9	7	17.7	7.36	47	.313	.396	0	—	0	-8	-8	0	-0.7
Bos-A	4	5	.444	37	0	0	0	8	81	91	5	25	32	13.1	3.44	114	.290	.346	0	—	0	1	4	-0	0.4
Yr	4	6	.400	52	0	0	0	9	99¹	116	7	34	39	13.8	4.17	92	.293	.352	0	—	0	-7	-4	-0	-0.3
1977 Bos-A	0	1	.000	16	0	0	0	0	30²	44	6	12	13	16.4	6.75	67	.338	.394	0	—	0	-9	-8	0	-0.6
Tor-A	2	1	.667	19	1	0	0	2	52	63	6	18	26	14.2	3.63	115	.304	.363	0	—	0	2	3	0	0.3
Yr	2	2	.500	35	1	0	0	2	82²	107	12	30	39	15.0	4.79	90	.317	.374	0	—	0	-7	-4	0	-0.3
1978 Tor-A	6	9	.400	50	0	0	0	7	94	87	11	37	36	11.9	3.93	100	.256	.329	0	—	0	-2	-0	2	0.2
1979 Tor-A	1	2	.333	10	0	0	0	0	18¹	24	1	8	6	15.2	5.40	80	.311	.378	0	—	0	-2	-2	1	0.0
Total 12	68	101	.402	439	147	22	3	59	1444	1425	123	493	621	12.3	3.78	94	.263	.332	42	.145	0	-32	-38	10	-1.7

■ WALTER MURPHY
Murphy, Walter Joseph   b: 9/27/07, New York, N.Y.   BR/TR, 6'1.5", 180 lbs.   Deb: 4/19/31

YEAR TM/L	W	L	PCT	G	GS	CG	SH	SV	IP	H	HR	BB	SO	RAT	ERA	ERA+	OAV	OOB	BH	AVG	PB	PR	/A	PD	TPI
1931 Bos-A	0	0	—	2	0	0	0	0	2	4	0	1	0	22.5	9.00	48	.444	.500	0	—	0	-1	-1	0	0.0

■ DALE MURRAY
Murray, Dale Albert   b: 2/2/50, Cuero, Tex.   BR/TR, 6'4", 205 lbs.   Deb: 7/07/74

YEAR TM/L	W	L	PCT	G	GS	CG	SH	SV	IP	H	HR	BB	SO	RAT	ERA	ERA+	OAV	OOB	BH	AVG	PB	PR	/A	PD	TPI
1974 Mon-N	1	1	.500	32	0	0	0	10	69²	46	1	23	31	8.9	1.03	371	.187	.257	0	.000	-1	20	22	0	2.3
1975 Mon-N	15	8	.652	63	0	0	0	9	111¹	134	0	39	43	14.2	3.96	97	.305	.365	3	.214	1	-4	-2	3	0.2
1976 Mon-N	4	9	.308	81	0	0	0	13	113¹	117	1	37	35	12.2	3.26	114	.277	.336	0	.000	-1	3	6	5	1.0
1977 Cin-N	7	2	.778	61	1	0	0	4	102	125	13	46	42	15.3	4.94	80	.314	.388	2	.167	-0	-12	-12	0	-1.0
1978 Cin-N	1	1	.500	15	0	0	0	2	32²	34	1	17	25	14.3	4.13	86	.272	.364	0	.000	-0	-2	-2	0	-0.1
NY-N	8	5	.615	53	0	0	0	5	86¹	85	4	36	37	12.8	3.65	96	.266	.345	0	.000	-0	-1	-2	2	0.0
Yr	9	6	.600	68	0	0	0	7	119	119	5	53	62	13.2	3.78	93	.266	.346	1	.100	-1	-3	-4	2	-0.1
1979 NY-N	4	8	.333	58	0	0	0	4	97	105	6	52	37	14.6	4.82	75	.287	.376	0	.000	-0	-12	-13	1	-1.1
Mon-N	1	2	.333	9	0	0	0	1	13¹	14	1	3	4	11.5	2.70	136	.292	.333	0	.000	-0	2	1	-0	0.1
Yr	5	10	.333	67	0	0	0	5	110¹	119	7	55	41	14.2	4.57	80	.285	.369	1	.125	-1	-10	-11	1	-1.0
1980 Mon-N	0	1	.000	16	0	0	0	0	29¹	39	3	12	16	15.6	6.14	58	.315	.375	0	—	-0	-8	-8	-1	-0.8
1981 Tor-A	1	0	1.000	11	0	0	0	0	15¹	12	1	5	12	10.0	1.17	336	.211	.274	0	—	-0	4	5	1	0.6
1982 Tor-A	8	7	.533	56	0	0	0	11	111	115	3	32	60	12.2	3.16	142	.268	.323	0	—	0	11	16	3	2.0
1983 NY-A	2	4	.333	40	0	0	0	1	94¹	113	6	22	45	13.0	4.48	87	.297	.337	0	—	0	-4	-6	0	-0.5
1984 NY-A	1	2	.333	19	0	0	0	0	23²	30	2	5	13	14.1	4.94	77	.306	.352	0	—	0	-3	-3	0	-0.2
1985 NY-A	0	0	—	3	0	0	0	0	2	4	0	0	0	18.0	13.50	30	.400	.400	0	—	0	-2	-2	0	-0.1
Tex-A	0	0	—	1	0	0	0	0	1	3	0	0	0	27.0	18.00	23	.750	.750	0	—	0	-2	-2	0	0.0
Yr	0	0	—	4	0	0	0	0	3	7	0	0	0	21.0	15.00	27	.500	.500	0	—	0	-4	-4	0	-0.1
Total 12	53	50	.515	518	1	0	0	60	902¹	976	40	329	400	13.2	3.85	100	.282	.346	5	.077	-3	-9	-1	15	2.4

■ GEORGE MURRAY
Murray, George King "Smiler"   b: 9/23/1898, Charlotte, N.C.   d: 10/18/55, Memphis, Tenn.   BR/TR, 6'2", 200 lbs.   Deb: 5/08/22

YEAR TM/L	W	L	PCT	G	GS	CG	SH	SV	IP	H	HR	BB	SO	RAT	ERA	ERA+	OAV	OOB	BH	AVG	PB	PR	/A	PD	TPI
1922 NY-A	4	2	.667	22	2	0	0	0	56²	53	0	26	14	12.7	3.97	101	.255	.340	5	.278	2	0	0	0	0.2
1923 Bos-A	7	11	.389	39	18	5	0	0	177²	190	9	87	40	14.4	4.91	84	.291	.380	9	.164	-3	-18	-16	-1	-1.8
1924 Bos-A	2	9	.182	28	7	0	0	0	80¹	97	6	32	27	15.2	6.72	65	.307	.383	4	.182	-1	-22	-21	0	-1.9
1926 Was-A	6	3	.667	12	12	5	0	0	81¹	89	1	37	28	14.6	5.64	69	.287	.374	5	.139	-2	-15	-16	-1	-1.6
1927 Was-A	1	1	.500	7	3	0	0	0	18	18	1	15	5	17.5	7.00	58	.265	.412	1	.167	-0	-6	-6	-1	-0.5
1933 Chi-A	0	0	—	2	0	0	0	0	2¹	3	0	2	0	19.3	7.71	55	.375	.500	0	—	0	-1	-1	0	0.0
Total 6	20	26	.435	110	42	10	0	0	416¹	450	17	199	114	14.5	5.38	76	.288	.376	24	.175	-4	-61	-59	-3	-5.6

■ JIM MURRAY
Murray, James Francis "Big Jim"   b: 12/31/1900, Scranton, Pa.   d: 7/15/73, New York, N.Y.   BB/TL, 6'2", 210 lbs.   Deb: 7/03/22

YEAR TM/L	W	L	PCT	G	GS	CG	SH	SV	IP	H	HR	BB	SO	RAT	ERA	ERA+	OAV	OOB	BH	AVG	PB	PR	/A	PD	TPI
1922 Bro-N	0	0	—	4	0	0	0	1	6	8	0	3	3	16.5	4.50	90	.320	.393	1	.500	0	-0	-0	0	0.0

■ AMBY MURRAY
Murray, Joseph Ambrose   b: 6/4/13, Fall River, Mass.   BL/TL, 5'7", 150 lbs.   Deb: 7/05/36

YEAR TM/L	W	L	PCT	G	GS	CG	SH	SV	IP	H	HR	BB	SO	RAT	ERA	ERA+	OAV	OOB	BH	AVG	PB	PR	/A	PD	TPI
1936 Bos-N	0	0	—	4	1	0	0	0	11	15	1	3	2	14.7	4.09	94	.319	.360	1	.250	0	-0	-0	0	0.0

■ JOE MURRAY
Murray, Joseph Ambrose   b: 11/11/20, Wilkes-Barre, Pa.   BL/TL, 6', 165 lbs.   Deb: 8/17/50

YEAR TM/L	W	L	PCT	G	GS	CG	SH	SV	IP	H	HR	BB	SO	RAT	ERA	ERA+	OAV	OOB	BH	AVG	PB	PR	/A	PD	TPI
1950 Phi-A	0	3	.000	8	2	0	0	0	30	34	1	21	8	16.5	5.70	80	.283	.390	0	.000	-2	-4	-4	1	-0.4

■ PAT MURRAY
Murray, Patrick Joseph   b: 7/18/1897, Scottsville, N.Y.   d: 11/5/83, Rochester, N.Y.   BR/TL, 6', 175 lbs.   Deb: 7/01/19

YEAR TM/L	W	L	PCT	G	GS	CG	SH	SV	IP	H	HR	BB	SO	RAT	ERA	ERA+	OAV	OOB	BH	AVG	PB	PR	/A	PD	TPI
1919 Phi-N	0	2	.000	8	2	1	0	0	34¹	50	0	12	11	17.3	6.29	51	.347	.412	0	—	-2	-13	-12	-0	-1.3

■ DENNIS MUSGRAVES
Musgraves, Dennis Eugene   b: 12/25/43, Indianapolis, Ind.   BR/TR, 6'4", 188 lbs.   Deb: 7/09/65

YEAR TM/L	W	L	PCT	G	GS	CG	SH	SV	IP	H	HR	BB	SO	RAT	ERA	ERA+	OAV	OOB	BH	AVG	PB	PR	/A	PD	TPI
1965 NY-N	0	0	—	5	1	0	0	0	16	11	0	7	11	11.3	0.56	627	.200	.313	0	.000	-0	5	5	-0	0.6

■ STAN MUSIAL
Musial, Stanley Frank "Stan The Man"   b: 11/21/20, Donora, Pa.   BL/TL, 6', 175 lbs.   Deb: 9/17/41   H♦

YEAR TM/L	W	L	PCT	G	GS	CG	SH	SV	IP	H	HR	BB	SO	RAT	ERA	ERA+	OAV	OOB	BH	AVG	PB	PR	/A	PD	TPI
1952 StL-N	0	0	—	1	0	0	0	0	0	0	0	0	0	—	—	—	.000	.000	194	.336	1	0	0	0	0.0

■ JEFF MUSSELMAN
Musselman, Jeffrey Joseph   b: 6/21/63, Doylestown, Pa.   BL/TL, 6', 180 lbs.   Deb: 9/02/86

YEAR TM/L	W	L	PCT	G	GS	CG	SH	SV	IP	H	HR	BB	SO	RAT	ERA	ERA+	OAV	OOB	BH	AVG	PB	PR	/A	PD	TPI
1986 Tor-A	0	0	—	6	0	0	0	0	5¹	8	1	5	4	21.9	10.13	42	.333	.448	0	—	0	-4	-4	0	-0.2
1987 Tor-A	12	5	.706	68	1	0	0	3	89	75	7	54	54	13.3	4.15	108	.237	.354	0	—	0	3	3	1	0.4

YEAR	TM/L	W	L	PCT	G	GS	CG	SH	SV	IP	H	HR	BB	SO	RAT	ERA	ERA+	OAV	OOB	BH	AVG	PB	PR	/A	PD	TPI
1988	Tor-A	8	5	.615	15	15	0	0	0	85	80	4	30	39	12.0	3.18	124	.252	.322	0	—	0	7	7	-1	0.6
1989	Tor-A	0	1	.000	5	3	0	0	0	11	19	2	9	3	22.9	10.64	35	.404	.500	0	—	0	-8	-8	0	-0.7
	NY-N	3	2	.600	20	0	0	0	0	26¹	27	1	14	11	14.0	3.08	106	.267	.357	0	—	0	1	1	2	0.3
1990	NY-N	0	2	.000	28	0	0	0	0	32	40	3	11	14	14.6	5.63	65	.310	.369	0	.000	-0	-7	-7	1	-0.6
Total	5	23	15	.605	142	19	0	0	3	248²	249	18	123	125	13.7	4.31	93	.266	.356	0	.000	0	-7	-8	3	-0.2

■ RON MUSSELMAN
Musselman, Ralph Ronald b: 11/11/54, Wilmington, N.C. BR/TR, 6'2", 185 lbs. Deb: 8/18/82

YEAR	TM/L	W	L	PCT	G	GS	CG	SH	SV	IP	H	HR	BB	SO	RAT	ERA	ERA+	OAV	OOB	BH	AVG	PB	PR	/A	PD	TPI
1982	Sea-A	1	0	1.000	12	0	0	0	0	15²	18	2	6	9	14.4	3.45	123	.300	.373	0	—	0	1	1	0	0.2
1984	Tor-A	0	2	.000	11	0	0	0	1	21¹	18	2	10	9	11.8	2.11	194	.225	.311	0	—	0	4	5	0	0.5
1985	Tor-A	3	0	1.000	25	4	0	0	1	52¹	59	2	24	29	14.3	4.47	94	.284	.358	0	—	0	-2	-2	-1	-0.1
Total	3	4	2	.667	48	4	0	0	1	89¹	95	6	40	47	13.7	3.73	112	.273	.350	0	—	0	4	5	-1	0.6

■ PAUL MUSSER
Musser, Paul b: 6/24/1889, Millheim, Pa. d: 7/7/73, State College, Pa. BR/TR, 6', 175 lbs. Deb: 6/06/12

YEAR	TM/L	W	L	PCT	G	GS	CG	SH	SV	IP	H	HR	BB	SO	RAT	ERA	ERA+	OAV	OOB	BH	AVG	PB	PR	/A	PD	TPI
1912	Was-A	0	0	—	7	2	0	0	2	20²	16	0	16	10	14.8	2.61	127	.225	.382	0	.000	-1	2	2	0	0.1
1919	Bos-A	0	2	.000	5	4	1	0	0	19²	26	0	8	14	15.6	4.12	73	.342	.405	0	.000	-1	-2	-2	-0	-0.3
Total	2	0	2	.000	12	6	1	0	2	40¹	42	0	24	24	15.2	3.35	95	.286	.393	0	.000	-2	-0	-1	0	-0.2

■ BARNEY MUSSILL
Mussill, Bernard James b: 10/1/19, Woodville, Pa. BR/TL, 6'1", 200 lbs. Deb: 4/20/44

YEAR	TM/L	W	L	PCT	G	GS	CG	SH	SV	IP	H	HR	BB	SO	RAT	ERA	ERA+	OAV	OOB	BH	AVG	PB	PR	/A	PD	TPI
1944	Phi-N	0	1	.000	16	0	0	0	0	19¹	20	1	13	5	15.4	6.05	60	.267	.375	0	.000	-0	-5	-5	0	-0.4

■ ALEX MUSTAIKIS
Mustaikis, Alexander Dominick b: 3/26/09, Chelsea, Mass. d: 1/17/70, Scranton, Pa. BR/TR, 6'3", 180 lbs. Deb: 7/07/40

YEAR	TM/L	W	L	PCT	G	GS	CG	SH	SV	IP	H	HR	BB	SO	RAT	ERA	ERA+	OAV	OOB	BH	AVG	PB	PR	/A	PD	TPI
1940	Bos-A	0	1	.000	6	1	0	0	0	15	15	1	15	6	18.0	9.00	50	.254	.405	2	.333	1	-8	-8	1	-0.4

■ ELMER MYERS
Myers, Elmer Glenn b: 3/2/1894, York Springs, Pa. d: 7/29/76, Collingwood, N.J. BR/TR, 6'2", 185 lbs. Deb: 10/06/15

YEAR	TM/L	W	L	PCT	G	GS	CG	SH	SV	IP	H	HR	BB	SO	RAT	ERA	ERA+	OAV	OOB	BH	AVG	PB	PR	/A	PD	TPI
1915	Phi-A	1	0	1.000	1	1	1	1	0	9	2	0	5	12	7.0	0.00	—	.074	.219	0	.000	-0	3	3	-0	0.2
1916	Phi-A	14	23	.378	44	35	31	2	1	315	280	7	168	182	13.2	3.66	79	.248	.353	27	.214	2	-29	-27	4	-2.1
1917	Phi-A	9	16	.360	38	23	13	2	3	201²	221	1	79	88	13.6	4.42	62	.283	.353	18	.247	2	-39	-37	1	-3.5
1918	Phi-A	4	8	.333	18	15	5	1	1	95¹	101	4	42	17	13.9	4.63	63	.264	.365	5	.143	2	-20	-18	2	-1.8
1919	Cle-A	8	7	.533	23	15	6	1	1	134²	134	3	43	38	12.5	3.74	89	.264	.334	11	.239	2	-8	-6	1	-0.2
1920	Cle-A	2	4	.333	16	7	2	0	1	71²	93	1	23	16	15.1	4.77	80	.316	.374	6	.240	0	-8	-8	-1	-0.6
	Bos-A	9	1	.900	12	10	9	1	0	97	90	1	24	34	10.8	2.13	171	.249	.299	12	.316	3	18	16	-1	1.9
	Yr	11	5	.688	28	17	11	1	1	168²	183	2	47	50	12.4	3.25	114	.277	.327	2	.032	3	10	9	-1	1.3
1921	Bos-A	8	12	.400	30	20	11	0	0	172	217	11	53	40	14.7	4.87	87	.315	.373	14	.215	-2	-11	-12	1	-1.2
1922	Bos-A	0	1	.000	3	1	0	0	0	5²	10	1	3	1	23.8	17.47	24	.370	.469	0	.000	-0	-8	-8	0	-0.6
Total	8	55	72	.433	185	127	78	8	7	1102	1148	29	440	428	13.4	4.06	81	.275	.352	93	.226	4	-102	-96	8	-7.9

■ HENRY MYERS
Myers, Henry C. b: 5/1858, Philadelphia, Pa. d: 4/18/1895, Philadelphia, Pa. BR/TR, 5'9", 159 lbs. Deb: 8/20/1881 M♦

YEAR	TM/L	W	L	PCT	G	GS	CG	SH	SV	IP	H	HR	BB	SO	RAT	ERA	ERA+	OAV	OOB	BH	AVG	PB	PR	/A	PD	TPI
1882	Bal-a	0	2	.000	6	2	1	0	0	26	30	2	4	7	11.8	6.58	42	.271	.296	53	.180	-1	-11	-11	-0	-0.8

■ JOSEPH MYERS
Myers, Joseph William b: 3/18/1882, Wilmington, Del. d: 2/11/56, Delaware City, Del BR/TR, 5'10.5", 205 lbs. Deb: 10/07/05

YEAR	TM/L	W	L	PCT	G	GS	CG	SH	SV	IP	H	HR	BB	SO	RAT	ERA	ERA+	OAV	OOB	BH	AVG	PB	PR	/A	PD	TPI
1905	Phi-A	0	0	—	1	1	1	0	0	5	3	0	3	5	10.8	3.60	74	.175	.298	0	.000	-0	-1	-1	0	0.0

■ RANDY MYERS
Myers, Randall Kirk b: 9/19/62, Vancouver, Wash. BL/TL, 6'1", 190 lbs. Deb: 10/06/85

YEAR	TM/L	W	L	PCT	G	GS	CG	SH	SV	IP	H	HR	BB	SO	RAT	ERA	ERA+	OAV	OOB	BH	AVG	PB	PR	/A	PD	TPI
1985	NY-N	0	0	—	1	0	0	0	0	2	0	1	2	4.5	0.00	—	.000	.143	0	—	0	1	1	0	0.1
1986	NY-N	0	0	—	10	0	0	0	0	10²	11	1	9	13	17.7	4.22	84	.256	.396	0	—	0	-1	-1	0	0.0
1987	NY-N	3	6	.333	54	0	0	0	6	75	61	6	30	92	10.9	3.96	95	.225	.302	2	.286	0	1	-2	-0	-0.1
1988	*NY-N	7	3	.700	55	0	0	0	26	68	45	5	17	69	8.5	1.72	187	.190	.250	1	.250	1	13	11	-1	1.2
1989	NY-N	7	4	.636	65	0	0	0	24	84¹	62	4	40	88	10.9	2.35	139	.206	.299	0	.000	0	11	9	-0	0.8
1990	*Cin-N	4	6	.400	66	0	0	0	31	86²	59	6	38	98	10.4	2.08	186	.193	.288	1	.250	0	17	17	-0	1.8
Total	6	21	19	.525	251	0	0	0	87	326²	238	22	135	362	10.4	2.56	138	.204	.290	4	.200	1	42	36	-2	3.8

■ BOB MYRICK
Myrick, Robert Howard b: 10/1/52, Hattiesburg, Miss. BR/TL, 6'1", 195 lbs. Deb: 5/28/76

YEAR	TM/L	W	L	PCT	G	GS	CG	SH	SV	IP	H	HR	BB	SO	RAT	ERA	ERA+	OAV	OOB	BH	AVG	PB	PR	/A	PD	TPI
1976	NY-N	1	1	.500	21	1	0	0	0	27²	34	2	13	11	15.3	3.25	101	.306	.379	0	.000	-0	1	0	1	0.0
1977	NY-N	2	2	.500	44	4	0	0	2	87¹	86	5	33	49	12.4	3.61	104	.265	.334	2	.182	-0	3	1	0	0.1
1978	NY-N	0	3	.000	17	0	0	0	0	24²	18	3	13	13	11.3	3.28	106	.207	.310	0	.000	-0	1	1	0	0.1
Total	3	3	6	.333	82	5	0	0	2	139²	138	10	59	73	12.8	3.48	104	.264	.340	2	.125	-1	4	2	1	0.2

■ CHRIS NABHOLZ
Nabholz, Christopher William b: 1/5/67, Harrisburg, Pa. BL/TL, 6'5", 210 lbs. Deb: 6/11/90

YEAR	TM/L	W	L	PCT	G	GS	CG	SH	SV	IP	H	HR	BB	SO	RAT	ERA	ERA+	OAV	OOB	BH	AVG	PB	PR	/A	PD	TPI
1990	Mon-N	6	2	.750	11	11	1	1	0	70	43	6	32	53	9.9	2.83	133	.176	.276	0	.000	-2	7	7	-0	0.6

■ JACK NABORS
Nabors, Herman John b: 11/19/1887, Montevallo, Ala. d: 11/20/23, Wilton, Ala. BR/TR, 6'3", 185 lbs. Deb: 8/09/15

YEAR	TM/L	W	L	PCT	G	GS	CG	SH	SV	IP	H	HR	BB	SO	RAT	ERA	ERA+	OAV	OOB	BH	AVG	PB	PR	/A	PD	TPI
1915	Phi-A	0	5	.000	10	7	2	0	0	54	58	1	35	18	16.3	5.50	54	.304	.424	2	.125	-1	-15	-15	0	-1.5
1916	Phi-A	1	20	.048	40	30	11	0	1	212²	206	2	95	74	12.9	3.47	83	.266	.349	7	.101	-4	-15	-14	-2	-2.1
1917	Phi-A	0	0	—	2	0	0	0	0	3	2	0	1	2	9.0	3.00	92	.200	.273	0	—	0	-0	-0	0	0.0
Total	3	1	25	.038	52	37	13	0	1	269²	266	3	131	94	13.5	3.87	75	.273	.364	9	.106	-6	-31	-29	-1	-3.6

■ BILL NAGEL
Nagel, William Taylor b: 8/19/15, Memphis, Tenn. d: 10/8/81, Freehold, N.J. BR/TR, 6'1", 190 lbs. Deb: 4/20/39 ♦

YEAR	TM/L	W	L	PCT	G	GS	CG	SH	SV	IP	H	HR	BB	SO	RAT	ERA	ERA+	OAV	OOB	BH	AVG	PB	PR	/A	PD	TPI
1939	Phi-A	0	0	—	1	0	0	0	0	3	7	1	1	0	24.0	12.00	39	.438	.471	86	.252	0	-2	-2	0	-0.1

■ JUDGE NAGLE
Nagle, Walter Harold "Lucky" b: 3/10/1880, Santa Rosa, Cal. d: 5/26/71, Santa Rosa, Cal. 6', 176 lbs. Deb: 4/26/11

YEAR	TM/L	W	L	PCT	G	GS	CG	SH	SV	IP	H	HR	BB	SO	RAT	ERA	ERA+	OAV	OOB	BH	AVG	PB	PR	/A	PD	TPI
1911	Pit-N	4	2	.667	8	3	1	0	1	27¹	33	3	6	11	13.2	3.62	95	.324	.367	1	.143	-0	-1	-1	0	0.0
	Bos-A	1	1	.500	5	1	0	0	0	27	27	2	6	12	11.0	3.33	98	.262	.303	1	.100	-1	0	-0	-1	-0.1

■ CHARLES NAGY
Nagy, Charles Harrison b: 5/5/67, Bridgeport, Conn. BL/TR, 6'3", 200 lbs. Deb: 6/29/90

YEAR	TM/L	W	L	PCT	G	GS	CG	SH	SV	IP	H	HR	BB	SO	RAT	ERA	ERA+	OAV	OOB	BH	AVG	PB	PR	/A	PD	TPI
1990	Cle-A	2	4	.333	9	8	0	0	0	45²	58	7	21	26	15.8	5.91	67	.315	.388	0	—	0	-10	-10	1	-0.8

■ STEVE NAGY
Nagy, Stephen b: 5/28/19, Franklin, N.J. BL/TL, 5'9", 174 lbs. Deb: 4/20/47

YEAR	TM/L	W	L	PCT	G	GS	CG	SH	SV	IP	H	HR	BB	SO	RAT	ERA	ERA+	OAV	OOB	BH	AVG	PB	PR	/A	PD	TPI
1947	Pit-N	1	3	.250	6	1	0	0	0	14	18	1	9	4	17.4	5.79	73	.310	.403	1	.250	0	-3	-2	0	-0.1
1950	Was-A	2	5	.286	9	9	2	0	0	53¹	69	5	29	17	16.5	6.58	68	.307	.386	5	.227	2	-12	-12	-0	-0.9
Total	2	3	8	.273	15	10	2	0	0	67¹	87	6	38	21	16.7	6.42	69	.307	.389	6	.231	2	-15	-15	-0	-1.0

■ MIKE NAGY
Nagy, Michael Timothy b: 3/25/48, Bronx, N.Y. BR/TR, 6'3", 195 lbs. Deb: 4/21/69

YEAR	TM/L	W	L	PCT	G	GS	CG	SH	SV	IP	H	HR	BB	SO	RAT	ERA	ERA+	OAV	OOB	BH	AVG	PB	PR	/A	PD	TPI
1969	Bos-A	12	2	.857	33	28	7	1	0	196²	183	10	106	84	13.7	3.11	122	.245	.347	5	.077	-2	11	15	1	1.5
1970	Bos-A	6	5	.545	23	20	4	0	0	128²	138	16	64	56	14.3	4.48	88	.275	.359	11	.250	2	-11	-7	-0	-0.4
1971	Bos-A	1	3	.250	12	7	0	0	0	38	46	4	20	9	15.6	6.63	56	.315	.398	1	.083	-1	-13	-12	-1	-1.2
1972	Bos-A	0	0	—	1	0	0	0	0	2	3	0	2	0	18.0	9.00	36	.375	.444	0	—	0	-1	-1	0	0.0
1973	StL-N	0	2	.000	9	7	0	0	0	40²	44	4	15	14	13.3	4.20	87	.282	.347	1	.091	-1	-2	-3	-0	-0.3
1974	Hou-N	1	1	.500	9	0	0	0	0	12²	17	3	5	5	16.3	8.53	41	.309	.377	0	—	0	-7	-7	0	-0.4
Total	6	20	13	.606	87	62	11	1	0	418²	431	37	210	170	14.1	4.15	92	.267	.357	18	.135	-2	-24	-16	0	-1.0

■ SAM NAHEM
Nahem, Samuel Ralph "Subway Sam" b: 10/19/15, New York, N.Y. BR/TR, 6'1.5", 190 lbs. Deb: 10/02/38

YEAR	TM/L	W	L	PCT	G	GS	CG	SH	SV	IP	H	HR	BB	SO	RAT	ERA	ERA+	OAV	OOB	BH	AVG	PB	PR	/A	PD	TPI
1938	Bro-N	1	0	1.000	1	1	1	0	0	9	6	0	4	2	10.0	3.00	130	.194	.286	2	.400	1	1	1	-0	0.1
1941	StL-N	5	2	.714	26	8	2	0	1	81²	76	2	38	31	12.8	2.98	126	.243	.329	4	.174	-1	6	7	1	0.8
1942	Phi-N	1	3	.250	35	2	0	0	0	74²	72	2	40	38	14.6	4.94	67	.250	.340	2	.100	-1	-13	-14	1	-1.3
1948	Phi-N	3	3	.500	28	1	0	0	0	59	68	4	45	30	17.7	7.02	56	.288	.408	2	.154	-0	-20	-20	-1	-2.0
Total	4	10	8	.556	90	12	3	0	1	224¹	222	8	127	101	14.3	4.69	78	.257	.357	10	.164	-2	-27	-26	1	-2.4

YEAR	TM/L	W	L	PCT	G	GS	CG	SH	SV	IP	H	HR	BB	SO	RAT	ERA	ERA+	OAV	OOB	BH	AVG	PB	PR	/A	PD	TPI

■ PETE NAKTENIS   Naktenis, Peter Ernest   b: 6/12/14, Aberdeen, Wash.   BL/TL, 6'1", 185 lbs.   Deb: 6/13/36

1936	Phi-A	0	1	.000	7	1	0	0	0	18²	24	2	27	18	25.6	12.54	41	.324	.515	1	.200	-0	-16	-15	-1	-1.2
1939	Cin-N	0	0	—	3	0	0	0	0	4	2	0	0	1	9.0	2.25	170	.154	.267	0	—	0	1	1	0	0.1
Total	2	0	1	.000	10	1	0	0	0	22²	26	2	27	19	22.6	10.72	45	.299	.483	1	.200	-0	-15	-15	-0	-1.1

■ BUDDY NAPIER   Napier, Skelton Le Roy   b: 12/18/1889, Byronville, Ga.   d: 3/29/68, Hutchins, Tex.   BR/TR, 5'11", 165 lbs.   Deb: 8/14/12

1912	StL-A	1	2	.333	7	2	0	0	0	25¹	33	0	5	10	14.6	4.97	67	.317	.366	0	.000	-1	-5	-5	0	-0.5
1918	Chi-N	0	0	—	1	0	0	0	0	6²	10	0	4	2	18.9	5.40	52	.357	.438	1	.333	0	-2	-2	0	-0.1
1920	Cin-N	4	2	.667	9	5	5	1	0	49	47	0	7	17	10.1	1.29	236	.254	.285	3	.214	1	10	10	0	1.2
1921	Cin-N	0	2	.000	22	6	1	0	1	56²	72	2	13	14	13.5	5.56	64	.329	.366	2	.143	1	-11	-12	1	-0.9
Total	4	5	6	.455	39	13	6	1	1	137²	162	2	29	43	12.7	3.92	84	.302	.343	6	.158	1	-8	-9	1	-0.3

■ GONZALO NARANJO   Naranjo, Lazaro Ramon Gonzalo   b: 11/25/34, Havana, Cuba   BL/TR, 5'11.5", 165 lbs.   Deb: 7/08/56

| 1956 | Pit-N | 1 | 2 | .333 | 17 | 3 | 0 | 0 | 0 | 34¹ | 37 | 7 | 17 | 26 | 14.4 | 4.46 | 85 | .282 | .369 | 1 | .143 | 0 | -3 | -3 | 1 | 0.0 |

■ RAY NARLESKI   Narleski, Raymond Edmond   b: 11/25/28, Camden, N.J.   BR/TR, 6'1", 175 lbs.   Deb: 4/17/54

1954	*Cle-A	3	3	.500	42	2	1	0	13	89	59	8	44	52	10.6	2.22	165	.189	.293	0	.000	-2	15	14	-1	1.2
1955	Cle-A	9	1	.900	**60**	1	1	0	**19**	111²	91	11	52	94	11.5	3.71	108	.220	.308	7	.292	1	3	3	-2	0.3
1956	Cle-A	3	2	.600	32	0	0	0	4	59¹	36	5	19	42	8.5	1.52	277	.170	.241	2	.250	0	**17**	**18**	-1	1.7
1957	Cle-A	11	5	.688	46	15	7	1	16	154¹	136	14	70	93	12.2	3.09	120	.235	.322	4	.093	-2	12	11	-4	0.5
1958	Cle-A	13	10	.565	44	24	7	0	1	183¹	179	21	91	102	13.4	4.07	90	.255	.343	11	.204	1	-6	-9	-3	-1.0
1959	Det-A	4	12	.250	42	10	1	0	5	104¹	105	21	59	71	14.2	5.78	70	.254	.348	2	.095	-1	-22	-20	-2	-2.2
Total	6	43	33	.566	266	52	17	1	58	702	606	80	335	454	12.2	3.60	106	.230	.320	26	.157	-2	19	18	-12	0.5

■ BUSTER NARUM   Narum, Leslie Ferdinand   b: 11/16/40, Philadelphia, Pa.   BR/TR, 6'1", 194 lbs.   Deb: 4/14/63

1963	Bal-A	0	0	—	7	0	0	0	0	9	8	0	5	5	13.0	3.00	118	.242	.342	1	1.000	1	1	1	0	0.2
1964	Was-A	9	15	.375	38	32	7	2	0	199	195	31	73	121	12.3	4.30	86	.259	.328	4	.061	-5	-15	-13	-3	-2.0
1965	Was-A	4	12	.250	46	24	2	0	0	173²	176	16	91	86	14.2	4.46	78	.267	.361	2	.043	-2	-19	-19	3	-2.0
1966	Was-A	0	0	—	3	0	0	0	0	3¹	11	2	4	0	40.5	21.60	16	.579	.652	0	—	0	-7	-7	0	-0.5
1967	Was-A	1	0	1.000	2	2	0	0	0	11²	8	1	4	8	9.3	3.09	103	.195	.267	0	—	-1	0	0	-0	0.0
Total	5	14	27	.341	96	58	9	2	0	396²	398	50	177	220	13.3	4.45	80	.264	.346	7	.059	-6	-40	-38	-1	-4.1

■ JIM NASH   Nash, James Edwin   b: 2/9/45, Hawthorne, Nev.   BR/TR, 6'5", 215 lbs.   Deb: 7/03/66

1966	KC-A	12	1	.923	18	17	5	0	1	127	95	6	47	98	10.1	2.06	165	.204	.277	5	.102	-2	19	19	-3	1.6
1967	KC-A	12	17	.414	37	34	8	2	0	222¹	200	21	87	186	11.8	3.76	85	.242	.317	7	.100	-2	-13	-14	-3	-1.9
1968	Oak-A	13	13	.500	34	33	12	6	0	228²	185	18	55	169	9.6	2.28	123	.219	.270	5	.068	-2	18	14	-3	1.0
1969	Oak-A	8	8	.500	26	19	3	1	0	115¹	112	17	30	75	11.2	3.67	94	.247	.296	4	.111	-1	-1	-3	-1	-0.4
1970	Atl-N	13	9	.591	34	33	6	2	0	212¹	211	22	90	153	13.0	4.07	105	.257	.334	7	.087	-3	-1	5	3	0.3
1971	Atl-N	9	7	.563	32	19	2	0	2	133	166	17	50	65	14.6	4.94	75	.314	.374	7	.149	-1	-22	-18	-1	-2.0
1972	Atl-N	1	1	.500	11	4	0	0	1	31¹	35	2	25	10	17.2	5.46	69	.307	.432	2	.222	-0	-7	-6	-0	-0.5
	Phi-N	0	8	.000	9	8	0	0	0	37¹	46	5	17	15	15.9	6.27	57	.311	.393	1	.100	-0	-12	-11	-0	-1.0
	Yr	1	9	.100	20	12	0	0	1	68²	81	7	42	25	16.5	5.90	62	.305	.405	1	.053	-0	-19	-17	0	-1.5
Total	7	68	64	.515	201	167	36	11	4	1107¹	1050	108	401	771	11.9	3.58	96	.250	.318	38	.101	-11	-18	-16	-10	-2.9

■ BILLY NASH   Nash, William Mitchell   b: 6/24/1865, Richmond, Va.   d: 11/15/29, E.Orange, N.J.   BR/TR, 5'8.5", 167 lbs.   Deb: 8/05/1884   MU♦

1889	Bos-N	0	0	—	1	0	0	0	0	1	0	0	1	0	9.0	0.00	—	.000	.252	132	.274	1	0	0	0	0.0
1890	Bos-P	0	0	—	1	0	0	0	0	0¹	1	0	0	0	27.0	0.00	—	.499	.499	130	.266	0	0	0	0	0.0
Total	2	0	0	—	2	0	0	0	0	1¹	1	0	1	0	13.5	0.00	—	.201	.335	1606	.275	1	1	1	0	0.0

■ PHILIP NASTU   Nastu, Philip   b: 3/8/55, Bridgeport, Conn.   BL/TL, 6'2", 180 lbs.   Deb: 9/15/78

1978	SF-N	0	1	.000	3	1	0	0	0	8	8	1	2	5	11.3	5.63	61	.258	.303	0	.000	-0	-2	-2	-0	-0.1
1979	SF-N	3	4	.429	25	14	1	0	0	100	105	14	41	47	13.3	4.32	81	.272	.345	1	.042	-1	-7	-9	-0	-0.9
1980	SF-N	0	0	—	6	0	0	0	0	6	10	1	5	1	22.5	6.00	59	.357	.455	0	—	0	-2	-2	0	-0.1
Total	3	3	5	.375	34	15	1	0	0	114	123	16	48	53	13.7	4.50	78	.276	.349	1	.040	-1	-10	-13	1	-1.0

■ JAIME NAVARRO   Navarro, Jaime (Cintron)   b: 3/27/67, Bayamon, P.R.   BR/TR, 6'4", 210 lbs.   Deb: 6/20/89

1989	Mil-A	7	8	.467	19	17	1	0	0	109²	119	6	32	56	12.5	3.12	123	.277	.328	0	—	0	9	9	-0	0.9
1990	Mil-A	8	7	.533	32	22	3	0	1	149¹	176	11	41	75	13.3	4.46	85	.293	.343	0	—	0	-9	-11	0	-1.0
Total	2	15	15	.500	51	39	4	0	1	259	295	17	73	131	13.0	3.89	98	.286	.337	0	—	0	-3	-0	-0	-0.1

■ JULIO NAVARRO   Navarro, Julio (Ventura) "Whiplash"   b: 1/9/36, Vieques, P.R.   BR/TR, 6', 175 lbs.   Deb: 9/03/62

1962	LA-A	1	1	.500	9	0	0	0	0	15¹	20	2	4	11	14.1	4.70	82	.317	.358	1	.500	0	-1	-1	0	0.0
1963	LA-A	4	5	.444	57	0	0	0	12	90¹	75	7	32	53	10.9	2.89	119	.228	.300	3	.200	1	7	5	1	0.8
1964	LA-A	0	0	—	5	0	0	0	1	9¹	5	0	5	8	11.6	1.93	170	.167	.324	0	.000	-0	2	1	0	0.1
	Det-A	2	1	.667	26	0	0	0	2	41	40	9	16	36	12.7	3.95	93	.250	.326	0	.000	-1	-1	-1	-0	-0.1
	Yr	2	1	.667	31	0	0	0	3	50¹	45	9	21	44	12.2	3.58	100	.234	.316	0	.000	-1	0	0	0	0.0
1965	Det-A	0	2	.000	15	1	0	0	1	30	25	5	12	22	11.1	4.20	83	.238	.316	0	.000	-0	-2	-2	0	-0.2
1966	Det-A	0	0	—	1	0	0	0	0	2	2	0	0	0	—	∞	—	1.000	1.000	0	—	0	-3	-3	0	-0.2
1970	Atl-N	0	0	—	17	0	0	0	1	26¹	24	7	1	21	8.9	4.10	105	.233	.248	1	.167	-0	-1	-1	0	0.0
Total	6	7	9	.438	130	1	0	0	17	212¹	191	32	70	151	11.4	3.65	99	.241	.309	5	.147	-0	1	-1	2	0.4

■ EARL NAYLOR   Naylor, Earl Eugene   b: 5/19/19, Kansas City, Mo.   d: 1/16/90, Winter Haven, Fla.   BR/TR, 6', 190 lbs.   Deb: 4/15/42   ♦

| 1942 | Phi-N | 0 | 5 | .000 | 20 | 4 | 1 | 0 | 0 | 60¹ | 68 | 5 | 29 | 19 | 14.5 | 6.12 | 54 | .286 | .363 | 33 | .196 | 1 | -19 | -19 | -0 | -1.8 |

■ ROLLIE NAYLOR   Naylor, Roleine Cecil   b: 2/4/1892, Crum, Tex.   d: 6/18/66, Fort Worth, Tex.   BR/TR, 6'1.5", 180 lbs.   Deb: 9/14/17

1917	Phi-A	2	2	.500	5	5	3	0	0	33	30	1	11	11	11.5	1.64	168	.265	.336	1	.091	-1	4	4	1	0.5
1919	Phi-A	5	18	.217	31	23	17	0	0	204²	210	2	64	68	12.2	3.34	103	.280	.339	12	.169	-2	-3	2	-0	0.0
1920	Phi-A	10	23	.303	42	36	20	0	0	251¹	306	7	86	90	14.3	3.47	116	.312	.371	14	.163	-6	9	15	2	1.1
1921	Phi-A	3	13	.188	32	19	6	0	0	169¹	214	10	53	39	14.4	4.84	92	.315	.367	6	.115	-4	-10	-7	-1	-1.0
1922	Phi-A	10	15	.400	35	26	11	0	0	171¹	212	7	51	37	14.0	4.73	90	.309	.359	11	.200	1	-13	-9	1	-0.6
1923	Phi-A	12	7	.632	26	20	9	2	0	143	149	5	59	27	13.1	3.46	119	.273	.344	11	.244	1	8	10	-1	1.0
1924	Phi-A	0	5	.000	10	7	1	0	0	38¹	53	2	20	10	17.1	6.34	68	.333	.408	3	.375	1	-9	-9	1	-0.6
Total	7	42	83	.336	181	136	67	2	0	1011	1174	34	344	282	13.7	3.93	102	.300	.359	58	.177	-11	-14	7	2	0.4

■ MIKE NAYMICK   Naymick, Michael John   b: 9/6/17, Berlin, Pa.   BR/TR, 6'8", 225 lbs.   Deb: 9/24/39

1939	Cle-A	0	1	.000	2	1	1	0	0	4²	3	0	5	3	15.4	1.93	228	.188	.381	0	.000	-0	1	1	-0	0.1
1940	Cle-A	1	2	.333	13	4	0	0	0	30	36	1	17	15	16.8	5.10	83	.290	.389	1	.167	-0	-2	-3	1	-0.1
1943	Cle-A	4	4	.500	29	4	0	0	2	62²	32	3	47	41	11.8	2.30	135	.160	.328	3	.188	-0	7	6	0	0.4
1944	Cle-A	0	0	—	7	0	0	0	0	13	16	1	10	4	18.0	9.69	34	.314	.426	0	.000	-0	-9	-9	-0	-0.8
	StL-N	0	0	—	1	0	0	0	0	2	2	0	1	1	13.5	4.50	78	.333	.429	0	—	0	-0	-0	0	0.0
Total	4	5	7	.417	52	9	1	0	2	112¹	89	5	80	64	14.0	3.93	89	.224	.362	4	.154	-0	-3	-6	1	-0.2

■ JACK NEAGLE   Neagle, John Henry   b: 1/2/1858, Syracuse, N.Y.   d: 9/20/04, Syracuse, N.Y.   BR/TR, 5'6", 155 lbs.   Deb: 7/08/1879   ♦

| 1879 | Cin-N | 0 | 1 | .000 | 2 | 2 | 1 | 0 | 0 | 13 | 13 | 0 | 5 | 4 | 12.5 | 3.46 | 67 | .244 | .309 | 2 | .167 | -0 | -1 | -2 | 0 | -0.1 |
| 1883 | Phi-N | 1 | 7 | .125 | 8 | 7 | 6 | 0 | 0 | 61¹ | 88 | 0 | 21 | 13 | 16.0 | 6.90 | 45 | .318 | .366 | 12 | .164 | -2 | -26 | -26 | -1 | -1.9 |

YEAR TM/L	W	L	PCT	G	GS	CG	SH	SV	IP	H	HR	BB	SO	RAT	ERA	ERA+	OAV	OOB	BH	AVG	PB	PR	/A	PD	TPI
Bal-a	1	4	.200	6	5	4	0	0	46	48	1	20	9	13.3	4.89	71	.252	.323	10	.286	1	-8	-7	-0	-0.3
Pit-a	3	12	.200	16	16	12	0	0	114	156	9	25	41	14.3	5.84	55	.306	.338	19	.188	-1	-32	-33	-1	-2.8
Yr	4	16	.200	22	21	16	0	0	160	204	10	45	50	14.0	5.57	59	.291	.334	7	.051	0	-40	-41	-1	-3.1
1884 Pit-a	11	26	.297	38	38	37	2	0	326	354	6	70	85	11.7	3.73	90	.262	.298	22	.149	-6	-17	-13	-2	-1.8
Total 3	16	50	.242	70	68	60	2	0	560¹	659	16	141	152	12.8	4.59	72	.277	.317	65	.176	-8	-85	-81	-4	-6.9

■ JOE NEALE
Neale, Joseph Hunt b: 5/7/1866, Wadsworth, Ohio d: 12/30/13, Akron, Ohio BR/TR, 5'8", 153 lbs. Deb: 6/21/1886 ♦

YEAR TM/L	W	L	PCT	G	GS	CG	SH	SV	IP	H	HR	BB	SO	RAT	ERA	ERA+	OAV	OOB	BH	AVG	PB	PR	/A	PD	TPI
1886 Lou-a	0	1	.000	1	1	0	0	0	7	11	0	7	0	23.1	7.71	47	.342	.459	0	.000	-0	-3	-3	1	-0.1
1887 Lou-a	1	4	.200	5	4	4	0	0	41¹	60	4	15	11	16.3	6.97	63	.327	.378	1	.053	-2	-12	-12	0	-0.9
1890 StL-a	5	3	.625	10	9	8	0	0	69	53	4	15	23	8.9	3.39	127	.206	.250	2	.067	-3	4	7	-1	0.3
1891 StL-a	6	4	.600	15	11	9	1	1	110¹	109	4	36	24	11.8	4.24	99	.249	.306	6	.118	-4	-6	-0	2	0.0
Total 4	12	12	.500	31	25	21	1	1	227²	233	12	73	58	12.1	4.59	93	.256	.311	9	.086	-9	-18	-8	2	-0.7

■ RON NECCIAI
Necciai, Ronald Andrew b: 6/18/32, Manown, Pa. BR/TR, 6'5", 185 lbs. Deb: 8/10/52

YEAR TM/L	W	L	PCT	G	GS	CG	SH	SV	IP	H	HR	BB	SO	RAT	ERA	ERA+	OAV	OOB	BH	AVG	PB	PR	/A	PD	TPI
1952 Pit-N	1	6	.143	12	9	0	0	0	54²	63	5	32	31	15.8	7.08	56	.296	.390	1	.059	-1	-20	-19	-1	-1.8

■ RON NEGRAY
Negray, Ronald Alvin b: 2/26/30, Akron, Ohio BR/TR, 6'1", 185 lbs. Deb: 9/14/52

YEAR TM/L	W	L	PCT	G	GS	CG	SH	SV	IP	H	HR	BB	SO	RAT	ERA	ERA+	OAV	OOB	BH	AVG	PB	PR	/A	PD	TPI
1952 Bro-N	0	0	—	4	1	0	0	0	13	15	0	5	5	13.8	3.46	105	.294	.357	0	.000	-0	0	0	0	0.0
1955 Phi-N	4	3	.571	19	10	2	0	0	71²	71	13	21	30	11.6	3.52	113	.257	.310	0	.000	-3	4	4	-0	0.0
1956 Phi-N	2	3	.400	39	4	0	0	3	66²	72	6	24	44	13.1	4.18	89	.280	.344	3	.429	1	-3	-3	0	-0.1
1958 LA-N	0	0	—	4	0	0	0	0	11¹	12	4	7	2	15.1	7.15	57	.279	.380	0	.000	-0	-4	-4	0	-0.3
Total 4	6	6	.500	66	15	2	0	3	162²	170	23	57	81	12.6	4.04	95	.271	.333	3	.086	-3	-3	-3	-0	-0.4

■ JIM NEHER
Neher, James Gilmore b: 2/5/1889, Rochester, N.Y. d: 11/11/51, Buffalo, N.Y. BR/TR, 5'11", 185 lbs. Deb: 9/10/12

YEAR TM/L	W	L	PCT	G	GS	CG	SH	SV	IP	H	HR	BB	SO	RAT	ERA	ERA+	OAV	OOB	BH	AVG	PB	PR	/A	PD	TPI
1912 Cle-A	0	0	—	1	0	0	0	0	1	0	0	0	0	0.0	0.00	—	.000	.000	0	—	0	0	0	0	0.0

■ ART NEHF
Nehf, Arthur Neukom b: 7/31/1892, Terre Haute, Ind. d: 12/18/60, Phoenix, Ariz. BL/TL, 5'9.5", 176 lbs. Deb: 8/13/15

YEAR TM/L	W	L	PCT	G	GS	CG	SH	SV	IP	H	HR	BB	SO	RAT	ERA	ERA+	OAV	OOB	BH	AVG	PB	PR	/A	PD	TPI
1915 Bos-N	5	4	.556	12	10	6	4	0	78¹	60	0	21	39	9.7	2.53	103	.214	.276	4	.143	-1	2	1	0	0.0
1916 Bos-N	7	5	.583	22	12	6	1	0	121	110	1	20	36	9.9	2.01	124	.244	.281	5	.125	-0	8	6	-0	0.7
1917 Bos-N	17	8	.680	38	23	17	5	0	233¹	197	4	39	101	9.3	2.16	118	.231	.268	12	.171	5	14	10	-0	1.6
1918 Bos-N	15	15	.500	32	31	**28**	2	0	284¹	274	2	76	96	11.3	2.69	100	.259	.312	16	.168	1	2	-0	3	0.5
1919 Bos-N	8	9	.471	22	19	13	1	0	168²	151	6	40	53	10.5	3.09	92	.242	.294	5	.206	-2	-3	-4	1	-0.1
NY-N	9	2	.818	13	12	9	2	0	102	70	2	19	24	8.0	1.50	187	.196	.240	8	.229	3	16	15	-1	2.1
Yr	17	11	.607	35	31	22	3	0	270²	221	8	59	77	9.4	2.49	114	.224	.269	6	.061	5	13	10	0	2.0
1920 NY-N	21	12	.636	40	33	22	4	0	280²	273	8	45	79	10.2	3.08	97	.260	.291	26	.268	5	2	-3	2	0.5
1921 *NY-N	20	10	.667	41	34	18	2	1	260²	266	18	55	67	11.2	3.63	101	.271	.311	18	.202	0	5	1	3	0.4
1922 *NY-N	19	13	.594	37	35	20	2	1	268¹	286	15	64	60	11.9	3.29	122	.276	.321	25	.255	4	24	21	1	2.4
1923 *NY-N	13	10	.565	34	27	7	1	2	196	219	14	49	50	12.4	4.50	85	.281	.326	12	.190	1	-11	-15	2	-1.1
1924 *NY-N	14	4	.778	30	20	11	0	2	171²	167	14	42	72	11.1	3.62	101	.254	.301	13	.228	5	5	1	2	0.8
1925 NY-N	11	9	.550	29	20	8	1	1	155	193	7	50	63	14.2	3.77	107	.308	.360	11	.216	1	9	5	2	0.7
1926 NY-N	0	0	—	2	0	0	0	0	1²	2	0	1	0	16.2	10.80	35	.286	.375	0	.000	-0	-1	-1	0	0.0
Cin-N	0	1	.000	7	0	0	0	0	17	25	0	5	4	16.4	3.71	100	.379	.431	1	.200	-0	0	-0	1	0.0
Yr	0	1	.000	9	0	0	0	0	18²	27	0	6	4	16.4	4.34	85	.370	.425	0	.000	-0	-1	-1	1	0.0
1927 Cin-N	3	5	.375	21	5	1	0	4	45¹	59	2	14	21	14.5	5.56	68	.319	.367	1	.077	-1	-8	-9	1	-0.8
Chi-N	1	1	.500	8	2	2	1	1	26¹	25	0	9	12	11.6	1.37	283	.260	.324	3	.429	1	7	7	0	0.9
Yr	4	6	.400	29	7	3	1	5	71²	84	2	23	33	13.4	4.02	95	.299	.352	1	.050	-1	-0	-2	1	0.1
1928 Chi-N	13	7	.650	31	21	10	2	0	176²	190	3	52	40	12.4	2.65	145	.281	.334	11	.190	2	26	23	1	2.7
1929 *Chi-N	8	5	.615	32	15	4	0	1	120²	148	11	39	27	14.1	5.59	83	.310	.365	13	.289	4	-12	-13	1	-0.7
Total 15	184	120	.605	451	319	182	28	13	2707²	2715	107	640	844	11.3	3.20	105	.265	.310	192	.210	33	85	45	18	10.6

■ GARY NEIBAUER
Neibauer, Gary Wayne b: 10/29/44, Billings, Mont. BR/TR, 6'3", 200 lbs. Deb: 4/12/69

YEAR TM/L	W	L	PCT	G	GS	CG	SH	SV	IP	H	HR	BB	SO	RAT	ERA	ERA+	OAV	OOB	BH	AVG	PB	PR	/A	PD	TPI
1969 *Atl-N	1	2	.333	29	4	0	0	0	57²	42	9	31	42	11.5	3.90	92	.204	.311	0	.000	-1	-2	-2	-0	-0.2
1970 Atl-N	0	3	.000	7	0	0	0	0	12²	11	0	8	9	13.5	4.97	86	.239	.352	0	.000	-0	-1	-1	-0	0.0
1971 Atl-N	1	0	1.000	6	1	0	0	1	21	14	3	9	6	10.3	2.14	173	.187	.282	0	.000	-1	3	4	0	0.4
1972 Atl-N	0	0	—	8	0	0	0	0	17¹	27	6	6	8	17.7	7.27	52	.360	.415	0	.000	-0	-7	-7	-0	-0.6
Phi-N	0	2	.000	9	2	0	0	0	18²	17	1	14	7	15.4	5.30	68	.239	.372	1	.250	0	-4	-4	-0	-0.3
Yr	0	2	.000	17	2	0	0	0	36	44	7	20	15	16.3	6.25	59	.297	.385	0	.000	-0	-11	-10	-0	-0.9
1973 Atl-N	2	1	.667	16	1	0	0	0	21¹	24	3	19	9	19.0	7.17	55	.282	.425	1	.250	1	-8	-8	-1	-0.6
Total 5	4	8	.333	75	4	0	0	1	148²	135	22	87	81	13.8	4.78	78	.242	.350	2	.069	-1	-20	-17	-1	-1.3

■ JIM NEIDLINGER
Neidlinger, James Llewellyn b: 9/24/64, Vallejo, Cal. BB/TR, 6'4", 180 lbs. Deb: 8/01/90

YEAR TM/L	W	L	PCT	G	GS	CG	SH	SV	IP	H	HR	BB	SO	RAT	ERA	ERA+	OAV	OOB	BH	AVG	PB	PR	/A	PD	TPI
1990 LA-N	5	3	.625	12	12	0	0	0	74	67	4	15	46	10.1	3.28	109	.241	.282	3	.120	-0	4	2	-1	0.2

■ AL NEIGER
Neiger, Alvin Edward b: 3/26/39, Wilmington, Del. BL/TL, 6', 195 lbs. Deb: 7/30/60

YEAR TM/L	W	L	PCT	G	GS	CG	SH	SV	IP	H	HR	BB	SO	RAT	ERA	ERA+	OAV	OOB	BH	AVG	PB	PR	/A	PD	TPI
1960 Phi-N	0	0	—	6	0	0	0	0	12²	16	2	4	3	15.6	5.68	68	.340	.415	1	.500	0	-3	-3	0	-0.1

■ ERNIE NEITZKE
Neitzke, Ernest Fredrich b: 11/13/1894, Toledo, Ohio d: 4/27/77, Sylvania, Ohio BR/TR, 5'10", 180 lbs. Deb: 6/02/21 ♦

YEAR TM/L	W	L	PCT	G	GS	CG	SH	SV	IP	H	HR	BB	SO	RAT	ERA	ERA+	OAV	OOB	BH	AVG	PB	PR	/A	PD	TPI
1921 Bos-A	0	0	—	2	0	0	0	0	7¹	8	0	4	1	14.7	6.14	69	.333	.429	6	.240	0	-2	-2	0	0.0

■ BOTS NEKOLA
Nekola, Francis Joseph b: 12/10/06, New York, N.Y. d: 3/11/87, Rockville Ctr., Md BL/TL, 5'11.5", 175 lbs. Deb: 7/19/29

YEAR TM/L	W	L	PCT	G	GS	CG	SH	SV	IP	H	HR	BB	SO	RAT	ERA	ERA+	OAV	OOB	BH	AVG	PB	PR	/A	PD	TPI
1929 NY-A	0	0	—	9	1	0	0	0	18²	21	0	15	2	17.4	4.34	89	.296	.419	2	.500	1	-0	-1	1	0.1
1933 Det-A	0	0	—	2	0	0	0	0	1¹	4	1	1	0	33.8	27.00	16	.500	.556	0	—	0	-3	-3	0	-0.2
Total 2	0	0	—	11	1	0	0	0	20	25	1	16	2	18.4	5.85	66	.316	.432	2	.500	1	-4	-4	1	-0.1

■ RED NELSON
Nelson, Albert Francis (b: Albert W. Horazdovsky)
b: 5/19/1886, Cleveland, Ohio d: 10/26/56, St.Petersburg, Fla BR/TR, 5'11", 190 lbs. Deb: 9/09/10

YEAR TM/L	W	L	PCT	G	GS	CG	SH	SV	IP	H	HR	BB	SO	RAT	ERA	ERA+	OAV	OOB	BH	AVG	PB	PR	/A	PD	TPI
1910 StL-A	5	1	.833	7	6	6	1	0	60	57	0	14	30	11.3	2.55	97	.261	.318	6	.261	2	-0	-1	4	0.6
1911 StL-A	3	9	.250	16	13	6	0	0	81	103	1	44	24	17.1	5.22	65	.324	.417	3	.111	-2	-17	-17	-1	-1.7
1912 StL-A	0	2	.000	8	3	0	0	1	18	21	0	13	9	17.0	7.00	47	.318	.430	1	.333	1	-7	-7	-1	-0.6
Phi-N	2	0	1.000	4	2	1	0	0	19¹	25	2	6	2	15.4	3.72	97	.301	.363	1	.100	-1	-1	-0	0	0.0
1913 Phi-N	0	0	—	2	0	0	0	0	8¹	9	1	4	3	14.0	2.16	154	.290	.371	1	.333	1	1	1	0	0.2
Cin-N	0	0	—	2	0	0	0	0	1²	6	0	4	0	59.4	37.80	9	.667	.786	0	—	0	-6	-6	0	-0.5
Yr	0	0	—	4	0	0	0	0	10	15	1	8	3	21.6	8.10	41	.375	.490	0	.000	0	-5	-5	0	-0.3
Total 4	10	12	.455	39	24	13	1	1	188¹	221	4	85	68	15.3	4.54	68	.305	.388	12	.182	-1	-31	-30	2	-2.0

■ ANDY NELSON
Nelson, Andrew "Peaches" TL, Deb: 5/26/08

YEAR TM/L	W	L	PCT	G	GS	CG	SH	SV	IP	H	HR	BB	SO	RAT	ERA	ERA+	OAV	OOB	BH	AVG	PB	PR	/A	PD	TPI
1908 Chi-A	0	0	—	2	1	0	0	0	9	11	0	4	1	16.0	2.00	116	.282	.364	0	.000	0	0	0	-0	0.0

■ EMMETT NELSON
Nelson, George Emmett "Ramrod" b: 2/26/05, Viborg, S.Dak. d: 8/25/67, Sioux Falls, S.D. BR/TR, 6'3", 180 lbs. Deb: 6/24/35

YEAR TM/L	W	L	PCT	G	GS	CG	SH	SV	IP	H	HR	BB	SO	RAT	ERA	ERA+	OAV	OOB	BH	AVG	PB	PR	/A	PD	TPI
1935 Cin-N	4	4	.500	19	7	3	1	1	60¹	70	2	23	14	14.2	4.33	92	.295	.363	2	.133	-1	-2	-2	1	-0.1
1936 Cin-N	1	0	1.000	6	1	0	0	0	17	24	1	4	3	15.4	3.18	120	.333	.377	1	.167	-0	2	1	0	0.1
Total 2	5	4	.556	25	8	3	1	1	77¹	94	3	27	17	14.4	4.07	97	.304	.366	3	.143	-1	-0	-1	1	0.0

■ JIM NELSON
Nelson, James Lorin b: 7/4/47, Birmingham, Ala. BR/TR, 6', 180 lbs. Deb: 5/30/70

YEAR TM/L	W	L	PCT	G	GS	CG	SH	SV	IP	H	HR	BB	SO	RAT	ERA	ERA+	OAV	OOB	BH	AVG	PB	PR	/A	PD	TPI
1970 Pit-N	4	2	.667	15	10	1	1	0	68¹	64	5	38	42	13.8	3.42	114	.255	.360	4	.200	0	5	4	-1	0.3
1971 Pit-N	2	2	.500	17	2	0	0	0	34²	27	0	26	11	15.1	2.34	145	.225	.384	3	.500	2	4	4	-0	0.6

YEAR TM/L	W	L	PCT	G	GS	CG	SH	SV	IP	H	HR	BB	SO	RAT	ERA	ERA+	OAV	OOB	BH	AVG	PB	PR	/A	PD	TPI
Total 2	6	4	.600	32	12	1	1	0	103	91	5	64	53	14.2	3.06	122	.245	.368	7	.269	2	9	8	-1	0.9

■ **LUKE NELSON**   Nelson, Luther Martin b: 12/4/1893, Cable, Ill. d: 11/14/85, Moline, Ill. BR/TR, 6', 180 lbs. Deb: 5/25/19

YEAR TM/L	W	L	PCT	G	GS	CG	SH	SV	IP	H	HR	BB	SO	RAT	ERA	ERA+	OAV	OOB	BH	AVG	PB	PR	/A	PD	TPI
1919 NY-A	3	0	1.000	9	1	0	0	0	24¹	22	1	11	11	12.6	2.96	108	.244	.333	1	.143	-0	1	1	-0	0.0

■ **LYNN NELSON**   Nelson, Lynn Bernard "Line Drive" b: 2/24/05, Sheldon, N.Dak. d: 2/15/55, Kansas City, Mo. BL/TR, 5'10.5", 170 lbs. Deb: 4/18/30 ◆

YEAR TM/L	W	L	PCT	G	GS	CG	SH	SV	IP	H	HR	BB	SO	RAT	ERA	ERA+	OAV	OOB	BH	AVG	PB	PR	/A	PD	TPI
1930 Chi-N	3	2	.600	37	3	0	0	0	81¹	97	10	28	29	14.5	5.09	96	.300	.367	4	.222	0	-1	-2	1	0.0
1933 Chi-N	5	5	.500	24	3	3	0	0	75²	65	2	30	20	11.3	3.21	102	.232	.306	5	.238	2	1	1	1	0.3
1934 Chi-N	0	1	.000	2	1	0	0	0	1	4	1	1	0	45.0	36.00	11	.667	.714	0	—	0	-4	-4	0	-0.2
1937 Phi-A	4	9	.308	30	4	1	0	2	116	140	12	51	49	15.0	5.90	80	.300	.371	40	.354	6	-16	-15	-2	-1.3
1938 Phi-A	10	11	.476	32	23	13	0	1	191	215	29	79	75	14.1	5.65	85	.277	.347	31	.277	4	-18	-17	-0	-1.4
1939 Phi-A	10	13	.435	35	24	12	2	1	197²	233	27	64	75	13.7	4.78	98	.292	.347	15	.188	-2	-4	-2	-1	-0.3
1940 Det-A	1	1	.500	6	2	0	0	0	14	23	5	9	7	20.6	10.93	44	.371	.451	8	.348	2	-10	-10	-0	-0.7
Total 7	33	42	.440	166	60	29	2	6	676²	777	86	262	255	14.0	5.25	88	.287	.353	103	.281	13	-52	-49	-0	-3.6

■ **MEL NELSON**   Nelson, Melvin Frederick b: 5/30/36, San Diego, Cal. BR/TL, 6', 185 lbs. Deb: 9/27/60

YEAR TM/L	W	L	PCT	G	GS	CG	SH	SV	IP	H	HR	BB	SO	RAT	ERA	ERA+	OAV	OOB	BH	AVG	PB	PR	/A	PD	TPI
1960 StL-N	0	1	.000	2	1	0	0	0	8	7	1	2	7	10.1	3.38	121	.226	.273	1	.500	0	0	1	0	0.1
1963 LA-A	2	3	.400	36	3	0	0	1	52²	55	7	32	41	15.2	5.30	65	.263	.366	1	.091	-1	-10	-11	1	-1.0
1965 Min-A	0	4	.000	28	3	0	0	3	54²	57	7	23	31	13.5	4.12	86	.261	.337	1	.111	-0	-4	-3	-0	-0.3
1967 Min-A	0	0	—	1	0	0	0	0	0¹	3	1	0	0	81.0	54.00	6	.750	.750	0	—	0	-2	-2	0	-0.1
1968 *StL-N	2	1	.667	18	4	1	0	0	52²	49	3	9	16	9.9	2.91	100	.254	.287	2	.167	0	-0	-0	0	0.0
1969 StL-N	0	1	.000	8	0	0	0	0	5¹	13	0	3	3	27.0	11.81	30	.520	.571	0	—	0	-5	-5	0	-0.4
Total 6	4	10	.286	93	11	1	0	5	173²	184	19	69	98	13.3	4.40	76	.271	.341	5	.147	-0	-20	-21	1	-1.7

■ **ROGER NELSON**   Nelson, Roger Eugene "Spider" b: 6/7/44, Altadena, Cal. BR/TR, 6'3", 200 lbs. Deb: 9/09/67

YEAR TM/L	W	L	PCT	G	GS	CG	SH	SV	IP	H	HR	BB	SO	RAT	ERA	ERA+	OAV	OOB	BH	AVG	PB	PR	/A	PD	TPI
1967 Chi-A	0	1	.000	5	0	0	0	0	7	4	1	0	4	7.7	1.29	241	.182	.250	0	—	0	2	1	0	0.2
1968 Bal-A	4	3	.571	19	6	0	0	0	71	49	3	26	70	9.6	2.41	121	.192	.270	1	.063	-0	5	4	-1	0.4
1969 KC-A	7	13	.350	29	29	8	1	0	193¹	170	12	65	82	11.2	3.31	112	.243	.313	8	.138	-1	7	8	-0	0.8
1970 KC-A	0	2	.000	4	2	0	0	0	9	18	3	0	3	19.0	10.00	37	.419	.432	0	—	0	-6	-6	0	-0.4
1971 KC-A	0	1	.000	13	1	0	0	0	34	35	1	5	29	10.6	5.29	65	.269	.296	2	.333	1	-7	-7	1	-0.5
1972 KC-A	11	6	.647	34	19	10	6	3	173¹	120	13	31	120	**7.9**	2.08	146	.196	**.236**	5	.093	-2	19	18	1	2.0
1973 *Cin-N	3	2	.600	14	8	1	0	0	54²	49	4	24	17	12.5	3.46	98	.246	.336	2	.111	-1	1	-0	1	0.0
1974 Cin-N	4	4	.500	14	12	1	0	1	85¹	67	7	35	42	10.9	3.38	103	.213	.293	5	.179	0	2	1	-0	0.1
1976 KC-A	0	0	—	3	0	0	0	0	8²	4	0	4	4	10.4	2.08	169	.138	.286	0	—	0	1	1	0	0.1
Total 9	29	32	.475	135	77	20	7	5	636¹	516	44	190	371	10.2	3.06	110	.224	.288	23	.128	-3	23	21	2	2.7

■ **GENE NELSON**   Nelson, Wayland Eugene b: 12/3/60, Tampa, Fla. BR/TR, 6', 172 lbs. Deb: 5/04/81

YEAR TM/L	W	L	PCT	G	GS	CG	SH	SV	IP	H	HR	BB	SO	RAT	ERA	ERA+	OAV	OOB	BH	AVG	PB	PR	/A	PD	TPI
1981 NY-A	3	1	.750	8	7	0	0	0	39¹	40	5	23	16	14.6	4.81	74	.261	.362	0	—	0	-5	-5	0	-0.4
1982 Sea-A	6	9	.400	22	19	2	1	0	122²	133	16	60	71	14.3	4.62	92	.279	.362	0	—	0	-7	-5	1	-0.3
1983 Sea-A	0	3	.000	10	5	1	0	0	32	38	6	21	11	16.9	7.88	54	.295	.397	0	—	0	-14	-13	1	-1.0
1984 Chi-A	3	5	.375	20	9	2	0	1	74²	72	9	17	36	10.8	4.46	93	.254	.299	0	—	0	-4	-3	0	-0.1
1985 Chi-A	10	10	.500	46	18	1	0	2	145²	144	23	67	101	13.5	4.26	101	.258	.345	0	.000	0	-2	1	0	0.1
1986 Chi-A	6	6	.500	54	1	0	0	6	114²	118	7	41	70	12.7	3.85	102	.271	.338	0	—	0	4	6	1	0.6
1987 Oak-A	6	5	.545	54	6	0	0	3	123²	120	12	35	94	11.6	3.93	105	.249	.307	0	—	0	7	3	-1	0.2
1988 *Oak-A	9	6	.600	54	1	0	0	3	111²	93	9	38	67	10.8	3.06	123	.228	.298	0	—	0	11	9	-1	0.8
1989 *Oak-A	3	5	.375	50	0	0	0	3	80	60	5	30	70	10.3	3.26	113	.203	.280	0	—	0	6	4	-2	0.2
1990 *Oak-A	3	3	.500	51	0	0	0	5	74²	55	5	17	38	9.0	1.57	238	.208	.263	0	—	0	19	18	-1	1.8
Total 10	49	53	.480	369	66	6	1	23	919	873	97	349	574	12.2	3.93	104	.250	.323	0	.000	0	16	14	-1	1.9

■ **BILL NELSON**   Nelson, William F. b: 9/28/1863, Terre Haute, Ind. d: 6/23/41, Terre Haute, Ind. TR, Deb: 9/03/1884

YEAR TM/L	W	L	PCT	G	GS	CG	SH	SV	IP	H	HR	BB	SO	RAT	ERA	ERA+	OAV	OOB	BH	AVG	PB	PR	/A	PD	TPI
1884 Pit-a	1	2	.333	3	3	3	0	0	26	26	1	8	6	11.8	4.50	75	.246	.300	2	.167	-1	-4	-3	-0	-0.3

■ **HAL NEUBAUER**   Neubauer, Harold Charles b: 5/13/02, Hoboken, N.J. d: 9/9/49, Barrington, R.I. BR/TR, 6'0.5", 185 lbs. Deb: 6/12/25

YEAR TM/L	W	L	PCT	G	GS	CG	SH	SV	IP	H	HR	BB	SO	RAT	ERA	ERA+	OAV	OOB	BH	AVG	PB	PR	/A	PD	TPI
1925 Bos-A	1	0	1.000	7	0	0	0	0	10¹	17	2	11	4	24.4	12.19	37	.378	.500	0	—	0	-9	-9	0	-0.7

■ **TEX NEUER**   Neuer, John S. b: 6/8/1877, Fremont, Ohio d: 1/14/66, Northumberland, Pa TL, Deb: 8/28/07

YEAR TM/L	W	L	PCT	G	GS	CG	SH	SV	IP	H	HR	BB	SO	RAT	ERA	ERA+	OAV	OOB	BH	AVG	PB	PR	/A	PD	TPI
1907 NY-A	4	2	.667	7	6	6	3	0	54	40	1	19	22	9.8	2.17	129	.208	.280	2	.095	-2	2	4	-1	0.1

■ **DAN NEUMEIER**   Neumeier, Daniel George b: 3/9/48, Shawano, Wis. BR/TR, 6'5", 205 lbs. Deb: 9/08/72

YEAR TM/L	W	L	PCT	G	GS	CG	SH	SV	IP	H	HR	BB	SO	RAT	ERA	ERA+	OAV	OOB	BH	AVG	PB	PR	/A	PD	TPI
1972 Chi-A	0	0	—	3	0	0	0	0	3	2	0	3	0	15.0	9.00	35	.200	.385	0	.000	-0	-2	-2	0	-0.1

■ **ERNIE NEVEL**   Nevel, Ernie Wyre b: 8/17/19, Charleston, Mo. d: 7/10/88, Springfield, Mo. BR/TR, 5'11", 190 lbs. Deb: 9/26/50

YEAR TM/L	W	L	PCT	G	GS	CG	SH	SV	IP	H	HR	BB	SO	RAT	ERA	ERA+	OAV	OOB	BH	AVG	PB	PR	/A	PD	TPI
1950 NY-A	0	1	.000	3	1	0	0	0	6¹	10	4	0	6	22.7	9.95	43	.345	.457	0	.000	-0	-4	-4	0	-0.2
1951 NY-A	0	0	—	1	0	0	0	1	4	1	0	1	1	4.5	0.00	—	.083	.154	0	.000	-0	2	2	-0	0.1
1953 Cin-N	0	0	—	10	0	0	0	0	10¹	16	0	1	5	14.8	6.10	71	.390	.405	0	—	0	-2	-2	-0	-0.1
Total 3	0	1	.000	14	1	0	0	1	20²	27	0	8	9	15.2	6.10	69	.329	.389	0	.000	0	-4	-4	0	-0.2

■ **ERNIE NEVERS**   Nevers, Ernest Alonzo b: 6/11/03, Willow River, Minn. d: 5/3/76, San Rafael, Cal. BR/TR, 6', 205 lbs. Deb: 4/26/26

YEAR TM/L	W	L	PCT	G	GS	CG	SH	SV	IP	H	HR	BB	SO	RAT	ERA	ERA+	OAV	OOB	BH	AVG	PB	PR	/A	PD	TPI
1926 StL-A	2	4	.333	11	7	4	0	0	74²	82	4	24	16	12.9	4.46	96	.290	.347	5	.185	-1	-4	-1	2	0.0
1927 StL-A	3	8	.273	27	5	2	0	2	94²	105	8	35	22	13.5	4.94	88	.311	.379	7	.219	-1	-8	-6	1	-0.4
1928 StL-A	1	0	1.000	6	0	0	0	0	9	9	1	2	1	11.0	3.00	140	.281	.324	0	.000	-0	1	1	0	0.1
Total 3	6	12	.333	44	12	6	0	2	178¹	196	13	61	39	13.1	4.64	93	.300	.363	12	.200	-2	-11	-6	4	-0.3

■ **DON NEWCOMBE**   Newcombe, Donald "Newk" b: 6/14/26, Madison, N.J. BL/TR, 6'4", 220 lbs. Deb: 5/20/49 ◆

YEAR TM/L	W	L	PCT	G	GS	CG	SH	SV	IP	H	HR	BB	SO	RAT	ERA	ERA+	OAV	OOB	BH	AVG	PB	PR	/A	PD	TPI
1949 *Bro-N	17	8	.680	38	31	19	**5**	1	244¹	223	17	73	149	11.0	3.17	129	.243	.301	22	.229	3	24	25	0	3.0
1950 Bro-N	19	11	.633	40	35	20	4	3	267¹	258	22	75	130	11.3	3.70	111	.254	.306	24	.247	7	13	12	1	1.9
1951 Bro-N	20	9	.690	40	36	18	3	0	272	261	19	91	164	11.0	3.28	120	.230	.297	23	.223	5	21	20	0	2.6
1954 Bro-N	9	8	.529	29	25	6	0	0	144¹	158	24	49	82	13.2	4.55	90	.274	.337	15	.319	-1	-8	-8	-1	-0.3
1955 *Bro-N	20	5	**.800**	34	31	17	1	0	233²	222	35	38	143	**10.1**	3.20	127	.249	.280	42	.359	20	22	22	0	**4.3**
1956 *Bro-N	27	7	.794	**38**	36	18	5	0	268	219	33	46	139	**9.0**	3.06	130	**.221**	**.257**	26	.234	9	21	**27**	0	**4.0**
1957 Bro-N	11	12	.478	28	28	12	4	0	198²	199	28	33	90	10.6	3.49	119	.258	.290	17	.230	5	9	15	2	2.3
1958 LA-N	0	6	.000	11	8	1	0	0	34¹	53	11	8	16	16.0	7.86	52	.346	.379	5	.417	2	-15	-14	0	-1.1
Cin-N	7	7	.500	20	18	7	0	1	133¹	159	20	28	53	12.7	3.85	108	.298	.335	21	.350	8	2	4	-1	1.2
Yr	7	13	.350	31	26	8	0	1	167²	212	31	36	69	13.4	4.67	89	.309	.344	10	.359	10	-13	-10	-1	0.1
1959 Cin-N	13	8	.619	30	29	17	2	1	222	216	25	27	100	10.1	3.16	128	.253	.280	32	.305	15	19	22	-1	2.3
1960 Cin-N	4	6	.400	16	15	1	0	0	82²	99	12	14	36	12.6	4.57	84	.304	.338	5	.139	-0	-7	-7	-1	-0.7
Cle-A	2	3	.400	20	2	0	0	0	54	64	9	12	21	11.5	4.33	86	.289	.315	6	.300	2	-3	-4	-1	-0.2
Total 10	149	90	.623	344	294	136	24	7	2154²	2102	252	490	1129	11.0	3.56	114	.254	.299	238	.271	81	97	116	-4	19.3

■ **TOM NEWELL**   Newell, Thomas Dean b: 5/17/63, Monrovia, Cal. BR/TR, 6'1", 185 lbs. Deb: 9/09/87

YEAR TM/L	W	L	PCT	G	GS	CG	SH	SV	IP	H	HR	BB	SO	RAT	ERA	ERA+	OAV	OOB	BH	AVG	PB	PR	/A	PD	TPI
1987 Phi-N	0	0	—	2	0	0	0	0	1	4	1	3	1	63.0	36.00	12	.571	.700	0	—	0	-4	-4	0	-0.2

■ **DON NEWHAUSER**   Newhauser, Donald Louis b: 11/7/47, Miami, Fla. BR/TR, 6'4", 200 lbs. Deb: 6/15/72

YEAR TM/L	W	L	PCT	G	GS	CG	SH	SV	IP	H	HR	BB	SO	RAT	ERA	ERA+	OAV	OOB	BH	AVG	PB	PR	/A	PD	TPI
1972 Bos-A	4	2	.667	31	0	0	0	4	37	30	2	25	27	13.9	2.43	132	.226	.356	0	.000	-0	3	3	0	0.3
1973 Bos-A	0	0	—	9	0	0	0	1	12	9	0	13	8	17.3	0.00	—	.205	.397	0	—	0	5	5	-0	0.5
1974 Bos-A	0	1	.000	2	0	0	0	0	3²	5	0	4	2	22.1	9.82	39	.357	.500	0	—	0	-3	-2	0	-0.1

YEAR TM/L	W	L	PCT	G	GS	CG	SH	SV	IP	H	HR	BB	SO	RAT	ERA	ERA+	OAV	OOB	BH	AVG	PB	PR	/A	PD	TPI
Total 3	4	3	.571	42	0	0	0	5	52²	44	2	42	37	15.2	2.39	144	.230	.377	0	.000	-0	5	6	-0	0.7

■ HAL NEWHOUSER
Newhouser, Harold   b: 5/20/21, Detroit, Mich.   BL/TL, 6'2", 180 lbs.   Deb: 9/29/39

YEAR TM/L	W	L	PCT	G	GS	CG	SH	SV	IP	H	HR	BB	SO	RAT	ERA	ERA+	OAV	OOB	BH	AVG	PB	PR	/A	PD	TPI
1939 Det-A	0	1	.000	1	1	1	0	0	5	3	0	4	4	12.6	5.40	91	.188	.350	0	.000	-0	-0	-0	0	0.0
1940 Det-A	9	9	.500	28	20	7	0	0	133¹	149	12	76	89	15.3	4.86	98	.282	.374	8	.200	-1	-7	-2	2	0.0
1941 Det-A	9	11	.450	33	27	5	1	0	173	166	6	137	106	15.8	4.79	95	.249	.378	9	.150	-2	-12	-5	1	-0.4
1942 Det-A	8	14	.364	38	23	11	1	5	183²	137	4	114	103	12.4	2.45	161	.207	.325	8	.154	-1	25	31	2	3.5
1943 Det-A	8	17	.320	37	25	10	1	1	195²	163	3	111	144	12.6	3.04	116	.224	.327	12	.185	-1	6	11	2	1.4
1944 Det-A	29	9	.763	47	34	25	6	2	312¹	264	6	102	187	10.6	2.22	161	.230	.293	29	.242	4	42	47	0	5.8
1945 *Det-A	25	9	.735	40	36	29	8	2	313¹	239	5	110	212	10.0	1.81	194	.211	.281	28	.257	5	54	59	2	7.9
1946 Det-A	26	9	.743	37	34	29	6	1	292²	215	10	98	275	9.7	1.94	189	.201	.269	13	.126	-1	51	56	0	6.4
1947 Det-A	17	17	.500	40	36	24	3	2	285	268	9	110	176	12.0	2.87	131	.249	.320	19	.198	2	26	28	2	3.6
1948 Det-A	21	12	.636	39	35	19	2	1	272¹	249	10	99	143	11.5	3.01	145	.242	.309	19	.207	1	39	41	1	4.5
1949 Det-A	18	11	.621	38	35	22	3	1	292	277	19	111	144	12.0	3.36	124	.251	.319	18	.198	2	27	26	2	3.0
1950 Det-A	15	13	.536	35	30	15	1	3	213²	232	23	81	87	13.4	4.34	108	.279	.346	13	.176	-2	6	8	-0	0.6
1951 Det-A	6	6	.500	15	14	7	1	0	96¹	98	10	19	37	11.2	3.92	106	.268	.310	9	.310	2	2	3	1	0.6
1952 Det-A	9	9	.500	25	19	8	0	0	154	148	13	47	57	11.4	3.74	102	.254	.310	10	.217	3	-1	1	1	0.6
1953 Det-A	0	1	.000	7	4	0	0	1	21²	31	4	8	6	17.0	7.06	58	.348	.414	4	.500	2	-7	-7	-0	-0.4
1954 *Cle-A	7	2	.778	26	1	0	0	7	46²	34	3	18	25	10.0	2.51	147	.209	.287	2	.154	-0	6	6	-0	0.6
1955 Cle-A	0	0	—	2	0	0	0	0	2¹	1	0	4	1	19.3	0.00	—	.125	.417	0	—	0	1	1	0	0.1
Total 17	207	150	.580	488	374	212	33	26	2993	2674	137	1249	1796	11.9	3.06	130	.239	.316	201	.201	12	257	305	16	37.8

■ FLOYD NEWKIRK
Newkirk, Floyd Elmo "Three-Finger"   b: 7/16/08, Norris City, Ill.   d: 4/15/76, Clayton, Mo.   BR/TR, 5'11", 178 lbs.   Deb: 8/21/34

YEAR TM/L	W	L	PCT	G	GS	CG	SH	SV	IP	H	HR	BB	SO	RAT	ERA	ERA+	OAV	OOB	BH	AVG	PB	PR	/A	PD	TPI
1934 NY-A	0	0	—	1	0	0	0	0	1	1	0	1	0	18.0	0.00	—	.333	.500	0	—	0	0	0	0	0.1

■ JOEL NEWKIRK
Newkirk, Joel Inez "Sailor"   b: 5/1/1896, Kyana, Ind.   d: 1/22/66, Eldorado, Ill.   BR/TR, 6', 180 lbs.   Deb: 8/20/19

YEAR TM/L	W	L	PCT	G	GS	CG	SH	SV	IP	H	HR	BB	SO	RAT	ERA	ERA+	OAV	OOB	BH	AVG	PB	PR	/A	PD	TPI
1919 Chi-N	0	0	—	1	0	0	0	0	2	2	0	3	1	27.0	13.50	21	.286	.545	0	.000	-0	-2	-2	0	-0.1
1920 Chi-N	0	1	.000	2	1	0	0	0	6²	8	1	6	2	18.9	5.40	59	.333	.467	0	.000	-0	-2	-2	-0	-0.2
Total 2	0	1	.000	3	1	0	0	0	8²	10	1	9	3	20.8	7.27	43	.323	.488	0	.000	-1	-4	-4	-0	-0.3

■ MAURY NEWLIN
Newlin, Maurice Milton   b: 6/22/14, Bloomingdale, Ind   d: 8/14/78, Houston, Tex.   BR/TR, 6', 176 lbs.   Deb: 9/20/40

YEAR TM/L	W	L	PCT	G	GS	CG	SH	SV	IP	H	HR	BB	SO	RAT	ERA	ERA+	OAV	OOB	BH	AVG	PB	PR	/A	PD	TPI
1940 StL-A	1	0	1.000	1	1	0	0	0	6	4	1	2	3	9.0	6.00	76	.190	.261	1	.500	0	-1	-1	-0	0.0
1941 StL-A	0	2	.000	14	0	0	0	1	27²	43	4	12	10	17.9	6.51	66	.361	.420	0	.000	-1	-7	-7	1	-0.6
Total 2	1	2	.333	15	1	0	0	1	33²	47	5	14	13	16.3	6.42	68	.336	.396	1	.125	-1	-8	-8	0	-0.6

■ FRED NEWMAN
Newman, Frederick William   b: 2/21/42, Boston, Mass.   d: 6/24/87, Framingham, Mass.   BR/TR, 6'3", 180 lbs.   Deb: 9/16/62

YEAR TM/L	W	L	PCT	G	GS	CG	SH	SV	IP	H	HR	BB	SO	RAT	ERA	ERA+	OAV	OOB	BH	AVG	PB	PR	/A	PD	TPI
1962 LA-A	0	1	.000	4	1	0	0	0	6¹	11	0	3	4	19.9	9.95	39	.393	.452	0	.000	-0	-4	-4	-0	-0.3
1963 LA-A	1	5	.167	12	8	0	0	0	44	56	6	15	16	14.9	5.32	64	.316	.376	4	.250	1	-8	-9	-0	-0.8
1964 LA-A	13	10	.565	32	28	7	2	0	190	177	9	39	83	10.6	2.75	120	.246	.291	11	.180	2	19	11	5	1.9
1965 Cal-A	14	16	.467	36	36	10	2	0	260²	225	15	64	109	10.0	2.93	116	.234	.282	7	.095	-0	15	13	9	2.4
1966 Cal-A	4	7	.364	21	19	1	0	0	102²	112	7	31	42	13.1	4.73	71	.289	.351	6	.200	1	-15	-16	1	-1.3
1967 Cal-A	1	0	1.000	3	1	0	0	0	6¹	8	1	2	0	15.6	1.42	221	.320	.393	0	.000	-0	1	1	-0	0.1
Total 6	33	39	.458	108	93	18	4	0	610	589	38	154	254	11.2	3.41	99	.256	.308	28	.153	3	8	-3	14	2.0

■ JEFF NEWMAN
Newman, Jeffrey Lynn   b: 9/11/48, Fort Worth, Tex.   BR/TR, 6'2", 215 lbs.   Deb: 6/30/76   MC♦

YEAR TM/L	W	L	PCT	G	GS	CG	SH	SV	IP	H	HR	BB	SO	RAT	ERA	ERA+	OAV	OOB	BH	AVG	PB	PR	/A	PD	TPI
1977 Oak-A	0	0	—	1	0	0	0	0	1	1	0	0	0	18.0	0.00	—	.250	.400	36	.222	0	0	0	0	0.0

■ RAY NEWMAN
Newman, Raymond Francis   b: 6/20/45, Evansville, Ind.   BL/TL, 6'5", 205 lbs.   Deb: 5/16/71

YEAR TM/L	W	L	PCT	G	GS	CG	SH	SV	IP	H	HR	BB	SO	RAT	ERA	ERA+	OAV	OOB	BH	AVG	PB	PR	/A	PD	TPI
1971 Chi-N	1	2	.333	30	0	0	0	2	38¹	30	4	17	35	11.0	3.52	112	.219	.305	0	.000	-1	-0	2	0	0.1
1972 Mil-A	0	0	—	4	0	0	0	1	7	4	0	2	1	7.7	0.00	—	.182	.250	1	1.000	0	2	2	0	0.4
1973 Mil-A	2	1	.667	11	0	0	0	1	18¹	19	2	5	10	11.8	2.95	128	.260	.308	0	—	0	2	2	1	0.2
Total 3	3	3	.500	45	0	0	0	4	63²	53	6	24	46	10.9	2.97	128	.228	.301	1	.143	-1	4	6	1	0.7

■ BOBO NEWSOM
Newsom, Louis Norman "Buck"   b: 8/11/07, Hartsville, S.C.   d: 12/7/62, Orlando, Fla.   BR/TR, 6'3", 200 lbs.   Deb: 9/11/29

YEAR TM/L	W	L	PCT	G	GS	CG	SH	SV	IP	H	HR	BB	SO	RAT	ERA	ERA+	OAV	OOB	BH	AVG	PB	PR	/A	PD	TPI
1929 Bro-N	0	3	.000	3	2	0	0	0	9¹	15	5	5	6	19.3	10.61	43	.375	.444	0	.000	-0	-6	-6	0	-0.4
1930 Bro-N	0	0	—	2	0	0	0	0	3	2	0	2	1	12.0	—	—	.167	.286	0	—	-0	2	2	0	0.1
1932 Chi-N	0	0	—	1	0	0	0	0	1	1	0	0	0	9.0	0.00	—	.333	.333	0	—	0	0	0	0	0.1
1934 StL-A	16	20	.444	47	32	15	2	5	262¹	259	15	149	135	14.0	4.01	124	.261	.358	17	.183	-3	14	29	-0	2.5
1935 StL-A	0	6	.000	7	6	1	0	1	42²	54	2	13	22	14.1	4.85	99	.303	.351	1	.091	-1	-2	-0	-0	0.0
Was-A	11	12	.478	28	23	17	2	2	198¹	222	9	84	65	14.1	4.45	97	.288	.361	22	.301	4	0	-3	-2	0.0
Yr	11	18	.379	35	29	18	2	3	241	276	11	97	87	14.1	4.52	97	.291	.359	23	.236	3	-2	-3	-2	0.0
1936 Was-A	17	15	.531	43	38	24	4	2	285²	294	13	146	156	14.0	4.32	111	.268	.355	23	.213	-1	23	15	0	1.2
1937 Was-A	3	4	.429	11	10	3	0	0	67²	76	4	48	39	16.9	5.85	76	.287	.402	3	.120	-1	-9	-11	-2	-0.9
Bos-A	13	10	.565	30	27	14	1	0	207²	193	14	119	127	13.7	4.46	106	.243	.344	19	.253	2	4	6	-2	0.7
Yr	16	14	.533	41	37	17	1	0	275¹	269	18	167	166	14.3	4.81	97	.253	.356	22	.030	3	-6	-4	-2	-0.2
1938 StL-A	20	16	.556	44	40	31	0	1	329²	334	30	192	226	14.5	5.08	98	.265	.364	31	.250	2	-11	-4	-4	-0.5
1939 StL-A	3	1	.750	6	6	3	0	0	45²	50	5	22	28	14.4	4.73	103	.266	.346	4	.222	-0	-1	1	0	0.0
Det-A	17	10	.630	35	31	21	3	2	246	222	14	104	164	12.0	3.37	145	.238	.316	18	.186	-4	34	42	-2	3.6
Yr	20	11	.645	41	37	24	3	2	291²	272	19	126	192	12.3	3.58	136	.243	.320	1	.009	-4	34	42	-2	3.6
1940 *Det-A	21	5	.808	36	34	20	3	0	264	235	19	100	164	11.5	2.83	168	.238	.310	23	.215	-1	46	56	-3	5.4
1941 Det-A	12	20	.375	43	36	12	2	2	250¹	265	15	118	175	13.9	4.60	99	.264	.343	9	.102	-6	-13	-2	-2	-0.8
1942 Was-A	11	17	.393	30	29	15	2	0	213²	236	6	92	113	13.9	4.93	74	.280	.353	12	.160	-2	-30	-30	-3	-3.3
Bro-N	2	2	.500	6	5	2	1	0	32	28	1	14	21	12.1	3.38	97	.235	.321	0	.000	-1	-0	-0	-1	-0.2
1943 Bro-N	9	4	.692	22	12	6	1	1	125	113	4	57	75	12.4	3.02	111	.244	.329	11	.250	1	5	5	0	0.6
StL-A	1	6	.143	10	9	0	0	0	52¹	69	7	35	37	18.1	7.39	45	.318	.415	5	.333	-1	-24	-24	-1	-2.2
Was-A	3	3	.500	6	6	2	0	0	40	38	1	21	11	13.7	3.82	84	.247	.345	2	.133	-1	-2	-3	-1	-0.4
Yr	4	9	.308	16	15	2	0	0	92¹	107	8	56	48	16.1	5.85	56	.288	.384	0	.000	0	-26	-26	-2	-2.6
1944 Phi-A	13	15	.464	37	33	18	2	1	265	243	11	82	142	11.2	2.82	123	.244	.304	10	.114	-6	18	19	-2	1.3
1945 Phi-A	8	20	.286	36	34	16	3	0	257¹	255	12	103	127	12.6	3.29	104	.260	.332	14	.163	-4	2	4	-5	-0.4
1946 Phi-A	3	5	.375	10	9	3	1	0	58²	61	7	30	32	14.7	3.38	105	.266	.364	2	.105	-1	1	1	-1	0.0
Was-A	11	8	.579	24	22	14	2	1	178	163	5	60	82	11.4	2.78	120	.242	.306	10	.161	-2	14	11	-3	0.6
Yr	14	13	.519	34	31	17	3	1	236²	224	7	90	114	12.0	2.93	116	.247	.316	0	.000	-3	15	12	-4	0.6
1947 Was-A	4	6	.400	14	13	1	0	0	83²	99	2	37	40	14.7	4.09	91	.296	.368	7	.241	1	-4	-3	-2	-0.4
*NY-A	7	5	.583	17	15	6	2	0	115²	109	8	30	42	11.0	2.80	126	.250	.301	4	.095	-3	12	9	-1	0.5
Yr	11	11	.500	31	28	7	2	0	199¹	208	10	67	82	12.5	3.34	108	.270	.330	0	.000	-1	8	6	-3	0.1
1948 NY-N	0	4	.000	11	4	0	0	0	25²	35	1	13	19	16.8	4.21	94	.330	.403	0	.429	-1	-1	-1	-0	-0.1
1952 Was-A	1	1	.500	10	0	0	0	2	12²	16	2	9	5	17.8	4.97	72	.302	.403	0	.000	-0	-2	-2	0	-0.1
Phi-A	3	3	.500	14	5	1	0	1	47²	38	2	23	22	11.9	3.59	110	.220	.318	2	.133	-1	2	2	0	0.2
Yr	4	4	.500	24	5	1	0	3	60¹	54	4	32	27	13.1	3.88	100	.239	.358	0	.000	-1	-1	0	1	0.1
1953 Phi-A	2	1	.667	17	2	1	0	0	38²	44	3	24	16	17.0	4.89	88	.282	.395	1	.167	-0	-4	-3	-0	-0.2
Total 20	211	222	.487	600	483	246	31	21	3759¹	3769	206	1732	2082	13.3	3.98	107	.261	.342	253	.189	-27	67	109	-34	7.0

■ DICK NEWSOME
Newsome, Heber Hampton   b: 12/13/09, Ahoskie, N.C.   d: 12/15/65, Ahoskie, N.C.   BR/TR, 6', 185 lbs.   Deb: 4/25/41

YEAR TM/L	W	L	PCT	G	GS	CG	SH	SV	IP	H	HR	BB	SO	RAT	ERA	ERA+	OAV	OOB	BH	AVG	PB	PR	/A	PD	TPI
1941 Bos-A	19	10	.655	36	29	17	2	0	213²	235	13	79	58	13.5	4.13	101	.277	.344	19	.244	3	0	1	4	0.7
1942 Bos-A	8	10	.444	24	23	11	0	0	158	174	11	67	40	13.7	5.01	74	.278	.348	13	.236	2	-24	-23	1	-1.8

YEAR TM/L	W	L	PCT	G	GS	CG	SH	SV	IP	H	HR	BB	SO	RAT	ERA	ERA+	OAV	OOB	BH	AVG	PB	PR	/A	PD	TPI
1943 Bos-A	8	13	.381	25	22	8	2	0	154¹	166	8	68	40	13.9	4.49	74	.274	.352	7	.146	-1	-20	-20	-1	-2.2
Total 3	35	33	.515	85	74	36	4	0	526	575	32	214	138	13.7	4.50	84	.276	.347	39	.215	3	-44	-42	4	-3.3

■ DOC NEWTON
Newton, Eustace James b: 10/26/1877, Indianapolis, Ind. d: 5/14/31, Memphis, Tenn. BL/TL, 6', 185 lbs. Deb: 4/27/00

YEAR TM/L	W	L	PCT	G	GS	CG	SH	SV	IP	H	HR	BB	SO	RAT	ERA	ERA+	OAV	OOB	BH	AVG	PB	PR	/A	PD	TPI
1900 Cin-N	9	15	.375	35	27	22	1	0	234²	255	4	100	88	13.6	4.14	89	.276	.347	17	.198	-1	-12	-12	-2	-1.3
1901 Cin-N	4	13	.235	20	18	17	0	0	168¹	190	6	59	65	14.0	4.12	78	.282	.352	9	.130	-4	-15	-17	1	-1.8
Bro-N	6	5	.545	13	12	9	0	0	105	110	1	30	45	12.6	2.83	119	.268	.328	9	.220	1	6	6	0	0.7
Yr	10	18	.357	33	30	26	0	0	273¹	300	7	89	110	13.0	3.62	90	.274	.332	4	.036	-3	-9	-11	1	-1.1
1902 Bro-N	15	14	.517	31	28	26	4	2	264¹	208	2	87	107	10.4	2.42	114	.217	.288	19	.174	-1	11	10	-2	0.8
1905 NY-A	2	2	.500	11	7	2	0	0	59²	61	1	24	15	12.8	2.11	139	.266	.335	3	.136	-1	4	5	-1	0.4
1906 NY-A	7	5	.583	21	15	6	2	0	125	118	3	33	52	10.9	3.17	94	.252	.302	9	.220	-0	-7	-3	2	0.0
1907 NY-A	7	10	.412	19	15	11	0	0	133	132	6	31	70	11.0	3.18	88	.261	.303	4	.108	-1	-9	-6	0	-0.6
1908 NY-A	4	5	.444	23	13	6	1	1	88¹	78	0	41	49	12.8	2.95	84	.242	.341	4	.160	-0	-5	-5	-0	-0.5
1909 NY-A	0	3	.000	4	4	1	0	0	22¹	27	0	11	11	16.5	2.82	90	.300	.394	1	.167	0	-1	-1	1	0.0
Total 8	54	72	.429	177	139	100	8	3	1200²	1179	17	416	502	12.2	3.22	95	.257	.324	75	.172	-8	-29	-19	-2	-2.3

■ KID NICHOLS
Nichols, Charles Augustus b: 9/14/1869, Madison, Wis. d: 4/11/53, Kansas City, Mo. BB/TR, 5'10.5", 175 lbs. Deb: 4/23/1890 MH

YEAR TM/L	W	L	PCT	G	GS	CG	SH	SV	IP	H	HR	BB	SO	RAT	ERA	ERA+	OAV	OOB	BH	AVG	PB	PR	/A	PD	TPI
1890 Bos-N	27	19	.587	48	47	47	7	0	424	374	8	112	222	10.3	2.23	168	.230	.280	43	.247	1	63	71	-0	7.0
1891 Bos-N	30	17	.638	52	48	45	5	3	425²	413	15	103	240	10.9	2.39	153	.245	.288	36	.197	-3	45	60	5	6.0
1892 *Bos-N	35	16	.686	53	51	49	5	0	453	404	15	121	187	10.4	2.84	124	.229	.279	39	.198	1	22	34	-1	3.4
1893 Bos-N	34	14	.708	52	44	43	1	1	425	426	15	118	94	11.5	3.52	141	.253	.302	39	.220	-2	55	67	-2	5.6
1894 Bos-N	32	13	.711	50	46	40	3	0	407	488	23	121	113	13.5	4.75	120	.304	.342	50	.294	3	26	42	0	3.7
1895 Bos-N	26	16	.619	47	42	42	1	3	379²	417	15	86	140	11.9	3.41	149	.275	.314	37	.236	-4	58	71	-1	5.8
1896 Bos-N	30	14	.682	49	43	37	3	1	372¹	387	14	101	102	11.4	2.83	161	.266	.313	28	.190	-4	63	71	1	6.3
1897 *Bos-N	31	11	.738	46	40	37	2	3	368	362	9	68	127	10.5	2.64	169	.255	.289	39	.265	3	68	75	-3	7.1
1898 Bos-N	31	12	.721	50	42	40	5	4	388	316	7	85	138	9.3	2.13	173	.221	.265	64	.241	4	64	67	-2	6.9
1899 Bos-N	21	19	.525	42	37	37	4	1	343¹	326	11	82	108	10.7	2.99	139	.250	.295	26	.191	-5	33	45	-1	3.9
1900 Bos-N	13	16	.448	29	27	25	4	0	231¹	215	11	72	53	11.2	3.07	134	.246	.303	18	.200	-2	16	27	-0	2.5
1901 Bos-N	19	16	.543	38	34	33	4	0	321	306	8	90	143	11.3	3.22	112	.250	.305	46	.282	11	4	14	-1	3.0
1904 StL-N	21	13	.618	36	35	35	3	1	317	268	3	50	134	9.2	2.02	134	.222	.256	17	.156	-1	25	24	-1	2.4
1905 StL-N	1	5	.167	7	7	5	0	0	52	64	1	18	16	14.2	5.37	56	.296	.350	5	.227	0	-14	-14	-1	-1.3
Phi-N	10	6	.625	17	16	15	1	0	139	129	1	28	50	10.4	2.27	129	.250	.294	10	.189	0	11	10	-4	0.7
Yr	11	11	.500	24	23	20	1	0	191	193	2	46	66	11.5	3.11	94	.264	.311	2	.027	-5	-2	-4	-5	-0.6
1906 Phi-N	0	1	.000	4	2	1	0	0	11	17	0	13	1	26.2	9.82	27	.386	.542	0	.000	-0	-9	-9	-0	-0.8
Total 15	361	208	.634	620	561	531	48	17	5057¹	4912	156	1268	1868	11.0	2.95	139	.250	.296	471	.226	1	531	653	-11	62.2

■ CHET NICHOLS
Nichols, Chester Raymond Jr. b: 2/22/31, Pawtucket, R.I. BB/TL, 6'1.5", 165 lbs. Deb: 4/19/51

YEAR TM/L	W	L	PCT	G	GS	CG	SH	SV	IP	H	HR	BB	SO	RAT	ERA	ERA+	OAV	OOB	BH	AVG	PB	PR	/A	PD	TPI
1951 Bos-N	11	8	.579	33	19	12	3	2	156	142	4	69	71	12.2	2.88	127	.246	.327	7	.137	-2	19	14	2	1.3
1954 Mil-N	9	11	.450	35	20	5	1	1	122¹	132	5	65	55	14.8	4.41	84	.286	.379	3	.086	-2	-5	-9	1	-1.0
1955 Mil-N	9	8	.529	34	21	6	0	1	144	139	20	67	44	12.9	4.00	94	.253	.335	8	.154	-2	1	-4	2	-0.3
1956 Mil-N	0	1	.000	2	0	0	0	0	4	9	1	3	2	27.0	6.75	51	.563	.632	0	.000	-0	-1	-1	0	0.0
1960 Bos-A	0	2	.000	6	1	0	0	0	12²	12	0	4	11	11.4	4.26	95	.240	.296	0	.000	-0	-0	-0	0	0.0
1961 Bos-A	3	2	.600	26	2	0	0	3	51²	40	3	26	20	11.5	2.09	199	.221	.319	1	.111	-0	11	12	3	1.5
1962 Bos-A	1	1	.500	29	1	0	0	3	57	61	3	22	33	13.1	3.00	138	.276	.342	0	.000	-1	6	7	1	0.8
1963 Bos-A	1	3	.250	21	7	0	0	0	52²	61	8	24	27	14.5	4.78	79	.298	.371	3	.231	0	-7	-6	0	-0.5
1964 Cin-N	0	0	—	3	0	0	0	0	3	4	1	0	3	12.0	6.00	60	.308	.308	0	—	0	-1	-0	0	0.0
Total 9	34	36	.486	189	71	23	4	10	603¹	600	45	280	266	13.2	3.64	105	.264	.346	22	.127	-8	22	11	10	1.8

■ CHET NICHOLS
Nichols, Chester Raymond Sr. "Nick" b: 7/3/1897, Woonsocket, R.I. d: 7/11/82, Pawtucket, R.I. BR/TR, 5'11", 160 lbs. Deb: 7/30/26

YEAR TM/L	W	L	PCT	G	GS	CG	SH	SV	IP	H	HR	BB	SO	RAT	ERA	ERA+	OAV	OOB	BH	AVG	PB	PR	/A	PD	TPI
1926 Pit-N	0	0	—	3	0	0	0	0	7²	13	0	5	2	21.1	8.22	48	.342	.419	1	.333	0	-4	-4	0	-0.2
1927 Pit-N	0	3	.000	8	0	0	0	0	27²	34	1	17	9	16.9	5.86	70	.309	.406	1	.111	-0	-6	-5	0	-0.5
1928 NY-N	0	0	—	3	0	0	0	0	2²	11	0	3	1	50.6	23.63	17	.611	.682	0	—	0	-6	-6	0	-0.4
1930 Phi-N	1	2	.333	16	5	1	0	0	59²	76	8	16	15	14.2	6.79	80	.306	.353	6	.300	0	-12	-9	1	-0.5
1931 Phi-N	0	1	.000	3	0	0	0	0	5²	10	0	1	1	17.5	9.53	45	.435	.458	0	.000	-0	-4	-3	0	-0.2
1932 Phi-N	0	2	.000	11	0	0	0	1	19¹	23	2	14	5	17.2	6.98	63	.299	.407	0	.000	-1	-7	-6	0	-0.4
Total 6	1	8	.111	44	5	1	0	1	122²	167	11	56	33	16.7	7.19	67	.325	.395	8	.211	-1	-38	-33	2	-2.2

■ DOLAN NICHOLS
Nichols, Dolan Levon "Nick" b: 2/28/30, Tishomingo, Miss. d: 11/20/89, Tupelo, Miss. BR/TR, 6', 195 lbs. Deb: 4/15/58

YEAR TM/L	W	L	PCT	G	GS	CG	SH	SV	IP	H	HR	BB	SO	RAT	ERA	ERA+	OAV	OOB	BH	AVG	PB	PR	/A	PD	TPI
1958 Chi-N	0	4	.000	24	0	0	0	1	41¹	46	1	16	9	13.7	5.01	78	.295	.364	0	.000	-1	-5	-5	1	-0.4

■ TRICKY NICHOLS
Nichols, Frederick C. b: 7/26/1850, Bridgeport, Conn. d: 8/22/1897, Bridgeport, Conn. BR/TR, 5'7.5", 150 lbs. Deb: 4/21/1875

YEAR TM/L	W	L	PCT	G	GS	CG	SH	SV	IP	H	HR	BB	SO	RAT	ERA	ERA+	OAV	OOB	BH	AVG	PB	PR	/A	PD	TPI
1875 NH-n	4	29	.121	34	33	30	0	0	288	319	2	10		10.3	3.03	74	.243	.248	23	.192	-2	-18	-25		-2.2
1876 Bos-N	1	0	1.000	1	1	1	0	0	9	7	0	0	0	7.0	1.00	226	.200	.200	0	.000	-1	1	1	0	0.1
1877 StL-N	18	23	.439	42	39	35	1	0	350	376	2	53	80	11.0	2.60	100	.259	.285	31	.167	-6	8	0	-0	-0.7
1878 Pro-N	4	7	.364	11	10	10	0	0	98	157	0	8	21	15.2	4.22	52	.345	.356	9	.184	-0	-21	-22	2	-1.7
1880 Wor-N	0	2	.000	2	2	2	0	0	17²	29	0	4	4	16.8	4.08	64	.350	.380	0	.000	-1	-3	-3	-0	-0.3
1882 Bal-a	1	12	.077	16	13	12	0	0	118¹	155	2	17	21	13.1	5.02	55	.296	.319	15	.158	-2	-31	-30	-2	-2.8
Total 5	24	44	.353	72	65	60	1	0	593	724	4	82	126	12.2	3.37	76	.284	.307	55	.161	-10	-45	-53	0	-5.4

■ ROD NICHOLS
Nichols, Rodney Lea b: 12/29/64, Burlington, Iowa BR/TR, 6'2", 190 lbs. Deb: 7/30/88

YEAR TM/L	W	L	PCT	G	GS	CG	SH	SV	IP	H	HR	BB	SO	RAT	ERA	ERA+	OAV	OOB	BH	AVG	PB	PR	/A	PD	TPI
1988 Cle-A	1	7	.125	11	10	3	0	0	69¹	73	5	23	31	12.7	5.06	81	.272	.334	0	—	0	-8	-7	0	-0.6
1989 Cle-A	4	6	.400	15	11	0	0	0	71²	81	9	24	42	13.4	4.40	90	.285	.345	0	—	0	-4	-3	-0	-0.3
1990 Cle-A	0	3	.000	4	2	0	0	0	16	24	5	6	3	18.0	7.88	51	.343	.410	0	—	0	-7	-7	0	-0.5
Total 3	5	16	.238	30	23	3	0	0	157	178	19	53	76	13.6	5.04	80	.286	.348	0	—	0	-20	-18	0	-1.4

■ FRANK NICHOLSON
Nicholson, Frank Collins b: 8/29/1889, Berlin, Pa. d: 11/10/72, Jersey Shore, Pa. BR/TR, 6'2", 175 lbs. Deb: 9/06/12

YEAR TM/L	W	L	PCT	G	GS	CG	SH	SV	IP	H	HR	BB	SO	RAT	ERA	ERA+	OAV	OOB	BH	AVG	PB	PR	/A	PD	TPI
1912 Phi-N	0	0	—	2	0	0	0	0	4	8	1	2	1	22.5	6.75	54	.471	.526	0	—	0	-1	-1	0	0.0

■ GEORGE NICOL
Nicol, George Edward b: 10/17/1870, Barry, Ill. d: 8/10/24, Milwaukee, Wis. TL, 5'7", 155 lbs. Deb: 9/23/1890 ♦

YEAR TM/L	W	L	PCT	G	GS	CG	SH	SV	IP	H	HR	BB	SO	RAT	ERA	ERA+	OAV	OOB	BH	AVG	PB	PR	/A	PD	TPI
1890 StL-a	2	1	.667	3	3	2	0	0	17	11	1	19	16	15.9	4.76	91	.179	.373	2	.286	1	-2	-1	-0	0.0
1891 Chi-N	0	1	.000	3	2	0	0	0	11	14	0	10	12	19.6	4.91	68	.299	.422	2	.333	1	-2	-2	-1	-0.1
1894 Pit-N	3	4	.429	8	5	3	0	0	44¹	57	2	33	11	18.3	6.50	81	.309	.413	9	.450	2	-6	-6	-1	-0.3
Lou-N	0	1	.000	1	1	1	0	0	9	19	2	5	3	24.0	15.00	34	.423	.481	38	.352	0	-10	-10	-0	-0.5
Yr	3	5	.375	9	6	4	0	0	53¹	76	4	38	14	19.2	7.93	66	.331	.426	2	.016	2	-15	-16	-1	-0.8
Total 3	5	7	.417	15	11	6	0	0	81¹	101	5	67	42	18.6	6.86	70	.299	.415	51	.362	5	-19	-19	-2	-0.9

■ TOM NIEDENFUER
Niedenfuer, Thomas Edward b: 8/13/59, St.Louis Park, Minn BR/TR, 6'5", 225 lbs. Deb: 8/15/81

YEAR TM/L	W	L	PCT	G	GS	CG	SH	SV	IP	H	HR	BB	SO	RAT	ERA	ERA+	OAV	OOB	BH	AVG	PB	PR	/A	PD	TPI
1981 *LA-N	3	1	.750	17	0	0	0	2	26	25	1	6	12	11.1	3.81	87	.258	.308	0	—	0	-1	-1	-0	-0.1
1982 LA-N	3	4	.429	55	0	0	0	9	69²	71	3	25	60	12.7	2.71	128	.269	.337	0	.000	-0	7	6	-1	0.5
1983 *LA-N	8	3	.727	66	0	0	0	11	94²	55	6	29	66	8.1	1.90	189	.170	.240	0	.000	-0	18	18	-1	1.7
1984 LA-N	2	5	.286	33	0	0	0	11	47¹	39	3	23	45	12.2	2.47	143	.227	.325	0	.000	-0	6	6	-1	0.5
1985 *LA-N	7	9	.438	64	0	0	0	19	106¹	86	6	24	102	9.4	2.71	128	.223	.289	1	—	0	10	9	-2	0.8
1986 LA-N	6	6	.500	60	0	0	0	11	80	86	11	29	55	13.0	3.71	93	.280	.344	2	.500	-1	-2	0	-0	-0.1
1987 LA-N	1	0	1.000	15	0	0	0	1	16¹	13	1	9	10	12.7	2.76	144	.220	.333	0	—	0	2	2	0	0.3
Bal-A	3	5	.375	45	0	0	0	13	52¹	55	11	22	37	13.4	4.99	88	.266	.339	0	—	0	-3	-3	-1	-0.3

YEAR TM/L	W	L	PCT	G	GS	CG	SH	SV	IP	H	HR	BB	SO	RAT	ERA	ERA+	OAV	OOB	BH	AVG	PB	PR	/A	PD	TPI
1988 Bal-A	3	4	.429	52	0	0	0	18	59	59	8	19	40	12.2	3.51	111	.259	.321	0	—	0	3	3	-1	0.2
1989 Sea-A	0	3	.000	25	0	0	0	0	36¹	46	7	15	15	15.4	6.69	60	.309	.376	0	—	0	-11	-11	0	-1.0
1990 StL-N	0	6	.000	52	0	0	0	2	65	66	3	25	32	12.6	3.46	113	.269	.337	0	.000	-0	2	3	-1	0.2
Total 10	36	46	.439	484	0	0	0	97	653	601	60	226	474	11.6	3.29	112	.247	.314	3	.115	-1	34	28	-5	2.7

■ DICK NIEHAUS
Niehaus, Richard J.   b: 10/24/1892, Covington, Ky.   d: 3/12/57, Atlanta, Ga.   BL/TL, 5'11", 165 lbs.   Deb: 9/09/13

YEAR TM/L	W	L	PCT	G	GS	CG	SH	SV	IP	H	HR	BB	SO	RAT	ERA	ERA+	OAV	OOB	BH	AVG	PB	PR	/A	PD	TPI
1913 StL-N	0	2	.000	3	3	2	0	0	24	20	1	13	4	12.4	4.13	78	.241	.344	2	.286	1	-2	-2	0	0.0
1914 StL-N	1	0	1.000	8	1	1	0	0	17¹	18	1	8	6	13.5	3.12	90	.269	.347	1	.250	1	-1	-1	-0	0.0
1915 StL-N	2	1	.667	15	2	0	0	0	45¹	48	2	22	21	14.1	3.97	70	.281	.366	1	.071	-1	-6	-6	0	-0.6
1920 Cle-N	1	2	.333	19	3	0	0	2	40	42	0	16	12	13.3	3.60	106	.269	.341	4	.444	2	1	1	-1	0.1
Total 4	4	5	.444	45	9	3	0	2	126²	128	4	59	43	13.4	3.77	85	.268	.351	8	.235	2	-8	-8	-1	-0.5

■ JOE NIEKRO
Niekro, Joseph Franklin   b: 11/7/44, Martins Ferry, Ohio   BR/TR, 6'1", 185 lbs.   Deb: 4/16/67

YEAR TM/L	W	L	PCT	G	GS	CG	SH	SV	IP	H	HR	BB	SO	RAT	ERA	ERA+	OAV	OOB	BH	AVG	PB	PR	/A	PD	TPI
1967 Chi-N	10	7	.588	36	22	7	2	0	169²	171	15	32	77	10.9	3.34	106	.257	.293	9	.196	1	1	4	-0	0.6
1968 Chi-N	14	10	.583	34	29	2	1	2	177	204	18	59	65	13.5	4.32	73	.294	.351	6	.100	-2	-26	-23	1	-2.4
1969 Chi-N	0	1	.000	4	3	0	0	0	19¹	24	3	6	7	14.0	3.72	108	.304	.353	1	.200	0	-0	1	1	0.2
SD-N	8	17	.320	37	31	8	3	0	202	213	15	45	55	11.5	3.70	96	.273	.312	6	.118	0	-2	-4	-1	-0.3
Yr	8	18	.308	41	34	8	3	0	221¹	237	18	51	62	11.7	3.70	97	.275	.316	6	.107	0	-3	-3	0	-0.1
1970 Det-A	12	13	.480	38	34	6	2	0	213	221	28	72	101	12.5	4.06	92	.266	.327	13	.197	4	-8	-8	2	-0.2
1971 Det-A	6	7	.462	31	15	0	0	1	122¹	136	13	49	43	13.8	4.49	80	.283	.352	4	.133	-0	-14	-12	1	-1.1
1972 Det-A	3	2	.600	18	7	1	0	1	47	62	3	8	24	13.6	3.83	82	.330	.360	3	.250	1	-4	-4	-0	-0.2
1973 Atl-N	2	4	.333	20	0	0	0	3	24	23	2	11	12	12.8	4.13	95	.277	.362	1	.333	1	-1	-1	1	0.0
1974 Atl-N	3	2	.600	27	2	0	0	0	43	36	5	18	31	11.7	3.56	106	.237	.326	0	.000	-1	0	1	1	0.1
1975 Hou-N	6	4	.600	40	4	1	1	4	88	79	3	39	54	12.3	3.07	110	.240	.324	3	.214	1	5	3	0	0.4
1976 Hou-N	4	8	.333	36	13	0	0	0	118	107	8	56	77	12.5	3.36	95	.238	.324	5	.185	2	2	-2	-1	0.0
1977 Hou-N	13	8	.619	44	14	9	2	5	180²	155	14	64	101	11.0	3.04	117	.237	.306	7	.140	-1	17	11	2	1.1
1978 Hou-N	14	14	.500	35	29	10	1	0	202²	190	13	73	97	12.1	3.86	86	.248	.321	9	.138	-1	-6	-13	-1	-1.4
1979 Hou-N	**21**	11	.656	38	38	11	**5**	0	263²	221	17	107	119	11.4	3.00	117	.228	.309	10	.120	-2	21	15	1	1.4
1980 *Hou-N	20	12	.625	37	36	11	2	0	256	268	12	79	127	12.3	3.55	93	.270	.326	22	.275	7	1	-8	0	0.0
1981 *Hou-N	9	9	.500	24	24	5	2	0	166	150	8	47	77	10.7	2.82	117	.243	.297	9	.176	1	12	9	-0	1.0
1982 Hou-N	17	12	.586	35	35	16	5	0	270	224	12	64	130	9.8	2.47	134	.229	.279	8	.090	-4	34	25	1	2.4
1983 Hou-N	15	14	.517	38	38	9	1	0	263²	238	15	101	152	11.7	3.48	98	.241	.313	8	.094	-3	4	-2	-2	-0.7
1984 Hou-N	16	12	.571	38	38	6	1	0	248¹	223	16	89	127	11.5	3.04	109	.241	.310	11	.133	-1	15	8	1	0.7
1985 Hou-N	9	12	.429	32	32	4	1	0	213	197	21	99	117	12.7	3.72	93	.247	.333	17	.250	3	-3	-6	1	-0.2
NY-A	2	1	.667	3	3	0	0	0	12¹	14	3	8	4	16.1	5.84	69	.280	.379	0	—	0	-2	-3	0	-0.1
1986 NY-A	9	10	.474	25	25	0	0	0	125²	139	15	63	59	14.5	4.87	84	.275	.356	0	—	0	-10	-11	-1	-1.0
1987 NY-A	3	4	.429	8	8	1	0	0	50²	40	4	19	30	11.2	3.55	123	.215	.301	0	—	0	5	5	-0	0.4
*Min-A	4	9	.308	19	18	0	0	0	96¹	115	11	45	54	15.5	6.26	74	.296	.378	0	—	0	-19	-18	-0	-1.5
Yr	7	13	.350	27	26	1	0	0	147	155	15	64	84	13.8	5.33	85	.268	.347	0	—	0	-14	-13	-1	-1.1
1988 Min-A	1	1	.500	5	2	0	0	0	11²	16	2	9	7	19.3	10.03	41	.320	.424	0	—	0	-8	-8	1	-0.6
Total 22	221	204	.520	702	500	107	29	16	3584	3466	276	1262	1747	12.0	3.59	97	.255	.321	152	.156	6	14	-38	6	-1.4

■ PHIL NIEKRO
Niekro, Philip Henry   b: 4/1/39, Blaine, Ohio   BR/TR, 6'1", 180 lbs.   Deb: 4/15/64

YEAR TM/L	W	L	PCT	G	GS	CG	SH	SV	IP	H	HR	BB	SO	RAT	ERA	ERA+	OAV	OOB	BH	AVG	PB	PR	/A	PD	TPI
1964 Mil-N	0	0	—	10	0	0	0	0	15	15	1	7	8	13.8	4.80	73	.273	.365	0	—	0	-2	-2	0	-0.1
1965 Mil-N	2	3	.400	41	1	0	0	6	74²	73	5	26	49	12.3	2.89	122	.258	.327	1	.100	-0	5	5	1	0.6
1966 Atl-N	4	3	.571	28	0	0	0	2	50¹	48	4	23	17	13.1	4.11	88	.249	.335	0	.000	-1	-3	-3	2	-0.1
1967 Atl-N	11	9	.550	46	20	10	1	9	207	164	9	55	129	9.8	**1.87**	178	.218	.277	7	.123	-0	35	33	1	3.9
1968 Atl-N	14	12	.538	37	34	15	5	2	257	228	16	45	140	9.7	2.59	116	.239	.277	8	.104	-1	11	11	3	1.6
1969 *Atl-N	23	13	.639	40	35	21	4	1	284¹	235	21	57	193	9.4	2.56	141	.221	.264	20	.211	3	33	33	2	4.2
1970 Atl-N	12	18	.400	34	32	10	3	0	229²	222	40	68	168	11.6	4.27	100	.248	.305	12	.152	-1	-6	0	2	0.1
1971 Atl-N	15	14	.517	42	36	18	4	2	268²	248	27	70	173	10.8	2.98	124	.245	.296	14	.152	-3	14	22	1	2.3
1972 Atl-N	16	12	.571	38	36	17	1	0	282¹	254	22	53	164	9.9	3.06	124	.236	.275	18	.194	1	12	23	1	2.9
1973 Atl-N	13	10	.565	42	30	9	1	4	245	214	21	89	131	11.3	3.31	119	.234	.306	10	.122	-2	10	17	2	2.0
1974 Atl-N	**20**	13	.606	41	39	**18**	6	1	302¹	249	19	88	195	10.2	2.38	159	.225	.286	20	.192	-0	42	47	0	**5.3**
1975 Atl-N	15	15	.500	39	37	13	1	0	275²	285	29	72	144	12.0	3.20	118	.269	.322	17	.172	-0	13	18	1	1.9
1976 Atl-N	17	11	.607	38	37	10	2	0	270²	249	18	101	173	11.9	3.29	115	.242	.315	18	.191	1	6	15	1	1.9
1977 Atl-N	16	20	.444	44	43	**20**	2	0	330¹	315	26	164	**262**	13.3	4.03	110	.255	.346	19	.174	-3	-5	15	1	1.5
1978 Atl-N	19	18	.514	44	42	**22**	4	1	334¹	295	16	102	248	11.0	2.88	141	.235	.299	27	.225	3	26	**43**	3	**5.8**
1979 Atl-N	21	20	.512	44	44	**23**	1	0	342	311	41	113	208	11.4	3.39	119	.241	.307	24	.195	2	13	25	3	**3.3**
1980 Atl-N	15	18	.455	40	38	11	3	1	275	256	30	85	176	11.3	3.63	103	.249	.308	12	.133	-2	-1	3	0	0.2
1981 Atl-N	7	7	.500	22	22	3	3	0	139¹	120	6	56	62	11.4	3.10	115	.233	.310	4	.077	-4	6	7	0	0.4
1982 *Atl-N	17	4	**.810**	35	35	4	2	0	234¹	225	23	73	144	11.6	3.61	103	.255	.314	17	.195	2	-0	3	1	0.7
1983 Atl-N	11	10	.524	34	33	2	0	0	201²	212	18	105	128	14.2	3.97	98	.276	.364	12	.185	0	-8	-2	0	0.0
1984 NY-A	16	8	.667	32	31	5	1	0	215²	219	15	76	136	12.4	3.09	123	.267	.331	0	—	0	22	17	2	2.0
1985 NY-A	16	12	.571	33	33	7	1	0	220	203	29	120	149	13.3	4.09	98	.245	.342	0	—	1	-2	-2	-0	-0.3
1986 Cle-A	11	11	.500	34	32	5	0	0	210¹	241	24	95	81	14.6	4.32	96	.287	.363	0	—	0	-3	-4	0	-0.3
1987 Tor-A	0	2	.000	3	3	0	0	0	12	15	4	7	7	16.5	8.25	54	.306	.393	0	—	0	-5	-5	-0	-0.4
Cle-A	7	11	.389	22	22	2	0	0	123²	142	18	53	57	14.5	5.89	77	.286	.359	0	—	0	-20	-19	0	-1.6
Yr	7	13	.350	25	25	2	0	0	135²	157	22	60	64	14.7	6.10	74	.288	.362	0	—	0	-25	-24	0	-2.0
Atl-N	0	0	—	1	1	0	0	0	3	6	0	6	0	36.0	15.00	29	.429	.600	0	.000	-0	-4	-4	0	-0.2
Total 24	318	274	.537	864	716	245	45	29	5404¹	5044	482	1809	3342	11.6	3.35	115	.247	.312	260	.169	-5	192	299	25	37.6

■ SCOTT NIELSEN
Nielsen, Jeffrey Scott   b: 12/18/58, Salt Lake City, Ut.   BR/TR, 6'1", 190 lbs.   Deb: 7/07/86

YEAR TM/L	W	L	PCT	G	GS	CG	SH	SV	IP	H	HR	BB	SO	RAT	ERA	ERA+	OAV	OOB	BH	AVG	PB	PR	/A	PD	TPI
1986 NY-A	4	4	.500	10	9	2	2	0	56	66	12	12	20	12.9	4.02	102	.299	.340	0	—	0	1	0	-1	0.0
1987 Chi-A	3	5	.375	19	7	1	1	2	66¹	83	9	25	23	14.8	6.24	73	.307	.368	0	—	0	-13	-12	-0	-1.1
1988 NY-A	1	2	.333	7	2	0	0	0	19²	27	5	13	4	18.3	6.86	57	.333	.426	0	—	0	-6	-6	1	-0.5
1989 NY-A	1	0	1.000	2	0	0	0	0	0²	2	0	1	0	40.5	13.50	29	.500	.600	0	—	0	-1	-1	0	0.0
Total 4	9	11	.450	38	18	3	3	2	142²	178	26	51	47	14.6	5.49	78	.309	.368	0	—	0	-19	-19	-0	-1.6

■ RANDY NIEMANN
Niemann, Randal Harold   b: 11/15/55, Scotia, Cal.   BL/TL, 6'4", 200 lbs.   Deb: 5/20/79

YEAR TM/L	W	L	PCT	G	GS	CG	SH	SV	IP	H	HR	BB	SO	RAT	ERA	ERA+	OAV	OOB	BH	AVG	PB	PR	/A	PD	TPI
1979 Hou-N	3	2	.600	26	7	3	2	1	67	68	1	22	24	12.2	3.76	93	.272	.333	2	.133	-0	-0	-2	-1	-0.2
1980 Hou-N	1	0	1.000	22	1	0	0	1	33	40	2	12	18	14.2	5.45	60	.299	.356	2	.333	1	-7	-8	1	-0.6
1982 Pit-N	1	1	.500	20	1	0	0	1	35¹	34	1	17	26	13.5	5.09	73	.254	.346	2	1.000	1	-6	-5	1	-0.3
1983 Pit-N	0	1	.000	8	1	0	0	0	13²	20	2	7	8	18.4	9.22	40	.357	.438	0	.000	-0	-8	-8	0	-0.7
1984 Chi-A	0	0	—	5	0	0	0	0	5¹	5	0	5	5	16.9	1.69	246	.263	.417	0	—	0	1	1	0	0.2
1985 NY-N	0	0	—	4	0	0	0	0	4²	5	0	4	2	9.6	0.00	—	.278	.278	0	—	0	2	2	0	0.2
1986 NY-N	2	3	.400	31	1	0	0	0	35²	44	2	12	18	14.1	3.79	93	.308	.361	2	.333	1	-0	-1	1	0.1
1987 Min-A	1	0	1.000	6	0	0	0	0	5¹	3	0	7	1	20.3	8.44	55	.158	.357	0	—	0	-2	-2	0	-0.1
Total 8	7	8	.467	122	10	3	2	3	200	219	8	82	102	13.8	4.64	77	.283	.357	8	.267	2	-21	-24	2	-1.4

■ JACK NIEMES
Niemes, Jacob Leland   b: 10/19/19, Cincinnati, Ohio   d: 3/4/66, Hamilton, Ohio   BR/TL, 6'1", 180 lbs.   Deb: 5/30/43

YEAR TM/L	W	L	PCT	G	GS	CG	SH	SV	IP	H	HR	BB	SO	RAT	ERA	ERA+	OAV	OOB	BH	AVG	PB	PR	/A	PD	TPI
1943 Cin-N	0	0	—	3	0	0	0	0	3	5	0	2	1	21.0	6.00	55	.385	.467	0	—	0	-1	-1	0	0.0

YEAR	TM/L	W	L	PCT	G	GS	CG	SH	SV	IP	H	HR	BB	SO	RAT	ERA	ERA+	OAV	OOB	BH	AVG	PB	PR	/A	PD	TPI

■ CHUCK NIESON
Nieson, Charles Bassett b: 9/24/42, Hanford, Cal. BR/TR, 6'2", 185 lbs. Deb: 9/18/64

YEAR	TM/L	W	L	PCT	G	GS	CG	SH	SV	IP	H	HR	BB	SO	RAT	ERA	ERA+	OAV	OOB	BH	AVG	PB	PR	/A	PD	TPI
1964	Min-A	0	0	—	2	0	0	0	0	2	1	1	1	5	9.0	4.50	79	.143	.250	0	—	0	-0	-0	0	0.0

■ JUAN NIEVES
Nieves, Juan Manuel (Cruz) b: 1/5/65, Las Lomas, P.R. BL/TL, 6'3", 175 lbs. Deb: 4/10/86

YEAR	TM/L	W	L	PCT	G	GS	CG	SH	SV	IP	H	HR	BB	SO	RAT	ERA	ERA+	OAV	OOB	BH	AVG	PB	PR	/A	PD	TPI
1986	Mil-A	11	12	.478	35	33	4	3	0	184²	224	17	77	116	14.7	4.92	88	.299	.366	0	—	0	-15	-12	-2	-1.3
1987	Mil-A	14	8	.636	34	33	3	1	0	195²	199	24	100	163	13.8	4.88	94	.264	.351	0	—	0	-9	-7	-2	-0.7
1988	Mil-A	7	5	.583	25	15	1	1	1	110¹	84	13	50	73	11.0	4.08	98	.208	.297	0	—	0	-1	-1	-0	-0.1
Total	3	32	25	.561	94	81	8	5	1	490²	507	54	227	352	13.5	4.71	92	.266	.345	0	—	0	-26	-20	-4	-2.1

■ JOHNNY NIGGELING
Niggeling, John Arnold b: 7/10/03, Remsen, Iowa d: 9/16/63, LeMars, Iowa BR/TR, 6', 170 lbs. Deb: 4/30/38

YEAR	TM/L	W	L	PCT	G	GS	CG	SH	SV	IP	H	HR	BB	SO	RAT	ERA	ERA+	OAV	OOB	BH	AVG	PB	PR	/A	PD	TPI
1938	Bos-N	1	0	1.000	2	0	0	0	0	2	4	0	1	1	22.5	9.00	38	.400	.455	0	—	0	-1	-1	0	0.0
1939	Cin-N	2	1	.667	10	5	2	1	0	40¹	51	2	13	20	14.7	5.80	66	.309	.367	2	.154	-0	-8	-9	-0	-0.8
1940	StL-A	7	11	.389	28	20	10	0	0	153²	148	9	69	82	13.0	4.45	103	.250	.333	9	.176	-1	-1	2	-1	0.0
1941	StL-A	7	9	.438	24	20	13	1	0	168¹	168	17	63	68	12.4	3.80	113	.255	.320	10	.167	-1	7	9	-1	0.7
1942	StL-A	15	11	.577	28	27	16	3	0	206²	173	10	93	107	12.1	2.66	139	.226	.319	10	.139	-2	23	24	-2	2.1
1943	StL-A	6	8	.429	20	20	7	0	0	150¹	122	7	57	73	11.1	3.17	105	.220	.299	3	.061	-4	2	3	-0	-0.2
	Was-A	4	2	.667	6	6	5	3	0	51	27	0	17	24	7.8	0.88	363	.153	.227	5	.278	1	14	13	0	1.9
	Yr	10	10	.500	26	26	12	3	0	201¹	149	7	74	97	10.0	2.59	127	.202	.275	3	.045	-3	16	16	-1	1.7
1944	Was-A	10	8	.556	24	24	14	2	0	206	164	5	88	121	11.2	2.32	141	.221	.307	9	.130	-2	25	21	-2	1.9
1945	Was-A	7	12	.368	26	25	8	2	0	176²	161	7	73	90	12.1	3.16	98	.240	.318	7	.119	-3	4	-1	-2	-0.7
1946	Was-A	3	2	.600	8	6	3	0	0	38	39	1	21	10	14.4	4.03	83	.265	.361	2	.182	0	-2	-3	-0	-0.2
	Bos-N	2	5	.286	8	8	3	0	0	58	54	2	21	24	11.8	3.26	105	.243	.311	2	.111	-1	1	1	0	0.0
Total	9	64	69	.481	184	161	81	12	0	1250²	1111	60	516	620	12.0	3.22	113	.236	.316	59	.140	-14	63	58	-9	4.7

■ AL NIPPER
Nipper, Albert Samuel b: 4/2/59, San Diego, Cal. BR/TR, 6', 188 lbs. Deb: 9/06/83

YEAR	TM/L	W	L	PCT	G	GS	CG	SH	SV	IP	H	HR	BB	SO	RAT	ERA	ERA+	OAV	OOB	BH	AVG	PB	PR	/A	PD	TPI
1983	Bos-A	1	1	.500	3	2	1	0	0	16	17	0	7	5	14.1	2.25	193	.293	.379	0	—	0	3	4	0	0.4
1984	Bos-A	11	6	.647	29	24	6	0	0	182²	183	18	52	84	11.9	3.89	107	.257	.313	0	—	0	2	5	3	0.9
1985	Bos-A	9	12	.429	25	25	5	0	0	162	157	14	82	85	13.8	4.06	106	.256	.352	0	—	0	2	4	3	0.7
1986	*Bos-A	10	12	.455	26	26	3	0	0	159	186	24	47	79	13.4	5.38	77	.290	.342	0	—	0	-21	-21	4	-1.6
1987	Bos-A	11	12	.478	30	30	6	0	0	174	196	30	62	89	13.7	5.43	84	.284	.349	0	—	0	-19	-17	2	-1.4
1988	Chi-N	2	4	.333	22	12	0	0	1	80	72	9	34	27	12.3	3.04	119	.238	.322	2	.087	-1	4	5	-1	0.3
1990	Cle-A	2	3	.400	9	5	0	0	0	24	35	2	19	12	21.0	6.75	59	.354	.467	0	—	0	-8	-7	-0	-0.7
Total	7	46	50	.479	144	124	21	0	1	797²	846	97	303	381	13.3	4.52	93	.271	.342	2	.087	-1	-37	-28	9	-1.4

■ MERLIN NIPPERT
Nippert, Merlin Lee b: 9/1/38, Mangum, Okla. BR/TR, 6'1", 175 lbs. Deb: 9/12/62

YEAR	TM/L	W	L	PCT	G	GS	CG	SH	SV	IP	H	HR	BB	SO	RAT	ERA	ERA+	OAV	OOB	BH	AVG	PB	PR	/A	PD	TPI
1962	Bos-A	0	0	—	4	0	0	0	0	6	4	1	4	3	12.0	4.50	92	.200	.333	0	—	0	-0	-0	0	0.0

■ RON NISCHWITZ
Nischwitz, Ronald Lee b: 7/1/37, Dayton, Ohio BB/TL, 6'3", 205 lbs. Deb: 9/04/61

YEAR	TM/L	W	L	PCT	G	GS	CG	SH	SV	IP	H	HR	BB	SO	RAT	ERA	ERA+	OAV	OOB	BH	AVG	PB	PR	/A	PD	TPI
1961	Det-A	0	1	.000	6	1	0	0	0	11¹	13	2	8	8	16.7	5.56	74	.295	.404	0	.000	-0	-2	-2	-0	-0.1
1962	Det-A	4	5	.444	48	0	0	0	4	64²	73	5	26	28	13.9	3.90	104	.285	.353	5	.417	2	1	1	0	0.4
1963	Cle-A	0	2	.000	14	0	0	0	0	16²	17	3	8	10	13.5	6.48	56	.262	.342	0	.000	-0	-5	-5	-0	-0.4
1965	Det-A	1	0	1.000	20	0	0	0	1	22²	21	2	6	12	10.7	2.78	125	.259	.310	0	.000	-0	2	2	0	0.1
Total	4	5	8	.385	88	1	0	0	6	115¹	124	12	48	58	13.5	4.21	92	.278	.349	5	.278	1	-5	-4	1	0.0

■ OTHO NITCHOLAS
Nitcholas, Otho James b: 9/13/08, McKinney, Tex. d: 9/11/86, McKinney, Tex. BR/TR, 6', 190 lbs. Deb: 4/18/45

YEAR	TM/L	W	L	PCT	G	GS	CG	SH	SV	IP	H	HR	BB	SO	RAT	ERA	ERA+	OAV	OOB	BH	AVG	PB	PR	/A	PD	TPI
1945	Bro-N	1	0	1.000	7	0	0	0	0	18²	19	4	1	4	9.6	5.30	71	.257	.267	1	.250	0	-3	-3	0	-0.2

■ WILLARD NIXON
Nixon, Willard Lee b: 6/17/28, Taylorsville, Ga. BL/TR, 6'2", 195 lbs. Deb: 7/07/50

YEAR	TM/L	W	L	PCT	G	GS	CG	SH	SV	IP	H	HR	BB	SO	RAT	ERA	ERA+	OAV	OOB	BH	AVG	PB	PR	/A	PD	TPI
1950	Bos-A	8	6	.571	22	15	2	0	2	101¹	126	8	58	57	16.5	6.04	81	.310	.398	5	.139	-1	-16	-13	-0	-1.2
1951	Bos-A	7	4	.636	33	14	2	1	1	125	136	12	56	70	14.3	4.90	91	.285	.368	13	.289	3	-11	-6	-0	-0.2
1952	Bos-A	5	4	.556	23	13	5	0	0	103²	115	12	61	50	15.6	4.86	81	.290	.390	11	.208	1	-14	-11	1	-0.8
1953	Bos-A	4	8	.333	23	15	5	1	0	116²	114	6	59	57	13.4	3.93	107	.254	.343	8	.190	0	1	4	-0	0.4
1954	Bos-A	11	12	.478	31	30	8	2	0	199²	182	16	87	102	13.2	4.06	101	.248	.335	18	.265	5	-7	1	1	0.9
1955	Bos-A	12	10	.545	31	31	7	3	0	208	207	10	85	95	12.8	4.07	105	.259	.333	18	.261	5	-2	5	3	1.4
1956	Bos-A	9	8	.529	23	22	9	1	0	145¹	142	9	57	74	12.8	4.21	110	.255	.333	11	.204	-1	-1	7	2	0.8
1957	Bos-A	12	13	.480	29	29	11	1	0	191	207	10	56	96	12.7	3.68	108	.281	.337	22	.293	5	2	7	-1	1.2
1958	Bos-A	1	7	.125	10	8	2	0	0	43¹	48	7	11	15	12.3	6.02	67	.281	.324	5	.294	1	-11	-10	-0	-0.7
Total	9	69	72	.489	225	177	51	9	3	1234	1277	90	530	616	13.5	4.39	97	.270	.349	111	.242	19	-59	-16	5	1.8

■ JUNIOR NOBOA
Noboa, Miliciades Arturo (Diaz) b: 11/10/64, Azua, D.R. BR/TR, 5'10", 155 lbs. Deb: 8/22/84 ◆

YEAR	TM/L	W	L	PCT	G	GS	CG	SH	SV	IP	H	HR	BB	SO	RAT	ERA	ERA+	OAV	OOB	BH	AVG	PB	PR	/A	PD	TPI
1990	Mon-N	0	0	—	1	0	0	0	0	0²	0	0	1	0	13.5	0.00	—	.000	.500	42	.266	0	0	0	0	0.0

■ THE ONLY NOLAN
Nolan, Edward Sylvester b: 11/7/1857, Paterson, N.J. d: 5/18/13, Paterson, N.J. BL/TR, 5'8", 171 lbs. Deb: 5/01/1878

YEAR	TM/L	W	L	PCT	G	GS	CG	SH	SV	IP	H	HR	BB	SO	RAT	ERA	ERA+	OAV	OOB	BH	AVG	PB	PR	/A	PD	TPI
1878	Ind-N	13	22	.371	38	38	37	1	0	347	357	1	56	125	10.7	2.57	79	.253	.281	37	.243	5	-10	-21	2	-1.4
1881	Cle-N	8	14	.364	22	21	20	0	0	180	183	3	38	54	11.1	3.05	86	.252	.290	41	.244	1	-6	-9	-1	-0.7
1883	Pit-a	0	7	.000	7	7	6	0	0	55	81	0	10	23	14.9	4.25	75	.322	.348	8	.308	1	-6	-6	-0	-0.4
1884	Wil-U	1	4	.200	5	5	5	0	0	40	44	1	7	52	11.5	2.93	113	.261	.291	9	.273	1	0	2	1	0.4
1885	Phi-N	1	5	.167	7	7	6	0	0	54	55	1	24	20	13.2	4.17	67	.252	.326	2	.077	-2	-8	-8	-1	-0.8
Total	5	23	52	.307	79	78	74	1	0	676	720	6	135	274	11.4	2.98	81	.259	.294	97	.240	7	-29	-44	2	-2.9

■ GARY NOLAN
Nolan, Gary Lynn b: 5/27/48, Herlong, Cal. BR/TR, 6'2.5", 197 lbs. Deb: 4/15/67

YEAR	TM/L	W	L	PCT	G	GS	CG	SH	SV	IP	H	HR	BB	SO	RAT	ERA	ERA+	OAV	OOB	BH	AVG	PB	PR	/A	PD	TPI
1967	Cin-N	14	8	.636	33	32	8	5	0	226²	193	18	62	206	10.3	2.58	145	.228	.284	7	.104	-2	20	29	-2	3.1
1968	Cin-N	9	4	.692	23	22	4	2	0	150	105	10	49	111	9.4	2.40	132	.196	.267	6	.130	2	10	13	-2	1.5
1969	Cin-N	8	8	.500	16	15	2	1	0	108²	102	11	40	83	11.8	3.56	106	.247	.313	8	.229	3	0	2	-2	0.4
1970	*Cin-N	18	7	.720	37	37	4	2	0	250²	226	25	96	181	11.6	3.27	123	.240	.311	13	.159	1	22	21	-2	2.1
1971	Cin-N	12	15	.444	35	35	9	0	0	244²	208	12	59	146	9.9	3.16	106	.227	.275	11	.147	-1	8	5	1	0.5
1972	*Cin-N	15	5	.750	25	25	6	2	0	176	147	13	30	90	9.1	1.99	161	.227	.262	7	.117	-1	29	24	-1	2.5
1973	Cin-N	0	1	.000	2	2	0	0	0	10¹	6	1	7	3	11.3	3.48	98	.167	.302	0	—	0	-0	-0	0	0.0
1975	*Cin-N	15	9	.625	32	32	5	1	0	210²	202	18	29	74	9.9	3.16	114	.251	.278	12	.176	2	11	10	-2	1.1
1976	*Cin-N	15	9	.625	34	34	7	1	0	239¹	232	28	27	113	9.8	3.46	101	.254	.276	8	.101	-3	1	1	-3	-0.5
1977	Cin-N	4	1	.800	9	8	0	0	0	39¹	53	5	12	28	14.9	4.81	82	.321	.367	1	.067	-1	-4	-4	-0	-0.4
	Cal-A	0	3	.000	5	5	0	0	0	18¹	31	5	2	4	16.2	8.84	44	.365	.379	0	—	0	-10	-10	-0	-0.8
Total	10	110	70	.611	250	247	45	14	0	1674²	1505	146	413	1039	10.4	3.08	116	.239	.287	73	.138	1	87	93	-13	9.5

■ DICK NOLD
Nold, Richard Louis b: 5/4/43, San Francisco, Cal. BR/TR, 6'2", 190 lbs. Deb: 8/19/67

YEAR	TM/L	W	L	PCT	G	GS	CG	SH	SV	IP	H	HR	BB	SO	RAT	ERA	ERA+	OAV	OOB	BH	AVG	PB	PR	/A	PD	TPI
1967	Was-A	0	2	.000	7	3	0	0	0	20¹	19	1	13	10	14.2	4.87	65	.241	.348	0	.000	-0	-4	-4	-0	-0.3

■ DICKIE NOLES
Noles, Dickie Ray b: 11/19/56, Charlotte, N.C. BR/TR, 6'2", 160 lbs. Deb: 7/05/79

YEAR	TM/L	W	L	PCT	G	GS	CG	SH	SV	IP	H	HR	BB	SO	RAT	ERA	ERA+	OAV	OOB	BH	AVG	PB	PR	/A	PD	TPI
1979	Phi-N	3	4	.429	14	14	1	0	0	90	80	6	38	42	12.0	3.80	101	.246	.329	3	.100	-1	-1	0	1	0.0
1980	*Phi-N	1	4	.200	48	3	0	0	6	81	80	5	42	57	13.7	3.89	97	.254	.344	4	.308	1	-3	-1	-0	0.0
1981	*Phi-N	2	2	.500	13	8	0	0	0	58¹	57	2	23	34	12.8	4.17	87	.260	.339	2	.105	-1	-4	-1	-0	-0.5
1982	Chi-N	10	13	.435	31	30	2	2	0	171	180	11	61	85	12.9	4.42	84	.274	.340	6	.107	-2	-16	-13	0	-1.4
1983	Chi-N	5	10	.333	24	18	1	1	0	116¹	133	6	37	59	13.2	4.72	80	.287	.341	9	.237	-0	-14	-12	-0	-1.0
1984	Chi-N	2	2	.500	21	1	0	0	0	50²	60	4	16	14	13.7	5.15	76	.305	.360	0	.000	-1	-9	-7	-1	-0.8
	Tex-A	2	3	.400	18	6	0	0	0	57²	60	6	30	39	14.8	5.15	80	.262	.360	0	—	0	-7	-6	-1	-0.7

YEAR TM/L	W	L	PCT	G	GS	CG	SH	SV	IP	H	HR	BB	SO	RAT	ERA	ERA+	OAV	OOB	BH	AVG	PB	PR	/A	PD	TPI
1985 Tex-A	4	8	.333	28	13	0	0	1	110¹	129	11	33	59	13.7	5.06	84	.289	.346	0	—	0	-11	-10	1	-0.8
1986 Cle-A	3	2	.600	32	0	0	0	0	54²	56	9	30	32	15.0	5.10	81	.269	.374	0	—	0	-6	-6	0	-0.5
1987 Chi-N	4	2	.667	41	1	0	0	2	64¹	59	1	27	33	12.7	3.50	122	.239	.326	0	.000	-1	4	6	1	0.6
Det-A	0	0	—	4	0	0	0	2	2	2	0	1	0	13.5	4.50	94	.250	.333	0	—	0	-0	-0	0	0.0
1988 Bal-A	0	2	.000	2	2	0	0	0	3¹	11	2	0	1	32.4	24.30	16	.500	.522	0	—	0	-8	-8	0	-0.5
1990 Phi-N	0	1	.000	1	0	0	0	0	0¹	2	0	0	0	54.0	27.00	14	.667	.667	0	—	0	-1	-1	0	0.0
Total 11	36	53	.404	277	96	3	3	11	860	909	66	338	455	13.4	4.56	86	.272	.345	24	.136	-4	-75	-61	-1	-5.6

■ ERIC NOLTE
Nolte, Eric Carl b: 4/28/64, Canoga Park, Cal. BL/TL, 6'3", 205 lbs. Deb: 8/01/87

YEAR TM/L	W	L	PCT	G	GS	CG	SH	SV	IP	H	HR	BB	SO	RAT	ERA	ERA+	OAV	OOB	BH	AVG	PB	PR	/A	PD	TPI
1987 SD-N	2	6	.250	12	12	1	0	0	67¹	57	6	36	44	12.7	3.21	123	.226	.328	2	.095	-1	7	6	-0	0.4
1988 SD-N	0	0	—	2	0	0	0	0	3	3	1	2	1	15.0	6.00	57	.273	.385	0	—	0	-1	-1	0	0.0
1989 SD-N	0	0	—	3	1	0	0	0	9	15	1	7	8	22.0	11.00	32	.375	.468	0	.000	-0	-8	-8	0	-0.6
Total 3	2	6	.250	17	13	1	0	0	79¹	75	8	45	53	13.8	4.20	92	.248	.349	2	.087	-1	-2	-3	-0	-0.2

■ JERRY NOPS
Nops, Jeremiah H. b: 6/23/1875, Toledo, Ohio d: 3/26/37, Camden, N.J. TL Deb: 9/07/1896

YEAR TM/L	W	L	PCT	G	GS	CG	SH	SV	IP	H	HR	BB	SO	RAT	ERA	ERA+	OAV	OOB	BH	AVG	PB	PR	/A	PD	TPI
1896 Phi-N	1	0	1.000	1	1	1	0	0	7	11	0	1	1	15.4	5.14	84	.354	.374	0	.000	-1	-1	-1	-0	0.0
Bal-N	2	1	.667	3	3	3	0	0	22	29	0	2	8	12.7	6.14	70	.315	.329	-1	.111	-1	-4	-5	-0	-0.3
Yr	3	1	.750	4	4	4	0	0	29	40	0	3	9	13.3	5.90	73	.325	.341	1	.077	-2	-5	-5	-0	-0.3
1897 *Bal-N	20	6	.769	30	25	23	1	0	220²	235	5	52	69	11.7	2.81	148	.271	.312	18	.196	-3	37	33	-2	2.5
1898 Bal-N	16	9	.640	33	29	23	2	0	235	241	5	78	91	12.2	3.56	101	.263	.321	20	.220	2	1	1	-5	-0.1
1899 Bal-N	17	11	.607	33	33	26	2	0	259	296	1	71	60	12.8	4.03	98	.287	.333	29	.276	1	-5	-2	-0	-0.1
1900 Bro-N	4	4	.500	9	8	6	1	0	68	79	1	18	22	12.8	3.84	100	.290	.334	4	.160	-1	-1	0	-1	-0.1
1901 Bal-A	12	10	.545	27	23	17	1	1	176²	192	5	59	43	12.8	4.08	95	.274	.330	13	.220	-0	-8	-4	-4	-0.6
Total 6	72	41	.637	136	122	99	7	1	988¹	1083	17	281	294	12.4	3.70	106	.277	.325	85	.221	-2	19	23	-15	1.3

■ WAYNE NORDHAGEN
Nordhagen, Wayne Oren b: 7/4/48, Thief River Falls, Minn. BR/TR, 6'2", 205 lbs. Deb: 7/16/76 ♦

YEAR TM/L	W	L	PCT	G	GS	CG	SH	SV	IP	H	HR	BB	SO	RAT	ERA	ERA+	OAV	OOB	BH	AVG	PB	PR	/A	PD	TPI
1979 Chi-A	0	0	—	2	0	0	0	0	2	2	0	1	2	13.5	9.00	47	.286	.375	54	.280	2	-1	-1	0	0.0

■ JOHN NORIEGA
Noriega, John Alan b: 12/20/43, Ogden, Utah BR/TR, 6'4", 185 lbs. Deb: 5/01/69

YEAR TM/L	W	L	PCT	G	GS	CG	SH	SV	IP	H	HR	BB	SO	RAT	ERA	ERA+	OAV	OOB	BH	AVG	PB	PR	/A	PD	TPI
1969 Cin-N	0	0	—	5	0	0	0	0	7²	12	1	3	4	17.6	5.87	64	.400	.455	0	—	0	-2	-2	-0	-0.1
1970 Cin-N	0	0	—	8	0	0	0	0	18	25	0	10	6	18.5	8.00	50	.333	.425	1	.250	0	-8	-8	1	-0.6
Total 2	0	0	—	13	0	0	0	0	25²	37	1	13	10	18.2	7.36	54	.352	.433	1	.250	0	-10	-10	1	-0.7

■ FRED NORMAN
Norman, Fredie Hubert b: 8/20/42, San Antonio, Tex. BB/TL, 5'8", 155 lbs. Deb: 9/21/62

YEAR TM/L	W	L	PCT	G	GS	CG	SH	SV	IP	H	HR	BB	SO	RAT	ERA	ERA+	OAV	OOB	BH	AVG	PB	PR	/A	PD	TPI
1962 KC-A	0	0	—	2	0	0	0	0	4	4	0	1	2	11.3	2.25	185	.250	.294	0	—	0	1	1	-0	0.1
1963 KC-A	0	1	.000	2	2	0	0	0	6¹	9	1	7	6	22.7	11.37	34	.346	.485	0	.000	-0	-5	-5	-0	-0.4
1964 Chi-N	0	4	.000	8	5	0	0	0	31²	34	9	21	20	15.9	6.54	57	.279	.389	1	.091	-1	-11	-10	-0	-1.0
1966 Chi-N	0	0	—	2	0	0	0	0	4	5	0	2	6	15.8	4.50	82	.313	.389	0	—	0	-0	-0	0	0.0
1967 Chi-N	0	0	—	1	0	0	0	0	1	0	0	0	3	0.0	0.00	—	.000	.000	0	—	0	0	0	0	0.0
1970 LA-N	2	0	1.000	30	0	0	0	1	62	65	8	33	47	14.5	5.23	73	.273	.366	1	.143	0	-8	-10	-1	-0.9
StL-N	0	0	—	1	0	0	0	0	1	1	0	0	0	9.0	0.00	—	.333	.333	0	—	0	0	0	0	0.1
Yr	2	0	1.000	31	0	0	0	1	63	66	8	33	47	14.1	5.14	75	.269	.356	2	.286	0	-8	-9	-1	-0.8
1971 StL-N	0	0	—	4	0	0	0	0	3²	7	1	7	4	34.4	12.27	29	.438	.609	0	—	0	-4	-4	-0	-0.3
SD-N	3	12	.200	20	18	5	0	0	127¹	114	7	56	77	12.2	3.32	99	.240	.323	9	.237	2	2	-0	-1	0.1
Yr	3	12	.200	24	18	5	0	0	131	121	8	63	81	12.8	3.57	95	.246	.334	3	.079	2	-2	-4	-1	-0.2
1972 SD-N	9	11	.450	42	28	10	6	2	211²	195	18	88	167	12.1	3.44	95	.244	.321	8	.125	1	0	-4	-1	-0.4
1973 SD-N	1	7	.125	12	11	7	1	0	74	72	9	29	49	12.4	4.26	82	.262	.334	3	.136	-0	-5	-6	1	-0.5
*Cin-N	12	6	.667	24	24	7	3	0	166¹	136	18	72	112	11.3	3.30	103	.224	.307	3	.052	-4	7	2	-1	-0.3
Yr	13	13	.500	36	35	8	3	0	240¹	208	27	101	161	11.6	3.60	95	.235	.314	4	.050	-4	2	-5	-1	-0.8
1974 Cin-N	13	12	.520	35	26	8	2	0	186¹	170	15	68	141	11.6	3.14	111	.241	.309	8	.131	-2	10	7	-3	0.1
1975 *Cin-N	12	4	.750	34	26	2	0	0	188	163	23	84	119	11.8	3.73	96	.235	.318	7	.117	-2	-2	-3	-2	-0.6
1976 *Cin-N	12	7	.632	33	24	8	3	0	180¹	153	10	70	126	11.3	3.09	113	.231	.308	7	.140	-1	8	8	-3	0.4
1977 Cin-N	14	13	.519	35	34	8	1	0	221¹	200	28	98	160	12.2	3.38	116	.241	.324	8	.110	-2	13	14	-1	1.1
1978 Cin-N	11	9	.550	36	31	0	0	1	177¹	173	19	82	111	13.1	3.70	96	.255	.338	9	.140	-1	-3	-3	-1	-0.4
1979 *Cin-N	11	13	.458	34	31	5	0	0	195¹	193	14	57	95	11.5	3.64	103	.258	.311	9	.153	0	2	2	-1	0.1
1980 Mon-N	4	4	.500	48	8	2	0	4	98	96	8	40	58	12.8	4.13	86	.259	.337	1	.050	-2	-6	-6	-1	-0.9
Total 16	104	103	.502	403	268	56	15	8	1939²	1790	188	815	1303	12.2	3.64	98	.246	.324	72	.125	-11	-0	-17	-16	-3.7

■ MIKE NORRIS
Norris, Michael Kelvin b: 3/19/55, San Francisco, Cal. BR/TR, 6'2", 175 lbs. Deb: 4/10/75

YEAR TM/L	W	L	PCT	G	GS	CG	SH	SV	IP	H	HR	BB	SO	RAT	ERA	ERA+	OAV	OOB	BH	AVG	PB	PR	/A	PD	TPI
1975 Oak-A	1	0	1.000	4	3	1	1	0	16²	6	0	8	5	7.6	0.00	—	.107	.219	0	—	0	7	7	0	0.8
1976 Oak-A	4	5	.444	24	19	1	1	0	96	91	10	56	44	14.0	4.78	70	.250	.353	0	—	0	-13	-15	3	-1.1
1977 Oak-A	2	7	.222	16	12	1	1	0	77¹	77	14	31	35	13.0	4.77	84	.260	.338	0	.000	0	-6	-6	1	-0.4
1978 Oak-A	0	5	.000	14	5	1	0	0	49	46	2	35	36	15.4	5.51	66	.249	.377	0	—	0	-10	-10	-0	-0.9
1979 Oak-A	5	8	.385	29	18	3	0	0	146¹	146	11	94	96	15.3	4.80	84	.265	.381	0	—	0	-9	-12	-1	-1.2
1980 Oak-A	22	9	.710	33	33	24	1	0	284¹	215	18	83	180	9.6	2.53	149	.209	.272	0	—	0	47	39	3	4.5
1981 *Oak-A	12	9	.571	23	23	12	2	0	173	145	17	63	78	11.3	3.75	93	.228	.308	0	—	0	-2	-5	-0	-0.5
1982 Oak-A	7	11	.389	28	28	7	1	0	166¹	154	25	84	83	13.2	4.76	82	.242	.336	0	—	0	-13	-16	-1	-1.4
1983 Oak-A	4	5	.444	16	16	2	0	0	88²	68	11	36	63	10.9	3.76	103	.213	.299	0	—	0	3	1	-2	0.0
1990 Oak-A	1	0	1.000	14	0	0	0	0	27	24	0	9	16	11.7	3.00	124	.242	.318	0	—	0	3	2	0	0.2
Total 10	58	59	.496	201	157	52	7	0	1124²	972	108	499	636	12.1	3.89	97	.233	.322	0	.000	0	7	-16	5	-0.0

■ LOU NORTH
North, Louis Alexander b: 6/15/1891, Elgin, Ill. d: 5/16/74, Shelton, Conn. BR/TR, 5'11", 175 lbs. Deb: 8/22/13

YEAR TM/L	W	L	PCT	G	GS	CG	SH	SV	IP	H	HR	BB	SO	RAT	ERA	ERA+	OAV	OOB	BH	AVG	PB	PR	/A	PD	TPI
1913 Det-A	0	1	.000	1	1	0	0	0	6	10	1	9	3	28.5	15.00	19	.357	.514	0	.000	-0	-8	-8	-0	-0.5
1917 StL-N	0	0	—	5	0	0	0	0	11¹	14	1	4	4	14.3	3.97	68	.350	.409	0	.000	-0	-2	-2	0	-0.1
1920 StL-N	3	2	.600	24	6	3	0	1	88	90	3	32	37	12.7	3.27	91	.278	.346	7	.226	0	-1	-3	-1	-0.3
1921 StL-N	4	4	.500	40	0	0	0	7	86¹	81	5	32	28	11.9	3.54	103	.256	.327	3	.158	-1	2	1	-2	-0.1
1922 StL-N	10	3	.769	53	11	4	0	4	149²	164	4	64	84	14.1	4.45	87	.283	.361	11	.234	2	-6	-10	-4	-0.3
1923 StL-N	3	4	.429	34	3	0	0	1	71²	90	8	31	24	15.6	5.15	76	.308	.380	4	.182	-1	-9	-10	0	-0.9
1924 StL-N	0	0	—	6	0	0	0	0	14²	15	1	9	8	14.7	6.75	56	.273	.375	1	.250	-0	-5	-5	-0	-0.4
Bos-N	1	2	.333	9	4	1	0	0	35¹	45	1	19	11	16.3	5.35	71	.321	.403	1	.111	-1	-6	-6	-1	-0.6
Yr	1	2	.333	15	4	1	0	0	50	60	2	28	19	15.8	5.76	66	.308	.395	0	.000	-1	-11	-11	-1	-1.0
Total 7	21	16	.568	172	25	8	0	13	463	509	24	200	199	14.0	4.43	82	.287	.363	27	.197	-1	-34	-42	-0	-3.2

■ JAKE NORTHROP
Northrop, George Howard "Jerky" b: 3/5/1888, Monroeton, Pa. d: 11/16/45, Monroeton, Pa. BL/TR, 5'11", 170 lbs. Deb: 7/29/18

YEAR TM/L	W	L	PCT	G	GS	CG	SH	SV	IP	H	HR	BB	SO	RAT	ERA	ERA+	OAV	OOB	BH	AVG	PB	PR	/A	PD	TPI
1918 Bos-N	5	1	.833	7	4	4	1	0	40	26	0	3	4	6.5	1.35	199	.183	.200	2	.154	-1	6	6	0	0.7
1919 Bos-N	1	5	.167	11	3	2	0	0	37¹	43	2	10	9	13.0	4.58	62	.301	.351	4	.500	3	-7	-7	1	-0.3
Total 2	6	6	.500	18	7	6	1	0	77¹	69	2	13	13	9.7	2.91	95	.242	.278	6	.286	2	-1	-1	2	0.4

■ EFFIE NORTON
Norton, Elisha Strong "Leiter" b: 8/17/1873, Conneaut, Ohio d: 3/5/50, Aspinwall, Pa. BR/TR, Deb: 8/08/1896

YEAR TM/L	W	L	PCT	G	GS	CG	SH	SV	IP	H	HR	BB	SO	RAT	ERA	ERA+	OAV	OOB	BH	AVG	PB	PR	/A	PD	TPI
1896 Was-N	3	1	.750	8	5	2	0	0	44	49	2	14	13	12.9	3.07	144	.280	.333	4	.211	-0	6	7	-0	0.5
1897 Was-N	2	1	.667	4	2	1	0	0	17	31	0	11	3	22.2	6.88	63	.388	.463	5	.278	1	-5	-5	-0	-0.2
Total 2	5	2	.714	12	7	3	0	0	61	80	2	25	16	15.5	4.13	106	.314	.375	9	.243	0	1	2	-1	0.3

■ TOM NORTON
Norton, Thomas John b: 4/26/50, Elyria, Ohio BR/TR, 6'1", 200 lbs. Deb: 4/18/72

YEAR TM/L	W	L	PCT	G	GS	CG	SH	SV	IP	H	HR	BB	SO	RAT	ERA	ERA+	OAV	OOB	BH	AVG	PB	PR	/A	PD	TPI
1972 Min-A	0	1	.000	21	0	0	0	0	32¹	31	1	14	22	12.8	2.78	115	.252	.333	0	—	0	1	2	1	0.3

YEAR	TM/L	W	L	PCT	G	GS	CG	SH	SV	IP	H	HR	BB	SO	RAT	ERA	ERA+	OAV	OOB	BH	AVG	PB	PR	/A	PD	TPI
■ **RANDY NOSEK**					Nosek, Randall William		b: 1/8/67, Omaha, Neb.		BR/TR, 6'4", 215 lbs.	Deb: 5/27/89																
1989	Det-A	0	2	.000	2	2	0	0	0	5¹	7	2	10	4	28.7	13.50	28	.333	.548	0	—	0	-6	-6	-0	-0.4
1990	Det-A	1	1	.500	3	2	0	0	0	7	7	1	9	3	20.6	7.71	51	.280	.471	0	—	0	-3	-3	-0	-0.2
Total	2	1	3	.250	5	4	0	0	0	12¹	14	3	19	7	24.1	10.22	38	.304	.508	0	—	0	-9	-9	-0	-0.6
■ **DON NOTTEBART**					Nottebart, Donald Edward		b: 1/23/36, West Newton, Mass.		BR/TR, 6'1", 190 lbs.	Deb: 7/01/60																
1960	Mil-N	1	0	1.000	5	1	0	0	1	15¹	14	0	15	8	17.0	4.11	83	.233	.387	0	.000	-1	-1	-1	1	0.0
1961	Mil-N	6	7	.462	38	11	2	0	3	126¹	117	11	48	66	11.9	4.06	92	.251	.323	7	.184	0	-0	-4	2	-0.2
1962	Mil-N	2	2	.500	39	0	0	0	2	64	64	4	20	36	12.4	3.23	117	.258	.324	2	.333	1	5	4	2	0.6
1963	Hou-N	11	8	.579	31	27	9	2	0	193	170	10	39	118	9.8	3.17	99	.234	.275	11	.167	0	3	-0	-0	0.0
1964	Hou-N	6	11	.353	28	24	2	0	0	157	165	12	37	90	11.6	3.90	88	.275	.319	3	.064	-2	-6	-8	4	-0.6
1965	Hou-N	4	15	.211	29	25	3	0	0	158	166	14	55	77	12.9	4.67	72	.273	.338	5	.104	-1	-20	-23	2	-2.1
1966	Cin-N	5	4	.556	59	1	0	0	11	111¹	97	11	43	69	11.5	3.07	127	.235	.311	4	.167	-0	7	10	1	1.2
1967	Cin-N	0	3	.000	47	0	0	0	4	79¹	75	4	19	48	10.9	1.93	194	.253	.303	0	.000	-0	13	16	1	1.8
1969	NY-A	0	0	—	4	0	0	0	0	6	6	1	0	5	10.5	4.50	77	.261	.292	0	—	0	-1	-1	0	0.0
	Chi-N	1	1	.500	16	0	0	0	0	18	28	2	7	8	17.5	7.00	58	.350	.402	0	.000	-0	-7	-6	-0	-0.5
Total	9	36	51	.414	296	89	16	2	21	928¹	902	69	283	525	11.7	3.65	96	.256	.315	32	.134	-3	-8	-13	12	0.2
■ **CHET NOURSE**					Nourse, Chester Linwood		b: 8/7/1887, Ipswich, Mass.		d: 4/20/58, Clearwater, Fla.		6'3", 185 lbs.	Deb: 7/27/09													
1909	Bos-A	0	0	—	3	0	0	0	0	5	5	0	5	3	18.0	7.20	35	.263	.417	0	.000	-0	-3	-3	0	-0.2
■ **RAFAEL NOVOA**					Novoa, Rafael Angel		b: 10/26/67, New York, N.Y.		BL/TL, 6', 180 lbs.	Deb: 7/31/90															
1990	SF-N	0	1	.000	7	2	0	0	1	18²	21	3	13	14	16.4	6.75	55	.284	.391	1	.200	0	-6	-6	-1	-0.5
■ **WIN NOYES**					Noyes, Winfield Charles		b: 6/16/1889, Pleasanton, Neb.		d: 4/8/69, Cashmere, Wash.		BR/TR, 6', 180 lbs.	Deb: 5/19/13													
1913	Bos-N	0	0	—	11	0	0	0	0	20²	22	1	6	5	13.9	4.79	69	.289	.372	1	.250	0	-4	-3	0	-0.2
1917	Phi-A	10	10	.500	27	22	11	1	1	171	156	5	77	64	12.5	2.95	93	.258	.345	6	.115	-2	-5	-4	-1	-0.6
1919	Phi-A	1	5	.167	10	6	3	0	0	49	66	1	15	20	15.1	5.69	60	.332	.381	2	.125	-1	-13	-12	0	-1.2
	Chi-A	0	0	—	1	1	0	0	0	6	10	0	0	4	15.0	7.50	42	.385	.385	1	.500	1	-3	-3	-0	-0.1
	Yr	1	5	.167	11	7	3	0	0	55	76	1	15	24	14.9	5.89	58	.336	.378	0	.000	-1	-16	-15	0	-1.3
Total	3	11	15	.423	49	29	14	1	1	246²	254	7	98	93	13.2	3.76	78	.280	.356	10	.135	-3	-25	-22	-1	-2.1
■ **ED NUNEZ**					Nunez, Edwin (Martinez)		b: 5/27/63, Humacao, P.R.		BR/TR, 6'5", 235 lbs.	Deb: 4/07/82															
1982	Sea-A	1	2	.333	8	5	0	0	0	35¹	36	7	16	27	13.2	4.58	92	.269	.347	0	—	0	-2	-1	0	0.0
1983	Sea-A	0	4	.000	14	5	0	0	0	37	40	3	22	35	15.8	4.38	97	.278	.385	0	—	0	-1	-0	0	0.0
1984	Sea-A	2	2	.500	37	0	0	0	7	67²	55	8	21	57	10.5	3.19	125	.218	.286	0	—	0	6	6	-1	0.5
1985	Sea-A	7	3	.700	70	0	0	0	16	90¹	79	13	34	58	11.3	3.09	136	.234	.305	0	—	0	11	11	0	1.1
1986	Sea-A	1	2	.333	14	1	0	0	0	21²	25	5	5	17	12.5	5.82	73	.284	.323	0	—	0	-4	-4	0	-0.3
1987	Sea-A	3	4	.429	48	0	0	0	12	47¹	45	7	18	34	12.2	3.80	124	.262	.335	0	—	0	3	5	-0	0.4
1988	Sea-A	1	4	.200	14	3	0	0	0	29¹	45	4	14	19	18.7	7.98	52	.366	.439	0	—	0	-13	-12	1	-1.0
	NY-N	1	0	1.000	10	0	0	0	0	14	21	1	3	8	15.4	4.50	72	.339	.369	0	—	0	-2	-2	0	-0.1
1989	Det-A	3	4	.429	27	0	0	0	1	54	49	6	36	41	14.2	4.17	92	.254	.371	0	—	0	-2	-2	-0	-0.1
1990	Det-A	3	1	.750	42	0	0	0	6	80¹	65	4	37	66	11.7	2.24	175	.218	.309	0	—	0	15	15	-1	1.5
Total	9	22	26	.458	284	14	0	0	42	477	460	58	206	362	12.8	3.83	107	.255	.335	0	—	0	11	15	-1	2.0
■ **JOSE NUNEZ**					Nunez, Jose (Jimenez)		b: 1/13/64, Jarabacoa, D.R.		BR/TR, 6'3", 175 lbs.	Deb: 4/09/87															
1987	Tor-A	5	2	.714	37	9	0	0	0	97	91	12	58	99	13.8	5.01	90	.256	.360	0	—	0	-6	-6	-1	-0.5
1988	Tor-A	0	1	.000	13	2	0	0	0	29¹	28	3	17	18	14.1	3.07	128	.259	.365	0	—	0	3	3	0	0.3
1989	Tor-A	0	0	—	6	1	0	0	0	10²	8	0	2	14	8.4	2.53	149	.200	.238	0	—	0	2	1	-0	0.1
1990	Chi-N	4	7	.364	21	10	0	0	0	60²	61	5	34	40	14.1	6.53	63	.270	.365	0	.000	-1	-18	-16	0	-1.5
Total	4	9	10	.474	77	22	0	0	0	197²	188	20	111	171	13.7	5.05	84	.258	.356	0	.000	-1	-20	-17	-1	-1.6
■ **HOWIE NUNN**					Nunn, Howard Ralph		b: 10/18/35, Westfield, N.C.		BR/TR, 6', 173 lbs.	Deb: 4/11/59															
1959	StL-N	2	2	.500	16	0	0	0	0	21¹	23	3	15	20	16.0	7.59	56	.291	.404	0	.000	-0	-9	-8	1	-0.6
1961	Cin-N	2	1	.667	24	0	0	0	0	37²	35	0	24	26	14.3	3.58	113	.252	.366	2	.250	-0	2	2	-0	0.2
1962	Cin-N	0	0	—	6	0	0	0	0	9²	15	0	3	4	16.8	5.59	72	.375	.419	0	.000	-0	-2	-2	0	-0.1
Total	3	4	3	.571	46	0	0	0	0	68²	73	3	42	50	15.2	5.11	80	.283	.385	2	.200	-0	-9	-8	1	-0.5
■ **JOE NUXHALL**					Nuxhall, Joseph Henry		b: 7/30/28, Hamilton, Ohio		BL/TL, 6'3", 195 lbs.	Deb: 6/10/44															
1944	Cin-N	0	0	—	1	0	0	0	0	0²	2	0	5	0	94.5	67.50	5	.500	.778	0	—	0	-5	-5	0	-0.3
1952	Cin-N	1	4	.200	37	5	2	0	1	92¹	83	4	42	52	12.5	3.22	117	.246	.334	2	.087	-2	5	6	1	0.6
1953	Cin-N	9	11	.450	30	17	5	1	2	141²	136	13	69	52	13.5	4.32	101	.252	.345	16	.327	8	-1	1	-2	0.6
1954	Cin-N	12	5	.706	35	14	5	1	0	166²	188	11	59	85	13.7	3.89	108	.292	.357	9	.173	4	3	6	-0	0.9
1955	Cin-N	17	12	.586	50	33	14	**5**	3	257	240	25	78	98	11.3	3.47	122	.249	.309	17	.198	4	16	22	-2	2.5
1956	Cin-N	13	11	.542	44	32	10	2	3	200²	196	18	87	120	13.0	3.72	107	.257	.338	11	.186	3	1	6	-1	0.8
1957	Cin-N	10	10	.500	39	28	6	2	1	174¹	192	24	53	99	13.0	4.75	87	.275	.332	14	.237	3	-17	-12	-2	-1.0
1958	Cin-N	12	11	.522	36	26	5	0	0	175²	169	15	63	111	11.9	3.79	109	.257	.323	13	.210	0	3	7	-0	0.6
1959	Cin-N	9	9	.500	28	21	6	1	1	131²	155	10	35	75	13.1	4.24	96	.292	.337	11	.250	3	-4	-3	-1	0.0
1960	Cin-N	1	8	.111	38	6	0	0	0	112	130	8	27	72	12.9	4.42	86	.297	.344	2	.077	-1	-8	-7	2	-0.6
1961	KC-A	5	8	.385	37	13	1	0	1	128	135	12	65	81	14.3	5.34	77	.268	.355	19	.292	8	-19	-17	-2	-1.0
1962	LA-A	0	0	—	5	0	0	0	0	5¹	7	0	5	2	21.9	10.13	38	.304	.448	0	—	0	-4	-4	0	-0.2
	Cin-N	5	0	1.000	12	9	1	0	1	66	59	4	25	57	11.6	2.45	164	.240	.313	7	.269	3	11	12	-1	1.4
1963	Cin-N	15	8	.652	35	29	14	2	2	217¹	194	19	39	169	9.9	2.61	128	.237	.277	12	.158	0	16	18	-1	1.8
1964	Cin-N	9	8	.529	32	22	7	4	2	154²	146	19	51	111	11.8	4.07	89	.250	.317	7	.130	-1	-9	-8	-2	-0.9
1965	Cin-N	11	4	.733	32	16	5	1	2	148²	142	18	31	117	10.7	3.45	109	.252	.295	8	.178	1	1	5	-3	0.3
1966	Cin-N	6	8	.429	35	16	2	1	0	130	136	14	42	71	12.9	4.50	87	.270	.338	4	.100	-2	-13	-9	-0	-1.0
Total	16	135	117	.536	526	287	83	20	19	2302²	2310	209	776	1372	12.3	3.90	102	.262	.327	152	.198	29	-21	16	-12	4.5
■ **RICH NYE**					Nye, Richard Raymond		b: 8/4/44, Oakland, Cal.		BL/TL, 6'4", 185 lbs.	Deb: 9/16/66															
1966	Chi-N	0	2	.000	3	2	0	0	0	17	16	1	7	9	12.2	2.12	174	.254	.329	1	.250	0	3	3	-0	0.3
1967	Chi-N	13	10	.565	35	30	7	0	0	205	179	15	52	119	10.2	3.20	111	.234	.284	16	.213	3	4	8	0	1.2
1968	Chi-N	7	12	.368	27	20	6	1	1	132²	145	16	34	74	12.2	3.80	83	.276	.321	8	.182	-0	-12	-9	-0	-1.0
1969	Chi-N	3	5	.375	34	5	1	0	3	68²	72	13	21	39	12.3	5.11	79	.271	.326	1	.063	-1	-12	-8	-0	-0.9
1970	StL-N	0	0	—	6	0	0	0	0	8	13	2	6	5	21.4	4.50	91	.371	.463	1	.500	1	-0	-0	0	0.0
	Mon-N	3	2	.600	8	6	2	0	0	46¹	47	3	20	21	13.0	4.08	101	.260	.333	3	.176	0	-0	-0	-0	0.0
	Yr	3	2	.600	14	6	2	0	0	54¹	60	5	26	26	14.2	4.14	99	.276	.354	2	.105	1	-1	-0	0	0.0
Total	5	26	31	.456	113	63	16	1	4	477²	472	50	140	267	11.6	3.71	96	.257	.311	30	.190	2	-17	-7	-1	-0.4
■ **JERRY NYMAN**					Nyman, Gerald Smith		b: 11/23/42, Logan, Utah		BL/TL, 5'10", 165 lbs.	Deb: 8/24/68															
1968	Chi-A	2	1	.667	8	7	1	1	0	40¹	38	1	16	27	12.0	2.01	151	.247	.318	2	.154	-0	4	5	-0	0.5
1969	Chi-A	4	4	.500	20	10	2	1	0	64²	58	7	39	40	13.5	5.29	73	.244	.350	1	.050	-1	-12	-10	-1	-1.1
1970	SD-N	0	2	.000	2	2	0	0	0	5¹	8	1	2	2	16.9	15.19	26	.364	.417	0	—	0	-7	-7	-0	-0.5
Total	3	6	7	.462	30	19	3	2	0	110¹	104	9	57	69	13.1	4.57	78	.251	.342	3	.091	-1	-14	-12	-1	-1.1

YEAR TM/L	W	L	PCT	G	GS	CG	SH	SV	IP	H	HR	BB	SO	RAT	ERA	ERA+	OAV	OOB	BH	AVG	PB	PR	/A	PD	TPI

■ PRINCE OANA
Oana, Henry Kauhane b: 1/22/08, Waipahu, Hawaii d: 6/19/76, Austin, Tex. BR/TR, 6'2", 193 lbs. Deb: 4/22/34 ◆

1943 Det-A	3	2	.600	10	0	0	0	0	34	34	4	19	15	14.6	4.50	78	.262	.364	10	.385	5	-5	-4	-0	-0.3
1945 Det-A	0	0	—	3	1	0	0	1	11¹	3	0	7	3	7.9	1.59	221	.086	.238	1	.200	-0	2	2	-0	0.2
Total 2	3	2	.600	13	1	0	0	1	45¹	37	4	26	18	12.9	3.77	93	.224	.337	16	.308	5	-2	-1	-0	-0.1

■ HENRY OBERBECK
Oberbeck, Henry A. b: 5/17/1858, Missouri d: 8/26/21, St.Louis, Mo. Deb: 5/07/1883 ◆

1884 Bal-U	0	0	—	2	1	0	0	0	6	9	0	2	1	16.5	3.00	110	.325	.371	23	.184	-0	0	-0	-0	0.0
KC-U	0	5	.000	6	4	3	0	0	29²	47	0	3	6	15.2	5.76	48	.337	.351	17	.189	-0	-9	-10	-0	-0.7
Yr	0	5	.000	8	5	3	0	0	35²	56	0	5	7	15.4	5.30	54	.335	.355	10	.047	-1	-9	-10	-0	-0.7

■ DOC OBERLANDER
Oberlander, Hartman Louis b: 5/12/1864, Waukegan, Ill. d: 11/14/22, Pryor, Montana Deb: 5/16/1888

| 1888 Cle-a | 1 | 2 | .333 | 3 | 3 | 3 | 0 | 0 | 25² | 27 | 2 | 18 | 23 | 15.8 | 5.26 | 59 | .261 | .370 | 3 | .214 | 0 | -6 | -6 | -0 | -0.4 |

■ FRANK OBERLIN
Oberlin, Frank Rufus "Flossie" b: 3/29/1876, Elsie, Mich. d: 1/6/52, Ashley, Ind. BR/TR, 6'1", 165 lbs. Deb: 9/20/06

1906 Bos-A	1	3	.250	4	4	4	0	0	34	38	0	13	13	13.5	3.18	87	.286	.349	2	.154	-0	-2	-2	1	0.0
1907 Bos-A	1	5	.167	12	4	2	0	0	46	48	2	24	18	14.1	4.30	60	.271	.357	2	.154	-0	-9	-9	-1	-0.9
Was-A	2	6	.250	11	8	3	0	0	48²	57	0	12	18	12.8	4.62	52	.294	.335	1	.056	-2	-11	-12	-1	-1.4
Yr	3	11	.214	23	12	5	0	0	94²	105	2	36	36	13.4	4.47	56	.283	.346	0	.000	-2	-20	-21	-1	-2.3
1909 Was-A	1	4	.200	9	4	1	0	0	41	41	1	16	13	13.8	3.73	65	.266	.358	2	.143	-1	-6	-6	-1	-0.7
1910 Was-A	0	6	.000	8	6	6	0	0	57¹	52	0	23	18	12.1	2.98	84	.259	.341	1	.053	-2	-3	-3	-0	-0.5
Total 4	5	24	.172	44	26	16	0	0	227	236	3	88	80	13.2	3.77	67	.275	.347	8	.104	-4	-31	-31	-2	-3.5

■ DAN O'BRIEN
O'Brien, Daniel Jogues b: 4/22/54, St.Petersburg, Fla. BR/TR, 6'4", 215 lbs. Deb: 9/04/78

1978 StL-N	0	2	.000	7	2	0	0	0	18	22	1	8	12	16.0	4.50	78	.301	.386	0	.000	-0	-2	-2	-0	-0.2
1979 StL-N	1	1	.500	6	0	0	0	0	11	21	0	3	5	19.6	8.18	46	.420	.453	0	.000	-0	-5	-5	-0	-0.5
Total 2	1	3	.250	13	2	0	0	0	29	43	1	11	17	17.4	5.90	61	.350	.412	0	.000	-1	-7	-7	-0	-0.7

■ EDDIE O'BRIEN
O'Brien, Edward Joseph b: 12/11/30, S.Amboy, N.J. BR/TR, 5'9", 165 lbs. Deb: 4/25/53 C◆

1956 Pit-N	0	0	—	1	0	0	0	0	2	1	0	0	0	9.0	0.00	—	.167		14	.264	0	1	1	0	0.1
1957 Pit-N	1	0	1.000	3	1	1	0	0	12¹	11	2	3	10	10.2	2.19	173	.229	.275	0	.000	-0	2	2	0	0.2
1958 Pit-N	0	0	—	1	0	0	0	0	2	4	1	1	1	22.5	13.50	29	.444	.500	0	—	0	-2	-2	-0	-0.1
Total 3	1	0	1.000	5	1	1	0	0	16¹	16	3	4	11	11.6	3.31	115	.254	.309	131	.236	-0	1	1	0	0.2

■ DARBY O'BRIEN
O'Brien, John F. b: 4/15/1867, Troy, N.Y. d: 3/11/1892, W.Troy, N.Y. BR/TR, 5'10", 165 lbs. Deb: 6/23/1888

1888 Cle-a	11	19	.367	30	30	30	1	0	259	245	5	99	135	12.0	3.30	94	.241	.308	20	.183	-3	-7	-6	2	-0.5
1889 Cle-N	22	17	.564	41	41	39	1	0	346²	345	9	167	122	13.3	4.15	97	.251	.332	35	.250	4	-5	-5	2	0.1
1890 Cle-P	8	16	.333	25	25	22	0	0	206¹	229	9	93	54	14.0	3.40	117	.269	.341	15	.156	-5	19	13	-1	0.4
1891 Bos-a	18	13	.581	40	30	22	0	2	268²	300	13	127	87	14.3	3.65	96	.273	.348	30	.234	1	2	-5	-2	-0.5
Total 4	59	65	.476	136	126	113	2	2	1080²	1119	36	486	398	13.4	3.68	100	.258	.332	100	.211	-4	9	-1	0	-0.5

■ JOHNNY O'BRIEN
O'Brien, John Thomas b: 12/11/30, S.Amboy, N.J. BR/TR, 5'9", 170 lbs. Deb: 4/19/53 ◆

1956 Pit-N	1	0	1.000	8	0	0	0	0	19	8	2	9	9	9.0	2.84	133	.133	.268	18	.173	-0	2	2	-1	0.2
1957 Pit-N	0	3	.000	16	1	0	0	0	40	46	7	24	19	16.0	6.07	62	.293	.390	11	.314	2	-10	-10	-1	-0.9
1958 StL-N	0	0	—	1	0	0	0	0	2	7	0	2	2	40.5	22.50	18	.538	.600	0	.000	0	-4	-4	0	-0.2
Total 3	1	3	.250	25	1	0	0	0	61	61	9	35	30	14.6	5.61	68	.265	.369	204	.250	2	-12	-12	-1	-0.9

■ BOB O'BRIEN
O'Brien, Robert Allen b: 4/23/49, Pittsburgh, Pa. BL/TL, 5'10", 170 lbs. Deb: 4/11/71

| 1971 LA-N | 2 | 2 | .500 | 14 | 4 | 1 | 1 | 0 | 42 | 42 | 4 | 13 | 15 | 12.0 | 3.00 | 108 | .262 | .322 | 1 | .111 | -0 | 2 | 1 | -1 | 0.0 |

■ TOM O'BRIEN
O'Brien, Thomas H. b: 6/22/1860, Salem, Mass. d: 4/21/21, Worcester, Mass. Deb: 6/14/1882 ◆

| 1887 NY-a | 0 | 0 | — | 1 | 0 | 0 | 0 | 0 | 3² | 4 | 0 | 5 | 0 | 22.1 | 7.36 | 58 | .268 | .451 | 25 | .194 | -0 | -1 | -1 | -0 | 0.0 |

■ BUCK O'BRIEN
O'Brien, Thomas Joseph b: 5/9/1882, Brockton, Mass. d: 7/25/59, Boston, Mass. BR/TR, 5'10", 188 lbs. Deb: 9/09/11

1911 Bos-A	5	1	.833	6	5	5	2	0	47²	30	0	21	31	9.8	0.38	868	.180	.275	2	.125	-1	16	15	1	1.7
1912 *Bos-A	20	13	.606	37	34	25	2	0	275²	237	3	90	115	11.0	2.58	132	.237	.306	13	.138	-5	23	25	1	2.3
1913 Bos-A	4	9	.308	15	12	6	0	0	90¹	103	0	35	54	13.7	3.69	80	.305	.370	5	.167	0	-8	-7	1	-0.6
Chi-A	0	2	.000	6	3	0	0	0	18¹	21	0	13	4	16.7	3.93	74	.318	.430	0	.000	-0	-2	-2	-0	-0.2
Yr	4	11	.267	21	15	6	0	0	108²	124	0	48	58	14.2	3.73	79	.307	.381	3	.091	-0	-10	-10	1	-0.8
Total 3	29	25	.537	64	54	36	4	0	432	391	3	159	204	11.7	2.63	125	.249	.322	20	.140	-6	29	31	2	3.2

■ DARBY O'BRIEN
O'Brien, William D. b: 9/1/1863, Peoria, Ill. d: 6/15/1893, Peoria, Ill. BR/TR, 6'1", 186 lbs. Deb: 4/16/1887 ◆

| 1887 NY-a | 0 | 0 | — | 1 | 0 | 0 | 0 | 0 | 1 | 1 | 0 | 1 | 0 | 18.0 | 0.00 | — | .251 | .401 | 157 | .301 | 0 | 0 | 0 | -0 | 0.0 |

■ BILLY O'BRIEN
O'Brien, William Smith b: 3/14/1860, Albany, N.Y. d: 5/26/11, Kansas City, Mo. BR , 6', 185 lbs. Deb: 9/27/1884 ◆

| 1884 StP-U | 1 | 0 | 1.000 | 2 | 0 | 0 | 0 | 0 | 10 | 8 | 0 | 3 | 7 | 9.9 | 1.80 | 91 | .205 | .261 | 7 | .233 | 1 | 1 | -0 | 0 | 0.0 |

■ WALTER OCKEY
Ockey, Walter Andrew "Footie" (b: Walter Andrew Okpych)
b: 1/4/20, New York, N.Y. d: 12/4/71, Staten Island, N.Y. BR/TR, 6', 175 lbs. Deb: 5/03/44

| 1944 NY-N | 0 | 0 | — | 2 | 0 | 0 | 0 | 0 | 2² | 2 | 1 | 2 | 1 | 13.5 | 3.38 | 109 | .200 | .333 | 0 | — | 0 | 0 | 0 | -0 | 0.0 |

■ PAT O'CONNELL
O'Connell, Patrick H. b: 6/10/1861, Bangor, Me. d: 1/24/43, Lewiston, Maine BR/TR, 5'10", 175 lbs. Deb: 7/22/1886 ◆

| 1886 Bal-a | 0 | 0 | — | 1 | 0 | 0 | 0 | 0 | 3 | 4 | 0 | 2 | 1 | 18.0 | 6.00 | 57 | .306 | .398 | 30 | .181 | -0 | -1 | -1 | 0 | 0.0 |

■ ANDY O'CONNOR
O'Connor, Andrew James b: 9/14/1884, Roxbury, Mass. d: 9/26/80, Norwood, Mass. 6', 160 lbs. Deb: 10/06/08

| 1908 NY-A | 0 | 1 | .000 | 1 | 1 | 0 | 0 | 0 | 8 | 15 | 0 | 7 | 5 | 28.1 | 10.13 | 25 | .429 | .556 | 0 | .000 | -0 | -7 | -7 | -0 | -0.5 |

■ FRANK O'CONNOR
O'Connor, Frank Henry b: 9/15/1870, Keeseville, N.Y. d: 12/26/13, Brattleboro, Vt. BL/TL, 6', 185 lbs. Deb: 8/03/1893

| 1893 Phi-N | 0 | 0 | — | 3 | 1 | 0 | 0 | 1 | 4 | 2 | 0 | 9 | 0 | 24.8 | 11.25 | 41 | .145 | .482 | 2 | 1.000 | 2 | -3 | -3 | 0 | 0.0 |

■ JACK O'CONNOR
O'Connor, Jack William b: 6/2/58, Twenty-Nine Palms, Cal. BL/TL, 6'3", 215 lbs. Deb: 4/09/81

1981 Min-A	3	2	.600	28	0	0	0	0	35¹	46	3	16	30	19.9	5.86	67	.336	.462	0	—	0	-9	-8	1	-0.6
1982 Min-A	8	9	.471	23	19	6	1	0	126	122	13	57	56	12.9	4.29	99	.255	.337	0	—	0	-3	-1	-3	-0.2
1983 Min-A	2	3	.400	27	8	0	0	0	83	107	13	36	56	15.5	5.86	73	.315	.380	0	—	0	-17	-15	-1	-1.5
1984 Min-A	0	0	—	2	0	0	0	0	4²	1	1	4	0	9.6	1.93	218	.067	.263	0	—	0	1	1	-0	0.1
1985 Mon-N	0	2	.000	20	1	0	0	0	23²	21	1	13	16	12.9	4.94	69	.239	.337	0	—	0	-4	-4	-1	-0.4
1987 Bal-A	1	1	.500	29	0	0	0	2	46	46	5	23	33	13.5	4.30	102	.263	.348	0	—	0	1	0	-1	0.0
Total 6	14	17	.452	129	28	6	1	2	318²	343	36	163	177	14.4	4.89	85	.278	.364	0	—	0	-30	-25	-5	-2.6

■ HANK O'DAY
O'Day, Henry Francis b: 7/8/1862, Chicago, Ill. d: 7/2/35, Chicago, Ill. TR , Deb: 5/02/1884 MU

1884 Tol-a	9	28	.243	41	40	35	2	1	326²	335	6	66	163	11.0	3.75	91	.251	.286	51	.211	-1	-18	-12	5	-0.2
1885 Pit-a	5	7	.417	12	12	10	0	0	103	110	4	16	36	11.0	3.67	88	.262	.289	12	.245	1	-5	-5	-1	-0.2
1886 Was-N	2	2	.500	6	6	6	0	0	49	41	1	17	47	10.7	1.65	198	.218	.283	1	.053	-2	9	9	1	0.7
1887 Was-N	8	20	.286	30	30	29	0	0	254²	255	15	109	86	12.9	4.17	97	.253	.326	23	.198	-3	-3	-4	1	-0.4
1888 Was-N	16	29	.356	46	46	43	3	0	403	400	8	117	186	10.6	3.10	90	.230	.284	23	.139	-6	-12	-14	-4	-2.3
1889 Was-N	2	10	.167	13	13	11	0	0	108	117	7	57	23	14.5	4.33	91	.267	.352	8	.182	-1	-4	-5	1	-0.3
*NY-N	9	1	.900	10	10	8	0	0	78	83	2	35	28	13.6	4.27	92	.264	.338	3	.097	-2	-2	-3	-0	-0.3
Yr	11	11	.500	23	23	19	0	0	186	200	9	92	51	14.1	4.31	92	.266	.346	7	.093	-2	-6	-7	0	-0.6

YEAR	TM/L	W	L	PCT	G	GS	CG	SH	SV	IP	H	HR	BB	SO	RAT	ERA	ERA+	OAV	OOB	BH	AVG	PB	PR	/A	PD	TPI
1890	NY-P	22	13	.629	43	35	32	1	3	329	356	11	163	94	14.2	4.21	108	.264	.344	34	.227	-2	1	12	-3	0.7
Total	7	73	110	.399	201	192	177	6	4	1651¹	1656	66	580	663	12.2	3.74	97	.251	.311	155	.190	-16	-35	-23	1	-2.7

■ PAUL O'DEA
O'Dea, Paul "Lefty" b: 7/3/20, Cleveland, Ohio d: 12/11/78, Cleveland, Ohio BL/TL, 6', 200 lbs. Deb: 4/19/44 ♦

YEAR	TM/L	W	L	PCT	G	GS	CG	SH	SV	IP	H	HR	BB	SO	RAT	ERA	ERA+	OAV	OOB	BH	AVG	PB	PR	/A	PD	TPI
1944	Cle-A	0	0	—	3	0	0	0	0	4¹	5	0	6	0	22.8	2.08	159	.333	.524	55	.318	1	1	1	-0	0.1
1945	Cle-A	0	0	—	1	0	0	0	0	2	4	0	2	0	27.0	13.50	24	.400	.500	52	.235	0	-2	-2	0	-0.1
Total	2	0	0	—	4	0	0	0	0	6¹	9	0	8	0	24.2	5.68	58	.360	.515	107	.272	1	-2	-2	-0	0.0

■ BILLY O'DELL
O'Dell, William Oliver b: 2/10/33, Whitmire, S.C. BB/TL, 5'11", 170 lbs. Deb: 6/20/54

YEAR	TM/L	W	L	PCT	G	GS	CG	SH	SV	IP	H	HR	BB	SO	RAT	ERA	ERA+	OAV	OOB	BH	AVG	PB	PR	/A	PD	TPI
1954	Bal-A	1	1	.500	7	2	1	0	0	16¹	15	0	5	6	11.0	2.76	130	.242	.299	0	.000	-0	2	1	0	0.2
1956	Bal-A	0	0	—	4	1	0	0	0	8	6	0	6	6	13.5	1.13	349	.222	.364	0	.000	-0	3	2	-0	0.2
1957	Bal-A	4	10	.286	35	15	2	1	4	140¹	107	12	39	97	9.7	2.69	133	.212	.276	5	.147	-1	17	14	-2	1.1
1958	Bal-A	14	11	.560	41	25	12	3	8	221¹	201	13	51	137	10.4	2.97	121	.241	.288	8	.111	-1	20	15	-1	1.5
1959	Bal-A	10	12	.455	38	24	6	2	1	199¹	163	18	67	88	10.4	2.93	129	.220	.286	5	.083	-3	21	19	2	1.8
1960	SF-N	8	13	.381	43	24	6	1	2	202²	198	16	72	145	12.1	3.20	109	.252	.317	6	.107	1	13	6	-1	0.5
1961	SF-N	7	5	.583	46	14	4	1	2	130¹	132	10	33	110	11.5	3.59	106	.260	.306	4	.103	-2	6	3	-1	0.0
1962	*SF-N	19	14	.576	43	39	20	2	0	280²	282	18	66	195	11.4	3.53	108	.258	.304	12	.133	-1	13	8	-2	0.4
1963	SF-N	14	10	.583	36	33	10	3	1	222¹	218	14	70	116	11.9	3.16	101	.253	.314	16	.205	4	3	1	-3	0.0
1964	SF-N	8	7	.533	36	8	1	0	2	85	82	10	35	54	12.8	5.40	66	.252	.332	0	.000	-2	-18	-17	-1	-2.0
1965	Mil-N	10	6	.625	62	1	0	0	18	111¹	87	10	30	78	9.6	2.18	161	.215	.272	4	.174	1	17	17	-0	1.8
1966	Atl-N	2	3	.400	24	0	0	0	6	41¹	44	3	18	20	13.9	2.40	152	.272	.352	2	.250	0	6	6	-0	0.6
	Pit-N	3	2	.600	37	2	0	0	4	71¹	74	3	23	47	12.7	2.78	129	.275	.341	1	.063	-1	7	6	-1	0.5
	Yr	5	5	.500	61	2	0	0	10	112²	118	6	41	67	13.0	2.64	136	.273	.341	1	.042	-1	12	12	-1	1.1
1967	Pit-N	5	6	.455	27	11	1	0	0	86²	88	10	41	34	13.7	5.82	58	.265	.351	3	.115	-0	-24	-24	-1	-2.4
Total	13	105	100	.512	479	199	63	13	48	1817	1697	137	556	1133	11.4	3.29	109	.246	.306	66	.125	-7	85	59	-12	4.2

■ TED ODENWALD
Odenwald, Theodore Joseph "Lefty" b: 1/4/02, Hudson, Wis. d: 10/23/65, Shakopee, Minn. BR/TL, 5'10", 147 lbs. Deb: 4/13/21

YEAR	TM/L	W	L	PCT	G	GS	CG	SH	SV	IP	H	HR	BB	SO	RAT	ERA	ERA+	OAV	OOB	BH	AVG	PB	PR	/A	PD	TPI
1921	Cle-A	1	0	1.000	10	0	0	0	0	17¹	16	0	6	4	11.9	1.56	274	.262	.338	0	.000	-1	5	5	0	0.5
1922	Cle-A	0	0	—	1	0	0	0	0	1¹	6	0	2	2	54.0	40.50	10	.600	.667	0	—	0	-5	-5	0	-0.3
Total	2	1	0	1.000	11	0	0	0	0	18²	22	0	8	6	14.9	4.34	98	.310	.387	0	.000	-1	-0	-0	0	0.2

■ DAVE ODOM
Odom, David Everett "Blimp" or "Porky" b: 6/5/18, Dinuba, Cal. BR/TL, 6'1", 220 lbs. Deb: 5/31/43

YEAR	TM/L	W	L	PCT	G	GS	CG	SH	SV	IP	H	HR	BB	SO	RAT	ERA	ERA+	OAV	OOB	BH	AVG	PB	PR	/A	PD	TPI
1943	Bos-N	0	3	.000	22	3	1	0	2	54²	54	3	30	17	14.5	5.27	65	.269	.374	0	.000	-2	-11	-11	-1	-1.4

■ BLUE MOON ODOM
Odom, Johnny Lee b: 5/29/45, Macon, Ga. BR/TR, 6', 178 lbs. Deb: 9/05/64 ♦

YEAR	TM/L	W	L	PCT	G	GS	CG	SH	SV	IP	H	HR	BB	SO	RAT	ERA	ERA+	OAV	OOB	BH	AVG	PB	PR	/A	PD	TPI
1964	KC-A	1	2	.333	5	5	1	1	0	17	29	5	11	10	21.2	10.06	38	.363	.440	0	.000	-0	-12	-12	0	-1.0
1965	KC-A	0	0	—	1	0	0	0	0	1	2	0	2	0	36.0	9.00	39	.400	.571	0	—	0	-1	-1	0	0.0
1966	KC-A	5	5	.500	14	14	4	2	0	90¹	70	1	53	47	12.5	2.49	136	.215	.328	3	.097	-1	9	9	2	1.1
1967	KC-A	3	8	.273	29	17	0	0	0	103²	94	9	68	67	14.3	5.04	63	.243	.360	8	.286	2	-21	-21	0	-1.9
1968	Oak-A	16	10	.615	32	31	9	4	0	231¹	179	9	98	143	11.0	2.45	115	.216	.304	17	.218	6	14	9	1	1.9
1969	Oak-A	15	6	.714	32	32	10	3	0	231¹	179	15	112	150	11.6	2.92	118	.215	.312	21	.266	11	18	13	1	2.6
1970	Oak-A	9	8	.529	29	29	4	1	0	156¹	128	14	100	88	13.6	3.80	93	.227	.351	13	.241	6	-1	-5	3	0.4
1971	Oak-A	10	12	.455	25	25	3	1	0	140²	147	13	71	69	13.9	4.29	78	.271	.355	8	.160	1	-13	-15	-0	-1.4
1972	*Oak-A	15	6	.714	31	30	4	2	0	194¹	164	10	87	86	11.8	2.50	114	.234	.321	0	.000	0	12	7	1	0.9
1973	*Oak-A	5	12	.294	30	24	3	0	0	150¹	153	14	67	83	13.3	4.49	79	.263	.341	0	.000	0	-11	-16	-1	-1.6
1974	*Oak-A	1	5	.167	34	5	1	0	1	87¹	85	4	52	52	14.4	3.81	87	.267	.375	0	—	0	-2	-5	1	-0.3
1975	Oak-A	0	2	.000	7	2	0	0	0	11	19	1	11	4	25.4	12.27	30	.422	.544	0	—	0	-10	-11	0	-0.9
	Cle-A	1	0	1.000	3	1	1	1	0	10¹	4	1	8	10	10.5	2.61	145	.118	.286	0	—	0	1	1	-0	0.1
	Yr	1	2	.333	10	3	1	1	0	21¹	23	2	19	14	17.7	7.59	49	.284	.420	0	—	0	-9	-9	-0	-0.8
	Atl-N	1	7	.125	15	10	0	0	0	56	78	5	28	30	17.0	7.07	53	.342	.414	1	.077	-1	-21	-21	0	-1.9
1976	Chi-A	2	2	.500	8	4	0	0	0	28	31	2	20	18	16.7	5.79	62	.282	.397	0	—	0	-7	-7	-1	-0.7
Total	13	84	85	.497	295	229	40	15	1	1509	1362	103	788	857	13.0	3.70	89	.244	.341	79	.195	25	-45	-71	7	-2.7

■ GEORGE O'DONNELL
O'Donnell, George Dana b: 5/27/29, Winchester, Ill. BR/TR, 6'3", 175 lbs. Deb: 4/18/54

YEAR	TM/L	W	L	PCT	G	GS	CG	SH	SV	IP	H	HR	BB	SO	RAT	ERA	ERA+	OAV	OOB	BH	AVG	PB	PR	/A	PD	TPI
1954	Pit-N	3	·9	.250	21	10	3	0	1	87¹	105	4	21	8	13.2	4.53	92	.315	.360	2	.087	-1	-4	-3	1	-0.2

■ JOHN O'DONOGHUE
O'Donoghue, John Eugene b: 10/7/39, Kansas City, Mo. BR/TL, 6'4", 203 lbs. Deb: 9/29/63

YEAR	TM/L	W	L	PCT	G	GS	CG	SH	SV	IP	H	HR	BB	SO	RAT	ERA	ERA+	OAV	OOB	BH	AVG	PB	PR	/A	PD	TPI
1963	KC-A	0	1	.000	1	1	0	0	0	6	2	0	2	1	12.0	1.50	256	.286	.348	0	.000	-0	1	2	-0	0.1
1964	KC-A	10	14	.417	39	32	2	1	0	173²	202	24	65	79	14.0	4.92	78	.286	.349	13	.236	2	-25	-21	0	-1.9
1965	KC-A	9	18	.333	34	30	4	1	0	177²	183	15	66	82	12.7	3.95	88	.267	.332	12	.218	3	-10	-9	1	-0.5
1966	Cle-A	6	8	.429	32	13	2	0	0	108	109	13	23	49	11.2	3.83	90	.264	.306	5	.152	-0	-5	-5	1	-0.3
1967	Cle-A	8	9	.471	33	17	5	2	2	130²	120	10	33	81	10.7	3.24	101	.247	.298	4	.100	-0	-0	0	3	0.4
1968	Bal-A	0	0	—	16	0	0	0	2	22	34	2	7	11	16.8	6.14	48	.374	.418	0	.000	-0	-8	-8	0	-0.8
1969	Sea-A	2	2	.500	55	0	0	0	6	70	58	5	37	48	12.6	2.96	123	.230	.336	1	.077	-1	5	5	-0	0.5
1970	Mil-A	2	0	1.000	25	0	0	0	0	23¹	29	4	9	13	14.7	5.01	76	.299	.358	0	.000	-0	-3	-3	1	-0.2
	Mon-N	2	3	.400	9	3	0	0	0	22¹	20	2	11	6	13.3	5.24	78	.263	.371	0	.000	-0	-3	-3	0	-0.2
1971	Mon-N	0	0	—	13	0	0	0	0	17¹	19	3	7	7	13.5	4.67	75	.271	.338	0	—	0	-2	-2	0	-0.1
Total	9	39	55	.415	257	96	13	4	10	751	780	78	260	377	12.6	4.07	87	.269	.332	35	.170	2	-49	-44	6	-3.0

■ LEFTY O'DOUL
O'Doul, Francis Joseph b: 3/4/1897, San Francisco, Cal. d: 12/7/69, San Francisco, Cal. BL/TL, 6', 180 lbs. Deb: 4/29/19 ♦

YEAR	TM/L	W	L	PCT	G	GS	CG	SH	SV	IP	H	HR	BB	SO	RAT	ERA	ERA+	OAV	OOB	BH	AVG	PB	PR	/A	PD	TPI
1919	NY-A	0	0	—	3	0	0	0	0	5	7	0	4	2	19.8	3.60	89	.304	.407	4	.250	0	-0	-0	-0	0.0
1920	NY-A	0	0	—	2	0	0	0	0	3²	4	0	2	2	17.2	4.91	78	.286	.412	2	.167	-0	-0	-0	0	0.0
1922	NY-A	0	0	—	6	0	0	0	0	16	24	0	12	5	20.3	3.38	119	.353	.450	3	.333	1	1	1	0	0.2
1923	Bos-A	1	1	.500	23	1	0	0	0	53	69	2	31	10	17.7	5.43	76	.337	.433	5	.143	-1	-9	-8	1	-0.7
Total	4	1	1	.500	34	1	0	0	0	77²	104	2	49	19	18.3	4.87	83	.335	.434	1140	.349	-1	-8	-7	1	-0.5

■ BRYAN OELKERS
Oelkers, Bryan Alois b: 3/11/61, Zaragoza, Spain BL/TL, 6'3", 192 lbs. Deb: 4/09/83

YEAR	TM/L	W	L	PCT	G	GS	CG	SH	SV	IP	H	HR	BB	SO	RAT	ERA	ERA+	OAV	OOB	BH	AVG	PB	PR	/A	PD	TPI
1983	Min-A	0	5	.000	10	8	0	0	0	34¹	56	7	17	13	19.1	8.65	49	.376	.440	0	—	0	-18	-17	-1	-1.5
1986	Cle-A	3	3	.500	35	4	0	0	1	69	70	13	40	33	15.1	4.70	88	.262	.371	0	—	0	-4	-4	-1	-0.4
Total	2	3	8	.273	45	12	0	0	1	103¹	126	20	57	46	16.5	6.01	70	.303	.395	0	—	0	-21	-21	-2	-1.9

■ JOE OESCHGER
Oeschger, Joseph Carl b: 5/24/1892, Chicago, Ill. d: 7/28/86, Rohnert Park, Cal BR/TR, 6' ", 190 lbs. Deb: 4/21/14

YEAR	TM/L	W	L	PCT	G	GS	CG	SH	SV	IP	H	HR	BB	SO	RAT	ERA	ERA+	OAV	OOB	BH	AVG	PB	PR	/A	PD	TPI
1914	Phi-N	4	8	.333	32	10	5	0	1	124	129	5	54	47	14.0	3.77	78	.279	.366	3	.075	-4	-14	-11	-1	-1.6
1915	Phi-N	1	0	1.000	6	1	1	0	0	23²	21	1	9	8	11.4	3.42	80	.247	.319	0	.000	-1	-2	-2	0	-0.2
1916	Phi-N	1	0	1.000	14	0	0	0	0	30¹	18	2	14	17	9.8	2.37	112	.184	.292	0	.000	-1	1	1	0	0.2
1917	Phi-N	15	14	.517	42	30	18	5	1	262	241	7	72	123	11.0	2.75	102	.249	.305	10	.114	-4	-1	2	-3	-0.5
1918	Phi-N	6	18	.250	30	23	13	2	3	184	159	3	83	60	12.2	3.03	99	.238	.328	5	.083	-4	-6	-1	-2	-0.6
1919	Phi-N	0	1	.000	5	4	2	0	0	38	52	1	16	5	16.6	5.92	54	.340	.409	0	.000	-2	-13	-11	0	-1.2
	NY-N	0	1	.000	5	1	0	0	0	8	12	0	2	3	15.8	4.50	62	.400	.438	0	.000	-0	-2	-0	-0	-0.1
	Bos-N	4	2	.667	7	7	4	1	0	56²	63	0	21	16	13.5	2.54	112	.300	.366	2	.091	-1	2	2	-1	0.0
	Yr	4	4	.500	17	12	6	1	0	102²	127	1	39	24	14.6	3.94	76	.322	.384	2	.053	-1	-12	-11	-1	-1.3
1920	Bos-N	15	13	.536	38	30	20	5	0	299	294	10	99	80	12.1	3.46	88	.265	.329	18	.178	-3	-14	-14	-3	-1.9
1921	Bos-N	20	14	.588	46	36	19	3	0	299	303	11	99	68	12.5	3.52	104	.274	.341	28	.255	2	9	4	3	0.8
1922	Bos-N	6	21	.222	46	23	10	1	1	195²	234	8	81	51	14.9	5.06	79	.303	.375	12	.190	-0	-21	-23	1	-2.0
1923	Bos-N	5	15	.250	44	19	6	1	2	166¹	227	4	54	33	15.5	5.68	70	.330	.383	12	.231	-0	-31	-31	0	-2.8

YEAR	TM/L	W	L	PCT	G	GS	CG	SH	SV	IP	H	HR	BB	SO	RAT	ERA	ERA+	OAV	OOB	BH	AVG	PB	PR	/A	PD	TPI
1924	NY-N	2	0	1.000	10	2	0	0	0	29	35	1	14	10	15.2	3.10	118	.287	.360	3	.429	1	2	2	-1	0.2
	Phi-N	2	7	.222	19	8	0	0	0	65¹	88	6	16	8	14.7	4.41	101	.333	.378	5	.250	-1	-4	0	0	0.0
	Yr	4	7	.364	29	10	0	0	0	94¹	123	7	30	18	14.9	4.01	105	.319	.372	0	.000	0	-1	2	-1	0.2
1925	Bro-N	1	2	.333	21	3	1	0	0	37	60	2	19	6	19.5	6.08	69	.382	.452	1	.125	-0	-7	-8	0	-0.7
Total	12	82	116	.414	365	197	99	18	8	1818	1936	61	651	535	13.1	3.81	88	.281	.349	99	.165	-19	-96	-89	-6	-10.5

■ JACK OGDEN
Ogden, John Mahlon b: 11/5/1897, Ogden, Pa. d: 11/9/77, Philadelphia, Pa. BR/TR, 6', 190 lbs. Deb: 6/22/18

YEAR	TM/L	W	L	PCT	G	GS	CG	SH	SV	IP	H	HR	BB	SO	RAT	ERA	ERA+	OAV	OOB	BH	AVG	PB	PR	/A	PD	TPI
1918	NY-N	0	0	—	5	0	0	0	0	8²	8	0	3	1	13.5	3.12	84	.296	.406	0	.000	-0	-0	-0	-0	0.0
1928	StL-A	15	16	.484	38	31	18	1	2	242²	257	23	80	67	12.5	4.15	101	.274	.331	17	.200	-1	-3	1	-3	-0.1
1929	StL-A	4	8	.333	34	14	7	0	0	131¹	154	8	44	32	13.6	4.93	90	.301	.357	11	.244	0	-10	-7	-0	-0.5
1931	Cin-N	4	8	.333	22	9	3	1	1	89	79	3	32	24	11.2	2.93	127	.242	.310	4	.148	-1	9	8	-1	0.6
1932	Cin-N	2	2	.500	24	3	1	0	0	57	72	5	22	20	14.8	5.21	74	.310	.370	2	.167	0	-8	-9	-0	-0.7
Total	5	25	34	.424	123	57	29	2	3	528²	570	39	181	144	12.8	4.24	97	.280	.340	34	.200	-1	-13	-8	-4	-0.7

■ CURLY OGDEN
Ogden, Warren Harvey b: 1/24/01, Ogden, Pa. d: 8/6/64, Chester, Pa. BR/TR, 6'1.5", 180 lbs. Deb: 7/18/22

YEAR	TM/L	W	L	PCT	G	GS	CG	SH	SV	IP	H	HR	BB	SO	RAT	ERA	ERA+	OAV	OOB	BH	AVG	PB	PR	/A	PD	TPI
1922	Phi-A	1	4	.200	15	6	4	0	0	72¹	59	4	33	20	12.1	3.11	137	.237	.338	7	.241	-0	8	9	-0	0.9
1923	Phi-A	1	2	.333	18	2	0	0	0	46¹	63	2	32	14	19.0	5.63	73	.330	.434	5	.294	1	-8	-8	-0	-0.6
1924	Phi-A	0	3	.000	5	1	0	0	0	12²	14	1	7	4	15.6	4.97	86	.275	.373	0	.000	-1	-1	-1	-0	-0.1
	*Was-A	9	5	.643	16	16	9	3	0	108	83	3	51	23	11.3	2.58	156	.221	.317	13	.277	2	20	17	-0	1.9
	Yr	9	8	.529	21	17	9	3	0	120²	97	4	58	27	11.7	2.83	143	.227	.322	1	.020	1	19	16	-0	1.8
1925	Was-A	3	1	.750	17	4	2	1	0	42	45	1	18	6	13.9	4.50	94	.288	.369	3	.250	-0	-0	-1	-0	0.0
1926	Was-A	4	4	.500	22	9	4	0	0	96¹	114	2	45	21	15.3	4.30	90	.305	.387	5	.185	-1	-3	-5	-1	-0.5
Total	5	18	19	.486	93	38	19	4	0	377²	378	13	186	88	13.9	3.79	108	.271	.364	33	.244	1	14	12	-1	1.6

■ JOE OGRODOWSKI
Ogrodowski, Joseph Anthony b: 11/20/06, Hoytville, Pa. d: 6/24/59, Elmira, N.Y. BR/TR, 5'11", 165 lbs. Deb: 4/27/25

YEAR	TM/L	W	L	PCT	G	GS	CG	SH	SV	IP	H	HR	BB	SO	RAT	ERA	ERA+	OAV	OOB	BH	AVG	PB	PR	/A	PD	TPI
1925	Bos-N	0	0	—	1	0	0	0	0	1	6	0	3	0	81.0	54.00	7	.600	.692	0	—	0	-6	-6	0	-0.3

■ BILL O'HARA
O'Hara, William Alexander b: 8/14/1883, Toronto, Ont., Can. d: 6/15/31, Jersey City, N.J. BL/TR, 5'10", Deb: 4/15/09 ◆

YEAR	TM/L	W	L	PCT	G	GS	CG	SH	SV	IP	H	HR	BB	SO	RAT	ERA	ERA+	OAV	OOB	BH	AVG	PB	PR	/A	PD	TPI
1910	StL-N	0	0	—	1	0	0	0	0	1	0	0	0	0	0.0	0.00	—	.000	.000	3	.150	-0	0	0	0	0.10

■ JOE OHL
Ohl, Joseph Earl b: 1/10/1888, Jobstown, N.J. d: 12/18/51, Camden, N.J. BL/TL, Deb: 7/29/09

YEAR	TM/L	W	L	PCT	G	GS	CG	SH	SV	IP	H	HR	BB	SO	RAT	ERA	ERA+	OAV	OOB	BH	AVG	PB	PR	/A	PD	TPI
1909	Was-A	0	0	—	4	0	0	0	0	8²	7	0	1	2	9.3	2.08	117	.194	.237	0	.000	-0	0	0	0	0.0

■ BOBBY OJEDA
Ojeda, Robert Michael b: 12/17/57, Los Angeles, Cal. BL/TL, 6'1", 185 lbs. Deb: 7/13/80

YEAR	TM/L	W	L	PCT	G	GS	CG	SH	SV	IP	H	HR	BB	SO	RAT	ERA	ERA+	OAV	OOB	BH	AVG	PB	PR	/A	PD	TPI
1980	Bos-A	1	1	.500	7	7	0	0	0	26	39	2	14	12	18.3	6.92	61	.361	.434	0	—	0	-8	-8	-0	-0.7
1981	Bos-A	6	2	.750	10	10	2	0	0	66¹	50	6	25	28	10.4	3.12	124	.212	.293	0	—	0	4	6	-0	0.6
1982	Bos-A	4	6	.400	22	14	0	0	0	78¹	95	13	29	52	14.4	5.63	76	.296	.356	0	—	0	-14	-12	-1	-1.1
1983	Bos-A	12	7	.632	29	28	5	0	0	173²	173	15	73	94	12.9	4.04	108	.265	.342	0	—	0	0	6	0	0.6
1984	Bos-A	12	12	.500	33	32	8	5	0	216²	211	17	96	137	12.8	3.99	104	.259	.338	0	—	0	0	4	1	0.5
1985	Bos-A	9	11	.450	39	22	5	0	0	157²	166	11	48	102	12.3	4.00	107	.273	.328	0	—	0	3	5	0	0.5
1986	*NY-N	18	5	**.783**	32	30	7	2	0	217¹	185	15	52	148	9.9	2.57	138	.230	.279	8	.113	-2	28	23	1	2.3
1987	NY-N	3	5	.375	10	7	0	0	0	46¹	45	5	10	21	10.7	3.88	97	.253	.293	1	.071	-0	1	-1	0	0.0
1988	NY-N	10	13	.435	29	29	5	5	0	190¹	158	6	33	133	9.2	2.88	112	.225	.264	10	.164	1	12	7	2	1.1
1989	NY-N	13	11	.542	31	31	5	2	0	192	179	16	78	95	12.1	3.47	94	.245	.319	7	.106	-2	1	-4	3	-0.3
1990	NY-N	7	6	.538	38	12	0	0	0	118	123	10	40	62	12.6	3.66	100	.272	.334	4	.133	-0	2	-0	3	0.3
Total	11	95	79	.546	280	222	37	14	0	1482²	1424	116	498	884	11.8	3.65	104	.254	.317	30	.124	-4	28	25	9	3.8

■ FRANK OKRIE
Okrie, Frank Anthony "Lefty" b: 10/28/1896, Detroit, Mich. d: 10/16/59, Detroit, Mich. BL/TL, 5'11", 175 lbs. Deb: 4/20/20

YEAR	TM/L	W	L	PCT	G	GS	CG	SH	SV	IP	H	HR	BB	SO	RAT	ERA	ERA+	OAV	OOB	BH	AVG	PB	PR	/A	PD	TPI
1920	Det-A	1	2	.333	21	1	1	0	0	41	44	2	18	9	14.7	5.27	71	.295	.390	1	.200	-0	-7	-7	6	0.0

■ RED OLDHAM
Oldham, John Cyrus b: 7/15/1893, Zion, Md. d: 1/28/61, Costa Mesa, Cal. BB/TL, 6' ", 176 lbs. Deb: 8/19/14

YEAR	TM/L	W	L	PCT	G	GS	CG	SH	SV	IP	H	HR	BB	SO	RAT	ERA	ERA+	OAV	OOB	BH	AVG	PB	PR	/A	PD	TPI
1914	Det-A	2	4	.333	9	7	3	0	0	45¹	42	1	8	23	10.5	3.38	83	.243	.288	4	.267	1	-3	-3	-1	-0.2
1915	Det-A	3	0	1.000	17	2	1	0	0	57²	52	1	17	17	11.4	2.81	108	.243	.311	2	.143	-0	1	1	-0	0.1
1920	Det-A	8	13	.381	39	22	10	1	1	215¹	248	5	91	62	14.4	3.85	97	.302	.376	12	.174	-1	-1	-3	4	0.0
1921	Det-A	11	14	.440	40	28	12	1	1	229¹	258	11	81	67	13.5	4.24	101	.288	.351	19	.224	2	1	1	1	0.4
1922	Det-A	10	13	.435	43	27	9	0	3	212	256	14	59	72	13.8	4.67	83	.305	.358	19	.260	4	-15	-19	1	-1.2
1925	*Pit-N	3	2	.600	11	4	3	0	1	53	66	2	18	10	14.6	3.91	114	.313	.372	6	.333	2	2	3	0	0.6
1926	Pit-N	2	2	.500	17	2	0	0	2	41²	56	1	18	16	16.2	5.62	70	.359	.429	2	.222	-1	-8	-8	0	-0.6
Total	7	39	48	.448	176	92	38	2	12	854¹	978	35	292	267	13.7	4.15	93	.295	.358	64	.226	9	-23	-26	5	-0.9

■ STEVE OLIN
Olin, Steven Robert b: 10/10/65, Portland, Ore. BR/TR, 6'3", 185 lbs. Deb: 7/29/89

YEAR	TM/L	W	L	PCT	G	GS	CG	SH	SV	IP	H	HR	BB	SO	RAT	ERA	ERA+	OAV	OOB	BH	AVG	PB	PR	/A	PD	TPI
1989	Cle-A	1	4	.200	25	0	0	0	1	36	35	1	14	24	12.3	3.75	106	.255	.325	0	—	0	1	1	0	0.1
1990	Cle-A	4	4	.500	50	1	0	0	1	92¹	96	3	26	64	12.5	3.41	117	.270	.331	0	—	0	5	6	2	0.8
Total	2	5	8	.385	75	1	0	0	2	128¹	131	4	40	88	12.4	3.51	113	.266	.329	0	—	0	6	7	2	0.9

■ OMAR OLIVARES
Olivares, Omar (Palqu) b: 7/6/67, Mayaguez, P.R. BR/TR, 6'1", 185 lbs. Deb: 8/18/90

YEAR	TM/L	W	L	PCT	G	GS	CG	SH	SV	IP	H	HR	BB	SO	RAT	ERA	ERA+	OAV	OOB	BH	AVG	PB	PR	/A	PD	TPI
1990	StL-N	1	1	.500	9	6	0	0	0	49¹	45	2	17	20	11.7	2.92	134	.249	.320	3	.176	1	5	5	1	0.8

■ FRANCISCO OLIVERAS
Oliveras, Francisco Javier (Noa) b: 1/31/63, Santurce, P.R. BR/TR, 5'10", 170 lbs. Deb: 5/03/89

YEAR	TM/L	W	L	PCT	G	GS	CG	SH	SV	IP	H	HR	BB	SO	RAT	ERA	ERA+	OAV	OOB	BH	AVG	PB	PR	/A	PD	TPI
1989	Min-A	3	4	.429	12	8	1	0	0	55²	64	8	15	24	12.9	4.53	91	.288	.336	0	—	-0	-4	-2	-1	-0.2
1990	SF-N	2	2	.500	33	2	0	0	2	55¹	47	5	21	41	11.4	2.77	135	.230	.308	0	.000	-1	6	6	-1	0.5
Total	2	5	6	.455	45	10	1	0	2	111	111	13	36	65	12.2	3.65	108	.261	.323	0	.000	-1	2	3	-1	0.3

■ DIOMEDES OLIVO
Olivo, Diomedes Antonio (Maldonado) b: 1/22?/19, Guayubin, D.R. d: 2/15/77, Santo Domingo, D.R. BL/TL, 6'1", 195 lbs. Deb: 9/05/60

YEAR	TM/L	W	L	PCT	G	GS	CG	SH	SV	IP	H	HR	BB	SO	RAT	ERA	ERA+	OAV	OOB	BH	AVG	PB	PR	/A	PD	TPI
1960	Pit-N	0	0	—	4	0	0	0	0	9²	8	1	5	10	12.1	2.79	134	.216	.310	0	.000	-0	1	1	-0	0.1
1962	Pit-N	5	1	.833	62	1	0	0	7	84¹	88	5	25	66	12.1	2.77	142	.277	.329	3	.188	1	11	11	-1	1.1
1963	StL-N	0	5	.000	19	0	0	0	0	13¹	16	1	9	9	17.6	5.40	66	.296	.406	0	—	0	-3	-3	-0	-0.2
Total	3	5	6	.455	85	1	0	0	7	107¹	112	7	39	85	12.7	3.10	125	.274	.339	3	.176	0	9	9	-0	1.0

■ CHI-CHI OLIVO
Olivo, Federico Emilio (Maldonado) b: 3/18/28, Guayubin, D.R. d: 2/3/77, Guaybin, D.R. BR/TR, 6'2", 215 lbs. Deb: 6/05/61

YEAR	TM/L	W	L	PCT	G	GS	CG	SH	SV	IP	H	HR	BB	SO	RAT	ERA	ERA+	OAV	OOB	BH	AVG	PB	PR	/A	PD	TPI
1961	Mil-N	0	0	—	3	0	0	0	0	2	3	1	5	1	36.0	18.00	21	.500	.727	0	—	0	-3	-3	0	-0.2
1964	Mil-N	2	1	.667	38	0	0	0	5	60	55	7	21	45	11.4	3.75	94	.247	.311	1	.250	0	-1	-2	0	0.0
1965	Mil-N	0	1	.000	8	0	0	0	0	13	12	1	5	11	11.8	1.38	254	.267	.340	0	—	0	3	3	-0	0.3
1966	Atl-N	5	4	.556	47	0	0	0	7	66	59	4	19	41	10.8	4.23	86	.240	.297	1	.111	-0	-5	-4	-1	-0.5
Total	4	7	6	.538	96	0	0	0	12	141	129	13	50	98	11.5	3.96	90	.248	.315	2	.154	-0	-6	-6	-0	-0.4

■ JIM OLLOM
Ollom, James Donald b: 7/8/45, Snohomish, Wash. BR/TL, 6'4", 210 lbs. Deb: 9/03/66

YEAR	TM/L	W	L	PCT	G	GS	CG	SH	SV	IP	H	HR	BB	SO	RAT	ERA	ERA+	OAV	OOB	BH	AVG	PB	PR	/A	PD	TPI
1966	Min-A	0	0	—	3	1	0	0	0	10	6	1	1	11	7.2	3.60	100	.167	.211	0	.000	-0	-0	-0	-0	0.0
1967	Min-A	0	1	.000	21	2	0	0	0	35	33	4	11	17	12.3	5.40	64	.258	.336	1	.200	-0	-8	-8	-0	-0.7
Total	2	0	1	.000	24	3	0	0	0	45	39	5	12	28	11.2	5.00	70	.238	.309	1	.143	-0	-9	-8	-0	-0.7

■ FRED OLMSTEAD
Olmstead, Frederic William b: 7/3/1881, Grand Rapids, Mich d: 10/22/36, Muskogee, Okla. BR/TR, 5'11", 170 lbs. Deb: 7/02/08

YEAR	TM/L	W	L	PCT	G	GS	CG	SH	SV	IP	H	HR	BB	SO	RAT	ERA	ERA+	OAV	OOB	BH	AVG	PB	PR	/A	PD	TPI
1908	Chi-A	0	0	—	1	0	0	0	0	2	6	0	1	1	31.5	13.50	17	.600	.636	0	.000	0	-2	-2	0	-0.1
1909	Chi-A	3	2	.600	8	6	5	0	0	54²	52	1	12	21	10.7	1.81	129	.277	.323	2	.095	-1	4	3	0	0.2
1910	Chi-A	10	12	.455	32	20	14	4	0	184¹	174	1	50	68	11.1	1.95	123	.260	.316	10	.154	-2	12	9	2	0.9
1911	Chi-A	6	6	.500	25	11	7	1	2	117²	146	3	30	45	13.9	4.21	77	.309	.358	7	.189	-0	-11	-13	-0	-1.2

YEAR TM/L	W	L	PCT	G	GS	CG	SH	SV	IP	H	HR	BB	SO	RAT	ERA	ERA+	OAV	OOB	BH	AVG	PB	PR	/A	PD	TPI
Total 4	19	20	.487	66	37	26	5	2	358²	378	5	93	135	12.1	2.74	97	.283	.334	19	.153	-3	2	-3	1	-0.2

■ AL OLMSTED
Olmsted, Alan Ray   b: 3/18/57, St.Louis, Mo.   BR/TL, 6'2", 195 lbs.   Deb: 9/12/80

YEAR TM/L	W	L	PCT	G	GS	CG	SH	SV	IP	H	HR	BB	SO	RAT	ERA	ERA+	OAV	OOB	BH	AVG	PB	PR	/A	PD	TPI
1980 StL-N	1	1	.500	5	5	0	0	0	34²	32	2	14	14	12.2	2.86	129	.244	.322	2	.182	-0	3	3	1	0.4

■ HANK OLMSTED
Olmsted, Henry Theodore   b: 1/12/1879, Saginaw Bay, Mich.   d: 1/6/69, Bradenton, Fla.   5'8.5", 147 lbs.   Deb: 7/15/05

YEAR TM/L	W	L	PCT	G	GS	CG	SH	SV	IP	H	HR	BB	SO	RAT	ERA	ERA+	OAV	OOB	BH	AVG	PB	PR	/A	PD	TPI
1905 Bos-A	1	2	.333	3	3	3	0	0	25	18	0	12	6	10.8	3.24	83	.203	.298	1	.125	-0	-2	-1	-0	-0.1

■ OLE OLSEN
Olsen, Arthur   b: 9/12/1894, S.Norwalk, Conn.   BR/TR, 5'10", 163 lbs.   Deb: 4/12/22

YEAR TM/L	W	L	PCT	G	GS	CG	SH	SV	IP	H	HR	BB	SO	RAT	ERA	ERA+	OAV	OOB	BH	AVG	PB	PR	/A	PD	TPI
1922 Det-A	7	6	.538	37	15	5	0	3	137	147	8	40	52	13.2	4.53	86	.281	.348	7	.179	-1	-7	-10	1	-0.9
1923 Det-A	1	1	.500	17	2	1	0	0	41¹	42	1	17	12	13.9	6.31	61	.290	.383	1	.125	-1	-11	-11	-1	-1.1
Total 2	8	7	.533	54	17	6	0	3	178¹	189	9	57	64	13.4	4.95	78	.283	.356	8	.170	-1	-18	-21	-0	-2.0

■ VERN OLSEN
Olsen, Vern Jarl   b: 3/16/18, Hillsboro, Ore.   d: 7/13/89, Maywood, Ill.   BR/TL, 6'0.5", 175 lbs.   Deb: 9/08/39

YEAR TM/L	W	L	PCT	G	GS	CG	SH	SV	IP	H	HR	BB	SO	RAT	ERA	ERA+	OAV	OOB	BH	AVG	PB	PR	/A	PD	TPI
1939 Chi-N	1	0	1.000	4	0	0	0	0	7²	2	0	7	3	10.6	0.00	—	.087	.300	0	.000	0	3	3	-0	0.4
1940 Chi-N	13	9	.591	34	20	9	4	0	172²	172	5	62	71	12.3	2.97	126	.260	.325	15	.263	3	17	15	4	2.3
1941 Chi-N	10	8	.556	37	23	10	2	1	185²	202	7	59	73	12.7	3.15	111	.276	.331	15	.238	3	10	7	2	1.3
1942 Chi-N	6	9	.400	32	17	4	1	1	140¹	161	6	55	46	13.9	4.49	71	.283	.347	9	.188	1	-18	-20	2	-1.7
1946 Chi-N	0	0	—	5	0	0	0	0	9²	10	0	9	8	17.7	2.79	119	.294	.442	0	—	0	1	1	0	0.1
Total 5	30	26	.536	112	60	23	7	2	516	547	18	192	201	13.0	3.40	103	.271	.335	39	.231	8	12	6	7	2.4

■ GREGG OLSON
Olson, Greggory William   b: 10/11/66, Scribner, Neb.   BR/TR, 6'4", 210 lbs.   Deb: 9/02/88

YEAR TM/L	W	L	PCT	G	GS	CG	SH	SV	IP	H	HR	BB	SO	RAT	ERA	ERA+	OAV	OOB	BH	AVG	PB	PR	/A	PD	TPI
1988 Bal-A	1	1	.500	10	0	0	0	0	11	10	1	10	9	16.4	3.27	119	.244	.392	0	—	0	1	1	0	0.1
1989 Bal-A	5	2	.714	64	0	0	0	27	85	57	1	46	90	11.0	1.69	224	.188	.296	0	—	0	21	20	-0	2.0
1990 Bal-A	6	5	.545	64	0	0	0	37	74¹	57	3	31	74	11.0	2.42	158	.213	.301	0	—	0	12	12	-1	1.1
Total 3	12	8	.600	138	0	0	0	64	170¹	124	5	87	173	11.4	2.11	180	.202	.305	0	—	0	34	32	-1	3.2

■ TED OLSON
Olson, Theodore Otto   b: 8/27/12, Quincy, Mass.   d: 12/9/80, Weymouth, Mass.   BR/TR, 6'2.5", 185 lbs.   Deb: 6/21/36

YEAR TM/L	W	L	PCT	G	GS	CG	SH	SV	IP	H	HR	BB	SO	RAT	ERA	ERA+	OAV	OOB	BH	AVG	PB	PR	/A	PD	TPI
1936 Bos-A	1	1	.500	5	3	1	0	0	18¹	24	3	8	5	15.7	7.36	72	.324	.390	1	.143	-0	-5	-4	0	-0.3
1937 Bos-A	0	0	—	11	0	0	0	0	32¹	42	4	15	11	15.9	7.24	66	.318	.388	3	.300	1	-9	-9	1	-0.5
1938 Bos-A	0	0	—	2	0	0	0	0	7	9	0	2	2	14.1	6.43	77	.310	.355	0	.000	-0	-1	-1	0	0.0
Total 3	1	1	.500	18	3	1	0	0	57²	75	7	25	18	15.6	7.18	69	.319	.385	4	.222	1	-15	-14	1	-0.8

■ ED OLWINE
Olwine, Edward R.   b: 5/28/58, Greenville, Ohio   BL/TL, 6'2", 165 lbs.   Deb: 6/02/86

YEAR TM/L	W	L	PCT	G	GS	CG	SH	SV	IP	H	HR	BB	SO	RAT	ERA	ERA+	OAV	OOB	BH	AVG	PB	PR	/A	PD	TPI
1986 Atl-N	0	0	—	37	0	0	0	1	47²	35	5	17	37	10.0	3.40	117	.207	.283	1	.333	1	2	3	0	0.3
1987 Atl-N	0	1	.000	27	0	0	0	1	23¹	25	4	8	12	13.1	5.01	87	.269	.333	0	—	0	-2	-2	-0	-0.1
1988 Atl-N	0	0	—	16	0	0	0	1	18²	22	4	4	5	13.0	6.75	54	.286	.329	0	—	0	-7	-6	-0	-0.6
Total 3	0	1	.000	80	0	0	0	3	89²	82	13	29	54	11.4	4.52	89	.242	.307	1	.333	1	-8	-5	-1	-0.4

■ SKINNY O'NEAL
O'Neal, Oran Herbert   b: 5/2/1899, Gatewood, Mo.   d: 6/2/81, Springfield, Mo.   BR/TR, 5'11", 160 lbs.   Deb: 4/18/25

YEAR TM/L	W	L	PCT	G	GS	CG	SH	SV	IP	H	HR	BB	SO	RAT	ERA	ERA+	OAV	OOB	BH	AVG	PB	PR	/A	PD	TPI
1925 Phi-N	0	0	—	11	1	0	0	0	20¹	35	2	12	6	20.8	9.30	51	.407	.480	1	.167	-0	-11	-10	-0	-0.8
1927 Phi-N	0	0	—	2	0	0	0	0	5	9	0	2	2	19.8	9.00	46	.409	.458	0	.000	-0	-3	-3	1	-0.1
Total 2	0	0	—	13	1	0	0	0	25¹	44	2	14	8	20.6	9.24	50	.407	.475	1	.143	-0	-14	-13	0	-0.9

■ RANDY O'NEAL
O'Neal, Randall Jeffrey   b: 8/30/60, Ashland, Ky.   BR/TR, 6'2", 195 lbs.   Deb: 9/12/84

YEAR TM/L	W	L	PCT	G	GS	CG	SH	SV	IP	H	HR	BB	SO	RAT	ERA	ERA+	OAV	OOB	BH	AVG	PB	PR	/A	PD	TPI
1984 Det-A	2	1	.667	4	3	0	0	0	18²	16	0	6	12	10.6	3.38	116	.222	.282	0	—	0	1	1	-0	0.1
1985 Det-A	5	5	.500	28	12	1	0	1	94¹	82	8	36	52	11.4	3.24	126	.240	.316	0	—	0	9	9	1	1.0
1986 Det-A	3	7	.300	37	11	1	0	2	122²	121	13	44	68	12.3	4.33	95	.260	.327	0	—	0	-2	-3	1	-0.1
1987 Atl-N	4	2	.667	16	10	0	0	0	61	79	12	24	33	15.5	5.61	78	.316	.380	2	.105	-1	-10	-9	1	-0.7
StL-N	0	0	—	1	1	0	0	0	5	2	0	2	4	7.2	1.80	231	.111	.200	1	1.000	0	1	1	0	0.2
Yr	4	2	.667	17	11	0	0	0	66	81	12	26	37	14.6	5.32	81	.298	.359	1	.050	-0	-9	-7	2	-0.5
1988 StL-N	2	3	.400	10	8	0	0	0	53	57	7	10	20	11.7	4.58	76	.274	.314	-2	—	-2	-7	-7	1	-0.6
1989 Phi-N	0	1	.000	20	1	0	0	0	39	46	5	9	29	12.7	6.23	57	.301	.340	0	.000	-1	-12	-12	1	-1.1
1990 SF-N	1	0	1.000	26	0	0	0	0	47	58	3	18	30	14.6	3.83	97	.314	.374	1	.167	-0	-1	0	0	0.0
Total 7	17	19	.472	142	46	2	0	3	440²	461	48	149	248	12.6	4.35	91	.272	.334	4	.080	-3	-19	-19	5	-1.2

■ ED O'NEIL
O'Neil, Edward J.   b: 3/11/1859, Fall River, Mass.   d: 9/30/1892, Fall River, Mass.   TR, 5'11", 180 lbs.   Deb: 6/20/1890

YEAR TM/L	W	L	PCT	G	GS	CG	SH	SV	IP	H	HR	BB	SO	RAT	ERA	ERA+	OAV	OOB	BH	AVG	PB	PR	/A	PD	TPI
1890 Tol-a	0	2	.000	2	2	0	0	0	16	27	0	13	2	22.5	7.88	50	.363	.458	0	.000	-2	-7	-7	0	-0.5
Phi-a	0	6	.000	6	6	6	0	0	52	84	0	32	17	20.1	9.69	39	.353	.430	5	.161	-1	-34	-34	1	-2.4
Yr	0	8	.000	8	8	8	0	0	68	111	0	45	19	20.6	9.26	42	.355	.436	3	.075	-2	-41	-41	1	-2.9

■ J. O'NEILL
O'Neill, J.   b: Bedford, Pa.   Deb: 8/20/1875

YEAR TM/L	W	L	PCT	G	GS	CG	SH	SV	IP	H	HR	BB	SO	RAT	ERA	ERA+	OAV	OOB	BH	AVG	PB	PR	/A	PD	TPI
1875 Atl-n	0	4	.000	5	4	3	0	0	34	56	2	0		14.8	4.76	48	.324	.324	3	.115	-1	-9	-9		-0.8

■ TIP O'NEILL
O'Neill, James Edward   b: 5/25/1858, Woodstock, Ont., Canada   d: 12/31/15, Montreal, Que., Can   BR/TR, 6'1.5", 167 lbs.   Deb: 5/05/1883 ◆

YEAR TM/L	W	L	PCT	G	GS	CG	SH	SV	IP	H	HR	BB	SO	RAT	ERA	ERA+	OAV	OOB	BH	AVG	PB	PR	/A	PD	TPI
1883 NY-N	5	12	.294	19	19	15	0	0	148	182	5	64	55	15.0	4.07	76	.286	.351	15	.197	-1	-15	-16	-1	-1.5
1884 StL-a	11	4	.733	17	14	14	0	0	141	125	3	51	36	11.2	2.68	122	.225	.290	82	.276	5	9	9	1	0.9
Total 2	16	16	.500	36	33	29	0	0	289	307	8	115	91	13.1	3.39	94	.257	.322	1386	.326	3	-6	-7	-0	-0.6

■ HARRY O'NEILL
O'Neill, Joseph Henry   b: 2/20/1897, Ridgetown, Ont., Canada   d: 9/5/69, Ridgetown, Ont., Can.   BR/TR, 6', 180 lbs.   Deb: 9/15/22

YEAR TM/L	W	L	PCT	G	GS	CG	SH	SV	IP	H	HR	BB	SO	RAT	ERA	ERA+	OAV	OOB	BH	AVG	PB	PR	/A	PD	TPI
1922 Phi-A	0	0	—	1	0	0	0	0	3	2	0	1	0	12.0	3.00	142	.200	.333	0	.000	-0	0	0	0	0.0
1923 Phi-A	0	0	—	3	0	0	0	0	2	1	0	3	2	18.0	0.00	—	.167	.444	0	—	0	1	1	0	0.1
Total 2	0	0	—	4	0	0	0	0	5	3	0	4	2	14.4	1.80	233	.188	.381	0	.000	-0	1	1	0	0.1

■ MIKE O'NEILL
O'Neill, Michael Joyce (a.k.a. Michael Joyce In 1901)   b: 9/7/1877, Galway, Ireland   d: 8/12/59, Scranton, Pa.   BR/TR, 5'11", 185 lbs.   Deb: 9/20/01 ◆

YEAR TM/L	W	L	PCT	G	GS	CG	SH	SV	IP	H	HR	BB	SO	RAT	ERA	ERA+	OAV	OOB	BH	AVG	PB	PR	/A	PD	TPI
1901 StL-N	2	2	.500	5	4	4	1	0	41	29	2	10	16	9.4	1.32	241	.198	.268	6	.400	3	9	8	-1	1.1
1902 StL-N	16	15	.516	36	32	29	2	2	288¹	297	3	66	105	11.7	2.90	94	.266	.314	43	.319	9	-4	-5	0	0.8
1903 StL-N	4	13	.235	19	17	12	0	0	145	184	4	43	39	14.5	3.79	86	.304	.356	25	.227	2	-8	-8	-0	-0.7
1904 StL-N	10	14	.417	25	24	23	1	0	220	229	1	50	68	11.5	2.09	129	.262	.304	21	.231	4	16	15	1	2.4
Total 4	32	44	.421	85	77	68	4	2	694¹	739	8	169	228	12.1	2.73	105	.269	.318	97	.255	18	13	10	1	3.6

■ PAUL O'NEILL
O'Neill, Paul Andrew   b: 2/25/63, Columbus, Ohio   BL/TL, 6'4", 200 lbs.   Deb: 9/03/85 ◆

YEAR TM/L	W	L	PCT	G	GS	CG	SH	SV	IP	H	HR	BB	SO	RAT	ERA	ERA+	OAV	OOB	BH	AVG	PB	PR	/A	PD	TPI
1987 Cin-N	0	0	—	1	0	0	0	0	2	2	1	4	2	27.0	13.50	31	.286	.545	41	.256	0	-2	-2	0	-0.1

■ EMMETT O'NEILL
O'Neill, Robert Emmett "Pinky"   b: 1/13/18, San Mateo, Cal.   BR/TR, 6'3", 185 lbs.   Deb: 8/03/43

YEAR TM/L	W	L	PCT	G	GS	CG	SH	SV	IP	H	HR	BB	SO	RAT	ERA	ERA+	OAV	OOB	BH	AVG	PB	PR	/A	PD	TPI
1943 Bos-A	1	4	.200	11	5	1	0	0	57²	56	3	46	20	16.1	4.53	73	.256	.387	3	.188	1	-8	-8	0	-0.6
1944 Bos-A	6	11	.353	28	22	8	1	0	151²	154	6	89	68	14.5	4.63	73	.256	.365	10	.182	-0	-20	-21	-2	-2.2
1945 Bos-A	8	11	.421	24	22	10	1	0	141²	134	5	117	55	16.3	5.15	66	.258	.399	9	.180	-1	-28	-27	-1	-2.4
1946 Chi-N	0	0	—	1	0	0	0	0	1	0	0	3	1	27.0	0.00	—	.000	.500	0	—	0	0	0	0	0.0
Chi-A	0	0	—	2	0	0	0	0	3²	4	0	5	0	22.1	0.00	—	.333	.529	0	.000	-0	1	1	0	0.1
Total 4	15	26	.366	66	49	19	2	0	355²	348	14	260	144	15.6	4.76	71	.261	.385	22	.180	-2	-54	-54	-2	-5.1

■ STEVE ONTIVEROS
Ontiveros, Steven   b: 3/5/61, Tularosa, N.Mex.   BR/TR, 6', 180 lbs.   Deb: 6/14/85

YEAR TM/L	W	L	PCT	G	GS	CG	SH	SV	IP	H	HR	BB	SO	RAT	ERA	ERA+	OAV	OOB	BH	AVG	PB	PR	/A	PD	TPI
1985 Oak-A	1	3	.250	39	0	0	0	8	74²	45	4	19	36	8.0	1.93	200	.174	.236	0	—	0	18	16	1	1.7
1986 Oak-A	2	2	.500	46	0	0	0	10	72²	72	10	25	54	12.1	4.71	82	.265	.329	0	—	0	-4	-7	0	-0.6
1987 Oak-A	10	8	.556	35	22	2	1	1	150²	141	19	50	97	11.6	4.00	103	.242	.306	0	—	0	8	2	2	0.4

YEAR TM/L	W	L	PCT	G	GS	CG	SH	SV	IP	H	HR	BB	SO	RAT	ERA	ERA+	OAV	OOB	BH	AVG	PB	PR	/A	PD	TPI
1988 Oak-A	3	4	.429	10	10	0	0	0	54²	57	4	21	30	12.8	4.61	82	.265	.331	0	—	0	-4	-5	1	-0.3
1989 Phi-N	2	1	.667	6	5	0	0	0	30²	34	2	15	12	14.4	3.82	93	.288	.368	1	.083	-0	-1	-1	1	0.0
1990 Phi-N	0	0	—	5	0	0	0	0	10	9	1	3	6	10.8	2.70	141	.225	.279	0	—	0	1	1	1	0.2
Total 6	18	18	.500	141	37	2	1	19	393¹	358	40	133	235	11.4	3.78	104	.241	.306	1	.083	-0	18	7	6	1.4

■ JOSE OQUENDO
Oquendo, Jose Manuel (Contreras) b: 7/4/63, Rio Piedras, P.R. BB/TR, 5'10", 160 lbs. Deb: 5/02/83 ◆

YEAR TM/L	W	L	PCT	G	GS	CG	SH	SV	IP	H	HR	BB	SO	RAT	ERA	ERA+	OAV	OOB	BH	AVG	PB	PR	/A	PD	TPI
1987 *StL-N	0	0		1	0	0	0	0	1	4	0	1	0	54.0	27.00	15	.571	.667	71	.286	0	-3	-3	0	-0.1
1988 StL-N	0	1	.000	1	0	0	0	0	4	4	0	6	1	22.5	4.50	77	.267	.476	125	.277	0	-0	-0	-0	0.0
Total 2	0	1	.000	2	0	0	0	0	5	8	0	7	1	28.8	9.00	40	.364	.533	629	.264	1	-3	-3	-0	-0.1

■ DON O'RILEY
O'Riley, Donald Lee b: 3/12/45, Topeka, Kan. BR/TR, 6'3", 205 lbs. Deb: 6/20/69

YEAR TM/L	W	L	PCT	G	GS	CG	SH	SV	IP	H	HR	BB	SO	RAT	ERA	ERA+	OAV	OOB	BH	AVG	PB	PR	/A	PD	TPI
1969 KC-A	1	1	.500	18	0	0	0	1	23¹	32	0	15	10	18.1	6.94	53	.311	.398	0	.000	-0	-9	-8	-0	-0.8
1970 KC-A	0	0	—	9	2	0	0	1	23¹	26	5	9	13	13.9	5.40	69	.277	.346	0	.000	-0	-4	-4	-0	-0.4
Total 2	1	1	.500	27	2	0	0	1	46²	58	5	24	23	16.0	6.17	60	.294	.374	0	.000	-1	-13	-13	-1	-1.2

■ JESSE OROSCO
Orosco, Jesse Russell b: 4/21/57, Santa Barbara, Cal. BR/TL, 6'2", 174 lbs. Deb: 4/05/79

YEAR TM/L	W	L	PCT	G	GS	CG	SH	SV	IP	H	HR	BB	SO	RAT	ERA	ERA+	OAV	OOB	BH	AVG	PB	PR	/A	PD	TPI
1979 NY-N	1	2	.333	18	2	0	0	0	35	33	4	22	22	14.7	4.89	74	.260	.377	0	.000	-1	-4	-5	1	-0.4
1981 NY-N	0	1	.000	8	0	0	0	1	17¹	13	2	6	18	9.9	1.56	224	.213	.284	0	.000	-0	4	4	0	0.4
1982 NY-N	4	10	.286	54	2	0	0	4	109¹	92	7	40	89	11.0	2.72	134	.230	.303	2	.143	-0	11	11	-0	1.1
1983 NY-N	13	7	.650	62	0	0	0	17	110	76	3	38	84	9.4	1.47	246	.197	.271	4	.333	1	26	26	0	3.0
1984 NY-N	10	6	.625	60	0	0	0	31	87	58	7	34	85	9.7	2.59	137	.185	.269	1	.250	0	10	9	-1	1.0
1985 NY-N	8	6	.571	54	0	0	0	17	79	66	6	34	68	11.4	2.73	126	.224	.304	3	.429	1	8	8	-1	0.7
1986 *NY-N	8	6	.571	58	0	0	0	21	81	64	6	35	62	11.3	2.33	151	.217	.306	0	.000	0	12	11	-1	1.1
1987 NY-N	3	9	.250	58	0	0	0	16	77	78	5	31	78	13.0	4.44	85	.266	.340	0	.000	-1	-3	-6	-0	-0.6
1988 *LA-N	3	2	.600	55	0	0	0	9	53	41	4	30	43	12.4	2.72	123	.215	.327	0	.000	-0	4	4	0	0.4
1989 Cle-A	3	4	.429	69	0	0	0	3	78	54	7	26	79	9.5	2.08	191	.198	.272	0	—	0	16	16	1	1.7
1990 Cle-A	5	4	.556	55	0	0	0	2	64²	58	9	38	55	13.4	3.90	102	.239	.342	0	—	0	1	1	0	0.1
Total 11	58	57	.504	551	4	0	0	121	791¹	633	60	334	683	11.2	2.76	132	.220	.305	10	.172	1	83	78	0	8.5

■ O'ROURKE
O'Rourke Deb: 7/09/1872

YEAR TM/L	W	L	PCT	G	GS	CG	SH	SV	IP	H	HR	BB	SO	RAT	ERA	ERA+	OAV	OOB	BH	AVG	PB	PR	/A	PD	TPI
1872 Eck-n	0	1	.000	1	1	1	0	0	9	16	0	1		17.0	6.00	58	.320	.333	0	.000	-1	-2	-3		-0.1

■ JIM O'ROURKE
O'Rourke, James Henry "Orator Jim" b: 9/1/1850, Bridgeport, Conn. d: 1/8/19, Bridgeport, Conn. BR/TR, 5'8", 185 lbs. Deb: 4/26/1872 MUH◆

YEAR TM/L	W	L	PCT	G	GS	CG	SH	SV	IP	H	HR	BB	SO	RAT	ERA	ERA+	OAV	OOB	BH	AVG	PB	PR	/A	PD	TPI
1883 Buf-N	0	0	—	2	0	0	0	0	7	10	0	1	1	14.1	6.43	49	.317	.338	143	.328	1	-3	-3	-0	-0.1
1884 Buf-N	0	1	.000	4	0	0	0	1	12²	7	0	1	3	5.7	2.84	110	.153	.171	162	.347	2	0	0	-0	0.0
Total 2	0	1	.000	6	0	0	0	2	19²	17	0	2	4	8.7	4.12	76	.220	.240	2304	.310	3	-2	-2	-0	-0.1

■ MIKE O'ROURKE
O'Rourke, Michael J. Deb: 9/01/1890

YEAR TM/L	W	L	PCT	G	GS	CG	SH	SV	IP	H	HR	BB	SO	RAT	ERA	ERA+	OAV	OOB	BH	AVG	PB	PR	/A	PD	TPI
1890 Bal-a	1	2	.333	5	5	5	0	0	41	45	0	10	8	12.1	3.95	103	.270	.312	3	.115	-0	-0	0	1	0.1

■ DAVE ORR
Orr, David L. b: 9/29/1859, New York, N.Y. d: 6/3/15, Brooklyn, N.Y. BL/TR, 5'11", 250 lbs. Deb: 5/17/1883 M◆

YEAR TM/L	W	L	PCT	G	GS	CG	SH	SV	IP	H	HR	BB	SO	RAT	ERA	ERA+	OAV	OOB	BH	AVG	PB	PR	/A	PD	TPI
1885 NY-a	0	0	—	3	0	0	0	0	10	11	2	5	1	14.4	7.20	41	.268	.347	152	.342	2	-4	-5	-0	-0.3

■ JOE ORRELL
Orrell, Forrest Gordon b: 10/6/17, National City, Cal. BR/TR, 6'4", 210 lbs. Deb: 8/12/43

YEAR TM/L	W	L	PCT	G	GS	CG	SH	SV	IP	H	HR	BB	SO	RAT	ERA	ERA+	OAV	OOB	BH	AVG	PB	PR	/A	PD	TPI
1943 Det-A	0	0	—	10	0	0	0	1	19¹	18	0	11	2	14.4	3.72	95	.257	.373	1	.250	0	-1	-0	0	0.0
1944 Det-A	2	1	.667	10	2	0	0	0	22¹	26	0	11	10	15.3	2.42	147	.286	.369	1	.250	0	3	3	1	0.4
1945 Det-A	2	3	.400	12	5	1	0	0	48	46	1	24	14	13.5	3.00	117	.260	.355	2	.133	-1	2	3	-0	0.2
Total 3	4	4	.500	32	7	1	0	1	89²	90	1	46	26	14.2	3.01	117	.266	.362	4	.174	-1	4	5	1	0.6

■ PHIL ORTEGA
Ortega, Filomeno Coronado "Kemo" b: 10/7/39, Gilbert, Ariz. BR/TR, 6'2", 170 lbs. Deb: 9/10/60

YEAR TM/L	W	L	PCT	G	GS	CG	SH	SV	IP	H	HR	BB	SO	RAT	ERA	ERA+	OAV	OOB	BH	AVG	PB	PR	/A	PD	TPI
1960 LA-N	0	0	—	3	1	0	0	0	6¹	12	1	5	4	24.2	17.05	23	.400	.486	0	.000	-0	-9	-9	0	-0.7
1961 LA-N	0	2	.000	4	2	1	0	0	13	10	6	2	15	8.3	5.54	78	.208	.240	1	.250	-0	-2	-2	-0	-0.1
1962 LA-N	0	2	.000	24	3	0	0	1	53²	60	8	39	30	17.1	6.88	53	.276	.394	0	.000	-1	-17	-19	-1	-1.9
1963 LA-N	0	0	—	1	0	0	0	0	1	2	1	0	1	18.0	18.00	17	.400	.400	0	—	0	-2	-2	-0	-0.1
1964 LA-N	7	9	.438	34	25	4	3	1	157¹	149	22	56	107	12.1	4.00	81	.249	.320	6	.136	4	-8	-13	-2	-1.6
1965 Was-A	12	15	.444	35	29	4	2	0	179²	176	33	97	88	13.9	5.11	68	.262	.359	11	.208	4	-33	-33	-1	-2.9
1966 Was-A	12	12	.500	33	31	5	1	0	197¹	158	29	53	122	9.9	3.92	88	.218	.276	3	.056	-2	-11	-10	-1	-1.3
1967 Was-A	10	10	.500	34	34	5	2	0	219²	189	16	57	122	10.3	3.03	104	.231	.286	4	.061	-3	5	3	-1	0.0
1968 Was-A	5	12	.294	31	16	1	1	0	115²	115	12	62	57	14.2	4.98	59	.263	.361	4	.167	1	-26	-27	-2	-2.6
1969 Cal-A	0	0	—	5	0	0	0	0	8	13	3	7	4	22.5	10.13	34	.333	.435	0	—	0	-6	-6	0	-0.5
Total 10	46	62	.426	204	141	20	9	2	951²	884	131	378	549	12.2	4.43	75	.246	.323	29	.115	-1	-109	-117	-5	-11.7

■ AL ORTH
Orth, Albert Lewis "Smiling Al" or "The Curveless Wonder" b: 9/5/1872, Tipton, Ind. d: 10/8/48, Lynchburg, Va. BL/TR, 6', 200 lbs. Deb: 8/15/1895 U◆

YEAR TM/L	W	L	PCT	G	GS	CG	SH	SV	IP	H	HR	BB	SO	RAT	ERA	ERA+	OAV	OOB	BH	AVG	PB	PR	/A	PD	TPI
1895 Phi-N	8	1	.889	11	10	9	0	1	88	103	0	22	25	12.8	3.89	123	.288	.329	16	.356	4	9	9	-1	0.9
1896 Phi-N	15	10	.600	25	23	19	0	1	196	244	10	46	23	13.3	4.41	98	.303	.340	21	.256	3	-1	-2	1	0.1
1897 Phi-N	14	19	.424	36	34	29	2	0	282¹	349	12	82	64	13.7	4.62	91	.301	.347	50	.329	7	-10	-13	1	-0.1
1898 Phi-N	15	13	.536	32	28	25	1	0	250	290	2	53	52	12.3	3.02	114	.288	.324	36	.293	7	16	11	0	1.9
1899 Phi-N	14	3	.824	21	15	13	3	1	144²	149	0	19	35	10.5	2.49	148	.266	.290	13	.210	1	22	19	-4	1.5
1900 Phi-N	14	14	.500	33	30	24	2	1	262	302	4	60	68	12.4	3.78	96	.288	.327	40	.310	6	-2	-5	1	0.3
1901 Phi-N	20	12	.625	35	33	30	6	1	281²	250	3	32	92	9.3	2.27	150	.236	.264	36	.281	6	33	35	3	4.8
1902 Was-A	19	18	.514	38	37	36	1	0	324	367	18	40	76	11.3	3.97	93	.286	.307	38	.217	2	-14	-10	1	-0.4
1903 Was-A	10	22	.313	36	32	30	2	2	279²	326	8	62	88	12.5	4.34	72	.290	.327	49	.302	9	-43	-38	0	-2.1
1904 Was-A	3	4	.429	10	7	7	0	0	73²	88	2	15	23	12.6	4.76	56	.297	.331	22	.216	0	-18	-17	1	-1.6
NY-A	11	6	.647	20	18	11	2	0	137²	122	0	19	47	9.2	2.68	101	.238	.266	19	.297	3	-1	0	1	0.6
Yr	14	10	.583	30	25	18	2	0	211¹	210	2	34	70	10.4	3.41	79	.260	.290	1	.006	3	-19	-17	2	-1.0
1905 NY-A	18	16	.529	40	37	26	6	0	305¹	273	8	61	121	9.8	2.86	103	.240	.279	24	.183	-1	-7	3	0	0.3
1906 NY-A	27	17	.614	45	39	36	3	0	338²	317	2	66	133	10.2	2.34	127	.251	.288	37	.274	6	13	24	-0	3.6
1907 NY-A	14	21	.400	36	33	21	2	0	248²	244	2	53	78	10.7	2.61	107	.259	.298	34	.324	7	-2	5	3	2.1
1908 NY-A	2	13	.133	21	17	8	1	0	139¹	134	4	30	22	10.9	3.42	72	.255	.300	20	.290	5	-16	-15	0	-1.0
1909 NY-A	0	0	—	1	1	0	0	0	3	6	0	1	1	21.0	12.00	21	.429	.467	9	.265	0	-3	-3	-0	-0.2
Total 15	204	189	.519	440	394	324	31	6	3354²	3564	75	661	948	11.4	3.37	101	.272	.308	464	.273	66	-23	15	7	10.7

■ BABY ORTIZ
Ortiz, Oliverio (Nunez) b: 12/5/19, Camaguey, Cuba d: 3/27/84, Central Senado, Camaguey, Cuba BR/TR, 6', 190 lbs. Deb: 9/23/44

YEAR TM/L	W	L	PCT	G	GS	CG	SH	SV	IP	H	HR	BB	SO	RAT	ERA	ERA+	OAV	OOB	BH	AVG	PB	PR	/A	PD	TPI
1944 Was-A	0	2	.000	2	2	1	0	0	13	13	0	6	4	13.2	6.23	52	.255	.333	1	.167	-0	-4	-4	-1	-0.4

■ OSSIE ORWOLL
Orwoll, Oswald Christian b: 11/17/1900, Portland, Ore. d: 5/8/67, Decorah, Iowa BL/TL, 6', 174 lbs. Deb: 4/13/28 ◆

YEAR TM/L	W	L	PCT	G	GS	CG	SH	SV	IP	H	HR	BB	SO	RAT	ERA	ERA+	OAV	OOB	BH	AVG	PB	PR	/A	PD	TPI
1928 Phi-A	6	5	.545	27	8	3	0	2	106	110	7	50	53	13.8	4.58	87	.274	.358	52	.306	7	-6	-7	-1	-0.6
1929 Phi-A	0	2	.000	12	0	0	0	0	30	32	6	6	12	11.4	4.80	88	.278	.314	13	.255	1	-2	-2	0	-0.1
Total 2	6	7	.462	39	8	3	0	3	136	142	13	56	65	13.2	4.63	88	.275	.348	65	.294	7	-8	-9	-1	-0.7

■ OZZIE OSBORN
Osborn, Danny Leon b: 6/19/46, Springfield, Mo. BR/TR, 6'2", 195 lbs. Deb: 4/26/75

YEAR TM/L	W	L	PCT	G	GS	CG	SH	SV	IP	H	HR	BB	SO	RAT	ERA	ERA+	OAV	OOB	BH	AVG	PB	PR	/A	PD	TPI
1975 Chi-A	3	0	1.000	24	0	0	0	0	58	57	2	37	38	14.9	4.50	86	.265	.378	0	—	0	-5	-4	-1	-0.4

■ BOB OSBORN
Osborn, John Bode b: 4/17/03, San Diego, Tex. d: 4/19/60, Paris, Ark. BR/TR, 6'1", 175 lbs. Deb: 9/16/25

YEAR TM/L	W	L	PCT	G	GS	CG	SH	SV	IP	H	HR	BB	SO	RAT	ERA	ERA+	OAV	OOB	BH	AVG	PB	PR	/A	PD	TPI
1925 Chi-N	0	0	—	1	0	0	0	0	2	6	0	0	0	27.0	0.00	—	.600	.600	0	—	0	1	1	0	0.1
1926 Chi-N	6	5	.545	31	15	6	0	1	136¹	157	3	58	43	14.2	3.63	106	.301	.371	6	.146	-3	3	3	2	0.3

YEAR	TM/L	W	L	PCT	G	GS	CG	SH	SV	IP	H	HR	BB	SO	RAT	ERA	ERA+	OAV	OOB	BH	AVG	PB	PR	/A	PD	TPI
1927	Chi-N	5	5	.500	24	12	2	0	0	107²	125	2	48	45	14.5	4.18	92	.294	.367	8	.205	-0	-3	-4	-1	-0.4
1929	Chi-N	0	0	—	3	1	0	0	0	9	8	0	2	1	10.0	3.00	154	.242	.286	1	.250	0	2	2	-0	0.1
1930	Chi-N	10	6	.625	35	13	3	0	1	126²	147	9	53	42	14.3	4.97	98	.300	.369	4	.095	-5	-0	-1	2	-0.2
1931	Pit-N	6	1	.857	27	2	0	0	0	64²	85	3	20	9	14.8	5.01	77	.316	.366	3	.167	-0	-8	-8	-1	-0.8
Total	6	27	17	.614	121	43	11	0	2	446¹	528	17	181	140	14.4	4.32	97	.302	.368	22	.153	-8	-6	-7	3	-0.9

■ PAT OSBORN
Osborn, Larry Patrick b: 5/4/49, Murray, Ky. BL/TL, 6'4", 195 lbs. Deb: 4/13/74

YEAR	TM/L	W	L	PCT	G	GS	CG	SH	SV	IP	H	HR	BB	SO	RAT	ERA	ERA+	OAV	OOB	BH	AVG	PB	PR	/A	PD	TPI
1974	Cin-N	0	0	—	6	0	0	0	0	9	11	2	4	4	15.0	8.00	44	.297	.366	0	.000	-0	-4	-5	0	-0.3
1975	Mil-A	0	1	.000	6	1	0	0	0	11²	19	2	9	1	23.1	5.40	71	.404	.517	0	—	0	-2	-2	0	-0.1
Total	2	0	1	.000	12	1	0	0	0	20²	30	4	13	5	19.6	6.53	56	.357	.455	0	.000	-0	-6	-7	1	-0.4

■ TINY OSBORNE
Osborne, Earnest Preston b: 4/9/1893, Porterdale, Ga. d: 1/5/69, Atlanta, Ga. BL/TR, 6'4.5", 215 lbs. Deb: 4/15/22

YEAR	TM/L	W	L	PCT	G	GS	CG	SH	SV	IP	H	HR	BB	SO	RAT	ERA	ERA+	OAV	OOB	BH	AVG	PB	PR	/A	PD	TPI
1922	Chi-N	9	5	.643	41	14	7	1	3	184	183	7	95	81	14.2	4.50	93	.271	.370	9	.134	-4	-8	-6	-3	-1.1
1923	Chi-N	8	15	.348	37	25	8	1	1	179²	174	14	89	69	13.3	4.56	88	.255	.342	12	.200	-1	-11	-11	-1	-1.2
1924	Chi-N	0	0	—	2	0	0	0	1	3	3	0	2	2	15.0	3.00	130	.300	.417	0	—	0	0	0	0	0.0
	Bro-N	6	5	.545	21	13	6	0	0	104¹	123	1	54	52	15.6	5.09	74	.298	.384	9	.250	1	-14	-16	-1	-1.4
	Yr	6	5	.545	23	13	6	0	1	107¹	126	1	56	54	15.6	5.03	75	.298	.385	1	.028	1	-14	-15	-1	-1.4
1925	Bro-N	8	15	.348	41	22	10	0	1	175	210	9	75	59	14.9	4.94	85	.304	.375	14	.246	1	-13	-15	-1	-1.3
Total	4	31	40	.437	142	74	31	2	6	646	693	31	315	263	14.3	4.72	86	.300	.367	44	.200	-3	-46	-47	-7	-5.0

■ FRED OSBORNE
Osborne, Frederick W. b: Hampton, Iowa Deb: 7/14/1890 ♦

YEAR	TM/L	W	L	PCT	G	GS	CG	SH	SV	IP	H	HR	BB	SO	RAT	ERA	ERA+	OAV	OOB	BH	AVG	PB	PR	/A	PD	TPI
1890	Pit-N	0	5	.000	8	5	5	0	0	58	82	6	45	14	19.7	8.38	39	.324	.426	40	.238	1	-31	-33	-0	-2.4

■ WAYNE OSBORNE
Osborne, Wayne Harold "Ossie" or "Fish Hook" b: 10/11/12, Watsonville, Cal. d: 3/13/87, Camas, Wash. BL/TR, 6'2.5", 172 lbs. Deb: 4/18/35

YEAR	TM/L	W	L	PCT	G	GS	CG	SH	SV	IP	H	HR	BB	SO	RAT	ERA	ERA+	OAV	OOB	BH	AVG	PB	PR	/A	PD	TPI
1935	Pit-N	0	0	—	2	0	0	0	0	1¹	1	0	1	0	6.8	6.75	61	.250	.250	0	—	0	-0	-0	0	0.0
1936	Bos-N	1	1	.500	5	3	0	0	0	20	31	1	9	8	18.0	5.85	66	.352	.412	2	.250	0	-4	-4	0	-0.3
Total	2	1	1	.500	7	3	0	0	0	21¹	32	1	9	9	17.3	5.91	65	.348	.406	2	.250	0	-4	-5	0	-0.3

■ CHARLIE OSGOOD
Osgood, Charles Benjamin b: 11/23/26, Somerville, Mass. BR/TR, 5'10", 180 lbs. Deb: 6/18/44

YEAR	TM/L	W	L	PCT	G	GS	CG	SH	SV	IP	H	HR	BB	SO	RAT	ERA	ERA+	OAV	OOB	BH	AVG	PB	PR	/A	PD	TPI
1944	Bro-N	0	0	—	1	0	0	0	0	3	2	0	3	0	18.0	3.00	118	.222	.462	0	—	0	0	0	0	0.0

■ DAN OSINSKI
Osinski, Daniel b: 11/17/33, Chicago, Ill. BR/TR, 6'1.5", 190 lbs. Deb: 4/11/62

YEAR	TM/L	W	L	PCT	G	GS	CG	SH	SV	IP	H	HR	BB	SO	RAT	ERA	ERA+	OAV	OOB	BH	AVG	PB	PR	/A	PD	TPI
1962	KC-A	0	0	—	4	0	0	0	0	4²	8	1	8	4	30.9	17.36	24	.381	.552	0	—	0	-7	-7	0	-0.5
	LA-A	6	4	.600	33	0	0	0	4	54¹	45	3	30	44	12.4	2.82	137	.223	.323	0	.000	-1	7	6	0	0.6
	Yr	6	4	.600	37	0	0	0	4	59	53	4	38	48	13.9	3.97	98	.237	.347	2	.182	-1	0	-1	0	0.1
1963	LA-A	8	8	.500	47	16	4	1	0	159¹	145	15	80	100	12.8	3.28	105	.242	.333	5	.111	-2	6	3	-1	0.0
1964	LA-A	3	3	.500	47	4	1	1	2	93	87	8	39	88	12.4	3.48	94	.244	.322	1	.056	-1	1	-2	1	-0.1
1965	Mil-N	0	3	.000	61	0	0	0	6	83	81	4	40	54	13.2	2.82	125	.261	.348	1	.167	-0	7	5	-0	0.6
1966	Bos-A	4	3	.571	44	1	0	0	2	67¹	68	8	28	44	13.0	3.61	105	.274	.350	2	.333	0	-1	1	-0	0.2
1967	*Bos-A	3	1	.750	34	0	0	0	2	63²	61	5	14	38	10.6	2.54	137	.243	.283	3	.333	1	5	7	-0	0.8
1969	Chi-A	5	5	.500	51	0	0	0	2	60²	56	3	23	27	11.7	3.56	108	.251	.321	0	.000	-0	0	2	2	0.4
1970	Hou-N	0	1	.000	3	0	0	0	0	3²	5	0	2	1	17.2	9.82	39	.357	.438	0	—	0	-2	-2	0	-0.1
Total	8	29	28	.509	324	21	5	2	18	589²	556	47	264	400	12.6	3.34	107	.250	.331	12	.122	-3	16	15	1	1.9

■ CLAUDE OSTEEN
Osteen, Claude Wilson b: 8/9/39, Caney Springs, Tenn. BL/TL, 5'11", 160 lbs. Deb: 7/06/57 C

YEAR	TM/L	W	L	PCT	G	GS	CG	SH	SV	IP	H	HR	BB	SO	RAT	ERA	ERA+	OAV	OOB	BH	AVG	PB	PR	/A	PD	TPI
1957	Cin-N	0	0	—	3	0	0	0	0	4	4	0	3	3	15.8	2.25	183	.250	.368	0	.000	-0	1	1	-0	0.1
1959	Cin-N	0	0	—	2	0	0	0	0	7²	11	1	9	3	23.5	7.04	58	.333	.476	0	.000	-0	-3	-3	0	-0.2
1960	Cin-N	0	1	.000	20	3	0	0	0	48¹	53	5	30	15	15.6	5.03	76	.293	.396	1	.083	-1	-7	-6	1	-0.6
1961	Cin-N	0	0	—	1	0	0	0	0	0¹	0	0	0	0	0.0	0.00	—	.000	.000	0	—	0	0	0	0	0.0
	Was-A	1	1	.500	3	3	0	0	0	18¹	14	3	9	14	11.8	4.91	82	.219	.324	1	.143	-0	-2	-2	0	-0.1
1962	Was-A	8	13	.381	28	22	7	2	1	150¹	140	12	47	59	11.4	3.65	111	.246	.309	10	.208	1	5	6	1	0.8
1963	Was-A	9	14	.391	40	29	8	2	0	212¹	222	23	60	109	12.0	3.35	111	.270	.320	12	.171	1	7	9	-1	0.9
1964	Was-A	15	13	.536	37	36	13	0	0	257	256	20	64	133	11.3	3.33	111	.259	.306	14	.156	1	8	11	2	1.5
1965	*LA-N	15	15	.500	40	40	9	1	0	287	253	19	78	162	10.5	2.79	117	.236	.290	12	.121	-1	24	15	7	2.2
1966	*LA-N	17	14	.548	39	38	8	3	0	240¹	238	6	65	137	11.4	2.85	116	.261	.312	16	.211	5	20	12	2	1.9
1967	LA-N	17	17	.500	39	39	14	5	0	288¹	269	19	52	152	11.0	3.22	90	.270	.304	18	.178	5	5	-4	0	0.1
1968	LA-N	12	18	.400	39	36	5	3	0	253²	267	14	54	119	11.6	3.09	90	.275	.316	15	.179	2	-3	-9	2	-0.6
1969	LA-N	20	15	.571	41	41	16	7	0	321	293	17	74	183	10.5	2.66	125	.245	.293	24	.216	6	33	24	3	3.5
1970	LA-N	16	14	.533	37	37	11	4	0	258²	280	24	52	114	11.7	3.83	100	.276	.313	19	.204	5	6	0	0	0.4
1971	LA-N	14	11	.560	38	38	11	4	0	259	262	25	63	109	11.4	3.51	92	.266	.312	16	.186	2	-1	-8	6	0.0
1972	LA-N	20	11	.645	33	33	14	4	0	252	232	16	69	100	10.9	2.64	126	.245	.299	24	.273	4	23	19	0	3.3
1973	LA-N	16	11	.593	33	33	12	3	0	236²	227	20	61	86	11.0	3.31	104	.258	.307	12	.154	-1	9	3	3	0.6
1974	Hou-N	9	9	.500	23	21	7	2	0	138¹	158	8	47	45	13.5	3.71	94	.292	.351	13	.283	3	-1	-4	0	0.0
	StL-N	0	2	.000	8	2	0	0	0	22²	26	1	11	6	14.7	4.37	82	.286	.363	0	.000	-0	-2	-2	0	-0.2
	Yr	9	11	.450	31	23	7	2	0	161	184	9	58	51	13.5	3.80	92	.288	.347	0	.000	2	-3	-6	1	-0.2
1975	Chi-A	7	16	.304	37	37	5	0	0	204¹	237	16	92	63	14.6	4.36	89	.294	.367	0	—	0	-13	-11	2	-0.8
Total	18	196	195	.501	541	488	140	40	1	3460¹	3471	249	940	1612	11.6	3.30	104	.263	.314	207	.188	37	110	50	28	12.8

■ DARRELL OSTEEN
Osteen, Milton Darrell b: 2/14/43, Oklahoma City, Okla BR/TR, 6'1", 170 lbs. Deb: 9/02/65

YEAR	TM/L	W	L	PCT	G	GS	CG	SH	SV	IP	H	HR	BB	SO	RAT	ERA	ERA+	OAV	OOB	BH	AVG	PB	PR	/A	PD	TPI
1965	Cin-N	0	0	—	3	0	0	0	0	3	2	0	4	1	18.0	0.00	—	.200	.429	0	—	0	1	1	0	0.1
1966	Cin-N	0	2	.000	13	0	0	0	0	15	26	3	9	17	21.0	12.00	33	.371	.443	1	.500	0	-14	-13	-0	-1.2
1967	Cin-N	0	2	.000	10	0	0	0	2	14¹	10	1	13	13	16.3	6.28	60	.196	.388	0	.000	-0	-5	-4	0	-0.3
1970	Oak-A	1	0	1.000	3	1	0	0	0	5²	9	0	3	3	19.1	6.35	56	.346	.414	0	.000	-0	-2	-2	-0	-0.1
Total	4	1	4	.200	29	1	0	0	3	38	47	4	29	34	18.7	8.05	47	.299	.418	1	.200	-0	-19	-18	0	-1.5

■ FRED OSTENDORF
Ostendorf, Frederick K. b: 8/5/1890, Baltimore, Md. d: 3/2/65, Keoughtan, Va. BL/TL, 6'.5 ", 169 lbs. Deb: 7/16/14

YEAR	TM/L	W	L	PCT	G	GS	CG	SH	SV	IP	H	HR	BB	SO	RAT	ERA	ERA+	OAV	OOB	BH	AVG	PB	PR	/A	PD	TPI
1914	Ind-F	0	0	—	1	0	0	0	0	2	5	0	2	0	36.0	22.50	15	.478	.594	0	.000	-0	-4	-4	0	-0.3

■ BILL OSTER
Oster, William Charles b: 1/2/33, New York, N.Y. BL/TL, 6'3", 198 lbs. Deb: 8/23/54

YEAR	TM/L	W	L	PCT	G	GS	CG	SH	SV	IP	H	HR	BB	SO	RAT	ERA	ERA+	OAV	OOB	BH	AVG	PB	PR	/A	PD	TPI
1954	Phi-A	0	1	.000	8	1	0	0	0	15²	19	2	12	5	17.8	6.32	62	.311	.425	1	.333	0	-5	-4	0	-0.3

■ FRITZ OSTERMUELLER
Ostermueller, Frederick Raymond b: 9/15/07, Quincy, Ill. d: 12/17/57, Quincy, Ill. BL/TL, 5'11", 175 lbs. Deb: 4/21/34

YEAR	TM/L	W	L	PCT	G	GS	CG	SH	SV	IP	H	HR	BB	SO	RAT	ERA	ERA+	OAV	OOB	BH	AVG	PB	PR	/A	PD	TPI
1934	Bos-A	10	13	.435	33	23	10	0	3	198²	200	7	99	75	13.6	3.49	138	.262	.348	13	.167	-2	22	29	3	3.0
1935	Bos-A	7	8	.467	22	19	10	0	1	137²	135	0	78	41	14.1	3.92	121	.257	.356	14	.286	1	8	13	0	1.4
1936	Bos-A	10	16	.385	43	23	7	1	2	180²	210	8	84	90	14.8	4.88	109	.288	.364	15	.234	0	3	9	2	1.1
1937	Bos-A	3	7	.300	25	7	2	0	0	86²	101	2	44	29	15.2	4.98	95	.286	.367	11	.333	3	-4	-2	1	0.1
1938	Bos-A	13	5	.722	31	18	10	1	2	176²	199	15	58	46	13.2	4.58	108	.275	.331	16	.216	2	4	7	0	0.8
1939	Bos-A	11	7	.611	34	20	8	0	4	159¹	173	6	58	61	13.2	4.24	112	.277	.341	9	.161	-2	7	9	-0	0.6
1940	Bos-A	5	9	.357	31	16	5	0	0	143²	166	7	70	80	14.8	4.95	91	.284	.361	17	.315	4	-9	-7	-1	-0.3
1941	StL-A	0	3	.000	15	2	0	0	0	46	45	3	23	20	13.3	4.50	96	.257	.343	3	.214	-0	-2	-1	0	0.0
1942	StL-A	3	1	.750	10	4	2	0	0	43²	46	4	17	21	13.0	3.71	100	.266	.332	3	.188	-0	-0	-0	1	0.0
1943	StL-A	3	2	.000	11	3	0	0	0	28²	34	1	9	11	13.5	5.02	66	.312	.382	2	—	-0	-5	-5	0	-0.4
	Bro-N	1	1	.500	7	1	0	0	0	27¹	21	0	12	15	10.9	3.29	102	.212	.297	0	.000	-1	0	0	0	0.0
1944	Bro-N	2	1	.667	10	4	3	0	1	41²	46	3	12	17	12.5	3.24	110	.267	.315	2	.154	-0	2	1	-0	0.1
	Pit-N	11	7	.611	28	24	14	1	1	204²	201	7	65	80	11.7	2.73	136	.260	.318	20	.250	2	20	23	-1	2.6

YEAR TM/L	W	L	PCT	G	GS	CG	SH	SV	IP	H	HR	BB	SO	RAT	ERA	ERA+	OAV	OOB	BH	AVG	PB	PR	/A	PD	TPI
Yr	13	8	.619	38	28	17	1	2	246¹	247	10	77	97	11.9	2.81	131	.261	.317	3	.032	2	22	24	-1	2.7
1945 Pit-N	5	4	.556	14	11	4	1	0	80²	74	6	37	29	12.6	4.57	86	.236	.321	9	.321	2	-7	-6	0	-0.2
1946 Pit-N	13	10	.565	27	25	16	2	0	193¹	193	5	56	57	11.7	2.84	124	.263	.318	21	.328	7	12	15	-1	2.3
1947 Pit-N	12	10	.545	26	24	12	3	0	183	181	18	68	66	12.3	3.84	110	.254	.320	12	.188	0	5	8	-1	0.7
1948 Pit-N	8	11	.421	23	22	10	2	0	134¹	143	13	41	43	12.4	4.42	92	.262	.315	8	.182	-0	-7	-5	-1	-0.6
Total 15	114	115	.498	390	246	113	11	15	2066²	2170	105	835	774	13.2	3.99	109	.268	.337	175	.234	17	49	85	-2	11.2

■ JOE OSTROWSKI
Ostrowski, Joseph Paul "Professor" or "Specs" b: 11/15/16, W.Wyoming, Pa. BL/TL, 6', 180 lbs. Deb: 7/18/48

YEAR TM/L	W	L	PCT	G	GS	CG	SH	SV	IP	H	HR	BB	SO	RAT	ERA	ERA+	OAV	OOB	BH	AVG	PB	PR	/A	PD	TPI
1948 StL-A	4	6	.400	26	9	3	0	3	78¹	108	6	17	20	14.4	5.97	76	.333	.367	4	.222	1	-15	-12	2	-0.8
1949 StL-A	8	8	.500	40	13	4	0	2	141	185	16	27	34	13.5	4.79	95	.307	.337	7	.189	2	-9	-4	-1	-0.1
1950 StL-A	2	4	.333	9	7	2	0	0	57¹	57	2	7	15	10.0	2.51	197	.251	.274	4	.222	2	13	16	-1	1.7
NY-A	1	1	.500	21	4	1	0	3	43²	50	11	15	15	13.4	5.15	83	.294	.351	1	.111	-0	-3	-4	0	-0.3
Yr	3	5	.375	30	11	3	0	3	101	107	13	22	30	11.5	3.65	128	.270	.308	6	.222	1	10	11	-0	1.4
1951 *NY-A	6	4	.600	34	3	2	0	5	95¹	103	4	18	30	11.5	3.49	110	.279	.314	3	.107	-2	7	4	-0	0.1
1952 NY-A	2	2	.500	20	1	0	0	2	40	56	5	14	17	16.0	5.62	59	.327	.382	0	.000	-1	-9	-10	-1	-1.1
Total 5	23	25	.479	150	37	12	0	15	455²	559	44	98	131	13.0	4.54	95	.300	.336	19	.161	2	-16	-12	0	-0.5

■ ALFONSO OSUNA
Osuna, Alfonso b: 8/10/65, Inglewood, Cal. BR/TL, 6'3", 200 lbs. Deb: 9/02/90

YEAR TM/L	W	L	PCT	G	GS	CG	SH	SV	IP	H	HR	BB	SO	RAT	ERA	ERA+	OAV	OOB	BH	AVG	PB	PR	/A	PD	TPI
1990 Hou-N	2	0	1.000	12	0	0	0	0	11¹	10	1	6	6	15.1	4.76	79	.270	.413	0	—	0	-1	-1	0	0.0

■ BILL OTEY
Otey, William Tilford "Steamboat Bill" b: 12/16/1886, Dayton, Ohio d: 4/23/31, Dayton, Ohio BL/TL, 6'2", 181 lbs. Deb: 9/27/07

YEAR TM/L	W	L	PCT	G	GS	CG	SH	SV	IP	H	HR	BB	SO	RAT	ERA	ERA+	OAV	OOB	BH	AVG	PB	PR	/A	PD	TPI
1907 Pit-N	0	1	.000	3	2	1	0	0	16¹	23	1	4	5	15.4	4.41	55	.319	.364	1	.250	0	-4	-4	-0	-0.3
1910 Was-A	0	1	.000	9	1	1	0	0	34²	40	1	6	12	12.2	3.38	74	.301	.336	5	.385	2	-3	-3	-1	-0.2
1911 Was-A	1	3	.250	12	2	0	0	0	49²	68	2	15	16	15.6	6.34	52	.333	.387	1	.059	-2	-17	-17	1	-1.5
Total 3	1	5	.167	24	5	2	0	0	100²	131	4	25	33	14.4	5.01	57	.320	.367	7	.206	0	-23	-24	-0	-2.0

■ HARRY OTIS
Otis, Harry George "Cannonball" b: 10/5/1886, W.New York, N.J. d: 1/29/76, Teaneck, N.J. TL, 6' ", 180 lbs. Deb: 9/05/09

YEAR TM/L	W	L	PCT	G	GS	CG	SH	SV	IP	H	HR	BB	SO	RAT	ERA	ERA+	OAV	OOB	BH	AVG	PB	PR	/A	PD	TPI
1909 Cle-A	2	2	.500	5	3	0	0	0	26¹	26	0	18	6	16.1	1.37	187	.283	.416	1	.111	-0	3	3	0	0.4

■ DENNIS O'TOOLE
O'Toole, Dennis Joseph b: 3/13/49, Chicago, Ill. BR/TR, 6'3", 195 lbs. Deb: 9/08/69

YEAR TM/L	W	L	PCT	G	GS	CG	SH	SV	IP	H	HR	BB	SO	RAT	ERA	ERA+	OAV	OOB	BH	AVG	PB	PR	/A	PD	TPI
1969 Chi-A	0	0	—	2	0	0	0	0	4	5	0	2	4	15.8	6.75	57	.333	.412	0	—	0	-1	-1	-0	0.0
1970 Chi-A	0	0	—	3	0	0	0	0	3¹	5	0	2	3	18.9	2.70	144	.357	.438	0	—	0	0	0	0	0.0
1971 Chi-A	0	0	—	1	0	0	0	0	2	0	0	1	2	4.5	0.00	—	.000	.143	0	—	0	1	1	0	0.1
1972 Chi-A	0	0	—	3	0	0	0	0	5	10	0	2	5	21.6	5.40	58	.417	.462	0	—	0	-1	-1	0	0.0
1973 Chi-A	0	0	—	6	0	0	0	0	16	23	3	3	8	14.6	5.63	70	.329	.356	0	—	0	-3	-3	0	-0.2
Total 5	0	0	—	15	0	0	0	0	30¹	43	3	10	22	15.7	5.04	75	.333	.381	0	—	0	-5	-4	-0	-0.1

■ JIM O'TOOLE
O'Toole, James Jerome b: 1/10/37, Chicago, Ill. BB/TL, 6', 190 lbs. Deb: 9/26/58

YEAR TM/L	W	L	PCT	G	GS	CG	SH	SV	IP	H	HR	BB	SO	RAT	ERA	ERA+	OAV	OOB	BH	AVG	PB	PR	/A	PD	TPI
1958 Cin-N	0	1	.000	1	1	0	0	0	7	4	0	5	4	11.6	1.29	322	.154	.290	0	.000	-0	2	2	-0	0.2
1959 Cin-N	5	8	.385	28	19	3	1	0	129¹	144	14	73	68	15.4	5.15	79	.287	.382	5	.135	-0	-17	-16	1	-1.4
1960 Cin-N	12	12	.500	34	31	7	2	1	196¹	198	14	66	124	12.3	3.80	100	.263	.325	7	.106	-3	-1	0	-3	-0.5
1961 *Cin-N	19	9	.679	39	35	11	3	2	252²	229	16	93	178	11.6	3.10	131	.240	.310	16	.172	-1	26	27	-0	2.6
1962 Cin-N	16	13	.552	36	34	11	3	0	251²	222	20	87	170	11.2	3.50	115	.238	.307	10	.110	-5	12	15	-2	0.8
1963 Cin-N	17	14	.548	33	32	12	5	0	234¹	208	13	57	146	10.3	2.88	116	.239	.288	11	.149	-1	11	12	-1	1.0
1964 Cin-N	17	7	.708	30	30	9	3	0	220	194	8	51	145	10.0	2.66	136	.235	.279	7	.100	-1	21	23	-2	2.3
1965 Cin-N	3	10	.231	29	22	2	0	1	127²	154	14	47	71	14.4	5.92	63	.294	.355	4	.089	-2	-34	-31	-1	-3.2
1966 Cin-N	5	7	.417	25	24	2	0	0	142	139	16	49	96	12.1	3.55	110	.254	.318	6	.128	-2	1	6	-1	0.4
1967 Chi-A	4	3	.571	15	10	1	1	0	54¹	53	4	18	37	11.9	2.82	110	.251	.313	1	.077	-1	3	2	-0	0.0
Total 10	98	84	.538	270	238	58	18	4	1615¹	1545	119	546	1039	11.8	3.57	106	.251	.315	67	.125	-16	24	40	-11	2.2

■ MARTY O'TOOLE
O'Toole, Martin James b: 11/27/1888, Wm.Penn, Pa. d: 2/18/49, Aberdeen, Wash. BR/TR, 5'11", 175 lbs. Deb: 9/21/08

YEAR TM/L	W	L	PCT	G	GS	CG	SH	SV	IP	H	HR	BB	SO	RAT	ERA	ERA+	OAV	OOB	BH	AVG	PB	PR	/A	PD	TPI
1908 Cin-N	1	0	1.000	3	2	1	0	0	15	15	0	7	5	13.2	2.40	96	.273	.355	1	.200	0	-0	-0	0	0.0
1911 Pit-N	3	2	.600	5	5	3	0	0	38	28	1	20	34	11.4	2.37	145	.215	.320	5	.357	2	4	4	0	0.7
1912 Pit-N	15	17	.469	37	36	17	5	0	275¹	237	4	159	150	13.0	2.71	120	.235	.340	22	.222	1	21	17	1	1.8
1913 Pit-N	6	8	.429	26	15	7	0	1	144²	148	3	55	58	12.8	3.30	91	.271	.341	7	.132	-2	-1	-5	0	-0.7
1914 Pit-N	1	8	.111	19	9	1	0	1	92¹	92	3	47	36	13.5	4.68	57	.270	.358	5	.167	0	-19	-21	-1	-2.1
NY-N	1	1	.500	10	5	2	0	0	34	34	0	12	13	12.2	4.24	63	.262	.324	3	.300	1	-5	-6	-0	-0.5
Yr	2	9	.182	29	14	3	0	1	126¹	126	3	59	49	13.2	4.56	58	.268	.349	0	.000	1	-25	-27	-1	-2.6
Total 5	27	36	.429	100	72	31	5	2	599¹	554	11	300	296	12.9	3.21	95	.251	.341	43	.204	2	-1	-10	-0	-0.8

■ JIM OTTEN
Otten, James Edward b: 7/1/51, Lewiston, Mont. BR/TR, 6'2", 195 lbs. Deb: 7/31/74

YEAR TM/L	W	L	PCT	G	GS	CG	SH	SV	IP	H	HR	BB	SO	RAT	ERA	ERA+	OAV	OOB	BH	AVG	PB	PR	/A	PD	TPI
1974 Chi-A	0	1	.000	5	1	0	0	0	16¹	22	0	12	11	19.3	5.51	68	.324	.432	0	—	0	-3	-3	-0	-0.2
1975 Chi-A	0	0	—	2	0	0	0	0	5¹	4	1	7	3	16.9	6.75	57	.235	.458	0	—	0	-2	-2	-0	-0.1
1976 Chi-A	0	0	—	2	0	0	0	0	6	9	0	2	3	16.5	4.50	79	.333	.379	0	—	0	-1	-1	-0	0.0
1980 StL-N	0	5	.000	31	4	0	0	0	55¹	71	3	26	38	16.1	5.53	67	.323	.399	1	.200	-0	-12	-11	0	-1.0
1981 StL-N	1	0	1.000	24	0	0	0	0	35²	44	3	20	20	16.1	5.30	67	.321	.408	0	.000	-0	-7	-7	-1	-0.8
Total 5	1	6	.143	64	5	0	0	0	118²	150	7	67	75	16.7	5.46	67	.320	.408	1	.143	-0	-25	-24	-1	-2.1

■ DAVE OTTO
Otto, David Alan b: 11/12/64, Chicago, Ill. BL/TL, 6'7", 210 lbs. Deb: 9/08/87

YEAR TM/L	W	L	PCT	G	GS	CG	SH	SV	IP	H	HR	BB	SO	RAT	ERA	ERA+	OAV	OOB	BH	AVG	PB	PR	/A	PD	TPI
1987 Oak-A	0	0	—	3	0	0	0	0	6	7	1	1	3	12.0	9.00	46	.304	.333	0	—	0	-3	-3	-0	-0.2
1988 Oak-A	0	0	—	3	2	0	0	0	10	9	0	6	7	13.5	1.80	210	.243	.349	0	—	0	2	2	0	0.2
1989 Oak-A	0	0	—	1	1	0	0	0	6²	6	0	2	4	10.8	2.70	136	.261	.320	0	—	0	1	1	0	0.1
1990 Oak-A	0	0	—	2	0	0	0	0	2¹	3	0	3	2	23.1	7.71	48	.300	.462	0	—	0	-1	-1	-0	-0.1
Total 4	0	0	—	9	3	0	0	0	25	25	1	12	16	13.3	4.32	89	.269	.352	0	—	0	-1	-1	0	0.1

■ ORVAL OVERALL
Overall, Orval b: 2/2/1881, Farmersville, Cal. d: 7/14/47, Fresno, Cal. BB/TR, 6'2", 214 lbs. Deb: 4/16/05

YEAR TM/L	W	L	PCT	G	GS	CG	SH	SV	IP	H	HR	BB	SO	RAT	ERA	ERA+	OAV	OOB	BH	AVG	PB	PR	/A	PD	TPI
1905 Cin-N	18	23	.439	42	39	32	2	0	318	290	4	147	173	12.8	2.86	116	.252	.343	17	.145	-3	5	16	-2	1.3
1906 Cin-N	4	5	.444	13	10	6	0	0	82¹	77	1	46	33	13.9	4.26	65	.253	.359	6	.194	0	-15	-14	-1	-1.4
*Chi-N	12	3	.800	18	14	13	2	1	144	116	1	51	94	11.0	1.88	141	.217	.290	9	.170	-1	12	12	-0	1.3
Yr	16	8	.667	31	24	19	2	1	226¹	193	2	97	127	11.7	2.74	98	.229	.311	2	.024	-0	-3	-2	-2	-0.1
1907 *Chi-N	23	7	.767	35	29	25	8	3	265¹	199	3	69	139	9.5	1.70	147	.206	.266	20	.213	4	23	24	1	3.4
1908 *Chi-N	15	11	.577	37	27	16	4	4	225	165	3	78	167	9.8	1.92	123	.208	.280	9	.125	-1	11	11	-2	0.9
1909 *Chi-N	20	11	.645	38	32	23	9	3	285	204	1	80	**205**	9.2	1.42	179	**.198**	.262	22	.229	8	37	36	-1	5.0
1910 *Chi-N	12	6	.667	23	21	11	4	1	144²	106	2	54	92	10.0	2.68	108	.212	.291	5	.122	-1	6	3	1	0.3
1913 Chi-N	4	5	.444	11	9	6	1	0	68	73	1	26	30	13.2	3.31	96	.284	.352	6	.250	2	-1	-1	1	0.2
Total 7	108	71	.603	217	181	132	30	12	1532¹	1230	16	551	933	10.7	2.24	123	.222	.298	94	.179	9	79	86	-4	11.0

■ STUBBY OVERMIRE
Overmire, Frank b: 5/16/19, Moline, Mich. d: 3/3/77, Lakeland, Fla. BR/TL, 5'7", 170 lbs. Deb: 4/25/43 C

YEAR TM/L	W	L	PCT	G	GS	CG	SH	SV	IP	H	HR	BB	SO	RAT	ERA	ERA+	OAV	OOB	BH	AVG	PB	PR	/A	PD	TPI
1943 Det-A	7	6	.538	29	18	8	3	1	147	135	5	38	48	10.7	3.18	111	.243	.293	7	.167	0	2	6	-1	0.6
1944 Det-A	11	11	.500	32	28	11	3	1	199²	214	4	41	57	11.6	3.07	116	.271	.309	11	.175	1	8	11	2	1.5
1945 *Det-A	9	9	.500	31	22	9	0	4	162¹	189	6	42	36	13.0	3.88	91	.294	.341	10	.189	0	-9	-7	1	-0.5
1946 Det-A	3	5	.417	24	13	3	0	0	97¹	106	6	29	34	12.5	4.62	79	.274	.325	5	.152	-1	-12	-10	2	-0.9
1947 Det-A	11	5	.688	28	17	7	3	0	140²	142	9	44	33	12.0	3.77	100	.259	.315	7	.149	-1	-1	-0	0	0.0
1948 Det-A	3	4	.429	37	4	0	0	3	66¹	89	5	31	14	16.3	5.97	73	.326	.395	1	.071	-1	-12	-12	1	-1.0
1949 Det-A	1	3	.250	14	1	0	0	0	17¹	29	2	9	3	20.3	9.87	42	.377	.448	1	.333	0	-11	-11	0	-0.9

YEAR	TM/L	W	L	PCT	G	GS	CG	SH	SV	IP	H	HR	BB	SO	RAT	ERA	ERA+	OAV	OOB	BH	AVG	PB	PR	/A	PD	TPI
1950	StL-A	9	12	.429	31	19	8	2	0	161	200	11	45	39	13.8	4.19	118	.298	.343	8	.167	1	7	14	-1	1.3
1951	StL-A	1	6	.143	8	7	3	0	0	53¹	61	5	21	13	13.8	3.54	124	.281	.345	1	.071	-1	3	5	-1	0.4
	NY-A	1	1	.500	15	4	1	0	0	44²	50	2	18	14	14.1	4.63	83	.287	.361	1	.143	0	-3	-4	0	-0.3
	Yr	2	7	.222	23	11	4	0	0	98	111	7	39	27	14.0	4.04	102	.284	.352	5	.238	-1	1	1	-0	0.1
1952	StL-A	0	3	.000	17	4	0	0	0	41	44	3	7	10	11.2	3.73	105	.270	.300	2	.182	-0	-0	1	1	0.2
Total	10	58	67	.464	266	137	50	11	10	1130²	1259	56	325	301	12.7	3.96	98	.280	.330	54	.161	-0	-28	-8	5	0.4

■ MIKE OVERY
Overy, Harry Michael b: 1/27/51, Clinton, Ill. BR/TR, 6'2", 190 lbs. Deb: 8/14/76

YEAR	TM/L	W	L	PCT	G	GS	CG	SH	SV	IP	H	HR	BB	SO	RAT	ERA	ERA+	OAV	OOB	BH	AVG	PB	PR	/A	PD	TPI
1976	Cal-A	0	2	.000	5	0	0	0	0	7¹	6	1	3	8	12.3	6.14	54	.214	.313	0	—	0	-2	-2	0	-0.1

■ ERNIE OVITZ
Ovitz, Ernest Gayheart b: 10/7/1885, Mineral Point, Wis. d: 9/11/80, Green Bay, Wis. 5'8.5", 156 lbs. Deb: 6/22/11

YEAR	TM/L	W	L	PCT	G	GS	CG	SH	SV	IP	H	HR	BB	SO	RAT	ERA	ERA+	OAV	OOB	BH	AVG	PB	PR	/A	PD	TPI
1911	Chi-A	0	0	—	1	0	0	0	0	2	3	0	3	0	27.0	4.50	74	.375	.545	0	—	0	-0	-0	0	0.0

■ BOB OWCHINKO
Owchinko, Robert Dennis b: 1/1/55, Detroit, Mich. BL/TL, 6'2", 190 lbs. Deb: 9/25/76

YEAR	TM/L	W	L	PCT	G	GS	CG	SH	SV	IP	H	HR	BB	SO	RAT	ERA	ERA+	OAV	OOB	BH	AVG	PB	PR	/A	PD	TPI
1976	SD-N	0	2	.000	2	2	0	0	0	4¹	11	0	3	4	29.1	16.62	20	.478	.538	0	.000	-0	-6	-6	0	-0.5
1977	SD-N	9	12	.429	30	28	3	2	0	170	191	20	67	101	13.7	4.45	80	.287	.352	4	.082	-2	-10	-17	-2	-2.0
1978	SD-N	10	13	.435	36	33	4	1	0	202¹	198	14	78	94	12.3	3.56	93	.263	.333	11	.175	1	0	-5	-1	-0.4
1979	SD-N	6	12	.333	42	20	2	0	0	149¹	144	16	55	66	12.1	3.74	94	.259	.328	4	.121	0	-0	-3	-0	-0.3
1980	Cle-A	2	9	.182	29	14	1	1	0	114¹	138	13	47	66	14.7	5.27	77	.301	.368	0	—	0	-16	-15	-1	-1.4
1981	•Oak-A	4	3	.571	29	0	0	0	2	39¹	34	2	19	26	12.4	3.20	109	.245	.340	0	—	0	2	1	-0	0.1
1982	Oak-A	2	4	.333	54	0	0	0	3	102	111	11	52	67	14.4	5.21	75	.275	.358	0	—	0	-13	-15	-1	-1.5
1983	Pit-N	0	0	—	1	0	0	0	0	0	2	1	0	0	—	∞	—	1.000	1.000	0	—	0	-1	-1	0	0.0
1984	Cin-N	3	5	.375	49	4	0	0	2	94	91	10	39	60	12.4	4.12	92	.253	.327	2	.167	1	-6	-4	-1	-0.2
1986	Mon-N	1	0	1.000	3	3	0	0	0	15	17	1	3	6	12.0	3.60	103	.288	.323	1	.200	0	0	0	0	0.0
Total	10	37	60	.381	275	104	10	4	7	890²	937	88	363	490	13.2	4.28	85	.274	.345	22	.135	0	-49	-66	-4	-6.2

■ FRANK OWEN
Owen, Frank Malcolm "Yip" b: 12/23/1879, Ypsilanti, Mich. d: 11/24/42, Dearborn, Mich. BL/TR, Deb: 4/29/01

YEAR	TM/L	W	L	PCT	G	GS	CG	SH	SV	IP	H	HR	BB	SO	RAT	ERA	ERA+	OAV	OOB	BH	AVG	PB	PR	/A	PD	TPI
1901	Det-A	1	3	.250	8	5	3	0	0	56	70	1	30	17	16.1	4.34	89	.302	.382	1	.050	-2	-4	-3	2	-0.2
1903	Chi-A	8	12	.400	26	20	15	1	1	167¹	167	1	44	66	11.3	3.50	80	.259	.307	7	.123	-1	-10	-13	4	-1.0
1904	Chi-A	21	15	.583	37	36	34	4	1	315	243	2	61	103	8.7	1.94	126	.214	.254	23	.215	5	23	18	7	3.4
1905	Chi-A	21	13	.618	42	38	32	3	0	334	276	6	56	125	8.9	2.10	118	.226	.260	18	.145	-3	21	14	4	1.5
1906	•Chi-A	22	13	.629	42	36	27	7	0	293	289	4	54	66	10.5	2.33	109	.261	.295	14	.136	-2	12	7	5	1.0
1907	Chi-A	2	3	.400	11	4	2	0	0	47	43	1	13	15	10.7	2.49	96	.245	.297	4	.250	1	0	-0	1	0.0
1908	Chi-A	6	7	.462	25	14	5	1	0	140	142	2	37	48	11.7	3.41	68	.260	.310	9	.180	1	-16	-17	2	-1.5
1909	Chi-A	1	1	.500	3	2	1	0	0	16	19	0	3	3	12.9	4.50	52	.279	.319	1	.167	-0	-4	-4	0	-0.3
Total	8	82	67	.550	194	155	119	16	2	1368¹	1249	17	298	443	10.2	2.55	100	.244	.286	77	.159	-2	22	1	24	2.9

■ JIM OWENS
Owens, James Philip "Bear" b: 1/16/34, Gifford, Pa. BR/TR, 5'11", 180 lbs. Deb: 4/19/55 C

YEAR	TM/L	W	L	PCT	G	GS	CG	SH	SV	IP	H	HR	BB	SO	RAT	ERA	ERA+	OAV	OOB	BH	AVG	PB	PR	/A	PD	TPI
1955	Phi-N	0	2	.000	3	2	0	0	0	8²	13	2	7	6	20.8	8.31	48	.382	.488	0	.000	-0	-4	-4	-0	-0.3
1956	Phi-N	0	4	.000	10	5	0	0	0	29³	35	3	22	22	17.9	7.28	51	.313	.434	1	.167	-0	-12	-12	0	-1.0
1958	Phi-N	1	0	1.000	1	1	0	0	0	7	4	1	5	3	11.6	2.57	154	.154	.290	0	.000	0	1	1	0	0.1
1959	Phi-N	12	12	.500	31	30	11	1	1	221¹	203	14	73	135	11.4	3.21	128	.244	.308	9	.120	-1	18	22	-1	2.1
1960	Phi-N	4	14	.222	31	22	6	0	0	150	182	21	64	83	14.8	5.04	77	.299	.367	3	.068	-3	-21	-19	-1	-2.2
1961	Phi-N	5	10	.333	20	17	3	0	0	106²	119	8	32	38	12.7	4.47	91	.287	.339	2	.074	-1	-5	-5	-1	-0.6
1962	Phi-N	2	4	.333	23	12	1	0	0	69²	90	12	33	21	15.9	6.33	61	.318	.389	2	.143	-1	-18	-19	-1	-1.8
1963	Cin-N	0	2	.000	19	3	0	0	4	42¹	42	6	24	29	14.0	5.31	63	.259	.355	1	.125	0	-10	-9	1	-0.8
1964	Hou-N	8	7	.533	48	11	0	0	6	118	115	7	32	88	11.2	3.28	104	.262	.312	3	.103	-1	3	2	-1	0.0
1965	Hou-N	6	5	.545	50	0	0	0	8	71¹	64	4	29	53	11.7	3.28	102	.238	.312	1	.125	-0	2	1	-0	0.0
1966	Hou-N	4	7	.364	40	0	0	0	2	50	53	5	17	32	12.8	4.68	73	.273	.335	0	.000	-0	-6	-7	1	-0.6
1967	Hou-N	0	1	.000	10	0	0	0	0	10²	12	1	2	6	11.8	4.22	78	.308	.341	0	—	0	-1	-1	-0	-0.1
Total	12	42	68	.382	286	103	21	1	21	885¹	932	84	340	516	13.0	4.31	88	.273	.340	22	.101	-7	-53	-51	-5	-5.2

■ RICK OWNBEY
Ownbey, Richard Wayne b: 10/20/57, Corona, Cal. BR/TR, 6'3", 185 lbs. Deb: 8/17/82

YEAR	TM/L	W	L	PCT	G	GS	CG	SH	SV	IP	H	HR	BB	SO	RAT	ERA	ERA+	OAV	OOB	BH	AVG	PB	PR	/A	PD	TPI
1982	NY-N	1	2	.333	8	8	2	0	0	50¹	44	3	43	28	15.6	3.75	97	.242	.387	3	.200	1	-1	-1	-1	0.0
1983	NY-N	1	3	.250	10	4	0	0	0	34²	31	4	21	19	13.8	4.67	78	.240	.351	1	.111	-0	-4	-4	0	-0.4
1984	StL-N	0	3	.000	4	4	0	0	0	19	23	1	8	11	14.7	4.74	73	.303	.369	0	.000	0	-2	-3	-0	-0.2
1986	StL-N	1	3	.250	17	3	0	0	0	42²	47	4	19	25	14.3	3.80	96	.294	.376	0	—	0	-1	-1	-1	-0.1
Total	4	3	11	.214	39	19	2	0	0	146²	145	12	91	83	14.7	4.11	88	.265	.373	4	.114	-1	-8	-8	-1	-0.7

■ DOC OZMER
Ozmer, Horace Robert b: 5/25/01, Atlanta, Ga. d: 12/28/70, Atlanta, Ga. BR/TR, 5'10.5", 185 lbs. Deb: 5/11/23

YEAR	TM/L	W	L	PCT	G	GS	CG	SH	SV	IP	H	HR	BB	SO	RAT	ERA	ERA+	OAV	OOB	BH	AVG	PB	PR	/A	PD	TPI
1923	Phi-A	0	0	—	1	0	0	0	0	2	1	0	1	1	9.0	4.50	91	.167	.286	0	—	0	-0	-0	0	0.0

■ CHARLIE PABOR
Pabor, Charles Henry b: 9/24/1846, New York, N.Y. d: 4/22/13, New Haven, Conn. TL, 5'8", 155 lbs. Deb: 5/04/1871 M♦

YEAR	TM/L	W	L	PCT	G	GS	CG	SH	SV	IP	H	HR	BB	SO	RAT	ERA	ERA+	OAV	OOB	BH	AVG	PB	PR	/A	PD	TPI
1871	Cle-n	0	2	.000	7	1	1	0	0	29¹	50	4	6	0	17.2	6.75	61	.325	.350	42	.296		-8	-9		-0.4
1872	Cle-n	1	1	.500	2	2	0	0	0	18	20	0	0		10.0	3.00	121	.244	.244	19	.211	-0	1	1		0.1
1875	Atl-n	0	1	.000	1	1	0	0	0	4	11	0	1		27.0	9.00	26	.440	.462	36	.235		-3	-3		-0.1
Total	3 n	1	4	.200	10	4	3	0	0	51¹	81	4	7	0	15.4	5.61	41	.310	.328	203	.286	-0	-18	-19		-0.4

■ JOHN PACELLA
Pacella, John Lewis b: 9/15/56, Brooklyn, N.Y. BR/TR, 6'3", 195 lbs. Deb: 9/15/77

YEAR	TM/L	W	L	PCT	G	GS	CG	SH	SV	IP	H	HR	BB	SO	RAT	ERA	ERA+	OAV	OOB	BH	AVG	PB	PR	/A	PD	TPI
1977	NY-N	0	0	—	3	0	0	0	0	4	2	0	2	1	9.0	0.00	—	.133	.235	0	—	0	2	2	-0	0.1
1979	NY-N	0	2	.000	4	3	0	0	0	16¹	16	0	4	12	11.0	4.41	83	.246	.290	0	.000	-0	-1	-1	-0	-0.1
1980	NY-N	3	4	.429	32	15	0	0	0	84	89	5	59	68	16.1	5.14	69	.280	.396	2	.100	-1	-14	-15	-1	-1.6
1982	NY-A	0	1	.000	3	1	0	0	0	10	13	0	9	2	20.7	7.20	55	.342	.479	0	—	0	-3	-4	0	-0.2
	Min-A	1	2	.333	21	1	0	0	2	51²	61	14	37	20	17.1	7.32	58	.299	.407	0	—	0	-19	-18	-1	-1.7
	Yr	1	3	.250	24	2	0	0	2	61²	74	14	46	22	17.5	7.30	58	.301	.411	0	—	0	-22	-21	-1	-1.9
1984	Bal-A	0	1	.000	6	1	0	0	0	14²	15	2	9	8	14.7	6.75	57	.268	.369	0	—	0	-4	-5	-0	-0.4
1986	Det-A	0	0	—	5	0	0	0	1	11	10	0	13	5	18.8	4.09	101	.294	.489	0	—	0	0	0	1	0.0
Total	6	4	10	.286	74	21	0	0	3	191²	206	21	133	116	16.1	5.73	67	.282	.395	2	.083	-1	-40	-41	-2	-3.8

■ PAT PACILLO
Pacillo, Patrick Michael b: 7/23/63, Jersey City, N.J. BR/TR, 6'2", 205 lbs. Deb: 5/23/87

YEAR	TM/L	W	L	PCT	G	GS	CG	SH	SV	IP	H	HR	BB	SO	RAT	ERA	ERA+	OAV	OOB	BH	AVG	PB	PR	/A	PD	TPI
1987	Cin-N	3	3	.500	12	7	0	0	0	39²	41	7	19	23	13.8	6.13	69	.270	.355	1	.091	-0	-9	-8	-0	-0.7
1988	Cin-N	1	0	1.000	6	0	0	0	0	10²	14	2	4	11	15.2	5.06	71	.318	.375	0	—	0	-2	-1	-0	-0.1
Total	2	4	3	.571	18	7	0	0	0	50¹	55	9	23	34	14.1	5.90	70	.281	.359	1	.083	-0	-11	-10	-0	-0.8

■ GENE PACKARD
Packard, Eugene Milo b: 7/13/1887, Colorado Springs Colorado d: 5/19/59, Riverside, Cal. BL/TL, 5'10", 155 lbs. Deb: 9/27/12

YEAR	TM/L	W	L	PCT	G	GS	CG	SH	SV	IP	H	HR	BB	SO	RAT	ERA	ERA+	OAV	OOB	BH	AVG	PB	PR	/A	PD	TPI
1912	Cin-N	1	0	1.000	1	1	0	0	0	9	7	0	4	2	11.0	3.00	112	.206	.289	1	.250	0	0	0	0	0.1
1913	Cin-N	7	11	.389	39	21	9	2	0	190²	208	2	64	73	13.2	2.97	109	.286	.350	11	.180	-0	5	6	-1	0.5
1914	KC-F	20	14	.588	42	34	24	4	5	302	282	5	88	154	11.3	2.89	107	.247	.306	28	.241	4	11	7	8	2.0
1915	KC-F	20	12	.625	42	31	21	5	2	281²	250	3	74	108	10.6	2.68	109	.242	.298	22	.232	3	11	7	7	1.8
1916	Chi-N	10	6	.625	37	15	5	2	5	155¹	154	4	38	36	11.3	2.78	105	.256	.304	7	.130	-1	-3	2	6	0.8
1917	•Chi-N	0	0	—	2	0	0	0	0	1²	3	1	0	1	16.2	10.80	27	.375	.375	0	—	0	-1	-1	0	0.0
	StL-N	9	6	.600	34	11	6	0	2	153¹	138	4	25	44	9.7	2.47	109	.246	.281	15	.288	3	3	3	2	0.8
	Yr	9	6	.600	36	11	6	0	2	155	141	5	25	45	9.8	2.55	105	.247	.283	2	.038	3	3	2	0	0.8
1918	StL-N	12	12	.500	30	23	10	1	2	182¹	184	6	33	46	11.0	3.50	77	.266	.304	12	.174	-1	-15	-16	-1	-1.8
1919	Phi-N	6	8	.429	21	16	10	1	1	134¹	167	3	30	24	13.5	4.15	78	.321	.363	7	.137	-2	-19	-14	0	-1.5

YEAR TM/L	W	L	PCT	G	GS	CG	SH	SV	IP	H	HR	BB	SO	RAT	ERA	ERA+	OAV	OOB	BH	AVG	PB	PR	/A	PD	TPI
Total 8	85	69	.552	248	152	86	15	17	1410¹	1393	28	356	488	11.4	3.01	99	.262	.313	103	.205	7	-7	-4	19	2.7

■ **JOE PACTWA**   Pactwa, Joseph Martin b: 6/2/48, Hammond, Ind. BL/TL, 5'11", 185 lbs. Deb: 9/15/75

YEAR TM/L	W	L	PCT	G	GS	CG	SH	SV	IP	H	HR	BB	SO	RAT	ERA	ERA+	OAV	OOB	BH	AVG	PB	PR	/A	PD	TPI
1975 Cal-A	1	0	1.000	4	3	0	0	0	16¹	23	0	10	3	18.2	3.86	92	.343	.429	0	—	0	-0	-1	0	0.0

■ **DAVE PAGAN**   Pagan, David Percy b: 9/15/49, Nipawin, Sask., Can. BR/TR, 6'2", 175 lbs. Deb: 7/01/73

YEAR TM/L	W	L	PCT	G	GS	CG	SH	SV	IP	H	HR	BB	SO	RAT	ERA	ERA+	OAV	OOB	BH	AVG	PB	PR	/A	PD	TPI
1973 NY-A	0	0	—	4	1	0	0	0	12²	16	1	1	9	12.1	2.84	129	.320	.333	0	—	0	1	1	0	0.1
1974 NY-A	1	3	.250	16	6	1	0	0	49¹	49	1	28	39	14.0	5.11	68	.265	.362	0	—	0	-8	-9	-0	-0.8
1975 NY-A	0	0	—	13	0	0	0	1	31	30	2	13	18	13.1	4.06	90	.256	.341	0	—	0	-1	-1	-0	-0.1
1976 NY-A	1	1	.500	7	2	1	0	0	23²	18	0	4	13	8.4	2.28	150	.222	.259	0	—	0	3	3	-0	0.3
Bal-A	1	4	.200	20	5	0	0	1	46²	54	2	23	34	15.0	5.98	55	.298	.380	0	—	0	-13	-14	-1	-1.4
Yr	2	5	.286	27	7	1	0	1	70¹	72	2	27	47	12.8	4.73	70	.273	.342	0	—	0	-9	-11	-2	-1.1
1977 Sea-A	1	1	.500	24	4	1	1	2	66	86	3	26	30	15.5	6.14	67	.323	.388	0	—	0	-15	-15	0	-1.3
Pit-N	0	0	—	1	0	0	0	0	3	1	0	0	4	3.0	0.00	—	.100	.100	0	—	0	1	1	0	0.2
Total 5	4	9	.308	85	18	3	1	4	232¹	254	9	95	147	13.7	4.96	74	.285	.358	0	—	0	-31	-34	-2	-3.0

■ **JOE PAGE**   Page, Joseph Francis "Fireman" b: 10/28/17, Cherry Valley, Pa. d: 4/21/80, Latrobe, Pa. BL/TL, 6'3", 200 lbs. Deb: 4/19/44

YEAR TM/L	W	L	PCT	G	GS	CG	SH	SV	IP	H	HR	BB	SO	RAT	ERA	ERA+	OAV	OOB	BH	AVG	PB	PR	/A	PD	TPI
1944 NY-A	5	7	.417	19	16	4	0	0	102²	100	3	52	63	13.6	4.56	76	.258	.351	5	.156	-0	-13	-12	-1	-1.3
1945 NY-A	6	3	.667	20	9	4	0	0	102	95	1	46	50	12.4	2.82	123	.246	.326	9	.250	1	6	7	-2	0.7
1946 NY-A	9	8	.529	31	17	6	1	3	136	126	7	72	77	13.4	3.57	97	.252	.351	7	.163	-0	-1	-2	-1	-0.2
1947 *NY-A	14	8	.636	56	2	0	0	17	141¹	105	5	72	116	11.3	2.48	142	.208	.308	10	.217	1	**19**	17	-1	1.7
1948 NY-A	7	8	.467	55	1	0	0	16	107²	116	6	66	77	15.3	4.26	96	.275	.374	7	.292	3	0	-2	-1	0.0
1949 *NY-A	13	8	.619	60	0	0	0	27	135¹	103	8	75	99	12.2	2.59	156	.215	.328	7	.175	-1	24	22	-2	1.8
1950 NY-A	3	7	.300	37	0	0	0	13	55¹	66	8	31	33	15.8	5.04	85	.295	.380	2	.250	1	-3	-5	-1	-0.3
1954 Pit-N	0	0	—	7	0	0	0	0	9²	16	4	7	4	22.3	11.17	37	.364	.462	0	—	0	-8	-8	-0	-0.6
Total 8	57	49	.538	285	45	14	1	76	790	727	42	421	519	13.2	3.53	106	.247	.344	47	.205	5	25	18	-9	1.8

■ **PHIL PAGE**   Page, Philippe Rausac b: 8/23/05, Springfield, Mass. d: 7/27/58, Springfield, Mass BR/TR, 6'2", 175 lbs. Deb: 9/18/28 C

YEAR TM/L	W	L	PCT	G	GS	CG	SH	SV	IP	H	HR	BB	SO	RAT	ERA	ERA+	OAV	OOB	BH	AVG	PB	PR	/A	PD	TPI
1928 Det-A	2	0	1.000	3	2	2	0	0	22	21	1	10	3	12.7	2.45	167	.256	.337	2	.222	-0	4	4	1	0.5
1929 Det-A	0	2	.000	10	4	1	0	0	25¹	29	1	19	6	17.4	8.17	53	.296	.415	1	.125	-1	-11	-11	-1	-1.0
1930 Det-A	0	1	.000	12	0	0	0	0	12	23	1	9	2	24.0	9.75	49	.434	.516	0	—	0	-7	-7	-0	-0.4
1934 Bro-N	1	0	1.000	6	0	0	0	0	10	13	1	6	4	17.1	5.40	72	.342	.432	0	.000	-0	-1	-2	1	0.0
Total 4	3	3	.500	31	6	3	0	0	69¹	86	4	44	15	17.0	6.23	68	.317	.415	3	.167	-1	-15	-15	1	-0.9

■ **SAM PAGE**   Page, Samuel Walter b: 2/11/16, Woodruff, S.C. BL/TR, 6', 172 lbs. Deb: 9/11/39

YEAR TM/L	W	L	PCT	G	GS	CG	SH	SV	IP	H	HR	BB	SO	RAT	ERA	ERA+	OAV	OOB	BH	AVG	PB	PR	/A	PD	TPI
1939 Phi-A	0	3	.000	4	3	1	0	0	22	34	1	15	11	20.0	6.95	68	.343	.430	3	.429	1	-6	-5	0	-0.2

■ **VANCE PAGE**   Page, Vance Linwood b: 9/15/05, Elm City, N.C. d: 7/14/51, Wilson, N.C. BR/TR, 6', 180 lbs. Deb: 8/06/38

YEAR TM/L	W	L	PCT	G	GS	CG	SH	SV	IP	H	HR	BB	SO	RAT	ERA	ERA+	OAV	OOB	BH	AVG	PB	PR	/A	PD	TPI
1938 *Chi-N	5	4	.556	13	9	3	0	1	68	90	4	13	18	13.6	3.84	100	.323	.353	4	.154	-1	-0	-0	3	0.2
1939 Chi-N	7	7	.500	27	17	8	1	1	139¹	169	8	37	43	13.4	3.88	98	.298	.342	12	.255	3	1	1	1	0.5
1940 Chi-N	1	3	.250	30	1	0	0	2	59	65	1	26	22	13.9	4.42	85	.271	.342	4	.308	2	-4	-4	0	-0.1
1941 Chi-N	2	2	.500	25	3	1	0	1	48¹	48	2	30	17	14.9	4.28	82	.254	.362	2	.286	1	-3	-4	1	-0.2
Total 4	15	16	.484	95	30	12	1	5	314²	372	15	106	100	13.8	4.03	95	.292	.348	22	.237	4	-7	-8	5	0.4

■ **PAT PAIGE**   Paige, George Lynn "Piggy" b: 5/5/1883, Paw Paw, Mich. d: 6/8/39, Berlin, Wis. BL/TL, 5'10", 175 lbs. Deb: 5/20/11

YEAR TM/L	W	L	PCT	G	GS	CG	SH	SV	IP	H	HR	BB	SO	RAT	ERA	ERA+	OAV	OOB	BH	AVG	PB	PR	/A	PD	TPI
1911 Cle-A	1	0	1.000	2	1	1	0	0	16	21	0	7	6	15.8	4.50	76	.339	.406	1	.143	-0	-2	-2	1	0.0

■ **SATCHEL PAIGE**   Paige, Leroy Robert b: 7/7/06, Mobile, Ala. d: 6/8/82, Kansas City, Mo. BR/TR, 6'3.5", 180 lbs. Deb: 7/09/48 CH

YEAR TM/L	W	L	PCT	G	GS	CG	SH	SV	IP	H	HR	BB	SO	RAT	ERA	ERA+	OAV	OOB	BH	AVG	PB	PR	/A	PD	TPI
1948 *Cle-A	6	1	.857	21	7	3	2	1	72²	61	2	25	45	10.8	2.48	164	.228	.297	2	.087	-2	15	13	-0	1.0
1949 Cle-A	4	7	.364	31	5	1	0	5	83	70	4	33	54	11.3	3.04	131	.230	.308	1	.063	-1	11	9	-1	0.7
1951 StL-A	3	4	.429	23	3	0	0	5	62	67	6	29	48	14.1	4.79	92	.276	.355	2	.125	-2	-5	-3	-1	-0.4
1952 StL-A	12	10	.545	46	6	3	2	10	138	116	5	57	91	11.5	3.07	128	.226	.307	5	.128	-2	9	13	-0	1.1
1953 StL-A	3	9	.250	57	4	0	0	11	117¹	114	12	39	51	11.8	3.53	119	.257	.319	2	.069	-3	6	9	-2	0.4
1965 KC-A	0	0	—	1	1	0	0	0	3	1	0	0	1	3.0	0.00	—	.100	.100	0	.000	-0	1	1	0	0.1
Total 6	28	31	.475	179	26	7	4	32	476	429	29	183	290	11.7	3.29	124	.241	.314	12	.097	-10	37	42	-4	2.9

■ **PHIL PAINE**   Paine, Phillips Steere "Flip" b: 6/8/30, Chepachet, R.I. d: 2/19/78, Lebanon, Pa. BR/TR, 6'2", 180 lbs. Deb: 7/14/51

YEAR TM/L	W	L	PCT	G	GS	CG	SH	SV	IP	H	HR	BB	SO	RAT	ERA	ERA+	OAV	OOB	BH	AVG	PB	PR	/A	PD	TPI
1951 Bos-N	2	0	1.000	21	0	0	0	0	35¹	36	2	20	17	15.3	3.06	120	.271	.382	0	.000	-0	4	2	-0	0.2
1954 Mil-N	1	0	1.000	11	0	0	0	0	14	14	1	12	11	17.4	3.86	97	.292	.443	0	—	0	-0	-0	-0	-0.1
1955 Mil-N	2	0	1.000	15	0	0	0	0	25¹	20	2	14	26	12.1	2.49	151	.225	.330	1	.333	0	4	4	0	0.4
1956 Mil-N	0	0	—	1	0	0	0	0	0	3	0	0	0	∞	∞	—	1.000	1.000	0	—	0	-2	-2	-0	-0.1
1957 Mil-N	0	0	—	1	0	0	0	0	2	1	0	3	2	18.0	0.00	—	.143	.400	0	—	0	1	1	0	0.1
1958 StL-N	5	1	.833	46	0	0	0	1	73¹	70	7	31	45	13.0	3.56	116	.256	.343	2	.286	-0	3	5	0	0.5
Total 6	10	1	.909	95	0	0	0	1	150	144	12	80	101	14.0	3.36	116	.260	.364	3	.214	-0	10	9	-0	1.1

■ **VICENTE PALACIOS**   Palacios, Vicente (Hernandez) b: 7/19/63, Verzcruz, Mex. BR/TR, 6'3", 165 lbs. Deb: 9/04/87

YEAR TM/L	W	L	PCT	G	GS	CG	SH	SV	IP	H	HR	BB	SO	RAT	ERA	ERA+	OAV	OOB	BH	AVG	PB	PR	/A	PD	TPI
1987 Pit-N	2	1	.667	6	4	0	0	0	29¹	27	1	9	13	11.4	4.30	96	.250	.314	1	.111	-0	-1	-1	-1	-0.1
1988 Pit-N	1	2	.333	7	3	0	0	0	24¹	28	3	15	15	15.9	6.66	51	.295	.391	0	.000	-0	-9	-9	-0	-0.8
1990 Pit-N	0	0	—	7	0	0	0	3	15	4	0	2	8	3.6	0.00	—	.083	.120	0	.000	-0	6	6	-0	0.6
Total 3	3	3	.500	20	7	0	0	3	68²	59	4	26	36	11.3	4.19	89	.235	.309	1	.048	-1	-3	-3	-0	-0.3

■ **MIKE PALAGYI**   Palagyi, Michael Raymond b: 7/4/17, Conneaut, Ohio BR/TR, 6'2", 185 lbs. Deb: 8/18/39

YEAR TM/L	W	L	PCT	G	GS	CG	SH	SV	IP	H	HR	BB	SO	RAT	ERA	ERA+	OAV	OOB	BH	AVG	PB	PR	/A	PD	TPI
1939 Was-A	0	0	—	1	0	0	0	0	0	0	0	3	0	∞	∞	—	—	1.000	0	—	0	-3	-3	0	-0.1

■ **ERV PALICA**   Palica, Ervin Martin (b: Ervin Martin Pavliecivich)
b: 2/9/28, Lomita, Cal. d: 5/29/82, Huntington Beach, Cal. BR/TR, 6'1.5", 180 lbs. Deb: 4/21/45 ♦

YEAR TM/L	W	L	PCT	G	GS	CG	SH	SV	IP	H	HR	BB	SO	RAT	ERA	ERA+	OAV	OOB	BH	AVG	PB	PR	/A	PD	TPI
1947 Bro-N	0	1	.000	3	0	0	0	0	3	2	0	2	1	15.0	3.00	138	.182	.357	0	—	0	0	0	0	0.0
1948 Bro-N	6	6	.500	41	10	0	0	3	125¹	111	13	58	74	12.4	4.45	94	.239	.327	5	.128	0	-7	-6	-1	-0.7
1949 *Bro-N	8	9	.471	49	1	0	0	6	97	93	6	49	44	13.3	3.62	113	.261	.352	3	.158	0	5	5	0	0.5
1950 Bro-N	13	8	.619	43	19	10	2	1	201¹	176	19	98	131	12.3	3.58	115	.237	.327	15	.221	2	13	12	-4	0.9
1951 Bro-N	2	6	.250	19	8	0	0	0	53	55	10	20	15	12.7	4.75	83	.259	.323	2	.154	0	-5	-5	-1	-0.3
1953 Bro-N	0	0	—	4	0	0	0	0	6	10	1	8	3	27.0	12.00	36	.370	.514	1	1.000	0	-5	-5	0	-0.3
1954 Bro-N	3	3	.500	25	3	0	0	0	67²	77	9	31	24	14.5	5.32	77	.285	.361	4	.250	1	-9	-9	-1	-0.9
1955 Bal-A	5	11	.313	33	25	5	1	0	169²	165	10	83	68	13.3	4.14	92	.260	.348	13	.236	2	-3	-6	-1	-0.8
1956 Bal-A	4	11	.267	29	14	2	0	0	116¹	117	10	50	62	13.0	4.49	87	.264	.339	5	.156	-2	-4	-7	0	-0.8
Total 9	41	55	.427	246	80	20	3	10	839¹	806	72	399	423	13.0	4.22	94	.255	.340	48	.198	5	-16	-22	-7	-2.0

■ **DONN PALL**   Pall, Donn Steven b: 1/11/62, Chicago, Ill. BR/TR, 6'2", 185 lbs. Deb: 8/01/88

YEAR TM/L	W	L	PCT	G	GS	CG	SH	SV	IP	H	HR	BB	SO	RAT	ERA	ERA+	OAV	OOB	BH	AVG	PB	PR	/A	PD	TPI
1988 Chi-A	0	2	.000	17	0	0	0	0	28²	39	1	8	16	14.8	3.45	115	.328	.370	0	—	0	2	2	1	0.2
1989 Chi-A	4	5	.444	53	0	0	0	6	87	90	9	19	58	12.1	3.31	115	.270	.325	0	—	0	6	5	-1	0.3
1990 Chi-A	3	5	.375	56	0	0	0	2	76	63	7	24	39	10.8	3.32	115	.232	.303	0	—	0	5	4	0	0.4
Total 3	7	12	.368	126	0	0	0	8	191²	192	17	51	113	12.0	3.33	115	.265	.324	0	—	0	12	11	-1	0.9

■ **MIKE PALM**   Palm, Richard Paul b: 2/13/25, Boston, Mass. BR/TR, 6'3.5", 190 lbs. Deb: 7/11/48

YEAR TM/L	W	L	PCT	G	GS	CG	SH	SV	IP	H	HR	BB	SO	RAT	ERA	ERA+	OAV	OOB	BH	AVG	PB	PR	/A	PD	TPI
1948 Bos-A	0	0	—	3	0	0	0	0	3	6	0	5	1	33.0	6.00	73	.400	.550	0	.000	-0	-1	-1	0	0.0

YEAR TM/L	W	L	PCT	G	GS	CG	SH	SV	IP	H	HR	BB	SO	RAT	ERA	ERA+	OAV	OOB	BH	AVG	PB	PR	/A	PD	TPI
■ **PALMER**			Palmer	b: St.Louis, Mo.					Deb: 5/28/1885																
1885 StL-N	0	4	.000	4	4	4	0	0	34	46	2	20	9	17.5	3.44	80	.309	.391	1	.091	-0	-2	-3	-1	-0.3
■ **DAVID PALMER**				Palmer, David William			b: 10/19/57, Glens Falls, N.Y.		BR/TR, 6'1", 195 lbs.			Deb: 9/09/78													
1978 Mon-N	0	1	.000	5	1	0	0	0	9²	9	1	2	7	10.2	2.79	126	.243	.282	0	.000	-0	1	1	1	0.1
1979 Mon-N	10	2	.833	36	11	2	1	2	122²	110	10	30	72	10.4	2.64	139	.237	.286	1	.032	-3	15	14	-0	1.2
1980 Mon-N	8	6	.571	24	19	3	1	0	129²	124	11	30	73	10.8	2.98	119	.255	.301	9	.200	1	9	8	1	1.2
1982 Mon-N	6	4	.600	13	13	1	0	0	73²	60	3	36	46	12.0	3.18	115	.224	.320	1	.042	-2	3	4	0	0.2
1984 Mon-N	7	3	.700	20	19	1	1	0	105¹	101	5	44	66	12.4	3.84	89	.256	.331	5	.152	1	-3	-5	1	-0.3
1985 Mon-N	7	10	.412	24	23	0	0	0	135²	128	5	67	106	13.1	3.71	91	.250	.341	4	.111	-1	-2	-5	1	-0.4
1986 Atl-N	11	10	.524	35	35	2	0	0	209²	181	17	102	170	12.4	3.65	109	.234	.327	12	.182	2	2	8	1	1.1
1987 Atl-N	8	11	.421	28	28	0	0	0	152¹	169	17	64	111	14.2	4.90	89	.281	.357	6	.125	-0	-14	-9	0	-0.8
1988 Phi-N	7	9	.438	22	22	1	1	0	129	129	8	48	85	12.3	4.47	80	.261	.327	10	.256	5	-15	-13	-1	-0.8
1989 Det-A	0	3	.000	5	5	0	0	0	17¹	25	1	11	12	18.7	7.79	49	.342	.429	0	—	0	-8	-8	-0	-0.6
Total 10	64	59	.520	212	176	10	4	2	1085	1036	78	434	748	12.4	3.78	99	.252	.327	48	.149	2	-11	-6	4	0.9
■ **JIM PALMER**				Palmer, James Alvin			b: 10/15/45, New York, N.Y.		BR/TR, 6'3", 190 lbs.			Deb: 4/17/65													
1965 Bal-A	5	4	.556	27	6	0	0	1	92	75	6	56	75	13.0	3.72	93	.229	.345	5	.192	1	-3	-3	0	0.0
1966 •Bal-A	15	10	.600	30	30	6	0	0	208¹	176	21	91	147	11.5	3.46	96	.231	.313	7	.096	-2	-0	-3	-1	-0.5
1967 Bal-A	3	1	.750	9	9	2	1	0	49	34	6	20	23	9.9	2.94	107	.199	.283	1	.077	0	2	1	0	0.2
1969 •Bal-A	16	4	**.800**	26	23	11	6	0	181	131	11	64	123	9.7	2.34	152	.200	.272	13	.203	2	26	25	-4	2.6
1970 •Bal-A	20	10	.667	39	39	17	**5**	0	305	263	21	100	199	10.7	2.71	134	.231	.294	17	.150	-1	**34**	32	-0	**3.3**
1971 •Bal-A	20	9	.690	37	37	20	3	0	282	231	19	106	184	10.9	2.68	125	.221	.295	20	.196	2	24	21	0	2.5
1972 Bal-A	21	10	.677	36	36	18	3	0	274¹	219	21	70	184	9.5	2.07	149	.217	.269	22	.224	4	30	31	-1	4.1
1973 •Bal-A	22	9	.710	38	37	19	6	1	296¹	225	16	113	158	10.4	**2.40**	156	.211	.289	0	—	0	47	44	-1	4.7
1974 •Bal-A	7	12	.368	26	26	5	2	0	178²	176	12	69	84	12.5	3.27	105	.257	.328	0	—	0	7	4	2	0.6
1975 Bal-A	**23**	11	.676	39	38	25	**10**	1	323	253	20	80	193	9.3	**2.09**	168	.216	.267	0	—	0	**61**	51	2	**5.8**
1976 Bal-A	**22**	13	.629	40	40	23	6	0	315	255	20	84	159	9.9	2.51	130	.224	.282	0	—	0	35	27	1	3.1
1977 Bal-A	**20**	11	.645	39	39	**22**	3	0	319	263	24	99	193	10.3	2.91	130	.229	.292	0	—	0	41	31	0	3.3
1978 Bal-A	21	12	.636	38	38	19	6	0	**296**	246	19	97	138	10.5	2.46	142	.227	.291	0	—	0	43	34	1	3.8
1979 •Bal-A	10	6	.625	23	22	7	0	0	155²	144	12	43	67	10.8	3.30	122	.246	.297	0	—	0	16	12	0	1.3
1980 Bal-A	16	10	.615	34	33	4	0	0	224	238	26	74	109	12.7	3.98	99	.275	.334	0	—	0	1	-1	1	0.1
1981 Bal-A	7	8	.467	22	22	5	0	0	127¹	117	14	46	35	11.7	3.75	97	.247	.316	0	—	0	-1	-2	2	0.0
1982 Bal-A	15	5	**.750**	36	32	8	2	1	227	195	22	63	103	10.4	3.13	129	.231	**.287**	0	—	0	24	23	1	2.5
1983 •Bal-A	5	4	.556	14	11	0	0	0	76²	86	11	19	34	12.3	4.23	94	.281	.323	0	—	0	-1	-2	-1	-0.2
1984 Bal-A	0	3	.000	5	3	0	0	0	17²	22	2	17	4	19.9	9.17	42	.319	.453	0	—	0	-10	-10	-0	-0.8
Total 19	268	152	.638	558	521	211	53	4	3948	3349	303	1311	2212	10.7	2.86	125	.230	.296	85	.174	7	374	315	3	36.4
■ **LOWELL PALMER**				Palmer, Lowell Raymond			b: 8/18/47, Sacramento, Cal.		BR/TR, 6'1", 190 lbs.			Deb: 6/21/69													
1969 Phi-N	2	8	.200	26	9	1	1	0	90	91	12	47	68	14.4	5.20	68	.264	.362	3	.136	1	-16	-17	-0	-1.5
1970 Phi-N	1	2	.333	38	5	0	0	0	102	98	15	55	85	13.9	5.47	73	.255	.355	4	.148	1	-16	-17	-1	-1.5
1971 Phi-N	0	0	—	3	1	0	0	0	15	13	3	13	6	18.0	6.00	59	.236	.417	1	.200	-0	-4	-4	-0	-0.3
1972 StL-N	0	3	.000	16	2	0	0	0	34²	30	7	26	25	14.8	3.89	88	.244	.380	0	.000	-1	-2	-2	0	0.0
Cle-A	0	0	—	1	0	0	0	0	2	2	0	2	3	18.0	4.50	71	.222	.364	0	—	0	-0	-0	0	0.0
1974 SD-N	2	5	.286	22	8	1	0	0	73	68	9	59	52	16.5	5.67	63	.256	.404	2	.087	-1	-17	-17	-1	-1.8
Total 5	5	18	.217	106	25	2	1	0	316²	302	41	202	239	15.0	5.29	69	.255	.374	10	.122	-0	-55	-57	-2	-5.3
■ **EMILIO PALMERO**				Palmero, Emilio Antonio "Pal"			b: 6/13/1895, Guanabacoa, Cuba		d: 7/15/70, Toledo, Ohio			BL/TL, 5'11", 157 lbs.		Deb: 9/21/15										
1915 NY-N	0	2	.000	3	2	1	0	0	11²	10	0	9	8	17.0	3.09	83	.233	.400	1	.250	0	-0	-1	0	0.0
1916 NY-N	0	3	.000	4	1	0	0	0	15²	17	2	8	8	14.9	8.04	30	.288	.382	0	.000	-0	-9	-10	1	-0.8
1921 StL-A	4	7	.364	24	9	4	0	0	90	109	1	49	26	16.4	5.00	90	.319	.413	8	.216	1	-7	-5	2	-0.2
1926 Was-A	2	2	.500	7	3	0	0	0	17	22	1	15	6	20.1	4.76	81	.344	.475	1	.333	0	-1	-2	-0	-0.1
1928 Bos-N	0	1	.000	3	1	0	0	0	6²	14	0	2	0	21.6	5.40	72	.452	.485	0	.000	-0	-1	-1	-0	-0.1
Total 5	6	15	.286	41	16	5	0	0	141	172	4	83	48	17.0	5.17	77	.319	.420	10	.208	1	-19	-19	2	-1.1
■ **ED PALMQUIST**				Palmquist, Edwin Lee			b: 6/10/33, Los Angeles, Cal.		BR/TR, 6'3", 195 lbs.			Deb: 6/10/60													
1960 LA-N	0	1	.000	22	0	0	0	0	39	34	6	16	23	11.8	2.54	156	.243	.325	0	.000	-1	5	6	0	0.6
1961 LA-N	0	0	—	5	0	0	0	1	8²	10	0	7	5	19.7	6.23	70	.333	.487	0	—	0	-2	-2	0	-0.1
Min-A	1	1	.500	9	2	0	0	0	21	33	7	13	13	21.0	9.43	45	.359	.454	0	—	0	-13	-12	-1	-1.0
Total 2	1	3	.250	36	2	0	0	1	68²	77	13	36	41	15.6	5.11	80	.294	.391	0	.000	-1	-9	-8	1	-0.5
■ **JIM PANTHER**				Panther, James Edward			b: 3/1/45, Burlington, Iowa		BR/TR, 6'1", 190 lbs.			Deb: 4/05/71													
1971 Oak-A	0	1	.000	4	0	0	0	0	5²	10	1	5	4	23.8	11.12	30	.385	.484	0	.000	-0	-5	-5	0	-0.4
1972 Tex-A	5	9	.357	58	4	0	0	0	93²	101	8	46	44	14.6	4.13	73	.277	.365	1	.125	0	-11	-12	0	-1.2
1973 Atl-N	2	3	.400	23	0	0	0	0	30²	45	3	9	8	15.8	7.63	52	.363	.406	0	—	0	-14	-13	-1	-1.3
Total 3	7	13	.350	85	4	0	0	0	130	156	12	60	56	15.3	5.26	61	.303	.381	1	.111	-0	-30	-29	-0	-2.9
■ **JOHN PAPA**				Papa, John Paul			b: 12/5/40, Bridgeport, Conn.		BR/TR, 5'11", 190 lbs.			Deb: 4/11/61													
1961 Bal-A	0	0	—	2	0	0	0	0	1	2	1	3	3	45.0	18.00	22	.400	.625	0	—	0	-2	-2	0	-0.1
1962 Bal-A	0	0	—	1	0	0	0	0	1	3	0	1	0	36.0	27.00	14	.600	.667	0	—	0	-3	-3	0	-0.1
Total 2	0	0	—	3	0	0	0	0	2	5	1	4	3	40.5	22.50	17	.500	.643	0	—	0	-4	-4	0	-0.2
■ **AL PAPAI**			Papai, Alfred Thomas			b: 5/7/19, Divernon, Ill.		BR/TR, 6'3", 185 lbs.			Deb: 4/24/48														
1948 StL-N	0	1	.000	10	0	0	0	0	16	14	3	7	8	11.8	5.06	81	.241	.323	0	.000	-0	-2	-2	0	-0.1
1949 StL-A	4	11	.267	42	15	6	0	2	142¹	175	8	81	31	16.3	5.06	90	.298	.384	3	.079	-2	-14	-8	3	-0.6
1950 Bos-A	4	2	.667	16	3	2	0	2	50²	61	5	28	19	15.8	6.75	73	.293	.377	3	.176	-0	-12	-10	-0	-0.9
StL-N	1	0	1.000	13	0	0	0	0	19	21	0	14	7	16.6	5.21	82	.300	.417	0	.000	-0	-2	-2	0	-0.1
1955 Chi-A	0	0	—	7	0	0	0	0	11²	10	1	8	5	13.9	3.86	102	.244	.367	0	.000	-0	0	0	1	0.1
Total 4	9	14	.391	88	18	8	0	4	239²	281	17	138	70	15.8	5.37	84	.291	.381	6	.097	-3	-30	-22	4	-1.6
■ **LARRY PAPE**				Pape, Laurence Albert			b: 7/21/1883, Norwood, Ohio		d: 7/21/18, Swissvale, Pa.		BR/TR, 5'11", 175 lbs.		Deb: 7/06/09											
1909 Bos-A	2	0	1.000	11	3	2	1	2	58¹	46	0	12	18	9.7	2.01	125	.218	.276	3	.143	-1	3	3	-2	0.0
1911 Bos-A	10	8	.556	27	19	10	1	0	176¹	167	3	63	49	11.9	2.45	134	.264	.335	13	.203	-1	18	16	6	2.1
1912 Bos-A	1	1	.500	13	2	1	0	1	48²	74	0	16	17	17.0	4.99	68	.366	.418	4	.235	1	-9	-9	1	-0.6
Total 3	13	9	.591	51	24	13	2	3	283¹	287	3	91	84	12.4	2.80	112	.275	.339	20	.196	-1	12	11	4	1.5
■ **FRANK PAPISH**				Papish, Frank Richard "Pap"			b: 10/21/17, Pueblo, Colo.		d: 8/30/65, Pueblo, Colo.		BR/TL, 6'2", 192 lbs.		Deb: 5/08/45											
1945 Chi-A	4	4	.500	19	5	3	0	1	84¹	75	3	40	45	12.3	3.74	89	.241	.328	6	.231	1	-3	-4	1	-0.1
1946 Chi-A	7	5	.583	31	15	6	2	0	138	122	7	63	66	12.1	2.74	125	.243	.328	8	.186	0	12	10	1	1.1
1947 Chi-A	12	12	.500	38	26	6	1	3	199	185	6	98	79	12.9	3.26	112	.245	.333	5	.086	-5	10	9	-0	0.3
1948 Chi-A	2	8	.200	32	14	2	0	4	95¹	97	7	75	41	16.5	5.00	85	.265	.394	5	.185	-0	-8	-8	-1	-0.8
1949 Cle-A	1	0	1.000	25	3	1	0	1	62	54	3	39	23	13.5	3.19	125	.240	.352	1	.125	-0	7	5	1	0.6
1950 Pit-N	0	0	—	4	1	0	0	0	2¹	8	1	4	1	46.3	27.00	16	.533	.632	0	—	0	-6	-6	0	-0.4
Total 6	26	29	.473	149	64	18	3	9	581	541	26	319	255	13.4	3.58	103	.249	.346	25	.154	-5	12	7	0	0.7

YEAR TM/L	W	L	PCT	G	GS	CG	SH	SV	IP	H	HR	BB	SO	RAT	ERA	ERA+	OAV	OOB	BH	AVG	PB	PR	/A	PD	TPI
■ JOHN PAPPALAU Pappalau, John Joseph b: 4/3/1875, Albany, N.Y. d: 5/12/44, Albany, N.Y. 6′, 175 lbs. Deb: 6/09/1897																									
1897 Cle-N	0	1	1.000	2	1	1	0	0	12	22	0	6	3	21.0	10.50	43	.390	.448	0	.000	-0	-8	-8	0	-0.5
■ MILT PAPPAS Pappas, Milton Stephen "Gimpy" (b: Miltiades Stergios Papastegios) b: 5/11/39, Detroit, Mich. BR/TR, 6′3″, 190 lbs. Deb: 8/10/57																									
1957 Bal-A	0	0	—	4	0	0	0	0	9	6	0	3	3	9.0	1.00	359	.200	.273	0	.000	-0	3	3	0	0.3
1958 Bal-A	10	10	.500	31	21	3	0	0	135¹	135	8	48	72	12.3	4.06	89	.262	.327	6	.143	-0	-4	-7	2	-0.5
1959 Bal-A	15	9	.625	33	27	15	4	3	209¹	175	8	75	120	10.9	3.27	116	.226	.298	11	.139	-3	14	12	-1	0.8
1960 Bal-A	15	11	.577	30	27	11	3	0	205²	184	15	83	126	11.9	3.37	113	.243	.323	5	.043	-5	12	10	1	0.6
1961 Bal-A	13	9	.591	26	23	11	4	1	177²	134	16	78	89	11.1	3.04	129	.208	.301	9	.136	1	19	17	3	2.1
1962 Bal-A	12	10	.545	35	32	9	1	0	205¹	200	31	75	130	12.1	4.03	93	.257	.324	6	.087	-0	-1	-6	2	-0.4
1963 Bal-A	16	9	.640	34	32	11	4	0	216²	186	21	69	120	10.8	3.03	116	.233	.298	9	.127	-1	14	12	3	1.5
1964 Bal-A	16	7	.696	37	36	13	7	0	251²	225	21	48	157	10.0	2.97	120	.239	.281	12	.129	-2	18	17	-1	1.6
1965 Bal-A	13	9	.591	34	34	9	3	0	221¹	192	22	52	127	10.0	2.60	133	.233	.281	5	.071	-3	21	21	-3	1.6
1966 Cin-N	12	11	.522	33	32	6	2	0	209²	224	23	39	133	11.4	4.29	91	.275	.310	8	.107	-2	-16	-9	1	-0.9
1967 Cin-N	16	13	.552	34	32	5	3	0	217²	218	19	38	129	10.8	3.35	112	.259	.295	7	.097	-2	1	10	1	1.0
1968 Cin-N	2	5	.286	15	11	0	0	0	62²	70	9	10	43	11.8	5.60	56	.275	.307	1	.063	-1	-18	-17	-0	-1.8
Atl-N	10	8	.556	22	19	3	1	0	121¹	111	8	22	75	10.1	2.37	126	.246	.285	6	.162	2	8	8	-1	1.1
Yr	12	13	.480	37	30	3	1	0	184	181	17	32	118	10.6	3.47	88	.255	.294	4	.075	1	-10	-9	-1	-0.7
1969 *Atl-N	6	10	.375	26	24	1	0	0	144	149	14	44	72	12.3	3.63	99	.267	.325	7	.156	3	-0	-0	0	0.2
1970 Atl-N	2	2	.500	11	3	1	0	0	35²	44	6	7	25	13.4	6.06	71	.293	.333	0	.000	-1	-8	-7	0	-0.7
Chi-N	10	8	.556	21	20	6	2	0	144²	135	14	36	80	10.6	2.68	168	.248	.294	12	.240	5	22	29	-0	3.7
Yr	12	10	.545	32	23	7	2	0	180¹	179	20	43	105	11.1	3.34	133	.256	.300	3	.050	3	14	22	-0	3.0
1971 Chi-N	17	14	.548	35	35	14	**5**	0	261¹	279	25	62	99	11.9	3.51	112	.274	.319	14	.154	-1	-1	12	-1	1.2
1972 Chi-N	17	7	.708	29	28	10	3	0	195	187	18	29	80	10.3	2.77	138	.251	.287	13	.191	2	15	23	1	3.0
1973 Chi-N	7	12	.368	30	29	1	1	0	162	192	20	40	48	13.1	4.28	92	.299	.344	3	.063	-3	-11	-6	0	-0.7
Total 17	209	164	.560	520	465	129	43	4	3186	3046	298	858	1728	11.2	3.40	110	.252	.306	132	.123	-14	86	123	5	13.6
■ JIM PARK Park, James b: 11/10/1892, Richmond, Ky. d: 12/17/70, Lexington, Ky. BR/TR, 6′2″, 175 lbs. Deb: 9/07/15																									
1915 StL-A	2	0	1.000	3	3	1	0	0	22²	18	1	9	5	10.7	1.19	241	.214	.290	4	.400	1	4	4	-0	0.6
1916 StL-A	1	4	.200	26	6	1	0	0	79	69	2	25	26	10.8	2.62	105	.244	.307	2	.100	-1	2	1	-1	-0.1
1917 StL-A	1	1	.500	13	0	0	0	0	20¹	27	1	12	9	17.3	6.64	39	.333	.419	0	.000	-0	-9	-9	-0	-0.9
Total 3	4	5	.444	42	9	2	0	0	122	114	4	46	40	11.9	3.02	91	.254	.325	6	.188	-0	-3	-4	-2	-0.4
■ DOC PARKER Parker, Harley Park b: 6/14/1872, Theresa, N.Y. d: 3/3/41, Chicago, Ill. BR/TR, 6′2″, 200 lbs. Deb: 7/11/1893																									
1893 Chi-N	0	0	—	1	0	0	0	1	2	5	0	1	0	27.0	13.50	34	.458	.503	0	.000	-0	-2	-2	0	-0.1
1895 Chi-N	4	2	.667	7	6	5	1	0	51¹	65	1	9	9	13.0	3.68	138	.304	.332	7	.318	1	6	8	0	0.8
1896 Chi-N	1	5	.167	9	7	7	0	0	73	100	3	27	15	15.7	6.16	74	.323	.377	10	.278	0	-15	-13	1	-0.9
1901 Cin-N	0	1	.000	1	1	1	0	0	8	26	1	2	0	31.5	15.75	20	.531	.550	0	.000	-0	-11	-11	0	-0.7
Total 4	5	8	.385	18	14	13	1	1	134¹	196	5	39	24	15.7	5.90	79	.336	.378	17	.274	0	-21	-18	1	-0.9
■ HARRY PARKER Parker, Harry William b: 9/14/47, Highland, Ill. BR/TR, 6′3″, 190 lbs. Deb: 8/08/70																									
1970 StL-N	1	1	.500	7	4	0	0	0	22¹	24	0	15	9	15.7	3.22	128	.276	.382	2	.250	0	2	2	0	0.3
1971 StL-N	0	0	—	4	0	0	0	0	5	6	2	2	2	14.4	7.20	50	.286	.348	0	—	0	-2	-2	-0	-0.1
1973 *NY-N	8	4	.667	38	9	0	0	5	96²	79	7	36	63	11.0	3.35	108	.217	.293	4	.174	-0	3	3	-0	0.2
1974 NY-N	4	12	.250	40	16	1	0	4	131	145	10	46	58	13.3	3.92	91	.281	.343	0	.000	-4	-4	-5	-1	-1.0
1975 NY-N	2	3	.400	18	1	0	0	2	34²	37	2	19	22	14.5	4.41	78	.272	.361	0	.000	1	-3	-4	-0	-0.4
StL-N	0	1	.000	14	0	0	0	1	18²	21	3	10	13	14.9	6.27	60	.288	.373	0	.000	-0	-5	-5	1	-0.4
Yr	2	4	.333	32	1	0	0	3	53¹	58	5	29	35	14.7	5.06	70	.278	.366	5	1.667	1	-9	-9	-0	-0.6
1976 Cle-A	0	0	—	3	0	0	0	0	7	3	0	0	5	3.9	0.00	—	.136	.136	0	—	0	3	3	0	0.3
Total 6	15	21	.417	124	30	1	0	12	315¹	315	24	128	172	12.8	3.85	94	.258	.332	6	.086	-3	-7	-8	-0	-0.9
■ CLAY PARKER Parker, James Clayton b: 12/19/62, Columbia, La. BR/TR, 6′1″, 185 lbs. Deb: 9/14/87																									
1987 Sea-A	0	0	—	3	1	0	0	0	7²	15	2	4	8	23.5	10.57	45	.405	.476	0	—	0	-5	-5	0	-0.3
1989 NY-A	4	5	.444	22	17	2	0	0	120	123	9	31	53	11.7	3.68	105	.264	.313	0	—	0	3	3	1	0.3
1990 NY-A	1	1	.500	5	2	0	0	0	22	19	5	7	20	10.6	4.50	87	.229	.289	0	—	0	-1	-1	-0	-0.1
Det-A	2	2	.500	24	1	0	0	0	51	45	6	25	20	12.5	3.18	124	.242	.335	0	—	0	4	4	1	0.5
Yr	3	3	.500	29	3	0	0	0	73	64	11	32	40	12.0	3.58	110	.237	.320	0	—	0	3	3	0	0.4
Total 3	7	8	.467	54	21	2	0	0	200²	202	22	67	101	12.2	3.90	101	.262	.324	0	—	0	0	1	0.4
■ JAY PARKER Parker, Jay b: 7/8/1874, Theresa, N.Y. d: 6/8/35, Hartford, Mich. BR/TR, 5′11″, 185 lbs. Deb: 9/27/1899																									
1899 Pit-N	0	0	—	1	1	0	0	0	0	0	0	2	0	—	∞	—	—	1.000	0	—	0	-2	-2	0	-0.1
■ ROY PARKER Parker, Roy W. b: 1897, BR/TR, 6′2″, 185 lbs. Deb: 9/10/19																									
1919 StL-N	0	0	—	2	0	0	0	0	2	6	0	1	0	36.0	31.50	9	.333	.400	0	—	0	-6	-6	0	-0.5
■ SLICKER PARKS Parks, Vernon Henry b: 11/10/1895, Dallas, Mich. d: 2/21/78, Royal Oak, Mich. BR/TR, 5′10″, 158 lbs. Deb: 7/11/21																									
1921 Det-A	3	2	.600	10	1	0	0	0	25¹	33	2	16	10	17.8	5.68	75	.306	.400	1	.111	-1	-4	-4	-1	-0.4
■ BILL PARKS Parks, William Robert b: 6/4/1849, Easton, Pa. d: 10/10/11, Easton, Pa. 5′8″, 150 lbs. Deb: 4/26/1875 ♦																									
1875 Was-n	4	8	.333	14	11	9	0	0	106²	148	5	6		13.0	4.05	65	.285	.293	20	.179	-3	-19	-17		-1.7
Phi-n	0	0	—	2	0	0	0	0	5¹	13	0	1		23.6	6.75	37	.419	.438	1	.167	-0	-3	-3		-0.1
Yr	4	8	.333	16	11	9	0	0	112	161	5	7		13.5	4.18	63	.292	.301	0	.000	-4	-21	-19		-1.8
■ ROY PARMELEE Parmelee, Le Roy Earl "Tarzan" b: 4/25/07, Lambertville, Mich d: 8/31/81, Monroe, Mich. BR/TR, 6′1″, 190 lbs. Deb: 9/28/29																									
1929 NY-N	1	0	1.000	2	1	0	0	0	7	13	1	3	1	21.9	9.00	51	.481	.548	1	.500	0	-3	-3	0	-0.2
1930 NY-N	0	1	.000	11	1	0	0	0	21	18	3	26	19	18.9	9.43	50	.228	.419	1	.250	-1	-10	-11	0	-0.8
1931 NY-N	2	2	.500	13	5	4	0	0	58²	47	1	33	30	12.7	3.68	100	.223	.336	4	.200	-0	1	0	0	0.0
1932 NY-N	0	3	.000	8	3	0	0	0	25¹	25	0	14	23	14.6	3.91	95	.250	.353	2	.400	1	-0	-1	0	0.0
1933 NY-N	13	8	.619	32	32	14	3	0	218¹	191	9	77	132	11.6	3.17	101	.232	.309	19	.235	4	1	1	-0	0.4
1934 NY-N	10	6	.625	22	20	7	2	0	152²	134	6	60	83	11.8	3.42	113	**.238**	.318	11	.200	2	11	8	2	1.0
1935 NY-N	14	10	.583	34	31	13	0	0	226	214	20	97	79	12.7	4.22	91	.249	.332	18	.209	3	-5	-9	2	-0.4
1936 StL-N	11	11	.500	37	28	9	0	2	221	226	13	107	79	14.0	4.56	86	.270	.360	15	.197	-0	-13	-15	-0	-1.4
1937 Chi-N	7	8	.467	33	18	8	0	0	145²	165	13	79	55	15.5	5.13	78	.286	.379	9	.173	0	-20	-19	1	-1.6
1939 Phi-A	1	6	.143	14	5	0	0	1	44²	42	2	35	13	16.1	6.45	73	.235	.369	2	.133	-1	-9	-9	0	-0.7
Total 10	59	55	.518	206	144	55	5	3	1120¹	1075	68	531	514	13.3	4.27	89	.253	.343	82	.207	9	-45	-58	4	-3.7
■ MEL PARNELL Parnell, Melvin Lloyd "Dusty" b: 6/13/22, New Orleans, La. BL/TL, 6′, 180 lbs. Deb: 4/20/47																									
1947 Bos-A	2	3	.400	15	5	1	0	0	50²	60	1	27	23	15.6	6.39	61	.296	.381	1	.056	-2	-15	-14	-1	-1.5
1948 Bos-A	15	8	.652	35	27	16	1	0	212	205	7	90	77	12.7	3.14	140	.252	.330	13	.162	-4	27	29	2	2.8
1949 Bos-A	**25**	7	.781	39	33	**27**	4	2	295¹	258	8	134	122	12.1	2.77	157	.237	.324	29	.254	2	**47**	**52**	-0	**5.7**
1950 Bos-A	18	10	.643	40	31	21	2	3	249	244	17	106	93	12.9	3.61	136	.259	.338	19	.194	-1	27	36	5	4.0
1951 Bos-A	18	11	.621	36	29	11	3	2	221	187	17	77	77	12.5	3.26	137	.230	.272	25	.309	4	21	30	0	**3.6**
1952 Bos-A	12	12	.500	33	29	15	3	2	214	207	16	89	107	12.7	3.62	109	.255	.332	8	.095	-4	1	8	1	0.6
1953 Bos-A	21	8	.724	38	34	12	5	0	241	217	15	116	136	12.6	3.06	137	.239	.328	21	.223	1	25	31	-2	3.2
1954 Bos-A	3	7	.300	19	15	4	1	0	92¹	104	7	35	38	13.6	3.70	111	.287	.352	3	.088	-2	0	4	0	0.3

YEAR TM/L	W	L	PCT	G	GS	CG	SH	SV	IP	H	HR	BB	SO	RAT	ERA	ERA+	OAV	OOB	BH	AVG	PB	PR	/A	PD	TPI
1955 Bos-A	2	3	.400	13	9	0	0	1	46	62	12	25	18	17.2	7.83	55	.318	.398	6	.316	1	-20	-18	0	-1.5
1956 Bos-A	7	6	.538	21	20	6	1	0	131¹	129	13	59	41	12.9	3.77	123	.256	.335	7	.152	-2	6	12	-0	1.0
Total 10	123	75	.621	289	232	113	20	10	1752²	1715	104	758	732	12.8	3.50	125	.257	.336	132	.198	-7	119	170	5	18.2

■ RUBE PARNHAM
Parnham, James Arthur   b: 2/1/1894, Heidelberg, Pa.   d: 11/25/63, McKeesport, Pa.   BR/TR, 6'3", 185 lbs.   Deb: 9/20/16

YEAR TM/L	W	L	PCT	G	GS	CG	SH	SV	IP	H	HR	BB	SO	RAT	ERA	ERA+	OAV	OOB	BH	AVG	PB	PR	/A	PD	TPI
1916 Phi-A	2	1	.667	4	3	2	0	0	24²	27	0	13	8	14.6	4.01	72	.300	.388	3	.273	1	-3	-3	1	-0.1
1917 Phi-A	0	1	.000	2	2	0	0	0	11	12	1	9	4	17.2	4.09	67	.316	.447	0	.000	-0	-2	-2	0	-0.1
Total 2	2	2	.500	6	5	2	0	0	35²	39	1	22	12	15.4	4.04	70	.305	.407	3	.214	0	-5	-5	1	-0.2

■ JEFF PARRETT
Parrett, Jeffrey Dale   b: 8/26/61, Indianapolis, Ind.   BR/TR, 6'4", 185 lbs.   Deb: 4/11/86

YEAR TM/L	W	L	PCT	G	GS	CG	SH	SV	IP	H	HR	BB	SO	RAT	ERA	ERA+	OAV	OOB	BH	AVG	PB	PR	/A	PD	TPI
1986 Mon-N	0	1	.000	12	0	0	0	0	20¹	19	3	13	21	14.2	4.87	76	.247	.356	1	.500	0	-3	-3	0	-0.1
1987 Mon-N	7	6	.538	45	0	0	0	6	62	53	8	30	56	12.0	4.21	100	.229	.318	0	.000	-1	-1	-0	-0	0.0
1988 Mon-N	12	4	.750	61	0	0	0	6	91²	66	8	45	62	11.0	2.65	136	.214	.316	0	—	0	8	10	-1	1.0
1989 Phi-N	12	6	.667	72	0	0	0	6	105²	90	6	44	98	11.4	2.98	119	.232	.310	0	.000	-1	6	7	-2	0.5
1990 Phi-N	4	9	.308	47	5	0	0	1	81²	92	10	36	69	14.2	5.18	74	.293	.368	0	.000	-1	-13	-12	-0	-1.3
Atl-N	1	1	.500	20	0	0	0	1	27	27	1	19	17	15.7	3.00	130	.281	.405	1	1.000	0	2	3	0	0.4
Yr	5	10	.333	67	5	0	0	2	108²	119	11	55	86	14.5	4.64	83	.289	.374	1	.000	-1	-10	-10	-0	-0.9
Total 5	36	27	.571	257	5	0	0	20	388¹	347	36	187	323	12.4	3.66	102	.245	.335	2	.087	-1	0	4	-3	0.5

■ MIKE PARROTT
Parrott, Michael Everett Arch   b: 12/6/54, Oxnard, Cal.   BR/TR, 6'4", 210 lbs.   Deb: 9/05/77

YEAR TM/L	W	L	PCT	G	GS	CG	SH	SV	IP	H	HR	BB	SO	RAT	ERA	ERA+	OAV	OOB	BH	AVG	PB	PR	/A	PD	TPI
1977 Bal-A	0	0	—	3	0	0	0	0	4¹	4	0	2	2	12.5	2.08	183	.250	.333	0	—	0	1	1	0	0.1
1978 Sea-A	1	5	.167	27	10	0	0	1	82¹	108	8	32	41	15.6	5.14	74	.316	.379	0	—	0	-13	-12	0	-1.1
1979 Sea-A	14	12	.538	38	30	13	2	0	229¹	231	17	86	127	12.7	3.77	116	.267	.338	0	—	0	11	15	2	1.8
1980 Sea-A	1	16	.059	27	16	1	0	3	94	136	16	42	53	17.1	7.28	57	.348	.412	0	—	0	-34	-33	3	-2.7
1981 Sea-A	3	6	.333	24	12	0	0	1	85	102	3	28	43	13.9	5.08	76	.299	.354	0	—	0	-13	-12	0	-1.1
Total 5	19	39	.328	119	68	14	2	5	495	581	44	190	266	14.2	4.87	85	.297	.363	0	—	0	-48	-41	6	-3.0

■ TOM PARROTT
Parrott, Thomas William "Tacky Tom"   b: 4/10/1868, Portland, Ore.   d: 1/1/32, Dundee, Ore.   BR/TR, 5'10.5", 170 lbs.   Deb: 6/18/1893 ◆

YEAR TM/L	W	L	PCT	G	GS	CG	SH	SV	IP	H	HR	BB	SO	RAT	ERA	ERA+	OAV	OOB	BH	AVG	PB	PR	/A	PD	TPI
1893 Chi-N	0	3	.000	4	3	2	0	0	27	35	1	17	7	17.3	6.67	69	.305	.394	7	.259	-0	-6	-6	-1	-0.4
Cin-N	10	7	.588	22	17	11	1	0	154	174	1	70	33	14.3	4.09	117	.276	.349	13	.191	-3	10	12	2	0.9
Yr	10	10	.500	26	20	13	1	0	181	209	2	87	40	14.7	4.48	106	.281	.356	2	.021	-3	4	6	1	0.5
1894 Cin-N	17	19	.472	41	36	31	1	1	308²	402	19	126	61	15.4	5.60	99	.311	.373	74	.323	8	-9	-1	3	1.3
1895 Cin-N	11	18	.379	41	31	23	0	3	263¹	382	8	76	57	15.7	5.47	91	.333	.375	69	.343	11	-20	-14	3	0.5
1896 StL-N	1	1	.500	7	2	2	0	0	42	62	4	18	8	17.1	6.21	70	.340	.399	138	.291	1	-9	-9	-0	-0.6
Total 4	39	48	.448	115	89	69	2	4	795	1055	33	307	166	15.4	5.33	96	.314	.371	301	.301	18	-34	-19	6	1.7

■ JIGGS PARSON
Parson, William Edwin   b: 12/28/1885, Parker, S.Dak.   d: 5/19/67, Los Angeles, Cal.   BR/TR, 6'2", 180 lbs.   Deb: 5/16/10

YEAR TM/L	W	L	PCT	G	GS	CG	SH	SV	IP	H	HR	BB	SO	RAT	ERA	ERA+	OAV	OOB	BH	AVG	PB	PR	/A	PD	TPI
1910 Bos-N	0	2	.000	10	4	0	0	0	35¹	35	2	26	7	16.0	3.82	87	.278	.409	1	.083	-1	-3	-2	0	-0.2
1911 Bos-N	0	1	.000	7	0	0	0	0	25	36	2	15	7	19.8	6.48	59	.375	.478	2	.200	-0	-9	-7	-0	-0.7
Total 2	0	3	.000	17	4	0	0	0	60¹	71	4	41	14	17.6	4.92	72	.320	.439	3	.136	-2	-12	-9	-0	-0.9

■ CHARLIE PARSONS
Parsons, Charles James   b: 7/18/1863, Cherry Flats, Pa.   d: 3/24/36, Mansfield, Pa.   TL, 5'10", 160 lbs.   Deb: 5/29/1886

YEAR TM/L	W	L	PCT	G	GS	CG	SH	SV	IP	H	HR	BB	SO	RAT	ERA	ERA+	OAV	OOB	BH	AVG	PB	PR	/A	PD	TPI
1886 Bos-N	0	2	.000	2	2	2	0	0	16	20	0	4	5	13.5	3.94	81	.294	.333	3	.375	-1	-1	-1	-0	0.0
1887 NY-a	1	1	.500	4	4	4	0	0	34	51	0	6	5	15.1	4.50	94	.334	.360	3	.200	-1	-1	-1	-0	0.0
1890 Cle-N	0	1	.000	2	1	0	0	0	9	12	0	6	2	18.0	6.00	60	.311	.404	3	.750	1	-2	-2	0	0.0
Total 3	1	4	.200	8	7	6	0	0	59	83	0	16	12	15.1	4.58	84	.320	.360	9	.333	2	-4	-5	-0	0.0

■ TOM PARSONS
Parsons, Thomas Anthony   b: 9/13/39, Lakeville, Conn.   BR/TR, 6'7", 210 lbs.   Deb: 9/05/63

YEAR TM/L	W	L	PCT	G	GS	CG	SH	SV	IP	H	HR	BB	SO	RAT	ERA	ERA+	OAV	OOB	BH	AVG	PB	PR	/A	PD	TPI
1963 Pit-N	0	1	.000	1	1	0	0	0	4¹	4	1	2	2	18.7	8.31	40	.368	.429	0	.000	-0	-2	-2	0	-0.1
1964 NY-N	1	2	.333	4	2	1	0	0	19¹	20	1	6	10	12.1	4.19	85	.274	.329	0	.000	-1	-1	-1	-0	-0.1
1965 NY-N	1	10	.091	35	11	1	1	1	90²	108	17	17	58	12.4	4.67	76	.290	.321	1	.056	-1	-11	-11	1	-1.1
Total 3	2	13	.133	40	14	2	1	1	114¹	135	19	25	70	12.6	4.72	75	.291	.327	1	.037	-2	-15	-15	1	-1.3

■ BILL PARSONS
Parsons, William Raymond   b: 8/17/48, Riverside, Cal.   BR/TR, 6'6", 195 lbs.   Deb: 4/13/71

YEAR TM/L	W	L	PCT	G	GS	CG	SH	SV	IP	H	HR	BB	SO	RAT	ERA	ERA+	OAV	OOB	BH	AVG	PB	PR	/A	PD	TPI
1971 Mil-A	13	17	.433	36	35	12	4	0	244²	219	19	93	139	11.6	3.20	108	.241	.315	12	.167	3	7	7	0	1.2
1972 Mil-A	13	13	.500	33	30	10	2	0	214	194	27	68	111	11.1	3.91	77	.240	.301	11	.164	0	-20	-21	-3	-2.4
1973 Mil-A	3	6	.333	20	17	0	0	0	59²	59	6	67	30	19.0	6.79	55	.257	.424	0	—	0	-20	-20	-0	-1.9
1974 Oak-A	0	0	—	4	0	0	0	0	2	1	0	3	2	18.0	0.00	—	.143	.400	0	—	0	1	1	0	0.1
Total 4	29	36	.446	93	82	22	6	0	520¹	473	52	231	282	12.3	3.89	85	.242	.325	23	.165	3	-32	-33	-3	-3.0

■ STAN PARTENHEIMER
Partenheimer, Stanwood Wendell "Party"   b: 10/21/22, Chicopee Falls, Mass.   d: 1/28/89, Wilson, N.C.   BR/TL, 5'11", 175 lbs.   Deb: 5/27/44

YEAR TM/L	W	L	PCT	G	GS	CG	SH	SV	IP	H	HR	BB	SO	RAT	ERA	ERA+	OAV	OOB	BH	AVG	PB	PR	/A	PD	TPI
1944 Bos-A	0	0	—	1	1	0	0	0	1	3	0	2	0	45.0	18.00	19	.500	.625	0	.000	-0	-2	-2	0	-0.1
1945 StL-N	0	0	—	8	2	0	0	0	13¹	12	2	16	6	18.9	6.08	62	.250	.438	0	.000	-0	-3	-3	0	-0.3
Total 2	0	0	—	9	3	0	0	0	14¹	15	2	18	6	20.7	6.91	54	.278	.458	0	.000	-1	-5	-5	0	-0.4

■ BILL PASCHALL
Paschall, William Herbert   b: 4/22/54, Norfolk, Va.   BR/TR, 6', 175 lbs.   Deb: 9/20/78

YEAR TM/L	W	L	PCT	G	GS	CG	SH	SV	IP	H	HR	BB	SO	RAT	ERA	ERA+	OAV	OOB	BH	AVG	PB	PR	/A	PD	TPI
1978 KC-A	0	1	.000	2	0	0	0	1	8	6	0	0	5	7.9	3.38	113	.207	.233	0	—	0	0	0	-0	0.0
1979 KC-A	0	1	.000	7	0	0	0	0	13²	18	2	5	3	16.5	6.59	65	.300	.373	0	—	0	-4	-4	0	-0.2
1981 KC-A	0	0	—	2	0	0	0	0	2	2	0	1	1	9.0	4.50	80	.286	.286	0	—	0	-0	-0	0	0.0
Total 3	0	2	.000	11	0	0	0	1	23²	26	2	5	9	12.9	5.32	76	.271	.327	0	—	0	-3	-3	-0	-0.2

■ CAMILO PASCUAL
Pascual, Camilo Alberto (Lus) "Little Potato"   b: 1/20/34, Havana, Cuba   BR/TR, 5'11", 170 lbs.   Deb: 4/15/54 C

YEAR TM/L	W	L	PCT	G	GS	CG	SH	SV	IP	H	HR	BB	SO	RAT	ERA	ERA+	OAV	OOB	BH	AVG	PB	PR	/A	PD	TPI
1954 Was-A	4	7	.364	48	4	1	0	3	119¹	126	7	61	60	14.6	4.22	84	.276	.368	4	.133	-0	-7	-9	3	-0.6
1955 Was-A	2	12	.143	43	16	1	0	0	129	158	5	70	82	16.3	6.14	62	.311	.401	7	.219	0	-31	-33	2	-2.9
1956 Was-A	6	18	.250	39	27	6	0	2	188²	194	33	89	162	13.8	5.87	74	.261	.345	8	.138	-2	-36	-32	0	-3.1
1957 Was-A	8	17	.320	29	26	8	2	0	175²	168	11	76	113	12.7	4.10	95	.258	.338	7	.140	-2	-6	-4	1	-0.4
1958 Was-A	8	12	.400	31	27	6	2	0	177¹	166	14	60	146	11.6	3.15	121	.248	.313	9	.158	-1	12	13	0	1.3
1959 Was-A	17	10	.630	32	30	**17**	**6**	0	238²	202	10	69	185	10.3	2.64	148	.226	.284	26	.302	6	32	34	4	**4.8**
1960 Was-A	12	8	.600	26	22	8	3	0	151²	139	11	53	143	11.5	3.03	128	.240	.306	9	.176	3	14	15	-1	1.7
1961 Min-A	15	16	.484	35	33	15	**8**	0	252¹	205	26	100	**221**	11.0	3.46	123	.217	.294	14	.165	0	16	22	0	2.3
1962 Min-A	20	11	.645	34	33	**18**	5	0	257²	236	25	59	**206**	10.4	3.32	123	.241	.286	26	.268	8	19	22	-0	3.2
1963 Min-A	21	9	.700	31	31	**18**	3	0	248¹	205	21	81	**202**	10.5	2.46	148	.224	.289	23	.250	6	32	**33**	-1	4.2
1964 Min-A	15	12	.556	36	36	14	1	0	267¹	245	30	98	213	11.6	3.30	108	.241	.309	11	.181	4	10	8	-0	1.2
1965 *Min-A	9	3	.750	27	27	5	1	0	156	126	12	63	96	11.2	3.35	106	.217	.299	12	.200	3	2	4	2	0.9
1966 Min-A	8	6	.571	21	19	2	0	0	103	113	9	30	56	12.7	4.89	73	.278	.330	8	.216	1	-17	-15	3	-1.1
1967 Was-A	12	10	.545	28	27	5	1	0	164²	147	15	43	106	10.5	3.28	96	.236	.289	9	.176	1	-1	-2	-0	0.0
1968 Was-A	13	12	.520	31	31	8	4	0	201	181	11	59	111	10.9	2.69	109	.239	.298	12	.185	1	7	5	2	0.9
1969 Was-A	2	5	.286	14	13	0	0	0	55¹	49	12	38	34	15.0	6.83	51	.239	.371	4	.235	0	-20	-21	0	-1.9
Cin-N	0	0	—	5	1	0	0	0	7¹	14	2	4	3	22.1	8.59	44	.424	.486	0	—	0	-4	-4	-0	-0.3
1970 LA-N	0	0	—	10	0	0	0	0	14	12	2	5	8	11.6	2.57	149	.231	.310	0	—	0	2	2	0	0.2
1971 Cle-A	2	2	.500	9	1	0	0	0	23¹	17	0	11	20	11.2	3.09	124	.205	.305	3	.600	1	1	2	1	0.4
Total 18	174	170	.506	529	404	132	36	10	2930²	2703	256	1069	2167	11.8	3.63	103	.244	.314	198	.205	30	26	38	13	10.7

■ CARLOS PASCUAL
Pascual, Carlos Alberto (Lus)   b: 3/13/31, Havana, Cuba   BR/TR, 5'6", 165 lbs.   Deb: 9/24/50

YEAR TM/L	W	L	PCT	G	GS	CG	SH	SV	IP	H	HR	BB	SO	RAT	ERA	ERA+	OAV	OOB	BH	AVG	PB	PR	/A	PD	TPI
1950 Was-A	1	1	.500	2	2	2	0	0	17	12	0	8	3	11.1	2.12	212	.194	.296	1	.250	0	5	4	-1	0.4

YEAR TM/L	W	L	PCT	G	GS	CG	SH	SV	IP	H	HR	BB	SO	RAT	ERA	ERA+	OAV	OOB	BH	AVG	PB	PR	/A	PD	TPI

■ LARRY PASHNICK
Pashnick, Larry John b: 4/25/56, Lincoln Park, Mich. BR/TR, 6'3", 205 lbs. Deb: 4/10/82

YEAR TM/L	W	L	PCT	G	GS	CG	SH	SV	IP	H	HR	BB	SO	RAT	ERA	ERA+	OAV	OOB	BH	AVG	PB	PR	/A	PD	TPI
1982 Det-A	4	4	.500	28	13	1	0	0	94^1	110	15	25	19	13.0	4.01	101	.297	.343	0	—	0	1	1	0	0.0
1983 Det-A	1	3	.250	12	6	0	0	0	37^2	48	5	18	17	16.5	5.26	74	.308	.390	0	—	0	-5	-6	1	-0.4
1984 Min-A	2	1	.667	13	1	0	0	0	38^1	38	3	11	10	12.0	3.52	119	.260	.321	0	—	0	2	3	0	0.3
Total 3	7	8	.467	53	20	1	0	0	170^1	196	25	54	46	13.5	4.17	97	.292	.350	0	—	0	-2	-2	1	-0.1

■ CLAUDE PASSEAU
Passeau, Claude William b: 4/9/09, Wayensboro, Miss. BR/TR, 6'3", 198 lbs. Deb: 9/29/35

YEAR TM/L	W	L	PCT	G	GS	CG	SH	SV	IP	H	HR	BB	SO	RAT	ERA	ERA+	OAV	OOB	BH	AVG	PB	PR	/A	PD	TPI
1935 Pit-N	0	1	.000	1	1	0	0	0	3	7	0	2	1	27.0	12.00	34	.500	.563	0	.000	-0	-3	-3	0	-0.1
1936 Phi-N	11	15	.423	49	21	8	2	3	217^1	247	7	55	85	12.7	3.48	130	.280	.325	22	.282	4	13	26	1	3.2
1937 Phi-N	14	18	.438	50	34	18	1	2	**292^1**	348	16	79	135	13.3	4.34	100	.296	.343	21	.196	-0	-14	-0	-0	0.1
1938 Phi-N	11	18	.379	44	33	15	0	1	239	281	8	93	100	14.4	4.52	86	.287	.354	13	.162	-2	-19	-17	3	-1.5
1939 Phi-N	2	4	.333	8	8	4	1	0	53^1	54	1	25	29	13.5	4.22	95	.263	.346	4	.200	-0	-2	-1	-0	-0.1
Chi-N	13	9	.591	34	27	13	1	3	221	215	8	48	108	10.9	3.05	129	.254	.297	12	.156	-1	21	22	1	2.2
Yr	15	13	.536	42	35	17	2	3	274^1	269	9	73	**137**	11.4	3.28	120	.255	.306	2	.021	-2	19	20	1	2.1
1940 Chi-N	20	13	.606	46	31	20	4	5	280^2	259	8	59	124	10.3	2.50	150	.237	.278	20	.204	6	42	39	1	4.8
1941 Chi-N	14	14	.500	34	30	20	3	0	231	262	10	52	80	12.3	3.35	105	.281	.320	19	.221	4	7	4	-0	0.8
1942 Chi-N	19	14	.576	35	34	24	3	0	278^1	284	13	74	89	11.7	2.68	119	.260	.309	19	.181	1	20	16	1	1.9
1943 Chi-N	15	12	.556	35	31	18	1	1	257	245	10	66	93	11.0	2.91	115	.249	.299	19	.198	1	14	12	1	1.5
1944 Chi-N	15	9	.625	34	27	18	2	3	227	234	8	50	89	11.3	2.89	122	.266	.306	13	.162	-1	18	16	1	1.7
1945 *Chi-N	17	9	.654	34	27	19	**5**	1	227	205	4	59	98	10.5	2.46	149	.238	.289	17	.187	1	34	**30**	3	**3.6**
1946 Chi-N	9	8	.529	21	21	10	2	0	129^1	118	5	42	47	11.2	3.13	106	.237	.298	10	.204	3	4	3	1	0.7
1947 Chi-N	2	6	.250	19	6	1	1	2	63^1	97	7	24	26	17.3	6.25	63	.353	.407	0	.000	-2	-19	-16	-1	-1.7
Total 13	162	150	.519	444	331	188	26	21	2719^2	2856	105	728	1104	12.0	3.32	113	.267	.316	189	.192	13	120	128	10	17.1

■ FRANK PASTORE
Pastore, Frank Enrico b: 8/21/57, Alhambra, Cal. BR/TR, 6'2", 188 lbs. Deb: 4/04/79

YEAR TM/L	W	L	PCT	G	GS	CG	SH	SV	IP	H	HR	BB	SO	RAT	ERA	ERA+	OAV	OOB	BH	AVG	PB	PR	/A	PD	TPI
1979 *Cin-N	6	7	.462	30	9	2	1	4	95^1	102	8	23	63	11.9	4.25	88	.271	.315	4	.160	-0	-5	-5	0	-0.5
1980 Cin-N	13	7	.650	27	27	9	2	0	184^2	161	13	42	110	9.9	3.27	109	.233	.277	10	.156	-1	7	6	-1	0.5
1981 Cin-N	4	9	.308	22	22	2	1	0	132	125	11	35	81	11.1	4.02	88	.247	.300	5	.114	-2	-8	-7	-2	-1.0
1982 Cin-N	8	13	.381	31	29	3	2	0	188^1	210	13	57	94	13.0	3.97	93	.286	.341	10	.172	1	-8	-6	-1	-0.5
1983 Cin-N	9	12	.429	36	29	4	1	0	184^1	207	20	64	93	13.3	4.88	78	.290	.349	11	.186	2	-26	-22	-1	-2.1
1984 Cin-N	3	8	.273	24	16	1	0	0	98^1	110	10	40	53	14.0	6.50	58	.285	.357	2	.071	-2	-32	-30	0	-2.9
1985 Cin-N	2	1	.667	17	6	1	0	0	54	60	1	16	29	12.8	3.83	99	.287	.341	2	.143	-0	-1	-0	-0	0.0
1986 Min-A	3	1	.750	33	1	0	0	2	49^1	54	4	24	18	14.2	4.01	107	.283	.363	0	—	0	1	2	-0	0.1
Total 8	48	58	.453	220	139	22	7	6	986^1	1029	80	301	541	12.3	4.29	87	.270	.326	44	.151	-2	-72	-62	-4	-6.4

■ JIM PASTORIUS
Pastorius, James W. "Sunny Jim" b: 7/12/1881, Pittsburgh, Pa. d: 5/10/41, Pittsburgh, Pa. BL/TL, 5'9", 165 lbs. Deb: 4/15/06

YEAR TM/L	W	L	PCT	G	GS	CG	SH	SV	IP	H	HR	BB	SO	RAT	ERA	ERA+	OAV	OOB	BH	AVG	PB	PR	/A	PD	TPI
1906 Bro-N	10	14	.417	29	24	16	3	0	211^2	225	4	69	58	12.6	3.61	70	.274	.333	10	.141	-0	-23	-26	-1	-2.8
1907 Bro-N	16	12	.571	28	26	20	4	0	222	218	2	77	70	12.2	2.35	100	.264	.331	15	.205	3	-3	-0	-0	0.2
1908 Bro-N	4	20	.167	28	25	16	2	0	213^2	171	5	74	54	10.6	2.44	96	.216	.288	8	.129	-0	-2	-2	1	-0.1
1909 Bro-N	1	9	.100	12	9	5	1	0	79^2	91	4	58	23	16.9	5.76	45	.313	.429	2	.080	-1	-28	-28	1	-2.6
Total 4	31	55	.360	97	84	57	10	0	727	705	15	278	205	12.4	3.12	78	.258	.330	35	.152	1	-50	-56	1	-5.3

■ JOE PATE
Pate, Joseph William b: 6/6/1892, Alice, Tex. d: 12/26/48, Fort Worth, Tex. BL/TL, 5'10", 184 lbs. Deb: 4/15/26

YEAR TM/L	W	L	PCT	G	GS	CG	SH	SV	IP	H	HR	BB	SO	RAT	ERA	ERA+	OAV	OOB	BH	AVG	PB	PR	/A	PD	TPI
1926 Phi-A	9	0	1.000	47	2	0	0	6	113	109	3	51	24	12.9	2.71	154	.262	.345	4	.148	-0	**16**	**18**	4	2.2
1927 Phi-A	0	3	.000	32	0	0	0	6	53^2	67	3	21	14	14.9	5.20	82	.318	.382	3	.300	1	-6	-6	0	-0.3
Total 2	9	3	.750	79	2	0	0	12	166^2	176	6	72	38	13.6	3.51	120	.281	.358	7	.189	1	10	13	4	1.9

■ CASE PATTEN
Patten, Case Lyman "Casey" b: 5/7/1876, Westport, N.Y. d: 5/31/35, Rochester, N.Y. BB/TL, 6', 175 lbs. Deb: 5/04/01

YEAR TM/L	W	L	PCT	G	GS	CG	SH	SV	IP	H	HR	BB	SO	RAT	ERA	ERA+	OAV	OOB	BH	AVG	PB	PR	/A	PD	TPI
1901 Was-A	18	10	.643	32	30	26	4	0	254^1	285	8	74	109	12.7	3.93	93	.280	.328	13	.135	-5	-7	-7	-1	-1.0
1902 Was-A	17	16	.515	36	34	33	1	1	299^2	331	11	89	92	12.6	4.05	91	.280	.331	12	.096	-10	-16	-12	-1	-2.0
1903 Was-A	11	22	.333	36	34	32	0	1	300	313	11	80	133	11.8	3.60	87	.268	.315	14	.132	-6	-21	-16	0	-2.0
1904 Was-A	14	23	.378	45	39	37	2	**3**	357^2	367	2	79	150	11.2	3.07	87	.266	.306	16	.127	-6	-19	-16	1	-2.2
1905 Was-A	14	22	.389	42	36	29	2	0	309^2	300	3	86	113	11.2	3.14	85	.255	.306	16	.155	-3	-16	-17	-2	-2.3
1906 Was-A	19	16	.543	38	32	28	7	0	282^2	253	2	79	96	10.6	2.17	122	.242	.296	11	.117	-4	17	15	-0	1.1
1907 Was-A	12	15	.429	36	29	20	1	0	237^1	272	5	63	58	12.7	3.56	68	.289	.334	11	.126	-3	-27	-30	-3	-3.8
1908 Was-A	0	2	.000	4	3	1	0	0	18	25	0	6	6	15.5	3.50	65	.333	.383	1	.200	-0	-2	-2	-0	-0.2
Bos-A	0	1	.000	1	1	0	0	0	3	8	0	1	0	27.0	15.00	16	.533	.563	0	.000	-0	-4	-4	0	-0.3
Yr	0	3	.000	5	4	1	0	0	21	33	0	7	6	17.1	5.14	45	.367	.412	1	.000	-0	-6	-7	-0	-0.6
Total 8	105	128	.451	270	238	206	17	5	2062^1	2154	40	557	757	11.8	3.36	88	.269	.317	94	.127	-37	-96	-91	-7	-12.7

■ DARYL PATTERSON
Patterson, Daryl Alan b: 11/21/43, Coalinga, Cal. BL/TR, 6'4", 192 lbs. Deb: 4/10/68

YEAR TM/L	W	L	PCT	G	GS	CG	SH	SV	IP	H	HR	BB	SO	RAT	ERA	ERA+	OAV	OOB	BH	AVG	PB	PR	/A	PD	TPI
1968 *Det-A	2	3	.400	38	1	0	0	7	68	53	3	27	49	11.1	2.12	142	.213	.300	0	.000	-1	7	7	-0	0.6
1969 Det-A	0	2	.000	18	0	0	0	0	22^1	15	2	19	12	13.7	2.82	132	.205	.370	0	.000	-0	2	2	-1	0.2
1970 Det-A	7	1	.875	43	0	0	0	2	78	81	9	39	55	14.4	4.85	77	.269	.362	0	.000	-1	-10	-10	-1	-1.1
1971 Det-A	0	1	.000	12	0	0	0	0	9^1	14	1	6	5	20.3	4.82	74	.359	.457	0	—	0	-1	-1	0	0.0
Oak-A	0	0	—	4	0	0	0	0	5^2	5	2	4	2	15.9	7.94	42	.238	.385	0	.000	-0	-3	-3	-0	-0.2
Yr	0	1	.000	16	0	0	0	0	15	19	3	10	7	18.0	6.00	58	.311	.417	0	.000	-0	-4	-4	-0	-0.2
StL-N	0	1	.000	13	2	0	0	1	26^2	20	3	15	11	11.8	4.39	82	.211	.318	0	.000	-0	-3	-2	-0	-0.2
1974 Pit-N	2	1	.667	14	0	0	0	1	21	35	3	9	8	18.9	7.29	47	.376	.431	0	.000	0	-9	-9	0	-0.8
Total 5	11	9	.550	142	3	0	0	11	231	223	23	119	142	13.8	4.09	85	.256	.353	0	.000	-3	-17	-16	-2	-1.5

■ DAVE PATTERSON
Patterson, David Glenn b: 7/25/56, Springfield, Mo. BR/TR, 6', 170 lbs. Deb: 6/09/79

YEAR TM/L	W	L	PCT	G	GS	CG	SH	SV	IP	H	HR	BB	SO	RAT	ERA	ERA+	OAV	OOB	BH	AVG	PB	PR	/A	PD	TPI
1979 LA-N	4	1	.800	36	0	0	0	6	53	62	5	22	34	14.3	5.26	69	.292	.359	1	.143	-0	-9	-10	0	-1.0

■ GIL PATTERSON
Patterson, Gilbert Thomas b: 9/5/55, Philadelphia, Pa. BR/TR, 6'1", 185 lbs. Deb: 4/19/77

YEAR TM/L	W	L	PCT	G	GS	CG	SH	SV	IP	H	HR	BB	SO	RAT	ERA	ERA+	OAV	OOB	BH	AVG	PB	PR	/A	PD	TPI
1977 NY-A	1	2	.333	10	6	0	0	1	33^1	38	3	20	29	16.5	5.40	73	.290	.396	0	—	0	-5	-5	0	-0.4

■ KEN PATTERSON
Patterson, Kenneth Brian b: 7/8/64, Costa Mesa, Cal. BL/TL, 6'4", 210 lbs. Deb: 7/09/88

YEAR TM/L	W	L	PCT	G	GS	CG	SH	SV	IP	H	HR	BB	SO	RAT	ERA	ERA+	OAV	OOB	BH	AVG	PB	PR	/A	PD	TPI
1988 Chi-A	0	2	.000	9	2	0	0	1	20^2	25	2	7	8	13.9	4.79	83	.294	.348	0	—	0	-2	-2	-0	-0.1
1989 Chi-A	6	1	.857	50	0	0	0	0	65^2	64	11	28	43	12.9	4.52	84	.257	.337	0	—	0	-5	-5	-1	-0.5
1990 Chi-A	2	1	.667	43	0	0	0	2	66^1	58	6	34	40	12.8	3.39	113	.242	.341	0	—	0	4	3	0	0.4
Total 3	8	4	.667	102	3	0	0	3	152^2	147	19	69	91	13.0	4.07	94	.256	.340	0	—	0	-3	-4	-1	-0.2

■ REGGIE PATTERSON
Patterson, Reginald Allen b: 11/7/58, Birmingham, Ala. BR/TR, 6'4", 180 lbs. Deb: 8/13/81

YEAR TM/L	W	L	PCT	G	GS	CG	SH	SV	IP	H	HR	BB	SO	RAT	ERA	ERA+	OAV	OOB	BH	AVG	PB	PR	/A	PD	TPI
1981 Chi-A	0	1	.000	6	1	0	0	0	7^1	14	1	6	2	24.5	13.50	26	.412	.500	0	—	0	-8	-8	0	-0.7
1983 Chi-N	1	2	.333	5	2	0	0	0	18^2	17	3	6	10	12.1	4.82	79	.246	.325	0	.000	-1	-2	-2	-0	-0.2
1984 Chi-N	0	1	.000	3	1	0	0	0	6	10	1	2	5	18.0	10.50	37	.357	.400	0	.000	-0	-5	-4	0	-0.3
1985 Chi-N	3	0	1.000	8	5	1	0	0	39	36	2	10	17	10.6	3.00	133	.250	.299	1	.100	-0	3	4	0	0.4
Total 4	4	4	.500	22	9	1	0	0	71	77	7	24	34	13.1	5.20	75	.280	.342	1	.056	-1	-13	-10	0	-0.8

■ BOB PATTERSON
Patterson, Robert Chandler b: 5/16/59, Jacksonville, Fla. BR/TR, 6'2", 185 lbs. Deb: 9/02/85

YEAR TM/L	W	L	PCT	G	GS	CG	SH	SV	IP	H	HR	BB	SO	RAT	ERA	ERA+	OAV	OOB	BH	AVG	PB	PR	/A	PD	TPI
1985 SD-N	0	0	—	3	0	0	0	0	4	13	2	3	3	16.0	24.75	14	.565	.615	0	—	0	-9	-9	-0	-0.8
1986 Pit-N	2	3	.400	11	5	0	0	0	36^1	49	5	9	20	13.4	4.95	77	.322	.344	1	.125	-0	-5	-5	1	-0.3
1987 Pit-N	1	4	.200	15	7	0	0	0	43	49	5	22	27	15.1	6.70	61	.290	.375	1	.083	-1	-13	-12	-0	-1.2
1989 Pit-N	4	3	.571	12	3	0	0	1	26^2	23	3	8	20	10.5	4.05	83	.232	.290	0	.000	0	-2	-2	-0	-0.2

YEAR TM/L	W	L	PCT	G	GS	CG	SH	SV	IP	H	HR	BB	SO	RAT	ERA	ERA+	OAV	OOB	BH	AVG	PB	PR	/A	PD	TPI
1990 *Pit-N	8	5	.615	55	5	0	0	5	94²	88	9	21	70	10.6	2.95	123	.249	.296	1	.053	-1	9	7	-0	0.6
Total 5	15	15	.500	96	20	0	0	6	204²	222	19	59	138	12.5	4.66	80	.279	.331	3	.071	-2	-20	-21	-0	-1.9

■ ROY PATTERSON
Patterson, Roy Lewis "Boy Wonder" b: 12/17/1876, Stoddard, Wis. d: 4/14/53, St.Croix Falls, Wis. BR/TR, 6', 185 lbs. Deb: 4/24/01

YEAR TM/L	W	L	PCT	G	GS	CG	SH	SV	IP	H	HR	BB	SO	RAT	ERA	ERA+	OAV	OOB	BH	AVG	PB	PR	/A	PD	TPI
1901 Chi-A	20	16	.556	41	35	30	4	0	312¹	345	11	62	127	11.7	3.37	103	.277	.311	26	.222	1	10	4	-0	0.3
1902 Chi-A	19	14	.576	34	30	26	2	0	268	262	5	67	61	11.0	3.06	111	.256	.302	20	.190	-2	15	10	2	0.9
1903 Chi-A	15	15	.500	34	30	26	2	1	293	275	5	69	89	10.6	2.70	104	.248	.292	11	.105	-5	8	3	2	0.0
1904 Chi-A	9	9	.500	22	17	14	4	0	165	148	1	24	64	9.4	2.29	107	.241	.269	6	.103	-3	6	3	-1	-0.1
1905 Chi-A	4	6	.400	13	9	7	0	0	88²	73	0	16	29	9.0	1.83	135	.226	.262	8	.267	2	8	6	1	1.0
1906 Chi-A	10	7	.588	21	18	12	3	1	142	119	1	47	45	8.6	2.09	121	.231	.255	3	.061	-4	9	7	1	0.4
1907 Chi-A	4	6	.400	19	13	4	1	0	96	105	0	18	27	11.5	2.63	92	.280	.313	3	.097	-2	-1	-2	1	-0.3
Total 7	81	73	.526	184	152	119	16	2	1365	1327	23	273	442	10.5	2.75	107	.255	.292	77	.156	-14	57	31	6	2.2

■ MARTY PATTIN
Pattin, Martin William b: 4/6/43, Charleston, Ill. BR/TR, 5'11", 180 lbs. Deb: 5/14/68 C

YEAR TM/L	W	L	PCT	G	GS	CG	SH	SV	IP	H	HR	BB	SO	RAT	ERA	ERA+	OAV	OOB	BH	AVG	PB	PR	/A	PD	TPI
1968 Cal-A	4	4	.500	52	4	0	0	3	84	67	7	37	66	11.4	2.79	104	.221	.310	1	.083	-1	2	1	-1	0.0
1969 Sea-A	7	12	.368	34	27	2	1	0	158²	166	29	71	126	13.6	5.62	65	.268	.345	9	.155	-1	-35	-35	-1	-3.6
1970 Mil-A	14	12	.538	37	29	11	0	0	233¹	204	20	71	161	10.8	3.39	112	.235	.298	9	.129	-2	8	10	2	1.0
1971 Mil-A	14	14	.500	36	36	9	5	0	264²	225	29	73	169	10.3	3.13	111	.235	.292	7	.084	-3	10	10	1	0.7
1972 Bos-A	17	13	.567	38	35	13	4	0	253	232	19	65	168	10.9	3.24	99	.243	.297	12	.140	0	-5	-1	1	0.1
1973 Bos-A	15	15	.500	34	30	11	2	1	219¹	238	31	69	119	12.9	4.31	93	.277	.337	0	—	0	-12	-7	1	-0.5
1974 KC-A	3	7	.300	25	11	2	0	0	117¹	121	10	28	50	11.6	3.99	96	.264	.309	0	—	0	-5	-2	-1	-0.2
1975 KC-A	10	10	.500	44	15	5	1	5	177	173	13	45	89	11.2	3.25	118	.253	.302	0	—	0	10	12	-1	1.1
1976 *KC-A	8	14	.364	44	15	4	1	5	141	114	9	38	65	9.9	2.49	141	.216	.273	0	—	0	16	16	-0	1.7
1977 *KC-A	10	3	.769	31	10	4	0	0	128¹	115	16	37	55	10.8	3.58	113	.242	.300	0	—	0	7	7	-0	0.6
1978 *KC-A	3	3	.500	32	5	2	0	4	78²	72	8	25	30	11.3	3.32	115	.248	.312	0	—	0	4	4	-2	0.3
1979 KC-A	5	2	.714	31	7	1	0	3	94¹	109	11	21	41	12.5	4.58	93	.293	.332	0	—	0	-4	-3	-1	-0.3
1980 *KC-A	4	0	1.000	37	0	0	0	4	89	97	7	23	40	12.2	3.64	111	.277	.324	0	—	0	4	4	-1	0.3
Total 13	114	109	.511	475	224	64	14	25	2038²	1933	209	603	1179	11.4	3.62	102	.250	.309	38	.123	-7	0	16	-5	1.2

■ JIMMY PATTISON
Pattison, James Wells b: 12/18/08, New York, N.Y. BL/TL, 6', 185 lbs. Deb: 4/18/29

YEAR TM/L	W	L	PCT	G	GS	CG	SH	SV	IP	H	HR	BB	SO	RAT	ERA	ERA+	OAV	OOB	BH	AVG	PB	PR	/A	PD	TPI
1929 Bro-N	0	1	.000	6	0	0	0	0	11²	9	1	4	5	10.0	4.63	100	.231	.302	1	.500	0	0	-0	-0	0.0

■ HARRY PATTON
Patton, Harry Claude b: 6/29/1884, Gillespie, Ill. d: 6/9/30, St.Louis, Mo. Deb: 8/22/10

YEAR TM/L	W	L	PCT	G	GS	CG	SH	SV	IP	H	HR	BB	SO	RAT	ERA	ERA+	OAV	OOB	BH	AVG	PB	PR	/A	PD	TPI
1910 StL-N	0	0	—	1	0	0	0	0	4	4	0	2	2	13.5	2.25	132	.267	.353	0	—	0	0	0	0	0.1

■ MIKE PAUL
Paul, Michael George b: 4/18/45, Detroit, Mich. BL/TL, 6', 175 lbs. Deb: 5/27/68 C

YEAR TM/L	W	L	PCT	G	GS	CG	SH	SV	IP	H	HR	BB	SO	RAT	ERA	ERA+	OAV	OOB	BH	AVG	PB	PR	/A	PD	TPI
1968 Cle-A	5	8	.385	36	7	0	0	3	91²	72	11	35	87	11.0	3.93	75	.213	.296	4	.167	0	-10	-10	-1	-1.1
1969 Cle-A	5	10	.333	47	12	0	0	2	117¹	104	12	54	98	12.3	3.61	104	.241	.328	0	.000	-3	0	2	-1	-0.1
1970 Cle-A	2	8	.200	30	15	1	0	0	88	91	13	45	70	13.9	4.81	82	.271	.357	4	.154	-1	-11	-8	-1	-1.0
1971 Cle-A	2	7	.222	17	12	1	0	0	62	78	8	14	33	14.1	5.95	64	.318	.367	1	.053	-1	-17	-15	-1	-1.6
1972 Tex-A	8	9	.471	49	20	2	1	1	161²	149	4	52	108	11.3	2.17	139	.246	.308	8	.167	1	16	15	-1	1.7
1973 Tex-A	5	4	.556	36	10	1	0	2	87¹	104	9	36	49	14.9	4.95	75	.295	.368	0	—	0	-11	-12	1	-1.0
Chi-N	0	1	.000	11	1	0	0	0	18¹	17	2	9	6	13.3	3.44	115	.258	.347	0	.000	-0	1	1	0	0.1
1974 Chi-N	0	1	.000	2	0	0	0	0	1¹	4	1	1	1	33.8	27.00	14	.500	.556	0	—	0	-3	-3	0	-0.2
Total 7	27	48	.360	228	77	5	1	8	627²	619	60	246	452	12.7	3.91	89	.260	.334	17	.115	-5	-35	-30	-4	-3.2

■ GENE PAULETTE
Paulette, Eugene Edward b: 5/26/1891, Centralia, Ill. d: 2/8/66, Little Rock, Ark. BR/TR, 6', 150 lbs. Deb: 6/16/11 ♦

YEAR TM/L	W	L	PCT	G	GS	CG	SH	SV	IP	H	HR	BB	SO	RAT	ERA	ERA+	OAV	OOB	BH	AVG	PB	PR	/A	PD	TPI
1918 StL-N	0	0	—	1	0	0	0	0	0¹	1	0	0	0	27.0	0.00	—	.500	.500	126	.273	0	0	0	0	0.0

■ GIL PAULSEN
Paulsen, Guilford Paul Hans b: 11/14/02, Graettinger, Iowa BR/TR, 6'2.5", 190 lbs. Deb: 10/03/25

YEAR TM/L	W	L	PCT	G	GS	CG	SH	SV	IP	H	HR	BB	SO	RAT	ERA	ERA+	OAV	OOB	BH	AVG	PB	PR	/A	PD	TPI
1925 StL-N	0	0	—	1	0	0	0	0	2	1	0	0	1	4.5	0.00	—	.125	.125	0	—	0	1	1	0	0.1

■ DAVE PAVLAS
Pavlas, David Lee b: 8/12/62, Frankfurt, W.Germany BR/TR, 6'7", 180 lbs. Deb: 8/21/90

YEAR TM/L	W	L	PCT	G	GS	CG	SH	SV	IP	H	HR	BB	SO	RAT	ERA	ERA+	OAV	OOB	BH	AVG	PB	PR	/A	PD	TPI
1990 Chi-N	2	0	1.000	13	0	0	0	0	21¹	23	2	6	12	12.2	2.11	196	.271	.319	0	.000	0	4	5	-0	0.5

■ JOHN PAWLOWSKI
Pawlowski, John b: 9/6/63, Johnson City, N.Y. BR/TR, 6'2", 175 lbs. Deb: 9/19/87

YEAR TM/L	W	L	PCT	G	GS	CG	SH	SV	IP	H	HR	BB	SO	RAT	ERA	ERA+	OAV	OOB	BH	AVG	PB	PR	/A	PD	TPI
1987 Chi-A	0	0	—	2	0	0	0	0	3²	7	0	3	2	24.5	4.91	93	.438	.526	0	—	0	-0	-0	0	0.0
1988 Chi-A	1	0	1.000	6	0	0	0	0	14	20	2	3	10	14.8	8.36	48	.328	.359	0	—	0	-7	-7	0	-0.5
Total 2	1	0	1.000	8	0	0	0	0	17²	27	2	6	12	16.8	7.64	54	.351	.398	0	—	0	-7	-7	0	-0.5

■ MIKE PAXTON
Paxton, Michael De Wayne b: 9/3/53, Memphis, Tenn. BR/TR, 5'11", 190 lbs. Deb: 5/25/77

YEAR TM/L	W	L	PCT	G	GS	CG	SH	SV	IP	H	HR	BB	SO	RAT	ERA	ERA+	OAV	OOB	BH	AVG	PB	PR	/A	PD	TPI
1977 Bos-A	10	5	.667	29	12	2	1	0	108	134	7	25	58	13.5	3.83	117	.311	.353	0	—	0	3	8	-0	0.7
1978 Cle-A	12	11	.522	33	27	5	2	1	191	179	13	63	96	11.8	3.86	97	.247	.314	0	—	0	-2	-3	-1	-0.3
1979 Cle-A	8	8	.500	33	24	3	0	0	159²	210	14	52	70	14.9	5.92	72	.315	.366	0	—	0	-30	-30	0	-2.6
1980 Cle-A	0	0	—	4	0	0	0	0	7²	13	4	6	6	22.3	12.91	32	.394	.487	0	—	0	-8	-8	0	-0.6
Total 4	30	24	.556	99	63	10	3	1	466¹	536	38	146	230	13.4	4.71	87	.289	.345	0	—	0	-37	-32	-1	-2.8

■ GEORGE PAYNE
Payne, George Washington b: 5/23/1890, Mt.Vernon, Ky. d: 1/24/59, Bellflower, Cal. BR/TR, 5'11", 172 lbs. Deb: 5/08/20

YEAR TM/L	W	L	PCT	G	GS	CG	SH	SV	IP	H	HR	BB	SO	RAT	ERA	ERA+	OAV	OOB	BH	AVG	PB	PR	/A	PD	TPI
1920 Chi-A	1	1	.500	12	0	0	0	0	29²	39	2	9	7	14.6	5.46	69	.312	.358	1	.125	-0	-5	-6	-1	-0.6

■ HARLEY PAYNE
Payne, Harley Fenwick "Lady" b: 1/9/1868, Windsor, Ont., Can. d: 12/29/35, Orwell, Ohio BB/TL, 6', 160 lbs. Deb: 4/18/1896

YEAR TM/L	W	L	PCT	G	GS	CG	SH	SV	IP	H	HR	BB	SO	RAT	ERA	ERA+	OAV	OOB	BH	AVG	PB	PR	/A	PD	TPI
1896 Bro-N	14	16	.467	34	28	24	2	0	241²	284	4	58	52	12.7	3.39	122	.290	.330	21	.214	0	26	20	3	2.0
1897 Bro-N	14	17	.452	40	38	30	1	0	280	350	8	71	86	13.5	4.63	89	.303	.344	26	.236	-1	-10	-16	1	-1.3
1898 Bro-N	1	0	1.000	1	1	1	0	0	9	11	0	3	2	14.0	4.00	90	.299	.352	3	.750	1	-0	-0	0	0.1
1899 Pit-N	1	3	.250	5	5	2	0	0	26¹	33	2	4	8	12.6	3.76	102	.306	.331	1	.100	-1	0	0	2	0.1
Total 4	30	36	.455	80	72	57	3	0	557	678	14	136	148	13.2	4.04	101	.298	.337	51	.230	1	16	3	6	0.9

■ MIKE PAYNE
Payne, Michael Earl b: 11/15/61, Woonsocket, R.I. BR/TR, 5'11", 165 lbs. Deb: 8/22/84

YEAR TM/L	W	L	PCT	G	GS	CG	SH	SV	IP	H	HR	BB	SO	RAT	ERA	ERA+	OAV	OOB	BH	AVG	PB	PR	/A	PD	TPI
1984 Atl-N	0	1	.000	3	1	0	0	0	5²	7	0	3	3	15.9	6.35	61	.333	.417	0	.000	-0	-2	-2	0	-0.1

■ MIKE PAZIK
Pazik, Michael Joseph b: 1/26/50, Lynn, Mass. BL/TL, 6'2", 195 lbs. Deb: 5/11/75

YEAR TM/L	W	L	PCT	G	GS	CG	SH	SV	IP	H	HR	BB	SO	RAT	ERA	ERA+	OAV	OOB	BH	AVG	PB	PR	/A	PD	TPI
1975 Min-A	0	4	.000	5	3	0	0	0	19²	28	5	10	8	17.4	8.24	47	.329	.400	0	—	0	-10	-10	-1	-0.8
1976 Min-A	0	0	—	5	0	0	0	0	9	13	0	4	6	18.0	7.00	51	.342	.419	0	—	0	-3	-3	-0	-0.3
1977 Min-A	1	0	1.000	3	3	0	0	0	18	18	1	6	6	12.0	2.50	159	.265	.324	0	—	0	3	3	0	0.3
Total 3	1	4	.200	13	6	0	0	0	46²	59	6	20	20	15.4	5.79	67	.309	.377	0	—	0	-10	-10	-1	-0.8

■ FRANK PEARCE
Pearce, Frank b: Louisville, Ky. Deb: 10/04/1876

YEAR TM/L	W	L	PCT	G	GS	CG	SH	SV	IP	H	HR	BB	SO	RAT	ERA	ERA+	OAV	OOB	BH	AVG	PB	PR	/A	PD	TPI
1876 Lou-N	0	0	—	1	0	0	0	0	4	5	0	1	4	13.5	4.50	60	.286	.325	0	.000	-0	-1	-1	-0	0.0

■ FRANK PEARCE
Pearce, Franklin Thomas b: 8/31/05, Middletown, Ky. d: 9/3/50, Van Buren, N.Y. BR/TR, 6', 170 lbs. Deb: 4/20/33

YEAR TM/L	W	L	PCT	G	GS	CG	SH	SV	IP	H	HR	BB	SO	RAT	ERA	ERA+	OAV	OOB	BH	AVG	PB	PR	/A	PD	TPI
1933 Phi-N	5	4	.556	20	7	3	1	0	82	78	5	29	18	11.7	3.62	105	.251	.315	5	.192	-1	-3	2	0	0.2
1934 Phi-N	0	2	.000	7	1	0	0	0	20	25	4	5	4	13.5	7.20	66	.301	.341	2	.667	-0	-7	-6	-0	-0.4
1935 Phi-N	0	0	—	5	0	0	0	0	13	22	0	6	7	19.4	8.31	55	.361	.418	2	.500	1	-6	-5	0	-0.3
Total 3	5	6	.455	32	8	3	1	0	115	125	9	40	29	12.9	4.77	85	.275	.333	9	.273	0	-16	-9	0	-0.5

■ GEORGE PEARCE
Pearce, George Thomas "Filbert" b: 1/10/1888, Aurora, Ill. d: 10/11/35, Joliet, Ill. BL/TL, 5'10.5", 175 lbs. Deb: 4/16/12

YEAR TM/L	W	L	PCT	G	GS	CG	SH	SV	IP	H	HR	BB	SO	RAT	ERA	ERA+	OAV	OOB	BH	AVG	PB	PR	/A	PD	TPI
1912 Chi-N	0	0	—	3	2	0	0	0	14²	15	0	12	9	16.6	5.52	60	.172	.273	1	.167	0	-3	-4	1	-0.2

YEAR	TM/L	W	L	PCT	G	GS	CG	SH	SV	IP	H	HR	BB	SO	RAT	ERA	ERA+	OAV	OOB	BH	AVG	PB	PR	/A	PD	TPI
1913	Chi-N	13	5	.722	25	21	15	3	0	163¹	137	4	59	73	11.0	2.31	137	.234	.308	4	.073	-3	16	16	-0	1.3
1914	Chi-N	9	12	.429	30	16	4	0	1	141	122	3	65	78	12.1	3.51	79	.239	.327	4	.089	-3	-11	-11	1	-1.3
1915	Chi-N	13	9	.591	36	20	8	2	0	176	158	1	77	96	12.2	3.32	84	.244	.328	11	.196	1	-11	-11	-0	-1.0
1916	Chi-N	0	0	—	4	1	0	0	0	4¹	6	0	1	0	14.5	2.08	140	.300	.333	0	—	0	0	0	0	0.0
1917	StL-N	1	1	.500	5	0	0	0	0	10¹	7	0	3	4	9.6	3.48	77	.184	.262	0	.000	-1	-1	-1	0	0.0
Total	6	36	27	.571	103	60	27	5	1	509²	445	8	217	260	11.9	3.11	94	.236	.318	20	.120	-6	-10	-10	2	-1.2

■ JIM PEARCE Pearce, James Madison b: 6/9/25, Zebulon, N.C. BR/TR, 6'6", 180 lbs. Deb: 9/08/49

YEAR	TM/L	W	L	PCT	G	GS	CG	SH	SV	IP	H	HR	BB	SO	RAT	ERA	ERA+	OAV	OOB	BH	AVG	PB	PR	/A	PD	TPI
1949	Was-A	0	1	.000	2	1	0	0	0	5¹	9	1	5	1	23.6	8.44	50	.375	.483	0	.000	-0	-3	-2	1	-0.1
1950	Was-A	2	1	.667	20	3	1	0	0	56²	58	2	37	18	15.2	6.04	74	.270	.379	2	.154	-1	-9	-10	-0	-0.9
1953	Was-A	0	1	.000	4	1	0	0	0	9¹	15	3	6	0	20.3	7.71	51	.405	.488	0	.000	-0	-4	-4	-0	-0.3
1954	Cin-N	1	0	1.000	2	1	1	0	0	11	7	0	5	3	10.6	0.00	—	.194	.310	0	.000	-0	5	5	0	0.6
1955	Cin-N	0	1	.000	2	1	0	0	0	3¹	8	0	0	0	21.6	10.80	39	.471	.471	0	—	0	-3	-2	0	-0.1
Total	5	3	4	.429	30	7	2	0	0	85²	97	6	53	22	16.0	5.78	76	.295	.396	2	.105	-2	-13	-13	1	-0.8

■ DICKEY PEARCE Pearce, Richard J. b: 2/29/1836, Brooklyn, N.Y. d: 10/12/08, Onset, Mass. BR/TR, 5'3.5", 161 lbs. Deb: 5/18/1871 MU♦

YEAR	TM/L	W	L	PCT	G	GS	CG	SH	SV	IP	H	HR	BB	SO	RAT	ERA	ERA+	OAV	OOB	BH	AVG	PB	PR	/A	PD	TPI
1875	StL-n	0	0	—	2	0	0	0	0	5¹	10	0	0		16.9	6.75	33	.357	.357	77	.247	0	-3	-3		-0.1

■ FRANK PEARS Pears, Frank H. b: 8/30/1866, Kentucky d: 11/29/23, St.Louis, Mo. TR , Deb: 10/06/1889 U

YEAR	TM/L	W	L	PCT	G	GS	CG	SH	SV	IP	H	HR	BB	SO	RAT	ERA	ERA+	OAV	OOB	BH	AVG	PB	PR	/A	PD	TPI
1889	KC-a	0	2	.000	3	2	2	0	0	22	21	2	9	5	12.3	4.91	85	.244	.315	1	.091	-1	-3	-2	-0	-0.2
1893	StL-N	0	0	—	1	0	0	0	0	4	9	0	2	0	24.8	13.50	35	.432	.482	0	.000	-0	-4	-4	0	-0.2
Total	2	0	2	.000	4	2	2	0	0	26	30	2	11	5	14.2	6.23	69	.280	.347	1	.077	-2	-7	-6	-0	-0.4

■ ALEX PEARSON Pearson, Alexander Franklin b: 3/9/1877, Greensboro, Pa. d: 10/30/66, Rochester, Pa. BR/TR, 5'10.5", 160 lbs. Deb: 8/01/02

YEAR	TM/L	W	L	PCT	G	GS	CG	SH	SV	IP	H	HR	BB	SO	RAT	ERA	ERA+	OAV	OOB	BH	AVG	PB	PR	/A	PD	TPI
1902	StL-N	2	6	.250	11	10	8	0	0	82	90	0	22	24	12.6	3.95	69	.279	.330	9	.265	1	-11	-11	0	-1.0
1903	Cle-A	1	2	.333	4	3	2	0	0	30¹	34	1	3	12	11.0	3.56	80	.282	.300	1	.083	-1	-2	-2	0	-0.2
Total	2	3	8	.273	15	13	10	0	0	112¹	124	1	25	36	12.2	3.85	72	.280	.322	10	.217	-0	-13	-13	0	-1.2

■ IKE PEARSON Pearson, Issac Overton b: 3/1/17, Grenada, Miss. d: 3/17/85, Sarasota, Fla. BR/TR, 6'1", 180 lbs. Deb: 6/06/39

YEAR	TM/L	W	L	PCT	G	GS	CG	SH	SV	IP	H	HR	BB	SO	RAT	ERA	ERA+	OAV	OOB	BH	AVG	PB	PR	/A	PD	TPI
1939	Phi-N	2	13	.133	26	13	4	0	0	125	144	15	56	29	14.8	5.76	70	.296	.374	2	.054	-3	-26	-24	1	-2.4
1940	Phi-N	3	14	.176	29	20	5	1	1	145¹	160	13	57	43	13.6	5.45	72	.275	.343	9	.205	1	-26	-25	1	-2.1
1941	Phi-N	4	14	.222	46	10	0	0	6	136	139	8	70	38	14.4	3.57	104	.266	.361	5	.125	-2	1	2	0	-0.4
1942	Phi-N	1	6	.143	35	7	0	0	0	85¹	87	4	50	21	14.9	4.54	73	.271	.376	1	.043	-2	-12	-12	0	-1.4
1946	Phi-N	1	0	1.000	5	2	1	1	0	14¹	16	1	8	6	15.7	3.77	91	.271	.368	1	.200	1	-1	-1	0	0.0
1948	Chi-A	2	3	.400	23	2	0	0	1	53	62	6	27	12	15.5	4.92	87	.292	.378	2	.200	-0	-4	-4	1	-0.2
Total	6	13	50	.206	164	54	10	2	8	559	608	49	268	149	14.5	4.83	79	.279	.363	20	.126	-6	-66	-64	3	-6.1

■ MONTE PEARSON Pearson, Montgomery Marcellus "Hoot" b: 9/2/09, Oakland, Cal. d: 1/27/78, Fresno, Cal. BR/TR, 6', 175 lbs. Deb: 4/22/32

YEAR	TM/L	W	L	PCT	G	GS	CG	SH	SV	IP	H	HR	BB	SO	RAT	ERA	ERA+	OAV	OOB	BH	AVG	PB	PR	/A	PD	TPI
1932	Cle-A	0	0	—	8	0	0	0	0	8	10	1	11	5	23.6	10.13	47	.323	.500	0	—	0	-5	-5	1	-0.3
1933	Cle-A	10	5	.667	19	16	10	0	0	135¹	111	6	55	54	11.0	2.33	191	.221	.297	13	.260	1	29	32	-1	3.3
1934	Cle-A	18	13	.581	39	33	19	0	2	254²	257	16	130	140	13.7	4.52	101	.260	.346	25	.272	6	-1	1	1	0.7
1935	Cle-A	8	13	.381	30	24	10	1	0	181²	199	19	103	90	15.0	4.90	92	.279	.371	11	.177	-0	-8	-2	2	-0.5
1936	*NY-A	19	7	.731	33	31	15	1	1	223	191	19	135	118	13.3	3.71	125	.233	.343	23	.253	6	33	23	2	2.6
1937	*NY-A	9	3	.750	22	20	7	1	1	144²	145	6	64	71	13.1	3.17	140	.261	.339	11	.216	1	23	20	-0	2.0
1938	*NY-A	16	7	.696	28	27	17	1	0	202	198	12	113	98	13.9	3.97	114	.258	.354	13	.171	1	18	13	1	1.3
1939	*NY-A	12	5	.706	22	20	8	0	0	146¹	151	9	70	76	13.7	4.49	97	.272	.354	17	.321	6	-2	-1	4	0.4
1940	NY-A	7	5	.583	16	16	7	1	0	109²	108	8	44	43	12.5	3.69	109	.262	.333	4	.121	-1	8	4	2	0.5
1941	Cin-N	1	3	.250	7	4	1	0	0	24¹	22	3	15	9	13.7	5.18	69	.242	.349	0	.000	-1	-4	-4	-0	-0.4
Total	10	100	61	.621	224	191	94	5	4	1429²	1392	82	740	703	13.5	4.00	112	.256	.346	117	.228	18	95	75	6	9.6

■ MARV PEASLEY Peasley, Marvin Warren b: 7/16/1888, Jonesport, Me. d: 12/27/48, San Francisco, Cal BL/TL, 6'1", 175 lbs. Deb: 9/27/10

YEAR	TM/L	W	L	PCT	G	GS	CG	SH	SV	IP	H	HR	BB	SO	RAT	ERA	ERA+	OAV	OOB	BH	AVG	PB	PR	/A	PD	TPI
1910	Det-A	0	1	.000	2	1	0	0	0	10	13	0	11	4	22.5	8.10	32	.295	.446	0	.000	0	-6	-6	0	-0.5

■ GEORGE PECHINEY Pechiney, George Adolphe "Pisch" b: 9/20/1861, Cincinnati, Ohio d: 7/14/43, Cincinnati, Ohio BR/TR, 5'9", 184 lbs. Deb: 8/04/1885

YEAR	TM/L	W	L	PCT	G	GS	CG	SH	SV	IP	H	HR	BB	SO	RAT	ERA	ERA+	OAV	OOB	BH	AVG	PB	PR	/A	PD	TPI
1885	Cin-a	7	4	.636	11	11	11	1	0	98	95	1	30	49	11.5	2.02	161	.244	.298	6	.150	-2	13	13	1	1.2
1886	Cin-a	15	21	.417	40	40	35	2	0	330¹	355	4	133	110	13.3	4.14	85	.262	.328	30	.208	-1	-25	-23	-2	-2.2
1887	Cle-a	1	9	.100	10	10	10	0	0	86	118	8	44	24	17.0	7.12	61	.315	.387	9	.250	-0	-27	-26	0	-1.9
Total	3	23	34	.404	61	61	56	3	0	514¹	568	13	207	183	13.6	4.23	85	.268	.333	45	.205	-3	-39	-36	-2	-2.9

■ STEVE PEEK Peek, Stephen George b: 7/30/14, Springfield, Mass BB/TR, 6'2", 195 lbs. Deb: 4/16/41

YEAR	TM/L	W	L	PCT	G	GS	CG	SH	SV	IP	H	HR	BB	SO	RAT	ERA	ERA+	OAV	OOB	BH	AVG	PB	PR	/A	PD	TPI
1941	NY-A	4	2	.667	17	8	2	0	0	80	85	6	39	18	13.9	5.06	78	.276	.357	1	.036	-3	-8	-10	4	-1.1

■ RED PEERY Peery, George Allan b: 8/15/06, Payson, Utah d: 5/6/85, Salt Lake City, Ut. BL/TL, 5'11", 160 lbs. Deb: 9/22/27

YEAR	TM/L	W	L	PCT	G	GS	CG	SH	SV	IP	H	HR	BB	SO	RAT	ERA	ERA+	OAV	OOB	BH	AVG	PB	PR	/A	PD	TPI
1927	Pit-N	0	0	—	1	0	0	0	0	1	0	0	1	0	9.0	0.00	—	.000	.200	0	—	0	0	0	0	0.1
1929	Bos-N	0	1	.000	9	1	0	0	0	44	53	1	9	3	12.7	5.11	91	.305	.339	3	.214	1	-2	-2	0	0.0
Total	2	0	1	.000	10	1	0	0	0	45	53	1	10	3	12.6	5.00	93	.298	.335	3	.214	1	-2	-2	0	0.1

■ HEINIE PEITZ Peitz, Henry Clement b: 11/28/1870, St.Louis, Mo. d: 10/23/43, Cincinnati, Ohio BR/TR, 5'11", 165 lbs. Deb: 10/15/1892 C♦

YEAR	TM/L	W	L	PCT	G	GS	CG	SH	SV	IP	H	HR	BB	SO	RAT	ERA	ERA+	OAV	OOB	BH	AVG	PB	PR	/A	PD	TPI
1894	StL-N	0	0	—	1	0	0	0	0	3	7	0	2	0	27.0	9.00	60	.448	.510	89	.263	0	-1	-1	0	0.0
1897	Cin-N	0	1	.000	2	1	1	0	0	8	9	0	4	3	14.6	7.88	58	.282	.361	78	.293	1	-3	-3	1	-0.1
1899	Cin-N	0	0	—	1	0	0	0	0	5	6	0	1	0	12.6	5.40	73	.297	.330	79	.272	0	-1	-1	0	0.0
Total	3	0	1	.000	4	1	1	0	0	16	22	0	7	3	16.3	7.31	62	.324	.388	1117	.271	1	-5	-5	1	-0.1

■ BARNEY PELTY Pelty, Barney b: 9/10/1880, Farmington, Mo. d: 5/24/39, Farmington, Mo. BR/TR, 5'9", 175 lbs. Deb: 8/20/03

YEAR	TM/L	W	L	PCT	G	GS	CG	SH	SV	IP	H	HR	BB	SO	RAT	ERA	ERA+	OAV	OOB	BH	AVG	PB	PR	/A	PD	TPI
1903	StL-A	3	3	.500	7	6	5	0	1	48²	49	1	15	20	11.8	2.40	121	.261	.316	3	.150	-0	3	3	-1	0.2
1904	StL-A	15	18	.455	39	35	31	2	0	301	270	7	77	126	10.4	2.84	87	.241	.289	15	.127	-6	-8	-12	-1	-2.2
1905	StL-A	14	14	.500	31	28	27	1	0	258²	222	3	68	114	10.1	2.75	93	.233	.284	15	.153	-3	-3	-6	3	-0.3
1906	StL-A	16	11	.593	34	30	25	4	2	260²	189	1	59	92	8.6	1.59	163	.206	.254	15	.163	-3	32	29	6	3.7
1907	StL-A	12	21	.364	36	31	29	5	1	273	234	1	64	85	9.8	2.57	98	.233	.279	16	.168	-1	-1	-2	2	0.0
1908	StL-A	7	4	.636	20	13	7	2	0	122	104	0	32	36	10.8	1.99	120	.241	.309	5	.119	-2	5	5	1	0.5
1909	StL-A	11	11	.500	27	23	17	5	0	199¹	158	2	53	88	9.8	2.30	105	.222	.281	15	.165	0	4	3	4	0.8
1910	StL-A	5	11	.313	27	18	12	3	0	165¹	157	3	70	48	12.8	3.48	71	.263	.348	5	.089	-4	-18	-19	5	-1.9
1911	StL-A	7	15	.318	28	22	18	1	0	197	197	4	69	59	12.3	2.97	114	.265	.331	9	.138	-3	8	9	1	0.7
1912	StL-A	1	5	.167	6	6	2	0	0	38²	40	0	15	10	14.2	5.59	59	.297	.374	0	.000	-2	-10	-10	0	-0.9
	Was-A	1	4	.200	11	4	1	0	0	43²	40	0	10	15	11.1	3.30	101	.250	.310	2	.222	0	0	-0	-0	0.0
	Yr	2	9	.182	17	10	3	0	0	82¹	83	0	25	25	12.2	4.37	76	.269	.332	1	.048	-2	-10	-10	0	-0.9
Total	10	92	117	.440	266	216	174	23	4	1908	1663	22	532	693	10.5	2.63	100	.239	.296	100	.143	-25	14	0	19	0.2

■ ALEJANDRO PENA Pena, Alejandro (Vasquez) b: 6/25/59, Cambiaso, D.R. BR/TR, 5'11", 165 lbs. Deb: 9/14/81

YEAR	TM/L	W	L	PCT	G	GS	CG	SH	SV	IP	H	HR	BB	SO	RAT	ERA	ERA+	OAV	OOB	BH	AVG	PB	PR	/A	PD	TPI
1981	*LA-N	1	1	.500	14	0	0	0	2	25¹	18	2	11	14	10.3	2.84	117	.194	.279	0	.000	-1	2	1	0	0.1
1982	LA-N	0	2	.000	29	0	0	0	0	35²	37	2	21	20	14.9	4.79	72	.272	.373	0	—	0	-5	-5	1	-0.3
1983	*LA-N	12	9	.571	34	26	4	3	1	177	152	7	51	120	10.4	2.75	131	.229	.285	6	.100	-2	17	17	2	1.7
1984	LA-N	12	6	.667	28	28	8	4	0	199¹	186	7	46	135	10.6	2.48	142	.246	.292	8	.121	-1	24	23	-1	2.3
1985	LA-N	0	1	.000	2	1	0	0	0	4¹	7	1	2	2	20.8	8.31	42	.350	.435	0	.000	-0	-2	-2	0	-0.1
1986	LA-N	1	2	.333	24	10	0	0	1	70	74	6	30	46	13.5	4.89	71	.270	.344	3	.176	0	-9	-11	-1	-1.1
1987	LA-N	2	7	.222	37	7	0	0	11	87¹	82	9	37	76	12.5	3.50	113	.251	.331	1	.077	-1	6	4	-2	0.1

YEAR TM/L	W	L	PCT	G	GS	CG	SH	SV	IP	H	HR	BB	SO	RAT	ERA	ERA+	OAV	OOB	BH	AVG	PB	PR	/A	PD	TPI
1988 *LA-N	6	7	.462	60	0	0	0	12	94¹	75	4	27	83	9.8	1.91	175	.218	.277	0	.000	-1	16	15	-1	1.5
1989 LA-N	4	3	.571	53	0	0	0	5	76	62	6	18	75	9.7	2.13	160	.220	.272	1	1.000	0	12	11	-2	1.0
1990 NY-N	3	3	.500	52	0	0	0	5	76	71	4	22	76	11.1	3.20	114	.245	.300	1	.167	0	5	4	-1	0.3
Total 10	41	41	.500	333	72	12	7	37	845¹	764	48	266	647	11.1	2.95	120	.240	.301	20	.114	-4	66	56	-5	5.5

■ HIPOLITO PENA   Pena, Hipolito (Concepcion)   b: 1/30/64, Fantino, D.R.   BL/TL, 6'3", 165 lbs.   Deb: 9/01/86

YEAR TM/L	W	L	PCT	G	GS	CG	SH	SV	IP	H	HR	BB	SO	RAT	ERA	ERA+	OAV	OOB	BH	AVG	PB	PR	/A	PD	TPI
1986 Pit-N	0	3	.000	10	1	0	0	1	8¹	7	3	3	6	11.9	8.64	44	.206	.289	0	—	0	-5	-4	0	-0.4
1987 Pit-N	0	3	.000	16	1	0	0	1	25²	16	2	26	16	14.7	4.56	90	.184	.372	1	.167	-0	-1	-1	0	-0.4
1988 NY-A	1	1	.500	16	0	0	0	0	14¹	10	1	9	10	11.9	3.14	125	.192	.311	0	—	0	1	1	0	0.1
Total 3	1	7	.125	42	2	0	0	2	48¹	33	6	38	32	13.4	4.84	83	.191	.340	1	.167	-0	-5	-4	0	-0.3

■ JOSE PENA   Pena, Jose (Gutierrez)   b: 12/3/42, Ciudad Juarez, Mex.   BR/TR, 6'2", 190 lbs.   Deb: 6/01/69

YEAR TM/L	W	L	PCT	G	GS	CG	SH	SV	IP	H	HR	BB	SO	RAT	ERA	ERA+	OAV	OOB	BH	AVG	PB	PR	/A	PD	TPI
1969 Cin-N	1	1	.500	6	0	0	0	0	5	10	1	0	5	3	27.0	18.00	21	.400	.500	0	—	0	-8	-8	0	-0.7
1970 LA-N	4	3	.571	29	0	0	0	4	57	51	8	29	31	13.1	4.42	87	.241	.340	1	.125	0	-2	-4	1	-0.2
1971 LA-N	2	0	1.000	21	0	0	0	1	43	32	7	18	44	10.7	3.56	91	.211	.298	2	.667	1	-0	-2	-1	-0.1
1972 LA-N	0	0	—	5	0	0	0	0	7¹	13	1	6	4	23.3	8.59	39	.371	.463	0	—	0	-4	-4	0	-0.4
Total 4	7	4	.636	61	0	0	0	5	112¹	106	16	58	82	13.5	4.97	72	.250	.346	3	.273	1	-15	-18	0	-1.4

■ ORLANDO PENA   Pena, Orlando Gregorio (Quevara)   b: 11/17/33, Victoria De Las Tunas, Cuba   BR/TR, 5'11", 154 lbs.   Deb: 8/24/58

YEAR TM/L	W	L	PCT	G	GS	CG	SH	SV	IP	H	HR	BB	SO	RAT	ERA	ERA+	OAV	OOB	BH	AVG	PB	PR	/A	PD	TPI
1958 Cin-N	1	0	1.000	9	0	0	0	3	15	10	0	4	11	8.4	0.60	691	.185	.241	0	—	0	6	6	-0	0.6
1959 Cin-N	5	9	.357	46	8	1	0	5	136	150	26	39	76	12.5	4.76	85	.280	.329	3	.088	-0	-12	-11	-1	-1.1
1960 Cin-N	0	1	.000	4	0	0	0	0	9¹	8	0	3	9	10.6	2.89	132	.222	.282	0	.000	-0	1	1	-0	0.0
1962 KC-A	6	4	.600	13	12	6	1	0	89²	71	9	27	56	9.9	3.01	138	.213	.274	5	.161	-0	10	11	-1	1.0
1963 KC-A	12	20	.375	35	33	9	3	0	217	218	24	53	128	11.4	3.69	104	.260	.308	9	.145	-0	-1	4	-2	0.3
1964 KC-A	12	14	.462	40	32	5	0	0	219¹	231	40	73	184	12.8	4.43	86	.268	.331	12	.160	0	-20	-15	-2	-1.6
1965 KC-A	0	6	.000	12	5	0	0	0	35¹	42	4	13	24	14.5	6.88	51	.302	.370	1	.111	-0	-13	-13	-0	-1.3
Det-A	4	6	.400	30	0	0	0	4	57¹	54	5	20	55	11.8	2.51	138	.252	.319	2	.250	1	6	6	-1	0.6
Yr	4	12	.250	42	5	0	0	4	92²	96	9	33	79	12.6	4.18	83	.270	.333	2	.118	1	-7	-7	-1	-0.7
1966 Det-A	4	2	.667	54	0	0	0	7	108	105	16	35	79	12.1	3.08	113	.252	.317	2	.111	-1	4	5	2	0.7
1967 Det-A	0	1	.000	2	0	0	0	0	2	5	0	0	2	27.0	13.50	24	.500	.545	0	—	0	-2	-2	-0	-0.1
Cle-A	0	3	.000	48	1	0	0	8	88¹	67	8	22	72	9.2	3.36	97	.208	.261	0	.000	-1	-1	-1	-0	-0.1
Yr	0	4	.000	50	1	0	0	8	90¹	72	8	22	74	9.5	3.59	91	.216	.266	0	.000	-1	-4	-3	-0	-0.2
1970 Pit-N	2	1	.667	23	0	0	0	2	37²	38	7	2	25	11.0	4.78	82	.268	.307	0	.000	-0	-3	-4	1	-0.3
1971 Bal-A	0	1	1.000	5	0	0	0	0	14²	16	0	5	4	12.9	3.07	109	.281	.339	0	.000	-0	1	0	0	0.0
1973 Bal-A	1	1	.500	11	2	0	0	1	44²	36	10	8	23	9.3	4.03	93	.218	.263	0	—	0	-1	-1	-0	-0.1
StL-N	4	4	.500	42	0	0	0	6	62	60	3	14	38	10.7	2.18	167	.251	.292	1	.143	-0	10	10	0	1.1
1974 StL-N	5	2	.714	42	0	0	0	1	45	45	0	20	23	13.2	2.60	137	.269	.351	1	.500	1	5	5	-0	0.5
Cal-A	0	0	—	4	0	0	0	3	8	6	0	1	5	7.9	0.00	—	.214	.241	0	—	0	3	3	0	0.4
1975 Cal-A	0	2	.000	7	0	0	0	0	12²	13	0	8	4	14.9	2.13	166	.283	.389	0	—	0	2	2	-0	0.2
Total 14	56	77	.421	427	93	21	4	40	1202	1175	151	352	818	11.6	3.71	101	.255	.312	36	.136	-3	-7	6	-6	0.8

■ RAMON PENA   Pena, Ramon Arturo (Padilla)   b: 5/5/62, Santiago, D.R.   BR/TR, 5'10", 155 lbs.   Deb: 4/27/89

YEAR TM/L	W	L	PCT	G	GS	CG	SH	SV	IP	H	HR	BB	SO	RAT	ERA	ERA+	OAV	OOB	BH	AVG	PB	PR	/A	PD	TPI
1989 Det-A	0	0	—	8	0	0	0	0	18	26	0	8	12	18.0	6.00	64	.338	.414	0	—	0	-4	-4	1	-0.3

■ RUSTY PENCE   Pence, Russell William   b: 3/11/1900, Marine, Ill.   d: 8/11/71, Hot Srpings, Ark.   BR/TR, 6', 185 lbs.   Deb: 5/13/21

YEAR TM/L	W	L	PCT	G	GS	CG	SH	SV	IP	H	HR	BB	SO	RAT	ERA	ERA+	OAV	OOB	BH	AVG	PB	PR	/A	PD	TPI
1921 Chi-A	0	0	—	4	0	0	0	0	5¹	6	0	7	2	23.6	8.44	50	.286	.483	0	.000	-0	-2	-2	0	-0.1

■ KEN PENNER   Penner, Kenneth William   b: 4/24/1896, Booneville, Ind.   d: 5/28/59, Sacramento, Cal.   BL/TR, 5'11.5", 170 lbs.   Deb: 9/11/16

YEAR TM/L	W	L	PCT	G	GS	CG	SH	SV	IP	H	HR	BB	SO	RAT	ERA	ERA+	OAV	OOB	BH	AVG	PB	PR	/A	PD	TPI
1916 Cle-A	1	0	1.000	4	2	0	0	0	12²	14	0	4	5	12.8	4.26	71	.304	.360	0	.000	-0	-2	-1	1	-0.1
1929 Chi-N	0	1	.000	5	0	0	0	0	12²	14	1	6	3	14.2	2.84	162	.280	.357	1	.250	0	3	2	0	0.2
Total 2	1	1	.500	9	2	0	0	0	25¹	28	1	10	8	13.5	3.55	108	.292	.358	1	.167	-0	1	1	1	0.1

■ KEWPIE PENNINGTON   Pennington, George Louis   b: 9/24/1896, New York, N.Y.   d: 5/3/53, Newark, N.J.   BR/TR, 5'8.5", 168 lbs.   Deb: 4/14/17

YEAR TM/L	W	L	PCT	G	GS	CG	SH	SV	IP	H	HR	BB	SO	RAT	ERA	ERA+	OAV	OOB	BH	AVG	PB	PR	/A	PD	TPI
1917 StL-A	0	0	—	1	0	0	0	0	1	1	0	0	0	9.0	0.00	—	.250	.250	0	—	0	0	0	0	0.0

■ HERB PENNOCK   Pennock, Herbert Jefferis "The Knight Of Kennett Square"   b: 2/19/1894, Kennett Square, Pa   d: 1/30/48, New York, N.Y.   BB/TL, 6', 160 lbs.   Deb: 5/14/12   CH

YEAR TM/L	W	L	PCT	G	GS	CG	SH	SV	IP	H	HR	BB	SO	RAT	ERA	ERA+	OAV	OOB	BH	AVG	PB	PR	/A	PD	TPI
1912 Phi-A	1	2	.333	17	2	1	0	2	50	48	1	30	38	14.6	4.50	68	.262	.375	2	.133	-1	-7	-8	0	-0.7
1913 Phi-A	2	1	.667	14	3	1	0	0	33¹	30	4	22	17	14.0	5.13	54	.248	.329	1	.111	-0	-8	-9	-0	-0.9
1914 *Phi-A	11	4	.733	28	14	8	3	3	151²	136	1	65	90	12.0	2.79	94	.248	.330	12	.214	2	-1	-3	-1	-0.1
1915 Phi-A	3	6	.333	11	8	3	1	1	44	46	2	29	24	15.8	5.32	55	.266	.377	5	.278	1	-12	-12	0	-1.0
Bos-A	0	0	—	5	1	0	0	0	14	23	0	10	7	21.2	9.64	29	.390	.478	1	.167	0	-10	-11	-1	-1.0
Yr	3	6	.333	16	9	3	1	1	58	69	2	39	31	16.8	6.36	46	.295	.396	1	.000	1	-22	-22	-0	-2.0
1916 Bos-A	0	2	.000	9	2	0	0	1	26²	23	0	8	12	10.8	3.04	91	.245	.311	1	.125	-0	-1	-1	-0	-0.1
1917 Bos-A	5	5	.500	24	5	4	1	1	100²	90	2	23	35	10.4	3.31	78	.243	.292	4	.167	2	-7	-8	-0	-0.6
1919 Bos-A	16	8	.667	32	26	16	5	0	219	223	2	48	70	11.3	2.71	111	.274	.316	13	.173	1	13	8	-2	0.6
1920 Bos-A	16	13	.552	37	31	19	4	2	242¹	244	9	61	68	11.5	3.68	99	.264	.312	20	.260	4	3	-1	-2	0.0
1921 Bos-A	12	14	.462	32	32	15	1	0	222²	268	7	59	91	13.3	4.04	105	.307	.352	18	.212	2	6	5	1	0.7
1922 Bos-A	10	17	.370	32	26	15	1	1	202	230	7	74	59	13.6	4.32	95	.297	.359	9	.138	-3	-6	-5	1	-0.5
1923 *NY-A	19	6	**.760**	35	27	21	1	3	238¹	235	11	66	93	11.5	3.13	126	.261	.314	16	.193	1	23	21	1	2.2
1924 NY-A	21	9	.700	40	34	25	4	3	286¹	302	13	64	101	11.5	2.83	147	.273	.314	16	.158	-2	45	**42**	-0	3.9
1925 *NY-A	16	17	.485	47	31	21	2	2	277	267	11	71	88	**11.0**	2.96	144	.254	**.303**	20	.202	-3	**44**	**40**	-3	3.3
1926 *NY-A	23	11	.676	40	33	19	1	2	266¹	294	11	43	78	**11.5**	3.62	107	.284	**.313**	18	.212	3	12	7	1	1.0
1927 *NY-A	19	8	.704	34	26	18	1	2	209²	225	5	48	51	11.8	3.00	128	.283	.325	15	.217	0	26	20	-2	1.7
1928 NY-A	17	6	.739	28	24	18	**5**	3	211	215	2	40	53	10.9	2.56	147	.267	.302	15	.203	-1	35	28	2	2.9
1929 NY-A	9	11	.450	27	23	8	1	2	157¹	205	11	28	49	13.5	4.92	78	.318	.349	9	.176	-1	-12	-19	0	-1.8
1930 NY-A	11	7	.611	25	19	11	1	0	156¹	194	8	20	46	12.3	4.32	100	.301	.322	11	.183	-2	6	-0	-1	-0.3
1931 NY-A	11	6	.647	25	25	12	1	0	189¹	247	7	30	65	13.2	4.28	93	.315	.342	10	.152	1	2	-7	-0	-0.5
1932 *NY-A	9	5	.643	22	21	9	1	0	146²	191	8	38	54	14.1	4.60	89	.310	.350	8	.151	0	-2	-9	-0	-0.7
1933 NY-A	7	4	.636	23	5	2	1	4	65	96	4	21	22	16.2	5.54	70	.342	.387	1	.238	-0	-9	-12	-1	-1.0
1934 Bos-A	2	0	1.000	30	2	1	0	1	62	68	2	16	16	12.2	3.05	158	.276	.321	3	.214	-0	**10**	**12**	-1	1.0
Total 22	240	162	.597	617	420	247	35	33	3571²	3900	128	916	1227	12.2	3.60	106	.281	.328	232	.191	3	150	82	-8	8.1

■ PAUL PENSON   Penson, Paul Eugene   b: 7/12/31, Kansas City, Kan.   BR/TR, 6'1", 185 lbs.   Deb: 4/21/54

YEAR TM/L	W	L	PCT	G	GS	CG	SH	SV	IP	H	HR	BB	SO	RAT	ERA	ERA+	OAV	OOB	BH	AVG	PB	PR	/A	PD	TPI
1954 Phi-N	1	1	.500	5	3	0	0	0	16	14	1	14	3	15.8	4.50	90	.237	.384	0	.000	-1	-1	-1	-1	-0.1

■ GENE PENTZ   Pentz, Eugene David   b: 6/21/53, Johnstown, Pa.   BR/TR, 6'1", 200 lbs.   Deb: 7/29/75

YEAR TM/L	W	L	PCT	G	GS	CG	SH	SV	IP	H	HR	BB	SO	RAT	ERA	ERA+	OAV	OOB	BH	AVG	PB	PR	/A	PD	TPI
1975 Det-A	0	4	.000	13	0	0	0	0	25¹	24	0	20	21	16.7	3.20	126	.293	.420	0	—	0	2	2	-0	0.2
1976 Hou-N	3	3	.500	40	0	0	0	5	63²	62	5	31	36	13.3	2.97	108	.259	.347	1	.200	0	4	2	1	0.3
1977 Hou-N	5	2	.714	41	4	0	0	2	87	76	8	44	51	12.5	3.83	93	.236	.330	0	.000	-1	1	-3	0	-0.3
1978 Hou-N	0	0	—	10	0	0	0	0	15	15	1	13	8	15.6	6.00	55	.214	.371	0	—	0	-4	-4	1	-0.3
Total 4	8	9	.471	104	4	0	0	7	191	177	14	108	116	13.6	3.63	96	.250	.351	1	.053	-1	2	-3	1	-0.1

■ JIMMY PEOPLES   Peoples, James Elsworth   b: 10/8/1863, Big Beaver, Mich.   d: 8/29/20, Detroit, Mich.   TR, 5'8", 200 lbs.   Deb: 5/29/1884   U♦

YEAR TM/L	W	L	PCT	G	GS	CG	SH	SV	IP	H	HR	BB	SO	RAT	ERA	ERA+	OAV	OOB	BH	AVG	PB	PR	/A	PD	TPI
1885 Cin-a	0	2	.000	2	2	1	0	0	15	30	0	2	4	19.2	12.00	27	.399	.415	4	.182	-0	-15	-15	1	-0.9

YEAR TM/L	W	L	PCT	G	GS	CG	SH	SV	IP	H	HR	BB	SO	RAT	ERA	ERA+	OAV	OOB	BH	AVG	PB	PR	/A	PD	TPI

■ LAURIN PEPPER   Pepper, Hugh McLaurin   b: 1/18/31, Vaughan, Miss.   BR/TR, 5'11", 190 lbs.   Deb: 7/04/54

YEAR TM/L	W	L	PCT	G	GS	CG	SH	SV	IP	H	HR	BB	SO	RAT	ERA	ERA+	OAV	OOB	BH	AVG	PB	PR	/A	PD	TPI
1954 Pit-N	1	5	.167	14	8	0	0	0	50²	63	4	43	17	18.8	7.99	52	.315	.436	4	.235	0	-22	-21	1	-1.7
1955 Pit-N	0	1	.000	14	1	0	0	0	20	30	5	25	7	25.6	10.35	40	.370	.528	0	.000	-0	-14	-14	-0	-1.2
1956 Pit-N	1	1	.500	11	7	0	0	0	30	30	1	25	12	16.5	3.00	126	.256	.387	0	.000	-0	3	3	-1	0.2
1957 Pit-N	0	1	.000	5	1	0	0	0	9	11	1	5	4	16.0	8.00	47	.297	.381	0	—	0	-4	-4	-0	-0.3
Total 4	2	8	.200	44	17	0	0	0	109²	134	11	98	40	19.2	7.06	57	.308	.437	4	.160	-0	-38	-37	0	-3.0

■ BOB PEPPER   Pepper, Robert Ernest   b: 5/3/1895, Rosston, Pa.   d: 4/8/68, Fort Cliff, Pa.   BR/TR, 6'2", 178 lbs.   Deb: 7/23/15

YEAR TM/L	W	L	PCT	G	GS	CG	SH	SV	IP	H	HR	BB	SO	RAT	ERA	ERA+	OAV	OOB	BH	AVG	PB	PR	/A	PD	TPI
1915 Phi-A	0	0	—	1	0	0	0	0	5	6	0	4	0	19.8	1.80	164	.333	.478	0	.000	-0	1	1	0	0.0

■ HARRISON PEPPERS   Peppers, Harrison (b: William Harrison Pepper)   b: 9/1866, Kentucky   d: 11/5/03, Webb City, Mo.   BL,   Deb: 6/30/1894

YEAR TM/L	W	L	PCT	G	GS	CG	SH	SV	IP	H	HR	BB	SO	RAT	ERA	ERA+	OAV	OOB	BH	AVG	PB	PR	/A	PD	TPI
1894 Lou-N	0	1	.000	2	1	0	0	0	8	10	0	4	0	15.8	6.75	75	.303	.378	0	.000	-1	-1	-1	0	-0.1

■ LUIS PERAZA   Peraza, Luis (Rios)   b: 6/17/42, Rio Piedras, P.R.   BR/TR, 5'11", 185 lbs.   Deb: 4/09/69

YEAR TM/L	W	L	PCT	G	GS	CG	SH	SV	IP	H	HR	BB	SO	RAT	ERA	ERA+	OAV	OOB	BH	AVG	PB	PR	/A	PD	TPI
1969 Phi-N	0	0	—	8	0	0	0	0	9	12	1	2	7	14.0	6.00	59	.364	.400	0	.000	-0	-2	-2	0	-0.2

■ OSWALD PERAZA   Peraza, Oswald Jose   b: 10/19/62, Puerto Cabello, Venez.   BR/TR, 6'4", 172 lbs.   Deb: 4/04/88

YEAR TM/L	W	L	PCT	G	GS	CG	SH	SV	IP	H	HR	BB	SO	RAT	ERA	ERA+	OAV	OOB	BH	AVG	PB	PR	/A	PD	TPI
1988 Bal-A	5	7	.417	19	15	1	0	0	86	98	10	37	61	14.3	5.55	70	.282	.355	0	—	0	-15	-16	0	-1.4

■ HUB PERDUE   Perdue, Herbert Rodney "The Gallatin Squash"   b: 6/7/1882, Bethpage, Tenn.   d: 10/31/68, Gallatin, Tex.   BR/TR, 5'10.5", 192 lbs.   Deb: 4/19/11

YEAR TM/L	W	L	PCT	G	GS	CG	SH	SV	IP	H	HR	BB	SO	RAT	ERA	ERA+	OAV	OOB	BH	AVG	PB	PR	/A	PD	TPI
1911 Bos-N	6	10	.375	24	19	9	0	1	137¹	180	10	41	40	14.7	4.98	77	.321	.372	10	.208	-1	-24	-18	-0	-1.6
1912 Bos-N	13	16	.448	37	30	20	1	3	249	295	11	54	101	12.7	3.80	94	.293	.331	12	.138	-6	-11	-6	-4	-1.4
1913 Bos-N	16	13	.552	38	32	16	3	1	212¹	201	7	39	91	10.3	3.26	101	.249	.287	7	.104	-5	-1	0	-7	-1.0
1914 Bos-N	2	5	.286	9	9	2	0	0	51	60	5	11	13	13.1	5.82	47	.311	.357	1	.071	-0	-17	-17	0	-1.6
StL-N	8	8	.500	22	19	12	0	1	153¹	160	3	35	43	11.7	2.82	99	.290	.338	8	.167	-1	-0	-0	-4	-0.4
Yr	10	13	.435	31	28	14	0	1	204¹	220	8	46	56	11.9	3.57	78	.295	.340	3	.048	-1	-18	-18	-3	-2.0
1915 StL-N	6	12	.333	31	13	5	1	1	115¹	141	7	19	29	12.6	4.21	66	.311	.341	4	.111	-1	-19	-18	0	-2.0
Total 5	51	64	.443	161	122	64	5	7	918¹	1037	43	199	317	12.3	3.85	85	.290	.331	42	.140	-14	-73	-60	-14	-8.0

■ GEORGE PEREZ   Perez, George Thomas   b: 12/29/37, San Fernando, Cal.   BR/TR, 6'2.5", 200 lbs.   Deb: 4/17/58

YEAR TM/L	W	L	PCT	G	GS	CG	SH	SV	IP	H	HR	BB	SO	RAT	ERA	ERA+	OAV	OOB	BH	AVG	PB	PR	/A	PD	TPI
1958 Pit-N	0	1	.000	4	0	0	0	1	8¹	9	1	4	2	14.0	5.40	72	.300	.382	0	.000	-0	-1	-1	-0	-0.1

■ MELIDO PEREZ   Perez, Melido Turpen Gross (b: Melido Turpen Gross (Perez))   b: 2/15/66, San Cristobal, D.R.   BR/TR, 6'4", 180 lbs.   Deb: 9/04/87

YEAR TM/L	W	L	PCT	G	GS	CG	SH	SV	IP	H	HR	BB	SO	RAT	ERA	ERA+	OAV	OOB	BH	AVG	PB	PR	/A	PD	TPI
1987 KC-A	1	1	.500	3	3	0	0	0	10¹	18	2	5	5	20.0	7.84	58	.375	.434	0	—	0	-4	-4	-0	-0.3
1988 Chi-A	12	10	.545	32	32	3	1	0	197	186	26	72	138	11.9	3.79	105	.248	.316	0	—	0	4	4	-2	0.2
1989 Chi-A	11	14	.440	31	31	2	0	0	183¹	187	23	90	141	13.7	5.01	76	.264	.350	0	—	0	-23	-25	-2	-2.4
1990 Chi-A	13	14	.481	35	35	3	3	0	197	177	14	86	161	12.1	4.61	83	.241	.322	0	—	0	-16	-17	-2	-1.8
Total 4	37	39	.487	101	101	8	4	0	587²	568	65	253	445	12.7	4.52	86	.254	.331	0	—	0	-38	-42	-6	-4.3

■ MIKE PEREZ   Perez, Michael Irvin   b: 10/19/64, Yauco, P.R.   BR/TR, 6', 185 lbs.   Deb: 9/05/90

YEAR TM/L	W	L	PCT	G	GS	CG	SH	SV	IP	H	HR	BB	SO	RAT	ERA	ERA+	OAV	OOB	BH	AVG	PB	PR	/A	PD	TPI
1990 StL-N	1	0	1.000	13	0	0	0	1	13²	12	0	3	5	9.9	3.95	99	.240	.283	0	.000	-0	-0	0	0	0.0

■ PASCUAL PEREZ   Perez, Pascual Gross (b: Pascual Gross (Perez))   b: 5/17/57, San Cristobal, D.R.   BR/TR, 6'2", 162 lbs.   Deb: 5/07/80

YEAR TM/L	W	L	PCT	G	GS	CG	SH	SV	IP	H	HR	BB	SO	RAT	ERA	ERA+	OAV	OOB	BH	AVG	PB	PR	/A	PD	TPI
1980 Pit-N	0	1	.000	2	2	0	0	0	12	15	0	2	7	14.3	3.75	97	.341	.396	1	.250	-0	-0	-0	0	0.0
1981 Pit-N	2	7	.222	17	13	2	0	0	86¹	92	5	34	46	13.4	3.96	91	.273	.345	3	.136	-0	-5	-4	0	-0.3
1982 *Atl-N	4	4	.500	16	11	0	0	0	79¹	85	4	17	29	11.6	3.06	122	.276	.314	3	.167	1	5	6	0	0.8
1983 Atl-N	15	8	.652	33	33	7	1	0	215¹	213	26	51	144	11.2	3.43	113	.260	.307	12	.160	-1	5	11	1	1.3
1984 Atl-N	14	8	.636	30	30	4	1	0	211²	208	26	51	145	11.1	3.74	103	.260	.307	5	.076	-2	-4	3	2	0.4
1985 Atl-N	1	13	.071	22	22	0	0	0	95¹	115	10	57	57	16.3	6.14	63	.297	.389	3	.120	-0	-27	-24	-1	-2.4
1987 Mon-N	7	0	1.000	10	10	2	0	0	70¹	52	5	16	58	8.8	2.30	182	.206	.257	1	.042	-2	14	15	1	1.5
1988 Mon-N	12	8	.600	27	27	4	2	0	188	133	15	44	131	8.8	2.44	147	.196	.253	2	.037	-3	21	24	2	2.6
1989 Mon-N	9	13	.409	33	28	2	0	0	198¹	178	15	45	152	10.3	3.31	107	.237	.283	11	.204	2	4	5	0	0.8
1990 NY-A	1	2	.333	3	3	0	0	0	14	8	0	3	12	7.1	1.29	309	.163	.212	0	—	0	4	4	-0	0.4
Total 10	65	64	.504	193	179	21	4	0	1170²	1099	100	320	781	11.1	3.45	109	.248	.303	41	.120	-5	17	39	6	5.1

■ CECIL PERKINS   Perkins, Cecil Boyce   b: 12/1/40, Baltimore, Md.   BR/TR, 6', 175 lbs.   Deb: 7/05/67

YEAR TM/L	W	L	PCT	G	GS	CG	SH	SV	IP	H	HR	BB	SO	RAT	ERA	ERA+	OAV	OOB	BH	AVG	PB	PR	/A	PD	TPI
1967 NY-A	0	1	.000	2	1	0	0	0	5	6	1	2	1	14.4	9.00	35	.316	.381	0	.000	-0	-3	-3	0	-0.2

■ CHARLIE PERKINS   Perkins, Charles Sullivan "Lefty"   b: 9/9/05, Ensley, Ala.   d: 5/25/88, Salem, Ore.   BR/TL, 6'1", 175 lbs.   Deb: 5/01/30

YEAR TM/L	W	L	PCT	G	GS	CG	SH	SV	IP	H	HR	BB	SO	RAT	ERA	ERA+	OAV	OOB	BH	AVG	PB	PR	/A	PD	TPI
1930 Phi-A	0	0	—	8	1	0	0	0	23²	25	0	15	15	15.2	6.46	72	.313	.421	1	.125	-1	-5	-5	0	-0.4
1934 Bro-N	0	3	.000	11	2	0	0	0	24¹	37	3	14	5	19.6	8.51	46	.336	.421	2	.286	-1	-12	-12	-1	-1.1
Total 2	0	3	.000	19	3	0	0	0	48	62	3	29	20	17.4	7.50	57	.326	.421	3	.200	-1	-17	-17	-1	-1.5

■ JOHN PERKOVICH   Perkovich, John Joseph "Perky"   b: 3/10/24, Chicago, Ill.   BR/TR, 5'11", 170 lbs.   Deb: 5/06/50

YEAR TM/L	W	L	PCT	G	GS	CG	SH	SV	IP	H	HR	BB	SO	RAT	ERA	ERA+	OAV	OOB	BH	AVG	PB	PR	/A	PD	TPI
1950 Chi-A	0	0	—	1	0	0	0	0	5	7	3	1	3	14.4	7.20	62	.318	.348	0	.000	-0	-1	-2	-0	-0.1

■ HARRY PERKOWSKI   Perkowski, Harry Walter   b: 9/6/22, Dante, Va.   BL/TL, 6'2.5", 196 lbs.   Deb: 9/13/47

YEAR TM/L	W	L	PCT	G	GS	CG	SH	SV	IP	H	HR	BB	SO	RAT	ERA	ERA+	OAV	OOB	BH	AVG	PB	PR	/A	PD	TPI
1947 Cin-N	0	0	—	3	1	0	0	0	7¹	12	1	3	2	18.4	3.68	111	.375	.429	0	.000	0	0	0	0	0.0
1949 Cin-N	1	1	.500	5	3	2	0	0	23²	21	2	14	3	13.3	4.56	92	.236	.340	3	.333	1	-1	-1	-0	0.0
1950 Cin-N	0	0	—	22	0	0	0	0	34¹	36	6	23	19	15.7	5.24	81	.286	.400	7	.318	2	-4	-4	1	0.0
1951 Cin-N	3	6	.333	35	7	1	0	1	102	96	2	46	56	12.6	2.82	144	.251	.333	1	.040	-3	13	14	0	1.2
1952 Cin-N	12	10	.545	33	24	11	1	0	194	197	9	89	86	13.4	3.80	99	.265	.347	12	.160	-0	-2	-1	1	0.0
1953 Cin-N	12	11	.522	33	25	7	2	2	193	204	26	62	70	12.5	4.52	96	.271	.327	14	.203	1	-5	-4	0	-0.1
1954 Cin-N	2	8	.200	28	12	3	1	0	95²	100	16	62	32	15.3	6.11	69	.276	.384	4	.160	-1	-22	-20	-1	-1.9
1955 Chi-N	3	4	.429	25	4	0	0	2	47²	53	3	25	28	14.7	5.29	77	.283	.368	2	.154	-0	-7	-6	1	-0.4
Total 8	33	40	.452	184	76	24	4	5	697²	719	65	324	296	13.5	4.37	94	.269	.350	43	.180	1	-27	-21	2	-1.2

■ JON PERLMAN   Perlman, Jonathan Samuel   b: 12/13/56, Dallas, Tex.   BL/TR, 6'3", 185 lbs.   Deb: 9/06/85

YEAR TM/L	W	L	PCT	G	GS	CG	SH	SV	IP	H	HR	BB	SO	RAT	ERA	ERA+	OAV	OOB	BH	AVG	PB	PR	/A	PD	TPI
1985 Chi-N	1	0	1.000	6	0	0	0	0	8²	10	3	8	4	18.7	11.42	35	.313	.450	0	.000	-0	-8	-7	0	-0.6
1987 SF-N	0	0	—	10	0	0	0	0	11¹	11	1	4	3	12.7	3.97	97	.256	.333	0	—	0	0	-0	0	0.0
1988 Cle-A	0	2	.000	10	0	0	0	0	19²	25	0	11	10	16.5	5.49	75	.309	.391	0	—	0	-3	-3	1	-0.1
Total 3	1	2	.333	26	0	0	0	0	39²	46	4	23	17	15.9	6.35	63	.295	.389	0	.000	-0	-11	-10	1	-0.7

■ LEN PERME   Perme, Leonard John   b: 11/25/17, Cleveland, Ohio   BL/TL, 6', 170 lbs.   Deb: 9/08/42

YEAR TM/L	W	L	PCT	G	GS	CG	SH	SV	IP	H	HR	BB	SO	RAT	ERA	ERA+	OAV	OOB	BH	AVG	PB	PR	/A	PD	TPI
1942 Chi-A	0	1	.000	4	1	1	0	0	13	5	0	4	4	6.9	1.38	260	.119	.213	1	.333	0	3	3	0	0.4
1946 Chi-A	0	0	—	4	0	0	0	0	4¹	6	0	7	2	27.0	8.31	41	.316	.500	0	—	0	-2	-2	0	-0.1
Total 2	0	1	.000	8	1	1	0	0	17¹	11	0	11	6	11.9	3.12	114	.180	.315	1	.333	0	1	1	0	0.3

■ HUB PERNOLL   Pernoll, Henry Hubbard   b: 3/14/1888, Grant's Pass, Ore.   d: 2/18/44, Grant's Pass, Ore.   BR/TL, 5'8", 175 lbs.   Deb: 4/25/10

YEAR TM/L	W	L	PCT	G	GS	CG	SH	SV	IP	H	HR	BB	SO	RAT	ERA	ERA+	OAV	OOB	BH	AVG	PB	PR	/A	PD	TPI
1910 Det-A	4	3	.571	11	5	4	0	0	54²	54	1	14	25	12.0	2.96	89	.270	.333	1	.063	-2	-3	-2	3	0.0
1912 Det-A	0	0	—	3	0	0	0	0	9	9	0	4	3	13.0	6.00	54	.265	.342	0	.000	-0	-3	-3	0	-0.2
Total 2	4	3	.571	14	5	4	0	0	63²	63	1	18	28	12.2	3.39	80	.269	.335	1	.053	-2	-5	-5	3	-0.2

■ RON PERRANOSKI   Perranoski, Ronald Peter (b: Ronald Peter Perzanowski)   b: 4/1/36, Paterson, N.J.   BL/TL, 6', 180 lbs.   Deb: 4/14/61   C

YEAR TM/L	W	L	PCT	G	GS	CG	SH	SV	IP	H	HR	BB	SO	RAT	ERA	ERA+	OAV	OOB	BH	AVG	PB	PR	/A	PD	TPI
1961 LA-N	7	5	.583	53	1	0	0	6	91²	82	5	41	56	12.5	2.65	164	.244	.333	1	.083	-0	14	17	0	1.7
1962 LA-N	6	6	.500	70	0	0	0	20	107¹	103	1	36	68	11.7	2.85	127	.255	.316	1	.071	-1	13	9	-0	0.8

YEAR TM/L	W	L	PCT	G	GS	CG	SH	SV	IP	H	HR	BB	SO	RAT	ERA	ERA+	OAV	OOB	BH	AVG	PB	PR	/A	PD	TPI
1963 *LA-N	16	3	**.842**	**69**	0	0	0	21	129	112	7	43	75	11.1	1.67	180	.231	.299	3	.125	0	**23**	19	0	2.2
1964 LA-N	5	7	.417	72	0	0	0	14	125^1	128	5	46	79	12.6	3.09	105	.263	.328	2	.105	-0	6	2	2	0.4
1965 *LA-N	6	6	.500	59	0	0	0	17	104^2	85	2	40	53	11.0	2.24	146	.226	.305	3	.158	1	15	12	-1	1.2
1966 *LA-N	6	7	.462	55	0	0	0	7	82	82	4	31	50	12.5	3.18	104	.269	.338	2	.250	1	4	1	2	0.5
1967 LA-N	6	7	.462	**70**	0	0	0	16	110	97	4	45	75	11.9	2.45	126	.240	.320	1	.100	-0	11	8	1	1.0
1968 Min-A	8	7	.533	66	0	0	0	6	87	86	5	38	65	12.8	3.10	100	.252	.327	0	.000	-1	-1	-0	0	0.0
1969 *Min-A	9	10	.474	75	0	0	0	**31**	119^2	85	4	52	62	10.4	2.11	173	.205	.295	2	.083	-1	20	**21**	1	2.2
1970 *Min-A	7	8	.467	67	0	0	0	**34**	111	108	7	42	55	12.2	2.43	153	.259	.328	1	.042	-2	16	16	-1	1.3
1971 Min-A	1	4	.200	36	0	0	0	5	42^2	60	2	28	21	19.2	6.75	53	.337	.435	0	.000	-0	-16	-15	0	-1.5
Det-A	0	1	.000	11	0	0	0	2	18	16	2	3	8	10.0	2.50	144	.254	.299	0	.000	-0	2	2	-0	0.2
Yr	1	5	.167	47	0	0	0	7	60^2	76	4	31	29	16.0	5.49	65	.309	.388	0	.000	-0	-14	-13	-0	-1.3
1972 Det-A	0	1	.000	17	0	0	0	0	18^2	23	2	8	10	15.4	7.71	41	.307	.381	0	.000	-0	-10	-9	-0	-1.0
LA-N	2	0	1.000	9	0	0	0	0	16^2	19	0	8	5	14.6	2.70	123	.292	.370	0	—	0	1	1	0	0.1
1973 Cal-A	0	2	.000	8	0	0	0	0	11	11	0	7	5	15.5	4.09	87	.282	.404	0	—	0	-0	-1	0	0.0
Total 13	79	74	.516	737	1	0	0	179	1174^2	1097	50	468	687	12.2	2.79	123	.250	.325	16	.096	-4	99	83	5	9.1

■ BILL PERRIN
Perrin, William Joseph "Lefty"   b: 6/23/10, New Orleans, La.   d: 6/30/74, New Orleans, La.   BR/TL, 5'11", 172 lbs.   Deb: 9/30/34

YEAR TM/L	W	L	PCT	G	GS	CG	SH	SV	IP	H	HR	BB	SO	RAT	ERA	ERA+	OAV	OOB	BH	AVG	PB	PR	/A	PD	TPI
1934 Cle-A	0	1	.000	1	0	0	0	0	5	13	0	2	3	28.8	14.40	32	.520	.571	0	—	-0	-6	-5	0	-0.3

■ GEORGE PERRING
Perring, George Wilson   b: 8/13/1884, Sharon, Wis.   d: 8/20/60, Beloit, Wis.   BR/TR, 6', 190 lbs.   Deb: 4/30/08 ♦

YEAR TM/L	W	L	PCT	G	GS	CG	SH	SV	IP	H	HR	BB	SO	RAT	ERA	ERA+	OAV	OOB	BH	AVG	PB	PR	/A	PD	TPI
1914 KC-F	0	0	—	1	0	0	0	0	0^2	2	0	1	0	40.5	13.50	23	.524	.623	138	.278	0	-1	-1	0	0.0

■ POL PERRITT
Perritt, William Dayton   b: 8/30/1892, Arcadia, La.   d: 10/15/47, Shreveport, La.   BR/TR, 6'2", 168 lbs.   Deb: 9/07/12

YEAR TM/L	W	L	PCT	G	GS	CG	SH	SV	IP	H	HR	BB	SO	RAT	ERA	ERA+	OAV	OOB	BH	AVG	PB	PR	/A	PD	TPI
1912 StL-N	1	1	.500	6	3	1	0	0	31	25	0	10	13	10.2	3.19	107	.229	.294	2	.222	-0	1	1	0	0.1
1913 StL-N	6	14	.300	36	21	8	0	0	175	205	9	64	64	14.2	5.25	62	.300	.367	12	.203	-1	-40	-39	0	-3.8
1914 StL-N	16	13	.552	41	32	18	3	2	286	248	7	93	115	11.2	2.36	118	.245	.318	13	.141	-2	14	14	-3	0.9
1915 NY-N	12	18	.400	35	30	16	4	0	220	226	6	59	91	12.1	2.66	96	.266	.323	11	.162	-0	2	-2	-4	-0.8
1916 NY-N	18	11	.621	40	28	17	5	2	251	243	11	56	115	11.0	2.62	93	.257	.304	7	.084	-4	0	-5	-2	-1.2
1917 *NY-N	17	7	.708	35	26	14	5	1	215	186	3	45	72	10.0	1.88	135	.237	.284	11	.157	-2	20	16	1	1.7
1918 NY-N	18	13	.581	35	31	19	6	0	233	212	5	38	60	9.7	2.74	96	.246	.278	14	.175	-1	1	-3	-3	-0.7
1919 NY-N	1	1	.500	11	3	0	0	1	19	27	0	12	12	19.4	7.11	39	.386	.488	0	.000	-1	-9	-9	0	-0.9
1920 NY-N	0	0	—	8	0	0	0	2	15	9	0	4	3	7.8	1.80	167	.167	.224	0	.000	-1	2	2	0	0.2
1921 NY-N	2	0	1.000	5	1	0	0	0	11^2	7	0	2	5	14.7	3.86	95	.321	.345	0	.000	-1	-0	-0	-1	-0.0
Det-A	1	0	1.000	4	2	0	0	0	13	18	0	7	3	18.0	4.85	88	.383	.473	2	.400	0	-1	-1	-0	-0.0
Total 10	92	78	.541	256	177	93	23	8	1469^2	1416	41	390	543	11.4	2.89	94	.259	.314	72	.151	-12	-10	-28	-10	-4.5

■ GAYLORD PERRY
Perry, Gaylord Jackson   b: 9/15/38, Williamston, N.C.   BR/TR, 6'4", 205 lbs.   Deb: 4/14/62

YEAR TM/L	W	L	PCT	G	GS	CG	SH	SV	IP	H	HR	BB	SO	RAT	ERA	ERA+	OAV	OOB	BH	AVG	PB	PR	/A	PD	TPI
1962 SF-N	3	1	.750	13	7	1	0	0	43	54	3	14	20	14.2	5.23	73	.310	.362	3	.231	0	-6	-7	-0	-0.6
1963 SF-N	1	6	.143	31	4	0	0	2	76	84	10	29	52	13.6	4.03	79	.279	.346	4	.222	1	-6	-7	-0	-0.6
1964 SF-N	12	11	.522	44	19	5	2	5	206^1	179	16	43	155	9.9	2.75	130	.232	.278	3	.054	-3	18	19	-2	1.5
1965 SF-N	8	12	.400	47	26	6	0	1	195^2	194	21	70	170	12.4	4.19	86	.256	.324	10	.156	-0	-14	-13	3	-1.0
1966 SF-N	21	8	.724	36	35	13	3	0	255^2	242	15	40	201	10.1	2.99	123	.247	.280	16	.186	-0	17	19	0	2.1
1967 SF-N	15	17	.469	39	37	18	3	1	293	231	20	84	230	9.8	2.61	126	.214	.274	13	.143	-1	25	22	3	2.7
1968 SF-N	16	15	.516	39	38	19	3	1	291	240	10	59	173	9.4	2.44	120	.222	.265	11	.113	-3	18	16	4	2.1
1969 SF-N	19	14	.576	40	39	26	3	0	325^1	290	23	91	233	10.8	2.49	141	.237	.295	14	.120	-2	40	37	3	4.2
1970 SF-N	**23**	13	.639	41	41	23	**5**	0	328^2	292	27	84	214	10.5	3.20	124	.237	.290	14	.117	-3	31	28	5	3.0
1971 *SF-N	16	12	.571	37	37	14	2	0	280	255	20	67	158	10.5	2.76	123	.242	.290	10	.102	-3	22	20	0	1.8
1972 Cle-A	**24**	16	.600	41	40	**29**	5	1	342^2	253	17	82	234	9.1	1.92	168	.205	.261	17	.155	1	**44**	49	2	**6.6**
1973 Cle-A	19	19	.500	41	41	**29**	7	0	344	315	34	115	238	11.4	3.38	116	.246	.311	0	—	0	17	21	1	2.3
1974 Cle-A	21	13	.618	37	37	28	4	0	322^1	230	25	99	216	9.4	2.51	**144**	.204	.272	0	—	0	40	**39**	0	**4.4**
1975 Cle-A	6	9	.400	15	15	10	1	0	121^2	120	16	34	85	11.5	3.55	106	.256	.308	0	—	0	3	3	1	0.4
Tex-A	12	8	.600	22	22	15	4	0	184	157	12	36	148	9.6	3.03	124	.227	.268	0	—	0	15	15	-1	1.4
Yr	18	17	.514	37	37	25	5	0	305^2	277	28	70	233	10.3	3.24	116	.238	.283	0	—	0	18	18	-0	1.8
1976 Tex-A	15	14	.517	32	32	21	2	0	250^1	232	14	52	143	10.2	3.24	111	.247	.287	0	—	0	8	10	-3	0.7
1977 Tex-A	15	12	.556	34	34	13	4	0	238	239	21	56	177	11.3	3.37	121	.262	.308	0	—	0	18	19	-2	1.8
1978 SD-N	**21**	6	**.778**	37	37	5	2	0	260^2	241	9	66	154	10.7	2.73	122	.248	.298	8	.092	-3	25	17	0	1.5
1979 SD-N	12	11	.522	32	32	10	0	0	232^2	225	12	67	140	11.4	3.06	115	.257	.313	6	.085	-2	17	12	1	1.2
1980 Tex-A	6	9	.400	24	24	6	2	0	155	159	12	46	107	12.3	3.43	114	.268	.328	0	—	0	10	8	1	0.9
NY-A	4	4	.500	10	8	0	0	0	50^2	65	2	18	28	14.9	4.44	88	.320	.378	0	—	0	-2	-3	0	-0.2
Yr	10	13	.435	34	32	6	2	0	205^2	224	14	64	135	12.6	3.68	106	.278	.332	0	—	0	8	5	1	0.7
1981 Atl-N	8	9	.471	23	23	3	0	0	150^2	182	9	24	60	12.5	3.94	91	.304	.335	12	.250	3	-8	-6	-1	-0.3
1982 Sea-A	10	12	.455	32	32	6	0	0	216^2	245	27	54	116	12.6	4.40	96	.287	.332	0	—	0	-8	-4	1	-0.2
1983 Sea-A	3	10	.231	16	16	2	0	0	102	116	18	23	42	12.5	4.94	86	.286	.329	0	—	0	-10	-8	1	-0.6
KC-A	4	4	.500	14	14	1	1	0	84^1	98	6	26	40	13.3	4.27	95	.292	.344	0	—	0	-2	-2	0	0.0
Yr	7	14	.333	30	30	3	1	0	186^1	214	24	49	82	12.8	4.64	90	.286	.331	0	—	0	-12	-10	1	-0.6
Total 22	314	265	.542	777	690	303	53	11	5350^1	4938	399	1379	3534	10.8	3.11	117	.245	.297	141	.131	-16	311	305	17	35.1

■ SCOTT PERRY
Perry, Herbert Scott   b: 4/17/1891, Dennison, Tex.   d: 10/27/59, Kansas City, Mo.   BR/TR, 6'1", 195 lbs.   Deb: 5/13/15

YEAR TM/L	W	L	PCT	G	GS	CG	SH	SV	IP	H	HR	BB	SO	RAT	ERA	ERA+	OAV	OOB	BH	AVG	PB	PR	/A	PD	TPI
1915 StL-A	0	0	—	1	1	0	0	0	2	5	0	1	0	31.5	13.50	21	.455	.538	0	—	0	-2	-2	0	-0.1
1916 Chi-N	2	1	.667	4	3	2	1	0	28^1	28	0	3	10	10.5	2.54	115	.291	.311	3	.273	1	0	1	0	0.3
1917 Cin-N	0	0	—	4	1	0	0	0	13^1	17	0	8	4	17.6	6.75	39	.321	.419	0	.000	-1	-6	-6	0	-0.6
1918 Phi-A	20	19	.513	44	36	**30**	3	2	332^1	295	1	111	81	11.0	1.98	148	.247	.312	15	.134	-6	30	35	2	3.6
1919 Phi-A	4	17	.190	25	21	12	0	1	183^2	193	4	72	38	13.1	3.58	96	.282	.352	8	.136	-3	-7	-3	7	0.1
1920 Phi-A	11	25	.306	42	34	20	1	1	263^2	310	14	65	79	13.0	3.62	111	.300	.345	13	.157	-4	5	12	0	0.8
1921 Phi-A	3	6	.333	12	8	5	0	1	70	77	4	24	19	13.1	4.11	108	.288	.349	1	.038	-4	1	3	1	0.0
Total 7	40	68	.370	132	104	69	5	5	893^1	927	23	284	231	12.3	3.07	113	.277	.336	40	.135	-17	21	40	10	4.1

■ JIM PERRY
Perry, James Evan   b: 10/30/36, Williamston, N.C.   BB/TR, 6'4", 190 lbs.   Deb: 4/23/59

YEAR TM/L	W	L	PCT	G	GS	CG	SH	SV	IP	H	HR	BB	SO	RAT	ERA	ERA+	OAV	OOB	BH	AVG	PB	PR	/A	PD	TPI
1959 Cle-A	12	10	.545	44	13	8	2	4	153	122	10	55	79	10.5	2.65	139	.225	.298	15	.300	3	21	18	0	2.2
1960 Cle-A	**18**	10	**.643**	41	36	10	**4**	1	261^1	257	35	91	120	12.1	3.62	103	.260	.324	22	.242	3	7	4	1	0.6
1961 Cle-A	10	17	.370	35	35	6	1	0	223^2	238	28	87	90	13.3	4.71	84	.273	.343	12	.164	-1	-17	-19	-1	-1.8
1962 Cle-A	12	12	.500	35	27	7	3	0	193^2	213	21	59	74	12.7	4.14	94	.285	.339	11	.183	0	-4	-6	2	-0.3
1963 Cle-A	0	0	—	5	0	0	0	0	10^1	12	0	2	7	12.2	5.23	69	.293	.326	0	.000	-0	-2	-2	0	-0.1
Min-A	9	9	.500	35	25	5	1	1	168^1	167	17	57	65	12.1	3.74	97	.256	.318	11	.216	1	-3	-2	0	0.1
Yr	9	9	.500	40	25	5	1	1	178^2	179	17	59	72	12.1	3.83	95	.258	.318	6	.113	3	-4	-4	0	0.1
1964 Min-A	6	3	.667	42	1	0	0	2	65^1	61	7	23	55	11.7	3.44	104	.245	.311	2	.154	-0	1	1	-0	0.0
1965 *Min-A	12	7	.632	36	19	4	1	0	167^2	142	18	47	88	10.3	2.63	135	.232	.290	9	.170	1	15	17	-1	2.0
1966 Min-A	11	7	.611	33	25	8	1	0	184^1	149	17	53	122	10.1	2.54	142	.222	.284	13	.220	5	18	22	-1	2.8
1967 Min-A	8	7	.533	37	11	3	2	0	130^2	123	8	50	94	12.1	3.03	114	.255	.328	8	.190	1	3	6	1	0.7
1968 Min-A	8	6	.571	32	18	3	2	1	139	113	8	26	69	9.3	2.27	136	.219	.263	6	.143	2	11	13	1	1.9
1969 *Min-A	20	6	.769	46	36	12	3	0	261^2	244	18	66	153	11.0	2.82	129	.247	.300	16	.172	1	23	24	-2	2.5
1970 *Min-A	**24**	12	.667	40	40	13	4	0	278^2	258	20	57	168	10.5	3.04	123	.243	.287	24	.247	5	21	21	1	3.0
1971 Min-A	17	17	.500	40	39	8	0	1	270	263	39	102	126	12.3	4.23	84	.259	.329	17	.185	1	-23	-20	1	-1.8
1972 Min-A	13	16	.448	35	35	5	2	0	217^2	191	14	60	85	10.7	3.35	96	.236	.295	11	.155	-1	-7	-3	-1	-0.4

YEAR	TM/L	W	L	PCT	G	GS	CG	SH	SV	IP	H	HR	BB	SO	RAT	ERA	ERA+	OAV	OOB	BH	AVG	PB	PR	/A	PD	TPI
1973	Det-A	14	13	.519	35	34	7	1	0	203	225	22	55	66	12.6	4.03	101	.282	.331	0	—	0	-5	1	1	0.2
1974	Cle-A	17	12	.586	36	36	8	3	0	252	242	11	64	71	11.1	2.96	122	.254	.304	0	—	0	18	18	0	2.0
1975	Cle-A	1	6	.143	8	6	0	0	0	37²	46	8	18	11	15.3	6.69	57	.309	.383	0	—	0	-12	-12	0	-1.0
	Oak-A	3	4	.429	15	11	2	1	0	67²	61	7	26	33	12.5	4.66	78	.237	.324	0	—	0	-7	-8	-1	-0.8
	Yr	4	10	.286	23	17	2	1	0	105¹	107	15	44	44	13.5	5.38	68	.264	.346	0	—	0	-19	-20	-1	-1.8
Total 17		215	174	.553	630	447	109	32	10	3285²	3127	308	998	1576	11.5	3.45	106	.252	.312	177	.199	24	61	75	0	11.8

■ PAT PERRY
Perry, William Patrick b: 2/4/59, Taylorsville, Ill. BL/TL, 6'1", 170 lbs. Deb: 9/12/85

YEAR	TM/L	W	L	PCT	G	GS	CG	SH	SV	IP	H	HR	BB	SO	RAT	ERA	ERA+	OAV	OOB	BH	AVG	PB	PR	/A	PD	TPI
1985	StL-N	1	0	1.000	6	0	0	0	0	12¹	3	0	3	6	4.4	0.00	—	.077	.143	1	.500	0	5	5	-0	0.5
1986	StL-N	2	3	.400	46	0	0	0	2	68²	59	5	34	29	12.2	3.80	96	.239	.331	0	.000	-1	-1	-1	1	0.0
1987	StL-N	4	2	.667	45	0	0	0	1	65²	54	7	21	33	10.6	4.39	95	.222	.289	1	.143	-0	-2	-2	1	0.0
	Cin-N	1	0	1.000	12	0	0	0	0	15¹	6	0	4	6	6.5	0.00	—	.122	.204	0	—	0	7	7	0	0.8
	Yr	5	2	.714	57	0	0	0	1	81	60	7	25	39	9.6	3.56	117	.203	.268	1	.143	-0	5	6	1	0.8
1988	Cin-N	2	2	.500	12	0	0	0	0	20²	21	4	9	11	13.1	5.66	63	.262	.337	0	.000	-0	-5	-5	-0	-0.4
	Chi-N	2	2	.500	35	0	0	0	1	38	40	5	7	24	11.4	3.32	109	.270	.308	1	1.000	1	1	1	-0	0.3
	Yr	4	4	.500	47	0	0	0	1	58²	61	9	16	35	12.0	4.14	87	.264	.315	0	.000	1	-5	-4	-0	-0.1
1989	Chi-N	0	1	.000	19	0	0	0	1	35²	23	2	16	20	9.8	1.77	213	.187	.281	1	.167	-0	7	8	-1	0.8
1990	LA-N	0	0	—	7	0	0	0	0	6²	9	0	5	2	20.3	8.10	44	.310	.429	0	.000	-0	-3	-3	-0	-0.3
Total 6		12	10	.545	182	0	0	0	6	263	215	23	99	131	11.5	3.46	110	.224	.300	4	.148	0	8	10	1	1.7

■ PARSON PERRYMAN
Perryman, Emmett Key b: 10/24/1888, Everett Springs, Ga. d: 9/12/66, Starke, Fla. BR/TR, 6'4.5", 193 lbs. Deb: 4/14/15

YEAR	TM/L	W	L	PCT	G	GS	CG	SH	SV	IP	H	HR	BB	SO	RAT	ERA	ERA+	OAV	OOB	BH	AVG	PB	PR	/A	PD	TPI
1915	StL-A	2	4	.333	24	3	0	0	0	50¹	52	2	16	19	12.3	3.93	73	.281	.342	0	.000	-1	-6	-6	1	-0.5

■ BILL PERTICA
Pertica, William Andrew b: 3/5/1897, Santa Barbara, Cal. d: 12/28/67, Los Angeles, Cal. BR/TR, 5'9", 165 lbs. Deb: 8/07/18

YEAR	TM/L	W	L	PCT	G	GS	CG	SH	SV	IP	H	HR	BB	SO	RAT	ERA	ERA+	OAV	OOB	BH	AVG	PB	PR	/A	PD	TPI
1918	Bos-A	0	0	—	1	0	0	0	0	3	3	0	0	1	9.0	3.00	89	.273	.273	0	—	0	-0	-0	0	0.0
1921	StL-N	14	10	.583	38	31	15	2	2	208¹	212	9	70	67	12.6	3.37	109	.267	.334	10	.143	-3	10	7	-3	0.1
1922	StL-N	8	8	.500	34	14	2	0	0	117¹	153	5	65	30	17.0	5.91	65	.333	.419	6	.182	-0	-24	-27	1	-2.3
1923	StL-N	0	0	—	1	1	0	0	0	2¹	2	0	3	0	23.1	3.86	101	.250	.500	0	.000	-0	0	0	0	0.0
Total 4		22	18	.550	74	46	17	2	2	331	370	14	138	98	14.2	4.27	87	.291	.367	16	.152	-4	-14	-20	-1	-2.2

■ STAN PERZANOWSKI
Perzanowski, Stanley b: 8/25/50, East Chicago, Ind. BB/TR, 6'2", 170 lbs. Deb: 6/20/71

YEAR	TM/L	W	L	PCT	G	GS	CG	SH	SV	IP	H	HR	BB	SO	RAT	ERA	ERA+	OAV	OOB	BH	AVG	PB	PR	/A	PD	TPI
1971	Chi-A	0	1	.000	5	0	0	0	1	6	14	1	3	5	25.5	12.00	30	.412	.459	0	.000	-0	-6	-6	0	-0.5
1974	Chi-A	0	0	—	2	1	0	0	0	2¹	8	1	2	2	38.6	19.29	15	.533	.588	0	—	0	-4	-4	0	-0.3
1975	Tex-A	3	3	.500	12	8	1	0	0	66	59	1	25	26	12.1	3.00	125	.246	.330	0	—	0	6	6	1	0.7
1976	Tex-A	0	0	—	5	0	0	0	0	11²	20	3	4	6	20.1	10.03	36	.385	.448	0	—	0	-8	-8	0	-0.7
1978	Min-A	2	7	.222	13	7	1	0	1	56²	59	1	26	31	14.1	5.24	73	.276	.365	0	—	0	-9	-9	0	-0.7
Total 5		5	11	.313	37	16	2	0	2	142²	160	7	60	70	14.6	5.11	74	.288	.369	0	.000	-0	-22	-21	2	-1.5

■ JEFF PETEREK
Peterek, Jeffrey Allen b: 9/22/63, Michigan City, Ind. BR/TR, 6'2", 195 lbs. Deb: 8/14/89

YEAR	TM/L	W	L	PCT	G	GS	CG	SH	SV	IP	H	HR	BB	SO	RAT	ERA	ERA+	OAV	OOB	BH	AVG	PB	PR	/A	PD	TPI
1989	Mil-A	2	2	.000	7	4	0	0	0	31¹	31	3	14	16	12.9	4.60	95	.252	.328	0	—	0	-0	-1	0	0.0

■ GARY PETERS
Peters, Gary Charles b: 4/21/37, Grove City, Pa. BL/TL, 6'2", 200 lbs. Deb: 9/10/59

YEAR	TM/L	W	L	PCT	G	GS	CG	SH	SV	IP	H	HR	BB	SO	RAT	ERA	ERA+	OAV	OOB	BH	AVG	PB	PR	/A	PD	TPI
1959	Chi-A	0	0	—	2	0	0	0	0	1	2	0	2	1	36.0	0.00	—	.400	.571	0	—	0	0	0	0	0.0
1960	Chi-A	0	0	—	2	0	0	0	0	3¹	4	0	1	4	13.5	2.70	140	.286	.333	0	—	0	0	0	0	0.0
1961	Chi-A	0	0	—	3	0	0	0	1	10¹	10	0	2	6	10.5	1.74	225	.270	.308	1	.333	0	3	2	1	0.4
1962	Chi-A	0	1	.000	5	0	0	0	0	6¹	8	0	1	4	14.2	5.68	69	.308	.357	0	—	0	-1	-1	0	-0.1
1963	Chi-A	19	8	.704	41	30	13	4	1	243	192	9	68	189	9.9	**2.33**	150	.216	.278	21	.259	9	**35**	32	-1	**4.3**
1964	Chi-A	**20**	8	.714	37	36	11	3	0	273²	217	20	104	205	10.8	2.50	138	.219	.297	25	.208	8	34	29	-0	4.1
1965	Chi-A	10	12	.455	33	30	1	0	0	176¹	181	19	63	95	12.7	3.62	88	.265	.331	13	.181	2	-3	-8	0	-0.6
1966	Chi-A	12	10	.545	30	27	11	4	0	204²	156	11	45	129	**9.0**	**1.98**	160	.212	**.261**	19	.235	6	**33**	27	1	**3.9**
1967	Chi-A	16	11	.593	38	36	11	3	0	260	187	15	91	215	10.0	2.28	136	**.199**	.277	21	.212	6	27	24	2	3.7
1968	Chi-A	4	13	.235	31	25	6	1	1	162²	146	7	60	110	11.8	3.76	80	.242	.318	15	.208	7	-14	-13	-0	-0.7
1969	Chi-A	10	15	.400	36	32	7	3	0	218²	238	21	78	140	13.2	4.53	85	.283	.347	12	.169	-2	-22	-16	-2	-1.5
1970	Bos-A	16	11	.593	34	34	10	4	0	221²	221	20	83	155	12.6	4.06	98	.257	.328	20	.244	7	-9	-2	-1	0.3
1971	Bos-A	14	11	.560	34	32	9	1	1	214	241	25	70	100	13.3	4.37	84	.288	.347	26	.271	9	-22	-16	-1	-0.8
1972	Bos-A	3	3	.500	33	4	0	0	1	85¹	91	10	38	67	13.7	4.32	74	.279	.360	6	.200	1	-12	-11	-1	-0.8
Total 14		124	103	.546	359	286	79	23	5	2081	1894	157	706	1420	11.5	3.25	106	.243	.311	179	.222	57	50	46	-2	12.1

■ JOHN PETERS
Peters, John Paul b: 4/8/1850, Louisiana, Mo. d: 1/4/24, St.Louis, Mo. BR/TR, 5'7", 180 lbs. Deb: 5/23/1874 ♦

YEAR	TM/L	W	L	PCT	G	GS	CG	SH	SV	IP	H	HR	BB	SO	RAT	ERA	ERA+	OAV	OOB	BH	AVG	PB	PR	/A	PD	TPI
1876	Chi-N	0	0	—	1	0	0	0	1	1	1	0	1	0	18.0	0.00	—	.243	.391	111	.351	0	0	0	0	0.0

■ RUBE PETERS
Peters, Oscar Casper b: 3/15/1885, Grandfork, Ill. d: 2/7/65, Pequannock, N.J. BR/TR, 6'1", 195 lbs. Deb: 4/13/12

YEAR	TM/L	W	L	PCT	G	GS	CG	SH	SV	IP	H	HR	BB	SO	RAT	ERA	ERA+	OAV	OOB	BH	AVG	PB	PR	/A	PD	TPI
1912	Chi-A	5	6	.455	28	11	4	0	0	108²	134	2	33	39	14.3	4.14	77	.309	.366	6	.194	-1	-10	-11	5	-0.6
1914	Bro-F	2	2	.500	11	3	1	0	0	37²	52	1	16	13	16.2	3.82	84	.336	.398	1	.091	-1	-3	-3	0	-0.2
Total 2		7	8	.467	39	14	5	0	0	146¹	186	3	49	52	14.8	4.06	79	.316	.374	7	.167	-1	-13	-14	5	-0.8

■ RAY PETERS
Peters, Raymond James b: 8/27/46, Buffalo, N.Y. BR/TR, 6'5.5", 210 lbs. Deb: 6/04/70

YEAR	TM/L	W	L	PCT	G	GS	CG	SH	SV	IP	H	HR	BB	SO	RAT	ERA	ERA+	OAV	OOB	BH	AVG	PB	PR	/A	PD	TPI
1970	Mil-A	0	2	.000	2	2	0	0	0	2	7	0	5	1	54.0	31.50	12	.583	.706	0	—	0	-6	-6	0	-0.4

■ STEVE PETERS
Peters, Steven Bradley b: 11/14/62, Oklahoma City, Okla BL/TL, 5'10", 170 lbs. Deb: 8/11/87

YEAR	TM/L	W	L	PCT	G	GS	CG	SH	SV	IP	H	HR	BB	SO	RAT	ERA	ERA+	OAV	OOB	BH	AVG	PB	PR	/A	PD	TPI
1987	StL-N	0	0	—	12	0	0	0	1	15	17	1	6	11	13.8	1.80	231	.298	.365	0	.000	-0	4	4	1	0.4
1988	StL-N	3	3	.500	44	0	0	0	1	45	57	8	22	30	15.8	6.40	54	.313	.387	0	.000	-0	-15	-15	-1	-1.5
Total 2		3	3	.500	56	0	0	0	1	60	74	9	28	41	15.3	5.25	69	.310	.382	0	.000	-1	-11	-11	0	-1.1

■ ADAM PETERSON
Peterson, Adam Charles b: 12/11/65, Long Beach, Cal. BR/TR, 6'3", 190 lbs. Deb: 9/19/87

YEAR	TM/L	W	L	PCT	G	GS	CG	SH	SV	IP	H	HR	BB	SO	RAT	ERA	ERA+	OAV	OOB	BH	AVG	PB	PR	/A	PD	TPI
1987	Chi-A	0	0	—	1	1	0	0	0	4	8	1	3	1	24.8	13.50	34	.444	.524	0	—	0	-4	-4	0	-0.2
1988	Chi-A	0	1	.000	2	2	0	0	0	6	6	0	5	6	18.0	13.50	29	.240	.387	0	—	0	-6	-6	-0	-0.5
1989	Chi-A	0	1	.000	3	2	0	0	0	5¹	13	1	2	3	25.3	15.19	25	.464	.500	0	—	0	-7	-7	-0	-0.5
1990	Chi-A	2	5	.286	20	11	2	0	0	85	90	12	26	29	12.5	4.55	84	.278	.335	0	—	0	-6	-7	-1	-0.7
Total 4		2	7	.222	26	16	2	0	0	100¹	117	14	37	38	14.0	6.01	64	.296	.359	0	—	0	-23	-24	-1	-1.9

■ FRITZ PETERSON
Peterson, Fritz Fred (b: Fred Ingels Peterson) b: 2/8/42, Chicago, Ill. BB/TL, 6', 185 lbs. Deb: 4/15/66

YEAR	TM/L	W	L	PCT	G	GS	CG	SH	SV	IP	H	HR	BB	SO	RAT	ERA	ERA+	OAV	OOB	BH	AVG	PB	PR	/A	PD	TPI
1966	NY-A	12	11	.522	34	32	11	2	0	215	196	15	40	96	10.0	3.31	101	.241	.279	15	.224	4	3	0	0	0.5
1967	NY-A	8	14	.364	36	30	6	1	0	181¹	179	11	43	102	11.2	3.47	90	.256	.302	7	.146	1	-5	-7	2	-0.4
1968	NY-A	12	11	.522	36	27	6	2	0	212¹	187	13	29	115	9.3	2.63	110	.241	.272	5	.079	-2	8	6	4	1.0
1969	NY-A	17	16	.515	37	37	16	4	0	272	228	15	43	150	9.1	2.55	136	.229	.263	9	.112	-0	32	28	2	3.3
1970	NY-A	20	11	.645	39	37	8	2	0	260¹	247	24	40	127	10.0	2.90	121	.248	.280	20	.222	5	23	18	2	2.6
1971	NY-A	15	13	.536	37	35	16	4	1	274	269	25	42	139	10.3	3.05	106	.258	.289	7	.082	-3	12	5	2	0.4
1972	NY-A	17	15	.531	35	35	12	3	0	250¹	270	17	44	100	11.5	3.24	91	.276	.310	19	.232	3	-5	-8	2	-0.3
1973	NY-A	8	15	.348	31	31	6	0	0	184¹	199	14	49	59	12.8	3.95	93	.286	.337	0	—	0	-3	-6	1	-0.4
1974	NY-A	0	0	—	3	3	0	0	0	7²	13	1	2	5	17.6	4.70	74	.361	.395	0	—	0	-1	-1	0	0.0
	Cle-A	9	14	.391	29	29	3	0	0	152²	187	16	37	52	13.4	4.36	83	.305	.349	0	—	0	-13	-13	1	-1.1
	Yr	9	14	.391	32	30	3	0	0	160¹	200	17	39	57	13.6	4.38	82	.308	.351	0	—	0	-14	-14	1	-1.1
1975	Cle-A	14	8	.636	25	25	6	2	0	146¹	154	15	40	47	12.3	3.94	96	.275	.331	0	—	0	-3	-3	1	-0.3
1976	Cle-A	0	3	.000	9	9	0	0	0	47	59	3	10	19	13.2	5.55	63	.309	.343	0	—	0	-11	-11	0	-1.0
	Tex-A	1	0	1.000	4	2	0	0	0	15	21	0	7	4	16.8	3.60	100	.344	.412	0	—	0	-0	-0	0	0.0

YEAR TM/L	W	L	PCT	G	GS	CG	SH	SV	IP	H	HR	BB	SO	RAT	ERA	ERA+	OAV	OOB	BH	AVG	PB	PR	/A	PD	TPI
Yr	1	3	.250	13	11	0	0	0	62	80	3	17	23	14.1	5.08	69	.316	.359	0	—	0	-11	-11	0	-1.0
Total 11	133	131	.504	355	330	90	20	1	2218¹	2217	173	426	1015	10.9	3.30	101	.261	.300	82	.159	8	40	10	17	4.5

■ JIM PETERSON
Peterson, James Niels b: 8/18/08, Philadelphia, Pa. d: 4/8/75, Palm Beach, Fla. BR/TR, 6'0.5", 200 lbs. Deb: 7/09/31

YEAR TM/L	W	L	PCT	G	GS	CG	SH	SV	IP	H	HR	BB	SO	RAT	ERA	ERA+	OAV	OOB	BH	AVG	PB	PR	/A	PD	TPI
1931 Phi-A	0	1	.000	6	1	1	0	0	13	18	0	4	7	15.2	6.23	72	.321	.367	1	.500	1	-3	-3	-0	-0.1
1933 Phi-A	2	5	.286	32	5	0	0	0	90²	114	6	36	18	14.9	4.96	86	.305	.366	4	.148	-1	-7	-7	3	-0.4
1937 Bro-N	0	0	—	3	0	0	0	0	5²	8	3	2	4	15.9	7.94	51	.333	.385	0	—	0	-3	-2	1	-0.1
Total 3	2	6	.250	41	6	1	0	0	109¹	140	9	42	29	15.0	5.27	82	.308	.367	5	.172	0	-12	-12	3	-0.6

■ KENT PETERSON
Peterson, Kent Franklin "Pete" b: 12/21/25, Goshen, Utah BR/TL, 5'10", 170 lbs. Deb: 7/15/44

YEAR TM/L	W	L	PCT	G	GS	CG	SH	SV	IP	H	HR	BB	SO	RAT	ERA	ERA+	OAV	OOB	BH	AVG	PB	PR	/A	PD	TPI
1944 Cin-N	0	0	—	1	0	0	0	0	1	0	0	0	0	0.00	—	.000	.000	0	—	0	0	0	0	0.0
1947 Cin-N	6	13	.316	37	17	3	1	2	152¹	156	8	62	78	13.1	4.25	96	.265	.338	3	.068	-3	-3	-3	-2	-0.7
1948 Cin-N	2	15	.118	43	17	2	0	1	137	146	10	59	64	13.9	4.60	85	.271	.350	5	.139	-2	-10	-10	0	-1.1
1949 Cin-N	4	5	.444	30	7	2	0	0	66¹	66	8	46	28	15.7	6.24	67	.261	.383	1	.056	-2	-16	-15	-1	-1.6
1950 Cin-N	0	3	.000	9	2	0	0	0	20	25	4	17	6	18.9	7.20	59	.305	.424	1	.333	-2	-7	-7	-1	-0.6
1951 Cin-N	1	1	.500	9	0	0	0	0	9²	13	0	8	5	20.5	6.52	63	.317	.440	0	.000	-0	-3	-3	0	-0.2
1952 Phi-N	0	0	—	3	0	0	0	2	7	2	0	2	7	5.1	0.00	—	.091	.167	0	.000	-0	3	3	0	0.3
1953 Phi-N	0	1	.000	15	0	0	0	0	27	26	3	21	20	16.0	6.67	63	.252	.384	0	.000	-1	-7	-7	-0	-0.7
Total 8	13	38	.255	147	43	7	1	5	420¹	434	33	215	208	14.2	4.95	82	.266	.357	10	.091	-8	-43	-42	-4	-4.6

■ SID PETERSON
Peterson, Sidney Herbert b: 1/31/18, Havelock, N.Dak. BR/TR, 6'3", 200 lbs. Deb: 5/04/43

YEAR TM/L	W	L	PCT	G	GS	CG	SH	SV	IP	H	HR	BB	SO	RAT	ERA	ERA+	OAV	OOB	BH	AVG	PB	PR	/A	PD	TPI
1943 StL-A	2	0	1.000	3	0	0	0	0	10	15	0	3	0	17.1	2.70	123	.341	.396	0	.000	-0	1	1	0	0.0

■ DAN PETRY
Petry, Daniel Joseph b: 11/13/58, Palo Alto, Cal. BR/TR, 6'4", 185 lbs. Deb: 7/08/79

YEAR TM/L	W	L	PCT	G	GS	CG	SH	SV	IP	H	HR	BB	SO	RAT	ERA	ERA+	OAV	OOB	BH	AVG	PB	PR	/A	PD	TPI
1979 Det-A	6	5	.545	15	15	2	0	0	98	90	11	33	43	11.7	3.95	110	.254	.325	0	—	0	3	4	-0	0.4
1980 Det-A	10	9	.526	27	25	4	3	0	164²	156	9	83	88	13.1	3.94	104	.253	.342	0	—	0	2	3	2	0.5
1981 Det-A	10	9	.526	23	22	7	2	0	141	115	10	57	79	11.0	3.00	126	.224	.302	0	—	0	10	12	1	1.5
1982 Det-A	15	9	.625	35	35	8	1	0	246	220	15	100	132	11.9	3.22	126	.241	.319	0	—	0	23	23	4	2.9
1983 Det-A	19	11	.633	38	38	9	2	0	266¹	256	37	99	122	12.2	3.92	100	.256	.327	0	—	0	4	-0	4	0.3
1984 *Det-A	18	8	.692	35	35	7	2	0	233¹	231	21	66	144	11.6	3.24	121	.259	.312	0	—	0	19	18	3	2.2
1985 Det-A	15	13	.536	34	34	8	0	0	238²	190	24	81	109	10.3	3.36	121	.217	.285	0	—	0	21	19	1	2.1
1986 Det-A	5	10	.333	20	20	2	0	0	116	122	15	53	56	14.0	4.66	89	.268	.350	0	—	0	-6	-7	1	-0.4
1987 *Det-A	9	7	.563	30	21	0	0	0	134²	148	22	76	93	15.6	5.61	75	.279	.379	0	—	0	-17	-21	1	-1.7
1988 Cal-A	3	9	.250	22	22	4	1	0	139²	139	18	59	64	13.1	4.38	88	.263	.344	0	—	0	-6	-8	3	-0.5
1989 Cal-A	3	2	.600	19	4	0	0	0	51	53	8	23	21	13.6	5.47	70	.275	.355	0	—	0	-9	-9	0	-0.8
1990 Det-A	10	9	.526	32	23	1	0	0	149²	144	14	77	73	13.6	4.45	88	.263	.353	0	—	0	-9	-9	2	-0.6
Total 12	123	101	.549	330	294	52	11	0	1979	1868	204	807	1024	12.4	3.89	103	.251	.328	0	—	0	35	25	22	5.9

■ JAY PETTIBONE
Pettibone, Harry Jonathan b: 6/21/57, Mt.Clemens, Mich. BR/TR, 6'4", 182 lbs. Deb: 9/11/83

YEAR TM/L	W	L	PCT	G	GS	CG	SH	SV	IP	H	HR	BB	SO	RAT	ERA	ERA+	OAV	OOB	BH	AVG	PB	PR	/A	PD	TPI
1983 Min-A	0	4	.000	4	4	1	0	0	27	28	8	8	10	12.7	5.33	80	.280	.345	0	—	0	-4	-3	0	-0.2

■ PAUL PETTIT
Pettit, George William Paul "Lefty" b: 11/29/31, Los Angeles, Cal. BL/TL, 6'2", 195 lbs. Deb: 5/04/51

YEAR TM/L	W	L	PCT	G	GS	CG	SH	SV	IP	H	HR	BB	SO	RAT	ERA	ERA+	OAV	OOB	BH	AVG	PB	PR	/A	PD	TPI
1951 Pit-N	0	0	—	2	0	0	0	0	2²	2	1	1	0	10.1	3.38	125	.200	.273	0	.000	-0	0	0	0	0.0
1953 Pit-N	1	2	.333	10	5	0	0	0	28	33	1	20	14	17.0	7.71	58	.297	.405	2	.250	1	-11	-10	0	-0.7
Total 2	1	2	.333	12	5	0	0	0	30²	35	2	21	14	16.4	7.34	61	.289	.394	2	.222	1	-10	-10	0	-0.7

■ LEON PETTIT
Pettit, Leon Arthur "Lefty" b: 6/23/02, Waynesburg, Pa. d: 11/21/74, Columbia, Tenn. BL/TL, 5'10.5", 165 lbs. Deb: 4/18/35

YEAR TM/L	W	L	PCT	G	GS	CG	SH	SV	IP	H	HR	BB	SO	RAT	ERA	ERA+	OAV	OOB	BH	AVG	PB	PR	/A	PD	TPI
1935 Was-A	8	5	.615	41	7	1	0	3	109	129	6	58	45	15.8	4.95	87	.301	.390	2	.080	0	-6	-8	-0	-0.6
1937 Phi-N	0	1	.000	3	1	0	0	0	4	6	1	4	0	22.5	11.25	39	.353	.476	0	—	0	-3	-3	0	-0.2
Total 2	8	6	.571	44	8	1	0	3	113	135	7	62	45	16.0	5.18	84	.303	.393	2	.080	0	-9	-11	-0	-0.8

■ BOB PETTIT
Pettit, Robert Henry b: 7/19/1861, Williamstown, Mass. d: 11/1/10, Derby, Conn. BL/TR, 5'9", 160 lbs. Deb: 9/03/1887 ◆

YEAR TM/L	W	L	PCT	G	GS	CG	SH	SV	IP	H	HR	BB	SO	RAT	ERA	ERA+	OAV	OOB	BH	AVG	PB	PR	/A	PD	TPI
1887 Chi-N	0	0	—	1	0	0	0	1	1	3	0	2	0	45.0	0.00	—	.504	.629	36	.261	0	0	0	0	0.0

■ CHARLIE PETTY
Petty, Charles E. b: 6/28/1866, Nashville, Tenn. TR , Deb: 7/30/1889

YEAR TM/L	W	L	PCT	G	GS	CG	SH	SV	IP	H	HR	BB	SO	RAT	ERA	ERA+	OAV	OOB	BH	AVG	PB	PR	/A	PD	TPI
1889 Cin-a	2	3	.400	5	5	5	0	0	44	44	3	20	10	13.1	5.52	71	.252	.329	6	.300	1	-8	-8	0	-0.4
1893 NY-N	5	2	.714	9	6	4	0	0	54	66	0	28	12	15.7	3.33	140	.292	.370	7	.318	2	8	8	-0	0.9
1894 Was-N	3	8	.273	16	12	8	0	0	103	156	4	32	14	16.4	5.59	94	.345	.388	1	.195	-2	-3	-4	-1	-0.4
Cle-N	0	2	.000	4	3	2	0	0	27	42	4	14	4	18.7	8.67	63	.351	.419	1	.083	-2	-10	-10	-1	-0.8
Yr	3	10	.231	20	15	10	0	0	130	198	8	46	18	16.9	6.23	85	.346	.395	4	.075	-4	-13	-13	-1	-1.2
Total 3	10	15	.400	34	26	19	0	0	228	308	11	94	40	15.9	5.41	90	.317	.377	22	.232	-0	-13	-13	-1	-0.7

■ JESSE PETTY
Petty, Jesse Lee "The Silver Fox" b: 11/23/1894, Orr, Okla. d: 10/23/71, St.Paul, Minn. BR/TL, 6', 195 lbs. Deb: 4/14/21

YEAR TM/L	W	L	PCT	G	GS	CG	SH	SV	IP	H	HR	BB	SO	RAT	ERA	ERA+	OAV	OOB	BH	AVG	PB	PR	/A	PD	TPI
1921 Cle-A	0	0	—	4	0	0	0	0	9	10	0	0	0	10.0	2.00	213	.345	.345	0	.000	-0	2	2	1	0.3
1925 Bro-N	9	9	.500	28	22	7	0	0	153	188	15	47	39	13.9	4.88	86	.304	.355	7	.140	-3	-10	-12	-1	-1.4
1926 Bro-N	17	17	.500	38	33	23	1	1	275²	246	9	79	101	10.7	2.84	135	**.240**	.296	17	.175	-3	30	30	-4	2.4
1927 Bro-N	13	18	.419	42	33	19	2	1	271²	263	13	53	101	10.6	2.98	133	.254	.293	9	.099	-7	28	30	-3	2.0
1928 Bro-N	15	15	.500	40	31	15	2	1	234	264	18	56	74	12.5	4.04	98	.289	.334	9	.111	-5	-1	-2	-1	-1.0
1929 Pit-N	11	10	.524	36	25	12	1	0	184¹	197	12	42	58	11.7	3.71	129	.277	.317	7	.104	-6	21	22	-2	1.3
1930 Pit-N	1	6	.143	10	7	0	0	1	41¹	67	8	13	16	17.9	8.27	60	.362	.410	1	.083	-1	-15	-15	-0	-1.3
Chi-N	1	3	.250	9	3	0	0	0	39¹	51	2	6	18	13.0	2.97	164	.317	.341	3	.231	0	9	8	0	0.8
Yr	2	9	.182	19	10	0	0	1	80²	118	10	19	34	15.3	5.69	87	.339	.373	4	.000	-1	-6	-7	-0	-0.5
Total 7	67	78	.462	207	154	76	6	4	1208¹	1286	77	296	407	11.9	3.68	113	.275	.320	53	.128	-25	63	63	-12	3.1

■ PRETZEL PEZZULLO
Pezzullo, John b: 12/10/10, Bridgeport, Conn. d: 5/16/90, Dallas, Tex. BL/TL, 5'11.5", 180 lbs. Deb: 4/18/35

YEAR TM/L	W	L	PCT	G	GS	CG	SH	SV	IP	H	HR	BB	SO	RAT	ERA	ERA+	OAV	OOB	BH	AVG	PB	PR	/A	PD	TPI
1935 Phi-N	3	5	.375	41	7	2	0	1	84¹	115	5	45	24	17.8	6.40	71	.321	.407	6	.250	1	-22	-18	-2	-1.7
1936 Phi-N	0	0	—	1	0	0	0	0	2	1	0	6	0	31.5	4.50	101	.167	.583	0	—	0	-0	-0	0	0.0
Total 2	3	5	.375	42	7	2	0	1	86¹	116	5	51	24	18.1	6.36	71	.319	.412	6	.250	1	-22	-18	-2	-1.7

■ JEFF PFEFFER
Pfeffer, Edward Joseph b: 3/4/1888, Seymour, Ill. d: 8/15/72, Chicago, Ill. BR/TR, 6'3", 210 lbs. Deb: 4/16/11

YEAR TM/L	W	L	PCT	G	GS	CG	SH	SV	IP	H	HR	BB	SO	RAT	ERA	ERA+	OAV	OOB	BH	AVG	PB	PR	/A	PD	TPI
1911 StL-A	0	0	—	2	0	0	0	0	10	11	0	4	4	13.5	7.20	47	.297	.366	0	.000	-1	-4	-4	-0	-0.3
1913 Bro-N	0	1	.000	5	2	1	0	0	24¹	28	0	13	13	16.6	3.33	99	.311	.421	0	.000	-1	-0	-0	0	0.0
1914 Bro-N	23	12	.657	43	34	27	3	4	315	264	9	91	135	10.3	1.97	145	.232	.293	23	.198	-1	29	31	-4	3.0
1915 Bro-N	19	14	.576	40	34	26	6	3	291²	243	8	76	84	10.4	2.10	132	.231	.293	27	.255	5	21	22	-4	2.6
1916 *Bro-N	25	11	.694	41	37	30	6	1	328²	274	5	63	128	9.7	1.92	140	.230	.278	34	.279	7	26	28	-4	3.8
1917 Bro-N	11	15	.423	30	30	24	3	0	266	225	4	66	115	10.4	2.23	125	.234	.294	13	.130	-5	14	17	-2	1.1
1918 Bro-N	1	0	1.000	1	1	1	0	0	9	2	0	3	1	5.0	0.00	—	.071	.161	1	.250	0	3	3	0	0.5
1919 Bro-N	17	13	.567	30	30	26	4	0	267	270	7	49	92	11.2	2.66	112	.267	.308	20	.206	1	7	9	1	0.3
1920 *Bro-N	16	9	.640	30	28	20	2	0	215	225	5	45	80	11.5	3.01	106	.273	.314	18	.243	1	3	5	-3	0.3
1921 Bro-N	1	5	.167	6	5	2	0	0	31²	36	0	9	8	13.1	4.55	86	.310	.365	0	.000	-2	-3	-2	-0	-0.3
StL-N	9	3	.750	18	13	7	1	0	98²	115	3	28	22	13.5	4.29	86	.305	.361	4	.138	-1	-6	-7	-1	-0.8
Yr	10	8	.556	24	18	9	1	0	130¹	151	3	37	30	13.3	4.35	86	.306	.360	3	.075	-2	-8	-9	-1	-1.1
1922 StL-N	19	12	.613	44	32	19	1	2	261¹	286	15	67	72	12.2	3.58	108	.279	.324	24	.245	4	15	8	1	1.2
1923 StL-N	8	9	.471	26	18	7	1	0	152¹	171	8	40	32	13.0	4.02	97	.287	.341	7	.127	-4	-0	-2	-1	-0.5
1924 StL-N	4	5	.444	16	12	3	0	0	78	102	3	30	20	15.3	5.31	71	.318	.378	3	.115	-2	-12	-13	-1	-1.4
Pit-N	5	3	.625	15	4	1	0	0	58²	68	3	17	19	13.0	3.07	125	.293	.341	6	.240	-0	5	5	-1	0.3

YEAR TM/L	W	L	PCT	G	GS	CG	SH	SV	IP	H	HR	BB	SO	RAT	ERA	ERA+	OAV	OOB	BH	AVG	PB	PR	/A	PD	TPI
Yr	9	8	.529	31	16	4	0	0	136²	170	6	47	39	14.3	4.35	88	.307	.361	0	.000	-3	-7	-8	-2	-1.1
Total 13	158	112	.585	347	280	194	28	10	2407¹	2320	67	592	836	11.3	2.77	114	.258	.311	180	.206	2	97	103	-18	10.6

■ BIG JEFF PFEFFER
Pfeffer, Francis Xavier b: 3/31/1882, Champaign, Ill. d: 12/19/54, Kankakee, Ill. BR/TR, 6'1", 185 lbs. Deb: 4/15/05

YEAR TM/L	W	L	PCT	G	GS	CG	SH	SV	IP	H	HR	BB	SO	RAT	ERA	ERA+	OAV	OOB	BH	AVG	PB	PR	/A	PD	TPI
1905 Chi-N	4	4	.500	15	11	9	0	0	101	84	2	36	56	11.0	2.50	120	.240	.318	8	.200	1	6	5	-1	0.5
1906 Bos-N	13	22	.371	35	35	33	4	0	302¹	270	4	114	158	11.9	2.95	91	.246	.325	31	.196	2	-11	-9	1	-0.4
1907 Bos-N	6	8	.429	19	16	12	1	0	144	129	3	61	65	12.3	3.00	85	.253	.341	15	.250	3	-8	-7	-1	-0.5
1908 Bos-N	0	0	—	4	0	0	0	0	10	18	1	8	3	23.4	12.60	19	.383	.473	0	.000	-0	-11	-11	-0	-1.1
1910 Chi-N	1	0	1.000	13	1	1	0	0	41¹	43	1	16	11	13.1	3.27	88	.281	.353	3	.176	1	-1	-2	-0	-0.1
1911 Bos-N	7	5	.583	26	6	4	1	2	97	116	3	57	24	16.1	4.73	81	.301	.391	9	.196	1	-14	-10	0	-0.6
Total 6	31	39	.443	112	69	59	6	2	695²	660	14	292	317	12.7	3.30	87	.260	.342	66	.204	7	-40	-34	-1	-2.2

■ FRED PFEFFER
Pfeffer, Nathaniel Frederick "Fritz" or "Dandelion"
b: 3/17/1860, Louisville, Ky. d: 4/10/32, Chicago, Ill. BR/TR, 5'10.5", 184 lbs. Deb: 5/01/1882 M♦

YEAR TM/L	W	L	PCT	G	GS	CG	SH	SV	IP	H	HR	BB	SO	RAT	ERA	ERA+	OAV	OOB	BH	AVG	PB	PR	/A	PD	TPI
1884 Chi-N	0	0	—	1	0	0	0	0	1	3	0	1	0	36.0	9.00	35	.495	.567	135	.289	0	-1	-1	0	0.0
1885 *Chi-N	2	1	.667	5	2	2	0	2	31²	26	1	8	13	9.7	2.56	119	.213	.262	113	.241	1	1	2	-0	0.2
1892 Lou-N	0	0	—	1	0	0	0	0	5	4	0	5	0	16.2	1.80	170	.211	.375	121	.257	0	1	1	0	0.1
1894 Lou-N	0	0	—	1	0	0	0	0	7	8	0	6	0	18.0	2.57	198	.284	.410	126	.308	0	2	2	0	0.2
Total 4	2	1	.667	8	2	2	0	2	44²	41	1	20	13	12.3	2.62	130	.234	.313	1671	.255	1	3	4	-0	0.5

■ JACK PFIESTER
Pfiester, John Albert "Jack The Giant Killer" (b: John Albert Hagenbush)
b: 5/24/1878, Cincinnati, Ohio d: 9/3/53, Loveland, Ohio BR/TL, 5'11", 180 lbs. Deb: 9/08/03

YEAR TM/L	W	L	PCT	G	GS	CG	SH	SV	IP	H	HR	BB	SO	RAT	ERA	ERA+	OAV	OOB	BH	AVG	PB	PR	/A	PD	TPI
1903 Pit-N	0	3	.000	3	3	2	0	0	19	26	0	15	18	18.0	6.16	53	.321	.409	0	.000	-1	-6	-6	-0	-0.5
1904 Pit-N	1	1	.500	3	2	1	0	0	20	28	0	9	6	16.6	7.20	38	.318	.381	2	.286	1	-10	-10	0	-0.7
1906 *Chi-N	20	8	.714	31	29	20	4	0	250²	173	3	63	153	8.9	1.51	175	.194	.258	4	.048	-7	31	32	-1	2.7
1907 *Chi-N	14	9	.609	30	22	13	3	0	195	143	1	48	90	9.0	1.15	216	.207	.263	6	.094	-2	29	29	-2	2.9
1908 *Chi-N	12	10	.545	33	29	18	3	0	252	204	0	70	117	10.2	2.00	118	.223	.287	8	.101	-3	10	10	-2	0.4
1909 Chi-N	17	6	.739	29	25	13	5	0	196²	179	1	49	73	10.7	2.43	105	.240	.291	11	.169	0	4	3	3	0.6
1910 *Chi-N	6	3	.667	14	13	5	2	0	100¹	82	0	26	34	9.8	1.79	161	.225	.279	3	.091	-2	14	12	-0	1.0
1911 Chi-N	1	4	.200	6	5	3	0	0	33²	34	0	18	15	14.4	4.01	83	.262	.360	2	.182	0	-2	-3	1	-0.1
Total 8	71	44	.617	149	128	75	17	0	1067¹	869	6	293	503	10.1	2.02	128	.223	.284	36	.103	-15	69	67	-2	6.3

■ DAN PFISTER
Pfister, Daniel Albin b: 12/20/36, Plainfield, N.J. BR/TR, 6', 187 lbs. Deb: 9/09/61

YEAR TM/L	W	L	PCT	G	GS	CG	SH	SV	IP	H	HR	BB	SO	RAT	ERA	ERA+	OAV	OOB	BH	AVG	PB	PR	/A	PD	TPI
1961 KC-A	0	0	—	2	0	0	0	0	2¹	5	2	4	3	34.7	15.43	27	.417	.563	0	—	0	-3	-3	0	-0.2
1962 KC-A	4	14	.222	41	25	2	0	1	196¹	175	27	106	123	13.3	4.54	92	.238	.341	12	.185	-1	-12	-8	1	-0.7
1963 KC-A	1	0	1.000	3	1	0	0	0	9¹	8	1	3	9	11.6	1.93	199	.229	.308	0	.000	-0	2	2	0	0.2
1964 KC-A	1	5	.167	19	3	0	0	0	41¹	50	10	29	21	18.5	6.53	58	.311	.434	0	.000	-0	-13	-12	-0	-1.2
Total 4	6	19	.240	65	29	2	0	1	249¹	238	40	142	156	14.3	4.87	84	.252	.359	12	.162	-2	-27	-22	1	-1.9

■ BILL PFLANN
Pflann, William F. b: Brooklyn, N.Y. 6', 205 lbs. Deb: 6/16/1894

YEAR TM/L	W	L	PCT	G	GS	CG	SH	SV	IP	H	HR	BB	SO	RAT	ERA	ERA+	OAV	OOB	BH	AVG	PB	PR	/A	PD	TPI
1894 Cin-N	0	1	.000	1	1	0	0	0	3	10	1	4	0	42.0	27.00	21	.537	.618	0	.000	-0	-7	-7	0	-0.3

■ LEE PFUND
Pfund, Le Roy Herbert b: 10/10/18, Oak Park, Ill. BR/TR, 6'1", 185 lbs. Deb: 4/21/45

YEAR TM/L	W	L	PCT	G	GS	CG	SH	SV	IP	H	HR	BB	SO	RAT	ERA	ERA+	OAV	OOB	BH	AVG	PB	PR	/A	PD	TPI
1945 Bro-N	3	2	.600	15	10	2	0	0	62¹	69	4	35	27	15.7	5.20	72	.274	.373	4	.182	0	-10	-10	0	-0.8

■ BILL PHEBUS
Phebus, Raymond William b: 8/9/09, Cherryvale, Kan. BR/TR, 5'9", 170 lbs. Deb: 9/06/36

YEAR TM/L	W	L	PCT	G	GS	CG	SH	SV	IP	H	HR	BB	SO	RAT	ERA	ERA+	OAV	OOB	BH	AVG	PB	PR	/A	PD	TPI
1936 Was-A	0	0	—	2	1	0	0	0	7¹	4	1	4	4	11.0	2.45	195	.114	.225	0	.000	0	2	2	-0	0.2
1937 Was-A	3	2	.600	6	5	4	1	1	40²	33	2	24	12	13.1	2.21	200	.232	.351	0	.000	1	11	10	-1	1.0
1938 Was-A	0	0	—	5	0	0	0	1	6¹	9	1	7	2	22.7	11.37	40	.346	.485	0	.000	-0	-5	-5	0	-0.3
Total 3	3	2	.600	13	6	4	1	2	54¹	46	4	35	18	13.9	3.31	135	.227	.349	0	.000	1	8	7	-1	0.9

■ RAY PHELPS
Phelps, Raymond Clifford b: 12/11/03, Dunlap, Tenn. d: 7/7/71, Fort Pierce, Fla. BR/TR, 6'2", 200 lbs. Deb: 4/23/30

YEAR TM/L	W	L	PCT	G	GS	CG	SH	SV	IP	H	HR	BB	SO	RAT	ERA	ERA+	OAV	OOB	BH	AVG	PB	PR	/A	PD	TPI
1930 Bro-N	14	7	.667	36	24	11	2	0	179²	198	21	52	64	12.7	4.11	119	.280	.332	10	.147	-2	17	16	2	1.4
1931 Bro-N	7	9	.438	28	26	3	1	0	149¹	184	3	44	50	14.0	5.00	76	.306	.357	8	.157	-1	-19	-20	1	-1.9
1932 Bro-N	4	5	.444	20	8	4	1	0	79¹	101	5	27	21	14.9	5.90	65	.323	.382	2	.087	-1	-18	-18	0	-1.7
1935 Chi-A	4	8	.333	27	17	4	0	1	125	126	10	55	38	13.2	4.82	96	.262	.341	5	.122	-4	-5	-3	2	-0.3
1936 Chi-A	4	6	.400	15	4	2	0	0	68²	91	9	42	17	17.7	6.03	86	.331	.423	6	.231	1	-8	-6	1	-0.3
Total 5	33	35	.485	126	79	24	4	1	602	700	48	220	190	14.0	4.93	90	.294	.358	31	.148	-8	-32	-32	6	-2.8

■ DEACON PHILLIPPE
Phillippe, Charles Louis b: 5/23/1872, Rural Retreat, Va. d: 3/30/52, Avalon, Pa. BR/TR, 6'0.5", 180 lbs. Deb: 4/21/1899

YEAR TM/L	W	L	PCT	G	GS	CG	SH	SV	IP	H	HR	BB	SO	RAT	ERA	ERA+	OAV	OOB	BH	AVG	PB	PR	/A	PD	TPI
1899 Lou-N	21	17	.553	42	38	33	2	1	321	331	10	64	68	11.1	3.17	122	.266	.302	26	.203	-1	24	25	-0	2.2
1900 *Pit-N	20	13	.606	38	33	29	1	0	279	274	7	42	75	10.2	2.84	128	.256	.285	19	.181	-3	27	25	-2	1.8
1901 Pit-N	22	12	.647	37	32	30	1	2	296	274	7	38	103	9.8	2.22	147	.244	.275	26	.230	5	36	34	3	4.4
1902 Pit-N	20	9	.690	31	30	29	5	0	272	265	1	26	122	9.7	2.05	133	.255	.275	25	.221	2	22	21	-2	2.3
1903 *Pit-N	25	9	.735	36	33	31	4	2	289¹	269	4	29	123	9.4	2.43	133	.241	.263	26	.210	-3	27	26	-3	2.5
1904 Pit-N	10	10	.500	21	19	17	3	1	166²	183	1	26	82	11.4	3.24	85	.272	.302	8	.123	-3	-9	-9	-1	-1.3
1905 Pit-N	20	13	.606	38	33	25	5	0	279	235	0	48	133	9.5	2.19	137	.233	.274	9	.093	-5	25	25	-2	2.0
1906 Pit-N	15	10	.600	33	24	19	3	0	218²	216	3	26	90	10.0	2.47	108	.252	.276	20	.244	3	4	5	1	0.8
1907 Pit-N	14	11	.560	35	26	17	1	2	214	214	2	36	61	10.7	2.61	93	.264	.300	12	.185	1	-3	-4	-1	-0.4
1908 Pit-N	0	0	—	5	0	0	0	0	12	20	0	3	1	17.3	11.25	20	.357	.390	1	.250	0	-12	-12	-1	-1.1
1909 *Pit-N	8	3	.727	22	12	7	1	0	131²	128	3	17	38	9.5	2.32	117	.253	.280	3	.071	-3	4	6	-2	0.1
1910 Pit-N	14	2	.875	31	8	5	1	4	121²	111	4	9	30	9.1	2.29	135	.239	.258	9	.220	1	10	11	-3	1.0
1911 Pit-N	0	0	—	3	0	0	0	0	6	5	0	2	3	10.5	7.50	46	.238	.304	1	1.000	1	-3	-3	0	0.0
Total 13	189	109	.634	372	288	242	27	12	2607	2518	41	363	929	10.1	2.59	120	.253	.282	185	.189	0	153	150	-13	14.3

■ BUZ PHILLIPS
Phillips, Albert Abernathy b: 5/25/04, Newton, N.C. d: 11/6/64, Baltimore, Md. BR/TR, 5'11.5", 185 lbs. Deb: 8/05/30

YEAR TM/L	W	L	PCT	G	GS	CG	SH	SV	IP	H	HR	BB	SO	RAT	ERA	ERA+	OAV	OOB	BH	AVG	PB	PR	/A	PD	TPI
1930 Phi-N	0	0	—	14	1	0	0	0	43²	68	6	18	9	17.9	8.04	68	.354	.412	6	.462	3	-15	-12	-1	-0.8

■ RED PHILLIPS
Phillips, Clarence Lemuel b: 11/3/08, Pauls Valley, Okla. d: 2/1/88, Wichita, Kan. BR/TR, 6'3.5", 195 lbs. Deb: 7/24/34

YEAR TM/L	W	L	PCT	G	GS	CG	SH	SV	IP	H	HR	BB	SO	RAT	ERA	ERA+	OAV	OOB	BH	AVG	PB	PR	/A	PD	TPI
1934 Det-A	2	0	1.000	7	1	1	0	1	23¹	31	1	16	3	18.1	6.17	77	.316	.412	3	.250	1	-4	-5	-1	-0.3
1936 Det-A	2	4	.333	22	6	3	0	0	87¹	124	12	22	15	15.0	6.49	76	.332	.370	10	.303	2	-14	-15	0	-1.0
Total 2	4	4	.500	29	7	4	0	1	110²	155	13	38	18	15.7	6.42	75	.329	.379	13	.289	3	-18	-20	-1	-1.3

■ JACK PHILLIPS
Phillips, Jack Dorn "Stretch" b: 9/6/21, Clarence, N.Y. BR/TR, 6'4", 193 lbs. Deb: 8/22/47 ♦

YEAR TM/L	W	L	PCT	G	GS	CG	SH	SV	IP	H	HR	BB	SO	RAT	ERA	ERA+	OAV	OOB	BH	AVG	PB	PR	/A	PD	TPI
1950 Pit-N	0	0	—	1	0	0	0	0	5	7	0	1	2	14.4	7.20	61	.333	.364	61	.293	0	-2	-2	0	0.0

■ JACK PHILLIPS
Phillips, John Stephen b: 5/24/19, St.Louis, Mo. d: 6/16/58, St.Louis, Mo. BR/TR, 6'1", 185 lbs. Deb: 7/13/45 ♦

YEAR TM/L	W	L	PCT	G	GS	CG	SH	SV	IP	H	HR	BB	SO	RAT	ERA	ERA+	OAV	OOB	BH	AVG	PB	PR	/A	PD	TPI
1945 NY-N	0	0	—	1	0	0	0	0	4¹	5	1	5	0	22.8	10.38	38	.313	.500	1	.500	0	-3	-3	0	-0.2

■ ED PHILLIPS
Phillips, Norman Edwin b: 9/20/44, Ardmore, Okla. BR/TR, 6'1", 190 lbs. Deb: 4/09/70

YEAR TM/L	W	L	PCT	G	GS	CG	SH	SV	IP	H	HR	BB	SO	RAT	ERA	ERA+	OAV	OOB	BH	AVG	PB	PR	/A	PD	TPI
1970 Bos-A	0	2	.000	18	0	0	0	0	23²	29	4	10	23	15.6	5.32	74	.312	.390	0	.000	-0	-4	-4	-1	-0.4

■ TOM PHILLIPS
Phillips, Thomas Gerald b: 4/5/1889, Phillipsburg, Pa. d: 4/12/29, Phillipsburg, Pa. BR/TR, 6'2", 190 lbs. Deb: 9/13/15

YEAR TM/L	W	L	PCT	G	GS	CG	SH	SV	IP	H	HR	BB	SO	RAT	ERA	ERA+	OAV	OOB	BH	AVG	PB	PR	/A	PD	TPI
1915 StL-A	1	3	.250	5	4	1	0	0	27¹	28	0	12	5	13.8	2.96	97	.283	.372	1	.111	-1	-0	-1	-0	-0.1
1919 Cle-A	1	1	.500	5	3	2	0	0	55	55	2	34	18	15.1	2.95	114	.272	.385	4	.364	1	2	2	-1	0.2
1921 Was-A	1	0	1.000	1	1	0	0	0	9	9	0	3	2	12.0	2.00	206	.290	.353	0	.000	0	2	2	-0	0.1
1922 Was-A	3	7	.300	17	7	2	1	0	70	72	2	22	19	12.6	4.89	79	.273	.338	3	.150	-1	-7	-8	-1	-0.8

YEAR	TM/L	W	L	PCT	G	GS	CG	SH	SV	IP	H	HR	BB	SO	RAT	ERA	ERA+	OAV	OOB	BH	AVG	PB	PR	/A	PD	TPI
Total	4	8	12	.400	45	15	6	1	0	161¹	164	4	71	44	13.6	3.74	95	.275	.361	8	.186	-1	-3	-3	-2	-0.6

■ BILL PHILLIPS
Phillips, William Corcoran "Whoa Bill" or "Silver Bill"
b: 11/9/1868, Allenport, Pa.   d: 10/25/41, Charleroi, Pa.   BR/TR, 5'11", 180 lbs.   Deb: 8/11/1890   M

YEAR	TM/L	W	L	PCT	G	GS	CG	SH	SV	IP	H	HR	BB	SO	RAT	ERA	ERA+	OAV	OOB	BH	AVG	PB	PR	/A	PD	TPI
1890	Pit-N	1	9	.100	10	10	9	0	0	82	123	8	29	25	16.7	7.57	43	.337	.386	11	.239	1	-37	-39	0	-2.9
1895	Cin-N	6	7	.462	18	9	6	0	2	109	126	6	44	15	14.0	6.03	83	.285	.350	15	.313	2	-15	-13	1	-0.7
1899	Cin-N	17	9	.654	33	27	18	1	1	227²	234	3	71	43	12.1	3.32	118	.265	.320	12	.130	-5	14	15	0	0.9
1900	Cin-N	9	11	.450	29	24	17	3	0	208¹	229	5	67	51	12.8	4.28	86	.279	.333	13	.165	-4	-13	-14	6	-1.0
1901	Cin-N	14	18	.438	37	36	29	1	0	281¹	364	7	67	109	14.1	4.64	69	.311	.353	22	.202	2	-41	-45	5	-3.5
1902	Cin-N	16	16	.500	33	33	30	0	0	269	267	3	55	85	11.0	2.51	119	.259	.301	39	.342	10	8	15	3	3.3
1903	Cin-N	7	6	.538	16	13	11	1	0	118¹	134	0	30	46	13.0	3.35	106	.279	.330	10	.175	-1	-1	3	2	0.4
Total	7	70	76	.479	176	152	120	6	3	1295²	1477	32	363	374	13.0	4.09	87	.284	.334	122	.224	4	-85	-77	18	-3.5

■ TAYLOR PHILLIPS
Phillips, William Taylor "Tay"   b: 6/18/33, Atlanta, Ga.   BL/TL, 5'11", 185 lbs.   Deb: 6/08/56

YEAR	TM/L	W	L	PCT	G	GS	CG	SH	SV	IP	H	HR	BB	SO	RAT	ERA	ERA+	OAV	OOB	BH	AVG	PB	PR	/A	PD	TPI
1956	Mil-N	5	3	.625	23	6	3	0	2	87²	69	6	33	36	11.2	2.26	153	.223	.311	0	.000	-2	15	12	2	1.2
1957	Mil-N	3	2	.600	27	6	0	0	2	73	82	3	40	36	15.2	5.55	63	.300	.392	2	.100	-1	-14	-17	0	-1.6
1958	Chi-N	7	10	.412	39	27	5	1	1	170¹	178	22	79	102	13.9	4.76	82	.266	.349	3	.056	-4	-15	-16	1	-1.8
1959	Chi-N	0	2	.000	7	2	0	0	0	16²	22	3	11	5	18.9	7.56	52	.319	.427	0	.000	-0	-7	-7	0	-0.6
	Phi-N	1	4	.200	32	3	1	0	1	63	72	4	31	35	15.3	5.00	82	.303	.392	1	.091	-1	-7	-6	0	-0.5
	Yr	1	6	.143	39	5	1	0	1	79²	94	7	42	40	15.8	5.54	74	.303	.393	0	.000	-1	-14	-13	1	-1.1
1960	Phi-N	0	1	.000	10	1	0	0	0	14	21	2	4	6	16.7	8.36	46	.356	.406	0	.000	-0	-7	-7	0	-0.6
1963	Chi-A	0	0	—	9	0	0	0	0	14	16	2	13	13	19.3	10.29	34	.302	.448	0	.000	-0	-10	-11	0	-1.0
Total	6	16	22	.421	147	45	9	1	6	438²	460	42	211	233	14.2	4.82	78	.275	.364	6	.053	-9	-46	-51	4	-4.9

■ TOM PHOEBUS
Phoebus, Thomas Harold   b: 4/7/42, Baltimore, Md.   BR/TR, 5'8", 185 lbs.   Deb: 9/15/66

YEAR	TM/L	W	L	PCT	G	GS	CG	SH	SV	IP	H	HR	BB	SO	RAT	ERA	ERA+	OAV	OOB	BH	AVG	PB	PR	/A	PD	TPI
1966	Bal-A	2	1	.667	3	3	2	2	0	22	16	0	6	17	9.0	1.23	271	.213	.272	1	.167	0	5	5	-0	0.6
1967	Bal-A	14	9	.609	33	33	7	4	0	208	177	16	114	179	12.6	3.33	95	.227	.326	11	.145	1	-2	-4	-2	-0.5
1968	Bal-A	15	15	.500	36	36	9	3	0	240²	186	10	105	193	11.0	2.62	112	.212	.299	15	.183	3	10	8	-1	0.2
1969	Bal-A	14	7	.667	35	33	6	2	0	202	180	23	87	117	12.1	3.52	101	.241	.324	15	.200	2	2	1	-1	0.2
1970	*Bal-A	5	5	.500	27	21	3	0	0	135	106	11	62	72	11.6	3.07	119	.219	.315	7	.163	-0	10	9	1	0.9
1971	SD-N	3	11	.214	29	21	2	0	0	133¹	144	14	64	80	14.2	4.45	74	.280	.363	6	.163	1	-15	-17	-1	-1.6
1972	SD-N	0	1	.000	1	1	0	0	0	5²	3	2	6	8	14.3	7.94	41	.150	.346	0	.000	-0	-3	-3	0	-0.2
	Chi-N	3	3	.500	37	1	0	0	6	83¹	76	9	45	59	13.3	3.78	101	.247	.346	2	.133	-1	-3	1	0	0.0
	Yr	3	4	.429	38	2	0	0	6	89	79	11	51	67	13.3	4.04	93	.241	.346	0	.000	-1	-6	-3	1	-0.2
Total	7	56	52	.519	201	149	29	11	6	1030	888	85	489	725	12.2	3.33	100	.233	.324	57	.170	5	4	-1	-3	0.6

■ BILL PHYLE
Phyle, William Joseph   b: 6/25/1875, Duluth, Minn.   d: 8/6/53, Los Angeles, Cal.   TR,   Deb: 9/17/1898   ♦

YEAR	TM/L	W	L	PCT	G	GS	CG	SH	SV	IP	H	HR	BB	SO	RAT	ERA	ERA+	OAV	OOB	BH	AVG	PB	PR	/A	PD	TPI
1898	Chi-N	2	1	.667	3	3	2	0	0	23	24	0	6	4	11.7	0.78	458	.267	.313	1	.111	-0	7	7	-0	0.7
1899	Chi-N	1	8	.111	10	9	9	0	1	83²	92	2	29	10	13.0	4.20	89	.279	.337	6	.176	-2	-3	-4	1	-0.4
1901	NY-N	7	10	.412	24	19	16	0	1	168²	208	2	54	62	14.2	4.27	77	.301	.356	12	.182	-1	-18	-18	2	-1.6
Total	3	10	19	.345	37	31	28	2	2	275¹	324	4	89	76	13.7	3.96	88	.292	.347	32	.176	-3	-14	-15	2	-1.3

■ WILEY PIATT
Piatt, Wiley Harold "Iron Man"   b: 7/13/1874, Blue Creek, Ohio   d: 9/20/46, Cincinnati, Ohio   BL/TL, 5'10", 175 lbs.   Deb: 4/22/1898

YEAR	TM/L	W	L	PCT	G	GS	CG	SH	SV	IP	H	HR	BB	SO	RAT	ERA	ERA+	OAV	OOB	BH	AVG	PB	PR	/A	PD	TPI
1898	Phi-N	24	14	.632	39	37	33	6	0	306	285	2	97	121	11.2	3.18	108	.245	.303	32	.262	4	15	9	-3	0.9
1899	Phi-N	23	15	.605	39	38	31	2	0	305	323	6	86	89	12.1	3.45	107	.271	.320	33	.270	4	14	8	-5	0.6
1900	Phi-N	9	10	.474	22	20	16	1	0	160²	194	5	71	47	14.8	4.71	77	.298	.367	17	.250	1	-18	-19	-3	-1.7
1901	Phi-A	5	12	.294	18	16	15	0	1	140	176	4	60	45	15.2	4.63	82	.303	.369	13	.224	0	-15	-13	-4	-1.3
	Chi-A	4	2	.667	7	6	4	1	0	51²	42	2	14	19	9.8	2.79	125	.220	.273	2	.118	-1	5	4	-1	0.1
	Yr	9	14	.391	25	22	19	1	1	191²	218	6	74	64	13.7	4.13	89	.283	.346	7	.093	-1	-10	-9	-5	-1.2
1902	Chi-A	12	12	.500	32	30	22	2	0	246	263	3	66	96	12.0	3.51	96	.274	.321	17	.200	1	2	-3	-4	-0.5
1903	Bos-N	9	14	.391	25	23	18	0	0	181	198	5	61	100	13.1	3.18	101	.280	.340	16	.225	1	2	1	-3	-0.0
Total	6	86	79	.521	182	170	139	12	1	1390¹	1481	27	455	517	12.6	3.61	97	.272	.329	130	.239	11	4	-15	-23	-2.0

■ RON PICHE
Piche, Ronald Jacques   b: 5/22/35, Verdun, Que., Canada   BR/TR, 5'11", 165 lbs.   Deb: 5/30/60   C

YEAR	TM/L	W	L	PCT	G	GS	CG	SH	SV	IP	H	HR	BB	SO	RAT	ERA	ERA+	OAV	OOB	BH	AVG	PB	PR	/A	PD	TPI
1960	Mil-N	3	5	.375	37	0	0	0	9	48	48	3	23	38	13.9	3.56	96	.258	.349	0	.000	-0	1	-1	-1	-0.1
1961	Mil-N	2	2	.500	12	1	1	0	1	23¹	20	1	16	16	13.9	3.47	108	.238	.360	0	.000	-1	1	1	0	0.0
1962	Mil-N	3	2	.600	14	8	2	0	0	52	54	6	29	28	14.9	4.85	78	.273	.374	1	.056	-1	-5	-6	1	-0.6
1963	Mil-N	1	1	.500	37	1	0	0	0	53	53	4	25	40	13.2	3.40	95	.256	.336	0	.000	-1	-1	-1	1	0.0
1965	Cal-A	0	3	.000	14	1	0	0	0	19²	20	5	12	14	14.6	6.86	50	.267	.368	0	.000	-0	-7	-8	0	-0.7
1966	StL-N	1	3	.250	20	0	0	0	2	25¹	21	4	18	21	14.2	4.26	84	.214	.342	0	.000	-0	-2	-2	-0	-0.1
Total	6	10	16	.385	134	11	3	0	12	221¹	216	23	123	157	14.1	4.19	84	.255	.354	1	.024	-3	-13	-16	1	-1.6

■ CHARLIE PICKETT
Pickett, Charles Albert   b: 3/1/1883, Delaware, Ohio   d: 5/20/69, Springfield, Ohio   BR/TR, 6'1", 175 lbs.   Deb: 6/21/10

YEAR	TM/L	W	L	PCT	G	GS	CG	SH	SV	IP	H	HR	BB	SO	RAT	ERA	ERA+	OAV	OOB	BH	AVG	PB	PR	/A	PD	TPI
1910	StL-N	0	0	—	2	0	0	0	0	6	7	0	2	2	13.5	1.50	199	.280	.333	0	—	0	1	1	0	0.1

■ CLARENCE PICKREL
Pickrel, Clarence Douglas   b: 3/28/11, Grenta, Va.   d: 11/4/83, Rocky Mount, Va.   BR/TR, 6'1", 180 lbs.   Deb: 4/22/33

YEAR	TM/L	W	L	PCT	G	GS	CG	SH	SV	IP	H	HR	BB	SO	RAT	ERA	ERA+	OAV	OOB	BH	AVG	PB	PR	/A	PD	TPI
1933	Phi-N	1	0	1.000	9	0	0	0	0	13²	20	0	3	6	15.8	3.95	97	.357	.400	0	.000	-0	-1	-0	-1	0.0
1934	Bos-N	0	0	—	10	1	0	0	0	16	24	0	7	9	17.4	5.06	76	.333	.392	0	.000	-0	-2	-2	-1	-0.2
Total	2	1	0	1.000	19	1	0	0	0	29²	44	0	10	15	16.7	4.55	85	.344	.396	0	.000	-0	-3	-2	-1	-0.2

■ JEFF PICO
Pico, Jeffrey Mark   b: 2/12/66, Antioch, Cal.   BR/TR, 6'1", 190 lbs.   Deb: 5/31/88

YEAR	TM/L	W	L	PCT	G	GS	CG	SH	SV	IP	H	HR	BB	SO	RAT	ERA	ERA+	OAV	OOB	BH	AVG	PB	PR	/A	PD	TPI
1988	Chi-N	6	7	.462	29	13	3	2	1	112²	108	6	37	57	11.6	4.15	87	.252	.312	5	.147	-0	-9	-7	0	-0.6
1989	Chi-N	3	1	.750	53	5	0	0	2	90²	99	8	31	38	12.9	3.77	100	.278	.336	1	.100	-1	-3	-0	2	0.1
1990	Chi-N	4	4	.500	31	8	0	0	2	92	120	7	37	37	15.5	4.79	86	.321	.383	6	.273	2	-10	-7	2	-0.2
Total	3	13	12	.520	113	26	3	2	5	295¹	327	21	105	132	13.2	4.24	90	.282	.343	12	.182	1	-22	-14	3	-0.7

■ MARIO PICONE
Picone, Mario Peter "Babe"   b: 7/5/26, Brooklyn, N.Y.   BR/TR, 5'11", 180 lbs.   Deb: 9/27/47

YEAR	TM/L	W	L	PCT	G	GS	CG	SH	SV	IP	H	HR	BB	SO	RAT	ERA	ERA+	OAV	OOB	BH	AVG	PB	PR	/A	PD	TPI
1947	NY-N	0	0	—	2	1	0	0	0	7	10	1	2	1	15.4	7.71	53	.345	.387	1	.500	1	-3	-3	0	-0.1
1952	NY-N	0	1	.000	2	1	0	0	0	9	11	2	5	3	16.0	7.00	53	.306	.390	0	.000	-0	-3	-3	0	-0.2
1954	NY-N	0	0	—	5	0	0	0	0	13²	13	1	11	6	15.8	5.27	77	.283	.421	0	.000	-0	-2	-2	-0	-0.1
	Cin-N	0	1	.000	4	1	0	0	0	10¹	9	3	7	1	13.9	6.10	69	.243	.364	0	.000	-0	-2	-2	1	0.0
	Yr	0	1	.000	9	1	0	0	0	24	22	4	18	7	15.0	5.63	73	.265	.396	2	1.000	0	-4	-4	0	-0.1
Total	3	0	2	.000	13	3	0	0	0	40	43	7	25	11	15.3	6.30	64	.291	.393	1	.167	1	-10	-10	1	-0.4

■ AL PIECHOTA
Piechota, Aloysius Edward "Pie"   b: 1/19/14, Chicago, Ill.   BR/TR, 6', 195 lbs.   Deb: 5/07/40

YEAR	TM/L	W	L	PCT	G	GS	CG	SH	SV	IP	H	HR	BB	SO	RAT	ERA	ERA+	OAV	OOB	BH	AVG	PB	PR	/A	PD	TPI
1940	Bos-N	2	5	.286	21	8	2	0	0	61	68	6	41	18	16.1	5.75	65	.278	.381	4	.200	1	-13	-14	-0	-1.2
1941	Bos-N	0	0	—	1	0	0	0	0	1	0	0	1	0	9.0	0.00	—	.000	.250	0	—	0	0	0	0	0.0
Total	2	2	5	.286	22	8	2	0	0	62	68	6	42	18	16.0	5.66	66	.274	.379	4	.200	1	-13	-13	-0	-1.2

■ CY PIEH
Pieh, Edwin John   b: 9/29/1886, Waunakee, Wis.   d: 9/12/45, Jacksonville, Fla   BR/TR, 6'2", 190 lbs.   Deb: 9/06/13

YEAR	TM/L	W	L	PCT	G	GS	CG	SH	SV	IP	H	HR	BB	SO	RAT	ERA	ERA+	OAV	OOB	BH	AVG	PB	PR	/A	PD	TPI
1913	NY-A	1	0	1.000	4	0	0	0	0	10¹	10	0	7	6	14.8	4.35	69	.250	.362	1	.250	0	-2	-2	1	0.0
1914	NY-A	4	4	.500	18	4	1	0	0	62¹	68	6	29	24	14.0	5.05	55	.289	.367	2	.118	-0	-16	-16	-1	-1.7
1915	NY-A	4	5	.444	21	8	3	2	0	94	78	2	39	46	11.7	2.87	102	.234	.324	2	.067	-3	1	1	0	-0.2
Total	3	9	9	.500	43	12	4	2	0	166²	156	8	75	76	12.7	3.78	76	.257	.343	5	.098	-3	-17	-17	0	-1.9

YEAR	TM/L	W	L	PCT	G	GS	CG	SH	SV	IP	H	HR	BB	SO	RAT	ERA	ERA+	OAV	OOB	BH	AVG	PB	PR	/A	PD	TPI

■ RAY PIERCE Pierce, Raymond Lester "Lefty" b: 6/6/1897, Emporia, Kan. d: 5/4/63, Denver, Colo. BL/TL, 5'7", 156 lbs. Deb: 5/12/24

1924	Chi-N	0	0	—	6	0	0	0	0	7¹	7	2	4	2	13.5	7.36	53	.269	.367	0	—	0	-3	-3	-0	-0.2
1925	Phi-N	5	4	.556	23	8	4	0	0	90	134	7	24	18	15.9	5.50	87	.356	.397	5	.179	-0	-12	-7	0	-0.5
1926	Phi-N	2	7	.222	37	7	1	0	0	84²	128	3	35	18	17.4	5.63	74	.348	.406	3	.125	-2	-17	-14	-1	-1.5
Total	3	7	11	.389	66	15	5	0	0	182	269	12	63	38	16.5	5.64	79	.349	.400	8	.154	-2	-32	-24	-0	-2.2

■ TONY PIERCE Pierce, Tony Michael b: 1/29/46, Brunswick, Ga. BR/TL, 6'1", 190 lbs. Deb: 4/14/67

1967	KC-A	3	4	.429	49	6	0	0	7	97²	79	6	30	61	10.5	3.04	105	.221	.290	0	.000	-2	2	2	-1	-0.1
1968	Oak-A	1	2	.333	17	3	0	0	1	32²	39	3	10	16	13.8	3.86	73	.295	.350	0	.000	-1	-3	-4	1	-0.3
Total	2	4	6	.400	66	9	0	0	8	130¹	118	9	40	77	11.3	3.25	95	.241	.306	0	.000	-3	-1	-2	-0	-0.4

■ BILLY PIERCE Pierce, Walter William b: 4/2/27, Detroit, Mich. BL/TL, 5'10", 160 lbs. Deb: 6/01/45

1945	Det-A	0	0	—	5	0	0	0	0	10	6	1	10	10	15.3	1.80	195	.182	.386	0	.000	-0	2	2	0	0.2
1948	Det-A	3	0	1.000	22	5	0	0	0	55¹	47	5	51	36	16.1	6.34	69	.234	.391	5	.294	2	-13	-12	-0	-0.9
1949	Chi-A	7	15	.318	32	26	8	0	0	171²	145	11	112	95	13.5	3.88	108	.228	.344	9	.176	-1	6	6	0	0.5
1950	Chi-A	12	16	.429	33	29	15	1	1	219¹	189	11	137	118	13.5	3.98	113	.228	.339	20	.260	4	15	12	-2	1.3
1951	Chi-A	15	14	.517	37	28	18	1	2	240¹	237	14	73	113	11.6	3.03	133	.258	.313	16	.203	1	29	27	-1	2.5
1952	Chi-A	15	12	.556	33	32	14	4	1	255¹	214	12	79	144	10.4	2.57	142	.227	.289	17	.187	0	31	31	0	3.3
1953	Chi-A	18	12	.600	40	33	19	7	3	271¹	216	20	102	**186**	10.6	2.72	148	**.218**	.292	11	.126	-4	38	39	-3	3.4
1954	Chi-A	9	10	.474	36	26	12	4	3	188²	179	15	86	148	12.8	3.48	107	.249	.332	11	.193	0	5	5	-3	0.3
1955	Chi-A	15	10	.600	33	26	16	6	1	205²	162	16	64	157	10.0	**1.97**	**200**	.213	**.277**	12	.171	-1	45	45	-2	**4.7**
1956	Chi-A	20	9	.690	35	33	**21**	1	1	276¹	261	24	100	192	10.9	3.32	123	.249	.316	16	.157	-4	26	24	-1	1.6
1957	Chi-A	**20**	12	.625	37	34	**16**	4	2	257	228	18	71	171	10.5	3.26	115	.234	.287	17	.172	-2	15	14	-1	1.2
1958	Chi-A	17	11	.607	35	32	**19**	3	2	245	204	33	66	144	10.0	2.68	136	.227	.280	17	.205	2	30	26	-3	2.7
1959	*Chi-A	14	15	.483	34	33	12	2	0	224	217	26	62	114	11.3	3.62	104	.253	.306	13	.191	3	6	4	0	0.6
1960	Chi-A	14	7	.667	32	30	8	1	0	196¹	201	24	46	108	11.3	3.62	104	.266	.308	12	.179	1	5	3	-1	0.3
1961	Chi-A	10	9	.526	39	28	5	1	3	180	190	17	54	106	12.3	3.80	103	.275	.328	8	.143	-2	4	2	-0	0.0
1962	*SF-N	16	6	.727	30	23	7	2	1	162¹	147	19	35	76	10.3	3.49	109	.239	.284	12	.214	2	8	5	-1	0.6
1963	SF-N	3	11	.214	38	13	3	1	8	99	106	12	20	52	11.5	4.27	75	.272	.309	4	.129	-0	-11	-12	1	-1.1
1964	SF-N	3	0	1.000	34	1	0	0	4	49	40	6	10	29	9.2	2.20	162	.222	.263	3	.333	1	7	7	-1	0.8
Total	18	211	169	.555	585	432	193	38	32	3306²	2989	284	1178	1999	11.4	3.27	119	.240	.307	203	.184	0	250	229	-19	22.0

■ BILL PIERCY Piercy, William Benton "Wild Bill" b: 5/2/1896, ElMonte, Cal. d: 8/28/51, Long Beach, Cal. BR/TR, 6'1.5", 170 lbs. Deb: 10/03/17

1917	NY-A	0	1	.000	1	1	1	0	0	9	9	0	2	4	11.0	3.00	90	.257	.297	0	.000	-0	-0	-0	0	0.0
1921	*NY-A	5	4	.556	14	10	5	1	0	81²	82	4	28	35	12.9	2.98	142	.263	.337	6	.214	0	12	11	-0	1.1
1922	Bos-A	3	9	.250	29	12	7	1	0	121¹	140	2	62	24	15.4	4.67	88	.304	.394	5	.147	-1	-8	-8	2	-0.5
1923	Bos-A	8	17	.320	30	24	11	0	0	187¹	193	5	73	51	13.5	3.41	121	.277	.357	7	.132	-3	12	15	3	1.5
1924	Bos-A	5	7	.417	23	18	3	0	0	121	156	6	46	20	17.3	5.95	73	.335	.429	6	.154	-2	-23	-21	2	-1.9
1926	Chi-N	6	5	.545	19	5	1	0	0	90¹	96	1	37	31	13.8	4.48	86	.280	.360	9	.257	1	-7	-6	0	-0.4
Total	6	27	43	.386	116	70	28	2	0	610²	676	16	268	165	14.5	4.26	97	.292	.376	33	.173	-5	-15	-10	8	-0.2

■ MARINO PIERETTI Pieretti, Marino Paul "Chick" b: 9/23/20, Lucca, Italy d: 1/30/81, San Francisco, Cal BR/TR, 5'7", 153 lbs. Deb: 4/19/45

1945	Was-A	14	13	.519	44	27	14	3	2	233¹	235	3	91	66	12.6	3.32	94	.257	.325	18	.222	2	1	-6	2	-0.2
1946	Was-A	2	2	.500	30	2	1	0	0	62	70	9	40	20	16.3	5.95	56	.292	.397	3	.214	0	-17	-18	1	-1.6
1947	Was-A	2	4	.333	23	10	2	1	0	83¹	97	3	47	32	15.8	4.21	88	.287	.377	6	.231	0	-5	-5	-0	-0.4
1948	Was-A	0	2	.000	8	1	0	0	0	11²	18	1	7	6	19.3	10.80	40	.375	.455	0	.000	-0	-8	-8	0	-0.7
	Chi-A	8	10	.444	21	18	4	0	1	120	117	6	52	28	12.7	4.95	86	.262	.339	7	.179	-1	-9	-9	2	-0.7
	Yr	8	12	.400	29	19	4	0	1	131²	135	7	59	34	13.3	5.47	78	.273	.351	4	.098	-1	-17	-18	2	-1.4
1949	Chi-N	4	6	.400	39	9	0	0	4	116	131	10	54	25	14.4	5.51	76	.289	.364	9	.237	1	-17	-17	2	-1.3
1950	Cle-A	0	1	.000	29	1	0	0	1	47¹	45	2	30	11	14.3	4.18	104	.253	.361	2	.286	0	2	1	1	0.2
Total	6	30	38	.441	194	68	21	4	8	673²	713	34	321	188	13.9	4.53	81	.272	.353	45	.217	2	-52	-63	7	-4.7

■ AL PIEROTTI Pierotti, Albert Felix b: 10/24/1895, Boston, Mass. d: 2/12/64, Everett, Mass. BR/TR, 5'10.5", 195 lbs. Deb: 8/09/20

1920	Bos-N	1	1	.500	6	2	2	0	0	25	23	2	9	12	11.5	2.88	106	.250	.317	2	.250	0	1	0	-0	0.0
1921	Bos-N	0	1	.000	2	0	0	0	0	1²	3	0	3	1	32.4	21.60	17	.375	.545	0	.000	-0	-3	-3	0	-0.2
Total	2	1	2	.333	8	2	2	0	0	26²	26	2	12	13	12.8	4.05	76	.260	.339	2	.222	-0	-3	-3	-0	-0.2

■ BILL PIERRO Pierro, William Leonard "Wild Bill" b: 4/15/26, Brooklyn, N.Y. BR/TR, 6'1", 155 lbs. Deb: 7/17/50

| 1950 | Pit-N | 0 | 2 | .000 | 12 | 3 | 0 | 0 | 0 | 29 | 33 | 2 | 28 | 13 | 19.6 | 10.55 | 42 | .289 | .438 | 2 | .222 | -0 | -21 | -20 | -1 | -1.7 |

■ DAVE PIERSON Pierson, David P. b: 8/20/1855, Wilkes-Barre, Pa. d: 11/11/22, Trenton, N.J. BR/TR, 5'7", 142 lbs. Deb: 4/25/1876 ♦

| 1876 | Cin-N | 0 | 1 | .000 | 1 | 1 | 0 | 0 | 0 | 0 | 2 | 1 | 0 | 0 | — | ∞ | — | 1.000 | 1.000 | 55 | .236 | -0 | -2 | -2 | 0 | -0.1 |

■ WILLIAM PIERSON Pierson, William Morris b: 6/14/1899, Atlantic City, N.J. d: 2/20/59, Atlantic City, N.J BL/TR, 6'2", 180 lbs. Deb: 7/04/18

1918	Phi-A	0	1	.000	8	1	0	0	0	21²	20	0	20	6	17.4	3.32	88	.286	.457	1	.250	-0	-1	-1	-1	-0.1
1919	Phi-A	0	0	—	2	1	0	0	0	7²	9	0	8	4	20.0	3.52	97	.333	.486	1	.333	0	-0	-0	0	0.0
1924	Phi-A	0	0	—	1	0	0	0	0	2²	3	0	3	0	20.3	3.38	127	.300	.462	0	—	0	0	0	0	0.0
Total	3	0	1	.000	11	2	0	0	0	32	32	0	31	10	18.3	3.38	94	.299	.464	2	.286	0	-1	-1	-0	-0.1

■ GEORGE PIKTUZIS Piktuzis, George Richard b: 1/3/32, Chicago, Ill. BR/TL, 6'2", 200 lbs. Deb: 4/25/56

| 1956 | Chi-N | 0 | 0 | — | 2 | 0 | 0 | 0 | 0 | 5 | 6 | 1 | 2 | 3 | 14.4 | 7.20 | 52 | .333 | .400 | 0 | — | 0 | -2 | -2 | -0 | -0.1 |

■ DUANE PILLETTE Pillette, Duane Xavier "Dee" b: 7/24/22, Detroit, Mich. BR/TR, 6'3", 195 lbs. Deb: 7/19/49

1949	NY-A	2	4	.333	12	3	2	0	0	37¹	43	6	19	9	14.9	4.34	93	.299	.380	0	.000	-1	-1	-1	1	0.0
1950	NY-A	0	0	—	4	0	0	0	0	7	9	0	3	4	15.4	1.29	334	.321	.387	0	—	0	3	2	-0	0.2
	StL-A	3	5	.375	24	7	1	0	2	73²	104	6	44	18	18.3	7.09	70	.337	.423	3	.136	-1	-21	-17	0	-1.6
	Yr	3	5	.375	28	7	1	0	2	80²	113	6	47	22	18.1	6.58	74	.335	.420	2	.091	-1	-18	-15	-0	-1.4
1951	StL-A	6	14	.300	35	24	6	1	0	191	205	14	115	65	15.3	4.99	88	.276	.376	8	.136	-4	-19	-13	-1	-1.5
1952	StL-A	10	13	.435	30	30	9	1	0	205¹	222	14	55	62	12.4	3.59	109	.274	.325	12	.182	0	2	7	-2	0.6
1953	StL-A	7	13	.350	31	25	7	1	0	166²	181	16	62	58	13.2	4.48	94	.277	.341	7	.132	-1	-9	-5	-1	-0.6
1954	Bal-A	10	14	.417	25	25	11	1	0	179	158	9	67	66	11.4	3.12	115	.234	.305	7	.132	-1	12	9	3	1.2
1955	Bal-A	0	3	.000	7	5	0	0	0	20²	31	0	14	13	16.6	6.53	58	.344	.433	1	.167	0	-6	-6	0	-0.5
1956	Phi-N	0	0	—	20	0	0	0	0	23¹	32	2	12	10	17.0	6.56	57	.330	.404	0	.000	-0	-7	-7	-0	-0.7
Total	8	38	66	.365	188	119	34	4	2	904	985	67	391	305	13.9	4.40	93	.277	.352	38	.140	-7	-45	-32	1	-2.9

■ HERMAN PILLETTE Pillette, Herman Polycarp "Old Folks" b: 12/26/1895, St.Paul, Ore. d: 4/30/60, Sacramento, Cal. BR/TR, 6'2", 190 lbs. Deb: 7/30/17

1917	Cin-N	0	0	—	1	0	0	0	0	1	4	0	0	0	36.0	18.00	15	.571	.571	0	—	0	-2	-2	0	-0.1
1922	Det-A	19	12	.613	40	37	18	4	1	274²	270	6	95	71	12.5	2.85	136	.258	.328	17	.172	-3	36	31	3	3.1
1923	Det-A	14	19	.424	47	36	14	0	1	250¹	280	7	83	64	13.3	3.85	100	.288	.347	21	.247	4	4	0	4	0.8
1924	Det-A	1	1	.500	19	3	1	0	1	37²	46	1	14	13	15.1	4.78	86	.297	.366	4	.364	1	-2	-3	0	-0.1
Total	4	34	32	.515	107	76	33	4	3	563²	600	14	192	148	13.0	3.45	113	.275	.340	42	.215	2	36	27	8	3.7

■ SQUIZ PILLION Pillion, Cecil Randolph b: 4/13/1894, Hartford, Conn. d: 9/30/62, Pittsburgh, Pa. TL, 6', 178 lbs. Deb: 8/20/15

| 1915 | Phi-A | 0 | 0 | — | 2 | 0 | 0 | 0 | 0 | 5¹ | 10 | 0 | 2 | 0 | 21.9 | 6.75 | 44 | .400 | .464 | 0 | .000 | -0 | -2 | -2 | 0 | -0.1 |

YEAR	TM/L	W	L	PCT	G	GS	CG	SH	SV	IP	H	HR	BB	SO	RAT	ERA	ERA+	OAV	OOB	BH	AVG	PB	PR	/A	PD	TPI

■ HORACIO PINA
Pina, Horacio (Garcia) b: 3/12/45, Coahuila, Mexico BR/TR, 6'2", 177 lbs. Deb: 8/14/68

1968	Cle-A	1	1	.500	12	3	0	0	2	31¹	24	0	15	24	11.5	1.72	172	.218	.317	0	.000	-1	4	4	0	0.4
1969	Cle-A	4	2	.667	31	4	0	0	1	46²	44	6	27	32	14.7	5.21	72	.256	.373	3	.500	1	-8	-7	0	-0.5
1970	Was-A	5	3	.625	61	0	0	0	6	71	66	4	35	41	13.2	2.79	127	.250	.344	0	.000	-0	7	6	1	0.7
1971	Was-A	1	1	.500	56	0	0	0	2	57²	47	2	31	38	12.8	3.59	92	.227	.339	0	.000	-0	-1	-2	1	0.0
1972	Tex-A	2	7	.222	60	0	0	0	15	76	61	3	43	60	13.3	3.20	94	.228	.352	1	.200	-1	-1	-2	2	0.1
1973	*Oak-A	6	3	.667	47	0	0	0	8	88	58	8	34	41	10.2	2.76	128	.193	.292	0	—	0	10	8	3	1.1
1974	Chi-N	3	4	.429	34	0	0	0	4	47¹	49	4	28	32	15.0	3.99	96	.268	.371	1	.200	-0	-2	-1	0	0.0
	Cal-N	1	2	.333	11	0	0	0	0	11²	9	1	3	6	9.3	2.31	149	.209	.261	0	—	-0	2	1	1	0.2
1978	Phi-N	0	0	—	2	0	0	0	0	2¹	0	0	0	4	0.0	0.00	—	.000	.000	0	.000	-0	1	1	0	0.1
Total	8	23	23	.500	314	7	0	0	38	432	358	28	216	278	12.6	3.25	106	.231	.336	5	.185	0	12	9	9	2.1

■ ED PINKHAM
Pinkham, Edward b: 1849, Brooklyn, N.Y. TL, 5'7", 142 lbs. Deb: 5/08/1871 ♦

| 1871 | Chi-n | 1 | 0 | 1.000 | 3 | 0 | 0 | 0 | 1 | 10¹ | 10 | 0 | 3 | 0 | 11.3 | 3.48 | 132 | .208 | .255 | 25 | .263 | 1 | 1 | 1 | | 0.1 |

■ GEORGE PINKNEY
Pinkney, George Burton b: 1/11/1862, Orange Prairie, Ill. d: 11/10/26, Peoria, Ill. BR/TR, 5'7", 160 lbs. Deb: 8/16/1884 ♦

| 1886 | Bro-a | 0 | 0 | — | 1 | 0 | 0 | 0 | 0 | 2 | 2 | 0 | 0 | 0 | 9.0 | 4.50 | 78 | .248 | .248 | 156 | .261 | 0 | -0 | -0 | 0 | 0.0 |

■ ED PINNANCE
Pinnance, Edward D. "Peanuts"
b: 10/22/1879, Walpole Island, Ont., Canada d: 12/12/44, Walpole Island, Ontario, Canada BL/TR, 6'1", 180 lbs. Deb: 9/14/03

| 1903 | Phi-A | 0 | 0 | — | 2 | 1 | 0 | 0 | 1 | 7 | 5 | 0 | 2 | 2 | 9.0 | 2.57 | 119 | .200 | .260 | 0 | .000 | -0 | 0 | 0 | 0 | 0.0 |

■ LERTON PINTO
Pinto, William Lerton b: 4/8/1899, Chillcothe, Ohio d: 5/13/83, Oxnard, Cal. BL/TL, 6', 190 lbs. Deb: 5/23/22

1922	Phi-N	0	1	.000	9	0	0	0	0	24²	31	1	14	4	16.4	5.11	91	.320	.405	1	.111	-1	-3	-1	-0	-0.1
1924	Phi-N	0	0	—	3	0	0	0	0	4	7	1	0	1	15.8	9.00	50	.467	.467	0	.000	-0	-2	-2	-0	-0.1
Total	2	0	1	.000	12	0	0	0	0	28²	38	2	14	5	16.3	5.65	82	.339	.413	1	.100	-1	-5	-3	-0	-0.2

■ ED PIPGRAS
Pipgras, Edward John b: 6/15/04, Schleswig, Iowa d: 4/13/64, Currie, Minn. BR/TR, 6'2.5", 175 lbs. Deb: 8/25/32

| 1932 | Bro-N | 0 | 1 | .000 | 5 | 1 | 0 | 0 | 0 | 10 | 16 | 2 | 6 | 5 | 19.8 | 5.40 | 71 | .348 | .423 | 0 | .000 | -0 | -2 | -2 | 0 | -0.1 |

■ GEORGE PIPGRAS
Pipgras, George William b: 12/20/1899, Ida Grove, Iowa d: 10/19/86, Gainesville, Fla. BR/TR, 6'1.5", 185 lbs. Deb: 6/09/23 U

1923	NY-A	1	3	.250	8	2	2	0	0	33¹	34	2	25	12	16.2	5.94	66	.276	.403	0	.000	-1	-7	-7	-0	-0.7
1924	NY-A	0	1	.000	9	1	0	0	1	15¹	19	0	18	4	24.7	9.98	42	.351	.532	1	.333	-0	-10	-10	-1	-0.7
1927	*NY-A	10	3	.769	29	21	9	1	0	166¹	148	2	77	81	12.2	4.11	94	.247	.334	16	.239	2	1	-5	-2	-0.4
1928	*NY-A	24	13	.649	46	38	22	4	3	300²	314	4	103	139	12.6	3.38	111	.272	.333	18	.157	-3	22	13	-5	0.3
1929	NY-A	18	12	.600	39	33	13	3	0	225¹	229	16	95	125	13.1	4.23	91	.264	.340	12	.143	-3	0	-9	-4	-1.5
1930	NY-A	15	15	.500	44	30	15	3	4	221	230	9	70	111	12.5	4.11	105	.263	.324	12	.150	-2	13	5	-3	0.0
1931	NY-A	7	6	.538	36	14	6	1	3	137²	134	8	58	59	12.7	3.79	105	.251	.327	1	.024	-5	9	3	-2	-0.4
1932	*NY-A	16	9	.640	32	27	14	2	0	219	235	15	87	111	13.5	4.19	97	.269	.340	18	.220	1	7	-3	-2	-0.3
1933	NY-A	2	2	.500	4	4	3	0	0	33	32	1	12	14	12.0	3.27	119	.252	.317	1	.091	-1	4	2	1	0.2
	Bos-A	9	8	.529	22	17	9	2	1	128¹	140	5	45	56	13.1	4.07	108	.276	.337	9	.196	-1	3	4	-2	0.2
	Yr	11	10	.524	26	21	12	2	1	161¹	172	6	57	70	12.9	3.90	110	.271	.333	4	.070	-1	7	7	-1	0.4
1934	Bos-A	0	0	—	2	1	0	0	0	3¹	4	1	3	0	18.9	8.10	59	.308	.438	0	.000	-0	-1	-1	0	0.0
1935	Bos-A	0	1	.000	5	1	0	0	0	5	9	3	5	2	27.0	14.40	33	.391	.517	0	—	0	-6	-5	0	-0.4
Total	11	102	73	.583	276	189	93	16	12	1488¹	1529	66	598	714	13.1	4.09	98	.266	.339	88	.163	-13	35	-14	-16	-3.7

■ COTTON PIPPEN
Pippen, Henry Harold b: 4/2/11, Cisco, Tex. d: 2/15/81, Williams, Cal. BR/TR, 6'2", 180 lbs. Deb: 8/28/36

1936	StL-N	0	2	.000	6	3	0	0	0	21	37	5	8	8	20.1	7.71	51	.402	.461	1	.167	0	-9	-9	1	-0.6
1939	Phi-A	4	11	.267	25	17	5	0	1	118²	169	13	40	33	15.9	5.99	79	.329	.378	3	.086	-2	-18	-17	2	-1.5
	Det-A	0	1	.000	3	2	0	0	0	14	18	1	6	5	15.4	7.07	69	.310	.375	2	.400	-0	-4	-3	-0	-0.2
	Yr	4	12	.250	28	19	5	0	1	132²	187	14	46	38	15.8	6.11	77	.326	.376	4	.100	-2	-22	-20	1	-1.7
1940	Det-A	1	2	.333	4	3	0	0	0	21¹	29	3	10	9	16.9	6.75	70	.326	.400	0	.000	-1	-6	-5	0	-0.4
Total	3	5	16	.238	38	25	5	0	1	175	253	22	64	55	16.5	6.38	73	.336	.391	6	.111	-3	-36	-34	2	-2.7

■ GERRY PIRTLE
Pirtle, Gerald Eugene b: 12/3/47, Tulsa, Okla. BR/TR, 6'1", 185 lbs. Deb: 7/02/78

| 1978 | Mon-N | 0 | 2 | .000 | 19 | 0 | 0 | 0 | 0 | 25² | 33 | 5 | 23 | 14 | 20.3 | 5.96 | 59 | .314 | .446 | 0 | — | 0 | -7 | -7 | 0 | -0.6 |

■ SKIP PITLOCK
Pitlock, Lee Patrick Thomas b: 11/6/47, Hillside, Ill. BL/TL, 6'2", 180 lbs. Deb: 6/12/70

1970	SF-N	5	5	.500	18	15	1	0	0	87	92	13	48	56	14.9	4.66	85	.274	.371	2	.080	-0	-6	-7	0	-0.5
1974	Chi-A	3	3	.500	40	5	0	0	1	105²	103	7	55	68	14.1	4.43	84	.257	.356	0	—	0	-10	-8	-1	-0.9
1975	Chi-A	0	0	—	1	0	0	0	0	0	1	0	0	0	—	—	—	1.000	1.000	0	—	0	0	0	0	0.0
Total	3	8	8	.500	59	20	1	0	1	192²	196	20	103	124	14.5	4.53	85	.266	.364	2	.080	-0	-15	-15	-1	-1.4

■ TOGIE PITTINGER
Pittinger, Charles Reno b: 1/13/1871, Greencastle, Pa. d: 1/14/09, Greencastle, Pa. BL/TR, 6'2", 175 lbs. Deb: 4/26/00

1900	Bos-N	2	9	.182	18	13	8	0	0	114	135	7	54	27	14.9	5.13	80	.294	.368	6	.130	-5	-18	-13	-1	-1.4
1901	Bos-N	13	16	.448	34	33	27	1	0	281³	288	7	76	129	11.9	3.01	120	.263	.315	11	.110	-9	10	19	3	1.4
1902	Bos-N	27	16	.628	46	40	36	7	0	389¹	360	4	128	174	11.7	2.52	112	.245	.313	20	.136	-9	11	13	-2	0.3
1903	Bos-N	18	22	.450	44	39	35	3	1	351²	396	12	143	140	14.2	3.48	92	.294	.369	14	.109	-8	-8	-11	-3	-2.0
1904	Bos-N	15	21	.417	38	38	35	5	0	335¹	298	1	144	146	12.2	2.66	104	.242	.329	14	.107	-8	3	4	5	0.0
1905	Phi-N	23	14	.622	46	37	29	4	2	337	311	3	104	136	11.5	3.10	94	.247	.313	19	.156	-3	-4	-7	-3	-1.3
1906	Phi-N	8	10	.444	20	16	9	2	0	129²	128	2	50	43	13.2	3.40	77	.252	.334	4	.091	-2	-11	-11	-1	-1.5
1907	Phi-N	9	5	.643	16	12	8	1	0	102	101	3	35	37	12.4	3.00	81	.261	.330	5	.139	-0	-6	-7	-0	-0.7
Total	8	115	113	.504	262	228	187	23	3	2040¹	2017	39	734	832	12.5	3.10	98	.260	.331	92	.124	-44	-23	-14	-3	-5.2

■ STAN PITULA
Pitula, Stanley b: 3/23/31, Hackensack, N.J. d: 8/15/65, Hackensack, N.J. BR/TR, 5'10", 170 lbs. Deb: 4/24/57

| 1957 | Cle-A | 2 | 2 | .500 | 23 | 5 | 1 | 0 | 0 | 59² | 67 | 8 | 32 | 17 | 15.2 | 4.98 | 75 | .296 | .388 | 3 | .200 | 0 | -8 | -8 | -0 | -0.8 |

■ JUAN PIZARRO
Pizarro, Juan Ramon (Cordova) b: 2/7/37, Santurce, P.R. BL/TL, 5'11", 170 lbs. Deb: 5/04/57

1957	*Mil-N	5	6	.455	24	10	3	0	0	99¹	99	16	51	68	13.7	4.62	76	.261	.350	9	.250	3	-8	-12	-1	-1.0
1958	*Mil-N	6	4	.600	16	10	7	1	1	96²	75	12	47	84	11.7	2.70	130	.212	.312	8	.250	3	13	9	0	1.2
1959	Mil-N	6	2	.750	29	14	6	2	0	133²	117	13	70	126	13.1	3.77	94	.237	.342	5	.122	0	3	-3	-1	-0.4
1960	Mil-N	6	7	.462	21	17	3	0	0	114²	105	13	72	88	14.2	4.55	75	.244	.357	11	.275	3	-10	-14	-1	-1.2
1961	Chi-A	14	7	.667	39	25	12	1	2	194²	164	17	89	188	11.9	3.05	128	.226	.314	17	.246	5	21	19	-2	2.2
1962	Chi-A	12	14	.462	36	32	9	1	1	203¹	182	16	97	173	12.4	3.81	103	.236	.322	11	.159	-0	4	2	-2	0.0
1963	Chi-A	16	8	.667	32	28	10	3	1	214²	177	14	63	163	10.2	2.39	147	.224	.284	13	.178	3	30	27	-3	2.9
1964	Chi-A	19	9	.679	33	33	11	4	0	239	193	23	55	162	9.5	2.56	135	.219	.267	19	.211	4	28	24	-1	2.9
1965	Chi-A	6	3	.667	18	18	2	1	0	97	96	9	37	65	12.4	3.43	93	.254	.322	8	.235	3	0	-3	0	0.0
1966	Chi-A	8	6	.571	34	9	1	0	0	88²	91	9	39	42	13.3	3.76	84	.269	.347	6	.154	0	-3	-6	-1	-0.4
1967	Pit-N	8	10	.444	50	11	1	1	9	107	99	10	52	96	12.9	3.95	85	.245	.334	7	.259	2	-7	-7	-2	-0.7
1968	Pit-N	1	1	.500	12	0	0	0	0	11	14	2	10	6	20.5	3.27	89	.311	.446	0	.000	-0	-0	-0	-0	0.0
	Bos-A	6	8	.429	19	12	6	0	2	107²	97	15	44	84	11.8	3.59	88	.242	.317	5	.161	1	-7	-5	2	-0.2
1969	Bos-A	0	1	.000	6	0	0	0	0	9	14	2	6	4	20.0	6.00	63	.359	.444	0	—	0	-2	-2	-0	-0.1
	Cle-A	3	3	.500	48	4	1	0	4	82²	67	6	49	44	12.8	3.16	119	.229	.343	3	.200	1	4	6	0	0.5
	Oak-A	1	1	.500	3	0	0	0	1	7²	3	1	3	4	7.0	2.35	146	.125	.222	1	.500	0	1	1	0	0.1
	Yr	4	5	.444	57	4	1	0	7	99¹	84	9	58	52	12.9	3.35	112	.230	.335	1	.050	1	3	4	1	0.7

YEAR	TM/L	W	L	PCT	G	GS	CG	SH	SV	IP	H	HR	BB	SO	RAT	ERA	ERA+	OAV	OOB	BH	AVG	PB	PR	/A	PD	TPI
1970	Chi-N	0	0	—	12	0	0	0	1	15²	16	2	9	14	14.9	4.60	98	.262	.366	0	.000	-0	-1	-0	0	0.0
1971	Chi-N	7	6	.538	16	14	6	3	0	101¹	78	10	40	67	10.7	3.46	114	.209	.289	6	.176	1	0	5	0	0.7
1972	Chi-N	4	5	.444	16	7	1	0	1	59¹	66	7	32	24	15.0	3.94	97	.293	.384	3	.143	-1	-3	-1	1	0.0
1973	Chi-N	0	1	.000	2	0	0	0	0	4	6	1	1	3	18.0	11.25	35	.353	.421	0	.000	-0	-3	-3	0	-0.2
	Hou-N	2	2	.500	15	1	0	0	0	23¹	28	1	11	10	15.4	6.56	55	.301	.381	0	.000	-0	-8	-8	1	-0.6
	Yr	2	3	.400	17	1	0	0	0	27¹	34	2	12	13	15.5	7.24	51	.304	.376	1	.250	-0	-11	-11	1	-0.8
1974	*Pit-N	1	1	.500	7	2	0	0	0	24	20	2	11	7	11.6	1.88	184	.220	.304	2	.333	0	5	4	-0	0.5
Total	18	131	105	.555	488	245	79	17	28	2034¹	1807	201	888	1522	12.1	3.43	104	.237	.320	133	.202	28	55	33	-9	6.5

■ GORDIE PLADSON
Pladson, Gordon Cecil b: 7/31/56, New Westminster, B.C., Canada   BR/TR, 6'4", 210 lbs. Deb: 9/07/79

YEAR	TM/L	W	L	PCT	G	GS	CG	SH	SV	IP	H	HR	BB	SO	RAT	ERA	ERA+	OAV	OOB	BH	AVG	PB	PR	/A	PD	TPI
1979	Hou-N	0	0	—	4	0	0	0	0	4	9	1	2	2	24.8	4.50	78	.450	.500	0	—	0	-0	-0	0	0.0
1980	Hou-N	0	4	.000	12	6	0	0	0	41¹	38	3	16	13	11.8	4.35	75	.244	.314	0	.000	-1	-3	-5	-0	-0.5
1981	Hou-N	0	0	—	2	0	0	0	0	4	9	0	3	3	27.0	9.00	37	.429	.500	0	—	0	-2	-3	-0	-0.2
1982	Hou-N	0	0	—	2	0	0	0	0	1¹	10	0	2	0	81.0	54.00	6	.769	.800	0	—	0	-7	-8	-0	-0.6
Total	4	0	4	.000	20	6	0	0	0	50²	66	4	23	18	15.8	6.04	55	.314	.382	0	.000	-1	-14	-15	0	-1.3

■ EMIL PLANETA
Planeta, Emil Joseph b: 1/31/09, Higganum, Conn. d: 2/2/63, Rocky Hill, Conn.   BR/TR, 6', 190 lbs. Deb: 9/20/31

YEAR	TM/L	W	L	PCT	G	GS	CG	SH	SV	IP	H	HR	BB	SO	RAT	ERA	ERA+	OAV	OOB	BH	AVG	PB	PR	/A	PD	TPI
1931	NY-N	0	0	—	2	0	0	0	0	5¹	7	0	4	0	18.6	10.13	37	.292	.393	0	.000	-0	-4	-4	-0	-0.3

■ ED PLANK
Plank, Edward Arthur b: 4/9/52, Chicago, Ill.   BR/TR, 6'1", 205 lbs. Deb: 9/06/78

YEAR	TM/L	W	L	PCT	G	GS	CG	SH	SV	IP	H	HR	BB	SO	RAT	ERA	ERA+	OAV	OOB	BH	AVG	PB	PR	/A	PD	TPI
1978	SF-N	0	0	—	5	0	0	0	0	6²	6	1	2	1	10.8	4.05	85	.273	.333	0	—	0	-0	-0	-0	0.0
1979	SF-N	0	0	—	4	0	0	0	0	3²	9	0	2	1	27.0	7.36	47	.450	.500	0	—	0	-1	-2	0	-0.1
Total	2	0	0	—	9	0	0	0	0	10¹	15	1	4	2	16.5	5.23	66	.357	.413	0	—	0	-2	-2	-0	-0.1

■ EDDIE PLANK
Plank, Edward Stewart "Gettysburg Eddie" b: 8/31/1875, Gettysburg, Pa. d: 2/24/26, Gettysburg, Pa.   BL/TL, 5'11.5", 175 lbs. Deb: 5/13/01 H

YEAR	TM/L	W	L	PCT	G	GS	CG	SH	SV	IP	H	HR	BB	SO	RAT	ERA	ERA+	OAV	OOB	BH	AVG	PB	PR	/A	PD	TPI
1901	Phi-A	17	13	.567	33	32	28	1	0	260²	254	2	68	90	11.1	3.31	114	.252	.300	18	.182	-4	10	13	-2	0.7
1902	Phi-A	20	15	.571	36	32	31	1	0	300	319	5	61	107	11.4	3.30	111	.273	.309	35	.292	6	9	12	-1	1.7
1903	Phi-A	23	16	.590	43	40	33	3	0	336	317	5	65	176	10.2	2.38	128	.249	.285	25	.187	-1	22	25	-1	2.5
1904	Phi-A	26	17	.605	44	43	37	7	0	357¹	311	2	86	201	10.0	2.17	124	.235	.282	31	.240	3	17	20	1	2.7
1905	*Phi-A	24	12	.667	41	41	35	4	0	346²	287	3	75	210	9.4	2.26	118	.227	.270	29	.230	3	15	15	-3	1.7
1906	Phi-A	19	6	.760	26	25	21	5	0	211²	173	1	51	108	9.5	2.25	121	.226	.275	17	.233	2	10	11	-2	1.2
1907	Phi-A	24	16	.600	43	40	33	8	0	343²	282	5	85	183	9.6	2.20	119	.226	.275	26	.211	2	13	16	-0	1.9
1908	Phi-A	14	16	.467	34	28	21	4	1	244²	202	1	46	135	9.5	2.17	118	.224	.269	16	.180	-1	6	11	-4	0.6
1909	Phi-A	19	10	.655	34	33	24	3	0	265¹	215	1	62	132	9.7	1.76	136	.224	.277	21	.219	4	21	19	1	2.8
1910	Phi-A	16	10	.615	38	32	22	1	2	250¹	218	3	55	123	10.1	2.01	118	.237	.286	11	.128	-3	14	10	-3	0.4
1911	*Phi-A	23	8	.742	40	30	24	6	4	256²	237	2	77	149	11.5	2.10	150	.255	.322	18	.191	-1	35	30	0	2.9
1912	Phi-A	26	6	.813	37	30	23	5	2	259²	234	1	83	110	11.2	2.22	139	.245	.309	24	.267	4	32	25	-1	2.8
1913	*Phi-A	18	10	.643	41	30	18	7	4	242²	211	3	57	151	10.1	2.60	106	.234	.283	8	.105	-0	9	4	-2	0.1
1914	*Phi-A	15	7	.682	34	22	12	4	3	185¹	178	2	42	110	11.0	2.87	92	.266	.315	9	.150	0	-3	-5	-3	-0.8
1915	StL-F	21	11	.656	42	31	23	6	3	268¹	212	1	54	147	9.0	2.08	154	.218	.262	24	.258	5	28	33	-3	4.0
1916	StL-A	16	15	.516	37	26	17	3	3	235²	203	2	67	88	10.5	2.33	118	.237	.297	15	.185	-0	13	11	-4	0.8
1917	StL-A	5	6	.455	20	14	8	1	1	131	105	2	38	26	10.0	1.79	146	.225	.287	4	.105	-1	13	12	-1	1.1
Total	17	326	194	.627	623	529	410	69	23	4495²	3958	41	1072	2246	10.2	2.35	122	.239	.288	331	.206	16	267	264	-29	27.1

■ BILL PLEIS
Pleis, William b: 8/5/37, St.Louis, Mo.   BL/TL, 5'10", 170 lbs. Deb: 4/16/61

YEAR	TM/L	W	L	PCT	G	GS	CG	SH	SV	IP	H	HR	BB	SO	RAT	ERA	ERA+	OAV	OOB	BH	AVG	PB	PR	/A	PD	TPI
1961	Min-A	4	2	.667	37	0	0	0	2	56¹	59	4	34	32	15.5	4.95	86	.266	.373	1	.111	-1	-6	-4	-1	-0.5
1962	Min-A	2	5	.286	21	4	0	0	3	45	46	7	14	31	12.2	4.40	93	.264	.323	4	.286	1	-2	-2	-1	0.0
1963	Min-A	6	2	.750	36	4	1	0	0	68	67	10	16	37	11.0	4.37	83	.258	.301	2	.125	0	-6	-5	-0	-0.5
1964	Min-A	4	1	.800	47	0	0	0	4	50²	43	6	31	42	13.3	3.91	92	.232	.346	1	.250	0	-2	-2	0	0.0
1965	*Min-A	4	4	.500	41	2	0	0	4	51¹	49	3	27	33	13.3	2.98	119	.250	.341	0	.000	-1	3	3	-0	0.2
1966	Min-A	1	2	.333	8	0	0	0	0	9¹	5	1	4	9	8.7	1.93	186	.152	.243	0	—	0	2	2	-0	0.2
Total	6	21	16	.568	190	10	1	0	13	280²	269	31	126	184	12.9	4.07	93	.251	.334	8	.160	0	-11	-8	-2	-0.6

■ DAN PLESAC
Plesac, Daniel Thomas b: 2/4/62, Gary, Ind.   BL/TL, 6'5", 205 lbs. Deb: 4/11/86

YEAR	TM/L	W	L	PCT	G	GS	CG	SH	SV	IP	H	HR	BB	SO	RAT	ERA	ERA+	OAV	OOB	BH	AVG	PB	PR	/A	PD	TPI
1986	Mil-A	10	7	.588	51	0	0	0	14	91	81	5	29	75	10.9	2.97	146	.240	.301	0	—	0	12	14	-1	1.3
1987	Mil-A	5	6	.455	57	0	0	0	23	79¹	63	8	23	89	10.1	2.61	175	.213	.276	0	—	0	16	17	-0	1.6
1988	Mil-A	1	2	.333	50	0	0	0	30	52¹	46	2	12	52	10.0	2.41	165	.234	.278	0	—	0	9	9	-0	0.9
1989	Mil-A	3	4	.429	52	0	0	0	33	61¹	47	6	17	52	9.4	2.35	163	.213	.269	0	—	0	10	10	-0	1.0
1990	Mil-A	3	7	.300	66	0	0	0	24	69	67	5	31	65	13.2	4.43	85	.257	.342	0	—	0	-4	-5	-1	-0.5
Total	5	22	26	.458	276	0	0	0	124	353	304	26	112	333	10.8	2.98	139	.232	.295	0	—	0	44	45	-2	4.3

■ NORMAN PLITT
Plitt, Norman William b: 2/21/1893, York, Pa. d: 2/1/54, New York, N.Y.   BR/TR, 5'11", 180 lbs. Deb: 4/26/18

YEAR	TM/L	W	L	PCT	G	GS	CG	SH	SV	IP	H	HR	BB	SO	RAT	ERA	ERA+	OAV	OOB	BH	AVG	PB	PR	/A	PD	TPI
1918	Bro-N	0	0	—	1	0	0	0	0	2	3	0	1	0	18.0	4.50	62	.429	.500	1	1.000	0	-0	-0	0	0.0
1927	Bro-N	2	6	.250	19	8	1	0	0	62¹	73	3	36	9	15.9	4.91	81	.303	.396	4	.222	-0	-7	-7	1	-0.5
	NY-N	1	0	1.000	3	0	0	0	0	7¹	9	0	1	0	13.5	3.68	105	.310	.355	0	.000	-0	0	0	1	0.0
	Yr	3	6	.333	22	8	1	0	0	69²	82	3	37	9	15.5	4.78	83	.303	.388	0	.000	-0	-7	-6	1	-0.5
Total	2	3	6	.333	23	8	1	0	0	71²	85	3	38	9	15.4	4.77	82	.307	.394	5	.250	0	-7	-7	1	-0.5

■ TIM PLODINEC
Plodinec, Timothy Alfred b: 1/27/47, Aliquippa, Pa.   BR/TR, 6'4", 190 lbs. Deb: 6/02/72

YEAR	TM/L	W	L	PCT	G	GS	CG	SH	SV	IP	H	HR	BB	SO	RAT	ERA	ERA+	OAV	OOB	BH	AVG	PB	PR	/A	PD	TPI
1972	StL-N	0	0	—	1	0	0	0	0	0¹	3	0	0	0	81.0	27.00	13	.750	.750	0	—	0	-1	-1	0	0.0

■ ERIC PLUNK
Plunk, Eric Vaughn b: 9/3/63, Wilmington, Cal.   BR/TR, 6'5", 210 lbs. Deb: 5/12/86

YEAR	TM/L	W	L	PCT	G	GS	CG	SH	SV	IP	H	HR	BB	SO	RAT	ERA	ERA+	OAV	OOB	BH	AVG	PB	PR	/A	PD	TPI
1986	Oak-A	4	7	.364	26	15	0	0	0	120¹	91	14	102	98	14.8	5.31	73	.214	.372	0	—	0	-15	-19	-2	-2.0
1987	Oak-A	4	6	.400	32	11	0	0	2	95	91	8	62	90	14.7	4.74	87	.253	.366	0	—	0	-3	-6	-1	-0.6
1988	*Oak-A	7	2	.778	49	0	0	0	5	78	62	6	39	79	11.8	3.00	126	.217	.313	0	—	0	8	7	-1	0.5
1989	Oak-A	1	1	.500	23	0	0	0	1	28²	17	1	24	24	9.4	2.20	167	.172	.268	0	—	0	5	5	-0	0.5
	NY-A	7	5	.583	27	7	0	0	0	75²	65	9	52	61	13.9	3.69	105	.237	.359	0	—	0	2	2	-2	0.0
	Yr	8	6	.571	50	7	0	0	1	104¹	82	10	64	85	12.6	3.28	116	.219	.333	0	—	0	7	6	-2	0.5
1990	NY-A	6	3	.667	47	0	0	0	0	72²	58	6	43	67	12.8	2.72	146	.225	.340	0	—	0	10	10	2	1.2
Total	5	29	24	.547	204	33	0	0	8	470¹	384	44	310	419	13.5	3.96	99	.226	.348	0	—	0	7	-2	-5	-0.4

■ RAY POAT
Poat, Raymond Willis b: 12/19/17, Chicago, Ill. d: 4/29/90, Oak Lawn, Ill.   BR/TR, 6'2", 200 lbs. Deb: 4/15/42

YEAR	TM/L	W	L	PCT	G	GS	CG	SH	SV	IP	H	HR	BB	SO	RAT	ERA	ERA+	OAV	OOB	BH	AVG	PB	PR	/A	PD	TPI
1942	Cle-A	1	3	.250	4	4	1	1	0	18¹	24	1	9	8	16.7	5.40	64	.296	.374	0	.000	-0	-4	-4	0	-0.3
1943	Cle-A	2	5	.286	17	4	1	0	0	45	44	3	20	31	12.8	4.40	71	.259	.337	2	.154	-0	-6	-6	-0	-0.7
1944	Cle-A	4	8	.333	36	6	1	0	0	80²	82	6	37	40	13.3	5.13	64	.265	.343	0	.000	-2	-15	-16	-0	-1.8
1947	NY-N	4	3	.571	7	7	5	0	0	60	53	8	13	25	9.9	2.55	160	.238	.280	4	.190	2	10	10	-0	1.3
1948	NY-N	11	10	.524	39	24	7	3	0	157²	162	21	67	57	13.2	4.34	91	.262	.337	7	.125	-1	-7	-7	-2	-0.9
1949	NY-N	0	0	—	2	0	0	0	0	2¹	8	0	1	0	34.7	19.29	21	.615	.643	0	—	0	-4	-4	0	-0.3
	Pit-N	0	1	.000	11	2	0	0	0	36	52	6	15	17	16.8	6.25	67	.335	.394	1	.100	-1	-9	-8	-0	-0.8
	Yr	0	1	.000	13	2	0	0	0	38¹	60	6	16	17	17.8	7.04	59	.357	.413	0	.000	-1	-13	-12	-0	-1.1
Total	6	22	30	.423	116	47	15	4	1	400	425	48	162	178	13.3	4.55	82	.271	.340	14	.115	-3	-34	-36	-3	-3.5

■ BUD PODBIELAN
Podbielan, Clarence Anthony b: 3/6/24, Curlew, Wash. d: 10/26/82, Syracuse, N.Y.   BR/TR, 6'1.5", 170 lbs. Deb: 4/25/49

YEAR	TM/L	W	L	PCT	G	GS	CG	SH	SV	IP	H	HR	BB	SO	RAT	ERA	ERA+	OAV	OOB	BH	AVG	PB	PR	/A	PD	TPI
1949	Bro-N	0	1	.000	7	1	0	0	0	12¹	9	1	9	5	13.9	3.65	112	.205	.352	0	.000	-0	1	1	1	0.1
1950	Bro-N	5	4	.556	20	10	2	0	1	72²	93	10	29	28	15.4	5.33	77	.307	.371	3	.107	-1	-10	-10	1	-0.9

YEAR	TM/L	W	L	PCT	G	GS	CG	SH	SV	IP	H	HR	BB	SO	RAT	ERA	ERA+	OAV	OOB	BH	AVG	PB	PR	/A	PD	TPI
1951	Bro-N	2	2	.500	27	5	1	0	0	79²	67	9	36	26	11.9	3.50	112	.233	.322	7	.304	1	4	4	1	0.6
1952	Bro-N	0	0	—	3	0	0	0	0	2	4	1	3	1	31.5	18.00	20	.444	.583	0	—	0	-3	-3	-0	-0.2
	Cin-N	4	5	.444	24	7	4	1	1	86²	78	8	26	22	10.9	2.80	135	.245	.304	4	.160	0	9	9	-1	0.9
	Yr	4	5	.444	27	7	4	1	1	88²	82	9	29	23	11.4	3.15	120	.251	.314	2	.080	0	6	6	-1	0.7
1953	Cin-N	6	16	.273	36	24	8	1	1	186¹	214	21	67	74	14.0	4.73	92	.290	.356	7	.125	-3	-9	-8	-0	-0.9
1954	Cin-N	7	10	.412	27	24	4	0	0	131	157	20	58	42	14.9	5.36	78	.300	.372	6	.143	-1	-19	-17	-1	-1.7
1955	Cin-N	1	2	.333	17	2	0	0	0	42	36	4	11	26	10.3	3.21	132	.234	.289	2	.400	1	4	5	0	0.6
1957	Cin-N	0	1	.000	5	3	1	0	0	16	18	4	4	13	12.4	6.19	66	.290	.333	0	.000	-1	-4	-4	-1	-0.4
1959	Cle-A	0	1	.000	6	0	0	0	0	12¹	17	1	2	5	13.9	5.84	63	.354	.380	0	.000	-0	-3	-3	0	-0.2
Total 9		25	42	.373	172	76	20	2	3	641	693	79	245	242	13.4	4.49	92	.279	.348	29	.154	-4	-30	-26	-1	-2.1

■ JOHNNY PODGAJNY — Podgajny, John Sigmund "Specs" b: 6/10/20, Chester, Pa. d: 3/2/71, Chester, Pa. BR/TR, 6'2", 173 lbs. Deb: 9/15/40

YEAR	TM/L	W	L	PCT	G	GS	CG	SH	SV	IP	H	HR	BB	SO	RAT	ERA	ERA+	OAV	OOB	BH	AVG	PB	PR	/A	PD	TPI
1940	Phi-N	1	3	.250	4	4	3	0	0	35	33	0	1	12	9.0	2.83	138	.250	.261	2	.167	-0	4	4	0	0.4
1941	Phi-N	9	12	.429	34	24	8	0	0	181¹	191	8	70	53	13.2	4.62	80	.270	.339	8	.129	-3	-20	-18	1	-1.9
1942	Phi-N	6	14	.300	43	23	6	0	0	186²	191	9	63	40	12.8	3.91	85	.268	.337	11	.183	-0	-12	-12	-1	-1.3
1943	Phi-N	4	4	.500	13	5	3	0	0	64	77	4	16	13	13.1	4.22	80	.310	.352	5	.250	1	-6	-6	1	-0.3
	Pit-N	0	4	.000	15	5	0	0	0	34¹	37	1	13	7	13.1	4.72	74	.266	.329	1	.143	-0	-5	-5	2	-0.3
	Yr	4	8	.333	28	10	3	0	0	98¹	114	5	29	20	13.1	4.39	78	.295	.344	1	.037	-0	-11	-11	3	-0.6
1946	Cle-A	0	0	—	6	0	0	0	0	9	13	0	2	4	15.0	5.00	66	.302	.333	0	—	0	-1	-2	0	-0.1
Total 5		20	37	.351	115	61	20	0	0	510¹	542	22	165	129	12.8	4.20	84	.273	.334	27	.168	-3	-41	-39	4	-3.5

■ JOHNNY PODRES — Podres, John Joseph b: 9/30/32, Witherbee, N.Y. BL/TL, 5'11", 170 lbs. Deb: 4/17/53 C

YEAR	TM/L	W	L	PCT	G	GS	CG	SH	SV	IP	H	HR	BB	SO	RAT	ERA	ERA+	OAV	OOB	BH	AVG	PB	PR	/A	PD	TPI
1953	*Bro-N	9	4	.692	33	18	3	1	0	115	126	12	64	82	14.9	4.23	101	.282	.373	11	.306	2	1	0	-0	0.2
1954	Bro-N	11	7	.611	29	21	6	2	0	151²	147	13	53	79	11.9	4.27	96	.255	.319	17	.283	5	-3	-3	-2	0.0
1955	*Bro-N	9	10	.474	27	24	5	2	0	159¹	160	15	57	114	12.5	3.95	103	.259	.326	11	.183	-0	1	2	-1	0.0
1957	Bro-N	12	9	.571	31	27	10	**6**	3	196	168	15	44	109	**9.8**	**2.66**	**156**	.230	**.274**	15	.208	1	26	33	0	3.7
1958	LA-N	13	15	.464	39	31	10	2	1	210¹	208	27	78	143	12.3	3.72	110	.261	.328	9	.127	-3	5	9	-2	0.4
1959	*LA-N	14	9	.609	34	29	6	2	0	195	192	23	74	145	12.4	4.11	103	.261	.331	16	.246	4	-3	3	1	0.8
1960	LA-N	14	12	.538	34	33	8	1	0	227²	217	25	71	159	11.4	3.08	129	.250	.308	9	.136	-1	17	22	-1	2.2
1961	LA-N	18	5	**.783**	32	29	6	1	0	182²	192	27	51	124	12.2	3.74	116	.271	.324	16	.232	1	6	12	-1	1.3
1962	LA-N	15	13	.536	40	40	8	0	0	255	270	20	71	178	12.1	3.81	95	.272	.323	14	.159	1	-4	-5	-4	-0.7
1963	*LA-N	14	12	.538	37	34	10	5	1	198¹	196	16	64	134	11.9	3.54	85	.257	.316	9	.141	1	-6	-11	-1	-1.1
1964	LA-N	0	2	.000	2	2	0	0	0	2²	5	1	3	0	27.0	16.88	19	.417	.533	0	—	0	-4	-4	0	-0.3
1965	LA-N	7	6	.538	27	22	2	1	1	134	126	17	39	63	11.2	3.43	95	.247	.303	8	.178	1	2	-2	-2	-0.3
1966	LA-N	0	0	—	1	0	0	0	0	1²	2	0	1	1	16.2	0.00	—	.400	.500	0	—	0	1	1	0	0.1
	Det-A	4	5	.444	36	13	2	1	4	107²	106	12	34	53	11.8	3.43	102	.259	.317	7	.233	2	0	1	-0	0.3
1967	Det-A	3	1	.750	21	8	0	0	1	63¹	58	12	11	34	9.9	3.84	85	.244	.280	2	.100	-1	-4	-4	-0	-0.5
1969	SD-N	5	6	.455	17	9	1	0	0	64²	64	7	28	17	13.2	4.31	82	.264	.341	1	.063	-1	-5	-6	-1	-0.7
Total 15		148	116	.561	440	340	77	24	11	2265	2239	242	743	1435	12.0	3.68	105	.259	.319	145	.190	12	37	45	-13	5.4

■ JOE POETZ — Poetz, Joseph Frank "Bull Montana" b: 6/22/1900, St.Louis, Mo. d: 2/7/42, St.Louis, Mo. BR/TR, 5'10.5", 175 lbs. Deb: 9/14/26

YEAR	TM/L	W	L	PCT	G	GS	CG	SH	SV	IP	H	HR	BB	SO	RAT	ERA	ERA+	OAV	OOB	BH	AVG	PB	PR	/A	PD	TPI
1926	NY-N	0	1	.000	2	1	0	0	0	8	5	2	8	0	15.8	3.38	111	.192	.400	0	.000	0	0	0	0	0.1

■ BOOTS POFFENBERGER — Poffenberger, Cletus Elwood b: 7/1/15, Williamsport, Md. BR/TR, 5'10", 178 lbs. Deb: 6/11/37

YEAR	TM/L	W	L	PCT	G	GS	CG	SH	SV	IP	H	HR	BB	SO	RAT	ERA	ERA+	OAV	OOB	BH	AVG	PB	PR	/A	PD	TPI
1937	Det-A	10	5	.667	29	16	5	0	3	137¹	147	8	79	35	15.1	4.65	100	.277	.375	11	.216	-0	-1	0	2	0.2
1938	Det-A	6	7	.462	25	15	8	1	1	125	147	8	66	28	15.5	4.82	104	.297	.382	8	.182	-1	-1	2	-1	0.0
1939	Bro-N	0	0	—	3	1	0	0	0	5	7	1	4	2	19.8	5.40	75	.318	.423	0	.000	-0	-1	-1	0	0.0
Total 3		16	12	.571	57	32	13	1	4	267¹	301	17	149	65	15.4	4.75	101	.287	.379	19	.198	-2	-2	2	1	0.2

■ TOM POHOLSKY — Poholsky, Thomas George b: 8/26/29, Detroit, Mich. BR/TR, 6'3", 205 lbs. Deb: 4/20/50

YEAR	TM/L	W	L	PCT	G	GS	CG	SH	SV	IP	H	HR	BB	SO	RAT	ERA	ERA+	OAV	OOB	BH	AVG	PB	PR	/A	PD	TPI
1950	StL-N	0	0	—	5	1	0	0	0	14²	16	2	3	2	11.7	3.68	117	.281	.317	0	.000	-0	1	1	-0	0.1
1951	StL-N	7	13	.350	38	26	10	1	1	195	204	15	68	70	12.6	4.43	89	.271	.331	14	.209	0	-10	-10	1	-0.7
1954	StL-N	5	7	.417	25	13	4	0	0	106	101	11	20	55	10.6	3.06	135	.254	.296	4	.148	-1	12	12	0	1.2
1955	StL-N	9	11	.450	30	24	8	2	0	151	143	26	35	66	10.7	3.81	106	.244	.289	8	.182	-0	4	4	-0	0.3
1956	StL-N	9	14	.391	33	29	7	2	0	203	210	27	44	95	11.5	3.59	105	.268	.311	11	.159	-1	4	4	1	0.4
1957	Chi-N	1	7	.125	28	11	1	0	0	84	117	9	22	28	15.1	4.93	79	.330	.372	2	.105	-1	-10	-10	1	-0.9
Total 6		31	52	.373	159	104	30	5	1	753²	791	90	192	316	11.9	3.93	101	.270	.317	39	.171	-3	1	2	3	0.4

■ JENNINGS POINDEXTER — Poindexter, Chester Jennings "Jinx" b: 9/30/10, Pauls Valley, Okla. d: 3/3/83, Norman, Okla. BL/TL, 5'10", 165 lbs. Deb: 9/15/36

YEAR	TM/L	W	L	PCT	G	GS	CG	SH	SV	IP	H	HR	BB	SO	RAT	ERA	ERA+	OAV	OOB	BH	AVG	PB	PR	/A	PD	TPI
1936	Bos-A	0	2	.000	3	3	0	0	0	10²	13	0	16	2	24.5	6.75	79	.302	.492	0	.000	-1	-2	-2	0	-0.1
1939	Phi-N	0	0	—	11	1	0	0	0	30¹	29	0	15	12	13.1	4.15	96	.250	.336	2	.200	-0	-1	-0	-0	0.0
Total 2		0	2	.000	14	4	0	0	0	41	42	0	31	14	16.0	4.83	90	.264	.384	2	.143	-1	-3	-2	-0	-0.1

■ LOU POLCHOW — Polchow, Louis William b: 3/14/1881, Mankato, Minn. d: 8/15/12, Good Thunder, Minn 5'9", Deb: 9/14/02

YEAR	TM/L	W	L	PCT	G	GS	CG	SH	SV	IP	H	HR	BB	SO	RAT	ERA	ERA+	OAV	OOB	BH	AVG	PB	PR	/A	PD	TPI
1902	Cle-A	0	1	.000	1	1	1	0	0	8	9	0	4	2	14.6	5.63	61	.284	.364	0	.000	-1	-2	-2	0	-0.1

■ DICK POLE — Pole, Richard Henry b: 10/13/50, Trout Creek, Mich. BR/TR, 6'3", 200 lbs. Deb: 8/03/73 C

YEAR	TM/L	W	L	PCT	G	GS	CG	SH	SV	IP	H	HR	BB	SO	RAT	ERA	ERA+	OAV	OOB	BH	AVG	PB	PR	/A	PD	TPI
1973	Bos-A	3	2	.600	12	7	0	0	0	54²	70	4	18	24	14.5	5.60	72	.318	.370	0	—	0	-11	-10	-0	-0.9
1974	Bos-A	1	1	.500	15	2	0	0	1	45	55	6	13	32	13.8	4.20	91	.304	.354	0	—	0	-3	-2	0	0.0
1975	*Bos-A	4	6	.400	18	11	2	1	0	89²	102	11	32	42	13.7	4.42	92	.290	.352	0	—	0	-6	-3	0	-0.2
1976	Bos-A	6	5	.545	31	15	1	0	0	120²	131	8	48	49	13.5	4.33	90	.279	.348	0	.000	0	-11	-6	-1	-0.6
1977	Sea-A	7	12	.368	25	24	3	0	0	122¹	127	16	57	51	14.0	5.15	80	.270	.356	0	—	0	-15	-14	-2	-1.5
1978	Sea-A	4	11	.267	21	18	2	0	0	98²	122	16	41	41	15.1	6.48	59	.306	.375	0	—	0	-30	-29	-1	-2.8
Total 6		25	37	.403	122	77	8	1	1	531	607	61	209	239	14.1	5.05	79	.290	.359	0	.000	0	-76	-63	-4	-6.0

■ KEN POLIVKA — Polivka, Kenneth Lyle "Soup" b: 1/21/21, Chicago, Ill. d: 7/23/88, Aurora, Ill. BL/TL, 5'10.5", 175 lbs. Deb: 4/18/47

YEAR	TM/L	W	L	PCT	G	GS	CG	SH	SV	IP	H	HR	BB	SO	RAT	ERA	ERA+	OAV	OOB	BH	AVG	PB	PR	/A	PD	TPI
1947	Cin-N	0	0	—	2	0	0	0	0	3	3	0	3	1	18.0	3.00	137	.250	.400	0	—	0	0	0	0	0.0

■ HOWIE POLLET — Pollet, Howard Joseph b: 6/26/21, New Orleans, La. d: 8/8/74, Houston, Tex. BL/TL, 6'1.5", 175 lbs. Deb: 8/20/41 C

YEAR	TM/L	W	L	PCT	G	GS	CG	SH	SV	IP	H	HR	BB	SO	RAT	ERA	ERA+	OAV	OOB	BH	AVG	PB	PR	/A	PD	TPI
1941	StL-N	5	2	.714	9	8	6	2	0	70	55	1	27	37	10.7	1.93	195	.212	.289	5	.179	-0	13	14	0	1.7
1942	*StL-N	7	5	.583	27	13	5	2	0	109¹	102	7	39	42	11.8	2.88	119	.242	.309	7	.226	3	5	7	-2	0.9
1943	StL-N	8	4	.667	16	14	12	5	0	118¹	83	2	32	61	8.9	1.75	192	.200	.261	7	.163	-1	21	21	-2	2.1
1946	*StL-N	21	10	.677	40	32	22	4	5	**266**	228	12	86	107	10.8	**2.10**	**165**	.234	.300	14	.161	-0	**39**	40	1	4.7
1947	StL-N	9	11	.450	37	24	9	0	2	176¹	195	11	87	73	14.5	4.34	95	.286	.369	15	.231	-2	-5	-4	0	0.0
1948	StL-N	13	8	.619	36	26	11	0	0	181¹	216	10	67	80	13.8	4.54	90	.289	.369	8	.118	-3	-12	-9	2	-0.9
1949	StL-N	20	9	.690	39	28	17	**5**	1	230²	228	9	59	108	11.3	2.77	150	.256	.304	16	.195	1	33	**36**	-2	3.7
1950	StL-N	14	13	.519	37	30	14	2	2	232¹	228	19	68	117	11.5	3.29	130	.256	.310	12	.143	-2	22	26	-0	2.4
1951	StL-N	0	3	.000	6	2	0	0	0	12¹	10	1	8	10	13.1	4.38	91	.208	.321	0	.000	1	-1	-1	0	0.0
	Pit-N	6	10	.375	21	21	4	1	0	128²	149	24	51	47	14.1	5.04	84	.294	.360	5	.139	-0	-15	-12	0	-1.0
	Yr	6	13	.316	27	23	4	1	1	141	159	25	59	57	14.0	4.98	84	.287	.357	8	.216	0	-16	-12	0	-1.0
1952	Pit-N	7	16	.304	31	30	9	1	0	214	217	22	77	90	12.2	4.12	97	.266	.327	7	.130	-0	-9	-9	-0	-0.7
1953	Pit-N	1	1	.500	5	2	0	0	0	12²	27	2	6	8	23.4	10.66	42	.482	.532	1	.333	-0	-9	-9	-0	-0.7
	Chi-N	5	6	.455	25	17	2	0	1	111¹	120	6	44	45	13.3	4.12	108	.271	.338	4	.129	-1	2	4	-1	0.2
	Yr	6	7	.462	30	19	2	0	1	124	147	8	50	53	14.4	4.79	93	.295	.360	3	.088	-1	-7	-5	-1	-0.5

YEAR	TM/L	W	L	PCT	G	GS	CG	SH	SV	IP	H	HR	BB	SO	RAT	ERA	ERA+	OAV	OOB	BH	AVG	PB	PR	/A	PD	TPI
1954	Chi-N	8	10	.444	20	20	4	2	0	128¹	131	4	54	58	13.0	3.58	117	.263	.335	13	.277	2	7	9	0	1.2
1955	Chi-N	4	3	.571	24	7	1	1	5	61	62	11	27	27	13.1	5.61	73	.265	.341	6	.400	3	-11	-10	1	-0.5
1956	Chi-A	3	1	.750	11	4	0	0	0	26¹	27	2	11	14	13.0	4.10	100	.252	.322	3	.375	1	0	-0	0	0.1
	Pit-N	0	4	.000	19	0	0	0	3	23¹	18	3	8	10	10.0	3.09	122	.212	.280	0	.000	0	2	2	0	0.2
Total	14	131	116	.530	403	278	116	25	20	2107¹	2096	146	745	934	12.2	3.51	113	.260	.324	129	.185	7	82	111	1	14.1

■ LOU POLLI   Polli, Louis Americo "Crip"   b: 7/9/01, Barre, Vt.   BR/TR, 5'10.5", 165 lbs.   Deb: 4/18/32

YEAR	TM/L	W	L	PCT	G	GS	CG	SH	SV	IP	H	HR	BB	SO	RAT	ERA	ERA+	OAV	OOB	BH	AVG	PB	PR	/A	PD	TPI
1932	StL-A	0	0	—	5	0	0	0	0	6²	13	0	3	5	21.6	5.40	90	.406	.457	1	.500	0	-1	-0	-0	0.0
1944	NY-N	0	2	.000	19	0	0	0	3	35²	42	3	20	6	15.6	4.54	81	.294	.380	0	.000	-1	-4	-3	0	-0.3
Total	2	0	2	.000	24	0	0	0	3	42¹	55	3	23	11	16.6	4.68	82	.314	.394	1	.125	-1	-4	-4	-0	-0.3

■ JOHN POLONI   Poloni, John Paul   b: 2/28/54, Dearborn, Mich.   BL/TL, 6'5", 210 lbs.   Deb: 9/16/77

YEAR	TM/L	W	L	PCT	G	GS	CG	SH	SV	IP	H	HR	BB	SO	RAT	ERA	ERA+	OAV	OOB	BH	AVG	PB	PR	/A	PD	TPI
1977	Tex-A	1	0	1.000	2	1	0	0	0	7	8	1	1	5	11.6	6.43	63	.286	.310	0	—	0	-2	-2	-0	-0.1

■ JOHN POMORSKI   Pomorski, John Leon   b: 12/30/05, Brooklyn, N.Y.   d: 12/6/77, Brampton, Ont., Can.   BR/TR, 6', 178 lbs.   Deb: 4/17/34

YEAR	TM/L	W	L	PCT	G	GS	CG	SH	SV	IP	H	HR	BB	SO	RAT	ERA	ERA+	OAV	OOB	BH	AVG	PB	PR	/A	PD	TPI
1934	Chi-A	0	0	—	3	0	0	0	0	1²	1	0	2	0	16.2	5.40	88	.143	.333	0	—	0	-0	-0	0	0.0

■ ARLIE POND   Pond, Erasmus Arlington   b: 1/19/1872, Rutland, Vt.   d: 9/19/30, Cebu, Philippines   TR , 5'10", 160 lbs.   Deb: 7/04/1895

YEAR	TM/L	W	L	PCT	G	GS	CG	SH	SV	IP	H	HR	BB	SO	RAT	ERA	ERA+	OAV	OOB	BH	AVG	PB	PR	/A	PD	TPI
1895	Bal-N	0	1	.000	6	1	1	0	2	13²	10	0	12	13	14.5	5.93	80	.202	.357	2	.333	1	-2	-2	-0	0.0
1896	Bal-N	16	8	.667	28	26	21	2	0	214¹	232	4	57	80	12.1	3.49	123	.274	.320	19	.235	0	21	19	-2	1.4
1897	Bal-N	18	9	.667	32	28	23	0	0	248	267	4	72	59	12.3	3.52	119	.273	.323	22	.244	2	22	18	-0	1.7
1898	Bal-N	1	1	.500	3	2	1	1	0	20	8	0	9	4	7.6	0.45	796	.122	.229	2	.286	1	7	7	-1	0.8
Total	4	35	19	.648	69	57	46	3	2	496	517	8	150	156	12.1	3.45	122	.266	.319	45	.245	3	48	42	-3	3.9

■ ELMER PONDER   Ponder, Charles Elmer   b: 6/26/1893, Reed, Okla.   d: 4/20/74, Albuquerque, N.Mex   BR/TR, 6', 178 lbs.   Deb: 9/18/17

YEAR	TM/L	W	L	PCT	G	GS	CG	SH	SV	IP	H	HR	BB	SO	RAT	ERA	ERA+	OAV	OOB	BH	AVG	PB	PR	/A	PD	TPI
1917	Pit-N	1	1	.500	3	2	1	1	0	21¹	12	0	6	11	8.0	1.69	168	.167	.241	0	.000	-1	2	3	-1	0.1
1919	Pit-N	0	5	.000	9	5	0	0	0	47¹	55	0	6	6	12.2	3.99	76	.297	.330	2	.133	-1	-6	-5	-1	-0.6
1920	Pit-N	11	15	.423	33	23	13	2	0	196	182	3	40	62	10.3	2.62	123	.246	.286	7	.119	-4	11	13	1	1.0
1921	Pit-N	2	0	1.000	8	1	1	0	0	24²	29	1	3	3	11.7	2.19	175	.305	.327	0	.000	-2	4	5	0	0.3
	Chi-N	3	6	.333	16	11	5	0	0	89¹	117	7	17	31	13.8	4.74	81	.321	.356	4	.121	-2	-9	-9	2	-0.8
	Yr	5	6	.455	24	12	6	0	0	114	146	8	20	34	13.3	4.18	91	.317	.350	0	.000	-4	-5	-5	2	-0.5
Total	4	17	27	.386	69	42	20	3	0	378²	395	11	72	113	11.3	3.21	105	.271	.309	13	.105	-10	3	6	1	0.0

■ ED POOLE   Poole, Edward I.   b: 9/7/1874, Canton, Ohio   d: 3/11/19, Malvern, Ohio   TR , 5'10", 175 lbs.   Deb: 10/06/00   ♦

YEAR	TM/L	W	L	PCT	G	GS	CG	SH	SV	IP	H	HR	BB	SO	RAT	ERA	ERA+	OAV	OOB	BH	AVG	PB	PR	/A	PD	TPI
1900	Pit-N	1	0	1.000	1	0	0	0	0	7	4	0	0	3	5.1	1.29	283	.167	.167	2	.500	1	2	2	0	0.2
1901	Pit-N	5	4	.556	12	10	8	1	0	80	78	3	30	26	12.9	3.60	91	.254	.334	16	.205	1	-2	-3	-0	-0.2
1902	Pit-N	0	0	—	1	0	0	0	0	8	7	0	3	2	11.3	1.13	243	.235	.305	1	.250	0	1	1	0	0.2
	Cin-N	12	4	.750	16	16	16	2	0	138	129	2	54	55	12.5	2.15	139	.247	.327	7	.115	-4	10	13	-0	0.9
	Yr	12	4	.750	17	16	16	2	0	146	136	2	57	57	12.4	2.10	142	.247	.326	0	.000	-4	11	14	-0	1.1
1903	Cin-N	7	13	.350	25	21	18	0	0	184	188	4	77	73	13.5	3.28	109	.270	.352	17	.243	-0	-0	6	2	0.9
1904	Bro-N	8	14	.364	25	23	19	1	1	178	178	4	74	67	13.1	3.39	81	.268	.349	8	.129	-3	-13	-13	3	-1.2
Total	5	33	35	.485	80	70	61	5	1	595	584	13	238	226	13.0	3.04	103	.260	.341	51	.183	-5	-2	6	6	0.8

■ JIM POOLE   Poole, James Richard   b: 4/28/66, Rochester, N.Y.   BL/TL, 6'2", 190 lbs.   Deb: 6/15/90

YEAR	TM/L	W	L	PCT	G	GS	CG	SH	SV	IP	H	HR	BB	SO	RAT	ERA	ERA+	OAV	OOB	BH	AVG	PB	PR	/A	PD	TPI
1990	LA-N	0	0	—	16	0	0	0	0	10²	7	1	8	6	12.7	4.22	84	.184	.326	0	—	0	-1	-1	-0	0.0

■ TOM POORMAN   Poorman, Thomas Iverson   b: 10/14/1857, Lock Haven, Pa.   d: 2/18/05, Lock Haven, Pa.   BL/TR, 5'10.5", 170 lbs.   Deb: 5/05/1880   ♦

YEAR	TM/L	W	L	PCT	G	GS	CG	SH	SV	IP	H	HR	BB	SO	RAT	ERA	ERA+	OAV	OOB	BH	AVG	PB	PR	/A	PD	TPI
1880	Buf-N	1	8	.111	11	9	9	0	1	85	117	3	19	13	14.4	4.13	59	.311	.345	11	.157	-3	-17	-16	1	-1.6
	Chi-N	2	0	1.000	2	1	0	0	0	15	12	0	8	0	12.0	2.40	101	.208	.305	5	.200	-0	-0	-0	1	0.0
	Yr	3	8	.273	13	10	9	0	1	100	129	3	27	13	14.0	3.87	63	.298	.339	0	.000	-3	-17	-16	1	-1.6
1884	Tol-a	0	1	.000	1	1	1	0	0	9	13	1	2	0	15.0	3.00	114	.321	.353	89	.233	0	0	0	0	0.0
1887	Phi-a	0	0	—	1	0	0	0	0	0²	5	1	1	1	81.0	40.50	11	.715	.751	155	.265	0	-3	-3	0	-0.1
Total	3	3	9	.250	15	11	10	0	1	109²	147	5	30	14	14.5	4.02	63	.306	.346	498	.244	-3	-19	-18	1	-1.7

■ BILL POPP   Popp, William Peter   b: 6/7/1877, St.Louis, Mo.   d: 9/5/09, St.Louis, Mo.   TR , 5'10.5", 170 lbs.   Deb: 4/19/02

YEAR	TM/L	W	L	PCT	G	GS	CG	SH	SV	IP	H	HR	BB	SO	RAT	ERA	ERA+	OAV	OOB	BH	AVG	PB	PR	/A	PD	TPI
1902	StL-N	2	6	.250	9	7	5	0	0	60¹	87	2	26	20	17.6	4.92	56	.337	.408	1	.048	-2	-14	-15	1	-1.5

■ ED PORRAY   Porray, Edmund Joseph   b: 12/5/1888, AtSea On Atlantic Ocean   d: 7/13/54, Lackawaxen, Pa.   BR/TR, 5'11", 170 lbs.   Deb: 4/17/14

YEAR	TM/L	W	L	PCT	G	GS	CG	SH	SV	IP	H	HR	BB	SO	RAT	ERA	ERA+	OAV	OOB	BH	AVG	PB	PR	/A	PD	TPI
1914	Buf-F	0	1	.000	3	3	0	0	0	10¹	18	2	7	7	21.8	4.35	76	.390	.470	0	.000	-1	-1	-1	1	0.0

■ CHUCK PORTER   Porter, Charles William   b: 1/12/56, Baltimore, Md.   BR/TR, 6'3", 187 lbs.   Deb: 9/14/81

YEAR	TM/L	W	L	PCT	G	GS	CG	SH	SV	IP	H	HR	BB	SO	RAT	ERA	ERA+	OAV	OOB	BH	AVG	PB	PR	/A	PD	TPI
1981	Mil-A	0	0	—	3	0	0	0	0	4¹	6	0	1	1	14.5	4.15	82	.316	.350	0	—	0	-0	-0	-0	0.0
1982	Mil-A	0	0	—	3	0	0	0	0	3²	3	0	1	3	9.8	4.91	77	.250	.308	0	—	0	-0	-0	0	0.0
1983	Mil-A	7	9	.438	25	21	6	1	0	134	162	9	38	76	13.6	4.50	83	.298	.346	0	—	0	-7	-11	-0	-1.0
1984	Mil-A	6	4	.600	17	12	1	0	0	81¹	92	8	12	48	11.5	3.87	99	.284	.310	0	—	0	1	-0	0	0.0
1985	Mil-A	0	0	—	6	1	0	0	0	13²	15	1	2	8	11.2	1.98	211	.273	.298	0	—	0	3	3	-0	0.3
Total	5	13	13	.500	54	34	7	1	0	237	278	18	54	136	12.7	4.14	92	.291	.331	0	—	0	-3	-9	0	-0.7

■ HENRY PORTER   Porter, Henry   b: 6/1858, Vergennes, Vt.   d: 12/30/06, Brockton, Mass.   BR/TR,   Deb: 9/27/1884

YEAR	TM/L	W	L	PCT	G	GS	CG	SH	SV	IP	H	HR	BB	SO	RAT	ERA	ERA+	OAV	OOB	BH	AVG	PB	PR	/A	PD	TPI
1884	Mil-U	3	3	.500	6	6	6	1	0	51	32	1	9	71	7.2	3.00	55	.168	.205	11	.275	2	0	-8	1	-0.4
1885	Bro-a	33	21	.611	54	54	53	2	0	481²	427	11	107	197	10.0	2.78	118	.227	.269	40	.205	-2	25	27	3	2.6
1886	Bro-a	27	19	.587	48	48	48	1	0	424	439	8	120	163	11.9	3.42	102	.255	.303	33	.179	-9	2	4	-1	-0.5
1887	Bro-a	15	24	.385	40	40	38	1	0	339²	416	7	96	74	13.6	4.21	102	.291	.335	28	.199	-2	3	3	-2	0.0
1888	KC-a	18	37	.327	55	54	53	4	0	474	527	16	120	145	12.3	4.16	83	.271	.314	28	.144	-13	-58	-38	4	-3.9
1889	KC-a	0	3	.000	4	4	3	0	0	23	52	0	14	9	25.8	12.52	33	.433	.492	1	.100	-1	-22	-21	0	-1.5
Total	6	96	107	.473	207	206	201	9	0	1793¹	1893	43	466	659	11.8	3.70	96	.260	.304	142	.184	-26	-50	-31	4	-3.7

■ NED PORTER   Porter, Ned Swindell   b: 5/6/05, Apalachicola, Fla.   d: 6/30/68, Gainesville, Fla.   BR/TR, 6', 173 lbs.   Deb: 8/07/26

YEAR	TM/L	W	L	PCT	G	GS	CG	SH	SV	IP	H	HR	BB	SO	RAT	ERA	ERA+	OAV	OOB	BH	AVG	PB	PR	/A	PD	TPI
1926	NY-N	0	0	—	2	0	0	0	0	2	2	1	0	1	9.0	4.50	83	.250	.250	0	—	0	-0	-0	0	0.0
1927	NY-N	0	0	—	1	0	0	0	0	2	3	0	1	0	18.0	0.00	—	.333	.400	0	—	0	1	1	-0	0.1
Total	2	0	0	—	3	0	0	0	0	4	5	1	1	1	13.5	2.25	169	.294	.333	0	—	0	1	1	-0	0.1

■ ODIE PORTER   Porter, Odie Oscar   b: 5/24/1877, Borden, Ind.   d: 5/2/03, Borden, Ind.   Deb: 6/16/02

YEAR	TM/L	W	L	PCT	G	GS	CG	SH	SV	IP	H	HR	BB	SO	RAT	ERA	ERA+	OAV	OOB	BH	AVG	PB	PR	/A	PD	TPI
1902	Phi-A	0	1	.000	1	1	1	0	0	8	12	0	5	2	19.1	3.38	109	.346	.428	0	.000	-0	0	0	0	0.0

■ BOB PORTERFIELD   Porterfield, Erwin Coolidge   b: 8/10/23, Newport, Va.   d: 4/28/80, Sealy, Tex.   BR/TR, 6', 190 lbs.   Deb: 8/08/48

YEAR	TM/L	W	L	PCT	G	GS	CG	SH	SV	IP	H	HR	BB	SO	RAT	ERA	ERA+	OAV	OOB	BH	AVG	PB	PR	/A	PD	TPI
1948	NY-A	5	3	.625	16	12	2	1	0	78	85	5	34	30	13.7	4.50	91	.273	.345	6	.250	0	-2	-4	-1	-0.3
1949	NY-A	2	5	.286	12	8	3	0	0	57²	53	3	29	25	13.0	4.06	100	.251	.344	1	.053	-2	1	-0	-0	-0.1
1950	NY-A	1	1	.500	10	2	0	0	0	19²	28	2	8	9	16.5	8.09	49	.341	.400	1	.333	-0	-9	-10	-0	-0.7
1951	NY-A	0	0	—	2	0	0	0	0	3	5	0	3	2	24.0	15.00	26	.385	.500	0	—	0	-4	-4	-0	-0.2
	Was-A	9	8	.529	19	19	10	3	0	133¹	109	8	54	53	11.0	3.24	126	.224	.302	6	.130	-3	13	13	-0	0.9
	Yr	9	8	.529	21	19	10	3	0	136¹	114	8	57	55	11.3	3.50	117	.228	.308	3	.065	-3	9	9	-0	0.7
1952	Was-A	13	14	.481	31	29	15	3	0	231²	222	7	85	80	12.2	2.72	131	.254	.323	15	.190	-3	24	21	-3	2.0
1953	Was-A	**22**	10	.688	34	32	**24**	**9**	0	255	243	19	73	77	11.2	3.35	116	.257	.310	25	.255	8	18	15	2	2.7
1954	Was-A	13	15	.464	32	31	**21**	2	0	244	249	14	77	82	12.1	3.32	107	.266	.324	9	.102	-3	11	6	4	0.7
1955	Was-A	10	17	.370	30	27	8	2	0	178	197	14	54	74	12.8	4.45	86	.282	.335	12	.190	1	-10	-12	-0	-1.1

YEAR	TM/L	W	L	PCT	G	GS	CG	SH	SV	IP	H	HR	BB	SO	RAT	ERA	ERA+	OAV	OOB	BH	AVG	PB	PR	/A	PD	TPI
1956	Bos-A	3	12	.200	25	18	4	1	0	126	127	21	64	53	13.7	5.14	90	.260	.347	14	.326	3	-14	-7	-1	-0.4
1957	Bos-A	4	4	.500	28	9	3	1	1	102¹	107	8	30	28	12.1	4.05	99	.272	.325	5	.172	0	-3	-1	1	0.0
1958	Bos-A	0	0	—	2	0	0	0	0	4	3	1	0	1	6.8	4.50	89	.214	.214	0	—	0	-0	-0	-0	0.0
	Pit-N	4	6	.400	37	6	2	1	5	87²	78	7	19	39	10.1	3.29	118	.241	.285	1	.050	-1	6	6	0	0.5
1959	Pit-N	0	0	—	6	0	0	0	0	5¹	6	1	2	1	13.5	1.69	229	.286	.348	0	—	0	1	1	-0	0.1
	Chi-N	0	0	—	4	0	0	0	0	6¹	14	1	3	0	24.2	11.37	35	.424	.472	0	.000	-0	-5	-5	0	-0.4
	Pit-N	1	2	.333	30	0	0	0	1	36	45	2	17	18	15.5	4.75	81	.321	.395	0	.000	-0	-3	-4	1	-0.2
	Yr	1	2	.333	40	0	0	0	1	47²	65	4	22	19	16.4	5.29	73	.335	.403	0	.000	-0	-7	-7	1	-0.5
Total	12	87	97	.473	318	193	92	23	8	1567²	1571	113	552	572	12.3	3.79	102	.263	.327	95	.184	4	26	16	3	3.5

■ AL PORTO
Porto, Alfred "Lefty" b: 6/27/26, Heilwood, Pa. BL/TL, 5'11", 176 lbs. Deb: 4/22/48

YEAR	TM/L	W	L	PCT	G	GS	CG	SH	SV	IP	H	HR	BB	SO	RAT	ERA	ERA+	OAV	OOB	BH	AVG	PB	PR	/A	PD	TPI
1948	Phi-N	0	0	—	3	0	0	0	0	4	2	0	1	0	6.8	0.00	—	.143	.200	0	—	0	2	2	-0	0.2

■ ARNIE PORTOCARRERO
Portocarrero, Arnold Mario b: 7/5/31, New York, N.Y. d: 6/21/86, Kansas City, Kan. BR/TR, 6'3", 196 lbs. Deb: 4/18/54

YEAR	TM/L	W	L	PCT	G	GS	CG	SH	SV	IP	H	HR	BB	SO	RAT	ERA	ERA+	OAV	OOB	BH	AVG	PB	PR	/A	PD	TPI
1954	Phi-A	9	18	.333	34	33	16	1	0	248	233	25	114	132	12.8	4.06	96	.249	.334	8	.107	-2	-9	-4	-4	-1.0
1955	KC-A	5	9	.357	24	20	4	1	0	111¹	109	12	67	34	14.6	4.77	88	.259	.366	4	.108	-2	-10	-7	-1	-0.8
1956	KC-A	0	1	.000	3	1	0	0	0	8	9	2	7	2	18.0	10.13	43	.300	.432	0	.000	-0	-5	-5	0	-0.4
1957	KC-A	4	9	.308	33	17	1	0	0	114²	103	10	34	42	11.0	3.92	101	.240	.300	3	.107	-1	-2	0	-1	0.0
1958	Bal-A	15	11	.577	32	27	10	3	2	204²	173	17	57	90	10.2	3.25	110	.229	.286	11	.164	0	12	8	-3	0.5
1959	Bal-A	2	7	.222	27	14	1	0	0	90	107	10	32	23	14.1	6.80	56	.294	.354	0	.000	-2	-29	-30	1	-2.9
1960	Bal-A	3	2	.600	13	5	1	0	0	40²	44	6	9	15	11.7	4.43	86	.275	.314	0	.000	-1	-2	-3	-1	-0.4
Total	7	38	57	.400	166	117	33	5	2	817¹	778	82	320	338	12.3	4.32	89	.252	.325	26	.108	-9	-47	-42	-8	-5.0

■ MARK PORTUGAL
Portugal, Mark Steven b: 10/30/62, Los Angeles, Cal. BR/TR, 6', 170 lbs. Deb: 8/14/85

YEAR	TM/L	W	L	PCT	G	GS	CG	SH	SV	IP	H	HR	BB	SO	RAT	ERA	ERA+	OAV	OOB	BH	AVG	PB	PR	/A	PD	TPI
1985	Min-A	1	3	.250	6	4	0	0	0	24¹	24	3	14	12	14.1	5.55	79	.270	.369	0	—	0	-4	-3	1	-0.1
1986	Min-A	6	10	.375	27	15	3	0	1	112²	112	10	50	67	13.0	4.31	100	.265	.345	0	—	0	-2	-0	-0	0.0
1987	Min-A	1	3	.250	13	7	0	0	0	44	58	13	24	28	17.0	7.77	59	.326	.409	0	—	0	-16	-15	0	-1.3
1988	Min-A	3	3	.500	26	0	0	0	3	57²	60	11	17	31	12.2	4.53	90	.274	.329	0	—	0	-4	-3	-2	-0.4
1989	Hou-N	7	1	.875	20	15	2	1	0	108	91	7	37	86	10.8	2.75	123	.232	.302	7	.206	3	9	8	0	1.1
1990	Hou-N	11	10	.524	32	32	1	0	0	196²	187	21	67	136	11.8	3.62	104	.250	.315	9	.136	-1	4	3	-0	0.1
Total	6	29	30	.492	124	73	6	1	4	543¹	532	65	209	360	12.4	4.11	95	.260	.331	16	.160	1	-13	-12	-1	-0.6

■ BILL POSEDEL
Posedel, William John "Sailor Bill" or "Barnacle Bill" b: 8/2/06, San Francisco, Cal. d: 11/28/89, Livermore, Cal. BR/TR, 5'11", 175 lbs. Deb: 4/23/38 C

YEAR	TM/L	W	L	PCT	G	GS	CG	SH	SV	IP	H	HR	BB	SO	RAT	ERA	ERA+	OAV	OOB	BH	AVG	PB	PR	/A	PD	TPI
1938	Bro-N	8	9	.471	33	17	6	1	1	140	178	14	46	49	14.5	5.66	69	.311	.365	10	.227	1	-29	-27	-1	-2.6
1939	Bos-N	15	13	.536	33	29	18	5	0	220²	221	8	78	73	12.2	3.92	94	.268	.331	8	.110	-3	0	-5	-1	-1.0
1940	Bos-N	12	17	.414	35	32	18	0	1	233	263	16	81	86	13.3	4.13	90	.288	.346	14	.171	1	-7	-11	-1	-0.9
1941	Bos-N	4	4	.500	18	9	3	0	0	57¹	61	6	30	10	14.4	4.87	73	.279	.368	8	.320	2	-8	-8	0	-0.5
1946	Bos-N	2	0	1.000	19	0	0	0	4	28¹	34	4	13	9	14.9	6.99	49	.304	.376	0	.000	-0	-11	-11	-0	-1.1
Total	5	41	43	.488	138	87	45	6	6	679¹	757	48	248	227	13.4	4.56	82	.286	.349	40	.176	0	-55	-63	-3	-6.1

■ BOB POSER
Poser, John Falk b: 3/16/10, Columbus, Wis. BL/TL, 6', 173 lbs. Deb: 4/17/32

YEAR	TM/L	W	L	PCT	G	GS	CG	SH	SV	IP	H	HR	BB	SO	RAT	ERA	ERA+	OAV	OOB	BH	AVG	PB	PR	/A	PD	TPI
1932	Chi-A	0	0	—	1	0	0	0	0	0²	3	0	2	1	67.5	27.00	16	.600	.714	0	.000	-0	-2	-2	0	0.0
1935	StL-A	1	1	.500	4	1	0	0	0	13²	26	0	4	1	19.8	9.22	52	.400	.435	1	.250	0	-7	-7	-0	-0.5
Total	2	1	1	.500	5	1	0	0	0	14¹	29	0	6	2	22.0	10.05	47	.414	.461	1	.143	0	-9	-8	-0	-0.5

■ LOU POSSEHL
Possehl, Louis Thomas b: 4/12/26, Chicago, Ill. BR/TR, 6'2", 180 lbs. Deb: 8/25/46

YEAR	TM/L	W	L	PCT	G	GS	CG	SH	SV	IP	H	HR	BB	SO	RAT	ERA	ERA+	OAV	OOB	BH	AVG	PB	PR	/A	PD	TPI
1946	Phi-N	1	2	.333	4	4	0	0	0	13²	19	0	10	4	19.8	5.93	58	.339	.448	0	.000	-0	-4	-4	0	-0.3
1947	Phi-N	0	0	—	2	0	0	0	0	4¹	5	0	1	1	12.5	4.15	96	.385	.429	0	—	0	-0	-0	0	0.1
1948	Phi-N	1	1	.500	3	2	1	0	0	14²	17	3	4	7	12.9	4.91	80	.304	.350	1	.250	-0	-2	-2	0	0.0
1951	Phi-N	0	1	.000	2	1	0	0	0	6	9	0	3	6	18.0	6.00	64	.333	.400	0	.000	-0	-1	-1	0	0.0
1952	Phi-N	0	1	.000	4	1	0	0	0	12²	12	3	7	4	13.5	4.97	73	.235	.328	0	.000	-0	-2	-2	-0	-0.1
Total	5	2	6	.286	15	8	1	0	0	51¹	62	6	24	22	15.4	5.26	71	.305	.384	1	.100	-0	-9	-9	0	-0.3

■ NELLIE POTT
Pott, Nelson Adolph "Lefty" b: 7/16/1899, Cincinnati, Ohio d: 12/3/63, Cincinnati, Ohio BL/TL, 6', 185 lbs. Deb: 4/19/22

YEAR	TM/L	W	L	PCT	G	GS	CG	SH	SV	IP	H	HR	BB	SO	RAT	ERA	ERA+	OAV	OOB	BH	AVG	PB	PR	/A	PD	TPI
1922	Cle-A	0	0	—	2	0	0	0	0	2	7	1	2	0	40.5	31.50	13	.583	.643	0	—	0	-6	-6	0	-0.4

■ DYKES POTTER
Potter, Maryland Dykes b: 9/7/10, Ashland, Ky. BR/TR, 6', 185 lbs. Deb: 4/26/38

YEAR	TM/L	W	L	PCT	G	GS	CG	SH	SV	IP	H	HR	BB	SO	RAT	ERA	ERA+	OAV	OOB	BH	AVG	PB	PR	/A	PD	TPI
1938	Bro-N	0	0	—	2	0	0	0	0	2	4	1	0	1	18.0	4.50	87	.400	.400	0	—	0	-0	-0	0	0.0

■ NELS POTTER
Potter, Nelson Thomas "Nellie" b: 8/23/11, Mt.Morris, Ill. d: 9/30/90, Mt.Morris, Ill. BL/TR, 5'11", 180 lbs. Deb: 4/25/36

YEAR	TM/L	W	L	PCT	G	GS	CG	SH	SV	IP	H	HR	BB	SO	RAT	ERA	ERA+	OAV	OOB	BH	AVG	PB	PR	/A	PD	TPI
1936	StL-N	0	0	—	1	0	0	0	0	1	0	0	0	0	0.0	0.00	—	.000	.000	0	—	0	0	0	0	0.0
1938	Phi-A	2	12	.143	35	9	4	0	5	111¹	139	15	49	43	15.4	6.47	75	.306	.376	10	.256	1	-21	-20	-1	-1.7
1939	Phi-A	8	12	.400	41	25	9	0	2	196¹	258	26	88	60	16.1	6.60	71	.321	.391	12	.179	-1	-43	-41	0	-3.6
1940	Phi-A	9	14	.391	31	25	13	0	0	200²	213	18	71	73	12.8	4.44	100	.269	.330	18	.254	2	-1	-0	-0	0.2
1941	Phi-A	1	1	.500	10	3	1	0	2	23¹	35	3	16	7	19.7	9.26	45	.337	.425	1	.167	-1	-13	-13	0	-1.1
	Bos-A	2	0	1.000	10	0	0	0	0	20	21	0	16	6	16.6	4.50	93	.284	.411	0	.000	-0	-1	-1	0	-0.1
	Yr	3	1	.750	20	3	1	0	2	43¹	56	3	32	13	18.3	7.06	59	.315	.419	2	.222	0	-14	-14	0	-1.1
1943	StL-A	10	5	.667	33	13	8	1	0	168¹	146	11	54	80	10.9	2.78	120	.235	.299	8	.145	-1	10	10	1	1.1
1944	*StL-A	19	7	.731	32	29	16	3	0	232	211	6	70	91	10.9	2.83	127	.244	.301	13	.159	-2	15	20	2	2.2
1945	StL-A	15	11	.577	32	32	21	3	0	255¹	212	10	68	129	9.9	2.47	143	.226	.279	28	.304	4	25	30	-1	3.8
1946	StL-A	8	9	.471	23	19	10	0	0	145	152	9	59	72	13.3	3.72	100	.268	.340	12	.231	2	-4	-0	-1	0.2
1947	StL-A	4	10	.286	32	10	3	0	2	122²	130	13	44	65	12.9	4.04	96	.277	.342	9	.257	1	-5	-2	1	0.2
1948	StL-A	1	1	.500	2	2	0	0	0	10¹	11	1	4	4	14.8	5.23	87	.262	.354	2	.500	1	-1	-1	1	0.0
	Phi-A	2	2	.500	8	0	0	0	1	18	17	1	5	13	11.0	4.00	107	.250	.301	1	.250	0	1	1	-0	0.0
	Yr	3	3	.500	10	2	0	0	1	28¹	28	2	9	17	11.8	4.45	99	.250	.306	1	.125	1	-0	-0	0	0.0
	*Bos-N	5	2	.714	18	7	3	0	2	85	77	4	8	47	9.0	2.33	165	.245	.264	11	.379	3	15	14	1	1.9
1949	Bos-N	6	11	.353	41	3	1	0	7	96²	99	6	30	57	12.1	4.19	90	.265	.321	3	.130	-0	-2	-4	0	-0.3
Total	12	92	97	.487	349	177	89	6	22	1686	1721	123	582	747	12.4	3.99	99	.265	.328	128	.228	12	-23	-6	2	2.9

■ SQUIRE POTTER
Potter, Squire b: 3/18/02, Flatwoods, Ky. d: 1/27/83, Ashland, Ky. BR/TR, 6'1", 185 lbs. Deb: 8/07/23

YEAR	TM/L	W	L	PCT	G	GS	CG	SH	SV	IP	H	HR	BB	SO	RAT	ERA	ERA+	OAV	OOB	BH	AVG	PB	PR	/A	PD	TPI
1923	Was-A	0	0	—	1	0	0	0	0	3	11	0	4	1	45.0	21.00	18	.688	.750	0	—	0	-6	-6	-0	-0.4

■ BILL POUNDS
Pounds, Jeared Wells b: 3/11/1878, Paterson, N.J. d: 7/7/36, Paterson, N.J. BR/TR, 5'10.5", 178 lbs. Deb: 5/02/03

YEAR	TM/L	W	L	PCT	G	GS	CG	SH	SV	IP	H	HR	BB	SO	RAT	ERA	ERA+	OAV	OOB	BH	AVG	PB	PR	/A	PD	TPI
1903	Cle-A	0	0	—	1	0	0	0	0	5	8	0	0	2	14.4	10.80	26	.359	.359	0	1.500	0	-4	-4	0	-0.3
	Bro-N	0	0	—	1	0	0	0	0	6	8	1	2	1	15.0	6.00	53	.348	.400	2	.667	1	-2	-2	0	0.0

■ ABNER POWELL
Powell, Charles Abner "Ab" b: 12/15/1860, Shenandoah, Pa. d: 8/7/53, New Orleans, La. BR/TR, 5'7", 160 lbs. Deb: 8/04/1884 ◆

YEAR	TM/L	W	L	PCT	G	GS	CG	SH	SV	IP	H	HR	BB	SO	RAT	ERA	ERA+	OAV	OOB	BH	AVG	PB	PR	/A	PD	TPI
1884	Was-U	6	12	.333	18	17	14	1	0	134	135	3	19	78	10.3	3.43	87	.245	.270	54	.283	3	-6	-7	2	-0.5
1886	Bal-a	2	5	.286	7	7	7	0	0	60	66	2	26	15	13.8	5.10	67	.267	.336	7	.179	-1	-11	-11	2	-0.7
	Cin-a	0	1	.000	4	1	1	0	0	15¹	16	0	9	4	14.7	4.70	75	.256	.350	4	.230	-0	-2	-2	-0	-0.1
	Yr	2	6	.250	11	8	8	0	0	75¹	82	2	35	19	14.0	5.02	69	.264	.339	5	.044	-1	-13	-13	2	-0.8
Total	2	8	18	.308	29	25	22	1	0	209¹	217	5	54	97	11.7	4.00	78	.252	.296	78	.257	3	-19	-20	4	-1.3

■ DENNIS POWELL
Powell, Dennis Clay b: 8/13/63, Moultrie, Ga. BR/TL, 6'3", 175 lbs. Deb: 7/07/85

YEAR	TM/L	W	L	PCT	G	GS	CG	SH	SV	IP	H	HR	BB	SO	RAT	ERA	ERA+	OAV	OOB	BH	AVG	PB	PR	/A	PD	TPI
1985	LA-N	1	1	.500	16	2	0	0	1	29¹	30	7	13	19	13.5	5.22	67	.263	.344	0	.000	-0	-5	-6	0	-0.5

YEAR	TM/L	W	L	PCT	G	GS	CG	SH	SV	IP	H	HR	BB	SO	RAT	ERA	ERA+	OAV	OOB	BH	AVG	PB	PR	/A	PD	TPI
1986	LA-N	2	7	.222	27	6	0	0	0	65¹	65	5	25	31	12.5	4.27	81	.272	.343	3	.214	1	-4	-6	-0	-0.4
1987	Sea-A	1	3	.250	16	3	0	0	0	34¹	32	3	15	17	12.3	3.15	150	.250	.329	0	—	0	5	6	0	0.6
1988	Sea-A	1	3	.250	12	2	0	0	0	18²	29	2	11	15	20.3	8.68	48	.363	.452	0	—	0	-10	-9	0	-0.8
1989	Sea-A	2	2	.500	43	1	0	0	2	45	49	6	21	27	14.4	5.00	81	.285	.369	0	—	0	-6	-5	1	-0.3
1990	Sea-A	0	0	—	2	0	0	0	0	3	5	0	2	0	24.0	9.00	44	.357	.471	0	—	0	-2	-2	0	-0.1
	Mil-A	0	4	.000	9	7	0	0	0	39¹	59	0	19	23	18.1	6.86	55	.341	.409	0	—	0	-13	-13	1	-1.1
	Yr	0	4	.000	11	7	0	0	0	42¹	64	0	21	23	18.3	7.02	54	.340	.410	0	—	0	-15	-15	1	-1.2
Total 6		7	20	.259	125	21	0	0	3	235	269	23	106	132	14.7	5.21	74	.292	.370	3	.176	1	-34	-35	2	-2.6

■ GROVER POWELL Powell, Grover David b: 10/10/40, Sayre, Pa. d: 5/21/85, Raleigh, N.C. BL/TL, 5'10", 175 lbs. Deb: 7/13/63

YEAR	TM/L	W	L	PCT	G	GS	CG	SH	SV	IP	H	HR	BB	SO	RAT	ERA	ERA+	OAV	OOB	BH	AVG	PB	PR	/A	PD	TPI
1963	NY-N	1	1	.500	20	4	1	1	0	49²	37	2	32	39	12.7	2.72	128	.202	.324	2	.200	1	3	4	0	0.5

■ JACK POWELL Powell, John Joseph "Red" b: 7/9/1874, Bloomington, Ill. d: 10/17/44, Chicago, Ill. BR/TR, 5'11", 195 lbs. Deb: 6/23/1897

YEAR	TM/L	W	L	PCT	G	GS	CG	SH	SV	IP	H	HR	BB	SO	RAT	ERA	ERA+	OAV	OOB	BH	AVG	PB	PR	/A	PD	TPI
1897	Cle-N	15	10	.600	27	26	24	2	0	225	245	2	62	61	12.3	3.16	142	.275	.322	20	.206	-4	29	33	-1	2.6
1898	Cle-N	23	15	.605	42	41	36	6	0	342	328	8	112	93	11.6	3.00	121	.251	.310	18	.132	-7	23	23	-2	1.4
1899	StL-N	23	19	.548	48	43	**40**	2	0	373	433	15	85	87	13.3	3.52	113	.290	.328	27	.201	-1	14	19	-2	1.4
1900	StL-N	17	16	.515	38	37	28	3	0	287²	325	9	77	77	12.6	4.44	82	.284	.329	31	.284	9	-24	-26	0	-1.4
1901	StL-N	19	19	.500	**45**	37	33	2	3	338¹	351	14	50	133	10.9	3.54	90	.266	.296	21	.176	1	-8	-14	-5	-1.6
1902	StL-A	22	17	.564	42	39	36	3	**2**	328¹	320	12	93	137	11.3	3.21	110	.256	.307	26	.205	3	13	12	-6	0.8
1903	StL-A	15	19	.441	38	34	33	4	**2**	306¹	294	11	58	169	10.3	2.91	100	.252	.287	25	.208	2	2	0	-2	0.0
1904	NY-A	23	19	.548	47	45	38	3	0	390¹	340	6	92	202	10.0	2.44	111	.235	.281	26	.178	-3	7	12	-6	-1.8
1905	NY-A	8	13	.381	37	23	13	1	1	203	214	4	57	84	12.0	3.50	84	.272	.321	12	.185	-0	-19	-13	-6	-1.8
	StL-A	2	1	.667	3	3	3	0	0	28	22	0	5	12	8.7	1.61	159	.218	.255	1	.100	-0	3	3	-1	0.2
	Yr	10	14	.417	40	26	16	1	1	231	236	4	62	96	11.6	3.27	88	.266	.314	5	.067	-0	-16	-10	-7	-1.6
1906	StL-A	13	14	.481	28	26	25	3	1	244	196	2	55	132	9.3	1.77	146	.223	.269	21	.233	3	25	22	-4	2.4
1907	StL-A	13	16	.448	32	31	27	4	1	255²	229	4	62	96	10.2	2.68	94	.241	.288	12	.132	-3	-4	-4	-3	-1.2
1908	StL-A	16	13	.552	33	32	23	5	1	256	208	1	47	85	9.2	2.11	114	.231	.274	21	.236	3	8	8	-6	0.6
1909	StL-A	12	16	.429	34	27	18	4	3	239	221	1	42	82	10.1	2.11	115	.250	.287	14	.179	0	10	8	-3	0.6
1910	StL-A	7	11	.389	21	18	8	3	0	129¹	121	0	28	52	10.4	2.30	108	.250	.292	7	.163	-1	3	3	-3	-0.2
1911	StL-A	8	19	.296	31	27	18	1	1	207²	224	7	44	52	11.9	3.29	102	.262	.304	12	.164	-3	1	2	-5	-0.5
1912	StL-A	9	17	.346	32	27	19	0	0	235¹	248	5	52	67	11.6	3.10	107	.276	.318	15	.183	0	6	6	-3	0.3
Total 16		245	254	.491	578	516	422	46	15	4389	4319	110	1021	1621	11.0	2.97	106	.258	.301	309	.192	-0	90	94	-57	4.0

■ JACK POWELL Powell, Reginald Bertrand b: 8/17/1891, Holcomb, Mo. d: 3/12/30, Memphis, Tenn. TR, 6'2", Deb: 6/14/13

YEAR	TM/L	W	L	PCT	G	GS	CG	SH	SV	IP	H	HR	BB	SO	RAT	ERA	ERA+	OAV	OOB	BH	AVG	PB	PR	/A	PD	TPI
1913	StL-A	0	0	—	2	0	0	0	0	2	1	0	2	0	13.5	0.00	—	.143	.333	0	—	0	1	1	1	0.1

■ BILL POWELL Powell, William Burris "Big Bill" b: 5/8/1885, Richmond, Va. d: 9/28/67, E.Liverpool, Ohio BR/TR, 6'2.5", 182 lbs. Deb: 4/16/09

YEAR	TM/L	W	L	PCT	G	GS	CG	SH	SV	IP	H	HR	BB	SO	RAT	ERA	ERA+	OAV	OOB	BH	AVG	PB	PR	/A	PD	TPI
1909	Pit-N	0	1	.000	3	1	0	0	0	7¹	7	0	6	2	17.2	3.68	74	.292	.452	1	.333		-1	-1	0	0.0
1910	Pit-N	4	6	.400	12	9	4	2	0	75	65	0	34	23	12.5	2.40	129	.242	.338	6	.261	1	5	6	2	0.9
1912	Chi-N	0	0	—	1	0	0	0	0	2	2	0	1	0	13.5	9.00	37	.250	.333	0	—	0	-1	-1	0	0.0
1913	Cin-N	0	1	.000	1	1	0	0	0	0¹	2	0	2	0	108.0	54.00	6	1.000	1.000	0	—	0	-2	-2	0	-0.1
Total 4		4	8	.333	17	11	4	2	0	84²	76	0	43	25	13.3	2.87	107	.251	.355	7	.269	1	1	2	2	0.8

■ TED POWER Power, Ted Henry b: 1/31/55, Guthrie, Okla. BR/TR, 6'4", 215 lbs. Deb: 9/09/81

YEAR	TM/L	W	L	PCT	G	GS	CG	SH	SV	IP	H	HR	BB	SO	RAT	ERA	ERA+	OAV	OOB	BH	AVG	PB	PR	/A	PD	TPI
1981	LA-N	1	3	.250	5	2	0	0	0	14¹	16	0	7	7	15.1	3.14	106	.286	.375	0	.000	-0	1	0	-0	0.0
1982	LA-N	1	1	.500	12	4	0	0	0	33²	38	4	23	15	16.3	6.68	52	.288	.394	0	.000	-1	-12	-12	0	-1.2
1983	Cin-N	5	6	.455	49	6	1	0	2	111	120	10	49	57	13.8	4.54	84	.286	.362	0	.000	-2	-11	-9	-2	-1.2
1984	Cin-N	9	7	.563	78	0	0	0	11	108²	93	4	46	81	11.5	2.82	134	.237	.317	0	.000	-0	9	12	0	1.2
1985	Cin-N	8	6	.571	64	0	0	0	27	80	65	2	45	42	12.5	2.70	140	.227	.334	0	—	0	8	10	-2	0.9
1986	Cin-N	10	6	.625	56	10	0	0	1	129	115	13	52	95	11.7	3.70	105	.245	.322	3	.125	0	2	0	0	0.3
1987	Cin-N	10	13	.435	34	34	2	1	0	204	213	28	71	133	12.7	4.50	94	.267	.329	7	.119	0	-10	-6	-3	-0.8
1988	KC-A	5	6	.455	22	12	2	2	0	80¹	98	7	30	44	14.7	5.94	67	.305	.370	0	—	0	-18	-17	-0	-1.6
	Det-A	1	1	.500	4	2	0	0	0	18²	23	1	8	13	14.9	5.79	66	.307	.373	0	—	0	-4	-4	0	-0.3
	Yr	6	7	.462	26	14	2	2	0	99	121	8	38	57	14.5	5.91	67	.300	.361	0	—	0	-21	-22	-0	-1.9
1989	StL-N	7	7	.500	23	15	0	0	0	97	96	7	21	43	10.9	3.71	98	.255	.296	3	.091	-2	-2	-1	-1	-0.3
1990	*Pit-N	1	3	.250	40	0	0	0	7	51²	50	5	17	42	11.7	3.66	99	.255	.315	1	.125	0	1	-0	-1	0.0
Total 10		58	59	.496	387	85	5	3	48	928¹	927	81	369	572	12.7	4.12	94	.263	.335	14	.091	-4	-37	-25	-10	-3.0

■ JIM POWERS Powers, James T. b: 1868, New York, N.Y. 5'10", 150 lbs. Deb: 4/18/1890

YEAR	TM/L	W	L	PCT	G	GS	CG	SH	SV	IP	H	HR	BB	SO	RAT	ERA	ERA+	OAV	OOB	BH	AVG	PB	PR	/A	PD	TPI
1890	Bro-a	1	2	.333	4	2	2	0	0	30	38	1	16	3	16.2	5.70	68	.300	.378	2	.154	-1	-6	-6	-0	-0.4

■ IKE POWERS Powers, John Lloyd b: 3/13/06, Hancock, Md. d: 12/22/68, Hancock, Md. BR/TR, 6'0.5", 188 lbs. Deb: 7/26/27

YEAR	TM/L	W	L	PCT	G	GS	CG	SH	SV	IP	H	HR	BB	SO	RAT	ERA	ERA+	OAV	OOB	BH	AVG	PB	PR	/A	PD	TPI
1927	Phi-A	1	1	.500	11	1	0	0	0	26	26	1	7	3	11.4	4.50	95	.271	.320	2	.400	1	-1	-1	0	0.0
1928	Phi-A	1	0	1.000	9	0	0	0	2	12	8	1	10	4	14.3	4.50	89	.222	.404	0	—	0	-1	-1	1	0.0
Total 2		2	1	.667	20	1	0	0	2	38	34	2	17	7	12.3	4.50	93	.258	.347	2	.400	1	-2	-1	1	0.0

■ WILLIE PRALL Prall, Wilfred Anthony b: 4/20/50, Hackensack, N.J. BL/TL, 6'3", 200 lbs. Deb: 9/03/75

YEAR	TM/L	W	L	PCT	G	GS	CG	SH	SV	IP	H	HR	BB	SO	RAT	ERA	ERA+	OAV	OOB	BH	AVG	PB	PR	/A	PD	TPI
1975	Chi-N	0	2	.000	3	3	0	0	0	14²	21	1	8	7	17.8	8.59	45	.339	.414	0	.000	-0	-8	-8	0	-0.6

■ AL PRATT Pratt, Albert George "Uncle Al" b: 11/19/1848, Allegheny, Pa. d: 11/21/37, Pittsburgh, Pa. 5'7", 140 lbs. Deb: 5/04/1871 MU

YEAR	TM/L	W	L	PCT	G	GS	CG	SH	SV	IP	H	HR	BB	SO	RAT	ERA	ERA+	OAV	OOB	BH	AVG	PB	PR	/A	PD	TPI
1871	Cle-n	10	17	.370	28	28	22	0	0	224²	296	9	47	**33**	13.7	3.77	110	.277	.307	34	.262	2	11	9		0.7
1872	Cle-n	2	9	.182	15	12	8	0	0	104²	150	3	13		14.0	4.39	83	.287	.305	18	.281	1	-8	-9		-0.5
Total 2 n		12	26	.316	43	40	30	0	0	329¹	446	12	60	33	13.8	3.96	92	.280	.306	52	.268	3	-9	-12		0.2

■ JOHN PREGENZER Pregenzer, John Arthur b: 8/2/35, Burlington, Wis. BR/TR, 6'5", 220 lbs. Deb: 4/20/63

YEAR	TM/L	W	L	PCT	G	GS	CG	SH	SV	IP	H	HR	BB	SO	RAT	ERA	ERA+	OAV	OOB	BH	AVG	PB	PR	/A	PD	TPI
1963	SF-N	0	0	—	6	0	0	0	1	9¹	8	0	5	16	16.4	4.82	66	.242	.405	0	—	0	-2	-2	0	-0.1
1964	SF-N	2	0	1.000	13	0	0	0	0	18¹	21	1	11	8	16.2	4.91	73	.296	.398	0	—	0	-3	-3	0	-0.2
Total 2		2	0	1.000	19	0	0	0	1	27²	29	1	19	13	16.3	4.88	70	.279	.400	0	—	0	-4	-4	0	-0.3

■ JIM PRENDERGAST Prendergast, James Bartholomew b: 8/23/17, Brooklyn, N.Y. BL/TL, 6'1", 208 lbs. Deb: 4/25/48

YEAR	TM/L	W	L	PCT	G	GS	CG	SH	SV	IP	H	HR	BB	SO	RAT	ERA	ERA+	OAV	OOB	BH	AVG	PB	PR	/A	PD	TPI
1948	Bos-N	1	1	.500	10	2	0	0	1	16²	30	1	5	3	18.9	10.26	37	.380	.417	0	.000	-1	-12	-12	1	-1.0

■ MIKE PRENDERGAST Prendergast, Michael Thomas b: 12/15/1888, Arlington, Ill. d: 11/18/67, Omaha, Neb. BR/TR, 5'9.5", 165 lbs. Deb: 4/26/14

YEAR	TM/L	W	L	PCT	G	GS	CG	SH	SV	IP	H	HR	BB	SO	RAT	ERA	ERA+	OAV	OOB	BH	AVG	PB	PR	/A	PD	TPI
1914	Chi-F	5	9	.357	30	19	7	1	0	136	131	6	40	71	11.5	2.38	124	.255	.313	4	.108	-2	12	9	-2	0.5
1915	Chi-F	14	12	.538	42	30	16	3	0	253²	220	6	67	95	10.3	2.48	112	.240	.295	6	.075	-7	15	9	-2	0.0
1916	Chi-N	6	11	.353	35	10	4	2	2	152	127	5	23	56	8.9	2.31	126	.228	.260	7	.152	-2	5	10	-0	1.0
1917	Chi-N	3	6	.333	35	8	1	0	1	99¹	112	6	21	43	12.1	3.35	86	.302	.339	7	.250	1	-7	-5	-0	-0.4
1918	Phi-N	13	14	.481	33	30	20	0	1	252¹	257	6	46	41	10.8	2.89	104	.273	.308	7	.082	-3	-4	-3	-1	-0.5
1919	Phi-N	0	1	.000	5	0	0	0	0	15	20	0	10	5	18.6	8.40	38	.351	.456	1	.333	0	-9	-9	-0	-0.7
Total 6		41	53	.436	180	97	48	6	4	908¹	867	29	207	311	10.7	2.74	107	.258	.304	32	.115	-17	13	18	-6	-0.1

■ GEORGE PRENTISS Prentiss, George Pepper (a.k.a. George Pepper Wilson in 1901)
b: 6/10/1876, Wilmington, Del. d: 9/8/02, Wilmington, Del. BB, 5'11", 175 lbs. Deb: 9/23/01

YEAR	TM/L	W	L	PCT	G	GS	CG	SH	SV	IP	H	HR	BB	SO	RAT	ERA	ERA+	OAV	OOB	BH	AVG	PB	PR	/A	PD	TPI
1901	Bos-A	1	0	1.000	2	1	1	0	0	10	7	0	6	6	11.7	1.80	196	.195	.311	1	.333	1	2	2	0	0.3
1902	Bos-A	2	2	.500	7	4	3	0	0	41	55	0	10	9	14.3	5.27	68	.321	.359	5	.313	1	-8	-8	0	-0.5
	Bal-A	0	1	.000	2	2	0	0	0	6²	14	1	5	1	25.7	10.80	35	.426	.501	0	.000	-1	-5	-5	-0	-0.4

YEAR TM/L	W	L	PCT	G	GS	CG	SH	SV	IP	H	HR	BB	SO	RAT	ERA	ERA+	OAV	OOB	BH	AVG	PB	PR	/A	PD	TPI
Yr	2	3	.400	9	6	3	0	0	47²	69	1	15	10	15.9	6.04	60	.338	.383	0	.000	-0	-13	-13	-0	-0.9
Total 2	3	3	.500	11	7	4	0	0	57²	76	1	21	10	15.1	5.31	68	.317	.372	6	.261	1	-11	-11	-0	-0.6

■ JOE PRESKO
Presko, Joseph Edward "Little Joe" b: 10/7/28, Kansas City, Mo. BR/TR, 5'9.5", 165 lbs. Deb: 5/03/51

YEAR TM/L	W	L	PCT	G	GS	CG	SH	SV	IP	H	HR	BB	SO	RAT	ERA	ERA+	OAV	OOB	BH	AVG	PB	PR	/A	PD	TPI
1951 StL-N	7	4	.636	15	12	5	0	2	88²	86	9	20	38	11.0	3.45	115	.251	.296	6	.162	-1	5	5	-1	0.3
1952 StL-N	7	10	.412	28	18	5	1	0	146²	140	15	57	63	12.1	4.05	92	.247	.317	4	.093	-2	-5	-5	-1	-0.7
1953 StL-N	6	13	.316	34	25	4	0	1	161²	165	19	65	56	13.1	5.01	85	.261	.335	13	.220	1	-13	-14	-1	-1.1
1954 StL-N	4	9	.308	37	6	1	1	0	71²	97	14	41	36	18.0	6.91	60	.327	.417	4	.250	0	-23	-22	-0	-2.0
1957 Det-A	1	1	.500	7	0	0	0	0	11	10	0	4	3	12.3	1.64	236	.278	.366	0	.000	-0	3	3	-0	0.2
1958 Det-A	0	0	—	7	0	0	0	2	10²	13	0	1	6	11.8	3.38	120	.317	.333	0	—	0	0	1	0	0.1
Total 6	25	37	.403	128	61	15	2	5	490¹	511	57	188	202	13.1	4.61	87	.267	.337	27	.173	-1	-33	-33	-3	-3.2

■ TOT PRESSNELL
Pressnell, Forest Charles b: 8/8/06, Findlay, Ohio BR/TR, 5'10", 175 lbs. Deb: 4/21/38

YEAR TM/L	W	L	PCT	G	GS	CG	SH	SV	IP	H	HR	BB	SO	RAT	ERA	ERA+	OAV	OOB	BH	AVG	PB	PR	/A	PD	TPI
1938 Bro-N	11	14	.440	43	19	6	1	3	192	209	11	56	57	12.8	3.56	110	.276	.332	9	.143	-1	5	7	-1	0.6
1939 Bro-N	9	7	.563	31	18	10	2	2	156²	171	8	33	43	11.8	4.02	100	.273	.311	10	.196	-1	-2	0	1	0.0
1940 Bro-N	6	5	.545	24	4	1	1	2	68¹	58	4	17	21	10.1	3.69	108	.221	.274	0	.000	-2	1	2	-1	0.0
1941 Chi-N	5	3	.625	29	1	0	0	1	70	69	2	23	27	12.3	3.09	114	.253	.320	3	.200	-1	4	3	-0	0.3
1942 Chi-N	1	1	.500	27	0	0	0	4	39¹	40	5	5	9	11.4	5.49	58	.260	.305	2	.667	1	-10	-10	-0	-0.8
Total 5	32	30	.516	154	42	17	4	12	526¹	547	30	134	157	12.0	3.80	101	.264	.315	24	.161	-3	-1	3	-1	0.1

■ JOE PRICE
Price, Joseph Walter b: 11/29/56, Inglewood, Cal. BR/TL, 6'4", 220 lbs. Deb: 6/14/80

YEAR TM/L	W	L	PCT	G	GS	CG	SH	SV	IP	H	HR	BB	SO	RAT	ERA	ERA+	OAV	OOB	BH	AVG	PB	PR	/A	PD	TPI
1980 Cin-N	7	3	.700	24	13	2	0	0	111¹	95	10	37	44	10.8	3.56	101	.236	.302	5	.128	-2	1	0	-1	-0.1
1981 Cin-N	6	1	.857	41	0	0	0	4	53²	42	3	18	41	10.1	2.52	141	.222	.290	0	.000	-0	6	6	1	0.7
1982 Cin-N	3	4	.429	59	1	0	0	3	72²	73	7	32	71	13.5	2.85	130	.263	.347	1	.333	-1	6	7	-1	0.6
1983 Cin-N	10	6	.625	21	21	5	0	0	144	118	12	46	83	10.3	2.88	132	.225	.287	4	.098	-1	12	15	0	1.5
1984 Cin-N	7	13	.350	30	30	3	1	0	171²	176	19	61	129	12.5	4.19	90	.261	.324	7	.146	-1	-12	-8	-3	-1.0
1985 Cin-N	2	2	.500	26	8	0	0	1	64²	59	10	23	52	11.4	3.90	97	.242	.307	0	.000	-1	-2	-1	-1	-0.2
1986 Cin-N	1	2	.333	25	2	0	0	1	41²	49	5	22	30	15.3	5.40	72	.293	.376	1	.143	-0	-8	-7	-1	-0.7
1987 *SF-N	2	2	.500	20	0	0	0	1	35	19	5	13	42	8.5	2.57	149	.154	.241	1	.167	-0	6	5	-1	0.4
1988 SF-N	1	6	.143	38	3	0	0	4	61²	59	5	27	49	12.7	3.94	83	.249	.328	0	.000	-0	-3	-5	-0	-0.5
1989 SF-N	1	1	.500	7	1	0	0	0	14	16	3	4	10	12.9	5.79	58	.314	.364	0	.000	-0	-4	-4	0	-0.3
Bos-A	2	5	.286	31	5	0	0	0	70¹	71	8	30	52	12.9	4.35	94	.262	.336	0	—	0	-4	-2	-1	-0.2
1990 Bal-A	3	4	.429	50	0	0	0	0	65¹	62	8	24	54	11.8	3.58	107	.253	.320	0	—	0	2	2	-1	0.1
Total 11	45	49	.479	372	84	10	1	13	906	839	95	337	657	11.8	3.65	102	.246	.316	19	.111	-5	0	9	-8	0.3

■ WILLIAM PRICE
Price, William b: Philadelphia, Pa. Deb: 4/27/1890

YEAR TM/L	W	L	PCT	G	GS	CG	SH	SV	IP	H	HR	BB	SO	RAT	ERA	ERA+	OAV	OOB	BH	AVG	PB	PR	/A	PD	TPI
1890 Phi-a	1	0	1.000	1	1	1	0	0	9	6	0	7	1	13.0	2.00	191	.184	.328	1	.250	-0	2	2	0	0.2

■ BOB PRIDDY
Priddy, Robert Simpson b: 12/10/39, Pittsburgh, Pa. BR/TR, 6'1", 200 lbs. Deb: 9/20/62

YEAR TM/L	W	L	PCT	G	GS	CG	SH	SV	IP	H	HR	BB	SO	RAT	ERA	ERA+	OAV	OOB	BH	AVG	PB	PR	/A	PD	TPI
1962 Pit-N	1	0	1.000	2	0	0	0	0	3	4	0	1	1	15.0	3.00	131	.308	.357	0	—	0	0	0	0	0.0
1964 Pit-N	1	2	.333	19	0	0	0	1	34¹	35	2	15	23	13.4	3.93	89	.282	.364	0	.000	0	-2	-2	-1	-0.2
1965 SF-N	1	0	1.000	8	0	0	0	0	10¹	6	1	2	7	7.0	1.74	207	.176	.222	0	.000	0	2	2	0	0.2
1966 SF-N	6	3	.667	38	3	0	0	1	91	88	8	28	51	11.8	3.96	93	.259	.321	3	.176	0	-4	-3	-1	-0.3
1967 Was-A	3	7	.300	46	8	1	0	4	110	98	12	33	57	10.7	3.44	92	.240	.297	4	.182	1	-3	-3	1	0.0
1968 Chi-A	3	11	.214	35	18	2	0	0	114	106	14	41	66	11.9	3.63	83	.244	.315	1	.042	-1	-8	-8	-2	-1.0
1969 Chi-A	0	0	—	4	0	0	0	0	8	10	2	2	5	13.5	4.50	86	.303	.343	0	—	0	-1	-1	0	0.0
Cal-A	0	1	.000	15	0	0	0	0	26¹	24	4	7	15	10.6	4.78	73	.242	.292	0	.000	0	-4	-4	0	-0.3
Yr	0	1	.000	19	0	0	0	0	34¹	34	6	9	20	11.3	4.72	76	.258	.305	1	.500	0	-4	-4	0	-0.3
Atl-N	0	0	—	1	0	0	0	0	2	1	0	1	1	9.0	0.00	—	.143	.250	0	—	0	1	1	0	0.1
1970 Atl-N	5	5	.500	41	0	0	0	8	73	75	9	24	32	12.6	5.42	79	.269	.333	3	.200	0	-11	-9	1	-0.7
1971 Atl-N	4	9	.308	40	0	0	0	4	64	71	8	44	36	16.3	4.22	88	.289	.399	2	.182	0	-5	-4	1	-0.2
Total 9	24	38	.387	249	29	3	0	18	536	518	60	198	294	12.2	4.00	87	.257	.327	13	.137	1	-33	-30	-1	-2.4

■ RAY PRIM
Prim, Raymond Lee "Pop" b: 12/30/06, Salitpa, Ala. BR/TL, 6', 178 lbs. Deb: 9/24/33

YEAR TM/L	W	L	PCT	G	GS	CG	SH	SV	IP	H	HR	BB	SO	RAT	ERA	ERA+	OAV	OOB	BH	AVG	PB	PR	/A	PD	TPI
1933 Was-A	0	1	.000	2	1	0	0	0	14¹	13	0	2	6	9.4	3.14	133	.232	.259	0	.000	-1	2	2	1	0.2
1934 Was-A	0	2	.000	8	1	0	0	0	14²	19	1	8	3	16.6	6.75	64	.339	.422	0	-00	-4	-4	0	-0	-0.2
1935 Phi-N	3	4	.429	29	6	1	0	0	73¹	110	4	15	27	15.3	5.77	79	.340	.369	2	.083	-3	-14	-10	-0	-1.1
1943 Chi-N	4	3	.571	29	5	0	0	1	60	67	2	14	27	12.2	2.55	131	.282	.321	2	.167	-0	6	5	2	0.7
1945 *Chi-N	13	8	.619	34	19	9	2	2	165¹	142	9	23	88	9.0	2.40	153	.228	.256	13	.255	3	26	23	-1	2.5
1946 Chi-N	2	3	.400	14	2	0	0	1	23¹	28	5	10	10	14.7	5.79	57	.289	.355	1	.200	-0	-6	-6	1	-0.5
Total 6	22	21	.512	116	34	10	2	4	351	379	21	72	161	11.6	3.56	107	.272	.308	18	.180	-0	9	9	2	1.6

■ DON PRINCE
Prince, Donald Mark b: 4/5/38, Clarkton, N.C. BR/TR, 6'4", 200 lbs. Deb: 9/21/62

YEAR TM/L	W	L	PCT	G	GS	CG	SH	SV	IP	H	HR	BB	SO	RAT	ERA	ERA+	OAV	OOB	BH	AVG	PB	PR	/A	PD	TPI
1962 Chi-N	0	0	—	1	0	0	0	0	1	0	0	1	0	18.0	0.00	—	.000	.500	0	—	0	0	0	0	0.1

■ JIM PROCTOR
Proctor, James Arthur b: 9/9/35, Brandywine, Md. BR/TR, 6', 165 lbs. Deb: 9/14/59

YEAR TM/L	W	L	PCT	G	GS	CG	SH	SV	IP	H	HR	BB	SO	RAT	ERA	ERA+	OAV	OOB	BH	AVG	PB	PR	/A	PD	TPI
1959 Det-A	0	1	.000	2	1	0	0	0	2²	8	0	3	0	37.1	16.88	24	.533	.611	0	—	0	-4	-4	0	-0.2

■ RED PROCTOR
Proctor, Noah Richard b: 10/27/1900, Williamsburg, Va. d: 12/17/54, Richmond, Va. BR/TR, 6'1", 165 lbs. Deb: 8/06/23

YEAR TM/L	W	L	PCT	G	GS	CG	SH	SV	IP	H	HR	BB	SO	RAT	ERA	ERA+	OAV	OOB	BH	AVG	PB	PR	/A	PD	TPI
1923 Chi-A	0	0	—	2	0	0	0	0	4	11	0	2	0	29.3	13.50	29	.550	.591	0	—	0	-4	-4	-0	-0.3

■ GEORGE PROESER
Proeser, George "Yatz" b: 5/30/1864, Cincinnati, Ohio d: 10/13/41, New Burlington, O. BL/TL, 5'10", 190 lbs. Deb: 9/15/1888 ◆

YEAR TM/L	W	L	PCT	G	GS	CG	SH	SV	IP	H	HR	BB	SO	RAT	ERA	ERA+	OAV	OOB	BH	AVG	PB	PR	/A	PD	TPI
1888 Cle-a	3	4	.429	7	7	7	1	0	59	53	4	30	20	12.7	3.81	82	.231	.320	7	.304	2	-5	-5	-1	-0.2

■ MIKE PROLY
Proly, Michael James b: 12/15/50, Jamaica, N.Y. BR/TR, 6', 185 lbs. Deb: 4/10/76

YEAR TM/L	W	L	PCT	G	GS	CG	SH	SV	IP	H	HR	BB	SO	RAT	ERA	ERA+	OAV	OOB	BH	AVG	PB	PR	/A	PD	TPI
1976 StL-N	1	0	1.000	14	0	0	0	0	17	21	0	6	4	14.3	3.71	95	.328	.386	0	—	0	-0	-0	0	0.0
1978 Chi-A	5	2	.714	14	6	2	0	1	65²	63	4	12	19	10.3	2.74	139	.250	.284	0	—	0	7	8	-0	0.8
1979 Chi-A	3	8	.273	38	6	0	0	9	88¹	89	6	40	32	13.2	3.87	110	.260	.339	0	—	0	3	4	1	0.4
1980 Chi-A	5	10	.333	62	3	0	0	8	146²	136	7	58	56	12.1	3.07	131	.253	.329	0	—	0	16	16	2	1.8
1981 Phi-N	2	1	.667	35	2	0	0	2	63	66	6	19	19	12.3	3.86	94	.282	.339	0	.000	-1	-3	-2	1	0.0
1982 Chi-N	5	3	.625	44	1	0	0	1	82	77	5	22	24	11.1	2.30	162	.257	.312	4	.286	1	12	13	1	1.6
1983 Chi-N	1	5	.167	60	0	0	0	1	83	79	5	38	31	12.8	3.58	106	.259	.343	1	.091	-0	2	0	0	0.2
Total 7	22	29	.431	267	18	2	0	22	545²	531	33	195	185	12.1	3.23	121	.261	.328	5	.156	-0	36	40	5	4.8

■ BILL PROUGH
Prough, Herschel Clinton "Clint" b: 11/28/1887, Markle, Ind. d: 12/29/36, Richmond, Ind. BR/TR, 6'3", 185 lbs. Deb: 4/27/12

YEAR TM/L	W	L	PCT	G	GS	CG	SH	SV	IP	H	HR	BB	SO	RAT	ERA	ERA+	OAV	OOB	BH	AVG	PB	PR	/A	PD	TPI
1912 Cin-N	0	0	—	1	0	0	0	0	3	7	0	1	0	24.0	6.00	56	.500	.533	0	.000	-0	-1	-1	-0	0.0

■ AUGIE PRUDHOMME
Prudhomme, John Olgus b: 11/20/02, Frierson, La. BR/TR, 6'2", 186 lbs. Deb: 4/19/29

YEAR TM/L	W	L	PCT	G	GS	CG	SH	SV	IP	H	HR	BB	SO	RAT	ERA	ERA+	OAV	OOB	BH	AVG	PB	PR	/A	PD	TPI
1929 Det-A	1	6	.143	34	6	2	0	1	94	119	7	53	26	16.7	6.22	69	.322	.410	5	.238	1	-21	-20	1	-1.6

■ HUB PRUETT
Pruett, Hubert Shelby "Shucks" b: 9/1/1900, Malden, Mo. d: 1/28/82, Ladue, Mo. BL/TL, 5'10.5", 165 lbs. Deb: 4/26/22

YEAR TM/L	W	L	PCT	G	GS	CG	SH	SV	IP	H	HR	BB	SO	RAT	ERA	ERA+	OAV	OOB	BH	AVG	PB	PR	/A	PD	TPI
1922 StL-A	7	7	.500	39	8	4	0	7	119²	99	2	59	70	12.3	2.33	178	.235	.336	5	.147	-1	23	24	2	2.5
1923 StL-A	4	7	.364	32	8	3	0	2	104¹	109	3	64	59	15.2	4.31	97	.271	.373	3	.130	-1	-4	-2	0	-0.1
1924 StL-A	3	4	.429	33	1	0	0	2	65	64	1	42	27	15.2	4.57	99	.270	.389	3	.200	-1	-2	-0	0	0.0
1927 Phi-N	7	17	.292	31	28	12	1	1	186	238	6	89	90	16.4	6.05	68	.314	.395	13	.217	1	-44	-40	3	-3.2
1928 Phi-N	2	4	.333	13	9	4	0	0	71¹	78	2	49	35	16.4	4.54	94	.291	.406	5	.208	-0	-4	-2	0	-0.1

YEAR TM/L	W	L	PCT	G	GS	CG	SH	SV	IP	H	HR	BB	SO	RAT	ERA	ERA+	OAV	OOB	BH	AVG	PB	PR	/A	PD	TPI
1930 NY-N	5	4	.556	45	8	1	0	3	135²	152	11	63	49	14.5	4.78	99	.287	.367	5	.135	-1	3	-1	1	0.0
1932 Bos-N	1	5	.167	18	7	4	0	0	63	76	3	30	27	16.0	5.14	73	.308	.396	2	.105	-1	-9	-10	2	-0.8
Total 7	29	48	.377	211	69	28	1	13	745	816	28	396	357	15.1	4.63	92	.286	.380	36	.170	-3	-38	-29	7	-1.7

■ TEX PRUIETT Pruiett, Charles Le Roy b: 4/10/1883, Osgood, Ind. d: 3/6/53, Ventura, Cal. BL/TR, Deb: 4/26/07

YEAR TM/L	W	L	PCT	G	GS	CG	SH	SV	IP	H	HR	BB	SO	RAT	ERA	ERA+	OAV	OOB	BH	AVG	PB	PR	/A	PD	TPI
1907 Bos-A	3	11	.214	35	17	6	2	3	173²	166	1	59	54	11.7	3.11	83	.254	.315	8	.157	-1	-11	-10	1	-0.9
1908 Bos-A	1	7	.125	13	6	1	1	2	58²	55	1	21	28	12.3	1.99	124	.259	.338	1	.063	-2	3	3	0	0.2
Total 2	4	18	.182	48	23	7	3	5	232¹	221	2	80	82	11.8	2.83	90	.255	.321	9	.134	-2	-8	-7	2	-0.7

■ TROY PUCKETT Puckett, Troy Levi b: 12/10/1889, Winchester, Ind. d: 4/13/71, Winchester, Ind. BL/TR, 6'2", 186 lbs. Deb: 10/04/11

YEAR TM/L	W	L	PCT	G	GS	CG	SH	SV	IP	H	HR	BB	SO	RAT	ERA	ERA+	OAV	OOB	BH	AVG	PB	PR	/A	PD	TPI
1911 Phi-N	0	0	—	1	0	0	0	0	2	4	0	2	1	31.5	13.50	26	.444	.583	0	—	0	-2	-2	0	-0.1

■ MIGUEL PUENTE Puente, Miguel Antonio (Aguilar) b: 5/8/48, San Luis Potosi, Mex BR/TR, 6', 160 lbs. Deb: 5/03/70

YEAR TM/L	W	L	PCT	G	GS	CG	SH	SV	IP	H	HR	BB	SO	RAT	ERA	ERA+	OAV	OOB	BH	AVG	PB	PR	/A	PD	TPI
1970 SF-N	1	3	.250	6	4	1	0	0	18²	25	5	11	14	17.4	8.20	48	.325	.409	0	.000	-1	-9	-9	0	-0.8

■ CHARLIE PULEO Puleo, Charles Michael b: 2/7/55, Glen Ridge, N.J. BR/TR, 6'2", 190 lbs. Deb: 9/16/81

YEAR TM/L	W	L	PCT	G	GS	CG	SH	SV	IP	H	HR	BB	SO	RAT	ERA	ERA+	OAV	OOB	BH	AVG	PB	PR	/A	PD	TPI
1981 NY-N	0	0	—	4	1	0	0	0	13¹	8	0	8	8	10.8	0.00	—	.182	.308	0	.000	-0	5	5	0	0.6
1982 NY-N	9	9	.500	36	24	1	1	1	171	179	13	90	98	14.3	4.47	81	.275	.364	6	.125	-1	-17	-16	3	-1.4
1983 Cin-N	6	12	.333	27	24	0	0	0	143²	145	18	91	71	15.1	4.89	78	.269	.379	5	.100	-2	-20	-17	-1	-1.9
1984 Cin-N	1	2	.333	5	4	0	0	0	22	27	2	15	6	17.2	5.73	66	.297	.396	1	.200	0	-5	-5	-1	-0.5
1986 Atl-N	1	2	.333	5	3	1	0	0	24¹	13	4	12	18	9.6	2.96	134	.160	.277	2	.333	0	2	3	-0	0.3
1987 Atl-N	6	8	.429	35	16	1	0	0	123¹	122	11	40	99	12.0	4.23	103	.262	.325	5	.179	1	-2	-2	0	0.1
1988 Atl-N	5	5	.500	53	3	0	0	1	106¹	101	9	47	70	12.8	3.47	106	.251	.333	3	.231	0	-0	2	-0	0.2
1989 Atl-N	1	1	.500	15	1	0	0	0	29	26	2	16	17	13.0	4.66	78	.245	.344	0	.000	-0	-4	-3	-1	-0.3
Total 8	29	39	.426	180	76	3	1	2	633	621	59	319	387	13.6	4.25	90	.261	.351	22	.144	-1	-41	-30	-1	-2.8

■ ALFONSO PULIDO Pulido, Alfonso (Manzo) b: 1/23/57, Veracruz, Mexico BL/TL, 5'11", 170 lbs. Deb: 9/05/83

YEAR TM/L	W	L	PCT	G	GS	CG	SH	SV	IP	H	HR	BB	SO	RAT	ERA	ERA+	OAV	OOB	BH	AVG	PB	PR	/A	PD	TPI
1983 Pit-N	0	0	—	1	1	0	0	0	2	4	2	1	1	22.5	9.00	41	.400	.455	0	—	0	-1	-1	0	0.0
1984 Pit-N	0	0	—	1	0	0	0	0	2	3	0	1	2	18.0	9.00	40	.333	.400	0	—	0	-1	-1	0	0.0
1986 NY-A	1	1	.500	10	3	0	0	0	30²	38	8	9	13	13.8	4.70	87	.306	.353	0	—	0	-2	-2	0	-0.1
Total 3	1	1	.500	12	4	0	0	0	34²	45	10	11	16	14.5	5.19	78	.315	.364	0	—	0	-4	-4	0	-0.1

■ SPENCER PUMPELLY Pumpelly, Spencer Armstrong b: 4/11/1893, Owego, N.Y. d: 12/5/73, Sayre, Pa. Deb: 7/11/25

YEAR TM/L	W	L	PCT	G	GS	CG	SH	SV	IP	H	HR	BB	SO	RAT	ERA	ERA+	OAV	OOB	BH	AVG	PB	PR	/A	PD	TPI
1925 Was-A	0	0	—	1	0	0	0	0	1	1	1	1	0	18.0	9.00	47	.333	.500	0	—	0	-1	-1	0	0.0

■ BLONDIE PURCELL Purcell, William Aloysius b: Paterson, N.J. 5'9.5", 159 lbs. Deb: 5/01/1879 M♦

YEAR TM/L	W	L	PCT	G	GS	CG	SH	SV	IP	H	HR	BB	SO	RAT	ERA	ERA+	OAV	OOB	BH	AVG	PB	PR	/A	PD	TPI
1879 Syr-N	4	15	.211	22	17	15	0	0	179²	245	1	19	28	13.2	3.76	63	.305	.321	72	.260	3	-25	-28	-2	-2.3
Cin-N	0	2	.000	2	2	2	0	0	18	27	0	2	3	14.5	4.00	58	.326	.342	11	.220	-0	-3	-3	-0	-0.2
Yr	4	17	.190	24	19	17	0	0	197²	272	1	21	31	13.3	3.78	63	.307	.323	3	.009	3	-28	-31	-2	-2.5
1880 Cin-N	3	17	.150	25	21	21	0	0	196	235	1	32	47	12.3	3.21	77	.283	.309	95	.292	4	-18	-16	0	-1.4
1881 Buf-N	4	1	.800	9	5	5	0	0	61²	62	2	9	15	10.4	2.77	100	.250	.277	33	.292	2	0	0	1	0.0
1882 Buf-N	2	1	.667	6	3	2	0	0	31	44	2	4	9	13.9	4.94	59	.316	.335	105	.276	1	-7	-7	1	-0.5
1883 Phi-N	2	6	.250	11	9	7	0	0	80	110	0	12	30	13.7	4.39	70	.309	.331	114	.268	2	-11	-12	1	-0.9
1884 Phi-N	0	0	—	1	0	0	0	0	4	3	1	0	1	6.8	2.25	133	.197	.197	108	.252	0	0	-0	-0	0.0
1885 Phi-a	0	1	.000	1	1	0	0	0	6	11	0	2	3	19.5	6.00	57	.378	.418	90	.296	0	-2	-2	0	0.0
1886 Bal-a	0	0	—	1	0	0	0	0	1	1	0	0	0	9.0	9.00	38	.248	.248	19	.224	0	-1	-1	0	0.0
1887 Bal-a	0	0	—	1	0	0	0	0	4	8	0	4	2	27.0	15.75	26	.401	.501	142	.250	0	-5	-5	-0	-0.3
Total 9	15	43	.259	79	57	52	0	0	581¹	746	7	84	138	12.8	3.73	70	.295	.318	1217	.267	12	-72	-73	-0	-5.6

■ JOHN PURDIN Purdin, John Nolan b: 7/16/42, Lynx, Ohio BR/TR, 6'2", 185 lbs. Deb: 9/16/64

YEAR TM/L	W	L	PCT	G	GS	CG	SH	SV	IP	H	HR	BB	SO	RAT	ERA	ERA+	OAV	OOB	BH	AVG	PB	PR	/A	PD	TPI
1964 LA-N	2	0	1.000	3	2	1	1	0	16	6	1	6	8	6.8	0.56	576	.115	.207	1	.200	0	5	5	-0	0.5
1965 LA-N	2	1	.667	11	2	0	0	0	22²	26	8	13	16	15.5	6.75	48	.283	.371	0	.000	-0	-8	-9	-1	-0.9
1968 LA-N	2	3	.400	35	1	0	0	2	55²	42	2	21	38	10.2	3.07	90	.206	.280	3	.500	1	-1	-2	-0	0.0
1969 LA-N	0	0	—	9	0	0	0	2	16¹	19	7	12	6	17.1	6.06	55	.292	.403	0	.000	-0	-4	-5	0	-0.4
Total 4	6	4	.600	58	5	1	1	2	110²	93	18	52	68	11.8	3.90	77	.225	.312	4	.250	1	-8	-11	-1	-0.8

■ BOB PURKEY Purkey, Robert Thomas b: 7/14/29, Pittsburgh, Pa. BR/TR, 6'2", 175 lbs. Deb: 4/14/54

YEAR TM/L	W	L	PCT	G	GS	CG	SH	SV	IP	H	HR	BB	SO	RAT	ERA	ERA+	OAV	OOB	BH	AVG	PB	PR	/A	PD	TPI
1954 Pit-N	3	8	.273	36	11	0	0	0	131¹	145	3	62	38	14.7	5.07	83	.293	.379	2	.077	-1	-15	-13	5	-0.7
1955 Pit-N	2	7	.222	14	10	2	0	0	67²	77	5	25	24	13.8	5.32	77	.287	.353	6	.316	2	-10	-9	1	-0.5
1956 Pit-N	0	0	—	2	0	0	0	0	4	2	1	0	1	4.5	2.25	168	.143	.143	0	—	0	1	1	0	0.1
1957 Pit-N	11	14	.440	48	21	6	1	2	179²	194	10	38	51	12.0	3.86	98	.278	.322	5	.111	-0	-0	1	0	-0.1
1958 Cin-N	17	11	.607	37	34	17	3	0	250	259	25	49	70	11.2	3.60	115	.268	.306	9	.111	-2	10	15	3	1.7
1959 Cin-N	13	18	.419	38	33	9	1	1	218	241	25	43	78	12.0	4.25	95	.279	.318	11	.167	3	-7	-5	0	0.0
1960 Cin-N	17	11	.607	41	33	11	1	0	252²	259	29	43	97	11.6	3.60	106	.265	.312	11	.133	-2	5	6	2	0.7
1961 *Cin-N	16	12	.571	36	34	13	1	1	246¹	245	27	51	116	11.0	3.73	109	.255	.297	8	.100	-3	8	9	7	1.3
1962 Cin-N	23	5	**.821**	37	37	18	2	0	288¹	260	28	64	141	10.6	2.81	143	.240	.291	11	.103	-3	36	**39**	3	4.2
1963 Cin-N	6	10	.375	21	21	4	1	0	137	143	12	33	55	11.7	3.55	94	.272	.318	4	.098	-1	-4	-3	2	-0.1
1964 Cin-N	11	9	.550	34	25	9	2	1	195²	181	16	49	78	10.9	3.04	119	.246	.299	3	.052	-4	11	13	3	1.3
1965 StL-N	10	9	.526	32	17	3	1	2	124¹	148	20	33	39	13.6	5.79	66	.294	.346	1	.029	-3	-31	-27	1	-2.7
1966 Pit-N	0	1	.000	10	0	0	0	1	19²	16	0	4	5	9.2	1.37	260	.235	.278	0	.000	-0	5	5	1	0.6
Total 13	129	115	.529	386	276	92	13	9	2114²	2170	195	510	793	11.7	3.79	103	.266	.315	71	.110	-13	9	30	28	5.8

■ OSCAR PURNER Purner, Oscar E. b: 1873, Washington, D.C. Deb: 9/02/1895

YEAR TM/L	W	L	PCT	G	GS	CG	SH	SV	IP	H	HR	BB	SO	RAT	ERA	ERA+	OAV	OOB	BH	AVG	PB	PR	/A	PD	TPI
1895 Was-N	0	0	—	1	0	0	0	0	2	4	1	3	0	31.5	9.00	53	.408	.547	0	.000	-0	-1	-1	0	0.0

■ AMBROSE PUTTMANN Puttmann, Ambrose Nicholas "Putty" or "Brose" b: 9/9/1880, Cincinnati, Ohio d: 6/21/36, Jamaica, N.Y. TL, 6'4", 185 lbs. Deb: 9/04/03

YEAR TM/L	W	L	PCT	G	GS	CG	SH	SV	IP	H	HR	BB	SO	RAT	ERA	ERA+	OAV	OOB	BH	AVG	PB	PR	/A	PD	TPI
1903 NY-A	2	0	1.000	3	2	1	0	0	19	16	0	4	8	9.5	0.95	330	.228	.270	1	.143	-0	4	5	1	0.6
1904 NY-A	2	0	1.000	9	3	2	1	0	49¹	40	0	17	26	10.4	2.74	99	.223	.290	5	.278	2	-1	-0	0	0.2
1905 NY-A	2	7	.222	17	9	5	1	1	86¹	79	2	37	39	12.1	4.27	69	.245	.322	10	.313	3	-15	-13	0	-0.9
1906 StL-N	2	2	.500	4	4	0	0	0	18²	23	2	9	12	16.4	5.30	90	.303	.391	2	.333	0	-6	-6	0	-0.4
Total 4	8	9	.471	33	18	8	2	1	173¹	158	4	67	85	11.8	3.58	80	.244	.316	18	.286	5	-18	-14	1	-0.5

■ JOHN PYECHA Pyecha, John Nicholas b: 11/25/31, Aliquippa, Pa. BR/TR, 6'5", 200 lbs. Deb: 4/24/54

YEAR TM/L	W	L	PCT	G	GS	CG	SH	SV	IP	H	HR	BB	SO	RAT	ERA	ERA+	OAV	OOB	BH	AVG	PB	PR	/A	PD	TPI
1954 Chi-N	0	1	.000	1	0	0	0	0	2²	4	1	2	2	20.3	10.13	41	.333	.429	0	.000	-0	-2	-2	0	-0.1

■ HARLAN PYLE Pyle, Harlan Albert "Firpo" b: 11/29/05, Burchard, Neb. BR/TR, 6'2", 180 lbs. Deb: 9/21/28

YEAR TM/L	W	L	PCT	G	GS	CG	SH	SV	IP	H	HR	BB	SO	RAT	ERA	ERA+	OAV	OOB	BH	AVG	PB	PR	/A	PD	TPI
1928 Cin-N	0	0	—	2	1	0	0	0	1¹	1	0	4	1	33.8	20.25	20	.143	.455	0	.000	-0	-2	-2	0	-0.1

■ SHADOW PYLE Pyle, Harry Thomas b: 10/30/1861, Reading, Pa. d: 11/26/08, Reading, Pa. 5'8", 136 lbs. Deb: 10/15/1884

YEAR TM/L	W	L	PCT	G	GS	CG	SH	SV	IP	H	HR	BB	SO	RAT	ERA	ERA+	OAV	OOB	BH	AVG	PB	PR	/A	PD	TPI
1884 Phi-N	0	1	.000	1	1	1	0	0	9	9	0	6	4	15.0	4.00	75	.246	.353	0	.000	-1	-1	-1	-0	-0.1
1887 Chi-N	1	3	.250	4	4	3	0	0	26²	32	1	21	5	17.9	4.73	94	.289	.403	3	.188	-0	-2	-1	1	0.0
Total 2	1	4	.200	5	5	4	0	0	35²	41	1	27	9	17.2	4.54	90	.279	.390	3	.150	-1	-3	-2	1	-0.1

■ EWALD PYLE Pyle, Herbert Ewald "Lefty" b: 8/27/10, St.Louis, Mo. BL/TL, 6'0.5", 175 lbs. Deb: 4/23/39

YEAR TM/L	W	L	PCT	G	GS	CG	SH	SV	IP	H	HR	BB	SO	RAT	ERA	ERA+	OAV	OOB	BH	AVG	PB	PR	/A	PD	TPI
1939 StL-A	0	2	.000	6	1	0	0	0	8¹	17	3	11	5	30.2	12.96	38	.405	.528	0	.000	-0	-8	-7	1	-0.5

YEAR	TM/L	W	L	PCT	G	GS	CG	SH	SV	IP	H	HR	BB	SO	RAT	ERA	ERA+	OAV	OOB	BH	AVG	PB	PR	/A	PD	TPI
1942	StL-A	0	0	—	2	0	0	0	0	5^1	6	0	4	1	16.9	6.75	55	.286	.400	0	.000	-0	-2	-2	-0	-0.1
1943	Was-A	4	8	.333	18	11	2	1	1	72^2	70	0	45	25	14.4	4.09	78	.254	.360	2	.100	-1	-6	-7	-1	-0.9
1944	NY-N	7	10	.412	31	21	3	0	0	164	152	12	68	79	12.4	4.34	85	.241	.321	8	.157	-0	-13	-12	-0	-1.2
1945	NY-N	0	0	—	6	1	0	0	0	6^1	16	0	4	2	28.4	17.05	23	.457	.513	0	.000	-0	-9	-9	1	-0.7
	Bos-N	0	1	.000	4	2	0	0	0	13^2	16	1	18	10	22.4	7.24	53	.302	.479	2	.333	1	-5	-5	-0	-0.4
	Yr	0	1	.000	10	3	0	0	0	20	32	1	22	12	24.3	10.35	37	.364	.491	0	.000	0	-15	-14	0	-1.1
Total 5		11	21	.344	67	36	5	1	1	270^1	277	16	150	122	14.4	5.03	71	.262	.357	12	.143	-2	-44	-43	-0	-3.8

■ TOM QUALTERS — Qualters, Thomas Francis "Money Bags" b: 4/1/35, McKeesport, Pa. BR/TR, 6'0.5", 190 lbs. Deb: 9/13/53

YEAR	TM/L	W	L	PCT	G	GS	CG	SH	SV	IP	H	HR	BB	SO	RAT	ERA	ERA+	OAV	OOB	BH	AVG	PB	PR	/A	PD	TPI
1953	Phi-N	0	0	—	1	0	0	0	0	0^1	4	1	1	0	162.0	162.00	3	.800	.857	0	—	0	-6	-6	0	-0.3
1957	Phi-N	0	0	—	6	0	0	0	0	7^1	12	0	4	6	19.6	7.36	52	.400	.471	0	—	0	-3	-3	0	-0.2
1958	Phi-N	0	0	—	1	0	0	0	0	2	2	0	1	0	13.5	4.50	88	.222	.300	0	—	0	-0	-0	0	-0.0
	Chi-A	0	0	—	26	0	0	0	0	43	45	1	20	14	13.6	4.19	87	.281	.361	0	.000	0	-2	-3	1	0.0
Total 3		0	0	—	34	0	0	0	0	52^2	63	2	26	20	15.4	5.64	65	.309	.390	0	.000	0	-11	-11	1	-0.5

■ BILL QUARLES — Quarles, William H. b: 1869, Petersburg, Va. d: 3/25/1897, Petersburg, Va. 6'3", Deb: 5/21/1891

YEAR	TM/L	W	L	PCT	G	GS	CG	SH	SV	IP	H	HR	BB	SO	RAT	ERA	ERA+	OAV	OOB	BH	AVG	PB	PR	/A	PD	TPI
1891	Was-a	1	1	.500	3	2	2	0	0	22	32	1	12	10	18.0	8.18	46	.328	.402	0	.000	-2	-11	-11	-0	-0.9
1893	Bos-N	2	1	.667	3	3	3	0	0	27	31	2	5	6	12.0	4.67	106	.280	.311	2	.222	-0	0	1	-0	0.1
Total 2		3	2	.600	6	5	5	0	0	49	63	3	17	16	14.7	6.24	70	.302	.355	2	.100	-2	-11	-10	-0	-0.8

■ MEL QUEEN — Queen, Melvin Douglas b: 3/26/42, Johnson City, N.Y. BL/TR, 6'1", 189 lbs. Deb: 4/13/64 C♦

YEAR	TM/L	W	L	PCT	G	GS	CG	SH	SV	IP	H	HR	BB	SO	RAT	ERA	ERA+	OAV	OOB	BH	AVG	PB	PR	/A	PD	TPI
1966	Cin-N	0	0	—	7	0	0	0	0	7	11	0	6	9	21.9	6.43	61	.367	.472	7	.127	0	-2	-2	0	-0.1
1967	Cin-N	14	8	.636	31	24	6	2	0	195^2	155	17	52	154	9.8	2.76	136	.215	.273	17	.210	3	13	22	-2	2.7
1968	Cin-N	0	1	.000	5	4	0	0	0	18^1	25	7	6	20	15.2	5.89	54	.333	.383	1	.125	-0	-6	-6	-0	-0.5
1969	Cin-N	1	0	1.000	2	1	0	0	0	12	7	2	3	7	8.3	2.25	167	.163	.234	1	.167	-0	2	2	-0	0.2
1970	Cal-A	3	6	.333	34	3	0	0	9	60	58	5	28	44	13.7	4.20	86	.261	.357	4	.250	1	-3	-4	-1	-0.4
1971	Cal-A	2	2	.500	44	0	0	0	4	65^2	49	3	29	53	11.8	1.78	182	.212	.321	0	.000	-1	12	11	-1	1.0
1972	Cal-A	0	0	—	17	0	0	0	0	31	31	2	19	19	15.4	4.35	67	.265	.381	0	.000	-0	-4	-5	-0	-0.5
Total 7		20	17	.541	140	33	6	2	14	389^2	336	36	143	306	11.6	3.14	113	.233	.313	49	.179	3	12	18	-4	2.4

■ MEL QUEEN — Queen, Melvin Joseph b: 3/4/18, Maxwell, Pa. d: 4/4/82, Fort Smith, Ark. BR/TR, 6'0.5", 204 lbs. Deb: 4/18/42

YEAR	TM/L	W	L	PCT	G	GS	CG	SH	SV	IP	H	HR	BB	SO	RAT	ERA	ERA+	OAV	OOB	BH	AVG	PB	PR	/A	PD	TPI
1942	NY-A	1	0	1.000	4	0	0	0	0	5^2	6	0	3	0	17.5	0.00	—	.300	.440	0	—	0	2	2	0	0.2
1944	NY-A	6	3	.667	10	10	4	1	0	81^2	68	7	34	30	11.4	3.31	105	.227	.308	6	.194	0	1	2	-2	0.0
1946	NY-A	1	1	.500	14	3	1	0	0	30^1	40	2	21	26	18.1	6.53	53	.315	.412	1	.143	-0	-10	-10	-1	-1.0
1947	NY-A	0	0	—	5	0	0	0	0	6^2	9	2	4	2	18.9	9.45	37	.321	.424	0	.000	-0	-4	-4	-0	-0.4
	Pit-N	3	7	.300	14	12	2	0	0	74	70	8	51	34	14.8	4.01	105	.244	.360	2	.077	-2	0	2	-1	-0.1
1948	Pit-N	4	4	.500	25	8	0	0	1	66^1	82	8	40	34	17.0	6.65	61	.308	.405	1	.059	-2	-20	-19	-1	-1.9
1950	Pit-N	5	14	.263	33	21	4	1	0	120^1	135	18	73	76	15.7	5.98	73	.284	.381	2	.057	-3	-25	-21	-2	-2.4
1951	Pit-N	7	9	.438	39	21	4	1	0	168^1	149	21	99	123	13.3	4.44	95	.233	.337	5	.106	-3	-9	-4	-4	-1.0
1952	Pit-N	0	2	.000	2	2	0	0	0	3^1	8	2	4	3	32.4	29.70	13	.381	.480	0	—	0	-10	-10	-0	-0.7
Total 8		27	40	.403	146	77	15	3	1	556^2	567	68	329	328	14.7	5.09	80	.262	.362	17	.104	-11	-74	-63	-10	-7.3

■ EDDIE QUICK — Quick, Edward b: Baltimore, Md. d: 6/19/13, Rocky Ford, Colo. TR, 5'11", Deb: 9/28/03

YEAR	TM/L	W	L	PCT	G	GS	CG	SH	SV	IP	H	HR	BB	SO	RAT	ERA	ERA+	OAV	OOB	BH	AVG	PB	PR	/A	PD	TPI
1903	NY-A	0	0	—	1	1	0	0	0	2	5	0	1	0	27.0	9.00	35	.467	.513	0	.000	-0	-1	-1	0	0.0

■ TAD QUINN — Quinn, Clarence Carr b: 9/21/1882, Torrington, Conn. d: 8/6/46, Waterbury, Conn. TR, 6'1", Deb: 9/27/02

YEAR	TM/L	W	L	PCT	G	GS	CG	SH	SV	IP	H	HR	BB	SO	RAT	ERA	ERA+	OAV	OOB	BH	AVG	PB	PR	/A	PD	TPI
1902	Phi-A	0	1	.000	1	1	0	0	0	8	12	1	1	3	14.6	4.50	82	.346	.364	0	.000	-0	-1	-1	-0	0.0
1903	Phi-A	0	0	—	2	0	0	0	0	9	11	0	5	1	16.0	5.00	61	.300	.384	2	.667	1	-2	-2	1	0.0
Total 2		0	1	.000	3	1	0	0	0	17	23	1	6	4	15.4	4.76	70	.322	.375	2	.333	1	-3	-3	0	0.0

■ FRANK QUINN — Quinn, Frank William b: 11/27/27, Springfield, Mass. BR/TR, 6'2", 180 lbs. Deb: 5/29/49

YEAR	TM/L	W	L	PCT	G	GS	CG	SH	SV	IP	H	HR	BB	SO	RAT	ERA	ERA+	OAV	OOB	BH	AVG	PB	PR	/A	PD	TPI
1949	Bos-A	0	0	—	8	0	0	0	0	22	18	2	9	4	11.5	2.86	152	.222	.308	1	.167	-0	3	4	0	0.3
1950	Bos-A	0	0	—	1	0	0	0	0	2	2	0	1	0	13.5	9.00	54	.250	.333	0	—	0	-1	-1	0	0.0
Total 2		0	0	—	9	0	0	0	0	24	20	2	10	4	11.6	3.38	131	.225	.310	1	.167	-0	2	3	0	0.3

■ JACK QUINN — Quinn, John Picus (b: John Quinn Picus) b: 7/5/1883, Janesville, Pa. d: 4/17/46, Pottsville, Pa. BR/TR, 6', 196 lbs. Deb: 4/15/09

YEAR	TM/L	W	L	PCT	G	GS	CG	SH	SV	IP	H	HR	BB	SO	RAT	ERA	ERA+	OAV	OOB	BH	AVG	PB	PR	/A	PD	TPI
1909	NY-A	9	5	.643	23	11	8	0	1	118^2	110	1	24	36	10.5	1.97	128	.252	.297	7	.156	0	7	7	4	1.3
1910	NY-A	18	12	.600	35	31	20	0	0	235^2	214	2	58	82	10.6	2.37	112	.247	.299	19	.232	4	4	8	8	2.2
1911	NY-A	8	10	.444	40	16	7	0	2	174^2	203	2	41	71	12.8	3.76	96	.297	.341	10	.164	-1	-8	-3	3	0.0
1912	NY-A	5	7	.417	18	11	7	0	0	102^2	139	4	23	47	14.6	5.79	62	.325	.365	8	.205	-1	-28	-25	2	-2.0
1913	Bos-N	4	3	.571	8	7	6	1	0	56^1	55	1	7	33	10.1	2.40	137	.261	.288	4	.200	1	5	6	2	1.0
1914	Bal-F	26	14	.650	46	42	27	4	1	342^2	335	3	65	164	10.7	2.60	130	.266	.307	33	.273	8	23	29	1	4.4
1915	Bal-F	9	22	.290	44	31	21	0	1	273^2	289	9	63	118	11.8	3.45	92	.278	.325	29	.264	4	-13	-8	3	0.0
1918	Chi-A	5	1	.833	6	5	5	0	0	51	38	0	7	22	7.9	2.29	119	.216	.246	4	.222	1	3	3	0	0.4
1919	NY-A	15	14	.517	38	31	18	4	0	266	242	8	65	97	10.6	2.61	123	.244	.295	19	.209	1	18	17	1	2.1
1920	NY-A	18	10	.643	41	32	17	2	3	253^1	271	8	48	101	11.4	3.20	119	.273	.308	8	.091	-5	17	18	2	1.4
1921	*NY-A	8	7	.533	33	13	6	0	0	119	158	2	32	44	14.7	3.78	112	.327	.375	9	.220	1	7	6	1	0.7
1922	Bos-A	13	16	.448	40	32	16	4	0	256	263	9	59	67	11.4	3.48	118	.267	.311	9	.099	-5	16	18	5	1.8
1923	Bos-A	7	17	.433	42	28	16	1	7	243	302	6	53	71	13.4	3.89	106	.291	.356	18	.225	0	3	6	-1	0.5
1924	Bos-A	12	13	.480	44	25	13	2	7	228^2	241	10	52	64	12.0	3.27	134	.273	.322	14	.179	-4	24	28	4	2.7
1925	Bos-A	7	8	.467	19	15	8	0	0	105	140	3	26	24	14.5	4.37	104	.315	.357	3	.094	-2	0	2	2	0.2
	Phi-A	6	3	.667	18	14	4	0	0	99^2	119	3	16	19	12.5	3.88	120	.296	.328	3	.097	-3	6	8	2	0.7
	Yr	13	11	.542	37	29	12	0	0	204^2	259	6	42	43	13.4	4.13	111	.305	.340	7	.111	-5	6	11	4	0.9
1926	Phi-A	10	11	.476	31	21	8	3	1	163^2	191	4	36	58	12.5	3.41	122	.296	.334	8	.174	-0	11	14	2	1.5
1927	Phi-A	15	10	.600	34	25	11	3	1	201^1	211	8	37	43	11.3	3.26	131	.278	.315	6	.091	-7	20	22	-0	1.5
1928	Phi-A	18	7	.720	31	28	18	4	1	211^1	239	3	34	43	11.9	2.90	139	.290	.320	13	.165	-3	27	26	2	2.5
1929	*Phi-A	11	9	.550	35	18	7	0	2	161	182	8	39	41	12.4	3.97	107	.290	.332	8	.133	-4	5	5	1	0.1
1930	*Phi-A	9	7	.563	35	7	0	0	6	89^2	109	6	22	28	13.2	4.42	106	.302	.344	9	.265	1	2	3	2	0.5
1931	Bro-N	5	4	.556	39	1	0	0	15	64^1	65	1	24	25	12.6	2.66	143	.266	.335	3	.200	0	9	8	1	0.9
1932	Bro-N	3	7	.300	42	0	0	0	8	87^1	102	1	24	28	13.1	3.30	116	.296	.343	4	.200	0	6	5	0	0.5
1933	Cin-N	0	1	.000	14	0	0	0	1	15^2	20	0	5	3	14.4	4.02	84	.323	.373	0	.000	-0	-1	-1	1	0.0
Total 23		247	218	.531	756	444	243	28	57	3920^1	4238	102	860	1329	11.9	3.29	114	.280	.323	248	.184	-13	162	204	46	25.0

■ WIMPY QUINN — Quinn, Wellington Hunt b: 5/12/18, Birmingham, Ala. d: 9/1/54, Santa Monica, Cal. BR/TR, 6'2", 187 lbs. Deb: 6/08/41

YEAR	TM/L	W	L	PCT	G	GS	CG	SH	SV	IP	H	HR	BB	SO	RAT	ERA	ERA+	OAV	OOB	BH	AVG	PB	PR	/A	PD	TPI
1941	Chi-N	0	0	—	3	0	0	0	0	5	3	0	3	2	10.8	7.20	49	.158	.273	1	.500	0	-2	-2	0	-0.1

■ LUIS QUINTANA — Quintana, Luis Joaquin (Santos) b: 12/25/51, Vega Baja, P.R. BL/TL, 6'2", 175 lbs. Deb: 7/09/74

YEAR	TM/L	W	L	PCT	G	GS	CG	SH	SV	IP	H	HR	BB	SO	RAT	ERA	ERA+	OAV	OOB	BH	AVG	PB	PR	/A	PD	TPI
1974	Cal-A	2	1	.667	18	0	0	0	0	12^2	17	0	14	11	22.0	4.26	81	.327	.470	0	—	0	-1	-1	-0	-0.1
1975	Cal-A	0	2	.000	4	0	0	0	0	7	13	2	6	5	24.4	6.43	55	.394	.487	0	—	0	-2	-2	-0	-0.1
Total 2		2	3	.400	22	0	0	0	0	19^2	30	2	20	16	22.9	5.03	69	.353	.476	0	—	0	-3	-3	-0	-0.1

■ ART QUIRK — Quirk, Arthur Lincoln b: 4/11/38, Providence, R.I. BR/TL, 5'11", 170 lbs. Deb: 4/17/62

YEAR	TM/L	W	L	PCT	G	GS	CG	SH	SV	IP	H	HR	BB	SO	RAT	ERA	ERA+	OAV	OOB	BH	AVG	PB	PR	/A	PD	TPI
1962	Bal-A	2	2	.500	7	5	0	0	0	27^1	36	3	18	18	17.8	5.93	63	.308	.400	1	.143	0	-6	-7	1	-0.5
1963	Was-A	1	0	1.000	7	3	0	0	0	21	23	3	8	12	13.3	4.29	87	.280	.344	1	.250	0	-2	-1	-0	-0.1
Total 2		3	2	.600	14	8	0	0	0	48^1	59	6	26	30	15.8	5.21	72	.296	.378	2	.182	0	-7	-8	1	-0.6

YEAR TM/L	W	L	PCT	G	GS	CG	SH	SV	IP	H	HR	BB	SO	RAT	ERA	ERA+	OAV	OOB	BH	AVG	PB	PR	/A	PD	TPI

■ DAN QUISENBERRY
Quisenberry, Daniel Raymond b: 2/7/53, Santa Monica, Cal. BR/TR, 6'2", 170 lbs. Deb: 7/08/79

YEAR TM/L	W	L	PCT	G	GS	CG	SH	SV	IP	H	HR	BB	SO	RAT	ERA	ERA+	OAV	OOB	BH	AVG	PB	PR	/A	PD	TPI
1979 KC-A	3	2	.600	32	0	0	0	5	40	42	5	7	13	11.0	3.15	135	.278	.310	0	—	0	5	5	1	0.5
1980 *KC-A	12	7	.632	**75**	0	0	0	**33**	128¹	129	5	27	37	11.0	3.09	131	.265	.305	0	—	0	14	14	3	1.7
1981 *KC-A	1	4	.200	40	0	0	0	18	62¹	59	1	15	20	10.8	1.73	208	.258	.306	0	—	0	13	13	3	1.7
1982 KC-A	9	7	.563	72	0	0	0	35	136²	126	12	12	46	9.1	2.57	159	.252	.270	0	—	0	23	23	6	3.0
1983 KC-A	5	3	.625	**69**	0	0	0	**45**	139	118	6	11	48	8.4	1.94	210	.229	.245	0	—	0	**33**	**33**	2	3.6
1984 *KC-A	6	3	.667	72	0	0	0	**44**	129¹	121	10	12	41	9.3	2.64	152	.247	.265	0	—	0	19	20	3	2.3
1985 *KC-A	8	9	.471	**84**	0	0	0	37	129	142	8	16	54	11.1	2.37	175	.280	.303	0	—	0	25	26	1	2.7
1986 KC-A	3	7	.300	62	0	0	0	12	81¹	92	2	24	36	13.2	2.77	154	.291	.347	0	—	0	13	13	2	1.6
1987 KC-A	4	1	.800	47	0	0	0	8	49	58	3	10	17	12.7	2.76	165	.287	.324	0	—	0	9	10	2	1.1
1988 KC-A	0	1	.000	20	0	0	0	1	25¹	32	0	5	9	13.1	3.55	112	.305	.336	0	—	0	1	1	1	0.2
StL-N	2	0	1.000	33	0	0	0	0	38	54	4	6	19	14.2	6.16	56	.344	.368	0	.000	0	-11	-11	0	-1.0
1989 StL-N	3	1	.750	63	0	0	0	6	78¹	78	2	14	37	10.6	2.64	137	.261	.294	1	.250	0	7	9	2	1.2
1990 SF-N	0	1	.000	5	0	0	0	0	6²	13	1	3	2	21.6	13.50	28	.419	.471	0	.000	-0	-7	-7	0	-0.6
Total 12	56	46	.549	674	0	0	0	244	1043¹	1064	59	162	379	10.6	2.76	146	.267	.297	1	.167	0	144	148	27	18.0

■ CHARLIE RABE
Rabe, Charles Henry b: 5/6/32, Boyce, Tex. BL/TL, 6'1", 180 lbs. Deb: 9/21/57

YEAR TM/L	W	L	PCT	G	GS	CG	SH	SV	IP	H	HR	BB	SO	RAT	ERA	ERA+	OAV	OOB	BH	AVG	PB	PR	/A	PD	TPI
1957 Cin-N	0	1	.000	2	1	0	0	0	8¹	5	2	0	6	5.4	2.16	190	.167	.167	0	.000	-0	2	2	-0	0.1
1958 Cin-N	0	3	.000	9	1	0	0	0	18²	25	3	9	10	16.4	4.34	96	.321	.391	0	.000	-1	-1	-0	0	0.0
Total 2	0	4	.000	11	2	0	0	0	27	30	5	9	16	13.0	3.67	113	.278	.333	0	.000	-1	1	1	0	0.1

■ STEVE RACHUNOK
Rachunok, Stephen Stepanovich "The Mad Russian" b: 12/5/16, Rittman, Ohio BR/TR, 6'4.5", 205 lbs. Deb: 9/17/40

YEAR TM/L	W	L	PCT	G	GS	CG	SH	SV	IP	H	HR	BB	SO	RAT	ERA	ERA+	OAV	OOB	BH	AVG	PB	PR	/A	PD	TPI
1940 Bro-N	0	1	.000	2	1	1	0	0	10	9	0	5	10	12.6	4.50	89	.243	.333	0	.000	0	-1	-1	0	0.0

■ DICK RADATZ
Radatz, Richard Raymond "The Monster" b: 4/2/37, Detroit, Mich. BR/TR, 6'6", 230 lbs. Deb: 4/10/62

YEAR TM/L	W	L	PCT	G	GS	CG	SH	SV	IP	H	HR	BB	SO	RAT	ERA	ERA+	OAV	OOB	BH	AVG	PB	PR	/A	PD	TPI
1962 Bos-A	9	6	.600	**62**	0	0	0	24	124²	95	9	40	144	10.0	2.24	184	.211	.281	3	.097	-2	**24**	**26**	-3	2.2
1963 Bos-A	15	6	.714	66	0	0	0	25	132¹	94	9	51	162	10.2	1.97	192	.201	.286	2	.069	-2	**24**	**27**	-3	2.4
1964 Bos-A	16	9	.640	79	0	0	0	**29**	157	103	13	58	181	9.6	2.29	168	.186	.271	6	.162	-0	23	**27**	-3	2.6
1965 Bos-A	9	11	.450	63	0	0	0	22	124¹	104	11	53	121	11.7	3.91	95	.227	.314	5	.185	1	-6	-3	-1	-0.2
1966 Bos-A	0	2	.000	16	0	0	0	4	19	24	3	11	19	16.6	4.74	80	.304	.389	0	.000	0	-3	-2	-1	-0.2
Cle-A	0	3	.000	39	0	0	0	10	56²	49	6	34	49	13.7	4.61	75	.233	.348	1	.111	-0	-7	-7	-1	-0.8
Yr	0	5	.000	55	0	0	0	14	75²	73	9	45	68	14.4	4.64	76	.253	.359	0	.000	-1	-10	-9	-2	-1.0
1967 Cle-A	0	0	—	3	0	0	0	0	3	5	1	2	1	21.0	6.00	54	.357	.438	0	—	0	-1	-1	0	0.0
Chi-N	1	0	1.000	20	0	0	0	5	23¹	12	4	24	18	15.8	6.56	54	.154	.383	1	.250	-0	-8	-8	-0	-0.8
1969 Det-A	2	2	.500	11	0	0	0	0	18²	14	3	5	18	9.2	3.38	111	.212	.268	0	.000	-0	1	1	0	0.1
Mon-N	0	4	.000	22	0	0	0	3	34²	32	6	18	32	13.2	5.71	64	.244	.340	1	.250	0	-8	-8	-1	-0.7
Total 7	52	43	.547	381	0	0	0	122	693²	532	65	296	745	11.1	3.13	122	.212	.303	19	.131	-3	38	53	-12	4.6

■ CHARLEY RADBOURN
Radbourn, Charles Gardner "Old Hoss" b: 12/11/1854, Rochester, N.Y. d: 2/5/1897, Bloomington, Ill. BR/TR, 5'9", 168 lbs. Deb: 5/05/1880 H♦

YEAR TM/L	W	L	PCT	G	GS	CG	SH	SV	IP	H	HR	BB	SO	RAT	ERA	ERA+	OAV	OOB	BH	AVG	PB	PR	/A	PD	TPI
1881 Pro-N	25	11	**.694**	41	36	34	3	0	325¹	309	1	64	117	10.3	2.43	109	.240	.276	59	.219	-1	12	8	3	0.7
1882 Pro-N	33	20	.623	55	52	51	**6**	0	474	429	6	51	**201**	9.1	2.09	134	.228	.248	78	.239	-1	**42**	**38**	0	3.3
1883 Pro-N	48	25	.658	**76**	68	66	4	1	632¹	563	7	56	315	**8.8**	2.05	151	.224	**.241**	108	.283	14	**76**	**73**	4	**8.5**
1884 *Pro-N	**59**	12	**.831**	75	73	**73**	11	1	**678²**	528	18	98	**441**	8.3	**1.38**	**205**	.203	.232	83	.230	6	121	109	-4	**10.4**
1885 Pro-N	28	21	.571	49	49	49	2	0	445²	423	4	83	154	10.2	2.20	121	.239	.273	58	.233	11	30	23	4	3.8
1886 Bos-N	27	31	.466	58	58	57	3	0	509¹	521	18	111	218	11.2	3.00	106	.254	.292	60	.237	9	17	10	3	1.9
1887 Bos-N	24	23	.511	50	50	48	1	0	425	505	20	133	87	13.5	4.55	89	.287	.337	40	.229	2	-24	-25	-2	-2.0
1888 Bos-N	7	16	.304	24	24	24	1	0	207	187	8	45	64	10.1	2.87	99	.232	.273	17	.215	1	-1	-1	-1	0.0
1889 Bos-N	20	11	.645	33	31	28	1	0	277	282	14	72	99	11.5	3.67	114	.255	.301	23	.189	-2	11	15	4	1.7
1890 Bos-P	27	12	.692	41	38	36	1	0	343	352	8	100	80	11.9	3.31	133	.254	.304	39	.253	0	35	42	3	3.8
1891 Cin-N	11	13	.458	26	24	23	2	0	218	238	7	63	62	12.3	4.25	79	.266	.314	17	.177	-1	-22	-21	-2	-2.0
Total 11	309	195	.613	528	503	489	35	2	4535¹	4335	117	875	1830	10.3	2.67	120	.240	.275	585	.235	38	298	265	11	30.1

■ GEORGE RADBOURN
Radbourn, George B. "Dordy" b: 4/8/1856, Bloomington, Ill. d: 1/1/04, Bloomington, Ill. Deb: 5/30/1883

YEAR TM/L	W	L	PCT	G	GS	CG	SH	SV	IP	H	HR	BB	SO	RAT	ERA	ERA+	OAV	OOB	BH	AVG	PB	PR	/A	PD	TPI
1883 Det-N	1	2	.333	3	3	2	0	0	22	38	1	7	2	18.4	6.55	47	.360	.399	2	.167	-1	-8	-8	0	-0.6

■ ROY RADEBAUGH
Radebaugh, Roy b: 2/22/1884, Champaign, Ill. d: 1/17/45, Cedar Rapids, Iowa BR/TR, 5'7", 160 lbs. Deb: 9/22/11

YEAR TM/L	W	L	PCT	G	GS	CG	SH	SV	IP	H	HR	BB	SO	RAT	ERA	ERA+	OAV	OOB	BH	AVG	PB	PR	/A	PD	TPI
1911 StL-N	0	0	—	2	1	0	0	0	10	6	0	4	1	9.0	2.70	125	.176	.263	0	.000	-0	1	1	0	0.1

■ DREW RADER
Rader, Drew Leon "Lefty" b: 5/14/01, Elmira, N.Y. d: 6/5/75, Catskill, N.Y. BR/TL, 6'2", 187 lbs. Deb: 7/18/21

YEAR TM/L	W	L	PCT	G	GS	CG	SH	SV	IP	H	HR	BB	SO	RAT	ERA	ERA+	OAV	OOB	BH	AVG	PB	PR	/A	PD	TPI
1921 Pit-N	0	0	—	1	0	0	0	0	2	2	0	0	0	9.0	0.00	—	.286	.286	0	.000	-0	1	1	0	0.1

■ PAUL RADFORD
Radford, Paul Revere "Shorty" b: 10/14/1861, Roxbury, Mass. d: 2/21/45, Boston, Mass. BR/TR, 5'6", 148 lbs. Deb: 5/01/1883 ♦

YEAR TM/L	W	L	PCT	G	GS	CG	SH	SV	IP	H	HR	BB	SO	RAT	ERA	ERA+	OAV	OOB	BH	AVG	PB	PR	/A	PD	TPI
1884 *Pro-N	0	2	.000	2	2	1	0	0	13	27	0	3	2	20.8	7.62	37	.404	.430	70	.197	0	-7	-7	0	-0.4
1885 Pro-N	0	2	.000	3	2	2	0	0	18¹	34	1	8	3	20.6	7.85	34	.380	.431	90	.243	1	-10	-11	0	-0.8
1887 NY-a	0	0	—	2	0	0	0	0	5	15	1	3	4	32.4	18.00	24	.501	.547	129	.265	1	-8	-8	0	-0.4
1890 Cle-P	0	0	—	1	0	0	0	0	5	7	1	1	3	14.4	3.60	110	.317	.347	136	.292	0	0	0	1	0.0
1891 Bos-a	0	0	—	1	0	0	0	0	1	0	0	0	0	0.0	0.00	—	.000	.000	118	.259	0	0	0	0	0.0
1893 Was-N	0	0	—	1	0	0	0	0	1	2	2	5	1	36.0	18.00	26	.403	.575	106	.228	0	-1	-1	0	0.0
Total 6	0	4	.000	10	4	3	0	0	43¹	85	5	17	13	21.2	8.52	36	.393	.437	1206	.242	2	-25	-26	1	-1.6

■ SCOTT RADINSKY
Radinsky, Scott David b: 3/3/68, Glendale, Cal. BL/TL, 6'3", 190 lbs. Deb: 4/09/90

YEAR TM/L	W	L	PCT	G	GS	CG	SH	SV	IP	H	HR	BB	SO	RAT	ERA	ERA+	OAV	OOB	BH	AVG	PB	PR	/A	PD	TPI
1990 Chi-A	6	1	.857	62	0	0	0	4	52¹	47	1	36	46	14.6	4.82	79	.241	.365	0	—	0	-5	-6	-0	-0.5

■ HAL RAETHER
Raether, Harold Herman "Bud" b: 10/10/32, Lake Mills, Wis. BR/TR, 6'1", 185 lbs. Deb: 7/04/54

YEAR TM/L	W	L	PCT	G	GS	CG	SH	SV	IP	H	HR	BB	SO	RAT	ERA	ERA+	OAV	OOB	BH	AVG	PB	PR	/A	PD	TPI
1954 Phi-A	0	0	—	1	0	0	0	0	2	1	0	4	0	22.5	4.50	87	.200	.556	0	—	0	-0	-0	0	0.0
1957 KC-A	0	0	—	1	0	0	0	0	2	2	1	0	0	9.0	9.00	44	.250	.250	0	—	0	-1	-1	0	0.0
Total 2	0	0	—	2	0	0	0	0	4	3	1	4	0	15.8	6.75	58	.231	.412	0	—	0	-1	-1	0	0.0

■ KEN RAFFENSBERGER
Raffensberger, Kenneth David b: 8/8/17, York, Pa. BR/TL, 6'2", 185 lbs. Deb: 4/25/39

YEAR TM/L	W	L	PCT	G	GS	CG	SH	SV	IP	H	HR	BB	SO	RAT	ERA	ERA+	OAV	OOB	BH	AVG	PB	PR	/A	PD	TPI
1939 StL-N	0	0	—	1	0	0	0	0	1	0	0	0	1	18.0	0.00	—	.400	.400	0	—	0	0	0	0	0.0
1940 Chi-N	7	9	.438	43	10	3	0	3	114²	120	10	29	55	11.9	3.38	111	.271	.319	5	.167	-1	6	5	-1	0.3
1941 Chi-N	0	1	.000	10	1	0	0	0	18	17	0	7	5	12.0	4.50	78	.262	.333	0	.000	-1	-2	-2	1	-0.1
1943 Phi-N	0	1	.000	1	1	0	0	0	8	7	0	2	3	10.1	1.13	300	.241	.290	0	.000	0	2	2	0	0.2
1944 Phi-N	13	20	.394	37	31	18	3	0	258²	257	9	45	136	10.6	3.06	118	.252	.285	11	.138	-3	16	16	-4	0.9
1945 Phi-N	0	3	.000	5	4	1	0	0	24¹	28	3	14	6	15.5	4.44	86	.283	.372	0	.000	-1	-2	-2	0	-0.2
1946 Phi-N	8	15	.348	39	23	14	2	**6**	196	203	10	39	73	11.2	3.63	95	.265	.302	10	.167	-1	-5	-4	-3	-0.7
1947 Phi-N	2	6	.250	10	7	3	1	0	41	50	4	8	16	13.0	5.49	73	.307	.343	4	.267	0	-7	-7	1	-0.4
Cin-N	6	5	.545	19	15	7	0	1	106²	132	11	29	38	13.6	4.13	99	.305	.348	6	.162	-1	-1	-0	-0	-0.1
Yr	8	11	.421	29	22	10	1	1	147²	182	15	37	54	13.3	4.51	90	.305	.345	1	.019	-0	-7	-7	0	-0.5
1948 Cin-N	11	12	.478	40	24	7	4	0	180¹	187	15	37	52	11.2	3.84	102	.259	.296	7	.113	-2	-5	-5	-0	-0.2
1949 Cin-N	18	17	.514	41	38	25	**5**	0	284	289	23	80	103	11.8	3.39	123	.264	.315	16	.178	-0	21	25	-3	2.3
1950 Cin-N	14	19	.424	38	35	18	4	0	239	271	34	40	87	11.8	4.26	100	.279	.308	11	.134	-2	-3	-1	-2	-0.3
1951 Cin-N	16	17	.485	42	33	14	5	5	248²	232	30	38	81	**10.0**	3.44	119	.246	.279	10	.122	-3	14	18	-4	1.1
1952 Cin-N	17	13	.567	38	33	18	**6**	1	247	247	18	45	93	10.7	2.81	134	.261	.295	8	.107	-2	25	27	-2	2.4

YEAR	TM/L	W	L	PCT	G	GS	CG	SH	SV	IP	H	HR	BB	SO	RAT	ERA	ERA+	OAV	OOB	BH	AVG	PB	PR	/A	PD	TPI
1953	Cin-N	7	14	.333	26	26	9	1	0	174	200	23	33	47	12.1	3.93	111	.289	.322	8	.140	-1	7	8	2	0.8
1954	Cin-N	0	2	.000	6	1	0	0	0	10¹	15	2	3	5	15.7	7.84	53	.333	.375	1	.500	0	-4	-4	-0	-0.3
Total	15	119	154	.436	396	282	133	31	16	2151²	2257	192	449	806	11.4	3.60	110	.267	.306	97	.141	-17	71	82	-16	5.7

■ AL RAFFO   Raffo, Albert Martin   b: 11/27/41, San Francisco, Cal.   BR/TR, 6'5", 210 lbs.   Deb: 4/29/69

YEAR	TM/L	W	L	PCT	G	GS	CG	SH	SV	IP	H	HR	BB	SO	RAT	ERA	ERA+	OAV	OOB	BH	AVG	PB	PR	/A	PD	TPI
1969	Phi-N	1	3	.250	45	0	0	0	1	72¹	81	6	25	38	13.7	4.11	86	.286	.353	1	.167	0	-4	-5	1	-0.3

■ PAT RAGAN   Ragan, Don Carlos Patrick   b: 11/15/1888, Blanchard, Iowa   d: 9/4/56, Los Angeles, Cal.   BR/TR, 5'10.5", 185 lbs.   Deb: 4/21/09   C

YEAR	TM/L	W	L	PCT	G	GS	CG	SH	SV	IP	H	HR	BB	SO	RAT	ERA	ERA+	OAV	OOB	BH	AVG	PB	PR	/A	PD	TPI
1909	Cin-N	0	1	.000	2	0	0	0	0	8	7	0	4	2	12.4	3.38	77	.259	.355	1	.500	0	-1	-1	-0	0.0
	Chi-N	0	0	—	2	0	0	0	0	3²	4	0	1	2	12.3	2.45	104	.286	.333	0	.000	-0	0	0	0	0.0
	Yr	0	1	.000	4	0	0	0	0	11²	11	0	5	4	12.3	3.09	84	.268	.348	0	.000	0	-1	-1	-0	0.0
1911	Bro-N	4	3	.571	22	7	5	1	1	93²	81	0	31	39	11.0	2.11	158	.252	.321	4	.138	-1	13	13	-1	1.1
1912	Bro-N	7	18	.280	36	26	12	1	1	208	211	7	65	101	12.1	3.63	92	.259	.317	4	.060	-7	-5	-7	-2	-1.4
1913	Bro-N	15	18	.455	44	32	14	0	0	264²	284	10	64	109	12.0	3.77	87	.281	.327	15	.165	-2	-17	-14	2	-1.4
1914	Bro-N	10	15	.400	38	26	14	1	3	208¹	214	5	85	106	13.0	2.98	96	.270	.343	10	.133	-3	-4	-3	-0	-0.6
1915	Bro-N	1	0	1.000	5	0	0	0	0	19²	11	0	8	7	8.7	0.92	304	.164	.253	1	.167	-0	4	4	0	0.4
	Bos-N	16	12	.571	33	26	13	3	0	227	208	2	59	81	10.9	2.46	105	.255	.311	12	.150	-0	7	3	-2	0.0
	Yr	17	12	.586	38	26	13	3	0	246²	219	2	67	88	10.7	2.34	112	.248	.306	5	.058	-1	11	7	-2	0.4
1916	Bos-N	9	9	.500	28	23	14	3	0	182	143	3	47	94	9.4	2.08	120	.218	.270	13	.217	3	11	8	1	1.3
1917	Bos-N	6	9	.400	30	13	5	1	1	147²	138	6	35	61	10.6	2.93	87	.250	.295	6	.125	-1	-4	-6	0	-0.7
1918	Bos-N	8	17	.320	30	25	15	2	0	206¹	212	4	54	68	11.8	3.23	83	.270	.320	13	.183	-2	-11	-12	-0	-1.5
1919	Bos-N	0	2	.000	4	3	0	0	0	12²	16	0	3	3	13.5	7.11	40	.281	.317	1	.250	0	-6	-6	0	-0.5
	NY-N	1	0	1.000	7	1	1	0	0	22²	19	0	14	7	13.1	1.59	177	.247	.363	3	.429	1	3	3	0	0.5
	Yr	1	2	.333	11	4	1	0	0	35¹	35	0	17	10	13.2	3.57	79	.261	.344	1	.091	1	-3	-3	0	0.0
	Chi-A	0	0	—	1	0	0	0	0	1	1	0	0	0	9.0	0.00	—	.250	.250	0	—	0	0	0	0	0.1
1923	Phi-N	0	0	—	1	0	0	0	0	3	6	1	0	0	18.0	6.00	77	.400	.400	1	.500	0	-1	-0	-0	0.0
Total	11	77	104	.425	283	182	93	12	6	1608¹	1555	38	470	680	11.5	2.99	97	.259	.315	84	.154	-12	-8	-18	-2	-2.7

■ FRANK RAGLAND   Ragland, Frank Roland   b: 5/26/04, Water Valley, Miss   d: 7/28/59, Paris, Miss.   BR/TR, 6'1", 186 lbs.   Deb: 4/17/32

YEAR	TM/L	W	L	PCT	G	GS	CG	SH	SV	IP	H	HR	BB	SO	RAT	ERA	ERA+	OAV	OOB	BH	AVG	PB	PR	/A	PD	TPI
1932	Was-A	1	0	1.000	12	1	0	0	0	37²	54	5	21	11	18.6	7.41	58	.346	.433	3	.273	1	-12	-13	0	-1.0
1933	Phi-N	0	4	.000	11	5	0	0	0	38¹	51	1	10	4	14.6	6.81	56	.317	.360	2	.200	0	-15	-13	1	-1.1
Total	2	1	4	.200	23	6	0	0	0	76	105	6	31	15	16.6	7.11	58	.331	.398	5	.238	1	-27	-25	1	-2.1

■ ERIC RAICH   Raich, Eric James   b: 11/1/51, Detroit, Mich.   BR/TR, 6'4", 225 lbs.   Deb: 5/24/75

YEAR	TM/L	W	L	PCT	G	GS	CG	SH	SV	IP	H	HR	BB	SO	RAT	ERA	ERA+	OAV	OOB	BH	AVG	PB	PR	/A	PD	TPI
1975	Cle-A	7	8	.467	18	17	2	0	0	92²	118	12	31	34	14.6	5.54	68	.320	.374	0	—	0	-18	-18	-1	-1.7
1976	Cle-A	0	0	—	1	0	0	0	0	2²	7	1	0	1	23.6	16.88	21	.467	.467	0	—	0	-4	-4	-0	-0.3
Total	2	7	8	.467	19	17	2	0	0	95¹	125	13	31	35	14.8	5.85	64	.326	.377	0	—	0	-22	-22	-1	-2.0

■ CHUCK RAINEY   Rainey, Charles David   b: 7/14/54, San Diego, Cal.   BR/TR, 5'11", 220 lbs.   Deb: 4/08/79

YEAR	TM/L	W	L	PCT	G	GS	CG	SH	SV	IP	H	HR	BB	SO	RAT	ERA	ERA+	OAV	OOB	BH	AVG	PB	PR	/A	PD	TPI
1979	Bos-A	8	5	.615	20	16	4	1	1	103²	97	7	41	41	12.2	3.82	116	.250	.326	0	—	0	5	7	1	0.8
1980	Bos-A	8	3	.727	16	13	2	1	0	87	92	7	41	43	14.0	4.86	87	.273	.355	0	—	0	-8	-6	-1	-0.6
1981	Bos-A	0	1	.000	11	2	0	0	0	40	39	2	13	20	11.7	2.70	143	.252	.310	0	—	0	4	5	1	0.6
1982	Bos-A	7	5	.583	27	25	3	3	0	129	146	14	63	57	14.7	5.02	86	.294	.376	0	—	0	-14	-10	1	-0.8
1983	Chi-N	14	13	.519	34	34	1	1	0	191	219	17	74	84	13.9	4.48	85	.295	.361	9	.161	1	-18	-15	3	-1.0
1984	Chi-N	5	7	.417	17	16	0	0	0	88¹	102	4	38	45	14.5	4.28	91	.290	.362	3	.097	-1	-7	-4	1	-0.3
	Oak-A	1	1	.500	16	0	0	0	1	30²	43	2	17	10	17.6	6.75	55	.333	.411	0	—	0	-9	-10	-0	-0.9
Total	6	43	35	.551	141	106	10	6	2	669²	738	53	287	300	13.9	4.50	90	.284	.358	12	.138	-1	-47	-33	6	-2.2

■ DAVE RAJSICH   Rajsich, David Christopher   b: 9/28/51, Youngstown, Ohio   BL/TL, 6'5", 175 lbs.   Deb: 7/02/78

YEAR	TM/L	W	L	PCT	G	GS	CG	SH	SV	IP	H	HR	BB	SO	RAT	ERA	ERA+	OAV	OOB	BH	AVG	PB	PR	/A	PD	TPI
1978	NY-A	0	0	—	4	2	0	0	0	13¹	16	0	6	9	14.9	4.05	89	.320	.393	0	—	0	-0	-1	-0	0.0
1979	Tex-A	1	3	.250	27	3	0	0	0	53²	56	7	18	32	12.4	3.52	118	.267	.325	0	—	0	4	4	1	0.4
1980	Tex-A	2	1	.667	24	1	0	0	2	48¹	56	7	22	35	15.1	5.96	65	.295	.377	0	—	0	-10	-11	0	-1.0
Total	3	3	4	.429	55	6	0	0	2	115¹	128	14	46	76	13.8	4.60	86	.284	.355	0	—	0	-7	-8	1	-0.6

■ ED RAKOW   Rakow, Edward Charles "Rock"   b: 5/30/36, Pittsburgh, Pa.   BB/TR, 5'11", 178 lbs.   Deb: 4/22/60

YEAR	TM/L	W	L	PCT	G	GS	CG	SH	SV	IP	H	HR	BB	SO	RAT	ERA	ERA+	OAV	OOB	BH	AVG	PB	PR	/A	PD	TPI
1960	LA-N	0	1	.000	9	2	0	0	0	22	30	5	11	9	16.8	7.36	54	.323	.394	2	.333	0	-9	-8	0	-0.7
1961	KC-A	2	8	.200	45	11	1	0	1	124²	131	14	49	81	13.6	4.76	86	.269	.346	3	.103	-2	-10	-9	0	-0.9
1962	KC-A	14	17	.452	42	35	11	2	1	235¹	232	31	98	159	12.8	4.25	98	.260	.336	8	.098	-5	-7	-2	1	-0.4
1963	KC-A	9	10	.474	34	26	7	1	0	174¹	173	18	61	104	12.3	3.92	98	.261	.328	6	.105	-2	-6	-2	1	-0.1
1964	Det-A	8	9	.471	42	13	1	0	3	152¹	155	14	59	96	13.0	3.72	98	.266	.340	0	.000	-4	-2	-1	2	-0.2
1965	Det-A	0	0	—	6	0	0	0	0	13¹	14	2	11	10	16.9	6.08	57	.280	.410	0	.000	-0	-4	-4	-1	-0.4
1967	Atl-N	3	2	.600	17	3	0	0	0	39¹	36	4	15	25	11.9	5.26	63	.247	.313	0	.000	-1	-8	-8	-1	-0.9
Total	7	36	47	.434	195	90	20	3	5	761¹	771	88	304	484	13.0	4.33	91	.264	.339	19	.084	-13	-46	-35	4	-3.6

■ JOHN RALEIGH   Raleigh, John Austin   b: 4/21/1890, Elkhorn, Wis.   d: 8/24/55, Escondido, Cal.   BR/TL,   Deb: 8/04/09

YEAR	TM/L	W	L	PCT	G	GS	CG	SH	SV	IP	H	HR	BB	SO	RAT	ERA	ERA+	OAV	OOB	BH	AVG	PB	PR	/A	PD	TPI
1909	StL-N	1	10	.091	15	10	3	0	0	80²	85	0	21	26	12.2	3.79	67	.285	.339	2	.087	-2	-11	-11	0	-1.3
1910	StL-N	0	0	—	3	1	0	0	0	5	8	0	0	2	14.4	9.00	33	.364	.364	0	.000	-0	-3	-3	0	-0.2
Total	2	1	10	.091	18	11	3	0	0	85²	93	0	21	28	12.3	4.10	62	.291	.340	2	.083	-2	-14	-15	0	-1.5

■ PEP RAMBERT   Rambert, Elmer Donald   b: 8/1/16, Cleveland, Ohio   d: 11/16/74, W.Palm Beach, Fla.   BR/TR, 6', 175 lbs.   Deb: 9/23/39

YEAR	TM/L	W	L	PCT	G	GS	CG	SH	SV	IP	H	HR	BB	SO	RAT	ERA	ERA+	OAV	OOB	BH	AVG	PB	PR	/A	PD	TPI
1939	Pit-N	0	0	—	2	0	0	0	0	3²	7	0	1	4	19.6	9.82	39	.389	.421	0	—	0	-2	-2	0	-0.1
1940	Pit-N	0	1	.000	3	1	0	0	0	8¹	12	0	4	0	20.5	7.56	50	.333	.442	0	.000	0	-3	-3	0	-0.3
Total	2	0	1	.000	5	1	0	0	0	12	19	0	5	4	20.3	8.25	46	.352	.435	0	.000	0	-6	-6	0	-0.3

■ PETE RAMBO   Rambo, Warren Dawson   b: 11/1/06, Thoroughfare, N.J.   BR/TR, 5'9", 150 lbs.   Deb: 9/16/26

YEAR	TM/L	W	L	PCT	G	GS	CG	SH	SV	IP	H	HR	BB	SO	RAT	ERA	ERA+	OAV	OOB	BH	AVG	PB	PR	/A	PD	TPI
1926	Phi-N	0	0	—	1	0	0	0	0	3²	6	0	4	4	24.5	14.73	28	.353	.476	1	1.000	0	-4	-4	0	-0.2

■ ALLAN RAMIREZ   Ramirez, Daniel Allan   b: 5/1/57, Victoria, Tex.   BR/TR, 5'10", 180 lbs.   Deb: 6/08/83

YEAR	TM/L	W	L	PCT	G	GS	CG	SH	SV	IP	H	HR	BB	SO	RAT	ERA	ERA+	OAV	OOB	BH	AVG	PB	PR	/A	PD	TPI
1983	Bal-A	4	4	.500	11	10	1	0	0	57	46	6	30	20	12.0	3.47	114	.229	.329	0	—	0	4	3	1	0.4

■ PEDRO RAMOS   Ramos, Pedro (Guerra) "Pete"   b: 4/28/35, Pinar Del Rio, Cuba   BB/TR, 6', 175 lbs.   Deb: 4/11/55   ♦

YEAR	TM/L	W	L	PCT	G	GS	CG	SH	SV	IP	H	HR	BB	SO	RAT	ERA	ERA+	OAV	OOB	BH	AVG	PB	PR	/A	PD	TPI
1955	Was-A	5	11	.313	45	9	3	1	5	130	121	13	39	34	11.8	3.88	99	.253	.323	3	.079	-2	1	-1	-0	-0.3
1956	Was-A	12	10	.545	37	18	4	0	0	152	178	23	76	54	15.2	5.27	82	.299	.381	9	.205	1	-19	-16	0	-1.4
1957	Was-A	12	16	.429	43	30	7	1	0	231	251	43	69	91	12.7	4.79	81	.271	.327	13	.171	0	-26	-23	0	-2.3
1958	Was-A	14	18	.438	43	37	10	4	3	259¹	277	38	77	132	12.5	4.23	90	.273	.327	21	.239	1	-13	-12	-0	-1.1
1959	Was-A	13	19	.406	37	35	11	0	0	233²	233	29	52	95	11.3	4.16	94	.257	.304	11	.147	-0	-8	-6	0	-0.6
1960	Was-A	11	18	.379	43	36	14	1	2	274	254	39	99	160	11.8	3.45	130	.245	.315	10	.116	-2	13	13	0	1.2
1961	Min-A	11	20	.355	42	34	9	3	2	264¹	265	39	79	174	11.8	3.95	107	.258	.313	16	.172	2	2	9	-3	0.8
1962	Cle-A	10	12	.455	37	27	7	2	1	201¹	189	28	85	96	12.5	3.71	104	.246	.326	10	.147	2	6	4	0	0.6
1963	Cle-A	9	8	.529	36	22	5	0	0	184²	159	29	41	169	9.8	3.12	116	.226	.273	6	.109	1	10	10	-2	0.9
1964	Cle-A	7	10	.412	36	19	3	1	0	133	144	18	26	98	11.8	5.14	70	.273	.312	7	.179	-2	-22	-23	-1	-2.1
	NY-A	1	0	1.000	13	0	0	0	8	21²	13	1	0	21	5.4	1.25	291	.183	.183	0	.000	-1	6	6	-1	0.5
	Yr	8	10	.444	49	19	3	1	8	154²	157	19	26	119	10.6	4.60	78	.259	.290	2	.045	1	-17	-17	-1	-1.6
1965	NY-A	5	5	.500	65	0	0	0	19	92¹	80	7	27	68	10.5	2.92	116	.237	.296	1	.083	-1	5	5	-0	0.4
1966	NY-A	3	9	.250	52	1	0	0	13	89²	98	10	18	58	11.7	3.61	92	.283	.321	2	.154	-0	-2	-3	-0	-0.3
1967	Phi-N	0	0	—	6	0	0	0	0	8	14	1	8	1	27.0	9.00	38	.412	.545	0	.000	-0	-5	-5	1	-0.4

YEAR	TM/L	W	L	PCT	G	GS	CG	SH	SV	IP	H	HR	BB	SO	RAT	ERA	ERA+	OAV	OOB	BH	AVG	PB	PR	/A	PD	TPI
1969	Pit-N	0	1	.000	5	0	0	0	0	6	8	2	0	4	12.0	6.00	58	.320	.320	0	.000	-0	-2	-2	0	-0.1
	Cin-N	4	3	.571	38	0	0	0	2	66¹	73	8	24	40	13.8	5.16	73	.284	.357	0	.000	-1	-12	-10	0	-1.0
	Yr	4	4	.500	43	0	0	0	2	72¹	81	10	24	44	13.7	5.23	72	.287	.354	1	.111	-1	-13	-12	0	-1.1
1970	Was-A	0	0		4	0	0	0	0	8¹	10	2	4	10	15.1	7.56	47	.294	.368	0	.000	-0	-4	-4	0	-0.3
Total	15	117	160	.422	582	268	73	13	55	2355²	2364	315	724	1305	12.1	4.08	95	.261	.320	109	.155	-0	-68	-58	-6	-5.5

■ WILLIE RAMSDELL
Ramsdell, James Willard "The Knuck" b: 4/4/16, Williamsburg, Kan. d: 10/8/69, Wichita, Kan. BR/TR, 5'11", 165 lbs. Deb: 9/24/47

YEAR	TM/L	W	L	PCT	G	GS	CG	SH	SV	IP	H	HR	BB	SO	RAT	ERA	ERA+	OAV	OOB	BH	AVG	PB	PR	/A	PD	TPI
1947	Bro-N	1	1	.500	2	0	0	0	0	2²	4	0	3	3	27.0	6.75	61	.333	.500	1	1.000	0	-1	-1	0	0.0
1948	Bro-N	4	4	.500	27	1	0	0	4	50¹	48	6	41	34	16.5	5.19	77	.251	.391	1	.091	-1	-7	-7	1	-0.5
1950	Bro-N	1	2	.333	5	0	0	0	1	6¹	7	0	2	2	14.2	2.84	144	.292	.370	0	.000	-0	1	1	0	0.1
	Cin-N	7	12	.368	27	22	8	1	0	157¹	151	17	75	83	13.0	3.72	114	.255	.341	10	.200	1	7	9	-1	0.9
	Yr	8	14	.364	32	22	8	1	1	163²	158	17	77	85	13.0	3.68	115	.256	.341	5	.094	0	8	10	-1	1.0
1951	Cin-N	9	17	.346	31	31	10	1	0	196	204	18	70	89	12.9	4.04	101	.266	.333	9	.155	-1	-2	1	-2	-0.1
1952	Chi-N	2	3	.400	19	4	0	0	0	67	41	5	24	30	9.4	2.42	159	.173	.263	1	.056	-1	10	11	-1	1.0
Total	5	24	39	.381	111	58	18	2	5	479²	455	46	215	240	12.9	3.83	107	.250	.335	22	.156	-2	9	14	-2	1.4

■ TOAD RAMSEY
Ramsey, Thomas A. b: 8/8/1864, Indianapolis, Ind. d: 3/27/06, Indianapolis, Ind. BR/TL, Deb: 9/05/1885

YEAR	TM/L	W	L	PCT	G	GS	CG	SH	SV	IP	H	HR	BB	SO	RAT	ERA	ERA+	OAV	OOB	BH	AVG	PB	PR	/A	PD	TPI
1885	Lou-a	3	6	.333	9	9	9	0	0	79	44	1	28	83	8.2	1.94	167	.156	.232	4	.129	-2	12	11	-1	0.8
1886	Lou-a	38	27	.585	67	67	**66**	3	0	**588²**	447	3	207	499	10.0	2.45	149	**.201**	.268	58	.241	-2	66	**78**	-5	6.6
1887	Lou-a	37	27	.578	65	64	61	0	0	561	544	9	167	**355**	11.4	3.43	128	.245	.298	43	.191	-9	54	60	-10	3.4
1888	Lou-a	8	30	.211	40	40	37	1	0	342¹	362	10	86	228	11.8	3.42	90	.262	.305	17	.120	-7	-13	-13	-5	-2.1
1889	Lou-a	1	16	.059	18	18	15	0	0	140	175	7	71	60	15.8	5.59	69	.297	.372	15	.263	0	-27	-27	-2	-2.2
	StL-a	3	1	.750	5	3	3	0	0	41	44	0	10	33	11.9	3.95	107	.266	.308	5	.294	1	-0	1	-1	0.1
	Yr	4	17	.190	23	21	18	0	0	181	219	7	81	93	14.9	5.22	75	.290	.359	2	.027	1	-28	-26	-2	-2.1
1890	StL-a	24	17	.585	44	40	34	1	0	348²	325	10	102	257	11.0	3.69	117	.239	.293	33	.228	-1	7	24	-7	1.7
Total	6	114	124	.479	248	241	225	5	0	2100²	1941	40	671	1515	11.2	3.29	117	.236	.294	175	.204	-22	97	134	-31	8.3

■ RIBS RANEY
Raney, Frank Robert Donald (b: Frank Robert Donald Raniszewski) b: 2/16/23, Detroit, Mich. BR/TR, 6'4", 190 lbs. Deb: 9/18/49

YEAR	TM/L	W	L	PCT	G	GS	CG	SH	SV	IP	H	HR	BB	SO	RAT	ERA	ERA+	OAV	OOB	BH	AVG	PB	PR	/A	PD	TPI
1949	StL-A	1	2	.333	3	3	1	0	0	16¹	23	2	12	5	19.3	7.71	59	.333	.432	0	.000	-1	-6	-6	-0	-0.5
1950	StL-A	0	1	.000	1	0	0	0	0	2	2	0	2	2	18.0	4.50	110	.250	.400	0	.000	-0	0	0	0	0.0
Total	2	1	3	.250	4	3	1	0	0	18¹	25	2	14	7	19.1	7.36	62	.325	.429	0	.000	-1	-6	-6	-0	-0.5

■ VIC RASCHI
Raschi, Victor John Angelo b: 3/28/19, W.Springfield, Mass. d: 10/14/88, Groveland, N.Y. BR/TR, 6'1", 205 lbs. Deb: 9/23/46

YEAR	TM/L	W	L	PCT	G	GS	CG	SH	SV	IP	H	HR	BB	SO	RAT	ERA	ERA+	OAV	OOB	BH	AVG	PB	PR	/A	PD	TPI
1946	NY-A	2	0	1.000	2	2	2	0	0	16	14	0	5	11	10.7	3.94	88	.230	.288	1	.250	0	-1	-1	0	0.0
1947	*NY-A	7	2	.778	15	14	6	1	0	104²	89	11	38	51	11.0	3.87	91	.226	.296	10	.250	2	-2	-4	-0	-0.2
1948	NY-A	19	8	.704	36	31	18	6	1	222²	208	15	74	124	11.5	3.84	106	.247	.310	19	.235	2	11	6	-1	0.6
1949	*NY-A	21	10	.677	38	37	21	3	0	274²	247	16	138	124	12.8	3.34	121	.241	.334	13	.157	1	26	21	1	2.3
1950	*NY-A	21	8	**.724**	33	32	17	2	1	256²	232	19	116	155	12.3	4.00	107	.243	.327	17	.198	1	17	8	-3	0.6
1951	*NY-A	21	10	.677	35	34	15	4	0	258¹	233	20	103	**164**	11.9	3.27	117	.242	.319	15	.176	-3	24	16	-3	1.0
1952	*NY-A	16	6	.727	31	31	13	4	0	223	174	13	91	127	10.9	2.78	119	.216	.300	13	.188	3	22	13	-4	1.2
1953	*NY-A	13	6	.684	28	26	7	4	1	181	150	11	55	76	**10.2**	3.33	111	.224	**.283**	9	.143	-2	13	7	-2	0.3
1954	StL-N	8	9	.471	30	29	6	2	0	179	182	24	71	73	12.7	4.73	87	.268	.337	9	.141	-2	-13	-12	2	-1.1
1955	StL-N	0	1	.000	1	1	0	0	0	1²	5	0	1	1	32.4	21.60	19	.556	.600	0	—	0	-3	-3	-0	-0.2
	KC-A	4	6	.400	20	18	1	0	0	101¹	132	10	35	38	14.9	5.42	77	.312	.366	6	.182	-0	-16	-14	1	-1.2
Total	10	132	66	.667	269	255	106	26	3	1819	1666	139	727	944	12.0	3.72	105	.244	.319	112	.184	3	78	38	-9	3.3

■ DENNIS RASMUSSEN
Rasmussen, Dennis Lee b: 4/18/59, Los Angles, Cal. BL/TL, 6'7", 230 lbs. Deb: 9/16/83

YEAR	TM/L	W	L	PCT	G	GS	CG	SH	SV	IP	H	HR	BB	SO	RAT	ERA	ERA+	OAV	OOB	BH	AVG	PB	PR	/A	PD	TPI
1983	SD-N	0	0	—	4	1	0	0	0	13²	10	1	8	13	11.9	1.98	176	.200	.310	0	.000	-0	3	2	0	0.3
1984	NY-A	9	6	.600	24	24	1	0	0	147²	127	16	60	110	11.6	4.57	83	.234	.315	0	—	0	-10	-13	-1	-1.3
1985	NY-A	3	5	.375	22	16	2	0	0	101²	97	10	42	63	12.4	3.98	100	.255	.331	0	—	0	2	0	0	0.0
1986	NY-A	18	6	.750	31	31	3	1	0	202	160	28	74	131	10.5	3.88	105	.217	.290	0	—	0	7	5	-1	0.4
1987	NY-A	9	7	.563	26	25	2	0	0	146	145	31	55	89	12.6	4.75	92	.260	.331	0	—	0	-5	-6	0	-0.5
	Cin-N	4	1	.800	7	7	0	0	0	45¹	39	5	12	39	10.3	3.97	107	.229	.284	1	.067	-1	1	1	0	0.1
1988	Cin-N	2	6	.250	11	11	1	1	0	56¹	68	8	22	27	14.7	5.75	62	.300	.367	5	.227	1	-14	-14	0	-1.1
	SD-N	14	4	.778	20	20	6	0	0	148¹	131	9	36	85	10.3	2.55	133	.238	.287	9	.188	2	15	14	2	2.0
	Yr	16	10	.615	31	31	7	1	0	204²	199	17	58	112	11.4	3.43	100	.254	.308	5	.071	3	0	0	2	0.9
1989	SD-N	10	10	.500	33	33	1	0	0	183²	190	18	72	87	13.0	4.26	82	.270	.340	11	.169	1	-16	-16	0	-1.5
1990	SD-N	11	15	.423	32	32	3	1	0	187²	217	28	62	86	13.5	4.51	85	.292	.349	18	.290	5	-15	-14	1	-0.7
Total	8	80	60	.571	210	200	19	3	0	1232¹	1184	154	443	730	12.0	4.13	93	.254	.322	44	.205	8	-33	-39	1	-2.3

■ ERIC RASMUSSEN
Rasmussen, Eric Ralph (Born Harold Ralph Rasmussen) b: 3/22/52, Racine, Wis. BR/TR, 6'3", 205 lbs. Deb: 7/21/75

YEAR	TM/L	W	L	PCT	G	GS	CG	SH	SV	IP	H	HR	BB	SO	RAT	ERA	ERA+	OAV	OOB	BH	AVG	PB	PR	/A	PD	TPI
1975	StL-N	5	5	.500	14	13	2	1	0	81	86	8	20	59	11.8	3.78	99	.264	.306	4	.154	-1	-1	-0	-0	0.0
1976	StL-N	6	12	.333	43	17	2	1	0	150¹	139	10	54	76	11.7	3.53	100	.247	.315	4	.105	-1	-1	0	3	0.2
1977	StL-N	11	17	.393	34	34	11	3	0	233	223	24	63	120	11.2	3.48	111	.254	.308	10	.139	0	11	10	-1	0.9
1978	StL-N	2	5	.286	10	10	2	1	0	60¹	61	4	20	32	12.1	4.18	84	.270	.329	2	.111	-1	-4	-4	0	-0.4
	SD-N	12	10	.545	27	24	3	2	0	146¹	154	16	43	59	12.2	4.06	82	.277	.331	7	.152	-1	-8	-12	1	-1.1
	Yr	14	15	.483	37	34	5	3	0	206²	215	20	63	91	12.1	4.09	83	.274	.329	0	.000	-2	-12	-16	1	-1.5
1979	SD-N	6	9	.400	45	20	5	3	3	156²	142	9	42	54	10.6	3.27	108	.244	.295	2	.056	-2	8	4	0	0.2
1980	SD-N	4	11	.267	40	14	0	0	1	111¹	130	9	42	50	13.4	4.37	79	.295	.349	2	.095	-1	-9	-12	-0	-1.2
1982	StL-N	1	2	.333	8	3	0	0	0	18¹	21	2	8	15	14.2	4.42	82	.288	.358	0	.000	-0	-2	-2	0	-0.1
1983	StL-N	0	0	—	6	0	0	0	1	7²	16	1	4	6	23.5	11.74	31	.444	.500	0	—	0	-7	-7	0	-0.6
	KC-A	3	6	.333	11	9	2	1	0	52²	61	4	22	18	14.2	4.78	85	.289	.356	0	—	0	-4	-4	-0	-0.3
Total	8	50	77	.394	238	144	27	12	5	1017²	1033	87	309	489	12.0	3.85	94	.266	.321	31	.119	-5	-17	-27	3	-2.4

■ HANS RASMUSSEN
Rasmussen, Henry Florian b: 4/18/1895, Chicago, Ill. d: 1/1/49, Chicago, Ill. BR/TR, 6'6", 220 lbs. Deb: 8/11/15

YEAR	TM/L	W	L	PCT	G	GS	CG	SH	SV	IP	H	HR	BB	SO	RAT	ERA	ERA+	OAV	OOB	BH	AVG	PB	PR	/A	PD	TPI
1915	Chi-F	0	0	—	2	0	0	0	0	2	3	0	2	2	22.5	13.50	21	.354	.478	0	.000	-0	-2	-2	0	-0.1

■ FRED RATH
Rath, Frederick Helsher b: 9/1/43, Little Rock, Ark. BR/TR, 6'3", 200 lbs. Deb: 9/10/68

YEAR	TM/L	W	L	PCT	G	GS	CG	SH	SV	IP	H	HR	BB	SO	RAT	ERA	ERA+	OAV	OOB	BH	AVG	PB	PR	/A	PD	TPI
1968	Chi-A	0	0	—	5	0	0	0	0	11¹	8	0	3	9	9.5	1.59	191	.182	.250	0	—	0	2	2	0	0.2
1969	Chi-A	0	2	.000	3	2	0	0	0	11²	11	4	8	4	14.7	7.71	50	.256	.373	0	.000	-0	-5	-5	0	-0.4
Total	2	0	2	.000	8	2	0	0	0	23	19	4	11	7	12.1	4.70	73	.218	.313	0	.000	-0	-4	-3	0	-0.2

■ STEVE RATZER
Ratzer, Steven Wayne b: 9/9/53, Paterson, N.J. BR/TR, 6'1", 192 lbs. Deb: 10/05/80

YEAR	TM/L	W	L	PCT	G	GS	CG	SH	SV	IP	H	HR	BB	SO	RAT	ERA	ERA+	OAV	OOB	BH	AVG	PB	PR	/A	PD	TPI
1980	Mon-N	0	0	—	1	1	0	0	0	4	9	0	2	0	24.8	11.25	32	.450	.500	0	.000	-0	-3	-3	0	-0.2
1981	Mon-N	1	1	.500	12	0	0	0	0	17¹	23	2	7	4	15.6	6.23	56	.311	.370	0	.000	-0	-5	-5	1	-0.4
Total	2	1	1	.500	13	1	0	0	0	21¹	32	2	9	4	17.3	7.17	49	.340	.398	0	.000	-0	-9	-9	1	-0.6

■ DOUG RAU
Rau, Douglas James b: 12/15/48, Columbus, Tex. BL/TL, 6'2", 175 lbs. Deb: 9/02/72

YEAR	TM/L	W	L	PCT	G	GS	CG	SH	SV	IP	H	HR	BB	SO	RAT	ERA	ERA+	OAV	OOB	BH	AVG	PB	PR	/A	PD	TPI
1972	LA-N	2	2	.500	7	3	0	0	0	32²	18	1	11	19	8.3	2.20	151	.159	.240	1	.143	1	5	4	0	0.6
1973	LA-N	4	2	.667	31	3	0	0	3	63²	64	5	28	51	13.1	3.96	87	.259	.337	1	.091	-1	-2	-4	-1	-0.4
1974	*LA-N	13	11	.542	36	35	3	1	0	198¹	191	20	70	126	12.0	3.72	91	.251	.318	9	.141	-1	-2	-7	-0	-0.8
1975	*LA-N	15	9	.625	38	38	8	2	0	257²	227	18	61	151	10.2	3.11	109	.236	.283	17	.195	2	15	8	-1	1.0
1976	LA-N	16	12	.571	34	32	8	3	0	231	221	18	69	98	11.6	2.57	132	.258	.318	9	.150	1	24	21	0	2.4
1977	*LA-N	14	8	.636	32	32	4	2	0	212¹	232	15	49	126	12.2	3.43	111	.282	.327	10	.141	-0	11	9	-1	0.7
1978	*LA-N	15	9	.625	30	30	7	2	0	199	219	17	68	95	13.1	3.26	108	.284	.344	9	.143	-1	7	6	-2	0.3

YEAR	TM/L	W	L	PCT	G	GS	CG	SH	SV	IP	H	HR	BB	SO	RAT	ERA	ERA+	OAV	OOB	BH	AVG	PB	PR	/A	PD	TPI
1979	LA-N	1	5	.167	11	11	1	1	0	56	73	3	22	28	15.9	5.30	69	.320	.390	2	.143	1	-10	-10	0	-0.8
1981	Cal-A	1	2	.333	3	3	0	0	0	10¹	14	2	4	3	15.7	8.71	42	.341	.400	0	—	0	-6	-6	-0	-0.5
Total	9	81	60	.574	222	187	33	11	3	1261	1259	99	382	697	11.9	3.35	104	.262	.320	58	.154	2	41	21	-4	2.5

■ BOB RAUCH
Rauch, Robert John b: 6/16/49, Brookings, S.D. BR/TR, 6'4", 200 lbs. Deb: 6/29/72

YEAR	TM/L	W	L	PCT	G	GS	CG	SH	SV	IP	H	HR	BB	SO	RAT	ERA	ERA+	OAV	OOB	BH	AVG	PB	PR	/A	PD	TPI
1972	NY-N	0	1	.000	19	0	0	0	1	27	27	3	21	23	16.0	5.00	67	.273	.400	0	.000	-0	-5	-5	0	-0.4

■ LANCE RAUTZHAN
Rautzhan, Clarence George b: 8/20/52, Pottsville, Pa. BR/TL, 6'1", 195 lbs. Deb: 7/23/77

YEAR	TM/L	W	L	PCT	G	GS	CG	SH	SV	IP	H	HR	BB	SO	RAT	ERA	ERA+	OAV	OOB	BH	AVG	PB	PR	/A	PD	TPI
1977	*LA-N	4	1	.800	25	0	0	0	2	20²	25	0	7	13	13.9	4.35	88	.313	.368	0	.000	-0	-1	-1	0	0.0
1978	*LA-N	2	1	.667	43	0	0	0	4	61¹	61	1	19	25	11.9	2.93	120	.263	.321	0	.000	-0	4	4	2	0.5
1979	LA-N	0	2	.000	12	0	0	0	1	9²	9	0	11	5	19.6	7.45	49	.273	.467	0	—	0	-4	-4	1	-0.3
	Mil-A	0	0	—	3	0	0	0	0	3	3	0	10	2	39.0	9.00	46	.300	.650	0	—	0	-2	-2	0	-0.1
Total	3	6	4	.600	83	0	0	0	7	94²	98	1	47	45	14.0	3.90	93	.276	.364	0	.000	-1	-2	-3	3	0.2

■ SHANE RAWLEY
Rawley, Shane William b: 7/27/55, Racine, Wis. BR/TL, 6', 170 lbs. Deb: 4/06/78

YEAR	TM/L	W	L	PCT	G	GS	CG	SH	SV	IP	H	HR	BB	SO	RAT	ERA	ERA+	OAV	OOB	BH	AVG	PB	PR	/A	PD	TPI
1978	Sea-A	4	9	.308	52	2	0	0	4	111¹	114	7	51	66	13.7	4.12	92	.275	.362	0	—	0	-4	-4	1	-0.2
1979	Sea-A	5	9	.357	48	3	0	0	11	84¹	88	2	40	48	13.8	3.84	113	.278	.361	0	—	0	3	5	1	0.5
1980	Sea-A	7	7	.500	59	0	0	0	13	113²	103	3	63	68	13.4	3.33	124	.257	.363	0	—	0	9	10	2	1.2
1981	Sea-A	4	6	.400	46	0	0	0	8	68¹	64	1	38	35	13.6	3.95	97	.257	.358	0	—	0	-2	-1	0	0.0
1982	NY-A	11	10	.524	47	17	3	0	3	164	165	10	54	111	12.1	4.06	98	.267	.328	0	—	0	-1	1	0	0.0
1983	NY-A	14	14	.500	34	33	13	2	1	238¹	246	19	79	124	12.4	3.78	103	.269	.329	0	—	0	8	3	0	0.3
1984	NY-A	2	3	.400	11	10	0	0	0	42	46	0	27	24	15.6	6.21	61	.272	.372	0	—	0	-10	-11	-0	-1.0
	Phi-N	10	6	.625	18	18	3	0	0	120¹	117	13	27	58	10.8	3.81	95	.257	.300	5	.116	-2	-3	-2	-1	-0.4
1985	Phi-N	13	8	.619	36	31	6	2	0	198²	188	16	81	106	12.3	3.31	111	.249	.323	8	.138	0	6	8	1	1.1
1986	Phi-N	11	7	.611	23	23	7	1	0	157²	166	13	50	73	12.4	3.54	109	.270	.326	9	.173	0	3	5	0	0.6
1987	Phi-N	17	11	.607	36	36	4	1	0	229²	250	23	86	123	13.4	4.39	97	.279	.346	12	.152	-0	-8	-4	-1	-0.4
1988	Phi-N	8	16	.333	32	32	4	1	0	198	220	27	78	87	13.7	4.18	85	.286	.355	6	.105	-1	-16	-14	0	-1.4
1989	Min-A	5	12	.294	27	25	1	0	0	145	167	19	60	68	14.1	5.21	79	.293	.361	0	—	0	-21	-17	-1	-1.7
Total	12	111	118	.485	469	230	41	7	40	1871¹	1934	153	734	991	13.0	4.02	97	.271	.341	40	.138	-3	-36	-22	4	-1.4

■ CARL RAY
Ray, Carl Grady b: 1/31/1889, Danbury, N.C. d: 4/3/70, Walnut Cove, N.C. BL/TL, 5'11", 170 lbs. Deb: 9/25/15

YEAR	TM/L	W	L	PCT	G	GS	CG	SH	SV	IP	H	HR	BB	SO	RAT	ERA	ERA+	OAV	OOB	BH	AVG	PB	PR	/A	PD	TPI
1915	Phi-A	0	1	.000	2	1	0	0	0	7¹	11	0	6	6	25.8	4.91	60	.333	.488	0	.000	0	-2	-2	-0	-0.1
1916	Phi-A	0	1	.000	3	1	0	0	0	9¹	9	0	14	5	23.1	4.82	60	.257	.480	0	.000	0	-2	-2	-0	-0.2
Total	2	0	2	.000	5	2	0	0	0	16²	20	0	20	11	24.3	4.86	60	.294	.484	0	.000	0	-4	-4	-0	-0.3

■ JIM RAY
Ray, James Francis "Sting" b: 12/1/44, Rock Hill, S.C. BR/TR, 6'1", 185 lbs. Deb: 9/16/65

YEAR	TM/L	W	L	PCT	G	GS	CG	SH	SV	IP	H	HR	BB	SO	RAT	ERA	ERA+	OAV	OOB	BH	AVG	PB	PR	/A	PD	TPI
1965	Hou-N	0	2	.000	3	2	0	0	0	7²	11	1	6	7	20.0	10.57	32	.355	.459	0	.000	-0	-6	-6	0	-0.5
1966	Hou-N	0	0	—	1	0	0	0	0	0	0	0	1	0	—	∞	—	—	1.000	0	—	0	-1	-1	0	0.0
1968	Hou-N	2	3	.400	41	2	1	0	1	80²	65	5	25	71	10.2	2.68	110	.220	.283	1	.067	-1	3	2	-1	0.1
1969	Hou-N	8	2	.800	40	13	0	0	0	115	105	11	48	115	12.1	3.91	90	.245	.324	3	.115	-1	-4	-5	-1	-0.4
1970	Hou-N	6	3	.667	52	2	0	0	5	105	97	13	49	67	12.5	3.26	119	.251	.336	5	.185	-0	9	7	0	0.7
1971	Hou-N	10	4	.714	47	1	0	0	3	97²	72	9	31	46	9.7	2.12	159	.211	.281	3	.167	0	15	14	-2	1.3
1972	Hou-N	10	9	.526	54	0	0	0	8	90¹	77	10	44	50	12.4	4.28	79	.227	.321	1	.063	-1	-8	-9	-1	-1.1
1973	Hou-N	6	4	.600	42	0	0	0	6	69	65	5	38	25	13.8	4.43	82	.253	.356	3	.231	0	-6	-6	-0	-0.5
1974	Det-A	1	3	.250	28	0	0	0	2	52¹	49	4	29	26	13.6	4.47	85	.254	.354	0	—	0	-5	-4	0	-0.3
Total	9	43	30	.589	308	20	1	0	25	617²	541	52	271	407	12.0	3.61	97	.238	.323	16	.137	-3	-4	-8	-5	-0.9

■ FARMER RAY
Ray, Robert Henry b: 9/17/1886, Ft.Lyon, Colo. d: 3/11/63, Electra, Tex. BL/TR, 5'11", 160 lbs. Deb: 6/13/10

YEAR	TM/L	W	L	PCT	G	GS	CG	SH	SV	IP	H	HR	BB	SO	RAT	ERA	ERA+	OAV	OOB	BH	AVG	PB	PR	/A	PD	TPI
1910	StL-A	4	10	.286	21	16	11	0	0	140²	146	3	49	35	12.9	3.58	69	.285	.356	7	.175	0	-17	-17	-3	-2.0

■ CURT RAYDON
Raydon, Curtis Lowell b: 11/18/33, Bloomington, Ill. BR/TR, 6'4", 190 lbs. Deb: 4/15/58

YEAR	TM/L	W	L	PCT	G	GS	CG	SH	SV	IP	H	HR	BB	SO	RAT	ERA	ERA+	OAV	OOB	BH	AVG	PB	PR	/A	PD	TPI
1958	Pit-N	8	4	.667	31	20	2	1	1	134¹	118	18	61	85	12.3	3.62	107	.236	.326	1	.026	-2	5	4	-3	-0.1

■ BUGS RAYMOND
Raymond, Arthur Lawrence b: 2/24/1882, Chicago, Ill. d: 9/7/12, Chicago, Ill. BR/TR, 5'10", 180 lbs. Deb: 9/23/04

YEAR	TM/L	W	L	PCT	G	GS	CG	SH	SV	IP	H	HR	BB	SO	RAT	ERA	ERA+	OAV	OOB	BH	AVG	PB	PR	/A	PD	TPI
1904	Det-A	0	1	.000	5	2	1	0	0	14²	14	0	6	7	12.3	3.07	83	.252	.325	0	.000	-1	-1	-1	1	0.0
1907	StL-N	2	4	.333	8	6	6	1	0	64²	56	3	21	34	10.9	1.67	150	.230	.294	2	.091	-0	6	6	0	0.7
1908	StL-N	15	25	.375	48	37	23	5	2	324¹	236	2	95	145	9.6	2.03	116	.207	.277	17	.189	1	12	12	3	1.9
1909	NY-N	18	12	.600	39	31	18	2	0	270	239	7	87	121	11.1	2.47	104	.245	.311	13	.146	0	4	3	2	0.5
1910	NY-N	4	11	.267	19	11	6	0	0	99¹	106	2	40	55	14.0	3.81	78	.280	.362	5	.156	-1	-9	-9	2	-0.7
1911	NY-N	6	4	.600	17	9	4	1	0	81²	73	1	33	39	11.9	3.31	102	.248	.328	5	.200	-0	1	1	1	0.1
Total	6	45	57	.441	136	96	58	9	2	854²	724	15	282	401	10.9	2.49	105	.235	.305	42	.160	-0	14	11	9	2.5

■ HARRY RAYMOND
Raymond, Harry H. "Jack" b: 2/20/1862, Utica, N.Y. d: 3/21/25, San Diego, Cal. 5'9", 179 lbs. Deb: 9/09/1888 ♦

YEAR	TM/L	W	L	PCT	G	GS	CG	SH	SV	IP	H	HR	BB	SO	RAT	ERA	ERA+	OAV	OOB	BH	AVG	PB	PR	/A	PD	TPI
1889	Lou-a	1	0	1.000	1	1	1	0	0	9	8	0	11	1	19.0	1.00	384	.231	.416	123	.239	0	3	3	-0	0.3

■ CLAUDE RAYMOND
Raymond, Joseph Claude Marc "Frenchy" b: 5/7/37, St.Jean, Que., Canada BR/TR, 5'10", 175 lbs. Deb: 4/15/59

YEAR	TM/L	W	L	PCT	G	GS	CG	SH	SV	IP	H	HR	BB	SO	RAT	ERA	ERA+	OAV	OOB	BH	AVG	PB	PR	/A	PD	TPI
1959	Chi-A	0	0	—	3	0	0	0	0	4	5	2	2	1	15.8	9.00	42	.333	.412	0	—	0	-2	-2	0	-0.1
1961	Mil-N	1	0	1.000	13	0	0	0	2	20¹	22	2	9	13	14.2	3.98	94	.275	.356	0	.000	-0	0	-1	0	0.0
1962	Mil-N	5	5	.500	26	0	0	0	10	42²	37	5	15	40	11.4	2.74	138	.236	.310	0	.000	-1	6	5	-1	0.3
1963	Mil-N	4	6	.400	45	0	0	0	5	53¹	57	12	27	44	14.9	5.40	60	.268	.361	2	.500	2	-13	-13	1	-1.0
1964	Hou-N	5	5	.500	38	0	0	0	5	79²	64	3	22	56	10.1	2.82	112	.229	.292	1	.071	-0	6	5	1	0.6
1965	Hou-N	7	4	.636	33	7	2	0	5	96¹	87	6	16	79	10.1	2.90	116	.244	.286	3	.115	-0	7	5	-1	0.4
1966	Hou-N	7	5	.583	62	0	0	0	16	92	85	10	25	73	11.2	3.13	109	.242	.300	1	.111	-0	5	3	-2	0.1
1967	Hou-N	0	4	.000	21	0	0	0	5	31	31	5	7	17	11.6	3.19	104	.256	.308	1	.200	0	1	0	-0	0.0
	Atl-N	4	1	.800	28	0	0	0	5	34¹	33	2	11	14	11.5	2.62	127	.260	.319	0	.000	0	3	3	0	0.3
	Yr	4	5	.444	49	0	0	0	10	65¹	64	7	18	31	11.3	2.89	115	.255	.305	1	.143	0	4	3	0	0.3
1968	Atl-N	3	5	.375	36	0	0	0	10	60¹	56	4	18	37	11.2	2.83	106	.256	.315	1	.143	-0	1	1	0	0.1
1969	Atl-N	2	2	.500	33	0	0	0	1	48	56	4	13	15	13.3	5.25	69	.289	.350	2	.286	-0	-9	-9	-0	-0.8
	Mon-N	1	2	.333	15	0	0	0	1	22	21	2	8	11	12.7	4.09	90	.256	.337	0	.000	-0	-1	-1	1	0.0
	Yr	3	4	.429	48	0	0	0	2	70	77	6	21	26	12.9	4.89	74	.281	.337	2	.000	-0	-10	-10	0	-0.8
1970	Mon-N	6	7	.462	59	0	0	0	23	83¹	76	13	27	68	11.3	4.43	93	.240	.303	0	.000	-1	-4	-3	-1	-0.4
1971	Mon-N	1	7	.125	37	0	0	0	0	53²	81	5	25	29	17.8	4.70	75	.373	.438	0	.000	-0	-7	-7	1	-0.5
Total	12	46	53	.465	449	7	2	0	83	721	711	75	225	497	12.0	3.66	96	.261	.324	11	.109	-2	-7	-13	-0	-1.0

■ BARRY RAZIANO
Raziano, Barry John b: 2/5/47, New Orleans, La. BB/TR, 5'10", 175 lbs. Deb: 8/18/73

YEAR	TM/L	W	L	PCT	G	GS	CG	SH	SV	IP	H	HR	BB	SO	RAT	ERA	ERA+	OAV	OOB	BH	AVG	PB	PR	/A	PD	TPI
1973	KC-A	0	0	—	2	0	0	0	0	5	6	1	1	0	14.4	5.40	76	.316	.381	0	—	0	-1	-1	0	0.0
1974	Cal-A	1	2	.333	13	0	0	0	1	16²	15	1	8	9	12.4	6.48	53	.246	.333	0	—	0	-5	-6	-0	-0.5
Total	2	1	2	.333	15	0	0	0	1	21²	21	2	9	9	12.9	6.23	58	.262	.344	0	—	0	-6	-6	-0	-0.5

■ RIP REAGAN
Reagan, Arthur (b: Arthur Edgar Ragan) b: 6/5/1878, Lincoln, Ill. d: 6/8/53, Kansas City, Mo. BR/TR, 5'11", 170 lbs. Deb: 9/19/03

YEAR	TM/L	W	L	PCT	G	GS	CG	SH	SV	IP	H	HR	BB	SO	RAT	ERA	ERA+	OAV	OOB	BH	AVG	PB	PR	/A	PD	TPI
1903	Cin-N	0	2	.000	3	2	2	0	0	18	40	0	7	7	24.0	6.00	59	.455	.500	2	.250	0	-5	-5	0	-0.3

■ JIM REARDON
Reardon, James Matthew b: 1866, Hoosick Falls, N.Y. d: 2/25/1891, Hoosick Falls, N.Y Deb: 7/17/1886

YEAR	TM/L	W	L	PCT	G	GS	CG	SH	SV	IP	H	HR	BB	SO	RAT	ERA	ERA+	OAV	OOB	BH	AVG	PB	PR	/A	PD	TPI
1886	StL-N	0	1	.000	1	1	1	0	0	8	10	1	5	0	16.9	6.75	48	.294	.384	1	.250	0	-3	-3	-0	-0.2
	Cin-a	0	1	.000	1	1	0	0	0	2	5	0	4	0	40.5	18.00	19	.452	.598	0	.000	-1	-3	-3	0	-0.2

YEAR TM/L	W	L	PCT	G	GS	CG	SH	SV	IP	H	HR	BB	SO	RAT	ERA	ERA+	OAV	OOB	BH	AVG	PB	PR	/A	PD	TPI
■ JEFF REARDON Reardon, Jeffrey James b: 10/1/55, Dalton, Mass. BR/TR, 6′, 190 lbs. Deb: 8/25/79																									
1979 NY-N	1	2	.333	18	0	0	0	2	20²	12	2	9	10	9.1	1.74	209	.174	.269	0	—	0	5	4	-0	0.4
1980 NY-N	8	7	.533	61	0	0	0	6	110¹	96	10	47	101	11.7	2.61	136	.231	.310	0	.000	-1	12	12	-3	0.9
1981 NY-N	1	0	1.000	18	0	0	0	2	28²	27	2	12	28	12.6	3.45	101	.245	.325	0	.000	-0	0	0	-1	0.0
*Mon-N	2	0	1.000	25	0	0	0	6	41²	21	3	9	21	6.7	1.30	269	.148	.204	0	.000	-0	10	10	-1	0.9
Yr	3	0	1.000	43	0	0	0	8	70¹	48	5	21	49	9.0	2.18	160	.189	.254	0	.000	-1	10	10	-2	0.9
1982 Mon-N	7	4	.636	75	0	0	0	26	109	87	6	36	86	10.3	2.06	176	.221	.289	1	.100	-0	19	19	-2	1.8
1983 Mon-N	7	9	.438	66	0	0	0	21	92	87	7	44	78	12.9	3.03	118	.250	.336	1	.125	-0	6	6	-2	0.3
1984 Mon-N	7	7	.500	68	0	0	0	23	87	70	5	37	79	11.4	2.90	118	.220	.307	0	.000	-1	7	5	-2	0.2
1985 Mon-N	2	8	.200	63	0	0	0	**41**	87²	68	7	26	67	9.8	3.18	107	.209	.270	2	.286	0	4	2	-1	0.2
1986 Mon-N	7	9	.438	62	0	0	0	35	89	83	12	26	67	11.1	3.94	94	.251	.307	1	.125	-0	-2	-3	-0	-0.2
1987 *Min-A	8	8	.500	63	0	0	0	31	80¹	70	14	28	83	11.3	4.48	103	.232	.303	0	—	0	-0	1	-1	0.0
1988 Min-A	2	4	.333	63	0	0	0	42	73	68	6	15	56	10.5	2.47	165	.245	.289	0	—	0	12	13	-2	1.1
1989 Min-A	5	4	.556	65	0	0	0	31	73	68	8	12	46	10.2	4.07	102	.246	.285	0	—	0	-2	1	-2	0.0
1990 *Bos-A	5	3	.625	47	0	0	0	21	51¹	39	5	19	33	10.3	3.16	129	.206	.282	0	—	0	4	5	-1	0.5
Total 12	62	65	.488	694	0	0	0	287	943²	796	87	320	755	10.8	3.03	124	.228	.296	5	.091	-2	75	75	-16	6.1
■ FRANK REBERGER Reberger, Frank Beall "Crane" b: 6/7/44, Caldwell, Idaho BL/TR, 6′5″, 200 lbs. Deb: 6/06/68																									
1968 Chi-N	0	1	.000	3	1	0	0	0	6	9	1	2	3	16.5	4.50	70	.346	.393	0	—	0	-1	-1	0	0.0
1969 SD-N	1	2	.333	67	0	0	0	6	87²	83	6	41	65	12.9	3.59	98	.258	.345	1	.200	0	0	-1	2	0.1
1970 SF-N	7	8	.467	45	18	3	0	2	152	178	13	98	117	16.8	5.57	71	.293	.397	11	.234	1	-26	-27	-0	-2.4
1971 SF-N	3	0	1.000	13	7	0	0	0	43²	37	5	19	21	12.0	3.92	87	.228	.317	3	.231	0	-2	-3	1	-0.1
1972 SF-N	3	4	.429	20	11	2	0	0	99¹	97	10	37	52	12.6	3.99	87	.257	.332	8	.229	2	-6	-6	1	-0.1
Total 5	14	15	.483	148	37	5	0	8	388²	404	35	197	258	14.3	4.52	81	.270	.361	23	.230	4	-35	-36	3	-2.5
■ JOHN RECCIUS Reccius, John b: 6/7/1862, Louisville, Ky. d: 9/1/30, Louisville, Ky. 5′6.5″. Deb: 5/02/1882 ♦																									
1882 Lou-a	4	6	.400	13	10	9	1	0	95	106	3	22	31	12.1	3.03	81	.264	.302	63	.237	3	-4	-6	-1	-0.4
1883 Lou-a	0	0	—	1	0	0	0	0	4	10	0	0	0	22.5	2.25	132	.446	.446	9	.143	-0	0	0	0	0.0
Total 2	4	6	.400	14	10	9	1	0	99	116	3	22	31	12.5	3.00	83	.274	.310	72	.219	3	-3	-6	-1	-0.4
■ PHIL RECCIUS Reccius, Phillip b: 6/7/1862, Louisville, Ky. d: 2/15/03, Louisville, Ky. 5′9″, 163 lbs. Deb: 9/25/1882 ♦																									
1884 Lou-a	6	7	.462	18	11	11	0	0	129¹	118	2	19	46	9.5	2.71	113	.230	.257	63	.240	2	8	5	0	0.5
1885 Lou-a	0	4	.000	7	5	4	0	1	40	46	0	11	10	12.8	3.82	84	.276	.321	97	.241	1	-3	-3	1	-0.1
1886 Lou-a	0	1	.000	1	1	0	0	0	3	7	0	3	0	30.0	9.00	41	.435	.524	4	.308	0	-2	-2	0	0.0
1887 Cle-a	0	0	—	1	0	0	0	0	7	8	0	5	0	16.7	7.71	57	.277	.383	47	.205	-0	-3	-3	0	-0.1
Total 4	6	12	.333	27	17	15	0	1	179¹	179	2	38	56	10.9	3.26	97	.247	.284	225	.231	3	1	-2	2	0.3
■ PHIL REDDING Redding, Philip Hayden b: 1/25/1890, Crystal Springs, Miss. d: 3/30/29, Greenwood, Miss. BL/TR, 5′11.5″, 190 lbs. Deb: 9/14/12																									
1912 StL-N	2	1	.667	3	3	2	0	0	25¹	31	2	11	9	14.9	4.97	69	.307	.375	0	.000	-1	-4	-4	-0	-0.4
1913 StL-N	0	0	—	1	0	0	0	0	2²	2	0	1	1	10.1	6.75	48	.286	.375	0	.000	-0	-1	-1	0	0.0
Total 2	2	1	.667	4	3	2	0	0	28	33	2	12	10	14.5	5.14	66	.306	.375	0	.000	-1	-5	-5	-0	-0.4
■ PETE REDFERN Redfern, Peter Irvine b: 8/25/54, Glendale, Cal. BR/TR, 6′2″, 195 lbs. Deb: 5/15/76																									
1976 Min-A	8	8	.500	23	23	1	1	0	118	105	6	63	74	13.0	3.51	103	.241	.341	0	—	0	0	1	-1	0.0
1977 Min-A	6	9	.400	30	28	1	0	0	137¹	164	13	66	73	15.3	5.18	77	.304	.384	0	—	0	-17	-18	1	-1.6
1978 Min-A	0	2	.000	3	2	0	0	0	9²	10	2	6	4	14.9	6.52	59	.294	.400	0	—	0	-3	-3	0	-0.2
1979 Min-A	7	3	.700	40	6	0	0	1	108¹	106	8	35	85	11.8	3.49	126	.258	.318	0	—	0	9	11	-1	0.9
1980 Min-A	7	7	.500	23	16	2	0	2	104²	117	11	33	73	12.9	4.56	96	.283	.336	0	—	0	-6	-2	-1	-0.2
1981 Min-A	9	8	.529	24	23	3	0	0	141²	140	12	52	77	12.3	4.07	97	.261	.328	0	—	0	-6	-2	-1	-0.2
1982 Min-A	5	11	.313	27	13	2	0	0	94¹	122	16	51	40	16.6	6.58	64	.322	.404	0	—	0	-26	-25	1	-2.2
Total 7	42	48	.467	170	111	9	1	3	714	764	68	306	426	13.6	4.54	89	.278	.353	0	—	0	-50	-38	-3	-3.5
■ HOWIE REED Reed, Howard Dean "Diz" b: 12/21/36, Dallas, Tex. d: 12/7/84, Corpus Christi, Tex. BR/TR, 6′1″, 195 lbs. Deb: 9/13/58																									
1958 KC-A	1	0	1.000	3	1	1	0	0	10¹	5	0	4	5	7.8	0.87	449	.132	.214	0	.000	0	3	3	-0	0.4
1959 KC-A	0	3	.000	6	3	0	0	0	20²	26	3	10	11	15.7	7.40	54	.313	.387	0	.000	-0	-8	-8	-0	-0.7
1960 KC-A	0	0	—	1	0	0	0	0	1²	2	1	0	1	10.8	0.00	—	.286	.286	0	—	0	1	1	0	0.1
1964 LA-N	3	4	.429	26	7	0	0	1	90	79	4	36	52	11.5	3.20	101	.236	.310	2	.100	-0	3	0	1	0.2
1965 *LA-N	7	5	.583	38	5	0	0	1	78	73	6	27	47	11.9	3.12	105	.243	.312	0	.000	0	4	1	1	0.2
1966 LA-N	0	0	—	1	0	0	0	0	1²	1	0	0	0	5.4	0.00	—	.167	.167	0	.000	0	1	1	0	0.1
Cal-A	1	1	.500	19	0	0	0	1	43	39	5	15	17	11.3	2.93	115	.247	.312	0	.000	-1	2	2	-0	0.1
1967 Hou-N	1	1	.500	4	2	0	0	0	18¹	19	0	2	9	10.3	3.44	96	.268	.288	0	.000	-0	-0	-0	-0	0.1
1969 Mon-N	6	7	.462	31	15	2	1	1	106	119	7	50	59	14.5	4.84	76	.290	.369	4	.125	1	-15	-14	3	-1.0
1970 Mon-N	6	5	.545	57	1	0	0	5	89	81	7	40	42	12.4	3.13	131	.252	.339	0	.000	0	9	10	0	1.0
1971 Mon-N	2	3	.500	43	0	0	0	0	56²	66	8	24	25	14.3	4.29	82	.296	.364	0	—	-0	-5	-5	0	-0.4
Total 10	26	29	.473	229	35	3	1	9	515¹	510	41	208	268	12.7	3.72	96	.261	.334	6	.066	-1	-5	-9	4	-0.1
■ JERRY REED Reed, Jerry Maxwell b: 10/8/55, Bryson City, N.C. BR/TR, 6′1″, 190 lbs. Deb: 9/11/81																									
1981 Phi-N	0	1	.000	4	0	0	0	0	4²	7	0	6	5	25.1	7.71	47	.333	.481	0	—	0	-2	-2	0	-0.1
1982 Phi-N	1	0	1.000	7	0	0	0	0	8²	11	0	3	1	15.6	5.19	71	.324	.395	0	—	0	-2	-1	-0	-0.1
Cle-A	1	1	.500	6	1	0	0	0	15²	15	1	3	10	10.3	3.45	118	.250	.286	0	—	0	1	1	0	0.1
1983 Cle-A	0	0	—	7	0	0	0	0	21¹	26	4	9	11	14.8	7.17	59	.310	.376	0	—	0	-7	-7	1	-0.5
1985 Cle-A	3	5	.375	33	5	0	0	8	72¹	67	12	19	37	11.1	4.11	101	.245	.302	0	—	0	0	0	1	0.1
1986 Sea-A	4	0	1.000	11	4	0	0	0	34²	38	3	13	16	13.2	3.12	136	.273	.336	0	—	0	4	4	-0	0.4
1987 Sea-A	1	2	.333	39	1	0	0	7	81²	79	7	24	51	11.7	3.42	138	.255	.315	0	—	0	9	12	1	1.1
1988 Sea-A	1	1	.500	46	0	0	0	1	86¹	82	8	33	48	12.2	3.96	105	.256	.330	0	—	0	0	2	1	0.3
1989 Sea-A	7	7	.500	52	1	0	0	0	101²	89	10	43	50	11.8	3.19	126	.235	.314	0	—	0	8	9	0	1.0
1990 Sea-A	0	1	.000	4	0	0	0	0	7¹	8	1	3	2	13.5	4.91	81	.286	.355	0	—	0	-1	-1	0	0.0
Bos-A	2	1	.667	29	0	0	0	2	45	55	1	16	17	14.2	4.80	85	.302	.359	0	—	0	-4	-4	0	-0.3
Yr	2	2	.500	33	0	0	0	2	52¹	63	2	19	19	14.1	4.82	84	.300	.358	0	—	0	-5	-4	0	-0.3
Total 9	20	19	.513	238	12	0	0	18	479¹	477	47	172	248	12.4	3.94	107	.261	.328	0	—	0	6	14	3	2.0
■ RICK REED Reed, Richard Allen b: 8/16/64, Huntington, W.Va. BR/TR, 6′, 195 lbs. Deb: 8/08/88																									
1988 Pit-N	1	0	1.000	2	2	0	0	0	12	10	1	2	6	9.0	3.00	113	.233	.267	0	.000	-0	1	1	0	0.0
1989 Pit-N	1	4	.200	15	7	0	0	0	54²	62	5	11	34	12.3	5.60	60	.290	.330	1	.077	-0	-13	-14	-0	-1.3
1990 Pit-N	2	3	.400	13	8	1	1	1	53²	62	6	12	27	12.6	4.36	83	.279	.319	4	.250	1	-3	-4	0	-0.3
Total 3	4	7	.364	30	17	1	1	1	120¹	134	12	25	67	12.1	4.79	73	.280	.320	5	.152	1	-16	-18	-1	-1.6
■ BOB REED Reed, Robert Edward b: 1/12/45, Boston, Mass. BR/TR, 5′10″, 175 lbs. Deb: 9/05/69																									
1969 Det-A	0	0	—	8	1	0	0	0	14²	9	0	8	9	10.4	1.84	203	.184	.298	1	.500	0	3	3	0	0.4
1970 Det-A	2	4	.333	16	4	0	0	2	46¹	54	5	14	26	13.2	4.86	77	.292	.342	1	.083	-0	-6	-6	-0	-0.6
Total 2	2	4	.333	24	5	0	0	2	61	63	5	22	35	12.5	4.13	90	.269	.332	2	.143	-0	-3	-3	-0	-0.2
■ RON REED Reed, Ronald Lee b: 11/2/42, LaPorte, Ind. BR/TR, 6′6″, 215 lbs. Deb: 9/26/66																									
1966 Atl-N	1	1	.500	2	2	0	0	0	8¹	7	1	4	6	11.9	2.16	168	.226	.314	0	.000	-0	1	1	-0	0.1
1967 Atl-N	1	1	.500	3	3	0	0	0	21¹	21	1	3	11	11.0	2.95	112	.262	.306	0	.000	-1	1	1	1	0.1

YEAR TM/L	W	L	PCT	G	GS	CG	SH	SV	IP	H	HR	BB	SO	RAT	ERA	ERA+	OAV	OOB	BH	AVG	PB	PR	/A	PD	TPI
1968 Atl-N	11	10	.524	35	28	6	1	0	201²	189	10	49	111	10.9	3.35	89	.246	.297	10	.161	1	-8	-8	0	-0.7
1969 *Atl-N	18	10	.643	36	33	7	1	0	241¹	227	24	56	160	10.8	3.47	104	.246	.294	10	.125	-2	3	4	-1	0.1
1970 Atl-N	7	10	.412	21	18	6	0	0	134²	140	16	39	68	12.1	4.41	97	.266	.319	4	.091	-3	-5	-2	1	-0.2
1971 Atl-N	13	14	.481	32	32	8	1	0	222¹	221	26	54	129	11.2	3.72	100	.261	.306	11	.149	-3	-6	-0	-1	-0.3
1972 Atl-N	11	15	.423	31	30	11	1	0	213	222	18	60	111	12.2	3.93	96	.270	.325	13	.178	-1	-11	-3	1	-0.1
1973 Atl-N	4	11	.267	20	19	2	0	0	116¹	133	7	31	64	12.9	4.41	89	.287	.335	9	.200	0	-10	-6	1	-0.4
1974 Atl-N	10	11	.476	28	28	6	2	0	186	171	16	41	78	10.4	3.39	112	.243	.286	6	.105	-3	5	8	-1	0.3
1975 Atl-N	4	5	.444	10	10	1	0	0	74²	93	1	16	40	13.1	4.22	89	.304	.339	6	.231	1	-5	-4	-0	-0.2
StL-N	9	8	.529	24	24	7	2	0	175²	181	4	37	99	11.4	3.23	116	.263	.305	9	.161	-0	8	10	-1	1.0
Yr	13	13	.500	34	34	8	2	0	250¹	274	5	53	139	11.9	3.52	107	.275	.314	2	.024	1	3	7	-1	0.8
1976 *Phi-N	8	7	.533	59	4	1	0	14	128	88	8	32	96	8.6	2.46	144	.193	.249	4	.167	-0	15	15	-1	1.5
1977 *Phi-N	7	5	.583	60	3	0	0	15	124¹	101	9	37	84	10.1	2.75	145	.223	.283	2	.111	-0	16	17	-1	1.7
1978 *Phi-N	3	4	.429	66	0	0	0	17	108²	87	6	23	85	9.5	2.24	160	.223	.275	0	.000	-0	16	16	-2	1.5
1979 Phi-N	13	8	.619	61	0	0	0	5	102	110	9	32	58	12.7	4.15	92	.278	.335	3	.300	1	-5	-4	-0	-0.2
1980 *Phi-N	7	5	.583	55	0	0	0	9	91¹	88	4	30	54	11.7	4.04	94	.253	.314	3	.300	1	-4	-3	1	0.0
1981 *Phi-N	5	3	.625	39	0	0	0	8	61¹	54	6	17	40	10.6	3.08	118	.237	.293	3	.500	1	3	4	-1	0.5
1982 Phi-N	5	5	.500	57	2	0	0	14	98	85	4	24	57	10.3	2.66	138	.235	.289	4	.333	2	10	11	2	1.6
1983 *Phi-N	9	1	.900	61	0	0	0	8	95²	89	5	34	73	11.7	3.48	102	.248	.315	1	.167	-0	2	1	-2	0.0
1984 Chi-A	0	6	.000	51	0	0	0	12	73	67	7	14	57	10.1	3.08	135	.248	.288	0	.000	0	7	9	0	0.9
Total 19	146	140	.510	751	236	55	8	103	2477²	2374	182	633	1481	11.1	3.46	107	.252	.303	98	.158	-6	32	68	-2	7.2

■ **BILL REEDER**   Reeder, William Edgar b: 2/20/22, Dike, Texas BR/TR, 6'5", 205 lbs. Deb: 4/23/49

YEAR TM/L	W	L	PCT	G	GS	CG	SH	SV	IP	H	HR	BB	SO	RAT	ERA	ERA+	OAV	OOB	BH	AVG	PB	PR	/A	PD	TPI
1949 StL-N	1	1	.500	21	1	0	0	0	33²	33	2	30	21	17.1	5.08	82	.270	.418	0	.000	-0	-4	-3	-0	-0.3

■ **STAN REES**   Rees, Stanley Milton "Nellie" b: 2/25/1899, Cynthiana, Ky. d: 8/30/37, Lexington, Ky. BL/TL, 6'3", 190 lbs. Deb: 6/12/18

YEAR TM/L	W	L	PCT	G	GS	CG	SH	SV	IP	H	HR	BB	SO	RAT	ERA	ERA+	OAV	OOB	BH	AVG	PB	PR	/A	PD	TPI
1918 Was-A	1	0	1.000	2	0	0	0	0	2	3	0	4	1	31.5	0.00	—	.500	.700	0	—	0	1	1	0	0.1

■ **BOBBY REEVES**   Reeves, Robert Edwin "Gunner" b: 6/24/04, Hill City, Tenn. BR/TR, 5'11", 170 lbs. Deb: 6/09/26 ♦

YEAR TM/L	W	L	PCT	G	GS	CG	SH	SV	IP	H	HR	BB	SO	RAT	ERA	ERA+	OAV	OOB	BH	AVG	PB	PR	/A	PD	TPI
1931 Bos-A	0	0	—	1	0	0	0	0	7¹	6	0	1	0	8.6	3.68	117	.214	.241	14	.167	0	1	1	0	0.0

■ **MIKE REGAN**   Regan, Michael Joseph b: 11/19/1887, Phoenix, N.Y. d: 5/22/61, Albany, N.Y. BR/TR, 5'11", 165 lbs. Deb: 5/13/17

YEAR TM/L	W	L	PCT	G	GS	CG	SH	SV	IP	H	HR	BB	SO	RAT	ERA	ERA+	OAV	OOB	BH	AVG	PB	PR	/A	PD	TPI
1917 Cin-N	11	10	.524	32	26	16	1	0	216	228	4	41	50	11.4	2.71	97	.273	.310	15	.200	1	0	-2	3	0.2
1918 Cin-N	5	5	.500	22	6	4	3	2	80	77	0	29	15	11.9	3.26	82	.262	.328	8	.296	2	-4	-5	-0	-0.3
1919 Cin-N	0	0	—	1	0	0	0	0	2¹	1	0	1	0	3.9	0.00	—	.143	.143	0	.000	-0	1	1	0	0.1
Total 3	16	15	.516	55	32	20	4	2	298¹	306	4	70	66	11.5	2.84	93	.269	.314	23	.223	3	-4	-7	3	-0.0

■ **PHIL REGAN**   Regan, Philip Raymond "The Vulture" b: 4/6/37, Otsego, Mich. BR/TR, 6'3", 200 lbs. Deb: 7/19/60 C

YEAR TM/L	W	L	PCT	G	GS	CG	SH	SV	IP	H	HR	BB	SO	RAT	ERA	ERA+	OAV	OOB	BH	AVG	PB	PR	/A	PD	TPI
1960 Det-A	0	4	.000	17	7	0	0	1	68	70	11	25	38	12.8	4.50	88	.267	.336	1	.059	-1	-5	-4	-1	-0.5
1961 Det-A	10	7	.588	32	16	6	0	2	120	134	19	41	46	13.2	5.25	78	.281	.339	3	.075	-2	-16	-15	-2	-1.8
1962 Det-A	11	9	.550	35	23	6	0	0	171¹	169	23	64	87	12.3	4.04	101	.254	.320	13	.206	1	-1	0	-2	0.0
1963 Det-A	15	9	.625	38	27	5	1	1	189	179	33	59	115	11.7	3.86	97	.245	.308	9	.143	-1	-5	-2	-3	-0.5
1964 Det-A	5	10	.333	32	21	2	0	1	146²	162	21	49	91	13.3	5.03	73	.282	.344	13	.317	5	-23	-22	0	-1.7
1965 Det-A	1	5	.167	16	7	1	0	0	51²	57	6	20	37	13.4	5.05	69	.282	.347	1	.083	-0	-9	-9	-0	-0.9
1966 *LA-N	14	1	.933	65	0	0	0	21	116²	85	6	24	88	8.4	1.62	203	.207	.251	3	.143	0	26	22	1	2.4
1967 LA-N	6	9	.400	55	3	0	0	6	96¹	108	2	32	53	13.3	2.99	104	.284	.343	1	.100	0	4	1	1	0.2
1968 LA-N	2	0	1.000	5	0	0	0	0	7²	10	1	1	7	12.9	3.52	78	.313	.333	0	.000	-0	-0	-1	-0	0.0
Chi-N	10	5	.667	68	0	0	0	25	127	109	9	24	60	9.6	2.20	144	.232	.272	3	.150	0	11	14	1	1.7
Yr	12	5	.706	73	0	0	0	25	134²	119	10	25	67	9.8	2.27	138	.237	.276	1	.048	0	11	13	0	1.7
1969 Chi-N	12	6	.667	71	0	0	0	17	112	120	6	35	56	12.6	3.70	109	.282	.339	1	.067	-0	-1	4	1	0.5
1970 Chi-N	5	9	.357	54	0	0	0	12	75²	81	8	32	31	13.6	4.76	95	.287	.362	0	.000	-1	-6	-2	2	0.0
1971 Chi-N	5	5	.500	48	1	0	0	6	73¹	84	4	33	28	14.6	3.93	100	.301	.379	1	.000	-1	-4	0	1	0.1
1972 Chi-N	0	1	.000	5	0	0	0	0	4	6	0	2	2	18.0	2.25	169	.400	.471	0	—	0	1	1	0	0.1
Chi-A	0	1	.000	10	0	0	0	0	13¹	18	1	6	4	16.9	4.05	77	.346	.424	1	1.000	0	-1	-1	0	0.0
Total 13	96	81	.542	551	105	20	1	92	1372²	1392	150	447	743	12.2	3.84	97	.265	.325	49	.153	1	-31	-16	-1	-0.4

■ **EARL REID**   Reid, Earl Percy b: 6/8/13, Bangor, Ala. d: 5/11/84, Cullman, Ala. BL/TR, 6'3", 190 lbs. Deb: 5/08/46

YEAR TM/L	W	L	PCT	G	GS	CG	SH	SV	IP	H	HR	BB	SO	RAT	ERA	ERA+	OAV	OOB	BH	AVG	PB	PR	/A	PD	TPI
1946 Bos-N	1	0	1.000	2	0	0	0	0	3	4	0	3	2	21.0	3.00	114	.308	.438	0	—	0	0	0	0	0.0

■ **BILL REIDY**   Reidy, William Joseph b: 10/9/1873, Cleveland, Ohio d: 10/14/15, Cleveland, Ohio BR/TR, 5'10", 175 lbs. Deb: 7/21/1896

YEAR TM/L	W	L	PCT	G	GS	CG	SH	SV	IP	H	HR	BB	SO	RAT	ERA	ERA+	OAV	OOB	BH	AVG	PB	PR	/A	PD	TPI
1896 NY-N	0	1	.000	2	1	1	0	1	13	24	1	2	1	18.0	7.62	55	.391	.411	0	.000	-1	-5	-5	0	-0.3
1899 Bro-N	1	0	1.000	2	1	1	0	1	7	9	0	2	2	14.1	2.57	152	.311	.356	0	.000	-1	1	1	0	0.1
1901 Mil-A	16	20	.444	37	33	28	2	0	301¹	364	14	62	50	12.7	4.21	85	.295	.329	16	.143	-6	-18	-21	-2	-2.5
1902 StL-A	3	5	.375	12	9	7	0	0	95	111	0	13	16	11.7	4.45	79	.292	.315	8	.195	-0	-9	-10	1	-0.7
1903 StL-A	1	4	.200	5	5	5	1	0	43	53	1	7	8	12.6	3.98	73	.302	.329	1	.067	-0	-5	-5	-1	-0.6
Bro-N	6	7	.462	15	13	11	0	0	104	130	6	14	21	13.0	3.46	92	.315	.346	9	.243	1	-2	-3	-1	-0.2
1904 Bro-N	0	4	.000	6	4	2	0	1	38¹	49	0	6	11	13.4	4.46	62	.293	.326	5	.156	-0	-7	-7	-0	-0.7
Total 6	27	41	.397	79	66	55	3	2	601²	740	15	106	109	12.8	4.17	82	.301	.332	39	.159	-9	-46	-50	-3	-4.9

■ **ART REINHART**   Reinhart, Arthur Conrad b: 5/29/1899, Ackley, Iowa d: 11/11/46, Houston, Tex. BL/TL, 6'1", 170 lbs. Deb: 4/26/19

YEAR TM/L	W	L	PCT	G	GS	CG	SH	SV	IP	H	HR	BB	SO	RAT	ERA	ERA+	OAV	OOB	BH	AVG	PB	PR	/A	PD	TPI
1919 StL-N	0	0	—	1	0	0	0	0	0	0	0	0	0	—	—	—	1.000		0	—	0	0	0	0	0.0
1925 StL-N	11	5	.688	20	16	15	1	0	144²	149	7	47	26	12.4	3.05	142	.278	.341	22	.328	5	20	20	0	2.6
1926 *StL-N	10	5	.667	27	11	9	0	0	143	159	5	47	26	13.2	4.22	93	.295	.355	20	.317	4	-6	-5	1	0.1
1927 StL-N	5	2	.714	21	9	4	2	1	81²	82	5	36	15	13.0	4.19	94	.267	.344	10	.313	2	-2	-2	-1	0.0
1928 StL-N	4	6	.400	23	9	3	1	2	75¹	80	3	27	12	12.8	2.87	139	.272	.333	4	.167	-0	9	9	-0	0.9
Total 5	30	18	.625	92	45	31	4	3	444²	470	20	157	79	12.9	3.60	113	.280	.345	56	.301	11	20	23	0	3.6

■ **JACK REIS**   Reis, Harrie Crane b: 6/14/1890, Cincinnati, Ohio d: 7/20/39, Cincinnati, Ohio BR/TR, 5'10.5", 160 lbs. Deb: 9/09/11

YEAR TM/L	W	L	PCT	G	GS	CG	SH	SV	IP	H	HR	BB	SO	RAT	ERA	ERA+	OAV	OOB	BH	AVG	PB	PR	/A	PD	TPI
1911 StL-N	0	0	—	3	0	0	0	0	9¹	5	0	8	4	12.5	0.96	350	.156	.325	0	.000	-0	3	3	0	0.3

■ **LAURIE REIS**   Reis, Lawrence P. b: 11/20/1858, Illinois d: 1/24/21, Chicago, Ill. BR/TR, 160 lbs. Deb: 10/01/1877

YEAR TM/L	W	L	PCT	G	GS	CG	SH	SV	IP	H	HR	BB	SO	RAT	ERA	ERA+	OAV	OOB	BH	AVG	PB	PR	/A	PD	TPI
1877 Chi-N	3	1	.750	4	4	4	1	0	36	29	1	6	11	8.8	0.75	396	.208	.240	2	.125	-2	8	9	-0	0.7
1878 Chi-N	1	3	.250	4	4	4	0	0	36	55	0	4	8	14.3	3.25	75	.334	.350	3	.150	-1	-4	-3	-1	-0.4
Total 2	4	4	.500	8	8	8	1	0	72	84	1	10	19	11.8	2.00	135	.276	.299	5	.139	-2	4	6	-2	0.3

■ **BOBBY REIS**   Reis, Robert Joseph Thomas b: 1/2/09, Woodside, N.Y. d: 5/1/73, St.Paul, Minn. BR/TR, 6'1", 175 lbs. Deb: 9/19/31 ♦

YEAR TM/L	W	L	PCT	G	GS	CG	SH	SV	IP	H	HR	BB	SO	RAT	ERA	ERA+	OAV	OOB	BH	AVG	PB	PR	/A	PD	TPI
1935 Bro-N	3	2	.600	14	2	1	0	2	41¹	46	0	24	7	15.5	2.83	140	.277	.372	21	.247	1	5	5	1	0.5
1936 Bos-N	6	5	.545	35	5	3	0	0	138²	152	7	74	25	15.0	4.48	86	.283	.375	13	.217	1	-7	-10	4	-0.4
1937 Bos-N	0	0	—	4	0	0	0	0	5	3	0	5	0	14.4	1.80	198	.158	.333	21	.244	1	1	1	0	0.1
1938 Bos-N	1	6	.143	16	2	1	0	0	57²	61	5	41	20	16.9	4.99	69	.271	.397	9	.184	-0	-8	-10	-0	-0.9
Total 4	10	13	.435	69	9	5	0	2	242²	262	12	144	52	15.5	4.27	88	.277	.379	70	.233	3	-8	-14	5	-0.7

■ **TOMMY REIS**   Reis, Thomas Edward b: 8/6/14, Newport, Ky. BR/TR, 6'2", 180 lbs. Deb: 4/27/38

YEAR TM/L	W	L	PCT	G	GS	CG	SH	SV	IP	H	HR	BB	SO	RAT	ERA	ERA+	OAV	OOB	BH	AVG	PB	PR	/A	PD	TPI
1938 Phi-N	0	1	.000	4	0	0	0	0	4²	8	0	8	2	30.9	19.29	20	.364	.533	0	.000	-0	-8	-8	0	-0.6
Bos-N	0	0	—	4	0	0	0	0	6¹	8	1	1	4	12.8	7.11	48	.296	.321	0	—	0	-2	-3	-0	-0.2
Yr	0	1	.000	8	0	0	0	0	11	16	1	9	6	20.5	12.27	30	.327	.431	0	.000	-0	-10	-11	-0	-0.8

YEAR TM/L	W	L	PCT	G	GS	CG	SH	SV	IP	H	HR	BB	SO	RAT	ERA	ERA+	OAV	OOB	BH	AVG	PB	PR	/A	PD	TPI
■ **BUGS REISIGL** Reisigl, Jacob b: 12/12/1887, Brooklyn, N.Y. d: 2/24/57, Amsterdam, N.Y. BR/TR, 5'10.5", 175 lbs. Deb: 9/20/11																									
1911 Cle-A	0	1	.000	2	1	1	0	0	13	13	1	3	6	11.1	6.23	55	.271	.314	0	.000	-1	-4	-4	0	-0.3
■ **DOC REISLING** Reisling, Frank Carl b: 7/25/1874, Martins Ferry, O. d: 3/4/55, Tulsa, Okla. BR/TR, 5'10", 180 lbs. Deb: 9/10/04																									
1904 Bro-N	3	4	.429	7	7	6	1	0	51	45	0	10	19	11.3	2.12	130	.238	.308	2	.154	-0	4	4	0	0.4
1905 Bro-N	0	1	.000	2	0	0	0	0	3	3	0	4	2	21.0	3.00	96	.273	.467	0	.000	0	0	-0	0	0.0
1909 Was-A	2	4	.333	10	6	6	1	0	66²	70	0	17	22	11.7	2.43	100	.270	.315	4	.167	0	0	0	-1	0.0
1910 Was-A	10	10	.500	30	20	13	2	1	191	185	3	44	57	11.0	2.54	98	.264	.312	12	.200	2	-1	-1	1	0.2
Total 4	15	19	.441	49	33	25	4	1	311²	303	3	75	100	11.3	2.45	103	.261	.314	18	.184	2	3	2	0	0.6
■ **WIN REMMERSWAAL** Remmerswaal, Wilhelmus Abraham b: 3/8/54, The Hague, Holland BR/TR, 6'2", 160 lbs. Deb: 8/03/79																									
1979 Bos-A	1	0	1.000	8	0	0	0	0	20¹	26	1	12	16	17.3	7.08	62	.317	.411	0	—	0	-6	-6	-0	-0.5
1980 Bos-A	2	1	.667	14	0	0	0	0	35¹	39	4	9	20	12.2	4.58	92	.295	.340	0	—	0	-2	-1	-1	-0.1
Total 2	3	1	.750	22	0	0	0	0	55²	65	5	21	36	14.1	5.50	78	.304	.369	0	—	0	-9	-7	-1	-0.6
■ **ALEX REMNEAS** Remneas, Alexander Norman b: 2/21/1886, Minneapolis, Minn. d: 8/27/75, Phoenix, Ariz. BR/TR, 6'1", 180 lbs. Deb: 4/15/12																									
1912 Det-A	0	0	—	1	0	0	0	0	1²	5	0	0	0	27.0	27.00	12	.455	.455	0	—	-0	-4	-4	0	-0.2
1915 StL-A	0	0	—	2	0	0	0	0	6	3	0	3	5	10.5	1.50	191	.136	.269	0	.000	-0	1	1	0	0.1
Total 2	0	0	—	3	0	0	0	0	7²	8	0	3	5	14.1	7.04	42	.242	.324	0	.000	0	-3	-3	0	-0.1
■ **ERWIN RENFER** Renfer, Erwin Arthur b: 12/11/1891, Elgin, Ill. d: 10/26/57, Sycamore, Ill. BR/TR, 6', 180 lbs. Deb: 9/18/13																									
1913 Det-A	0	1	.000	1	1	0	0	0	6	5	0	3	1	13.5	6.00	49	.227	.346	0	.000	-0	-2	-2	0	-0.1
■ **MARSHALL RENFROE** Renfroe, Marshall Daniel b: 5/25/36, Century, Fla. d: 12/10/70, Pensacola, Fla. BL/TL, 6', 180 lbs. Deb: 9/27/59																									
1959 SF-N	0	0	—	1	1	0	0	0	2	3	1	3	3	27.0	27.00	14	.333	.500	0	.000	-0	-5	-5	0	-0.3
■ **HAL RENIFF** Reniff, Harold Eugene "Porky" b: 7/2/38, Warren, Ohio BR/TR, 6', 215 lbs. Deb: 6/08/61																									
1961 NY-A	2	0	1.000	25	0	0	0	2	45¹	31	1	31	21	12.3	2.58	144	.197	.330	0	.000	-1	7	6	-0	0.5
1962 NY-A	0	0	—	2	0	0	0	0	3²	6	0	5	1	29.5	7.36	51	.400	.571	0	—	-0	-1	-1	-0	-0.1
1963 *NY-A	4	3	.571	48	0	0	0	18	89¹	63	3	42	56	10.8	2.62	134	.202	.301	0	.000	-1	10	9	3	1.1
1964 *NY-A	6	4	.600	41	0	0	0	9	69¹	47	3	30	38	10.0	3.12	116	.199	.289	1	.100	-1	4	4	0	0.4
1965 NY-A	3	4	.429	51	0	0	0	3	85¹	74	4	48	74	13.4	3.80	90	.232	.341	0	.000	-0	-3	-4	-1	-0.4
1966 NY-A	3	7	.300	56	0	0	0	9	95¹	80	2	49	79	12.7	3.21	104	.229	.333	4	.286	1	2	1	-1	0.1
1967 NY-A	0	2	.000	24	0	0	0	0	40	40	0	14	24	12.8	4.27	73	.256	.329	0	.000	-0	-5	-5	-0	-0.5
NY-N	3	3	.500	29	0	0	0	4	43	42	1	23	21	13.8	3.35	101	.266	.363	0	.000	-0	0	0	-1	0.0
Total 7	21	23	.477	276	0	0	0	45	471¹	383	14	242	314	12.3	3.27	106	.225	.327	5	.096	-2	14	10	-0	1.1
■ **JIM RENINGER** Reninger, James David b: 3/7/13, Aurora, Ill. BR/TR, 6'3", 210 lbs. Deb: 9/17/38																									
1938 Phi-A	0	2	.000	4	4	1	0	0	22²	28	3	14	9	16.7	7.15	68	.295	.385	0	.000	-0	-6	-6	0	-0.4
1939 Phi-A	0	2	.000	4	2	0	0	0	16¹	24	3	12	3	19.8	7.71	61	.369	.468	1	.167	-0	-6	-5	0	-0.4
Total 2	0	4	.000	8	6	1	0	0	39	52	6	26	12	18.0	7.38	65	.325	.419	1	.077	-1	-12	-11	0	-0.8
■ **STEVE RENKO** Renko, Steven b: 12/10/44, Kansas City, Kan. BR/TR, 6'5", 230 lbs. Deb: 6/27/69																									
1969 Mon-N	6	7	.462	18	15	4	0	0	103¹	94	14	50	68	12.7	4.01	92	.243	.333	6	.167	1	-5	-4	-1	-0.3
1970 Mon-N	13	11	.542	41	33	7	1	1	222²	203	27	104	142	12.7	4.32	95	.241	.329	16	.200	2	-7	-5	-0	-0.2
1971 Mon-N	15	14	.517	40	37	9	3	0	275²	256	24	135	129	12.9	3.75	94	.247	.336	21	.210	4	-9	-7	-1	-0.3
1972 Mon-N	1	10	.091	30	12	0	0	0	97	96	11	67	66	15.1	5.20	68	.262	.376	7	.292	1	-19	-18	1	-1.5
1973 Mon-N	15	11	.577	36	34	9	0	1	249²	201	26	108	164	11.2	2.81	136	.218	.300	24	.273	8	24	28	-2	3.8
1974 Mon-N	12	16	.429	37	35	8	1	0	227²	222	17	81	138	12.0	4.03	95	.257	.321	17	.210	3	-10	-5	3	0.2
1975 Mon-N	6	12	.333	31	25	3	1	1	170¹	175	20	76	99	13.3	4.07	94	.265	.341	15	.278	5	-8	-5	-0	0.1
1976 Mon-N	0	1	.000	5	1	0	0	0	13	15	2	3	4	12.5	5.54	67	.288	.327	1	.333	-0	-3	-3	-0	-0.2
Chi-N	8	11	.421	28	27	4	1	0	163¹	164	12	43	112	11.4	3.86	100	.258	.305	5	.094	-4	-6	0	-1	-0.4
Yr	8	12	.400	33	28	4	1	0	176¹	179	14	46	116	11.5	3.98	97	.260	.307	6	—	-3	-9	-3	-2	-0.6
1977 Chi-N	2	2	.500	13	8	0	0	1	51¹	51	10	21	34	12.8	4.56	96	.258	.332	2	.167	0	-4	-1	-1	-0.1
Chi-A	5	0	1.000	8	8	0	0	0	53¹	55	3	17	36	12.3	3.54	115	.274	.333	0	—	0	3	3	0	0.3
1978 Oak-A	6	12	.333	27	25	3	1	0	151	152	10	67	89	13.2	4.29	85	.265	.344	0	—	0	-9	-11	-0	-1.0
1979 Bos-A	11	9	.550	27	27	4	1	0	171	174	22	53	99	12.1	4.11	107	.260	.317	0	—	0	2	6	-1	0.5
1980 Bos-A	9	9	.500	32	23	1	0	0	165¹	180	17	56	90	12.9	4.19	101	.281	.340	0	—	0	-3	0	-1	0.0
1981 Cal-A	8	4	.667	22	15	0	0	1	102	93	7	42	50	12.0	3.44	106	.250	.328	0	—	0	2	2	-2	0.1
1982 Cal-A	11	6	.647	31	23	4	0	0	156	163	17	51	81	12.4	4.44	91	.269	.327	0	—	0	-6	-7	-2	-0.7
1983 KC-A	6	11	.353	25	17	1	0	1	121¹	144	9	36	54	13.4	4.30	95	.293	.341	0	—	0	-3	-3	-1	-0.3
Total 15	134	146	.479	451	365	57	9	6	2494	2438	248	1010	1455	12.5	3.99	98	.256	.329	114	.215	21	-62	-27	-8	0.0
■ **ANDY REPLOGLE** Replogle, Andrew David b: 10/7/53, South Bend, Ind. BR/TR, 6'5", 205 lbs. Deb: 4/11/78																									
1978 Mil-A	9	5	.643	32	18	3	2	0	149¹	177	14	47	41	13.6	3.92	96	.301	.353	0	—	0	-3	-3	-2	-0.4
1979 Mil-A	0	0	—	3	0	0	0	0	8	13	0	2	2	16.9	5.63	74	.382	.417	0	—	0	-1	-1	0	0.0
Total 2	9	5	.643	35	18	3	2	0	157¹	190	14	49	43	13.7	4.00	94	.305	.357	0	—	0	-4	-4	-2	-0.4
■ **XAVIER RESCIGNO** Rescigno, Xavier Frederick "Mr. X" b: 10/13/13, New York, N.Y. BR/TR, 5'10.5", 175 lbs. Deb: 4/22/43																									
1943 Pit-N	6	9	.400	37	14	5	1	2	132²	125	6	45	41	11.7	2.98	117	.252	.317	5	.143	0	6	7	-2	0.6
1944 Pit-N	10	8	.556	48	6	2	0	5	124	146	9	34	45	13.1	4.35	85	.291	.337	2	.091	-1	-10	-9	-0	-0.9
1945 Pit-N	3	5	.375	44	1	0	0	9	78²	95	6	34	29	14.9	5.72	69	.303	.372	2	.133	-0	-17	-16	-1	-1.5
Total 3	19	22	.463	129	21	7	1	16	335¹	366	21	113	115	13.0	4.13	89	.279	.338	9	.125	-1	-21	-17	-3	-1.8
■ **GEORGE RETTGER** Rettger, George Edward b: 7/29/1868, Cleveland, Ohio d: 6/5/21, Lakewood, Ohio TR, 5'11", 175 lbs. Deb: 8/13/1891																									
1891 StL-a	7	3	.700	14	12	10	1	1	92²	85	4	51	49	13.2	3.40	124	.236	.330	3	.071	-4	3	8	-1	0.4
1892 Cle-N	1	3	.250	6	5	3	0	0	38	32	2	31	12	14.9	4.26	80	.219	.356	2	.133	-0	-4	-4	-0	-0.3
Cin-N	1	0	1.000	1	1	1	0	0	9	8	0	10	1	18.0	4.00	82	.229	.400	1	.125	-0	-1	-1	0	0.0
Yr	2	3	.400	7	6	4	0	0	47	40	2	41	13	15.5	4.21	80	.221	.365	4	.174	-0	-5	-4	-0	-0.3
Total 2	9	6	.600	21	18	14	1	1	139²	125	6	92	62	14.0	3.67	107	.231	.342	6	.092	-4	-1	4	-1	0.1
■ **OTTO RETTIG** Rettig, Adolph John b: 1/29/1894, New York, N.Y. d: 6/16/77, Stuart, Fla. BR/TR, 5'11", 165 lbs. Deb: 7/19/22																									
1922 Phi-A	1	2	.333	4	4	1	0	0	18¹	18	0	12	3	15.2	4.91	87	.265	.383	0	.000	-1	-2	-1	0	-0.1
■ **ED REULBACH** Reulbach, Edward Marvin "Big Ed" b: 12/1/1882, Detroit, Mich. d: 7/17/61, Glens Falls, N.Y. BR/TR, 6'1", 190 lbs. Deb: 5/16/05																									
1905 Chi-N	18	14	.563	34	29	28	5	1	292	208	1	73	152	9.2	1.42	210	**.201**	.266	14	.127	-5	51	51	-2	4.9
1906 *Chi-N	19	4	**.826**	33	24	20	6	3	218	129	2	92	94	9.7	1.65	160	.175	.278	13	.157	-2	24	24	2	2.9
1907 *Chi-N	17	4	**.810**	27	22	16	4	0	192	147	1	64	96	10.3	1.69	148	.217	.294	11	.175	-0	17	17	0	2.1
1908 *Chi-N	24	7	**.774**	46	35	25	7	1	297²	227	4	106	133	10.4	2.03	116	.214	.292	23	.232	7	11	11	-1	1.9
1909 Chi-N	19	10	.655	35	32	23	6	0	262²	194	1	82	105	9.8	1.78	143	.212	.285	12	.140	-1	24	22	5	3.0
1910 *Chi-N	12	8	.600	24	23	14	1	0	173¹	162	1	49	56	11.4	3.12	92	.251	.313	6	.107	-3	-2	-5	-1	-0.6
1911 Chi-N	16	9	.640	33	29	15	2	0	221²	191	3	103	79	12.1	2.96	112	.236	.325	6	.090	-1	11	9	3	1.1
1912 Chi-N	10	6	.625	39	19	8	0	4	169	161	7	60	75	12.2	3.78	88	.252	.323	6	.109	-3	-7	-8	4	-0.6
1913 Chi-N	1	3	.250	10	2	1	0	0	38²	41	1	21	10	14.7	4.42	72	.281	.375	3	.250	0	-5	-5	0	-0.4
Bro-N	7	6	.538	15	12	8	2	0	110	77	3	34	46	9.4	2.05	161	.202	.274	3	.103	0	14	15	-1	1.6

YEAR	TM/L	W	L	PCT	G	GS	CG	SH	SV	IP	H	HR	BB	SO	RAT	ERA	ERA+	OAV	OOB	BH	AVG	PB	PR	/A	PD	TPI
	Yr	8	9	.471	25	14	9	2	0	148²	118	4	55	56	10.7	2.66	123	.223	.301	8	.195	0	9	10	-0	1.2
1914	Bro-N	11	18	.379	44	29	14	3	3	256	228	5	83	119	11.3	2.64	108	.242	.310	9	.122	-0	4	6	1	0.8
1915	New-F	21	10	.677	33	30	23	4	1	270	233	3	69	117	10.2	2.23	127	.236	.287	18	.196	-0	24	18	1	2.1
1916	Bos-N	7	6	.538	21	11	6	0	0	109¹	99	4	47	11	11.9	2.47	101	.251	.328	3	.091	-1	2	0	5	0.5
1917	Bos-N	0	1	.000	5	2	0	0	0	22¹	21	0	15	9	14.9	2.82	90	.256	.378	0	.000	1	-0	-1	1	0.1
Total	13	182	106	.632	399	299	201	40	13	2632²	2118	33	892	1138	10.7	2.28	123	.224	.298	127	.147	-9	168	156	22	19.4

■ PAUL REUSCHEL

Reuschel, Paul Richard   b: 1/12/47, Quincy, Ill.   BR/TR, 6'4", 225 lbs.   Deb: 7/25/75

YEAR	TM/L	W	L	PCT	G	GS	CG	SH	SV	IP	H	HR	BB	SO	RAT	ERA	ERA+	OAV	OOB	BH	AVG	PB	PR	/A	PD	TPI
1975	Chi-N	1	3	.250	28	0	0	0	5	36	44	1	13	12	14.5	3.50	110	.312	.374	0	.000	-0	0	1	0	0.1
1976	Chi-N	4	2	.667	50	2	0	0	3	87	94	12	33	55	13.2	4.55	85	.278	.344	2	.154	-0	-10	-7	1	-0.5
1977	Chi-N	5	6	.455	69	0	0	0	4	107	105	9	40	62	12.2	4.37	100	.262	.329	0	.000	-2	-6	0	2	0.1
1978	Chi-N	2	0	1.000	16	0	0	0	0	28	29	4	13	13	13.8	5.14	78	.269	.352	0	.000	-1	-5	-3	0	-0.3
	Cle-A	2	4	.333	18	6	1	0	0	89²	95	5	22	24	11.9	3.11	120	.271	.318	0	—	0	6	6	1	0.8
1979	Cle-A	2	1	.667	17	1	0	0	1	45¹	73	7	11	22	16.7	7.94	54	.365	.398	0	—	0	-19	-19	1	-1.6
Total	5	16	16	.500	198	9	1	0	13	393	440	38	132	188	13.2	4.51	89	.286	.344	2	.063	-2	-32	-21	5	-1.4

■ RICK REUSCHEL

Reuschel, Rickey Eugene   b: 5/16/49, Quincy, Ill.   BR/TR, 6'3", 215 lbs.   Deb: 6/19/72

YEAR	TM/L	W	L	PCT	G	GS	CG	SH	SV	IP	H	HR	BB	SO	RAT	ERA	ERA+	OAV	OOB	BH	AVG	PB	PR	/A	PD	TPI
1972	Chi-N	10	8	.556	21	18	5	4	0	129	127	3	29	87	11.0	2.93	130	.259	.303	6	.136	-1	7	13	-0	1.3
1973	Chi-N	14	15	.483	36	36	7	3	0	237	244	15	62	168	11.8	3.00	131	.263	.312	9	.123	-3	17	25	4	2.7
1974	Chi-N	13	12	.520	41	38	8	2	0	240²	262	18	83	160	13.1	4.30	89	.276	.338	19	.221	2	-18	-13	4	-0.6
1975	Chi-N	11	17	.393	38	37	6	0	1	234	244	17	67	155	12.2	3.73	103	.268	.323	16	.208	3	-3	3	3	0.8
1976	Chi-N	14	12	.538	38	37	9	2	1	260	260	17	64	146	11.5	3.46	111	.265	.315	19	.229	4	1	11	3	2.2
1977	Chi-N	20	10	.667	39	37	8	4	1	252	233	14	74	166	11.1	2.79	157	.247	.305	18	.207	2	31	45	3	5.6
1978	Chi-N	14	15	.483	35	35	9	1	0	242²	235	16	54	115	10.9	3.41	118	.254	.299	10	.137	-1	4	17	2	2.0
1979	Chi-N	18	12	.600	36	36	5	1	0	239	251	16	75	125	12.7	3.62	114	.274	.335	13	.165	1	3	13	5	2.1
1980	Chi-N	11	13	.458	38	38	6	0	0	257	281	13	76	140	12.6	3.40	115	.286	.340	13	.159	-1	6	15	5	2.1
1981	Chi-N	4	7	.364	13	13	1	0	0	85²	87	4	23	53	12.0	3.47	107	.263	.323	2	.080	-2	0	2	1	0.2
	*NY-A	4	4	.500	12	11	3	0	0	70²	75	4	10	22	11.0	2.67	134	.280	.308	0	—	0	8	7	1	0.9
1983	Chi-N	1	1	.500	4	4	0	0	0	20²	18	1	10	9	12.2	3.92	97	.234	.322	1	.143	-0	-1	-0	1	0.1
1984	Chi-N	5	5	.500	19	14	1	0	0	92¹	123	7	23	43	14.5	5.17	76	.339	.363	3	.241	2	-16	-13	1	-0.8
1985	Pit-N	14	8	.636	31	26	9	1	1	194	153	7	52	138	9.6	2.27	157	.215	.272	10	.169	1	28	28	4	3.9
1986	Pit-N	9	16	.360	35	34	4	2	0	215²	232	20	57	125	12.4	3.96	97	.274	.326	11	.157	0	-6	-3	3	0.0
1987	Pit-N	8	6	.571	25	25	9	3	0	177	163	9	35	80	10.4	2.75	150	.246	.290	9	.150	2	26	27	2	3.2
	*SF-N	5	3	.625	9	8	3	1	0	50	44	1	7	27	9.5	4.32	89	.230	.265	2	.105	-0	-1	-3	0	-0.1
	Yr	13	9	.591	34	33	**12**	**4**	0	227	207	13	42	107	**10.0**	3.09	131	.239	.276	5	.063	2	25	24	2	3.1
1988	SF-N	19	11	.633	36	36	7	2	0	245	242	11	42	92	10.7	3.12	104	.260	.297	8	.110	-1	9	4	-1	0.0
1989	*SF-N	17	8	.680	32	32	2	0	0	208¹	195	18	54	111	10.8	2.94	115	.247	.297	10	.164	1	13	10	0	1.1
1990	SF-N	3	6	.333	15	13	0	0	1	87	102	8	31	49	13.9	3.93	95	.297	.357	4	.154	0	-1	-2	0	-0.1
Total	18	214	189	.531	553	528	102	26	5	3537²	3571	221	928	2011	11.7	3.37	114	.264	.315	187	.168	9	109	185	41	26.6

■ JERRY REUSS

Reuss, Jerry   b: 6/19/49, St.Louis, Mo.   BL/TL, 6'5", 200 lbs.   Deb: 9/27/69

YEAR	TM/L	W	L	PCT	G	GS	CG	SH	SV	IP	H	HR	BB	SO	RAT	ERA	ERA+	OAV	OOB	BH	AVG	PB	PR	/A	PD	TPI
1969	StL-N	1	0	1.000	1	1	0	0	0	7	2	0	3	3	9.0	0.00	—	.091	.259	1	.333	0	3	3	0	0.4
1970	StL-N	7	8	.467	20	20	5	2	0	127¹	132	9	49	74	12.9	4.10	100	.271	.339	2	.050	-3	-1	-0	-0	-0.1
1971	StL-N	14	14	.500	36	35	7	2	0	211	228	15	109	131	14.7	4.78	75	.279	.368	8	.123	0	-31	-28	-2	-2.9
1972	Hou-N	9	13	.409	33	30	4	1	1	192	177	14	83	174	12.7	4.17	81	.246	.332	7	.106	-1	-15	-17	-1	-1.9
1973	Hou-N	16	13	.552	41	40	12	3	0	279¹	271	17	117	177	12.6	3.74	97	.256	.332	13	.137	-1	-2	-3	-2	-0.6
1974	*Pit-N	16	11	.593	35	35	14	1	0	260	259	20	101	105	12.5	3.50	99	.261	.339	13	.151	0	4	-1	-1	-0.3
1975	*Pit-N	18	11	.621	32	32	15	6	0	237¹	224	10	78	131	11.5	2.54	139	.253	.314	14	.197	2	28	26	2	3.4
1976	Pit-N	14	9	.609	31	29	11	3	2	209¹	209	16	51	108	11.3	3.53	99	.256	.301	16	.242	6	-1	-1	-2	0.3
1977	Pit-N	10	13	.435	33	33	8	2	0	208	225	11	71	116	13.0	4.11	97	.280	.341	12	.171	1	-5	-3	1	0.0
1978	Pit-N	3	2	.600	23	12	3	1	0	82²	97	5	23	42	13.4	4.90	76	.297	.348	5	.185	0	-12	-11	-0	-1.0
1979	LA-N	7	14	.333	39	21	4	1	3	160	178	4	60	83	13.6	3.54	103	.282	.347	7	.167	1	3	2	2	0.4
1980	LA-N	18	6	.750	37	29	10	**6**	3	229¹	193	12	40	111	9.1	2.51	139	.227	.261	6	.088	-1	28	25	2	2.8
1981	*LA-N	10	4	.714	22	22	8	2	0	152²	138	6	27	51	10.0	2.30	144	.243	.282	10	.196	0	20	17	3	2.4
1982	LA-N	18	11	.621	39	37	8	4	0	254²	232	11	50	138	10.0	3.11	111	.240	.278	17	.221	3	14	10	2	1.6
1983	*LA-N	12	11	.522	32	31	7	0	0	223¹	233	12	50	143	11.5	2.94	122	.271	.313	20	.282	5	17	16	4	2.8
1984	LA-N	5	7	.417	30	15	2	0	1	99	102	4	31	44	12.1	3.82	92	.266	.321	4	.167	1	-3	-0	-0	-0.1
1985	*LA-N	14	10	.583	34	33	5	3	0	212²	210	13	58	84	11.5	2.92	119	.260	.312	10	.135	-1	16	13	-1	1.1
1986	LA-N	2	6	.250	19	13	0	0	1	74	96	13	17	29	14.0	5.84	59	.313	.353	5	.250	2	-17	-20	1	-1.6
1987	LA-N	0	0	—	1	0	0	0	0	2	2	0	0	2	9.0	4.50	88	.333	.333	0	—	0	-0	-0	0	0.0
	Cin-N	0	5	.000	7	7	0	0	0	34²	52	2	12	10	16.9	7.79	54	.351	.404	1	.125	0	-14	-14	-0	-1.2
	Yr	0	5	.000	8	7	0	0	0	36²	54	2	12	12	16.4	7.61	56	.348	.399	0	.000	0	-14	-14	-0	-1.2
	Cal-A	4	5	.444	17	16	1	1	0	82¹	112	16	17	37	14.3	5.25	82	.327	.362	0	—	0	-7	-9	2	-0.6
1988	Chi-A	13	9	.591	32	29	2	0	0	183	183	15	43	73	11.3	3.44	115	.263	.309	0	—	0	11	11	0	1.1
1989	Chi-A	8	5	.615	23	19	1	1	0	106²	135	12	21	27	13.4	5.06	75	.308	.344	0	—	0	-14	-15	-2	-1.5
	Mil-A	1	4	.200	7	7	0	0	0	33²	36	7	13	13	13.4	5.35	72	.273	.342	0	—	0	-5	-6	0	-0.5
	Yr	9	9	.500	30	26	1	1	0	140¹	171	19	34	40	13.2	5.13	74	.295	.336	0	—	0	-19	-21	-2	-2.0
1990	Pit-N	0	0	—	4	1	0	0	0	7²	8	1	3	1	12.9	3.52	103	.267	.333	0	—	0	0	0	0	0.0
Total	22	220	191	.535	628	547	127	39	11	3669²	3734	245	1127	1907	12.1	3.64	100	.265	.322	171	.167	15	16	-7	8	4.0

■ ALLIE REYNOLDS

Reynolds, Allie Pierce "Superchief"   b: 2/10/15, Bethany, Okla.   BR/TR, 6', 195 lbs.   Deb: 9/17/42

YEAR	TM/L	W	L	PCT	G	GS	CG	SH	SV	IP	H	HR	BB	SO	RAT	ERA	ERA+	OAV	OOB	BH	AVG	PB	PR	/A	PD	TPI
1942	Cle-A	0	0	—	2	0	0	0	0	5	5	0	4	2	16.2	0.00	—	.250	.375	0	.000	-0	2	2	-0	0.2
1943	Cle-A	11	12	.478	34	21	11	3	3	198²	140	3	109	**151**	11.6	2.99	104	**.202**	.316	10	.149	-1	7	3	-2	0.0
1944	Cle-A	11	8	.579	28	21	5	1	1	158	141	2	91	84	13.4	3.30	100	.240	.346	7	.123	-3	2	-0	-2	-0.4
1945	Cle-A	18	12	.600	44	30	16	2	4	247¹	227	7	130	112	13.2	3.20	101	.247	.343	8	.094	-7	5	1	-1	-0.6
1946	Cle-A	11	15	.423	31	28	9	3	0	183¹	180	10	108	107	14.2	3.88	85	.259	.359	14	.222	1	-8	-12	-1	-1.1
1947	*NY-A	19	8	.704	34	30	17	4	2	241²	207	23	123	129	12.4	3.20	110	.227	.322	13	.146	-2	13	9	-2	0.5
1948	NY-A	16	7	.696	39	31	11	1	3	236¹	240	17	111	101	13.5	3.77	108	.268	.351	16	.193	0	14	8	-3	0.5
1949	*NY-A	17	6	.739	35	31	4	2	1	213²	200	15	123	105	13.8	4.00	101	.250	.353	17	.218	5	5	1	0	0.6
1950	NY-A	16	12	.571	35	29	14	2	2	240²	215	12	138	160	13.5	3.74	115	.242	.349	15	.185	1	22	15	-1	1.3
1951	*NY-A	17	8	.680	40	26	16	**7**	**7**	221	171	12	100	126	11.2	3.05	125	**.213**	.313	14	.184	0	26	19	-3	1.6
1952	*NY-A	20	8	.714	35	29	24	**6**	6	244¹	194	10	97	**160**	11.0	2.06	161	.218	.300	13	.153	0	**44**	34	-2	3.4
1953	*NY-A	13	7	.650	41	15	5	1	13	145	140	9	61	86	12.8	3.41	108	.253	.333	5	.122	1	9	4	-2	0.2
1954	*NY-A	13	4	.765	36	18	5	4	7	157	133	13	66	100	11.6	3.32	104	.233	.316	8	.160	-0	7	2	-1	0.1
Total	13	182	107	.630	434	309	137	36	49	2492¹	2193	133	1261	1423	12.7	3.30	110	.238	.333	140	.163	-4	149	87	-19	6.3

■ ARCHIE REYNOLDS

Reynolds, Archie Edward   b: 1/3/46, Glendale, Cal.   BR/TR, 6'2", 205 lbs.   Deb: 8/15/68

YEAR	TM/L	W	L	PCT	G	GS	CG	SH	SV	IP	H	HR	BB	SO	RAT	ERA	ERA+	OAV	OOB	BH	AVG	PB	PR	/A	PD	TPI
1968	Chi-N	0	1	.000	7	1	0	0	0	13¹	14	1	7	6	14.9	6.75	47	.259	.355	1	.500	1	-6	-5	-0	-0.4
1969	Chi-N	0	1	.000	2	2	0	0	0	7¹	11	1	7	4	22.1	2.45	164	.379	.500	0	.000	0	1	1	0	0.2
1970	Chi-N	0	2	.000	7	1	0	0	0	15	17	2	9	16	16.2	6.60	68	.298	.403	0	.000	0	-4	-3	-0	-0.3
1971	Cal-A	0	3	.000	15	1	0	0	0	27¹	32	2	18	15	16.5	4.61	70	.305	.407	0	—	-0	-3	-4	0	-0.3
1972	Mil-A	0	1	.000	5	2	0	0	0	18²	26	2	8	13	16.4	7.23	42	.338	.400	2	.500	1	-9	-9	-1	-0.8
Total	5	0	8	.000	36	7	0	0	0	81²	100	8	49	47	16.6	5.73	61	.311	.405	3	.273	2	-21	-21	-0	-1.6

YEAR TM/L	W	L	PCT	G	GS	CG	SH	SV	IP	H	HR	BB	SO	RAT	ERA	ERA+	OAV	OOB	BH	AVG	PB	PR	/A	PD	TPI
■ CHARLIE REYNOLDS							Reynolds, Charles E.	b: 7/31/1857, Allegany, N.Y.	d: 5/1/13, Buffalo, N.Y.						Deb: 5/18/1882										
1882 Phi-a	1	1	.500	2	2	1	0	0	12	18	0	3	4	15.8	5.25	57	.325	.360	1	.125	-1	-3	-3	-1	-0.3
■ CRAIG REYNOLDS							Reynolds, Gordon Craig	b: 12/27/52, Houston, Tex.	BL/TR, 6'1", 175 lbs.						Deb: 8/01/75 ♦										
1986 *Hou-N	0	0	—	1	0	0	0	0	1	3	0	2	1	45.0	27.00	13	.500	.625	78	.249	0	-3	-3	0	-0.1
1989 Hou-N	0	0	—	1	0	0	0	0	1	3	0	1	0	45.0	27.00	13	.500	.625	38	.201	0	-3	-3	0	-0.1
Total 2	0	0	—	2	0	0	0	0	2	6	0	3	1	45.0	27.00	13	.500	.625	1142	.256	0	-5	-5	0	-0.2
■ KEN REYNOLDS							Reynolds, Kenneth Lee	b: 1/4/47, Trevose, Pa.	BL/TL, 6', 180 lbs.						Deb: 9/05/70										
1970 Phi-N	0	0	—	4	0	0	0	0	2¹	3	0	4	1	27.0	0.00	—	.333	.538	0	—	0	1	1	0	0.1
1971 Phi-N	5	9	.357	35	25	2	1	0	162¹	163	11	82	81	13.9	4.49	78	.269	.361	10	.200	2	-19	-17	-1	-1.6
1972 Phi-N	2	15	.118	33	23	2	0	0	154¹	149	17	60	87	12.2	4.26	84	.258	.329	8	.200	1	-14	-11	0	-1.0
1973 Mil-A	0	1	.000	2	1	0	0	0	7¹	5	1	10	3	19.6	7.36	51	.200	.444	0	—	0	-3	-3	1	-0.1
1975 StL-N	0	1	.000	10	0	0	0	0	17	12	0	11	7	12.2	1.59	236	.214	.343	0	.000	-0	4	4	1	0.5
1976 SD-N	0	3	.000	19	2	0	0	1	32¹	38	0	29	18	18.6	6.40	51	.309	.441	0	.000	-1	-10	-11	-0	-1.2
Total 6	7	29	.194	103	51	4	1	1	375²	370	29	196	197	13.8	4.46	80	.265	.358	18	.186	2	-41	-38	1	-3.3
■ BOB REYNOLDS							Reynolds, Robert Allen	b: 1/21/47, Seattle, Wash.	BR/TR, 6', 205 lbs.						Deb: 9/19/69										
1969 Mon-N	0	0	—	1	1	0	0	0	1¹	3	0	3	2	40.5	20.25	18	.429	.600	0	—	0	-2	-2	0	-0.1
1971 StL-N	0	0	—	4	0	0	0	0	7	15	2	6	4	28.3	10.29	35	.441	.537	0	.000	-0	-5	-5	0	-0.4
Mil-A	0	1	.000	3	0	0	0	0	6	4	0	3	4	10.5	3.00	116	.222	.333	0	.000	-0	0	0	0	0.0
1972 Bal-A	0	0	—	3	0	0	0	0	9²	8	0	7	5	14.0	1.86	165	.258	.395	0	.000	-0	1	1	-0	0.1
1973 *Bal-A	7	5	.583	42	1	0	0	9	111	88	3	31	31	9.6	1.95	192	.219	.275	0	—	0	23	22	-3	2.0
1974 *Bal-A	7	5	.583	54	0	0	0	7	69¹	75	4	14	43	11.7	2.73	127	.278	.316	0	—	0	7	6	-0	0.5
1975 Bal-A	0	1	.000	7	0	0	0	0	6	11	1	1	1	18.0	9.00	39	.423	.444	0	—	0	-3	-4	-0	-0.3
Det-A	0	2	.000	21	0	0	0	3	34²	40	8	14	26	14.3	4.67	86	.288	.357	0	—	0	-3	-3	0	-0.1
Cle-A	0	2	.000	5	0	0	0	2	9²	11	0	3	5	13.0	4.66	81	.289	.341	0	—	0	-1	-1	0	0.0
Yr	0	5	.000	33	0	0	0	5	50¹	62	9	18	32	14.3	5.19	75	.301	.357	0	—	0	-8	-7	0	-0.4
Total 6	14	16	.467	140	2	0	0	21	254²	255	18	82	167	12.0	3.15	116	.264	.324	0	.000	-0	16	14	-3	1.7
■ ROSS REYNOLDS							Reynolds, Ross Ernest "Doc"	b: 8/20/1887, Barksdale, Tex.	d: 6/23/70, Ada, Okla.	BR/TR, 6'2", 185 lbs.					Deb: 5/02/14										
1914 Det-A	5	3	.625	26	7	3	1	0	78	62	0	39	31	12.3	2.08	135	.230	.340	1	.048	-2	6	6	-1	0.4
1915 Det-A	0	1	.000	4	2	0	0	0	11¹	17	0	5	2	18.3	6.35	48	.378	.451	0	.000	-0	-4	-4	0	-0.3
Total 2	5	4	.556	30	9	3	1	0	89¹	79	0	44	33	13.1	2.62	108	.251	.355	1	.042	-3	1	2	-0	0.1
■ FLINT RHEM							Rhem, Charles Flint "Shad"	b: 1/24/01, Rhems, S.C.	d: 7/30/69, Columbia, S.C.	BR/TR, 6'2", 180 lbs.					Deb: 9/06/24										
1924 StL-N	2	2	.500	6	3	3	0	1	32¹	31	1	17	20	13.4	4.45	85	.254	.345	2	.167	-0	-2	-2	0	-0.2
1925 StL-N	8	13	.381	30	23	8	1	1	170	204	16	58	66	14.1	4.92	88	.299	.357	14	.237	1	-12	-11	0	-0.8
1926 *StL-N	20	7	.741	34	34	20	1	0	258	241	12	75	72	11.1	3.21	122	.250	.305	18	.188	2	18	20	1	2.0
1927 StL-N	10	12	.455	27	26	9	2	0	169¹	189	6	54	51	13.1	4.41	90	.285	.342	4	.068	-6	-9	-9	-3	-1.5
1928 *StL-N	11	8	.579	28	22	9	0	3	169²	199	13	71	47	14.5	4.14	97	.296	.365	11	.164	-1	-3	-3	2	-0.2
1930 *StL-N	12	8	.600	26	19	9	0	0	139²	173	11	37	47	13.7	4.45	113	.306	.352	12	.231	-1	8	9	-2	0.5
1931 *StL-N	11	10	.524	33	26	10	2	1	207¹	214	17	60	72	12.0	3.56	111	.268	.321	9	.130	-4	7	9	-1	0.4
1932 StL-N	4	2	.667	6	6	5	1	0	50	48	3	10	18	10.4	3.06	129	.257	.294	3	.188	0	5	5	0	0.5
Phi-N	11	7	.611	26	20	10	0	1	168²	177	13	49	35	12.1	3.74	118	.269	.319	7	.113	-5	3	13	0	0.9
Yr	15	9	.625	32	26	15	1	1	218²	225	16	59	53	11.7	3.58	120	.266	.314	1	.013	-5	7	18	0	1.4
1933 Phi-N	5	14	.263	28	19	3	0	2	125	182	10	33	27	15.6	6.62	58	.340	.381	4	.087	-4	-46	-39	0	-4.0
1934 StL-N	1	0	1.000	5	1	0	0	1	15²	26	0	7	6	19.0	4.60	92	.394	.452	0	.000	-0	-1	-1	0	0.0
Bos-N	8	8	.500	25	20	5	1	0	152²	164	5	38	56	11.9	3.60	106	.273	.317	3	.058	-5	8	4	1	0.0
Yr	9	8	.529	30	21	5	1	1	168¹	190	5	45	62	12.6	3.69	105	.285	.331	1	.019	-5	7	3	1	0.0
1935 Bos-N	0	5	.000	10	6	0	0	0	40¹	61	4	11	10	16.1	5.36	71	.341	.379	0	.000	-1	-6	-7	0	-0.7
1936 StL-N	2	1	.667	10	4	0	0	0	26²	49	2	9	7	19.6	6.75	58	.405	.446	1	.125	-0	-8	-8	-0	-0.7
Total 12	105	97	.520	294	229	91	8	10	1725¹	1958	113	529	534	13.1	4.20	98	.287	.340	88	.144	-29	-39	-20	-2	-3.8
■ BILLY RHINES							Rhines, William Pearl "Bunker"	b: 3/14/1869, Ridgway, Pa.	d: 1/30/22, Ridgway, Pa.	5'11", 168 lbs.					Deb: 4/22/1890										
1890 Cin-N	28	17	.622	46	45	45	6	0	401¹	337	6	113	182	10.1	1.95	182	.221	.275	29	.188	-5	72	71	0	6.4
1891 Cin-N	17	24	.415	48	43	40	1	1	372²	364	4	124	138	11.8	2.87	117	.246	.305	18	.122	-9	20	21	3	1.3
1892 Cin-N	4	7	.364	12	10	8	0	0	83²	113	0	36	12	16.0	5.06	65	.310	.373	5	.167	1	-16	-17	-1	-1.4
1893 Lou-N	1	4	.200	5	5	3	0	0	31	49	3	19	0	19.7	8.71	51	.348	.426	1	.091	-1	-14	-15	0	-1.1
1895 Cin-N	19	10	.655	38	33	25	0	0	267²	322	4	76	72	13.4	4.81	103	.293	.339	25	.221	-4	-1	5	-1	0.1
1896 Cin-N	8	6	.571	19	17	11	3	0	143	128	1	48	32	11.1	2.45	188	.238	.300	10	.192	-3	30	34	0	2.9
1897 Cin-N	21	15	.583	41	32	26	1	0	288²	311	4	86	65	12.4	4.08	112	.273	.324	17	.159	-7	7	15	-2	0.6
1898 Pit-N	12	16	.429	31	29	27	2	0	258	289	0	61	48	12.2	3.52	101	.281	.321	15	.150	-5	2	1	5	0.2
1899 Pit-N	4	4	.500	9	9	4	0	0	54	59	3	13	6	12.0	6.00	64	.278	.319	10	.435	4	-13	-13	-1	-0.8
Total 9	114	103	.525	249	223	189	13	1	1900	1972	25	576	555	12.1	3.47	114	.262	.315	130	.176	-28	88	101	4	8.2
■ BOB RHOADS							Rhoads, Robert Barton "Dusty"	b: 10/4/1879, Wooster, Ohio	d: 2/12/67, San Bernardino, Cal.	TR, 6'1", 215 lbs.					Deb: 4/19/02										
1902 Chi-N	4	8	.333	16	12	12	1	1	118	131	1	42	43	13.7	3.20	84	.281	.348	10	.222	0	-6	-7	-1	-0.6
1903 StL-N	5	8	.385	17	13	12	1	0	129	154	3	47	52	14.2	4.60	71	.303	.366	1	.140	-2	-19	-17	-2	-2.0
Cle-A	2	3	.400	5	5	5	0	0	41	55	2	3	21	12.7	5.27	54	.320	.332	2	.118	-1	-10	-11	-0	-1.0
1904 Cle-A	10	9	.526	22	19	18	0	0	175¹	175	1	48	72	11.4	2.87	88	.261	.310	18	.196	0	-5	-7	-0	-0.7
1905 Cle-A	16	9	.640	28	26	24	4	0	235	219	4	55	61	10.5	2.83	93	.248	.292	21	.221	4	-5	-5	1	0.0
1906 Cle-A	22	10	.688	38	34	31	7	0	315	259	5	92	89	10.0	1.80	146	.237	.285	19	.161	-4	31	29	-1	2.8
1907 Cle-A	15	14	.517	35	31	23	5	1	275	258	0	84	76	11.2	2.29	110	.250	.306	17	.185	-1	8	7	-0	0.5
1908 Cle-A	18	12	.600	37	30	20	1	0	270	229	2	73	62	10.3	1.77	135	.239	.298	20	.222	4	19	19	3	3.0
1909 Cle-A	5	9	.357	20	15	9	2	0	133¹	124	1	50	46	12.2	2.90	88	.281	.361	7	.163	-0	-6	-5	1	-0.4
Total 8	97	82	.542	218	185	154	21	2	1691²	1604	19	494	522	11.3	2.61	100	.256	.312	121	.188	1	7	1	1	1.6
■ RICK RHODEN							Rhoden, Richard Alan	b: 5/16/53, Boynton Beach, Fla.	BR/TR, 6'3", 195 lbs.						Deb: 7/05/74										
1974 LA-N	1	0	1.000	4	0	0	0	0	9	5	1	4	7	9.0	2.00	170	.161	.257	1	.500	0	2	1	0	0.2
1975 LA-N	3	3	.500	26	11	1	0	0	99¹	94	8	32	40	11.5	3.08	110	.253	.314	2	.071	-2	6	4	0	0.2
1976 LA-N	12	3	.800	27	26	10	3	0	181	165	17	53	77	10.9	2.98	113	.242	.298	20	.308	7	10	8	-2	1.4
1977 *LA-N	16	10	.615	31	31	4	1	0	216¹	223	20	63	122	12.0	3.74	102	.270	.323	18	.231	5	4	2	0	0.4
1978 *LA-N	10	8	.556	30	23	6	3	0	164²	160	13	51	79	11.7	3.66	96	.255	.314	7	.135	-0	-2	-3	-1	-0.3
1979 Pit-N	0	1	.000	1	1	0	0	0	5	5	0	2	2	12.6	7.20	54	.263	.333	1	1.000	0	-2	-2	0	0.0
1980 Pit-N	7	5	.583	20	19	2	0	0	126²	133	9	40	70	12.5	3.84	95	.273	.323	15	.375	6	-3	-3	0	0.4
1981 Pit-N	9	4	.692	21	21	4	2	0	136¹	147	6	53	76	13.3	3.89	92	.283	.352	9	.188	1	-6	-5	1	-0.2
1982 Pit-N	11	14	.440	35	35	6	1	0	230¹	239	14	70	128	12.2	4.14	89	.267	.321	22	.265	9	-14	-11	3	0.0
1983 Pit-N	13	13	.500	36	35	7	2	1	244¹	256	13	68	153	12.0	3.09	120	.276	.327	13	.151	-2	14	17	1	1.9
1984 Pit-N	14	9	.609	33	33	6	3	0	238¹	216	13	62	136	10.5	2.72	132	.243	.293	28	.333	10	23	23	2	3.9
1985 Pit-N	10	15	.400	35	35	2	0	0	213¹	254	18	69	128	13.9	4.47	80	.296	.352	14	.189	2	-21	-21	-0	-1.9
1986 Pit-N	15	12	.556	34	34	12	1	0	253²	211	9	76	159	10.3	2.84	135	.228	.288	25	.278	9	25	28	1	4.2
1987 NY-A	16	10	.615	30	29	4	0	0	181²	184	22	61	107	12.3	3.86	113	.268	.330	0	—	0	12	10	0	1.0
1988 NY-A	12	12	.500	30	30	5	1	0	197	206	20	56	94	12.3	4.29	92	.269	.325	0	.000	0	-7	-8	-0	-0.7

YEAR	TM/L	W	L	PCT	G	GS	CG	SH	SV	IP	H	HR	BB	SO	RAT	ERA	ERA+	OAV	OOB	BH	AVG	PB	PR	/A	PD	TPI
1989	Hou-N	2	6	.250	20	17	0	0	0	96²	108	7	41	41	14.2	4.28	79	.289	.364	6	.207	1	-8	-10	1	-0.7
Total	16	151	125	.547	413	380	69	17	1	2593²	2606	198	801	1419	12.0	3.59	103	.264	.321	181	.238	46	33	32	4	9.6

■ CHARLIE RHODES
Rhodes, Charles Anderson "Dusty" b: 4/7/1885, Caney, Kan. d: 10/26/18, Caney, Kan. BR/TR, 5'7", 180 lbs. Deb: 7/26/06

YEAR	TM/L	W	L	PCT	G	GS	CG	SH	SV	IP	H	HR	BB	SO	RAT	ERA	ERA+	OAV	OOB	BH	AVG	PB	PR	/A	PD	TPI
1906	StL-N	3	4	.429	9	6	3	0	0	45	37	0	20	32	12.6	3.40	77	.223	.328	3	.188	0	-4	-4	0	-0.3
1908	Cin-N	0	0	—	1	0	0	0	0	4	1	0	2	4	9.0	0.00	—	.077	.250	0	.000	-0	1	1	0	0.2
	StL-N	1	2	.333	4	4	3	0	0	33	23	2	12	15	9.8	3.00	79	.200	.281	3	.250	1	-2	-2	1	0.0
	Yr	1	2	.333	5	4	3	0	0	37	24	2	14	19	9.5	2.68	88	.186	.271	0	.000	1	-1	-1	1	0.2
1909	StL-N	3	5	.375	12	10	4	0	0	61	55	0	33	25	13.3	3.98	64	.256	.360	4	.211	1	-9	-10	2	-0.6
Total	3	7	11	.389	26	20	10	0	0	143	116	2	67	76	12.1	3.46	73	.228	.329	10	.208	2	-14	-15	3	-0.7

■ GORDON RHODES
Rhodes, John Gordon "Dusty" b: 8/11/07, Winnemucca, Nev. d: 3/24/60, Long Beach, Cal. BR/TR, 6', 187 lbs. Deb: 4/29/29

YEAR	TM/L	W	L	PCT	G	GS	CG	SH	SV	IP	H	HR	BB	SO	RAT	ERA	ERA+	OAV	OOB	BH	AVG	PB	PR	/A	PD	TPI
1929	NY-A	0	4	.000	10	4	0	0	0	42²	57	3	16	13	15.8	4.85	80	.333	.397	3	.300	1	-3	-5	-0	-0.3
1930	NY-A	0	0	—	3	0	0	0	0	2	3	0	4	1	31.5	9.00	48	.500	.700	0	—	0	-1	-1	0	0.0
1931	NY-A	6	3	.667	18	11	4	0	0	87	82	3	52	36	13.9	3.41	116	.235	.334	6	.214	1	9	5	0	0.6
1932	NY-A	1	2	.333	10	2	1	0	0	24	25	0	21	15	17.3	7.88	52	.275	.411	2	.286	0	-9	-10	1	-0.6
	Bos-A	1	8	.111	12	11	4	0	0	79¹	79	5	31	22	12.5	5.11	88	.261	.329	2	.074	-2	-6	-5	-0	-0.6
	Yr	2	10	.167	22	13	5	0	0	103¹	104	5	52	37	13.6	5.75	76	.264	.350	0	.000	-2	-15	-16	1	-1.2
1933	Bos-A	12	15	.444	34	29	14	0	0	232	242	13	93	85	13.0	4.03	109	.265	.334	23	.267	5	6	9	-1	1.2
1934	Bos-A	12	12	.500	44	31	10	0	2	219	247	10	98	79	14.3	4.56	105	.285	.360	10	.133	-4	-2	6	1	0.3
1935	Bos-A	2	10	.167	34	19	1	0	2	146¹	195	14	60	44	15.7	5.41	88	.324	.387	7	.146	-4	-16	-11	-0	-1.2
1936	Phi-A	9	20	.310	35	28	13	1	1	216¹	266	26	102	61	15.4	5.74	89	.304	.378	16	.213	-2	-17	-15	-3	-1.6
Total	8	43	74	.368	200	135	47	1	5	1048²	1196	74	477	356	14.4	4.85	95	.286	.361	69	.194	-5	-37	-28	-2	-2.2

■ BILL RHODES
Rhodes, William Clarence b: Pottstown, Pa. Deb: 6/14/1893

YEAR	TM/L	W	L	PCT	G	GS	CG	SH	SV	IP	H	HR	BB	SO	RAT	ERA	ERA+	OAV	OOB	BH	AVG	PB	PR	/A	PD	TPI
1893	Lou-N	5	12	.294	20	19	17	0	0	151²	244	10	66	22	18.4	7.60	58	.352	.409	9	.129	-3	-49	-54	-2	-4.3

■ DENNIS RIBANT
Ribant, Dennis Joseph b: 9/20/41, Detroit, Mich. BR/TR, 5'11", 165 lbs. Deb: 8/09/64

YEAR	TM/L	W	L	PCT	G	GS	CG	SH	SV	IP	H	HR	BB	SO	RAT	ERA	ERA+	OAV	OOB	BH	AVG	PB	PR	/A	PD	TPI
1964	NY-N	1	5	.167	14	7	1	1	1	57²	65	8	9	35	11.5	5.15	69	.281	.308	2	.100	-0	-10	-10	-1	-1.0
1965	NY-N	1	3	.250	19	1	0	0	3	35¹	29	5	6	13	8.9	3.82	92	.228	.263	0	.000	-1	-1	-0	-0.1
1966	NY-N	11	9	.550	39	26	10	1	3	188¹	184	20	40	84	10.8	3.20	114	.254	.294	12	.197	0	8	9	1	1.1
1967	Pit-N	9	8	.529	38	22	2	0	0	172	186	16	40	75	12.0	4.08	82	.280	.324	16	.267	5	-14	-14	2	-0.6
1968	Det-A	2	2	.500	14	0	0	0	1	24¹	20	1	10	7	11.5	2.22	136	.217	.301	1	.200	-0	2	2	0	0.3
	Chi-A	0	2	.000	17	0	0	0	0	31¹	42	3	17	20	17.5	6.03	50	.318	.404	0	.000	-1	-11	-10	0	-1.1
	Yr	2	4	.333	31	0	0	0	2	55²	62	4	27	27	14.7	4.37	69	.276	.358	1	.083	-0	-9	-8	0	-0.8
1969	StL-N	0	0	—	1	0	0	0	0	1¹	4	1	1	0	33.8	13.50	26	.571	.625	0	—	0	-1	-1	0	0.0
	Cin-N	0	0	—	7	0	0	0	0	8¹	6	1	3	7	9.7	1.08	348	.188	.257	0	—	0	2	2	-0	0.2
	Yr	0	0	—	8	0	0	0	0	9²	10	2	4	7	13.0	2.79	134	.250	.318	0	—	0	1	1	-0	0.2
Total	6	24	29	.453	149	56	13	2	9	518²	536	55	126	241	11.6	3.87	90	.267	.312	31	.195	4	-24	-23	1	-1.2

■ FRANK RICCELLI
Riccelli, Frank Joseph b: 2/24/53, Syracuse, N.Y. BL/TL, 6'3", 205 lbs. Deb: 9/11/76

YEAR	TM/L	W	L	PCT	G	GS	CG	SH	SV	IP	H	HR	BB	SO	RAT	ERA	ERA+	OAV	OOB	BH	AVG	PB	PR	/A	PD	TPI
1976	SF-N	1	1	.500	4	3	0	0	0	16	16	1	5	11	11.8	5.63	64	.258	.313	1	.167	-0	-4	-4	-0	-0.3
1978	Hou-N	0	0	—	2	0	0	0	0	3	1	0	0	1	3.0	0.00	—	.100	.100	0	—	0	1	1	0	0.1
1979	Hou-N	2	2	.500	11	2	0	0	0	22	22	0	18	20	16.4	4.09	86	.262	.392	2	.333	1	-1	-1	0	-0.2
Total	3	3	3	.500	17	5	0	0	0	41	39	1	23	32	13.6	4.39	81	.250	.346	3	.250	1	-3	-4	0	-0.2

■ SAM RICE
Rice, Edgar Charles b: 2/20/1890, Morocco, Ind. d: 10/13/74, Rossmor, Md. BL/TR, 5'9", 150 lbs. Deb: 8/07/15 H♦

YEAR	TM/L	W	L	PCT	G	GS	CG	SH	SV	IP	H	HR	BB	SO	RAT	ERA	ERA+	OAV	OOB	BH	AVG	PB	PR	/A	PD	TPI
1915	Was-A	1	0	1.000	4	2	1	0	0	18	13	0	9	9	11.0	2.00	146	.213	.314	3	.375	1	2	2	0	0.3
1916	Was-A	0	1	.000	5	1	0	0	0	21¹	18	0	10	3	11.8	2.95	93	.237	.326	59	.299	2	-0	-0	0	0.0
Total	2	1	1	.500	9	3	1	0	0	39¹	31	0	19	12	11.4	2.52	113	.226	.321	2987	.322	2	2	1	0	0.3

■ WOODY RICH
Rich, Woodrow Earl b: 3/9/16, Morganton, N.C. d: 4/18/83, Morganton, N.C. BL/TR, 6'2", 185 lbs. Deb: 4/22/39

YEAR	TM/L	W	L	PCT	G	GS	CG	SH	SV	IP	H	HR	BB	SO	RAT	ERA	ERA+	OAV	OOB	BH	AVG	PB	PR	/A	PD	TPI
1939	Bos-A	4	3	.571	21	12	3	0	1	77	78	2	35	24	13.8	4.91	96	.264	.352	7	.259	0	-2	-2	2	0.0
1940	Bos-A	1	0	1.000	3	1	1	0	0	11²	9	2	1	8	7.7	0.77	583	.214	.233	0	.000	-1	5	5	-0	0.4
1941	Bos-A	0	0	—	2	1	0	0	0	3²	8	1	2	4	24.5	17.18	24	.421	.476	0	—	0	-5	-5	-0	-0.3
1944	Bos-N	1	1	.500	7	2	1	0	0	25	32	3	12	6	16.9	5.76	66	.327	.416	1	.125	-1	-6	-5	0	-0.5
Total	4	6	4	.600	33	16	5	0	1	117¹	127	8	50	42	14.2	5.06	89	.280	.361	8	.205	-1	-9	-7	2	-0.4

■ J.R. RICHARD
Richard, James Rodney b: 3/7/50, Vienna, La. BR/TR, 6'8", 222 lbs. Deb: 9/05/71

YEAR	TM/L	W	L	PCT	G	GS	CG	SH	SV	IP	H	HR	BB	SO	RAT	ERA	ERA+	OAV	OOB	BH	AVG	PB	PR	/A	PD	TPI
1971	Hou-N	2	1	.667	4	4	1	0	0	21	17	1	16	29	14.1	3.43	98	.215	.347	0	.000	-1	0	-0	0	0.0
1972	Hou-N	1	0	1.000	4	1	0	0	0	6	10	0	8	8	30.0	13.50	25	.385	.556	0	—	0	-7	-7	0	-0.5
1973	Hou-N	6	2	.750	16	10	2	1	0	72	54	2	38	75	11.6	4.00	91	.210	.314	5	.179	-0	-3	-3	-1	-0.4
1974	Hou-N	2	3	.400	15	9	0	0	0	64²	58	3	36	42	13.2	4.18	83	.243	.344	3	.143	0	-4	-5	-1	-0.5
1975	Hou-N	12	10	.545	33	31	7	1	0	203	178	8	138	176	14.2	4.39	77	.238	.359	15	.203	4	-17	-23	-3	-2.1
1976	Hou-N	20	15	.571	39	39	14	3	0	291	221	14	151	214	11.6	2.75	114	**.212**	.314	14	.140	0	24	14	-1	1.3
1977	Hou-N	18	12	.600	36	36	13	3	0	267	212	18	104	214	10.7	2.97	120	.218	.293	20	.230	6	28	18	2	2.6
1978	Hou-N	18	11	.621	36	36	16	3	0	275¹	192	12	141	**303**	11.0	3.11	107	**.196**	.299	18	.178	1	14	6	1	0.7
1979	Hou-N	18	13	.581	38	38	19	4	0	292¹	220	13	98	**313**	9.9	**2.71**	130	**.209**	.278	12	.126	-0	**33**	**26**	-3	2.4
1980	Hou-N	10	4	.714	17	17	4	4	0	113²	65	2	40	119	8.3	1.90	173	.166	.244	6	.154	1	21	18	-1	1.9
Total	10	107	71	.601	238	221	76	19	0	1606	1227	73	770	1493	11.3	3.15	108	.212	.306	93	.168	11	91	44	-7	5.4

■ DUANE RICHARDS
Richards, Duane Lee b: 12/16/36, Spartanburg, Ind. BR/TR, 6'3", 200 lbs. Deb: 9/25/60

YEAR	TM/L	W	L	PCT	G	GS	CG	SH	SV	IP	H	HR	BB	SO	RAT	ERA	ERA+	OAV	OOB	BH	AVG	PB	PR	/A	PD	TPI
1960	Cin-N	0	0	—	2	0	0	0	0	3	5	0	2	2	21.0	9.00	42	.385	.467	0	—	0	-2	-2	0	-0.1

■ RUSTY RICHARDS
Richards, Russell Earl b: 1/27/65, Houston, Tex. BL/TR, 6'4", 200 lbs. Deb: 9/20/89

YEAR	TM/L	W	L	PCT	G	GS	CG	SH	SV	IP	H	HR	BB	SO	RAT	ERA	ERA+	OAV	OOB	BH	AVG	PB	PR	/A	PD	TPI
1989	Atl-N	0	0	—	2	2	0	0	0	9¹	10	2	6	6	16.4	4.82	76	.278	.395	0	.000	-0	-1	-1	0	0.0
1990	Atl-N	0	0	—	1	0	0	0	0	1	2	1	1	0	27.0	27.00	14	.400	.500	0	—	0	-3	-3	0	-0.1
Total	2	0	0	—	3	2	0	0	0	10¹	12	3	7	4	17.4	6.97	53	.293	.408	0	.000	-0	-4	-4	0	-0.1

■ HARDY RICHARDSON
Richardson, Abram Harding "Old True Blue" b: 4/21/1855, Clarksboro, N.J. d: 1/14/31, Utica, N.Y. BR/TR, 5'9.5", 170 lbs. Deb: 5/01/1879 ♦

YEAR	TM/L	W	L	PCT	G	GS	CG	SH	SV	IP	H	HR	BB	SO	RAT	ERA	ERA+	OAV	OOB	BH	AVG	PB	PR	/A	PD	TPI
1885	Buf-N	0	0	—	1	0	0	0	0	4	5	0	3	1	18.0	2.25	132	.292	.398	136	.319	0	0	0	0	0.0
1886	Det-N	3	0	1.000	4	0	0	0	0	12	11	1	10	5	15.8	4.50	74	.234	.368	189	.351	2	-2	-2	0	0.0
Total	2	3	0	1.000	5	0	0	0	0	16	16	1	13	6	16.3	3.94	82	.249	.376	1688	.299	3	-1	-1	0	0.0

■ DANNY RICHARDSON
Richardson, Daniel b: 1/25/1863, Elmira, N.Y. d: 9/12/26, New York, N.Y. BR/TR, 5'8", 165 lbs. Deb: 5/22/1884 M♦

YEAR	TM/L	W	L	PCT	G	GS	CG	SH	SV	IP	H	HR	BB	SO	RAT	ERA	ERA+	OAV	OOB	BH	AVG	PB	PR	/A	PD	TPI
1885	NY-N	7	1	.875	9	8	7	1	0	75	58	0	18	21	9.1	2.40	111	.204	.251	52	.263	2	3	2	-1	0.2
1886	NY-N	0	2	.000	5	1	1	0	0	25	33	1	11	17	15.8	5.76	56	.305	.370	55	.232	1	-7	-7	1	-0.5
1887	NY-N	0	0	—	1	0	0	0	0	0	0	0	1	0	—	—	—	—	1.000	125	.278	0	0	0	0	0.0
Total	3	7	3	.700	15	9	8	1	0	100	91	1	30	38	10.9	3.24	86	.232	.286	1129	.254	3	-3	-5	0	-0.3

■ GORDIE RICHARDSON
Richardson, Gordon Clark b: 7/19/38, Colquitt, Ga. BR/TL, 6', 185 lbs. Deb: 7/26/64

YEAR	TM/L	W	L	PCT	G	GS	CG	SH	SV	IP	H	HR	BB	SO	RAT	ERA	ERA+	OAV	OOB	BH	AVG	PB	PR	/A	PD	TPI
1964	*StL-N	4	2	.667	19	6	1	0	2	47	45	5	15	28	10.7	2.30	166	.251	.296	1	.077	-0	6	8	-1	0.7
1965	NY-N	2	2	.500	35	0	0	0	1	52¹	41	5	16	43	10.1	3.78	93	.224	.294	0	.000	-1	-1	-1	-1	-0.2
1966	NY-N	0	2	.000	15	1	0	0	1	18²	24	7	6	15	14.5	9.16	40	.312	.361	0	.000	-0	-12	-11	0	-1.1
Total	3	6	6	.500	69	7	1	0	4	118	105	14	37	86	11.1	4.04	90	.242	.307	1	.048	-1	-6	-5	-2	-0.6

YEAR TM/L	W	L	PCT	G	GS	CG	SH	SV	IP	H	HR	BB	SO	RAT	ERA	ERA+	OAV	OOB	BH	AVG	PB	PR	/A	PD	TPI

■ JEFF RICHARDSON Richardson, Jeffrey Scott b: 8/29/63, Wichita, Kan. BR/TR, 6'3", 185 lbs. Deb: 9/19/90

YEAR TM/L	W	L	PCT	G	GS	CG	SH	SV	IP	H	HR	BB	SO	RAT	ERA	ERA+	OAV	OOB	BH	AVG	PB	PR	/A	PD	TPI
1990 Cal-A	0	0	—	1	0	0	0	0	0¹	1	0	0	0	27.0	0.00	—	.500	.500	0	—	0	0	0	0	0.0

■ JACK RICHARDSON Richardson, John William b: 10/3/1891, Central City, Ill. d: 1/18/70, Marion, Ill. BB/TR, 6'3", 197 lbs. Deb: 9/17/15

YEAR TM/L	W	L	PCT	G	GS	CG	SH	SV	IP	H	HR	BB	SO	RAT	ERA	ERA+	OAV	OOB	BH	AVG	PB	PR	/A	PD	TPI
1915 Phi-A	0	1	.000	3	3	2	0	0	24	21	0	14	11	13.5	2.63	112	.253	.367	0	.000	-1	1	1	-0	0.0
1916 Phi-A	0	0	—	1	0	0	0	0	0²	2	0	1	1	40.5	40.50	7	.667	.750	0	—	0	-3	-3	0	-0.2
Total 2	0	1	.000	4	3	2	0	0	24²	23	0	15	12	14.2	3.65	81	.267	.382	0	.000	-1	-2	-2	-0	-0.2

■ PETE RICHERT Richert, Peter Gerard b: 10/29/39, Floral Park, N.Y. BL/TL, 5'11", 165 lbs. Deb: 4/12/62

YEAR TM/L	W	L	PCT	G	GS	CG	SH	SV	IP	H	HR	BB	SO	RAT	ERA	ERA+	OAV	OOB	BH	AVG	PB	PR	/A	PD	TPI
1962 LA-N	5	4	.556	19	12	1	0	0	81¹	77	6	45	75	13.6	3.87	94	.249	.346	2	.080	-1	1	-2	0	-0.2
1963 LA-N	5	3	.625	20	12	1	0	0	78	80	7	28	54	12.6	4.50	67	.262	.326	4	.182	1	-11	-13	-1	-1.3
1964 LA-N	2	3	.400	8	6	1	1	0	34²	38	2	18	25	15.1	4.15	78	.271	.363	1	.091	-0	-2	-4	1	-0.2
1965 Was-A	15	12	.556	34	29	6	0	0	194	146	18	84	161	10.8	2.60	134	.210	.297	10	.156	-0	19	19	-1	1.9
1966 Was-A	14	14	.500	36	34	7	0	0	245²	196	36	69	195	9.7	3.37	103	.215	.271	14	.163	2	2	2	-3	0.1
1967 Was-A	2	6	.250	11	10	1	1	0	54¹	49	5	15	41	10.8	4.64	68	.237	.291	1	.059	-1	-8	-9	-1	-1.1
Bal-A	7	10	.412	26	19	5	1	2	132¹	107	11	41	90	10.1	2.99	105	.220	.282	4	.108	-1	4	2	1	0.2
Yr	9	16	.360	37	29	6	2	2	186²	156	16	56	131	10.3	3.47	91	.223	.282	1	.019	-2	-5	-7	-1	-0.9
1968 Bal-A	6	3	.667	36	0	0	0	6	62¹	51	7	12	47	9.5	3.47	84	.225	.273	2	.200	-0	-3	-4	1	-0.2
1969 *Bal-A	7	4	.636	44	0	0	0	12	57¹	42	7	14	54	8.8	2.20	162	.202	.252	1	.125	-0	9	9	-1	0.8
1970 Bal-A	7	2	.778	50	0	0	0	13	54²	36	5	24	66	10.0	1.98	185	.194	.289	0	.000	-0	11	10	-0	1.0
1971 Bal-A	3	5	.375	35	0	0	0	4	36¹	26	3	22	35	12.1	3.47	97	.205	.327	0	—	0	-0	0	0	0.0
1972 LA-N	2	3	.400	37	0	0	0	6	52	42	3	18	38	10.6	2.25	148	.219	.289	3	.500	1	7	6	-0	0.7
1973 LA-N	3	3	.500	39	0	0	0	7	51	44	5	19	31	11.3	3.18	108	.234	.308	1	.200	0	3	1	1	0.2
1974 StL-N	0	0	—	13	0	0	0	1	11¹	10	1	4	16	16.7	2.38	150	.244	.404	0	—	0	2	2	-0	0.1
Phi-N	2	1	.667	21	0	0	0	0	20¹	15	0	4	9	8.4	2.21	171	.205	.247	0	—	0	3	4	0	0.4
Yr	2	1	.667	34	0	0	0	1	31²	25	1	15	13	11.4	2.27	163	.216	.305	0	—	0	5	5	-0	0.5
Total 13	80	73	.523	429	122	22	3	51	1165²	959	116	424	925	10.8	3.19	106	.223	.295	43	.145	-1	34	24	-5	2.4

■ LEW RICHIE Richie, Lewis A. b: 8/23/1883, Ambler, Pa. d: 8/15/36, South Mountain, Pa. BR/TR, 5'8", 165 lbs. Deb: 5/08/06

YEAR TM/L	W	L	PCT	G	GS	CG	SH	SV	IP	H	HR	BB	SO	RAT	ERA	ERA+	OAV	OOB	BH	AVG	PB	PR	/A	PD	TPI
1906 Phi-N	9	11	.450	33	22	14	3	0	205²	170	3	79	65	11.2	2.41	109	.230	.309	3	.050	-3	5	5	-3	0.0
1907 Phi-N	6	6	.500	25	12	9	2	0	117	88	0	38	40	10.1	1.77	137	.215	.290	7	.163	0	9	8	-1	0.9
1908 Phi-N	7	10	.412	25	15	13	1	1	157²	125	1	49	58	10.3	1.83	133	.233	.304	11	.212	2	9	10	-1	1.3
1909 Phi-N	1	1	.500	11	1	0	0	1	45	40	0	18	11	12.0	2.00	130	.263	.349	4	.250	1	3	3	-0	0.4
Bos-N	7	7	.500	22	13	9	2	2	131¹	118	2	44	42	11.1	2.32	121	.247	.312	5	.114	-2	4	7	-3	0.2
Yr	8	8	.500	33	14	9	2	3	176²	158	2	62	53	11.3	2.24	123	.250	.318	9	.033	-1	7	10	-3	0.6
1910 Bos-N	0	3	.000	4	2	0	0	0	16¹	20	0	9	7	16.0	2.76	121	.317	.403	0	.000	-1	1	1	1	0.1
*Chi-N	11	4	.733	30	11	8	3	4	130	117	1	51	52	11.8	2.70	107	.257	.336	9	.225	3	5	3	1	0.6
Yr	11	7	.611	34	13	8	3	4	146¹	137	1	60	59	12.3	2.71	108	.264	.344	9	.068	2	5	4	1	0.7
1911 Chi-N	15	11	.577	36	28	18	4	1	253	213	6	103	78	11.3	2.31	143	.235	.315	14	.154	-3	31	28	1	2.7
1912 Chi-N	16	8	.667	39	27	15	4	0	238	222	5	74	69	11.4	2.95	113	.249	.310	10	.132	-3	12	10	-1	0.5
1913 Chi-N	2	4	.333	16	6	0	0	0	65	77	3	30	15	15.0	5.82	58	.304	.380	2	.118	-0	-19	-19	-1	-1.9
Total 8	74	65	.532	241	137	86	20	9	1359¹	1190	21	495	437	11.4	2.54	115	.244	.317	65	.147	-6	60	58	-8	4.8

■ BERYL RICHMOND Richmond, Beryl Justice b: 8/24/07, Glen Easton, W.Va. d: 4/24/80, Cameron, W.Va. BB/TL, 6'1", 185 lbs. Deb: 4/21/33

YEAR TM/L	W	L	PCT	G	GS	CG	SH	SV	IP	H	HR	BB	SO	RAT	ERA	ERA+	OAV	OOB	BH	AVG	PB	PR	/A	PD	TPI
1933 Chi-N	0	0	—	4	0	0	0	0	4²	10	0	2	2	23.1	1.93	170	.455	.500	0	.000	-0	1	1	-0	0.0
1934 Cin-N	1	2	.333	6	2	1	0	0	19¹	23	0	10	9	15.4	3.72	110	.303	.384	0	.000	-1	1	1	-0	0.0
Total 2	1	2	.333	10	2	1	0	0	24	33	0	12	11	16.9	3.38	116	.337	.409	0	.000	-1	1	1	-0	0.0

■ LEE RICHMOND Richmond, J. Lee b: 5/5/1857, Sheffield, Ohio d: 10/1/29, Toledo, Ohio TL, 5'10", 142 lbs. Deb: 9/27/1879 ♦

YEAR TM/L	W	L	PCT	G	GS	CG	SH	SV	IP	H	HR	BB	SO	RAT	ERA	ERA+	OAV	OOB	BH	AVG	PB	PR	/A	PD	TPI
1879 Bos-N	1	0	1.000	1	1	1	0	0	9	4	0	1	11	5.0	2.00	124	.125	.152	2	.333	0	0	0	0	0.1
1880 Wor-N	32	32	.500	74	66	57	5	3	590²	541	7	74	243	9.4	2.15	121	.231	.255	70	.227	-4	15	29	-6	2.3
1881 Wor-N	25	26	.490	53	52	50	3	0	462¹	547	7	68	156	12.0	3.39	89	.282	.306	63	.250	-1	-31	-19	2	-1.3
1882 Wor-N	14	33	.298	48	46	44	0	0	411	525	11	88	123	13.4	3.74	83	.294	.327	64	.281	8	-39	-29	3	-1.3
1883 Pro-N	3	7	.300	12	12	8	0	0	92	122	2	27	13	14.6	3.33	93	.301	.345	55	.284	3	-2	-2	0	-0.1
1886 Cin-a	0	2	.000	3	2	1	0	0	18	24	0	11	6	17.5	8.00	44	.306	.391	8	.276	0	-9	-9	0	-0.6
Total 6	75	100	.429	191	179	161	8	3	1583	1763	27	269	552	11.6	3.06	95	.268	.297	262	.257	7	-66	-29	-2	-0.9

■ RAY RICHMOND Richmond, Raymond Sinclair b: 6/15/1896, Fillmore, Ill. d: 10/21/69, DeSoto, Mo. BR/TR, 6', 175 lbs. Deb: 9/25/20

YEAR TM/L	W	L	PCT	G	GS	CG	SH	SV	IP	H	HR	BB	SO	RAT	ERA	ERA+	OAV	OOB	BH	AVG	PB	PR	/A	PD	TPI
1920 StL-A	2	0	1.000	2	2	1	0	0	17	18	0	9	4	14.3	6.35	62	.273	.360	1	.167	-0	-5	-5	0	-0.3
1921 StL-A	0	1	.000	6	2	0	0	0	14¹	21	1	13	6	23.2	11.30	40	.362	.500	0	.000	-1	-11	-11	0	-0.9
Total 2	2	1	.667	8	4	1	0	0	31¹	39	1	22	10	18.4	8.62	48	.315	.430	1	.100	-1	-16	-15	0	-1.2

■ REGGIE RICHTER Richter, Emil Henry b: 9/14/1888, Dusseldorf, Germany d: 8/2/34, Winfield, Ill. BR/TR, 6'2", 180 lbs. Deb: 5/30/11

YEAR TM/L	W	L	PCT	G	GS	CG	SH	SV	IP	H	HR	BB	SO	RAT	ERA	ERA+	OAV	OOB	BH	AVG	PB	PR	/A	PD	TPI
1911 Chi-N	1	3	.250	22	5	0	0	2	54²	62	1	20	34	14.0	3.13	106	.307	.378	1	.100	-1	2	1	-0	0.0

■ DICK RICKETTS Ricketts, Richard James b: 12/4/33, Pottstown, Pa. d: 3/6/88, Rochester, N.Y. BL/TR, 6'7", 215 lbs. Deb: 6/14/59

YEAR TM/L	W	L	PCT	G	GS	CG	SH	SV	IP	H	HR	BB	SO	RAT	ERA	ERA+	OAV	OOB	BH	AVG	PB	PR	/A	PD	TPI
1959 StL-N	1	6	.143	12	9	0	0	0	55²	68	7	30	25	15.8	5.82	73	.301	.383	1	.056	-2	-12	-10	-2	-1.1

■ ELMER RIDDLE Riddle, Elmer Ray b: 7/31/14, Columbus, Ga. d: 5/14/84, Columbus, Ga. BR/TR, 5'11.5", 170 lbs. Deb: 10/01/39

YEAR TM/L	W	L	PCT	G	GS	CG	SH	SV	IP	H	HR	BB	SO	RAT	ERA	ERA+	OAV	OOB	BH	AVG	PB	PR	/A	PD	TPI
1939 Cin-N	0	0	—	1	0	0	0	0	2	1	0	0	0	4.5	0.00	—	.143	.143	0	—	0	1	1	0	0.1
1940 *Cin-N	1	2	.333	15	1	1	0	2	33²	30	0	17	9	12.6	1.87	202	.250	.343	1	.143	0	7	7	0	0.8
1941 Cin-N	19	4	**.826**	33	22	15	4	1	216²	180	8	59	80	10.1	2.24	160	.224	.282	16	.225	3	33	33	-0	3.8
1942 Cin-N	7	11	.389	29	19	7	1	0	158¹	157	7	79	78	13.6	3.69	89	.260	.349	15	.259	3	-7	-7	-1	-0.5
1943 Cin-N	**21**	11	.656	36	33	19	5	3	260¹	235	6	107	69	11.9	2.63	126	.245	.322	18	.194	1	22	20	-0	2.2
1944 Cin-N	2	2	.500	4	4	2	0	0	26²	25	0	12	6	12.5	4.05	86	.250	.330	1	.125	-0	-1	-2	1	0.0
1945 Cin-N	1	4	.200	12	3	0	0	0	29²	39	4	27	5	20.0	8.19	46	.333	.458	3	.273	4	-14	-15	-1	-1.2
1947 Cin-N	1	0	1.000	16	3	0	0	0	30¹	42	5	31	8	22.0	8.31	49	.333	.468	0	.000	-0	-14	-14	-1	-1.3
1948 Pit-N	12	10	.545	28	27	12	3	1	191	184	20	67	63	12.6	3.49	117	.250	.327	12	.188	1	10	12	0	1.5
1949 Pit-N	1	8	.111	16	12	1	0	0	74¹	91	9	45	24	15.7	5.33	79	.281	.386	3	.136	-1	-11	-9	-1	-1.0
Total 10	65	52	.556	190	124	57	13	8	1023	974	59	458	342	12.8	3.40	107	.252	.335	69	.204	7	26	25	-2	4.4

■ DENNY RIDDLEBERGER Riddleberger, Dennis Michael b: 11/22/45, Clifton Forge, Va. BR/TL, 6'3", 195 lbs. Deb: 9/15/70

YEAR TM/L	W	L	PCT	G	GS	CG	SH	SV	IP	H	HR	BB	SO	RAT	ERA	ERA+	OAV	OOB	BH	AVG	PB	PR	/A	PD	TPI
1970 Was-A	0	0	—	8	0	0	0	0	9¹	7	1	2	5	8.7	0.96	369	.219	.265	0	—	0	3	3	-0	0.2
1971 Was-A	3	1	.750	57	0	0	0	1	69²	67	9	32	56	12.9	3.23	102	.260	.344	0	.000	0	2	1	-0	0.0
1972 Cle-A	1	3	.250	38	0	0	0	1	54	45	5	22	34	11.5	2.50	129	.237	.322	0	.000	-0	3	4	-0	0.4
Total 3	4	4	.500	103	0	0	0	2	133	119	15	56	95	12.0	2.77	119	.248	.330	0	.000	-0	8	8	-1	0.6

■ DORSEY RIDDLEMOSER Riddlemoser, Dorsey Lee b: 3/25/1875, Frederick, Md. d: 5/11/54, Frederick, Md. BR/TR, Deb: 8/22/1899

YEAR TM/L	W	L	PCT	G	GS	CG	SH	SV	IP	H	HR	BB	SO	RAT	ERA	ERA+	OAV	OOB	BH	AVG	PB	PR	/A	PD	TPI
1899 Was-N	0	1	.000	1	1	0	0	0	2	7	0	2	0	40.5	18.00	22	.552	.613	0	.000	0	-3	-3	0	-0.2

■ JACK RIDGWAY Ridgway, Jacob A. b: 7/23/1889, Philadelphia, Pa. d: 2/23/28, Philadelphia, Pa. BL/TR, 5'11", 174 lbs. Deb: 5/20/14

YEAR TM/L	W	L	PCT	G	GS	CG	SH	SV	IP	H	HR	BB	SO	RAT	ERA	ERA+	OAV	OOB	BH	AVG	PB	PR	/A	PD	TPI
1914 Bal-F	0	1	.000	4	1	0	0	0	9	20	1	3	2	24.0	11.00	31	.449	.494	0	.000	-0	-8	-8	0	-0.6

■ STEVE RIDZIK Ridzik, Stephen George b: 4/29/29, Yonkers, N.Y. BR/TR, 5'11", 170 lbs. Deb: 9/04/50

YEAR TM/L	W	L	PCT	G	GS	CG	SH	SV	IP	H	HR	BB	SO	RAT	ERA	ERA+	OAV	OOB	BH	AVG	PB	PR	/A	PD	TPI
1950 Phi-N	0	0	—	1	0	0	0	0	3	3	1	1	2	12.0	6.00	67	.300	.364	0	—	0	-1	-1	0	0.0

YEAR	TM/L	W	L	PCT	G	GS	CG	SH	SV	IP	H	HR	BB	SO	RAT	ERA	ERA+	OAV	OOB	BH	AVG	PB	PR	/A	PD	TPI
1952	Phi-N	4	2	.667	24	9	2	0	0	92²	74	10	37	43	10.9	3.01	121	.218	.297	3	.136	0	7	7	-2	0.5
1953	Phi-N	9	6	.600	42	12	1	0	0	124	119	15	48	53	12.5	3.77	112	.256	.332	7	.194	2	7	6	-0	0.7
1954	Phi-N	4	5	.444	35	6	0	0	0	80²	72	7	44	45	12.9	4.13	98	.233	.329	5	.227	1	-1	-1	0	0.0
1955	Phi-N	0	1	.000	3	1	0	0	0	11	7	1	8	6	14.7	2.45	162	.179	.360	0	.000	-1	2	2	0	0.1
	Cin-N	0	3	.000	13	2	0	0	0	30	35	4	14	6	15.0	4.50	94	.299	.379	1	.167	-0	-1	-1	-0	-0.1
	Yr	0	4	.000	16	3	0	0	0	41	42	5	22	12	14.3	3.95	105	.264	.357	0	.000	-1	0	1	-0	0.0
1956	NY-N	6	2	.750	41	5	1	1	0	92¹	80	7	65	53	14.6	3.80	99	.240	.371	7	.250	1	-0	-0	-0	0.0
1957	NY-N	0	2	.000	15	0	0	0	0	26²	19	3	19	13	13.5	4.73	83	.213	.364	1	.200	-0	-3	-2	0	-0.1
1958	Cle-A	0	2	.000	6	0	0	0	0	8²	9	1	5	6	14.5	2.08	176	.257	.350	0	.000	-0	2	2	0	0.2
1963	Was-A	5	6	.455	20	10	0	0	1	89²	82	16	35	47	12.2	4.82	77	.240	.319	5	.172	0	-12	-11	0	-1.0
1964	Was-A	5	5	.500	49	3	0	0	2	112	96	10	31	60	10.8	2.89	128	.236	.301	6	.222	1	9	10	-1	1.1
1965	Was-A	6	4	.600	63	0	0	0	8	109²	108	18	43	72	13.0	4.02	86	.257	.335	3	.167	0	-7	-7	0	-0.5
1966	Phi-N	0	0	—	2	0	0	0	0	2¹	5	0	1	0	23.1	7.71	47	.455	.500	0	—	0	-1	-1	0	0.0
Total	12	39	38	.506	314	48	4	1	11	782²	709	93	351	406	12.6	3.79	101	.243	.332	38	.192	4	2	3	-3	0.9

■ ELMER RIEGER
Rieger, Elmer Jay b: 2/25/1889, Perris, Cal. d: 10/21/59, Los Angeles, Cal. BB/TR, 6′, 175 lbs. Deb: 4/20/10

YEAR	TM/L	W	L	PCT	G	GS	CG	SH	SV	IP	H	HR	BB	SO	RAT	ERA	ERA+	OAV	OOB	BH	AVG	PB	PR	/A	PD	TPI
1910	StL-N	0	2	.000	13	2	0	0	0	21¹	26	1	7	9	14.3	5.48	54	.325	.386	0	.000	0	-6	-6	0	-0.5

■ DAVE RIGHETTI
Righetti, David Allan b: 11/28/58, San Jose, Cal. BL/TL, 6′2″, 170 lbs. Deb: 9/16/79

YEAR	TM/L	W	L	PCT	G	GS	CG	SH	SV	IP	H	HR	BB	SO	RAT	ERA	ERA+	OAV	OOB	BH	AVG	PB	PR	/A	PD	TPI
1979	NY-A	0	1	.000	3	3	0	0	0	17¹	10	2	10	13	10.4	3.63	112	.182	.308	0	—	0	1	1	0	0.1
1981	*NY-A	8	4	.667	15	15	2	0	0	105¹	75	1	38	89	9.7	2.05	174	.196	.269	0	—	0	19	18	-1	1.8
1982	NY-A	11	10	.524	33	27	4	0	1	183	155	11	108	163	13.2	3.79	105	.229	.340	0	—	0	6	4	-2	0.2
1983	NY-A	14	8	.636	31	31	7	2	0	217	194	12	67	169	10.9	3.44	113	.237	.297	0	—	0	15	11	-2	0.9
1984	NY-A	5	6	.455	64	0	0	0	31	96¹	79	5	37	90	10.8	2.34	162	.223	.296	0	—	0	18	16	-0	1.5
1985	NY-A	12	7	.632	74	0	0	0	29	107	96	5	45	92	11.9	2.78	144	.241	.318	0	—	0	16	15	-1	1.4
1986	NY-A	8	8	.500	74	0	0	0	**46**	106²	88	4	35	83	10.5	2.45	167	.226	.293	0	—	0	20	19	-1	1.8
1987	NY-A	8	6	.571	60	0	0	0	31	95	95	9	44	77	13.4	3.51	125	.262	.346	0	—	0	10	9	-1	0.8
1988	NY-A	5	4	.556	60	0	0	0	25	87	86	5	37	70	12.8	3.52	112	.257	.332	0	—	0	4	4	-1	0.3
1989	NY-A	2	6	.250	55	0	0	0	25	69	73	3	26	51	13.0	3.00	129	.277	.344	0	—	0	7	7	-1	0.6
1990	NY-A	1	1	.500	53	0	0	0	36	53	48	8	26	43	12.9	3.57	111	.234	.326	0	—	0	2	2	-1	0.1
Total	11	74	61	.548	522	76	13	2	224	1136²	999	65	473	940	11.8	3.11	127	.236	.315	0	—	0	118	105	-11	9.5

■ JOHNNY RIGNEY
Rigney, John Dungan b: 10/28/14, Oak Park, Ill. d: 10/21/84, Lombard, Ill. BR/TR, 6′2″, 190 lbs. Deb: 4/21/37

YEAR	TM/L	W	L	PCT	G	GS	CG	SH	SV	IP	H	HR	BB	SO	RAT	ERA	ERA+	OAV	OOB	BH	AVG	PB	PR	/A	PD	TPI
1937	Chi-A	2	5	.286	22	4	0	0	1	90²	107	10	46	38	15.5	4.96	93	.290	.373	5	.167	-0	-3	-4	-1	-0.3
1938	Chi-A	9	9	.500	38	12	7	1	1	167	164	16	72	84	12.8	3.56	138	.256	.333	8	.145	-3	23	25	0	2.0
1939	Chi-A	15	8	.652	35	29	11	2	0	218²	208	10	84	119	12.1	3.70	128	.247	.316	16	.200	-1	22	25	-2	2.1
1940	Chi-A	14	18	.438	39	33	19	2	3	280²	240	22	90	141	10.6	3.11	142	.230	.302	20	.215	1	40	41	-2	4.0
1941	Chi-A	13	13	.500	30	29	18	3	0	237	224	21	92	119	12.1	3.84	107	.249	.320	17	.202	2	8	7	-0	0.7
1942	Chi-A	3	3	.500	7	7	6	0	0	59	40	2	16	34	8.7	3.20	112	.185	.245	1	.053	-1	3	3	0	0.1
1946	Chi-A	5	5	.500	15	11	3	2	0	82²	76	6	35	51	12.3	4.03	85	.240	.319	4	.154	-1	-5	-6	-1	-0.6
1947	Chi-A	2	3	.400	11	7	2	0	0	50²	42	3	15	19	10.1	1.95	187	.228	.286	0	.000	-2	10	10	1	1.0
Total	8	63	64	.496	197	132	66	10	5	1186¹	1101	90	450	605	11.9	3.59	121	.244	.314	71	.177	-6	98	100	-4	9.0

■ JOSE RIJO
Rijo, Jose Antonio (Abreu) b: 5/13/65, San Cristobal, D.R. BR/TR, 6′1″, 200 lbs. Deb: 4/05/84

YEAR	TM/L	W	L	PCT	G	GS	CG	SH	SV	IP	H	HR	BB	SO	RAT	ERA	ERA+	OAV	OOB	BH	AVG	PB	PR	/A	PD	TPI
1984	NY-A	2	8	.200	24	5	0	0	2	62¹	74	5	33	47	15.6	4.76	80	.298	.383	0	—	0	-5	-7	1	-0.5
1985	Oak-A	6	4	.600	12	9	0	0	0	63²	57	6	28	65	12.2	3.53	109	.239	.322	0	—	0	4	2	-1	0.1
1986	Oak-A	9	11	.450	39	26	4	0	1	193²	172	24	108	176	13.2	4.65	83	.237	.339	0	—	0	-10	-17	-2	-1.7
1987	Oak-A	2	7	.222	21	14	1	0	0	82¹	106	10	41	67	16.3	5.90	70	.305	.381	0	—	0	-13	-16	0	-1.4
1988	Cin-N	13	8	.619	49	19	0	0	0	162	120	7	63	160	10.3	2.39	150	.209	.291	2	.054	-2	19	21	-1	2.1
1989	Cin-N	7	6	.538	19	19	1	1	0	111	101	6	48	86	12.2	2.84	127	.249	.332	8	.211	1	8	9	-0	1.2
1990	*Cin-N	14	8	.636	29	29	7	1	0	197	151	10	78	152	10.6	2.70	144	.212	.292	10	.161	0	24	26	1	2.9
Total	7	53	52	.505	193	121	13	2	3	872	781	68	399	753	12.3	3.60	106	.240	.326	20	.146	-1	27	21	-2	2.7

■ GEORGE RILEY
Riley, George Michael b: 10/6/56, Philadelphia, Pa. BL/TL, 6′2″, 210 lbs. Deb: 9/15/79

YEAR	TM/L	W	L	PCT	G	GS	CG	SH	SV	IP	H	HR	BB	SO	RAT	ERA	ERA+	OAV	OOB	BH	AVG	PB	PR	/A	PD	TPI
1979	Chi-N	0	1	.000	4	1	0	0	0	13	16	1	6	5	16.6	5.54	74	.320	.414	0	.000	-0	-3	-2	0	-0.1
1980	Chi-N	0	4	.000	22	0	0	0	0	36	41	2	20	18	15.8	5.75	68	.293	.389	0	.000	-0	-9	-7	1	-0.6
1984	SF-N	1	0	1.000	5	4	0	0	0	29¹	39	1	7	12	14.7	3.99	88	.315	.361	1	.100	-0	-1	-2	-0	-0.1
1986	Mon-N	0	0	—	10	0	0	0	0	8²	7	0	8	5	16.6	4.15	89	.212	.381	0	—	0	-0	-0	-0	-0.1
Total	4	1	5	.167	41	5	0	0	0	87	103	4	41	40	15.6	4.97	76	.297	.382	1	.077	-1	-13	-11	1	-0.8

■ ANDY RINCON
Rincon, Andrew John b: 3/5/59, Monterey Park, Cal. BR/TR, 6′3″, 195 lbs. Deb: 9/15/80

YEAR	TM/L	W	L	PCT	G	GS	CG	SH	SV	IP	H	HR	BB	SO	RAT	ERA	ERA+	OAV	OOB	BH	AVG	PB	PR	/A	PD	TPI
1980	StL-N	3	1	.750	4	4	1	0	0	31	23	1	7	22	8.7	2.61	141	.215	.263	3	.250	0	3	4	0	0.5
1981	StL-N	3	1	.750	5	5	1	1	0	35²	27	0	5	13	8.6	1.77	201	.214	.258	5	.231	1	7	7	-0	0.9
1982	StL-N	2	3	.400	11	6	1	0	0	40	35	1	25	11	13.5	4.72	77	.241	.353	1	.100	-0	-5	-5	-0	-0.5
Total	3	8	5	.615	20	15	3	1	0	106²	85	2	37	46	10.5	3.12	116	.225	.297	7	.200	1	5	6	-0	0.9

■ JEFF RINEER
Rineer, Jeffrey Alan b: 7/3/55, Lancaster, Pa. BL/TL, 6′4″, 205 lbs. Deb: 9/30/79

YEAR	TM/L	W	L	PCT	G	GS	CG	SH	SV	IP	H	HR	BB	SO	RAT	ERA	ERA+	OAV	OOB	BH	AVG	PB	PR	/A	PD	TPI
1979	Bal-A	0	0	—	1	0	0	0	0	1	0	0	0	0	0.0	0.00	—	.000	.000	0	—	0	0	0	0	0.0

■ JIMMY RING
Ring, James Joseph b: 2/15/1895, Brooklyn, N.Y. d: 7/6/65, New York, N.Y. BR/TR, 6′1″, 170 lbs. Deb: 4/13/17

YEAR	TM/L	W	L	PCT	G	GS	CG	SH	SV	IP	H	HR	BB	SO	RAT	ERA	ERA+	OAV	OOB	BH	AVG	PB	PR	/A	PD	TPI
1917	Cin-N	3	7	.300	24	7	3	0	2	88	90	2	35	33	12.9	4.40	60	.272	.343	2	.077	-2	-16	-17	0	-1.9
1918	Cin-N	9	5	.643	21	18	13	4	0	142¹	130	5	48	26	11.4	2.85	94	.247	.314	6	.120	-3	-1	-3	-3	-0.8
1919	*Cin-N	10	9	.526	32	18	12	2	3	183	150	1	51	61	10.0	2.26	123	.232	.291	6	.097	-5	13	10	3	0.9
1920	Cin-N	17	16	.515	42	33	18	1	1	266²	268	4	92	73	12.3	3.54	86	.264	.329	19	.198	-0	-12	-15	1	-1.5
1921	Phi-N	10	19	.345	34	30	21	0	1	246	258	8	88	88	12.8	4.24	100	.274	.340	12	.145	-5	-13	-0	2	-0.1
1922	Phi-N	12	18	.400	40	33	17	0	1	249¹	292	19	103	116	14.4	4.58	102	.297	.365	13	.148	-5	-13	2	3	0.2
1923	Phi-N	18	16	.529	39	36	23	0	0	304¹	336	13	115	112	13.4	3.87	119	.283	.347	12	.106	-10	4	25	3	1.9
1924	Phi-N	10	12	.455	32	31	16	1	0	215¹	236	10	108	72	14.5	3.97	112	.286	.371	17	.230	-1	-2	12	2	1.5
1925	Phi-N	14	16	.467	38	37	21	1	0	270	325	14	119	93	14.8	4.37	109	.284	.367	11	.109	-8	-3	12	2	0.7
1926	NY-N	11	10	.524	39	23	5	0	2	183¹	207	12	74	76	13.8	4.57	82	.290	.357	8	.143	-3	-15	-17	-2	-2.0
1927	StL-N	0	4	.000	13	3	1	0	0	33	39	3	17	13	15.5	6.55	60	.300	.385	3	.375	1	-10	-10	1	-0.6
1928	Phi-N	4	17	.190	35	25	4	0	1	179	214	13	103	72	16.6	6.40	67	.316	.407	11	.183	-2	-46	-41	1	-3.8
Total	12	118	149	.442	389	294	154	9	11	2354¹	2545	104	953	835	13.5	4.12	95	.281	.351	120	.147	-42	-115	-50	13	-5.5

■ ALLEN RIPLEY
Ripley, Allen Stevens b: 10/18/52, Norwood, Mass. BR/TR, 6′3″, 190 lbs. Deb: 4/10/78

YEAR	TM/L	W	L	PCT	G	GS	CG	SH	SV	IP	H	HR	BB	SO	RAT	ERA	ERA+	OAV	OOB	BH	AVG	PB	PR	/A	PD	TPI
1978	Bos-A	2	5	.286	15	11	1	0	0	73	92	10	22	26	14.4	5.55	74	.311	.364	0	—	0	-14	-12	-1	-1.1
1979	Bos-A	3	1	.750	16	3	0	0	1	64²	77	9	25	34	14.6	5.15	86	.295	.363	0	—	0	-7	-5	-1	-0.5
1980	SF-N	9	10	.474	23	20	2	0	0	112²	119	10	36	65	12.7	4.15	85	.274	.335	6	.150	-0	-7	-8	0	-0.7
1981	SF-N	4	4	.500	19	14	1	0	0	90²	103	5	27	47	13.2	4.07	84	.289	.345	4	.133	-1	-6	-6	1	-0.6
1982	Chi-N	5	7	.417	28	19	0	0	0	122²	130	12	38	57	12.5	4.18	89	.285	.343	5	.132	-2	-8	-6	1	-0.6
Total	5	23	27	.460	101	67	4	0	1	463²	521	46	148	229	13.3	4.50	84	.289	.348	15	.139	-3	-42	-37	0	-3.5

■ WALT RIPLEY
Ripley, Walter Franklin b: 11/26/16, Worcester, Mass. d: 10/7/90, Attleboro, Mass. BR/TR, 6′, 168 lbs. Deb: 8/17/35

YEAR	TM/L	W	L	PCT	G	GS	CG	SH	SV	IP	H	HR	BB	SO	RAT	ERA	ERA+	OAV	OOB	BH	AVG	PB	PR	/A	PD	TPI
1935	Bos-A	0	0	—	2	0	0	0	0	4	7	0	3	0	22.5	9.00	53	.412	.500	0	—	0	-2	-2	-0	-0.1

YEAR TM/L	W	L	PCT	G	GS	CG	SH	SV	IP	H	HR	BB	SO	RAT	ERA	ERA+	OAV	OOB	BH	AVG	PB	PR	/A	PD	TPI

■ **RAY RIPPELMEYER** Rippelmeyer, Raymond Roy b: 7/9/33, Valmeyer, Ill. BR/TR, 6'3", 200 lbs. Deb: 4/14/62 C

| 1962 Was-A | 1 | 2 | .333 | 18 | 1 | 0 | 0 | 0 | 39¹ | 47 | 7 | 17 | 17 | 14.6 | 5.49 | 74 | .294 | .362 | 3 | .500 | 2 | -7 | -6 | 2 | -0.1 |

■ **CHARLIE RIPPLE** Ripple, Charles Dawson b: 12/1/21, Bolton, N.C. d: 5/6/79, Wilmington, N.C. BL/TL, 6'2", 210 lbs. Deb: 9/25/44

1944 Phi-N	0	0	—	1	1	0	0	0	2¹	6	0	4	2	38.6	15.43	23	.500	.625	1	1.000	0	-3	-3	0	-0.1
1945 Phi-N	0	1	.000	4	0	0	0	0	7²	7	0	10	5	20.0	7.04	54	.241	.436	0	.000	-0	-3	-3	-0	-0.2
1946 Phi-N	1	0	1.000	6	0	0	0	0	3¹	5	0	6	3	29.7	10.80	32	.385	.579	0	—	0	-3	-3	-0	-0.2
Total 3	1	1	.500	11	1	0	0	0	13¹	18	0	20	10	25.7	9.45	39	.333	.514	1	.500	0	-9	-9	-0	-0.5

■ **JAY RITCHIE** Ritchie, Jay Seay b: 11/20/36, Salisbury, N.C. BR/TR, 6'4", 175 lbs. Deb: 8/04/64

1964 Bos-A	1	1	.500	21	0	0	0	0	46	43	4	14	35	11.2	2.74	141	.249	.305	1	.111	-1	5	6	0	0.6
1965 Bos-A	1	2	.333	44	0	0	0	2	71	83	3	26	55	13.9	3.17	118	.302	.364	1	.200	-1	2	4	0	0.5
1966 Atl-N	0	1	.000	22	0	0	0	4	35¹	32	3	12	33	11.2	4.08	89	.241	.303	2	.500	1	-2	-2	0	0.0
1967 Atl-N	4	6	.400	52	0	0	0	2	82¹	75	6	29	57	11.8	3.17	105	.245	.319	3	.300	1	2	1	1	0.4
1968 Cin-N	2	3	.400	28	2	0	0	0	56²	68	7	13	32	13.0	4.61	69	.293	.333	0	—	-1	-10	-9	-1	-1.1
Total 5	8	13	.381	167	2	0	0	8	291¹	301	23	94	212	12.4	3.49	101	.269	.329	7	.200	1	-3	1	0	0.4

■ **WALLY RITCHIE** Ritchie, Wallace Reid b: 7/12/65, Glendale, Cal. BL/TL, 6'2", 180 lbs. Deb: 5/01/87

1987 Phi-N	3	2	.600	49	0	0	0	3	62¹	60	8	29	45	13.0	3.75	113	.254	.338	1	.250	0	2	3	-0	0.3
1988 Phi-N	0	0	—	19	0	0	0	0	26	19	1	17	8	12.8	3.12	114	.207	.336	0	—	0	1	1	-0	0.1
Total 2	3	2	.600	68	0	0	0	3	88¹	79	9	46	53	12.9	3.57	113	.241	.338	1	.250	0	3	5	-0	0.4

■ **REGGIE RITTER** Ritter, Reggie Blake b: 1/23/60, Malvern, Ark. BL/TR, 6'2", 195 lbs. Deb: 5/17/86

1986 Cle-A	0	0	—	5	0	0	0	0	10	14	1	4	6	17.1	6.30	66	.341	.413	0	—	0	-2	-2	0	-0.1
1987 Cle-A	1	1	.500	14	0	0	0	0	26²	33	5	16	11	16.5	6.08	74	.300	.389	0	—	0	-5	-5	-0	-0.3
Total 2	1	1	.500	19	0	0	0	0	36²	47	6	20	17	16.7	6.14	72	.311	.395	0	—	0	-7	-7	1	-0.4

■ **HANK RITTER** Ritter, William Herbert b: 10/12/1893, McCoysville, Pa. d: 9/3/64, Akron, Ohio BR/TR, 6', 180 lbs. Deb: 8/03/12

1912 Phi-N	0	0	—	3	0	0	0	0	6	5	0	5	1	15.0	4.50	81	.185	.313	0	.000	-0	-1	-1	-0	0.0
1914 NY-N	1	0	1.000	1	0	0	0	0	8	4	0	4	4	9.0	1.13	236	.160	.276	0	.000	-0	1	1	-0	0.1
1915 NY-N	2	1	.667	22	2	0	0	2	58¹	66	4	15	35	13.3	4.63	55	.291	.348	2	.125	-1	-12	-13	-1	-1.5
1916 NY-N	1	0	1.000	3	0	0	0	0	5	3	0	3	3	7.2	0.00	—	.200	.250	0	—	0	1	1	0	0.2
Total 4	4	1	.800	29	2	0	0	2	77¹	78	4	27	43	12.6	3.96	67	.265	.333	2	.100	-1	-10	-11	-1	-1.2

■ **JIM RITTWAGE** Rittwage, James Michael b: 10/23/44, Cleveland, Ohio BR/TR, 6'3", 190 lbs. Deb: 9/07/70

| 1970 Cle-A | 1 | 1 | .500 | 8 | 3 | 1 | 0 | 0 | 26 | 18 | 0 | 21 | 16 | 13.5 | 4.15 | 95 | .194 | .342 | 3 | .375 | 1 | -1 | -1 | 0 | 0.1 |

■ **KEVIN RITZ** Ritz, Kevin D b: 6/8/65, Eatonstown, N.J. BR/TR, 6'4", 195 lbs. Deb: 7/15/89

1989 Det-A	4	6	.400	12	12	1	0	0	74	75	2	44	56	14.6	4.38	87	.265	.366	0	—	0	-4	-5	-0	-0.4
1990 Det-A	0	4	.000	4	4	0	0	0	7¹	14	0	14	3	34.4	11.05	36	.400	.571	0	—	0	-6	-6	1	-0.4
Total 2	4	10	.286	16	16	1	0	0	81¹	89	2	58	59	16.4	4.98	77	.280	.393	0	—	0	-10	-10	1	-0.8

■ **TINK RIVIERE** Riviere, Arthur Bernard b: 8/2/1899, Liberty, Tex. d: 9/27/65, Liberty, Tex. BR/TR, 5'10", 167 lbs. Deb: 4/15/21

1921 StL-N	1	0	1.000	18	2	0	0	0	38¹	45	2	20	15	15.7	6.10	60	.280	.366	3	.375	2	-10	-10	-2	-0.9
1925 Chi-A	0	0	—	3	0	0	0	0	4²	6	0	7	1	27.0	13.50	31	.429	.636	0	.000	-0	-5	-5	1	-0.3
Total 2	1	0	1.000	21	2	0	0	0	43	51	2	27	16	17.0	6.91	54	.291	.395	3	.333	2	-15	-15	-1	-1.2

■ **EPPA RIXEY** Rixey, Eppa "Jephta" b: 5/3/1891, Culpeper, Va. d: 2/28/63, Cincinnati, Ohio BR/TL, 6'5", 210 lbs. Deb: 6/21/12 H

1912 Phi-N	10	10	.500	23	20	10	3	0	162	147	2	54	59	11.3	2.50	145	.247	.312	9	.170	-2	16	20	-1	1.9
1913 Phi-N	9	5	.643	35	19	9	1	2	155²	148	4	56	75	12.1	3.12	107	.258	.331	9	.191	-0	1	4	-0	0.3
1914 Phi-N	2	11	.154	24	15	2	0	0	103	124	0	45	41	15.0	4.37	67	.313	.387	1	.038	-1	-18	-16	1	-1.7
1915 *Phi-N	11	12	.478	29	22	10	2	1	176²	163	2	64	88	11.7	2.39	115	.250	.319	9	.164	-0	7	7	0	0.8
1916 Phi-N	22	10	.688	38	33	20	3	0	287	239	2	74	134	10.0	1.85	143	.229	.284	15	.155	-2	25	26	3	3.2
1917 Phi-N	16	21	.432	39	36	23	4	1	281¹	249	1	67	121	10.3	2.27	124	.241	.290	18	.191	-2	14	17	4	2.3
1919 Phi-N	6	12	.333	23	18	11	1	0	154	160	4	50	63	12.4	3.97	81	.278	.339	7	.149	-2	-18	-13	1	-1.3
1920 Phi-N	11	22	.333	41	33	25	0	2	284¹	288	5	69	109	11.4	3.48	98	.274	.321	25	.248	2	-11	-2	3	0.3
1921 Cin-N	19	18	.514	40	36	21	2	1	301	324	1	66	76	11.8	2.78	129	.282	.324	13	.129	-5	**34**	27	4	2.5
1922 Cin-N	25	13	.658	40	38	26	2	0	313¹	337	13	45	80	11.1	3.53	113	.275	.303	21	.193	-1	20	16	0	1.4
1923 Cin-N	20	15	.571	42	37	23	3	1	309	334	3	65	97	11.7	2.80	138	.280	.320	17	.159	-4	41	37	3	3.3
1924 Cin-N	15	14	.517	35	29	15	4	1	238¹	219	3	47	57	10.1	2.76	137	.246	.285	18	.214	1	29	27	0	2.8
1925 Cin-N	21	11	.656	39	36	22	2	1	287¹	302	8	47	69	11.2	2.88	143	.273	.307	22	.214	-1	44	39	-1	3.6
1926 Cin-N	14	8	.636	37	29	14	3	1	233	231	12	58	61	11.2	3.40	109	.265	.313	19	.226	0	11	8	-1	0.6
1927 Cin-N	12	10	.545	34	29	11	1	1	219²	240	3	43	42	11.7	3.48	109	.287	.325	20	.247	4	11	7	0	1.0
1928 Cin-N	19	18	.514	43	37	17	3	2	291¹	317	4	67	58	12.0	3.43	115	.288	.330	18	.173	-1	18	17	0	1.5
1929 Cin-N	10	13	.435	35	24	11	0	1	201	235	6	60	37	13.3	4.16	110	.296	.348	6	.231	-0	12	9	-1	0.7
1930 Cin-N	9	13	.409	32	21	5	0	0	164	207	11	47	37	14.3	5.10	95	.317	.370	11	.200	-1	-2	-5	-0	-0.5
1931 Cin-N	4	7	.364	22	17	4	0	0	126²	143	4	30	22	12.3	3.91	96	.291	.332	6	.150	-1	-1	-2	4	0.0
1932 Cin-N	5	5	.500	25	11	6	2	0	111²	108	3	16	14	10.3	2.66	145	.254	.288	9	.265	1	15	15	1	1.7
1933 Cin-N	6	3	.667	16	12	5	1	0	94¹	118	1	12	10	12.4	3.15	108	.298	.319	9	.257	2	2	3	2	0.6
Total 21	266	251	.515	692	552	290	37	14	4494²	4633	92	1082	1350	11.6	3.15	116	.272	.318	291	.191	-14	250	248	19	25.0

■ **JOHN ROACH** Roach, John F. b: Farrensville, Pa. d: 3/1/15, Sandusky, Ohio TL, 5'9", 175 lbs. Deb: 5/14/1887

| 1887 NY-N | 0 | 1 | .000 | 1 | 1 | 1 | 0 | 0 | 8 | 18 | 0 | 4 | 3 | 24.8 | 11.25 | 33 | .433 | .482 | 1 | .250 | -0 | -6 | -7 | 0 | -0.4 |

■ **SKELL ROACH** Roach, Skell (b: Rudolph C. Weichbrodt) b: 10/20/1871, Germany d: 3/9/58, Oak Park, Ill. BR/TR, Deb: 8/09/1899

| 1899 Chi-N | 1 | 0 | 1.000 | 1 | 1 | 1 | 0 | 0 | 9 | 13 | 0 | 1 | 0 | 14.0 | 3.00 | 125 | .337 | .354 | 0 | .000 | -1 | 1 | 1 | -0 | 0.0 |

■ **BRUCE ROBBINS** Robbins, Bruce Duane b: 9/10/59, Portland, Ind. BL/TL, 6'1", 190 lbs. Deb: 7/28/79

1979 Det-A	3	3	.500	10	8	0	0	0	46	45	3	21	22	12.9	3.91	111	.265	.346	0	—	0	2	2	-0	0.2
1980 Det-A	4	2	.667	15	6	0	0	0	51²	60	12	28	23	15.3	6.62	62	.287	.371	0	—	0	-15	-14	0	-1.3
Total 2	7	5	.583	25	14	0	0	0	97²	105	15	49	45	14.2	5.34	79	.277	.360	0	—	0	-13	-12	-0	-1.1

■ **BERT ROBERGE** Roberge, Bertrand Roland b: 10/3/54, Lewiston, Maine BR/TR, 6'4", 190 lbs. Deb: 5/28/79

1979 Hou-N	3	0	1.000	26	0	0	0	4	32	20	0	17	33	10.4	1.69	208	.196	.311	0	.000	-0	7	6	-0	0.6
1980 Hou-N	2	0	1.000	14	0	0	0	0	24¹	24	7	10	9	13.3	5.92	56	.261	.346	0	.000	-0	-6	-7	-0	-0.6
1982 Hou-N	1	2	.333	22	0	0	0	3	25²	29	6	18	12.3	4.21	79	.284	.324	0	.000	-0	-2	-3	0	-0.2
1984 Chi-A	3	3	.500	21	0	0	0	0	40²	36	2	15	25	12.0	3.76	111	.240	.321	0	.000	-0	1	2	1	0.3
1985 Mon-N	3	3	.500	42	0	0	0	2	68	58	5	22	34	10.9	3.44	99	.232	.299	0	.000	-0	1	-0	0	0.0
1986 Mon-N	0	4	.000	21	0	0	0	1	28²	33	2	10	20	13.8	6.28	59	.295	.358	0	.000	-0	-8	-8	-0	-0.8
Total 6	12	12	.500	146	0	0	0	10	219¹	200	11	80	119	11.8	3.98	90	.248	.321	0	.000	-1	-7	-10	2	-0.7

■ **DALE ROBERTS** Roberts, Dale "Mountain Man" b: 4/12/42, Owenton, Ky. BR/TL, 6'4", 180 lbs. Deb: 9/09/67

| 1967 NY-A | 0 | 0 | — | 2 | 0 | 0 | 0 | 0 | 2 | 3 | 0 | 2 | 0 | 31.5 | 9.00 | 35 | .429 | .636 | 0 | — | 0 | -1 | -1 | 0 | 0.0 |

■ **DAVE ROBERTS** Roberts, David Arthur b: 9/11/44, Gallipolis, Ohio BL/TL, 6'3", 195 lbs. Deb: 7/06/69

| 1969 SD-N | 0 | 3 | .000 | 22 | 5 | 0 | 0 | 1 | 48² | 65 | 5 | 19 | 19 | 16.1 | 4.81 | 74 | .322 | .388 | 4 | .267 | 1 | -7 | -7 | 1 | -0.5 |

YEAR	TM/L	W	L	PCT	G	GS	CG	SH	SV	IP	H	HR	BB	SO	RAT	ERA	ERA+	OAV	OOB	BH	AVG	PB	PR	/A	PD	TPI
1970	SD-N	8	14	.364	43	21	3	2	1	181²	182	16	43	102	11.2	3.81	104	.261	.305	9	.153	1	5	3	0	0.4
1971	SD-N	14	17	.452	37	34	14	2	0	269²	238	9	61	135	10.1	2.10	157	.240	.288	19	.221	2	41	36	1	4.4
1972	Hou-N	12	7	.632	35	28	7	3	2	192	227	18	57	111	13.4	4.50	75	.296	.346	16	.239	5	-22	-24	-0	-2.0
1973	Hou-N	17	11	.607	39	36	12	6	0	249¹	264	15	62	119	11.8	2.85	127	.271	.316	11	.129	-3	22	22	0	2.0
1974	Hou-N	10	12	.455	34	30	8	2	1	204	216	6	65	72	12.5	3.40	102	.271	.333	16	.219	5	5	1	3	0.9
1975	Hou-N	8	14	.364	32	27	7	0	1	198¹	182	16	73	101	11.7	4.27	79	.244	.313	9	.143	0	-14	-20	2	-1.8
1976	Det-A	16	17	.485	36	36	18	4	0	252	254	16	63	79	11.5	4.00	93	.264	.312	0	—	0	-13	-8	3	-0.5
1977	Det-A	4	10	.286	22	22	5	0	0	129¹	143	20	41	46	12.9	5.15	83	.274	.330	0	—	0	-16	-12	0	-1.1
	Chi-N	1	1	.500	17	6	1	0	1	53	55	1	12	23	11.5	3.23	136	.275	.319	1	.059	-2	4	7	2	0.7
1978	Chi-N	6	8	.429	35	20	2	1	1	142¹	159	17	56	54	13.8	5.25	77	.288	.357	17	.327	7	-26	-19	2	-1.0
1979	SF-N	0	2	.000	26	1	0	0	3	42	42	3	18	23	13.1	2.57	136	.262	.341	0	.000	-1	5	4	1	0.4
	*Pit-N	5	2	.714	21	3	0	0	1	38²	47	1	12	15	14.0	3.26	119	.318	.373	0	.000	-1	2	3	1	0.3
	Yr	5	4	.556	47	4	0	0	4	80²	89	4	30	38	13.4	2.90	127	.287	.352	0	.000	-1	7	7	1	0.7
1980	Pit-N	0	1	.000	2	0	0	0	0	2¹	2	0	1	1	11.6	3.86	94	.250	.333	0	—	0	-0	-0	0	0.0
	Sea-A	4	10	.286	37	4	0	0	3	80¹	86	7	27	47	12.8	4.37	95	.270	.329	0	—	0	-3	-2	-1	-0.3
1981	NY-N	0	3	.000	7	4	0	0	0	15¹	26	5	5	10	18.2	9.39	37	.366	.408	1	.250	-0	-10	-10	0	-0.5
Total	13	103	125	.452	445	277	77	20	15	2099	2188	155	615	957	12.2	3.78	97	.270	.324	103	.194	15	-27	-28	12	1.0

■ JIM ROBERTS
Roberts, James Newson "Big Jim" b: 10/13/1895, Artesia, Miss. d: 6/24/84, Columbus, Miss. BR/TR, 6'3", 205 lbs. Deb: 7/27/24

YEAR	TM/L	W	L	PCT	G	GS	CG	SH	SV	IP	H	HR	BB	SO	RAT	ERA	ERA+	OAV	OOB	BH	AVG	PB	PR	/A	PD	TPI
1924	Bro-N	0	3	.000	11	5	0	0	0	25¹	41	1	8	10	18.1	7.46	50	.360	.411	1	.143	-0	-10	-10	0	-0.9
1925	Bro-N	0	0	—	1	0	0	0	0	1	1	0	0	0	9.0	0.00	—	.500	.500	0	—	0	0	0	0	0.0
Total	2	0	3	.000	12	5	0	0	0	26¹	42	1	8	10	17.8	7.18	52	.362	.413	1	.143	-0	-10	-10	0	-0.9

■ LEON ROBERTS
Roberts, Leon Kauffman b: 1/22/51, Vicksburg, Mich. BR/TR, 6'3", 200 lbs. Deb: 9/03/74 ◆

YEAR	TM/L	W	L	PCT	G	GS	CG	SH	SV	IP	H	HR	BB	SO	RAT	ERA	ERA+	OAV	OOB	BH	AVG	PB	PR	/A	PD	TPI
1984	KC-A	0	0	—	1	0	0	0	0	1	4	1	1	1	45.0	27.00	15	.571	.625	10	.222	0	-3	-3	0	-0.1

■ RAY ROBERTS
Roberts, Raymond b: 8/25/1895, Cruger, Miss. d: 1/30/62, Cruger, Miss. BL/TR, 5'11", 180 lbs. Deb: 9/12/19

YEAR	TM/L	W	L	PCT	G	GS	CG	SH	SV	IP	H	HR	BB	SO	RAT	ERA	ERA+	OAV	OOB	BH	AVG	PB	PR	/A	PD	TPI
1919	Phi-A	0	2	.000	3	2	0	0	0	14	21	0	3	2	15.4	7.71	44	.368	.400	1	.250	-0	-7	-7	-0	-0.5

■ ROBIN ROBERTS
Roberts, Robin Evan b: 9/30/26, Springfield, Ill. BB/TR, 6', 190 lbs. Deb: 6/18/48 H

YEAR	TM/L	W	L	PCT	G	GS	CG	SH	SV	IP	H	HR	BB	SO	RAT	ERA	ERA+	OAV	OOB	BH	AVG	PB	PR	/A	PD	TPI
1948	Phi-N	7	9	.438	20	20	9	0	0	146²	148	10	61	84	13.1	3.19	124	.278	.356	11	.250	4	12	12	-3	1.5
1949	Phi-N	15	15	.500	43	31	11	3	4	226²	229	15	75	95	12.3	3.69	107	.273	.337	5	.075	-3	9	6	-4	0.0
1950	*Phi-N	20	11	.645	40	39	21	**5**	1	304¹	282	29	77	146	10.7	3.02	134	.248	.297	12	.118	-3	**38**	35	0	3.2
1951	Phi-N	21	15	.583	44	39	22	6	2	**315**	284	20	64	127	10.0	3.03	127	.237	**.278**	15	.172	5	33	29	-3	3.2
1952	Phi-N	**28**	7	.800	39	37	**30**	3	2	**330**	292	22	45	148	9.3	2.59	141	.234	.263	14	.125	2	**42**	**39**	-3	4.1
1953	Phi-N	**23**	16	.590	44	41	**33**	5	2	**346²**	324	30	61	**198**	10.0	2.75	153	.242	.276	22	.179	2	59	**56**	-2	5.9
1954	Phi-N	23	15	.605	45	38	**29**	4	4	**336²**	289	35	56	**185**	**9.4**	2.97	136	.231	**.267**	15	.123	-3	41	40	-4	3.4
1955	Phi-N	**23**	14	.622	41	38	**26**	1	3	305	292	41	53	160	10.2	3.28	121	.246	**.280**	27	.252	14	26	24	-5	3.3
1956	Phi-N	19	18	.514	43	37	**22**	1	3	297¹	328	46	40	157	11.2	4.45	84	.282	.307	20	.200	4	-22	-24	-0	-1.9
1957	Phi-N	10	22	.313	39	32	14	2	2	249²	246	40	43	128	10.5	4.07	93	.252	.284	13	.162	0	-5	-7	1	-0.6
1958	Phi-N	17	14	.548	35	34	21	1	0	269²	270	30	51	130	10.8	3.24	122	.259	.294	20	.202	4	21	22	2	2.4
1959	Phi-N	15	17	.469	35	35	19	2	0	257¹	267	34	35	137	10.7	4.27	96	.263	.291	17	.191	3	-9	-5	0	0.0
1960	Phi-N	12	16	.429	35	35	13	2	1	237¹	256	31	34	122	11.1	4.02	97	.275	.302	12	.152	-1	-7	-4	-3	-0.6
1961	Phi-N	1	10	.091	26	18	2	0	0	117	154	19	23	54	13.8	5.85	70	.326	.360	3	.091	-2	-24	-23	-1	-2.4
1962	Bal-A	10	9	.526	27	25	6	0	0	191¹	176	17	41	102	10.4	2.78	135	.244	.289	10	.192	2	25	21	-1	2.3
1963	Bal-A	14	13	.519	35	35	9	2	0	251¹	230	35	40	124	9.8	3.33	106	.240	**.272**	16	.203	2	8	6	-1	0.7
1964	Bal-A	13	7	.650	31	31	8	4	0	204	203	18	52	109	11.4	2.91	123	.261	.310	9	.132	-1	16	15	-1	1.4
1965	Bal-A	5	7	.417	20	15	5	1	0	114²	110	17	20	63	10.3	3.38	103	.252	.286	6	.171	1	1	1	-1	0.1
	Hou-N	5	2	.714	10	10	3	2	0	76	61	1	10	34	8.4	1.89	177	.216	.243	5	.238	3	14	12	-2	1.6
1966	Hou-N	3	5	.375	13	12	1	1	1	63²	79	7	10	26	12.7	3.82	90	.307	.336	1	.063	-1	-1	-3	-0	-0.3
	Chi-N	2	3	.400	11	9	1	0	0	48¹	62	8	11	28	13.6	6.14	60	.313	.349	2	.200	1	-14	-13	0	-1.1
	Yr	5	8	.385	24	21	2	1	1	112	141	15	21	54	13.0	4.82	73	.307	.337	4	.154	0	-15	-16	-0	-1.4
Total	19	286	245	.539	676	609	305	45	25	4688²	4582	505	902	2357	10.6	3.41	113	.255	.293	255	.167	34	264	239	-32	26.2

■ CHARLIE ROBERTSON
Robertson, Charles Culbertson b: 1/31/1896, Dexter, Tex. d: 8/23/84, Fort Worth, Tex. BL/TR, 6', 175 lbs. Deb: 5/13/19

YEAR	TM/L	W	L	PCT	G	GS	CG	SH	SV	IP	H	HR	BB	SO	RAT	ERA	ERA+	OAV	OOB	BH	AVG	PB	PR	/A	PD	TPI
1919	Chi-A	0	1	.000	1	1	0	0	0	2	5	0	1	0	22.5	9.00	35	.556	.556	0	—	0	-1	-1	0	0.0
1922	Chi-A	14	15	.483	37	34	21	3	0	272	294	9	89	83	12.8	3.64	112	.286	.345	16	.184	-2	12	13	-4	0.7
1923	Chi-A	13	18	.419	38	34	18	1	0	255	262	8	104	91	13.1	3.81	104	.272	.346	21	.247	0	5	4	-2	0.2
1924	Chi-A	4	10	.286	17	14	5	0	0	97¹	108	2	54	29	15.0	4.99	83	.293	.383	6	.182	-1	-8	-9	-2	-1.0
1925	Chi-A	8	12	.400	24	23	6	2	0	137	181	8	47	27	15.1	5.26	79	.327	.381	10	.222	0	-13	-17	-1	-1.5
1926	StL-A	1	2	.333	8	7	1	0	0	28	38	4	21	13	19.6	8.36	51	.333	.445	3	.300	1	-13	-13	0	-1.0
1927	Bos-N	7	17	.292	28	22	6	0	0	154¹	188	2	46	49	13.9	4.72	79	.308	.360	12	.240	1	-14	-17	-1	-1.7
1928	Bos-N	2	5	.286	13	7	3	0	1	59¹	73	5	16	17	13.5	5.31	74	.308	.352	0	.000	-1	-9	-9	-1	-0.9
Total	8	49	80	.380	166	142	60	6	1	1005	1149	38	377	310	13.8	4.44	90	.296	.361	68	.208	-2	-42	-49	-12	-5.2

■ JERRY ROBERTSON
Robertson, Jerry Lee b: 10/13/43, Winchester, Kan. BB/TR, 6'2", 205 lbs. Deb: 4/08/69

YEAR	TM/L	W	L	PCT	G	GS	CG	SH	SV	IP	H	HR	BB	SO	RAT	ERA	ERA+	OAV	OOB	BH	AVG	PB	PR	/A	PD	TPI
1969	Mon-N	5	16	.238	38	27	3	0	1	179²	186	17	81	133	13.6	3.96	93	.272	.352	5	.089	-3	-7	-6	-3	-1.0
1970	Det-A	0	0	—	11	0	0	0	0	14²	19	1	5	11	14.7	3.68	101	.306	.358	0	—	0	0	0	-0	0.0
Total	2	5	16	.238	49	27	3	0	1	194¹	205	18	86	144	13.7	3.94	93	.274	.352	5	.089	-3	-7	-6	-3	-1.0

■ DICK ROBERTSON
Robertson, Preston b: 1891, Washington, D.C. d: 10/2/44, New Orleans, La. BR/TR, 5'9", 160 lbs. Deb: 9/16/13

YEAR	TM/L	W	L	PCT	G	GS	CG	SH	SV	IP	H	HR	BB	SO	RAT	ERA	ERA+	OAV	OOB	BH	AVG	PB	PR	/A	PD	TPI
1913	Cin-N	0	1	.000	2	1	1	0	0	10	13	0	9	1	19.8	7.20	45	.342	.468	0	.000	-0	-4	-4	-0	-0.4
1918	Bro-N	6	6	.333	13	9	7	1	0	87	87	0	28	18	11.9	2.59	108	.272	.330	9	.300	2	2	2	0	0.4
1919	Was-A	0	1	.000	7	4	0	0	0	27²	25	1	9	7	11.1	2.28	141	.253	.315	0	.000	-1	3	3	0	0.2
Total	3	3	8	.273	22	14	8	1	0	124²	125	1	46	26	12.3	2.89	101	.274	.340	9	.225	0	0	0	0	0.2

■ RICH ROBERTSON
Robertson, Richard Paul b: 10/14/44, Albany, Cal. BR/TR, 6'2", 210 lbs. Deb: 9/10/66

YEAR	TM/L	W	L	PCT	G	GS	CG	SH	SV	IP	H	HR	BB	SO	RAT	ERA	ERA+	OAV	OOB	BH	AVG	PB	PR	/A	PD	TPI
1966	SF-N	0	0	—	1	0	0	0	0	2¹	3	0	2	3	19.3	7.71	48	.300	.417	0	—	0	-1	-1	0	0.0
1967	SF-N	0	0	—	1	0	0	0	0	2	3	0	1	3	13.5	4.50	73	.333	.333	0	—	0	-0	-0	0	0.0
1968	SF-N	2	0	1.000	3	1	0	0	0	9	9	0	3	8	12.0	6.00	49	.265	.324	1	.500	0	-3	-3	0	-0.2
1969	SF-N	1	3	.250	17	7	1	1	0	44¹	53	4	21	20	15.2	5.48	64	.298	.375	0	.000	-1	-9	-10	-0	-0.9
1970	SF-N	8	9	.471	41	26	6	0	1	183²	199	22	96	121	14.5	4.85	82	.277	.363	6	.102	-0	-16	-18	-0	-1.7
1971	SF-N	2	2	.500	23	6	1	0	1	61	66	5	31	32	14.6	4.57	74	.267	.354	1	.067	-1	-8	-8	-1	-0.9
Total	6	13	14	.481	86	40	8	1	2	302¹	333	31	153	184	14.6	4.94	76	.278	.362	8	.093	-2	-38	-40	-1	-3.7

■ DEWEY ROBINSON
Robinson, Dewey Everett b: 4/28/55, Evanston, Ill. BR/TR, 6', 180 lbs. Deb: 4/06/79

YEAR	TM/L	W	L	PCT	G	GS	CG	SH	SV	IP	H	HR	BB	SO	RAT	ERA	ERA+	OAV	OOB	BH	AVG	PB	PR	/A	PD	TPI
1979	Chi-A	0	1	.000	11	0	0	0	0	14¹	11	1	9	5	12.6	6.28	68	.212	.328	0	—	0	-3	-3	-0	-0.2
1980	Chi-A	1	1	.500	15	0	0	0	0	35	26	2	16	28	10.8	3.09	131	.215	.307	0	—	0	4	4	0	0.4
1981	Chi-A	1	0	1.000	4	0	0	0	0	4	5	1	3	2	18.0	4.50	79	.357	.471	0	—	0	-0	-0	0	0.0
Total	3	2	2	.500	30	0	0	0	0	53¹	42	4	28	35	11.8	4.05	100	.225	.326	0	—	0	0	0	0	0.2

■ DON ROBINSON
Robinson, Don Allen b: 6/8/57, Ashland, Ky. BR/TR, 6'4", 225 lbs. Deb: 4/10/78

YEAR	TM/L	W	L	PCT	G	GS	CG	SH	SV	IP	H	HR	BB	SO	RAT	ERA	ERA+	OAV	OOB	BH	AVG	PB	PR	/A	PD	TPI
1978	Pit-N	14	6	.700	35	32	9	1	1	228¹	203	20	57	135	10.4	3.47	107	.236	.286	20	.235	2	3	6	-1	0.8
1979	*Pit-N	8	8	.500	29	25	4	0	0	160²	171	12	52	96	12.7	3.87	100	.277	.337	10	.204	1	-2	0	-3	-0.1
1980	Pit-N	7	10	.412	29	24	3	2	1	160¹	157	14	45	103	11.6	3.99	91	.257	.314	19	.333	7	-7	-6	0	0.0

YEAR TM/L	W	L	PCT	G	GS	CG	SH	SV	IP	H	HR	BB	SO	RAT	ERA	ERA+	OAV	OOB	BH	AVG	PB	PR	/A	PD	TPI
1981 Pit-N	0	3	.000	16	2	0	0	2	38¹	47	4	23	17	16.4	5.87	61	.313	.405	3	.250	1	-10	-10	1	-0.7
1982 Pit-N	15	13	.536	38	30	6	0	0	227	213	26	103	165	12.6	4.28	87	.250	.333	24	.282	9	-17	-15	-2	-0.7
1983 Pit-N	2	2	.500	9	6	0	0	0	36¹	43	5	21	28	15.9	4.46	83	.297	.386	2	.154	1	-3	-3	0	-0.1
1984 Pit-N	5	6	.455	51	1	0	0	10	122	99	6	49	110	10.9	3.02	119	.226	.304	8	.290	4	8	8	0	1.3
1985 Pit-N	5	11	.313	44	6	0	0	3	95¹	95	6	42	65	13.1	3.87	92	.255	.334	5	.238	3	-3	-3	-0	0.0
1986 Pit-N	3	4	.429	50	0	0	0	14	69¹	61	5	27	53	11.7	3.38	114	.237	.315	4	.667	2	3	4	0	0.6
1987 Pit-N	6	6	.500	42	0	0	0	12	65¹	66	6	22	53	12.1	3.86	107	.267	.327	1	.143	0	2	2	0	0.2
*SF-N	5	1	.833	25	0	0	0	7	42²	39	1	18	26	12.0	2.74	140	.239	.315	2	.273	2	6	5	-0	0.7
Yr	11	7	.611	67	0	0	0	19	108	105	7	40	79	12.1	3.42	117	.255	.322	3	.173	2	8	7	-1	0.9
1988 SF-N	10	5	.667	51	19	3	2	6	176²	152	11	49	122	10.4	2.45	133	.231	.287	9	.173	2	20	16	-2	1.8
1989 *SF-N	12	11	.522	34	32	5	1	0	197	184	22	37	96	10.2	3.43	98	.248	.285	15	.185	4	2	-1	-4	-0.1
1990 SF-N	10	7	.588	26	25	4	0	0	157²	173	18	41	78	12.3	4.57	81	.280	.326	9	.143	1	-14	-15	-1	-1.4
Total 13	102	93	.523	479	202	34	6	56	1777	1703	156	586	1147	11.7	3.70	98	.253	.315	133	.232	38	-14	-12	-12	2.3

■ HUMBERTO ROBINSON
Robinson, Humberto Valentino b: 6/25/30, Colon, Panama BR/TR, 6'1", 155 lbs. Deb: 4/20/55

YEAR TM/L	W	L	PCT	G	GS	CG	SH	SV	IP	H	HR	BB	SO	RAT	ERA	ERA+	OAV	OOB	BH	AVG	PB	PR	/A	PD	TPI
1955 Mil-N	3	1	.750	13	2	1	0	2	38	31	1	25	19	14.2	3.08	122	.235	.373	1	.077	-1	4	3	0	0.2
1956 Mil-N	0	0	—	1	0	0	0	0	2	1	0	2	0	13.5	0.00	—	.167	.375	0	—	0	1	1	0	0.1
1958 Mil-N	2	4	.333	19	0	0	0	1	41²	30	4	13	26	9.7	3.02	116	.203	.276	1	.167	-1	4	2	1	0.4
1959 Cle-A	1	0	1.000	5	0	0	0	0	8²	9	0	4	6	13.5	4.15	89	.281	.361	0	—	0	-0	-0	0	0.0
Phi-N	2	4	.333	31	4	1	0	1	73	70	6	24	32	11.6	3.33	123	.251	.310	3	.231	1	5	6	1	0.8
1960 Phi-N	0	4	.000	33	1	0	0	0	49²	48	6	22	31	12.7	3.44	113	.255	.333	1	.167	-0	2	2	0	0.2
Total 5	8	13	.381	102	7	2	0	4	213	189	17	90	114	12.0	3.25	119	.241	.323	6	.158	0	16	14	2	1.7

■ JEFF ROBINSON
Robinson, Jeffrey Daniel b: 12/13/60, Santa Ana, Cal. BR/TR, 6'4", 195 lbs. Deb: 4/07/84

YEAR TM/L	W	L	PCT	G	GS	CG	SH	SV	IP	H	HR	BB	SO	RAT	ERA	ERA+	OAV	OOB	BH	AVG	PB	PR	/A	PD	TPI
1984 SF-N	7	15	.318	34	33	1	1	0	171²	195	12	52	102	13.3	4.56	77	.288	.345	7	.115	-2	-19	-20	0	-2.1
1985 SF-N	0	0	—	8	0	0	0	0	12¹	16	2	10	8	19.0	5.11	67	.333	.448	0	—	0	-2	-2	-0	-0.2
1986 SF-N	6	3	.667	64	1	0	0	8	104¹	92	8	32	90	10.8	3.36	105	.234	.293	1	.067	-1	4	2	-1	0.0
1987 SF-N	6	8	.429	63	0	0	0	10	96²	69	10	48	82	11.0	2.79	138	.207	.309	2	.111	-1	14	11	1	1.1
Pit-N	2	1	.667	18	0	0	0	4	26²	20	1	6	19	8.8	3.04	135	.215	.263	1	.250	1	3	3	0	0.5
Yr	8	9	.471	81	0	0	0	14	123¹	89	11	54	101	10.4	2.85	137	.206	.295	0	.000	0	17	14	1	1.6
1988 Pit-N	11	5	.688	75	0	0	0	9	124²	113	6	39	87	11.2	3.03	112	.244	.307	3	.188	0	6	5	0	0.6
1989 Pit-N	7	13	.350	50	19	0	0	4	141¹	161	14	59	95	14.1	4.58	73	.283	.351	8	.229	2	-17	-19	1	-1.6
1990 NY-A	3	6	.333	54	4	1	0	0	88²	82	8	34	43	11.9	3.45	115	.248	.320	0	—	0	4	5	2	0.7
Total 7	42	51	.452	366	57	2	1	35	766¹	748	61	280	526	12.2	3.76	95	.257	.325	22	.148	0	-7	-15	3	-1.0

■ JEFF ROBINSON
Robinson, Jeffrey Mark b: 12/14/61, Ventura, Cal. BR/TR, 6'6", 210 lbs. Deb: 4/12/87

YEAR TM/L	W	L	PCT	G	GS	CG	SH	SV	IP	H	HR	BB	SO	RAT	ERA	ERA+	OAV	OOB	BH	AVG	PB	PR	/A	PD	TPI
1987 *Det-A	9	6	.600	29	21	2	1	0	127¹	132	16	54	98	13.6	5.37	79	.262	.342	0	—	0	-13	-16	-1	-1.5
1988 Det-A	13	6	.684	24	23	6	2	0	172	121	19	72	114	10.3	2.98	128	.197	.284	0	—	0	19	16	-0	1.7
1989 Det-A	4	5	.444	16	16	1	1	0	78	76	10	46	40	14.2	4.73	81	.259	.361	0	—	0	-7	-8	-1	-0.8
1990 Det-A	10	9	.526	27	27	1	1	0	145	141	23	88	76	14.6	5.96	66	.255	.364	0	—	0	-33	-33	-0	-3.1
Total 4	36	26	.581	96	87	10	5	0	522¹	470	68	260	328	12.9	4.65	85	.239	.333	0	—	0	-35	-41	-3	-3.7

■ JACK ROBINSON
Robinson, John Edward b: 2/20/21, Orange, N.J. BR/TR, 6', 175 lbs. Deb: 5/04/49

YEAR TM/L	W	L	PCT	G	GS	CG	SH	SV	IP	H	HR	BB	SO	RAT	ERA	ERA+	OAV	OOB	BH	AVG	PB	PR	/A	PD	TPI
1949 Bos-A	0	0	—	3	0	0	0	0	4	1	1	1	3	13.5	2.25	194	.267	.353	0	—	0	1	1	0	0.1

■ HANK ROBINSON
Robinson, John Henry "Rube" (b: John Henry Roberson)
b: 8/16/1889, Floyd, Ark. d: 7/3/65, N.Little Rock, Ark BR/TL, 5'11.5", 160 lbs. Deb: 9/02/11

YEAR TM/L	W	L	PCT	G	GS	CG	SH	SV	IP	H	HR	BB	SO	RAT	ERA	ERA+	OAV	OOB	BH	AVG	PB	PR	/A	PD	TPI
1911 Pit-N	0	1	.000	5	0	0	0	0	13	13	0	5	8	13.2	2.77	124	.283	.365	0	.000	-0	1	1	1	0.1
1912 Pit-N	12	7	.632	33	16	11	0	2	175	146	3	30	79	9.6	2.26	144	.230	.276	15	.254	2	22	19	-0	2.1
1913 Pit-N	14	9	.609	43	23	8	1	0	196¹	184	1	41	50	10.6	2.38	126	.255	.301	11	.180	-1	18	14	-1	1.2
1914 StL-N	7	8	.467	26	16	6	1	0	126	128	1	32	30	11.7	3.00	93	.274	.325	6	.171	-0	-3	-3	2	0.0
1915 StL-N	7	8	.467	32	15	6	1	0	143	128	1	35	57	10.7	2.45	114	.245	.301	5	.106	-2	5	5	1	0.4
1918 NY-A	2	4	.333	11	3	1	0	0	48	47	0	16	14	12.4	3.00	94	.269	.340	0	.000	-1	-1	-1	0	-0.2
Total 6	42	37	.532	150	73	32	3	2	701¹	646	6	159	238	10.7	2.53	118	.252	.303	37	.170	-3	42	36	3	3.6

■ RON ROBINSON
Robinson, Ronald Dean b: 3/24/62, Exeter, Cal. BR/TR, 6'4", 235 lbs. Deb: 8/14/84

YEAR TM/L	W	L	PCT	G	GS	CG	SH	SV	IP	H	HR	BB	SO	RAT	ERA	ERA+	OAV	OOB	BH	AVG	PB	PR	/A	PD	TPI
1984 Cin-N	1	2	.333	12	5	1	0	0	39²	35	3	13	24	10.9	2.72	139	.232	.293	0	.000	-1	4	5	0	0.4
1985 Cin-N	7	7	.500	33	12	0	0	1	108¹	107	11	32	76	11.6	3.99	95	.259	.314	2	.091	-1	-5	-2	1	-0.2
1986 Cin-N	10	3	.769	70	0	0	0	14	116²	110	10	43	117	12.0	3.24	119	.253	.323	1	.071	-1	6	8	1	0.8
1987 Cin-N	7	5	.583	48	18	0	0	4	154	148	14	43	99	11.2	3.68	115	.256	.308	7	.194	0	7	10	-2	0.8
1988 Cin-N	3	7	.300	17	16	0	0	0	78²	88	5	26	38	13.3	4.12	87	.285	.344	5	.200	1	-6	-5	0	-0.3
1989 Cin-N	5	3	.625	15	15	0	0	0	83¹	80	8	28	36	11.9	3.35	108	.252	.317	6	.214	1	1	2	0	0.4
1990 Cin-N	2	2	.500	6	5	0	0	0	31¹	36	2	14	14	14.4	4.88	79	.295	.368	1	.091	-1	-4	-4	0	-0.3
Mil-A	12	5	.706	22	22	7	2	0	148¹	158	5	37	57	12.2	2.91	130	.275	.326	0	—	0	16	14	0	1.5
Total 7	47	34	.580	223	93	8	2	19	760¹	762	58	236	461	12.0	3.52	110	.263	.321	22	.153	-2	20	29	-0	3.1

■ BILL ROBINSON
Robinson, William (b: William Anderson) b: Taylorsville, Ky. Deb: 8/12/1889

YEAR TM/L	W	L	PCT	G	GS	CG	SH	SV	IP	H	HR	BB	SO	RAT	ERA	ERA+	OAV	OOB	BH	AVG	PB	PR	/A	PD	TPI
1889 Lou-a	0	1	.000	1	1	1	0	0	8	10	2	6	2	18.0	10.13	38	.297	.403	1	.333	0	-6	-6	0	-0.3

■ YANK ROBINSON
Robinson, William H. b: 9/19/1859, Philadelphia, Pa. d: 8/25/1894, St.Louis, Mo. BR/TR, 5'6.5", 170 lbs. Deb: 8/24/1882 ♦

YEAR TM/L	W	L	PCT	G	GS	CG	SH	SV	IP	H	HR	BB	SO	RAT	ERA	ERA+	OAV	OOB	BH	AVG	PB	PR	/A	PD	TPI
1882 Det-N	0	0	—	1	0	0	0	0	2	0	0	1	0	4.5	0.00	—	.000	.140	7	.179	-0	1	1	0	0.1
1884 Bal-U	3	3	.500	11	3	3	0	0	75	96	1	18	61	13.7	3.48	95	.291	.328	111	.267	2	-4	-1	-3	0.0
1886 *StL-a	0	1	.000	1	1	0	0	0	9	10	0	7	1	18.0	3.00	115	.269	.384	132	.274	0	0	0	0	0.0
1887 *StL-a	0	0	—	1	0	0	0	1	3	3	0	3	0	18.0	3.00	151	.251	.401	131	.305	0	0	1	0	0.0
Total 4	3	4	.429	14	4	4	0	1	89	109	1	29	62	14.0	3.34	101	.283	.334	825	.241	2	-2	0	-3	0.1

■ CHICK ROBITAILLE
Robitaille, Joseph Anthony b: 3/2/1879, Whitehall, N.Y. d: 7/30/47, Waterford, N.Y. BR/TR, 5'8", 150 lbs. Deb: 9/02/04

YEAR TM/L	W	L	PCT	G	GS	CG	SH	SV	IP	H	HR	BB	SO	RAT	ERA	ERA+	OAV	OOB	BH	AVG	PB	PR	/A	PD	TPI
1904 Pit-N	4	3	.571	9	8	8	0	0	66	52	1	13	34	9.0	1.91	144	.208	.250	2	.095	-2	6	6	-1	0.3
1905 Pit-N	8	5	.615	17	12	10	0	0	120	126	1	28	32	11.8	2.93	103	.276	.322	6	.133	-2	1	1	0	0.0
Total 2	12	8	.600	26	20	18	0	0	186	178	2	41	66	10.8	2.56	114	.252	.297	8	.121	-4	7	7	-1	0.3

■ ARMANDO ROCHE
Roche, Armando (Baez) b: 12/7/26, Havana, Cuba BR/TR, 6', 190 lbs. Deb: 5/10/45

YEAR TM/L	W	L	PCT	G	GS	CG	SH	SV	IP	H	HR	BB	SO	RAT	ERA	ERA+	OAV	OOB	BH	AVG	PB	PR	/A	PD	TPI
1945 Was-A	0	0	—	2	0	0	0	0	6	10	0	2	0	18.0	6.00	52	.400	.444	0	.000	-0	-2	-2	0	-0.1

■ MIKE ROCHFORD
Rochford, Michael Joseph b: 3/14/63, Methuen, Mass. BL/TL, 6'4", 205 lbs. Deb: 9/03/88

YEAR TM/L	W	L	PCT	G	GS	CG	SH	SV	IP	H	HR	BB	SO	RAT	ERA	ERA+	OAV	OOB	BH	AVG	PB	PR	/A	PD	TPI
1988 Bos-A	0	0	—	2	0	0	0	0	2¹	4	0	1	1	19.3	0.00	—	.364	.417	0	—	0	1	1	0	0.2
1989 Bos-A	0	0	—	4	0	0	0	0	4	4	1	4	1	18.0	6.75	61	.267	.421	0	—	0	-1	-1	0	0.0
1990 Bos-A	0	1	.000	2	1	0	0	0	4	10	1	4	0	31.5	18.00	23	.526	.609	0	—	0	-6	-6	0	-0.5
Total 3	0	1	.000	8	1	0	0	0	10¹	18	2	9	2	23.5	9.58	43	.400	.500	0	—	0	-7	-6	0	-0.3

■ RICH RODAS
Rodas, Richard Martin b: 11/7/59, Roseville, Cal. BL/TL, 6'1", 180 lbs. Deb: 9/06/83

YEAR TM/L	W	L	PCT	G	GS	CG	SH	SV	IP	H	HR	BB	SO	RAT	ERA	ERA+	OAV	OOB	BH	AVG	PB	PR	/A	PD	TPI
1983 LA-N	0	0	—	7	0	0	0	0	4²	4	0	3	5	13.5	1.93	186	.222	.333	0	—	0	1	1	0	0.1
1984 LA-N	0	0	—	3	0	0	0	0	5	5	1	1	1	10.8	5.40	65	.250	.286	0	.000	-0	-1	-1	0	0.0
Total 2	0	0	—	10	0	0	0	0	9²	9	2	4	6	12.1	3.72	96	.237	.310	0	.000	-0	-0	-0	0	0.1

YEAR TM/L	W	L	PCT	G	GS	CG	SH	SV	IP	H	HR	BB	SO	RAT	ERA	ERA+	OAV	OOB	BH	AVG	PB	PR	/A	PD	TPI
■ **EDUARDO RODRIGUEZ** Rodriguez, Eduardo (Reyes) b: 3/6/52, Barceloneta, P.R. BR/TR, 6', 180 lbs. Deb: 6/20/73																								
1973 Mil-A	9	7	.563	30	6	2	0	5	76¹	71	6	47	49	14.1	3.30	114	.247	.357	1	1.000	1	4	4	-0	0.5
1974 Mil-A	7	4	.636	43	6	0	0	4	111²	97	7	51	58	12.3	3.63	100	.240	.333	0	—	0	-0	-0	-0	0.0
1975 Mil-A	7	0	1.000	43	1	0	0	7	87²	77	9	44	65	12.9	3.49	110	.235	.334	0	—	0	3	3	-2	0.1
1976 Mil-A	5	13	.278	45	12	3	0	8	136	124	10	65	77	12.7	3.64	96	.249	.339	0	—	0	-2	-2	-1	-0.2
1977 Mil-A	5	6	.455	42	5	1	1	4	142²	126	15	56	104	11.7	4.35	93	.236	.311	0	—	0	-5	-5	-1	-0.5
1978 Mil-A	5	5	.500	32	8	0	0	2	105¹	107	9	26	51	11.5	3.93	96	.262	.310	0	—	0	-2	-2	-0	-0.2
1979 KC-A	4	1	.800	29	1	1	0	2	74¹	79	9	34	26	14.0	4.84	88	.276	.359	0	—	0	-5	-5	-1	-0.5
Total 7	42	36	.538	264	39	7	1	32	734	681	65	323	430	12.6	3.89	98	.248	.332	1	1.000	1	-7	-7	-6	-0.8
■ **FREDDY RODRIGUEZ** Rodriguez, Fernando Pedro (Borrego) b: 4/29/24, Havana, Cuba BR/TR, 6', 180 lbs. Deb: 4/18/58																								
1958 Chi-N	0	0	—	7	0	0	0	2	7¹	8	2	5	5	17.2	7.36	53	.267	.389	0	.000	-0	-3	-3	-0	-0.2
1959 Phi-N	0	0	—	1	0	0	0	0	2	4	1	0	1	22.5	13.50	30	.400	.455	0	—	0	-2	-2	0	-0.1
Total 2	0	0	—	8	0	0	0	2	9¹	12	3	5	6	18.3	8.68	46	.300	.404	0	.000	-0	-5	-5	-0	-0.3
■ **RICK RODRIGUEZ** Rodriguez, Ricardo b: 9/21/60, Oakland, Cal. BR/TR, 6'3", 190 lbs. Deb: 9/17/86																								
1986 Oak-A	1	2	.333	3	3	0	0	0	16¹	17	4	7	2	13.2	6.61	58	.262	.333	0	—	0	-4	-5	0	-0.3
1987 Oak-A	1	0	1.000	15	0	0	0	0	24¹	32	1	15	9	17.8	2.96	139	.337	.432	0	—	0	4	3	1	0.4
1988 Cle-A	1	2	.333	10	5	0	0	0	33	43	4	17	9	16.6	7.09	58	.323	.404	0	—	0	-11	-11	0	-0.8
1990 SF-N	0	0	—	3	0	0	0	0	3¹	5	0	2	2	18.9	8.10	46	.357	.438	0	—	0	-2	-2	0	-0.1
Total 4	3	4	.429	31	8	0	0	0	77	97	9	41	22	16.4	5.73	71	.316	.400	0	—	0	-13	-14	2	-0.8
■ **RICH RODRIGUEZ** Rodriguez, Richard Anthony b: 3/1/63, Los Angeles, Cal. BL/TL, 5'10", 194 lbs. Deb: 6/30/90																								
1990 SD-N	1	1	.500	32	0	0	0	1	47²	52	2	16	22	13.0	2.83	136	.287	.348	0	.000	-0	5	5	1	0.6
■ **ROSARIO RODRIGUEZ** Rodriguez, Rosario Isabel (Echavarria) b: 7/8/69, Los Mochis, Mexico BR/TL, 6', 185 lbs. Deb: 9/01/89																								
1989 Cin-N	1	1	.500	7	0	0	0	0	4¹	3	0	3	0	12.5	4.15	87	.188	.316	0	—	0	-0	-0	0	0.0
1990 Cin-N	0	0	—	9	0	0	0	0	10¹	15	3	2	8	15.7	6.10	64	.357	.400	0	—	0	-3	-3	0	-0.1
Total 2	1	1	.500	16	0	0	0	0	14²	18	3	5	8	14.7	5.52	69	.310	.375	0	—	0	-3	-3	1	-0.1
■ **ROBERTO RODRIQUEZ** Rodriquez, Roberto (Munoz) b: 11/29/41, Caracas, Venez. BR/TR, 6'3", 185 lbs. Deb: 5/13/67																								
1967 KC-A	1	1	.500	15	5	0	0	2	40¹	42	4	14	29	12.7	3.57	89	.268	.331	0	.000	-1	-2	-2	-0	-0.2
1970 Oak-A	0	0	—	6	0	0	0	0	12¹	10	2	3	8	9.5	2.92	121	.227	.277	0	.000	-0	1	1	0	0.1
SD-N	0	0	—	10	0	0	0	3	16¹	26	1	5	8	17.1	6.61	60	.366	.408	0	—	0	-5	-5	0	-0.4
Chi-N	3	2	.600	26	0	0	0	2	43¹	50	6	15	46	13.5	5.82	77	.289	.346	1	.125	1	-9	-6	-0	-0.5
Yr	3	2	.600	36	0	0	0	5	59²	76	7	20	54	14.5	6.03	72	.311	.364	1	.091	0	-13	-11	-0	-0.9
Total 2	4	3	.571	57	5	0	0	7	112¹	128	13	37	91	13.3	4.81	80	.288	.344	1	.048	-1	-14	-12	-1	-1.0
■ **PREACHER ROE** Roe, Elwin Charles b: 2/26/15, Ash Flat, Ark. BR/TL, 6'2", 170 lbs. Deb: 8/22/38																								
1938 StL-N	0	0	—	1	0	0	0	0	2²	6	0	2	1	27.0	13.50	29	.429	.500	0	.000	-0	-3	-3	0	-0.2
1944 Pit-N	13	11	.542	39	25	7	1	1	185¹	182	7	59	88	11.8	3.11	120	.253	.311	7	.132	-2	10	13	-2	0.9
1945 Pit-N	14	13	.519	33	31	15	3	1	235	228	11	46	**148**	10.5	2.87	137	.259	.296	8	.107	-4	24	28	-0	2.6
1946 Pit-N	3	8	.273	21	10	1	0	2	70	83	5	25	28	14.1	5.14	69	.294	.356	1	.067	-1	-13	-13	-0	-1.3
1947 Pit-N	4	15	.211	38	22	4	1	2	144	156	19	63	59	13.7	5.25	80	.276	.348	5	.125	-2	-19	-16	-1	-1.8
1948 Bro-N	12	8	.600	34	22	8	2	2	177²	156	14	33	86	9.7	2.63	152	.233	.271	5	.098	-2	26	27	-1	2.5
1949 *Bro-N	15	6	**.714**	30	27	13	3	1	212²	201	25	44	109	10.5	2.79	147	.252	.293	8	.114	-2	29	31	-2	2.8
1950 Bro-N	19	11	.633	36	32	16	2	1	250²	245	34	66	125	11.3	3.30	124	.257	.308	14	.154	-3	23	22	-2	1.8
1951 Bro-N	22	3	**.880**	34	33	19	2	0	257²	247	30	64	113	10.9	3.04	129	.258	.304	10	.112	-5	26	25	-1	2.0
1952 *Bro-N	11	2	.846	27	25	8	2	0	158²	163	16	39	83	11.6	3.12	117	.270	.317	4	.070	-3	11	9	-1	0.5
1953 *Bro-N	11	3	.786	25	24	9	1	0	157	171	27	40	85	12.2	4.36	98	.278	.323	3	.053	-1	-2	1	-0	-0.4
1954 Bro-N	3	4	.429	15	10	1	0	0	63	69	11	23	31	13.1	5.00	82	.279	.341	3	.143	-0	-7	-6	-0	-0.5
Total 12	127	84	.602	333	261	101	17	10	1914¹	1907	199	504	956	11.4	3.43	116	.261	.310	68	.110	-27	108	115	-8	8.9
■ **CLAY ROE** Roe, James Clay "Shad" b: 1/7/04, Green Briar, Tenn. d: 4/4/56, Cleveland, Miss. BL/TL, 6'1", 180 lbs. Deb: 10/03/23																								
1923 Was-A	0	1	.000	1	1	0	0	0	1²	3	0	6	2	32.4	0.00	—	.000	.500	0	—	0	1	1	0	0.1
■ **ED ROEBUCK** Roebuck, Edward Jack b: 7/3/31, East Millsboro, Pa. BR/TR, 6'2", 185 lbs. Deb: 4/18/55																								
1955 *Bro-N	5	6	.455	47	0	0	0	12	84	96	14	24	33	13.2	4.71	86	.288	.342	2	.111	-1	-6	-6	1	-0.5
1956 *Bro-N	5	4	.556	43	0	0	0	1	89¹	83	15	29	60	11.5	3.93	101	.251	.315	6	.333	2	-2	0	1	0.3
1957 Bro-N	8	2	.800	44	1	0	0	8	96¹	70	9	46	73	11.0	2.71	154	.205	.303	5	.238	3	13	**16**	2	0.2
1958 LA-N	0	1	.000	32	0	0	0	5	44	45	9	15	26	12.7	3.48	118	.271	.339	2	.500	1	2	3	0	0.4
1960 LA-N	8	3	.727	58	0	0	0	8	116²	109	13	38	77	11.3	2.78	143	.256	.317	4	.167	-0	13	15	2	1.9
1961 LA-N	2	1	.667	5	0	0	0	0	9	12	1	2	9	14.0	5.00	87	.324	.359	0	.000	-0	-1	-1	0	0.0
1962 LA-N	10	2	.833	64	0	0	0	9	119¹	102	11	54	72	12.2	3.09	117	.232	.325	6	.214	1	11	7	1	0.8
1963 LA-N	2	4	.333	29	0	0	0	0	40¹	54	4	21	26	17.2	4.24	71	.321	.403	1	.250	0	-4	-5	1	-0.4
Was-A	2	1	.667	26	0	0	0	4	57¹	63	5	29	25	14.8	3.30	113	.284	.372	2	.182	0	2	3	1	0.4
1964 Was-A	0	0	—	2	0	0	0	0	1	0	0	2	0	18.0	9.00	41	.000	.333	0	—	0	-1	-1	0	0.0
Phi-N	5	3	.625	60	0	0	0	12	77¹	55	7	25	42	9.8	2.21	157	.196	.272	0	.000	-1	11	11	1	1.2
1965 Phi-N	5	3	.625	44	0	0	0	3	50¹	55	2	15	29	13.4	3.40	102	.288	.355	0	.000	-0	1	0	-1	0.0
1966 Phi-N	0	2	.000	6	0	0	0	0	6	9	0	2	5	16.5	6.00	60	.333	.379	0	—	0	-2	-2	-0	-0.1
Total 11	52	31	.627	460	1	0	0	62	791	753	90	302	477	12.3	3.35	114	.254	.329	28	.204	4	38	41	8	6.2
■ **MIKE ROESLER** Roesler, Michael Joseph b: 9/12/63, Fort Wayne, Ind. BR/TR, 6'5", 195 lbs. Deb: 8/09/89																								
1989 Cin-N	0	1	.000	17	0	0	0	0	25	22	4	9	14	11.2	3.96	91	.239	.307	0	—	0	-1	-1	-1	-0.1
1990 Pit-N	1	0	1.000	5	0	0	0	0	6	5	1	2	4	10.5	3.00	121	.217	.280	0	.000	-0	1	0	-0	0.0
Total 2	1	1	.500	22	0	0	0	0	31	27	5	11	18	11.0	3.77	96	.235	.302	0	.000	-0	-1	-1	-1	-0.1
■ **OSCAR ROETTGER** Roettger, Oscar Frederick Louis "Okkie" b: 2/19/1900, St.Louis, Mo. d: 7/4/86, St.Louis, Mo. BR/TR, 6', 170 lbs. Deb: 7/07/23 ♦																								
1923 NY-A	0	0	—	5	0	0	0	1	11²	16	3	12	7	22.4	8.49	46	.340	.483	0	.000	-0	-6	-6	0	-0.5
1924 NY-A	0	0	—	1	0	0	0	0	0	1	0	2	0	—	—	—	1.000	1.000	0	—	0	0	0	0	0.0
Total 2	0	0	—	6	0	0	0	1	11²	17	3	14	7	24.7	8.49	46	.354	.508	14	.212	0	-6	-6	0	-0.5
■ **JOE ROGALSKI** Rogalski, Joseph Anthony b: 7/15/12, Ashland, Wis. d: 11/20/51, Ashland, Wis. BR/TR, 6'2", 187 lbs. Deb: 9/14/38																								
1938 Det-A	0	0	—	2	0	0	0	0	7	12	0	0	2	15.4	2.57	194	.400	.400	0	.000	-0	2	2	-0	0.1
■ **KEN ROGERS** Rogers, Kenneth Scott b: 11/10/64, Savannah, Ga. BL/TL, 6'1", 200 lbs. Deb: 4/06/89																								
1989 Tex-A	3	4	.429	73	0	0	0	2	73²	60	2	42	63	13.0	2.93	135	.232	.348	0	—	0	8	8	2	1.1
1990 Tex-A	10	6	.625	69	3	0	0	15	97²	93	6	42	74	12.5	3.13	127	.249	.326	0	—	0	8	9	2	1.1
Total 2	13	10	.565	142	3	0	0	17	171¹	153	8	84	137	12.7	3.05	130	.242	.335	0	—	0	16	18	4	2.2
■ **LEE ROGERS** Rogers, Lee Otis "Buck" b: 10/8/13, Tuscaloosa, Ala. BR/TL, 5'11", 170 lbs. Deb: 4/27/38																								
1938 Bos-A	1	1	.500	14	2	0	0	0	27²	32	4	18	7	16.3	6.51	76	.302	.403	0	.000	-0	-5	-5	1	-0.2
Bro-N	0	2	.000	12	2	0	0	0	23²	23	0	10	11	12.9	5.70	68	.256	.337	0	.000	-0	-5	-5	1	-0.2
■ **BUCK ROGERS** Rogers, Orlin Woodrow "Lefty" b: 11/5/12, Spring Garden, Va. BR/TL, 5'8.5", 164 lbs. Deb: 9/15/35																								
1935 Was-A	0	1	.000	2	1	0	0	0	10	16	0	6	7	19.8	7.20	60	.340	.415	0	.000	-0	-3	-3	-0	-0.3

YEAR	TM/L	W	L	PCT	G	GS	CG	SH	SV	IP	H	HR	BB	SO	RAT	ERA	ERA+	OAV	OOB	BH	AVG	PB	PR	/A	PD	TPI

■ STEVE ROGERS
Rogers, Stephen Douglas b: 10/26/49, Jefferson City, Mo. BR/TR, 6'2", 175 lbs. Deb: 7/18/73

YEAR	TM/L	W	L	PCT	G	GS	CG	SH	SV	IP	H	HR	BB	SO	RAT	ERA	ERA+	OAV	OOB	BH	AVG	PB	PR	/A	PD	TPI
1973	Mon-N	10	5	.667	17	17	7	3	0	134	93	5	49	64	9.6	1.54	247	.199	.276	4	.098	-1	31	34	1	4.1
1974	Mon-N	15	22	.405	38	38	11	1	0	253²	255	19	80	154	12.1	4.47	86	.265	.324	11	.139	-1	-24	-18	2	-1.5
1975	Mon-N	11	12	.478	35	35	12	3	0	251²	248	13	88	137	12.2	3.29	116	.260	.325	13	.169	1	9	15	1	1.8
1976	Mon-N	7	17	.292	33	32	8	4	1	230	212	10	69	150	11.2	3.21	116	.250	.309	11	.149	-2	7	13	5	1.8
1977	Mon-N	17	16	.515	40	40	17	4	0	301²	272	16	81	206	10.7	3.10	123	.242	.296	10	.104	-4	27	24	3	2.3
1978	Mon-N	13	10	.565	30	29	11	1	1	219	186	12	64	126	10.4	2.47	143	.235	.294	8	.113	-2	27	26	1	2.7
1979	Mon-N	13	12	.520	37	37	13	5	0	248²	232	14	78	143	11.4	3.00	122	.251	.312	12	.156	1	20	18	2	2.2
1980	Mon-N	16	11	.593	37	37	14	4	0	281	247	16	85	147	10.7	2.98	120	.238	.298	13	.160	1	19	18	-1	2.0
1981	*Mon-N	12	8	.600	22	22	7	3	0	160²	149	7	41	87	10.8	3.42	102	.248	.298	8	.145	-1	1	1	-1	0.0
1982	Mon-N	19	8	.704	35	35	14	4	0	277	245	12	65	179	10.3	**2.40**	**151**	.237	.286	11	.129	0	**37**	**38**	0	**4.3**
1983	Mon-N	17	12	.586	36	36	13	5	0	273	258	10	78	146	11.2	3.23	111	.252	.308	12	.146	-1	12	11	-1	0.9
1984	Mon-N	6	15	.286	31	28	1	0	0	169¹	171	12	78	64	13.3	4.31	80	.267	.348	7	.143	1	-13	-17	1	-1.5
1985	Mon-N	2	4	.333	8	7	1	0	0	38	51	1	20	18	16.8	5.68	60	.329	.406	2	.143	0	-9	-10	1	-0.7
Total	13	158	152	.510	399	393	129	37	2	2837²	2619	151	876	1621	11.2	3.17	115	.248	.308	122	.138	-8	146	154	15	18.4

■ TOM ROGERS
Rogers, Thomas Andrew "Shotgun" b: 2/12/1892, Sparta, Tenn. d: 3/7/36, Nashville, Tenn. BR/TR, 6'0.5", 180 lbs. Deb: 4/14/17

YEAR	TM/L	W	L	PCT	G	GS	CG	SH	SV	IP	H	HR	BB	SO	RAT	ERA	ERA+	OAV	OOB	BH	AVG	PB	PR	/A	PD	TPI
1917	StL-A	3	6	.333	24	8	3	0	0	108²	112	2	44	27	13.2	3.89	67	.277	.352	5	.172	-1	-15	-16	-0	-1.7
1918	StL-A	8	10	.444	29	16	11	0	2	154	148	3	49	29	11.7	3.27	84	.267	.330	13	.245	2	-8	-9	2	-0.5
1919	StL-A	0	1	.000	2	0	0	0	0	1	7	0	0	1	63.0	27.00	12	.700	.700	0	—	0	-3	-3	0	-0.2
	Phi-A	4	12	.250	23	18	7	1	0	140	152	9	60	37	13.8	4.31	80	.292	.369	11	.224	-0	-17	-14	4	-0.8
	Yr	4	13	.235	25	18	7	1	0	141	159	9	60	38	14.2	4.47	77	.300	.374	0	.000	-0	-19	-16	4	-1.0
1921	*NY-A	0	1	.000	5	0	0	0	1	11	12	1	9	0	18.0	7.36	58	.300	.440	1	.333	0	-4	-4	1	-0.1
Total	4	15	30	.333	83	42	21	1	3	414²	431	15	162	94	13.1	3.95	75	.282	.354	30	.224	1	-46	-45	7	-3.3

■ CLINT ROGGE
Rogge, Francis Clinton b: 7/19/1889, Memphis, Mich. d: 1/6/69, Mt.Clemens, Mich. BL/TR, 5'10", 185 lbs. Deb: 4/11/15

YEAR	TM/L	W	L	PCT	G	GS	CG	SH	SV	IP	H	HR	BB	SO	RAT	ERA	ERA+	OAV	OOB	BH	AVG	PB	PR	/A	PD	TPI
1915	Pit-F	17	11	.607	37	31	17	5	0	254¹	240	6	93	93	12.1	2.55	118	.257	.330	14	.173	0	14	13	1	1.6
1921	Cin-N	1	2	.333	6	3	0	0	0	35¹	43	2	9	12	13.2	4.08	88	.307	.349	1	.100	0	-1	-2	0	-0.1
Total	2	18	13	.581	43	34	17	5	0	289²	283	8	102	105	12.2	2.73	113	.264	.336	15	.165	0	13	11	1	1.5

■ GARRY ROGGENBURK
Roggenburk, Garry Earl b: 4/16/40, Cleveland, Ohio BR/TL, 6'6", 195 lbs. Deb: 4/20/63

YEAR	TM/L	W	L	PCT	G	GS	CG	SH	SV	IP	H	HR	BB	SO	RAT	ERA	ERA+	OAV	OOB	BH	AVG	PB	PR	/A	PD	TPI
1963	Min-A	2	4	.333	36	2	0	0	4	50	47	3	22	24	13.3	2.16	169	.253	.347	1	.143	0	8	8	1	1.0
1965	Min-A	1	0	1.000	12	0	0	0	2	21	21	1	12	6	14.1	3.43	104	.266	.363	0	.000	-0	0	0	-0	0.0
1966	Min-A	1	2	.333	12	0	0	0	1	12¹	14	4	10	3	17.5	5.84	62	.292	.414	0	—	0	-3	-3	0	-0.2
	Bos-A	0	0	—	1	0	0	0	0	0¹	1	0	1	0	54.0	0.00	—	.500	.667	0	—	0	0	0	0	0.0
	Yr	1	2	.333	13	0	0	0	1	12²	15	4	11	3	18.5	5.68	63	.300	.426	0	—	0	-3	-3	0	-0.2
1968	Bos-A	0	0	—	4	0	0	0	0	8¹	9	0	3	4	13.0	2.16	146	.257	.316	0	—	0	1	1	-0	0.1
1969	Bos-A	0	1	.000	7	0	0	0	0	9²	13	1	5	8	17.7	8.38	45	.342	.432	0	.000	-0	-5	-5	-0	-0.4
	Sea-A	2	2	.500	7	4	1	0	0	24¹	27	6	11	11	14.4	4.44	82	.276	.355	1	.125	-0	-2	-2	-0	-0.2
	Yr	2	3	.400	14	4	1	0	0	34	40	7	16	19	15.1	5.56	66	.292	.370	0	.000	-1	-7	-7	0	-0.6
Total	5	6	9	.400	79	6	1	0	7	126	132	15	64	56	14.5	3.64	99	.272	.364	2	.100	-1	-1	-1	1	0.3

■ SAUL ROGOVIN
Rogovin, Saul Walter b: 10/10/23, Brooklyn, N.Y. BR/TR, 6'2", 205 lbs. Deb: 4/28/49

YEAR	TM/L	W	L	PCT	G	GS	CG	SH	SV	IP	H	HR	BB	SO	RAT	ERA	ERA+	OAV	OOB	BH	AVG	PB	PR	/A	PD	TPI
1949	Det-A	0	1	.000	5	0	0	0	0	5²	13	1	7	2	31.8	14.29	29	.464	.571	0	—	0	-6	-6	-0	-0.5
1950	Det-A	2	1	.667	11	5	1	0	0	40	39	5	26	11	15.1	4.50	104	.258	.374	3	.188	0	0	1	-0	0.1
1951	Det-A	1	1	.500	5	4	0	0	0	24	23	4	7	5	11.3	5.25	80	.247	.300	2	.286	1	-3	-3	1	0.0
	Chi-A	11	7	.611	22	22	17	3	0	192²	166	11	67	77	10.9	2.48	163	.234	.301	15	.203	-0	35	33	-1	3.4
	Yr	12	8	.600	27	26	17	3	0	216²	189	15	74	82	11.0	**2.78**	**146**	.235	.301	6	.074	1	32	**31**	-0	3.4
1952	Chi-A	14	9	.609	33	30	12	3	1	231²	224	14	79	121	11.9	3.85	95	.255	.318	17	.202	3	-4	-5	0	-0.7
1953	Chi-A	7	12	.368	22	19	4	1	1	131	151	17	48	62	13.8	5.22	77	.289	.351	5	.135	-0	-18	-17	0	-1.6
1955	Bal-A	1	8	.111	14	12	1	0	0	71	79	5	27	35	13.7	4.56	84	.288	.358	2	.091	-1	-5	-6	-0	-0.7
	Phi-N	5	3	.625	12	11	5	2	0	73	60	3	17	27	9.5	3.08	129	.230	.277	6	.250	2	8	7	-1	0.9
1956	Phi-N	7	6	.538	22	18	3	0	0	106²	122	22	27	48	12.6	4.98	75	.282	.325	4	.111	-2	-14	-15	-1	-1.7
1957	Phi-N	0	0	—	4	0	0	0	0	8	11	1	3	0	15.8	9.00	42	.333	.389	0	—	0	-5	-5	-0	-0.4
Total	8	48	48	.500	150	121	43	9	2	883²	888	83	308	388	12.3	4.06	96	.262	.326	54	.180	2	-12	-16	-3	-0.7

■ LES ROHR
Rohr, Leslie Norvin b: 3/5/46, Lowestoft, England BL/TL, 6'5", 205 lbs. Deb: 9/19/67

YEAR	TM/L	W	L	PCT	G	GS	CG	SH	SV	IP	H	HR	BB	SO	RAT	ERA	ERA+	OAV	OOB	BH	AVG	PB	PR	/A	PD	TPI
1967	NY-N	2	1	.667	3	3	0	0	0	17	13	1	9	15	11.6	2.12	160	.224	.328	0	.000	-1	2	2	-1	0.1
1968	NY-N	0	2	.000	2	1	0	0	0	6	9	0	7	5	24.0	4.50	67	.333	.471	0	—	0	-1	-1	0	0.0
1969	NY-N	0	0	—	1	0	0	0	0	1¹	5	0	1	0	40.5	20.25	18	.625	.667	0	—	0	-2	-2	0	-0.1
Total	3	2	3	.400	6	4	0	0	0	24¹	27	1	17	20	16.3	3.70	90	.290	.400	0	.000	-0	-1	-1	-1	0.0

■ BILLY ROHR
Rohr, William Joseph b: 7/1/45, San Diego, Cal. BL/TL, 6'3", 170 lbs. Deb: 4/14/67

YEAR	TM/L	W	L	PCT	G	GS	CG	SH	SV	IP	H	HR	BB	SO	RAT	ERA	ERA+	OAV	OOB	BH	AVG	PB	PR	/A	PD	TPI
1967	Bos-A	2	3	.400	10	8	2	1	0	42¹	43	4	22	16	14.2	5.10	68	.256	.349	0	.000	-1	-9	-8	-0	-0.8
1968	Cle-A	1	0	1.000	17	0	0	0	0	18¹	18	5	10	5	13.7	6.87	43	.265	.359	0	.000	-0	-8	-8	-0	-0.8
Total	2	3	3	.500	27	8	2	1	1	60²	61	9	32	21	14.1	5.64	59	.258	.352	0	.000	-1	-17	-16	0	-1.6

■ MEL ROJAS
Rojas, Melquiades (Medrano) b: 12/10/66, Haina, D.R. BR/TR, 5'11", 175 lbs. Deb: 8/01/90

YEAR	TM/L	W	L	PCT	G	GS	CG	SH	SV	IP	H	HR	BB	SO	RAT	ERA	ERA+	OAV	OOB	BH	AVG	PB	PR	/A	PD	TPI
1990	Mon-N	3	1	.750	23	0	0	0	1	40	34	5	24	26	13.5	3.60	104	.234	.351	0	.000	-0	1	1	-0	0.0

■ MINNIE ROJAS
Rojas, Minervino Alejandro (Landin) b: 11/26/38, Remidios, Las Villas, Cuba BR/TR, 6'1", 170 lbs. Deb: 5/30/66

YEAR	TM/L	W	L	PCT	G	GS	CG	SH	SV	IP	H	HR	BB	SO	RAT	ERA	ERA+	OAV	OOB	BH	AVG	PB	PR	/A	PD	TPI
1966	Cal-A	7	4	.636	47	2	0	0	10	84¹	83	9	15	37	10.6	2.88	117	.262	.297	1	.071	-0	5	4	-1	0.3
1967	Cal-A	12	9	.571	72	0	0	0	27	121²	106	7	38	83	10.9	2.52	125	.232	.296	1	.059	-1	10	8	-2	0.6
1968	Cal-A	4	3	.571	38	0	0	0	6	55	55	11	15	33	11.5	4.25	68	.252	.300	1	.100	-0	-8	-8	-1	-1.0
Total	3	23	16	.590	157	2	0	0	43	261	244	27	68	153	10.9	3.00	105	.246	.297	3	.073	-2	7	5	-3	-0.1

■ COOKIE ROJAS
Rojas, Octavio Victor (Rivas) b: 3/6/39, Havana, Cuba BR/TR, 5'10", 160 lbs. Deb: 4/10/62 MC♦

YEAR	TM/L	W	L	PCT	G	GS	CG	SH	SV	IP	H	HR	BB	SO	RAT	ERA	ERA+	OAV	OOB	BH	AVG	PB	PR	/A	PD	TPI
1967	Phi-N	0	0	—	1	0	0	0	0	1	1	0	0	0	9.0	0.00	—	.200	.200	137	.259	0	0	0	0	0.0

■ JIM ROLAND
Roland, James Ivan b: 12/14/42, Franklin, N.C. BR/TL, 6'3", 175 lbs. Deb: 9/20/62

YEAR	TM/L	W	L	PCT	G	GS	CG	SH	SV	IP	H	HR	BB	SO	RAT	ERA	ERA+	OAV	OOB	BH	AVG	PB	PR	/A	PD	TPI
1962	Min-A	0	0	—	1	0	0	0	0	2	1	0	0	1	4.5	0.00	—	.143	.143	0	—	0	1	1	0	0.1
1963	Min-A	4	1	.800	10	7	2	1	0	49	32	4	27	34	10.8	2.57	142	.185	.295	0	.000	-2	6	6	0	0.5
1964	Min-A	2	6	.250	30	13	1	0	3	94¹	76	12	55	63	12.9	4.10	87	.218	.332	4	.148	-1	-5	-6	-1	-0.7
1966	Min-A	0	0	—	1	0	0	0	0	2	0	0	0	1	0.0	0.00	—	.000	.000	0	—	0	1	1	0	0.1
1967	Min-A	0	1	.000	25	0	0	0	2	35²	33	3	17	16	12.6	3.03	114	.244	.329	0	.000	-0	1	2	0	0.1
1968	Min-A	4	1	.800	28	4	1	0	0	61²	55	3	24	36	11.8	3.50	88	.238	.315	0	.000	-0	-4	-3	1	-0.2
1969	Oak-A	5	1	.833	39	3	2	0	1	86¹	59	2	46	48	11.6	2.19	157	.197	.316	2	.095	-1	14	12	0	1.2
1970	Oak-A	3	3	.500	28	2	0	0	2	43¹	28	2	23	26	10.6	2.70	131	.181	.287	0	.000	-0	5	4	1	0.4
1971	Oak-A	1	3	.250	31	0	0	0	1	45¹	34	4	19	30	11.5	3.18	105	.214	.312	0	.000	-0	1	1	-0	0.0
1972	Oak-A	0	0	—	2	0	0	0	0	2¹	5	0	0	4	19.3	3.86	74	.455	.455	0	—	0	-0	-0	-0	0.0
	NY-A	0	1	.000	16	0	0	0	0	25	27	3	16	13	15.8	5.04	58	.287	.396	0	.000	-0	-6	-6	-0	-0.6
	Tex-A	0	0	—	5	0	0	0	0	3¹	7	1	2	4	27.0	8.10	37	.412	.500	0	—	-0	-2	-2	-0	-0.1
	Yr	0	1	.000	23	0	0	0	0	30²	39	4	18	17	17.0	5.28	56	.317	.408	0	.000	-0	-8	-8	-0	-0.8
Total	10	19	17	.528	216	29	6	1	9	450¹	357	34	229	272	12.1	3.22	106	.218	.321	6	.071	-5	12	10	0	0.8

YEAR TM/L	W	L	PCT	G	GS	CG	SH	SV	IP	H	HR	BB	SO	RAT	ERA	ERA+	OAV	OOB	BH	AVG	PB	PR	/A	PD	TPI
■ JOSE ROMAN Roman, Jose Rafael (Sarita) b: 5/21/63, Santo Domingo, D.R. BR/TR, 6', 175 lbs. Deb: 9/05/84																									
1984 Cle-A	0	2	.000	3	2	0	0	0	6	9	1	11	3	30.0	18.00	23	.391	.588	0	—	0	-9	-9	-0	-0.7
1985 Cle-A	0	4	.000	5	3	0	0	0	16¹	13	3	14	12	14.9	6.61	63	.200	.342	0	—	0	-4	-4	-0	-0.3
1986 Cle-A	1	2	.333	6	5	0	0	0	22	23	3	17	9	16.8	6.55	63	.280	.410	0	—	0	-6	-6	-1	-0.5
Total 3	1	8	.111	14	10	0	0	0	44¹	45	7	42	24	17.9	8.12	51	.265	.413	0	—	0	-20	-20	-1	-1.5
■ RON ROMANICK Romanick, Ronald James b: 11/6/60, Burley, Idaho BR/TR, 6'4", 195 lbs. Deb: 4/05/84																									
1984 Cal-A	12	12	.500	33	33	8	2	0	229²	240	23	61	87	12.0	3.76	105	.270	.320	0	—	0	6	5	-1	0.4
1985 Cal-A	14	9	.609	31	31	6	1	0	195	210	29	62	64	12.7	4.11	100	.280	.338	0	—	0	1	0	-2	-0.1
1986 Cal-A	5	8	.385	18	18	1	1	0	106¹	124	13	44	38	14.2	5.50	75	.297	.364	0	—	0	-16	-16	-0	-1.5
Total 3	31	29	.517	82	82	15	4	0	531	574	65	167	189	12.7	4.24	96	.279	.336	0	—	0	-9	-11	-4	-1.2
■ JIM ROMANO Romano, James King b: 4/6/27, Brooklyn, N.Y. d: 9/12/90, New York, N.Y. BR/TR, 6'4", 190 lbs. Deb: 9/21/50																									
1950 Bro-N	0	0	—	3	1	0	0	0	6¹	8	0	2	8	14.2	5.68	72	.296	.345	0	.000	-0	-1	-1	0	0.0
■ DUTCH ROMBERGER Romberger, Allen Isaiah b: 5/26/27, Klingerstown, Pa. d: 5/26/83, Weikert, Pa. BR/TR, 6', 185 lbs. Deb: 5/31/54																									
1954 Phi-A	1	1	.500	10	0	0	0	0	15²	28	3	12	6	23.0	11.49	34	.406	.494	0	.000	0	-14	-13	-0	-1.2
■ RAMON ROMERO Romero, Ramon (De Los Santos) b: 1/8/59, San Pedro De Macoris, D.R. BL/TL, 6'4", 170 lbs. Deb: 9/18/84																									
1984 Cle-A	0	0	—	1	0	0	0	0	3	0	0	0	3	3.0	0.00	—	.000	.111	0	—	0	1	1	0	0.1
1985 Cle-A	2	3	.400	19	10	0	0	0	64¹	69	13	38	38	15.7	6.58	63	.276	.382	0	—	0	-17	-17	-1	-1.6
Total 2	2	3	.400	20	10	0	0	0	67¹	69	13	38	41	15.1	6.28	66	.267	.374	0	—	0	-16	-16	-1	-1.5
■ EDDIE ROMMEL Rommel, Edwin Americus b: 9/13/1897, Baltimore, Md. d: 8/26/70, Baltimore, Md. BR/TR, 6'2", 197 lbs. Deb: 4/19/20 CU																									
1920 Phi-A	7	7	.500	33	12	8	2	1	173²	165	5	43	43	11.0	2.85	141	.259	.309	11	.216	-0	18	23	5	2.8
1921 Phi-A	16	23	.410	46	32	20	0	3	285¹	312	21	87	71	12.6	3.94	113	.284	.337	18	.191	-2	11	16	4	1.6
1922 Phi-A	**27**	13	.675	**51**	33	22	3	2	294	294	21	63	54	11.1	3.28	130	.267	.309	17	.181	-3	25	32	4	3.3
1923 Phi-A	18	19	.486	**56**	31	19	5	1	297²	306	14	108	76	12.6	3.27	126	.271	.336	24	.238	1	24	28	6	**3.6**
1924 Phi-A	18	15	.545	43	34	21	3	1	278	302	8	94	72	12.9	3.95	108	.284	.344	15	.158	-6	9	10	8	1.1
1925 Phi-A	**21**	10	.677	52	28	14	1	3	261	285	10	95	67	13.3	3.69	126	.281	.345	15	.185	-1	20	28	6	3.2
1926 Phi-A	11	11	.500	37	26	12	3	0	219	225	10	54	52	11.5	3.08	135	.268	.314	6	.098	-4	23	26	3	2.6
1927 Phi-A	11	3	.786	30	17	8	2	1	146²	166	6	48	33	13.3	4.36	98	.286	.343	8	.157	-3	-4	-2	3	0.0
1928 Phi-A	13	5	.722	43	11	6	0	4	173²	177	11	26	37	10.6	3.06	131	.266	.295	12	.255	3	19	18	3	2.4
1929 *Phi-A	12	2	.857	32	6	4	0	4	113²	135	10	34	25	13.5	2.85	148	.294	.344	8	.205	-0	18	17	1	1.7
1930 Phi-A	9	4	.692	35	9	5	0	3	130¹	142	11	27	35	11.7	4.28	109	.277	.315	10	.263	3	5	6	2	1.0
1931 *Phi-A	7	5	.583	25	10	8	1	0	118	136	5	27	18	12.5	2.97	151	.291	.331	14	.259	2	18	20	0	2.3
1932 Phi-A	1	2	.333	17	0	0	0	2	65¹	84	6	18	16	14.1	5.51	82	.315	.358	6	.300	2	-7	-7	2	-0.2
Total 13	171	119	.590	500	249	147	18	29	2556¹	2729	138	724	599	12.3	3.54	122	.277	.329	164	.199	-8	179	217	48	25.4
■ ENRIQUE ROMO Romo, Enrique (Navarro) b: 7/15/47, Santa Rosalia, Mex BR/TR, 5'11", 185 lbs. Deb: 4/07/77																									
1977 Sea-A	8	10	.444	58	3	0	0	16	114¹	93	8	39	105	11.8	2.83	145	.227	.302	0	—	0	16	16	0	1.7
1978 Sea-A	11	7	.611	56	0	0	0	10	107¹	88	12	39	62	11.1	3.69	103	.227	.306	0	—	0	1	1	-1	0.0
1979 *Pit-N	10	5	.667	84	0	0	0	5	129¹	122	11	43	106	11.7	2.99	130	.253	.318	2	.167	-0	11	13	2	1.5
1980 Pit-N	5	5	.500	74	0	0	0	11	123²	117	10	28	82	10.6	3.27	111	.250	.296	5	.455	3	4	5	1	0.9
1981 Pit-N	1	3	.250	33	0	0	0	9	41²	47	5	18	23	14.0	4.54	79	.288	.359	0	.000	-0	-5	-4	-0	-0.5
1982 Pit-N	9	3	.750	45	0	0	0	1	86²	81	11	36	58	12.3	4.36	85	.245	.322	3	.300	1	-7	-6	-0	-0.5
Total 6	44	33	.571	350	3	0	0	52	603	548	57	203	436	11.4	3.45	111	.245	.312	10	.270	4	19	25	1	3.1
■ VICENTE ROMO Romo, Vicente (Navarro) "Huevo" b: 4/12/43, Santa Rosalia, Mex. BR/TR, 6'1", 180 lbs. Deb: 4/11/68																									
1968 LA-N	0	0	—	1	0	0	0	0	1	1	0	0	0	9.0	0.00	—	.250	.250	0	—	0	0	0	0	0.0
Cle-A	5	3	.625	40	1	0	0	12	83¹	43	5	32	54	8.3	1.62	183	.154	.245	2	.143	-0	13	12	0	1.4
1969 Cle-A	1	1	.500	3	0	0	0	0	8	7	0	3	7	11.3	2.25	167	.233	.303	1	.500	0	1	1	-0	0.2
Bos-A	7	9	.438	52	11	4	1	11	127¹	116	14	50	89	11.8	3.18	120	.247	.321	4	.129	-1	6	9	0	0.9
Yr	8	10	.444	55	11	4	1	11	135¹	123	14	53	96	11.8	3.13	122	.246	.319	1	.030	-0	7	10	1	1.1
1970 Bos-A	7	3	.700	48	10	0	0	6	108	115	14	43	71	13.2	4.08	97	.273	.340	4	.148	0	-4	-1	1	0.0
1971 Chi-A	1	7	.125	45	2	0	0	5	72	52	9	37	48	11.1	3.38	106	.202	.303	1	.364	1	1	2	1	0.5
1972 Chi-A	3	0	1.000	28	0	0	0	1	51²	47	5	18	46	11.5	3.31	94	.246	.314	0	.000	-1	-1	-1	-0	-0.1
1973 SD-N	2	3	.400	49	1	0	0	9	87²	85	11	46	51	13.4	3.70	94	.260	.351	2	.125	-0	-0	-2	0	-0.1
1974 SD-N	5	5	.500	54	1	0	0	9	71	78	6	37	26	14.8	4.56	78	.290	.380	0	.000	-1	-7	-8	2	-0.6
1982 LA-N	1	2	.333	15	6	0	0	1	35²	32	1	14	24	10.3	3.03	114	.195	.285	1	.200	0	2	2	1	0.2
Total 8	32	33	.492	335	32	4	1	52	645²	569	61	280	416	11.9	3.36	106	.239	.322	18	.149	-5	10	13	6	2.4
■ JOHN ROMONOSKY Romonosky, John b: 7/7/29, Harrisburg, Ill. BR/TR, 6'2", 195 lbs. Deb: 9/06/53																									
1953 StL-N	0	0	—	2	2	0	0	0	7²	9	1	4	3	16.4	4.70	91	.281	.378	0	.000	-0	-0	-0	-0	0.0
1958 Was-A	2	4	.333	18	5	1	0	0	55¹	52	6	28	38	13.0	6.51	59	.243	.331	4	.308	2	-17	-17	0	-1.3
1959 Was-A	1	0	1.000	12	2	0	0	0	38¹	36	4	19	22	13.6	3.29	119	.254	.354	2	.182	0	2	3	0	0.3
Total 3	3	4	.429	32	9	1	0	0	101¹	97	11	51	63	13.5	5.15	75	.250	.343	6	.231	2	-15	-14	-0	-1.0
■ GILBERTO RONDON Rondon, Gilberto b: 11/18/53, Bronx, N.Y. BR/TR, 6'2", 200 lbs. Deb: 4/10/76																									
1976 Hou-N	2	2	.500	19	7	0	0	0	53²	70	6	39	21	18.3	5.70	56	.315	.418	4	.286	1	-13	-15	-1	-1.4
1979 Chi-A	0	0	—	4	0	0	0	0	9²	11	2	6	3	15.8	3.72	114	.282	.378	0	—	0	1	1	-0	0.0
Total 2	2	2	.500	23	7	0	0	0	63¹	81	8	45	24	17.9	5.40	62	.310	.412	4	.286	1	-13	-14	-1	-1.4
■ JIM ROOKER Rooker, James Phillip b: 9/23/41, Lakeview, Ore. BR/TL, 6', 195 lbs. Deb: 6/30/68																									
1968 Det-A	0	0	—	2	0	0	0	0	4²	4	0	1	4	9.6	3.86	78	.235	.278	0	.000	-0	-0	-0	0	0.0
1969 KC-A	4	16	.200	28	22	8	1	0	158¹	136	13	73	108	11.9	3.75	98	.229	.315	16	.281	8	-2	-1	-1	0.6
1970 KC-A	10	15	.400	38	29	6	3	1	203²	190	11	102	117	12.9	3.54	106	.252	.341	14	.200	3	4	5	0	0.8
1971 KC-A	2	7	.222	20	7	1	1	0	54	59	2	24	31	14.0	5.33	64	.284	.361	0	.000	-0	-11	-11	-1	-1.2
1972 KC-A	5	6	.455	18	10	4	2	0	72	78	3	24	44	12.9	4.38	69	.280	.339	2	.100	-1	-11	-11	-1	-1.1
1973 Pit-N	10	6	.625	41	18	6	3	5	170¹	143	12	52	122	10.4	2.85	123	.229	.290	12	.245	3	15	13	0	1.3
1974 *Pit-N	15	11	.577	33	33	15	1	0	262²	228	11	83	139	10.8	2.78	124	.238	.301	29	.305	10	25	20	1	3.3
1975 *Pit-N	13	11	.542	28	28	7	1	0	196²	177	16	76	102	11.7	2.97	119	.238	.311	6	.095	-3	14	12	0	1.0
1976 Pit-N	15	8	.652	30	29	10	1	1	198²	201	12	72	92	12.5	3.35	104	.263	.328	16	.216	3	3	3	-0	0.6
1977 Pit-N	14	9	.609	30	30	7	2	0	204¹	196	24	64	89	11.5	3.08	129	.253	.310	13	.186	0	19	20	-1	2.1
1978 Pit-N	9	11	.450	28	28	1	0	0	163¹	160	11	81	76	13.4	4.24	87	.259	.348	9	.161	0	-12	-10	1	-0.8
1979 Pit-N	4	7	.364	19	17	1	0	0	103²	106	11	39	44	12.6	4.60	84	.266	.331	4	.121	-1	-10	-8	-0	-0.9
1980 Pit-N	2	2	.500	4	4	0	0	0	18	16	0	12	8	14.0	3.50	104	.262	.384	1	.143	1	0	0	0	0.0
Total 13	103	109	.486	319	255	66	15	7	1810¹	1694	128	703	976	12.0	3.46	104	.249	.321	122	.201	22	34	30	-0	6.1
■ CHARLIE ROOT Root, Charles Henry "Chinski" b: 3/17/1899, Middletown, Ohio d: 11/5/70, Hollister, Cal. BR/TR, 5'10.5", 190 lbs. Deb: 4/18/23 C																									
1923 StL-A	0	4	.000	27	2	0	0	0	60	68	4	18	27	13.8	5.70	73	.302	.369	1	.077	-1	-11	-10	-1	-1.0
1926 Chi-N	18	17	.514	42	32	21	2	2	271¹	267	10	62	127	11.1	2.82	136	.264	.310	13	.143	-4	30	31	-2	2.6
1927 Chi-N	**26**	15	.634	**48**	36	21	4	2	**309**	296	16	117	145	12.3	3.76	103	.254	.326	27	.221	3	6	4	-0	0.2
1928 Chi-N	14	18	.438	40	30	13	1	2	237	214	15	73	122	11.2	3.57	108	.242	.305	13	.178	-0	11	7	-3	0.4
1929 *Chi-N	19	6	**.760**	43	31	19	4	5	272	286	12	83	124	12.3	3.47	133	.275	.330	15	.156	0	38	35	-5	2.8

YEAR	TM/L	W	L	PCT	G	GS	CG	SH	SV	IP	H	HR	BB	SO	RAT	ERA	ERA+	OAV	OOB	BH	AVG	PB	PR	/A	PD	TPI
1930	Chi-N	16	14	.533	37	30	15	4	3	220¹	247	17	63	124	12.9	4.33	113	.281	.334	21	.262	5	16	14	-3	1.3
1931	Chi-N	17	14	.548	39	31	19	3	2	251	240	17	71	131	11.4	3.48	111	.252	.309	20	.222	3	11	11	-3	1.0
1932	*Chi-N	15	10	.600	39	23	11	0	3	216¹	211	10	55	96	11.3	3.58	105	.253	.303	13	.171	-1	7	5	-3	0.0
1933	Chi-N	15	10	.600	35	30	20	2	0	242¹	232	14	61	86	11.3	2.60	126	.252	.306	8	.094	-4	20	18	-3	1.2
1934	Chi-N	4	7	.364	34	9	2	0	0	117²	141	8	53	46	15.2	4.28	90	.298	.375	7	.175	1	-3	-5	-0	-0.3
1935	*Chi-N	15	8	.652	38	18	11	1	2	201¹	193	15	47	94	10.9	3.08	127	.252	.298	14	.203	2	21	19	-3	1.8
1936	Chi-N	3	6	.333	33	4	0	0	1	73²	81	3	20	32	12.6	4.15	96	.280	.331	5	.333	1	-1	-1	-1	0.0
1937	Chi-N	13	5	.722	43	15	5	0	5	178²	173	18	32	74	10.5	3.38	118	.253	.290	12	.179	0	11	12	-0	1.2
1938	*Chi-N	8	7	.533	44	11	5	0	8	160²	163	10	30	70	10.9	2.86	134	.258	.294	8	.167	-0	17	17	-2	1.5
1939	Chi-N	8	8	.500	35	16	8	0	4	167¹	189	11	30	65	12.1	4.03	98	.286	.323	10	.175	2	-2	-2	-3	-0.2
1940	Chi-N	2	4	.333	36	8	1	0	1	112	118	9	33	50	12.2	3.86	97	.265	.317	4	.129	-1	-0	-1	-0	-0.1
1941	Chi-N	8	7	.533	19	15	6	0	0	106²	133	8	37	46	14.3	5.40	65	.306	.360	5	.152	2	-21	-22	-1	-2.0
Total	17	201	160	.557	632	341	177	21	40	3197¹	3252	187	889	1459	11.9	3.59	110	.264	.318	196	.180	8	148	129	-37	10.4

■ CHUCK ROSE   Rose, Charles Alfred b: 9/1/1885, Macon, Mo. d: 8/4/61, Salina, Kan. BL/TL, 5'8.5", 158 lbs. Deb: 9/13/09

YEAR	TM/L	W	L	PCT	G	GS	CG	SH	SV	IP	H	HR	BB	SO	RAT	ERA	ERA+	OAV	OOB	BH	AVG	PB	PR	/A	PD	TPI
1909	StL-A	1	2	.333	3	3	3	0	0	25	32	1	7	6	15.1	5.40	45	.330	.393	0	.000	-1	-8	-8	-1	-0.8

■ DON ROSE   Rose, Donald Gary b: 3/19/47, Covina, Cal. BR/TR, 6'3", 195 lbs. Deb: 9/15/71

YEAR	TM/L	W	L	PCT	G	GS	CG	SH	SV	IP	H	HR	BB	SO	RAT	ERA	ERA+	OAV	OOB	BH	AVG	PB	PR	/A	PD	TPI
1971	NY-N	0	0	—	1	0	0	0	0	2	2	0	0	1	9.0	0.00	—	.286	.286	0	—	0	1	1	0	0.1
1972	Cal-A	1	4	.200	16	4	0	0	0	42²	49	9	19	39	14.3	4.22	69	.283	.354	2	.200	1	-5	-6	-1	-0.5
1974	SF-N	0	0	—	2	0	0	0	0	1	4	0	1	0	45.0	9.00	42	.667	.714	0	—	0	-1	-1	0	0.0
Total	3	1	4	.200	19	4	0	0	0	45²	55	9	20	40	14.8	4.14	71	.296	.364	2	.200	1	-5	-6	-1	-0.4

■ ZEKE ROSEBRAUGH   Rosebraugh, Eli Ethelbert b: 9/8/70, Charleston, Ill. d: 7/16/30, Fresno, Cal. L, Deb: 9/21/1898

YEAR	TM/L	W	L	PCT	G	GS	CG	SH	SV	IP	H	HR	BB	SO	RAT	ERA	ERA+	OAV	OOB	BH	AVG	PB	PR	/A	PD	TPI
1898	Pit-N	0	2	.000	4	2	2	0	0	21²	23	0	9	6	13.3	3.32	107	.270	.340	3	.375	1	1	1	-0	0.1
1899	Pit-N	0	1	.000	2	2	0	0	0	6	14	0	3	2	25.5	9.00	42	.451	.499	0	.000	-0	-3	-3	0	-0.2
Total	2	0	3	.000	6	4	2	0	0	27²	37	0	12	8	15.9	4.55	79	.318	.382	3	.300	1	-3	-3	-0	-0.1

■ CHIEF ROSEMAN   Roseman, James John b: 1856, New York, N.Y. d: 7/4/38, Brooklyn, N.Y. BR/TR, 5'7", 167 lbs. Deb: 5/01/1882 M♦

YEAR	TM/L	W	L	PCT	G	GS	CG	SH	SV	IP	H	HR	BB	SO	RAT	ERA	ERA+	OAV	OOB	BH	AVG	PB	PR	/A	PD	TPI
1885	NY-a	0	1	.000	1	1	0	0	0	1	3	0	2	0	45.0	27.00	11	.499	.624	114	.278	0	-3	-3	-0	-0.1
1886	NY-a	0	0	—	1	0	0	0	0	7	6	0	0	0	7.7	5.14	66	.221	.221	127	.227	0	-1	-1	0	-0.0
1887	NY-a	0	0	—	2	0	0	0	0	8	11	0	5	1	18.0	7.88	54	.315	.401	55	.228	-0	-3	-3	-0	-0.1
Total	3	0	1	.000	4	1	0	0	0	16	20	0	7	1	15.2	7.88	48	.294	.360	726	.263	0	-7	-7	0	-0.2

■ STEVE ROSENBERG   Rosenberg, Steven Allen b: 10/31/64, Brooklyn, N.Y. BL/TL, 6', 186 lbs. Deb: 6/04/88

YEAR	TM/L	W	L	PCT	G	GS	CG	SH	SV	IP	H	HR	BB	SO	RAT	ERA	ERA+	OAV	OOB	BH	AVG	PB	PR	/A	PD	TPI
1988	Chi-A	0	1	.000	33	0	0	0	1	46	53	5	19	28	14.1	4.30	92	.298	.365	0	—	0	-2	-2	-0	-0.1
1989	Chi-A	4	13	.235	38	21	2	0	0	142	148	14	58	77	13.1	4.94	77	.273	.344	0	—	0	-17	-18	-1	-1.7
1990	Chi-A	1	0	1.000	6	0	0	0	0	10	10	2	5	4	13.5	5.40	71	.256	.341	0	—	0	-2	-2	-0	-0.1
Total	3	5	14	.263	77	21	2	0	1	198	211	21	82	109	13.4	4.82	80	.278	.349	0	—	0	-20	-21	0	-1.9

■ STEVE ROSER   Roser, Emerson Corey b: 1/25/18, Rome, N.Y. BR/TR, 6'4", 220 lbs. Deb: 5/05/44

YEAR	TM/L	W	L	PCT	G	GS	CG	SH	SV	IP	H	HR	BB	SO	RAT	ERA	ERA+	OAV	OOB	BH	AVG	PB	PR	/A	PD	TPI
1944	NY-A	4	3	.571	16	6	1	0	1	84	80	3	34	34	12.2	3.86	90	.256	.329	3	.100	-2	-4	-3	-1	-0.5
1945	NY-A	0	0	—	11	0	0	0	0	27	27	1	8	11	13.1	3.67	94	.262	.315	1	.125	-0	-1	-1	-0	0.0
1946	NY-A	1	1	.500	4	1	0	0	0	3¹	7	0	4	1	29.7	16.20	21	.438	.550	0	—	0	-5	-5	-0	-0.4
	Bos-N	1	1	.500	14	1	0	0	1	35	33	1	18	18	13.1	3.60	95	.250	.340	0	.000	-1	-1	-1	-0	-0.1
Total	3	6	5	.545	45	8	1	0	2	149¹	147	5	64	64	12.7	4.04	86	.261	.336	4	.093	-3	-10	-9	-0	-1.0

■ BUSTER ROSS   Ross, Chester Franklin b: 3/11/03, Kuttawa, Ky. d: 4/24/82, Mayfield, Ky. BL/TL, 6'1", 195 lbs. Deb: 6/15/24

YEAR	TM/L	W	L	PCT	G	GS	CG	SH	SV	IP	H	HR	BB	SO	RAT	ERA	ERA+	OAV	OOB	BH	AVG	PB	PR	/A	PD	TPI
1924	Bos-A	4	3	.571	30	2	1	1	1	93¹	109	3	30	16	13.4	3.47	126	.307	.361	5	.200	-0	8	9	-1	0.8
1925	Bos-A	3	8	.273	33	8	0	0	0	94¹	119	9	40	15	15.6	6.20	73	.313	.386	3	.125	-1	-19	-17	-1	-1.7
1926	Bos-A	0	1	.000	1	0	0	0	0	2²	5	0	4	0	30.4	16.88	24	.385	.529	0	.000	-0	-4	-4	0	-0.2
Total	3	7	12	.368	64	10	1	1	1	190¹	233	12	74	31	14.8	5.01	89	.311	.377	8	.160	-2	-15	-12	-2	-1.1

■ CLIFF ROSS   Ross, Clifford Davis b: 8/3/28, Philadelphia, Pa. BL/TL, 6'4", 195 lbs. Deb: 9/11/54

YEAR	TM/L	W	L	PCT	G	GS	CG	SH	SV	IP	H	HR	BB	SO	RAT	ERA	ERA+	OAV	OOB	BH	AVG	PB	PR	/A	PD	TPI
1954	Cin-N	0	0	—	4	0	0	0	1	2²	0	0	0	1	0.0	0.00	—	.000	.000	0	—	0	1	1	0	0.1

■ ERNIE ROSS   Ross, Ernest Bertram "Curly" b: 3/31/1880, Toronto, Ont., Can. d: 3/28/50, Toronto, Ont., Can. 5'8", 150 lbs. Deb: 9/17/02

YEAR	TM/L	W	L	PCT	G	GS	CG	SH	SV	IP	H	HR	BB	SO	RAT	ERA	ERA+	OAV	OOB	BH	AVG	PB	PR	/A	PD	TPI
1902	Bal-A	1	1	.500	2	2	2	0	0	17	20	0	12	2	16.9	7.41	51	.293	.399	0	.000	-1	-7	-7	-1	-0.6

■ BOB ROSS   Ross, Floyd Robert b: 11/2/28, Fullerton, Cal. BR/TL, 6', 165 lbs. Deb: 6/16/50

YEAR	TM/L	W	L	PCT	G	GS	CG	SH	SV	IP	H	HR	BB	SO	RAT	ERA	ERA+	OAV	OOB	BH	AVG	PB	PR	/A	PD	TPI
1950	Was-A	0	1	.000	6	2	0	0	0	12²	15	1	15	2	21.3	8.53	53	.300	.462	0	.000	-0	-6	-6	0	-0.4
1951	Was-A	0	1	.000	11	1	0	0	0	31²	36	3	21	23	16.2	6.54	63	.295	.399	1	.111	-0	-8	-9	-1	-0.8
1956	Phi-N	0	0	—	3	0	0	0	0	3¹	4	1	2	4	16.2	8.10	46	.333	.429	0	—	0	-2	-2	0	0.0
Total	3	0	2	.000	20	3	0	0	0	47²	55	5	38	29	17.6	7.17	58	.299	.419	1	.083	-1	-16	-16	-0	-1.2

■ GARY ROSS   Ross, Gary Douglas b: 9/16/47, McKeesport, Pa. BR/TR, 6'1", 185 lbs. Deb: 6/28/68

YEAR	TM/L	W	L	PCT	G	GS	CG	SH	SV	IP	H	HR	BB	SO	RAT	ERA	ERA+	OAV	OOB	BH	AVG	PB	PR	/A	PD	TPI
1968	Chi-N	1	1	.500	13	5	1	0	0	41	44	1	25	31	15.1	4.17	76	.288	.388	1	.091	-1	-5	-5	0	-0.5
1969	Chi-N	0	0	—	2	1	0	0	0	2	1	0	2	2	13.5	13.50	30	.143	.333	0	—	0	-2	-2	0	-0.1
	SD-N	3	12	.200	46	7	0	0	3	109²	104	5	56	58	13.5	4.19	84	.252	.348	0	.000	-2	-7	-8	2	-0.8
	Yr	3	12	.200	48	8	0	0	3	111²	105	5	58	60	13.5	4.35	81	.250	.348	1	.043	-2	-9	-10	2	-0.9
1970	SD-N	2	3	.400	33	2	0	0	1	62¹	72	8	36	39	16.0	5.20	76	.305	.404	4	.500	2	-8	-8	1	-0.5
1971	SD-N	1	3	.250	13	0	0	0	0	24¹	27	0	11	13	14.4	2.96	111	.300	.382	0	.000	-0	1	1	0	0.1
1972	SD-N	4	3	.571	60	0	0	0	3	91²	87	2	49	46	13.7	2.45	134	.261	.363	2	.154	-0	10	8	1	1.0
1973	SD-N	4	4	.500	58	0	0	0	0	76¹	93	8	33	44	15.3	5.42	64	.304	.379	0	.000	-0	-15	-17	0	-1.6
1974	SD-N	0	0	—	9	0	0	0	0	18	23	1	6	11	14.5	4.50	79	.315	.367	0	.000	-0	-2	-2	-0	-0.1
1975	Cal-A	0	1	.000	1	1	0	0	0	5	6	1	1	4	12.6	5.40	66	.273	.304	0	—	0	-1	-1	-0	0.0
1976	Cal-A	8	16	.333	34	31	7	2	0	225	224	12	58	100	11.5	3.00	111	.258	.308	0	—	0	13	8	6	1.5
1977	Cal-A	2	4	.333	14	12	0	0	0	58¹	72	8	11	30	14.8	5.55	70	.337	.371	0	—	0	-10	-11	1	-0.9
Total	10	25	47	.347	283	59	8	2	7	713²	764	48	288	378	13.6	3.92	89	.278	.352	7	.115	-2	-26	-36	11	-1.9

■ GEORGE ROSS   Ross, George Sidney b: 6/27/1892, San Rafael, Cal. d: 4/22/35, Amityville, N.Y. BL/TL, 5'10.5", 175 lbs. Deb: 6/27/18

YEAR	TM/L	W	L	PCT	G	GS	CG	SH	SV	IP	H	HR	BB	SO	RAT	ERA	ERA+	OAV	OOB	BH	AVG	PB	PR	/A	PD	TPI
1918	NY-N	0	0	—	1	0	0	0	1	2¹	2	0	3	2	19.3	0.00	—	.222	.417	0	—	0	1	1	0	0.1

■ BUCK ROSS   Ross, Lee Ravon b: 2/2/15, Norwood, N.C. d: 11/23/78, Charlotte, N.C. BR/TR, 6'2", 170 lbs. Deb: 5/07/36

YEAR	TM/L	W	L	PCT	G	GS	CG	SH	SV	IP	H	HR	BB	SO	RAT	ERA	ERA+	OAV	OOB	BH	AVG	PB	PR	/A	PD	TPI
1936	Phi-A	9	14	.391	30	27	12	1	0	200²	253	17	83	47	15.1	5.83	88	.304	.367	12	.169	-1	-18	-16	-1	-1.5
1937	Phi-A	5	10	.333	28	22	7	1	0	147¹	183	12	63	37	15.1	4.89	96	.306	.373	5	.102	-3	-4	-3	0	-0.4
1938	Phi-A	9	16	.360	29	28	10	0	0	184¹	218	23	80	54	15.5	5.32	91	.289	.357	12	.190	-0	-11	-10	-0	-0.8
1939	Phi-A	6	14	.300	29	28	6	1	0	174	216	17	95	43	16.1	6.00	78	.302	.384	12	.207	-1	-27	-25	-2	-2.3
1940	Phi-A	5	10	.333	24	19	10	0	1	156¹	160	15	60	43	12.7	4.38	102	.256	.322	7	.132	-2	0	1	-1	-0.1
1941	Phi-A	0	1	.000	1	1	0	0	0	4	10	2	2	0	27.0	18.00	23	.435	.482	0	—	0	-6	-6	-0	-0.4
	Chi-A	3	8	.273	20	11	7	0	0	108¹	99	6	43	30	11.9	3.16	130	.239	.312	7	.219	1	12	11	-1	1.1
	Yr	3	9	.250	21	12	7	0	0	112¹	109	8	45	30	12.4	3.69	111	.249	.321	2	.061	1	6	5	-1	0.7
1942	Chi-A	5	7	.417	22	14	4	2	1	113¹	118	6	39	37	12.5	5.00	72	.264	.323	6	.158	0	-17	-18	-2	-1.9
1943	Chi-A	11	7	.611	21	21	7	1	0	149¹	140	6	56	41	11.9	3.19	105	.253	.324	4	.087	-1	8	7	-1	0.7
1944	Chi-A	2	7	.222	20	9	2	0	0	90¹	97	7	35	20	13.4	5.18	66	.280	.350	2	.077	-2	-18	-18	-2	-2.1
1945	Chi-A	1	1	.500	13	2	0	0	0	37¹	51	3	17	8	16.4	5.79	57	.327	.393	2	.182	-0	-10	-10	-0	-1.0

YEAR	TM/L	W	L	PCT	G	GS	CG	SH	SV	IP	H	HR	BB	SO	RAT	ERA	ERA+	OAV	OOB	BH	AVG	PB	PR	/A	PD	TPI
Total	10	56	95	.371	237	182	65	6	2	1365¹	1545	114	573	360	14.0	4.94	88	.283	.351	69	.154	-11	-97	-91	-11	-9.4

■ MARK ROSS
Ross, Mark Joseph b: 8/8/54, Galveston, Tex.   BR/TR, 6', 195 lbs.   Deb: 9/12/82

YEAR	TM/L	W	L	PCT	G	GS	CG	SH	SV	IP	H	HR	BB	SO	RAT	ERA	ERA+	OAV	OOB	BH	AVG	PB	PR	/A	PD	TPI
1982	Hou-N	0	0	—	4	0	0	0	0	6	3	0	0	4	4.5	1.50	221	.143	.143	0	—	0	1	1	0	0.1
1984	Hou-N	1	0	1.000	2	0	0	0	0	2¹	1	0	0	1	3.9	0.00	—	.125	.125	0	—	0	1	1	0	0.1
1985	Hou-N	0	2	.000	8	0	0	0	1	13	12	2	2	3	9.7	4.85	71	.240	.269	0	.000	-0	-2	-2	0	-0.1
1987	Pit-N	0	0	—	1	0	0	0	0	1	1	1	0	0	9.0	9.00	46	.250	.250	0	—	0	-1	-1	0	0.0
1988	Tor-A	0	0	—	3	0	0	0	0	7¹	5	0	4	4	11.0	4.91	80	.185	.290	0	—	0	-1	-1	-0	0.0
1990	Pit-N	1	0	1.000	9	0	0	0	0	12²	11	2	4	5	10.7	3.55	102	.244	.306	0	.000	-0	0	0	0	0.0
Total	6	2	2	.500	27	0	0	0	1	42¹	33	5	10	17	9.1	3.83	93	.213	.261	0	.000	-0	-0	-1	1	0.1

■ FRANK ROSSO
Rosso, Francis James b: 3/1/21, Agawam, Mass.   d: 1/26/80, Ulrichsville, O.   BR/TR, 5'11", 180 lbs.   Deb: 9/15/44

YEAR	TM/L	W	L	PCT	G	GS	CG	SH	SV	IP	H	HR	BB	SO	RAT	ERA	ERA+	OAV	OOB	BH	AVG	PB	PR	/A	PD	TPI
1944	NY-N	0	0	—	2	0	0	0	0	4	11	0	3	1	31.5	9.00	41	.550	.609	0	—	0	-2	-2	0	-0.1

■ MARV ROTBLATT
Rotblatt, Marvin "Rotty" b: 10/18/27, Chicago, Ill.   BB/TL, 5'7", 160 lbs.   Deb: 7/04/48

YEAR	TM/L	W	L	PCT	G	GS	CG	SH	SV	IP	H	HR	BB	SO	RAT	ERA	ERA+	OAV	OOB	BH	AVG	PB	PR	/A	PD	TPI
1948	Chi-A	0	1	.000	7	2	0	0	0	18¹	19	0	23	4	21.1	7.85	54	.271	.457	0	.000	-0	-7	-7	-0	-0.6
1950	Chi-A	0	0	—	2	0	0	0	0	8²	11	2	5	6	16.6	6.23	72	.344	.432	0	.000	-0	-2	-2	0	0.0
1951	Chi-A	4	2	.667	26	2	0	0	2	47²	44	4	23	20	12.8	3.40	119	.244	.333	0	.000	-2	4	3	1	0.3
Total	3	4	3	.571	35	4	0	0	2	74²	74	6	51	30	15.3	4.82	86	.262	.379	0	.000	-2	-5	-6	1	-0.3

■ JACK ROTHROCK
Rothrock, John Houston b: 3/14/05, Long Beach, Cal.   d: 2/2/80, San Bernardino, Cal   BB/TR, 5'11.5", 165 lbs.   Deb: 7/28/25 ♦

YEAR	TM/L	W	L	PCT	G	GS	CG	SH	SV	IP	H	HR	BB	SO	RAT	ERA	ERA+	OAV	OOB	BH	AVG	PB	PR	/A	PD	TPI
1928	Bos-A	0	0	—	1	0	0	0	0	1	0	0	0	0	0.0	0.00	—	.000	.000	92	.267	0	0	0	0	0.0

■ LARRY ROTHSCHILD
Rothschild, Lawrence Lee b: 3/12/54, Chicago, Ill.   BL/TR, 6'2", 180 lbs.   Deb: 9/11/81 C

YEAR	TM/L	W	L	PCT	G	GS	CG	SH	SV	IP	H	HR	BB	SO	RAT	ERA	ERA+	OAV	OOB	BH	AVG	PB	PR	/A	PD	TPI
1981	Det-A	0	0	—	5	0	0	0	1	5²	4	0	6	1	15.9	1.59	237	.200	.385	0	—	0	1	1	1	0.2
1982	Det-A	0	0	—	2	0	0	0	0	2²	4	1	2	0	20.3	13.50	30	.333	.429	0	—	0	-3	-3	0	-0.2
Total	2	0	0	—	7	0	0	0	1	8¹	8	1	8	1	17.3	5.40	72	.250	.400	0	—	0	-1	-1	1	0.0

■ GENE ROUNSAVILLE
Rounsaville, Virle Gene b: 9/27/44, Konawa, Okla.   BR/TR, 6'3", 205 lbs.   Deb: 4/07/70

YEAR	TM/L	W	L	PCT	G	GS	CG	SH	SV	IP	H	HR	BB	SO	RAT	ERA	ERA+	OAV	OOB	BH	AVG	PB	PR	/A	PD	TPI
1970	Chi-A	0	1	.000	8	0	0	0	0	6¹	10	1	2	3	17.1	9.95	39	.357	.400	0	—	0	-4	-4	0	-0.3

■ JACK ROWAN
Rowan, John Albert b: 6/16/1887, New Castle, Pa.   d: 9/29/66, Dayton, Ohio   BR/TR, 6'1", 210 lbs.   Deb: 9/06/06

YEAR	TM/L	W	L	PCT	G	GS	CG	SH	SV	IP	H	HR	BB	SO	RAT	ERA	ERA+	OAV	OOB	BH	AVG	PB	PR	/A	PD	TPI
1906	Det-A	0	1	.000	1	1	1	0	0	9	15	0	6	0	21.0	11.00	25	.373	.455	1	.250	0	-8	-8	-0	-0.5
1908	Cin-N	3	3	.500	8	7	4	1	0	49¹	46	0	16	24	11.3	1.82	126	.253	.313	1	.071	-0	3	3	0	0.3
1909	Cin-N	11	12	.478	38	23	14	0	0	225²	185	0	104	81	11.6	2.79	93	.233	.324	6	.092	-1	-5	-5	-1	-1.1
1910	Cin-N	14	13	.519	42	30	18	4	1	261	242	4	105	108	12.3	2.93	99	.254	.334	19	.229	3	3	-0	-4	-0.2
1911	Phi-N	2	4	.333	12	6	2	0	0	45²	59	3	20	17	15.8	4.73	73	.316	.385	1	.077	-1	-7	-7	1	-0.6
	Chi-N	0	0	—	1	0	0	0	0	2	1	0	2	0	18.0	4.50	74	.143	.400	-0	-0	-0	-0	-0	0	0.0
	Yr	2	4	.333	13	6	2	0	0	47²	60	3	22	17	15.7	4.72	73	.308	.381	1	.071	-1	-7	-7	1	-0.6
1913	Cin-N	0	4	.000	5	5	5	0	0	39	37	0	9	21	10.8	3.00	108	.264	.313	2	.182	1	1	1	-0	0.2
1914	Cin-N	1	3	.250	12	2	0	0	0	39	38	1	10	16	11.1	3.46	85	.262	.310	0	.000	-1	-3	-2	-0	-0.3
Total	7	31	40	.437	119	74	44	5	3	670²	623	8	272	267	12.2	3.07	92	.255	.333	30	.151	1	-16	-19	-8	-2.2

■ DAVE ROWE
Rowe, David E. b: 2/1856, Jacksonville, Ill.   BR , 5'9", 180 lbs.   Deb: 5/30/1877   M♦

YEAR	TM/L	W	L	PCT	G	GS	CG	SH	SV	IP	H	HR	BB	SO	RAT	ERA	ERA+	OAV	OOB	BH	AVG	PB	PR	/A	PD	TPI
1877	Chi-N	0	1	.000	1	1	0	0	0	1	3	0	2	0	45.0	18.00	17	.494	.619	2	.286	0	-2	-2	0	0.0
1882	Cle-N	0	1	.000	1	1	1	0	0	9	29	3	7	0	36.0	12.00	23	.512	.566	25	.258	0	-9	-9	-0	-0.5
1883	Bal-a	0	0	—	1	0	0	0	0	4	12	1	2	1	31.5	20.25	17	.492	.530	80	.313	0	-8	-7	-0	-0.4
1884	StL-U	1	0	1.000	1	1	1	0	0	9	10	0	0	2	10.0	2.00	148	.263	.263	142	.293	0	1	1	0	0.1
Total	4	1	2	.333	4	3	2	0	0	23	54	4	11	3	25.4	9.78	30	.432	.478	383	.263	1	-17	-17	-0	-0.8

■ DON ROWE
Rowe, Donald Howard b: 4/3/36, Brawley, Cal.   BL/TL, 6', 180 lbs.   Deb: 4/09/63   C

YEAR	TM/L	W	L	PCT	G	GS	CG	SH	SV	IP	H	HR	BB	SO	RAT	ERA	ERA+	OAV	OOB	BH	AVG	PB	PR	/A	PD	TPI
1963	NY-N	0	0	—	26	1	0	0	0	54²	59	6	21	27	13.3	4.28	81	.280	.348	3	.231	0	-6	-5	-1	-0.5

■ KEN ROWE
Rowe, Kenneth Darrell b: 12/31/33, Ferndale, Mich.   BR/TR, 6'2", 185 lbs.   Deb: 4/14/63   C

YEAR	TM/L	W	L	PCT	G	GS	CG	SH	SV	IP	H	HR	BB	SO	RAT	ERA	ERA+	OAV	OOB	BH	AVG	PB	PR	/A	PD	TPI
1963	LA-N	1	1	.500	14	0	0	0	1	27²	28	2	11	12	13.0	2.93	103	.264	.339	0	.000	-0	1	0	0	0.0
1964	Bal-A	1	0	1.000	6	0	0	0	0	4¹	10	1	1	4	22.8	8.31	43	.455	.478	0	—	0	-2	-2	0	-0.1
1965	Bal-A	0	0	—	6	0	0	0	0	13¹	17	0	2	3	12.8	3.38	103	.321	.345	1	1.000	0	0	0	-1	0.0
Total	3	2	1	.667	26	0	0	0	1	45¹	55	3	14	19	13.9	3.57	90	.304	.357	1	.167	0	-1	-2	-0	-0.1

■ SCHOOLBOY ROWE
Rowe, Lynwood Thomas b: 1/11/10, Waco, Tex.   d: 1/8/61, ElDorado, Ark.   BR/TR, 6'4.5", 210 lbs.   Deb: 4/15/33   C♦

YEAR	TM/L	W	L	PCT	G	GS	CG	SH	SV	IP	H	HR	BB	SO	RAT	ERA	ERA+	OAV	OOB	BH	AVG	PB	PR	/A	PD	TPI
1933	Det-A	7	4	.636	19	15	8	1	0	123¹	129	7	31	75	11.7	3.58	121	.269	.315	11	.220	-0	10	10	1	1.1
1934	*Det-A	24	8	.750	45	30	20	3	1	266	259	12	81	149	11.5	3.45	127	.256	.312	33	.303	12	31	28	-1	3.7
1935	*Det-A	19	13	.594	42	34	21	6	3	275²	272	11	68	140	11.2	3.69	113	.255	.301	34	.312	13	23	15	-2	2.4
1936	Det-A	19	10	.655	41	35	19	4	3	245¹	266	15	64	115	12.2	4.51	110	.275	.321	23	.256	7	14	12	2	1.4
1937	Det-A	1	4	.200	10	2	1	0	0	31¹	49	7	9	6	16.9	8.62	54	.350	.393	2	.200	-0	-14	-14	1	-1.0
1938	Det-A	0	2	.000	4	3	0	0	0	21	20	1	11	4	13.3	3.00	167	.256	.348	1	.167	-0	4	5	1	0.5
1939	Det-A	10	12	.455	28	24	8	1	0	164	192	17	61	51	14.0	4.99	98	.291	.353	15	.246	2	-2	-1	0	0.1
1940	*Det-A	16	3	.842	27	23	11	1	0	169	170	15	43	61	11.4	3.46	137	.259	.305	18	.269	5	17	24	3	3.0
1941	Det-A	8	6	.571	27	14	4	0	1	139	155	6	33	54	12.2	4.14	110	.278	.318	15	.273	5	0	6	1	1.3
1942	Det-A	1	0	1.000	2	1	0	0	0	10¹	9	0	2	7	9.6	0.00	—	.220	.256	-0	-0	-1	4	5	0	0.5
	Bro-N	1	0	1.000	9	2	0	0	0	30¹	36	2	12	6	14.5	5.34	61	.288	.355	4	.211	0	-7	-7	-0	-0.6
1943	Phi-N	14	8	.636	27	25	11	3	1	199	194	7	29	52	10.2	2.94	115	.247	.276	36	.300	16	10	10	1	1.0
1946	Phi-N	11	4	.733	17	16	9	2	0	136	112	3	21	51	9.2	2.12	162	.224	.263	11	.180	2	20	20	-2	2.3
1947	Phi-N	14	10	.583	31	28	15	1	1	195²	232	22	45	74	12.9	4.32	93	.292	.333	22	.278	10	-6	-7	-1	0.1
1948	Phi-N	10	10	.500	30	20	8	0	0	148	167	5	31	46	12.2	4.07	97	.281	.319	10	.192	1	-2	-1	0	0.0
1949	Phi-N	3	7	.300	23	6	2	0	0	65¹	68	2	17	22	12.0	4.82	82	.300	.354	4	.235	2	-6	-6	1	-0.3
Total	15	158	101	.610	382	278	137	22	12	2219¹	2330	132	558	913	11.8	3.87	110	.268	.314	239	.263	76	93	96	3	16.0

■ MIKE ROWLAND
Rowland, Michael Evan b: 1/31/53, Chicago, Ill.   BR/TR, 6'3", 205 lbs.   Deb: 7/25/80

YEAR	TM/L	W	L	PCT	G	GS	CG	SH	SV	IP	H	HR	BB	SO	RAT	ERA	ERA+	OAV	OOB	BH	AVG	PB	PR	/A	PD	TPI
1980	SF-N	1	1	.500	19	0	0	0	0	27	20	2	8	8	9.7	2.33	152	.206	.274	0	—	0	4	4	0	0.4
1981	SF-N	0	1	.000	9	1	0	0	0	15²	13	1	6	8	11.5	3.45	100	.232	.317	1	1.000	0	0	-0	0	0.0
Total	2	1	2	.333	28	1	0	0	0	42²	33	3	14	16	10.3	2.74	128	.216	.290	1	1.000	0	4	4	0	0.4

■ CHARLIE ROY
Roy, Charles Robert b: 6/22/1884, Beaulieu, Minn.   d: 2/10/50, Blackfoot, Idaho   5'10", 190 lbs.   Deb: 6/27/06

YEAR	TM/L	W	L	PCT	G	GS	CG	SH	SV	IP	H	HR	BB	SO	RAT	ERA	ERA+	OAV	OOB	BH	AVG	PB	PR	/A	PD	TPI
1906	Phi-N	0	1	.000	7	1	0	0	0	18¹	24	0	5	6	14.7	4.91	53	.316	.366	0	.000	-1	-5	-5	-0	-0.5

■ EMILE ROY
Roy, Emile Arthur b: 5/26/07, Brighton, Mass.   BR/TR, 5'11", 180 lbs.   Deb: 9/30/33

YEAR	TM/L	W	L	PCT	G	GS	CG	SH	SV	IP	H	HR	BB	SO	RAT	ERA	ERA+	OAV	OOB	BH	AVG	PB	PR	/A	PD	TPI
1933	Phi-A	0	1	.000	1	1	0	0	0	2¹	4	0	4	3	30.9	27.00	16	.364	.533	0	—	0	-6	-6	-0	-0.3

■ JEAN-PIERRE ROY
Roy, Jean-Pierre b: 6/26/20, Montreal, Que., Can.   BB/TR, 5'10", 160 lbs.   Deb: 5/05/46

YEAR	TM/L	W	L	PCT	G	GS	CG	SH	SV	IP	H	HR	BB	SO	RAT	ERA	ERA+	OAV	OOB	BH	AVG	PB	PR	/A	PD	TPI
1946	Bro-N	0	0	—	3	1	0	0	0	6¹	5	2	5	6	14.2	9.95	34	.200	.333	0	.000	-0	-5	-5	-0	-0.4

■ LUTHER ROY
Roy, Luther Franklin b: 7/29/02, Ooltewah, Tenn.   d: 7/24/63, Grand Rapids, Mich.   BR/TR, 5'10.5", 161 lbs.   Deb: 6/12/24

YEAR	TM/L	W	L	PCT	G	GS	CG	SH	SV	IP	H	HR	BB	SO	RAT	ERA	ERA+	OAV	OOB	BH	AVG	PB	PR	/A	PD	TPI
1924	Cle-A	0	5	.000	16	5	2	0	0	48²	62	3	31	14	17.2	7.77	55	.318	.412	4	.267	0	-19	-19	1	-1.6
1925	Cle-A	0	0	—	6	1	0	0	0	10	14	1	11	1	22.5	3.60	123	.368	.510	0	.000	-0	1	1	-0	0.0
1927	Chi-N	3	1	.750	11	0	0	0	0	19²	14	0	11	5	11.9	2.29	169	.209	.329	1	.333	0	4	3	0	0.4

YEAR TM/L	W	L	PCT	G	GS	CG	SH	SV	IP	H	HR	BB	SO	RAT	ERA	ERA+	OAV	OOB	BH	AVG	PB	PR	/A	PD	TPI
1929 Phi-N	3	6	.333	21	12	1	0	0	88²	137	11	37	16	18.0	8.42	62	.350	.411	9	.281	2	-37	-32	1	-2.3
Bro-N	0	0	—	2	0	0	0	0	3²	4	0	2	0	14.7	4.91	94	.286	.375	0	.000	-0	-0	-0	0	0.0
Yr	3	6	.333	23	12	1	0	0	92¹	141	11	39	16	17.5	8.29	62	.346	.403	7	.212	2	-37	-32	1	-2.3
Total 4	6	12	.333	56	18	3	0	0	170²	231	15	92	36	17.2	7.17	66	.328	.408	14	.264	2	-51	-47	1	-3.5

■ NORMIE ROY
Roy, Norman Brooks "Jumbo" b: 11/15/28, Newton, Mass. BR/TR, 6', 200 lbs. Deb: 4/23/50

YEAR TM/L	W	L	PCT	G	GS	CG	SH	SV	IP	H	HR	BB	SO	RAT	ERA	ERA+	OAV	OOB	BH	AVG	PB	PR	/A	PD	TPI
1950 Bos-N	4	3	.571	19	6	2	0	1	59²	72	7	39	25	17.0	5.13	75	.305	.408	3	.167	0	-7	-8	0	-0.7

■ DICK ROZEK
Rozek, Richard Louis b: 3/27/27, Cedar Rapids, Iowa BL/TL, 6'0.5", 190 lbs. Deb: 4/29/50

YEAR TM/L	W	L	PCT	G	GS	CG	SH	SV	IP	H	HR	BB	SO	RAT	ERA	ERA+	OAV	OOB	BH	AVG	PB	PR	/A	PD	TPI
1950 Cle-A	0	0	—	12	0	0	0	0	25¹	28	3	19	14	16.7	4.97	87	.283	.398	0	.000	-1	-1	-2	-1	-0.2
1951 Cle-A	0	0	—	7	1	0	0	0	15¹	18	1	11	5	17.6	2.93	129	.286	.400	1	.333	-0	2	1	0	0.1
1952 Cle-A	1	0	1.000	10	1	0	0	0	12²	11	0	13	5	17.1	4.97	67	.224	.387	0	.000	-0	-2	-2	0	-0.2
1953 Phi-A	0	0	—	2	0	0	0	0	10²	8	3	9	2	14.3	5.06	85	.222	.378	0	.000	-0	-1	-1	-0	0.0
1954 Phi-A	0	0	—	2	0	0	0	0	1¹	0	0	3	0	27.0	6.75	58	.000	.571	0	—	0	-0	-0	0	0.0
Total 5	1	0	1.000	33	4	0	0	0	65¹	65	7	55	26	16.8	4.55	88	.260	.397	1	.083	-1	-3	-4	-1	-0.3

■ DAVE ROZEMA
Rozema, David Scott b: 8/5/56, Grand Rapids, Mich. BR/TR, 6'4", 185 lbs. Deb: 4/11/77

YEAR TM/L	W	L	PCT	G	GS	CG	SH	SV	IP	H	HR	BB	SO	RAT	ERA	ERA+	OAV	OOB	BH	AVG	PB	PR	/A	PD	TPI
1977 Det-A	15	7	.682	28	28	16	1	0	218¹	222	25	34	92	10.8	3.09	139	.265	.299	0	—	0	23	29	1	3.1
1978 Det-A	9	12	.429	28	28	11	2	0	209¹	205	17	41	57	10.7	3.14	123	.260	.298	0	—	0	15	17	-1	1.7
1979 Det-A	4	4	.500	16	16	4	1	0	97¹	101	12	30	33	12.7	3.51	123	.270	.334	0	—	0	8	9	1	1.0
1980 Det-A	6	9	.400	42	13	2	1	4	144²	152	11	49	49	12.8	3.92	105	.277	.342	0	—	0	2	3	1	0.4
1981 Det-A	5	5	.500	28	9	2	2	3	104	99	12	25	46	11.0	3.63	104	.256	.306	0	—	0	0	2	-0	0.1
1982 Det-A	3	0	1.000	8	2	0	0	1	27²	17	2	7	15	8.1	1.63	250	.179	.243	0	—	0	8	7	1	0.9
1983 Det-A	8	3	.727	29	16	1	0	0	105	100	10	29	63	11.1	3.43	114	.248	.300	0	—	0	7	6	1	0.7
1984 Det-A	7	6	.538	29	16	0	0	0	101	110	13	18	48	11.6	3.74	105	.274	.309	0	—	0	3	2	1	0.3
1985 Tex-A	3	7	.300	34	4	0	0	7	88	100	10	22	42	12.7	4.19	101	.287	.333	0	—	0	-0	0	1	0.1
1986 Tex-A	0	0	—	6	0	0	0	0	10²	19	1	3	3	18.6	5.91	73	.404	.440	0	—	0	-2	-2	-0	-0.1
Total 10	60	53	.531	248	132	36	7	17	1106	1125	113	258	448	11.5	3.47	117	.266	.313	0	—	0	63	73	5	8.2

■ JORGE RUBIO
Rubio, Jorge Jesus (Chavez) b: 4/23/45, Mexicali, Mexico BR/TR, 6'3", 200 lbs. Deb: 4/21/66

YEAR TM/L	W	L	PCT	G	GS	CG	SH	SV	IP	H	HR	BB	SO	RAT	ERA	ERA+	OAV	OOB	BH	AVG	PB	PR	/A	PD	TPI
1966 Cal-A	2	1	.667	7	4	1	1	0	27¹	22	2	16	27	12.8	2.96	113	.220	.333	0	.000	-1	1	1	-1	0.0
1967 Cal-A	0	2	.000	3	3	0	0	0	15	18	2	9	4	18.6	3.60	87	.316	.443	1	.333	1	-1	-1	0	0.0
Total 2	2	3	.400	10	7	1	1	0	42¹	40	4	25	31	14.9	3.19	103	.255	.374	1	.091	-0	1	0	-0	0.0

■ DAVE RUCKER
Rucker, David Michael b: 9/1/57, San Bernardino, Cal BL/TL, 6'1", 185 lbs. Deb: 4/12/81

YEAR TM/L	W	L	PCT	G	GS	CG	SH	SV	IP	H	HR	BB	SO	RAT	ERA	ERA+	OAV	OOB	BH	AVG	PB	PR	/A	PD	TPI
1981 Det-A	0	0	—	2	0	0	0	0	3²	3	0	1	2	12.3	7.36	51	.188	.278	0	—	0	-2	-1	0	-0.1
1982 Det-A	5	6	.455	27	4	1	0	0	64	62	4	23	31	12.2	3.38	120	.251	.320	0	—	0	5	5	0	0.5
1983 Det-A	1	2	.333	4	3	0	0	0	9	18	2	8	6	27.0	17.00	23	.419	.519	0	—	0	-13	-13	0	-1.0
StL-N	5	3	.625	34	0	0	0	0	37	36	1	18	22	13.4	2.68	135	.263	.353	0	.000	-0	4	4	0	0.4
1984 StL-N	2	3	.400	50	0	0	0	0	73	62	0	34	38	12.0	2.10	166	.237	.327	1	.143	-0	12	11	-1	1.1
1985 Phi-N	3	2	.600	39	3	0	0	1	79¹	83	6	40	41	14.2	4.31	85	.279	.368	4	.333	2	-6	-6	1	-0.3
1986 Phi-N	0	2	.000	19	0	0	0	0	25	34	4	14	14	17.3	5.76	67	.340	.421	0	.000	-0	-6	-5	0	-0.4
1988 Pit-N	0	2	.000	31	0	0	0	0	28¹	39	2	9	16	15.2	4.76	71	.328	.375	0	.000	-0	-4	-4	0	-0.4
Total 7	16	20	.444	206	10	1	0	1	319¹	337	19	147	170	13.9	3.97	93	.276	.357	5	.192	1	-10	-10	1	-0.2

■ NAP RUCKER
Rucker, George Napoleon b: 9/30/1884, Crabapple, Ga. d: 12/19/70, Alpharetta, Ga. BR/TL, 5'11", 190 lbs. Deb: 4/15/07

YEAR TM/L	W	L	PCT	G	GS	CG	SH	SV	IP	H	HR	BB	SO	RAT	ERA	ERA+	OAV	OOB	BH	AVG	PB	PR	/A	PD	TPI
1907 Bro-N	15	13	.536	37	30	26	4	0	275¹	242	3	80	131	10.8	2.06	114	.242	.303	15	.155	-1	13	9	-2	0.6
1908 Bro-N	17	19	.472	42	35	30	6	1	333¹	265	1	125	199	11.0	2.08	113	.231	.317	21	.179	-1	11	10	3	1.3
1909 Bro-N	13	19	.406	38	33	28	6	1	309¹	245	6	101	201	10.5	2.24	116	.228	.303	12	.119	-5	12	12	-4	0.4
1910 Bro-N	17	18	.486	41	39	**27**	**6**	0	320¹	293	5	84	147	10.8	2.58	117	.251	.306	23	.209	-1	16	16	-2	1.3
1911 Bro-N	22	18	.550	48	33	23	5	4	315²	255	12	110	190	10.6	2.71	123	.226	.300	21	.202	2	24	22	0	2.4
1912 Bro-N	18	21	.462	45	34	23	**6**	4	297²	272	6	72	151	10.5	2.21	152	.242	.289	25	.245	2	40	38	2	4.3
1913 Bro-N	14	15	.483	41	33	16	4	3	260	236	3	67	111	10.7	2.87	115	.249	.304	21	.241	2	10	12	-4	1.1
1914 Bro-N	7	6	.538	16	16	5	0	0	103²	113	2	27	35	12.3	3.39	84	.275	.323	9	.265	2	-7	-6	1	-0.3
1915 Bro-N	9	4	.692	19	15	7	1	1	122²	134	3	38	120	12.0	2.42	115	.279	.322	9	.214	1	4	5	2	0.9
1916 *Bro-N	2	1	.667	9	4	1	0	0	37	34	0	14	10	14.1	1.69	159	.241	.282	1	.091	-1	4	4	0	0.4
Total 10	134	134	.500	336	272	186	38	14	2375¹	2089	41	701	1217	10.8	2.42	119	.242	.305	157	.195	1	127	121	-5	12.4

■ ERNIE RUDOLPH
Rudolph, Ernest William b: 2/13/10, Black River Falls Wis. BL/TR, 5'8", 165 lbs. Deb: 6/16/45

YEAR TM/L	W	L	PCT	G	GS	CG	SH	SV	IP	H	HR	BB	SO	RAT	ERA	ERA+	OAV	OOB	BH	AVG	PB	PR	/A	PD	TPI
1945 Bro-N	1	0	1.000	7	0	0	0	0	8²	12	1	7	3	19.7	5.19	72	.333	.442	0	—	1	-1	-1	0	0.0

■ DON RUDOLPH
Rudolph, Frederick Donald b: 8/16/31, Baltimore, Md. d: 9/12/68, Granada Hills, Cal BL/TL, 5'11", 195 lbs. Deb: 9/21/57

YEAR TM/L	W	L	PCT	G	GS	CG	SH	SV	IP	H	HR	BB	SO	RAT	ERA	ERA+	OAV	OOB	BH	AVG	PB	PR	/A	PD	TPI
1957 Chi-A	1	0	1.000	5	0	0	0	0	12	6	2	2	2	6.0	2.25	166	.146	.186	1	.500	1	2	2	-0	0.2
1958 Chi-A	1	0	1.000	7	0	0	0	1	7	4	0	5	2	11.6	2.57	141	.190	.346	0	—	0	1	1	0	0.1
1959 Chi-A	0	0	—	4	0	0	0	1	3	4	0	2	0	18.0	0.00	—	.333	.429	0	—	0	1	1	0	0.2
Cin-N	0	0	—	5	0	0	0	0	7¹	13	1	3	8	19.6	4.91	83	.394	.444	0	.000	-0	-1	-1	0	0.0
1962 Cle-A	0	0	—	1	0	0	0	0	0¹	1	0	0	0	27.0	0.00	—	1.000	1.000	0	—	0	0	0	0	0.0
Was-A	8	10	.444	37	23	6	2	0	176¹	187	13	42	68	11.8	3.62	111	.274	.319	10	.175	1	7	8	-0	1.0
Yr	8	10	.444	38	23	6	2	0	176²	188	13	42	68	11.9	3.62	112	.275	.320	4	.070	1	7	8	-0	1.0
1963 Was-A	7	19	.269	37	26	4	0	1	174	189	28	36	70	11.9	4.55	82	.275	.317	8	.178	2	-18	-16	-0	-1.4
1964 Was-A	1	3	.250	28	4	0	0	0	70¹	81	10	12	32	11.9	4.09	90	.290	.320	1	.067	-1	-4	-3	-0	-0.3
Total 6	18	32	.360	124	57	10	2	3	450¹	485	54	102	182	11.9	4.00	96	.276	.319	20	.167	3	-11	-8	0	-0.2

■ DICK RUDOLPH
Rudolph, Richard "Baldy" b: 8/25/1887, New York, N.Y. d: 10/20/49, Bronx, N.Y. BR/TR, 5'9.5", 160 lbs. Deb: 9/30/10 C

YEAR TM/L	W	L	PCT	G	GS	CG	SH	SV	IP	H	HR	BB	SO	RAT	ERA	ERA+	OAV	OOB	BH	AVG	PB	PR	/A	PD	TPI
1910 NY-N	0	1	.000	3	1	1	0	2	12	21	0	2	9	17.3	7.50	40	.350	.371	1	.250	0	-6	-6	-0	-0.5
1911 NY-N	0	0	—	1	0	0	0	0	2	2	0	0	0	9.0	9.00	37	.250	.250	1	1.000	0	-1	-1	0	0.0
1913 Bos-N	14	13	.519	33	22	17	2	0	249¹	258	4	59	109	11.5	2.92	112	.276	.320	21	.239	4	8	10	5	2.0
1914 *Bos-N	27	10	.730	42	36	31	6	0	336¹	288	9	61	138	**9.4**	2.35	117	.238	.276	15	.125	-1	16	15	2	1.7
1915 Bos-N	22	19	.537	44	43	30	3	1	341¹	304	4	64	147	9.9	2.37	109	.242	.282	23	.198	6	14	8	1	1.6
1916 Bos-N	19	12	.613	41	38	27	5	3	312	266	7	38	133	**8.9**	2.16	115	.235	**.261**	16	.158	1	16	11	6	2.0
1917 Bos-N	13	13	.500	31	30	21	1	0	242²	252	1	54	96	11.5	3.41	75	.272	.314	20	.230	3	-19	-23	1	-2.1
1918 Bos-N	9	10	.474	21	20	15	3	0	154	144	2	30	48	10.2	2.57	104	.255	.292	10	.185	-1	3	2	1	0.2
1919 Bos-N	13	18	.419	37	32	24	2	2	273²	282	2	54	76	11.1	2.17	132	.276	.314	17	.193	3	23	21	0	2.8
1920 Bos-N	4	8	.333	18	12	3	0	0	89	104	4	24	24	13.3	4.04	75	.294	.346	5	.185	-0	-9	-10	0	-0.9
1922 Bos-N	0	2	.000	3	3	1	0	0	16	22	1	5	3	15.2	5.06	79	.328	.375	2	.400	0	-2	-2	0	0.0
1923 Bos-N	1	2	.333	4	4	1	1	0	19¹	27	0	10	3	17.7	3.72	107	.333	.413	0	.000	-1	1	1	0	0.0
1927 Bos-N	0	0	—	1	0	0	0	0	1¹	1	0	1	0	13.5	0.00	—	.200	.333	0	—	0	1	1	0	0.1
Total 13	122	108	.530	279	241	172	27	8	2049	1971	35	402	786	10.5	2.66	104	.258	.298	131	.188	13	44	25	16	6.9

■ DUTCH RUETHER
Ruether, Walter Henry b: 9/13/1893, Alameda, Cal. d: 5/16/70, Phoenix, Ariz. BL/TL, 6'1.5", 180 lbs. Deb: 4/13/17 ♦

YEAR TM/L	W	L	PCT	G	GS	CG	SH	SV	IP	H	HR	BB	SO	RAT	ERA	ERA+	OAV	OOB	BH	AVG	PB	PR	/A	PD	TPI
1917 Chi-N	2	0	1.000	10	4	1	0	0	36¹	37	0	12	23	12.9	2.48	117	.285	.359	12	.273	2	1	2	0	0.2
Cin-N	1	2	.333	7	4	1	0	0	35²	43	0	14	12	14.9	3.53	74	.323	.396	5	.208	1	-3	-4	-0	-0.3
Yr	3	2	.600	17	8	2	1	0	72	80	0	26	35	13.5	3.00	92	.301	.367	11	.162	3	-2	-2	-0	-0.1
1918 Cin-N	0	1	.000	2	2	1	0	0	10	10	0	4	3	12.6	2.70	99	.244	.311	0	.000	-0	0	-0	-0	0.0
1919 *Cin-N	19	6	**.760**	33	29	20	3	0	242²	195	1	83	78	10.6	1.82	153	.223	.295	24	.261	5	30	26	-3	3.3

YEAR	TM/L	W	L	PCT	G	GS	CG	SH	SV	IP	H	HR	BB	SO	RAT	ERA	ERA+	OAV	OOB	BH	AVG	PB	PR	/A	PD	TPI
1920	Cin-N	16	12	.571	37	33	23	5	3	265^2	235	2	96	99	11.5	2.47	123	.247	.321	20	.192	-1	20	17	0	1.7
1921	Bro-N	10	13	.435	36	27	12	1	2	211^1	247	7	67	78	13.7	4.26	91	.299	.356	34	.351	12	-11	-9	-1	0.3
1922	Bro-N	21	12	.636	35	35	26	2	0	267^1	290	11	92	89	13.1	3.53	115	.282	.345	26	.208	6	17	16	-0	2.0
1923	Bro-N	15	14	.517	34	34	20	0	0	275	308	11	86	87	13.1	4.22	92	.287	.343	32	.274	4	-7	-10	-2	-0.6
1924	Bro-N	8	13	.381	30	21	13	2	3	168	190	4	45	63	12.9	3.91	96	.282	.332	15	.242	2	-1	-3	2	0.0
1925	*Was-A	18	7	.720	30	29	16	1	0	223^1	241	5	105	68	14.3	3.87	109	.281	.365	36	.333	6	13	9	-2	1.6
1926	Was-A	12	6	.667	23	23	9	0	0	169^1	214	5	66	48	15.1	4.84	80	.311	.375	23	.250	4	-15	-18	-2	-1.6
	*NY-A	2	3	.400	5	5	1	0	0	36	32	0	18	8	12.8	3.50	110	.248	.345	2	.095	-2	2	1	0	0.1
	Yr	14	9	.609	28	28	10	0	0	205^1	246	5	84	56	14.5	4.60	84	.300	.366	7	.062	3	-13	-17	-2	-1.5
1927	NY-A	13	6	.684	27	26	12	3	0	184	202	9	52	45	12.8	3.38	114	.287	.343	21	.262	5	16	10	1	1.4
Total	11	137	95	.591	309	272	155	18	8	2124^2	2244	55	739	708	12.9	3.50	104	.277	.342	250	.258	45	60	36	-7	8.1

■ BRUCE RUFFIN

Ruffin, Bruce Wayne   b: 10/4/63, Lubbock, Tex   BB/TL, 6'2", 205 lbs.   Deb: 6/28/86

YEAR	TM/L	W	L	PCT	G	GS	CG	SH	SV	IP	H	HR	BB	SO	RAT	ERA	ERA+	OAV	OOB	BH	AVG	PB	PR	/A	PD	TPI
1986	Phi-N	9	4	.692	21	21	6	0	0	146^1	138	6	44	70	11.3	2.46	157	.251	.308	4	.073	-3	20	23	-1	2.0
1987	Phi-N	11	14	.440	35	35	3	1	0	204^2	236	17	73	93	13.7	4.35	97	.298	.359	4	.055	-5	-6	-3	-0	-0.6
1988	Phi-N	6	10	.375	55	15	3	0	3	144^1	151	7	80	82	14.6	4.43	80	.275	.370	4	.121	-0	-16	-14	-1	-1.3
1989	Phi-N	6	10	.375	24	23	1	0	0	125^2	152	10	62	70	15.3	4.44	80	.301	.377	6	.176	2	-13	-13	2	-0.8
1990	Phi-N	6	13	.316	32	25	2	1	0	149	178	14	62	79	14.6	5.38	71	.297	.364	3	.068	-2	-26	-26	0	-2.6
Total	5	38	51	.427	167	119	15	2	3	770	855	54	321	394	13.8	4.22	91	.286	.356	21	.088	-8	-41	-32	3	-3.3

■ RED RUFFING

Ruffing, Charles Herbert   b: 5/3/04, Granville, Ill.   d: 2/17/86, Mayfield Hts., O.   BR/TR, 6'1.5", 205 lbs.   Deb: 5/31/24   CH♦

YEAR	TM/L	W	L	PCT	G	GS	CG	SH	SV	IP	H	HR	BB	SO	RAT	ERA	ERA+	OAV	OOB	BH	AVG	PB	PR	/A	PD	TPI
1924	Bos-A	0	0	—	8	2	0	0	0	23	29	0	9	10	16.0	6.65	66	.333	.414	1	.143	0	-6	-6	-1	-0.5
1925	Bos-A	9	18	.333	37	27	13	3	1	217^1	253	10	75	64	13.7	5.01	91	.299	.357	17	.215	-0	-15	-11	-1	-1.0
1926	Bos-A	6	15	.286	37	22	6	0	2	166	169	4	68	58	13.1	4.39	93	.274	.351	10	.196	0	-7	-6	-1	-0.6
1927	Bos-A	5	13	.278	26	18	10	0	2	158^1	160	7	87	77	14.3	4.66	91	.277	.375	14	.255	1	-9	-8	-0	-0.5
1928	Bos-A	10	25	.286	42	34	**25**	1	2	289^1	303	8	96	118	12.7	3.89	106	.275	.339	38	.314	12	5	7	-3	1.5
1929	Bos-A	9	22	.290	35	30	18	1	1	244^1	280	17	118	109	14.7	4.86	88	.297	.376	35	.307	5	-17	-16	-2	-0.7
1930	Bos-A	0	3	.000	4	3	1	0	0	24	32	1	6	14	14.6	6.38	72	.323	.368	3	.273	1	-5	-5	-1	-0.3
	NY-A	15	5	.750	34	25	12	2	1	197^2	200	10	62	117	12.0	4.14	104	.260	.317	37	.374	16	11	3	-3	1.4
	Yr	15	8	.652	38	28	13	2	1	221^2	232	11	68	131	12.3	4.38	99	.267	.322	7	.064	17	7	-1	-4	1.1
1931	NY-A	16	14	.533	37	30	19	1	2	237	240	11	87	132	12.6	4.41	90	.256	.323	36	.330	10	-1	-12	-3	-0.2
1932	*NY-A	18	7	.720	35	29	22	3	2	259	219	16	115	**190**	11.7	3.09	132	**.226**	.311	38	.306	13	40	28	-3	3.6
1933	NY-A	9	14	.391	35	28	18	0	3	235	230	7	93	122	12.5	3.91	99	.258	.330	29	.252	8	10	-1	0	0.5
1934	NY-A	19	11	.633	36	31	19	5	0	256^1	232	18	104	149	11.8	3.93	103	.236	.310	28	.248	6	16	4	-3	0.5
1935	NY-A	16	11	.593	30	29	19	2	0	222	201	17	76	81	11.3	3.12	130	.239	.303	37	.339	13	33	23	-2	3.2
1936	*NY-A	20	12	.625	33	33	25	3	0	271	274	22	90	102	12.2	3.85	121	.263	.323	37	.291	15	36	24	2	3.7
1937	*NY-A	20	7	.741	31	31	22	4	0	256^1	242	17	68	131	10.9	2.98	149	.247	.296	26	.202	3	47	42	-4	3.9
1938	*NY-A	**21**	7	**.750**	31	31	22	3	0	247^1	246	16	82	127	11.9	3.31	137	.258	.317	**41**	.344	10	41	34	-2	3.9
1939	*NY-A	21	7	.750	28	28	22	**5**	0	233^1	211	15	75	95	11.1	2.93	149	.240	.301	35	.307	3	44	37	-1	4.3
1940	NY-A	15	12	.556	30	30	20	3	0	226	218	24	76	97	11.8	3.38	119	.252	.314	11	.124	-2	25	16	-3	1.0
1941	*NY-A	15	6	.714	23	23	13	2	0	185^2	177	13	54	60	11.2	3.54	111	.252	.306	27	.303	11	13	8	-3	1.6
1942	*NY-A	14	7	.667	24	24	16	4	0	193^2	183	10	41	80	10.5	3.21	107	.250	.292	20	.250	6	10	5	-2	1.0
1945	NY-A	7	3	.700	11	11	8	1	0	87^1	85	2	20	24	10.9	2.89	120	.251	.294	10	.217	1	5	6	-1	0.5
1946	NY-A	5	1	.833	8	8	4	2	0	61	37	2	23	19	8.9	1.77	195	.171	.251	3	.120	-1	12	11	-1	1.1
1947	Chi-A	3	5	.375	9	9	1	0	0	53	60	7	16	11	13.4	6.11	60	.290	.339	5	.208	-0	-14	-14	-0	-1.3
Total	22	273	225	.548	624	536	335	45	16	4344	4284	254	1541	1987	12.2	3.80	109	.258	.323	521	.269	135	272	174	-36	26.6

■ VERN RUHLE

Ruhle, Vernon Gerald   b: 1/25/51, Coleman, Mich.   BR/TR, 6'1", 185 lbs.   Deb: 9/09/74

YEAR	TM/L	W	L	PCT	G	GS	CG	SH	SV	IP	H	HR	BB	SO	RAT	ERA	ERA+	OAV	OOB	BH	AVG	PB	PR	/A	PD	TPI
1974	Det-A	2	0	1.000	5	3	1	0	0	33	35	1	6	10	11.5	2.73	139	.273	.311	0	—	0	3	4	-0	0.4
1975	Det-A	11	12	.478	32	31	8	3	0	190	199	17	65	67	12.8	4.03	100	.266	.330	0	—	0	-5	-0	-2	-0.1
1976	Det-A	9	12	.429	32	32	5	1	0	199^2	227	19	59	88	13.1	3.92	95	.288	.340	0	—	0	-9	-5	0	-0.4
1977	Det-A	3	5	.375	14	10	0	0	0	66^1	83	9	15	27	13.7	5.70	75	.305	.348	0	—	0	-12	-10	-1	-0.9
1978	Hou-N	3	3	.500	13	10	2	2	0	68	57	0	20	27	10.3	2.12	156	.224	.283	1	.056	-1	11	9	-1	0.8
1979	Hou-N	2	6	.250	13	10	2	2	0	66^1	64	9	8	33	10.0	4.07	86	.249	.277	1	.053	-1	-2	-4	-1	-0.5
1980	*Hou-N	12	4	.750	28	22	6	2	0	159^1	148	7	29	55	10.2	2.37	139	.251	.289	12	.245	4	22	16	-1	2.1
1981	*Hou-N	4	6	.400	20	15	1	0	1	102	97	6	20	39	10.4	2.91	113	.250	.289	6	.250	3	7	4	0	0.7
1982	Hou-N	9	13	.409	31	21	3	2	1	149	169	12	24	56	11.9	3.93	84	.289	.321	4	.098	-0	-5	-10	0	-1.1
1983	Hou-N	8	5	.615	41	9	0	0	3	114^2	107	13	36	43	11.5	3.69	92	.249	.312	2	.105	0	-1	-4	1	-0.2
1984	Hou-N	1	9	.100	40	6	0	0	2	90^1	112	5	29	60	14.3	4.58	72	.309	.365	1	.083	-1	-10	-13	1	-1.1
1985	Cle-A	2	10	.167	42	16	1	0	3	125	139	16	30	54	12.3	4.32	96	.283	.326	0	—	0	-2	-3	-0	-0.5
1986	*Cal-A	1	3	.250	16	3	0	0	1	47^2	46	5	7	23	10.2	4.15	96	.247	.278	0	—	0	0	-0	1	0.0
Total	13	67	88	.432	327	188	29	12	11	1411^1	1483	119	348	582	11.9	3.73	97	.270	.318	27	.148	5	-3	-16	-3	-0.5

■ ANDY RUSH

Rush, Jesse Howard   b: 12/26/1889, Longton, Kan.   d: 3/16/69, Fresno, Cal.   BR/TR, 6'3", 180 lbs.   Deb: 4/16/25

YEAR	TM/L	W	L	PCT	G	GS	CG	SH	SV	IP	H	HR	BB	SO	RAT	ERA	ERA+	OAV	OOB	BH	AVG	PB	PR	/A	PD	TPI
1925	Bro-N	0	1	.000	4	2	0	0	0	9^2	16	3	5	4	19.6	9.31	45	.364	.429	0	.000	-0	-5	-6	0	-0.4

■ BOB RUSH

Rush, Robert Ransom   b: 12/21/25, Battle Creek, Mich   BR/TR, 6'4", 205 lbs.   Deb: 4/22/48

YEAR	TM/L	W	L	PCT	G	GS	CG	SH	SV	IP	H	HR	BB	SO	RAT	ERA	ERA+	OAV	OOB	BH	AVG	PB	PR	/A	PD	TPI
1948	Chi-N	5	11	.313	36	16	4	0	0	133^1	153	8	37	72	12.9	3.92	100	.287	.335	5	.128	-2	1	-0	1	0.0
1949	Chi-N	10	18	.357	35	27	9	1	4	201	197	10	79	80	12.4	4.07	99	.255	.324	2	.032	-7	-1	-1	1	-0.6
1950	Chi-N	13	20	.394	39	34	19	1	1	254^2	261	11	93	93	12.7	3.71	113	.265	.332	15	.167	-1	12	14	2	1.6
1951	Chi-N	11	12	.478	37	29	12	2	2	211^1	212	16	68	129	12.1	3.83	107	.254	.312	13	.191	-0	3	6	0	0.7
1952	Chi-N	17	13	.567	34	32	17	4	0	250^1	205	14	81	157	10.5	2.70	143	.216	.282	28	.292	7	29	32	2	**4.6**
1953	Chi-N	9	14	.391	29	28	8	1	0	166^2	177	17	66	84	13.4	4.54	98	.270	.341	6	.111	-2	-5	-2	1	-0.2
1954	Chi-N	13	15	.464	33	32	11	0	0	236^1	213	12	103	124	12.2	3.77	111	.243	.326	23	.277	7	8	11	3	2.2
1955	Chi-N	13	11	.542	33	33	14	3	0	234	204	19	73	130	10.7	3.50	117	.234	.295	9	.110	-3	14	15	1	1.3
1956	Chi-N	13	10	.565	32	32	13	1	0	239^2	210	30	59	104	10.2	3.19	118	.233	.282	9	.098	-3	15	15	-1	1.1
1957	Chi-N	6	16	.273	31	29	5	0	0	205^1	211	16	66	103	12.2	4.38	88	.265	.323	14	.203	2	-12	-12	-1	-1.1
1958	*Mil-N	10	6	.625	28	20	5	2	0	147^1	142	13	31	84	10.6	3.42	103	.253	.289	9	.200	1	9	2	-0	0.1
1959	Mil-N	5	6	.455	31	9	1	1	0	101^1	102	5	23	64	11.2	2.40	148	.257	.299	6	.188	0	17	13	-1	1.2
1960	Mil-N	2	0	1.000	10	0	0	0	1	15	24	2	5	8	17.4	4.20	82	.369	.414	1	.333	1	-1	-1	0	0.0
	Chi-A	0	0	—	9	0	0	0	0	6	12	1	9	6	13.2	5.65	67	.302	.362	1	1.000	0	-3	-3	0	0.1
Total	13	127	152	.455	417	321	118	16	8	2410^2	2327	177	789	1244	11.8	3.65	109	.251	.313	140	.173	0	88	90	6	10.8

■ AMOS RUSIE

Rusie, Amos Wilson "The Hoosier Thunderbolt"   b: 5/30/1871, Mooresville, Ind.   d: 12/6/42, Seattle, Wash.   BR/TR, 6'1", 200 lbs.   Deb: 5/09/1889   H

YEAR	TM/L	W	L	PCT	G	GS	CG	SH	SV	IP	H	HR	BB	SO	RAT	ERA	ERA+	OAV	OOB	BH	AVG	PB	PR	/A	PD	TPI
1889	Ind-N	12	10	.545	33	22	19	1	0	225	246	12	116	109	14.5	5.32	79	.269	.352	18	.175	-4	-32	-29	-3	-2.7
1890	NY-N	29	34	.460	67	63	56	4	1	548^2	436	3	289	**341**	11.9	2.56	137	**.212**	.309	79	.278	11	61	57	5	6.8
1891	NY-N	33	20	.623	61	57	52	**6**	1	500^1	391	7	262	**337**	11.7	2.55	125	**.207**	.304	54	.245	4	44	36	1	3.6
1892	NY-N	31	31	.500	64	61	58	2	0	532	405	7	267	288	11.4	2.88	112	.202	.296	53	.210	-0	24	20	5	2.3
1893	NY-N	33	21	.611	**56**	52	**50**	4	1	482	451	15	218	208	12.5	3.23	144	**.240**	.319	57	.269	3	77	77	2	**7.1**
1894	*NY-N	**36**	13	.735	54	50	45	3	1	444	426	10	200	195	12.7	**2.78**	**189**	.250	.329	52	.280	2	126	122	7	**10.9**
1895	NY-N	23	23	.500	49	47	42	4	0	393^1	384	9	159	**201**	12.7	3.73	124	.252	.333	44	.246	-5	46	40	2	3.3
1897	NY-N	28	10	.737	38	37	35	2	0	322^1	314	6	87	135	11.2	2.54	164	.253	.302	40	.278	2	64	58	2	5.7
1898	NY-N	20	11	.645	37	36	33	4	1	300	288	6	103	114	11.7	3.03	115	.251	.312	29	.210	-1	19	15	0	1.3
1901	Cin-N	0	1	.000	3	2	2	0	0	22	43	1	3	6	18.8	8.59	37	.405	.422	1	.125	-1	-13	-13	0	-1.0

YEAR TM/L	W	L	PCT	G	GS	CG	SH	SV	IP	H	HR	BB	SO	RAT	ERA	ERA+	OAV	OOB	BH	AVG	PB	PR	/A	PD	TPI
Total 10	245	174	.585	462	427	392	30	5	3769²	3384	76	1704	1934	12.1	3.07	130	.234	.315	427	.247	13	416	381	21	37.0

■ SCOTT RUSKIN
Ruskin, Scott Drew   b: 6/8/63, Jacksonville, Fla.   BB/TL, 6'2", 185 lbs.   Deb: 4/09/90

YEAR TM/L	W	L	PCT	G	GS	CG	SH	SV	IP	H	HR	BB	SO	RAT	ERA	ERA+	OAV	OOB	BH	AVG	PB	PR	/A	PD	TPI
1990 Pit-N	2	2	.500	44	0	0	0	2	47²	50	2	28	34	15.1	3.02	120	.269	.370	2	.333	1	4	3	0	0.5
Mon-N	1	0	1.000	23	0	0	0	0	27²	25	2	10	23	11.4	2.28	165	.243	.310	0	.000	-0	5	5	0	0.5
Yr	3	2	.600	67	0	0	0	2	75¹	75	4	38	57	13.5	2.75	133	.256	.341	0	.000	1	9	8	0	1.0

■ ALLAN RUSSELL
Russell, Allan E. "Rubberarm"   b: 7/31/1893, Baltimore, Md.   d: 10/20/72, Baltimore, Md.   BB/TR, 5'11", 165 lbs.   Deb: 9/13/15

YEAR TM/L	W	L	PCT	G	GS	CG	SH	SV	IP	H	HR	BB	SO	RAT	ERA	ERA+	OAV	OOB	BH	AVG	PB	PR	/A	PD	TPI
1915 NY-A	1	2	.333	5	3	1	0	0	27	21	1	21	21	14.3	2.67	110	.228	.377	2	.250	0	1	1	-0	0.0
1916 NY-A	6	10	.375	34	18	8	1	6	171¹	138	8	75	104	11.6	3.20	90	.232	.324	2	.044	-3	-7	-6	-0	-0.9
1917 NY-A	7	8	.467	25	10	6	0	2	104¹	89	3	39	55	11.6	2.24	120	.236	.319	10	.323	4	5	5	-1	0.8
1918 NY-A	7	11	.389	27	18	7	2	4	141	139	6	73	54	13.9	3.26	87	.267	.363	7	.167	-1	-7	-7	-1	-0.9
1919 NY-A	5	5	.500	23	9	4	1	1	90²	89	6	32	50	12.2	3.47	92	.251	.317	7	.233	0	-2	-3	0	-0.2
Bos-A	10	4	.714	21	11	9	1	4	121¹	105	0	39	63	10.8	2.52	120	.246	.310	5	.122	-1	10	7	-1	0.4
Yr	15	9	.625	44	20	13	2	5	212	194	6	71	113	11.3	2.93	106	.248	.311	4	.056	-1	7	4	-1	0.2
1920 Bos-A	5	6	.455	16	10	7	0	1	107²	100	3	38	53	11.8	3.01	121	.251	.321	5	.122	-2	9	8	1	0.6
1921 Bos-A	7	11	.389	39	13	7	0	3	173	204	10	77	60	15.1	4.11	103	.303	.382	7	.123	-5	3	2	0	-0.2
1922 Bos-A	6	7	.462	34	11	1	0	2	125²	152	6	57	34	15.3	5.01	82	.314	.392	3	.079	-3	-14	-13	2	-1.2
1923 Was-A	10	7	.588	52	5	4	0	9	181¹	177	9	77	67	12.7	3.03	124	.270	.348	10	.200	2	19	15	-3	1.2
1924 *Was-A	5	1	.833	37	0	0	0	8	82¹	83	1	45	17	14.1	4.37	92	.282	.379	5	.278	2	-1	-3	-0	-0.1
1925 Was-A	2	4	.333	32	2	0	0	2	68²	85	6	37	25	16.1	5.77	73	.315	.399	2	.143	-1	-10	-12	2	-0.9
Total 11	71	76	.483	345	110	54	5	42	1394¹	1382	59	610	603	13.1	3.52	99	.269	.351	65	.157	-10	5	-4	-2	-1.4

■ LEFTY RUSSELL
Russell, Clarence Dickson   b: 7/8/1890, Baltimore, Md.   d: 1/22/62, Baltimore, Md.   BL/TL, 6'1", 165 lbs.   Deb: 10/01/10

YEAR TM/L	W	L	PCT	G	GS	CG	SH	SV	IP	H	HR	BB	SO	RAT	ERA	ERA+	OAV	OOB	BH	AVG	PB	PR	/A	PD	TPI
1910 Phi-A	1	0	1.000	1	1	1	1	0	9	8	0	2	5	10.0	0.00	—	.258	.303	0	.000	-0	3	2	0	0.3
1911 Phi-A	0	3	.000	7	2	0	0	0	31²	45	1	18	7	19.3	7.67	41	.357	.456	5	.385	1	-15	-16	1	-1.1
1912 Phi-A	0	2	.000	5	2	1	0	0	17¹	18	1	14	9	18.2	7.27	42	.265	.412	0	.000	-0	-8	-8	0	-0.7
Total 3	1	5	.167	13	5	2	1	0	58	71	2	34	21	17.5	6.36	47	.316	.423	5	.250	1	-20	-22	1	-1.5

■ REB RUSSELL
Russell, Ewell Albert   b: 4/12/1889, Jackson, Miss.   d: 9/30/73, Indianapolis, Ind   BL/TL, 5'11", 185 lbs.   Deb: 4/18/13   ♦

YEAR TM/L	W	L	PCT	G	GS	CG	SH	SV	IP	H	HR	BB	SO	RAT	ERA	ERA+	OAV	OOB	BH	AVG	PB	PR	/A	PD	TPI
1913 Chi-A	22	16	.579	52	36	26	8	4	316²	250	2	79	122	9.5	1.90	154	.219	.273	20	.189	3	36	36	-5	3.7
1914 Chi-A	8	12	.400	38	23	8	1	1	167¹	168	3	33	79	11.0	2.90	92	.268	.308	17	.266	4	-3	-4	0	0.0
1915 Chi-A	11	10	.524	41	25	10	3	2	229¹	215	0	47	90	10.5	2.59	115	.249	.292	21	.244	4	9	10	-2	1.3
1916 Chi-A	18	11	.621	56	25	16	5	3	264¹	207	1	42	112	8.5	2.42	114	.220	.254	13	.143	-3	12	10	-1	0.5
1917 *Chi-A	15	5	.750	35	24	11	5	3	189¹	170	1	32	54	9.6	1.95	137	.245	.279	19	.279	5	15	15	-0	2.3
1918 Chi-A	7	5	.583	19	15	10	2	0	124²	117	0	33	38	10.8	2.60	105	.252	.302	7	.140	-1	2	2	-1	-0.1
1919 Chi-A	0	0	—	1	0	0	0	0	1	1	0	1	0	—	—	—	1.000	1.000	0	—	0	0	0	0	0.0
Total 7	81	59	.579	242	148	81	24	13	1291²	1128	7	267	495	9.8	2.33	120	.238	.281	262	.268	10	72	69	-9	7.7

■ JACK RUSSELL
Russell, Jack Erwin   b: 10/24/05, Paris, Tex.   BR/TR, 6'1.5", 178 lbs.   Deb: 5/05/26

YEAR TM/L	W	L	PCT	G	GS	CG	SH	SV	IP	H	HR	BB	SO	RAT	ERA	ERA+	OAV	OOB	BH	AVG	PB	PR	/A	PD	TPI
1926 Bos-A	0	5	.000	36	5	1	0	0	98	94	2	24	17	10.9	3.58	114	.268	.316	4	.190	-0	5	5	4	0.9
1927 Bos-A	4	9	.308	34	15	4	1	0	147	172	5	40	25	13.3	4.10	103	.298	.348	6	.125	-3	1	2	2	0.1
1928 Bos-A	11	14	.440	32	26	10	2	0	201¹	233	6	41	27	12.4	3.84	107	.294	.332	13	.210	-0	4	6	2	0.7
1929 Bos-A	6	18	.250	35	32	13	0	0	227¹	263	12	40	37	12.1	3.92	109	.290	.322	9	.129	-4	8	9	5	0.9
1930 Bos-A	9	20	.310	35	30	15	0	0	229²	302	11	53	35	14.0	5.45	85	.321	.359	14	.177	-3	-20	-21	2	-1.8
1931 Bos-A	10	18	.357	36	31	13	0	0	232	298	7	65	45	14.2	5.16	83	.310	.355	16	.195	-0	-20	-22	3	-1.6
1932 Bos-A	1	7	.125	11	6	1	0	0	39²	61	2	15	7	17.2	6.81	66	.343	.394	1	.091	-1	-10	-10	0	-0.9
Cle-A	5	7	.417	18	11	6	0	1	113	146	5	27	27	13.9	4.70	101	.310	.349	12	.300	2	-3	1	2	0.5
Yr	6	14	.300	29	17	7	0	1	152²	207	7	42	34	14.7	5.25	89	.319	.361	2	.039	1	-13	-10	2	-0.4
1933 *Was-A	12	6	.667	50	3	2	0	13	124	119	3	32	28	11.0	2.69	156	.255	.305	5	.147	-1	22	21	4	2.3
1934 Was-A	5	10	.333	54	9	3	0	7	157²	179	6	56	38	13.5	4.17	104	.287	.348	7	.159	3	6	3	3	0.7
1935 Was-A	4	9	.308	43	7	2	0	3	126	170	10	37	30	14.9	5.71	76	.324	.371	7	.200	1	-18	-20	3	-1.4
1936 Was-A	3	2	.600	18	5	1	0	3	49²	66	3	25	6	16.5	6.34	75	.317	.391	0	.000	-2	-7	-9	1	-0.7
Bos-A	0	3	.000	23	2	0	0	0	40	57	2	16	9	16.4	5.62	94	.345	.403	1	.286	-0	-3	-1	2	0.1
Yr	3	5	.375	41	7	1	0	3	89²	123	5	41	15	16.5	6.02	83	.330	.396	1	.045	-1	-10	-10	2	-0.6
1937 Det-A	2	5	.286	25	0	0	0	4	40¹	63	4	20	10	18.7	7.59	62	.362	.431	0	.000	-1	-13	-13	1	-1.0
1938 *Chi-N	6	1	.857	42	0	0	0	3	102¹	100	1	30	29	11.5	3.34	115	.258	.313	7	.219	1	5	6	3	1.0
1939 Chi-N	4	3	.571	39	0	0	0	3	68²	78	3	24	32	13.4	3.67	107	.282	.339	0	.000	-2	2	2	2	0.1
1940 StL-N	3	4	.429	26	0	0	0	1	54	53	1	26	16	13.2	2.50	160	.252	.335	0	.000	-2	8	9	1	0.9
Total 15	85	141	.376	557	182	71	3	38	2050²	2454	83	571	418	13.4	4.46	97	.299	.346	103	.167	-11	-33	-33	40	0.8

■ JEFF RUSSELL
Russell, Jeffrey Lee   b: 9/2/61, Cincinnati, Ohio   BR/TR, 6'4", 200 lbs.   Deb: 8/13/83

YEAR TM/L	W	L	PCT	G	GS	CG	SH	SV	IP	H	HR	BB	SO	RAT	ERA	ERA+	OAV	OOB	BH	AVG	PB	PR	/A	PD	TPI
1983 Cin-N	4	5	.444	10	10	2	0	0	68¹	58	7	22	40	10.5	3.03	126	.233	.295	3	.143	1	5	6	-0	0.7
1984 Cin-N	6	18	.250	33	30	4	2	0	181²	186	15	65	101	12.6	4.26	89	.263	.329	8	.140	-0	-14	-10	1	-0.7
1985 Tex-A	3	6	.333	13	13	0	0	0	62	85	10	27	44	16.5	7.55	56	.324	.392	0	—	0	-23	-23	1	-1.9
1986 Tex-A	5	2	.714	37	0	0	0	0	82	74	11	31	54	11.6	3.40	126	.244	.316	0	—	0	7	8	2	1.0
1987 Tex-A	5	4	.556	52	2	0	0	3	97¹	109	9	52	56	15.1	4.44	101	.285	.373	0	—	0	0	0	2	0.2
1988 Tex-A	10	9	.526	34	24	5	0	0	188²	183	15	66	88	12.2	3.82	107	.257	.326	0	.000	0	3	6	2	0.8
1989 Tex-A	6	4	.600	71	0	0	0	38	72²	45	4	24	77	8.9	1.98	200	.182	.263	0	—	0	15	16	1	1.8
1990 Tex-A	1	5	.167	27	0	0	0	10	25¹	23	1	16	16	13.9	4.26	93	.253	.364	0	—	0	-1	-1	0	0.0
Total 8	40	53	.430	277	79	11	2	53	778	763	72	303	476	12.6	4.03	101	.258	.331	11	.139	1	-8	3	9	1.9

■ JOHN RUSSELL
Russell, John Albert   b: 10/20/1894, San Mateo, Cal.   d: 11/19/30, Ely, Nev.   BL/TL, 6'2", 195 lbs.   Deb: 7/04/17

YEAR TM/L	W	L	PCT	G	GS	CG	SH	SV	IP	H	HR	BB	SO	RAT	ERA	ERA+	OAV	OOB	BH	AVG	PB	PR	/A	PD	TPI
1917 Bro-N	0	1	.000	5	1	1	0	0	16	12	1	6	1	10.1	4.50	62	.222	.300	1	.250	0	-3	-3	-0	-0.2
1918 Bro-N	0	0	—	1	0	0	0	0	1	2	0	1	0	27.0	18.00	15	.500	.600	0	—	0	-2	-2	0	-0.1
1921 Chi-A	2	5	.286	11	9	4	0	0	66¹	82	3	35	15	16.0	5.29	80	.314	.397	10	.400	3	-7	-8	-0	-0.4
1922 Chi-A	0	1	.000	4	1	0	0	1	6²	7	0	4	3	14.9	6.75	60	.280	.379	0	.000	-0	-2	-2	0	-0.1
Total 4	2	7	.222	21	11	5	0	1	90	103	4	46	19	15.0	5.40	73	.299	.384	11	.367	3	-14	-14	0	-0.8

■ JOHN RUSSELL
Russell, John William   b: 1/5/61, Oklahoma City, Okla.   BR/TR, 6', 200 lbs.   Deb: 6/22/84   ♦

YEAR TM/L	W	L	PCT	G	GS	CG	SH	SV	IP	H	HR	BB	SO	RAT	ERA	ERA+	OAV	OOB	BH	AVG	PB	PR	/A	PD	TPI
1989 Atl-N	0	0	—	1	0	0	0	0	0¹	0	0	0	0	0.0	0.00	—	.000	.000	29	.182	0	0	0	0	0.0

■ MARIUS RUSSO
Russo, Marius Ugo "Lefty"   b: 7/19/14, Brooklyn, N.Y.   BR/TL, 6'1", 190 lbs.   Deb: 6/06/39

YEAR TM/L	W	L	PCT	G	GS	CG	SH	SV	IP	H	HR	BB	SO	RAT	ERA	ERA+	OAV	OOB	BH	AVG	PB	PR	/A	PD	TPI
1939 NY-A	8	3	.727	21	11	9	2	2	116	86	6	41	55	9.9	2.41	181	.210	.283	10	.244	1	29	25	2	2.8
1940 NY-A	14	8	.636	30	24	15	0	1	189¹	181	17	55	87	11.3	3.28	123	.249	.303	12	.188	2	23	16	3	2.0
1941 *NY-A	14	10	.583	28	27	17	3	1	209²	195	8	87	105	12.1	3.09	127	.244	.322	18	.231	2	25	20	1	2.3
1942 NY-A	4	1	.800	9	5	2	0	0	45¹	41	2	14	15	11.1	2.78	124	.244	.306	4	.235	1	4	3	0	0.5
1943 *NY-A	5	10	.333	24	14	5	1	1	101²	89	7	45	42	12.0	3.72	87	.235	.319	6	.194	1	-5	-6	1	-0.4
1946 NY-A	0	2	.000	8	3	0	0	0	18²	26	1	11	7	17.8	4.34	80	.333	.416	0	.000	-1	-2	-2	1	-0.1
Total 6	45	34	.570	120	84	48	6	5	680²	618	41	253	311	11.6	3.13	124	.242	.312	50	.213	7	74	57	8	7.1

■ RUST
Rust   b: Louisville, Ky.   Deb: 7/04/1882   ♦

YEAR TM/L	W	L	PCT	G	GS	CG	SH	SV	IP	H	HR	BB	SO	RAT	ERA	ERA+	OAV	OOB	BH	AVG	PB	PR	/A	PD	TPI
1882 Bal-a	0	1	.000	1	1	0	0	0	5	10	1	0	0	19.8	7.20	38	.391	.414	1	.333	0	-3	-2	0	-0.1

YEAR TM/L	W	L	PCT	G	GS	CG	SH	SV	IP	H	HR	BB	SO	RAT	ERA	ERA+	OAV	OOB	BH	AVG	PB	PR	/A	PD	TPI
■ DICK RUSTECK Rusteck, Richard Frank b: 7/12/41, Chicago, Ill. BR/TL, 6'1", 175 lbs. Deb: 6/10/66
1966 NY-N	1	2	.333	8	3	1	1	0	24	24	1	8	9	12.0	3.00	121	.276	.337	0	.000	-1	2	2	0	0.1
■ BABE RUTH Ruth, George Herman "The Bambino" or "The Sultan Of Swat" b: 2/6/1895, Baltimore, Md. d: 8/16/48, New York, N.Y. BL/TL, 6'2", 215 lbs. Deb: 7/11/14 CH♦
1914 Bos-A	2	1	.667	4	3	1	0	0	23	21	1	7	3	11.0	3.91	69	.236	.292	2	.200	0	-3	-3	0	-0.2
1915 *Bos-A	18	8	.692	32	28	16	1	0	217²	166	3	85	112	10.6	2.44	114	.212	.294	29	.315	15	12	8	1	2.6
1916 *Bos-A	23	12	.657	44	41	23	9	1	323²	230	0	118	170	9.9	1.75	158	.201	.280	37	.272	13	39	37	-0	5.9
1917 Bos-A	24	13	.649	41	38	35	6	2	326¹	244	2	108	128	10.0	2.01	128	.211	.284	40	.325	17	24	21	2	4.6
1918 *Bos-A	13	7	.650	20	19	18	1	0	166¹	125	1	49	40	9.5	2.22	121	.214	.277	95	.300	12	10	9	4	1.0
1919 Bos-A	9	5	.643	17	15	12	0	1	133¹	148	2	58	30	14.0	2.97	102	.290	.365	139	.322	13	4	1	1	0.1
1920 NY-A	1	0	1.000	1	1	0	0	0	4	3	0	2	0	11.3	4.50	85	.200	.294	172	.376	1	-0	-0	0	0.0
1921 *NY-A	2	0	1.000	2	1	0	0	0	9	14	1	9	2	23.0	9.00	47	.350	.469	204	.378	2	-5	-5	0	-0.3
1930 NY-A	1	0	1.000	1	1	1	0	0	9	11	0	2	3	13.0	3.00	143	.306	.342	186	.359	1	2	1	1	0.1
1933 NY-A	1	0	1.000	1	1	1	0	0	9	12	0	3	0	15.0	5.00	78	.308	.357	138	.301	1	-1	-1	0	0.0
Total 10	94	46	.671	163	148	107	17	4	1221¹	974	10	441	488	10.6	2.28	122	.221	.297	2873	.342	75	82	67	8	13.8
■ JOHNNY RUTHERFORD Rutherford, John William "Doc" b: 5/5/25, Belleville, Ont., Canada BL/TR, 5'10.5", 170 lbs. Deb: 4/30/52
1952 *Bro-N	7	7	.500	22	11	4	0	2	97¹	97	9	29	29	11.8	4.25	86	.262	.319	9	.290	2	-6	-7	1	-0.2
■ DICK RUTHVEN Ruthven, Richard David b: 3/27/51, Sacramento, Cal. BR/TR, 6'3", 190 lbs. Deb: 4/17/73
1973 Phi-N	6	9	.400	25	23	3	1	1	128¹	125	10	75	98	14.2	4.21	90	.257	.360	5	.132	-1	-8	-6	0	-0.6
1974 Phi-N	9	13	.409	35	35	6	0	0	212²	182	11	116	153	12.7	4.02	94	.231	.332	13	.191	-1	-10	-6	-1	-0.7
1975 Phi-N	2	2	.500	11	7	0	0	0	40²	37	2	22	26	13.3	4.20	89	.243	.343	2	.154	-0	-2	-0	-0	-0.2
1976 Atl-N	14	17	.452	36	36	8	4	0	240¹	255	14	90	142	13.2	4.19	90	.275	.345	13	.171	-0	-19	-11	2	-0.8
1977 Atl-N	7	13	.350	25	23	6	2	0	151	158	14	62	84	13.2	4.23	105	.267	.338	12	.267	3	-5	4	-1	0.6
1978 Atl-N	2	6	.250	13	13	2	1	0	81	78	8	28	45	11.8	4.11	98	.257	.319	2	.083	-2	-5	-1	-0	-0.1
*Phi-N	13	5	.722	20	20	9	2	0	150²	136	13	28	75	9.9	2.99	119	.248	.285	15	.283	4	10	10	-0	1.5
Yr	15	11	.577	33	33	11	3	0	231²	214	21	56	120	10.5	3.38	111	.250	.297	1	.013	3	5	9	-0	1.4
1979 Phi-N	7	5	.583	20	20	3	2	0	122¹	121	10	37	58	11.8	4.27	90	.256	.313	6	.146	-0	-7	-6	-2	-0.7
1980 *Phi-N	17	10	.630	33	33	6	1	0	223¹	241	16	74	86	12.8	3.55	107	.283	.342	16	.235	4	1	0	1	1.1
1981 *Phi-N	12	7	.632	23	22	5	0	0	146²	162	10	54	80	13.4	5.15	70	.281	.346	7	.140	-2	-27	-25	-0	-2.5
1982 Phi-N	11	11	.500	33	31	8	2	0	204¹	189	18	59	115	11.2	3.79	97	.246	.305	7	.109	-2	-4	-3	-2	-0.7
1983 Phi-N	1	3	.250	7	7	0	0	0	33²	46	5	10	26	15.0	5.61	64	.333	.378	1	.111	-0	-7	-8	-0	-0.7
Chi-N	12	9	.571	25	25	5	2	0	149¹	156	17	28	73	11.3	4.10	92	.269	.306	12	.226	2	-8	-5	2	0.0
Yr	13	12	.520	32	32	5	2	0	183	202	22	38	99	12.0	4.38	86	.279	.318	2	.032	2	-15	-13	2	-0.7
1984 Chi-N	6	10	.375	23	22	0	0	0	126²	154	14	41	55	14.1	5.04	77	.302	.359	7	.159	0	-21	-16	0	-1.4
1985 Chi-N	4	7	.364	20	15	0	0	0	87¹	103	6	37	26	14.4	4.53	88	.299	.367	5	.208	-0	-9	-5	-0	-0.5
1986 Chi-N	0	0	—	6	0	0	0	0	10²	12	4	6	3	15.2	5.06	80	.293	.383	0	.000	-0	-2	-1	-0	-0.1
Total 14	123	127	.492	355	332	61	17	1	2109	2155	165	767	1145	12.6	4.14	92	.267	.333	123	.183	6	-123	-75	-2	-5.8
■ CYCLONE RYAN Ryan, Daniel R. b: 1866, Capperwhite, Ireland d: 1/30/17, Medfield, Mass. TR, 6', Deb: 8/08/1887 ♦
1887 NY-a	0	1	.000	2	1	0	0	0	2¹	5	1	6	0	42.4	23.14	18	.418	.612	7	.219	-0	-5	-5	0	-0.3
1891 Bos-N	0	0	—	1	0	0	0	0	3	2	0	1	0	9.0	0.00	—	.182	.251	0	.000	-0	1	1	0	0.1
Total 2	0	1	.000	3	1	0	0	0	5¹	7	1	7	0	23.6	10.13	39	.305	.468	7	.212	-0	-4	-4	0	-0.2
■ JACK RYAN Ryan, Jack "Gulfport" b: 9/19/1884, Lawrenceville, Ill. d: 10/16/49, Hondsboro, Miss. TR, 5'10", 165 lbs. Deb: 7/02/08
1908 Cle-A	1	1	.500	8	1	1	0	0	35²	27	3	2	7	7.6	2.27	105	.220	.238	1	.091	0	0	0	0	0.1
1909 Bos-A	4	3	.571	13	8	2	0	0	61¹	65	0	20	24	13.1	3.23	77	.281	.349	4	.211	0	-5	-5	-0	-0.5
1911 Bro-N	0	1	.000	3	1	0	0	0	6	9	1	4	1	21.0	3.00	111	.375	.483	0	.000	0	0	0	0	0.0
Total 3	5	5	.500	24	10	3	0	1	103	101	4	26	32	11.6	2.88	87	.267	.324	5	.161	1	-4	-4	0	-0.4
■ JIMMY RYAN Ryan, James Edward "Pony" b: 2/11/1863, Clinton, Mass. d: 10/26/23, Chicago, Ill. BR/TL, 5'9", 162 lbs. Deb: 10/08/1885 ♦
1886 *Chi-N	0	0	—	5	0	0	0	1	23¹	19	2	13	15	12.3	4.63	79	.213	.314	100	.306	1	-3	-3	0	-0.1
1887 Chi-N	2	1	.667	8	3	2	0	0	45	53	3	17	14	14.0	4.20	106	.285	.345	145	.285	2	-1	1	2	0.1
1888 Chi-N	4	0	1.000	8	2	1	0	0	38¹	47	2	12	11	13.9	3.05	99	.291	.340	182	.332	5	-1	-0	0	0.0
1891 Chi-N	0	0	—	2	0	0	0	1	5²	11	0	2	2	20.6	1.59	209	.394	.434	140	.277	1	1	1	-0	0.1
1893 Chi-N	0	0	—	1	0	0	0	0	4²	3	0	0	1	5.8	0.00	—	.178	.178	102	.299	0	2	2	0	0.2
Total 5	6	1	.857	24	5	3	0	2	117	133	7	44	43	13.6	3.62	104	.277	.337	2502	.306	9	-2	2	2	0.3
■ JOHNNY RYAN Ryan, John Joseph b: 10/1853, Philadelphia, Pa. d: 3/22/02, Philadelphia, Pa. 5'7.5", 150 lbs. Deb: 8/19/1873 ♦
1874 Bal-n	0	0	—	1	0	0	0	0	1¹	9	0	0		60.8	13.50	23	.643	.643	33	.179	-0	-2	-2		0.0
1875 NH-n	1	5	.167	10	6	4	0	0	59¹	69	1	9		11.8	3.34	68	.256	.280	23	.158	-1	-6	-7		-0.5
1876 Lou-N	0	0	—	1	0	0	0	0	8	22	0	0	1	24.8	5.63	48	.469	.469	61	.253	-0	-3	-3	-0	-0.3
Total 2 n	1	5	.167	11	6	4	0	0	60²	78	1	9		12.9	3.56	64	.275	.297	58	.172	-1	-7	-9		-0.5
■ JOHN RYAN Ryan, John M. b: Hamilton, Ohio Deb: 4/19/1884
1884 Bal-U	3	2	.600	6	6	5	0	0	51	61	1	16	33	13.6	3.35	99	.278	.327	2	.080	-3	-2	-0	0	-0.1
■ NOLAN RYAN Ryan, Lynn Nolan b: 1/31/47, Refugio, Tex. BR/TR, 6'2", 170 lbs. Deb: 9/11/66
1966 NY-N	0	1	.000	2	1	0	0	0	3	5	1	3	6	24.0	15.00	24	.357	.471	0	—	0	-4	-4	0	-0.3
1968 NY-N	6	9	.400	21	18	3	0	0	134	93	12	75	133	11.6	3.09	98	.200	.317	2	.114	-1	-2	-1	-3	-0.4
1969 *NY-N	6	3	.667	25	10	2	0	1	89¹	60	3	53	92	11.5	3.53	104	.189	.307	3	.103	-1	1	1	-3	-0.2
1970 NY-N	7	11	.389	27	19	5	2	1	131²	86	10	97	125	12.8	3.42	118	.188	.335	8	.178	-1	9	9	-2	0.7
1971 NY-N	10	14	.417	30	26	3	0	0	152	125	8	116	137	15.2	3.97	86	.219	.365	6	.128	-0	-8	-9	-2	-1.1
1972 Cal-A	19	16	.543	39	39	20	9	0	284	166	14	157	329	10.6	2.28	128	.171	.292	13	.135	0	25	20	-4	1.9
1973 Cal-A	21	16	.568	41	39	26	4	1	326	238	18	162	383	11.2	2.87	123	.203	.304	0	—	0	34	24	-4	2.1
1974 Cal-A	22	16	.579	42	41	26	3	0	332²	221	18	202	367	11.7	2.89	119	.190	.314	0	—	0	27	20	-0	2.1
1975 Cal-A	14	12	.538	28	28	10	5	0	198	152	13	132	186	13.2	3.45	103	.213	.342	0	—	0	7	2	-2	0.0
1976 Cal-A	17	18	.486	39	39	21	7	0	284¹	193	13	183	327	12.1	3.36	99	.195	.323	0	—	0	5	-1	-2	-0.2
1977 Cal-A	19	16	.543	37	37	22	4	0	299	198	12	204	341	12.4	2.77	141	.193	.331	0	—	0	43	38	-2	3.8
1978 Cal-A	10	13	.435	31	31	14	3	0	234²	183	12	148	260	12.8	3.72	97	.220	.340	0	—	0	-1	-3	-1	-0.3
1979 *Cal-A	16	14	.533	34	34	17	5	0	222²	169	15	114	223	11.7	3.60	113	.212	.314	0	—	0	15	12	-1	1.0
1980 *Hou-N	11	10	.524	35	35	4	2	0	233²	205	10	98	200	11.8	3.35	98	.236	.316	6	.086	-1	6	-2	-2	-0.5
1981 *Hou-N	11	5	.688	21	21	5	3	0	149	99	2	68	140	10.1	1.69	195	.188	.281	11	.216	3	30	27	-1	3.2
1982 Hou-N	16	12	.571	35	35	10	3	0	250¹	196	20	109	245	11.3	3.16	105	.213	.302	10	.120	-1	12	4	-2	0.1
1983 Hou-N	14	9	.609	29	29	5	2	0	196¹	134	9	101	183	11.0	2.98	114	.195	.302	5	.072	-3	14	9	-1	0.4
1984 Hou-N	12	11	.522	30	30	5	2	0	183²	143	12	69	197	10.6	3.04	109	.211	.288	6	.098	-1	11	6	-4	0.0
1985 Hou-N	10	12	.455	35	35	4	0	0	232	205	12	95	209	12.0	3.80	91	.239	.322	6	.111	-1	-5	-9	-4	-1.4
1986 *Hou-N	12	8	.600	30	30	1	0	0	178	119	14	82	194	10.4	3.34	108	.188	.285	6	.102	-2	8	5	-2	0.0
1987 Hou-N	8	16	.333	34	34	0	0	0	211²	154	14	87	270	10.4	2.76	142	.199	.284	4	.062	-3	31	27	-2	2.2
1988 Hou-N	12	11	.522	33	33	4	1	0	220	186	18	87	228	11.5	3.52	94	.227	.307	4	.057	-3	-2	-5	-4	-1.2
1989 Tex-A	16	10	.615	32	32	6	2	0	239¹	162	17	98	301	10.1	3.20	124	.187	.286	0	—	0	18	20	-3	1.8
1990 Tex-A	13	9	.591	30	30	5	2	0	204	137	18	74	232	9.6	3.44	116	.188	.269	0	—	0	11	12	-3	1.0
Total 24	302	272	.526	740	706	218	59	3	4989¹	3629	295	2614	5308	11.5	3.16	112	.203	.310	94	.110	-16	287	203	-52	14.7

YEAR	TM/L	W	L	PCT	G	GS	CG	SH	SV	IP	H	HR	BB	SO	RAT	ERA	ERA+	OAV	OOB	BH	AVG	PB	PR	/A	PD	TPI

■ ROSY RYAN Ryan, Wilfred Patrick Dolan b: 3/15/1898, Worcester, Mass. d: 12/10/80, Scottsdale, Ariz. BL/TR, 6', 185 lbs. Deb: 9/07/19

1919	NY-N	1	2	.333	4	3	1	0	0	20¹	20	0	9	7	13.3	3.10	91	.260	.345	0	.000	-1	-0	-1	-0	-0.1
1920	NY-N	0	1	.000	3	1	1	0	0	15¹	14	1	4	5	10.6	1.76	170	.259	.310	0	.000	-1	2	2	0	0.2
1921	NY-N	7	10	.412	36	16	5	0	3	147¹	140	6	32	58	10.6	3.73	98	.255	.297	9	.200	1	1	-1	-1	-0.1
1922	*NY-N	17	12	.586	46	20	12	1	3	191²	194	5	74	75	12.7	3.01	133	.269	.338	12	.194	1	23	21	-1	1.9
1923	*NY-N	16	5	.762	45	15	7	0	4	172²	169	8	46	58	11.3	3.49	109	.257	.308	11	.208	0	10	6	0	0.6
1924	*NY-N	8	6	.571	37	9	2	0	5	124²	137	1	37	36	12.7	4.26	86	.285	.339	5	.139	-1	-5	-8	-2	-1.0
1925	Bos-N	2	8	.200	37	7	1	0	2	122²	152	7	52	48	15.0	6.31	64	.303	.368	11	.282	3	-28	-31	-1	-2.6
1926	Bos-N	0	2	.000	7	2	0	0	0	19	29	1	7	1	17.1	7.58	47	.392	.444	1	.200	-0	-8	-9	-0	-0.7
1928	NY-A	0	0	—	3	0	0	0	0	6	17	1	1	5	27.0	16.50	23	.486	.500	0	.000	-1	-8	-8	-0	-0.7
1933	Bro-N	1	1	.500	30	0	0	0	2	61¹	69	3	16	22	12.9	4.55	71	.276	.327	2	.154	0	-8	-9	-0	-0.9
Total	10	52	47	.525	248	73	29	1	19	881	941	33	278	315	12.6	4.14	91	.277	.333	51	.190	1	-22	-38	-6	-3.4

■ MIKE RYBA Ryba, Dominic Joseph b: 6/9/03, DeLancey, Pa. d: 12/13/71, Brookline Station Mo. BR/TR, 5'11.5", 180 lbs. Deb: 9/22/35 C

1935	StL-N	1	1	.500	2	1	1	0	0	16	15	0	1	6	9.0	3.38	121	.242	.254	2	.400	1	1	1	0	0.2
1936	StL-N	5	1	.833	14	0	0	0	0	45	55	3	16	25	14.6	5.40	73	.294	.356	3	.167	-0	-7	-7	-1	-0.7
1937	StL-N	9	6	.600	38	8	5	0	0	135	152	8	40	57	12.9	4.13	96	.284	.336	15	.313	4	-3	-2	0	0.3
1938	StL-N	1	1	.500	3	0	0	0	0	5	8	0	1	6	16.2	5.40	73	.348	.375	0	—	0	-1	-1	0	0.0
1941	Bos-A	7	3	.700	40	3	0	0	6	121	143	14	42	54	13.8	4.46	93	.297	.353	8	.216	1	-4	-4	2	0.0
1942	Bos-A	3	3	.500	18	0	0	0	3	44¹	49	5	13	16	12.8	3.86	97	.278	.332	5	.294	1	-1	-1	1	0.1
1943	Bos-A	7	5	.583	40	8	4	1	2	143²	142	4	57	50	12.5	3.26	102	.262	.333	8	.186	1	1	1	-1	0.0
1944	Bos-A	12	7	.632	42	7	2	0	2	138	119	7	39	50	10.3	3.33	102	.233	.287	6	.146	-0	2	1	3	0.3
1945	Bos-A	7	6	.538	34	9	4	1	2	123	122	5	33	44	11.5	2.49	137	.259	.310	9	.250	2	12	13	-1	1.5
1946	*Bos-A	0	1	.000	9	0	0	0	1	12²	12	1	5	5	12.1	3.55	103	.261	.333	2	1.000	1	-0	0	-0	0.1
Total	10	52	34	.605	240	36	16	2	16	783²	817	47	247	307	12.3	3.66	100	.269	.326	58	.235	9	-1	1	3	1.8

■ GARY RYERSON Ryerson, Gary Lawrence b: 6/7/48, Los Angeles, Cal. BR/TL, 6'1", 175 lbs. Deb: 6/28/72

1972	Mil-A	3	8	.273	20	14	4	1	0	102	119	9	21	45	12.4	3.62	84	.290	.324	1	.042	-1	-6	-7	-1	-0.9
1973	Mil-A	0	1	.000	9	4	0	0	0	23	32	0	7	10	15.3	7.83	48	.327	.371	0	—	0	-10	-10	0	-0.9
Total	2	3	9	.250	29	18	4	1	0	125	151	9	28	55	12.9	4.39	72	.297	.333	1	.042	-1	-17	-17	-1	-1.8

■ BRET SABERHAGEN Saberhagen, Bret William b: 4/11/64, Chicago Heights, Ill. BR/TR, 6'1", 160 lbs. Deb: 4/04/84

1984	*KC-A	10	11	.476	38	18	2	1	1	157²	138	13	36	73	10.0	3.48	116	.237	.283	0	—	0	9	10	1	1.0
1985	*KC-A	20	6	.769	32	32	10	1	0	235¹	211	19	38	158	9.6	2.87	145	.241	.273	0	—	0	33	34	2	3.8
1986	KC-A	7	12	.368	30	25	4	2	0	156	165	15	29	112	11.3	4.15	102	.268	.303	0	—	0	0	2	1	0.3
1987	KC-A	18	10	.643	33	33	15	4	0	257	246	27	53	163	10.7	3.36	135	.252	.295	0	—	0	31	34	1	3.5
1988	KC-A	14	16	.467	35	35	9	0	0	260²	271	18	59	171	11.5	3.80	105	.269	.312	0	—	0	5	5	0	0.5
1989	KC-A	23	6	.793	36	35	12	4	0	262¹	209	13	43	193	8.7	2.16	178	.217	.252	0	—	0	50	49	0	5.5
1990	KC-A	5	9	.357	20	20	5	0	0	135	146	9	28	87	11.7	3.27	116	.279	.316	0	—	0	10	8	3	1.2
Total	7	97	70	.581	224	198	57	12	1	1464	1386	114	286	957	10.4	3.23	127	.250	.289	0	—	0	139	141	7	15.8

■ RAY SADECKI Sadecki, Raymond Michael b: 12/26/40, Kansas City, Kan. BL/TL, 5'11", 180 lbs. Deb: 5/19/60

1960	StL-N	9	9	.500	26	26	7	1	0	157¹	148	15	86	95	13.4	3.78	109	.249	.345	12	.211	-0	-0	6	-2	0.5
1961	StL-N	14	10	.583	31	31	13	0	0	222²	196	28	102	114	12.2	3.72	118	.238	.324	22	.253	2	8	17	-5	1.6
1962	StL-N	6	8	.429	22	17	4	1	1	102¹	121	13	43	50	14.7	5.54	77	.296	.367	3	.081	-2	-18	-14	-1	-1.6
1963	StL-N	10	10	.500	36	28	4	1	0	193¹	198	25	78	136	13.0	4.10	87	.266	.339	9	.141	-1	-17	-12	-3	-1.5
1964	*StL-N	20	11	.645	37	32	9	2	1	220	232	16	60	119	12.0	3.68	103	.273	.322	12	.160	2	-4	-3	-3	0.3
1965	StL-N	6	15	.286	36	28	4	0	1	172²	192	26	64	122	13.3	5.21	74	.284	.346	11	.200	2	-32	-26	-2	-2.5
1966	StL-N	2	1	.667	5	3	1	0	0	24¹	16	2	9	21	9.2	2.22	162	.188	.266	3	.429	2	4	4	0	0.6
	SF-N	3	7	.300	26	19	3	1	0	105	125	20	39	62	14.4	5.40	68	.293	.358	11	.324	6	-21	-20	-2	-1.5
	Yr	5	8	.385	31	22	4	1	0	129¹	141	22	48	83	13.4	4.80	76	.283	.343	1	.024	7	-17	-17	-2	-0.9
1967	SF-N	12	6	.667	35	24	10	2	0	188	165	8	58	145	10.9	2.78	118	.238	.301	18	.247	4	13	11	-1	1.5
1968	SF-N	12	18	.400	38	36	13	6	0	254	225	14	70	206	10.6	2.91	101	.237	.292	8	.094	-1	2	1	-3	-0.3
1969	SF-N	5	8	.385	29	17	4	3	0	138¹	137	18	53	104	12.5	4.23	83	.259	.329	5	.125	2	-10	-11	1	-0.8
1970	NY-N	8	4	.667	28	19	4	0	0	138²	134	18	52	89	12.1	3.89	103	.255	.322	8	.205	1	2	2	-2	0.0
1971	NY-N	7	7	.500	34	20	5	2	0	163¹	139	14	44	120	10.3	2.92	117	.229	.285	10	.200	1	10	9	-1	0.9
1972	NY-N	2	1	.667	34	2	0	0	0	75²	73	3	31	38	12.6	3.09	109	.257	.334	2	.154	-0	3	2	-1	0.1
1973	*NY-N	5	4	.556	31	11	1	0	1	116²	109	11	41	87	11.6	3.39	107	.248	.314	7	.226	1	3	3	-3	0.1
1974	NY-N	8	8	.500	34	10	3	1	0	103	107	7	35	46	12.6	3.41	105	.274	.337	7	.259	1	2	2	0	0.3
1975	StL-N	1	0	1.000	8	0	0	0	0	11	13	0	7	8	16.4	3.27	115	.289	.385	0	—	0	0	1	-0	0.0
	Atl-N	2	3	.400	25	5	0	0	1	66¹	73	3	21	24	13.3	4.21	90	.286	.350	3	.200	1	-4	-3	-1	-0.3
	Yr	3	3	.500	33	5	0	0	1	77¹	86	3	28	32	13.7	4.07	93	.285	.353	3	.200	1	-4	-3	-1	-0.3
	KC-A	1	0	1.000	5	0	0	0	0	3	5	0	3	0	24.0	3.00	128	.333	.444	0	—	0	0	0	0	0.0
1976	KC-A	0	0	—	3	0	0	0	0	4²	7	1	2	3	19.3	0.00	—	.368	.455	0	—	0	2	2	-0	0.2
	Mil-A	2	0	1.000	36	0	0	0	1	37¹	38	2	20	27	14.7	4.34	81	.262	.363	0	—	0	-3	-4	-1	-0.4
	Yr	2	0	1.000	39	0	0	0	1	42	45	2	23	28	15.2	3.86	91	.274	.374	0	—	0	-2	-2	-1	-0.2
1977	NY-N	0	1	.000	4	0	0	0	0	3	3	1	3	0	18.0	6.00	62	.300	.462	0	—	0	-1	-1	0	0.0
Total	18	135	131	.508	563	328	85	20	7	2500²	2456	240	922	1614	12.3	3.78	97	.258	.326	151	.191	19	-61	-32	-28	-2.8

■ JIM SADOWSKI Sadowski, James Michael b: 8/7/51, Pittsburgh, Pa. BR/TR, 6'3", 195 lbs. Deb: 4/27/74

| 1974 | Pit-N | 0 | 1 | .000 | 4 | 0 | 0 | 0 | 0 | 9 | 7 | 1 | 9 | 1 | 16.0 | 6.00 | 57 | .233 | .410 | 0 | .000 | 0 | -2 | -3 | -1 | -0.1 |

■ BOB SADOWSKI Sadowski, Robert b: 2/19/38, Pittsburgh, Pa. BR/TR, 6'2", 195 lbs. Deb: 6/19/63

1963	Mil-N	5	7	.417	19	18	5	1	0	116²	99	8	30	72	10.3	2.62	123	.231	.289	2	.057	-2	9	8	1	0.7
1964	Mil-N	9	10	.474	51	18	5	0	5	166²	159	18	56	96	12.0	4.10	86	.251	.319	8	.154	0	-11	-11	3	-0.8
1965	Mil-N	5	9	.357	34	13	3	0	3	123	117	11	35	78	11.3	4.32	82	.250	.306	3	.086	-2	-11	-11	-1	-1.3
1966	Bos-A	1	1	.500	11	5	0	0	0	33¹	41	4	9	11	13.8	5.40	70	.311	.359	0	.000	-1	-7	-6	0	-0.6
Total	4	20	27	.426	115	54	13	1	8	439²	416	41	130	257	11.5	3.87	90	.250	.311	13	.101	-4	-20	-20	3	-2.0

■ TED SADOWSKI Sadowski, Theodore b: 4/1/36, Pittsburgh, Pa. BR/TR, 6'1.5", 190 lbs. Deb: 9/02/60

1960	Was-A	1	0	1.000	9	1	0	0	1	17¹	17	4	9	12	14.0	5.19	75	.258	.355	0	.000	-0	-3	-3	-0	-0.2
1961	Min-A	0	2	.000	15	1	0	0	0	33	49	6	11	12	16.6	6.82	62	.348	.399	0	.000	-1	-10	-9	1	-0.8
1962	Min-A	1	1	.500	19	0	0	0	0	34	37	6	11	15	13.0	5.03	81	.301	.363	2	.500	1	-4	-4	0	-0.2
Total	3	2	3	.400	43	2	0	0	1	84¹	103	16	31	39	14.6	5.76	71	.312	.376	2	.154	-0	-17	-16	1	-1.2

■ JOHNNY SAIN Sain, John Franklin b: 9/25/17, Havana, Ark. BR/TR, 6'2", 185 lbs. Deb: 4/24/42 C

1942	Bos-N	4	7	.364	40	3	0	0	0	97	79	8	63	68	13.6	3.90	86	.228	.354	2	.074	-2	-6	-6	0	-0.7
1946	Bos-N	20	14	.588	37	34	24	3	2	265	225	8	87	129	10.7	2.21	155	.230	.294	28	.298	5	35	36	3	5.1
1947	Bos-N	21	12	.636	38	35	22	3	1	266	265	19	79	132	11.8	3.52	111	.255	.310	37	.346	12	16	11	1	2.4
1948	*Bos-N	24	15	.615	42	39	28	4	1	314²	297	19	83	137	11.0	2.60	147	.245	.296	25	.217	2	47	43	-2	4.6
1949	Bos-N	10	17	.370	37	36	16	1	0	243	285	15	75	73	13.5	4.81	78	.291	.344	20	.206	1	-21	-28	-1	-2.6
1950	Bos-N	20	13	.606	37	37	25	3	0	278¹	294	34	70	96	11.8	3.94	98	.269	.314	21	.206	4	6	-3	-2	-0.1
1951	Bos-N	5	13	.278	26	22	6	1	1	160¹	195	16	45	63	13.6	4.21	87	.299	.347	11	.212	3	-4	-10	0	-0.6
	*NY-A	2	1	.667	7	4	3	0	0	37	41	5	8	21	11.9	4.14	93	.281	.318	4	.286	1	-0	-1	1	0.0

YEAR TM/L	W	L	PCT	G	GS	CG	SH	SV	IP	H	HR	BB	SO	RAT	ERA	ERA+	OAV	OOB	BH	AVG	PB	PR	/A	PD	TPI
1952 *NY-A	11	6	.647	35	16	8	0	7	148¹	149	15	38	57	11.5	3.46	96	.261	.310	19	.268	6	4	-2	-1	0.2
1953 *NY-A	14	7	.667	40	19	10	1	9	189	189	16	45	84	11.3	3.00	123	.262	.308	17	.250	4	21	15	0	1.9
1954 NY-A	6	6	.500	45	0	0	0	22	77	66	11	15	33	9.5	3.16	109	.229	.267	6	.353	2	5	2	-0	0.5
1955 NY-A	0	0	—	3	0	0	0	0	5¹	6	4	1	5	11.8	6.75	55	.300	.333	0	.000	-0	-2	-2	0	-0.1
KC-A	2	5	.286	25	0	0	0	1	44²	54	10	10	12	12.9	5.44	77	.297	.333	0	—	-1	-7	-6	-0	-0.7
Yr	2	5	.286	28	0	0	0	1	50	60	14	11	17	12.8	5.58	74	.297	.333	0	.000	-1	-9	-8	-0	-0.8
Total 11	139	116	.545	412	245	140	16	51	2125²	2145	180	619	910	11.8	3.49	106	.261	.315	190	.245	38	94	50	-1	9.9

■ RANDY ST. CLAIRE

St. Claire, Randy Anthony b: 8/23/60, Glens Falls, N.Y. BR/TR, 6'3", 180 lbs. Deb: 9/11/84

YEAR TM/L	W	L	PCT	G	GS	CG	SH	SV	IP	H	HR	BB	SO	RAT	ERA	ERA+	OAV	OOB	BH	AVG	PB	PR	/A	PD	TPI
1984 Mon-N	0	0	—	4	0	0	0	0	8	11	0	2	4	15.8	4.50	76	.344	.400	0	—	0	-1	-1	0	0.0
1985 Mon-N	5	3	.625	42	0	0	0	0	68²	69	3	26	25	12.6	3.93	86	.265	.334	1	.200	1	-3	-4	1	-0.2
1986 Mon-N	2	0	1.000	11	0	0	0	1	19	13	2	6	21	9.0	2.37	156	.186	.250	0	.000	-0	3	3	0	0.3
1987 Mon-N	3	3	.500	44	0	0	0	7	67	64	9	20	43	11.4	4.03	104	.249	.306	2	.333	1	0	1	-0	0.2
1988 Mon-N	0	0	—	6	0	0	0	0	7¹	11	2	5	6	19.6	6.14	59	.344	.432	0	—	0	-2	-2	0	-0.1
Cin-N	1	0	1.000	10	0	0	0	0	13²	13	3	5	8	11.9	2.63	136	.241	.305	0	.000	-0	1	1	0	0.1
Yr	1	0	1.000	16	0	0	0	0	21	24	5	10	14	14.6	3.86	93	.276	.351	0	.000	-0	-1	-1	0	0.0
1989 Min-A	1	0	1.000	14	0	0	0	1	22¹	19	4	10	14	12.5	5.24	79	.226	.323	0	—	-0	-3	-3	0	-0.2
Total 6	12	6	.667	131	0	0	0	9	206	200	23	74	121	12.2	3.98	95	.253	.321	3	.231	1	-5	-5	1	0.1

■ JIM ST. VRAIN

St. Vrain, James Marcellin b: 6/6/1871, Ralls County, Mo. d: 6/12/37, Butte, Montana BR/TL, 5'9", 175 lbs. Deb: 4/20/02

YEAR TM/L	W	L	PCT	G	GS	CG	SH	SV	IP	H	HR	BB	SO	RAT	ERA	ERA+	OAV	OOB	BH	AVG	PB	PR	/A	PD	TPI
1902 Chi-N	4	6	.400	12	11	10	1	0	95	88	0	25	51	11.1	2.08	130	.246	.302	3	.097	-2	7	7	0	0.5

■ LUIS SALAZAR

Salazar, Luis Ernesto (Garcia) b: 5/19/56, Barcelona, Venez. BR/TR, 6', 185 lbs. Deb: 8/15/80 ♦

YEAR TM/L	W	L	PCT	G	GS	CG	SH	SV	IP	H	HR	BB	SO	RAT	ERA	ERA+	OAV	OOB	BH	AVG	PB	PR	/A	PD	TPI
1987 SD-N	0	0	—	2	0	0	0	0	2	0	1	2	1	13.5	4.50	88	.250	.333	48	.254	0	-0	-0	0	0.0

■ FREDDY SALE

Sale, Frederick Link b: 5/2/02, Chester, S.C. d: 5/27/56, Hermosa Beach, Cal BR/TR, 5'9", 160 lbs. Deb: 6/30/24

YEAR TM/L	W	L	PCT	G	GS	CG	SH	SV	IP	H	HR	BB	SO	RAT	ERA	ERA+	OAV	OOB	BH	AVG	PB	PR	/A	PD	TPI
1924 Pit-N	0	0	—	1	0	0	0	0	1	2	0	0	0	18.0	0.00	—	.500	.500	0	—	0	0	0	0	0.0

■ HARRY SALISBURY

Salisbury, Henry H. b: 5/15/1855, Providence, R.I. d: 3/29/33, Chicago, Ill. BL , Deb: 8/28/1879

YEAR TM/L	W	L	PCT	G	GS	CG	SH	SV	IP	H	HR	BB	SO	RAT	ERA	ERA+	OAV	OOB	BH	AVG	PB	PR	/A	PD	TPI
1879 Tro-N	4	6	.400	10	10	9	0	0	89	103	0	11	31	11.5	2.22	112	.272	.292	2	.056	-4	3	3	2	0.0
1882 Pit-a	20	18	.526	38	38	38	1	0	335	315	1	37	135	9.5	2.63	99	.232	.253	22	.152	-6	2	-1	-2	-0.8
Total 2	24	24	.500	48	48	47	1	0	424	418	1	48	166	9.9	2.55	102	.241	.261	24	.133	-10	5	2	-1	-0.8

■ BILL SALISBURY

Salisbury, William Ansel "Solly" b: 11/12/1876, Algona, Iowa d: 1/17/52, Rowena, Ore. BR/TR, 6', 180 lbs. Deb: 4/19/02

YEAR TM/L	W	L	PCT	G	GS	CG	SH	SV	IP	H	HR	BB	SO	RAT	ERA	ERA+	OAV	OOB	BH	AVG	PB	PR	/A	PD	TPI
1902 Phi-N	0	0	—	2	1	0	0	0	6	15	1	2	0	25.5	13.50	21	.468	.499	0	.000	-0	-7	-7	-0	-0.6

■ SLIM SALLEE

Sallee, Harry Franklin "Scatter" b: 2/3/1885, Higginsport, Ohio d: 3/23/50, Higginsport, Ohio BL/TL, 6'3", 180 lbs. Deb: 4/16/08

YEAR TM/L	W	L	PCT	G	GS	CG	SH	SV	IP	H	HR	BB	SO	RAT	ERA	ERA+	OAV	OOB	BH	AVG	PB	PR	/A	PD	TPI
1908 StL-N	3	8	.273	25	12	7	1	0	128²	144	1	36	39	12.8	3.15	75	.274	.324	2	.049	-3	-11	-11	0	-1.5
1909 StL-N	10	11	.476	32	27	12	1	0	219	223	3	59	55	11.8	2.42	104	.264	.315	8	.113	-2	4	3	0	0.0
1910 StL-N	7	8	.467	18	13	9	1	2	115	112	4	24	46	10.7	2.97	100	.251	.290	4	.108	-2	1	0	0	-0.1
1911 StL-N	15	9	.625	36	30	18	1	3	245	234	6	64	74	11.1	2.76	123	.257	.309	15	.169	-1	18	17	-2	1.3
1912 StL-N	16	17	.485	48	32	20	3	6	294	289	6	72	108	11.2	2.60	132	.257	.305	14	.136	-4	26	27	-2	1.9
1913 StL-N	19	15	.559	50	31	18	3	5	276	257	11	60	106	10.5	2.71	119	.255	.301	20	.211	2	15	16	0	1.9
1914 StL-N	18	17	.514	46	30	18	3	6	282¹	252	5	72	105	10.6	2.10	133	.246	.302	21	.231	2	22	22	-1	2.4
1915 StL-N	13	17	.433	46	33	17	2	3	275¹	245	6	57	91	10.0	2.84	98	.238	.280	11	.120	-4	-3	-2	-0	-0.5
1916 StL-N	5	5	.500	16	7	4	2	1	70	75	2	23	28	12.9	3.47	76	.290	.352	3	.167	-0	-7	-6	-1	-0.8
NY-N	9	4	.692	15	11	7	2	0	111²	96	2	10	35	8.5	1.37	178	.234	.252	9	.257	2	15	13	-2	1.5
Yr	14	9	.609	31	18	11	4	1	181²	171	4	33	63	10.1	2.18	115	.255	.290	3	.057	-2	9	7	-4	0.7
1917 *NY-N	18	7	.720	34	24	18	1	4	215²	199	4	34	54	9.8	2.17	118	.249	.280	17	.221	1	13	9	3	0.7
1918 NY-N	8	8	.500	18	16	12	1	2	132	122	3	12	33	**9.1**	2.25	117	.241	**.259**	5	.122	-2	8	6	-2	0.2
1919 *Cin-N	21	7	.750	29	28	22	4	0	227²	221	4	20	24	9.6	2.06	135	.258	.276	14	.189	2	22	18	-4	1.8
1920 Cin-N	5	6	.455	21	12	6	0	2	116	129	4	16	13	11.4	3.34	91	.293	.320	6	.171	-1	-3	-4	-3	-0.7
NY-N	1	0	1.000	5	1	1	0	0	17	16	0	0	2	8.5	1.59	189	.239	.239	1	.333	0	3	3	0	0.3
Yr	6	6	.500	26	13	7	0	2	133	145	4	16	15	10.9	3.11	97	.284	.306	4	.105	-0	0	-1	-3	-0.4
1921 NY-N	6	4	.600	37	0	0	0	2	96¹	115	7	14	23	12.1	3.64	101	.307	.332	8	.364	2	1	0	-1	0.1
Total 14	174	143	.549	476	307	189	25	36	2821²	2729	68	573	836	10.7	2.56	114	.257	.298	158	.171	-8	125	110	-21	8.7

■ ROGER SALMON

Salmon, Roger Elliott b: 5/11/1891, Newark, N.J. d: 6/17/74, Belfast, Me. BL/TL, 6'2", 170 lbs. Deb: 5/03/12

YEAR TM/L	W	L	PCT	G	GS	CG	SH	SV	IP	H	HR	BB	SO	RAT	ERA	ERA+	OAV	OOB	BH	AVG	PB	PR	/A	PD	TPI
1912 Phi-A	1	0	1.000	2	0	0	0	0	5	7	0	4	5	19.8	9.00	34	.318	.423	0	.000	-0	-3	-3	-0	-0.2

■ GUS SALVE

Salve, Augustus William b: 12/29/1885, Boston, Mass. d: 3/29/71, Providence, R.I. TL , 6', 190 lbs. Deb: 9/14/08

YEAR TM/L	W	L	PCT	G	GS	CG	SH	SV	IP	H	HR	BB	SO	RAT	ERA	ERA+	OAV	OOB	BH	AVG	PB	PR	/A	PD	TPI
1908 Phi-A	0	1	.000	2	1	0	0	0	15¹	17	1	9	6	15.8	4.11	62	.266	.365	0	.000	-1	-3	-3	-1	-0.3

■ JACK SALVESON

Salveson, John Theodore b: 1/5/14, Fullerton, Cal. d: 12/28/74, Norwalk, Cal. BR/TR, 6'0.5", 180 lbs. Deb: 6/03/33

YEAR TM/L	W	L	PCT	G	GS	CG	SH	SV	IP	H	HR	BB	SO	RAT	ERA	ERA+	OAV	OOB	BH	AVG	PB	PR	/A	PD	TPI
1933 NY-N	0	2	.000	8	2	2	0	0	30²	30	4	14	8	12.9	3.82	84	.252	.331	1	.111	-1	-2	-2	0	-0.1
1934 NY-N	3	1	.750	12	4	0	0	0	38¹	43	2	13	18	13.1	3.52	110	.281	.337	3	.300	0	2	1	0	0.2
1935 Pit-N	0	1	.000	5	0	0	0	0	7	11	1	5	2	21.9	9.00	46	.306	.405	0	.000	-0	-4	-4	1	-0.2
Chi-A	1	2	.333	20	2	2	0	1	66²	79	6	23	22	13.8	4.86	95	.298	.354	6	.300	2	-3	-2	-0	0.0
1943 Cle-A	5	3	.625	23	11	4	3	3	86	87	5	26	24	11.9	3.35	93	.266	.322	6	.231	2	-0	-2	2	0.0
1945 Cle-A	0	0	—	19	0	0	0	0	44	52	3	6	11	12.1	3.68	88	.294	.321	4	.400	3	-2	-2	1	0.2
Total 5	9	9	.500	87	19	8	3	4	272²	302	21	87	85	12.9	3.99	91	.280	.336	20	.260	6	-8	-11	2	0.1

■ MANNY SALVO

Salvo, Manuel "Gyp" b: 6/30/13, Sacramento, Cal. BR/TR, 6'4", 210 lbs. Deb: 4/22/39

YEAR TM/L	W	L	PCT	G	GS	CG	SH	SV	IP	H	HR	BB	SO	RAT	ERA	ERA+	OAV	OOB	BH	AVG	PB	PR	/A	PD	TPI
1939 NY-N	4	10	.286	32	18	4	0	1	136	150	11	75	69	15.2	4.63	85	.285	.380	4	.098	-2	-11	-11	1	-1.0
1940 Bos-N	10	9	.526	21	20	14	5	0	160²	151	9	43	60	11.0	3.08	121	.248	.300	6	.103	-2	14	11	-2	0.7
1941 Bos-N	7	16	.304	35	27	11	2	0	195	192	9	93	67	13.3	4.06	88	.255	.340	7	.113	-0	-9	-11	-0	-1.1
1942 Bos-N	7	8	.467	25	14	6	1	0	130²	129	7	41	25	12.0	3.03	110	.260	.322	5	.122	-1	4	4	-1	0.3
1943 Bos-N	0	1	.000	1	1	0	0	0	5	5	0	6	1	19.8	7.20	47	.250	.423	2	1.000	2	-2	-2	-0	0.0
Phi-N	0	0	—	1	0	0	0	0	0¹	2	0	1	0	81.0	27.00	12	.667	.750	0	—	0	-1	-1	0	0.0
Bos-N	5	6	.455	20	13	5	1	0	93²	94	6	25	25	11.5	3.27	105	.261	.311	6	.214	0	1	2	-0	0.2
Yr	5	7	.417	22	14	5	1	0	99	101	6	32	26	12.2	3.55	96	.264	.322	8	.257	2	-2	-1	-1	0.2
Total 5	33	50	.398	135	93	40	9	1	721¹	723	42	284	247	12.8	3.69	98	.261	.334	30	.129	-4	-4	-7	-2	-0.9

■ JOE SAMBITO

Sambito, Joseph Charles b: 6/28/52, Brooklyn, N.Y. BL/TL, 6'1", 185 lbs. Deb: 7/20/76

YEAR TM/L	W	L	PCT	G	GS	CG	SH	SV	IP	H	HR	BB	SO	RAT	ERA	ERA+	OAV	OOB	BH	AVG	PB	PR	/A	PD	TPI
1976 Hou-N	3	2	.600	20	4	1	1	1	53¹	45	4	14	26	10.0	3.54	90	.237	.289	2	.222	1	-0	-2	1	0.0
1977 Hou-N	5	5	.500	54	1	0	0	7	89	77	6	24	67	10.2	2.33	153	.235	.287	2	.154	-0	16	12	1	1.3
1978 Hou-N	4	9	.308	62	0	0	0	11	88	85	5	32	96	12.0	3.07	108	.260	.326	1	.167	-0	5	2	1	0.4
1979 Hou-N	8	7	.533	63	0	0	0	22	91¹	80	4	23	83	10.5	1.77	198	.235	.292	2	.286	2	**20**	18	0	2.1
1980 *Hou-N	8	4	.667	64	0	0	0	17	90¹	65	3	22	75	8.9	2.19	150	.200	.255	0	.000	-1	14	11	0	1.1
1981 *Hou-N	5	5	.500	49	0	0	0	10	63²	43	4	22	41	9.5	1.84	179	.192	.270	0	.000	-1	12	10	1	1.1
1982 Hou-N	0	0	—	9	0	0	0	0	12²	7	0	2	7	6.4	0.71	467	.159	.196	0	.000	-0	4	4	0	0.4
1984 Hou-N	0	0	—	32	0	0	0	0	47²	39	5	16	26	10.4	3.02	110	.228	.294	0	.000	-0	3	2	-1	0.0
1985 NY-N	0	0	—	8	0	0	0	0	10²	21	1	8	6	24.5	12.66	27	.420	.500	0	—	0	-11	-11	-0	-0.9
1986 *Bos-A	2	0	1.000	53	0	0	0	12	44²	52	6	30	14.5	4.84	86	.298	.362	0	—	-0	-3	-3	0	-0.2
1987 Bos-A	2	6	.250	47	0	0	0	0	37²	46	8	16	35	14.8	6.93	65	.301	.367	0	—	0	-10	-10	-0	-0.9
Total 11	37	38	.493	461	5	1	1	84	629	562	48	195	489	11.0	3.03	115	.241	.302	7	.135	2	49	32	3	4.4

YEAR	TM/L	W	L	PCT	G	GS	CG	SH	SV	IP	H	HR	BB	SO	RAT	ERA	ERA+	OAV	OOB	BH	AVG	PB	PR	/A	PD	TPI

■ BILL SAMPEN   Sampen, William Albert b: 1/18/63, Lincoln, Ill.   BR/TR, 6'1", 185 lbs.   Deb: 4/10/90

| 1990 | Mon-N | 12 | 7 | .632 | 59 | 4 | 0 | 0 | 2 | 90¹ | 94 | 7 | 33 | 69 | 12.9 | 2.99 | 126 | .268 | .334 | 0 | .000 | -1 | 8 | 8 | -1 | 0.6 |

■ JOE SAMUELS   Samuels, Joseph Jonas "Skabotch" b: 3/21/05, Scranton, Pa.   BR/TR, 6'1.5", 196 lbs.   Deb: 4/23/30

| 1930 | Det-A | 0 | 0 | — | 2 | 0 | 0 | 0 | 0 | 6 | 10 | 1 | 6 | 1 | 24.0 | 16.50 | 29 | .417 | .533 | 0 | .000 | -0 | -8 | -8 | -0 | -0.5 |

■ ROGER SAMUELS   Samuels, Roger Howard b: 1/3/61, San Jose, Cal.   BL/TL, 6'5", 210 lbs.   Deb: 7/20/88

1988	SF-N	1	2	.333	15	0	0	0	0	23¹	17	4	7	22	9.6	3.47	94	.202	.272	0	.000	-0	-0	-1	0	0.0
1989	Pit-N	0	0	—	5	0	0	0	0	3²	9	1	4	2	31.9	9.82	34	.474	.565	0	—	0	-3	-3	-0	-0.2
Total	2	1	2	.333	20	0	0	0	0	27	26	5	11	24	12.7	4.33	76	.252	.330	0	.000	-0	-3	-3	-0	-0.2

■ ALEX SANCHEZ   Sanchez, Alex Anthony b: 4/8/66, Concord, Cal.   BR/TR, 6'2", 185 lbs.   Deb: 5/23/89

| 1989 | Tor-A | 0 | 1 | .000 | 4 | 3 | 0 | 0 | 0 | 11² | 16 | 1 | 14 | 4 | 23.1 | 10.03 | 38 | .356 | .508 | 0 | — | 0 | -8 | -8 | 1 | -0.6 |

■ ISRAEL SANCHEZ   Sanchez, Israel (Matos) b: 8/20/63, Falcon Lasvias, Cuba   BL/TL, 5'9", 170 lbs.   Deb: 7/07/88

1988	KC-A	3	2	.600	19	1	0	0	1	35²	36	0	18	14	13.6	4.54	88	.265	.351	0	—	0	-2	-2	0	-0.1
1990	KC-A	0	0	—	11	0	0	0	0	9²	16	1	3	5	18.6	8.38	45	.381	.435	0	—	0	-5	-5	0	-0.4
Total	2	3	2	.600	30	1	0	0	1	45¹	52	1	21	19	14.7	5.36	74	.292	.370	0	—	0	-7	-7	0	-0.5

■ LUIS SANCHEZ   Sanchez, Luis Mercedes (b: Luis Mercedes Escoba (Sanchez)) b: 8/24/53, Cariaco, Sucre, Ven.   BR/TR, 6'2", 170 lbs.   Deb: 4/10/81

1981	Cal-A	0	2	.000	17	0	0	0	2	33²	39	4	11	13	13.6	2.94	124	.287	.345	0	—	0	3	3	-0	0.3
1982	*Cal-A	7	4	.636	46	0	0	0	5	92²	89	3	34	58	12.6	3.21	126	.259	.339	0	—	0	9	9	1	0.9
1983	Cal-A	10	8	.556	56	1	0	0	7	98¹	92	6	40	49	12.4	3.66	110	.254	.333	0	—	0	4	4	2	0.5
1984	Cal-A	9	7	.563	49	0	0	0	11	83²	84	10	33	62	12.9	3.33	119	.268	.343	0	—	0	6	6	-1	0.5
1985	Cal-A	2	0	1.000	26	0	0	0	2	61¹	67	9	27	34	13.9	5.72	72	.283	.358	0	—	0	-11	-11	0	-0.9
Total	5	28	21	.571	194	1	0	0	27	369²	371	32	145	216	12.9	3.75	107	.267	.342	0	—	0	11	10	2	1.3

■ RAUL SANCHEZ   Sanchez, Raul Guadalupe (Rodriguez) b: 12/12/30, Mariano, Cuba   BR/TR, 6', 150 lbs.   Deb: 4/17/52

1952	Was-A	1	1	.500	3	2	1	1	0	12²	13	0	7	6	14.2	3.55	100	.260	.351	0	.000	-1	0	0	0	0.0
1957	Cin-N	3	2	.600	38	0	0	0	5	62¹	61	7	25	37	13.0	4.76	86	.262	.344	2	.286	1	-6	-5	0	-0.3
1960	Cin-N	1	0	1.000	8	0	0	0	0	14²	12	1	11	5	16.0	4.91	78	.226	.388	1	.500	0	-2	-2	0	0.0
Total	3	5	3	.625	49	2	1	1	5	89²	86	8	43	48	13.7	4.62	86	.256	.352	3	.214	0	-8	-6	1	-0.3

■ BEN SANDERS   Sanders, Alexander Bennett b: 2/16/1865, Catharpen, Va.   d: 8/29/30, Memphis, Tenn.   BR/TR, 6', 210 lbs.   Deb: 6/06/1888 ♦

1888	Phi-N	19	10	.655	31	29	28	8	0	275¹	240	3	33	121	8.9	1.90	156	.226	.249	58	.246	5	29	32	4	5.2
1889	Phi-N	19	18	.514	44	39	34	1	1	349¹	406	9	96	123	12.9	3.55	123	.281	.326	47	.278	6	18	31	-2	3.4
1890	Phi-P	19	18	.514	43	40	37	2	1	346²	412	13	69	107	12.5	3.76	114	.283	.315	59	.312	10	18	20	1	2.7
1891	Phi-a	11	5	.688	19	18	15	0	0	145	157	3	37	40	12.0	3.79	101	.267	.310	39	.250	2	-1	1	-0	0.0
1892	Lou-N	12	19	.387	31	31	30	3	0	268¹	281	6	62	77	11.5	3.22	95	.259	.299	54	.273	10	2	-5	-1	0.9
Total	5	80	70	.533	168	157	144	14	2	1385	1496	34	297	468	11.7	3.24	116	.265	.302	257	.271	33	66	78	2	12.2

■ DEE SANDERS   Sanders, Dee Wilma b: 4/8/21, Quitman, Tex.   BR/TR, 6'3", 195 lbs.   Deb: 8/12/45

| 1945 | StL-A | 0 | 0 | — | 2 | 0 | 0 | 0 | 0 | 1¹ | 7 | 0 | 1 | 1 | 54.0 | 40.50 | 9 | .700 | .727 | 0 | — | 0 | -6 | -5 | 0 | -0.4 |

■ KEN SANDERS   Sanders, Kenneth George "Daffy" b: 7/8/41, St.Louis, Mo.   BR/TR, 5'11", 168 lbs.   Deb: 8/06/64

1964	KC-A	0	2	.000	21	0	0	0	1	27	23	2	17	18	13.7	3.67	104	.232	.350	0	—	0	-0	0	1	0.1
1966	Bos-A	3	6	.333	24	0	0	0	2	47¹	36	2	28	33	12.5	3.80	100	.214	.333	0	.000	-0	-2	-2	-0	0.0
	KC-A	3	4	.429	38	1	0	0	1	65¹	59	7	48	41	14.9	3.72	91	.250	.379	2	.250	-2	-2	-1	1	-0.1
	Yr	6	10	.375	62	1	0	0	3	112²	95	9	76	74	13.7	3.75	95	.233	.355	2	.143	-2	-4	-2	1	-0.1
1968	Oak-A	0	1	.000	7	0	0	0	0	10²	8	1	8	6	13.5	3.38	84	.229	.372	0	—	0	-0	-1	0	0.0
1970	Mil-A	5	2	.714	50	0	0	0	13	92¹	64	8	25	64	9.1	1.75	216	.201	.268	3	.231	1	20	21	1	2.5
1971	Mil-A	7	12	.368	83	0	0	0	31	136¹	111	9	34	80	9.8	1.91	181	.227	.282	0	.000	-1	23	24	2	2.7
1972	Mil-A	2	9	.182	62	0	0	0	17	92¹	88	10	31	51	11.8	3.12	97	.245	.309	1	.143	0	-1	-1	1	0.0
1973	Min-A	2	4	.333	27	0	0	0	8	44¹	53	4	21	19	15.4	6.09	65	.299	.382	0	—	0	-11	-11	1	-0.9
	Cle-A	5	1	.833	15	0	0	0	5	27¹	18	2	9	14	8.9	1.65	238	.188	.257	0	—	0	7	7	0	0.7
	Yr	7	5	.583	42	0	0	0	13	71²	71	6	30	33	12.7	4.40	90	.255	.328	0	—	0	-5	-4	1	-0.2
1974	Cle-A	0	1	.000	11	0	0	0	1	11	21	5	5	5	21.3	9.82	37	.404	.456	0	—	0	-8	-8	0	-0.7
	Cal-A	0	0	—	9	0	0	0	1	9²	10	0	3	4	12.1	2.79	123	.278	.333	0	—	0	1	1	1	0.1
	Yr	0	1	.000	18	0	0	0	2	20²	31	5	8	8	17.0	6.53	54	.352	.406	0	—	0	-7	-7	1	-0.6
1975	NY-N	1	1	.500	29	0	0	0	5	43	31	2	14	8	9.4	2.30	150	.205	.273	0	.000	-0	6	5	0	0.6
1976	NY-N	1	2	.333	31	0	0	0	1	47	39	4	12	16	10.0	2.87	115	.231	.286	0	.000	-0	3	2	1	0.3
	KC-A	0	0	—	3	0	0	0	0	3	3	0	3	2	18.0	0.00	—	.273	.429	0	—	0	1	1	0	0.1
Total	10	29	45	.392	408	1	0	0	86	656²	564	49	258	360	11.5	2.97	118	.235	.314	6	.115	-0	38	39	8	5.4

■ ROY SANDERS   Sanders, Roy Garvin "Butch" or "Pepe" b: 8/1/1892, Stafford, Kan.   d: 1/17/50, Kansas City, Mo.   BR/TR, 6'0.5", 195 lbs.   Deb: 4/16/17

1917	Cin-N	0	1	.000	2	2	0	0	0	14	12	0	16	3	18.6	4.50	58	.273	.475	0	.000	-1	-3	-3	1	-0.2
1918	Pit-N	7	9	.438	28	14	6	1	1	156	135	1	52	55	10.9	2.60	111	.239	.305	8	.151	-1	3	5	1	0.6
Total	2	7	10	.412	30	16	7	1	1	170	147	1	68	58	11.5	2.75	104	.241	.321	8	.136	-2	0	2	2	0.4

■ ROY SANDERS   Sanders, Roy L. "Simon" b: 1894,   BR/TR, 6', 185 lbs.   Deb: 8/06/18

1918	NY-A	0	2	.000	6	2	0	0	0	25²	28	0	16	8	16.1	4.21	67	.301	.414	0	.000	-1	-4	-4	-1	-0.5
1920	StL-A	1	1	.500	8	1	0	0	0	17¹	20	1	17	2	19.7	5.19	75	.313	.463	0	.000	-1	-3	-2	-0	-0.2
Total	2	1	3	.250	14	3	0	0	0	43	48	1	33	10	17.6	4.60	71	.306	.435	0	.000	-2	-7	-6	-1	-0.7

■ WAR SANDERS   Sanders, Warren Williams b: 8/2/1877, Maynardville, Tenn.   d: 8/3/62, Chattanooga, Tenn.   BR/TL, 5'10", 160 lbs.   Deb: 4/18/03

1903	StL-N	1	6	.143	8	6	3	0	0	40	48	0	21	9	16.0	6.07	54	.286	.372	1	.067	-2	-12	-12	-0	-1.2
1904	StL-N	1	2	.333	4	3	1	0	0	19	25	1	1	11	12.4	4.74	57	.298	.314	0	.000	-1	-4	-4	0	-0.4
Total	2	2	8	.200	12	9	4	0	0	59	73	1	22	20	14.9	5.64	55	.290	.354	1	.048	-2	-17	-17	-0	-1.6

■ SCOTT SANDERSON   Sanderson, Scott Douglas b: 7/22/56, Dearborn, Mich.   BR/TR, 6'5", 195 lbs.   Deb: 8/06/78

1978	Mon-N	4	2	.667	10	9	1	1	0	61	52	3	21	50	10.9	2.51	140	.232	.301	2	.105	-1	7	7	-1	0.5
1979	Mon-N	9	8	.529	34	24	5	3	1	168	148	16	54	138	11.0	3.43	107	.236	.300	8	.160	-0	6	4	-2	0.2
1980	Mon-N	16	11	.593	33	33	7	3	0	211¹	206	16	56	125	11.3	3.11	115	.257	.308	5	.078	-3	12	11	-2	0.6
1981	*Mon-N	9	7	.563	22	22	4	1	0	137¹	122	10	31	77	10.1	2.95	118	.236	.281	4	.114	2	8	8	-2	0.9
1982	Mon-N	12	12	.500	32	32	7	0	0	224	212	24	58	158	11.0	3.46	105	.251	.301	8	.140	1	4	5	-4	0.2
1983	Mon-N	6	7	.462	18	16	0	0	1	81¹	98	12	20	55	13.1	4.65	77	.303	.344	4	.143	-1	-9	-10	-1	-1.0
1984	*Chi-N	8	5	.615	24	24	3	0	0	140²	140	6	24	76	10.6	3.14	125	.264	.298	5	.119	-1	7	12	1	1.4
1985	Chi-N	5	6	.455	19	19	2	0	0	121	100	13	27	80	9.4	3.12	128	.228	.273	2	.065	-2	6	12	1	1.2
1986	Chi-N	9	11	.450	37	28	1	1	1	169²	165	21	37	124	10.8	4.19	96	.255	.297	3	.059	-4	-9	-3	-1	-0.6
1987	Chi-N	8	9	.471	32	22	0	0	0	144²	156	23	50	106	13.0	4.29	100	.274	.336	3	.075	-1	-3	-0	-1	-0.1
1988	Chi-N	1	2	.333	11	0	0	0	0	15¹	13	1	3	6	9.4	5.28	68	.232	.271	0	—	0	-3	-3	-0	-0.2
1989	*Chi-N	11	9	.550	37	23	2	0	0	146¹	155	16	31	86	11.6	3.94	95	.273	.313	2	.047	-2	-7	-3	-2	-0.6
1990	*Oak-A	17	11	.607	34	34	2	1	0	206¹	205	26	66	128	12.0	3.88	96	.255	.315	0	—	0	1	-3	-2	-0.5
Total	13	115	100	.535	343	286	34	10	5	1827	1772	189	478	1209	11.2	3.59	105	.255	.305	46	.100	-11	18	37	-16	2.0

YEAR	TM/L	W	L	PCT	G	GS	CG	SH	SV	IP	H	HR	BB	SO	RAT	ERA	ERA+	OAV	OOB	BH	AVG	PB	PR	/A	PD	TPI
■ FRED SANFORD	Sanford, John Frederick b: 8/9/19, Garfield, Utah BB/TR, 6'1", 200 lbs. Deb: 5/05/43																									
1943	StL-A	0	0	—	3	0	0	0	0	9¹	7	0	4	2	10.6	1.93	172	.219	.306	0	—	0	1	1	0	0.2
1946	StL-A	2	1	.667	3	3	2	2	0	22	19	0	9	8	11.5	2.05	182	.235	.311	2	.286	1	4	4	0	0.6
1947	StL-A	7	16	.304	34	23	9	0	4	186²	186	17	76	62	12.6	3.71	104	.261	.332	11	.204	-0	-0	3	-1	0.2
1948	StL-A	12	21	.364	42	33	9	1	2	227	250	19	91	79	13.6	4.64	98	.279	.347	11	.151	-2	-9	-2	1	-0.2
1949	NY-A	7	3	.700	29	11	3	0	0	95¹	100	9	57	51	14.8	3.87	105	.270	.367	4	.118	-2	3	2	-0	0.0
1950	NY-A	5	4	.556	26	12	2	0	0	112²	103	9	79	54	14.6	4.55	94	.252	.374	8	.229	1	0	-3	3	0.0
1951	NY-A	0	3	.000	11	2	0	0	0	26²	15	2	25	10	13.5	3.71	103	.169	.351	0	.000	-1	1	0	1	0.0
	Was-A	2	3	.400	7	7	0	0	0	37	51	5	27	12	19.0	6.57	62	.329	.429	1	.071	-1	-10	-10	-1	-1.0
	StL-A	2	4	.333	9	7	1	0	0	27¹	37	6	23	7	19.8	10.21	43	.308	.420	2	.286	-1	-18	-18	-0	-1.4
	Yr	4	10	.286	27	16	1	0	0	91	103	13	75	29	17.6	6.82	60	.283	.405	4	.154	-1	-27	-27	0	-2.4
Total	7	37	55	.402	164	98	26	3	6	744	768	67	391	285	14.1	4.45	94	.268	.357	39	.170	-4	-28	-21	3	-1.6
■ JACK SANFORD	Sanford, John Stanley b: 5/18/29, Wellesley Hills, Mass. BR/TR, 6', 190 lbs. Deb: 9/16/56 C																									
1956	Phi-N	1	0	1.000	3	1	0	0	0	13	7	0	13	6	14.5	1.38	269	.184	.404	1	.333	0	3	3	0	0.4
1957	Phi-N	19	8	.704	33	33	15	3	0	236²	194	22	94	**188**	11.1	3.08	124	**.221**	.298	15	.169	-1	21	19	-1	1.7
1958	Phi-N	10	13	.435	38	27	7	2	0	186¹	197	15	81	106	13.6	4.44	89	.274	.350	10	.169	1	-10	-10	-2	-0.9
1959	SF-N	15	12	.556	36	31	10	0	1	222¹	198	22	70	132	11.1	3.16	121	.235	.300	8	.111	1	20	16	-1	1.4
1960	SF-N	12	14	.462	37	34	11	6	0	219	199	11	99	125	12.3	3.82	91	.243	.326	13	.176	1	-1	-8	-1	-0.7
1961	SF-N	13	9	.591	38	33	6	0	0	217¹	203	22	87	112	12.2	4.22	90	.249	.325	16	.216	5	-5	-10	-0	-0.4
1962	*SF-N	24	7	.774	39	38	13	2	0	265¹	233	23	92	147	11.1	3.43	111	.234	.301	15	.153	0	15	11	2	1.3
1963	SF-N	16	13	.552	42	42	11	0	0	284¹	273	21	76	158	11.2	3.51	91	.251	.303	13	.138	3	-7	-10	-3	-0.4
1964	SF-N	5	7	.417	18	17	3	1	1	106¹	91	7	37	64	11.2	3.30	108	.228	.300	4	.133	1	3	3	1	0.5
1965	SF-N	4	5	.444	23	16	0	0	2	91	92	11	30	43	12.8	3.96	91	.256	.325	3	.120	-0	-4	-4	0	-0.3
	Cal-A	1	2	.333	9	5	0	0	1	29¹	35	2	10	13	13.8	4.60	74	.324	.381	1	.143	0	-4	-4	1	-0.3
1966	Cal-A	13	7	.650	50	6	0	0	5	108	108	11	27	54	11.6	3.83	88	.271	.323	3	.136	1	-5	-6	1	-0.3
1967	Cal-A	3	2	.600	12	9	0	0	1	48¹	53	6	7	21	11.2	4.47	70	.288	.314	3	.200	1	-7	-7	1	-0.4
	KC-A	1	2	.333	10	1	0	0	0	22	24	1	14	13	16.4	6.55	49	.296	.412	0	.000	-0	-8	-8	1	-0.7
	Yr	4	4	.500	22	10	0	0	1	70¹	77	7	21	34	12.8	5.12	62	.288	.345	2	.111	-1	-15	-15	2	-1.1
Total	12	137	101	.576	388	293	76	14	11	2049¹	1907	174	737	1182	11.8	3.69	98	.247	.316	105	.158	11	11	-14	5	0.9
■ JOSE SANTIAGO	Santiago, Jose Guillermo (Guzman) "Pants" b: 9/4/28, Coamo, P.R. BR/TR, 5'10", 175 lbs. Deb: 4/17/54																									
1954	Cle-A	0	0	—	1	0	0	0	0	1²	0	0	2	1	10.8	0.00	—	.000	.286	0	—	0	1	1	-0	0.1
1955	Cle-A	2	0	1.000	17	0	0	0	0	32²	31	1	14	19	13.8	2.48	161	.256	.357	2	.500	1	5	5	0	0.7
1956	KC-A	1	2	.333	9	5	0	0	0	21²	36	8	17	9	24.1	8.31	52	.387	.504	2	.400	0	-10	-10	0	-0.7
Total	3	3	2	.600	27	5	0	0	0	56	67	9	33	29	17.7	4.66	88	.306	.420	4	.444	2	-4	-3	0	0.1
■ JOSE SANTIAGO	Santiago, Jose Rafael (Alfonso) b: 8/15/40, Juana Diaz, P.R. BR/TR, 6'2", 185 lbs. Deb: 9/09/63																									
1963	KC-A	1	0	1.000	4	0	0	0	0	7	8	4	2	6	12.9	9.00	43	.276	.323	0	—	0	-4	-4	0	-0.3
1964	KC-A	0	6	.000	34	8	0	0	0	83²	84	9	35	64	13.2	4.73	81	.258	.337	0	.000	-2	-10	-9	-1	-1.0
1965	KC-A	0	0	—	4	0	0	0	0	5	8	1	4	8	21.6	9.00	39	.364	.462	0	—	0	-3	-3	0	-0.2
1966	Bos-A	12	13	.480	35	28	7	1	2	172	155	17	58	119	11.3	3.66	104	.238	.302	11	.196	0	-4	3	-1	0.3
1967	*Bos-A	12	4	.750	50	11	2	0	5	145¹	138	14	47	109	11.6	3.59	97	.251	.313	8	.190	2	-6	-2	0	0.1
1968	Bos-A	9	4	.692	18	18	7	2	0	124	96	9	42	86	10.2	2.25	140	.215	.287	7	.163	1	10	13	-0	1.6
1969	Bos-A	0	0	—	10	0	0	0	0	7²	11	2	4	4	17.6	3.52	108	.324	.395	0	—	0	0	0	-0	0.0
1970	Bos-A	0	2	.000	8	0	0	0	1	11¹	18	0	8	8	20.6	10.32	38	.353	.441	2	.667	1	-8	-8	-0	-0.6
Total	8	34	29	.540	163	65	16	3	8	556	518	56	200	404	11.8	3.74	96	.246	.314	28	.173	3	-26	-10	-2	-0.1
■ AL SANTORINI	Santorini, Alan Joel b: 5/19/48, Irvington, N.J. BR/TR, 6', 190 lbs. Deb: 9/10/68																									
1968	Atl-N	0	1	.000	1	1	0	0	0	3	4	1	0	0	12.0	0.00	—	.286	.286	0	—	0	1	1	0	0.1
1969	SD-N	8	14	.364	32	30	2	1	0	184²	194	11	73	111	13.4	3.95	90	.270	.343	7	.111	-1	-7	-8	1	-0.9
1970	SD-N	1	8	.111	21	12	0	0	0	75²	91	11	43	41	16.3	6.07	66	.294	.385	0	.000	-2	-17	-18	-1	-1.8
1971	SD-N	0	2	.000	18	3	0	0	0	38¹	43	4	11	21	12.7	3.76	88	.285	.333	2	.400	1	-1	-2	-1	-0.1
	StL-N	0	2	.000	19	5	0	0	2	49²	51	2	19	21	12.9	3.81	95	.270	.340	3	.300	1	-2	-1	-0	0.0
	Yr	0	4	.000	37	8	0	0	2	88	94	6	30	42	12.8	3.78	92	.275	.335	5	.231	1	-3	-3	-1	-0.1
1972	StL-N	8	11	.421	30	19	3	3	0	133²	136	6	46	72	12.3	4.11	83	.263	.324	3	.075	-2	-10	-10	-1	-1.3
1973	StL-N	0	0	—	6	0	0	0	0	8¹	14	1	2	2	18.4	5.40	67	.400	.447	0	.000	-0	-2	-2	-0	-0.1
Total	6	17	38	.309	127	70	5	4	3	493¹	533	36	194	268	13.5	4.29	83	.276	.346	15	.109	-4	-38	-40	-2	-4.1
■ MANNY SARMIENTO	Sarmiento, Manuel Eduardo (Aponte) b: 2/2/56, Cagua, Venez. BR/TR, 6', 170 lbs. Deb: 7/30/76																									
1976	*Cin-N	5	1	.833	22	0	0	0	0	43²	36	1	12	20	10.1	2.06	170	.222	.280	0	.000	-1	7	7	-1	0.6
1977	Cin-N	0	0	—	24	0	0	0	1	40¹	28	6	11	23	8.7	2.45	160	.196	.253	0	.000	-0	7	7	-1	0.6
1978	Cin-N	9	7	.563	63	4	0	0	5	127¹	109	16	54	72	11.6	4.38	81	.234	.315	0	.000	-1	-11	-12	-0	-1.3
1979	Cin-N	0	4	.000	23	1	0	0	0	38²	47	2	7	23	12.8	4.66	80	.311	.346	0	.000	-1	-4	-4	-0	-0.4
1980	Sea-A	0	1	.000	9	0	0	0	1	14²	14	2	6	15	12.3	3.68	112	.255	.328	0	—	0	1	1	-0	0.0
1982	Pit-N	9	4	.692	35	17	4	0	1	164²	153	7	46	81	10.9	3.39	109	.246	.298	9	.191	1	4	6	-2	0.5
1983	Pit-N	3	5	.375	52	0	0	0	4	84¹	74	8	36	49	11.7	2.99	124	.243	.324	0	.000	-1	6	7	-1	0.6
Total	7	26	22	.542	228	22	4	0	12	513²	461	42	172	283	11.1	3.49	106	.242	.306	9	.103	-3	9	11	-5	0.6
■ KEVIN SAUCIER	Saucier, Kevin Andrew b: 8/9/56, Pensacola, Fla. BR/TL, 6'1", 190 lbs. Deb: 10/01/78																									
1978	Phi-N	0	1	.000	1	0	0	0	0	2	4	0	1	2	27.0	18.00	20	.400	.500	0	—	0	-3	-3	0	-0.2
1979	Phi-N	1	4	.200	29	2	0	0	1	62¹	68	4	33	21	15.0	4.19	91	.291	.385	1	.100	-1	-3	-3	1	-0.2
1980	*Phi-N	7	3	.700	40	0	0	0	0	50	50	2	20	25	13.3	3.42	111	.281	.366	0	.000	-1	1	2	0	0.2
1981	Det-A	4	2	.667	38	0	0	0	13	49	26	1	21	23	9.6	1.65	228	.160	.277	0	—	0	11	12	0	1.3
1982	Det-A	3	1	.750	31	1	0	0	5	40¹	35	0	29	23	14.7	3.12	130	.254	.391	0	—	0	4	4	0	0.4
Total	5	15	11	.577	139	3	0	0	19	203²	183	7	104	94	13.3	3.31	116	.253	.359	1	.056	-2	10	12	1	1.5
■ DENNIS SAUNDERS	Saunders, Dennis James b: 1/4/49, Alhambra, Cal. BB/TR, 6'3", 195 lbs. Deb: 5/21/70																									
1970	Det-A	1	1	.500	8	0	0	0	1	14	16	1	5	8	14.1	3.21	116	.286	.355	0	.000	-1	1	1	1	0.1
■ RICH SAUVEUR	Sauveur, Richard Daniel b: 11/23/63, Arlington, Va. BL/TL, 6'4", 163 lbs. Deb: 7/01/86																									
1986	Pit-N	0	0	—	3	3	0	0	0	12	17	3	6	6	18.8	6.00	64	.354	.446	1	.333	0	-3	-3	1	-0.1
1988	Mon-N	0	0	—	4	0	0	0	0	3	3	1	2	3	15.0	6.00	60	.250	.357	0	—	0	-1	-1	0	0.0
Total	2	0	0	—	7	3	0	0	0	15	20	4	8	9	18.0	6.00	63	.333	.429	1	.333	0	-4	-4	1	-0.1
■ JACK SAVAGE	Savage, John Joseph b: 4/22/64, Louisville, Ky. BR/TR, 6'3", 190 lbs. Deb: 9/14/87																									
1987	LA-N	0	0	—	3	0	0	0	0	3¹	4	0	0	0	10.8	2.70	147	.286	.286	0	—	0	1	1	.0	0.0
1990	Min-A	0	2	.000	17	0	0	0	1	26	37	3	11	12	16.6	8.31	50	.339	.400	0	—	0	-13	-12	0	-1.1
Total	2	0	2	.000	20	0	0	0	1	29¹	41	3	11	12	16.0	7.67	54	.333	.388	0	—	0	-12	-11	0	-1.1
■ BOB SAVAGE	Savage, John Robert b: 12/1/21, Manchester, N.H. BR/TR, 6'2", 180 lbs. Deb: 6/24/42																									
1942	Phi-A	0	1	.000	8	3	0	0	0	30²	24	0	31	10	16.1	3.23	117	.220	.393	1	.111	0	1	2	-0	0.2
1946	Phi-A	3	15	.167	40	19	7	1	2	164	164	5	93	78	14.2	4.06	87	.259	.355	5	.122	1	-10	-9	-3	-1.1
1947	Phi-A	8	10	.444	44	8	2	1	2	146	135	8	55	56	11.7	3.76	101	.245	.314	2	.050	-4	-1	1	-2	-0.4
1948	Phi-A	5	1	.833	33	1	1	0	5	75¹	98	9	33	26	15.7	6.21	69	.318	.384	1	.077	-1	-16	-16	-1	-1.5

YEAR	TM/L	W	L	PCT	G	GS	CG	SH	SV	IP	H	HR	BB	SO	RAT	ERA	ERA+	OAV	OOB	BH	AVG	PB	PR	/A	PD	TPI
1949	StL-A	0	0	—	4	0	0	0	0	7	12	1	3	1	19.3	6.43	70	.400	.455	0	.000	-0	-2	-1	0	0.0
Total 5		16	27	.372	129	31	10	2	9	423	433	23	215	171	13.8	4.32	88	.265	.352	9	.087	-4	-27	-24	-6	-2.8

■ DON SAVIDGE
Savidge, Donald Snyder b: 8/28/08, Berwick, Pa. d: 3/22/83, Santa Barbara, Cal BR/TR, 6'1", 180 lbs. Deb: 8/06/29

YEAR	TM/L	W	L	PCT	G	GS	CG	SH	SV	IP	H	HR	BB	SO	RAT	ERA	ERA+	OAV	OOB	BH	AVG	PB	PR	/A	PD	TPI
1929	Was-A	0	0	—	3	0	0	0	0	6	12	1	2	2	21.0	9.00	47	.414	.452	0		0	-3	-3	0	-0.2

■ RALPH SAVIDGE
Savidge, Ralph Austin "The Human Whipcord" b: 2/3/1879, Jerseytown, Pa. d: 7/22/59, Berwick, Pa. BR/TR, 6'2", 210 lbs. Deb: 9/22/08

YEAR	TM/L	W	L	PCT	G	GS	CG	SH	SV	IP	H	HR	BB	SO	RAT	ERA	ERA+	OAV	OOB	BH	AVG	PB	PR	/A	PD	TPI
1908	Cin-N	0	1	.000	4	1	1	0	0	21	18	0	8	7	11.1	2.57	90	.247	.321	0	.000	-1	-0	-1	-1	-0.1
1909	Cin-N	0	0	—	1	0	0	0	0	4	10	1	3	2	31.5	22.50	12	.588	.667	0	.000	-0	-9	-9	0	-0.6
Total 2		0	1	.000	5	1	1	0	0	25	28	1	11	9	14.4	5.76	41	.311	.392	0	.000	-1	-9	-9	-1	-0.7

■ MOE SAVRANSKY
Savransky, Morris b: 1/13/29, Cleveland, Ohio BL/TL, 5'11", 175 lbs. Deb: 4/23/54

YEAR	TM/L	W	L	PCT	G	GS	CG	SH	SV	IP	H	HR	BB	SO	RAT	ERA	ERA+	OAV	OOB	BH	AVG	PB	PR	/A	PD	TPI
1954	Cin-N	0	2	.000	16	0	0	0	0	24	23	6	8	7	12.4	4.88	86	.247	.320	1	.500	1	-2	-2	1	0.0

■ RICK SAWYER
Sawyer, Richard Clyde b: 4/7/48, Bakersfield, Cal. BR/TR, 6'2", 205 lbs. Deb: 4/28/74

YEAR	TM/L	W	L	PCT	G	GS	CG	SH	SV	IP	H	HR	BB	SO	RAT	ERA	ERA+	OAV	OOB	BH	AVG	PB	PR	/A	PD	TPI
1974	NY-A	0	0	—	1	0	0	0	0	1²	2	0	1	1	16.2	16.20	22	.500	.600	0	—	0	-2	-2	-0	-0.1
1975	NY-A	0	0	—	4	0	0	0	0	6	7	0	2	3	13.5	3.00	121	.304	.360	0	—	0	1	0	-0	0.0
1976	SD-N	5	3	.625	13	11	4	2	0	81²	84	2	38	33	13.6	2.53	129	.272	.353	5	.208	1	9	7	-0	0.8
1977	SD-N	7	6	.538	56	9	0	0	0	111	136	15	55	45	16.1	5.84	61	.316	.402	3	.150	1	-24	-28	1	-2.5
Total 4		12	9	.571	74	20	4	2	0	200¹	229	17	96	82	15.0	4.49	76	.299	.382	8	.182	2	-17	-24	1	-1.8

■ WILL SAWYER
Sawyer, Willard Newton b: 7/29/1864, Brimfield, Ohio d: 1/5/36, Kent, Ohio BL/TL, Deb: 7/21/1883

YEAR	TM/L	W	L	PCT	G	GS	CG	SH	SV	IP	H	HR	BB	SO	RAT	ERA	ERA+	OAV	OOB	BH	AVG	PB	PR	/A	PD	TPI
1883	Cle-N	4	10	.286	17	15	15	0	0	141	119	1	47	76	10.6	2.36	133	.215	.277	1	.021	-7	12	12	-3	0.2

■ BILL SAYLES
Sayles, William Nisbeth b: 7/27/17, Portland, Ore. BR/TR, 6'2", 175 lbs. Deb: 7/17/39

YEAR	TM/L	W	L	PCT	G	GS	CG	SH	SV	IP	H	HR	BB	SO	RAT	ERA	ERA+	OAV	OOB	BH	AVG	PB	PR	/A	PD	TPI
1939	Bos-A	0	0	—	5	0	0	0	0	14	14	1	13	9	17.4	7.07	67	.264	.409	1	.143	-0	-4	-4	0	-0.3
1943	NY-N	1	3	.250	18	3	1	0	0	53	60	1	23	38	14.1	4.75	72	.284	.355	4	.308	1	-8	-8	-0	-0.7
	Bro-N	0	0	—	5	0	0	0	0	11²	13	0	10	5	17.7	7.71	44	.271	.397	1	.500	0	-6	-6	-0	-0.5
	Yr	1	3	.250	23	3	1	0	0	64²	73	1	33	43	14.8	5.29	65	.282	.363	0	.000	1	-14	-13	-1	-1.2
Total 2		1	3	.250	28	3	1	0	0	78²	87	2	46	52	15.2	5.61	65	.279	.372	6	.273	1	-17	-17	-1	-1.5

■ PHIL SAYLOR
Saylor, Philip Andrew "Lefty" b: 1/2/1871, Van Wert Co., Ohio d: 7/23/37, W.Alexandria, O. TL, Deb: 7/11/1891

YEAR	TM/L	W	L	PCT	G	GS	CG	SH	SV	IP	H	HR	BB	SO	RAT	ERA	ERA+	OAV	OOB	BH	AVG	PB	PR	/A	PD	TPI
1891	Phi-N	0	0	—	1	0	0	0	0	3	2	1	0	0	6.0	6.00	57	.182	.182	0	.000	-0	-1	-1	0	0.0

■ FRANK SCANLAN
Scanlan, Frank Aloysius b: 4/28/1890, Syracuse, N.Y. d: 4/9/69, Brooklyn, N.Y. 6'1.5", 175 lbs. Deb: 8/06/09

YEAR	TM/L	W	L	PCT	G	GS	CG	SH	SV	IP	H	HR	BB	SO	RAT	ERA	ERA+	OAV	OOB	BH	AVG	PB	PR	/A	PD	TPI
1909	Phi-N	0	0	—	6	0	0	0	1	11	8	0	5	5	10.6	1.64	159	.211	.302	0	.000	-1	1	1	-0	0.0

■ DOC SCANLAN
Scanlan, William Dennis b: 3/7/1881, Syracuse, N.Y. d: 5/29/49, Brooklyn, N.Y. BL/TR, 5'8", 165 lbs. Deb: 9/24/03

YEAR	TM/L	W	L	PCT	G	GS	CG	SH	SV	IP	H	HR	BB	SO	RAT	ERA	ERA+	OAV	OOB	BH	AVG	PB	PR	/A	PD	TPI
1903	Pit-N	0	1	.000	1	1	1	0	0	9	5	0	6	0	11.0	4.00	81	.167	.306	0	.000	0	-1	-1	-0	0.0
1904	Pit-N	1	3	.250	4	3	1	0	0	22	21	0	20	10	17.6	4.91	56	.236	.387	0	.000	-1	-5	-5	-0	-0.5
	Bro-N	6	6	.500	13	12	11	3	0	104	94	0	40	40	11.0	2.16	127	.242	.316	5	.143	-1	7	7	-2	0.3
	Yr	7	9	.438	17	15	12	3	0	126	115	0	60	50	12.6	2.64	104	.240	.327	2	.049	-2	1	1	-2	-0.2
1905	Bro-N	14	12	.538	33	28	22	2	0	250	220	4	104	135	12.0	2.92	99	.237	.319	16	.167	-1	2	-1	-3	-0.5
1906	Bro-N	18	13	.581	38	33	28	6	2	288	230	5	127	120	11.3	3.19	79	.214	.301	18	.186	3	-18	-21	-8	-2.8
1907	Bro-N	6	8	.429	17	15	10	2	0	107	90	1	61	59	13.0	3.20	73	.239	.349	9	.265	5	-9	-10	-2	-0.8
1909	Bro-N	8	7	.533	19	17	12	2	0	141¹	125	2	65	72	12.4	2.93	89	.252	.343	12	.273	5	-5	-5	-1	-0.1
1910	Bro-N	9	11	.450	34	25	14	0	2	217¹	175	1	106	103	12.3	2.61	116	.234	.341	14	.203	1	10	10	-2	0.9
1911	Bro-N	3	10	.231	22	15	3	0	1	113²	101	2	69	45	13.9	3.64	92	.256	.374	4	.121	-2	-3	-4	-0	-0.6
Total 8		65	71	.478	181	149	102	15	5	1252¹	1061	15	608	584	12.3	3.00	93	.234	.330	78	.188	8	-21	-31	-19	-4.1

■ PAT SCANTLEBURY
Scantlebury, Patrico Athelstan b: 11/11/25, Gatun, Canal Zone BL/TL, 6'1", 180 lbs. Deb: 4/19/56

YEAR	TM/L	W	L	PCT	G	GS	CG	SH	SV	IP	H	HR	BB	SO	RAT	ERA	ERA+	OAV	OOB	BH	AVG	PB	PR	/A	PD	TPI
1956	Cin-N	0	1	.000	6	2	0	0	0	19	24	5	5	10	13.7	6.63	60	.293	.333	0	.000	-0	-6	-6	0	-0.5

■ RANDY SCARBERY
Scarbery, Randy James b: 6/22/52, Fresno, Cal. BB/TR, 6'1", 185 lbs. Deb: 4/16/79

YEAR	TM/L	W	L	PCT	G	GS	CG	SH	SV	IP	H	HR	BB	SO	RAT	ERA	ERA+	OAV	OOB	BH	AVG	PB	PR	/A	PD	TPI
1979	Chi-A	2	8	.200	45	5	0	0	4	101¹	102	9	34	45	12.3	4.62	92	.262	.326	0	—	0	-5	-4	0	-0.3
1980	Chi-A	1	2	.333	15	0	0	0	2	28²	24	1	7	18	10.4	4.08	99	.238	.300	0	—	0	-0	-0	-0	0.0
Total 2		3	10	.231	60	5	0	0	6	130	126	10	41	63	11.9	4.50	93	.257	.320	0	—	0	-5	-4	0	-0.3

■ RAY SCARBOROUGH
Scarborough, Ray Wilson (b: Rae Wilson Scarborough) b: 7/23/17, Mt.Gilead, N.C. d: 7/1/82, Mount Olive, N.C. BR/TR, 6', 185 lbs. Deb: 6/26/42 C

YEAR	TM/L	W	L	PCT	G	GS	CG	SH	SV	IP	H	HR	BB	SO	RAT	ERA	ERA+	OAV	OOB	BH	AVG	PB	PR	/A	PD	TPI
1942	Was-A	2	1	.667	17	5	1	1	0	63¹	68	2	32	16	14.2	4.12	89	.272	.355	4	.190	0	-3	-3	1	-0.2
1943	Was-A	4	4	.500	24	6	2	0	3	86	93	2	46	43	14.5	2.83	113	.273	.359	8	.333	2	5	4	-0	0.6
1946	Was-A	7	11	.389	32	20	6	1	1	155²	176	8	74	46	14.5	4.05	83	.286	.364	7	.140	-2	-9	-12	2	-1.1
1947	Was-A	6	13	.316	33	18	8	2	0	161	165	5	67	63	13.0	3.41	109	.267	.339	6	.120	-3	5	6	-0	0.2
1948	Was-A	15	8	.652	31	26	9	0	1	185¹	166	10	72	76	11.7	2.82	154	.233	.307	14	.219	-0	30	31	1	3.3
1949	Was-A	13	11	.542	34	27	11	1	0	199²	204	10	88	81	13.5	4.60	93	.265	.346	13	.194	-0	-9	-8	1	-0.6
1950	Was-A	3	5	.375	8	8	4	2	0	58¹	62	1	22	24	13.3	4.01	112	.276	.345	2	.100	-1	4	3	1	0.2
	Chi-A	10	13	.435	27	23	8	1	1	149¹	160	10	62	70	13.6	5.30	85	.274	.347	8	.174	-1	-12	-14	-1	-1.3
	Yr	13	18	.419	35	31	12	3	1	207²	222	11	84	94	13.4	4.94	91	.273	.344	4	.061	-3	-8	-10	-0	-1.1
1951	Bos-A	12	9	.571	37	22	8	0	0	184	201	21	61	71	13.5	5.09	88	.275	.342	13	.191	-1	-20	-13	1	-1.2
1952	Bos-A	1	5	.167	28	8	1	1	4	76²	79	8	35	29	13.9	4.81	82	.266	.351	4	.222	-0	-10	-7	-0	-0.6
	*NY-A	5	1	.833	9	4	0	1	0	34	27	4	15	13	11.4	2.91	114	.223	.314	5	.357	2	3	2	-0	0.3
	Yr	6	6	.500	37	12	1	1	4	110²	106	12	50	42	12.8	4.23	89	.251	.332	2	.063	-7	-6	-0	0.3
1953	NY-A	2	2	.500	25	1	0	0	2	54²	52	4	26	20	13.5	3.29	112	.250	.345	1	.083	0	4	2	0	0.3
	Det-A	0	2	.000	13	0	0	0	2	20²	34	3	11	12	20.9	8.27	49	.354	.436	0	.000	-0	-10	-10	-0	-0.9
	Yr	2	4	.333	38	1	0	0	4	75¹	86	7	37	32	15.1	4.66	81	.279	.362	0	.000	-0	-6	-7	-0	-0.6
Total 10		80	85	.485	318	168	59	9	12	1428²	1487	88	611	564	13.5	4.13	97	.267	.344	85	.186	-6	-22	-19	5	-1.0

■ MAC SCARCE
Scarce, Guerrant McCurdy b: 4/8/49, Danville, Va. BL/TL, 6'3", 180 lbs. Deb: 7/10/72

YEAR	TM/L	W	L	PCT	G	GS	CG	SH	SV	IP	H	HR	BB	SO	RAT	ERA	ERA+	OAV	OOB	BH	AVG	PB	PR	/A	PD	TPI
1972	Phi-N	1	2	.333	31	0	0	0	6	36²	30	6	20	40	12.8	3.44	105	.222	.331	0	.000	-1	0	1	1	0.0
1973	Phi-N	1	8	.111	52	0	0	0	12	70²	54	3	47	57	13.0	2.42	157	.220	.347	0	.000	-1	10	11	-1	1.0
1974	Phi-N	3	8	.273	58	0	0	0	5	70¹	72	6	35	50	13.9	4.99	76	.275	.365	0	.000	-1	-11	-9	-1	-1.1
1975	NY-N	0	0	—	1	0	0	0	0	0	1	0	0	0	—	—	—	1.000	1.000	0	—	0	0	0	0	0.0
1978	Min-A	1	1	.500	17	0	0	0	0	32	35	5	15	17	14.9	3.94	97	.292	.384	0	—	0	-1	-0	-1	0.0
Total 5		6	19	.240	159	0	0	0	21	209²	192	20	117	164	13.6	3.69	102	.251	.357	0	.000	-2	-2	2	-3	-0.1

■ AL SCHACHT
Schacht, Alexander b: 11/11/1892, New York, N.Y. d: 7/14/84, Waterbury, Conn. BR/TR, 5'11", 142 lbs. Deb: 9/18/19 C

YEAR	TM/L	W	L	PCT	G	GS	CG	SH	SV	IP	H	HR	BB	SO	RAT	ERA	ERA+	OAV	OOB	BH	AVG	PB	PR	/A	PD	TPI
1919	Was-A	2	0	1.000	2	2	1	0	0	15	14	0	4	4	10.8	2.40	134	.233	.281	0	.000	0	1	1	-0	0.1
1920	Was-A	6	4	.600	22	11	5	1	1	99¹	130	4	30	19	14.6	4.44	88	.319	.367	5	.192	1	-7	-8	-2	-0.4
1921	Was-A	6	6	.500	29	5	2	0	1	82²	110	0	27	15	15.1	4.90	84	.332	.386	5	.227	1	-6	-7	-3	-0.8
Total 3		14	10	.583	53	18	8	1	2	197	254	4	61	38	14.5	4.48	86	.318	.368	10	.196	2	-11	-14	-1	-1.1

■ SID SCHACHT
Schacht, Sidney b: 2/3/18, Bogota, N.J. BR/TR, 5'11", 170 lbs. Deb: 4/23/50

YEAR	TM/L	W	L	PCT	G	GS	CG	SH	SV	IP	H	HR	BB	SO	RAT	ERA	ERA+	OAV	OOB	BH	AVG	PB	PR	/A	PD	TPI
1950	StL-A	0	0	—	8	1	0	0	0	10²	24	5	14	7	32.1	16.03	31	.429	.543	0	.000	-0	-14	-13	-0	-1.1
1951	StL-A	0	0	—	6	0	0	0	0	6	14	1	5	4	28.5	21.00	21	.452	.528	0	—	0	-11	-11	-0	-0.9
	Bos-N	0	2	.000	5	0	0	0	0	4²	6	0	2	1	15.4	1.93	191	.300	.364	0	—	0	1	1	-0	0.1

YEAR	TM/L	W	L	PCT	G	GS	CG	SH	SV	IP	H	HR	BB	SO	RAT	ERA	ERA+	OAV	OOB	BH	AVG	PB	PR	/A	PD	TPI
Total	2	0	2	.000	19	1	0	0	1	21¹	44	6	21	12	27.4	14.34	31	.411	.508	0	.000	-0	-24	-23	-0	-1.9

■ HAL SCHACKER Schacker, Harold b: 4/6/25, Brooklyn, N.Y. BR/TR, 6′, 190 lbs. Deb: 5/09/45

YEAR	TM/L	W	L	PCT	G	GS	CG	SH	SV	IP	H	HR	BB	SO	RAT	ERA	ERA+	OAV	OOB	BH	AVG	PB	PR	/A	PD	TPI
1945	Bos-N	0	1	.000	6	0	0	0	0	15¹	14	2	9	6	13.5	5.28	73	.241	.343	0	.000	0	-3	-2	-0	-0.2

■ GERMANY SCHAEFER Schaefer, Herman A. b: 2/4/1877, Chicago, Ill. d: 5/16/19, Saranac Lake, N.Y. BR/TR, 5′9″, 175 lbs. Deb: 10/05/01 ♦

YEAR	TM/L	W	L	PCT	G	GS	CG	SH	SV	IP	H	HR	BB	SO	RAT	ERA	ERA+	OAV	OOB	BH	AVG	PB	PR	/A	PD	TPI
1912	Was-A	0	0	—	1	0	0	0	0	0²	1	0	0	0	13.5	0.00	—	.333	.333	41	.247	0	0	0	0	0.0
1913	Was-A	0	0	—	1	0	0	0	0	0¹	2	1	0	0	54.0	54.00	5	.667	.667	32	.320	0	-2	-2	0	-0.1
Total	2	0	0	—	2	0	0	0	0	1	3	1	0	0	27.0	18.00	18	.500	.500	972	.257	0	-2	-2	0	-0.1

■ HARRY SCHAEFFER Schaeffer, Harry Edward "Lefty" b: 6/23/24, Reading, Pa. BL/TL, 6′2.5″, 175 lbs. Deb: 7/28/52

YEAR	TM/L	W	L	PCT	G	GS	CG	SH	SV	IP	H	HR	BB	SO	RAT	ERA	ERA+	OAV	OOB	BH	AVG	PB	PR	/A	PD	TPI
1952	NY-A	0	1	.000	5	2	0	0	0	17	18	2	18	15	19.1	5.29	63	.265	.419	0	.000	-0	-3	-4	0	-0.3

■ MARK SCHAEFFER Schaeffer, Mark Philip b: 6/5/48, Santa Monica, Cal. BL/TL, 6′5″, 215 lbs. Deb: 4/18/72

YEAR	TM/L	W	L	PCT	G	GS	CG	SH	SV	IP	H	HR	BB	SO	RAT	ERA	ERA+	OAV	OOB	BH	AVG	PB	PR	/A	PD	TPI
1972	SD-N	2	0	1.000	41	0	0	0	1	41	52	3	28	25	18.0	4.61	71	.319	.425	0	.000	-0	-5	-6	1	-0.5

■ JOE SCHAFFERNOTH Schaffernoth, Joseph Arthur b: 8/6/37, Trenton, N.J. BR/TR, 6′4.5″, 195 lbs. Deb: 4/15/59

YEAR	TM/L	W	L	PCT	G	GS	CG	SH	SV	IP	H	HR	BB	SO	RAT	ERA	ERA+	OAV	OOB	BH	AVG	PB	PR	/A	PD	TPI
1959	Chi-N	1	0	1.000	5	1	0	0	0	7²	11	1	4	3	17.6	8.22	48	.355	.429	0	.000	-0	-4	-4	0	-0.3
1960	Chi-N	2	3	.400	33	0	0	0	3	55	46	2	17	33	10.5	2.78	136	.235	.299	2	.286	0	6	6	0	0.7
1961	Chi-N	0	4	.000	21	0	0	0	0	38¹	43	7	18	23	14.6	6.34	66	.293	.373	0	.000	-1	-10	-9	0	-0.9
	Cle-A	0	1	.000	15	0	0	0	0	17	16	2	14	9	16.4	4.76	83	.242	.383	0	.000	-0	-1	-2	1	0.0
Total	3	3	8	.273	74	1	0	0	3	118	116	12	53	68	13.1	4.58	86	.264	.347	2	.125	-1	-9	-8	1	-0.5

■ ART SCHALLOCK Schallock, Arthur Lawrence b: 4/25/24, Mill Valley, Cal. BL/TL, 5′9″, 160 lbs. Deb: 7/16/51

YEAR	TM/L	W	L	PCT	G	GS	CG	SH	SV	IP	H	HR	BB	SO	RAT	ERA	ERA+	OAV	OOB	BH	AVG	PB	PR	/A	PD	TPI
1951	NY-A	3	1	.750	11	6	1	0	0	46¹	50	3	20	19	13.8	3.88	99	.272	.346	5	.294	1	1	-0	0	0.1
1952	NY-A	0	0	—	2	0	0	0	0	2	3	0	2	1	22.5	9.00	37	.375	.500	0	—	0	-1	-1	0	-0.1
1953	*NY-A	0	0	—	7	1	0	0	1	21¹	30	2	15	13	19.4	2.95	125	.345	.447	2	.333	0	2	2	-0	0.2
1954	NY-A	0	1	.000	6	1	1	0	0	17¹	20	3	11	9	16.6	4.15	83	.282	.386	0	.000	-0	-1	-1	-0	-0.1
1955	NY-A	0	0	—	2	0	0	0	0	3	4	1	1	1	15.0	6.00	62	.333	.385	0	—	0	-1	-1	0	0.0
	Bal-A	3	5	.375	30	6	1	0	0	80¹	92	2	42	33	15.2	4.15	92	.294	.381	2	.105	-1	-2	-3	-1	-0.3
Yr	3	5	.375	32	6	1	0	0	83¹	96	3	43	35	15.2	4.21	90	.295	.381	2	.105	-1	-2	-4	-1	-0.3
Total	5	6	7	.462	58	14	3	0	1	170¹	199	11	91	77	15.6	4.02	94	.295	.383	9	.200	0	-1	-5	-1	-0.1

■ CHARLEY SCHANZ Schanz, Charley Murrell b: 6/8/19, Anacortes, Wash. BR/TR, 6′3.5″, 215 lbs. Deb: 4/20/44

YEAR	TM/L	W	L	PCT	G	GS	CG	SH	SV	IP	H	HR	BB	SO	RAT	ERA	ERA+	OAV	OOB	BH	AVG	PB	PR	/A	PD	TPI
1944	Phi-N	13	16	.448	40	30	13	1	3	241¹	231	6	103	84	12.7	3.32	109	.254	.334	12	.148	-1	8	8	-0	0.7
1945	Phi-N	4	15	.211	35	21	5	1	3	144²	165	5	87	56	16.2	4.35	88	.285	.387	6	.154	-0	-9	-8	1	-0.7
1946	Phi-N	6	6	.500	32	15	4	0	4	116¹	130	8	71	47	15.9	5.80	59	.286	.389	3	.083	-2	-31	-31	1	-3.1
1947	Phi-N	2	4	.333	34	6	1	0	2	101²	107	7	47	42	13.9	4.16	96	.295	.380	4	.148	-1	-1	-2	0	-0.2
1950	Bos-N	3	2	.600	14	0	0	0	2	22²	25	3	24	14	19.9	8.34	59	.281	.439	1	.091	-1	-9	-9	0	-0.8
Total	5	28	43	.394	155	72	23	2	14	626²	658	29	332	243	14.6	4.34	86	.275	.369	26	.134	-5	-43	-42	1	-4.1

■ JOHN SCHAPPERT Schappert, John b: Brooklyn, N.Y. d: 7/29/16, Rockaway Beach, N.Y. BR/TR, 5′10″, 170 lbs. Deb: 5/03/1882

YEAR	TM/L	W	L	PCT	G	GS	CG	SH	SV	IP	H	HR	BB	SO	RAT	ERA	ERA+	OAV	OOB	BH	AVG	PB	PR	/A	PD	TPI
1882	StL-a	8	7	.533	15	14	13	0	0	128	131	2	32	38	11.5	3.52	80	.248	.291	9	.180	0	-12	-10	-2	-0.9

■ BILL SCHARDT Schardt, Wilbur "Big Bill" b: 1/20/1886, Cleveland, Ohio d: 7/20/64, Vermilion, Ohio BR/TR, 6′4″, 210 lbs. Deb: 4/14/11

YEAR	TM/L	W	L	PCT	G	GS	CG	SH	SV	IP	H	HR	BB	SO	RAT	ERA	ERA+	OAV	OOB	BH	AVG	PB	PR	/A	PD	TPI
1911	Bro-N	5	15	.250	39	22	10	1	4	195¹	190	4	91	77	13.3	3.59	93	.266	.355	10	.169	0	-4	-6	0	-0.5
1912	Bro-N	0	1	.000	7	0	0	0	1	20²	25	1	6	7	14.4	4.35	77	.301	.363	0	.000	-1	-2	-2	2	0.0
Total	2	5	16	.238	46	22	10	1	5	216	215	5	97	84	13.4	3.67	91	.269	.356	10	.154	-1	-6	-8	2	-0.5

■ JEFF SCHATTINGER Schattinger, Jeffrey Charles b: 10/25/55, Fresno, Cal. BL/TR, 6′5″, 200 lbs. Deb: 9/21/81

YEAR	TM/L	W	L	PCT	G	GS	CG	SH	SV	IP	H	HR	BB	SO	RAT	ERA	ERA+	OAV	OOB	BH	AVG	PB	PR	/A	PD	TPI
1981	KC-A	0	0	—	1	0	0	0	0	3	2	0	1	1	15.0	0.00	—	.182	.357	0	—	0	1	1	0	0.1

■ DAN SCHATZEDER Schatzeder, Daniel Ernest b: 12/1/54, Elmhurst, Ill. BL/TL, 6′, 185 lbs. Deb: 9/04/77

YEAR	TM/L	W	L	PCT	G	GS	CG	SH	SV	IP	H	HR	BB	SO	RAT	ERA	ERA+	OAV	OOB	BH	AVG	PB	PR	/A	PD	TPI
1977	Mon-N	2	1	.667	6	3	1	1	0	21²	16	0	13	14	12.0	2.49	153	.203	.315	2	.333	0	3	3	0	0.4
1978	Mon-N	7	7	.500	29	18	2	0	0	143²	108	10	68	69	11.2	3.07	115	.213	.308	10	.222	3	8	7	-2	0.9
1979	Mon-N	10	5	.667	32	21	3	0	1	162	136	17	59	106	10.9	2.83	129	.225	.295	11	.216	4	16	15	-3	1.7
1980	Det-A	11	13	.458	32	26	9	2	0	192²	178	23	58	94	11.2	4.02	102	.246	.304	0	—	0	2	-2	0	0.0
1981	Det-A	6	8	.429	17	14	1	0	0	71¹	74	13	29	20	13.2	6.06	62	.265	.339	0	—	0	-19	-18	-0	-1.7
1982	SF-N	1	4	.200	13	3	0	0	0	33¹	47	3	12	18	15.9	7.29	49	.333	.386	1	.125	-0	-14	-14	0	-1.3
	Mon-N	0	2	.000	26	1	0	0	0	36	37	1	12	15	12.8	3.50	104	.276	.345	2	.400	1	0	1	-0	0.1
Yr	1	6	.143	39	4	0	0	0	69¹	84	4	24	33	14.3	5.32	68	.304	.364	3	.077	1	-13	-13	-0	-1.2
1983	Mon-N	5	2	.714	58	2	0	0	2	87	88	3	25	48	12.2	3.21	112	.265	.326	2	.200	0	4	4	-1	0.3
1984	Mon-N	7	7	.500	36	14	1	1	1	136	112	13	36	89	9.9	2.71	126	.224	.278	11	.314	5	13	11	-3	1.3
1985	Mon-N	3	5	.375	24	15	1	0	0	104¹	101	13	31	64	11.4	3.80	89	.259	.314	6	.194	3	-2	-5	-0	-0.1
1986	Mon-N	3	2	.600	30	1	0	0	1	59	53	6	19	33	11.0	3.20	115	.240	.300	9	.429	6	3	3	-1	0.9
	Phi-N	3	3	.500	25	0	0	0	1	29¹	28	3	16	14	13.5	3.38	114	.252	.346	1	.200	0	1	2	-0	0.2
Yr	6	5	.545	55	1	0	0	2	88¹	81	9	35	47	11.8	3.26	115	.243	.314	5	.192	7	4	5	-1	1.1
1987	Phi-N	3	1	.750	26	0	0	0	0	37²	40	4	14	28	12.9	4.06	104	.278	.342	2	.167	0	0	1	-1	0.0
	*Min-A	3	1	.750	30	1	0	0	0	43²	64	8	18	30	17.1	6.39	72	.342	.403	0	—	0	-9	-9	-0	-0.7
1988	Cle-A	0	2	.000	15	0	0	0	0	16	26	6	2	10	16.3	9.56	43	.351	.377	0	—	0	-10	-10	-0	-0.9
	Min-A	0	1	.000	10	0	0	0	3	10¹	8	1	5	7	12.2	1.74	234	.216	.326	0	—	0	3	3	0	0.3
Yr	0	3	.000	25	0	0	0	3	26¹	34	7	7	17	14.4	6.49	63	.304	.350	0	—	0	-7	-7	-0	-0.6
1989	Hou-N	4	1	.800	36	0	0	0	1	56²	64	2	28	46	15.1	4.45	76	.287	.374	0	.000	-1	-6	-7	-0	-0.7
1990	Hou-N	1	3	.250	45	2	0	0	0	64	61	2	23	37	11.8	2.39	157	.261	.327	1	.250	0	10	10	-0	1.0
	NY-N	0	0	—	6	0	0	0	0	5²	5	0	0	2	7.9	0.00	—	.263	.263	0	—	0	2	2	0	0.2
Yr	1	3	.250	51	2	0	0	0	69²	66	2	23	39	11.5	2.20	170	.256	.317	0	.000	0	12	12	-0	1.2
Total	14	69	68	.504	496	121	18	4	10	1310¹	1246	128	468	744	11.9	3.72	100	.252	.320	58	.240	22	5	0	-12	1.9

■ RUBE SCHAUER Schauer, Alexander John (b: Dimitri Ivanovich Dimitrihoff) b: 3/19/1891, Odessa, Russia d: 4/15/57, Minneapolis, Minn. BR/TR, 6′2″, 192 lbs. Deb: 8/27/13

YEAR	TM/L	W	L	PCT	G	GS	CG	SH	SV	IP	H	HR	BB	SO	RAT	ERA	ERA+	OAV	OOB	BH	AVG	PB	PR	/A	PD	TPI
1913	NY-N	0	1	.000	3	1	1	0	0	12	14	0	9	7	17.3	7.50	42	.292	.404	0	.000	-0	-6	-6	0	-0.5
1914	NY-N	0	0	—	6	0	0	0	0	22¹	16	2	8	6	9.7	3.22	82	.205	.279	1	.143	-0	-1	-1	-0	-0.1
1915	NY-N	2	8	.200	32	7	4	0	0	105¹	101	4	35	65	11.8	3.50	73	.258	.322	2	.077	-2	-9	-11	-1	-1.4
1916	NY-N	1	4	.200	19	3	1	0	0	45²	44	0	16	24	12.2	2.96	82	.257	.328	2	.222	0	-2	-3	-0	-0.2
1917	Phi-N	7	16	.304	33	21	10	0	1	215	209	6	69	62	11.8	3.14	88	.263	.324	11	.145	-3	-11	-9	1	-1.1
Total	5	10	29	.256	93	32	16	0	1	400¹	384	12	137	164	11.9	3.35	80	.259	.324	16	.132	-4	-29	-30	-1	-3.3

■ OWEN SCHEETZ Scheetz, Owen Franklin b: 12/24/13, New Bedford, Ohio BR/TR, 6′, 190 lbs. Deb: 4/22/43

YEAR	TM/L	W	L	PCT	G	GS	CG	SH	SV	IP	H	HR	BB	SO	RAT	ERA	ERA+	OAV	OOB	BH	AVG	PB	PR	/A	PD	TPI
1943	Was-A	0	0	—	6	0	0	0	1	9	16	0	4	5	20.0	7.00	46	.381	.435	0	.000	-0	-4	-4	0	-0.3

■ LEFTY SCHEGG Schegg, Gilbert Eugene (b: Gilbert Eugene Price) b: 8/28/1889, Leesville, Ohio d: 2/27/63, Niles, Ohio TL, 5′11″, 180 lbs. Deb: 8/20/12

YEAR	TM/L	W	L	PCT	G	GS	CG	SH	SV	IP	H	HR	BB	SO	RAT	ERA	ERA+	OAV	OOB	BH	AVG	PB	PR	/A	PD	TPI
1912	Was-A	0	0	—	2	1	0	0	0	5¹	7	0	4	3	18.6	3.38	99	.333	.440	0	.000	-0	-0	-0	-0	0.0

■ CARL SCHEIB Scheib, Carl Alvin b: 1/1/27, Gratz, Pa. BR/TR, 6′1″, 192 lbs. Deb: 9/06/43

YEAR	TM/L	W	L	PCT	G	GS	CG	SH	SV	IP	H	HR	BB	SO	RAT	ERA	ERA+	OAV	OOB	BH	AVG	PB	PR	/A	PD	TPI
1943	Phi-A	0	1	.000	6	0	0	0	0	18²	24	4	3	3	13.5	4.34	78	.308	.341	0	.000	-1	-2	-2	-1	-0.2
1944	Phi-A	0	0	—	15	0	0	0	0	36¹	36	1	11	13	12.6	4.21	83	.257	.329	3	.300	1	-3	-3	1	0.0

YEAR TM/L	W	L	PCT	G	GS	CG	SH	SV	IP	H	HR	BB	SO	RAT	ERA	ERA+	OAV	OOB	BH	AVG	PB	PR	/A	PD	TPI
1945 Phi-A	0	0	—	4	0	0	0	0	8^2	6	0	4	2	10.4	3.12	110	.207	.303	0	.000	-0	0	0	0	0.0
1947 Phi-A	4	6	.400	21	12	6	2	0	116	121	11	55	26	13.8	5.04	76	.274	.357	6	.133	-3	-17	-16	-1	-1.8
1948 Phi-A	14	8	.636	32	24	15	1	0	198^2	219	14	76	44	13.4	3.94	109	.286	.351	31	.298	7	8	8	1	2.0
1949 Phi-A	9	12	.429	38	23	11	2	0	182^2	191	16	118	43	15.3	5.12	80	.275	.382	17	.236	3	-19	-21	-2	-1.8
1950 Phi-A	3	10	.231	43	8	1	0	3	106	138	13	70	37	17.7	7.22	63	.317	.411	13	.250	2	-31	-31	-1	-2.6
1951 Phi-A	1	12	.077	46	11	3	0	10	143	132	7	71	49	13.3	4.47	96	.250	.347	21	.396	8	-6	-3	4	1.0
1952 Phi-A	11	7	.611	30	19	8	1	2	158	153	21	50	42	11.8	4.39	90	.253	.314	18	.220	-1	-12	-8	1	-0.6
1953 Phi-A	3	7	.300	28	8	3	0	2	96	99	9	29	25	12.7	4.88	88	.261	.325	8	.195	-1	-9	-6	0	-0.6
1954 Phi-A	0	1	.000	1	1	0	0	0	2	5	0	1	1	31.5	22.50	17	.500	.583	0	—	0	-4	-4	0	-0.3
StL-N	0	1	.000	3	1	0	0	0	4^2	6	3	5	5	21.2	11.57	36	.300	.440	0	.000	-0	-4	-4	0	-0.3
Total 11	45	65	.409	267	107	47	6	17	1070^2	1130	99	493	290	13.9	4.88	85	.274	.355	117	.250	16	-100	-89	3	-5.2

■ FRANK SCHEIBECK
Scheibeck, Frank S. b: 6/28/1865, Detroit, Mich. d: 10/22/56, Detroit, Mich. BR/TR, 5'7", 145 lbs. Deb: 5/09/1887 ♦

YEAR TM/L	W	L	PCT	G	GS	CG	SH	SV	IP	H	HR	BB	SO	RAT	ERA	ERA+	OAV	OOB	BH	AVG	PB	PR	/A	PD	TPI
1887 Cle-a	0	1	.000	1	1	1	0	0	9	17	1	4	3	21.0	12.00	36	.387	.439	2	.222	0	-8	-8	-0	-0.4

■ JACK SCHEIBLE
Scheible, John G. b: 2/16/1866, Youngstown, Ohio d: 8/9/1897, Youngstown, Ohio TL , Deb: 9/08/1893

YEAR TM/L	W	L	PCT	G	GS	CG	SH	SV	IP	H	HR	BB	SO	RAT	ERA	ERA+	OAV	OOB	BH	AVG	PB	PR	/A	PD	TPI
1893 Cle-N	1	1	.500	2	2	2	1	0	18	15	0	11	1	13.0	2.00	245	.220	.328	1	.143	-0	5	6	0	0.5
1894 Phi-N	0	1	.000	1	1	0	0	0	0^1	6	0	2	0	216.0	189.00	3	.862	.893	0	—	0	-7	-7	0	-0.3
Total 2	1	2	.333	3	3	2	1	0	18^1	21	0	13	1	16.7	5.40	91	.279	.385	1	.143	-0	-1	-1	0	0.2

■ JIM SCHELLE
Schelle, Gerard Anthony b: 4/13/17, Baltimore, Md. BR/TR, 6'3", 204 lbs. Deb: 7/23/39

YEAR TM/L	W	L	PCT	G	GS	CG	SH	SV	IP	H	HR	BB	SO	RAT	ERA	ERA+	OAV	OOB	BH	AVG	PB	PR	/A	PD	TPI
1939 Phi-A	0	0	—	1	0	0	0	0	0	1	0	3	0	—	∞	—	1.000	1.000	0	—	0	-3	-3	0	-0.1

■ FRED SCHEMANSKE
Schemanske, Frederick George "Buck" b: 4/28/03, Detroit, Mich. d: 2/18/60, Detroit, Mich. BR/TR, 6'2", 190 lbs. Deb: 9/15/23 ♦

YEAR TM/L	W	L	PCT	G	GS	CG	SH	SV	IP	H	HR	BB	SO	RAT	ERA	ERA+	OAV	OOB	BH	AVG	PB	PR	/A	PD	TPI
1923 Was-A	0	0	—	1	0	0	0	0	1	3	0	0	0	27.0	27.00	14	.600	.600	2	1.000	1	-3	-3	0	-0.1

■ BILL SCHENCK
Schenck, William G. b: Brooklyn, N.Y. 5'7", 171 lbs. Deb: 5/29/1882 ♦

YEAR TM/L	W	L	PCT	G	GS	CG	SH	SV	IP	H	HR	BB	SO	RAT	ERA	ERA+	OAV	OOB	BH	AVG	PB	PR	/A	PD	TPI
1882 Lou-a	1	0	1.000	2	1	1	0	0	10	6	0	1	4	6.3	0.90	274	.162	.184	60	.260	0	2	2	-0	0.2

■ JOHN SCHENEBERG
Scheneberg, John Bluford b: 11/20/1887, Guyandotte, W.Va. d: 9/26/50, Huntington, W.Va. BB/TR, 6'1", 180 lbs. Deb: 9/23/13

YEAR TM/L	W	L	PCT	G	GS	CG	SH	SV	IP	H	HR	BB	SO	RAT	ERA	ERA+	OAV	OOB	BH	AVG	PB	PR	/A	PD	TPI
1913 Pit-N	0	1	.000	1	1	0	0	0	6	10	0	2	1	18.0	6.00	50	.400	.444	1	.500	0	-2	-2	0	0.0
1920 StL-A	0	0	—	1	0	0	0	0	2	7	0	1	0	36.0	27.00	15	.583	.615	0	—	0	-5	-5	-0	-0.3
Total 2	0	1	.000	2	1	0	0	0	8	17	0	3	1	22.5	11.25	29	.459	.500	1	.500	0	-7	-7	0	-0.3

■ FRED SCHERMAN
Scherman, Frederick John b: 7/25/44, Dayton, Ohio BL/TL, 6'1", 195 lbs. Deb: 4/26/69

YEAR TM/L	W	L	PCT	G	GS	CG	SH	SV	IP	H	HR	BB	SO	RAT	ERA	ERA+	OAV	OOB	BH	AVG	PB	PR	/A	PD	TPI
1969 Det-A	1	0	1.000	4	0	0	0	0	4	6	2	0	3	13.5	6.75	55	.333	.333	0	—	0	-1	-1	0	0.0
1970 Det-A	4	4	.500	48	0	0	0	1	69^2	61	5	28	58	11.6	3.23	115	.237	.315	2	.167	-0	4	4	0	0.4
1971 Det-A	11	6	.647	69	1	1	0	20	113	91	11	49	46	11.5	2.71	133	.226	.318	5	.208	1	9	11	1	1.5
1972 *Det-A	7	3	.700	57	3	0	0	12	94	91	5	53	53	14.3	3.64	86	.269	.376	2	.091	-1	-6	-5	-0	-0.6
1973 Det-A	2	2	.500	34	0	0	0	1	61^2	59	6	30	28	13.4	4.23	97	.258	.351	0	—	0	-3	-1	-1	-0.1
1974 Hou-N	2	5	.286	53	0	0	0	4	61^1	67	5	26	35	14.7	4.11	84	.284	.372	0	.000	-0	-3	-4	-0	-0.4
1975 Hou-N	0	1	.000	16	0	0	0	0	16^1	21	4	4	13	14.3	4.96	68	.318	.366	0	.000	-0	-2	-3	0	-0.2
Mon-N	4	3	.571	34	7	0	0	0	76^1	84	3	41	43	15.3	3.54	108	.283	.379	1	.063	-1	1	2	1	0.3
Yr	4	4	.500	50	7	0	0	0	92^2	105	7	45	56	15.1	3.79	99	.288	.373	1	.059	-1	-2	-0	1	0.1
1976 Mon-N	2	2	.500	31	0	0	0	1	30	42	5	14	18	13.3	4.95	75	.261	.331	1	.250	0	-6	-5	-0	-0.5
Total 8	33	26	.559	346	11	1	0	39	536^1	522	46	245	297	13.4	3.66	99	.260	.350	11	.134	-1	-9	-3	0	0.4

■ BILL SCHERRER
Scherrer, William Joseph b: 1/20/58, Tonawanda, N.Y. BL/TL, 6'4", 170 lbs. Deb: 9/07/82

YEAR TM/L	W	L	PCT	G	GS	CG	SH	SV	IP	H	HR	BB	SO	RAT	ERA	ERA+	OAV	OOB	BH	AVG	PB	PR	/A	PD	TPI
1982 Cin-N	0	1	.000	5	2	0	0	0	17^1	17	0	0	7	8.8	2.60	142	.250	.250	1	.500	1	2	2	0	0.3
1983 Cin-N	2	3	.400	73	0	0	0	10	92	73	6	33	57	10.4	2.74	139	.225	.296	1	.091	-0	9	11	1	1.2
1984 Cin-N	1	1	.500	36	0	0	0	1	52^1	64	6	15	35	13.6	4.99	76	.300	.346	0	.000	-0	-8	-7	0	-0.6
*Det-A	1	0	1.000	18	0	0	0	0	19	14	1	8	16	10.4	1.89	207	.206	.289	0	—	0	4	4	-0	0.4
1985 Det-A	3	2	.600	48	0	0	0	0	66	62	10	41	46	14.2	4.36	93	.248	.356	0	—	0	-2	-2	1	0.0
1986 Det-A	0	1	.000	13	0	0	0	0	21	19	3	22	16	18.0	7.29	57	.244	.416	0	—	0	-7	-7	0	-0.6
1987 Cin-N	1	1	.500	23	0	0	0	0	33	43	3	16	24	16.1	4.36	97	.328	.401	0	.000	-0	-1	-0	-0	0.0
1988 Bal-A	0	1	.000	4	0	0	0	0	4	8	2	3	3	24.8	13.50	29	.400	.478	0	—	0	-4	-4	0	-0.3
Phi-N	0	0	—	8	0	0	0	0	6^2	7	0	2	3	12.2	5.40	66	.269	.321	0	—	0	-1	-1	0	0.0
Total 7	8	10	.444	228	2	0	0	11	311^1	307	31	140	207	13.0	4.08	96	.260	.340	2	.118	-0	-8	-5	1	0.4

■ DUTCH SCHESLER
Schesler, Charles b: 6/1/1900, Frankfurt, Germany d: 11/19/53, Harrisburg, Pa. BR/TR, 6'2", 185 lbs. Deb: 4/16/31

YEAR TM/L	W	L	PCT	G	GS	CG	SH	SV	IP	H	HR	BB	SO	RAT	ERA	ERA+	OAV	OOB	BH	AVG	PB	PR	/A	PD	TPI
1931 Phi-N	0	0	—	17	0	0	0	0	38^1	65	4	18	14	20.4	7.28	58	.385	.455	1	.111	-0	-15	-13	0	-1.1

■ LOU SCHETTLER
Schettler, Louis Martin b: 6/12/1886, Pittsburgh, Pa. d: 5/1/60, Youngstown, Ohio BR/TR, 5'11", 160 lbs. Deb: 4/25/10

YEAR TM/L	W	L	PCT	G	GS	CG	SH	SV	IP	H	HR	BB	SO	RAT	ERA	ERA+	OAV	OOB	BH	AVG	PB	PR	/A	PD	TPI
1910 Phi-N	2	6	.250	27	7	3	0	1	107	96	2	51	62	12.5	3.20	98	.247	.337	7	.171	-1	-2	-1	-1	-0.3

■ CURT SCHILLING
Schilling, Curtis Montague b: 11/14/66, Anchorage, Al. BR/TR, 6'5", 205 lbs. Deb: 9/07/88

YEAR TM/L	W	L	PCT	G	GS	CG	SH	SV	IP	H	HR	BB	SO	RAT	ERA	ERA+	OAV	OOB	BH	AVG	PB	PR	/A	PD	TPI
1988 Bal-A	0	3	.000	4	4	0	0	0	14^2	22	1	10	4	20.3	9.82	40	.355	.452	0	—	0	-10	-10	-1	-0.8
1989 Bal-A	0	1	.000	5	1	0	0	0	8^2	10	4	3	6	13.5	6.23	61	.286	.342	0	—	0	-2	-2	-0	-0.2
1990 Bal-A	1	2	.333	35	0	0	0	3	46	38	1	19	32	11.2	2.54	150	.229	.308	0	—	0	7	7	-1	0.6
Total 3	1	6	.143	44	5	0	0	3	69^1	70	6	32	42	13.4	4.54	84	.266	.348	0	—	0	-5	-5	-1	-0.4

■ RED SCHILLINGS
Schillings, Elbert Isaiah b: 3/29/1900, Deport, Tex. d: 1/7/54, Oklahoma City, Okla BR/TR, 5'10", 180 lbs. Deb: 9/11/22

YEAR TM/L	W	L	PCT	G	GS	CG	SH	SV	IP	H	HR	BB	SO	RAT	ERA	ERA+	OAV	OOB	BH	AVG	PB	PR	/A	PD	TPI
1922 Phi-A	0	0	—	4	0	0	0	0	8	10	1	11	4	23.6	6.75	63	.313	.488	0	.000	-0	-2	-2	0	-0.2

■ CALVIN SCHIRALDI
Schiraldi, Calvin Drew b: 6/16/62, Houston, Tex. BR/TR, 6'4", 200 lbs. Deb: 9/01/84

YEAR TM/L	W	L	PCT	G	GS	CG	SH	SV	IP	H	HR	BB	SO	RAT	ERA	ERA+	OAV	OOB	BH	AVG	PB	PR	/A	PD	TPI
1984 NY-N	0	2	.000	5	3	0	0	0	17^1	20	3	10	16	15.6	5.71	62	.286	.375	0	.000	-0	-4	-4	0	-0.3
1985 NY-N	2	1	.667	10	4	0	0	0	26^1	43	4	11	21	19.5	8.89	39	.368	.435	1	.125	-0	-15	-16	0	-1.4
1986 *Bos-A	4	2	.667	25	0	0	0	9	51	36	5	15	55	9.2	1.41	295	.201	.267	0	—	0	16	16	-1	1.5
1987 Bos-A	8	5	.615	62	1	0	0	6	83^2	75	15	40	93	12.5	4.41	103	.240	.328	0	—	0	1	1	-0	0.1
1988 Chi-N	9	13	.409	29	27	2	1	1	166^1	166	16	63	140	12.5	4.38	82	.257	.325	6	.100	-2	-17	-14	-3	-1.9
1989 Chi-N	3	6	.333	54	0	0	0	4	78^2	60	7	50	54	12.7	3.78	100	.209	.328	0	.000	-1	-2	-0	-1	-0.1
SD-N	3	1	.750	5	4	0	0	0	21^1	12	1	13	17	10.5	2.53	138	.162	.287	1	.143	1	2	2	-0	0.3
Yr	6	7	.462	59	4	0	0	4	100	72	8	63	71	12.2	3.51	105	.198	.316	1	.063	0	0	2	-1	0.2
1990 SD-N	3	8	.273	42	8	0	0	1	104	105	11	60	74	14.4	4.41	87	.264	.362	4	.190	2	-7	-7	-1	-0.5
Total 7	32	38	.457	232	47	2	1	21	548^2	517	59	262	470	12.9	4.22	91	.248	.335	12	.111	-1	-28	-22	-6	-2.3

■ BIFF SCHLITZER
Schlitzer, Victor Joseph b: 12/4/1884, Rochester, N.Y. d: 1/4/48, Wellesley Hills, Mass. BR/TR, 5'11", 175 lbs. Deb: 4/17/08

YEAR TM/L	W	L	PCT	G	GS	CG	SH	SV	IP	H	HR	BB	SO	RAT	ERA	ERA+	OAV	OOB	BH	AVG	PB	PR	/A	PD	TPI
1908 Phi-A	6	8	.429	24	18	11	2	0	131	110	1	45	57	10.8	3.16	81	.234	.303	9	.196	-1	-11	-9	-2	-1.1
1909 Phi-A	0	3	.000	4	3	0	0	0	13^1	13	0	7	6	15.5	5.40	45	.245	.365	1	.250	0	-4	-4	1	-0.3
Bos-A	4	4	.500	13	8	5	0	1	69^2	68	0	17	23	11.1	3.49	72	.234	.279	4	.154	1	-8	-8	1	-0.6
Yr	4	7	.364	17	11	5	0	1	83	81	0	24	29	11.5	3.80	65	.234	.286	5	.167	1	-12	-12	2	-0.9
1914 Buf-F	0	0	—	3	0	0	0	0	3^1	7	3	2	1	24.3	16.20	20	.435	.497	1	1.000	0	-5	-5	0	-0.3
Total 3	10	15	.400	44	29	16	2	1	217^1	198	4	71	87	11.4	3.60	71	.239	.303	15	.195	-0	-28	-25	-2	-2.3

■ GEORGE SCHMEES
Schmees, George Edward "Rocky" b: 9/6/24, Cincinnati, Ohio BL/TL, 6', 190 lbs. Deb: 4/15/52 ♦

YEAR TM/L	W	L	PCT	G	GS	CG	SH	SV	IP	H	HR	BB	SO	RAT	ERA	ERA+	OAV	OOB	BH	AVG	PB	PR	/A	PD	TPI
1952 Bos-A	0	0	—	2	1	0	0	0	6	9	0	2	2	16.5	3.00	131	.346	.393	13	.203	0	0	1	1	0.1

YEAR TM/L	W	L	PCT	G	GS	CG	SH	SV	IP	H	HR	BB	SO	RAT	ERA	ERA+	OAV	OOB	BH	AVG	PB	PR	/A	PD	TPI
■ AL SCHMELZ Schmelz, Alan George b: 11/12/43, Whittier, Cal. BR/TR, 6'4", 210 lbs. Deb: 9/07/67																									
1967 NY-N	0	0	—	2	0	0	0	0	3	4	1	1	2	15.0	3.00	113	.364	.417	0	—	0	0	0	0	0.0
■ BUTCH SCHMIDT Schmidt, Charles John "Butcher Boy" b: 7/19/1886, Baltimore, Md. d: 9/4/52, Baltimore, Md. BL/TL, 6'1.5", 200 lbs. Deb: 5/11/09 ♦																									
1909 NY-A	0	0	—	1	0	0	0	0	5	10	0	1	2	19.8	7.20	35	.435	.458	0	.000	-0	-3	-3	-0	-0.2
■ DAVE SCHMIDT Schmidt, David Joseph b: 4/22/57, Niles, Mich. BR/TR, 6'1", 185 lbs. Deb: 5/01/81																									
1981 Tex-A	0	1	.000	14	1	0	0	1	31²	31	1	11	13	12.2	3.13	111	.258	.326	0	—	0	2	1	0	0.1
1982 Tex-A	4	6	.400	33	8	0	0	6	109²	118	5	25	69	12.1	3.20	121	.279	.327	0	—	0	11	8	-0	0.8
1983 Tex-A	3	3	.500	31	0	0	0	2	46¹	42	3	14	29	11.1	3.88	103	.241	.302	0	—	0	1	1	0	0.1
1984 Tex-A	6	6	.500	43	0	0	0	12	70¹	69	3	20	46	11.4	2.56	162	.262	.314	0	—	0	11	12	1	1.4
1985 Tex-A	7	6	.538	51	4	1	1	5	85²	81	6	22	46	10.8	3.15	134	.246	.293	0	—	0	9	10	1	1.2
1986 Chi-A	3	6	.333	49	1	0	0	8	92¹	94	10	27	67	12.3	3.31	130	.264	.325	0	—	0	9	10	-1	0.9
1987 Bal-A	10	5	.667	35	14	2	2	1	124	128	13	26	70	11.3	3.77	117	.263	.302	0	—	0	9	9	-1	0.8
1988 Bal-A	8	5	.615	41	9	0	0	2	129²	129	14	38	67	11.8	3.40	115	.262	.319	0	—	0	8	7	2	0.9
1989 Bal-A	10	13	.435	38	26	2	0	0	156²	196	24	36	46	13.4	5.69	67	.310	.349	0	—	0	-31	-33	2	-3.0
1990 Mon-N	3	3	.500	34	0	0	0	13	48	58	3	13	22	13.3	4.31	87	.297	.341	0	.000	-0	-3	-3	0	-0.2
Total 10	54	54	.500	369	63	5	3	50	894¹	946	82	232	475	12.1	3.79	106	.273	.321	0	.000	-0	26	23	4	3.0
■ FREDDY SCHMIDT Schmidt, Frederick Albert b: 2/9/16, Hartford, Conn. BR/TR, 6'1", 185 lbs. Deb: 4/25/44																									
1944 *StL-N	7	3	.700	37	9	3	2	5	114¹	94	5	58	58	12.0	3.15	112	.222	.317	7	.206	-0	6	5	-1	0.4
1946 StL-N	1	0	1.000	16	0	0	0	0	27¹	27	0	15	14	14.8	3.29	105	.276	.388	0	.000	-0	0	0	0	0.1
1947 StL-N	0	0	—	2	0	0	0	0	4	5	1	1	2	13.5	2.25	184	.333	.375	0	—	0	1	1	-0	0.1
Phi-N	5	8	.385	29	5	0	0	0	76²	74	4	43	24	14.4	4.70	85	.285	.392	1	.050	-2	-5	-6	-1	-0.7
Chi-N	0	0	—	1	1	0	0	0	3	4	0	5	0	27.0	9.00	44	.333	.529	0	.000	-0	-2	-2	-0	-0.1
Yr	5	8	.385	32	6	0	0	0	83²	85	5	49	26	14.4	4.73	85	.285	.386	0	.000	-2	-6	-7	-1	-0.7
Total 3	13	11	.542	85	15	3	2	5	225¹	206	10	122	98	13.4	3.75	98	.252	.355	8	.140	-2	-0	-1	-1	-0.2
■ PETE SCHMIDT Schmidt, Friedrich Christoph Herman b: 7/23/1890, Lowden, Iowa d: 3/11/73, Pembroke, Ont., Can BR/TR, 5'11", 175 lbs. Deb: 7/14/13																									
1913 StL-A	0	0	—	1	0	0	0	1	2	3	0	2	0	22.5	4.50	65	.333	.455	0	—	0	-0	-0	0	0.0
■ HENRY SCHMIDT Schmidt, Henry Martin b: 6/26/1873, Brownsville, Tex. d: 4/23/26, Nashville, Tenn. 5'11", 170 lbs. Deb: 4/17/03																									
1903 Bro-N	22	13	.629	40	36	29	5	2	301	321	5	120	96	13.8	3.83	83	.280	.359	21	.196	3	-19	-21	6	-1.0
■ WILLARD SCHMIDT Schmidt, Willard Raymond b: 5/29/28, Hays, Kan. BR/TR, 6'1", 187 lbs. Deb: 4/19/52																									
1952 StL-N	2	3	.400	18	3	0	0	1	34²	36	6	18	30	14.5	5.19	72	.267	.361	1	.125	-0	-6	-6	1	-0.4
1953 StL-N	0	2	.000	6	2	0	0	0	17²	21	1	13	11	17.8	9.17	46	.288	.402	0	.000	-1	-10	-10	0	-0.8
1955 StL-N	7	6	.538	20	15	8	1	0	129²	89	7	57	86	10.3	2.78	146	.197	.291	5	.119	-3	18	19	1	1.7
1956 StL-N	6	8	.429	33	21	2	0	1	147²	131	18	78	52	12.8	3.84	99	.246	.344	10	.233	1	-1	-1	2	0.2
1957 StL-N	10	3	.769	40	8	1	0	0	116²	146	13	49	63	15.2	4.78	83	.312	.380	7	.212	0	-12	-11	1	-0.9
1958 Cin-N	3	5	.375	41	2	0	0	0	69¹	60	8	33	41	12.2	2.86	145	.235	.325	1	.091	-1	8	10	1	1.1
1959 Cin-N	3	2	.600	36	4	0	0	0	70²	80	4	30	40	14.1	3.95	103	.296	.369	1	.083	0	-0	1	1	0.2
Total 7	31	29	.517	194	55	11	1	2	586¹	563	57	278	323	13.1	3.93	101	.258	.344	25	.163	-2	-1	2	6	1.1
■ CRAZY SCHMIT Schmit, Frederick M. "Germany" b: 2/13/1866, Chicago, Ill. d: 10/5/40, Chicago, Ill. BL/TL, 5'10.5", 165 lbs. Deb: 4/21/1890																									
1890 Pit-N	1	9	.100	11	10	9	1	0	83¹	108	3	42	35	16.2	5.83	56	.305	.379	2	.061	-3	-21	-24	-0	-2.1
1892 Bal-N	1	4	.200	6	6	6	0	0	47¹	37	0	26	17	12.0	3.23	107	.207	.307	1	.105	-1	0	1	1	0.1
1893 Bal-N	3	2	.600	9	6	4	0	0	49	67	1	22	10	16.3	6.61	72	.316	.380	5	.238	0	-11	-10	-1	-0.7
NY-N	0	2	.000	4	4	1	0	0	20²	30	0	17	5	20.5	7.40	63	.329	.435	4	.444	1	-6	-6	0	-0.3
Yr	3	4	.429	13	10	5	0	0	69²	97	1	39	15	17.6	6.85	69	.320	.397	2	.067	1	-17	-16	-1	-1.0
1899 Cle-N	2	17	.105	20	19	16	0	0	138¹	197	3	62	24	16.9	5.86	63	.334	.397	11	.157	-2	-31	-33	2	-2.8
1901 Bal-A	0	2	.000	4	3	1	0	0	22²	25	0	16	2	16.3	1.99	195	.276	.385	2	.222	0	4	5	1	0.6
Total 5	7	36	.163	54	48	37	1	0	361¹	464	7	185	93	16.2	5.45	69	.306	.381	26	.161	-4	-64	-68	2	-5.2
■ JOHNNY SCHMITZ Schmitz, John Albert "Bear Tracks" b: 11/27/20, Wausau, Wis. BR/TL, 6', 170 lbs. Deb: 9/06/41																									
1941 Chi-N	2	0	1.000	5	3	1	0	0	20²	12	0	9	11	9.6	1.31	269	.182	.289	4	.571	2	5	5	1	0.9
1942 Chi-N	3	7	.300	23	10	1	0	2	86²	70	3	45	51	12.3	3.43	93	.230	.335	4	.154	-1	-1	-2	4	0.1
1946 Chi-N	11	11	.500	41	31	14	2	2	224¹	184	6	94	**135**	11.2	2.61	127	**.221**	.302	9	.129	-2	20	18	1	1.9
1947 Chi-N	13	18	.419	38	28	10	3	4	207	209	8	80	97	12.7	3.22	123	.262	.330	9	.132	-2	19	17	2	1.6
1948 Chi-N	18	13	.581	34	30	18	2	1	242	186	11	97	100	10.6	2.64	148	**.215**	.295	11	.131	-2	35	34	5	3.9
1949 Chi-N	11	13	.458	36	31	9	3	3	207	227	11	92	75	14.0	4.35	93	.287	.363	10	.143	-1	-7	-7	5	-0.2
1950 Chi-N	10	16	.385	39	27	8	3	0	193	217	23	91	75	14.5	4.99	84	.284	.363	8	.119	-3	-18	-17	5	-1.3
1951 Chi-N	1	2	.333	8	3	0	0	0	18	22	1	15	6	18.5	8.00	51	.301	.420	1	.167	-0	-8	-8	1	-0.5
Bro-N	1	4	.200	16	7	0	0	0	55²	55	4	28	20	13.7	5.34	74	.259	.351	4	.222	2	-9	-9	1	-0.5
Yr	2	6	.250	24	10	0	0	0	73²	77	5	43	26	14.9	5.99	66	.270	.370	1	.042	1	-17	-17	3	-1.0
1952 Bro-N	1	1	.500	10	3	1	0	0	33¹	29	3	18	11	13.0	4.32	84	.238	.340	1	.125	-0	-2	-3	2	0.0
NY-A	1	1	.500	5	2	1	0	1	15	15	0	9	3	15.0	3.60	92	.263	.373	3	.600	2	0	-0	0	0.2
Cin-N	1	0	1.000	3	0	0	0	0	5	3	0	3	3	10.8	0.00	—	.188	.316	0	—	0	2	2	0	0.2
1953 NY-A	0	0	—	3	0	0	0	2	4¹	2	1	3	0	10.4	2.08	178	.143	.294	0	—	0	1	1	0	0.1
Was-A	2	7	.222	24	13	5	0	4	107²	118	9	37	39	13.3	3.68	106	.286	.351	2	.059	-4	4	3	1	0.0
Yr	2	7	.222	27	13	5	0	6	112	120	10	40	39	13.2	3.62	108	.282	.349	0	.000	-4	5	3	1	0.1
1954 Was-A	11	8	.579	29	23	12	2	1	185¹	176	6	64	56	11.8	2.91	122	.255	.321	7	.117	-3	17	13	3	1.3
1955 Was-A	7	10	.412	32	21	6	1	1	165	187	8	54	49	13.5	3.71	103	.291	.352	10	.185	0	5	2	3	0.5
1956 Bos-N	0	0	—	2	0	0	0	0	4¹	5	0	4	0	18.7	0.00	—	.278	.409	0	.000	-0	2	2	0	0.2
Bal-A	0	3	.000	18	3	0	0	0	38¹	49	3	14	15	15.0	3.99	98	.318	.379	0	.000	-1	1	-0	1	0.0
Yr	0	3	.000	20	3	0	0	0	42²	54	3	18	15	15.4	3.59	111	.314	.382	0	.000	-1	3	2	1	0.2
Total 13	93	114	.449	366	235	86	16	21	1812²	1766	97	757	746	12.7	3.55	107	.258	.335	83	.141	-14	66	50	35	8.4
■ CHARLIE SCHMUTZ Schmutz, Charles Otto "King" b: 1/1/1890, San Diego, Cal. d: 6/27/62, Seattle, Wash. BR/TR, 6'1.5", 195 lbs. Deb: 5/13/14																									
1914 Bro-N	1	3	.250	18	5	1	0	0	57¹	57	1	13	21	11.1	3.30	87	.265	.310	3	.188	1	-3	-3	0	-0.1
1915 Bro-N	0	0	—	1	0	0	0	0	4	7	0	1	1	18.0	6.75	41	.438	.471	0	.000	-0	-2	-2	0	-0.1
Total 2	1	3	.250	19	5	1	0	0	61¹	64	1	14	22	11.6	3.52	81	.277	.321	3	.176	0	-5	-5	1	-0.2
■ FRANK SCHNEIBERG Schneiberg, Frank Frederick b: 3/12/1882, Milwaukee, Wis. d: 5/18/48, Milwaukee, Wis. TR , Deb: 6/08/10																									
1910 Bro-N	0	0	—	1	0	0	0	0	1	5	0	4	0	81.0	63.00	5	.625	.750	0	—	0	-7	-7	0	-0.4
■ DAN SCHNEIDER Schneider, Daniel Louis b: 8/29/42, Evansville, Ind. BL/TL, 6'3", 170 lbs. Deb: 5/12/63																									
1963 Mil-N	0	1	1.000	30	3	0	0	0	43²	36	2	20	19	11.5	3.09	104	.225	.311	0	.000	-1	1	1	-1	0.0
1964 Mil-N	1	2	.333	13	5	0	0	0	36¹	38	6	13	14	12.6	5.45	65	.270	.331	0	.000	-1	-8	-8	1	-0.7
1966 Atl-N	0	0	—	14	0	0	0	0	26¹	35	1	5	11	14.0	3.42	106	.324	.360	4	.500	1	1	1	-0	0.0
1967 Hou-N	0	2	.000	54	0	0	0	2	52²	60	5	27	39	15.2	4.96	67	.296	.384	1	.200	-0	-9	-10	1	-0.8
1969 Hou-N	0	1	.000	6	0	0	0	0	7¹	16	2	5	3	25.8	13.50	26	.485	.553	0	.000	-0	-8	-8	0	-0.7
Total 5	2	5	.286	117	8	0	0	2	166¹	185	16	70	86	14.0	4.71	72	.287	.359	5	.172	-0	-24	-24	2	-2.0

YEAR TM/L	W	L	PCT	G	GS	CG	SH	SV	IP	H	HR	BB	SO	RAT	ERA	ERA+	OAV	OOB	BH	AVG	PB	PR	/A	PD	TPI

■ JEFF SCHNEIDER Schneider, Jeffrey Theodore b: 12/6/52, Bremerton, Wash. BB/TL, 6'3", 195 lbs. Deb: 8/12/81

| 1981 Bal-A | 0 | 0 | — | 11 | 0 | 0 | 0 | 1 | 24 | 27 | 4 | 12 | 17 | 15.0 | 4.88 | 74 | .290 | .377 | 0 | — | 0 | -3 | -3 | -0 | -0.3 |

■ PETE SCHNEIDER Schneider, Peter Joseph b: 8/20/1895, Los Angeles, Cal. d: 6/1/57, Los Angeles, Cal. BR/TR, 6'1", 194 lbs. Deb: 6/20/14

1914 Cin-N	5	13	.278	29	20	11	1	1	144¹	143	1	56	62	12.8	2.81	104	.269	.347	8	.178	1	-0	2	-1	0.2
1915 Cin-N	14	19	.424	48	35	16	5	2	275²	254	4	104	108	11.9	2.48	115	.251	.325	23	.245	5	8	12	-0	1.9
1916 Cin-N	10	19	.345	44	31	16	2	1	274¹	259	4	82	117	11.6	2.69	96	.255	.319	21	.236	2	-3	-3	-0.3
1917 Cin-N	20	19	.513	46	42	24	0	0	333²	311	4	117	138	11.8	2.10	124	.255	.326	19	.167	0	23	19	-5	1.5
1918 Cin-N	10	15	.400	33	30	17	2	0	217	213	2	117	51	14.1	3.53	76	.272	.374	24	.289	6	-18	-21	-3	-1.8
1919 NY-A	0	1	.000	7	4	0	0	0	29	19	1	22	11	13.7	3.41	94	.192	.355	1	.111	-1	-1	-1	-1	-0.1
Total 6	59	86	.407	207	162	84	10	4	1274	1199	16	498	487	12.4	2.66	102	.257	.336	96	.221	14	9	8	-12	1.4

■ KARL SCHNELL Schnell, Karl Otto b: 9/20/1899, Los Angeles, Cal. BR/TR, 6'1", 176 lbs. Deb: 4/24/22

1922 Cin-N	0	0	—	10	0	0	0	0	20	21	0	18	5	17.5	2.70	148	.300	.443	1	.250	0	3	3	0	0.3
1923 Cin-N	0	0	—	1	0	0	0	0	1	2	0	2	0	36.0	36.00	11	.667	.800	0	—	0	-4	-4	0	-0.2
Total 2	0	0	—	11	0	0	0	0	21	23	0	20	5	18.4	4.29	93	.315	.462	1	.250	0	-0	-1	0	0.1

■ GERRY SCHOEN Schoen, Gerald Thomas b: 1/15/47, New Orleans, La. BR/TR, 6'3", 215 lbs. Deb: 9/14/68

| 1968 Was-A | 0 | 1 | .000 | 1 | 1 | 0 | 0 | 0 | 3² | 6 | 1 | 1 | 1 | 17.2 | 7.36 | 40 | .400 | .438 | 0 | .000 | -0 | -2 | -2 | -0 | -0.1 |

■ JUMBO SCHOENECK Schoeneck, Louis N. b: 3/3/1862, Chicago, Ill. d: 1/20/30, Chicago, Ill. BR/TR, 6'3", 223 lbs. Deb: 4/20/1884 ♦

| 1888 Ind-N | 0 | 0 | — | 2 | 0 | 0 | 0 | 0 | 4¹ | 5 | 0 | 1 | 1 | 12.5 | 0.00 | — | .279 | .317 | 40 | .237 | 0 | 1 | 1 | -0 | 0.1 |

■ MIKE SCHOOLER Schooler, Michael Ralph b: 8/10/62, Anaheim, Cal. BR/TR, 6'3", 220 lbs. Deb: 6/10/88

1988 Sea-A	5	8	.385	40	0	0	0	15	48¹	45	4	24	54	13.0	3.54	118	.245	.335	0	—	0	2	3	-0	0.3
1989 Sea-A	1	7	.125	67	0	0	0	33	77	81	2	19	69	11.9	2.81	144	.266	.314	0	—	0	9	10	1	1.2
1990 Sea-A	1	4	.200	49	0	0	0	30	56	47	5	16	45	10.3	2.25	176	.227	.286	0	.000	0	10	11	0	1.1
Total 3	7	19	.269	156	0	0	0	78	181¹	173	11	59	168	11.7	2.83	143	.249	.311	0	.000	0	22	24	1	2.6

■ ED SCHORR Schorr, Edward Walter b: 2/14/1891, Bremen, Ohio d: 9/12/69, Atlantic City, N.J. BR/TR, 6'2.5", 180 lbs. Deb: 4/26/15

| 1915 Chi-N | 0 | 0 | — | 2 | 0 | 0 | 0 | 0 | 6 | 9 | 0 | 5 | 3 | 21.0 | 7.50 | 37 | .409 | .519 | 1 | .500 | 0 | -3 | -3 | 0 | -0.2 |

■ GENE SCHOTT Schott, Eugene Arthur b: 7/14/13, Batavia, Ohio BR/TR, 6'2", 185 lbs. Deb: 4/16/35 ♦

1935 Cin-N	8	11	.421	33	19	9	1	0	159	153	5	64	49	12.3	3.91	102	.253	.326	12	.200	1	2	1	3	0.5
1936 Cin-N	11	11	.500	31	22	8	0	1	180	184	7	73	65	13.1	3.80	101	.262	.335	18	.300	7	4	0	1	0.8
1937 Cin-N	4	13	.235	37	17	7	2	1	154¹	150	7	48	56	11.6	2.97	125	.253	.310	7	.143	-1	16	13	2	1.3
1938 Cin-N	5	5	.500	31	4	0	0	2	83	89	8	32	21	13.2	4.45	82	.279	.347	3	.125	-1	-6	-7	1	-0.6
1939 Phi-N	0	1	.000	4	0	0	0	0	11	14	0	5	1	17.2	4.91	82	.326	.420	2	.333	1	-1	-1	-0	0.0
Total 5	28	41	.406	136	62	24	3	4	587¹	590	22	222	192	12.6	3.72	103	.261	.329	42	.211	6	15	6	7	2.0

■ BARNEY SCHREIBER Schreiber, David Henry b: 5/8/1882, Waverly, Ohio d: 10/6/64, Chillicothe, Ohio BL/TL, 6', 185 lbs. Deb: 5/15/11

| 1911 Cin-N | 0 | 0 | — | 3 | 0 | 0 | 0 | 1 | 10 | 19 | 2 | 5 | 2 | 18.9 | 5.40 | 61 | .413 | .438 | 0 | .000 | 0 | -2 | -2 | -0 | -0.2 |

■ PAUL SCHREIBER Schreiber, Paul Frederick "Von" b: 10/8/02, Jacksonville, Fla. d: 1/28/82, Sarasota, Fla. BR/TR, 6'2", 180 lbs. Deb: 9/02/22 C

1922 Bro-N	0	0	—	1	0	0	0	0	1	2	0	0	0	18.0	0.00	—	.500	.500	0	—	0	0	0	0	0.1
1923 Bro-N	0	0	—	9	0	0	0	1	15	16	1	8	4	15.6	4.20	92	.276	.382	0	.000	-0	-0	-1	-0	0.0
1945 NY-A	0	0	—	2	0	0	0	0	4¹	4	0	2	1	12.5	4.15	83	.267	.353	0	.000	-0	-0	-0	1	0.0
Total 3	0	0	—	12	0	0	0	1	20¹	22	1	10	5	15.0	3.98	96	.286	.382	0	.000	-0	-0	-0	1	0.1

■ AL SCHROLL Schroll, Albert Bringhurst "Bull" b: 3/22/32, New Orleans, La. BR/TR, 6'2", 210 lbs. Deb: 4/20/58

1958 Bos-A	0	0	—	5	0	0	0	0	10	6	1	4	7	9.0	4.50	89	.176	.263	1	1.000	0	-1	-1	0	0.0
1959 Phi-N	1	1	.500	3	0	0	0	0	9¹	12	1	6	4	17.4	8.68	47	.353	.450	1	.250	0	-5	-5	0	-0.3
Bos-A	1	4	.200	14	5	1	0	0	46	47	3	22	26	13.7	4.70	86	.269	.354	1	.111	-0	-4	-3	-0	-0.2
1960 Chi-N	0	0	—	2	0	0	0	0	2²	3	1	5	2	27.0	10.13	37	.273	.500	1	1.000	0	-2	-2	-0	-0.1
1961 Min-A	4	4	.500	11	8	2	0	0	50	53	5	27	24	14.8	5.22	81	.266	.360	5	.278	2	-7	-5	-0	-0.2
Total 4	6	9	.400	35	13	3	0	0	118	121	11	64	63	14.3	5.34	77	.267	.362	9	.273	4	-19	-16	-0	-0.8

■ KEN SCHROM Schrom, Kenneth Marvin b: 11/23/54, Grangeville, Idaho BR/TR, 6'2", 195 lbs. Deb: 8/08/80

1980 Tor-A	1	0	1.000	17	0	0	0	1	31	32	2	19	13	14.8	5.23	82	.274	.375	0	—	0	-4	-3	0	-0.2
1982 Tor-A	1	0	1.000	6	0	0	0	0	15¹	13	3	5	8	16.4	5.87	76	.232	.394	0	—	0	-3	-2	-0	-0.2
1983 Min-A	15	8	.652	33	28	6	1	0	196¹	196	14	80	80	13.1	3.71	114	.266	.345	0	—	0	8	12	-3	0.9
1984 Min-A	5	11	.313	25	21	3	0	0	137	156	15	41	49	13.0	4.47	94	.285	.336	0	—	0	-7	-4	-2	-0.5
1985 Min-A	9	12	.429	29	26	6	0	0	160²	164	28	59	74	12.5	4.99	88	.272	.337	0	—	0	-15	-10	1	-0.8
1986 Cle-A	14	7	.667	34	33	3	1	0	206	217	34	49	87	12.1	4.54	91	.271	.322	0	—	0	-8	-9	-3	-1.1
1987 Cle-A	6	13	.316	32	29	4	1	0	153²	185	29	57	61	14.3	6.50	70	.298	.360	0	—	0	-35	-34	-2	-3.1
Total 7	51	51	.500	176	137	22	3	1	900	963	125	320	372	13.1	4.81	89	.276	.342	0	—	0	-65	-51	-8	-5.0

■ RON SCHUELER Schueler, Ronald Richard b: 4/18/48, Catherine, Kan. BR/TR, 6'4", 205 lbs. Deb: 4/16/72 C

1972 Atl-N	5	8	.385	37	18	3	0	2	144²	122	16	60	96	11.4	3.67	103	.227	.307	8	.190	0	-3	2	-1	0.1
1973 Atl-N	8	7	.533	39	20	4	2	2	186	179	24	66	124	11.3	3.87	102	.255	.319	11	.177	-1	-4	1	-1	0.0
1974 Phi-N	11	16	.407	44	27	5	0	1	203¹	202	17	98	109	13.5	3.72	102	.264	.351	6	.118	-2	-2	1	-2	-0.3
1975 Phi-N	4	4	.500	46	6	1	0	0	92²	88	6	40	69	12.5	5.24	71	.258	.338	2	.154	-0	-17	-16	1	-1.4
1976 Phi-N	1	0	1.000	35	0	0	0	3	49²	44	4	16	43	11.2	2.90	122	.243	.312	0	.000	-0	3	4	-1	0.3
1977 Min-A	8	7	.533	52	7	0	0	3	134²	131	16	61	77	13.2	4.41	90	.260	.347	0	—	0	-5	-6	1	-0.2
1978 Chi-A	3	5	.375	30	7	0	0	0	81²	76	10	39	39	13.4	4.30	88	.251	.350	0	—	0	-5	-5	0	-0.3
1979 Chi-A	0	1	.000	8	1	0	0	0	19²	19	3	13	6	15.6	7.32	58	.264	.391	0	—	0	-7	-7	0	-0.5
Total 8	40	48	.455	291	86	13	2	11	912¹	861	96	393	563	12.6	4.08	94	.253	.334	27	.159	-3	-40	-25	-2	-2.5

■ DAVE SCHULER Schuler, David Paul b: 10/4/53, Framingham, Mass. BR/TL, 6'4", 210 lbs. Deb: 9/17/79

1979 Cal-A	0	0	—	1	0	0	0	0	1²	2	1	0	0	10.8	10.80	38	.333	.333	0	—	0	-1	-1	0	0.0
1980 Cal-A	0	1	.000	8	0	0	0	0	12²	13	3	2	7	10.7	3.55	111	.271	.300	0	—	0	1	1	-0	0.0
1985 Atl-N	0	0	—	9	0	0	0	0	10²	19	4	3	10	18.6	6.75	57	.404	.440	0	—	0	-4	-3	-0	-0.3
Total 3	0	1	.000	18	0	0	0	0	25	34	8	5	17	14.0	5.40	72	.337	.368	0	—	0	-4	-4	-0	-0.3

■ BUDDY SCHULTZ Schultz, Charles Budd b: 9/19/50, Cleveland, Ohio BR/TL, 6', 170 lbs. Deb: 9/03/75

1975 Chi-N	2	0	1.000	6	0	0	0	0	5²	11	0	5	4	25.4	6.35	60	.367	.457	0	—	0	-2	-2	-0	-0.1
1976 Chi-N	1	1	.500	29	0	0	0	2	23²	37	3	9	15	17.5	6.08	63	.356	.407	0	.000	-0	-7	-6	0	-0.5
1977 StL-N	6	1	.857	40	3	0	0	1	85¹	76	5	24	66	10.5	2.32	166	.245	.299	2	.167	0	15	14	-1	1.4
1978 StL-N	2	4	.333	62	0	0	0	6	83	68	6	36	70	11.3	3.80	93	.226	.309	1	.200	1	-2	-3	-1	-0.2
1979 StL-N	4	3	.571	31	0	0	0	3	42¹	40	7	14	38	11.5	4.46	84	.256	.318	0	.000	-0	-3	-3	-0	-0.3
Total 5	15	9	.625	168	3	0	0	12	240	232	21	88	193	12.0	3.68	101	.257	.324	3	.120	0	1	1	-2	0.3

■ BARNEY SCHULTZ Schultz, George Warren b: 8/15/26, Beverly, N.J. BR/TR, 6'2", 200 lbs. Deb: 4/12/55 C

1955 StL-N	1	2	.333	19	0	0	0	4	29²	28	5	15	19	14.3	7.89	52	.259	.370	0	.000	-1	-13	-13	1	-1.1
1959 Det-A	1	2	.333	13	0	0	0	0	18¹	17	1	14	17	15.7	4.42	92	.254	.390	2	1.000	1	-1	-1	-0	0.0
1961 Chi-N	7	6	.538	41	0	0	0	7	66²	57	6	25	59	11.6	2.70	155	.228	.308	1	.100	-1	10	11	-1	1.0

YEAR TM/L	W	L	PCT	G	GS	CG	SH	SV	IP	H	HR	BB	SO	RAT	ERA	ERA+	OAV	OOB	BH	AVG	PB	PR	/A	PD	TPI
1962 Chi-N	5	5	.500	51	0	0	0	5	77^2	66	7	23	58	10.8	3.82	108	.231	.297	0	.000	-0	1	3	-0	0.2
1963 Chi-N	1	0	1.000	15	0	0	0	2	27^1	25	5	9	18	11.2	3.62	97	.263	.327	0	.000	-0	-1	-0	-0	0.0
StL-N	2	0	1.000	24	0	0	0	1	35^1	36	5	8	26	11.7	3.57	99	.263	.313	0	—	0	-1	-0	-0	0.0
Yr	3	0	1.000	39	0	0	0	3	62^2	61	10	17	44	11.5	3.59	98	.263	.319	0	.000	-0	-2	-0	-0	0.0
1964 *StL-N	1	3	.250	30	0	0	0	14	49^1	35	1	11	29	8.4	1.64	232	.201	.249	1	.167	-0	10	12	-1	1.2
1965 StL-N	2	2	.500	34	0	0	0	2	42^1	39	8	11	38	10.6	3.83	100	.242	.291	0	.000	-0	-1	0	0	0.0
Total 7	20	20	.500	227	0	0	0	35	346^2	303	38	116	264	11.3	3.63	109	.237	.308	4	.121	-1	4	12	-1	1.3

■ BOB SCHULTZ
Schultz, Robert Duffy b: 11/27/23, Louisville, Ky. d: 3/31/79, Nashville, Tenn. BR/TL, 6'3", 200 lbs. Deb: 4/20/51

YEAR TM/L	W	L	PCT	G	GS	CG	SH	SV	IP	H	HR	BB	SO	RAT	ERA	ERA+	OAV	OOB	BH	AVG	PB	PR	/A	PD	TPI
1951 Chi-N	3	6	.333	17	10	2	0	0	77^1	75	9	51	27	14.9	5.24	78	.251	.364	4	.138	-1	-11	-10	-1	-1.1
1952 Chi-N	6	3	.667	29	5	1	0	0	74	63	3	51	31	14.1	4.01	96	.232	.357	4	.222	1	-2	-1	-2	-0.2
1953 Chi-N	0	2	.000	7	2	0	0	0	11^2	13	2	11	4	19.3	5.40	82	.289	.439	0	.000	-0	-1	-1	-1	-0.1
Pit-N	0	2	.000	11	2	0	0	0	18^2	26	3	10	5	18.3	8.20	55	.321	.409	0	.000	0	-8	-8	-0	-0.6
Yr	0	4	.000	18	4	0	0	0	30^1	39	5	21	9	18.4	7.12	63	.307	.413	1	.200	-0	-10	-9	-1	-0.7
1955 Det-A	0	0	—	1	0	0	0	0	1^1	2	0	2	0	27.0	20.25	19	.333	.500	0	—	0	-2	-2	-0	-0.1
Total 4	9	13	.409	65	19	3	0	0	183	179	17	125	67	15.3	5.16	79	.255	.372	8	.154	-1	-25	-23	-3	-2.1

■ WEBB SCHULTZ
Schultz, Webb Carl b: 1/31/1898, Wautoma, Wis. d: 7/26/86, Delavan, Wis. BR/TR, 5'11", 172 lbs. Deb: 8/03/24

YEAR TM/L	W	L	PCT	G	GS	CG	SH	SV	IP	H	HR	BB	SO	RAT	ERA	ERA+	OAV	OOB	BH	AVG	PB	PR	/A	PD	TPI
1924 Chi-A	0	0	—	1	0	0	0	0	1	1	0	0	0	9.0	9.00	46	.250	.250	0	—	0	-1	-1	0	0.0

■ MIKE SCHULTZ
Schultz, William Michael b: 12/17/20, Syracuse, N.Y. BL/TL, 6'1", 175 lbs. Deb: 4/20/47

YEAR TM/L	W	L	PCT	G	GS	CG	SH	SV	IP	H	HR	BB	SO	RAT	ERA	ERA+	OAV	OOB	BH	AVG	PB	PR	/A	PD	TPI
1947 Cin-N	0	0	—	1	0	0	0	0	2	4	0	2	0	27.0	4.50	91	.444	.545	0	—	0	-0	-0	0	0.0

■ JOHN SCHULTZE
Schultze, John F. b: Burlington, N.J. 6'0.5", 165 lbs. Deb: 5/06/1891

YEAR TM/L	W	L	PCT	G	GS	CG	SH	SV	IP	H	HR	BB	SO	RAT	ERA	ERA+	OAV	OOB	BH	AVG	PB	PR	/A	PD	TPI
1891 Phi-N	0	1	.000	6	1	0	0	0	15	18	1	11	4	17.4	6.60	52	.286	.393	1	.167	-0	-5	-5	-0	-0.4

■ AL SCHULZ
Schulz, Albert Christopher b: 5/12/1889, Toledo, Ohio d: 12/13/31, Gallipolis, Ohio BR/TL, 6', 182 lbs. Deb: 9/25/12

YEAR TM/L	W	L	PCT	G	GS	CG	SH	SV	IP	H	HR	BB	SO	RAT	ERA	ERA+	OAV	OOB	BH	AVG	PB	PR	/A	PD	TPI
1912 NY-A	1	1	.500	3	1	1	0	0	16^1	11	0	11	8	12.1	2.20	163	.183	.310	0	.000	-0	2	3	1	0.3
1913 NY-A	7	13	.350	38	22	9	0	0	193	197	4	69	77	12.6	3.73	80	.266	.333	11	.175	0	-17	-16	-1	-1.6
1914 NY-A	1	3	.250	6	4	1	0	0	28^1	27	0	10	18	12.4	4.76	58	.237	.310	0	.000	-0	-6	-6	1	-0.5
Buf-F	9	12	.429	27	23	10	0	2	171	160	3	77	87	12.6	3.37	98	.259	.343	10	.179	-0	-3	-1	1	0.0
1915 Buf-F	21	14	.600	42	38	25	5	0	309^2	264	8	149	160	12.2	3.08	101	.238	.332	18	.165	-2	-2	1	0	0.0
1916 Cin-N	8	19	.296	44	22	10	0	2	215	208	4	93	95	12.8	3.14	83	.268	.350	8	.125	-3	-12	-13	0	-1.8
Total 5	47	62	.431	160	110	56	5	4	933^1	867	19	409	445	12.5	3.32	90	.254	.337	47	.155	-6	-39	-33	2	-3.6

■ WALT SCHULZ
Schulz, Walter Frederick b: 4/16/1900, St.Louis, Mo. d: 2/27/28, Prescott, Ark. BR/TR, 6', 170 lbs. Deb: 9/24/20

YEAR TM/L	W	L	PCT	G	GS	CG	SH	SV	IP	H	HR	BB	SO	RAT	ERA	ERA+	OAV	OOB	BH	AVG	PB	PR	/A	PD	TPI
1920 StL-N	0	0	—	2	0	0	0	0	6	10	0	2	0	18.0	6.00	50	.370	.414	0	.000	-0	-2	-2	0	-0.1

■ DON SCHULZE
Schulze, Donald Arthur b: 9/27/62, Roselle, Ill. BR/TR, 6'3", 215 lbs. Deb: 9/13/83

YEAR TM/L	W	L	PCT	G	GS	CG	SH	SV	IP	H	HR	BB	SO	RAT	ERA	ERA+	OAV	OOB	BH	AVG	PB	PR	/A	PD	TPI
1983 Chi-N	0	1	.000	4	3	0	0	0	14	19	1	7	8	17.4	7.07	54	.322	.403	0	.000	0	-5	-5	0	-0.4
1984 Chi-N	0	0	—	1	1	0	0	0	3	8	0	1	2	27.0	12.00	33	.571	.600	0	—	0	-3	-3	0	-0.1
Cle-A	3	6	.333	19	14	2	0	0	85^2	105	9	27	39	13.9	4.83	85	.302	.352	0	—	0	-8	-7	-0	-0.6
1985 Cle-A	4	10	.286	19	18	1	0	0	94^1	128	10	19	37	14.4	6.01	69	.322	.360	0	—	0	-20	-20	1	-1.7
1986 Cle-A	4	4	.500	19	13	1	0	0	84^2	88	9	34	33	13.5	5.00	83	.266	.343	0	—	0	-8	-8	-1	-0.8
1987 NY-N	1	2	.333	5	4	0	0	0	21^2	24	4	6	5	12.9	6.23	61	.296	.352	0	.000	0	-5	-6	1	-0.3
1989 NY-A	1	1	.500	2	2	0	0	0	11	12	1	5	5	14.7	4.09	95	.300	.391	0	—	0	-0	-0	0	0.0
SD-N	2	1	.667	7	4	0	0	0	24^1	38	6	6	15	16.3	5.55	63	.352	.386	0	.000	-0	-6	-6	1	-0.5
Total 6	15	25	.375	76	59	4	0	0	338^2	422	40	105	144	14.3	5.47	74	.306	.361	0	.000	0	-54	-54	1	-4.4

■ HAL SCHUMACHER
Schumacher, Harold Henry "Prince Hal" b: 11/23/10, Hinckley, N.Y. BR/TR, 6', 190 lbs. Deb: 4/15/31

YEAR TM/L	W	L	PCT	G	GS	CG	SH	SV	IP	H	HR	BB	SO	RAT	ERA	ERA+	OAV	OOB	BH	AVG	PB	PR	/A	PD	TPI
1931 NY-N	1	1	.500	8	2	1	0	0	18^1	31	3	14	11	22.1	10.80	34	.387	.479	1	.143	-0	-14	-14	1	-1.2
1932 NY-N	5	6	.455	27	13	2	1	0	101^1	119	3	39	38	14.2	3.55	104	.288	.352	7	.226	1	4	2	2	0.5
1933 *NY-N	19	12	.613	35	33	21	7	1	258^2	199	9	84	96	9.9	2.16	149	**.214**	.280	21	.214	1	34	30	4	3.9
1934 NY-N	23	10	.697	41	36	18	2	0	297	299	16	89	112	11.8	3.18	122	.259	.313	28	.239	9	29	23	3	3.5
1935 NY-N	19	9	.679	33	33	19	3	0	261^2	235	11	70	79	10.7	2.89	133	.238	.292	11	.196	2	33	28	7	3.8
1936 *NY-N	11	13	.458	35	30	9	3	1	215^1	234	15	69	75	12.7	3.47	112	.280	.336	16	.216	2	13	10	4	1.5
1937 *NY-N	13	12	.520	38	29	10	1	1	217^2	222	11	89	100	12.9	3.60	108	.264	.335	18	.222	3	8	7	1	1.1
1938 NY-N	13	8	.619	28	28	12	3	0	185	178	12	50	54	11.2	3.50	108	.248	.299	16	.239	4	6	5	2	1.2
1939 NY-N	13	10	.565	29	27	8	0	0	181^2	199	14	89	58	14.4	4.81	82	.276	.358	14	.203	1	-18	-18	-0	-1.6
1940 NY-N	13	13	.500	34	30	12	1	1	227	218	14	96	123	12.4	3.25	119	.251	.325	15	.192	2	15	16	4	2.3
1941 NY-N	12	10	.545	30	26	12	3	1	206	187	11	79	63	11.8	3.36	110	.243	.317	10	.152	-1	6	8	-0	0.7
1942 NY-N	12	13	.480	29	29	12	3	0	216	208	12	82	49	12.2	3.04	111	.251	.321	13	.173	1	7	8	2	1.2
1946 NY-N	4	4	.500	24	13	2	0	1	96^2	95	8	52	48	13.7	3.91	88	.255	.347	1	.038	-2	-5	-5	2	-0.4
Total 13	158	121	.566	391	329	138	27	7	2482^1	2424	139	902	906	12.1	3.36	111	.255	.321	181	.202	23	117	100	32	16.5

■ HACK SCHUMANN
Schumann, Carl J. b: 8/13/1884, Buffalo, N.Y. d: 3/25/46, Millgrove, N.Y. TR , 6'2", 230 lbs. Deb: 9/19/06

YEAR TM/L	W	L	PCT	G	GS	CG	SH	SV	IP	H	HR	BB	SO	RAT	ERA	ERA+	OAV	OOB	BH	AVG	PB	PR	/A	PD	TPI
1906 Phi-A	0	2	.000	4	2	1	0	0	18	21	0	8	9	14.5	4.00	68	.294	.365	0	.000	-1	-3	-3	-0	-0.3

■ FERDIE SCHUPP
Schupp, Ferdinand Maurice b: 1/16/1891, Louisville, Ky. d: 12/16/71, Los Angeles, Cal. BR/TR, 5'10", 150 lbs. Deb: 4/19/13

YEAR TM/L	W	L	PCT	G	GS	CG	SH	SV	IP	H	HR	BB	SO	RAT	ERA	ERA+	OAV	OOB	BH	AVG	PB	PR	/A	PD	TPI
1913 NY-N	0	0	—	5	1	0	0	0	12	10	0	3	2	9.8	0.75	416	.244	.295	1	.333	1	3	3	0	0.4
1914 NY-N	0	0	—	8	0	0	0	1	17	19	0	9	9	15.9	5.82	46	.306	.411	0	.000	-0	-6	-6	-0	-0.6
1915 NY-N	1	0	1.000	23	1	0	0	0	54^2	57	1	29	28	14.7	5.10	50	.281	.379	2	.200	0	-14	-15	-1	-1.5
1916 NY-N	9	3	.750	30	11	8	4	1	140^1	79	1	37	86	7.8	0.90	271	.167	.235	4	.098	-2	27	24	-3	2.2
1917 *NY-N	21	7	**.750**	36	32	25	6	0	272	202	7	70	147	9.1	1.95	131	**.209**	.265	15	.161	1	23	18	-4	1.7
1918 NY-N	0	1	.000	10	2	1	0	0	33^1	42	1	27	22	19.4	7.56	35	.328	.456	1	.111	-0	-18	-18	-0	-1.8
1919 NY-N	1	3	.250	9	4	0	0	1	32	32	2	18	17	14.1	5.63	50	.269	.365	2	.333	0	-10	-10	-1	-1.0
StL-N	4	4	.500	10	9	6	0	0	69^2	55	2	30	37	11.1	3.75	75	.221	.307	1	.050	-0	-6	-7	-1	-0.8
Yr	5	7	.417	19	13	6	0	1	101^2	87	4	48	54	12.0	4.34	64	.236	.326	3	.115	-0	-16	-17	-2	-1.8
1920 StL-N	16	13	.552	38	37	17	0	0	250^2	246	5	127	119	13.7	3.52	85	.265	.358	22	.256	5	-11	-15	-3	-1.2
1921 StL-N	2	0	1.000	9	4	1	0	1	37^1	42	5	21	22	15.7	4.10	89	.276	.371	4	.286	0	-1	-2	-1	-0.1
Bro-N	3	4	.429	20	7	1	0	2	61	75	2	27	26	15.3	4.57	85	.310	.384	1	.083	-1	-5	-5	0	-0.4
Yr	5	4	.556	29	11	2	0	3	98^1	117	7	48	48	15.3	4.39	87	.295	.374	2	.077	-1	-7	-6	-0	-0.5
1922 Chi-A	4	4	.500	18	12	3	1	0	74	79	4	66	38	17.9	6.08	67	.284	.425	5	.217	1	-17	-17	-0	-1.5
Total 10	61	39	.610	216	120	62	11	6	1054	938	30	464	553	12.3	3.32	87	.244	.331	58	.182	5	-35	-51	-12	-4.6

■ WAYNE SCHURR
Schurr, Wayne Allen b: 8/6/37, Garrett, Ind. BR/TR, 6'4", 185 lbs. Deb: 4/15/64

YEAR TM/L	W	L	PCT	G	GS	CG	SH	SV	IP	H	HR	BB	SO	RAT	ERA	ERA+	OAV	OOB	BH	AVG	PB	PR	/A	PD	TPI
1964 Chi-N	0	0	—	26	0	0	0	0	48^1	57	3	11	29	12.7	3.72	100	.298	.337	0	.000	-0	-1	-0	-0	0.0

■ MIKE SCHWABE
Schwabe, Michael Scott b: 7/12/64, Ft.Dodge, Iowa BR/TR, 6'4", 200 lbs. Deb: 5/27/89

YEAR TM/L	W	L	PCT	G	GS	CG	SH	SV	IP	H	HR	BB	SO	RAT	ERA	ERA+	OAV	OOB	BH	AVG	PB	PR	/A	PD	TPI
1989 Det-A	2	4	.333	13	4	0	0	0	44^2	58	6	16	13	15.1	6.04	63	.307	.364	0	—	0	-11	-11	1	-0.9
1990 Det-A	0	0	—	1	0	0	0	0	3^2	5	0	0	1	12.3	2.45	160	.357	.357	0	—	0	1	1	0	0.1
Total 2	2	4	.333	14	4	0	0	0	48^1	63	6	16	14	14.9	5.77	66	.310	.364	0	—	0	-10	-10	1	-0.8

■ DON SCHWALL
Schwall, Donald Bernard b: 3/2/36, Wilkes-Barre, Pa. BR/TR, 6'6", 200 lbs. Deb: 5/21/61

YEAR TM/L	W	L	PCT	G	GS	CG	SH	SV	IP	H	HR	BB	SO	RAT	ERA	ERA+	OAV	OOB	BH	AVG	PB	PR	/A	PD	TPI
1961 Bos-A	15	7	.682	25	25	10	2	0	178^2	167	8	110	91	14.3	3.22	129	.255	.368	11	.180	-0	16	19	1	2.0
1962 Bos-A	9	15	.375	33	32	5	1	0	182^1	180	18	121	89	15.4	4.94	84	.260	.378	9	.136	-2	-20	-16	1	-1.6

YEAR TM/L	W	L	PCT	G	GS	CG	SH	SV	IP	H	HR	BB	SO	RAT	ERA	ERA+	OAV	OOB	BH	AVG	PB	PR	/A	PD	TPI
1963 Pit-N	6	12	.333	33	24	3	2	0	167^2	158	13	74	86	12.8	3.33	99	.255	.340	8	.160	-0	-1	-1	2	0.1
1964 Pit-N	4	3	.571	15	9	0	0	0	49^2	53	1	15	36	12.3	4.35	81	.269	.321	5	.263	2	-4	-5	0	-0.2
1965 Pit-N	9	6	.600	43	1	0	0	4	77	77	5	30	55	12.7	2.92	120	.269	.343	0	.000	-2	5	5	1	0.5
1966 Pit-N	3	2	.600	11	4	0	0	0	41^2	31	3	21	24	11.4	2.16	165	.209	.312	1	.100	-0	7	7	0	0.7
Atl-N	3	3	.500	11	8	0	0	0	45^1	44	2	19	27	12.9	4.37	83	.256	.337	0	.000	-2	-4	-4	-0	-0.5
Yr	6	5	.545	22	12	0	0	0	87	75	5	40	51	12.1	3.31	109	.234	.322	1	.043	-2	3	3	-0	0.2
1967 Atl-N	0	0	—	1	0	0	0	0	0^2	0	0	1	0	13.5	0.00	—	.000	.500	0	—	0	0	0	0	0.0
Total 7	49	48	.505	172	103	18	5	4	743	710	50	391	408	13.7	3.72	102	.257	.354	34	.145	-5	-1	5	5	1.0

■ BLACKIE SCHWAMB
Schwamb, Ralph Richard b: 8/6/26, Lancaster, Cal. d: 12/21/89, Los Angeles, Cal. BR/TR, 6'5.5", 198 lbs. Deb: 7/25/48

YEAR TM/L	W	L	PCT	G	GS	CG	SH	SV	IP	H	HR	BB	SO	RAT	ERA	ERA+	OAV	OOB	BH	AVG	PB	PR	/A	PD	TPI
1948 StL-A	1	1	.500	12	5	0	0	0	31^2	44	3	21	7	18.5	8.53	53	.331	.422	3	.300	1	-15	-14	1	-1.1

■ RUDY SCHWENCK
Schwenck, Rudolph Christian b: 4/6/1884, Louisville, Ky. d: 11/27/41, Anchorage, Ky. 6', 174 lbs. Deb: 9/23/09

YEAR TM/L	W	L	PCT	G	GS	CG	SH	SV	IP	H	HR	BB	SO	RAT	ERA	ERA+	OAV	OOB	BH	AVG	PB	PR	/A	PD	TPI
1909 Chi-N	1	1	.500	3	2	0	0	0	4	16	0	3	3	45.0	13.50	19	.308	.357	1	.250	0	-5	-5	1	-0.3

■ HAL SCHWENK
Schwenk, Harold Edward b: 8/23/1890, Schuylkill Haven, Pa. d: 9/3/55, Kansas City, Mo. BL/TL, 6', 185 lbs. Deb: 9/04/13

YEAR TM/L	W	L	PCT	G	GS	CG	SH	SV	IP	H	HR	BB	SO	RAT	ERA	ERA+	OAV	OOB	BH	AVG	PB	PR	/A	PD	TPI
1913 StL-A	1	0	1.000	2	1	1	0	0	11	12	0	4	3	13.1	3.27	90	.333	.400	1	.333	1	-0	-0	-0	0.0

■ JIM SCOGGINS
Scoggins, Lynn J. "Lefty" b: 7/19/1891, Killeen, Tex. d: 8/16/23, Columbia, S.C. BL/TL, 5'11", 165 lbs. Deb: 8/26/13

YEAR TM/L	W	L	PCT	G	GS	CG	SH	SV	IP	H	HR	BB	SO	RAT	ERA	ERA+	OAV	OOB	BH	AVG	PB	PR	/A	PD	TPI
1913 Chi-A	0	1	.000	1	1	0	0	0	1	1	0	0	1	0	—	.000	.500	0	—	0	0	0	0	0.0

■ HERB SCORE
Score, Herbert Jude b: 6/7/33, Rosedale, N.Y. BL/TL, 6'2", 185 lbs. Deb: 4/15/55

YEAR TM/L	W	L	PCT	G	GS	CG	SH	SV	IP	H	HR	BB	SO	RAT	ERA	ERA+	OAV	OOB	BH	AVG	PB	PR	/A	PD	TPI
1955 Cle-A	16	10	.615	33	32	11	2	0	227^1	158	18	154	**245**	12.4	2.85	140	.194	.323	10	.119	-4	28	29	-5	2.0
1956 Cle-A	20	9	.690	35	33	16	**5**	0	249^1	162	18	129	**263**	10.6	2.53	**166**	**.186**	.292	16	.184	1	**45**	**46**	-5	4.4
1957 Cle-A	2	1	.667	5	5	3	1	0	36	18	0	26	39	11.3	2.00	186	.149	.304	1	.091	-0	7	7	0	0.7
1958 Cle-A	2	3	.400	12	5	2	1	3	41	29	1	34	48	13.8	3.95	92	.197	.348	1	.091	-0	-1	-1	-1	-0.2
1959 Cle-A	9	11	.450	30	25	9	1	0	160^2	123	28	115	147	13.4	4.71	78	**.210**	.341	5	.096	-3	-15	-18	-4	-2.3
1960 Chi-A	5	10	.333	23	22	5	1	0	113^2	91	10	87	78	14.3	3.72	102	.226	.366	3	.100	-0	2	1	-1	0.0
1961 Chi-A	1	2	.333	8	5	1	0	0	24^1	22	3	24	14	17.0	6.66	59	.259	.422	0	.000	-1	-7	-7	0	-0.7
1962 Chi-A	0	0	—	4	0	0	0	0	6	6	1	4	3	15.0	4.50	87	.261	.370	0	—	-0	-0	-0	-0	-0.0
Total 8	55	46	.545	150	127	47	11	3	858^1	609	79	573	837	12.5	3.36	117	.200	.328	36	.128	-7	59	55	-16	3.9

■ DICK SCOTT
Scott, Amos Richard b: 2/5/1883, Bethel, Ohio d: 1/18/11, Chicago, Ill. BR/TR, 6', 180 lbs. Deb: 6/26/01

YEAR TM/L	W	L	PCT	G	GS	CG	SH	SV	IP	H	HR	BB	SO	RAT	ERA	ERA+	OAV	OOB	BH	AVG	PB	PR	/A	PD	TPI
1901 Cin-N	0	2	.000	3	2	2	0	0	21	26	2	9	7	16.3	5.14	62	.302	.387	0	.000	-1	-4	-5	-1	-0.5

■ ED SCOTT
Scott, Edward b: 8/12/1870, Walbridge, Ohio d: 11/1/33, Toledo, Ohio BR/TR, 6'3", Deb: 4/19/00

YEAR TM/L	W	L	PCT	G	GS	CG	SH	SV	IP	H	HR	BB	SO	RAT	ERA	ERA+	OAV	OOB	BH	AVG	PB	PR	/A	PD	TPI
1900 Cin-N	17	21	.447	43	36	32	0	1	323	380	9	66	92	12.4	3.82	96	.292	.327	20	.157	-5	-4	-5	9	0.0
1901 Cle-A	8	6	.571	17	16	11	0	1	124^2	149	2	38	23	13.5	4.40	81	.293	.342	10	.208	1	-10	-12	2	-0.8
Total 2	25	27	.481	60	52	43	0	2	447^2	529	11	104	115	12.7	3.98	87	.292	.331	30	.171	-5	-14	-17	11	-0.8

■ GEORGE SCOTT
Scott, George William b: 11/17/1896, Trenton, Mo. BR/TR, 6'1", 175 lbs. Deb: 9/13/20

YEAR TM/L	W	L	PCT	G	GS	CG	SH	SV	IP	H	HR	BB	SO	RAT	ERA	ERA+	OAV	OOB	BH	AVG	PB	PR	/A	PD	TPI
1920 StL-N	0	0	—	2	0	0	0	0	6	4	0	3	1	10.5	4.50	66	.200	.304	0	.000	-0	-1	-1	-0	-0.1

■ JIM SCOTT
Scott, James "Death Valley Jim" b: 4/23/1888, Deadwood, S.Dak. d: 4/7/57, Palm Springs, Cal. BR/TR, 6'1", 235 lbs. Deb: 4/25/09

YEAR TM/L	W	L	PCT	G	GS	CG	SH	SV	IP	H	HR	BB	SO	RAT	ERA	ERA+	OAV	OOB	BH	AVG	PB	PR	/A	PD	TPI
1909 Chi-A	12	12	.500	36	29	20	4	0	250^1	194	0	93	135	10.9	2.30	102	.223	.310	9	.106	-1	5	1	-2	-0.2
1910 Chi-A	8	18	.308	41	23	14	2	1	229^2	182	5	86	135	10.7	2.43	99	.226	.303	15	.203	1	2	-1	3	0.3
1911 Chi-A	14	11	.560	39	26	14	3	0	222	195	3	81	128	11.4	2.39	135	.240	.311	11	.155	-2	24	21	-4	1.4
1912 Chi-A	2	2	.500	6	4	2	1	0	37^2	36	0	15	23	12.4	2.15	149	.265	.342	0	.000	-2	5	4	-0	0.2
1913 Chi-A	20	20	.500	48	38	25	4	1	312^1	252	2	86	158	10.0	1.90	154	.221	.281	7	.072	-7	36	36	-1	3.1
1914 Chi-A	14	18	.438	43	33	12	2	1	253^1	228	5	75	138	10.9	2.84	94	.246	.306	14	.163	-0	-3	-4	2	-0.3
1915 Chi-A	24	11	.686	48	35	23	7	2	296^1	256	3	78	120	10.3	2.03	146	.238	.292	12	.126	-5	30	31	3	3.2
1916 Chi-A	7	14	.333	32	21	8	1	3	165^1	155	3	53	71	11.5	2.72	101	.258	.321	6	.115	-3	2	1	-0	1.1
1917 Chi-A	6	7	.462	24	17	6	2	1	125	126	0	42	37	12.5	1.87	142	.272	.341	5	.119	-2	11	11	0	1.1
Total 9	107	113	.486	317	226	124	26	9	1892	1624	21	609	945	10.9	2.30	120	.238	.305	79	.129	-20	111	99	2	8.5

■ JACK SCOTT
Scott, John William b: 4/18/1892, Ridgeway, N.C. d: 11/30/59, Durham, N.C. BL/TR, 6'2.5", 199 lbs. Deb: 9/06/16

YEAR TM/L	W	L	PCT	G	GS	CG	SH	SV	IP	H	HR	BB	SO	RAT	ERA	ERA+	OAV	OOB	BH	AVG	PB	PR	/A	PD	TPI
1916 Pit-N	0	0	—	1	0	0	0	0	5	5	1	3	4	14.4	10.80	25	.278	.381	0	.000	0	-5	-5	0	-0.3
1917 Bos-N	1	2	.333	7	3	3	0	0	39^2	36	0	5	21	10.0	1.82	141	.255	.295	2	.125	-1	4	3	-1	0.2
1919 Bos-N	6	6	.500	19	12	7	0	1	103^2	109	3	39	44	12.9	3.13	91	.275	.341	7	.175	-1	-2	-3	-3	-0.7
1920 Bos-N	10	21	.323	44	32	22	3	1	291	308	6	85	94	12.6	3.53	87	.277	.336	21	.212	0	-13	-15	-4	-2.0
1921 Bos-N	15	13	.536	**47**	29	16	2	3	233^2	258	9	57	83	12.4	3.70	93	.289	.330	30	.341	10	2	-1	-2	0.6
1922 Cin-N	0	0	—	1	0	0	0	0	1	2	0	1	0	27.0	9.00	44	.500	.600	0	.000	-1	-1	-1	0	0.0
*NY-N	8	2	.800	17	10	5	0	2	79^2	83	7	23	37	12.2	4.41	91	.265	.320	8	.267	1	-3	-4	-1	-0.3
Yr	8	2	.800	18	10	5	0	2	80^2	85	7	24	37	12.4	4.46	90	.268	.324	8	.032	1	-3	-4	-1	-0.3
1923 *NY-N	16	7	.696	40	25	9	3	1	220	223	15	65	79	11.9	3.89	98	.267	.323	25	.316	7	3	-2	-2	0.3
1925 NY-N	14	15	.483	36	28	18	2	3	239^2	251	10	55	87	11.6	3.15	128	.269	.313	21	.241	5	30	24	2	2.9
1926 NY-N	13	15	.464	**50**	22	13	0	5	226	242	13	59	82	11.9	4.34	86	.276	.319	28	.337	9	-13	-15	-1	-0.6
1927 Phi-N	9	21	.300	**48**	25	17	1	1	233^1	304	15	69	69	14.5	5.09	81	.330	.379	30	.289	-0	-30	-25	-0	-1.5
1928 NY-N	4	1	.800	16	3	3	0	1	50^1	59	3	11	17	12.9	3.58	109	.295	.338	4	.267	1	2	2	0	0.3
1929 NY-N	7	6	.538	30	6	2	0	1	91^2	89	12	27	40	11.4	3.53	130	.260	.314	8	.308	3	12	11	1	1.3
Total 12	103	109	.486	356	195	115	11	19	1814^2	1969	94	493	657	12.4	3.85	96	.281	.332	187	.275	43	-13	-30	-11	0.2

■ LEFTY SCOTT
Scott, Marshall b: 7/15/15, Roswell, N.Mex. d: 3/3/64, Houston, Tex. BR/TL, 6'0.5", 165 lbs. Deb: 6/15/45

YEAR TM/L	W	L	PCT	G	GS	CG	SH	SV	IP	H	HR	BB	SO	RAT	ERA	ERA+	OAV	OOB	BH	AVG	PB	PR	/A	PD	TPI
1945 Phi-N	0	2	.000	8	2	0	0	0	22^1	29	1	12	5	16.5	4.43	86	.312	.390	0	.000	-0	-2	-1	-0	-0.1

■ MIKE SCOTT
Scott, Michael Warren b: 4/26/55, Santa Monica, Cal. BR/TR, 6'2", 210 lbs. Deb: 4/18/79

YEAR TM/L	W	L	PCT	G	GS	CG	SH	SV	IP	H	HR	BB	SO	RAT	ERA	ERA+	OAV	OOB	BH	AVG	PB	PR	/A	PD	TPI
1979 NY-N	1	3	.250	18	9	0	0	0	52^1	59	4	20	21	13.6	5.33	68	.289	.353	0	.000	-1	-9	-10	-0	-1.0
1980 NY-N	1	1	.500	6	6	1	0	0	29^1	40	4	8	13	14.7	4.30	83	.331	.372	1	.111	0	-2	-2	0	-0.1
1981 NY-N	5	10	.333	23	23	1	0	0	136	130	11	34	54	10.9	3.90	89	.261	.309	3	.073	-2	-6	-6	4	-0.4
1982 NY-N	7	13	.350	37	22	1	0	3	147	185	13	60	63	15.1	5.14	71	.321	.387	7	.146	0	-25	-25	4	-1.0
1983 Hou-N	10	6	.625	24	24	2	2	0	145	143	6	46	73	12.0	3.72	91	.258	.320	8	.167	1	-2	-5	1	-0.3
1984 Hou-N	5	11	.313	31	29	0	0	0	154	179	7	43	83	13.1	4.68	71	.293	.343	6	.128	0	-19	-23	0	-2.3
1985 Hou-N	18	8	.692	36	35	4	2	0	221^2	194	20	80	137	11.2	3.29	105	.235	.304	11	.153	2	7	4	-2	0.5
1986 *Hou-N	18	10	.643	37	37	7	**5**	0	275^1	182	17	72	**306**	8.4	2.22	162	**.186**	.244	12	.126	-0	46	42	1	4.6
1987 Hou-N	16	13	.552	36	36	8	3	0	247^2	199	21	79	233	10.2	3.23	121	.217	**.282**	10	.125	-1	23	19	-0	1.7
1988 Hou-N	14	8	.636	32	32	8	5	0	218^2	162	19	53	190	9.2	2.92	114	.204	.261	6	.085	-3	13	10	-1	0.6
1989 Hou-N	**20**	10	.667	33	32	9	2	0	229	180	23	62	172	9.6	3.10	109	.212	.268	10	.133	-0	10	7	-2	0.4
1990 Hou-N	9	13	.409	32	32	4	2	0	205^2	194	27	66	121	11.4	3.81	98	.246	.305	7	.130	-0	-0	-1	-2	-0.3
Total 12	124	106	.539	345	317	45	22	3	2061^2	1847	171	623	1466	10.9	3.51	101	.239	.299	81	.124	-6	36	9	2	1.4

■ MILT SCOTT
Scott, Milton Parker "Mikado Milt" b: 1/17/1866, Chicago, Ill. d: 11/3/38, Baltimore, Md. 5'9", 160 lbs. Deb: 9/30/1882 ♦

YEAR TM/L	W	L	PCT	G	GS	CG	SH	SV	IP	H	HR	BB	SO	RAT	ERA	ERA+	OAV	OOB	BH	AVG	PB	PR	/A	PD	TPI
1886 Bal-a	0	0	—	1	0	0	0	0	3	2	0	2	0	12.0	3.00	114	.180	.306	92	.190	-0	0	0	0	0.0

■ MICKEY SCOTT
Scott, Ralph Robert b: 7/25/47, Weimar, Germany BL/TL, 6'1", 155 lbs. Deb: 5/06/72

YEAR TM/L	W	L	PCT	G	GS	CG	SH	SV	IP	H	HR	BB	SO	RAT	ERA	ERA+	OAV	OOB	BH	AVG	PB	PR	/A	PD	TPI
1972 Bal-A	0	1	.000	15	0	0	0	0	23	23	2	5	11	11.3	2.74	112	.277	.326	0	.000	1	1	1	-0	0.1
1973 Bal-A	0	0	—	1	0	0	0	0	1^2	2	1	2	2	21.6	5.40	69	.286	.444	0	—	0	-0	-0	0	0.0

YEAR	TM/L	W	L	PCT	G	GS	CG	SH	SV	IP	H	HR	BB	SO	RAT	ERA	ERA+	OAV	OOB	BH	AVG	PB	PR	/A	PD	TPI
	Mon-N	1	2	.333	22	0	0	0	0	24	27	3	9	11	14.3	5.25	73	.287	.362	0	.000	-0	-4	-4	0	-0.3
1975	Cal-A	4	2	.667	50	0	0	0	1	68¹	59	8	18	31	10.3	3.29	108	.233	.287	0	—	0	4	2	-0	0.2
1976	Cal-A	3	0	1.000	33	0	0	0	3	39	47	3	12	10	13.6	3.23	103	.307	.358	0	—	0	1	0	-0	0.0
1977	Cal-A	0	2	.000	12	0	0	0	0	16	19	1	4	5	12.9	5.63	70	.302	.343	0	—	0	-3	-3	-0	-0.2
Total 5		8	7	.533	133	0	0	0	4	172	177	18	50	70	12.1	3.72	94	.271	.327	0	.000	0	-2	-4	-0	-0.2

■ DICK SCOTT
Scott, Richard Lewis b: 3/15/33, Portsmouth, N.H. BR/TL, 6'2", 185 lbs. Deb: 5/08/63

YEAR	TM/L	W	L	PCT	G	GS	CG	SH	SV	IP	H	HR	BB	SO	RAT	ERA	ERA+	OAV	OOB	BH	AVG	PB	PR	/A	PD	TPI
1963	LA-N	0	0	—	9	0	0	0	2	12	17	6	3	6	15.0	6.75	45	.340	.377	0	—	0	-5	-5	0	-0.4
1964	Chi-N	0	0	—	3	0	0	0	0	4¹	10	2	1	1	22.8	12.46	30	.417	.440	0	—	0	-4	-4	0	-0.3
Total 2		0	0	—	12	0	0	0	2	16¹	27	8	4	7	17.1	8.27	39	.365	.397	0	—	0	-9	-9	0	-0.7

■ SCOTT SCUDDER
Scudder, William Scott b: 2/14/68, Paris, Tex. BR/TR, 6'2", 180 lbs. Deb: 6/06/89

YEAR	TM/L	W	L	PCT	G	GS	CG	SH	SV	IP	H	HR	BB	SO	RAT	ERA	ERA+	OAV	OOB	BH	AVG	PB	PR	/A	PD	TPI
1989	Cin-N	4	9	.308	23	17	0	0	0	100¹	91	14	61	66	13.7	4.49	80	.239	.346	4	.167	1	-11	-10	-1	-1.0
1990	*Cin-N	5	5	.500	21	10	0	0	0	71²	74	12	30	42	13.4	4.90	79	.265	.343	1	.056	-1	-9	-8	-1	-0.9
Total 2		9	14	.391	44	27	0	0	0	172	165	26	91	108	13.6	4.66	80	.250	.345	5	.119	0	-20	-18	-2	-1.9

■ ROD SCURRY
Scurry, Rodney Grant b: 3/17/56, Sacramento, Cal. BL/TL, 6'2", 180 lbs. Deb: 4/17/80

YEAR	TM/L	W	L	PCT	G	GS	CG	SH	SV	IP	H	HR	BB	SO	RAT	ERA	ERA+	OAV	OOB	BH	AVG	PB	PR	/A	PD	TPI
1980	Pit-N	0	2	.000	20	0	0	0	0	37²	23	2	17	28	10.0	2.15	169	.176	.280	1	.250	0	6	6	-0	0.7
1981	Pit-N	4	5	.444	27	7	0	0	7	74	74	6	40	65	14.2	3.77	95	.261	.358	3	.158	0	-2	-1	-1	-0.2
1982	Pit-N	4	5	.444	76	0	0	0	14	103²	79	3	64	94	12.8	1.74	213	.212	.334	5	.238	1	21	23	-1	2.5
1983	Pit-N	4	9	.308	61	0	0	0	7	68	63	6	53	67	15.9	5.56	67	.249	.387	0	.000	-1	-15	-14	-0	-1.5
1984	Pit-N	5	6	.455	43	0	0	0	4	46¹	28	1	22	48	9.7	2.53	143	.175	.275	0	.000	-0	5	6	0	0.6
1985	Pit-N	0	1	1.000	30	0	0	0	2	47²	42	4	28	43	13.2	3.21	111	.236	.340	0	.000	-0	2	2	0	0.2
	NY-A	1	0	1.000	5	0	0	0	1	12²	5	2	10	17	10.7	2.84	141	.125	.300	0	—	0	2	2	-0	0.1
1986	NY-A	1	2	.333	31	0	0	0	2	39¹	38	1	22	36	14.2	3.66	112	.252	.354	0	—	0	2	2	0	0.2
1988	Sea-A	0	2	.000	39	0	0	0	2	31¹	32	6	18	33	15.5	4.02	103	.258	.370	0	—	0	-0	0	0	0.1
Total 8		19	32	.373	332	7	0	0	39	460²	384	31	274	431	13.2	3.24	115	.227	.341	9	.164	0	22	25	-2	2.7

■ JOHNNIE SEALE
Seale, Johnny Ray "Durango Kid" b: 11/14/38, Edgewater, Colo. BL/TL, 5'10", 155 lbs. Deb: 9/20/64

YEAR	TM/L	W	L	PCT	G	GS	CG	SH	SV	IP	H	HR	BB	SO	RAT	ERA	ERA+	OAV	OOB	BH	AVG	PB	PR	/A	PD	TPI
1964	Det-A	1	0	1.000	4	0	0	0	0	10	6	1	4	5	9.0	3.60	102	.171	.256	0	.000	-0	0	0	1	0.1
1965	Det-A	0	0	—	4	0	0	0	0	3	7	1	2	3	27.0	12.00	29	.500	.563	0	—	0	-3	-3	0	-0.2
Total 2		1	0	1.000	8	0	0	0	0	13	13	2	6	8	13.2	5.54	65	.265	.345	0	.000	-0	-3	-3	1	-0.1

■ KIM SEAMAN
Seaman, Kim Michael b: 5/6/57, Pascagoula, Miss. BL/TL, 6'4", 205 lbs. Deb: 9/28/79

YEAR	TM/L	W	L	PCT	G	GS	CG	SH	SV	IP	H	HR	BB	SO	RAT	ERA	ERA+	OAV	OOB	BH	AVG	PB	PR	/A	PD	TPI
1979	StL-N	0	0	—	1	0	0	0	0	2	0	0	2	3	9.0	0.00	—	.000	.250	0	—	0	1	1	0	0.1
1980	StL-N	3	2	.600	26	0	0	0	4	23²	16	2	13	10	11.0	3.42	108	.188	.296	0	.000	-0	0	1	-0	0.0
Total 2		3	2	.600	27	0	0	0	4	25²	16	2	15	13	10.9	3.16	117	.176	.292	0	.000	-0	1	2	-0	0.1

■ RUDY SEANEZ
Seanez, Rudy Caballero b: 10/20/68, Brawley, Cal. BR/TR, 6', 70 lbs. Deb: 90/7 /89

YEAR	TM/L	W	L	PCT	G	GS	CG	SH	SV	IP	H	HR	BB	SO	RAT	ERA	ERA+	OAV	OOB	BH	AVG	PB	PR	/A	PD	TPI
1989	Cle-A	0	0	—	5	0	0	0	0	5	1	0	4	7	9.0	3.60	110	.071	.278	0	—	0	0	0	-0	0.0
1990	Cle-A	2	1	.667	24	0	0	0	0	27¹	22	2	25	24	15.8	5.60	71	.220	.381	0	—	0	-5	-5	-1	-0.5
Total 2		2	1	.667	29	0	0	0	0	32¹	23	2	29	31	14.8	5.29	75	.202	.368	0	—	0	-5	-5	-1	-0.5

■ RAY SEARAGE
Searage, Raymond Mark b: 5/1/55, Freeport, N.Y. BL/TL, 6'1", 180 lbs. Deb: 6/11/81

YEAR	TM/L	W	L	PCT	G	GS	CG	SH	SV	IP	H	HR	BB	SO	RAT	ERA	ERA+	OAV	OOB	BH	AVG	PB	PR	/A	PD	TPI
1981	NY-N	1	0	1.000	26	0	0	0	1	36²	34	2	17	16	12.5	3.68	95	.252	.336	1	1.000	0	-1	-1	-0	0.0
1984	Mil-A	2	1	.667	21	0	0	0	6	38¹	20	0	16	29	8.7	0.70	546	.155	.253	0	—	0	14	13	-0	1.4
1985	Mil-A	1	4	.200	33	0	0	0	1	38	54	2	24	36	18.5	5.92	70	.338	.424	0	—	0	-7	-7	-1	-0.7
1986	Mil-A	0	1	.000	17	0	0	0	1	22	29	6	9	10	16.0	6.95	62	.315	.382	0	—	0	-7	-6	0	-0.5
	Chi-A	1	0	1.000	29	0	0	0	0	29	15	1	19	26	10.6	0.62	694	.156	.296	0	—	0	11	12	0	1.2
	Yr	1	1	.500	46	0	0	0	1	51	44	7	28	36	12.7	3.35	129	.233	.332	0	—	0	5	5	0	0.7
1987	Chi-A	2	3	.400	58	0	0	0	2	55²	56	9	24	33	13.1	4.20	109	.264	.342	0	—	0	2	2	0	0.2
1989	LA-N	3	4	.429	41	0	0	0	0	35²	29	1	18	24	11.9	3.53	97	.225	.320	0	—	0	-0	-0	1	0.0
1990	LA-N	1	0	1.000	29	0	0	0	0	32¹	30	1	10	19	11.1	2.78	128	.250	.308	0	.000	-0	4	3	1	0.3
Total 7		11	13	.458	254	0	0	0	11	287²	267	22	137	193	12.7	3.50	113	.249	.336	1	.333	0	15	15	1	1.9

■ STEVE SEARCY
Searcy, William Steven b: 6/4/64, Knoxville, Tenn. BL/TL, 6'1", 190 lbs. Deb: 8/29/88

YEAR	TM/L	W	L	PCT	G	GS	CG	SH	SV	IP	H	HR	BB	SO	RAT	ERA	ERA+	OAV	OOB	BH	AVG	PB	PR	/A	PD	TPI
1988	Det-A	0	2	.000	2	2	0	0	0	8	8	3	4	5	13.5	5.63	68	.242	.324	0	—	0	-1	-2	0	-0.1
1989	Det-A	1	1	.500	8	2	0	0	0	22¹	27	3	12	11	15.7	6.04	63	.307	.390	0	—	0	-5	-6	-0	-0.5
1990	Det-A	2	7	.222	16	12	1	0	0	75¹	76	9	51	66	15.2	4.66	84	.270	.381	0	—	0	-6	-6	-1	-0.6
Total 3		3	10	.231	26	16	1	0	0	105²	111	15	67	82	15.2	5.03	77	.275	.379	0	—	0	-13	-13	-1	-1.2

■ TOM SEATON
Seaton, Thomas Gordon b: 8/30/1887, Blair, Neb. d: 4/10/40, ElPaso, Tex. BB/TR, 6', 175 lbs. Deb: 4/13/12

YEAR	TM/L	W	L	PCT	G	GS	CG	SH	SV	IP	H	HR	BB	SO	RAT	ERA	ERA+	OAV	OOB	BH	AVG	PB	PR	/A	PD	TPI
1912	Phi-N	16	12	.571	44	27	16	2	2	255	246	8	106	118	12.7	3.28	111	.255	.334	18	.217	-0	4	10	-1	0.8
1913	Phi-N	27	12	.692	52	35	21	5	1	322¹	262	6	136	**168**	11.4	2.60	128	.226	.313	12	.109	-5	22	26	1	2.4
1914	Bro-F	25	14	.641	44	38	26	7	2	302²	299	6	102	172	12.3	3.03	105	.259	.326	22	.206	4	6	5	-0	0.9
1915	Bro-F	12	11	.522	32	23	13	0	3	189¹	199	6	99	86	14.3	4.56	66	.273	.362	16	.242	4	-32	-32	1	-2.7
	New-F	2	6	.250	12	10	7	0	1	75	61	1	21	28	10.1	2.28	125	.224	.285	4	.154	0	6	5	1	0.7
	Yr	14	17	.452	44	33	20	0	4	264¹	260	7	120	114	13.0	3.92	76	.259	.339	20	.204	4	-26	-28	2	-2.0
1916	Chi-N	6	6	.500	31	14	4	0	1	121	108	3	43	45	11.5	3.27	89	.246	.319	7	.184	0	-9	-5	1	-0.3
1917	Chi-N	5	4	.556	16	9	3	1	1	74²	60	0	23	27	10.1	2.53	114	.227	.292	5	.238	1	1	3	1	0.6
Total 6		93	65	.589	231	156	90	15	11	1340	1235	30	530	644	12.1	3.14	103	.248	.325	84	.186	4	-2	12	3	2.4

■ TOM SEATS
Seats, Thomas Edward b: 9/24/11, Farmington, N.C. BR/TL, 5'11", 190 lbs. Deb: 5/04/40

YEAR	TM/L	W	L	PCT	G	GS	CG	SH	SV	IP	H	HR	BB	SO	RAT	ERA	ERA+	OAV	OOB	BH	AVG	PB	PR	/A	PD	TPI
1940	Det-A	2	2	.500	26	2	0	0	1	55²	64	4	21	25	14.2	4.69	101	.290	.349	1	.083	-1	-2	0	0	0.0
1945	Bro-N	10	7	.588	31	18	6	2	0	121²	127	8	37	44	12.5	4.36	86	.261	.320	9	.209	0	-8	-8	0	-0.7
Total 2		12	9	.571	57	20	6	2	1	177¹	194	12	58	69	13.0	4.47	91	.271	.329	10	.182	-1	-10	-8	1	-0.7

■ TOM SEAVER
Seaver, George Thomas "Tom Terrific" b: 11/17/44, Fresno, Cal. BR/TR, 6'1", 195 lbs. Deb: 4/13/67

YEAR	TM/L	W	L	PCT	G	GS	CG	SH	SV	IP	H	HR	BB	SO	RAT	ERA	ERA+	OAV	OOB	BH	AVG	PB	PR	/A	PD	TPI
1967	NY-N	16	13	.552	35	34	18	2	0	251	224	19	78	170	11.0	2.76	123	.241	.303	11	.143	2	17	18	-0	2.2
1968	NY-N	16	12	.571	36	35	14	5	1	277²	224	15	48	205	9.1	2.20	137	.222	.262	15	.158	1	24	25	1	3.3
1969	*NY-N	**25**	7	**.781**	36	35	18	5	0	273¹	202	24	82	208	9.6	2.21	166	**.207**	.273	11	.121	-0	42	44	2	5.3
1970	NY-N	18	12	.600	37	36	19	2	0	290²	230	21	83	**283**	9.8	**2.82**	**143**	.214	.273	17	.179	4	40	39	1	4.7
1971	NY-N	20	10	.667	36	35	21	4	0	286¹	210	18	61	**289**	8.6	**1.76**	**194**	.206	.253	18	.196	4	54	52	0	6.7
1972	NY-N	21	12	.636	35	35	13	3	0	262	215	23	77	249	10.2	2.92	115	.224	.285	13	.146	4	16	13	1	1.9
1973	*NY-N	19	10	.655	36	36	**18**	3	0	290	219	23	64	251	8.9	2.08	174	**.206**	.254	15	.161	2	51	50	-1	5.9
1974	NY-N	11	11	.500	32	32	12	5	0	236	199	19	75	201	10.6	3.20	111	.230	.293	7	.099	-2	11	9	2	0.9
1975	NY-N	**22**	9	.710	36	36	15	5	0	280¹	217	11	88	**243**	9.9	2.38	145	.214	.280	17	.179	3	39	33	1	4.1
1976	NY-N	14	11	.560	35	34	13	5	0	271	211	14	77	**235**	9.7	2.59	127	.213	.273	7	.085	-2	27	21	1	2.6
1977	NY-N	7	3	.700	13	13	5	3	0	96	79	7	28	72	10.0	3.00	125	.221	.277	5	.161	-0	10	8	1	0.9
	Cin-N	14	3	.824	20	20	14	4	0	165¹	120	12	38	124	8.6	2.34	168	.201	.249	12	.218	4	29	29	-2	3.5
	Yr	21	6	.778	33	33	19	7	0	261¹	199	19	66	196	**9.1**	2.58	149	**.208**	**.259**	17	.192	4	39	37	-1	4.4
1978	Cin-N	16	14	.533	36	36	8	1	0	259²	218	26	89	226	10.6	2.88	123	.227	.292	9	.122	-0	20	19	-3	1.8
1979	*Cin-N	16	6	**.727**	32	32	9	**5**	0	215	187	16	61	131	10.4	3.14	119	.236	.291	12	.158	2	14	14	0	1.7
1980	Cin-N	10	8	.556	26	26	5	1	0	168	140	24	59	101	10.7	3.64	98	.225	.293	6	.130	1	-1	-1	1	0.1
1981	Cin-N	**14**	2	**.875**	23	23	6	1	0	166¹	120	10	66	87	10.2	2.54	140	.205	.289	11	.200	4	17	19	-1	2.5

YEAR	TM/L	W	L	PCT	G	GS	CG	SH	SV	IP	H	HR	BB	SO	RAT	ERA	ERA+	OAV	OOB	BH	AVG	PB	PR	/A	PD	TPI
1982	Cin-N	5	13	.278	21	21	0	0	0	111¹	136	14	44	62	14.8	5.50	67	.302	.368	6	.176	1	-23	-22	-1	-2.1
1983	NY-N	9	14	.391	34	34	5	2	0	231	201	18	86	135	11.3	3.55	102	.235	.308	10	.156	2	2	2	-1	0.3
1984	Chi-A	15	11	.577	34	33	10	4	0	236²	216	27	61	131	10.6	3.95	105	.240	.290	0	—	0	1	5	2	0.7
1985	Chi-A	16	11	.593	35	33	6	1	0	238²	223	22	69	134	11.3	3.17	136	.248	.307	0	—	0	26	30	3	3.5
1986	Chi-A	2	6	.250	12	12	1	0	0	72	66	9	27	31	12.3	4.38	99	.242	.321	0	—	0	-2	-1	-1	0.0
	Bos-A	5	7	.417	16	16	1	0	0	104¹	114	8	29	72	12.5	3.80	110	.278	.329	0	—	0	4	4	-0	0.4
	Yr	7	13	.350	28	28	2	0	0	176¹	180	17	56	103	12.1	4.03	105	.261	.318	0	—	0	3	4	-1	0.4
Total	20	311	205	.603	656	647	231	61	1	4782²	3971	380	1390	3640	10.2	2.86	127	.226	.285	202	.154	28	419	411	6	50.4

■ BOB SEBRA
Sebra, Robert Bush   b: 12/11/61, Ridgewood, N.J.   BR/TR, 6'2", 200 lbs.   Deb: 6/26/85

YEAR	TM/L	W	L	PCT	G	GS	CG	SH	SV	IP	H	HR	BB	SO	RAT	ERA	ERA+	OAV	OOB	BH	AVG	PB	PR	/A	PD	TPI
1985	Tex-A	0	2	.000	7	4	0	0	0	20¹	26	4	14	13	18.1	7.52	56	.306	.410	0	—	0	-8	-7	-0	-0.6
1986	Mon-N	5	5	.500	17	13	3	1	0	91¹	82	9	25	66	10.8	3.55	104	.239	.296	6	.207	1	2	1	-1	0.2
1987	Mon-N	6	15	.286	36	27	4	1	0	177¹	184	15	67	156	12.9	4.42	95	.272	.340	8	.157	0	-7	-4	-1	-0.4
1988	Phi-N	1	2	.333	3	3	0	0	0	11¹	15	0	10	7	19.9	7.94	48	.333	.455	0	.000	-1	-6	-6	-0	-0.5
1989	Phi-N	2	3	.400	6	5	0	0	0	34¹	41	6	10	21	14.4	4.46	80	.295	.359	0	.000	-0	-4	-3	-0	-0.6
	Cin-N	0	0	—	15	0	0	0	1	21	24	2	18	14	19.3	6.43	56	.296	.441	0	.000	-0	-7	-7	-0	-0.6
	Yr	2	3	.400	21	5	0	0	1	55¹	65	8	28	35	15.6	5.20	68	.289	.375	2	.182	-1	-11	-10	-0	-0.9
1990	Mil-A	1	2	.333	10	0	0	0	0	11	20	1	5	4	21.3	8.18	46	.408	.473	0	—	0	-5	-5	1	-0.4
Total	6	15	29	.341	94	52	7	2	1	366²	392	37	149	281	13.6	4.71	84	.276	.351	14	.146	-0	-34	-31	-1	-2.6

■ DOC SECHRIST
Sechrist, Theodore O'Hara   b: 2/10/1876, Williamstown, Ky.   d: 4/2/50, Louisville, Ky.   BR/TR, 5'9", 160 lbs.   Deb: 4/28/1899

YEAR	TM/L	W	L	PCT	G	GS	CG	SH	SV	IP	H	HR	BB	SO	RAT	ERA	ERA+	OAV	OOB	BH	AVG	PB	PR	/A	PD	TPI
1899	NY-N	0	0	—	1	0	0	0	0	0	0	0	2	0	—	—	—	—	1.000	0	—	0	0	0	0	0.0

■ DON SECRIST
Secrist, Donald Laverne   b: 2/26/44, Seattle, Wash.   BL/TL, 6'2", 195 lbs.   Deb: 4/11/69

YEAR	TM/L	W	L	PCT	G	GS	CG	SH	SV	IP	H	HR	BB	SO	RAT	ERA	ERA+	OAV	OOB	BH	AVG	PB	PR	/A	PD	TPI
1969	Chi-A	0	1	.000	19	0	0	0	0	40	35	7	14	23	11.2	6.07	63	.227	.296	1	.143	0	-11	-10	0	-0.9
1970	Chi-A	0	0	—	9	0	0	0	0	14²	19	2	12	9	19.0	5.52	71	.333	.449	0	—	0	-3	-3	0	-0.2
Total	2	0	1	.000	28	0	0	0	0	54²	54	9	26	32	13.3	5.93	65	.256	.340	1	.143	0	-14	-13	0	-1.1

■ DUKE SEDGWICK
Sedgwick, Henry Kenneth   b: 6/1/1898, Martins Ferry, O.   d: 12/4/82, Clearwater, Fla.   BR/TR, 6', 175 lbs.   Deb: 7/12/21

YEAR	TM/L	W	L	PCT	G	GS	CG	SH	SV	IP	H	HR	BB	SO	RAT	ERA	ERA+	OAV	OOB	BH	AVG	PB	PR	/A	PD	TPI
1921	Phi-N	1	3	.250	16	5	1	0	0	71¹	81	3	32	21	14.8	4.92	86	.283	.363	5	.208	-1	-9	-5	-1	-0.6
1923	Was-A	0	1	.000	5	2	1	0	0	16	27	1	6	4	18.6	7.88	48	.415	.465	0	.000	-1	-7	-7	1	-0.6
Total	2	1	4	.200	21	7	2	0	0	87¹	108	4	38	25	15.5	5.46	76	.308	.382	5	.172	-2	-16	-13	-0	-1.2

■ CHARLIE SEE
See, Charles Henry "Chad"   b: 10/13/1896, Pleasantville, N.Y   d: 7/19/48, Bridgeport, Conn.   BL/TR, 5'10.5", 175 lbs.   Deb: 8/06/19 ♦

YEAR	TM/L	W	L	PCT	G	GS	CG	SH	SV	IP	H	HR	BB	SO	RAT	ERA	ERA+	OAV	OOB	BH	AVG	PB	PR	/A	PD	TPI
1920	Cin-N	0	0	—	1	0	0	0	0	6	6	0	4	3	15.0	6.00	51	.286	.400	25	.305	0	-2	-2	-0	-0.1

■ CHUCK SEELBACH
Seelbach, Charles Frederick   b: 3/20/48, Lakewood, Ohio   BR/TR, 6', 180 lbs.   Deb: 6/29/71

YEAR	TM/L	W	L	PCT	G	GS	CG	SH	SV	IP	H	HR	BB	SO	RAT	ERA	ERA+	OAV	OOB	BH	AVG	PB	PR	/A	PD	TPI
1971	Det-A	0	0	—	5	0	0	0	0	4	6	2	7	1	31.5	13.50	27	.375	.583	0	—	0	-4	-4	0	-0.4
1972	*Det-A	9	8	.529	61	3	0	0	14	112	96	6	39	76	11.1	2.89	109	.238	.310	3	.143	1	2	3	-1	0.4
1973	Det-A	1	0	1.000	5	0	0	0	0	7	7	1	2	2	11.6	3.86	106	.250	.300	0	—	0	-0	0	1	0.1
1974	Det-A	0	0	—	4	0	0	0	0	7²	9	2	3	0	15.3	4.70	81	.300	.382	0	—	0	-1	-1	0	0.0
Total	4	10	8	.556	75	3	0	0	14	130²	118	11	51	79	12.0	3.38	96	.247	.326	3	.143	1	-3	-2	0	0.1

■ EMMETT SEERY
Seery, John Emmett   b: 2/13/1861, Princeville, Ill.   BL/TR,   Deb: 4/17/1884 ♦

YEAR	TM/L	W	L	PCT	G	GS	CG	SH	SV	IP	H	HR	BB	SO	RAT	ERA	ERA+	OAV	OOB	BH	AVG	PB	PR	/A	PD	TPI
1886	StL-N	0	0	—	2	0	0	0	0	7	8	1	3	2	14.1	7.71	42	.276	.344	108	.238	0	-3	-3	-0	-0.2

■ HERMAN SEGELKE
Segelke, Herman Neils   b: 4/24/58, San Mateo, Cal.   BR/TR, 6'4", 200 lbs.   Deb: 4/07/82

YEAR	TM/L	W	L	PCT	G	GS	CG	SH	SV	IP	H	HR	BB	SO	RAT	ERA	ERA+	OAV	OOB	BH	AVG	PB	PR	/A	PD	TPI
1982	Chi-N	0	0	—	3	0	0	0	0	4¹	6	1	6	2	24.9	8.31	45	.316	.480	0	—	0	-2	-2	0	-0.1

■ DIEGO SEGUI
Segui, Diego Pablo (Gonzalez)   b: 8/17/37, Holguin, Cuba   BR/TR, 6', 190 lbs.   Deb: 4/12/62

YEAR	TM/L	W	L	PCT	G	GS	CG	SH	SV	IP	H	HR	BB	SO	RAT	ERA	ERA+	OAV	OOB	BH	AVG	PB	PR	/A	PD	TPI
1962	KC-A	8	5	.615	37	13	2	0	6	116²	89	16	46	71	10.5	3.86	108	.211	.291	8	.235	2	1	4	0	0.6
1963	KC-A	9	6	.600	38	23	4	1	0	167	173	17	73	116	13.4	3.77	102	.267	.343	12	.218	1	-3	1	1	0.3
1964	KC-A	8	17	.320	40	35	5	2	0	217	219	30	94	155	13.0	4.56	84	.260	.335	11	.155	0	-23	-18	2	-1.5
1965	KC-A	5	15	.250	40	25	5	1	0	163	166	18	67	119	13.0	4.64	75	.261	.334	9	.191	2	-21	-21	-1	-1.9
1966	Was-A	3	7	.300	21	13	1	1	0	72	82	8	24	54	13.3	5.00	69	.291	.346	2	.111	-1	-13	-12	-1	-1.3
1967	KC-A	3	4	.429	36	3	0	0	1	70	62	4	31	52	12.2	3.09	103	.238	.324	0	.000	-1	1	1	-0	0.0
1968	Oak-A	6	5	.545	52	0	0	0	6	83	51	7	32	72	9.0	2.39	118	.173	.255	1	.111	0	5	4	-1	0.3
1969	Sea-A	12	6	.667	66	8	2	0	12	142¹	127	14	61	113	12.0	3.35	108	.238	.319	4	.148	-0	4	4	0	0.5
1970	Oak-A	10	10	.500	47	19	3	2	2	162	130	9	68	95	11.1	**2.56**	**138**	.222	.305	5	.116	-2	21	18	-1	1.5
1971	*Oak-A	10	8	.556	26	21	5	0	0	146¹	122	13	63	81	11.6	3.14	106	.229	.316	4	.085	-1	5	3	-0	0.1
1972	Oak-A	0	1	.000	7	3	0	0	0	22²	25	2	7	11	12.7	3.57	80	.287	.340	1	.143	-0	-1	-2	-0	-0.2
	StL-N	3	1	.750	33	0	0	0	9	55²	47	2	32	54	12.8	3.07	111	.229	.333	1	.143	0	2	2	0	0.0
1973	StL-N	7	6	.538	65	0	0	0	17	100¹	78	6	53	93	11.8	2.78	131	.211	.310	0	.000	-1	10	10	-2	0.7
1974	Bos-A	6	8	.429	58	0	0	0	10	108	106	9	49	76	13.0	4.00	96	.257	.337	0	—	0	-5	-2	-1	-0.2
1975	*Bos-A	2	5	.286	33	1	1	0	6	71	71	10	43	45	14.5	4.82	85	.270	.373	0	—	0	-8	-6	-1	-0.6
1977	Sea-A	0	7	.000	40	7	0	0	2	110²	108	20	43	91	12.4	5.69	72	.251	.321	0	—	0	-20	-19	-0	-1.8
Total	15	92	111	.453	639	171	28	7	71	1807²	1656	185	786	1298	12.2	3.81	96	.243	.323	58	.151	-0	-43	-34	-4	-3.2

■ JOSE SEGURA
Segura, Jose Altagracia (Mota)   b: 1/26/63, Fundacion, D.R.   BR/TR, 5'11", 180 lbs.   Deb: 4/10/88

YEAR	TM/L	W	L	PCT	G	GS	CG	SH	SV	IP	H	HR	BB	SO	RAT	ERA	ERA+	OAV	OOB	BH	AVG	PB	PR	/A	PD	TPI
1988	Chi-A	0	0	—	4	0	0	0	0	8²	19	1	8	2	28.0	13.50	29	.432	.519	0	—	0	-9	-9	0	-0.7
1989	Chi-A	0	1	.000	7	0	0	0	0	6	13	2	3	4	24.0	15.00	25	.464	.516	0	—	0	-7	-7	0	-0.6
Total	2	0	1	.000	11	0	0	0	0	14²	32	3	11	6	26.4	14.11	28	.444	.518	0	—	0	-17	-17	1	-1.3

■ SOCKS SEIBOLD
Seibold, Harry   b: 4/3/1896, Philadelphia, Pa.   d: 9/21/65, Philadelphia, Pa.   BR/TR, 5'8.5", 162 lbs.   Deb: 9/18/15 ♦

YEAR	TM/L	W	L	PCT	G	GS	CG	SH	SV	IP	H	HR	BB	SO	RAT	ERA	ERA+	OAV	OOB	BH	AVG	PB	PR	/A	PD	TPI
1916	Phi-A	1	2	.333	3	2	1	1	0	21²	22	0	9	5	12.9	4.15	69	.272	.344	2	.167	-0	-3	-3	1	-0.1
1917	Phi-A	4	16	.200	33	15	9	1	1	160	141	1	85	55	12.9	3.94	70	.243	.343	13	.220	2	-23	-21	-1	-2.1
1919	Phi-A	2	3	.400	14	4	1	0	0	45²	58	2	26	19	17.3	5.32	64	.322	.419	2	.154	-1	-11	-10	-0	-0.9
1929	Bos-N	12	17	.414	33	27	16	1	1	205²	228	17	80	54	13.6	4.73	99	.285	.352	20	.286	4	-0	-1	-1	0.2
1930	Bos-N	15	16	.484	36	33	20	1	2	251	288	16	85	70	13.4	4.12	120	.290	.348	19	.211	0	24	23	-3	1.8
1931	Bos-N	10	18	.357	33	29	10	3	0	206¹	226	12	65	50	12.8	4.67	81	.279	.335	9	.129	-4	-18	-20	0	-2.2
1932	Bos-N	3	10	.231	28	20	6	1	0	136²	173	12	41	33	14.2	4.68	80	.309	.358	7	.152	-1	-12	-14	2	-1.2
1933	Bos-N	1	4	.200	11	5	1	0	1	36²	43	0	14	10	14.0	3.68	83	.295	.356	1	.111	0	-1	-3	0	-0.1
Total	8	48	86	.358	191	135	64	8	5	1063²	1179	60	405	296	13.5	4.43	91	.284	.350	76	.192	-0	-45	-48	-0	-4.6

■ EPP SELL
Sell, Lester Elwood   b: 4/26/1897, Llewellyn, Pa.   d: 2/19/61, Reading, Pa.   BR/TR, 6', 175 lbs.   Deb: 9/01/22

YEAR	TM/L	W	L	PCT	G	GS	CG	SH	SV	IP	H	HR	BB	SO	RAT	ERA	ERA+	OAV	OOB	BH	AVG	PB	PR	/A	PD	TPI
1922	StL-N	4	2	.667	7	5	0	0	0	33	47	3	6	5	15.0	6.82	57	.338	.374	4	.333	1	-10	-11	1	-0.7
1923	StL-N	0	1	.000	5	1	0	0	0	15	16	1	8	2	14.4	6.00	65	.291	.381	0	.000	-1	-3	-3	-0	-0.3
Total	2	4	3	.571	12	6	0	0	0	48	63	4	14	7	14.8	6.56	59	.325	.376	4	.211	1	-13	-14	1	-1.0

■ JEFF SELLERS
Sellers, Jeffrey Doyle   b: 5/11/64, Compton, Cal.   BR/TR, 6'1", 175 lbs.   Deb: 9/15/85

YEAR	TM/L	W	L	PCT	G	GS	CG	SH	SV	IP	H	HR	BB	SO	RAT	ERA	ERA+	OAV	OOB	BH	AVG	PB	PR	/A	PD	TPI
1985	Bos-A	2	0	1.000	4	4	1	0	0	22¹	24	1	7	6	12.5	3.63	118	.273	.326	0	—	0	1	2	0	0.2
1986	Bos-A	3	7	.300	14	13	1	0	0	82	90	13	40	51	14.6	4.94	84	.282	.367	0	—	0	-7	-7	-0	-0.6
1987	Bos-A	7	8	.467	25	22	4	2	0	139²	161	10	61	99	14.5	5.28	86	.298	.373	0	—	0	-13	-12	1	-0.9
1988	Bos-A	1	7	.125	18	12	1	0	0	85²	89	9	56	70	15.5	4.83	85	.268	.379	0	—	0	-8	-7	-0	-0.6
Total	4	13	22	.371	61	51	7	2	0	329²	364	33	164	226	14.7	4.97	87	.285	.370	0	—	0	-27	-24	1	-1.9

YEAR	TM/L	W	L	PCT	G	GS	CG	SH	SV	IP	H	HR	BB	SO	RAT	ERA	ERA+	OAV	OOB	BH	AVG	PB	PR	/A	PD	TPI

■ DAVE SELLS
Sells, David Wayne b: 9/18/46, Vacaville, Cal. BR/TR, 5'11", 175 lbs. Deb: 8/02/72

1972	Cal-A	2	0	1.000	10	0	0	0	0	16	11	0	5	2	9.0	2.81	103	.196	.262	0	—	0	0	0	1	0.1
1973	Cal-A	7	2	.778	51	0	0	0	10	68	72	2	35	25	14.8	3.71	96	.277	.373	0	—	0	1	-1	0	0.0
1974	Cal-A	2	3	.400	20	0	0	0	2	39	48	3	16	14	15.5	3.69	93	.312	.387	0	—	0	-0	-1	1	0.0
1975	Cal-A	0	0	—	4	0	0	0	0	8¹	9	3	8	7	18.4	8.64	41	.250	.386	0	—	0	-5	-5	0	-0.3
	LA-N	0	2	.000	5	0	0	0	0	7	6	2	3	1	11.6	3.86	88	.222	.300	1	1.000	0	-0	-0	0	0.0
Total 4		11	7	.611	90	0	0	0	12	138¹	146	10	67	49	14.4	3.90	88	.274	.363	1	1.000	0	-4	-7	2	-0.2

■ DICK SELMA
Selma, Richard Jay b: 11/4/43, Santa Ana, Cal. BR/TR, 5'11", 160 lbs. Deb: 9/02/65

1965	NY-N	2	1	.667	4	4	1	1	0	26²	22	2	9	26	10.8	3.71	95	.229	.302	2	.222	0	-1	-1	0	0.0
1966	NY-N	4	6	.400	30	7	0	0	1	80²	84	11	39	58	14.1	4.24	86	.274	.361	1	.071	0	-6	-5	1	-0.3
1967	NY-N	2	4	.333	38	4	0	0	2	81¹	71	3	36	52	12.1	2.77	122	.241	.328	2	.091	-1	6	6	1	0.6
1968	NY-N	9	10	.474	33	23	4	3	0	169²	148	11	54	117	11.0	2.76	110	.233	.298	12	.207	2	4	5	2	1.0
1969	SD-N	2	2	.500	4	3	1	0	0	22	19	3	9	20	11.5	4.09	86	.229	.304	2	.286	0	-1	-1	0	0.0
	Chi-N	10	8	.556	36	25	4	2	1	168²	137	13	72	161	11.3	3.63	111	.222	.307	8	.154	-0	-1	7	-1	0.7
	Yr	12	10	.545	40	28	5	2	1	190²	156	16	81	181	11.3	3.68	108	.223	.307	10	.017	-1	-2	6	-1	0.7
1970	Phi-N	8	9	.471	73	0	0	0	22	134¹	108	8	59	153	11.5	2.75	145	.226	.317	3	.150	1	**19**	**19**	1	2.0
1971	Phi-N	0	2	.000	17	0	0	0	1	24²	21	2	8	15	11.3	3.28	107	.231	.307	1	1.000	0	0	1	0	0.1
1972	Phi-N	2	9	.182	46	10	1	0	3	98²	91	13	73	58	15.4	5.56	65	.249	.381	4	.200	1	-23	-22	1	-2.0
1973	Phi-N	1	1	.500	6	0	0	0	0	8	6	1	5	4	12.4	5.63	67	.240	.367	0	—	0	-2	-2	1	-0.3
1974	Cal-A	2	2	.500	18	0	0	0	1	23	22	2	17	15	15.7	5.09	68	.272	.404	0	—	0	-4	-4	1	-0.3
	Mil-A	0	0	—	2	0	0	0	0	2¹	5	0	0	2	23.1	19.29	19	.455	.500	0	—	0	-4	-4	0	-0.3
	Yr	2	2	.500	20	0	0	0	1	25¹	27	2	17	17	16.0	6.39	54	.290	.405	0	—	0	-8	-8	1	-0.6
Total 10		42	54	.438	307	76	11	6	31	840	734	69	381	681	12.2	3.62	100	.238	.327	35	.172	2	-11	-2	6	1.5

■ FRANK SELMAN
Selman, Frank C. (a.k.a. Frank C. Williams 1871-75) b: Baltimore, Md. Deb: 5/04/1871 ♦

| 1873 | Mar-n | 0 | 1 | .000 | 1 | 1 | 1 | 0 | 0 | 9 | 21 | 0 | 0 | | 21.0 | 10.00 | 36 | .350 | .350 | 1 | .250 | -0 | -6 | -6 | | -0.3 |

■ CARROLL SEMBERA
Sembera, Carroll William b: 7/26/41, Shiner, Tex. BR/TR, 6', 155 lbs. Deb: 9/28/65

1965	Hou-N	0	1	.000	2	1	0	0	0	7¹	5	0	3	4	9.8	3.68	91	.185	.267	0	.000	-0	-0	-0	0	0.0
1966	Hou-N	1	2	.333	24	0	0	0	1	33	36	3	16	21	14.2	3.00	114	.288	.369	0	.000	-0	2	2	0	0.2
1967	Hou-N	2	6	.250	45	0	0	0	3	59²	66	7	19	48	13.0	4.83	69	.269	.325	1	.143	-1	-10	-10	1	-0.9
1969	Mon-N	0	2	.000	23	0	0	0	2	33	28	1	24	15	14.7	3.55	104	.246	.386	1	.250	0	0	0	0	0.1
1970	Mon-N	0	0	—	5	0	0	0	0	6²	14	2	11	6	35.1	18.90	22	.424	.578	0	—	0	-11	-11	0	-0.9
Total 5		3	11	.214	99	1	0	0	6	139²	149	13	73	94	14.6	4.70	74	.274	.364	2	.133	-0	-18	-19	1	-1.5

■ RAY SEMPROCH
Semproch, Roman Anthony "Baby" b: 1/7/31, Cleveland, Ohio BR/TR, 5'11", 180 lbs. Deb: 4/15/58

1958	Phi-N	13	11	.542	36	30	12	2	0	204¹	211	25	58	92	12.1	3.92	101	.264	.319	7	.095	-5	1	1	-0	-0.3
1959	Phi-N	3	10	.231	30	18	2	0	3	111²	119	12	59	54	14.6	5.40	76	.277	.368	6	.176	-0	-18	-16	1	-1.4
1960	Det-A	3	0	1.000	17	0	0	0	0	27	29	2	16	9	15.0	4.00	99	.269	.363	0	.000	-0	-0	-1	1	0.1
1961	LA-A	0	0	—	2	0	0	0	0	1	1	0	3	1	36.0	9.00	50	.333	.667	0	—	0	-1	-0	0	0.0
Total 4		19	21	.475	85	48	14	2	3	344	360	39	136	156	13.2	4.42	91	.269	.340	13	.116	-5	-18	-16	2	-1.6

■ STEVE SENTENEY
Senteney, Stephen Leonard b: 8/7/55, Indianapolis, Ind. d: 6/19/89, Colusa, Cal. BR/TR, 6'2", 205 lbs. Deb: 6/06/82

| 1982 | Tor-A | 0 | 0 | — | 11 | 0 | 0 | 0 | 0 | 22 | 23 | 5 | 6 | 20 | 11.9 | 4.91 | 91 | .247 | .293 | 0 | — | 0 | -2 | -1 | -0 | 0.0 |

■ MANNY SEOANE
Seoane, Manuel Modesto b: 6/26/55, Tampa, Fla. BR/TR, 6'3", 187 lbs. Deb: 9/18/77

1977	Phi-N	0	0	—	2	1	0	0	0	6	11	0	3	4	21.0	6.00	67	.407	.467	1	.500	0	-1	-1	-0	0.0
1978	Chi-N	1	0	1.000	7	1	0	0	0	8¹	11	0	6	5	18.4	5.40	75	.297	.395	0	—	0	-2	-1	-0	-0.1
Total 2		1	0	1.000	9	2	0	0	0	14¹	22	0	9	9	19.5	5.65	71	.344	.425	1	.500	0	-3	-3	-0	-0.1

■ BILLY SERAD
Serad, William I. b: 1863, Philadelphia, Pa. d: 11/1/25, Chester, Pa. BR/TR, 5'7", 156 lbs. Deb: 5/05/1884

1884	Buf-N	16	20	.444	37	37	34	2	0	308	373	21	111	150	14.1	4.27	73	.284	.339	24	.175	-7	-44	-39	-3	-3.9
1885	Buf-N	7	21	.250	30	29	27	0	0	241¹	299	5	80	90	14.1	4.10	72	.264	.342	16	.154	-6	-34	-31	-3	-3.4
1887	Cin-a	10	11	.476	22	21	20	2	1	187¹	201	7	80	34	13.5	4.08	106	.264	.334	14	.177	-4	4	5	-0	0.1
1888	Cin-a	2	3	.400	6	5	5	0	0	50²	62	1	19	4	14.4	3.55	89	.291	.349	3	.130	-1	-3	-2	-0	-0.2
Total 4		35	55	.389	95	92	86	4	1	787¹	935	34	290	278	14.0	4.13	82	.282	.340	57	.166	-18	-77	-66	-6	-7.4

■ GARY SERUM
Serum, Gary Wayne b: 10/24/56, Fargo, N.D. BR/TR, 6'1", 180 lbs. Deb: 7/22/77

1977	Min-A	0	0	—	8	0	0	0	0	22²	22	4	10	14	13.5	4.37	91	.268	.362	0	—	0	-1	-1	-0	0.0
1978	Min-A	9	9	.500	34	23	6	1	1	184¹	188	14	44	80	11.5	4.10	93	.266	.311	0	—	0	-7	-6	0	-0.5
1979	Min-A	1	3	.250	20	5	0	0	0	64	93	10	20	31	15.9	6.61	66	.354	.399	0	—	0	-17	-16	0	-1.4
Total 3		10	12	.455	62	28	6	1	1	271	303	28	74	125	12.7	4.72	84	.288	.337	0	—	0	-25	-23	-0	-1.9

■ SCOTT SERVICE
Service, Scott David b: 2/26/67, Cincinnati, Ohio BR/TR, 6'6", 230 lbs. Deb: 9/05/88

| 1988 | Phi-N | 0 | 0 | — | 5 | 0 | 0 | 0 | 0 | 5¹ | 7 | 0 | 1 | 6 | 15.2 | 1.69 | 211 | .333 | .391 | 0 | — | 0 | 1 | 1 | -0 | 0.1 |

■ MERLE SETTLEMIRE
Settlemire, Edgar Merle "Lefty" b: 1/19/03, Santa Fe, Ohio d: 6/12/88, Russell's Point, Ohio BL/TL, 5'9", 156 lbs. Deb: 4/13/28

| 1928 | Bos-A | 0 | 6 | .000 | 30 | 9 | 0 | 0 | 0 | 82¹ | 116 | 2 | 34 | 12 | 17.1 | 5.47 | 75 | .345 | .415 | 3 | .176 | -1 | -13 | -12 | 2 | -0.9 |

■ AL SEVERINSEN
Severinsen, Albert Henry b: 11/9/44, Brooklyn, N.Y. BR/TR, 6'3", 220 lbs. Deb: 7/01/69

1969	Bal-A	1	1	.500	12	0	0	0	0	19²	14	2	10	13	11.0	2.29	156	.206	.308	1	.333	0	3	3	0	0.4
1971	SD-N	2	5	.286	59	0	0	0	8	70	77	4	30	31	14.0	3.47	95	.292	.368	0	.000	-0	-0	-1	2	0.0
1972	SD-N	0	1	.000	17	0	0	0	1	21¹	13	1	7	9	9.3	2.53	130	.173	.262	0	.000	-0	2	2	0	0.2
Total 3		3	7	.300	88	0	0	0	9	111	104	7	47	53	12.6	3.08	108	.256	.338	1	.200	0	5	3	2	0.6

■ ED SEWARD
Seward, Edward William (b: Edward William Sourhardt)
b: 6/29/1867, Cleveland, Ohio d: 7/30/47, Cleveland, Ohio TR , 5'7", 175 lbs. Deb: 9/30/1885 U♦

1885	Pro-N	0	0	—	1	0	0	0	0	6	2	0	0	1	3.0	0.00	—	.099	.099	0	.000	-0	2	2	1	0.2
1887	Phi-a	25	25	.500	55	52	52	3	0	470²	445	7	140	155	11.2	4.13	104	.240	.294	50	.188	-5	9	8	-2	0.0
1888	Phi-a	35	19	.648	57	57	57	6	0	518²	388	4	127	**272**	8.9	2.01	149	.200	.250	32	.142	-4	61	56	3	5.2
1889	Phi-a	21	15	.583	39	38	35	3	0	320	353	8	101	102	12.8	3.97	95	.271	.324	31	.217	6	-4	-7	-1	-0.4
1890	Phi-a	6	12	.333	21	19	15	1	0	154	165	4	72	55	13.9	4.73	81	.266	.342	10	.139	-1	-15	-16	-0	-1.4
1891	Cle-N	2	1	.667	3	3	0	0	0	17	16	0	1	4	9.4	3.86	90	.247	.258	4	.211	0	-1	-1	-0	-0.0
Total 6		89	72	.553	176	169	159	13	0	1485²	1369	23	441	589	11.0	3.40	108	.236	.290	127	.174	-4	51	43	-1	4.0

■ FRANK SEWARD
Seward, Frank Martin b: 4/7/21, Pennsauken, N.J. BR/TR, 6'3", 200 lbs. Deb: 9/28/43

1943	NY-N	0	1	.000	1	1	0	0	0	9	12	0	5	2	17.0	3.00	115	.324	.405	0	.000	-1	0	0	-0	0.0
1944	NY-N	3	2	.600	25	7	2	0	0	78¹	98	8	32	16	15.2	5.40	68	.306	.373	2	.083	-2	-16	-15	-1	-1.7
Total 2		3	3	.500	26	8	3	0	0	87¹	110	8	37	18	15.4	5.15	71	.308	.376	2	.071	-2	-15	-15	-1	-1.7

■ RIP SEWELL
Sewell, Truett Banks b: 5/11/07, Decatur, Ala. d: 9/3/89, Plant City, Fla. BL/TR, 6'1", 180 lbs. Deb: 6/14/32 C

1932	Det-A	0	0	—	5	0	0	0	0	10²	19	2	8	2	22.8	12.66	37	.388	.474	1	.500	0	-10	-9	0	-0.7
1938	Pit-N	0	1	.000	17	0	0	0	1	38¹	41	3	21	17	15.0	4.23	90	.275	.372	1	.083	-1	-2	-2	1	-0.1
1939	Pit-N	10	9	.526	52	12	5	1	2	176¹	177	10	73	69	12.8	4.08	94	.265	.339	11	.200	1	-3	-5	3	0.0
1940	Pit-N	16	5	.762	33	23	14	2	1	189²	169	6	67	60	11.3	2.80	136	.238	.307	14	.192	2	22	21	2	2.7

YEAR TM/L	W	L	PCT	G	GS	CG	SH	SV	IP	H	HR	BB	SO	RAT	ERA	ERA+	OAV	OOB	BH	AVG	PB	PR	/A	PD	TPI
1941 Pit-N	14	17	.452	39	32	18	2	2	249	225	18	84	76	11.3	3.72	97	.235	.299	16	.174	0	-2	-3	2	0.0
1942 Pit-N	17	15	.531	40	33	18	5	2	248	259	13	72	69	12.1	3.41	99	.265	.317	13	.149	-2	-3	-1	0	-0.1
1943 Pit-N	21	9	.700	35	31	25	2	3	265¹	267	6	75	65	11.7	2.54	137	.260	.312	30	.286	6	25	28	1	4.0
1944 Pit-N	21	12	.636	38	33	24	3	2	286	263	15	99	87	11.5	3.18	117	.240	.304	25	.223	3	14	17	-1	2.1
1945 Pit-N	11	9	.550	33	24	9	1	1	188	212	9	91	60	14.6	4.07	97	.279	.357	20	.313	6	-6	-3	0	0.4
1946 Pit-N	8	12	.400	25	20	11	2	0	149¹	140	6	53	33	11.7	3.68	96	.245	.310	9	.180	0	-4	-3	-1	-0.2
1947 Pit-N	6	4	.600	24	12	4	1	0	121	121	11	36	36	11.9	3.57	118	.263	.321	5	.125	-1	7	9	1	0.9
1948 Pit-N	13	3	.813	21	17	7	0	0	121²	126	9	37	36	12.1	3.48	117	.262	.317	6	.143	1	6	8	0	0.9
1949 Pit-N	6	1	.857	28	6	2	1	1	76	82	8	32	26	13.5	3.91	108	.280	.351	1	.063	-0	1	2	-0	0.2
Total 13	143	97	.596	390	243	137	20	15	2119¹	2101	116	748	636	12.2	3.48	107	.256	.320	152	.203	16	45	60	8	10.1

■ ELMER SEXAUER
Sexauer, Elmer George b: 5/21/26, St.Louis Co., Mo.   BR/TR, 6'4", 220 lbs.   Deb: 9/06/48

YEAR TM/L	W	L	PCT	G	GS	CG	SH	SV	IP	H	HR	BB	SO	RAT	ERA	ERA+	OAV	OOB	BH	AVG	PB	PR	/A	PD	TPI
1948 Bro-N	0	0	—	2	0	0	0	0	0²	0	0	2	0	27.0	13.50	30	.000	.500	0	—	0	-1	-1	0	0.0

■ FRANK SEXTON
Sexton, Frank Joseph b: 7/8/1872, Brockton, Mass.   d: 1/4/38, Brighton, Mass.   Deb: 6/21/1895

YEAR TM/L	W	L	PCT	G	GS	CG	SH	SV	IP	H	HR	BB	SO	RAT	ERA	ERA+	OAV	OOB	BH	AVG	PB	PR	/A	PD	TPI
1895 Bos-N	1	5	.167	7	5	4	0	0	49	59	2	22	14	14.9	5.69	90	.293	.363	5	.227	-1	-5	-3	-0	-0.3

■ GORDON SEYFRIED
Seyfried, Gordon Clay b: 7/4/37, Long Beach, Cal.   BR/TR, 6', 185 lbs.   Deb: 9/13/63

YEAR TM/L	W	L	PCT	G	GS	CG	SH	SV	IP	H	HR	BB	SO	RAT	ERA	ERA+	OAV	OOB	BH	AVG	PB	PR	/A	PD	TPI
1963 Cle-A	0	1	.000	3	1	0	0	0	7¹	9	0	3	1	14.7	1.23	295	.300	.364	0	.000	-0	2	2	0	0.2
1964 Cle-A	0	0	—	2	0	0	0	0	2¹	4	0	0	0	15.4	0.00	—	.444	.444	0	—	0	1	1	0	0.1
Total 2	0	1	.000	5	1	0	0	0	9²	13	0	3	1	14.9	0.93	388	.333	.381	0	.000	-0	3	3	0	0.3

■ JAKE SEYMOUR
Seymour, Jacob (b: Jacob Semer) b: 1854, Pittsburgh, Pa.   d: 8/1/1897, Allegheny, Pa.   Deb: 9/23/1882

YEAR TM/L	W	L	PCT	G	GS	CG	SH	SV	IP	H	HR	BB	SO	RAT	ERA	ERA+	OAV	OOB	BH	AVG	PB	PR	/A	PD	TPI
1882 Pit-a	0	1	.000	1	1	1	0	0	8	16	0	2	2	20.3	7.88	33	.391	.420	0	.000	-1	-5	-5	0	-0.3

■ CY SEYMOUR
Seymour, James Bentley b: 12/9/1872, Albany, N.Y.   d: 9/20/19, New York, N.Y.   BL/TL, 6', 200 lbs.   Deb: 4/22/1896 ◆

YEAR TM/L	W	L	PCT	G	GS	CG	SH	SV	IP	H	HR	BB	SO	RAT	ERA	ERA+	OAV	OOB	BH	AVG	PB	PR	/A	PD	TPI
1896 NY-N	2	4	.333	11	8	4	0	0	70¹	75	8	51	33	16.1	6.40	66	.271	.384	7	.219	-1	-16	-17	1	-1.4
1897 NY-N	18	14	.563	38	33	28	2	1	277²	254	4	164	149	13.5	3.37	123	.242	.344	33	.241	1	29	24	7	2.8
1898 NY-N	25	19	.568	45	43	39	4	0	356²	313	4	213	239	13.3	3.18	109	.234	.340	82	.276	7	17	12	7	2.9
1899 NY-N	14	18	.438	32	32	31	0	0	268¹	247	5	170	142	14.0	3.56	106	.245	.353	52	.327	8	9	6	4	2.0
1900 NY-N	2	1	.667	13	7	2	0	0	53	58	4	54	19	19.0	6.96	52	.278	.426	12	.300	1	-19	-20	1	-1.3
1902 Cin-N	0	0	—	1	0	0	0	0	3	4	0	3	2	21.0	9.00	33	.319	.451	83	.340	0	-2	-2	-0	-0.1
Total 6	61	56	.521	140	123	104	6	1	1029	951	25	655	584	14.0	3.76	101	.244	.353	1723	.303	16	18	3	19	4.9

■ JOHN SHAFFER
Shaffer, John W. "Cannon Ball" b: 2/18/1864, Lock Haven, Pa.   d: 11/21/26, Endicott, N.Y.   Deb: 9/13/1886

YEAR TM/L	W	L	PCT	G	GS	CG	SH	SV	IP	H	HR	BB	SO	RAT	ERA	ERA+	OAV	OOB	BH	AVG	PB	PR	/A	PD	TPI
1886 NY-a	5	3	.625	8	8	8	1	0	69	40	0	29	36	9.0	1.96	175	.161	.248	6	.240	1	11	11	-1	1.0
1887 NY-a	2	11	.154	13	13	13	0	0	112	148	3	53	22	16.2	6.19	69	.307	.375	8	.167	-3	-24	-24	2	-1.8
Total 2	7	14	.333	21	21	21	1	0	181	188	3	82	58	13.4	4.57	86	.257	.332	14	.192	-2	-12	-13	1	-0.8

■ GUS SHALLIX
Shallix, August (b: August Schallick)
b: 3/29/1858, Paderborn, Westphalia, Germany   d: 10/28/37, Cincinnati, Ohio   BR/TR, 5'11", 165 lbs.   Deb: 6/22/1884

YEAR TM/L	W	L	PCT	G	GS	CG	SH	SV	IP	H	HR	BB	SO	RAT	ERA	ERA+	OAV	OOB	BH	AVG	PB	PR	/A	PD	TPI
1884 Cin-a	11	10	.524	23	23	23	0	0	199²	163	6	53	78	9.7	3.70	90	.211	.261	3	.036	-11	-10	-8	1	-1.4
1885 Cin-a	6	4	.600	13	12	7	0	0	91¹	95	1	33	15	12.6	3.25	100	.257	.318	5	.128	-2	-0	0	1	0.0
Total 2	17	14	.548	36	35	30	0	0	291	258	7	86	93	10.6	3.56	93	.226	.280	8	.065	-13	-10	-8	2	-1.4

■ GREG SHANAHAN
Shanahan, Paul Gregory b: 12/11/47, Eureka, Cal.   BR/TR, 6'2", 190 lbs.   Deb: 9/04/73

YEAR TM/L	W	L	PCT	G	GS	CG	SH	SV	IP	H	HR	BB	SO	RAT	ERA	ERA+	OAV	OOB	BH	AVG	PB	PR	/A	PD	TPI
1973 LA-N	0	0	—	7	0	0	0	1	15²	14	2	4	11	10.3	3.45	100	.230	.277	0	.000	0	-0	-0	0	0.0
1974 LA-N	0	0	—	4	0	0	0	0	7	7	1	5	2	15.4	3.86	88	.259	.375	0	—	0	-0	-0	0	0.0
Total 2	0	0	—	11	0	0	0	1	22²	21	3	9	13	11.9	3.57	96	.239	.309	0	.000	0	0	-0	0	0.0

■ HARVEY SHANK
Shank, Harvey Tillman b: 7/29/46, Toronto, Ont., Can.   BR/TR, 6'4", 220 lbs.   Deb: 5/16/70

YEAR TM/L	W	L	PCT	G	GS	CG	SH	SV	IP	H	HR	BB	SO	RAT	ERA	ERA+	OAV	OOB	BH	AVG	PB	PR	/A	PD	TPI
1970 Cal-A	0	0	—	1	0	0	0	0	3	2	0	2	1	12.0	0.00	—	.182	.308	0	—	0	1	1	0	0.1

■ BILL SHANNER
Shanner, Wilfred William b: 11/4/1894, Oakland City, Ind.   d: 12/18/86, Evansville, Ind.   BL/TR,   Deb: 10/01/20

YEAR TM/L	W	L	PCT	G	GS	CG	SH	SV	IP	H	HR	BB	SO	RAT	ERA	ERA+	OAV	OOB	BH	AVG	PB	PR	/A	PD	TPI
1920 Phi-A	0	0	—	1	0	0	0	0	4	6	2	1	1	15.8	6.75	60	.353	.389	0	.000	-0	-1	-1	0	0.0

■ BOBBY SHANTZ
Shantz, Robert Clayton b: 9/26/25, Pottstown, Pa.   BR/TL, 5'6", 139 lbs.   Deb: 5/01/49

YEAR TM/L	W	L	PCT	G	GS	CG	SH	SV	IP	H	HR	BB	SO	RAT	ERA	ERA+	OAV	OOB	BH	AVG	PB	PR	/A	PD	TPI
1949 Phi-A	6	8	.429	33	7	4	1	2	127	100	9	74	58	12.5	3.40	121	.221	.334	7	.189	1	11	10	4	1.4
1950 Phi-A	8	14	.364	36	23	6	1	0	214²	251	18	85	93	14.4	4.61	99	.294	.362	11	.167	-0	-1	-4	0	0.2
1951 Phi-A	18	10	.643	32	25	13	3	0	205¹	213	15	70	77	12.6	3.94	108	.270	.333	18	.250	2	4	8	3	1.3
1952 Phi-A	24	7	.774	33	33	27	5	0	279²	230	21	63	152	9.6	2.48	160	.225	.272	19	.198	2	37	46	1	5.6
1953 Phi-A	5	9	.357	16	16	6	0	0	105²	107	10	26	58	11.3	4.09	105	.263	.307	9	.237	1	-1	2	1	0.6
1954 Phi-A	1	0	1.000	2	1	0	0	0	8	12	2	3	3	18.0	7.88	50	.364	.432	1	.333	0	-4	-4	0	-0.2
1955 KC-A	5	10	.333	23	17	4	1	0	125	124	8	66	58	13.8	4.54	92	.264	.356	6	.146	-2	-8	-5	1	-0.4
1956 KC-A	2	7	.222	45	2	1	0	9	101¹	95	12	37	67	12.0	4.35	99	.248	.319	2	.091	-1	-2	-0	1	0.0
1957 *NY-A	11	5	.688	30	21	9	1	5	173	157	15	40	72	10.6	2.45	147	.248	.299	10	.179	2	26	22	7	3.4
1958 NY-A	7	6	.538	33	13	3	0	1	126	127	8	35	80	11.7	3.36	105	.262	.315	8	.229	2	6	2	3	0.8
1959 NY-A	7	3	.700	33	4	2	2	3	94²	64	4	33	66	9.2	2.38	153	.189	.261	5	.217	2	16	13	1	1.6
1960 *NY-A	5	4	.556	42	0	0	0	11	67²	57	5	24	54	11.0	2.79	128	.235	.309	1	.100	-0	8	6	1	0.6
1961 Pit-N	6	3	.667	43	6	2	1	2	89¹	91	5	26	61	12.2	3.32	120	.271	.331	7	.438	3	7	7	1	1.1
1962 Hou-N	1	1	.500	3	3	1	0	0	20²	15	1	5	14	8.7	1.31	286	.208	.260	0	.000	-1	6	6	2	0.6
StL-N	5	3	.625	28	0	0	0	4	57²	45	7	20	47	10.3	2.18	195	.211	.282	2	.154	0	11	13	1	1.4
Yr	6	4	.600	31	3	1	0	4	78¹	60	8	25	61	9.9	1.95	211	.210	.276	0	.000	-1	17	19	3	2.0
1963 StL-N	6	4	.600	55	0	0	0	11	79	55	6	17	70	8.4	2.62	135	.192	.243	1	.143	0	6	8	2	1.2
1964 StL-N	1	3	.250	16	0	0	0	0	17¹	14	2	7	12	10.9	3.12	122	.226	.304	0	—	0	1	1	1	0.3
Chi-N	0	1	.000	20	0	0	0	1	11¹	15	2	6	12	16.7	5.56	67	.319	.396	0	—	0	-3	-2	0	-0.1
Phi-N	1	1	.500	14	0	0	0	0	32	23	1	6	18	8.2	2.25	154	.204	.244	0	.000	-0	5	4	2	0.7
Yr	2	5	.286	50	0	0	0	1	60²	52	5	19	42	10.5	3.12	116	.233	.293	2	.400	0	3	3	4	0.7
Total 16	119	99	.546	537	171	78	15	48	1935¹	1795	151	643	1072	11.5	3.38	119	.248	.313	107	.195	11	125	137	37	20.1

■ GEORGE SHARROTT
Sharrott, George Oscar b: 11/2/1869, W.New Brighton, S.I., N.Y.   d: 1/6/32, Jamaica, N.Y.   BL/TL,   Deb: 7/27/1893

YEAR TM/L	W	L	PCT	G	GS	CG	SH	SV	IP	H	HR	BB	SO	RAT	ERA	ERA+	OAV	OOB	BH	AVG	PB	PR	/A	PD	TPI
1893 Bro-N	4	6	.400	13	10	10	0	1	95	114	3	58	24	16.3	5.87	75	.289	.380	9	.231	0	-13	-15	-1	-1.2
1894 Bro-N	0	1	.000	2	2	1	0	0	9	7	0	5	2	12.0	7.00	71	.213	.316	1	.333	0	-2	-2	-0	-0.1
Total 2	4	7	.364	15	12	11	0	1	104	121	3	63	26	15.9	5.97	75	.283	.375	10	.238	0	-14	-17	-1	-1.3

■ JACK SHARROTT
Sharrott, John Henry b: 8/13/1869, Bangor, Me.   d: 12/31/27, Los Angeles, Cal.   BR/TR, 5'9", 165 lbs.   Deb: 4/22/1890 ◆

YEAR TM/L	W	L	PCT	G	GS	CG	SH	SV	IP	H	HR	BB	SO	RAT	ERA	ERA+	OAV	OOB	BH	AVG	PB	PR	/A	PD	TPI
1890 NY-N	11	10	.524	25	20	18	0	0	184	162	3	88	84	12.2	2.89	121	.230	.315	22	.202	-2	14	12	3	1.1
1891 NY-N	5	5	.500	10	9	6	0	1	69¹	47	2	35	41	10.6	2.60	123	.185	.283	10	.333	4	6	5	1	0.8
1892 NY-N	0	0	—	1	0	0	0	0	2	2	0	1	1	13.5	4.50	72	.250	.333	1	.125	-0	-0	-0	0	0.0
1893 Phi-N	4	2	.667	12	4	2	0	0	56	53	1	33	11	13.8	4.50	102	.242	.342	38	.250	1	1	0	0	0.0
Total 4	20	17	.541	48	33	26	0	1	311¹	264	6	157	137	12.2	3.12	116	.222	.313	71	.237	2	20	17	3	1.9

■ JOE SHAUTE
Shaute, Joseph Benjamin "Lefty" b: 8/1/1899, Peckville, Pa.   d: 2/21/70, Scranton, Pa.   BL/TL, 6', 190 lbs.   Deb: 7/06/22

YEAR TM/L	W	L	PCT	G	GS	CG	SH	SV	IP	H	HR	BB	SO	RAT	ERA	ERA+	OAV	OOB	BH	AVG	PB	PR	/A	PD	TPI
1922 Cle-A	0	0	—	2	0	0	0	0	3²	7	2	3	3	24.5	19.64	20	.389	.476	0	.000	-0	-6	-6	-0	-0.4
1923 Cle-A	10	8	.556	33	16	7	0	0	172	176	4	53	61	12.0	3.51	113	.275	.332	11	.162	-4	9	9	-2	0.3
1924 Cle-A	20	17	.541	46	34	21	2	2	283	317	8	83	68	12.9	3.75	114	.287	.340	34	.318	9	15	16	-2	2.3

YEAR	TM/L	W	L	PCT	G	GS	CG	SH	SV	IP	H	HR	BB	SO	RAT	ERA	ERA+	OAV	OOB	BH	AVG	PB	PR	/A	PD	TPI
1925	Cle-A	4	12	.250	26	17	10	1	4	131	160	6	44	34	14.1	5.43	81	.304	.358	16	.302	3	-15	-15	-1	-1.1
1926	Cle-A	14	10	.583	34	25	15	1	1	206²	215	9	65	47	12.3	3.53	115	.278	.337	20	.274	4	11	12	-5	1.1
1927	Cle-A	9	16	.360	45	28	14	0	2	230¹	255	9	75	63	13.0	4.22	100	.286	.343	27	.325	6	-2	-0	-2	0.4
1928	Cle-A	13	17	.433	36	31	21	1	2	253²	295	6	68	81	13.1	4.04	102	.299	.348	21	.228	3	-0	3	1	0.7
1929	Cle-A	8	8	.500	26	24	8	0	0	162	211	6	52	43	14.7	4.28	104	.320	.370	17	.293	3	-1	3	-2	0.4
1930	Cle-A	0	0	—	4	0	0	0	0	4²	8	0	4	2	23.1	15.43	31	.333	.429	0	—	0	-6	-5	0	-0.4
1931	Bro-N	11	8	.579	25	19	6	0	0	128²	162	9	32	50	13.6	4.83	79	.305	.346	8	.178	-0	-14	-15	0	-1.3
1932	Bro-N	7	7	.500	34	9	1	0	4	117	147	8	21	32	13.1	4.54	84	.301	.333	9	.200	1	-9	-9	-1	-0.8
1933	Bro-N	3	4	.429	41	4	0	0	2	108¹	125	4	31	26	13.0	3.49	92	.287	.336	6	.222	1	-2	-3	-1	-0.1
1934	Cin-N	0	2	.000	8	1	0	0	1	17¹	19	1	3	2	11.4	4.15	98	.268	.297	1	.250	0	-0	-0	-1	0.0
Total	13	99	109	.476	360	208	103	5	18	1818¹	2097	75	534	512	13.1	4.15	99	.293	.345	170	.258	26	-18	-12	-13	1.1

■ JEFF SHAVER
Shaver, Jeffrey Thomas b: 7/30/63, Beaver, Pa. BR/TR, 6'3", 195 lbs. Deb: 7/06/88

YEAR	TM/L	W	L	PCT	G	GS	CG	SH	SV	IP	H	HR	BB	SO	RAT	ERA	ERA+	OAV	OOB	BH	AVG	PB	PR	/A	PD	TPI
1988	Oak-A	0	0	—	1	0	0	0	0	1	1	0	0	0	9.0	0.00	—	.000	.333	0	—	0	0	0	0	0.0

■ DON SHAW
Shaw, Donald Wellington b: 2/23/44, Pittsburgh, Pa. BL/TL, 6', 180 lbs. Deb: 4/11/67

YEAR	TM/L	W	L	PCT	G	GS	CG	SH	SV	IP	H	HR	BB	SO	RAT	ERA	ERA+	OAV	OOB	BH	AVG	PB	PR	/A	PD	TPI
1967	NY-N	4	5	.444	40	0	0	0	3	51¹	40	5	23	44	11.0	2.98	114	.219	.306	0	.000	-	2	2	-1	0.2
1968	NY-N	0	0	—	7	0	0	0	0	12¹	3	1	5	11	5.8	0.73	414	.086	.200	0	—	0	3	3	0	0.4
1969	Mon-N	2	5	.286	35	1	0	0	1	65²	61	9	37	45	13.7	5.21	71	.254	.358	0	.000	-0	-12	-11	1	-1.0
1971	StL-N	7	2	.778	45	0	0	0	2	51	45	1	31	19	13.6	2.65	136	.237	.347	0	.000	-0	5	5	0	0.6
1972	StL-N	0	1	.000	8	0	0	0	0	3	5	1	3	0	24.0	9.00	38	.417	.533	0	—	-0	-2	-2	-0	-0.1
	Oak-A	0	1	.000	3	0	0	0	0	5¹	12	2	2	4	23.6	16.88	17	.500	.538	0	—	0	-8	-8	-0	-0.7
Total	5	13	14	.481	138	1	0	0	6	188²	166	19	101	123	12.9	4.01	87	.243	.343	0	.000	-0	-12	-11	-0	-0.6

■ DUPEE SHAW
Shaw, Frederick Lander b: 5/31/1859, Charlestown, Mass. d: 6/11/38, Everett, Mass. BL/TL, 5'8", 165 lbs. Deb: 6/11/1883

YEAR	TM/L	W	L	PCT	G	GS	CG	SH	SV	IP	H	HR	BB	SO	RAT	ERA	ERA+	OAV	OOB	BH	AVG	PB	PR	/A	PD	TPI
1883	Det-N	10	15	.400	26	25	23	1	0	227	238	3	44	73	11.2	2.50	124	.254	.288	29	.206	-3	16	15	0	1.0
1884	Det-N	9	18	.333	28	28	25	0	0	227²	219	8	72	142	11.5	3.04	95	.239	.295	26	.191	-1	-2	-4	1	-0.3
	Bos-U	21	15	.583	39	38	35	5	0	315²	227	1	37	309	7.5	1.77	166	.188	.212	37	.242	1	44	41	-1	3.7
1885	Pro-N	23	26	.469	49	49	47	6	0	399²	343	7	99	194	10.0	2.57	104	.221	.268	22	.133	-9	11	4	-3	-0.7
1886	Was-N	13	31	.295	45	44	43	1	0	385²	384	12	91	117	11.1	3.34	98	.249	.291	13	.088	-10	-1	-2	-1	-1.1
1887	Was-N	7	13	.350	21	20	20	0	0	181¹	263	8	46	47	15.3	6.45	63	.330	.366	13	.186	-2	-48	-49	-2	-3.9
1888	Was-N	0	3	.000	3	3	3	0	0	25	36	2	7	8	15.5	6.48	43	.326	.366	0	.000	-1	-10	-10	-1	-0.9
Total	6	83	121	.407	211	207	196	13	0	1762	1710	41	396	950	10.8	3.10	99	.242	.282	140	.170	-25	10	-5	-6	-2.2

■ JIM SHAW
Shaw, James Aloysius "Grunting Jim" b: 8/19/1893, Pittsburgh, Pa. d: 1/27/62, Washington, D.C. BR/TR, 6', 180 lbs. Deb: 9/15/13

YEAR	TM/L	W	L	PCT	G	GS	CG	SH	SV	IP	H	HR	BB	SO	RAT	ERA	ERA+	OAV	OOB	BH	AVG	PB	PR	/A	PD	TPI
1913	Was-A	0	1	.000	2	1	0	0	0	13	8	0	7	14	11.1	2.08	142	.205	.340	0	.000	-0	1	1	1	0.2
1914	Was-A	15	17	.469	48	31	15	5	4	257	198	3	137	164	12.0	2.70	103	.216	.324	10	.118	-3	1	2	1	0.0
1915	Was-A	6	11	.353	25	18	7	1	1	133	102	1	76	78	12.2	2.50	117	.220	.333	10	.233	1	6	6	-1	0.7
1916	Was-A	3	8	.273	26	9	5	2	1	106¹	86	1	50	44	11.7	2.62	105	.227	.320	5	.156	-0	2	2	-3	0.0
1917	Was-A	15	14	.517	47	31	15	2	1	266¹	233	1	123	118	12.1	3.21	82	.242	.328	14	.154	-2	-16	-17	-3	-2.3
1918	Was-A	16	12	.571	41	30	14	4	1	241¹	201	2	90	129	10.9	2.42	113	.228	.300	11	.133	-4	9	8	-5	-0.1
1919	Was-A	17	17	.500	45	37	23	3	5	306²	274	5	101	128	11.2	2.73	118	.244	.309	17	.160	-1	17	16	-6	1.0
1920	Was-A	11	18	.379	38	32	17	0	1	236¹	285	12	87	88	14.3	4.27	87	.314	.376	14	.189	0	-12	-14	-4	-1.6
1921	Was-A	1	0	1.000	15	4	0	0	3	40¹	59	2	17	4	17.0	7.36	56	.345	.404	5	.417	-2	-14	-15	0	-1.0
Total	9	84	98	.462	287	193	96	17	17	1600¹	1446	28	688	767	12.1	3.07	98	.247	.329	86	.163	-8	-4	-10	-20	-3.1

■ JEFF SHAW
Shaw, Jeffrey Lee b: 7/7/66, Washington Court House, Ohio BR/TR, 6'2", 185 lbs. Deb: 4/30/90

YEAR	TM/L	W	L	PCT	G	GS	CG	SH	SV	IP	H	HR	BB	SO	RAT	ERA	ERA+	OAV	OOB	BH	AVG	PB	PR	/A	PD	TPI
1990	Cle-A	3	4	.429	12	9	0	0	0	48²	73	11	20	25	17.2	6.66	60	.356	.413	0	—	0	-15	-14	0	-1.3

■ BOB SHAW
Shaw, Robert John b: 6/29/33, Bronx, N.Y. BR/TR, 6'2", 195 lbs. Deb: 8/11/57 C

YEAR	TM/L	W	L	PCT	G	GS	CG	SH	SV	IP	H	HR	BB	SO	RAT	ERA	ERA+	OAV	OOB	BH	AVG	PB	PR	/A	PD	TPI
1957	Det-A	0	1	.000	7	0	0	0	0	9²	11	2	7	4	16.8	7.45	52	.289	.400	0	.000	-0	-4	-4	0	-0.3
1958	Det-A	1	2	.333	11	2	0	0	0	26²	32	2	13	17	15.2	5.06	80	.302	.378	3	.375	1	-4	-3	1	0.0
	Chi-A	4	2	.667	29	3	0	0	1	64	67	8	28	18	13.6	4.64	78	.271	.350	0	.000	-1	-6	-7	2	-0.5
	Yr	5	4	.556	40	5	0	0	1	90²	99	10	41	35	14.1	4.76	79	.280	.358	4	.182	0	-10	-10	3	-0.5
1959	*Chi-A	18	6	.750	47	26	8	3	3	230²	217	15	54	89	10.8	2.69	140	.249	.297	9	.123	-2	30	27	2	2.8
1960	Chi-A	13	13	.500	36	32	7	1	0	192²	221	16	62	46	13.4	4.06	93	.292	.348	8	.138	-0	-4	-6	0	-0.6
1961	Chi-A	3	4	.429	14	10	3	0	0	71¹	85	11	20	31	13.4	3.79	103	.302	.351	0	.000	-1	2	1	0	0.0
	KC-A	9	10	.474	26	24	6	0	0	150¹	165	13	58	60	13.8	4.31	95	.281	.352	11	.200	-1	-5	-3	0	-0.2
	Yr	12	14	.462	40	34	9	0	0	221²	250	24	78	91	13.6	4.14	98	.286	.349	3	.041	-2	-3	-2	0	-0.2
1962	Mil-N	15	9	.625	38	29	12	3	2	225	223	20	44	124	11.2	2.80	136	.260	.305	10	.137	1	29	25	0	2.6
1963	Mil-N	7	11	.389	48	16	3	3	13	159	144	10	55	105	11.5	2.66	121	.243	.312	5	.122	0	11	10	-1	0.9
1964	SF-N	7	6	.538	61	1	0	0	11	93¹	105	5	31	57	13.6	3.76	95	.286	.350	0	.000	-1	-2	-2	-1	-0.4
1965	SF-N	16	9	.640	42	33	6	1	2	235	213	17	53	148	10.3	2.64	136	.236	.280	8	.101	-3	23	25	1	2.6
1966	SF-N	1	4	.200	13	6	0	0	0	31²	45	9	7	21	14.8	6.25	59	.324	.356	0	.000	-1	-9	-9	-0	-0.9
	NY-N	11	10	.524	26	25	7	2	0	167²	171	12	42	104	11.8	3.92	93	.261	.313	13	.260	3	-6	-5	1	-0.1
	Yr	12	14	.462	39	31	7	2	0	199¹	216	21	49	125	12.3	4.29	85	.272	.320	4	.071	2	-15	-14	0	-1.0
1967	NY-N	3	9	.250	23	13	3	1	0	98²	105	9	28	49	12.3	4.29	79	.273	.326	1	.040	-1	-10	-10	-1	-1.2
	Chi-N	0	2	.000	9	3	0	0	0	22¹	33	0	9	7	18.5	6.04	59	.351	.430	1	.250	0	-7	-6	0	-0.6
	Yr	3	11	.214	32	16	3	1	0	121	138	9	37	56	13.3	4.61	74	.286	.342	2	.069	-1	-17	-16	-2	-1.8
Total	11	108	98	.524	430	223	55	14	32	1778	1837	149	511	880	12.2	3.52	105	.267	.323	69	.133	-7	38	33	1	4.1

■ SAM SHAW
Shaw, Samuel E. b: 5/1864, Baltimore, Md. BR/TR, 5'5", 140 lbs. Deb: 5/03/1888

YEAR	TM/L	W	L	PCT	G	GS	CG	SH	SV	IP	H	HR	BB	SO	RAT	ERA	ERA+	OAV	OOB	BH	AVG	PB	PR	/A	PD	TPI
1888	Bal-a	2	4	.333	6	6	6	0	0	53	65	2	15	22	13.6	3.40	88	.291	.336	3	.150	-1	-2	-2	-1	-0.2
1893	Chi-N	1	0	1.000	2	2	1	0	0	16	12	2	13	1	14.1	5.63	82	.202	.346	2	.286	-0	-2	-2	0	-0.1
Total	2	3	4	.429	8	8	7	0	0	69	77	4	28	23	13.7	3.91	86	.273	.338	5	.185	-1	-4	-4	-1	-0.3

■ BOB SHAWKEY
Shawkey, James Robert b: 12/4/1890, Sigel, Pa. d: 12/31/80, Syracuse, N.Y. BR/TR, 5'11", 168 lbs. Deb: 7/16/13 MC

YEAR	TM/L	W	L	PCT	G	GS	CG	SH	SV	IP	H	HR	BB	SO	RAT	ERA	ERA+	OAV	OOB	BH	AVG	PB	PR	/A	PD	TPI
1913	Phi-A	6	5	.545	18	15	8	1	0	111¹	92	2	50	52	11.7	2.34	118	.207	.291	6	.136	-2	7	5	1	0.5
1914	*Phi-A	16	8	.667	38	31	18	5	2	237	223	4	75	89	11.4	2.73	96	.262	.323	17	.205	2	0	-3	-1	-0.2
1915	Phi-A	6	6	.500	17	13	7	1	0	100	103	3	38	56	12.8	4.05	73	.278	.346	4	.129	-1	-12	-12	-0	-1.3
	NY-A	4	7	.364	16	9	5	1	0	85²	78	2	35	31	12.1	3.26	90	.265	.347	7	.241	1	-3	-3	-1	-0.2
	Yr	10	13	.435	33	22	12	2	0	185²	181	5	73	87	12.4	3.68	80	.272	.345	11	.050	1	-15	-15	-1	-1.5
1916	NY-A	24	14	.632	53	27	21	4	8	276²	204	4	81	122	9.5	2.21	131	.209	.273	17	.183	-1	19	21	0	2.2
1917	NY-A	13	15	.464	32	26	16	2	0	236¹	207	2	72	97	10.9	2.44	110	.243	.306	16	.190	-0	6	7	3	1.1
1918	NY-A	1	1	.500	3	2	1	1	0	16	7	0	10	3	9.6	1.13	251	.143	.288	3	.750	2	3	3	0	0.6
1919	NY-A	20	11	.645	41	27	22	3	5	261¹	218	7	92	122	10.8	2.72	117	.231	.303	22	.234	-0	15	14	-1	1.3
1920	NY-A	20	13	.606	38	31	20	5	2	267²	246	10	85	126	11.2	2.45	156	.248	.308	23	.230	-0	40	41	-3	3.7
1921	*NY-A	18	12	.600	38	31	18	3	2	245	245	15	86	126	12.4	4.08	104	.263	.329	27	.300	4	6	4	-5	0.3
1922	*NY-A	20	12	.625	39	34	22	3	1	299²	286	16	98	130	11.5	2.91	138	.256	.316	21	.183	-3	38	36	-1	3.3
1923	*NY-A	16	11	.593	36	31	17	1	1	258²	232	17	102	125	11.8	3.51	112	.246	.322	20	.202	-3	14	12	1	0.6
1924	NY-A	16	11	.593	38	25	10	1	0	207²	226	11	74	114	13.1	4.12	101	.286	.350	22	.319	7	3	1	-2	0.6
1925	NY-A	6	14	.300	33	20	9	1	0	186	209	12	67	81	13.6	4.11	104	.294	.359	10	.147	-4	6	3	-2	-0.1
1926	*NY-A	8	7	.533	29	16	3	1	0	104¹	102	8	37	63	12.2	3.62	106	.263	.330	9	.257	-2	1	0	-3	0.3
1927	NY-A	2	3	.400	19	2	0	0	4	43²	44	1	16	23	12.6	2.89	134	.262	.330	1	.091	-1	6	5	0	0.3
Total	15	196	150	.566	488	334	197	33	28	2937	2722	114	1018	1360	11.6	3.09	114	.251	.319	225	.214	4	151	137	-13	13.2

YEAR TM/L	W	L	PCT	G	GS	CG	SH	SV	IP	H	HR	BB	SO	RAT	ERA	ERA+	OAV	OOB	BH	AVG	PB	PR	/A	PD	TPI

■ SPEC SHEA
Shea, Francis Joseph "The Naugatuck Nugget" (b: Francis Joseph O'shea) b: 10/2/20, Naugatuck, Conn. BR/TR, 6', 195 lbs. Deb: 4/19/47

YEAR TM/L	W	L	PCT	G	GS	CG	SH	SV	IP	H	HR	BB	SO	RAT	ERA	ERA+	OAV	OOB	BH	AVG	PB	PR	/A	PD	TPI
1947 *NY-A	14	5	.737	27	23	13	3	1	178²	127	10	89	89	11.1	3.07	115	.200	.303	11	.196	2	13	9	-3	0.8
1948 NY-A	9	10	.474	28	22	8	3	1	155²	117	10	87	71	11.9	3.41	120	.208	.316	7	.149	1	15	12	-2	0.9
1949 NY-A	1	1	.500	20	3	0	0	1	52¹	48	5	43	22	15.6	5.33	76	.250	.387	3	.250	1	-7	-7	0	-0.6
1951 NY-A	5	5	.500	25	11	2	2	0	95²	112	11	50	38	15.6	4.33	88	.300	.389	6	.214	1	-2	-5	0	-0.4
1952 Was-A	11	7	.611	22	21	12	2	0	169	144	6	92	65	12.7	2.93	121	.231	.331	15	.238	2	14	12	-1	1.4
1953 Was-A	12	7	.632	23	23	11	1	0	164²	151	11	75	38	12.6	3.94	99	.244	.329	11	.177	-1	1	-1	-1	-0.1
1954 Was-A	2	9	.182	23	11	1	0	0	71¹	97	9	34	22	16.8	6.18	58	.340	.414	1	.050	-2	-19	-21	1	-2.0
1955 Was-A	2	2	.500	27	4	1	1	2	56¹	53	4	27	16	12.9	3.99	96	.251	.339	4	.400	2	-0	-1	-1	0.0
Total 8	56	46	.549	195	118	48	12	5	943²	849	66	497	361	13.0	3.80	99	.243	.340	58	.195	6	14	-3	-6	-0.0

■ JOHN SHEA
Shea, John Michael Joseph "Lefty" b: 12/27/04, Everett, Mass. d: 11/30/56, Malden, Mass. BL/TL, 5'10.5", 171 lbs. Deb: 6/30/28

YEAR TM/L	W	L	PCT	G	GS	CG	SH	SV	IP	H	HR	BB	SO	RAT	ERA	ERA+	OAV	OOB	BH	AVG	PB	PR	/A	PD	TPI
1928 Bos-A	0	0	—	1	0	0	0	0	1	1	0	1	0	18.0	18.00	23	.250	.400	0	—	0	-2	-2	0	0.0

■ MIKE SHEA
Shea, Michael J. b: 3/10/1867, New Orleans, La. 5'10", 170 lbs. Deb: 4/20/1887

YEAR TM/L	W	L	PCT	G	GS	CG	SH	SV	IP	H	HR	BB	SO	RAT	ERA	ERA+	OAV	OOB	BH	AVG	PB	PR	/A	PD	TPI
1887 Cin-a	1	1	.500	2	2	2	0	0	16²	26	0	10	0	19.4	7.02	61	.343	.420	2	.250	0	-5	-5	1	-0.2

■ RED SHEA
Shea, Patrick Henry b: 11/29/1898, Ware, Mass. d: 11/17/81, Stafford Springs, Conn. BR/TR, 6', 165 lbs. Deb: 5/06/18

YEAR TM/L	W	L	PCT	G	GS	CG	SH	SV	IP	H	HR	BB	SO	RAT	ERA	ERA+	OAV	OOB	BH	AVG	PB	PR	/A	PD	TPI
1918 Phi-A	0	0	—	3	0	0	0	0	9	14	0	2	2	16.0	4.00	73	.378	.410	1	.000	-0	-1	-1	-0	-0.1
1921 NY-N	5	2	.714	9	2	1	0	0	32	28	2	2	10	9.3	3.09	119	.239	.270	1	.111	-1	2	2	-1	0.1
1922 NY-N	0	3	.000	11	2	0	0	0	23	22	2	11	5	12.9	4.70	85	.256	.340	0	.000	-1	-2	-2	1	-0.1
Total 3	5	5	.500	23	4	1	0	0	64	64	4	15	17	11.5	3.80	97	.267	.318	1	.053	-2	-0	-1	-0	-0.1

■ STEVE SHEA
Shea, Steven Francis b: 12/5/42, Worcester, Mass. BR/TR, 6'3", 215 lbs. Deb: 7/14/68

YEAR TM/L	W	L	PCT	G	GS	CG	SH	SV	IP	H	HR	BB	SO	RAT	ERA	ERA+	OAV	OOB	BH	AVG	PB	PR	/A	PD	TPI
1968 Hou-N	4	4	.500	30	0	0	0	6	34²	27	0	11	15	10.6	3.38	88	.229	.311	0	.000	-1	-2	-2	1	-0.1
1969 Mon-N	0	0	—	10	0	0	0	0	15²	18	2	8	11	14.9	2.87	128	.300	.382	0	—	0	1	1	0	0.1
Total 2	4	4	.500	40	0	0	0	6	50¹	45	2	19	26	12.0	3.22	99	.253	.335	0	.000	-1	-0	-0	1	0.0

■ AL SHEALY
Shealy, Albert Berley b: 3/20/1900, Chapin, S.C. d: 3/7/67, Hagerstown, Md. BR/TR, 5'11", 175 lbs. Deb: 4/13/28

YEAR TM/L	W	L	PCT	G	GS	CG	SH	SV	IP	H	HR	BB	SO	RAT	ERA	ERA+	OAV	OOB	BH	AVG	PB	PR	/A	PD	TPI
1928 NY-A	8	6	.571	23	12	3	0	2	96	124	4	42	39	15.7	5.06	74	.308	.375	9	.237	2	-11	-14	0	-1.1
1930 Chi-N	0	0	—	24	0	0	0	0	27	37	2	14	14	17.0	8.00	63	.327	.402	3	.600	1	-9	-9	-0	-0.6
Total 2	8	6	.571	47	12	3	0	2	123	161	6	56	53	16.0	5.71	70	.313	.381	12	.279	3	-20	-23	-0	-1.7

■ JOHN SHEARON
Shearon, John M. b: 1870, Pittsburgh, Pa. d: 2/1/23, Bradford, Pa. Deb: 7/28/1891 ♦

YEAR TM/L	W	L	PCT	G	GS	CG	SH	SV	IP	H	HR	BB	SO	RAT	ERA	ERA+	OAV	OOB	BH	AVG	PB	PR	/A	PD	TPI
1891 Cle-N	1	3	.250	6	5	4	0	0	46	57	2	24	19	15.8	3.52	98	.293	.371	30	.242	-0	-1	-0	0	0.0

■ GEORGE SHEARS
Shears, George Penfield b: 4/13/1890, Marshall, Mo. d: 11/12/78, Loveland, Colo. BR/TL, 6'3", 180 lbs. Deb: 4/24/12

YEAR TM/L	W	L	PCT	G	GS	CG	SH	SV	IP	H	HR	BB	SO	RAT	ERA	ERA+	OAV	OOB	BH	AVG	PB	PR	/A	PD	TPI
1912 NY-A	0	0	—	4	0	0	0	0	15	24	1	11	9	21.0	5.40	67	.364	.455	1	.167	0	-3	-3	0	-0.1

■ TOM SHEEHAN
Sheehan, Thomas Clancy b: 3/31/1894, Grand Ridge, Ill. d: 10/29/82, Chillicothe, Ohio BR/TR, 6'2.5", 190 lbs. Deb: 7/14/15 MC

YEAR TM/L	W	L	PCT	G	GS	CG	SH	SV	IP	H	HR	BB	SO	RAT	ERA	ERA+	OAV	OOB	BH	AVG	PB	PR	/A	PD	TPI
1915 Phi-A	4	9	.308	15	13	8	1	0	102	131	1	38	22	15.0	4.15	71	.335	.395	4	.118	-3	-14	-14	-0	-1.6
1916 Phi-A	1	16	.059	38	17	8	0	0	188	197	2	94	54	14.0	3.69	78	.287	.374	7	.125	-2	-18	-17	4	-1.5
1921 NY-A	1	0	1.000	12	1	0	0	1	33	43	1	19	7	17.2	5.45	78	.326	.414	5	.625	2	-4	-4	2	0.0
1924 Cin-N	9	11	.450	39	16	8	2	1	166²	170	6	54	52	12.1	3.24	116	.269	.328	18	.310	4	12	10	-2	1.1
1925 Cin-N	1	0	1.000	10	3	1	0	1	29	37	3	12	5	15.2	8.07	51	.298	.360	1	.200	1	-12	-13	-0	-1.0
Pit-N	1	1	.500	23	0	0	0	2	57¹	63	2	13	13	11.9	2.67	167	.286	.326	3	.150	-1	10	11	0	1.0
Yr	2	1	.667	33	3	1	0	3	86¹	100	5	25	18	13.0	4.48	97	.291	.339	4	.160	-0	-2	-1	-0	0.0
1926 Pit-N	0	2	.000	9	4	1	0	0	31	36	0	12	16	14.5	6.68	59	.298	.370	1	.111	-1	-10	-9	-0	-0.9
Total 6	17	39	.304	146	54	26	3	5	607	677	14	242	169	13.7	4.00	87	.294	.362	39	.205	-0	-36	-36	3	-2.9

■ ROLLIE SHELDON
Sheldon, Roland Frank b: 12/17/36, Putnam, Conn. BR/TR, 6'4", 185 lbs. Deb: 4/23/61

YEAR TM/L	W	L	PCT	G	GS	CG	SH	SV	IP	H	HR	BB	SO	RAT	ERA	ERA+	OAV	OOB	BH	AVG	PB	PR	/A	PD	TPI
1961 NY-A	11	5	.688	35	21	6	2	0	162²	149	17	55	84	11.4	3.60	103	.246	.311	7	.125	-2	8	2	1	0.1
1962 NY-A	7	8	.467	34	16	2	0	1	118	136	12	28	54	12.6	5.49	68	.289	.331	2	.077	0	-20	-23	-2	-2.3
1964 *NY-A	5	2	.714	19	12	3	0	1	102¹	92	18	18	57	9.8	3.61	100	.243	.279	3	.088	-2	0	0	1	0.0
1965 NY-A	0	0	—	3	0	0	0	0	6¹	5	0	1	7	8.5	1.42	240	.238	.273	0	.000	-0	1	1	0	0.2
KC-A	10	8	.556	32	29	4	1	0	186²	180	22	56	105	11.7	3.95	88	.251	.312	4	.078	-3	-10	-10	0	-1.2
Yr	10	8	.556	35	29	4	1	0	193	185	22	57	112	11.6	3.87	90	.251	.310	2	.038	-3	-9	-8	0	-1.0
1966 KC-A	4	7	.364	14	13	1	1	0	69	73	3	26	26	13.0	3.13	109	.275	.342	2	.087	-1	2	2	1	0.1
Bos-A	1	6	.143	23	10	1	0	0	79²	106	15	23	38	14.8	4.97	77	.320	.368	2	.111	-1	-14	-10	1	-1.0
Yr	5	13	.278	37	23	2	1	0	148²	179	18	49	64	13.9	4.12	88	.297	.352	0	.000	-2	-11	-8	1	-0.9
Total 5	38	36	.514	160	101	17	4	2	724²	741	87	207	371	11.9	4.09	89	.266	.320	20	.096	-9	-32	-36	2	-4.1

■ FRANK SHELLENBACK
Shellenback, Frank Victor b: 12/16/1898, Joplin, Mo. d: 8/17/69, Newton, Mass. BR/TR, 6'2", 192 lbs. Deb: 5/08/18 C

YEAR TM/L	W	L	PCT	G	GS	CG	SH	SV	IP	H	HR	BB	SO	RAT	ERA	ERA+	OAV	OOB	BH	AVG	PB	PR	/A	PD	TPI
1918 Chi-A	9	12	.429	28	21	10	2	2	182²	180	1	74	47	12.7	2.66	103	.262	.338	7	.130	-1	2	2	-5	-0.4
1919 Chi-A	1	3	.250	8	4	2	0	0	35	40	1	16	10	14.4	5.14	62	.303	.378	1	.091	-0	-7	-8	-0	-0.7
Total 2	10	15	.400	36	25	12	2	2	217²	220	2	90	57	13.0	3.06	92	.269	.344	8	.123	-1	-5	-6	-5	-1.1

■ JIM SHELLENBACK
Shellenback, James Philip b: 11/18/43, Riverside, Cal. BL/TL, 6'2", 200 lbs. Deb: 9/15/66 C

YEAR TM/L	W	L	PCT	G	GS	CG	SH	SV	IP	H	HR	BB	SO	RAT	ERA	ERA+	OAV	OOB	BH	AVG	PB	PR	/A	PD	TPI
1966 Pit-N	0	0	—	2	0	0	0	0	3	3	2	3	0	18.0	9.00	40	.300	.462	0	—	0	-2	-2	0	-0.1
1967 Pit-N	1	1	.500	6	2	1	0	0	23¹	23	1	12	11	13.9	2.70	125	.250	.343	1	.167	-0	2	2	0	0.2
1969 Pit-N	0	0	—	8	0	0	0	0	16²	14	1	4	7	9.7	3.24	108	.233	.281	0	.000	-0	1	0	1	0.2
Was-A	4	7	.364	30	11	2	0	1	84²	87	8	48	50	14.5	4.04	86	.268	.364	5	.185	-0	-4	-5	2	-0.3
1970 Was-A	6	7	.462	39	14	2	1	0	117¹	107	6	51	57	12.1	3.68	97	.246	.325	2	.067	-2	0	-2	-0	-0.3
1971 Was-A	3	11	.214	40	15	3	1	0	120	123	10	49	47	13.1	3.53	94	.267	.342	5	.167	-0	-1	-3	1	-0.1
1972 Tex-A	2	4	.333	22	6	0	0	1	57	46	6	16	30	10.1	3.47	87	.221	.283	1	.100	-0	-3	-3	-1	-0.3
1973 Tex-A	0	0	—	2	0	0	0	0	1²	0	0	0	3	0.0	0.00	—	.000	.000	0	—	0	1	1	0	0.1
1974 Tex-A	0	0	—	11	0	0	0	0	24²	30	5	12	14	15.7	5.84	61	.306	.387	0	—	0	-6	-6	0	-0.5
1977 Min-A	0	0	—	5	0	0	0	0	5²	10	1	5	3	23.8	7.94	50	.385	.484	0	—	0	-2	-2	0	-0.1
Total 9	16	30	.348	165	48	8	2	2	454	443	40	200	222	12.9	3.81	89	.258	.338	14	.135	-2	-14	-21	4	-1.2

■ BERT SHEPARD
Shepard, Robert Earl b: 6/28/20, Dana, Ind. BL/TL, 5'11", 185 lbs. Deb: 8/04/45

YEAR TM/L	W	L	PCT	G	GS	CG	SH	SV	IP	H	HR	BB	SO	RAT	ERA	ERA+	OAV	OOB	BH	AVG	PB	PR	/A	PD	TPI
1945 Was-A	0	0	—	1	0	0	0	0	5¹	3	0	1	2	8.4	1.69	184	.167	.250	0	.000	-0	1	1	0	0.1

■ BILL SHERDEL
Sherdel, William Henry "Wee Willie" b: 8/15/1896, McSherrystown, Pa d: 11/14/68, McSherrystown, Pa BL/TL, 5'10", 160 lbs. Deb: 4/22/18

YEAR TM/L	W	L	PCT	G	GS	CG	SH	SV	IP	H	HR	BB	SO	RAT	ERA	ERA+	OAV	OOB	BH	AVG	PB	PR	/A	PD	TPI
1918 StL-N	6	12	.333	35	17	9	1	0	182¹	174	3	49	40	11.2	2.71	100	.259	.313	15	.242	3	1	-0	-1	0.2
1919 StL-N	5	9	.357	36	10	7	0	1	137¹	137	3	42	52	11.9	3.47	80	.270	.328	13	.271	2	-9	-10	1	-0.7
1920 StL-N	11	10	.524	43	7	4	0	6	170	183	14	70	74	12.4	3.28	91	.297	.350	14	.222	2	-3	-6	1	-0.2
1921 StL-N	9	8	.529	38	8	5	1	1	144¹	137	7	38	57	11.1	3.18	115	.247	.299	5	.114	-2	10	8	0	0.6
1922 StL-N	17	13	.567	47	31	15	3	2	242	298	12	62	79	13.6	3.87	100	.303	.348	17	.193	1	6	-0	-3	-0.2
1923 StL-N	15	13	.536	39	26	14	0	2	225	270	15	59	78	13.4	4.32	90	.296	.343	28	.337	8	-8	-10	-3	-0.5
1924 StL-N	12	15	.444	35	10	6	0	3	168²	188	9	38	57	12.3	3.42	111	.291	.335	15	.200	2	8	7	-2	0.7
1925 StL-N	15	6	.714	32	21	17	2	1	200	216	8	42	53	11.7	3.11	139	.277	.316	15	.205	2	26	27	-0	2.8
1926 *StL-N	16	12	.571	34	29	17	3	0	234²	255	6	49	59	11.9	3.49	112	.278	.318	22	.244	2	9	11	-3	1.0
1927 StL-N	17	12	.586	39	28	18	0	6	232¹	241	17	48	59	11.3	3.53	112	.269	.308	14	.194	1	10	11	-4	0.9
1928 *StL-N	21	10	.677	38	27	20	0	5	248²	251	17	56	72	11.2	2.86	140	.261	.303	19	.226	4	31	31	-5	3.1

YEAR	TM/L	W	L	PCT	G	GS	CG	SH	SV	IP	H	HR	BB	SO	RAT	ERA	ERA+	OAV	OOB	BH	AVG	PB	PR	/A	PD	TPI
1929	StL-N	10	15	.400	33	22	11	1	0	195²	278	14	58	69	15.5	5.93	79	.337	.382	16	.229	2	-26	-28	-2	-2.4
1930	StL-N	3	2	.600	13	7	1	0	0	64	86	5	13	29	14.1	4.64	108	.325	.358	2	.105	-1	2	3	-1	0.1
	Bos-N	6	5	.545	21	14	7	0	1	119¹	131	10	30	26	12.3	4.75	104	.283	.329	4	.095	-4	3	2	-0	-0.1
	Yr	9	7	.563	34	21	8	0	1	183¹	217	15	43	55	12.9	4.71	105	.298	.339	5	.082	-5	5	5	-1	0.0
1931	Bos-N	6	10	.375	27	16	8	0	0	137²	163	13	35	34	13.0	4.25	89	.294	.337	14	.304	3	-6	-7	-2	-0.5
1932	Bos-N	0	0	—	1	0	0	0	0	1²	3	0	1	0	21.6	0.00	—	.375	.444	0	—	0	1	1	0	0.1
	StL-N	0	0	—	3	0	0	0	0	5²	7	0	1	1	12.7	4.76	83	.304	.333	1	1.000	1	-1	-1	0	0.0
	Yr	0	0	—	4	0	0	0	0	7¹	10	0	2	1	14.7	3.68	106	.323	.364	0	.000	1	0	0	0	0.1
Total	15	165	146	.531	514	273	159	11	26	2709¹	3018	149	661	839	12.4	3.72	103	.285	.330	214	.223	27	55	38	-24	4.9

■ ROY SHERID
Sherid, Royden Richard   b: 1/25/07, Norristown, Pa.   d: 2/28/82, Parker Ford, Pa.   BR/TR, 6'2", 185 lbs.   Deb: 5/11/29

YEAR	TM/L	W	L	PCT	G	GS	CG	SH	SV	IP	H	HR	BB	SO	RAT	ERA	ERA+	OAV	OOB	BH	AVG	PB	PR	/A	PD	TPI
1929	NY-A	6	6	.500	33	15	9	0	1	154²	165	6	55	51	13.1	3.61	107	.277	.343	9	.180	-0	11	4	-1	0.2
1930	NY-A	12	13	.480	37	21	8	0	4	184	214	13	87	59	15.0	5.23	82	.289	.368	7	.101	-6	-12	-19	-1	-2.2
1931	NY-A	5	5	.500	17	8	3	0	2	74¹	94	4	24	39	14.7	5.69	70	.306	.362	10	.333	2	-11	-14	0	-1.0
Total	3	23	24	.489	87	44	20	0	7	413	473	23	166	149	14.2	4.71	87	.288	.358	26	.174	-4	-12	-29	-1	-3.0

■ JOE SHERMAN
Sherman, Joel Powers   b: 11/4/1890, Yarmouth, Mass.   d: 12/21/87, Cape Coral, Fla.   BR/TR, 6', 165 lbs.   Deb: 9/24/15

YEAR	TM/L	W	L	PCT	G	GS	CG	SH	SV	IP	H	HR	BB	SO	RAT	ERA	ERA+	OAV	OOB	BH	AVG	PB	PR	/A	PD	TPI
1915	Phi-A	1	0	1.000	2	1	1	0	0	15	15	0	1	5	10.8	2.40	123	.259	.295	2	.333	1	1	1	-0	0.1

■ DAN SHERMAN
Sherman, Lester Daniel "Babe"   b: 5/9/1890, Hubbardsville, N.Y.   d: 9/16/55, Highland Park, Mich.   BR/TR, 5'6", 145 lbs.   Deb: 6/04/14

YEAR	TM/L	W	L	PCT	G	GS	CG	SH	SV	IP	H	HR	BB	SO	RAT	ERA	ERA+	OAV	OOB	BH	AVG	PB	PR	/A	PD	TPI
1914	Chi-F	0	1	.000	1	1	0	0	0	0¹	0	0	2	0	54.0	0.00	—	.000	.687	0	—	0	0	0	0	0.0

■ TIM SHERRILL
Sherrill, Timothy Shawn   b: 9/10/65, Harrison, Ark.   BL/TL, 5'11", 170 lbs.   Deb: 8/14/90

YEAR	TM/L	W	L	PCT	G	GS	CG	SH	SV	IP	H	HR	BB	SO	RAT	ERA	ERA+	OAV	OOB	BH	AVG	PB	PR	/A	PD	TPI
1990	StL-N	0	0	—	8	0	0	0	0	4¹	10	0	3	3	27.0	6.23	63	.476	.542	0	—	0	-1	-1	0	0.0

■ FRED SHERRY
Sherry, Fred Peter (b: Fred Peter Schuerholz)   b: 1/13/1889, Honesdale, Pa.   d: 7/27/75, Honesdale, Pa.   BR/TR, 6', 170 lbs.   Deb: 4/25/11

YEAR	TM/L	W	L	PCT	G	GS	CG	SH	SV	IP	H	HR	BB	SO	RAT	ERA	ERA+	OAV	OOB	BH	AVG	PB	PR	/A	PD	TPI
1911	Was-A	0	4	.000	10	3	2	0	0	52¹	63	1	19	20	14.1	4.30	76	.310	.369	3	.158	-0	-6	-6	0	-0.5

■ LARRY SHERRY
Sherry, Lawrence   b: 7/25/35, Los Angeles, Cal.   BR/TR, 6'2", 180 lbs.   Deb: 4/17/58   C

YEAR	TM/L	W	L	PCT	G	GS	CG	SH	SV	IP	H	HR	BB	SO	RAT	ERA	ERA+	OAV	OOB	BH	AVG	PB	PR	/A	PD	TPI
1958	LA-N	0	0	—	5	0	0	0	0	4¹	10	0	7	2	37.4	12.46	33	.476	.621	0	—	0	-4	-4	0	-0.3
1959	*LA-N	7	2	.778	23	9	1	1	3	94¹	75	9	43	72	11.4	2.19	193	.218	.308	7	.219	2	18	21	-1	2.5
1960	LA-N	14	10	.583	57	3	1	0	7	142¹	125	14	82	114	13.5	3.79	105	.238	.347	6	.162	1	1	3	1	0.5
1961	LA-N	4	4	.500	53	1	0	0	15	94²	90	10	39	79	12.6	3.90	111	.252	.333	2	.154	-1	1	5	-2	0.3
1962	LA-N	7	3	.700	58	0	0	0	11	90	81	8	44	71	13.1	3.20	113	.241	.339	2	.118	-0	7	4	-0	0.3
1963	LA-N	2	6	.250	36	3	0	0	3	79²	82	8	24	47	12.4	3.73	81	.265	.325	1	.111	1	-4	-6	-0	-0.5
1964	Det-A	7	5	.583	38	0	0	0	11	66¹	52	7	37	58	12.5	3.66	100	.216	.327	0	.000	-2	-0	-0	-0	-0.1
1965	Det-A	3	6	.333	39	0	0	0	5	78¹	71	5	40	46	12.9	3.10	112	.254	.349	3	.300	2	3	3	1	0.6
1966	Det-A	8	5	.615	55	0	0	0	20	77²	66	8	36	63	12.2	3.82	91	.232	.325	4	.400	2	-3	-3	-1	-0.1
1967	Det-A	0	1	.000	20	0	0	0	1	28	35	3	7	20	13.8	6.43	51	.289	.333	0	.000	-0	-10	-10	-0	-0.9
	Hou-N	1	2	.333	29	0	0	0	6	40²	53	4	13	32	14.8	4.87	68	.327	.381	0	.000	-1	-7	-7	1	-0.6
1968	Cal-A	0	0	—	3	0	0	0	0	3	7	2	2	2	27.0	6.00	49	.467	.529	0	—	0	-1	-1	0	0.0
Total	11	53	44	.546	416	16	2	1	82	799¹	747	78	374	606	13.0	3.67	101	.249	.339	25	.169	5	0	5	-2	1.7

■ BEN SHIELDS
Shields, Benjamin Cowan "Big Ben" or "Lefty"   b: 6/17/03, Huntersville, N.C   d: 1/24/82, Woodruff, S.C.   BR/TL, 6'1.5", 195 lbs.   Deb: 4/17/24

YEAR	TM/L	W	L	PCT	G	GS	CG	SH	SV	IP	H	HR	BB	SO	RAT	ERA	ERA+	OAV	OOB	BH	AVG	PB	PR	/A	PD	TPI
1924	NY-A	0	0	—	2	0	0	0	0	2	6	0	2	3	36.0	27.00	15	.545	.615	0	—	0	-5	-5	0	-0.3
1925	NY-A	3	0	1.000	4	2	2	0	0	24	24	2	12	5	14.3	4.88	87	.267	.365	1	.125	-1	-1	-2	-0	-0.2
1930	Bos-A	0	0	—	3	0	0	0	0	10	16	0	6	1	19.8	9.00	51	.400	.478	0	.000	-1	-5	-5	0	-0.3
1931	Phi-N	1	0	1.000	4	0	0	0	0	5¹	9	1	7	0	27.0	15.19	28	.391	.533	0	.000	-0	-7	-6	0	-0.5
Total	4	4	0	1.000	13	2	2	0	0	41¹	55	3	27	9	18.3	8.27	53	.335	.435	1	.077	-2	-18	-18	-0	-1.3

■ CHARLIE SHIELDS
Shields, Charles S.   b: 12/10/1879, Jackson, Tenn.   d: 8/27/53, Memphis, Tenn.   BL/TL,   Deb: 4/23/02

YEAR	TM/L	W	L	PCT	G	GS	CG	SH	SV	IP	H	HR	BB	SO	RAT	ERA	ERA+	OAV	OOB	BH	AVG	PB	PR	/A	PD	TPI
1902	Bal-A	4	11	.267	23	15	10	1	1	142¹	201	7	32	28	14.5	4.24	89	.333	.366	8	.167	-1	-10	-7	-4	-1.0
	StL-A	3	0	1.000	4	4	3	0	0	30	37	1	7	6	13.2	3.30	107	.303	.341	6	.462	2	1	1	-0	0.3
	Yr	7	11	.389	27	19	13	1	1	172¹	238	8	39	34	14.5	4.07	92	.328	.362	6	.098	1	-10	-7	-4	-0.7
1907	StL-N	0	2	.000	3	2	0	0	0	6²	12	0	7	1	28.4	9.45	26	.444	.583	0	.000	-0	-5	-5	-0	-0.4
Total	2	7	13	.350	30	21	13	1	1	179	250	8	46	35	15.0	4.27	86	.332	.372	14	.222	1	-15	-12	-4	-1.1

■ STEVE SHIELDS
Shields, Stephen Mack   b: 11/30/58, Gasden, Ala.   BR/TR, 6'5", 220 lbs.   Deb: 6/01/85

YEAR	TM/L	W	L	PCT	G	GS	CG	SH	SV	IP	H	HR	BB	SO	RAT	ERA	ERA+	OAV	OOB	BH	AVG	PB	PR	/A	PD	TPI
1985	Atl-N	1	2	.333	23	6	0	0	0	68	86	9	32	29	15.8	5.16	75	.320	.394	2	.111	-1	-12	-10	-1	-1.0
1986	Atl-N	0	0	—	6	0	0	0	0	12²	13	4	7	6	14.2	7.11	56	.271	.364	0	.000	-0	-5	-4	-0	-0.4
	KC-A	0	0	—	3	0	0	0	0	8²	3	1	4	2	7.3	2.08	205	.111	.226	0	—	0	2	2	0	0.2
1987	Sea-A	2	0	1.000	20	0	0	0	3	30	43	7	12	22	16.5	6.60	71	.333	.390	0	—	0	-7	-6	0	-0.5
1988	NY-A	5	5	.500	39	0	0	0	0	82¹	96	8	30	55	14.0	4.37	90	.298	.362	0	—	0	-4	-4	0	-0.3
1989	Min-A	0	1	.000	11	0	0	0	0	17¹	28	3	6	12	17.7	7.79	53	.354	.400	0	—	0	-8	-7	0	-0.6
Total	5	8	8	.500	102	6	0	0	3	219	269	32	91	126	14.9	5.26	77	.308	.375	2	.105	-1	-33	-29	-1	-2.6

■ VINCE SHIELDS
Shields, Vincent William   b: 11/18/1900, Fredericton, N.B., Canada   d: 10/17/52, Plaster Rock, N.B. Canada   BL/TR, 5'11", 185 lbs.   Deb: 9/20/24

YEAR	TM/L	W	L	PCT	G	GS	CG	SH	SV	IP	H	HR	BB	SO	RAT	ERA	ERA+	OAV	OOB	BH	AVG	PB	PR	/A	PD	TPI
1924	StL-N	1	1	.500	2	1	0	0	0	12	10	1	3	4	12.0	3.00	126	.227	.320	2	.400	0	1	1	-0	0.1

■ GARLAND SHIFFLETT
Shifflett, Garland Jessie "Duck"   b: 3/28/35, Elkton, Va.   BR/TR, 5'10.5", 165 lbs.   Deb: 4/22/57

YEAR	TM/L	W	L	PCT	G	GS	CG	SH	SV	IP	H	HR	BB	SO	RAT	ERA	ERA+	OAV	OOB	BH	AVG	PB	PR	/A	PD	TPI
1957	Was-A	0	0	—	6	1	0	0	0	8	6	0	10	2	18.0	10.13	38	.222	.432	0	—	0	-6	-6	0	-0.5
1964	Min-A	0	2	.000	10	0	0	0	1	17²	22	1	7	8	15.3	4.58	78	.297	.366	0	.000	-0	-2	-2	1	-0.1
Total	2	0	2	.000	16	1	0	0	1	25²	28	1	17	10	16.1	6.31	58	.277	.387	0	.000	-0	-8	-8	1	-0.6

■ RAY SHINES
Shines, Anthony Raymond   b: 7/18/56, Durham, N.C.   BB/TR, 6'1", 210 lbs.   Deb: 9/09/83 ♦

YEAR	TM/L	W	L	PCT	G	GS	CG	SH	SV	IP	H	HR	BB	SO	RAT	ERA	ERA+	OAV	OOB	BH	AVG	PB	PR	/A	PD	TPI
1985	Mon-N	0	0	—	1	0	0	0	0	1	1	0	0	0	9.0	0.00	—	.250	.250	6	.120	-0	0	0	0	0.0

■ DAVE SHIPANOFF
Shipanoff, David Noel   b: 11/13/59, Edmonton, Alb., Can.   BR/TR, 6'2", 185 lbs.   Deb: 8/09/85

YEAR	TM/L	W	L	PCT	G	GS	CG	SH	SV	IP	H	HR	BB	SO	RAT	ERA	ERA+	OAV	OOB	BH	AVG	PB	PR	/A	PD	TPI
1985	Phi-N	1	2	.333	26	0	0	0	3	36¹	33	3	16	26	12.4	3.22	114	.231	.313	0	.000	-0	1	2	-0	0.1

■ JOE SHIPLEY
Shipley, Joseph Clark "Moses"   b: 5/9/35, Morristown, Tenn.   BR/TR, 6'4", 210 lbs.   Deb: 7/14/58

YEAR	TM/L	W	L	PCT	G	GS	CG	SH	SV	IP	H	HR	BB	SO	RAT	ERA	ERA+	OAV	OOB	BH	AVG	PB	PR	/A	PD	TPI
1958	SF-N	0	0	—	1	0	0	0	0	1¹	3	0	3	0	54.0	33.75	11	.429	.667	0	—	0	-4	-4	0	-0.3
1959	SF-N	0	0	—	10	1	0	0	0	18	16	2	17	11	17.0	4.50	85	.239	.400	0	.000	-1	-1	-1	-0	-0.1
1960	SF-N	0	0	—	15	0	0	0	0	20	22	0	9	9	14.4	5.40	64	.274	.376	0	—	0	-4	-4	1	-0.3
1963	Chi-A	0	1	.000	3	0	0	0	0	4²	7	2	6	3	28.9	5.79	61	.409	.536	0	.000	-0	-1	-1	0	0.0
Total	4	0	1	.000	29	1	0	0	0	44	48	4	35	23	18.2	5.93	61	.284	.424	0	.000	-1	-10	-11	0	-0.7

■ DUKE SHIREY
Shirey, Clair Lee   b: 6/20/1898, Jersey Shore, Pa.   d: 9/1/62, Hagerstown, Pa.   BR , 6'1", 175 lbs.   Deb: 9/28/20

YEAR	TM/L	W	L	PCT	G	GS	CG	SH	SV	IP	H	HR	BB	SO	RAT	ERA	ERA+	OAV	OOB	BH	AVG	PB	PR	/A	PD	TPI
1920	Was-A	0	1	.000	2	1	0	0	0	4	5	0	2	0	18.0	6.75	55	.313	.421	0	.000	-0	-1	-1	-0	-0.1

■ TEX SHIRLEY
Shirley, Alvis Newman   b: 4/25/18, Birthright, Tex.   BB/TR, 6'1", 175 lbs.   Deb: 9/06/41

YEAR	TM/L	W	L	PCT	G	GS	CG	SH	SV	IP	H	HR	BB	SO	RAT	ERA	ERA+	OAV	OOB	BH	AVG	PB	PR	/A	PD	TPI
1941	Phi-A	0	1	.000	5	0	0	0	1	7¹	8	1	6	1	17.2	2.45	171	.286	.412	0	.000	-0	1	1	0	0.2
1942	Phi-A	0	1	.000	15	1	0	0	1	35²	37	1	22	10	15.4	5.30	71	.272	.381	0	.000	-1	-7	-6	-0	-0.7
1944	*StL-A	5	4	.556	23	11	2	1	0	80¹	74	6	64	35	13.9	4.15	87	.203	.348	4	.163	-6	-5	-1	-0.7
1945	StL-A	8	12	.400	32	24	10	2	0	183²	191	8	93	77	14.0	3.63	97	.274	.360	20	.286	2	-5	-2	0	-1.0
1946	StL-A	6	12	.333	27	18	7	0	0	139²	148	7	105	45	16.4	4.96	75	.273	.391	10	.196	-0	-23	-19	-0	-1.9

YEAR TM/L	W	L	PCT	G	GS	CG	SH	SV	IP	H	HR	BB	SO	RAT	ERA	ERA+	OAV	OOB	BH	AVG	PB	PR	/A	PD	TPI
Total 5	19	30	.388	102	54	19	3	2	446²	443	20	290	168	14.9	4.25	85	.261	.371	34	.214	-1	-39	-31	-3	-3.1

■ BOB SHIRLEY
Shirley, Robert Charles b: 6/25/54, Cushing, Okla. BR/TL, 5'11", 180 lbs. Deb: 4/10/77

YEAR TM/L	W	L	PCT	G	GS	CG	SH	SV	IP	H	HR	BB	SO	RAT	ERA	ERA+	OAV	OOB	BH	AVG	PB	PR	/A	PD	TPI
1977 SD-N	12	18	.400	39	35	1	0	0	214	215	22	100	146	13.4	3.70	96	.259	.341	9	.122	-2	5	-4	1	-0.5
1978 SD-N	8	11	.421	50	20	2	0	5	166	164	10	61	102	12.4	3.69	90	.262	.330	5	.125	0	-2	-7	2	-0.5
1979 SD-N	8	16	.333	49	25	4	1	0	205	196	15	59	117	11.5	3.38	104	.257	.316	5	.091	-2	8	3	0	0.1
1980 SD-N	11	12	.478	59	12	3	0	7	137	143	12	54	67	12.9	3.55	97	.276	.344	1	.033	-2	1	-2	2	-0.1
1981 StL-N	6	4	.600	28	11	1	0	0	79¹	78	6	34	36	12.8	4.08	87	.260	.337	3	.136	-1	-5	-5	-1	-0.6
1982 Cin-N	8	13	.381	41	20	1	0	0	152²	138	17	73	89	12.6	3.60	103	.248	.338	6	.143	-1	0	2	1	0.2
1983 NY-A	5	8	.385	25	17	1	1	0	108	122	10	36	53	13.2	5.08	77	.293	.350	0	—	0	-12	-14	1	-1.2
1984 NY-A	3	3	.500	41	7	1	0	0	114¹	119	8	38	48	12.4	3.38	112	.274	.333	0	—	0	8	5	0	0.6
1985 NY-A	5	5	.500	48	8	2	0	2	109	103	5	26	55	10.7	2.64	151	.251	.295	0	—	0	18	16	-0	1.6
1986 NY-A	0	4	.000	39	6	0	0	3	105¹	108	13	40	64	12.9	5.04	81	.271	.342	0	—	0	-10	-11	1	-0.9
1987 NY-A	1	0	1.000	12	1	0	0	0	34	36	4	16	12	13.8	4.50	97	.277	.356	0	—	0	-0	-0	-0	-0.0
KC-A	0	0	—	3	0	0	0	0	7¹	10	5	6	1	19.6	14.73	31	.323	.432	0	—	0	-8	-8	0	-0.6
Yr	1	0	1.000	15	1	0	0	0	41¹	46	9	22	13	14.8	6.31	70	.275	.360	0	—	0	-9	-9	-0	-0.6
Total 11	67	94	.416	434	162	16	2	18	1432	1432	127	543	790	12.5	3.82	96	.264	.334	29	.110	-7	2	-24	6	-1.9

■ STEVE SHIRLEY
Shirley, Steven Brian b: 10/12/56, San Francsico, Cal. BL/TL, 6', 185 lbs. Deb: 6/21/82

YEAR TM/L	W	L	PCT	G	GS	CG	SH	SV	IP	H	HR	BB	SO	RAT	ERA	ERA+	OAV	OOB	BH	AVG	PB	PR	/A	PD	TPI
1982 LA-N	1	1	.500	11	0	0	0	0	12²	15	1	7	8	15.6	4.26	81	.300	.386	1	1.000	0	-1	-1	0	0.0

■ GEORGE SHOCH
Shoch, George Quintus b: 1/6/1859, Philadelphia, Pa. d: 9/30/37, Philadelphia, Pa. BR/TR, Deb: 9/10/1886 ♦

YEAR TM/L	W	L	PCT	G	GS	CG	SH	SV	IP	H	HR	BB	SO	RAT	ERA	ERA+	OAV	OOB	BH	AVG	PB	PR	/A	PD	TPI
1888 Was-N	0	0	—	1	0	0	0	0	3	2	0	1	0	9.0	0.00	—	.183	.251	58	.183	0	1	1	0	0.1

■ URBAN SHOCKER
Shocker, Urban James (b: Urbain Jacques Shockcor) b: 8/22/1890, Cleveland, Ohio d: 9/9/28, Denver, Colo. BR/TR, 5'10", 170 lbs. Deb: 4/24/16

YEAR TM/L	W	L	PCT	G	GS	CG	SH	SV	IP	H	HR	BB	SO	RAT	ERA	ERA+	OAV	OOB	BH	AVG	PB	PR	/A	PD	TPI
1916 NY-A	4	3	.571	12	9	4	1	0	82¹	67	2	32	43	11.5	2.62	110	.230	.319	4	.190	1	2	2	-1	0.4
1917 NY-A	8	5	.615	26	13	7	0	1	145	124	5	46	68	10.6	2.61	103	.241	.303	8	.178	-1	1	1	2	0.2
1918 StL-A	6	5	.545	14	9	7	0	2	94²	69	0	40	33	10.5	1.81	152	.209	.296	11	.324	4	10	10	1	-1.7
1919 StL-A	13	11	.542	30	25	14	5	0	211	193	6	55	86	10.7	2.69	123	.244	.296	8	.138	-0	13	15	-2	1.4
1920 StL-A	20	10	.667	38	28	22	5	5	245²	224	10	70	107	10.9	2.71	145	.248	.305	18	.225	3	30	33	-1	3.5
1921 StL-A	27	12	.692	47	38	30	4	4	326²	345	21	86	132	12.0	3.55	126	.270	.319	27	.260	6	26	34	2	4.0
1922 StL-A	24	17	.585	48	38	29	2	3	348	365	22	57	**149**	11.0	2.97	139	.272	.304	22	.191	2	41	45	-3	4.5
1923 StL-A	20	12	.625	43	35	24	3	5	277¹	292	12	49	109	**11.2**	3.41	122	.272	**.306**	16	.200	2	18	24	-3	2.2
1924 StL-A	16	13	.552	40	33	17	4	1	246¹	270	11	52	88	11.9	4.20	107	.277	.315	16	.239	5	1	9	-2	1.2
1925 NY-A	12	12	.500	41	30	15	2	2	244¹	278	17	58	74	12.5	3.65	117	.294	.336	11	.172	5	20	17	-1	1.9
1926 *NY-A	19	11	.633	41	32	18	0	2	258²	272	13	71	59	12.0	3.38	114	.269	.318	13	.171	1	18	14	-1	1.3
1927 NY-A	18	6	.750	31	27	13	2	0	200	207	8	41	35	11.2	2.84	136	.268	.306	13	.241	3	29	23	-1	2.4
1928 NY-A	0	0	—	1	0	0	0	0	2	5	0	0	0	13.5	0.00	—	.429	.429	0	—	0	1	1	0	0.1
Total 13	187	117	.615	412	317	200	28	25	2681²	2709	127	657	983	11.4	3.17	124	.265	.311	167	.209	29	210	226	-10	24.8

■ MILT SHOFFNER
Shoffner, Milburn James b: 11/13/05, Sherman, Tex. d: 1/19/78, Madison, Ohio BL/TL, 6'1.5", 184 lbs. Deb: 7/20/29

YEAR TM/L	W	L	PCT	G	GS	CG	SH	SV	IP	H	HR	BB	SO	RAT	ERA	ERA+	OAV	OOB	BH	AVG	PB	PR	/A	PD	TPI
1929 Cle-A	2	3	.400	11	3	1	0	0	44²	46	4	22	15	14.3	5.04	88	.284	.380	0	.000	-3	-4	-3	0	-0.4
1930 Cle-A	3	4	.429	24	10	1	0	0	84²	129	8	50	17	19.1	7.97	61	.362	.442	7	.212	1	-31	-30	0	-2.3
1931 Cle-A	2	3	.400	12	4	1	0	0	41	55	4	26	12	18.2	7.24	64	.320	.415	1	.077	-1	-13	-12	0	-1.1
1937 Bos-N	3	1	.750	6	5	3	1	0	42²	38	1	9	13	10.1	2.53	142	.239	.284	2	.125	1	7	5	1	0.6
1938 Bos-N	8	7	.533	26	15	9	1	1	139²	147	7	36	49	11.9	3.54	97	.270	.317	12	.211	3	4	-2	-2	-0.1
1939 Bos-N	4	6	.400	25	11	7	0	1	132¹	133	4	42	51	12.0	3.13	118	.265	.324	7	.159	-0	12	8	0	0.8
Cin-N	2	2	.500	10	3	0	0	0	37²	43	3	11	6	13.4	3.35	115	.289	.346	1	.091	-1	2	2	-0	0.1
Yr	6	8	.429	35	14	7	0	1	170	176	7	53	57	12.2	3.18	117	.270	.327	5	.091	-1	14	10	0	0.9
1940 Cin-N	1	0	1.000	20	0	0	0	0	54¹	56	3	18	17	12.3	5.63	67	.268	.326	2	.125	-1	-11	-11	-0	-1.1
Total 7	25	26	.490	134	51	22	2	3	577	647	34	214	180	13.6	4.59	85	.287	.352	32	.156	-1	-35	-43	-2	-3.5

■ ERNIE SHORE
Shore, Ernest Grady b: 3/24/1891, East Bend, N.C. d: 9/24/80, Winston-Salem, N.C. BR/TR, 6'4", 220 lbs. Deb: 6/20/12

YEAR TM/L	W	L	PCT	G	GS	CG	SH	SV	IP	H	HR	BB	SO	RAT	ERA	ERA+	OAV	OOB	BH	AVG	PB	PR	/A	PD	TPI
1912 NY-N	0	0	—	1	0	0	0	0	1	8	1	1	1	81.0	27.00	13	.667	.692	0	—	0	-3	-3	-0	-0.1
1914 Bos-A	10	5	.667	20	16	10	1	1	139²	103	1	34	51	9.2	2.00	135	.204	.261	5	.102	-3	12	11	2	1.1
1915 *Bos-A	19	8	.704	38	32	17	4	0	247	207	3	66	102	10.1	1.64	169	.228	.283	8	.101	-3	36	31	4	3.6
1916 *Bos-A	16	10	.615	38	28	10	3	1	225²	221	1	49	62	10.9	2.63	105	.259	.302	7	.091	-5	5	3	6	0.5
1917 Bos-A	13	10	.565	29	27	14	1	1	226²	201	1	55	57	10.6	2.22	116	.240	.297	13	.167	-1	11	9	3	1.2
1919 NY-A	5	8	.385	20	13	3	0	0	95	105	4	44	24	14.2	4.17	77	.288	.366	4	.143	-1	-10	-10	0	-1.1
1920 NY-A	2	2	.500	14	5	2	0	1	44¹	61	1	21	12	16.8	4.87	78	.333	.405	2	.182	0	-5	-5	1	-0.3
Total 7	65	43	.602	160	121	56	9	5	979¹	906	12	270	309	11.1	2.47	113	.247	.304	39	.121	-13	45	36	17	4.9

■ RAY SHORE
Shore, Raymond Everett b: 6/9/21, Cincinnati, Ohio BR/TR, 6'3", 210 lbs. Deb: 9/21/46 C

YEAR TM/L	W	L	PCT	G	GS	CG	SH	SV	IP	H	HR	BB	SO	RAT	ERA	ERA+	OAV	OOB	BH	AVG	PB	PR	/A	PD	TPI
1946 StL-A	0	0	—	1	0	0	0	0	1	3	0	1	1	36.0	18.00	21	.500	.571	0	—	0	-2	-2	0	-0.1
1948 StL-A	1	2	.333	17	4	0	0	0	38	40	2	35	12	18.7	6.39	71	.270	.422	0	.000	-2	-9	-8	0	-0.7
1949 StL-A	0	1	.000	13	0	0	0	0	23¹	27	3	31	13	23.1	10.80	42	.297	.484	0	.000	-1	-17	-16	0	-1.4
Total 3	1	3	.250	31	4	0	0	0	62¹	70	5	67	26	20.6	8.23	55	.286	.450	0	.000	-2	-28	-26	1	-2.2

■ BILL SHORES
Shores, William David b: 5/26/04, Abilene, Tex. d: 2/19/84, Purcell, Okla. BR/TR, 6', 185 lbs. Deb: 4/11/28

YEAR TM/L	W	L	PCT	G	GS	CG	SH	SV	IP	H	HR	BB	SO	RAT	ERA	ERA+	OAV	OOB	BH	AVG	PB	PR	/A	PD	TPI
1928 Phi-A	1	1	.500	3	2	1	0	0	14	13	0	7	5	12.9	3.21	125	.250	.339	1	1.000	-1	1	1	-0	0.0
1929 Phi-A	11	6	.647	39	13	5	1	7	152²	150	9	59	49	12.5	3.60	118	.262	.334	5	.125	-2	11	11	-1	0.8
1930 *Phi-A	12	4	.750	31	19	7	1	0	159	169	11	70	48	13.7	4.19	112	.276	.353	11	.193	-2	8	9	1	0.6
1931 Phi-A	0	3	.000	6	2	0	0	0	16	26	3	10	2	20.3	5.06	89	.361	.439	1	.333	0	-1	-1	0	0.0
1933 NY-N	2	1	.667	8	3	1	0	0	36²	41	4	14	20	13.5	3.93	82	.291	.355	3	.273	1	-2	-3	1	0.0
1936 Chi-A	0	0	—	9	0	0	0	0	17	26	1	8	5	18.0	9.53	55	.356	.420	1	.200	-0	-8	-8	0	-0.6
Total 6	26	15	.634	96	39	14	2	7	395¹	425	28	168	129	13.6	4.17	105	.279	.353	21	.174	-4	8	8	1	0.8

■ CHRIS SHORT
Short, Christopher Joseph b: 9/19/37, Milford, Del. BR/TL, 6'4", 205 lbs. Deb: 4/19/59

YEAR TM/L	W	L	PCT	G	GS	CG	SH	SV	IP	H	HR	BB	SO	RAT	ERA	ERA+	OAV	OOB	BH	AVG	PB	PR	/A	PD	TPI
1959 Phi-N	0	0	—	3	2	0	0	0	14¹	19	3	10	8	18.8	8.16	50	.317	.423	0	.000	-1	-7	-6	0	-0.5
1960 Phi-N	6	9	.400	42	10	2	0	3	107¹	101	8	52	54	13.1	3.94	99	.249	.339	0	.000	-3	-2	-1	0	-0.3
1961 Phi-N	6	12	.333	39	16	1	0	1	127¹	157	12	71	80	16.3	5.94	69	.304	.391	6	.162	-1	-27	-26	-1	-2.6
1962 Phi-N	11	9	.550	47	12	4	0	3	142	149	13	56	91	13.5	3.42	113	.272	.348	8	.222	1	8	7	0	0.8
1963 Phi-N	9	12	.429	38	27	6	3	0	198	185	14	69	160	11.7	2.95	109	.248	.315	7	.106	-2	7	6	3	0.8
1964 Phi-N	17	9	.654	42	31	12	4	2	220²	174	10	51	181	9.3	2.20	158	.217	.268	7	.108	-1	33	31	-1	3.1
1965 Phi-N	18	11	.621	47	40	15	5	2	297¹	260	18	89	237	10.7	2.82	123	.235	.295	13	.131	-2	24	21	-3	1.7
1966 Phi-N	20	10	.667	42	39	19	4	0	272	257	26	68	177	11.1	3.54	102	.250	.302	22	.208	1	2	2	0	0.3
1967 Phi-N	9	11	.450	29	26	8	2	1	199¹	163	9	74	142	10.9	2.39	142	.225	.300	6	.091	-2	22	22	0	2.3
1968 Phi-N	19	13	.594	42	36	9	2	1	269²	236	25	81	202	10.9	2.94	102	.236	.299	12	.152	0	1	2	-1	0.1
1969 Phi-N	0	0	—	2	2	0	0	0	10	11	2	4	5	14.4	7.20	49	.282	.364	0	.000	-0	-4	-4	0	-0.3
1970 Phi-N	9	16	.360	36	34	7	2	1	199	211	13	66	133	12.8	4.30	93	.272	.334	3	.049	-5	-6	-7	-2	-1.3
1971 Phi-N	7	14	.333	31	26	5	2	1	173	182	22	63	95	12.9	3.85	92	.274	.339	4	.083	-1	7	-6	-0	-0.8
1972 Phi-N	1	1	.500	19	0	0	0	1	23	24	3	8	20	12.5	3.91	92	.267	.327	0	—	0	-1	-1	-0	0.0
1973 Mil-A	3	5	.375	42	7	0	0	2	72	86	5	44	44	16.5	5.13	73	.299	.395	0	—	0	-10	-11	-0	-1.0
Total 15	135	132	.506	501	308	88	24	18	2325	2215	183	806	1629	11.9	3.43	103	.252	.319	88	.126	-17	33	30	-5	2.3

YEAR	TM/L	W	L	PCT	G	GS	CG	SH	SV	IP	H	HR	BB	SO	RAT	ERA	ERA+	OAV	OOB	BH	AVG	PB	PR	/A	PD	TPI

■ BILL SHORT
Short, William Ross b: 11/27/37, Kingston, N.Y. BL/TL, 5'9", 170 lbs. Deb: 4/23/60

1960	NY-A	3	5	.375	10	10	2	0	0	47	49	5	30	14	15.3	4.79	75	.282	.390	3	.200	1	-5	-6	-0	-0.5
1962	Bal-A	0	0	—	5	0	0	0	0	4	8	0	6	3	33.8	15.75	24	.381	.536	0	.000	-0	-5	-5	0	-0.4
1966	Bal-A	2	3	.400	6	6	1	1	0	37²	34	2	10	27	10.5	2.87	116	.239	.289	1	.091	-1	2	2	1	0.2
	Bos-A	0	0	—	8	0	0	0	0	8¹	10	1	2	2	13.0	4.32	88	.294	.333	0	.000	-0	-1	-0	0	0.0
	Yr	2	3	.400	14	6	1	1	0	46	44	3	12	29	11.0	3.13	109	.247	.295	0	.000	-1	2	1	1	0.2
1967	Pit-N	0	0	—	6	0	0	0	1	2¹	1	0	1	1	7.7	3.86	87	.143	.250	0	.000	-0	-0	-0	0	0.0
1968	NY-N	0	3	.000	34	0	0	0	1	30¹	24	0	14	24	11.6	4.75	64	.220	.315	0	.000	-0	-6	-6	1	-0.5
1969	Cin-N	0	0	—	4	0	0	0	0	2¹	4	0	1	0	19.3	15.43	24	.400	.455	0	.000	-0	-3	-3	0	-0.2
Total	6	5	11	.313	73	16	3	1	2	132	130	8	64	71	13.4	4.70	73	.262	.349	4	.125	-1	-18	-19	2	-1.4

■ CLYDE SHOUN
Shoun, Clyde Mitchell "Hardrock" b: 3/20/12, Mountain City, Tenn. d: 3/20/68, Mountain Home, Tenn. BL/TL, 6'1", 188 lbs. Deb: 8/07/35

1935	Chi-N	1	0	1.000	5	0	0	0	0	12²	14	2	5	5	13.5	2.84	138	.298	.365	0	.000	-0	2	2	-0	0.1
1936	Chi-N	0	0	—	4	0	0	0	0	4¹	3	0	6	1	18.7	12.46	32	.200	.429	0	—	0	-4	-4	0	-0.3
1937	Chi-N	7	7	.500	37	9	2	0	0	93	118	9	45	43	15.8	5.61	71	.309	.382	4	.138	-1	-18	-17	-1	-1.7
1938	StL-N	6	6	.500	40	12	3	0	1	117¹	130	8	43	37	13.3	4.14	96	.283	.345	8	.258	0	-2	-1	-0	-0.2
1939	StL-N	3	1	.750	53	2	0	0	9	103	98	4	42	50	12.4	3.76	109	.248	.323	3	.115	-1	2	4	-1	0.3
1940	StL-N	13	11	.542	54	19	13	1	5	197¹	193	13	46	82	11.0	3.92	102	.255	.299	12	.190	-1	-2	1	-0	0.0
1941	StL-N	3	5	.375	26	6	0	0	0	70	98	9	20	34	15.2	5.66	67	.337	.379	4	.182	0	-16	-15	1	-1.2
1942	StL-N	0	0	—	2	0	0	0	0	1²	1	0	0	0	5.4	0.00	—	.167	.167	0	—	0	1	1	0	0.1
	Cin-N	1	3	.250	34	0	0	0	0	72²	55	2	24	32	9.8	2.23	147	.216	.283	4	.308	1	9	9	1	1.1
	Yr	1	3	.250	36	0	0	0	0	74¹	56	2	24	32	9.7	2.18	151	.215	.281	0	.000	1	9	9	1	1.2
1943	Cin-N	14	5	.737	45	5	2	0	7	147	131	5	46	61	10.8	3.06	108	.241	.300	13	.310	3	5	4	1	0.9
1944	Cin-N	13	10	.565	38	21	12	1	2	202²	193	10	42	55	10.6	3.02	116	.248	.290	15	.224	1	13	11	-3	0.8
1946	Cin-N	1	6	.143	27	5	0	0	0	79	87	3	26	20	13.0	4.10	82	.292	.351	2	.095	-1	-6	-7	-2	-1.0
1947	Cin-N	0	0	—	10	0	0	0	0	14¹	16	2	5	7	13.8	5.02	82	.320	.393	0	—	0	-2	-1	0	0.0
	Bos-N	5	3	.625	26	3	1	1	1	73²	73	6	21	23	11.5	4.40	89	.254	.305	3	.158	-1	-3	-4	-1	-0.5
	Yr	5	3	.625	36	3	1	1	1	88	89	8	26	30	11.8	4.50	87	.263	.316	0	.000	-1	-4	-6	-1	-0.5
1948	Bos-N	5	1	.833	36	2	1	0	4	74	77	7	20	25	11.8	4.01	96	.267	.315	4	.190	0	-0	-1	-2	-0.2
1949	Bos-N	0	0	—	1	0	0	0	0	1	1	0	0	0	9.0	0.00	—	.250	.250	0	—	0	0	0	0	0.0
	Chi-A	1	1	.500	16	0	0	0	0	23¹	37	1	13	8	19.3	5.79	72	.370	.442	1	.200	0	-4	-4	0	-0.3
Total	14	73	59	.553	454	85	34	3	29	1287	1325	81	404	483	12.2	3.91	96	.267	.324	73	.202	1	-27	-25	-8	-2.1

■ ERIC SHOW
Show, Eric Vaughn b: 5/19/56, Riverside, Cal. BR/TR, 6'1", 185 lbs. Deb: 9/02/81

1981	SD-N	1	3	.250	15	0	0	0	3	23	17	2	9	22	10.6	3.13	104	.213	.300	0	—	0	1	0	-0	0.0
1982	SD-N	10	6	.625	47	14	2	2	3	150	117	10	48	88	10.2	2.64	130	.217	.287	6	.146	-1	16	13	1	1.4
1983	SD-N	15	12	.556	35	33	4	2	0	200²	201	25	74	120	12.6	4.17	84	.263	.333	11	.172	1	-12	-15	-2	-1.6
1984	*SD-N	15	9	.625	32	32	3	1	0	206²	175	18	88	104	11.6	3.40	105	.234	.317	17	.246	6	4	4	-1	1.0
1985	SD-N	12	11	.522	35	35	5	2	0	233	212	27	87	141	11.7	3.09	114	.243	.316	10	.127	-1	13	11	-3	0.8
1986	SD-N	9	5	.643	24	22	2	0	0	136¹	109	11	69	94	11.9	2.97	123	.225	.326	7	.163	1	11	10	-2	1.0
1987	SD-N	8	16	.333	34	34	5	3	0	206¹	188	26	85	117	12.3	3.84	103	.241	.323	5	.071	-4	6	3	-1	-0.2
1988	SD-N	16	11	.593	32	32	13	1	0	234²	201	22	53	144	10.0	3.26	104	.231	.280	12	.148	-0	5	4	-4	0.0
1989	SD-N	8	6	.571	16	16	1	0	0	106¹	113	9	39	66	13.0	4.23	83	.274	.340	8	.235	2	-9	-9	-1	-0.8
1990	SD-N	6	8	.429	39	12	0	0	1	106¹	131	16	41	55	14.9	5.76	67	.306	.372	5	.200	1	-23	-23	-0	-2.1
Total	10	100	87	.535	309	230	35	11	7	1603¹	1464	166	593	951	11.8	3.59	100	.245	.318	81	.160	3	12	-1	-11	-0.5

■ LEV SHREVE
Shreve, Leven Lawrence b: 1/14/1869, Louisville, Ky. d: 10/18/42, Detroit, Mich. TR, 5'11", 150 lbs. Deb: 5/02/1887

1887	Bal-a	3	1	.750	5	5	4	1	0	38	33	0	19	13	12.3	3.79	108	.225	.314	4	.167	-1	2	1	0	0.0
	Ind-N	5	9	.357	14	14	14	1	0	122	141	5	65	22	15.2	4.72	87	.281	.364	13	.265	0	-9	-8	-1	-0.7
1888	Ind-N	11	24	.314	35	35	34	1	0	297²	352	23	93	101	13.5	4.63	64	.284	.334	21	.183	-1	-59	-56	-0	-5.0
1889	Ind-N	0	3	.000	3	3	1	0	0	15²	25	3	12	5	21.3	13.79	30	.350	.443	0	.000	-1	-17	-17	0	-1.1
Total	3	19	37	.339	57	57	53	3	0	473¹	551	31	189	141	14.1	4.89	69	.281	.344	38	.195	-2	-83	-79	-0	-6.8

■ HARRY SHRIVER
Shriver, Harry Graydon "Pop" b: 9/2/1896, Wadestown, W.Va. d: 1/21/70, Morgantown, W.Va. BR/TR, 6'2", 180 lbs. Deb: 4/14/22

1922	Bro-N	4	6	.400	25	14	4	2	0	108¹	114	5	48	38	13.6	2.99	136	.287	.367	1	.037	-3	13	13	-2	0.7
1923	Bro-N	0	0	—	1	1	0	0	0	4	8	0	0	1	18.0	6.75	58	.444	.444	0	.000	-0	-1	-1	-0	0.0
Total	2	4	6	.400	26	15	4	2	0	112¹	122	5	48	39	13.8	3.12	130	.294	.370	1	.036	-3	12	12	-2	0.7

■ TOOTS SHULTZ
Shultz, Wallace Luther b: 10/10/1888, Homestead, Pa. d: 1/30/59, McKeesport, Pa. BR/TR, 5'10", 175 lbs. Deb: 5/05/11

1911	Phi-N	0	3	.000	5	3	2	0	0	25	30	5	15	9	17.6	9.36	37	.300	.412	2	.250	0	-17	-16	0	-1.3
1912	Phi-N	1	4	.200	22	4	1	0	1	59	75	2	35	20	17.2	4.58	79	.316	.411	5	.238	0	-8	-6	0	-0.4
Total	2	1	7	.125	27	7	3	0	1	84	105	7	50	29	17.4	6.00	60	.312	.411	7	.241	0	-24	-23	1	-1.7

■ HARRY SHUMAN
Shuman, Harry b: 3/5/16, Philadelphia, Pa. BR/TR, 6'2", 195 lbs. Deb: 9/14/42

1942	Pit-N	0	0	—	1	0	0	0	0	2	0	0	1	0	4.5	0.00	—	.000	.167	0	—	0	1	1	0	0.1
1943	Pit-N	0	0	—	11	0	0	0	0	22	30	0	8	5	16.4	5.32	65	.337	.404	0	.000	-0	-5	-4	1	-0.3
1944	Phi-N	0	0	—	18	0	0	0	0	26²	26	1	11	4	12.5	4.05	89	.245	.316	0	.000	-0	-1	-1	0	0.0
Total	3	0	0	—	30	0	0	0	0	50²	56	1	20	10	13.9	4.44	80	.280	.351	0	.000	-0	-5	-5	1	-0.2

■ PAUL SIEBERT
Siebert, Paul Edward b: 6/5/53, Minneapolis, Minn. BL/TL, 6'2", 205 lbs. Deb: 9/07/74

1974	Hou-N	1	1	.500	5	5	1	1	0	25¹	21	3	11	10	11.4	3.55	97	.236	.320	0	.000	-1	0	-0	1	0.0
1975	Hou-N	0	2	.000	7	2	0	1	0	18¹	20	0	6	6	13.3	2.95	114	.294	.360	0	.000	-0	1	1	1	0.1
1976	Hou-N	0	2	.000	19	2	0	0	0	25²	29	0	18	10	16.8	3.16	101	.296	.410	0	.000	-0	1	0	-0	0.0
1977	SD-N	0	0	—	4	0	0	0	0	3²	3	1	4	1	17.2	2.45	144	.214	.389	0	—	0	1	0	-0	0.0
	NY-N	2	1	.667	25	0	0	0	0	28	27	0	13	20	13.2	3.86	97	.257	.345	0	.000	-0	-0	-0	-0	0.0
	Yr	2	1	.667	29	0	0	0	0	31²	30	1	17	21	13.6	3.69	101	.250	.348	0	.000	-0	1	0	-0	0.0
1978	NY-N	0	2	.000	27	0	0	0	3	28	30	2	21	12	16.7	5.14	68	.283	.406	0	.000	-0	-5	-5	0	-0.4
Total	5	3	8	.273	87	7	1	1	3	129	130	6	73	59	14.4	3.77	92	.271	.372	0	.000	-2	-4	-4	1	-0.3

■ SONNY SIEBERT
Siebert, Wilfred Charles b: 1/14/37, St.Mary's, Mo. BR/TR, 6'3", 190 lbs. Deb: 4/26/64

1964	Cle-A	7	9	.438	41	14	3	1	3	156	142	15	57	144	11.6	3.23	111	.243	.313	13	.265	5	7	6	-2	1.0
1965	Cle-A	16	8	.667	39	27	4	1	1	188²	139	14	46	191	9.1	2.43	143	.206	.262	7	.106	-2	22	22	1	2.3
1966	Cle-A	16	8	.667	34	32	11	1	1	241	193	25	62	163	9.7	2.80	123	.221	.278	11	.129	-2	17	17	2	1.9
1967	Cle-A	10	12	.455	34	26	7	1	4	185¹	136	17	54	136	9.5	2.38	137	.202	.268	7	.135	1	18	18	-2	2.1
1968	Cle-A	12	10	.545	31	30	8	4	0	206	145	12	88	146	10.5	2.97	100	.198	.290	11	.157	1	0	-1	0	0.2
1969	Cle-A	0	1	.000	2	2	0	0	0	14	10	1	8	6	11.6	3.21	117	.196	.305	1	.250	0	1	1	0	0.1
	Bos-A	14	10	.583	43	22	2	0	5	163¹	151	21	68	127	12.3	3.80	100	.245	.324	8	.151	1	-3	-0	2	0.3
	Yr	14	11	.560	45	24	2	0	5	177¹	161	22	76	133	12.2	3.76	101	.241	.322	4	.070	1	-3	1	2	0.4
1970	Bos-A	15	8	.652	33	33	7	2	0	222²	207	29	60	142	11.0	3.44	115	.248	.303	10	.130	-2	7	13	0	1.3
1971	Bos-A	16	10	.615	32	32	12	4	0	235¹	220	20	60	131	10.8	2.91	127	.245	.294	21	.266	10	15	21	1	3.7
1972	Bos-A	12	12	.500	32	30	7	3	0	196¹	204	17	59	102	12.0	3.80	84	.264	.322	17	.236	6	-16	-13	2	-0.5
1973	Bos-A	0	1	.000	2	2	0	0	0	2¹	5	1	1	5	23.1	7.71	52	.417	.462	0	—	0	-1	-0	0	0.0
	Tex-A	7	11	.389	25	20	1	1	2	119²	120	11	37	76	12.0	3.99	93	.258	.317	0	—	0	-2	-4	2	0.0
	Yr	7	12	.368	27	20	1	1	2	122	125	12	38	81	12.2	4.06	92	.262	.320	0	—	0	-3	-4	2	0.0

YEAR	TM/L	W	L	PCT	G	GS	CG	SH	SV	IP	H	HR	BB	SO	RAT	ERA	ERA+	OAV	OOB	BH	AVG	PB	PR	/A	PD	TPI
1974	StL-N	8	8	.500	28	20	5	3	0	133²	150	8	51	68	13.7	3.84	93	.288	.355	5	.114	-2	-3	-4	-1	-0.6
1975	SD-N	3	2	.600	6	6	0	0	0	26²	37	2	10	10	16.2	4.39	79	.330	.390	3	.375	2	-2	-3	0	0.0
	Oak-A	4	4	.500	17	13	0	0	0	61	60	4	31	44	13.4	3.69	98	.252	.338	0	.000	0	1	-0	-1	-0.1
Total	12	140	114	.551	399	307	67	21	16	2152	1919	197	692	1512	11.1	3.21	110	.238	.303	114	.173	19	57	73	6	11.7

■ DWIGHT SIEBLER
Siebler, Dwight Leroy b: 8/5/37, Columbus, Neb. BR/TR, 6'2", 184 lbs. Deb: 8/26/63

YEAR	TM/L	W	L	PCT	G	GS	CG	SH	SV	IP	H	HR	BB	SO	RAT	ERA	ERA+	OAV	OOB	BH	AVG	PB	PR	/A	PD	TPI
1963	Min-A	2	1	.667	7	5	2	0	0	38²	25	6	12	22	8.8	2.79	130	.182	.253	2	.133	-0	4	4	-1	0.3
1964	Min-A	0	0	—	9	0	0	0	0	11	10	1	6	10	13.1	4.91	73	.256	.356	0	—	0	-2	-2	-0	-0.1
1965	Min-A	0	0	—	7	1	0	0	0	15	11	2	11	15	13.2	4.20	85	.193	.324	0	.000	-0	-1	-1	0	0.0
1966	Min-A	2	2	.500	23	2	0	0	1	49²	47	6	14	24	11.2	3.44	104	.253	.308	0	.000	-1	-0	1	-1	0.0
1967	Min-A	0	0	—	2	0	0	0	0	3	4	0	1	0	15.0	3.00	115	.364	.417	0	—	0	0	0	0	0.0
Total	5	4	3	.571	48	8	2	0	1	117¹	97	15	44	71	11.0	3.45	104	.226	.300	2	.074	-1	1	2	-1	0.2

■ CANDY SIERRA
Sierra, Ulises (Pizarro) b: 3/27/67, Rio Piedras, P.R. BR/TR, 6'2", 190 lbs. Deb: 4/06/88

YEAR	TM/L	W	L	PCT	G	GS	CG	SH	SV	IP	H	HR	BB	SO	RAT	ERA	ERA+	OAV	OOB	BH	AVG	PB	PR	/A	PD	TPI
1988	SD-N	0	1	.000	15	0	0	0	0	23²	36	2	11	20	17.9	5.70	60	.379	.443	0	.000	-0	-6	-6	-0	-0.6
	Cin-N	0	0	—	1	0	0	0	0	4	5	0	1	4	13.5	4.50	80	.294	.333	0	.000	-0	-0	0	0	0.0
	Yr	0	1	.000	16	0	0	0	0	27²	41	2	12	24	17.2	5.53	62	.363	.424	0	.000	-0	-6	-6	-0	-0.6

■ ED SIEVER
Siever, Edward T. b: 4/2/1877, Goodard, Kan. d: 2/4/20, Detroit, Mich. BL/TL, 5'11.5", 190 lbs. Deb: 4/26/01

YEAR	TM/L	W	L	PCT	G	GS	CG	SH	SV	IP	H	HR	BB	SO	RAT	ERA	ERA+	OAV	OOB	BH	AVG	PB	PR	/A	PD	TPI
1901	Det-A	19	15	.559	38	33	30	2	0	288²	334	9	65	85	12.4	3.24	119	.286	.324	18	.168	-5	14	19	-1	1.3
1902	Det-A	8	11	.421	25	23	17	4	1	188¹	166	0	32	36	9.5	**1.91**	**191**	.237	.271	10	.152	-4	35	36	-4	2.9
1903	StL-A	13	14	.481	31	27	24	1	0	254	245	6	39	90	10.1	2.48	117	.253	.282	13	.140	-4	14	12	3	1.1
1904	StL-A	10	15	.400	29	24	19	2	0	217	235	3	65	77	12.4	2.65	93	.277	.328	11	.155	-1	-1	-4	1	-0.5
1906	Det-A	14	11	.560	30	25	20	1	0	222²	240	5	45	71	11.5	2.71	102	.278	.314	12	.156	-3	-0	1	-2	-0.3
1907	*Det-A	18	11	.621	39	33	22	3	1	274²	256	1	52	88	10.1	2.16	121	.249	.285	15	.160	-3	12	14	-4	0.8
1908	Det-A	2	6	.250	11	9	4	1	0	61²	74	0	13	23	12.7	3.50	69	.302	.337	3	.167	-1	-8	-7	-1	-0.8
Total	7	84	83	.503	203	174	136	14	2	1507	1550	24	311	470	11.1	2.60	116	.266	.303	82	.156	-21	65	70	-8	4.5

■ WALTER SIGNER
Signer, Walter Donald Aloysius b: 10/12/10, New York, N.Y. d: 7/23/74, Greenwich, Conn. BR/TR, 6', 185 lbs. Deb: 9/18/43

YEAR	TM/L	W	L	PCT	G	GS	CG	SH	SV	IP	H	HR	BB	SO	RAT	ERA	ERA+	OAV	OOB	BH	AVG	PB	PR	/A	PD	TPI
1943	Chi-N	2	1	.667	4	2	1	0	0	25	24	3	4	5	10.1	2.88	116	.245	.275	2	.250	0	1	1	0	0.2
1945	Chi-N	0	0	—	6	0	0	0	1	8	11	1	5	0	18.0	3.38	108	.256	.333	0	.000	-0	0	0	0	0.0
Total	2	2	1	.667	10	2	1	0	1	33	35	4	9	5	12.0	3.00	114	.248	.293	2	.222	0	2	2	0	0.2

■ SETH SIGSBY
Sigsby, Seth De Witt (b: Seth De Witt) b: 4/30/1874, Cobleskill, N.Y. d: 9/15/53, Schenectady, N.Y 6', 175 lbs. Deb: 6/27/1893

YEAR	TM/L	W	L	PCT	G	GS	CG	SH	SV	IP	H	HR	BB	SO	RAT	ERA	ERA+	OAV	OOB	BH	AVG	PB	PR	/A	PD	TPI
1893	NY-N	0	0	—	1	0	0	0	0	3	1	0	4	2	15.0	9.00	52	.101	.360	0	.000	-0	-1	-1	0	0.0

■ AL SIMA
Sima, Albert b: 10/7/22, Mahwah, N.J. BR/TL, 6', 187 lbs. Deb: 6/28/50

YEAR	TM/L	W	L	PCT	G	GS	CG	SH	SV	IP	H	HR	BB	SO	RAT	ERA	ERA+	OAV	OOB	BH	AVG	PB	PR	/A	PD	TPI
1950	Was-A	4	5	.444	17	9	1	0	0	77	89	9	26	23	13.6	4.79	94	.291	.348	3	.115	-2	-2	-3	-1	-0.5
1951	Was-A	3	7	.300	18	8	1	0	0	77	79	5	41	26	14.0	4.79	85	.261	.349	3	.176	1	-6	-6	-0	-0.4
1953	Was-A	2	3	.400	31	5	1	0	1	68¹	63	7	31	25	12.8	3.42	114	.249	.338	2	.118	-1	4	4	1	0.4
1954	Chi-A	0	1	.000	5	1	0	0	1	7	11	1	2	1	16.7	5.14	73	.393	.433	0	.000	-0	-1	-1	0	0.0
	Phi-A	2	5	.286	29	7	1	0	2	79¹	101	9	32	36	15.1	5.22	75	.309	.370	1	.050	-2	-13	-12	-1	-1.3
	Yr	2	6	.250	34	8	1	0	3	86¹	112	10	34	37	15.2	5.21	75	.315	.375	0	.000	-2	-14	-13	-1	-1.3
Total	4	11	21	.344	100	30	4	0	4	308²	343	31	132	111	14.0	4.61	89	.282	.354	9	.110	-5	-18	-17	-1	-1.8

■ CURT SIMMONS
Simmons, Curtis Thomas b: 5/19/29, Egypt, Pa. BL/TL, 5'11", 175 lbs. Deb: 9/28/47

YEAR	TM/L	W	L	PCT	G	GS	CG	SH	SV	IP	H	HR	BB	SO	RAT	ERA	ERA+	OAV	OOB	BH	AVG	PB	PR	/A	PD	TPI
1947	Phi-N	1	0	1.000	1	1	1	0	0	9	5	0	6	9	11.0	1.00	401	.161	.297	1	.500	0	3	3	-0	0.4
1948	Phi-N	7	13	.350	31	22	7	0	0	170	169	8	108	86	14.8	4.87	81	.266	.374	7	.137	-1	-17	-17	0	-1.7
1949	Phi-N	4	10	.286	38	14	2	0	1	131¹	133	7	55	83	13.0	4.59	86	.275	.350	7	.171	-1	-8	-9	-1	-1.0
1950	Phi-N	17	8	.680	31	27	11	2	1	214²	178	19	88	146	11.2	3.40	119	.223	.302	12	.156	-1	18	16	-1	1.3
1952	Phi-N	14	8	.636	28	28	15	**6**	0	201¹	170	11	70	141	10.8	2.82	130	.227	.294	11	.164	2	20	19	-3	1.8
1953	Phi-N	16	13	.552	32	30	19	4	0	238	211	17	82	138	11.2	3.21	131	.236	.302	13	.140	-3	28	26	-3	2.0
1954	Phi-N	14	15	.483	34	33	21	3	1	253	226	14	98	125	11.7	2.81	144	.239	.314	16	.176	-1	35	35	-3	3.1
1955	Phi-N	8	8	.500	25	22	3	0	0	130	148	15	50	58	13.9	4.92	81	.290	.356	8	.174	-1	-13	-14	-1	-1.4
1956	Phi-N	15	10	.600	33	27	14	0	0	198	186	17	65	88	11.5	3.36	111	.248	.311	17	.236	3	9	8	0	1.1
1957	Phi-N	12	11	.522	32	29	9	2	0	212	214	19	50	92	11.3	3.44	111	.264	.309	17	.239	4	10	9	-2	1.0
1958	Phi-N	7	14	.333	29	27	7	1	1	168¹	196	11	40	78	12.8	4.38	90	.293	.336	12	.203	-0	-8	-8	-1	-0.8
1959	Phi-N	0	0	—	7	0	0	0	0	10	16	2	0	4	15.3	4.50	91	.400	.415	0	—	0	-1	-0	0	0.0
1960	Phi-N	0	0	—	4	2	0	0	0	4	13	3	4	4	42.8	18.00	22	.542	.633	0	—	0	-6	-6	-0	-0.5
	StL-N	7	4	.636	23	17	3	1	0	152	149	11	31	63	10.7	2.66	154	.257	.295	10	.213	1	19	24	1	2.9
	Yr	7	4	.636	27	19	3	1	0	156	162	14	37	67	11.5	3.06	134	.269	.311	4	.085	1	12	18	1	2.4
1961	StL-N	9	10	.474	30	29	6	2	0	195²	203	14	64	99	12.5	3.13	**141**	.269	.329	20	.303	6	20	**28**	0	**3.6**
1962	StL-N	10	10	.500	31	22	9	4	0	154	167	18	32	74	11.8	3.51	122	.280	.320	8	.160	0	7	13	-0	1.4
1963	StL-N	15	9	.625	32	32	11	6	0	232²	209	13	48	127	10.2	2.48	143	.239	.283	13	.160	-0	21	28	-3	2.9
1964	*StL-N	18	9	.667	34	34	12	3	0	244	233	24	49	104	10.6	3.43	111	.249	.290	10	.106	-3	3	10	-0	0.8
1965	StL-N	9	15	.375	34	32	5	0	0	203	229	19	54	96	12.7	4.08	94	.283	.331	3	.047	-5	-12	-5	-1	-1.0
1966	StL-N	1	1	.500	10	5	1	0	0	33¹	35	3	14	13	13.2	4.59	78	.269	.340	1	.125	0	-4	-4	-1	-0.3
	Chi-N	4	7	.364	19	10	3	1	0	77¹	79	7	21	24	11.8	4.07	90	.268	.319	2	.111	-0	-4	-3	2	-0.2
	Yr	5	8	.385	29	15	4	1	0	110²	114	10	35	38	12.2	4.23	86	.268	.325	3	.115	-0	-8	-7	1	-0.5
1967	Chi-N	3	7	.300	17	14	3	0	0	82	100	10	23	31	13.7	4.94	72	.300	.349	4	.143	-1	-14	-13	0	-1.3
	Cal-A	2	1	.667	14	4	1	1	1	34²	44	1	9	13	14.3	2.60	121	.321	.372	2	.222	1	2	2	-0	0.2
Total	20	193	183	.513	569	461	163	36	5	3348¹	3313	255	1063	1697	11.9	3.54	111	.259	.319	194	.171	2	109	142	-18	14.3

■ PAT SIMMONS
Simmons, Patrick Clement (b: Patrick Clement Simoni) b: 11/29/08, Watervliet, N.Y. d: 7/3/68, Albany, N.Y. BR/TR, 5'11", 172 lbs. Deb: 4/18/28

YEAR	TM/L	W	L	PCT	G	GS	CG	SH	SV	IP	H	HR	BB	SO	RAT	ERA	ERA+	OAV	OOB	BH	AVG	PB	PR	/A	PD	TPI
1928	Bos-A	0	2	.000	31	3	0	0	1	69	69	4	38	16	14.1	4.04	102	.271	.367	2	.133	-1	0	**1**	-0	0.0
1929	Bos-A	0	0	—	2	0	0	0	1	7	6	0	3	2	11.6	0.00	—	.231	.310	0	.000	-0	3	3	0	0.3
Total	2	0	2	.000	33	3	0	0	2	76	75	4	41	18	13.9	3.67	112	.267	.362	2	.125	-1	3	4	0	0.3

■ JOE SIMPSON
Simpson, Joe Allen b: 12/31/51, Purcell, Okla. BL/TL, 6'3", 175 lbs. Deb: 9/02/75 ◆

YEAR	TM/L	W	L	PCT	G	GS	CG	SH	SV	IP	H	HR	BB	SO	RAT	ERA	ERA+	OAV	OOB	BH	AVG	PB	PR	/A	PD	TPI
1983	KC-A	0	0	—	2	0	0	0	0	3	4	0	2	1	18.0	3.00	136	.308	.400	20	.168	1	0	0	0	0.0

■ STEVE SIMPSON
Simpson, Steven Edward b: 8/30/48, St.Joseph, Mo. d: 11/2/89, Omaha, Neb. BR/TR, 6'3", 200 lbs. Deb: 9/10/72

YEAR	TM/L	W	L	PCT	G	GS	CG	SH	SV	IP	H	HR	BB	SO	RAT	ERA	ERA+	OAV	OOB	BH	AVG	PB	PR	/A	PD	TPI
1972	SD-N	0	2	.000	9	0	0	0	2	11¹	10	0	8	9	14.3	4.76	69	.238	.360	0	—	0	-2	-2	-0	-0.1

■ DUKE SIMPSON
Simpson, Thomas Leo b: 9/15/27, Columbus, Ohio BR/TR, 6'1.5", 190 lbs. Deb: 5/06/53

YEAR	TM/L	W	L	PCT	G	GS	CG	SH	SV	IP	H	HR	BB	SO	RAT	ERA	ERA+	OAV	OOB	BH	AVG	PB	PR	/A	PD	TPI
1953	Chi-N	1	2	.333	30	1	0	0	0	45	60	8	25	21	17.2	8.00	56	.314	.396	2	.250	0	-19	-18	-0	-1.6

■ WAYNE SIMPSON
Simpson, Wayne Kirby b: 12/2/48, Los Angeles, Cal. BR/TR, 6'3", 220 lbs. Deb: 4/09/70

YEAR	TM/L	W	L	PCT	G	GS	CG	SH	SV	IP	H	HR	BB	SO	RAT	ERA	ERA+	OAV	OOB	BH	AVG	PB	PR	/A	PD	TPI
1970	Cin-N	14	3	.824	26	26	10	2	0	176	125	15	81	119	11.0	3.02	134	**.198**	.298	6	.094	-4	20	20	2	1.9
1971	Cin-N	4	7	.364	22	21	1	0	0	117¹	106	9	77	61	14.3	4.76	71	.244	.361	1	.031	-2	-17	-18	2	-1.8
1972	Cin-N	8	5	.615	24	22	1	0	0	130¹	124	17	49	70	12.1	4.14	78	.247	.316	3	.063	-3	-10	-13	-3	-1.0
1973	KC-A	3	4	.429	16	10	1	0	0	59²	66	1	35	29	15.4	5.73	72	.284	.381	0	—	0	-13	-11	-0	-1.0
1975	Phi-N	1	0	1.000	7	5	0	0	0	30²	31	1	11	19	12.6	3.23	116	.263	.331	2	.222	0	1	2	0	0.3
1977	Cal-A	6	12	.333	27	23	0	0	0	122	154	14	62	55	16.5	5.83	67	.308	.392	0	—	0	-24	-26	-1	-2.4
Total	6	36	31	.537	122	107	13	2	0	636	606	57	315	353	13.4	4.37	85	.251	.343	12	.078	-8	-42	-47	1	-4.9

YEAR	TM/L	W	L	PCT	G	GS	CG	SH	SV	IP	H	HR	BB	SO	RAT	ERA	ERA+	OAV	OOB	BH	AVG	PB	PR	/A	PD	TPI

■ PETE SIMS
Sims, Clarence   b: 5/24/1891, Crown City, Ohio   d: 12/2/68, Dallas, Tex.   BR/TR, 5'11.5", 165 lbs.   Deb: 9/16/15

YEAR	TM/L	W	L	PCT	G	GS	CG	SH	SV	IP	H	HR	BB	SO	RAT	ERA	ERA+	OAV	OOB	BH	AVG	PB	PR	/A	PD	TPI
1915	StL-A	1	0	1.000	3	2	0	0	0	8¹	6	0	6	4	13.0	4.32	66	.214	.353	1	1.000	1	-1	-1	-0	0.0

■ BERT SINCOCK
Sincock, Herbert Sylvester   b: 9/8/1887, Barkerville, B.C. Canada   d: 8/1/46, Houghton, Mich.   5'10.5", 165 lbs.   Deb: 6/25/08

YEAR	TM/L	W	L	PCT	G	GS	CG	SH	SV	IP	H	HR	BB	SO	RAT	ERA	ERA+	OAV	OOB	BH	AVG	PB	PR	/A	PD	TPI
1908	Cin-N	0	0	—	1	0	0	0	0	4²	3	0	0	1	5.8	3.86	60	.176	.176	0	.000	-0	-1	-1	0	0.0

■ BILL SINGER
Singer, William Robert "The Singer Throwing Machine"   b: 4/24/44, Los Angeles, Cal.   BR/TR, 6'4", 184 lbs.   Deb: 9/24/64

YEAR	TM/L	W	L	PCT	G	GS	CG	SH	SV	IP	H	HR	BB	SO	RAT	ERA	ERA+	OAV	OOB	BH	AVG	PB	PR	/A	PD	TPI
1964	LA-N	0	1	.000	2	2	0	0	0	14	11	0	12	3	14.8	3.21	101	.216	.365	1	.167	0	1	0	0	0.0
1965	LA-N	0	0	—	2	0	0	0	0	1	2	0	2	1	36.0	0.00	—	.400	.571	0	—	0	0	0	0	0.0
1966	LA-N	0	0	—	3	0	0	0	0	4	4	0	2	4	13.5	0.00	—	.286	.375	0	—	0	2	1	0	0.2
1967	LA-N	12	8	.600	32	29	7	3	0	204¹	185	5	61	169	11.2	2.64	117	.239	.301	6	.090	-3	17	10	0	0.8
1968	LA-N	13	17	.433	37	36	12	6	0	256¹	227	14	78	227	10.9	2.88	96	.237	.298	12	.148	3	3	-3	-1	-0.1
1969	LA-N	20	12	.625	41	40	16	2	1	315²	244	22	74	247	9.4	2.34	142	.210	.263	11	.102	-4	44	35	-2	3.0
1970	LA-N	8	5	.615	16	16	5	3	0	106¹	79	10	32	93	9.6	3.13	122	.203	.267	5	.132	-0	11	8	-1	0.7
1971	LA-N	10	17	.370	31	31	8	1	0	203¹	195	19	71	144	12.0	4.16	78	.252	.318	6	.103	-0	-16	-21	-2	-2.3
1972	LA-N	6	16	.273	26	25	4	3	0	169¹	148	8	60	101	11.3	3.67	91	.237	.309	4	.073	-3	-4	-6	1	-0.8
1973	Cal-A	20	14	.588	40	40	19	2	0	315²	280	15	130	241	11.9	3.22	110	.235	.314	0	—	0	21	11	-2	0.9
1974	Cal-A	7	4	.636	14	14	8	0	0	108²	102	3	43	77	12.1	2.98	115	.250	.323	0	—	0	8	5	0	0.6
1975	Cal-A	7	15	.318	29	27	8	0	1	179	171	18	81	78	13.0	4.98	71	.257	.343	0	—	0	-24	-28	0	-2.6
1976	Tex-A	4	1	.800	10	10	2	1	0	64²	56	4	27	34	12.2	3.48	103	.239	.331	0	—	0	0	1	-0	0.0
	Min-A	9	9	.500	26	26	5	3	0	172	177	9	69	63	13.2	3.77	96	.274	.349	0	—	0	-5	-3	-1	-0.4
	Yr	13	10	.565	36	36	7	4	0	236²	233	13	96	97	12.7	3.69	97	.262	.338	0	—	0	-4	-2	-2	-0.4
1977	Tor-A	2	8	.200	13	12	0	0	0	59²	71	5	39	33	16.9	6.79	62	.296	.399	0	—	0	-18	-17	0	-1.5
Total	14	118	127	.482	322	308	94	24	2	2174	1952	132	781	1515	11.6	3.39	99	.240	.311	45	.109	-6	39	-7	-8	-1.5

■ ELMER SINGLETON
Singleton, Bert Elmer "Smoky"   b: 6/26/18, Ogden, Utah   BR/TR, 6'2", 174 lbs.   Deb: 8/20/45

YEAR	TM/L	W	L	PCT	G	GS	CG	SH	SV	IP	H	HR	BB	SO	RAT	ERA	ERA+	OAV	OOB	BH	AVG	PB	PR	/A	PD	TPI
1945	Bos-N	1	4	.200	7	5	1	0	0	37¹	35	1	14	14	12.1	4.82	79	.248	.321	0	.000	-2	-4	-4	-0	-0.5
1946	Bos-N	0	1	.000	15	2	0	0	0	33²	27	3	21	17	13.1	3.74	92	.221	.340	0	.000	-1	-1	-1	0	-0.1
1947	Pit-N	2	2	.500	36	3	0	0	1	67	70	9	39	24	14.9	6.31	67	.267	.366	4	.308	1	-17	-16	0	-1.2
1948	Pit-N	4	6	.400	38	5	1	0	2	92¹	90	11	40	53	12.8	4.97	82	.253	.330	2	.087	-2	-10	-9	1	-0.9
1950	Was-A	1	2	.333	21	1	0	0	0	36¹	39	4	17	19	13.9	5.20	86	.291	.371	3	.429	1	-3	-3	1	0.0
1957	Chi-N	0	1	.000	5	2	0	0	0	13¹	20	3	2	6	14.9	6.75	57	.333	.355	0	.000	-0	-4	-4	0	-0.3
1958	Chi-N	1	0	1.000	2	0	0	0	0	4²	1	0	1	2	3.9	0.00	—	.071	.133	0	.000	-0	2	2	0	0.2
1959	Chi-N	2	1	.667	21	1	0	0	0	43	40	2	12	25	10.9	2.72	145	.252	.304	0	.000	-0	6	6	1	0.6
Total	8	11	17	.393	145	19	2	0	4	327²	322	33	146	160	13.0	4.83	83	.258	.338	9	.132	-3	-32	-29	3	-2.2

■ JOHN SINGLETON
Singleton, John Edward "Sheriff"   b: 11/27/1896, Gallipolis, Ohio   d: 10/23/37, Dayton, Ohio   BR/TL, 5'11", 171 lbs.   Deb: 6/08/22

YEAR	TM/L	W	L	PCT	G	GS	CG	SH	SV	IP	H	HR	BB	SO	RAT	ERA	ERA+	OAV	OOB	BH	AVG	PB	PR	/A	PD	TPI
1922	Phi-N	1	10	.091	22	9	3	1	0	93	127	6	38	27	16.5	5.90	79	.346	.415	5	.139	-3	-19	-13	-1	-1.3

■ DOUG SISK
Sisk, Douglas Randall   b: 9/26/57, Benton, Wash.   BR/TR, 6'2", 210 lbs.   Deb: 9/06/82

YEAR	TM/L	W	L	PCT	G	GS	CG	SH	SV	IP	H	HR	BB	SO	RAT	ERA	ERA+	OAV	OOB	BH	AVG	PB	PR	/A	PD	TPI
1982	NY-N	0	1	.000	8	0	0	0	1	8²	5	1	4	4	10.4	1.04	349	.172	.294	0	—	0	2	2	0	0.3
1983	NY-N	5	4	.556	67	0	0	0	11	104¹	88	1	59	33	13.0	2.24	162	.235	.346	3	.500	1	16	16	-0	1.8
1984	NY-N	1	3	.250	50	0	0	0	15	77²	57	1	54	32	13.2	2.09	169	.215	.354	1	.091	-0	13	12	0	1.3
1985	NY-N	4	5	.444	42	0	0	0	2	73	86	3	40	26	15.8	5.30	65	.291	.379	0	.000	-1	-14	-15	1	-1.5
1986	•NY-N	4	2	.667	41	0	0	0	1	70²	77	0	31	31	14.4	3.06	116	.282	.366	0	.000	-0	5	4	-0	0.4
1987	NY-N	3	1	.750	55	0	0	0	3	78	83	5	22	37	12.5	3.46	109	.270	.325	0	.000	-0	5	3	2	0.4
1988	Bal-A	3	3	.500	52	0	0	0	0	94¹	109	3	45	26	14.9	3.72	105	.306	.387	0	—	0	3	2	1	0.3
1990	Atl-N	0	0	—	3	0	0	0	0	2¹	1	0	4	1	19.3	3.86	101	.143	.455	0	—	0	-0	-0	0	0.0
Total	8	20	19	.513	318	0	0	0	33	509	506	14	259	190	13.9	3.22	114	.265	.359	4	.105	-1	31	25	3	2.9

■ TOMMIE SISK
Sisk, Tommie Wayne   b: 4/12/42, Ardmore, Okla.   BR/TR, 6'3", 195 lbs.   Deb: 7/19/62

YEAR	TM/L	W	L	PCT	G	GS	CG	SH	SV	IP	H	HR	BB	SO	RAT	ERA	ERA+	OAV	OOB	BH	AVG	PB	PR	/A	PD	TPI
1962	Pit-N	0	2	.000	5	3	1	0	0	17²	18	1	8	6	13.8	4.08	97	.257	.342	1	.200	0	-0	-0	-0	0.0
1963	Pit-N	1	3	.250	57	4	1	0	1	108	85	6	45	73	10.9	2.92	113	.222	.305	1	.063	-0	4	5	1	0.5
1964	Pit-N	1	4	.200	42	4	0	0	1	61¹	91	4	29	35	18.0	6.16	57	.364	.436	0	.000	-1	-18	-18	2	-1.7
1965	Pit-N	7	3	.700	38	12	1	1	0	111¹	103	6	50	66	12.4	3.40	103	.248	.330	2	.061	-2	2	1	-1	0.0
1966	Pit-N	10	5	.667	34	23	4	1	1	150	146	14	52	60	12.1	4.14	86	.256	.323	5	.098	-1	-9	-9	1	-1.0
1967	Pit-N	13	13	.500	37	31	11	2	1	207²	196	6	78	85	12.0	3.34	101	.253	.324	7	.101	-2	1	1	1	0.0
1968	Pit-N	5	5	.500	33	11	0	0	0	96	101	3	35	41	13.0	3.28	89	.282	.351	2	.083	-1	-3	-4	1	-0.3
1969	SD-N	2	13	.133	53	13	1	0	6	143	160	11	48	59	13.2	4.78	74	.285	.342	3	.120	0	-19	-20	1	-1.8
1970	Chi-A	1	1	.500	17	1	0	0	0	33¹	37	6	13	16	13.5	5.40	72	.276	.340	1	.250	0	-6	-6	1	-0.4
Total	9	40	49	.449	316	99	19	4	10	928¹	937	57	358	441	12.7	3.92	88	.266	.337	22	.094	-7	-48	-50	5	-4.7

■ DAVE SISLER
Sisler, David Michael   b: 10/16/31, St.Louis, Mo.   BR/TR, 6'4", 200 lbs.   Deb: 4/21/56

YEAR	TM/L	W	L	PCT	G	GS	CG	SH	SV	IP	H	HR	BB	SO	RAT	ERA	ERA+	OAV	OOB	BH	AVG	PB	PR	/A	PD	TPI
1956	Bos-A	9	8	.529	39	14	3	0	3	142¹	120	13	72	93	12.6	4.62	100	.227	.328	5	.119	-3	-7	0	0	-0.1
1957	Bos-A	7	8	.467	22	19	5	0	1	122¹	135	15	61	55	14.6	4.71	85	.280	.363	7	.167	-0	-12	-10	1	-0.8
1958	Bos-A	8	9	.471	30	25	4	1	0	149¹	157	22	79	71	14.3	4.94	81	.276	.366	9	.196	-0	-19	-16	-1	-1.5
1959	Bos-A	0	0	—	3	0	0	0	0	6²	9	3	1	3	13.5	6.75	60	.310	.333	1	.500	-0	-2	-2	-0	-0.1
	Det-A	1	3	.250	32	0	0	0	7	51²	46	4	36	29	14.5	4.01	101	.242	.366	1	.200	-0	-1	0	-1	0.0
	Yr	1	3	.250	35	0	0	0	7	58¹	55	7	37	32	14.3	4.32	94	.251	.362	0	.000	-0	-3	-2	-1	-0.1
1960	Det-A	7	5	.583	41	0	0	0	6	80	56	3	45	47	11.6	2.47	160	.199	.314	2	.125	-0	12	13	1	1.5
1961	Was-A	2	8	.200	45	1	0	0	11	60¹	55	6	48	30	15.8	4.18	96	.251	.393	0	.000	-0	-1	-1	0	0.0
1962	Cin-N	4	3	.571	35	0	0	0	1	43²	44	4	26	27	14.4	3.92	103	.270	.370	0	—	0	0	1	-0	0.0
Total	7	38	44	.463	247	59	12	1	29	656¹	622	70	368	355	13.8	4.33	95	.253	.354	25	.157	-3	-31	-15	1	-1.0

■ GEORGE SISLER
Sisler, George Harold "Georgeous George"   b: 3/24/1893, Manchester, Ohio   d: 3/26/73, Richmond Heights, Mo.   BL/TL, 5'11", 170 lbs.   Deb: 6/28/15   MCH♦

YEAR	TM/L	W	L	PCT	G	GS	CG	SH	SV	IP	H	HR	BB	SO	RAT	ERA	ERA+	OAV	OOB	BH	AVG	PB	PR	/A	PD	TPI
1915	StL-A	4	4	.500	15	8	6	0	0	70	62	0	38	41	13.4	2.83	101	.247	.355	78	.285	3	1	0	0	0.0
1916	StL-A	1	2	.333	3	3	3	1	0	27	18	0	6	12	8.3	1.00	275	.198	.255	177	.305	1	5	5	0	0.7
1918	StL-A	0	0	—	2	1	0	0	1	8	10	0	4	4	16.9	4.50	61	.286	.375	154	.341	1	-2	-2	0	-0.1
1920	StL-A	0	0	—	1	0	0	0	1	1	0	0	0	2	0.0	0.00	—	.000	.000	257	.407	1	0	0	0	0.0
1925	StL-A	0	0	—	1	0	0	0	0	2	1	0	1	1	9.0	0.00	—	.167	.286	224	.345	0	1	1	0	0.1
1926	StL-A	0	0	—	1	0	0	0	1	2	0	0	2	3	9.0	0.00	—	.000	.286	178	.290	0	1	1	0	0.1
1928	Bos-N	0	0	—	1	0	0	0	0	1	0	0	1	0	9.0	0.00	—	.000	.333	167	.340	0	0	0	0	0.0
Total	7	5	6	.455	24	12	9	1	3	111	91	0	52	63	12.1	2.35	123	.231	.330	2812	.340	7	8	7	1	0.8

■ CARL SITTON
Sitton, Carl Vetter   b: 9/22/1882, Pendleton, S.C.   d: 9/11/31, Valdosta, Ga.   TR, 5'10.5", 170 lbs.   Deb: 4/24/09

YEAR	TM/L	W	L	PCT	G	GS	CG	SH	SV	IP	H	HR	BB	SO	RAT	ERA	ERA+	OAV	OOB	BH	AVG	PB	PR	/A	PD	TPI
1909	Cle-A	3	2	.600	14	5	3	0	0	50	50	1	16	16	12.2	2.88	89	.263	.327	2	.154	0	-2	-2	-1	-0.1

■ PETE SIVESS
Sivess, Peter   b: 9/23/13, South River, N.J.   BR/TR, 6'3.5", 195 lbs.   Deb: 6/13/36

YEAR	TM/L	W	L	PCT	G	GS	CG	SH	SV	IP	H	HR	BB	SO	RAT	ERA	ERA+	OAV	OOB	BH	AVG	PB	PR	/A	PD	TPI
1936	Phi-N	3	4	.429	17	6	2	0	0	65	84	6	36	22	16.8	4.57	99	.310	.393	3	.120	-2	-4	-0	-1	-0.3
1937	Phi-N	1	1	.500	6	2	1	0	0	23	30	5	11	4	16.0	7.04	62	.330	.402	0	.000	-1	-8	-7	-1	-0.7
1938	Phi-N	3	6	.333	39	8	2	0	3	116	143	12	69	32	16.5	5.51	71	.306	.397	6	.188	-1	-22	-21	-0	-2.1
Total	3	7	11	.389	62	16	5	0	3	204	257	23	116	58	16.5	5.38	77	.310	.396	9	.143	-4	-34	-28	-2	-3.1

YEAR TM/L	W	L	PCT	G	GS	CG	SH	SV	IP	H	HR	BB	SO	RAT	ERA	ERA+	OAV	OOB	BH	AVG	PB	PR	/A	PD	TPI
■ JIM SIWY Siwy, James b: 9/20/58, Central Falls, R.I BR/TR, 6'4", 200 lbs. Deb: 8/20/82																									
1982 Chi-A	0	0	—	2	1	0	0	0	7	10	1	5	3	19.3	10.29	39	.385	.484	0	—	0	-5	-5	-0	-0.4
1984 Chi-A	0	0	—	1	0	0	0	0	4¹	3	0	2	1	10.4	2.08	200	.231	.333	0	—	0	1	1	0	0.1
Total 2	0	0	—	3	1	0	0	0	11¹	13	1	7	4	15.9	7.15	57	.333	.435	0	—	0	-4	-4	0	-0.3
■ JOE SKALSKI Skalski, Joseph Douglas b: 9/26/64, Burnham, Ill. BR/TR, 6'3", 190 lbs. Deb: 4/10/89																									
1989 Cle-A	0	2	.000	2	1	0	0	0	6²	7	0	4	3	17.6	6.75	59	.259	.394	0	—	0	-2	-2	0	-0.1
■ DAVE SKAUGSTAD Skaugstad, David Wendell b: 1/10/40, Algona, Iowa BL/TL, 6'1", 179 lbs. Deb: 9/25/57																									
1957 Cin-N	0	0	—	2	0	0	0	0	5²	4	0	6	4	15.9	1.59	259	.190	.370	0	.000	0	1	2	0	0.2
■ DAVE SKEELS Skeels, David b: 12/29/1892, Washington State d: 12/2/26, Spokane, Wash. BL/TR, 6'1", 187 lbs. Deb: 9/14/10																									
1910 Det-A	0	0	—	1	1	0	0	0	6	9	0	4	2	21.0	12.00	22	.333	.438	0	.000	-0	-6	-6	0	-0.4
■ CRAIG SKOK Skok, Craig Richard b: 9/1/47, Dobbs Ferry, N.Y. BR/TL, 6', 190 lbs. Deb: 5/04/73																									
1973 Bos-A	0	1	.000	11	0	0	0	1	28²	35	2	11	22	14.4	6.28	64	.304	.365	0	—	0	-8	-7	-0	-0.7
1976 Tex-A	0	1	.000	9	0	0	0	0	5	13	2	3	5	28.8	12.60	28	.481	.533	0	—	0	-5	-5	-0	-0.4
1978 Atl-N	3	2	.600	43	0	0	0	2	62	64	8	27	28	13.2	4.35	93	.266	.340	2	.250	0	-5	-2	-0	-0.1
1979 Atl-N	1	3	.250	44	0	0	0	2	54¹	58	7	17	30	12.9	3.98	102	.282	.345	0	.000	-0	-1	0	0	0.1
Total 4	4	7	.364	107	0	0	0	5	150	170	19	58	85	13.9	4.86	83	.289	.355	2	.182	0	-20	-14	-0	-1.1
■ JOHN SKOPEC Skopec, John S. "Buckshot" b: 5/8/1880, Chicago, Ill. d: 10/12/12, Chicago.Ill. BR/TL, 5'10", 190 lbs. Deb: 4/25/01																									
1901 Chi-A	6	3	.667	9	9	6	0	0	68¹	62	1	45	24	14.1	3.16	110	.239	.352	10	.333	3	4	2	3	0.8
1903 Det-A	2	2	.500	6	5	3	0	0	39¹	46	0	13	14	13.5	3.43	85	.291	.345	2	.154	-0	-2	-2	0	-0.1
Total 2	8	5	.615	15	14	9	0	0	107²	108	1	58	38	13.9	3.26	101	.259	.349	12	.279	3	2	0	3	0.7
■ JOHN SLAGLE Slagle, John A. b: Lawrence, Ind. BL/TR, Deb: 4/30/1891																									
1891 Cin-a	0	0	—	1	0	0	0	1	1¹	3	0	1	1	27.0	0.00	—	.431	.502	0	.000	-0	1	1	0	0.0
■ ROGER SLAGLE Slagle, Roger Lee b: 11/4/53, Wichita, Kan. BR/TR, 6'3", 190 lbs. Deb: 9/07/79																									
1979 NY-A	0	0	—	1	0	0	0	0	2	0	0	0	2	0.0	0.00	—	.000	.000	0	—	0	1	1	0	0.1
■ WALT SLAGLE Slagle, Walter Jennings b: 12/15/1878, Kenton, Ohio d: 6/17/74, San Gabriel, Cal. BB/TR, 6', 165 lbs. Deb: 5/04/10																									
1910 Cin-N	0	0	—	1	0	0	0	0	1	1	0	3	0	36.0	9.00	32	.000	.571	0	—	0	-1	-1	0	0.0
■ CY SLAPNICKA Slapnicka, Cyril Charles b: 3/23/1886, Cedar Rapids, Iowa d: 10/20/79, Cedar Rapids, Iowa BB/TR, 5'10", 165 lbs. Deb: 9/26/11																									
1911 Chi-N	0	2	.000	3	2	1	0	0	24	21	0	7	10	11.6	3.38	98	.236	.313	2	.222	-0	0	-0	1	0.1
1918 Pit-N	1	4	.200	7	6	4	0	1	49¹	50	2	22	3	14.0	4.74	61	.269	.362	1	.071	-1	-11	-10	-0	-1.0
Total 2	1	6	.143	10	8	5	0	1	73¹	71	2	29	13	13.3	4.30	70	.258	.346	3	.130	-1	-11	-10	1	-0.9
■ JOHN SLAPPEY Slappey, John Henry b: 8/8/1898, Albany, Ga. d: 6/10/57, Marietta, Ga. BL/TL, 6'4", 170 lbs. Deb: 8/23/20																									
1920 Phi-A	0	1	.000	3	1	0	0	0	6¹	15	0	4	1	27.0	7.11	57	.441	.500	1	.500	1	-2	-2	0	-0.1
■ JIM SLATON Slaton, James Michael b: 6/19/50, Long Beach, Cal. BR/TR, 6', 185 lbs. Deb: 4/14/71																									
1971 Mil-A	10	8	.556	26	23	5	4	0	147²	140	16	71	63	12.9	3.78	92	.253	.339	5	.109	-1	-5	-5	-2	-0.8
1972 Mil-A	1	6	.143	9	8	0	0	0	44	50	3	21	17	14.7	5.52	55	.287	.367	1	.091	-1	-12	-12	1	-1.2
1973 Mil-A	13	15	.464	38	38	13	3	0	276¹	266	30	99	134	11.9	3.71	101	.251	.316	0	—	0	3	1	-3	-0.1
1974 Mil-A	13	16	.448	40	35	10	3	0	250	255	22	102	126	13.0	3.92	92	.268	.341	0	—	0	-9	-9	0	-0.8
1975 Mil-A	11	18	.379	37	33	10	3	0	217	238	28	90	119	13.7	4.52	85	.276	.346	0	—	0	-18	-17	0	-1.5
1976 Mil-A	14	15	.483	38	38	12	2	0	292²	287	14	94	138	11.9	3.44	101	.269	.320	0	—	0	2	2	-0	0.1
1977 Mil-A	10	14	.417	32	31	7	1	0	221	223	25	77	104	12.7	3.58	113	.266	.336	0	—	0	12	12	0	1.2
1978 Det-A	17	11	.607	35	34	11	2	0	233²	235	27	85	92	12.6	4.12	94	.263	.332	0	—	0	-9	-7	-1	-0.7
1979 Mil-A	15	9	.625	32	31	12	3	0	213	229	15	54	80	12.0	3.63	115	.278	.323	0	—	0	14	13	1	1.3
1980 Mil-A	1	1	.500	3	3	0	0	0	16¹	17	3	5	4	12.1	4.41	88	.270	.324	0	—	0	-1	-1	0	0.0
1981 *Mil-A	5	7	.417	24	21	0	0	0	117¹	120	10	50	47	13.2	4.37	78	.273	.350	0	—	0	-9	-12	1	-1.2
1982 *Mil-A	10	6	.625	39	7	0	0	6	117²	117	14	41	59	12.2	3.29	115	.264	.327	0	—	0	10	6	-0	0.6
1983 Mil-A	14	6	.700	46	0	0	0	5	112¹	112	12	56	38	13.7	4.33	86	.272	.363	0	—	0	-3	-7	-0	-0.6
1984 Cal-A	7	10	.412	32	22	5	1	0	163	192	22	56	67	13.8	4.97	80	.295	.353	0	—	0	-18	-18	1	-1.6
1985 Cal-A	6	10	.375	29	24	1	0	1	148¹	162	22	63	60	13.8	4.37	94	.284	.357	0	—	0	-4	-4	0	-0.3
1986 Cal-A	4	6	.400	14	12	0	0	0	73¹	84	9	29	31	14.1	5.65	73	.295	.364	0	—	0	-12	-13	1	-1.0
Det-A	0	0	—	22	0	0	0	2	40	46	5	11	12	13.0	4.05	102	.287	.337	0	—	0	1	0	1	0.1
Yr	4	6	.400	36	12	0	0	2	113¹	130	14	40	43	13.6	5.08	81	.287	.346	0	—	0	-11	-12	1	-0.9
Total 16	151	158	.489	496	360	86	22	14	2683²	2773	277	1004	1191	12.8	4.03	94	.270	.337	6	.105	-2	-58	-70	-2	-6.5
■ PHIL SLATTERY Slattery, Philip Ryan b: 2/25/1893, Harper, Iowa d: 3/2/68, Long Beach, Cal. BR/TL, 5'11", 160 lbs. Deb: 9/16/15																									
1915 Pit-N	0	0	—	3	0	0	0	0	8	5	0	1	1	9.0	0.00	—	.185	.267	0	.000	-0	2	2	-0	0.2
■ BARNEY SLAUGHTER Slaughter, Byron Atkins b: 10/6/1884, Smyrna, Del. d: 5/17/61, Philadelphia, Pa. BR/TR, 5'11.5", 165 lbs. Deb: 8/09/10																									
1910 Phi-N	0	1	.000	8	1	0	0	1	18	21	0	11	7	16.0	5.50	57	.318	.416	1	.200	0	-5	-5	0	-0.3
■ STERLING SLAUGHTER Slaughter, Sterling Feore b: 11/18/41, Danville, Ill. BR/TR, 5'11", 165 lbs. Deb: 4/19/64																									
1964 Chi-N	2	4	.333	20	6	1	0	0	51²	64	8	32	32	16.7	5.75	65	.305	.397	1	.083	-0	-13	-12	-1	-1.3
■ BILL SLAYBACK Slayback, William Grover b: 2/21/48, Hollywood, Cal. BR/TR, 6'4", 200 lbs. Deb: 6/26/72																									
1972 Det-A	5	6	.455	23	13	3	1	0	81²	74	4	25	65	11.0	3.20	98	.239	.298	4	.174	-0	-1	-0	1	0.0
1973 Det-A	0	0	—	3	0	0	0	0	2	5	0	1	1	27.0	4.50	91	.417	.462	0	—	0	-0	-0	-0	0.0
1974 Det-A	1	3	.250	16	4	0	0	0	54²	57	1	26	23	14.2	4.77	80	.273	.361	0	—	0	-7	-6	-0	-0.5
Total 3	6	9	.400	42	17	3	1	0	138¹	136	5	51	89	12.5	3.84	89	.256	.327	4	.174	-0	-8	-7	0	-0.5
■ STEVE SLAYTON Slayton, Foster Herbert b: 4/26/02, Barre, Vt. d: 12/20/84, Manchester, N.H. BR/TR, 6', 163 lbs. Deb: 7/21/28																									
1928 Bos-A	0	0	—	3	0	0	0	0	7	6	0	3	2	11.6	3.86	107	.240	.321	0	.000	-0	0	0	-0	0.0
■ LOU SLEATER Sleater, Louis Mortimer b: 9/8/26, St.Louis, Mo. BL/TL, 5'10", 185 lbs. Deb: 4/25/50																									
1950 StL-A	0	0	—	1	0	0	0	0	1	0	0	0	1	0.0	0.00	—	.000	.000	0	—	0	1	1	0	0.0
1951 StL-A	1	9	.100	20	8	4	0	1	81	88	7	53	33	16.2	5.11	86	.271	.381	7	.226	0	-9	-6	-1	-0.6
1952 StL-A	0	1	.000	4	2	0	0	0	8²	9	1	5	1	14.5	7.27	54	.265	.359	0	.000	-0	-3	-3	0	-0.2
Was-A	4	2	.667	14	9	3	1	0	57	56	4	30	22	13.9	3.63	98	.260	.356	1	.050	-2	0	-0	-1	-0.3
Yr	4	3	.571	18	11	3	1	0	65²	65	5	35	23	14.0	4.11	88	.261	.357	1	.040	-2	-3	-4	-1	-0.5
1955 KC-A	1	1	.500	16	1	0	0	0	25²	33	3	21	11	18.9	7.71	54	.324	.439	2	.154	-1	-11	-10	-0	-0.9
1956 Mil-N	2	2	.500	25	1	0	0	2	45²	42	6	27	32	13.6	3.15	110	.240	.342	5	.500	2	3	2	1	0.4
1957 Det-A	3	3	.500	41	0	0	0	2	69¹	61	9	28	43	11.7	3.76	102	.237	.315	5	.250	3	0	1	-0	0.4
1958 Det-A	0	0	—	4	0	0	0	0	5¹	3	2	2	6	14.5	6.75	60	.158	.360	1	1.000	1	-2	-2	0	-0.0
Bal-A	1	0	1.000	6	0	0	0	0	7	14	0	2	5	20.6	12.86	28	.438	.471	0	.000	-1	-7	-7	-0	-0.7
Yr	1	0	1.000	10	0	0	0	0	12¹	17	2	4	11	18.2	10.22	37	.333	.424	1	.000	1	-9	-9	-0	-0.7
Total 7	12	18	.400	131	21	7	1	5	300²	306	32	172	152	14.5	4.70	83	.263	.362	21	.204	3	-28	-26	-2	-1.9

YEAR	TM/L	W	L	PCT	G	GS	CG	SH	SV	IP	H	HR	BB	SO	RAT	ERA	ERA+	OAV	OOB	BH	AVG	PB	PR	/A	PD	TPI

■ **LEFTY SLOAT**   Sloat, Dwain Clifford   b: 12/1/18, Nokomis, Ill.   BR/TL, 6′, 168 lbs.   Deb: 4/24/48

YEAR	TM/L	W	L	PCT	G	GS	CG	SH	SV	IP	H	HR	BB	SO	RAT	ERA	ERA+	OAV	OOB	BH	AVG	PB	PR	/A	PD	TPI
1948	Bro-N	0	1	.000	4	1	0	0	0	7¹	7	0	8	1	18.4	6.14	65	.280	.455	0	.000	-0	-2	-2	1	0.0
1949	Chi-N	0	0	—	5	1	0	0	0	9	14	0	3	3	17.0	7.00	58	.400	.447	0	—	0	-3	-3	0	-0.2
Total	2	0	1	.000	9	2	0	0	0	16¹	21	0	11	4	17.6	6.61	61	.350	.451	0	.000	-0	-5	-5	1	-0.2

■ **WALT SMALLWOOD**   Smallwood, Walter Clayton   b: 4/24/1893, Dayton, Md.   d: 4/29/67, Baltimore, Md.   BR/TR, 6′2″, 190 lbs.   Deb: 9/19/17

YEAR	TM/L	W	L	PCT	G	GS	CG	SH	SV	IP	H	HR	BB	SO	RAT	ERA	ERA+	OAV	OOB	BH	AVG	PB	PR	/A	PD	TPI
1917	NY-A	0	0	—	2	0	0	0	0	2	1	0	1	1	9.0	0.00	—	.167	.286	0	—	0	1	1	0	0.1
1919	NY-A	0	0	—	6	0	0	0	0	21²	20	1	9	6	12.9	4.98	64	.263	.356	0	.000	-1	-4	-4	-0	-0.4
Total	2	0	0	—	8	0	0	0	0	23²	21	1	10	7	12.5	4.56	69	.256	.351	0	.000	-1	-4	-4	-0	-0.3

■ **JOHN SMILEY**   Smiley, John Patrick   b: 3/17/65, Phoenixville, Pa.   BL/TL, 6′4″, 180 lbs.   Deb: 9/01/86

YEAR	TM/L	W	L	PCT	G	GS	CG	SH	SV	IP	H	HR	BB	SO	RAT	ERA	ERA+	OAV	OOB	BH	AVG	PB	PR	/A	PD	TPI
1986	Pit-N	1	0	1.000	12	0	0	0	0	11²	4	2	4	9	6.2	3.86	99	.105	.190	0	—	0	-0	-0	0	0.0
1987	Pit-N	5	5	.500	63	0	0	0	4	75	69	7	50	58	14.3	5.76	71	.244	.357	1	.143	0	-14	-14	0	-1.2
1988	Pit-N	13	11	.542	34	32	5	1	0	205	185	15	46	129	10.3	3.25	105	.241	.287	5	.079	-2	5	3	-1	0.1
1989	Pit-N	12	8	.600	28	28	8	1	0	205¹	174	22	49	123	9.9	2.81	120	.226	.276	9	.138	1	16	13	-2	1.2
1990	*Pit-N	9	10	.474	26	25	2	0	0	149¹	161	15	36	86	12.0	4.64	78	.275	.319	6	.122	-0	-14	-17	0	-1.6
Total	5	40	34	.541	163	85	15	2	4	646¹	593	61	185	405	11.0	3.73	94	.243	.298	21	.114	-2	-8	-15	-2	-1.5

■ **SMITH**   Smith   Deb: 6/09/1884

YEAR	TM/L	W	L	PCT	G	GS	CG	SH	SV	IP	H	HR	BB	SO	RAT	ERA	ERA+	OAV	OOB	BH	AVG	PB	PR	/A	PD	TPI
1884	Bal-U	0	0	—	1	1	0	0	0	6	12	0	2	2	21.0	9.00	37	.391	.429	1	.200	-0	-4	-4	-0	-0.2

■ **AL SMITH**   Smith, Alfred John   b: 10/12/07, Belleville, Ill.   d: 4/28/77, Brownsville, Tex.   BL/TL, 5′11″, 180 lbs.   Deb: 5/05/34   C

YEAR	TM/L	W	L	PCT	G	GS	CG	SH	SV	IP	H	HR	BB	SO	RAT	ERA	ERA+	OAV	OOB	BH	AVG	PB	PR	/A	PD	TPI
1934	NY-N	3	5	.375	30	5	0	0	5	66²	70	2	21	27	12.3	4.32	90	.266	.320	4	.286	0	-2	-3	0	-0.2
1935	NY-N	10	8	.556	40	10	4	1	5	124	125	6	32	44	11.9	3.41	113	.263	.319	4	.118	-0	8	6	-0	0.5
1936	*NY-N	14	13	.519	43	30	9	4	2	209¹	217	16	69	89	12.5	3.78	103	.274	.335	10	.137	-1	6	3	-1	0.0
1937	*NY-N	5	4	.556	33	9	2	0	0	85²	91	8	30	41	12.9	4.20	93	.275	.339	3	.120	-2	-3	-3	-1	-0.4
1938	Phi-N	1	4	.200	37	1	0	0	1	86	115	4	40	46	16.2	6.28	62	.320	.388	0	.000	-2	-24	-23	0	-2.3
1939	Phi-N	0	0	—	5	0	0	0	0	9	11	1	5	2	18.0	4.00	100	.314	.429	0	.000	-0	0	0	0	0.0
1940	Cle-A	15	7	.682	31	24	11	1	2	183	187	12	55	46	12.2	3.44	122	.270	.329	19	.306	7	19	16	3	2.4
1941	Cle-A	12	13	.480	29	27	13	2	0	206²	204	12	75	76	12.2	3.83	103	.256	.321	11	.155	2	7	2	2	0.6
1942	Cle-A	10	15	.400	30	24	7	1	0	168¹	163	9	71	66	12.8	3.96	87	.251	.329	15	.250	3	-6	-9	-1	-0.7
1943	Cle-A	17	7	.708	29	27	14	3	1	208¹	186	7	72	72	11.1	2.55	122	.239	.303	14	.206	3	17	13	-0	1.8
1944	Cle-A	7	13	.350	28	26	7	1	0	181²	197	6	69	44	13.3	3.42	96	.280	.347	10	.156	-1	0	-2	2	-0.1
1945	Cle-A	5	12	.294	21	19	8	3	1	133²	141	8	48	34	12.9	3.84	85	.275	.340	12	.293	4	-7	-9	2	-0.2
Total	12	99	101	.495	356	202	75	16	17	1662¹	1707	94	587	587	12.6	3.72	99	.267	.332	102	.191	13	17	-10	6	1.4

■ **AL SMITH**   Smith, Alfred Kendricks   b: 12/13/03, Norristown, Pa.   BR/TR, 6′, 170 lbs.   Deb: 6/18/26

YEAR	TM/L	W	L	PCT	G	GS	CG	SH	SV	IP	H	HR	BB	SO	RAT	ERA	ERA+	OAV	OOB	BH	AVG	PB	PR	/A	PD	TPI
1926	NY-N	0	0	—	1	0	0	0	0	2	4	0	2	0	27.0	9.00	42	.444	.545	0	—	0	-1	-1	0	0.0

■ **ART SMITH**   Smith, Arthur Laird   b: 6/21/06, Boston, Mass.   BR/TR, 6′, 175 lbs.   Deb: 6/09/32

YEAR	TM/L	W	L	PCT	G	GS	CG	SH	SV	IP	H	HR	BB	SO	RAT	ERA	ERA+	OAV	OOB	BH	AVG	PB	PR	/A	PD	TPI
1932	Chi-A	0	1	.000	3	2	0	0	0	7	17	1	4	1	27.0	11.57	37	.500	.553	0	.000	-0	-6	-6	1	-0.3

■ **BILLY SMITH**   Smith, Billy Lavern   b: 9/13/54, LaMarque, Tex.   BR/TR, 6′7″, 200 lbs.   Deb: 6/09/81

YEAR	TM/L	W	L	PCT	G	GS	CG	SH	SV	IP	H	HR	BB	SO	RAT	ERA	ERA+	OAV	OOB	BH	AVG	PB	PR	/A	PD	TPI
1981	*Hou-N	1	1	.500	10	1	0	0	1	20²	20	3	3	3	10.0	3.05	108	.263	.291	0	.000	-0	1	1	0	0.1

■ **BRYN SMITH**   Smith, Bryn Nelson   b: 8/11/55, Marietta, Ga.   BR/TR, 6′2″, 200 lbs.   Deb: 9/08/81

YEAR	TM/L	W	L	PCT	G	GS	CG	SH	SV	IP	H	HR	BB	SO	RAT	ERA	ERA+	OAV	OOB	BH	AVG	PB	PR	/A	PD	TPI
1981	Mon-N	1	0	1.000	7	0	0	0	0	13	14	1	3	9	11.8	2.77	126	.280	.321	0	.000	-0	1	1	-0	0.1
1982	Mon-N	2	4	.333	47	1	0	0	3	79¹	81	5	23	50	11.8	4.20	87	.264	.315	0	.000	-0	-5	-5	0	-0.4
1983	Mon-N	6	11	.353	49	12	5	3	3	155¹	142	13	43	101	11.0	2.49	144	.248	.306	5	.167	-0	20	19	0	2.1
1984	Mon-N	12	13	.480	28	28	4	2	0	179	178	15	51	101	11.7	3.32	103	.259	.313	7	.132	1	5	2	2	0.5
1985	Mon-N	18	5	.783	32	32	4	2	0	222¹	193	12	41	127	9.5	2.91	116	.232	.269	14	.194	3	17	12	-1	1.5
1986	Mon-N	10	8	.556	30	30	1	0	0	187¹	182	15	63	105	12.1	3.94	94	.251	.316	8	.138	1	-5	-5	3	0.0
1987	Mon-N	10	9	.526	26	26	2	0	0	150¹	164	16	31	94	11.8	4.37	96	.271	.312	6	.136	-0	-5	-3	0	-0.2
1988	Mon-N	12	10	.545	32	32	1	0	0	198	179	15	32	122	10.0	3.00	120	.243	.284	6	.109	-1	10	13	-2	1.1
1989	Mon-N	10	11	.476	33	32	3	1	0	215²	177	16	54	129	9.8	2.84	124	.223	.276	4	.065	-2	16	17	3	1.9
1990	StL-N	9	8	.529	26	25	0	0	0	141¹	160	11	30	78	12.4	4.27	92	.286	.327	10	.256	3	-7	-5	-1	-0.2
Total	10	90	79	.533	310	218	20	8	6	1541²	1470	119	371	916	11.0	3.37	108	.251	.299	60	.142	5	46	45	5	6.4

■ **CHARLIE SMITH**   Smith, Charles Edwin   b: 4/20/1880, Cleveland, Ohio   d: 1/3/29, Wickliffe, Ohio   BR/TR, 6′1″, 185 lbs.   Deb: 8/06/02

YEAR	TM/L	W	L	PCT	G	GS	CG	SH	SV	IP	H	HR	BB	SO	RAT	ERA	ERA+	OAV	OOB	BH	AVG	PB	PR	/A	PD	TPI
1902	Cle-A	2	1	.667	3	3	2	1	0	20	23	0	5	5	12.6	4.05	85	.289	.331	1	.125	-0	-1	-1	0	-0.1
1906	Was-A	9	16	.360	33	22	17	2	0	235¹	250	2	75	105	12.4	2.91	91	.275	.331	16	.184	-0	-6	-7	-2	-1.0
1907	Was-A	10	20	.333	36	31	21	3	0	258²	254	0	51	119	10.6	2.61	93	.259	.295	12	.143	-3	-2	-5	3	-0.6
1908	Was-A	9	13	.409	26	23	13	1	1	184	166	2	60	83	11.2	2.40	96	.247	.311	8	.123	-2	0	-2	-1	-0.4
1909	Was-A	3	12	.200	23	15	7	1	0	145²	140	4	37	72	11.2	3.27	74	.250	.303	7	.156	-1	-13	-14	0	-1.5
	Bos-A	3	0	1.000	3	3	2	0	0	25	23	2	2	11	9.4	2.16	116	.237	.260	3	.300	1	1	1	0	0.2
	Yr	6	12	.333	26	18	9	1	0	170²	163	6	39	83	10.7	3.11	78	.247	.290	2	.036	-0	-12	-13	1	-1.3
1910	Bos-A	11	6	.647	24	18	11	0	1	156¹	141	4	35	53	10.2	2.30	111	.248	.294	5	.114	-2	4	4	-2	0.0
1911	Bos-A	0	0	—	1	1	0	0	0	2	2	1	1	0	13.5	9.00	36	.250	.333	0	—	0	-1	-1	0	0.0
	Chi-N	3	2	.600	7	5	3	1	0	38	31	0	7	11	9.2	1.42	233	.228	.271	1	.077	-1	8	8	-1	0.6
1912	Chi-N	7	4	.636	20	5	1	0	0	94	92	2	31	47	12.1	4.21	79	.254	.318	9	.257	1	-8	-9	1	-0.6
1913	Chi-N	7	9	.438	20	17	8	1	0	137²	138	2	34	47	11.5	2.55	125	.274	.325	4	.089	-3	10	10	0	0.7
1914	Chi-N	2	4	.333	16	5	1	0	0	53¹	49	3	15	17	10.9	3.86	72	.251	.308	1	.091	-1	-6	-6	-1	-0.7
Total	10	66	87	.431	212	148	86	10	3	1350¹	1309	22	353	570	11.2	2.81	94	.258	.309	67	.150	-13	-14	-24	-1	-3.6

■ **POP SMITH**   Smith, Charles Marvin   b: 10/12/1856, Digby, N.S., Canada   d: 4/18/27, Boston, Mass.   BR/TR, 5′11″, 170 lbs.   Deb: 5/01/1880 ♦

YEAR	TM/L	W	L	PCT	G	GS	CG	SH	SV	IP	H	HR	BB	SO	RAT	ERA	ERA+	OAV	OOB	BH	AVG	PB	PR	/A	PD	TPI
1883	Col-a	0	0	—	3	0	0	0	0	5²	10	0	0	0	15.9	6.35	48	.362	.362	106	.262	1	-2	-2	-0	-0.1

■ **POP-BOY SMITH**   Smith, Clarence Ossie   b: 5/23/1892, Newport, Tenn.   d: 2/16/24, Sweetwater, Tenn.   BR/TR, 6′1″, 176 lbs.   Deb: 4/19/13

YEAR	TM/L	W	L	PCT	G	GS	CG	SH	SV	IP	H	HR	BB	SO	RAT	ERA	ERA+	OAV	OOB	BH	AVG	PB	PR	/A	PD	TPI
1913	Chi-A	0	1	.000	15	0	0	0	0	32	31	0	11	13	12.7	3.38	87	.261	.338	0	.000	-0	-2	-2	1	0.0
1916	Cle-A	1	2	.333	5	3	0	0	1	25²	25	1	11	4	13.0	3.86	78	.253	.333	2	.286	0	-3	-2	-0	-0.2
1917	Cle-A	0	1	.000	6	0	0	0	0	8²	14	0	4	3	19.7	8.31	34	.368	.442	0	.000	-0	-5	-5	1	-0.3
Total	3	1	4	.200	26	5	0	0	1	66¹	70	1	26	20	13.7	4.21	70	.273	.352	2	.154	-1	-10	-9	2	-0.5

■ **CLAY SMITH**   Smith, Clay Jamieson   b: 9/11/14, Cambridge, Kan.   BR/TR, 6′2″, 190 lbs.   Deb: 9/13/38

YEAR	TM/L	W	L	PCT	G	GS	CG	SH	SV	IP	H	HR	BB	SO	RAT	ERA	ERA+	OAV	OOB	BH	AVG	PB	PR	/A	PD	TPI
1938	Cle-A	0	0	—	4	0	0	0	0	11	18	1	2	3	16.4	6.55	71	.367	.392	0	.000	-0	-2	-2	0	-0.1
1940	*Det-A	1	1	.500	14	1	0	0	0	28¹	32	3	13	14	14.6	5.08	94	.283	.362	0	.000	-1	-2	-1	1	0.0
Total	2	1	1	.500	18	1	0	0	0	39¹	50	4	15	17	15.1	5.49	86	.309	.371	0	.000	-1	-4	-3	1	-0.1

■ **DARYL SMITH**   Smith, Daryl Clinton   b: 7/29/60, Baltimore, Md.   BR/TR, 6′4″, 185 lbs.   Deb: 9/18/90

YEAR	TM/L	W	L	PCT	G	GS	CG	SH	SV	IP	H	HR	BB	SO	RAT	ERA	ERA+	OAV	OOB	BH	AVG	PB	PR	/A	PD	TPI
1990	KC-A	0	1	.000	2	1	0	0	0	6²	5	0	4	6	12.2	4.05	94	.238	.360	0	—	0	-0	-0	-0	0.0

■ **DAVE SMITH**   Smith, David Merwin   b: 12/17/14, Sellers, S.C.   BR/TR, 5′10″, 170 lbs.   Deb: 6/16/38

YEAR	TM/L	W	L	PCT	G	GS	CG	SH	SV	IP	H	HR	BB	SO	RAT	ERA	ERA+	OAV	OOB	BH	AVG	PB	PR	/A	PD	TPI
1938	Phi-A	2	1	.667	21	0	0	0	0	44¹	50	0	28	13	16.0	5.08	95	.284	.385	0	.000	-1	-1	-1	0	-0.1
1939	Phi-A	0	0	—	1	0	0	0	0	0	1	0	2	0	—	—	—	1.000	1.000	0	—	0	0	0	0	0.0
Total	2	2	1	.667	22	0	0	0	0	44¹	51	0	30	13	16.6	5.08	95	.288	.394	0	.000	-1	-1	-1	0	-0.1

YEAR	TM/L	W	L	PCT	G	GS	CG	SH	SV	IP	H	HR	BB	SO	RAT	ERA	ERA+	OAV	OOB	BH	AVG	PB	PR	/A	PD	TPI

■ DAVE SMITH
Smith, David Stanley b: 1/21/55, Richmond, Cal. BR/TR, 6'1", 195 lbs. Deb: 4/11/80

YEAR	TM/L	W	L	PCT	G	GS	CG	SH	SV	IP	H	HR	BB	SO	RAT	ERA	ERA+	OAV	OOB	BH	AVG	PB	PR	/A	PD	TPI
1980	*Hou-N	7	5	.583	57	0	0	0	10	102²	90	1	32	85	11.0	1.93	170	.237	.304	0	.000	-1	19	15	-1	1.4
1981	*Hou-N	5	3	.625	42	0	0	0	8	75	54	2	23	52	9.5	2.76	119	.198	.265	2	.250	0	6	4	-0	0.5
1982	Hou-N	5	4	.556	49	1	0	0	11	63¹	69	4	31	28	14.2	3.84	86	.285	.366	0	.000	-0	-2	-4	-1	-0.4
1983	Hou-N	3	1	.750	42	0	0	0	6	72²	72	2	36	41	13.4	3.10	110	.258	.343	0	.000	-1	4	2	-2	0.0
1984	Hou-N	5	4	.556	53	0	0	0	5	77¹	60	5	20	45	9.4	2.21	150	.214	.269	0	.000	-0	12	10	-0	1.0
1985	Hou-N	9	5	.643	64	0	0	0	27	79¹	69	3	17	40	9.9	2.27	153	.235	.280	0	.000	0	12	11	-1	1.0
1986	*Hou-N	4	7	.364	54	0	0	0	33	56	39	5	22	46	10.0	2.73	132	.200	.284	0	.000	-0	6	5	-0	0.5
1987	Hou-N	2	3	.400	50	0	0	0	24	60	39	0	21	73	9.2	1.65	237	.182	.258	1	.500	1	16	15	-1	1.5
1988	Hou-N	4	5	.444	51	0	0	0	27	57¹	60	1	19	38	12.6	2.67	124	.268	.328	0	.000	-0	5	4	-0	0.4
1989	Hou-N	3	4	.429	52	0	0	0	25	58	49	1	19	31	10.7	2.64	128	.233	.300	0	.000	-0	6	5	1	0.6
1990	Hou-N	6	6	.500	49	0	0	0	23	60¹	45	4	20	50	9.7	2.39	157	.210	.278	0	.000	0	9	9	-1	0.8
Total 11		53	47	.530	563	1	0	0	199	762	646	28	260	529	10.8	2.53	136	.230	.299	3	.070	-2	93	77	-6	7.3

■ DAVE SMITH
Smith, David Wayne b: 8/30/57, Tomball, Tex. BR/TR, 6'1", 190 lbs. Deb: 9/18/84

YEAR	TM/L	W	L	PCT	G	GS	CG	SH	SV	IP	H	HR	BB	SO	RAT	ERA	ERA+	OAV	OOB	BH	AVG	PB	PR	/A	PD	TPI
1984	Cal-A	0	0	—	1	0	0	0	0	1	4	1	0	0	36.0	18.00	22	.571	.571	0	—	0	-2	-2	0	0.0
1985	Cal-A	0	0	—	4	0	0	0	0	5	5	1	1	3	10.8	7.20	57	.278	.316	0	—	0	-2	-2	-0	-0.1
Total 2		0	0	—	5	0	0	0	0	6	9	2	1	3	15.0	9.00	45	.360	.385	0	—	0	-3	-3	0	-0.1

■ DOUG SMITH
Smith, Douglass Weldon b: 5/25/1892, Millers Falls, Mass. d: 9/18/73, Greenfield, Mass. BL/TL, 5'10", 168 lbs. Deb: 7/10/12

YEAR	TM/L	W	L	PCT	G	GS	CG	SH	SV	IP	H	HR	BB	SO	RAT	ERA	ERA+	OAV	OOB	BH	AVG	PB	PR	/A	PD	TPI
1912	Bos-A	0	0	—	1	0	0	0	0	3	4	0	0	1	12.0	3.00	113	.364	.364	0	—	0	0	0	-0	0.0

■ EDDIE SMITH
Smith, Edgar b: 12/14/13, Columbus, N.J. BB/TL, 5'10", 174 lbs. Deb: 9/20/36

YEAR	TM/L	W	L	PCT	G	GS	CG	SH	SV	IP	H	HR	BB	SO	RAT	ERA	ERA+	OAV	OOB	BH	AVG	PB	PR	/A	PD	TPI
1936	Phi-A	1	1	.500	2	2	2	0	0	19	22	3	8	7	14.2	1.89	269	.275	.341	1	.125	-1	7	7	0	0.6
1937	Phi-A	4	17	.190	38	23	14	1	5	196²	178	18	90	79	12.4	3.94	120	.242	.327	17	.233	1	15	17	-2	1.6
1938	Phi-A	3	10	.231	43	7	0	0	4	130²	151	13	76	78	15.9	5.92	82	.287	.381	12	.286	3	-16	-16	-0	-1.1
1939	Phi-A	1	0	1.000	3	0	0	0	0	3²	7	0	2	3	22.1	9.82	48	.412	.474	0	—	0	-2	-2	-0	-0.1
	Chi-A	9	11	.450	29	22	7	1	0	176²	161	11	90	67	13.0	3.67	129	.247	.342	6	.115	-1	19	21	-2	1.7
	Yr	10	11	.476	32	22	7	1	0	180¹	168	11	92	70	13.2	3.79	125	.251	.346	9	.173	-1	17	19	-2	1.6
1940	Chi-A	14	9	.609	32	28	12	0	0	207¹	179	16	95	119	12.0	3.21	138	.228	.313	15	.217	2	27	28	-1	2.8
1941	Chi-A	13	17	.433	34	33	21	1	1	263¹	243	13	114	111	12.4	3.18	129	.246	.328	19	.216	4	28	27	0	3.1
1942	Chi-A	7	20	.259	29	28	18	2	1	215	223	17	86	78	13.1	3.98	90	.269	.341	9	.123	-2	-8	-9	2	-0.8
1943	Chi-A	11	11	.500	25	25	14	2	0	187²	197	2	76	66	13.3	3.69	90	.277	.351	11	.159	-1	-8	-7	1	-0.7
1946	Chi-A	8	11	.421	24	21	3	1	1	145¹	135	6	60	59	12.3	2.85	120	.246	.325	8	.178	0	11	9	-0	1.0
1947	Chi-A	1	3	.250	15	5	0	0	0	33¹	40	1	24	12	17.3	7.29	50	.299	.405	1	.167	-0	-13	-13	-1	-1.3
	Bos-A	1	3	.250	8	3	0	0	0	17	18	3	18	15	19.1	7.41	52	.269	.424	1	.167	0	-7	-7	-0	-0.6
	Yr	2	6	.250	23	8	0	0	0	50¹	58	4	42	27	17.9	7.33	51	.289	.412	1	.083	-0	-20	-20	-1	-1.9
Total 10		73	113	.392	282	197	91	8	12	1595²	1554	106	739	694	13.1	3.82	108	.256	.340	100	.188	5	51	53	-4	6.2

■ EDGAR SMITH
Smith, Edgar Eugene b: 6/12/1862, Providence, R.I. d: 11/3/1892, Providence, R.I. BR/TR, 5'10", 160 lbs. Deb: 5/25/1883 ◆

YEAR	TM/L	W	L	PCT	G	GS	CG	SH	SV	IP	H	HR	BB	SO	RAT	ERA	ERA+	OAV	OOB	BH	AVG	PB	PR	/A	PD	TPI
1883	Phi-N	0	1	.000	1	1	0	0	0	7	18	0	3	2	27.0	15.43	20	.455	.494	3	.750	1	-10	-10	-0	-0.5
1884	Was-a	0	2	.000	3	2	2	0	0	22	27	0	5	4	13.1	4.91	62	.286	.322	5	.088	-1	-4	-5	0	-0.3
1885	Pro-N	1	0	1.000	1	1	1	0	0	9	9	0	0	1	9.0	1.00	266	.248	.248	1	.250	0	2	2	0	0.2
1890	Cle-N	1	4	.200	6	6	5	0	0	44	42	1	10	11	10.6	4.30	83	.244	.286	7	.292	2	-4	-4	2	0.0
Total 4		2	7	.222	11	10	8	0	0	82	96	1	18	18	12.5	5.05	65	.281	.317	18	.184	2	-15	-16	1	-0.6

■ ELMER SMITH
Smith, Elmer Ellsworth b: 3/23/1868, Pittsburgh, Pa. d: 11/3/45, Pittsburgh, Pa. BL/TL, 5'11", 178 lbs. Deb: 5/31/1886 ◆

YEAR	TM/L	W	L	PCT	G	GS	CG	SH	SV	IP	H	HR	BB	SO	RAT	ERA	ERA+	OAV	OOB	BH	AVG	PB	PR	/A	PD	TPI
1886	Cin-a	4	5	.444	10	10	9	0	0	81²	65	1	54	41	13.1	3.75	94	.208	.325	9	.281	4	-3	-2	-2	0.0
1887	Cin-a	34	17	.667	52	52	49	3	0	447¹	400	5	126	176	10.6	**2.94**	**147**	**.230**	.283	47	.253	5	68	**68**	-6	5.7
1888	Cin-a	22	17	.564	40	40	37	5	0	348¹	309	1	89	154	10.3	2.74	115	.229	.277	29	.225	5	13	16	-5	1.5
1889	Cin-a	9	12	.429	29	22	16	0	0	203	253	1	101	104	15.7	4.88	80	.296	.370	23	.277	5	-23	-22	-4	-1.6
1892	Pit-N	6	7	.462	17	13	12	1	0	134	140	2	58	51	13.3	3.63	91	.258	.330	140	.274	6	-5	-5	-1	-0.4
1894	Pit-N	0	0	—	1	0	0	0	0	4	6	0	1	0	15.8	4.50	116	.342	.378	174	.356	0	0	0	-0	0.0
1898	Cin-N	0	0	—	1	0	0	0	0	2	2	0	3	0	45.0	18.00	21	.411	.635	166	.342	0	-2	-2	0	0.0
Total 7		75	58	.564	150	137	123	9	0	1219¹	1175	20	432	526	11.9	3.35	112	.244	.306	1455	.310	26	48	55	-19	5.2

■ FRANK SMITH
Smith, Frank Elmer "Nig" or "Piano Mover" (b: Frank Elmer Schmidt)
b: 10/28/1879, Pittsburgh, Pa. d: 11/3/52, Pittsburgh, Pa. BR/TR, 5'10.5", 194 lbs. Deb: 4/22/04

YEAR	TM/L	W	L	PCT	G	GS	CG	SH	SV	IP	H	HR	BB	SO	RAT	ERA	ERA+	OAV	OOB	BH	AVG	PB	PR	/A	PD	TPI
1904	Chi-A	16	9	.640	26	23	22	4	0	202¹	157	0	58	107	9.6	2.09	117	.215	.273	18	.250	4	11	8	-3	1.0
1905	Chi-A	19	13	.594	39	31	27	4	0	291²	215	0	107	171	9.9	2.13	116	.207	.281	24	.226	6	17	11	-1	1.6
1906	Chi-A	5	5	.500	20	13	8	1	1	122	124	3	37	53	11.9	3.39	75	.267	.321	12	.293	5	-10	-12	1	-0.6
1907	Chi-A	23	10	.697	41	37	29	3	0	310	280	3	111	139	11.4	2.47	97	.243	.309	18	.196	5	3	-2	4	0.6
1908	Chi-A	16	17	.485	41	35	24	3	1	297²	213	2	73	129	8.7	2.03	114	.203	.268	20	.189	2	12	10	3	1.7
1909	Chi-A	25	17	.595	51	40	37	7	1	365	278	1	70	177	8.7	1.80	130	.214	.257	22	.173	5	27	22	10	**4.3**
1910	Chi-A	4	9	.308	19	15	9	3	0	128²	91	1	40	50	9.3	2.03	118	.204	.272	8	.186	2	7	5	4	1.3
	Bos-A	1	2	.333	4	3	2	0	0	28	22	0	11	8	10.9	4.82	53	.234	.321	1	.111	-0	-7	-7	0	-0.6
	Yr	5	11	.313	23	18	11	3	0	156²	113	1	51	58	9.5	2.53	96	.208	.277	8	.154	2	-0	-2	4	0.7
1911	Bos-A	0	0	—	1	1	0	0	0	2¹	6	0	3	1	34.7	15.43	21	.500	.600	0	—	0	-3	-3	0	-0.1
	Cin-N	10	14	.417	34	18	10	0	1	176¹	198	1	55	67	13.1	3.98	83	.289	.345	12	.214	3	-11	-13	5	-0.5
1912	Cin-N	1	1	.500	7	3	1	0	0	22²	34	1	15	5	19.5	6.35	53	.351	.438	0	.000	-0	-7	-8	-0	-0.7
1914	Bal-F	10	8	.556	39	22	9	1	2	174²	180	8	47	83	11.7	2.99	113	.259	.306	12	.203	1	4	7	2	1.2
1915	Bal-F	4	4	.500	17	9	2	0	0	88²	108	5	31	37	14.1	4.67	68	.312	.369	5	.172	1	-16	-15	0	-1.3
	Bro-F	5	2	.714	15	5	4	1	0	63	69	2	18	24	12.4	3.14	96	.290	.340	4	.200	1	-1	-1	1	0.1
	Yr	9	6	.600	32	14	6	1	0	151²	177	7	49	61	13.4	4.04	77	.303	.357	3	.061	2	-17	-15	1	-1.2
Total 11		139	111	.556	354	255	184	27	6	2273	1975	27	676	1051	10.6	2.59	100	.237	.295	156	.204	33	27	2	26	8.0

■ FRANK SMITH
Smith, Frank Thomas b: 4/4/28, Pierrepont Manor, N.Y. BR/TR, 6'3", 195 lbs. Deb: 4/18/50

YEAR	TM/L	W	L	PCT	G	GS	CG	SH	SV	IP	H	HR	BB	SO	RAT	ERA	ERA+	OAV	OOB	BH	AVG	PB	PR	/A	PD	TPI
1950	Cin-N	2	7	.222	38	4	0	0	0	90²	73	12	39	55	11.9	3.87	109	.216	.312	2	.095	-2	3	4	-1	0.1
1951	Cin-N	5	5	.500	50	0	0	0	11	76	65	7	22	34	10.8	3.20	128	.230	.295	0	.000	-1	6	7	0	0.7
1952	Cin-N	12	11	.522	53	2	1	0	7	122¹	109	13	41	77	11.6	3.75	101	.242	.315	5	.172	0	-0	-0	-2	-0.1
1953	Cin-N	8	1	.889	50	1	0	0	2	83²	89	15	25	42	12.6	5.49	79	.272	.330	2	.154	-1	-11	-11	0	-0.9
1954	Cin-N	5	8	.385	50	0	0	0	20	81	60	15	29	51	10.2	2.67	157	.211	.291	1	.100	1	13	14	-0	1.4
1955	StL-N	3	1	.750	28	0	0	0	1	39	27	3	23	17	12.7	3.23	126	.205	.344	0	.000	-1	3	4	0	0.3
1956	Cin-N	0	0	—	2	0	0	0	0	3	3	2	2	1	15.0	12.00	33	.300	.417	0	—	0	-3	-3	0	-0.2
Total 7		35	33	.515	271	7	1	0	44	495²	426	67	181	277	11.6	3.81	107	.234	.313	10	.115	-3	11	16	-2	1.3

■ FRED SMITH
Smith, Frederick b: 11/24/1878, New Diggins, Wis. d: 2/4/64, Los Angeles, Cal. BL/TR, 6', 186 lbs. Deb: 6/14/07

YEAR	TM/L	W	L	PCT	G	GS	CG	SH	SV	IP	H	HR	BB	SO	RAT	ERA	ERA+	OAV	OOB	BH	AVG	PB	PR	/A	PD	TPI
1907	Cin-N	2	7	.222	18	9	5	0	1	85¹	90	3	24	19	12.4	2.85	91	.274	.331	3	.107	-2	-4	-2	0	-0.3

■ FRED SMITH
Smith, Frederick C. b: 3/25/1863, Greene, N.Y. d: 1/9/41, Syracuse, N.Y. BL/TR, 5'11", 156 lbs. Deb: 4/18/1890

YEAR	TM/L	W	L	PCT	G	GS	CG	SH	SV	IP	H	HR	BB	SO	RAT	ERA	ERA+	OAV	OOB	BH	AVG	PB	PR	/A	PD	TPI
1890	Tol-a	19	13	.594	35	34	31	2	0	286	273	13	90	116	11.4	3.27	121	.244	.300	21	.167	-2	19	22	3	2.0

■ GEORGE SMITH
Smith, George Allen "Columbia George" b: 5/31/1892, Byram, Conn. d: 1/7/65, Greenwich, Conn. BR/TR, 6'2", 163 lbs. Deb: 8/09/16

YEAR	TM/L	W	L	PCT	G	GS	CG	SH	SV	IP	H	HR	BB	SO	RAT	ERA	ERA+	OAV	OOB	BH	AVG	PB	PR	/A	PD	TPI
1916	NY-N	3	0	1.000	9	1	0	0	0	20²	14	0	6	9	9.1	2.61	93	.197	.269	0	.000	-0	-0	-0	0	0.0
1917	NY-N	0	3	.000	14	1	1	0	0	38	38	1	11	16	11.8	2.84	90	.270	.327	0	.000	-1	-1	-1	0	-0.2

YEAR TM/L	W	L	PCT	G	GS	CG	SH	SV	IP	H	HR	BB	SO	RAT	ERA	ERA+	OAV	OOB	BH	AVG	PB	PR	/A	PD	TPI
1918 Cin-N	2	3	.400	10	6	4	1	0	55¹	71	3	11	19	13.3	4.07	66	.329	.361	0	.000	-2	-8	-9	0	-1.0
NY-N	2	3	.400	5	2	1	0	0	26²	26	0	6	4	11.1	4.05	65	.255	.303	2	.250	0	-4	-4	-1	-0.4
Bro-N	4	1	.800	8	5	4	0	0	50	43	0	5	18	9.0	2.34	119	.249	.278	3	.200	0	2	2	1	0.4
Yr	8	7	.533	23	13	9	1	0	132	140	3	22	41	11.2	3.41	79	.285	.318	3	.075	-2	-9	-10	0	-1.0
1919 NY-N	0	2	.000	3	2	0	0	0	11	18	1	4	0	18.0	5.73	49	.383	.431	0	.000	-0	-3	-4	-0	-0.3
Phi-N	5	11	.313	31	20	11	1	0	184²	194	7	46	42	11.8	3.22	100	.278	.326	8	.133	-3	-6	0	-0	-0.2
Yr	5	13	.278	34	22	11	1	0	195²	212	8	50	42	12.2	3.36	95	.285	.332	2	.032	-4	-10	-3	-0	-0.5
1920 Phi-N	13	18	.419	43	28	10	1	2	250²	265	10	51	51	11.6	3.45	99	.283	.324	7	.097	-6	-9	-1	-1	-0.7
1921 Phi-N	4	20	.167	39	28	12	1	1	221¹	303	12	52	45	14.6	4.76	89	.335	.373	4	.056	-9	-24	-13	-1	-2.0
1922 Phi-N	5	14	.263	42	18	6	1	0	194	250	16	35	44	13.5	4.78	98	.316	.350	5	.076	-8	-15	-2	-1	-0.9
1923 Bro-N	3	6	.333	25	7	3	0	1	91	99	3	28	15	12.9	3.66	106	.278	.336	5	.192	-1	3	2	-2	0.0
Total 8	41	81	.336	229	118	52	5	4	1143¹	1321	53	255	263	12.6	3.89	94	.298	.340	34	.097	-31	-63	-31	-5	-5.3

■ HEINIE SMITH
Smith, George Henry b: 10/24/1871, Pittsburgh, Pa. d: 6/25/39, Buffalo, N.Y. BR/TR, 5'9.5", 160 lbs. Deb: 9/08/1897 M♦

YEAR TM/L	W	L	PCT	G	GS	CG	SH	SV	IP	H	HR	BB	SO	RAT	ERA	ERA+	OAV	OOB	BH	AVG	PB	PR	/A	PD	TPI
1901 NY-N	0	1	.000	2	1	1	0	0	13¹	24	0	5	5	22.3	8.10	41	.386	.463	6	.207	-0	-7	-7	-0	-0.5

■ GERMANY SMITH
Smith, George J. b: 4/21/1863, Pittsburgh, Pa. d: 12/1/27, Altoona, Pa. BR/TR, 6', 175 lbs. Deb: 4/17/1884 ♦

YEAR TM/L	W	L	PCT	G	GS	CG	SH	SV	IP	H	HR	BB	SO	RAT	ERA	ERA+	OAV	OOB	BH	AVG	PB	PR	/A	PD	TPI
1884 Alt-U	0	0	—	1	0	0	0	0	1	3	0	0	1	27.0	9.00	36	.491	.491	34	.315	0	-1	-1	0	0.0

■ GEORGE SMITH
Smith, George Shelby b: 10/27/01, Louisville, Ky. d: 5/26/81, Richmond, Va. BR/TR, 6'1", 175 lbs. Deb: 4/21/26

YEAR TM/L	W	L	PCT	G	GS	CG	SH	SV	IP	H	HR	BB	SO	RAT	ERA	ERA+	OAV	OOB	BH	AVG	PB	PR	/A	PD	TPI
1926 Det-A	1	2	.333	23	1	0	0	0	44	55	3	33	15	18.4	6.95	58	.318	.433	0	.000	-0	-14	-14	-1	-1.3
1927 Det-A	4	1	.800	29	0	0	0	0	71¹	62	3	50	32	14.4	3.91	108	.240	.368	7	.368	3	2	2	-1	0.5
1928 Det-A	1	1	.500	39	2	0	0	3	106	103	3	50	54	13.0	4.42	93	.263	.346	3	.111	-2	-4	-4	-2	-0.7
1929 Det-A	3	2	.600	14	2	1	0	0	35²	42	1	36	13	19.7	5.80	74	.307	.451	5	.417	2	-6	-6	1	-0.2
1930 Bos-A	1	2	.333	27	2	0	0	0	73²	92	7	49	21	17.3	6.60	70	.317	.418	8	.333	2	-16	-16	-0	-1.2
Total 5	10	8	.556	132	7	1	0	3	330²	354	17	218	135	15.7	5.28	81	.283	.392	23	.264	4	-39	-38	-3	-2.9

■ HAL SMITH
Smith, Harold Laverne b: 6/30/02, Creston, Iowa BR/TR, 6'3", 195 lbs. Deb: 9/14/32

YEAR TM/L	W	L	PCT	G	GS	CG	SH	SV	IP	H	HR	BB	SO	RAT	ERA	ERA+	OAV	OOB	BH	AVG	PB	PR	/A	PD	TPI
1932 Pit-N	1	0	1.000	2	1	1	1	0	12	9	0	2	4	8.3	0.75	508	.209	.244	0	.000	-0	4	4	0	0.4
1933 Pit-N	8	7	.533	28	19	8	2	1	145	149	5	31	40	11.5	2.86	116	.261	.305	6	.128	-2	8	7	-2	0.4
1934 Pit-N	3	4	.429	20	5	1	0	0	50	72	3	18	15	16.9	7.20	57	.343	.405	1	.059	-2	-17	-17	-0	-1.7
1935 Pit-N	0	0	—	1	0	0	0	0	3	2	0	1	0	9.0	3.00	137	.200	.273	0	—	0	0	0	0	0.0
Total 4	12	11	.522	51	25	10	3	1	210	232	8	52	59	12.6	3.77	94	.279	.328	7	.104	-4	-5	-5	-2	-0.9

■ HARRY SMITH
Smith, Harrison Morton b: 8/15/1889, Union, Neb. d: 7/26/64, Dunbar, Neb. BR/TR, 5'9", 160 lbs. Deb: 10/06/12

YEAR TM/L	W	L	PCT	G	GS	CG	SH	SV	IP	H	HR	BB	SO	RAT	ERA	ERA+	OAV	OOB	BH	AVG	PB	PR	/A	PD	TPI
1912 Chi-A	1	0	1.000	1	1	0	0	0	5	6	0	0	1	10.8	1.80	178	.333	.333	0	.000	-0	1	1	0	0.1

■ JACK SMITH
Smith, Jack Hatfield b: 11/15/35, Pikeville, Ky. BR/TR, 6', 185 lbs. Deb: 9/10/62

YEAR TM/L	W	L	PCT	G	GS	CG	SH	SV	IP	H	HR	BB	SO	RAT	ERA	ERA+	OAV	OOB	BH	AVG	PB	PR	/A	PD	TPI
1962 LA-N	0	0	—	8	0	0	0	1	10	10	0	4	7	12.6	4.50	81	.263	.333	0	.000	-0	-1	-1	-0	0.0
1963 LA-N	0	0	—	4	0	0	0	0	8¹	10	2	2	5	15.1	7.56	40	.303	.378	0	.000	-0	-4	-4	0	-0.3
1964 Mil-N	2	2	.500	22	0	0	0	0	31	28	3	11	19	11.3	3.77	93	.237	.302	1	.333	0	-1	-1	1	0.0
Total 3	2	2	.500	34	0	0	0	1	49¹	48	5	17	31	12.2	4.56	76	.254	.322	1	.167	-0	-5	-6	1	-0.3

■ JAKE SMITH
Smith, Jacob (b: Jacob Schmidt) b: 6/21/1887, Dravosburg, Pa d: 11/7/48, E.McKeesport, Pa. BB/TR, 6'5", 200 lbs. Deb: 10/03/11

YEAR TM/L	W	L	PCT	G	GS	CG	SH	SV	IP	H	HR	BB	SO	RAT	ERA	ERA+	OAV	OOB	BH	AVG	PB	PR	/A	PD	TPI
1911 Phi-N	0	0	—	2	0	0	0	0	5	3	0	2	1	9.0	0.00	—	.176	.263	0	.000	-0	2	2	0	0.2

■ PHENOMENAL SMITH
Smith, John Francis (b: John Francis Gammon)
b: 12/12/1864, Philadelphia, Pa. d: 4/3/52, Manchester, N.H. BL/TL, 5'6.5", 161 lbs. Deb: 4/18/1884

YEAR TM/L	W	L	PCT	G	GS	CG	SH	SV	IP	H	HR	BB	SO	RAT	ERA	ERA+	OAV	OOB	BH	AVG	PB	PR	/A	PD	TPI
1884 Bal-U	3	4	.429	9	8	5	0	0	62	86	2	17	13	15.0	3.48	95	.308	.348	5	.147	-3	-3	-1	-1	-0.3
Phi-a	0	1	.000	1	1	1	0	0	9	14	0	1	3	15.0	4.00	85	.337	.353	1	.250	-0	-1	-1	0	0.0
Pit-a	0	1	.000	1	1	1	0	0	8	11	0	2	4	14.6	9.00	37	.310	.347	0	.000	-1	-5	-5	0	-0.3
Yr	0	2	.000	2	2	2	0	0	17	25	0	3	7	14.8	6.35	57	.325	.350	0	.000	-1	-6	-6	0	-0.3
1885 Bro-a	0	1	.000	1	1	1	0	0	8	12	0	6	2	20.3	12.38	27	.332	.428	1	.333	0	-8	-8	0	-0.4
Phi-a	0	1	.000	1	1	0	0	0	4	7	0	4	7	24.8	9.00	38	.368	.477	0	.000	-0	-3	-2	0	-0.1
Yr	0	2	.000	2	2	1	0	0	12	19	0	10	9	21.8	11.25	30	.345	.445	0	.000	-0	-11	-11	0	-0.5
1886 Det-N	1	1	.500	3	3	3	0	0	25	16	0	8	15	8.6	2.16	153	.176	.242	1	.111	-1	3	3	-1	0.2
1887 Bal-a	25	30	.455	58	55	54	1	0	491¹	526	7	176	206	12.9	3.79	108	.264	.324	48	.234	-8	28	17	-1	1.8
1888 Bal-a	14	19	.424	35	32	31	0	0	292	249	5	137	152	11.9	3.61	83	.222	.307	27	.248	8	-18	-20	-4	-1.4
Phi-a	2	1	.667	3	3	3	0	0	22	21	0	10	19	12.7	2.86	104	.242	.321	3	.333	1	0	0	0	0.1
Yr	16	20	.444	38	35	34	0	0	314	270	5	147	171	12.0	3.55	84	.224	.308	12	.102	9	-17	-20	-4	-1.3
1889 Phi-a	2	3	.400	5	5	5	0	0	43	53	2	25	12	16.3	4.40	86	.294	.380	3	.188	0	-3	-3	-1	-0.2
1890 Phi-N	8	12	.400	24	20	19	1	0	204	209	5	89	81	13.1	4.28	88	.258	.331	24	.279	4	-16	-14	-2	-0.9
Pit-N	1	3	.250	5	5	5	0	0	44	39	0	13	15	10.6	3.07	107	.231	.286	7	.412	2	2	1	-0	0.2
Yr	9	15	.375	29	25	24	1	0	248	248	5	102	96	12.7	4.06	88	.253	.323	11	.107	6	-14	-13	-2	-0.6
1891 Phi-N	1	1	.500	3	2	0	0	0	19	20	1	8	3	13.3	4.26	80	.260	.330	3	.375	1	-2	-2	-1	0.0
Total 8	57	78	.422	149	137	128	2	0	1231¹	1263	22	496	532	12.9	3.87	94	.256	.324	123	.243	20	-25	-34	-10	-1.2

■ CHICK SMITH
Smith, John William (b: Jan Smadt) b: 12/2/1892, Dayton, Ky. d: 10/11/35, Dayton, Ohio BL/TL, 5'8", 165 lbs. Deb: 4/12/13

YEAR TM/L	W	L	PCT	G	GS	CG	SH	SV	IP	H	HR	BB	SO	RAT	ERA	ERA+	OAV	OOB	BH	AVG	PB	PR	/A	PD	TPI
1913 Cin-N	0	1	.000	5	1	0	0	0	17²	15	1	11	11	13.2	3.57	91	.238	.351	0	.000	-1	-1	-1	0	0.0

■ LEE SMITH
Smith, Lee Arthur b: 12/4/57, Shreveport, La. BR/TR, 6'5", 220 lbs. Deb: 9/01/80

YEAR TM/L	W	L	PCT	G	GS	CG	SH	SV	IP	H	HR	BB	SO	RAT	ERA	ERA+	OAV	OOB	BH	AVG	PB	PR	/A	PD	TPI
1980 Chi-N	2	0	1.000	18	0	0	0	0	21²	21	0	14	17	14.5	2.91	135	.259	.368	0	—	0	2	2	-0	0.2
1981 Chi-N	3	6	.333	40	1	0	0	1	66²	57	2	31	50	12.0	3.51	105	.239	.330	0	.000	-1	-0	1	-0	0.0
1982 Chi-N	2	5	.286	72	5	0	0	17	117	105	5	37	99	11.2	2.69	139	.245	.309	1	.063	-0	12	14	-1	1.3
1983 Chi-N	4	10	.286	66	0	0	0	**29**	103¹	70	5	41	91	9.8	1.65	229	.194	.279	1	.111	-1	23	25	-1	2.5
1984 *Chi-N	9	7	.563	69	0	0	0	33	101	98	6	35	86	11.9	3.65	107	.255	.317	1	.077	-1	-1	3	-0	0.2
1985 Chi-N	7	4	.636	65	0	0	0	33	97²	87	9	32	112	11.1	3.04	131	.242	.305	0	.000	-0	6	10	-1	0.9
1986 Chi-N	9	9	.500	66	0	0	0	31	90¹	69	7	42	93	11.1	3.09	131	.215	.306	0	.000	-1	6	10	-1	0.9
1987 Chi-N	4	10	.286	62	0	0	0	36	83²	84	4	32	96	12.5	3.12	137	.259	.326	0	.000	-0	9	11	-1	1.0
1988 *Bos-A	4	5	.444	64	0	0	0	29	83²	72	5	37	96	11.8	2.80	147	.225	.307	0	—	0	11	12	-1	1.1
1989 Bos-A	6	1	.857	64	0	0	0	25	70²	53	6	33	96	11.0	3.57	115	.209	.301	0	—	0	2	4	-2	0.5
1990 Bos-A	2	1	.667	11	0	0	0	4	14¹	13	0	9	17	13.8	1.88	216	.236	.344	0	—	0	3	3	0	0.4
StL-N	3	4	.429	53	0	0	0	27	68²	58	3	20	70	10.2	2.10	187	.227	.284	0	.000	-0	13	14	-2	1.2
Total 11	55	62	.470	650	6	0	0	265	918²	787	54	363	923	11.3	2.88	137	.233	.309	3	.048	-4	86	109	-11	9.9

■ ROY SMITH
Smith, Le Roy Purdy b: 9/6/61, Mt.Vernon, N.Y. BR/TR, 6'3", 200 lbs. Deb: 6/23/84

YEAR TM/L	W	L	PCT	G	GS	CG	SH	SV	IP	H	HR	BB	SO	RAT	ERA	ERA+	OAV	OOB	BH	AVG	PB	PR	/A	PD	TPI
1984 Cle-A	5	5	.500	22	14	0	0	0	86¹	91	14	40	55	13.8	4.59	89	.270	.349	0	—	0	-6	-5	-2	-0.5
1985 Cle-A	1	4	.200	12	11	1	0	0	62¹	84	8	17	28	14.7	5.34	77	.321	.364	0	—	0	-8	-8	-1	-0.8
1986 Min-A	0	2	.000	5	0	0	0	0	10¹	13	1	5	8	16.5	6.97	62	.295	.380	0	—	0	-3	-3	0	-0.2
1987 Min-A	1	0	1.000	7	1	0	0	0	16¹	20	3	6	8	15.4	4.96	93	.290	.364	0	—	0	-1	-1	0	0.0
1988 Min-A	0	0	—	3	0	0	0	0	37	29	3	12	17	10.2	2.68	152	.210	.278	0	—	0	5	6	-0	0.6
1989 Min-A	10	6	.625	32	26	2	0	1	172¹	180	22	51	92	12.3	3.92	106	.269	.326	0	—	0	-1	4	-2	0.2
1990 Min-A	5	10	.333	32	23	1	1	0	153¹	191	20	47	87	14.0	4.81	87	.313	.362	0	—	0	-15	-11	-2	-1.2
Total 7	25	27	.481	119	79	4	1	1	538	608	71	178	295	13.3	4.45	93	.285	.344	0	—	0	-29	-17	-7	-2.0

YEAR TM/L	W	L	PCT	G	GS	CG	SH	SV	IP	H	HR	BB	SO	RAT	ERA	ERA+	OAV	OOB	BH	AVG	PB	PR	/A	PD	TPI
MARK SMITH					Smith, Mark Christopher b: 11/23/55, Arlington, Va. BR/TR, 6'2", 215 lbs. Deb: 8/12/83																			
1983 Oak-A	1	0	1.000	8	1	0	0	0	14²	24	0	6	10	19.0	6.75	57	.387	.449	0	—	0	-4	-5	-0	-0.4
MIKE SMITH					Smith, Michael Anthony b: 2/23/61, Hinds, Miss. BR/TR, 6', 175 lbs. Deb: 4/06/84																			
1984 Cin-N	1	0	1.000	8	0	0	0	0	10¹	12	1	5	7	14.8	5.23	72	.286	.362	0	—	0	-2	-2	-0	-0.1
1985 Cin-N	0	0	—	2	0	0	0	0	3¹	2	2	1	2	8.1	5.40	70	.167	.231	0	—	0	-1	-1	0	0.0
1986 Cin-N	0	0	—	2	1	0	0	0	3¹	7	0	1	1	21.6	13.50	29	.412	.444	0	—	0	-4	-4	0	-0.2
1988 Mon-N	0	0	—	5	0	0	0	1	8²	6	0	5	4	11.4	3.12	115	.207	.324	0	.000	-0	0	0	0	0.0
1989 Pit-N	0	1	.000	16	0	0	0	0	24	28	1	10	12	14.3	3.75	89	.301	.369	0	.000	-0	-1	-1	1	0.0
Total 5	1	1	.500	33	1	0	0	1	49²	55	4	22	26	14.0	4.71	75	.285	.358	0	.000	-1	-7	-6	1	-0.3
MIKE SMITH					Smith, Michael Anthony b: 10/31/63, San Antonio, Tex. BR/TR, 6'3", 180 lbs. Deb: 6/30/89																			
1989 Bal-A	2	0	1.000	13	1	0	0	0	20	25	3	14	12	17.5	7.65	50	.313	.415	0	—	0	-8	-9	0	-0.7
1990 Bal-A	0	0	—	2	0	0	0	0	3	4	2	1	2	15.0	12.00	32	.308	.357	0	—	0	-3	-3	0	-0.2
Total 2	2	0	1.000	15	1	0	0	0	23	29	5	15	14	17.2	8.22	46	.312	.407	0	—	0	-11	-11	0	-0.9
PETE SMITH					Smith, Peter John b: 2/27/66, Abington, Mass. BR/TR, 6'2", 185 lbs. Deb: 9/08/87																			
1987 Atl-N	1	2	.333	6	6	0	0	0	31²	39	3	14	11	15.1	4.83	90	.307	.376	1	.091	-1	-3	-2	-1	-0.2
1988 Atl-N	7	15	.318	32	32	5	3	0	195¹	183	15	88	124	12.5	3.69	100	.250	.331	6	.113	-2	-5	-0	-3	-0.3
1989 Atl-N	5	14	.263	28	27	1	0	0	142	144	13	57	115	12.7	4.75	77	.263	.333	4	.098	-0	-20	-17	-1	-1.9
1990 Atl-N	5	6	.455	13	13	3	0	0	77	77	11	24	56	11.8	4.79	82	.260	.316	2	.087	-1	-9	-8	-1	-0.8
Total 4	18	37	.327	79	78	9	3	0	446	443	42	183	306	12.7	4.30	87	.260	.332	13	.102	-4	-36	-27	-6	-3.2
PETE SMITH					Smith, Peter Luke b: 3/19/40, Natick, Mass. BR/TR, 6'2", 190 lbs. Deb: 9/13/62																			
1962 Bos-A	0	1	.000	1	1	0	0	0	3²	7	3	2	1	22.1	19.64	21	.438	.500	0	.000	-0	-6	-6	0	-0.4
1963 Bos-A	0	0	—	6	1	0	0	0	15	11	2	6	6	10.2	3.60	105	.212	.293	0	.000	-0	0	0	0	0.0
Total 2	0	1	.000	7	2	0	0	0	18²	18	5	8	7	12.5	6.75	57	.265	.342	0	.000	-0	-6	-6	0	-0.4
REGGIE SMITH					Smith, Reginald b: Louisville, Ky. Deb: 7/11/1886																			
1886 Phi-a	0	1	.000	1	1	1	0	0	9	15	0	5	4	20.0	7.00	50	.355	.423	0	.000	-1	-4	-3	0	-0.2
ED SMITH					Smith, Rhesa Edward b: 2/21/1879, Mentone, Ind. d: 3/20/55, Tarpon Springs, Fla. BR/TR, 5'11", 170 lbs. Deb: 4/27/06																			
1906 StL-A	8	11	.421	19	18	13	0	0	154²	153	3	53	45	12.0	3.72	69	.261	.323	11	.204	2	-18	-20	1	-1.7
BOB SMITH					Smith, Robert Ashley b: 7/19/1890, Hardwick, Vt. BR/TR, 5'11", 160 lbs. Deb: 4/19/13																			
1913 Chi-A	0	0	—	1	0	0	0	0	2	3	1	3	1	27.0	13.50	22	.273	.429	0	—	0	-2	-2	0	-0.1
1915 Buf-F	0	0	—	1	0	0	0	0	1	1	0	2	0	36.0	18.00	17	.268	.594	0	—	0	-2	-2	0	0.0
Total 2	0	0	—	2	0	0	0	0	3	4	1	5	1	30.0	15.00	20	.271	.482	0	—	0	-4	-4	0	-0.1
BOB SMITH					Smith, Robert Eldridge b: 4/22/1895, Rogersville, Tenn. d: 7/19/87, Waycross, Ga. BR/TR, 5'10", 175 lbs. Deb: 4/19/23 ♦																			
1925 Bos-N	5	3	.625	13	10	6	0	0	92²	110	6	36	19	14.2	4.47	90	.304	.367	49	.282	2	-2	-5	0	-0.3
1926 Bos-N	10	13	.435	33	23	14	4	1	201¹	199	10	75	44	12.2	3.75	94	.269	.336	25	.298	7	2	-5	3	0.4
1927 Bos-N	10	18	.357	41	32	16	1	3	260²	297	9	75	81	12.9	3.76	99	.301	.351	27	.248	4	4	-1	2	0.4
1928 Bos-N	13	17	.433	38	25	14	0	2	244¹	274	11	74	59	12.9	3.87	101	.289	.342	23	.250	3	3	1	3	0.6
1929 Bos-N	11	17	.393	34	29	19	1	3	231	256	20	71	65	12.8	4.68	100	.285	.338	17	.172	-1	1	0	1	0.1
1930 Bos-N	10	14	.417	38	24	14	2	5	219²	247	25	85	84	13.7	4.26	116	.290	.357	19	.235	-1	17	16	1	1.5
1931 Chi-N	15	12	.556	36	29	18	2	2	240¹	239	10	62	63	11.3	3.22	120	.256	.303	19	.218	2	17	17	1	2.0
1932 *Chi-N	4	3	.571	34	11	4	1	2	119	148	4	36	35	14.1	4.61	82	.303	.355	10	.238	2	-10	-11	1	-0.7
1933 Cin-N	4	4	.500	16	6	4	0	0	73²	75	3	11	18	10.5	2.20	154	.260	.287	5	.200	0	9	10	-0	1.1
Bos-N	4	3	.571	14	4	3	1	1	58²	68	3	7	16	11.5	3.22	95	.296	.316	4	.200	1	1	-1	1	0.0
Yr	8	7	.533	30	10	7	1	1	132¹	143	6	18	34	10.9	2.65	123	.276	.300	1	.022	1	10	9	1	1.1
1934 Bos-N	6	9	.400	39	5	3	0	5	121²	133	9	36	26	12.5	4.66	82	.277	.328	9	.250	1	-8	-11	1	-0.8
1935 Bos-N	8	18	.308	46	20	8	2	5	203¹	232	13	61	58	13.1	3.94	96	.285	.337	17	.270	2	2	-3	-1	-0.1
1936 Bos-N	6	7	.462	35	11	5	2	8	136	142	3	35	36	11.8	3.77	102	.264	.311	10	.222	0	4	1	1	0.2
1937 Bos-N	0	1	.000	18	0	0	0	3	44	52	6	14	12	12.3	4.09	88	.295	.326	2	.200	0	-1	-2	-1	-0.2
Total 13	106	139	.433	435	229	128	16	40	2246¹	2472	132	670	618	12.7	3.94	100	.283	.335	409	.242	22	40	4	14	4.2
BOB SMITH					Smith, Robert Gilchrist b: 2/1/31, Woodsville, N.H. BR/TL, 6'1.5", 190 lbs. Deb: 4/29/55																			
1955 Bos-A	0	0	—	1	0	0	0	0	1²	1	0	1	1	10.8	0.00	—	.200	.333	0	—	0	1	1	0	0.1
1957 StL-N	0	0	—	6	0	0	0	1	9²	12	0	6	11	17.7	4.66	85	.267	.365	0	.000	-0	-1	-1	0	0.0
Pit-N	2	4	.333	20	4	2	0	0	55	48	2	25	35	12.1	3.11	122	.229	.314	1	.077	-1	5	4	-1	0.2
Yr	2	4	.333	26	4	2	0	1	64²	60	2	31	46	12.8	3.34	114	.234	.319	1	.091	-1	4	3	-1	0.2
1958 Pit-N	2	2	.500	35	4	0	0	0	61	61	6	31	24	13.9	4.43	87	.262	.353	1	.091	-1	-3	-4	1	-0.3
1959 Pit-N	0	0	—	20	0	0	0	0	28¹	32	1	17	12	15.6	3.49	111	.291	.386	0	.000	-0	1	1	-0	0.1
Det-A	0	3	.000	9	0	0	0	0	11	20	5	3	10	18.8	8.18	50	.417	.451	0	—	0	-5	-5	-0	-0.4
Total 4	4	9	.308	91	8	2	0	2	166²	174	14	83	93	14.1	4.05	95	.267	.354	2	.069	-2	-3	-3	-0	-0.3
BOB SMITH					Smith, Robert Walkay "Riverboat" b: 5/13/28, Clarence, Mo. BL/TL, 6', 185 lbs. Deb: 4/22/58																			
1958 Bos-A	4	3	.571	17	7	1	0	0	66²	61	4	45	43	14.3	3.78	106	.248	.364	2	.105	-1	-0	2	1	0.2
1959 Chi-N	0	0	—	1	0	0	0	0	0²	5	0	2	0	94.5	81.00	5	.833	.875	0	—	0	-6	-6	0	-0.3
Cle-A	0	1	.000	12	3	0	0	0	29¹	31	2	12	17	13.2	5.22	71	.282	.352	0	.000	-0	-4	-5	0	-0.5
Total 2	4	4	.500	30	10	1	0	0	96²	97	6	59	60	14.5	4.75	82	.268	.371	2	.080	-2	-10	-9	1	-0.6
RUFUS SMITH					Smith, Rufus Frazier "Shirt" b: 1/24/05, Guilford College, N.C. d: 8/21/84, Aiken, S.C. BR/TL, 5'8", 165 lbs. Deb: 10/02/27																			
1927 Det-A	0	0	—	1	1	0	0	0	8	8	0	3	2	13.5	3.38	125	.242	.324	0	.000	-1	1	1	-0	0.0
SHERRY SMITH					Smith, Sherrod Malone b: 2/18/1891, Monticello, Ga. d: 9/12/49, Reidsville, Ga. BR/TL, 6'1", 170 lbs. Deb: 5/11/11																			
1911 Pit-N	0	0	—	1	0	0	0	0	0²	4	0	1	0	67.5	54.00	6	.667	.714	0	—	0	-4	-4	0	-0.2
1912 Pit-N	0	0	—	3	0	0	0	1	4	6	0	1	3	15.8	6.75	48	.600	.636	0	—	0	-1	-2	-0	-0.1
1915 Bro-N	14	8	.636	29	20	11	2	2	173²	169	3	42	52	11.2	2.59	107	.264	.315	14	.246	3	3	4	0	0.7
1916 *Bro-N	14	10	.583	36	23	15	4	1	219	193	5	45	62	9.9	2.34	114	.239	.282	21	.273	6	7	8	1	1.8
1917 Bro-N	12	12	.500	38	23	15	0	1	211¹	210	5	51	58	11.2	3.32	84	.265	.311	15	.195	2	-14	-12	4	-0.5
1919 Bro-N	7	12	.368	30	19	13	2	1	173	181	3	29	40	11.1	2.24	133	.278	.313	8	.148	-2	13	14	3	1.8
1920 *Bro-N	11	9	.550	33	12	6	2	3	136¹	134	1	36	41	10.8	1.85	173	.264	.304	10	.233	2	19	21	6	3.2
1921 Bro-N	7	11	.389	35	17	9	0	4	175¹	232	4	34	36	13.7	3.90	100	.319	.350	13	.228	1	-2	-0	5	0.6
1922 Bro-N	4	8	.333	28	9	3	1	2	108²	128	6	35	15	14.1	4.56	89	.309	.373	9	.257	2	-5	-6	2	-0.1
Cle-A	1	0	1.000	2	1	0	0	0	15²	18	0	3	4	12.1	3.45	116	.295	.328	2	.333	1	1	1	0	0.2
1923 Cle-A	9	6	.600	30	16	10	1	1	124	129	4	37	23	12.2	3.27	121	.269	.324	11	.244	1	10	10	2	1.3
1924 Cle-A	12	14	.462	39	27	20	2	1	247²	267	5	42	34	11.5	3.02	142	.277	.312	18	.202	-1	33	35	4	3.6
1925 Cle-A	11	14	.440	31	30	22	1	1	237	296	11	48	30	13.3	4.86	91	.306	.342	28	.304	7	-12	-12	0	-0.3
1926 Cle-A	11	10	.524	27	24	16	1	0	188¹	214	8	31	25	11.9	3.73	109	.292	.324	14	.215	2	6	7	4	1.2
1927 Cle-A	1	4	.200	11	2	1	0	1	38	53	2	14	8	15.9	5.45	77	.342	.396	2	.167	-0	-6	-5	0	-0.4
Total 14	114	118	.491	373	224	142	16	21	2052²	2234	57	440	428	11.9	3.32	108	.282	.324	165	.233	23	48	59	32	12.8

YEAR TM/L	W	L	PCT	G	GS	CG	SH	SV	IP	H	HR	BB	SO	RAT	ERA	ERA+	OAV	OOB	BH	AVG	PB	PR	/A	PD	TPI
■ **TOM SMITH**				Smith, Thomas E.		b: 12/5/1871, Boston, Mass.					d: 3/2/29, Dorchester, Mass.				BR/TR, 180 lbs.		Deb: 6/06/1894								
1894 Bos-N	0	0	—	2	0	0	0	1	6	8	2	6	2	21.0	15.00	38	.316	.448	0	.000	-0	-6	-6	-0	-0.4
1895 Phi-N	2	3	.400	11	7	4	0	0	68	76	1	53	21	17.1	6.88	70	.278	.396	8	.242	-0	-16	-16	-1	-1.2
1896 Lou-N	2	3	.400	11	5	4	0	0	55	73	2	25	14	16.0	5.40	80	.316	.383	8	.205	-0	-6	-7	1	-0.4
1898 StL-N	0	1	.000	1	1	1	0	0	9	9	0	5	1	14.0	2.00	189	.258	.352	1	.500	1	2	2	0	0.3
Total 4	4	7	.364	25	13	9	0	1	138	166	5	89	38	16.6	6.33	72	.294	.390	17	.224	-0	-27	-27	0	-1.7
■ **BILL SMITH**				Smith, William Garland		b: 6/8/34, Washington, D.C.					BL/TL, 6', 190 lbs.		Deb: 9/13/58												
1958 StL-N	0	1	.000	2	1	0	0	0	9²	12	0	4	4	14.9	6.52	63	.324	.390	0	.000	-0	-3	-3	0	-0.2
1959 StL-N	0	0	—	6	0	0	0	1	8¹	11	0	3	4	15.1	1.08	393	.333	.389	0	.000	-0	3	3	0	0.3
1962 Phi-N	1	5	.167	24	5	0	0	0	50¹	59	8	10	26	12.5	4.29	90	.295	.332	2	.182	1	-2	-2	-0	-0.1
Total 3	1	6	.143	32	6	0	0	1	68¹	82	8	17	34	13.2	4.21	94	.304	.347	2	.143	0	-2	-2	-0	-0.0
■ **BILL SMITH**				Smith, William S.		b: 1851, Guelph, Ont., Canada					d: 10/27/1897, Guelph, Ont., Can.		6', 168 lbs.		Deb: 7/06/1886									
1886 Det-N	5	4	.556	9	9	9	0	0	77	81	0	30	36	13.0	4.09	81	.259	.324	7	.184	-1	-7	-7	-1	-0.6
■ **WILLIE SMITH**				Smith, Willie		b: 2/11/39, Anniston, Ala.					BL/TL, 6', 182 lbs.		Deb: 6/18/63 ♦												
1963 Det-A	1	0	1.000	11	2	0	0	2	21²	24	2	13	16	15.4	4.57	82	.300	.398	1	.125	-0	-2	-2	0	-0.1
1964 LA-A	1	4	.200	15	1	0	0	0	31²	34	5	10	20	12.8	2.84	116	.293	.354	108	.301	6	3	2	0	0.2
1968 Cle-A	0	0	—	2	0	0	0	0	5	2	0	1	1	5.4	0.00	—	.125	.176	6	.143	0	2	2	0	0.2
Chi-N	0	0	—	1	0	0	0	0	2²	0	0	0	2	0.0	0.00	—	.000	.000	39	.275	0	1	1	0	0.1
Total 3	2	4	.333	29	3	0	0	2	61	60	7	24	39	12.5	3.10	110	.273	.347	410	.248	6	3	2	1	0.4
■ **ZANE SMITH**				Smith, Zane William		b: 12/28/60, Madison, Wis.					BL/TL, 6'2", 185 lbs.		Deb: 9/10/84												
1984 Atl-N	1	0	1.000	3	3	0	0	0	20	16	1	13	16	13.0	2.25	171	.219	.337	5	.556	2	3	4	0	0.7
1985 Atl-N	9	10	.474	42	18	2	2	0	147	135	4	80	85	13.3	3.80	101	.254	.355	6	.162	-0	-3	1	2	0.3
1986 Atl-N	8	16	.333	38	32	3	1	1	204²	209	14	105	139	14.0	4.05	98	.275	.367	5	.085	-3	-2	3	-0.1	-0.9
1987 Atl-N	15	10	.600	36	36	9	3	0	242	245	19	91	130	12.7	4.09	106	.266	.335	10	.132	-1	-0	7	2	0.2
1988 Atl-N	5	10	.333	23	22	3	0	0	140¹	159	8	44	59	13.2	4.30	86	.292	.348	7	.167	0	-13	-10	3	-0.5
1989 Atl-N	1	12	.077	17	17	0	0	0	99	102	5	33	58	12.5	4.45	82	.267	.329	5	.179	-0	-11	-9	2	-0.6
Mon-N	0	1	.000	31	0	0	0	2	48	39	2	19	35	11.1	1.50	235	.220	.299	1	.250	0	11	11	1	1.3
Yr	1	13	.071	48	17	0	0	2	147	141	7	52	93	11.9	3.49	103	.249	.313	0	.000	0	0	2	3	0.7
1990 Mon-N	6	7	.462	22	21	1	0	0	139¹	141	11	41	80	11.9	3.23	116	.266	.322	7	.175	1	9	8	1	1.1
*Pit-N	6	2	.750	11	10	3	2	0	76	55	4	9	50	7.6	1.30	278	.203	.229	4	.143	0	21	20	-0	2.3
Yr	12	9	.571	33	31	4	2	0	215¹	196	15	50	130	10.3	2.55	145	.243	.287	1	.015	1	30	28	1	3.4
Total 7	51	68	.429	223	159	21	8	3	1116¹	1101	62	435	652	12.6	3.66	107	.263	.335	50	.155	-1	8	30	14	5.4
■ **MIKE SMITHSON**				Smithson, Billy Mike		b: 1/21/55, Centerville, Tenn.					BL/TR, 6'8", 215 lbs.		Deb: 8/27/82												
1982 Tex-A	3	4	.429	8	8	3	0	0	46²	51	5	13	24	12.9	5.01	77	.282	.340	0	—	0	-5	-6	-1	-0.5
1983 Tex-A	10	14	.417	33	33	10	0	0	223¹	233	14	71	135	12.6	3.91	102	.269	.330	0	—	0	4	2	1	0.4
1984 Min-A	15	13	.536	36	36	10	1	0	252	246	35	54	144	11.0	3.68	114	.252	.296	0	—	0	9	15	-1	1.4
1985 Min-A	15	14	.517	37	37	8	0	0	257	264	25	78	127	12.5	4.34	101	.270	.333	0	—	0	-6	2	-1	0.1
1986 Min-A	13	14	.481	34	33	8	1	0	198	234	26	57	114	13.9	4.77	90	.294	.352	0	—	0	-13	-10	1	-0.8
1987 Min-A	4	7	.364	21	20	0	0	0	109	126	17	38	53	14.3	5.94	78	.286	.355	0	—	0	-18	-16	-1	-1.4
1988 *Bos-A	9	6	.600	31	18	1	0	0	126²	149	25	37	73	13.6	5.97	69	.292	.347	0	—	0	-28	-26	-1	-2.5
1989 Bos-A	7	14	.333	40	19	1	1	2	143²	170	21	35	61	13.5	4.95	83	.297	.348	0	—	0	-17	-14	0	-1.2
Total 8	76	86	.469	240	204	41	6	2	1356¹	1473	168	383	731	12.8	4.58	92	.277	.334	0	—	0	-74	-53	-2	-4.5
■ **LEFTY SMOLL**				Smoll, Clyde Hetrick		b: 4/17/14, Quakertown, Pa.					d: 8/31/85, Quakertown, Pa.		BB/TL, 5'10", 175 lbs.		Deb: 4/26/40									
1940 Phi-N	2	8	.200	33	9	0	0	0	109	145	6	36	31	15.3	5.37	73	.322	.378	5	.161	-1	-18	-18	-1	-1.9
■ **JOHN SMOLTZ**				Smoltz, John Andrew		b: 5/15/67, Detroit, Mich.					BR/TR, 6'3", 210 lbs.		Deb: 7/23/88												
1988 Atl-N	2	7	.222	12	12	0	0	0	64	74	10	33	37	15.3	5.48	67	.285	.369	2	.118	-0	-14	-13	-1	-1.3
1989 Atl-N	12	11	.522	29	29	5	0	0	208	160	15	72	168	10.1	2.94	124	.212	.282	7	.113	1	13	16	1	2.1
1990 Atl-N	14	11	.560	34	34	6	2	0	231¹	206	20	90	170	11.6	3.85	102	.240	.313	12	.162	1	-2	2	1	0.4
Total 3	28	29	.491	75	75	11	2	0	503¹	440	45	195	375	11.4	3.68	102	.235	.309	21	.137	1	-4	5	1	1.2
■ **HARRY SMYTHE**				Smythe, William Henry		b: 10/24/04, Augusta, Ga.					d: 8/28/80, Augusta, Ga.		BL/TL, 5'10.5", 179 lbs.		Deb: 7/21/29									
1929 Phi-N	4	6	.400	19	7	2	0	1	68²	94	3	15	12	14.4	5.24	99	.330	.365	5	.192	-1	-4	-0	2	0.1
1930 Phi-N	0	3	.000	25	3	0	0	2	49²	84	3	31	9	21.4	7.79	70	.368	.450	4	.286	-0	-16	-13	-0	-1.0
1934 NY-A	0	2	.000	8	0	0	0	1	15	24	1	8	7	19.2	7.80	52	.381	.451	1	.200	-0	-6	-6	1	-0.4
Bro-N	1	1	.500	8	0	0	0	0	21¹	30	3	8	5	16.5	5.91	66	.337	.398	3	.333	1	-4	-5	1	-0.2
Total 3	5	12	.294	60	10	2	0	4	154²	232	10	62	33	17.4	6.40	78	.349	.408	13	.241	-0	-29	-24	3	-1.5
■ **NAT SNELL**				Snell, Nathaniel		b: 9/2/52, Orangeburg, S.C.					BR/TR, 6'4", 190 lbs.		Deb: 9/20/84												
1984 Bal-A	1	1	.500	5	0	0	0	0	7²	8	1	1	7	10.6	2.35	165	.258	.281	0	—	0	1	1	-0	0.1
1985 Bal-A	3	2	.600	43	0	0	0	5	100¹	100	4	30	41	11.8	2.69	150	.260	.315	0	—	0	16	15	2	1.7
1986 Bal-A	2	1	.667	34	0	0	0	0	72¹	69	9	22	29	11.4	3.86	107	.257	.316	0	—	0	3	2	1	0.3
1987 Det-A	1	2	.333	22	2	0	0	0	38²	39	5	19	19	13.5	3.96	107	.267	.352	0	—	0	2	1	-0	0.1
Total 4	7	6	.538	104	2	0	0	5	219	216	19	72	96	11.9	3.29	125	.260	.321	0	—	0	22	20	2	2.2
■ **FRANK SNOOK**				Snook, Frank Walter		b: 3/28/49, Somerville, N.J.					BR/TR, 6'2", 180 lbs.		Deb: 7/13/73												
1973 SD-N	0	2	.000	18	0	0	0	1	27¹	19	4	18	13	12.2	3.62	96	.200	.327	0	.000	-0	0	-0	1	0.0
■ **COLONEL SNOVER**				Snover, Colonel Lester "Bosco"		b: 5/16/1895, Hallstead, Pa.					d: 4/30/69, Rochester, N.Y.		BL/TL, 6'0.5", 200 lbs.		Deb: 9/18/19									
1919 NY-N	0	1	.000	2	1	0	0	0	9	7	0	3	4	11.0	1.00	281	.212	.297	0	.000	0	2	2	-0	0.2
■ **BRIAN SNYDER**				Snyder, Brian Robert		b: 2/20/58, Flemington, N.J.					BL/TL, 6'3", 185 lbs.		Deb: 5/25/85												
1985 Sea-A	1	2	.333	15	6	0	0	1	35¹	44	2	19	23	16.3	6.37	66	.306	.390	0	—	0	-9	-8	1	-0.7
1989 Oak-A	0	0	—	2	0	0	0	0	0²	2	1	2	1	54.0	27.00	14	.500	.667	0	—	0	-2	-2	0	-0.1
Total 2	1	2	.333	17	6	0	0	1	36	46	3	21	24	17.0	6.75	62	.311	.400	0	—	0	-10	-10	1	-0.8
■ **GENE SNYDER**				Snyder, Gene Walter		b: 3/31/31, York, Pa.					BR/TL, 5'11", 175 lbs.		Deb: 4/26/59												
1959 LA-N	1	1	.500	11	1	0	0	0	26¹	32	1	20	20	17.8	5.47	77	.299	.409	0	.000	-0	-4	-4	-0	-0.3
■ **GEORGE SNYDER**				Snyder, George T.		b: 1849, Philadelphia, Pa.					d: 8/2/05, Philadelphia, Pa.		Deb: 9/30/1882											
1882 Phi-a	1	0	1.000	1	1	0	0	0	9	4	0	2	0	6.0	0.00	—	.125	.177	1	.333	0	3	3	0	0.4
■ **BILL SNYDER**				Snyder, William Nicholas		b: 1/28/1898, Mansfield, Ohio					d: 10/8/34, Vicksburg, Mich.		BR/TR,		Deb: 9/04/19										
1919 Was-A	0	1	.000	2	1	0	0	0	8	6	0	3	5	10.1	1.13	285	.200	.273	0	.000	-0	2	2	-0	0.1
1920 Was-A	2	1	.667	16	4	1	0	1	54	59	1	28	17	15.5	4.17	90	.280	.380	6	.316	1	-2	-3	-1	-0.2
Total 2	2	2	.500	18	5	1	0	1	62	65	1	31	22	14.8	3.77	97	.270	.367	6	.286	1	-0	-1	-1	-0.1
■ **RAY SOFF**				Soff, Raymond John		b: 10/31/58, Adrian, Mich.					BR/TR, 6', 185 lbs.		Deb: 7/17/86												
1986 StL-N	4	2	.667	30	0	0	0	0	38¹	37	4	13	22	11.7	3.29	111	.255	.316	0	.000	-0	2	1	0	0.2
1987 StL-N	1	0	1.000	12	0	0	0	0	15¹	18	3	5	9	14.1	6.46	64	.295	.358	0	.000	-0	-4	-4	0	-0.3

YEAR TM/L	W	L	PCT	G	GS	CG	SH	SV	IP	H	HR	BB	SO	RAT	ERA	ERA+	OAV	OOB	BH	AVG	PB	PR	/A	PD	TPI
Total 2	5	2	.714	42	0	0	0	0	53²	55	7	18	31	12.4	4.19	90	.267	.329	0	.000	-0	-2	-2	0	-0.1

■ JULIO SOLANO
Solano, Julio Cesar   b: 1/8/60, Aqua Blanca, D.R.   BR/TR, 6'1", 160 lbs.   Deb: 4/05/83

YEAR TM/L	W	L	PCT	G	GS	CG	SH	SV	IP	H	HR	BB	SO	RAT	ERA	ERA+	OAV	OOB	BH	AVG	PB	PR	/A	PD	TPI
1983 Hou-N	0	2	.000	4	0	0	0	0	6	5	1	4	3	13.5	6.00	57	.217	.333	0	—	0	-2	-2	0	-0.1
1984 Hou-N	1	3	.250	31	0	0	0	0	50²	31	3	18	33	8.7	1.95	170	.179	.257	1	.333	0	9	8	-1	0.8
1985 Hou-N	2	2	.500	20	0	0	0	0	33²	34	5	13	17	12.6	3.48	100	.262	.329	0	.000	-0	0	-0	-1	0.0
1986 Hou-N	3	1	.750	16	1	0	0	0	32	39	5	22	21	18.0	7.59	47	.310	.424	0	.000	-1	-14	-14	-0	-1.4
1987 Hou-N	0	0	—	11	0	0	0	0	20	25	5	9	12	15.3	7.65	51	.298	.366	0	.000	-0	-8	-8	0	-0.7
1988 Sea-A	0	0	—	17	0	0	0	3	22	22	3	12	10	13.9	4.09	102	.268	.362	0	—	0	-0	0	0	0.1
1989 Sea-A	0	0	—	7	0	0	0	0	9²	6	1	4	6	10.2	5.59	72	.176	.282	0	—	0	-2	-2	0	0.0
Total 7	6	8	.429	106	1	0	0	3	174	162	23	82	102	12.8	4.55	79	.248	.336	1	.077	-1	-16	-18	-1	-1.3

■ MARCELINO SOLIS
Solis, Marcelino   b: 7/19/30, San Luis Potosi, Mexico   BL/TL, 6'1", 185 lbs.   Deb: 7/16/58

YEAR TM/L	W	L	PCT	G	GS	CG	SH	SV	IP	H	HR	BB	SO	RAT	ERA	ERA+	OAV	OOB	BH	AVG	PB	PR	/A	PD	TPI
1958 Chi-N	3	3	.500	15	4	0	0	0	52	74	5	20	15	17.0	6.06	65	.339	.405	5	.250	1	-12	-12	0	-1.0

■ BUDDY SOLOMON
Solomon, Eddie   b: 2/9/51, Perry, Ga.   d: 1/12/86, Macon, Ga.   BR/TR, 6'2", 185 lbs.   Deb: 9/02/73

YEAR TM/L	W	L	PCT	G	GS	CG	SH	SV	IP	H	HR	BB	SO	RAT	ERA	ERA+	OAV	OOB	BH	AVG	PB	PR	/A	PD	TPI
1973 LA-N	0	0	—	4	0	0	0	0	6¹	10	3	4	6	21.3	7.11	48	.357	.455	0	.000	-0	-2	-3	0	-0.2
1974 *LA-N	0	0	—	4	0	0	0	1	6	5	1	2	2	10.5	1.50	227	.217	.280	0	—	0	1	1	0	0.2
1975 Chi-N	0	0	—	6	0	0	0	0	6²	7	1	6	3	17.6	1.35	285	.269	.406	0	—	0	2	2	0	0.2
1976 StL-N	1	1	.500	26	2	0	0	0	37	45	2	16	19	15.1	4.86	73	.306	.378	2	.400	1	-6	-5	1	-0.3
1977 Atl-N	6	6	.500	18	16	0	0	0	88²	110	10	34	54	14.8	4.57	97	.305	.368	4	.129	-1	-6	-1	-0	-0.1
1978 Atl-N	4	6	.400	37	8	0	0	2	106	98	12	50	64	12.7	4.08	99	.247	.335	4	.138	-1	-6	-0	-0	0.0
1979 Atl-N	7	14	.333	31	30	4	0	0	186	184	19	51	66	11.7	4.21	96	.254	.308	13	.203	-1	-10	-3	-1	-0.2
1980 Pit-N	7	3	.700	26	12	2	0	0	100¹	96	8	37	35	12.3	2.69	135	.253	.325	7	.219	-1	10	11	0	1.3
1981 Pit-N	8	6	.571	22	17	2	0	1	127	133	10	27	38	11.6	3.12	115	.278	.321	7	.163	-1	5	7	-0	0.6
1982 Pit-N	2	6	.250	11	10	0	0	0	46²	69	9	18	18	17.0	6.75	55	.347	.404	2	.133	-1	-16	-16	-1	-1.6
Chi-A	1	0	1.000	6	0	0	0	0	7¹	7	1	2	2	11.0	3.68	110	.241	.290	0	—	0	0	0	0	0.0
Total 10	36	42	.462	191	95	8	0	4	718	764	76	247	337	12.9	4.00	97	.274	.337	39	.177	-1	-28	-8	-1	-0.1

■ JOE SOMMER
Sommer, Joseph John   b: 11/20/1858, Covington, Ky.   d: 1/16/38, Cincinnati, Ohio   BR/TR,   Deb: 7/08/1880 ♦

YEAR TM/L	W	L	PCT	G	GS	CG	SH	SV	IP	H	HR	BB	SO	RAT	ERA	ERA+	OAV	OOB	BH	AVG	PB	PR	/A	PD	TPI
1883 Cin-a	0	0	—	1	0	0	0	0	5	9	0	1	2	18.0	5.40	60	.367	.392	115	.278	0	-1	-1	-0	0.0
1885 Bal-a	0	0	—	2	0	0	0	1	3	6	0	0	0	18.0	9.00	36	.399	.399	118	.251	0	-2	-2	0	-0.1
1886 Bal-a	0	0	—	1	0	0	0	0	4	14	0	1	3	38.3	18.00	19	.536	.584	117	.209	-0	-6	-6	0	-0.4
1887 Bal-a	0	0	—	1	0	0	0	0	1	2	0	1	0	27.0	9.00	46	.401	.501	123	.266	0	-1	-1	0	0.0
1890 Cle-N	0	0	—	1	0	0	0	0	1	2	1	2	0	36.0	0.00	—	.404	.575	8	.229	-0	0	0	0	0.0
Total 5	0	0	—	6	0	0	0	1	14	33	1	7	3	25.7	9.64	35	.437	.484	911	.248	1	-10	-10	-0	-0.5

■ RUDY SOMMERS
Sommers, Rudolph   b: 10/30/1888, Cincinnati, Ohio   d: 3/18/49, Louisville, Ky.   BB/TL, 5'11", 165 lbs.   Deb: 9/08/12

YEAR TM/L	W	L	PCT	G	GS	CG	SH	SV	IP	H	HR	BB	SO	RAT	ERA	ERA+	OAV	OOB	BH	AVG	PB	PR	/A	PD	TPI
1912 Chi-N	0	1	.000	1	0	0	0	0	3	4	0	2	2	18.0	3.00	111	.308	.400				0	0	-0	0.0
1914 Bro-F	2	7	.222	23	8	2	0	2	82	88	2	34	40	13.7	4.06	79	.282	.358	6	.250	2	-8	-8	-1	-0.5
1926 Bos-A	0	0	—	2	0	0	0	0	2	3	0	3	0	27.0	13.50	30	.333	.500	0	—	0	-2	-2	-0	-0.1
1927 Bos-A	0	0	—	7	0	0	0	0	14	18	2	14	2	20.6	8.36	51	.353	.492	1	.500	0	-7	-6	1	-0.4
Total 4	2	8	.200	33	8	2	0	2	101	113	4	53	44	15.1	4.81	70	.294	.383	7	.259	3	-16	-16	0	-1.0

■ ANDY SOMMERVILLE
Sommerville, Andrew Henry (b: Henry Travers Summersgill)   b: 2/6/1876, Brooklyn, N.Y.   d: 6/16/31, Richmond Hill, N.Y.   Deb: 8/08/1894

YEAR TM/L	W	L	PCT	G	GS	CG	SH	SV	IP	H	HR	BB	SO	RAT	ERA	ERA+	OAV	OOB	BH	AVG	PB	PR	/A	PD	TPI
1894 Bro-N	0	1	.000	1	1	0	0	0	0¹	1	0	5	0	162.0	162.00	3	.510	.862	0	—	0	-6	-6	0	-0.3

■ DON SONGER
Songer, Donald C.   b: 1/31/1900, Walnut, Kan.   d: 10/3/62, Kansas City, Mo.   BL/TL, 6', 165 lbs.   Deb: 9/21/24

YEAR TM/L	W	L	PCT	G	GS	CG	SH	SV	IP	H	HR	BB	SO	RAT	ERA	ERA+	OAV	OOB	BH	AVG	PB	PR	/A	PD	TPI
1924 Pit-N	0	0	—	4	1	0	0	1	9¹	14	1	3	3	16.4	6.75	57	.333	.378	0	.000	-0	-3	-3	0	-0.2
1925 Pit-N	0	1	.000	8	0	0	0	0	11²	14	0	8	4	17.0	2.31	193	.298	.400	0	.000	-0	3	3	0	0.2
1926 Pit-N	7	8	.467	35	14	5	1	2	126¹	118	4	52	27	12.9	3.13	126	.252	.340	4	.105	-2	10	11	1	1.0
1927 Pit-N	0	0	—	2	0	0	0	0	4²	10	0	4	1	28.9	11.57	36	.526	.625	0	.000	-0	-4	-4	0	-0.3
NY-N	3	5	.375	22	1	0	0	1	50¹	48	4	31	9	14.3	2.86	135	.261	.370	3	.300	1	6	6	1	0.8
Yr	3	5	.375	24	1	0	0	1	55	58	4	35	10	15.4	3.60	108	.284	.392	2	.182	1	2	2	1	0.5
Total 4	10	14	.417	71	16	5	1	4	202¹	204	9	98	44	14.0	3.38	117	.268	.361	7	.132	-2	11	13	2	1.5

■ LARY SORENSEN
Sorensen, Lary Alan   b: 10/4/55, Detroit, Mich.   BR/TR, 6'2", 200 lbs.   Deb: 6/07/77

YEAR TM/L	W	L	PCT	G	GS	CG	SH	SV	IP	H	HR	BB	SO	RAT	ERA	ERA+	OAV	OOB	BH	AVG	PB	PR	/A	PD	TPI
1977 Mil-A	7	10	.412	23	20	9	0	0	142¹	147	10	36	57	11.6	4.36	93	.270	.316	0	—	0	-5	-5	1	-0.2
1978 Mil-A	18	12	.600	37	36	17	3	1	280²	277	14	50	78	10.6	3.21	117	.259	.295	0	—	0	17	17	1	1.9
1979 Mil-A	15	14	.517	34	34	16	2	0	235¹	250	30	42	63	11.3	3.98	105	.275	.310	0	—	0	6	5	1	0.6
1980 Mil-A	12	10	.545	35	29	8	2	1	195²	242	13	45	54	13.3	3.68	105	.311	.351	0	—	0	8	4	1	0.5
1981 StL-N	7	7	.500	23	23	3	1	0	140¹	149	3	26	52	11.3	3.27	109	.271	.305	3	.065	-3	3	4	0	0.2
1982 Cle-A	10	15	.400	32	30	6	1	0	189¹	251	19	55	62	14.7	5.61	73	.322	.369	0	—	0	-32	-32	0	-3.0
1983 Cle-A	12	11	.522	36	34	8	1	0	222²	238	21	65	76	12.3	4.24	100	.276	.328	0	—	0	-5	-0	2	0.2
1984 Oak-A	6	13	.316	46	21	2	0	1	183¹	240	21	44	63	14.2	4.91	76	.317	.359	0	—	0	-19	-24	-1	-2.3
1985 Chi-N	3	7	.300	45	3	0	0	0	82¹	86	8	24	34	12.5	4.26	94	.274	.333	0	.000	-0	-6	-3	0	-0.2
1987 Mon-N	3	4	.429	23	5	0	0	1	47²	56	7	12	21	13.4	4.72	89	.286	.336	0	.000	-1	-3	-3	-0	-0.3
1988 SF-N	0	0	—	12	0	0	0	2	16²	24	1	3	9	14.6	4.86	67	.329	.355	0	.000	-0	-3	-3	-0	-0.2
Total 11	93	103	.474	346	235	69	10	6	1736¹	1960	147	402	569	12.4	4.15	95	.287	.329	3	.049	-4	-38	-38	6	-2.8

■ VIC SORRELL
Sorrell, Victor Garland   b: 4/9/01, Morrisville, N.C.   d: 5/4/72, Raleigh, N.C.   BR/TR, 5'10", 180 lbs.   Deb: 4/22/28

YEAR TM/L	W	L	PCT	G	GS	CG	SH	SV	IP	H	HR	BB	SO	RAT	ERA	ERA+	OAV	OOB	BH	AVG	PB	PR	/A	PD	TPI
1928 Det-A	8	11	.421	29	23	8	0	0	171	182	9	83	67	14.2	4.79	86	.277	.363	6	.109	-5	-14	-13	-3	-1.8
1929 Det-A	14	15	.483	36	31	13	1	1	226	270	15	106	81	15.1	5.18	83	.302	.377	12	.145	-6	-23	-22	-1	-2.6
1930 Det-A	16	11	.593	35	30	14	2	1	233¹	245	13	106	97	13.5	3.86	124	.274	.351	15	.188	-3	21	24	-3	1.7
1931 Det-A	13	14	.481	35	32	19	1	1	245	267	8	114	90	14.0	4.15	110	.278	.355	14	.159	-4	6	12	1	0.8
1932 Det-A	14	14	.500	32	31	13	1	0	234¹	234	11	77	84	12.1	4.03	117	.259	.319	9	.118	-4	12	17	-2	1.2
1933 Det-A	11	15	.423	36	28	13	1	1	232²	233	18	78	75	12.1	3.79	114	.260	.321	11	.149	-2	13	13	0	1.1
1934 Det-A	6	9	.400	28	19	6	1	2	129²	146	13	45	46	13.5	4.79	92	.283	.345	4	.108	-1	-4	-6	2	-0.4
1935 Det-A	4	3	.571	12	6	4	0	0	51¹	65	2	25	22	16.1	4.03	103	.319	.398	0	.000	-3	2	1	0	-0.1
1936 Det-A	6	7	.462	30	14	5	1	3	131¹	153	9	64	37	15.0	5.28	94	.294	.373	6	.154	1	-3	-5	2	-0.1
1937 Det-A	0	2	.000	7	2	0	0	1	17	25	3	8	11	17.5	9.00	52	.338	.402	0	.000	-0	-8	-8	0	-0.7
Total 10	92	101	.477	280	216	95	8	10	1671²	1820	101	706	619	13.7	4.43	102	.279	.351	77	.139	-28	-0	14	-3	-0.9

■ ELIAS SOSA
Sosa, Elias (Martinez)   b: 6/10/50, LaVega, D.R.   BR/TR, 6'2", 186 lbs.   Deb: 9/08/72

YEAR TM/L	W	L	PCT	G	GS	CG	SH	SV	IP	H	HR	BB	SO	RAT	ERA	ERA+	OAV	OOB	BH	AVG	PB	PR	/A	PD	TPI
1972 SF-N	0	1	.000	8	0	0	0	3	15²	10	0	12	10	12.6	2.30	152	.189	.338	0	.000	-0	2	2	-0	0.2
1973 SF-N	10	4	.714	71	1	0	0	18	107	95	7	41	70	11.8	3.28	116	.241	.318	1	.071	-0	5	6	-1	0.5
1974 SF-N	9	7	.563	68	0	0	0	6	101	94	8	45	48	12.5	3.48	109	.252	.334	1	.067	-1	2	4	0	0.2
1975 StL-N	0	3	.000	14	1	0	0	0	27¹	22	3	14	15	12.2	3.95	95	.227	.330	1	.125	-0	-1	-1	0	0.0
Atl-N	2	2	.500	43	0	0	0	2	62¹	70	3	29	31	14.7	4.48	84	.294	.378	1	.143	-0	-6	-5	0	-0.4
Yr	2	5	.286	57	1	0	0	2	89²	92	6	43	46	13.9	4.32	87	.271	.358	0	.000	-1	-7	-5	0	-0.4
1976 Atl-N	4	4	.500	21	0	0	0	3	35¹	41	3	13	32	14.0	5.35	71	.287	.350	1	.143	-0	-7	-6	-0	-0.6
LA-N	2	4	.333	24	0	0	0	1	33²	30	0	12	20	11.2	3.48	97	.242	.309	0	—	0	-0	-0	-0	0.0
Yr	6	8	.429	45	0	0	0	4	69	71	3	25	52	12.5	4.43	81	.263	.325	0	.000	-0	-7	-6	-0	-0.6
1977 *LA-N	2	2	.500	44	0	0	0	1	63²	42	7	12	47	7.8	1.98	193	.189	.234	1	.250	-0	14	13	-0	1.3
1978 Oak-A	8	2	.800	68	0	0	0	14	109	106	5	44	61	12.5	2.64	138	.264	.338	0	—	0	14	12	0	1.3

YEAR	TM/L	W	L	PCT	G	GS	CG	SH	SV	IP	H	HR	BB	SO	RAT	ERA	ERA+	OAV	OOB	BH	AVG	PB	PR	/A	PD	TPI
1979	Mon-N	8	7	.533	62	0	0	0	18	96²	77	2	37	59	10.8	1.96	187	.219	.297	2	.154	0	19	18	-1	1.7
1980	Mon-N	9	6	.600	67	0	0	0	9	93²	104	5	19	58	11.9	3.07	116	.286	.323	1	.091	-1	5	5	-0	0.4
1981	*Mon-N	1	2	.333	32	0	0	0	3	39¹	46	3	8	18	12.6	3.66	95	.297	.335	2	1.000	1	-1	-1	0	0.1
1982	Det-A	3	3	.500	38	0	0	0	4	61	64	11	18	24	12.4	4.43	92	.270	.327	0	—	0	-2	-2	1	-0.1
1983	SD-N	1	4	.200	41	1	0	0	1	72¹	72	7	30	45	13.1	4.35	80	.268	.348	1	.143	-0	-6	-7	-1	-0.7
Total 12		59	51	.536	601	3	0	0	83	918	873	64	334	538	12.0	3.32	111	.255	.325	12	.130	-3	37	39	-2	3.9

■ JOSE SOSA
Sosa, Jose Ynocencio (b: Jose Ynocencio (Sosa)) b: 12/28/52, Santo Domingo, D.R.   BR/TR, 5'11", 158 lbs.   Deb: 7/22/75

YEAR	TM/L	W	L	PCT	G	GS	CG	SH	SV	IP	H	HR	BB	SO	RAT	ERA	ERA+	OAV	OOB	BH	AVG	PB	PR	/A	PD	TPI
1975	Hou-N	1	3	.250	25	2	0	0	1	47	51	5	23	31	14.4	4.02	84	.291	.377	3	.333	2	-2	-3	-1	-0.2
1976	Hou-N	0	0	—	9	0	0	0	0	11²	16	0	6	5	19.3	6.94	46	.340	.446	0	—	0	-4	-5	1	-0.3
Total 2		1	3	.250	34	2	0	0	1	58²	67	5	29	36	15.3	4.60	72	.302	.392	3	.333	2	-7	-8	-0	-0.5

■ ALLEN SOTHORON
Sothoron, Allen Sutton b: 4/27/1893, Bradford, Ohio d: 6/17/39, St.Louis, Mo.   BB/TR, 5'11", 182 lbs.   Deb: 9/17/14   MC

YEAR	TM/L	W	L	PCT	G	GS	CG	SH	SV	IP	H	HR	BB	SO	RAT	ERA	ERA+	OAV	OOB	BH	AVG	PB	PR	/A	PD	TPI
1914	StL-A	0	0	—	1	0	0	0	0	6	6	0	4	3	15.0	6.00	45	.261	.307	0	.000	-0	-2	-2	-0	-0.1
1915	StL-A	0	1	.000	3	1	0	0	0	3²	8	0	5	2	31.9	7.36	39	.400	.520	0	.000	-0	-2	-2	0	-0.1
1917	StL-A	14	19	.424	48	32	17	3	4	276²	259	2	96	85	11.8	2.83	92	.251	.320	20	.217	3	-5	-7	-1	-0.5
1918	StL-A	12	12	.500	29	24	14	2	0	209	152	3	67	71	9.6	1.94	141	.205	.274	10	.159	-2	20	19	-3	1.5
1919	StL-A	20	13	.606	40	30	21	3	3	270	256	4	87	106	11.8	2.20	151	.246	.311	17	.175	-3	31	34	-7	2.6
1920	StL-A	8	15	.348	36	26	12	1	2	218¹	263	6	89	81	14.8	4.70	83	.307	.376	16	.222	-1	-22	-19	-2	-2.0
1921	StL-A	1	2	.333	5	4	1	0	0	27²	33	0	8	9	13.7	5.20	86	.314	.368	1	.111	-1	-3	-2	0	-0.2
	Bos-A	0	2	.000	2	2	0	0	0	6	15	0	5	2	30.0	13.50	31	.455	.526	1	.500	1	-6	-6	0	-0.4
	Cle-A	12	4	.750	22	16	10	2	0	144²	146	0	58	61	13.1	3.24	132	.279	.358	16	.276	2	17	17	-2	1.5
	Yr	13	8	.619	29	22	11	2	0	178¹	194	0	71	72	13.7	3.89	111	.293	.367	2	.029	2	8	8	-2	0.9
1922	Cle-A	1	3	.250	6	4	2	0	0	25¹	26	1	14	8	14.9	6.39	63	.274	.378	4	.444	1	-7	-7	-0	-0.4
1924	StL-N	10	16	.385	29	28	16	4	0	196²	209	9	84	62	13.9	3.57	106	.275	.354	14	.194	-2	7	5	-3	0.0
1925	StL-N	10	10	.500	28	23	8	2	0	155²	173	7	63	67	14.0	4.05	107	.280	.353	11	.196	-1	4	5	-5	0.0
1926	StL-N	3	3	.500	15	4	1	0	0	42²	37	2	16	19	11.2	4.22	93	.247	.319	3	.231	0	-2	-1	-1	-0.1
Total 11		91	100	.476	264	194	102	17	9	1582¹	1583	34	596	576	12.7	3.31	105	.264	.336	113	.207	-2	29	30	-24	1.8

■ MARIO SOTO
Soto, Mario Melvin b: 7/12/56, Bani, D.R.   BR/TR, 6', 174 lbs.   Deb: 7/21/77

YEAR	TM/L	W	L	PCT	G	GS	CG	SH	SV	IP	H	HR	BB	SO	RAT	ERA	ERA+	OAV	OOB	BH	AVG	PB	PR	/A	PD	TPI
1977	Cin-N	2	6	.250	12	10	2	1	0	60²	60	12	26	44	13.2	5.34	74	.258	.340	1	.077	-0	-10	-10	-0	-0.8
1978	Cin-N	1	0	1.000	5	1	0	0	0	18	13	1	13	13	13.0	2.50	142	.197	.329	0	.000	-0	2	2	-0	0.2
1979	*Cin-N	3	2	.600	25	0	0	0	0	37¹	33	2	30	32	15.4	5.30	70	.243	.383	4	.571	2	-7	-7	-1	-0.5
1980	Cin-N	10	8	.556	53	12	3	1	4	190¹	126	11	84	182	10.0	3.07	116	.187	.274	2	.043	-4	11	11	-1	0.6
1981	Cin-N	12	9	.571	25	25	10	3	0	175	142	13	61	151	10.6	3.29	108	.220	.290	4	.068	-4	4	5	-2	0.0
1982	Cin-N	14	13	.519	35	34	13	2	0	257²	202	19	71	274	9.7	2.79	132	.215	.273	14	.167	1	23	26	-3	2.7
1983	Cin-N	17	13	.567	34	34	18	3	0	273²	207	28	95	242	10.1	2.70	141	.208	.280	11	.125	-2	28	34	-2	3.3
1984	Cin-N	18	7	.720	33	33	13	0	0	237¹	181	26	87	185	10.4	3.53	107	.209	.286	18	.207	3	2	7	-3	0.8
1985	Cin-N	12	15	.444	36	36	9	1	0	256²	196	30	104	214	10.6	3.58	106	.211	.292	11	.133	-2	0	6	-1	0.3
1986	Cin-N	5	10	.333	19	19	1	1	0	105	113	15	46	67	13.7	4.71	82	.280	.355	3	.111	-1	-12	-10	-0	-1.0
1987	Cin-N	3	2	.600	6	6	0	0	0	32¹	34	7	12	11	12.8	5.01	85	.279	.343	1	.083	-1	-3	-3	-0	-0.2
1988	Cin-N	3	7	.300	14	14	3	1	0	87	88	8	28	34	12.2	4.66	77	.267	.328	1	.045	-1	-12	-10	-0	-1.1
Total 12		100	92	.521	297	224	72	13	4	1731	1395	172	657	1449	10.8	3.47	108	.220	.296	70	.132	-10	28	51	-12	4.3

■ MARK SOUZA
Souza, Kenneth Mark b: 2/1/55, Redwood City, Cal.   BL/TL, 6', 180 lbs.   Deb: 4/22/80

YEAR	TM/L	W	L	PCT	G	GS	CG	SH	SV	IP	H	HR	BB	SO	RAT	ERA	ERA+	OAV	OOB	BH	AVG	PB	PR	/A	PD	TPI
1980	Oak-A	0	0	—	5	0	0	0	0	7	9	1	5	2	18.0	7.71	49	.310	.412	0	—	0	-3	-3	-0	-0.2

■ JOHN SOWDERS
Sowders, John b: 12/10/1866, Louisville, Ky. d: 7/29/08, Indianapolis, Ind   BR/TL, 6',   Deb: 6/28/1887 ◆

YEAR	TM/L	W	L	PCT	G	GS	CG	SH	SV	IP	H	HR	BB	SO	RAT	ERA	ERA+	OAV	OOB	BH	AVG	PB	PR	/A	PD	TPI
1887	Ind-N	0	0	—	1	0	0	0	0	3	11	0	5	0	48.0	21.00	20	.554	.644	0	.000	-0	-6	-6	-0	-0.3
1889	KC-a	6	16	.273	25	23	20	0	1	185	204	9	105	104	15.0	4.82	87	.271	.360	19	.218	-2	-20	-13	-2	-1.2
1890	Bro-P	19	16	.543	39	37	28	1	0	309	358	3	161	91	15.1	3.82	117	.278	.358	25	.189	-4	14	22	-2	1.4
Total 3		25	32	.439	65	60	48	1	1	497	573	12	271	195	15.3	4.29	102	.278	.362	44	.199	-7	-11	4	-4	-0.1

■ BILL SOWDERS
Sowders, William Jefferson "Little Bill" b: 11/29/1864, Louisville, Ky. d: 2/2/51, Indianapolis, Ind.   BR/TR, 6',   Deb: 4/24/1888

YEAR	TM/L	W	L	PCT	G	GS	CG	SH	SV	IP	H	HR	BB	SO	RAT	ERA	ERA+	OAV	OOB	BH	AVG	PB	PR	/A	PD	TPI
1888	Bos-N	19	15	.559	36	35	34	2	0	317	278	3	73	132	10.0	2.07	137	.227	.271	18	.148	-4	27	27	1	2.4
1889	Bos-N	1	2	.333	7	4	3	0	2	42	53	3	23	10	16.3	5.14	81	.298	.379	4	.235	0	-5	-5	1	-0.2
	Pit-N	6	5	.545	13	11	9	0	0	52²	94	1	29	33	21.0	7.35	51	.376	.440	13	.271	2	-19	-21	2	-1.3
	Yr	7	7	.500	20	15	12	0	2	94²	147	4	52	43	18.9	6.37	62	.344	.415	4	.062	2	-25	-26	3	-1.5
1890	Pit-N	3	8	.273	15	11	9	0	0	106	117	1	24	30	12.0	4.42	74	.272	.310	9	.180	-2	-10	-13	-2	-1.4
Total 3		29	30	.492	71	61	55	2	2	517²	542	8	149	205	12.0	3.34	94	.260	.310	44	.186	-4	-8	-12	2	-0.5

■ BOB SPADE
Spade, Robert b: 1/4/1877, Akron, Ohio d: 9/7/24, Cincinnati, Ohio   BR/TR, 5'10", 190 lbs.   Deb: 9/22/07

YEAR	TM/L	W	L	PCT	G	GS	CG	SH	SV	IP	H	HR	BB	SO	RAT	ERA	ERA+	OAV	OOB	BH	AVG	PB	PR	/A	PD	TPI
1907	Cin-N	1	2	.333	3	3	3	1	0	27	21	0	9	7	10.3	1.00	260	.219	.292	2	.286	1	4	5	-1	0.7
1908	Cin-N	17	12	.586	35	28	22	2	1	249¹	230	2	85	74	11.6	2.74	84	.250	.317	17	.195	1	-11	-12	-4	-1.6
1909	Cin-N	5	5	.500	14	13	8	0	0	98	91	0	39	31	12.3	2.85	91	.236	.313	10	.294	4	-3	-3	-4	-0.3
1910	Cin-N	1	2	.333	3	3	1	0	0	17¹	35	1	9	1	23.4	6.75	43	.479	.542	0	.000	-1	-7	-7	-0	-0.6
	StL-A	1	3	.250	7	5	2	1	0	34²	34	1	17	8	13.5	4.41	56	.270	.361	3	.273	2	-7	-7	-0	-0.6
Total 4		25	24	.510	62	52	36	4	1	426¹	411	4	159	121	12.3	2.96	82	.257	.329	32	.222	7	-23	-25	-9	-2.4

■ WARREN SPAHN
Spahn, Warren Edward b: 4/23/21, Buffalo, N.Y.   BL/TL, 6', 172 lbs.   Deb: 4/19/42   CH

YEAR	TM/L	W	L	PCT	G	GS	CG	SH	SV	IP	H	HR	BB	SO	RAT	ERA	ERA+	OAV	OOB	BH	AVG	PB	PR	/A	PD	TPI
1942	Bos-N	0	0	—	4	2	1	0	0	15²	25	0	11	7	20.7	5.74	58	.368	.456	1	.167	-0	-4	-4	-0	-0.4
1946	Bos-N	8	5	.615	24	16	8	0	1	125²	107	6	36	67	10.3	2.94	117	.228	.285	7	.163	-1	7	7	-2	0.4
1947	Bos-N	21	10	.677	40	35	22	7	3	289²	245	15	84	123	10.3	2.33	167	.226	.283	16	.163	1	56	50	-2	5.1
1948	*Bos-N	15	12	.556	36	35	16	3	1	257	237	19	77	114	11.0	3.71	103	.242	.298	15	.167	1	7	3	0	0.5
1949	Bos-N	21	14	.600	38	38	25	4	0	302¹	283	27	86	151	11.1	3.07	123	.245	.299	18	.162	0	33	24	-3	2.1
1950	Bos-N	21	17	.553	41	39	25	1	1	293	248	22	111	191	11.1	3.16	123	.227	.299	23	.217	4	32	22	-1	2.3
1951	Bos-N	22	14	.611	39	36	26	7	0	310²	278	20	109	164	11.2	2.98	123	.238	.304	22	.190	5	34	24	-2	2.6
1952	Bos-N	14	19	.424	40	35	19	5	3	290	263	19	73	183	10.6	2.98	121	.240	.291	18	.161	2	24	20	1	2.5
1953	Mil-N	23	7	.767	35	32	24	5	3	265²	211	14	70	148	9.6	2.10	187	.217	.270	23	.219	4	65	54	2	6.2
1954	Mil-N	21	12	.636	39	34	23	1	0	283¹	262	24	86	136	11.1	3.14	118	.245	.302	21	.208	6	29	18	1	2.5
1955	Mil-N	17	14	.548	39	32	16	1	1	245²	249	25	65	110	11.6	3.26	115	.265	.314	17	.210	5	21	14	1	1.9
1956	Mil-N	20	11	.645	39	35	20	3	3	281¹	249	26	52	128	9.7	2.78	124	.238	.276	22	.210	6	31	21	-1	2.7
1957	*Mil-N	21	11	.656	39	35	18	4	3	271	241	23	78	111	10.7	2.69	130	.237	.293	13	.138	1	36	24	1	2.7
1958	*Mil-N	22	11	.667	38	36	23	2	1	290	257	29	76	150	10.4	3.07	115	.237	.288	36	.333	16	28	14	4	3.5
1959	Mil-N	21	15	.583	40	36	21	4	0	292	282	21	70	143	10.9	2.96	120	.253	.298	24	.231	7	32	19	-1	2.4
1960	Mil-N	21	10	.677	40	33	18	4	2	267²	254	24	74	154	11.2	3.50	98	.250	.303	14	.147	3	8	-2	3	0.2
1961	Mil-N	21	13	.618	38	34	21	4	0	262²	236	24	64	115	10.4	3.02	124	.243	.293	21	.223	1	30	21	3	3.4
1962	Mil-N	18	14	.563	34	34	22	0	0	269¹	248	25	55	118	10.2	3.04	125	.246	.287	18	.184	4	27	23	2	2.9
1963	Mil-N	23	7	.767	33	33	22	7	0	259²	241	23	49	102	10.1	2.60	124	.240	.284	16	.178	5	20	18	5	3.2
1964	Mil-N	6	13	.316	38	25	4	1	4	173²	204	23	52	78	13.4	5.29	67	.297	.348	11	.186	2	-34	-34	0	-3.2
1965	NY-N	4	12	.250	20	19	5	0	0	126	140	18	35	56	12.6	4.36	81	.281	.331	4	.114	1	-11	-12	0	-1.0
	SF-N	3	4	.429	16	11	3	0	0	71²	70	8	21	34	11.6	3.39	106	.256	.312	3	.143	0	1	2	1	0.3
	Yr	7	16	.304	36	30	8	0	0	197²	210	26	56	90	12.2	4.01	89	.271	.321	10	.179	2	-10	-10	1	-0.7
Total 21		363	245	.597	750	665	382	63	29	5243²	4830	434	1434	2583	10.8	3.09	118	.244	.297	363	.194	82	470	330	11	43.0

YEAR TM/L	W	L	PCT	G	GS	CG	SH	SV	IP	H	HR	BB	SO	RAT	ERA	ERA+	OAV	OOB	BH	AVG	PB	PR	/A	PD	TPI
■ **AL SPALDING**			Spalding, Albert Goodwill			b: 9/2/1850, Byron, Ill.			d: 9/9/15, San Diego, Cal.			BR/TR, 6'1", 170 lbs.			Deb: 5/05/1871 MH♦										
1871 Bos-n	**19**	10	.655	31	31	22	**1**	0	257¹	333	2	38	23	13.0	3.36	124	.268	.290	39	.271	2	25	23		1.6
1872 Bos-n	**38**	8	**.826**	48	48	41	**3**	0	404²	412	0	28		9.8	**1.98**	**188**	.241	.253	87	.357	19	**78**	**79**		**7.2**
1873 Bos-n	**41**	14	**.745**	**60**	55	48	1	1	**500²**	648	5	28		12.2	2.97	124	.285	.294	107	.331	20	35	39		**4.4**
1874 Bos-n	**52**	16	**.765**	**71**	69	**65**	**4**	0	**616¹**	753	1	23		11.3	2.35	126	.273	.279	119	.331	22	44	42		**5.0**
1875 Bos-n	**55**	5	**.917**	**72**	63	52	**7**	**8**	575	572	1	14		9.2	**1.52**	156	.245	.249	107	.312	21	**60**	**54**		**6.6**
1876 Chi-N	**47**	12	**.797**	61	60	54	9	0	528²	542	6	26	39	9.7	1.75	139	.247	.256	91	.312	10	33	41	4	5.3
1877 Chi-N	1	0	1.000	4	1	0	0	1	11	17	0	0	2	13.9	3.27	91	.335	.335	65	.256	0	-1	-0	1	0.0
Total 5 n	205	53	.795	282	266	228	16	9	2354	2718	9	131	23	10.9	2.32	139	.263	.272	459	.325	84	242	235		24.8
Total 2	48	12	.800	65	61	54	9	1	539²	559	6	26	41	9.8	1.78	138	.249	.258	158	.287	84	32	40	5	5.3
■ **BILL SPANSWICK**			Spanswick, William Henry			b: 7/8/38, Springfield, Mass.			BL/TL, 6'3", 195 lbs.			Deb: 4/18/64												
1964 Bos-A	2	3	.400	29	7	0	0	0	65¹	75	9	44	55	16.8	6.89	56	.306	.418	4	.286	1	-24	-22	1	-1.9
■ **TULLY SPARKS**			Sparks, Thomas Frank			b: 12/12/1874, Aetna, Ga.			d: 7/15/37, Anniston, Ala.			BR/TR,		Deb: 9/15/1897										
1897 Phi-N	0	1	.000	1	1	1	0	0	8	12	0	4	0	18.0	10.13	41	.343	.411	0	.000	-1	-5	-5	0	-0.3
1899 Pit-N	8	6	.571	28	17	8	0	0	170	180	1	82	53	13.9	3.86	99	.271	.351	1	.129	-1	-0	-1	-0	-0.2
1901 Mil-A	7	16	.304	29	26	18	0	0	210	228	5	93	62	13.8	3.51	102	.273	.346	12	.169	-2	4	2	-0	-0.4
1902 NY-N	4	10	.286	15	13	11	0	0	115	123	2	40	40	13.1	3.76	75	.273	.338	5	.135	-1	-12	-12	3	-0.9
Bos-A	7	9	.438	17	15	15	1	0	142²	151	4	40	37	12.0	3.47	103	.272	.321	8	.154	-1	2	2	0	0.1
1903 Phi-N	11	15	.423	28	28	27	0	0	248	248	3	56	88	11.3	2.72	120	.263	.310	10	.109	-5	15	15	-2	0.8
1904 Phi-N	7	16	.304	26	25	19	3	0	200²	208	1	43	67	11.5	2.65	101	.260	.302	8	.105	-4	2	1	-4	-0.7
1905 Phi-N	14	11	.560	34	26	20	3	1	260	217	2	73	98	10.3	2.18	134	.236	.298	12	.128	-2	24	21	-6	1.4
1906 Phi-N	19	16	.543	42	37	29	6	3	316²	244	4	62	114	9.0	2.16	121	.211	.257	16	.154	0	17	16	-4	1.4
1907 Phi-N	22	8	.733	33	31	24	3	1	265	221	2	51	90	9.5	2.00	121	.228	.271	3	.034	-8	14	12	-5	0.0
1908 Phi-N	16	15	.516	33	31	24	2	2	263¹	251	3	51	85	10.6	2.60	93	.257	.300	4	.052	-5	-7	-5	-2	-1.3
1909 Phi-N	6	11	.353	24	16	6	1	0	121²	126	4	32	40	11.9	2.96	88	.280	.332	5	.139	-1	-5	-5	-0	-0.6
1910 Phi-N	0	2	.000	3	3	0	0	0	15	22	2	2	4	15.6	6.00	52	.324	.361	0	.000	-1	-5	-5	0	-0.4
Total 12	121	136	.471	313	269	202	19	8	2336	2231	33	629	778	11.2	2.79	105	.253	.307	91	.114	-32	42	37	-19	-0.7
■ **JOE SPARMA**			Sparma, Joseph Blase			b: 2/4/42, Massillon, Ohio			d: 5/14/86, Columbus, Ohio			BR/TR, 6'1", 190 lbs.			Deb: 5/20/64									
1964 Det-A	5	6	.455	21	11	3	2	0	84	62	4	45	71	11.8	3.00	122	.207	.316	4	.160	1	6	6	1	0.9
1965 Det-A	13	8	.619	30	28	6	0	0	167	142	13	75	127	11.9	3.18	109	.228	.314	7	.135	-0	5	6	-1	0.5
1966 Det-A	2	7	.222	29	13	0	0	0	91²	103	14	52	61	15.5	5.30	66	.288	.383	5	.217	1	-19	-19	-1	-1.9
1967 Det-A	16	9	.640	37	37	11	5	0	217²	186	20	85	153	11.5	3.76	87	.227	.306	4	.054	-5	-13	-12	-2	-1.9
1968 *Det-A	10	10	.500	34	31	7	1	0	182¹	169	14	77	110	12.5	3.70	81	.246	.328	8	.133	-1	-15	-14	-2	-1.8
1969 Det-A	6	8	.429	23	16	3	2	0	92²	78	5	77	41	15.2	4.76	78	.231	.375	4	.138	-1	-12	-11	-1	-1.1
1970 Mon-N	0	4	.000	9	6	1	0	0	29¹	34	7	25	23	18.7	7.06	58	.296	.430	0	.000	-0	-10	-10	-0	-0.9
Total 7	52	52	.500	183	142	31	10	0	864²	774	77	436	586	12.9	3.94	86	.239	.334	32	.119	-6	-57	-53	-6	-6.2
■ **TRIS SPEAKER**			Speaker, Tristram E "The Grey Eagle"			b: 4/4/1888, Hubbard, Tex.			d: 12/8/58, Lake Whitney, Tex.			BL/TL, 5'11.5", 193 lbs.			Deb: 9/14/07 MH♦							
1914 Bos-A	0	0	—	1	0	0	0	0	1	2	0	0	0	18.0	9.00	30	.500	.500	193	.338	1	-1	-1	0	0.0
■ **CLIFF SPECK**			Speck, Robert Clifford			b: 8/8/56, Portland, Ore.			BR/TR, 6'4", 195 lbs.			Deb: 7/30/86										
1986 Atl-N	2	1	.667	13	1	0	0	0	28¹	25	2	15	21	13.0	4.13	96	.238	.339	0	.000	-0	-1	-0	0	0.0
■ **BY SPEECE**			Speece, Byron Franklin			b: 1/6/1897, West Baden, Ind.			d: 9/29/74, Elgin, Ore.			BR/TR, 5'11", 170 lbs.			Deb: 4/21/24								
1924 *Was-A	2	1	.667	21	1	0	0	0	54¹	60	0	27	15	14.7	2.65	152	.303	.392	3	.150	-1	**10**	**8**	1	0.9
1925 Cle-A	3	5	.375	28	3	3	0	1	90¹	106	0	28	26	13.6	4.28	103	.297	.353	5	.161	-2	1	1	0	0.0
1926 Cle-A	0	0	—	2	0	0	0	0	3	1	0	2	1	9.0	0.00	—	.125	.300	0	—	0	1	1	0	0.2
1930 Phi-N	0	0	—	11	0	0	0	0	19²	41	1	4	9	20.6	13.27	41	.432	.455	1	.333	0	-18	-17	0	-1.3
Total 4	5	6	.455	62	4	3	0	1	167¹	208	1	61	51	14.7	4.73	93	.316	.378	9	.167	-2	-6	-6	2	-0.2
■ **FLOYD SPEER**			Speer, Floyd Vernie			b: 1/27/13, Booneville, Ark.			d: 3/22/69, Little Rock, Ark.			BR/TR, 6', 180 lbs.			Deb: 4/25/43								
1943 Chi-A	0	0	—	1	0	0	0	0	1	1	0	2	1	27.0	9.00	37	.250	.500	0	—	0	-1	-1	0	0.0
1944 Chi-A	0	0	—	2	0	0	0	0	2	4	0	0	1	18.0	9.00	38	.500	.500	0	—	0	-1	-1	0	0.0
Total 2	0	0	—	3	0	0	0	0	3	5	0	2	2	21.0	9.00	38	.417	.500	0	—	0	-2	-2	0	0.0
■ **KID SPEER**			Speer, George Nathan			b: 6/16/1886, Corning, Mo.			d: 1/13/46, Edmonton, Alberta, Canada			BL/TL,		Deb: 4/24/09								
1909 Det-A	4	4	.500	12	8	4	0	1	76¹	88	2	13	12	12.4	2.83	89	.293	.331	3	.120	-0	-3	-3	1	-0.1
■ **HACK SPENCER**			Spencer, Fred Calvin			b: 4/25/1885, St.Cloud, Minn.			d: 2/5/69, St.Anthony, Minn.			BR/TR, 5'10.5", 172 lbs.			Deb: 4/18/12							
1912 StL-A	0	0	—	1	0	0	0	0	1²	2	0	0	0	10.8	0.00	—	.286	.286	0	—	0	1	1	0	0.1
■ **GEORGE SPENCER**			Spencer, George Elwell			b: 7/7/26, Columbus, Ohio			BR/TR, 6'1", 215 lbs.			Deb: 8/17/50									
1950 NY-N	1	0	1.000	10	1	0	0	0	25¹	12	3	7	5	6.8	2.49	165	.141	.207	0	.000	-1	5	5	0	0.4
1951 *NY-N	10	4	.714	57	4	2	0	6	132	125	21	56	36	12.4	3.75	104	.254	.332	4	.125	-1	3	2	1	0.3
1952 NY-N	3	5	.375	35	4	0	0	3	60	57	13	21	27	12.2	5.55	67	.251	.323	2	.200	0	-12	-12	0	-1.2
1953 NY-N	0	0	—	1	0	0	0	0	2¹	3	0	2	1	19.3	7.71	56	.300	.417	0	—	0	-1	-1	0	0.0
1954 NY-N	1	0	1.000	6	0	0	0	0	12¹	9	1	8	4	12.4	3.65	111	.209	.333	0	.000	-0	1	1	1	0.1
1955 NY-N	0	0	—	1	0	0	0	0	1²	1	1	3	0	21.6	5.40	75	.167	.444	0	—	0	-0	-0	0	0.0
1958 Det-A	1	0	1.000	7	0	0	0	0	10	11	1	4	5	13.5	2.70	149	.289	.357	0	—	0	1	1	0	0.2
1960 Det-A	0	1	.000	5	0	0	0	0	7²	10	1	5	4	17.6	3.52	112	.323	.417	0	.000	-0	0	0	0	0.0
Total 8	16	10	.615	122	9	2	0	9	251¹	228	41	106	82	12.1	4.05	96	.245	.324	6	.120	-2	-3	-4	3	-0.2
■ **GLENN SPENCER**			Spencer, Glenn Edward			b: 9/11/05, Corning, N.Y.			d: 12/30/58, Binghamton, N.Y.			BR/TR, 5'11", 155 lbs.			Deb: 4/11/28							
1928 Pit-N	0	0	—	4	0	0	0	0	5²	4	0	3	2	11.1	1.59	255	.200	.304	0	.000	-0	2	2	-0	0.1
1930 Pit-N	8	9	.471	41	10	5	0	4	156²	185	16	63	60	14.4	5.40	90	.305	.372	6	.113	-4	-7	-7	-2	-1.1
1931 Pit-N	11	12	.478	38	18	11	1	3	186²	180	8	65	51	12.1	3.42	112	.260	.328	5	.096	-3	9	9	-0	0.6
1932 Pit-N	4	8	.333	39	13	5	1	1	137²	167	10	44	35	14.0	4.97	77	.288	.341	6	.162	-1	-17	-18	-1	-1.8
1933 NY-N	0	2	.000	17	3	1	0	0	47¹	52	3	26	14	15.0	5.13	63	.284	.376	2	.167	-1	-9	-10	1	-0.9
Total 5	23	31	.426	139	44	22	2	8	534	588	37	201	162	13.5	4.53	91	.282	.349	19	.123	-9	-23	-25	-3	-3.1
■ **BOB SPICER**			Spicer, Robert Oberton			b: 4/11/25, Richmond, Va.			BL/TR, 5'10", 173 lbs.			Deb: 4/17/55									
1955 KC-A	0	0	—	2	0	0	0	0	2²	9	2	4	2	47.3	33.75	12	.529	.636	0	.000	-0	-9	-9	0	-0.6
1956 KC-A	0	0	—	2	0	0	0	0	2¹	6	1	1	0	30.9	19.29	22	.545	.615	0	—	0	-4	-4	0	-0.2
Total 2	0	0	—	4	0	0	0	0	5	15	3	5	2	39.6	27.00	16	.536	.629	0	.000	-0	-13	-13	0	-0.8
■ **DAN SPILLNER**			Spillner, Daniel Ray			b: 11/27/51, Casper, Wyo.			BR/TR, 6'1", 190 lbs.			Deb: 5/21/74									
1974 SD-N	9	11	.450	30	25	5	2	0	148	153	15	70	95	13.6	4.01	89	.267	.346	1	.023	-4	-7	-8	-1	-1.2
1975 SD-N	5	13	.278	37	25	3	0	1	166²	194	14	63	104	14.8	4.27	81	.293	.356	6	.133	1	-12	-15	-1	-1.4
1976 SD-N	2	11	.154	32	14	0	0	0	106²	120	11	55	57	14.8	5.06	65	.291	.374	1	.040	-1	-19	-21	1	-2.1
1977 SD-N	7	6	.538	76	0	0	0	6	123	130	12	60	74	14.0	3.73	95	.280	.363	2	.118	1	2	-3	-2	-0.4
1978 SD-N	1	0	1.000	17	0	0	0	0	25²	32	2	7	16	13.7	4.56	73	.317	.361	0	—	0	-3	-4	-0	-0.3
Cle-A	3	1	.750	36	0	0	0	3	56¹	54	2	21	48	12.1	3.67	102	.254	.323	0	—	0	1	0	-1	0.0

YEAR TM/L	W	L	PCT	G	GS	CG	SH	SV	IP	H	HR	BB	SO	RAT	ERA	ERA+	OAV	OOB	BH	AVG	PB	PR	/A	PD	TPI
1979 Cle-A	9	5	.643	49	13	3	0	1	157²	153	16	64	97	12.6	4.62	92	.256	.331	0	—	0	-7	-6	-1	-0.6
1980 Cle-A	16	11	.593	34	30	7	1	0	194¹	225	23	74	100	14.0	5.28	77	.288	.352	0	—	0	-27	-26	-2	-2.6
1981 Cle-A	4	4	.500	32	5	1	0	7	97¹	86	3	39	59	11.6	3.14	115	.240	.314	0	—	0	6	5	0	0.6
1982 Cle-A	12	10	.545	65	0	0	0	21	133²	117	9	45	90	10.9	2.49	164	.235	.299	0	—	0	**24**	**24**	-3	2.1
1983 Cle-A	2	9	.182	60	0	0	0	8	92¹	117	7	38	48	15.3	5.07	84	.315	.382	0	—	0	-10	-9	-1	-0.9
1984 Cle-A	0	5	.000	14	8	0	0	1	51	70	3	22	23	16.2	5.65	72	.332	.395	0	—	0	-9	-9	1	-0.6
Chi-A	1	0	1.000	22	0	0	0	1	48¹	51	7	14	26	12.3	4.10	101	.276	.330	0	—	0	-1	0	-0	0.0
Yr	1	5	.167	36	8	0	0	2	99¹	121	10	36	49	14.3	4.89	84	.301	.360	0	—	0	-10	-9	1	-0.6
1985 Chi-A	4	3	.571	52	3	0	0	1	91²	83	10	33	41	11.4	3.44	126	.245	.312	0	—	0	7	9	-2	0.7
Total 12	75	89	.457	556	123	19	3	50	1492²	1585	134	605	878	13.3	4.21	91	.275	.345	10	.077	-3	-55	-62	-12	-6.7

■ SCIPIO SPINKS
Spinks, Scipio Ronald b: 7/12/47, Chicago, Ill. BR/TR, 6'1", 183 lbs. Deb: 9/16/69

YEAR TM/L	W	L	PCT	G	GS	CG	SH	SV	IP	H	HR	BB	SO	RAT	ERA	ERA+	OAV	OOB	BH	AVG	PB	PR	/A	PD	TPI
1969 Hou-N	0	0	—	1	0	0	0	0	2	1	0	1	4	9.0	0.00	—	.143	.250	0	—	0	1	1	0	0.1
1970 Hou-N	0	1	.000	5	2	0	0	0	13²	17	5	9	6	17.1	9.88	39	.293	.388	0	.000	-0	-9	-9	-0	-0.8
1971 Hou-N	1	0	1.000	5	3	1	0	0	29¹	22	2	13	26	11.0	3.68	91	.210	.303	2	.222	0	-1	-1	0	0.0
1972 StL-N	5	5	.500	16	16	6	0	0	118	96	5	59	93	12.0	2.67	127	.221	.317	7	.167	-1	10	10	0	1.0
1973 StL-N	1	5	.167	8	8	0	0	0	38²	39	4	25	25	14.9	4.89	75	.269	.376	2	.182	1	-5	-5	1	-0.3
Total 5	7	11	.389	35	29	7	0	0	201²	175	16	107	154	12.7	3.70	94	.234	.332	11	.169	0	-4	-5	1	0.0

■ PAUL SPLITTORFF
Splittorff, Paul William b: 10/8/46, Evansville, Ind. BL/TL, 6'3", 205 lbs. Deb: 9/23/70

YEAR TM/L	W	L	PCT	G	GS	CG	SH	SV	IP	H	HR	BB	SO	RAT	ERA	ERA+	OAV	OOB	BH	AVG	PB	PR	/A	PD	TPI
1970 KC-A	0	1	.000	2	1	0	0	0	8²	16	1	5	10	21.8	7.27	51	.390	.457	1	.500	0	-3	-3	0	-0.2
1971 KC-A	8	9	.471	22	22	6	3	0	144¹	129	4	35	80	10.5	2.68	128	.243	.295	5	.104	-1	13	12	2	1.4
1972 KC-A	12	12	.500	35	33	12	2	0	216	189	11	67	140	10.8	3.13	97	.241	.304	16	.225	4	-2	-2	3	0.5
1973 KC-A	20	11	.645	38	38	12	3	0	262	279	19	78	110	12.4	3.98	103	.272	.327	0	—	0	-5	4	1	0.5
1974 KC-A	13	19	.406	36	36	8	1	0	226	252	23	75	90	13.1	4.10	93	.285	.342	0	—	0	-12	-7	1	-0.6
1975 KC-A	9	10	.474	35	23	6	3	1	159	156	10	56	76	12.1	3.17	121	.257	.321	0	—	0	11	12	2	1.5
1976 *KC-A	11	8	.579	26	23	5	1	0	158²	169	11	59	59	13.1	3.97	88	.277	.343	0	—	0	-8	-8	2	-0.8
1977 *KC-A	16	6	**.727**	37	37	6	2	0	229	243	11	83	99	12.9	3.69	109	.278	.342	0	—	0	9	9	0	0.9
1978 *KC-A	19	13	.594	39	38	13	2	0	262	244	22	60	76	10.5	3.40	112	.247	.293	0	—	0	11	12	2	1.5
1979 KC-A	15	17	.469	36	35	11	0	0	240	248	25	77	77	12.4	4.24	101	.268	.328	0	—	0	-1	1	-2	-0.1
1980 *KC-A	14	11	.560	34	33	4	0	0	204	236	17	43	53	12.4	4.15	98	.296	.333	0	—	0	-3	-2	0	-0.1
1981 KC-A	5	5	.500	21	15	1	0	0	99	111	12	23	48	12.3	4.36	83	.294	.337	0	—	0	-8	-8	1	-0.7
1982 KC-A	10	10	.500	29	28	0	0	0	162	166	14	57	74	12.6	4.28	95	.266	.330	0	—	0	-4	-4	0	-0.2
1983 KC-A	13	8	.619	27	27	4	0	0	156	159	9	52	61	12.2	3.63	112	.262	.322	0	—	0	7	8	0	0.8
1984 KC-A	1	3	.250	12	3	0	0	0	28	47	3	10	4	18.3	7.71	52	.376	.422	0	—	0	-12	-11	1	-0.9
Total 15	166	143	.537	429	392	88	17	1	2554²	2644	192	780	1057	12.2	3.81	101	.270	.326	22	.182	3	-6	10	13	3.8

■ CARL SPONGBERG
Spongberg, Carl Gustav b: 5/21/1884, Idaho Falls, Idaho d: 7/21/38, Los Angeles, Cal. BR/TR, 6'2", 208 lbs. Deb: 8/01/08

YEAR TM/L	W	L	PCT	G	GS	CG	SH	SV	IP	H	HR	BB	SO	RAT	ERA	ERA+	OAV	OOB	BH	AVG	PB	PR	/A	PD	TPI
1908 Chi-N	0	0	—	1	0	0	0	0	7	9	1	6	4	21.9	9.00	26	.321	.472	2	.667	1	-5	-5	0	-0.3

■ KARL SPOONER
Spooner, Karl Benjamin b: 6/23/31, Oriskany Falls, N.Y. d: 4/10/84, Vero Beach, Fla. BR/TL, 6', 185 lbs. Deb: 9/22/54

YEAR TM/L	W	L	PCT	G	GS	CG	SH	SV	IP	H	HR	BB	SO	RAT	ERA	ERA+	OAV	OOB	BH	AVG	PB	PR	/A	PD	TPI
1954 Bro-N	2	0	1.000	2	2	2	2	0	18	7	0	6	27	6.5	0.00	—	.113	.191	1	.167	0	8	8	-1	1.1
1955 *Bro-N	8	6	.571	29	14	2	1	2	98²	79	8	41	78	11.4	3.65	111	.215	.302	8	.286	3	4	5	-1	0.7
Total 2	10	6	.625	31	16	4	3	2	116²	86	8	47	105	10.6	3.09	132	.200	.286	9	.265	3	12	13	-1	1.8

■ HOMER SPRAGINS
Spragins, Homer Franklin b: 11/9/20, Grenada, Miss. BR/TR, 6'1", 190 lbs. Deb: 9/13/47

YEAR TM/L	W	L	PCT	G	GS	CG	SH	SV	IP	H	HR	BB	SO	RAT	ERA	ERA+	OAV	OOB	BH	AVG	PB	PR	/A	PD	TPI
1947 Phi-N	0	0	—	4	0	0	0	0	5¹	3	0	3	3	10.1	6.75	59	.158	.273	0	—	0	-2	-2	0	-0.1

■ CHARLIE SPRAGUE
Sprague, Charles Wellington b: 10/10/1864, Cleveland, Ohio d: 12/31/12, Des Moines, Iowa 5'11", 150 lbs. Deb: 9/17/1887 ♦

YEAR TM/L	W	L	PCT	G	GS	CG	SH	SV	IP	H	HR	BB	SO	RAT	ERA	ERA+	OAV	OOB	BH	AVG	PB	PR	/A	PD	TPI
1887 Chi-N	1	0	1.000	3	3	2	0	0	22	24	1	13	9	15.1	4.91	91	.270	.363	2	.154	-1	-2	-1	-0	-0.1
1889 Cle-N	0	2	.000	2	2	2	0	0	17	27	0	10	8	19.6	8.47	48	.349	.423	1	.143	-0	-8	-8	1	-0.5
1890 Tol-a	9	5	.643	19	12	9	0	0	122²	111	0	78	59	13.9	3.89	102	.234	.342	47	.236	3	-0	1	-2	0.1
Total 3	10	7	.588	24	17	13	0	0	161²	162	1	101	76	14.6	4.51	89	.253	.355	50	.228	1	-11	-9	-2	-0.5

■ ED SPRAGUE
Sprague, Edward Nelson b: 9/16/45, Boston, Mass. BR/TR, 6'4", 195 lbs. Deb: 4/10/68

YEAR TM/L	W	L	PCT	G	GS	CG	SH	SV	IP	H	HR	BB	SO	RAT	ERA	ERA+	OAV	OOB	BH	AVG	PB	PR	/A	PD	TPI
1968 Oak-A	3	4	.429	47	1	0	0	4	68²	51	5	34	34	11.4	3.28	86	.209	.311	0	.000	-1	-2	-3	1	-0.2
1969 Oak-A	1	1	.500	27	0	0	0	2	46¹	47	4	31	20	15.5	4.47	77	.267	.383	1	.200	0	-4	-5	2	-0.2
1971 Cin-N	1	0	1.000	7	0	0	0	0	11	8	0	1	7	7.4	0.00	—	.195	.214	0	.000	-0	4	4	0	0.4
1972 Cin-N	3	3	.500	33	1	0	0	0	56²	55	6	26	25	13.3	4.13	78	.261	.350	0	.000	-1	-4	-6	-1	-0.7
1973 Cin-N	1	3	.250	28	0	0	0	1	38²	35	3	22	19	13.7	5.12	66	.246	.355	0	.000	-0	-6	-7	1	-0.6
StL-N	0	0	—	8	0	0	0	0	8	8	1	4	2	13.5	2.25	162	.276	.364	0	—	0	1	1	0	0.2
Yr	1	3	.250	36	0	0	0	1	46²	43	4	26	21	13.3	4.63	74	.247	.345	0	.000	-0	-5	-6	1	-0.4
Mil-A	0	1	.000	7	0	0	0	0	9²	13	0	14	3	27.0	9.31	40	.317	.509	0	—	0	-6	-6	0	-0.5
1974 Mil-A	7	2	.778	20	10	3	0	0	94	94	3	31	57	12.4	2.39	151	.266	.332	0	—	0	13	13	-1	1.3
1975 Mil-A	1	7	.125	18	11	0	0	1	67¹	81	5	40	21	16.4	4.68	82	.297	.390	0	—	0	-7	-6	-0	-0.6
1976 Mil-A	0	2	.000	3	0	0	0	0	7²	14	0	3	0	20.0	7.04	50	.438	.486	0	—	0	-3	-3	1	-0.1
Total 8	17	23	.425	198	23	3	0	9	408	406	27	206	188	13.9	3.84	89	.263	.356	1	.045	-1	-15	-19	3	-1.0

■ JACK SPRING
Spring, Jack Russell b: 3/11/33, Spokane, Wash. BR/TL, 6'1", 175 lbs. Deb: 4/16/55

YEAR TM/L	W	L	PCT	G	GS	CG	SH	SV	IP	H	HR	BB	SO	RAT	ERA	ERA+	OAV	OOB	BH	AVG	PB	PR	/A	PD	TPI
1955 Phi-N	0	1	.000	2	0	0	0	0	2²	2	2	1	2	10.1	6.75	59	.200	.273	0	.000	-0	-1	-1	0	0.0
1957 Bos-A	0	0	—	1	0	0	0	0	1	0	0	0	2	0.0	0.00	—	.000	.000	0	—	0	0	0	0	0.0
1958 Was-A	0	0	—	3	1	0	0	0	7	16	1	7	1	29.6	14.14	27	.457	.548	0	.000	-0	-8	-8	0	-0.6
1961 LA-A	3	0	1.000	18	4	0	0	0	38	35	4	15	27	12.6	4.26	106	.243	.327	0	.000	-1	-1	1	0	0.0
1962 LA-A	4	2	.667	57	0	0	0	6	65	66	7	30	31	13.6	4.02	96	.270	.355	1	.091	-1	-0	-1	1	0.0
1963 LA-A	3	0	1.000	45	0	0	0	2	38¹	40	3	9	13	11.5	3.05	112	.268	.310	1	.333	0	2	2	1	0.3
1964 LA-A	1	0	1.000	6	0	0	0	0	3¹	3	1	3	0	16.2	2.70	122	.273	.429	0	—	0	0	0	0	0.0
Chi-N	0	0	—	7	0	0	0	0	6	4	0	2	1	9.0	6.00	62	.200	.273	0	—	0	-2	-2	0	0.0
StL-N	0	0	—	2	0	0	0	0	3	8	1	1	0	27.0	3.00	127	.471	.500	0	—	0	0	0	0	0.0
Yr	0	0	—	9	0	0	0	0	9	12	1	3	1	15.0	5.00	75	.316	.366	0	—	0	-1	-1	0	0.0
1965 Cle-A	1	2	.333	14	0	0	0	0	21²	21	2	10	9	12.9	3.74	93	.259	.341	1	.333	0	-1	-1	-0	0.0
Total 8	12	5	.706	155	5	0	0	8	186	195	21	78	86	13.5	4.26	90	.273	.349	3	.107	-1	-9	-9	2	-0.3

■ BRAD SPRINGER
Springer, Bradford Louis b: 5/9/04, Detroit, Mich. d: 1/4/70, Birmingham, Mich. BL/TL, 6', 155 lbs. Deb: 5/01/25

YEAR TM/L	W	L	PCT	G	GS	CG	SH	SV	IP	H	HR	BB	SO	RAT	ERA	ERA+	OAV	OOB	BH	AVG	PB	PR	/A	PD	TPI
1925 StL-A	0	0	—	2	0	0	0	0	3	1	0	7	0	24.0	3.00	156	.200	.667	0	—	0	0	1	0	0.1
1926 Cin-N	0	0	—	1	0	0	0	0	1¹	2	0	2	1	33.8	6.75	55	.286	.500	0	.000	-0	-0	-0	0	0.0
Total 2	0	0	—	3	0	0	0	0	4¹	3	0	9	1	27.0	4.15	105	.250	.591	0	.000	-0	0	0	0	0.1

■ ED SPRINGER
Springer, Edward H. b: 2/9/1861, California d: 4/24/26, Los Angeles Co., Cal. 6'2", 187 lbs. Deb: 7/12/1889

YEAR TM/L	W	L	PCT	G	GS	CG	SH	SV	IP	H	HR	BB	SO	RAT	ERA	ERA+	OAV	OOB	BH	AVG	PB	PR	/A	PD	TPI
1889 Lou-a	0	1	.000	1	1	1	0	0	5	8	0	2	1	18.0	9.00	43	.351	.403	0	.000	-0	-3	-3	-0	-0.2

■ CHARLIE SPROULL
Sproull, Charles William b: 1/9/19, Taylorsville, Ga. d: 1/13/80, Rockford, Ill. BR/TR, 6'3", 185 lbs. Deb: 4/19/45

YEAR TM/L	W	L	PCT	G	GS	CG	SH	SV	IP	H	HR	BB	SO	RAT	ERA	ERA+	OAV	OOB	BH	AVG	PB	PR	/A	PD	TPI
1945 Phi-N	4	10	.286	34	19	2	0	1	130¹	158	10	80	47	16.4	5.94	65	.298	.390	5	.143	-1	-31	-31	-1	-3.0

■ BOB SPROUT
Sprout, Robert Samiel b: 12/5/41, Florin, Pa. BL/TL, 6', 165 lbs. Deb: 9/27/61

YEAR TM/L	W	L	PCT	G	GS	CG	SH	SV	IP	H	HR	BB	SO	RAT	ERA	ERA+	OAV	OOB	BH	AVG	PB	PR	/A	PD	TPI
1961 LA-A	0	0	—	1	1	0	0	0	4	4	0	3	2	15.8	4.50	100	.267	.389	0	—	0	-0	0	-0	0.0

YEAR TM/L	W	L	PCT	G	GS	CG	SH	SV	IP	H	HR	BB	SO	RAT	ERA	ERA+	OAV	OOB	BH	AVG	PB	PR	/A	PD	TPI

■ BOBBY SPROWL   Sprowl, Robert John b: 4/14/56, Sandusky, Ohio   BL/TL, 6'2", 190 lbs.   Deb: 9/05/78

YEAR TM/L	W	L	PCT	G	GS	CG	SH	SV	IP	H	HR	BB	SO	RAT	ERA	ERA+	OAV	OOB	BH	AVG	PB	PR	/A	PD	TPI
1978 Bos-A	0	2	.000	3	3	0	0	0	12²	12	3	10	10	15.6	6.39	64	.245	.373	0	—	0	-4	-3	-0	-0.2
1979 Hou-N	0	0	—	3	0	0	0	0	4	1	0	2	3	6.8	0.00	—	.083	.214	0	—	0	2	2	0	0.2
1980 Hou-N	0	0	—	1	0	0	0	0	1	1	0	1	3	18.0	0.00	—	.250	.400	0	—	0	0	0	0	0.0
1981 Hou-N	0	1	.000	15	1	0	0	0	28²	40	1	14	18	17.0	5.97	55	.333	.403	1	.167	-0	-8	-9	-0	-0.8
Total 4	0	3	.000	22	4	0	0	0	46¹	54	4	27	34	15.7	5.44	65	.292	.382	1	.167	-0	-10	-10	-0	-0.8

■ MIKE SQUIRES   Squires, Michael Lynn b: 3/5/52, Kalamazoo, Mich.   BL/TL, 5'11", 185 lbs.   Deb: 9/01/75   C♦

YEAR TM/L	W	L	PCT	G	GS	CG	SH	SV	IP	H	HR	BB	SO	RAT	ERA	ERA+	OAV	OOB	BH	AVG	PB	PR	/A	PD	TPI
1984 Chi-A	0	0	—	1	0	0	0	0	0¹	0	0	0	0	0.0	0.00	—	.000	.000	15	.183	0	0	0	0	0.0

■ GEORGE STABLEIN   Stablein, George Charles b: 10/29/57, Inglewood, Cal.   BR/TR, 6'4", 185 lbs.   Deb: 9/20/80

YEAR TM/L	W	L	PCT	G	GS	CG	SH	SV	IP	H	HR	BB	SO	RAT	ERA	ERA+	OAV	OOB	BH	AVG	PB	PR	/A	PD	TPI
1980 SD-N	0	1	.000	4	2	0	0	0	11²	16	0	3	4	14.7	3.09	111	.340	.380	0	.000	-0	1	0	-0	-0.1

■ EDDIE STACK   Stack, William Edward b: 10/24/1887, Chicago, Ill. d: 8/28/58, Chicago, Ill.   BR/TR, 6', 175 lbs.   Deb: 6/07/10

YEAR TM/L	W	L	PCT	G	GS	CG	SH	SV	IP	H	HR	BB	SO	RAT	ERA	ERA+	OAV	OOB	BH	AVG	PB	PR	/A	PD	TPI
1910 Phi-N	6	7	.462	20	16	8	1	0	117	115	7	34	48	11.8	4.00	78	.266	.326	3	.083	-3	-13	-11	-1	-1.4
1911 Phi-N	5	5	.500	13	10	5	0	0	77²	67	3	41	36	13.2	3.59	96	.234	.342	2	.083	-2	-2	-1	1	-0.1
1912 Bro-N	7	5	.583	28	17	4	0	1	142	139	3	55	45	12.9	3.36	100	.257	.336	7	.135	-3	1	-0	-0	-0.3
1913 Bro-N	4	4	.500	23	9	4	1	0	87	79	0	32	34	11.6	2.38	138	.250	.321	4	.160	-1	8	9	-2	0.6
Chi-N	4	2	.667	11	7	3	1	1	51	56	1	15	28	12.9	4.24	75	.280	.336	1	.063	-1	-6	-6	-1	-0.7
Yr	8	6	.571	34	16	7	2	1	138	135	1	47	62	12.0	3.07	106	.261	.325	1	.024	-2	2	3	-3	-0.1
1914 Chi-N	0	1	.000	7	1	0	0	0	16¹	13	0	11	9	13.2	4.96	56	.220	.343	0	.000	-0	-4	-4	0	-0.3
Total 5	26	24	.520	102	60	24	3	2	491	469	14	188	200	12.4	3.52	93	.256	.332	17	.108	-10	-15	-14	-3	-2.2

■ GENERAL STAFFORD   Stafford, James Joseph "Jamsey" b: 7/9/1868, Webster, Mass. d: 9/11/23, Worcester, Mass.   BR/TR, 5'8", 165 lbs.   Deb: 8/27/1890 ♦

YEAR TM/L	W	L	PCT	G	GS	CG	SH	SV	IP	H	HR	BB	SO	RAT	ERA	ERA+	OAV	OOB	BH	AVG	PB	PR	/A	PD	TPI
1890 Buf-P	3	9	.250	12	12	11	0	0	98	123	8	43	21	15.2	5.14	80	.294	.360	7	.143	-1	-10	-11	-1	-1.0

■ JOHN STAFFORD   Stafford, John Henry "Doc" b: 4/8/1870, Dudley, Mass. d: 7/3/40, Worcester, Mass.   BR/TR, 5'10", 170 lbs.   Deb: 6/15/1893

YEAR TM/L	W	L	PCT	G	GS	CG	SH	SV	IP	H	HR	BB	SO	RAT	ERA	ERA+	OAV	OOB	BH	AVG	PB	PR	/A	PD	TPI
1893 Cle-N	0	1	.000	2	0	0	0	0	7	12	1	7	4	24.4	14.14	35	.367	.478	0	.000	-1	-7	-7	-0	-0.5

■ BILL STAFFORD   Stafford, William Charles b: 8/13/39, Catskill, N.Y.   BR/TR, 6'1", 188 lbs.   Deb: 4/17/60

YEAR TM/L	W	L	PCT	G	GS	CG	SH	SV	IP	H	HR	BB	SO	RAT	ERA	ERA+	OAV	OOB	BH	AVG	PB	PR	/A	PD	TPI
1960 *NY-A	3	1	.750	11	8	2	1	0	60	50	3	18	36	10.4	2.25	159	.226	.287	1	.045	-2	11	9	1	0.8
1961 *NY-A	14	9	.609	36	25	8	3	2	195	168	13	59	101	10.7	2.68	139	.232	.294	12	.179	2	29	23	-0	2.4
1962 *NY-A	14	9	.609	35	33	7	2	0	213¹	188	23	77	109	11.3	3.67	102	.233	.303	17	.218	3	7	2	-1	0.3
1963 NY-A	4	8	.333	28	14	0	0	3	89²	104	16	42	52	15.0	6.02	58	.287	.366	7	.292	3	-24	-25	-0	-2.2
1964 NY-A	5	0	1.000	31	1	0	0	4	60²	50	4	22	39	11.0	2.67	136	.231	.308	1	.077	-1	6	6	0	0.6
1965 NY-A	3	8	.273	22	15	1	0	0	111¹	93	16	31	71	10.2	3.56	96	.229	.286	0	.000	-3	-1	-2	0	-0.4
1966 KC-A	0	4	.000	9	8	0	0	0	39²	42	2	12	31	12.7	4.99	68	.273	.333	0	.000	-1	-7	-7	-1	-0.8
1967 KC-A	0	1	.000	14	0	0	0	0	16	12	0	9	10	11.8	1.69	189	.214	.323	0	.000	-0	3	3	0	0.3
Total 8	43	40	.518	186	104	18	6	9	785²	707	77	270	449	11.4	3.52	103	.240	.308	38	.155	0	24	9	-1	1.0

■ CHICK STAHL   Stahl, Charles Sylvester b: 1/10/1873, Avila, Ind. d: 3/28/07, W.Baden, Ind.   BL/TL, 5'10", 160 lbs.   Deb: 4/19/1897   M♦

YEAR TM/L	W	L	PCT	G	GS	CG	SH	SV	IP	H	HR	BB	SO	RAT	ERA	ERA+	OAV	OOB	BH	AVG	PB	PR	/A	PD	TPI
1899 Bos-N	0	0	—	1	0	0	0	0	2	2	0	3	0	22.5	9.00	46	.260	.468	202	.351	0	-1	-1	0	0.0

■ GERRY STALEY   Staley, Gerald Lee b: 8/21/20, Brush Prairie, Wash.   BR/TR, 6', 195 lbs.   Deb: 4/20/47

YEAR TM/L	W	L	PCT	G	GS	CG	SH	SV	IP	H	HR	BB	SO	RAT	ERA	ERA+	OAV	OOB	BH	AVG	PB	PR	/A	PD	TPI
1947 StL-N	1	0	1.000	18	1	1	0	0	29¹	33	2	8	14	12.9	2.76	150	.287	.339	0	.000	-1	4	4	1	0.5
1948 StL-N	4	4	.500	31	3	0	0	0	52	61	5	21	23	14.2	6.92	59	.288	.352	2	.222	1	-17	-16	1	-1.3
1949 StL-N	10	10	.500	45	17	5	2	6	171¹	154	7	41	55	10.4	2.73	152	.238	.286	5	.122	-0	25	27	4	3.1
1950 StL-N	13	13	.500	42	22	7	1	3	169²	201	14	61	62	14.3	4.99	86	.300	.365	4	.145	-1	-16	-13	4	-0.9
1951 StL-N	19	13	.594	42	30	10	4	3	227	244	14	74	67	12.9	3.81	104	.275	.337	13	.160	-1	4	4	3	0.5
1952 StL-N	17	14	.548	35	33	15	0	0	239²	238	21	52	93	11.2	3.27	114	.256	.301	13	.153	-2	12	12	4	1.5
1953 StL-N	18	9	.667	40	32	10	1	4	230	243	31	54	88	12.3	3.99	107	.269	.322	8	.103	-4	8	7	3	0.5
1954 StL-N	7	13	.350	48	20	3	1	2	155²	198	21	47	50	14.5	5.26	78	.308	.361	5	.139	-2	-21	-20	3	-1.6
1955 Cin-N	5	8	.385	30	18	2	0	0	119²	146	22	28	40	13.3	4.66	91	.308	.351	2	.056	-4	-8	-6	1	-0.7
NY-A	0	0	—	2	0	0	0	0	2	5	1	1	0	27.0	13.50	28	.417	.462	0	—	0	-2	-2	0	-0.1
1956 NY-A	0	0	—	1	0	0	0	0	0¹	4	0	1	0	108.0	108.00	4	.800	.800	0	—	0	-4	-4	0	-0.2
Chi-A	8	3	.727	26	10	5	0	0	101²	98	11	20	25	11.0	2.92	140	.251	.298	3	.094	-2	14	13	1	1.2
Yr	8	3	.727	27	10	5	0	0	102	102	11	20	26	11.3	3.26	126	.258	.304	2	.061	-2	10	9	1	1.0
1957 Chi-A	5	1	.833	47	0	0	0	7	105	95	7	27	44	10.5	2.06	182	.244	.293	1	.045	-1	20	20	2	2.2
1958 Chi-A	4	5	.444	50	0	0	0	8	85¹	81	10	24	27	11.1	3.16	115	.259	.312	0	.000	-1	6	4	3	0.7
1959 *Chi-A	8	5	.615	67	0	0	0	14	116¹	111	5	25	54	10.5	2.24	167	.259	.300	2	.154	-3	21	20	2	2.0
1960 Chi-A	13	8	.619	64	0	0	0	10	115¹	94	8	25	52	9.5	2.42	156	.227	.276	4	.235	1	19	17	3	2.2
1961 Chi-A	0	3	.000	16	0	0	0	0	18	17	3	5	8	11.0	5.00	78	.246	.297	0	—	0	-2	-2	0	-0.1
KC-A	1	1	.500	23	0	0	0	2	30	32	4	10	16	13.2	3.60	114	.278	.346	0	.000	-0	1	2	1	0.3
Det-A	1	1	.500	13	0	0	0	2	13¹	15	1	6	8	14.2	3.38	121	.288	.362	0	.000	-0	1	1	0	0.1
Yr	2	5	.286	52	0	0	0	4	61¹	64	8	21	32	12.5	3.96	102	.267	.326	1	.500	0	1	1	1	0.3
Total 15	134	111	.547	640	186	58	9	61	1981²	2070	187	529	727	12.1	3.70	108	.270	.322	66	.126	-16	65	68	33	9.9

■ HARRY STALEY   Staley, Henry E. b: 11/3/1866, Jacksonville, Ill. d: 1/12/10, Battle Creek, Mich   BR/TR, 5'10", 175 lbs.   Deb: 6/23/1888

YEAR TM/L	W	L	PCT	G	GS	CG	SH	SV	IP	H	HR	BB	SO	RAT	ERA	ERA+	OAV	OOB	BH	AVG	PB	PR	/A	PD	TPI
1888 Pit-N	12	12	.500	25	24	24	2	0	207¹	185	6	53	89	10.3	2.69	98	.230	.278	11	.129	-3	3	-1	-1	-0.5
1889 Pit-N	21	26	.447	49	47	46	1	1	420	433	11	116	159	11.8	3.51	107	.258	.306	30	.161	-6	24	11	2	0.5
1890 Pit-P	21	25	.457	46	46	44	3	0	387²	392	5	74	145	10.8	3.23	121	.251	.285	34	.207	1	43	29	-3	2.1
1891 Pit-N	4	5	.444	9	7	6	0	0	71²	77	4	11	25	11.1	2.89	114	.264	.271	7	.226	1	4	3	0	0.4
Bos-N	20	8	.714	31	30	26	1	0	252¹	236	11	69	114	10.9	2.50	146	.238	.288	17	.167	-2	24	33	-1	2.9
Yr	24	13	.649	40	37	32	1	0	324	313	15	80	139	10.9	2.58	138	.244	.289	11	.083	-1	28	36	-1	3.3
1892 *Bos-N	22	10	.688	37	35	31	3	0	299²	273	10	97	93	11.1	3.03	116	.233	.292	16	.131	-6	8	16	-1	0.9
1893 Bos-N	18	10	.643	36	31	23	0	0	263	344	22	81	61	14.5	5.13	96	.307	.353	30	.265	3	-14	-6	-1	-0.1
1894 Bos-N	12	10	.545	27	21	18	0	0	208²	305	15	61	32	15.8	6.81	83	.337	.379	20	.235	0	-35	-26	-3	-1.9
1895 StL-N	6	13	.316	23	16	13	0	0	158²	223	8	39	28	14.9	5.22	93	.326	.363	9	.134	-6	-8	-7	-2	-1.1
Total 8	136	119	.533	283	257	231	10	1	2269	2468	92	601	746	12.2	3.80	105	.268	.313	174	.182	-18	51	51	-9	3.2

■ TRACY STALLARD   Stallard, Evan Tracy b: 8/31/37, Coeburn, Va.   BR/TR, 6'5", 204 lbs.   Deb: 9/24/60

YEAR TM/L	W	L	PCT	G	GS	CG	SH	SV	IP	H	HR	BB	SO	RAT	ERA	ERA+	OAV	OOB	BH	AVG	PB	PR	/A	PD	TPI
1960 Bos-A	0	0	—	4	0	0	0	0	4	2	0	6	4	6.5	0.00	—	.000	.133	0	—	0	2	2	0	0.2
1961 Bos-A	2	7	.222	43	14	1	0	2	132²	110	15	96	109	14.0	4.88	85	.229	.359	3	.083	-3	-13	-11	-2	-1.4
1962 Bos-A	0	0	—	1	0	0	0	0	1	1	0	0	0	0.0	0.00	—	.000	.000	0	—	0	0	0	0	0.0
1963 NY-N	6	17	.261	39	23	5	0	1	154²	156	23	77	110	13.6	4.71	74	.262	.347	3	.063	-3	-24	-21	-2	-2.5
1964 NY-N	10	20	.333	36	34	11	2	0	225²	213	20	73	118	11.6	3.79	94	.252	.316	15	.190	2	-6	-5	-2	-0.5
1965 StL-N	11	8	.579	40	26	4	1	0	194¹	172	25	70	99	11.5	3.38	114	.235	.307	6	.088	-4	3	10	-1	-0.5
1966 StL-N	1	5	.167	20	7	0	0	1	52¹	65	9	25	35	15.8	5.68	63	.305	.383	0	.000	-2	-12	-12	0	-1.3
Total 7	30	57	.345	183	104	21	3	4	764²	716	92	343	477	12.7	4.17	90	.248	.332	27	.110	-10	-50	-37	-7	-5.0

■ CHARLEY STANCEU   Stanceu, Charles b: 1/9/16, Canton, Ohio d: 4/3/69, Canton, Ohio   BR/TR, 6'2", 190 lbs.   Deb: 4/16/41

YEAR TM/L	W	L	PCT	G	GS	CG	SH	SV	IP	H	HR	BB	SO	RAT	ERA	ERA+	OAV	OOB	BH	AVG	PB	PR	/A	PD	TPI
1941 NY-A	3	3	.500	22	2	0	0	0	58	58	3	35	21	17.6	5.63	70	.296	.405	0	.000	-2	-8	-9	-1	-1.0
1946 NY-A	0	0	—	3	0	0	0	0	4	6	0	5	3	24.8	9.00	38	.316	.458	0	—	0	-2	-2	0	-0.1
Phi-N	2	4	.333	14	11	1	0	0	70¹	71	4	39	23	14.1	4.22	81	.270	.364	0	.000	-2	-6	-6	-1	-0.8
Total 2	5	7	.417	39	13	1	0	0	122¹	135	7	79	47	15.8	4.93	74	.282	.385	0	.000	-3	-17	-18	-1	-1.9

YEAR TM/L	W	L	PCT	G	GS	CG	SH	SV	IP	H	HR	BB	SO	RAT	ERA	ERA+	OAV	OOB	BH	AVG	PB	PR	/A	PD	TPI
■ PETE STANDRIDGE							Standridge, Alfred Peter		b: 4/25/1891, Black Diamond, Wash.				d: 8/2/63, San Francisco, Cal.				BR/TR, 5'10.5", 165 lbs.		Deb: 9/19/11					
1911 StL-N	0	0	—	2	0	0	0	0	4²	10	0	4	3	28.9	9.64	35	.435	.536	0	.000	-0	-3	-3	0	-0.2
1915 Chi-N	4	1	.800	29	3	2	0	0	112¹	120	2	36	42	12.7	3.61	77	.274	.332	9	.225	3	-11	-10	1	-0.7
Total 2	4	1	.800	31	3	2	0	0	117	130	2	40	45	13.3	3.85	73	.282	.343	9	.220	3	-14	-14	1	-0.9
■ AL STANEK					Stanek, Albert Wilfred "Lefty"		b: 12/24/43, Springfield, Mass.			BL/TL, 5'11.5", 190 lbs.		Deb: 4/26/63												
1963 SF-N	0	0	—	11	0	0	0	0	13¹	10	1	12	5	14.9	4.73	68	.217	.379	0	.000	-0	-2	-2	1	-0.1
■ KEVIN STANFIELD					Stanfield, Kevin Bruce		b: 12/19/55, Huron, S.Dak.			BL/TL, 6', 190 lbs.		Deb: 9/14/79												
1979 Min-A	0	0	—	3	0	0	0	0	3	2	0	0	0	6.0	6.00	73	.200	.200	0	—	0	-1	-1	0	0.0
■ LEE STANGE					Stange, Albert Lee		b: 10/27/36, Chicago, Ill.			BR/TR, 5'10", 170 lbs.		Deb: 4/15/61 C												
1961 Min-A	1	0	1.000	7	0	0	0	0	12¹	15	1	10	10	18.2	2.92	145	.294	.410	0	.000	-0	2	2	0	0.2
1962 Min-A	4	3	.571	44	6	1	0	3	95	98	14	39	70	13.1	4.45	92	.271	.343	1	.059	-1	-5	-4	-0	-0.4
1963 Min-A	12	5	.706	32	20	7	2	0	164²	145	21	43	100	10.3	2.62	139	.233	.283	5	.096	-1	18	19	-0	1.8
1964 Min-A	3	6	.333	14	11	2	0	0	79²	78	13	19	54	11.0	4.74	75	.255	.298	1	.040	-1	-10	-10	1	-0.9
Cle-A	4	8	.333	23	14	0	0	0	91²	98	14	31	78	12.8	4.12	87	.270	.329	2	.080	-1	-5	-5	-0	-0.6
Yr	7	14	.333	37	25	2	0	0	171¹	176	27	50	132	11.9	4.41	81	.262	.314	8	.160	-2	-15	-16	0	-1.5
1965 Cle-A	8	4	.667	41	12	4	2	0	132	122	13	26	80	10.2	3.34	104	.247	.286	3	.107	1	2	2	-2	0.2
1966 Cle-A	1	0	1.000	8	2	1	0	0	16	17	1	3	8	11.8	2.81	122	.279	.323	1	.250	1	1	1	-0	0.1
Bos-A	7	9	.438	28	19	8	2	0	153¹	140	17	43	77	10.8	3.35	114	.246	.300	3	.063	-4	2	8	-1	0.4
Yr	8	9	.471	36	21	9	2	0	169¹	157	18	46	85	10.8	3.30	114	.248	.300	2	.038	-3	3	9	-1	0.5
1967 *Bos-A	8	10	.444	35	24	6	2	1	181²	171	14	32	101	10.2	2.77	126	.246	.282	3	.061	-3	9	14	-2	1.1
1968 Bos-A	5	5	.500	50	2	1	0	12	103	89	10	25	53	10.0	3.93	86	.237	.286	2	.133	0	-11	-9	-1	-1.0
1969 Bos-A	6	9	.400	41	15	2	0	3	137	137	14	56	59	13.1	3.68	103	.256	.333	3	.086	-2	-1	2	-1	0.0
1970 Bos-A	2	2	.500	20	0	0	0	2	27¹	34	5	12	14	15.8	5.60	71	.301	.378	0	.000	-0	-6	-5	0	-0.4
Chi-A	1	0	1.000	16	0	0	0	0	22¹	28	5	5	14	13.3	5.24	74	.295	.330	0	.000	-0	-4	-3	0	-0.3
Yr	3	2	.600	36	0	0	0	2	49²	62	10	17	28	14.3	5.44	72	.291	.343	1	.167	-0	-10	-8	0	-0.7
Total 10	62	61	.504	359	125	32	8	21	1216	1172	142	344	718	11.3	3.56	102	.252	.306	24	.079	-12	-8	12	-6	0.2
■ DON STANHOUSE					Stanhouse, Donald Joseph		b: 2/12/51, DuQuoin, Ill.			BR/TR, 6'2.5", 185 lbs.		Deb: 4/19/72												
1972 Tex-A	2	9	.182	24	16	1	0	1	104²	83	8	73	78	13.5	3.78	80	.223	.351	4	.129	-0	-8	-9	2	-0.7
1973 Tex-A	1	7	.125	21	5	1	0	1	70	70	5	44	42	14.9	4.76	78	.262	.371	0	—	0	-7	-8	2	-0.5
1974 Tex-A	1	1	.500	18	0	0	0	0	31¹	38	4	17	26	16.4	4.88	73	.302	.393	0	—	0	-4	-5	1	-0.3
1975 Mon-N	0	0	—	4	3	0	0	0	13	19	1	11	5	20.8	8.31	46	.345	.455	1	.333	-0	-7	-6	0	-0.5
1976 Mon-N	9	12	.429	34	26	8	1	1	184	182	7	92	79	13.6	3.77	99	.263	.352	11	.212	2	-5	-1	3	0.5
1977 Mon-N	10	10	.500	47	16	1	1	10	158¹	147	12	84	89	13.4	3.41	112	.251	.349	9	.191	1	9	7	-1	0.7
1978 Bal-A	6	9	.400	56	0	0	0	24	74²	60	0	52	42	13.5	2.89	121	.230	.358	0	—	0	7	5	0	0.5
1979 *Bal-A	7	3	.700	52	0	0	0	21	72²	49	4	51	34	12.5	2.85	141	.202	.342	0	—	0	11	9	1	1.0
1980 LA-N	2	2	.500	21	0	0	0	7	25	30	4	16	5	16.6	5.04	69	.306	.404	0	.000	0	-4	-4	1	-0.2
1982 Bal-A	0	1	.000	17	0	0	0	0	26²	29	3	15	8	15.5	5.40	75	.276	.377	0	—	0	-4	-4	0	-0.3
Total 10	38	54	.413	294	66	11	2	64	760¹	707	48	455	408	13.9	3.84	105	.252	.359	25	.185	4	-13	-16	9	0.2
■ JOE STANKA					Stanka, Joe Donald		b: 7/23/31, Hammon, Okla.			BR/TR, 6'5", 201 lbs.		Deb: 9/02/59												
1959 Chi-A	1	0	1.000	2	0	0	0	0	5¹	2	1	4	3	10.1	3.38	111	.111	.273	1	.333	0	0	0	-0	0.0
■ BUCK STANLEY					Stanley, John Leonard		b: 11/13/1889, Washington, D.C.			d: 8/13/40, Norfolk, Va.		BL/TL, 5'10", 160 lbs.		Deb: 9/12/11										
1911 Phi-N	0	0	—	4	0	0	0	0	11¹	14	0	9	5	18.3	6.35	54	.326	.442	0	.000	-1	-4	-4	-1	-0.4
■ JOE STANLEY					Stanley, Joseph Bernard		b: 4/2/1881, Washington, D.C.			d: 9/13/67, Detroit, Mich.		BB/TR, 5'9.5", 150 lbs.		Deb: 9/11/1897 ◆									
1897 Was-N	0	0	—	1	0	0	0	0	0²	0	0	0	0	0.0	0.00	—	.000	.000	0	.000	-0	0	0	0	0.0
1903 Bos-N	0	0	—	1	0	0	0	0	4	4	0	4	4	20.3	9.00	36	.286	.474	77	.250	0	-3	-3	-0	-0.1
1906 Was-A	0	0	—	1	0	0	0	0	3	3	1	1	0	12.0	12.00	22	.263	.323	36	.163	-0	-3	-3	0	-0.2
Total 3	0	0	—	3	0	0	0	0	7²	7	1	5	4	15.3	9.39	33	.256	.390	148	.213	-0	-5	-5	-0	-0.3
■ BOB STANLEY					Stanley, Robert William		b: 11/10/54, Portland, Maine			BR/TR, 6'4", 210 lbs.		Deb: 4/16/77												
1977 Bos-A	8	7	.533	41	13	3	1	3	151	176	10	43	44	13.2	3.99	112	.294	.344	0	—	0	1	8	4	1.2
1978 Bos-A	15	2	.882	52	3	0	0	10	141²	142	5	34	38	11.2	2.60	158	.266	.312	0	—	0	18	24	3	2.8
1979 Bos-A	16	12	.571	40	30	9	4	1	216²	250	14	44	56	12.4	3.99	114	.294	.332	0	—	0	5	10	3	1.3
1980 Bos-A	10	8	.556	52	17	5	1	14	175	186	11	52	71	12.6	3.39	124	.278	.337	0	—	0	12	16	4	2.0
1981 Bos-A	10	8	.556	35	1	0	0	0	98²	110	3	38	28	14.0	3.83	101	.294	.368	0	—	0	-2	0	4	0.4
1982 Bos-A	12	7	.632	48	0	0	0	14	168¹	161	11	50	83	11.5	3.10	139	.255	.313	0	—	0	18	23	4	2.8
1983 Bos-A	8	10	.444	64	0	0	0	33	145¹	145	7	38	65	11.5	2.85	153	.266	.317	0	—	0	20	24	-0	2.4
1984 Bos-A	9	10	.474	57	0	0	0	22	106²	113	9	23	52	11.6	3.54	117	.267	.308	0	—	0	5	7	3	1.0
1985 Bos-A	6	6	.500	48	0	0	0	10	87²	76	7	30	46	11.1	2.87	149	.237	.306	0	—	0	12	14	0	1.4
1986 *Bos-A	6	6	.500	66	1	0	0	16	82¹	109	9	22	54	14.3	4.37	95	.322	.364	0	—	0	-2	-2	1	0.0
1987 Bos-A	4	15	.211	34	20	4	1	0	152²	198	17	42	67	14.2	5.01	91	.321	.366	0	—	0	-9	-8	-1	-0.5
1988 *Bos-A	6	4	.600	57	0	0	0	5	101²	90	6	29	57	11.2	3.19	129	.242	.309	0	—	0	9	10	0	1.1
1989 Bos-A	5	2	.714	43	0	0	0	4	79¹	90	4	26	32	14.6	4.88	84	.321	.374	0	—	0	-9	-7	1	-0.5
Total 13	115	97	.542	637	85	21	7	132	1707	1858	113	471	693	12.5	3.64	117	.282	.334	0	—	0	80	121	26	15.4
■ MIKE STANTON					Stanton, Michael Thomas		b: 9/25/52, Phenix City, Ala.			BB/TR, 6'2", 205 lbs.		Deb: 7/09/75												
1975 Hou-N	0	2	.000	7	2	0	0	1	17¹	20	1	20	16	20.8	7.27	46	.290	.449	1	.250	0	-7	-8	0	-0.6
1980 Cle-A	1	3	.250	51	0	0	0	5	85²	98	5	44	74	15.2	5.46	75	.297	.385	0	—	0	-14	-13	1	-1.1
1981 Cle-A	3	3	.500	24	0	0	0	2	43¹	43	4	18	34	12.7	4.36	83	.262	.335	0	—	0	-3	-4	-1	-0.3
1982 Sea-A	2	4	.333	56	1	0	0	7	71¹	70	5	21	49	11.5	4.16	102	.260	.314	0	—	0	-1	1	1	0.2
1983 Sea-A	2	3	.400	50	0	0	0	7	65	65	3	28	47	13.0	3.32	128	.273	.352	0	—	0	5	7	0	0.6
1984 Sea-A	4	4	.500	54	0	0	0	8	61	55	3	22	55	11.7	3.54	113	.241	.313	0	—	0	3	3	-1	0.2
1985 Sea-A	1	2	.333	24	0	0	0	1	29	32	4	21	17	17.4	5.28	80	.278	.403	0	—	0	-4	-3	1	-0.2
Chi-A	0	1	.000	11	0	0	0	0	11²	15	2	8	12	17.7	9.26	47	.294	.390	0	—	0	-7	-6	-0	-0.5
Yr	1	3	.250	35	0	0	0	1	40²	47	6	29	29	16.8	6.42	66	.278	.384	0	—	0	-10	-10	1	-0.7
Total 7	13	22	.371	277	3	0	0	31	384¹	398	27	182	304	13.8	4.61	88	.272	.356	1	.250	0	-27	-24	1	-1.7
■ MIKE STANTON					Stanton, William Michael		b: 6/2/67, Galena Park, Tex.			BL/TL, 6'1", 190 lbs.		Deb: 8/24/89												
1989 Atl-N	0	1	.000	20	0	0	0	7	24	17	0	8	27	9.4	1.50	243	.207	.278	0	—	0	5	6	-0	0.6
1990 Atl-N	0	3	.000	7	0	0	0	2	7	16	1	4	7	27.0	18.00	22	.444	.512	0	—	0	-11	-11	0	-0.9
Total 2	0	4	.000	27	0	0	0	9	31	33	1	12	34	13.4	5.23	71	.280	.351	0	—	0	-6	-5	-0	-0.3
■ DAVE STAPLETON					Stapleton, David Earl		b: 10/16/61, Miami, Arizona			BL/TL, 6'1", 185 lbs.		Deb: 9/14/87												
1987 Mil-A	2	0	1.000	4	0	0	0	0	14²	13	0	3	14	9.8	1.84	248	.241	.281	0	—	0	4	4	0	0.4
1988 Mil-A	0	0	—	6	0	0	0	0	13²	20	1	9	6	19.8	5.93	67	.339	.435	0	—	0	-3	-3	0	-0.2
Total 2	2	0	1.000	10	0	0	0	0	28¹	33	1	12	20	14.6	3.81	112	.292	.365	0	—	0	1	1	0	0.2
■ CON STARKEL					Starkel, Conrad		b: 11/16/1880, Germany			d: 1/19/33, Tacoma, Wash.		BR/TR, 6', 200 lbs.		Deb: 4/19/06										
1906 Was-A	0	0	—	1	0	0	0	0	3	7	1	2	1	27.0	18.00	15	.455	.518	0	—	0	-5	-5	-0	-0.3

YEAR	TM/L	W	L	PCT	G	GS	CG	SH	SV	IP	H	HR	BB	SO	RAT	ERA	ERA+	OAV	OOB	BH	AVG	PB	PR	/A	PD	TPI

■ RAY STARR   Starr, Raymond Francis "Iron Man"   b: 4/23/06, Nowata, Okla.   d: 2/9/63, Baylis, Ill.   BR/TR, 6'1", 178 lbs.   Deb: 9/11/32

YEAR	TM/L	W	L	PCT	G	GS	CG	SH	SV	IP	H	HR	BB	SO	RAT	ERA	ERA+	OAV	OOB	BH	AVG	PB	PR	/A	PD	TPI
1932	StL-N	1	1	.500	3	2	1	1	0	20	19	2	10	6	13.5	2.70	146	.284	.385	1	.250	0	3	3	1	0.3
1933	NY-N	0	1	.000	6	2	0	0	0	13¹	19	0	10	2	20.3	5.40	59	.339	.448	0	.000	-0	-3	-3	0	-0.3
	Bos-N	0	1	.000	9	1	0	0	0	28	32	4	9	15	13.5	3.86	79	.296	.356	1	.143	0	-2	-2	0	-0.1
	Yr	0	2	.000	15	3	0	0	0	41¹	51	4	19	17	15.5	4.35	71	.309	.384	1	.100	-0	-5	-6	0	-0.4
1941	Cin-N	3	2	.600	7	4	3	2	0	34	28	1	6	11	9.3	2.65	136	.219	.259	2	.182	-0	4	4	0	0.4
1942	Cin-N	15	13	.536	37	33	17	4	0	276²	228	10	106	83	11.0	2.67	123	.226	.301	8	.091	-4	20	19	-1	1.5
1943	Cin-N	11	10	.524	36	33	9	2	1	217¹	201	9	91	62	12.3	3.64	91	.248	.328	9	.122	-4	-6	-8	0	-1.1
1944	Pit-N	6	5	.545	27	12	5	0	3	89²	116	6	36	25	15.4	5.02	74	.314	.377	3	.136	1	-14	-13	-1	-1.2
1945	Pit-N	0	2	.000	4	0	0	0	0	6²	10	0	4	0	18.9	9.45	42	.370	.452	1	1.000	1	-4	-4	0	-0.2
	Chi-N	1	0	1.000	9	1	0	0	0	13¹	17	1	7	5	16.2	7.43	49	.298	.375	1	.500	0	-5	-6	0	-0.4
	Yr	1	2	.333	13	1	0	0	0	20	27	1	11	5	17.1	8.10	46	.321	.400	2	.667	1	-10	-10	0	-0.6
Total	7	37	35	.514	138	88	35	9	4	699	670	33	279	189	12.4	3.53	96	.255	.329	26	.123	-7	-8	-11	0	-1.1

■ DICK STARR   Starr, Richard Eugene   b: 3/2/21, Kittanning, Pa.   BR/TR, 6'3", 190 lbs.   Deb: 9/05/47

YEAR	TM/L	W	L	PCT	G	GS	CG	SH	SV	IP	H	HR	BB	SO	RAT	ERA	ERA+	OAV	OOB	BH	AVG	PB	PR	/A	PD	TPI
1947	NY-A	1	0	1.000	4	1	1	0	0	12¹	12	1	8	1	14.6	1.46	242	.250	.357	1	.333	1	3	3	0	0.4
1948	NY-A	0	0	—	1	0	0	0	0	2	0	0	2	2	9.0	4.50	91	.000	.250	0	—	0	-0	-0	0	0.0
1949	StL-A	1	7	.125	30	8	1	1	0	83¹	96	6	48	44	15.7	4.32	105	.292	.384	2	.087	-1	-1	2	-1	0.0
1950	StL-A	7	5	.583	32	16	4	1	2	123²	140	11	74	30	16.1	5.02	99	.287	.389	5	.139	-3	-6	-1	-1	-0.3
1951	StL-A	2	5	.286	15	9	0	0	0	62	66	10	42	26	16.0	7.40	59	.273	.385	4	.222	0	-23	-21	-1	-1.8
	Was-A	1	7	.125	11	11	1	0	0	61¹	76	12	24	17	14.7	5.58	73	.304	.365	3	.176	1	-10	-10	-1	-1.0
	Yr	3	12	.200	26	20	1	0	0	123¹	142	22	66	43	15.2	6.49	65	.287	.371	5	.143	1	-33	-31	-2	-2.8
Total	5	12	24	.333	93	45	7	2	2	344²	390	40	198	120	15.6	5.25	86	.286	.381	15	.155	-3	-37	-27	-4	-2.7

■ HERMAN STARRETTE   Starrette, Herman Paul   b: 11/20/38, Statesville, N.C.   BR/TR, 6', 175 lbs.   Deb: 7/01/63   C

YEAR	TM/L	W	L	PCT	G	GS	CG	SH	SV	IP	H	HR	BB	SO	RAT	ERA	ERA+	OAV	OOB	BH	AVG	PB	PR	/A	PD	TPI
1963	Bal-A	0	1	.000	18	0	0	0	0	26	26	1	7	13	12.1	3.46	102	.271	.333	0	.000	0	0	0	1	0.1
1964	Bal-A	1	0	1.000	5	0	0	0	0	11	9	0	6	5	12.3	1.64	218	.250	.357	0	.000	-0	2	2	-0	0.2
1965	Bal-A	0	0	—	4	0	0	0	0	9	8	0	3	3	11.0	1.00	347	.258	.324	0	.000	-0	2	2	0	0.3
Total	3	1	1	.500	27	0	0	0	0	46	43	1	16	21	11.9	2.54	139	.264	.337	0	.000	-0	5	5	1	0.6

■ ED STAUFFER   Stauffer, Charles Edward   b: 1/10/1898, Emsworth, Pa.   d: 7/2/79, St.Petersburg, Fla   BR/TR, 5'11", 185 lbs.   Deb: 4/26/23

YEAR	TM/L	W	L	PCT	G	GS	CG	SH	SV	IP	H	HR	BB	SO	RAT	ERA	ERA+	OAV	OOB	BH	AVG	PB	PR	/A	PD	TPI
1923	Chi-N	0	0	—	1	0	0	0	0	2	5	0	1	0	27.0	13.50	30	.556	.600	0	—	0	-2	-2	0	-0.1
1925	StL-A	0	1	.000	20	1	0	0	0	30¹	34	1	21	13	16.3	5.34	87	.283	.390	1	.250	-0	-3	-2	-1	-0.2
Total	2	0	1	.000	21	1	0	0	0	32¹	39	1	22	13	17.0	5.85	79	.302	.404	1	.250	-0	-5	-4	-1	-0.3

■ BILL STEARNS   Stearns, William E.   b: 3/20/1853, Washington, D.C.   d: 12/30/1898, Washington, D.C.   Deb: 6/26/1871

YEAR	TM/L	W	L	PCT	G	GS	CG	SH	SV	IP	H	HR	BB	SO	RAT	ERA	ERA+	OAV	OOB	BH	AVG	PB	PR	/A	PD	TPI
1871	Oly-n	2	0	1.000	2	2	2	0	0	18	10	0	8	0	9.0	2.50	167	.149	.240	0	.000	-1	3	3		0.1
1872	Nat-n	0	11	.000	11	11	11	0	0	99	194	2	5		18.1	6.91	68	.340	.346	11	.234	-4	-35	-24		-1.6
1873	Was-n	7	25	.219	32	32	32	0	0	283	475	8	11		15.5	5.02	74	.326	.331	24	.179	-7	-45	-42		-3.1
1874	Har-n	2	14	.125	22	18	14	0	1	164	255	1	13		14.7	4.50	70	.311	.322	21	.159	-5	-27	-24		-2.2
1875	Was-n	1	14	.067	17	16	14	0	0	141	243	1	4		15.8	5.36	49	.332	.335	20	.260	-1	-45	-43		-3.2
Total	5 n	12	64	.158	84	79	73	0	1	705	1177	12	41	0	15.5	5.17	51	.323	.330	76	.190	-17	-212	-200		-10.0

■ CHARLIE STECHER   Stecher, Charles   b: Bordentown, N.J.   Deb: 9/06/1890

YEAR	TM/L	W	L	PCT	G	GS	CG	SH	SV	IP	H	HR	BB	SO	RAT	ERA	ERA+	OAV	OOB	BH	AVG	PB	PR	/A	PD	TPI
1890	Phi-a	0	10	.000	10	10	9	0	0	68	111	1	60	18	22.6	10.32	37	.355	.459	7	.241	1	-49	-49	2	-3.4

■ ELMER STEELE   Steele, Elmer Rae   b: 5/17/1886, Muitzeskill, N.Y.   d: 3/9/66, Rhinebeck, N.Y.   BB/TR, 5'11", 200 lbs.   Deb: 9/12/07

YEAR	TM/L	W	L	PCT	G	GS	CG	SH	SV	IP	H	HR	BB	SO	RAT	ERA	ERA+	OAV	OOB	BH	AVG	PB	PR	/A	PD	TPI
1907	Bos-A	0	1	.000	4	1	0	0	0	11¹	11	0	4	10	9.5	1.59	163	.256	.273	0	.000	-1	1	1	0	0.1
1908	Bos-A	5	7	.417	16	13	9	1	0	118	85	1	13	37	7.7	1.83	135	.209	.239	2	.051	-4	7	8	-1	0.5
1909	Bos-A	4	4	.500	16	8	2	0	1	75²	75	1	15	30	10.8	2.85	88	.255	.294	6	.250	-1	-3	-3	0	-0.1
1910	Pit-N	0	3	.000	3	3	2	0	0	24	19	0	3	7	8.3	2.25	138	.221	.247	0	.000	-1	2	2	1	0.3
1911	Pit-N	9	9	.500	31	16	7	2	2	166	153	5	31	52	10.2	2.60	132	.256	.297	11	.180	-0	15	15	2	1.7
	Bro-N	0	0	—	5	2	0	0	0	23	24	0	5	9	11.3	3.13	107	.258	.296	0	.000	-1	1	1	0	0.0
	Yr	9	9	.500	36	18	7	2	2	189	177	5	36	61	10.1	2.67	128	.255	.292	5	.071	-1	15	16	3	1.7
Total	5	18	24	.429	75	43	20	3	3	418	367	7	68	147	9.5	2.41	122	.241	.278	19	.132	-5	23	25	4	2.5

■ BOB STEELE   Steele, Robert Wesley   b: 1/5/1894, Cassburn, Ont., Can.   d: 1/27/62, Ocala, Fla.   BB/TL, 5'10.5", 175 lbs.   Deb: 4/17/16

YEAR	TM/L	W	L	PCT	G	GS	CG	SH	SV	IP	H	HR	BB	SO	RAT	ERA	ERA+	OAV	OOB	BH	AVG	PB	PR	/A	PD	TPI
1916	StL-N	5	15	.250	29	22	7	1	0	148	156	6	42	67	12.2	3.41	78	.285	.340	10	.196	-1	-13	-13	-3	-1.7
1917	StL-N	1	3	.250	12	6	1	0	0	42	33	1	19	23	11.1	3.21	84	.223	.311	5	.385	2	-2	-2	-1	-0.1
	Pit-N	5	11	.313	27	19	13	1	1	179²	158	0	53	82	10.8	2.76	103	.237	.298	17	.224	1	-1	2	-2	0.0
	Yr	6	14	.300	39	25	14	1	1	221²	191	1	72	105	10.9	2.84	99	.235	.301	0	.000	2	-3	-1	-3	-0.1
1918	Pit-N	2	3	.400	10	4	2	1	1	49	44	2	17	21	11.6	3.31	87	.240	.312	2	.125	-0	-3	-2	-0	-0.2
	NY-N	3	5	.375	12	7	5	1	1	66	56	1	11	24	9.5	2.59	101	.226	.267	6	.286	2	1	0	-3	0.0
	Yr	5	8	.385	22	11	7	2	2	115	100	3	28	45	10.3	2.90	94	.231	.282	3	.081	2	-2	-2	-3	-0.2
1919	NY-N	0	1	.000	1	0	0	0	0	3	3	0	2	0	15.0	6.00	47	.250	.357	0	.000	-0	-1	-1	-0	0.0
Total	4	16	38	.296	91	58	28	4	3	487²	450	10	144	217	11.2	3.05	90	.249	.310	40	.225	3	-19	-16	-9	-2.0

■ BILL STEELE   Steele, William Mitchell "Big Bill"   b: 10/5/1885, Milford, Pa.   d: 10/19/49, Overland, Pa.   BR/TR, 5'11", 200 lbs.   Deb: 9/10/10

YEAR	TM/L	W	L	PCT	G	GS	CG	SH	SV	IP	H	HR	BB	SO	RAT	ERA	ERA+	OAV	OOB	BH	AVG	PB	PR	/A	PD	TPI
1910	StL-N	4	4	.500	9	8	6	1	0	71²	71	1	24	51	12.7	3.27	91	.264	.338	8	.258	1	-2	-2	1	0.0
1911	StL-N	18	19	.486	43	34	23	1	3	287¹	287	8	113	115	12.8	3.73	91	.269	.345	21	.208	4	-10	-11	3	-0.3
1912	StL-N	9	13	.409	40	25	7	0	2	194	245	5	66	67	14.8	4.69	73	.307	.366	11	.180	1	-27	-27	4	-2.0
1913	StL-N	4	4	.500	12	9	2	0	0	54	58	3	18	10	13.2	5.00	65	.286	.353	1	.056	-1	-11	-11	-0	-1.1
1914	StL-N	1	2	.333	17	2	0	0	0	53¹	55	3	7	16	11.0	2.70	104	.274	.308	5	.294	2	1	1	0	0.4
	Bro-N	1	1	.500	8	1	0	0	1	16¹	17	1	7	3	13.2	5.51	52	.258	.329	1	.333	1	-5	-5	-0	-0.3
	Yr	2	3	.400	25	3	0	0	1	69²	72	4	14	19	11.1	3.36	84	.267	.303	2	.100	3	-4	-4	1	0.1
Total	5	37	43	.463	129	79	40	1	7	676²	733	21	235	236	13.3	4.02	82	.282	.348	47	.203	8	-55	-55	8	-3.3

■ BILL STEEN   Steen, William John   b: 11/11/1887, Pittsburgh, Pa.   d: 3/13/79, Signal Hill, Cal.   BR/TR, 6'0.5", 180 lbs.   Deb: 4/15/12

YEAR	TM/L	W	L	PCT	G	GS	CG	SH	SV	IP	H	HR	BB	SO	RAT	ERA	ERA+	OAV	OOB	BH	AVG	PB	PR	/A	PD	TPI
1912	Cle-A	9	8	.529	26	16	6	1	0	143¹	163	3	45	61	13.1	3.77	90	.298	.352	13	.271	2	-7	-6	-1	-0.4
1913	Cle-A	4	5	.444	22	13	7	2	2	128¹	113	3	49	57	11.6	2.45	124	.237	.313	7	.171	-0	7	8	-0	0.9
1914	Cle-A	9	14	.391	30	22	13	1	0	200²	201	0	68	97	12.2	2.60	111	.272	.337	14	.200	1	3	6	0	0.8
1915	Cle-A	1	4	.200	10	7	2	0	0	45¹	51	1	15	22	13.5	4.96	61	.290	.352	1	.188	-0	-10	-10	2	-0.7
	Det-A	5	1	.833	20	7	3	0	4	79¹	83	0	22	28	12.0	2.72	111	.269	.319	5	.179	-1	2	3	2	0.4
	Yr	6	5	.545	30	14	5	0	4	124²	134	1	37	50	12.4	3.54	86	.275	.328	1	.023	-1	-8	-7	4	-0.3
Total	4	28	32	.467	108	65	31	4	6	597	611	7	199	265	12.4	3.05	101	.272	.334	42	.207	1	-6	2	3	1.0

■ MILT STEENGRAFE   Steengrafe, Milton Henry   b: 5/26/1900, San Francisco, Cal   d: 6/2/77,   BR/TR, 6', 170 lbs.   Deb: 5/05/24

YEAR	TM/L	W	L	PCT	G	GS	CG	SH	SV	IP	H	HR	BB	SO	RAT	ERA	ERA+	OAV	OOB	BH	AVG	PB	PR	/A	PD	TPI
1924	Chi-A	0	0	—	3	0	0	0	0	5²	15	0	4	3	30.2	12.71	32	.484	.543	0	.000	-0	-5	-5	0	-0.4
1926	Chi-A	1	1	.500	13	1	0	0	0	38¹	43	1	19	10	15.0	3.99	97	.295	.383	0	.000	-2	0	-1	-0	-0.2
Total	2	1	1	.500	16	1	0	0	0	44	58	1	23	13	17.0	5.11	76	.328	.411	0	.000	-2	-5	-6	-0	-0.6

■ MORRIE STEEVENS   Steevens, Morris Dale   b: 10/7/40, Salem, Ill.   BL/TL, 6'2", 175 lbs.   Deb: 4/13/62

YEAR	TM/L	W	L	PCT	G	GS	CG	SH	SV	IP	H	HR	BB	SO	RAT	ERA	ERA+	OAV	OOB	BH	AVG	PB	PR	/A	PD	TPI
1962	Chi-N	0	1	.000	12	1	0	0	0	15	10	0	11	5	13.2	2.40	173	.196	.349	0	.000	-0	3	3	0	0.3
1964	Phi-N	0	0	—	4	0	0	0	0	2²	5	0	4	3	20.3	3.38	103	.385	.429	0	—	0	0	0	0	0.0
1965	Phi-N	0	1	.000	6	0	0	0	0	2²	5	1	4	3	30.4	16.88	20	.417	.563	0	—	0	-4	-4	0	-0.3

YEAR TM/L	W	L	PCT	G	GS	CG	SH	SV	IP	H	HR	BB	SO	RAT	ERA	ERA+	OAV	OOB	BH	AVG	PB	PR	/A	PD	TPI
Total 3	0	2	.000	22	1	0	0	0	20¹	20	1	16	11	16.4	4.43	90	.263	.398	0	.000	-0	-1	-1	0	0.0

ED STEIN
Stein, Edward F.   b: 9/5/1869, Detroit, Mich.   d: 5/10/28, Detroit, Mich.   BR/TR, 5'11", 170 lbs.   Deb: 7/24/1890

YEAR TM/L	W	L	PCT	G	GS	CG	SH	SV	IP	H	HR	BB	SO	RAT	ERA	ERA+	OAV	OOB	BH	AVG	PB	PR	/A	PD	TPI
1890 Chi-N	12	6	.667	20	18	14	1	0	160²	147	9	83	65	12.9	3.81	96	.236	.326	9	.153	-2	-4	-3	-1	-0.4
1891 Chi-N	7	6	.538	14	10	9	1	0	101	99	7	57	38	13.9	3.74	89	.247	.341	7	.163	-1	-4	-5	2	-0.3
1892 Bro-N	27	16	.628	48	42	38	6	1	377¹	310	5	150	190	11.0	2.84	111	.215	.289	31	.215	4	19	14	1	1.7
1893 Bro-N	19	15	.559	37	34	28	1	0	298¹	294	4	119	81	12.5	3.77	118	.250	.351	25	.212	-3	30	22	2	1.6
1894 Bro-N	27	14	.659	45	41	38	2	1	359	396	10	171	84	14.2	4.54	109	.277	.354	40	.267	5	31	16	0	1.5
1895 Bro-N	15	13	.536	32	27	24	1	1	255¹	282	9	93	55	13.2	4.72	93	.276	.336	26	.250	1	2	-9	1	-0.5
1896 Bro-N	3	6	.333	17	10	6	0	0	90¹	130	6	51	16	18.0	4.88	84	.334	.411	10	.256	0	-5	-8	0	-0.5
1898 Bro-N	0	2	.000	3	2	2	0	0	23	39	0	9	6	18.8	5.48	65	.372	.421	4	.400	1	-5	-5	-0	-0.3
Total 8	110	78	.585	216	184	159	12	3	1665	1697	50	733	535	13.1	3.96	104	.258	.332	152	.228	5	63	26	5	2.8

IRV STEIN
Stein, Irvin Michael   b: 5/21/11, Madisonville, La.   d: 1/7/81, Covington, La.   BR/TR, 6'2", 170 lbs.   Deb: 7/07/32

YEAR TM/L	W	L	PCT	G	GS	CG	SH	SV	IP	H	HR	BB	SO	RAT	ERA	ERA+	OAV	OOB	BH	AVG	PB	PR	/A	PD	TPI
1932 Phi-A	0	0	—	1	0	0	0	0	3	7	2	1	0	24.0	12.00	38	.500	.533	0	.000	-0	-3	-2	0	-0.1

RANDY STEIN
Stein, William Randolph   b: 3/7/53, Pomona, Cal.   BR/TR, 6'4", 210 lbs.   Deb: 4/17/78

YEAR TM/L	W	L	PCT	G	GS	CG	SH	SV	IP	H	HR	BB	SO	RAT	ERA	ERA+	OAV	OOB	BH	AVG	PB	PR	/A	PD	TPI
1978 Mil-A	3	2	.600	31	1	0	0	1	72²	78	5	39	42	15.0	5.33	71	.280	.376	0	—	0	-13	-13	0	-1.2
1979 Sea-A	2	3	.400	23	1	0	0	0	41¹	48	7	27	39	16.5	5.88	74	.291	.394	0	—	0	-8	-7	-1	-0.7
1981 Sea-A	0	1	.000	5	0	0	0	0	9¹	18	1	8	6	25.1	10.61	36	.429	.520	0	—	0	-7	-7	0	-0.6
1982 Chi-N	0	0	—	6	0	0	0	0	10¹	7	2	7	6	12.2	3.48	107	.200	.333	0	—	0	0	0	-0	0.0
Total 4	5	6	.455	65	2	0	0	1	133²	151	15	81	93	16.0	5.72	69	.290	.390	0	—	0	-27	-26	-1	-2.5

RAY STEINEDER
Steineder, Raymond J.   b: 11/13/1895, Salem, N.J.   d: 8/25/82, Vineland, N.J.   BR/TR, 6'0.5", 160 lbs.   Deb: 7/16/23

YEAR TM/L	W	L	PCT	G	GS	CG	SH	SV	IP	H	HR	BB	SO	RAT	ERA	ERA+	OAV	OOB	BH	AVG	PB	PR	/A	PD	TPI
1923 Pit-N	2	0	1.000	15	2	1	0	0	55	58	3	18	23	12.8	4.75	85	.278	.341	7	.467	3	-5	-4	-1	-0.2
1924 Pit-N	1	1	.000	5	0	0	0	0	2²	6	0	5	0	37.1	13.50	28	.400	.550	0	—	0	-3	-3	0	-0.2
Phi-N	1	1	.500	9	0	0	0	0	28²	29	1	16	11	14.1	4.40	101	.266	.360	3	.300	0	-2	0	0	0.1
Yr	1	2	.333	14	0	0	0	0	31¹	35	1	21	11	16.1	5.17	85	.282	.386	0	.000	0	-5	-3	0	-0.1
Total 2	3	2	.600	29	2	1	0	0	86¹	93	4	39	34	14.0	4.90	85	.279	.358	10	.400	3	-9	-7	-1	-0.3

RICK STEIRER
Steirer, Ricky Francis   b: 8/27/56, Baltimore, Md.   BR/TR, 6'4", 200 lbs.   Deb: 8/05/82

YEAR TM/L	W	L	PCT	G	GS	CG	SH	SV	IP	H	HR	BB	SO	RAT	ERA	ERA+	OAV	OOB	BH	AVG	PB	PR	/A	PD	TPI
1982 Cal-A	1	0	1.000	10	1	0	0	0	26¹	25	2	11	14	12.6	3.76	108	.243	.322	0	—	0	1	1	0	0.1
1983 Cal-A	3	2	.600	19	5	0	0	0	61²	77	3	18	25	14.3	4.82	83	.302	.355	0	—	0	-5	-6	1	-0.4
1984 Cal-A	0	1	.000	1	1	0	0	0	2²	6	0	2	2	27.0	16.88	24	.500	.571	0	—	0	-4	-4	0	-0.2
Total 3	4	3	.571	30	7	0	0	0	90²	108	5	31	41	14.2	4.86	83	.292	.353	0	—	0	-8	-8	1	-0.5

BILL STELLBERGER
Stellberger, William F.   b: 4/22/1865, Detroit, Mich.   d: 11/9/36, Detroit, Mich.   BL/TL,   Deb: 10/01/1885

YEAR TM/L	W	L	PCT	G	GS	CG	SH	SV	IP	H	HR	BB	SO	RAT	ERA	ERA+	OAV	OOB	BH	AVG	PB	PR	/A	PD	TPI
1885 Pro-N	0	1	.000	1	1	1	0	0	8	14	0	4	0	20.3	7.88	34	.366	.426	0	.000	-1	-4	-5	0	-0.3

JEFF STEMBER
Stember, Jeffrey Alan   b: 3/2/58, Elizabeth, N.J.   BR/TR, 6'5", 220 lbs.   Deb: 8/05/80

YEAR TM/L	W	L	PCT	G	GS	CG	SH	SV	IP	H	HR	BB	SO	RAT	ERA	ERA+	OAV	OOB	BH	AVG	PB	PR	/A	PD	TPI
1980 SF-N	0	0	—	1	1	0	0	0	3	2	1	2	0	12.0	3.00	118	.167	.286	0	.000	-0	0	0	0	0.0

BILL STEMMEYER
Stemmeyer, William "Cannon Ball"   b: 5/6/1865, Cleveland, Ohio   d: 5/3/45, Cleveland, Ohio   BR/TR, 6'2", 190 lbs.   Deb: 10/03/1885

YEAR TM/L	W	L	PCT	G	GS	CG	SH	SV	IP	H	HR	BB	SO	RAT	ERA	ERA+	OAV	OOB	BH	AVG	PB	PR	/A	PD	TPI
1885 Bos-N	1	1	.500	2	2	2	1	0	11	7	0	11	8	14.7	0.00	—	.174	.351	3	.429	1	3	3	0	0.5
1886 Bos-N	22	18	.550	41	41	41	0	0	348²	300	11	144	239	11.5	3.02	105	.223	.298	41	.277	9	11	6	-4	1.0
1887 Bos-N	6	8	.429	15	14	14	0	1	119¹	138	4	41	41	13.5	5.20	77	.282	.337	12	.255	2	-15	-16	-2	-1.1
1888 Cle-a	0	2	.000	2	2	2	0	0	16	37	0	9	7	25.9	9.00	35	.437	.491	4	.400	1	-11	-10	-0	-0.6
Total 4	29	29	.500	60	59	59	1	1	495	482	15	205	295	12.5	3.67	92	.246	.317	60	.283	13	-11	-17	-5	-0.2

DAVE STENHOUSE
Stenhouse, David Rotchford   b: 9/12/33, Westerly, R.I.   BR/TR, 6', 195 lbs.   Deb: 4/18/62

YEAR TM/L	W	L	PCT	G	GS	CG	SH	SV	IP	H	HR	BB	SO	RAT	ERA	ERA+	OAV	OOB	BH	AVG	PB	PR	/A	PD	TPI
1962 Was-A	11	12	.478	34	26	9	2	0	197	169	24	90	123	11.9	3.65	110	.234	.320	3	.052	-5	7	8	1	0.5
1963 Was-A	3	9	.250	16	16	2	1	0	87	90	12	45	47	14.1	4.55	82	.260	.347	2	.080	-1	-9	-8	0	-0.8
1964 Was-A	2	7	.222	26	14	1	0	1	88	80	12	39	44	12.3	4.81	77	.239	.320	6	.300	2	-12	-11	0	-0.8
Total 3	16	28	.364	76	56	12	3	1	372	339	48	174	214	12.5	4.14	94	.241	.327	11	.107	-4	-14	-11	1	-1.1

BUZZ STEPHEN
Stephen, Louis Roberts   b: 7/13/44, Porterville, Cal.   BR/TR, 6'4", 205 lbs.   Deb: 9/20/68

YEAR TM/L	W	L	PCT	G	GS	CG	SH	SV	IP	H	HR	BB	SO	RAT	ERA	ERA+	OAV	OOB	BH	AVG	PB	PR	/A	PD	TPI
1968 Min-A	1	1	.500	2	2	0	0	0	11¹	11	0	7	4	15.1	4.76	65	.275	.396	0	.000	0	-2	-2	0	-0.2

BRYAN STEPHENS
Stephens, Bryan Maris   b: 7/14/20, Fayetteville, Ark   BR/TR, 6'4", 175 lbs.   Deb: 5/15/47

YEAR TM/L	W	L	PCT	G	GS	CG	SH	SV	IP	H	HR	BB	SO	RAT	ERA	ERA+	OAV	OOB	BH	AVG	PB	PR	/A	PD	TPI
1947 Cle-A	5	10	.333	31	5	1	0	1	92	79	6	39	34	11.7	4.01	87	.230	.312	3	.111	-2	-3	-5	-1	-0.8
1948 StL-A	3	6	.333	43	12	2	0	3	122²	141	14	67	35	15.6	6.02	76	.289	.379	4	.125	-1	-24	-20	-0	-1.9
Total 2	8	16	.333	74	17	3	0	4	214²	220	20	106	69	13.9	5.16	79	.264	.352	7	.119	-3	-27	-26	-1	-2.7

CLARENCE STEPHENS
Stephens, Clarence Wright   b: 8/19/1863, Cincinnati, Ohio   d: 2/28/45, Cincinnati, Ohio   TR,   Deb: 10/08/1886

YEAR TM/L	W	L	PCT	G	GS	CG	SH	SV	IP	H	HR	BB	SO	RAT	ERA	ERA+	OAV	OOB	BH	AVG	PB	PR	/A	PD	TPI
1886 Cin-a	1	0	1.000	1	1	1	0	0	8	9	0	5	6	15.8	5.63	62	.271	.366	3	.600	1	-2	-2	0	0.0
1891 Cin-N	0	1	.000	1	1	0	0	0	8	9	1	3	3	13.5	7.88	43	.273	.334	0	.000	-0	-4	-4	-0	-0.3
1892 Cin-N	0	1	.000	1	1	1	0	0	7	12	0	4	1	20.6	1.29	254	.364	.432	0	.000	0	2	2	1	0.2
Total 3	1	2	.333	3	3	2	0	0	23	30	1	12	10	16.4	5.09	67	.303	.378	3	.300	0	-4	-4	1	-0.1

BEN STEPHENS
Stephens, George Benjamin   b: 9/28/1867, Romeo, Mich.   d: 8/5/1896, Armada, Mich.   5'10.5", 170 lbs.   Deb: 8/05/1892

YEAR TM/L	W	L	PCT	G	GS	CG	SH	SV	IP	H	HR	BB	SO	RAT	ERA	ERA+	OAV	OOB	BH	AVG	PB	PR	/A	PD	TPI
1892 Bal-N	1	1	.500	5	2	2	0	1	29	37	2	9	14	14.3	2.79	124	.298	.346	0	.000	-2	2	2	0	0.0
1893 Was-N	0	6	.000	9	6	6	0	0	63²	83	1	31	14	16.1	5.80	80	.306	.377	3	.103	-3	-8	-8	1	-0.8
1894 Was-N	0	0	—	3	2	1	0	0	11	19	1	8	1	22.1	4.91	107	.375	.460	1	.250	-0	1	0	0	0.0
Total 3	1	7	.125	17	10	9	0	1	103²	139	4	48	22	16.2	4.86	90	.312	.378	4	.087	-5	-6	-5	1	-0.8

EARL STEPHENSON
Stephenson, Chester Earl   b: 7/31/47, Benson, N.C.   BL/TL, 6'3", 175 lbs.   Deb: 4/07/71

YEAR TM/L	W	L	PCT	G	GS	CG	SH	SV	IP	H	HR	BB	SO	RAT	ERA	ERA+	OAV	OOB	BH	AVG	PB	PR	/A	PD	TPI
1971 Chi-N	1	0	1.000	16	0	0	0	0	20¹	24	1	11	11	15.5	4.43	89	.316	.402	0	.000	-0	-2	-1	0	0.0
1972 Mil-A	3	5	.375	35	8	1	0	0	80¹	79	5	33	33	12.9	3.25	93	.262	.340	0	.000	-2	-2	-2	0	-0.3
1977 Bal-A	0	0	—	1	0	0	0	0	3	5	1	0	2	15.0	9.00	42	.357	.357	0	—	0	-2	-2	-0	-0.1
1978 Bal-A	0	0	—	2	0	0	0	0	9²	10	0	5	4	14.0	2.79	125	.294	.385	0	—	0	1	1	-0	0.0
Total 4	4	5	.444	54	8	1	0	1	113¹	118	7	49	50	13.5	3.57	91	.277	.356	0	.000	-2	-4	-4	0	-0.4

JERRY STEPHENSON
Stephenson, Jerry Joseph   b: 10/6/43, Detroit, Mich.   BL/TR, 6'2", 185 lbs.   Deb: 4/14/63

YEAR TM/L	W	L	PCT	G	GS	CG	SH	SV	IP	H	HR	BB	SO	RAT	ERA	ERA+	OAV	OOB	BH	AVG	PB	PR	/A	PD	TPI
1963 Bos-A	0	0	—	1	1	0	0	0	2¹	5	0	2	3	27.0	7.71	49	.556	.636	0	.000	-0	-1	-1	0	0.0
1965 Bos-A	1	5	.167	15	8	0	0	0	52	62	7	33	49	16.6	6.23	60	.287	.384	3	.231	1	-16	-14	0	-1.3
1966 Bos-A	2	5	.286	15	11	1	0	0	66¹	68	6	44	50	15.3	5.83	65	.264	.373	2	.118	-1	-18	-15	1	-1.5
1967 *Bos-A	3	1	.750	8	6	0	0	1	39²	32	4	16	24	11.1	3.86	90	.227	.310	4	.250	0	-3	-2	0	0.0
1968 Bos-A	2	8	.200	23	7	2	0	0	68²	81	4	42	51	16.4	5.64	56	.295	.392	6	.353	2	-20	-19	1	-1.7
1969 Sea-A	0	0	—	2	0	0	0	0	2²	6	0	3	1	33.8	10.13	36	.429	.556	0	—	0	-2	-2	0	-0.1
1970 LA-N	0	0	—	3	0	0	0	0	6²	11	0	5	6	21.6	9.45	41	.379	.471	0	.000	-0	-4	-4	0	-0.3
Total 7	8	19	.296	67	33	3	0	1	238¹	265	21	145	184	15.7	5.70	62	.281	.381	15	.231	2	-64	-57	1	-4.9

JOHN STERLING
Sterling, John A.   b: Philadelphia, Pa.   Deb: 10/12/1890

YEAR TM/L	W	L	PCT	G	GS	CG	SH	SV	IP	H	HR	BB	SO	RAT	ERA	ERA+	OAV	OOB	BH	AVG	PB	PR	/A	PD	TPI
1890 Phi-a	0	1	.000	1	1	1	0	0	5	16	1	4	1	36.0	21.60	18	.519	.575	0	.000	-0	-10	-10	-0	-0.6

RANDY STERLING
Sterling, Randall Wayne   b: 4/21/51, Key West, Fla.   BB/TR, 6'2", 195 lbs.   Deb: 9/16/74

YEAR TM/L	W	L	PCT	G	GS	CG	SH	SV	IP	H	HR	BB	SO	RAT	ERA	ERA+	OAV	OOB	BH	AVG	PB	PR	/A	PD	TPI
1974 NY-N	1	1	.500	3	2	0	0	0	9¹	13	0	3	2	16.4	4.82	74	.351	.415	0	.000	0	-1	-1	0	0.0

YEAR TM/L	W	L	PCT	G	GS	CG	SH	SV	IP	H	HR	BB	SO	RAT	ERA	ERA+	OAV	OOB	BH	AVG	PB	PR	/A	PD	TPI

■ JIM STEVENS
Stevens, James Arthur "Steve" b: 8/25/1889, Williamsburg, Md. d: 9/25/66, Baltimore, Md. BR/TR, 5'11", 180 lbs. Deb: 8/24/14

YEAR TM/L	W	L	PCT	G	GS	CG	SH	SV	IP	H	HR	BB	SO	RAT	ERA	ERA+	OAV	OOB	BH	AVG	PB	PR	/A	PD	TPI
1914 Was-A	0	0	—	2	0	0	0	0	3	4	0	2	0	21.0	9.00	31	.364	.500	0	.000	-0	-2	-2	-0	-0.1

■ DAVE STEWART
Stewart, David Keith b: 2/19/57, Oakland, Cal. BR/TR, 6'2", 200 lbs. Deb: 9/22/78

YEAR TM/L	W	L	PCT	G	GS	CG	SH	SV	IP	H	HR	BB	SO	RAT	ERA	ERA+	OAV	OOB	BH	AVG	PB	PR	/A	PD	TPI
1978 LA-N	0	0	—	1	0	0	0	0	2	1	0	1	1	4.5	0.00	—	.167	.167	0	—	0	1	1	0	0.1
1981 *LA-N	4	3	.571	32	0	0	0	6	43¹	40	3	14	29	11.2	2.49	133	.250	.310	2	.400	2	5	4	0	0.6
1982 LA-N	9	8	.529	45	14	0	0	1	146¹	137	14	49	80	11.6	3.81	91	.249	.313	7	.179	1	-3	-6	-1	-0.5
1983 LA-N	5	2	.714	46	1	0	0	8	76	67	4	33	54	12.1	2.96	121	.237	.321	1	.143	-0	6	5	-0	0.5
Tex-A	5	2	.714	8	8	2	0	0	59	50	2	17	24	10.5	2.14	188	.233	.295	0	—	0	13	12	1	1.4
1984 Tex-A	7	14	.333	32	27	3	0	0	192¹	193	26	87	119	13.3	4.73	88	.258	.339	0	—	0	-16	-12	-1	-1.3
1985 Tex-A	0	6	.000	42	5	0	0	4	81¹	86	13	37	62	13.3	5.42	78	.273	.353	0	—	0	-12	-11	-0	-1.0
Phi-N	0	0	—	4	0	0	0	0	4¹	5	0	4	2	18.7	6.23	59	.278	.409	0	—	0	-1	-1	-0	-0.1
1986 Phi-N	0	0	—	8	0	0	0	0	12¹	15	1	4	9	13.9	6.57	59	.306	.358	0	—	0	-4	-4	-0	-0.3
Oak-A	9	5	.643	29	17	4	1	0	149¹	137	15	65	102	12.4	3.74	103	.241	.322	0	—	0	7	2	-0	0.2
1987 Oak-A	20	13	.606	37	37	8	1	0	261¹	224	24	105	205	11.5	3.68	112	.229	.307	0	—	0	22	13	-3	1.0
1988 *Oak-A	21	12	.636	37	37	**14**	2	0	**275²**	240	14	110	192	11.5	3.23	117	.234	.310	0	—	0	22	17	-4	1.4
1989 *Oak-A	21	9	.700	36	36	8	0	0	257²	260	23	69	155	11.7	3.32	111	.263	.315	0	—	0	16	10	-1	1.0
1990 *Oak-A	22	11	.667	36	36	**11**	**4**	0	267	226	16	83	166	10.6	2.56	146	.231	.294	0	—	0	40	35	-2	3.6
Total 11	123	85	.591	393	218	50	8	19	1828	1681	155	677	1202	11.8	3.52	109	.244	.315	10	.196	2	96	66	-11	6.6

■ FRANK STEWART
Stewart, Frank "Stewy" b: 9/8/06, Minneapolis, Minn. BR/TR, 6'1.5", 180 lbs. Deb: 10/02/27

YEAR TM/L	W	L	PCT	G	GS	CG	SH	SV	IP	H	HR	BB	SO	RAT	ERA	ERA+	OAV	OOB	BH	AVG	PB	PR	/A	PD	TPI
1927 Chi-A	0	1	.000	1	1	0	0	0	4	5	0	4	0	20.3	9.00	45	.357	.500	0	.000	-0	-2	-2	1	-0.1

■ JOE STEWART
Stewart, Joseph Lawrence "Ace" b: 3/11/1879, Monroe, N.C. d: 2/9/13, Youngstown, Ohio TR, 5'11", 175 lbs. Deb: 9/13/04

YEAR TM/L	W	L	PCT	G	GS	CG	SH	SV	IP	H	HR	BB	SO	RAT	ERA	ERA+	OAV	OOB	BH	AVG	PB	PR	/A	PD	TPI
1904 Bos-N	0	0	—	2	0	0	0	0	9¹	12	0	4	1	16.4	9.64	29	.286	.362	1	.200	-0	-7	-7	-0	-0.6

■ SAMMY STEWART
Stewart, Samuel Lee b: 10/28/54, Asheville, N.C. BR/TR, 6'3", 200 lbs. Deb: 9/01/78

YEAR TM/L	W	L	PCT	G	GS	CG	SH	SV	IP	H	HR	BB	SO	RAT	ERA	ERA+	OAV	OOB	BH	AVG	PB	PR	/A	PD	TPI
1978 Bal-A	1	1	.500	2	2	0	0	0	11¹	10	0	3	11	10.3	3.18	110	.238	.289	0	—	0	1	0	0	0.0
1979 *Bal-A	8	5	.615	31	3	1	0	1	117²	96	11	71	71	13.2	3.52	114	.232	.351	0	—	0	9	6	2	0.9
1980 Bal-A	7	7	.500	33	3	2	0	3	118²	103	9	60	78	12.5	3.56	111	.235	.330	0	—	0	6	5	-1	0.5
1981 Bal-A	4	8	.333	29	3	0	0	4	112¹	89	8	57	57	11.9	**2.32**	**156**	.225	.327	0	—	0	17	16	1	1.8
1982 Bal-A	10	9	.526	38	12	1	1	5	139	140	9	62	69	13.2	4.14	97	.263	.342	0	—	0	-1	-2	1	0.0
1983 *Bal-A	9	4	.692	58	1	0	0	7	144¹	138	7	47	96	12.8	3.62	109	.253	.336	0	—	0	7	5	-1	0.5
1984 Bal-A	7	4	.636	60	0	0	0	13	93	81	7	47	56	12.5	3.29	118	.241	.336	0	—	0	7	6	-0	0.6
1985 Bal-A	5	7	.417	56	1	0	0	9	129²	117	15	66	77	12.8	3.61	112	.246	.339	0	—	0	8	6	-1	0.5
1986 Bos-A	4	1	.800	27	0	0	0	0	63²	64	7	48	47	15.8	4.38	95	.266	.388	0	—	0	-1	-2	-0	-0.1
1987 Cle-A	4	2	.667	25	0	0	0	3	27	25	4	21	25	15.7	5.67	80	.234	.364	0	—	0	-4	-3	0	-0.2
Total 10	59	48	.551	359	25	4	1	45	956²	863	77	502	586	13.0	3.59	110	.245	.341	0	—	0	49	39	1	4.5

■ BUNKY STEWART
Stewart, Veston Goff b: 1/7/31, Jasper, N.C. BL/TL, 6', 154 lbs. Deb: 5/04/52

YEAR TM/L	W	L	PCT	G	GS	CG	SH	SV	IP	H	HR	BB	SO	RAT	ERA	ERA+	OAV	OOB	BH	AVG	PB	PR	/A	PD	TPI
1952 Was-A	0	0	—	1	0	0	0	0	1	2	0	1	1	27.0	18.00	20	.500	.600	0	—	0	-2	-2	0	0.0
1953 Was-A	0	2	.000	2	2	1	0	0	15¹	17	1	11	3	17.0	4.70	83	.283	.403	1	.200	-0	-1	-1	-0	-0.1
1954 Was-A	0	0	.000	29	2	0	0	1	50²	67	3	27	27	17.4	7.64	47	.324	.412	0	.000	-0	-22	-23	1	-2.1
1955 Was-A	0	0	—	7	1	0	0	0	15¹	18	0	6	10	14.1	4.11	93	.295	.358	0	.000	-0	-0	-0	0	0.0
1956 Was-A	5	7	.417	33	9	1	0	2	105	111	15	82	36	17.0	5.57	78	.276	.405	7	.250	-0	-16	-15	1	-1.2
Total 5	5	11	.313	72	14	2	0	3	187¹	215	19	127	77	16.9	6.01	67	.293	.404	8	.211	-0	-42	-41	2	-3.4

■ LEFTY STEWART
Stewart, Walter Cleveland b: 9/23/1900, Sparta, Tenn. d: 9/26/74, Knoxville, Tenn. BR/TL, 5'10", 160 lbs. Deb: 4/20/21

YEAR TM/L	W	L	PCT	G	GS	CG	SH	SV	IP	H	HR	BB	SO	RAT	ERA	ERA+	OAV	OOB	BH	AVG	PB	PR	/A	PD	TPI
1921 Det-A	0	0	—	5	0	0	0	1	9	20	0	5	4	25.0	12.00	36	.455	.510	0	.000	-0	-8	-8	0	-0.6
1927 StL-A	8	11	.421	27	19	11	0	1	155²	187	7	43	43	13.4	4.28	102	.310	.357	15	.306	3	-2	1	2	0.5
1928 StL-A	7	9	.438	29	17	7	1	3	142²	173	5	32	25	13.1	4.67	90	.310	.350	14	.275	3	-10	-7	0	-0.3
1929 StL-A	9	6	.600	23	18	8	1	0	149²	137	11	49	47	11.4	3.25	136	.246	.312	6	.118	-4	17	20	-0	1.5
1930 StL-A	20	12	.625	35	33	23	1	0	271	281	21	70	79	11.7	3.45	141	.268	.315	22	.244	2	36	43	1	4.5
1931 StL-A	14	17	.452	36	33	20	1	0	258	287	17	85	89	13.1	4.40	105	.277	.334	22	.250	6	-0	7	1	1.4
1932 StL-A	15	19	.441	41	32	18	2	1	259²	269	22	99	86	12.9	4.61	105	.270	.338	12	.146	-2	-4	7	-1	0.5
1933 *Was-A	15	6	.714	34	31	11	1	0	230²	227	19	60	69	11.2	3.82	109	.256	.304	11	.143	1	12	9	1	1.0
1934 Was-A	7	11	.389	24	22	7	1	0	152	184	8	36	36	13.1	4.03	107	.303	.343	7	.156	-1	8	5	-0	0.3
1935 Was-A	0	1	.000	1	1	0	0	0	2²	8	1	2	1	33.8	13.50	32	.533	.588	0	.000	-0	-3	-3	0	-0.1
Cle-A	6	6	.500	24	10	2	0	2	91	122	6	17	24	13.8	5.44	83	.312	.342	6	.200	-1	-10	-9	-1	-0.9
Yr	6	7	.462	25	11	2	0	2	93²	130	7	19	25	14.4	5.67	79	.320	.352	1	.032	-1	-13	-12	-1	-1.0
Total 10	101	98	.508	279	216	107	8	8	1722	1895	117	498	503	12.6	4.19	108	.281	.332	115	.204	7	35	64	2	7.8

■ MACK STEWART
Stewart, William Macklin b: 9/23/14, Stevenson, Ala. d: 3/21/60, Macon, Ga. BR/TR, 6', 167 lbs. Deb: 7/07/44

YEAR TM/L	W	L	PCT	G	GS	CG	SH	SV	IP	H	HR	BB	SO	RAT	ERA	ERA+	OAV	OOB	BH	AVG	PB	PR	/A	PD	TPI
1944 Chi-N	0	0	—	8	0	0	0	0	12¹	11	1	4	3	10.9	1.46	242	.239	.300	0	.000	-0	3	3	-0	0.3
1945 Chi-N	0	1	.000	16	1	0	0	0	28¹	37	0	14	9	16.2	4.76	77	.322	.395	1	.333	0	-3	-4	0	-0.2
Total 2	0	1	.000	24	1	0	0	0	40²	48	1	18	12	14.6	3.76	96	.298	.369	1	.250	0	-0	-1	0	0.1

■ DAVE STIEB
Stieb, David Andrew b: 7/22/57, Santa Ana, Cal. BR/TR, 6', 185 lbs. Deb: 6/29/79

YEAR TM/L	W	L	PCT	G	GS	CG	SH	SV	IP	H	HR	BB	SO	RAT	ERA	ERA+	OAV	OOB	BH	AVG	PB	PR	/A	PD	TPI
1979 Tor-A	8	8	.500	18	18	7	1	0	129¹	139	11	48	52	13.3	4.31	101	.276	.344	0	—	0	-1	0	3	0.3
1980 Tor-A	12	15	.444	34	32	14	4	0	242²	232	12	83	108	11.9	3.71	116	.260	.327	0	.000	0	9	16	6	2.2
1981 Tor-A	11	10	.524	25	25	11	2	0	183²	148	10	61	89	10.8	3.19	124	.223	.299	0	—	0	10	15	2	1.9
1982 Tor-A	17	14	.548	38	38	**19**	**5**	0	**288¹**	271	27	75	141	11.0	3.25	138	.248	.299	0	—	0	27	**39**	4	**4.6**
1983 Tor-A	17	12	.586	36	36	14	4	0	278	223	21	93	187	10.7	3.04	141	.219	.293	0	—	0	31	**39**	6	**4.1**
1984 Tor-A	16	8	.667	35	35	11	2	0	267	215	19	88	198	10.6	2.83	**145**	**.221**	.293	0	—	0	34	37	1	**4.1**
1985 *Tor-A	14	13	.519	36	36	8	2	0	265	206	22	96	167	10.6	**2.48**	**170**	**.213**	.290	0	—	0	49	51	5	**6.1**
1986 Tor-A	7	12	.368	37	34	1	1	1	205	239	29	87	127	15.0	4.74	89	.297	.376	0	—	0	-13	-12	2	-0.9
1987 Tor-A	13	9	.591	33	31	3	1	0	185	164	16	87	115	12.6	4.09	110	.239	.331	0	—	0	8	8	1	0.9
1988 Tor-A	16	8	.667	32	31	8	4	0	207¹	157	15	79	147	10.8	3.04	129	.210	.296	0	—	0	21	21	1	2.2
1989 *Tor-A	17	8	.680	33	33	3	2	0	206²	164	12	76	101	11.0	3.35	112	.219	.302	0	—	0	12	10	0	1.0
1990 Tor-A	18	6	.750	33	33	2	2	0	208²	179	11	64	125	10.9	2.93	129	.230	.297	0	—	0	23	20	3	2.5
Total 12	166	123	.574	390	382	101	30	1	2666²	2337	205	937	1557	11.4	3.34	125	.237	.310	0	.000	0	209	245	27	29.0

■ FRED STIELY
Stiely, Fred Warren "Lefty" b: 6/1/01, Pillow, Pa. d: 1/6/81, Valley View, Pa. BL/TL, 5'8", 170 lbs. Deb: 10/06/29

YEAR TM/L	W	L	PCT	G	GS	CG	SH	SV	IP	H	HR	BB	SO	RAT	ERA	ERA+	OAV	OOB	BH	AVG	PB	PR	/A	PD	TPI
1929 StL-A	1	0	1.000	1	1	0	0	0	9	11	0	3	2	15.0	0.00	—	.297	.366	2	.667	1	4	4	0	0.8
1930 StL-A	0	1	.000	4	2	1	0	0	19	27	4	8	5	17.1	8.53	57	.346	.414	3	.429	2	-8	-8	-0	-0.4
1931 StL-A	0	0	—	4	0	0	0	0	6²	7	0	3	2	14.9	6.75	69	.269	.367	0	—	0	-2	-2	-0	-0.1
Total 3	1	1	.500	9	3	2	0	0	34²	45	4	14	9	16.1	5.97	79	.319	.392	5	.500	3	-6	-5	0	0.3

■ DICK STIGMAN
Stigman, Richard Lewis b: 1/24/36, Nimrod, Minn. BR/TL, 6'3", 200 lbs. Deb: 4/22/60

YEAR TM/L	W	L	PCT	G	GS	CG	SH	SV	IP	H	HR	BB	SO	RAT	ERA	ERA+	OAV	OOB	BH	AVG	PB	PR	/A	PD	TPI
1960 Cle-A	5	11	.313	41	18	3	0	9	133²	118	13	87	104	13.8	4.51	83	.238	.352	8	.222	2	-9	-11	-2	-1.1
1961 Cle-A	2	5	.286	22	6	0	0	0	64¹	65	9	25	48	12.6	4.62	85	.264	.332	2	.125	-1	-4	-5	0	-0.4
1962 Min-A	12	5	.706	40	15	6	0	3	142²	119	19	64	116	11.9	3.66	112	.233	.319	2	.044	-0	5	7	-2	0.0
1963 Min-A	15	15	.500	33	33	15	3	0	241	210	32	81	193	10.9	3.25	112	.231	.294	9	.107	-2	10	11	-5	0.4
1964 Min-A	6	15	.286	32	29	5	1	0	190	160	31	70	159	11.1	4.03	89	.225	.299	7	.101	-3	-8	-9	-3	-1.5
1965 Min-A	4	2	.667	33	8	0	0	4	70	59	14	33	70	11.8	4.37	81	.227	.314	2	.133	-0	-7	-6	-1	-0.7

YEAR	TM/L	W	L	PCT	G	GS	CG	SH	SV	IP	H	HR	BB	SO	RAT	ERA	ERA+	OAV	OOB	BH	AVG	PB	PR	/A	PD	TPI
1966	Bos-A	2	1	.667	34	10	1	1	0	81	85	15	46	65	14.7	5.44	70	.268	.363	2	.118	-1	-18	-15	-1	-1.7
Total	7	46	54	.460	235	119	30	5	16	922^2	819	133	406	755	12.0	4.03	93	.237	.318	32	.113	-8	-32	-29	-14	-5.0

■ ROLLIE STILES
Stiles, Rolland Mays "Lena"   b: 11/17/06, Ratcliff, Ark.   BR/TR, 6'1.5", 180 lbs.   Deb: 6/19/30

YEAR	TM/L	W	L	PCT	G	GS	CG	SH	SV	IP	H	HR	BB	SO	RAT	ERA	ERA+	OAV	OOB	BH	AVG	PB	PR	/A	PD	TPI
1930	StL-A	3	6	.333	20	7	3	0	0	102	136	10	41	25	15.7	5.91	82	.337	.399	10	.270	0	-14	-12	-0	-0.9
1931	StL-A	3	1	.750	34	2	0	0	0	81	112	2	60	32	19.3	7.22	64	.352	.458	1	.045	-2	-26	-23	-0	-2.2
1933	StL-A	3	7	.300	31	9	6	1	0	115	154	4	47	29	15.9	5.01	93	.337	.390	2	.061	-3	-9	-5	-1	-0.7
Total	3	9	14	.391	85	18	9	1	1	298	402	16	148	86	16.8	5.92	80	.337	.412	13	.141	-5	-49	-40	-1	-3.8

■ ARCHIE STIMMEL
Stimmel, Archibald May "Lumbago"   b: 5/30/1873, Woodsboro, Md.   d: 8/18/58, Frederick, Md.   BR/TR, 6', 175 lbs.   Deb: 7/03/00

YEAR	TM/L	W	L	PCT	G	GS	CG	SH	SV	IP	H	HR	BB	SO	RAT	ERA	ERA+	OAV	OOB	BH	AVG	PB	PR	/A	PD	TPI
1900	Cin-N	1	1	.500	2	1	1	0	0	13	18	1	4	2	15.2	6.92	53	.327	.373	1	.200	-0	-5	-5	-0	-0.3
1901	Cin-N	4	14	.222	20	18	14	1	0	153^1	170	10	44	55	13.1	4.11	78	.279	.338	5	.081	-4	-13	-15	-2	-2.0
1902	Cin-N	0	4	.000	4	3	3	0	0	26	37	1	12	7	17.7	3.46	87	.334	.408	2	.200	-0	-2	-1	-0	-0.1
Total	3	5	19	.208	26	22	18	1	0	192^1	225	12	60	64	13.9	4.21	76	.290	.350	8	.104	-4	-20	-21	-3	-2.4

■ CARL STIMSON
Stimson, Carl Remus   b: 7/18/1894, Hamburg, Iowa   d: 11/9/36, Omaha, Neb.   BB/TR, 6'5", 190 lbs.   Deb: 6/06/23

YEAR	TM/L	W	L	PCT	G	GS	CG	SH	SV	IP	H	HR	BB	SO	RAT	ERA	ERA+	OAV	OOB	BH	AVG	PB	PR	/A	PD	TPI
1923	Bos-A	0	0	—	2	0	0	0	0	4	12	0	5	1	40.5	22.50	18	.750	.818	0	.000	-0	-8	-8	0	-0.6

■ HARRY STINE
Stine, Harry C.   b: 2/20/1864, Shenandoah, Pa.   d: 6/5/24, Niagara Falls, N.Y   TL, 5'6", 150 lbs.   Deb: 7/22/1890

YEAR	TM/L	W	L	PCT	G	GS	CG	SH	SV	IP	H	HR	BB	SO	RAT	ERA	ERA+	OAV	OOB	BH	AVG	PB	PR	/A	PD	TPI
1890	Phi-a	0	1	.000	1	1	1	0	0	8	17	0	4	1	23.6	9.00	42	.418	.470	0	.000	-0	-5	-5	-0	-0.3

■ LEE STINE
Stine, Lee Elbert   b: 11/17/13, Stillwater, Okla.   BR/TR, 5'11", 185 lbs.   Deb: 4/17/34

YEAR	TM/L	W	L	PCT	G	GS	CG	SH	SV	IP	H	HR	BB	SO	RAT	ERA	ERA+	OAV	OOB	BH	AVG	PB	PR	/A	PD	TPI
1934	Chi-A	0	0	—	4	0	0	0	0	11	11	2	10	8	18.0	8.18	58	.268	.423	0	.000	0	-5	-4	-0	-0.3
1935	Chi-A	0	0	—	1	0	0	0	0	2	2	1	3	1	22.5	9.00	51	.286	.500	0	—	0	-1	-1	1	0.0
1936	Cin-N	3	8	.273	40	13	5	1	2	121^2	157	6	41	26	15.2	5.03	76	.318	.379	8	.296	3	-14	-16	2	-1.0
1938	NY-A	0	0	—	4	0	0	0	0	8^2	9	0	1	4	10.4	1.04	437	.333	.357	1	.500	0	4	3	-0	0.3
Total	4	3	8	.273	49	13	5	1	2	143^1	179	9	55	39	15.3	5.09	78	.315	.384	9	.300	3	-16	-18		-1.0

■ JACK STIVETTS
Stivetts, John Elmer "Happy Jack"   b: 3/31/1868, Ashland, Pa.   d: 4/18/30, Ashland, Pa.   BR/TR, 6'2", 185 lbs.   Deb: 6/26/1889 ♦

YEAR	TM/L	W	L	PCT	G	GS	CG	SH	SV	IP	H	HR	BB	SO	RAT	ERA	ERA+	OAV	OOB	BH	AVG	PB	PR	/A	PD	TPI
1889	StL-a	12	7	.632	26	20	18	2	1	191^2	153	4	68	143	10.4	2.25	188	.212	.280	18	.228	-1	34	42	-1	3.8
1890	StL-a	27	21	.563	54	46	41	3	0	419^1	399	14	179	289	12.4	3.52	123	.243	.318	65	.288	16	16	37	2	5.9
1891	StL-a	33	22	.600	64	56	40	3	1	440	357	15	232	259	12.0	2.86	147	.214	.310	92	.305	11	42	66	2	8.1
1892	*Bos-N	35	16	.686	54	48	45	3	1	415^2	346	12	171	180	11.2	3.03	116	.217	.293	71	.296	16	12	22	1	4.5
1893	Bos-N	20	12	.625	38	34	29	1	1	283^2	315	17	115	61	13.6	4.41	112	.273	.339	51	.297	8	8	17	-2	2.2
1894	Bos-N	26	14	.650	45	39	30	0	0	338	429	27	127	76	14.8	4.90	116	.306	.364	80	.328	11	16	29	-3	3.7
1895	Bos-N	17	17	.500	38	34	30	0	0	291	341	15	89	111	13.3	4.64	110	.288	.338	30	.190	-8	5	15	-2	0.5
1896	Bos-N	22	14	.611	42	36	31	2	0	329	353	20	99	71	12.4	4.10	111	.272	.324	76	.344	12	9	16	-3	2.9
1897	*Bos-N	11	4	.733	18	15	10	0	0	129^1	147	5	43	27	13.2	3.41	131	.284	.339	73	.367	7	13	15	1	1.3
1898	Bos-N	0	1	.000	2	1	1	0	0	12	12	2	7	1	18.0	8.25	45	.331	.411	28	.252	0	-6	-6	0	-0.4
1899	Cle-N	0	4	.000	7	4	3	0	0	38	48	0	25	5	17.3	5.68	65	.308	.403	8	.205	1	-8	-8	2	-0.6
Total	11	203	132	.606	388	333	278	14	4	2887^2	2905	131	1155	1223	12.7	3.74	121	.255	.324	592	.297	72	142	247	-1	31.9

■ CHUCK STOBBS
Stobbs, Charles Klein   b: 7/2/29, Wheeling, W.Va.   BL/TL, 6'1", 185 lbs.   Deb: 9/15/47

YEAR	TM/L	W	L	PCT	G	GS	CG	SH	SV	IP	H	HR	BB	SO	RAT	ERA	ERA+	OAV	OOB	BH	AVG	PB	PR	/A	PD	TPI
1947	Bos-A	0	1	.000	4	1	0	0	0	9	10	0	10	5	20.0	6.00	65	.294	.455	0	.000	-0	-2	-2	-0	-0.1
1948	Bos-A	0	0	—	6	0	0	0	0	7	9	0	7	4	20.6	6.43	68	.321	.457	0	.000	-0	-2	-2	0	0.0
1949	Bos-A	11	6	.647	26	19	10	0	0	152	145	10	75	70	13.1	4.03	108	.254	.343	11	.208	0	3	6	-1	0.5
1950	Bos-A	12	7	.632	32	21	6	0	1	169^1	158	17	88	78	13.3	5.10	96	.250	.346	14	.246	3	-10	-4	1	0.1
1951	Bos-A	10	9	.526	34	25	6	0	0	170	180	15	74	75	13.7	4.76	94	.271	.349	11	.180	-2	-12	-6	-2	-0.8
1952	Chi-A	7	12	.368	38	17	2	0	1	135	118	9	72	73	13.0	3.13	116	.237	.339	3	.079	-1	8	8	1	0.7
1953	Was-A	11	8	.579	27	20	8	0	0	153	146	11	44	67	11.2	3.29	118	.246	.299	10	.227	1	12	10	-1	1.1
1954	Was-A	11	11	.500	31	24	10	3	0	182	189	6	67	67	12.7	4.10	87	.270	.335	7	.137	0	-8	-11	1	-0.9
1955	Was-A	4	14	.222	41	16	2	0	3	140^1	169	13	57	60	14.6	5.00	77	.302	.368	6	.171	2	-16	-18	2	-1.4
1956	Was-A	15	15	.500	37	33	15	1	1	240	264	29	54	97	12.0	3.60	120	.279	.318	15	.179	-2	15	19	1	1.8
1957	Was-A	8	20	.286	42	31	5	2	1	211^2	235	28	80	114	13.6	5.36	73	.279	.345	16	.211	1	-37	-34	-3	-3.4
1958	Was-A	2	6	.250	19	8	0	0	0	56^2	87	7	16	23	16.7	6.04	63	.369	.413	0	.000	-0	-14	-14	0	-1.4
	StL-N	1	3	.250	17	0	0	0	1	39^2	40	4	14	25	12.3	3.63	114	.261	.323	1	.250	0	1	2	1	0.3
1959	Was-A	1	8	.111	41	7	0	0	7	90^2	82	13	24	50	10.7	2.98	131	.238	.291	2	.105	-1	9	9	0	0.8
1960	Was-A	12	7	.632	40	13	1	1	2	119^1	115	13	38	72	11.8	3.32	117	.252	.313	3	.088	-2	7	8	-2	0.4
1961	Min-A	2	3	.400	24	3	0	0	1	44^2	56	8	15	17	14.7	7.46	57	.311	.371	3	.375	1	-17	-16	-1	-1.4
Total	15	107	130	.451	459	238	65	7	19	1920^1	2003	183	735	897	13.0	4.29	95	.269	.338	102	.176	-1	-63	-46	-2	-3.7

■ WES STOCK
Stock, Wesley Gay   b: 4/10/34, Longview, Wash.   BR/TR, 6'2", 188 lbs.   Deb: 4/19/59   C

YEAR	TM/L	W	L	PCT	G	GS	CG	SH	SV	IP	H	HR	BB	SO	RAT	ERA	ERA+	OAV	OOB	BH	AVG	PB	PR	/A	PD	TPI
1959	Bal-A	0	0	—	7	0	0	0	0	12^2	16	1	2	8	12.8	3.55	107	.302	.327	0	.000	-0	0	0	-0	0.0
1960	Bal-A	2	2	.500	17	0	0	0	2	34^1	26	2	14	23	10.7	2.88	132	.218	.306	0	.000	-1	4	4	1	0.3
1961	Bal-A	5	0	1.000	35	1	0	0	3	71^2	58	3	27	47	10.9	3.01	130	.225	.303	0	.000	-1	8	7	2	0.8
1962	Bal-A	3	2	.600	53	0	0	0	1	65	50	7	36	34	12.0	4.43	85	.217	.326	0	.000	-0	-3	-5	3	-0.1
1963	Bal-A	7	0	1.000	47	0	0	0	1	75^1	69	11	31	55	11.9	3.94	89	.246	.321	0	.000	-1	-3	-3	0	-0.3
1964	Bal-A	2	0	1.000	14	0	0	0	0	20^2	17	5	8	14	10.9	3.92	91	.233	.309	0	.000	-0	-1	-1	0	0.0
	KC-A	6	3	.667	50	0	0	0	5	93	69	10	34	101	10.4	1.94	197	.213	.296	3	.200	0	17	19	-1	2.0
	Yr	8	3	.727	64	0	0	0	5	113^2	86	15	42	115	10.5	2.30	164	.216	.297	1	.053	-0	17	19	-1	2.0
1965	KC-A	0	4	.000	62	2	0	0	4	99^2	96	18	40	52	12.6	5.24	67	.251	.328	0	.000	-1	-20	-19	2	-1.8
1966	KC-A	2	2	.500	35	0	0	0	3	44	30	3	21	31	11.0	2.66	128	.199	.309	0	.000	-0	4	4	-0	0.2
1967	KC-A	0	0	—	1	0	0	0	0	1	3	0	2	0	45.0	18.00	18	.500	.625	0	—	0	-2	-2	0	0.0
Total	9	27	13	.675	321	3	0	0	22	517^1	434	60	215	365	11.6	3.60	102	.231	.315	3	.051	-4	6	4	7	1.2

■ OTIS STOCKSDALE
Stocksdale, Otis Hinkley "Old Gray Fox"   b: 8/7/1871, Near Arcadia, Md.   d: 3/15/33, Pennsville, N.J.   BL/TR, 5'10.5", 180 lbs.   Deb: 7/24/1893

YEAR	TM/L	W	L	PCT	G	GS	CG	SH	SV	IP	H	HR	BB	SO	RAT	ERA	ERA+	OAV	OOB	BH	AVG	PB	PR	/A	PD	TPI
1893	Was-N	2	8	.200	11	11	7	0	0	69	111	4	32	12	18.7	8.22	56	.352	.412	12	.300	2	-27	-27	1	-1.8
1894	Was-N	5	9	.357	18	14	11	0	0	117^1	176	10	42	10	16.7	5.06	104	.342	.392	23	.324	1	3	3	0	0.3
1895	Was-N	6	11	.353	20	17	11	0	1	136	199	7	52	23	16.6	6.09	79	.335	.389	23	.311	3	-20	-19	0	-1.2
	Bos-N	2	2	.500	4	4	1	0	0	23	31	2	8	2	15.3	5.87	87	.317	.369	4	.267	-0	-3	-2	-0	-0.1
	Yr	8	13	.381	24	21	12	0	1	159	230	9	60	25	16.4	6.06	80	.333	.386	27	.304	3	-23	-21	-0	-1.3
1896	Bal-N	0	1	.000	1	0	0	0	0	1^2	4	0	2	1	32.4	16.20	26	.455	.556	1	.333	1	-2	-2	0	-0.1
Total	4	15	31	.326	54	46	30	0	1	347	521	23	136	48	17.0	6.20	80	.341	.395	63	.310	5	-48	-48	2	-2.9

■ BOB STODDARD
Stoddard, Robert Lyle   b: 3/8/57, San Jose, Cal.   BR/TR, 6'1", 190 lbs.   Deb: 9/04/81

YEAR	TM/L	W	L	PCT	G	GS	CG	SH	SV	IP	H	HR	BB	SO	RAT	ERA	ERA+	OAV	OOB	BH	AVG	PB	PR	/A	PD	TPI
1981	Sea-A	2	1	.667	5	5	1	0	0	34^2	35	3	9	22	11.7	2.60	148	.269	.321	0	—	0	4	5	-0	0.5
1982	Sea-A	3	3	.500	9	9	2	1	0	67^1	48	7	18	24	9.2	2.41	179	.205	.271	0	—	0	12	14	1	1.6
1983	Sea-A	9	17	.346	35	23	2	1	0	175^2	182	29	58	87	12.5	4.41	97	.274	.336	0	—	0	-7	-3	0	0.0
1984	Sea-A	2	3	.400	27	6	0	0	0	79	86	10	37	39	14.2	5.13	78	.278	.359	0	—	0	-10	-10	1	-0.8
1985	Det-A	0	0	—	8	0	0	0	0	13^1	16	3	5	11	13.5	6.75	60	.268	.328	0	—	0	-4	-4	1	-0.2
1986	SD-N	1	0	1.000	18	0	0	0	1	23^1	20	1	11	17	12.3	2.31	158	.227	.320	0	.000	-0	4	3	0	0.3
1987	KC-A	1	3	.250	17	2	0	0	1	40	51	3	22	23	17.1	4.27	107	.313	.404	0	—	0	1	1	1	0.2
Total	7	18	27	.400	119	45	5	2	3	433^1	437	56	160	223	12.7	4.03	103	.266	.336	0	.000	-0	0	6	6	1.6

YEAR TM/L	W	L	PCT	G	GS	CG	SH	SV	IP	H	HR	BB	SO	RAT	ERA	ERA+	OAV	OOB	BH	AVG	PB	PR	/A	PD	TPI
■ **TIM STODDARD**				Stoddard, Timothy Paul b: 1/24/53, E.Chicago, Ind. BR/TR, 6'7", 230 lbs. Deb: 9/07/75																				
1975 Chi-A	0	0	—	1	0	0	0	0	1	2	1	0	0	18.0	9.00	43	.400	.400	0	—	0	-1	-1	0	0.0
1978 Bal-A	0	1	.000	8	0	0	0	0	18	22	3	8	14	16.0	6.00	58	.301	.386	0	—	0	-4	-5	0	-0.4
1979 *Bal-A	3	1	.750	29	0	0	0	3	58	44	3	19	47	9.8	1.71	235	.212	.278	0	—	0	16	15	-0	1.5
1980 Bal-A	5	3	.625	64	0	0	0	26	86	72	2	38	64	11.6	2.51	157	.233	.319	0	—	0	15	14	-1	1.3
1981 Bal-A	4	2	.667	31	0	0	0	7	37¹	38	6	18	32	14.0	3.86	94	.268	.358	0	—	0	-1	-1	-0	0.0
1982 Bal-A	3	4	.429	50	0	0	0	12	56	53	4	29	42	13.3	4.02	100	.249	.342	0	—	0	0	0	-1	0.0
1983 Bal-A	4	3	.571	47	0	0	0	9	57²	65	10	29	50	14.8	6.09	65	.293	.377	0	—	0	-13	-14	-0	-1.3
1984 *Chi-N	10	6	.625	58	0	0	0	7	92	77	9	57	87	13.2	3.82	102	.236	.352	1	.091	-1	-2	1	-1	0.0
1985 SD-N	1	6	.143	44	0	0	0	1	60	63	3	37	42	15.0	4.65	76	.269	.369	0	.000	-1	-7	-7	-1	-0.8
1986 SD-N	1	3	.250	30	0	0	0	0	45¹	33	4	34	47	13.3	3.77	97	.200	.337	1	.250	1	-0	-1	0	0.0
NY-A	4	1	.800	24	0	0	0	0	49¹	41	6	23	34	11.7	3.83	107	.232	.320	0	—	0	2	1	0	0.1
1987 NY-A	4	3	.571	57	0	0	0	8	92²	83	13	30	78	11.0	3.50	125	.235	.295	0	—	0	10	9	-1	0.8
1988 NY-A	2	2	.500	28	0	0	0	3	55	62	5	27	33	14.9	6.38	62	.286	.370	0	—	0	-15	-15	-0	-1.4
1989 Cle-A	0	0	—	14	0	0	0	0	21¹	25	1	7	12	13.5	2.95	134	.313	.368	0	—	0	2	2	0	0.3
Total 13	41	35	.539	485	0	0	0	76	729²	680	72	356	582	12.9	3.95	100	.250	.339	2	.100	-0	2	-0	-4	0.1
■ **ART STOKES**				Stokes, Arthur Milton b: 9/13/1896, Emmitsburg, Md. d: 6/3/62, Titusville, Pa. BR/TR, 5'10.5", 155 lbs. Deb: 5/05/25																				
1925 Phi-A	1	1	.500	12	0	0	0	0	24¹	24	0	10	7	13.3	4.07	114	.270	.356	0	.000	-0	1	2	-0	0.1
■ **DICK STONE**				Stone, Charles Richard b: 12/5/11, Oklahoma City, Okla d: 2/18/1880, Oklahoma City, Okla. BL/TL, 5'9", 153 lbs. Deb: 8/26/45																				
1945 Was-A	0	0	—	3	0	0	0	0	5	6	0	2	0	14.4	0.00	—	.316	.381	0	—	0	2	2	0	0.2
■ **DEAN STONE**				Stone, Darrah Dean b: 9/1/30, Moline, Ill. BL/TL, 6'4", 205 lbs. Deb: 9/13/53																				
1953 Was-A	0	1	.000	3	1	0	0	0	8²	13	0	5	5	18.7	8.31	47	.361	.439	0	.000	-0	-4	-4	0	-0.3
1954 Was-A	12	10	.545	31	23	10	2	0	178²	161	7	69	87	11.6	3.22	110	.240	.312	5	.096	-0	10	7	-3	0.3
1955 Was-A	6	13	.316	43	24	5	1	1	180	180	14	114	84	14.9	4.15	92	.267	.375	2	.043	-3	-4	-6	-2	-1.1
1956 Was-A	5	7	.417	41	21	2	0	3	132	148	10	93	86	16.9	6.27	69	.282	.397	3	.088	-1	-31	-29	-2	-2.8
1957 Was-A	0	0	—	3	0	0	0	0	3¹	5	0	2	3	18.9	8.10	48	.357	.438	0	—	0	-2	-2	0	-0.1
Bos-A	1	3	.250	17	8	0	0	1	51¹	56	5	35	32	16.0	5.08	78	.284	.392	0	.000	-1	-7	-6	1	-0.6
Yr	1	3	.250	20	8	0	0	1	54²	61	5	37	35	16.1	5.27	76	.288	.394	2	.143	-1	-9	-8	1	-0.7
1959 StL-N	0	1	.000	18	1	0	0	1	30	30	4	16	17	13.8	4.20	101	.273	.365	0	.000	-0	-1	0	-0	0.0
1962 Hou-N	3	2	.600	15	7	2	2	0	52¹	61	4	20	31	14.1	4.47	84	.295	.360	4	.250	1	-3	-4	-0	-0.2
Chi-A	1	0	1.000	27	0	0	0	5	30¹	28	3	9	23	11.3	3.26	120	.255	.317	1	.500	1	2	2	-0	0.2
1963 Bal-A	1	2	.333	17	0	0	0	1	19¹	23	0	10	12	15.4	5.12	69	.307	.388	0	—	0	-3	-3	-0	-0.2
Total 8	29	39	.426	215	85	19	5	12	686	705	47	373	380	14.3	4.47	86	.269	.363	15	.088	-6	-43	-46	-5	-4.8
■ **DWIGHT STONE**				Stone, Dwight Ely b: 8/2/1886, Holt Co., Neb. d: 6/3/76, Glendale, Cal. BR/TR, 6'1.5", 170 lbs. Deb: 4/13/13																				
1913 StL-A	2	6	.250	18	7	4	1	0	91	94	0	46	37	14.5	3.56	82	.267	.363	9	.273	2	-6	-6	1	-0.3
1914 KC-F	8	14	.364	39	22	6	0	0	186²	205	8	77	88	14.0	4.34	71	.281	.356	7	.121	-2	-23	-26	1	-2.7
Total 2	10	20	.333	57	29	10	1	0	277²	299	8	123	125	14.2	4.08	74	.276	.358	16	.176	-1	-30	-32	2	-3.0
■ **ARNIE STONE**				Stone, Edwin Arnold b: 10/9/1892, North Creek, N.Y. d: 7/29/48, Hudson Falls, N.Y BR/TL, 6', 180 lbs. Deb: 8/07/23																				
1923 Pit-N	0	1	.000	9	0	0	0	0	12¹	19	0	4	2	16.8	8.03	50	.352	.397	0	.000	-0	-6	-6	-0	-0.5
1924 Pit-N	4	2	.667	26	2	1	0	0	64	57	0	15	7	10.1	2.95	130	.259	.306	2	.133	-1	6	6	0	0.5
Total 2	4	3	.571	35	2	1	0	0	76¹	76	0	19	9	11.2	3.77	102	.277	.324	2	.125	-1	1	1	-0	0.0
■ **GEORGE STONE**				Stone, George Heard b: 7/9/46, Ruston, La. BL/TL, 6'3", 205 lbs. Deb: 9/15/67																				
1967 Atl-N	0	0	—	2	1	0	0	0	7¹	8	0	1	5	11.0	4.91	68	.267	.290	0	.000	-0	-1	-1	0	-0.1
1968 Atl-N	7	4	.636	17	10	2	0	0	75	63	9	19	52	9.8	2.76	108	.222	.271	9	.333	3	2	2	-1	0.4
1969 *Atl-N	13	10	.565	36	20	3	0	3	165¹	166	20	48	102	11.9	3.65	99	.260	.317	11	.186	1	-1	-1	-0	0.0
1970 Atl-N	11	11	.500	35	30	9	2	0	207¹	218	27	50	131	11.9	3.86	111	.267	.314	17	.236	4	4	10	3	1.8
1971 Atl-N	6	8	.429	27	24	4	2	0	172²	186	19	35	110	11.8	3.60	103	.274	.315	11	.177	-0	-3	-2	-0	0.2
1972 Atl-N	6	11	.353	31	16	2	1	1	111	143	18	44	63	15.5	5.51	69	.315	.380	5	.200	2	-25	-21	1	-1.8
1973 *NY-N	12	3	.800	27	20	2	0	1	148	157	16	31	77	11.4	2.80	129	.274	.311	13	.271	2	14	13	1	1.8
1974 NY-N	2	7	.222	15	13	1	0	0	77	103	10	21	29	14.5	5.03	71	.322	.364	3	.115	-1	-12	-13	1	-1.2
1975 NY-N	3	3	.500	13	11	1	0	0	57	75	3	21	21	15.2	5.05	68	.323	.379	3	.167	-1	-9	-10	1	-0.8
Total 9	60	57	.513	203	145	24	5	5	1020²	1119	122	270	590	12.4	3.89	96	.278	.326	72	.212	10	-31	-19	5	0.3
■ **ROCKY STONE**				Stone, John Vernon b: 8/23/18, Redding, Cal. d: 11/12/86, Fountain Valley, Cal. BR/TR, 6', 200 lbs. Deb: 5/02/43																				
1943 Cin-N	0	1	.000	13	0	0	0	0	24²	23	0	8	11	11.3	4.38	76	.237	.295	1	.250	0	-3	-3	-1	-0.3
■ **STEVE STONE**				Stone, Steven Michael b: 7/14/47, Euclid, Ohio BR/TR, 5'10", 175 lbs. Deb: 4/08/71																				
1971 SF-N	5	9	.357	24	19	2	2	0	110²	110	9	55	63	13.7	4.15	82	.259	.349	0	.000	-2	-8	-9	2	-1.0
1972 SF-N	6	8	.429	27	16	4	1	0	123²	97	11	49	85	10.8	2.98	117	.218	.298	4	.118	-1	6	7	0	0.6
1973 Chi-A	6	11	.353	36	22	3	0	1	176¹	163	11	82	138	12.9	4.24	93	.245	.335	0	—	0	-8	-5	-0	-0.5
1974 Chi-A	8	6	.571	38	23	1	0	0	169²	185	19	64	90	13.4	4.14	92	.278	.345	7	.121	-3	-10	-6	1	-0.7
1975 Chi-N	12	8	.600	33	32	6	1	0	214¹	198	24	80	139	11.9	3.95	97	.245	.317	8	.111	-2	-8	-3	0	-0.4
1976 Chi-N	3	6	.333	17	15	1	1	0	75	70	6	21	33	11.3	4.08	95	.250	.309	3	.143	-1	-5	-2	-1	-0.3
1977 Chi-A	15	12	.556	31	31	8	1	0	207¹	228	25	80	124	13.6	4.51	90	.281	.350	0	—	0	-10	-10	-0	-0.9
1978 Chi-A	12	12	.500	30	30	6	1	0	212	196	19	84	118	12.0	4.37	87	.247	.321	0	—	0	-14	-13	-1	-1.3
1979 *Bal-A	11	7	.611	32	32	3	0	0	186	173	31	73	96	12.0	3.77	106	.248	.320	0	—	0	9	5	1	0.6
1980 Bal-A	25	7	.781	37	37	9	1	0	250²	224	22	101	149	11.9	3.23	122	.240	.319	0	—	0	22	20	-2	1.8
1981 Bal-A	4	7	.364	15	12	0	0	0	62²	63	7	27	30	13.1	4.60	79	.266	.343	0	—	0	-7	-7	-0	-0.6
Total 11	107	93	.535	320	269	43	7	1	1788¹	1707	184	716	1065	12.4	3.97	97	.253	.328	22	.100	-10	-32	-22	-0	-2.7
■ **TIGE STONE**				Stone, William Arthur b: 9/18/01, Macon, Ga. d: 1/1/60, Jacksonville, Fla. 5'8", 145 lbs. Deb: 8/23/23 ◆																				
1923 StL-N	0	0	—	1	0	0	0	0	3	5	1	3	1	24.0	12.00	33	.455	.571	1	1.000	0	-3	-3	0	-0.1
■ **BILL STONEMAN**				Stoneman, William Hambly b: 4/7/44, Oak Park, Ill. BR/TR, 5'10", 170 lbs. Deb: 7/16/67																				
1967 Chi-N	2	4	.333	28	2	0	0	4	63	51	7	22	52	10.4	3.29	108	.223	.291	0	.000	-1	1	2	-1	0.0
1968 Chi-N	0	1	.000	18	0	0	0	0	29¹	36	5	14	18	15.3	5.52	57	.310	.391	0	.000	-0	-8	-8	-0	-0.8
1969 Mon-N	11	19	.367	42	36	8	5	0	235²	233	26	123	185	14.1	4.39	84	.261	.358	4	.055	-3	-21	-19	-1	-2.2
1970 Mon-N	7	15	.318	40	30	5	3	0	207²	209	26	109	176	14.4	4.59	90	.263	.361	6	.100	-2	-13	-11	-2	-1.4
1971 Mon-N	17	16	.515	39	39	20	3	0	294²	243	20	146	251	12.0	3.15	112	.225	.321	12	.129	-1	10	12	1	1.2
1972 Mon-N	12	14	.462	36	35	13	4	0	250²	213	15	102	171	11.4	2.98	119	.229	.308	6	.080	-4	13	16	-0	1.3
1973 Mon-N	4	8	.333	29	17	0	0	1	96²	120	12	55	48	16.9	6.80	56	.310	.404	1	.050	-1	-34	-32	0	-3.1
1974 Cal-A	1	8	.111	13	11	0	0	0	58²	78	8	31	33	17.0	6.14	66	.322	.404	0	—	0	-16	-18	-0	-1.6
Total 8	54	85	.388	245	170	46	15	5	1236¹	1182	120	602	934	13.3	4.08	90	.253	.344	29	.086	-13	-68	-57	-4	-6.6
■ **LIL STONER**				Stoner, Ulysses Simpson Grant b: 2/28/1899, Bowie, Tex. d: 6/26/66, Enid, Okla. BR/TR, 5'9.5", 180 lbs. Deb: 4/15/22																				
1922 Det-A	4	4	.500	17	7	2	0	0	62²	79	3	35	18	16.4	7.04	55	.315	.409	2	.100	-1	-21	-22	1	-1.9
1924 Det-A	11	11	.500	36	25	10	1	0	215²	271	13	65	66	14.2	4.72	87	.316	.367	15	.195	1	-12	-14	-1	-1.2
1925 Det-A	10	9	.526	34	18	8	0	1	152	166	6	53	51	13.5	4.26	101	.283	.352	16	.291	4	2	1	-3	0.1
1926 Det-A	7	10	.412	32	22	7	0	0	159²	179	11	63	57	13.8	5.47	74	.291	.359	9	.170	-2	-26	-25	-0	-2.4

YEAR	TM/L	W	L	PCT	G	GS	CG	SH	SV	IP	H	HR	BB	SO	RAT	ERA	ERA+	OAV	OOB	BH	AVG	PB	PR	/A	PD	TPI
1927	Det-A	10	13	.435	38	24	13	0	5	215	251	9	77	63	13.9	3.98	106	.301	.362	8	.108	-6	4	6	-2	-0.1
1928	Det-A	5	8	.385	36	11	4	0	4	126¹	151	16	42	29	14.0	4.35	95	.296	.353	7	.179	-1	-4	-3	-2	-0.5
1929	Det-A	3	3	.500	24	3	1	0	4	53	57	7	31	12	15.3	5.26	82	.288	.390	1	.067	-2	-6	-6	2	-0.4
1930	Pit-N	0	0	—	5	0	0	0	0	5²	7	2	3	1	15.9	4.76	105	.318	.400	0	—	0	0	0	0	0.0
1931	Phi-N	0	0	—	7	1	0	0	0	13²	22	0	5	2	17.8	6.59	64	.373	.422	0	.000	-1	-4	-4	0	-0.3
Total 9		50	58	.463	229	111	45	1	14	1003²	1180	62	374	299	14.2	4.76	87	.301	.366	58	.172	-7	-66	-67	-4	-6.7

■ MEL STOTTLEMYRE
Stottlemyre, Melvin Leon b: 11/13/41, Hazelton, Mo. BR/TR, 6'1", 178 lbs. Deb: 8/12/64 C

YEAR	TM/L	W	L	PCT	G	GS	CG	SH	SV	IP	H	HR	BB	SO	RAT	ERA	ERA+	OAV	OOB	BH	AVG	PB	PR	/A	PD	TPI
1964	*NY-A	9	3	.750	13	12	5	2	0	96	77	3	35	49	10.7	2.06	176	.219	.294	9	.243	2	17	17	1	2.3
1965	NY-A	20	9	.690	37	37	**18**	4	0	**291**	250	18	88	155	10.7	2.63	129	.233	.295	13	.131	1	27	25	7	3.6
1966	NY-A	12	20	.375	37	35	9	3	1	251	239	18	82	146	11.5	3.80	87	.253	.313	11	.138	1	-10	-13	4	-0.8
1967	NY-A	15	15	.500	36	36	10	4	0	255	235	20	88	151	11.5	2.96	105	.248	.313	8	.098	-3	8	5	6	0.7
1968	NY-A	21	12	.636	36	36	19	6	0	278²	243	21	65	140	10.0	2.45	118	.234	.281	13	.143	2	16	14	2	2.1
1969	NY-A	20	14	.588	39	39	**24**	3	0	303	267	19	97	113	11.0	2.82	123	.239	.303	18	.178	5	27	22	9	3.8
1970	NY-A	15	13	.536	37	37	14	0	0	271	262	23	84	126	11.7	3.09	114	.255	.315	16	.188	8	19	13	3	2.5
1971	NY-A	16	12	.571	35	35	19	7	0	269²	234	16	69	132	10.2	2.87	113	.233	.285	16	.170	2	18	11	3	1.7
1972	NY-A	14	18	.438	36	36	9	7	0	260	250	13	85	110	11.7	3.22	92	.254	.316	16	.200	3	-5	-8	3	-0.1
1973	NY-A	16	16	.500	38	38	19	4	0	273	259	13	79	95	11.3	3.07	119	.253	.310	0	—	0	23	18	2	2.2
1974	NY-A	6	7	.462	16	15	6	0	0	113	119	7	37	40	12.7	3.58	97	.272	.335	0	—	0	0	-1	-0	-0.1
Total 11		164	139	.541	360	356	152	40	1	2661¹	2435	171	809	1257	11.1	2.97	112	.245	.304	120	.160	20	139	102	39	17.9

■ MEL STOTTLEMYRE
Stottlemyre, Melvin Leon Jr. b: 12/28/63, Prosser, Wash. BR/TR, 6', 190 lbs. Deb: 7/17/90

YEAR	TM/L	W	L	PCT	G	GS	CG	SH	SV	IP	H	HR	BB	SO	RAT	ERA	ERA+	OAV	OOB	BH	AVG	PB	PR	/A	PD	TPI
1990	KC-A	0	1	.000	13	2	0	0	0	31¹	35	3	12	14	13.5	4.88	78	.280	.343	0	—	0	-3	-4	0	-0.3

■ TODD STOTTLEMYRE
Stottlemyre, Todd Vernon b: 5/20/65, Sunnyside, Wash. BL/TR, 6'3", 195 lbs. Deb: 4/06/88

YEAR	TM/L	W	L	PCT	G	GS	CG	SH	SV	IP	H	HR	BB	SO	RAT	ERA	ERA+	OAV	OOB	BH	AVG	PB	PR	/A	PD	TPI
1988	Tor-A	4	8	.333	28	16	0	0	0	98	109	15	46	67	14.6	5.69	69	.283	.366	0	—	0	-19	-19	-0	-1.8
1989	*Tor-A	7	7	.500	27	18	0	0	0	127²	137	11	44	63	13.1	3.88	97	.282	.348	0	—	0	-2	-1	-0.2	-1.0
1990	Tor-A	13	17	.433	33	33	4	0	0	203	214	18	69	115	12.9	4.34	87	.274	.339	0	—	0	-10	-12	1	-1.0
Total 3		24	32	.429	88	67	4	0	0	428²	460	44	159	245	13.4	4.51	85	.278	.348	0	—	0	-29	-33	0	-3.0

■ ALLYN STOUT
Stout, Allyn McClelland "Fish Hook" b: 10/31/04, Peoria, Ill. d: 12/22/74, Sikestown, Mo. BR/TR, 5'10", 167 lbs. Deb: 5/16/31

YEAR	TM/L	W	L	PCT	G	GS	CG	SH	SV	IP	H	HR	BB	SO	RAT	ERA	ERA+	OAV	OOB	BH	AVG	PB	PR	/A	PD	TPI
1931	StL-N	6	0	1.000	30	3	1	0	3	72²	87	2	34	40	15.1	4.21	93	.305	.381	2	.105	-1	-3	-2	1	-0.2
1932	StL-N	4	5	.444	36	3	1	0	1	73²	87	5	28	32	14.5	4.40	89	.305	.375	2	.100	-1	-4	-4	1	-0.3
1933	StL-N	0	0	—	1	0	0	0	0	2	1	0	1	1	9.0	0.00	—	.167	.286	0	—	0	1	1	0	0.1
	Cin-N	2	3	.400	23	5	2	0	0	71¹	85	3	26	29	14.0	3.79	90	.295	.354	4	.182	-0	-4	-3	-1	-0.4
	Yr	2	3	.400	24	5	2	0	0	73¹	86	3	27	30	13.9	3.68	92	.293	.352	4	.045	-0	-3	-2	-1	-0.3
1934	Cin-N	6	8	.429	41	16	4	0	1	140²	170	10	47	51	14.1	4.86	84	.297	.354	8	.186	-0	-13	-12	-0	-1.1
1935	NY-N	1	4	.200	40	2	0	0	5	88	99	7	37	29	14.3	4.91	79	.289	.365	2	.133	-0	-9	-10	-1	-1.0
1943	Bos-N	1	0	1.000	9	0	0	0	1	9¹	17	1	4	3	20.3	6.75	51	.378	.429	0	.000	-0	-3	-3	0	-0.3
Total 6		20	20	.500	180	29	8	0	11	457²	546	28	177	185	14.5	4.54	85	.299	.365	18	.149	-3	-35	-34	-0	-3.2

■ JESSE STOVALL
Stovall, Jesse Cramer "Scout" b: 7/24/1875, Independence, Mo. d: 7/12/55, San Diego, Cal. BL/TR, 6', 175 lbs. Deb: 8/31/03

YEAR	TM/L	W	L	PCT	G	GS	CG	SH	SV	IP	H	HR	BB	SO	RAT	ERA	ERA+	OAV	OOB	BH	AVG	PB	PR	/A	PD	TPI
1903	Cle-A	5	1	.833	6	6	6	2	0	57	44	0	21	12	10.3	2.05	139	.213	.286	1	.045	-2	6	5	-0	0.3
1904	Det-A	3	13	.188	22	17	13	1	0	146²	170	3	45	41	13.2	4.42	58	.291	.341	11	.196	0	-30	-30	1	-2.9
Total 2		8	14	.364	28	23	19	3	0	203²	214	3	66	53	12.4	3.76	70	.270	.327	12	.154	-2	-24	-25	1	-2.6

■ HARRY STOVEY
Stovey, Harry Duffield (b: Harry Duffield Stowe)
b: 12/20/1856, Philadelphia, Pa. d: 9/20/37, New Bedford, Mass BR/TR, 5'11.5", 175 lbs. Deb: 5/01/1880 M♦

YEAR	TM/L	W	L	PCT	G	GS	CG	SH	SV	IP	H	HR	BB	SO	RAT	ERA	ERA+	OAV	OOB	BH	AVG	PB	PR	/A	PD	TPI
1880	Wor-N	0	0	—	2	0	0	0	0	6	8	0	3	3	16.5	4.50	58	.305	.376	94	.265	0	-1	-1	-0	0.0
1883	Phi-a	0	0	—	1	0	0	0	0	3	5	0	0	4	15.0	9.00	39	.349	.349	127	.302	0	-2	-2	0	-0.1
1886	Phi-a	0	0	—	1	0	0	0	0	0¹	2	0	0	0	54.0	27.00	13	.665	.665	144	.294	0	-1	-1	0	0.0
Total 3		0	0	—	4	0	0	0	0	9¹	15	0	3	7	17.4	6.75	43	.344	.386	1769	.288	1	-4	-4	-0	-0.1

■ HAL STOWE
Stowe, Harold Rudolph b: 8/29/37, Gastonia, N.C. BL/TL, 6', 170 lbs. Deb: 9/30/60

YEAR	TM/L	W	L	PCT	G	GS	CG	SH	SV	IP	H	HR	BB	SO	RAT	ERA	ERA+	OAV	OOB	BH	AVG	PB	PR	/A	PD	TPI
1960	NY-A	0	0	—	1	0	0	0	0	1	1	0	1	0	9.0	9.00	40	.000	.500	0	—	0	-1	-1	0	0.0

■ MIKE STRAHLER
Strahler, Michael Wayne b: 3/14/47, Chicago, Ill. BR/TR, 6'4", 180 lbs. Deb: 9/12/70

YEAR	TM/L	W	L	PCT	G	GS	CG	SH	SV	IP	H	HR	BB	SO	RAT	ERA	ERA+	OAV	OOB	BH	AVG	PB	PR	/A	PD	TPI
1970	LA-N	1	1	.500	6	0	0	0	1	18²	13	1	10	11	11.1	1.45	265	.194	.299	2	.250	0	5	5	0	0.5
1971	LA-N	0	0	—	6	0	0	0	0	12²	10	1	8	7	12.8	2.84	114	.217	.333	0	.000	-0	1	1	-0	0.0
1972	LA-N	1	2	.333	19	2	1	0	0	47	42	5	22	25	12.4	3.26	102	.237	.325	2	.182	1	1	0	-0	0.1
1973	Det-A	4	5	.444	22	11	1	0	0	80¹	84	7	39	37	13.9	4.37	94	.273	.356	0	—	0	-5	-3	-1	-0.2
Total 4		6	8	.429	53	13	2	0	1	158²	149	14	79	80	13.0	3.57	105	.249	.339	4	.200	1	2	3	-1	0.4

■ DICK STRAHS
Strahs, Richard Bernard b: 12/4/24, Evanston, Ill. BL/TR, 6', 192 lbs. Deb: 7/24/54

YEAR	TM/L	W	L	PCT	G	GS	CG	SH	SV	IP	H	HR	BB	SO	RAT	ERA	ERA+	OAV	OOB	BH	AVG	PB	PR	/A	PD	TPI
1954	Chi-A	0	0	—	9	0	0	0	1	14¹	16	0	8	8	15.1	5.65	66	.271	.358	0	.000	0	-3	-3	0	-0.2

■ LES STRAKER
Straker, Lester Paul (Bolnalda) b: 10/10/59, Ciudad Bolivar, Ven BR/TR, 6'1", 193 lbs. Deb: 4/11/87

YEAR	TM/L	W	L	PCT	G	GS	CG	SH	SV	IP	H	HR	BB	SO	RAT	ERA	ERA+	OAV	OOB	BH	AVG	PB	PR	/A	PD	TPI
1987	*Min-A	8	10	.444	31	26	1	0	0	154¹	150	24	59	76	12.3	4.37	106	.257	.328	0	—	0	1	4	-1	0.3
1988	Min-A	2	5	.286	16	14	1	1	1	82²	86	8	25	23	12.1	3.92	104	.276	.329	0	—	0	0	1	1	0.2
Total 2		10	15	.400	47	40	2	1	1	237	236	32	84	99	12.2	4.22	105	.264	.328	0	—	0	2	5	-0	0.5

■ BOB STRAMPE
Strampe, Robert Edwin b: 6/13/50, Janesville, Wis. BB/TR, 6'1", 185 lbs. Deb: 5/10/72

YEAR	TM/L	W	L	PCT	G	GS	CG	SH	SV	IP	H	HR	BB	SO	RAT	ERA	ERA+	OAV	OOB	BH	AVG	PB	PR	/A	PD	TPI
1972	Det-A	0	0	—	7	0	0	0	0	4²	6	0	7	4	25.1	11.57	27	.300	.481	0	—	0	-4	-4	-0	-0.4

■ PAUL STRAND
Strand, Paul Edward b: 12/19/1893, Carbonado, Wash. d: 7/2/74, Salt Lake City, Utah BR/TL, 6'0.5", 190 lbs. Deb: 5/15/13 ♦

YEAR	TM/L	W	L	PCT	G	GS	CG	SH	SV	IP	H	HR	BB	SO	RAT	ERA	ERA+	OAV	OOB	BH	AVG	PB	PR	/A	PD	TPI
1913	Bos-N	0	0	—	7	0	0	0	0	17	22	1	12	6	18.0	2.12	155	.393	.500	1	.167	-0	2	2	0	0.2
1914	Bos-N	5	2	.714	16	3	1	0	1	55¹	47	1	23	33	11.5	2.44	113	.235	.317	8	.333	2	2	2	-1	0.4
1915	Bos-N	1	1	.500	6	2	2	0	1	22²	26	0	3	13	11.5	2.38	109	.295	.319	2	.091	-0	1	1	-1	0.1
Total 3		6	3	.667	29	5	3	0	2	95	95	2	38	52	12.7	2.37	119	.276	.350	49	.224	2	5	5	-1	0.7

■ SCOTT STRATTON
Stratton, C. Scott b: 10/2/1869, Campbellsburg, Ky. d: 3/8/39, Louisville, Ky. BL/TR, 6', 180 lbs. Deb: 4/21/1888 ♦

YEAR	TM/L	W	L	PCT	G	GS	CG	SH	SV	IP	H	HR	BB	SO	RAT	ERA	ERA+	OAV	OOB	BH	AVG	PB	PR	/A	PD	TPI
1888	Lou-a	10	17	.370	33	28	28	2	0	269²	287	7	53	97	11.3	3.64	85	.263	.297	64	.257	4	-17	-17	0	-1.4
1889	Lou-a	3	13	.188	19	17	13	0	1	133²	157	6	42	42	13.4	3.23	119	.284	.334	66	.288	4	9	9	2	0.8
1890	*Lou-a	34	14	**.708**	50	49	44	4	0	431	398	3	61	207	9.6	2.36	163	.238	.264	61	.323	15	**72**	71	6	**9.1**
1891	Pit-N	0	2	.000	2	2	2	0	0	18¹	16	0	5	5	10.3	2.45	134	.226	.277	1	.125	2	2	1	0	0.2
	Lou-a	6	13	.316	20	20	20	1	0	172	204	10	34	52	12.5	4.08	90	.285	.317	27	.235	1	-7	-8	3	-0.2
1892	Lou-N	21	19	.525	42	40	39	2	0	351²	342	1	70	93	10.5	2.92	105	.245	.281	56	.256	9	14	6	2	1.9
1893	Lou-N	12	24	.333	38	36	35	1	0	323²	451	8	104	44	15.4	5.45	81	.320	.367	50	.226	3	-28	-38	6	-2.2
1894	Lou-N	1	5	.167	7	5	4	0	0	43	72	3	13	3	17.8	8.37	61	.368	.407	12	.324	2	-15	-16	1	-0.8
	Chi-N	8	5	.615	15	12	11	0	0	119¹	198	5	40	23	17.9	6.03	93	.366	.409	36	.375	7	-9	-6	1	-0.3
	Yr	9	10	.474	22	17	15	0	0	162¹	270	8	53	26	17.9	6.65	82	.366	.409	10	.075	9	-24	-21	1	-0.3
1895	Chi-N	2	3	.400	5	5	3	0	0	30	51	1	14	4	19.5	9.60	53	.370	.428	7	.292	1	-16	-15	1	-1.0
Total 8		97	115	.458	231	214	199	10	1	1892¹	2176	44	436	570	12.4	3.88	99	.279	.318	380	.274	46	6	-12	22	6.9

■ MONTY STRATTON
Stratton, Monty Franklin Pierce "Gander" b: 5/21/12, Celeste, Tex. d: 9/29/82, Greenville, Tex. BR/TR, 6'5", 180 lbs. Deb: 6/02/34 C

YEAR	TM/L	W	L	PCT	G	GS	CG	SH	SV	IP	H	HR	BB	SO	RAT	ERA	ERA+	OAV	OOB	BH	AVG	PB	PR	/A	PD	TPI
1934	Chi-A	0	0	—	1	0	0	0	0	3¹	4	0	1	0	13.5	5.40	88	.333	.385	0	.000	-0	-0	-0	0	0.0

YEAR	TM/L	W	L	PCT	G	GS	CG	SH	SV	IP	H	HR	BB	SO	RAT	ERA	ERA+	OAV	OOB	BH	AVG	PB	PR	/A	PD	TPI
1935	Chi-A	1	2	.333	5	5	2	0	0	38	40	4	9	8	12.1	4.03	115	.274	.325	2	.143	-1	2	3	0	0.2
1936	Chi-A	5	7	.417	16	14	3	0	0	95	117	8	46	37	15.5	5.21	100	.305	.381	8	.216	1	-2	-0	1	0.2
1937	Chi-A	15	5	.750	22	21	14	5	0	164²	142	6	37	69	**9.9**	2.40	**191**	.234	**.280**	12	.200	-0	41	40	1	4.1
1938	Chi-A	15	9	.625	26	22	17	0	2	186¹	186	18	56	82	12.0	4.01	122	.255	.315	21	.266	5	16	18	-0	2.2
Total	5	36	23	.610	70	62	36	5	2	487¹	489	32	149	196	12.0	3.71	130	.261	.319	43	.224	5	56	61	2	6.7

■ ED STRATTON   Stratton, William Edward b: Baltimore, Md.   Deb: 5/14/1873

YEAR	TM/L	W	L	PCT	G	GS	CG	SH	SV	IP	H	HR	BB	SO	RAT	ERA	ERA+	OAV	OOB	BH	AVG	PB	PR	/A	PD	TPI
1873	Mar-n	0	3	.000	3	3	3	0	0	27	75	3	0		25.0	10.00	36	.410	.410	2	.125	-1	-19	-19		-1.1

■ JOE STRAUSS   Strauss, Joseph "Dutch" or "The Socker" (b: Joseph Strasser) b: 11/1858, Ohio d: 6/25/06, Cincinnati, Ohio   BR/TR,   Deb: 7/27/1884 ◆

YEAR	TM/L	W	L	PCT	G	GS	CG	SH	SV	IP	H	HR	BB	SO	RAT	ERA	ERA+	OAV	OOB	BH	AVG	PB	PR	/A	PD	TPI
1886	Lou-a	0	0	—	2	0	0	1	0	4	6	0	3	0	20.3	4.50	81	.331	.426	64	.215	-0	-0	-0	0	0.0

■ OSCAR STREIT   Streit, Oscar William b: 7/7/1873, Florence, Ala. d: 10/10/35, Birmingham, Ala.   BL/TL, 6'5", 190 lbs.   Deb: 4/21/1899

YEAR	TM/L	W	L	PCT	G	GS	CG	SH	SV	IP	H	HR	BB	SO	RAT	ERA	ERA+	OAV	OOB	BH	AVG	PB	PR	/A	PD	TPI
1899	Bos-N	1	0	1.000	2	1	1	0	0	14²	15	1	15	0	18.4	6.75	62	.264	.418	0	.000	-1	-5	-4	0	-0.3
1902	Cle-A	0	7	.000	8	7	4	0	0	51²	72	3	25	10	16.9	5.23	66	.330	.398	4	.211	1	-9	-10	-1	-0.8
Total	2	1	7	.125	10	8	5	0	0	66¹	87	4	40	10	17.2	5.56	65	.316	.403	4	.154	-0	-14	-14	-1	-1.1

■ ED STRELECKI   Strelecki, Edward Henry b: 4/10/05, Newark, N.J. d: 1/9/68, Newark, N.J.   BR/TR, 5'11.5", 180 lbs.   Deb: 4/16/28

YEAR	TM/L	W	L	PCT	G	GS	CG	SH	SV	IP	H	HR	BB	SO	RAT	ERA	ERA+	OAV	OOB	BH	AVG	PB	PR	/A	PD	TPI
1928	StL-A	0	2	.000	22	2	1	0	1	50¹	49	4	17	8	12.0	4.29	98	.269	.335	2	.200	0	-1	-1	0	0.0
1929	StL-A	1	1	.500	7	0	0	0	0	11	12	1	6	2	15.5	4.91	90	.279	.380	0	.000	-0	-1	-1	0	0.0
1931	Cin-N	0	0	—	13	0	0	0	0	24¹	37	2	9	3	18.1	9.25	40	.394	.462	1	.200	0	-15	-15	1	-1.2
Total	3	1	3	.250	42	2	1	0	1	85²	98	7	32	13	14.2	5.78	71	.307	.379	3	.176	0	-17	-16	1	-1.2

■ PHIL STREMMEL   Stremmel, Philip b: 4/16/1880, Zanesville, Ohio d: 12/26/47, Chicago, Ill.   BR/TR, 6', 175 lbs.   Deb: 9/16/09

YEAR	TM/L	W	L	PCT	G	GS	CG	SH	SV	IP	H	HR	BB	SO	RAT	ERA	ERA+	OAV	OOB	BH	AVG	PB	PR	/A	PD	TPI
1909	StL-A	0	2	.000	2	2	2	0	0	18	20	0	4	6	12.5	4.50	54	.308	.357	0	.000	-1	-4	-4	1	-0.3
1910	StL-A	0	2	.000	5	2	2	0	0	29	31	0	16	7	14.6	3.72	66	.287	.379	1	.125	-0	-4	-4	2	-0.2
Total	2	0	4	.000	7	4	4	0	0	47	51	0	20	13	13.8	4.02	61	.295	.371	1	.071	-1	-8	-8	2	-0.5

■ CUB STRICKER   Stricker, John A. (b: John A. Streaker)   b: 2/15/1860, Philadelphia, Pa. d: 11/19/37, Philadelphia, Pa.   BR/TR, 5'3", 138 lbs.   Deb: 5/02/1882 M◆

YEAR	TM/L	W	L	PCT	G	GS	CG	SH	SV	IP	H	HR	BB	SO	RAT	ERA	ERA+	OAV	OOB	BH	AVG	PB	PR	/A	PD	TPI
1882	Phi-a	1	0	1.000	2	0	0	0	0	7	3	0	1	2	5.1	1.29	232	.121	.155	59	.217	-0	1	1	-0	0.1
1884	Phi-a	0	0	—	1	0	0	0	0	3	6	0	1	1	21.0	6.00	57	.395	.433	92	.231	0	-1	-1	-0	0.0
1887	Cle-a	0	0	—	3	0	0	0	1	5²	5	0	7	2	19.1	3.18	137	.228	.415	141	.264	0	1	1	0	0.1
1888	Cle-a	1	0	1.000	2	0	0	0	0	12	16	0	2	5	13.5	4.50	69	.309	.335	115	.233	0	-2	-2	0	-0.1
Total	4	2	0	1.000	8	0	0	0	1	27²	30	0	11	10	13.3	3.58	94	.264	.329	1107	.239	1	-1	-1	0	0.1

■ JIM STRICKLAND   Strickland, James Michael b: 6/12/46, Los Angeles, Cal.   BL/TL, 6', 175 lbs.   Deb: 5/19/71

YEAR	TM/L	W	L	PCT	G	GS	CG	SH	SV	IP	H	HR	BB	SO	RAT	ERA	ERA+	OAV	OOB	BH	AVG	PB	PR	/A	PD	TPI
1971	Min-A	1	0	1.000	24	0	0	0	1	31¹	20	2	18	21	11.5	1.44	247	.183	.310	0	.000	0	7	7	0	0.8
1972	Min-A	3	1	.750	25	0	0	0	3	36	28	7	19	30	11.8	2.50	128	.214	.313	1	.333	1	2	3	0	0.4
1973	Min-A	0	1	.000	7	0	0	0	0	5¹	11	0	5	6	27.0	11.81	34	.440	.533	0	—	0	-5	-5	0	-0.4
1975	Cle-A	0	0	—	4	0	0	0	1	4²	4	0	2	3	13.5	1.93	196	.222	.333	0	—	0	1	1	-0	0.1
Total	4	4	2	.667	60	0	0	0	5	77¹	63	9	44	60	12.8	2.68	128	.223	.333	1	.250	1	6	7	0	0.9

■ BILL STRICKLAND   Strickland, William Goss b: 3/29/08, Nashville, Ga.   BR/TR, 6'2", 170 lbs.   Deb: 9/16/37

YEAR	TM/L	W	L	PCT	G	GS	CG	SH	SV	IP	H	HR	BB	SO	RAT	ERA	ERA+	OAV	OOB	BH	AVG	PB	PR	/A	PD	TPI
1937	StL-A	0	0	—	9	0	0	0	0	21¹	28	2	15	6	19.0	5.91	82	.341	.455	1	.167	-0	-3	-3	-0	-0.2

■ ELMER STRICKLETT   Stricklett, Elmer Griffin "Spitball" b: 8/29/1876, Glasco, Kan. d: 6/7/64, Santa Cruz, Cal.   TR , 5'6", 140 lbs.   Deb: 4/22/04

YEAR	TM/L	W	L	PCT	G	GS	CG	SH	SV	IP	H	HR	BB	SO	RAT	ERA	ERA+	OAV	OOB	BH	AVG	PB	PR	/A	PD	TPI
1904	Chi-A	0	1	.000	1	1	0	0	0	7	12	0	2	3	18.0	10.29	24	.377	.414	0	.000	-0	-6	-6	0	-0.4
1905	Bro-N	9	18	.333	33	28	25	1	1	237	259	0	71	77	13.1	3.34	87	.282	.343	13	.148	-1	-9	-12	9	-0.3
1906	Bro-N	14	18	.438	41	35	28	5	5	291²	273	2	77	88	11.0	2.72	93	.253	.306	20	.206	5	-3	-6	9	0.8
1907	Bro-N	12	14	.462	29	26	25	4	0	229²	211	1	65	69	11.1	2.27	103	.255	.315	12	.148	1	5	2	7	1.1
Total	4	35	51	.407	104	90	78	10	6	765¹	755	3	215	237	11.7	2.85	91	.264	.322	45	.167	4	-12	-23	26	1.2

■ JOHN STRIKE   Strike, John b: 1865, Pennsylvania   Deb: 5/18/1882 ◆

YEAR	TM/L	W	L	PCT	G	GS	CG	SH	SV	IP	H	HR	BB	SO	RAT	ERA	ERA+	OAV	OOB	BH	AVG	PB	PR	/A	PD	TPI
1886	Phi-N	1	1	.500	2	2	1	0	0	15	19	1	7	11	15.6	4.80	69	.297	.366	0	.000	-1	-2	-3	-1	-0.3

■ JAKE STRIKER   Striker, Wilbur Scott b: 10/23/33, New Washington, O.   BL/TL, 6'2", 200 lbs.   Deb: 9/25/59

YEAR	TM/L	W	L	PCT	G	GS	CG	SH	SV	IP	H	HR	BB	SO	RAT	ERA	ERA+	OAV	OOB	BH	AVG	PB	PR	/A	PD	TPI
1959	Cle-A	1	0	1.000	1	1	0	0	0	6²	8	0	4	5	16.2	2.70	136	.296	.387	0	.000	1	1	1	0	0.1
1960	Chi-A	0	0	—	2	0	0	0	0	3²	5	1	1	1	17.2	4.91	77	.357	.438	0	—	0	-0	-0	-0	0.0
Total	2	1	0	1.000	3	1	0	0	0	10¹	13	1	5	6	16.5	3.48	107	.317	.404	0	.000	1	0	0	-0	0.1

■ NICK STRINCEVICH   Strincevich, Nicholas Mihailovich "Jumbo"   b: 3/1/15, Gary, Ind.   BR/TR, 6'1", 180 lbs.   Deb: 4/23/40

YEAR	TM/L	W	L	PCT	G	GS	CG	SH	SV	IP	H	HR	BB	SO	RAT	ERA	ERA+	OAV	OOB	BH	AVG	PB	PR	/A	PD	TPI
1940	Bos-N	4	8	.333	32	14	5	0	1	128²	142	17	63	54	14.9	5.53	67	.278	.367	5	.116	-2	-24	-26	-2	-2.8
1941	Bos-N	0	0	—	3	0	0	0	0	3¹	7	0	6	1	37.8	10.80	33	.412	.583	0	—	0	-3	-3	0	-0.1
	Pit-N	1	2	.333	12	3	0	0	0	31	35	4	13	12	14.2	5.23	69	.280	.353	3	.429	1	-5	-6	0	-0.4
	Yr	1	2	.333	15	3	0	0	0	34¹	42	4	19	13	16.3	5.77	63	.294	.380	0	.000	1	-8	-8	0	-0.5
1942	Pit-N	0	0	—	7	1	0	0	0	22¹	19	2	9	10	11.7	2.82	120	.229	.312	0	.000	-1	1	1	-0	0.1
1944	Pit-N	14	7	.667	40	26	11	0	2	190	190	5	37	47	10.9	3.08	121	.257	.296	9	.158	-1	11	13	6	1.9
1945	Pit-N	16	10	.615	36	29	18	1	2	228¹	235	7	49	49	11.3	3.31	119	.260	.301	17	.202	0	12	16	-1	1.5
1946	Pit-N	10	15	.400	32	22	11	3	1	176	185	7	44	49	11.9	3.58	98	.268	.316	8	.154	1	-3	-1	-2	-0.1
1947	Pit-N	1	6	.143	32	7	1	0	0	89	111	9	37	22	15.2	5.26	80	.316	.385	1	.048	-2	-12	-10	0	-1.0
1948	Pit-N	0	0	—	3	0	0	0	0	4¹	9	1	1	2	20.8	8.31	49	.444	.500	0	—	0	-2	-2	0	-0.1
	Phi-N	0	1	.000	6	1	0	0	0	16²	26	1	10	4	19.4	9.18	43	.347	.424	0	.000	-1	-10	-10	-0	-1.0
	Yr	0	1	.000	9	1	0	0	0	21	34	1	12	5	19.7	9.00	44	.366	.438	0	.000	-1	-12	-12	-0	-1.0
Total	8	46	49	.484	203	103	46	4	6	889²	958	52	270	274	12.7	4.05	93	.273	.329	43	.158	-4	-34	-26	1	-1.9

■ JOHN STROHMAYER   Strohmayer, John Emery b: 10/13/46, Belle Fourche, S.D.   BR/TR, 6'1", 181 lbs.   Deb: 4/29/70

YEAR	TM/L	W	L	PCT	G	GS	CG	SH	SV	IP	H	HR	BB	SO	RAT	ERA	ERA+	OAV	OOB	BH	AVG	PB	PR	/A	PD	TPI
1970	Mon-N	3	1	.750	42	0	0	0	0	76	85	7	39	74	14.9	4.86	85	.279	.364	1	.167	-0	-7	-6	-1	-0.6
1971	Mon-N	7	5	.583	27	14	2	0	1	114	124	16	31	56	12.6	4.34	81	.281	.333	8	.229	1	-11	-10	-1	-1.0
1972	Mon-N	1	2	.333	48	0	0	0	3	76²	73	6	31	50	12.3	3.52	101	.256	.331	0	.000	0	-1	0	1	0.1
1973	Mon-N	0	1	.000	17	3	0	0	0	34²	34	4	22	15	14.8	5.19	73	.260	.370	1	.200	0	-6	-5	-0	-0.4
	NY-N	0	0	—	7	0	0	0	0	10	13	2	4	5	15.3	8.10	45	.310	.370	0	—	0	-5	-5	-0	-0.4
	Yr	0	1	.000	24	3	0	0	0	44²	47	6	26	20	14.7	5.84	65	.270	.365	1	.200	0	-11	-10	-0	-0.8
1974	NY-N	0	0	—	1	0	0	0	0	1	0	0	1	0	9.0	0.00	—	.000	.250	0	—	0	0	0	0	0.0
Total	5	11	9	.550	142	17	2	0	4	312¹	329	35	128	200	13.4	4.47	83	.272	.346	10	.200	1	-29	-26	-0	-2.3

■ BRENT STROM   Strom, Brent Terry b: 10/14/48, San Diego, Cal.   BR/TL, 6'3", 189 lbs.   Deb: 7/31/72

YEAR	TM/L	W	L	PCT	G	GS	CG	SH	SV	IP	H	HR	BB	SO	RAT	ERA	ERA+	OAV	OOB	BH	AVG	PB	PR	/A	PD	TPI
1972	NY-N	0	3	.000	11	5	0	0	0	30¹	34	7	15	20	14.5	6.82	49	.296	.377	0	.000	-1	-11	-12	-1	-1.2
1973	Cle-A	2	10	.167	27	18	2	0	0	123	134	18	47	91	13.5	4.61	85	.278	.346	0	—	0	-11	-9	0	-0.8
1975	SD-N	8	8	.500	18	16	6	2	0	120¹	103	6	33	56	10.3	2.54	137	.233	.289	3	.100	-1	14	12	1	1.3
1976	SD-N	12	16	.429	36	33	8	1	0	210²	188	15	73	103	11.2	3.29	99	.239	.305	4	.063	-2	5	-0	0	-0.2
1977	SD-N	0	2	.000	8	3	0	0	0	16²	25	5	12	8	18.9	12.42	28	.329	.427	1	.333	0	-16	-16	0	-1.4
Total	5	22	39	.361	100	75	16	3	0	501	482	51	180	278	12.0	3.95	88	.254	.321	8	.078	-3	-19	-26	0	-2.3

■ FLOYD STROMME   Stromme, Floyd Marvin "Rock" b: 8/1/16, Copperstown, N.Dak.   BR/TR, 5'11", 170 lbs.   Deb: 7/05/39

YEAR	TM/L	W	L	PCT	G	GS	CG	SH	SV	IP	H	HR	BB	SO	RAT	ERA	ERA+	OAV	OOB	BH	AVG	PB	PR	/A	PD	TPI
1939	Cle-A	0	1	.000	5	0	0	0	0	13	13	1	13	4	18.0	4.85	91	.265	.419	1	.333	0	-0	-1	-0	0.0

YEAR TM/L	W	L	PCT	G	GS	CG	SH	SV	IP	H	HR	BB	SO	RAT	ERA	ERA+	OAV	OOB	BH	AVG	PB	PR	/A	PD	TPI

■ **SAILOR STROUD**   Stroud, Ralph Vivian   b: 5/15/1885, Ironia, N.J.   d: 4/11/70, Stockton, Cal.   BR/TR, 6′, 160 lbs.   Deb: 4/29/10

1910 Det-A	5	9	.357	28	15	7	3	1	130¹	123	9	41	63	11.8	3.25	81	.257	.325	1	.026	-4	-11	-9	-4	-1.7
1915 NY-N	12	9	.571	32	22	8	0	1	184	194	3	35	62	11.5	2.79	92	.281	.321	9	.161	-1	-1	-5	1	-0.5
1916 NY-N	3	2	.600	10	4	0	0	1	46²	47	1	9	16	11.0	2.70	90	.266	.305	1	.071	-1	-0	-1	-0	-0.2
Total 3	20	20	.500	70	41	15	3	3	361	364	13	85	141	11.5	2.94	88	.271	.321	11	.101	-6	-12	-15	-4	-2.4

■ **STEAMBOAT STRUSS**   Struss, Clarence Herbert   b: 2/24/09, Riverdale, Ill.   d: 9/12/85, Grand Rapids, Mich.   BR/TR, 5′11″, 163 lbs.   Deb: 9/30/34

| 1934 Pit-N | 0 | 1 | .000 | 1 | 1 | 0 | 0 | 0 | 7 | 7 | 0 | 6 | 3 | 16.7 | 6.43 | 64 | .250 | .382 | 1 | .333 | 0 | -2 | -2 | 0 | 0.0 |

■ **DUTCH STRYKER**   Stryker, Sterling Alpa   b: 7/29/1895, Atlantic Highlands, N.J.   d: 11/5/64, Red Bank, N.J.   BR/TR, 5′11.5″, 180 lbs.   Deb: 4/16/24

1924 Bos-N	3	8	.273	20	10	2	0	0	73¹	90	4	22	22	13.9	6.01	64	.314	.365	5	.217	-0	-17	-18	2	-1.4
1926 Bro-N	0	0	—	2	0	0	0	0	2	8	0	1	0	40.5	27.00	14	.571	.600	0	—	0	-5	-5	0	-0.4
Total 2	3	8	.273	22	10	2	0	0	75¹	98	4	23	22	14.6	6.57	58	.326	.375	5	.217	-0	-23	-23	2	-1.8

■ **JOHNNY STUART**   Stuart, John Davis "Stud"   b: 4/27/01, Clinton, Tenn.   d: 5/13/70, Charleston, W.Va.   BR/TR, 5′11″, 170 lbs.   Deb: 7/27/22

1922 StL-N	0	0	—	2	1	0	0	0	2	2	0	2	1	22.5	9.00	43	.222	.417	0	—	0	-1	-1	0	0.0
1923 StL-N	9	5	.643	37	10	7	1	3	149²	139	11	70	55	13.1	4.27	91	.252	.345	14	.246	1	-4	-6	-1	-0.6
1924 StL-N	9	11	.450	28	22	13	0	0	159	167	12	60	54	13.1	4.75	80	.273	.343	11	.204	-1	-16	-17	-3	-2.0
1925 StL-N	2	2	.500	15	1	1	0	0	47	52	6	24	14	14.9	6.13	71	.278	.366	4	.250	1	-10	-9	-0	-0.7
Total 4	20	18	.526	82	34	21	1	3	357²	360	29	156	124	13.4	4.76	82	.265	.348	29	.228	1	-31	-34	-5	-3.3

■ **MARLIN STUART**   Stuart, Marlin Henry   b: 8/8/18, Paragould, Ark.   BL/TR, 6′2″, 185 lbs.   Deb: 4/26/49

1949 Det-A	0	2	.000	14	2	0	0	0	29²	39	3	35	14	22.4	9.10	46	.348	.503	2	.333	1	-16	-16	0	-1.3
1950 Det-A	3	1	.750	19	1	0	0	2	43²	59	6	22	19	16.9	5.56	84	.330	.406	1	.083	-1	-5	-4	0	-0.4
1951 Det-A	4	6	.400	29	15	5	0	0	124	119	9	71	46	14.3	3.77	111	.258	.365	10	.233	1	5	6	1	0.7
1952 Det-A	3	2	.600	30	9	2	0	1	91¹	91	8	48	32	14.0	4.93	77	.265	.360	2	.087	-1	-13	-11	0	-1.1
StL-A	1	2	.333	12	2	0	0	1	26	26	3	9	13	12.1	4.15	94	.260	.321	0	.000	-1	-1	-1	-0	-0.1
Yr	4	4	.500	42	11	2	0	2	117¹	117	11	57	45	13.3	4.76	81	.262	.346	4	.138	-2	-14	-12	-1	-1.2
1953 StL-A	8	2	.800	60	2	0	0	7	114¹	136	6	44	46	14.2	3.94	107	.300	.363	5	.192	-1	1	3	-0	0.3
1954 Bal-A	1	2	.333	22	0	0	0	2	38¹	46	2	15	13	14.8	4.46	80	.303	.373	0	.000	-0	-3	-4	1	-0.3
NY-A	3	0	1.000	10	0	0	0	1	18¹	28	0	12	2	19.6	5.40	64	.350	.435	2	.333	0	-3	-4	1	-0.3
Yr	4	2	.667	32	0	0	0	3	56²	74	2	27	15	16.0	4.76	74	.316	.387	0	.000	0	-7	-8	1	-0.5
Total 6	23	17	.575	196	31	7	0	15	485²	544	37	256	185	15.1	4.65	87	.289	.378	22	.176	-1	-36	-31	1	-2.4

■ **GEORGE STUELAND**   Stueland, George Anton   b: 3/2/1899, Algona, Iowa   d: 9/9/64, Onawa, Iowa   BB/TR, 6′1.5″, 174 lbs.   Deb: 9/15/21

1921 Chi-N	0	1	.000	2	1	0	0	0	11	11	0	7	4	14.7	5.73	67	.282	.391	1	.333	0	-2	-2	0	-0.1
1922 Chi-N	9	4	.692	35	12	4	0	0	113	129	9	49	44	14.6	5.81	72	.297	.374	4	.129	-2	-22	-20	-1	-2.1
1923 Chi-N	0	1	.000	6	0	0	0	0	8	11	0	5	2	18.0	5.63	71	.478	.571	0	—	0	-1	-1	0	0.0
1925 Chi-N	0	0	—	2	0	0	0	0	3	2	0	3	2	15.0	3.00	144	.182	.357	1	1.000	0	0	0	0	0.1
Total 4	9	6	.600	45	13	4	0	0	135	153	9	64	52	14.8	5.73	73	.301	.385	6	.171	-1	-25	-24	-1	-2.1

■ **PAUL STUFFEL**   Stuffel, Paul Harrington "Stu"   b: 3/22/27, Canton, Ohio   BR/TR, 6′2″, 185 lbs.   Deb: 9/16/50

1950 Phi-N	0	0	—	3	0	0	0	0	5	4	0	3	3	10.8	1.80	225	.211	.286	0	—	0	1	1	0	0.1
1952 Phi-N	1	0	1.000	2	1	0	0	0	6	5	0	7	3	18.0	3.00	122	.217	.400	0	.000	-0	0	0	0	0.1
1953 Phi-N	0	0	—	2	0	0	0	0	0	0	0	4	0	—	∞	—	—	1.000	0	—	0	-4	-4	0	-0.3
Total 3	1	0	1.000	7	1	0	0	0	11	9	0	12	6	18.0	5.73	67	.214	.400	0	.000	-0	-2	-2	0	-0.1

■ **GEORGE STULTZ**   Stultz, George Irvin   b: 6/30/1873, Louisville, Ky.   d: 3/19/55, Louisville, Ky.   5′10″, 150 lbs.   Deb: 9/22/1894

| 1894 Bos-N | 1 | 0 | 1.000 | 1 | 1 | 1 | 0 | 0 | 9 | 4 | 0 | 5 | 1 | 9.0 | 0.00 | — | .134 | .258 | 1 | .333 | -0 | 5 | 6 | 1 | 0.6 |

■ **JIM STUMP**   Stump, James Gilbert   b: 2/10/32, Lansing, Mich.   BR/TR, 6′, 188 lbs.   Deb: 8/29/57

1957 Det-A	1	0	1.000	6	0	0	0	0	13¹	11	0	8	2	12.8	2.03	190	.220	.328	1	.500	0	3	3	0	0.4
1959 Det-A	0	0	—	5	0	0	0	0	11¹	12	1	4	6	12.7	2.38	170	.279	.340	1	1.000	1	2	2	0	0.3
Total 2	1	0	1.000	11	0	0	0	0	24²	23	1	12	8	12.8	2.19	180	.247	.333	2	.667	1	4	5	0	0.7

■ **JOHN STUPER**   Stuper, John Anton   b: 5/9/57, Butler, Pa.   BR/TR, 6′2″, 200 lbs.   Deb: 6/01/82

1982 ★StL-N	9	7	.563	23	21	2	0	0	136²	137	8	55	53	12.6	3.36	108	.266	.337	5	.119	-1	4	4	-3	0.0
1983 StL-N	12	11	.522	40	30	6	1	1	198	202	15	71	81	12.5	3.68	98	.265	.329	8	.136	-1	-1	-1	-1	-0.2
1984 StL-N	3	5	.375	15	12	0	0	0	61¹	73	4	20	19	13.9	5.28	66	.297	.354	1	.063	-1	-12	-12	1	-1.2
1985 Cin-N	8	5	.615	33	13	1	0	0	99	116	8	37	38	13.9	4.55	83	.303	.364	1	.059	-0	-10	-8	0	-0.8
Total 4	32	28	.533	111	76	9	1	1	495	528	35	183	191	13.0	3.96	92	.277	.341	15	.112	-3	-20	-18	-3	-2.2

■ **TOM STURDIVANT**   Sturdivant, Thomas Virgil "Snake"   b: 4/28/30, Gordon, Kan.   BL/TR, 6′0.5″, 170 lbs.   Deb: 4/14/55

1955 ★NY-A	1	3	.250	33	6	1	0	0	68¹	48	6	42	48	12.1	3.16	118	.203	.329	1	.083	-1	6	4	-0	0.3
1956 ★NY-A	16	8	.667	32	17	6	2	5	158¹	134	15	52	110	10.8	3.30	117	.224	**.291**	20	.313	4	15	10	-2	1.1
1957 ★NY-A	16	6	**.727**	28	28	7	2	0	201²	170	14	80	118	11.3	2.54	141	.232	.311	13	.183	1	28	23	-2	2.4
1958 NY-A	3	6	.333	15	10	0	0	0	70²	77	6	38	41	15.0	4.20	84	.274	.366	4	.190	0	-3	-5	-2	-0.6
1959 NY-A	0	2	.000	7	3	0	0	0	25¹	20	4	9	16	10.3	4.97	73	.222	.293	0	.000	-1	-3	-4	-0	-0.3
KC-A	2	6	.250	36	3	0	0	5	71²	70	9	34	57	13.8	4.65	86	.258	.354	1	.059	-2	-6	-5	1	-0.5
Yr	2	8	.200	43	6	0	0	5	97	90	13	43	73	12.9	4.73	83	.249	.338	0	.000	-3	-9	-9	1	-0.8
1960 Bos-A	3	3	.500	40	3	0	0	1	101¹	106	16	45	67	13.6	4.97	81	.279	.358	4	.182	-1	-12	-10	-0	-1.0
1961 Was-A	2	6	.250	15	10	1	1	0	80	67	6	40	39	12.4	4.61	87	.233	.332	2	.077	-1	-5	-5	1	-0.5
Pit-N	5	2	.714	13	11	6	1	1	85²	81	6	17	45	10.4	2.84	141	.249	.289	8	.250	1	11	11	-0	1.1
1962 Pit-N	9	5	.643	49	12	2	1	2	125¹	120	12	39	76	11.6	3.73	105	.260	.321	6	.182	0	3	3	0	0.3
1963 Pit-N	0	0	—	3	0	0	0	0	8¹	8	1	4	6	13.0	6.48	50	.267	.353	0	.000	-0	-3	-3	0	-0.2
Det-A	1	2	.333	28	0	0	0	2	55	43	7	24	36	11.1	3.76	99	.221	.309	0	.000	-1	-1	-0	0	0.0
KC-A	1	2	.333	17	3	0	0	0	53	47	3	17	26	11.0	3.74	103	.237	.301	0	.000	-1	-1	1	0	0.0
Yr	2	4	.333	45	3	0	0	2	108	90	10	41	62	11.0	3.75	101	.226	.300	0	.050	-2	-1	1	1	0.0
1964 KC-A	0	0	—	3	0	0	0	0	3²	4	0	1	1	17.2	9.82	39	.308	.438	1	1.000	0	-3	-2	-0	-0.1
NY-N	0	0	—	16	0	0	0	1	28²	34	2	7	18	13.5	5.97	60	.306	.358	0	.000	-0	-8	-8	-0	-0.7
Total 10	59	51	.536	335	101	22	7	17	1137	1029	107	449	704	12.0	3.74	102	.244	.322	60	.183	-2	18	10	-4	1.3

■ **DICK SUCH**   Such, Richard Stanley   b: 10/15/44, Sanford, N.C.   BL/TR, 6′4″, 190 lbs.   Deb: 4/06/70   C

| 1970 Was-A | 1 | 5 | .167 | 21 | 5 | 0 | 0 | 0 | 50 | 48 | 8 | 45 | 41 | 17.3 | 7.56 | 47 | .258 | .410 | 3 | .231 | 1 | -21 | -22 | -0 | -2.0 |

■ **CHARLEY SUCHE**   Suche, Charles Morris   b: 8/5/15, Cranes Mill, Tex.   d: 2/11/84, San Antonio, Tex.   BR/TL, 6′2″, 190 lbs.   Deb: 9/18/38

| 1938 Cle-A | 0 | 0 | — | 1 | 0 | 0 | 0 | 0 | 1¹ | 4 | 0 | 3 | 1 | 47.3 | 27.00 | 17 | .571 | .700 | 1 | 1.000 | 1 | -3 | -3 | 0 | -0.1 |

■ **JIM SUCHECKI**   Suchecki, James Joseph   b: 8/25/27, Chicago, Ill.   BR/TR, 6′, 185 lbs.   Deb: 5/20/50

1950 Bos-A	0	0	—	4	0	0	0	0	4	3	0	4	3	15.8	4.50	109	.231	.412	0	—	0	0	0	-0	0.0
1951 StL-A	0	6	.000	29	6	0	0	0	89²	113	8	42	47	15.7	5.42	81	.299	.371	2	.100	-2	-13	-10	-1	-1.1
1952 Pit-N	0	0	—	5	0	0	0	0	10	14	1	4	6	17.1	5.40	74	.326	.396	0	.000	0	-2	-2	0	-0.1
Total 3	0	6	.000	38	6	0	0	0	103²	130	9	50	56	15.8	5.38	81	.300	.374	2	.091	-2	-15	-12	-1	-1.2

■ **WILLIE SUDHOFF**   Sudhoff, John William "Wee Willie"   b: 9/17/1874, St.Louis, Mo.   d: 5/25/17, St.Louis, Mo.   TR, 5′7″, 165 lbs.   Deb: 8/20/1897

| 1897 StL-N | 2 | 7 | .222 | 11 | 9 | 9 | 0 | 0 | 92² | 126 | 8 | 21 | 19 | 14.3 | 4.47 | 99 | .321 | .356 | 10 | .238 | -1 | -2 | -1 | 2 | 0.0 |

YEAR	TM/L	W	L	PCT	G	GS	CG	SH	SV	IP	H	HR	BB	SO	RAT	ERA	ERA+	OAV	OOB	BH	AVG	PB	PR	/A	PD	TPI
1898	StL-N	11	27	.289	41	38	35	0	1	315	355	11	102	65	13.1	4.34	87	.282	.336	19	.158	-6	-26	-19	8	-1.5
1899	Cle-N	3	8	.273	11	10	8	0	0	86¹	131	3	25	10	16.3	6.98	53	.348	.388	2	.065	-2	-30	-32	2	-2.5
	StL-N	13	10	.565	26	24	18	0	0	189¹	203	6	67	33	12.8	3.61	110	.274	.334	14	.206	0	5	8	4	1.1
	Yr	16	18	.471	37	34	26	0	0	275²	334	9	92	43	13.9	4.67	83	.299	.352	12	.121	-2	-25	-24	6	-1.4
1900	StL-N	6	8	.429	16	14	13	2	0	127	128	2	37	29	11.7	2.76	132	.261	.313	20	.189	-0	13	12	1	1.2
1901	StL-N	17	11	.607	38	26	25	1	2	276¹	281	4	92	78	12.7	3.52	90	.262	.330	19	.176	3	-6	-10	3	-0.4
1902	StL-A	12	12	.500	30	25	20	0	0	220	213	6	67	42	11.5	2.86	123	.255	.310	13	.169	-2	17	16	3	1.8
1903	StL-A	21	15	.583	38	35	30	5	0	293²	262	4	56	104	9.7	2.27	128	.238	.275	20	.182	-1	23	21	3	2.5
1904	StL-A	8	15	.348	27	24	20	1	0	222¹	232	8	54	63	11.6	3.76	66	.269	.313	14	.165	-0	-29	-32	6	-2.7
1905	StL-A	10	20	.333	32	30	23	1	0	244	222	8	78	70	11.1	2.99	85	.244	.303	16	.186	2	-9	-12	5	-0.5
1906	Was-A	0	2	.000	9	5	0	0	0	19²	30	1	9	7	17.8	9.15	29	.353	.415	3	.429	1	-14	-14	1	-1.2
Total	10	103	135	.433	279	240	201	10	3	2086¹	2183	61	608	520	12.1	3.56	92	.269	.321	150	.179	-6	-57	-65	38	-2.2

■ **JOE SUGDEN**   Sugden, Joseph   b: 7/31/1870, Philadelphia, Pa.   d: 6/28/59, Philadelphia, Pa.   BB/TR, 5'10", 180 lbs.   Deb: 7/20/1893   C◆

YEAR	TM/L	W	L	PCT	G	GS	CG	SH	SV	IP	H	HR	BB	SO	RAT	ERA	ERA+	OAV	OOB	BH	AVG	PB	PR	/A	PD	TPI
1902	StL-A	0	0	—	1	0	0	0	0	1	1	0	0	0	9.0	0.00	—	.261	.261	50	.250		0	0	0	0.0

■ **GEORGE SUGGS**   Suggs, George Franklin   b: 7/7/1882, Kinston, N.C.   d: 4/4/49, Kinston, N.C.   BR/TR, 5'7.5", 168 lbs.   Deb: 4/21/08

YEAR	TM/L	W	L	PCT	G	GS	CG	SH	SV	IP	H	HR	BB	SO	RAT	ERA	ERA+	OAV	OOB	BH	AVG	PB	PR	/A	PD	TPI
1908	Det-A	1	1	.500	6	1	1	0	1	27	32	0	4	8	11.3	1.67	145	.299	.312	2	.200	0	2	2	-1	0.2
1909	Det-A	1	3	.250	9	4	2	0	1	44¹	34	1	10	18	9.5	2.03	124	.228	.290	1	.067	-1	2	2	-0	0.1
1910	Cin-N	20	12	.625	35	30	23	2	3	266	248	6	48	91	10.5	2.40	121	.253	.297	14	.165	2	19	15	1	1.9
1911	Cin-N	15	13	.536	36	29	17	1	0	260²	258	3	79	91	12.0	3.00	110	.268	.330	23	.256	6	12	9	4	1.9
1912	Cin-N	19	16	.543	42	36	25	5	3	303	320	6	56	104	11.5	2.94	110	.269	.308	17	.160	-1	16	14	2	1.4
1913	Cin-N	8	15	.348	36	22	9	2	2	199	220	6	35	73	11.8	4.03	81	.292	.329	17	.254	-2	-18	-17	3	-1.1
1914	Bal-F	24	14	.632	46	38	26	6	4	319¹	322	6	57	132	11.0	2.90	116	.266	.304	21	.212	4	11	17	6	2.9
1915	Bal-F	11	17	.393	35	25	12	0	3	232²	288	13	68	71	14.0	4.14	77	.318	.370	17	.221	2	-29	-25	2	-2.0
Total	8	99	91	.521	245	185	115	16	17	1652	1722	41	355	588	11.7	3.11	103	.275	.320	112	.204	14	14	18	17	5.3

■ **ED SUKLA**   Sukla, Edward Anthony   b: 3/3/43, Long Beach, Cal.   BR/TR, 5'11", 170 lbs.   Deb: 9/17/64

YEAR	TM/L	W	L	PCT	G	GS	CG	SH	SV	IP	H	HR	BB	SO	RAT	ERA	ERA+	OAV	OOB	BH	AVG	PB	PR	/A	PD	TPI
1964	LA-A	0	1	.000	2	0	0	0	0	2²	2	1	1	3	10.1	6.75	49	.200	.273	0	—	0	-1	-1	0	0.0
1965	Cal-A	2	3	.400	25	0	0	0	3	32	32	3	10	15	12.1	4.50	76	.264	.326	0	—	0	-4	-4	1	-0.2
1966	Cal-A	1	1	.500	12	0	0	0	1	16²	18	4	6	8	13.0	6.48	52	.281	.343	0	.000	-0	-6	-6	-0	-0.6
Total	3	3	5	.375	39	0	0	0	4	51¹	52	8	17	26	12.3	5.26	64	.267	.329	0	.000	-0	-10	-11	0	-0.8

■ **CHARLIE SULLIVAN**   Sullivan, Charles Edward   b: 5/23/03, Yadkin Valley, N.C   d: 5/28/35, Maiden, N.C.   BL/TL, 6'1", 185 lbs.   Deb: 4/21/28

YEAR	TM/L	W	L	PCT	G	GS	CG	SH	SV	IP	H	HR	BB	SO	RAT	ERA	ERA+	OAV	OOB	BH	AVG	PB	PR	/A	PD	TPI
1928	Det-A	0	2	.000	3	2	0	0	0	12¹	18	1	6	2	17.5	6.57	63	.360	.429	0	.000	-1	-3	-3	0	-0.3
1930	Det-A	1	5	.167	40	3	2	0	5	93²	112	9	53	38	16.0	6.53	73	.311	.401	7	.292	2	-20	-18	1	-1.3
1931	Det-A	3	2	.600	31	4	2	0	0	95	109	6	46	28	14.8	4.93	93	.288	.366	4	.167	-1	-6	-4	0	-0.3
Total	3	4	9	.308	74	9	4	0	5	201	239	16	105	68	15.5	5.78	81	.303	.386	11	.212	-0	-29	-25	1	-1.9

■ **FLEURY SULLIVAN**   Sullivan, Florence P.   b: 1862, E.St.Louis, Ill.   d: 2/15/1897, E.St.Louis, Ill.   Deb: 5/03/1884

YEAR	TM/L	W	L	PCT	G	GS	CG	SH	SV	IP	H	HR	BB	SO	RAT	ERA	ERA+	OAV	OOB	BH	AVG	PB	PR	/A	PD	TPI
1884	Pit-a	16	35	.314	51	51	51	2	0	441	496	15	96	189	12.1	4.20	80	.269	.305	29	.153	-9	-47	-41	0	-4.3

■ **FRANK SULLIVAN**   Sullivan, Franklin Leal   b: 1/23/30, Hollywood, Cal.   BR/TR, 6'6.5", 215 lbs.   Deb: 7/31/53

YEAR	TM/L	W	L	PCT	G	GS	CG	SH	SV	IP	H	HR	BB	SO	RAT	ERA	ERA+	OAV	OOB	BH	AVG	PB	PR	/A	PD	TPI
1953	Bos-A	1	1	.500	14	0	0	0	0	25²	24	3	11	17	12.6	5.61	75	.264	.350	1	.250	0	-5	-4	-0	-0.3
1954	Bos-A	15	12	.556	36	26	11	3	1	206¹	185	18	66	124	11.2	3.14	131	.240	.305	7	.103	-3	13	22	1	2.2
1955	Bos-A	**18**	13	.581	35	35	16	3	0	260	235	23	100	129	11.8	2.91	147	.241	.316	10	.112	-5	30	40	3	3.9
1956	Bos-A	14	7	.667	34	33	12	1	0	242	253	22	82	116	12.8	3.42	135	.268	.332	12	.141	-6	20	32	0	2.9
1957	Bos-A	14	11	.560	31	30	14	3	0	240²	206	16	48	127	**9.8**	2.73	146	.230	**.275**	13	.165	-2	28	34	2	**3.8**
1958	Bos-A	13	9	.591	32	29	10	2	3	199¹	216	12	49	103	12.1	3.57	112	.278	.324	11	.164	-1	4	10	-1	0.9
1959	Bos-A	9	11	.450	30	26	5	2	1	177²	172	17	67	107	12.5	3.95	103	.258	.332	12	.200	-1	-2	2	-1	0.1
1960	Bos-A	6	16	.273	40	22	4	0	1	153²	164	12	52	98	13.0	5.10	79	.269	.332	5	.125	-1	-21	-18	-2	-1.9
1961	Phi-N	3	16	.158	49	18	1	1	6	159¹	161	19	55	114	12.5	4.29	95	.262	.327	5	.152	-1	-5	-4	1	-0.2
1962	Phi-N	0	2	.000	19	0	0	0	0	23	38	2	12	12	20.3	6.26	62	.396	.473	0	—	0	-6	-6	0	-0.5
	Min-A	4	1	.800	21	0	0	0	5	33¹	33	3	13	10	12.4	3.24	126	.258	.326	0	.000	-0	3	3	0	0.3
1963	Min-A	0	1	.000	10	0	0	0	1	11	15	1	4	2	15.5	5.73	64	.349	.404	0	—	0	-3	-3	0	-0.1
Total	11	97	100	.492	351	219	73	15	18	1732	1702	148	559	959	12.0	3.60	116	.257	.320	76	.144	-18	59	108	2	11.1

■ **HARRY SULLIVAN**   Sullivan, Harry Andrew   b: 4/12/1888, Rockford, Ill.   d: 9/22/19, Rockford, Ill.   BL/TL,   Deb: 8/11/09

YEAR	TM/L	W	L	PCT	G	GS	CG	SH	SV	IP	H	HR	BB	SO	RAT	ERA	ERA+	OAV	OOB	BH	AVG	PB	PR	/A	PD	TPI
1909	StL-N	0	0	—	2	1	0	0	0	1	4	1	2	1	54.0	36.00	7	.500	.600	0	.000	-0	-4	-4	0	-0.3

■ **JIM SULLIVAN**   Sullivan, James E.   b: 4/25/1869, Charlestown, Mass.   d: 11/30/01, Roxbury, Mass.   BR/TR, 5'10", 155 lbs.   Deb: 4/22/1891

YEAR	TM/L	W	L	PCT	G	GS	CG	SH	SV	IP	H	HR	BB	SO	RAT	ERA	ERA+	OAV	OOB	BH	AVG	PB	PR	/A	PD	TPI
1891	Bos-N	0	0	—	1	0	0	0	0	0	2	0	5	0	∞	∞	—	1.000	1.000	0	.000	-0	-3	-3	0	-0.1
	Col-a	0	1	.000	1	1	1	0	0	9	10	1	5	1	15.0	4.00	86	.272	.359	0	.000	-1	-0	-1	1	0.0
1895	Bos-N	11	9	.550	21	19	16	0	0	179¹	236	10	58	46	14.8	4.82	106	.312	.361	15	.176	-6	-1	6	-2	0.4
1896	Bos-N	11	12	.478	31	26	21	1	1	225¹	268	12	68	33	13.4	4.03	113	.293	.342	19	.216	-3	8	13	-3	0.7
1897	*Bos-N	4	5	.444	13	9	8	1	2	89	91	1	26	17	11.8	3.94	113	.263	.314	6	.182	-3	4	5	-1	0.2
Total	4	26	27	.491	67	55	46	2	3	502²	607	24	162	97	13.8	4.35	108	.295	.347	40	.190	-12	8	20	-5	0.8

■ **JIM SULLIVAN**   Sullivan, James Richard   b: 4/5/1894, Mine Run, Va.   d: 2/12/72, Burtonsville, Md.   BR/TR, 5'11", 165 lbs.   Deb: 9/27/21

YEAR	TM/L	W	L	PCT	G	GS	CG	SH	SV	IP	H	HR	BB	SO	RAT	ERA	ERA+	OAV	OOB	BH	AVG	PB	PR	/A	PD	TPI
1921	Phi-A	0	2	.000	2	2	2	0	0	17	20	0	7	8	14.3	3.18	140	.294	.360	0	.000	-1	2	2	-0	0.1
1922	Phi-A	0	2	.000	20	2	1	0	0	51¹	76	3	25	15	17.9	5.44	78	.373	.443	1	.091	-2	-8	-7	-0	-0.6
1923	Cle-A	0	1	.000	3	0	0	0	0	5	10	0	5	4	28.8	14.40	28	.476	.593	0	.000	-0	-6	-6	-0	-0.4
Total	3	0	5	.000	25	4	3	0	0	73¹	106	3	37	27	17.8	5.52	78	.362	.437	1	.056	-2	-12	-10	-0	-0.9

■ **JOHN SULLIVAN**   Sullivan, John Jeremiah "Lefty"   b: 5/31/1894, Chicago, Ill.   d: 7/7/58, Chicago, Ill.   BL/TL, 5'11", 165 lbs.   Deb: 7/18/19

YEAR	TM/L	W	L	PCT	G	GS	CG	SH	SV	IP	H	HR	BB	SO	RAT	ERA	ERA+	OAV	OOB	BH	AVG	PB	PR	/A	PD	TPI
1919	Chi-A	0	1	.000	4	2	1	0	0	15	24	0	8	9	19.8	4.20	76	.364	.440	0	.000	-0	-2	-2	-1	-0.2

■ **JOE SULLIVAN**   Sullivan, Joe   b: 9/26/10, Mason City, Ill.   d: 4/8/85, Sequim, Wash.   BL/TL, 5'11", 175 lbs.   Deb: 4/20/35

YEAR	TM/L	W	L	PCT	G	GS	CG	SH	SV	IP	H	HR	BB	SO	RAT	ERA	ERA+	OAV	OOB	BH	AVG	PB	PR	/A	PD	TPI
1935	Det-A	6	6	.500	25	12	5	0	2	125²	119	4	71	53	13.8	3.51	119	.244	.344	7	.163	-1	13	9	-0	0.7
1936	Det-A	2	5	.286	26	4	1	0	1	79²	111	4	40	32	17.3	6.78	73	.331	.406	5	.179	-1	-15	-16	-1	-1.4
1939	Bos-N	6	9	.400	31	11	7	0	2	113²	114	9	50	46	13.1	3.64	101	.266	.346	12	.300	3	3	1	0	0.4
1940	Bos-N	10	14	.417	36	22	7	0	1	177¹	157	9	89	64	12.9	3.55	105	.240	.339	14	.197	-0	6	3	0	0.3
1941	Bos-N	2	2	.500	16	2	0	0	0	52¹	60	3	26	11	15.1	4.13	86	.290	.374	1	.067	-1	-3	-3	1	-0.2
	Pit-N	4	1	.800	16	4	0	0	1	39¹	40	2	22	10	14.2	2.97	121	.258	.350	4	.364	1	3	3	0	0.4
	Yr	6	3	.667	32	6	0	0	1	91²	100	5	48	21	14.5	3.63	99	.275	.359	5	.038	-0	0	-0	1	0.2
Total	5	30	37	.448	150	55	20	0	5	588	601	25	298	216	14.0	4.01	99	.265	.355	43	.207	1	7	-3	0	0.2

■ **MARTY SULLIVAN**   Sullivan, Martin C.   b: 10/20/1862, Lowell, Mass.   d: 1/6/1894, Lowell, Mass.   BR/TR,   Deb: 4/30/1887   ◆

YEAR	TM/L	W	L	PCT	G	GS	CG	SH	SV	IP	H	HR	BB	SO	RAT	ERA	ERA+	OAV	OOB	BH	AVG	PB	PR	/A	PD	TPI
1887	Chi-N	0	0	—	1	0	0	0	0	2¹	6	0	1	1	27.0	7.71	58	.466	.504	134	.284	0	-1	-1	0	0.0

■ **MIKE SULLIVAN**   Sullivan, Michael Joseph "Big Mike"   b: 10/23/1866, Boston, Mass.   d: 6/14/06, Boston, Mass.   BL, 6'1", 210 lbs.   Deb: 6/17/1889

YEAR	TM/L	W	L	PCT	G	GS	CG	SH	SV	IP	H	HR	BB	SO	RAT	ERA	ERA+	OAV	OOB	BH	AVG	PB	PR	/A	PD	TPI
1889	Was-N	0	3	.000	9	3	3	0	0	41	47	2	32	15	17.3	7.24	55	.279	.394	1	.053	-2	-15	-15	-0	-1.3
1890	Chi-N	5	6	.455	12	12	10	0	0	96	108	3	58	33	15.6	4.59	79	.276	.369	5	.125	-3	-11	-10	-0	-1.0
1891	Phi-a	0	2	.000	2	2	1	0	0	18	17	2	10	7	13.5	3.50	109	.241	.335	0	.000	-1	0	1	-0	0.0
	NY-N	1	2	.333	3	3	3	0	0	24	24	0	8	11	12.0	3.38	95	.251	.308	2	.200	-0	-0	-0	0	0.0
1892	Cin-N	12	4	.750	21	16	15	0	0	166¹	179	8	74	56	13.7	3.08	106	.264	.336	13	.176	-3	4	3	-2	0.0

YEAR	TM/L	W	L	PCT	G	GS	CG	SH	SV	IP	H	HR	BB	SO	RAT	ERA	ERA+	OAV	OOB	BH	AVG	PB	PR	/A	PD	TPI
1893	Cin-N	8	11	.421	27	18	14	0	1	183²	200	5	103	40	14.8	5.05	95	.269	.358	16	.203	-3	-8	-5	-0	-0.6
1894	Was-N	2	10	.167	20	12	11	0	1	117²	166	10	74	21	18.4	6.58	80	.329	.415	9	.158	-4	-16	-17	-0	-1.5
	Cle-N	6	5	.545	13	11	9	0	0	90²	128	4	47	19	17.4	6.35	86	.329	.401	13	.295	0	-10	-9	-1	-0.6
	Yr	8	15	.348	33	23	20	0	1	208¹	294	14	121	40	17.9	6.48	83	.329	.409	4	.040	-4	-27	-26	-1	-2.1
1895	Cle-N	1	2	.333	4	3	2	0	0	31	42	1	16	5	16.8	8.42	59	.318	.392	2	.133	-2	-13	-12	-0	-0.8
1896	NY-N	10	13	.435	25	22	18	0	0	185¹	188	3	71	42	12.6	4.66	90	.261	.327	16	.208	-3	-6	-9	0	-1.0
1897	NY-N	8	7	.533	23	16	11	1	2	148²	183	6	71	35	15.4	5.09	82	.300	.373	18	.273	0	-13	-15	1	-1.1
1898	Bos-N	0	1	.000	3	2	0	0	0	12	19	1	9	1	21.0	12.00	31	.356	.449	1	.333	0	-11	-11	-0	-0.8
1899	Bos-N	1	0	1.000	1	1	1	0	0	9	10	1	4	1	14.0	5.00	83	.281	.354	1	.333	0	-1	-1	-0	0.0
Total	11	54	66	.450	163	121	99	1	4	1123¹	1311	46	577	286	15.1	5.11	84	.285	.365	97	.196	-20	-100	-102	-3	-8.8

■ PAT SULLIVAN
Sullivan, Patrick J.   b: 12/22/1862, Milwaukee, Wis.   TR , 5'11", 165 lbs.   Deb: 8/30/1884 ♦

YEAR	TM/L	W	L	PCT	G	GS	CG	SH	SV	IP	H	HR	BB	SO	RAT	ERA	ERA+	OAV	OOB	BH	AVG	PB	PR	/A	PD	TPI
1884	KC-U	0	1	.000	1	1	0	0	0	7	15	1	5	1	25.7	11.57	24	.408	.479	22	.193	-0	-7	-7	-0	-0.4

■ LEFTY SULLIVAN
Sullivan, Paul Thomas   b: 9/7/16, Nashville, Tenn.   d: 11/1/88, Scottsdale, Ariz.   BL/TL, 6'3", 204 lbs.   Deb: 5/06/39

| 1939 | Cle-A | 0 | 1 | .000 | 7 | 1 | 0 | 0 | 0 | 12² | 9 | 0 | 9 | 4 | 13.5 | 4.26 | 103 | .214 | .365 | 0 | .000 | -0 | 1 | 0 | -1 | 0.0 |

■ SUTER SULLIVAN
Sullivan, Suter G.   b: 10/14/1872, Baltimore, Md.   d: 4/19/25, Baltimore, Md.   Deb: 7/24/1898 ♦

| 1898 | StL-N | 0 | 0 | — | 1 | 0 | 0 | 0 | 0 | 6 | 10 | 0 | 4 | 3 | 21.0 | 1.50 | 253 | .367 | .449 | 32 | .222 | -0 | 1 | 2 | -0 | 0.2 |

■ TOM SULLIVAN
Sullivan, Thomas   b: 3/1/1860, New York, N.Y.   d: 4/12/47, Cincinnati, Ohio   Deb: 9/27/1884

1884	Col-a	2	2	.500	4	4	4	0	0	31	42	2	3	12	13.1	4.06	75	.307	.322	1	.091	-1	-3	-4	-1	-0.3
1886	Lou-a	2	7	.222	9	9	8	0	0	75	94	6	33	27	15.2	3.96	92	.293	.359	3	.111	-2	-4	-3	0	-0.2
1888	KC-a	8	16	.333	24	24	24	0	0	214²	227	2	68	84	12.4	3.40	101	.262	.315	10	.109	-6	-8	1	5	0.0
1889	KC-a	2	8	.200	10	10	10	0	0	87¹	111	2	48	24	16.4	5.67	74	.300	.381	5	.152	-1	-18	-14	-1	-1.1
Total	4	14	33	.298	47	47	46	0	0	408	474	12	152	147	13.8	4.04	89	.280	.339	19	.117	-10	-33	-20	4	-1.6

■ TOM SULLIVAN
Sullivan, Thomas Augustin   b: 10/18/1895, Boston, Mass.   d: 9/23/62, Boston, Mass.   BL/TL, 5'11", 178 lbs.   Deb: 5/15/22

| 1922 | Phi-N | 0 | 0 | — | 3 | 0 | 0 | 0 | 0 | 8 | 16 | 0 | 5 | 2 | 24.8 | 11.25 | 41 | .410 | .489 | 1 | .250 | 1 | -6 | -6 | 0 | -0.3 |

■ SLEEPER SULLIVAN
Sullivan, Thomas Jefferson "Old Iron Hands"   b: St.Louis, Mo.   d: 9/25/1899, Camden, N.J.   TR , 175 lbs.   Deb: 5/03/1881 ♦

1882	StL-a	0	1	.000	1	1	1	0	0	9	15	0	1	0	16.0	8.00	35	.349	.364	34	.181	-0	-5	-5	-1	-0.3
1884	StL-U	1	0	1.000	1	1	0	0	0	6	10	0	3	3	15.0	4.50	66	.349	.349	1	.111	-0	-1	-1	0	0.0
Total	2	1	1	.500	2	2	1	0	0	15	25	0	1	3	15.6	6.60	44	.349	.358	64	.186	-1	-6	-6	-1	-0.3

■ BILL SULLIVAN
Sullivan, William T.   Deb: 4/19/1890

| 1890 | Syr-a | 1 | 4 | .200 | 6 | 6 | 4 | 0 | 0 | 42 | 51 | 2 | 27 | 13 | 16.7 | 7.93 | 45 | .291 | .385 | 2 | .091 | -2 | -19 | -20 | -0 | -1.6 |

■ ED SUMMERS
Summers, Oron Edgar "Kickapoo Ed" or "Chief"   b: 12/5/1884, Ladoga, Ind.   d: 5/12/53, Indianapolis, Ind.   BB/TR, 6'2", 180 lbs.   Deb: 4/16/08

1908	*Det-A	24	12	.667	40	32	23	5	1	301	271	3	55	103	10.3	1.64	147	.242	.290	14	.124	-6	25	26	-0	2.3
1909	*Det-A	19	9	.679	35	32	24	3	1	281²	243	4	52	107	9.7	2.24	113	.227	.269	10	.106	-4	8	9	1	0.4
1910	Det-A	13	12	.520	30	25	18	1	0	220¹	211	8	60	82	11.3	2.53	104	.254	.308	14	.184	-0	-0	2	1	0.4
1911	Det-A	11	11	.500	30	20	13	0	1	179¹	189	3	51	65	12.6	3.66	95	.274	.334	16	.254	1	-6	-4	-1	-0.3
1912	Det-A	1	1	.500	3	3	1	0	0	16²	16	1	3	5	10.3	4.86	67	.250	.284	3	.500	1	-3	-3	0	-0.1
Total	5	68	45	.602	138	112	79	9	3	999	930	19	221	362	10.8	2.42	111	.246	.296	57	.162	-8	23	30	0	2.9

■ BILLY SUNDAY
Sunday, William Ashley "Parson" or "The Evangelist"   b: 11/19/1862, Ames, Iowa   d: 11/6/35, Chicago, Ill.   BL , 5'10", 160 lbs.   Deb: 5/22/1883 ♦

| 1890 | Pit-N | 0 | 0 | — | 1 | 0 | 0 | 0 | 0 | 2 | 2 | 0 | 2 | 0 | — | ∞ | — | 1.000 | 1.000 | 92 | .257 | 0 | -2 | -2 | -0 | -0.1 |

■ GORDIE SUNDIN
Sundin, Gordon Vincent   b: 10/10/37, Minneapolis, Minn.   BR/TR, 6'4", 215 lbs.   Deb: 9/19/56

| 1956 | Bal-A | 0 | 0 | — | 1 | 0 | 0 | 0 | 0 | 0 | 0 | 0 | 2 | 0 | — | ∞ | — | — | 1.000 | 0 | — | 0 | -1 | -1 | 0 | 0.0 |

■ STEVE SUNDRA
Sundra, Stephen Richard "Smokey"   b: 3/27/10, Luxor, Pa.   d: 3/23/52, Cleveland, Ohio   BR/TR, 6'2", 190 lbs.   Deb: 4/17/36

1936	NY-A	0	0	—	1	0	0	0	0	2	2	0	2	1	18.0	0.00	—	.286	.444	0	.000	-0	1	1	0	0.1
1938	NY-A	6	4	.600	25	8	3	0	0	93²	107	7	43	33	14.4	4.80	94	.291	.365	6	.182	1	-0	-3	1	0.0
1939	*NY-A	11	1	.917	24	11	8	1	0	120²	110	7	56	27	12.4	2.76	158	.240	.323	13	.265	9	25	21	1	2.5
1940	NY-A	4	6	.400	27	8	2	0	2	99¹	121	11	42	26	14.9	5.53	73	.299	.366	4	.138	-1	-13	-16	1	-1.4
1941	Was-A	9	13	.409	28	23	11	0	0	168¹	203	11	61	50	14.2	5.29	76	.294	.352	13	.217	2	-21	-23	-0	-1.9
1942	Was-A	1	3	.250	6	4	2	0	0	33²	43	1	15	5	15.8	5.61	65	.305	.376	2	.167	-0	-7	-7	0	-0.6
	StL-A	8	3	.727	20	13	6	0	0	110²	122	2	29	26	12.3	3.82	97	.275	.319	9	.225	3	-2	-1	0	0.1
	Yr	9	6	.600	26	17	8	0	0	144¹	165	3	44	31	13.0	4.24	87	.282	.332	1	.019	2	-9	-9	0	-0.5
1943	StL-A	15	11	.577	32	29	13	3	0	208	212	10	66	44	12.0	3.25	103	.266	.322	16	.219	1	1	2	1	0.4
1944	StL-A	2	0	1.000	3	3	2	0	0	19	15	1	4	1	9.0	1.42	253	.211	.253	0	.000	-0	4	5	-0	0.5
1946	StL-A	0	0	—	2	0	0	0	0	4	9	1	3	1	27.0	11.25	33	.409	.480	0	—	0	-3	-3	0	-0.2
Total	9	56	41	.577	168	99	47	4	2	859¹	944	50	321	214	13.3	4.17	94	.277	.340	63	.209	10	-16	-24	3	-0.5

■ TOM SUNKEL
Sunkel, Thomas Jacob "Lefty"   b: 8/9/12, Paris, Ill.   BL/TL, 6'1", 190 lbs.   Deb: 8/26/37

1937	StL-N	0	0	—	9	1	0	0	1	29¹	24	0	11	9	10.7	2.76	144	.214	.285	1	.111	-1	4	4	-0	0.3
1939	StL-N	4	4	.500	20	11	2	1	0	85¹	79	4	56	54	14.3	4.22	98	.242	.354	9	.321	2	-3	-1	-2	-0.0
1941	NY-N	1	1	.500	2	2	1	1	0	15¹	7	0	12	14	11.7	2.93	126	.140	.317	2	.333	0	1	1	-0	0.1
1942	NY-N	3	6	.333	19	11	3	0	0	63²	65	5	41	29	15.0	4.81	70	.269	.375	2	.105	-1	-11	-10	-2	-1.3
1943	NY-N	0	1	.000	1	1	0	0	0	2²	4	1	3	0	23.6	10.13	34	.308	.438	0	—	-0	-2	-2	-0	-0.1
1944	Bro-N	1	3	.250	12	3	0	0	1	24	39	1	10	6	18.4	7.50	47	.368	.422	0	.000	-1	-10	-11	-1	-1.1
Total	6	9	15	.375	63	29	6	2	2	220¹	218	11	133	112	14.4	4.53	83	.256	.358	14	.212	0	-21	-19	-4	-2.1

■ RICK SURHOFF
Surhoff, Richard Clifford   b: 10/3/62, Bronx, N.Y.   BR/TR, 6'3", 210 lbs.   Deb: 9/08/85

| 1985 | Phi-N | 1 | 0 | 1.000 | 2 | 0 | 0 | 0 | 0 | 1 | 2 | 0 | 0 | 1 | 18.0 | 0.00 | — | .500 | .500 | 0 | — | 0 | 0 | 0 | 0 | 0.0 |
| | Tex-A | 0 | 1 | .000 | 7 | 0 | 0 | 0 | 2 | 8¹ | 12 | 3 | 3 | 8 | 16.2 | 7.56 | 56 | .343 | .395 | 0 | — | 0 | -3 | -3 | -0 | -0.2 |

■ MAX SURKONT
Surkont, Matthew Constantine   b: 6/16/22, Central Falls, R.I.   d: 10/8/86, Largo, Fla.   BR/TR, 6'1", 195 lbs.   Deb: 4/19/49

1949	Chi-A	3	5	.375	44	2	0	0	4	96	92	9	60	38	14.5	4.78	87	.255	.366	1	.045	-0	-6	-7	-1	-0.8
1950	Bos-N	5	2	.714	9	6	2	0	0	55²	63	5	20	21	13.7	3.23	119	.285	.350	10	.435	5	6	4	-0	0.8
1951	Bos-N	12	16	.429	37	33	11	2	1	237	230	21	89	110	12.4	3.99	92	.252	.323	11	.151	0	-1	-8	-3	-1.0
1952	Bos-N	12	13	.480	31	29	12	3	0	215	201	19	76	125	11.7	3.77	96	.245	.311	7	.111	-1	-4	-4	-1	-0.5
1953	Mil-N	11	5	.688	28	24	11	2	0	170	168	22	64	83	12.3	4.18	94	.255	.321	16	.286	6	2	-1	0	0.2
1954	Pit-N	9	18	.333	33	29	11	0	0	208¹	216	25	78	78	12.9	4.41	95	.268	.335	10	.167	-0	-8	-5	0	-0.3
1955	Pit-N	7	14	.333	35	22	5	0	2	166¹	194	23	78	84	14.9	5.57	74	.298	.376	7	.140	-1	-28	-27	-2	-2.7
1956	Pit-N	0	0	—	1	0	0	0	0	2	2	0	3	1	22.5	4.50	84	.333	.556	0	—	-0	-0	-0	0	0.0
	StL-N	0	0	—	5	0	0	0	0	5²	10	3	2	5	19.1	9.53	40	.417	.462	0	.000	-0	-4	-4	-0	-0.3
	NY-N	2	2	.500	8	4	1	0	1	32	24	5	9	18	9.3	4.78	79	.202	.258	1	.111	-0	-4	-4	-0	-0.3
	Yr	2	2	.500	14	4	1	0	1	39²	36	8	14	24	11.3	5.45	69	.240	.305	1	.100	-0	-7	-7	-0	-0.6
1957	NY-N	0	1	.000	5	0	0	0	0	6¹	9	2	2	8	15.6	9.95	40	.321	.367	0	—	-0	-4	-4	0	-0.3
Total	9	61	76	.445	236	149	53	7	8	1194¹	1209	134	481	571	12.9	4.38	89	.262	.335	63	.176	8	-48	-63	-5	-5.2

YEAR	TM/L	W	L	PCT	G	GS	CG	SH	SV	IP	H	HR	BB	SO	RAT	ERA	ERA+	OAV	OOB	BH	AVG	PB	PR	/A	PD	TPI
GEORGE SUSCE					Susce, George Daniel b: 9/13/31, Pittsburgh, Pa. BR/TR, 6'1", 180 lbs. Deb: 4/15/55																					
1955	Bos-A	9	7	.563	29	15	6	1	1	144¹	123	12	49	60	11.2	3.06	140	.232	.306	7	.143	-2	15	20	0	1.9
1956	Bos-A	2	4	.333	21	6	0	0	0	69²	71	14	44	26	15.4	6.20	74	.262	.373	4	.222	1	-16	-12	-0	-0.9
1957	Bos-A	7	3	.700	29	5	0	0	1	88¹	93	6	41	40	14.0	4.28	93	.274	.358	3	.120	-1	-5	-3	-1	-0.3
1958	Bos-A	0	0	—	2	0	0	0	0	2	6	1	1	0	31.5	18.00	22	.600	.636	0	—	0	-3	-3	0	-0.2
	Det-A	4	3	.571	27	10	2	0	1	90²	90	7	26	42	11.8	3.67	110	.259	.316	3	.125	-1	1	4	-2	0.2
	Yr	4	3	.571	29	10	2	0	1	92²	96	8	27	42	12.2	3.98	101	.268	.325	2	.083	-1	-2	1	-2	0.0
1959	Det-A	0	0	—	9	0	0	0	0	14²	24	4	9	9	21.5	12.89	32	.358	.449	0	.000	-0	-15	-14	-0	-1.3
Total	5	22	17	.564	117	36	8	1	3	409²	407	44	170	177	13.1	4.42	95	.260	.340	17	.145	-2	-23	-9	-3	-0.6
RICK SUTCLIFFE					Sutcliffe, Richard Lee b: 6/21/56, Independence, Mo. BL/TR, 6'7", 215 lbs. Deb: 9/29/76																					
1976	LA-N	0	0	—	1	1	0	0	0	5	2	0	1	3	5.4	0.00	—	.125	.176	0	.000	-0	2	2	-0	0.2
1978	LA-N	0	0	—	2	0	0	0	0	1²	2	0	1	0	21.6	0.00	—	.286	.444	0	—	0	1	1	0	0.1
1979	LA-N	17	10	.630	39	30	5	1	0	242	217	16	97	117	11.8	3.46	105	.243	.319	21	.247	5	7	5	-2	0.8
1980	LA-N	3	9	.250	42	10	1	1	5	110	122	10	55	59	14.6	5.56	63	.285	.368	4	.148	-0	-24	-25	-1	-2.6
1981	LA-N	2	2	.500	14	6	0	0	0	47	41	5	20	16	12.1	4.02	83	.238	.325	2	.182	1	-3	-4	1	-0.2
1982	Cle-A	14	8	.636	34	27	6	1	1	216	174	16	98	142	11.5	**2.96**	138	**.226**	.317	0	—	0	27	27	1	2.9
1983	Cle-A	17	11	.607	36	35	10	2	0	243¹	251	23	102	160	13.3	4.29	99	.268	.344	0	—	0	-6	-1	1	0.0
1984	Cle-A	4	5	.444	15	15	2	0	0	94¹	111	7	46	58	15.2	5.15	79	.298	.378	0	—	0	-12	-11	-0	-1.0
	*Chi-N	16	1	**.941**	20	20	7	3	0	150¹	123	9	39	155	9.8	2.69	145	.220	.272	14	.250	3	15	20	1	2.8
1985	Chi-N	8	8	.500	20	20	6	3	0	130	119	12	44	102	11.5	3.18	125	.240	.306	10	.233	2	6	12	1	1.7
1986	Chi-N	5	14	.263	28	27	4	1	0	176²	166	18	96	122	13.4	4.64	87	.252	.348	11	.208	3	-18	-12	1	-0.7
1987	Chi-N	18	10	.643	34	34	6	1	0	237¹	223	24	106	174	12.6	3.68	116	.252	.335	12	.148	2	11	16	4	2.3
1988	Chi-N	13	14	.481	32	32	12	2	0	226	232	18	70	144	12.1	3.86	93	.269	.325	12	.160	3	-10	-6	1	-0.1
1989	*Chi-N	16	11	.593	35	34	5	1	0	229	202	18	69	153	10.7	3.66	103	.240	.299	10	.143	1	-4	3	1	0.6
1990	Chi-N	0	2	.000	5	5	0	0	0	21¹	25	2	12	7	15.6	5.91	70	.305	.394	0	.000	-0	-5	-4	1	-0.3
Total	14	133	105	.559	357	296	64	16	6	2130	2010	178	856	1412	12.2	3.83	102	.252	.327	96	.189	20	-15	21	8	6.5
HARRY SUTER					Suter, Harry Richard "Handsome Harry" or "Rube" b: 9/15/1887, Independence, Mo. d: 7/24/71, Topeka, Kan. BL/TL, 5'10", 190 lbs. Deb: 4/16/09																					
1909	Chi-A	2	3	.400	18	7	3	1	1	87¹	72	2	28	53	10.7	2.47	95	.199	.264	3	.094	-1	0	-1	-1	-0.3
DARRELL SUTHERLAND					Sutherland, Darrell Wayne b: 11/14/41, Glendale, Cal. BR/TR, 6'4", 169 lbs. Deb: 6/28/64																					
1964	NY-N	0	3	.000	10	4	0	0	0	26²	32	1	12	9	15.5	7.76	46	.302	.383	1	.200	0	-13	-12	1	-1.0
1965	NY-N	3	1	.750	18	2	0	0	0	48	33	4	17	16	10.1	2.81	125	.199	.289	2	.154	0	4	4	2	0.7
1966	NY-N	2	0	1.000	31	0	0	0	1	44¹	60	6	25	23	17.7	4.87	75	.339	.426	2	.667	1	-6	-6	1	-0.3
1968	Cle-A	0	0	—	3	0	0	0	0	3¹	6	0	4	2	27.0	8.10	37	.375	.500	0	—	0	-2	-2	0	-0.1
Total	4	5	4	.556	62	6	0	0	1	122¹	131	11	58	50	14.5	4.78	75	.282	.371	5	.238	1	-17	-17	4	-0.7
SUDS SUTHERLAND					Sutherland, Harvey Scott b: 2/20/1894, Beaverton, Ore. d: 5/11/72, Portland, Ore. BR/TR, 6', 180 lbs. Deb: 4/14/21																					
1921	Det-A	6	2	.750	13	8	3	0	0	58	80	1	18	18	15.2	4.97	86	.328	.374	11	.407	2	-4	-4	2	0.1
DIZZY SUTHERLAND					Sutherland, Howard Alvin b: 4/9/23, Washington, D.C. d: 8/26/79, Washington, D.C. BL/TL, 6', 200 lbs. Deb: 9/20/49																					
1949	Was-A	0	1	.000	1	1	0	0	0	1	2	0	6	0	72.0	45.00	9	.400	.727	0	—	0	-5	-5	0	-0.3
BRUCE SUTTER					Sutter, Howard Bruce b: 1/8/53, Lancaster, Pa. BR/TR, 6'2", 190 lbs. Deb: 5/09/76																					
1976	Chi-N	6	3	.667	52	0	0	0	10	83¹	63	4	26	73	9.6	2.70	143	.209	.272	0	.000	-1	7	11	-1	1.0
1977	Chi-N	7	3	.700	62	0	0	0	31	107¹	69	5	23	129	7.8	1.34	327	.183	.232	3	.150	-0	31	**36**	0	3.8
1978	Chi-N	8	10	.444	64	0	0	0	27	99	82	10	34	106	10.6	3.18	127	.220	.287	1	.077	-0	4	9	-1	0.9
1979	Chi-N	6	6	.500	62	0	0	0	**37**	101¹	67	3	32	110	8.8	2.22	185	.186	.252	3	.250	-1	17	**21**	0	2.4
1980	Chi-N	5	8	.385	60	0	0	0	**28**	102¹	90	5	34	76	11.0	2.64	148	.242	.307	1	.111	-1	11	14	-0	1.5
1981	StL-N	3	5	.375	48	0	0	0	**25**	82¹	64	5	24	57	9.7	2.62	136	.218	.279	0	.000	-1	8	9	-1	0.7
1982	*StL-N	9	8	.529	70	0	0	0	**36**	102¹	88	8	34	61	11.0	2.90	125	.235	.303	1	.125	-0	8	8	0	0.8
1983	StL-N	9	10	.474	60	0	0	0	21	89¹	90	8	30	64	12.2	4.23	86	.262	.324	0	.000	-1	-6	-6	1	-0.5
1984	StL-N	5	7	.417	71	0	0	0	**45**	122²	109	9	23	77	9.8	1.54	225	.245	.284	0	.000	-1	28	26	1	2.8
1985	Atl-N	7	7	.500	58	0	0	0	23	88¹	91	13	29	52	12.5	4.48	86	.267	.330	0	.000	-0	-9	-6	-0	-0.6
1986	Atl-N	2	0	1.000	16	0	0	0	3	18²	17	3	9	16	12.5	4.34	92	.243	.329	0	.000	0	-1	-1	0	0.0
1988	Atl-N	1	4	.200	38	0	0	0	14	45¹	49	4	11	40	12.1	4.76	77	.275	.321	0	.000	0	-7	-5	-0	-0.5
Total	12	68	71	.489	661	0	0	0	300	1042¹	879	77	309	861	10.4	2.83	135	.230	.289	9	.088	-5	91	116	0	12.3
JACK SUTTHOFF					Sutthoff, John Gerhard "Sunny Jack" b: 6/29/1873, Cincinnati, Ohio d: 8/3/42, Cincinnati, Ohio BL/TR, 5'9", 175 lbs. Deb: 9/15/1898																					
1898	Was-N	0	0	—	2	1	0	0	0	8¹	16	1	8	3	25.9	12.96	28	.401	.501	1	.333	0	-9	-9	0	-0.5
1899	StL-N	0	2	.000	2	2	1	0	0	13	19	0	10	4	20.1	10.38	38	.339	.440	0	.000	0	-9	-9	1	-0.6
1901	Cin-N	1	6	.143	10	4	4	0	0	70¹	82	2	39	12	15.9	5.50	58	.289	.381	3	.107	-2	-17	-18	-1	-1.8
1903	Cin-N	16	9	.640	30	27	21	3	0	224²	207	2	79	76	12.1	2.80	127	.246	.323	12	.143	-3	12	19	-1	1.5
1904	Cin-N	5	6	.455	12	10	8	0	0	90	83	1	43	27	12.9	2.30	127	.255	.348	6	.182	-0	4	6	-2	0.5
	Phi-N	6	13	.316	19	18	17	0	0	163²	172	2	71	46	13.9	3.68	73	.272	.354	10	.164	-0	-17	-18	-1	-1.9
	Yr	11	19	.367	31	28	25	0	0	253²	255	3	114	73	13.4	3.19	87	.266	.349	4	.043	-0	-13	-12	-3	-1.4
1905	Phi-N	3	4	.429	13	6	4	1	0	78	82	2	36	26	14.1	3.81	77	.290	.378	2	.080	-1	-7	-8	0	-0.7
Total	6	31	40	.437	88	68	55	4	0	648	661	10	286	194	13.6	3.65	86	.269	.353	34	.142	-7	-43	-37	-4	-3.5
DON SUTTON					Sutton, Donald Howard b: 4/2/45, Clio, Ala. BR/TR, 6'1", 185 lbs. Deb: 4/14/66																					
1966	LA-N	12	12	.500	37	35	6	2	0	225²	192	19	52	209	9.9	2.99	110	.228	.276	15	.183	1	15	8	-1	0.8
1967	LA-N	11	15	.423	37	34	11	3	1	232²	223	18	57	169	11.1	3.95	79	.250	.300	10	.133	-0	-15	-22	-2	-2.5
1968	LA-N	11	15	.423	35	27	7	2	1	207²	179	6	59	162	10.4	2.60	106	.232	.288	11	.177	1	9	4	-2	0.3
1969	LA-N	17	18	.486	41	41	11	4	0	293¹	269	25	91	217	11.1	3.47	96	.242	.301	15	.153	-1	4	-5	-0	-0.6
1970	LA-N	15	13	.536	38	38	10	4	0	260¹	251	38	78	201	11.7	4.08	94	.249	.310	13	.155	3	-1	-7	-2	-0.5
1971	LA-N	17	12	.586	38	37	12	4	1	265¹	231	10	55	194	9.9	2.54	127	.238	.282	19	.216	3	27	20	-1	2.4
1972	LA-N	19	9	.679	33	33	18	**9**	0	272²	186	13	63	207	**8.4**	2.08	160	**.189**	**.240**	13	.143	-1	42	38	-1	4.1
1973	LA-N	18	10	.643	33	33	14	3	0	256¹	196	18	56	200	9.0	2.42	142	.209	.258	10	.119	-1	35	29	-1	2.8
1974	*LA-N	19	9	.679	40	40	10	5	0	276	241	23	80	179	10.7	3.23	105	.229	.288	18	.184	1	12	5	-1	0.4
1975	LA-N	16	13	.552	35	35	11	4	0	254¹	202	17	62	175	9.4	2.87	119	.213	**.264**	11	.138	-1	21	15	-2	1.3
1976	LA-N	21	10	.677	35	34	15	4	0	267²	231	22	82	161	10.6	3.06	111	.234	.295	7	.083	-3	13	10	-3	0.4
1977	LA-N	14	8	.636	33	33	9	3	0	240¹	207	23	69	150	10.4	3.18	120	.233	.291	11	.151	1	19	17	-1	1.7
1978	*LA-N	15	11	.577	34	34	12	2	0	238¹	228	29	54	154	10.8	3.55	99	.250	.295	6	.083	-3	1	-1	-3	-0.6
1979	LA-N	12	15	.444	33	32	6	1	1	226	201	21	61	146	10.5	3.82	95	.239	.291	11	.143	-2	-2	-5	-1	-0.7
1980	LA-N	13	5	.722	32	31	4	2	1	212¹	163	20	47	128	**9.0**	2.20	159	.211	**.258**	4	.078	-4	33	30	-0	2.9
1981	Hou-N	11	9	.550	23	23	6	3	0	158²	132	6	29	104	**9.2**	2.61	126	.230	**.268**	7	.137	-0	16	12	0	1.4
1982	Hou-N	13	8	.619	27	27	4	0	0	195	169	10	46	139	10.0	3.00	111	.232	.279	11	.162	-0	13	7	-1	0.5
	*Mil-A	4	1	.800	7	7	2	1	0	54²	55	8	18	36	12.0	3.29	115	.263	.322	0	—	0	5	3	0	0.3
1983	Mil-A	8	13	.381	31	31	4	0	0	220¹	209	21	54	134	10.9	4.08	93	.246	.295	0	—	0	-9	-2	-0	-0.9
1984	Mil-A	14	12	.538	33	33	1	0	0	212²	224	24	51	143	11.8	3.77	102	.266	.310	0	—	0	5	2	-2	0.0
1985	Oak-A	13	8	.619	29	29	1	1	0	194¹	194	19	51	91	11.3	3.89	99	.256	.302	0	—	0	6	-1	0	0.0
	Cal-A	2	2	.500	5	5	0	0	0	31²	27	6	8	16	9.9	3.69	111	.233	.282	0	—	0	2	1	-1	0.1
	Yr	15	10	.600	34	34	1	1	0	226	221	25	59	107	11.2	3.86	101	.251	.298	0	—	0	7	-1	-1	0.1

YEAR	TM/L	W	L	PCT	G	GS	CG	SH	SV	IP	H	HR	BB	SO	RAT	ERA	ERA+	OAV	OOB	BH	AVG	PB	PR	/A	PD	TPI
1986	*Cal-A	15	11	.577	34	34	3	1	0	207	192	31	49	116	10.6	3.74	110	.242	.288	0	—	0	10	9	-2	0.6
1987	Cal-A	11	11	.500	35	34	1	0	0	191²	199	38	41	99	11.6	4.70	92	.269	.313	0	—	0	-5	-8	-2	-0.9
1988	LA-N	3	6	.333	16	16	0	0	0	87¹	91	7	30	44	12.6	3.92	85	.270	.332	2	.087	-1	-5	-6	-0	-0.6
Total	23	324	256	.559	774	756	178	58	5	5282¹	4692	472	1343	3574	10.4	3.26	108	.236	.287	195	.144	-7	259	146	-29	12.7

■ EZRA SUTTON
Sutton, Ezra Ballou b: 9/17/1850, Palmyra, N.Y. d: 6/20/07, Braintree, Mass. BR/TR, 5'8.5", 153 lbs. Deb: 5/04/1871 ♦

YEAR	TM/L	W	L	PCT	G	GS	CG	SH	SV	IP	H	HR	BB	SO	RAT	ERA	ERA+	OAV	OOB	BH	AVG	PB	PR	/A	PD	TPI
1875	Ath-n	0	0	—	2	0	0	0	0	6	14	0	0		21.0	7.50	35	.412	.412	116	.324	1	-3	-3		-0.2

■ JOHN SUTTON
Sutton, Johnny Ike b: 11/13/52, Dallas, Tex. BR/TR, 5'11", 185 lbs. Deb: 4/07/77

YEAR	TM/L	W	L	PCT	G	GS	CG	SH	SV	IP	H	HR	BB	SO	RAT	ERA	ERA+	OAV	OOB	BH	AVG	PB	PR	/A	PD	TPI
1977	StL-N	2	1	.667	14	0	0	0	0	24¹	28	1	9	9	13.7	2.59	149	.315	.378	0	.000	-0	4	3	0	0.4
1978	Min-A	0	0		17	0	0	0	0	44¹	46	3	15	18	12.6	3.45	111	.264	.326	0	—	0	2	2	-0	0.1
Total	2	2	1	.667	31	0	0	0	0	68²	74	4	24	27	13.0	3.15	122	.281	.344	0	.000	-0	5	5	0	0.5

■ BILL SWABACH
Swabach, William Deb: 7/09/1887

YEAR	TM/L	W	L	PCT	G	GS	CG	SH	SV	IP	H	HR	BB	SO	RAT	ERA	ERA+	OAV	OOB	BH	AVG	PB	PR	/A	PD	TPI
1887	NY-N	0	2	.000	2	2	2	0	0	16	27	1	6	6	18.6	5.06	74	.364	.411	0	.000	-1	-2	-2	0	-0.2

■ BILL SWAGGERTY
Swaggerty, William David b: 12/5/56, Sanford, Fla. BR/TR, 6'2", 186 lbs. Deb: 8/13/83

YEAR	TM/L	W	L	PCT	G	GS	CG	SH	SV	IP	H	HR	BB	SO	RAT	ERA	ERA+	OAV	OOB	BH	AVG	PB	PR	/A	PD	TPI
1983	Bal-A	1	1	.500	7	2	0	0	0	21²	23	1	6	7	12.0	2.91	136	.267	.315	0	—	0	3	3	1	0.4
1984	Bal-A	3	2	.600	23	6	0	0	0	57	68	7	21	18	14.1	5.21	74	.302	.362	0	—	0	-8	-8	-0	-0.8
1985	Bal-A	0	0	—	1	0	0	0	0	1²	3	0	2	2	27.0	5.40	75	.375	.500	0	—	0	-0	-0	0	0.0
1986	Bal-A	0	0	—	1	0	0	0	0	1	6	0	1	1	63.0	18.00	23	.750	.778	0	—	0	-2	-2	0	0.0
Total	4	4	3	.571	32	8	0	0	0	81¹	100	8	30	28	14.4	4.76	82	.306	.364	0	—	0	-7	-8	1	-0.4

■ CY SWAIM
Swaim, John Hillary b: 3/11/1874, Cadwallader, Ohio 6'6", 180 lbs. Deb: 5/03/1897

YEAR	TM/L	W	L	PCT	G	GS	CG	SH	SV	IP	H	HR	BB	SO	RAT	ERA	ERA+	OAV	OOB	BH	AVG	PB	PR	/A	PD	TPI
1897	Was-N	10	11	.476	27	20	16	0	0	194	227	5	61	55	13.4	4.41	99	.290	.341	17	.227	-3	-2	-1	-3	-0.5
1898	Was-N	3	11	.214	16	13	9	0	1	101¹	119	4	28	30	13.1	4.26	86	.290	.336	5	.143	-3	-7	-7	-1	-0.9
Total	2	13	22	.371	43	33	25	0	1	295¹	346	9	89	85	13.3	4.36	94	.290	.339	22	.200	-6	-9	-8	-4	-1.4

■ CRAIG SWAN
Swan, Craig Steven b: 11/30/50, Van Nuys, Cal. BR/TR, 6'3", 215 lbs. Deb: 9/03/73

YEAR	TM/L	W	L	PCT	G	GS	CG	SH	SV	IP	H	HR	BB	SO	RAT	ERA	ERA+	OAV	OOB	BH	AVG	PB	PR	/A	PD	TPI
1973	NY-N	0	1	.000	3	1	0	0	0	8¹	16	2	2	4	19.4	8.64	42	.432	.462	0	.000	-0	-5	-5	-0	-0.4
1974	NY-N	1	3	.250	7	5	0	0	0	30¹	28	1	21	10	14.5	4.45	80	.255	.374	4	.364	1	-3	-3	0	-0.4
1975	NY-N	1	3	.250	6	6	0	0	0	31	38	4	13	19	15.1	6.39	54	.302	.371	0	.000	-1	-10	-10	-1	-1.0
1976	NY-N	6	9	.400	23	22	2	1	0	132¹	129	11	44	89	12.1	3.54	93	.254	.320	4	.103	-1	-4	-1	-0	-0.4
1977	NY-N	9	10	.474	26	24	1	0	0	146²	153	10	56	71	12.9	4.23	88	.268	.334	9	.188	-0	-5	-8	-2	-1.0
1978	NY-N	9	6	.600	29	28	5	1	0	207¹	164	12	58	125	**9.7**	**2.43**	**143**	.219	.277	10	.154	-0	26	24	0	2.7
1979	NY-N	14	13	.519	35	35	10	3	0	251¹	241	20	57	145	10.7	3.29	110	.255	.299	10	.123	-1	12	10	-1	0.7
1980	NY-N	5	9	.357	21	21	4	1	0	128¹	117	20	30	79	10.3	3.58	99	.247	.292	7	.219	2	-0	-2	-0	0.0
1981	NY-N	0	2	.000	5	3	0	0	0	13²	10	0	1	9	7.2	3.29	106	.204	.220	0	.000	-0	0	0	0	0.0
1982	NY-N	11	7	.611	37	21	2	0	1	166¹	165	13	37	67	10.9	3.35	108	.256	.297	8	.182	3	5	5	-1	0.8
1983	NY-N	2	8	.200	27	18	0	0	1	96¹	112	14	42	43	14.4	5.51	66	.299	.369	2	.077	-2	-20	-20	-1	-2.2
1984	NY-N	1	0	1.000	10	0	0	0	0	18²	18	5	7	10	12.1	8.20	43	.247	.313	0	—	0	-10	-10	-0	-0.2
	Cal-A	0	1	.000	2	1	0	0	0	5	8	3	0	2	14.4	10.80	37	.348	.348	0	—	0	-4	-4	0	-0.2
Total	12	59	72	.450	231	185	25	7	2	1235²	1199	115	368	673	11.5	3.74	95	.256	.312	54	.151	1	-13	-24	-8	-1.9

■ DUCKY SWAN
Swan, Harry Gordon b: 8/11/1887, Lancaster, Pa. d: 5/8/46, Pittsburgh, Pa. BR/TR, 5'10", 165 lbs. Deb: 4/28/14

YEAR	TM/L	W	L	PCT	G	GS	CG	SH	SV	IP	H	HR	BB	SO	RAT	ERA	ERA+	OAV	OOB	BH	AVG	PB	PR	/A	PD	TPI
1914	KC-F	0	0	—	1	0	0	0	0	1	0	0	1	1	9.0	0.00	—	.000	.268	0	—	0	0	0	0	0.0

■ RUSS SWAN
Swan, Russell Howard b: 1/3/64, Fremont, Cal. BL/TL, 6'4", 210 lbs. Deb: 8/03/89

YEAR	TM/L	W	L	PCT	G	GS	CG	SH	SV	IP	H	HR	BB	SO	RAT	ERA	ERA+	OAV	OOB	BH	AVG	PB	PR	/A	PD	TPI
1989	SF-N	0	2	.000	2	2	0	0	0	6²	11	4	4	2	20.3	10.80	31	.393	.469	0	.000	-0	-5	-6	0	-0.4
1990	SF-N	0	1	.000	2	1	0	0	0	2¹	6	0	4	1	38.6	3.86	96	.429	.556	0	.000	-0	-0	-0	0	0.0
	Sea-A	2	3	.400	11	8	0	0	0	47	42	3	18	15	11.5	3.64	109	.244	.316	0	—	0	1	2	0	0.2
Total	2	2	6	.250	15	11	0	0	0	56	59	7	26	18	13.7	4.50	86	.276	.354	0	.000	-0	-4	-4	1	-0.2

■ RED SWANSON
Swanson, Arthur Leonard b: 10/15/36, Baton Rouge, La. BR/TR, 6'1.5", 175 lbs. Deb: 9/10/55

YEAR	TM/L	W	L	PCT	G	GS	CG	SH	SV	IP	H	HR	BB	SO	RAT	ERA	ERA+	OAV	OOB	BH	AVG	PB	PR	/A	PD	TPI
1955	Pit-N	0	0	—	1	0	0	0	0	2	2	1	3	0	22.5	18.00	23	.286	.500	0	—	0	-3	-3	-0	-0.2
1956	Pit-N	0	0	—	9	0	0	0	0	11²	21	1	8	5	22.4	10.03	38	.438	.518	0	—	0	-8	-8	1	-0.6
1957	Pit-N	3	3	.500	32	8	1	0	0	72²	68	9	31	29	12.4	3.72	102	.248	.327	0	.000	-1	1	1	-1	-0.1
Total	3	3	3	.500	42	8	1	0	0	86¹	91	11	42	34	14.0	4.90	77	.277	.360	0	.000	-1	-10	-11	-0	-0.9

■ ED SWARTWOOD
Swartwood, Cyrus Edward b: 1/12/1859, Rockford, Ill. d: 5/15/24, Pittsburgh, Pa. TR , 198 lbs. Deb: 8/11/1881 U♦

YEAR	TM/L	W	L	PCT	G	GS	CG	SH	SV	IP	H	HR	BB	SO	RAT	ERA	ERA+	OAV	OOB	BH	AVG	PB	PR	/A	PD	TPI
1884	Pit-a	0	0	—	1	0	0	0	0	2¹	6	0	1	0	27.0	11.57	29	.457	.495	115	.288	0	-2	-2	0	-0.1
1890	Tol-a	0	0	—	1	0	0	0	0	3	2	0	0	1	6.0	3.00	132	.184	.184	151	.327	0	0	0	0	0.0
Total	2	0	0	—	2	0	0	0	0	5¹	8	0	1	1	15.2	6.75	53	.333	.360	861	.299	1	-2	-2	0	-0.1

■ BUD SWARTZ
Swartz, Sherwin Merle b: 6/13/29, Tulsa, Okla. BL/TL, 6'2.5", 180 lbs. Deb: 7/12/47

YEAR	TM/L	W	L	PCT	G	GS	CG	SH	SV	IP	H	HR	BB	SO	RAT	ERA	ERA+	OAV	OOB	BH	AVG	PB	PR	/A	PD	TPI
1947	StL-A	0	0	—	5	0	0	0	0	5¹	9	1	7	1	27.0	6.75	57	.360	.500	1	1.000	0	-2	-2	-0	0.0

■ MONTY SWARTZ
Swartz, Vernon Monroe "Dazzy" b: 1/1/1897, Farmersville, Ohio d: 1/13/80, Germantown, Ohio BR/TR, 5'11", 182 lbs. Deb: 10/03/20

YEAR	TM/L	W	L	PCT	G	GS	CG	SH	SV	IP	H	HR	BB	SO	RAT	ERA	ERA+	OAV	OOB	BH	AVG	PB	PR	/A	PD	TPI
1920	Cin-N	0	1	.000	1	1	1	0	0	12	17	0	2	2	14.3	4.50	68	.333	.358	2	.500	1	-2	-2	0	0.0

■ PARK SWARTZEL
Swartzel, Park B. b: 11/21/1865, Knightstown, Ind. d: 1/3/40, Los Angeles, Cal. BR/TR, Deb: 4/17/1889

YEAR	TM/L	W	L	PCT	G	GS	CG	SH	SV	IP	H	HR	BB	SO	RAT	ERA	ERA+	OAV	OOB	BH	AVG	PB	PR	/A	PD	TPI
1889	KC-a	19	27	.413	48	47	45	0	1	410¹	481	21	117	147	13.1	4.32	97	.283	.330	25	.144	-10	-22	-6	9	-0.3

■ CHARLIE SWEENEY
Sweeney, Charles J. b: 4/13/1863, San Francisco, Cal d: 4/4/02, San Francisco, Cal. BR , 5'10.5", 181 lbs. Deb: 5/11/1882 ♦

YEAR	TM/L	W	L	PCT	G	GS	CG	SH	SV	IP	H	HR	BB	SO	RAT	ERA	ERA+	OAV	OOB	BH	AVG	PB	PR	/A	PD	TPI
1883	Pro-N	7	7	.500	20	18	14	0	0	146²	142	3	28	48	10.4	3.13	99	.239	.274	19	.218	-1	0	-1	2	0.0
1884	Pro-N	17	8	.680	27	24	22	4	1	221	153	4	29	145	**7.4**	1.55	183	**.185**	**.212**	50	.298	8	35	31	1	4.2
	StL-U	24	7	.774	33	33	32	2	0	271	207	2	13	192	7.3	1.83	162	.197	.207	54	.316	11	36	34	5	5.0
1885	StL-N	11	21	.344	35	35	32	2	0	275	276	6	50	84	10.7	3.93	70	.249	.281	55	.206	0	-34	-36	0	-3.1
1886	StL-N	5	6	.455	11	11	11	0	0	93	108	9	39	28	14.2	4.16	77	.279	.345	16	.250	1	-9	-10	1	-0.6
1887	Cle-a	0	3	.000	3	3	3	0	0	24	42	0	13	8	20.6	8.25	58	.369	.434	30	.226	0	-11	-10	0	-0.7
Total	5	64	52	.552	129	123	113	8	1	1030²	928	24	172	505	9.6	2.87	103	.227	.259	224	.251	19	18	8	8	4.8

■ BILL SWEENEY
Sweeney, William J. b: Philadelphia, Pa. d: 8/2/03, Philadelphia, Pa. TR , Deb: 6/27/1882

YEAR	TM/L	W	L	PCT	G	GS	CG	SH	SV	IP	H	HR	BB	SO	RAT	ERA	ERA+	OAV	OOB	BH	AVG	PB	PR	/A	PD	TPI
1882	Phi-a	9	10	.474	20	20	18	0	0	170	178	4	42	48	11.6	2.91	102	.252	.294	14	.159	-3	-4	1	-1	-0.1
1884	Bal-U	**40**	21	.656	**62**	60	**58**	4	0	**538**	522	13	74	374	10.0	2.59	128	.238	.263	71	.240	-5	25	**43**	1	3.8
Total	2	49	31	.613	82	80	76	4	0	708	700	17	116	422	10.4	2.67	121	.241	.270	85	.221	-8	21	44	0	3.7

■ LES SWEETLAND
Sweetland, Lester Leo (Born Leo Sweetland) b: 8/15/01, St.Ignace, Mich. d: 3/4/74, Melbourne, Fla. BR/TL, 5'11.5", 155 lbs. Deb: 7/04/27

YEAR	TM/L	W	L	PCT	G	GS	CG	SH	SV	IP	H	HR	BB	SO	RAT	ERA	ERA+	OAV	OOB	BH	AVG	PB	PR	/A	PD	TPI
1927	Phi-N	2	10	.167	21	13	6	0	0	103²	147	3	53	21	17.6	6.16	67	.348	.425	12	.316	4	-26	-23	5	-1.3
1928	Phi-N	3	15	.167	37	18	9	0	0	135¹	163	19	97	23	18.3	6.58	65	.306	.426	9	.191	0	-39	-35	3	-2.8
1929	Phi-N	13	11	.542	43	25	10	2	2	204¹	255	23	87	47	15.5	5.11	102	.316	.389	26	.292	3	-9	2	4	0.9
1930	Phi-N	7	15	.318	34	25	8	1	0	167	271	24	60	36	18.1	7.71	71	.373	.425	16	.281	4	-51	-42	1	-2.9
1931	Chi-N	8	7	.533	26	14	5	0	2	130¹	156	0	61	32	15.3	5.04	77	.297	.375	15	.268	5	-17	-17	0	-1.0
Total	5	33	58	.363	161	95	38	3	4	740²	992	68	358	159	16.9	6.10	77	.329	.407	78	.272	17	-142	-116	13	-7.1

■ STEVE SWETONIC
Swetonic, Stephen Albert b: 8/13/03, Mt.Pleasant, Pa. d: 4/22/74, Canonsburg, Pa. BR/TR, 5'11", 185 lbs. Deb: 4/17/29 ♦

YEAR	TM/L	W	L	PCT	G	GS	CG	SH	SV	IP	H	HR	BB	SO	RAT	ERA	ERA+	OAV	OOB	BH	AVG	PB	PR	/A	PD	TPI
1929	Pit-N	8	10	.444	41	12	3	0	5	143²	172	6	50	35	14.2	4.82	99	.299	.360	13	.271	3	-2	-1	2	0.4

YEAR TM/L	W	L	PCT	G	GS	CG	SH	SV	IP	H	HR	BB	SO	RAT	ERA	ERA+	OAV	OOB	BH	AVG	PB	PR	/A	PD	TPI
1930 Pit-N	6	6	.500	23	6	3	1	5	96²	107	7	27	35	12.5	4.47	111	.276	.323	4	.111	-3	5	5	-1	0.2
1931 Pit-N	0	2	.000	14	0	0	0	1	27²	28	0	16	8	14.3	3.90	99	.264	.361	1	.143	-0	-0	-0	-0	0.0
1932 Pit-N	11	6	.647	24	19	11	**4**	0	162²	134	11	55	39	10.5	2.82	135	**.221**	.286	5	.093	-4	19	18	-1	1.3
1933 Pit-N	12	12	.500	31	21	8	3	0	164²	166	10	64	37	12.7	3.50	95	.260	.330	11	.200	1	-3	-3	-1	-0.2
Total 5	37	36	.507	133	58	25	8	11	595¹	607	34	212	154	12.5	3.81	107	.262	.326	34	.170	-2	20	19	-1	1.7

■ BILL SWIFT
Swift, William Charles b: 10/27/61, Portland, Maine   BR/TR, 6', 170 lbs.   Deb: 6/07/85

YEAR TM/L	W	L	PCT	G	GS	CG	SH	SV	IP	H	HR	BB	SO	RAT	ERA	ERA+	OAV	OOB	BH	AVG	PB	PR	/A	PD	TPI
1985 Sea-A	6	10	.375	23	21	0	0	0	120²	131	8	48	55	13.7	4.77	88	.279	.352	0	—	0	-8	-8	1	-0.6
1986 Sea-A	2	9	.182	29	17	1	0	0	115¹	148	5	55	55	16.4	5.46	78	.319	.399	0	—	0	-16	-16	2	-1.2
1988 Sea-A	8	12	.400	38	24	6	1	0	174²	199	10	65	47	14.0	4.59	91	.294	.363	0	—	0	-12	-8	3	-0.4
1989 Sea-A	7	3	.700	37	16	0	0	1	130	140	7	38	45	12.5	4.43	91	.278	.331	0	—	0	-8	-6	5	0.0
1990 Sea-A	6	4	.600	55	8	0	0	6	128	135	4	21	42	11.5	2.39	166	.272	.311	0	—	0	22	22	1	2.4
Total 5	29	38	.433	182	86	7	1	7	668²	753	34	227	244	13.6	4.32	95	.289	.352	0	—	0	-23	-15	12	0.2

■ BILL SWIFT
Swift, William Vincent b: 1/10/08, Elmira, N.Y.   d: 2/23/69, Bartow, Fla.   BR/TR, 6'1.5", 192 lbs.   Deb: 4/12/32

YEAR TM/L	W	L	PCT	G	GS	CG	SH	SV	IP	H	HR	BB	SO	RAT	ERA	ERA+	OAV	OOB	BH	AVG	PB	PR	/A	PD	TPI
1932 Pit-N	14	10	.583	39	23	11	0	4	214¹	205	15	26	64	9.8	3.61	106	.248	.272	15	.192	-1	6	5	-4	0.0
1933 Pit-N	14	10	.583	37	29	13	2	0	218¹	214	11	36	64	10.5	3.13	106	.251	.285	20	.244	3	5	5	-2	0.6
1934 Pit-N	11	13	.458	37	24	13	1	0	212²	244	15	46	81	12.6	3.98	103	.284	.326	18	.214	2	2	3	-1	0.4
1935 Pit-N	15	8	.652	39	21	11	3	1	203²	193	6	37	74	10.2	2.70	152	.247	.282	19	.244	3	30	32	-4	3.1
1936 Pit-N	16	16	.500	45	31	17	0	2	262¹	275	18	63	92	11.8	4.01	101	.265	.310	31	.295	9	0	1	-4	0.6
1937 Pit-N	9	10	.474	36	17	9	0	3	164	160	14	34	44	10.8	3.95	98	.256	.297	9	.167	-1	-1	-2	-3	-0.4
1938 Pit-N	7	5	.583	36	9	2	0	4	150	155	9	40	77	11.9	3.24	117	.271	.323	10	.200	2	9	9	-1	0.9
1939 Pit-N	5	7	.417	36	8	2	1	4	129²	150	6	28	56	12.6	3.89	99	.293	.333	10	.238	2	0	-1	-3	-0.1
1940 Bos-N	1	1	.500	4	0	0	0	1	9¹	12	0	7	7	18.3	2.89	129	.308	.413	0	.000	-0	1	1	0	0.0
1941 Bro-N	3	0	1.000	9	0	0	0	1	22	26	4	7	9	13.5	3.27	112	.289	.340	1	.200	-0	1	1	-0	0.1
1943 Chi-A	0	2	.000	18	1	0	0	0	51¹	48	5	27	28	14.2	4.21	79	.246	.355	1	.100	1	-5	-5	-2	-0.6
Total 11	95	82	.537	336	163	78	7	20	1637¹	1682	103	351	636	11.4	3.58	108	.263	.305	134	.227	18	49	49	-24	4.6

■ OAD SWIGART
Swigart, Oadis Vaughn b: 2/13/15, Archie, Mo.   BL/TR, 6', 175 lbs.   Deb: 9/14/39

YEAR TM/L	W	L	PCT	G	GS	CG	SH	SV	IP	H	HR	BB	SO	RAT	ERA	ERA+	OAV	OOB	BH	AVG	PB	PR	/A	PD	TPI
1939 Pit-N	1	1	.500	3	3	1	1	0	24¹	27	1	6	8	12.2	4.44	87	.293	.337	2	.250	0	-1	-2	-0	-0.1
1940 Pit-N	0	2	.000	7	2	0	0	0	22¹	27	1	10	9	14.9	4.43	86	.297	.366	1	.200	-0	-1	-2	0	0.0
Total 2	1	3	.250	10	5	1	1	0	46²	54	2	16	17	13.5	4.44	86	.295	.352	3	.231	-0	-3	-3	-0	-0.1

■ AD SWIGLER
Swigler, Adam William "Doc" b: 9/21/1895, Philadelphia, Pa.   d: 2/5/75, Philadelphia, Pa.   5'10", 180 lbs.   Deb: 9/25/17

YEAR TM/L	W	L	PCT	G	GS	CG	SH	SV	IP	H	HR	BB	SO	RAT	ERA	ERA+	OAV	OOB	BH	AVG	PB	PR	/A	PD	TPI
1917 NY-N	0	1	.000	1	1	0	0	0	6	7	0	8	4	22.5	6.00	43	.333	.517	0	.000	-0	-2	-2	0	-0.1

■ GREG SWINDELL
Swindell, Forrest Gregory b: 1/2/65, Houston, Tex.   BR/TL, 6'2", 225 lbs.   Deb: 8/21/86

YEAR TM/L	W	L	PCT	G	GS	CG	SH	SV	IP	H	HR	BB	SO	RAT	ERA	ERA+	OAV	OOB	BH	AVG	PB	PR	/A	PD	TPI
1986 Cle-A	5	2	.714	9	9	1	0	0	61²	57	9	15	46	10.7	4.23	98	.243	.291	0	—	0	-0	-1	1	0.0
1987 Cle-A	3	8	.273	16	15	4	1	0	102¹	112	18	37	97	13.2	5.10	89	.283	.346	0	—	0	-7	-7	-1	-0.6
1988 Cle-A	18	14	.563	33	33	12	4	0	242	234	18	45	180	10.4	3.20	129	.252	.287	0	—	0	21	25	-1	2.4
1989 Cle-A	13	6	.684	28	28	5	2	0	184¹	170	16	51	129	10.8	3.37	118	.246	.298	0	—	0	11	12	-1	1.2
1990 Cle-A	12	9	.571	34	34	3	0	0	214²	245	27	47	135	12.3	4.40	90	.288	.326	0	—	0	-12	-10	-2	-1.1
Total 5	51	39	.567	120	119	25	7	0	805	818	88	195	587	11.4	3.88	106	.264	.308	0	—	0	12	19	-4	1.9

■ JOSH SWINDELL
Swindell, Joshua Ernest b: 7/5/1883, Rose Hill, Kan.   d: 3/19/69, Fruita, Colo.   TR, 6', 180 lbs.   Deb: 9/16/11 ♦

YEAR TM/L	W	L	PCT	G	GS	CG	SH	SV	IP	H	HR	BB	SO	RAT	ERA	ERA+	OAV	OOB	BH	AVG	PB	PR	/A	PD	TPI
1911 Cle-A	0	1	.000	4	1	1	0	0	17¹	19	0	4	6	12.5	2.08	164	.257	.304	1	.250	-0	2	3	-0	0.2

■ LEN SWORMSTEDT
Swormstedt, Leonard Jordan b: 10/6/1878, Cincinnati, Ohio   d: 7/19/64, Salem, Mass.   BR/TR, 5'11.5", 165 lbs.   Deb: 9/29/01

YEAR TM/L	W	L	PCT	G	GS	CG	SH	SV	IP	H	HR	BB	SO	RAT	ERA	ERA+	OAV	OOB	BH	AVG	PB	PR	/A	PD	TPI
1901 Cin-N	2	1	.667	3	3	3	0	0	26	19	2	5	13	8.7	1.73	185	.203	.251	0	.000	-1	5	4	0	0.3
1902 Cin-N	0	2	.000	2	2	1	0	0	18	22	1	5	3	13.5	4.00	75	.301	.345	0	.000	-1	-2	-2	-0	-0.2
1906 Bos-A	1	1	.500	3	2	2	0	0	21	17	0	0	6	7.3	1.29	214	.224	.224	1	.125	-1	3	3	-1	0.3
Total 3	3	4	.429	8	7	7	0	0	65	58	3	10	22	9.6	2.22	136	.239	.272	1	.043	-3	5	6	-1	0.4

■ BOB SYKES
Sykes, Robert Joseph b: 12/11/54, Neptune, N.J.   BB/TL, 6'1", 195 lbs.   Deb: 4/09/77

YEAR TM/L	W	L	PCT	G	GS	CG	SH	SV	IP	H	HR	BB	SO	RAT	ERA	ERA+	OAV	OOB	BH	AVG	PB	PR	/A	PD	TPI
1977 Det-A	5	7	.417	32	20	3	0	0	132²	141	15	50	58	13.1	4.41	97	.271	.337	0	—	0	-5	-2	-0	-0.1
1978 Det-A	6	6	.500	22	10	3	2	2	93²	99	14	34	58	12.9	3.94	98	.275	.339	0	—	0	-2	-1	-2	-0.2
1979 StL-N	4	3	.571	13	11	0	0	0	67	86	11	34	35	16.3	6.18	61	.315	.393	2	.095	-0	-18	-18	-1	-1.7
1980 StL-N	6	10	.375	27	19	4	3	0	126	134	12	54	50	13.4	4.64	79	.277	.350	4	.103	-2	-15	-13	-1	-1.6
1981 StL-N	2	0	1.000	22	1	0	0	0	37¹	37	2	18	14	13.5	4.58	78	.266	.354	0	.000	-0	-5	-4	1	-0.3
Total 5	23	26	.469	116	61	10	5	2	456²	497	54	190	215	13.6	4.65	84	.280	.351	6	.097	-2	-44	-38	-4	-3.9

■ LOU SYLVESTER
Sylvester, Louis J. b: 2/14/1855, Springfield, Ill.   BR/TR, 5'3", 165 lbs.   Deb: 4/18/1884 ♦

YEAR TM/L	W	L	PCT	G	GS	CG	SH	SV	IP	H	HR	BB	SO	RAT	ERA	ERA+	OAV	OOB	BH	AVG	PB	PR	/A	PD	TPI
1884 Cin-U	0	1	.000	6	1	0	1	0	32²	32	0	6	7	10.5	3.58	88	.239	.272	89	.267	1	-2	-2	1	0.0

■ LEFTY TABER
Taber, Edward Timothy b: 1/11/1900, Rock Island, Ill.   d: 11/5/83, Lincoln, Neb.   BL/TL, 6', 180 lbs.   Deb: 9/04/26

YEAR TM/L	W	L	PCT	G	GS	CG	SH	SV	IP	H	HR	BB	SO	RAT	ERA	ERA+	OAV	OOB	BH	AVG	PB	PR	/A	PD	TPI
1926 Phi-N	0	0	—	6	0	0	0	0	8¹	8	0	5	0	16.2	7.56	55	.242	.375	0	.000	-0	-3	-3	0	-0.2
1927 Phi-N	0	1	.000	3	1	0	0	0	3¹	8	0	5	0	37.8	18.90	22	.533	.667	0	.000	-0	-6	-5	0	-0.4
Total 2	0	1	.000	9	1	0	0	0	11²	16	0	10	0	22.4	10.80	38	.333	.475	0	.000	-0	-9	-9	0	-0.6

■ JOHN TABER
Taber, John Pardon b: 6/28/1868, Acushnet, Mass.   d: 2/21/40, Boston, Mass.   BR/TR, 5'8", Deb: 4/30/1890

YEAR TM/L	W	L	PCT	G	GS	CG	SH	SV	IP	H	HR	BB	SO	RAT	ERA	ERA+	OAV	OOB	BH	AVG	PB	PR	/A	PD	TPI
1890 Bos-N	0	1	.000	2	1	1	0	1	13	11	0	8	3	13.2	4.15	90	.223	.331	0	.000	-1	-1	-1	1	0.0

■ JOHN TAFF
Taff, John Gallatin b: 6/3/1890, Austin, Tex.   d: 5/15/61, Houston, Tex.   BR/TR, 6', 170 lbs.   Deb: 5/11/13

YEAR TM/L	W	L	PCT	G	GS	CG	SH	SV	IP	H	HR	BB	SO	RAT	ERA	ERA+	OAV	OOB	BH	AVG	PB	PR	/A	PD	TPI
1913 Phi-A	0	1	.000	7	1	0	0	1	17²	22	0	5	9	13.8	6.62	42	.293	.338	1	.200	-0	-7	-8	0	-0.7

■ DOUG TAITT
Taitt, Douglas John "Poco" b: 8/3/02, Bay City, Mich.   d: 12/12/70, Portland, Ore.   BL/TR, 6', 176 lbs.   Deb: 4/10/28 ♦

YEAR TM/L	W	L	PCT	G	GS	CG	SH	SV	IP	H	HR	BB	SO	RAT	ERA	ERA+	OAV	OOB	BH	AVG	PB	PR	/A	PD	TPI
1928 Bos-A	0	0	—	1	0	0	0	0	1	2	0	2	1	36.0	27.00	15	.400	.571	144	.299	0	-3	-3	0	-0.1

■ FRED TALBOT
Talbot, Frederick Lealand "Bubby" b: 6/28/41, Washington, D.C.   BR/TR, 6'2", 195 lbs.   Deb: 9/28/63

YEAR TM/L	W	L	PCT	G	GS	CG	SH	SV	IP	H	HR	BB	SO	RAT	ERA	ERA+	OAV	OOB	BH	AVG	PB	PR	/A	PD	TPI
1963 Chi-A	0	0	—	1	0	0	0	0	3	2	0	4	2	18.0	3.00	117	.222	.462	0	.000	-0	0	0	0	0.0
1964 Chi-A	4	5	.444	17	12	3	2	0	75¹	83	7	20	34	12.8	3.70	93	.288	.343	5	.263	3	-1	-2	-1	0.0
1965 KC-A	10	12	.455	39	33	2	1	0	198	188	25	86	117	12.7	4.14	84	.251	.333	14	.200	3	-15	-14	-0	-1.1
1966 KC-A	4	4	.500	11	11	0	0	0	67²	65	6	28	37	12.6	4.79	71	.248	.325	3	.150	0	-10	-10	0	-0.9
NY-A	7	7	.500	23	19	3	0	0	124²	123	16	45	48	12.4	4.13	81	.262	.331	5	.143	1	-10	-11	0	-0.9
Yr	11	11	.500	34	30	3	0	0	192	188	22	73	85	12.4	4.36	77	.256	.326	7	.127	1	-20	-22	0	-1.8
1967 NY-A	6	8	.429	29	22	2	0	0	138²	132	20	54	61	12.5	4.22	74	.252	.329	6	.158	3	-15	-17	3	-1.1
1968 NY-A	1	9	.100	29	11	1	0	0	99	89	6	42	67	12.1	3.36	86	.241	.322	2	.118	1	-4	-5	1	-0.3
1969 NY-A	0	0	—	8	0	0	0	0	12¹	13	1	6	7	13.9	5.11	68	.283	.365	0	.000	-0	-2	-2	0	-0.1
Sea-A	5	8	.385	25	16	1	1	0	114²	125	12	41	67	13.3	4.16	87	.278	.343	6	.162	2	-7	-7	0	-0.4
Oak-A	1	2	.333	12	2	0	0	1	19	22	2	7	9	13.7	5.21	66	.297	.358	1	.333	0	-3	-4	0	-0.3
Yr	6	10	.375	45	18	1	1	1	146	160	15	54	83	13.2	4.38	82	.277	.339	3	.073	2	-12	-13	0	-0.8
1970 Oak-A	0	1	.000	1	0	0	0	0	1²	2	1	1	0	16.2	10.80	33	.286	.375	0	—	0	-1	-1	0	0.0
Total 8	38	56	.404	195	126	12	4	1	853²	844	96	334	449	12.7	4.12	81	.260	.334	42	.174	13	-68	-74	3	-5.1

■ ROY TALCOTT
Talcott, Le Roy Everett b: 1/16/20, Brookline, Mass.   BR/TR, 6'1.5", 180 lbs.   Deb: 6/24/43

YEAR TM/L	W	L	PCT	G	GS	CG	SH	SV	IP	H	HR	BB	SO	RAT	ERA	ERA+	OAV	OOB	BH	AVG	PB	PR	/A	PD	TPI
1943 Bos-N	0	0	—	1	0	0	0	0	0²	1	0	2	0	40.5	27.00	13	.333	.600	0	—	0	-2	-2	0	-0.1

YEAR	TM/L	W	L	PCT	G	GS	CG	SH	SV	IP	H	HR	BB	SO	RAT	ERA	ERA+	OAV	OOB	BH	AVG	PB	PR	/A	PD	TPI

■ VITO TAMULIS Tamulis, Vitautis Casimurus b: 7/11/11, Cambridge, Mass. d: 5/5/74, Nashville, Tenn. BL/TL, 5'9", 170 lbs. Deb: 9/25/34

1934	NY-A	1	0	1.000	1	1	1	1	0	9	7	0	1	5	8.0	0.00	—	.219	.242	1	.250	0	4	4	0	0.5
1935	NY-A	10	5	.667	30	19	9	3	1	160²	178	7	55	57	13.2	4.09	99	.280	.339	14	.246	4	7	-1	-0	0.2
1938	StL-A	0	3	.000	3	2	0	0	0	15¹	26	2	10	11	21.1	7.63	65	.366	.444	2	.400	1	-5	-5	0	-0.2
	Bro-N	12	6	.667	38	18	9	0	2	159²	181	11	40	70	12.6	3.83	102	.288	.333	7	.127	-3	-1	1	-2	-0.2
1939	Bro-N	9	8	.529	39	17	8	1	4	158²	177	10	45	83	13.0	4.37	92	.287	.343	10	.182	-1	-8	-6	0	-0.6
1940	Bro-N	8	5	.615	41	12	4	1	2	154¹	147	5	34	55	10.7	3.09	129	.244	.288	6	.130	-1	13	16	-1	1.4
1941	Phi-N	0	1	.000	6	1	0	0	0	12	21	1	7	5	21.8	9.00	41	.382	.460	0	.000	-0	-7	-7	0	-0.6
	Bro-N	0	0	—	12	0	0	0	1	22	21	1	10	8	12.7	3.68	100	.244	.323	0	.000	-1	-0	-0	0	0.0
	Yr	0	1	.000	18	1	0	0	1	34	42	2	17	13	15.6	5.56	66	.296	.371	0	.000	-1	-7	-7	0	-0.6
Total	6	40	28	.588	170	70	31	6	10	691²	758	37	202	294	12.7	3.97	101	.278	.331	40	.175	-1	3	4	-2	0.5

■ FRANK TANANA Tanana, Frank Daryl b: 7/3/53, Detroit, Mich. BL/TL, 6'2", 180 lbs. Deb: 9/09/73

1973	Cal-A	2	2	.500	4	4	2	1	0	26¹	20	2	8	22	9.6	3.08	115	.200	.259	0	—	0	2	1	0	0.2
1974	Cal-A	14	19	.424	39	35	12	4	0	268²	262	27	77	180	11.6	3.12	110	.255	.312	0	—	0	15	10	0	1.1
1975	Cal-A	16	9	.640	34	33	16	5	0	257¹	211	21	73	**269**	10.2	2.62	135	.226	.288	0	—	0	33	26	1	3.0
1976	Cal-A	19	10	.655	34	34	23	2	0	288¹	212	24	73	261	**9.2**	2.43	137	.203	**.261**	0	—	0	35	29	0	3.3
1977	Cal-A	15	9	.625	31	31	20	**7**	0	241¹	201	19	61	205	10.2	**2.54**	**154**	.227	.286	0	—	0	41	37	1	**4.0**
1978	Cal-A	18	12	.600	33	33	10	4	0	239	239	26	60	137	11.6	3.65	99	.258	.309	0	—	0	3	-1	-2	-0.2
1979	*Cal-A	7	5	.583	18	17	2	1	0	90¹	93	9	25	46	12.0	3.89	105	.264	.317	0	—	0	3	2	-0	0.1
1980	Cal-A	11	12	.478	32	31	7	0	0	204	223	18	45	113	12.2	4.15	95	.277	.322	0	—	0	-3	-5	-1	-0.5
1981	Bos-A	4	10	.286	24	23	5	2	0	141¹	142	17	43	78	12.0	4.01	96	.265	.324	0	—	0	-6	-2	1	-0.1
1982	Tex-A	7	18	.280	30	30	7	0	0	194¹	199	16	55	87	12.1	4.21	92	.264	.320	0	—	0	-3	-7	0	-0.6
1983	Tex-A	7	9	.438	29	22	3	0	0	159¹	144	14	49	108	11.3	3.16	127	.240	.304	0	—	0	16	15	3	1.8
1984	Tex-A	15	15	.500	35	35	9	1	0	246¹	234	30	81	141	11.7	3.25	127	.245	.308	0	—	0	20	24	1	2.7
1985	Tex-A	2	7	.222	13	13	0	0	0	77²	89	15	23	52	13.1	5.91	72	.287	.338	0	—	0	-15	-15	0	-1.2
	Det-A	10	7	.588	20	20	4	0	0	137¹	131	13	34	107	10.9	3.34	122	.250	.298	0	—	0	12	11	0	1.2
	Yr	12	14	.462	33	33	4	0	0	215	220	28	57	159	11.7	4.27	97	.262	.311	0	—	0	-3	-3	1	0.0
1986	Det-A	12	9	.571	32	31	3	1	0	188¹	196	23	65	119	12.6	4.16	99	.268	.330	0	—	0	0	-1	1	0.0
1987	*Det-A	15	10	.600	34	34	5	3	0	218²	216	27	56	146	11.4	3.91	108	.256	.306	0	—	0	13	8	1	0.8
1988	Det-A	14	11	.560	32	32	2	0	0	203	213	25	64	127	12.5	4.21	91	.267	.324	0	—	0	-6	-9	1	-0.7
1989	Det-A	10	14	.417	33	33	6	1	0	223²	227	21	74	147	12.4	3.58	107	.265	.329	0	—	0	7	6	2	0.8
1990	Det-A	9	8	.529	34	29	1	0	1	176¹	196	25	66	114	13.5	5.31	74	.280	.352	0	—	0	-27	-27	1	-2.5
Total	18	207	196	.514	541	520	137	32	1	3581²	3442	372	1032	2459	11.5	3.58	107	.252	.310	0	—	0	142	101	10	13.2

■ JESSE TANNEHILL Tannehill, Jesse Niles "Powder" b: 7/14/1874, Dayton, Ky. d: 9/22/56, Dayton, Ky. BB/TL, 5'8", 150 lbs. Deb: 6/17/1894 C◆

1894	Cin-N	1	0	1.000	5	1	1	0	1	29	37	1	16	7	16.4	7.14	78	.307	.388	0	.000	-2	-6	-5	-1	-0.5
1897	Pit-N	9	9	.500	21	16	11	1	1	142	172	1	24	40	12.4	4.25	98	.297	.325	49	.266	3	1	-1	3	0.0
1898	Pit-N	25	13	.658	43	38	34	5	2	326²	338	2	63	93	11.0	2.95	121	.265	.300	44	.289	7	24	22	3	3.4
1899	Pit-N	24	14	.632	40	35	32	3	1	313	354	4	51	61	11.6	2.73	140	.285	.313	34	.258	4	39	38	4	4.5
1900	Pit-N	20	6	.769	29	27	23	2	0	234	247	3	43	50	11.2	2.88	126	.270	.303	37	.336	8	21	19	1	2.8
1901	Pit-N	18	10	.643	32	30	25	4	1	252¹	240	1	36	118	10.2	**2.18**	150	.249	.283	33	.244	5	32	31	-4	3.4
1902	Pit-N	20	6	.769	26	24	23	2	0	231	203	0	25	100	9.3	1.95	140	.236	.266	43	.291	7	21	20	-0	3.7
1903	NY-A	15	15	.500	32	31	22	2	0	239²	258	3	34	106	11.0	3.27	96	.274	.299	26	.234	5	-8	-4	2	0.5
1904	Bos-A	21	11	.656	33	31	30	4	0	281²	256	5	33	116	9.2	2.04	131	.243	.266	24	.197	3	17	20	3	3.2
1905	Bos-A	22	9	.710	37	32	27	6	0	271²	238	7	59	113	9.8	2.48	109	.237	.279	21	.226	6	5	7	3	1.7
1906	Bos-A	13	11	.542	27	26	18	2	0	196¹	207	9	39	82	11.3	3.16	87	.274	.309	22	.278	6	-10	-9	-0	-0.2
1907	Bos-A	6	7	.462	18	16	10	2	1	131	131	3	20	29	10.4	2.47	104	.262	.291	10	.196	1	1	2	1	0.3
1908	Bos-A	0	0	—	1	1	0	0	0	5	4	0	3	2	12.6	3.60	68	.200	.304	1	.500	0	-1	-1	0	0.0
	Was-A	2	4	.333	10	9	5	0	0	71²	77	0	23	14	13.3	3.77	61	.278	.346	11	.256	2	-11	-12	2	-1.1
	Yr	2	4	.333	11	10	5	0	0	76²	81	0	26	16	13.3	3.76	61	.273	.343	2	.044	2	-12	-12	2	-1.1
1909	Was-A	1	1	.500	3	2	2	1	0	21	19	1	5	8	10.7	3.43	71	.268	.325	6	.167	0	-2	-2	1	-0.2
1911	Cin-N	0	0	—						4¹	6	0	3	1	18.7	6.23	53	.316	.409	0	.000	-0	-1	-1	0	0.0
Total	15	197	116	.629	358	319	263	34	7	2750¹	2787	40	477	940	10.8	2.79	115	.263	.296	361	.256	55	123	125	18	21.5

■ BRUCE TANNER Tanner, Bruce Matthew b: 12/9/61, New Castle, Pa. BL/TR, 6'3", 220 lbs. Deb: 6/12/85

| 1985 | Chi-A | 1 | 2 | .333 | 10 | 4 | 0 | 0 | 0 | 27 | 34 | 1 | 13 | 9 | 16.3 | 5.33 | 81 | .309 | .392 | 0 | — | 0 | -4 | -3 | 1 | -0.1 |

■ KEVIN TAPANI Tapani, Kevin Ray b: 2/18/64, Des Moines, Iowa BR/TR, 6', 180 lbs. Deb: 7/04/89

1989	NY-N	0	0	—	3	0	0	0	0	7¹	5	1	4	2	11.0	3.68	89	.192	.300	0	.000	-0	-0	-0	0	0.0
	Min-A	2	2	.500	5	5	0	0	0	32²	34	2	8	21	11.6	3.86	107	.266	.309	0	—	0	0	1	-0	0.1
1990	Min-A	12	8	.600	28	28	1	1	0	159¹	164	12	29	101	11.0	4.07	103	.264	.299	0	—	0	-3	2	0	0.2
Total	2	14	10	.583	36	33	1	1	0	199¹	203	15	41	124	11.1	4.02	103	.262	.301	0	.000	-0	-3	3	0	0.3

■ AL TATE Tate, Alvin Walter b: 7/1/18, Coleman, Okla. BR/TR, 6', 180 lbs. Deb: 9/27/46

| 1946 | Pit-N | 0 | 1 | .000 | 2 | 1 | 0 | 0 | 0 | 9 | 8 | 0 | 7 | 2 | 15.0 | 5.00 | 70 | .267 | .405 | 1 | .333 | -0 | -2 | -1 | 0 | 0.0 |

■ RANDY TATE Tate, Randall Lee b: 10/23/52, Florence, Ala. BR/TR, 6'3", 190 lbs. Deb: 4/14/75

| 1975 | NY-N | 5 | 13 | .278 | 26 | 23 | 2 | 0 | 0 | 137² | 121 | 8 | 86 | 99 | 13.9 | 4.45 | 78 | .240 | .356 | 0 | .000 | -4 | -13 | -15 | 0 | -1.9 |

■ STU TATE Tate, Stuart Douglas b: 6/17/62, Huntsville, Ala. BR/TR, 6'3", 205 lbs. Deb: 9/20/89

| 1989 | SF-N | 0 | 0 | — | 2 | 0 | 0 | 0 | 0 | 2² | 3 | 0 | 0 | 4 | 10.1 | 3.38 | 100 | .250 | .250 | 0 | — | 0 | 0 | -0 | 0 | 0.0 |

■ KEN TATUM Tatum, Kenneth Ray b: 4/25/44, Alexandria, La. BR/TR, 6'2", 205 lbs. Deb: 5/28/69

1969	Cal-A	7	2	.778	45	0	0	0	22	86¹	51	1	39	65	9.8	1.36	257	.172	.277	6	.286	4	**22**	20	-0	2.5
1970	Cal-A	7	4	.636	62	0	0	0	17	88²	68	12	26	50	10.0	2.94	123	.208	.277	2	.182	1	8	7	0	0.8
1971	Bos-A	2	4	.333	36	1	0	0	9	53²	50	3	25	21	13.9	4.19	88	.255	.362	3	.300	2	-4	-3	1	0.0
1972	Bos-A	0	2	.000	22	0	0	0	4	29¹	32	3	15	15	15.0	3.07	105	.283	.377	0	.000	0	0	0	-0	0.0
1973	Bos-A	0	0	—	1	0	0	0	0	4	6	2	3	0	20.3	9.00	45	.462	.563	0	—	0	-2	-2	0	-0.1
1974	Chi-A	0	0	—	10	1	0	0	0	20²	23	3	9	5	13.9	4.79	78	.274	.344	0	.000	0	-3	-2	1	-0.1
Total	6	16	12	.571	176	2	0	0	52	282²	230	24	117	156	11.7	2.93	122	.224	.314	11	.244	7	20	20	1	3.1

■ WALT TAUSCHER Tauscher, Walter Edward b: 11/22/01, LaSalle, Ill. BR/TR, 6'1", 186 lbs. Deb: 4/19/28

1928	Pit-N	0	0	—	17	0	0	0	1	29¹	28	0	12	7	13.2	4.91	83	.280	.374	1	.167	-0	-3	-3	-0	-0.2
1931	Was-A	1	0	1.000	6	0	0	0	0	12	24	2	4	5	21.0	7.50	57	.429	.467	0	—	0	-4	-4	2	-0.2
Total	2	1	0	1.000	23	0	0	0	1	41¹	52	2	16	12	15.5	5.66	73	.333	.406	1	.167	-0	-7	-7	1	-0.4

■ ARLAS TAYLOR Taylor, Arlas Walter "Lefty" or "Foxy" b: 3/16/1896, Warick County, Ind d: 9/10/58, Dade City, Fla. BR/TL, 5'11", Deb: 9/15/21

| 1921 | Phi-A | 0 | 1 | .000 | 1 | 1 | 0 | 0 | 0 | 2 | 7 | 1 | 2 | 1 | 40.5 | 22.50 | 20 | .636 | .692 | 0 | — | 0 | -4 | -4 | 0 | -0.2 |

■ BEN TAYLOR Taylor, Benjamin Harrison b: 4/2/1889, Paoli, Ind. d: 11/3/46, Martin County, Ind. BR/TR, 5'11", 163 lbs. Deb: 6/28/12

| 1912 | Cin-N | 0 | 0 | — | 2 | 0 | 0 | 0 | 0 | 5² | 9 | 0 | 3 | 2 | 20.6 | 3.18 | 106 | .346 | .433 | 0 | .000 | 0 | 0 | 0 | 0 | 0.0 |

■ BRUCE TAYLOR Taylor, Bruce Bell b: 4/16/53, Holden, Mass. BR/TR, 6', 178 lbs. Deb: 8/05/77

| 1977 | Det-A | 1 | 0 | 1.000 | 19 | 0 | 0 | 0 | 2 | 29¹ | 23 | 2 | 10 | 19 | 10.4 | 3.38 | 127 | .219 | .293 | 0 | — | 0 | 2 | 3 | 0 | 0.3 |

YEAR TM/L	W	L	PCT	G	GS	CG	SH	SV	IP	H	HR	BB	SO	RAT	ERA	ERA+	OAV	OOB	BH	AVG	PB	PR	/A	PD	TPI
1978 Det-A	0	0	—	1	0	0	0	0	1	0	0	0	0	0.0	0.00	—	.000	.000	0	—	0	0	0	0	0.0
1979 Det-A	1	2	.333	10	0	0	0	0	18²	16	1	7	8	12.1	4.82	90	.242	.333	0	—	0	-1	-1	0	0.0
Total 3	2	2	.500	30	0	0	0	2	49	39	3	17	27	10.8	3.86	111	.224	.304	0	—	0	1	2	0	0.3

■ CHUCK TAYLOR
Taylor, Charles Gilbert b: 4/18/42, Murfreesboro, Tenn. BR/TR, 6'2", 195 lbs. Deb: 5/27/69

YEAR TM/L	W	L	PCT	G	GS	CG	SH	SV	IP	H	HR	BB	SO	RAT	ERA	ERA+	OAV	OOB	BH	AVG	PB	PR	/A	PD	TPI
1969 StL-N	7	5	.583	27	13	5	1	0	126²	108	8	30	62	10.0	2.56	140	.235	.287	7	.179	1	15	14	-1	1.5
1970 StL-N	6	7	.462	56	7	1	1	8	124¹	116	5	31	64	10.8	3.11	132	.256	.306	3	.115	-1	13	14	1	1.4
1971 StL-N	3	1	.750	43	1	0	0	3	71¹	72	7	25	46	12.4	3.53	102	.267	.331	2	.167	0	-1	1	0	0.1
1972 NY-N	0	0	—	20	0	0	0	2	31	44	2	9	9	15.7	5.52	61	.341	.388	0	.000	-0	-7	-7	1	-0.6
Mil-A	0	0	—	5	0	0	0	1	11²	8	0	3	5	9.3	1.54	196	.200	.273	1	.500	0	2	2	0	0.3
1973 Mon-N	2	0	1.000	8	0	0	0	0	20¹	17	3	2	10	8.4	1.77	215	.230	.250	0	.000	-0	4	5	1	0.5
1974 Mon-N	6	2	.750	61	0	0	0	11	107²	101	8	25	43	10.8	2.17	177	.256	.305	3	.300	1	17	20	2	2.2
1975 Mon-N	2	2	.500	54	0	0	0	6	74	72	6	24	29	11.8	3.53	108	.264	.326	0	.000	-0	1	2	0	0.2
1976 Mon-N	2	3	.400	31	0	0	0	0	40	38	4	13	14	11.5	4.50	83	.273	.336	0	.000	-0	-4	-3	0	-0.3
Total 8	28	20	.583	305	21	6	2	31	607	576	43	162	282	11.1	3.07	123	.258	.312	16	.158	0	40	47	2	5.3

■ DORN TAYLOR
Taylor, Donald Clyde b: 8/11/58, Abington, Pa. BR/TR, 6'2", 180 lbs. Deb: 4/30/87

YEAR TM/L	W	L	PCT	G	GS	CG	SH	SV	IP	H	HR	BB	SO	RAT	ERA	ERA+	OAV	OOB	BH	AVG	PB	PR	/A	PD	TPI
1987 Pit-N	2	3	.400	14	8	0	0	0	53¹	48	10	28	37	13.0	5.74	72	.247	.345	3	.167	-0	-10	-10	-0	-0.9
1989 Pit-N	1	1	.500	9	0	0	0	0	10²	14	0	5	3	16.0	5.06	66	.333	.404	0	.000	-0	-2	-2	-0	-0.1
1990 Bal-A	0	1	.000	4	0	0	0	0	3²	4	0	2	4	14.7	2.45	156	.250	.333	0	—	-0	1	1	0	0.0
Total 3	3	5	.375	27	8	0	0	0	67²	66	10	35	44	13.6	5.45	73	.262	.354	3	.158	-0	-11	-11	-1	-1.0

■ ED TAYLOR
Taylor, Edgar Ruben "Rube" b: 3/23/1877, Palestine, Tex. d: 1/31/12, Dallas, Tex. TL , Deb: 8/08/03

YEAR TM/L	W	L	PCT	G	GS	CG	SH	SV	IP	H	HR	BB	SO	RAT	ERA	ERA+	OAV	OOB	BH	AVG	PB	PR	/A	PD	TPI
1903 StL-N	0	0	—	1	0	0	0	0	3	0	0	0	1	0.0	0.00	—	.000	.000	0	.000	-0	1	1	0	0.1

■ GARY TAYLOR
Taylor, Gary William b: 10/19/45, Detroit, Mich. BR/TR, 6'2", 190 lbs. Deb: 9/02/69

YEAR TM/L	W	L	PCT	G	GS	CG	SH	SV	IP	H	HR	BB	SO	RAT	ERA	ERA+	OAV	OOB	BH	AVG	PB	PR	/A	PD	TPI
1969 Det-A	0	1	.000	7	0	0	0	0	10¹	10	2	6	3	13.9	5.23	71	.244	.340	0	.000	-0	-2	-2	0	-0.1

■ HARRY TAYLOR
Taylor, Harry Evans b: 12/2/35, San Angelo, Tex. BR/TR, 6', 185 lbs. Deb: 9/17/57

YEAR TM/L	W	L	PCT	G	GS	CG	SH	SV	IP	H	HR	BB	SO	RAT	ERA	ERA+	OAV	OOB	BH	AVG	PB	PR	/A	PD	TPI
1957 KC-A	0	0	—	2	0	0	0	0	8²	11	0	4	4	16.6	3.12	127	.314	.400	1	.250	0	1	1	-0	0.1

■ HARRY TAYLOR
Taylor, James Harry b: 5/20/19, E.Glenn, Ind. BR/TR, 6'1", 175 lbs. Deb: 9/22/46

YEAR TM/L	W	L	PCT	G	GS	CG	SH	SV	IP	H	HR	BB	SO	RAT	ERA	ERA+	OAV	OOB	BH	AVG	PB	PR	/A	PD	TPI
1946 Bro-N	0	0	—	4	0	0	0	1	4²	1	0	1	6	11.6	3.86	88	.313	.353	0	—	0	-0	-0	0	0.0
1947 *Bro-N	10	5	.667	33	20	10	2	1	162	130	10	83	58	12.1	3.11	133	.225	.327	8	.129	-2	17	18	1	1.8
1948 Bro-N	2	7	.222	17	13	2	0	0	80²	90	8	61	32	17.2	5.36	75	.288	.408	6	.273	1	-13	-12	2	-0.8
1950 Bos-A	2	0	1.000	3	2	2	1	0	19	13	0	8	8	9.9	1.42	345	.197	.284	2	.286	0	7	7	0	0.8
1951 Bos-A	4	9	.308	31	8	1	0	2	81¹	100	6	42	22	15.8	5.75	78	.307	.388	3	.103	-3	-15	-12	1	-1.1
1952 Bos-A	1	0	1.000	2	1	1	0	0	10	6	1	6	1	11.7	1.80	219	.176	.317	1	.250	0	2	2	0	0.3
Total 6	19	21	.475	90	44	16	3	4	357²	344	25	201	127	14.0	4.10	102	.258	.359	20	.161	-3	-2	4	5	1.0

■ JACK TAYLOR
Taylor, John Budd "Brewery Jack" b: 5/23/1873, W.New Brighton, N.Y. d: 2/7/1900, Staten Island, N.Y. 6'1", 190 lbs. Deb: 9/16/1891

YEAR TM/L	W	L	PCT	G	GS	CG	SH	SV	IP	H	HR	BB	SO	RAT	ERA	ERA+	OAV	OOB	BH	AVG	PB	PR	/A	PD	TPI
1891 NY-N	0	1	.000	1	1	1	0	0	8	4	1	3	3	7.9	1.13	285	.143	.226	0	.000	-0	2	2	-0	0.2
1892 Phi-N	1	0	1.000	3	3	2	0	0	26	28	2	10	7	13.2	1.38	234	.264	.328	2	.167	-0	5	5	-1	0.4
1893 Phi-N	10	9	.526	25	16	14	0	1	170	189	8	77	41	14.1	4.24	108	.273	.346	20	.215	-2	8	7	2	0.5
1894 Phi-N	23	13	.639	41	34	31	1	1	298	347	13	96	76	13.4	4.08	125	.288	.340	48	.333	8	41	34	2	3.4
1895 Phi-N	26	14	.650	41	37	33	1	1	335	403	7	83	93	13.1	4.49	107	.293	.334	45	.290	7	11	11	4	1.9
1896 Phi-N	20	21	.488	45	41	35	1	1	359	459	17	112	97	14.3	4.79	90	.308	.357	29	.185	-6	-17	-19	4	-1.7
1897 Phi-N	16	20	.444	40	37	35	2	2	317¹	376	5	76	88	12.8	4.23	99	.292	.332	35	.252	2	3	-1	2	0.3
1898 StL-N	15	29	.341	50	47	42	0	1	397¹	465	14	83	89	12.4	3.90	97	.290	.325	42	.242	4	-13	-15	8	-0.8
1899 Cin-N	9	10	.474	24	18	15	2	2	168¹	197	7	41	34	12.7	4.12	95	.292	.332	17	.250	-0	-5	-4	-1	-0.3
Total 9	120	117	.506	270	234	208	7	9	2079	2468	74	581	528	13.2	4.23	103	.292	.337	234	.252	12	37	34	20	5.5

■ JACK TAYLOR
Taylor, John W. b: 1/14/1874, New Straightsville, Ohio d: 3/4/38, Columbus, Ohio BR/TR, 5'10", 170 lbs. Deb: 9/25/1898

YEAR TM/L	W	L	PCT	G	GS	CG	SH	SV	IP	H	HR	BB	SO	RAT	ERA	ERA+	OAV	OOB	BH	AVG	PB	PR	/A	PD	TPI
1898 Chi-N	5	0	1.000	5	5	5	0	0	41	32	0	10	11	9.2	2.20	163	.214	.263	3	.200	1	6	6	-0	0.7
1899 Chi-N	18	21	.462	41	39	39	1	0	354²	380	6	84	67	11.8	3.76	100	.274	.315	37	.266	9	4	-0	2	0.9
1900 Chi-N	10	17	.370	28	26	25	2	1	222¹	226	4	58	57	11.5	2.55	141	.263	.310	19	.235	2	28	26	2	2.4
1901 Chi-N	13	19	.406	33	31	30	0	0	275²	341	5	44	68	12.9	3.36	96	.301	.334	23	.217	2	-1	-4	3	0.1
1902 Chi-N	23	11	.676	36	33	33	7	1	324²	271	2	43	83	9.0	1.33	203	.227	.259	44	.237	3	52	49	4	6.9
1903 Chi-N	21	14	.600	37	33	33	1	1	312¹	277	2	57	83	9.8	2.45	128	.235	.273	28	.222	4	28	24	1	2.9
1904 StL-N	20	19	.513	41	39	39	2	1	352	297	5	82	103	10.0	2.22	121	.220	.271	28	.211	4	20	19	2	2.6
1905 StL-N	15	21	.417	37	34	34	3	1	309	302	10	85	102	11.6	3.44	87	.259	.315	23	.190	3	-15	-16	-2	-1.4
1906 StL-N	8	9	.471	17	17	17	1	0	155	133	4	47	27	10.9	2.15	122	.227	.292	11	.208	3	8	8	1	1.4
Chi-N	12	3	.800	17	16	15	2	0	147¹	116	1	39	34	9.8	1.83	144	.223	.285	11	.208	2	13	13	1	1.9
Yr	20	12	.625	34	33	32	3	0	302¹	249	4	86	61	10.2	1.99	132	.224	.283	14	.132	5	21	21	2	3.3
1907 Chi-N	7	5	.583	18	13	8	0	0	123	127	3	33	22	11.8	3.29	76	.268	.318	9	.191	0	-11	-11	2	-0.9
Total 10	152	139	.522	310	286	278	19	5	2617	2502	41	582	657	10.8	2.66	115	.250	.296	236	.223	34	134	116	12	17.5

■ DUMMY TAYLOR
Taylor, Luther Haden b: 2/21/1875, Oskaloosa, Kan. d: 8/22/58, Jacksonville, Ill. BR/TR, 6'1", 160 lbs. Deb: 8/27/00

YEAR TM/L	W	L	PCT	G	GS	CG	SH	SV	IP	H	HR	BB	SO	RAT	ERA	ERA+	OAV	OOB	BH	AVG	PB	PR	/A	PD	TPI
1900 NY-N	4	3	.571	11	7	6	0	0	62¹	74	0	24	16	14.1	2.45	147	.294	.356	3	.136	-1	9	8	-2	0.5
1901 NY-N	19	27	.413	45	43	37	4	0	353¹	377	8	112	136	12.8	3.18	104	.271	.332	18	.132	-8	5	5	1	-0.1
1902 Cle-A	1	3	.250	4	4	4	1	0	34	37	0	8	8	11.9	1.59	217	.277	.318	1	.100	-1	8	7	1	0.8
NY-N	7	15	.318	26	25	18	0	0	200²	194	4	55	87	11.7	2.29	123	.254	.314	6	.092	-5	11	12	-1	0.6
1903 NY-N	13	13	.500	33	31	18	1	0	244²	306	6	89	94	14.7	4.23	79	.314	.374	12	.146	-2	-26	-24	-0	-2.3
1904 NY-N	21	15	.583	37	36	29	5	0	296¹	231	6	75	138	9.6	2.34	117	.214	.270	16	.157	-1	13	13	3	1.6
1905 NY-N	16	9	.640	32	28	18	4	0	213	200	5	51	91	10.9	2.66	110	.247	.298	9	.130	-1	8	6	2	0.7
1906 NY-N	17	9	.654	31	27	13	2	0	213	186	4	51	90	10.5	2.20	119	.233	.289	14	.184	-1	10	10	-1	1.0
1907 NY-N	11	7	.611	28	21	11	3	1	171	145	1	46	56	10.2	2.42	102	.232	.288	6	.125	-0	1	1	-0	0.4
1908 NY-N	8	5	.615	27	15	6	1	2	127²	127	5	34	50	11.6	2.33	104	.253	.306	8	.229	2	1	1	0	0.4
Total 9	117	106	.525	274	237	160	21	3	1916	1877	39	551	767	11.7	2.75	107	.256	.313	93	.144	-16	40	39	4	3.2

■ WILEY TAYLOR
Taylor, Philip Wiley b: 3/18/1888, Wamego, Kan. d: 7/8/54, Westmoreland, Kan. BR/TR, 6'1", 175 lbs. Deb: 9/06/11

YEAR TM/L	W	L	PCT	G	GS	CG	SH	SV	IP	H	HR	BB	SO	RAT	ERA	ERA+	OAV	OOB	BH	AVG	PB	PR	/A	PD	TPI
1911 Det-A	0	2	.000	3	2	1	0	0	19	18	0	10	9	13.7	3.79	91	.247	.345	0	.000	-1	-1	-1	-0	-0.1
1912 Chi-A	0	1	.000	3	3	0	0	0	20	21	0	14	4	15.7	4.95	65	.309	.427	0	.000	-1	-4	-4	0	-0.3
1913 StL-A	0	2	.000	5	4	1	0	0	31²	33	0	16	12	13.9	4.83	61	.280	.366	0	.000	-1	-7	-7	0	-0.6
1914 StL-A	2	5	.286	16	8	2	1	0	50	41	0	25	20	12.2	3.42	79	.209	.305	2	.167	-0	-4	-4	-0	-0.4
Total 4	2	10	.167	27	17	4	1	0	120²	113	0	65	45	13.5	4.10	72	.248	.346	2	.061	-3	-15	-15	-0	-1.4

■ RON TAYLOR
Taylor, Ronald Wesley b: 12/13/37, Toronto, Ont., Can. BR/TR, 6'1", 195 lbs. Deb: 4/11/62

YEAR TM/L	W	L	PCT	G	GS	CG	SH	SV	IP	H	HR	BB	SO	RAT	ERA	ERA+	OAV	OOB	BH	AVG	PB	PR	/A	PD	TPI
1962 Cle-A	2	2	.500	8	4	1	0	0	37	36	6	15	13	13.5	5.94	65	.281	.352	3	.273	0	-7	-8	-0	-0.6
1963 StL-N	9	7	.563	54	9	2	0	11	133¹	119	10	30	91	10.3	2.84	125	.243	.293	1	.031	-3	7	11	-2	0.6
1964 *StL-N	8	4	.667	63	2	0	0	7	101¹	109	15	33	69	12.7	4.62	82	.274	.331	2	.133	-0	-12	-9	2	-0.7
1965 StL-N	2	1	.667	25	0	0	0	1	43²	45	6	15	26	12.2	4.53	85	.261	.326	2	.400	1	-5	-3	0	-0.2
Hou-N	1	5	.167	32	1	0	0	4	57²	68	5	16	37	13.9	6.40	52	.305	.365	0	.000	-1	-18	-19	-1	-2.1
Yr	3	6	.333	57	1	0	0	5	101¹	111	11	31	63	13.1	5.60	64	.283	.343	0	.000	-0	-23	-23	-1	-2.3
1966 Hou-N	2	3	.400	36	1	0	0	0	64²	89	5	10	29	14.5	5.71	60	.333	.369	2	.167	0	-15	-16	-1	-1.7

YEAR TM/L	W	L	PCT	G	GS	CG	SH	SV	IP	H	HR	BB	SO	RAT	ERA	ERA+	OAV	OOB	BH	AVG	PB	PR	/A	PD	TPI
1967 NY-N	4	6	.400	50	0	0	0	8	73	60	1	23	46	10.4	2.34	145	.230	.295	0	.000	-1	8	8	0	0.9
1968 NY-N	1	5	.167	58	0	0	0	13	76²	64	4	18	49	9.7	2.70	112	.228	.277	0	.000	-1	2	3	1	0.3
1969 *NY-N	9	4	.692	59	0	0	0	13	76	61	7	24	42	10.2	2.72	134	.228	.294	1	.250	-0	7	8	0	0.9
1970 NY-N	5	4	.556	57	0	0	0	13	66¹	65	5	16	28	11.0	3.93	102	.265	.310	0	.000	-0	1	1	1	0.1
1971 NY-N	2	2	.500	45	0	0	0	2	69	71	7	11	32	10.8	3.65	93	.269	.301	1	.250	-0	-1	-2	0	-0.1
1972 SD-N	0	0	—	4	0	0	0	0	5	9	5	0	0	16.2	12.60	26	.375	.375	0	—	0	-5	-5	0	-0.4
Total 11	45	43	.511	491	17	3	0	72	800	794	76	209	464	11.5	3.93	91	.264	.316	12	.103	-5	-39	-32	-0	-3.0

■ TERRY TAYLOR   Taylor, Terry Derrell b: 7/28/64, Crestview, Fla. BR/TR, 6'1", 180 lbs. Deb: 8/19/88

YEAR TM/L	W	L	PCT	G	GS	CG	SH	SV	IP	H	HR	BB	SO	RAT	ERA	ERA+	OAV	OOB	BH	AVG	PB	PR	/A	PD	TPI
1988 Sea-A	0	1	.000	5	5	0	0	0	23	26	2	11	9	14.5	6.26	66	.295	.374	0	—	0	-6	-5	-1	-0.5

■ PETE TAYLOR   Taylor, Vernon Charles b: 11/26/27, Severn, Md. BR/TR, 6'1", 170 lbs. Deb: 5/02/52

YEAR TM/L	W	L	PCT	G	GS	CG	SH	SV	IP	H	HR	BB	SO	RAT	ERA	ERA+	OAV	OOB	BH	AVG	PB	PR	/A	PD	TPI
1952 StL-A	0	0	—	1	0	0	0	0	2	4	0	3	0	31.5	13.50	29	.500	.636	0	—	0	-2	-2	0	-0.1

■ BILLY TAYLOR   Taylor, William Henry "Bollicky Bill" b: 1855, Washington, D.C. d: 5/14/1900, Jacksonville, Fla. TR, 5'11.5", 204 lbs. Deb: 5/21/1881 ♦

YEAR TM/L	W	L	PCT	G	GS	CG	SH	SV	IP	H	HR	BB	SO	RAT	ERA	ERA+	OAV	OOB	BH	AVG	PB	PR	/A	PD	TPI
1881 Wor-N	0	1	.000	1	1	1	0	0	8	15	0	6	0	23.6	7.88	38	.384	.466	3	.107	-0	-5	-4	0	-0.2
Cle-N	0	0	—	1	0	0	0	0	3	0	0	1	2	3.0	0.00	—	.000	.100	25	.243	-0	1	1	0	0.1
Yr	0	1	.000	2	1	1	0	0	11	15	0	7	2	18.0	5.73	51	.312	.399	0	.000	-1	-4	-3	0	-0.1
1882 Pit-a	0	1	.000	1	0	0	0	0	5	11	0	4	1	27.0	16.20	16	.414	.491	84	.281	0	-8	-8	-0	-0.4
1883 Pit-a	4	7	.364	19	9	8	0	0	127	166	4	34	41	14.2	5.39	60	.296	.337	96	.260	3	-29	-31	-2	-2.4
1884 StL-U	25	4	.862	33	29	29	2	4	263	222	2	40	154	9.0	1.68	177	.213	.243	68	.366	19	39	38	-1	5.7
Phi-a	18	12	.600	30	30	30	1	0	260	232	8	44	130	9.6	2.53	134	.226	.258	28	.252	3	21	25	2	3.0
1885 Phi-a	1	5	.167	6	6	6	0	0	52¹	68	0	9	11	13.2	3.27	105	.301	.328	4	.190	-1	-0	1	-1	0.0
1886 Bal-a	1	6	.143	8	8	8	0	0	72¹	87	1	20	37	13.3	5.72	60	.284	.328	12	.308	1	-18	-18	-0	-1.3
1887 Phi-a	1	0	1.000	1	1	1	0	0	9	10	1	7	0	17.0	3.00	143	.271	.387	1	.250	-0	1	1	-0	0.1
Total 7	50	36	.581	100	84	83	3	4	799²	811	11	165	376	11.0	3.17	102	.248	.284	323	.277	25	2	5	-3	4.6

■ BUD TEACHOUT   Teachout, Arthur John b: 2/27/04, Los Angeles, Cal. d: 5/11/85, Laguna Beach, Cal BR/TL, 6'2", 183 lbs. Deb: 5/12/30

YEAR TM/L	W	L	PCT	G	GS	CG	SH	SV	IP	H	HR	BB	SO	RAT	ERA	ERA+	OAV	OOB	BH	AVG	PB	PR	/A	PD	TPI
1930 Chi-N	11	4	.733	40	16	6	0	0	153	178	16	48	59	13.3	4.06	120	.296	.348	17	.270	3	16	14	-0	1.4
1931 Chi-N	1	2	.333	27	3	1	0	0	61¹	79	6	28	14	15.8	5.72	67	.305	.375	5	.238	0	-13	-13	1	-1.0
1932 StL-N	0	0	—	1	0	0	0	0	1	2	0	0	0	18.0	0.00	—	.400	.400	0	—	0	0	0	0	0.0
Total 3	12	6	.667	68	19	7	0	0	215¹	259	22	76	73	14.0	4.51	102	.299	.356	22	.262	3	3	2	1	0.4

■ GEORGE TEBEAU   Tebeau, George E. "White Wings" b: 12/26/1861, St.Louis, Mo. d: 2/4/23, Denver, Colo. BR/TR, 5'9", 175 lbs. Deb: 4/16/1887 ♦

YEAR TM/L	W	L	PCT	G	GS	CG	SH	SV	IP	H	HR	BB	SO	RAT	ERA	ERA+	OAV	OOB	BH	AVG	PB	PR	/A	PD	TPI
1887 Cin-a	0	1	.000	1	1	0	0	0	8	21	0	3	1	27.0	13.50	32	.468	.501	94	.296	0	-8	-8	0	-0.4
1890 Tol-a	0	0	—	1	0	0	0	0	5	9	0	5	0	25.2	9.00	44	.378	.486	102	.268	0	-3	-3	-0	-0.1
Total 2	0	1	.000	2	1	0	0	0	13	30	0	8	1	26.3	11.77	35	.437	.495	622	.269	1	-11	-11	0	-0.5

■ PATSY TEBEAU   Tebeau, Oliver Wendell b: 12/5/1864, St.Louis, Mo. d: 5/15/18, St.Louis, Mo. BR/TR, 5'8", 163 lbs. Deb: 9/20/1887 M♦

YEAR TM/L	W	L	PCT	G	GS	CG	SH	SV	IP	H	HR	BB	SO	RAT	ERA	ERA+	OAV	OOB	BH	AVG	PB	PR	/A	PD	TPI
1896 *Cle-N	0	0	—	1	0	0	0	0	0	1	0	0	0	—	—	—	1.000	1.000	146	.269	0	0	0	0	0.0

■ AL TEDROW   Tedrow, Allen Seymour b: 12/14/1891, Westerville, Ohio d: 1/23/58, Westerville, Ohio BR/TL, 6', 180 lbs. Deb: 9/15/14

YEAR TM/L	W	L	PCT	G	GS	CG	SH	SV	IP	H	HR	BB	SO	RAT	ERA	ERA+	OAV	OOB	BH	AVG	PB	PR	/A	PD	TPI
1914 Cle-A	1	2	.333	4	3	1	0	0	19	14		4	14	14.5	1.21	239	.235	.367	1	.167	0	4	4	0	0.5

■ KENT TEKULVE   Tekulve, Kenton Charles b: 3/5/47, Cincinnati, Ohio BR/TR, 6'4", 180 lbs. Deb: 5/20/74

YEAR TM/L	W	L	PCT	G	GS	CG	SH	SV	IP	H	HR	BB	SO	RAT	ERA	ERA+	OAV	OOB	BH	AVG	PB	PR	/A	PD	TPI
1974 Pit-N	1	1	.500	8	0	0	0	0	9	12	1	5	6	18.0	6.00	57	.343	.439	0	—	0	-2	-3	1	-0.1
1975 *Pit-N	1	2	.333	34	0	0	0	5	56	43	2	23	28	10.8	2.25	157	.215	.299	1	.091	-0	9	8	2	1.0
1976 Pit-N	5	3	.625	64	0	0	0	9	102²	91	3	25	68	10.2	2.45	142	.241	.288	0	.000	-1	12	12	2	1.3
1977 Pit-N	10	1	.909	72	0	0	0	7	103	89	5	33	59	10.7	3.06	130	.236	.299	3	.250	-0	10	11	4	1.5
1978 Pit-N	8	7	.533	91	0	0	0	31	135	115	5	55	77	11.5	2.33	159	.228	.306	2	.095	-1	19	21	3	2.5
1979 *Pit-N	10	8	.556	94	0	0	0	31	134¹	109	5	49	75	10.7	2.75	141	.222	.296	2	.133	-0	15	17	2	1.9
1980 Pit-N	8	12	.400	78	0	0	0	21	93	96	6	40	47	13.3	3.39	107	.267	.342	0	.000	-1	2	3	1	0.3
1981 Pit-N	5	5	.500	45	0	0	0	3	65	61	1	17	34	10.9	2.49	144	.250	.302	0	.000	-0	7	8	1	1.0
1982 Pit-N	12	8	.600	85	0	0	0	20	128²	113	7	46	66	11.3	2.87	129	.237	.309	1	.071	-1	10	12	2	1.4
1983 Pit-N	7	5	.583	76	0	0	0	18	99	78	1	36	52	10.4	1.64	226	.223	.296	0	.000	-1	22	23	1	2.4
1984 Pit-N	3	9	.250	72	0	0	0	13	88	86	4	33	36	12.3	2.66	135	.262	.331	0	.000	-1	9	9	3	1.2
1985 Pit-N	0	0	—	3	0	0	0	0	3¹	7	1	5	4	32.4	16.20	22	.467	.600	0	—	0	-5	-5	0	-0.3
Phi-N	4	10	.286	58	0	0	0	14	72¹	67	4	25	36	11.7	2.99	123	.246	.314	0	.000	-0	5	6	0	0.6
Yr	4	10	.286	61	0	0	0	14	75²	74	5	30	40	12.6	3.57	103	.258	.332	0	.000	-0	0	1	0	0.3
1986 Phi-N	11	5	.688	73	0	0	0	4	110	99	2	25	57	10.1	2.54	152	.240	.283	0	.000	-0	14	16	1	1.7
1987 Phi-N	6	4	.600	90	0	0	0	3	105	96	8	29	60	10.7	3.09	137	.243	.295	0	.000	-0	12	13	1	1.5
1988 Phi-N	3	7	.300	70	0	0	0	0	80	87	3	22	43	12.5	3.60	99	.276	.327	0	.000	-0	-1	-0	1	0.0
1989 Cin-N	0	3	.000	37	0	0	0	1	52	56	5	23	31	13.7	5.02	72	.272	.345	1	.500	0	-9	-8	0	-0.7
Total 16	94	90	.511	1050	0	0	0	184	1436¹	1305	63	491	779	11.4	2.85	131	.244	.309	10	.083	-6	128	141	23	17.2

■ ANTHONY TELFORD   Telford, Anthony Charles b: 3/6/66, San Jose, Cal. BR/TR, 6', 175 lbs. Deb: 8/19/90

YEAR TM/L	W	L	PCT	G	GS	CG	SH	SV	IP	H	HR	BB	SO	RAT	ERA	ERA+	OAV	OOB	BH	AVG	PB	PR	/A	PD	TPI
1990 Bal-A	3	3	.500	8	8	0	0	0	36¹	43	4	19	20	15.6	4.95	77	.295	.380	0	—	0	-4	-5	0	-0.3

■ TOM TELLMANN   Tellmann, Thomas John b: 3/29/54, Warren, Pa. BR/TR, 6'3", 195 lbs. Deb: 6/09/79

YEAR TM/L	W	L	PCT	G	GS	CG	SH	SV	IP	H	HR	BB	SO	RAT	ERA	ERA+	OAV	OOB	BH	AVG	PB	PR	/A	PD	TPI
1979 SD-N	0	0	—	1	0	0	0	0	2²	7	1	0	1	23.6	16.88	21	.467	.467	0	.000	-0	-4	-4	0	-0.2
1980 SD-N	3	0	1.000	6	2	2	0	1	22¹	23	0	8	9	12.5	1.61	213	.264	.326	1	.125	-0	5	5	0	0.5
1983 Mil-A	9	4	.692	44	0	0	0	8	99²	95	7	35	48	11.9	2.80	133	.259	.327	0	—	0	14	10	3	1.3
1984 Mil-A	6	3	.667	50	0	0	0	4	81	82	6	31	28	12.7	2.78	138	.272	.342	0	—	0	11	10	1	1.1
1985 Oak-A	0	0	—	11	0	0	0	0	21¹	33	3	9	8	18.1	5.06	76	.347	.410	0	—	0	-2	-3	0	-0.2
Total 5	18	7	.720	112	2	2	0	13	227	240	17	83	94	13.0	3.05	123	.277	.343	1	.111	-0	24	18	4	2.5

■ CHUCK TEMPLETON   Templeton, Charles Sherman b: 6/1/32, Detroit, Mich. BR/TL, 6'3", 210 lbs. Deb: 9/09/55

YEAR TM/L	W	L	PCT	G	GS	CG	SH	SV	IP	H	HR	BB	SO	RAT	ERA	ERA+	OAV	OOB	BH	AVG	PB	PR	/A	PD	TPI
1955 Bro-N	0	1	.000	4	0	0	0	0	4²	5	2	5	3	21.2	11.57	35	.294	.478	0	—	0	-4	-4	0	-0.3
1956 Bro-N	0	1	.000	6	2	0	0	0	16¹	20	2	10	8	16.5	6.61	60	.294	.385	0	.000	-0	-5	-5	-0	-0.4
Total 2	0	2	.000	10	2	0	0	0	21	25	4	15	11	17.6	7.71	52	.294	.406	0	.000	-0	-9	-9	-0	-0.7

■ JOHN TENER   Tener, John Kinley b: 7/25/1863, County Tyrone, Ireland d: 5/19/46, Pittsburgh, Pa. BR/TR, 6'4", 180 lbs. Deb: 6/08/1885 ♦

YEAR TM/L	W	L	PCT	G	GS	CG	SH	SV	IP	H	HR	BB	SO	RAT	ERA	ERA+	OAV	OOB	BH	AVG	PB	PR	/A	PD	TPI
1888 Chi-N	7	5	.583	12	12	11	1	0	102	90	6	25	39	10.1	2.74	110	.228	.274	9	.196	-1	1	3	1	0.4
1889 Chi-N	15	15	.500	35	30	28	1	0	287	302	16	105	105	12.8	3.64	114	.262	.323	41	.273	6	12	17	3	2.4
1890 Pit-P	3	11	.214	14	14	13	0	0	117	160	6	70	30	17.7	7.31	53	.312	.395	12	.190	1	-40	-44	4	-2.8
Total 3	25	31	.446	61	56	52	2	0	506	552	28	200	174	13.4	4.30	90	.268	.333	62	.236	6	-27	-23	8	0.0

■ JIM TENNANT   Tennant, James McDonnell b: 3/3/07, Shepherdstown, W.Va d: 4/16/67, Trumbull, Conn. BR/TR, 6'1", 190 lbs. Deb: 9/28/29

YEAR TM/L	W	L	PCT	G	GS	CG	SH	SV	IP	H	HR	BB	SO	RAT	ERA	ERA+	OAV	OOB	BH	AVG	PB	PR	/A	PD	TPI
1929 NY-N	0	0	—	1	0	0	0	0	1	1	0	0	1	9.0	0.00	—	.333	.333	0	—	0	1	1	0	0.0

■ FRED TENNEY   Tenney, Fred Clay b: 7/9/1859, Marlborough, N.H. d: 6/15/19, Fall River, Mass. Deb: 4/28/1884 ♦

YEAR TM/L	W	L	PCT	G	GS	CG	SH	SV	IP	H	HR	BB	SO	RAT	ERA	ERA+	OAV	OOB	BH	AVG	PB	PR	/A	PD	TPI
1884 Bos-U	3	1	.750	4	4	4	0	0	35	31	0	5	18	9.3	2.31	127	.222	.248	2	.118	-2	3	2	-1	0.0
Wil-U	0	1	.000	1	1	1	0	0	8	6	0	4	10	11.3	1.13	293	.194	.287	0	.000	-1	2	2	0	0.1
Yr	3	2	.600	5	5	5	0	0	43	37	0	9	28	9.6	2.09	144	.217	.256	0	.000	-2	4	4	-1	0.1

YEAR TM/L	W	L	PCT	G	GS	CG	SH	SV	IP	H	HR	BB	SO	RAT	ERA	ERA+	OAV	OOB	BH	AVG	PB	PR	/A	PD	TPI

■ FRED TENNEY
Tenney, Frederick b: 11/26/1871, Georgetown, Mass. d: 7/3/52, Boston, Mass. BL/TL, 5'9", 155 lbs. Deb: 6/16/1894 M♦

YEAR TM/L	W	L	PCT	G	GS	CG	SH	SV	IP	H	HR	BB	SO	RAT	ERA	ERA+	OAV	OOB	BH	AVG	PB	PR	/A	PD	TPI
1905 Bos-N	0	0	—	1	0	0	0	0	2	5	0	1	0	27.0	4.50	69	.417	.462	158	.288	0	-0	-0	0	0.0

■ BOB TERLECKI
Terlecki, Robert Joseph b: 2/14/45, Trenton, N.J. BR/TR, 5'8", 185 lbs. Deb: 8/16/72

YEAR TM/L	W	L	PCT	G	GS	CG	SH	SV	IP	H	HR	BB	SO	RAT	ERA	ERA+	OAV	OOB	BH	AVG	PB	PR	/A	PD	TPI
1972 Phi-N	0	0	—	9	0	0	0	0	13¹	16	2	10	5	17.6	4.73	76	.308	.419	0	—	0	-2	-2	0	-0.1

■ GREG TERLECKY
Terlecky, Gregory John b: 3/20/52, Culver City, Cal. BR/TR, 6'3", 200 lbs. Deb: 6/12/75

YEAR TM/L	W	L	PCT	G	GS	CG	SH	SV	IP	H	HR	BB	SO	RAT	ERA	ERA+	OAV	OOB	BH	AVG	PB	PR	/A	PD	TPI
1975 StL-N	0	1	.000	20	0	0	0	0	30¹	38	4	12	13	14.8	4.45	84	.306	.368	1	.333	0	-3	-2	0	-0.1

■ JEFF TERPKO
Terpko, Jeffrey Michael b: 10/16/50, Sayre, Pa. BR/TR, 6', 180 lbs. Deb: 9/21/74

YEAR TM/L	W	L	PCT	G	GS	CG	SH	SV	IP	H	HR	BB	SO	RAT	ERA	ERA+	OAV	OOB	BH	AVG	PB	PR	/A	PD	TPI
1974 Tex-A	0	0	—	3	0	0	0	0	7	6	0	4	3	12.9	1.29	277	.231	.333	0	—	0	2	2	-0	0.2
1976 Tex-A	3	3	.500	32	0	0	0	0	52²	42	3	29	24	12.1	2.39	150	.223	.327	0	—	0	7	7	0	0.7
1977 Mon-N	0	1	.000	13	0	0	0	0	20²	28	2	15	14	18.7	5.66	67	.346	.448	0	.000	-0	-4	-4	-0	-0.4
Total 3	3	4	.429	48	0	0	0	0	80¹	76	5	48	41	13.9	3.14	116	.258	.362	0	.000	-0	4	5	-1	0.5

■ WALT TERRELL
Terrell, Charles Walter b: 5/11/58, Jeffersonville, Ind BL/TR, 6'2", 205 lbs. Deb: 9/08/82

YEAR TM/L	W	L	PCT	G	GS	CG	SH	SV	IP	H	HR	BB	SO	RAT	ERA	ERA+	OAV	OOB	BH	AVG	PB	PR	/A	PD	TPI
1982 NY-N	0	3	.000	3	3	0	0	0	21	22	2	14	8	15.4	3.43	106	.268	.375	2	.400	1	0	0	-0	0.1
1983 NY-N	8	8	.500	21	20	4	2	0	133²	123	7	55	59	12.1	3.57	102	.251	.329	8	.182	3	1	1	-0	0.4
1984 NY-N	11	12	.478	33	33	3	1	0	215	232	16	80	114	13.2	3.52	101	.282	.348	6	.080	-4	2	0	1	-0.1
1985 Det-A	15	10	.600	34	34	5	3	0	229	221	21	95	130	12.6	3.85	106	.255	.332	0	—	0	7	6	4	0.9
1986 Det-A	15	12	.556	34	33	9	2	0	217¹	199	30	98	93	12.4	4.56	90	.245	.329	0	—	0	-9	-10	2	-0.7
1987 *Det-A	17	10	.630	35	35	10	1	0	244²	254	30	94	143	12.9	4.05	104	.268	.336	0	—	0	11	5	-1	0.4
1988 Det-A	7	16	.304	29	29	11	1	0	206¹	199	20	78	84	12.2	3.97	96	.258	.328	0	—	0	-0	-4	1	-0.1
1989 SD-N	5	13	.278	19	19	4	1	0	123¹	134	14	26	63	11.7	4.01	87	.277	.314	4	.100	-0	-7	-7	3	-0.3
NY-A	6	5	.545	13	13	1	1	0	83	102	9	24	30	13.9	5.20	74	.307	.358	0	—	0	-12	-12	0	-1.1
1990 Pit-N	2	7	.222	16	16	0	0	0	82²	98	13	33	34	14.7	5.88	62	.295	.366	3	.107	-1	-19	-21	1	-1.9
Det-A	6	4	.600	13	12	0	0	0	75¹	86	7	24	30	14.1	4.54	86	.290	.359	0	—	0	-5	-5	-0	-0.5
Total 9	92	100	.479	250	247	47	12	0	1631¹	1670	157	621	788	12.8	4.13	94	.268	.337	23	.120	-1	-31	-47	11	-2.9

■ JERRY TERRELL
Terrell, Jerry Wayne b: 7/13/46, Waseca, Minn. BR/TR, 5'11", 165 lbs. Deb: 4/14/73 ♦

YEAR TM/L	W	L	PCT	G	GS	CG	SH	SV	IP	H	HR	BB	SO	RAT	ERA	ERA+	OAV	OOB	BH	AVG	PB	PR	/A	PD	TPI
1979 KC-A	0	0	—	1	0	0	0	0	1	0	0	0	0	0.0	0.00	—	.000	.000	12	.300	0	0	0	0	0.0
1980 KC-A	0	0	—	1	0	0	0	0	1	1	0	1	0	18.0	0.00	—	.250	.400	1	.063	0	0	0	0	0.0
Total 2	0	0	—	2	0	0	0	0	2	1	0	1	0	9.0	0.00	—	.143	.250	412	.253	1	1	1	0	0.0

■ JOHN TERRY
Terry, John Burchard b: 11/1/1879, Waterbury, Conn. d: 4/27/33, Kansas City, Mo. Deb: 9/17/02

YEAR TM/L	W	L	PCT	G	GS	CG	SH	SV	IP	H	HR	BB	SO	RAT	ERA	ERA+	OAV	OOB	BH	AVG	PB	PR	/A	PD	TPI
1902 Det-A	0	1	.000	1	1	1	0	0	5	8	0	1	0	16.2	3.60	101	.361	.388	0	.000	-0	-0	-0	-0	0.0
1903 StL-A	1	1	.500	3	1	1	0	0	17²	21	0	4	2	12.7	2.55	114	.294	.332	0	.000	-1	1	1	-0	0.0
Total 2	1	2	.333	4	2	2	0	0	22²	29	0	5	2	13.5	2.78	111	.310	.345	0	.000	-2	1	1	-0	0.0

■ YANK TERRY
Terry, Lancelot Yank b: 2/11/11, Bedford, Ind. d: 11/4/79, Bloomington, Ind. BR/TR, 6'1", 180 lbs. Deb: 8/03/40

YEAR TM/L	W	L	PCT	G	GS	CG	SH	SV	IP	H	HR	BB	SO	RAT	ERA	ERA+	OAV	OOB	BH	AVG	PB	PR	/A	PD	TPI
1940 Bos-A	1	0	1.000	4	1	0	0	0	19¹	24	2	11	9	16.3	8.84	51	.304	.389	2	.250	0	-10	-9	0	-0.7
1942 Bos-A	6	5	.545	20	11	3	0	1	85	82	5	43	37	13.4	3.92	95	.248	.339	3	.111	-1	-2	-2	-0	-0.2
1943 Bos-A	7	9	.438	30	22	7	0	1	163²	147	8	63	63	11.6	3.52	94	.242	.314	3	.067	-3	-4	-4	0	-0.6
1944 Bos-A	6	10	.375	27	17	3	0	0	132²	142	10	65	30	14.2	4.21	81	.276	.361	11	.234	1	-11	-12	0	-0.9
1945 Bos-A	0	4	.000	12	4	1	0	0	56²	68	8	14	28	13.0	4.13	82	.296	.336	2	.111	-2	-5	-5	-1	-0.6
Total 5	20	28	.417	93	55	14	0	2	457¹	463	33	196	167	13.1	4.09	85	.263	.339	21	.145	-4	-32	-31	-0	-3.0

■ RALPH TERRY
Terry, Ralph Willard b: 1/9/36, Big Cabin, Okla. BR/TR, 6'3", 195 lbs. Deb: 8/06/56

YEAR TM/L	W	L	PCT	G	GS	CG	SH	SV	IP	H	HR	BB	SO	RAT	ERA	ERA+	OAV	OOB	BH	AVG	PB	PR	/A	PD	TPI
1956 NY-A	1	2	.333	3	3	0	0	0	13¹	17	2	11	8	18.9	9.45	41	.347	.467	1	.167	-0	-8	-8	-0	-0.7
1957 NY-A	1	1	.500	7	2	1	1	0	20²	18	1	8	7	11.3	3.05	118	.240	.313	1	.250	0	2	1	0	0.2
KC-A	4	11	.267	21	19	3	1	0	130²	119	15	47	80	11.7	3.38	117	.239	.310	6	.143	-2	6	8	-0	0.6
Yr	5	12	.294	28	21	4	2	0	151¹	137	16	55	87	11.7	3.33	117	.239	.310	1	.022	-2	8	10	0	0.8
1958 KC-A	11	13	.458	40	33	8	3	2	216²	217	29	61	134	11.6	4.24	92	.262	.314	14	.197	-0	-11	-8	-2	-1.0
1959 KC-A	2	4	.333	9	7	2	0	0	46¹	56	9	19	35	14.8	5.24	76	.308	.376	3	.176	-1	-7	-6	1	-0.5
NY-A	3	7	.300	24	16	5	1	0	127¹	130	7	30	55	11.5	3.39	107	.270	.316	4	.098	-3	7	4	0	0.1
Yr	5	11	.313	33	23	7	1	0	173²	186	16	49	90	12.3	3.89	96	.280	.331	1	.017	-3	-0	-3	1	-0.4
1960 *NY-A	10	8	.556	35	23	7	3	1	166²	149	15	52	92	11.1	3.40	105	.237	.300	6	.122	-2	9	3	0	0.1
1961 *NY-A	16	3	.842	31	27	9	2	0	188¹	162	19	42	86	9.8	3.15	118	.232	.277	15	.227	2	18	12	1	1.5
1962 *NY-A	23	12	.657	43	39	14	3	2	298²	257	40	57	176	9.6	3.19	117	.231	.270	20	.189	1	26	18	-4	1.5
1963 *NY-A	17	15	.531	40	37	**18**	3	1	268	246	29	39	114	9.7	3.22	109	.242	.273	7	.080	-5	12	9	-0	0.3
1964 *NY-A	7	11	.389	27	14	2	1	4	115	130	20	31	77	12.7	4.54	80	.283	.329	7	.200	1	-12	-12	0	-1.0
1965 Cle-A	11	6	.647	30	26	6	2	0	165²	154	22	23	84	9.7	3.69	94	.242	.269	7	.143	2	-4	-4	-3	-0.4
1966 KC-A	1	5	.167	15	10	0	0	0	64	65	7	15	33	11.4	3.80	89	.263	.308	3	.214	1	-3	-3	-0	-0.2
NY-N	0	1	.000	11	1	0	0	1	24²	27	1	11	14	13.9	4.74	77	.293	.369	1	.167	-0	-3	-3	-0	-0.2
1967 NY-N	0	0	—	2	0	0	0	0	3¹	1	0	0	5	2.7	0.00	—	.091	.091	0	—	0	1	1	0	0.2
Total 12	107	99	.519	338	257	75	20	11	1849¹	1748	216	446	1000	10.8	3.62	102	.249	.296	95	.160	-6	32	13	-8	0.5

■ SCOTT TERRY
Terry, Scott Ray b: 11/21/59, Hobbs, N.Mex. BR/TR, 5'11", 195 lbs. Deb: 4/09/86

YEAR TM/L	W	L	PCT	G	GS	CG	SH	SV	IP	H	HR	BB	SO	RAT	ERA	ERA+	OAV	OOB	BH	AVG	PB	PR	/A	PD	TPI
1986 Cin-N	1	2	.333	28	3	0	0	0	55²	66	8	32	32	15.8	6.14	63	.300	.389	1	.250	0	-15	-14	0	-1.3
1987 StL-N	0	0	—	11	0	0	0	0	13¹	13	0	8	9	14.2	3.38	123	.260	.362	0	.000	-0	1	1	0	0.1
1988 StL-N	9	6	.600	51	11	1	0	3	129¹	119	5	34	65	10.6	2.92	119	.247	.297	7	.250	2	8	8	0	1.1
1989 StL-N	8	10	.444	31	24	1	0	2	148²	142	14	43	69	11.4	3.57	102	.253	.310	7	.156	2	1	1	2	0.5
1990 StL-N	2	6	.250	50	2	0	0	2	72	75	7	27	35	13.3	4.75	82	.264	.337	5	.455	2	-8	-7	1	-0.3
Total 5	20	24	.455	171	40	2	0	7	419	415	34	144	210	12.2	3.91	94	.260	.324	20	.222	6	-15	-11	3	0.1

■ ADONIS TERRY
Terry, William H b: 8/7/1864, Westfield, Mass. d: 2/24/15, Milwaukee, Wis. BR/TR, 5'11.5", 168 lbs. Deb: 5/01/1884 U♦

YEAR TM/L	W	L	PCT	G	GS	CG	SH	SV	IP	H	HR	BB	SO	RAT	ERA	ERA+	OAV	OOB	BH	AVG	PB	PR	/A	PD	TPI
1884 Bro-a	19	35	.352	56	55	54	2	0	476	487	10	72	230	10.6	3.55	93	.251	.277	55	.233	3	-16	-12	-4	-1.0
1885 Bro-a	6	17	.261	25	23	23	0	1	209	213	9	42	96	11.0	4.26	77	.253	.288	45	.170	-3	-24	-22	1	-1.9
1886 Bro-a	18	16	.529	34	34	32	5	0	288¹	263	1	115	162	11.8	3.09	113	.232	.302	71	.237	2	12	13	4	1.1
1887 Bro-a	16	16	.500	40	35	35	1	3	318	331	10	99	138	12.2	4.02	107	.258	.312	103	.293	7	10	10	4	0.8
1888 Bro-a	13	8	.619	23	23	20	2	0	195	145	2	67	138	9.8	2.03	147	**.199**	.267	29	.252	3	22	21	-0	2.3
1889 *Bro-a	22	15	.595	41	39	35	2	0	326	285	6	126	186	11.3	3.29	113	.228	.298	48	.300	12	20	16	5	3.0
1890 *Bro-N	26	16	.619	46	44	38	1	0	370	362	6	133	185	12.0	2.94	117	.249	.312	101	.278	14	25	20	1	1.8
1891 Bro-N	6	16	.273	25	22	18	1	1	194	207	5	80	65	13.3	4.22	78	.263	.331	19	.209	3	-19	-20	-1	-1.3
1892 Bal-N	0	1	.000	1	1	1	0	0	9	7	0	7	3	14.0	4.00	86	.206	.342	0	.000	-1	-1	-1	0	0.0
Pit-N	18	7	.720	30	26	24	2	1	240	185	3	106	95	10.9	2.51	131	.204	.288	16	.160	1	21	21	0	2.2
Yr	18	8	.692	31	27	25	2	1	249	192	3	113	98	11.0	2.57	129	.205	.290	16	.096	1	20	20	1	2.2
1893 Pit-N	12	6	.600	26	19	14	0	0	170	177	5	99	52	14.6	4.45	103	.260	.354	18	.254	2	4	2	0	0.4
1894 Pit-N	1	0	1.000	1	1	0	0	0	0²	2	0	4	0	81.0	67.50	8	.510	.758	0	—	0	-5	-5	-0	-0.2
Chi-N	5	11	.313	23	21	16	0	0	163¹	232	12	123	39	19.6	5.84	96	.330	.430	33	.347	5	-9	-4	-0	0.2
Yr	5	12	.294	24	22	16	0	0	164	234	12	127	39	19.8	6.09	92	.331	.433	11	.116	5	-14	-9	-1	0.0
1895 Chi-N	21	14	.600	38	34	31	0	0	311¹	346	14	84	88	13.8	4.80	106	.277	.346	30	.219	-6	-1	10	2	0.6
1896 Chi-N	15	14	.517	30	28	25	1	0	235²	268	6	88	74	13.6	4.28	106	.284	.345	26	.263	2	2	7	-2	0.7
1897 Chi-N	0	1	.000	1	1	0	0	0	8	11	0	6	1	19.1	10.13	44	.324	.425	0	.000	-1	-5	-5	0	-0.3
Total 14	197	196	.501	440	406	367	17	6	3514	3521	76	1298	1552	12.3	3.73	103	.252	.316	594	.249	45	38	47	9	8.4

YEAR	TM/L	W	L	PCT	G	GS	CG	SH	SV	IP	H	HR	BB	SO	RAT	ERA	ERA+	OAV	OOB	BH	AVG	PB	PR	/A	PD	TPI

■ DICK TERWILLIGER
Terwilliger, Richard Martin b: 6/27/06, Sand Lake, Mich. d: 1/21/69, Greenville, Mich. BR/TR, 5'11", 178 lbs. Deb: 8/18/32

YEAR TM/L	W	L	PCT	G	GS	CG	SH	SV	IP	H	HR	BB	SO	RAT	ERA	ERA+	OAV	OOB	BH	AVG	PB	PR	/A	PD	TPI
1932 StL-N	0	0	—	1	0	0	0	0	3	1	0	2	2	12.0	0.00	—	.143	.400	0	.000	-0	1	1	0	0.2

■ JEFF TESREAU
Tesreau, Charles Monroe b: 3/5/1889, Silver Mine, Mo. d: 9/24/46, Hanover, N.H. BR/TR, 6'2", 218 lbs. Deb: 4/12/12

YEAR TM/L	W	L	PCT	G	GS	CG	SH	SV	IP	H	HR	BB	SO	RAT	ERA	ERA+	OAV	OOB	BH	AVG	PB	PR	/A	PD	TPI
1912 *NY-N	17	7	.708	36	28	19	3	1	243	177	2	106	119	10.9	1.96	172	.199	.292	12	.146	-2	39	38	1	3.8
1913 *NY-N	22	13	.629	41	38	17	1	0	282	222	7	119	167	11.1	2.17	144	.220	.306	21	.221	2	32	30	-0	3.4
1914 NY-N	26	10	.722	42	40	26	8	1	322¹	238	8	128	189	10.4	2.37	112	.209	.293	28	.239	5	15	10	-3	1.3
1915 NY-N	19	16	.543	43	38	24	8	3	306	235	4	75	176	9.3	2.29	112	.215	.269	24	.233	5	16	9	1	1.5
1916 NY-N	14	14	.500	40	33	23	5	2	268¹	249	6	65	113	10.7	2.92	83	.250	.300	18	.191	2	-9	-14	0	-1.4
1917 *NY-N	13	8	.619	33	20	11	1	2	183²	168	9	58	85	11.2	3.09	83	.249	.312	14	.230	2	-8	-11	1	-0.9
1918 NY-N	4	4	.500	12	9	3	1	0	73²	61	1	21	31	10.0	2.32	113	.227	.283	7	.318	2	4	3	1	0.6
Total 7	115	72	.615	247	206	123	27	9	1679	1350	37	572	880	10.5	2.43	114	.223	.294	124	.216	16	89	63	0	8.3

■ BOB TEWKSBURY
Tewksbury, Robert Alan b: 11/30/60, Concord, N.H. BR/TR, 6'4", 200 lbs. Deb: 4/11/86

YEAR TM/L	W	L	PCT	G	GS	CG	SH	SV	IP	H	HR	BB	SO	RAT	ERA	ERA+	OAV	OOB	BH	AVG	PB	PR	/A	PD	TPI
1986 NY-A	9	5	.643	23	20	2	0	0	130¹	144	8	31	49	12.4	3.31	123	.282	.329	0	—	0	12	11	2	1.4
1987 NY-A	1	4	.200	8	6	0	0	0	33¹	47	5	7	12	14.9	6.75	65	.338	.374	0	—	0	-9	-9	0	-0.7
Chi-N	0	4	.000	7	3	0	0	0	18	32	1	13	10	22.5	6.50	66	.421	.506	0	.000	-1	-5	-4	-0	-0.4
1988 Chi-N	0	0	—	1	1	0	0	0	3¹	6	1	2	1	21.6	8.10	45	.400	.471	0	.000	-0	-2	-2	0	-0.1
1989 StL-N	1	0	1.000	7	4	1	1	0	30	25	2	10	17	11.1	3.30	110	.225	.301	1	.111	-0	1	1	-0	0.0
1990 StL-N	10	9	.526	28	20	3	2	1	145¹	151	7	15	50	10.5	3.47	113	.267	.290	7	.171	1	5	7	-0	0.9
Total 5	21	22	.488	74	54	6	3	1	360¹	405	24	78	139	12.3	3.90	103	.286	.328	8	.140	0	3	5	2	1.1

■ GRANT THATCHER
Thatcher, Ulysses Grant b: 2/23/1877, Maytown, Pa. d: 3/17/36, Lancaster, Pa. TR, 5'10.5", 180 lbs. Deb: 9/09/03

YEAR TM/L	W	L	PCT	G	GS	CG	SH	SV	IP	H	HR	BB	SO	RAT	ERA	ERA+	OAV	OOB	BH	AVG	PB	PR	/A	PD	TPI
1903 Bro-N	3	1	.750	4	4	4	0	0	28	33	1	7	9	12.9	2.89	110	.292	.333	2	.182	0	1	1	0	0.1
1904 Bro-N	1	0	1.000	1	0	0	0	0	9	9	0	2	4	11.0	4.00	69	.281	.324	1	.250	0	-1	-1	-0	0.0
Total 2	4	1	.800	5	4	4	0	0	37	42	1	9	13	12.4	3.16	98	.290	.331	3	.200	0	-0	-0	0	0.1

■ GREG THAYER
Thayer, Gregory Allen b: 10/23/49, Cedar Rapids, Iowa BR/TR, 5'11", 182 lbs. Deb: 4/07/78

YEAR TM/L	W	L	PCT	G	GS	CG	SH	SV	IP	H	HR	BB	SO	RAT	ERA	ERA+	OAV	OOB	BH	AVG	PB	PR	/A	PD	TPI
1978 Min-A	1	1	.500	20	0	0	0	0	45	40	5	30	30	14.6	3.80	101	.258	.388	0	—	0	-0	0	-0	0.0

■ JACK THEIS
Theis, John Louis b: 7/23/1891, Georgetown, Ohio d: 7/6/41, Georgetown, Ohio BR/TR, 6', 190 lbs. Deb: 7/05/20

YEAR TM/L	W	L	PCT	G	GS	CG	SH	SV	IP	H	HR	BB	SO	RAT	ERA	ERA+	OAV	OOB	BH	AVG	PB	PR	/A	PD	TPI
1920 Cin-N	0	0	—	1	0	0	0	0	2	1	0	3	0	18.0	0.00	—	.143	.400	0	—	0	1	1	0	0.1

■ DUANE THEISS
Theiss, Duane Charles b: 11/20/53, Zanesville, Ohio BR/TR, 6'3", 185 lbs. Deb: 8/05/77

YEAR TM/L	W	L	PCT	G	GS	CG	SH	SV	IP	H	HR	BB	SO	RAT	ERA	ERA+	OAV	OOB	BH	AVG	PB	PR	/A	PD	TPI
1977 Atl-N	1	1	.500	17	0	0	0	0	20²	26	1	16	7	18.7	6.53	68	.338	.457	0	.000	-0	-6	-5	0	-0.4
1978 Atl-N	0	0	—	3	0	0	0	0	6¹	3	0	3	3	9.9	1.42	285	.158	.304	0	.000	-0	2	2	0	0.2
Total 2	1	1	.500	20	0	0	0	0	27	29	1	19	10	16.7	5.33	82	.302	.427	0	.000	-0	-5	-3	0	-0.2

■ JUG THESENGA
Thesenga, Arnold Joseph b: 4/27/14, Jefferson, S.Dak. BR/TR, 6', 200 lbs. Deb: 9/01/44

YEAR TM/L	W	L	PCT	G	GS	CG	SH	SV	IP	H	HR	BB	SO	RAT	ERA	ERA+	OAV	OOB	BH	AVG	PB	PR	/A	PD	TPI
1944 Was-A	0	0	—	5	1	0	0	0	12¹	18	0	12	2	21.9	5.11	64	.340	.462	0	.000	-0	-2	-3	0	-0.2

■ BERT THIEL
Thiel, Maynard Bert b: 5/4/26, Marion, Wis. BR/TR, 5'10", 185 lbs. Deb: 4/17/52

YEAR TM/L	W	L	PCT	G	GS	CG	SH	SV	IP	H	HR	BB	SO	RAT	ERA	ERA+	OAV	OOB	BH	AVG	PB	PR	/A	PD	TPI
1952 Bos-N	1	1	.500	4	0	0	0	0	7	11	1	4	6	21.9	7.71	47	.344	.447	0	—	0	-3	-3	0	-0.2

■ HENRY THIELMAN
Thielman, Henry Joseph b: 10/3/1880, St.Cloud, Minn. d: 9/2/42, New York, N.Y. BR/TR, 5'11", 175 lbs. Deb: 4/17/02 ♦

YEAR TM/L	W	L	PCT	G	GS	CG	SH	SV	IP	H	HR	BB	SO	RAT	ERA	ERA+	OAV	OOB	BH	AVG	PB	PR	/A	PD	TPI
1902 NY-N	0	1	.000	2	2	0	0	0	6	8	0	6	5	21.0	1.50	187	.319	.451	1	.111	-0	1	1	0	0.1
Cin-N	9	15	.375	25	23	22	0	1	211	201	2	78	49	12.7	3.24	92	.251	.332	12	.132	-4	-11	-6	-0	-0.9
Yr	9	16	.360	27	25	22	0	1	217	209	2	84	54	12.9	3.19	94	.253	.336	7	.070	-4	-10	-5	0	-0.8
1903 Bro-N	0	3	.000	4	3	3	0	0	29	31	3	14	10	14.6	4.66	69	.330	.427	5	.217	1	-4	-5	1	-0.3
Total 2	9	19	.321	31	28	25	0	1	246	240	5	98	64	13.1	3.37	90	.261	.346	18	.146	-3	-14	-9	1	-1.1

■ JAKE THIELMAN
Thielman, John Peter b: 5/20/1879, St.Cloud, Minn. d: 1/28/28, Minneapolis, Minn. BR/TR, 5'11", 175 lbs. Deb: 4/23/05

YEAR TM/L	W	L	PCT	G	GS	CG	SH	SV	IP	H	HR	BB	SO	RAT	ERA	ERA+	OAV	OOB	BH	AVG	PB	PR	/A	PD	TPI
1905 StL-N	15	16	.484	32	29	26	0	0	242	265	4	62	87	12.6	3.50	85	.281	.333	21	.231	8	-13	-14	3	-0.2
1906 StL-N	0	1	.000	1	1	0	0	0	5	5	0	2	0	12.6	3.60	73	.263	.333	1	.500	0	-1	-1	0	0.0
1907 Cle-A	11	8	.579	20	18	18	3	0	166	151	2	34	56	10.0	2.33	108	.284	.284	12	.203	1	4	3	-2	0.2
1908 Cle-A	4	3	.571	11	8	5	0	0	61²	59	2	9	15	10.5	3.65	66	.260	.300	8	.348	4	-9	-9	2	-0.2
Bos-A	0	0	—	1	0	0	0	0	0²	3	1	0	0	40.5	40.50	6	.600	.600	0	—	0	-3	-3	0	-0.2
Yr	4	3	.571	12	8	5	0	0	62¹	62	3	9	15	10.3	4.04	59	.263	.290	5	.217	4	-11	-11	2	-0.4
Total 4	30	28	.517	65	56	49	3	0	475¹	483	9	107	158	11.5	3.16	86	.266	.313	42	.240	13	-21	-23	3	-0.4

■ DAVE THIES
Thies, David Robert b: 3/21/37, Minneapolis, Minn. BR/TR, 6'4", 205 lbs. Deb: 4/20/63

YEAR TM/L	W	L	PCT	G	GS	CG	SH	SV	IP	H	HR	BB	SO	RAT	ERA	ERA+	OAV	OOB	BH	AVG	PB	PR	/A	PD	TPI
1963 KC-A	0	1	.000	9	2	0	0	0	25¹	26	2	12	9	14.2	4.62	83	.274	.367	2	.333	1	-3	-2	0	0.0

■ JAKE THIES
Thies, Vernon Arthur b: 4/1/26, St.Louis, Mo. BR/TR, 5'11", 170 lbs. Deb: 4/24/54

YEAR TM/L	W	L	PCT	G	GS	CG	SH	SV	IP	H	HR	BB	SO	RAT	ERA	ERA+	OAV	OOB	BH	AVG	PB	PR	/A	PD	TPI
1954 Pit-N	3	9	.250	33	18	3	1	0	130¹	120	13	49	57	11.9	3.87	108	.244	.317	1	.030	-2	3	5	0	0.3
1955 Pit-N	0	1	.000	1	1	0	0	0	3²	5	0	3	0	22.1	4.91	84	.357	.500	0	—	0	-0	-0	-0	0.0
Total 2	3	10	.231	34	19	3	1	0	134	125	13	52	57	12.2	3.90	107	.248	.323	1	.030	-2	3	4	0	0.3

■ BOBBY THIGPEN
Thigpen, Robert Thomas b: 7/17/63, Tallahassee, Fla. BR/TR, 6'3", 195 lbs. Deb: 8/06/86

YEAR TM/L	W	L	PCT	G	GS	CG	SH	SV	IP	H	HR	BB	SO	RAT	ERA	ERA+	OAV	OOB	BH	AVG	PB	PR	/A	PD	TPI
1986 Chi-A	2	0	1.000	20	0	0	0	7	35²	26	1	12	20	9.8	1.77	244	.205	.279	0	—	0	10	10	0	1.0
1987 Chi-A	7	5	.583	51	0	0	0	16	89	86	10	24	52	11.4	2.73	168	.256	.311	0	—	0	17	18	0	1.8
1988 Chi-A	5	8	.385	68	0	0	0	34	90	96	6	33	62	13.3	3.30	120	.273	.342	0	—	0	7	7	0	0.7
1989 Chi-A	2	6	.250	61	0	0	0	34	79	62	10	40	47	11.7	3.76	101	.218	.316	0	—	0	1	0	-1	0.0
1990 Chi-A	4	6	.400	77	0	0	0	57	88²	60	5	32	70	9.4	1.83	209	.195	.274	0	—	0	20	20	-0	2.0
Total 5	20	25	.444	277	0	0	0	148	382¹	330	32	141	251	11.3	2.78	147	.235	.309	0	—	0	55	55	-0	5.5

■ DICK THOENEN
Thoenen, Richard Crispin b: 1/9/44, Mexico, Mo. BR/TR, 6'6", 215 lbs. Deb: 9/16/67

YEAR TM/L	W	L	PCT	G	GS	CG	SH	SV	IP	H	HR	BB	SO	RAT	ERA	ERA+	OAV	OOB	BH	AVG	PB	PR	/A	PD	TPI
1967 Phi-N	0	0	—	1	0	0	0	0	1	2	0	0	0	18.0	9.00	38	.500	.500	0	—	0	-1	-1	0	0.0

■ TOMMY THOMAS
Thomas, Alphonse b: 12/23/1899, Baltimore, Md. d: 4/27/88, Dallastown, Pa. BR/TR, 5'10", 175 lbs. Deb: 4/17/26

YEAR TM/L	W	L	PCT	G	GS	CG	SH	SV	IP	H	HR	BB	SO	RAT	ERA	ERA+	OAV	OOB	BH	AVG	PB	PR	/A	PD	TPI
1926 Chi-A	15	12	.556	44	32	13	2	2	249	225	7	110	127	12.1	3.80	102	.244	.325	16	.186	-1	6	2	-3	-0.2
1927 Chi-A	19	16	.543	40	36	24	3	1	307²	271	16	94	107	10.7	2.98	136	.244	.303	14	.147	-3	40	36	-5	2.7
1928 Chi-A	17	16	.515	36	32	24	3	2	283	277	16	76	129	11.4	3.08	131	.259	.310	21	.219	3	30	30	-3	2.9
1929 Chi-A	14	18	.438	36	31	24	2	1	259²	270	17	60	62	11.4	3.19	134	.269	.310	25	.255	2	30	32	-3	3.0
1930 Chi-A	5	13	.278	34	27	7	0	0	169	229	13	44	58	14.6	5.22	89	.323	.364	7	.125	-4	-11	-11	0	-1.2
1931 Chi-A	10	14	.417	43	36	11	2	2	245¹	298	17	69	72	13.6	4.73	90	.292	.340	21	.241	1	-10	-13	-1	-1.1
1932 Chi-A	3	3	.500	12	3	1	0	0	43²	55	6	15	11	14.6	6.18	70	.307	.364	1	.077	-1	-9	-10	-0	-0.8
Was-A	8	7	.533	18	14	7	1	0	117	114	5	46	36	12.3	3.54	122	.255	.325	10	.238	1	12	10	-2	1.0
Yr	11	10	.524	30	17	8	1	0	160²	169	11	61	47	12.9	4.26	101	.270	.334	2	.036	0	4	1	-2	0.0
1933 *Was-A	7	7	.500	35	14	2	0	3	135	149	9	49	35	13.3	4.80	87	.273	.336	10	.238	1	-8	-9	-2	-0.8
1934 Was-A	8	9	.471	33	18	7	1	1	133¹	154	9	58	42	14.5	5.47	79	.294	.368	7	.184	-0	-14	-17	-2	-1.7
1935 Was-A	0	0	—	1	0	0	0	0	0¹	3	0	0	0	81.0	54.00	8	.750	.750	0	—	0	-2	-2	0	-0.1
Phi-N	0	1	.000	4	1	0	0	0	12	15	2	3	3	15.0	5.25	86	.313	.377	0	.000	-0	-2	-2	0	-0.2
1936 StL-A	11	9	.550	36	21	8	1	0	179²	219	25	72	40	14.8	5.26	87	.290	.362	8	.138	-0	-4	2	-2	-0.1
1937 StL-A	0	1	.000	17	2	0	0	0	30²	46	2	10	10	16.7	7.04	69	.348	.399	0	.000	-1	-8	-8	0	-0.6
Bos-A	0	2	.000	9	0	0	0	0	11	16	2	4	4	17.2	4.09	116	.340	.404	1	.250	-0	1	1	0	0.1

YEAR TM/L	W	L	PCT	G	GS	CG	SH	SV	IP	H	HR	BB	SO	RAT	ERA	ERA+	OAV	OOB	BH	AVG	PB	PR	/A	PD	TPI
Yr	0	3	.000	26	2	0	0	0	41²	62	4	14	14	16.6	6.26	77	.344	.395	0	.000	-1	-8	-7	0	-0.5
Total 12	117	128	.478	398	267	128	15	12	2176¹	2341	144	712	736	12.7	4.11	104	.275	.333	141	.195	-5	52	43	-23	2.9

■ BLAINE THOMAS
Thomas, Blaine M. "Baldy" b: 1888, Glendora, Cal. d: 8/21/15, Glendora, Cal. BR/TR, 5'10", 165 lbs. Deb: 8/25/11

YEAR TM/L	W	L	PCT	G	GS	CG	SH	SV	IP	H	HR	BB	SO	RAT	ERA	ERA+	OAV	OOB	BH	AVG	PB	PR	/A	PD	TPI
1911 Bos-A	0	0	—	2	2	0	0	0	4²	3	0	7	0	21.2	0.00	—	.273	.579	1	.500	0	2	2	0	0.2

■ CARL THOMAS
Thomas, Carl Leslie b: 5/28/32, Minneapolis, Minn. BR/TR, 6'5", 245 lbs. Deb: 4/19/60

YEAR TM/L	W	L	PCT	G	GS	CG	SH	SV	IP	H	HR	BB	SO	RAT	ERA	ERA+	OAV	OOB	BH	AVG	PB	PR	/A	PD	TPI
1960 Cle-A	1	0	1.000	4	0	0	0	0	9²	8	1	10	5	17.7	7.45	50	.229	.413	1	.333	1	-4	-4	0	-0.2

■ LEFTY THOMAS
Thomas, Clarence Fletcher b: 10/4/03, Glade Springs, Va. d: 3/21/52, Charlottesville, Va. BL/TL, 6', 183 lbs. Deb: 9/26/25

YEAR TM/L	W	L	PCT	G	GS	CG	SH	SV	IP	H	HR	BB	SO	RAT	ERA	ERA+	OAV	OOB	BH	AVG	PB	PR	/A	PD	TPI
1925 Was-A	0	2	.000	2	2	1	0	0	13	14	0	7	10	14.5	2.08	204	.264	.350	0	.000	-1	3	3	0	0.2
1926 Was-A	0	0	—	6	0	0	0	0	8²	8	0	10	3	18.7	5.19	74	.267	.450	0	.000	0	-1	-1	-0	-0.1
Total 2	0	2	.000	8	2	1	0	0	21²	22	0	17	13	16.2	3.32	123	.265	.390	0	.000	-1	2	2	-0	0.1

■ CLAUDE THOMAS
Thomas, Claude Alfred "Lefty" b: 5/15/1890, Stanberry, Mo. d: 3/6/46, Sulphur, Okla. BL/TL, 6'1", 180 lbs. Deb: 9/14/16

YEAR TM/L	W	L	PCT	G	GS	CG	SH	SV	IP	H	HR	BB	SO	RAT	ERA	ERA+	OAV	OOB	BH	AVG	PB	PR	/A	PD	TPI
1916 Was-A	1	2	.333	7	4	1	1	0	28¹	27	1	12	7	13.0	4.13	67	.265	.353	1	.100	-1	-4	-4	0	-0.5

■ FAY THOMAS
Thomas, Fay Wesley "Scow" b: 10/10/04, Holyrood, Kan. d: 8/16/90, Chatsworth, Cal. BR/TR, 6'2", 195 lbs. Deb: 6/27/27

YEAR TM/L	W	L	PCT	G	GS	CG	SH	SV	IP	H	HR	BB	SO	RAT	ERA	ERA+	OAV	OOB	BH	AVG	PB	PR	/A	PD	TPI
1927 NY-N	0	0	—	9	0	0	0	0	16¹	19	3	4	11	13.2	3.31	117	.302	.353	0	.000	-0	1	1	-1	0.0
1931 Cle-A	2	4	.333	16	2	1	0	0	48²	63	2	32	25	17.8	5.18	89	.323	.421	2	.154	-1	-4	-3	-1	-0.3
1932 Bro-N	0	1	.000	7	2	0	0	0	17	22	0	8	9	15.9	7.41	51	.306	.375	0	.000	-0	-7	-7	0	-0.6
1935 StL-A	7	15	.318	49	19	4	0	1	147	165	11	89	67	15.7	4.78	100	.289	.388	4	.105	-3	-5	0	2	0.0
Total 4	9	20	.310	81	23	5	0	1	229	269	16	133	112	16.0	4.95	93	.299	.392	6	.107	-5	-15	-9	1	-0.9

■ FROSTY THOMAS
Thomas, Forrest b: 5/23/1881, Faucett, Mo. d: 3/18/70, St.Joseph, Mo. BR/TR, 6', 185 lbs. Deb: 5/01/05

YEAR TM/L	W	L	PCT	G	GS	CG	SH	SV	IP	H	HR	BB	SO	RAT	ERA	ERA+	OAV	OOB	BH	AVG	PB	PR	/A	PD	TPI
1905 Det-A	0	1	.000	2	1	0	0	0	6	10	0	3	5	19.5	7.50	37	.371	.434	0	.000	-0	-3	-3	0	-0.2

■ BUD THOMAS
Thomas, Luther Baxter b: 9/9/10, Faber, Va. BR/TR, 6', 180 lbs. Deb: 9/13/32

YEAR TM/L	W	L	PCT	G	GS	CG	SH	SV	IP	H	HR	BB	SO	RAT	ERA	ERA+	OAV	OOB	BH	AVG	PB	PR	/A	PD	TPI
1932 Was-A	0	0	—	2	0	0	0	0	3	1	0	2	1	9.0	0.00	—	.100	.250	0	—	0	1	1	0	0.1
1933 Was-A	0	0	—	2	0	0	0	0	4	11	1	2	1	31.5	15.75	27	.550	.609	0	.000	-0	-5	-5	0	-0.3
1937 Phi-A	8	15	.348	35	26	6	1	0	169²	208	15	52	54	13.8	4.99	95	.295	.344	6	.128	-1	-7	-5	-3	-0.7
1938 Phi-A	9	14	.391	42	29	7	1	0	212¹	259	23	62	48	13.7	4.92	98	.299	.347	9	.130	-3	-3	-2	-0	-0.4
1939 Phi-A	0	1	.000	2	0	0	0	0	4	8	2	1	0	20.3	15.75	30	.421	.450	0	.000	-0	-5	-5	0	-0.3
Was-A	0	0	—	4	0	0	0	0	9	11	0	4	2	13.0	6.00	72	.306	.342	0	.000	-0	-1	-2	0	-0.1
Det-A	7	0	1.000	27	0	0	0	1	47¹	45	7	20	14	12.4	4.18	117	.254	.330	1	.111	-1	2	4	1	0.3
Yr	7	1	.875	33	2	0	0	1	60¹	64	9	23	14	13.0	5.22	92	.276	.341	0	.000	-2	-4	-3	1	-0.1
1940 Det-A	0	1	.000	3	0	0	0	0	4	8	1	3	0	24.8	9.00	53	.421	.500	0	—	0	-2	-2	1	0.0
1941 Det-A	1	3	.250	26	1	0	0	2	72²	74	4	22	17	11.9	4.21	108	.260	.313	2	.105	-1	-1	3	2	0.4
Total 7	25	34	.424	143	58	13	2	3	526	625	53	166	135	13.6	4.96	96	.292	.345	18	.120	-7	-20	-13	1	-1.0

■ MYLES THOMAS
Thomas, Myles Lewis b: 10/22/1897, State College, Pa. d: 12/12/63, Toledo, Ohio BR/TR, 5'9.5", 170 lbs. Deb: 4/18/26

YEAR TM/L	W	L	PCT	G	GS	CG	SH	SV	IP	H	HR	BB	SO	RAT	ERA	ERA+	OAV	OOB	BH	AVG	PB	PR	/A	PD	TPI
1926 *NY-A	6	6	.500	33	13	3	0	0	140¹	140	6	65	38	13.3	4.23	91	.271	.356	5	.116	-3	-3	-6	1	-0.7
1927 NY-A	7	4	.636	21	9	3	0	0	88²	111	4	43	25	15.7	4.87	79	.322	.398	9	.333	2	-7	-10	0	-0.7
1928 NY-A	1	0	1.000	12	1	0	0	0	31²	33	3	9	10	11.9	3.41	110	.277	.328	4	.400	1	2	1	0	0.2
1929 NY-A	0	2	.000	5	1	0	0	0	15	27	1	9	3	21.6	10.80	36	.409	.480	1	.143	-0	-11	-12	1	-0.9
Was-A	7	8	.467	22	14	7	0	2	125¹	139	3	48	33	13.4	3.52	121	.288	.352	14	.292	2	10	10	1	1.2
Yr	7	10	.412	27	15	7	0	2	140¹	166	4	57	36	14.3	4.30	98	.302	.368	2	.036	1	-1	-2	1	0.3
1930 Was-A	2	2	.500	12	2	0	0	0	33²	49	3	15	12	17.1	8.29	55	.358	.421	2	.182	-1	-14	-14	-1	-1.2
Total 5	23	22	.511	105	40	11	0	2	434²	499	20	189	121	14.3	4.64	87	.299	.372	35	.240	-1	-23	-30	1	-2.1

■ ROY THOMAS
Thomas, Roy Allen b: 3/24/1874, Norristown, Pa. d: 11/20/59, Norristown, Pa. BL/TL, 5'11", 150 lbs. Deb: 4/14/1899 C♦

YEAR TM/L	W	L	PCT	G	GS	CG	SH	SV	IP	H	HR	BB	SO	RAT	ERA	ERA+	OAV	OOB	BH	AVG	PB	PR	/A	PD	TPI
1900 Phi-N	0	0	—	1	0	0	0	0	2²	4	0	0	0	13.5	3.38	107	.345	.345	168	.316	0	0	0	-0	0.0

■ ROY THOMAS
Thomas, Roy Justin b: 6/22/53, Quantico, Va. BR/TR, 6'5", 215 lbs. Deb: 9/21/77

YEAR TM/L	W	L	PCT	G	GS	CG	SH	SV	IP	H	HR	BB	SO	RAT	ERA	ERA+	OAV	OOB	BH	AVG	PB	PR	/A	PD	TPI
1977 Hou-N	0	0	—	4	0	0	0	0	6¹	5	0	3	4	11.4	2.84	125	.208	.296	0	—	0	1	1	0	0.1
1978 StL-N	1	1	.500	16	1	0	0	3	28¹	21	0	16	16	11.8	3.81	92	.216	.327	1	.250	0	-1	-1	1	0.0
1979 StL-N	3	4	.429	26	6	0	0	1	77	66	9	44	44	10.5	2.92	129	.237	.298	1	.059	-1	7	7	1	0.7
1980 StL-N	2	3	.400	24	5	0	0	0	55	59	3	25	22	14.2	4.75	78	.274	.358	2	.154	-0	-7	-6	1	-0.5
1983 Sea-A	3	1	.750	43	0	0	0	1	88²	95	3	32	77	13.1	3.45	123	.275	.340	0	—	0	6	8	-0	0.7
1984 Sea-A	3	2	.600	21	1	0	0	0	49²	52	8	37	42	16.9	5.26	76	.280	.410	0	—	0	-7	-7	0	-0.6
1985 Sea-A	7	0	1.000	40	0	0	0	1	93²	66	8	48	70	11.1	3.36	125	.202	.309	0	—	0	8	9	-1	0.8
1987 Sea-A	1	0	1.000	8	0	0	0	1	20²	23	2	11	14	15.2	5.23	90	.299	.393	0	—	0	-2	-1	-0	-0.1
Total 8	20	11	.645	182	13	0	0	7	419¹	387	33	196	289	12.8	3.82	105	.250	.339	4	.118	-1	5	9	1	1.1

■ STAN THOMAS
Thomas, Stanley Brown b: 7/11/49, Rumford, Me. BR/TR, 6'2", 185 lbs. Deb: 7/05/74

YEAR TM/L	W	L	PCT	G	GS	CG	SH	SV	IP	H	HR	BB	SO	RAT	ERA	ERA+	OAV	OOB	BH	AVG	PB	PR	/A	PD	TPI
1974 Tex-A	0	0	—	12	0	0	0	0	13²	22	1	6	8	18.4	6.59	54	.379	.438	0	—	0	-5	-5	0	-0.3
1975 Tex-A	4	4	.500	46	1	0	0	3	81¹	72	2	34	46	12.1	3.10	121	.239	.322	0	—	0	6	6	0	0.7
1976 Cle-A	4	4	.500	37	7	2	0	6	105²	88	5	41	54	11.3	2.30	152	.229	.310	0	—	0	14	14	3	1.8
1977 Sea-A	2	6	.250	13	9	1	0	0	58¹	74	8	25	14	15.7	6.02	68	.310	.382	0	—	0	-13	-12	0	-1.1
NY-A	1	0	1.000	3	0	0	0	0	6¹	7	0	4	1	15.6	7.11	55	.280	.379	0	—	0	-2	-2	-0	-0.1
Yr	3	6	.333	16	9	1	0	0	64²	81	8	29	15	15.3	6.12	67	.300	.368	0	—	0	-15	-15	0	-1.2
Total 4	11	14	.440	111	17	3	0	9	265¹	263	16	110	123	13.0	3.70	101	.261	.340	0	—	0	1	1	4	1.0

■ TOM THOMAS
Thomas, Thomas R. "Savage Tom" b: 12/27/1873, Shawnee, Ohio d: 9/23/42, Shawnee, Ohio 6'4", 195 lbs. Deb: 9/30/1899

YEAR TM/L	W	L	PCT	G	GS	CG	SH	SV	IP	H	HR	BB	SO	RAT	ERA	ERA+	OAV	OOB	BH	AVG	PB	PR	/A	PD	TPI
1899 StL-N	1	1	.500	4	2	2	0	0	25	22	1	4	8	9.4	2.52	158	.236	.268	3	.250	0	4	4	0	0.4
1900 StL-N	2	2	.500	5	1	1	0	0	26¹	38	2	4	7	14.4	3.76	97	.336	.359	1	.091	-1	-0	-0	-1	-0.1
Total 2	3	3	.500	9	3	3	0	0	51¹	60	3	8	15	11.9	3.16	120	.291	.318	4	.174	-0	4	4	-1	0.3

■ ERSKINE THOMASON
Thomason, Melvin Erskine b: 8/13/48, Laurens, S.C. BR/TR, 6'1", 190 lbs. Deb: 9/18/74

YEAR TM/L	W	L	PCT	G	GS	CG	SH	SV	IP	H	HR	BB	SO	RAT	ERA	ERA+	OAV	OOB	BH	AVG	PB	PR	/A	PD	TPI
1974 Phi-N	0	0	—	1	0	0	0	0	1	0	0	0	0	0.0	0.00	—	.000	.000	0	—	0	0	0	0	0.0

■ ART THOMPSON
Thompson, Arthur J. Deb: 6/17/1884

YEAR TM/L	W	L	PCT	G	GS	CG	SH	SV	IP	H	HR	BB	SO	RAT	ERA	ERA+	OAV	OOB	BH	AVG	PB	PR	/A	PD	TPI
1884 Was-U	0	1	.000	1	1	1	0	0	8	10	0	3	8	14.6	6.75	44	.287	.343	0	.000	-1	-3	-3	0	-0.2

■ FORREST THOMPSON
Thompson, David Forrest b: 3/3/18, Mooresville, N.C. d: 2/26/79, Charlotte, N.C. BL/TL, 5'11", 195 lbs. Deb: 4/26/48

YEAR TM/L	W	L	PCT	G	GS	CG	SH	SV	IP	H	HR	BB	SO	RAT	ERA	ERA+	OAV	OOB	BH	AVG	PB	PR	/A	PD	TPI
1948 Was-A	6	10	.375	46	7	0	0	4	131¹	134	9	54	40	13.0	3.84	113	.262	.334	10	.286	2	7	7	-0	0.9
1949 Was-A	1	3	.250	9	1	1	0	0	16¹	22	1	9	8	17.6	4.41	97	.328	.416	3	.600	2	-0	-0	0	0.2
Total 2	7	13	.350	55	8	1	0	4	147²	156	10	63	48	13.5	3.90	111	.270	.344	13	.325	4	6	7	-0	1.1

■ JUNIOR THOMPSON
Thompson, Eugene Earl b: 6/7/17, Latham, Ill. BR/TR, 6'1", 185 lbs. Deb: 4/26/39

YEAR TM/L	W	L	PCT	G	GS	CG	SH	SV	IP	H	HR	BB	SO	RAT	ERA	ERA+	OAV	OOB	BH	AVG	PB	PR	/A	PD	TPI
1939 *Cin-N	13	5	.722	42	11	5	3	2	152¹	130	6	55	87	11.1	2.54	151	.236	.309	11	.229	0	23	22	-2	2.1
1940 Cin-N	16	9	.640	33	31	17	3	0	225¹	197	10	96	103	11.8	3.32	114	.233	.313	18	.228	3	13	12	-1	1.4
1941 Cin-N	6	6	.500	27	15	4	0	1	109	117	6	57	46	14.6	4.87	74	.272	.361	7	.233	1	-15	-15	2	-1.1
1942 Cin-N	4	7	.364	29	10	1	0	0	101²	86	5	53	35	12.5	3.36	98	.226	.324	8	.267	2	-1	-1	4	0.5
1946 NY-N	4	6	.400	39	1	0	0	4	62²	36	5	40	31	10.9	1.29	266	.190	.332	1	.143	0	15	15	2	1.8
1947 NY-N	4	2	.667	15	0	0	0	0	35²	36	3	27	13	16.1	4.29	95	.279	.408	0	.000	-1	-1	-1	1	0.0

YEAR	TM/L	W	L	PCT	G	GS	CG	SH	SV	IP	H	HR	BB	SO	RAT	ERA	ERA+	OAV	OOB	BH	AVG	PB	PR	/A	PD	TPI
Total	6	47	35	.573	185	68	27	6	7	686²	602	35	328	315	12.3	3.26	113	.239	.329	45	.225	6	35	32	5	4.7

■ FULLER THOMPSON　Thompson, Fuller Weidner b: 5/1/1889, Los Angeles, Cal. d: 2/19/72, Los Angeles, Cal. BR/TR, 5'11.5", 164 lbs. Deb: 8/19/11

YEAR	TM/L	W	L	PCT	G	GS	CG	SH	SV	IP	H	HR	BB	SO	RAT	ERA	ERA+	OAV	OOB	BH	AVG	PB	PR	/A	PD	TPI
1911	Bos-N	0	0	—	3	0	0	0	0	4²	5	0	2	0	13.5	3.86	99	.294	.368	0	—	0	-0	-0	0	0.0

■ HARRY THOMPSON　Thompson, Harold b: 9/9/1889, Nanticoke, Pa. d: 2/14/51, Reno, Nev. BL/TL, 5'8", 150 lbs. Deb: 4/24/19

YEAR	TM/L	W	L	PCT	G	GS	CG	SH	SV	IP	H	HR	BB	SO	RAT	ERA	ERA+	OAV	OOB	BH	AVG	PB	PR	/A	PD	TPI
1919	Was-A	0	3	.000	12	2	0	0	1	43¹	48	0	8	10	12.0	3.53	91	.293	.333	8	.250	1	-1	-2	1	0.1
	Phi-A	0	1	.000	3	0	0	0	0	12	16	4	3	1	14.3	6.75	51	.327	.365	0	.000	-1	-5	-4	0	-0.4
	Yr	0	4	.000	15	2	0	0	1	55¹	64	4	11	11	12.2	4.23	77	.298	.332	3	.079	0	-6	-6	1	-0.3

■ LEE THOMPSON　Thompson, John Dudley "Lefty" b: 2/26/1898, Smithfield, Utah d: 2/17/63, Santa Barbara, Cal BL/TL, 6'1", 185 lbs. Deb: 9/04/21

YEAR	TM/L	W	L	PCT	G	GS	CG	SH	SV	IP	H	HR	BB	SO	RAT	ERA	ERA+	OAV	OOB	BH	AVG	PB	PR	/A	PD	TPI
1921	Chi-A	0	3	.000	4	4	0	0	0	20²	32	0	6	4	16.5	8.27	51	.333	.373	2	.286	0	-9	-9	-1	-0.7

■ GUS THOMPSON　Thompson, John Gustav b: 6/22/1877, Humboldt, Iowa d: 3/28/58, Kalispell, Mont. 6'2", 185 lbs. Deb: 8/31/03

YEAR	TM/L	W	L	PCT	G	GS	CG	SH	SV	IP	H	HR	BB	SO	RAT	ERA	ERA+	OAV	OOB	BH	AVG	PB	PR	/A	PD	TPI
1903	*Pit-N	2	2	.500	5	4	3	0	0	43	52	1	16	22	14.4	3.56	91	.295	.358	4	.250	0	-1	-2	-1	-0.1
1906	StL-N	2	11	.154	17	12	8	0	0	103	111	2	25	36	12.3	4.28	61	.285	.336	6	.176	-1	-19	-19	1	-1.8
Total	2	4	13	.235	22	16	11	0	0	146	163	3	41	58	12.9	4.07	69	.288	.343	10	.200	-1	-20	-20	0	-1.9

■ JOCKO THOMPSON　Thompson, John Samuel b: 1/17/17, Beverly, Mass. d: 2/3/88, Olney, Md. BL/TL, 6', 185 lbs. Deb: 9/21/48

YEAR	TM/L	W	L	PCT	G	GS	CG	SH	SV	IP	H	HR	BB	SO	RAT	ERA	ERA+	OAV	OOB	BH	AVG	PB	PR	/A	PD	TPI
1948	Phi-N	1	0	1.000	2	2	1	0	0	13	10	0	9	7	13.2	2.77	142	.233	.365	0	.000	0	2	2	-0	0.2
1949	Phi-N	1	3	.250	8	5	1	0	0	31¹	38	6	11	12	14.1	6.89	57	.314	.371	2	.182	-0	-10	-10	-0	-0.9
1950	Phi-N	0	0	—	2	0	0	0	0	4	1	0	4	2	11.3	0.00	—	.077	.294	0	—	0	2	2	0	0.2
1951	Phi-N	4	8	.333	29	14	3	2	0	119¹	102	12	59	60	12.3	3.85	100	.231	.325	4	.103	-1	2	0	-1	-0.1
Total	4	6	11	.353	41	21	5	2	0	167²	151	18	83	81	12.7	4.24	91	.244	.336	6	.113	-1	-5	-7	-1	-0.6

■ MIKE THOMPSON　Thompson, Michael Wayne b: 9/6/49, Denver, Colo. BR/TR, 6'3", 190 lbs. Deb: 5/19/71

YEAR	TM/L	W	L	PCT	G	GS	CG	SH	SV	IP	H	HR	BB	SO	RAT	ERA	ERA+	OAV	OOB	BH	AVG	PB	PR	/A	PD	TPI
1971	Was-A	1	6	.143	16	12	0	0	0	66²	53	3	54	41	14.9	4.86	68	.222	.372	2	.118	0	-10	-12	0	-1.0
1973	StL-N	0	0	—	2	2	0	0	0	4	1	0	5	3	13.5	0.00	—	.077	.333	0	.000	-0	2	2	0	0.1
1974	StL-N	0	3	.000	19	4	0	0	0	38¹	37	1	35	25	17.4	5.63	63	.274	.430	0	.000	-1	-9	-9	0	-0.9
	Atl-N	0	0	—	1	1	0	0	0	4	7	0	2	2	20.3	4.50	84	.412	.474	1	1.000	0	0	0	0	0.0
	Yr	0	3	.000	20	5	0	0	0	42¹	44	1	37	27	17.2	5.53	65	.286	.424	0	.000	-1	-9	-9	0	-0.9
1975	Atl-N	0	6	.000	16	10	0	0	0	51²	60	2	32	42	16.0	4.70	80	.305	.402	1	.071	-1	-6	-5	0	-0.5
Total	4	1	15	.063	54	29	0	0	0	164²	158	6	128	113	15.9	4.86	73	.263	.396	4	.098	-1	-24	-24	1	-2.3

■ RICH THOMPSON　Thompson, Richard Neil b: 11/1/58, New York, N.Y. BB/TR, 6'3", 225 lbs. Deb: 4/28/85

YEAR	TM/L	W	L	PCT	G	GS	CG	SH	SV	IP	H	HR	BB	SO	RAT	ERA	ERA+	OAV	OOB	BH	AVG	PB	PR	/A	PD	TPI
1985	Cle-A	3	8	.273	57	0	0	0	5	80	95	8	48	30	16.8	6.30	66	.303	.405	0		0	-19	-19	-1	-1.9
1989	Mon-N	0	2	.000	19	1	0	0	0	33	27	2	11	15	10.9	2.18	162	.241	.320	0	.000	0	5	5	-0	0.5
1990	Mon-N	0	0	—	1	0	0	0	0	1	1	0	0	0	9.0	0.00	—	.250	.250	0	—	0	0	0	0	0.0
Total	3	3	10	.231	77	1	0	0	5	114	123	10	59	45	15.0	5.05	78	.286	.382	0	.000	0	-14	-14	-2	-1.4

■ THOMAS THOMPSON　Thompson, Thomas Carl b: 11/7/1889, Spring City, Tenn. d: 1/16/80, LaJolla, Cal. BR/TR, 5'9.5", 170 lbs. Deb: 6/05/12

YEAR	TM/L	W	L	PCT	G	GS	CG	SH	SV	IP	H	HR	BB	SO	RAT	ERA	ERA+	OAV	OOB	BH	AVG	PB	PR	/A	PD	TPI
1912	NY-A	0	2	.000	7	2	1	0	0	32²	43	0	13	15	16.3	6.06	59	.341	.415	3	.300	1	-10	-9	-0	-0.7

■ WILL THOMPSON　Thompson, Will McLain b: 8/30/1870, Pittsburgh, Pa. d: 6/9/62, Pittsburgh, Pa. BR/TR, 5'11.5", 190 lbs. Deb: 7/09/1892

YEAR	TM/L	W	L	PCT	G	GS	CG	SH	SV	IP	H	HR	BB	SO	RAT	ERA	ERA+	OAV	OOB	BH	AVG	PB	PR	/A	PD	TPI
1892	Pit-N	0	1	.000	1	1	0	0	0	3	3	0	5	2	24.0	3.00	110	.250	.471	0	—	0	0	0	0	0.0

■ HANK THORMAHLEN　Thormahlen, Herbert Ehler "Lefty" b: 7/5/1896, Jersey City, N.J. d: 2/6/55, Los Angeles, Cal. BL/TL, 6', 180 lbs. Deb: 9/29/17

YEAR	TM/L	W	L	PCT	G	GS	CG	SH	SV	IP	H	HR	BB	SO	RAT	ERA	ERA+	OAV	OOB	BH	AVG	PB	PR	/A	PD	TPI
1917	NY-A	0	1	.000	1	1	0	0	0	8	9	0	4	5	15.8	2.25	119	.281	.378	0	.000	-0	0	-0	0	0.0
1918	NY-A	7	3	.700	16	12	5	2	0	112²	85	1	52	22	11.4	2.48	114	.217	.318	3	.077	-4	4	4	1	0.2
1919	NY-A	12	10	.545	30	25	13	2	1	188²	155	10	61	62	10.5	2.62	122	.228	.295	11	.186	-0	13	12	-1	1.1
1920	NY-A	9	6	.600	29	15	6	0	1	143¹	178	5	43	35	14.0	4.14	92	.302	.362	10	.222	1	-6	-5	2	-0.1
1921	Bos-A	1	7	.125	23	9	3	0	0	96¹	101	3	34	17	13.2	4.48	94	.277	.349	4	.174	-1	-2	-3	0	-0.2
1925	Bro-N	0	3	.000	5	2	0	0	0	16	22	0	9	7	18.6	3.94	106	.333	.429	1	.200	0	1	0	0	0.1
Total	6	29	30	.492	104	64	27	4	2	565	550	19	203	148	12.3	3.33	105	.261	.332	29	.168	-3	10	9	2	1.1

■ PAUL THORMODSGARD　Thormodsgard, Paul Gayton b: 11/10/53, San Francisco, Cal. BR/TR, 6'2", 190 lbs. Deb: 4/10/77

YEAR	TM/L	W	L	PCT	G	GS	CG	SH	SV	IP	H	HR	BB	SO	RAT	ERA	ERA+	OAV	OOB	BH	AVG	PB	PR	/A	PD	TPI
1977	Min-A	11	15	.423	37	37	8	1	0	218	236	25	65	94	12.6	4.62	86	.280	.333	0	—	0	-14	-16	-1	-1.5
1978	Min-A	1	6	.143	12	12	1	0	0	66	81	7	17	23	13.5	5.05	76	.308	.352	0	—	0	-9	-9	-0	-0.8
1979	Min-A	0	0	—	1	0	0	0	0	1	3	1	0	1	27.0	9.00	49	.500	.500	0	—	0	-1	-1	0	0.0
Total	3	12	21	.364	50	49	9	1	0	285	320	33	82	118	12.8	4.74	83	.288	.339	0	—	0	-24	-25	-1	-2.3

■ JOHN THORNTON　Thornton, John b: 1870, Washington, D.C. d: 8/31/1893, Pensacola, Fla. 5'10.5", 175 lbs. Deb: 8/14/1889 ♦

YEAR	TM/L	W	L	PCT	G	GS	CG	SH	SV	IP	H	HR	BB	SO	RAT	ERA	ERA+	OAV	OOB	BH	AVG	PB	PR	/A	PD	TPI
1889	Was-N	0	1	.000	1	1	1	0	0	9	8	0	7	3	15.0	5.00	79	.231	.360	0	.000	-1	-1	-1	-0	0.0
1891	Phi-N	15	16	.484	37	32	23	1	2	269	268	3	115	52	12.8	3.68	93	.250	.323	17	.138	-7	-10	-8	2	-1.1
1892	Phi-N	0	2	.000	3	2	1	0	0	12	16	1	17	2	24.8	12.75	25	.308	.478	5	.385	1	-13	-13	0	-0.8
Total	3	15	19	.441	41	35	25	1	2	290	292	4	139	57	13.4	4.10	83	.252	.332	22	.154	-7	-24	-22	2	-1.9

■ WALTER THORNTON　Thornton, Walter Miller b: 2/18/1875, Lewiston, Maine d: 7/14/60, Los Angeles, Cal. TL, 6'1", 180 lbs. Deb: 7/01/1895 ♦

YEAR	TM/L	W	L	PCT	G	GS	CG	SH	SV	IP	H	HR	BB	SO	RAT	ERA	ERA+	OAV	OOB	BH	AVG	PB	PR	/A	PD	TPI
1895	Chi-N	2	0	1.000	7	2	2	0	1	40	58	3	31	13	20.0	6.07	84	.333	.434	7	.318	2	-6	-4	-1	-0.1
1896	Chi-N	2	1	.667	5	5	2	0	0	23²	30	1	13	10	16.4	5.70	80	.306	.388	8	.364	2	-4	-3	-1	0.0
1897	Chi-N	6	7	.462	16	16	15	0	0	130¹	164	4	51	55	14.8	4.70	95	.305	.365	85	.321	4	-6	-3	-0	-0.2
1898	Chi-N	13	10	.565	28	25	21	2	0	215¹	226	4	56	56	11.8	3.34	107	.268	.313	62	.295	6	6	6	-1	0.5
Total	4	23	18	.561	56	48	40	2	1	409¹	478	12	151	134	13.8	4.18	97	.289	.349	162	.312	14	-8	-6	-2	0.2

■ BOB THORPE　Thorpe, Robert Joseph b: 1/12/35, San Diego, Cal. d: 3/17/60, San Diego, Cal. BR/TR, 6'1", 170 lbs. Deb: 4/17/55

YEAR	TM/L	W	L	PCT	G	GS	CG	SH	SV	IP	H	HR	BB	SO	RAT	ERA	ERA+	OAV	OOB	BH	AVG	PB	PR	/A	PD	TPI
1955	Chi-N	0	0	—	2	0	0	0	0	3	4	0	0	0	12.0	3.00	136	.333	.333	0	—	0	0	0	0	0.1

■ GEORGE THROOP　Throop, George Lynford b: 11/24/50, Pasadena, Cal. BR/TR, 6'7", 205 lbs. Deb: 9/07/75

YEAR	TM/L	W	L	PCT	G	GS	CG	SH	SV	IP	H	HR	BB	SO	RAT	ERA	ERA+	OAV	OOB	BH	AVG	PB	PR	/A	PD	TPI
1975	KC-A	0	0	—	7	0	0	0	2	9	8	1	2	8	10.0	4.00	96	.250	.294	0	—	0	-0	-0	0	0.0
1977	KC-A	0	0	—	4	0	0	0	0	5¹	1	1	4	1	8.4	3.38	120	.059	.238	0	—	0	0	0	0	0.1
1978	KC-A	1	0	1.000	1	0	0	0	0	3	2	0	3	2	15.0	0.00	—	.222	.417	0	—	0	1	1	0	0.2
1979	KC-A	0	0	—	4	0	0	0	0	2²	7	0	5	1	40.5	13.50	32	.467	.600	0	—	0	-3	-3	0	-0.2
	Hou-N	1	0	1.000	14	0	0	0	1	22¹	23	4	11	15	14.5	3.22	109	.271	.361	0	.000	0	1	1	-0	0.0
Total	4	2	0	1.000	30	0	0	0	3	42¹	41	6	25	27	14.2	3.83	97	.259	.364	0	.000	0	-0	-1	0	0.1

■ LOU THUMAN　Thuman, Louis Charles Frank b: 12/13/16, Baltimore, Md. BR/TR, 6'2", 185 lbs. Deb: 9/08/39

YEAR	TM/L	W	L	PCT	G	GS	CG	SH	SV	IP	H	HR	BB	SO	RAT	ERA	ERA+	OAV	OOB	BH	AVG	PB	PR	/A	PD	TPI
1939	Was-A	0	0	—	3	0	0	0	0	4	5	0	2	1	15.8	9.00	48	.278	.350	0	—	0	-2	-2	0	0.0
1940	Was-A	0	1	.000	2	0	0	0	0	5	10	0	7	0	30.6	14.40	29	.400	.531	0	.000	-0	-6	-6	0	-0.4
Total	2	0	1	.000	5	0	0	0	0	9	15	0	9	1	24.0	12.00	35	.349	.462	0	.000	-0	-8	-8	0	-0.4

■ MARK THURMOND　Thurmond, Mark Anthony b: 9/12/56, Houston, Tex. BL/TL, 6', 180 lbs. Deb: 5/14/83

YEAR	TM/L	W	L	PCT	G	GS	CG	SH	SV	IP	H	HR	BB	SO	RAT	ERA	ERA+	OAV	OOB	BH	AVG	PB	PR	/A	PD	TPI
1983	SD-N	7	3	.700	21	18	2	0	0	115¹	104	3	49	10.8	2.65	131	.248	.306	2	.054	-2	12	11	1	1.0	
1984	*SD-N	14	8	.636	32	29	1	1	0	178²	174	12	55	57	11.5	2.97	120	.256	.311	11	.190	1	12	12	2	1.7
1985	SD-N	7	11	.389	36	23	1	1	2	138¹	154	9	44	57	13.1	3.97	89	.291	.349	3	.088	-2	-6	-7	1	-0.6
1986	SD-N	3	7	.300	17	15	2	0	0	70²	96	7	27	32	15.7	6.50	58	.325	.382	6	.250	1	-22	-22	0	-1.9
	Det-A	4	1	.800	25	4	0	0	3	51²	44	7	17	17	10.6	1.92	215	.234	.298	0	—	0	13	13	-0	1.2
1987	*Det-A	0	1	.000	48	0	0	0	5	61²	83	5	24	21	15.6	4.23	100	.331	.389	0	—	0	2	-0	0	0.0

YEAR	TM/L	W	L	PCT	G	GS	CG	SH	SV	IP	H	HR	BB	SO	RAT	ERA	ERA+	OAV	OOB	BH	AVG	PB	PR	/A	PD	TPI
1988	Bal-A	1	8	.111	43	6	0	0	3	74²	80	10	27	29	13.1	4.58	85	.277	.343	0	—	0	-5	-6	-1	-0.5
1989	Bal-A	2	4	.333	49	2	0	0	4	90	102	6	17	34	13.1	3.90	97	.288	.323	0	—	0	-0	-1	-1	-0.1
1990	SF-N	2	3	.400	43	0	0	0	4	56²	53	6	18	24	11.3	3.34	112	.257	.317	0	.000	-1	3	2	2	0.4
Total	8	40	46	.465	314	97	6	3	21	837²	890	69	262	320	12.5	3.69	101	.277	.333	22	.139	-1	9	2	4	1.2

■ SLOPPY THURSTON
Thurston, Hollis John   b: 6/2/1899, Fremont, Neb.   d: 9/14/73, Los Angeles, Cal.   BR/TR, 5'11", 165 lbs.   Deb: 4/19/23

YEAR	TM/L	W	L	PCT	G	GS	CG	SH	SV	IP	H	HR	BB	SO	RAT	ERA	ERA+	OAV	OOB	BH	AVG	PB	PR	/A	PD	TPI
1923	StL-A	0	0	—	2	1	0	0	0	4	8	0	2	0	22.5	6.75	62	.421	.476	0	—	0	-1	-1	0	0.0
	Chi-A	7	8	.467	44	12	8	0	4	191²	223	11	36	55	12.2	3.05	130	.316	.341	25	.316	6	20	19	-0	2.5
	Yr	7	8	.467	46	13	8	0	4	195²	231	11	38	55	12.4	3.13	127	.310	.345	2	.025	6	19	18	-0	2.5
1924	Chi-A	20	14	.588	38	36	28	1	1	291	330	17	60	37	12.2	3.80	108	.290	.329	31	.254	4	14	10	1	1.6
1925	Chi-A	10	14	.417	36	25	9	0	1	183	250	14	47	35	14.9	5.95	70	.335	.378	24	.286	6	-32	-37	3	-2.4
1926	Chi-A	6	8	.429	31	13	6	1	3	134¹	164	10	36	35	13.5	5.02	77	.311	.356	19	.311	5	-15	-17	-1	-1.2
1927	Was-A	13	13	.500	29	28	13	2	0	205¹	254	16	60	38	13.9	4.47	91	.308	.356	29	.315	9	-8	-9	-0	0.0
1930	Bro-N	6	4	.600	24	11	5	2	1	106	110	4	17	26	10.8	3.40	144	.266	.346	10	.200	-0	19	18	2	1.8
1931	Bro-N	9	9	.500	24	17	11	0	0	143	175	3	39	23	13.5	3.97	96	.301	.346	13	.217	2	-2	-2	0	0.0
1932	Bro-N	12	8	.600	28	20	10	2	0	153	174	14	38	35	12.5	4.06	94	.287	.330	17	.304	5	-3	-4	1	0.2
1933	Bro-N	6	8	.429	32	15	5	0	3	131¹	171	4	34	22	14.5	4.52	71	.319	.366	7	.159	-1	-17	-19	2	-1.8
Total	9	89	86	.509	288	178	95	8	13	1542²	1859	93	369	306	13.1	4.24	94	.304	.346	175	.270	37	-25	-43	7	0.7

■ LUIS TIANT
Tiant, Luis Clemente (Vega)   b: 11/23/40, Marianao, Cuba   BR/TR, 6', 180 lbs.   Deb: 7/19/64

YEAR	TM/L	W	L	PCT	G	GS	CG	SH	SV	IP	H	HR	BB	SO	RAT	ERA	ERA+	OAV	OOB	BH	AVG	PB	PR	/A	PD	TPI
1964	Cle-A	10	4	.714	19	16	9	3	1	127	94	13	47	105	10.1	2.83	127	.207	.284	5	.111	-1	11	11	0	1.0
1965	Cle-A	11	11	.500	41	30	10	2	1	196¹	166	20	66	152	10.8	3.53	99	.228	.295	6	.088	-2	-2	-1	0	-0.2
1966	Cle-A	12	11	.522	46	16	7	5	8	155	121	16	50	145	10.0	2.79	123	.213	.279	4	.111	-1	11	11	-1	0.9
1967	Cle-A	12	9	.571	33	29	9	1	2	213²	177	24	67	219	10.3	2.74	119	.221	.282	18	.254	5	12	13	-3	1.6
1968	Cle-A	21	9	.700	34	32	19	9	0	258¹	152	16	73	264	8.0	**1.60**	**185**	**.168**	**.233**	7	.080	-4	40	39	-3	3.8
1969	Cle-A	9	20	.310	38	37	9	1	0	249²	229	37	129	156	13.2	3.71	101	.246	.343	19	.235	6	-3	1	-0	0.8
1970	*Min-A	7	3	.700	18	17	2	1	0	92²	84	12	41	50	12.3	3.40	109	.246	.330	13	.406	5	3	3	0	1.0
1971	Bos-A	1	7	.125	21	10	1	0	0	72¹	73	8	32	59	13.2	4.85	76	.259	.337	3	.158	-0	-11	-9	-0	-0.9
1972	Bos-A	15	6	.714	43	19	12	6	3	179	128	7	65	123	9.7	**1.91**	**168**	.202	.277	6	.107	-2	23	26	-1	2.8
1973	Bos-A	20	13	.606	35	35	23	0	0	272	217	32	78	206	**10.0**	3.34	120	.219	**.281**	0	—	0	14	20	-1	2.0
1974	Bos-A	22	13	.629	38	38	25	7	0	311¹	281	21	82	176	10.6	2.92	132	.241	.293	0	—	0	24	32	-3	3.2
1975	*Bos-A	18	14	.563	35	35	18	2	0	260	262	25	72	142	11.7	4.02	101	.264	.316	0	.000	0	-7	2	-4	-0.1
1976	Bos-A	21	12	.636	38	38	19	3	0	279	274	25	64	131	11.0	3.06	128	.260	.304	0	.000	0	14	26	-2	2.6
1977	Bos-A	12	8	.600	32	32	3	3	0	188²	210	26	51	124	12.5	4.53	99	.279	.327	0	—	0	-10	-1	-2	-0.2
1978	Bos-A	13	8	.619	32	31	12	5	0	212¹	185	26	57	114	10.5	3.31	124	.234	.290	0	—	0	11	19	-2	1.8
1979	NY-A	13	8	.619	30	30	5	1	0	195²	190	22	53	104	11.2	3.91	104	.251	.300	0	—	0	7	4	-0	0.3
1980	NY-A	8	9	.471	25	25	3	0	0	136¹	139	10	50	84	12.5	4.89	80	.265	.330	0	—	0	-13	-15	1	-1.2
1981	Pit-N	2	5	.286	9	9	1	0	0	57¹	54	3	19	32	11.5	3.92	92	.243	.303	3	.188	1	-3	-2	-1	-0.1
1982	Cal-A	2	2	.500	6	5	0	0	0	29²	39	3	8	30	14.3	5.76	70	.310	.351	0	—	0	-6	-6	-1	-0.5
Total	19	229	172	.571	573	484	187	49	15	3486¹	3075	346	1104	2416	10.9	3.30	113	.236	.298	84	.164	6	116	173	-23	18.6

■ JAY TIBBS
Tibbs, Jay Lindsey   b: 1/4/62, Birmingham, Ala.   BR/TR, 6'3", 185 lbs.   Deb: 7/15/84

YEAR	TM/L	W	L	PCT	G	GS	CG	SH	SV	IP	H	HR	BB	SO	RAT	ERA	ERA+	OAV	OOB	BH	AVG	PB	PR	/A	PD	TPI
1984	Cin-N	6	2	.750	14	14	3	1	0	100²	87	4	33	40	10.7	2.86	132	.238	.302	5	.139	-1	8	10	-1	0.9
1985	Cin-N	10	16	.385	35	34	5	2	0	218	216	14	83	98	12.3	3.92	97	.262	.329	6	.092	-3	-8	-3	2	-0.4
1986	Mon-N	7	9	.438	35	31	3	2	0	190¹	181	12	70	117	12.0	3.97	93	.256	.326	7	.130	-0	-5	-6	-0	-0.6
1987	Mon-N	4	5	.444	19	12	0	0	0	83	95	10	34	54	14.0	4.99	84	.289	.355	3	.120	0	-8	-7	-0	-0.6
1988	Bal-A	4	15	.211	30	24	1	0	0	158²	184	18	63	82	14.2	5.39	72	.293	.360	0	—	0	-25	-26	0	-2.4
1989	Bal-A	5	0	1.000	10	8	1	0	0	54¹	62	2	20	30	13.6	2.82	135	.287	.347	0	—	0	6	6	-0	0.6
1990	Bal-A	2	7	.222	10	10	0	0	0	50²	55	8	14	23	12.3	5.68	67	.279	.327	0	—	0	-10	-10	1	-0.9
	Pit-N	1	0	1.000	5	0	0	0	0	7	7	0	2	4	11.6	2.57	141	.259	.310	0	—	0	1	1	0	0.1
Total	7	39	54	.419	158	133	13	5	0	862²	887	68	319	448	12.6	4.20	91	.269	.335	21	.117	-4	-41	-36	0	-3.3

■ DICK TIDROW
Tidrow, Richard William   b: 5/14/47, San Francisco, Cal.   BR/TR, 6'4", 210 lbs.   Deb: 4/18/72

YEAR	TM/L	W	L	PCT	G	GS	CG	SH	SV	IP	H	HR	BB	SO	RAT	ERA	ERA+	OAV	OOB	BH	AVG	PB	PR	/A	PD	TPI
1972	Cle-A	14	15	.483	39	34	10	3	0	237¹	200	24	70	123	10.5	2.77	116	.230	.291	7	.100	-3	8	12	-3	0.6
1973	Cle-A	14	16	.467	42	40	13	2	0	274²	289	31	95	138	12.8	4.42	89	.270	.334	0	—	0	-19	-15	-1	-1.6
1974	Cle-A	1	3	.250	4	4	0	0	0	19	21	4	13	8	17.1	7.11	51	.276	.396	0	—	0	-7	-7	0	-0.6
	NY-A	11	9	.550	33	25	5	0	1	190²	205	14	53	100	12.4	3.87	90	.279	.331	0	—	0	-5	-8	-1	-0.9
	Yr	12	12	.500	37	29	5	0	1	209²	226	18	66	108	12.7	4.16	84	.278	.335	0	—	0	-13	-15	-1	-1.5
1975	NY-A	6	3	.667	37	0	0	0	0	69¹	65	5	31	38	12.9	3.12	117	.256	.344	0	—	0	5	4	-1	0.3
1976	*NY-A	4	5	.444	47	2	0	0	10	92¹	80	5	24	65	10.2	2.63	130	.233	.285	0	—	0	9	8	-1	0.7
1977	*NY-A	11	4	.733	49	7	0	0	5	151	143	20	41	83	11.1	3.16	125	.250	.303	0	—	0	15	13	-1	1.3
1978	*NY-A	7	11	.389	31	25	4	0	0	185¹	191	13	53	73	12.1	3.84	94	.267	.322	0	—	0	-2	-4	-2	-0.5
1979	NY-A	2	1	.667	14	0	0	0	2	22²	38	5	4	7	16.7	7.94	51	.409	.433	0	—	0	-9	-10	1	-0.7
	Chi-N	11	5	.688	63	0	0	0	4	102¹	86	5	42	68	11.4	2.72	151	.231	.313	2	.200	1	12	16	1	1.9
1980	Chi-N	6	5	.545	**84**	0	0	0	6	116	97	10	53	97	12.0	2.79	140	.229	.322	0	.000	-1	10	14	-1	1.4
1981	Chi-N	3	10	.231	51	0	0	0	9	74²	73	6	30	39	12.5	5.06	73	.256	.329	0	.000	-1	-13	-11	-1	-1.3
1982	Chi-N	8	3	.727	65	0	0	0	6	103²	106	6	29	62	12.0	3.39	110	.265	.319	0	.000	-1	2	4	-2	0.1
1983	*Chi-A	2	4	.333	50	1	0	0	7	91²	86	13	34	66	11.9	4.22	99	.242	.310	0	—	0	-2	-0	1	0.0
1984	NY-N	0	0	—	11	0	0	0	0	15²	25	5	7	8	18.4	9.19	38	.357	.416	0	—	0	-10	-10	0	-0.8
Total	13	100	94	.515	620	138	32	5	55	1746²	1705	163	579	975	12.0	3.68	101	.257	.321	9	.095	-5	-5	6	-9	-0.1

■ BOBBY TIEFENAUER
Tiefenauer, Bobby Gene   b: 10/10/29, Desloge, Mo.   BR/TR, 6'2", 185 lbs.   Deb: 7/14/52   C

YEAR	TM/L	W	L	PCT	G	GS	CG	SH	SV	IP	H	HR	BB	SO	RAT	ERA	ERA+	OAV	OOB	BH	AVG	PB	PR	/A	PD	TPI
1952	StL-N	0	0	—	6	0	0	0	0	8	12	1	7	3	21.4	7.88	47	.343	.452	0	.000	-0	-4	-4	0	-0.3
1955	StL-N	1	4	.200	18	0	0	0	0	32¹	31	6	10	16	12.4	4.41	92	.261	.338	0	.000	-0	-1	-1	0	0.0
1960	Cle-A	0	1	.000	6	0	0	0	0	9	8	0	3	2	11.0	2.00	187	.242	.306	0	.000	0	2	2	0	0.2
1961	StL-N	0	0	—	3	0	0	0	0	4¹	9	0	4	3	27.0	6.23	71	.450	.542	0	—	0	-1	-1	-0	0.0
1962	Hou-N	2	4	.333	43	0	0	0	1	85	91	6	21	60	12.1	4.34	86	.277	.324	1	.111	0	-4	-6	-2	-0.6
1963	Mil-N	1	1	.500	12	0	0	0	2	29²	20	1	4	22	7.3	1.21	265	.194	.224	0	.000	-0	7	7	1	0.8
1964	Mil-N	4	6	.400	46	0	0	0	13	73	61	6	15	48	9.7	3.21	110	.225	.273	0	.000	-1	3	3	-1	0.1
1965	Mil-N	0	1	.000	7	0	0	0	0	7	8	1	3	7	15.4	7.71	46	.286	.375	0	—	0	-3	-3	0	-0.2
	NY-A	1	1	.500	10	0	0	0	2	20¹	19	3	5	15	11.1	3.54	96	.253	.309	0	.000	-0	-0	-0	0	0.0
	Cle-A	0	5	.000	15	0	0	0	4	22¹	24	3	10	13	14.1	4.84	72	.273	.354	0	.000	-0	-3	-3	-0	-0.3
	Yr	1	6	.143	25	0	0	0	6	42²	43	6	15	28	12.4	4.22	82	.259	.324	1	.333	-0	-4	-4	-0	-0.3
1967	Cle-A	0	1	.000	5	0	0	0	0	11¹	9	0	3	6	9.5	0.79	411	.225	.279	0	—	0	3	3	0	0.3
1968	Chi-N	0	1	.000	15	0	0	0	1	13¹	20	2	2	9	15.4	6.08	52	.351	.373	0	.000	-0	-5	-4	-0	-0.4
Total	10	9	25	.265	179	0	0	0	23	316	312	29	87	204	11.7	3.84	94	.260	.317	1	.026	-2	-7	-9	-1	-0.4

■ VERLE TIEFENTHALER
Tiefenthaler, Verle Matthew   b: 7/11/37, Breda, Iowa   BL/TR, 6'1", 190 lbs.   Deb: 4/19/62

YEAR	TM/L	W	L	PCT	G	GS	CG	SH	SV	IP	H	HR	BB	SO	RAT	ERA	ERA+	OAV	OOB	BH	AVG	PB	PR	/A	PD	TPI
1962	Chi-A	0	0	—	3	0	0	0	0	3²	6	1	7	1	31.9	9.82	40	.353	.542	0	—	0	-2	-2	-0	-0.1

■ EDDIE TIEMEYER
Tiemeyer, Edward Carl   b: 5/9/1885, Cincinnati, Ohio   d: 9/27/46, Cincinnati, Ohio   BR/TR, 5'11.5", 185 lbs.   Deb: 8/19/06 ♦

YEAR	TM/L	W	L	PCT	G	GS	CG	SH	SV	IP	H	HR	BB	SO	RAT	ERA	ERA+	OAV	OOB	BH	AVG	PB	PR	/A	PD	TPI
1906	Cin-N	0	0	—	1	0	0	0	0	1	1	0	1	1	18.0	0.00	—	.500	.667	2	.182	0	0	0	0	0.0

■ MIKE TIERNAN
Tiernan, Michael Joseph "Silent Mike"   b: 1/21/1867, Trenton, N.J.   d: 11/9/18, New York, N.Y.   BL/TL, 5'11", 165 lbs.   Deb: 4/30/1887 ♦

YEAR	TM/L	W	L	PCT	G	GS	CG	SH	SV	IP	H	HR	BB	SO	RAT	ERA	ERA+	OAV	OOB	BH	AVG	PB	PR	/A	PD	TPI
1887	NY-N	1	2	.333	5	0	0	0	1	19²	33	2	7	3	18.3	8.69	43	.363	.408	117	.287	2	-10	-11	0	-0.7

YEAR TM/L	W	L	PCT	G	GS	CG	SH	SV	IP	H	HR	BB	SO	RAT	ERA	ERA+	OAV	OOB	BH	AVG	PB	PR	/A	PD	TPI

■ LES TIETJE — Tietje, Leslie William "Toots" b: 9/11/11, Sumner, Iowa BR/TR, 6'0.5", 178 lbs. Deb: 9/18/33

YEAR TM/L	W	L	PCT	G	GS	CG	SH	SV	IP	H	HR	BB	SO	RAT	ERA	ERA+	OAV	OOB	BH	AVG	PB	PR	/A	PD	TPI
1933 Chi-A	2	0	1.000	3	3	1	0	0	22¹	16	1	15	9	12.5	2.42	175	.203	.330	1	.125	0	5	5	0	0.5
1934 Chi-A	5	14	.263	34	22	6	1	0	176	174	20	96	81	13.9	4.81	98	.257	.351	1	.017	-8	-6	-1	1	-0.6
1935 Chi-A	9	15	.375	30	21	9	1	0	169²	184	14	81	64	14.2	4.30	108	.277	.357	12	.197	-1	3	6	-2	0.3
1936 Chi-A	0	0	—	2	0	0	0	0	2¹	6	0	5	3	42.4	27.00	19	.462	.611	0	—	0	-6	-6	0	-0.3
StL-A	3	5	.375	14	7	2	0	0	50¹	65	2	30	16	17.3	6.62	81	.310	.401	1	.067	-2	-9	-7	1	-0.6
Yr	3	5	.375	16	7	2	0	0	52²	71	2	35	19	18.5	7.52	71	.318	.415	2	.133	-1	-15	-13	1	-0.9
1937 StL-A	1	2	.333	5	4	2	0	0	30	32	0	17	5	14.7	4.20	115	.283	.377	0	.000	-2	1	2	-0	0.0
1938 StL-A	2	5	.286	17	8	2	1	0	62	83	8	38	15	17.6	7.55	66	.327	.414	2	.111	-1	-19	-18	0	-1.5
Total 6	22	41	.349	105	65	22	3	0	512²	560	45	282	193	14.9	5.11	93	.279	.369	17	.099	-13	-31	-19	0	-2.2

■ RAY TIFT — Tift, Raymond Frank b: 6/21/1884, Fitchburg, Mass. d: 3/29/45, Verona, N.J. TR , Deb: 8/07/07

YEAR TM/L	W	L	PCT	G	GS	CG	SH	SV	IP	H	HR	BB	SO	RAT	ERA	ERA+	OAV	OOB	BH	AVG	PB	PR	/A	PD	TPI
1907 NY-A	0	0	—	4	1	0	0	0	19	33	0	4	6	17.5	4.74	59	.382	.409	0	.000	-1	-5	-4	-0	-0.4

■ JOHNNY TILLMAN — Tillman, John Lawrence "Ducky" b: 10/6/1893, Bridgeport, Conn. d: 4/7/64, Harrisburg, Pa. BB/TR, 5'11", 170 lbs. Deb: 9/20/15

YEAR TM/L	W	L	PCT	G	GS	CG	SH	SV	IP	H	HR	BB	SO	RAT	ERA	ERA+	OAV	OOB	BH	AVG	PB	PR	/A	PD	TPI
1915 StL-A	1	0	1.000	2	1	0	0	0	10	6	0	4	6	9.0	0.90	319	.176	.263	0	.000	-0	2	2	0	0.2

■ THAD TILLOTSON — Tillotson, Thaddeus Asa b: 12/20/40, Merced, Cal. BR/TR, 6'2.5", 195 lbs. Deb: 4/14/67

YEAR TM/L	W	L	PCT	G	GS	CG	SH	SV	IP	H	HR	BB	SO	RAT	ERA	ERA+	OAV	OOB	BH	AVG	PB	PR	/A	PD	TPI
1967 NY-A	3	9	.250	43	5	1	0	2	98¹	99	9	39	62	12.8	4.03	78	.261	.333	1	.063	-0	-9	-10	0	-1.0
1968 NY-A	1	0	1.000	7	0	0	0	0	10¹	11	0	7	1	15.7	4.35	67	.282	.391	0	.000	-0	-2	-2	0	-0.1
Total 2	4	9	.308	50	5	1	0	2	108²	110	9	46	63	13.1	4.06	77	.263	.339	1	.059	-1	-10	-11	1	-1.1

■ GARY TIMBERLAKE — Timberlake, Gary Dale b: 8/8/48, Laconia, Ind. BR/TL, 6'2", 205 lbs. Deb: 6/18/69

YEAR TM/L	W	L	PCT	G	GS	CG	SH	SV	IP	H	HR	BB	SO	RAT	ERA	ERA+	OAV	OOB	BH	AVG	PB	PR	/A	PD	TPI
1969 Sea-A	0	0	—	2	2	0	0	0	6	7	0	9	4	24.0	7.50	48	.269	.457	0	.000	-0	-3	-3	-0	-0.2

■ TOM TIMMERMANN — Timmermann, Thomas Henry b: 5/12/40, Breese, Ill. BR/TR, 6'4", 215 lbs. Deb: 6/18/69

YEAR TM/L	W	L	PCT	G	GS	CG	SH	SV	IP	H	HR	BB	SO	RAT	ERA	ERA+	OAV	OOB	BH	AVG	PB	PR	/A	PD	TPI
1969 Det-A	4	3	.571	31	1	1	0	1	55²	50	1	26	42	12.6	2.75	136	.238	.328	1	.111	-0	5	6	-1	0.5
1970 Det-A	6	7	.462	61	0	0	0	27	85¹	90	3	34	49	13.3	4.11	91	.273	.344	0	.000	-2	-4	-4	-0	-0.5
1971 Det-A	7	6	.538	52	2	0	0	4	84	82	6	37	51	13.1	3.86	93	.262	.346	1	.053	-1	-4	-2	0	-0.3
1972 Det-A	8	10	.444	34	25	3	2	0	149²	121	12	41	88	10.0	2.89	109	.216	.276	6	.136	-0	3	4	-1	0.3
1973 Det-A	1	1	.500	17	1	0	0	1	39	39	4	11	21	11.5	3.69	111	.258	.309	0	—	0	1	2	-0	0.1
Cle-A	8	7	.533	29	15	4	0	2	124¹	117	15	54	62	12.6	4.92	80	.251	.332	0	—	0	-15	-14	0	-1.3
Yr	9	8	.529	46	16	4	0	3	163¹	156	19	65	83	12.3	4.63	86	.252	.327	0	—	0	-15	-12	-0	-1.2
1974 Cle-A	1	1	.500	4	0	0	0	0	10	9	1	5	2	12.6	5.40	67	.250	.341	0	—	0	-2	-2	1	0.0
Total 6	35	35	.500	228	44	8	2	35	548	508	42	208	315	12.0	3.78	96	.246	.319	8	.091	-4	-16	-10	-1	-1.2

■ BEN TINCUP — Tincup, Austin Ben b: 12/14/1890, Adair, Okla. d: 7/5/80, Claremore, Okla. BL/TR, 6'1", 180 lbs. Deb: 5/22/14 C♦

YEAR TM/L	W	L	PCT	G	GS	CG	SH	SV	IP	H	HR	BB	SO	RAT	ERA	ERA+	OAV	OOB	BH	AVG	PB	PR	/A	PD	TPI
1914 Phi-N	8	10	.444	28	17	9	3	2	155	165	0	62	108	13.4	2.61	113	.286	.359	9	.170	-1	3	6	0	0.6
1915 Phi-N	0	0	—	10	0	0	0	0	31	26	1	9	10	10.2	2.03	135	.263	.324	0	.000	-1	2	2	1	0.2
1918 Phi-N	0	1	.000	8	1	0	0	0	16²	24	0	6	6	16.2	7.56	40	.329	.380	1	.125	-0	-9	-8	1	-0.7
1928 Chi-N	0	0	—	2	0	0	0	0	9	14	0	1	3	15.0	7.00	55	.378	.395	0	.000	-0	-3	-3	0	-0.2
Total 4	8	11	.421	48	18	9	3	2	211²	229	1	78	127	13.2	3.10	95	.291	.358	10	.135	-3	-6	-3	2	-0.1

■ BUD TINNING — Tinning, Lyle Forrest b: 3/12/06, Pilger, Neb. d: 1/17/61, Evansville, Ind. BB/TR, 5'11", 198 lbs. Deb: 4/20/32

YEAR TM/L	W	L	PCT	G	GS	CG	SH	SV	IP	H	HR	BB	SO	RAT	ERA	ERA+	OAV	OOB	BH	AVG	PB	PR	/A	PD	TPI
1932 *Chi-N	5	3	.625	24	7	2	0	0	93¹	93	3	24	30	11.5	2.80	135	.263	.313	2	.087	-1	11	10	0	0.9
1933 Chi-N	13	6	.684	32	21	10	3	1	175¹	169	3	60	59	12.0	3.18	103	.255	.320	14	.209	1	3	2	-2	0.0
1934 Chi-N	4	6	.400	39	7	1	1	3	129¹	134	9	46	44	12.6	3.34	116	.269	.332	7	.179	-1	10	8	-1	0.6
1935 StL-N	0	0	—	4	0	0	0	0	7²	9	1	5	2	17.6	5.87	70	.300	.417	0	.000	-0	-2	-2	0	-0.1
Total 4	22	15	.595	99	35	13	4	4	405²	405	16	135	135	12.2	3.19	113	.262	.325	23	.177	-1	23	18	-3	1.4

■ DAN TIPPLE — Tipple, Daniel E. "Big Dan" or "Rusty" b: 2/13/1890, Rockford, Ill. d: 3/26/60, Omaha, Neb. BR/TR, 6', 176 lbs. Deb: 9/18/15

YEAR TM/L	W	L	PCT	G	GS	CG	SH	SV	IP	H	HR	BB	SO	RAT	ERA	ERA+	OAV	OOB	BH	AVG	PB	PR	/A	PD	TPI
1915 NY-A	1	1	.500	3	2	2	0	0	19	14	1	11	14	11.8	0.95	309	.203	.313	0	.000	-1	4	4	-1	0.3

■ JACK TISING — Tising, Johnnie Joseph b: 10/9/03, High Point, Mo. d: 9/5/67, Leadville, Ohio BL/TR, 6'2", 180 lbs. Deb: 4/24/36

YEAR TM/L	W	L	PCT	G	GS	CG	SH	SV	IP	H	HR	BB	SO	RAT	ERA	ERA+	OAV	OOB	BH	AVG	PB	PR	/A	PD	TPI
1936 Pit-N	1	3	.250	10	6	1	0	0	47	52	5	24	27	14.6	4.21	96	.272	.353	3	.273	0	-1	-1	-0	0.0

■ CANNONBALL TITCOMB — Titcomb, Ledell b: 8/21/1866, W.Baldwin, Me. d: 6/8/50, Kingston, N.H. BL/TL, 5'6", 157 lbs. Deb: 5/05/1886

YEAR TM/L	W	L	PCT	G	GS	CG	SH	SV	IP	H	HR	BB	SO	RAT	ERA	ERA+	OAV	OOB	BH	AVG	PB	PR	/A	PD	TPI
1886 Phi-N	0	5	.000	5	5	5	0	0	41	43	1	24	24	14.7	3.73	88	.259	.352	1	.063	-2	-2	-2	1	-0.2
1887 Phi-a	1	2	.333	3	3	3	0	0	24	31	1	19	16	18.8	6.00	71	.302	.411	0	.000	-1	-5	-5	-1	-0.4
NY-N	4	3	.571	9	9	9	0	0	72	68	3	37	34	13.1	4.13	91	.242	.331	2	.069	-4	-1	-3	-1	-0.5
1888 *NY-N	14	8	.636	23	23	22	4	0	197	149	4	46	129	8.9	2.24	122	.202	.249	10	.122	-4	13	11	-4	0.2
1889 NY-N	1	2	.333	3	3	3	0	0	26	27	1	16	7	14.9	6.58	60	.259	.358	1	.083	-0	-7	-8	-0	-0.6
1890 Roc-a	10	9	.526	20	19	19	1	0	168²	168	6	97	73	14.1	3.74	95	.252	.347	8	.107	-5	3	-3	-3	-0.9
Total 5	30	29	.508	63	62	61	5	0	528²	486	16	239	283	12.3	3.47	95	.236	.316	22	.098	-16	1	-10	-8	-2.4

■ DAVE TOBIK — Tobik, David Vance b: 3/2/53, Euclid, Ohio BR/TR, 6'1", 190 lbs. Deb: 8/26/78

YEAR TM/L	W	L	PCT	G	GS	CG	SH	SV	IP	H	HR	BB	SO	RAT	ERA	ERA+	OAV	OOB	BH	AVG	PB	PR	/A	PD	TPI
1978 Det-A	0	0	—	5	0	0	0	0	12	12	1	3	11	11.3	3.75	103	.261	.306	0	—	0	0	0	-0	0.0
1979 Det-A	3	5	.375	37	0	0	0	3	68²	59	12	25	48	11.0	4.33	100	.231	.300	0	—	0	-1	-0	-1	0.0
1980 Det-A	1	0	1.000	17	1	0	0	0	61	61	7	21	34	12.1	3.98	103	.266	.328	0	—	0	0	1	-0	0.1
1981 Det-A	2	2	.500	27	0	0	0	1	60¹	47	7	33	32	11.9	2.69	140	.215	.317	0	—	0	7	7	-1	0.6
1982 Det-A	4	9	.308	51	1	0	0	9	98²	86	8	38	63	11.4	3.56	114	.241	.316	0	—	0	6	6	-1	0.5
1983 Tex-A	2	1	.667	27	0	0	0	9	44	36	2	13	30	10.0	3.68	109	.222	.280	0	—	0	2	2	0	0.2
1984 Tex-A	1	6	.143	24	0	0	0	0	42¹	44	5	17	30	13.2	3.61	115	.265	.337	0	—	0	2	2	0	0.3
1985 Sea-A	1	0	1.000	8	0	0	0	1	9	10	2	3	8	13.0	6.00	70	.286	.342	0	—	0	-2	-2	-0	-0.1
Total 8	14	23	.378	196	2	0	0	28	396	355	44	153	256	11.6	3.70	110	.242	.314	0	—	0	13	16	-3	1.6

■ JIM TOBIN — Tobin, James Anthony "Abba Dabba" b: 12/27/12, Oakland, Cal. d: 5/19/69, Oakland, Cal. BR/TR, 6', 185 lbs. Deb: 4/30/37 ♦

YEAR TM/L	W	L	PCT	G	GS	CG	SH	SV	IP	H	HR	BB	SO	RAT	ERA	ERA+	OAV	OOB	BH	AVG	PB	PR	/A	PD	TPI
1937 Pit-N	6	3	.667	20	8	7	0	1	87	74	1	28	37	10.7	3.00	129	.226	.289	15	.441	7	9	8	-2	1.4
1938 Pit-N	14	12	.538	40	33	14	2	0	241¹	254	17	66	70	12.0	3.47	109	.270	.321	25	.243	7	9	9	-1	1.4
1939 Pit-N	9	9	.500	25	19	8	0	0	145¹	194	7	33	43	14.2	4.52	85	.319	.356	18	.243	5	-10	-11	-1	-0.6
1940 Bos-N	7	3	.700	15	11	9	0	0	96¹	102	8	24	29	11.8	3.83	97	.264	.307	12	.300	0	-1	-1	0	0.1
1941 Bos-N	12	12	.500	33	26	20	3	0	238	229	12	60	61	10.9	3.10	115	.253	.300	19	.184	3	14	12	5	2.1
1942 Bos-N	12	21	.364	37	33	**28**	1	0	**287²**	283	20	96	71	12.0	3.97	84	.257	.320	28	.246	14	-21	-20	6	0.0
1943 Bos-N	14	14	.500	33	30	24	1	0	250	241	12	69	54	11.2	2.66	128	.251	.303	30	.280	6	20	21	2	3.6
1944 Bos-N	18	19	.486	43	36	**28**	5	3	299¹	271	18	97	83	11.2	3.01	127	.240	.302	22	.190	6	20	27	7	4.4
1945 Bos-N	9	14	.391	27	25	16	0	0	196²	220	10	56	38	12.9	3.84	100	.282	.334	11	.143	5	-1	-0	3	0.7
*Det-A	4	5	.444	14	6	2	0	1	58¹	61	2	28	14	14.3	3.55	99	.274	.365	3	.120	0	-1	-0	1	0.1
Total 9	105	112	.484	287	227	156	12	5	1900	1929	107	557	498	11.9	3.44	106	.262	.316	183	.230	54	39	45	19	13.2

■ PAT TOBIN — Tobin, Marion Brooks b: 1/28/16, Hermitage, Ark. d: 1/21/75, Shreveport, La. BR/TR, 6'1", 198 lbs. Deb: 8/21/41

YEAR TM/L	W	L	PCT	G	GS	CG	SH	SV	IP	H	HR	BB	SO	RAT	ERA	ERA+	OAV	OOB	BH	AVG	PB	PR	/A	PD	TPI
1941 Phi-A	0	0	—	1	0	0	0	0	1	4	0	2	0	54.0	36.00	12	.571	.667	0	—	0	-4	-4	0	-0.2

■ FRANK TODD — Todd, George Franklin b: 10/18/1869, Aberdeen, Md. d: 8/11/19, Havre De Grace, Md. TL, Deb: 7/14/1898

YEAR TM/L	W	L	PCT	G	GS	CG	SH	SV	IP	H	HR	BB	SO	RAT	ERA	ERA+	OAV	OOB	BH	AVG	PB	PR	/A	PD	TPI
1898 Lou-N	0	2	.000	4	2	0	0	0	11	23	0	8	5	25.4	13.91	26	.422	.496	1	.200	0	-13	-13	-1	-1.0

YEAR TM/L	W	L	PCT	G	GS	CG	SH	SV	IP	H	HR	BB	SO	RAT	ERA	ERA+	OAV	OOB	BH	AVG	PB	PR	/A	PD	TPI

■ JACKSON TODD   Todd, Jackson A   b: 11/20/51, Tulsa, Okla.   BR/TR, 6'2", 180 lbs.   Deb: 5/05/77

1977	NY-N	3	6	.333	19	10	0	0	0	71²	78	8	20	39	12.6	4.77	78	.273	.325	1	.059	-1	-7	-8	0	-0.8
1979	Tor-A	0	1	.000	12	1	0	0	0	32¹	40	7	7	14	13.4	5.85	74	.299	.338	0	—	0	-6	-5	0	-0.4
1980	Tor-A	5	2	.714	12	12	4	0	0	85	90	14	30	44	12.9	4.02	107	.276	.341	0	—	0	0	3	1	0.4
1981	Tor-A	2	7	.222	21	13	3	0	0	97²	94	10	31	41	11.9	3.96	99	.251	.315	0	—	0	-3	-0	1	0.1
Total	4	10	16	.385	64	36	7	0	0	286²	302	39	88	138	12.5	4.40	92	.270	.328	1	.059	-1	-16	-11	2	-0.7

■ JIM TODD   Todd, James Richard   b: 9/21/47, Lancaster, Pa.   BL/TR, 6'2", 190 lbs.   Deb: 4/29/74

1974	Chi-N	4	2	.667	43	6	0	0	3	88	82	7	41	42	12.9	3.89	98	.252	.341	1	.063	-2	-3	-1	1	0.0
1975	*Oak-A	8	3	.727	58	0	0	0	12	122	104	4	33	50	10.3	2.29	159	.234	.292	0	—	0	20	18	4	2.3
1976	Oak-A	7	8	.467	49	0	0	0	4	82²	87	6	34	22	13.8	3.81	88	.276	.358	0	—	0	-3	-4	2	-0.1
1977	Chi-N	1	1	.500	20	0	0	0	0	30²	47	1	19	17	20.0	9.10	48	.336	.422	0	.000	-0	-18	-16	0	-1.4
1978	Sea-A	3	4	.429	49	2	0	0	3	106²	113	4	61	37	14.7	3.88	98	.280	.375	0	—	0	-1	-1	0	0.0
1979	Oak-A	2	5	.286	51	0	0	0	2	81	108	12	51	26	17.9	6.56	62	.329	.423	0	—	0	-21	-23	1	-2.0
Total	6	25	23	.521	270	8	0	0	24	511	541	34	239	194	14.0	4.23	89	.277	.360	1	.059	-2	-25	-26	8	-1.2

■ HAL TOENES   Toenes, William Harrel   b: 10/8/17, Mobile, Ala.   BR/TR, 5'11.5", 175 lbs.   Deb: 9/17/47

| 1947 | Was-A | 0 | 1 | .000 | 3 | 1 | 0 | 0 | 0 | 6² | 11 | 0 | 2 | 5 | 17.6 | 6.75 | 55 | .379 | .419 | 0 | .000 | 0 | -2 | -2 | -0 | -0.1 |

■ FREDDIE TOLIVER   Toliver, Freddie Lee   b: 2/3/61, Natchez, Miss.   BR/TR, 6'1", 165 lbs.   Deb: 9/15/84

1984	Cin-N	0	0	—	3	1	0	0	0	10	7	0	4	4	12.6	0.90	420	.206	.341	0	.000	-0	3	3	-0	0.3
1985	Phi-N	0	4	.000	11	3	0	0	0	25	27	2	17	23	15.8	4.68	79	.273	.379	2	.500	1	-3	-3	-0	-0.1
1986	Phi-N	0	2	.000	5	5	0	0	0	25²	28	0	11	20	13.7	3.51	110	.286	.358	0	.000	-0	1	1	0	0.1
1987	Phi-N	1	1	.500	10	4	0	0	0	30¹	34	2	17	25	15.4	5.64	75	.291	.385	0	.000	-1	-5	-5	-0	-0.4
1988	Min-A	7	6	.538	21	19	0	0	0	114²	116	8	52	69	13.3	4.24	96	.270	.350	0	—	0	-3	-2	0	-0.1
1989	Min-A	1	3	.250	7	5	0	0	0	29	39	2	15	11	17.1	7.76	53	.317	.396	0	—	0	-12	-12	2	-0.9
	SD-N	0	0	—	9	0	0	0	0	14	17	5	9	14	17.4	7.07	49	.321	.429	0	—	0	-6	-6	-0	-0.5
Total	6	9	16	.360	66	37	0	0	1	248²	268	19	128	166	14.5	4.81	83	.281	.368	2	.125	0	-26	-23	2	-1.6

■ DICK TOMANEK   Tomanek, Richard Carl "Bones"   b: 1/6/31, Avon Lake, Ohio   BL/TL, 6'1", 175 lbs.   Deb: 9/25/53

1953	Cle-A	1	0	1.000	1	1	1	0	0	9	6	1	6	6	13.0	2.00	188	.176	.317	0	.000	-1	2	2	-0	0.1
1954	Cle-A	0	0	—	1	0	0	0	0	1²	1	1	1	0	10.8	5.40	68	.167	.286	0	—	0	-0	-0	0	0.0
1957	Cle-A	2	1	.667	34	2	0	0	0	69²	67	13	37	55	13.6	5.68	65	.248	.341	3	.231	0	-15	-15	0	-1.4
1958	Cle-A	2	3	.400	18	6	2	0	0	57²	61	8	28	42	14.2	5.62	65	.276	.363	2	.118	-0	-12	-13	0	-1.1
	KC-A	5	5	.500	36	2	1	0	5	72¹	69	9	28	50	12.1	3.61	108	.252	.321	3	.231	1	1	2	0	0.3
	Yr	7	8	.467	54	8	3	0	5	130	130	13	56	92	12.9	4.50	84	.261	.336	2	.067	1	-11	-10	-0	-0.8
1959	KC-A	0	1	.000	16	0	0	0	2	20²	27	6	12	13	17.9	6.53	61	.310	.406	1	.500	0	-6	-6	-0	-0.4
Total	5	10	10	.500	106	11	4	0	7	231	231	34	112	166	13.6	4.95	77	.259	.346	9	.180	1	-30	-30	0	-2.5

■ ANDY TOMASIC   Tomasic, Andrew John   b: 12/10/19, Hokendauqua, Pa.   BR/TR, 6', 175 lbs.   Deb: 4/28/49

| 1949 | NY-N | 0 | 1 | .000 | 2 | 0 | 0 | 0 | 0 | 5 | 9 | 2 | 5 | 2 | 25.2 | 18.00 | 22 | .375 | .483 | 0 | .000 | -0 | -8 | -8 | -0 | -0.6 |

■ DAVE TOMLIN   Tomlin, David Allen   b: 6/22/49, Maysville, Ky.   BL/TL, 6'2", 180 lbs.   Deb: 9/02/72

1972	Cin-N	0	0	—	3	0	0	0	0	4	7	2	1	2	18.0	9.00	36	.412	.444	0	—	0	-2	-3	0	-0.2
1973	*Cin-N	1	2	.333	16	0	0	0	1	27²	24	5	15	20	12.7	4.88	70	.238	.336	0	.000	-0	-4	-5	0	-0.4
1974	SD-N	2	0	1.000	47	0	0	0	2	58	59	4	30	29	14.1	4.34	82	.271	.364	0	.000	-0	-5	-5	1	-0.4
1975	SD-N	4	2	.667	67	0	0	0	1	83	87	5	31	48	13.0	3.25	107	.275	.344	1	.200	1	3	2	3	0.6
1976	SD-N	0	1	.000	49	1	0	0	0	73	62	4	20	43	10.2	2.84	115	.235	.291	0	.000	-1	5	4	2	0.6
1977	SD-N	4	4	.500	76	0	0	0	3	101²	98	3	32	55	11.7	3.01	118	.259	.320	2	.286	0	10	6	1	0.8
1978	Cin-N	9	1	.900	57	0	0	0	4	62¹	88	3	30	32	17.5	5.78	61	.326	.399	1	.200	0	-15	-15	1	-1.4
1979	*Cin-N	2	2	.500	53	0	0	0	1	58¹	59	3	18	30	12.0	2.62	142	.269	.328	1	.500	1	7	7	0	0.8
1980	Cin-N	3	0	1.000	27	0	0	0	0	26	38	2	11	6	17.0	5.54	65	.355	.415	0	—	0	-6	-6	1	-0.4
1982	Mon-N	0	0	—	1	0	0	0	0	2	1	0	1	2	9.0	4.50	81	.167	.286	0	—	0	-0	-0	0	0.0
1983	Pit-N	0	0	—	5	0	0	0	0	4	6	0	1	5	15.8	6.75	55	.316	.350	0	—	0	-1	-1	0	-0.1
1985	Pit-N	0	0	—	1	0	0	0	0	1	1	0	1	0	18.0	0.00	—	.333	.500	0	—	0	0	0	0	0.0
1986	Mon-N	0	0	—	7	0	0	0	0	10¹	13	1	7	6	18.3	5.23	71	.317	.429	0	—	0	-2	-2	0	-0.1
Total	13	25	12	.676	409	1	0	0	12	511¹	543	32	198	278	13.3	3.82	92	.277	.347	5	.147	1	-9	-17	10	-0.1

■ RANDY TOMLIN   Tomlin, Randy Leon   b: 6/14/66, Bainbridge, Md.   BL/TL, 5'11", 179 lbs.   Deb: 8/06/90

| 1990 | Pit-N | 4 | 4 | .500 | 12 | 12 | 2 | 0 | 0 | 77² | 62 | 5 | 12 | 42 | 8.7 | 2.55 | 142 | .221 | .256 | 1 | .040 | -1 | 11 | 9 | 1 | 1.0 |

■ CHUCK TOMPKINS   Tompkins, Charles Herbert   b: 9/1/1889, Prescott, Ark.   d: 9/20/75, Prescott, Ark.   BR/TR, 6', 185 lbs.   Deb: 6/25/12

| 1912 | Cin-N | 0 | 0 | — | 1 | 0 | 0 | 0 | 0 | 3 | 5 | 0 | 1 | 0 | 15.0 | 0.00 | — | .357 | .357 | 1 | 1.000 | 0 | 1 | 1 | 0 | 0.2 |

■ RON TOMPKINS   Tompkins, Ronald Everett "Stretch"   b: 11/27/44, San Diego, Cal.   BR/TR, 6'4", 198 lbs.   Deb: 9/09/65

1965	KC-A	0	0	—	5	1	0	0	0	10¹	9	0	3	4	11.3	3.48	100	.237	.310	0	.000	-0	-0	0	0	0.0
1971	Chi-N	0	2	.000	35	0	0	0	3	39²	31	3	21	20	12.5	4.08	96	.214	.325	0	—	0	-3	-1	1	0.1
Total	2	0	2	.000	40	1	0	0	3	50	40	3	24	24	12.2	3.96	97	.219	.322	0	.000	-0	-3	-1	1	0.1

■ TOMMY TOMS   Toms, Thomas Howard   b: 10/15/51, Charlottesville, Va   BR/TR, 6'4", 195 lbs.   Deb: 5/04/75

1975	SF-N	0	1	.000	7	0	0	0	0	10¹	13	1	6	6	16.5	6.10	62	.317	.404	0	—	0	-3	-3	0	-0.2
1976	SF-N	0	1	.000	7	0	0	0	1	8²	13	1	1	4	14.5	6.23	58	.351	.368	0	—	0	-3	-3	0	-0.2
1977	SF-N	0	1	.000	4	0	0	0	0	4	7	0	2	2	20.3	2.25	174	.333	.391	0	—	0	1	1	0	0.1
Total	3	0	3	.000	18	0	0	0	1	23	33	2	9	12	16.4	5.48	69	.333	.389	0	—	0	-5	-4	0	-0.3

■ FRED TONEY   Toney, Fred Alexandra   b: 12/11/1888, Nashville, Tenn.   d: 3/11/53, Nashville, Tenn.   BR/TR, 6'1", 195 lbs.   Deb: 4/15/11

1911	Chi-N	1	1	.500	18	4	1	0	0	67	55	2	35	27	12.8	2.42	137	.229	.339	2	.111	-1	7	7	1	0.6
1912	Chi-N	1	2	.333	9	2	0	0	0	24	21	0	11	9	12.4	5.25	63	.239	.330	0	.000	-0	-5	-5	-1	-0.5
1913	Chi-N	2	2	.500	7	5	2	0	0	39	52	1	22	12	17.3	6.00	53	.327	.412	3	.250	1	-12	-12	0	-0.9
1915	Cin-N	17	6	.739	36	23	18	6	2	222²	160	1	73	108	9.5	1.58	181	.207	.278	7	.095	-5	29	32	1	3.2
1916	Cin-N	14	17	.452	41	38	21	3	1	300	247	7	78	146	10.0	2.28	114	.231	.288	12	.121	-4	11	11	-4	0.2
1917	Cin-N	24	16	.600	43	42	31	7	1	339²	300	4	77	123	10.1	2.20	119	.238	.286	13	.112	-6	19	16	-4	0.5
1918	Cin-N	6	10	.375	21	19	9	1	2	136²	148	2	31	32	11.8	2.90	92	.282	.322	9	.214	0	-2	-3	-1	-0.2
	NY-N	6	2	.750	11	9	7	1	1	85¹	55	1	7	19	6.8	1.69	156	.192	.216	6	.188	-1	10	9	-1	0.9
	Yr	12	12	.500	32	28	16	2	3	222	203	3	38	51	9.9	2.43	109	.250	.285	15	.000	-0	8	5	0	0.7
1919	NY-N	13	6	.684	24	20	14	4	1	181	157	6	35	40	9.6	1.84	152	.235	.276	15	.227	1	22	19	-3	2.0
1920	NY-N	21	11	.656	42	37	17	4	1	278¹	266	8	57	81	10.6	2.65	113	.259	.302	23	.240	3	15	11	-2	1.2
1921	*NY-N	18	11	.621	42	32	16	1	3	249¹	274	14	65	63	12.4	3.61	102	.289	.338	18	.209	2	5	2	-1	0.2
1922	NY-N	5	6	.455	13	12	6	0	0	86¹	94	5	31	10	12.9	4.17	96	.277	.343	2	.067	-3	-1	-2	-1	-0.4
1923	StL-N	11	12	.478	29	28	16	1	0	196²	211	8	61	48	12.7	3.84	102	.282	.341	8	.116	-5	3	1	4	0.2
Total	12	139	102	.577	336	271	158	28	12	2206	2037	59	583	718	10.9	2.69	113	.251	.305	118	.159	-17	102	85	-11	6.8

■ DOC TONKIN   Tonkin, Harry Glenville   b: 8/11/1881, Concord, N.H.   d: 5/30/59, Miami, Fla.   BL/TL, 5'9", 165 lbs.   Deb: 8/19/07

| 1907 | Was-A | 0 | 0 | — | 1 | 0 | 0 | 0 | 0 | 2² | 6 | 0 | 5 | 0 | 37.1 | 6.75 | 36 | .444 | .594 | 2 | 1.000 | 1 | -1 | -1 | 0 | 0.0 |

YEAR	TM/L	W	L	PCT	G	GS	CG	SH	SV	IP	H	HR	BB	SO	RAT	ERA	ERA+	OAV	OOB	BH	AVG	PB	PR	/A	PD	TPI

■ STEVE TOOLE
Toole, Stephen John b: 4/9/1859, New Orleans, La. d: 3/28/19, Pittsburgh, Pa. BR/TL, 6', 170 lbs. Deb: 4/20/1886 U

1886	Bro-a	6	6	.500	13	12	11	0	0	104	100	0	64	48	14.2	4.41	79	.241	.343	20	.351	4	-11	-11	2	-0.3
1887	Bro-a	14	10	.583	24	24	22	1	0	194	186	1	106	48	13.5	4.31	100	.243	.335	24	.233	-1	-0	-0	-1	0.0
1888	KC-a	5	6	.455	12	10	10	0	0	91²	124	4	50	35	17.1	6.68	51	.312	.389	10	.208	-0	-37	-33	0	-2.5
1890	Bro-a	2	4	.333	6	6	6	0	0	53¹	47	0	39	10	14.5	4.05	96	.229	.353	6	.300	1	-1	-1	1	0.1
Total	4	27	26	.509	55	52	49	1	0	443	457	5	259	141	14.5	4.79	81	.256	.351	60	.263	5	-49	-44	2	-2.7

■ RUPE TOPPIN
Toppin, Ruperto b: 12/7/41, Panama City, Panama BR/TR, 6', 185 lbs. Deb: 7/28/62

| 1962 | KC-A | 0 | 0 | — | 2 | 0 | 0 | 0 | 0 | 2 | 1 | 0 | 5 | 1 | 27.0 | 13.50 | 31 | .167 | .545 | 1 | 1.000 | 0 | -2 | -2 | 0 | -0.1 |

■ RED TORKELSON
Torkelson, Chester Leroy b: 3/19/1894, Chicago, Ill. d: 9/22/64, Chicago, Ill. BR/TR, 6', 175 lbs. Deb: 8/29/17

| 1917 | Cle-A | 2 | 1 | .667 | 4 | 3 | 0 | 0 | 0 | 22¹ | 33 | 1 | 13 | 10 | 19.3 | 7.66 | 37 | .333 | .421 | 2 | .222 | -0 | -12 | -12 | 0 | -1.0 |

■ PABLO TORREALBA
Torrealba, Pablo Arnoldo (Torrealba) b: 4/28/48, Barquisimento, Ven. BL/TL, 5'10", 173 lbs. Deb: 4/09/75

1975	Atl-N	0	1	.000	6	0	0	0	0	6²	7	0	3	5	13.5	1.35	279	.250	.323	1	1.000	0	2	2	0	0.3
1976	Atl-N	0	2	.000	36	0	0	0	2	53	67	0	22	33	15.6	3.57	106	.315	.387	0	.000	-0	-0	1	1	0.2
1977	Oak-A	4	6	.400	41	10	3	0	2	116²	127	5	38	51	12.9	2.62	153	.279	.337	0	—	0	19	18	2	2.0
1978	Chi-A	2	4	.333	25	3	1	1	1	57¹	69	6	39	23	17.4	4.71	81	.301	.410	0	—	0	-6	-6	-1	-0.6
1979	Chi-A	0	0	—	3	0	0	0	0	5²	5	1	2	1	11.1	1.59	268	.250	.318	0	—	0	2	2	0	0.2
Total	5	6	13	.316	111	13	4	1	5	239¹	275	12	104	113	14.6	3.27	120	.291	.366	1	.200	-0	16	17	2	2.1

■ ANGEL TORRES
Torres, Angel Rafael (Ruiz) b: 10/24/52, Las Ciengas, Azua, D.R. BL/TL, 5'11", 168 lbs. Deb: 9/12/77

| 1977 | Cin-N | 0 | 0 | — | 5 | 0 | 0 | 0 | 0 | 8¹ | 7 | 2 | 8 | 8 | 16.2 | 2.16 | 182 | .233 | .395 | 0 | — | 0 | 2 | 2 | 0 | 0.2 |

■ GIL TORRES
Torres, Don Gilberto (Nunez) b: 8/23/15, Regla, Cuba d: 1/11/83, Regla, Cuba BR/TR, 6', 155 lbs. Deb: 4/25/40 ♦

1940	Was-A	0	0	—	2	0	0	0	0	2²	3	0	0	1	10.1	0.00	—	.273	.273	0	—	0	1	1	0	0.1
1946	Was-A	0	0	—	3	0	0	0	1	7	9	0	3	2	15.4	7.71	43	.310	.375	47	.254	1	-3	-3	-0	-0.2
Total	2	0	0	—	5	0	0	0	1	9²	12	0	3	3	14.0	5.59	64	.300	.349	320	.252	1	-2	-2	0	-0.1

■ HECTOR TORRES
Torres, Hector Epitacio (Marroquin) b: 9/16/45, Monterrey, Mexico BR/TR, 6', 175 lbs. Deb: 4/10/68 ♦

| 1972 | Mon-N | 0 | 0 | — | 1 | 0 | 0 | 0 | 0 | 0² | 5 | 0 | 0 | 0 | 67.5 | 27.00 | 13 | .714 | .714 | 28 | .155 | 0 | -2 | -2 | 0 | -0.1 |

■ MIKE TORREZ
Torrez, Michael Augustine b: 8/28/46, Topeka, Kan. BR/TR, 6'5", 220 lbs. Deb: 9/10/67

1967	StL-N	0	1	.000	3	1	0	0	0	5²	5	0	1	5	11.1	3.18	103	.238	.304	0	.000	-0	0	0	-0	0.0
1968	StL-N	2	1	.667	5	2	0	0	0	19¹	20	1	12	6	15.4	2.79	104	.286	.398	2	.286	0	0	0	0	0.1
1969	StL-N	10	4	.714	24	15	3	0	0	107²	96	7	62	61	13.5	3.59	99	.240	.346	3	.073	-2	-0	-0	1	-0.1
1970	StL-N	8	10	.444	30	28	5	1	0	179¹	168	12	103	100	13.8	4.22	98	.248	.350	17	.270	4	-3	-2	-0	0.2
1971	StL-N	1	2	.333	9	6	0	0	0	36	41	2	30	8	18.0	6.00	60	.304	.434	1	.143	1	-10	-10	0	-0.7
	Mon-N	0	0	—	1	0	0	0	0	3	4	0	1	2	15.0	0.00	—	.308	.357	0	—	0	1	1	0	0.2
	Yr	1	2	.333	10	6	0	0	0	39	45	2	31	10	17.5	5.54	65	.300	.420	3	.429	1	-9	-8	1	-0.5
1972	Mon-N	16	12	.571	34	33	13	0	0	243¹	215	15	103	112	12.0	3.33	107	.242	.325	15	.176	0	3	6	3	1.0
1973	Mon-N	9	12	.429	35	34	3	1	0	208	207	17	115	90	14.1	4.46	86	.262	.359	12	.174	-1	-18	-15	2	-1.2
1974	Mon-N	15	8	.652	32	30	6	1	0	186¹	184	16	84	92	13.1	3.57	107	.257	.337	8	.125	-3	1	5	5	0.8
1975	Bal-A	20	9	.690	36	36	16	2	0	270²	238	15	133	119	12.5	3.06	115	.239	.332	0	—	0	22	14	1	1.5
1976	Oak-A	16	12	.571	39	39	13	4	0	266¹	231	15	87	115	10.9	2.50	134	.235	.301	0	—	0	30	25	-1	2.7
1977	Oak-A	3	1	.750	4	4	2	0	0	26¹	23	3	11	12	12.0	4.44	91	.242	.327	0	—	0	-1	-1	0	0.0
	*NY-A	14	12	.538	31	31	15	2	0	217	212	20	75	90	12.2	3.82	103	.259	.326	0	—	0	6	3	-1	0.1
	Yr	17	13	.567	35	35	17	2	0	243¹	235	23	86	102	12.1	3.88	102	.256	.324	0	—	0	5	2	-1	0.1
1978	Bos-A	16	13	.552	36	36	15	2	0	250	272	19	99	120	13.5	3.96	104	.281	.349	0	—	0	-6	4	2	0.2
1979	Bos-A	16	13	.552	36	36	12	1	0	252¹	254	20	121	125	13.6	4.49	98	.264	.349	0	—	0	-8	-2	-0	-0.1
1980	Bos-A	9	16	.360	36	32	6	1	0	207¹	256	18	75	97	14.4	5.08	83	.313	.371	0	—	0	-24	-20	2	-1.7
1981	Bos-A	10	3	.769	22	22	6	1	0	127¹	130	11	51	54	12.8	3.68	105	.267	.337	0	—	0	0	3	1	0.2
1982	Bos-A	9	9	.500	31	31	1	0	0	175²	196	20	74	84	14.1	5.23	82	.282	.356	0	—	0	-22	-18	-2	-1.8
1983	NY-N	10	17	.370	39	34	5	0	0	222¹	227	16	113	94	13.8	4.37	83	.271	.358	3	.046	-5	-18	-18	1	-2.2
1984	NY-N	1	5	.167	9	8	0	0	0	37²	55	3	18	16	17.9	5.02	70	.369	.444	3	.300	1	-6	-6	0	-0.4
	Oak-A	0	0	—	2	0	0	0	0	2¹	5	0	9	3	46.3	27.00	14	.563	.632	0	—	0	-1	-1	0	-0.1
Total	18	185	160	.536	494	458	117	15	0	3044	3043	223	1371	1404	13.2	3.96	97	.264	.345	64	.155	-4	-60	-38	8	-1.6

■ LOU TOST
Tost, Louis Eugene b: 6/1/11, Cumberland, Wash. d: 2/22/67, Santa Clara, Cal. BL/TL, 6', 175 lbs. Deb: 4/20/42

1942	Bos-N	10	10	.500	35	22	5	1	0	147²	146	12	52	43	12.3	3.53	94	.256	.322	9	.176	0	-4	-3	-1	-0.4
1943	Bos-N	0	1	.000	3	1	0	0	0	6²	10	2	4	3	18.9	5.40	63	.357	.438	0	.000	-0	-1	-1	0	-0.1
1947	Pit-N	0	0	—	1	0	0	0	0	1	3	0	0	0	27.0	9.00	47	.600	.600	0	—	0	-1	-1	0	0.0
Total	3	10	11	.476	39	23	5	1	0	155¹	159	14	56	46	12.7	3.65	92	.263	.330	9	.173	-0	-6	-5	-1	-0.5

■ PAUL TOTH
Toth, Paul Louis b: 6/30/35, McRoberts, Ky. BR/TR, 6'1", 175 lbs. Deb: 4/22/62

1962	StL-N	1	0	1.000	6	1	0	0	0	16²	18	1	4	5	11.9	5.40	79	.295	.338	2	.400	1	-3	-2	-0	-0.1
	Chi-N	3	1	.750	6	4	1	0	0	34	29	2	10	11	10.9	4.24	98	.240	.308	2	.182	0	-1	-0	0	0.0
	Yr	4	1	.800	12	5	2	0	0	50²	47	3	14	16	11.2	4.62	91	.257	.317	1	.063	1	-4	-2	-0	-0.1
1963	Chi-N	5	9	.357	27	14	3	2	0	130¹	115	9	35	66	10.5	3.10	113	.240	.294	1	.026	-3	3	6	-1	0.2
1964	Chi-N	0	2	.000	4	2	0	0	0	10²	15	2	5	0	16.9	8.44	44	.341	.408	1	.333	0	-6	-6	0	-0.4
Total	3	9	12	.429	43	21	5	2	0	192	177	14	54	82	11.0	3.80	97	.251	.308	6	.103	-2	-7	-2	-1	-0.3

■ CLAY TOUCHSTONE
Touchstone, Clayland Maffitt b: 1/24/03, Moore, Pa. d: 4/28/49, Beaumont, Tex. BR/TR, 5'9", 175 lbs. Deb: 9/04/28

1928	Bos-N	0	0	—	5	0	0	0	0	8	15	0	2	1	20.3	4.50	87	.417	.462	0	.000	-0	-0	-1	0	0.0
1929	Bos-N	0	0	—	1	0	0	0	0	2²	6	1	0	1	20.3	16.88	28	.429	.429	1	1.000	0	-4	-4	-0	-0.2
1945	Chi-A	0	0	—	6	0	0	0	0	10	14	1	6	4	18.9	5.40	61	.311	.404	0	.000	-0	-2	-2	0	-0.2
Total	3	0	0	—	12	0	0	0	0	20²	35	2	8	6	19.6	6.53	57	.368	.429	1	.250	0	-6	-6	0	-0.4

■ CESAR TOVAR
Tovar, Cesar Leonardo "Pepito" (b: Cesar Leonard Perez (Tovar)) b: 7/3/40, Caracas, Venez. BR/TR, 5'9", 155 lbs. Deb: 4/12/65 ♦

| 1968 | Min-A | 0 | 0 | — | 1 | 1 | 0 | 0 | 0 | 1 | 0 | 0 | 1 | 0 | 9.0 | 0.00 | — | .000 | .250 | 167 | .272 | 0 | 0 | 0 | 0 | 0.0 |

■ IRA TOWNSEND
Townsend, Ira Dance "Pat" b: 1/9/1894, Weimar, Tex. d: 7/21/65, Schulenberg, Tex. BR/TR, 6'1", 180 lbs. Deb: 8/25/20

1920	Bos-N	0	0	—	4	1	0	0	0	6²	10	0	2	1	17.6	1.35	226	.370	.433	0	.000	-0	1	1	0	0.1
1921	Bos-N	0	0	—	4	0	0	0	0	7¹	11	1	4	0	20.9	6.14	59	.344	.447	0	.000	-0	-2	-2	0	-0.1
Total	2	0	0	—	8	1	0	0	0	14	21	1	6	1	19.3	3.86	87	.356	.441	0	.000	-1	-1	-1	0	0.0

■ HAPPY TOWNSEND
Townsend, John b: 4/9/1879, Townsend, Del. d: 12/21/63, Wilmington, Del. BR/TR, 6', 190 lbs. Deb: 4/19/01

1901	Phi-N	9	6	.600	19	16	14	2	0	143²	118	3	64	72	11.7	3.45	99	.223	.312	7	.109	-4	-2	-1	-2	-0.6
1902	Was-A	9	16	.360	27	26	22	0	0	220¹	233	12	89	71	13.2	4.45	83	.272	.340	23	.264	3	-21	-18	-1	-1.4
1903	Was-A	2	11	.154	20	13	10	0	0	126²	145	3	48	54	13.7	4.76	66	.286	.348	2	.045	-4	-25	-23	0	-2.5
1904	Was-A	5	26	.161	36	34	31	2	0	291¹	319	3	100	143	12.9	3.58	74	.279	.337	20	.168	-2	-32	-30	-2	-3.5
1905	Was-A	7	16	.304	34	24	22	0	0	263	247	2	84	102	11.3	2.63	101	.250	.308	15	.181	1	1	1	-3	-0.1
1906	Cle-A	3	7	.300	17	12	8	1	0	92²	92	1	31	31	11.9	2.91	90	.262	.322	4	.133	-1	-2	-3	0	-0.4
Total	6	35	82	.299	153	125	107	5	0	1137²	1154	24	416	473	12.5	3.59	84	.264	.328	71	.166	-8	-82	-75	-8	-8.5

YEAR TM/L	W	L	PCT	G	GS	CG	SH	SV	IP	H	HR	BB	SO	RAT	ERA	ERA+	OAV	OOB	BH	AVG	PB	PR	/A	PD	TPI

■ LEO TOWNSEND Townsend, Leo Alphonse "Lefty" b: 1/15/1891, Mobile, Ala. d: 12/3/76, Mobile, Ala. BL/TL, 5'10", 160 lbs. Deb: 9/08/20

1920 Bos-N	2	2	.500	7	1	1	0	0	24¹	18	1	2	0	7.4	1.48	206	.220	.238	1	.167	0	4	4	0	0.5
1921 Bos-N	0	1	.000	1	1	0	0	0	1¹	2	0	3	0	33.8	27.00	14	.400	.625	0	—	0	-3	-3	0	-0.2
Total 2	2	3	.400	8	2	1	0	0	25²	20	1	5	0	8.8	2.81	110	.230	.272	1	.167	0	1	1	1	0.3

■ BILL TOZER Tozer, William Louis b: 7/3/1882, St.Louis, Mo. d: 2/23/55, Belmont, Cal. BR/TR, 6', 200 lbs. Deb: 4/16/08

| 1908 Cin-N | 0 | 0 | — | 4 | 0 | 0 | 0 | 0 | 10² | 11 | 0 | 4 | 5 | 13.5 | 1.69 | 137 | .268 | .348 | 0 | .000 | -0 | 1 | 1 | 0 | 0.1 |

■ FRED TRAUTMAN Trautman, Frederick Orlando b: 3/24/1892, Bucyrus, Ohio d: 2/15/64, Bucyrus, Ohio BR/TR, 6'1", 175 lbs. Deb: 4/27/15

| 1915 New-F | 0 | 0 | — | 1 | 0 | 0 | 0 | 0 | 3 | 4 | 0 | 1 | 2 | 18.0 | 6.00 | 47 | .328 | .422 | 0 | .000 | -0 | -1 | -1 | -0 | 0.0 |

■ JOHN TRAUTWEIN Trautwein, John Howard b: 8/7/62, Lafayette Hills, Pa. BR/TR, 6'3", 205 lbs. Deb: 4/07/88

| 1988 Bos-A | 0 | 1 | .000 | 9 | 0 | 0 | 0 | 0 | 16 | 26 | 2 | 9 | 8 | 20.3 | 9.00 | 46 | .382 | .462 | 0 | — | 0 | -9 | -9 | 0 | -0.7 |

■ ALLAN TRAVERS Travers, Aloysius Joseph "Joe" b: 5/7/1892, Philadelphia, Pa. d: 4/19/68, Philadelphia, Pa. BR/TR, 6'1", 180 lbs. Deb: 5/18/12

| 1912 Det-A | 0 | 1 | .000 | 1 | 1 | 1 | 0 | 0 | 8 | 26 | 0 | 7 | 1 | 37.1 | 15.75 | 21 | .605 | .660 | 0 | .000 | -0 | -11 | -11 | 1 | -0.6 |

■ BILL TRAVERS Travers, William Edward b: 10/27/52, Norwood, Mass. BL/TL, 6'4", 187 lbs. Deb: 5/19/74

1974 Mil-A	2	3	.400	23	1	0	0	0	53	59	6	30	31	15.3	4.92	73	.296	.391	0	—	0	-8	-8	0	-0.7
1975 Mil-A	6	11	.353	28	23	5	0	1	136¹	130	15	60	57	13.3	4.29	89	.252	.342	0	—	0	-8	-7	-1	-0.7
1976 Mil-A	15	16	.484	34	34	15	3	0	240	211	21	95	120	11.8	2.81	124	.237	.316	0	—	0	19	18	-1	1.9
1977 Mil-A	4	12	.250	19	19	2	1	0	121²	140	13	57	49	15.1	5.25	77	.291	.374	0	—	0	-16	-16	0	-1.4
1978 Mil-A	12	11	.522	28	28	8	3	0	175²	184	20	58	66	12.7	4.41	85	.268	.331	0	—	0	-13	-13	1	-1.1
1979 Mil-A	14	8	.636	30	27	9	2	0	187¹	196	33	45	74	11.7	3.89	107	.270	.315	0	—	0	7	6	1	0.4
1980 Mil-A	12	6	.667	29	25	7	1	0	154¹	147	20	47	62	11.7	3.91	99	.249	.311	0	—	0	2	-1	-1	0.0
1981 Cal-A	0	1	.000	4	4	0	0	0	9²	14	2	4	5	16.8	8.38	44	.333	.391	0	—	0	-5	-5	0	-0.4
1983 Cal-A	0	3	.000	10	7	0	0	0	42²	58	4	19	24	16.7	5.91	68	.331	.403	0	—	0	-9	-9	0	-0.7
Total 9	65	71	.478	205	168	46	10	1	1120²	1139	134	415	488	12.8	4.10	93	.265	.335	0	—	0	-30	-34	-2	-2.7

■ HARRY TREKELL Trekell, Harry Roy b: 11/18/1892, Breda, Ill. d: 11/4/65, Spokane, Wash. BR/TR, 6'1.5", 170 lbs. Deb: 8/16/13

| 1913 StL-N | 0 | 1 | .000 | 7 | 1 | 1 | 0 | 0 | 30 | 25 | 2 | 8 | 15 | 10.5 | 4.50 | 72 | .221 | .285 | 1 | .111 | -0 | -4 | -4 | -0 | -0.4 |

■ BILL TREMEL Tremel, William Leonard "Mumbles" b: 7/4/29, Lilly, Pa. BR/TR, 5'11", 180 lbs. Deb: 6/12/54

1954 Chi-N	1	2	.333	33	0	0	0	4	51¹	45	3	28	21	12.8	4.21	100	.243	.343	2	.250	0	-1	-0	-1	0.0
1955 Chi-N	3	0	1.000	23	0	0	0	2	38²	33	2	18	13	11.9	3.72	110	.239	.327	2	.286	0	1	2	-0	0.2
1956 Chi-N	0	0	—	1	0	0	0	0	1	3	0	0	0	27.0	9.00	42	.600	.600	0	—	0	-1	-1	0	0.0
Total 3	4	2	.667	57	0	0	0	6	91	81	5	46	34	12.6	4.05	102	.247	.340	4	.267	1	-0	1	-1	0.2

■ BOB TRICE Trice, Robert Lee b: 8/28/26, Newton, Ga. d: 9/16/88, Weirton, W.Va. BR/TR, 6'3", 190 lbs. Deb: 9/13/53

1953 Phi-A	2	1	.667	3	3	1	0	0	23	25	4	6	4	12.1	5.48	78	.275	.320	1	.143	0	-4	-3	1	-0.1
1954 Phi-A	7	8	.467	19	18	8	1	0	119	146	14	48	22	14.7	5.60	70	.305	.369	12	.286	5	-25	-22	1	-1.6
1955 KC-A	0	0	—	4	0	0	0	0	10	14	4	6	2	18.0	9.00	46	.326	.408	2	.667	1	-6	-5	1	-0.3
Total 3	9	9	.500	26	21	9	1	0	152	185	22	60	28	14.5	5.80	69	.302	.365	15	.288	5	-34	-31	3	-2.0

■ JOE TRIMBLE Trimble, Joseph Gerard b: 10/12/30, Providence, R.I. BR/TR, 6'1", 190 lbs. Deb: 4/29/55

1955 Bos-A	0	0	—	2	0	0	0	0	2	0	0	3	1	13.5	0.00	—	.000	.375	0	—	0	1	1	0	0.1
1957 Pit-N	0	2	.000	5	4	0	0	0	19²	23	7	13	9	16.9	8.24	46	.291	.398	1	.143	-0	-10	-10	0	-0.8
Total 2	0	2	.000	7	4	0	0	0	21²	23	7	16	10	16.6	7.48	51	.274	.396	1	.143	-0	-9	-9	0	-0.7

■ KEN TRINKLE Trinkle, Kenneth Wayne b: 12/15/19, Paoli, Ind. d: 5/10/76, Paoli, Ind. BR/TR, 6'1.5", 175 lbs. Deb: 4/25/43

1943 NY-N	1	5	.167	11	6	1	0	0	45²	51	3	15	10	13.2	3.74	92	.276	.333	3	.250	1	-2	-2	2	0.1
1946 NY-N	7	14	.333	48	13	2	0	2	151	146	8	74	49	13.2	3.87	89	.253	.340	3	.079	-2	-8	-7	0	-0.9
1947 NY-N	8	4	.667	62	0	0	0	10	93²	100	3	48	37	14.3	3.75	109	.278	.364	3	.188	-0	3	3	2	0.5
1948 NY-N	4	5	.444	53	0	0	0	7	70²	66	6	41	20	14.0	3.18	124	.244	.350	2	.250	-0	6	6	1	0.8
1949 Phi-N	1	1	.500	42	0	0	0	2	74¹	79	3	30	14	13.6	4.00	99	.299	.377	0	.000	-0	0	0	2	0.1
Total 5	21	29	.420	216	19	3	0	21	435¹	442	23	208	130	13.6	3.74	100	.267	.352	11	.138	-2	0	0	6	0.6

■ RICH TROEDSON Troedson, Richard La Monte b: 5/1/50, Palo Alto, Cal. BL/TL, 6'1", 170 lbs. Deb: 4/09/73

1973 SD-N	7	9	.438	50	18	2	0	1	152¹	167	12	59	81	13.4	4.25	82	.284	.351	7	.175	0	-10	-13	2	-1.1
1974 SD-N	1	1	.500	15	1	0	0	1	18²	24	6	8	11	15.9	8.68	41	.300	.371	0	.000	-0	-10	-11	0	-0.9
Total 2	8	10	.444	65	19	2	0	2	171	191	18	67	92	13.7	4.74	73	.286	.353	7	.171	-0	-21	-24	2	-2.0

■ HAL TROSKY Trosky, Harold Arthur Jr. "Hoot" (b: Harold Arthur Troyavesky Jr.) b: 9/29/36, Cleveland, Ohio BR/TR, 6'3", 205 lbs. Deb: 9/25/58

| 1958 Chi-A | 1 | 0 | 1.000 | 2 | 0 | 0 | 0 | 0 | 3 | 5 | 0 | 2 | 1 | 21.0 | 6.00 | 61 | .385 | .467 | 0 | — | 0 | -1 | -1 | 0 | 0.0 |

■ BILL TROTTER Trotter, William Felix b: 8/10/08, Cisne, Ill. d: 8/26/84, Arlington, Mass. BR/TR, 6'2", 195 lbs. Deb: 4/23/37

1937 StL-A	2	9	.182	34	12	3	0	1	122¹	150	14	50	37	15.2	5.81	83	.304	.376	1	.030	-3	-16	-13	-1	-1.5
1938 StL-A	0	1	.000	1	1	1	0	0	8	8	0	0	1	9.0	5.63	88	.242	.242	0	.000	-0	-1	-1	1	0.0
1939 StL-A	6	13	.316	41	13	4	0	0	156²	205	16	54	61	15.2	5.34	91	.318	.376	4	.108	-1	-13	-8	-1	-0.7
1940 StL-A	7	6	.538	36	4	1	0	2	98	117	5	31	29	13.7	3.77	122	.300	.353	1	.045	-2	7	9	1	0.7
1941 StL-A	4	2	.667	29	0	0	0	0	49²	68	2	19	17	16.1	5.98	72	.332	.394	0	.000	-1	-10	-9	1	-0.8
1942 StL-A	0	1	.000	3	0	0	0	0	2	5	0	2	0	31.5	18.00	21	.385	.467	0	—	0	-3	-3	0	-0.2
Was-A	3	1	.750	17	0	0	0	0	40²	52	4	14	13	14.6	5.75	63	.304	.357	0	.000	-0	-9	-9	0	-0.8
Yr	3	2	.600	20	0	0	0	0	42²	57	4	16	13	15.4	6.33	58	.310	.365	2	.250	-0	-13	-13	1	-1.0
1944 StL-N	0	1	.000	2	1	0	0	0	6	14	5	4	0	27.0	13.50	26	.467	.529	0	.000	-0	-7	-7	0	-0.5
Total 7	22	34	.393	163	31	9	0	3	483¹	619	46	174	158	15.0	5.40	85	.313	.373	6	.055	-7	-52	-42	2	-3.8

■ DIZZY TROUT Trout, Paul Howard b: 6/29/15, Sandcut, Ind. d: 2/28/72, Harvey, Ill. BR/TR, 6'2.5", 195 lbs. Deb: 4/25/39

1939 Det-A	9	10	.474	33	22	6	0	2	162	168	7	74	72	13.7	3.61	135	.270	.351	12	.211	-0	18	23	-1	2.1
1940 *Det-A	3	7	.300	33	10	1	0	2	100²	125	4	54	64	16.3	4.47	106	.307	.392	4	.129	-2	-1	3	2	0.3
1941 Det-A	9	9	.500	37	18	6	1	2	151²	144	7	84	88	13.6	3.74	122	.252	.350	9	.180	0	7	14	1	1.5
1942 Det-A	12	18	.400	35	29	13	1	0	223	214	15	89	91	12.4	3.43	115	.249	.322	16	.213	2	6	13	4	2.1
1943 Det-A	20	12	.625	44	30	18	5	6	246²	204	6	101	111	11.1	2.48	142	.227	.305	20	.220	2	22	29	4	4.1
1944 Det-A	27	14	.659	49	40	33	7	0	352¹	314	6	83	144	10.2	2.12	168	.237	.284	36	.271	12	51	57	7	8.9
1945 *Det-A	18	15	.545	41	31	18	4	2	246¹	252	8	79	97	12.1	3.14	112	.267	.324	25	.245	4	6	10	4	2.0
1946 Det-A	17	13	.567	38	32	23	5	3	276¹	244	11	97	151	11.2	2.34	156	.236	.306	20	.194	3	36	40	4	5.5
1947 Det-A	10	11	.476	32	26	9	2	2	186¹	186	6	65	74	12.3	3.48	108	.261	.325	11	.162	3	5	6	4	1.4
1948 Det-A	10	14	.417	32	23	11	2	2	183²	193	6	73	91	13.1	3.43	127	.269	.338	15	.217	2	18	19	2	2.3
1949 Det-A	3	6	.333	33	0	0	0	0	59¹	68	7	21	19	13.5	4.40	95	.292	.350	2	.143	0	-1	-2	2	0.0
1950 Det-A	13	5	.722	34	20	11	1	4	184²	190	13	64	88	12.6	3.75	125	.267	.332	12	.190	1	17	19	3	2.3
1951 Det-A	9	14	.391	42	22	7	0	5	191²	172	13	75	89	11.6	4.04	103	.240	.312	14	.269	5	2	3	4	1.2
1952 Det-A	1	5	.167	10	2	0	0	1	27	30	4	19	20	16.3	5.33	71	.286	.395	3	.333	1	-5	-5	1	-0.2
Bos-A	9	8	.529	26	17	2	0	1	133²	133	8	68	57	13.7	3.84	108	.263	.354	6	.136	-1	1	5	1	0.5
Yr	10	13	.435	36	19	2	0	2	160²	163	7	87	77	14.2	3.92	100	.267	.361	1	.019	-1	-4	-0	2	0.3
1957 Bal-A	0	0	—	2	0	0	0	0	0¹	4	0	0	0	108.0	81.00	4	.800	.800	0	—	0	-3	-3	0	-0.2
Total 15	170	161	.514	521	322	158	28	35	2725²	2641	112	1046	1256	12.3	3.23	124	.255	.325	205	.213	32	177	232	39	33.8

■ STEVE TROUT
Trout, Steven Russell b: 7/30/57, Detroit, Mich. BL/TL, 6'4", 195 lbs. Deb: 7/01/78

YEAR TM/L	W	L	PCT	G	GS	CG	SH	SV	IP	H	HR	BB	SO	RAT	ERA	ERA+	OAV	OOB	BH	AVG	PB	PR	/A	PD	TPI
1978 Chi-A	3	0	1.000	4	3	1	0	0	22¹	19	0	11	11	12.1	4.03	94	.229	.319	0	—	0	-1	-1	0	0.0
1979 Chi-A	11	8	.579	34	18	6	2	4	155	165	10	59	76	13.3	3.89	109	.273	.343	0	—	0	6	6	2	0.8
1980 Chi-A	9	16	.360	32	30	7	2	0	199²	229	14	49	89	12.9	3.70	109	.290	.338	0	—	0	8	7	3	1.0
1981 Chi-A	8	7	.533	20	18	3	0	0	124²	122	7	38	54	11.8	3.47	103	.261	.322	0	—	0	3	2	1	0.2
1982 Chi-A	6	9	.400	25	19	2	0	0	120¹	130	9	50	62	13.6	4.26	95	.273	.344	0	—	0	-3	-3	0	-0.2
1983 Chi-N	10	14	.417	34	32	1	0	0	180	217	13	59	80	13.9	4.65	82	.305	.360	12	.194	1	-20	-17	3	-1.3
1984 *Chi-N	13	7	.650	32	31	6	2	0	190	205	7	59	81	12.6	3.41	115	.285	.341	8	.131	-1	4	10	4	1.5
1985 Chi-N	9	7	.563	24	24	3	1	0	140²	142	8	63	44	13.2	3.39	118	.270	.350	5	.109	-2	3	9	3	1.2
1986 Chi-N	5	7	.417	37	25	0	0	0	161	184	6	78	69	14.7	4.75	85	.298	.378	9	.209	1	-19	-13	1	-0.9
1987 Chi-N	6	3	.667	11	11	3	2	0	75	72	3	27	32	12.0	3.00	143	.260	.328	4	.154	-1	9	11	1	1.1
NY-A	0	4	.000	14	9	0	0	0	46¹	51	4	37	27	17.3	6.60	66	.274	.397	0	—	0	-11	-11	0	-0.9
1988 Sea-A	4	7	.364	15	13	0	0	0	56¹	86	6	31	14	19.5	7.83	53	.361	.445	0	—	0	-24	-23	0	-2.0
1989 Sea-A	4	3	.571	19	3	0	0	0	30	43	3	17	17	18.0	6.60	61	.333	.411	0	—	0	-9	-9	0	-0.7
Total 12	88	92	.489	301	236	32	9	4	1501¹	1665	90	578	656	13.6	4.18	96	.286	.354	38	.160	-2	-55	-30	17	-0.2

■ BOB TROWBRIDGE
Trowbridge, Robert b: 6/27/30, Hudson, N.Y. d: 4/3/80, Hudson, N.Y. BR/TR, 6'1", 180 lbs. Deb: 4/22/56

YEAR TM/L	W	L	PCT	G	GS	CG	SH	SV	IP	H	HR	BB	SO	RAT	ERA	ERA+	OAV	OOB	BH	AVG	PB	PR	/A	PD	TPI
1956 Mil-N	3	2	.600	19	4	1	0	0	50²	38	4	34	40	13.1	2.66	130	.210	.341	0	.000	-0	6	4	0	0.4
1957 *Mil-N	7	5	.583	32	16	3	1	1	126	118	9	52	75	12.2	3.64	96	.248	.323	4	.103	-1	3	-2	-1	-0.4
1958 Mil-N	1	3	.250	27	4	0	0	0	55	53	4	26	31	13.1	3.93	90	.252	.338	1	.111	-0	0	-2	-1	-0.3
1959 Mil-N	1	0	1.000	16	0	0	0	1	30¹	45	2	10	22	16.3	5.93	60	.344	.390	0	.000	-0	-7	-8	-0	-0.8
1960 KC-A	1	3	.250	22	1	0	0	2	68¹	70	6	34	33	13.8	4.61	86	.281	.370	1	.056	-1	-6	-5	0	-0.5
Total 5	13	13	.500	116	25	4	1	5	330¹	324	25	156	201	13.2	3.95	91	.260	.344	6	.078	-4	-3	-13	-1	-1.6

■ BUN TROY
Troy, Robert b: 8/22/1888, Germany d: 10/7/18, Meuse, France BR/TR, 6'4", 195 lbs. Deb: 9/15/12

YEAR TM/L	W	L	PCT	G	GS	CG	SH	SV	IP	H	HR	BB	SO	RAT	ERA	ERA+	OAV	OOB	BH	AVG	PB	PR	/A	PD	TPI
1912 Det-A	0	1	.000	1	1	0	0	0	6²	9	0	3	1	17.6	5.40	60	.346	.433	0	.000	-0	-2	-2	-0	-0.1

■ VIRGIL TRUCKS
Trucks, Virgil Oliver "Fire" b: 4/26/19, Birmingham, Ala. BR/TR, 5'11", 198 lbs. Deb: 9/27/41 C

YEAR TM/L	W	L	PCT	G	GS	CG	SH	SV	IP	H	HR	BB	SO	RAT	ERA	ERA+	OAV	OOB	BH	AVG	PB	PR	/A	PD	TPI
1941 Det-A	0	0	—	1	0	0	0	0	2	4	0	0	3	18.0	9.00	50	.500	.500	0	—	0	-1	-1	0	0.0
1942 Det-A	14	8	.636	28	20	8	2	0	167²	147	3	74	91	12.0	2.74	144	.231	.314	8	.123	-4	17	23	-2	1.9
1943 Det-A	16	10	.615	33	25	10	2	2	202²	170	11	52	118	9.9	2.84	124	.225	.276	13	.181	-2	10	15	-3	1.3
1945 *Det-A	0	0	—	1	1	0	0	0	5¹	3	0	2	3	8.4	1.69	208	.176	.263	0	.000	-0	1	1	0	0.1
1946 Det-A	14	9	.609	32	29	15	2	0	236²	217	23	75	161	11.2	3.23	113	.241	.302	17	.179	-1	7	11	-1	1.0
1947 Det-A	10	12	.455	36	26	8	2	2	180²	186	14	79	108	13.3	4.53	83	.263	.339	19	.271	2	-17	-15	-1	-1.3
1948 Det-A	14	13	.519	43	26	7	0	2	211²	190	14	85	123	11.8	3.78	115	.240	.315	13	.165	-3	12	14	-1	0.9
1949 Det-A	19	11	.633	41	32	17	6	4	275	209	16	124	153	11.0	2.81	148	.211	.301	12	.120	-6	42	41	-4	3.2
1950 Det-A	3	1	.750	7	7	2	1	0	48¹	45	6	21	25	12.5	3.54	133	.243	.324	3	.150	-1	6	6	1	0.6
1951 Det-A	13	8	.619	37	18	6	1	1	153²	153	9	75	89	13.6	4.33	96	.262	.350	13	.236	-1	-4	-3	1	-0.1
1952 Det-A	5	19	.208	35	29	8	3	1	197	190	12	82	129	12.7	3.97	96	.251	.330	12	.188	-0	-7	-4	2	-0.1
1953 StL-A	5	4	.556	16	12	4	2	2	88	83	4	32	47	12.2	3.07	137	.249	.322	4	.160	-1	9	11	-1	1.0
Chi-A	15	6	.714	24	21	13	3	1	176¹	151	14	67	102	11.3	2.86	141	.232	.306	15	.238	2	22	23	1	2.7
Yr	20	10	.667	40	33	17	5	3	264¹	234	18	99	149	11.4	2.93	139	.237	.308	1	.011	-1	31	34	-0	3.7
1954 Chi-A	19	12	.613	40	33	16	5	3	264²	224	13	95	152	10.9	2.79	134	.228	.297	17	.183	-1	27	28	1	2.9
1955 Chi-A	13	8	.619	32	26	7	3	0	175	176	19	61	91	12.3	3.96	100	.260	.323	8	.125	-3	0	-0	1	-0.2
1956 Det-A	6	5	.545	22	16	3	1	1	120	104	15	63	43	13.0	3.83	108	.239	.343	11	.244	1	4	4	-0	0.3
1957 KC-A	9	7	.563	48	7	0	0	7	116	106	12	62	55	13.2	3.03	131	.248	.346	4	.143	-1	10	12	0	1.1
1958 KC-A	0	1	.000	16	0	0	0	3	22	18	2	15	15	13.5	2.05	191	.222	.344	0	.000	-0	4	5	0	0.5
NY-A	2	1	.667	25	0	0	0	0	39²	40	1	24	26	15.0	4.54	78	.265	.373	2	.250	1	-3	-4	-0	-0.4
Yr	2	2	.500	41	0	0	0	4	61²	58	3	39	41	14.4	3.65	100	.249	.361	0	.000	0	1	0	-0	0.1
Total 17	177	135	.567	517	328	124	33	30	2682¹	2416	188	1088	1534	11.9	3.39	117	.240	.317	171	.180	-20	141	167	-7	15.4

■ MIKE TRUJILLO
Trujillo, Michael Andrew b: 1/12/60, Denver, Colo. BR/TR, 6'1", 180 lbs. Deb: 4/14/85

YEAR TM/L	W	L	PCT	G	GS	CG	SH	SV	IP	H	HR	BB	SO	RAT	ERA	ERA+	OAV	OOB	BH	AVG	PB	PR	/A	PD	TPI
1985 Bos-A	4	4	.500	27	7	1	0	0	84	112	7	23	19	14.8	4.82	89	.320	.367	0	—	0	-6	-5	2	-0.2
1986 Bos-A	0	0	—	3	0	0	0	0	5²	7	0	6	4	20.6	9.53	44	.304	.448	0	—	0	-3	-3	1	-0.2
Sea-A	3	2	.600	11	4	1	1	1	41¹	32	5	15	19	10.2	2.40	177	.215	.287	0	—	0	8	8	0	0.9
Yr	3	2	.600	14	4	1	1	1	47	39	5	21	23	11.5	3.26	130	.227	.311	0	—	0	5	5	1	0.7
1987 Sea-A	4	4	.500	28	7	0	0	1	65²	70	12	26	36	13.4	6.17	76	.277	.349	0	—	0	-12	-11	-1	-1.0
1988 Det-A	0	0	—	6	0	0	0	0	12¹	11	2	5	5	11.7	5.11	75	.234	.308	0	—	0	-2	-2	0	0.0
1989 Det-A	1	2	.333	8	4	1	0	0	25²	35	3	13	13	16.8	5.96	64	.333	.407	0	—	0	-6	-6	0	-0.5
Total 5	12	12	.500	83	22	3	1	3	234²	267	29	88	96	13.8	5.02	86	.288	.353	0	—	0	-21	-19	2	-1.0

■ ED TRUMBULL
Trumbull, Edward J. (b: Edward J. Trembly) b: 11/3/1860, Chicopee, Mass. Deb: 5/10/1884 ♦

YEAR TM/L	W	L	PCT	G	GS	CG	SH	SV	IP	H	HR	BB	SO	RAT	ERA	ERA+	OAV	OOB	BH	AVG	PB	PR	/A	PD	TPI
1884 Was-a	1	9	.100	10	10	10	0	0	84	108	4	31	43	14.9	4.71	64	.296	.351	10	.116	-2	-14	-16	-1	-1.2

■ JOHN TSITOURIS
Tsitouris, John Philip b: 5/4/36, Monroe, N.C. BR/TR, 6', 175 lbs. Deb: 6/13/57

YEAR TM/L	W	L	PCT	G	GS	CG	SH	SV	IP	H	HR	BB	SO	RAT	ERA	ERA+	OAV	OOB	BH	AVG	PB	PR	/A	PD	TPI
1957 Det-A	1	0	1.000	2	0	0	0	0	3¹	8	0	2	2	27.0	8.10	48	.500	.556	0	.000	-0	-2	-2	0	-0.1
1958 KC-A	0	0	—	1	1	0	0	0	3	2	0	2	1	12.0	3.00	130	.182	.308	0	.000	-0	0	0	0	0.0
1959 KC-A	4	3	.571	24	10	0	0	0	83¹	90	3	35	50	13.8	4.97	81	.271	.346	3	.150	-1	-10	-9	-1	-0.9
1960 KC-A	0	2	.000	14	2	0	0	0	33	38	3	21	12	18.3	6.55	61	.297	.427	0	.000	-1	-10	-9	-1	-0.9
1962 Cin-N	1	0	1.000	4	2	1	1	0	21¹	13	0	7	7	9.7	0.84	477	.181	.280	0	.000	-1	7	8	0	0.8
1963 Cin-N	12	8	.600	30	21	8	3	0	191	167	20	38	113	10.2	3.16	106	.232	.281	5	.081	-3	3	4	-3	-0.1
1964 Cin-N	9	13	.409	37	24	6	1	2	175¹	178	20	75	146	13.2	3.80	95	.263	.340	11	.190	2	-5	-4	-1	-0.2
1965 Cin-N	6	9	.400	31	20	3	0	1	131	134	18	65	91	14.3	4.95	76	.265	.359	3	.070	-2	-20	-17	-1	-2.0
1966 Cin-N	0	0	—	1	0	0	0	0	1	3	0	1	0	36.0	18.00	22	.750	.800	0	—	0	-2	-2	0	-0.1
1967 Cin-N	1	0	1.000	2	1	0	0	0	8	4	1	6	4	11.3	3.38	111	.154	.313	0	—	0	0	0	0	0.1
1968 Cin-N	0	3	.000	3	3	0	0	0	12²	16	6	8	6	17.8	7.11	44	.302	.403	0	.000	-0	-6	-6	0	-0.4
Total 11	34	38	.472	149	84	18	5	3	663	653	71	260	432	12.9	4.13	88	.257	.335	22	.111	-6	-44	-36	-4	-3.8

■ TOMMY TUCKER
Tucker, Thomas Joseph "Foghorn" b: 10/28/1863, Holyoke, Mass. d: 10/22/35, Montague, Mass. BB/TR, 5'11", 165 lbs. Deb: 4/16/1887 ♦

YEAR TM/L	W	L	PCT	G	GS	CG	SH	SV	IP	H	HR	BB	SO	RAT	ERA	ERA+	OAV	OOB	BH	AVG	PB	PR	/A	PD	TPI
1888 Bal-a	0	0	—	1	0	0	0	0	2¹	4	0	0	2	15.4	3.86	77	.365	.365	149	.287	0	-0	-0	0	0.0
1891 Bos-N	0	0	—	1	0	0	0	0	1	3	0	0	0	27.0	9.00	41	.501	.501	148	.270	0	-1	-1	0	0.0
Total 2	0	0	—	2	0	0	0	0	3¹	7	0	0	2	18.9	5.40	59	.413	.413	1882	.290	0	-1	-1	0	0.0

■ TOM TUCKEY
Tuckey, Thomas H. "Tabasco Tom" b: 10/7/1883, Connecticut d: 10/17/50, New York, N.Y. TL, 6'3", Deb: 8/11/08

YEAR TM/L	W	L	PCT	G	GS	CG	SH	SV	IP	H	HR	BB	SO	RAT	ERA	ERA+	OAV	OOB	BH	AVG	PB	PR	/A	PD	TPI
1908 Bos-N	3	3	.500	8	8	3	1	0	72	60	2	20	26	10.5	2.50	96	.265	.336	1	.050	-2	-1	-1	0	-0.2
1909 Bos-N	0	9	.000	17	10	4	0	0	90²	104	1	22	16	12.8	4.27	66	.295	.342	4	.138	-2	-17	-15	1	-1.5
Total 2	3	12	.200	25	18	7	1	0	162²	164	3	42	42	11.8	3.49	76	.284	.340	5	.102	-3	-18	-15	1	-1.7

■ JOHN TUDOR
Tudor, John Thomas b: 2/2/54, Schenectady, N.Y. BL/TL, 6', 185 lbs. Deb: 8/16/79

YEAR TM/L	W	L	PCT	G	GS	CG	SH	SV	IP	H	HR	BB	SO	RAT	ERA	ERA+	OAV	OOB	BH	AVG	PB	PR	/A	PD	TPI
1979 Bos-A	1	2	.333	6	6	1	0	0	28	39	2	9	11	15.4	6.43	69	.345	.393	0	—	0	-7	-6	1	-0.4
1980 Bos-A	8	5	.615	16	13	5	0	0	92²	81	4	31	45	11.2	3.02	140	.238	.307	0	—	0	10	12	2	1.5
1981 Bos-A	4	3	.571	18	11	2	0	1	78²	74	11	28	44	12.0	4.58	85	.252	.323	0	—	0	-8	-6	1	-0.5
1982 Bos-A	13	10	.565	32	30	6	1	0	195²	215	20	59	146	13.0	3.63	119	.280	.338	0	—	0	10	15	2	1.7
1983 Bos-A	13	12	.520	34	34	7	2	0	242	236	32	81	136	11.9	4.09	106	.255	.317	0	—	0	-1	7	-1	0.5
1984 Pit-N	12	11	.522	32	32	6	1	0	212	200	19	56	117	10.9	3.27	110	.248	.297	16	.211	2	8	8	-0	1.1

YEAR	TM/L	W	L	PCT	G	GS	CG	SH	SV	IP	H	HR	BB	SO	RAT	ERA	ERA+	OAV	OOB	BH	AVG	PB	PR	/A	PD	TPI
1985	*StL-N	21	8	.724	36	36	14	**10**	0	275	209	14	49	169	**8.6**	1.93	183	.209	**.249**	13	.138	1	51	49	1	5.8
1986	StL-N	13	7	.650	30	30	3	0	0	219	197	22	53	107	10.3	2.92	125	.244	.291	11	.153	-0	19	18	1	1.9
1987	*StL-N	10	2	.833	16	16	0	0	0	96	100	11	32	54	12.5	3.84	108	.272	.333	7	.200	1	3	3	1	0.5
1988	StL-N	6	5	.545	21	21	4	1	0	145¹	131	5	31	55	10.1	2.29	152	.247	.290	5	.109	-1	19	19	1	2.3
	*LA-N	4	3	.571	9	9	1	0	0	52¹	58	5	10	32	11.7	2.41	138	.284	.318	0	.000	-1	6	5	0	0.5
	Yr	10	8	.556	30	30	5	1	0	197²	189	10	41	87	10.5	2.32	148	.255	.294	4	.068	-2	25	24	2	2.8
1989	LA-N	0	0	—	6	3	0	0	0	14¹	17	1	6	9	14.4	3.14	109	.309	.377	0	.000	-0	1	0	0	0.0
1990	StL-N	12	4	.750	25	22	1	1	0	146¹	120	10	30	63	9.3	2.40	163	.225	.269	7	.152	0	23	25	2	3.0
Total	12	117	72	.619	281	263	50	16	1	1797	1677	156	475	988	10.9	3.12	124	.248	.301	59	.154	2	132	147	10	17.9

■ OSCAR TUERO
Tuero, Oscar (Monzon) (b: Oscar Tuero Monzon) b: 12/17/1898, Canada d: 10/21/60, Houston, Tex. BR/TR, 5'8.5", 158 lbs. Deb: 5/30/18

YEAR	TM/L	W	L	PCT	G	GS	CG	SH	SV	IP	H	HR	BB	SO	RAT	ERA	ERA+	OAV	OOB	BH	AVG	PB	PR	/A	PD	TPI
1918	StL-N	1	2	.333	11	3	2	0	0	44¹	32	0	10	13	9.1	1.02	267	.208	.269	3	.250	0	9	8	-0	0.9
1919	StL-N	5	7	.417	**45**	17	4	0	**4**	154²	137	4	42	45	11.0	3.20	87	.242	.306	8	.205	1	-5	-7	-0	-0.6
1920	StL-N	0	0	—	2	0	0	0	0	0²	5	0	1	0	81.0	54.00	6	.833	.857	0	—	0	-4	-4	0	-0.3
Total	3	6	9	.400	58	20	6	0	4	199²	174	4	53	58	10.8	2.88	96	.240	.303	11	.216	1	-0	-2	-0	-0.0

■ BOB TUFTS
Tufts, Robert Malcolm b: 11/2/55, Medford, Mass. BL/TL, 6'5", 215 lbs. Deb: 8/10/81

YEAR	TM/L	W	L	PCT	G	GS	CG	SH	SV	IP	H	HR	BB	SO	RAT	ERA	ERA+	OAV	OOB	BH	AVG	PB	PR	/A	PD	TPI
1981	SF-N	0	0	—	11	0	0	0	0	15¹	20	1	6	12	15.8	3.52	97	.308	.375	0	.000	-0	-0	-0	1	0.0
1982	KC-A	2	0	1.000	10	0	0	0	2	20	24	3	3	13	12.1	4.50	91	.293	.318	0	—	0	-1	-1	-1	-0.1
1983	KC-A	0	0	—	6	0	0	0	0	6²	16	1	5	3	29.7	8.10	50	.444	.524	0	—	0	-3	-3	0	-0.2
Total	3	2	0	1.000	27	0	0	0	2	42	60	5	14	28	16.3	4.71	81	.328	.382	0	.000	-0	-4	-4	0	-0.3

■ LEE TUNNELL
Tunnell, Byron Lee b: 10/30/60, Tyler, Tex. BR/TR, 6'1", 180 lbs. Deb: 9/04/82

YEAR	TM/L	W	L	PCT	G	GS	CG	SH	SV	IP	H	HR	BB	SO	RAT	ERA	ERA+	OAV	OOB	BH	AVG	PB	PR	/A	PD	TPI
1982	Pit-N	1	1	.500	5	3	0	0	0	18¹	17	1	5	4	11.8	3.93	94	.254	.324	0	.000	-0	-1	-0	0	0.0
1983	Pit-N	11	6	.647	35	25	5	3	0	177²	167	15	58	95	11.5	3.65	102	.252	.314	7	.121	-1	-0	1	3	0.3
1984	Pit-N	1	7	.125	26	6	0	0	1	68¹	81	6	40	51	15.9	5.27	68	.298	.388	1	.083	-1	-13	-13	1	-1.1
1985	Pit-N	4	10	.286	24	23	0	0	0	132¹	126	11	57	74	12.5	4.01	89	.251	.329	4	.085	-2	-6	-6	1	-0.7
1987	*StL-N	4	4	.500	32	9	0	0	0	74¹	90	5	34	49	15.1	4.84	86	.307	.381	4	.235	-1	-6	-6	0	-0.4
1989	Min-A	1	0	1.000	10	0	0	0	0	12	18	1	6	7	18.0	6.00	69	.340	.407	0	—	0	-3	-2	-0	-0.2
Total	6	22	28	.440	132	66	5	3	1	483	499	39	200	280	13.1	4.23	88	.270	.343	16	.116	-4	-29	-27	5	-2.1

■ GEORGE TURBEVILLE
Turbeville, George Elkins b: 8/24/14, Turbeville, S.C. d: 10/5/83, Salisbury, N.C. BR/TL, 6'1", 175 lbs. Deb: 7/20/35

YEAR	TM/L	W	L	PCT	G	GS	CG	SH	SV	IP	H	HR	BB	SO	RAT	ERA	ERA+	OAV	OOB	BH	AVG	PB	PR	/A	PD	TPI
1935	Phi-A	0	3	.000	19	6	2	0	0	63²	74	2	69	20	20.2	7.63	60	.312	.467	2	.105	-2	-22	-22	-1	-2.1
1936	Phi-A	2	5	.286	12	6	2	0	0	43²	42	4	32	10	16.5	6.39	80	.258	.398	2	.143	-1	-7	-6	-0	-0.5
1937	Phi-A	0	4	.000	31	3	0	0	0	77¹	80	2	56	17	15.8	4.77	99	.266	.381	6	.231	0	-1	-1	-1	0.0
Total	3	2	12	.143	62	15	4	0	0	184²	196	10	157	47	17.5	6.14	77	.280	.416	10	.169	-2	-30	-29	-1	-2.6

■ LUCAS TURK
Turk, Lucas Newton "Harlem" or "Chief" b: 5/2/1898, Homer, Ga. BR/TR, 6', 165 lbs. Deb: 6/07/22

YEAR	TM/L	W	L	PCT	G	GS	CG	SH	SV	IP	H	HR	BB	SO	RAT	ERA	ERA+	OAV	OOB	BH	AVG	PB	PR	/A	PD	TPI
1922	Was-A	0	0	—	5	0	0	0	0	11²	16	0	5	1	16.2	6.94	56	.340	.404	1	.250	0	-4	-4	-1	-0.3

■ BOB TURLEY
Turley, Robert Lee "Bullet Bob" b: 9/19/30, Troy, Ill. BR/TR, 6'2", 215 lbs. Deb: 9/29/51 C

YEAR	TM/L	W	L	PCT	G	GS	CG	SH	SV	IP	H	HR	BB	SO	RAT	ERA	ERA+	OAV	OOB	BH	AVG	PB	PR	/A	PD	TPI
1951	StL-A	0	1	.000	1	1	0	0	0	7¹	11	0	3	5	17.2	7.36	60	.355	.412	0	.000	-0	-3	-2	0	-0.1
1953	StL-A	2	6	.250	10	7	3	1	0	60¹	39	4	44	61	12.7	3.28	128	.184	.329	5	.278	2	5	6	-1	0.7
1954	Bal-A	14	15	.483	35	35	14	0	0	247¹	178	7	181	**185**	13.3	3.46	104	**.203**	.343	11	.136	-2	-7	3	-2	0.0
1955	*NY-A	17	13	.567	36	34	13	6	1	246²	168	16	177	210	12.8	3.06	122	**.193**	.333	11	.134	-0	25	19	-3	1.5
1956	*NY-A	8	4	.667	27	21	5	1	1	132	138	13	103	91	16.7	5.05	70	.273	.400	8	.174	-0	-13	-17	-1	-1.7
1957	*NY-A	13	6	.684	32	23	9	4	3	176¹	120	17	85	152	10.9	2.71	133	**.194**	.300	5	.088	-1	21	17	-1	1.5
1958	*NY-A	**21**	7	**.750**	33	31	**19**	6	1	245¹	178	24	128	168	11.5	2.97	119	**.206**	.313	12	.136	-1	22	15	-2	1.3
1959	NY-A	8	11	.421	33	22	7	3	0	154¹	141	15	83	111	13.2	4.32	84	.245	.343	4	.087	-2	-8	-11	-1	-1.4
1960	*NY-A	9	3	.750	34	24	4	1	5	173¹	138	14	87	87	11.9	3.27	110	.222	.322	4	.073	-3	12	6	-1	0.1
1961	NY-A	3	5	.375	15	12	1	0	0	72	74	11	51	48	16.1	5.75	65	.269	.391	2	.095	-1	-14	-16	-1	-1.6
1962	NY-A	3	3	.500	24	8	0	0	1	69	68	8	47	42	15.5	4.57	82	.263	.384	0	.000	-1	-5	-6	1	-0.6
1963	LA-A	2	7	.222	19	12	3	2	0	87¹	71	5	51	70	12.8	3.30	104	.222	.332	4	.160	1	3	1	-0	0.1
	Bos-A	1	4	.200	11	7	0	0	0	41¹	42	6	28	35	15.5	6.10	62	.256	.368	3	.214	-1	-11	-11	-0	-1.0
	Yr	3	11	.214	30	19	3	2	0	128²	113	11	79	105	13.5	4.20	84	.232	.340	0	.000	1	-8	-9	-1	-0.9
Total	12	101	85	.543	310	237	78	24	12	1712²	1366	140	1068	1265	13.1	3.64	101	.220	.340	69	.126	-11	41	4	-13	-1.2

■ TUCK TURNER
Turner, George A. b: 2/13/1873, W.New Brighton, N.Y. d: 7/16/45, Staten Island, N.Y. BB/TL, Deb: 8/18/1893 ♦

YEAR	TM/L	W	L	PCT	G	GS	CG	SH	SV	IP	H	HR	BB	SO	RAT	ERA	ERA+	OAV	OOB	BH	AVG	PB	PR	/A	PD	TPI
1894	Phi-N	0	0	—	1	0	0	0	0	6	9	1	2	3	16.5	7.50	68	.342	.389	141	.416	1	-1	-2	-0	0.0

■ JIM TURNER
Turner, James Riley "Milkman Jim" b: 8/6/03, Antioch, Tenn. BL/TR, 6', 185 lbs. Deb: 4/30/37 C

YEAR	TM/L	W	L	PCT	G	GS	CG	SH	SV	IP	H	HR	BB	SO	RAT	ERA	ERA+	OAV	OOB	BH	AVG	PB	PR	/A	PD	TPI
1937	Bos-N	20	11	.645	33	30	**24**	**5**	1	256²	228	13	52	69	**9.8**	2.38	150	.235	**.274**	24	.250	4	**44**	34	0	**3.9**
1938	Bos-N	14	18	.438	35	34	22	3	0	268	267	21	54	71	10.9	3.46	99	.259	.299	22	.229	4	10	-1	4	0.6
1939	Bos-N	4	11	.267	25	22	9	0	0	157²	181	10	51	50	13.5	4.28	86	.293	.351	13	.236	2	-6	-10	1	-0.6
1940	*Cin-N	14	7	.667	24	23	11	0	0	187	187	9	32	53	10.5	2.89	131	.264	.296	18	.240	3	20	19	-1	2.3
1941	Cin-N	6	4	.600	23	10	3	0	0	113	120	5	24	34	11.5	3.11	116	.277	.317	6	.146	-1	7	6	2	0.7
1942	Cin-N	0	0	—	3	0	0	0	0	3¹	5	1	3	0	21.6	10.80	30	.333	.444	0	.000	-0	-3	-3	0	-0.2
	*NY-A	1	1	.500	5	0	0	0	1	7	4	0	1	2	6.4	1.29	268	.167	.200	0	.000	-0	2	2	0	0.2
1943	NY-A	3	0	1.000	18	0	0	0	1	43¹	44	1	13	15	11.8	3.53	91	.260	.313	1	.077	-1	-1	-2	-0	-0.2
1944	NY-A	4	4	.500	35	0	0	0	7	41²	42	3	22	13	13.8	3.46	101	.264	.354	2	.200	-1	-0	0	-1	0.0
1945	NY-A	3	4	.429	30	0	0	0	**10**	54¹	45	4	31	22	12.6	3.64	95	.225	.329	1	.091	-1	-2	-1	1	-0.1
Total	9	69	60	.535	231	119	69	8	20	1132	1123	67	283	329	11.3	3.22	111	.260	.307	87	.218	11	70	45	8	6.6

■ KEN TURNER
Turner, Kenneth Charles b: 8/17/43, Framingham, Mass. BR/TL, 6'2", 190 lbs. Deb: 6/11/67

YEAR	TM/L	W	L	PCT	G	GS	CG	SH	SV	IP	H	HR	BB	SO	RAT	ERA	ERA+	OAV	OOB	BH	AVG	PB	PR	/A	PD	TPI
1967	Cal-A	1	2	.333	13	1	0	0	0	17¹	16	4	4	6	10.9	4.15	76	.239	.292	0	.000	-0	-2	-2	0	-0.1

■ TED TURNER
Turner, Theodore Holhot b: 5/4/1892, Lawrenceburg, Ky. d: 2/4/58, Lexington, Ky. BR/TR, 6', 180 lbs. Deb: 4/20/20

YEAR	TM/L	W	L	PCT	G	GS	CG	SH	SV	IP	H	HR	BB	SO	RAT	ERA	ERA+	OAV	OOB	BH	AVG	PB	PR	/A	PD	TPI
1920	Chi-N	0	0	—	1	0	0	0	0	1¹	2	0	1	0	20.3	13.50	24	.400	.500	0	.000	-0	-2	-2	0	-0.1

■ TINK TURNER
Turner, Thomas Lovatt b: 2/20/1890, Swarthmore, Pa. d: 2/25/62, Philadelphia, Pa. BR/TR, 6'1", 190 lbs. Deb: 9/24/15

YEAR	TM/L	W	L	PCT	G	GS	CG	SH	SV	IP	H	HR	BB	SO	RAT	ERA	ERA+	OAV	OOB	BH	AVG	PB	PR	/A	PD	TPI
1915	Phi-A	0	1	.000	1	1	0	0	0	2	5	1	3	0	36.0	22.50	13	.500	.615	0	—	0	-4	-4	-1	-0.3

■ ELMER TUTWILER
Tutwiler, Elmer Strange b: 11/19/05, Carbon Hill, Ala. d: 5/3/76, Pensacola, Fla. BR/TR, 5'11", 158 lbs. Deb: 8/20/28

YEAR	TM/L	W	L	PCT	G	GS	CG	SH	SV	IP	H	HR	BB	SO	RAT	ERA	ERA+	OAV	OOB	BH	AVG	PB	PR	/A	PD	TPI
1928	Pit-N	0	0	—	2	0	0	0	0	3²	4	0	0	1	9.8	4.91	83	.267	.267	0	.000	-0	-0	-0	0	0.0

■ TWINK TWINING
Twining, Howard Earle "Doc" b: 5/30/1894, Horsham, Pa. d: 6/14/73, Lansdale, Pa. BR/TR, 6', 168 lbs. Deb: 7/09/16

YEAR	TM/L	W	L	PCT	G	GS	CG	SH	SV	IP	H	HR	BB	SO	RAT	ERA	ERA+	OAV	OOB	BH	AVG	PB	PR	/A	PD	TPI
1916	Cin-N	0	0	—	1	0	0	0	0	2	4	1	1	0	27.0	13.50	19	.444	.545	0	—	0	-2	-2	0	-0.1

■ LARRY TWITCHELL
Twitchell, Lawrence Grant b: 2/18/1864, Cleveland, Ohio d: 8/23/30, Cleveland, Ohio BR/TR, 6', 185 lbs. Deb: 4/30/1886 ♦

YEAR	TM/L	W	L	PCT	G	GS	CG	SH	SV	IP	H	HR	BB	SO	RAT	ERA	ERA+	OAV	OOB	BH	AVG	PB	PR	/A	PD	TPI
1886	Det-N	0	2	.000	4	4	2	0	0	25	35	1	12	6	16.9	6.48	51	.318	.385	1	.063	-2	-9	-9	1	-0.7
1887	*Det-N	11	1	.917	15	12	11	0	**1**	112¹	120	3	36	24	12.5	4.33	93	.266	.320	88	.333	4	-3	-4	-1	-0.2
1888	Det-N	0	0	—	2	0	0	0	1	4	6	1	0	3	13.5	6.75	41	.335	.335	128	.244	0	-2	-2	0	-0.1
1889	Cle-N	0	0	—	1	0	0	0	0	1	0	0	1	0	0.00	—	.000	.252	151	.275	0	0	0	0	0.0
1890	Buf-P	5	7	.417	13	12	12	0	0	104¹	112	3	72	29	15.9	4.57	90	.263	.369	38	.221	1	-4	-5	2	-0.3
1891	Col-a	1	1	.500	6	1	1	0	0	31	29	1	13	8	12.2	4.06	85	.239	.313	62	.277	2	-1	-2	0	-0.1
1894	Lou-N	0	0	—	1	0	0	0	0	3	5	1	1	0	18.0	6.00	85	.367	.410	56	.267	0	-0	-0	0	0.0

YEAR TM/L	W	L	PCT	G	GS	CG	SH	SV	IP	H	HR	BB	SO	RAT	ERA	ERA+	OAV	OOB	BH	AVG	PB	PR	/A	PD	TPI
Total 7	17	11	.607	42	29	26	0	2	280^2	307	10	135	70	14.2	4.62	85	.268	.346	676	.263	6	-19	-22	2	-1.4

■ WAYNE TWITCHELL   Twitchell, Wayne Lee   b: 3/10/48, Portland, Ore.   BR/TR, 6'6", 215 lbs.   Deb: 9/07/70

YEAR TM/L	W	L	PCT	G	GS	CG	SH	SV	IP	H	HR	BB	SO	RAT	ERA	ERA+	OAV	OOB	BH	AVG	PB	PR	/A	PD	TPI
1970 Mil-A	0	0	—	2	0	0	0	0	1^2	3	0	1	5	21.6	10.80	35	.333	.400	0	—	0	-1	-1	0	0.0
1971 Phi-N	1	0	1.000	6	1	0	0	0	16	8	1	10	15	10.7	0.00	—	.145	.288	0	.000	-0	6	6	-0	0.7
1972 Phi-N	5	9	.357	49	15	1	1	1	139^2	138	6	56	112	12.6	4.06	88	.259	.332	2	.071	-2	-9	-7	-1	-1.0
1973 Phi-N	13	9	.591	34	28	10	5	0	223^1	172	16	99	169	11.3	2.50	152	.219	.314	7	.097	-4	29	32	-4	2.7
1974 Phi-N	6	9	.400	25	18	2	0	0	112^1	122	11	65	72	15.5	5.21	73	.276	.377	6	.171	-1	-20	-18	-1	-1.9
1975 Phi-N	5	10	.333	36	20	0	0	0	134^1	132	10	78	101	14.1	4.42	84	.261	.361	3	.088	-2	-12	-10	-3	-1.4
1976 Phi-N	3	1	.750	26	2	0	0	1	61^2	55	3	18	67	11.1	1.75	203	.241	.305	1	.167	0	12	12	-0	1.3
1977 Phi-N	0	5	.000	12	8	0	0	0	45^2	50	3	25	37	14.8	4.53	88	.287	.377	1	.091	-0	-3	-3	0	-0.2
Mon-N	6	5	.545	22	22	2	0	0	139	116	18	49	93	11.0	4.21	90	.230	.304	8	.205	2	-5	-6	-1	-0.4
Yr	6	10	.375	34	30	2	0	0	184^2	166	21	74	130	11.9	4.29	90	.244	.323	6	.120	2	-8	-9	-0	-0.6
1978 Mon-N	4	12	.250	33	15	0	0	0	112	121	16	71	69	15.8	5.38	65	.286	.395	2	.083	-1	-22	-23	-1	-2.5
1979 NY-N	5	3	.625	33	2	0	0	0	63^2	55	6	55	44	16.1	5.23	70	.243	.400	3	.375	1	-11	-11	-0	-1.0
Sea-A	0	2	.000	4	2	0	0	0	13^2	11	2	10	5	15.1	5.27	83	.220	.371	0	—	0	-2	-1	0	0.0
Total 10	48	65	.425	282	133	15	6	2	1063	983	92	537	789	13.2	3.98	94	.250	.346	33	.127	-7	-38	-31	-11	-3.7

■ JEFF TWITTY   Twitty, Jeffrey Dean   b: 11/10/57, Lancaster, S.C.   BL/TL, 6'2", 185 lbs.   Deb: 7/05/80

YEAR TM/L	W	L	PCT	G	GS	CG	SH	SV	IP	H	HR	BB	SO	RAT	ERA	ERA+	OAV	OOB	BH	AVG	PB	PR	/A	PD	TPI
1980 KC-A	2	1	.667	13	0	0	0	0	22^1	33	4	7	9	16.1	6.04	67	.351	.396	0	—	0	-5	-5	0	-0.4

■ CY TWOMBLY   Twombly, Edwin Parker   b: 6/15/1897, Groveland, Mass.   d: 12/3/74, Savannah, Ga.   BL/TL, 5'10.5", 170 lbs.   Deb: 6/25/21

YEAR TM/L	W	L	PCT	G	GS	CG	SH	SV	IP	H	HR	BB	SO	RAT	ERA	ERA+	OAV	OOB	BH	AVG	PB	PR	/A	PD	TPI
1921 Chi-A	1	2	.333	7	4	0	0	0	27^2	26	1	25	7	17.2	5.86	72	.283	.445	0	.000	-2	-5	-5	1	-0.5

■ LEFTY TYLER   Tyler, George Albert   b: 12/14/1889, Derry, N.H.   d: 9/29/53, Lowell, Mass.   BL/TL, 6', 175 lbs.   Deb: 9/20/10

YEAR TM/L	W	L	PCT	G	GS	CG	SH	SV	IP	H	HR	BB	SO	RAT	ERA	ERA+	OAV	OOB	BH	AVG	PB	PR	/A	PD	TPI
1910 Bos-N	0	0	—	2	0	0	0	0	11^1	11	1	6	6	13.5	2.38	140	.275	.370	2	.500	1	1	1	-0	0.2
1911 Bos-N	7	10	.412	28	20	10	1	0	165^1	150	11	109	90	14.6	5.06	76	.243	.365	10	.164	-1	-31	-23	2	-1.8
1912 Bos-N	12	22	.353	42	29	18	1	0	256^1	262	8	126	144	14.0	4.18	86	.267	.356	19	.198	-1	-22	-17	3	-1.4
1913 Bos-N	16	17	.485	39	34	**28**	4	2	290^1	245	2	108	143	11.3	2.79	118	.235	.313	21	.206	4	13	16	7	2.8
1914 *Bos-N	16	13	.552	38	34	21	5	2	271^1	247	7	101	140	12.0	2.69	103	.249	.327	19	.202	1	3	2	-2	0.0
1915 Bos-N	10	9	.526	32	24	15	1	0	204^2	182	6	84	89	11.9	2.86	91	.243	.327	23	.261	7	-2	-6	-1	0.0
1916 Bos-N	17	9	.654	34	28	21	6	1	249^1	200	6	58	117	9.4	2.02	123	.226	.276	19	.204	7	17	13	2	2.5
1917 Bos-N	14	12	.538	32	28	22	4	1	239	203	1	86	98	11.1	2.52	101	.240	.314	31	.231	4	5	1	3	1.2
1918 *Chi-N	19	8	.704	33	30	22	6	1	269^1	218	1	67	102	9.7	2.00	139	.226	.279	21	.210	1	23	23	3	3.3
1919 Chi-N	2	2	.500	6	5	3	0	0	30	20	0	13	9	9.9	2.10	137	.196	.287	1	.143	1	3	3	1	0.5
1920 Chi-N	11	12	.478	27	27	18	2	0	193	193	6	57	57	11.8	3.31	97	.268	.324	17	.262	5	-4	-2	3	0.6
1921 Chi-N	3	2	.600	10	4	0	0	0	50	59	2	14	8	13.1	3.24	118	.294	.340	6	.231	1	3	3	-0	0.4
Total 12	127	116	.523	323	265	182	30	7	2230	1990	51	829	1003	11.6	2.95	101	.244	.319	189	.217	29	9	11	20	8.3

■ JIM TYNG   Tyng, James Alexander   b: 3/27/1856, Philadelphia, Pa.   d: 10/30/31, New York, N.Y.   5'9", 155 lbs.   Deb: 9/23/1879

YEAR TM/L	W	L	PCT	G	GS	CG	SH	SV	IP	H	HR	BB	SO	RAT	ERA	ERA+	OAV	OOB	BH	AVG	PB	PR	/A	PD	TPI
1879 Bos-N	1	2	.333	3	3	3	0	0	27	35	0	6	7	13.7	5.00	50	.295	.329	5	.357	1	-8	-8	0	-0.4
1888 Phi-N	0	0	—	1	0	0	0	1	4	8	0	2	2	22.5	4.50	66	.401	.456	0	.000	-0	-1	-1	0	0.0
Total 2	1	2	.333	4	3	3	0	1	31	43	0	8	9	14.8	4.94	52	.310	.348	5	.333	1	-8	-8	0	-0.4

■ DAVE TYRIVER   Tyriver, David Burton   b: 10/31/37, Oshkosh, Wis.   d: 10/28/88, Oshkosh, Wis.   BR/TR, 6' ", 175 lbs.   Deb: 8/21/62

YEAR TM/L	W	L	PCT	G	GS	CG	SH	SV	IP	H	HR	BB	SO	RAT	ERA	ERA+	OAV	OOB	BH	AVG	PB	PR	/A	PD	TPI
1962 Cle-A	0	0	—	4	0	0	0	0	10^2	10	2	7	7	15.2	4.22	92	.250	.375	0	.000	-0	-0	-0	0	0.0

■ JIMMY UCHRINSCKO   Uchrinscko, James Emerson   b: 10/20/1900, W.Newton, Pa.   BL/TR, 6', 180 lbs.   Deb: 7/20/26

YEAR TM/L	W	L	PCT	G	GS	CG	SH	SV	IP	H	HR	BB	SO	RAT	ERA	ERA+	OAV	OOB	BH	AVG	PB	PR	/A	PD	TPI
1926 Was-A	0	0	—	3	0	0	0	0	8	13	0	8	0	23.6	10.13	38	.433	.553	0	.000	-0	-5	-6	0	-0.4

■ GEORGE UHLE   Uhle, George Ernest "The Bull"   b: 9/18/1898, Cleveland, Ohio   d: 2/26/85, Lakewood, Ohio   BR/TR, 6', 190 lbs.   Deb: 4/30/19   C♦

YEAR TM/L	W	L	PCT	G	GS	CG	SH	SV	IP	H	HR	BB	SO	RAT	ERA	ERA+	OAV	OOB	BH	AVG	PB	PR	/A	PD	TPI
1919 Cle-A	10	5	.667	26	12	7	1	0	127	129	1	43	50	12.7	2.91	115	.261	.329	13	.302	3	5	6	0	1.0
1920 *Cle-A	4	5	.444	27	6	2	0	1	84^2	98	3	29	27	14.4	5.21	73	.296	.367	11	.344	2	-13	-13	0	-0.9
1921 Cle-A	16	13	.552	41	28	13	2	2	238	288	9	63	63	13.4	4.01	106	.306	.352	23	.245	3	7	7	-2	0.7
1922 Cle-A	22	16	.579	50	40	23	5	3	287^1	328	6	89	82	13.5	4.07	98	.290	.348	29	.266	9	-1	-2	-3	0.2
1923 Cle-A	26	16	.619	54	44	**29**	1	5	357^2	378	8	102	109	12.4	3.77	105	.271	.326	52	.361	16	8	8	0	2.4
1924 Cle-A	9	15	.375	28	25	15	0	1	196^1	238	6	75	57	14.9	4.77	90	.308	.376	33	.308	7	-12	-11	1	-0.9
1925 Cle-A	13	11	.542	29	26	17	1	0	210^2	218	5	78	68	13.0	4.10	108	.268	.339	29	.287	6	7	7	-3	1.0
1926 Cle-A	27	11	**.711**	39	36	**32**	3	1	318^1	300	7	118	159	12.2	2.83	143	.253	.328	30	.227	4	42	43	-5	**4.7**
1927 Cle-A	8	9	.471	25	22	10	1	1	153^1	187	3	59	69	15.0	4.34	97	.310	.344	21	.266	4	-3	-2	-1	0.0
1928 Cle-A	12	17	.414	31	28	18	2	1	214^1	252	8	48	74	12.9	4.07	102	.300	.344	28	.286	7	-1	2	2	1.1
1929 Det-A	15	11	.577	32	30	23	1	0	249	283	9	58	100	12.4	4.08	105	.287	.328	37	.343	4	4	6	-3	1.1
1930 Det-A	12	12	.500	33	29	18	1	3	239	239	18	75	117	12.0	3.65	131	.264	.323	36	.308	8	26	30	-3	3.4
1931 Det-A	11	12	.478	29	18	15	2	2	193	190	10	49	63	11.3	3.50	131	.255	.304	22	.244	5	19	23	-1	2.7
1932 Det-A	6	6	.500	33	15	6	1	5	146^2	152	15	42	51	12.1	4.48	105	.266	.320	10	.182	1	-0	4	-1	0.4
1933 Det-A	0	0	—	1	0	0	0	0	0^2	2	1	0	1	27.0	27.00	16	.500	.500	0	—	0	-2	-2	0	-0.1
NY-N	1	1	.500	6	1	0	0	0	13^2	16	1	6	4	14.5	7.90	41	.302	.373	0	.000	-0	-7	-7	0	-0.6
NY-A	6	1	.857	12	6	4	0	0	61	63	4	20	26	12.7	5.16	75	.257	.321	8	.400	4	-6	-9	-1	-0.4
1934 NY-A	2	4	.333	16	2	0	0	0	16^1	16	3	7	10	20.4	9.92	41	.400	.451	2	—		-10	-11	-0	-0.7
1936 Cle-A	0	1	.000	7	0	0	0	0	12^2	26	2	5	5	22.0	8.53	59	.419	.463	4	.381	4	-5	-5	-0	-0.3
Total 17	200	166	.546	513	368	232	21	25	3119^2	3417	119	966	1135	13.0	3.99	105	.281	.340	393	.289	93	60	74	-16	14.8

■ BOB UHL   Uhl, Robert Ellwood "Lefty"   b: 9/17/13, San Francisco, Cal.   d: 8/21/90, Santa Rosa, Cal.   BB/TL, 5'11", 175 lbs.   Deb: 5/08/38

YEAR TM/L	W	L	PCT	G	GS	CG	SH	SV	IP	H	HR	BB	SO	RAT	ERA	ERA+	OAV	OOB	BH	AVG	PB	PR	/A	PD	TPI
1938 Chi-A	0	0	—	1	0	0	0	0	2	1	0	0	0	4.5	0.00	—	.167	.167	0	—	0	1	1	0	0.1
1940 Det-A	0	0	—	1	0	0	0	0	0	4	0	2	0	—	∞	—	1.000	1.000	0	—	0	-4	-4	0	-0.2
Total 2	0	0	—	2	0	0	0	0	2	5	0	2	0	31.5	18.00	27	.500	.583	0	—	0	-3	-3	0	-0.1

■ JERRY UJDUR   Ujdur, Gerald Raymond   b: 3/5/57, Duluth, Minn.   BR/TR, 6'1", 195 lbs.   Deb: 8/17/80

YEAR TM/L	W	L	PCT	G	GS	CG	SH	SV	IP	H	HR	BB	SO	RAT	ERA	ERA+	OAV	OOB	BH	AVG	PB	PR	/A	PD	TPI
1980 Det-A	1	0	1.000	9	2	0	0	0	21^1	36	5	10	9	19.8	7.59	54	.383	.448	0	—	0	-8	-8	-1	-0.7
1981 Det-A	0	0	—	4	4	0	0	0	14	19	2	5	5	15.4	6.43	59	.322	.375	0	—	0	-4	-4	0	-0.3
1982 Det-A	10	10	.500	25	25	7	0	0	178	150	29	69	86	11.2	3.69	110	.230	.306	0	—	0	8	7	-1	0.7
1983 Det-A	0	4	.000	11	6	0	0	0	34	44	6	20	13	16.4	7.15	55	.293	.385	0	—	0	-12	-12	-1	-1.1
1984 Cle-A	1	2	.333	4	3	0	0	0	14^1	22	1	6	5	18.8	6.91	59	.355	.429	0	—	0	-5	-4	-1	-0.4
Total 5	12	16	.429	53	40	7	0	0	261^2	268	43	110	118	13.2	4.78	84	.266	.342	0	—	0	-21	-22	-2	-1.8

■ SANDY ULLRICH   Ullrich, Carlos Santiago (Castello)   b: 7/25/21, Havana, Cuba   BR/TR, 6'1", 180 lbs.   Deb: 5/03/44

YEAR TM/L	W	L	PCT	G	GS	CG	SH	SV	IP	H	HR	BB	SO	RAT	ERA	ERA+	OAV	OOB	BH	AVG	PB	PR	/A	PD	TPI
1944 Was-A	0	0	—	3	0	0	0	0	9^2	17	2	4	2	20.5	9.31	35	.386	.449	1	.333	0	-6	-7	0	-0.5
1945 Was-A	3	3	.500	28	6	0	0	1	81^2	91	3	34	26	13.8	4.54	88	.276	.343	6	.273	1	-11	-13	2	-1.0
Total 2	3	3	.500	31	6	0	0	1	91	108	5	38	28	14.5	5.04	62	.289	.356	7	.280	1	-17	-19	2	-1.5

■ DUTCH ULRICH   Ulrich, Frank W.   b: 11/18/1899, Baltimore, Md.   d: 2/11/29, Baltimore, Md.   BR/TR, 6'2", 195 lbs.   Deb: 4/18/25

YEAR TM/L	W	L	PCT	G	GS	CG	SH	SV	IP	H	HR	BB	SO	RAT	ERA	ERA+	OAV	OOB	BH	AVG	PB	PR	/A	PD	TPI
1925 Phi-N	3	3	.500	21	4	2	1	0	65	73	6	12	29	11.9	3.05	157	.285	.320	2	.125	-1	9	12	1	1.2
1926 Phi-N	8	13	.381	45	17	8	1	1	147^2	178	9	37	52	13.2	4.08	101	.304	.347	12	.245	2	-4	1	-0	0.3
1927 Phi-N	8	11	.421	32	18	14	1	1	193^1	201	6	40	42	11.2	3.17	131	.271	.308	9	.123	-6	16	21	-2	1.3
Total 3	19	27	.413	98	39	24	3	2	406	452	21	89	123	12.0	3.48	122	.286	.324	23	.167	-5	21	34	-2	2.8

YEAR	TM/L	W	L	PCT	G	GS	CG	SH	SV	IP	H	HR	BB	SO	RAT	ERA	ERA+	OAV	OOB	BH	AVG	PB	PR	/A	PD	TPI

■ ARNOLD UMBACH Umbach, Arnold William b: 12/6/42, Williamsburg, Va. BR/TR, 6'1", 180 lbs. Deb: 10/03/64

YEAR	TM/L	W	L	PCT	G	GS	CG	SH	SV	IP	H	HR	BB	SO	RAT	ERA	ERA+	OAV	OOB	BH	AVG	PB	PR	/A	PD	TPI
1964	Mil-N	1	0	1.000	1	1	0	0	0	8¹	11	0	4	7	16.2	3.24	109	.333	.405	0	.000	0	0	0	0	0.0
1966	Atl-N	0	2	.000	22	3	0	0	0	40²	40	1	18	23	13.3	3.10	117	.256	.341	1	.200	0	2	2	-0	0.3
Total 2		1	2	.333	23	4	0	0	0	49	51	1	22	30	13.8	3.12	116	.270	.352	1	.125	0	3	3	-0	0.3

■ JIM UMBARGER Umbarger, James Harold b: 2/17/53, Burbank, Cal. BL/TL, 6'6", 200 lbs. Deb: 4/08/75

YEAR	TM/L	W	L	PCT	G	GS	CG	SH	SV	IP	H	HR	BB	SO	RAT	ERA	ERA+	OAV	OOB	BH	AVG	PB	PR	/A	PD	TPI
1975	Tex-A	8	7	.533	56	12	3	2	2	131	134	11	59	50	13.4	4.12	91	.276	.357	0	—	0	-5	-5	1	-0.3
1976	Tex-A	10	12	.455	30	30	10	3	0	197¹	208	12	54	105	12.0	3.15	114	.274	.324	0	—	0	8	10	-0	1.0
1977	Oak-A	1	5	.167	12	8	1	0	0	44	62	3	28	24	19.2	6.55	61	.354	.454	0	—	0	-12	-12	0	-1.0
	Tex-A	1	1	.500	3	2	0	0	0	13	14	2	4	5	12.5	5.54	74	.275	.327	0	—	0	-2	-2	-0	-0.1
	Yr	2	6	.250	15	10	1	0	0	57	76	5	32	29	17.1	6.32	64	.326	.408	0	—	0	-14	-14	0	-1.1
1978	Tex-A	5	8	.385	32	9	1	0	1	97²	116	9	36	60	14.2	4.88	77	.299	.362	0	—	0	-12	-12	1	-1.1
Total 4		25	33	.431	133	61	15	5	3	483	534	37	181	244	13.5	4.14	90	.287	.354	0	—	0	-23	-22	2	-1.5

■ JIM UMBRICHT Umbricht, James b: 9/17/30, Chicago, Ill. d: 4/8/64, Houston, Tex. BR/TR, 6'4", 215 lbs. Deb: 9/26/59

YEAR	TM/L	W	L	PCT	G	GS	CG	SH	SV	IP	H	HR	BB	SO	RAT	ERA	ERA+	OAV	OOB	BH	AVG	PB	PR	/A	PD	TPI
1959	Pit-N	0	0	—	1	1	0	0	0	7	7	3	4	3	14.1	6.43	60	.259	.355	0	.000	-0	-2	-2	0	-0.1
1960	Pit-N	1	2	.333	17	3	0	0	1	40²	40	5	27	26	14.8	5.09	74	.270	.383	2	.333	0	-6	-6	-1	-0.6
1961	Pit-N	0	0	—	1	0	0	0	0	3¹	5	0	2	1	18.9	2.70	148	.333	.412	1	1.000	0	0	0	0	0.1
1962	Hou-N	4	0	1.000	34	0	0	0	0	67	51	3	17	55	9.4	2.01	185	.213	.270	1	.111	-0	14	13	0	1.3
1963	Hou-N	4	3	.571	35	3	0	0	0	76	52	6	21	48	8.8	2.61	121	.195	.256	1	.111	-0	6	5	1	0.5
Total 5		9	5	.643	88	7	0	0	3	194	155	17	71	133	10.6	3.06	115	.222	.297	5	.179	-0	13	10	0	1.2

■ WILLIE UNDERHILL Underhill, Willie Vern b: 9/6/04, Yowell, Tex. d: 10/26/70, Bay City, Tex. BR/TR, 6'2", 185 lbs. Deb: 9/08/27

YEAR	TM/L	W	L	PCT	G	GS	CG	SH	SV	IP	H	HR	BB	SO	RAT	ERA	ERA+	OAV	OOB	BH	AVG	PB	PR	/A	PD	TPI
1927	Cle-A	0	2	.000	4	1	0	0	0	8¹	12	0	11	4	24.8	9.72	43	.375	.535	0	.000	-0	-5	-5	0	-0.4
1928	Cle-A	1	2	.333	11	3	1	0	0	28	33	0	20	16	17.4	4.50	92	.306	.419	4	.364	2	-1	-1	0	0.0
Total 2		1	4	.200	15	4	1	0	0	36¹	45	0	31	20	19.1	5.70	73	.321	.448	4	.333	1	-7	-6	0	-0.4

■ FRED UNDERWOOD Underwood, Frederick Theodore b: 10/14/1868, St.Louis Co., Mo. d: 1/26/06, Kansas City, Mo. Deb: 7/18/1894

YEAR	TM/L	W	L	PCT	G	GS	CG	SH	SV	IP	H	HR	BB	SO	RAT	ERA	ERA+	OAV	OOB	BH	AVG	PB	PR	/A	PD	TPI
1894	Bro-N	2	4	.333	7	6	5	0	0	47	80	1	30	10	21.1	7.85	63	.371	.448	7	.389	2	-13	-15	-0	-0.9

■ PAT UNDERWOOD Underwood, Patrick John b: 2/9/57, Kokomo, Ind. BL/TL, 6', 175 lbs. Deb: 5/31/79

YEAR	TM/L	W	L	PCT	G	GS	CG	SH	SV	IP	H	HR	BB	SO	RAT	ERA	ERA+	OAV	OOB	BH	AVG	PB	PR	/A	PD	TPI
1979	Det-A	6	4	.600	27	15	1	0	0	121²	126	17	29	83	11.6	4.59	94	.269	.314	0	—	0	-5	-4	-1	-0.4
1980	Det-A	3	6	.333	49	7	0	0	5	112²	121	12	35	60	12.6	3.59	114	.277	.333	0	—	0	6	6	0	0.6
1982	Det-A	4	8	.333	33	12	2	0	3	99	108	17	22	43	11.8	4.73	86	.269	.307	0	—	0	-7	-7	1	-0.5
1983	Det-A	0	0	—	4	0	0	0	0	10¹	11	1	6	2	14.8	8.71	45	.289	.386	0	—	0	-5	-6	-0	-0.4
Total 4		13	18	.419	113	34	3	0	8	343²	366	47	92	188	12.1	4.43	94	.272	.320	0	—	0	-12	-10	-0	-0.7

■ TOM UNDERWOOD Underwood, Thomas Gerald b: 12/22/53, Kokomo, Ind. BR/TL, 5'11", 170 lbs. Deb: 8/19/74

YEAR	TM/L	W	L	PCT	G	GS	CG	SH	SV	IP	H	HR	BB	SO	RAT	ERA	ERA+	OAV	OOB	BH	AVG	PB	PR	/A	PD	TPI
1974	Phi-N	1	0	1.000	7	0	0	0	0	13	15	1	5	8	13.8	4.85	78	.313	.377	0	.000	-0	-2	-2	-0	-0.1
1975	Phi-N	14	13	.519	35	35	7	2	0	219¹	221	12	84	123	12.8	4.14	90	.262	.333	9	.122	-2	-13	-10	-3	-1.5
1976	*Phi-N	10	5	.667	33	25	3	0	2	155²	154	9	63	94	12.6	3.53	101	.260	.332	5	.109	-1	-0	0	-2	-0.2
1977	Phi-N	3	2	.600	14	0	0	0	1	33¹	44	2	18	20	16.7	5.13	78	.328	.408	0	.000	-0	-5	-4	-0	-0.4
	StL-N	6	9	.400	19	17	1	0	0	100	104	7	57	66	14.6	4.95	78	.278	.375	4	.133	-0	-12	-12	-1	-1.2
	Yr	9	11	.450	33	17	1	0	1	133¹	148	9	75	86	15.1	4.99	78	.290	.382	4	.121	-0	-16	-16	-2	-1.6
1978	Tor-A	6	14	.300	31	30	7	1	0	197²	201	23	87	139	13.2	4.10	96	.263	.340	0	—	0	-7	-4	-3	-0.6
1979	Tor-A	9	16	.360	33	32	12	1	0	227	213	23	95	127	12.6	3.69	118	.253	.335	0	—	0	13	17	-1	1.6
1980	*NY-A	13	9	.591	38	27	2	2	2	187	163	15	66	116	11.2	3.66	107	.237	.307	0	—	0	8	5	-0	0.5
1981	NY-A	1	4	.200	9	6	0	0	0	32²	32	2	13	29	12.4	4.41	81	.262	.333	0	—	0	-3	-3	-0	-0.2
	*Oak-A	3	2	.600	16	5	1	0	1	51	37	4	25	46	11.3	3.18	109	.202	.305	0	—	0	3	2	-0	0.2
	Yr	4	6	.400	25	11	1	0	1	83²	69	6	38	75	11.7	3.66	96	.226	.316	0	—	0	-0	-1	-0	0.0
1982	Oak-A	10	6	.625	56	10	2	0	5	153	136	11	68	79	12.1	3.29	119	.241	.324	0	—	0	13	10	-2	0.8
1983	Oak-A	9	7	.563	51	15	0	0	4	144²	156	13	50	62	12.9	4.04	95	.277	.338	0	—	0	0	-3	-2	-0.4
1984	Bal-A	1	0	1.000	37	1	0	0	1	71²	78	8	31	39	13.3	3.52	110	.282	.354	0	—	0	4	3	1	0.4
Total 11		86	87	.497	379	203	35	6	18	1586	1554	130	662	948	12.7	3.89	100	.259	.336	18	.117	-4	-0	-0	-15	-1.1

■ WOODY UPCHURCH Upchurch, Jefferson Woodrow b: 4/13/11, Buies Creek, N.C. d: 10/23/71, Buies Creek, N.C. BR/TL, 6', 180 lbs. Deb: 9/14/35

YEAR	TM/L	W	L	PCT	G	GS	CG	SH	SV	IP	H	HR	BB	SO	RAT	ERA	ERA+	OAV	OOB	BH	AVG	PB	PR	/A	PD	TPI
1935	Phi-A	0	2	.000	3	3	1	0	0	21¹	23	3	12	2	14.8	5.06	90	.271	.361	2	.286	0	-1	-1	-0	0.0
1936	Phi-A	0	2	.000	7	2	1	0	0	22¹	36	7	14	6	20.1	9.67	53	.353	.431	1	.143	-0	-12	-11	-1	-0.9
Total 2		0	4	.000	10	5	2	0	0	43²	59	10	26	8	17.5	7.42	65	.316	.399	3	.214	-0	-13	-13	-1	-0.9

■ JOHN UPHAM Upham, John Leslie b: 12/29/41, Windsor, Ont., Can. BL/TL, 6', 180 lbs. Deb: 4/16/67 ♦

YEAR	TM/L	W	L	PCT	G	GS	CG	SH	SV	IP	H	HR	BB	SO	RAT	ERA	ERA+	OAV	OOB	BH	AVG	PB	PR	/A	PD	TPI
1967	Chi-N	0	1	.000	5	0	0	0	0	1¹	4	1	2	2	40.5	33.75	11	.571	.667	2	.667	1	-5	-4	0	-0.3
1968	Chi-N	0	0	—	2	0	0	0	0	7	2	0	3	2	7.7	0.00	—	.087	.222	2	.200	0	2	2	0	0.3
Total 2		0	1	.000	7	0	0	0	0	8¹	6	1	5	4	13.0	5.40	60	.200	.333	4	.308	1	-2	-2	0	0.0

■ BILL UPHAM Upham, William Lawrence b: 4/4/1888, Akron, Ohio d: 9/14/59, Newark, N.J. BB/TR, 6', 178 lbs. Deb: 4/10/15

YEAR	TM/L	W	L	PCT	G	GS	CG	SH	SV	IP	H	HR	BB	SO	RAT	ERA	ERA+	OAV	OOB	BH	AVG	PB	PR	/A	PD	TPI
1915	Bro-F	6	8	.429	33	11	4	2	5	121	129	0	40	46	12.6	3.05	99	.274	.331	4	.111	-2	-0	-0	2	0.0
1918	Bos-N	1	1	.500	3	2	2	0	0	20²	28	2	1	8	12.6	5.23	51	.326	.333	2	.222	0	-6	-6	0	-0.5
Total 2		7	9	.438	36	13	6	2	5	141²	157	2	41	54	12.6	3.37	88	.282	.332	6	.133	-2	-6	-6	2	-0.5

■ JERRY UPP Upp, George Henry b: 12/10/1883, Sandusky, Ohio d: 6/30/37, Sandusky, Ohio TL, Deb: 9/02/09

YEAR	TM/L	W	L	PCT	G	GS	CG	SH	SV	IP	H	HR	BB	SO	RAT	ERA	ERA+	OAV	OOB	BH	AVG	PB	PR	/A	PD	TPI
1909	Cle-A	2	1	.667	7	4	2	0	0	26²	26	0	12	13	12.8	1.69	152	.260	.339	2	.222	0	2	3	1	0.4

■ CECIL UPSHAW Upshaw, Cecil Lee b: 10/22/42, Spearsville, La. BR/TR, 6'6", 205 lbs. Deb: 10/01/66

YEAR	TM/L	W	L	PCT	G	GS	CG	SH	SV	IP	H	HR	BB	SO	RAT	ERA	ERA+	OAV	OOB	BH	AVG	PB	PR	/A	PD	TPI
1966	Atl-N	0	0	—	1	0	0	0	0	3	0	0	3	2	9.0	0.00	—	.000	.273	1	1.000	0	1	1	0	0.2
1967	Atl-N	2	3	.400	30	0	0	0	8	45¹	42	4	8	31	10.7	2.58	129	.247	.297	1	.167	1	4	4	0	0.5
1968	Atl-N	8	7	.533	52	0	0	0	13	116²	98	6	24	74	9.7	2.47	121	.229	.276	4	.174	0	7	7	-0	0.8
1969	*Atl-N	6	4	.600	62	0	0	0	27	105¹	102	7	29	57	11.3	2.91	124	.259	.311	5	.238	2	8	8	1	1.1
1971	Atl-N	11	6	.647	49	0	0	0	9	82	95	5	28	56	13.7	3.51	106	.292	.352	0	.000	-2	-0	2	-1	0.0
1972	Atl-N	3	5	.375	42	0	0	0	13	53²	50	5	19	23	11.7	3.69	103	.249	.317	1	.143	-0	-1	1	1	0.1
1973	Atl-N	0	1	.000	5	0	0	0	0	3²	8	0	2	3	24.5	9.82	40	.444	.500	0	—	0	-3	-2	0	-0.1
	Hou-N	2	3	.400	35	0	0	0	1	38¹	38	3	15	21	12.7	4.46	81	.259	.331	0	.000	-0	-3	-4	1	-0.2
	Yr	2	4	.333	40	0	0	0	1	42	46	3	17	24	13.7	4.93	74	.277	.348	0	.000	-0	-6	-6	1	-0.3
1974	Cle-A	0	1	.000	7	0	0	0	0	8	10	1	4	7	15.8	3.38	107	.345	.424	0	—	-0	0	0	-0	0.0
	NY-A	1	5	.167	36	0	0	0	6	59²	53	1	24	27	12.1	3.02	116	.254	.339	0	—	0	4	3	1	0.4
	Yr	1	6	.143	43	0	0	0	6	67²	63	2	28	34	12.5	3.06	115	.262	.347	0	—	0	4	3	1	0.4
1975	Chi-A	1	1	.500	29	0	0	0	1	47¹	49	5	21	22	14.1	3.23	120	.271	.359	0	—	-0	3	3	-0	0.3
Total 9		34	36	.486	348	0	0	0	86	563	545	37	177	323	11.9	3.13	112	.258	.322	12	.160	1	19	23	2	3.1

■ BILL UPTON Upton, William Ray b: 7/18/29, Esther, Mo. BR/TR, 6', 167 lbs. Deb: 4/13/54

YEAR	TM/L	W	L	PCT	G	GS	CG	SH	SV	IP	H	HR	BB	SO	RAT	ERA	ERA+	OAV	OOB	BH	AVG	PB	PR	/A	PD	TPI
1954	Phi-A	0	0	—	2	0	0	0	1	5	6	1	1	2	12.6	1.80	217	.300	.333	0	—	0	1	1	0	0.1

■ JACK URBAN Urban, Jack Elmer b: 12/5/28, Omaha, Neb. BR/TR, 5'8", 155 lbs. Deb: 6/13/57

YEAR	TM/L	W	L	PCT	G	GS	CG	SH	SV	IP	H	HR	BB	SO	RAT	ERA	ERA+	OAV	OOB	BH	AVG	PB	PR	/A	PD	TPI
1957	KC-A	7	4	.636	31	13	3	0	0	129¹	111	7	45	55	10.9	3.34	118	.237	.305	11	.282	2	6	9	2	1.4
1958	KC-A	8	11	.421	30	24	5	1	1	132	150	17	51	54	13.8	5.93	66	.286	.351	7	.152	-2	-32	-30	-1	-3.0

YEAR	TM/L	W	L	PCT	G	GS	CG	SH	SV	IP	H	HR	BB	SO	RAT	ERA	ERA+	OAV	OOB	BH	AVG	PB	PR	/A	PD	TPI
1959	StL-N	0	0	—	8	0	0	0	0	10^2	18	1	7	4	21.1	9.28	46	.409	.490	0	.000	-0	-6	-6	-0	-0.5
Total 3		15	15	.500	69	37	8	1	1	272	279	25	103	113	12.7	4.83	82	.269	.337	18	.209	0	-32	-27	1	-2.1

■ JOHN URREA
Urrea, John Godoy b: 2/9/55, Los Angeles, Cal. BR/TR, 6'3", 200 lbs. Deb: 4/10/77

YEAR	TM/L	W	L	PCT	G	GS	CG	SH	SV	IP	H	HR	BB	SO	RAT	ERA	ERA+	OAV	OOB	BH	AVG	PB	PR	/A	PD	TPI
1977	StL-N	7	6	.538	41	12	2	1	4	139^2	126	13	35	81	10.4	3.16	122	.244	.292	4	.138	2	12	11	0	1.3
1978	StL-N	4	9	.308	27	12	1	0	0	98^2	108	4	47	61	14.8	5.38	65	.284	.373	3	.125	-1	-20	-20	0	-2.0
1979	StL-N	0	0	—	3	2	0	0	0	11^1	13	0	9	5	17.5	3.97	95	.310	.431	1	.250	0	-0	-0	0	0.0
1980	StL-N	4	1	.800	30	1	0	0	3	64^2	57	2	41	36	13.9	3.48	106	.239	.356	3	.231	0	1	2	-1	0.1
1981	SD-N	2	2	.500	38	0	0	0	2	49	43	1	28	19	13.6	2.39	136	.239	.351	1	.250	0	6	5	-1	0.4
Total 5		17	18	.486	139	27	3	1	9	363^1	347	20	160	202	12.9	3.74	97	.256	.339	12	.162	2	-2	-4	-1	-0.2

■ BOB VAIL
Vail, Robert Garfield "Doc" b: 9/24/1881, Linneus, Maine d: 3/22/42, Philadelphia, Pa. 5'10", 165 lbs. Deb: 8/27/08

YEAR	TM/L	W	L	PCT	G	GS	CG	SH	SV	IP	H	HR	BB	SO	RAT	ERA	ERA+	OAV	OOB	BH	AVG	PB	PR	/A	PD	TPI
1908	Pit-N	1	2	.333	4	1	0	0	0	15	15	1	9	7	13.8	6.00	38	.268	.359	1	.333	1	-6	-6	-1	-0.6

■ EFRAIN VALDEZ
Valdez, Efrain Antonio b: 7/11/66, Nizao Bani, D.R. BL/TL, 5'11", 180 lbs. Deb: 8/13/90

YEAR	TM/L	W	L	PCT	G	GS	CG	SH	SV	IP	H	HR	BB	SO	RAT	ERA	ERA+	OAV	OOB	BH	AVG	PB	PR	/A	PD	TPI
1990	Cle-A	1	1	.500	13	0	0	0	0	23^2	20	2	14	13	12.9	3.04	131	.233	.340	0	—	0	2	2	0	0.2

■ RAFAEL VALDEZ
Valdez, Rafael Emilio (Diaz) b: 12/17/67, Nizao Boni, D.R. BR/TR, 5'11", 165 lbs. Deb: 4/18/90

YEAR	TM/L	W	L	PCT	G	GS	CG	SH	SV	IP	H	HR	BB	SO	RAT	ERA	ERA+	OAV	OOB	BH	AVG	PB	PR	/A	PD	TPI
1990	SD-N	0	1	.000	3	0	0	0	0	5^2	11	4	2	3	20.6	11.12	35	.393	.433	0	.000	-0	-5	-5	-0	-0.4

■ RENE VALDEZ
Valdez, Rene Gutierrez (b: Rene Gutierrez (Valdez)) b: 6/2/29, Guanabacoa, Cuba BR/TR, 6'3", 175 lbs. Deb: 4/21/57

YEAR	TM/L	W	L	PCT	G	GS	CG	SH	SV	IP	H	HR	BB	SO	RAT	ERA	ERA+	OAV	OOB	BH	AVG	PB	PR	/A	PD	TPI
1957	Bro-N	1	1	.500	5	1	0	0	0	13	13	1	7	10	13.8	5.54	75	.265	.357	0	.000	0	-2	-2	-0	-0.1

■ SERGIO VALDEZ
Valdez, Sergio Sanchez (b: Sergio Sanchez (Valdez)) b: 9/7/64, Elias Pina, D.R. BR/TR, 6', 165 lbs. Deb: 9/10/86

YEAR	TM/L	W	L	PCT	G	GS	CG	SH	SV	IP	H	HR	BB	SO	RAT	ERA	ERA+	OAV	OOB	BH	AVG	PB	PR	/A	PD	TPI
1986	Mon-N	0	4	.000	5	5	0	0	0	25	39	2	11	20	18.4	6.84	54	.361	.425	1	.125	-0	-9	-9	-0	-0.8
1989	Atl-N	1	2	.333	19	1	0	0	0	32^2	31	5	17	26	13.2	6.06	60	.246	.336	1	1.000	0	-9	-9	-0	-0.8
1990	Atl-N	0	0	—	6	0	0	0	0	5^1	6	0	3	3	15.2	6.75	58	.273	.360	0	—	0	-2	-2	0	-0.0
	Cle-A	6	6	.500	24	13	0	0	0	102^1	109	17	35	63	12.8	4.75	84	.276	.336	0	—	0	-10	-9	-0	-0.8
Total 3		7	12	.368	54	19	0	0	0	165^1	185	24	66	112	13.8	5.39	72	.284	.352	2	.222	0	-29	-28	-1	-2.4

■ CORKY VALENTINE
Valentine, Harold Lewis b: 1/4/29, Troy, Ohio BR/TR, 6'1", 203 lbs. Deb: 4/17/54

YEAR	TM/L	W	L	PCT	G	GS	CG	SH	SV	IP	H	HR	BB	SO	RAT	ERA	ERA+	OAV	OOB	BH	AVG	PB	PR	/A	PD	TPI
1954	Cin-N	12	11	.522	36	28	7	3	1	194^1	211	24	60	73	12.7	4.45	94	.282	.339	9	.138	-2	-8	-5	-2	-0.8
1955	Cin-N	2	1	.667	10	5	0	0	0	26^2	29	5	16	14	15.5	7.43	57	.276	.377	0	.000	-1	-10	-9	1	-0.8
Total 2		14	12	.538	46	33	7	3	1	221	240	29	76	87	13.1	4.81	87	.282	.344	9	.125	-3	-18	-15	-1	-1.6

■ JOHN VALENTINE
Valentine, John Gill b: 11/21/1855, Brooklyn, N.Y. d: 10/10/03, Central Islip, N.Y Deb: 5/03/1883

YEAR	TM/L	W	L	PCT	G	GS	CG	SH	SV	IP	H	HR	BB	SO	RAT	ERA	ERA+	OAV	OOB	BH	AVG	PB	PR	/A	PD	TPI
1883	Col-a	2	10	.167	13	12	11	0	0	102	130	0	17	13	13.0	3.53	87	.291	.317	17	.283	3	-3	-5	1	0.0

■ VITO VALENTINETTI
Valentinetti, Vito John b: 9/16/28, W.New York, N.J. BR/TR, 6', 195 lbs. Deb: 6/20/54

YEAR	TM/L	W	L	PCT	G	GS	CG	SH	SV	IP	H	HR	BB	SO	RAT	ERA	ERA+	OAV	OOB	BH	AVG	PB	PR	/A	PD	TPI
1954	Chi-A	0	0	—	1	0	0	0	0	1	4	1	2	1	54.0	54.00	7	.571	.667	0	—	0	-6	-6	0	-0.4
1956	Chi-N	6	4	.600	42	2	0	0	1	95^1	84	10	36	26	11.4	3.78	100	.243	.317	2	.100	-1	-0	-0	-1	-0.2
1957	Chi-N	0	0	—	9	0	0	0	0	12	12	1	7	8	14.3	2.25	172	.255	.352	0	.000	0	2	2	0	0.2
	Cle-A	2	2	.500	11	2	1	0	0	23^2	26	3	13	9	15.2	4.94	75	.289	.385	1	.200	-0	-3	-3	0	-0.2
1958	Det-A	1	0	1.000	15	0	0	0	2	18^2	18	4	5	10	11.6	3.38	120	.257	.316	0	—	0	1	1	-0	0.1
	Was-A	4	6	.400	23	10	2	0	0	95^2	106	16	49	33	14.8	5.08	75	.286	.373	9	.321	2	-14	-13	2	-0.9
	Yr	5	6	.455	38	10	2	0	2	114^1	124	20	54	43	14.2	4.80	80	.281	.362	9	.036	2	-13	-12	2	-0.9
1959	Was-A	0	2	.000	7	1	0	0	0	10^2	16	0	10	7	22.8	10.13	39	.356	.482	0	—	0	-7	-7	0	-0.5
Total 5		13	14	.481	108	15	3	0	3	257	266	35	122	94	13.8	4.73	81	.273	.358	12	.218	1	-27	-26	1	-1.9

■ FERNANDO VALENZUELA
Valenzuela, Fernando (Anguamea) b: 11/1/60, Navoja, Mexico BL/TL, 5'11", 180 lbs. Deb: 9/15/80

YEAR	TM/L	W	L	PCT	G	GS	CG	SH	SV	IP	H	HR	BB	SO	RAT	ERA	ERA+	OAV	OOB	BH	AVG	PB	PR	/A	PD	TPI
1980	LA-N	2	0	1.000	10	0	0	0	0	17^2	8	0	5	16	6.6	0.00	—	.136	.203	0	—	-0	7	7	0	0.7
1981	*LA-N	13	7	.650	25	25	11	8	0	192^1	140	11	61	180	9.5	2.48	134	.205	.271	16	.250	3	22	18	1	2.4
1982	LA-N	19	13	.594	37	37	18	4	0	285	247	13	83	199	10.5	2.87	121	.236	.294	16	.168	1	23	19	4	2.6
1983	*LA-N	15	10	.600	35	35	9	4	0	257	245	16	99	189	12.2	3.75	96	.255	.327	17	.187	2	-3	-4	4	0.1
1984	LA-N	12	17	.414	34	34	12	2	0	261	218	14	106	240	11.2	3.03	116	.229	.308	15	.190	4	16	14	3	2.3
1985	*LA-N	17	10	.630	35	35	14	5	0	272^1	211	14	101	208	10.3	2.45	142	.214	.288	21	.216	4	35	31	1	3.9
1986	LA-N	21	11	.656	34	34	20	3	0	269^1	226	18	85	242	10.4	3.14	110	.226	.288	24	.220	4	17	9	3	1.7
1987	LA-N	14	14	.500	34	34	12	1	0	251	254	25	124	190	13.7	3.98	100	.262	.349	13	.141	-1	3	-0	3	0.2
1988	LA-N	5	8	.385	23	22	3	0	1	142^1	142	11	76	64	13.8	4.24	79	.268	.360	8	.182	1	-12	-14	2	-0.9
1989	LA-N	10	13	.435	31	31	3	0	0	196^2	185	11	98	116	13.0	3.43	99	.251	.340	12	.182	1	1	-0	2	0.2
1990	LA-N	13	13	.500	33	33	5	2	0	204	223	19	77	115	13.2	4.59	78	.276	.339	21	.304	8	-18	-23	0	-1.5
Total 11		141	116	.549	331	320	107	29	2	2348^2	2099	152	915	1759	11.6	3.31	106	.240	.314	163	.202	28	90	56	24	11.7

■ JULIO VALERA
Valera, Julio Enrique b: 10/13/68, San Sebastian, P.R. BR/TR, 6'2", 185 lbs. Deb: 9/01/90

YEAR	TM/L	W	L	PCT	G	GS	CG	SH	SV	IP	H	HR	BB	SO	RAT	ERA	ERA+	OAV	OOB	BH	AVG	PB	PR	/A	PD	TPI
1990	NY-N	1	1	.500	3	3	0	0	0	13	20	1	7	4	18.7	6.92	53	.351	.422	1	.200	0	-5	-5	-0	-0.4

■ CLAY Van ALSTYNE
Van Alstyne, Clayton Emory "Spike" b: 5/24/1900, Stuyvesant, N.Y. d: 1/5/60, Hudson, N.Y. BR/TR, 5'11", 180 lbs. Deb: 8/20/27

YEAR	TM/L	W	L	PCT	G	GS	CG	SH	SV	IP	H	HR	BB	SO	RAT	ERA	ERA+	OAV	OOB	BH	AVG	PB	PR	/A	PD	TPI
1927	Was-A	0	0	—	2	0	0	0	0	3	3	0	0	0	9.0	3.00	136	.250	.250	0	—	0	0	0	-0	0.0
1928	Was-A	0	0	—	4	0	0	0	0	21^1	26	0	13	5	16.9	5.48	73	.329	.430	2	.250	1	-3	-3	1	0.0
Total 2		0	0	—	6	0	0	0	0	24^1	29	0	13	5	15.9	5.18	78	.319	.410	2	.250	1	-3	-3	1	0.0

■ RUSS Van ATTA
Van Atta, Russell "Sheriff" b: 6/21/06, Augusta, N.J. d: 10/10/86, Andover, N.J. BL/TL, 6', 184 lbs. Deb: 4/25/33

YEAR	TM/L	W	L	PCT	G	GS	CG	SH	SV	IP	H	HR	BB	SO	RAT	ERA	ERA+	OAV	OOB	BH	AVG	PB	PR	/A	PD	TPI
1933	NY-A	12	4	.750	26	22	10	2	1	157	160	8	63	76	12.8	4.18	93	.282	.332	17	.283	4	2	-5	0	-0.1
1934	NY-A	3	5	.375	28	9	0	0	0	88	107	3	46	39	15.9	6.34	64	.307	.390	6	.207	1	-18	-22	-1	-1.9
1935	NY-A	0	0	—	5	0	0	0	0	4^2	5	0	4	3	17.4	3.86	105	.263	.391	0	.000	-0	0	0	-0	0.0
	StL-A	9	16	.360	53	17	1	0	3	170^1	201	10	86	87	15.3	5.34	90	.292	.373	9	.214	-1	-17	-10	-2	-1.1
	Yr	9	16	.360	58	17	1	0	3	175	206	10	90	90	15.4	5.30	90	.291	.373	1	.023	-1	-16	-10	-2	-1.1
1936	StL-A	4	7	.364	52	9	2	0	2	122^2	164	9	68	59	17.2	6.60	81	.320	.401	5	.172	-1	-21	-17	1	-1.3
1937	StL-A	1	2	.333	16	6	1	0	0	58^2	74	2	32	34	16.3	5.52	87	.307	.388	6	.462	3	-6	-5	0	0.0
1938	StL-A	4	7	.364	25	12	3	1	0	104	118	7	61	35	15.6	6.06	82	.289	.382	4	.133	-2	-15	-13	1	-1.1
1939	StL-A	0	0	—	2	1	0	0	0	7	9	0	7	6	21.9	11.57	42	.310	.459	0	.000	-0	-5	-5	-0	-0.4
Total 7		33	41	.446	207	76	17	3	6	712^1	838	39	367	339	15.4	5.60	82	.293	.375	47	.228	4	-80	-78	-1	-5.9

■ OZZIE Van BRABANT
Van Brabant, Camille Oscar b: 9/28/26, Kingsville, Ont., Canada BR/TR, 6'1", 165 lbs. Deb: 4/13/54

YEAR	TM/L	W	L	PCT	G	GS	CG	SH	SV	IP	H	HR	BB	SO	RAT	ERA	ERA+	OAV	OOB	BH	AVG	PB	PR	/A	PD	TPI
1954	Phi-A	0	2	.000	9	2	0	0	0	26^2	35	3	18	10	18.2	7.09	55	.347	.450	1	.200	1	-10	-9	1	-0.7
1955	KC-A	0	0	—	2	0	0	0	0	2	4	1	2	1	27.0	18.00	23	.400	.500	0	—	0	-3	-3	0	-0.2
Total 2		0	2	.000	11	2	0	0	0	28^2	39	4	20	11	18.8	7.85	50	.351	.455	1	.200	1	-13	-13	1	-0.9

■ DAZZY VANCE
Vance, Clarence Arthur b: 3/4/1891, Orient, Iowa d: 2/16/61, Homosassa Springs Fla BR/TR, 6'2", 200 lbs. Deb: 4/16/15 H

YEAR	TM/L	W	L	PCT	G	GS	CG	SH	SV	IP	H	HR	BB	SO	RAT	ERA	ERA+	OAV	OOB	BH	AVG	PB	PR	/A	PD	TPI
1915	Pit-N	0	1	.000	1	1	0	0	0	2^2	3	0	5	0	30.4	10.13	27	.375	.643	0	—	-0	-2	-2	0	-0.1
	NY-A	0	3	.000	8	3	1	0	0	28	23	1	16	18	13.2	3.54	83	.232	.350	2	.667	2	-2	-0	-0	0.0
1918	NY-A	0	0	—	2	0	0	0	0	2^1	9	0	2	0	42.4	15.43	18	.692	.733	0	—	0	-3	-3	0	-0.2
1922	Bro-N	18	12	.600	36	30	16	5	0	245^2	259	9	94	134	13.2	3.70	110	.276	.347	20	.225	1	11	10	-0	1.1
1923	Bro-N	18	15	.545	37	35	21	3	0	280^1	263	9	100	197	12.0	3.50	111	.250	.322	7	.084	-3	16	12	-1	0.7
1924	Bro-N	28	6	.824	35	34	30	3	0	308^2	238	11	77	262	9.4	2.16	174	.213	.269	16	.151	-2	59	55	-2	5.4
1925	Bro-N	22	9	.710	31	31	26	4	0	265^1	247	8	66	221	11.0	3.53	118	.250	.304	14	.143	-0	22	19	-1	1.7

YEAR	TM/L	W	L	PCT	G	GS	CG	SH	SV	IP	H	HR	BB	SO	RAT	ERA	ERA+	OAV	OOB	BH	AVG	PB	PR	/A	PD	TPI
1926	Bro-N	9	10	.474	24	22	12	0	1	169	172	7	58	**140**	12.3	3.89	98	.271	.333	10	.182	-1	-1	-1	0	-0.1
1927	Bro-N	16	15	.516	34	32	**25**	2	1	273¹	242	12	69	184	10.4	2.70	147	**.239**	.291	15	.167	-2	37	38	-3	3.5
1928	Bro-N	22	10	.688	38	32	24	4	2	280¹	226	11	72	**200**	9.8	2.09	190	**.221**	**.277**	17	.177	2	59	59	-0	**6.4**
1929	Bro-N	14	13	.519	31	26	17	1	0	231¹	244	15	47	126	11.7	3.89	119	.274	.316	10	.135	-2	21	19	0	1.5
1930	Bro-N	17	15	.531	35	31	20	4	0	258²	241	15	55	173	10.5	2.61	188	**.246**	**.289**	12	.135	-5	68	66	-2	**5.6**
1931	Bro-N	11	13	.458	30	29	12	2	0	218²	221	12	53	150	11.3	3.38	113	.261	.304	9	.134	-2	12	11	-0	0.8
1932	Bro-N	12	11	.522	27	24	9	1	1	175²	171	10	57	103	11.7	4.20	91	.256	.315	5	.089	-4	-6	-7	-1	-1.1
1933	StL-N	6	2	.750	28	11	2	0	3	99	105	3	28	67	12.2	3.55	98	.267	.318	5	.179	-1	-2	-1	-1	-0.2
1934	Cin-N	0	2	.000	6	2	0	0	0	18	28	1	11	9	20.0	7.50	54	.350	.435	1	.250	-0	-7	-7	-0	-0.5
	*StL-N	1	1	.500	19	4	1	0	1	59	62	4	14	33	11.9	3.66	115	.271	.318	2	.133	-0	3	4	-0	0.3
	Yr	1	3	.250	25	6	1	0	1	77	90	5	25	42	13.7	4.56	92	.290	.347	0	.000	-0	-4	-3	-0	-0.2
1935	Bro-N	3	2	.600	20	0	0	0	2	51	55	3	16	28	13.1	4.41	90	.268	.330	1	.059	-2	-2	-2	-0	-0.3
Total 16		197	140	.585	442	347	216	29	11	2967	2809	131	840	2045	11.3	3.24	125	.251	.308	146	.150	-17	281	266	-11	24.5

■ SANDY VANCE

Vance, Gene Covington   b: 1/5/47, Lamar, Colo.   BR/TR, 6'2", 180 lbs.   Deb: 4/26/70

YEAR	TM/L	W	L	PCT	G	GS	CG	SH	SV	IP	H	HR	BB	SO	RAT	ERA	ERA+	OAV	OOB	BH	AVG	PB	PR	/A	PD	TPI
1970	LA-N	7	7	.500	20	18	2	0	0	115	109	9	37	45	11.5	3.13	122	.248	.308	7	.189	1	12	9	-2	0.7
1971	LA-N	2	1	.667	10	3	0	0	0	26	38	1	9	11	16.3	6.92	47	.355	.405	0	.000	-0	-10	-11	-0	-1.0
Total 2		9	8	.529	30	21	2	0	0	141	147	10	46	56	12.4	3.83	97	.269	.327	7	.167	0	2	-2	-2	-0.3

■ JOE VANCE

Vance, Joseph Albert "Sandy"   b: 9/16/05, Devine, Tex.   d: 7/4/78, Devine, Tex.   BR/TR, 6'1.5", 190 lbs.   Deb: 4/18/35

YEAR	TM/L	W	L	PCT	G	GS	CG	SH	SV	IP	H	HR	BB	SO	RAT	ERA	ERA+	OAV	OOB	BH	AVG	PB	PR	/A	PD	TPI
1935	Chi-A	2	2	.500	10	0	0	0	0	31	36	1	21	12	16.5	6.68	69	.295	.399	2	.182	-1	-8	-7	0	-0.6
1937	NY-A	1	0	1.000	2	2	0	0	0	15	11	2	9	3	12.0	3.00	148	.204	.317	0	.000	-1	3	2	1	0.2
1938	NY-A	0	0	—	3	1	0	0	0	11¹	20	2	4	2	19.1	7.15	63	.408	.453	3	.750	2	-3	-3	0	0.0
Total 3		3	2	.600	15	3	0	0	0	57¹	67	5	34	17	15.9	5.81	79	.298	.390	5	.250	1	-8	-8	1	-0.4

■ CHRIS Van CUYK

Van Cuyk, Christian Gerald   b: 3/1/27, Kimberly, Wis.   BL/TL, 6'6", 215 lbs.   Deb: 7/16/50

YEAR	TM/L	W	L	PCT	G	GS	CG	SH	SV	IP	H	HR	BB	SO	RAT	ERA	ERA+	OAV	OOB	BH	AVG	PB	PR	/A	PD	TPI
1950	Bro-N	1	3	.250	12	4	1	0	0	33¹	33	3	12	21	12.4	4.86	84	.266	.336	1	.100	-1	-3	-3	-1	-0.3
1951	Bro-N	1	2	.333	9	6	0	0	0	29¹	33	4	11	16	14.7	5.52	71	.295	.378	2	.250	0	-5	-5	0	-0.4
1952	Bro-N	5	6	.455	23	16	4	0	1	97²	104	12	40	66	13.7	5.16	71	.271	.347	8	.242	2	-16	-17	-1	-1.5
Total 3		7	11	.389	44	26	5	0	1	160¹	170	19	63	103	13.6	5.16	73	.274	.351	11	.216	1	-23	-25	-2	-2.2

■ JOHNNY Van CUYK

Van Cuyk, John Henry   b: 7/7/21, Little Chute, Wis.   BL/TL, 6'1", 190 lbs.   Deb: 9/18/47

YEAR	TM/L	W	L	PCT	G	GS	CG	SH	SV	IP	H	HR	BB	SO	RAT	ERA	ERA+	OAV	OOB	BH	AVG	PB	PR	/A	PD	TPI
1947	Bro-N	0	0	—	2	0	0	0	0	3¹	5	0	1	2	16.2	5.40	77	.357	.400	0	—	0	-0	-0	0	0.0
1948	Bro-N	0	0	—	3	0	0	0	0	5	4	1	1	1	9.0	3.60	111	.200	.238	0	—	0	0	0	0	0.0
1949	Bro-N	0	0	—	2	0	0	0	0	2	3	0	1	0	18.0	9.00	46	.429	.500	0	—	0	-1	-1	0	0.0
Total 3		0	0	—	7	0	0	0	0	10¹	12	1	3	3	13.1	5.23	78	.293	.341	0	—	0	-1	-1	0	0.0

■ ED VANDE BERG

Vande Berg, Edward John   b: 10/26/58, Redlands, Cal.   BR/TL, 6'2", 175 lbs.   Deb: 4/07/82

YEAR	TM/L	W	L	PCT	G	GS	CG	SH	SV	IP	H	HR	BB	SO	RAT	ERA	ERA+	OAV	OOB	BH	AVG	PB	PR	/A	PD	TPI
1982	Sea-A	9	4	.692	**78**	0	0	0	5	76	54	5	32	60	10.4	2.37	179	.207	.298	0	—	0	14	16	2	1.8
1983	Sea-A	2	4	.333	68	0	0	0	5	64¹	59	6	22	49	11.5	3.36	127	.246	.312	0	—	0	5	6	0	0.6
1984	Sea-A	8	12	.400	50	17	2	0	7	130¹	165	18	50	71	14.8	4.76	84	.313	.373	0	—	0	-11	-11	0	-1.0
1985	Sea-A	2	1	.667	76	0	0	0	3	67²	71	4	31	34	13.7	3.72	113	.274	.354	0	—	0	3	4	1	0.4
1986	LA-N	1	5	.167	60	0	0	0	0	71¹	83	8	33	42	14.8	3.41	101	.290	.366	0	.000	-0	2	0	1	0.1
1987	Cle-A	1	0	1.000	55	0	0	0	0	72¹	96	9	21	40	14.6	5.10	89	.325	.370	0	—	0	-5	-5	0	-0.3
1988	Tex-A	2	2	.500	26	0	0	0	0	37	44	2	11	18	13.4	4.14	99	.308	.357	0	—	0	-1	-0	-0	0.0
Total 7		25	28	.472	413	17	2	0	22	519	572	52	200	314	13.5	3.92	104	.284	.351	0	.000	-0	8	10	4	1.6

■ HY VANDENBERG

Vandenberg, Harold Harris   b: 3/17/06, Abilene, Kan.   BR/TR, 6'2.5", 190 lbs.   Deb: 6/08/35

YEAR	TM/L	W	L	PCT	G	GS	CG	SH	SV	IP	H	HR	BB	SO	RAT	ERA	ERA+	OAV	OOB	BH	AVG	PB	PR	/A	PD	TPI
1935	Bos-A	0	0	—	3	0	0	0	0	5¹	15	1	4	2	32.1	20.25	23	.500	.559	1	1.000	0	-9	-9	0	-0.6
1937	NY-N	0	1	.000	1	1	1	0	0	8	10	0	6	2	18.0	7.88	49	.313	.421	0	.000	-1	-4	-4	1	-0.2
1938	NY-N	0	1	.000	6	1	0	0	0	18	28	2	12	7	20.0	7.50	50	.368	.455	0	.000	-1	-7	-7	1	-0.6
1939	NY-N	0	0	—	2	1	0	0	0	6¹	10	0	6	3	22.7	5.68	69	.345	.457	0	.000	-0	-1	-1	0	0.0
1940	NY-N	1	1	.500	13	3	1	0	1	32¹	27	2	16	17	12.2	3.90	100	.227	.324	1	.125	-0	-0	-0	-0	0.0
1944	Chi-N	7	4	.636	35	9	2	0	2	126¹	123	8	51	54	12.5	3.63	97	.255	.327	9	.237	1	-0	-1	0	0.0
1945	*Chi-N	7	3	.700	30	7	3	1	2	95¹	91	4	33	35	12.1	3.49	105	.259	.330	4	.125	-1	3	2	0	0.1
Total 7		15	10	.600	90	22	7	1	5	291²	304	17	128	120	13.5	4.32	85	.271	.349	15	.169	-1	-19	-21	2	-1.3

■ JOHNNY VANDER MEER

Vander Meer, John Samuel "Double No-Hit" or "The Dutch Master"   b: 11/2/14, Prospect Park, N.J.   BB/TL, 6'1", 190 lbs.   Deb: 4/22/37

YEAR	TM/L	W	L	PCT	G	GS	CG	SH	SV	IP	H	HR	BB	SO	RAT	ERA	ERA+	OAV	OOB	BH	AVG	PB	PR	/A	PD	TPI
1937	Cin-N	3	5	.375	19	9	4	0	0	84¹	63	0	69	52	14.3	3.84	97	.209	.359	5	.217	1	1	-1	2	0.1
1938	Cin-N	15	10	.600	32	29	16	3	0	225¹	177	12	103	125	11.3	3.12	117	**.213**	.302	15	.181	-2	17	13	-2	0.9
1939	Cin-N	5	9	.357	30	21	8	0	0	129	128	7	95	102	15.7	4.67	82	.264	.387	4	.111	-1	-11	-12	-2	-1.4
1940	*Cin-N	3	1	.750	10	7	2	0	1	48	38	3	41	41	15.0	3.75	101	.211	.360	6	.300	2	1	0	-0	0.2
1941	Cin-N	16	13	.552	33	32	18	6	0	226¹	172	8	126	**202**	11.9	2.82	127	.214	.321	10	.132	-3	20	19	0	1.8
1942	Cin-N	18	12	.600	33	33	21	4	0	244	188	6	102	**186**	10.7	2.43	135	.208	.290	11	.147	-1	24	23	-1	2.4
1943	Cin-N	15	16	.484	36	36	21	3	0	289	228	5	162	**174**	12.2	2.87	116	.224	.332	13	.137	-2	17	14	1	1.5
1946	Cin-N	10	12	.455	29	25	11	4	0	204¹	175	11	78	94	11.1	3.17	105	.233	.305	18	.247	2	5	4	-2	0.4
1947	Cin-N	9	14	.391	30	29	9	3	0	186	186	11	87	79	13.4	4.40	93	.261	.343	5	.088	-3	-7	-6	-1	-0.8
1948	Cin-N	17	14	.548	33	33	14	3	0	232	204	15	124	120	12.8	3.41	115	.239	.336	11	.141	0	14	13	-1	1.2
1949	Cin-N	5	10	.333	28	24	7	3	0	159²	172	7	85	76	14.6	4.90	85	.281	.370	4	.077	-3	-15	-13	1	-1.3
1950	Chi-N	3	4	.429	32	6	0	0	1	73²	60	10	59	41	14.8	3.79	111	.221	.363	2	.125	-0	3	3	-0	0.3
1951	Cle-A	0	1	.000	1	1	0	0	0	3	8	1	1	2	27.0	18.00	21	.500	.529	0	.000	-0	-5	-5	1	-0.3
Total 13		119	121	.496	346	285	131	29	2	2104²	1799	100	1132	1294	12.6	3.44	107	.232	.332	104	.152	-9	63	53	-3	5.0

■ BEN Van DYKE

Van Dyke, Benjamin Harrison   b: 8/15/1888, Clintonville, Pa.   d: 10/22/73, Sarasota, Fla.   BR/TL, 6'1", 150 lbs.   Deb: 5/11/09

YEAR	TM/L	W	L	PCT	G	GS	CG	SH	SV	IP	H	HR	BB	SO	RAT	ERA	ERA+	OAV	OOB	BH	AVG	PB	PR	/A	PD	TPI
1909	Phi-N	0	0	—	2	0	0	0	0	7¹	7	0	4	5	13.5	3.68	71	.269	.367	0	.000	-0	-1	-1	-0	-0.1
1912	Bos-A	0	0	—	3	1	0	0	0	14¹	13	0	7	8	13.2	3.14	108	.245	.344	1	.250	-0	0	0	-0	0.0
Total 2		0	0	—	5	1	0	0	0	21²	20	0	11	13	13.3	3.32	94	.253	.352	1	.143	-0	-1	-0	-1	-0.1

■ ELAM VANGILDER

Vangilder, Elam Russell   b: 4/23/1896, Cape Girardeau, Mo   d: 4/30/77, Cape Girardeau, Mo   BR/TR, 6'1", 192 lbs.   Deb: 9/18/19

YEAR	TM/L	W	L	PCT	G	GS	CG	SH	SV	IP	H	HR	BB	SO	RAT	ERA	ERA+	OAV	OOB	BH	AVG	PB	PR	/A	PD	TPI
1919	StL-A	1	0	1.000	3	1	0	0	0	13	15	0	3	6	12.5	2.08	160	.306	.346	2	.667	1	2	2	1	0.3
1920	StL-A	3	8	.273	24	13	4	0	0	104²	131	7	40	25	15.0	5.50	71	.310	.373	4	.133	-2	-20	-18	0	-1.8
1921	StL-A	11	12	.478	31	21	10	1	0	180¹	196	10	67	48	13.2	3.94	114	.278	.342	13	.200	-2	7	11	0	0.9
1922	StL-A	19	13	.594	43	30	19	3	4	245	248	13	48	63	11.1	3.42	121	.270	.310	32	.344	13	17	20	-2	3.2
1923	StL-A	16	17	.485	41	35	20	4	1	282¹	276	11	120	74	12.8	3.06	136	.266	.345	24	.218	-0	29	**35**	-3	3.3
1924	StL-A	5	10	.333	43	18	5	0	1	145¹	183	10	55	49	15.3	5.64	80	.317	.385	13	.295	4	-23	-18	-1	-1.1
1925	StL-A	14	8	.636	52	16	4	1	6	193¹	225	11	92	61	15.0	4.70	99	.303	.385	13	.183	-3	-7	-1	-0	-0.2
1926	StL-A	9	11	.450	42	19	8	1	1	181	196	12	98	40	14.7	5.17	83	.285	.376	11	.190	1	-23	-18	-2	-1.7
1927	StL-A	10	12	.455	44	23	12	3	1	203	245	13	102	62	15.6	4.79	91	.310	.392	19	.279	3	-15	-10	-4	-0.9
1928	Det-A	11	10	.524	38	11	7	0	5	156¹	163	4	67	43	13.4	3.91	105	.272	.348	15	.259	2	2	3	0	0.5
1929	Det-A	0	1	.000	6	0	0	0	0	11¹	16	1	7	3	18.3	6.35	68	.348	.434	0	.000	-0	-3	-3	1	-0.1
Total 11		99	102	.493	367	187	90	13	19	1715²	1894	92	699	474	13.8	4.28	100	.288	.360	146	.243	16	-33	3	-7	2.4

■ GEORGE Van HALTREN

Van Haltren, George Edward Martin "Rip"   b: 3/30/1866, St.Louis, Mo.   d: 9/29/45, Oakland, Cal.   BL/TL, 5'11", 170 lbs.   Deb: 6/27/1887   M♦

YEAR	TM/L	W	L	PCT	G	GS	CG	SH	SV	IP	H	HR	BB	SO	RAT	ERA	ERA+	OAV	OOB	BH	AVG	PB	PR	/A	PD	TPI
1887	Chi-N	11	7	.611	20	18	18	1	1	161	177	7	66	76	13.6	3.86	116	.271	.338	35	.203	-2	3	11	-0	0.9
1888	Chi-N	13	13	.500	30	24	24	4	1	245²	263	15	60	139	11.8	3.52	86	.264	.306	90	.283	11	-19	-14	2	-1.2

YEAR TM/L	W	L	PCT	G	GS	CG	SH	SV	IP	H	HR	BB	SO	RAT	ERA	ERA+	OAV	OOB	BH	AVG	PB	PR	/A	PD	TPI
1890 Bro-P	15	10	.600	28	25	23	0	2	223	272	8	89	48	14.6	4.28	104	.288	.349	126	.335	10	-1	4	4	0.3
1891 Bal-a	0	1	.000	6	1	0	0	0	23	38	1	10	7	18.8	5.09	73	.357	.412	180	.318	3	-3	-3	0	-0.2
1892 Bal-N	0	0	—	4	0	0	0	0	14²	28	1	7	5	21.5	9.20	38	.389	.443	168	.302	2	-10	-9	0	-0.7
1895 NY-N	0	0	—	1	0	0	0	0	5	13	0	2	1	27.0	12.60	37	.473	.509	177	.340	0	-4	-4	0	-0.2
1896 NY-N	1	0	1.000	2	0	0	0	0	8	5	1	1	3	6.8	2.25	187	.179	.207	197	.351	1	2	2	0	0.2
1900 NY-N	0	0	—	1	0	0	0	0	3	1	0	3	0	12.0	0.00	—	.105	.319	180	.315	0	1	1	-0	0.1
1901 NY-N	0	0	—	1	0	0	0	0	6	12	0	6	2	28.5	3.00	110	.411	.525	182	.335	0	0	0	1	0.1
Total 9	40	31	.563	93	68	65	5	4	689¹	809	33	244	281	13.8	4.05	96	.282	.339	2532	.316	27	-31	-13	7	-0.8

■ IKE Van ZANDT
Van Zandt, Charles Isaac b: 1877, Brooklyn, N.Y. d: 9/14/08, Nashua, N.H. BL , Deb: 8/05/01 ◆

YEAR TM/L	W	L	PCT	G	GS	CG	SH	SV	IP	H	HR	BB	SO	RAT	ERA	ERA+	OAV	OOB	BH	AVG	PB	PR	/A	PD	TPI
1901 NY-N	0	0	—	2	0	0	0	0	12²	16	0	8	2	17.8	7.11	47	.306	.408	1	.167	-0	-5	-5	-1	-0.4
1905 StL-A	0	0	—	1	0	0	0	0	6²	2	0	2	3	5.4	0.00	—	.096	.175	75	.233	0	2	2	0	0.2
Total 2	0	0	—	3	0	0	0	0	19¹	18	0	10	5	13.5	4.66	65	.246	.345	76	.224	-0	-3	-3	-1	-0.2

■ ANDY VARGA
Varga, Andrew William b: 12/11/30, Chicago, Ill. BR/TL, 6'4", 187 lbs. Deb: 9/09/50

YEAR TM/L	W	L	PCT	G	GS	CG	SH	SV	IP	H	HR	BB	SO	RAT	ERA	ERA+	OAV	OOB	BH	AVG	PB	PR	/A	PD	TPI
1950 Chi-N	0	0	—	1	0	0	0	0	1	1	0	1	0	9.0	0.00	—	.000	.333	0	—	0	0	0	0	0.0
1951 Chi-N	0	0	—	2	0	0	0	0	3	2	0	6	1	24.0	3.00	136	.200	.500	0	—	0	0	0	0	0.0
Total 2	0	0	—	3	0	0	0	0	4	2	0	7	1	20.3	2.25	183	.167	.474	0	—	0	1	1	0	0.0

■ ROBERTO VARGAS
Vargas, Roberto Enrique b: 5/29/29, Santurce, P.R. BL/TL, 5'11", 170 lbs. Deb: 4/17/55

YEAR TM/L	W	L	PCT	G	GS	CG	SH	SV	IP	H	HR	BB	SO	RAT	ERA	ERA+	OAV	OOB	BH	AVG	PB	PR	/A	PD	TPI
1955 Mil-N	0	0	—	25	0	0	0	2	24²	39	4	14	13	19.7	8.76	43	.355	.432	1	.500	0	-13	-14	1	-1.1

■ BILL VARGUS
Vargus, William Fay b: 11/11/1899, N.Scituate, Mass. d: 2/12/79, Hyannis, Mass. BL/TL, 6', 165 lbs. Deb: 6/23/25

YEAR TM/L	W	L	PCT	G	GS	CG	SH	SV	IP	H	HR	BB	SO	RAT	ERA	ERA+	OAV	OOB	BH	AVG	PB	PR	/A	PD	TPI
1925 Bos-N	1	1	.500	11	2	1	0	0	36¹	45	1	13	5	14.9	3.96	102	.302	.366	3	.250	0	1	0	0	0.0
1926 Bos-N	0	0	—	4	0	0	0	0	3	4	0	1	0	15.0	3.00	118	.333	.385	0	—	0	0	0	0	0.0
Total 2	1	1	.500	15	2	1	0	0	39¹	49	1	14	5	14.9	3.89	102	.304	.367	3	.250	0	2	0	0	0.0

■ DIKE VARNEY
Varney, Lawrence Delano b: 8/9/1880, Dover, N.H. d: 4/23/50, Long Island City, N.Y. TL , 6', 165 lbs. Deb: 7/03/02

YEAR TM/L	W	L	PCT	G	GS	CG	SH	SV	IP	H	HR	BB	SO	RAT	ERA	ERA+	OAV	OOB	BH	AVG	PB	PR	/A	PD	TPI
1902 Cle-A	1	1	.500	3	3	0	0	0	14²	14	0	12	7	16.0	6.14	56	.252	.385	1	.167	-0	-4	-4	0	-0.3

■ CAL VASBINDER
Vasbinder, Moses Calhoun b: 7/19/1880, Scio, Ohio d: 12/22/50, Cadiz, Ohio BR/TR, 6'2", Deb: 4/27/02

YEAR TM/L	W	L	PCT	G	GS	CG	SH	SV	IP	H	HR	BB	SO	RAT	ERA	ERA+	OAV	OOB	BH	AVG	PB	PR	/A	PD	TPI
1902 Cle-A	0	0	—	2	0	0	0	0	5	5	1	8	2	23.4	9.00	38	.261	.478	1	.500	0	-3	-3	0	-0.1

■ RAFAEL VASQUEZ
Vasquez, Rafael b: 6/28/58, LaRomana, D.R. BR/TR, 6', 160 lbs. Deb: 4/06/79

YEAR TM/L	W	L	PCT	G	GS	CG	SH	SV	IP	H	HR	BB	SO	RAT	ERA	ERA+	OAV	OOB	BH	AVG	PB	PR	/A	PD	TPI
1979 Sea-A	1	0	1.000	9	0	0	0	0	16	23	4	6	9	16.9	5.06	86	.354	.417	0	—	0	-2	-1	-0	-0.1

■ PORTER VAUGHAN
Vaughan, Cecil Porter "Lefty" b: 5/11/19, Stevensville, Va. BR/TL, 6'1", 178 lbs. Deb: 6/16/40

YEAR TM/L	W	L	PCT	G	GS	CG	SH	SV	IP	H	HR	BB	SO	RAT	ERA	ERA+	OAV	OOB	BH	AVG	PB	PR	/A	PD	TPI
1940 Phi-A	2	9	.182	18	15	5	0	2	99¹	104	9	61	46	15.2	5.35	83	.264	.367	8	.235	0	-11	-10	-1	-0.9
1941 Phi-A	0	2	.000	5	3	1	0	0	22²	32	3	12	6	17.5	7.94	53	.327	.400	1	.143	0	-10	-9	0	-0.8
1946 Phi-A	0	0	—	1	0	0	0	0	0	1	0	1	0	—	—	—	1.000	1.000	0	—	0	0	0	0	0.0
Total 3	2	11	.154	24	18	6	0	2	122	137	12	74	52	15.8	5.83	75	.278	.375	9	.220	-0	-20	-19	-1	-1.7

■ CHARLIE VAUGHAN
Vaughan, Charles Wayne b: 10/6/47, Mercedes, Tex. BR/TL, 6'1.5", 185 lbs. Deb: 9/03/66

YEAR TM/L	W	L	PCT	G	GS	CG	SH	SV	IP	H	HR	BB	SO	RAT	ERA	ERA+	OAV	OOB	BH	AVG	PB	PR	/A	PD	TPI
1966 Atl-N	1	0	1.000	1	1	0	0	0	7	8	0	3	6	14.1	2.57	141	.296	.367	1	.250	0	1	1	0	0.1
1969 Atl-N	0	0	—	1	0	0	0	0	1	1	0	3	1	36.0	18.00	20	.250	.571	0	—	0	-2	-2	0	0.0
Total 2	1	0	1.000	2	1	0	0	0	8	9	0	6	7	16.9	4.50	81	.290	.405	1	.250	0	-1	-1	0	0.1

■ ROY VAUGHN
Vaughn, Clarence Leroy b: 9/4/11, Sedalia, Mo. d: 3/1/37, Martinsville, Va. BB/TR, 6'0.5", 178 lbs. Deb: 7/01/34

YEAR TM/L	W	L	PCT	G	GS	CG	SH	SV	IP	H	HR	BB	SO	RAT	ERA	ERA+	OAV	OOB	BH	AVG	PB	PR	/A	PD	TPI
1934 Phi-A	0	0	—	2	0	0	0	0	4¹	3	1	3	1	12.5	2.08	211	.176	.300	0	.000	-0	1	1	-0	0.1

■ DE WAYNE VAUGHN
Vaughn, De Wayne Mathew b: 7/22/59, Oklahoma City, Okla BR/TR, 5'11", 180 lbs. Deb: 4/17/88

YEAR TM/L	W	L	PCT	G	GS	CG	SH	SV	IP	H	HR	BB	SO	RAT	ERA	ERA+	OAV	OOB	BH	AVG	PB	PR	/A	PD	TPI
1988 Tex-A	0	0	—	8	0	0	0	0	15¹	24	4	4	8	16.4	7.63	53	.348	.384	0	—	0	-6	-6	-0	-0.5

■ FARMER VAUGHN
Vaughn, Harry Francis b: 3/1/1864, Rural Dale, Ohio d: 2/21/14, Cincinnati, Ohio BR/TR, 6'3", 177 lbs. Deb: 10/07/1886 ◆

YEAR TM/L	W	L	PCT	G	GS	CG	SH	SV	IP	H	HR	BB	SO	RAT	ERA	ERA+	OAV	OOB	BH	AVG	PB	PR	/A	PD	TPI
1891 Cin-a	0	0	—	1	0	0	0	0	7	12	0	1	0	16.7	3.86	107	.366	.384	45	.257	-0	-0	0	-0	0.0

■ HIPPO VAUGHN
Vaughn, James Leslie b: 4/9/1888, Weatherford, Tex. d: 5/29/66, Chicago, Ill. BB/TL, 6'4", 215 lbs. Deb: 6/19/08

YEAR TM/L	W	L	PCT	G	GS	CG	SH	SV	IP	H	HR	BB	SO	RAT	ERA	ERA+	OAV	OOB	BH	AVG	PB	PR	/A	PD	TPI
1908 NY-A	0	0	—	2	0	0	0	0	2¹	1	0	4	2	19.3	3.86	64	.167	.500	0	.000	-0	-0	-0	0	0.0
1910 NY-A	13	11	.542	30	25	18	5	1	221²	190	1	58	107	10.5	1.83	146	.237	.297	10	.133	-3	17	20	-0	2.1
1911 NY-A	8	10	.444	26	18	11	0	0	145²	158	2	54	74	13.5	4.39	82	.284	.354	7	.143	-1	-17	-13	0	-1.1
1912 NY-A	2	8	.200	15	10	5	1	0	63	66	1	37	46	14.9	5.14	70	.264	.361	2	.095	-2	-13	-11	1	-1.0
Was-A	4	3	.571	12	8	4	0	0	81	75	0	43	49	13.6	2.89	115	.253	.356	6	.200	-1	4	4	2	0.5
Yr	6	11	.353	27	18	9	1	0	144	141	1	80	95	14.1	3.88	89	.258	.358	8	.157	-3	-9	-7	3	-0.5
1913 Chi-N	5	1	.833	7	6	5	2	0	56	37	0	27	36	10.6	1.45	220	.182	.284	4	.190	-1	11	11	0	1.1
1914 Chi-N	21	13	.618	42	35	23	4	1	293²	236	1	109	165	10.8	2.05	135	.222	.299	14	.144	-0	24	24	-1	2.5
1915 Chi-N	20	12	.625	41	34	18	4	1	269²	240	4	77	148	10.9	2.87	97	.238	.296	14	.163	1	-4	-3	-1	-0.3
1916 Chi-N	17	16	.515	44	35	21	4	1	294	269	4	67	144	10.5	2.20	132	.250	.298	14	.135	-4	14	23	0	2.3
1917 Chi-N	23	13	.639	41	39	27	5	0	295²	255	3	91	195	10.5	2.01	144	.235	.300	16	.160	-1	23	29	2	3.7
1918 *Chi-N	22	10	.688	35	33	27	8	0	290¹	216	4	76	148	9.3	1.74	160	.208	.266	23	.240	4	33	34	-2	4.4
1919 Chi-N	21	14	.600	38	37	25	4	1	306²	264	3	62	141	9.7	1.79	161	.234	.278	17	.173	-0	38	37	-3	4.0
1920 Chi-N	19	16	.543	40	38	24	4	0	301	301	8	81	131	11.7	2.54	126	.264	.318	22	.216	-3	20	22	-3	2.6
1921 Chi-N	3	11	.214	17	14	7	0	0	109¹	153	8	31	30	15.6	6.01	64	.341	.390	10	.244	2	-27	-27	-1	-2.3
Total 13	178	138	.563	390	332	215	41	5	2730	2461	39	817	1416	11.1	2.49	120	.244	.306	159	.173	-1	123	152	-6	18.5

■ AL VEACH
Veach, Alvis Lindell b: 8/6/09, Maylene, Ala. BR/TR, 5'11", 178 lbs. Deb: 9/22/35

YEAR TM/L	W	L	PCT	G	GS	CG	SH	SV	IP	H	HR	BB	SO	RAT	ERA	ERA+	OAV	OOB	BH	AVG	PB	PR	/A	PD	TPI
1935 Phi-A	0	2	.000	2	2	1	0	0	10	20	1	9	3	26.1	11.70	39	.417	.509	0	.000	-1	-8	-8	0	-0.6

■ BOBBY VEACH
Veach, Robert Hayes b: 6/29/1888, Island, Ky. d: 8/7/45, Detroit, Mich. BL/TR, 5'11", 160 lbs. Deb: 8/06/12 ◆

YEAR TM/L	W	L	PCT	G	GS	CG	SH	SV	IP	H	HR	BB	SO	RAT	ERA	ERA+	OAV	OOB	BH	AVG	PB	PR	/A	PD	TPI
1918 Det-A	0	0	—	1	0	0	0	1	2	2	0	2	0	18.0	4.50	59	.286	.444	139	.279	0	-0	-0	0	0.0

■ PEEK-A-BOO VEACH
Veach, William Walter b: 6/15/1862, Indianapolis, Ind d: 11/12/37, Indianapolis, Ind. Deb: 8/24/1884 ◆

YEAR TM/L	W	L	PCT	G	GS	CG	SH	SV	IP	H	HR	BB	SO	RAT	ERA	ERA+	OAV	OOB	BH	AVG	PB	PR	/A	PD	TPI
1884 KC-U	3	9	.250	12	12	12	0	0	104	95	1	10	62	9.1	2.42	114	.227	.245	11	.134	-1	7	4	1	0.3
1887 Lou-a	0	1	.000	1	1	1	0	0	9	5	1	8	2	13.0	4.00	110	.157	.326	0	.000	-0	0	0	0	0.0
Total 2	3	10	.231	13	13	13	0	0	113	100	2	18	64	9.4	2.55	113	.222	.252	76	.215	-1	7	4	1	0.3

■ BOB VEALE
Veale, Robert Andrew b: 10/28/35, Birmingham, Ala. BB/TR, 6'6", 212 lbs. Deb: 4/16/62

YEAR TM/L	W	L	PCT	G	GS	CG	SH	SV	IP	H	HR	BB	SO	RAT	ERA	ERA+	OAV	OOB	BH	AVG	PB	PR	/A	PD	TPI
1962 Pit-N	2	2	.500	11	6	2	0	1	45²	39	2	25	42	12.6	3.74	105	.235	.335	4	.250	1	1	1	-1	0.1
1963 Pit-N	5	2	.714	34	7	3	2	3	77²	59	1	40	68	11.6	1.04	316	.215	.317	2	.087	-0	19	19	-0	2.1
1964 Pit-N	18	12	.600	40	38	14	1	0	279²	222	8	124	250	11.2	2.74	128	.217	.303	15	.156	-4	25	24	-2	2.3
1965 Pit-N	17	12	.586	39	37	14	7	0	266	221	5	119	276	11.7	2.84	124	.225	.313	8	.086	-4	21	20	-4	1.3
1966 Pit-N	16	12	.571	38	37	12	3	0	268¹	228	18	102	229	11.2	3.02	118	.232	.307	13	.138	-2	18	17	-3	1.2
1967 Pit-N	16	8	.667	33	31	6	1	0	203	184	12	119	179	13.7	3.64	93	.245	.352	3	.043	-5	-6	-0	-1	-1.1
1968 Pit-N	13	14	.481	36	33	13	4	0	245¹	187	13	94	171	10.4	2.05	142	.211	.288	9	.110	-2	25	24	-2	2.3
1969 Pit-N	13	14	.481	34	34	9	1	0	225²	232	8	91	213	13.0	3.23	108	.267	.338	4	.051	-5	9	6	-1	0.0
1970 Pit-N	10	15	.400	34	32	5	1	0	202	189	15	94	178	12.7	3.92	100	.246	.331	11	.164	1	3	-0	-3	-0.1

YEAR TM/L	W	L	PCT	G	GS	CG	SH	SV	IP	H	HR	BB	SO	RAT	ERA	ERA+	OAV	OOB	BH	AVG	PB	PR	/A	PD	TPI
1971 *Pit-N	6	0	1.000	37	0	0	0	2	46¹	59	5	24	40	16.1	6.99	48	.314	.392	3	.333	1	-18	-19	-2	-1.9
1972 Pit-N	0	0	—	5	0	0	0	0	9	10	0	7	6	17.0	6.00	55	.313	.436	0	.000	-0	-3	-3	-0	-0.2
Bos-A	2	0	1.000	6	0	0	0	2	8	2	0	3	10	5.6	0.00	—	.083	.185	0	.000	-0	3	3	0	0.3
1973 Bos-A	2	3	.400	32	0	0	0	11	36¹	37	2	12	25	12.1	3.47	116	.268	.327	0	—	0	1	2	1	0.3
1974 Bos-A	0	1	.000	18	0	0	0	2	13	15	2	4	16	13.2	5.54	69	.283	.333	0	—	0	-2	-0	-0	-0.2
Total 13	120	95	.558	397	255	78	20	21	1926	1684	91	858	1703	12.0	3.07	113	.236	.320	72	.114	-16	96	86	-16	6.5

■ LOU VEDDER
Vedder, Louis Edward   b: 4/20/1897, Oakville, Mich.   d: 3/9/90, Lake Placid, Fla.   BR/TR, 5'10.5", 175 lbs.   Deb: 9/18/20

YEAR TM/L	W	L	PCT	G	GS	CG	SH	SV	IP	H	HR	BB	SO	RAT	ERA	ERA+	OAV	OOB	BH	AVG	PB	PR	/A	PD	TPI
1920 Det-A	0	0	—	1	0	0	0	0	2	0	0	0	1	0.0	0.00	—	.000	.000	0	—	0	1	1	0	0.1

■ AL VEIGEL
Veigel, Allen Francis   b: 1/30/17, Dover, Ohio   BR/TR, 6'1", 180 lbs.   Deb: 9/21/39

YEAR TM/L	W	L	PCT	G	GS	CG	SH	SV	IP	H	HR	BB	SO	RAT	ERA	ERA+	OAV	OOB	BH	AVG	PB	PR	/A	PD	TPI
1939 Bos-N	0	1	.000	2	2	0	0	0	2²	3	0	5	1	27.0	6.75	55	.250	.471	0	.000	-0	-1	-1	-0	0.0

■ BUCKY VEIL
Veil, Frederick William   b: 8/2/1881, Tyrone, Pa.   d: 4/16/31, Altoona, Pa.   BR/TR, 5'10", 165 lbs.   Deb: 4/19/03

YEAR TM/L	W	L	PCT	G	GS	CG	SH	SV	IP	H	HR	BB	SO	RAT	ERA	ERA+	OAV	OOB	BH	AVG	PB	PR	/A	PD	TPI
1903 *Pit-N	5	3	.625	12	6	4	0	0	70²	70	1	36	20	13.8	3.82	85	.269	.362	6	.207	-0	-4	-5	-0	-0.4
1904 Pit-N	0	0	—	1	1	0	0	0	4²	4	0	4	1	17.4	5.79	47	.250	.429	1	1.000	0	-2	-2	0	0.0
Total 2	5	3	.625	13	7	4	0	0	75¹	74	1	40	21	14.0	3.94	81	.268	.367	7	.233	0	-6	-6	-0	-0.4

■ CARLOS VELAZQUEZ
Velazquez, Carlos (Quinones)   b: 3/22/48, Loiza, P.R.   BR/TR, 5'11", 180 lbs.   Deb: 7/20/73

YEAR TM/L	W	L	PCT	G	GS	CG	SH	SV	IP	H	HR	BB	SO	RAT	ERA	ERA+	OAV	OOB	BH	AVG	PB	PR	/A	PD	TPI
1973 Mil-A	2	2	.500	18	0	0	0	2	38¹	46	5	10	12	13.1	2.58	146	.297	.339	0	—	0	5	5	0	0.5

■ JOE VERBANIC
Verbanic, Joseph Michael   b: 4/24/43, Washington, Pa.   BR/TR, 6', 155 lbs.   Deb: 7/22/66

YEAR TM/L	W	L	PCT	G	GS	CG	SH	SV	IP	H	HR	BB	SO	RAT	ERA	ERA+	OAV	OOB	BH	AVG	PB	PR	/A	PD	TPI
1966 Phi-N	1	1	.500	17	0	0	0	0	14	12	2	10	7	14.1	5.14	70	.226	.349	0	—	0	-2	-2	0	-0.2
1967 NY-A	4	3	.571	28	6	1	1	2	80¹	74	6	21	39	10.9	2.80	112	.249	.303	2	.111	-0	4	3	2	0.5
1968 NY-A	6	7	.462	40	11	2	1	4	97	104	6	41	40	14.0	3.15	92	.284	.366	2	.080	-1	-2	-3	1	-0.2
1970 NY-A	1	0	1.000	7	0	0	0	0	15²	20	1	12	8	19.0	4.60	76	.323	.440	1	.333	0	-2	-2	1	0.0
Total 4	12	11	.522	92	17	3	2	6	207	210	15	84	94	13.2	3.26	95	.270	.348	5	.109	-1	-2	-4	4	0.1

■ AL VERDEL
Verdel, Albert Alfred "Stumpy"   b: 6/10/21, Punxsutawney, Pa.   BR/TR, 5'9.5", 186 lbs.   Deb: 4/20/44

YEAR TM/L	W	L	PCT	G	GS	CG	SH	SV	IP	H	HR	BB	SO	RAT	ERA	ERA+	OAV	OOB	BH	AVG	PB	PR	/A	PD	TPI
1944 Phi-N	0	0	—	1	0	0	0	0	1	0	0	0	0	0.0	0.00	—	.000	.000	0	—	0	0	0	0	0.0

■ RANDY VERES
Veres, Randolf Ruhland   b: 11/25/65, Sacramento, Cal.   BR/TR, 6'3", 190 lbs.   Deb: 7/01/89

YEAR TM/L	W	L	PCT	G	GS	CG	SH	SV	IP	H	HR	BB	SO	RAT	ERA	ERA+	OAV	OOB	BH	AVG	PB	PR	/A	PD	TPI
1989 Mil-A	0	1	.000	3	1	0	0	0	8¹	9	0	4	8	14.0	4.32	89	.290	.371	0	—	0	-0	-0	0	0.0
1990 Mil-A	0	3	.000	26	0	0	0	1	41²	38	5	16	16	11.9	3.67	103	.247	.322	0	—	0	1	1	1	0.2
Total 2	0	4	.000	29	1	0	0	1	50	47	5	20	24	12.2	3.78	100	.254	.330	0	—	0	1	0	1	0.2

■ TOMMY VEREKER
Vereker, John James   b: 12/2/1893, Baltimore, Md.   d: 4/2/74, Baltimore, Md.   5'10", 185 lbs.   Deb: 6/17/15

YEAR TM/L	W	L	PCT	G	GS	CG	SH	SV	IP	H	HR	BB	SO	RAT	ERA	ERA+	OAV	OOB	BH	AVG	PB	PR	/A	PD	TPI
1915 Bal-F	0	0	—	2	0	0	0	0	3	3	1	2	1	18.0	15.00	21	.268	.422	0	—	0	-4	-4	0	-0.3

■ JOHN VERHOEVEN
Verhoeven, John C   b: 7/3/53, Long Beach, Cal.   BR/TR, 6'5", 200 lbs.   Deb: 7/06/76

YEAR TM/L	W	L	PCT	G	GS	CG	SH	SV	IP	H	HR	BB	SO	RAT	ERA	ERA+	OAV	OOB	BH	AVG	PB	PR	/A	PD	TPI
1976 Cal-A	0	2	.000	21	0	0	0	4	37¹	35	2	14	23	11.8	3.38	99	.252	.320	0	—	0	1	-0	1	0.1
1977 Cal-A	0	2	.000	3	0	0	0	0	4²	4	0	4	3	17.4	3.86	101	.222	.391	0	—	0	0	0	0	0.0
Chi-A	0	0	—	6	0	0	0	0	10¹	9	0	2	6	9.6	2.61	156	.231	.268	0	—	0	2	2	1	0.2
Yr	0	2	.000	9	0	0	0	0	15	13	0	6	9	11.4	3.00	134	.224	.297	0	—	0	2	2	1	0.2
1980 Min-A	3	4	.429	44	0	0	0	4	99²	109	10	29	42	12.7	3.97	110	.289	.345	0	—	0	1	4	0	0.4
1981 Min-A	0	0	—	25	0	0	0	0	52	57	4	14	16	12.6	3.98	99	.288	.341	0	—	0	-2	-0	0	0.0
Total 4	3	8	.273	99	0	0	0	4	204	214	16	63	90	12.5	3.79	106	.278	.337	0	—	0	1	5	2	0.7

■ JOE VERNON
Vernon, Joseph Henry   b: 11/25/1889, Mansfield, Mass.   d: 3/13/55, Philadelphia, Pa.   BR/TR, 5'11", 160 lbs.   Deb: 7/20/12

YEAR TM/L	W	L	PCT	G	GS	CG	SH	SV	IP	H	HR	BB	SO	RAT	ERA	ERA+	OAV	OOB	BH	AVG	PB	PR	/A	PD	TPI
1912 Chi-N	0	0	—	1	0	0	0	0	4	4	0	6	1	24.8	11.25	30	.286	.524	0	.000	-0	-3	-4	-0	-0.2
1914 Bro-F	0	0	—	1	1	0	0	0	3¹	4	0	5	0	24.3	10.80	30	.305	.497	0	.000	-0	-3	-3	0	-0.2
Total 2	0	0	—	2	1	0	0	0	7¹	8	0	11	1	24.5	11.05	30	.295	.512	0	.000	-0	-6	-6	-0	-0.4

■ BOB VESELIC
Veselic, Robert Michael   b: 9/27/55, Pittsburgh, Pa.   BR/TR, 6', 175 lbs.   Deb: 9/18/80

YEAR TM/L	W	L	PCT	G	GS	CG	SH	SV	IP	H	HR	BB	SO	RAT	ERA	ERA+	OAV	OOB	BH	AVG	PB	PR	/A	PD	TPI
1980 Min-A	0	0	—	1	0	0	0	0	4	3	1	1	2	9.0	4.50	97	.214	.267	0	—	0	-0	-0	0	0.0
1981 Min-A	1	1	.500	5	0	0	0	0	22²	22	1	12	13	13.5	3.18	124	.250	.340	0	—	0	1	2	-1	0.1
Total 2	1	1	.500	6	0	0	0	0	26²	25	2	13	15	12.8	3.38	119	.245	.330	0	—	0	1	2	-1	0.1

■ LEE VIAU
Viau, Leon A.   b: 7/5/1866, Corinth, Vt.   d: 12/17/47, Hopewell, N.J.   BR/TR, 5'4", 160 lbs.   Deb: 4/22/1888

YEAR TM/L	W	L	PCT	G	GS	CG	SH	SV	IP	H	HR	BB	SO	RAT	ERA	ERA+	OAV	OOB	BH	AVG	PB	PR	/A	PD	TPI
1888 Cin-a	27	14	.659	42	42	42	1	0	387²	331	7	110	164	10.2	2.65	119	.222	.276	13	.087	-11	18	22	-2	0.9
1889 Cin-a	22	20	.524	47	42	38	1	1	373	379	8	136	152	12.4	3.79	103	.255	.318	21	.143	-9	3	5	-2	-0.4
1890 Cin-N	7	5	.583	13	10	7	1	0	90	97	8	39	41	13.6	4.50	79	.267	.338	5	.139	-2	-9	-9	1	-0.8
Cle-N	4	9	.308	13	13	13	1	0	107	101	4	42	30	12.0	3.36	106	.242	.311	7	.163	-2	2	2	-1	0.0
Yr	11	14	.440	26	23	20	2	0	197	198	12	81	71	12.7	3.88	92	.254	.324	7	.089	-4	-7	-7	0	-0.8
1891 Cle-N	18	17	.514	45	38	31	0	0	343²	367	3	138	130	13.2	3.01	115	.263	.329	23	.160	-3	13	17	1	1.4
1892 Cle-N	0	1	.000	1	1	0	0	0	1	5	0	1	0	54.0	36.00	9	.625	.667	0	—	0	-4	-4	0	-0.2
Lou-N	4	11	.267	16	15	14	1	0	130²	156	7	56	36	14.6	3.99	77	.285	.351	13	.197	1	-10	-13	2	-0.8
Bos-N	1	0	1.000	1	1	1	0	0	9	5	0	4	1	9.0	0.00	—	.156	.250	0	.000	-1	3	4	0	0.3
Yr	5	12	.294	18	17	15	1	0	140²	166	7	61	37	14.5	3.97	78	.282	.350	7	.101	0	-11	-14	3	-0.7
Total 5	83	77	.519	178	162	146	5	1	1442	1441	37	526	554	12.3	3.33	104	.251	.314	82	.139	-26	16	23	-0	0.4

■ RUBE VICKERS
Vickers, Harry Porter   b: 5/17/1878, St.Marys, Ont., Can   d: 12/9/58, Belleville, Mich.   BL/TR, 6'2", 225 lbs.   Deb: 9/21/02

YEAR TM/L	W	L	PCT	G	GS	CG	SH	SV	IP	H	HR	BB	SO	RAT	ERA	ERA+	OAV	OOB	BH	AVG	PB	PR	/A	PD	TPI
1902 Cin-N	0	3	.000	3	3	3	0	0	21	31	0	8	6	17.1	6.00	50	.342	.401	4	.364	-1	-8	-7	-0	-0.5
1903 Bro-N	0	1	.000	4	1	1	0	0	14	27	0	9	5	23.8	10.93	29	.415	.493	1	.100	-1	-12	-12	1	-0.9
1907 Phi-A	2	2	.500	10	4	3	1	0	50¹	44	1	12	21	10.0	3.40	77	.237	.283	3	.150	-1	-5	-4	1	-0.4
1908 Phi-A	18	19	.486	53	34	21	6	1	317	264	0	71	156	9.8	2.21	116	.231	.282	17	.160	-1	6	12	-3	1.1
1909 Phi-A	2	2	.500	18	3	1	0	1	55²	60	0	19	25	13.1	3.40	71	.274	.338	1	.063	-1	-6	-6	-1	-0.9
Total 5	22	27	.449	88	45	29	7	2	458	426	1	119	213	11.0	2.93	89	.250	.305	26	.160	-3	-23	-17	-2	-1.6

■ TOM VICKERY
Vickery, Thomas Gill "Vinegar Tom"   b: 5/5/1867, Milford, N.J.   d: 3/21/21, Burlington, N.J.   6', 170 lbs.   Deb: 4/21/1890

YEAR TM/L	W	L	PCT	G	GS	CG	SH	SV	IP	H	HR	BB	SO	RAT	ERA	ERA+	OAV	OOB	BH	AVG	PB	PR	/A	PD	TPI
1890 Phi-N	24	22	.522	46	46	41	2	0	382	405	8	184	162	13.9	3.44	106	.264	.343	33	.208	-4	5	9	-2	0.3
1891 Chi-N	6	5	.545	14	12	7	0	0	79²	72	4	44	39	13.1	4.07	81	.232	.327	7	.179	-1	-6	-7	1	-0.6
1892 Bal-N	8	10	.444	24	21	17	0	0	176	189	3	87	49	14.1	3.53	98	.264	.343	18	.243	2	-5	-1	-1	0.0
1893 Phi-N	4	5	.444	13	11	7	0	0	80	100	4	37	15	15.4	5.40	85	.297	.367	11	.314	1	-6	-7	3	-0.2
Total 4	42	42	.500	97	90	72	2	0	717²	766	16	352	265	14.0	3.75	98	.264	.344	69	.225	-3	-12	-6	-0	-0.5

■ BOB VINES
Vines, Robert Earl   b: 2/25/1897, Waxahachie, Tex.   d: 10/18/82, Orlando, Fla.   BR/TR, 6'4", 184 lbs.   Deb: 9/03/24

YEAR TM/L	W	L	PCT	G	GS	CG	SH	SV	IP	H	HR	BB	SO	RAT	ERA	ERA+	OAV	OOB	BH	AVG	PB	PR	/A	PD	TPI
1924 StL-N	0	0	—	2	0	0	0	0	10²	23	1	0	0	19.4	9.28	41	.426	.426	0	.000	-1	-6	-7	-0	-0.5
1925 Phi-N	0	0	—	3	0	0	0	0	4	9	0	3	0	27.0	11.25	42	.450	.522	0	—	0	-3	-3	0	-0.2
Total 2	0	0	—	5	0	0	0	0	14²	32	1	3	0	21.5	9.82	45	.432	.455	0	.000	-1	-10	-9	-0	-0.7

■ DAVE VINEYARD
Vineyard, David Kent   b: 2/25/41, Clay, W.Va.   BR/TR, 6'3", 195 lbs.   Deb: 7/18/64

YEAR TM/L	W	L	PCT	G	GS	CG	SH	SV	IP	H	HR	BB	SO	RAT	ERA	ERA+	OAV	OOB	BH	AVG	PB	PR	/A	PD	TPI
1964 Bal-A	2	5	.286	19	6	1	0	0	54	57	5	27	50	14.0	4.17	86	.274	.357	2	.167	0	-3	-4	-1	-0.3

■ BILL VINTON
Vinton, William Miller   b: 4/27/1865, Winthrop, Mass.   d: 9/3/1893, Pawtucket, R.I.   BR/TR, 6'1", 160 lbs.   Deb: 7/03/1884

YEAR TM/L	W	L	PCT	G	GS	CG	SH	SV	IP	H	HR	BB	SO	RAT	ERA	ERA+	OAV	OOB	BH	AVG	PB	PR	/A	PD	TPI
1884 Phi-N	10	10	.500	21	21	20	0	0	182	166	6	35	105	9.9	2.23	134	.230	.265	9	.115	-6	15	15	2	1.0
1885 Phi-N	3	6	.333	9	9	8	0	0	77	90	0	23	21	13.2	3.04	92	.279	.327	2	.067	-3	-2	-2	0	-0.4

YEAR	TM/L	W	L	PCT	G	GS	CG	SH	SV	IP	H	HR	BB	SO	RAT	ERA	ERA+	OAV	OOB	BH	AVG	PB	PR	/A	PD	TPI
	Phi-a	4	3	.571	7	7	6	2	0	55	46	1	15	34	10.0	2.45	140	.217	.269	4	.154	-0	5	6	-0	0.5
Total	2	17	19	.472	37	37	34	2	0	314	302	7	73	160	10.7	2.46	122	.240	.282	15	.112	-10	18	19	2	1.1

■ FRANK VIOLA
Viola, Frank John   b: 4/19/60, Hempstead, N.Y.   BL/TL, 6'4", 200 lbs.   Deb: 6/06/82

YEAR	TM/L	W	L	PCT	G	GS	CG	SH	SV	IP	H	HR	BB	SO	RAT	ERA	ERA+	OAV	OOB	BH	AVG	PB	PR	/A	PD	TPI
1982	Min-A	4	10	.286	22	22	3	1	0	126	152	22	38	84	13.6	5.21	81	.302	.351	0	—	0	-16	-14	-1	-1.3
1983	Min-A	7	15	.318	35	34	4	0	0	210	242	34	92	127	14.7	5.49	77	.287	.363	0	—	0	-33	-29	-2	-2.8
1984	Min-A	18	12	.600	35	35	10	4	0	257²	225	28	73	149	10.5	3.21	131	.233	.290	0	—	0	22	28	-3	2.7
1985	Min-A	18	14	.563	36	36	9	0	0	250²	262	26	68	135	11.9	4.09	108	.268	.316	0	—	0	1	9	-2	0.7
1986	Min-A	16	13	.552	37	37	7	1	0	245²	257	37	83	191	12.6	4.51	96	.268	.329	0	—	0	-9	-5	-3	-0.7
1987	*Min-A	17	10	.630	36	36	7	1	0	251²	230	29	66	197	10.8	2.90	159	.241	.294	0	—	0	44	48	-1	4.8
1988	Min-A	**24**	7	**.774**	35	35	7	2	0	255¹	236	20	54	193	10.3	2.64	154	.245	.288	0	—	0	38	**40**	-2	4.2
1989	Min-A	8	12	.400	24	24	7	1	0	175²	171	17	47	138	11.3	3.79	109	.256	.308	0	—	0	2	7	-0	0.7
	NY-N	5	5	.500	12	12	2	1	0	85¹	75	5	27	73	10.9	3.38	97	.236	.298	3	.130	-0	1	-1	-1	-0.1
1990	NY-N	20	12	.625	35	35	7	3	0	**249²**	227	15	60	182	10.4	2.67	137	.242	.289	13	.153	-1	**31**	27	0	2.8
Total	9	137	110	.555	307	306	63	14	0	2107²	2077	233	608	1469	11.6	3.70	113	.257	.311	16	.148	-1	81	109	-14	11.0

■ JAKE VIRTUE
Virtue, Jacob Kitchline "Guesses"   b: 3/2/1865, Philadelphia, Pa.   d: 2/3/43, Camden, N.J.   BB/TR, 5'9.5", 165 lbs.   Deb: 7/21/1890 ♦

YEAR	TM/L	W	L	PCT	G	GS	CG	SH	SV	IP	H	HR	BB	SO	RAT	ERA	ERA+	OAV	OOB	BH	AVG	PB	PR	/A	PD	TPI
1893	Cle-N	0	0	—	1	0	0	0	0	5	3	0	3	2	10.8	1.80	272	.169	.289	100	.265	0	2	2	-0	0.2
1894	Cle-N	0	0	—	1	0	0	0	0	0	0	0	1	0	—	—	—	—	1.000	23	.258	0	0	0	0	0.0
Total	2	0	0	—	2	0	0	0	0	5	3	0	4	2	12.6	1.80	272	.169	.321	483	.274	0	2	2	-0	0.2

■ JOE VITELLI
Vitelli, Antonio Joseph   b: 4/12/08, Mckees Rocks, Pa.   d: 2/7/67, Pittsburgh, Pa.   BR/TR, 6'1", 195 lbs.   Deb: 5/30/44 ♦

YEAR	TM/L	W	L	PCT	G	GS	CG	SH	SV	IP	H	HR	BB	SO	RAT	ERA	ERA+	OAV	OOB	BH	AVG	PB	PR	/A	PD	TPI
1944	Pit-N	0	0	—	4	0	0	0	0	7	5	1	7	2	16.7	2.57	145	.185	.371	0	.000	-0	1	1	0	0.1

■ OLLIE VOIGT
Voigt, Olen Edward "Ode"   b: 1/29/1900, Wheaton, Ill.   d: 4/7/70, Scottsdale, Ariz.   BL/TR, 6'1", 170 lbs.   Deb: 4/19/24

YEAR	TM/L	W	L	PCT	G	GS	CG	SH	SV	IP	H	HR	BB	SO	RAT	ERA	ERA+	OAV	OOB	BH	AVG	PB	PR	/A	PD	TPI
1924	StL-A	1	0	1.000	8	1	0	0	0	16¹	21	1	13	4	18.7	5.51	82	.356	.472	1	.250	1	-2	-2	1	0.0

■ BILL VOISELLE
Voiselle, William Symmes "Big Bill" or "Ninety-Six"   b: 1/29/19, Greenwood, S.C.   BR/TR, 6'4", 200 lbs.   Deb: 9/01/42

YEAR	TM/L	W	L	PCT	G	GS	CG	SH	SV	IP	H	HR	BB	SO	RAT	ERA	ERA+	OAV	OOB	BH	AVG	PB	PR	/A	PD	TPI
1942	NY-N	0	1	.000	2	1	0	0	0	9	6	1	4	5	10.0	2.00	168	.176	.263	0	.000	0	1	1	0	0.2
1943	NY-N	1	2	.333	4	4	3	0	0	31	18	1	14	19	9.3	2.03	170	.154	.244	1	.111	-1	5	5	-1	0.4
1944	NY-N	21	16	.568	43	41	25	1	0	312²	276	31	118	**161**	11.5	3.02	121	.232	.303	22	.210	3	20	22	-4	2.2
1945	NY-N	14	14	.500	41	35	14	4	0	232¹	249	15	97	115	13.6	4.49	87	.273	.345	10	.127	-3	-18	-15	-0	-1.7
1946	NY-N	9	15	.375	36	25	10	2	0	178	171	14	85	89	12.9	3.74	92	.248	.330	9	.164	-1	-7	-6	-1	-0.7
1947	NY-N	1	4	.200	11	5	1	0	0	42²	44	4	22	20	14.1	4.64	88	.284	.376	2	.133	-1	-3	-3	0	-0.2
	Bos-N	8	7	.533	22	20	7	0	0	131¹	146	10	51	59	13.6	4.32	90	.280	.345	9	.170	-1	-4	-6	-0	-0.5
	Yr	9	11	.450	33	25	8	0	0	174	190	14	73	79	13.7	4.40	90	.280	.351	0	.000	-1	-7	-9	0	-0.7
1948	*Bos-N	13	13	.500	37	30	9	2	2	215²	226	18	90	89	13.3	3.63	106	.272	.345	7	.097	-4	8	5	-2	0.0
1949	Bos-N	7	8	.467	30	22	5	4	1	169¹	170	14	78	63	13.2	4.04	94	.263	.343	7	.115	-2	0	-5	1	-0.5
1950	Chi-N	0	4	.000	19	7	0	0	0	51¹	64	7	29	25	16.5	5.79	73	.303	.390	1	.077	-1	-9	-9	-1	-0.9
Total	9	74	84	.468	245	190	74	13	3	1373¹	1370	115	588	645	12.9	3.83	98	.258	.334	68	.147	-10	-6	-10	-7	-1.7

■ JAKE VOLZ
Volz, Jacob Phillip "Silent Jake"   b: 4/4/1878, San Antonio, Tex.   d: 8/11/62, San Antonio, Tex.   BR/TR, 5'10", 175 lbs.   Deb: 9/28/01

YEAR	TM/L	W	L	PCT	G	GS	CG	SH	SV	IP	H	HR	BB	SO	RAT	ERA	ERA+	OAV	OOB	BH	AVG	PB	PR	/A	PD	TPI
1901	Bos-A	1	0	1.000	1	1	1	0	0	7	6	2	9	5	19.3	9.00	39	.229	.426	0	.000	-1	-4	-4	-1	-0.3
1905	Bos-N	0	2	.000	3	2	1	0	0	8²	12	0	8	1	21.8	10.38	30	.364	.500	0	.000	-0	-7	-7	-0	-0.6
1908	Cin-N	1	2	.333	7	4	1	0	0	22²	16	1	12	6	11.9	3.57	65	.195	.313	1	.250	0	-3	-3	-1	-0.4
Total	3	2	4	.333	11	7	2	0	0	38¹	34	3	29	12	15.5	6.10	44	.241	.381	1	.100	-1	-14	-14	-2	-1.3

■ TONY Von FRICKEN
Von Fricken, Anthony   b: 5/30/1870, Brooklyn, N.Y.   d: 3/22/47, Troy, N.Y.   BB/TR, 5'11.5", 160 lbs.   Deb: 5/09/1890

YEAR	TM/L	W	L	PCT	G	GS	CG	SH	SV	IP	H	HR	BB	SO	RAT	ERA	ERA+	OAV	OOB	BH	AVG	PB	PR	/A	PD	TPI
1890	Bos-N	0	1	.000	1	1	1	0	0	8	23	0	8	2	34.9	10.13	37	.493	.567	0	.000	-1	-6	-6	0	-0.4

■ BRUCE Von HOFF
Von Hoff, Bruce Frederick   b: 11/17/43, Oakland, Cal.   BR/TR, 6', 187 lbs.   Deb: 9/28/65

YEAR	TM/L	W	L	PCT	G	GS	CG	SH	SV	IP	H	HR	BB	SO	RAT	ERA	ERA+	OAV	OOB	BH	AVG	PB	PR	/A	PD	TPI
1965	Hou-N	0	0	—	3	0	0	0	0	3	3	0	2	1	15.0	9.00	37	.250	.357	0	—	0	-2	-2	-0	-0.1
1967	Hou-N	0	3	.000	10	10	0	0	0	50¹	52	3	28	22	14.3	4.83	69	.268	.360	1	.067	-1	-8	-8	-1	-0.9
Total	2	0	3	.000	13	10	0	0	0	53¹	55	3	30	23	14.3	5.06	65	.267	.360	1	.067	-1	-10	-10	-1	-1.0

■ DAVE Von OHLEN
Von Ohlen, David   b: 10/25/58, Flushing, N.Y.   BL/TL, 6'2", 200 lbs.   Deb: 5/13/83

YEAR	TM/L	W	L	PCT	G	GS	CG	SH	SV	IP	H	HR	BB	SO	RAT	ERA	ERA+	OAV	OOB	BH	AVG	PB	PR	/A	PD	TPI
1983	StL-N	3	2	.600	46	0	0	0	2	68¹	71	3	25	21	13.0	3.29	110	.280	.351	1	.143	0	3	2	-0	0.3
1984	StL-N	1	0	1.000	27	0	0	0	1	34²	39	0	8	19	12.2	3.12	111	.300	.341	1	1.000	0	2	1	1	0.3
1985	Cle-A	3	2	.600	26	0	0	0	0	43¹	47	3	20	12	13.9	2.91	142	.288	.366	0	—	0	6	6	1	0.7
1986	Oak-A	0	3	.000	24	0	0	0	1	15¹	18	0	7	4	14.7	3.52	110	.300	.373	0	—	0	1	1	1	0.1
1987	Oak-A	0	0	—	4	0	0	0	0	6	10	1	1	3	16.5	7.50	55	.400	.423	0	—	0	-2	-2	-0	-0.1
Total	5	7	7	.500	127	0	0	0	4	167²	185	7	61	59	13.4	3.33	113	.293	.358	2	.250	1	9	8	2	1.3

■ CY VORHEES
Vorhees, Henry Bert   b: 9/30/1874, Lodi, Ohio   d: 2/8/10, Perry, Ohio   6'3", 200 lbs.   Deb: 4/17/02

YEAR	TM/L	W	L	PCT	G	GS	CG	SH	SV	IP	H	HR	BB	SO	RAT	ERA	ERA+	OAV	OOB	BH	AVG	PB	PR	/A	PD	TPI
1902	Phi-N	3	3	.500	10	4	3	1	0	53²	63	1	20	24	14.1	3.86	73	.292	.355	7	.350	2	-6	-6	-1	-0.4
	Was-A	0	1	.000	1	1	1	0	0	8	10	0	2	1	13.5	4.50	82	.306	.346	2	.667	1	-1	-1	0	0.0

■ ED VOSBERG
Vosberg, Edward John   b: 9/28/61, Tucson, Ariz.   BL/TL, 6'1", 190 lbs.   Deb: 9/17/86

YEAR	TM/L	W	L	PCT	G	GS	CG	SH	SV	IP	H	HR	BB	SO	RAT	ERA	ERA+	OAV	OOB	BH	AVG	PB	PR	/A	PD	TPI
1986	SD-N	0	1	.000	5	3	0	0	0	13²	17	1	9	8	17.1	6.59	55	.304	.400	0	.000	-0	-4	-4	-0	-0.4
1990	SF-N	1	1	.500	18	0	0	0	0	24¹	21	3	12	12	12.2	5.55	67	.233	.324	0	—	0	-5	-5	0	-0.4
Total	2	1	2	.333	23	3	0	0	0	38	38	4	21	20	14.0	5.92	62	.260	.353	0	.000	-0	-9	-9	0	-0.8

■ ALEX VOSS
Voss, Alexander   b: 1855, Roswell, Ga.   d: 8/31/06, Cincinnati, Ohio   BR/TR, 6'1", 180 lbs.   Deb: 4/17/1884 ♦

YEAR	TM/L	W	L	PCT	G	GS	CG	SH	SV	IP	H	HR	BB	SO	RAT	ERA	ERA+	OAV	OOB	BH	AVG	PB	PR	/A	PD	TPI
1884	Was-U	5	14	.263	27	20	18	0	0	186¹	206	2	32	112	11.5	3.57	83	.262	.291	47	.192	-3	-12	-13	3	-1.0
	KC-U	0	6	.000	7	6	6	0	0	53	74	2	7	17	13.8	4.25	65	.310	.329	4	.089	-2	-7	-9	1	-0.6
	Yr	5	20	.200	34	26	24	0	0	239¹	280	4	39	129	12.0	3.72	78	.273	.300	5	.017	-6	-19	-21	4	-1.6

■ RIP VOWINKEL
Vowinkel, John Henry   b: 11/18/1884, Oswego, N.Y.   d: 7/13/66, Oswego, N.Y.   BR/TR, 5'10", 195 lbs.   Deb: 9/05/05

YEAR	TM/L	W	L	PCT	G	GS	CG	SH	SV	IP	H	HR	BB	SO	RAT	ERA	ERA+	OAV	OOB	BH	AVG	PB	PR	/A	PD	TPI
1905	Cin-N	3	3	.500	6	6	4	0	0	45	52	2	10	7	12.6	4.20	79	.302	.344	1	.071	-0	-6	-4	-1	-0.5

■ PETE VUCKOVICH
Vuckovich, Peter Dennis   b: 10/27/52, Johnstown, Pa.   BR/TR, 6'4", 215 lbs.   Deb: 8/03/75

YEAR	TM/L	W	L	PCT	G	GS	CG	SH	SV	IP	H	HR	BB	SO	RAT	ERA	ERA+	OAV	OOB	BH	AVG	PB	PR	/A	PD	TPI
1975	Chi-A	0	1	.000	4	2	0	0	0	10¹	17	0	7	5	20.9	13.06	30	.386	.471	0	—	0	-11	-11	0	-0.8
1976	Chi-A	7	4	.636	33	7	1	0	0	110¹	122	9	60	62	15.2	4.65	77	.287	.380	0	—	0	-14	-13	-1	-1.3
1977	Tor-A	7	7	.500	53	8	3	1	8	148	143	13	59	123	12.6	3.47	121	.257	.333	0	—	0	10	12	0	1.2
1978	StL-N	12	12	.500	45	23	6	2	1	198¹	187	9	59	149	11.3	2.54	138	.253	.310	8	.138	-1	23	21	1	2.3
1979	StL-N	15	10	.600	34	32	9	0	0	233	229	22	64	145	11.4	3.59	105	.260	.312	12	.152	-2	4	4	-1	0.1
1980	StL-N	12	9	.571	32	30	7	3	1	222¹	203	18	68	132	11.1	3.40	109	.247	.306	13	.183	1	0	5	-1	0.9
1981	*Mil-A	**14**	4	**.778**	24	23	2	1	0	149²	137	9	57	84	11.9	3.55	96	.249	.324	0	—	0	-2	-1	0	0.0
1982	*Mil-A	18	6	**.750**	30	30	9	1	0	223²	234	14	102	105	13.7	3.34	113	.275	.356	0	—	0	18	11	1	1.2
1983	Mil-A	0	0	—	3	3	0	0	0	14²	19	0	10	10	16.0	4.91	76	.259	.377	0	—	0	-2	-2	-0	-0.1
1985	Mil-A	6	10	.375	22	22	1	0	0	112²	134	16	48	55	15.1	5.51	76	.298	.374	0	—	0	-17	-17	-1	-1.6
1986	Mil-A	2	4	.333	6	6	0	0	0	32¹	33	3	11	12	12.8	3.06	141	.273	.343	0	—	0	4	5	1	0.5
Total	11	93	69	.574	286	186	38	8	10	1455¹	1454	107	545	882	12.6	3.66	103	.264	.334	33	.159	-2	22	16	1	2.4

■ PAUL WACHTEL
Wachtel, Paul Horine   b: 4/30/1888, Myersville, Md.   d: 12/15/64, San Antonio, Tex.   BR/TR, 5'11", 175 lbs.   Deb: 9/18/17

YEAR	TM/L	W	L	PCT	G	GS	CG	SH	SV	IP	H	HR	BB	SO	RAT	ERA	ERA+	OAV	OOB	BH	AVG	PB	PR	/A	PD	TPI
1917	Bro-N	0	0	—	2	0	0	0	0	6	9	0	4	3	19.5	10.50	27	.375	.464	1	.333	0	-5	-5	-0	-0.4

YEAR TM/L	W	L	PCT	G	GS	CG	SH	SV	IP	H	HR	BB	SO	RAT	ERA	ERA+	OAV	OOB	BH	AVG	PB	PR	/A	PD	TPI
■ **CHARLIE WACKER**				Wacker, Charles James b: 12/8/1883, Jeffersonville, Ind d: 8/7/48, Evansville, Ind. BL/TL, 5'9", Deb: 4/28/09																				
1909 Pit-N	0	0	—	1	0	0	0	0	2	2	0	1	0	13.5	0.00	—	.400	.500	0	—	0	1	1	0	0.1
■ **RUBE WADDELL**				Waddell, George Edward b: 10/13/1876, Bradford, Pa. d: 4/1/14, San Antonio, Tex. BR/TL, 6'1.5", 196 lbs. Deb: 9/08/1897 H																				
1897 Lou-N	0	1	.000	2	1	1	0	0	14	17	0	6	5	14.8	3.21	133	.297	.364	0	.000	-1	2	2	0	0.1
1899 Lou-N	7	2	.778	10	9	9	1	1	79	69	4	14	44	9.5	3.08	125	.235	.270	8	.235	-0	7	7	-1	0.5
1900 *Pit-N	8	13	.381	29	22	16	2	0	208²	176	3	55	**130**	10.0	**2.37**	**153**	**.229**	**.280**	14	.173	-2	31	29	0	2.6
1901 Pit-N	0	2	.000	2	2	0	0	0	7²	10	0	9	4	23.5	9.39	35	.313	.476	0	.000	-0	-5	-5	0	-0.4
Chi-N	14	14	.500	29	28	26	0	0	243²	239	5	66	168	11.6	2.81	115	.255	.309	25	.255	6	14	12	2	2.0
Yr	14	16	.467	31	30	26	0	0	251¹	249	5	75	172	11.9	3.01	108	.257	.315	2	.020	6	9	6	3	1.6
1902 Phi-A	24	7	.774	33	27	26	3	0	276¹	224	7	64	**210**	9.4	2.05	179	.222	.269	32	.286	8	47	50	-3	5.7
1903 Phi-A	21	16	.568	39	38	**34**	4	0	324	274	3	85	**302**	10.0	2.44	125	.229	.280	14	.122	-7	19	22	-1	4.4
1904 Phi-A	25	19	.568	46	46	39	8	0	383	307	5	91	**349**	9.4	1.62	**165**	.221	.269	17	.122	-7	**42**	45	-1	4.4
1905 Phi-A	**27**	10	**.730**	**46**	34	27	7	0	328²	231	5	90	**287**	8.8	**1.48**	180	**.199**	.257	20	.172	-0	**43**	43	-2	**4.6**
1906 Phi-A	15	18	.455	43	34	22	8	0	272²	221	1	92	**196**	10.3	2.21	123	.225	.291	14	.163	-0	15	16	-3	1.4
1907 Phi-A	19	13	.594	44	33	20	7	0	284²	234	2	73	**232**	9.7	2.15	121	.226	.277	12	.119	-5	13	15	-4	0.6
1908 StL-A	19	14	.576	43	36	25	5	0	285²	223	0	90	232	10.1	1.89	127	.213	.281	10	.110	-1	16	16	-3	1.3
1909 StL-A	11	14	.440	31	28	16	5	0	220¹	204	1	57	141	10.9	2.37	102	.267	.323	5	.067	-5	3	1	-2	-0.6
1910 StL-A	3	1	.750	10	2	0	0	1	33	31	1	11	16	11.7	3.55	70	.242	.307	1	.111	-0	-4	-4	-1	-0.5
Total 13	193	144	.573	407	340	261	50	5	2961²	2460	37	803	2316	10.0	2.16	135	.228	.283	172	.161	-17	241	248	-19	23.1
■ **TOM WADDELL**				Waddell, Thomas David b: 9/17/58, Dundee, Scotland BR/TR, 6'1", 185 lbs. Deb: 4/15/84																				
1984 Cle-A	7	4	.636	58	0	0	0	6	97	68	12	37	59	9.8	3.06	133	.202	.283	0	—	0	10	11	-1	1.1
1985 Cle-A	8	6	.571	49	9	1	0	9	112²	104	20	39	53	11.5	4.87	85	.246	.312	0	—	0	-9	-9	0	-0.8
1987 Cle-A	0	1	.000	6	0	0	0	0	5²	7	1	7	6	23.8	14.29	32	.292	.469	0	—	0	-6	-6	-0	-0.5
Total 3	15	11	.577	113	9	1	0	15	215¹	179	33	83	118	11.1	4.30	96	.229	.305	0	—	0	-5	-4	-1	-0.2
■ **BEN WADE**				Wade, Benjamin Styron b: 11/26/22, Morehead City, N.C BR/TR, 6'3", 195 lbs. Deb: 4/30/48																				
1948 Chi-N	0	1	.000	2	0	0	0	0	5	4	0	4	1	14.4	7.20	54	.211	.348	0	.000	-0	-2	-2	0	-0.1
1952 Bro-N	11	9	.550	37	24	5	1	3	180	166	19	94	118	13.1	3.60	101	.246	.340	7	.117	1	3	1	-2	0.0
1953 *Bro-N	7	5	.583	32	0	0	0	3	90¹	79	15	33	65	11.6	3.79	113	.232	.308	4	.167	0	5	5	-2	0.3
1954 Bro-N	1	1	.500	23	0	0	0	3	45	62	9	21	25	16.6	8.20	50	.339	.407	0	.000	-1	-21	-21	-1	-2.0
StL-N	0	0	—	13	0	0	0	0	23	27	3	15	19	17.2	5.48	75	.303	.415	0	.000	-0	-4	-3	0	-0.3
Yr	1	1	.500	36	0	0	0	3	68	89	12	36	44	16.8	7.28	56	.319	.401	0	.000	-1	-24	-24	-1	-2.3
1955 Pit-N	0	1	.000	11	1	0	0	1	28	26	3	14	7	13.2	3.21	128	.252	.347	0	.000	-0	3	3	0	0.2
Total 5	19	17	.528	118	25	5	1	10	371¹	364	49	181	235	13.4	4.34	90	.259	.347	11	.112	0	-16	-18	-5	-1.9
■ **JAKE WADE**				Wade, Jacob Fields "Whistling Jake" b: 4/1/12, Morehead City, N.C. BL/TL, 6'2", 175 lbs. Deb: 4/22/36																				
1936 Det-A	4	5	.444	13	11	4	1	0	78¹	93	7	52	30	16.8	5.29	94	.296	.398	5	.172	-0	-2	-3	-1	-0.2
1937 Det-A	7	10	.412	33	25	7	1	0	165¹	160	13	107	69	14.7	5.39	87	.257	.368	11	.186	-1	-14	-13	0	-1.2
1938 Det-A	3	2	.600	27	2	0	0	0	70	73	9	48	23	15.6	6.56	76	.268	.378	1	.048	-2	-14	-12	0	-1.2
1939 Bos-A	1	4	.200	20	6	1	0	0	47²	68	1	37	21	19.8	6.23	76	.358	.463	0	.000	-2	-9	-8	-0	-0.8
StL-A	0	2	.000	4	2	1	0	0	16¹	26	1	19	9	24.8	11.02	44	.356	.489	0	.000	-1	-12	-11	0	-0.9
Yr	1	6	.143	24	8	2	0	0	64	94	2	56	30	21.1	7.45	64	.357	.470	0	.000	-3	-20	-19	0	-1.7
1942 Chi-A	5	5	.500	15	10	3	0	0	85²	84	2	56	32	14.7	4.10	88	.259	.363	7	.241	1	-4	-5	1	-0.2
1943 Chi-A	3	7	.300	21	9	3	1	0	83²	66	3	54	41	13.3	3.01	111	.222	.349	4	.148	-0	3	3	-1	0.2
1944 Chi-A	2	4	.333	19	5	1	0	2	74²	75	3	41	35	14.0	4.82	71	.261	.354	7	.292	1	-12	-12	-2	-1.2
1946 NY-A	2	1	.667	13	1	0	0	1	35¹	33	2	14	22	12.2	2.29	151	.250	.327	1	.111	-0	5	5	0	0.5
Was-A	0	0	—	6	0	0	0	0	11¹	12	1	12	9	19.1	4.76	70	.279	.436	0	.000	-0	-2	-2	-0	-0.1
Yr	2	1	.667	19	1	0	0	1	46²	45	3	26	31	13.7	2.89	118	.256	.351	1	.100	-0	3	3	0	0.4
Total 8	27	40	.403	171	71	20	3	3	668¹	690	42	440	291	15.3	5.00	84	.269	.378	36	.167	-5	-60	-58	-2	-5.1
■ **JACK WADSWORTH**				Wadsworth, John L. b: 12/17/1867, Wellington, Ohio d: 7/8/41, Elyria, Ohio BL/TR, 180 lbs. Deb: 5/01/1890																				
1890 Cle-N	2	16	.111	20	19	19	0	0	169²	202	6	81	26	15.0	5.20	69	.287	.361	12	.176	-3	-31	-31	-0	-2.7
1893 Bal-N	0	3	.000	3	3	0	0	0	16	37	0	8	2	25.3	11.25	42	.439	.487	3	.429	1	-12	-12	-0	-0.7
1894 Lou-N	4	18	.182	22	22	20	0	0	173	261	10	103	57	18.9	7.60	67	.344	.422	19	.257	-0	-44	-48	-0	-3.4
1895 Lou-N	0	1	.000	2	0	0	0	0	9	24	0	7	2	31.0	16.00	29	.479	.543	1	.250	-0	-11	-11	0	-0.7
Total 4	6	38	.136	47	44	39	0	0	367²	524	16	199	87	17.7	6.85	64	.328	.403	35	.229	-2	-97	-101	-1	-7.5
■ **CHARLIE WAGNER**				Wagner, Charles Thomas "Broadway" b: 12/3/12, Reading, Pa. BR/TR, 5'11", 170 lbs. Deb: 4/19/38 C																				
1938 Bos-A	1	3	.250	13	6	1	0	0	36²	47	5	24	14	17.7	8.35	59	.309	.407	2	.167	-1	-14	-14	-1	-1.2
1939 Bos-A	3	1	.750	9	5	0	0	0	38¹	49	3	14	13	14.8	4.23	112	.320	.377	1	.071	-2	2	2	0	0.0
1940 Bos-A	1	0	1.000	12	1	0	0	0	29¹	45	5	8	13	16.3	5.52	81	.344	.381	1	.200	-0	-4	-3	0	-0.2
1941 Bos-A	12	8	.600	29	25	12	3	0	187¹	175	14	85	51	12.5	3.07	136	.245	.326	10	.159	-1	22	23	0	2.2
1942 Bos-A	14	11	.560	29	26	17	2	0	205¹	184	6	95	52	12.4	3.29	113	.247	.336	5	.077	-5	8	10	1	0.2
1946 Bos-A	1	0	1.000	8	4	0	0	0	30²	32	6	19	14	15.0	5.87	62	.276	.378	1	.091	-1	-8	-8	-0	-0.7
Total 6	32	23	.582	100	67	30	5	0	527²	532	38	245	157	13.4	3.91	104	.264	.346	20	.118	-9	6	10	1	0.8
■ **GARY WAGNER**				Wagner, Gary Edward b: 6/28/40, Bridgeport, Ill. BR/TR, 6'4", 185 lbs. Deb: 4/18/65																				
1965 Phi-N	7	7	.500	59	0	0	0	7	105	87	6	49	91	11.8	3.00	115	.233	.325	1	.077	-0	6	5	1	0.6
1966 Phi-N	0	1	.000	5	1	0	0	0	6¹	8	1	5	2	18.5	8.53	42	.333	.448	0	—	0	-3	-3	-0	-0.3
1967 Phi-N	0	0	—	1	0	0	0	0	2	1	0	1	1	4.5	0.00	—	.167	.167	0	—	0	1	1	0	0.1
1968 Phi-N	4	4	.500	44	0	0	0	8	78	69	6	31	43	12.1	3.00	100	.243	.328	1	.083	-1	-0	0	1	0.1
1969 Phi-N	0	3	.000	9	2	0	0	0	19¹	31	3	7	8	17.7	7.91	45	.365	.413	0	.000	-0	-9	-9	-1	-0.9
Bos-A	3	1	.250	6	1	0	0	0	16¹	18	1	15	9	18.2	6.06	63	.300	.440	0	.000	-0	-4	-4	0	-0.3
1970 Bos-A	3	1	.750	38	0	0	0	7	40¹	36	3	19	20	12.7	3.35	118	.232	.324	1	.167	-0	2	3	-0	0.2
Total 6	15	19	.441	162	4	0	0	22	267¹	250	14	126	174	13.0	3.70	93	.253	.343	3	.081	-2	-9	-8	1	-0.5
■ **HECTOR WAGNER**				Wagner, Hector Raul b: 11/26/68, Santo Domingo, D.R. BR/TR, 6'3", 185 lbs. Deb: 9/10/90																				
1990 KC-A	0	2	.000	5	5	0	0	0	23¹	32	4	11	14	16.6	8.10	47	.323	.391	0	—	0	-11	-11	0	-0.9
■ **HONUS WAGNER**				Wagner, John Peter "The Flying Dutchman"																				
				b: 2/24/1874, Mansfield, Pa. d: 12/6/55, Carnegie, Pa. BR/TR, 5'11", 200 lbs. Deb: 7/19/1897 MCH♦																				
1900 *Pit-N	0	0	—	1	0	0	0	0	3	3	0	4	1	21.0	0.00	—	.260	.450	201	.381	1	1	1	-0	0.1
1902 Pit-N	0	0	—	1	0	0	0	0	5¹	4	0	2	5	10.1	0.00	—	.209	.284	176	.330	0	2	2	-0	0.2
Total 2	0	0	—	2	0	0	0	0	8¹	7	0	6	6	14.0	0.00	—	.228	.354	3415	.327	1	3	3	-0	0.3
■ **MARK WAGNER**				Wagner, Mark Duane b: 3/4/54, Conneaut, Ohio BR/TR, 6', 165 lbs. Deb: 8/20/76 ♦																				
1984 Oak-A	0	0	—	1	0	0	0	0	1²	2	0	1	1	16.2	0.00	—	.400	.500	20	.230	-0	1	1	0	0.1
■ **BULL WAGNER**				Wagner, William George b: 1/1/1888, Lilley, Mich. d: 10/2/67, Muskegon, Mich. BR/TR, 6'0.5", 225 lbs. Deb: 6/02/13																				
1913 Bro-N	4	2	.667	18	1	0	0	0	70²	77	5	30	11	14.0	5.48	60	.285	.363	6	.231	1	-18	-17	-1	-1.6
1914 Bro-N	0	1	.000	6	0	0	0	0	12¹	14	0	12	4	19.7	6.57	44	.311	.466	0	.000	-0	-5	-5	0	-0.4
Total 2	4	3	.571	24	1	0	0	0	83	91	5	42	15	14.9	5.64	57	.289	.380	6	.222	0	-23	-22	-1	-2.0

YEAR	TM/L	W	L	PCT	G	GS	CG	SH	SV	IP	H	HR	BB	SO	RAT	ERA	ERA+	OAV	OOB	BH	AVG	PB	PR	/A	PD	TPI

■ RICK WAITS
Waits, Michael Richard b: 5/15/52, Atlanta, Ga. BL/TL, 6'3", 194 lbs. Deb: 9/17/73

YEAR	TM/L	W	L	PCT	G	GS	CG	SH	SV	IP	H	HR	BB	SO	RAT	ERA	ERA+	OAV	OOB	BH	AVG	PB	PR	/A	PD	TPI
1973	Tex-A	0	0	—	1	0	0	0	1	1	1	0	1	0	18.0	9.00	41	.333	.500	0	—	0	-1	-1	0	0.0
1975	Cle-A	6	2	.750	16	7	3	0	1	70¹	57	3	25	34	10.6	2.94	128	.221	.292	0	—	0	7	7	0	0.7
1976	Cle-A	7	9	.438	26	22	4	2	0	123²	143	7	54	65	14.3	4.00	87	.297	.368	0	—	0	-7	-7	1	-0.6
1977	Cle-A	9	7	.563	37	16	1	0	2	135¹	132	8	64	62	13.1	3.99	99	.262	.347	0	—	0	1	-1	0	0.0
1978	Cle-A	13	15	.464	34	33	15	2	0	230¹	206	16	86	97	11.5	3.20	117	.240	.310	0	—	0	14	14	4	1.8
1979	Cle-A	16	13	.552	34	34	8	3	0	231	230	26	91	91	12.7	4.44	96	.264	.336	0	—	0	-6	-5	2	-0.2
1980	Cle-A	13	14	.481	33	33	9	2	0	224¹	231	18	82	109	12.6	4.45	91	.270	.335	0	—	0	-10	-10	-1	-0.9
1981	Cle-A	8	10	.444	22	21	5	1	0	126¹	173	7	44	51	15.5	4.92	74	.330	.383	0	—	0	-18	-18	2	-1.5
1982	Cle-A	2	13	.133	25	21	2	0	0	115	128	13	57	44	14.6	5.40	76	.290	.372	0	—	0	-17	-17	1	-1.4
1983	Cle-A	0	1	.000	8	0	0	0	0	19²	23	1	9	13	14.6	4.58	93	.307	.381	0	—	0	-1	-1	0	0.0
	Mil-A	0	2	.000	10	2	0	0	0	30	39	1	11	20	15.0	5.10	73	.320	.376	0	—	0	-3	-5	-0	-0.4
	Yr	0	3	.000	18	2	0	0	0	49²	62	2	20	33	14.9	4.89	80	.308	.371	0	—	0	-5	-5	-0	-0.4
1984	Mil-A	2	4	.333	47	1	0	0	3	73	84	7	24	49	13.3	3.58	108	.297	.352	0	—	0	3	2	0	0.2
1985	Mil-A	3	2	.600	24	0	0	0	1	47	67	3	20	24	16.7	6.51	64	.340	.401	0	.000	0	-12	-12	0	-1.1
Total	12	79	92	.462	317	190	47	10	8	1427	1514	110	568	659	13.2	4.25	92	.277	.346	0	.000	0	-50	-53	10	-3.4

■ BILL WAKEFIELD
Wakefield, William Sumner b: 5/24/41, Kansas City, Mo. BR/TR, 6', 175 lbs. Deb: 4/18/64

YEAR	TM/L	W	L	PCT	G	GS	CG	SH	SV	IP	H	HR	BB	SO	RAT	ERA	ERA+	OAV	OOB	BH	AVG	PB	PR	/A	PD	TPI
1964	NY-N	3	5	.375	62	4	0	0	2	119²	103	10	61	61	13.0	3.61	99	.235	.341	4	.167	-0	-1	-0	0	0.0

■ RUBE WALBERG
Walberg, George Elvin b: 7/27/1896, Pine City, Minn. d: 10/27/78, Tempe, Ariz. BL/TL, 6'1.5", 190 lbs. Deb: 4/29/23

YEAR	TM/L	W	L	PCT	G	GS	CG	SH	SV	IP	H	HR	BB	SO	RAT	ERA	ERA+	OAV	OOB	BH	AVG	PB	PR	/A	PD	TPI
1923	NY-N	0	0	—	2	0	0	0	0	5	4	0	1	1	9.0	1.80	212	.211	.250	0	.000	-0	1	1	0	0.1
	Phi-A	4	8	.333	26	10	4	0	0	115	122	10	60	38	14.4	5.32	77	.280	.369	13	.317	3	-17	-16	0	-1.0
1924	Phi-A	0	0	—	6	2	0	0	0	7	10	0	10	3	25.7	12.86	33	.345	.513	1	.500	-0	-7	-7	-0	-0.5
1925	Phi-A	8	14	.364	53	20	7	0	7	191²	197	11	77	82	13.0	3.99	117	.269	.340	10	.156	-4	9	14	1	1.0
1926	Phi-A	12	10	.545	40	19	5	2	2	151	168	4	60	72	13.9	2.80	149	.292	.365	7	.152	-2	20	23	-1	2.0
1927	Phi-A	16	12	.571	46	34	15	0	4	249¹	257	18	91	136	12.7	3.93	108	.271	.337	18	.207	3	6	9	-1	1.2
1928	Phi-A	17	12	.586	38	30	15	3	1	235²	236	19	64	112	11.6	3.55	113	.265	.317	18	.209	1	13	12	1	1.3
1929	*Phi-A	18	11	.621	40	33	20	3	4	267²	256	22	99	94	11.9	3.60	118	.254	.320	23	.223	-0	19	19	-1	1.7
1930	*Phi-A	13	12	.520	38	30	12	2	1	205¹	207	6	85	100	12.9	4.69	100	.262	.335	12	.164	-3	-1	-0	-1	-0.3
1931	*Phi-A	20	12	.625	44	35	19	1	3	291	298	16	109	106	12.6	3.74	120	.266	.331	13	.124	-6	21	24	-1	1.6
1932	*Phi-A	17	10	.630	41	34	19	3	1	272	305	16	103	96	13.5	4.73	96	.282	.344	16	.170	-3	-8	-6	0	-0.7
1933	Phi-A	9	13	.409	40	20	10	1	4	201	224	12	95	68	14.3	4.88	88	.278	.354	9	.132	-1	-13	-13	1	-1.2
1934	Bos-A	6	7	.462	30	10	2	0	1	104²	118	5	41	38	13.8	4.04	119	.284	.350	6	.188	-1	5	9	1	0.9
1935	Bos-A	5	9	.357	44	10	4	0	3	142²	152	10	54	44	13.1	3.91	121	.273	.340	6	.162	-2	9	13	-1	1.0
1936	Bos-A	5	4	.556	24	9	5	0	0	100¹	98	7	36	49	12.1	4.40	121	.257	.323	5	.156	-1	7	10	0	0.8
1937	Bos-A	5	7	.417	32	11	3	0	1	104²	143	7	46	46	16.5	5.59	85	.332	.400	5	.147	-1	-11	-10	-0	-0.9
Total	15	155	141	.524	544	307	140	15	32	2644	2795	163	1031	1085	13.1	4.16	107	.273	.341	162	.179	-18	53	82	-1	7.0

■ DOC WALDBAUER
Waldbauer, Albert Charles b: 2/22/1892, Richmond, Va. d: 7/16/69, Yakima, Wash. BR/TR, 6', 172 lbs. Deb: 9/24/17

YEAR	TM/L	W	L	PCT	G	GS	CG	SH	SV	IP	H	HR	BB	SO	RAT	ERA	ERA+	OAV	OOB	BH	AVG	PB	PR	/A	PD	TPI
1917	Was-A	0	0	—	2	0	0	0	1	5	10	0	2	2	21.6	7.20	37	.476	.522	0	.000	-0	-3	-3	0	-0.1

■ BOB WALK
Walk, Robert Vernon b: 11/26/56, Van Nuys, Cal. BR/TR, 6'3", 185 lbs. Deb: 5/26/80

YEAR	TM/L	W	L	PCT	G	GS	CG	SH	SV	IP	H	HR	BB	SO	RAT	ERA	ERA+	OAV	OOB	BH	AVG	PB	PR	/A	PD	TPI
1980	*Phi-N	11	7	.611	27	27	2	0	0	151²	163	8	71	94	14.0	4.57	83	.276	.356	7	.140	-0	-16	-13	-1	-1.3
1981	Atl-N	1	4	.200	12	8	0	0	0	43¹	41	6	23	16	13.3	4.57	78	.250	.342	1	.143	-0	-5	-5	-1	-0.5
1982	*Atl-N	11	9	.550	32	27	3	1	0	164¹	179	19	59	84	13.4	4.87	77	.280	.347	10	.196	2	-23	-21	-2	-2.1
1983	Atl-N	0	0	—	1	1	0	0	0	3²	7	0	2	4	22.1	7.36	53	.412	.474	0	.000	-0	-2	-1	0	0.0
1984	Pit-N	1	1	.500	2	2	0	0	0	10¹	8	1	4	10	10.5	2.61	138	.200	.273	0	.000	0	1	1	0	0.0
1985	Pit-N	2	3	.400	9	9	1	1	0	58²	60	3	18	40	12.0	3.68	97	.265	.320	0	.000	-1	-1	-1	-1	-0.2
1986	Pit-N	7	8	.467	44	15	1	1	2	141²	129	14	64	78	12.5	3.75	102	.251	.337	6	.154	0	0	3	3	0.3
1987	Pit-N	8	2	.800	39	12	1	1	0	117	107	11	51	78	12.4	3.31	124	.245	.329	6	.231	1	10	10	1	1.2
1988	Pit-N	12	10	.545	32	32	1	1	0	212²	183	6	65	81	10.6	2.71	126	.230	.290	6	.087	-2	17	16	1	1.7
1989	Pit-N	13	10	.565	33	31	2	0	0	196	208	15	65	83	12.7	4.41	76	.271	.331	13	.186	2	-20	-23	1	-1.9
1990	*Pit-N	7	5	.583	26	24	1	1	1	129²	136	17	36	73	12.2	3.75	97	.270	.324	6	.162	1	-2	-1	-0	0.0
Total	11	73	59	.553	257	188	12	6	3	1229	1221	100	458	641	12.5	3.91	93	.260	.329	55	.149	2	-38	-37	1	-3.0

■ ED WALKER
Walker, Edward Harrison b: 8/11/1874, Cambois, England d: 9/29/47, Akron, Ohio BL/TL, 6'5", 242 lbs. Deb: 9/26/02

YEAR	TM/L	W	L	PCT	G	GS	CG	SH	SV	IP	H	HR	BB	SO	RAT	ERA	ERA+	OAV	OOB	BH	AVG	PB	PR	/A	PD	TPI
1902	Cle-A	0	1	.000	1	1	1	0	0	8	11	0	3	1	15.8	3.38	102	.327	.382	1	.333	0	0	0	0	0.0
1903	Cle-A	0	0	—	3	3	0	0	0	12	13	0	10	4	17.3	5.25	54	.275	.402	0	.000	-0	-3	-3	-1	-0.3
Total	2	0	1	.000	4	4	1	0	0	20	24	0	13	5	16.6	4.50	69	.297	.394	1	.167	0	-3	-3	-1	-0.3

■ DIXIE WALKER
Walker, Ewart Gladstone b: 6/1/1887, Brownsville, Pa. d: 11/14/65, Leeds, Ala. BL/TR, 6', 192 lbs. Deb: 9/17/09

YEAR	TM/L	W	L	PCT	G	GS	CG	SH	SV	IP	H	HR	BB	SO	RAT	ERA	ERA+	OAV	OOB	BH	AVG	PB	PR	/A	PD	TPI
1909	Was-A	3	1	.750	4	4	4	0	0	36	31	0	6	25	9.3	2.50	97	.217	.248	2	.154	-0	-0	-0	-1	0.0
1910	Was-A	11	11	.500	29	26	16	3	0	199¹	177	2	68	84	11.4	3.30	76	.245	.317	9	.130	-3	-17	-18	-1	-2.2
1911	Was-A	8	13	.381	32	24	15	2	0	185²	205	2	50	65	12.7	3.39	97	.286	.339	20	.303	4	-1	-2	-1	0.1
1912	Was-A	3	6	.333	9	8	5	0	0	60	72	2	18	29	14.1	5.25	63	.300	.359	2	.125	1	-13	-13	0	-1.0
Total	4	25	31	.446	74	62	40	5	0	481	485	6	142	203	12.1	3.52	82	.266	.326	33	.201	2	-31	-33	-2	-3.1

■ MYSTERIOUS WALKER
Walker, Frederick Mitchell b: 3/21/1884, Utica, Neb. d: 2/1/58, Oak Park, Ill. BR/TR, 5'10.5", 185 lbs. Deb: 6/28/10

YEAR	TM/L	W	L	PCT	G	GS	CG	SH	SV	IP	H	HR	BB	SO	RAT	ERA	ERA+	OAV	OOB	BH	AVG	PB	PR	/A	PD	TPI
1910	Cin-N	0	0	—	1	0	0	0	0	3	4	0	4	1	24.0	3.00	97	.333	.500	0	.000	-0	-0	0	0	0.0
1912	Cle-A	0	0	—	1	0	0	0	0	1	0	0	1	0	9.0	0.00	—	.000	.200	0	—	0	0	0	0	0.0
1913	Bro-N	1	3	.250	11	8	3	0	0	58¹	44	3	35	35	13.0	3.55	93	.233	.367	3	.167	-0	-2	-2	1	0.0
1914	Pit-F	4	16	.200	35	21	12	0	0	169¹	197	3	74	79	14.6	4.31	74	.294	.367	6	.113	-2	-21	-21	3	-2.0
1915	Bro-F	2	4	.333	13	7	2	0	1	65²	61	3	22	28	11.4	3.70	82	.242	.303	6	.222	1	-5	-5	1	-0.2
Total	5	7	23	.233	61	36	17	0	1	297¹	306	9	136	143	13.6	4.00	79	.272	.354	15	.152	-1	-27	-27	6	-2.2

■ GEORGE WALKER
Walker, George A. b: 1863, Hamilton, Ontario, Canada TR, 5'9", 184 lbs. Deb: 8/01/1888

YEAR	TM/L	W	L	PCT	G	GS	CG	SH	SV	IP	H	HR	BB	SO	RAT	ERA	ERA+	OAV	OOB	BH	AVG	PB	PR	/A	PD	TPI
1888	Bal-a	1	3	.250	4	4	4	1	0	35	36	2	14	18	12.9	5.91	50	.256	.324	1	.077	-1	-11	-11	-0	-1.0

■ LUKE WALKER
Walker, James Luke b: 9/2/43, DeKalb, Tex. BL/TL, 6'2", 190 lbs. Deb: 9/07/65

YEAR	TM/L	W	L	PCT	G	GS	CG	SH	SV	IP	H	HR	BB	SO	RAT	ERA	ERA+	OAV	OOB	BH	AVG	PB	PR	/A	PD	TPI
1965	Pit-N	0	0	—	2	0	0	0	0	5	2	0	1	5	5.4	0.00	—	.118	.167	0	—	0	2	2	0	0.2
1966	Pit-N	0	1	.000	10	1	0	0	0	10	8	0	15	7	21.6	4.50	79	.205	.436	0	.000	-0	-1	-0	0	0.0
1968	Pit-N	0	3	.000	39	2	0	0	3	61²	42	1	39	66	12.0	2.04	143	.190	.314	0	.000	-1	6	6	0	0.6
1969	Pit-N	4	6	.400	31	15	3	1	0	118²	98	5	57	96	11.9	3.64	96	.226	.319	0	.000	-3	-1	-2	1	-0.4
1970	*Pit-N	15	6	.714	42	19	5	3	3	163	129	6	89	124	12.1	3.04	128	.219	.323	6	.130	-1	18	16	-0	1.5
1971	*Pit-N	10	8	.556	28	24	4	2	0	159²	157	9	53	86	11.9	3.55	95	.262	.324	1	.022	-3	-2	-3	-2	-0.7
1972	*Pit-N	4	6	.400	26	12	2	0	2	92²	98	4	34	48	12.8	3.40	98	.278	.342	2	.083	-1	1	-1	-0	-0.2
1973	Pit-N	7	12	.368	37	18	2	1	1	122	129	9	66	74	14.5	4.65	76	.270	.360	2	.067	-2	-13	-15	-1	-1.8
1974	Det-A	5	5	.500	28	9	0	0	0	92	100	9	54	52	15.3	4.99	76	.278	.375	0	—	-0	-14	-12	-0	-1.2
Total	9	45	47	.489	243	100	16	7	9	824²	763	43	408	558	12.9	3.65	97	.247	.337	11	.059	-11	-3	-11	-3	-2.0

■ ROY WALKER
Walker, James Roy "Dixie" b: 4/13/1893, Lawrenceburg, Tenn d: 2/10/62, New Orleans, La. BR/TR, 6'1.5", 180 lbs. Deb: 8/22/12

YEAR	TM/L	W	L	PCT	G	GS	CG	SH	SV	IP	H	HR	BB	SO	RAT	ERA	ERA+	OAV	OOB	BH	AVG	PB	PR	/A	PD	TPI
1912	Cle-A	0	0	—	1	0	0	0	0	2	0	0	2	2	9.0	0.00	—	.000	.250	0	—	0	1	1	0	0.1
1915	Cle-A	4	9	.308	25	15	4	0	1	131	122	1	65	57	13.3	3.98	77	.261	.360	5	.132	-2	-15	-14	-2	-1.8
1917	Chi-N	0	1	.000	2	1	0	0	0	7	8	0	5	4	16.7	3.86	75	.286	.394	0	.000	-0	-1	-1	-0	0.0

YEAR	TM/L	W	L	PCT	G	GS	CG	SH	SV	IP	H	HR	BB	SO	RAT	ERA	ERA+	OAV	OOB	BH	AVG	PB	PR	/A	PD	TPI
1918	Chi-N	1	3	.250	13	7	2	0	1	43¹	50	1	15	20	13.7	2.70	103	.298	.359	0	.000	-1	0	0	0	0.0
1921	StL-N	11	12	.478	38	24	11	0	3	170²	194	10	53	52	13.1	4.22	87	.293	.347	11	.204	-0	-8	-10	-1	-1.1
1922	StL-N	1	2	.333	12	2	0	0	0	32	34	1	15	14	13.8	4.78	81	.293	.374	1	.143	-0	-2	-3	-1	-0.4
Total 6		17	27	.386	91	49	17	0	5	386	408	13	155	148	13.3	3.99	85	.282	.355	17	.153	-4	-26	-26	-5	-3.2

■ JERRY WALKER
Walker, Jerry Allen b: 2/12/39, Ada, Okla. BB/TR, 6'1", 195 lbs. Deb: 7/06/57 C

YEAR	TM/L	W	L	PCT	G	GS	CG	SH	SV	IP	H	HR	BB	SO	RAT	ERA	ERA+	OAV	OOB	BH	AVG	PB	PR	/A	PD	TPI
1957	Bal-A	1	0	1.000	13	3	1	1	1	27²	24	1	14	13	12.4	2.93	123	.245	.339	0	.000	-1	3	2	0	0.1
1958	Bal-A	0	0	—	6	0	0	0	0	10¹	16	2	5	6	18.3	6.97	52	.340	.404	0	.000	-0	-4	-4	-0	-0.3
1959	Bal-A	11	10	.524	30	22	7	2	4	182	160	13	52	100	10.6	2.92	130	.240	.297	11	.169	-1	19	18	-0	1.7
1960	Bal-A	3	4	.429	29	18	1	0	5	118	107	15	56	48	12.7	3.74	102	.247	.337	14	.368	5	2	1	1	0.7
1961	KC-A	8	14	.364	36	24	4	0	2	168	161	23	96	56	14.3	4.82	85	.253	.359	16	.250	3	-15	-13	1	-0.8
1962	KC-A	8	9	.471	31	21	3	1	0	143¹	165	27	78	57	15.7	5.90	70	.288	.381	15	.263	5	-31	-28	2	-1.9
1963	Cle-A	6	6	.500	39	2	0	0	1	88	92	15	36	41	13.3	4.91	74	.265	.338	2	.105	-0	-13	-13	-0	-1.2
1964	Cle-A	0	1	.000	6	0	0	0	0	9²	9	1	4	5	12.1	4.66	77	.257	.333	0	.000	-0	-1	-1	-0	-0.1
Total 8		37	44	.457	190	90	16	4	13	747	734	97	341	326	13.3	4.36	89	.259	.343	58	.230	10	-39	-38	3	-1.8

■ MARTY WALKER
Walker, Martin Van Buren "Buddy" b: 3/27/1899, Philadelphia, Pa. d: 4/24/78, Philadelphia, Pa. BL/TL, 6', 170 lbs. Deb: 9/30/28

YEAR	TM/L	W	L	PCT	G	GS	CG	SH	SV	IP	H	HR	BB	SO	RAT	ERA	ERA+	OAV	OOB	BH	AVG	PB	PR	/A	PD	TPI
1928	Phi-N	0	1	.000	1	1	0	0	0	0	2	0	3	0	—	∞	—	1.000	1.000	0	—	0	-2	-2	0	-0.1

■ MIKE WALKER
Walker, Michael Charles b: 10/4/66, Chicago, Ill. BR/TR, 6'2", 195 lbs. Deb: 9/09/88

YEAR	TM/L	W	L	PCT	G	GS	CG	SH	SV	IP	H	HR	BB	SO	RAT	ERA	ERA+	OAV	OOB	BH	AVG	PB	PR	/A	PD	TPI
1988	Cle-A	0	1	.000	3	1	0	0	0	8²	8	0	10	7	18.7	7.27	57	.258	.439	0	—	0	-3	-3	0	-0.2
1990	Cle-A	2	6	.250	18	11	0	0	0	75²	82	6	42	34	15.5	4.88	82	.277	.378	0	—	0	-8	-8	-0	-0.7
Total 2		2	7	.222	21	12	0	0	0	84¹	90	6	52	41	15.8	5.12	78	.275	.384	0	—	0	-11	-11	0	-0.9

■ TOM WALKER
Walker, Robert Thomas b: 11/7/48, Tampa, Fla. BR/TR, 6'1", 188 lbs. Deb: 4/23/72

YEAR	TM/L	W	L	PCT	G	GS	CG	SH	SV	IP	H	HR	BB	SO	RAT	ERA	ERA+	OAV	OOB	BH	AVG	PB	PR	/A	PD	TPI
1972	Mon-N	2	2	.500	46	0	0	0	2	74²	71	4	22	42	11.3	2.89	123	.248	.304	0	.000	-0	5	5	0	0.5
1973	Mon-N	7	5	.583	54	0	0	0	4	91²	95	7	42	68	13.7	3.63	105	.274	.357	0	.000	-1	0	2	-0	0.1
1974	Mon-N	4	5	.444	33	8	1	0	2	91²	96	7	28	70	12.4	3.83	100	.266	.322	3	.188	0	-2	-0	-1	0.0
1975	Det-A	3	8	.273	36	9	1	0	0	115¹	116	16	40	60	12.6	4.45	90	.261	.329	0	—	0	-9	-6	-1	-0.6
1976	StL-N	1	2	.333	10	0	0	0	0	19²	22	2	3	11	11.4	4.12	86	.265	.291	2	.400	1	-1	-1	-1	0.0
1977	Mon-N	1	1	.500	11	0	0	0	3	19	15	2	7	10	10.4	4.74	80	.221	.293	0	.000	-0	-2	-2	-0	-0.1
	Cal-A	0	0	—	1	0	0	0	0	2	3	2	0	1	13.5	9.00	43	.375	.375	0	—	0	-1	-1	0	0.0
Total 6		18	23	.439	191	17	2	0	11	414	418	40	142	262	12.4	3.87	99	.262	.326	5	.152	-0	-10	-3	-3	-0.1

■ TOM WALKER
Walker, Thomas William b: 8/1/1881, Philadelphia, Pa. d: 7/10/44, Woodbury Heights N.J. BR/TR, 5'11", 170 lbs. Deb: 9/27/02

YEAR	TM/L	W	L	PCT	G	GS	CG	SH	SV	IP	H	HR	BB	SO	RAT	ERA	ERA+	OAV	OOB	BH	AVG	PB	PR	/A	PD	TPI
1902	Phi-A	0	1	.000	1	1	1	0	0	8	10	0	0	2	11.3	5.63	65	.306	.306	1	.250	-0	-2	-2	1	0.0
1904	Cin-N	15	8	.652	24	24	22	2	0	217	196	2	53	64	11.1	2.24	131	.238	.299	9	.117	-5	12	17	-1	1.2
1905	Cin-N	9	7	.563	23	19	12	1	0	145	171	3	44	28	13.7	3.23	102	.305	.362	7	.137	-1	-4	1	0	0.1
Total 3		24	16	.600	48	44	35	3	0	370	377	5	97	94	12.1	2.70	115	.266	.324	17	.129	-6	7	16	-0	1.3

■ BILL WALKER
Walker, William Henry b: 10/7/03, E.St.Louis, Ill. d: 6/14/66, E.St.Louis, Ill. BR/TL, 6', 175 lbs. Deb: 9/13/27

YEAR	TM/L	W	L	PCT	G	GS	CG	SH	SV	IP	H	HR	BB	SO	RAT	ERA	ERA+	OAV	OOB	BH	AVG	PB	PR	/A	PD	TPI
1927	NY-N	0	0	—	3	0	0	0	0	4	6	0	5	4	24.8	9.00	43	.429	.579	0	—	0	-2	-2	-0	-0.1
1928	NY-N	3	6	.333	22	8	1	0	0	76¹	79	9	31	39	13.1	4.72	83	.275	.348	2	.091	-2	-6	-7	-1	-0.8
1929	NY-N	14	7	.667	29	23	13	1	0	177²	188	11	57	65	12.6	3.09	148	.274	.334	7	.115	-3	32	30	-3	2.1
1930	NY-N	17	15	.531	39	34	13	2	1	245¹	258	19	88	105	12.9	3.93	121	.268	.334	16	.186	-1	29	22	-1	1.7
1931	NY-N	16	9	.640	37	28	19	6	3	239¹	212	6	64	121	10.5	2.26	164	.231	.283	5	.065	-6	43	38	-4	2.9
1932	NY-N	8	12	.400	31	22	9	0	2	163	177	23	55	74	13.0	4.14	90	.274	.334	7	.135	-2	-5	-8	1	-0.7
1933	StL-N	9	10	.474	29	20	6	2	0	158	168	8	67	41	13.4	3.42	102	.273	.346	7	.132	-2	-1	1	2	0.1
1934	*StL-N	12	4	.750	24	19	10	1	0	153	160	11	66	76	13.4	3.12	136	.270	.345	4	.093	-4	16	19	-1	1.3
1935	StL-N	13	8	.619	37	25	8	2	1	193¹	222	7	78	79	14.2	3.82	107	.288	.357	6	.102	-4	4	6	-0	0.2
1936	StL-N	5	6	.455	21	13	4	1	1	79²	106	5	27	22	15.3	5.87	67	.318	.373	7	.280	2	-16	-17	1	-1.3
Total 10		97	77	.557	272	192	83	15	8	1489²	1576	99	538	626	12.9	3.59	114	.271	.335	62	.127	-23	93	83	-6	5.4

■ JIM WALKUP
Walkup, James Elton b: 12/14/09, Havana, Ark. BR/TR, 6'1", 170 lbs. Deb: 9/22/34

YEAR	TM/L	W	L	PCT	G	GS	CG	SH	SV	IP	H	HR	BB	SO	RAT	ERA	ERA+	OAV	OOB	BH	AVG	PB	PR	/A	PD	TPI
1934	StL-A	0	0	—	3	0	0	0	0	8¹	6	0	5	6	11.9	2.16	231	.200	.314	1	.333	0	2	3	-0	0.2
1935	StL-A	6	9	.400	55	20	4	1	0	181¹	226	17	104	44	16.5	6.25	77	.305	.392	6	.128	-3	-36	-29	-1	-2.9
1936	StL-A	0	3	.000	5	2	0	0	0	15²	20	1	6	5	14.9	8.04	67	.308	.366	0	.000	-1	-5	-5	1	-0.3
1937	StL-A	9	12	.429	27	18	6	0	0	150¹	218	16	83	46	18.0	7.36	66	.347	.423	14	.241	-1	-46	-42	2	-3.4
1938	StL-A	1	12	.077	18	13	1	0	0	94	127	13	53	28	17.5	6.80	73	.329	.414	4	.138	-2	-21	-19	1	-1.7
1939	StL-A	0	1	.000	1	0	0	0	0	0²	2	0	1	0	40.5	0.00	—	.500	.600	0	—	0	0	0	0	0.0
	Det-A	0	1	.000	7	0	0	0	0	12	15	3	8	5	17.3	7.50	65	.319	.418	1	.500	0	-4	-3	-0	-0.2
	Yr	0	2	.000	8	0	0	0	0	12²	17	3	9	5	18.5	7.11	69	.333	.433	0	.000	-0	-3	-3	0	-0.2
Total 6		16	38	.296	116	53	11	1	0	462¹	614	49	260	134	17.1	6.74	72	.323	.406	26	.182	-6	-110	-96	2	-8.3

■ JIM WALKUP
Walkup, James Huey b: 11/3/1895, Havana, Ark. d: 6/12/90, Duncan, Okla. BR/TL, 5'8", 150 lbs. Deb: 4/30/27

YEAR	TM/L	W	L	PCT	G	GS	CG	SH	SV	IP	H	HR	BB	SO	RAT	ERA	ERA+	OAV	OOB	BH	AVG	PB	PR	/A	PD	TPI
1927	Det-A	0	0	—	2	0	0	0	0	1²	3	0	0	0	16.2	5.40	78	.429	.429	0	.000	-0	-0	-0	0	0.0

■ MURRAY WALL
Wall, Murray Wesley b: 9/19/26, Dallas, Tex. d: 10/8/71, Lone Oak, Tex. BR/TR, 6'3", 185 lbs. Deb: 7/04/50

YEAR	TM/L	W	L	PCT	G	GS	CG	SH	SV	IP	H	HR	BB	SO	RAT	ERA	ERA+	OAV	OOB	BH	AVG	PB	PR	/A	PD	TPI
1950	Bos-N	0	0	—	1	0	0	0	0	4	6	0	2	2	18.0	9.00	43	.333	.400	0	.000	-0	-2	-2	0	-0.1
1957	Bos-A	3	0	1.000	11	0	0	0	1	24¹	21	3	2	13	8.5	3.33	120	.233	.250	2	.333	0	1	2	1	0.4
1958	Bos-A	8	9	.471	52	1	0	0	10	114¹	109	14	33	53	11.6	3.62	111	.255	.316	3	.107	-2	2	5	3	0.6
1959	Bos-A	1	4	.200	15	0	0	0	3	31²	31	5	15	8	13.1	5.40	75	.267	.351	0	.000	-1	-5	-5	1	-0.4
	Was-A	0	0	—	1	0	0	0	0	1¹	3	1	0	0	20.3	6.75	58	.600	.600	0	.000	-0	-0	-0	0	0.0
	Bos-A	1	1	.500	11	0	0	0	0	17¹	26	2	11	6	19.7	5.71	71	.371	.463	0	.000	-0	-4	-3	-0	-0.3
	Yr	2	5	.286	27	0	0	0	3	50¹	60	8	26	14	15.6	5.54	73	.313	.397	0	.000	-2	-9	-8	1	-0.7
Total 4		13	14	.481	91	1	0	0	14	193	196	25	63	82	12.4	4.20	96	.270	.333	5	.109	-3	-8	-4	5	0.2

■ STAN WALL
Wall, Stanley Arthur b: 6/16/51, Butler, Mo. BL/TL, 6'1", 175 lbs. Deb: 7/19/75

YEAR	TM/L	W	L	PCT	G	GS	CG	SH	SV	IP	H	HR	BB	SO	RAT	ERA	ERA+	OAV	OOB	BH	AVG	PB	PR	/A	PD	TPI
1975	LA-N	0	1	.000	10	0	0	0	1	16	12	0	7	6	11.3	1.69	201	.222	.323	0	—	0	3	3	0	0.3
1976	LA-N	2	2	.500	31	0	0	0	1	50	50	5	15	27	12.1	3.60	94	.269	.330	0	.000	-0	-1	-1	-0	-0.1
1977	LA-N	2	3	.400	25	0	0	0	1	32	36	3	13	22	14.1	5.34	72	.279	.350	0	.000	-0	-5	-5	-1	-0.5
Total 3		4	6	.400	66	0	0	0	1	98	98	8	35	55	12.6	3.86	91	.266	.336	0	.000	-1	-2	-4	-1	-0.3

■ DAVE WALLACE
Wallace, David William b: 9/7/47, Waterbury, Conn. BR/TR, 5'10", 185 lbs. Deb: 7/18/73

YEAR	TM/L	W	L	PCT	G	GS	CG	SH	SV	IP	H	HR	BB	SO	RAT	ERA	ERA+	OAV	OOB	BH	AVG	PB	PR	/A	PD	TPI
1973	Phi-N	0	0	—	4	0	0	0	0	3²	13	1	2	2	36.8	22.09	17	.591	.625	0	—	0	-8	-7	0	-0.6
1974	Phi-N	0	1	.000	3	0	0	0	0	3	4	2	3	3	21.0	9.00	42	.308	.438	0	—	0	-2	-2	0	-0.1
1978	Tor-A	0	0	—	6	0	0	0	0	14	12	1	11	7	14.8	3.86	102	.245	.383	0	—	0	0	-0	0	0.0
Total 3		0	1	.000	13	0	0	0	0	20²	29	4	16	12	19.6	7.84	49	.345	.450	0	—	0	-9	-9	0	-0.7

■ HUCK WALLACE
Wallace, Harry Clinton "Lefty" b: 7/27/1882, Richmond, Ind. d: 7/6/51, Cleveland, Ohio BL/TL, 5'6", 160 lbs. Deb: 6/05/12

YEAR	TM/L	W	L	PCT	G	GS	CG	SH	SV	IP	H	HR	BB	SO	RAT	ERA	ERA+	OAV	OOB	BH	AVG	PB	PR	/A	PD	TPI
1912	Phi-N	0	0	—	4	0	0	0	0	4²	7	0	4	4	21.2	0.00	—	.350	.458	0	—	0	2	2	0	0.2

■ LEFTY WALLACE
Wallace, James Harold b: 8/12/21, Evansville, Ind. d: 7/28/82, Evansville, Ind. BL/TL, 5'11", 160 lbs. Deb: 5/05/42

YEAR	TM/L	W	L	PCT	G	GS	CG	SH	SV	IP	H	HR	BB	SO	RAT	ERA	ERA+	OAV	OOB	BH	AVG	PB	PR	/A	PD	TPI
1942	Bos-N	1	3	.250	19	3	1	0	0	49¹	39	3	24	20	11.9	3.83	87	.217	.316	2	.143	-0	-3	-3	-1	-0.3
1945	Bos-N	1	0	1.000	5	3	1	0	0	20	18	1	9	4	12.6	4.50	85	.240	.329	0	.000	-1	-2	-1	0	-0.1
1946	Bos-N	3	3	.500	27	8	2	0	0	75¹	76	5	31	27	12.9	4.18	82	.253	.325	1	.056	-1	-6	-6	2	-0.5

YEAR TM/L	W	L	PCT	G	GS	CG	SH	SV	IP	H	HR	BB	SO	RAT	ERA	ERA+	OAV	OOB	BH	AVG	PB	PR	/A	PD	TPI
Total 3	5	6	.455	51	14	4	0	0	144²	133	9	64	51	12.5	4.11	84	.240	.323	3	.079	-2	-11	-10	1	-0.9

■ MIKE WALLACE   Wallace, Michael Sherman   b: 2/3/51, Gastonia, N.C.   BL/TL, 6'2", 190 lbs.   Deb: 6/27/73

YEAR TM/L	W	L	PCT	G	GS	CG	SH	SV	IP	H	HR	BB	SO	RAT	ERA	ERA+	OAV	OOB	BH	AVG	PB	PR	/A	PD	TPI
1973 Phi-N	1	1	.500	20	3	1	0	1	33¹	38	1	15	20	14.3	3.78	100	.304	.379	0	.000	-0	-0	0	-0	0.0
1974 Phi-N	1	0	1.000	8	0	0	0	0	8¹	12	0	2	1	15.1	5.40	70	.324	.359	0	—	0	-2	-2	-0	-0.1
NY-A	6	0	1.000	23	1	0	0	0	52¹	42	3	35	34	13.2	2.41	145	.222	.344	0	—	0	7	6	-1	0.6
1975 NY-A	0	0	—	3	0	0	0	0	4¹	11	1	1	2	24.9	14.54	25	.458	.480	0	—	0	-5	-5	0	-0.4
StL-N	0	0	—	9	0	0	0	0	8²	9	0	5	6	14.5	2.08	181	.281	.378	0	—	0	1	2	0	0.2
1976 StL-N	3	2	.600	49	0	0	0	2	66¹	66	3	39	40	14.2	4.07	87	.264	.363	1	.333	0	-4	-4	0	-0.3
1977 Tex-A	0	0	—	5	0	0	0	0	8¹	10	1	10	2	21.6	7.56	54	.323	.488	0	—	0	-3	-3	0	-0.2
Total 5	11	3	.786	117	4	1	0	3	181²	188	9	107	105	14.6	3.91	92	.273	.371	1	.143	0	-6	-6	-1	-0.2

■ BOBBY WALLACE   Wallace, Roderick John   b: 11/4/1873, Pittsburgh, Pa.   d: 11/3/60, Torrance, Cal.   BR/TR, 5'8", 170 lbs.   Deb: 9/15/1894   MUCH♦

YEAR TM/L	W	L	PCT	G	GS	CG	SH	SV	IP	H	HR	BB	SO	RAT	ERA	ERA+	OAV	OOB	BH	AVG	PB	PR	/A	PD	TPI
1894 Cle-N	2	1	.667	4	3	3	0	0	26¹	28	1	22	10	17.1	5.47	100	.270	.397	2	.154	-1	-0	-0	1	0.0
1895 Cle-N	12	14	.462	30	28	22	1	1	228²	271	3	87	63	14.1	4.09	122	.290	.351	21	.214	-3	17	23	3	2.0
1896 *Cle-N	10	7	.588	22	16	13	2	0	145¹	167	2	49	46	13.4	3.34	136	.286	.341	35	.235	1	16	19	-0	1.7
1902 StL-A	0	0	—	1	1	0	0	0	2	3	0	0	1	13.5	0.00	—	.346	.346	141	.285	0	1	1	0	0.1
Total 4	24	22	.522	57	48	38	3	1	402¹	469	6	158	120	14.0	3.89	125	.288	.351	2309	.268	-4	34	43	4	3.8

■ TIM WALLACH   Wallach, Timothy Charles   b: 9/14/57, Huntington Park, Cal.   BR/TR, 6'3", 220 lbs.   Deb: 9/06/80   ♦

YEAR TM/L	W	L	PCT	G	GS	CG	SH	SV	IP	H	HR	BB	SO	RAT	ERA	ERA+	OAV	OOB	BH	AVG	PB	PR	/A	PD	TPI
1987 Mon-N	0	0	—	1	0	0	0	0	1	1	0	0	0	9.0	0.00	—	.333	.333	177	.298	1	0	0	0	0.0
1989 Mon-N	0	0	—	1	0	0	0	0	1	2	0	0	0	18.0	9.00	39	.500	.500	159	.277	0	-1	-1	0	0.0
Total 2	0	0	—	2	0	0	0	0	2	3	0	0	0	13.5	4.50	86	.429	.429	1444	.267	1	-0	-0	0	0.0

■ RED WALLER   Waller, John Francis   b: 6/16/1883, Washington, D.C.   d: 2/9/15, Secaucus, N.J.   Deb: 4/27/09

YEAR TM/L	W	L	PCT	G	GS	CG	SH	SV	IP	H	HR	BB	SO	RAT	ERA	ERA+	OAV	OOB	BH	AVG	PB	PR	/A	PD	TPI
1909 NY-N	0	0	—	1	0	0	0	0	1	3	0	0	1	36.0	0.00	—	.429	.500	0	—	0	0	0	0	0.1

■ AUGIE WALSH   Walsh, August Sothley   b: 8/9/04, Wilmington, Del.   d: 11/12/85, San Rafael, Cal.   BR/TR, 6', 175 lbs.   Deb: 10/02/27

YEAR TM/L	W	L	PCT	G	GS	CG	SH	SV	IP	H	HR	BB	SO	RAT	ERA	ERA+	OAV	OOB	BH	AVG	PB	PR	/A	PD	TPI
1927 Phi-N	0	1	.000	1	1	1	0	0	10	12	3	5	0	15.3	4.50	92	.333	.415	1	.250	-0	-1	-0	-0	0.0
1928 Phi-N	4	9	.308	38	11	2	0	2	122¹	160	13	40	38	15.1	6.18	69	.321	.378	10	.256	2	-30	-26	-2	-2.3
Total 2	4	10	.286	39	12	3	0	2	132¹	172	16	45	38	15.1	6.05	70	.322	.380	11	.256	2	-30	-26	-2	-2.3

■ CONNIE WALSH   Walsh, Cornelius R.   b: 4/23/1882, St.Louis, Mo.   d: 4/5/53, St.Louis, Mo.   Deb: 9/16/07

YEAR TM/L	W	L	PCT	G	GS	CG	SH	SV	IP	H	HR	BB	SO	RAT	ERA	ERA+	OAV	OOB	BH	AVG	PB	PR	/A	PD	TPI
1907 Pit-N	0	0	—	1	0	0	0	0	1	1	0	1	0	18.0	9.00	27	.250	.400	0	—	0	-1	-1	0	0.0

■ DAVE WALSH   Walsh, David Peter   b: 9/25/60, Arlington, Mass.   BL/TL, 6'1", 185 lbs.   Deb: 8/13/90

YEAR TM/L	W	L	PCT	G	GS	CG	SH	SV	IP	H	HR	BB	SO	RAT	ERA	ERA+	OAV	OOB	BH	AVG	PB	PR	/A	PD	TPI
1990 LA-N	1	0	1.000	20	0	0	0	1	16¹	15	1	6	15	11.6	3.86	92	.242	.309	0	—	0	-0	-1	0	0.0

■ ED WALSH   Walsh, Edward Arthur   b: 2/11/05, Meriden, Conn.   d: 10/31/37, Meriden, Conn.   BR/TR, 6'1", 180 lbs.   Deb: 7/04/28

YEAR TM/L	W	L	PCT	G	GS	CG	SH	SV	IP	H	HR	BB	SO	RAT	ERA	ERA+	OAV	OOB	BH	AVG	PB	PR	/A	PD	TPI
1928 Chi-A	4	7	.364	14	10	3	0	0	78	86	2	42	32	15.3	4.96	82	.290	.387	3	.111	-2	-8	-8	-1	-0.9
1929 Chi-A	6	11	.353	24	20	7	0	0	129	156	9	64	31	15.6	5.65	76	.312	.394	10	.233	2	-20	-20	1	-1.5
1930 Chi-A	1	4	.200	37	4	0	0	0	103²	131	8	30	37	14.3	5.38	86	.316	.367	9	.265	1	-8	-9	1	-0.6
1932 Chi-A	0	2	.000	4	4	1	0	0	20¹	26	3	13	7	17.3	8.41	51	.299	.390	2	.286	0	-9	-9	0	-0.7
Total 4	11	24	.314	79	38	11	0	0	331	399	22	149	107	15.3	5.57	78	.307	.384	24	.216	1	-45	-45	1	-3.7

■ ED WALSH   Walsh, Edward Augustine "Big Ed"   b: 5/14/1881, Plains, Pa.   d: 5/26/59, Pompano Beach, Fla   BR/TR, 6'1", 193 lbs.   Deb: 5/07/04   MUCH

YEAR TM/L	W	L	PCT	G	GS	CG	SH	SV	IP	H	HR	BB	SO	RAT	ERA	ERA+	OAV	OOB	BH	AVG	PB	PR	/A	PD	TPI
1904 Chi-A	6	3	.667	18	8	6	1	1	110²	90	1	32	57	9.9	2.60	94	.223	.280	9	.220	3	-0	-2	0	0.1
1905 Chi-A	8	3	.727	22	13	9	1	0	136²	121	0	29	71	9.9	2.17	114	.239	.280	9	.155	-0	7	5	0	0.4
1906 *Chi-A	17	13	.567	41	31	24	**10**	1	278¹	215	1	58	171	8.8	1.88	135	.216	.260	14	.141	-2	25	21	6	2.8
1907 Chi-A	24	18	.571	**56**	46	**37**	5	4	**422¹**	341	3	87	206	9.1	**1.60**	**150**	.223	.265	25	.162	-1	**45**	**38**	21	**6.7**
1908 Chi-A	**40**	15	.727	**66**	49	**42**	11	6	**464**	343	6	**56**	**269**	7.9	1.42	164	.203	.232	27	.172	2	**51**	**47**	12	**7.2**
1909 Chi-A	15	11	.577	31	28	20	**8**	2	230¹	166	0	50	127	**8.6**	1.41	166	.203	**.253**	18	.214	4	**27**	24	6	4.2
1910 Chi-A	18	20	.474	**45**	36	33	7	**5**	369²	242	4	61	258	**7.5**	**1.27**	**189**	**.187**	.226	30	.217	4	**52**	46	8	**7.0**
1911 Chi-A	27	18	.600	**56**	37	33	5	4	**368²**	327	4	72	**255**	9.9	2.22	145	.239	.280	34	.215	-2	46	41	14	5.4
1912 Chi-A	27	17	.614	**62**	41	32	6	**10**	**393**	332	6	94	254	9.8	2.15	149	.231	.279	33	.243	5	51	46	6	6.0
1913 Chi-A	8	3	.727	16	14	7	1	1	97²	91	1	39	34	12.3	2.58	113	.243	.321	5	.156	-1	4	4	1	0.4
1914 Chi-A	2	3	.400	8	5	3	1	0	44²	33	0	20	15	10.9	2.82	95	.212	.305	1	.063	-1	-0	-1	1	0.0
1915 Chi-A	0	1	1.000	3	3	3	1	0	27	19	0	7	12	8.7	1.33	223	.202	.257	4	.364	1	5	5	-1	0.6
1916 Chi-A	0	1	.000	2	1	0	0	0	3¹	4	0	3	3	18.9	2.70	102	.286	.412	0	—	0	0	0	0	0.0
1917 Bos-N	0	1	.000	4	3	1	0	0	18	22	0	9	4	16.0	3.50	73	.314	.400	1	.250	1	-2	-2	0	0.0
Total 14	195	126	.607	430	315	250	57	34	2964¹	2346	22	617	1736	9.1	1.82	145	.218	.263	210	.193	13	310	270	75	40.8

■ JUNIOR WALSH   Walsh, James Gerald   b: 3/7/19, Newark, N.J.   BR/TR, 5'11", 185 lbs.   Deb: 9/14/46

YEAR TM/L	W	L	PCT	G	GS	CG	SH	SV	IP	H	HR	BB	SO	RAT	ERA	ERA+	OAV	OOB	BH	AVG	PB	PR	/A	PD	TPI
1946 Pit-N	0	1	.000	4	2	0	0	0	10¹	9	0	10	2	17.4	5.23	67	.237	.408	0	.000	-1	-2	-2	0	-0.2
1948 Pit-N	1	0	1.000	2	0	0	0	0	4¹	4	1	5	0	18.7	10.38	39	.235	.409	0	.000	-0	-3	-3	0	-0.2
1949 Pit-N	1	4	.200	9	7	1	1	0	42²	40	5	16	24	11.8	5.06	83	.244	.311	0	.000	-1	-5	-4	-1	-0.5
1950 Pit-N	1	1	.500	38	2	0	0	2	62¹	56	6	34	33	13.1	5.05	87	.246	.346	1	.167	-1	-6	-5	0	-0.3
1951 Pit-N	1	4	.200	36	1	0	0	0	73¹	92	9	46	32	17.1	6.87	61	.304	.397	1	.143	-1	-24	-22	0	-2.0
Total 5	4	10	.286	89	12	1	1	2	193	201	21	111	91	14.7	5.88	72	.268	.365	2	.065	-1	-40	-35	-0	-3.2

■ JIM WALSH   Walsh, James Thomas   b: 7/10/1894, Roxbury, Mass.   d: 5/13/67, Boston, Mass.   BL/TL, 5'11", 175 lbs.   Deb: 8/25/21

YEAR TM/L	W	L	PCT	G	GS	CG	SH	SV	IP	H	HR	BB	SO	RAT	ERA	ERA+	OAV	OOB	BH	AVG	PB	PR	/A	PD	TPI
1921 Det-A	0	0	—	3	0	0	0	0	4	2	0	1	3	6.8	2.25	190	.125	.176	0	—	0	1	1	-0	0.1

■ DEE WALSH   Walsh, Leo Thomas   b: 3/28/1890, St.Louis, Mo.   d: 7/14/71, St.Louis, Mo.   BB/TR, 5'9.5", 165 lbs.   Deb: 4/10/13   ♦

YEAR TM/L	W	L	PCT	G	GS	CG	SH	SV	IP	H	HR	BB	SO	RAT	ERA	ERA+	OAV	OOB	BH	AVG	PB	PR	/A	PD	TPI
1915 StL-A	0	0	—	1	0	0	0	0	2	2	0	2	0	18.0	13.50	21	.222	.364	33	.220	0	-2	-2	0	-0.1

■ JIMMY WALSH   Walsh, Michael Timothy "Runt"   b: 3/25/1886, Lima, Ohio   d: 1/21/47, Baltimore, Md.   BR/TR, 5'9", 174 lbs.   Deb: 4/25/10   ♦

YEAR TM/L	W	L	PCT	G	GS	CG	SH	SV	IP	H	HR	BB	SO	RAT	ERA	ERA+	OAV	OOB	BH	AVG	PB	PR	/A	PD	TPI
1911 Phi-N	0	1	.000	1	0	0	0	0	2²	7	1	1	1	27.0	13.50	26	.500	.533	78	.270	0	-3	-3	-0	-0.2

■ GENE WALTER   Walter, Gene Winston   b: 11/22/60, Chicago, Ill.   BL/TL, 6'4", 200 lbs.   Deb: 8/09/85

YEAR TM/L	W	L	PCT	G	GS	CG	SH	SV	IP	H	HR	BB	SO	RAT	ERA	ERA+	OAV	OOB	BH	AVG	PB	PR	/A	PD	TPI
1985 SD-N	0	2	.000	15	0	0	0	3	22	12	0	8	18	8.2	2.05	173	.158	.238	0	.000	0	4	4	0	0.4
1986 SD-N	2	2	.500	57	0	0	0	1	98	89	7	49	84	13.0	3.86	95	.247	.343	2	.200	1	-2	-2	1	0.0
1987 NY-N	3	1	.333	21	0	0	0	0	19²	18	1	13	11	14.6	3.20	118	.243	.364	0	.000	0	2	1	0	0.1
1988 NY-N	0	1	.000	19	0	0	0	0	16²	21	0	11	14	17.3	3.78	85	.309	.405	0	—	0	-1	-1	-0	0.0
Sea-A	1	0	1.000	16	0	0	0	0	26¹	21	0	15	13	13.0	5.13	81	.216	.333	0	—	0	-3	-3	0	-0.2
Total 4	6	7	.364	128	0	0	0	4	182²	161	8	96	140	13.0	3.74	98	.238	.339	2	.167	1	0	-1	0	0.3

■ BERNIE WALTER   Walter, James Bernard   b: 8/15/08, Dover, Tenn.   d: 10/30/88, Nashville, Tenn.   BR/TR, 6'1", 175 lbs.   Deb: 8/16/30

YEAR TM/L	W	L	PCT	G	GS	CG	SH	SV	IP	H	HR	BB	SO	RAT	ERA	ERA+	OAV	OOB	BH	AVG	PB	PR	/A	PD	TPI
1930 Pit-N	0	0	—	1	0	0	0	0	1	0	0	0	0	0.00	—	.000	.000	0	—	0	1	1	0	0.1

■ CHARLIE WALTERS   Walters, Charles Leonard   b: 2/21/47, Minneapolis, Minn.   BR/TR, 6'4", 190 lbs.   Deb: 4/11/69

YEAR TM/L	W	L	PCT	G	GS	CG	SH	SV	IP	H	HR	BB	SO	RAT	ERA	ERA+	OAV	OOB	BH	AVG	PB	PR	/A	PD	TPI
1969 Min-A	0	0	—	6	0	0	0	0	6²	6	1	3	2	13.5	5.40	68	.240	.345	0	—	0	-1	-1	0	0.0

■ MIKE WALTERS   Walters, Michael Charles   b: 10/18/57, St.Louis, Mo.   BR/TR, 6'5", 203 lbs.   Deb: 7/08/83

YEAR TM/L	W	L	PCT	G	GS	CG	SH	SV	IP	H	HR	BB	SO	RAT	ERA	ERA+	OAV	OOB	BH	AVG	PB	PR	/A	PD	TPI
1983 Min-A	1	1	.500	23	0	0	0	2	59	52	4	20	21	11.3	4.12	103	.243	.314	0	—	0	-0	1	0	0.1
1984 Min-A	0	3	.000	23	0	0	0	2	29	31	1	14	10	14.3	3.72	113	.287	.374	0	—	0	1	2	-0	0.1
Total 2	1	4	.200	46	0	0	0	4	88	83	5	34	31	12.3	3.99	106	.258	.334	0	—	0	0	2	0	0.2

YEAR TM/L	W	L	PCT	G	GS	CG	SH	SV	IP	H	HR	BB	SO	RAT	ERA	ERA+	OAV	OOB	BH	AVG	PB	PR	/A	PD	TPI
■ **BUCKY WALTERS**				Walters, William Henry b: 4/19/09, Philadelphia, Pa. BR/TR, 6'1", 180 lbs. Deb: 9/18/31 MC◆																				
1934 Phi-N	0	0	—	2	1	0	0	0	7	8	1	2	7	14.1	1.29	367	.296	.367	78	.260	0	2	3	0	0.3
1935 Phi-N	9	9	.500	24	22	8	2	0	151	168	9	68	40	14.5	4.17	109	.289	.370	24	.250	2	-3	6	2	0.6
1936 Phi-N	11	21	.344	40	33	15	4	0	258	284	11	115	66	14.1	4.26	107	.277	.353	29	.240	3	-7	8	9	2.3
1937 Phi-N	14	15	.483	37	34	15	3	0	246¹	292	14	86	87	13.9	4.75	91	.295	.353	38	.277	4	-23	-11	5	0.2
1938 Phi-N	4	8	.333	12	12	9	1	0	82²	91	8	42	28	14.8	5.23	74	.276	.363	10	.286	3	-13	-12	0	-0.8
Cin-N	11	6	.647	27	22	11	2	1	168¹	168	5	66	65	12.6	3.69	99	.255	.324	9	.141	-0	2	-1	3	0.1
Yr	15	14	.517	39	34	20	3	1	251	259	13	108	93	13.2	4.20	89	.261	.335	9	.091	3	-11	-13	3	-0.7
1939 *Cin-N	27	11	.711	39	36	31	2	0	319	250	15	109	137	10.3	2.29	168	.220	.291	39	.325	13	58	55	4	8.0
1940 *Cin-N	22	10	.688	36	36	29	3	0	305	241	19	92	115	10.0	2.48	153	.220	.283	24	.205	2	46	44	-1	5.0
1941 Cin-N	19	15	.559	37	35	27	5	2	302	292	10	88	129	11.4	2.83	127	.255	.309	20	.189	2	27	26	2	3.2
1942 Cin-N	15	14	.517	34	32	21	2	0	253²	223	8	73	109	10.7	2.66	123	.231	.289	24	.242	6	18	18	1	2.9
1943 Cin-N	15	15	.500	34	34	21	5	0	246¹	244	8	109	80	12.9	3.54	94	.264	.342	24	.267	8	-4	-6	1	0.2
1944 Cin-N	23	8	.742	34	32	27	6	1	285	233	10	87	77	10.2	2.40	145	.219	.281	30	.280	8	38	34	0	4.7
1945 Cin-N	10	10	.500	22	22	12	3	0	168	166	6	51	45	11.7	2.68	140	.259	.316	14	.230	5	21	20	0	2.7
1946 Cin-N	10	7	.588	22	22	10	2	0	151¹	146	9	64	60	12.6	2.56	131	.258	.336	7	.127	-1	14	13	2	1.5
1947 Cin-N	8	8	.500	20	20	5	2	0	122	137	15	49	43	13.9	5.75	71	.278	.347	12	.267	3	-23	-22	-1	-1.8
1948 Cin-N	0	3	.000	7	5	1	0	0	35	42	6	18	19	15.4	4.63	84	.316	.397	4	.267	-0	-3	-3	1	0.0
1950 Bos-N	0	0	—	1	0	0	0	0	4	5	0	2	0	15.8	4.50	86	.313	.389	0	.000	-0	-0	-0	-0	-0.1
Total 16	198	160	.553	428	398	242	42	4	3104²	2990	154	1121	1107	12.1	3.30	115	.253	.321	477	.243	58	152	168	29	29.1
■ **DICK WANTZ**				Wantz, Richard Carter b: 4/11/40, South Gate, Cal. d: 5/13/65, Inglewood, Cal. BR/TR, 6'5", 175 lbs. Deb: 4/13/65																				
1965 Cal-A	0	0	—	1	0	0	0	0	1	3	0	0	2	27.0	18.00	19	.500	.500	0	—	0	-2	-2	0	-0.1
■ **STEVE WAPNICK**				Wapnick, Steven Lee b: 9/25/65, Panorama City, Cal. BR/TR, 6'2", 200 lbs. Deb: 4/14/90																				
1990 Det-A	0	0	—	4	0	0	0	0	7	8	0	10	6	23.1	6.43	61	.296	.486	0	—	0	-2	-2	-0	-0.1
■ **WARD**				Ward Deb: N/A.																				
1885 Pro-N	0	1	.000	1	1	1	0	0	8	10	0	1	3	12.4	4.50	59	.292	.312	0	.000	-0	-1	-2	0	-0.1
■ **COLIN WARD**				Ward, Colin Norval b: 11/22/60, Los Angeles, Cal. BL/TL, 6'3", 190 lbs. Deb: 9/21/85																				
1985 SF-N	0	0	—	6	2	0	0	0	12¹	10	0	7	8	12.4	4.38	78	.233	.340	0	.000	-0	-1	-1	0	-0.1
■ **MONTE WARD**				Ward, John Montgomery b: 3/3/1860, Bellefonte, Pa. d: 3/4/25, Augusta, Ga. BL/TL, 5'9", 165 lbs. Deb: 7/15/1878 MH◆																				
1878 Pro-N	22	13	.629	37	37	37	6	0	334	308	3	34	116	9.2	1.51	146	.233	.252	27	.196	2	30	26	1	2.7
1879 Pro-N	47	19	.712	70	60	58	2	1	587	571	5	36	239	9.3	2.15	110	.239	.250	104	.286	17	23	14	4	3.2
1880 Pro-N	39	24	.619	70	67	59	8	1	595	501	5	45	230	8.3	1.74	127	.217	.232	81	.228	1	42	31	5	3.3
1881 Pro-N	18	18	.500	39	35	32	3	0	330	326	2	53	119	10.3	2.13	125	.247	.276	87	.244	3	24	19	5	1.9
1882 Pro-N	19	12	.613	33	32	29	4	1	278	261	6	36	72	9.6	2.59	108	.234	.234	87	.245	1	9	7	5	0.6
1883 NY-N	16	13	.552	34	25	24	1	0	277	278	3	31	121	10.0	2.70	115	.246	.266	97	.255	6	14	12	4	1.1
1884 NY-N	3	3	.500	9	5	5	0	0	60²	72	2	18	23	13.4	3.41	87	.280	.327	122	.253	1	-3	-3	1	-0.2
Total 7	164	102	.617	292	261	244	24	3	2461²	2317	26	253	920	9.4	2.10	118	.235	.254	2105	.275	31	138	104	24	12.6
■ **DICK WARD**				Ward, Richard Ole b: 5/21/09, Herrick, S.Dak. d: 5/30/66, Freeland, Wash. BR/TR, 6'1", 198 lbs. Deb: 5/03/34																				
1934 Chi-N	0	0	—	3	0	0	0	0	6	9	0	2	1	16.5	3.00	129	.375	.423	0	.000	-0	1	1	0	0.0
1935 StL-N	0	0	—	1	0	0	0	0	0	0	0	1	0	—	—	—	—	1.000	0	—	0	0	0	0	0.0
Total 2	0	0	—	4	0	0	0	0	6	9	0	3	1	18.0	3.00	129	.375	.444	0	.000	-0	1	1	0	0.0
■ **COLBY WARD**				Ward, Robert Colby b: 1/2/64, Lansing, Mich. BR/TR, 6'2", 185 lbs. Deb: 7/27/90																				
1990 Cle-A	1	3	.250	22	0	0	0	1	36	31	3	21	23	13.3	4.25	94	.238	.349	0	—	0	-1	-1	-0	0.0
■ **DUANE WARD**				Ward, Roy Duane b: 5/28/64, Park View, N.Mex. BR/TR, 6'4", 185 lbs. Deb: 4/12/86																				
1986 Atl-N	0	1	.000	10	0	0	0	0	16	22	2	8	8	16.9	7.31	54	.349	.423	0	.000	-0	-6	-6	1	-0.4
Tor-A	0	1	.000	2	1	0	0	0	2	3	0	4	1	36.0	13.50	31	.300	.533	0	—	0	-2	-2	0	-0.1
1987 Tor-A	1	0	1.000	12	1	0	0	0	11²	14	0	12	10	20.1	6.94	65	.304	.473	0	—	0	-3	-3	0	-0.2
1988 Tor-A	9	3	.750	64	0	0	0	15	111²	101	5	60	91	13.4	3.30	119	.245	.347	0	—	0	8	8	-1	0.7
1989 *Tor-A	4	10	.286	66	0	0	0	15	114²	94	4	58	122	12.3	3.77	100	.230	.333	0	—	0	1	0	1	0.1
1990 Tor-A	2	8	.200	73	0	0	0	11	127²	101	9	42	112	10.2	3.45	110	.221	.288	0	—	0	6	5	0	0.5
Total 5	16	23	.410	227	2	0	0	41	383²	335	20	184	344	12.5	3.82	101	.240	.334	0	.000	-0	4	1	1	0.6
■ **JON WARDEN**				Warden, Jonathan Edgar "Warbler" b: 10/1/46, Columbus, Ohio BB/TL, 6', 205 lbs. Deb: 4/11/68																				
1968 Det-A	4	1	.800	28	0	0	0	3	37¹	30	5	15	25	10.8	3.62	83	.217	.294	0	.000	-0	-3	-3	-1	-0.3
■ **CURT WARDLE**				Wardle, Curtis Ray b: 11/16/60, Downey, Cal. BL/TL, 6'5", 220 lbs. Deb: 8/30/84																				
1984 Min-A	0	0	—	2	0	0	0	0	4	3	2	0	5	6.8	4.50	93	.200	.200	0	—	0	-0	-0	0	0.0
1985 Min-A	1	3	.250	35	0	0	0	1	49	49	9	28	47	14.3	5.51	80	.266	.366	0	—	0	-7	-6	1	-0.4
Cle-A	7	6	.538	15	12	0	0	0	66	78	11	34	37	15.4	6.68	62	.297	.379	0	—	0	-19	-19	-1	-1.8
Yr	8	9	.471	50	12	0	0	1	115	127	20	62	84	14.9	6.18	69	.283	.371	0	—	0	-26	-25	-0	-2.2
Total 2	8	9	.471	52	12	0	0	1	119	130	22	62	89	14.7	6.13	69	.281	.369	0	—	0	-26	-25	-0	-2.2
■ **JACK WARHOP**				Warhop, John Milton "Chief" or "Crab" (b: John Milton Wauhop) b: 7/4/1884, Hinton, W.Va. d: 10/4/60, Freeport, Ill. BR/TR, 5'9.5", 168 lbs. Deb: 9/19/08																				
1908 NY-A	1	2	.333	5	4	3	0	0	36¹	40	0	8	11	12.9	4.46	56	.292	.349	1	.063	-1	-8	-8	0	-0.8
1909 NY-A	13	15	.464	36	23	21	3	2	243¹	197	2	81	95	11.2	2.40	105	.233	.319	11	.128	-2	2	3	2	0.3
1910 NY-A	14	14	.500	37	27	20	0	2	243	219	1	79	75	11.7	3.00	89	.246	.320	14	.177	-1	-13	-9	-3	-1.2
1911 NY-A	12	13	.480	31	25	17	1	0	209²	239	6	44	71	12.8	4.16	86	.286	.333	12	.156	-4	-19	-13	-1	-1.6
1912 NY-A	10	19	.345	39	32	16	0	3	258	256	3	59	110	11.5	2.86	126	.266	.319	19	.207	-1	13	21	-2	2.0
1913 NY-A	4	6	.400	15	7	1	0	0	62¹	69	1	33	11	16.5	3.75	80	.292	.406	3	.130	-1	-6	-5	-2	-0.7
1914 NY-A	8	15	.348	37	23	15	0	0	216²	182	8	44	56	9.8	2.37	117	.235	.286	10	.141	-1	9	9	-1	0.8
1915 NY-A	7	9	.438	21	19	12	0	0	141¹	164	7	52	34	14.3	3.96	74	.309	.384	7	.137	-2	-16	-16	-2	-1.9
Total 8	69	93	.426	221	160	105	4	7	1412²	1366	28	400	463	12.0	3.12	96	.262	.328	77	.156	-12	-38	-19	-8	-3.1
■ **CY WARMOTH**				Warmoth, Wallace Walter b: 2/2/1893, Bone Gap, Ill. d: 6/20/57, Mt.Carmel, Ill. BL/TL, 5'11", 158 lbs. Deb: 8/31/16																				
1916 StL-N	0	0	—	3	0	0	0	0	5	12	0	4	1	30.6	14.40	18	.500	.586	0	—	-0	-7	-7	-0	-0.6
1922 Was-A	1	0	1.000	5	1	1	0	0	19	15	0	9	8	11.4	1.42	272	.205	.293	1	.143	-0	6	5	0	0.5
1923 Was-A	7	5	.583	21	13	4	0	0	105	103	4	76	45	15.4	4.29	88	.261	.381	8	.222	2	-4	-6	0	-0.3
Total 3	8	5	.615	29	14	5	0	0	129	130	4	89	54	15.4	4.26	88	.264	.379	9	.200	1	-5	-7	-0	-0.4
■ **LON WARNEKE**				Warneke, Lonnie "The Arkansas Hummingbird" b: 3/28/09, Mt.Ida, Ark. d: 6/23/76, Hot Springs, Ark. BR/TR, 6'2", 185 lbs. Deb: 4/18/30 U																				
1930 Chi-N	0	0	—	1	0	0	0	0	2	5	0	5	0	47.3	33.75	14	.400	.700	0	—	0	-4	-4	0	-0.2
1931 Chi-N	2	4	.333	20	7	3	0	0	64¹	67	1	37	27	15.0	3.22	120	.269	.370	5	.263	1	5	5	-1	0.4
1932 *Chi-N	22	6	.786	35	32	25	4	0	277	247	12	64	106	10.2	2.37	159	.237	.283	19	.192	-0	46	43	0	4.5
1933 Chi-N	18	13	.581	36	34	26	4	1	287¹	262	8	75	133	10.6	2.00	163	.244	.295	30	.300	10	43	40	2	6.2
1934 Chi-N	22	10	.688	43	35	23	3	3	291¹	273	6	66	143	10.5	3.21	121	.244	.287	22	.195	-0	27	21	0	2.9
1935 *Chi-N	20	13	.606	42	30	20	1	4	261²	257	17	50	120	10.7	3.06	128	.257	.294	20	.220	1	28	25	-1	2.5
1936 Chi-N	16	13	.552	40	29	13	4	1	240¹	246	10	76	113	12.2	3.45	116	.264	.322	17	.202	0	15	14	-1	1.4

YEAR	TM/L	W	L	PCT	G	GS	CG	SH	SV	IP	H	HR	BB	SO	RAT	ERA	ERA+	OAV	OOB	BH	AVG	PB	PR	/A	PD	TPI
1937	StL-N	18	11	.621	36	33	18	2	0	238²	280	32	69	87	13.2	4.53	88	.287	.335	21	.262	5	-16	-14	-3	-1.1
1938	StL-N	13	8	.619	31	26	12	4	0	197	199	14	64	89	12.1	3.97	100	.256	.314	23	.324	5	-4	-0	-2	0.4
1939	StL-N	13	7	.650	34	21	6	2	2	162	160	14	49	59	11.7	3.78	109	.259	.316	10	.192	1	3	6	-0	0.7
1940	StL-N	16	10	.615	33	31	17	1	0	232	235	17	47	85	11.1	3.14	127	.257	.296	18	.209	2	18	22	1	2.7
1941	StL-N	17	9	.654	37	30	12	4	0	246	227	19	82	83	11.4	3.15	120	.249	.313	9	.117	-2	13	17	-1	1.5
1942	StL-N	6	4	.600	12	12	5	0	0	82	76	8	15	31	10.0	3.29	104	.238	.272	10	.333	3	0	1	-1	0.4
	Chi-N	5	7	.417	15	12	8	1	2	99	97	2	21	28	10.7	2.27	141	.259	.298	6	.188	-0	11	10	0	1.1
	Yr	11	11	.500	27	24	13	1	2	181	173	10	36	59	10.4	2.73	121	.249	.286	3	.048	3	12	11	-1	1.5
1943	Chi-N	4	5	.444	21	10	4	0	0	88¹	82	3	18	30	10.2	3.16	106	.246	.285	5	.192	1	2	2	1	0.4
1945	Chi-N	0	1	.000	9	1	0	0	0	14	16	0	1	6	10.9	3.86	95	.267	.279	0	.000	0	-0	-0	0	0.0
Total	15	192	121	.613	445	343	192	30	13	2782¹	2726	175	739	1140	11.3	3.18	119	.255	.304	215	.223	28	188	188	-4	23.0

■ ED WARNER
Warner, Edward Emory   b: 6/20/1889, Fitchburg, Mass.   d: 2/5/54, New York, N.Y.   BR/TL, 5'10.5", 165 lbs.   Deb: 7/02/12

YEAR	TM/L	W	L	PCT	G	GS	CG	SH	SV	IP	H	HR	BB	SO	RAT	ERA	ERA+	OAV	OOB	BH	AVG	PB	PR	/A	PD	TPI
1912	Pit-N	1	1	.500	11	3	1	0	0	45	40	0	18	13	12.2	3.60	91	.238	.323	2	.133	-1	-1	-2	1	-0.1

■ JACK WARNER
Warner, Jack Dyer   b: 7/12/40, Brandywine, W.Va.   BR/TR, 5'11", 190 lbs.   Deb: 4/10/62

YEAR	TM/L	W	L	PCT	G	GS	CG	SH	SV	IP	H	HR	BB	SO	RAT	ERA	ERA+	OAV	OOB	BH	AVG	PB	PR	/A	PD	TPI
1962	Chi-N	0	0	—	7	0	0	0	0	7	9	3	0	3	11.6	7.71	54	.321	.321	0	—	0	-3	-3	0	-0.1
1963	Chi-N	0	1	.000	8	0	0	0	0	22²	21	1	8	7	11.5	2.78	126	.256	.322	1	.250	0	1	2	-0	0.2
1964	Chi-N	0	0	—	7	0	0	0	0	9¹	12	0	4	6	15.4	2.89	128	.333	.400	0	—	0	1	1	0	0.1
1965	Chi-N	0	1	.000	11	0	0	0	0	15²	22	1	9	7	17.8	8.62	43	.355	.437	0	.000	-0	-9	-9	0	-0.8
Total	4	0	2	.000	33	0	0	0	0	54²	64	5	21	23	14.0	5.10	72	.308	.371	1	.200	0	-10	-9	1	-0.6

■ MIKE WARREN
Warren, Michael Bruce   b: 3/26/61, Inglewood, Cal.   BR/TR, 6'1", 175 lbs.   Deb: 6/12/83

YEAR	TM/L	W	L	PCT	G	GS	CG	SH	SV	IP	H	HR	BB	SO	RAT	ERA	ERA+	OAV	OOB	BH	AVG	PB	PR	/A	PD	TPI
1983	Oak-A	5	3	.625	12	9	3	1	0	65²	51	4	18	30	9.6	4.11	94	.215	.273	0	—	0	-0	-2	-1	-0.2
1984	Oak-A	3	6	.333	24	12	0	0	0	90	104	11	44	61	15.1	4.90	76	.291	.373	0	—	0	-9	-12	-2	-1.3
1985	Oak-A	1	4	.200	16	6	0	0	0	49	52	13	38	48	17.3	6.61	58	.261	.390	0	—	0	-13	-15	-1	-1.4
Total	3	9	13	.409	52	27	3	1	0	204²	207	28	100	139	13.9	5.06	75	.261	.349	0	—	0	-23	-28	-4	-2.9

■ TOMMY WARREN
Warren, Thomas Gentry   b: 7/5/17, Tulsa, Okla.   d: 1/2/68, Tulsa, Okla.   BB/TL, 6'1", 190 lbs.   Deb: 4/18/44

YEAR	TM/L	W	L	PCT	G	GS	CG	SH	SV	IP	H	HR	BB	SO	RAT	ERA	ERA+	OAV	OOB	BH	AVG	PB	PR	/A	PD	TPI
1944	Bro-N	1	4	.200	22	4	2	0	0	68²	74	4	40	18	14.9	4.98	71	.270	.363	11	.256	1	-10	-11	0	-0.8

■ DAN WARTHEN
Warthen, Daniel Dean   b: 12/1/52, Omaha, Neb.   BB/TL, 6', 200 lbs.   Deb: 5/18/75

YEAR	TM/L	W	L	PCT	G	GS	CG	SH	SV	IP	H	HR	BB	SO	RAT	ERA	ERA+	OAV	OOB	BH	AVG	PB	PR	/A	PD	TPI
1975	Mon-N	8	6	.571	40	18	2	0	3	167²	130	8	87	128	11.7	3.11	123	.217	.317	6	.118	-2	9	13	0	1.2
1976	Mon-N	2	10	.167	23	16	2	1	0	90	76	8	66	67	14.4	5.30	70	.232	.364	0	.000	-3	-18	-16	-0	-1.8
1977	Mon-N	2	3	.400	12	6	1	0	0	35	33	7	38	26	18.3	7.97	48	.262	.433	1	.111	-0	-16	-16	-1	-1.4
	Phi-N	0	1	.000	3	0	0	0	0	3²	4	0	5	1	22.1	0.00	—	.267	.450	0	—	-0	2	2	0	0.2
	Yr	2	4	.333	15	6	1	0	0	38²	37	7	43	27	18.6	7.22	53	.261	.432	1	.111	-0	-14	-15	-1	-1.2
1978	Hou-N	0	1	.000	5	1	0	0	0	10²	10	3	2	2	10.1	4.22	78	.250	.286	0	.000	-0	-1	-1	0	0.0
Total	4	12	21	.364	83	41	5	1	3	307	253	26	198	224	13.3	4.31	88	.228	.347	7	.079	-6	-23	-18	0	-1.8

■ GEORGE WASHBURN
Washburn, George Edward   b: 10/6/14, Solon, Me.   d: 1/5/79, Baton Rouge, La.   BL/TR, 6'1", 175 lbs.   Deb: 5/04/41

YEAR	TM/L	W	L	PCT	G	GS	CG	SH	SV	IP	H	HR	BB	SO	RAT	ERA	ERA+	OAV	OOB	BH	AVG	PB	PR	/A	PD	TPI
1941	NY-A	0	1	.000	1	1	0	0	0	2	2	0	5	1	31.5	13.50	29	.286	.583	0	.000	-0	-2	-2	0	-0.1

■ GREG WASHBURN
Washburn, Gregory James   b: 12/3/46, Coal City, Ill.   BR/TR, 6', 190 lbs.   Deb: 6/07/69

YEAR	TM/L	W	L	PCT	G	GS	CG	SH	SV	IP	H	HR	BB	SO	RAT	ERA	ERA+	OAV	OOB	BH	AVG	PB	PR	/A	PD	TPI
1969	Cal-A	0	2	.000	8	2	0	0	0	11¹	21	0	5	4	21.4	7.94	44	.404	.466	0	—	0	-5	-6	0	-0.4

■ LIBE WASHBURN
Washburn, Libeus   b: 6/16/1874, Lyme, N.H.   d: 3/22/40, Malone, N.Y.   BB/TL, 5'10", 180 lbs.   Deb: 5/30/02 ♦

YEAR	TM/L	W	L	PCT	G	GS	CG	SH	SV	IP	H	HR	BB	SO	RAT	ERA	ERA+	OAV	OOB	BH	AVG	PB	PR	/A	PD	TPI
1903	Phi-N	0	4	.000	4	4	4	0	0	35	44	0	11	9	14.1	4.37	75	.326	.377	3	.167	-0	-4	-4	-0	-0.3

■ RAY WASHBURN
Washburn, Ray Clark   b: 5/31/38, Pasco, Wash.   BR/TR, 6'1", 205 lbs.   Deb: 9/20/61

YEAR	TM/L	W	L	PCT	G	GS	CG	SH	SV	IP	H	HR	BB	SO	RAT	ERA	ERA+	OAV	OOB	BH	AVG	PB	PR	/A	PD	TPI
1961	StL-N	1	1	.500	3	2	1	0	0	20¹	10	1	7	12	8.0	1.77	248	.152	.243	1	.125	-1	5	6	0	0.6
1962	StL-N	12	9	.571	34	25	2	1	0	175²	187	25	58	109	12.7	4.10	104	.273	.332	10	.179	1	-3	3	1	0.5
1963	StL-N	5	3	.625	11	11	4	2	0	64¹	50	5	14	47	9.1	3.08	115	.212	.259	1	.053	-1	2	3	1	0.4
1964	StL-N	3	4	.429	15	10	0	0	2	60	60	7	17	28	12.3	4.05	94	.264	.329	2	.133	-0	-3	-2	1	0.0
1965	StL-N	9	11	.450	28	16	1	1	2	119¹	114	15	28	67	10.8	3.62	106	.254	.300	5	.152	-0	-1	3	-0	0.3
1966	StL-N	11	9	.550	27	26	4	1	0	170	183	15	44	98	12.1	3.76	95	.280	.326	5	.093	-1	-3	-3	1	-0.3
1967	★StL-N	10	7	.588	27	27	3	1	0	186¹	190	14	42	98	11.4	3.53	93	.265	.309	6	.091	-2	-3	-5	2	-0.4
1968	★StL-N	14	8	.636	31	30	8	4	0	215	191	9	47	124	10.0	2.26	128	.239	.283	5	.083	-1	17	15	-2	1.6
1969	StL-N	3	8	.273	28	16	2	0	1	132¹	133	9	49	80	12.4	3.06	117	.261	.327	3	.081	-2	8	8	1	0.7
1970	★Cin-N	4	4	.500	28	2	0	0	0	66¹	90	7	48	37	18.3	6.92	58	.324	.423	0	.000	-1	-21	-21	1	-2.0
Total	10	72	64	.529	239	166	25	10	5	1209²	1208	107	354	700	11.8	3.53	101	.261	.316	38	.105	-7	-3	6	6	1.4

■ BUCK WASHER
Washer, William   b: 10/11/1882, Akron, Ohio   d: 12/8/55, Akron, Ohio   TR, 5'10", 175 lbs.   Deb: 4/25/05

YEAR	TM/L	W	L	PCT	G	GS	CG	SH	SV	IP	H	HR	BB	SO	RAT	ERA	ERA+	OAV	OOB	BH	AVG	PB	PR	/A	PD	TPI
1905	Phi-N	0	0	—	1	0	0	0	0	3	4	0	5	0	27.0	6.00	49	—	1.800	0	.000	-0	-1	-1	0	0.0

■ GARY WASLEWSKI
Waslewski, Gary Lee   b: 7/21/41, Meriden, Conn.   BR/TR, 6'4", 190 lbs.   Deb: 6/11/67

YEAR	TM/L	W	L	PCT	G	GS	CG	SH	SV	IP	H	HR	BB	SO	RAT	ERA	ERA+	OAV	OOB	BH	AVG	PB	PR	/A	PD	TPI
1967	★Bos-A	2	2	.500	12	8	0	0	0	42	34	3	20	20	11.8	3.21	108	.225	.320	1	.091	-1	0	1	0	0.1
1968	Bos-A	4	7	.364	34	11	2	0	2	105¹	108	9	40	59	13.2	3.67	86	.269	.344	1	.038	-2	-8	-6	2	-0.6
1969	StL-N	0	2	.000	12	0	0	0	1	20²	19	3	8	16	12.2	3.92	91	.244	.322	0	.000	-0	-1	-1	1	0.0
	Mon-N	3	7	.300	30	14	3	1	1	109¹	102	5	63	63	14.2	3.29	112	.252	.364	1	.033	-2	4	5	1	0.3
	Yr	3	9	.250	42	14	3	1	2	130	121	8	71	79	13.8	3.39	108	.250	.355	1	.032	-2	3	4	1	0.3
1970	Mon-N	0	2	.000	6	4	0	0	0	24²	23	3	15	19	13.9	5.11	80	.247	.352	0	.000	-0	-3	-3	0	-0.2
	NY-A	2	2	.500	26	5	0	0	0	55	42	4	27	27	11.9	3.11	113	.219	.327	1	.100	-1	4	2	1	0.3
1971	NY-A	0	1	.000	24	0	0	0	1	35²	28	2	16	17	11.4	3.28	98	.214	.304	0	.000	-0	1	-0	0	0.0
1972	Oak-A	0	3	.000	8	0	0	0	0	17²	12	3	8	8	10.2	2.04	140	.190	.282	0	.000	-0	2	2	0	0.2
Total	6	11	26	.297	152	42	5	1	5	410¹	368	32	197	229	12.9	3.44	100	.243	.338	4	.045	-6	-2	1	5	0.1

■ STEVE WATERBURY
Waterbury, Steven Craig   b: 4/6/52, Carbondale, Ill.   BR/TR, 6'5", 190 lbs.   Deb: 9/14/76

YEAR	TM/L	W	L	PCT	G	GS	CG	SH	SV	IP	H	HR	BB	SO	RAT	ERA	ERA+	OAV	OOB	BH	AVG	PB	PR	/A	PD	TPI
1976	StL-N	0	0	—	5	0	0	0	0	6	7	0	3	4	15.0	6.00	59	.304	.385	0	—	0	-2	-2	0	-0.1

■ FRED WATERS
Waters, Fred Warren   b: 2/2/27, Benton, Miss.   d: 8/28/89, Pensacola, Fla.   BL/TL, 5'11", 185 lbs.   Deb: 9/20/55

YEAR	TM/L	W	L	PCT	G	GS	CG	SH	SV	IP	H	HR	BB	SO	RAT	ERA	ERA+	OAV	OOB	BH	AVG	PB	PR	/A	PD	TPI
1955	Pit-N	0	0	—	2	0	0	0	0	5	7	1	2	0	16.2	3.60	114	.318	.375	0	.000	-0	0	0	0	0.0
1956	Pit-N	2	2	.500	23	5	1	0	0	51	48	3	30	14	13.9	2.82	134	.258	.364	1	.050	-1	5	5	-1	0.3
Total	2	2	2	.500	25	5	1	0	0	56	55	4	32	14	14.1	2.89	131	.264	.365	1	.048	-1	6	6	-1	0.3

■ BOB WATKINS
Watkins, Robert Cecil   b: 3/12/48, San Francisco, Cal.   BR/TR, 6'1", 170 lbs.   Deb: 9/06/69

YEAR	TM/L	W	L	PCT	G	GS	CG	SH	SV	IP	H	HR	BB	SO	RAT	ERA	ERA+	OAV	OOB	BH	AVG	PB	PR	/A	PD	TPI
1969	Hou-N	0	0	—	5	0	0	0	0	15²	13	1	13	11	14.9	5.17	68	.241	.388	0	.000	-0	-3	-3	-0	-0.2

■ DOC WATSON
Watson, Charles John   b: 1/30/1886, Kensington, Ohio   d: 12/30/49, San Diego, Cal.   BR/TL, 6', 170 lbs.   Deb: 9/03/13

YEAR	TM/L	W	L	PCT	G	GS	CG	SH	SV	IP	H	HR	BB	SO	RAT	ERA	ERA+	OAV	OOB	BH	AVG	PB	PR	/A	PD	TPI
1913	Chi-N	1	0	1.000	1	1	1	0	0	9	8	0	6	1	15.0	1.00	318	.242	.375	0	.000					
1914	Chi-F	9	8	.529	26	18	10	3	1	172	145	2	49	69	10.3	2.04	145	.236	.295	5	.0					
	StL-F	3	4	.429	9	7	4	2	0	56	41	1	24	18	11.1	1.93	175	.211	.311	2	.2					
	Yr	12	12	.500	35	25	14	5	1	228	186	3	73	87	10.4	2.01	152	.229	.296	3	.04					
1915	StL-F	9	9	.500	33	20	6	0	0	135²	132	1	58	45	12.9	3.98	80	.273	.355	5	.125					
Total	3	22	21	.512	69	46	21	5	1	372²	326	4	137	133	11.5	2.70	115	.246	.322	12	.107					

YEAR TM/L	W	L	PCT	G	GS	CG	SH	SV	IP	H	HR	BB	SO	RAT	ERA	ERA+	OAV	OOB	BH	AVG	PB	PR	/A	PD	TPI
■ **MULE WATSON** Watson, John Reeves b: 10/15/1896, Homer, La. d: 8/25/49, Shreveport, La. BR/TR, 6'1.5", 185 lbs. Deb: 7/04/18																									
1918 Phi-A	7	10	.412	21	19	11	3	0	141²	139	0	44	30	11.8	3.37	87	.288	.350	6	.128	-3	-9	-7	-2	-1.1
1919 Phi-A	0	1	.000	4	2	0	0	0	14¹	17	2	7	6	15.1	6.91	50	.309	.387	0	.000	-1	-6	-6	1	-0.4
1920 Bos-N	0	0	—	1	0	0	0	0	3	0	0	0	0	0.0	0.00	—	.000	.000	0	.000	-0	1	1	0	0.1
Pit-N	0	0	—	5	0	0	0	0	11¹	15	2	7	1	17.5	8.74	37	.326	.415	0	.000	-0	-7	-7	0	-0.6
Bos-N	5	4	.556	12	10	4	2	0	71²	79	0	17	16	12.2	3.77	81	.298	.343	3	.130	-1	-5	-6	0	-0.6
Yr	5	4	.556	18	10	4	2	0	86	94	2	24	17	12.5	4.29	72	.294	.345	3	.037	-2	-11	-12	0	-1.1
1921 Bos-N	14	13	.519	44	31	15	1	2	259¹	269	11	57	48	11.6	3.85	95	.270	.314	12	.138	-4	-2	-6	-0	-0.9
1922 Bos-N	8	14	.364	41	29	8	1	1	201	262	9	59	53	14.6	4.70	85	.317	.366	13	.197	-0	-13	-16	-0	-1.4
1923 Bos-N	1	2	.333	11	4	1	0	1	31¹	42	2	20	10	17.8	5.17	77	.339	.431	2	.250	-0	-4	-4	0	-0.3
*NY-N	8	5	.615	17	15	8	0	0	108¹	117	11	21	26	11.5	3.41	112	.280	.316	8	.174	-1	7	5	-1	0.3
Yr	9	7	.563	28	19	9	0	1	139²	159	13	41	36	13.0	3.80	101	.293	.344	0	.000	-1	3	1	-1	0.0
1924 *NY-N	7	4	.636	22	16	6	1	0	99²	122	7	24	18	13.3	3.79	97	.303	.343	9	.257	4	1	-1	-1	0.2
Total 7	50	53	.485	178	126	53	8	4	941²	1062	44	256	208	12.8	4.03	89	.293	.342	53	.165	-8	-38	-45	-2	-4.7
■ **MILT WATSON** Watson, Milton Wilson "Mule" b: 1/10/1890, Flovilla, Ga. d: 4/10/62, Pine Bluff, Ark. BR/TR, 6'1", 180 lbs. Deb: 7/26/16																									
1916 StL-N	4	6	.400	18	13	5	2	0	103	109	3	33	27	12.8	3.06	86	.283	.346	7	.219	0	-5	-5	-0	-0.5
1917 StL-N	10	13	.435	41	20	5	3	0	161¹	149	3	51	45	11.7	3.51	77	.252	.321	5	.098	-4	-14	-15	2	-1.8
1918 Phi-N	5	7	.417	23	11	6	0	0	112²	126	1	36	29	13.1	3.43	87	.293	.350	4	.075	-4	-8	-5	-1	-1.0
1919 Phi-N	2	4	.333	8	4	3	0	0	47	51	3	19	12	13.8	5.17	62	.282	.356	1	.063	-2	-12	-10	0	-1.1
Total 4	21	30	.412	90	48	19	5	0	424	435	10	139	113	12.5	3.57	79	.274	.339	16	.115	-9	-40	-35	1	-4.4
■ **MOTHER WATSON** Watson, Walter L. b: 1/27/1865, Middleport, Ohio d: 11/23/1898, Middleport, Ohio 5'9", 145 lbs. Deb: 5/19/1887																									
1887 Cin-a	0	1	.000	2	2	1	0	0	14	22	0	6	1	18.0	5.79	75	.345	.401	1	.125	-1	-2	-2	-1	-0.1
■ **EDDIE WATT** Watt, Edward Dean b: 4/4/41, Lamoni, Iowa BR/TR, 5'10", 183 lbs. Deb: 4/12/66																									
1966 Bal-A	9	7	.563	43	13	1	0	4	145²	123	11	44	102	10.6	3.83	87	.230	.295	14	.304	6	-6	-8	-2	-0.4
1967 Bal-A	3	5	.375	49	0	0	0	8	103²	67	5	37	93	9.3	2.26	140	.183	.263	4	.182	2	11	10	-0	1.3
1968 Bal-A	5	5	.500	59	0	0	0	11	83¹	63	1	35	72	10.8	2.27	129	.209	.295	0	.000	-0	7	6	0	0.6
1969 *Bal-A	5	2	.714	56	0	0	0	16	71	49	3	26	46	9.8	1.65	216	.194	.274	0	.000	-0	16	15	-0	1.6
1970 *Bal-A	7	7	.500	53	0	0	0	12	55¹	44	3	29	33	12.7	3.25	112	.239	.358	1	.125	-0	3	2	0	0.3
1971 *Bal-A	3	1	.750	35	0	0	0	11	39²	39	1	8	26	10.7	1.82	185	.260	.297	0	.000	-0	7	7	-0	0.6
1972 Bal-A	2	3	.400	38	0	0	0	7	45²	30	2	20	23	10.2	2.17	142	.191	.291	0	.000	-0	5	5	0	0.5
1973 *Bal-A	3	4	.429	30	0	0	0	5	71	62	8	21	38	10.8	3.30	113	.235	.296	0	—	0	4	3	-1	0.2
1974 Phi-N	1	1	.500	42	0	0	0	6	38¹	39	3	26	23	15.7	3.99	95	.275	.394	0	.000	-0	-2	-1	0	0.0
1975 Chi-N	0	1	.000	6	0	0	0	0	6	14	0	8	6	34.5	13.50	28	.452	.575	0	—	0	-7	-6	0	-0.5
Total 10	38	36	.514	411	13	1	0	80	659²	530	37	254	462	11.0	2.91	116	.222	.304	19	.190	6	38	33	-3	4.2
■ **FRANK WATT** Watt, Frank Marion "Kilo" b: 12/15/02, Washington, D.C. d: 8/31/56, Washington, D.C. BR/TR, 6'1", 205 lbs. Deb: 4/14/31																									
1931 Phi-N	5	5	.500	38	12	5	0	2	122²	147	5	49	25	14.6	4.84	88	.296	.362	8	.205	0	-13	-8	-1	-0.8
■ **JIM WAUGH** Waugh, James Elden b: 11/25/33, Lancaster, Ohio BR/TR, 6'3", 185 lbs. Deb: 4/19/52																									
1952 Pit-N	1	6	.143	17	7	1	0	0	52¹	61	4	32	18	16.3	6.36	63	.285	.383	1	.100	-0	-15	-14	0	-1.3
1953 Pit-N	4	5	.444	29	11	1	0	0	90¹	108	21	56	23	16.3	6.48	69	.295	.389	5	.227	0	-22	-20	-0	-1.8
Total 2	5	11	.313	46	18	2	0	0	142²	169	25	88	41	16.3	6.43	67	.291	.387	6	.188	0	-37	-34	-0	-3.1
■ **FRANK WAYENBERG** Wayenberg, Frank b: 8/27/1898, Franklin, Kan. d: 4/16/75, Zanesville, Ohio BR/TR, 6'0.5", 172 lbs. Deb: 8/25/24																									
1924 Cle-A	0	0	—	2	1	0	0	0	6²	7	0	5	3	17.6	5.40	79	.259	.394	1	.500	0	-1	-1	-0	0.0
■ **GARY WAYNE** Wayne, Gary Anthony b: 11/30/62, Dearborn, Mich. BL/TL, 6'3", 185 lbs. Deb: 4/07/89																									
1989 Min-A	3	4	.429	60	0	0	0	1	71	55	4	36	41	11.7	3.30	126	.212	.311	0	—	0	5	7	0	0.7
1990 Min-A	1	1	.500	38	0	0	0	1	38²	38	5	13	28	12.1	4.19	100	.255	.319	0	—	0	-1	-0	-0	0.0
Total 2	4	5	.444	98	0	0	0	2	109²	93	9	49	69	11.8	3.61	115	.228	.314	0	—	0	3	7	-0	0.7
■ **HAL WEAFER** Weafer, Kenneth Albert "Al" b: 2/6/14, Woburn, Mass. BR/TR, 6'0.5", 183 lbs. Deb: 5/29/36																									
1936 Bos-N	0	0	—	1	0	0	0	0	3	6	1	3	0	27.0	12.00	32	.375	.474	0	.000	-0	-3	-3	-0	-0.2
■ **FLOYD WEAVER** Weaver, David Floyd b: 5/12/41, Ben Franklin, Tex. BR/TR, 6'4", 195 lbs. Deb: 9/30/62																									
1962 Cle-A	1	0	1.000	1	1	0	0	0	5	3	1	0	8	5.4	1.80	215	.167	.167	1	.500	0	1	1	-0	0.1
1965 Cle-A	2	2	.500	32	1	0	0	1	61¹	61	10	24	37	13.2	5.43	64	.265	.347	1	.091	0	-13	-13	0	-1.3
1970 Chi-A	1	2	.333	31	0	0	0	0	61²	52	7	31	52	12.4	4.38	89	.233	.332	0	.000	-1	-5	-3	-1	-0.4
1971 Mil-A	0	1	.000	21	0	0	0	0	27¹	33	3	18	12	17.1	7.24	48	.320	.426	0	—	0	-11	-11	-0	-1.1
Total 4	4	5	.444	85	5	0	0	1	155¹	149	21	73	108	13.3	5.21	70	.260	.351	2	.100	-0	-28	-27	-1	-2.7
■ **HARRY WEAVER** Weaver, Harry Abraham b: 2/26/1892, Clarendon, Pa. d: 5/30/83, Rochester, N.Y. BR/TR, 5'11", 160 lbs. Deb: 9/18/15																									
1915 Phi-A	0	2	.000	2	2	2	0	0	18	18	1	10	1	14.5	3.00	98	.290	.397	1	.167	0	-0	-0	1	0.1
1916 Phi-A	0	0	—	3	0	0	0	0	8	14	0	5	2	21.4	10.13	28	.424	.500	1	.500	0	-6	-6	0	-0.5
1917 Chi-N	1	1	.500	4	2	1	0	0	19²	17	0	7	8	11.0	2.75	105	.230	.296	1	.200	-0	-0	0	1	0.1
1918 Chi-N	2	2	.500	8	3	1	1	1	32²	27	1	7	9	9.4	2.20	126	.227	.270	2	.250	-1	2	2	1	0.4
1919 Chi-N	0	1	.000	2	1	0	0	0	3¹	6	0	2	1	24.3	10.80	27	.375	.474	0	.000	-0	-3	-3	-0	-0.2
Total 5	3	6	.333	19	8	4	1	1	81²	82	2	31	21	12.7	3.64	79	.270	.341	5	.227	0	-8	-7	3	-0.1
■ **JIM WEAVER** Weaver, James Brian "Fluff" b: 2/19/39, Lancaster, Pa. BL/TL, 6', 178 lbs. Deb: 8/13/67																									
1967 Cal-A	3	0	1.000	13	2	0	0	1	30¹	26	2	9	20	10.7	2.67	118	.232	.295	0	.000	-1	2	2	2	0.3
1968 Cal-A	0	1	.000	14	0	0	0	0	22²	22	4	10	8	12.7	2.38	122	.259	.337	0	.000	-0	2	1	-0	0.1
Total 2	3	1	.750	27	2	0	0	1	53	48	6	19	28	11.5	2.55	119	.244	.313	0	.000	-1	3	3	1	0.4
■ **JIM WEAVER** Weaver, James Dement "Big Jim" b: 11/25/03, Obion County, Ky. d: 12/12/83, Lakeland, Fla. BR/TR, 6'6", 230 lbs. Deb: 8/27/28																									
1928 Was-A	0	0	—	3	0	0	0	0	6	2	0	6	2	13.5	1.50	267	.143	.429	0	.000	-0	2	2	0	0.1
1931 NY-A	2	1	.667	17	5	2	0	0	57²	66	1	29	28	15.0	5.31	75	.280	.361	1	.050	-2	-6	-9	-0	-0.9
1934 StL-A	2	0	1.000	5	5	2	0	0	19²	17	3	20	11	16.9	6.41	78	.236	.402	1	.143	-0	-4	-3	1	-0.1
Chi-N	11	9	.550	27	20	8	1	0	159	163	5	54	98	12.5	3.91	99	.263	.326	3	.058	-5	3	-1	-1	-0.5
1935 Pit-N	14	8	.636	33	22	11	4	0	176¹	177	9	58	87	12.1	3.42	120	.254	.313	4	.071	-4	12	13	0	1.0
1936 Pit-N	14	8	.636	38	31	11	1	0	225²	239	12	74	108	12.5	4.31	94	.272	.329	8	.101	-5	-7	-6	-2	-1.2
1937 Pit-N	8	5	.615	32	9	2	1	0	109²	106	2	31	44	11.2	3.20	121	.255	.307	4	.148	-0	9	8	-2	0.6
1938 StL-A	0	1	.000	1	1	0	0	0	7	9	0	9	4	23.1	9.00	55	.321	.486	0	.000	-0	-3	-3	0	-0.2
Cin-N	4	6	.600	30	15	2	0	3	129¹	109	6	54	64	11.4	3.13	117	.227	.306	9	.205	-0	9	7	-1	0.7
1939 Cin-N	0	0	—	3	0	0	0	0	3	3	0	1	3	12.0	3.00	128	.250	.308	0	.000	-0	0	0	0	0.0
Total 8	57	36	.613	189	108	38	7	3	893¹	891	38	336	449	12.5	3.88	102	.258	.326	30	.104	-17	14	9	-4	-0.5
■ **MONTE WEAVER** Weaver, Montgomery Morton "Prof" b: 6/15/06, Hilton, N.C. BL/TR, 6', 170 lbs. Deb: 9/20/31																									
₃1 Was-A	1	0	1.000	3	1	1	0	0	10	11	0	6	6	15.3	4.50	95	.268	.362	0	.000	-0	-0	-0	0	0.0
Was-A	22	10	.688	43	30	13	1	2	234	236	9	112	83	13.4	4.08	106	.261	.342	27	.287	6	10	6	-2	0.9
Was-A	10	5	.667	23	21	12	1	0	152¹	147	6	53	45	11.9	3.25	129	.257	.322	7	.125	-3	17	16	-1	1.2
Was-A	11	15	.423	31	31	11	0	0	204²	255	16	63	51	14.0	4.79	90	.306	.355	13	.162	-2	-7	-11	-2	-1.3

YEAR	TM/L	W	L	PCT	G	GS	CG	SH	SV	IP	H	HR	BB	SO	RAT	ERA	ERA+	OAV	OOB	BH	AVG	PB	PR	/A	PD	TPI
1935	Was-A	1	1	.500	5	2	0	0	0	12	16	1	6	4	16.5	5.25	82	.320	.393	1	.333	0	-1	-1	0	0.0
1936	Was-A	6	4	.600	26	5	3	0	1	91	92	3	38	15	12.9	4.35	110	.262	.334	5	.200	1	7	4	0	0.4
1937	Was-A	12	9	.571	30	26	9	0	0	188^2	197	21	70	44	12.7	4.20	105	.266	.330	14	.206	1	9	5	1	0.6
1938	Was-A	7	6	.538	31	18	7	0	0	139	157	9	74	43	15.2	5.24	86	.282	.370	12	.267	4	-7	-11	-0	-0.7
1939	Bos-A	1	0	1.000	9	1	1	0	1	20^1	26	0	13	6	17.7	6.64	71	.321	.421	1	.000	-1	-5	-4	-1	-0.7
Total 9		71	50	.587	201	135	57	2	4	1052	1137	62	435	297	13.5	4.36	101	.276	.345	79	.209	5	24	3	-4	0.7

■ ORLIE WEAVER
Weaver, Orville Forest b: 6/4/1886, Newport, Ky. d: 11/28/70, New Orleans, La. BR/TR, 6', 180 lbs. Deb: 9/14/10

YEAR	TM/L	W	L	PCT	G	GS	CG	SH	SV	IP	H	HR	BB	SO	RAT	ERA	ERA+	OAV	OOB	BH	AVG	PB	PR	/A	PD	TPI
1910	Chi-N	1	1	.500	7	2	2	0	0	32	34	2	15	22	14.1	3.66	79	.270	.352	2	.154	-1	-2	-3	-1	-0.4
1911	Chi-N	2	2	.500	6	4	1	1	0	43^2	29	0	17	20	10.3	2.06	161	.196	.296	1	.059	-1	7	6	-0	0.4
	Bos-N	3	12	.200	27	17	4	0	0	121	140	9	84	50	17.2	6.47	59	.303	.418	5	.122	-2	-41	-36	-2	-3.6
	Yr	5	14	.263	33	21	5	1	0	164^2	169	9	101	70	15.1	5.30	70	.275	.384	4	.069	-4	-35	-29	-3	-3.2
Total 2		6	15	.286	40	23	7	1	0	196^2	203	11	116	92	15.1	5.03	71	.276	.383	8	.113	-4	-37	-32	-4	-3.6

■ ROGER WEAVER
Weaver, Roger Edward b: 10/6/54, Amsterdam, N.Y. BR/TR, 6'3", 190 lbs. Deb: 6/06/80

YEAR	TM/L	W	L	PCT	G	GS	CG	SH	SV	IP	H	HR	BB	SO	RAT	ERA	ERA+	OAV	OOB	BH	AVG	PB	PR	/A	PD	TPI
1980	Det-A	3	4	.429	19	6	0	0	0	63^2	56	5	34	42	12.9	4.10	100	.247	.347	0	—	0	-0	0	0	0.0

■ SAM WEAVER
Weaver, Samuel H. b: 7/10/1855, Philadelphia, Pa. d: 2/1/14, Philadelphia, Pa. BR/TR, 185 lbs. Deb: 10/25/1875

YEAR	TM/L	W	L	PCT	G	GS	CG	SH	SV	IP	H	HR	BB	SO	RAT	ERA	ERA+	OAV	OOB	BH	AVG	PB	PR	/A	PD	TPI
1875	Phi-n	1	0	1.000	1	1	1	0	0	6	6	0	2		12.0	1.50	168	.240	.296	1	.250	0	1	1		0.1
1878	Mil-N	12	31	.279	45	43	39	1	0	383	371	2	21	95	9.2	1.95	134	.242	.252	34	.200	-3	15	29	0	2.8
1882	Phi-a	26	15	.634	42	41	41	2	0	371	374	6	35	104	9.9	2.74	109	.245	.262	36	.232	1	-2	10	1	1.4
1883	Lou-a	26	22	.542	48	48	47	4	0	418^2	468	3	38	116	10.9	3.70	80	.265	.280	39	.192	1	-18	-34	0	-3.0
1884	Phi-U	5	10	.333	17	17	14	0	0	136	206	3	11	40	14.4	5.76	50	.327	.339	18	.214	-1	-41	-44	-0	-3.5
1886	Phi-a	0	2	.000	2	2	1	0	0	11	30	0	2	2	26.2	14.73	24	.474	.490	1	.143	-1	-14	-14	0	-1.0
Total 5		69	80	.463	154	151	142	7	0	1319^2	1449	14	107	357	10.6	3.23	90	.262	.276	128	.207	-3	-61	-46	2	-3.2

■ LEFTY WEBB
Webb, Cleon Earl b: 3/1/1885, Mt.Gilead, Ohio d: 1/12/58, Circleville, Ohio BB/TL, 5'11", 165 lbs. Deb: 5/23/10

YEAR	TM/L	W	L	PCT	G	GS	CG	SH	SV	IP	H	HR	BB	SO	RAT	ERA	ERA+	OAV	OOB	BH	AVG	PB	PR	/A	PD	TPI
1910	Pit-N	2	1	.667	7	3	2	0	0	27	29	0	9	6	13.3	5.67	55	.266	.333	2	.200	-0	-8	-8	0	-0.7

■ HANK WEBB
Webb, Henry Gaylon Matthew b: 5/21/50, Copiague, N.Y. BR/TR, 6'3", 175 lbs. Deb: 9/05/72

YEAR	TM/L	W	L	PCT	G	GS	CG	SH	SV	IP	H	HR	BB	SO	RAT	ERA	ERA+	OAV	OOB	BH	AVG	PB	PR	/A	PD	TPI
1972	NY-N	0	0	—	6	2	0	0	0	18^1	18	1	9	15	13.3	4.42	76	.261	.346	0	.000	-1	-2	-2	1	-0.1
1973	NY-N	0	0	—	2	0	0	0	0	1^2	2	1	2	1	21.6	10.80	33	.286	.444	0	—	0	-1	-1	0	0.0
1974	NY-N	0	2	.000	3	2	0	0	0	10	15	1	10	8	23.4	7.20	49	.341	.473	0	.000	-0	-4	-4	-0	-0.3
1975	NY-N	7	6	.538	29	15	3	1	0	115	102	12	62	38	12.9	4.07	85	.236	.333	8	.258	2	-6	-8	-1	-0.6
1976	NY-N	0	1	.000	8	0	0	0	0	16	17	2	7	7	14.6	4.50	73	.274	.366	0	.000	0	-2	-2	-0	-0.1
1977	LA-N	0	0	—	5	0	0	0	0	8	5	1	1	2	7.9	2.25	170	.192	.250	0	—	0	1	1	0	0.1
Total 6		7	9	.438	53	19	3	1	0	169	159	18	91	71	13.6	4.31	80	.248	.346	8	.200	1	-13	-16	-0	-1.0

■ RED WEBB
Webb, Samuel Henry b: 9/25/24, Washington, D.C. BL/TR, 6', 175 lbs. Deb: 9/15/48

YEAR	TM/L	W	L	PCT	G	GS	CG	SH	SV	IP	H	HR	BB	SO	RAT	ERA	ERA+	OAV	OOB	BH	AVG	PB	PR	/A	PD	TPI
1948	NY-N	2	1	.667	5	3	2	0	0	28	27	2	10	9	12.2	3.21	122	.248	.317	2	.222	0	2	2	0	0.3
1949	NY-N	1	1	.500	20	0	0	0	0	44^2	41	3	21	9	12.5	4.03	99	.248	.333	4	.400	2	0	-0	2	0.4
Total 2		3	2	.600	25	3	2	0	0	72^2	68	5	31	18	12.4	3.72	107	.248	.327	6	.316	2	2	2	2	0.7

■ BILL WEBB
Webb, William Frederick b: 12/12/13, Atlanta, Ga. BR/TR, 6'2", 180 lbs. Deb: 5/15/43

YEAR	TM/L	W	L	PCT	G	GS	CG	SH	SV	IP	H	HR	BB	SO	RAT	ERA	ERA+	OAV	OOB	BH	AVG	PB	PR	/A	PD	TPI
1943	Phi-N	0	0	—	1	1	0	0	0	1	1	1	0	0	18.0	9.00	37	.333	.500	0	—	0	-1	-1	0	0.0

■ LES WEBBER
Webber, Lester Elmer b: 5/6/15, Kelseyville, Cal. d: 11/13/86, Santa Maria, Cal. BR/TR, 6'0.5", 185 lbs. Deb: 5/17/42

YEAR	TM/L	W	L	PCT	G	GS	CG	SH	SV	IP	H	HR	BB	SO	RAT	ERA	ERA+	OAV	OOB	BH	AVG	PB	PR	/A	PD	TPI
1942	Bro-N	3	2	.600	19	3	1	0	1	51^2	46	2	22	23	11.8	2.96	110	.230	.306	1	.071	-1	2	2	1	0.2
1943	Bro-N	2	2	.500	54	0	0	0	10	115^2	112	6	69	24	14.5	3.81	88	.264	.373	3	.120	-1	-6	-6	3	-0.4
1944	Bro-N	7	8	.467	48	9	1	0	3	140^1	157	9	64	42	14.2	4.94	72	.282	.357	8	.205	1	-21	-22	4	-1.6
1945	Bro-N	7	3	.700	17	7	5	0	0	75^1	69	3	25	30	11.3	3.58	105	.237	.300	2	.091	-1	2	1	-1	0.0
1946	Bro-N	3	3	.500	11	4	0	0	0	43	34	5	15	16	10.3	2.30	147	.225	.295	1	.100	-1	5	5	0	0.4
	Cle-A	1	1	.500	4	2	0	0	0	5^1	13	0	5	5	30.4	23.63	14	.464	.545	0	.000	0	-12	-12	0	-0.9
1948	Cle-A	0	0	—	1	0	0	0	0	0^2	3	0	1	1	54.0	40.50	10	.750	.800	0	—	0	-3	-3	0	-0.1
Total 6		23	19	.548	154	25	7	0	14	432	434	25	201	141	13.4	4.19	83	.262	.345	15	.135	-2	-32	-34	6	-2.4

■ CHARLIE WEBER
Weber, Charles P. "Count" b: 10/22/1868, Cincinnati, Ohio d: 6/13/14, Beaumont, Tex. Deb: 7/30/1898

YEAR	TM/L	W	L	PCT	G	GS	CG	SH	SV	IP	H	HR	BB	SO	RAT	ERA	ERA+	OAV	OOB	BH	AVG	PB	PR	/A	PD	TPI
1898	Was-N	0	1	.000	1	1	0	0	0	4	9	0	1	0	22.5	15.75	23	.440	.466	0	.000	-0	-5	-5	0	-0.3

■ MIKE WEGENER
Wegener, Michael Denis b: 10/8/46, Denver, Colo. BR/TR, 6'4", 215 lbs. Deb: 4/09/69

YEAR	TM/L	W	L	PCT	G	GS	CG	SH	SV	IP	H	HR	BB	SO	RAT	ERA	ERA+	OAV	OOB	BH	AVG	PB	PR	/A	PD	TPI
1969	Mon-N	5	14	.263	32	26	4	1	0	165^2	150	10	96	124	13.6	4.40	84	.243	.349	13	.241	2	-15	-13	1	-0.9
1970	Mon-N	3	6	.333	25	16	1	0	0	104^1	100	16	56	35	13.8	5.26	78	.252	.350	4	.118	-2	-14	-13	0	-1.4
Total 2		8	20	.286	57	42	5	1	0	270	250	26	152	159	13.7	4.73	81	.247	.349	17	.193	0	-29	-27	1	-2.3

■ BILL WEGMAN
Wegman, William Edward b: 12/19/62, Cincinnati, Ohio BR/TR, 6'5", 200 lbs. Deb: 9/14/85

YEAR	TM/L	W	L	PCT	G	GS	CG	SH	SV	IP	H	HR	BB	SO	RAT	ERA	ERA+	OAV	OOB	BH	AVG	PB	PR	/A	PD	TPI
1985	Mil-A	2	0	1.000	3	3	0	0	0	17^2	17	3	6	10	10.2	3.57	117	.246	.278	0	—	0	1	1	-0	0.1
1986	Mil-A	5	12	.294	35	32	2	0	0	198^1	217	32	43	82	12.1	5.13	84	.279	.323	0	—	0	-21	-18	-0	-1.6
1987	Mil-A	12	11	.522	34	33	7	0	0	225	229	31	53	102	11.5	4.24	108	.265	.312	0	—	0	5	8	1	0.9
1988	Mil-A	13	13	.500	32	31	4	1	0	199	207	24	50	84	11.8	4.12	97	.265	.313	0	—	0	-3	-3	-0	-0.2
1989	Mil-A	2	6	.250	11	8	0	0	0	51	69	6	21	27	15.9	6.71	57	.321	.381	0	—	0	-16	-16	1	-1.4
1990	Mil-A	2	2	.500	8	5	1	1	0	29^2	37	6	6	20	13.0	4.85	78	.298	.331	0	—	0	-3	-4	-0	-0.3
Total 6		36	44	.450	123	112	14	2	0	720^2	776	102	176	321	12.1	4.63	92	.274	.321	0	—	0	-37	-31	0	-2.5

■ BIGGS WEHDE
Wehde, Wilbur b: 11/23/06, Holstein, Iowa d: 9/21/70, Sioux Falls, S.Dak. BR/TR, 5'10.5", 180 lbs. Deb: 9/15/30

YEAR	TM/L	W	L	PCT	G	GS	CG	SH	SV	IP	H	HR	BB	SO	RAT	ERA	ERA+	OAV	OOB	BH	AVG	PB	PR	/A	PD	TPI
1930	Chi-A	0	0	—	4	0	0	0	0	6^1	7	1	7	3	21.3	9.95	46	.304	.484	0	.000	-0	-4	-4	1	-0.2
1931	Chi-A	1	0	1.000	8	0	0	0	0	16	19	0	10	3	17.4	6.75	63	.333	.449	0	.000	-0	-4	-4	1	-0.3
Total 2		1	0	1.000	12	0	0	0	0	22^1	26	1	17	6	18.5	7.66	57	.325	.460	0	.000	-1	-8	-8	1	-0.5

■ HERM WEHMEIER
Wehmeier, Herman Ralph b: 2/18/27, Cincinnati, Ohio d: 5/21/73, Dallas, Tex. BR/TR, 6'2", 185 lbs. Deb: 9/07/45

YEAR	TM/L	W	L	PCT	G	GS	CG	SH	SV	IP	H	HR	BB	SO	RAT	ERA	ERA+	OAV	OOB	BH	AVG	PB	PR	/A	PD	TPI
1945	Cin-N	0	1	.000	2	2	0	0	0	5	10	0	4	0	25.2	12.60	30	.435	.519	0	.000	-0	-5	-5	0	-0.3
1947	Cin-N	0	0	—	1	0	0	0	0	5	1	0	0	0	0.0	0.00	—	.000	.000	0	—	0	0	0	0	0.0
1948	Cin-N	11	8	.579	33	24	6	1	0	147^1	179	14	75	56	15.6	5.86	67	.299	.379	5	.091	-3	-31	-32	0	-3.3
1949	Cin-N	11	12	.478	33	29	11	1	0	213^1	202	20	117	80	13.8	4.68	89	.253	.353	20	.256	2	-15	-12	-2	-1.0
1950	Cin-N	10	18	.357	41	32	12	0	4	230	255	27	135	121	15.4	5.67	75	.281	.376	14	.152	-3	-39	-37	-3	-3.9
1951	Cin-N	7	10	.412	39	22	10	2	2	184^2	167	15	89	93	12.7	3.70	110	.241	.330	17	.288	3	5	8	-2	0.9
1952	Cin-N	9	11	.450	33	26	6	1	0	190^1	197	23	103	83	14.5	5.15	73	.269	.365	12	.188	2	-30	-29	-4	-2.9
1953	Cin-N	1	6	.143	28	10	2	0	0	81^2	100	20	47	32	16.2	7.16	61	.299	.385	4	.200	-0	-26	-25	-1	-2.4
1954	Cin-N	0	3	.000	12	3	0	0	2	33^2	36	6	21	13	15.5	6.68	63	.271	.374	0	.000	-1	-10			
	Phi-N	10	8	.556	25	17	10	2	0	138	117	10	51	49	11.0	3.85	105	.231	.302	6	.120	-2				
	Yr	10	11	.476	37	20	10	2	2	171^2	153	16	72	62	11.8	4.40	92	.238	.316	2						
1955	Phi-N	10	12	.455	31	29	10	1	0	193^2	176	21	67	85	11.4	4.41	90	.241	.307	20						
1956	Phi-N	0	2	.000	3	3	0	0	0	20	18	2	11	8	13.0	4.05	92	.240	.337	0						
	StL-N	12	9	.571	31	19	7	2	1	170^2	150	14	71	68	11.7	3.69	102	.240	.319	13						
	Yr	12	11	.522	37	22	7	2	1	190^2	168	16	82	76	11.8	3.73	101	.240	.320	2	.030					
1957	StL-N	10	7	.588	36	18	5	0	0	165	165	25	54	91	12.1	4.31	92	.253	.312	12	.203					
1958	StL-N	0	1	.000	3	3	0	0	0	6	13	2	2	4	22.5	13.50	31	.448	.484	1	.500					

YEAR TM/L	W	L	PCT	G	GS	CG	SH	SV	IP	H	HR	BB	SO	RAT	ERA	ERA+	OAV	OOB	BH	AVG	PB	PR	/A	PD	TPI
Det-A	1	0	1.000	7	3	0	0	0	22²	21	2	5	11	10.3	2.38	169	.241	.283	0	.000	-1	3	4	0	0.4
Total 13	92	108	.460	361	240	79	9	9	1803	1806	210	852	794	13.4	4.80	84	.260	.344	124	.196	5	-165	-156	-13	-14.3

■ DAVE WEHRMEISTER
Wehrmeister, David Thomas   b: 11/9/52, Berwyn, Ill.   BR/TR, 6'4", 195 lbs.   Deb: 4/16/76

YEAR TM/L	W	L	PCT	G	GS	CG	SH	SV	IP	H	HR	BB	SO	RAT	ERA	ERA+	OAV	OOB	BH	AVG	PB	PR	/A	PD	TPI
1976 SD-N	0	4	.000	7	4	0	0	0	19¹	27	0	11	10	17.7	7.45	44	.333	.413	0	.000	-1	-8	-9	0	-0.8
1977 SD-N	1	3	.250	30	6	0	0	0	69²	81	8	44	32	16.5	6.07	58	.293	.396	2	.167	0	-17	-20	-1	-1.8
1978 SD-N	1	0	1.000	4	0	0	0	0	7¹	8	1	5	2	16.0	6.14	54	.276	.382	0	—	0	-2	-2	-0	-0.2
1981 NY-A	0	0	—	5	0	0	0	0	7	6	0	7	7	16.7	5.14	69	.240	.406	0	—	0	-1	-1	0	0.0
1984 Phi-N	0	0	—	7	0	0	0	0	15	18	1	7	13	15.6	7.20	50	.300	.382	0	.000	-0	-6	-6	0	-0.5
1985 Chi-A	2	2	.500	23	0	0	0	2	39¹	35	4	10	32	11.0	3.43	126	.241	.304	0	—	0	3	4	-0	0.3
Total 6	4	9	.308	76	10	0	0	2	157²	175	14	84	96	15.2	5.65	65	.284	.376	2	.100	-1	-31	-34	-0	-3.0

■ STUMP WEIDMAN
Weidman, George E.   b: 2/17/1861, Rochester, N.Y.   d: 3/2/05, New York, N.Y.   BR/TR,   Deb: 8/26/1880   U♦

YEAR TM/L	W	L	PCT	G	GS	CG	SH	SV	IP	H	HR	BB	SO	RAT	ERA	ERA+	OAV	OOB	BH	AVG	PB	PR	/A	PD	TPI
1880 Buf-N	0	9	.000	17	13	9	0	0	113²	141	1	9	25	11.9	3.40	72	.290	.302	8	.103	-6	-13	-12	-1	-1.7
1881 Det-N	8	5	.615	13	13	13	1	0	115	108	1	12	26	**9.4**	**1.80**	**162**	.238	**.257**	12	.255	0	12	14	-1	1.3
1882 Det-N	25	20	.556	46	45	43	4	0	411	391	10	39	161	9.4	2.63	111	.237	.254	42	.218	-5	12	14	-0	0.7
1883 Det-N	20	24	.455	52	47	41	3	2	402¹	435	8	72	183	11.3	3.53	88	.260	.291	58	.185	-8	-18	-19	-0	-2.7
1884 Det-N	4	21	.160	26	26	24	0	0	212²	257	9	57	96	13.3	3.72	78	.283	.326	49	.163	-4	-18	-20	-1	-1.6
1885 Det-N	14	24	.368	38	38	37	3	0	330	343	7	63	149	11.1	3.14	90	.256	.289	24	.157	-4	-12	-11	-3	-1.6
1886 KC-N	12	36	.250	51	51	48	1	0	427²	549	11	112	168	13.9	4.50	84	.299	.340	30	.168	-11	-57	-35	4	-3.2
1887 Det-N	13	7	.650	21	21	20	0	0	183	221	6	60	56	13.8	5.36	75	.290	.342	17	.207	-3	-27	-27	-0	-2.3
NY-a	4	8	.333	12	12	11	1	0	97	122	3	25	37	13.6	4.64	92	.296	.337	7	.152	-2	-4	-4	1	-0.4
NY-N	0	1	.000	1	1	1	0	0	8	10	0	2	4	13.5	1.13	333	.298	.337	1	.333	0	3	2	-0	0.2
1888 NY-N	1	1	.500	2	2	2	0	0	18	17	2	8	5	12.5	3.50	78	.240	.318	0	.000	-0	-1	-2	-0	-0.1
Total 9	101	156	.393	279	269	249	13	2	2318¹	2594	61	459	910	11.9	3.60	89	.269	.303	248	.177	-42	-122	-100	-1	-11.4

■ DICK WEIK
Weik, Richard Henry "Legs"   b: 11/17/27, Waterloo, Iowa   BR/TR, 6'3.5", 184 lbs.   Deb: 9/08/48 ♦

YEAR TM/L	W	L	PCT	G	GS	CG	SH	SV	IP	H	HR	BB	SO	RAT	ERA	ERA+	OAV	OOB	BH	AVG	PB	PR	/A	PD	TPI
1948 Was-A	1	2	.333	3	3	0	0	0	12²	14	1	22	8	25.6	5.68	76	.311	.537	3	.750	2	-2	-2	0	0.0
1949 Was-A	3	12	.200	27	14	2	2	1	95¹	78	5	103	58	17.1	5.38	79	.230	.410	5	.179	-1	-13	-12	1	-1.0
1950 Was-A	1	3	.250	14	5	1	0	0	44	38	2	47	26	17.4	4.30	105	.236	.409	2	.154	-1	1	1	-1	0.0
Cle-A	1	3	.250	11	2	0	0	0	26	18	1	26	16	15.6	3.81	114	.205	.391	1	.200	0	2	2	0	0.2
Yr	2	6	.250	25	7	1	0	0	70	56	3	73	42	16.7	4.11	108	.225	.402	0	.000	-1	4	2	-1	0.2
1953 Det-A	0	1	.000	12	1	0	0	0	19¹	32	3	23	6	25.6	13.97	29	.386	.519	1	.500	1	-21	-21	0	-1.8
1954 Det-A	0	1	.000	9	1	0	0	0	16¹	23	3	16	9	22.0	7.16	52	.348	.482	0	.000	-0	-6	-6	-0	-0.6
Total 5	6	22	.214	76	26	3	2	1	213²	203	15	237	123	18.6	5.90	72	.260	.433	12	.226	1	-39	-39	0	-3.2

■ ED WEILAND
Weiland, Edwin Nicholas   b: 11/26/14, Evanston, Ill.   d: 7/12/71, Chicago, Ill.   BL/TR, 5'11", 180 lbs.   Deb: 5/01/40

YEAR TM/L	W	L	PCT	G	GS	CG	SH	SV	IP	H	HR	BB	SO	RAT	ERA	ERA+	OAV	OOB	BH	AVG	PB	PR	/A	PD	TPI
1940 Chi-A	0	0	—	5	0	0	0	0	14¹	15	5	7	3	13.8	8.79	50	.263	.344	1	.200	-0	-7	-7	-0	-0.6
1942 Chi-A	0	0	—	5	0	0	0	0	9²	18	0	3	4	19.6	7.45	48	.383	.420	0	.000	-0	-4	-4	-0	-0.4
Total 2	0	0	—	10	0	0	0	0	24	33	5	10	7	16.1	8.25	50	.317	.377	1	.143	-0	-11	-11	-1	-1.0

■ BOB WEILAND
Weiland, Robert George "Lefty"   b: 12/14/05, Chicago, Ill.   d: 11/9/88, Chicago, Ill.   BL/TL, 6'4", 215 lbs.   Deb: 9/30/28

YEAR TM/L	W	L	PCT	G	GS	CG	SH	SV	IP	H	HR	BB	SO	RAT	ERA	ERA+	OAV	OOB	BH	AVG	PB	PR	/A	PD	TPI
1928 Chi-A	1	0	1.000	1	1	1	1	0	9	7	0	5	9	13.0	0.00	—	.212	.333	1	.333	0	4	4	-0	0.5
1929 Chi-A	2	4	.333	15	9	1	0	1	62	62	3	43	25	15.7	5.81	74	.268	.390	2	.111	-1	-11	-10	-1	-1.1
1930 Chi-A	0	4	.000	14	3	0	0	0	32²	38	1	21	15	16.8	6.61	70	.297	.404	0	.000	-1	-7	-7	-0	-0.7
1931 Chi-A	2	7	.222	15	8	3	0	0	75	75	3	46	38	15.0	5.16	83	.259	.368	4	.182	1	-7	-8	0	-0.4
1932 Bos-A	6	16	.273	43	27	7	0	1	195²	231	11	97	63	15.4	4.51	100	.295	.377	9	.148	-1	-1	-0	3	0.1
1933 Bos-A	8	14	.364	39	27	12	0	3	216¹	197	19	100	97	12.6	3.87	113	.244	.331	7	.108	-4	10	12	-2	0.6
1934 Bos-A	1	5	.167	11	7	2	0	0	55²	63	4	27	29	14.6	5.50	87	.293	.372	2	.105	-1	-6	-4	-0	-0.4
Cle-A	1	5	.167	16	7	2	0	0	70	71	5	30	42	13.0	4.11	111	.262	.336	3	.125	-0	3	3	-1	0.2
Yr	2	10	.167	27	14	4	0	0	125²	134	9	57	71	13.7	4.73	99	.276	.352	1	.023	-2	-3	-1	-0	-0.2
1935 StL-A	0	2	.000	14	4	0	0	0	32	39	6	31	11	20.0	9.56	50	.298	.436	0	.000	-1	-18	-17	-1	-1.5
1937 StL-N	15	14	.517	41	34	21	2	0	264¹	283	14	94	105	13.0	3.54	112	.276	.339	15	.169	0	11	13	-1	1.2
1938 StL-N	16	11	.593	35	29	11	1	1	228¹	248	14	67	117	12.6	3.59	110	.272	.324	11	.138	-3	5	9	-1	0.5
1939 StL-N	10	12	.455	32	23	6	3	1	146¹	146	9	50	63	12.4	3.57	115	.264	.331	3	.065	-5	6	9	-1	0.3
1940 StL-N	0	0	—	1	0	0	0	0	1	3	1	0	0	27.0	27.00	15	.600	.600	0	—	0	-3	-3	-0	-0.1
Total 12	62	94	.397	277	179	66	7	7	1388¹	1463	85	611	614	13.7	4.24	100	.272	.350	57	.129	-17	-13	2	-5	-0.8

■ CARL WEILMAN
Weilman, Carl Woolworth "Zeke" (b: Carl Woolworth Weilenmann)
b: 11/29/1889, Hamilton, Ohio   d: 5/25/24, Hamilton, Ohio   BL/TL, 6'5.5", 187 lbs.   Deb: 8/24/12

YEAR TM/L	W	L	PCT	G	GS	CG	SH	SV	IP	H	HR	BB	SO	RAT	ERA	ERA+	OAV	OOB	BH	AVG	PB	PR	/A	PD	TPI
1912 StL-A	2	4	.333	8	6	5	2	1	48¹	42	0	3	24	8.4	2.79	119	.227	.239	2	.118	-1	3	3	0	0.3
1913 StL-A	10	20	.333	39	28	17	2	0	251²	262	2	60	79	11.7	3.40	86	.281	.328	12	.146	-3	-13	-13	1	-1.4
1914 StL-A	18	13	.581	44	36	20	3	1	299	260	1	84	119	10.7	2.08	130	.237	.298	15	.149	-1	22	21	1	2.3
1915 StL-A	18	19	.486	47	31	19	3	4	295²	240	6	83	125	9.9	2.34	122	.229	.287	23	.230	2	19	17	-1	1.9
1916 StL-A	17	18	.486	46	31	19	1	2	276	237	3	76	91	10.5	2.15	128	.242	.301	14	.154	-1	21	18	-3	1.5
1917 StL-A	1	2	.333	5	3	0	0	0	19	19	1	6	9	11.8	1.89	137	.268	.325	0	.000	-1	2	1	1	0.2
1919 StL-A	10	6	.625	20	20	12	3	0	148	133	3	45	44	11.0	2.07	160	.244	.305	9	.191	0	19	21	0	2.3
1920 StL-A	9	13	.409	30	24	13	1	2	183¹	201	6	61	45	13.0	4.47	88	.291	.351	11	.175	-2	-14	-11	2	-1.0
Total 8	85	95	.472	239	179	105	15	10	1521	1394	22	418	536	10.9	2.67	112	.251	.307	86	.170	-7	59	56	2	6.1

■ JAKE WEIMER
Weimer, Jacob "Tornado Jake"   b: 11/29/1873, Ottumwa, Iowa   d: 6/19/28, Chicago, Ill.   BR/TL, 5'11", 175 lbs.   Deb: 4/17/03

YEAR TM/L	W	L	PCT	G	GS	CG	SH	SV	IP	H	HR	BB	SO	RAT	ERA	ERA+	OAV	OOB	BH	AVG	PB	PR	/A	PD	TPI
1903 Chi-N	20	8	.714	35	33	27	3	0	282	241	4	104	128	11.4	2.30	136	**.225**		21	.196	-2	30	26	-2	2.6
1904 Chi-N	20	14	.588	37	37	31	5	0	307	241	1	97	177	9.8	1.91	140	.204	.272	21	.183	-1	28	26	2	2.8
1905 Chi-N	18	12	.600	33	30	26	2	1	250	212	1	80	107	10.9	2.27	131	.229	.299	19	.207	2	20	20	-1	2.2
1906 Cin-N	20	14	.588	41	39	31	6	1	304²	263	0	99	141	11.1	2.22	124	.236	.306	29	.269	6	14	18	1	2.9
1907 Cin-N	11	14	.440	29	26	19	3	0	209	165	6	63	67	10.8	2.41	108	.226	.308	14	.194	2	1	4	3	1.0
1908 Cin-N	8	7	.533	15	15	9	2	0	116²	110	2	50	36	12.8	2.39	96	.255	.341	11	.244	2	-0	-1	1	0.2
1909 NY-N	0	0	—	1	0	0	0	0	3	7	0	0	1	24.0	9.00	28	.467	.500	0	.000	-0	-2	-2	0	-0.1
Total 7	97	69	.584	191	180	143	21	2	1472¹	1227	14	493	657	11.0	2.23	125	.227	.300	115	.213	12	92	92	4	11.6

■ LEFTY WEINERT
Weinert, Phillip Walter   b: 4/21/02, Philadelphia, Pa.   d: 4/17/73, Rockledge, Fla.   BL/TL, 6'1", 195 lbs.   Deb: 9/24/19

YEAR TM/L	W	L	PCT	G	GS	CG	SH	SV	IP	H	HR	BB	SO	RAT	ERA	ERA+	OAV	OOB	BH	AVG	PB	PR	/A	PD	TPI
1919 Phi-N	0	0	—	1	0	0	0	0	4	11	0	2	1	29.3	18.00	18	.478	.520	2	1.000	1	-7	-7	0	-0.3
1920 Phi-N	1	1	.500	10	2	0	0	0	22	27	1	19	10	19.2	6.14	56	.333	.465	0	.000	-1	-7	-7	-0	-0.7
1921 Phi-N	1	0	1.000	8	0	0	0	0	12¹	8	1	5	2	10.2	1.46	290	.216	.326	1	1.000	0	3	4	-1	0.4
1922 Phi-N	8	11	.421	34	22	10	0	1	166²	189	10	70	58	14.3	3.40	137	.289	.362	14	.241	0	13	23	-2	2.2
1923 Phi-N	4	17	.190	38	20	8	0	1	156	207	10	81	46	17.1	5.42	85	.327	.410	19	.322	3	-25	-14	-3	-1.2
1924 Phi-N	0	1	.000	8	1	0	0	0	14²	10	0	11	7	12.9	2.45	182	.204	.350	0	.000	-1	2	3	0	0.3
1927 Chi-N	1	1	.500	5	3	1	0	0	19²	21	2	6	5	12.4	4.58	84	.259	.310	1	.200	0	-1	-2	-0	-0.1
1928 Chi-N	1	0	1.000	10	1	0	0	0	17	24	0	9	8	18.0	5.29	73	.393	.479	0	.000	-0	-2	-3	-1	-0.3
1931 NY-A	2	2	.500	17	0	0	0	0	24²	31	2	19	24	20.1	6.20	64	.316	.451	0	.000	-0	-5	-6	-0	-0.5
Total 9	18	33	.353	131	49	19	0	2	437	528	26	222	160	15.9	4.59	97	.308	.393	37	.261	3	-29	-7	-6	-0.2

■ ...Y WEIR
Weir, William Franklin "Bill"   b: 2/25/11, Portland, Maine   BL/TL, 5'8.5", 170 lbs.   Deb: 6/25/36

YEAR TM/L	W	L	PCT	G	GS	CG	SH	SV	IP	H	HR	BB	SO	RAT	ERA	ERA+	OAV	OOB	BH	AVG	PB	PR	/A	PD	TPI
...s-N	4	3	.571	12	7	3	2	0	57¹	53	0	24	29	12.1	2.83	136	.241	.316	5	.278	2	8	6	1	0.9
...-N	1	1	.500	10	4	1	0	0	33	27	0	19	8	12.5	3.82	94	.227	.333	0	.000	-1	0	-1	1	0.0

YEAR	TM/L	W	L	PCT	G	GS	CG	SH	SV	IP	H	HR	BB	SO	RAT	ERA	ERA+	OAV	OOB	BH	AVG	PB	PR	/A	PD	TPI
1938	Bos-N	1	0	1.000	5	0	0	0	0	13^1	14	4	6	3	13.5	6.75	51	.269	.345	1	.333	0	-4	-5	0	-0.3
1939	Bos-N	0	0	—	2	0	0	0	0	2^2	1	0	1	2	6.8	0.00	—	.125	.222	0	.000	-0	1	1	0	0.1
Total	4	6	4	.600	29	11	4	2	0	106^1	95	4	50	42	12.3	3.55	104	.238	.323	6	.188	1	5	2	2	0.7

■ CURT WELCH
Welch, Curtis Benton   b: 2/11/1862, E.Liverpool, Ohio   d: 8/29/1896, E.Liverpool, Ohio   BR , 5'10", 175 lbs.   Deb: 5/01/1884 ♦

YEAR	TM/L	W	L	PCT	G	GS	CG	SH	SV	IP	H	HR	BB	SO	RAT	ERA	ERA+	OAV	OOB	BH	AVG	PB	PR	/A	PD	TPI
1890	Phi-a	0	0	—	1	0	0	0	0	1	6	0	0	1	54.0	54.00	7	.670	.670	106	.268	0	-6	-6	0	-0.3

■ TED WELCH
Welch, Floyd John   b: 10/17/1892, Coyville, Kan.   d: 1/6/43, Great Bend, Kan.   BL/TR, 5'9.5", 160 lbs.   Deb: 5/15/14

YEAR	TM/L	W	L	PCT	G	GS	CG	SH	SV	IP	H	HR	BB	SO	RAT	ERA	ERA+	OAV	OOB	BH	AVG	PB	PR	/A	PD	TPI
1914	StL-F	0	0	—	3	0	0	0	0	6	6	0	3	2	18.0	6.00	56	.268	.423	0	.000	-0	-2	-2	0	-0.1

■ JOHNNY WELCH
Welch, John Vernon   b: 12/2/06, Washington, D.C.   d: 9/2/40, St.Louis, Mo.   BL/TR, 6'3", 184 lbs.   Deb: 5/22/26

YEAR	TM/L	W	L	PCT	G	GS	CG	SH	SV	IP	H	HR	BB	SO	RAT	ERA	ERA+	OAV	OOB	BH	AVG	PB	PR	/A	PD	TPI
1926	Chi-N	0	0	—	3	0	0	0	0	4^1	5	0	1	0	12.5	2.08	185	.357	.400	1	1.000	0	1	1	-0	0.1
1927	Chi-N	0	0	—	1	0	0	0	0	1	0	0	3	1	27.0	9.00	43	.000	.500	0	—	0	-1	-1	0	0.0
1928	Chi-N	0	0	—	3	0	0	0	0	4	13	0	0	2	29.3	15.75	24	.591	.591	0	—	0	-5	-5	0	-0.4
1931	Chi-N	2	1	.667	8	3	1	0	0	33^2	39	2	10	7	13.4	3.74	103	.291	.345	5	.417	2	0	0	0	0.3
1932	Bos-A	4	6	.400	20	8	3	1	0	72^1	93	3	38	26	16.7	5.23	86	.312	.395	9	.250	2	-6	-6	0	-0.3
1933	Bos-A	4	9	.308	47	7	1	0	3	129	142	6	67	68	14.7	4.60	95	.283	.370	6	.162	-1	-5	-3	1	-0.3
1934	Bos-A	13	15	.464	41	22	8	1	0	206^1	223	14	76	91	13.4	4.49	107	.274	.342	15	.203	-1	0	7	0	0.6
1935	Bos-A	10	9	.526	31	19	10	1	2	143	155	4	53	48	13.3	4.47	106	.273	.339	9	.180	-0	4	4	-0	0.4
1936	Bos-A	2	1	.667	9	3	1	0	0	32^2	43	4	8	9	14.1	5.51	96	.305	.342	3	.273	1	-2	-1	0	-0.1
	Pit-N	0	0	—	9	1	0	0	1	22	22	3	6	5	11.5	4.50	90	.265	.315	2	.286	1	-1	-1	-0	0.0
Total	9	35	41	.461	172	63	24	3	6	648^1	735	36	262	257	14.1	4.66	99	.285	.355	50	.219	3	-18	-4	1	0.4

■ MICKEY WELCH
Welch, Michael Francis "Smiling Mickey"   b: 7/4/1859, Brooklyn, N.Y.   d: 7/30/41, Concord, N.H.   BR/TR, 5'8", 160 lbs.   Deb: 5/01/1880   H

YEAR	TM/L	W	L	PCT	G	GS	CG	SH	SV	IP	H	HR	BB	SO	RAT	ERA	ERA+	OAV	OOB	BH	AVG	PB	PR	/A	PD	TPI
1880	Tro-N	34	30	.531	65	64	64	4	0	574	575	7	80	123	10.3	2.54	99	.248	.273	72	.287	11	-11	-1	-6	0.5
1881	Tro-N	21	18	.538	40	40	40	4	0	368	371	7	78	104	11.0	2.67	111	.251	.288	30	.203	-4	4	12	-6	0.2
1882	Tro-N	14	16	.467	33	33	30	5	0	281	334	7	62	53	12.7	3.46	81	.279	.315	37	.245	1	-18	-20	-2	-1.9
1883	NY-N	25	23	.521	54	52	46	4	0	426	431	11	66	144	10.5	2.73	114	.247	.275	75	.234	3	20	18	-6	1.4
1884	NY-N	39	21	.650	65	65	62	4	0	557^1	528	12	146	345	10.9	2.50	119	.236	.283	60	.241	9	29	29	-6	3.3
1885	NY-N	44	11	.800	56	55	55	7	1	492	372	4	131	258	9.2	1.66	160	.200	.253	41	.206	5	63	55	-8	4.9
1886	NY-N	33	22	.600	59	59	56	1	0	500	514	13	163	272	12.2	2.99	107	.255	.311	46	.216	1	18	12	-3	0.8
1887	NY-N	22	15	.595	40	40	39	2	0	346	339	7	91	115	11.2	3.36	112	.249	.296	36	.243	4	27	15	-2	1.3
1888	*NY-N	26	19	.578	47	47	47	5	0	425^1	328	12	108	167	9.2	1.93	141	.205	.256	32	.189	1	43	38	-2	3.7
1889	*NY-N	27	12	.692	45	41	39	3	2	375	340	14	149	125	11.7	3.02	131	.234	.305	30	.192	-2	42	38	-2	3.0
1890	NY-N	17	14	.548	37	37	33	2	0	292^1	268	5	122	97	12.0	2.99	117	.237	.311	22	.179	-3	19	16	-2	1.0
1891	NY-N	5	9	.357	22	15	14	0	1	160	176	7	97	46	15.4	4.27	75	.269	.363	10	.141	-4	-16	-19	-2	-2.1
1892	NY-N	0	0	—	1	1	0	0	0	5	11	0	4	1	27.0	14.40	22	.423	.500	1	.333	0	-6	-6	0	-0.3
Total	13	307	210	.594	564	549	525	41	4	4802	4587	106	1297	1850	11.0	2.71	113	.241	.289	492	.224	22	213	193	-47	15.5

■ BOB WELCH
Welch, Robert Lynn   b: 11/3/56, Detroit, Mich.   BR/TR, 6'3", 190 lbs.   Deb: 6/20/78

YEAR	TM/L	W	L	PCT	G	GS	CG	SH	SV	IP	H	HR	BB	SO	RAT	ERA	ERA+	OAV	OOB	BH	AVG	PB	PR	/A	PD	TPI
1978	*LA-N	7	4	.636	23	13	4	3	3	111^1	92	6	26	66	9.6	2.02	174	.229	.277	5	.172	0	19	18	-1	1.9
1979	LA-N	5	6	.455	25	12	1	0	5	81^1	82	7	32	64	12.9	3.98	91	.265	.340	3	.158	-0	-2	-3	-1	-0.3
1980	LA-N	14	9	.609	32	32	3	2	0	213^2	190	15	79	141	11.5	3.29	106	.242	.314	17	.243	3	7	5	-1	0.0
1981	*LA-N	9	5	.643	23	23	2	1	0	141^1	141	11	41	88	11.8	3.44	96	.259	.315	10	.222	2	1	-2	-1	0.0
1982	LA-N	16	11	.593	36	36	9	3	0	235^2	199	19	81	176	10.9	3.36	103	.229	.299	12	.141	-1	6	3	-2	0.0
1983	*LA-N	15	12	.556	31	31	4	3	0	204	164	13	72	156	10.5	2.65	136	.222	.294	7	.096	-2	22	21	-0	2.0
1984	LA-N	13	13	.500	31	29	3	1	0	178^2	191	11	58	126	12.6	3.78	93	.273	.331	4	.078	-3	-4	-5	2	-0.5
1985	*LA-N	14	4	.778	23	23	8	3	0	167^1	141	16	35	96	9.8	2.31	150	.225	.273	9	.180	1	24	22	1	2.6
1986	LA-N	7	13	.350	33	33	7	3	0	235^2	227	14	55	183	11.0	3.28	105	.251	.299	8	.105	-0	11	4	-1	0.2
1987	LA-N	15	9	.625	35	35	6	4	0	251^2	204	21	86	196	10.5	3.22	123	.221	.291	13	.157	1	24	21	2	2.4
1988	*Oak-A	17	9	.654	36	36	4	2	0	244^2	237	22	81	158	12.1	3.64	104	.257	.323	0	—	0	9	4	0	0.4
1989	*Oak-A	17	8	.680	33	33	1	0	0	209^2	191	13	78	137	11.8	3.00	122	.241	.314	0	—	0	20	16	-0	1.6
1990	*Oak-A	27	6	.818	35	35	2	2	0	238	214	26	77	127	11.2	2.95	127	.242	.306	0	—	0	25	21	0	2.2
Total	13	176	109	.618	396	371	54	27	8	2513	2273	194	801	1714	11.2	3.16	114	.242	.305	88	.151	2	164	125	-3	13.3

■ DON WELCHEL
Welchel, Donald Ray   b: 2/3/57, Atlanta, Tex.   BR/TR, 6'4", 205 lbs.   Deb: 9/15/82

YEAR	TM/L	W	L	PCT	G	GS	CG	SH	SV	IP	H	HR	BB	SO	RAT	ERA	ERA+	OAV	OOB	BH	AVG	PB	PR	/A	PD	TPI
1982	Bal-A	1	0	1.000	2	0	0	0	0	4^1	6	0	2	3	16.6	8.31	49	.300	.364	0	—	0	-2	-2	0	-0.1
1983	Bal-A	0	2	.000	11	0	0	0	0	26^2	33	1	10	16	14.5	5.40	73	.297	.355	0	—	0	-4	-4	-0	-0.3
Total	2	1	2	.333	13	0	0	0	0	31	39	1	12	19	14.8	5.81	68	.298	.357	0	—	0	-6	-6	-0	-0.4

■ DAVID WELLS
Wells, David Lee   b: 5/20/63, Torrance, Cal.   BL/TL, 6'3", 187 lbs.   Deb: 6/30/87

YEAR	TM/L	W	L	PCT	G	GS	CG	SH	SV	IP	H	HR	BB	SO	RAT	ERA	ERA+	OAV	OOB	BH	AVG	PB	PR	/A	PD	TPI
1987	Tor-A	4	3	.571	18	2	0	0	1	29^1	37	0	12	32	15.0	3.99	113	.311	.374	0	—	0	2	2	0	0.2
1988	Tor-A	3	5	.375	41	0	0	0	4	64^1	65	12	31	56	13.7	4.62	85	.269	.356	0	—	0	-5	-5	-0	-0.4
1989	*Tor-A	7	4	.636	54	0	0	0	2	86^1	66	5	28	78	9.8	2.40	157	.207	.271	0	—	0	14	13	0	1.4
1990	Tor-A	11	6	.647	43	25	0	0	3	189	165	14	45	115	10.1	3.14	121	.235	.283	0	—	0	16	14	1	1.5
Total	4	25	18	.581	156	27	0	0	10	369	333	31	116	281	11.0	3.29	117	.241	.302	0	—	0	27	23	1	2.7

■ ED WELLS
Wells, Edwin Lee "Satchelfoot"   b: 6/7/1900, Ashland, Ohio   d: 5/1/86, Birmingham, Ala.   BL/TL, 6'1.5", 183 lbs.   Deb: 6/16/23

YEAR	TM/L	W	L	PCT	G	GS	CG	SH	SV	IP	H	HR	BB	SO	RAT	ERA	ERA+	OAV	OOB	BH	AVG	PB	PR	/A	PD	TPI
1923	Det-A	0	0	—	7	0	0	0	0	10	11	0	6	6	15.3	5.40	72	.306	.405	0	.000	-0	-2	-2	-0	-0.1
1924	Det-A	6	8	.429	29	15	5	0	4	102	117	2	42	33	14.1	4.06	101	.291	.360	7	.212	-1	2	1	1	0.1
1925	Det-A	6	9	.400	35	14	5	0	2	134^1	190	8	62	45	17.0	6.23	69	.345	.413	12	.279	2	-27	-29	0	-2.3
1926	Det-A	12	10	.545	36	26	9	4	0	178	201	7	76	58	14.1	4.15	98	.297	.370	15	.205	0	-2	-2	-3	-0.3
1927	Det-A	0	1	.000	8	1	0	0	1	20	28	3	5	5	14.8	6.75	62	.333	.371	2	.286	0	-6	-6	1	-0.4
1929	NY-A	13	9	.591	31	23	10	3	0	193^1	179	19	81	78	12.1	4.33	89	.248	.324	17	.230	2	-2	-10	-4	-1.2
1930	NY-A	12	3	.800	27	21	7	0	0	150^2	185	11	49	46	14.2	5.20	83	.302	.358	15	.259	0	-9	-15	-2	-1.4
1931	NY-A	9	5	.643	27	10	6	0	2	116^2	130	7	37	34	13.0	4.32	92	.286	.341	10	.222	1	1	-5	-1	-0.4
1932	NY-A	3	3	.500	22	0	0	0	2	31^2	38	1	12	13	14.2	4.26	96	.302	.362	0	.000	-1	1	-1	0	0.0
1933	StL-A	6	14	.300	36	22	10	0	1	203^2	220	13	63	58	13.0	4.20	111	.278	.330	14	.197	-1	2	10	-2	0.1
1934	StL-A	1	7	.125	33	8	2	0	1	92	108	7	35	27	14.0	4.79	104	.292	.353	1	.045	-2	-3	2	1	0.1
Total	11	68	69	.496	291	140	54	7	13	1232^1	1417	78	468	403	13.9	4.65	91	.291	.355	93	.215	1	-46	-55	-8	-5.2

■ JOHN WELLS
Wells, John Frederick   b: 11/25/22, Junction City, Kan   BR/TR, 5'11.5", 180 lbs.   Deb: 9/14/44

YEAR	TM/L	W	L	PCT	G	GS	CG	SH	SV	IP	H	HR	BB	SO	RAT	ERA	ERA+	OAV	OOB	BH	AVG	PB	PR	/A	PD	TPI
1944	Bro-N	0	2	.000	4	2	0	0	0	15	18	1	11	7	17.4	5.40	66	.316	.426	1	.250	0	-3	-3	0	-0.2

■ TERRY WELLS
Wells, Terry   b: 9/10/63, Kankakee, Ill.   BL/TL, 6'3", 205 lbs.   Deb: 7/03/90

YEAR	TM/L	W	L	PCT	G	GS	CG	SH	SV	IP	H	HR	BB	SO	RAT	ERA	ERA+	OAV	OOB	BH	AVG	PB	PR	/A	PD	TPI
1990	LA-N	1	2	.333	5	5	0	0	0	20^2	25	4	14	18	17.0	7.84	45	.287	.386	0	.000	-1	-9	-10	-1	-0.9

■ CHRIS WELSH
Welsh, Christopher Charles   b: 4/14/55, Wilmington, Del.   BL/TL, 6'2", 185 lbs.   Deb: 4/12/81

YEAR	TM/L	W	L	PCT	G	GS	CG	SH	SV	IP	H	HR	BB	SO	RAT	ERA	ERA+	OAV	OOB	BH	AVG	PB	PR	/A	PD	TPI
1981	SD-N	6	7	.462	22	19	4	2	0	123^2	122	9	41	51	11.9	3.78	86	.264	.325	6	.146	0	-4	-7	2	-0.5
1982	SD-N	8	8	.500	28	20	3	1	0	139^1	146	16	63	48	13.7	4.91	86	.268	.347	11	.262	1	-20	-23	1	-1.8
1983	SD-N	1	0	1.000	7	1	0	0	0	14^1	13	2	2	5	9.4	2.51	139	.236	.263	0	.000	-0	2	2	-0	0.1
	Mon-N	0	1	.000	16	5	0	0	0	44^2	46	5	18	17	13.7	5.04	71	.267	.351	4	.286	1	-7	-7	0	-0.4
	Yr	0	2	.000	23	6	0	0	0	59	59	7	20	22	12.7	4.42	81	.260	.331	4	.056	1	-5	-6	1	-0.3
1985	Tex-A	2	5	.286	25	6	0	0	0	76^1	101	11	25	31	15.3	4.13	102	.316	.372	0	—	0	0	1	-0	0.1
1986	Cin-N	6	9	.400	24	24	1	0	0	139^1	163	9	40	44	13.3	4.78	81	.301	.353	5	.119	0	-16	-14	0	-1.2

YEAR TM/L	W	L	PCT	G	GS	CG	SH	SV	IP	H	HR	BB	SO	RAT	ERA	ERA+	OAV	OOB	BH	AVG	PB	PR	/A	PD	TPI
Total 5	22	31	.415	122	75	8	3	0	537²	591	52	189	192	13.3	4.45	81	.282	.346	26	.182	5	-46	-49	4	-3.7

■ DICK WELTEROTH
Welteroth, Richard John b: 8/3/27, Williamsport, Pa. BR/TR, 5'11", 165 lbs. Deb: 5/16/48

1948 Was-A	2	1	.667	33	2	0	0	1	65¹	73	6	50	16	17.1	5.51	79	.286	.405	1	.100	-1	-9	-8	-0	-0.8
1949 Was-A	2	5	.286	52	2	0	0	2	95¹	107	6	89	37	18.6	7.36	58	.296	.437	1	.059	-1	-34	-33	0	-3.1
1950 Was-A	0	0	—	5	0	0	0	0	6	5	0	6	2	16.5	3.00	150	.217	.379	0	—	0	1	1	0	0.1
Total 3	4	6	.400	90	4	0	0	3	166²	185	12	145	55	17.9	6.48	66	.290	.422	2	.074	-2	-41	-40	0	-3.8

■ TONY WELZER
Welzer, Anton Frank b: 4/5/1899, Germany d: 3/18/71, Milwaukee, Wis. BR/TR, 5'11", 160 lbs. Deb: 4/13/26

1926 Bos-A	4	3	.571	39	6	1	1	0	139	167	5	53	29	14.4	4.86	84	.308	.373	8	.211	2	-13	-12	4	-0.5
1927 Bos-A	6	11	.353	37	19	8	0	1	171²	214	10	71	56	15.2	4.72	89	.318	.386	4	.095	-2	-11	-9	0	-0.9
Total 2	10	14	.417	76	25	9	1	1	310²	381	15	124	85	14.8	4.78	87	.313	.380	12	.150	-0	-24	-22	4	-1.4

■ BUTCH WENSLOFF
Wensloff, Charles William b: 12/3/15, Sausalito, Cal. BR/TR, 5'11", 185 lbs. Deb: 5/02/43

1943 NY-A	13	11	.542	29	27	18	1	1	223¹	179	7	70	105	10.1	2.54	127	.219	.282	14	.177	-0	19	17	-1	1.7
1947 *NY-A	3	1	.750	11	5	1	0	0	51²	41	3	22	18	11.0	2.61	135	.217	.299	5	.263	-1	6	5	-1	0.6
1948 Cle-A	0	1	.000	1	0	0	0	0	1²	2	1	3	2	27.0	10.80	38	.286	.500	0	—	0	-1	-1	0	0.0
Total 3	16	13	.552	41	32	19	1	1	276²	222	11	95	125	10.3	2.60	126	.219	.287	19	.194	0	24	21	-1	2.3

■ FRED WENZ
Wenz, Frederick Charles "Fireball" b: 8/26/41, Bound Brook, N.J. BR/TR, 6'3", 214 lbs. Deb: 6/04/68

1968 Bos-A	0	0	—	1	0	0	0	0	1	0	0	2	3	18.0	0.00	—	.000	.400	0	—	0	0	0	0	0.0
1969 Bos-A	1	0	1.000	8	0	0	0	0	11	9	7	10	11	15.5	5.73	66	.225	.380	0	—	0	-3	-2	-0	-0.1
1970 Phi-N	2	0	1.000	22	0	0	0	1	30¹	27	2	13	24	12.2	4.45	90	.237	.320	0	.000	-1	-1	-2	-1	-0.2
Total 3	3	0	1.000	31	0	0	0	1	42¹	36	9	25	38	13.2	4.68	84	.229	.339	0	.000	-0	-4	-4	-1	-0.3

■ PERRY WERDEN
Werden, Percival Wheritt b: 7/21/1865, St.Louis, Mo. d: 1/9/34, Minneapolis, Minn. BR/TR, 6'2", 220 lbs. Deb: 4/24/1884 ♦

1884 StL-U	12	1	.923	16	16	12	1	0	141¹	113	1	22	51	8.6	1.97	150	.204	.235	18	.237	-0	16	15	1	1.5

■ BILL WERLE
Werle, William George "Bugs" b: 12/21/20, Oakland, Cal. BL/TL, 6'2.5", 182 lbs. Deb: 4/22/49

1949 Pit-N	12	13	.480	35	29	10	2	0	221	243	22	51	106	12.3	4.24	99	.278	.324	9	.117	-3	-5	-1	1	-0.2
1950 Pit-N	8	16	.333	48	22	6	0	8	215¹	249	25	65	78	13.4	4.60	95	.290	.344	13	.194	1	-11	-5	4	0.0
1951 Pit-N	8	6	.571	59	9	2	0	6	149²	181	20	51	57	14.3	5.65	75	.304	.364	12	.300	4	-28	-24	-1	-1.5
1952 Pit-N	0	0	—	5	0	0	0	0	4	9	1	1	1	22.5	9.00	44	.429	.455	0	—	0	-2	-2	0	-0.1
StL-N	1	2	.333	19	0	0	0	1	39	40	6	15	23	12.9	4.85	77	.268	.339	1	.111	-0	-5	-5	1	-0.3
Yr	1	2	.333	24	0	0	0	1	43	49	7	16	24	13.8	5.23	71	.288	.353	0	.000	-0	-7	-7	2	-0.4
1953 Bos-A	0	1	.000	5	0	0	0	0	11²	7	1	4	4	6.2	1.54	273	.179	.200	0	.000	-0	3	3	1	0.5
1954 Bos-A	0	1	.000	14	0	0	0	0	24²	41	5	10	14	19.3	4.38	94	.376	.438	0	.000	-0	-2	-1	-0	0.0
Total 6	29	39	.426	185	60	18	2	15	665¹	770	80	194	283	13.4	4.69	90	.291	.345	35	.176	1	-50	-34	10	-1.6

■ GEORGE WERLEY
Werley, George William b: 9/8/38, St.Louis, Mo. BR/TR, 6'2", 196 lbs. Deb: 9/29/56

1956 Bal-A	0	0	—	1	0	0	0	0	1	1	0	2	0	27.0	9.00	44	.250	.500	0	—	0	-1	-1	0	0.0

■ JOHNNY WERTS
Werts, Henry Levi b: 4/20/1898, Pomaria, S.C. d: 9/24/90, Newberry, S.C. BR/TR, 5'10", 180 lbs. Deb: 4/14/26

1926 Bos-N	11	9	.550	32	23	7	1	0	189¹	212	6	47	65	12.8	3.28	108	.287	.338	17	.266	4	11	6	2	1.1
1927 Bos-N	4	10	.286	42	15	4	0	1	164¹	204	5	52	39	14.2	4.55	82	.315	.369	7	.163	-0	-11	-15	-1	-1.5
1928 Bos-N	0	2	.000	10	2	0	0	0	18¹	31	2	8	5	19.1	10.31	38	.369	.424	1	.333	0	-13	-13	0	-1.1
1929 Bos-N	0	0	—	4	0	0	0	1	6	13	1	4	2	25.5	10.50	45	.433	.500	1	1.000	0	-4	-4	0	-0.2
Total 4	15	21	.417	88	40	11	1	2	378	460	14	111	111	13.9	4.29	85	.307	.360	26	.234	4	-17	-27	2	-1.7

■ DAVID WEST
West, David Lee b: 9/1/64, Memphis, Tenn. BL/TL, 6'6", 205 lbs. Deb: 9/24/88

1988 NY-N	1	0	1.000	2	1	0	0	0	6	6	0	3	3	13.5	3.00	107	.273	.360	2	1.000	1	0	0	0	0.1
1989 NY-N	0	2	.000	11	2	0	0	0	24¹	25	4	14	19	14.8	7.40	44	.260	.360	1	.200	0	-11	-11	-1	-1.1
Min-A	3	2	.600	10	5	0	0	0	39¹	48	5	19	31	15.8	6.41	65	.306	.388	0	—	0	-11	-10	-1	-1.0
1990 Min-A	7	9	.438	29	27	2	0	0	146¹	142	21	78	92	13.8	5.10	82	.256	.352	0	—	0	-19	-15	-1	-1.5
Total 3	11	13	.458	52	35	2	0	0	216	221	30	114	145	14.3	5.54	73	.267	.360	3	.429	1	-41	-36	-3	-3.5

■ FRANK WEST
West, Frank b: 1873, Wilmerding, Pa. Deb: 7/11/1894

1894 Bos-N	0	0	—	1	0	0	0	0	3	5	0	2	1	21.0	9.00	63	.367	.448	0	.000	-0	-1	-1	0	0.0

■ HI WEST
West, James Hiram b: 8/8/1884, Roseville, Ill. d: 5/25/63, Los Angeles, Cal. BR/TR, 6', 185 lbs. Deb: 9/08/05

1905 Cle-A	2	2	.500	6	4	4	1	0	33	43	0	10	15	14.5	4.09	64	.316	.363	1	.077	-1	-5	-5	-2	-0.7
1911 Cle-A	3	4	.429	13	8	3	0	1	64²	84	1	18	17	14.6	3.76	91	.343	.395	3	.130	-2	-3	-2	-1	-0.4
Total 2	5	6	.455	19	12	7	1	1	97²	127	1	28	32	14.6	3.87	81	.333	.383	4	.111	-3	-8	-8	-2	-1.1

■ LEFTY WEST
West, Weldon Edison b: 9/3/15, Gibsonville, N.C. d: 7/23/79, Hendersonville, N.C. BR/TL, 6', 165 lbs. Deb: 4/30/44

1944 StL-A	0	0	—	11	0	0	0	0	24¹	34	1	19	11	20.0	6.29	57	.366	.414	1	.143	-0	-8	-7	-0	-0.7
1945 StL-A	3	4	.429	24	8	1	0	0	74¹	71	2	31	38	12.3	3.63	97	.245	.318	2	.074	-3	-2	-1	-2	-0.5
Total 2	3	4	.429	35	8	1	0	0	98²	105	3	50	49	14.2	4.29	83	.274	.359	3	.088	-3	-10	-8	-2	-1.2

■ HUYLER WESTERVELT
Westervelt, Huyler b: 10/1/1870, Piermont, N.Y. Deb: 4/21/1894

1894 NY-N	7	10	.412	23	18	11	1	0	141	170	4	76	35	15.7	5.04	104	.295	.377	8	.143	-5	4	3	0	0.0

■ MICKEY WESTON
Weston, Michael Lee b: 3/26/61, Flint, Mich. BR/TR, 6'1", 180 lbs. Deb: 6/18/89

1989 Bal-A	1	0	1.000	7	0	0	0	1	13	18	1	2	7	14.5	5.54	68	.346	.382	0	—	0	-2	-3	-0	-0.2
1990 Bal-A	0	1	1.000	9	2	0	0	0	21	28	6	6	9	14.6	7.71	50	.322	.366	0	—	0	-9	-9	-0	-0.8
Total 2	1	1	.500	16	2	0	0	1	34	46	7	8	16	14.6	6.88	55	.331	.372	0	—	0	-11	-12	-1	-1.0

■ JOHN WETTELAND
Wetteland, John Karl b: 8/21/66, San Mateo, Cal. BR/TR, 6'2", 195 lbs. Deb: 5/31/89

1989 LA-N	5	8	.385	31	12	0	0	1	102²	81	8	34	96	10.1	3.77	91	.218	.284	3	.143	-0	-3	-4	-2	-0.5
1990 LA-N	2	4	.333	22	5	0	0	0	43	44	6	17	36	13.6	4.81	74	.263	.346	1	.143	1	-5	-6	-1	-0.5
Total 2	7	12	.368	53	17	0	0	1	145²	125	14	51	132	11.1	4.08	85	.232	.304	4	.143	1	-8	-10	-2	-1.0

■ BUZZ WETZEL
Wetzel, Charles Edward b: 8/25/1894, Jay, Okla. d: 3/7/41, Globe, Ariz. BR/TR, 6'1", 162 lbs. Deb: 7/25/27

1927 Phi-A	0	0	—	2	1	0	0	0	4²	8	0	5	0	25.1	7.71	55	.400	.520	1	1.000	0	-2	-2	0	0.0

■ SHORTY WETZEL
Wetzel, George William b: 1868, Philadelphia, Pa. d: 2/25/1899, Dayton, Ohio Deb: 8/26/1885

1885 Bal-a	0	2	.000	2	2	2	0	0	18	27	0	9	6	18.0	8.00	41	.332	.399	0	.000	-1	-10	-9	1	-0.6

■ STEFAN WEVER
Wever, Stefan Matthew b: 4/22/58, Marburg, W.Germ BR/TR, 6'8", 245 lbs. Deb: 9/17/82

1982 NY-A	0	1	.000	1	1	0	0	0	2²	6	1	3	2	30.4	27.00	15	.429	.529	0	—	0	-7	-7	0	-0.4

■ GUS WEYHING
Weyhing, August "Cannonball" b: 9/29/1866, Louisville, Ky. d: 9/4/55, Louisville, Ky. BR/TR, 5'10", 145 lbs. Deb: 5/02/1887

1887 Phi-a	26	28	.481	55	55	53	2	0	466¹	465	13	191	193	12.2	4.27	101	.250	.312	42	.201	-8	2	1	-2	-0.7
1888 Phi-a	28	18	.609	47	47	45	3	0	404	314	4	111	204	9.5	2.25	133	.207	.261	40	.217	4	36	33	1	3.6
1889 Phi-a	30	21	.588	54	53	50	4	0	449	382	15	212	213	11.9	2.95	128	.223	.309	25	.131	-14	45	42	-3	2.0
1890 Bro-P	30	16	.652	49	46	38	3	0	390	419	10	179	177	13.8	3.60	124	.263	.337	27	.164	-6	27	37	-10	1.8
1891 Phi-a	31	20	.608	52	51	51	3	0	450	428	12	161	219	11.8	3.18	120	.242	.306	22	.111	-16	27	32	-5	1.0

YEAR	TM/L	W	L	PCT	G	GS	CG	SH	SV	IP	H	HR	BB	SO	RAT	ERA	ERA+	OAV	OOB	BH	AVG	PB	PR	/A	PD	TPI
1892	Phi-N	32	21	.604	59	49	46	6	3	469²	411	9	168	202	11.1	2.66	122	.226	.291	29	.136	-9	33	30	-9	0.9
1893	Phi-N	23	16	.590	42	40	33	2	0	345¹	399	10	145	101	14.2	4.74	97	.281	.347	22	.150	-9	-3	-6	-2	-1.4
1894	Phi-N	16	14	.533	38	34	25	2	1	266¹	365	12	116	81	16.3	5.81	88	.322	.385	20	.174	-8	-14	-21	-3	-2.4
1895	Phi-N	0	2	.000	2	2	0	0	0	9	23	0	13	5	36.0	20.00	24	.469	.580	0	.000	-1	-15	-15	0	-0.9
	Pit-N	1	0	1.000	1	1	1	0	0	9	10	0	5	3	15.0	1.00	452	.277	.365	1	.250	0	4	4	1	0.4
	Lou-N	7	19	.269	28	25	22	1	0	213	285	9	66	53	14.8	5.41	86	.316	.362	20	.225	0	-15	-18	0	-1.4
	Yr	8	21	.276	31	28	23	1	0	231	318	9	84	61	15.7	5.81	80	.322	.375	11	.113	-1	-26	-30	1	-1.9
1896	Lou-N	2	3	.400	5	5	4	0	0	42	62	6	15	9	16.5	6.64	65	.340	.390	2	.133	-1	-11	-11	1	-0.7
1898	Was-N	15	26	.366	45	42	39	0	0	361	428	10	84	92	12.8	4.51	81	.292	.331	25	.177	-5	-36	-34	-2	-3.6
1899	Was-N	17	21	.447	43	38	34	2	0	334²	414	8	76	96	13.2	4.54	86	.303	.340	26	.206	-1	-26	-24	-6	-2.6
1900	StL-N	3	2	.600	7	5	3	0	0	46²	60	2	21	6	15.6	4.63	79	.311	.379	2	.095	-2	-5	-5	-0	-0.6
	Bro-N	3	4	.429	8	8	3	0	0	48	66	1	20	8	16.1	4.31	89	.326	.386	4	.222	-0	-3	-3	-1	-0.2
	Yr	6	6	.500	15	13	6	0	0	94²	126	3	41	14	15.9	4.47	84	.319	.383	1	.026	-2	-8	-8	-1	-0.8
1901	Cle-A	0	0	—	2	1	0	0	0	11¹	16	0	5	0	19.9	7.94	45	.379	.433	0	.000	-1	-5	-6	0	-0.4
	Cin-N	0	1	.000	1	1	1	0	0	9	11	0	2	3	15.0	3.00	107	.299	.368	0	.000	-0	0	0	-0	0.0
Total	14	264	232	.532	538	503	448	28	4	4324¹	4562	120	1566	1665	12.8	3.89	102	.264	.325	307	.166	-79	41	38	-41	-5.2

■ JOHN WEYHING
Weyhing, John b: 6/24/1869, Louisville, Ky. d: 6/20/1890, Louisville, Ky. BL/TL, 6′2″, 185 lbs. Deb: 7/13/1888

YEAR	TM/L	W	L	PCT	G	GS	CG	SH	SV	IP	H	HR	BB	SO	RAT	ERA	ERA+	OAV	OOB	BH	AVG	PB	PR	/A	PD	TPI
1888	Cin-a	3	4	.429	8	8	7	0	0	65²	52	0	17	30	9.5	1.23	256	.210	.260	3	.130	-2	13	14	-1	1.2
1889	Col-a	0	0	—	1	0	0	0	0	1	1	0	4	0	45.0	27.00	13	.252	.628	0	—	0	-3	-3	0	-0.1
Total	2	3	4	.429	9	8	7	0	0	66²	53	0	21	30	10.0	1.62	195	.210	.271	3	.130	-2	11	11	-1	1.1

■ LEE WHEAT
Wheat, Leroy William b: 9/15/29, Edwardsville, Ill BR/TR, 6′4″, 200 lbs. Deb: 4/21/54

YEAR	TM/L	W	L	PCT	G	GS	CG	SH	SV	IP	H	HR	BB	SO	RAT	ERA	ERA+	OAV	OOB	BH	AVG	PB	PR	/A	PD	TPI
1954	Phi-A	0	2	.000	8	1	0	0	0	28¹	38	1	9	7	15.2	5.72	68	.304	.356	1	.125	-0	-6	-6	0	-0.5
1955	KC-A	0	0	—	3	0	0	0	0	2	8	1	3	1	49.5	22.50	19	.533	.611	0	—	0	-4	-4	0	-0.3
Total	2	0	2	.000	11	1	0	0	0	30¹	46	2	12	8	17.5	6.82	57	.329	.386	1	.125	-0	-10	-10	0	-0.8

■ CHARLIE WHEATLEY
Wheatley, Charles b: 6/27/1893, Rosedale, Kan. d: 12/10/82, Tulsa, Okla. BR/TR, 5′11″, 174 lbs. Deb: 9/06/12

YEAR	TM/L	W	L	PCT	G	GS	CG	SH	SV	IP	H	HR	BB	SO	RAT	ERA	ERA+	OAV	OOB	BH	AVG	PB	PR	/A	PD	TPI
1912	Det-A	1	4	.200	5	5	2	0	0	35	45	1	17	14	16.5	6.17	53	.331	.413	0	.000	-2	-11	-11	0	-1.0

■ WOODY WHEATON
Wheaton, Elwood Pierce b: 10/3/14, Philadelphia, Pa. BL/TL, 5′8.5″, 160 lbs. Deb: 9/28/43 ♦

YEAR	TM/L	W	L	PCT	G	GS	CG	SH	SV	IP	H	HR	BB	SO	RAT	ERA	ERA+	OAV	OOB	BH	AVG	PB	PR	/A	PD	TPI
1944	Phi-A	0	1	.000	11	1	1	0	0	38	36	1	20	15	13.5	3.55	98	.255	.352	11	.186	0	-1	-0	-1	0.0

■ RIP WHEELER
Wheeler, Floyd Clark b: 3/2/1898, Marion, Ky. d: 9/18/68, Marion, Ky. BR/TR, 6′, 180 lbs. Deb: 9/30/21

YEAR	TM/L	W	L	PCT	G	GS	CG	SH	SV	IP	H	HR	BB	SO	RAT	ERA	ERA+	OAV	OOB	BH	AVG	PB	PR	/A	PD	TPI
1921	Pit-N	0	0	—	1	0	0	0	0	3	6	0	1	0	24.0	9.00	43	.500	.571	0	.000	-0	-2	-2	0	-0.1
1922	Pit-N	0	0	—	1	0	0	0	0	1	1	0	2	0	27.0	0.00	—	.333	.600	0	—	0	0	0	0	0.0
1923	Chi-N	1	2	.333	3	3	1	0	0	24	28	2	5	5	13.5	4.88	82	.298	.353	1	.111	-1	-2	-2	1	-0.1
1924	Chi-N	3	6	.333	29	4	0	0	0	101¹	103	8	21	16	11.0	3.91	100	.265	.303	7	.219	-1	-0	-0	1	0.0
Total	4	4	8	.333	34	7	1	0	0	129¹	138	10	29	21	11.9	4.18	94	.278	.323	8	.190	-2	-4	-4	2	-0.1

■ GEORGE WHEELER
Wheeler, George L. (b: George L. Heroux) b: 8/3/1869, Methuen, Mass. d: 3/23/46, Santa Ana, Cal. BB/TB, Deb: 9/18/1896

YEAR	TM/L	W	L	PCT	G	GS	CG	SH	SV	IP	H	HR	BB	SO	RAT	ERA	ERA+	OAV	OOB	BH	AVG	PB	PR	/A	PD	TPI
1896	Phi-N	1	1	.500	3	2	2	0	0	16¹	18	0	5	2	12.7	3.86	112	.277	.329	1	.111	-1	1	1	0	0.0
1897	Phi-N	11	10	.524	26	19	17	0	0	191	229	3	62	35	13.7	3.96	106	.295	.347	16	.203	-1	8	5	1	0.4
1898	Phi-N	6	8	.429	15	13	10	0	0	112¹	155	1	36	20	15.3	4.17	82	.325	.372	8	.186	-1	-7	-9	3	-0.6
1899	Phi-N	3	1	.750	6	5	3	0	0	39	44	1	13	3	13.2	6.00	61	.284	.339	4	.235	1	-9	-10	0	-0.6
Total	4	21	20	.512	50	39	32	0	0	358²	446	5	116	60	14.1	4.24	92	.303	.353	29	.196	-2	-8	-13	5	-0.8

■ HARRY WHEELER
Wheeler, Harry Eugene b: 3/3/1858, Versailles, Ind. d: 10/9/1900, Cincinnati, Ohio BR/TR, 5′11″, 165 lbs. Deb: 6/19/1878 M♦

YEAR	TM/L	W	L	PCT	G	GS	CG	SH	SV	IP	H	HR	BB	SO	RAT	ERA	ERA+	OAV	OOB	BH	AVG	PB	PR	/A	PD	TPI
1878	Pro-N	6	1	.857	7	6	6	0	0	62	70	1	25	25	13.8	3.48	63	.271	.335	4	.148	-1	-8	-9	-2	-0.9
1879	Cin-N	0	1	.000	1	1	0	0	0	1	6	0	4	0	90.0	81.00	3	.659	.763	0	.000	-0	-9	-9	0	-0.5
1882	Cin-a	1	2	.333	4	1	1	0	0	21²	21	0	12	10	13.7	5.40	49	.238	.329	86	.250	1	-7	-7	-0	-0.5
1883	Col-a	0	1	.000	1	1	0	0	0	5	13	0	2	0	27.0	7.20	43	.456	.492	84	.226	0	-2	-2	0	-0.1
1884	KC-U	0	1	.000	1	1	1	0	0	8	7	0	0	6	7.9	1.13	245	.220	.220	16	.258	0	2	1	0	0.1
Total	5	7	6	.538	14	10	8	0	0	97²	117	1	43	41	14.7	4.70	51	.281	.348	256	.228	-0	-24	-25	-2	-1.9

■ GARY WHEELOCK
Wheelock, Gary Richard b: 11/29/51, Bakersfield, Cal. BR/TR, 6′3″, 205 lbs. Deb: 9/17/76

YEAR	TM/L	W	L	PCT	G	GS	CG	SH	SV	IP	H	HR	BB	SO	RAT	ERA	ERA+	OAV	OOB	BH	AVG	PB	PR	/A	PD	TPI
1976	Cal-A	0	0	—	2	0	0	0	0	2	6	0	1	2	36.0	27.00	12	.500	.571	0	—	0	-5	-5	0	-0.4
1977	Sea-A	6	9	.400	17	17	2	0	0	88¹	94	16	26	47	12.4	4.89	84	.268	.322	0	—	0	-8	-8	-1	-0.7
1980	Sea-A	0	0	—	1	1	0	0	0	3	4	0	1	1	15.0	6.00	69	.333	.385	0	—	0	-1	-1	0	0.0
Total	3	6	9	.400	20	18	2	0	0	93¹	104	16	28	50	13.0	5.40	76	.277	.333	0	—	0	-14	-14	-0	-1.1

■ JACK WHILLOCK
Whillock, Jack Franklin b: 11/4/42, Clinton, Ark. BR/TR, 6′3″, 195 lbs. Deb: 8/29/71

YEAR	TM/L	W	L	PCT	G	GS	CG	SH	SV	IP	H	HR	BB	SO	RAT	ERA	ERA+	OAV	OOB	BH	AVG	PB	PR	/A	PD	TPI
1971	Det-A	0	2	.000	7	0	0	0	1	8	10	0	2	6	13.5	5.63	64	.323	.364	0	.000	-0	-2	-2	0	-0.1

■ PAT WHITAKER
Whitaker, William H. b: 11/1864, St.Louis, Mo. d: 7/15/02, St.Louis, Mo. TR, Deb: 10/11/1888

YEAR	TM/L	W	L	PCT	G	GS	CG	SH	SV	IP	H	HR	BB	SO	RAT	ERA	ERA+	OAV	OOB	BH	AVG	PB	PR	/A	PD	TPI
1888	Bal-a	1	1	.500	2	2	2	0	0	14	13	0	6	5	12.2	5.14	58	.237	.313	0	.000	-1	-3	-3	2	-0.1
1889	Bal-a	1	0	1.000	1	1	1	0	0	9	10	0	4	1	14.0	2.00	197	.273	.344	1	.250	-0	2	2	0	0.2
Total	2	2	1	.667	3	3	3	0	0	23	23	0	10	6	12.9	3.91	86	.251	.325	1	.100	-1	-1	-1	2	0.1

■ BILL WHITBY
Whitby, William Edward b: 7/29/43, Crewe, Va. BR/TR, 6′1″, 190 lbs. Deb: 6/17/64

YEAR	TM/L	W	L	PCT	G	GS	CG	SH	SV	IP	H	HR	BB	SO	RAT	ERA	ERA+	OAV	OOB	BH	AVG	PB	PR	/A	PD	TPI
1964	Min-A	0	0	—	4	0	0	0	0	6¹	8	3	1	2	12.8	8.53	42	.308	.333	0	.000	-0	-3	-3	0	-0.3

■ BOB WHITCHER
Whitcher, Robert Arthur b: 4/29/17, Berlin, N.H. BL/TL, 5′8″, 165 lbs. Deb: 8/20/45

YEAR	TM/L	W	L	PCT	G	GS	CG	SH	SV	IP	H	HR	BB	SO	RAT	ERA	ERA+	OAV	OOB	BH	AVG	PB	PR	/A	PD	TPI
1945	Bos-N	0	2	.000	6	3	0	0	0	15²	12	1	12	6	13.8	2.87	133	.235	.381	1	.333	0	2	2	0	0.2

■ ABE WHITE
White, Adel b: 5/16/04, Winder, Ga. d: 10/1/78, Atlanta, Ga. BR/TL, 6′, 185 lbs. Deb: 7/10/37

YEAR	TM/L	W	L	PCT	G	GS	CG	SH	SV	IP	H	HR	BB	SO	RAT	ERA	ERA+	OAV	OOB	BH	AVG	PB	PR	/A	PD	TPI
1937	StL-N	0	1	.000	5	0	0	0	0	9¹	14	1	3	2	16.4	6.75	59	.341	.386	1	1.000	0	-3	-3	0	-0.1

■ ERNIE WHITE
White, Ernest Daniel b: 9/5/16, Pacolet Mills, S.C d: 5/22/74, Augusta, Ga. BR/TL, 5′11.5″, 175 lbs. Deb: 5/09/40 C

YEAR	TM/L	W	L	PCT	G	GS	CG	SH	SV	IP	H	HR	BB	SO	RAT	ERA	ERA+	OAV	OOB	BH	AVG	PB	PR	/A	PD	TPI
1940	StL-N	1	1	.500	8	1	0	0	0	21²	29	0	14	15	18.3	4.15	96	.315	.411	3	.429	1	-1	-0	1	0.1
1941	StL-N	17	7	.708	32	25	12	3	2	210	169	12	70	117	10.5	2.40	157	.217	.287	15	.190	0	29	32	-4	3.1
1942	*StL-N	7	5	.583	26	19	7	1	2	128¹	113	11	41	67	10.9	2.52	136	.232	.294	8	.195	0	11	13	-2	1.2
1943	*StL-N	5	5	.500	14	10	5	1	0	78²	78	4	33	28	12.8	3.78	89	.257	.332	6	.214	0	-3	-4	-1	-0.3
1946	Bos-N	0	1	.000	12	1	0	0	0	23²	22	1	12	8	12.9	4.18	82	.256	.347	1	.250	0	-2	-2	-1	-0.2
1947	Bos-N	0	0	—	1	1	0	0	0	4	1	0	1	0	4.5	0.00	—	.083	.154	1	1.000	0	2	2	0	0.2
1948	Bos-N	0	2	.000	15	0	0	0	2	23	13	0	17	9	11.7	1.96	196	.167	.316	0	.000	0	5	5	-1	0.4
Total	7	30	21	.588	108	57	24	5	6	489¹	425	28	188	244	11.5	2.78	130	.231	.306	34	.209	2	41	45	-8	4.5

■ DEKE WHITE
White, George Frederick b: 9/8/1872, Albany, N.Y. d: 11/5/57, Ilion, N.Y. BB/TL, Deb: 9/14/1895

YEAR	TM/L	W	L	PCT	G	GS	CG	SH	SV	IP	H	HR	BB	SO	RAT	ERA	ERA+	OAV	OOB	BH	AVG	PB	PR	/A	PD	TPI
1895	Phi-N	1	0	1.000	3	1	1	0	1	17¹	17	1	13	6	15.6	9.87	49	.253	.374	1	.125	-1	-10	-10	-0	-0.7

■ DOC WHITE
White, Guy Harris b: 4/9/1879, Washington, D.C. d: 2/19/69, Silver Spring, Md. BL/TL, 6′1″, 150 lbs. Deb: 4/22/01 ♦

YEAR	TM/L	W	L	PCT	G	GS	CG	SH	SV	IP	H	HR	BB	SO	RAT	ERA	ERA+	OAV	OOB	BH	AVG	PB	PR	/A	PD	TPI
1901	Phi-N	14	13	.519	31	27	22	0	0	236²	241	2	56	132	11.8	3.19	106	.262	.314	27	.276	5	3	5	2	1.2
1902	Phi-N	16	20	.444	36	35	34	3	1	306	273	6	72	185	10.6	2.53	114	.242	.294	47	.263	5	9	10	1	2.1
1903	Chi-A	17	16	.515	37	36	29	1	0	300	258	4	69	114	9.8	2.13	132	.232	.277	20	.202	6	28	23	2	3.2
1904	Chi-A	16	12	.571	30	30	23	7	0	228	201	6	68	115	10.6	1.78	138	.238	.294	12	.158	1	21	17	0	2.0

YEAR	TM/L	W	L	PCT	G	GS	CG	SH	SV	IP	H	HR	BB	SO	RAT	ERA	ERA+	OAV	OOB	BH	AVG	PB	PR	/A	PD	TPI
1905	Chi-A	17	13	.567	36	33	25	4	0	260¹	204	2	58	120	9.1	1.76	140	.217	.263	15	.167	0	26	21	-0	2.2
1906	*Chi-A	18	6	.750	28	24	20	7	0	219¹	160	2	38	95	**8.1**	**1.52**	**167**	.207	**.244**	12	.185	3	29	25	2	3.6
1907	Chi-A	**27**	13	.675	46	35	24	6	1	291	270	3	38	141	9.5	2.26	106	.248	.273	9	.222	4	9	5	5	1.4
1908	Chi-A	18	13	.581	41	37	24	5	0	296	267	3	69	126	10.5	2.55	91	.244	.295	25	.229	4	-5	-8	7	0.4
1909	Chi-A	11	9	.550	24	21	14	3	0	177²	149	1	31	77	9.5	1.72	136	.226	.269	45	.234	6	15	12	-1	1.4
1910	Chi-A	15	13	.536	33	29	20	2	1	236²	219	2	50	111	10.7	2.66	90	.243	.291	25	.198	2	-4	-7	3	0.0
1911	Chi-A	10	14	.417	34	29	16	4	2	214¹	219	2	35	72	11.0	2.98	108	.271	.309	20	.256	3	9	6	0	0.9
1912	Chi-A	8	10	.444	32	19	9	1	0	172	172	1	47	57	11.9	3.24	99	.267	.325	7	.125	-1	1	-1	-0	-0.2
1913	Chi-A	2	4	.333	19	8	2	0	0	103	106	1	39	39	13.1	3.50	84	.278	.353	3	.120	-1	-6	-7	3	-0.4
Total	13	189	156	.548	427	363	262	45	5	3041	2743	32	670	1384	10.3	2.39	112	.242	.289	278	.217	37	134	100	23	17.8

■ HAL WHITE
White, Harold George b: 3/18/19, Utica, N.Y.   BR/TR, 5'10", 165 lbs.   Deb: 4/22/41

YEAR	TM/L	W	L	PCT	G	GS	CG	SH	SV	IP	H	HR	BB	SO	RAT	ERA	ERA+	OAV	OOB	BH	AVG	PB	PR	/A	PD	TPI
1941	Det-A	0	0	—	4	0	0	0	0	9	11	0	6	2	17.0	6.00	76	.306	.405	0	.000	-0	-2	-1	0	-0.1
1942	Det-A	12	12	.500	34	25	12	4	1	216²	212	6	82	93	12.4	2.91	136	.252	.323	13	.169	-1	18	25	1	2.7
1943	Det-A	7	12	.368	32	24	7	2	2	177²	150	6	71	58	11.2	3.39	104	.228	.304	8	.140	-1	-2	3	1	0.3
1946	Det-A	1	1	.500	11	1	1	0	0	27¹	34	5	15	12	16.1	5.60	65	.312	.395	0	.000	-1	-6	-6	1	-0.5
1947	Det-A	4	5	.444	35	5	0	0	2	84²	91	5	47	33	14.9	3.61	104	.279	.373	3	.167	0	1	1	1	0.4
1948	Det-A	2	1	.667	27	0	0	0	1	42²	46	2	26	17	15.4	6.12	71	.272	.372	2	.154	0	-9	-8	-1	-0.7
1949	Det-A	1	0	1.000	9	0	0	0	2	12	5	0	4	4	6.8	0.00	—	.125	.205	1	.333	0	6	6	1	0.6
1950	Det-A	9	6	.600	42	8	3	1	1	111	96	7	65	53	13.1	4.54	103	.239	.347	4	.121	-2	0	2	0	0.0
1951	Det-A	3	4	.429	38	4	0	0	4	76	74	7	49	23	14.8	4.74	88	.264	.378	4	.250	-0	-5	-5	2	-0.2
1952	Det-A	1	8	.111	41	0	0	0	5	63¹	53	1	39	18	13.1	3.69	103	.237	.350	2	.182	-0	-0	1	1	0.2
1953	StL-A	0	0	—	10	0	0	0	0	10¹	8	1	3	2	10.5	2.61	161	.205	.279	0	.000	0	2	2	0	0.2
	StL-N	6	5	.545	49	0	0	0	7	84²	84	5	39	32	13.1	2.98	143	.272	.353	0	.000	-2	12	12	1	1.1
1954	StL-N	0	0	—	4	0	0	0	0	5	11	2	4	2	28.8	19.80	21	.440	.533	0	.000	-0	-9	-9	0	-0.7
Total	12	46	54	.460	336	67	23	7	25	920¹	875	47	450	349	13.1	3.78	106	.253	.342	37	.145	-7	6	23	8	3.3

■ DEACON WHITE
White, James Laurie b: 12/7/1847, Caton, N.Y.   d: 7/7/39, Aurora, Ill.   BL/TR, 5'11", 175 lbs.   Deb: 5/04/1871 M♦

YEAR	TM/L	W	L	PCT	G	GS	CG	SH	SV	IP	H	HR	BB	SO	RAT	ERA	ERA+	OAV	OOB	BH	AVG	PB	PR	/A	PD	TPI
1876	Chi-N	0	0	—	1	0	0	0	1	2	1	0	0	3	4.5	0.00	—	.138	.138	104	.343	0	1	1	0	0.0
1890	Buf-P	0	0	—	1	0	0	0	0	8	18	0	2	0	22.5	9.00	46	.427	.453	114	.260	0	-4	-4	-0	-0.2
Total	2	0	0	—	2	0	0	0	1	10	19	0	2	3	18.9	7.20	53	.385	.409	1619	.303	0	-4	-4	-0	-0.2

■ LARRY WHITE
White, Larry David b: 9/25/58, San Fernando, Cal.   BR/TR, 6'5", 190 lbs.   Deb: 9/20/83

YEAR	TM/L	W	L	PCT	G	GS	CG	SH	SV	IP	H	HR	BB	SO	RAT	ERA	ERA+	OAV	OOB	BH	AVG	PB	PR	/A	PD	TPI
1983	LA-N	0	0	—	4	0	0	0	0	7	4	0	3	5	9.0	1.29	279	.174	.269	0	—	0	2	2	0	0.2
1984	LA-N	0	1	.000	7	1	0	0	0	12	9	2	6	10	11.3	3.00	118	.209	.306	0	.000	-0	1	1	-0	0.0
Total	2	0	1	.000	11	1	0	0	0	19	13	2	9	15	10.4	2.37	150	.197	.293	0	.000	-0	3	3	0	0.2

■ KIRBY WHITE
White, Oliver Kirby "Red" or "Buck" b: 1/3/1884, Hillsboro, Ohio   d: 4/22/43, Hillsboro, Ohio   BL/TR, 6', 190 lbs.   Deb: 5/04/09

YEAR	TM/L	W	L	PCT	G	GS	CG	SH	SV	IP	H	HR	BB	SO	RAT	ERA	ERA+	OAV	OOB	BH	AVG	PB	PR	/A	PD	TPI
1909	Bos-N	6	13	.316	23	19	11	0	0	148¹	134	5	80	53	13.0	3.22	88	.245	.343	8	.160	-1	-10	-6	-1	-0.8
1910	Bos-N	1	2	.333	3	3	3	0	0	26	15	2	12	6	10.4	1.38	240	.188	.316	2	.333	1	5	6	0	0.8
	Pit-N	10	9	.526	30	21	7	3	2	153¹	142	2	75	42	13.0	3.46	90	.258	.352	12	.261	4	-7	-6	-3	-0.4
	Yr	11	11	.500	33	24	10	3	2	179¹	157	4	87	48	12.5	3.16	99	.248	.343	8	.154	4	-3	-1	-2	0.4
1911	Pit-N	0	1	.000	2	1	0	0	0	3	3	1	1	1	12.0	9.00	38	.250	.308	0	.000	-0	-2	-2	0	-0.1
Total	3	17	25	.405	58	44	21	3	2	330¹	294	10	168	102	12.8	3.24	93	.247	.345	22	.214	3	-15	-9	-3	-0.5

■ STEVE WHITE
White, Stephen Vincent b: 12/21/1884, Dorchester, Mass.   d: 1/29/75, Braintree, Mass.   BR/TR, 5'10", 160 lbs.   Deb: 5/29/12

YEAR	TM/L	W	L	PCT	G	GS	CG	SH	SV	IP	H	HR	BB	SO	RAT	ERA	ERA+	OAV	OOB	BH	AVG	PB	PR	/A	PD	TPI
1912	Was-A	0	0	—	1	0	0	0	0	0²	2	1	0	1	27.0	0.00	—	.667	.667	0	—	0	0	0	0	0.0
	Bos-N	0	0	—	3	0	0	0	0	6	9	0	5	2	22.5	6.00	60	.391	.517	0	.000	-0	-2	-2	0	-0.1

■ BILL WHITE
White, William Dighton b: 5/1/1860, Bridgeport, Ohio   d: 12/29/24, Bellaire, Ohio   TR ,   Deb: 5/03/1884 ♦

YEAR	TM/L	W	L	PCT	G	GS	CG	SH	SV	IP	H	HR	BB	SO	RAT	ERA	ERA+	OAV	OOB	BH	AVG	PB	PR	/A	PD	TPI
1886	Lou-a	0	0	—	1	0	0	0	0	1	2	0	2	1	36.0	9.00	41	.398	.569	143	.257	0	-1	-1	0	0.0

■ WILL WHITE
White, William Henry "Whoop-La" b: 10/11/1854, Caton, N.Y.   d: 8/31/11, Port Carling, Ont. Canada   BB/TR, 5'9.5", 175 lbs.   Deb: 7/20/1877 M

YEAR	TM/L	W	L	PCT	G	GS	CG	SH	SV	IP	H	HR	BB	SO	RAT	ERA	ERA+	OAV	OOB	BH	AVG	PB	PR	/A	PD	TPI
1877	Bos-N	2	1	.667	3	3	3	1	0	27	27	0	2	7	9.7	3.00	94	.245	.259	3	.200	-1	-1	-1	-1	-0.1
1878	Cin-N	30	21	.588	52	52	52	5	0	468	477	1	45	169	10.0	1.79	119	.251	.268	28	.142	-7	27	18	-2	0.6
1879	Cin-N	43	31	.581	**76**	75	**75**	4	0	**680**	676	10	68	232	9.8	1.99	117	.243	.261	40	.136	-15	**39**	26	-7	0.1
1880	Cin-N	18	42	.300	62	62	58	3	0	517¹	550	9	56	161	10.5	2.14	116	.259	.278	35	.169	-10	13	20	-7	0.4
1881	Det-N	0	2	.000	2	2	2	0	0	18	24	0	2	5	13.0	5.00	58	.307	.324	0	.000	-1	-4	-4	-0	-0.4
1882	Cin-a	**40**	12	**.769**	54	54	**52**	8	0	480	411	3	71	122	9.0	1.54	173	.216	.244	55	.266	6	**61**	60	13	**7.7**
1883	Cin-a	**43**	22	.662	65	64	64	**6**	0	577	473	16	104	141	9.0	**2.09**	156	.209	.244	54	.225	3	**78**	75	-3	**6.9**
1884	Cin-a	34	18	.654	52	52	52	**7**	0	456	479	16	74	118	10.9	3.32	101	.256	.284	35	.190	-2	-3	1	-6	-0.5
1885	Cin-a	18	15	.545	34	34	33	2	0	293¹	295	9	64	80	11.0	3.53	92	.250	.289	20	.169	-3	-9	-9	-3	-1.3
1886	Cin-a	1	2	.333	3	3	3	0	0	26	28	1	10	6	13.2	4.15	84	.262	.326	1	.111	-1	-2	-2	-0	-0.1
Total	10	229	166	.580	403	401	394	36	0	3542²	3440	65	496	1041	10.0	2.28	120	.240	.266	271	.183	-32	198	181	-16	13.3

■ JOHN WHITEHEAD
Whitehead, John Henderson "Silent John" b: 4/27/09, Coleman, Tex.   d: 10/20/64, Bonham, Tex.   BR/TR, 6'2", 195 lbs.   Deb: 4/19/35

YEAR	TM/L	W	L	PCT	G	GS	CG	SH	SV	IP	H	HR	BB	SO	RAT	ERA	ERA+	OAV	OOB	BH	AVG	PB	PR	/A	PD	TPI
1935	Chi-A	13	13	.500	28	27	18	1	0	222¹	209	17	101	72	12.6	3.72	124	.250	.332	12	.146	-5	18	22	3	1.9
1936	Chi-A	13	13	.500	34	32	15	1	1	230²	254	9	98	70	13.9	4.64	112	.276	.349	21	.241	1	10	14	3	1.7
1937	Chi-A	11	8	.579	26	24	8	4	0	165²	191	14	56	45	13.7	4.07	113	.294	.354	13	.224	1	10	10	-1	0.9
1938	Chi-A	10	11	.476	32	24	10	2	2	183¹	218	12	80	38	14.8	4.76	103	.299	.370	6	.100	-4	1	3	-0	0.0
1939	Chi-A	0	3	.000	7	4	0	0	0	32	60	4	5	9	18.3	8.16	58	.408	.428	0	.000	-1	-13	-12	0	-1.0
	StL-A	1	3	.250	26	4	0	0	1	66	88	10	17	9	14.6	5.86	83	.321	.365	1	.059	-2	-9	-7	1	-0.6
	Yr	1	6	.143	33	8	0	0	1	98	148	14	22	18	15.8	6.61	73	.352	.387	2	.077	-3	-22	-20	1	-1.6
1940	StL-A	1	3	.250	15	4	1	1	0	40	46	3	14	11	13.5	5.40	85	.286	.343	2	.167	-1	-5	-4	-0	-0.3
1942	StL-A	0	0	—	4	0	0	0	0	4	8	0	1	0	22.5	6.75	55	.421	.476	0	—	-0	-1	-1	0	0.0
Total	7	49	54	.476	172	119	52	9	4	944	1074	69	372	254	14.0	4.60	105	.287	.355	55	.169	-11	11	24	6	2.6

■ MILT WHITEHEAD
Whitehead, Milton P. b: 1862, Canada   d: 8/15/01, Highland Township San Bernardino County, Cal.   Deb: 4/20/1884 ♦

YEAR	TM/L	W	L	PCT	G	GS	CG	SH	SV	IP	H	HR	BB	SO	RAT	ERA	ERA+	OAV	OOB	BH	AVG	PB	PR	/A	PD	TPI
1884	StL-U	0	1	.000	1	1	1	0	0	8	14	0	2	2	18.0	9.00	33	.360	.391	83	.211	-0	-5	-5	0	-0.3

■ EARL WHITEHILL
Whitehill, Earl Oliver b: 2/7/1900, Cedar Rapids, Iowa   d: 10/22/54, Omaha, Neb.   BL/TL, 5'9.5", 174 lbs.   Deb: 9/15/23 C

YEAR	TM/L	W	L	PCT	G	GS	CG	SH	SV	IP	H	HR	BB	SO	RAT	ERA	ERA+	OAV	OOB	BH	AVG	PB	PR	/A	PD	TPI
1923	Det-A	2	0	1.000	8	3	1	0	0	33	22	2	15	19	10.9	2.73	142	.188	.296	4	.364	1	5	4	-0	0.5
1924	Det-A	17	9	.654	35	32	16	2	0	233	260	8	79	65	13.6	3.86	106	.288	.353	19	.213	1	10	6	0	0.6
1925	Det-A	11	11	.500	35	33	15	1	2	239¹	267	13	88	83	13.7	4.66	92	.293	.361	19	.218	0	-7	-9	-1	-0.9
1926	Det-A	16	13	.552	36	34	13	0	0	252²	271	7	79	109	12.8	3.99	102	.277	.336	23	.253	4	1	2	-1	0.5
1927	Det-A	16	14	.533	41	31	17	3	3	236	238	4	105	95	13.4	3.36	125	.267	.350	16	.205	-0	21	22	-3	1.9
1928	Det-A	11	16	.407	31	30	12	1	0	196¹	214	8	78	93	13.4	4.31	95	.277	.344	13	.194	-1	-6	-4	0	-0.4
1929	Det-A	14	15	.483	38	28	18	1	1	245¹	267	16	96	103	13.4	4.62	93	.280	.348	23	.256	5	-10	-9	-1	-0.9
1930	Det-A	17	13	.567	34	31	16	0	1	220²	248	8	80	109	13.7	4.24	113	.285	.351	16	.193	-4	10	14	-2	-0.7
1931	Det-A	13	16	.448	34	34	22	0	0	271¹	287	22	118	81	13.6	4.08	112	.274	.351	15	.155	-5	9	15	3	1.3
1932	Det-A	16	12	.571	33	33	19	2	0	244	255	17	93	81	13.0	4.54	104	.281	.337	22	.244	-2	-5	-1	0	0.5
1933	*Was-A	22	8	.733	39	37	19	2	1	270	271	9	100	96	12.5	3.33	125	.262	.329	24	.222	2	28	25	-2	2.4
1934	Was-A	14	11	.560	32	31	15	0	0	235	269	16	94	96	14.0	4.52	96	.290	.357	17	.200	4	-1	-5	-1	-0.2
1935	Was-A	14	13	.519	34	34	19	1	0	279¹	318	16	104	102	13.8	4.29	101	.289	.354	19	.183	-1	5	1	1	0.1
1936	Was-A	14	11	.560	28	28	14	0	0	212¹	252	17	89	63	14.5	4.87	98	.294	.362	13	.169	-0	4	-2	-1	-0.2

YEAR	TM/L	W	L	PCT	G	GS	CG	SH	SV	IP	H	HR	BB	SO	RAT	ERA	ERA+	OAV	OOB	BH	AVG	PB	PR	/A	PD	TPI
1937	Cle-A	8	8	.500	33	22	6	1	2	147	189	9	80	53	16.8	6.49	71	.322	.409	11	.224	1	-31	-31	2	-2.4
1938	Cle-A	9	8	.529	26	23	4	0	0	160¹	187	18	83	60	15.7	5.56	83	.289	.378	7	.125	-2	-14	-16	-1	-1.6
1939	Chi-N	4	7	.364	24	11	2	1	1	89¹	102	8	50	42	15.8	5.14	77	.292	.389	3	.103	-2	-12	-12	-1	-1.3
Total 17		218	185	.541	541	473	226	16	11	3564²	3917	192	1431	1350	13.8	4.36	100	.282	.353	264	.204	4	10	6	-10	1.1

■ CHARLIE WHITEHOUSE — Whitehouse, Charles Evis "Lefty" b: 1/25/1894, Charleston, Ill. d: 7/19/60, Indianapolis, Ind BB/TL, 6', 152 lbs. Deb: 8/29/14

YEAR	TM/L	W	L	PCT	G	GS	CG	SH	SV	IP	H	HR	BB	SO	RAT	ERA	ERA+	OAV	OOB	BH	AVG	PB	PR	/A	PD	TPI
1914	Ind-F	2	0	1.000	8	2	2	0	0	26	34	0	5	10	13.8	4.85	72	.324	.361	0	.000	-1	-5	-4	0	-0.4
1915	New-F	2	2	.500	11	3	1	0	0	39²	46	0	17	18	15.4	4.31	66	.298	.385	0	.000	-1	-6	-6	-1	-0.7
1919	Was-A	0	1	.000	6	1	0	0	0	12	13	1	6	5	14.3	4.50	71	.283	.365	0	.000	-0	-2	-2	-0	-0.1
Total 3		4	3	.571	25	6	3	0	0	77²	93	1	28	33	14.7	4.52	69	.304	.374	0	.000	-2	-12	-12	-1	-1.2

■ GIL WHITEHOUSE — Whitehouse, Gilbert Arthur b: 10/15/1893, Somerville, Mass. d: 2/14/26, Brewer, Me. BB/TR, 5'10", 170 lbs. Deb: 6/20/12 ♦

YEAR	TM/L	W	L	PCT	G	GS	CG	SH	SV	IP	H	HR	BB	SO	RAT	ERA	ERA+	OAV	OOB	BH	AVG	PB	PR	/A	PD	TPI
1915	New-F	0	0	—	1	0	0	0	0	1	0	0	1	0	9.0	0.00	—	.000	.268	27	.225	0	0	0	0	0.0

■ LEN WHITEHOUSE — Whitehouse, Leonard Joseph b: 9/10/57, Burlington, Vt. BL/TL, 5'11", 175 lbs. Deb: 9/01/81

YEAR	TM/L	W	L	PCT	G	GS	CG	SH	SV	IP	H	HR	BB	SO	RAT	ERA	ERA+	OAV	OOB	BH	AVG	PB	PR	/A	PD	TPI
1981	Tex-A	0	1	.000	2	1	0	0	0	3¹	8	1	2	2	27.0	16.20	21	.500	.556	0	—	0	-5	-5	0	-0.3
1983	Min-A	7	1	.875	60	0	0	0	2	73²	70	6	44	44	14.2	4.15	102	.261	.369	0	—	0	-1	1	-1	0.0
1984	Min-A	2	2	.500	30	0	0	0	1	31¹	29	3	17	18	13.8	3.16	133	.254	.361	0	—	0	3	4	-0	0.3
1985	Min-A	0	0	—	5	0	0	0	1	7¹	12	4	2	4	17.2	11.05	40	.353	.389	0	—	0	-6	-5	0	-0.4
Total 4		9	4	.692	97	1	0	0	4	115²	119	14	65	68	14.6	4.67	90	.275	.375	0	—	0	-8	-6	-1	-0.4

■ WALLY WHITEHURST — Whitehurst, Walter Richard b: 4/11/64, Shreveport, La. BR/TR, 6'3", 180 lbs. Deb: 7/17/89

YEAR	TM/L	W	L	PCT	G	GS	CG	SH	SV	IP	H	HR	BB	SO	RAT	ERA	ERA+	OAV	OOB	BH	AVG	PB	PR	/A	PD	TPI
1989	NY-N	0	1	.000	9	1	0	0	0	14	17	2	5	9	14.1	4.50	73	.293	.349	0	.000	0	-2	-2	-0	-0.1
1990	NY-N	1	0	1.000	38	0	0	0	2	65²	63	5	9	46	9.9	3.29	111	.251	.277	2	.250	0	4	3	0	0.3
Total 2		1	1	.500	47	1	0	0	2	79²	80	7	14	55	10.6	3.50	102	.259	.291	2	.222	1	2	1	0	0.2

■ JESSE WHITING — Whiting, Jesse W. b: 5/30/1879, Philadelphia, Pa. d: 10/28/37, Philadelphia, Pa. Deb: 9/27/02

YEAR	TM/L	W	L	PCT	G	GS	CG	SH	SV	IP	H	HR	BB	SO	RAT	ERA	ERA+	OAV	OOB	BH	AVG	PB	PR	/A	PD	TPI
1902	Phi-N	0	1	.000	1	1	1	0	0	9	13	0	6	0	19.0	5.00	56	.337	.426	1	.333	0	-2	-2	0	-0.1
1906	Bro-N	1	1	.500	3	2	2	1	0	24²	26	0	6	7	12.0	2.92	86	.286	.337	3	.300	1	-1	-1	1	0.0
1907	Bro-N	0	0	—	1	0	0	0	0	3	3	0	3	2	18.0	12.00	20	.273	.429	0	.000	-0	-3	-3	0	-0.2
Total 3		1	2	.333	5	3	3	1	0	36²	42	0	15	9	14.2	4.17	62	.299	.370	4	.267	0	-6	-6	1	-0.3

■ ART WHITNEY — Whitney, Arthur Wilson b: 1/16/1858, Brockton, Mass. d: 8/15/43, Lowell, Mass. BR/TR, 5'8", 155 lbs. Deb: 5/01/1880 ♦

YEAR	TM/L	W	L	PCT	G	GS	CG	SH	SV	IP	H	HR	BB	SO	RAT	ERA	ERA+	OAV	OOB	BH	AVG	PB	PR	/A	PD	TPI
1882	Det-N	0	1	.000	3	2	1	0	0	18	31	1	8	11	19.5	6.00	49	.359	.414	21	.183	-1	-6	-6	-0	-0.4
1886	Pit-a	0	0	—	1	0	0	0	0	6	7	0	3	2	15.0	3.00	113	.278	.355	122	.239	0	0	0	-0	0.0
1889	*NY-N	0	1	.000	1	0	0	0	0	6	7	0	3	3	15.0	3.00	132	.282	.360	103	.218	0	1	1	-0	0.1
Total 3		0	2	.000	5	2	1	0	0	30	45	1	14	16	17.7	4.80	67	.330	.393	820	.223	-1	-5	-5	-1	-0.3

■ JIM WHITNEY — Whitney, James Evans "Grasshopper Jim" b: 11/10/1857, Conklin, N.Y. d: 5/21/1891, Binghamton, N.Y. BL/TR, 6'2", 172 lbs. Deb: 5/02/1881 ♦

YEAR	TM/L	W	L	PCT	G	GS	CG	SH	SV	IP	H	HR	BB	SO	RAT	ERA	ERA+	OAV	OOB	BH	AVG	PB	PR	/A	PD	TPI
1881	Bos-N	31	33	.484	66	63	57	6	0	552¹	548	6	90	162	10.4	2.48	107	.248	.277	72	.255	11	18	11	-4	1.7
1882	Bos-N	24	21	.533	49	48	46	3	0	420	404	3	41	180	9.5	2.64	108	.239	.257	81	.323	23	12	10	2	3.7
1883	Bos-N	37	21	.638	62	56	54	1	2	514	492	7	35	345	9.2	2.24	138	.237	.250	115	.281	20	51	49	0	7.3
1884	Bos-N	23	14	.622	38	37	35	6	0	336	272	12	27	270	8.0	2.09	138	.209	.225	70	.259	9	33	30	3	4.5
1885	Bos-N	18	32	.360	51	50	50	2	0	441¹	503	14	37	200	11.0	2.98	90	.274	.288	68	.234	7	-8	-15	6	0.0
1886	KC-N	12	32	.273	46	44	42	3	0	393	465	9	55	167	11.9	4.49	84	.283	.306	59	.239	6	-52	-31	6	-0.9
1887	Was-N	24	21	.533	47	47	46	3	0	404²	430	16	42	146	10.5	3.22	125	.265	.283	53	.264	10	37	36	4	4.6
1888	Was-N	18	21	.462	39	39	37	2	0	325	317	7	54	79	10.3	3.05	91	.246	.277	24	.170	-1	-8	-9	-1	-1.0
1889	Ind-N	2	7	.222	9	8	7	0	0	70	106	4	19	16	16.1	6.81	61	.338	.376	12	.375	5	-22	-20	-1	-1.1
1890	Phi-a	2	2	.500	6	4	3	0	0	41	60	11	14	16	16.2	5.17	74	.340	.378	5	.238	0	-6	-6	0	-0.4
Total 10		191	204	.484	413	396	377	26	2	3496¹	3598	79	411	1571	10.3	2.97	104	.254	.275	559	.261	89	57	51	16	18.4

■ BILL WHITROCK — Whitrock, William Franklin b: 3/4/1870, Cincinnati, Ohio d: 7/26/35, Derby, Conn. TR, 5'7.5", 170 lbs. Deb: 5/03/1890

YEAR	TM/L	W	L	PCT	G	GS	CG	SH	SV	IP	H	HR	BB	SO	RAT	ERA	ERA+	OAV	OOB	BH	AVG	PB	PR	/A	PD	TPI
1890	StL-a	5	6	.455	16	11	10	0	1	105	104	2	40	39	12.3	3.51	123	.251	.316	7	.146	-3	4	9	1	0.7
1893	Lou-N	2	4	.333	6	6	4	0	0	37²	54	3	14	7	16.2	7.88	56	.326	.379	6	.286	1	-13	-15	0	-0.9
1894	Lou-N	0	1	.000	1	1	0	0	0	4	8	0	2	0	22.5	9.00	57	.410	.465	0	.000	-0	-2	-2	-0	-0.1
	Cin-N	2	6	.250	10	8	8	0	0	70¹	110	7	39	9	19.1	6.65	84	.352	.424	13	.217	-2	-10	-9	-0	-0.8
	Yr	2	7	.222	11	9	8	0	0	74¹	118	7	41	9	19.3	6.78	82	.355	.426	2	.032	-3	-12	-10	-0	-0.9
1896	Phi-N	0	1	.000	2	1	1	0	0	9	10	0	3	1	13.0	3.00	144	.279	.335	0	.000	-1	1	1	-0	0.1
Total 4		9	18	.333	35	27	23	0	1	226	286	12	98	56	15.3	5.30	90	.302	.367	26	.194	-5	-20	-14	1	-1.0

■ EDDIE WHITSON — Whitson, Eddie Lee b: 5/19/55, Johnson City, Tenn. BR/TR, 6'3", 195 lbs. Deb: 9/04/77

YEAR	TM/L	W	L	PCT	G	GS	CG	SH	SV	IP	H	HR	BB	SO	RAT	ERA	ERA+	OAV	OOB	BH	AVG	PB	PR	/A	PD	TPI
1977	Pit-N	1	0	1.000	5	2	0	0	0	15²	11	0	9	10	11.5	3.45	116	.204	.317	0	.000	-1	1	1	-0	0.0
1978	Pit-N	5	6	.455	43	0	0	0	0	74¹	66	5	37	64	12.7	3.27	113	.243	.338	2	.182	-0	3	4	-1	0.3
1979	Pit-N	2	3	.400	19	7	0	0	1	57²	53	6	36	31	14.0	4.37	89	.238	.346	0	.000	-1	-4	-3	-0	-0.4
	SF-N	5	8	.385	18	17	2	0	0	100¹	98	5	39	62	12.6	3.95	89	.254	.329	5	.156	-0	-2	-5	-0	-0.5
	Yr	7	11	.389	37	24	2	0	1	158	151	11	75	93	13.1	4.10	89	.248	.334	1	.022	-2	-6	-8	-1	-0.9
1980	SF-N	11	13	.458	34	34	6	2	0	211²	222	7	56	90	12.0	3.10	114	.271	.321	6	.091	-4	12	10	-2	0.5
1981	SF-N	6	9	.400	22	22	2	1	0	123	130	10	47	65	13.1	4.02	85	.273	.340	3	.091	-1	-7	-8	-2	-1.0
1982	Cle-A	4	2	.667	40	9	1	1	2	107²	91	6	58	61	12.5	3.26	125	.231	.330	0	—	0	10	10	-2	0.8
1983	SD-N	5	7	.417	31	21	2	0	1	144¹	143	23	50	81	12.1	4.30	81	.256	.318	8	.182	1	-11	-13	-4	-1.5
1984	*SD-N	14	8	.636	31	31	1	0	0	189	181	16	42	103	10.8	3.24	110	.255	.299	3	.049	-5	7	7	2	0.4
1985	NY-A	10	8	.556	30	30	2	2	0	158²	201	19	43	89	14.0	4.88	82	.309	.354	0	—	0	-13	-15	-1	-1.5
1986	NY-A	5	2	.714	14	4	0	0	0	37	54	5	23	27	18.7	7.54	54	.335	.418	0	—	0	-14	-14	0	-1.2
	SD-N	1	7	.125	17	12	0	0	0	75²	85	8	37	46	14.5	5.59	65	.287	.366	3	.167	-0	-16	-16	0	-1.5
1987	SD-N	10	13	.435	36	34	3	1	0	205²	197	36	64	135	11.6	4.73	84	.251	.310	8	.123	-1	-15	-18	-2	-2.0
1988	SD-N	13	11	.542	34	33	3	1	0	205¹	202	17	45	118	10.9	3.77	90	.259	.301	11	.167	1	-7	-9	-1	-0.8
1989	SD-N	16	11	.593	33	33	5	1	0	227	198	22	48	117	10.0	2.66	132	.235	.281	10	.139	1	21	21	-2	2.2
1990	SD-N	14	9	.609	32	32	6	3	0	228²	215	13	47	127	10.4	2.60	148	.251	.291	10	.149	1	30	32	3	3.9
Total 14		122	117	.510	439	321	33	12	8	2161²	2147	198	681	1226	11.9	3.75	98	.260	.318	69	.125	-10	-6	-17	-11	-2.3

■ WALT WHITTAKER — Whittaker, Walter Elton "Doc" b: 6/11/1894, Chelsea, Mass. d: 8/9/65, Pembroke, Mass. BL/TR, 5'9.5", 165 lbs. Deb: 7/06/16

YEAR	TM/L	W	L	PCT	G	GS	CG	SH	SV	IP	H	HR	BB	SO	RAT	ERA	ERA+	OAV	OOB	BH	AVG	PB	PR	/A	PD	TPI
1916	Phi-A	0	0	—	1	0	0	0	0	2	3	0	2	0	22.5	4.50	64	.375	.500	0	—	0	-0	-0	0	0.0

■ KEVIN WICKANDER — Wickander, Kevin Dean b: 1/5/65, Fort Dodge, Iowa BL/TL, 6'2", 202 lbs. Deb: 8/10/89

YEAR	TM/L	W	L	PCT	G	GS	CG	SH	SV	IP	H	HR	BB	SO	RAT	ERA	ERA+	OAV	OOB	BH	AVG	PB	PR	/A	PD	TPI
1989	Cle-A	0	0	—	2	0	0	0	0	2²	6	0	2	0	27.0	3.38	117	.462	.533	0	—	0	0	0	0	0.0
1990	Cle-A	0	1	.000	10	0	0	0	0	12¹	14	0	4	10	13.9	3.65	109	.304	.373	0	—	0	0	0	-0	0.0
Total 2		0	1	.000	12	0	0	0	0	15	20	0	6	10	16.2	3.60	110	.339	.409	0	—	0	1	1	-0	0.0

■ KEMP WICKER — Wicker, Kemp Caswell (b: Kemp Caswell Whicker) b: 8/13/06, Kernersville, N.C. d: 6/11/73, Kernersville, N.C BR/TL, 5'11", 182 lbs. Deb: 8/14/36

YEAR	TM/L	W	L	PCT	G	GS	CG	SH	SV	IP	H	HR	BB	SO	RAT	ERA	ERA+	OAV	OOB	BH	AVG	PB	PR	/A	PD	TPI
1936	NY-A	1	2	.333	7	0	0	0	0	20	31	2	11	5	18.9	7.65	61	.356	.429	1	.143	-0	-6	-7	0	-0.5
1937	*NY-A	7	3	.700	16	10	6	1	0	88	107	8	26	14	13.6	4.40	101	.296	.343	4	.114	-3	2	0	-2	-0.3
1938	NY-A	1	0	1.000	1	1	0	0	0	1	0	0	1	0	9.0	0.00	—	.000	.250	0	—	0	1	1	0	0.0
1941	Bro-N	1	2	.333	16	2	0	0	1	32	30	3	14	8	12.4	3.66	100	.252	.331	1	.250	0	-0	0	0	0.0
Total 4		10	7	.588	40	13	6	1	1	141	168	13	52	27	14.0	4.66	92	.294	.353	6	.130	-2	-3	-5	-2	-0.8

■ BOB WICKER
Wicker, Robert Kitridge b: 5/24/1878, Bedford, Ind. d: 1/22/55, Evanston, Ill. BR/TR, 6'2", 180 lbs. Deb: 8/11/01

YEAR TM/L	W	L	PCT	G	GS	CG	SH	SV	IP	H	HR	BB	SO	RAT	ERA	ERA+	OAV	OOB	BH	AVG	PB	PR	/A	PD	TPI
1901 StL-N	0	0	—	1	0	0	0	0	3	4	0	1	2	15.0	0.00	—	.317	.368	1	.333	0	1	1	-0	0.1
1902 StL-N	5	12	.294	22	16	14	1	0	152¹	159	1	45	78	12.1	3.19	86	.269	.321	18	.234	1	-7	-8	2	-0.4
1903 StL-N	0	0	—	1	0	0	0	0	5	4	0	3	3	12.6	0.00	—	.174	.269	0	.000	-0	2	2	1	0.2
Chi-N	20	9	.690	32	27	24	1	1	247	236	3	74	110	11.4	3.02	104	.253	.311	24	.245	5	7	3	-5	0.2
Yr	20	9	.690	33	27	24	1	1	252	240	3	77	110	11.4	2.96	106	.252	.309	4	.040	5	9	5	-5	0.4
1904 Chi-N	17	9	.654	30	27	23	4	0	229	201	6	58	99	10.3	2.67	100	.232	.282	34	.219	1	2	-0	-5	-0.4
1905 Chi-N	13	6	.684	22	22	17	4	0	178	139	3	47	86	9.5	2.02	147	.221	.276	10	.139	-2	19	19	-3	1.5
1906 Chi-N	3	5	.375	10	8	5	0	0	72¹	70	0	19	25	11.1	2.99	88	.257	.306	2	.100	-1	-3	-3	-1	-0.4
Cin-N	6	11	.353	20	17	14	0	0	150	150	3	46	69	11.8	2.70	102	.263	.319	9	.180	2	-1	1	-4	0.0
Yr	9	16	.360	30	25	19	0	0	222¹	220	3	65	94	11.6	2.79	97	.261	.315	7	.100	1	-4	-2	-5	-0.4
Total 6	64	52	.552	138	117	97	10	1	1036²	963	16	293	472	11.0	2.73	105	.247	.301	98	.205	6	20	16	-15	0.8

■ DAVE WICKERSHAM
Wickersham, David Clifford b: 9/27/35, Erie, Pa. BR/TR, 6'3", 188 lbs. Deb: 9/18/60

YEAR TM/L	W	L	PCT	G	GS	CG	SH	SV	IP	H	HR	BB	SO	RAT	ERA	ERA+	OAV	OOB	BH	AVG	PB	PR	/A	PD	TPI
1960 KC-A	0	0	—	5	0	0	0	2	8¹	4	0	1	3	5.4	1.08	369	.148	.179	0	.000	-0	3	3	0	0.3
1961 KC-A	2	1	.667	17	0	0	0	2	21	25	0	5	10	13.7	5.14	80	.309	.364	2	.667	1	-3	-2	0	0.0
1962 KC-A	11	4	.733	30	9	3	0	1	110	105	13	43	61	12.8	4.17	100	.257	.340	2	.057	-3	-2	-0	1	-0.1
1963 KC-A	12	15	.444	38	34	4	1	1	237²	244	21	79	118	12.6	4.09	94	.268	.333	11	.138	-3	-12	-6	1	-0.8
1964 Det-A	19	12	.613	40	36	11	1	1	254	224	28	81	164	11.2	3.44	106	.232	.299	6	.073	-5	5	6	0	0.1
1965 Det-A	9	14	.391	34	27	8	3	0	195¹	179	12	61	109	11.6	3.78	92	.241	.308	4	.069	-4	-7	-7	1	-0.8
1966 Det-A	8	3	.727	38	14	3	0	1	140²	139	14	54	93	12.9	3.20	109	.261	.338	2	.044	-3	4	4	1	0.3
1967 Det-A	4	5	.444	36	4	0	0	4	85¹	72	6	33	44	11.5	2.74	119	.235	.318	0	.000	-2	5	5	1	0.5
1968 Pit-N	1	0	1.000	11	0	0	0	1	20²	21	0	13	9	14.8	3.48	84	.276	.382	1	.333	-1	-1	-0	0	0.0
1969 KC-A	2	3	.400	34	0	0	0	5	50	58	6	14	27	13.3	3.96	93	.294	.347	0	.000	0	-2	-2	0	0.0
Total 10	68	57	.544	283	124	29	5	18	1123	1071	100	384	638	12.1	3.66	100	.252	.323	28	.086	-18	-11	-0	6	-0.5

■ AL WIDMAR
Widmar, Albert Joseph b: 3/20/25, Cleveland, Ohio BR/TR, 6'3", 185 lbs. Deb: 4/25/47 C

YEAR TM/L	W	L	PCT	G	GS	CG	SH	SV	IP	H	HR	BB	SO	RAT	ERA	ERA+	OAV	OOB	BH	AVG	PB	PR	/A	PD	TPI
1947 Bos-A	0	0	—	2	0	0	0	0	1¹	1	1	2	1	20.3	13.50	29	.200	.429	0	—	0	-1	-1	0	0.0
1948 StL-A	2	6	.250	49	0	0	0	1	82²	88	4	48	34	14.8	4.46	102	.275	.370	3	.300	1	-2	1	2	0.3
1950 StL-A	7	15	.318	36	26	8	1	4	194²	211	16	74	78	13.3	4.76	104	.271	.337	10	.149	-4	-4	4	0	0.1
1951 StL-A	4	9	.308	26	16	4	0	0	107²	157	19	52	28	17.6	6.52	67	.344	.414	5	.167	-1	-29	-25	1	-2.2
1952 Chi-A	0	0	—	1	0	0	0	0	2	4	1	0	2	18.0	4.50	81	.444	.444	0	—	-0	-0	-0	0	0.0
Total 5	13	30	.302	114	42	12	1	5	388¹	461	41	176	143	14.9	5.21	90	.294	.367	18	.168	-4	-36	-22	3	-1.8

■ WILD BILL WIDNER
Widner, William Waterfield b: 6/3/1867, Cincinnati, Ohio d: 12/10/08, Cincinnati, Ohio BR/TR, 6', 180 lbs. Deb: 6/08/1887

YEAR TM/L	W	L	PCT	G	GS	CG	SH	SV	IP	H	HR	BB	SO	RAT	ERA	ERA+	OAV	OOB	BH	AVG	PB	PR	/A	PD	TPI
1887 Cin-a	1	0	1.000	1	1	1	0	0	9	11	2	2	10	13.0	5.00	86	.290	.326	1	.250	-0	-1	-1	0	0.0
1888 Was-N	5	7	.417	13	13	13	0	0	115	111	7	22	33	10.4	2.82	99	.244	.279	12	.200	-1	0	-0	-0	0.0
1889 Col-a	12	20	.375	41	34	25	2	1	294	368	11	85	63	13.9	5.20	70	.297	.342	28	.211	-1	-44	-52	2	-4.1
1890 Col-a	4	8	.333	13	10	8	1	0	96	103	3	24	14	11.9	3.28	109	.266	.309	8	.195	-1	6	3	3	0.4
1891 Cin-a	0	1	.000	1	1	1	0	0	8	13	0	4	2	19.1	7.88	52	.353	.417	1	.250	-0	-4	-3	0	-0.2
Total 5	22	36	.379	69	59	48	3	1	522	606	23	137	110	12.8	4.36	79	.281	.324	50	.207	-3	-42	-52	4	-3.9

■ TED WIEAND
Wieand, Franklin Delano Roosevelt b: 4/4/33, Walnutport, Pa. BR/TR, 6'2", 195 lbs. Deb: 9/27/58

YEAR TM/L	W	L	PCT	G	GS	CG	SH	SV	IP	H	HR	BB	SO	RAT	ERA	ERA+	OAV	OOB	BH	AVG	PB	PR	/A	PD	TPI
1958 Cin-N	0	0	—	1	0	0	0	0	2	4	1	0	2	18.0	9.00	46	.400	.400	0	—	0	-1	-1	0	0.0
1960 Cin-N	0	1	.000	5	0	0	0	0	4¹	4	2	5	3	18.0	10.38	37	.250	.429	0	—	0	-3	-3	0	-0.2
Total 2	0	1	.000	6	0	0	0	0	6¹	8	3	5	5	18.5	9.95	39	.308	.419	0	—	0	-4	-4	0	-0.2

■ CHARLIE WIEDEMEYER
Wiedemeyer, Charles John "Chick" b: 1/31/14, Chicago, Ill. d: 10/27/79, Lake Geneva, Fla. BL/TL, 6'3", 180 lbs. Deb: 9/09/34

YEAR TM/L	W	L	PCT	G	GS	CG	SH	SV	IP	H	HR	BB	SO	RAT	ERA	ERA+	OAV	OOB	BH	AVG	PB	PR	/A	PD	TPI
1934 Chi-N	0	0	—	4	1	0	0	0	8¹	16	0	4	2	22.7	9.72	40	.432	.500	0	.000	-0	-5	-5	0	-0.4

■ JACK WIENEKE
Wieneke, John b: 3/10/1894, Saltzburg, Pa. d: 3/16/33, Pleasant Ridge, Mich. BR/TL, 6', 182 lbs. Deb: 7/04/21

YEAR TM/L	W	L	PCT	G	GS	CG	SH	SV	IP	H	HR	BB	SO	RAT	ERA	ERA+	OAV	OOB	BH	AVG	PB	PR	/A	PD	TPI
1921 Chi-A	0	1	.000	10	3	0	0	0	25¹	39	4	17	10	20.3	8.17	52	.351	.442	1	.111	-1	-11	-11	0	-0.9

■ BOB WIESLER
Wiesler, Robert George b: 8/13/30, St.Louis, Mo. BB/TL, 6'3", 188 lbs. Deb: 8/03/51

YEAR TM/L	W	L	PCT	G	GS	CG	SH	SV	IP	H	HR	BB	SO	RAT	ERA	ERA+	OAV	OOB	BH	AVG	PB	PR	/A	PD	TPI
1951 NY-A	0	2	.000	4	3	0	0	0	9¹	13	0	11	3	23.1	13.50	28	.361	.511	0	.000	-0	-10	-10	0	-0.8
1954 NY-A	3	2	.600	6	5	0	0	0	30¹	28	0	30	25	17.2	4.15	83	.259	.420	3	.273	1	-1	-2	-1	-0.1
1955 NY-A	0	0	—	16	7	0	0	0	53	39	1	49	22	15.1	3.91	96	.212	.380	2	.143	-1	0	-1	1	0.0
1956 Was-A	3	12	.200	37	21	3	0	0	123	141	11	112	49	18.7	6.44	67	.300	.438	3	.091	-3	-31	-29	2	-2.7
1957 Was-A	1	1	.500	3	2	1	0	0	16¹	15	2	11	9	14.9	4.41	88	.250	.375	1	.167	0	-1	-1	0	-0.2
1958 Was-A	0	0	—	4	0	0	0	0	9¹	14	2	5	5	19.3	6.75	56	.359	.444	0	.000	-0	-3	-3	1	-0.2
Total 6	7	19	.269	70	38	4	0	0	241¹	250	16	218	113	17.7	5.74	70	.279	.423	9	.130	-4	-46	-46	3	-3.8

■ WHITEY WIETELMANN
Wietelmann, William Frederick b: 3/15/19, Zanesville, Ohio BB/TR, 6', 170 lbs. Deb: 9/06/39 C♦

YEAR TM/L	W	L	PCT	G	GS	CG	SH	SV	IP	H	HR	BB	SO	RAT	ERA	ERA+	OAV	OOB	BH	AVG	PB	PR	/A	PD	TPI
1945 Bos-N	0	0	—	1	0	0	0	0	1	6	0	2	0	72.0	54.00	7	.667	.727	116	.271	0	-6	-6	0	-0.3
1946 Bos-N	0	0	—	3	0	0	0	0	6²	9	1	4	2	18.9	8.10	42	.310	.412	16	.205	0	-3	-3	-0	-0.2
Total 2	0	0	—	4	0	0	0	0	7²	15	1	6	2	25.8	14.09	25	.395	.489	409	.232	1	-9	-9	-0	-0.5

■ JIMMY WIGGS
Wiggs, James Alvin "Big Jim" b: 9/1/1876, Trondheim, Norway d: 1/20/63, Xenia, Ohio BB/TR, 6'4", 200 lbs. Deb: 4/23/03

YEAR TM/L	W	L	PCT	G	GS	CG	SH	SV	IP	H	HR	BB	SO	RAT	ERA	ERA+	OAV	OOB	BH	AVG	PB	PR	/A	PD	TPI
1903 Cin-N	0	1	.000	2	1	0	0	0	5	12	0	2	2	27.0	5.40	66	.500	.556	0	.000	-0	-1	-1	0	0.0
1905 Det-A	3	3	.500	7	7	4	0	0	41¹	30	0	29	37	12.8	3.27	84	.204	.336	2	.133	-2	-3	-2	-1	-0.3
1906 Det-A	0	0	—	4	1	0	0	0	10¹	11	1	7	7	15.7	5.23	53	.276	.384	1	.333	0	-3	-3	0	-0.2
Total 3	3	4	.429	13	9	4	0	0	56²	53	1	38	46	14.6	3.81	74	.252	.369	3	.158	-0	-7	-6	-0	-0.5

■ BILL WIGHT
Wight, William Robert "Lefty" b: 4/12/22, Rio Vista, Cal. BL/TL, 6'1", 180 lbs. Deb: 4/17/46

YEAR TM/L	W	L	PCT	G	GS	CG	SH	SV	IP	H	HR	BB	SO	RAT	ERA	ERA+	OAV	OOB	BH	AVG	PB	PR	/A	PD	TPI
1946 NY-A	2	2	.500	14	4	1	0	0	40¹	44	4	30	11	16.7	4.46	77	.289	.410	0	.000	-1	-4	-5	0	-0.4
1947 NY-A	1	0	1.000	3	1	1	0	0	9	2	0	3	2	10.0	1.00	353	.242	.286	0	.000	0	3	3	0	0.4
1948 Chi-A	9	20	.310	34	32	7	1	1	223¹	238	9	135	68	15.1	4.80	89	.278	.377	6	.082	-7	-13	-13	1	-1.7
1949 Chi-A	15	13	.536	35	33	14	3	1	245	254	9	96	78	12.9	3.31	126	.275	.343	14	.165	-1	24	24	0	2.2
1950 Chi-A	10	16	.385	30	28	13	3	0	206	213	10	79	62	12.8	3.58	125	.270	.336	0	.000	-8	23	21	2	1.3
1951 Bos-A	7	7	.500	34	17	4	2	0	118¹	128	5	63	38	14.5	5.10	88	.282	.369	3	.073	-5	-13	-8	2	-1.0
1952 Bos-A	2	1	.667	10	2	0	0	0	24¹	14	3	14	5	10.7	2.96	133	.169	.296	1	.143	-0	2	3	0	0.3
Det-A	5	9	.357	23	19	8	1	0	143²	167	7	55	65	13.9	3.88	98	.291	.354	11	.220	1	-3	-1	2	0.2
Yr	7	10	.412	33	21	8	3	0	168	181	10	69	70	13.4	3.75	102	.275	.344	3	.035	1	-1	1	3	0.5
1953 Det-A	0	3	.000	13	4	0	0	0	25¹	35	4	14	10	17.4	8.88	46	.333	.412	3	.429	1	-14	-14	-1	-1.2
Cle-A	2	1	.667	20	0	0	0	1	26²	29	1	16	14	15.2	3.71	101	.282	.378	0	.000	-1	1	0	0	0.0
Yr	2	4	.333	33	4	0	0	1	52	64	5	30	24	16.3	6.23	63	.308	.395	0	.000	0	-13	-14	-1	-1.2
1955 Cle-A	0	0	—	17	0	0	0	1	24	24	0	9	12	12.4	2.63	152	.261	.327	0	—	0	4	4	2	0.6
Bal-A	6	8	.429	19	14	8	2	2	117¹	111	6	39	54	11.6	2.45	155	.252	.315	3	.083	-2	20	18	2	1.9
Yr	6	8	.429	36	14	8	2	3	141¹	135	6	48	63	11.7	2.48	155	.254	.317	1	.028	-1	23	21	4	2.5
1956 Bal-A	9	12	.429	35	26	7	1	0	174²	198	7	72	84	14.2	4.02	98	.289	.362	12	.200	-1	3	-2	-1	-0.3
1957 Bal-A	6	6	.500	27	17	2	0	0	121	122	4	54	50	13.4	3.64	99	.271	.354	1	.029	-3	2	-1	-0	-0.4
1958 Cin-N	0	1	.000	7	0	0	0	0	6²	7	1	4	5	14.9	4.05	102	.292	.393	0	—	0	-0	0	0	0.0
StL-N	3	0	1.000	28	1	1	0	2	57¹	64	7	32	18	15.1	5.02	82	.290	.379	1	.100	-0	-7	-6	1	-0.4
Yr	3	1	.750	35	1	1	0	2	64	71	8	36	23	15.0	4.92	84	.290	.381	1	.100	-0	-7	-6	1	-0.4
Total 12	77	99	.438	347	198	66	15	8	1563	1656	74	714	574	13.7	3.95	103	.277	.355	55	.115	-28	27	22	11	1.5

■ FRED WIGINGTON

Wigington, Fred Thomas   b: 12/16/1897, Rogers, Neb.   d: 5/8/80, Mesa, Ariz.   BR/TR, 5'10", 168 lbs.   Deb: 4/20/23

YEAR TM/L	W	L	PCT	G	GS	CG	SH	SV	IP	H	HR	BB	SO	RAT	ERA	ERA+	OAV	OOB	BH	AVG	PB	PR	/A	PD	TPI
1923 StL-N	0	0	—	4	0	0	0	0	8^1	11	0	5	2	17.3	3.24	121	.367	.457	0	.000	-0	1	1	0	0.1

■ SANDY WIHTOL

Wihtol, Alexander Ames   b: 6/1/55, Palo Alto, Cal.   BR/TR, 6'1", 195 lbs.   Deb: 9/07/79

YEAR TM/L	W	L	PCT	G	GS	CG	SH	SV	IP	H	HR	BB	SO	RAT	ERA	ERA+	OAV	OOB	BH	AVG	PB	PR	/A	PD	TPI
1979 Cle-A	0	0	—	5	0	0	0	0	10^2	10	0	3	6	11.0	3.38	126	.238	.289	0	—	0	1	1	0	0.1
1980 Cle-A	1	0	1.000	17	0	0	0	0	35^1	35	2	14	20	13.0	3.57	114	.257	.336	0	—	0	2	2	-1	0.1
1982 Cle-A	0	0	—	6	0	0	0	0	11^2	9	1	7	8	13.1	4.63	88	.220	.347	0	—	0	-1	-1	-0	0.0
Total 3	1	0	1.000	28	0	0	0	1	57^2	54	3	24	34	12.6	3.75	110	.247	.329	0	—	0	2	2	-1	0.2

■ MILT WILCOX

Wilcox, Milton Edward   b: 4/20/50, Honolulu, Hawaii   BR/TR, 6'2", 185 lbs.   Deb: 9/05/70

YEAR TM/L	W	L	PCT	G	GS	CG	SH	SV	IP	H	HR	BB	SO	RAT	ERA	ERA+	OAV	OOB	BH	AVG	PB	PR	/A	PD	TPI
1970 *Cin-N	3	1	.750	5	2	1	1	1	22^1	19	2	7	13	10.9	2.42	167	.229	.297	1	.200	0	4	4	0	0.5
1971 Cin-N	2	2	.500	18	3	0	0	1	43^1	43	2	17	21	12.9	3.32	101	.269	.346	0	.000	-1	1	0	0	0.0
1972 Cle-A	7	14	.333	32	27	4	2	0	156	145	18	72	90	12.8	3.40	94	.251	.339	9	.200	1	-6	-3	-2	-0.4
1973 Cle-A	8	10	.444	26	19	4	0	0	134^1	143	14	68	82	14.7	5.83	67	.275	.367	0	—	0	-30	-29	1	-2.6
1974 Cle-A	2	2	.500	41	2	1	0	4	71^1	74	10	24	33	13.0	4.67	77	.271	.341	0	—	0	-8	-8	1	-0.7
1975 Chi-N	0	1	.000	25	0	0	0	0	38^1	50	4	17	21	16.0	5.63	68	.323	.393	1	.333	0	-9	-8	0	-0.6
1977 Det-A	6	2	.750	20	13	1	0	0	106^1	96	13	37	82	11.3	3.64	118	.241	.307	0	—	0	5	8	-1	0.7
1978 Det-A	13	12	.520	29	27	16	2	0	215^1	208	22	68	132	11.9	3.76	103	.255	.318	0	—	0	2	0	0	0.3
1979 Det-A	12	10	.545	33	29	7	0	0	196^1	201	18	73	109	13.1	4.35	99	.267	.341	0	—	0	-3	-1	3	0.2
1980 Det-A	13	11	.542	32	31	13	1	0	198^2	201	24	68	97	12.5	4.48	92	.262	.327	0	—	0	-10	-8	1	-0.6
1981 Det-A	12	9	.571	24	24	8	1	0	166^1	152	10	52	79	11.4	3.03	124	.247	.312	0	—	0	12	14	1	1.6
1982 Det-A	12	10	.545	29	29	9	1	0	193^2	187	18	85	112	13.0	3.62	112	.257	.340	0	—	0	10	9	2	1.2
1983 Det-A	11	10	.524	26	26	9	2	0	186	164	19	74	101	11.7	3.97	98	.237	.314	0	—	0	2	-1	3	0.2
1984 *Det-A	17	8	.680	33	33	0	0	0	193^2	183	13	66	119	11.9	4.00	98	.252	.321	0	—	0	-0	-2	1	0.0
1985 Det-A	1	3	.250	8	8	0	0	0	39	51	6	14	20	15.0	4.85	84	.315	.369	0	—	0	-3	-3	1	-0.1
1986 Sea-A	0	8	.000	13	10	0	0	0	55^2	74	11	28	26	16.7	5.50	77	.327	.404	0	—	0	-8	-8	1	-0.6
Total 16	119	113	.513	394	283	73	10	6	2016^2	1991	204	770	1137	12.7	4.07	96	.260	.334	11	.177	0	-44	-33	13	-0.9

■ RANDY WILES

Wiles, Randall E   b: 9/10/51, Fort Belvoir, Va.   BL/TL, 6'1", 185 lbs.   Deb: 8/07/77

YEAR TM/L	W	L	PCT	G	GS	CG	SH	SV	IP	H	HR	BB	SO	RAT	ERA	ERA+	OAV	OOB	BH	AVG	PB	PR	/A	PD	TPI
1977 Chi-A	1	1	.500	5	0	0	0	0	2^2	5	1	3	0	27.0	10.13	40	.417	.533	0	—	0	-2	-2	0	-0.1

■ MARK WILEY

Wiley, Mark Eugene   b: 2/28/48, National City, Cal.   BR/TR, 6'1", 200 lbs.   Deb: 6/17/75   C

YEAR TM/L	W	L	PCT	G	GS	CG	SH	SV	IP	H	HR	BB	SO	RAT	ERA	ERA+	OAV	OOB	BH	AVG	PB	PR	/A	PD	TPI
1975 Min-A	1	3	.250	15	3	1	0	2	38^2	50	4	13	15	14.9	6.05	64	.325	.381	0	—	0	-10	-9	-0	-0.9
1978 SD-N	1	0	1.000	4	1	0	0	0	7^2	11	1	1	1	14.1	5.87	57	.324	.343	0	.000	-0	-2	-2	0	-0.2
Tor-A	0	0	—	2	0	0	0	0	2^2	3	0	1	2	13.5	6.75	58	.273	.333	0	—	0	-1	-1	0	0.0
Total 2	2	3	.400	21	4	1	0	2	49	64	5	15	18	14.7	6.06	62	.322	.372	0	.000	-0	-13	-12	-0	-1.1

■ HARRY WILHELM

Wilhelm, Harry Lester   b: 4/7/1874, Uniontown, Pa.   d: 2/20/44, Republic, Pa.   BR/TR, 5'7", 155 lbs.   Deb: 8/12/1899

YEAR TM/L	W	L	PCT	G	GS	CG	SH	SV	IP	H	HR	BB	SO	RAT	ERA	ERA+	OAV	OOB	BH	AVG	PB	PR	/A	PD	TPI
1899 Lou-N	1	1	.500	5	3	2	0	0	25	36	1	3	6	14.0	6.12	63	.336	.354	3	.250	2	-6	-6	0	-0.3

■ KAISER WILHELM

Wilhelm, Irvin Key   b: 1/26/1874, Wooster, Ohio   d: 5/21/36, Rochester, N.Y.   BR/TR, 6', 162 lbs.   Deb: 4/18/03   MUC

YEAR TM/L	W	L	PCT	G	GS	CG	SH	SV	IP	H	HR	BB	SO	RAT	ERA	ERA+	OAV	OOB	BH	AVG	PB	PR	/A	PD	TPI
1903 Pit-N	5	3	.625	12	9	7	1	0	86	88	0	25	20	12.1	3.24	100	.264	.321	3	.088	-2	0	-0	2	0.0
1904 Bos-N	14	20	.412	39	36	30	3	0	288	316	8	74	73	12.4	3.69	75	.285	.333	7	.070	-8	-30	-30	2	-3.5
1905 Bos-N	3	23	.115	34	27	23	0	0	242	287	7	75	76	13.6	4.54	68	.295	.349	16	.160	-2	-41	-39	2	-3.7
1908 Bro-N	16	22	.421	42	36	33	6	0	332	266	3	83	99	9.6	1.87	125	.217	.271	12	.108	-4	18	18	3	1.9
1909 Bro-N	3	13	.188	22	17	14	1	0	163	176	3	59	45	13.1	3.26	80	.289	.353	13	.228	2	-12	-12	2	-0.8
1910 Bro-N	3	7	.300	15	5	0	0	0	68^1	88	3	18	17	14.1	4.74	64	.314	.358	6	.316	2	-13	-13	1	-0.9
1914 Bal-F	12	17	.414	47	27	11	1	5	243^2	263	10	81	113	12.7	4.03	84	.291	.349	21	.250	2	-22	-18	3	-1.1
1915 Bal-F	0	0	—	1	0	0	0	0	1	0	0	0	0	0.0	0.00	—	.000	.000	0	—	0	0	0	0	0.0
1921 Phi-N	0	0	—	4	0	0	0	0	8	11	0	3	1	15.8	3.38	125	.393	.452	0	.000	-0	0	1	0	0.0
Total 9	56	105	.348	216	157	118	12	5	1432	1495	34	418	444	12.2	3.44	83	.274	.328	78	.154	-10	-99	-93	15	-8.1

■ HOYT WILHELM

Wilhelm, James Hoyt   b: 7/26/23, Huntersville, N.C.   BR/TR, 6', 190 lbs.   Deb: 4/19/52   H

YEAR TM/L	W	L	PCT	G	GS	CG	SH	SV	IP	H	HR	BB	SO	RAT	ERA	ERA+	OAV	OOB	BH	AVG	PB	PR	/A	PD	TPI
1952 NY-N	15	3	**.833**	**71**	0	0	0	11	159^1	127	12	57	108	10.7	**2.43**	**152**	.220	.296	6	.158	0	**23**	23	0	2.4
1953 NY-N	7	8	.467	**68**	0	0	0	15	145	127	13	77	71	12.9	3.04	141	.238	.339	5	.152	1	**20**	20	-1	2.0
1954 *NY-N	12	4	.750	57	0	0	0	7	111^1	77	5	52	64	10.8	2.10	192	.198	.300	1	.048	-2	**24**	24	1	2.3
1955 NY-N	4	1	.800	59	0	0	0	0	103	104	10	40	71	12.8	3.93	102	.266	.337	3	.158	-1	1	2	0	0.1
1956 NY-N	4	9	.308	64	0	0	0	8	89^1	97	7	43	71	14.3	3.83	99	.280	.362	2	.222	-1	-1	-0	1	0.1
1957 StL-N	1	4	.200	40	0	0	0	11	55	52	7	21	29	12.4	4.25	93	.254	.332	0	.000	-1	-2	-2	-0	-0.2
Cle-A	1	0	1.000	2	0	0	0	1	3^2	2	1	1	0	9.8	2.45	154	.154	.267	0	—	0	1	1	-0	0.1
1958 Cle-A	2	7	.222	30	6	1	0	9	90^1	70	4	35	57	10.6	2.49	146	.215	.294	2	.095	-1	13	12	1	1.1
Bal-A	1	3	.250	9	4	3	1	0	40^2	25	2	10	35	8.0	1.99	180	.179	.238	1	.091	-1	8	7	-0	0.7
Yr	3	10	.231	39	10	4	1	5	131	95	6	45	92	9.7	2.34	155	.203	.274	1	.031	-2	21	19	0	1.8
1959 Bal-A	15	11	.577	32	27	13	3	0	226	178	13	77	139	10.6	**2.19**	**173**	.224	.301	4	.053	-6	**42**	40	-1	3.5
1960 Bal-A	11	8	.579	41	11	3	1	7	147	125	13	39	107	10.1	3.31	115	.228	.280	3	.071	-3	9	8	1	0.6
1961 Bal-A	9	7	.563	51	1	0	0	18	109^2	89	5	41	87	11.0	2.30	170	.219	.296	1	.050	-1	21	20	1	1.9
1962 Bal-A	7	10	.412	52	0	0	0	15	93	64	5	34	90	9.8	1.94	194	.197	.279	2	.125	-0	21	19	-0	1.9
1963 Chi-A	5	8	.385	55	3	0	0	21	136^1	106	8	30	111	9.2	2.64	133	.215	.265	2	.069	-0	15	13	0	1.3
1964 Chi-A	12	9	.571	73	0	0	0	27	131^1	94	7	30	95	8.6	1.99	174	.202	.254	3	.143	-0	24	21	-1	2.0
1965 Chi-A	7	7	.500	66	0	0	0	20	144	88	11	32	106	7.6	1.81	176	.177	.229	0	.000	-2	**26**	22	-1	2.1
1966 Chi-A	5	2	.714	46	0	0	0	21	81^1	50	6	17	61	7.5	1.66	191	.178	.227	1	.125	-0	16	14	-1	1.4
1967 Chi-A	8	3	.727	49	0	0	0	12	89	58	2	34	76	9.7	1.31	236	.183	.270	1	.077	-1	**19**	18	-1	1.8
1968 Chi-A	4	4	.500	72	0	0	0	12	93^2	69	4	24	72	9.1	1.73	175	.205	.262	0	.000	-0	13	13	-1	1.4
1969 Cal-A	5	7	.417	44	0	0	0	10	65^2	45	4	18	53	9.0	2.47	141	.194	.261	0	.000	-1	8	7	-0	0.6
Atl-N	2	0	1.000	8	0	0	0	4	12^1	5	0	4	14	7.3	0.73	494	.119	.213	0	.000	-0	4	4	0	0.4
1970 Atl-N	6	4	.600	50	0	0	0	13	78^1	69	7	39	67	12.5	3.10	138	.234	.325	1	.091	-0	8	10	0	1.1
Chi-N	0	1	1.000	3	0	0	0	0	3^2	4	1	3	1	17.2	9.82	46	.286	.412	0	—	0	-2	-2	1	-0.1
Yr	6	5	.545	53	0	0	0	13	82	73	8	42	68	12.6	3.40	126	.234	.325	2	.182	-0	6	8	1	1.0
1971 Atl-N	0	0	—	3	0	0	0	0	2^1	6	2	1	1	27.0	15.43	24	.500	.538	0	—	0	-3	-3	0	-0.2
LA-N	0	1	.000	9	0	0	0	3	17^2	6	1	4	15	5.1	1.02	317	.111	.172	0	.000	-0	5	4	-0	0.4
Yr	0	1	.000	12	0	0	0	3	20	12	3	5	16	7.6	2.70	122	.182	.239	0	.000	-0	2	1	0	0.2
1972 LA-N	0	1	.000	16	0	0	0	1	25^1	20	0	15	9	12.4	4.62	72	.217	.327	0	.000	-0	-3	-4	0	-0.2
Total 21	143	122	.540	1070	52	20	5	227	2254^1	1757	150	778	1610	10.4	2.52	146	.216	.290	38	.088	-20	310	289	1	28.7

■ LEFTY WILKIE

Wilkie, Aldon Jay   b: 10/30/14, Zealandia, Sask., Canada   BL/TL, 5'11.5", 175 lbs.   Deb: 4/22/41

YEAR TM/L	W	L	PCT	G	GS	CG	SH	SV	IP	H	HR	BB	SO	RAT	ERA	ERA+	OAV	OOB	BH	AVG	PB	PR	/A	PD	TPI
1941 Pit-N	2	4	.333	26	6	2	1	2	79	90	1	40	16	14.9	4.56	79	.289	.372	7	.292	1	-8	-8	1	-0.5
1942 Pit-N	6	7	.462	35	6	3	0	1	107^1	112	4	37	18	12.6	4.19	81	.269	.330	10	.263	2	-10	-10	2	-0.5
1946 Pit-N	0	0	—	7	0	0	0	0	7^2	13	0	3	3	18.8	10.57	33	.382	.432	0	—	0	-6	-6	-0	-0.5
Total 3	8	11	.421	68	12	5	1	3	194	215	5	80	37	13.8	4.59	76	.283	.352	17	.274	3	-25	-24	3	-1.5

■ DEAN WILKINS

Wilkins, Dean Allan   b: 8/24/66, Blue Island, Ill.   BR/TR, 6'1", 170 lbs.   Deb: 8/21/89

YEAR TM/L	W	L	PCT	G	GS	CG	SH	SV	IP	H	HR	BB	SO	RAT	ERA	ERA+	OAV	OOB	BH	AVG	PB	PR	/A	PD	TPI
1989 Chi-N	1	0	1.000	11	0	0	0	0	15^2	13	2	9	14	12.6	4.60	82	.228	.333	0	.000	-0	-2	-1	0	-0.1
1990 Chi-N	0	0	—	7	0	0	0	1	7^1	11	1	7	3	23.3	9.82	42	.333	.463	0	—	0	-5	-5	-0	-0.4
Total 2	1	0	1.000	18	0	0	0	1	23	24	3	16	17	16.0	6.26	62	.267	.383	0	.000	-0	-7	-6	0	-0.5

YEAR	TM/L	W	L	PCT	G	GS	CG	SH	SV	IP	H	HR	BB	SO	RAT	ERA	ERA+	OAV	OOB	BH	AVG	PB	PR	/A	PD	TPI

■ ERIC WILKINS Wilkins, Eric Lamoine b: 12/9/56, St.Louis, Mo. BR/TR, 6'1", 190 lbs. Deb: 4/11/79

| 1979 | Cle-A | 2 | 4 | .333 | 16 | 14 | 0 | 0 | 0 | 69² | 77 | 4 | 38 | 52 | 15.4 | 4.39 | 97 | .289 | .386 | 0 | — | 0 | -1 | -1 | 0 | 0.0 |

■ ROY WILKINSON Wilkinson, Roy Hamilton b: 5/8/1893, Canandaigua, N.Y. d: 7/2/56, Louisville, Ky. BR/TR, 6'1", 170 lbs. Deb: 4/29/18

1918	Cle-A	0	0	—	1	0	0	0	0	1	0	0	0	0	0.0	0.00	—	.000	.000	0	—	0	0	0	0	0.0
1919	*Chi-A	1	1	.500	4	1	1	1	0	22	21	0	10	5	12.7	2.05	156	.266	.348	3	.375	2	3	3	1	0.6
1920	Chi-A	7	9	.438	34	11	8	0	2	145	162	6	48	30	13.2	4.03	93	.297	.356	7	.146	-3	-4	-4	-2	-0.8
1921	Chi-A	4	20	.167	36	23	11	0	3	198¹	259	4	78	50	13.5	5.13	83	.334	.397	8	.123	-4	-19	-20	6	-1.6
1922	Chi-A	0	1	.000	4	1	0	0	1	14¹	24	1	6	3	19.5	8.79	46	.393	.456	0	.000	-0	-8	-8	0	-0.6
Total	5	12	31	.279	79	36	20	1	6	380²	466	11	142	88	14.5	4.66	86	.318	.381	18	.145	-5	-27	-28	4	-2.4

■ BILL WILKINSON Wilkinson, William Carl b: 8/10/64, Greybull, Wyoming BR/TL, 5'10", 160 lbs. Deb: 6/13/85

1985	Sea-A	0	2	.000	2	2	0	0	0	6	8	2	6	5	21.0	13.50	31	.333	.467	0	—	0	-6	-6	0	-0.4
1987	Sea-A	3	4	.429	56	0	0	0	10	76¹	61	8	21	73	9.7	3.66	129	.223	.278	0	—	0	7	9	-1	0.7
1988	Sea-A	2	2	.500	30	0	0	0	2	31	28	3	15	25	12.5	3.48	119	.233	.319	0	—	0	2	2	-1	0.2
Total	3	5	8	.385	88	2	0	0	12	113¹	97	13	42	103	11.0	4.13	110	.232	.302	0	—	0	2	5	-2	0.5

■ TED WILKS Wilks, Theodore "Cork" b: 11/13/15, Fulton, N.Y. d: 8/21/89, Houston, Tex. BR/TR, 5'9.5", 178 lbs. Deb: 4/25/44 C

1944	*StL-N	17	4	.810	36	21	16	4	0	207²	173	12	49	70	**9.7**	2.64	133	.227	**.275**	9	.141	-1	22	20	-4	1.6
1945	StL-N	4	7	.364	18	16	4	1	0	98¹	103	3	29	28	12.2	2.93	128	.270	.324	4	.133	-0	10	9	-2	0.7
1946	*StL-N	8	0	1.000	40	4	0	0	1	95	88	13	38	40	12.1	3.41	101	.248	.324	5	.208	0	0	0	-1	0.0
1947	StL-N	4	0	1.000	37	0	0	0	5	50¹	57	10	11	28	12.5	5.01	83	.279	.323	1	.167	0	-5	-5	0	-0.4
1948	StL-N	6	6	.500	57	2	1	0	13	130²	113	5	39	71	10.5	2.62	156	.235	.293	5	.167	0	**19**	**21**	-1	2.1
1949	StL-N	10	3	.769	59	0	0	0	9	118¹	105	7	38	71	10.9	3.73	112	.240	.301	1	.037	-3	4	6	-3	0.0
1950	StL-N	2	0	1.000	18	0	0	0	0	24¹	27	4	9	15	13.7	6.66	65	.287	.356	0	.000	-1	-7	-6	0	-0.6
1951	StL-N	0	0	—	17	0	0	0	1	18	19	1	5	5	12.0	3.00	132	.279	.329	0	.000	-0	2	2	-0	0.1
	Pit-N	3	5	.375	48	1	1	0	12	82²	69	6	24	43	10.3	2.83	149	.231	.292	1	.083	-1	10	13	0	1.3
	Yr	3	5	.375	65	1	1	0	13	100²	88	7	29	48	10.6	2.86	146	.240	.299	1	.077	-1	12	15	0	1.4
1952	Pit-N	5	5	.500	44	0	0	0	4	72¹	65	9	31	24	12.2	3.61	111	.245	.329	1	.125	-0	1	3	-1	0.2
	Cle-A	0	0	—	7	0	0	0	1	11²	8	0	7	6	11.6	3.86	87	.186	.300	0	—	0	-0	-1	0	0.0
1953	Cle-A	0	0	—	4	0	0	0	0	3²	5	0	3	2	19.6	7.36	51	.278	.381	0	—	0	-1	-1	-0	-0.1
Total	10	59	30	.663	385	44	22	5	46	913	832	76	283	403	11.1	3.26	118	.244	.304	27	.131	-5	55	61	-10	4.9

■ ED WILLETT Willett, Robert Edgar b: 3/7/1884, Norfolk, Va. d: 5/10/34, Wellington, Kan. BR/TR, 6', 183 lbs. Deb: 9/05/06

1906	Det-A	0	3	.000	3	3	3	0	0	25	24	0	8	16	11.5	3.96	70	.256	.314	0	.000	-1	-4	-3	1	-0.3
1907	Det-A	1	5	.167	10	6	1	0	0	48²	47	0	20	27	12.4	3.70	71	.256	.329	1	.077	-1	-6	-6	1	-0.6
1908	Det-A	15	8	.652	30	22	18	2	1	197¹	186	2	60	77	11.9	2.28	106	.261	.331	11	.164	-2	3	3	4	0.6
1909	*Det-A	21	10	.677	41	34	25	3	1	292³	239	5	76	89	10.1	2.34	108	.221	.281	22	.196	4	5	6	-1	1.0
1910	Det-A	16	11	.593	37	25	18	4	0	224¹	175	2	74	65	10.7	2.37	111	.217	.296	11	.133	-2	4	7	7	1.3
1911	Det-A	13	14	.481	38	27	15	2	1	231¹	261	5	80	86	13.8	3.66	95	.295	.363	22	.268	7	-8	-5	3	0.5
1912	Det-A	17	15	.531	37	31	28	1	0	284¹	281	3	84	89	12.1	3.29	99	.262	.326	19	.165	-2	1	-1	6	0.3
1913	Det-A	13	14	.481	34	30	19	0	0	242	237	0	89	59	12.5	3.09	95	.260	.333	26	.283	7	-4	-5	4	0.7
1914	StL-F	4	16	.200	27	21	14	0	0	175	208	5	56	73	14.1	4.22	80	.295	.355	15	.234	3	-20	-16	5	-0.7
1915	StL-F	2	3	.400	17	2	1	0	2	52²	61	2	18	19	14.0	4.61	69	.295	.360	3	.200	1	-9	-8	0	-0.7
Total	10	102	99	.507	274	201	142	12	5	1773¹	1719	24	565	600	12.1	3.08	95	.258	.326	130	.199	13	-39	-29	30	2.1

■ CARL WILLEY Willey, Carlton Francis b: 6/6/31, Cherryfield, Me. BR/TR, 6', 175 lbs. Deb: 4/30/58

1958	*Mil-N	9	7	.563	23	19	9	**4**	0	140	110	14	53	74	10.6	2.70	130	.215	.291	5	.104	-2	19	13	-2	0.9
1959	Mil-N	5	9	.357	26	15	5	2	0	117	126	12	31	51	12.2	4.15	85	.273	.322	4	.103	-1	-3	-8	-1	-0.9
1960	Mil-N	6	7	.462	28	21	2	1	0	144²	136	19	65	109	12.9	4.35	79	.248	.335	7	.146	1	-10	-15	-2	-1.5
1961	Mil-N	6	12	.333	35	22	4	0	0	159²	147	20	65	91	12.1	3.83	98	.247	.323	1	.019	-6	4	-2	3	-0.4
1962	Mil-N	2	5	.286	30	6	0	0	1	73¹	95	9	20	40	14.2	5.40	70	.319	.364	3	.273	1	-12	-13	0	-1.1
1963	NY-N	9	14	.391	30	28	7	4	0	183	149	24	69	101	10.9	3.10	113	.220	.296	6	.111	-1	4	8	0	0.8
1964	NY-N	0	2	.000	14	3	0	0	0	30	37	5	8	14	13.8	3.60	99	.301	.348	0	.000	-0	-0	-0	-1	-0.1
1965	NY-N	1	2	.333	13	3	1	0	0	28	30	2	15	13	15.1	4.18	84	.270	.367	0	.000	-1	-2	-2	0	-0.2
Total	8	38	58	.396	199	117	28	11	1	875²	830	105	326	493	12.1	3.76	95	.250	.320	26	.099	-8	1	-17	-2	-2.5

■ NICK WILLHITE Willhite, Jon Nicholas b: 1/27/41, Tulsa, Okla. BL/TL, 6'2", 190 lbs. Deb: 6/16/63

1963	LA-N	2	3	.400	8	8	1	1	0	38	44	5	10	28	12.8	3.79	80	.286	.329	3	.300	1	-2	-3	-1	-0.2
1964	LA-N	2	4	.333	10	7	2	0	0	43²	43	4	13	24	11.5	3.71	87	.264	.318	0	.000	-0	-1	-2	1	-0.1
1965	Was-A	0	0	—	5	0	0	0	0	6¹	10	2	4	3	19.9	7.11	49	.345	.424	0	—	0	-3	-3	0	-0.2
	LA-N	2	2	.500	15	6	0	0	1	42	47	7	22	28	15.2	5.36	61	.288	.380	4	.400	3	-8	-10	0	-0.7
1966	LA-N	0	0	—	6	0	0	0	0	4¹	3	0	5	4	16.6	2.08	159	.214	.421	0	—	0	1	1	0	0.1
1967	Cal-A	0	2	.000	10	7	0	0	0	39¹	39	8	16	22	12.6	4.35	72	.258	.329	0	.000	-1	-5	-5	0	-0.6
	NY-N	0	1	.000	4	1	0	0	0	8¹	9	1	5	9	15.1	8.64	39	.257	.350	0	.000	-0	-5	-5	0	-0.4
Total	5	6	12	.333	58	29	3	1	1	182	195	27	75	118	13.5	4.55	70	.275	.346	7	.163	2	-23	-27	1	-2.1

■ ALBERT WILLIAMS Williams, Albert Hamilton (De Souza) b: 5/6/54, Pearl Lagoon, Nic. BR/TR, 6'4", 190 lbs. Deb: 5/07/80

1980	Min-A	6	2	.750	18	9	3	0	1	77	73	9	30	35	12.0	3.51	124	.253	.323	0	—	0	5	7	-0	0.7
1981	Min-A	6	10	.375	23	22	4	0	0	150	160	11	52	76	12.8	4.08	97	.276	.337	0	—	0	-7	-2	-0	-0.4
1982	Min-A	9	7	.563	26	26	3	0	0	153²	166	18	55	61	12.9	4.22	101	.276	.337	0	—	0	-2	0	1	0.1
1983	Min-A	11	14	.440	36	29	4	1	1	193¹	196	21	68	68	12.5	4.14	103	.262	.327	0	—	0	-2	2	-1	0.1
1984	Min-A	3	5	.375	17	11	1	0	0	68²	75	9	22	22	13.6	5.77	73	.284	.355	0	—	0	-14	-12	0	-1.0
Total	5	35	38	.479	120	97	15	1	2	642²	670	68	227	262	12.7	4.24	99	.270	.334	0	—	0	-20	-4	-3	-0.5

■ AL WILLIAMS Williams, Almon Edward b: 5/11/14, Valhermosa Springs, Ala. d: 7/19/49, Groves, Tex. BR/TR, 6'3", 200 lbs. Deb: 4/19/37

1937	Phi-A	4	1	.800	16	8	2	0	1	75¹	88	0	49	27	16.5	5.38	88	.300	.402	2	.083	-2	-6	-6	0	-0.6
1938	Phi-A	0	7	.000	30	8	1	0	0	93¹	128	6	54	25	17.6	6.94	70	.324	.407	1	.040	-3	-22	-22	0	-2.0
Total	2	4	8	.333	46	16	3	0	1	168²	216	6	103	52	17.1	6.24	77	.314	.405	3	.061	-5	-29	-27	0	-2.6

■ GUS WILLIAMS Williams, Augustine H. b: 1870, New York, N.Y. d: 10/14/1890, New York, N.Y. 5'11", 170 lbs. Deb: 4/18/1890

| 1890 | Bro-a | 0 | 1 | .000 | 2 | 2 | 1 | 0 | 0 | 12 | 13 | 0 | 12 | 2 | 18.8 | 7.50 | 52 | .268 | .413 | 2 | .500 | 1 | -5 | -5 | -1 | -0.3 |

■ CHARLIE WILLIAMS Williams, Charles Prosek b: 10/11/47, Flushing, N.Y. BR/TR, 6'2", 200 lbs. Deb: 4/23/71

1971	NY-N	5	6	.455	31	9	1	0	0	90¹	92	7	41	53	13.5	4.78	71	.267	.348	2	.087	-1	-13	-14	-1	-1.5
1972	SF-N	0	2	.000	3	2	0	0	0	9¹	14	3	3	3	16.4	8.68	40	.350	.378	0	.000	-0	-5	-5	-0	-0.5
1973	SF-N	3	0	1.000	12	2	0	0	0	23	32	2	7	11	15.3	6.65	57	.330	.375	1	.333	0	-8	-7	0	-0.6
1974	SF-N	1	3	.250	39	7	0	0	0	100¹	93	6	31	48	11.3	2.78	137	.250	.311	3	.136	-1	9	11	3	1.4
1975	SF-N	5	3	.625	55	2	0	0	3	98	94	2	66	45	15.1	3.49	109	.261	.381	2	.125	-0	1	3	2	0.6
1976	SF-N	2	0	1.000	48	2	0	0	1	85	80	4	39	34	12.8	2.96	122	.256	.343	1	.125	-0	5	6	1	0.7
1977	SF-N	6	5	.545	55	8	1	0	0	119	116	9	60	41	13.5	4.01	98	.262	.354	4	.222	0	-1	-1	0	0.0
1978	SF-N	1	3	.250	25	1	0	0	0	48	60	5	28	22	16.7	5.44	63	.314	.405	0	.000	-1	-10	-11	0	-1.0
Total	8	23	22	.511	268	33	2	0	4	573	581	38	275	257	13.7	3.97	93	.269	.355	13	.134	-2	-22	-17	4	-0.9

YEAR TM/L	W	L	PCT	G	GS	CG	SH	SV	IP	H	HR	BB	SO	RAT	ERA	ERA+	OAV	OOB	BH	AVG	PB	PR	/A	PD	TPI
■ **LEFTY WILLIAMS** Williams, Claude Preston b: 3/9/1893, Aurora, Mo. d: 11/4/59, Laguna Beach, Cal. BR/TL, 5'9", 160 lbs. Deb: 9/17/13																								
1913 Det-A	1	3	.250	5	4	3	0	1	29	34	0	4	9	12.1	4.97	59	.286	.315	1	.100	-0	-7	-7	-1	-0.7
1914 Det-A	0	1	.000	1	1	0	0	0	1	3	0	2	0	45.0	0.00	—	.429	.556	0	—	0	0	0	0	0.0
1916 Chi-A	13	7	.650	43	26	10	2	1	224¹	220	5	65	138	11.8	2.89	96	.267	.327	10	.135	-0	-1	-3	-5	-0.9
1917 *Chi-A	17	8	.680	45	29	8	1	1	230	221	3	81	85	12.2	2.97	90	.252	.321	6	.090	-3	-8	-8	-5	-1.6
1918 Chi-A	6	4	.600	15	14	7	2	1	105²	76	0	47	30	10.9	2.73	100	.209	.308	5	.132	-2	1	0	-2	-0.4
1919 *Chi-A	23	11	.676	41	40	27	5	1	297	265	8	58	125	10.1	2.64	121	.244	.289	17	.181	1	20	18	-6	1.4
1920 Chi-A	22	14	.611	39	38	25	0	0	299	302	15	90	128	12.2	3.91	96	.271	.332	22	.218	0	-4	-5	-4	-0.8
Total 7	82	48	.631	189	152	80	10	5	1186	1121	31	347	515	11.5	3.13	99	.255	.316	61	.159	-4	1	-4	-22	-3.0
■ **MUTT WILLIAMS** Williams, David Carter b: 7/31/1891, Ozark, Ark. d: 3/30/62, Fayetteville, Ark. BR/TR, 6'3.5", 195 lbs. Deb: 10/04/13																								
1913 Was-A	1	0	1.000	1	1	0	0	0	4	4	1	2	1	13.5	4.50	66	.286	.375	1	.500	0	-1	-1	0	0.0
1914 Was-A	0	0	—	5	0	0	0	1	7	5	0	4	3	11.6	5.14	54	.227	.346	0	—	0	-2	-2	-0	-0.1
Total 2	1	0	1.000	6	1	0	0	1	11	9	1	6	4	12.3	4.91	58	.250	.357	1	.500	0	-3	-3	-0	-0.1
■ **DAVE WILLIAMS** Williams, David Owen b: 1879, Scranton, Pa. d: 4/25/18, Hot Springs, Ark. TL, Deb: 7/02/02																								
1902 Bos-A	0	0	—	3	0	0	0	0	18²	22	0	11	7	15.9	5.30	67	.294	.384	3	.333	1	-4	-4	-1	-0.2
■ **DON WILLIAMS** Williams, Donald Fred b: 9/14/31, Floyd, Va. BR/TR, 6'2", 180 lbs. Deb: 9/12/58																								
1958 Pit-N	0	0	—	2	0	0	0	0	4	6	1	1	3	15.8	6.75	57	.375	.412	0	—	0	-1	-1	0	0.0
1959 Pit-N	0	0	—	6	0	0	0	0	12	17	1	3	3	15.0	6.75	57	.362	.400	1	.333	1	-4	-4	-0	-0.2
1962 KC-A	0	0	—	3	0	0	0	0	4	6	0	0	1	15.8	9.00	46	.353	.389	0	.000	-0	-2	-2	0	-0.1
Total 3	0	0	—	11	0	0	0	0	20	29	2	4	7	15.3	7.20	55	.363	.400	1	.250	1	-7	-7	-0	-0.3
■ **DON WILLIAMS** Williams, Donald Reid "Dino" b: 9/2/35, Los Angeles, Cal. BR/TR, 6'5", 218 lbs. Deb: 8/04/63																								
1963 Min-A	0	0	—	3	0	0	0	0	4¹	8	1	6	2	29.1	10.38	35	.381	.519	0	—	0	-3	-3	0	-0.2
■ **DALE WILLIAMS** Williams, Elisha Alphonso b: 10/6/1855, Ludlow, Ky. d: 10/22/39, Covington, Ky. BR/TR, 5'9", 175 lbs. Deb: 8/12/1876																								
1876 Cin-N	1	8	.111	9	9	9	0	0	83	123	1	4	9	13.8	4.23	52	.322	.329	7	.200	-2	-18	-19	-0	-1.6
■ **FRANK WILLIAMS** Williams, Frank Lee b: 2/13/58, Seattle, Wash. BR/TR, 6'1", 180 lbs. Deb: 4/05/84																								
1984 SF-N	9	4	.692	61	1	1	1	3	106¹	88	2	51	91	12.0	3.55	99	.226	.321	4	.222	1	0	-1	3	0.4
1985 SF-N	2	4	.333	49	0	0	0	0	73	65	5	35	54	13.1	4.19	82	.242	.342	0	.000	-0	-5	-6	0	-0.6
1986 SF-N	3	1	.750	36	0	0	0	1	52¹	35	0	21	33	10.3	1.20	292	.212	.316	1	.500	0	15	13	1	1.5
1987 Cin-N	4	0	1.000	85	0	0	0	2	105²	101	5	39	60	12.1	2.30	185	.254	.324	0	.000	-1	21	23	1	2.4
1988 Cin-N	3	2	.600	60	0	0	0	1	62²	59	6	35	43	13.8	2.59	139	.252	.354	0	.000	-0	6	7	0	0.8
1989 Det-A	3	3	.500	42	0	0	0	1	71²	70	5	46	33	14.9	3.64	105	.254	.366	0	—	0	2	1	-0	0.1
Total 6	24	14	.632	333	1	1	1	8	471²	418	23	227	314	12.7	3.00	124	.242	.336	5	.172	1	39	38	5	4.6
■ **JOHNNIE WILLIAMS** Williams, John Brodie "Honolulu Johnnie" b: 7/16/1889, Honolulu, Hawaii d: 9/8/63, Long Beach, Cal. BR/TR, 6', 180 lbs. Deb: 4/21/14																								
1914 Det-A	0	2	.000	4	3	1	0	0	11¹	17	0	5	4	17.5	6.35	44	.378	.440	0	.000	-0	-5	-4	-0	-0.4
■ **LEON WILLIAMS** Williams, Leon Theo "Lefty" b: 12/2/05, Macon, Ga. BL/TL, 5'10.5", 154 lbs. Deb: 6/02/26																								
1926 Bro-N	0	0	—	8	0	0	0	0	8¹	16	0	2	3	19.4	5.40	71	.421	.450	1	.200	0	-1	-1	1	0.0
■ **MARSH WILLIAMS** Williams, Marshall McDiarmid "Cap" b: 2/21/1893, Faison, N.C. d: 2/22/35, Tucson, Ariz. BR/TR, 6', 180 lbs. Deb: 7/07/16																								
1916 Phi-A	0	6	.000	10	4	3	0	0	51¹	71	4	31	17	17.9	7.89	36	.350	.436	2	.105	-1	-29	-29	-1	-2.7
■ **MATT WILLIAMS** Williams, Matthew Evan b: 7/25/59, Houston, Tex. BR/TR, 6'1", 200 lbs. Deb: 8/02/83																								
1983 Tor-A	1	1	.500	4	3	0	0	0	8	13	5	7	5	23.6	14.63	29	.361	.477	0	—	0	-9	-9	0	-0.7
1985 Tex-A	2	1	.667	6	3	0	0	0	26	20	3	10	22	10.4	2.42	175	.211	.286	0	—	0	5	5	-1	0.5
Total 2	3	2	.600	10	6	0	0	0	34	33	8	17	27	13.5	5.29	80	.252	.342	0	—	0	-4	-4	-0	-0.2
■ **MITCH WILLIAMS** Williams, Mitchell Steven b: 11/17/64, Santa Ana, Cal. BL/TL, 6'3", 180 lbs. Deb: 4/09/86																								
1986 Tex-A	8	6	.571	**80**	0	0	0	8	98	69	8	79	90	14.6	3.58	120	.202	.369	0	—	0	6	8	-1	0.7
1987 Tex-A	8	6	.571	85	1	0	0	6	108²	63	9	94	129	13.6	3.23	138	.175	.355	0	—	0	15	15	0	1.4
1988 Tex-A	2	7	.222	67	0	0	0	18	68	48	4	47	61	13.4	4.63	88	.203	.349	0	—	0	-5	-4	0	-0.3
1989 *Chi-N	4	4	.500	**76**	0	0	0	36	81²	71	6	52	67	14.4	2.76	136	.238	.366	1	.200	1	7	9	-1	1.0
1990 Chi-N	1	8	.111	59	2	0	0	16	66¹	60	4	50	55	15.1	3.93	105	.239	.368	0	.000	-1	-1	-1	-1	0.0
Total 5	23	31	.426	367	3	0	0	84	422²	311	31	322	402	14.2	3.56	118	.209	.362	1	.100	1	22	30	-3	2.8
■ **STEAMBOAT WILLIAMS** Williams, Rees Gephardt b: 1/31/1892, Cascade, Mont. d: 6/29/79, Deer River, Minn. BL/TR, 5'11", 170 lbs. Deb: 7/12/14																								
1914 StL-N	0	1	.000	5	1	0	0	0	11	13	1	6	2	15.5	6.55	43	.295	.380	0	.000	-0	-5	-5	0	-0.4
1916 StL-N	6	7	.462	36	8	5	0	1	105	121	6	27	25	12.8	4.20	63	.291	.336	5	.208	1	-18	-18	0	-1.8
Total 2	6	8	.429	41	9	5	0	1	116	134	7	33	27	13.0	4.42	60	.291	.340	5	.200	1	-23	-23	0	-2.2
■ **RICK WILLIAMS** Williams, Richard Allen b: 11/9/52, Merced, Cal. BR/TR, 6'1", 180 lbs. Deb: 6/12/78																								
1978 Hou-N	1	2	.333	17	1	0	0	0	34²	43	2	10	17	13.8	4.67	71	.301	.346	0	.000	-1	-4	-5	0	-0.5
1979 Hou-N	4	7	.364	31	16	2	2	0	121¹	122	6	30	37	11.4	3.26	108	.261	.308	8	.258	3	6	3	1	0.7
Total 2	5	9	.357	48	17	2	2	0	156	165	8	40	54	11.9	3.58	97	.270	.317	8	.222	2	2	-2	1	0.2
■ **ACE WILLIAMS** Williams, Robert Fulton b: 3/18/17, Montclair, N.J. BR/TL, 6'2", 174 lbs. Deb: 7/15/40																								
1940 Bos-N	0	0	—	5	0	0	0	0	9	21	0	12	5	34.0	16.00	23	.375	.493	0	.000	-0	-12	-12	0	-1.0
1946 Bos-N	0	0	—	1	0	0	0	0	1	1	0	1	0	—	—	—	1.000	1.000	0	—	0	0	0	0	0.0
Total 2	0	0	—	6	0	0	0	0	9	22	0	13	5	36.0	16.00	23	.386	.507	0	.000	-0	-12	-12	0	-1.0
■ **STAN WILLIAMS** Williams, Stanley Wilson b: 9/14/36, Enfield, N.H. BR/TR, 6'5", 230 lbs. Deb: 5/17/58 C																								
1958 LA-N	9	7	.563	27	21	3	2	0	119	99	10	65	80	12.9	4.01	102	.228	.338	2	.050	-3	-1	1	0	-0.1
1959 *LA-N	5	5	.500	35	15	2	0	0	124²	102	12	86	89	14.2	3.97	106	.228	.363	7	.194	1	-0	4	0	0.5
1960 LA-N	14	10	.583	38	30	9	2	1	207¹	162	26	72	175	10.4	3.00	133	.210	.282	9	.141	0	18	22	1	2.5
1961 LA-N	15	12	.556	41	35	6	2	0	235¹	213	21	108	205	12.5	3.90	111	.242	.329	13	.167	-0	3	12	-1	1.1
1962 LA-N	14	12	.538	40	28	4	1	1	185²	184	16	98	108	13.7	4.46	81	.253	.341	5	.076	-2	-11	-17	-1	-1.8
1963 *NY-A	9	8	.529	29	21	6	1	0	146	137	7	57	98	12.3	3.21	110	.249	.326	5	.102	-1	7	5	1	0.5
1964 NY-A	1	5	.167	21	10	1	0	0	82	76	7	38	54	12.5	3.84	94	.248	.330	3	.143	-0	-2	-2	-1	-0.1
1965 Cle-A	0	0	—	3	0	0	0	0	4¹	6	1	3	1	18.7	6.23	56	.353	.450	0	—	0	-1	-1	0	0.0
1967 Cle-A	6	4	.600	16	8	2	1	1	79	64	6	24	75	10.1	2.62	125	.218	.279	2	.091	-1	5	6	-2	0.3
1968 Cle-A	13	11	.542	44	24	6	2	9	194¹	163	14	51	147	10.4	2.50	118	.225	.285	9	.161	-1	10	10	-0	1.2
1969 Cle-A	6	14	.300	61	15	3	0	12	178¹	155	25	67	139	11.8	3.94	96	.235	.317	4	.100	-1	-6	-3	-1	-0.4
1970 *Min-A	10	1	.909	68	0	0	0	15	113¹	85	8	32	76	9.7	1.99	187	.208	.274	0	.000	-2	22	22	-1	1.9
1971 Min-A	4	5	.444	46	1	0	0	4	78	63	7	44	47	13.3	4.15	86	.220	.340	0	.000	-1	-6	-5	-1	-0.6
StL-N	3	0	1.000	10	0	0	0	0	12²	13	0	2	8	12.1	1.42	253	.265	.321	0	.000	-0	3	3	0	0.4
1972 Bos-A	0	0	—	3	0	0	0	0	4	5	0	1	3	13.5	6.75	48	.294	.333	0	—	0	-2	-2	0	-0.1
Total 14	109	94	.537	482	208	42	11	43	1764	1527	160	748	1305	12.0	3.48	108	.232	.317	59	.118	-10	39	53	-3	5.3
■ **TED WILLIAMS** Williams, Theodore Samuel "The Kid", "The Thumper" or "The Splendid Splinter" b: 8/30/18, San Diego, Cal. BL/TR, 6'3", 205 lbs. Deb: 4/20/39 MH♦																								
1940 Bos-A	0	0	—	1	0	0	0	0	2	3	0	0	1	13.5	4.50	100	.333	.333	193	.344	1	-0	-0	P0	0.0

YEAR TM/L	W	L	PCT	G	GS	CG	SH	SV	IP	H	HR	BB	SO	RAT	ERA	ERA+	OAV	OOB	BH	AVG	PB	PR	/A	PD	TPI

■ TOM WILLIAMS   Williams, Thomas C.   b: 8/19/1870, Minersville, Ohio   d: 7/27/40, Columbus, Ohio   Deb: 5/01/1892

YEAR TM/L	W	L	PCT	G	GS	CG	SH	SV	IP	H	HR	BB	SO	RAT	ERA	ERA+	OAV	OOB	BH	AVG	PB	PR	/A	PD	TPI
1892 Cle-N	1	0	1.000	2	1	1	0	0	9	9	1	1	3	10.0	3.00	113	.250	.270	1	.100	-1	0	0	0	0.0
1893 Cle-N	1	1	.500	5	2	2	0	0	24	33	1	10	6	16.1	4.88	100	.317	.377	5	.278	1	-1	0	0	0.1
Total 2	2	1	.667	7	3	3	0	0	33	42	2	11	9	14.5	4.36	103	.300	.351	6	.214	-0	-0	0	0	0.1

■ POP WILLIAMS   Williams, Walter Merrill   b: 5/19/1874, Bowdoinham, Me.   d: 8/4/59, Topsham, Maine   BL/TR, 5'11", 190 lbs.   Deb: 9/14/1898

YEAR TM/L	W	L	PCT	G	GS	CG	SH	SV	IP	H	HR	BB	SO	RAT	ERA	ERA+	OAV	OOB	BH	AVG	PB	PR	/A	PD	TPI
1898 Was-N	0	2	.000	2	2	2	0	0	17	32	0	7	3	20.6	8.47	43	.396	.444	3	.375	1	-9	-9	-0	-0.6
1902 Chi-N	11	16	.407	31	31	26	1	0	254¹	259	2	63	94	11.6	2.51	107	.264	.312	23	.198	2	8	5	2	1.1
1903 Chi-N	0	1	.000	1	1	1	0	0	5	9	0	0	2	16.2	5.40	58	.409	.409	0	.000	-0	-1	-1	0	0.0
Phi-N	1	1	.500	2	2	2	0	0	18	21	0	6	8	14.0	3.00	109	.304	.368	2	.286	-0	1	1	1	0.2
Bos-N	4	5	.444	10	10	9	1	0	83	97	3	37	20	15.5	4.12	78	.295	.381	10	.238	0	-8	-8	-0	-0.7
Yr	5	7	.417	13	13	12	1	0	106	127	3	43	30	15.2	3.99	81	.302	.378	0	.000	-0	-8	-9	1	-0.5
Total 3	16	25	.390	46	46	40	2	0	377¹	418	5	113	127	13.0	3.20	90	.282	.339	38	.217	3	-10	-13	3	0.0

■ WASH WILLIAMS   Williams, Washington J.   b: Philadelphia, Pa.   d: 1/1890, Philadelphia, Pa.   5'11", 180 lbs.   Deb: 8/05/1884 ♦

YEAR TM/L	W	L	PCT	G	GS	CG	SH	SV	IP	H	HR	BB	SO	RAT	ERA	ERA+	OAV	OOB	BH	AVG	PB	PR	/A	PD	TPI
1885 Chi-N	0	0	—	1	1	0	0	0	2	2	0	5	0	31.5	13.50	22	.248	.536	1	.250	-0	-2	-2	0	-0.1

■ NED WILLIAMSON   Williamson, Edward Nagle   b: 10/24/1857, Philadelphia, Pa.   d: 3/3/1894, Willow Springs, Ark   BR/TR, 5'11", 170 lbs.   Deb: 5/01/1878 ♦

YEAR TM/L	W	L	PCT	G	GS	CG	SH	SV	IP	H	HR	BB	SO	RAT	ERA	ERA+	OAV	OOB	BH	AVG	PB	PR	/A	PD	TPI
1881 Chi-N	1	1	.500	3	1	1	0	0	18	14	0	0	2	7.0	2.00	137	.205	.205	92	.268	1	1	-1	0	0.1
1882 Chi-N	0	0	—	1	0	0	0	0	3	9	1	1	0	30.0	6.00	48	.494	.521	98	.282	0	-1	-1	0	0.0
1883 Chi-N	0	0	—	1	0	0	0	0	1	1	0	1	1	18.0	9.00	36	.245	.394	111	.276	0	-1	-1	0	0.0
1884 Chi-N	0	0	—	2	0	0	0	0	2	8	0	2	0	45.0	18.00	17	.567	.620	116	.278	1	-3	-3	0	-0.2
1885 *Chi-N	0	0	—	2	0	0	0	2	6	2	0	0	3	3.0	0.00	—	.099	.099	97	.238	0	2	2	0	0.2
1886 *Chi-N	0	0	—	2	0	0	0	1	3	2	0	1	6	13.5	0.00	—	.182	.182	93	.216	0	1	1	0	0.1
1887 Chi-N	0	0	—	1	0	0	0	0	2	2	0	1	0	13.5	9.00	50	.253	.337	117	.267	0	-1	-1	0	0.0
Total 7	1	1	.500	12	1	1	0	3	35	38	1	5	7	11.1	3.34	90	.264	.289	1159	.255	3	-2	-1	0	0.2

■ MARK WILLIAMSON   Williamson, Mark Alan   b: 7/21/59, Corpus Christi, Tex.   BR/TR, 6'", 155 lbs.   Deb: 4/08/87

YEAR TM/L	W	L	PCT	G	GS	CG	SH	SV	IP	H	HR	BB	SO	RAT	ERA	ERA+	OAV	OOB	BH	AVG	PB	PR	/A	PD	TPI
1987 Bal-A	8	9	.471	61	2	0	0	3	125	122	12	41	73	12.0	4.03	109	.261	.324	0	—	0	6	5	1	0.6
1988 Bal-A	5	8	.385	37	10	2	0	2	117²	125	14	40	69	12.8	4.90	80	.272	.333	0	—	0	-12	-13	-0	-1.2
1989 Bal-A	10	5	.667	65	0	0	0	9	107¹	105	4	30	55	11.5	2.93	129	.261	.315	0	—	0	11	10	-1	1.0
1990 Bal-A	8	2	.800	49	0	0	0	1	85¹	65	8	28	60	9.8	2.21	173	.215	.282	0	—	0	16	15	1	1.7
Total 4	31	24	.564	212	12	2	0	15	435¹	417	38	139	257	11.6	3.64	110	.256	.317	0	—	0	21	18	1	2.1

■ AL WILLIAMSON   Williamson, Silas Albert   b: 2/20/1900, Bucksville, Ark.   d: 11/29/78, Hot Springs, Ark.   BR/TR, 5'11", 160 lbs.   Deb: 4/27/28

YEAR TM/L	W	L	PCT	G	GS	CG	SH	SV	IP	H	HR	BB	SO	RAT	ERA	ERA+	OAV	OOB	BH	AVG	PB	PR	/A	PD	TPI
1928 Chi-A	0	0	—	1	0	0	0	0	2	1	0	0	0	4.5	0.00	—	.167	.167	0	—	0	1	1	0	0.1

■ CARL WILLIS   Willis, Carl Blake   b: 12/28/60, Danville, Va.   BL/TR, 6'4", 210 lbs.   Deb: 6/09/84

YEAR TM/L	W	L	PCT	G	GS	CG	SH	SV	IP	H	HR	BB	SO	RAT	ERA	ERA+	OAV	OOB	BH	AVG	PB	PR	/A	PD	TPI
1984 Det-A	0	2	.000	10	2	0	0	0	16	25	1	5	4	16.9	7.31	54	.362	.405	0	—	0	-6	-6	0	-0.5
Cin-N	0	1	.000	7	0	0	0	1	9²	8	1	2	3	9.3	3.72	101	.222	.263	0	—	0	-0	0	0	0.0
1985 Cin-N	1	0	1.000	11	0	0	0	1	13²	21	3	5	6	17.1	9.22	41	.344	.394	0	.000	0	-9	-8	-0	-0.7
1986 Cin-N	1	3	.250	29	0	0	0	0	52¹	54	4	32	24	15.0	4.47	87	.278	.383	1	.333	0	-4	-4	1	-0.2
1988 Chi-A	0	0	—	6	0	0	0	0	12	17	3	7	6	18.0	8.25	48	.362	.444	0	—	0	-6	-6	0	-0.5
Total 4	2	6	.250	63	2	0	0	2	103²	125	12	51	43	15.4	5.90	66	.307	.386	1	.250	0	-25	-23	1	-1.9

■ LEFTY WILLIS   Willis, Charles William   b: 11/4/05, Leetown, W.Va.   d: 5/10/62, Bethesda, Md.   BL/TL, 6'1", 175 lbs.   Deb: 10/03/25

YEAR TM/L	W	L	PCT	G	GS	CG	SH	SV	IP	H	HR	BB	SO	RAT	ERA	ERA+	OAV	OOB	BH	AVG	PB	PR	/A	PD	TPI
1925 Phi-A	0	0	—	1	1	0	0	0	5	9	2	2	3	19.8	10.80	43	.409	.458	0	.000	-1	-4	-3	0	-0.2
1926 Phi-A	0	0	—	13	1	0	0	1	32¹	31	0	12	13	12.2	1.39	300	.270	.344	2	.222	-0	9	10	-0	1.0
1927 Phi-A	3	1	.750	15	2	1	0	0	27	32	2	11	7	14.3	5.67	75	.308	.374	0	.000	-1	-5	-4	1	-0.3
Total 3	3	1	.750	29	4	1	0	1	64¹	72	4	25	23	13.7	3.92	108	.299	.367	2	.111	-1	1	2	1	0.5

■ DALE WILLIS   Willis, Dale Jerome   b: 5/29/38, Calhoun, Ga.   BR/TR, 5'11", 165 lbs.   Deb: 4/14/63

YEAR TM/L	W	L	PCT	G	GS	CG	SH	SV	IP	H	HR	BB	SO	RAT	ERA	ERA+	OAV	OOB	BH	AVG	PB	PR	/A	PD	TPI
1963 KC-A	0	2	.000	25	0	0	0	1	44²	46	3	25	47	15.1	5.04	76	.266	.371	1	.167	-0	-7	-6	0	-0.5

■ JIM WILLIS   Willis, James Gladden   b: 3/20/27, Doyline, La.   BL/TR, 6'3", 175 lbs.   Deb: 4/22/53

YEAR TM/L	W	L	PCT	G	GS	CG	SH	SV	IP	H	HR	BB	SO	RAT	ERA	ERA+	OAV	OOB	BH	AVG	PB	PR	/A	PD	TPI
1953 Chi-N	2	1	.667	13	3	2	0	0	43¹	37	1	17	15	11.8	3.12	143	.228	.313	0	.000	-1	6	6	1	0.7
1954 Chi-N	0	1	.000	14	1	0	0	0	23	22	1	18	5	16.8	3.91	107	.256	.402	0	.000	-1	0	1	1	0.1
Total 2	2	2	.500	27	4	2	0	0	66¹	59	2	35	20	13.6	3.39	129	.238	.346	0	.000	-2	6	7	2	0.8

■ JOE WILLIS   Willis, Joseph Denk   b: 4/9/1890, Coal Grove, Ohio   d: 12/4/66, Ironton, Ohio   BR/TL, 6'1", 185 lbs.   Deb: 5/03/11

YEAR TM/L	W	L	PCT	G	GS	CG	SH	SV	IP	H	HR	BB	SO	RAT	ERA	ERA+	OAV	OOB	BH	AVG	PB	PR	/A	PD	TPI
1911 StL-A	0	1	.000	1	1	0	0	0	7	8	0	3	0	14.1	5.14	66	.308	.379	0	.000	0	-1	-1	-0	0.0
StL-N	0	1	.000	2	2	1	0	0	15	13	0	4	5	10.2	4.20	80	.232	.283	0	.000	-1	-1	-1	0	-0.1
1912 StL-N	4	9	.308	31	17	4	0	2	129²	143	3	62	55	14.6	4.44	77	.278	.361	6	.158	-2	-15	-15	-1	-1.6
1913 StL-N	0	0	—	7	0	0	0	1	9²	9	0	11	6	18.6	7.45	43	.257	.435	0	.000	-0	-5	-5	-0	-0.4
Total 3	4	11	.267	41	20	5	0	3	161¹	173	3	80	66	14.4	4.63	74	.274	.360	6	.125	-2	-22	-22	-1	-2.1

■ LES WILLIS   Willis, Lester Evans "Wimpy" or "Lefty"   b: 1/17/08, Nacogdoches, Tex.   d: 1/22/82, Jasper, Tex.   BL/TL, 5'9.5", 195 lbs.   Deb: 4/28/47

YEAR TM/L	W	L	PCT	G	GS	CG	SH	SV	IP	H	HR	BB	SO	RAT	ERA	ERA+	OAV	OOB	BH	AVG	PB	PR	/A	PD	TPI
1947 Cle-A	0	2	.000	22	2	0	0	1	44	58	3	24	10	16.8	3.48	100	.324	.404	1	.091	-1	1	0	-0	-0.1

■ MIKE WILLIS   Willis, Michael Henry   b: 12/26/50, Oklahoma City, Okla   BL/TL, 6'2", 205 lbs.   Deb: 4/13/77

YEAR TM/L	W	L	PCT	G	GS	CG	SH	SV	IP	H	HR	BB	SO	RAT	ERA	ERA+	OAV	OOB	BH	AVG	PB	PR	/A	PD	TPI
1977 Tor-A	2	6	.250	43	3	0	0	5	107¹	105	15	38	59	12.0	3.94	106	.260	.324	0	—	0	1	3	1	0.4
1978 Tor-A	3	7	.300	44	2	1	0	7	100²	104	11	39	52	12.8	4.56	86	.271	.338	0	—	0	-9	-7	0	-0.6
1979 Tor-A	0	3	.000	17	1	0	0	0	26²	35	1	16	8	17.6	8.44	51	.333	.426	0	—	0	-13	-12	0	-1.0
1980 Tor-A	2	1	.667	20	0	0	0	3	26¹	25	3	11	14	12.6	1.71	252	.248	.327	0	—	0	7	8	0	0.8
1981 Tor-A	0	4	.000	20	0	0	0	0	35	43	6	20	16	16.5	5.91	67	.301	.390	0	—	0	-9	-8	0	-0.7
Total 5	7	21	.250	144	6	1	0	15	296	312	36	124	149	13.3	4.59	89	.274	.347	0	—	0	-22	-16	1	-1.1

■ RON WILLIS   Willis, Ronald Earl   b: 7/12/43, Willisville, Tenn.   d: 11/21/77, Memphis, Tenn.   BR/TR, 6'2", 185 lbs.   Deb: 9/20/66

YEAR TM/L	W	L	PCT	G	GS	CG	SH	SV	IP	H	HR	BB	SO	RAT	ERA	ERA+	OAV	OOB	BH	AVG	PB	PR	/A	PD	TPI
1966 StL-N	0	0	—	4	0	0	0	0	3	1	0	1	2	6.0	0.00	—	.100	.182	0	—	0	1	1	0	0.1
1967 *StL-N	6	5	.545	65	0	0	0	10	81	76	3	43	42	13.6	2.67	123	.257	.357	3	.375	1	6	6	2	1.0
1968 *StL-N	2	3	.400	48	0	0	0	4	63²	46	4	28	39	11.2	3.39	85	.213	.299	0	.000	-1	3	4	1	-0.3
1969 StL-N	1	2	.333	26	0	0	0	0	32¹	26	4	19	23	12.8	4.18	86	.224	.338	1	1.000	0	-2	-2	1	0.0
Hou-N	0	0	—	3	0	0	0	0	2¹	3	0	0	2	11.6	0.00	—	.300	.300	0	—	0	1	1	0	0.1
Yr	1	2	.333	29	0	0	0	0	34²	29	4	19	25	12.5	3.89	92	.223	.322	0	.000	-1	-1	-1	1	0.1
1970 SD-N	2	2	.500	42	0	0	0	4	56	53	4	28	20	13.7	4.02	99	.247	.344	0	.000	-1	0	-0	2	0.1
Total 5	11	12	.478	188	0	0	0	19	238¹	209	15	119	128	12.7	3.32	102	.237	.334	4	.160	0	4	2	5	1.0

■ VIC WILLIS   Willis, Victor Gazaway   b: 4/12/1876, Cecil Co., Md.   d: 8/3/47, Elkton, Md.   BR/TR, 6'2", 185 lbs.   Deb: 4/20/1898

YEAR TM/L	W	L	PCT	G	GS	CG	SH	SV	IP	H	HR	BB	SO	RAT	ERA	ERA+	OAV	OOB	BH	AVG	PB	PR	/A	PD	TPI
1898 Bos-N	25	13	.658	41	38	29	1	0	311	264	5	148	160	11.9	2.84	130	.228	.316	17	.145	-6	27	30	-1	2.2
1899 Bos-N	27	8	.771	41	38	35	5	2	342²	277	6	117	120	10.3	2.50	167	.221	.288	29	.216	-4	52	63	-0	5.9
1900 Bos-N	10	17	.370	32	29	22	2	0	236	258	11	106	53	13.9	4.19	98	.277	.351	12	.136	-6	-13	-2	-1	-0.6
1901 Bos-N	20	17	.541	38	35	33	6	0	305¹	262	6	78	133	10.3	2.36	153	.230	.286	20	.187	-1	33	43	-1	4.3
1902 Bos-N	27	20	.574	51	46	45	4	3	410	372	6	101	225	10.7	2.20	129	.242	.295	23	.153	-6	27	29	3	2.9
1903 Bos-N	12	18	.400	33	32	29	2	0	278	256	3	88	125	11.5	2.98	108	.251	.317	24	.188	-1	9	7	3	0.7

YEAR	TM/L	W	L	PCT	G	GS	CG	SH	SV	IP	H	HR	BB	SO	RAT	ERA	ERA+	OAV	OOB	BH	AVG	PB	PR	/A	PD	TPI
1904	Bos-N	18	25	.419	43	43	**39**	2	0	350	357	7	109	196	12.3	2.85	97	.266	.327	27	.182	1	-4	-4	6	0.3
1905	Bos-N	12	29	.293	41	41	36	4	0	342	340	7	107	149	12.1	3.21	97	.265	.328	20	.153	-3	-8	-4	6	0.0
1906	Pit-N	23	13	.639	41	36	32	6	1	322	295	0	76	124	10.5	1.73	154	.250	.298	20	.174	-1	32	34	6	4.5
1907	Pit-N	21	11	.656	39	37	27	6	1	292²	234	4	69	107	9.5	2.34	104	.219	.271	14	.136	-2	4	3	2	0.3
1908	Pit-N	23	11	.676	41	38	25	7	0	304²	239	2	69	97	9.3	2.07	111	.213	.262	17	.165	-1	10	8	-0	0.7
1909	*Pit-N	22	11	.667	39	35	24	4	1	289²	243	3	83	95	10.3	2.24	122	.231	.289	14	.136	-2	12	16	1	1.6
1910	StL-N	9	12	.429	33	23	12	1	3	212	224	6	61	67	12.1	3.35	89	.275	.326	11	.167	-2	-8	-9	3	-0.8
Total	13	249	205	.548	513	471	388	50	11	3996	3621	66	1212	1651	11.1	2.63	118	.243	.304	248	.166	-33	172	208	24	22.0

■ **CLAUDE WILLOUGHBY**   Willoughby, Claude William "Flunky" or "Weeping Willie"
b: 11/14/1898, Fredonia, Kan. d: 8/14/73, McPherson, Kan.   BR/TR, 5'9.5", 165 lbs. Deb: 9/18/25

YEAR	TM/L	W	L	PCT	G	GS	CG	SH	SV	IP	H	HR	BB	SO	RAT	ERA	ERA+	OAV	OOB	BH	AVG	PB	PR	/A	PD	TPI
1925	Phi-N	2	1	.667	3	3	1	0	0	23	26	0	11	6	14.9	1.96	244	.295	.380	0	.000	-1	6	7	-0	0.6
1926	Phi-N	8	12	.400	47	18	6	0	1	168	218	7	71	37	15.8	5.95	70	.327	.396	11	.212	-1	-40	-34	3	-2.9
1927	Phi-N	3	7	.300	35	6	1	1	2	97²	126	7	53	14	16.7	6.54	63	.321	.404	2	.077	-2	-28	-26	-0	-2.6
1928	Phi-N	6	5	.545	35	13	5	1	1	130²	180	6	83	26	18.3	5.30	80	.340	.432	6	.150	-1	-19	-15	-0	-1.4
1929	Phi-N	15	14	.517	49	34	14	1	4	243¹	288	15	108	50	14.8	4.99	104	.296	.370	13	.143	-5	-7	5	5	0.5
1930	Phi-N	4	17	.190	41	24	5	1	1	153	241	17	68	38	18.3	7.59	72	.369	.430	5	.104	-4	-44	-36	2	-3.1
1931	Pit-N	0	2	.000	9	2	1	0	0	25²	32	4	12	4	15.4	6.31	61	.305	.376	2	.286	0	-7	-7	0	-0.5
Total	7	38	58	.396	219	100	33	4	9	841¹	1111	56	406	175	16.4	5.84	81	.326	.401	39	.143	-15	-140	-106	9	-9.4

■ **JIM WILLOUGHBY**   Willoughby, James Arthur b: 1/31/49, Salinas, Cal.   BR/TR, 6'2", 185 lbs. Deb: 9/05/71

YEAR	TM/L	W	L	PCT	G	GS	CG	SH	SV	IP	H	HR	BB	SO	RAT	ERA	ERA+	OAV	OOB	BH	AVG	PB	PR	/A	PD	TPI
1971	SF-N	0	1	.000	2	1	0	0	0	4	8	1	3	20.3	9.00	38	.400	.429	0	.000	-0	-2	-2	0	-0.1	
1972	SF-N	6	4	.600	11	11	7	0	0	87²	72	8	14	40	9.0	2.36	148	.222	.259	5	.185	0	11	11	0	1.3
1973	SF-N	4	5	.444	39	12	1	1	1	123	138	21	37	60	13.0	4.68	82	.295	.350	4	.143	1	-14	-12	-1	-1.1
1974	SF-N	1	4	.200	18	4	0	0	0	40²	51	7	9	12	13.3	4.65	82	.304	.339	1	.100	-0	-5	-4	1	-0.2
1975	*Bos-A	5	2	.714	24	0	0	0	8	48¹	46	6	16	29	11.9	3.54	115	.247	.314	0	—	0	1	3	0	0.3
1976	Bos-A	3	12	.200	54	0	0	0	10	99	94	4	31	37	12.1	2.82	139	.256	.328	0	.000	0	8	12	1	1.4
1977	Bos-A	6	2	.750	31	0	0	0	2	54²	54	5	18	33	12.2	4.94	91	.258	.323	0	—	0	-5	-3	1	-0.1
1978	Chi-A	1	6	.143	59	0	0	0	13	93¹	95	6	19	36	11.4	3.86	99	.275	.320	0	—	0	-1	-1	2	0.1
Total	8	26	36	.419	238	28	8	1	34	550²	558	57	145	250	11.8	3.79	102	.267	.321	10	.149	1	-8	4	5	1.6

■ **FRANK WILLS**   Wills, Frank Lee b: 10/26/58, New Orleans, La.   BR/TR, 6'2", 200 lbs. Deb: 7/31/83

YEAR	TM/L	W	L	PCT	G	GS	CG	SH	SV	IP	H	HR	BB	SO	RAT	ERA	ERA+	OAV	OOB	BH	AVG	PB	PR	/A	PD	TPI
1983	KC-A	2	1	.667	6	4	0	0	0	34²	35	2	15	23	13.0	4.15	98	.259	.333	0	—	0	-0	-0	-0	0.0
1984	KC-A	2	3	.400	10	5	0	0	0	37	39	3	13	21	12.6	5.11	79	.271	.331	0	—	0	-5	-4	-1	-0.4
1985	Sea-A	5	11	.313	24	18	1	0	1	123	122	18	68	67	14.1	6.00	70	.266	.365	0	—	0	-25	-24	0	-2.2
1986	Cle-A	4	4	.500	26	0	0	0	4	40¹	43	6	16	32	13.2	4.91	84	.272	.339	0	—	0	-3	-3	0	-0.2
1987	Cle-A	0	1	.000	6	0	0	0	0	5¹	3	0	7	4	16.9	5.06	89	.176	.417	0	—	0	-0	-0	-0	-0.0
1988	Tor-A	0	0	—	10	0	0	0	0	20²	22	2	6	19	12.2	5.23	75	.272	.322	0	—	0	-3	-3	-0	-0.2
1989	Tor-A	3	1	.750	24	4	0	0	0	71¹	65	4	30	41	12.1	3.66	103	.242	.320	0	—	0	2	1	0	0.1
1990	Tor-A	6	4	.600	44	4	0	0	0	99	101	13	38	72	12.7	4.73	80	.266	.334	0	—	0	-9	-10	-0	-0.9
Total	8	22	25	.468	150	35	1	0	6	431¹	430	48	193	279	13.1	4.95	81	.262	.341	0	—	0	-44	-45	-0	-3.8

■ **TED WILLS**   Wills, Theodore Carl b: 2/9/34, Fresno, Cal.   BL/TL, 6'2", 200 lbs. Deb: 5/24/59

YEAR	TM/L	W	L	PCT	G	GS	CG	SH	SV	IP	H	HR	BB	SO	RAT	ERA	ERA+	OAV	OOB	BH	AVG	PB	PR	/A	PD	TPI
1959	Bos-A	2	6	.250	9	8	2	0	0	56¹	68	9	24	24	14.9	5.27	77	.302	.372	4	.250	1	-9	-8	-0	-0.5
1960	Bos-A	1	1	.500	15	0	0	0	0	30¹	38	4	16	28	16.9	7.42	55	.317	.410	2	.250	1	-12	-11	0	-0.9
1961	Bos-A	3	2	.600	17	0	0	0	0	19²	24	2	19	11	19.7	5.95	70	.304	.439	0	.000	-0	-4	-4	0	-0.3
1962	Bos-A	0	0	—	1	0	0	0	0	2	2	0	1	0	—	∞		1.000	1.000	0	—	0	-1	-1	0	0.0
	Cin-N	0	2	.000	26	5	0	0	3	61	61	12	23	58	13.1	5.31	76	.266	.346	5	.313	1	-9	-9	-0	-0.7
1965	Chi-A	2	0	1.000	15	0	0	0	1	19	17	2	14	12	15.2	2.84	112	.258	.395	0	.000	0	1	1	0	0.1
Total	5	8	11	.421	83	13	2	0	5	186¹	210	29	97	133	15.3	5.51	72	.291	.383	11	.250	3	-34	-32	0	-2.3

■ **PAUL WILMET**   Wilmet, Paul Richard b: 11/8/58, Green Bay, Wis.   BR/TR, 5'11", 170 lbs. Deb: 7/25/89

YEAR	TM/L	W	L	PCT	G	GS	CG	SH	SV	IP	H	HR	BB	SO	RAT	ERA	ERA+	OAV	OOB	BH	AVG	PB	PR	/A	PD	TPI
1989	Tex-A	0	0	—	3	0	0	0	0	2¹	5	0	2	1	27.0	15.43	26	.417	.500	0	—	0	-3	-3	0	-0.2

■ **WHITEY WILSHERE**   Wilshere, Vernon Sprague b: 8/3/12, Poplar Ridge, N.Y. d: 5/23/85, Cooperstown, N.Y.   BL/TL, 6', 180 lbs. Deb: 6/24/34

YEAR	TM/L	W	L	PCT	G	GS	CG	SH	SV	IP	H	HR	BB	SO	RAT	ERA	ERA+	OAV	OOB	BH	AVG	PB	PR	/A	PD	TPI
1934	Phi-A	0	1	.000	9	2	0	0	0	21²	39	0	15	19	22.8	12.05	36	.394	.478	0	.000	-0	-18	-18	-1	-1.6
1935	Phi-A	9	9	.500	27	18	7	3	1	142¹	136	8	78	80	14.2	4.05	112	.253	.358	4	.093	-4	6	8	-1	0.3
1936	Phi-A	1	2	.333	5	3	0	0	0	18¹	21	1	19	4	19.6	6.87	74	.288	.435	0	.000	-0	-4	-4	0	-0.2
Total	3	10	12	.455	41	23	7	3	1	182¹	196	9	112	103	15.7	5.28	87	.276	.383	4	.080	-4	-15	-14	-2	-1.5

■ **TERRY WILSHUSEN**   Wilshusen, Terry Wayne b: 3/22/49, Atascadero, Cal.   BR/TR, 6'2", 210 lbs. Deb: 4/07/73

YEAR	TM/L	W	L	PCT	G	GS	CG	SH	SV	IP	H	HR	BB	SO	RAT	ERA	ERA+	OAV	OOB	BH	AVG	PB	PR	/A	PD	TPI
1973	Cal-A	0	0	—	1	0	0	0	0	0¹	0	0	2	0	81.0	81.00	4	.000	.750	0	—	0	-3	-3	0	-0.2

■ **DON WILSON**   Wilson, Donald Edward b: 2/12/45, Monroe, La. d: 1/5/75, Houston, Tex.   BR/TR, 6'2.5", 195 lbs. Deb: 9/29/66

YEAR	TM/L	W	L	PCT	G	GS	CG	SH	SV	IP	H	HR	BB	SO	RAT	ERA	ERA+	OAV	OOB	BH	AVG	PB	PR	/A	PD	TPI
1966	Hou-N	1	0	1.000	1	0	0	0	0	6	5	1	1	7	9.0	3.00	114	.238	.273	1	.500	1	0	0	0	0.1
1967	Hou-N	10	9	.526	31	28	7	3	0	184	141	10	69	159	10.6	2.79	119	.209	.289	6	.091	-2	12	11	-3	0.7
1968	Hou-N	13	16	.448	33	30	9	3	0	208²	187	9	70	175	11.3	3.28	90	.236	.302	15	.214	4	-7	-7	-2	-0.6
1969	Hou-N	16	12	.571	34	34	13	1	0	225	210	16	97	235	12.6	4.00	89	.245	.328	8	.099	-1	-10	-11	-1	-1.3
1970	Hou-N	11	6	.647	29	27	3	0	0	184¹	188	15	66	94	12.7	3.91	99	.259	.327	8	.116	-2	3	-1	-2	-0.4
1971	Hou-N	16	10	.615	35	34	18	3	0	268	195	15	79	180	9.4	2.45	137	**.202**	.268	14	.154	-1	30	27	-3	2.5
1972	Hou-N	15	10	.600	33	33	13	3	0	228	196	16	66	172	10.4	2.68	125	.233	.290	11	.105	-2	20	17	1	1.7
1973	Hou-N	11	16	.407	37	32	10	3	2	239¹	187	21	92	149	10.8	3.20	114	.213	.293	14	.177	1	12	12	-2	1.1
1974	Hou-N	11	13	.458	33	27	5	4	0	204²	170	16	100	112	12.0	3.08	112	.227	.321	13	.206	2	12	9	-3	0.8
Total	9	104	92	.531	266	245	78	20	2	1748¹	1479	119	640	1283	11.2	3.15	109	.228	.301	87	.146	-1	73	57	-15	4.6

■ **DUANE WILSON**   Wilson, Duane Lewis b: 6/29/34, Wichita, Kan.   BL/TL, 6'1", 185 lbs. Deb: 7/03/58

YEAR	TM/L	W	L	PCT	G	GS	CG	SH	SV	IP	H	HR	BB	SO	RAT	ERA	ERA+	OAV	OOB	BH	AVG	PB	PR	/A	PD	TPI
1958	Bos-A	0	0	—	2	2	0	0	0	6¹	10	0	7	3	24.2	5.68	70	.400	.531	0	.000	-0	-1	-1	0	0.0

■ **FIN WILSON**   Wilson, Finis Elbert b: 12/9/1889, East Fork, Ky. d: 3/9/59, Coral Gables, Fla.   BL/TL, 6'1", 194 lbs. Deb: 9/26/14

YEAR	TM/L	W	L	PCT	G	GS	CG	SH	SV	IP	H	HR	BB	SO	RAT	ERA	ERA+	OAV	OOB	BH	AVG	PB	PR	/A	PD	TPI
1914	Bro-F	0	1	.000	2	1	1	0	0	7	7	0	11	4	23.1	7.71	41	.268	.485	1	.500	1	-4	-4	-0	-0.2
1915	Bro-F	1	8	.111	18	11	5	0	0	102¹	85	1	53	47	12.5	3.78	80	.249	.356	11	.314	3	-9	-9	-0	-0.5
Total	2	1	9	.100	20	12	6	0	0	109¹	92	1	64	51	13.2	4.03	75	.250	.367	12	.324	3	-12	-12	-0	-0.7

■ **ZEKE WILSON**   Wilson, Frank Ealton b: 12/24/1869, Benton, Ala. d: 4/26/28, Montgomery, Ala.   BR/TR, 5'10", Deb: 4/23/1895

YEAR	TM/L	W	L	PCT	G	GS	CG	SH	SV	IP	H	HR	BB	SO	RAT	ERA	ERA+	OAV	OOB	BH	AVG	PB	PR	/A	PD	TPI
1895	Bos-N	2	4	.333	6	6	4	0	0	45	54	1	27	5	16.2	5.20	98	.293	.383	6	.316	1	-2	-0	1	0.1
	Cle-N	3	1	.750	8	7	3	0	0	44²	63	3	20	16	16.7	4.23	118	.327	.391	2	.111	-2	3	4	0	0.1
	Yr	5	5	.500	14	13	7	0	0	89²	117	4	47	21	16.5	4.72	107	.310	.387	1	.027	-2	1	3	1	0.2
1896	Cle-N	17	9	.654	33	29	20	1	1	240	265	9	81	56	13.0	4.01	113	.278	.334	27	.270	2	9	14	6	2.0
1897	Cle-N	16	11	.593	34	30	26	1	0	263²	323	9	83	69	13.9	4.16	108	.299	.349	26	.224	-3	4	10	1	0.7
1898	Cle-N	13	18	.419	33	31	28	1	0	254²	307	4	51	45	12.7	3.60	100	.296	.329	21	.178	-4	0	0	5	0.1
1899	StL-N	1	1	.500	5	2	2	0	0	26	30	0	4	3	11.8	4.50	88	.289	.315	0	.000	-1	-2	-2	1	0.0
Total	5	52	44	.542	119	105	83	3	1	874	1042	26	266	194	13.5	4.03	106	.293	.343	82	.215	-8	13	25	14	3.0

■ **GARY WILSON**   Wilson, Gary Steven b: 11/21/54, Camden, Ark.   BR/TR, 6'2", 185 lbs. Deb: 4/13/79

YEAR	TM/L	W	L	PCT	G	GS	CG	SH	SV	IP	H	HR	BB	SO	RAT	ERA	ERA+	OAV	OOB	BH	AVG	PB	PR	/A	PD	TPI
1979	Hou-N	0	0	—	6	0	0	0	0	7¹	15	2	6	6	25.8	12.27	29	.441	.525	0	—	0	-7	-7	-0	-0.6

YEAR TM/L	W	L	PCT	G	GS	CG	SH	SV	IP	H	HR	BB	SO	RAT	ERA	ERA+	OAV	OOB	BH	AVG	PB	PR	/A	PD	TPI
■ GLENN WILSON Wilson, Glenn Dwight b: 12/22/58, Baytown, Tex. BR/TR, 6'1", 190 lbs. Deb: 4/15/82 ♦																									
1987 Phi-N	0	0	—	1	0	0	0	0	1	0	0	0	1	0.0	0.00	—	.000	.000	150	.264	0	0	0	0	0.0
■ TEX WILSON Wilson, Gomer Russell b: 7/8/01, Trenton, Tex. d: 9/15/46, Sulphur Springs, Tex. BR/TL, 5'10", 170 lbs. Deb: 9/02/24																									
1924 Bro-N	0	0	—	2	0	0	0	0	3²	7	0	1	1	19.6	14.73	25	.412	.444	0	.000	-0	-4	-4	0	-0.3
■ HIGHBALL WILSON Wilson, Howard Paul b: 8/9/1878, Philadelphia, Pa. d: 10/16/34, Havre-De-Grace, Md TR, Deb: 9/13/1899																									
1899 Cle-N	0	1	.000	1	1	1	0	0	8	12	0	5	1	19.1	9.00	41	.345	.428	1	.333	0	-5	-5	0	-0.2
1902 Phi-A	7	5	.583	13	10	8	0	0	96¹	103	1	19	18	11.4	2.43	151	.274	.309	6	.171	-1	12	13	-1	1.2
1903 Was-A	7	18	.280	30	28	25	1	0	242¹	269	7	43	56	11.6	3.31	95	.280	.311	17	.200	2	-9	-5	-3	-0.4
1904 Was-A	0	3	.000	3	3	3	0	0	25	33	0	4	11	13.3	4.68	57	.318	.343	2	.222	1	-6	-6	0	-0.4
Total 4	14	27	.341	47	42	37	1	0	371¹	417	8	71	86	11.8	3.29	99	.283	.316	26	.197	2	-7	-2	-4	0.2
■ JIM WILSON Wilson, James Alger b: 2/20/22, San Diego, Cal. d: 9/2/86, Newport Beach, Cal BR/TR, 6'1.5", 200 lbs. Deb: 4/18/45																									
1945 Bos-A	6	8	.429	23	21	8	2	0	144¹	121	7	88	50	13.1	3.30	103	.228	.339	13	.245	2	1	2	-2	0.1
1946 Bos-A	0	0	—	1	0	0	0	0	0²	2	1	0	0	27.0	27.00	14	.500	.500	0	—	0	-2	-2	0	-0.1
1948 StL-A	0	0	—	4	0	0	0	0	2²	5	0	5	1	33.8	13.50	34	.417	.588	0	—	0	-3	-3	0	-0.1
1949 Phi-A	0	0	—	2	0	0	0	0	5	7	2	5	2	21.6	14.40	29	.350	.480	0	.000	-0	-6	-6	0	-0.4
1951 Bos-N	7	7	.500	20	15	5	0	1	110	131	14	40	33	14.3	5.40	68	.294	.357	7	.179	0	-18	-21	-1	-2.0
1952 Bos-N	12	14	.462	33	33	14	0	0	234	234	16	90	104	12.6	4.23	85	.262	.333	14	.163	-0	-13	-16	-1	-1.7
1953 Mil-N	4	9	.308	20	18	5	0	0	114	110	16	43	71	12.1	4.34	90	.243	.315	6	.167	1	-1	-5	1	-0.3
1954 Mil-N	8	2	.800	27	19	6	4	0	127²	129	12	36	52	12.0	3.52	106	.266	.323	7	.159	0	8	3	1	0.4
1955 Bal-A	12	18	.400	34	31	14	4	0	235¹	200	17	87	96	11.1	3.44	111	.228	.300	15	.169	-1	14	10	-0	0.8
1956 Bal-A	4	2	.667	7	7	1	0	0	48¹	49	5	16	31	12.5	5.03	78	.268	.333	4	.267	2	-5	-6	-0	-0.3
Chi-A	9	12	.429	28	21	6	3	0	159²	149	15	70	82	12.5	4.06	101	.248	.329	19	.306	4	2	1	-0	0.5
Yr	13	14	.481	35	28	7	3	0	208	198	20	86	113	12.4	4.28	95	.252	.327	5	.065	6	-3	-5	0	0.2
1957 Chi-A	15	8	.652	30	29	12	5	0	201²	189	22	65	100	11.5	3.48	107	.249	.310	10	.147	-0	7	6	-2	0.4
1958 Chi-A	9	9	.500	28	23	4	1	1	155²	156	21	63	70	12.7	4.10	89	.268	.341	4	.078	-3	-6	-8	-1	-1.1
Total 12	86	89	.491	257	217	75	19	2	1539	1479	151	608	692	12.4	4.01	93	.254	.327	99	.181	4	-21	-45	-4	-3.8
■ JACK WILSON Wilson, John Francis "Black Jack" b: 4/12/12, Portland, Ore. BR/TR, 5'11", 210 lbs. Deb: 9/09/34																									
1934 Phi-A	0	1	.000	2	2	1	0	0	9	15	1	9	2	24.0	12.00	37	.405	.522	0	.000	-0	-8	-8	0	-0.5
1935 Bos-A	3	4	.429	23	6	2	0	1	64	72	0	36	19	15.5	4.22	112	.290	.385	5	.313	2	2	4	1	0.7
1936 Bos-A	6	8	.429	43	9	2	0	3	136¹	152	4	86	74	15.8	4.42	120	.284	.384	11	.220	-0	9	13	-0	1.2
1937 Bos-A	16	10	.615	51	21	14	1	7	221¹	209	13	119	137	13.5	3.70	128	.249	.344	14	.165	-3	23	26	1	2.2
1938 Bos-A	15	15	.500	37	27	11	3	1	194²	200	16	91	96	13.5	4.30	115	.262	.342	15	.221	0	11	14	-1	1.2
1939 Bos-A	11	11	.500	36	22	6	0	2	177¹	198	10	75	80	13.9	4.67	101	.281	.351	10	.159	-4	-1	1	-0	-0.2
1940 Bos-A	12	6	.667	41	16	9	0	5	157²	170	17	87	102	14.8	5.08	89	.270	.362	18	.273	4	-12	-10	-2	-0.7
1941 Bos-A	4	13	.235	27	12	4	1	1	116¹	140	7	70	55	16.6	5.03	83	.300	.397	7	.159	-1	-11	-11	2	-0.9
1942 Was-A	1	4	.200	12	6	1	0	0	42	57	2	23	18	17.4	6.64	55	.322	.403	2	.118	-1	-14	-14	-0	-1.4
Det-A	0	0	—	9	0	0	0	0	13	20	3	5	7	17.3	4.85	81	.351	.403	0	.000	-0	-2	-1	0	0.0
Yr	1	4	.200	21	6	1	0	0	55	77	5	28	25	17.2	6.22	60	.328	.399	0	.000	-1	-16	-15	-0	-1.4
Total 9	68	72	.486	281	121	50	5	20	1131²	1233	73	601	590	14.7	4.59	102	.277	.365	82	.199	-3	-4	13	-0	1.6
■ JOHN WILSON Wilson, John Nicodemus b: 6/15/1890, Boonsboro, Md. d: 9/23/54, Annapolis, Md. BR/TL, 6'1", 185 lbs. Deb: 6/11/13																									
1913 Was-A	0	0	—	3	0	0	0	0	4	4	0	3	1	15.8	4.50	66	.267	.389	0	—	0	-1	-1	0	0.0
■ JOHN WILSON Wilson, John Samuel b: 4/25/03, Coal City, Ala. d: 8/27/80, Chattanooga, Tenn. BR/TR, 6'2", 164 lbs. Deb: 5/09/27																									
1927 Bos-A	0	2	.000	5	2	2	0	0	25¹	31	1	13	8	15.6	3.55	119	.326	.407	1	.111	-1	2	2	-0	0.1
1928 Bos-A	0	0	—	2	0	0	0	0	5	6	0	6	1	21.6	9.00	46	.333	.500	0	.000	-0	-3	-3	0	-0.1
Total 2	0	2	.000	7	2	2	0	0	30¹	37	1	19	9	16.6	4.45	94	.327	.424	1	.100	-1	-1	-1	-0	0.0
■ MAX WILSON Wilson, Max b: 6/3/16, Haw River, N.C. d: 1/2/77, Greensboro, N.C. BL/TL, 5'7", 160 lbs. Deb: 9/10/40																									
1940 Phi-N	0	0	—	3	0	0	0	0	7	16	1	2	3	23.1	12.86	30	.444	.474	0	.000	-0	-7	-7	0	-0.5
1946 Was-A	0	1	.000	9	0	0	0	0	12²	16	1	9	8	17.8	7.11	47	.320	.424	0	.000	0	-5	-5	-0	-0.5
Total 2	0	1	.000	12	0	0	0	0	19²	32	2	11	11	19.7	9.15	39	.372	.443	0	.000	-0	-12	-12	0	-1.0
■ PETE WILSON Wilson, Peter Alex b: 10/9/1885, Springfield, Mass. d: 6/5/57, St.Petersburg, Fla TL, Deb: 9/15/08																									
1908 NY-A	3	3	.500	6	6	4	1	0	39	27	0	33	28	14.1	3.46	72	.191	.349	1	.071	-1	-5	-4	-1	-0.5
1909 NY-A	6	5	.545	14	12	7	1	0	93²	82	2	43	44	12.4	3.17	80	.230	.320	4	.118	-1	-7	-7	-1	-0.8
Total 2	9	8	.529	20	18	11	2	0	132²	109	2	76	72	12.9	3.26	77	.219	.329	5	.104	-2	-12	-11	-1	-1.3
■ EARL WILSON Wilson, Robert Earl (Name Changed From Wilson, Earl Lawrence) b: 10/2/34, Ponchatoula, La. BR/TR, 6'3", 216 lbs. Deb: 7/28/59																									
1959 Bos-A	1	1	.500	9	4	0	0	0	23²	21	2	31	17	19.8	6.08	67	.241	.441	4	.500	2	-6	-5	0	-0.2
1960 Bos-A	3	2	.600	13	9	2	0	0	65	61	4	48	40	15.1	4.71	86	.247	.369	4	.174	-0	-6	-5	0	-0.4
1962 Bos-A	12	8	.600	31	28	4	1	0	191¹	163	21	111	137	13.2	3.90	106	.231	.340	12	.174	3	1	5	-1	0.7
1963 Bos-A	11	16	.407	37	34	6	3	0	210²	184	18	105	123	12.4	3.76	101	.234	.325	15	.208	5	-3	1	1	0.8
1964 Bos-A	11	12	.478	33	31	6	0	0	202¹	213	37	73	166	12.8	4.49	86	.269	.332	15	.205	8	-20	-14	0	-0.5
1965 Bos-A	13	14	.481	36	36	8	1	0	230²	221	27	77	164	11.8	3.98	94	.250	.313	14	.177	9	-13	-7	-1	0.2
1966 Bos-A	5	5	.500	15	14	5	1	0	100²	88	14	36	67	11.3	3.84	99	.235	.306	8	.250	-0	-5	-0	-0	0.4
Det-A	13	6	.684	23	23	8	2	0	163¹	126	16	38	133	9.3	2.59	134	.213	.265	15	.234	9	15	16	2	3.1
Yr	18	11	.621	38	37	13	3	0	264	214	30	74	200	10.0	3.07	117	.220	.278	23	.094	9	11	16	1	3.5
1967 Det-A	22	11	.667	39	38	12	0	0	264	216	34	92	184	10.6	3.27	100	.224	.294	20	.185	7	-1	-0	2	1.0
1968 *Det-A	13	12	.520	34	33	10	3	0	224¹	192	20	65	168	10.3	2.85	106	.231	.287	20	.227	10	3	4	1	1.8
1969 Det-A	12	10	.545	35	35	9	1	0	214²	209	23	69	150	11.8	3.31	113	.256	.317	10	.132	-0	7	10	1	1.2
1970 Det-A	4	6	.400	18	16	4	1	0	96	87	15	32	74	11.3	4.41	85	.238	.303	6	.194	2	-7	-7	-0	-0.5
SD-N	1	6	.143	15	9	0	0	0	65	82	5	19	29	14.3	4.85	82	.309	.360	1	.059	-0	-6	-6	-1	-0.6
Total 11	121	109	.526	338	310	69	13	0	2051²	1863	236	796	1452	11.8	3.69	99	.242	.315	144	.195	60	-39	-10	3	7.0
■ ROY WILSON Wilson, Roy Edward "Lefty" b: 9/13/1896, Foster, Iowa d: 12/3/69, Clarion, Iowa BL/TL, 6', 175 lbs. Deb: 4/18/28																									
1928 Chi-A	0	0	—	1	0	0	0	0	3¹	2	0	3	2	13.5	0.00	—	.167	.333	0	.000	-0	1	2	0	0.2
■ STEVE WILSON Wilson, Stephen Douglas b: 12/13/64, Victoria, B.C., Can. BL/TL, 6'4", 205 lbs. Deb: 9/16/88																									
1988 Tex-A	0	0	—	3	0	0	0	0	7²	7	1	4	1	12.9	5.87	70	.259	.355	0	—	0	-2	-2	-0	-0.1
1989 *Chi-N	6	4	.600	53	8	0	0	2	85²	83	6	31	65	12.1	4.20	89	.257	.324	1	.063	-1	-7	-4	0	-0.4
1990 Chi-N	4	9	.308	45	15	1	0	1	139	140	17	43	95	12.0	4.79	86	.258	.316	6	.162	-0	-15	-10	-1	-1.0
Total 3	10	13	.435	101	23	1	0	3	232¹	230	24	78	161	12.0	4.61	87	.258	.320	7	.132	-0	-24	-16	-1	-1.5
■ TREVOR WILSON Wilson, Trevor Kirk b: 6/7/66, Torrance, Cal. BL/TL, 6', 190 lbs. Deb: 9/05/88																									
1988 SF-N	0	2	.000	4	4	0	0	0	22	25	1	8	15	13.5	4.09	80	.298	.359	2	.286	0	-2	-2	-0	-0.1
1989 SF-N	2	3	.400	14	4	0	0	0	39¹	28	2	24	22	12.8	4.35	78	.207	.344	2	.250	1	-4	-4	-0	-0.2
1990 SF-N	8	7	.533	27	17	3	2	0	110¹	87	11	49	66	11.2	4.00	90	.218	.305	4	.138	-0	-3	-3	2	-0.1
Total 3	10	12	.455	45	25	3	2	0	171²	140	14	81	103	11.8	4.09	88	.227	.321	8	.182	1	-8	-10	1	-0.4

YEAR TM/L	W	L	PCT	G	GS	CG	SH	SV	IP	H	HR	BB	SO	RAT	ERA	ERA+	OAV	OOB	BH	AVG	PB	PR	/A	PD	TPI

■ WALTER WILSON   Wilson, Walter Wood   b: 11/24/13, Glenn, Ga.   BL/TR, 6'4", 190 lbs.   Deb: 4/17/45

| 1945 Det-A | 1 | 3 | .250 | 25 | 4 | 1 | 0 | 0 | 70¹ | 76 | 4 | 35 | 28 | 14.6 | 4.61 | 76 | .284 | .373 | 1 | .053 | -2 | -10 | -9 | 1 | -0.9 |

■ WILLY WILSON   Wilson, William   b: 1/7/1884, Columbus, Ohio   d: 10/28/25, Seattle, Wash.   BR/TR,   Deb: 10/03/06

| 1906 Was-A | 0 | 1 | .000 | 1 | 1 | 1 | 0 | 0 | 7 | 3 | 0 | 2 | 1 | 6.4 | 2.57 | 102 | .133 | .203 | 0 | .000 | -0 | 0 | 0 | 0 | 0.0 |

■ MUTT WILSON   Wilson, William Clarence "Lank"   b: 7/20/1896, Kiser, N.C.   d: 8/31/62, Wildwood, Fla.   BR/TR, 6'3", 167 lbs.   Deb: 9/11/20

| 1920 Det-A | 1 | 1 | .500 | 3 | 2 | 1 | 0 | 0 | 13 | 12 | 0 | 5 | 4 | 11.8 | 3.46 | 108 | .240 | .309 | 1 | .250 | -0 | 0 | 0 | -1 | 0.0 |

■ BILL WILSON   Wilson, William Donald   b: 11/6/28, Central City, Neb.   BR/TR, 6'2", 200 lbs.   Deb: 9/24/50 ♦

| 1955 KC-A | 0 | 0 | — | 1 | 0 | 0 | 0 | 0 | 1 | 1 | 0 | 1 | 1 | 18.0 | 0.00 | — | .250 | .400 | 61 | .223 | 0 | 0 | 0 | 0 | 0.0 |

■ BILL WILSON   Wilson, William Harlan   b: 9/21/42, Pomeroy, Ohio   BR/TR, 6'2", 195 lbs.   Deb: 4/08/69

1969 Phi-N	2	5	.286	37	0	0	0	6	62¹	53	6	36	48	13.0	3.32	107	.231	.338	0	.000	-0	2	2	-1	0.0
1970 Phi-N	1	0	1.000	37	0	0	0	6	58¹	57	5	33	41	13.9	4.78	83	.263	.360	1	.250	0	-5	-5	-0	-0.4
1971 Phi-N	4	6	.400	38	0	0	0	7	58²	39	4	22	40	9.5	3.07	115	.188	.268	1	.100	-1	3	3	1	0.4
1972 Phi-N	1	1	.500	23	0	0	0	0	30	26	1	11	18	11.1	3.30	109	.234	.303	0	—	0	1	1	0	0.1
1973 Phi-N	1	3	.250	44	0	0	0	4	48²	54	7	29	24	15.3	6.66	57	.293	.390	0	.000	-0	-16	-15	-0	-1.6
Total 5	9	15	.375	179	0	0	0	17	258	229	23	131	171	12.6	4.22	88	.241	.335	2	.083	-1	-16	-15	0	-1.5

■ HOOKS WILTSE   Wiltse, George Leroy   b: 9/7/1880, Hamilton, N.Y.   d: 1/21/59, Long Beach, N.Y.   BR/TL, 6', 185 lbs.   Deb: 4/21/04   C

1904 NY-N	13	3	.813	24	16	14	2	3	164²	150	8	61	105	11.8	2.84	96	.240	.313	15	.224	3	-2	-2	2	0.4
1905 NY-N	15	6	.714	32	19	18	1	4	197	158	5	61	120	10.2	2.47	119	.219	.284	20	.278	7	12	10	5	2.4
1906 NY-N	16	11	.593	38	26	21	4	6	249¹	227	3	58	125	10.4	2.27	115	.241	.288	18	.191	1	10	9	-1	1.1
1907 NY-N	13	12	.520	33	21	14	3	2	190¹	171	3	48	79	10.6	2.18	114	.241	.294	9	.134	-0	6	6	2	1.0
1908 NY-N	23	14	.622	44	38	30	7	2	330	266	4	73	118	9.5	2.24	108	.224	.274	26	.236	6	5	7	1	1.5
1909 NY-N	20	11	.645	37	30	22	4	3	269¹	228	9	51	119	9.5	2.00	128	.233	.275	19	.200	2	18	17	-2	1.9
1910 NY-N	14	12	.538	36	30	18	2	2	235¹	232	4	52	88	10.9	2.72	109	.261	.303	13	.176	0	8	7	-2	0.4
1911 *NY-N	12	9	.571	30	24	11	4	0	187¹	177	7	39	92	10.5	3.27	103	.251	.292	13	.188	-1	3	2	1	0.1
1912 NY-N	9	6	.600	28	17	5	0	3	134	140	7	28	58	11.4	3.16	107	.265	.303	15	.326	4	4	3	2	0.9
1913 *NY-N	0	0	—	17	2	0	0	3	57²	53	1	8	25	9.7	1.56	200	.237	.266	5	.208	0	11	10	0	1.1
1914 NY-N	1	1	.500	20	0	0	0	1	38	41	2	12	19	12.6	2.84	93	.289	.344	2	.667	1	-0	-1	0	0.1
1915 Bro-F	3	5	.375	18	3	1	0	0	59¹	49	1	7	17	8.8	2.28	133	.226	.257	1	.045	-2	5	5	-1	0.2
Total 12	139	90	.607	357	226	154	27	34	2112¹	1892	54	498	965	10.4	2.47	113	.241	.289	156	.210	22	79	74	8	11.1

■ HAL WILTSE   Wiltse, Harold James "Whitey"   b: 8/6/03, Clay City, Ill.   d: 11/2/83, Bunkie, La.   BL/TL, 5'9", 168 lbs.   Deb: 4/13/26

1926 Bos-A	8	15	.348	37	29	9	1	0	196¹	201	6	99	59	14.0	4.22	97	.273	.363	5	.085	-5	-4	-3	0	-0.6
1927 Bos-A	10	18	.357	36	29	13	1	0	219	276	5	76	47	14.6	5.10	83	.321	.379	16	.208	-2	-23	-21	2	-1.8
1928 Bos-A	0	2	.000	2	2	1	0	0	12	16	1	1	5	15.0	9.00	46	.314	.364	0	.000	-1	-7	-7	-0	-0.5
StL-A	2	5	.286	26	5	0	0	0	72	93	4	35	23	16.4	5.25	80	.316	.395	5	.227	0	-10	-8	0	-0.6
Yr	2	7	.222	28	7	1	0	0	84	109	5	36	28	15.9	5.79	72	.313	.382	0	.000	-1	-16	-15	-0	-1.1
1931 Phi-N	0	0	—	1	0	0	0	0	1	3	0	0	0	27.0	9.00	47	.600	.600	0	—	0	-1	-1	0	0.0
Total 4	20	40	.333	102	65	23	2	1	500¹	589	16	211	134	14.7	4.87	85	.303	.375	26	.160	-7	-44	-40	2	-3.5

■ SNAKE WILTSE   Wiltse, Lewis De Witt   b: 12/5/1871, Bouckville, N.Y.   d: 8/25/28, Harrisburg, Pa.   BR/TL,   Deb: 5/05/01

1901 Pit-N	1	4	.200	7	5	3	0	0	44¹	57	2	13	10	15.0	4.26	77	.310	.368	3	.158	-1	-5	-5	1	-0.4
Phi-A	13	5	.722	19	19	18	2	0	166	185	1	35	40	11.9	3.58	105	.279	.315	25	.373	9	2	4	1	1.3
1902 Phi-A	8	8	.500	19	17	13	0	1	138	182	7	41	28	14.5	5.15	71	.318	.363	10	.175	-1	-24	-23	-0	-2.1
Bal-A	7	11	.389	19	18	13	0	0	164	215	4	51	37	14.6	5.10	74	.316	.364	39	.295	6	-28	-24	-0	-1.0
Yr	15	19	.441	38	35	31	0	1	302	397	11	92	65	14.6	5.13	73	.317	.364	10	.053	5	-52	-47	-1	-3.1
1903 NY-A	0	3	.000	4	3	2	0	0	25	35	1	6	6	14.8	5.40	58	.329	.365	2	.222	0	-7	-6	0	-0.5
Total 3	29	31	.483	68	62	54	2	2	537¹	674	15	146	121	13.8	4.59	80	.305	.350	79	.278	13	-62	-55	2	-2.7

■ FRED WINCHELL   Winchell, Frederick Russell (b: Frederick Cook)   b: 1/23/1882, Arlington, Mass.   d: 8/8/58, Toronto, Ont., Can.   TL, 5'8",   Deb: 9/16/09

| 1909 Cle-A | 0 | 3 | .000 | 4 | 3 | 0 | 0 | 1 | 14¹ | 16 | 0 | 2 | 7 | 11.3 | 6.28 | 41 | .296 | .321 | 1 | .200 | 0 | -6 | -6 | -0 | -0.5 |

■ ED WINEAPPLE   Wineapple, Edward "Lefty"   b: 8/10/05, Boston, Mass.   BL/TL, 6', 210 lbs.   Deb: 9/15/29

| 1929 Was-A | 0 | 0 | — | 1 | 0 | 0 | 0 | 0 | 4 | 7 | 0 | 3 | 1 | 22.5 | 4.50 | 94 | .467 | .556 | 0 | .000 | -0 | -0 | -0 | -0 | 0.0 |

■ RALPH WINEGARNER   Winegarner, Ralph Lee   b: 10/29/09, Benton, Kan.   d: 88, Benton, Kan.   BR/TR, 6', 182 lbs.   Deb: 9/20/30   C♦

1932 Cle-A	1	0	1.000	5	1	1	0	0	17¹	7	0	13	5	10.4	1.04	457	.123	.286	1	.143	-1	7	7	-0	0.6
1934 Cle-A	5	4	.556	22	6	4	0	0	78¹	91	1	39	32	15.2	5.51	82	.289	.371	10	.196	1	-9	-8	0	-0.6
1935 Cle-A	2	2	.500	25	4	2	0	0	67¹	89	10	29	41	15.9	5.75	78	.313	.379	26	.310	4	-10	-9	-0	-0.8
1936 Cle-A	0	0	—	9	0	0	0	0	14²	18	0	6	3	14.7	4.91	103	.295	.358	2	.125	-1	0	0	-0	0.0
1949 StL-A	0	0	—	9	0	0	0	0	16²	24	2	2	8	14.0	7.56	60	.329	.347	2	.400	2	-6	-6	-0	-0.3
Total 5	8	6	.571	70	11	7	0	0	194¹	229	13	89	89	14.9	5.33	86	.290	.364	51	.276	5	-18	-16	-1	-1.1

■ JIM WINFORD   Winford, James Head "Cowboy"   b: 10/9/09, Shelbyville, Tenn.   d: 12/16/70, Miami, Okla.   BR/TR, 6'1", 180 lbs.   Deb: 9/10/32

1932 StL-N	1	1	.500	4	1	0	0	0	8¹	9	0	5	4	15.1	6.48	61	.273	.368	2	.667	1	-2	-2	0	0.0
1934 StL-N	0	2	.000	5	1	0	0	0	12²	17	0	6	3	17.8	7.82	54	.327	.417	0	.000	0	-5	-5	-0	-0.3
1935 StL-N	0	0	—	2	1	0	0	0	11¹	13	1	5	7	14.3	3.97	103	.283	.353	0	.000	-0	0	0	-0	0.0
1936 StL-N	11	10	.524	39	23	10	1	3	192	203	10	68	72	12.9	3.80	104	.269	.333	5	.085	-4	5	3	-4	-0.4
1937 StL-N	2	4	.333	16	4	0	0	0	46¹	56	2	27	17	16.1	5.83	68	.311	.401	1	.125	-1	-10	-10	-0	-0.9
1938 Bro-N	0	1	.000	2	1	0	0	0	5²	9	1	4	4	20.6	11.12	35	.346	.433	0	.000	0	-5	-5	-0	-0.3
Total 6	14	18	.438	68	31	10	1	3	276¹	307	14	115	107	14.0	4.56	87	.281	.353	8	.108	-3	-17	-18	-5	-1.9

■ ERNIE WINGARD   Wingard, Ernest James "Jim"   b: 10/17/1900, Prattville, Ala.   d: 1/17/77, Prattville, Ala.   BL/TL, 6'2", 176 lbs.   Deb: 5/01/24

1924 StL-A	13	12	.520	36	26	14	0	1	218	215	6	85	23	12.5	3.51	129	.262	.334	18	.234	2	17	24	-2	2.4
1925 StL-A	9	10	.474	32	18	8	0	0	145	183	10	77	20	16.3	5.52	85	.319	.403	15	.288	4	-18	-14	2	-0.6
1926 StL-A	5	8	.385	39	16	7	0	3	169	188	9	76	30	14.3	3.57	120	.290	.369	14	.230	1	8	14	3	1.8
1927 StL-A	2	13	.133	38	17	7	0	0	156¹	213	7	79	28	16.9	6.56	68	.340	.415	10	.179	2	-42	-38	2	-3.0
Total 4	29	43	.403	145	77	36	0	4	688¹	799	32	317	101	14.8	4.64	96	.299	.377	57	.232	8	-34	-14	6	0.6

■ TED WINGFIELD   Wingfield, Frederick Davis   b: 8/7/1899, Bedford, Va.   d: 7/18/75, Johnson City, Tenn.   BR/TR, 5'11", 168 lbs.   Deb: 9/23/23

1923 Was-A	0	0	—	1	0	0	0	0	1	0	0	1	0	0.0	0.00	—	.000	.000	0	—	0	0	0	0	0.0
1924 Was-A	0	0	—	4	0	0	0	0	7	9	0	4	2	16.7	2.57	157	.300	.382	0	.000	-0	1	1	-0	0.1
Bos-A	0	2	.000	4	3	2	0	0	25²	23	0	8	4	10.9	2.45	178	.240	.298	3	.333	1	5	5	0	0.6
Yr	0	2	.000	8	3	2	0	0	32²	32	0	12	6	12.1	2.48	173	.254	.319	1	.091	0	6	7	0	0.7
1925 Bos-A	12	19	.387	41	26	18	2	2	254¹	267	11	92	30	13.0	3.96	115	.278	.346	23	.245	1	12	16	7	2.4
1926 Bos-A	11	16	.407	43	20	9	1	3	190²	220	11	50	30	12.8	4.44	92	.298	.344	15	.217	-0	-9	-8	2	-0.5
1927 Bos-A	1	7	.125	20	8	2	0	0	74²	105	2	27	1	16.3	5.06	83	.357	.417	6	.200	0	-8	-7	3	-0.3
Total 5	24	44	.353	113	57	31	3	5	553¹	624	24	181	68	13.3	4.18	103	.294	.353	45	.234	1	3	9	12	2.3

■ LAVE WINHAM   Winham, Lafayette Sharkey "Lefty"   b: 10/23/1881, Brooklyn, N.Y.   d: 9/12/51, Brooklyn, N.Y.   BL/TL, 5'11", 200 lbs.   Deb: 4/21/02

| 1902 Bro-N | 0 | 0 | — | 1 | 0 | 0 | 0 | 0 | 3 | 4 | 0 | 2 | 1 | 18.0 | 0.00 | — | .319 | .413 | 0 | .000 | -0 | 1 | 1 | 0 | 0.1 |
| 1903 Pit-N | 3 | 1 | .750 | 5 | 4 | 3 | 1 | 0 | 36 | 33 | 0 | 21 | 22 | 13.5 | 2.25 | 144 | .231 | .329 | 1 | .071 | -1 | 4 | 4 | -1 | 0.1 |

YEAR TM/L	W	L	PCT	G	GS	CG	SH	SV	IP	H	HR	BB	SO	RAT	ERA	ERA+	OAV	OOB	BH	AVG	PB	PR	/A	PD	TPI
Total 2	3	1	.750	6	4	3	1	0	39	37	0	23	23	13.8	2.08	154	.238	.336	1	.063	-2	5	5	-1	0.2

■ GEORGE WINKELMAN Winkelman, George Edward b: 2/18/1865, Washington, D.C. d: 5/19/60, Washington, D.C. BL/TL, Deb: 8/04/1883 ♦

YEAR TM/L	W	L	PCT	G	GS	CG	SH	SV	IP	H	HR	BB	SO	RAT	ERA	ERA+	OAV	OOB	BH	AVG	PB	PR	/A	PD	TPI
1886 Was-N	0	1	.000	1	1	0	0	0	6	12	0	5	4	25.5	10.50	31	.400	.485	1	.200	-0	-5	-5	-0	-0.3

■ GEORGE WINN Winn, George Benjamin "Breezy" or "Lefty" b: 10/26/1897, Perry, Ga. d: 11/1/69, Roberta, Ga. BL/TL, 5'11", 170 lbs. Deb: 4/29/19

YEAR TM/L	W	L	PCT	G	GS	CG	SH	SV	IP	H	HR	BB	SO	RAT	ERA	ERA+	OAV	OOB	BH	AVG	PB	PR	/A	PD	TPI
1919 Bos-A	0	0	—	3	0	0	0	0	4²	6	0	1	0	13.5	7.71	39	.353	.389	0	.000	-0	-2	-2	-0	-0.2
1922 Cle-A	1	2	.333	8	3	1	0	0	33²	44	2	5	7	13.1	4.54	88	.317	.340	3	.333	1	-2	-2	0	0.0
1923 Cle-A	0	0	—	1	0	0	0	0	2	0	0	1	0	4.5	0.00	—	.000	.143	0	—	0	1	1	0	0.1
Total 3	1	2	.333	12	3	1	0	0	40¹	50	2	7	7	12.7	4.69	83	.309	.337	3	.300	1	-3	-4	-0	-0.1

■ JIM WINN Winn, James Francis b: 9/23/59, Stockton, Cal. BR/TR, 6'3", 210 lbs. Deb: 4/10/83

YEAR TM/L	W	L	PCT	G	GS	CG	SH	SV	IP	H	HR	BB	SO	RAT	ERA	ERA+	OAV	OOB	BH	AVG	PB	PR	/A	PD	TPI
1983 Pit-N	0	0	—	7	0	0	0	0	11	12	2	6	3	14.7	7.36	50	.267	.353	0	—	0	-5	-4	0	-0.3
1984 Pit-N	1	0	1.000	9	0	0	0	1	18²	19	2	9	11	13.5	3.86	93	.264	.346	0	.000	-0	-1	-1	0	0.0
1985 Pit-N	3	6	.333	30	7	0	0	0	75²	77	4	31	22	13.1	5.23	68	.266	.341	2	.111	-0	-14	-14	2	-1.1
1986 Pit-N	3	5	.375	50	3	0	0	3	88	85	9	38	70	12.8	3.58	107	.258	.338	1	.063	-1	1	2	1	0.3
1987 Chi-A	4	6	.400	56	0	0	0	6	94	95	10	62	44	15.6	4.79	96	.271	.390	0	—	0	-3	-2	3	0.1
1988 Min-A	1	0	1.000	9	0	0	0	0	21	33	4	10	9	18.4	6.00	68	.355	.417	0	—	0	-5	-5	0	-0.3
Total 6	12	17	.414	161	10	0	0	10	308¹	321	31	156	159	14.2	4.67	85	.272	.362	3	.086	-1	-26	-23	6	-1.3

■ TOM WINSETT Winsett, John Thomas "Long Tom" b: 11/24/09, McKenzie, Tenn. BL/TR, 6'2", 190 lbs. Deb: 4/20/30 ♦

YEAR TM/L	W	L	PCT	G	GS	CG	SH	SV	IP	H	HR	BB	SO	RAT	ERA	ERA+	OAV	OOB	BH	AVG	PB	PR	/A	PD	TPI
1937 Bro-N	0	0	—	1	0	0	0	0	1	3	0	2	0	45.0	18.00	22	.600	.714	83	.237	0	-2	-2	0	0.0

■ HANK WINSTON Winston, Henry Rudolph b: 6/15/04, Youngville, N.C. d: 2/4/74, Jacksonville, Fla. BL/TR, 6'3.5", 226 lbs. Deb: 9/30/33

YEAR TM/L	W	L	PCT	G	GS	CG	SH	SV	IP	H	HR	BB	SO	RAT	ERA	ERA+	OAV	OOB	BH	AVG	PB	PR	/A	PD	TPI
1933 Phi-A	0	0	—	1	0	0	0	0	6²	7	0	6	2	17.6	6.75	63	.280	.419	0	.000	-0	-2	-2	0	-0.1
1936 Bro-N	1	3	.250	14	0	0	0	0	32¹	40	2	16	8	15.9	6.12	67	.301	.380	1	.091	-1	-8	-7	0	-0.7
Total 2	1	3	.250	15	0	0	0	0	39	47	2	22	10	16.2	6.23	67	.297	.387	1	.071	-1	-9	-9	0	-0.8

■ GEORGE WINTER Winter, George Lovington "Sassafras" b: 4/27/1878, New Providence, Pa d: 5/26/51, Franklin Lakes, N.J. TR, 5'8", 155 lbs. Deb: 6/15/01

YEAR TM/L	W	L	PCT	G	GS	CG	SH	SV	IP	H	HR	BB	SO	RAT	ERA	ERA+	OAV	OOB	BH	AVG	PB	PR	/A	PD	TPI
1901 Bos-A	16	12	.571	28	28	26	1	0	241	234	4	66	63	11.2	2.80	126	.252	.301	19	.190	-4	23	20	1	1.4
1902 Bos-A	11	9	.550	20	20	18	0	0	168¹	149	2	53	51	10.8	2.99	119	.238	.297	10	.164	-2	11	11	0	0.8
1903 Bos-A	9	8	.529	24	19	14	0	0	178¹	182	4	37	64	11.1	3.08	99	.264	.301	7	.106	-2	-1	-0	-0	-0.4
1904 Bos-A	8	4	.667	20	16	12	1	0	135²	126	4	27	31	10.1	2.32	115	.247	.285	5	.116	-2	4	5	-1	0.3
1905 Bos-A	16	17	.485	35	27	24	2	0	264¹	249	5	54	119	10.3	2.96	91	.250	.289	24	.261	3	-9	-8	1	-0.3
1906 Bos-A	6	18	.250	29	22	18	1	2	207²	215	6	38	72	11.0	4.12	67	.270	.303	17	.246	2	-33	-32	0	-3.0
1907 Bos-A	12	15	.444	35	27	21	4	1	256²	198	2	61	88	9.1	2.07	125	.215	.264	21	.223	1	14	15	-1	1.6
1908 Bos-A	4	14	.222	22	17	8	0	0	147²	150	3	36	55	11.6	3.05	81	.275	.324	9	.184	-1	-11	-10	0	-1.1
*Det-A	1	5	.167	7	6	5	0	1	56¹	49	0	7	25	9.4	1.60	152	.240	.276	2	.111	-1	5	5	1	0.6
Yr	5	19	.208	29	23	13	0	1	204	199	3	43	80	10.8	2.65	93	.264	.306	11	.000	-2	-6	-4	1	-0.5
Total 8	83	102	.449	220	182	146	9	4	1656	1552	32	379	568	10.5	2.87	101	.250	.293	114	.193	-8	2	7	-1	-0.1

■ CLARENCE WINTERS Winters, Clarence John b: 9/7/1898, Detroit, Mich. d: 6/29/45, Detroit, Mich. Deb: 8/28/24

YEAR TM/L	W	L	PCT	G	GS	CG	SH	SV	IP	H	HR	BB	SO	RAT	ERA	ERA+	OAV	OOB	BH	AVG	PB	PR	/A	PD	TPI
1924 Bos-A	0	1	.000	4	2	0	0	0	7	22	0	4	3	33.4	20.57	21	.512	.553	1	.333	0	-13	-13	-0	-1.0

■ JESSE WINTERS Winters, Jesse Franklin "Buck" or "T-Bone" b: 12/22/1893, Stephenville, Tex. d: 6/5/86, Abilene, Texas BR/TR, 6'1", 165 lbs. Deb: 5/03/19

YEAR TM/L	W	L	PCT	G	GS	CG	SH	SV	IP	H	HR	BB	SO	RAT	ERA	ERA+	OAV	OOB	BH	AVG	PB	PR	/A	PD	TPI
1919 NY-N	1	2	.333	16	2	0	0	3	28	39	1	13	6	17.7	5.46	51	.339	.420	0	.000	-0	-8	-8	-0	-0.8
1920 NY-N	0	0	—	21	0	0	0	0	46¹	37	1	28	14	13.4	3.50	86	.233	.361	0	.000	-1	-2	-3	1	-0.2
1921 Phi-N	5	10	.333	18	14	10	0	0	114	142	4	28	22	13.7	3.63	116	.310	.355	5	.128	-3	2	8	2	0.7
1922 Phi-N	6	6	.500	34	9	4	0	2	138¹	176	8	56	29	15.4	5.33	87	.319	.386	11	.256	-0	-19	-10	-1	-0.7
1923 Phi-N	1	6	.143	21	6	1	0	1	78¹	116	7	39	23	18.3	7.35	63	.348	.423	4	.160	-1	-29	-24	-0	-2.2
Total 5	13	24	.351	110	31	15	0	6	405	510	21	164	94	15.4	5.04	83	.316	.385	20	.171	-5	-56	-39	3	-3.2

■ ALAN WIRTH Wirth, Alan Lee b: 12/8/56, Mesa, Ariz. BR/TR, 6'4", 190 lbs. Deb: 4/09/78

YEAR TM/L	W	L	PCT	G	GS	CG	SH	SV	IP	H	HR	BB	SO	RAT	ERA	ERA+	OAV	OOB	BH	AVG	PB	PR	/A	PD	TPI
1978 Oak-A	5	6	.455	16	14	2	1	0	81¹	72	6	34	31	12.1	3.43	106	.252	.337	0	—	0	3	2	-0	0.1
1979 Oak-A	1	0	1.000	5	1	0	0	0	12	14	2	8	7	17.3	6.00	67	.298	.411	0	—	0	-2	-3	0	-0.1
1980 Oak-A	0	0	—	2	0	0	0	0	2	3	0	0	1	13.5	4.50	84	.333	.333	0	—	0	-0	-0	0	0.0
Total 3	6	6	.500	23	15	2	1	0	95¹	89	8	42	39	12.7	3.78	98	.260	.348	0	—	0	1	-1	-0	0.0

■ ARCHIE WISE Wise, Archibald Edwin b: 7/31/12, Waxahachie, Tex. d: 2/2/78, Dallas, Tex. BR/TR, 6', 165 lbs. Deb: 7/24/32

YEAR TM/L	W	L	PCT	G	GS	CG	SH	SV	IP	H	HR	BB	SO	RAT	ERA	ERA+	OAV	OOB	BH	AVG	PB	PR	/A	PD	TPI
1932 Chi-A	0	0	—	2	0	0	0	0	7¹	8	1	5	2	17.2	4.91	88	.258	.378	0	.000	-1	-0	-0	0	0.0

■ RICK WISE Wise, Richard Charles b: 9/13/45, Jackson, Mich. BR/TR, 6'1", 180 lbs. Deb: 4/18/64

YEAR TM/L	W	L	PCT	G	GS	CG	SH	SV	IP	H	HR	BB	SO	RAT	ERA	ERA+	OAV	OOB	BH	AVG	PB	PR	/A	PD	TPI
1964 Phi-N	5	3	.625	25	8	0	0	0	69	78	7	25	39	13.8	4.04	86	.277	.342	5	.294	2	-4	-4	-1	-0.3
1966 Phi-N	5	6	.455	22	13	3	0	0	99¹	100	5	24	58	11.5	3.71	97	.262	.311	0	.000	-1	-1	-0	-0.5
1967 Phi-N	11	11	.500	36	25	6	3	0	181¹	177	8	45	111	11.2	3.28	104	.259	.308	11	.208	3	2	3	1	0.7
1968 Phi-N	9	15	.375	30	30	7	1	0	182	210	12	37	97	12.5	4.55	66	.292	.332	14	.241	7	-32	-31	1	-2.4
1969 Phi-N	15	13	.536	33	31	14	4	0	220	215	17	61	144	11.4	3.23	110	.257	.309	20	.270	1	9	8	1	1.7
1970 Phi-N	13	14	.481	35	34	5	1	0	220¹	253	16	65	113	13.1	4.17	96	.287	.338	15	.200	4	-3	-4	1	0.1
1971 Phi-N	17	14	.548	38	37	17	4	0	272¹	261	20	70	155	11.1	2.88	123	.254	.304	23	.237	10	18	20	0	3.4
1972 StL-N	16	16	.500	35	35	20	2	0	269	250	16	71	142	10.8	3.11	109	.251	.301	16	.172	1	10	9	3	1.3
1973 StL-N	16	12	.571	35	34	14	5	0	259	259	18	59	144	11.2	3.37	108	.257	.308	17	.193	6	8	8	-0	1.5
1974 Bos-A	3	4	.429	9	9	1	0	0	49	47	2	16	25	11.8	3.86	100	.251	.314	0	—	0	-1	-0	-0	0.0
1975 *Bos-A	19	12	.613	35	35	17	1	0	255¹	262	34	72	141	11.9	3.95	103	.263	.315	0	—	0	-5	-4	-1	0.2
1976 Bos-A	14	11	.560	34	34	11	4	0	224¹	218	18	48	93	10.8	3.53	111	.255	.296	0	—	0	-0	9	2	1.2
1977 Bos-A	11	5	.688	26	20	4	2	0	128¹	151	19	28	85	12.8	4.77	94	.291	.332	0	—	0	-10	-4	1	-0.2
1978 Cle-A	9	19	.321	33	31	9	1	0	211²	226	22	59	106	12.2	4.34	86	.275	.325	0	—	0	-14	-14	0	-1.3
1979 Cle-A	15	10	.600	34	34	9	2	0	231²	229	24	68	108	11.6	3.73	114	.256	.309	0	—	0	12	13	5	1.8
1980 SD-N	6	8	.429	27	27	1	0	0	154¹	172	14	37	59	12.2	3.67	93	.285	.326	8	.138	-1	-1	-4	-0	-0.5
1981 SD-N	4	8	.333	18	18	0	0	0	98	116	10	19	27	12.4	3.77	86	.296	.328	1	.040	-1	-3	-6	1	-0.6
1982 SD-N	0	0	—	1	0	0	0	0	2	3	0	0	0	13.5	9.00	38	.333	.333	0	—	0	-1	-1	0	0.0
Total 18	188	181	.509	506	455	138	30	0	3127	3227	261	804	1647	11.7	3.69	100	.267	.315	130	.195	34	-15	2	12	6.1

■ ROY WISE Wise, Roy Ogden b: 11/18/24, Springfield, Ill. BB/TR, 6'2", 170 lbs. Deb: 5/13/44

YEAR TM/L	W	L	PCT	G	GS	CG	SH	SV	IP	H	HR	BB	SO	RAT	ERA	ERA+	OAV	OOB	BH	AVG	PB	PR	/A	PD	TPI
1944 Pit-N	0	0	—	2	0	0	0	0	3	4	0	3	1	21.0	9.00	41	.333	.467	0	—	0	-2	-2	0	-0.1

■ BILL WISE Wise, William E. b: 3/15/1861, Washington, D.C. d: 5/5/40, Washington, D.C. Deb: 5/02/1882

YEAR TM/L	W	L	PCT	G	GS	CG	SH	SV	IP	H	HR	BB	SO	RAT	ERA	ERA+	OAV	OOB	BH	AVG	PB	PR	/A	PD	TPI
1882 Bal-a	1	2	.333	3	3	3	0	0	26	30	1	4	9	11.8	2.77	99	.271	.296	2	.100	-1	-0	-0	-0	-0.1
1884 Was-U	23	18	.561	50	41	34	3	0	364¹	383	5	60	268	10.9	3.04	98	.253	.281	79	.233	2	-1	-3	4	0.3
1886 Was-N	0	1	.000	1	1	0	0	0	3	6	0	2	0	24.0	9.00	36	.400	.470	0	.000	-0	-2	-2	0	-0.1
Total 3	24	21	.533	54	45	37	3	0	393¹	419	6	66	277	11.1	3.07	96	.255	.284	81	.224	1	-3	-5	4	0.1

■ JACK WISNER Wisner, John Henry b: 11/5/1899, Grand Rapids, Mich. d: 12/15/81, Jackson, Mich. BR/TR, 6'3", 195 lbs. Deb: 9/12/19

YEAR TM/L	W	L	PCT	G	GS	CG	SH	SV	IP	H	HR	BB	SO	RAT	ERA	ERA+	OAV	OOB	BH	AVG	PB	PR	/A	PD	TPI
1919 Pit-N	1	0	1.000	4	1	0	0	0	18²	12	0	7	4	9.6	0.96	313	.185	.274	0	.000	-1	4	4	0	0.4
1920 Pit-N	1	3	.250	17	2	1	0	0	44²	46	1	10	13	11.5	3.43	94	.274	.318	0	.000	-1	-1	-1	1	0.0
1925 NY-N	0	0	—	25	0	0	0	0	40¹	33	6	14	13	10.9	3.79	106	.228	.304	0	.000	-1	2	1	0	0.0
1926 NY-N	2	2	.500	5	3	2	0	0	28	21	4	10	5	10.0	3.54	106	.208	.279	2	.200	-0	1	1	0	0.0

YEAR TM/L	W	L	PCT	G	GS	CG	SH	SV	IP	H	HR	BB	SO	RAT	ERA	ERA+	OAV	OOB	BH	AVG	PB	PR	/A	PD	TPI
Total 4	4	5	.444	51	6	4	0	0	131²	112	9	41	35	10.7	3.21	111	.234	.300	2	.065	-3	6	5	1	0.4

■ WHITEY WISTERT
Wistert, Francis Michael b: 2/20/12, Chicago, Ill. d: 4/23/85, Painesville, Ohio BR/TR, 6'4", 210 lbs. Deb: 9/11/34

YEAR TM/L	W	L	PCT	G	GS	CG	SH	SV	IP	H	HR	BB	SO	RAT	ERA	ERA+	OAV	OOB	BH	AVG	PB	PR	/A	PD	TPI
1934 Cin-N	0	1	.000	2	1	0	0	0	8	5	1	5	1	11.3	1.13	363	.185	.313	0	.000	-0	3	3	-0	0.2

■ WITHEROW
Witherow Deb: 7/01/1875

YEAR TM/L	W	L	PCT	G	GS	CG	SH	SV	IP	H	HR	BB	SO	RAT	ERA	ERA+	OAV	OOB	BH	AVG	PB	PR	/A	PD	TPI
1875 Was-n	0	1	.000	1	1	0	0	0	1	5	0	0		45.0	18.00	15	.625	.625	0	.000	-0	-2	-2		0.0

■ ROY WITHERUP
Witherup, Foster Leroy b: 7/26/1886, N.Washington, Pa. d: 12/23/41, New Bethlehem, Pa. 6', 185 lbs. Deb: 5/14/06

YEAR TM/L	W	L	PCT	G	GS	CG	SH	SV	IP	H	HR	BB	SO	RAT	ERA	ERA+	OAV	OOB	BH	AVG	PB	PR	/A	PD	TPI
1906 Bos-N	0	3	.000	8	3	3	0	0	46	59	2	19	14	15.5	6.26	43	.322	.389	2	.133	-1	-19	-18	-1	-1.8
1908 Was-A	2	4	.333	6	6	4	0	0	48¹	51	0	8	31	11.2	2.98	77	.264	.297	3	.167	-1	-3	-4	0	-0.4
1909 Was-A	1	5	.167	12	8	5	0	0	68	79	1	20	26	13.1	4.24	57	.306	.356	1	.053	-2	-13	-14	-1	-1.6
Total 3	3	12	.200	26	17	12	0	0	162¹	189	3	47	71	13.2	4.44	55	.298	.348	6	.115	-3	-35	-36	-2	-3.8

■ RED WITT
Witt, George Adrian b: 11/9/33, Long Beach, Cal. BR/TR, 6'3", 185 lbs. Deb: 9/21/57

YEAR TM/L	W	L	PCT	G	GS	CG	SH	SV	IP	H	HR	BB	SO	RAT	ERA	ERA+	OAV	OOB	BH	AVG	PB	PR	/A	PD	TPI
1957 Pit-N	0	1	.000	1	1	0	0	0	1¹	4	1	5	1	60.8	40.50	9	.500	.692	0	—	0	-5	-5	0	-0.3
1958 Pit-N	9	2	.818	18	15	5	3	0	106	78	2	59	81	11.8	1.61	240	.209	.320	6	.154	-1	28	27	-1	2.7
1959 Pit-N	0	7	.000	15	11	0	0	0	50²	58	7	32	30	16.2	6.93	56	.293	.394	0	.000	-1	-17	-17	-0	-1.7
1960 *Pit-N	1	2	.333	10	6	0	0	0	30	33	3	12	15	13.5	4.20	89	.300	.369	0	.000	-1	-1	-1	-0	-0.2
1961 Pit-N	0	1	.000	9	1	0	0	0	15²	17	5	5	9	12.6	6.32	63	.274	.328	1	.500	1	-4	-4	-0	-0.3
1962 LA-A	1	1	.500	5	2	0	0	0	10	15	4	5	10	18.0	8.10	48	.349	.417	1	.333	0	-5	-5	-0	-0.3
Hou-N	0	2	.000	8	2	0	0	0	15¹	20	2	9	10	17.6	7.04	53	.339	.435	1	.250	0	-5	-6	0	-0.4
Total 6	11	16	.407	66	38	5	3	0	229	225	24	127	156	14.0	4.32	89	.263	.361	9	.130	-2	-10	-12	-2	-0.5

■ MIKE WITT
Witt, Michael Atwater b: 7/20/60, Fullerton, Cal. BR/TR, 6'7", 185 lbs. Deb: 4/11/81

YEAR TM/L	W	L	PCT	G	GS	CG	SH	SV	IP	H	HR	BB	SO	RAT	ERA	ERA+	OAV	OOB	BH	AVG	PB	PR	/A	PD	TPI
1981 Cal-A	8	9	.471	22	21	7	1	0	129	123	9	47	75	12.6	3.28	111	.251	.330	0	—	0	5	5	-1	0.4
1982 *Cal-A	8	6	.571	33	26	5	1	0	179²	177	8	47	85	11.6	3.51	116	.260	.314	0	—	0	11	11	-0	1.1
1983 Cal-A	7	14	.333	43	19	2	0	5	154	173	14	75	77	14.8	4.91	82	.293	.379	0	—	0	-14	-15	0	-1.4
1984 Cal-A	15	11	.577	34	34	9	2	0	246²	227	17	84	196	11.5	3.47	114	.244	.310	0	—	0	14	14	-2	1.2
1985 Cal-A	15	9	.625	35	35	6	1	0	250	228	22	98	180	11.9	3.56	115	.243	.317	0	—	0	16	15	-1	1.5
1986 *Cal-A	18	10	.643	34	34	14	3	0	269	218	22	73	208	9.8	2.84	144	.221	.277	0	—	0	40	38	2	4.1
1987 Cal-A	16	14	.533	36	36	10	0	0	247	252	34	84	192	12.4	4.01	107	.261	.323	0	—	0	12	8	-1	0.7
1988 Cal-A	13	16	.448	34	34	12	2	0	249²	263	14	87	133	12.8	4.15	93	.272	.335	0	—	0	-5	-8	-0	-0.7
1989 Cal-A	9	15	.375	33	33	5	0	0	220	252	26	48	123	12.4	4.54	84	.292	.330	0	—	0	-16	-18	4	-1.3
1990 Cal-A	0	3	.000	10	0	0	0	1	20¹	19	1	13	14	14.6	1.77	220	.250	.367	0	—	0	5	5	0	0.6
NY-A	5	6	.455	16	16	2	1	0	96²	87	8	34	60	11.6	4.47	89	.240	.312	0	—	0	-6	-5	-0	-0.4
Yr	5	9	.357	26	16	2	1	1	117	106	9	47	74	12.1	4.00	99	.240	.319	0	—	0	-1	-1	1	0.2
Total 10	114	113	.502	330	288	72	11	6	2062	2019	175	690	1343	12.1	3.79	106	.257	.321	0	—	0	63	49	2	5.8

■ BOBBY WITT
Witt, Robert Andrew b: 5/11/64, Arlington, Mass. BR/TR, 6'2", 190 lbs. Deb: 4/10/86

YEAR TM/L	W	L	PCT	G	GS	CG	SH	SV	IP	H	HR	BB	SO	RAT	ERA	ERA+	OAV	OOB	BH	AVG	PB	PR	/A	PD	TPI
1986 Tex-A	11	9	.550	31	31	0	0	0	157²	130	18	143	174	15.8	5.48	78	.223	.379	0	—	0	-23	-21	-0	-1.9
1987 Tex-A	8	10	.444	26	25	1	0	0	143	114	10	140	160	16.2	4.91	91	.219	.388	0	.000	0	-7	-7	-0	-0.6
1988 Tex-A	8	10	.444	22	22	13	2	0	174¹	134	13	101	148	12.2	3.92	104	.216	.326	0	—	0	1	3	-1	0.2
1989 Tex-A	12	13	.480	31	31	5	1	0	194¹	182	14	114	166	13.8	5.14	77	.248	.351	0	—	0	-27	-25	-1	-2.4
1990 Tex-A	17	10	.630	33	32	7	1	0	222	197	12	110	221	12.6	3.36	118	.238	.330	0	—	0	13	15	-2	1.4
Total 5	56	52	.519	143	141	26	4	0	891¹	757	67	608	869	13.9	4.48	92	.230	.353	0	.000	0	-43	-35	-4	-3.3

■ JOHNNIE WITTIG
Wittig, John Carl "Hans" b: 6/16/14, Baltimore, Md. BR/TR, 6', 180 lbs. Deb: 8/04/38

YEAR TM/L	W	L	PCT	G	GS	CG	SH	SV	IP	H	HR	BB	SO	RAT	ERA	ERA+	OAV	OOB	BH	AVG	PB	PR	/A	PD	TPI
1938 NY-N	2	3	.400	13	6	2	0	0	39¹	41	4	26	14	15.3	4.81	78	.263	.368	0	.000	-1	-4	-5	-1	-0.6
1939 NY-N	0	2	.000	5	2	1	0	0	16²	19	0	14	4	17.8	7.56	52	.281	.418	0	.000	-1	-7	-7	0	-0.6
1941 NY-N	3	5	.375	25	9	0	0	0	85¹	111	5	45	47	16.6	5.59	66	.319	.398	5	.200	-0	-19	-18	-2	-1.8
1943 NY-N	5	15	.250	40	22	4	1	4	164	171	14	76	56	13.6	4.23	82	.272	.350	5	.098	-3	-15	-14	-3	-2.0
1949 Bos-A	0	0	—	1	0	0	0	0	2	2	0	2	0	18.0	9.00	48	.286	.444	0	—	0	-1	-1	0	0.0
Total 5	10	25	.286	84	39	7	1	4	307¹	343	23	163	121	14.9	4.89	73	.285	.371	10	.110	-6	-46	-44	-5	-5.0

■ PETE WOJEY
Wojey, Peter Paul b: 12/1/19, Stowe, Pa. BR/TR, 5'11", 185 lbs. Deb: 7/02/54

YEAR TM/L	W	L	PCT	G	GS	CG	SH	SV	IP	H	HR	BB	SO	RAT	ERA	ERA+	OAV	OOB	BH	AVG	PB	PR	/A	PD	TPI
1954 Bro-N	1	1	.500	14	1	0	0	1	27²	24	3	14	21	13.0	3.25	126	.242	.348	0	.000	-0	3	3	1	0.3
1956 Det-A	0	0	—	2	0	0	0	0	4	2	0	1	1	6.8	2.25	183	.167	.231	0	—	0	1	1	0	0.1
1957 Det-A	0	0	—	2	0	0	0	0	1¹	1	0	0	0	6.8	0.00	—	.200	.200	0	—	0	1	1	0	0.1
Total 3	1	1	.500	18	1	0	0	1	33	27	3	15	22	12.0	3.00	136	.233	.331	0	.000	-0	4	4	1	0.5

■ ED WOJNA
Wojna, Edward David b: 8/20/60, Bridgeport, Conn. BR/TR, 6'1", 185 lbs. Deb: 6/16/85

YEAR TM/L	W	L	PCT	G	GS	CG	SH	SV	IP	H	HR	BB	SO	RAT	ERA	ERA+	OAV	OOB	BH	AVG	PB	PR	/A	PD	TPI
1985 SD-N	2	4	.333	15	7	0	0	0	42	53	6	19	18	16.1	5.79	61	.312	.391	2	.167	-0	-10	-11	0	-1.0
1986 SD-N	2	2	.500	7	7	1	0	0	39	42	2	16	19	13.6	3.23	113	.268	.339	2	.143	-0	2	2	-0	0.1
1987 SD-N	0	3	.000	5	3	0	0	0	18¹	25	2	6	13	15.7	5.89	67	.333	.390	0	.000	-1	-4	-4	1	-0.3
1989 Cle-A	0	1	.000	9	3	0	0	0	33	31	0	14	10	12.3	4.09	97	.254	.331	0	—	0	-1	-0	1	0.0
Total 4	4	10	.286	36	20	1	0	0	132¹	151	10	55	60	14.4	4.62	81	.288	.361	4	.129	-1	-13	-13	1	-1.2

■ ERNIE WOLF
Wolf, Ernest Adolph b: 2/2/1889, Newark, N.J. d: 5/23/64, Atlantic Highlands, N.J. BR/TR, 5'11", 174 lbs. Deb: 9/10/12

YEAR TM/L	W	L	PCT	G	GS	CG	SH	SV	IP	H	HR	BB	SO	RAT	ERA	ERA+	OAV	OOB	BH	AVG	PB	PR	/A	PD	TPI
1912 Cle-A	0	0	—	1	0	0	0	0	5²	8	0	4	1	19.1	6.35	54	.348	.444	0	.000	-0	-2	-2	-0	-0.1

■ WALLY WOLF
Wolf, Walter Beck b: 1/5/42, Los Angeles, Cal. BR/TR, 6'0.5", 191 lbs. Deb: 9/27/69

YEAR TM/L	W	L	PCT	G	GS	CG	SH	SV	IP	H	HR	BB	SO	RAT	ERA	ERA+	OAV	OOB	BH	AVG	PB	PR	/A	PD	TPI
1969 Cal-A	0	0	—	2	0	0	0	0	2¹	3	1	3	2	23.1	11.57	30	.333	.500	0	—	0	-2	-2	0	-0.1
1970 Cal-A	0	0	—	4	0	0	0	0	5¹	3	1	4	5	11.8	5.06	76	.176	.333	0	—	0	-1	-1	-0	0.0
Total 2	0	0	—	6	0	0	0	0	7²	6	2	7	7	15.3	7.04	51	.231	.394	0	—	0	-3	-3	-0	-0.1

■ LEFTY WOLF
Wolf, Walter Francis b: 6/10/1900, Hartford, Conn. d: 9/25/71, New Orleans, La. BR/TL, 5'10", 163 lbs. Deb: 7/04/21

YEAR TM/L	W	L	PCT	G	GS	CG	SH	SV	IP	H	HR	BB	SO	RAT	ERA	ERA+	OAV	OOB	BH	AVG	PB	PR	/A	PD	TPI
1921 Phi-A	0	0	—	8	0	0	0	0	15	15	0	16	11	19.8	7.20	62	.273	.452	1	.250	-0	-5	-5	-0	-0.4

■ JIMMY WOLF
Wolf, William Van Winkle "Chicken" b: 5/12/1862, Louisville, Ky. d: 5/16/03, Louisville, Ky. BR, 5'9", 190 lbs. Deb: 5/02/1882 M♦

YEAR TM/L	W	L	PCT	G	GS	CG	SH	SV	IP	H	HR	BB	SO	RAT	ERA	ERA+	OAV	OOB	BH	AVG	PB	PR	/A	PD	TPI
1882 Lou-a	0	0	—	1	0	0	0	0	6	11	0	3	1	21.0	9.00	27	.371	.429	95	.299	0	-4	-4	-0	-0.2
1885 Lou-a	0	0	—	1	0	0	0	0	1	1	0	0	1	9.0	9.00	36	.249	.249	141	.292	0	-1	-1	0	0.0
1886 Lou-a	0	0	—	1	0	0	0	0	3	7	0	0	0	21.0	15.00	24	.435	.435	148	.272	0	-4	-4	-0	-0.2
Total 3	0	0	—	3	0	0	0	0	10	19	0	3	2	19.8	10.80	27	.382	.417	1440	.290	1	-9	-9	-0	-0.4

■ CHUCK WOLFE
Wolfe, Charles Hunt b: 2/15/1897, Wolfsburg, Pa. d: 11/27/57, Schellsburg, Pa. BL/TR, 5'7", 175 lbs. Deb: 8/02/23

YEAR TM/L	W	L	PCT	G	GS	CG	SH	SV	IP	H	HR	BB	SO	RAT	ERA	ERA+	OAV	OOB	BH	AVG	PB	PR	/A	PD	TPI
1923 Phi-A	0	0	—	3	0	0	0	0	9²	6	1	8	1	13.0	3.72	110	.194	.359	1	.333	0	0	0	-0	0.0

■ ED WOLFE
Wolfe, Edward Anthony b: 1/2/29, Los Angeles, Cal. BR/TR, 6'3", 185 lbs. Deb: 4/19/52

YEAR TM/L	W	L	PCT	G	GS	CG	SH	SV	IP	H	HR	BB	SO	RAT	ERA	ERA+	OAV	OOB	BH	AVG	PB	PR	/A	PD	TPI
1952 Pit-N	0	0	—	3	0	0	0	0	3²	7	1	5	1	31.9	7.36	54	.467	.619	0	—	0	-1	-1	0	0.0

■ BARNEY WOLFE
Wolfe, Wilbert Otto b: 1/9/1876, Independence, Pa. d: 2/27/53, N.Charleroi, Pa. BR/TR, 6'1", Deb: 4/24/03

YEAR TM/L	W	L	PCT	G	GS	CG	SH	SV	IP	H	HR	BB	SO	RAT	ERA	ERA+	OAV	OOB	BH	AVG	PB	PR	/A	PD	TPI
1903 NY-A	6	9	.400	20	16	12	1	0	148¹	143	1	26	48	10.3	2.97	105	.253	.285	4	.075	-4	-0	2	0	-0.1
1904 NY-A	0	3	.000	7	3	2	0	0	33²	31	1	4	8	9.4	3.21	85	.246	.269	0	.000	-1	-2	-2	0	-0.2
Was-A	6	9	.400	17	16	13	2	0	126²	131	0	22	44	10.9	3.27	81	.268	.299	5	.119	-2	-9	-9	-2	-1.1
Yr	6	12	.333	24	19	15	2	0	160¹	162	1	26	52	10.6	3.26	82	.263	.293	6	.115	-3	-12	-10	-1	-1.3

YEAR TM/L	W	L	PCT	G	GS	CG	SH	SV	IP	H	HR	BB	SO	RAT	ERA	ERA+	OAV	OOB	BH	AVG	PB	PR	/A	PD	TPI
1905 Was-A	9	13	.409	28	23	17	1	1	182	162	1	37	52	9.8	2.57	103	.240	.279	8	.127	-2	2	2	-2	-0.1
1906 Was-A	0	3	.000	4	3	2	0	0	20	17	0	10	8	12.1	4.05	65	.233	.326	2	.286	0	-3	-3	-0	-0.2
Total 4	21	37	.362	76	61	46	4	1	510²	484	3	99	160	10.3	2.96	94	.251	.287	19	.109	-9	-13	-10	-3	-1.7

■ BILL WOLFE
Wolfe, William b: Jersey City, N.J.   Deb: 9/10/02

YEAR TM/L	W	L	PCT	G	GS	CG	SH	SV	IP	H	HR	BB	SO	RAT	ERA	ERA+	OAV	OOB	BH	AVG	PB	PR	/A	PD	TPI
1902 Phi-N	0	1	.000	1	1	1	0	0	9	11	0	4	3	16.0	4.00	70	.301	.385	1	.333	0	-1	-1	0	0.0

■ ROGER WOLFF
Wolff, Roger Francis b: 4/10/11, Evansville, Ill.   BR/TR, 6'0.5", 208 lbs.   Deb: 9/20/41

YEAR TM/L	W	L	PCT	G	GS	CG	SH	SV	IP	H	HR	BB	SO	RAT	ERA	ERA+	OAV	OOB	BH	AVG	PB	PR	/A	PD	TPI
1941 Phi-A	0	2	.000	2	2	2	0	0	17	15	0	4	2	10.1	3.18	132	.231	.275	1	.200	-0	2	2	-0	0.2
1942 Phi-A	12	15	.444	32	25	15	2	3	214¹	206	16	69	94	11.7	3.32	114	.249	.309	6	.088	-3	8	11	-0	0.8
1943 Phi-A	10	15	.400	41	26	13	2	6	221	232	11	72	91	12.5	3.54	96	.274	.334	9	.122	-4	-6	-4	-3	-1.0
1944 Was-A	4	15	.211	33	21	5	0	2	155	186	9	60	73	14.6	4.99	65	.295	.362	12	.218	1	-27	-30	2	-2.7
1945 Was-A	20	10	.667	33	29	21	4	2	250	200	7	53	108	9.1	2.12	146	.215	**.258**	9	.107	-4	35	27	-1	2.3
1946 Was-A	5	8	.385	21	17	6	0	0	122	115	8	30	50	11.1	2.58	130	.249	.302	4	.103	-1	12	10	-1	0.9
1947 Cle-A	0	0	—	7	2	0	0	0	16	15	1	10	5	15.2	3.94	88	.259	.386	-0	.000	-0	-0	-1	1	0.0
Pit-N	1	4	.200	13	6	1	0	0	30	49	4	18	7	20.4	8.70	49	.368	.447	0	.000	-1	-15	-15	-1	-1.4
Total 7	52	69	.430	182	128	63	8	13	1025¹	1018	56	316	430	11.9	3.41	100	.258	.316	41	.122	-12	8	1	-3	-0.9

■ MELLIE WOLFGANG
Wolfgang, Meldon John "Red" b: 3/20/1890, Albany, N.Y. d: 6/30/47, Albany, N.Y.   BR/TR, 5'9", 160 lbs.   Deb: 4/18/14

YEAR TM/L	W	L	PCT	G	GS	CG	SH	SV	IP	H	HR	BB	SO	RAT	ERA	ERA+	OAV	OOB	BH	AVG	PB	PR	/A	PD	TPI
1914 Chi-A	9	5	.643	24	11	9	2	0	119¹	96	0	32	50	9.7	1.89	142	.219	.272	7	.175	-0	11	11	4	1.7
1915 Chi-A	2	2	.500	17	2	0	0	0	53²	39	0	12	21	8.7	1.84	161	.211	.263	2	.118	-1	7	7	-1	0.5
1916 Chi-A	4	6	.400	27	14	6	1	0	127	103	2	42	36	10.4	1.98	139	.228	.296	9	.225	0	12	11	2	1.5
1917 Chi-A	0	0	—	5	0	0	0	0	17²	18	1	6	3	12.7	5.09	52	.305	.379	0	.000	-1	-5	-5	-0	-0.5
1918 Chi-A	0	1	.000	4	0	0	0	0	8¹	12	0	3	1	16.2	5.40	51	.333	.385	1	.500	-1	-2	-2	-0	-0.1
Total 5	15	14	.517	77	27	15	3	0	326	268	3	95	111	10.1	2.18	127	.229	.289	19	.184	-1	23	21	5	3.1

■ HARRY WOLTER
Wolter, Harry Meigs b: 7/11/1884, Monterey, Cal. d: 7/7/70, Palo Alto, Cal.   BL/TL, 5'10", 175 lbs.   Deb: 5/14/07 ♦

YEAR TM/L	W	L	PCT	G	GS	CG	SH	SV	IP	H	HR	BB	SO	RAT	ERA	ERA+	OAV	OOB	BH	AVG	PB	PR	/A	PD	TPI
1907 Pit-N	0	0	—	1	0	0	0	0	2	3	0	2	0	22.5	4.50	54	.333	.455	0	.000	-0	-0	-0	0	0.0
StL-N	0	2	.000	3	3	1	0	0	23	27	1	18	8	18.4	4.30	58	.318	.448	16	.340	1	-5	-5	-1	-0.4
Yr	0	2	.000	4	3	1	0	0	25	30	1	20	8	18.7	4.32	58	.319	.448	3	.063	-1	-5	-5	-1	-0.4
1909 Bos-A	4	4	.500	11	6	0	0	0	59	66	0	30	21	15.3	3.51	71	.303	.397	30	.246	2	-7	-7	-1	-0.6
Total 2	4	6	.400	15	9	1	0	0	84	96	1	50	29	16.3	3.75	67	.308	.413	515	.270	3	-12	-12	-1	-1.0

■ RYNIE WOLTERS
Wolters, Reinder Albertus b: 12/18/1842, U.S.A. d: 1/3/17, Newark, N.J.   TR, 6', 165 lbs.   Deb: 5/18/1871

YEAR TM/L	W	L	PCT	G	GS	CG	SH	SV	IP	H	HR	BB	SO	RAT	ERA	ERA+	OAV	OOB	BH	AVG	PB	PR	/A	PD	TPI
1871 Mut-n	16	16	.500	**32**	32	**31**	1	0	**283**	345	7	39	22	12.2	3.43	110	**.263**	.285	51	.370	18	25	11		1.7
1872 Cle-n	3	6	.333	12	8	5	0	0	76¹	119	3	6		14.7	5.19	70	.301	.312	16	.232	-0	-12	-13		-0.9
1873 Res-n	0	1	.000	1	1	1	0	0	9	14	0	1		15.0	9.00	41	.233	.246	-0	.000	-1	-5	-5		-0.3
Total 3 n	19	23	.452	45	41	37	1	0	368¹	478	10	46	22	12.8	3.93	94	.271	.289	67	.318	17	-14	-9		0.5

■ DOOLEY WOMACK
Womack, Horace Guy b: 8/25/39, Columbia, S.C.   BL/TR, 6', 170 lbs.   Deb: 4/14/66

YEAR TM/L	W	L	PCT	G	GS	CG	SH	SV	IP	H	HR	BB	SO	RAT	ERA	ERA+	OAV	OOB	BH	AVG	PB	PR	/A	PD	TPI
1966 NY-A	7	3	.700	42	1	0	0	4	75	52	6	23	50	9.4	2.64	126	.198	.270	1	.200	0	7	6	2	0.9
1967 NY-A	5	6	.455	65	0	0	0	18	97	80	6	35	57	10.9	2.41	130	.230	.306	4	.286	1	9	8	4	1.4
1968 NY-A	3	7	.300	45	0	0	0	2	61²	53	6	29	27	12.1	3.21	90	.244	.336	1	.200	-0	-2	-2	0	0.1
1969 Hou-N	2	1	.667	30	0	0	0	0	51¹	49	1	20	32	12.6	3.51	101	.259	.340	1	.167	-0	0	0	2	0.2
Sea-A	2	1	.667	9	0	0	0	0	14¹	15	0	3	8	11.3	2.51	145	.273	.310	0	.000	-0	2	2	0	0.2
1970 Oak-A	0	0	—	2	0	0	0	0	3	4	2	1	3	15.0	15.00	24	.308	.357	0	—	-4	-4	-0	-0.2	
Total 5	19	18	.514	193	1	0	0	24	302¹	253	21	111	177	11.1	2.95	110	.233	.310	7	.226	1	12	9	11	2.6

■ SPADES WOOD
Wood, Charles Asher b: 1/13/09, Spartanburg, S.C. d: 5/18/86, Wichita, Kan.   BL/TL, 5'10.5", 150 lbs.   Deb: 8/16/30

YEAR TM/L	W	L	PCT	G	GS	CG	SH	SV	IP	H	HR	BB	SO	RAT	ERA	ERA+	OAV	OOB	BH	AVG	PB	PR	/A	PD	TPI
1930 Pit-N	4	3	.571	9	7	4	2	0	58	61	4	32	23	14.4	5.12	97	.270	.360	5	.250	1	-1	-1	-2	-0.1
1931 Pit-N	2	6	.250	15	10	2	0	0	64	69	2	46	33	16.3	6.05	64	.273	.387	5	.227	1	-16	-16	-0	-1.4
Total 2	6	9	.400	24	17	6	2	0	122	130	6	78	56	15.4	5.61	78	.271	.375	10	.238	1	-16	-17	-2	-1.5

■ GEORGE WOOD
Wood, George A. "Dandy" b: 11/9/1858, Boston, Mass. d: 4/4/24, Harrisburg, Pa.   BL/TR, 5'10.5", 175 lbs.   Deb: 5/01/1880   MU♦

YEAR TM/L	W	L	PCT	G	GS	CG	SH	SV	IP	H	HR	BB	SO	RAT	ERA	ERA+	OAV	OOB	BH	AVG	PB	PR	/A	PD	TPI
1883 Det-N	0	0	—	1	0	0	0	0	5	8	0	3	0	19.8	7.20	43	.342	.417	133	.302	0	-2	-2	0	-0.1
1885 Det-N	0	0	—	1	0	0	0	0	4	5	0	1	1	13.5	0.00	—	.292	.331	105	.290	0	1	1	0	0.1
1888 Phi-N	0	0	—	2	0	0	0	2	2	3	0	1	0	18.0	4.50	66	.335	.401	99	.229	0	-0	-0	0	0.0
1889 Phi-N	0	0	—	1	0	0	0	0	1	2	0	0	2	18.0	18.00	24	.403	.403	106	.251	0	-2	-2	0	-0.1
Total 4	0	0	—	5	0	0	0	2	12	18	0	5	3	17.3	5.25	59	.331	.387	1467	.273	1	-3	-3	0	0.0

■ JOHN WOOD
Wood, John B. b: 1871, 5'7", 142 lbs.   Deb: 5/09/1896

YEAR TM/L	W	L	PCT	G	GS	CG	SH	SV	IP	H	HR	BB	SO	RAT	ERA	ERA+	OAV	OOB	BH	AVG	PB	PR	/A	PD	TPI
1896 StL-N	0	0	—	1	0	0	0	0	0	1	0	2	0	—	∞	—	1.000	1.000	0	—	0	-1	-1	-0	0.0

■ JOE WOOD
Wood, Joseph "Smokey Joe" (b: Howard Ellsworth Wood)
b: 10/25/1889, Kansas City, Mo. d: 7/27/85, West Haven, Conn   BR/TR, 5'11", 180 lbs.   Deb: 8/24/08 ♦

YEAR TM/L	W	L	PCT	G	GS	CG	SH	SV	IP	H	HR	BB	SO	RAT	ERA	ERA+	OAV	OOB	BH	AVG	PB	PR	/A	PD	TPI
1908 Bos-A	1	1	.500	6	2	1	1	0	22²	14	0	16	11	12.3	2.38	103	.161	.298	0	.000	-1	0	0	-0	0.0
1909 Bos-A	11	7	.611	24	19	13	4	0	160²	121	1	43	88	9.5	2.18	114	.209	.270	9	.164	-0	5	6	-4	0.1
1910 Bos-A	12	13	.480	35	17	14	3	0	198²	155	3	56	145	10.0	1.68	152	.220	.287	18	.261	5	19	19	1	2.9
1911 Bos-A	23	17	.575	44	33	25	5	3	275²	226	2	76	231	10.2	2.02	162	.223	.284	23	.261	8	40	38	0	4.9
1912 *Bos-A	**34**	5	**.872**	43	38	**35**	10	1	344	267	2	82	258	9.4	1.91	178	.216	.272	36	.290	11	54	57	6	8.3
1913 Bos-A	11	5	.688	23	18	12	1	2	145²	120	0	61	123	11.7	2.29	129	.229	.319	15	.268	4	10	11	3	2.0
1914 Bos-A	9	3	.750	18	14	11	1	1	113¹	94	1	34	67	10.2	2.62	103	.229	.288	6	.140	-0	2	1	0	0.1
1915 Bos-A	15	5	**.750**	25	16	10	3	2	157¹	120	1	44	63	9.4	**1.49**	187	.216	.275	14	.259	4	25	23	1	3.1
1917 Cle-A	0	1	.000	5	1	0	0	1	15²	17	0	7	2	13.8	3.45	82	.309	.387	0	.000	-1	-1	-1	0	0.0
1919 Cle-A	0	0	—	1	0	0	0	0	0²	0	0	0	0	0.0	0.00	—	.000	.000	49	.255	0	0	0	0	0.0
1920 *Cle-A	0	0	—	1	0	0	0	0	2	4	0	2	1	27.0	22.50	17	.444	.545	37	.270	0	-4	-4	0	-0.2
Total 11	116	57	.671	225	158	121	28	11	1436¹	1138	10	421	989	10.1	2.03	146	.220	.285	553	.283	31	150	150	7	21.2

■ JOE WOOD
Wood, Joseph Frank b: 5/20/16, Shoshola, Pa.   BR/TR, 6', 190 lbs.   Deb: 5/01/44

YEAR TM/L	W	L	PCT	G	GS	CG	SH	SV	IP	H	HR	BB	SO	RAT	ERA	ERA+	OAV	OOB	BH	AVG	PB	PR	/A	PD	TPI
1944 Bos-A	0	1	.000	3	1	0	0	0	9²	13	0	5	5	14.9	6.52	52	.317	.364	0	.000	-0	-3	-3	0	-0.2

■ PETE WOOD
Wood, Peter Burke b: 2/1/1857, Hamilton, Ont., Can. d: 3/15/23, Chicago, Ill.   TR, 5'7", 185 lbs.   Deb: 7/15/1885

YEAR TM/L	W	L	PCT	G	GS	CG	SH	SV	IP	H	HR	BB	SO	RAT	ERA	ERA+	OAV	OOB	BH	AVG	PB	PR	/A	PD	TPI
1885 Buf-N	8	15	.348	24	22	21	0	0	198²	235	8	66	38	13.6	4.44	67	.281	.334	23	.221	-1	-36	-33	-1	-2.9
1889 Phi-N	1	1	.500	3	2	2	0	0	19	28	0	3	8	14.7	5.21	84	.332	.355	0	.000	-1	-3	-2	0	-0.1
Total 2	9	16	.360	27	24	23	0	0	217²	263	8	69	46	13.7	4.51	68	.286	.336	23	.205	-2	-38	-34	-1	-3.1

■ WILBUR WOOD
Wood, Wilbur Forrester b: 10/22/41, Cambridge, Mass.   BR/TL, 6', 180 lbs.   Deb: 6/30/61

YEAR TM/L	W	L	PCT	G	GS	CG	SH	SV	IP	H	HR	BB	SO	RAT	ERA	ERA+	OAV	OOB	BH	AVG	PB	PR	/A	PD	TPI
1961 Bos-A	0	0	—	6	1	0	0	0	13	14	2	7	7	14.5	5.54	75	.269	.356	0	.000	-0	-2	-2	-0	-0.2
1962 Bos-A	0	0	—	1	1	0	0	0	7²	6	0	3	3	10.6	3.52	117	.214	.290	0	.000	0	0	1	0	0.0
1963 Bos-A	0	5	.000	25	6	0	0	0	64²	67	10	13	28	11.1	3.76	101	.270	.314	0	.000	-2	-1	0	-0	-0.1
1964 Bos-A	0	0	—	4	0	0	0	0	5²	13	1	3	5	25.4	17.47	22	.433	.485	0	.000	-0	-9	-9	-0	-0.7
Pit-N	0	2	.000	3	2	1	0	0	17¹	16	0	11	7	15.1	3.63	97	.246	.372	0	.000	-0	-0	-1	-1	0.0
1965 Pit-N	0	0	—	34	1	0	0	0	51¹	46	5	19	29	10.7	3.16	111	.237	.300	0	.000	-0	2	2	-1	0.1
1967 Chi-A	4	2	.667	51	8	0	0	4	95¹	95	7	28	47	11.7	2.45	126	.260	.315	1	.063	-0	8	7	-0	0.7
1968 Chi-A	13	12	.520	**88**	2	0	0	16	159¹	127	8	33	74	9.2	1.87	162	.222	.268	2	.091	-1	**20**	20	-0	2.3
1969 Chi-A	10	11	.476	**76**	0	0	0	15	119²	113	13	40	73	11.7	3.01	128	.248	.313	0	.000	-2	8	11	0	1.1

YEAR	TM/L	W	L	PCT	G	GS	CG	SH	SV	IP	H	HR	BB	SO	RAT	ERA	ERA+	OAV	OOB	BH	AVG	PB	PR	/A	PD	TPI
1970	Chi-A	9	13	.409	77	0	0	0	21	121²	118	7	36	85	11.5	2.81	139	.258	.315	2	.111	-1	12	15	2	1.7
1971	Chi-A	22	13	.629	44	42	22	7	1	334	272	21	62	210	9.2	1.91	**188**	.222	.264	5	.052	-5	**57**	**62**	2	**7.1**
1972	Chi-A	**24**	17	.585	49	49	20	8	0	**376²**	325	28	74	193	9.7	2.51	125	.235	.277	17	.136	-2	23	26	4	3.3
1973	Chi-A	**24**	20	.545	49	48	21	4	0	**359¹**	381	25	91	199	12.0	3.46	114	.270	.318	0	—	0	14	20	1	2.2
1974	Chi-A	20	19	.513	42	42	22	1	0	320¹	305	27	80	169	11.1	3.60	104	.254	.305	0	—	0	1	5	3	0.8
1975	Chi-A	16	20	.444	43	43	14	2	0	291¹	309	26	92	140	12.5	4.11	94	.272	.329	0	—	0	-11	-8	1	-0.5
1976	Chi-A	4	3	.571	7	7	5	1	0	56¹	51	3	11	31	9.9	2.24	159	.242	.279	0	—	0	8	8	1	1.0
1977	Chi-A	7	8	.467	24	18	5	1	0	122²	139	10	50	42	14.6	4.99	82	.293	.373	0	—	0	-13	-12	3	-0.9
1978	Chi-A	10	10	.500	28	27	4	0	0	168	187	23	74	69	14.1	5.20	73	.285	.361	0	—	0	-27	-26	2	-2.2
Total	17	164	156	.512	651	297	114	24	57	2684	2582	209	724	1411	11.3	3.24	112	.254	.308	27	.084	-14	92	120	18	15.7

■ GENE WOODBURN
Woodburn, Eugene Stewart b: 8/20/1886, Bellaire, Ohio d: 1/18/61, Sandusky, Ohio BR/TR, 6', 175 lbs. Deb: 7/27/11

YEAR	TM/L	W	L	PCT	G	GS	CG	SH	SV	IP	H	HR	BB	SO	RAT	ERA	ERA+	OAV	OOB	BH	AVG	PB	PR	/A	PD	TPI
1911	StL-N	1	5	.167	11	6	1	0	0	38¹	22	0	40	23	16.0	5.40	63	.167	.382	1	.167	1	-9	-9	1	-0.6
1912	StL-N	1	4	.200	20	5	1	0	0	48¹	60	0	42	25	19.7	5.59	61	.305	.436	0	.000	-2	-12	-12	-1	-1.2
Total	2	2	9	.182	31	11	2	0	0	86²	82	0	82	48	18.1	5.50	62	.249	.413	1	.053	-0	-20	-20	-0	-1.8

■ FRED WOODCOCK
Woodcock, Fred Wayland b: 5/17/1868, Winchendon, Mass. d: 8/11/43, Ashburnham, Mass. BL/TL, 6'2", 190 lbs. Deb: 5/17/1892

YEAR	TM/L	W	L	PCT	G	GS	CG	SH	SV	IP	H	HR	BB	SO	RAT	ERA	ERA+	OAV	OOB	BH	AVG	PB	PR	/A	PD	TPI
1892	Pit-N	1	2	.333	5	4	3	0	0	33	42	1	17	8	16.1	3.55	93	.298	.373	3	.200	0	-1	-1	0	0.0

■ GEORGE WOODEND
Woodend, George Anthony b: 12/9/17, Hartford, Conn. d: 2/6/80, Hartford, Conn. BR/TR, 6', 200 lbs. Deb: 4/22/44

YEAR	TM/L	W	L	PCT	G	GS	CG	SH	SV	IP	H	HR	BB	SO	RAT	ERA	ERA+	OAV	OOB	BH	AVG	PB	PR	/A	PD	TPI
1944	Bos-N	0	0	—	3	0	0	0	0	2	5	0	5	0	45.0	13.50	28	.556	.714	0	—	0	-2	-2	0	-0.1

■ HAL WOODESHICK
Woodeshick, Harold Joseph b: 8/24/32, Wilkes-Barre, Pa. BR/TL, 6'3", 200 lbs. Deb: 9/14/56

YEAR	TM/L	W	L	PCT	G	GS	CG	SH	SV	IP	H	HR	BB	SO	RAT	ERA	ERA+	OAV	OOB	BH	AVG	PB	PR	/A	PD	TPI
1956	Det-A	0	2	.000	2	2	0	0	0	5¹	12	1	3	1	25.3	13.50	30	.444	.500	0	—	0	-6	-6	0	-0.4
1958	Cle-A	6	6	.500	14	9	3	0	0	71²	71	4	25	27	12.8	3.64	100	.265	.341	4	.167	-1	1	0	3	0.2
1959	Was-A	2	4	.333	31	3	0	0	0	61	58	2	36	30	14.0	3.69	106	.253	.357	0	.000	-1	1	2	1	0.1
1960	Was-A	4	5	.444	41	14	1	0	4	115	131	7	60	46	15.2	4.70	83	.289	.375	2	.069	-2	-11	-10	2	-0.9
1961	Was-A	3	2	.600	7	6	1	0	0	40¹	38	3	24	24	14.5	4.02	100	.257	.371	2	.125	-1	0	-0	1	-0.0
	Det-A	1	1	.500	12	2	0	0	0	18¹	25	3	17	13	20.6	7.85	52	.316	.438	0	.000	-0	-8	-8	1	-0.6
	Yr	4	3	.571	19	8	1	0	0	58²	63	6	41	37	16.0	5.22	77	.273	.382	1	.050	-1	-8	-8	2	-0.6
1962	Hou-N	5	16	.238	31	26	2	1	0	139¹	161	6	54	82	14.1	4.39	85	.290	.356	3	.081	-0	-7	-10	3	-1.0
1963	Hou-N	11	9	.550	55	0	0	0	10	114	75	3	42	94	9.7	1.97	160	.186	.273	3	.130	-0	17	15	3	1.9
1964	Hou-N	2	9	.182	61	0	0	0	23	78¹	73	3	32	58	12.9	2.76	124	.249	.337	0	.000	-0	7	6	1	0.7
1965	Hou-N	3	4	.429	27	0	0	0	3	32¹	27	3	18	22	12.5	3.06	110	.227	.328	1	.167	-0	2	1	1	0.2
	StL-N	3	2	.600	51	0	0	0	15	59²	47	1	27	37	11.5	1.81	212	.221	.314	0	.000	-1	11	13	2	1.6
	Yr	6	6	.500	78	0	0	0	18	92	74	4	45	59	11.8	2.25	163	.223	.319	1	.071	-1	13	15	2	1.8
1966	StL-N	2	1	.667	59	0	0	0	4	70¹	57	5	23	30	10.4	1.92	187	.224	.290	1	.200	0	13	13	3	1.8
1967	*StL-N	2	1	.667	36	0	0	0	2	41²	41	2	28	20	15.6	5.18	63	.252	.371	0	.000	-0	-8	-9	1	-0.8
Total	11	44	62	.415	427	62	7	1	61	847¹	816	40	389	484	13.2	3.56	102	.254	.342	16	.092	-7	13	7	18	2.8

■ DAN WOODMAN
Woodman, Daniel Courtenay "Cocoa" b: 7/8/1893, Danvers, Mass. d: 12/14/62, Danvers, Mass. BR/TR, 5'8", 160 lbs. Deb: 7/10/14

YEAR	TM/L	W	L	PCT	G	GS	CG	SH	SV	IP	H	HR	BB	SO	RAT	ERA	ERA+	OAV	OOB	BH	AVG	PB	PR	/A	PD	TPI
1914	Buf-F	0	0	—	13	0	0	0	1	33²	30	0	11	13	11.2	2.41	137	.246	.314	1	.143	-0	3	3	-1	0.2
1915	Buf-F	0	0	—	5	1	0	0	0	15¹	14	0	9	1	13.5	4.11	76	.250	.354	1	.250	-0	-2	-2	1	0.0
Total	2	0	0	—	18	1	0	0	1	49	44	0	20	14	11.9	2.94	110	.247	.327	2	.182	-0	1	2	1	0.2

■ CLARENCE WOODS
Woods, Clarence Cofield b: 6/11/1892, Woods Ridge, Ohio County, Ind. d: 7/2/69, Rising Sun, Ind. BR/TR, 6'5", 230 lbs. Deb: 8/08/14

YEAR	TM/L	W	L	PCT	G	GS	CG	SH	SV	IP	H	HR	BB	SO	RAT	ERA	ERA+	OAV	OOB	BH	AVG	PB	PR	/A	PD	TPI
1914	Ind-F	0	0	—	2	0	0	0	1	2	1	0	2	1	13.5	4.50	77	.155	.355	0	—	0	-0	-0	0	0.0

■ PINKY WOODS
Woods, George Rowland b: 5/22/15, Waterbury, Conn. d: 10/30/82, Los Angeles, Cal. BR/TR, 6'5", 225 lbs. Deb: 6/20/43

YEAR	TM/L	W	L	PCT	G	GS	CG	SH	SV	IP	H	HR	BB	SO	RAT	ERA	ERA+	OAV	OOB	BH	AVG	PB	PR	/A	PD	TPI
1943	Bos-A	5	6	.455	23	12	2	0	1	100²	109	6	55	32	14.8	4.92	67	.284	.375	8	.222	-0	-18	-18	0	-1.8
1944	Bos-A	4	8	.333	38	20	5	1	0	170²	171	4	88	56	14.0	3.27	104	.266	.360	7	.146	-1	3	2	2	0.3
1945	Bos-A	4	7	.364	24	12	3	0	2	107¹	108	3	63	36	14.4	4.19	81	.268	.368	9	.214	1	-10	-9	1	-0.7
Total	3	13	21	.382	85	44	10	1	3	378²	388	13	206	124	14.3	3.97	85	.272	.366	24	.190	-1	-25	-25	3	-2.2

■ JOHN WOODS
Woods, John Fulton "Abe" b: 1/18/1898, Princeton, W.Va. d: 10/4/46, Norfolk, Va. BR/TR, 6', 175 lbs. Deb: 9/16/24

YEAR	TM/L	W	L	PCT	G	GS	CG	SH	SV	IP	H	HR	BB	SO	RAT	ERA	ERA+	OAV	OOB	BH	AVG	PB	PR	/A	PD	TPI
1924	Bos-A	0	0	—	1	0	0	0	0	1	0	0	3	0	27.0	0.00	—	.000	.500	0	—	0	0	0	0	0.0

■ WALT WOODS
Woods, Walter Sydney b: 4/28/1875, Rye, N.H. d: 10/30/51, Portsmouth, N.H. BR/TR, 5'9.5", 165 lbs. Deb: 4/20/1898

YEAR	TM/L	W	L	PCT	G	GS	CG	SH	SV	IP	H	HR	BB	SO	RAT	ERA	ERA+	OAV	OOB	BH	AVG	PB	PR	/A	PD	TPI
1898	Chi-N	9	13	.409	27	22	18	3	0	215	224	7	59	26	11.8	3.14	114	.266	.315	27	.175	-4	11	11	2	0.5
1899	Lou-N	9	13	.409	26	21	17	0	0	186¹	216	9	37	21	12.2	3.28	117	.290	.323	19	.151	-3	12	12	5	1.1
1900	Pit-N	0	0	—	1	0	0	0	0	3	9	0	1	1	30.0	21.00	17	.513	.539	0	.000	-0	-6	-6	-0	-0.3
Total	3	18	26	.409	54	43	35	3	0	404¹	449	16	97	48	12.2	3.34	111	.280	.321	46	.164	-7	17	17	6	1.3

■ DICK WOODSON
Woodson, Richard Lee b: 3/30/45, Oelwein, Iowa BR/TR, 6'5", 205 lbs. Deb: 4/08/69

YEAR	TM/L	W	L	PCT	G	GS	CG	SH	SV	IP	H	HR	BB	SO	RAT	ERA	ERA+	OAV	OOB	BH	AVG	PB	PR	/A	PD	TPI
1969	*Min-A	7	5	.583	44	10	2	0	1	110¹	99	11	49	66	12.3	3.67	99	.237	.322	2	.074	-1	-1	-0	1	0.0
1970	*Min-A	1	2	.333	21	0	0	0	1	30²	29	2	19	22	14.1	3.82	98	.244	.348	0	.000	-0	-0	-0	0	0.0
1972	Min-A	14	14	.500	36	36	9	3	0	251²	193	19	101	150	10.6	2.72	118	.211	.291	7	.080	-5	10	14	1	1.1
1973	Min-A	10	8	.556	23	23	4	2	0	141¹	137	12	68	53	13.2	3.95	100	.254	.339	0	—	0	-2	0	-1	0.0
1974	Min-A	1	1	.500	5	4	0	0	0	27	30	5	4	12	11.7	4.33	87	.273	.304	0	—	0	-2	-2	1	0.0
	NY-A	1	2	.333	8	3	0	0	0	28	34	6	12	12	15.1	5.79	60	.301	.373	0	—	0	-7	-7	-1	-0.7
	Yr	2	3	.400	13	7	0	0	0	55	64	11	16	24	13.3	5.07	71	.286	.336	0	—	0	-9	-9	-0	-0.7
Total	5	34	32	.515	137	76	15	5	2	589	522	55	253	315	12.0	3.47	102	.236	.317	9	.077	-7	-2	5	1	0.4

■ FRANK WOODWARD
Woodward, Frank Russell b: 5/17/1894, New Haven, Conn. d: 6/11/61, New Haven, Conn. BR/TR, 5'10", 175 lbs. Deb: 4/17/18

YEAR	TM/L	W	L	PCT	G	GS	CG	SH	SV	IP	H	HR	BB	SO	RAT	ERA	ERA+	OAV	OOB	BH	AVG	PB	PR	/A	PD	TPI
1918	Phi-N	0	0	—	2	0	0	0	0	6	6	0	4	4	15.0	6.00	50	.250	.357	1	.333	0	-2	-2	-0	-0.1
1919	Phi-N	6	9	.400	17	12	6	0	0	100²	109	5	35	27	13.3	4.74	68	.291	.359	6	.207	1	-20	-17	-2	-1.7
	StL-N	3	5	.375	17	7	2	0	1	72	65	1	28	18	11.8	2.63	106	.248	.323	1	.048	-2	2	1	0	0.0
	Yr	9	14	.391	34	19	8	0	1	172²	174	6	63	45	12.4	3.86	79	.271	.337	5	.100	-1	-18	-16	-2	-1.7
1921	Was-A	0	0	—	3	1	0	0	0	10²	11	0	3	4	11.8	5.91	70	.282	.333	1	.333	-0	-2	-2	0	-0.1
1922	Was-A	0	0	—	1	0	0	0	0	2¹	3	0	3	2	23.1	11.57	33	.375	.545	0	.000	-0	-2	-2	0	-0.1
1923	Chi-A	0	1	.000	2	1	0	0	0	2	5	0	1	0	27.0	13.50	29	.500	.545	0	—	0	-2	-2	0	-0.1
Total	5	9	15	.375	42	21	8	0	1	193²	199	6	74	55	13.0	4.23	74	.277	.350	9	.158	-1	-26	-24	-1	-2.1

■ BOB WOODWARD
Woodward, Robert John b: 9/28/62, Hanover, N.H. BR/TR, 6'3", 185 lbs. Deb: 9/05/85

YEAR	TM/L	W	L	PCT	G	GS	CG	SH	SV	IP	H	HR	BB	SO	RAT	ERA	ERA+	OAV	OOB	BH	AVG	PB	PR	/A	PD	TPI
1985	Bos-A	1	0	1.000	5	2	0	0	0	26²	17	0	9	16	9.5	1.69	254	.168	.250	0	—	0	7	8	-1	0.8
1986	Bos-A	2	3	.400	9	6	0	0	0	35²	46	4	11	14	14.6	5.30	79	.313	.365	0	—	0	-4	-5	1	-0.3
1987	Bos-A	1	1	.500	9	6	0	0	0	37	53	6	15	15	16.8	7.05	64	.338	.399	0	—	0	-11	-10	-1	-0.9
1988	Bos-A	0	0	—	1	0	0	0	0	0²	2	0	1	0	40.5	13.50	30	.500	.600	0	—	0	-1	-1	0	0.0
Total	4	4	4	.500	24	14	0	0	0	100	118	10	36	45	14.2	5.04	86	.289	.352	0	—	0	-9	-8	-1	-0.4

■ FLOYD WOOLDRIDGE
Wooldridge, Floyd Lewis b: 8/25/28, Jerico Springs, Mo BR/TR, 6'1", 185 lbs. Deb: 5/01/55

YEAR	TM/L	W	L	PCT	G	GS	CG	SH	SV	IP	H	HR	BB	SO	RAT	ERA	ERA+	OAV	OOB	BH	AVG	PB	PR	/A	PD	TPI
1955	StL-N	2	4	.333	18	8	2	0	0	57²	64	9	27	14	14.4	4.84	84	.281	.359	4	.222	0	-5	-5	1	-0.5

■ JUNIOR WOOTEN
Wooten, Earl Hazwell b: 1/16/24, Pelzer, S.C. BR/TL, 5'11", 160 lbs. Deb: 9/16/47 ♦

YEAR	TM/L	W	L	PCT	G	GS	CG	SH	SV	IP	H	HR	BB	SO	RAT	ERA	ERA+	OAV	OOB	BH	AVG	PB	PR	/A	PD	TPI
1948	Was-A	0	0	—	1	0	0	0	0	2	2	0	2	1	18.0	9.00	48	.250	.400	66	.256	0	-1	-1	0	0.0

YEAR TM/L	W	L	PCT	G	GS	CG	SH	SV	IP	H	HR	BB	SO	RAT	ERA	ERA+	OAV	OOB	BH	AVG	PB	PR	/A	PD	TPI

■ FRED WORDEN   Worden, Fred B.   b: 9/4/1894, St.Louis, Mo.   d: 11/9/41, St.Louis, Mo.   BR/TR,   Deb: 9/28/14

| 1914 Phi-A | 0 | 0 | — | 1 | 0 | 0 | 0 | 0 | 2 | 8 | 0 | 0 | 1 | 36.0 | 18.00 | 15 | .615 | .615 | 0 | .000 | -0 | -3 | -3 | 0 | -0.2 |

■ HOGE WORKMAN   Workman, Harry Hall   b: 9/25/1899, Huntington, W.Va.   d: 5/20/72, Ft.Myers, Fla.   BR/TR, 5'11", 170 lbs.   Deb: 6/27/24

| 1924 Bos-A | 0 | 0 | — | 11 | 0 | 0 | 0 | 0 | 18 | 25 | 2 | 11 | 7 | 19.0 | 8.50 | 51 | .325 | .422 | 0 | .000 | -0 | -9 | -8 | 0 | -0.7 |

■ RALPH WORKS   Works, Ralph Talmadge "Judge"   b: 3/16/1888, Payson, Ill.   d: 8/8/41, Pasadena, Cal.   BL/TR, 6'2.5", 185 lbs.   Deb: 5/01/09

1909 *Det-A	4	1	.800	16	4	4	0	2	64	62	0	17	31	11.3	1.97	128	.261	.313	1	.059	-2	4	4	-1	0.2
1910 Det-A	3	6	.333	18	10	5	0	1	85²	73	1	39	36	12.2	3.57	74	.235	.328	8	.267	1	-10	-9	-1	-0.8
1911 Det-A	11	5	.688	30	15	9	3	0	167¹	173	3	67	68	13.2	3.87	89	.268	.342	9	.148	-3	-10	-8	-4	-1.4
1912 Det-A	5	10	.333	27	16	9	1	1	157	185	1	66	64	14.8	4.24	77	.308	.383	8	.143	-3	-16	-17	0	-1.8
Cin-N	1	1	.500	3	1	1	0	0	9²	4	0	5	5	9.3	2.79	120	.133	.278	1	.200	-0	1	1	0	0.0
1913 Cin-N	0	1	.000	5	2	0	0	0	15	15	0	8	4	15.6	7.80	42	.242	.356	1	.167	-0	-8	-8	0	-0.6
Total 5	24	24	.500	99	48	28	4	4	498²	512	5	202	208	13.3	3.79	83	.271	.348	28	.160	-8	-39	-37	-6	-4.4

■ TODD WORRELL   Worrell, Todd Roland   b: 9/28/59, Arcadia, Cal.   BR/TR, 6'5", 215 lbs.   Deb: 8/28/85

1985 *StL-N	3	0	1.000	17	0	0	0	5	21²	17	2	7	17	10.0	2.91	122	.215	.279	0	.000	-0	2	2	-0	0.1
1986 StL-N	9	10	.474	74	0	0	0	36	103²	86	9	41	73	11.1	2.08	175	.229	.307	1	.143	0	19	18	-2	1.7
1987 *StL-N	8	6	.571	75	0	0	0	33	94²	86	8	34	92	11.4	2.66	156	.242	.308	1	.100	-0	15	16	-0	1.5
1988 StL-N	5	9	.357	68	0	0	0	32	90	69	7	34	78	10.4	3.00	116	.214	.291	0	.000	-0	4	5	-1	0.4
1989 StL-N	3	5	.375	47	0	0	0	20	51²	42	4	26	41	11.8	2.96	123	.222	.316	0	.000	-0	3	4	1	0.4
Total 5	28	30	.483	281	0	0	0	126	361²	300	30	142	301	11.0	2.64	141	.227	.303	2	.080	-1	43	44	-3	4.1

■ RICH WORTHAM   Wortham, Richard Cooper   b: 10/22/53, Odessa, Tex.   BR/TL, 6', 185 lbs.   Deb: 5/03/78

1978 Chi-A	3	2	.600	8	8	2	0	0	59	59	1	23	25	12.5	3.05	125	.267	.336	0	—	0	5	5	-0	0.5
1979 Chi-A	14	14	.500	34	33	5	0	0	204	195	21	100	119	13.1	4.90	87	.255	.343	0	—	0	-15	-15	-2	-1.5
1980 Chi-A	4	7	.364	41	10	0	0	1	92	102	4	58	45	15.9	5.97	67	.285	.389	0	—	0	-20	-20	1	-1.8
1983 Oak-A	0	0	—	1	0	0	0	0	0	3	0	1	0	—	∞	—	1.000	1.000	0	—	0	-1	-1	0	0.0
Total 4	21	23	.477	84	51	7	0	1	355	359	26	182	189	13.9	4.89	84	.266	.356	0	—	0	-32	-31	-1	-2.8

■ AL WORTHINGTON   Worthington, Allan Fulton "Red"   b: 2/5/29, Birmingham, Ala.   BR/TR, 6'2", 195 lbs.   Deb: 7/06/53   C

1953 NY-N	4	8	.333	20	17	5	2	0	102	103	6	54	52	14.0	3.44	125	.258	.349	2	.065	-2	10	10	0	0.8
1954 NY-N	0	2	.000	10	1	0	0	0	18	21	0	15	8	18.0	3.50	115	.333	.462	0	.000	-1	1	1	0	0.1
1956 NY-N	7	14	.333	28	24	4	0	0	165²	158	20	74	95	12.8	3.97	95	.254	.338	12	.235	2	-4	-3	2	0.0
1957 NY-N	8	11	.421	55	12	1	1	4	157²	140	19	56	90	11.5	4.22	93	.237	.309	4	.100	-2	-6	-5	-0	-0.6
1958 SF-N	11	7	.611	54	12	1	0	6	151¹	152	17	57	76	12.5	3.63	105	.255	.322	8	.182	0	5	3	0	0.3
1959 SF-N	2	3	.400	42	3	0	0	2	73¹	68	8	37	45	13.5	3.68	103	.253	.354	1	.077	-1	2	1	1	0.1
1960 Bos-N	0	1	.000	6	0	0	0	0	11²	17	1	11	7	21.6	7.71	52	.340	.459	0	.000	-0	-5	-5	0	-0.4
Chi-A	1	1	.500	4	0	0	0	0	5¹	3	0	4	1	11.8	3.38	112	.176	.333	2	1.000	1	0	0	0	0.1
Yr	1	2	.333	10	0	0	0	0	17	20	1	15	8	18.5	6.35	62	.299	.427	0	.000	1	-5	-5	0	-0.3
1963 Cin-N	4	4	.500	50	0	0	0	10	81¹	75	6	31	55	12.1	2.99	112	.248	.324	1	.083	-0	3	3	2	0.5
1964 Cin-N	1	0	1.000	6	0	0	0	0	7	14	0	2	6	21.9	10.29	35	.400	.447	0	—	0	-5	-5	-0	-0.4
Min-A	5	6	.455	41	0	0	0	14	72¹	47	4	28	59	9.3	1.37	261	.183	.263	1	.063	-1	18	18	1	1.8
1965 *Min-A	10	7	.588	62	0	0	0	21	80¹	57	4	41	59	11.3	2.13	167	.207	.316	1	.100	-1	12	13	2	1.6
1966 Min-A	6	3	.667	65	0	0	0	16	91¹	66	6	27	93	9.3	2.46	146	.199	.261	3	.273	1	10	11	0	1.4
1967 Min-A	8	9	.471	59	0	0	0	16	92	77	6	38	80	11.3	2.84	122	.229	.309	0	.000	-1	4	6	-0	0.6
1968 Min-A	4	5	.444	54	0	0	0	18	76¹	67	1	32	57	11.7	2.71	114	.238	.315	0	.000	-1	2	3	0	0.3
1969 *Min-A	4	1	.800	46	0	0	0	3	61	65	7	20	51	12.5	4.57	80	.278	.335	0	.000	-1	-6	-6	-1	-0.7
Total 14	75	82	.478	602	69	11	3	110	1246²	1130	105	527	834	12.2	3.39	110	.243	.323	35	.137	-5	41	46	6	5.5

■ GENE WRIGHT   Wright, Clarence Eugene "Big Gene"   b: 12/11/1878, Cleveland, Ohio   d: 10/29/30, Barberton, Ohio   BR/TR, 6'2", 185 lbs.   Deb: 10/05/01

1901 Bro-N	1	0	1.000	1	1	1	0	0	9	6	0	1	6	7.0	1.00	335	.189	.213	1	.333	0	2	2	-0	0.3
1902 Cle-A	7	11	.389	21	18	15	1	1	148	150	6	75	52	13.7	3.95	87	.263	.349	10	.143	-2	-6	-8	-2	-1.1
1903 Cle-A	3	9	.250	15	12	8	0	0	101²	122	1	58	42	15.9	5.75	50	.296	.383	9	.209	2	-32	-33	2	-2.6
StL-A	3	5	.375	8	8	7	1	0	61	73	2	16	37	13.1	3.69	79	.296	.338	1	.143	-1	-5	-5	1	-0.4
Yr	6	14	.300	23	20	15	1	0	162²	195	3	74	79	14.9	4.98	58	.296	.367	1	.016	1	-36	-38	2	-3.0
1904 StL-A	0	1	.000	1	1	0	0	0	4	10	0	2	3	27.0	13.50	18	.469	.515	0	.000	-0	-5	-5	1	-0.3
Total 4	14	26	.350	46	40	31	2	1	323²	361	9	152	140	14.3	4.50	70	.282	.358	23	.167	-1	-45	-49	1	-4.1

■ CLYDE WRIGHT   Wright, Clyde   b: 2/20/41, Jefferson City, Tenn.   BR/TL, 6'1", 180 lbs.   Deb: 6/15/66

1966 Cal-A	4	7	.364	20	13	3	1	0	91¹	92	11	25	37	11.6	3.74	90	.265	.316	3	.103	-1	-3	-4	1	-0.4
1967 Cal-A	5	5	.500	20	11	1	0	0	77¹	76	5	24	35	11.8	3.26	96	.260	.319	6	.273	2	-0	-1	1	0.1
1968 Cal-A	10	6	.625	41	13	2	1	3	125²	123	13	44	71	12.1	3.94	74	.256	.321	8	.216	2	-13	-14	-1	-1.4
1969 Cal-A	1	8	.111	37	5	0	0	0	63²	66	4	30	31	13.7	4.10	85	.278	.362	2	.182	0	-3	-4	0	-0.3
1970 Cal-A	22	12	.647	39	39	7	2	0	260²	226	24	88	110	11.1	2.83	128	.232	.300	18	.171	2	26	23	-1	2.6
1971 Cal-A	16	17	.485	37	37	10	2	0	276²	225	17	82	135	10.1	2.99	108	.226	.287	14	.154	2	14	8	5	1.4
1972 Cal-A	18	11	.621	35	35	15	2	0	251	229	14	80	87	11.2	2.98	98	.246	.308	18	.217	7	2	-4	1	1.0
1973 Cal-A	11	19	.367	37	36	13	1	0	257	273	26	76	65	12.3	3.68	96	.273	.326	0	—	0	4	-4	6	0.2
1974 Mil-A	9	20	.310	38	32	15	0	0	232	264	22	54	64	12.3	4.42	82	.284	.323	0	—	0	-21	-21	2	-1.8
1975 Tex-A	4	6	.400	25	14	1	0	0	93¹	105	7	47	32	14.8	4.44	85	.294	.378	0	—	0	-7	-7	2	-0.4
Total 10	100	111	.474	329	235	67	9	3	1728²	1679	143	550	667	11.7	3.50	96	.256	.316	69	.183	14	-1	-27	19	1.0

■ DAVE WRIGHT   Wright, David William   b: 8/27/1875, Dennison, Ohio   d: 1/18/46, Dennison, Ohio   BR/TR, 6', 185 lbs.   Deb: 7/22/1895

1895 Pit-N	0	0	—	1	0	0	0	0	2	6	0	4	0	31.5	27.00	17	.509	.547	0	.000	-0	-5	-5	0	-0.3
1897 Chi-N	1	0	1.000	1	1	1	0	0	7	17	1	2	4	24.4	15.43	29	.458	.486	1	.333	0	-9	-9	-0	-0.4
Total 2	1	0	1.000	2	1	1	0	0	9	23	1	6	4	26.0	18.00	25	.470	.501	1	.250	0	-14	-14	0	-0.7

■ GEORGE WRIGHT   Wright, George   b: 1/28/1847, Yonkers, N.Y.   d: 8/21/37, Boston, Mass.   BR/TR, 5'9.5", 150 lbs.   Deb: 5/05/1871   MH♦

| 1875 Bos-n | 0 | 1 | .000 | 2 | 0 | 0 | 0 | 0 | 4 | 5 | 0 | 0 | 0 | 11.3 | 2.25 | 105 | .263 | .263 | 135 | .333 | 1 | 0 | 0 | | 0.0 |
| 1876 Bos-N | 0 | 0 | — | 1 | 0 | 0 | 0 | 0 | 1 | 1 | 0 | 1 | 0 | 9.0 | 0.00 | — | .243 | .243 | 100 | .299 | 0 | 0 | 0 | | 0.0 |

■ ED WRIGHT   Wright, Henderson Edward   b: 5/15/19, Dyersburg, Tenn.   BR/TR, 6'1", 180 lbs.   Deb: 7/29/45

1945 Bos-N	8	3	.727	15	12	7	1	0	111¹	104	7	33	24	11.1	2.51	153	.254	.310	5	.128	-2	16	16	-1	1.4
1946 Bos-N	12	9	.571	36	21	8	2	0	176¹	164	8	71	44	12.1	3.52	97	.250	.325	18	.305	6	-2	-2	1	0.5
1947 Bos-N	3	3	.500	23	6	1	0	0	64²	80	9	35	14	16.3	6.40	61	.305	.391	3	.130	-0	-17	-18	-0	-1.6
1948 Bos-N	0	0	—	3	0	0	0	0	4²	10	0	2	2	21.2	1.93	199	.474	.524	0	—	0	1	1	0	0.1
1952 Phi-A	2	1	.667	24	0	0	0	1	41¹	55	6	20	9	17.0	6.53	61	.320	.400	1	.143	-0	-13	-12	-1	-1.1
Total 5	25	16	.610	101	39	16	3	1	398¹	412	30	161	93	13.1	4.00	92	.271	.344	27	.211	3	-15	-14	-1	-0.7

■ JIM WRIGHT   Wright, James "Jiggs"   b: 9/19/1900, Hyde, England   d: 4/10/63, Oakland, Cal.   BR/TR, 6'2.5", 195 lbs.   Deb: 9/14/27

1927 StL-A	1	0	1.000	2	1	1	0	0	12	8	0	4	4	9.0	4.50	97	.182	.250	0	.000	-0	-0	-0	-0	0.0
1928 StL-A	0	0	—	2	0	0	0	0	2	3	0	2	2	22.5	13.50	31	.375	.500	0	—	0	-2	-2	0	-0.1
Total 2	1	0	1.000	4	1	1	0	0	14	11	0	6	6	10.9	5.79	75	.212	.293	0	.000	-0	-3	-2	0	-0.1

YEAR	TM/L	W	L	PCT	G	GS	CG	SH	SV	IP	H	HR	BB	SO	RAT	ERA	ERA+	OAV	OOB	BH	AVG	PB	PR	/A	PD	TPI

■ **JIM WRIGHT**   Wright, James Clifton b: 12/21/50, Reed City, Mich. Deb: 4/15/78   BR/TR, 6'1", 165 lbs.

1978	Bos-A	8	4	.667	24	16	5	3	0	116	122	8	24	56	11.9	3.57	115	.276	.323	0	—	0	2	7	-1	0.6
1979	Bos-A	1	0	1.000	11	1	0	0	0	23	19	5	7	15	11.3	5.09	87	.226	.309	0	—	0	-2	-2	-0	-0.1
Total	2	9	4	.692	35	17	5	3	0	139	141	13	31	71	11.8	3.82	109	.268	.321	0	—	0	0	5	-2	0.5

■ **JIM WRIGHT**   Wright, James Leon b: 3/3/55, St.Joseph, Mo. Deb: 4/22/81   BR/TR, 6'5", 205 lbs.

1981	KC-A	2	3	.400	17	4	0	0	0	52	57	5	21	27	13.8	3.46	104	.277	.349	0	—	0	1	1	-1	0.0
1982	KC-A	0	0	—	7	0	0	0	0	23²	32	3	6	9	14.5	5.32	77	.320	.358	0	—	0	-3	-3	-0	-0.3
Total	2	2	3	.400	24	4	0	0	0	75²	89	8	27	36	14.0	4.04	93	.291	.352	0	—	0	-2	-2	-1	-0.3

■ **RICKY WRIGHT**   Wright, James Richard b: 11/22/58, Paris, Tex. Deb: 7/28/82   BL/TL, 6'3", 175 lbs.

1982	LA-N	2	1	.667	14	5	0	0	0	32²	28	1	20	24	13.2	3.03	114	.233	.343	1	.125	0	2	2	0	0.2
1983	LA-N	0	0	—	6	0	0	0	0	6¹	5	0	2	5	9.9	2.84	126	.227	.292	0	—	0	1	1	-0	0.0
	Tex-A	0	0	—	1	0	0	0	0	2	0	0	1	2	4.5	0.00	—	.000	.167	0	—	0	1	1	-0	0.1
1984	Tex-A	0	2	.000	8	1	0	0	0	14²	20	3	11	6	19.0	6.14	68	.357	.463	0	—	0	-3	-3	-0	-0.2
1985	Tex-A	0	0	—	5	0	0	0	0	7²	5	0	5	7	11.7	4.70	90	.185	.313	0	—	0	-0	-0	0	0.0
1986	Tex-A	1	0	1.000	21	1	0	0	0	39¹	44	1	21	23	14.9	5.03	85	.284	.369	0	—	0	-4	-3	1	-0.2
Total	5	3	3	.500	55	7	0	0	0	102²	102	5	60	67	14.2	4.30	92	.265	.364	1	.125	0	-4	-4	1	-0.1

■ **KEN WRIGHT**   Wright, Kenneth Warren b: 9/4/46, Pensacola, Fla. Deb: 4/10/70   BR/TR, 6'2", 210 lbs.

1970	KC-A	1	2	.333	47	0	0	0	0	53¹	49	2	29	30	14.3	5.23	71	.261	.379	0	.000	-0	-9	-9	-0	-0.9
1971	KC-A	3	6	.333	21	12	1	1	1	78	66	6	47	56	13.4	3.69	93	.230	.344	2	.091	-1	-2	-2	0	-0.2
1972	KC-A	1	2	.333	17	0	0	0	4	18¹	15	0	15	18	15.2	4.91	62	.231	.383	0	.000	-0	-4	-4	-0	-0.4
1973	KC-A	6	5	.545	25	12	1	0	0	80²	60	6	82	75	15.8	4.91	84	.210	.386	0	—	0	-10	-7	-2	-0.8
1974	NY-A	0	0	—	3	0	0	0	0	5²	5	0	7	2	19.1	3.18	110	.227	.414	0	—	0	0	0	0	0.0
Total	5	11	15	.423	113	24	2	1	8	236	195	14	180	181	14.7	4.54	81	.230	.372	2	.071	-2	-24	-22	-1	-2.3

■ **MEL WRIGHT**   Wright, Melvin James b: 5/11/28, Manila, Ark. d: 5/16/83, Montreal, Que. Deb: 4/17/54 C   BR/TR, 6'3", 210 lbs.

1954	StL-N	0	0	—	9	0	0	0	0	10¹	16	2	11	4	25.3	10.45	39	.348	.492	0	.000	-0	-7	-7	0	-0.6
1955	StL-N	2	2	.500	29	0	0	0	1	36¹	44	4	9	18	13.4	6.19	66	.308	.353	0	.000	-1	-9	-9	-0	-0.8
1960	Chi-N	0	1	.000	9	0	0	0	2	16¹	17	1	3	8	11.0	4.96	76	.279	.313	0	.000	-0	-2	-2	-0	-0.2
1961	Chi-N	0	1	.000	11	0	0	0	0	21	42	3	4	6	19.7	10.71	39	.416	.438	0	.000	-0	-16	-15	1	-1.3
Total	4	2	4	.333	58	0	0	0	3	84	119	10	27	36	16.0	7.61	53	.339	.391	0	.000	-2	-34	-33	1	-2.9

■ **BOB WRIGHT**   Wright, Robert Cassius b: 12/13/1891, Greensburg, Ind. Deb: 9/21/15   BR/TR, 6'1.5", 175 lbs.

| 1915 | Chi-N | 0 | 0 | — | 2 | 0 | 0 | 0 | 0 | 4 | 6 | 0 | 0 | 3 | 13.5 | 2.25 | 123 | .353 | .353 | 0 | — | 0 | 0 | 0 | 0 | 0.0 |

■ **ROY WRIGHT**   Wright, Roy Earl b: 9/26/33, Buchtel, Ohio Deb: 9/30/56   BR/TR, 6'2", 170 lbs.

| 1956 | NY-N | 0 | 1 | .000 | 1 | 1 | 0 | 0 | 0 | 2² | 8 | 1 | 2 | 0 | 33.8 | 16.88 | 22 | .533 | .588 | 0 | .000 | -0 | -4 | -4 | 0 | -0.2 |

■ **RASTY WRIGHT**   Wright, Wayne Bromley b: 11/5/1895, Ceredo, W.Va. d: 6/12/48, Columbus, Ohio Deb: 6/22/17   BR/TR, 5'11", 160 lbs.

1917	StL-A	0	1	.000	16	1	0	0	0	39²	48	0	10	5	13.4	5.45	48	.300	.345	2	.200	0	-12	-13	0	-1.1
1918	StL-A	8	2	.800	18	13	6	1	0	111¹	99	1	18	25	9.9	2.51	109	.244	.285	10	.294	3	3	3	-1	0.6
1919	StL-A	0	5	.000	24	5	2	0	0	63¹	79	1	20	14	14.2	5.54	60	.315	.368	1	.083	-1	-16	-16	0	-1.5
1922	StL-A	9	7	.563	31	16	5	0	5	154	148	7	50	44	12.0	2.92	142	.262	.331	7	.140	-2	19	21	1	2.0
1923	StL-A	7	4	.636	20	8	4	0	0	82²	107	6	34	26	15.9	6.42	65	.317	.387	6	.222	1	-22	-21	1	-1.8
Total	5	24	19	.558	109	43	17	1	5	451	481	15	132	114	12.6	4.05	87	.280	.338	26	.195	1	-28	-26	1	-1.8

■ **HARRY WRIGHT**   Wright, William Henry b: 1/10/1835, Sheffield, England d: 10/3/1895, Atlantic City, N.J. Deb: 5/05/1871 MH♦   BR/TR, 5'9.5", 157 lbs.

1871	Bos-n	1	0	1.000	9	0	0	0	3	18²	34	0	4	0	18.3	6.27	66	.337	.362	44	.299	1	-4	-4		-0.2
1872	Bos-n	1	0	1.000	7	0	0	0	1	25²	26	0	0		9.1	2.10	177	.241	.241	54	.260	0	'5	5		0.3
1873	Bos-n	2	2	.500	12	5	0	0	5	35¹	62	0	6		17.3	4.84	76	.337	.358	67	.251	1	-5	-5		-0.2
1874	Bos-n	0	2	.000	6	2	0	0	3	16²	24	0	4		15.1	2.70	110	.338	.373	56	.304	2	1	0		0.0
Total	4 n	4	4	.500	34	7	0	0	12	96¹	146	0	14	0	14.9	4.02	74	.315	.335	222	.274	4	-11	-11		-0.1

■ **LUCKY WRIGHT**   Wright, William Simmons "William The Red" or "Deacon"
b: 2/21/1880, Tontogany, Ohio d: 7/6/41, Tontogany, Ohio Deb: 4/18/09   BR/TR, 6', 178 lbs.

| 1909 | Cle-A | 0 | 4 | .000 | 5 | 4 | 3 | 0 | 0 | 28 | 21 | 0 | 7 | 5 | 9.0 | 3.21 | 80 | .223 | .277 | 0 | .000 | -1 | -2 | -2 | 0 | -0.2 |

■ **FRANK WURM**   Wurm, Frank James b: 4/27/24, Cambridge, N.Y. Deb: 9/04/44   BB/TL, 6'1", 175 lbs.

| 1944 | Bro-N | 0 | 0 | — | 1 | 1 | 0 | 0 | 0 | 0¹ | 1 | 0 | 5 | 1 | 162.0 | 108.00 | 3 | .500 | .857 | 0 | — | 0 | -4 | -4 | 0 | -0.2 |

■ **JOHN WYATT**   Wyatt, John Thomas b: 4/19/35, Chicago, Ill. Deb: 9/08/61   BR/TR, 5'11.5", 200 lbs.

1961	KC-A	0	0	—	5	0	0	0	0	7¹	8	0	4	6	16.0	2.45	168	.308	.419	0	—	0	1	1	0	0.1
1962	KC-A	10	7	.588	59	9	0	0	11	125	121	12	80	106	14.8	4.46	93	.253	.366	3	.103	-2	-7	-4	-1	-0.6
1963	KC-A	6	4	.600	63	0	0	0	21	92	83	12	43	81	12.3	3.13	123	.239	.323	0	.000	-1	5	7	-1	0.6
1964	KC-A	9	8	.529	81	0	0	0	20	128	111	23	52	74	11.5	3.59	106	.236	.314	0	.000	-1	3	3	-1	0.1
1965	KC-A	2	6	.250	65	0	0	0	18	88²	78	8	53	70	13.7	3.25	107	.241	.354	0	.000	-0	2	2	0	0.2
1966	KC-A	0	3	.000	19	0	0	0	2	23²	19	3	16	25	14.1	5.32	64	.213	.346	0	—	0	-5	-5	0	-0.4
	Bos-A	3	4	.429	42	0	0	0	8	71²	59	3	27	63	11.3	3.14	121	.229	.311	0	.000	-0	2	5	-2	0.3
	Yr	3	7	.300	61	0	0	0	10	95¹	78	6	43	88	11.8	3.68	101	.223	.316	0	.000	-0	-3	0	-1	-0.1
1967	*Bos-A	10	7	.588	60	0	0	0	20	93¹	71	6	39	68	10.8	2.60	134	.217	.304	1	.083	-0	7	9	1	1.1
1968	Bos-A	1	2	.333	8	0	0	0	0	10²	9	2	6	11	13.5	4.22	75	.231	.348	0	—	0	-1	-1	0	0.0
	NY-A	0	2	.000	7	0	0	0	0	8¹	7	1	9	6	17.3	2.16	134	.219	.390	0	.000	-0	1	1	0	0.1
	Det-A	1	0	1.000	22	0	0	0	2	30¹	26	2	11	25	11.3	2.37	127	.236	.311	0	.000	-0	2	2	0	0.2
	Yr	2	4	.333	37	0	0	0	2	49¹	42	5	26	42	12.6	2.74	110	.230	.329	0	.000	-0	1	2	0	0.3
1969	Oak-A	0	1	.000	8	0	0	0	0	8¹	8	0	6	5	17.3	5.40	64	.250	.400	0	—	0	-2	-2	0	-0.1
Total	9	42	44	.488	435	9	0	0	103	687¹	600	72	346	540	12.7	3.47	107	.237	.334	4	.048	-7	6	19	-3	1.6

■ **WHIT WYATT**   Wyatt, John Whitlow b: 9/27/07, Kensington, Ga. Deb: 9/16/29 C   BR/TR, 6'1", 185 lbs.

1929	Det-A	0	1	.000	4	4	1	0	0	25¹	30	1	18	14	17.4	6.75	64	.309	.422	1	.100	-1	-7	-7	0	-0.6
1930	Det-A	4	5	.444	21	7	2	0	2	85²	76	6	35	68	12.0	3.57	134	.239	.320	12	.353	3	10	12	-0	1.4
1931	Det-A	0	2	.000	4	1	1	0	0	20¹	30	2	12	8	19.0	8.85	52	.361	.448	2	.286	0	-10	-10	-1	-0.7
1932	Det-A	9	13	.409	43	22	10	0	1	205²	228	12	102	82	14.6	5.03	86	.286	.369	15	.192	-0	-13	-8	-1	-0.7
1933	Det-A	0	1	.000	10	0	0	0	0	17	20	1	9	9	16.4	4.24	102	.299	.397	0	.000	-0	0	0	-0	0.0
	Chi-A	3	4	.429	26	7	2	0	1	87²	91	7	45	31	14.2	4.62	92	.266	.355	6	.214	-1	-3	-4	0	-0.2
	Yr	3	5	.375	36	7	2	0	1	104²	111	8	54	40	14.4	4.56	93	.270	.358	6	.214	-1	-3	-4	-0	-0.2
1934	Chi-A	4	11	.267	23	6	2	0	2	67²	83	10	37	36	16.1	7.18	66	.303	.388	6	.231	1	-20	-18	0	-1.5
1935	Chi-A	4	3	.571	30	1	0	0	3	52	65	6	25	22	15.9	6.75	68	.308	.387	3	.231	1	-13	-12	1	-0.8
1936	Chi-A	0	0	—	3	0	0	0	0	3	3	0	0	0	9.0	0.00	—	.273	.273	0	—	0	0	0	0	0.1
1937	Cle-A	2	3	.400	29	4	2	0	0	73	67	3	40	52	13.2	4.44	104	.244	.340	7	.389	3	1	1	-0	0.4
1939	Bro-N	8	3	.727	16	14	6	2	0	109	88	3	39	52	10.7	2.31	174	.224	.297	6	.167	-0	19	21	1	2.3
1940	Bro-N	15	14	.517	37	34	16	**5**	0	239¹	233	6	62	124	11.3	3.46	116	.254	.304	14	.175	-0	10	14	-3	1.2
1941	*Bro-N	22	10	.688	38	35	23	**7**	1	288¹	223	10	82	176	**9.6**	2.34	157	**.212**	**.270**	26	.239	7	**41**	**42**	-2	**5.3**
1942	Bro-N	19	7	.731	31	30	16	0	0	217¹	185	9	63	104	10.6	2.73	119	.225	.286	14	.182	1	14	13	-1	1.3

YEAR	TM/L	W	L	PCT	G	GS	CG	SH	SV	IP	H	HR	BB	SO	RAT	ERA	ERA+	OAV	OOB	BH	AVG	PB	PR	/A	PD	TPI
1943	Bro-N	14	5	.737	26	26	13	3	0	180²	139	5	43	80	**9.1**	2.49	135	**.207**	**.255**	17	.283	4	18	17	-2	2.2
1944	Bro-N	2	6	.250	9	9	1	0	0	37²	51	1	16	4	16.5	7.17	50	.311	.379	2	.154	-0	-15	-15	0	-1.4
1945	Phi-N	0	7	.000	10	10	2	0	0	51¹	72	3	14	10	15.1	5.26	73	.330	.371	2	.125	0	-8	-8	1	-0.6
Total	16	106	95	.527	360	210	97	17	13	1761	1684	98	642	872	12.1	3.79	105	.251	.319	133	.219	18	27	39	-8	7.7

■ JOHN WYCKOFF
Wyckoff, John Weldon b: 2/19/1892, Williamsport, Pa. d: 5/8/61, Sheboygan Falls, Wis. BR/TR, 6'1", 175 lbs. Deb: 4/19/13

YEAR	TM/L	W	L	PCT	G	GS	CG	SH	SV	IP	H	HR	BB	SO	RAT	ERA	ERA+	OAV	OOB	BH	AVG	PB	PR	/A	PD	TPI
1913	Phi-A	2	4	.333	17	7	4	0	0	61²	56	1	46	31	15.3	4.38	63	.233	.363	4	.190	-0	-10	-11	0	-1.0
1914	*Phi-A	11	7	.611	32	20	11	0	2	185	153	2	103	86	12.6	3.02	87	.228	.334	11	.147	-0	-6	-8	-5	-1.2
1915	Phi-A	10	22	.313	43	34	20	1	0	276	238	1	165	157	13.3	3.52	84	.246	.359	12	.125	-4	-18	-18	1	-2.1
1916	Phi-A	0	1	.000	7	2	1	0	0	21¹	20	1	20	4	17.3	5.48	52	.247	.402	3	.375	1	-6	-6	0	-0.4
	Bos-A	0	0	—	8	0	0	0	1	22²	19	0	18	18	14.7	4.76	58	.232	.370	1	.167	-0	-5	-5	-1	-0.6
	Yr	0	1	.000	15	2	1	0	1	44	39	1	38	22	15.8	5.11	55	.238	.381	0	.000	1	-11	-11	-1	-1.0
1917	Bos-A	0	0	—	1	0	0	0	0	5	4	0	4	1	16.2	1.80	144	.222	.391	0	.000	-0	0	0	0	0.1
1918	Bos-A	0	0	—	1	0	0	0	0	1	2	0	2	1	22.5	0.00	—	.400	.455	0	.000	-1	1	1	0	0.0
Total	6	23	34	.404	109	63	36	1	3	573²	494	5	357	299	13.6	3.55	79	.239	.355	31	.149	-4	-44	-47	-4	-5.2

■ FRANK WYMAN
Wyman, Frank H. b: 5/10/1862, Haverhill, Mass. d: 2/4/16, Everett, Mass. Deb: 6/24/1884 ♦

YEAR	TM/L	W	L	PCT	G	GS	CG	SH	SV	IP	H	HR	BB	SO	RAT	ERA	ERA+	OAV	OOB	BH	AVG	PB	PR	/A	PD	TPI
1884	KC-U	0	1	.000	3	1	1	0	0	21	37	0	3	9	17.1	6.86	40	.362	.380	27	.218	-0	-9	-10	-0	-0.6

■ EARLY WYNN
Wynn, Early "Gus" b: 1/6/20, Hartford, Ala. BB/TR, 6', 190 lbs. Deb: 9/13/39 CH♦

YEAR	TM/L	W	L	PCT	G	GS	CG	SH	SV	IP	H	HR	BB	SO	RAT	ERA	ERA+	OAV	OOB	BH	AVG	PB	PR	/A	PD	TPI
1939	Was-A	0	2	.000	3	3	1	0	0	20¹	26	0	10	1	15.9	5.75	76	.313	.387	1	.167	0	-3	-3	-1	-0.2
1941	Was-A	3	1	.750	5	5	4	0	0	40	35	1	10	15	10.1	1.57	257	.226	.273	2	.133	-0	11	11	0	1.2
1942	Was-A	10	16	.385	30	28	10	1	0	190	246	6	73	58	15.3	5.12	71	.314	.374	15	.217	2	-31	-31	-1	-2.8
1943	Was-A	18	12	.600	37	33	12	3	0	256²	232	15	83	89	11.1	2.91	110	.240	.301	29	.296	7	11	8	-2	1.5
1944	Was-A	8	17	.320	33	25	19	2	2	207²	221	3	67	65	12.6	3.38	96	.277	.334	19	.207	2	1	-3	-2	-0.3
1946	Was-A	8	5	.615	17	12	9	0	0	107	112	8	33	36	12.4	3.11	108	.267	.325	15	.319	6	5	3	0	1.0
1947	Was-A	17	15	.531	33	31	22	2	0	247	251	13	90	73	12.6	3.64	102	.262	.329	33	.275	7	2	2	-1	0.9
1948	Was-A	8	19	.296	33	31	15	1	0	198	236	18	94	49	15.0	5.82	75	.295	.370	23	.217	3	-34	-32	-1	-2.9
1949	Cle-A	11	7	.611	26	23	6	0	0	164²	186	8	57	62	13.3	4.15	96	.282	.340	10	.143	-1	1	-3	1	-0.3
1950	Cle-A	18	8	.692	32	28	14	2	0	213²	166	20	101	143	**11.4**	**3.20**	135	**.212**	**.305**	18	.234	7	33	27	-0	3.2
1951	Cle-A	20	13	.606	37	34	21	3	1	274¹	227	18	107	133	11.1	3.02	126	.225	.301	20	.185	2	**34**	23	-1	2.3
1952	Cle-A	23	12	.657	42	33	19	4	3	285²	239	23	132	153	11.7	2.90	115	.231	.318	22	.222	5	25	14	-1	1.8
1953	Cle-A	17	12	.586	36	34	16	1	0	251²	234	19	107	138	12.3	3.93	95	.245	.324	25	.275	8	2	-5	-1	0.2
1954	*Cle-A	**23**	11	.676	40	36	20	3	2	**270**	225	21	83	155	10.2	2.73	135	.225	.284	17	.183	1	30	29	-4	2.8
1955	Cle-A	17	11	.607	32	31	16	6	0	230	207	19	80	122	11.3	2.82	142	.240	.307	15	.179	2	29	30	-2	3.1
1956	Cle-A	20	9	.690	38	35	18	4	2	277²	233	19	91	158	10.7	2.72	154	.228	.294	23	.228	3	44	46	1	**5.3**
1957	Cle-A	14	17	.452	40	37	13	1	1	263	270	32	104	**184**	13.0	4.31	86	.265	.336	10	.116	-2	-15	-17	-1	-2.0
1958	Chi-A	14	16	.467	40	34	11	4	2	239²	214	27	104	**179**	12.2	4.13	88	.242	.325	15	.200	3	-10	-13	-3	-1.3
1959	*Chi-A	**22**	10	.688	37	37	14	5	0	**255²**	202	20	119	179	11.6	3.17	119	.216	.310	22	.244	9	20	17	-2	2.4
1960	Chi-A	13	12	.520	36	35	13	**4**	1	237¹	220	20	112	158	12.7	3.49	108	.247	.334	15	.200	6	10	8	-3	1.1
1961	Chi-A	8	2	.800	17	16	5	0	0	110¹	88	11	47	64	11.1	3.51	112	.220	.304	6	.162	-0	6	5	-2	0.3
1962	Chi-A	7	15	.318	27	26	11	3	0	167²	171	15	56	91	12.3	4.46	88	.264	.326	7	.130	0	-9	-10	-2	-1.1
1963	Cle-A	1	2	.333	20	5	1	0	1	55¹	50	2	15	29	10.6	2.28	159	.250	.302	3	.273	1	8	8	-0	1.0
Total	23	300	244	.551	691	612	290	49	15	4564	4291	338	1775	2334	12.1	3.54	106	.248	.321	365	.214	70	170	112	-25	17.2

■ BILLY WYNNE
Wynne, Billy Vernon b: 7/31/43, Williamston, N.C. BL/TR, 6'3", 205 lbs. Deb: 8/06/67

YEAR	TM/L	W	L	PCT	G	GS	CG	SH	SV	IP	H	HR	BB	SO	RAT	ERA	ERA+	OAV	OOB	BH	AVG	PB	PR	/A	PD	TPI
1967	NY-N	0	0	—	6	1	0	0	0	8²	12	0	2	4	14.5	3.12	109	.324	.359	0	.000	-0	0	0	-0	0.0
1968	Chi-A	0	0	—	1	0	0	0	0	2	2	0	2	1	18.0	4.50	67	.250	.400	0	—	0	-0	-0	0	0.0
1969	Chi-A	7	7	.500	20	20	6	1	0	128²	143	14	50	67	13.7	4.06	95	.283	.351	5	.122	-1	-6	-3	0	-0.2
1970	Chi-A	1	4	.200	12	9	0	0	0	44	54	8	22	19	15.8	5.32	73	.298	.377	1	.077	-1	-8	-7	1	-0.6
1971	Cal-A	0	0	—	3	0	0	0	0	3²	6	0	2	6	19.6	4.91	66	.375	.444	0	—	0	-1	-1	0	0.0
Total	5	8	11	.421	42	30	6	1	0	187	217	22	78	97	14.4	4.33	88	.290	.361	6	.109	-2	-15	-11	1	-0.8

■ BILL WYNNE
Wynne, William Andrew b: 3/27/1869, Neuse, N.C. d: 8/7/51, Raleigh, N.C. BR/TR, 5'11.5", 161 lbs. Deb: 8/31/1894

YEAR	TM/L	W	L	PCT	G	GS	CG	SH	SV	IP	H	HR	BB	SO	RAT	ERA	ERA+	OAV	OOB	BH	AVG	PB	PR	/A	PD	TPI
1894	Was-N	0	1	.000	1	1	1	0	0	8	10	0	8	2	20.3	6.75	78	.303	.439	0	.000	-0	-1	-1	0	0.0

■ HANK WYSE
Wyse, Henry Washington "Hooks" b: 3/1/18, Lunsford, Ark. BR/TR, 5'11.5", 185 lbs. Deb: 9/07/42

YEAR	TM/L	W	L	PCT	G	GS	CG	SH	SV	IP	H	HR	BB	SO	RAT	ERA	ERA+	OAV	OOB	BH	AVG	PB	PR	/A	PD	TPI
1942	Chi-N	2	1	.667	4	4	1	1	0	28	33	1	6	8	12.5	1.93	166	.287	.322	1	.125	-0	4	4	-0	0.4
1943	Chi-N	9	7	.563	38	15	8	2	5	156	160	4	34	45	11.3	2.94	113	.266	.307	4	.080	-3	8	7	4	0.7
1944	Chi-N	16	15	.516	41	34	14	3	1	257²	277	9	57	86	11.8	3.15	112	.278	.318	16	.178	-1	13	11	0	1.1
1945	*Chi-N	22	10	.688	38	34	23	2	0	278¹	272	17	55	77	10.7	2.68	136	.256	.296	17	.168	-2	**35**	30	3	3.1
1946	Chi-N	14	12	.538	40	27	12	2	1	201	206	7	52	52	11.7	2.68	124	.265	.313	18	.243	1	16	14	2	1.9
1947	Chi-N	6	9	.400	37	19	5	1	1	142	158	12	64	53	14.4	4.31	92	.286	.363	5	.111	-1	-4	-6	1	-0.5
1950	Phi-A	9	14	.391	41	23	4	0	0	170²	192	16	87	33	15.1	5.85	78	.287	.376	9	.153	-3	-24	-25	1	-2.4
1951	Phi-A	1	2	.333	9	1	0	0	0	14²	24	0	8	5	19.6	7.98	54	.381	.451	1	.250	-0	-6	-6	0	-0.5
	Was-A	0	0	—	3	2	0	0	0	9¹	17	0	10	3	27.0	9.64	42	.378	.500	0	.000	-1	-6	-6	0	-0.5
	Yr	1	2	.333	12	3	0	0	0	24	41	0	18	8	22.5	8.63	49	.380	.472	1	.000	-1	-12	-12	0	-1.0
Total	8	79	70	.530	251	159	67	11	8	1257²	1339	66	373	362	12.4	3.52	105	.274	.329	71	.163	-11	36	24	11	3.3

■ BIFF WYSONG
Wysong, Harlan b: 4/13/05, Clarksville, Ohio d: 8/8/51, Xenia, Ohio BL/TL, 6'3", 195 lbs. Deb: 8/10/30

YEAR	TM/L	W	L	PCT	G	GS	CG	SH	SV	IP	H	HR	BB	SO	RAT	ERA	ERA+	OAV	OOB	BH	AVG	PB	PR	/A	PD	TPI
1930	Cin-N	0	1	.000	1	1	0	0	0	2¹	6	0	3	1	34.7	19.29	25	.545	.643	0	—	0	-4	-4	0	-0.2
1931	Cin-N	0	2	.000	12	2	0	0	0	21²	25	2	23	5	19.9	7.89	47	.298	.449	1	.250	-0	-10	-10	-0	-0.9
1932	Cin-N	1	0	1.000	7	0	0	0	0	12¹	13	0	8	5	15.3	3.65	106	.277	.382	0	.000	-0	0	0	0	0.0
Total	3	1	3	.250	20	3	0	0	0	36¹	44	2	34	11	19.3	7.18	54	.310	.443	1	.167	-0	-13	-13	-0	-1.1

■ RUSTY YARNALL
Yarnall, Waldo William b: 10/22/02, Chicago, Ill. d: 10/9/85, Lowell, Mass. BR/TR, 6', 175 lbs. Deb: 6/30/26

YEAR	TM/L	W	L	PCT	G	GS	CG	SH	SV	IP	H	HR	BB	SO	RAT	ERA	ERA+	OAV	OOB	BH	AVG	PB	PR	/A	PD	TPI
1926	Phi-N	0	1	.000	1	0	0	0	0	1	3	0	1	0	36.0	18.00	23	.500	.571	0	.000	-0	-2	-2	0	0.0

■ RUBE YARRISON
Yarrison, Byron Wardsworth b: 3/9/1896, Montgomery, Pa. d: 4/22/77, Williamsport, Pa. BR/TR, 5'11", 165 lbs. Deb: 4/13/22

YEAR	TM/L	W	L	PCT	G	GS	CG	SH	SV	IP	H	HR	BB	SO	RAT	ERA	ERA+	OAV	OOB	BH	AVG	PB	PR	/A	PD	TPI
1922	Phi-A	1	2	.333	18	1	0	0	0	33²	50	4	12	10	17.1	8.29	51	.362	.421	1	.167	-0	-16	-15	0	-1.3
1924	Bro-N	0	2	.000	3	2	0	0	0	11	12	0	3	2	13.1	6.55	57	.267	.327	0	.000	-0	-3	-3	0	-0.2
Total	2	1	4	.200	21	3	0	0	0	44²	62	4	15	12	16.1	7.86	53	.339	.398	1	.125	-0	-19	-19	0	-1.5

■ EMIL YDE
Yde, Emil Ogden b: 1/28/1900, Great Lakes, Ill. d: 12/4/68, Leesburg, Fla. BB/TL, 5'11", 165 lbs. Deb: 4/21/24

YEAR	TM/L	W	L	PCT	G	GS	CG	SH	SV	IP	H	HR	BB	SO	RAT	ERA	ERA+	OAV	OOB	BH	AVG	PB	PR	/A	PD	TPI
1924	Pit-N	16	3	**.842**	33	22	14	**4**	0	194	171	3	62	53	11.1	2.83	136	.244	.311	21	.239	2	22	22	1	2.6
1925	*Pit-N	17	9	.654	33	28	13	0	0	207	254	11	75	41	14.4	4.13	108	.309	.369	17	.191	-2	3	8	0	0.6
1926	Pit-N	8	7	.533	37	22	12	1	0	187¹	181	3	81	34	12.7	3.65	108	.260	.339	17	.230	3	4	6	0	0.9
1927	*Pit-N	1	3	.250	9	2	0	0	0	29²	44	1	15	9	18.8	9.71	42	.375	.453	3	.167	-0	-19	-18	1	-1.5
1929	Det-A	7	3	.700	29	6	4	1	0	86²	100	8	63	23	16.9	5.30	81	.296	.406	16	.333	2	-10	-10	-1	-0.5
Total	5	49	25	.662	141	80	43	6	0	704²	751	26	296	160	13.5	4.02	102	.281	.355	74	.233	5	-0	7	2	2.1

■ JOE YEAGER
Yeager, Joseph F. "Little Joe" b: 8/28/1875, Philadelphia, Pa. d: 7/2/37, Detroit, Mich. BR/TR, Deb: 4/22/1898 ♦

YEAR	TM/L	W	L	PCT	G	GS	CG	SH	SV	IP	H	HR	BB	SO	RAT	ERA	ERA+	OAV	OOB	BH	AVG	PB	PR	/A	PD	TPI
1898	Bro-N	12	22	.353	36	33	32	0	0	291¹	333	4	80	70	12.8	3.65	98	.285	.331	23	.172	-3	-1	-2	5	0.0
1899	Bro-N	2	2	.500	10	4	2	1	1	47²	56	1	16	6	13.6	4.72	83	.292	.347	9	.191	0	-5	-4	1	-0.3
1900	Bro-N	1	1	.500	2	2	2	0	0	17	21	1	5	2	13.8	6.88	56	.303	.349	3	.333	0	-6	-6	-0	-0.4

YEAR	TM/L	W	L	PCT	G	GS	CG	SH	SV	IP	H	HR	BB	SO	RAT	ERA	ERA+	OAV	OOB	BH	AVG	PB	PR	/A	PD	TPI
1901	Det-A	12	11	.522	26	25	22	2	1	199²	209	4	46	38	11.5	2.61	147	.266	.307	37	.296	5	23	27	2	3.8
1902	Det-A	6	12	.333	19	15	14	0	0	140	171	5	41	28	13.6	4.82	76	.301	.348	39	.242	2	-19	-18	3	-1.6
1903	Det-A	0	1	.000	1	1	1	0	0	9	15	0	0	1	15.0	4.00	73	.369	.369	103	.256	0	-1	-1	0	0.0
Total	6	33	49	.402	94	80	73	3	2	704²	805	15	188	145	12.7	3.74	99	.285	.330	467	.252	4	-9	-4	11	1.5

■ AL YEARGIN
Yeargin, James Almond b: 10/16/01, Mauldin, S.C. d: 5/8/37, Greenville, S.C. BR/TR, 5'11", 170 lbs. Deb: 10/01/22

YEAR	TM/L	W	L	PCT	G	GS	CG	SH	SV	IP	H	HR	BB	SO	RAT	ERA	ERA+	OAV	OOB	BH	AVG	PB	PR	/A	PD	TPI
1922	Bos-N	0	1	.000	1	1	1	0	0	7	5	1	2	1	9.0	1.29	311	.192	.250	0	.000	-0	2	2	0	0.2
1924	Bos-N	1	11	.083	32	12	6	0	0	141¹	162	7	42	34	13.2	5.09	75	.293	.346	6	.143	-2	-19	-20	4	-1.7
Total	2	1	12	.077	33	13	7	0	0	148¹	167	8	44	35	13.0	4.91	78	.288	.342	6	.133	-2	-17	-18	4	-1.5

■ LARRY YELLEN
Yellen, Lawrence Alan b: 1/4/43, Brooklyn, N.Y. BR/TR, 5'11", 190 lbs. Deb: 9/26/63

YEAR	TM/L	W	L	PCT	G	GS	CG	SH	SV	IP	H	HR	BB	SO	RAT	ERA	ERA+	OAV	OOB	BH	AVG	PB	PR	/A	PD	TPI
1963	Hou-N	0	0	—	1	1	0	0	0	5	7	0	1	3	14.4	3.60	88	.280	.308	0	.000	-0	-0	-0	0	0.0
1964	Hou-N	0	0	—	13	1	0	0	0	21	27	4	10	9	15.9	6.86	50	.297	.366	0	.000	-0	-8	-8	0	-0.8
Total	2	0	0	—	14	2	0	0	0	26	34	4	11	12	15.6	6.23	54	.293	.354	0	.000	-0	-8	-8	0	-0.8

■ CHIEF YELLOWHORSE
Yellowhorse, Moses J. b: 1/28/1898, Pawnee, Okla. d: 4/10/64, Pawnee, Okla. BR/TR, 5'10", 180 lbs. Deb: 4/15/21

YEAR	TM/L	W	L	PCT	G	GS	CG	SH	SV	IP	H	HR	BB	SO	RAT	ERA	ERA+	OAV	OOB	BH	AVG	PB	PR	/A	PD	TPI
1921	Pit-N	5	3	.625	10	4	1	0	1	48¹	45	1	13	19	10.8	2.98	129	.254	.305	0	.000	-2	4	5	-2	0.0
1922	Pit-N	3	1	.750	28	5	2	0	0	77²	92	0	20	24	13.2	4.52	90	.305	.352	6	.316	1	-4	-4	-0	-0.2
Total	2	8	4	.667	38	9	3	0	1	126	137	1	33	43	12.3	3.93	101	.286	.335	6	.167	-2	1	1	-2	-0.2

■ CARROLL YERKES
Yerkes, Charles Carroll "Lefty" b: 6/13/03, McSherrystown, Pa. d: 12/20/50, Oakland, Cal. BR/TL, 5'11", 180 lbs. Deb: 5/31/27

YEAR	TM/L	W	L	PCT	G	GS	CG	SH	SV	IP	H	HR	BB	SO	RAT	ERA	ERA+	OAV	OOB	BH	AVG	PB	PR	/A	PD	TPI
1927	Phi-A	0	0	—	1	0	0	0	0	1	1	0	1	0	9.0	0.00	—	.000	.333	0	—	0	0	0	0	0.1
1928	Phi-A	0	1	.000	2	1	1	0	0	8²	7	0	2	1	9.3	2.08	193	.233	.281	0	.000	-0	2	2	1	0.2
1929	Phi-A	1	0	1.000	19	2	0	0	1	37¹	47	0	13	11	14.7	4.58	92	.329	.389	0	.000	-2	-1	-1	3	0.2
1932	Chi-N	0	0	—	2	0	0	0	0	9	5	2	3	4	8.0	3.00	126	.167	.242	1	.333	0	1	1	-0	0.1
1933	Chi-N	0	0	—	1	0	0	0	0	2	2	0	1	0	13.5	4.50	73	.286	.375	0	—	-0	-0	-0	0	0.0
Total	5	1	1	.500	25	3	1	0	1	58	61	2	20	16	12.7	3.88	106	.288	.352	1	.063	-2	2	1	3	0.4

■ STAN YERKES
Yerkes, Stanley Lewis "Yank" b: 11/28/1874, Cheltenham, Pa. d: 7/28/40, Boston, Mass. 5'10", Deb: 5/03/01

YEAR	TM/L	W	L	PCT	G	GS	CG	SH	SV	IP	H	HR	BB	SO	RAT	ERA	ERA+	OAV	OOB	BH	AVG	PB	PR	/A	PD	TPI
1901	Bal-A	0	1	.000	1	1	1	0	0	8	12	0	2	4	15.8	6.75	57	.342	.377	1	.333	0	-3	-3	0	-0.1
	StL-N	3	1	.750	4	4	4	0	0	34	35	2	6	15	10.9	3.18	100	.264	.296	1	.083	-1	1	0	-0	0.0
1902	StL-N	12	21	.364	39	37	27	1	0	272²	341	1	79	81	13.9	3.66	75	.306	.353	12	.132	-3	-27	-28	-2	-3.2
1903	StL-N	0	1	.000	1	1	0	0	0	5	8	0	0	3	14.4	1.80	181	.333	.333	0	.000	-0	1	1	-0	0.0
Total	3	15	24	.385	45	43	32	1	0	319²	396	3	87	103	13.7	3.66	77	.303	.347	14	.130	-4	-28	-30	-3	-3.3

■ RICH YETT
Yett, Richard Martin b: 10/6/62, Pomona, Cal. BR/TR, 6'2", 187 lbs. Deb: 4/13/85

YEAR	TM/L	W	L	PCT	G	GS	CG	SH	SV	IP	H	HR	BB	SO	RAT	ERA	ERA+	OAV	OOB	BH	AVG	PB	PR	/A	PD	TPI
1985	Min-A	0	0	—	1	1	0	0	0	0¹	1	0	2	0	81.0	27.00	16	.333	.600	0	—	0	-1	-1	0	0.0
1986	Cle-A	5	3	.625	39	3	1	1	1	78²	84	10	37	50	14.0	5.15	80	.275	.355	0	—	0	-8	-9	-1	-0.9
1987	Cle-A	3	9	.250	37	11	2	0	1	97²	96	21	49	59	13.6	5.25	86	.257	.347	0	—	0	-9	-8	-1	-0.7
1988	Cle-A	9	6	.600	23	22	0	0	0	134¹	146	11	55	71	13.5	4.62	89	.275	.344	0	—	0	-10	-8	-2	-0.8
1989	Cle-A	5	6	.455	32	12	1	0	0	99	111	10	47	47	14.5	5.00	79	.283	.363	0	—	0	-12	-11	-1	-1.2
1990	Min-A	0	0	—	4	0	0	0	0	4¹	6	1	1	2	14.5	2.08	202	.353	.389	0	—	0	1	1	0	0.1
Total	6	22	24	.478	136	49	4	1	2	414¹	444	53	191	229	13.9	4.95	84	.274	.353	0	—	0	-39	-36	-4	-3.5

■ EARL YINGLING
Yingling, Earl Hershey "Chink" b: 10/29/1888, Chillicothe, Ohio d: 10/2/62, Columbus, Ohio BL/TL, 5'11.5", 180 lbs. Deb: 4/12/11

YEAR	TM/L	W	L	PCT	G	GS	CG	SH	SV	IP	H	HR	BB	SO	RAT	ERA	ERA+	OAV	OOB	BH	AVG	PB	PR	/A	PD	TPI
1911	Cle-A	1	0	1.000	4	3	1	0	0	22¹	30	1	9	6	16.1	4.43	77	.326	.392	3	.273	0	-3	-3	0	-0.1
1912	Bro-N	6	11	.353	25	16	12	0	0	163	186	10	56	51	13.4	3.59	93	.284	.342	16	.250	3	-3	-4	-1	-0.2
1913	Bro-N	8	8	.500	26	13	8	2	0	146²	158	2	10	40	10.4	2.58	128	.280	.295	23	.383	8	10	12	-1	2.1
1914	Cin-N	9	13	.409	34	27	8	3	0	198	207	6	54	80	12.1	3.45	85	.274	.328	23	.192	1	-15	-12	-2	-1.0
1918	Was-A	1	2	.333	5	2	2	0	0	38	30	0	12	15	9.9	2.13	128	.238	.304	7	.467	3	3	3	1	0.8
Total	5	25	34	.424	94	61	31	5	0	568	611	19	141	192	12.1	3.22	98	.279	.325	72	.267	16	-8	-4	-2	1.6

■ JOE YINGLING
Yingling, Joseph Granville b: 7/23/1866, Westminster, Md. d: 10/24/46, Manchester, Md. BR/TL, 5'7.5", 145 lbs. Deb: 5/28/1886 ♦

YEAR	TM/L	W	L	PCT	G	GS	CG	SH	SV	IP	H	HR	BB	SO	RAT	ERA	ERA+	OAV	OOB	BH	AVG	PB	PR	/A	PD	TPI
1886	Was-N	0	0	—	1	0	0	0	0	3	7	0	1	1	24.0	12.00	27	.437	.470	0	.000	-0	-3	-3	0	-0.2

■ LEN YOCHIM
Yochim, Leonard Joseph b: 10/16/28, New Orleans, La. BL/TL, 6'2", 200 lbs. Deb: 9/18/51

YEAR	TM/L	W	L	PCT	G	GS	CG	SH	SV	IP	H	HR	BB	SO	RAT	ERA	ERA+	OAV	OOB	BH	AVG	PB	PR	/A	PD	TPI
1951	Pit-N	1	1	.500	2	2	0	0	0	8²	10	0	11	5	22.8	8.31	51	.278	.458	0	.000	-0	-4	-4	0	-0.3
1954	Pit-N	0	1	.000	10	1	0	0	0	19²	30	2	8	7	17.4	7.32	57	.361	.418	1	.500	-0	-7	-7	1	-0.5
Total	2	1	2	.333	12	3	0	0	0	28¹	40	2	19	12	19.1	7.62	55	.336	.432	1	.200	-0	-11	-11	1	-0.8

■ RAY YOCHIM
Yochim, Raymond Austin Aloysius b: 7/19/22, New Orleans, La. BR/TR, 6'1", 170 lbs. Deb: 5/02/48

YEAR	TM/L	W	L	PCT	G	GS	CG	SH	SV	IP	H	HR	BB	SO	RAT	ERA	ERA+	OAV	OOB	BH	AVG	PB	PR	/A	PD	TPI
1948	StL-N	0	0	—	1	0	0	0	0	1	0	0	3	1	27.0	0.00	—	.000	.500	0	—	0	0	0	0	0.0
1949	StL-N	0	0	—	3	0	0	0	0	2¹	3	1	4	3	27.0	15.43	27	.273	.467	0	—	0	-3	-3	0	-0.2
Total	2	0	0	—	4	0	0	0	0	3¹	3	1	7	4	27.0	10.80	38	.214	.476	0	—	0	-3	-2	0	-0.2

■ LEFTY YORK
York, James Edward b: 11/1/1892, West Fork, Ark. d: 4/9/61, York, Pa. BL/TL, 5'10", 185 lbs. Deb: 9/12/19

YEAR	TM/L	W	L	PCT	G	GS	CG	SH	SV	IP	H	HR	BB	SO	RAT	ERA	ERA+	OAV	OOB	BH	AVG	PB	PR	/A	PD	TPI
1919	Phi-N	0	2	.000	2	2	0	0	0	4¹	11	0	5	2	37.4	24.92	14	.500	.581	0	.000	-0	-10	-10	0	-0.8
1921	Chi-N	5	9	.357	40	10	4	1	1	139	170	5	63	57	15.4	4.73	81	.308	.384	5	.128	-2	-15	-14	-3	-1.8
Total	2	5	11	.313	42	12	4	1	1	143¹	183	5	68	59	16.1	5.34	71	.317	.393	5	.125	-2	-25	-24	-3	-2.6

■ JIM YORK
York, James Harlan b: 8/27/47, Maywood, Cal. BR/TR, 6'3", 200 lbs. Deb: 9/21/70

YEAR	TM/L	W	L	PCT	G	GS	CG	SH	SV	IP	H	HR	BB	SO	RAT	ERA	ERA+	OAV	OOB	BH	AVG	PB	PR	/A	PD	TPI
1970	KC-A	1	1	.500	4	0	0	0	0	8	5	2	2	6	7.9	3.38	111	.179	.233	0	.000	-0	0	0	-0	0.0
1971	KC-A	5	5	.500	53	0	0	0	3	93¹	70	7	44	103	11.3	2.89	119	.203	.299	2	.118	1	6	6	-1	0.6
1972	Hou-N	0	1	.000	26	0	0	0	0	36	45	3	18	25	16.0	5.25	64	.321	.403	0	.000	-0	-7	-8	0	-0.7
1973	Hou-N	3	4	.429	41	0	0	0	6	53	65	4	20	22	14.6	4.42	82	.305	.368	0	.000	-0	-4	-5	0	-0.4
1974	Hou-N	2	2	.500	28	0	0	0	1	38¹	48	1	19	15	16.0	3.29	105	.298	.376	0	.000	-0	1	1	0	0.0
1975	Hou-N	4	4	.500	19	4	0	0	0	46²	43	1	25	17	14.1	3.86	87	.251	.363	1	.091	-0	-1	-3	-1	-0.3
1976	NY-A	1	0	1.000	3	0	0	0	0	9²	14	1	4	6	17.7	5.59	61	.333	.404	0	—	0	-2	-2	-0	-0.2
Total	7	16	17	.485	174	4	0	0	10	285	290	19	132	194	13.7	3.79	91	.264	.349	3	.075	-1	-7	-10	-1	-1.0

■ MIKE YORK
York, Michael David b: 9/6/64, Oak Park, Ill. BR/TR, 6'1", 187 lbs. Deb: 8/17/90

YEAR	TM/L	W	L	PCT	G	GS	CG	SH	SV	IP	H	HR	BB	SO	RAT	ERA	ERA+	OAV	OOB	BH	AVG	PB	PR	/A	PD	TPI
1990	Pit-N	1	1	.500	4	1	0	0	0	12²	13	0	5	4	13.5	2.84	127	.277	.358	1	.333	0	1	1	0	0.2

■ GUS YOST
Yost, August 6'5", Deb: 6/12/1893

YEAR	TM/L	W	L	PCT	G	GS	CG	SH	SV	IP	H	HR	BB	SO	RAT	ERA	ERA+	OAV	OOB	BH	AVG	PB	PR	/A	PD	TPI
1893	Chi-N	0	1	.000	1	1	0	0	0	2²	3	0	8	1	37.1	13.50	34	.275	.582	0	.000	-0	-3	-3	0	-0.1

■ FLOYD YOUMANS
Youmans, Floyd Everett b: 5/11/64, Tampa, Fla. BR/TR, 6'2", 180 lbs. Deb: 7/01/85

YEAR	TM/L	W	L	PCT	G	GS	CG	SH	SV	IP	H	HR	BB	SO	RAT	ERA	ERA+	OAV	OOB	BH	AVG	PB	PR	/A	PD	TPI
1985	Mon-N	4	3	.571	14	12	0	0	0	77	57	3	49	54	12.5	2.45	138	.206	.327	1	.053	-0	10	8	-2	0.6
1986	Mon-N	13	12	.520	33	32	6	2	0	219	145	14	118	202	11.0	3.53	104	.188	.299	12	.160	2	4	4	-4	0.2
1987	Mon-N	9	8	.529	23	23	3	3	0	116¹	112	13	47	94	12.4	4.64	91	.251	.324	6	.150	1	-7	-6	-0	-0.4
1988	Mon-N	3	6	.333	14	13	1	1	0	84	64	8	41	54	11.5	3.21	112	.213	.311	4	.154	-0	2	4	-0	0.3
1989	Phi-N	1	5	.167	10	10	0	0	0	42²	50	7	25	20	16.2	5.70	62	.299	.397	1	.077	-1	-10	-10	0	-1.0
Total	5	30	34	.469	94	90	10	6	0	539	428	45	280	424	12.0	3.74	100	.218	.319	24	.139	1	-1	-1	-6	-0.2

■ CHARLIE YOUNG
Young, Charles "Cy" b: 1/12/1893, Philadelphia, Pa. d: 5/12/52, Riverside, N.J. BB/TR, 5'10.5", 155 lbs. Deb: 9/05/15

YEAR	TM/L	W	L	PCT	G	GS	CG	SH	SV	IP	H	HR	BB	SO	RAT	ERA	ERA+	OAV	OOB	BH	AVG	PB	PR	/A	PD	TPI
1915	Bal-F	2	3	.400	9	5	1	0	0	35	39	0	21	13	16.5	5.91	54	.289	.401	2	.222	0	-11	-11	2	-0.8

YEAR TM/L	W	L	PCT	G	GS	CG	SH	SV	IP	H	HR	BB	SO	RAT	ERA	ERA+	OAV	OOB	BH	AVG	PB	PR	/A	PD	TPI

■ CLIFF YOUNG Young, Clifford Raphael b: 8/2/64, Willis, Tex. BL/TL, 6'4", 200 lbs. Deb: 7/14/90

| 1990 Cal-A | 1 | 1 | .500 | 17 | 0 | 0 | 0 | 0 | 30² | 40 | 2 | 7 | 19 | 14.1 | 3.52 | 111 | .325 | .366 | 0 | — | 0 | 1 | 1 | 0 | 0.1 |

■ CURT YOUNG Young, Curtis Allen b: 4/16/60, Saginaw, Mich. BR/TL, 6'1", 175 lbs. Deb: 6/24/83

1983 Oak-A	0	1	.000	8	2	0	0	0	9	17	1	5	5	23.0	16.00	24	.386	.460	0	—	0	-12	-12	-0	-1.0
1984 Oak-A	9	4	.692	20	17	2	1	0	108²	118	9	31	41	13.0	4.06	92	.274	.334	0	—	0	-1	-4	-0	-0.3
1985 Oak-A	0	4	.000	19	7	0	0	0	46	57	15	22	19	15.7	7.24	53	.300	.376	0	—	0	-16	-17	-0	-1.6
1986 Oak-A	13	9	.591	29	27	5	2	0	198	176	19	57	116	10.9	3.45	112	.236	.297	0	—	0	16	9	1	1.0
1987 Oak-A	13	7	.650	31	31	6	0	0	203	194	38	44	124	10.7	4.08	101	.252	.295	0	.000	0	8	1	1	0.1
1988 *Oak-A	11	8	.579	26	26	1	0	0	156¹	162	23	50	69	12.4	4.14	91	.275	.336	0	—	0	-3	-6	-1	-0.6
1989 Oak-A	5	9	.357	25	20	1	0	0	111	117	10	47	55	13.5	3.73	99	.264	.338	0	—	0	2	-1	-1	0.0
1990 Oak-A	9	6	.600	26	21	0	0	0	124¹	124	17	53	56	13.0	4.85	77	.266	.344	0	—	0	-13	-15	2	-1.3
Total 8	60	48	.556	184	151	15	3	0	956¹	965	132	309	485	12.3	4.28	90	.262	.324	0	.000	0	-18	-45	0	-3.7

■ CY YOUNG Young, Denton True b: 3/29/1867, Gilmore, Ohio d: 11/4/55, Newcomerstown, Ohio BR/TR, 6'2", 210 lbs. Deb: 8/06/1890 MH

1890 Cle-N	9	7	.563	17	16	16	0	0	147²	145	6	32	36	10.8	3.47	103	.249	.289	8	.123	-6	1	2	2	-0.1
1891 Cle-N	27	22	.551	55	46	43	0	2	423²	431	4	140	147	12.1	2.85	122	.254	.311	29	.167	-3	24	29	-1	2.3
1892 *Cle-N	36	12	.750	53	49	48	9	0	453	363	8	118	168	9.6	1.93	176	.211	.261	31	.158	-8	68	74	5	7.1
1893 Cle-N	34	16	.680	53	46	42	1	1	422²	442	10	103	102	11.6	3.36	145	.261	.303	44	.235	-6	61	72	4	6.2
1894 Cle-N	26	21	.553	52	47	44	2	1	408²	488	19	106	108	13.1	3.94	139	.293	.335	40	.215	-8	63	69	7	5.4
1895 *Cle-N	35	10	.778	47	40	36	4	0	369²	363	10	75	121	10.7	3.26	153	.253	.290	30	.214	-4	62	71	8	6.5
1896 *Cle-N	28	15	.651	51	46	42	5	3	414¹	477	7	62	140	11.7	3.24	140	.286	.312	52	.289	7	52	60	8	6.9
1897 Cle-N	21	19	.525	46	38	35	2	0	333²	391	7	49	88	11.9	3.80	118	.290	.315	34	.222	-4	19	25	2	2.1
1898 Cle-N	25	13	.658	46	41	40	1	0	377²	387	6	41	101	10.2	2.53	143	.263	.283	39	.253	5	45	46	7	5.7
1899 StL-N	26	16	.619	44	42	40	4	1	369¹	368	10	44	111	10.0	2.58	154	.259	.282	32	.216	-1	52	57	5	6.0
1900 StL-N	19	19	.500	41	35	32	4	0	321¹	337	7	36	115	10.4	3.00	121	.269	.290	22	.177	-2	25	23	-0	1.9
1901 Bos-A	33	10	.767	43	41	38	5	0	371¹	324	6	37	158	8.7	1.62	217	.232	.252	32	.209	1	84	79	1	7.8
1902 Bos-A	32	11	.744	45	43	41	3	0	384²	350	6	53	160	9.4	2.15	166	.243	.270	34	.230	3	61	61	-6	5.8
1903 *Bos-A	28	9	.757	40	35	34	7	2	341²	294	6	37	176	8.7	2.08	146	.232	.254	44	.321	13	34	36	-4	5.1
1904 Bos-A	26	16	.619	43	41	40	10	1	380	327	6	29	200	8.4	1.97	136	.233	.249	33	.223	2	27	30	-6	3.1
1905 Bos-A	18	19	.486	38	33	31	4	0	320²	248	3	30	210	7.8	1.82	148	.215	.235	18	.150	-1	30	31	-3	3.1
1906 Bos-A	13	21	.382	39	34	28	0	2	287²	288	3	25	140	9.8	3.19	86	.264	.280	16	.154	-2	-16	-14	-2	-1.8
1907 Bos-A	21	15	.583	43	37	33	6	2	343¹	286	6	51	147	8.8	1.99	130	.228	.259	27	.216	0	21	23	-7	1.8
1908 Bos-A	21	11	.656	36	33	30	3	2	299	230	1	37	150	8.1	1.26	195	.213	.240	26	.226	1	38	40	-6	4.2
1909 Cle-A	19	15	.559	35	34	30	3	0	295	267	4	59	109	10.2	2.26	113	.250	.294	21	.196	-0	7	10	-1	1.0
1910 Cle-A	7	10	.412	21	20	14	1	0	163¹	149	0	27	58	9.9	2.53	102	.252	.289	8	.145	-0	-0	1	1	0.2
1911 Cle-A	3	4	.429	7	7	4	0	0	46¹	54	2	13	20	13.2	3.88	88	.298	.349	1	.063	-2	-3	-2	0	-0.3
Bos-N	4	5	.444	11	11	8	2	0	80	83	4	15	35	11.4	3.71	103	.268	.308	2	.080	-3	-3	1	0	-0.1
Total 22	511	316	.618	906	815	749	76	17	7354²	7092	138	1219	2800	10.2	2.63	138	.252	.283	623	.210	-20	753	819	13	79.9

■ HARLEY YOUNG Young, Harlan Edward "Cy The Third" b: 9/28/1883, Portland, Ind. d: 3/26/75, Jacksonville, Fla. BR/TR, 6'2". Deb: 4/21/08

1908 Pit-N	0	2	.000	8	3	0	0	0	48¹	40	0	10	17	10.2	2.23	103	.234	.296	1	.083	-0	1	0	1	0.1
Bos-N	0	1	.000	6	2	1	0	0	27¹	29	0	4	12	11.9	3.29	73	.269	.313	2	.200	-0	-3	-3	-0	-0.2
Yr	0	3	.000	14	5	1	0	0	75²	69	0	14	29	10.2	2.62	89	.243	.286	1	.045	-0	-2	-2	1	-0.1

■ IRV YOUNG Young, Irving Melrose "Young Cy" or "Cy The Second" b: 7/21/1877, Columbia Falls, Maine d: 1/14/35, Brewer, Maine BL/TL, 5'10", 170 lbs. Deb: 4/14/05

1905 Bos-N	20	21	.488	43	42	41	7	0	378	337	6	71	156	9.9	2.90	107	.241	.282	14	.103	-8	4	8	4	0.4
1906 Bos-N	16	25	.390	43	41	37	4	0	358¹	349	7	83	151	11.0	2.91	92	.263	.309	12	.096	-7	-11	-9	3	-1.4
1907 Bos-N	10	23	.303	40	32	22	3	1	245¹	287	5	58	86	13.1	3.96	64	.306	.354	13	.162	-1	-41	-38	1	-4.0
1908 Bos-N	4	9	.308	16	11	7	1	0	85	94	2	19	32	12.2	2.86	84	.289	.332	5	.156	-1	-5	-4	1	-0.6
Pit-N	4	3	.571	16	7	3	1	1	89²	73	1	21	31	9.9	2.01	115	.225	.283	6	.200	1	4	3	-1	0.4
Yr	8	12	.400	32	18	10	2	1	174²	167	3	40	63	10.9	2.42	97	.257	.305	2	.032	0	-1	-1	-2	-0.2
1910 Chi-A	4	8	.333	27	17	7	4	0	135²	122	0	39	64	10.9	2.72	88	.247	.306	5	.114	-2	-3	-5	-0	-0.7
1911 Chi-A	5	6	.455	24	11	3	1	2	92²	99	2	25	40	12.0	4.37	74	.229	.271	5	.179	-0	-11	-12	1	-1.0
Total 6	63	95	.399	209	161	120	21	4	1384²	1361	23	316	560	11.1	3.11	88	.260	.307	60	.126	-18	-62	-57	7	-6.9

■ J. B. YOUNG Young, J. B. b: Mt.Carmel, Pa. Deb: 6/10/1892

| 1892 StL-N | 0 | 0 | — | 1 | 0 | 0 | 0 | 0 | 2 | 9 | 0 | 2 | 1 | 49.5 | 22.50 | 14 | .600 | .647 | 0 | .000 | -0 | -4 | -4 | 0 | -0.3 |

■ KIP YOUNG Young, Kip Lane b: 10/29/54, Georgetown, Ohio BR/TR, 5'11", 175 lbs. Deb: 7/21/78

1978 Det-A	6	7	.462	14	13	7	0	0	105²	94	9	30	49	10.7	2.81	137	.246	.304	0	—	0	11	12	-2	1.2
1979 Det-A	2	2	.500	13	7	0	0	0	43²	60	11	11	22	14.8	6.39	68	.323	.364	0	—	0	-11	-10	1	-0.8
Total 2	8	9	.471	27	20	7	0	0	149¹	154	20	41	71	11.9	3.86	103	.271	.324	0	—	0	1	2	-1	0.4

■ MATT YOUNG Young, Matthew John b: 8/9/58, Pasadena, Cal. BL/TL, 6'3", 205 lbs. Deb: 4/06/83

1983 Sea-A	11	15	.423	33	32	5	2	0	203²	178	17	79	130	11.7	3.27	130	.236	.315	0	—	0	18	22	2	2.5
1984 Sea-A	6	8	.429	22	22	1	0	0	113¹	141	11	57	73	15.8	5.72	70	.307	.384	0	—	0	-22	-22	1	-1.9
1985 Sea-A	12	19	.387	37	35	5	2	1	218¹	242	23	76	136	13.4	4.91	86	.282	.345	0	—	0	-18	-17	-2	-1.7
1986 Sea-A	8	6	.571	65	5	1	0	13	103²	108	9	46	82	14.1	3.82	111	.272	.359	0	—	0	4	5	-2	0.3
1987 LA-N	5	8	.385	47	0	0	0	11	54¹	62	3	17	42	13.1	4.47	89	.288	.341	0	.000	-0	-2	-3	-2	-0.4
1989 *Oak-A	1	4	.200	26	4	0	0	0	37¹	42	3	21	27	17.6	6.75	55	.286	.410	0	—	0	-12	-13	-1	-1.1
1990 Sea-A	8	18	.308	34	33	7	1	0	225¹	198	15	107	176	12.4	3.51	113	.237	.328	0	—	0	10	11	-0	1.1
Total 7	51	78	.395	264	131	19	5	25	956	971	80	413	666	13.3	4.26	96	.265	.344	0	.000	-0	-23	-16	-2	-1.2

■ CHIEF YOUNGBLOOD Youngblood, Albert Clyde b: 6/13/1900, Hillsboro, Tex. d: 7/6/68, Amarillo, Tex. BL/TR, 6'3", 202 lbs. Deb: 7/16/22

| 1922 Was-A | 0 | 0 | — | 2 | 0 | 0 | 0 | 0 | 4¹ | 9 | 0 | 7 | 0 | 37.4 | 14.54 | 27 | .429 | .600 | 0 | .000 | -0 | -5 | -5 | 0 | -0.4 |

■ DUCKY YOUNT Yount, Herbert Macon "Hub" b: 12/7/1885, Iredell Co., N.C. d: 5/9/70, Winston-Salem, N.C. BR/TR, 6'2", 178 lbs. Deb: 5/28/14

| 1914 Bal-F | 1 | 1 | .500 | 13 | 1 | 1 | 0 | 0 | 41¹ | 44 | 2 | 19 | 19 | 14.2 | 4.14 | 81 | .281 | .366 | 1 | .083 | -1 | -4 | -4 | 1 | -0.3 |

■ LARRY YOUNT Yount, Lawrence King b: 2/15/50, Houston, Tex. BR/TR, 6'2", 185 lbs. Deb: 9/15/71

| 1971 Hou-N | 0 | 0 | — | 1 | 0 | 0 | 0 | 0 | 0 | 0 | 0 | 0 | 0 | — | — | — | — | — | 0 | — | 0 | 0 | 0 | 0 | 0.0 |

■ CARL YOWELL Yowell, Carl Columbus "Sundown" b: 12/20/02, Madison Va. d: 7/27/85, Jacksonville, Tex. BL/TL, 6'4", 180 lbs. Deb: 9/05/24

1924 Cle-A	1	1	.500	4	2	2	0	0	27	37	1	13	8	16.7	6.67	64	.343	.413	2	.182	-1	-7	-7	-0	-0.6
1925 Cle-A	2	3	.400	12	4	1	0	0	36¹	40	1	17	12	14.4	4.46	99	.310	.395	1	.125	-1	-0	-0	0	0.0
Total 2	3	4	.429	16	6	3	0	0	63¹	77	2	30	20	15.3	5.40	81	.325	.403	3	.158	-1	-8	-7	-0	-0.6

■ EDDIE YUHAS Yuhas, John Edward b: 8/5/24, Youngstown, Ohio d: 7/6/86, Winston-Salem, N.C BR/TR, 6'1", 180 lbs. Deb: 4/17/52

1952 StL-N	12	2	.857	54	2	0	0	6	99¹	90	5	36	39	11.5	2.72	137	.243	.312	4	.190	1	11	11	-1	1.2
1953 StL-N	0	0	—	2	0	0	0	0	1	3	0	0	0	27.0	18.00	24	.500	.500	0	—	0	-2	-2	0	0.0
Total 2	12	2	.857	56	2	0	0	6	100¹	93	5	36	39	11.7	2.87	130	.247	.315	4	.190	1	10	9	-1	1.2

■ ADRIAN ZABALA Zabala, Adrian (Rodriguez) b: 8/26/16, San Antonio De Los Banos, Cuba BL/TL, 5'11", 165 lbs. Deb: 8/11/45

| 1945 NY-N | 2 | 4 | .333 | 11 | 5 | 1 | 0 | 0 | 43¹ | 46 | 2 | 20 | 14 | 13.7 | 4.78 | 82 | .284 | .363 | 3 | .231 | 1 | -5 | -4 | 0 | -0.2 |

YEAR	TM/L	W	L	PCT	G	GS	CG	SH	SV	IP	H	HR	BB	SO	RAT	ERA	ERA+	OAV	OOB	BH	AVG	PB	PR	/A	PD	TPI
1949	NY-N	2	3	.400	15	4	2	1	1	41	44	5	10	13	12.1	5.27	76	.278	.325	1	.077	-1	-6	-6	-1	-0.7
Total	2	4	7	.364	26	9	3	1	1	84¹	90	7	30	27	12.9	5.02	79	.281	.345	4	.154	-0	-10	-10	-1	-0.9

■ ZIP ZABEL

Zabel, George Washington b: 2/18/1891, Wetmore, Kan. d: 5/31/70, Beloit, Wis. BR/TR, 6'1.5", 185 lbs. Deb: 10/05/13

YEAR	TM/L	W	L	PCT	G	GS	CG	SH	SV	IP	H	HR	BB	SO	RAT	ERA	ERA+	OAV	OOB	BH	AVG	PB	PR	/A	PD	TPI
1913	Chi-N	1	0	1.000	1	1	0	0	0	5	3	0	1	0	7.2	0.00	—	.167	.211	0	.000	0	2	2	0	0.2
1914	Chi-N	4	4	.500	29	7	2	0	3	128	104	5	45	50	10.6	2.18	128	.235	.309	7	.184	-1	9	9	-1	0.8
1915	Chi-N	7	10	.412	36	17	8	3	0	163	124	3	64	60	11.7	3.20	87	.218	.323	4	.074	-4	-8	-8	4	-0.7
Total	3	12	14	.462	66	25	10	3	3	296	231	8	130	110	11.2	2.71	103	.224	.315	11	.117	-4	2	3	3	0.3

■ CHINK ZACHARY

Zachary, Albert Myron (b: Albert Myron Zarski) b: 10/19/17, Brooklyn, N.Y. BR/TR, 5'11", 182 lbs. Deb: 4/23/44

YEAR	TM/L	W	L	PCT	G	GS	CG	SH	SV	IP	H	HR	BB	SO	RAT	ERA	ERA+	OAV	OOB	BH	AVG	PB	PR	/A	PD	TPI
1944	Bro-N	0	2	.000	4	2	0	0	0	10¹	10	2	7	3	15.7	9.58	37	.238	.360	0	.000	-0	-7	-7	-0	-0.6

■ TOM ZACHARY

Zachary, Jonathan Thompson Walton (a.k.a. Zach Walton In 1918) b: 5/7/1896, Graham, N.C. d: 1/24/69, Burlington, N.C. BL/TL, 6'1", 187 lbs. Deb: 7/11/18

YEAR	TM/L	W	L	PCT	G	GS	CG	SH	SV	IP	H	HR	BB	SO	RAT	ERA	ERA+	OAV	OOB	BH	AVG	PB	PR	/A	PD	TPI
1918	Phi-A	2	0	1.000	2	2	0	0	0	8	9	0	7	1	18.0	5.63	52	.321	.457	2	.500	1	-3	-2	0	-0.1
1919	Was-A	1	5	.167	17	7	0	0	0	61²	68	0	20	9	13.0	2.92	110	.292	.350	5	.333	2	2	2	-0	0.4
1920	Was-A	15	16	.484	44	31	19	3	2	262²	289	7	78	53	12.7	3.77	99	.285	.339	29	.261	6	1	-1	1	0.4
1921	Was-A	18	16	.529	39	31	17	2	1	250	314	10	59	53	13.6	3.96	104	.319	.361	23	.256	3	9	4	0	0.7
1922	Was-A	15	10	.600	32	25	13	1	1	184²	190	6	43	37	11.5	3.12	124	.275	.321	21	.296	5	19	15	0	2.0
1923	Was-A	10	16	.385	35	29	10	0	0	204¹	270	9	63	40	14.8	4.49	84	.321	.372	15	.192	-0	-12	-17	0	-1.6
1924	*Was-A	15	9	.625	33	27	13	1	2	202²	198	6	53	45	11.3	2.75	147	.264	.315	22	.306	4	33	29	2	3.4
1925	*Was-A	12	15	.444	38	33	11	1	2	217²	247	10	74	58	13.4	3.85	110	.296	.355	12	.174	-2	13	9	0	0.7
1926	StL-A	14	15	.483	34	31	18	3	0	247¹	264	14	97	53	13.4	3.60	119	.288	.359	23	.267	5	11	19	3	2.7
1927	StL-A	4	6	.400	13	12	6	0	0	78¹	110	4	27	13	15.7	4.37	100	.345	.396	3	.107	-2	-2	-0	-0	-0.2
	Was-A	4	7	.364	15	14	5	1	0	102²	116	2	30	13	13.0	3.94	103	.290	.343	5	.139	-2	2	1	-2	-0.2
	Yr	8	13	.381	28	26	11	1	0	181	226	6	57	26	14.2	4.13	102	.314	.366	4	.063	-4	0	1	-3	-0.4
1928	Was-A	6	9	.400	20	14	5	1	0	102²	130	5	40	19	15.0	5.44	74	.322	.384	10	.303	1	-16	-16	0	-1.2
	*NY-A	3	3	.500	7	6	3	0	1	45²	54	1	15	7	13.6	3.94	95	.320	.375	2	.133	-0	1	-1	1	0.0
	Yr	9	12	.429	27	20	8	1	1	148¹	184	6	55	26	14.5	4.98	79	.321	.380	1	.021	1	-15	-17	2	-1.2
1929	NY-A	12	0	1.000	26	11	7	2	2	119²	131	5	30	35	12.3	2.48	155	.277	.323	10	.238	1	23	18	-2	1.6
1930	NY-A	1	1	.500	3	3	0	0	0	16²	18	0	9	1	14.6	6.48	66	.269	.355	2	.250	1	-3	-4	1	-0.2
	Bos-N	11	5	.688	24	22	10	1	0	151¹	192	9	50	57	14.4	4.58	108	.317	.369	13	.241	2	7	6	-1	0.6
1931	Bos-N	11	15	.423	33	28	16	3	2	229	243	8	53	64	11.7	3.10	122	.272	.314	14	.167	-1	19	17	3	1.9
1932	Bos-N	12	11	.522	32	24	12	1	0	212	231	6	55	67	12.2	3.10	121	.280	.326	21	.273	5	18	16	-2	1.9
1933	Bos-N	7	9	.438	26	20	6	2	2	125	134	1	35	22	12.2	3.53	87	.276	.325	5	.119	-2	-3	-6	0	-0.7
1934	Bos-N	1	2	.333	5	4	2	1	0	24	27	1	8	4	13.1	3.38	113	.278	.333	0	.000	-1	2	1	0	0.0
	Bro-N	5	6	.455	22	12	4	0	2	101²	122	5	21	28	12.8	4.43	88	.301	.339	7	.184	1	-4	-6	-1	-0.4
	Yr	6	8	.429	27	16	6	1	2	125²	149	6	29	32	12.9	4.23	92	.297	.338	6	.130	0	-2	-5	-1	-0.4
1935	Bro-N	7	12	.368	25	21	9	1	4	158	193	10	35	33	13.1	3.59	111	.297	.335	7	.135	-1	8	7	1	0.6
1936	Bro-N	0	0	—	1	0	0	0	0	0¹	2	0	1	0	81.0	54.00	8	1.000	1.000	0	—	0	-2	-2	0	-0.1
	Phi-N	0	3	.000	7	2	0	0	1	20¹	28	2	11	8	17.3	7.97	57	.329	.406	3	.333	1	-9	-8	0	-0.5
	Yr	0	3	.000	8	2	0	0	1	20²	30	2	12	8	18.3	8.71	52	.345	.424	2	.222	1	-11	-10	0	-0.6
Total	19	186	191	.493	533	409	186	24	22	3126¹	3580	119	914	720	13.1	3.73	106	.294	.345	254	.226	25	116	82	4	11.7

■ CHRIS ZACHARY

Zachary, William Christopher b: 2/19/44, Knoxville, Tenn. BL/TR, 6'2", 200 lbs. Deb: 4/11/63

YEAR	TM/L	W	L	PCT	G	GS	CG	SH	SV	IP	H	HR	BB	SO	RAT	ERA	ERA+	OAV	OOB	BH	AVG	PB	PR	/A	PD	TPI
1963	Hou-N	2	2	.500	22	7	0	0	0	57	62	5	22	42	13.7	4.89	64	.272	.344	0	.000	-1	-10	-11	1	-1.1
1964	Hou-N	0	1	.000	1	1	0	0	0	4	6	1	1	2	15.8	9.00	38	.333	.368	0	.000	-0	-2	-2	0	-0.1
1965	Hou-N	0	2	.000	4	2	0	0	0	10²	12	0	6	4	15.2	4.22	80	.273	.360	0	.000	-0	-1	-1	0	0.0
1966	Hou-N	3	5	.375	10	8	0	0	0	55	44	1	32	37	12.6	3.44	100	.222	.322	4	.222	1	1	-0	-0	0.0
1967	Hou-N	1	6	.143	9	7	0	0	0	36¹	42	5	12	18	13.9	5.70	58	.290	.352	1	.100	-0	-9	-10	-0	-0.9
1969	KC-A	0	1	.000	8	2	0	0	0	18¹	27	4	7	6	16.7	7.85	47	.346	.400	1	.500	0	-9	-8	-0	-0.7
1971	StL-N	3	10	.231	23	12	1	1	0	89²	114	3	26	48	14.5	5.32	68	.316	.368	8	.242	1	-18	-17	0	-1.6
1972	*Det-A	1	1	.500	25	1	0	0	1	38¹	27	2	15	21	10.1	1.41	223	.201	.287	1	.500	1	7	7	0	0.9
1973	Pit-N	0	1	.000	6	0	0	0	1	12	10	1	1	6	8.3	3.00	117	.222	.239	0	.000	-0	1	1	-0	0.0
Total	9	10	29	.256	108	40	1	1	2	321¹	344	22	122	184	13.4	4.57	74	.275	.344	15	.181	1	-41	-42	0	-3.5

■ PAT ZACHRY

Zachry, Patrick Paul b: 4/24/52, Richmond, Tex. BR/TR, 6'5", 180 lbs. Deb: 4/11/76

YEAR	TM/L	W	L	PCT	G	GS	CG	SH	SV	IP	H	HR	BB	SO	RAT	ERA	ERA+	OAV	OOB	BH	AVG	PB	PR	/A	PD	TPI
1976	*Cin-N	14	7	.667	38	28	6	1	0	204	170	8	83	143	11.3	2.74	128	.228	.307	7	.113	-2	17	17	-2	1.5
1977	Cin-N	3	7	.300	12	12	3	0	0	75	78	7	29	36	13.0	5.04	78	.273	.342	3	.136	-1	-9	-9	-2	-0.7
	NY-N	7	6	.538	19	19	2	1	0	119²	129	14	48	63	13.5	3.76	99	.278	.350	6	.143	-1	2	-0	-1	-0.2
	Yr	10	13	.435	31	31	5	1	0	194²	207	21	77	99	13.3	4.25	90	.274	.344	1	.016	-2	-7	-10	0	-0.9
1978	NY-N	10	6	.625	21	21	5	2	0	138	120	9	60	78	11.8	3.33	105	.236	.318	3	.070	-2	4	2	1	0.1
1979	NY-N	5	1	.833	7	7	1	0	0	42²	44	3	21	17	14.1	3.59	101	.267	.356	2	.125	-1	1	0	0	0.0
1980	NY-N	6	10	.375	28	26	7	3	0	164²	145	16	58	88	11.4	3.01	118	.240	.312	2	.043	-4	11	10	-1	0.5
1981	NY-N	7	14	.333	24	24	3	0	0	139	151	13	56	76	13.7	4.14	84	.282	.354	6	.158	0	-10	-10	1	-0.9
1982	NY-N	6	9	.400	36	16	2	0	1	137²	149	10	57	69	13.5	4.05	90	.279	.349	3	.079	-2	-7	-6	-0	-0.8
1983	*LA-N	6	1	.857	40	1	0	0	0	61¹	63	4	21	36	12.5	2.49	144	.278	.341	2	.500	1	8	7	0	0.9
1984	LA-N	5	6	.455	58	0	0	0	2	82²	84	3	51	55	14.9	3.81	93	.267	.372	2	.333	1	-2	-3	1	0.0
1985	Phi-N	0	0	—	10	0	0	0	0	12²	14	1	11	8	17.8	4.26	86	.280	.410	0	.000	-0	-1	-1	1	0.0
Total	10	69	67	.507	293	154	29	7	3	1177¹	1147	88	495	669	12.7	3.52	102	.259	.336	36	.113	-11	13	8	0	0.4

■ GEORGE ZACKERT

Zackert, George Carl "Zeke" b: 12/24/1884, Buchanan Co., Mo. d: 2/18/77, Burlington, Iowa BL/TL, 6', 177 lbs. Deb: 9/22/11

YEAR	TM/L	W	L	PCT	G	GS	CG	SH	SV	IP	H	HR	BB	SO	RAT	ERA	ERA+	OAV	OOB	BH	AVG	PB	PR	/A	PD	TPI
1911	StL-N	0	2	.000	4	1	0	0	0	7¹	17	0	6	6	28.2	11.05	31	.486	.561	0	.000	-0	-6	-6	0	-0.5
1912	StL-N	0	0	—	1	0	0	0	0	1	2	0	1	0	36.0	18.00	19	.500	.667	0	—	0	-2	-2	0	0.0
Total	2	0	2	.000	5	1	0	0	0	8¹	19	0	7	6	29.2	11.88	28	.487	.574	0	.000	-0	-8	-8	1	-0.5

■ GEOFF ZAHN

Zahn, Geoffrey Clayton b: 12/19/45, Baltimore, Md. BL/TL, 6'1", 180 lbs. Deb: 9/02/73

YEAR	TM/L	W	L	PCT	G	GS	CG	SH	SV	IP	H	HR	BB	SO	RAT	ERA	ERA+	OAV	OOB	BH	AVG	PB	PR	/A	PD	TPI
1973	LA-N	1	0	1.000	6	1	0	0	0	13¹	5	2	2	9	4.7	1.35	255	.116	.156	0	.000	-0	3	3	0	0.3
1974	LA-N	3	5	.375	21	10	1	0	0	79²	78	3	16	33	10.8	2.03	167	.254	.295	4	.174	-0	14	12	0	1.3
1975	LA-N	0	1	.000	2	0	0	0	0	3	2	0	5	1	21.0	9.00	38	.222	.500	0	—	0	-2	-2	0	-0.1
	Chi-N	2	7	.222	16	10	1	0	1	62²	67	2	26	21	13.4	4.45	86	.282	.352	2	.133	-1	-6	-4	1	-0.3
	Yr	2	8	.200	18	10	1	0	1	65²	69	2	31	22	13.7	4.66	82	.279	.360	0	.000	-1	-8	-6	1	-0.4
1976	Chi-N	0	1	.000	3	2	0	0	0	8¹	16	0	2	4	20.5	10.80	36	.410	.452	0	.000	-0	-7	-6	0	-0.5
1977	Min-A	12	14	.462	34	32	7	1	0	198	234	20	66	88	13.9	4.68	85	.299	.358	0	—	0	-14	-15	3	-1.2
1978	Min-A	14	14	.500	35	35	12	1	0	252¹	260	18	81	106	12.3	3.03	126	.274	.334	0	—	0	20	22	0	2.4
1979	Min-A	13	7	.650	26	24	4	0	0	169	183	14	48	51	11.8	3.57	123	.279	.322	0	—	0	12	15	2	1.7
1980	Min-A	14	18	.438	38	35	13	5	0	232²	273	17	66	96	13.2	4.41	99	.302	.351	0	—	0	-10	-1	2	-0.3
1981	Cal-A	10	11	.476	25	25	9	1	0	161¹	181	18	43	52	12.5	4.41	83	.285	.330	0	—	0	-13	-14	1	-1.2
1982	*Cal-A	18	8	.692	34	34	12	4	0	229¹	225	18	65	81	11.5	3.73	109	.259	.314	0	—	0	9	8	-1	0.8
1983	Cal-A	11	11	.450	29	28	11	3	0	203	212	22	51	81	11.7	3.33	121	.269	.314	0	—	0	17	16	-1	1.4
1984	Cal-A	13	10	.565	28	27	9	5	0	199¹	200	11	48	61	11.2	3.12	127	.263	.308	0	—	0	19	19	1	2.1
1985	Cal-A	2	2	.500	7	7	1	1	0	37	44	5	14	14	14.1	4.38	94	.299	.360	0	—	0	-1	-1	1	0.0
Total	13	111	109	.505	304	270	79	20	1	1849	1978	149	526	705	12.3	3.74	107	.278	.329	6	.140	-2	43	51	7	6.7

YEAR TM/L	W	L	PCT	G	GS	CG	SH	SV	IP	H	HR	BB	SO	RAT	ERA	ERA+	OAV	OOB	BH	AVG	PB	PR	/A	PD	TPI

■ PAUL ZAHNISER Zahniser, Paul Vernon b: 9/6/1896, Sac City, Iowa d: 9/26/64, Klamath Falls, Ore. BR/TR, 5'10.5", 170 lbs. Deb: 5/18/23

1923 Was-A	9	10	.474	33	21	10	1	0	177	201	7	76	52	14.2	3.86	97	.291	.364	5	.096	-1	2	-2	-2	-0.5
1924 Was-A	5	7	.417	24	14	5	1	0	92	98	2	49	28	14.8	4.40	92	.283	.378	4	.129	-2	-2	-4	-1	-0.6
1925 Bos-A	5	12	.294	37	21	7	1	1	176²	232	6	89	30	16.4	5.15	88	.327	.403	8	.138	-4	-15	-12	-2	-1.5
1926 Bos-A	6	18	.250	30	24	7	1	0	172	213	5	69	35	14.9	4.97	82	.321	.387	8	.163	-1	-18	-17	3	-1.3
1929 Cin-N	0	0	—	1	0	0	0	0	1	2	1	1	0	27.0	27.00	17	.400	.500	0	—	0	-2	-2	-0	-0.1
Total 5	25	47	.347	125	80	29	4	1	618²	746	21	284	145	15.1	4.66	88	.309	.384	25	.132	-8	-35	-37	-2	-4.0

■ CARL ZAMLOCH Zamloch, Carl Eugene b: 10/6/1889, Oakland, Cal. d: 8/19/63, Santa Barbara, Cal BR/TR, 6'1", 176 lbs. Deb: 5/07/13

| 1913 Det-A | 1 | 6 | .143 | 17 | 5 | 3 | 0 | 1 | 69² | 66 | 1 | 23 | 28 | 11.9 | 2.45 | 119 | .257 | .325 | 4 | .182 | -1 | 4 | 4 | -1 | 0.2 |

■ OSCAR ZAMORA Zamora, Oscar Jose (Sosa) b: 9/23/44, Camaguey, Cuba BR/TR, 5'10", 178 lbs. Deb: 6/18/74

1974 Chi-N	3	9	.250	56	0	0	0	10	83²	82	6	19	38	10.9	3.12	122	.264	.306	2	.182	-0	5	6	0	0.7
1975 Chi-N	5	2	.714	52	0	0	0	10	71	84	17	15	28	12.5	5.07	76	.298	.333	1	.167	-0	-11	-10	-0	-0.9
1976 Chi-N	5	3	.625	40	2	0	0	3	55	70	8	17	27	14.4	5.24	74	.317	.368	0	.000	-1	-11	-8	-1	-1.0
1978 Hou-N	0	0	—	10	0	0	0	0	15	20	2	7	6	16.2	7.20	46	.328	.397	0	.000	-0	-6	-6	-0	-0.6
Total 4	13	14	.481	158	2	0	0	23	224²	256	33	58	99	12.6	4.53	84	.293	.337	3	.107	-2	-23	-18	-1	-1.8

■ DOM ZANNI Zanni, Dominick Thomas b: 3/1/32, Bronx, N.Y. BR/TR, 5'11", 180 lbs. Deb: 9/28/58

1958 SF-N	1	0	1.000	1	0	0	0	0	4	7	1	1	3	18.0	2.25	169	.412	.444	0	.000	-0	1	1	-0	0.0
1959 SF-N	0	0	—	9	0	0	0	0	11	12	2	8	11	17.2	6.55	58	.273	.396	0	—	0	-3	-3	1	-0.1
1961 SF-N	1	0	1.000	8	0	0	0	0	13²	13	1	12	11	16.5	3.95	96	.277	.424	0	—	0	0	-0	0	0.0
1962 Chi-A	6	5	.545	44	2	0	0	5	86¹	67	12	31	66	10.3	3.75	104	.214	.287	5	.278	2	2	1	2	0.5
1963 Chi-A	0	0	—	5	0	0	0	0	4¹	5	1	4	2	18.7	8.31	42	.294	.429	0	—	0	-2	-2	0	-0.1
Cin-N	1	1	.500	31	1	0	0	5	43	39	2	21	40	13.4	4.19	80	.247	.350	1	.333	0	-4	-4	1	-0.2
1965 Cin-N	0	0	—	8	0	0	0	0	13¹	7	1	5	10	8.1	1.35	278	.159	.245	0	.000	0	3	4	0	0.4
1966 Cin-N	0	0	—	5	0	0	0	0	7¹	5	0	3	5	11.0	0.00	—	.192	.300	1	1.000	0	3	3	-0	0.4
Total 7	9	6	.600	111	3	0	0	10	183	155	20	85	148	12.1	3.79	99	.233	.326	7	.280	2	-1	-1	3	0.9

■ JEFF ZASKE Zaske, Lloyd Jeffrey b: 10/6/60, Seattle, Wash. BR/TR, 6'5", 180 lbs. Deb: 7/21/84

| 1984 Pit-N | 0 | 0 | — | 3 | 0 | 0 | 0 | 0 | 5 | 4 | 0 | 1 | 2 | 9.0 | 0.00 | — | .211 | .250 | 0 | — | 0 | 2 | 2 | -0 | 0.2 |

■ CLINT ZAVARAS Zavaras, Clinton Wayne b: 1/4/67, Denver, Colo. BR/TR, 6'1", 175 lbs. Deb: 6/03/89

| 1989 Sea-A | 1 | 6 | .143 | 10 | 10 | 0 | 0 | 0 | 52 | 49 | 4 | 30 | 31 | 14.0 | 5.19 | 78 | .253 | .358 | 0 | — | 0 | -8 | -7 | -0 | -0.6 |

■ ZAY   Zay   Deb: 10/07/1886 ♦

| 1886 Bal-a | 0 | 1 | .000 | 1 | 1 | 0 | 0 | 0 | 2 | 4 | 0 | 4 | 2 | 36.0 | 9.00 | 38 | .398 | .569 | 0 | .000 | -0 | -1 | -1 | 0 | 0.0 |

■ MATT ZEISER Zeiser, Matthew J. b: 9/25/1888, Chicago, Ill. d: 6/10/42, Norwood Park, Ill BR/TR, 5'10", 170 lbs. Deb: 4/27/14

| 1914 Bos-A | 0 | 0 | — | 2 | 0 | 0 | 0 | 0 | 10 | 9 | 0 | 8 | 0 | 16.2 | 1.80 | 150 | .281 | .439 | 0 | .000 | -0 | 1 | 1 | -0 | 0.0 |

■ BILL ZEPP Zepp, William Clinton b: 7/22/46, Detroit, Mich. BR/TR, 6'2", 185 lbs. Deb: 8/12/69

1969 Min-A	0	0	—	4	0	0	0	0	5¹	6	1	4	2	16.9	6.75	54	.286	.400	0	.000	-0	-2	-2	0	-0.1
1970 •Min-A	9	4	.692	43	20	1	1	2	151	154	9	51	64	12.8	3.22	116	.266	.335	6	.136	-1	8	8	-1	0.6
1971 Det-A	1	1	.500	16	4	0	0	2	31²	41	2	17	15	17.3	5.12	70	.328	.421	0	.000	-0	-6	-5	0	-0.5
Total 3	10	5	.667	63	24	1	1	4	188	201	12	72	81	13.6	3.64	102	.278	.353	6	.122	-2	1	1	-1	0.0

■ GEORGE ZETTLEIN Zettlein, George "Charmer" b: 7/18/1844, Brooklyn, N.Y. d: 5/23/05, Patchogue, N.Y. BR/TR, 5'9", 162 lbs. Deb: 5/08/1871

1871 Chi-n	18	9	.667	28	28	25	0	0	240²	298	6	25	22	12.1	2.73	168	.267	.283	32	.250	-8	40	50		3.0
1872 Tro-n	14	8	.636	25	22	17	2	0	187²	209	2	8		10.4	2.54	146	.250	.257	29	.250	-0	25	24		1.7
Eck-n	1	8	.111	9	9	8	0	0	75¹	105	1	6		13.3	2.99	116	.298	.310	3	.088	-4	6	4		0.0
Yr	15	16	.484	34	31	25	2	0	263	314	3	14		11.2	2.67	136	.265	.273	0	.000	-4	31	28		1.7
1873 Phi-n	36	15	.706	51	51	49	0	0	460	594	3	41		12.4	2.88	127	.285	.298	50	.207	-8	37	39		2.3
1874 Chi-n	27	30	.474	57	57	57	3	0	515²	653	3	46		12.2	3.07	99	.280	.294	47	.193	-11	-4	-1		-0.7
1875 Chi-n	17	14	.548	31	31	29	6	0	282	269	0	6		8.8	1.82	138	.232	.236	29	.223	-3	20	22		1.7
Phi-n	12	8	.600	21	21	20	1	0	180¹	208	0	10		10.9	2.40	105	.263	.272	15	.179	-4	1	2		0.0
Yr	29	22	.569	52	52	49	7	0	462¹	477	0	16		9.6	2.04	123	.245	.251	0	.000	-7	21	24		1.7
1876 Phi-N	4	20	.167	28	25	23	1	2	234	358	2	6	10	14.0	3.88	62	.329	.333	27	.211	-5	-41	-38	-1	-3.5
Total 5 n	125	92	.576	222	219	205	12	0	1941²	2336	15	142	22	11.5	2.68	124	.269	.281	205	.210	-38	124	139		8.0

■ BOB ZICK Zick, Robert George b: 4/26/27, Chicago, Ill. BL/TR, 6', 168 lbs. Deb: 5/02/54

| 1954 Chi-N | 0 | 0 | — | 8 | 0 | 0 | 0 | 0 | 16¹ | 23 | 1 | 7 | 9 | 16.5 | 8.27 | 51 | .343 | .405 | 1 | .250 | 0 | -8 | -7 | -0 | -0.6 |

■ GEORGE ZIEGLER Ziegler, George J. b: 1872, Chicago, Ill. d: 7/22/16, Kankakee, Ill. Deb: 6/19/1890

| 1890 Pit-N | 0 | 1 | .000 | 1 | 1 | 0 | 0 | 0 | 6 | 12 | 0 | 4 | 1 | 18.0 | 10.50 | 31 | .404 | .404 | 0 | .000 | -0 | -5 | -5 | 0 | -0.3 |

■ STEVE ZIEM Ziem, Stephen Graeling b: 10/24/61, Milwaukee, Wis. BR/TR, 6'2", 210 lbs. Deb: 4/30/87

| 1987 Atl-N | 0 | 1 | .000 | 2 | 0 | 0 | 0 | 0 | 2¹ | 4 | 0 | 1 | 0 | 19.3 | 7.71 | 56 | .364 | .417 | 0 | — | 0 | -1 | -1 | 0 | 0.0 |

■ WALTER ZINK Zink, Walter Noble b: 11/21/1899, Pittsfield, Mass. d: 6/12/64, Quincy, Mass. BR/TR, 6', 165 lbs. Deb: 7/06/21

| 1921 NY-N | 0 | 0 | — | 2 | 0 | 0 | 0 | 0 | 4 | 4 | 0 | 3 | 1 | 15.8 | 2.25 | 163 | .235 | .350 | 0 | .000 | -0 | 1 | 1 | -0 | 0.0 |

■ JIMMY ZINN Zinn, James Edward b: 1/21/1895, Benton, Ark. BL/TR, 6'0.5", 195 lbs. Deb: 9/04/19

1919 Phi-A	1	3	.250	5	3	2	0	0	25²	38	1	10	9	17.2	6.31	54	.365	.426	4	.308	2	-9	-8	0	-0.7
1920 Pit-N	1	1	.500	6	3	2	0	0	31	32	2	5	18	11.0	3.48	92	.260	.295	3	.200	0	-1	-1	-0	0.0
1921 Pit-N	7	6	.538	32	9	5	1	4	127¹	159	3	30	49	13.5	3.68	104	.318	.359	11	.224	0	2	2	-2	0.0
1922 Pit-N	0	0	—	5	0	0	0	1	9²	11	1	2	3	12.1	1.86	219	.297	.333	0	.000	-0	2	2	0	0.2
1929 Cle-A	4	6	.400	18	11	6	1	2	105¹	150	8	33	29	15.9	5.04	88	.340	.390	16	.381	7	-9	-7	-0	0.0
Total 5	13	16	.448	66	26	15	2	7	299	390	15	80	108	14.4	4.30	92	.324	.369	34	.283	9	-15	-12	-2	-0.5

■ BILL ZINSER Zinser, William Francis b: 1/6/18, Astoria, N.Y. BR/TR, 6'1", 185 lbs. Deb: 8/19/44

| 1944 Was-A | 0 | 0 | — | 2 | 0 | 0 | 0 | 0 | 0² | 1 | 0 | 5 | 1 | 81.0 | 27.00 | 12 | .333 | .750 | 0 | — | 0 | -2 | -2 | 0 | -0.1 |

■ ED ZMICH Zmich, Edward Albert b: 10/1/1884, Cleveland, Ohio d: 8/20/50, Cleveland, Ohio BL/TL, 6', 180 lbs. Deb: 7/23/10

1910 StL-N	0	5	.000	9	6	2	0	0	36	38	0	29	19	17.5	6.25	48	.304	.446	1	.077	-1	-13	-13	1	-1.2
1911 StL-N	1	0	1.000	4	0	0	0	0	12²	8	0	8	4	12.1	2.13	158	.182	.321	0	.000	-1	2	2	-0	0.0
Total 2	1	5	.167	13	6	2	0	0	48²	46	0	37	23	16.1	5.18	60	.272	.414	1	.059	-2	-11	-11	0	-1.2

■ SAM ZOLDAK Zoldak, Samuel Walter "Sad Sam" b: 12/8/18, Brooklyn, N.Y. d: 8/25/66, New Hyde Park, N.Y BL/TL, 5'11.5", 185 lbs. Deb: 5/13/44

1944 StL-A	0	0	—	18	0	0	0	0	38²	49	1	19	15	15.8	3.72	97	.310	.384	2	.333	0	-1	-1	0	0.0
1945 StL-A	3	2	.600	26	1	1	0	0	69²	74	3	18	19	11.9	3.36	105	.267	.312	1	.050	-3	0	1	-1	-0.1
1946 StL-A	9	11	.450	35	21	9	2	2	170¹	166	11	57	51	11.8	3.43	109	.256	.317	9	.173	-0	1	6	1	0.7
1947 StL-A	9	10	.474	35	19	6	1	1	171	162	7	76	36	12.5	3.47	112	.254	.334	10	.172	-1	4	8	3	1.1
1948 StL-A	2	4	.333	11	9	0	0	0	54	64	4	19	13	14.0	4.67	98	.296	.356	6	.273	0	-2	-1	0	0.1
Cle-A	9	6	.600	23	12	4	1	0	105²	104	6	24	17	10.9	2.81	144	.261	.303	5	.139	-2	17	15	2	1.5
Yr	11	10	.524	34	21	4	1	0	159²	168	10	43	30	11.9	3.44	123	.273	.321	1	.017	-1	15	14	2	1.6

YEAR TM/L	W	L	PCT	G	GS	CG	SH	SV	IP	H	HR	BB	SO	RAT	ERA	ERA+	OAV	OOB	BH	AVG	PB	PR	/A	PD	TPI
1949 Cle-A	1	2	.333	27	0	0	0	0	53	60	4	18	11	13.2	4.25	94	.291	.348	3	.375	1	-0	-1	3	0.2
1950 Cle-A	4	2	.667	33	3	0	0	4	63²	64	6	21	15	12.2	3.96	109	.259	.320	3	.188	0	4	3	0	0.3
1951 Phi-A	6	10	.375	26	18	8	1	0	128	127	9	24	18	10.6	3.16	135	.257	.292	7	.156	-3	14	16	-1	1.2
1952 Phi-A	0	6	.000	16	10	2	0	1	75¹	86	3	25	12	13.3	4.06	97	.290	.345	4	.174	-1	-3	-1	2	0.1
Total 9	43	53	.448	250	93	30	5	8	929¹	956	54	301	207	12.2	3.54	112	.267	.325	50	.175	-8	34	45	9	5.1

■ BILL ZUBER

Zuber, William Henry "Goober" b: 3/26/13, Middle Amana, Iowa d: 11/2/82, Cedar Rapids, Iowa BR/TR, 6'2", 195 lbs. Deb: 9/16/36

YEAR TM/L	W	L	PCT	G	GS	CG	SH	SV	IP	H	HR	BB	SO	RAT	ERA	ERA+	OAV	OOB	BH	AVG	PB	PR	/A	PD	TPI
1936 Cle-A	1	1	.500	2	2	1	0	0	13²	14	0	15	5	19.1	6.59	76	.269	.433	1	.200	-0	-2	-2	0	-0.1
1938 Cle-A	0	3	.000	15	0	0	0	1	28²	33	0	20	14	16.6	5.02	92	.295	.402	0	.000	-1	-1	-1	-0	-0.1
1939 Cle-A	2	0	1.000	16	1	0	0	0	31²	41	2	19	16	17.3	5.97	74	.323	.415	1	.200	0	-5	-6	1	-0.3
1940 Cle-A	1	1	.500	17	0	0	0	0	24	25	3	14	12	14.6	5.63	75	.260	.355	1	.333	0	-3	-4	-0	-0.3
1941 Was-A	6	4	.600	36	7	1	0	2	96¹	110	5	61	51	16.2	5.42	75	.291	.392	0	.000	-3	-14	-15	-2	-1.7
1942 Was-A	9	9	.500	37	7	3	1	1	126²	115	5	82	64	14.0	3.84	95	.243	.355	6	.154	0	-3	-3	-3	-0.4
1943 NY-A	8	4	.667	20	13	7	0	1	118	100	3	74	57	13.3	3.89	83	.234	.347	7	.184	2	-8	-9	-2	-0.8
1944 NY-A	5	7	.417	22	13	2	1	0	107	101	5	54	59	13.1	4.21	83	.255	.346	4	.129	-2	-9	-9	-1	-1.1
1945 NY-A	5	11	.313	21	14	7	0	1	127	121	2	56	50	12.5	3.19	109	.259	.338	7	.167	-1	2	4	-1	0.1
1946 NY-A	0	1	.000	3	0	0	0	0	5²	10	2	3	3	20.6	12.71	27	.385	.448	0	.000	-0	-6	-6	-0	-0.5
*Bos-A	5	1	.833	15	7	2	1	0	56²	37	4	39	29	12.1	2.54	144	.187	.321	2	.111	-1	6	7	0	0.7
Yr	5	2	.714	18	7	2	1	0	62¹	47	6	42	32	12.9	3.47	105	.210	.335	1	.050	-1	0	1	0	0.2
1947 Bos-A	1	0	1.000	20	1	0	0	0	50²	60	4	31	23	16.2	5.33	73	.311	.406	2	.154	-0	-9	-8	-0	-0.8
Total 11	43	42	.506	224	65	23	3	6	786	767	35	468	383	14.2	4.28	87	.260	.362	31	.135	-6	-51	-50	-8	-5.3

■ GEORGE ZUVERINK

Zuverink, George b: 8/20/24, Holland, Mich. BR/TR, 6'4", 195 lbs. Deb: 4/21/51

YEAR TM/L	W	L	PCT	G	GS	CG	SH	SV	IP	H	HR	BB	SO	RAT	ERA	ERA+	OAV	OOB	BH	AVG	PB	PR	/A	PD	TPI
1951 Cle-A	0	0	—	16	0	0	0	0	25¹	24	2	13	14	13.5	5.33	71	.253	.349	0	—	0	-3	-4	0	-0.3
1952 Cle-A	0	0	—	1	0	0	0	0	1¹	1	0	0	1	6.8	0.00	—	.200	.200	0	—	0	1	0	0	0.1
1954 Cin-N	0	0	—	2	0	0	0	0	6	10	1	1	2	16.5	9.00	47	.385	.407	1	.500	0	-3	-3	-0	-0.2
Det-A	9	13	.409	35	25	9	2	4	203	201	22	62	70	12.0	3.59	103	.257	.318	8	.125	-3	3	2	3	0.2
1955 Det-A	0	5	.000	14	1	0	0	0	28¹	38	6	14	13	16.8	6.99	55	.309	.384	0	.000	-1	-10	-10	0	-0.9
Bal-A	4	3	.571	28	5	0	0	4	86¹	80	5	17	31	10.5	2.19	174	.264	.312	5	.217	1	17	16	1	1.8
Yr	4	8	.333	42	6	0	0	4	114²	118	11	31	44	12.0	3.38	113	.276	.331	5	.185	0	7	6	1	0.9
1956 Bal-A	7	6	.538	62	0	0	0	16	97¹	112	6	34	33	13.8	4.16	94	.294	.356	2	.118	-1	-0	-3	1	-0.2
1957 Bal-A	10	6	.625	56	0	0	0	9	112²	105	9	39	36	11.8	2.48	145	.257	.327	3	.130	-0	16	14	1	1.6
1958 Bal-A	2	2	.500	45	0	0	0	7	69	74	4	17	22	12.7	3.39	106	.286	.344	2	.222	1	3	2	2	0.4
1959 Bal-A	0	1	.000	6	0	0	0	0	13	15	1	6	1	14.5	4.15	91	.306	.382	0	—	1	-0	-1	0	0.0
Total 8	32	36	.471	265	31	9	2	40	642¹	660	56	203	223	12.5	3.54	105	.271	.334	21	.148	-2	23	13	9	2.5

The Fielding Register

The Fielding Register

The Fielding Register consists of the full fielding statistics, broken down by position, of every man who played at least 100 games at any single position since 1871, excepting those players who were primarily pitchers.

The players are listed alphabetically by surname and, when more than one player bears the name, alphabetically by *given* name—not by "use name," by which we mean the name that may have been applied to him during his playing career.

Each page of the Fielding Register is topped at the corner by a finding aid: the surname of, first, the player whose entry heads up the page and, second, the player whose entry concludes it. Boldface numerals indicate a league-leading total. Condensed type appears occasionally throughout this section; it has no special significance but is designed simply to accommodate unusually wide figures.

The record for each man who played in more than one season is given in a line for each season at each position, plus a career total line for that position. No attempt is made to combine totals from different positions, for such totals would be meaningless. If a man played for more than one team in a given year, his totals for each team are stated on separate lines. And if the teams for which he played in his "traded year" are in the same league, then his full record is stated in both separate and combined fashion for that position. (In the odd case of a man playing for three or more clubs in one year, with some of these clubs in the same league, the combined total line will reflect only his play in that league.) A man who played in only one year will have no additional career total line, since it would be identical to his seasonal listing.

Fielding records for the National Association are not yet available; SABR research in this area is ongoing. Gaps remain elsewhere in the official record of baseball for hitting, pitching, and baserunning data, but fielding data has always been available. The problem with this data, however, is that it is often wrong. Modern research has corrected the errors and reconstructed from newspaper accounts the fielding stats of nonregular players that might not have been recorded in year-end summaries.

As indicated in the Introduction to Part Two and the chapter on sabermetrics that follow, the editors are skeptical about the usefulness of the raw fielding data offered here. As a rule, the significant stat for outfielders is putouts and for infielders (even first basemen) assists. Outfield assists are of enormous defensive value, but they are four times less prevalent today than at the dawn of big-league play, when the less resilient ball of the turn of the century permitted outfielders to play shallow and thus pile up assists. The top fifteen outfielders in lifetime assists, excepting Max Carey and Sam Rice, played all or most of their games before 1920; they did not all have better arms than Roberto Clemente. And again because of the dead ball and styles of play (little free swinging and consequently few strikeouts), infield assist totals of the early years are also astronomical. Barehand play and later the use of small, unconstructed gloves made error totals higher years ago compared with today, at all positions. Chances accepted (putouts plus assists, usually measured on a per-game basis) are more meaningful than the fielding percentage, with its well-known reward for immobility.

So what do the traditional fielding stats mean? Without historical context and manipulation, not a lot. But that is not to say fielding itself is unimportant. A run saved in the field is the same as a run saved from the mound, or one gained at the bat or on the basepaths. That is why the editors advocate the use of Linear Weights Fielding Runs, modified substantially for this second edition of *Total Baseball*. Its various formulas normalize to the league average the number of chances accepted at each position (isolating left field, center field, and right field for more accurate comparisons); are calculated on a per-inning rather than a per-game basis; encompass within the formulas double plays and errors as well as putouts and assists; and for catchers Fielding Runs now give credit for handling a pitching staff. For more on this, see the Glossary.

For a key to the team and league abbreviations used in the Fielding Register, flip to the last page of this volume. The stat abbreviations used at the top of the columns are:

YEAR   Year of play (when a space in the column is blank, the man has played for two or more clubs in the last year stated in the column; if those clubs were in the same league, then the player will also have a combined total line for the position and year under review, beginning with the abbreviation "Yr" placed in the TM/L column)

Yr   Year's totals for play with two or more clubs in same league (see comments for YEAR)

TM/L   Team and League (see comments for YEAR)

PCT   Fielding Percentage (putouts plus assists divided by putouts plus assists plus errors)

G   Games

PO   Putouts

A   Assists

E   Errors

DP   Double Plays

FR   Fielding Runs (the Linear Weights measure of runs saved *beyond* what a league-average player at that position might have saved, defined as zero; this stat is calculated to take into account the particular demands of the different positions; see Glossary for formulas)

Hank Aaron OF

YEAR	TM/L	PCT	G	PO	A	E	DP	FR
1954	Mil-N	.970	116	223	5	7	0	-3
1955	Mil-N	.967	126	254	9	9	2	0
1956	Mil-N	.962	152	316	17	13	4	8
1957	Mil-N	.983	150	346	9	6	0	9
1958	Mil-N	.984	153	305	12	5	0	4
1959	Mil-N	.982	152	261	12	5	3	-2
1960	Mil-N	.982	153	320	13	6	6	8
1961	Mil-N	.982	154	377	13	7	3	0
1962	Mil-N	.980	153	340	11	7	1	-5
1963	Mil-N	.979	161	267	10	6	1	-4
1964	Mil-N	.983	139	270	13	5	5	11
1965	Mil-N	.987	148	298	9	4	2	9
1966	Atl-N	.988	158	315	12	4	5	11
1967	Atl-N	.979	152	321	12	7	3	12
1968	Atl-N	.991	151	330	13	3	2	14
1969	Atl-N	.982	144	267	11	5	3	5
1970	Atl-N	.977	125	246	6	6	1	3
1971	Atl-N	.981	60	104	2	2	0	-4
1972	Atl-N	.914	15	28	4	3	0	1
1973	Atl-N	.977	105	206	5	5	0	-2
1974	Atl-N	.986	89	142	3	2	0	-10
1975	Mil-A	1.000	3	2	0	0	0	0
1976	Mil-A	1.000	1	1	0	0	0	0
Total	23	.980	2760	5539	201	117	41	65

1B

YEAR	TM/L	PCT	G	PO	A	E	DP	FR
1962	Mil-N	1.000	1	1	0	0	0	0
1968	Atl-N	.979	14	88	7	2	8	-1
1969	Atl-N	1.000	4	32	2	0	3	0
1970	Atl-N	.987	11	73	4	1	6	-1
1971	Atl-N	.996	71	629	38	3	56	-5
1972	Atl-N	.987	109	968	66	14	79	-2
Total	6	.990	210	1791	117	0	152	-9

2B

YEAR	TM/L	PCT	G	PO	A	E	DP	FR
1955	Mil-N	.966	27	86	84	6	23	6
1960	Mil-N	1.000	2	1	0	0	0	0
1964	Mil-N	.967	11	14	15	1	2	-3
1966	Atl-N	—	2	0	0	0	0	0
1967	Atl-N	1.000	1	1	0	0	0	0
Total	5	.966	43	102	99	7	25	3

3B

YEAR	TM/L	PCT	G	PO	A	E	DP	FR
1959	Mil-N	1.000	5	2	10	0	0	0
1961	Mil-N	1.000	2	2	2	0	0	0
Total	2	1.000	7	4	12	0	0	0

Tommie Aaron 1B

YEAR	TM/L	PCT	G	PO	A	E	DP	FR
1962	Mil-N	.989	110	507	45	6	55	3
1963	Mil-N	1.000	45	197	9	0	26	0
1965	Mil-N	.961	6	45	4	2	3	0
1968	Atl-N	1.000	28	209	17	0	12	-1
1969	Atl-N	1.000	16	48	2	0	5	0
1970	Atl-N	.955	16	40	2	2	1	-1
1971	Atl-N	.974	11	70	6	2	16	0
Total	7	.990	232	1116	85	2	118	1

OF

YEAR	TM/L	PCT	G	PO	A	E	DP	FR
1962	Mil-N	.943	42	65	1	4	0	-2
1963	Mil-N	.917	14	11	0	1	0	-4
1968	Atl-N	.942	62	78	3	5	1	-3
1969	Atl-N	1.000	8	17	0	0	0	1
1970	Atl-N	1.000	12	13	0	0	0	0
Total	5	.949	138	184	4	0	1	-8

3B

YEAR	TM/L	PCT	G	PO	A	E	DP	FR
1962	Mil-N	1.000	1	0	1	0	1	0
1963	Mil-N	1.000	1	1	0	0	0	-1
1968	Atl-N	—	1	0	0	0	0	0
1971	Atl-N	1.000	7	4	13	0	2	2
Total	4	1.000	10	5	15	0	3	1

2B

YEAR	TM/L	PCT	G	PO	A	E	DP	FR
1962	Mil-N	1.000	1	0	1	0	0	0
1963	Mil-N	1.000	6	12	8	0	2	-4
Total	2	1.000	7	12	9	0	2	-4

Ed Abbaticchio 2B

YEAR	TM/L	PCT	G	PO	A	E	DP	FR
1897	Phi-N	.875	3	0	7	1	0	-2
1898	Phi-N	.882	4	9	6	2	0	-2
1903	Bos-N	.934	116	316	325	45	35	7
1907	Pit-N	.951	147	320	380	36	37	-23
1908	Pit-N	.969	144	268	423	22	42	-12
1909	Pit-N	.750	4	11	7	6	0	-3
1910	Bos-N	1.000	1	4	1	0	0	0
Total	7	.949	419	928	1149	112	114	-35

SS

YEAR	TM/L	PCT	G	PO	A	E	DP	FR
1903	Bos-N	.870	17	45	42	13	8	-4
1904	Bos-N	.915	154	367	473	78	47	2
1905	Bos-N	.919	152	386	468	75	53	-12
1909	Pit-N	.966	18	45	67	4	6	5
1910	Pit-N	.500	1	0	1	1	0	0
	Bos-N	.910	46	73	149	22	19	-3
	Yr	.907	47	73	150	23	19	-3
Total	5	.916	388	916	1200	193	133	-12

3B

YEAR	TM/L	PCT	G	PO	A	E	DP	FR
1898	Phi-N	.818	20	26	19	10	0	-11

OF

YEAR	TM/L	PCT	G	PO	A	E	DP	FR
1898	Phi-N	—	1	0	0	0	0	0
1905	Bos-N	1.000	1	1	0	0	0	0
1909	Pit-N	1.000	1	1	0	0	0	0
Total	3	1.000	3	2	0	0	0	0

Charlie Abbey OF

YEAR	TM/L	PCT	G	PO	A	E	DP	FR
1893	Was-N	.937	31	68	6	5	1	2
1894	Was-N	.909	129	344	26	37	6	13
1895	Was-N	.903	132	275	32	33	7	10
1896	Was-N	.879	78	104	12	16	3	-6
1897	Was-N	.946	80	126	14	8	1	2
Total	5	.910	450	917	90	9	18	21

Fred Abbott C

YEAR	TM/L	PCT	G	PO	A	E	DP	FR
1903	Cle-A	.958	71	337	97	19	9	9
1904	Cle-A	.953	33	144	37	9	2	-3
1905	Phi-N	.954	34	145	41	9	5	0
Total	3	.956	138	626	175	7	16	6

1B

YEAR	TM/L	PCT	G	PO	A	E	DP	FR
1903	Cle-A	1.000	3	20	4	0	1	1
1904	Cle-A	.987	7	72	4	1	3	0
1905	Phi-N	.963	5	50	2	2	6	-1
Total	3	.981	15	142	10	3	10	0

Shawn Abner OF

YEAR	TM/L	PCT	G	PO	A	E	DP	FR
1987	SD-N	.926	14	23	2	2	1	1
1988	SD-N	.982	35	55	1	1	1	1
1989	SD-N	1.000	51	67	0	0	0	2
1990	SD-N	.991	62	108	1	1	0	2
Total	4	.985	162	253	4	4	2	6

Cal Abrams OF

YEAR	TM/L	PCT	G	PO	A	E	DP	FR
1949	Bro-N	.833	7	9	1	2	0	-1
1950	Bro-N	1.000	15	17	0	0	0	0
1951	Bro-N	.944	34	64	3	4	1	-3
1952	Bro-N	—	1	0	0	0	0	0
	Cin-N	1.000	46	87	1	0	1	0
	Yr	1.000	47	87	1	0	1	0
1953	Pit-N	.973	112	205	13	6	3	1
1954	Pit-N	1.000	13	23	2	0	0	0
	Bal-A	.977	115	248	6	6	1	1
1955	Bal-A	.985	96	191	7	3	1	0
1956	Chi-A	1.000	2	2	0	0	0	0
Total	8	.977	441	846	33	1	7	-2

1B

YEAR	TM/L	PCT	G	PO	A	E	DP	FR
1955	Bal-A	1.000	4	4	0	0	0	0

Bill Abstein 1B

YEAR	TM/L	PCT	G	PO	A	E	DP	FR
1909	Pit-N	.982	135	1412	65	27	70	-5
1910	StL-N	.963	23	268	20	11	13	2
Total	2	.979	158	1680	85	8	83	-3

2B

YEAR	TM/L	PCT	G	PO	A	E	DP	FR
1906	Pit-N	.769	3	3	7	3	0	-2

OF

YEAR	TM/L	PCT	G	PO	A	E	DP	FR
1906	Pit-N	1.000	2	2	1	0	0	0

Merito Acosta OF

YEAR	TM/L	PCT	G	PO	A	E	DP	FR
1913	Was-A	.714	9	5	0	2	0	-3
1914	Was-A	.857	25	24	6	5	1	-2
1915	Was-A	.963	53	75	4	3	2	-4
1916	Was-A	1.000	4	10	1	0	0	1
1918	Phi-A	.944	45	77	7	5	2	-3
Total	5	.933	136	191	18	5	5	-11

Jerry Adair 2B

YEAR	TM/L	PCT	G	PO	A	E	DP	FR
1958	Bal-A	.833	1	1	4	1	2	1
1959	Bal-A	.932	11	24	17	3	4	-3
1960	Bal-A	1.000	3	3	4	0	2	0
1961	Bal-A	.987	107	233	237	6	57	-1
1962	Bal-A	.975	34	79	77	4	17	-3
1963	Bal-A	.985	103	242	268	8	67	0
1964	Bal-A	.994	153	395	422	5	107	9
1965	Bal-A	.986	157	395	446	12	99	12
1966	Bal-A	.969	13	30	33	2	7	-1
	Chi-A	.984	50	89	92	3	19	-2
	Yr	.980	63	119	125	5	26	-3
1967	Chi-A	.985	27	70	61	2	21	0
	Bos-A	.961	23	33	41	3	10	-3
	Yr	.976	50	103	102	5	31	-3
1968	Bos-A	.978	12	19	25	1	6	1
1969	KC-A	.984	109	223	261	8	41	-21
1970	KC-A	1.000	7	24	20	0	6	2
Total	13	.985	810	1860	2008	8	465	-9

SS

YEAR	TM/L	PCT	G	PO	A	E	DP	FR
1958	Bal-A	.967	10	10	19	1	3	1
1959	Bal-A	.800	1	2	2	1	1	-1
1961	Bal-A	.946	27	26	61	5	5	0
1962	Bal-A	.969	113	216	285	16	72	-7
1966	Chi-A	.975	75	109	236	9	35	0
1967	Bos-A	1.000	30	38	68	0	12	-4
1968	Bos-A	.976	46	62	104	4	15	-6
1969	KC-A	.970	8	14	18	1	1	-1
Total	8	.972	310	477	793	7	144	-18

3B

YEAR	TM/L	PCT	G	PO	A	E	DP	FR
1961	Bal-A	1.000	2	0	1	0	0	0
1962	Bal-A	—	1	0	0	0	0	0
1967	Bos-A	.952	35	34	66	5	8	-2
1968	Bos-A	.813	7	4	9	3	1	-1
1969	KC-A	—	1	0	0	0	0	0
Total	5	.934	46	38	76	8	9	-3

1B

YEAR	TM/L	PCT	G	PO	A	E	DP	FR
1968	Bos-A	1.000	1	5	1	0	0	0

Sparky Adams 2B

YEAR	TM/L	PCT	G	PO	A	E	DP	FR
1922	Chi-N	.914	11	18	35	5	5	-4
1924	Chi-N	.976	19	55	66	3	15	2
1925	Chi-N	.983	144	354	551	16	90	25
1926	Chi-N	.965	136	324	485	29	93	18
1927	Chi-N	.994	60	149	194	2	34	-5
1928	Pit-N	.971	107	265	343	18	54	-12
1929	Pit-N	.942	20	33	48	5	5	-1
1930	StL-N	.974	25	62	85	4	25	3
1934	Cin-N	.979	29	61	81	3	11	-1
Total	9	.974	551	1321	1888	5	332	25

3B

YEAR	TM/L	PCT	G	PO	A	E	DP	FR
1926	Chi-N	.959	19	12	35	2	4	-1
1927	Chi-N	.962	53	45	107	6	12	1
1929	Pit-N	.939	15	7	24	2	1	-2
1930	StL-N	.966	104	66	159	8	18	-13
1931	StL-N	.963	138	118	223	13	29	-8
1932	StL-N	.931	30	25	42	5	11	-4
1933	StL-N	.750	3	0	6	2	1	0
	Cin-N	.963	132	121	272	15	15	-2
	Yr	.959	135	121	278	17	16	-2
1934	Cin-N	.955	38	31	75	5	10	-1
Total	8	.959	532	425	943	8	101	-30

SS

YEAR	TM/L	PCT	G	PO	A	E	DP	FR
1923	Chi-N	.935	79	153	248	28	44	-7
1924	Chi-N	.941	88	169	277	28	62	-10
1925	Chi-N	1.000	5	13	22	0	5	3
1926	Chi-N	1.000	2	2	3	0	0	0
1927	Chi-N	.957	40	82	142	10	23	5
1928	Pit-N	.993	27	52	97	1	14	2
1929	Pit-N	.901	30	33	58	10	8	-12
1930	StL-N	.889	7	12	20	4	3	-3
1931	StL-N	.833	6	9	16	5	1	-3
1933	StL-N	.955	5	5	16	1	2	-2
	Cin-N	1.000	8	6	17	0	1	-1
	Yr	.978	13	11	33	1	3	-3
Total	10	.943	297	536	916	7	163	-30

OF

YEAR	TM/L	PCT	G	PO	A	E	DP	FR
1923	Chi-N	1.000	1	3	1	0	1	1
1928	Pit-N	—	1	0	0	0	0	0
1929	Pit-N	1.000	2	2	0	0	0	0
Total	3	1.000	4	5	1	0	1	1

Buster Adams OF

YEAR	TM/L	PCT	G	PO	A	E	DP	FR
1943	StL-N	1.000	6	11	0	0	0	0
	Phi-N	.984	107	298	6	5	1	-1
	Yr	.984	113	309	6	5	1	-1
1944	Phi-N	.979	151	449	14	10	1	8
1945	Phi-N	1.000	14	26	0	0	0	-2
	StL-N	.978	140	382	9	9	3	-5
	Yr	.979	154	408	9	9	3	-7
1946	StL-N	.990	58	95	1	1	1	-2
1947	Phi-N	.954	51	78	5	4	2	-4
Total	5	.979	527	1339	35	9	8	-6

Glenn Adams OF

YEAR	TM/L	PCT	G	PO	A	E	DP	FR
1975	SF-N	.941	25	31	1	2	0	-1
1976	SF-N	1.000	6	3	0	0	0	-1
1977	Min-A	.969	44	60	3	2	1	-1
1978	Min-A	1.000	5	6	0	0	0	0
1979	Min-A	.958	53	66	2	3	0	-5
1980	Min-A	.947	12	18	0	1	0	-1
Total	6	.959	145	183	6	8	1	-9

Bert Adams C

YEAR	TM/L	PCT	G	PO	A	E	DP	FR
1910	Cle-A	.964	5	12	15	1	1	3
1911	Cle-A	.900	2	6	3	1	0	-1
1912	Cle-A	.942	20	85	28	7	3	2
1915	Phi-N	.974	23	32	6	1	0	-4
1916	Phi-N	.929	11	20	6	2	1	1
1917	Phi-N	.994	38	130	40	1	4	1
1918	Phi-N	.976	76	261	69	8	8	-1
1919	Phi-N	.966	73	249	90	12	15	-2
Total	8	.970	248	795	257	3	32	-1

1B

YEAR	TM/L	PCT	G	PO	A	E	DP	FR
1915	Phi-N	.667	1	2	0	1	0	0
1917	Phi-N	1.000	1	5	0	0	0	0
1919	Phi-N	—	1	0	0	0	0	0
Total	3	.875	3	7	0	1	0	0

Bobby Adams 3B

YEAR	TM/L	PCT	G	PO	A	E	DP	FR
1946	Cin-N	1.000	1	0	1	0	0	0
1948	Cin-N	1.000	7	7	12	0	1	1
1949	Cin-N	.947	14	14	22	2	0	-1
1950	Cin-N	.923	42	46	62	9	4	-6
1951	Cin-N	.956	60	72	122	9	8	-3
1952	Cin-N	.962	154	176	328	20	28	9
1953	Cin-N	.951	150	159	324	25	39	8
1954	Cin-N	.951	93	127	186	16	24	2
1955	Cin-N	.969	42	35	88	4	11	3
	Chi-A	.933	9	5	9	1	0	3
1956	Bal-A	.984	24	23	40	1	5	0
1957	Chi-N	.949	47	43	68	6	5	-8
1958	Chi-N	1.000	9	4	6	0	0	0
Total	12	.955	652	711	1268	3	125	8

2B

YEAR	TM/L	PCT	G	PO	A	E	DP	FR
1946	Cin-N	.967	74	190	251	15	67	25
1947	Cin-N	.967	69	172	177	12	46	14
1948	Cin-N	.965	64	160	143	11	33	-13
1949	Cin-N	.984	63	162	138	5	29	-8
1950	Cin-N	.981	53	124	138	5	30	-3
1951	Cin-N	.958	42	112	93	9	25	4
1954	Cin-N	1.000	2	7	3	0	1	-1
1955	Cin-N	1.000	5	4	4	0	1	0
	Chi-A	1.000	1	3	4	0	1	2
1956	Bal-A	.941	18	39	25	4	7	-6
1957	Chi-N	1.000	1	1	0	0	0	0
1958	Chi-N	.966	7	5	13	1	5	-2
Total	11	.970	399	989	989	2	245	2

1B

YEAR	TM/L	PCT	G	PO	A	E	DP	FR
1958	Chi-N	.961	11	44	5	2	1	0
1959	Chi-N	.667	1	2	0	1	0	0
Total	2	.944	12	46	5	3	1	0

OF

YEAR	TM/L	PCT	G	PO	A	E	DP	FR
1946	Cin-N	1.000	2	2	0	0	0	0
1951	Cin-N	—	1	0	0	0	0	0
Total	2	1.000	3	2	0	0	0	0

Joe Adcock 1B

YEAR	TM/L	PCT	G	PO	A	E	DP	FR
1950	Cin-N	.989	24	169	11	2	13	-1
1952	Cin-N	1.000	17	117	3	0	7	0
1953	Mil-N	.991	157	1389	96	13	146	-1
1954	Mil-N	.995	133	1229	67	6	125	-11
1955	Mil-N	.990	78	725	44	8	68	-5
1956	Mil-N	.995	129	1086	75	6	109	-6
1957	Mil-N	.996	56	477	30	2	60	-3
1958	Mil-N	.989	71	525	36	6	55	-2
1959	Mil-N	.989	89	761	80	2	67	10
1960	Mil-N	.993	136	1229	104	9	105	3
1961	Mil-N	.993	148	1471	102	11	133	-5
1962	Mil-N	.997	112	907	57	3	72	-4
1963	Cle-A	.995	78	608	36	3	46	-4
1964	LA-A	.993	105	959	54	7	94	-4

YEAR	TM/L	PCT	G	PO	A	E	DP	FR
1965	Cal-A	.996	97	789	45	3	68	-3
1966	Cal-A	.997	71	565	39	2	60	0
Total	16	.994	1501	13006	879	3	1228	-41

OF

YEAR	TM/L	PCT	G	PO	A	E	DP	FR
1950	Cin-N	.968	75	177	6	6	3	4
1951	Cin-N	.983	107	221	8	4	2	0
1952	Cin-N	.985	85	189	5	3	1	3
1958	Mil-N	.976	22	39	1	1	0	-2
1959	Mil-N	.904	21	46	1	5	0	-1
Total	5	.973	310	672	21	9	6	4

■ Bob Addis OF

YEAR	TM/L	PCT	G	PO	A	E	DP	FR
1950	Bos-N	1.000	7	7	0	0	0	-1
1951	Bos-N	.982	46	107	1	2	1	0
1952	Chi-N	.988	79	160	8	2	2	2
1953	Chi-N	1.000	3	7	1	0	1	2
Total	4	.986	135	281	10	4	4	3

■ Tommie Agee OF

YEAR	TM/L	PCT	G	PO	A	E	DP	FR
1962	Cle-A	1.000	3	4	0	0	0	-1
1963	Cle-A	1.000	13	10	2	0	1	1
1964	Cle-A	1.000	12	5	0	0	0	0
1965	Chi-A	1.000	9	13	0	0	0	0
1966	Chi-A	.982	159	376	12	7	7	9
1967	Chi-A	.969	152	337	6	11	2	-4
1968	NY-N	.978	127	216	6	5	2	-12
1969	NY-N	.986	146	334	7	5	0	2
1970	NY-N	.967	150	374	4	13	3	9
1971	NY-N	.978	107	265	7	6	0	7
1972	NY-N	.962	109	273	6	11	1	3
1973	Hou-N	.983	67	114	2	2	2	2
	StL-N	.981	19	50	1	1	0	4
	Yr	.982	86	164	3	3	2	6
Total	12	.975	1073	2371	53	1	18	20

■ Harry Agganis 1B

YEAR	TM/L	PCT	G	PO	A	E	DP	FR
1954	Bos-A	.990	119	1064	89	12	101	7
1955	Bos-A	.987	20	208	14	3	15	0
Total	2	.989	139	1272	103	5	116	7

■ Joe Agler 1B

YEAR	TM/L	PCT	G	PO	A	E	DP	FR
1912	Was-A	—	1	0	0	0	0	0
1914	Buf-F	.985	76	734	49	12	44	4
1915	Buf-F	1.000	1	4	0	0	0	0
	Bal-F	.981	58	573	44	12	42	5
	Yr	.981	59	577	44	12	42	5
Total	3	.983	136	1311	93	4	86	9

OF

YEAR	TM/L	PCT	G	PO	A	E	DP	FR
1914	Buf-F	.963	54	97	8	4	3	1
1915	Buf-F	.973	20	36	0	1	0	-2
	Bal-F	1.000	4	5	0	0	0	-1
	Yr	.976	24	41	0	1	0	-3
Total	2	.967	78	138	8	5	3	-2

2B

YEAR	TM/L	PCT	G	PO	A	E	DP	FR
1915	Bal-F	.900	3	8	10	2	2	1

■ Sam Agnew C

YEAR	TM/L	PCT	G	PO	A	E	DP	FR
1913	StL-A	.952	103	383	170	28	17	2
1914	StL-A	.961	115	451	163	25	10	3
1915	StL-A	.934	102	398	153	39	16	6
1916	Bos-A	.952	38	110	47	8	4	8
1917	Bos-A	.965	85	297	88	14	5	-11
1918	Bos-A	.965	72	254	104	13	10	11
1919	Was-A	.974	36	141	48	5	5	8
Total	7	.955	551	2034	773	132	67	27

■ Luis Aguayo SS

YEAR	TM/L	PCT	G	PO	A	E	DP	FR
1980	Phi-N	1.000	5	3	9	0	1	1
1981	Phi-N	.976	21	12	28	1	6	-3
1982	Phi-N	.867	15	4	9	2	2	0
1983	Phi-N	1.000	2	3	0	0	0	-2
1984	Phi-N	.917	10	3	8	1	1	0
1985	Phi-N	.957	60	61	117	8	21	-2
1986	Phi-N	.967	20	25	33	2	9	-5
1987	Phi-N	.971	78	81	154	7	29	-11
1988	Phi-N	.967	27	32	55	3	12	2
	NY-A	.889	6	2	6	1	1	-1
1989	Cle-A	.912	15	8	23	3	3	1
Total	10	.960	259	234	442	8	85	-20

2B

YEAR	TM/L	PCT	G	PO	A	E	DP	FR
1980	Phi-N	.962	14	41	35	3	9	0
1981	Phi-N	.938	21	27	33	4	8	-2
1982	Phi-N	.966	21	21	36	2	3	3
1984	Phi-N	1.000	12	14	28	0	5	5
1985	Phi-N	.981	17	27	25	-1	5	3
1986	Phi-N	.967	31	32	57	3	10	-2
1987	Phi-N	1.000	6	4	16	0	1	1
1988	Phi-N	1.000	2	6	7	0	3	1
	NY-A	.946	13	14	21	2	3	-1
1989	Cle-A	1.000	10	17	28	0	7	3
Total	9	.970	147	203	286	5	54	11

3B

YEAR	TM/L	PCT	G	PO	A	E	DP	FR
1981	Phi-N	1.000	3	0	2	0	1	0
1982	Phi-N	1.000	5	2	4	0	0	1
1984	Phi-N	.909	14	1	19	2	1	2
1985	Phi-N	1.000	7	4	16	0	1	2
1986	Phi-N	—	1	0	0	0	0	0
1987	Phi-N	1.000	2	1	2	0	0	0
1988	Phi-N	.846	13	9	13	4	1	-1
	NY-A	.961	33	20	54	3	4	1
1989	Cle-A	.950	19	9	29	2	1	1
Total	8	.944	97	46	139	1	9	6

■ Willie Aikens 1B

YEAR	TM/L	PCT	G	PO	A	E	DP	FR
1977	Cal-A	.971	13	94	8	3	10	0
1979	Cal-A	.996	55	462	31	2	49	-2
1980	KC-A	.990	138	1081	65	12	95	-9
1981	KC-A	.992	99	844	56	7	79	-5
1982	KC-A	.994	128	1048	75	7	95	-3
1983	KC-A	.989	112	884	64	11	101	-1
1984	Tor-A	1.000	2	12	1	0	1	0

YEAR	TM/L	PCT	G	PO	A	E	DP	FR
Total	7	.991	547	4425	300	2	430	-20

■ Eddie Ainsmith C

YEAR	TM/L	PCT	G	PO	A	E	DP	FR
1910	Was-A	.963	30	131	52	7	4	-3
1911	Was-A	.952	47	208	71	14	2	1
1912	Was-A	.958	59	415	85	22	5	16
1913	Was-A	.967	79	418	82	17	10	6
1914	Was-A	.969	51	290	55	11	5	8
1915	Was-A	.988	42	209	47	3	2	5
1916	Was-A	.959	46	207	50	11	9	13
1917	Was-A	.971	119	580	154	22	15	15
1918	Was-A	.975	89	413	131	14	13	8
1919	Det-A	.962	106	456	107	22	7	-11
1920	Det-A	.955	61	219	55	13	4	-3
1921	Det-A	.947	34	99	25	7	0	-4
	StL-N	.956	23	70	17	4	2	2
1922	StL-N	.963	116	428	99	20	14	-3
1923	StL-N	.980	80	235	57	6	3	-8
	Bro-N	1.000	2	16	1	0	1	1
	Yr	.981	82	251	58	6	4	-7
1924	NY-N	1.000	9	5	0	0	0	0
Total	15	.966	993	4399	1088	193	96	43

1B

YEAR	TM/L	PCT	G	PO	A	E	DP	FR
1920	Det-A	1.000	1	3	0	0	0	0
1921	StL-N	1.000	1	8	0	0	0	0
Total	2	1.000	2	11	0	0	0	0

■ Mike Aldrete OF

YEAR	TM/L	PCT	G	PO	A	E	DP	FR
1986	SF-N	.978	31	43	1	1	0	-1
1987	SF-N	.986	79	141	3	2	1	-1
1988	SF-N	.982	115	211	5	4	1	-4
1989	Mon-N	.980	37	47	2	1	0	0
1990	Mon-N	.982	38	51	4	1	0	1
Total	5	.983	300	493	15	9	2	-5

1B

YEAR	TM/L	PCT	G	PO	A	E	DP	FR
1986	SF-N	1.000	37	274	35	0	34	5
1987	SF-N	.995	33	187	15	1	20	0
1988	SF-N	1.000	10	61	3	0	2	0
1989	Mon-N	1.000	10	62	7	0	8	1
1990	Mon-N	1.000	18	109	8	0	16	0
Total	5	.999	108	693	68	1	80	6

■ Dale Alexander 1B

YEAR	TM/L	PCT	G	PO	A	E	DP	FR
1929	Det-A	.988	155	1443	90	18	129	-4
1930	Det-A	.985	154	1338	71	22	132	-7
1931	Det-A	.987	126	1197	53	16	97	-8
1932	Det-A	1.000	2	4	0	0	0	0
	Bos-A	.992	101	1051	67	9	93	2
	Yr	.992	103	1055	67	9	93	2
1933	Bos-A	.992	79	728	47	6	51	3
Total	5	.988	617	5761	328	1	502	-14

OF

YEAR	TM/L	PCT	G	PO	A	E	DP	FR
1931	Det-A	1.000	4	8	0	0	0	0

■ Gary Alexander C

YEAR	TM/L	PCT	G	PO	A	E	DP	FR
1975	SF-N	1.000	2	2	0	0	0	-1
1976	SF-N	.964	23	92	16	4	0	-3
1977	SF-N	.968	33	174	8	6	0	-8
1978	Oak-A	—	1	0	0	0	0	0
	Cle-A	.983	66	305	34	6	3	-9
	Yr	.983	67	305	34	6	3	-9
1979	Cle-A	.961	91	404	40	18	5	-18
1980	Cle-A	.971	13	31	2	1	0	0
Total	6	.969	229	1008	100	5	8	-39

OF

YEAR	TM/L	PCT	G	PO	A	E	DP	FR
1977	SF-N	—	1	0	0	0	0	0
1978	Oak-A	1.000	6	16	0	0	0	0
1979	Cle-A	—	2	0	0	0	0	0
1980	Cle-A	1.000	2	3	0	0	0	0
1981	Pit-N	.941	8	12	4	1	0	2
Total	5	.972	19	31	4	1	0	2

1B

YEAR	TM/L	PCT	G	PO	A	E	DP	FR
1978	Oak-A	—	1	0	0	0	0	0
1981	Pit-N	.964	9	52	2	2	4	-1
Total	2	.964	10	52	2	2	4	-1

■ Walt Alexander C

YEAR	TM/L	PCT	G	PO	A	E	DP	FR
1912	StL-A	.969	37	140	46	6	2	-3
1913	StL-A	.947	43	125	71	11	7	4
1915	StL-A	—	1	0	0	0	0	0
	NY-A	.967	24	132	44	6	5	9
	Yr	.967	25	132	44	6	5	9
1916	NY-A	.960	27	100	43	6	2	1
1917	NY-A	.951	20	82	16	5	2	0
Total	5	.959	152	579	220	4	18	11

■ Andy Allanson C

YEAR	TM/L	PCT	G	PO	A	E	DP	FR
1986	Cle-A	.960	99	446	33	20	4	-6
1987	Cle-A	.986	50	252	22	4	3	-7
1988	Cle-A	.986	133	691	60	11	11	0
1989	Cle-A	.986	111	570	53	9	4	4
Total	4	.980	393	1959	168	4	22	-9

■ Nick Allen C

YEAR	TM/L	PCT	G	PO	A	E	DP	FR
1914	Buf-F	.969	26	93	30	4	5	2
1915	Buf-F	.956	80	347	110	21	8	8
1916	Chi-N	.958	4	19	4	1	1	0
1918	Cin-N	.950	31	105	47	8	7	8
1919	Cin-N	.958	12	36	10	2	2	3
1920	Cin-N	.961	36	107	39	6	5	6
Total	6	.958	189	707	240	2	28	27

■ Bernie Allen 2B

YEAR	TM/L	PCT	G	PO	A	E	DP	FR
1962	Min-A	.983	158	357	394	13	109	-17
1963	Min-A	.976	128	236	256	12	65	-24
1964	Min-A	.979	71	161	173	7	40	-11
1965	Min-A	1.000	10	18	19	0	6	-2
1966	Min-A	.974	89	191	214	11	46	-7
1967	Was-A	.990	75	177	200	4	57	19
1968	Was-A	.991	110	263	271	5	63	4
1969	Was-A	.974	110	239	281	14	70	4

YEAR	TM/L	PCT	G	PO	A	E	DP	FR
1970	Was-A	.969	80	169	175	11	47	-2
1971	Was-A	.961	41	54	69	5	10	-7
1972	NY-A	.980	20	50	47	2	17	2
1973	NY-A	.985	13	30	35	1	7	3
	Mon-N	.970	9	15	17	1	2	-1
Total	12	.980	914	1960	2151	6	539	-39

3B

YEAR	TM/L	PCT	G	PO	A	E	DP	FR
1965	Min-A	1.000	1	0	3	0	0	0
1966	Min-A	1.000	2	0	2	0	1	0
1968	Was-A	1.000	2	0	1	0	0	0
1969	Was-A	.900	6	4	5	1	0	3
1970	Was-A	1.000	12	7	29	0	2	2
1971	Was-A	.946	34	31	57	5	6	-4
1972	NY-A	.940	44	25	85	7	9	-2
1973	Mon-N	.947	8	4	14	1	1	0
Total	8	.950	109	71	196	4	19	-1

■ Ethan Allen OF

YEAR	TM/L	PCT	G	PO	A	E	DP	FR
1926	Cin-N	1.000	9	9	0	0	0	1
1927	Cin-N	.988	98	250	6	3	3	-8
1928	Cin-N	.981	129	348	12	7	4	0
1929	Cin-N	.988	137	393	12	5	2	-1
1930	Cin-N	.969	15	31	0	1	0	0
	NY-N	.985	62	122	6	2	0	0
	Yr	.981	77	153	6	3	0	0
1931	NY-N	.975	77	151	2	4	1	-5
1932	NY-N	.957	24	44	1	2	0	0
1933	StL-N	.984	67	179	8	3	1	12
1934	Phi-N	.978	145	337	19	8	3	11
1935	Phi-N	.980	156	412	26	9	6	12
1936	Phi-N	.954	30	82	1	4	0	2
	Chi-N	.980	89	191	2	4	2	-2
	Yr	.972	119	273	3	8	2	0
1937	StL-N	.980	78	186	8	4	1	5
1938	StL-A	1.000	7	11	0	0	0	0
Total	13	.981	1123	2746	103	6	23	27

■ Hank Allen OF

YEAR	TM/L	PCT	G	PO	A	E	DP	FR
1966	Was-A	.917	9	22	0	2	0	0
1967	Was-A	.980	99	148	1	3	1	-1
1968	Was-A	.895	25	17	0	2	0	-1
1969	Was-A	.933	91	120	6	9	2	-10
1970	Was-A	1.000	17	17	1	0	0	0
	Mil-A	1.000	14	19	2	0	0	1
	Yr	1.000	31	36	3	0	0	1
1973	Chi-A	1.000	5	5	0	0	0	0
Total	6	.957	260	348	10	6	3	-11

3B

YEAR	TM/L	PCT	G	PO	A	E	DP	FR
1968	Was-A	.884	16	8	30	5	3	0
1969	Was-A	.900	6	4	5	1	0	3
1972	Chi-A	.905	6	4	15	2	5	3
1973	Chi-A	1.000	9	1	9	0	0	1
Total	4	.905	37	17	59	8	8	7

2B

YEAR	TM/L	PCT	G	PO	A	E	DP	FR
1968	Was-A	1.000	11	26	11	0	3	-2
1969	Was-A	.667	3	2	0	1	0	-1
1970	Mil-A	1.000	5	4	8	0	2	0
1973	Chi-A	1.000	1	1	0	0	0	0
Total	4	.981	20	33	19	1	5	-3

1B

YEAR	TM/L	PCT	G	PO	A	E	DP	FR
1970	Mil-A	1.000	4	25	1	0	2	0
1973	Chi-A	.974	8	35	3	1	1	0
Total	2	.985	12	60	4	1	3	0

C

YEAR	TM/L	PCT	G	PO	A	E	DP	FR
1973	Chi-A	—	1	0	0	0	0	0

■ Myron Allen OF

YEAR	TM/L	PCT	G	PO	A	E	DP	FR
1887	Cle-a	.894	115	222	22	29	6	8
1888	KC-a	.931	35	72	9	6	1	6
Total	2	.903	150	294	31	5	7	14

3B

YEAR	TM/L	PCT	G	PO	A	E	DP	FR
1887	Cle-a	1.000	3	5	7	0	1	1

SS

YEAR	TM/L	PCT	G	PO	A	E	DP	FR
1887	Cle-a	.750	2	3	3	2	0	0

2B

YEAR	TM/L	PCT	G	PO	A	E	DP	FR
1886	Bos-N	1.000	1	2	2	0	0	0

■ Dick Allen 1B

YEAR	TM/L	PCT	G	PO	A	E	DP	FR
1969	Phi-N	.985	117	1024	54	16	100	-9
1970	StL-N	.993	79	676	41	5	67	-5
1971	LA-N	.993	28	258	13	2	26	-3
1972	Chi-A	.995	143	1234	67	7	94	-4
1973	Chi-A	.994	67	597	43	4	55	1
1974	Chi-A	.986	125	998	49	15	112	-10
1975	Phi-N	.982	113	900	70	18	79	-1
1976	Phi-N	.989	85	671	44	8	71	-3
1977	Oak-A	.984	50	389	37	7	36	2
Total	9	.989	807	6747	418	2	640	-32

3B

YEAR	TM/L	PCT	G	PO	A	E	DP	FR
1963	Phi-N	—	1	0	0	0	0	0
1964	Phi-N	.921	162	154	325	41	30	7
1965	Phi-N	.943	160	129	305	26	29	-2
1966	Phi-N	.967	91	81	180	9	15	-6
1967	Phi-N	.908	121	95	249	35	23	-5
1968	Phi-N	.786	10	7	15	6	4	-3
1970	StL-N	.895	38	27	67	11	3	-7
1971	LA-N	.918	67	36	133	15	12	-4
1972	Chi-A	1.000	2	1	2	0	0	0
Total	9	.927	652	530	1276	143	116	-20

OF

YEAR	TM/L	PCT	G	PO	A	E	DP	FR
1963	Phi-N	.833	7	10	0	2	0	-1
1966	Phi-N	.931	47	65	2	5	0	-4
1968	Phi-N	.973	139	208	5	6	0	-11
1970	StL-N	.750	3	5	1	2	0	0
1971	LA-N	.959	60	88	5	4	0	-5
Total	5	.953	256	376	13	9	0	-21

2B

YEAR	TM/L	PCT	G	PO	A	E	DP	FR
1967	Phi-N	—	1	0	0	0	0	0
1973	Chi-A	1.000	2	4	3	0	0	-1

YEAR	TM/L	PCT	G	PO	A	E	DP	FR
1974	Chi-A	.500	1	0	1	1	0	-1
Total	3	.889	4	4	4	1	0	-2
SS								
1965	Phi-N	1.000	2	1	0	0	0	0
1967	Phi-N	—	1	0	0	0	0	0
Total	2	1.000	3	1	0	0	0	0
■ Bob Allen SS								
1890	Phi-N	.924	133	**337**	**500**	69	**68**	**39**
1891	Phi-N	.896	118	258	426	79	50	13
1892	Phi-N	.919	**152**	331	537	77	**67**	18
1893	Phi-N	.919	124	**302**	447	66	65	18
1894	Phi-N	.915	40	87	129	20	15	-2
1897	Bos-N	.924	32	78	117	16	12	8
1900	Cin-N	.864	5	6	13	3	1	-1
Total	7	.915	604	1399	2169	330	278	93
OF								
1897	Bos-N	1.000	1	1	0	0	0	0
2B								
1897	Bos-N	1.000	1	3	2	0	0	-1
■ Gary Allenson C								
1979	Bos-A	.980	104	407	40	9	3	10
1980	Bos-A	.981	24	99	6	2	0	4
1981	Bos-A	.969	47	235	18	8	3	1
1982	Bos-A	.992	91	454	39	4	8	**8**
1983	Bos-A	.984	84	393	29	7	6	4
1984	Bos-A	.987	35	135	12	2	4	0
1985	Tor-A	1.000	14	39	2	0	0	-2
Total	7	.984	399	1762	146	2	24	25
3B								
1979	Bos-A	1.000	3	3	2	0	1	0
1980	Bos-A	1.000	5	1	2	0	1	0
Total	2	1.000	8	4	4	0	2	0
■ Gene Alley SS								
1963	Pit-N	.923	4	10	14	2	4	0
1964	Pit-N	.966	61	100	211	11	43	**24**
1965	Pit-N	.968	110	163	376	18	79	16
1966	Pit-N	.979	143	235	472	15	**128**	13
1967	Pit-N	.967	146	**257**	**500**	26	**105**	8
1968	Pit-N	.974	109	162	394	15	86	**23**
1969	Pit-N	.953	25	36	66	5	17	-3
1970	Pit-N	.975	108	202	381	15	84	**31**
1971	Pit-N	.958	108	187	316	22	55	-16
1972	Pit-N	.970	114	181	339	16	88	-5
1973	Pit-N	.981	49	76	129	4	20	4
Total	11	.970	977	1609	3198	149	709	95
2B								
1963	Pit-N	1.000	4	5	8	0	1	0
1964	Pit-N	1.000	1	1	0	0	1	0
1965	Pit-N	.965	40	80	140	8	34	14
1968	Pit-N	.992	24	47	81	1	11	3
1969	Pit-N	.977	53	109	147	6	39	10
1970	Pit-N	1.000	8	13	30	0	4	2
Total	6	.978	130	255	406	5	89	29
3B								
1963	Pit-N	.947	7	5	13	1	2	0
1964	Pit-N	1.000	3	1	2	0	2	1
1965	Pit-N	—	1	0	0	0	0	0
1969	Pit-N	.889	5	1	7	1	0	0
1970	Pit-N	1.000	2	1	1	0	0	0
1971	Pit-N	1.000	1	0	1	0	0	0
1972	Pit-N	1.000	4	0	1	0	0	0
1973	Pit-N	1.000	8	7	12	0	3	1
Total	8	.963	31	15	37	2	7	2
■ Bob Allison OF								
1958	Was-A	1.000	11	24	0	0	0	1
1959	Was-A	.974	149	333	8	9	1	-10
1960	Was-A	.965	140	290	10	**11**	3	6
1961	Min-A	.975	150	300	14	8	3	7
1962	Min-A	.977	147	287	10	7	1	6
1963	Min-A	.971	147	326	11	10	4	11
1964	Min-A	.992	61	114	3	1	1	3
1965	Min-A	.972	122	231	11	7	4	8
1966	Min-A	.967	56	86	3	3	0	-1
1967	Min-A	.978	145	220	6	5	0	-6
1968	Min-A	.966	117	166	4	6	0	-8
1969	Min-A	1.000	58	91	2	0	1	0
1970	Min-A	1.000	17	18	0	0	0	-1
Total	13	.975	1320	2486	82	7	18	16
1B								
1960	Was-A	1.000	4	21	3	0	1	1
1961	Min-A	.984	18	117	4	2	9	-2
1964	Min-A	.986	93	715	55	11	63	-1
1965	Min-A	1.000	3	16	1	0	1	0
1968	Min-A	.988	17	150	12	2	14	1
1969	Min-A	1.000	3	5	1	0	0	0
1970	Min-A	.952	7	36	4	2	2	0
Total	7	.985	145	1060	80	7	90	-1
■ Mel Almada OF								
1933	Bos-A	1.000	13	27	1	0	0	0
1934	Bos-A	.985	23	60	4	1	0	4
1935	Bos-A	.968	149	337	22	12	3	-7
1936	Bos-A	.987	81	144	9	2	2	-2
1937	Bos-A	.927	27	37	1	3	0	-4
	Was-A	.964	100	308	16	12	3	10
	Yr	.960	127	345	17	15	3	6
1938	Was-A	.968	47	147	5	5	1	9
	StL-A	.966	101	247	9	9	1	-3
	Yr	.967	148	394	14	14	2	6
1939	StL-A	.987	34	75	2	1	0	3
	Bro-N	.977	32	84	2	2	1	5
Total	7	.970	607	1466	71	7	12	12
1B								
1935	Bos-A	1.000	3	17	1	0	1	0
1937	Bos-A	.939	4	31	0	2	3	-1
Total	2	.961	7	48	1	2	4	-1

YEAR	TM/L	PCT	G	PO	A	E	DP	FR
■ Bill Almon SS								
1974	SD-N	.915	14	13	30	4	4	-2
1975	SD-N	1.000	2	6	5	0	0	1
1976	SD-N	.962	14	23	52	3	8	1
1977	SD-N	.954	155	**303**	538	**41**	87	18
1978	SD-N	.970	15	9	23	1	4	3
1979	SD-N	.958	25	26	43	3	11	6
1980	Mon-N	.911	12	17	24	4	1	-2
	NY-N	.967	22	30	57	3	14	6
	Yr	.948	34	47	81	7	15	4
1981	Chi-A	.969	103	190	340	17	78	14
1982	Chi-A	.949	108	164	317	**26**	72	**26**
1983	Oak-A	.941	52	51	93	9	14	-16
1984	Oak-A	1.000	1	0	1	0	0	0
1985	Pit-N	.987	43	50	101	2	19	-15
1986	Pit-N	.870	19	8	12	3	1	-4
1987	Pit-N	.944	4	9	8	1	3	2
	NY-N	.972	22	8	27	1	3	-2
	Yr	.963	26	17	35	2	6	0
1988	Phi-N	.857	5	4	2	1	1	0
Total	15	.956	616	911	1673	119	320	36
3B								
1978	SD-N	.933	114	72	221	21	20	-1
1980	NY-N	1.000	9	0	3	0	0	1
1983	Oak-A	.911	40	34	58	9	5	-10
1984	Oak-A	1.000	4	1	0	0	0	0
1985	Pit-N	.857	7	2	4	1	0	-2
1986	Pit-N	.921	28	9	26	3	3	-4
1987	Pit-N	—	1	0	0	0	0	0
1988	Phi-N	.944	9	4	13	1	0	1
Total	8	.927	212	122	325	5	28	-15
OF								
1979	SD-N	—	1	0	0	0	0	0
1983	Oak-A	.971	23	33	0	1	0	-1
1984	Oak-A	1.000	48	70	1	0	1	2
1985	Pit-N	1.000	32	27	2	0	0	-1
1986	Pit-N	.983	54	53	5	1	0	0
1987	Pit-N	—	2	0	0	0	0	0
	NY-N	—	1	0	0	0	0	0
	Yr	—	3	0	0	0	0	0
Total	6	.990	161	183	8	2	1	0
2B								
1978	SD-N	.970	7	21	11	1	2	-2
1979	SD-N	.985	61	116	150	4	37	11
1980	Mon-N	.750	1	1	2	1	1	0
	NY-N	.952	18	31	48	4	9	3
	Yr	.943	19	32	50	5	10	3
1983	Oak-A	1.000	5	1	4	0	0	0
1987	NY-N	.917	10	4	7	1	1	-1
Total	5	.973	102	174	222	1	50	11
1B								
1983	Oak-A	.996	38	208	21	1	14	0
1984	Oak-A	.990	44	184	13	2	18	-2
1985	Pit-N	.929	7	25	1	2	3	-1
1986	Pit-N	.923	4	10	2	1	0	0
1987	NY-N	1.000	2	5	0	0	0	0
1988	Phi-N	1.000	1	12	0	0	1	0
Total	6	.988	96	444	37	6	36	-3
C								
1984	Oak-A	1.000	1	0	0	0	0	0
■ Roberto Alomar 2B								
1988	SD-N	.980	143	319	459	16	88	**17**
1989	SD-N	.967	**157**	341	472	**28**	91	6
1990	SD-N	.976	137	311	392	17	73	0
Total	3	.974	437	971	1323	1	252	23
SS								
1990	SD-N	.895	5	5	12	2	4	-2
■ Sandy Alomar C								
1989	SD-N	1.000	6	33	1	0	1	0
1990	Cle-A	.981	129	686	46	**14**	6	-13
Total	2	.982	135	719	47	4	7	-13
■ Sandy Alomar 2B								
1965	Mil-N	.987	19	30	45	1	8	7
1966	Atl-N	.981	21	24	28	1	11	3
1967	NY-N	1.000	2	1	1	0	0	0
	Chi-A	1.000	2	2	3	0	2	1
1968	Chi-A	.958	99	188	221	**18**	48	-19
1969	Chi-A	.980	22	50	47	2	15	3
	Cal-A	.969	134	294	354	21	94	-10
	Yr	.970	156	344	401	23	**109**	-7
1970	Cal-A	.979	153	375	460	18	119	11
1971	Cal-A	.989	137	350	432	9	100	**20**
1972	Cal-A	.977	**154**	350	388	17	92	4
1973	Cal-A	.979	110	244	267	11	70	-1
1974	Cal-A	.974	15	16	21	1	3	4
	NY-A	.976	76	184	192	9	45	-12
	Yr	**.976**	91	200	213	10	48	-8
1975	NY-A	.985	150	340	368	11	93	-12
1976	NY-A	.970	38	85	108	6	17	-3
1977	Tex-A	.973	18	33	40	2	10	11
1978	Tex-A	.950	6	13	1	2	3	3
Total	14	.977	1156	2572	2988	128	729	10
SS								
1964	Mil-N	.967	19	27	60	3	8	8
1965	Mil-N	.964	39	38	69	4	11	7
1966	Atl-N	1.000	5	6	6	0	0	0
1967	NY-N	1.000	10	15	16	0	2	2
	Chi-A	.952	8	9	11	1	5	1
1968	Chi-A	1.000	1	1	16	0	6	2
1970	Cal-A	.949	10	16	21	2	5	-2
1971	Cal-A	.946	28	43	98	8	15	1
1972	Cal-A	1.000	4	3	6	0	1	0
1973	Cal-A	.957	31	47	88	6	16	-7
1974	Cal-A	.977	19	18	25	1	8	5
1975	NY-A	1.000	1	1	2	0	1	0

YEAR	TM/L	PCT	G	PO	A	E	DP	FR
1976	NY-A	1.000	6	5	3	0	1	-1
1977	Tex-A	.950	6	9	10	1	2	3
1978	Tex-A	1.000	2	1	2	0	1	1
Total	14	.963	197	249	433	6	82	20
3B								
1967	NY-N	1.000	3	0	1	0	0	0
1968	Chi-A	.950	27	11	27	2	1	2
1970	Cal-A	—	1	0	0	0	0	0
1974	Cal-A	1.000	5	4	3	0	0	0
1976	NY-A	.800	3	2	2	1	0	-1
1977	Tex-A	1.000	1	0	1	0	0	0
1978	Tex-A	1.000	3	3	2	0	0	0
Total	7	.949	43	20	36	3	1	1
1B								
1976	NY-A	1.000	1	3	1	0	0	0
1977	Tex-A	1.000	4	9	1	0	1	0
1978	Tex-A	.975	9	35	4	1	4	1
Total	3	.981	14	47	6	1	5	1
OF								
1968	Chi-A	—	1	0	0	0	0	0
1974	Cal-A	—	1	0	0	0	0	0
1976	NY-A	—	1	0	0	0	0	0
1977	Tex-A	1.000	5	1	0	0	0	0
Total	4	1.000	8	1	0	0	0	0
■ Felipe Alou OF								
1958	SF-N	.985	70	126	2	2	1	-4
1959	SF-N	.974	69	111	2	3	0	-3
1960	SF-N	.958	95	156	5	7	0	-5
1961	SF-N	.990	122	196	10	2	1	-1
1962	SF-N	.971	150	262	7	8	3	-1
1963	SF-N	.986	153	279	9	4	2	2
1964	Mil-N	.975	92	191	2	5	0	-5
1965	Mil-N	.980	91	148	2	3	0	-4
1966	Atl-N	.983	79	164	8	3	0	5
1967	Atl-N	.970	56	90	6	3	0	-2
1968	Atl-N	.980	158	379	8	8	2	4
1969	Atl-N	.989	116	260	4	3	1	-2
1970	Oak-A	.977	145	287	11	7	3	6
1971	Oak-A	1.000	2	7	0	0	0	0
	NY-A	.985	80	129	3	2	0	-9
	Yr	.986	82	136	3	2	0	-9
1972	NY-A	1.000	15	21	0	0	0	-1
1973	NY-A	.979	22	45	1	1	0	-1
	Mon-N	1.000	15	28	2	0	0	2
1974	Mil-A	1.000	1	0	1	0	0	0
Total	17	.979	1531	2879	82	2	13	-19
1B								
1964	Mil-N	1.000	18	138	10	0	12	0
1965	Mil-N	.994	69	476	37	3	39	2
1966	Atl-N	.988	90	769	53	10	63	-1
1967	Atl-N	.993	85	774	28	6	67	-10
1970	Oak-A	1.000	1	3	0	0	1	0
1971	NY-A	.995	42	377	20	2	23	-3
1972	NY-A	.990	95	648	54	7	69	3
1973	NY-A	.988	67	467	30	6	43	-3
	Mon-N	1.000	1	2	1	0	0	0
Total	8	.991	468	3654	233	4	317	-12
3B								
1965	Mil-N	1.000	2	0	1	0	0	0
1966	Atl-N	1.000	3	1	1	0	0	0
Total	2	1.000	5	1	2	0	0	0
SS								
1965	Mil-N	1.000	1	2	3	0	0	-1
1966	Atl-N	1.000	1	1	2	0	0	0
Total	2	1.000	2	3	5	0	0	-1
■ Jesus Alou OF								
1963	SF-N	.875	12	7	0	1	0	-1
1964	SF-N	.973	108	172	8	5	2	-1
1965	SF-N	.980	136	238	7	5	0	1
1966	SF-N	.967	100	141	4	5	1	-8
1967	SF-N	.948	123	195	5	11	2	-7
1968	SF-N	.975	105	175	10	2	2	0
1969	Hou-N	.928	112	173	8	14	1	-1
1970	Hou-N	.962	108	169	6	7	2	-6
1971	Hou-N	.983	109	229	7	4	3	4
1972	Hou-N	.970	23	32	0	1	0	-1
1973	Hou-N	.941	14	16	0	1	0	-2
	Oak-A	1.000	21	40	1	0	1	0
1974	NY-A	.963	20	23	3	1	0	0
1978	Hou-N	.976	28	40	1	1	0	-4
1979	Hou-N	1.000	6	6	0	0	0	0
Total	15	.968	1050	1691	63	8	15	-24
1B								
1979	Hou-N	1.000	1	2	0	0	1	0
■ Matty Alou OF								
1960	SF-N	1.000	1	1	0	0	0	0
1961	SF-N	.978	58	85	2	2	0	-3
1962	SF-N	.976	57	80	3	2	0	-2
1963	SF-N	.952	20	19	1	1	0	1
1964	SF-N	.976	80	120	2	3	1	-5
1965	SF-N	.986	103	139	6	2	1	-6
1966	Pit-N	.972	136	264	11	8	3	-7
1967	Pit-N	.989	134	249	9	3	3	-6
1968	Pit-N	.984	144	298	8	5	0	-5
1969	Pit-N	.977	**162**	327	10	8	4	-1
1970	Pit-N	.975	153	297	15	8	1	0
1971	StL-N	.981	94	203	8	4	0	6
1972	StL-N	.976	39	52	4	0	0	-1
	Oak-A	1.000	32	48	2	0	0	-4
1973	NY-A	.974	85	146	6	4	2	-4
	StL-N	1.000	1	0	1	0	0	0
1974	SD-N	.947	13	18	0	1	0	-2
Total	15	.979	1312	2346	88	1	15	-38

YEAR	TM/L	PCT	G	PO	A	E	DP	FR
		1B						
1967	Pit-N	1.000	1	3	0	0	0	0
1971	StL-N	.991	57	507	27	5	42	-4
1972	StL-N	.988	66	535	40	7	53	-5
	Oak-A	1.000	1	9	1	0	1	0
1973	NY-A	.980	40	376	20	8	44	-3
	StL-N	1.000	1	3	0	0	0	0
1974	SD-N	1.000	2	15	0	0	0	0
Total	5	.987	168	1448	88	20	140	-7

■ Whitey Alperman 2B

YEAR	TM/L	PCT	G	PO	A	E	DP	FR
1906	Bro-N	.940	103	245	308	35	25	1
1907	Bro-N	.953	115	298	378	33	41	19
1908	Bro-N	.934	42	74	110	13	8	-3
1909	Bro-N	.931	108	266	297	**42**	32	9
Total	4	.941	368	883	1093	123	106	26
		SS						
1906	Bro-N	.921	24	62	78	12	4	0
1907	Bro-N	.860	12	27	22	8	4	-7
1908	Bro-N	.867	2	7	6	2	0	0
Total	3	.902	38	96	106	2	8	-7
		3B						
1906	Bro-N	1.000	1	5	2	0	0	1
1907	Bro-N	.927	14	14	37	4	0	2
1908	Bro-N	.853	9	10	19	5	0	-1
Total	3	.906	24	29	58	9	0	2
		OF						
1908	Bro-N	.714	5	5	0	2	0	-1

■ Dell Alston OF

YEAR	TM/L	PCT	G	PO	A	E	DP	FR
1977	NY-A	1.000	2	2	1	0	0	1
1978	Oak-A	.956	50	86	0	4	0	-6
1979	Cle-A	.969	30	29	2	1	0	1
1980	Cle-A	.947	26	35	1	2	0	4
Total	4	.957	108	152	4	7	0	0
		1B						
1978	Oak-A	1.000	9	20	0	0	2	-1

■ Dave Altizer SS

YEAR	TM/L	PCT	G	PO	A	E	DP	FR
1906	Was-A	.931	113	257	323	43	31	-22
1907	Was-A	.927	78	155	251	32	23	-10
1908	Was-A	—	1	0	0	0	0	0
	Cle-A	.857	3	6	12	3	0	0
	Yr	.857	4	6	12	3	0	0
1910	Cin-N	.933	3	7	7	1	1	-2
1911	Cin-N	.907	23	37	60	10	4	0
Total	5	.926	221	462	653	9	59	-34
		OF						
1906	Was-A	1.000	2	6	1	0	0	1
1907	Was-A	.982	19	54	0	1	0	2
1908	Cle-A	.952	24	55	5	3	2	4
1909	Chi-A	.949	61	99	12	6	1	4
1911	Cin-N	1.000	1	2	0	0	0	0
Total	5	.959	107	216	18	0	3	11
		1B						
1907	Was-A	.981	50	479	24	10	18	-2
1908	Was-A	1.000	4	21	0	0	0	0
1909	Chi-A	.992	46	441	33	4	24	4
1911	Cin-N	1.000	1	1	0	0	0	0
Total	4	.986	101	942	57	4	42	2
		2B						
1908	Was-A	.959	38	68	119	8	12	0
1911	Cin-N	1.000	1	3	1	0	2	0
Total	2	.960	39	71	120	8	14	0
		3B						
1908	Was-A	.900	16	19	26	5	1	-2

■ George Altman OF

YEAR	TM/L	PCT	G	PO	A	E	DP	FR
1959	Chi-N	.990	121	278	7	3	2	-3
1960	Chi-N	.993	79	144	2	1	0	-4
1961	Chi-N	.978	130	258	11	6	2	6
1962	Chi-N	.972	129	234	8	7	3	1
1963	StL-N	.979	124	220	8	5	1	1
1964	NY-N	.968	109	202	12	7	3	6
1965	Chi-N	.943	45	66	0	4	0	-4
1966	Chi-N	.958	42	42	4	2	0	-3
1967	Chi-N	1.000	4	2	0	0	0	0
Total	9	.977	783	1446	52	5	11	0
		1B						
1960	Chi-N	.994	21	164	14	1	15	1
1961	Chi-N	1.000	3	20	1	0	3	0
1962	Chi-N	1.000	16	121	8	0	13	0
1965	Chi-N	1.000	2	12	0	0	1	0
1966	Chi-N	1.000	4	27	2	0	1	0
1967	Chi-N	1.000	1	2	0	0	1	0
Total	6	.997	47	346	25	1	34	1

■ George Alusik OF

YEAR	TM/L	PCT	G	PO	A	E	DP	FR
1958	Det-A	1.000	1	1	0	0	0	0
1961	Det-A	—	1	0	0	0	0	0
1962	KC-A	.968	50	87	3	3	0	-1
1963	KC-A	1.000	63	98	5	0	1	-2
1964	KC-A	.984	44	61	1	1	1	-4
Total	5	.985	159	247	9	4	2	-7
		1B						
1962	KC-A	1.000	1	2	0	0	0	0
1964	KC-A	.989	12	89	5	1	9	-2
Total	2	.990	13	91	5	1	9	-2

■ Luis Alvarado SS

YEAR	TM/L	PCT	G	PO	A	E	DP	FR
1968	Bos-A	.976	11	14	26	1	6	-3
1969	Bos-A	1.000	5	4	6	0	2	2
1970	Bos-A	.980	27	25	75	2	15	5
1971	Chi-A	.959	71	89	189	12	34	10
1972	Chi-A	.957	81	98	213	14	28	0
1973	Chi-A	.935	18	20	38	4	6	0
1974	Chi-A	.667	4	2	2	2	0	-1
	StL-N	.980	17	16	33	1	8	-2
	Cle-A	.864	7	4	15	3	2	0
Total	7	.957	241	272	597	9	101	11

YEAR	TM/L	PCT	G	PO	A	E	DP	FR
		2B						
1971	Chi-A	.988	16	31	49	1	12	6
1972	Chi-A	.962	16	8	17	1	1	1
1973	Chi-A	.980	45	91	107	4	24	3
1974	Chi-A	1.000	1	1	4	0	1	0
	Cle-A	.972	46	81	93	5	23	11
	Yr	.973	47	82	97	5	24	11
1976	StL-N	.936	16	22	22	3	3	-9
1977	NY-N	1.000	1	1	2	0	0	0
Total	6	.974	141	235	294	4	64	12
		3B						
1970	Bos-A	.929	29	20	59	6	2	0
1972	Chi-A	1.000	2	1	4	0	1	1
1973	Chi-A	.958	10	10	13	1	1	2
1974	Chi-A	—	1	0	0	0	0	0
1977	Det-A	—	2	0	0	0	0	0
Total	5	.939	44	31	76	7	4	3

■ Max Alvis 3B

YEAR	TM/L	PCT	G	PO	A	E	DP	FR
1962	Cle-A	.935	12	13	16	2	1	-4
1963	Cle-A	.942	158	**170**	285	28	32	-5
1964	Cle-A	.955	105	83	191	13	18	-7
1965	Cle-A	.958	156	**169**	264	19	17	-19
1966	Cle-A	.958	**157**	**180**	280	20	24	-6
1967	Cle-A	.965	**161**	**169**	304	17	20	-8
1968	Cle-A	.960	128	114	202	13	18	-17
1969	Cle-A	.973	58	49	96	4	10	-1
1970	Mil-A	.909	36	15	55	7	4	2
Total	9	.956	971	962	1693	123	144	-65
		SS						
1969	Cle-A	—	1	0	0	0	0	0

■ Billy Alvord 3B

YEAR	TM/L	PCT	G	PO	A	E	DP	FR
1885	StL-N	.714	2	4	1	2	0	-1
1889	KC-a	.877	34	34	94	18	8	6
1890	Tol-a	.872	116	203	252	**67**	13	4
1891	Cle-N	.814	13	20	28	11	1	-2
	Was-a	.862	81	147	210	57	10	**17**
1893	Cle-N	.875	3	5	2	1	0	-2
Total	5	.865	249	413	587	156	32	22
		SS						
1889	KC-a	.702	8	12	28	17	5	-1
		2B						
1889	KC-a	.857	8	20	28	8	4	0

■ Brant Alyea OF

YEAR	TM/L	PCT	G	PO	A	E	DP	FR
1965	Was-A	—	1	0	0	0	0	0
1968	Was-A	1.000	39	76	0	0	0	-1
1969	Was-A	.938	69	84	6	6	0	-5
1970	Min-N	.980	75	93	4	2	0	-7
1971	Min-N	.962	48	47	3	2	0	-6
1972	Oak-A	1.000	8	20	3	0	0	4
	StL-N	1.000	3	5	1	0	1	1
Total	6	.972	243	325	17	0	1	-14
		1B						
1965	Was-A	1.000	3	17	0	0	0	-1
1969	Was-A	1.000	3	6	0	0	0	0
Total	2	1.000	6	23	0	0	0	-1

■ Joey Amalfitano 2B

YEAR	TM/L	PCT	G	PO	A	E	DP	FR
1954	NY-N	—	1	0	0	0	0	0
1960	SF-N	.976	33	54	70	3	16	0
1961	SF-N	.970	95	201	223	13	48	-22
1962	Hou-N	.967	110	230	268	17	72	2
1963	SF-N	.980	37	59	88	3	12	-3
1964	Chi-N	.964	86	201	254	17	47	3
1965	Chi-N	.989	24	28	65	1	9	5
1966	Chi-N	.977	12	23	19	1	5	2
Total	8	.970	398	796	987	5	209	-13
		3B						
1954	NY-N	1.000	4	2	5	0	1	2
1955	NY-N	.818	2	4	5	2	1	3
1960	SF-N	.935	63	45	114	11	8	3
1961	SF-N	1.000	6	3	13	0	0	0
1962	Hou-N	.750	5	1	2	1	0	0
1963	SF-N	1.000	7	2	4	0	1	0
1966	Chi-N	—	3	0	0	0	0	0
Total	7	.935	90	57	143	4	11	8
		SS						
1955	NY-N	.957	5	8	14	1	2	9
1960	SF-N	1.000	3	1	3	0	0	0
1964	Chi-N	—	1	0	0	0	0	0
1965	Chi-N	.833	4	3	2	1	0	-1
1966	Chi-N	—	2	0	0	0	0	0
Total	5	.939	15	12	19	2	2	8
		OF						
1960	SF-N	1.000	1	3	0	0	0	0
		1B						
1964	Chi-N	—	1	0	0	0	0	0

■ Ruben Amaro SS

YEAR	TM/L	PCT	G	PO	A	E	DP	FR
1958	StL-N	.948	36	44	65	6	18	3
1960	Phi-N	.965	92	153	230	14	47	-8
1961	Phi-N	.970	132	243	379	19	91	**14**
1962	Phi-N	.968	78	143	224	12	50	6
1963	Phi-N	.950	63	90	121	11	24	-3
1964	Phi-N	.971	79	141	191	10	44	-9
1965	Phi-N	.957	60	86	114	9	23	-4
1966	NY-A	.977	14	17	25	1	8	5
1967	NY-A	.973	123	212	374	16	73	9
1968	NY-A	.962	23	16	34	2	8	-1
1969	Cal-A	1.000	5	1	5	0	1	1
Total	11	.967	705	1146	1762	100	387	13
		1B						
1961	Phi-N	1.000	3	11	0	0	1	0
1962	Phi-N	1.000	1	1	0	0	1	0
1963	Phi-N	1.000	5	6	0	0	1	0
1964	Phi-N	1.000	58	154	9	0	11	0
1965	Phi-N	.990	60	86	12	1	9	2
1967	NY-A	1.000	2	14	2	0	2	0

YEAR	TM/L	PCT	G	PO	A	E	DP	FR
1968	NY-A	1.000	22	38	3	0	3	0
1969	Cal-A	1.000	18	29	0	0	1	-1
Total	8	.997	169	339	26	1	28	1
		3B						
1963	Phi-N	.969	45	15	48	2	4	5
1964	Phi-N	—	3	0	0	0	0	0
1967	NY-A	.714	3	2	3	2	0	-1
1969	Cal-A	1.000	2	2	1	0	0	0
Total	4	.947	53	19	52	4	4	4
		2B						
1958	StL-N	1.000	1	1	1	0	0	0
1961	Phi-N	1.000	1	0	1	0	0	0
1964	Phi-N	.857	3	3	3	1	0	-1
1965	Phi-N	.958	6	15	8	1	2	0
1969	Cal-A	.952	9	9	11	1	0	0
Total	5	.945	20	28	24	3	2	-1
		OF						
1964	Phi-N	—	1	0	0	0	0	0

■ Wayne Ambler SS

YEAR	TM/L	PCT	G	PO	A	E	DP	FR
1938	Phi-A	.942	116	209	310	32	54	-22
1939	Phi-A	.954	77	126	184	15	31	-1
Total	2	.946	193	335	494	7	85	-23
		2B						
1937	Phi-A	.955	56	107	149	12	34	-4
1938	Phi-A	1.000	4	12	16	0	4	2
1939	Phi-A	.941	19	24	24	3	3	-2
Total	3	.957	79	143	189	5	41	-4

■ Sandy Amoros OF

YEAR	TM/L	PCT	G	PO	A	E	DP	FR
1952	Bro-N	1.000	10	18	0	0	0	-1
1954	Bro-N	.987	70	149	6	2	1	4
1955	Bro-N	.972	109	201	10	6	1	0
1956	Bro-N	.955	86	123	3	6	0	-10
1957	Bro-N	.966	66	122	2	2	0	-2
1960	LA-N	1.000	3	5	1	0	0	1
	Det-A	1.000	10	17	0	0	0	1
Total	6	.976	354	635	22	6	2	-7

■ Alf Anderson SS

YEAR	TM/L	PCT	G	PO	A	E	DP	FR
1941	Pit-N	.931	58	96	161	19	29	-6
1942	Pit-N	.942	48	77	103	11	17	-15
Total	2	.936	106	173	264	0	46	-21

■ Brady Anderson OF

YEAR	TM/L	PCT	G	PO	A	E	DP	FR
1988	Bos-A	.989	41	87	3	1	1	0
	Bal-A	.981	49	156	1	3	0	7
	Yr	.984	90	243	4	4	1	7
1989	Bal-A	.985	79	191	3	3	0	5
1990	Bal-A	.987	63	149	3	2	1	4
Total	3	.985	232	583	10	9	2	16

■ Dave Anderson SS

YEAR	TM/L	PCT	G	PO	A	E	DP	FR
1983	LA-N	.969	53	56	100	5	19	4
1984	LA-N	.965	111	169	334	18	63	17
1985	LA-N	.973	25	29	78	3	9	6
1986	LA-N	.940	34	53	89	9	15	2
1987	LA-N	.977	65	91	169	6	29	3
1988	LA-N	.986	82	128	225	5	49	13
1989	LA-N	.990	33	46	49	1	13	0
1990	SF-N	1.000	29	17	38	0	5	-4
Total	8	.973	432	589	1082	7	202	41
		3B						
1983	LA-N	—	1	0	0	0	0	0
1984	LA-N	.970	11	7	25	1	4	2
1985	LA-N	.957	51	28	107	6	10	12
1986	LA-N	.976	51	20	63	2	6	7
1987	LA-N	.978	35	11	33	1	4	3
1988	LA-N	1.000	12	3	5	0	1	0
1989	LA-N	1.000	18	9	11	0	1	0
1990	SF-N	1.000	2	0	1	0	0	0
Total	8	.970	181	78	245	0	26	24
		2B						
1985	LA-N	1.000	2	4	2	0	1	0
1986	LA-N	1.000	5	4	7	0	0	1
1987	LA-N	1.000	5	1	5	0	0	0
1988	LA-N	1.000	11	8	14	0	3	1
1989	LA-N	1.000	7	6	13	0	1	1
1990	SF-N	.964	13	7	20	1	3	-1
Total	6	.989	43	30	61	1	8	2
		1B						
1990	SF-N	1.000	3	9	0	0	2	0

■ George Anderson OF

YEAR	TM/L	PCT	G	PO	A	E	DP	FR
1914	Bro-F	.946	92	176	15	11	2	4
1915	Bro-F	.956	134	200	16	10	5	-8
1918	StL-N	.956	35	62	3	3	1	-5
Total	3	.952	261	438	34	4	8	-9

■ Harry Anderson OF

YEAR	TM/L	PCT	G	PO	A	E	DP	FR
1957	Phi-N	.986	109	213	5	3	1	1
1958	Phi-N	.975	87	155	4	4	1	-4
1959	Phi-N	.980	137	283	**17**	6	4	14
1960	Phi-N	1.000	16	25	1	0	0	0
	Cin-N	1.000	4	4	0	0	0	0
	Yr	1.000	20	29	1	0	0	0
Total	4	.982	353	680	27	3	6	11
		1B						
1958	Phi-N	.979	49	397	29	9	39	-3
1960	Phi-N	.989	12	81	6	1	3	-1
	Cin-N	.990	15	93	7	1	6	-1
	Yr	.989	27	174	13	2	9	-2
Total	2	.982	76	571	42	1	48	-5

■ Jim Anderson SS

YEAR	TM/L	PCT	G	PO	A	E	DP	FR
1978	Cal-A	.955	47	72	99	8	21	3
1979	Cal-A	.949	82	126	189	17	42	0
1980	Sea-A	.956	65	87	188	12	38	5
1981	Sea-A	.947	68	88	181	15	44	1
1983	Tex-A	.962	27	17	60	3	7	2
1984	Tex-A	.989	31	35	53	1	13	9

YEAR	TM/L	PCT	G	PO	A	E	DP	FR
Total	6	.955	320	425	770	6	165	20
		3B						
1979	Cal-A	1.000	10	4	8	0	0	-1
1980	Sea-A	.906	33	31	65	10	7	0
1981	Sea-A	1.000	2	0	3	0	1	1
1983	Tex-A	1.000	3	0	1	0	0	0
1984	Tex-A	1.000	6	2	4	0	0	1
Total	5	.922	54	37	81	0	8	1
		2B						
1978	Cal-A	—	1	0	0	0	0	0
1979	Cal-A	1.000	6	5	8	0	2	1
1980	Sea-A	1.000	2	1	1	0	0	0
1983	Tex-A	.971	17	26	41	2	6	4
1984	Tex-A	1.000	1	0	1	0	0	0
Total	5	.976	27	32	51	2	8	5
		C						
1979	Cal-A	1.000	3	6	0	0	0	0
1980	Sea-A	1.000	1	1	1	0	0	0
1983	Tex-A	1.000	1	1	0	0	0	0
Total	3	1.000	5	8	1	0	0	0
		OF						
1983	Tex-A	1.000	3	2	0	0	0	0

■ John Anderson   OF

YEAR	TM/L	PCT	G	PO	A	E	DP	FR
1894	Bro-N	.778	16	21	0	6	0	-5
1895	Bro-N	.882	101	205	11	29	4	-6
1896	Bro-N	.942	68	121	9	8	4	-2
1897	Bro-N	.936	115	253	11	18	2	1
1898	Bro-N	1.000	5	12	0	0	0	0
	Was-N	.948	93	200	20	12	3	9
	Bro-N	.966	17	25	3	1	1	1
	Yr	.952	115	237	23	13	4	8
1899	Bro-N	.933	76	148	6	11	2	-6
1901	Mil-A	.976	13	40	1	1	0	3
1902	StL-A	1.000	3	2	0	0	0	-1
1903	StL-A	1.000	7	7	1	0	0	-1
1904	NY-A	.956	112	186	9	9	1	-5
1905	NY-A	.900	22	33	3	4	0	-2
	Was-A	.960	97	161	7	7	1	0
	Yr	.949	119	194	10	11	1	-2
1906	Was-A	.953	151	286	19	15	2	5
1907	Was-A	.967	26	56	2	2	0	2
1908	Chi-A	.963	87	96	9	4	7	-6
Total	14	.939	1009	1852	111	127	27	-15
		1B						
1896	Bro-N	.982	42	417	19	8	26	-1
1897	Bro-N	.900	3	26	1	3	1	-1
1898	Was-N	.953	17	154	8	8	12	-1
	Bro-N	.947	2	16	2	1	3	0
	Yr	.952	19	170	10	9	15	-1
1899	Bro-N	.981	41	389	24	8	25	2
1901	Mil-A	.982	125	1310	66	25	81	2
1902	StL-A	.985	126	1361	47	22	78	-8
1903	StL-A	.986	133	1416	91	22	71	5
1904	NY-A	.985	33	368	33	6	21	5
1905	NY-A	1.000	3	32	2	0	0	0
	Was-A	.956	4	40	3	2	0	0
	Yr	.975	7	72	5	2	0	0
1907	Was-A	.983	61	615	32	11	13	-2
1908	Chi-A	.988	9	80	4	1	4	0
Total	11	.982	599	6224	332	117	335	1
		3B						
1894	Bro-N	1.000	1	1	1	0	0	0

■ Mike Anderson   OF

YEAR	TM/L	PCT	G	PO	A	E	DP	FR
1971	Phi-N	.986	26	67	1	1	0	2
1972	Phi-N	.987	35	68	6	1	1	5
1973	Phi-N	.981	67	99	4	2	1	2
1974	Phi-N	.980	133	238	12	5	3	1
1975	Phi-N	.977	105	161	6	4	0	-8
1976	StL-N	.982	58	106	5	2	1	3
1977	StL-N	.980	77	96	4	2	0	5
1978	Bal-A	.962	47	25	0	1	0	1
1979	Phi-N	.973	70	68	3	2	1	6
Total	9	.980	618	928	41	0	7	17
		1B						
1974	Phi-N	1.000	1	2	0	0	0	0
1975	Phi-N	1.000	3	9	0	0	1	0
1976	StL-N	.970	5	30	2	1	3	0
Total	3	.977	9	41	2	1	4	0

■ Ed Andrews   OF

YEAR	TM/L	PCT	G	PO	A	E	DP	FR
1885	Phi-N	.921	99	175	11	16	1	2
1886	Phi-N	.903	104	189	24	23	2	4
1887	Phi-N	.902	99	203	18	24	1	-2
1888	Phi-N	.903	124	210	23	25	5	-6
1889	Phi-N	.808	9	20	1	5	0	-1
	Ind-N	.885	40	67	10	10	1	-4
	Yr	.867	49	87	11	15	1	-5
1890	Bro-P	.912	94	220	17	23	3	1
1891	Cin-a	.961	83	173	25	8	4	17
Total	7	.912	652	1257	129	134	17	11
		2B						
1884	Phi-N	.891	109	239	326	69	37	-23
1885	Phi-N	.786	5	9	13	6	3	-2
1886	Phi-N	.824	3	7	7	3	1	-2
1887	Phi-N	.788	7	16	10	7	1	-5
1889	Phi-N	.750	1	3	0	1	0	-1
	Ind-N	1.000	1	1	1	0	0	0
	Yr	.833	2	4	1	1	0	-1
Total	5	.880	126	275	357	6	42	-33
		1B						
1887	Phi-N	1.000	1	2	0	0	0	0

■ Mike Andrews   2B

YEAR	TM/L	PCT	G	PO	A	E	DP	FR
1966	Bos-A	1.000	5	11	18	0	2	2
1967	Bos-A	.976	139	303	345	16	63	-5
1968	Bos-A	.976	139	330	375	17	93	3
1969	Bos-A	.972	120	297	334	18	82	5
1970	Bos-A	.973	148	342	350	19	74	-30
1971	Chi-A	.956	76	177	191	17	51	-2
1972	Chi-A	.973	145	354	325	19	69	-14
1973	Chi-A	1.000	6	13	7	0	2	-2
	Oak-A	.944	9	11	6	1	2	-1
	Yr	.974	15	24	13	1	4	-3
Total	8	.973	787	1838	1951	107	438	-44
		1B						
1971	Chi-A	.981	25	197	11	4	17	-1
1972	Chi-A	1.000	5	33	2	0	7	0
1973	Chi-A	1.000	9	61	3	0	1	0
Total	3	.987	39	291	16	4	25	-1
		SS						
1967	Bos-A	.750	6	2	1	1	0	-1
1968	Bos-A	.933	4	9	5	1	1	-2
Total	2	.895	10	11	6	2	1	-3
		3B						
1968	Bos-A	1.000	1	0	3	0	0	0
1973	Chi-A	1.000	5	7	2	0	0	-1
Total	2	1.000	6	7	5	0	0	-1

■ Rob Andrews   2B

YEAR	TM/L	PCT	G	PO	A	E	DP	FR
1975	Hou-N	.982	94	191	237	8	65	6
1976	Hou-N	.977	107	228	354	14	66	8
1977	SF-N	.964	115	225	314	20	66	-12
1978	SF-N	.977	62	120	131	6	23	9
1979	SF-N	.956	53	96	101	9	21	4
Total	5	.972	431	860	1137	7	241	15
		SS						
1975	Hou-N	.875	6	2	12	2	2	0
1976	Hou-N	1.000	3	0	2	0	0	0
1978	SF-N	1.000	1	3	4	0	0	0
Total	3	.920	10	5	18	2	2	0
		3B						
1979	SF-N	1.000	3	1	1	0	0	0

■ Cap Anson   1B

YEAR	TM/L	PCT	G	PO	A	E	DP	FR
1879	Chi-N	.975	51	620	8	16	26	0
1880	Chi-N	.978	81	866	15	20	28	1
1881	Chi-N	.975	84	892	43	24	48	8
1882	Chi-N	.949	82	810	27	45	42	0
1883	Chi-N	.964	98	1031	41	40	59	4
1884	Chi-N	.956	112	1211	40	58	86	0
1885	Chi-N	.958	112	1253	39	57	62	-4
1886	Chi-N	.963	125	1188	66	48	69	7
1887	Chi-N	.973	122	1232	70	36	75	10
1888	Chi-N	.986	134	1314	65	20	85	9
1889	Chi-N	.982	134	1409	79	27	73	9
1890	Chi-N	.978	135	1345	49	31	61	2
1891	Chi-N	.981	136	1407	79	29	86	8
1892	Chi-N	.973	146	1491	67	44	62	-5
1893	Chi-N	.981	101	997	44	20	59	-4
1894	Chi-N	.990	82	739	47	8	52	3
1895	Chi-N	.985	122	1176	60	19	82	-1
1896	Chi-N	.983	98	880	54	16	67	2
1897	Chi-N	.975	103	933	62	25	67	2
Total	19	.974	2058	20794	955	583	1189	51
		3B						
1876	Chi-N	.849	66	135	147	50	8	13
1877	Chi-N	.883	40	74	77	20	9	6
1878	Chi-N	.625	3	0	5	3	0	-1
1880	Chi-N	.875	9	14	14	4	1	1
Total	4	.858	118	223	243	7	18	19
		C						
1876	Chi-N	1.000	2	2	0	0	0	0
1877	Chi-N	.867	31	103	41	22	5	2
1878	Chi-N	.947	3	13	5	1	3	1
1881	Chi-N	1.000	2	2	0	0	0	0
1882	Chi-N	.750	1	3	0	1	0	-1
1883	Chi-N	.500	1	2	0	2	0	-1
1884	Chi-N	.727	3	4	4	3	0	-1
1885	Chi-N	1.000	1	2	0	0	0	0
1886	Chi-N	.909	12	32	18	5	1	2
1887	Chi-N	.500	1	1	0	1	0	0
1890	Chi-N	1.000	3	9	2	0	0	0
1891	Chi-N	1.000	2	2	1	0	0	0
1896	Chi-N	.879	10	21	8	4	0	-2
1897	Chi-N	.961	11	36	13	2	2	0
Total	14	.888	83	232	92	1	11	0
		OF						
1878	Chi-N	.825	48	60	6	14	0	-4
1883	Chi-N	1.000	1	1	0	0	0	0
Total	2	.827	49	61	6	4	0	-4
		2B						
1878	Chi-N	.873	9	22	26	7	4	-3
1880	Chi-N	—	1	0	0	0	0	0
1890	Chi-N	.923	2	7	5	1	0	-1
1894	Chi-N	1.000	1	4	1	0	0	0
Total	4	.890	13	33	32	8	4	-4
		SS						
1880	Chi-N	.750	1	2	1	1	0	-1
1881	Chi-N	—	1	0	0	0	0	0
1884	Chi-N	.800	1	1	3	1	0	0
Total	3	.778	3	3	4	2	0	-1

■ John Antonelli   3B

YEAR	TM/L	PCT	G	PO	A	E	DP	FR
1944	StL-N	1.000	3	3	5	0	0	1
1945	StL-N	.667	1	2	0	1	0	0
	Phi-N	.959	108	129	201	14	24	-3
	Yr	.957	109	131	201	15	24	-3
Total	2	.958	112	134	206	5	24	-2
		2B						
1944	StL-N	1.000	2	2	2	0	0	0
1945	Phi-N	.950	23	47	49	5	7	-7
Total	2	.952	25	49	51	5	7	-7
		1B						
1944	StL-N	1.000	3	23	3	0	2	1
1945	Phi-N	1.000	1	2	0	0	0	0
Total	2	1.000	4	25	3	0	2	1
		SS						
1945	Phi-N	1.000	1	1	1	0	1	0

■ Luis Aparicio   SS

YEAR	TM/L	PCT	G	PO	A	E	DP	FR
1956	Chi-A	.954	152	250	474	35	91	0
1957	Chi-A	.972	142	246	449	20	85	-13
1958	Chi-A	.973	145	289	463	21	90	9
1959	Chi-A	.970	152	282	460	23	87	-4
1960	Chi-A	.979	153	305	551	18	117	30
1961	Chi-A	.962	156	264	487	30	86	6
1962	Chi-A	.973	152	280	452	20	102	10
1963	Bal-A	.983	145	275	403	12	76	-5
1964	Bal-A	.979	145	260	437	15	98	3
1965	Bal-A	.971	141	238	439	20	87	3
1966	Bal-A	.978	151	303	441	17	104	10
1967	Bal-A	.957	131	221	333	25	67	-20
1968	Chi-A	.977	154	269	535	19	92	25
1969	Chi-A	.976	154	248	563	20	94	29
1970	Chi-A	.976	146	251	483	18	99	9
1971	Bos-A	.971	121	194	338	16	56	-18
1972	Bos-A	.968	109	183	304	16	54	-17
1973	Bos-A	.966	132	190	404	21	68	-16
Total	18	.972	2581	4548	8016	366	1553	50

■ Luke Appling   SS

YEAR	TM/L	PCT	G	PO	A	E	DP	FR
1930	Chi-A	.879	6	12	17	4	1	-1
1931	Chi-A	.900	76	147	232	42	37	-5
1932	Chi-A	.929	85	195	287	37	66	14
1933	Chi-A	.939	151	314	534	55	18	117	11
1934	Chi-A	.945	110	243	341	34	55	-6
1935	Chi-A	.958	153	335	556	39	93	21
1936	Chi-A	.951	137	320	471	41	119	15
1937	Chi-A	.944	154	280	541	49	111	14
1938	Chi-A	.953	78	149	258	20	37	1
1939	Chi-A	.951	148	289	461	39	78	-2
1940	Chi-A	.953	150	307	436	37	83	-2
1941	Chi-A	.948	154	294	473	42	95	0
1942	Chi-A	.948	141	269	418	38	77	-7
1943	Chi-A	.957	155	300	500	36	115	7
1945	Chi-A	.930	17	37	56	7	7	-1
1946	Chi-A	.951	149	252	505	39	99	7
1947	Chi-A	.949	129	232	422	35	86	-7
1948	Chi-A	.945	64	133	210	20	50	1
1949	Chi-A	.964	141	253	450	26	95	-1
1950	Chi-A	.967	20	37	50	3	13	-1
Total	20	.948	2218	4398	7218	643	1424	58
		3B						
1932	Chi-A	.854	14	13	22	6	2	-2
1947	Chi-A	1.000	2	1	1	0	0	0
1948	Chi-A	.943	72	84	163	15	13	11
Total	3	.931	88	98	186	1	15	9
		2B						
1931	Chi-A	.833	1	4	1	1	0	-1
1932	Chi-A	.966	30	62	110	6	16	6
1934	Chi-A	.974	8	21	16	1	4	-3
1950	Chi-A	—	1	0	0	0	0	0
Total	4	.964	40	87	127	8	20	2
		1B						
1950	Chi-A	1.000	13	91	12	0	16	2

■ Jimmy Archer   C

YEAR	TM/L	PCT	G	PO	A	E	DP	FR
1904	Pit-N	.919	7	25	9	3	0	1
1907	Det-A	.975	17	62	16	2	0	3
1909	Chi-N	.960	80	408	97	21	7	-5
1910	Chi-N	.970	49	239	80	10	6	5
1911	Chi-N	.977	102	476	124	14	11	-1
1912	Chi-N	.966	118	504	149	23	15	-5
1913	Chi-N	.969	103	455	138	19	6	1
1914	Chi-N	.973	76	367	105	13	8	6
1915	Chi-N	.977	88	419	124	13	11	-1
1916	Chi-N	.979	61	236	84	7	5	-4
1918	Pit-N	.989	21	63	30	1	4	4
	Bro-N	.968	7	17	13	1	0	1
	Cin-N	1.000	7	22	10	0	3	2
	Yr	.987	35	102	53	2	7	7
Total	11	.971	736	3293	979	127	76	7
		1B						
1910	Chi-N	.975	40	381	17	10	25	-2
1911	Chi-N	.989	10	84	4	1	6	0
1913	Chi-N	.969	8	58	5	2	4	0
1915	Chi-N	1.000	4	28	2	0	0	0
1918	Pit-N	1.000	1	4	0	0	1	0
	Cin-N	.923	1	11	1	1	1	0
	Yr	.941	2	15	1	1	1	0
Total	5	.977	64	566	29	4	36	-2
		2B						
1907	Det-A	.857	1	2	4	1	0	0
1911	Chi-N	—	1	0	0	0	0	0
Total	2	.857	2	2	4	1	0	0
		OF						
1904	Pit-N	—	1	0	0	0	0	0
		3B						
1916	Chi-N	—	1	0	0	0	0	0

■ Jose Arcia   SS

YEAR	TM/L	PCT	G	PO	A	E	DP	FR
1968	Chi-N	.920	7	8	15	2	1	2
1969	SD-N	.944	37	29	55	5	8	-1
1970	SD-N	.955	67	89	146	11	32	8
Total	3	.950	111	126	216	8	41	9
		2B						
1968	Chi-N	1.000	10	22	19	0	2	0
1969	SD-N	.977	68	162	176	8	33	6
1970	SD-N	.980	20	44	40	0	15	6
Total	3	.983	98	228	235	8	50	12
		OF						
1968	Chi-N	1.000	17	19	0	0	0	1
1969	SD-N	1.000	4	1	0	0	0	0
1970	SD-N	1.000	7	3	0	0	0	0

YEAR	TM/L	PCT	G	PO	A	E	DP	FR
Total	3	1.000	28	23	0	0	0	1
3B								
1968	Chi-N	—	1	0	0	0	0	0
1969	SD-N	.875	8	1	6	1	3	1
1970	SD-N	.500	9	1	3	4	0	-2
Total	3	.688	18	2	9	5	3	-1
1B								
1969	SD-N	.500	1	1	0	1	0	0

■ Joe Ardner   2B

YEAR	TM/L	PCT	G	PO	A	E	DP	FR
1884	Cle-N	.866	25	53	70	19	6	-5
1890	Cle-N	.920	84	205	257	40	42	-5
Total	2	.908	109	258	327	9	48	-10
3B								
1884	Cle-N	.750	1	2	1	1	0	0

■ Hank Arft   1B

YEAR	TM/L	PCT	G	PO	A	E	DP	FR
1948	StL-A	.995	69	598	43	3	81	-1
1950	StL-A	.995	84	701	51	4	59	2
1951	StL-A	.989	97	820	86	10	100	8
1952	StL-A	.985	10	63	4	1	11	0
Total	4	.992	260	2182	184	8	251	9

■ Tony Armas   OF

YEAR	TM/L	PCT	G	PO	A	E	DP	FR
1976	Pit-N	1.000	2	3	0	0	0	0
1977	Oak-A	.981	112	294	9	6	4	2
1978	Oak-A	.991	85	214	3	2	0	8
1979	Oak-A	.976	80	194	7	5	2	8
1980	Oak-A	.975	158	374	17	10	2	12
1981	Oak-A	.993	109	259	8	2	2	6
1982	Oak-A	.983	135	333	9	6	2	8
1983	Bos-A	.985	116	326	5	5	0	2
1984	Bos-A	.974	126	329	4	9	2	-5
1985	Bos-A	.983	79	173	3	3	1	-3
1986	Bos-A	.969	117	247	4	8	0	-12
1987	Cal-A	1.000	27	36	0	0	0	-3
1988	Cal-A	.986	113	212	5	3	1	-6
1989	Cal-A	.990	47	97	4	1	1	5
Total	14	.981	1306	3091	78	0	17	22
1B								
1989	Cal-A	.833	2	4	1	1	2	0
SS								
1977	Oak-A	—	1	0	0	0	0	0

■ Charlie Armbruster   C

YEAR	TM/L	PCT	G	PO	A	E	DP	FR
1905	Bos-A	.944	35	154	30	11	0	-6
1906	Bos-A	.955	66	262	99	17	6	1
1907	Bos-A	.935	21	80	36	8	4	2
	Chi-A	1.000	1	9	1	0	0	1
	Yr	.940	22	89	37	8	4	3
Total	3	.949	123	505	166	6	10	-2
1B								
1906	Bos-A	1.000	1	8	1	0	0	0

■ Morrie Arnovich   OF

YEAR	TM/L	PCT	G	PO	A	E	DP	FR
1936	Phi-N	1.000	13	37	1	0	0	2
1937	Phi-N	.972	107	237	10	7	5	6
1938	Phi-N	.983	133	327	18	6	0	18
1939	Phi-N	.983	132	335	10	6	0	12
1940	Phi-N	.959	37	91	3	4	0	1
	Cin-N	1.000	60	129	5	0	0	3
	Yr	.983	97	220	8	4	0	4
1941	NY-N	.982	61	103	5	2	0	0
1946	NY-N	1.000	1	1	0	0	0	0
Total	7	.981	544	1260	52	5	5	42

■ Richie Ashburn   OF

YEAR	TM/L	PCT	G	PO	A	E	DP	FR
1948	Phi-N	.981	116	344	14	7	2	13
1949	Phi-N	.980	154	514	13	11	3	19
1950	Phi-N	.988	147	405	8	5	2	3
1951	Phi-N	.988	154	538	15	7	6	25
1952	Phi-N	.980	154	428	23	9	5	13
1953	Phi-N	.990	156	496	18	5	4	22
1954	Phi-N	.984	153	483	12	8	2	13
1955	Phi-N	.983	140	387	10	7	3	6
1956	Phi-N	.983	154	503	11	9	3	21
1957	Phi-N	.987	156	502	18	7	7	27
1958	Phi-N	.984	152	495	8	8	2	15
1959	Phi-N	.971	149	359	4	11	1	-3
1960	Chi-N	.976	146	317	11	8	2	-8
1961	Chi-N	.978	76	131	4	3	0	-8
1962	NY-N	.975	97	187	9	5	1	5
Total	15	.983	2104	6089	178	110	43	163
2B								
1962	NY-N	.900	2	5	4	1	1	-1

■ Alan Ashby   C

YEAR	TM/L	PCT	G	PO	A	E	DP	FR
1973	Cle-A	.978	11	45	0	1	0	-2
1974	Cle-A	1.000	9	12	0	0	0	1
1975	Cle-A	.990	87	441	43	5	6	4
1976	Cle-A	.987	86	475	51	7	7	5
1977	Tor-A	.984	124	619	71	11	11	-7
1978	Tor-A	.986	81	399	38	6	6	-9
1979	Hou-N	.987	105	548	57	8	5	-1
1980	Hou-N	.991	114	608	60	6	10	4
1981	Hou-N	.982	81	434	58	9	6	7
1982	Hou-N	.977	95	530	55	14	5	-4
1983	Hou-N	.974	85	435	56	13	2	-12
1984	Hou-N	.986	63	303	42	5	3	-1
1985	Hou-N	.978	60	312	37	8	1	2
1986	Hou-N	.985	103	632	43	10	2	4
1987	Hou-N	.993	110	778	46	6	6	-4
1988	Hou-N	.991	66	414	23	4	4	-11
1989	Hou-N	1.000	19	101	4	0	0	-3
Total	17	.986	1299	7086	684	113	74	-35
1B								
1975	Cle-A	1.000	2	8	0	0	1	0
1976	Cle-A	1.000	2	1	1	0	0	0
Total	2	1.000	4	9	1	0	1	0
3B								
1975	Cle-A	.500	1	1	0	1	0	0

YEAR	TM/L	PCT	G	PO	A	E	DP	FR
1976	Cle-A	—	1	0	0	0	0	0
Total	2	.500	2	1	0	1	0	0

■ Tucker Ashford   3B

YEAR	TM/L	PCT	G	PO	A	E	DP	FR
1976	SD-N	1.000	1	1	2	0	0	0
1977	SD-N	.937	74	32	145	12	14	4
1978	SD-N	.917	32	15	18	3	2	-7
1980	Tex-A	.943	12	9	24	2	1	3
1983	NY-N	.957	15	5	17	1	2	0
1984	KC-A	.909	9	2	8	1	1	0
Total	6	.936	143	64	214	9	20	0
2B								
1977	SD-N	.833	4	2	3	1	0	-1
1978	SD-N	.970	18	33	32	2	9	-9
1981	NY-A	—	2	0	0	0	0	0
1983	NY-N	1.000	13	8	14	0	4	-1
Total	4	.968	37	43	49	3	13	-11
1B								
1978	SD-N	.984	14	60	3	1	11	-1
SS								
1977	SD-N	.929	10	15	11	2	2	0
1980	Tex-A	1.000	2	1	1	0	0	0
Total	2	.933	12	16	12	2	2	0
C								
1983	NY-N	1.000	1	1	0	0	0	0

■ Ken Aspromonte   2B

YEAR	TM/L	PCT	G	PO	A	E	DP	FR
1957	Bos-A	.965	24	46	65	4	14	-3
1958	Bos-A	.952	6	13	7	1	3	-3
	Was-A	.964	72	139	184	12	49	2
	Yr	.963	78	152	191	13	52	-1
1959	Was-A	.960	52	101	137	10	25	-6
1960	Cle-A	.976	80	192	215	10	63	-4
1961	LA-A	.970	62	156	196	11	55	18
	Cle-A	.963	21	29	50	3	8	-2
	Yr	.969	83	185	246	14	63	16
1962	Cle-A	1.000	6	10	6	0	2	-1
	Mil-N	1.000	12	24	29	0	6	-1
1963	Chi-N	.951	7	14	25	2	4	3
Total	7	.969	342	724	914	3	229	3
3B								
1958	Was-A	1.000	11	6	13	0	1	0
1960	Cle-A	.892	36	46	53	12	8	-8
1962	Cle-A	.889	3	3	5	1	1	0
	Mil-N	.955	6	9	12	1	1	1
Total	3	.913	56	64	83	4	11	-7
SS								
1958	Was-A	1.000	1	1	0	0	0	0
1959	Was-A	.933	12	15	27	3	5	-4
Total	2	.935	13	16	27	3	5	-4
1B								
1959	Was-A	1.000	1	10	0	0	0	0
1963	Chi-N	1.000	2	5	1	0	0	0
Total	2	1.000	3	15	1	0	0	0
OF								
1959	Was-A	1.000	1	1	0	0	0	0

■ Bob Aspromonte   3B

YEAR	TM/L	PCT	G	PO	A	E	DP	FR
1960	LA-N	.867	4	5	8	2	1	0
1961	LA-N	.917	9	2	9	1	0	0
1962	Hou-N	.967	142	150	233	13	21	3
1963	Hou-N	.938	131	134	213	23	4	-16
1964	Hou-N	.973	155	133	261	11	10	-15
1965	Hou-N	.962	146	123	281	16	25	1
1966	Hou-N	.962	149	149	261	16	18	-10
1967	Hou-N	.963	133	130	237	14	17	-4
1968	Hou-N	.973	75	67	148	6	8	0
1969	Atl-N	.913	23	29	34	6	1	-5
1970	Atl-N	.938	30	27	49	5	5	0
1971	NY-N	.965	97	76	145	8	10	-5
Total	12	.960	1094	1025	1879	121	120	-51
OF								
1968	Hou-N	.923	36	43	5	4	1	-1
1969	Atl-N	.975	24	38	1	1	0	0
1970	Atl-N	1.000	1	1	0	0	0	0
Total	3	.946	61	82	6	5	1	-1
SS								
1960	LA-N	.933	15	11	17	2	4	-2
1961	LA-N	1.000	4	6	9	0	0	1
1962	Hou-N	.947	11	13	23	2	3	-1
1965	Hou-N	.933	4	8	6	1	2	-1
1966	Hou-N	.750	2	0	3	1	0	0
1968	Hou-N	1.000	1	0	1	0	0	0
1969	Atl-N	.923	18	3	9	1	1	-2
1970	Atl-N	1.000	4	1	4	0	0	0
Total	8	.942	59	42	72	7	10	-5
1B								
1963	Hou-N	1.000	1	3	0	0	0	0
1965	Hou-N	.981	6	47	5	1	3	1
1966	Hou-N	.833	2	5	0	1	1	0
1968	Hou-N	1.000	1	6	1	0	0	0
1970	Atl-N	—	1	0	0	0	0	0
Total	5	.971	11	61	6	2	4	1
2B								
1961	LA-N	—	2	0	0	0	0	0
1962	Hou-N	1.000	1	5	1	0	1	0
1969	Atl-N	1.000	2	4	2	0	0	0
Total	3	1.000	5	9	3	0	1	0

■ Brian Asselstine   OF

YEAR	TM/L	PCT	G	PO	A	E	DP	FR
1976	Atl-N	1.000	9	19	0	0	0	0
1977	Atl-N	.983	35	57	1	1	0	3
1978	Atl-N	.968	35	60	1	2	0	-1
1979	Atl-N	1.000	1	1	0	0	0	0
1980	Atl-N	.962	61	102	0	4	0	-6
1981	Atl-N	.958	16	22	1	1	1	-1
Total	6	.971	157	261	3	8	1	-5

■ Joe Astroth   C

YEAR	TM/L	PCT	G	PO	A	E	DP	FR
1945	Phi-A	.857	8	20	4	4	0	0
1946	Phi-A	.889	4	7	1	1	0	0
1949	Phi-A	.979	44	163	24	4	4	2
1950	Phi-A	.985	38	123	9	2	3	-6
1951	Phi-A	.992	57	228	18	2	2	4
1952	Phi-A	.992	102	436	36	4	9	-4
1953	Phi-A	.987	79	341	47	5	13	7
1954	Phi-A	.988	71	300	39	4	5	-2
1955	KC-A	.989	100	420	50	5	9	-3
1956	KC-A	1.000	8	19	5	0	1	2
Total	10	.987	511	2057	233	1	46	0

■ Toby Atwell   C

YEAR	TM/L	PCT	G	PO	A	E	DP	FR
1952	Chi-N	.977	101	451	50	12	2	-6
1953	Chi-N	.940	24	108	17	8	0	1
	Pit-N	.967	45	187	20	7	2	-2
	Yr	.957	69	295	37	15	2	-1
1954	Pit-N	.990	88	360	39	4	4	-2
1955	Pit-N	.992	67	334	24	3	3	5
1956	Pit-N	1.000	9	27	2	0	0	1
	Mil-N	1.000	10	32	4	0	1	-1
	Yr	1.000	19	59	6	0	1	0
Total	5	.980	344	1499	156	4	12	-4

■ Bill Atwood   C

YEAR	TM/L	PCT	G	PO	A	E	DP	FR
1936	Phi-N	.972	53	184	27	6	3	-1
1937	Phi-N	.968	80	290	48	11	5	-14
1938	Phi-N	.969	94	350	53	13	12	1
1939	Phi-N	1.000	2	7	0	0	1	0
1940	Phi-N	.989	69	238	43	3	3	1
Total	5	.974	298	1069	171	3	24	-13

■ Jake Atz   2B

YEAR	TM/L	PCT	G	PO	A	E	DP	FR
1902	Was-A	1.000	3	2	11	0	1	0
1908	Chi-A	.936	46	82	137	15	12	-3
1909	Chi-A	.954	114	202	311	25	40	-9
Total	3	.949	163	286	459	0	53	-12
SS								
1908	Chi-A	.958	18	19	50	3	3	0
1909	Chi-A	1.000	1	2	1	0	0	0
Total	2	.960	19	21	51	3	3	0
OF								
1907	Chi-A	—	1	0	0	0	0	0
1909	Chi-A	1.000	3	4	3	0	0	2
Total	2	1.000	4	4	3	0	0	2
3B								
1907	Chi-A	1.000	2	0	8	0	1	1
1908	Chi-A	1.000	1	0	1	0	0	0
Total	2	1.000	3	0	9	0	1	1

■ Rick Auerbach   SS

YEAR	TM/L	PCT	G	PO	A	E	DP	FR
1971	Mil-A	.963	78	120	193	12	31	-10
1972	Mil-A	.959	153	256	452	30	90	-21
1973	Mil-A	.833	2	4	6	2	0	0
1974	LA-N	.950	19	12	26	2	4	1
1975	LA-N	.960	81	77	137	9	17	-16
1976	LA-N	.943	12	23	27	3	8	6
1977	Cin-N	.913	12	18	24	4	3	2
1978	Cin-N	.971	26	24	42	2	8	9
1979	Cin-N	.974	16	27	48	2	5	6
1980	Cin-N	1.000	3	3	11	0	1	0
1981	Sea-A	.979	38	44	99	3	26	2
Total	11	.960	440	608	1065	9	193	-21
2B								
1974	LA-N	.903	16	25	31	6	2	1
1975	LA-N	1.000	1	5	0	0	1	0
1976	LA-N	.973	7	16	20	1	4	5
1977	Cin-N	.976	19	19	22	1	4	4
1978	Cin-N	.875	10	3	4	1	1	1
1979	Cin-N	.667	3	2	0	1	0	-1
1980	Cin-N	1.000	1	1	0	0	0	0
Total	7	.937	57	71	77	0	12	10
3B								
1974	LA-N	1.000	3	1	3	0	0	0
1975	LA-N	—	1	0	0	0	0	0
1976	LA-N	.714	8	2	3	2	1	0
1978	Cin-N	1.000	3	2	1	0	0	0
1979	Cin-N	.933	18	2	26	2	2	1
1980	Cin-N	.750	3	0	3	1	0	-1
Total	6	.896	36	7	36	5	3	0

■ Doug Ault   1B

YEAR	TM/L	PCT	G	PO	A	E	DP	FR
1976	Tex-A	1.000	4	23	0	0	1	-1
1977	Tor-A	.987	122	1113	103	16	91	7
1978	Tor-A	.979	25	178	10	4	13	0
1980	Tor-A	1.000	32	198	20	0	21	3
Total	4	.988	183	1512	133	0	126	9
OF								
1978	Tor-A	.857	7	12	0	2	0	0
1980	Tor-A	1.000	1	2	0	0	0	0
Total	2	.875	8	14	0	2	0	0

■ Jimmy Austin   3B

YEAR	TM/L	PCT	G	PO	A	E	DP	FR
1909	NY-A	.928	111	176	236	32	19	12
1910	NY-A	.942	133	204	284	30	10	4
1911	StL-A	.931	148	228	337	42	27	16
1912	StL-A	.911	149	219	292	50	22	-1
1913	StL-A	.944	142	216	288	30	21	7
1914	StL-A	.935	127	183	249	30	18	1
1915	StL-A	.917	141	188	264	41	32	10
1916	StL-A	.939	124	128	274	26	21	-7
1917	StL-A	.947	121	159	248	23	22	7
1918	StL-A	.921	48	56	83	12	7	-4
1919	StL-A	.939	98	161	207	24	15	7
1920	StL-A	.943	75	108	171	17	14	2
1921	StL-A	1.000	2	1	4	0	0	1
1922	StL-A	.957	9	13	9	1	0	-2
1925	StL-A	1.000	1	1	0	0	0	0
1926	StL-A	1.000	1	1	1	0	0	1
1929	StL-A	1.000	1	0	2	0	0	1
Total	17	.933	1431	2042	2949	358	229	48

YEAR	TM/L	PCT	G	PO	A	E	DP	FR
SS								
1909	NY-A	.905	23	49	65	12	8	2
1917	StL-A	.921	6	10	25	3	3	2
1918	StL-A	.939	57	117	158	18	13	-13
1921	StL-A	.938	14	29	32	4	0	-3
Total	4	.929	100	205	280	7	24	-12
2B								
1909	NY-A	—	1	0	0	0	0	0
1921	StL-A	1.000	6	13	10	0	3	-1
1922	StL-A	—	2	0	0	0	0	-1
Total	3	1.000	9	13	10	0	3	-2

■ Earl Averill C

YEAR	TM/L	PCT	G	PO	A	E	DP	FR
1956	Cle-A	.994	34	157	15	1	2	3
1959	Chi-A	.963	32	173	11	7	1	1
1960	Chi-A	.979	34	130	8	3	1	-9
	Chi-A	1.000	5	24	2	0	0	2
1961	LA-A	.991	88	542	38	5	6	-3
1962	LA-A	1.000	6	15	5	0	0	0
1963	Phi-N	.966	20	77	9	3	0	1
Total	6	.984	219	1118	88	9	10	-5
OF								
1959	Chi-N	.833	5	5	0	1	0	0
1960	Chi-N	1.000	1	1	0	0	0	0
1961	LA-A	1.000	9	6	0	0	0	0
1962	LA-A	1.000	49	70	2	0	0	-3
1963	Phi-N	1.000	8	9	0	0	0	0
Total	5	.989	72	91	2	1	0	-3
3B								
1958	Cle-A	.863	17	10	34	7	3	0
1959	Chi-N	.906	13	16	32	5	2	2
1960	Chi-N	—	1	0	0	0	0	0
1963	Phi-N	.714	1	2	3	2	0	0
Total	4	.874	32	28	69	4	5	2
2B								
1959	Cle-A	1.000	2	3	6	0	1	1
1961	LA-A	—	1	0	0	0	0	0
Total	2	1.000	3	3	6	0	1	1
1B								
1963	Phi-N	1.000	1	1	0	0	0	0

■ Earl Averill OF

YEAR	TM/L	PCT	G	PO	A	E	DP	FR
1929	Cle-A	.966	**151**	**384**	14	14	3	-4
1930	Cle-A	.949	134	345	11	**19**	**5**	2
1931	Cle-A	.976	**155**	398	9	10	3	0
1932	Cle-A	.964	153	412	12	16	3	-4
1933	Cle-A	.971	149	390	8	12	3	0
1934	Cle-A	.970	**154**	**410**	12	13	3	5
1935	Cle-A	.982	139	371	6	7	2	-6
1936	Cle-A	.969	150	369	11	12	2	-8
1937	Cle-A	.976	**156**	362	11	9	3	-13
1938	Cle-A	.975	131	331	14	9	2	1
1939	Cle-A	1.000	11	12	0	0	0	-3
	Det-A	.976	80	157	3	4	0	-4
	Yr	.977	91	169	3	4	0	-7
1940	Det-A	.962	22	23	2	1	0	-3
1941	Bos-N	1.000	4	5	2	0	0	1
Total	13	.970	1589	3969	115	126	29	-36

■ Bobby Avila 2B

YEAR	TM/L	PCT	G	PO	A	E	DP	FR
1949	Cle-A	1.000	5	5	7	0	1	10
1950	Cle-A	.983	62	153	135	5	46	-5
1951	Cle-A	.982	136	349	417	14	87	-1
1952	Cle-A	.966	149	355	431	**28**	81	-18
1953	Cle-A	**.986**	140	346	**445**	11	114	**13**
1954	Cle-A	.976	141	356	**406**	**19**	100	11
1955	Cle-A	.982	141	348	342	13	108	-3
1956	Cle-A	.977	135	322	351	16	83	-10
1957	Cle-A	.983	107	280	254	9	72	-13
1958	Cle-A	.986	82	175	177	5	62	-19
1959	Bal-A	.950	8	9	10	1	2	-3
	Bos-A	.975	11	19	20	1	8	-2
	Mil-N	.967	51	103	131	8	21	-12
	Yr	.966	59	112	141	9	23	-15
Total	11	.979	1168	2820	3126	130	785	-52
3B								
1957	Cle-A	.935	16	13	16	2	2	-2
1958	Cle-A	.943	33	18	48	4	6	-2
1959	Bal-A	1.000	1	0	1	0	0	0
Total	3	.941	50	31	65	6	8	-4
OF								
1959	Bal-A	1.000	10	12	0	0	0	-1
SS								
1950	Cle-A	1.000	2	4	2	0	1	0
1954	Cle-A	.818	7	5	4	2	2	-2
Total	2	.882	9	9	6	2	3	-2

■ Benny Ayala OF

YEAR	TM/L	PCT	G	PO	A	E	DP	FR
1974	NY-N	.927	20	37	1	3	1	-1
1976	NY-N	.889	7	7	1	1	0	1
1977	StL-N	1.000	1	6	1	0	1	2
1979	Bal-A	.974	24	38	0	1	0	1
1980	Bal-A	1.000	19	20	2	0	1	1
1981	Bal-A	1.000	4	3	2	0	0	1
1982	Bal-A	.972	25	35	0	1	0	1
1983	Bal-A	.953	24	41	0	2	0	3
1984	Bal-A	1.000	13	10	0	0	0	0
1985	Cle-A	.917	20	21	1	2	0	0
Total	10	.958	157	218	8	0	3	10
1B								
1982	Bal-A	1.000	3	24	0	0	2	-1

■ Joe Azcue C

YEAR	TM/L	PCT	G	PO	A	E	DP	FR
1960	Cin-N	1.000	14	66	6	0	0	5
1962	KC-A	.985	70	363	42	6	5	4
1963	KC-A	1.000	1	5	0	0	0	0
	Cle-A	.992	91	564	42	5	13	4
	Yr	.992	92	569	42	5	13	4
1964	Cle-A	.993	76	510	36	4	2	2
1965	Cle-A	.994	108	714	53	5	2	0
1966	Cle-A	.989	97	588	40	7	3	-7
1967	Cle-A	**.999**	86	636	57	1	4	7
1968	Cle-A	**.996**	97	699	50	3	11	11
1969	Cle-A	.980	6	46	4	1	2	1
	Bos-A	.981	19	90	14	2	3	3
	Cal-A	.992	80	437	52	4	10	5
	Yr	.989	105	573	70	7	15	9
1970	Cal-A	.991	112	587	51	6	10	-4
1972	Cal-A	1.000	2	4	0	0	0	1
	Mil-A	1.000	9	20	5	0	2	2
	Yr	1.000	11	24	5	0	2	3
Total	11	.992	868	5329	452	4	67	34

■ Charlie Babb SS

YEAR	TM/L	PCT	G	PO	A	E	DP	FR
1903	NY-N	.912	113	238	343	56	35	-3
1904	Bro-N	.927	151	**370**	459	65	44	-3
1905	Bro-N	.923	36	74	119	16	8	0
Total	3	.921	300	682	921	137	87	-6
1B								
1905	Bro-N	.977	31	314	31	8	24	4
3B								
1903	NY-N	.889	8	12	20	4	2	2
1905	Bro-N	.850	5	11	6	3	1	0
Total	2	.875	13	23	26	7	3	2
2B								
1905	Bro-N	1.000	2	2	3	0	1	1

■ Loren Babe 3B

YEAR	TM/L	PCT	G	PO	A	E	DP	FR
1952	NY-A	.909	9	4	16	2	3	2
1953	NY-A	.920	5	8	15	2	3	3
	Phi-A	.950	93	114	192	16	24	2
	Yr	.948	98	122	207	18	27	5
Total	2	.946	107	126	223	0	30	7
SS								
1953	Phi-A	—	1	0	0	0	0	0

■ Wally Backman 2B

YEAR	TM/L	PCT	G	PO	A	E	DP	FR
1980	NY-N	1.000	20	48	43	0	7	-8
1981	NY-N	.946	11	14	21	2	2	-3
1982	NY-N	.964	88	169	202	14	30	-9
1983	NY-N	1.000	14	11	12	0	2	-2
1984	NY-N	.981	115	218	294	10	72	-11
1985	NY-N	**.989**	140	272	370	7	76	-9
1986	NY-N	.966	113	186	290	17	56	-3
1987	NY-N	.983	87	131	210	6	44	-7
1988	NY-N	.989	92	128	219	4	36	-9
1989	Min-A	.982	84	146	187	6	37	-22
1990	Pit-N	1.000	15	22	32	0	5	-6
Total	11	.980	779	1345	1880	6	367	-89
3B								
1981	NY-N	—	1	0	0	0	0	0
1982	NY-N	.846	6	4	7	2	0	-2
1983	NY-N	.800	2	5	3	2	0	0
1990	Pit-N	.920	71	34	104	12	5	-12
Total	4	.908	80	43	114	6	5	-14
SS								
1980	NY-N	.963	8	14	12	1	4	-3
1982	NY-N	—	1	0	0	0	0	0
1984	NY-N	1.000	8	5	12	0	1	-1
1985	NY-N	1.000	1	1	0	0	0	0
Total	4	.978	18	20	24	1	5	-4
OF								
1982	NY-N	1.000	4	3	1	0	0	1

■ Gene Bailey OF

YEAR	TM/L	PCT	G	PO	A	E	DP	FR
1917	Phi-A	.833	4	5	0	1	0	-1
1919	Bos-N	1.000	3	5	0	0	0	0
1920	Bos-N	.929	8	12	1	1	0	0
	Bos-A	.986	40	67	3	1	0	-4
1923	Bro-N	.959	100	245	10	11	0	7
1924	Bro-N	1.000	17	39	2	0	1	3
Total	5	.965	172	373	16	4	1	5
1B								
1923	Bro-N	.980	5	46	4	1	2	1

■ Mark Bailey C

YEAR	TM/L	PCT	G	PO	A	E	DP	FR
1984	Hou-N	.983	108	629	56	12	4	0
1985	Hou-N	.979	110	565	51	**13**	6	-9
1986	Hou-N	.989	53	318	33	4	3	1
1987	Hou-N	.985	27	126	7	2	0	-1
1988	Hou-N	.981	8	48	3	1	0	-1
1990	SF-N	1.000	1	3	0	0	0	0
Total	6	.983	307	1689	150	2	13	-10
1B								
1985	Hou-N	1.000	1	1	1	0	0	0
1986	Hou-N	1.000	1	4	0	0	0	0
Total	2	1.000	3	5	1	0	0	0

■ Ed Bailey C

YEAR	TM/L	PCT	G	PO	A	E	DP	FR
1953	Cin-N	1.000	2	6	0	0	0	-1
1954	Cin-N	.973	61	194	20	6	2	-12
1955	Cin-N	.962	11	42	8	2	3	3
1956	Cin-N	.984	106	511	52	9	**10**	3
1957	Cin-N	.985	115	542	41	5	5	-13
1958	Cin-N	.988	99	438	44	6	6	-4
1959	Cin-N	.990	117	549	64	6	6	1
1960	Cin-N	.989	129	621	52	7	8	-13
1961	Cin-N	.967	12	54	5	2	0	-4
	SF-N	.985	103	629	40	10	4	-2
	Yr	.984	115	683	45	12	4	-6
1962	SF-N	.987	75	419	25	6	3	-6
1963	SF-N	.987	88	560	44	8	3	-2
1964	Mil-N	.982	80	416	28	8	3	-10
1965	SF-N	1.000	12	49	4	0	1	3
	Chi-N	.981	54	237	23	5	3	-6
	Yr	.984	66	286	27	5	4	-3
Total	13	.986	1064	5267	450	0	57	-63
1B								
1965	SF-N	.933	2	12	2	1	1	0
	Chi-N	1.000	3	4	0	0	1	0
	Yr	.947	5	16	2	1	2	0
OF								
1961	SF-N	1.000	1	1	0	0	0	0

■ Bob Bailey 3B

YEAR	TM/L	PCT	G	PO	A	E	DP	FR
1962	Pit-N	.921	12	10	25	3	2	0
1963	Pit-N	.933	153	113	332	32	**38**	6
1964	Pit-N	.943	105	81	218	18	19	8
1965	Pit-N	.939	142	96	243	22	25	-16
1966	Pit-N	.956	96	57	201	12	20	1
1967	LA-N	.941	65	40	152	12	11	3
1968	LA-N	.953	90	81	164	12	14	-2
1969	Mon-N	—	1	0	0	0	0	0
1970	Mon-N	.953	48	31	71	5	5	-11
1971	Mon-N	**.960**	120	69	194	11	14	-12
1972	Mon-N	.938	134	83	250	22	21	-8
1973	Mon-N	.956	146	93	275	17	25	-4
1974	Mon-N	.956	68	34	117	7	7	-14
1975	Mon-N	1.000	3	1	6	0	1	0
1976	Cin-N	.889	10	4	12	2	1	-1
1978	Bos-A	1.000	1	0	2	0	0	0
Total	16	.946	1194	793	2262	175	203	-50
OF								
1964	Pit-N	.913	35	36	6	4	0	0
1965	Pit-N	.964	28	23	4	1	0	1
1966	Pit-N	1.000	20	24	1	0	0	0
1967	LA-N	.949	27	37	0	2	0	-1
1968	LA-N	—	1	0	0	0	0	0
1969	Mon-N	.846	12	11	0	2	0	0
1970	Mon-N	.963	44	50	2	2	1	-3
1971	Mon-N	.985	51	58	7	1	0	2
1972	Mon-N	1.000	5	7	1	0	0	0
1973	Mon-N	1.000	2	1	0	0	0	0
1974	Mon-N	.974	78	105	8	3	3	-6
1975	Mon-N	.979	61	88	4	2	1	-5
1976	Cin-N	.974	31	35	2	1	1	-1
1977	Cin-N	1.000	3	2	0	0	0	0
1978	Bos-A	1.000	1	2	0	0	0	0
Total	15	.966	399	479	35	8	6	-14
1B								
1967	LA-N	.947	4	17	1	1	1	0
1969	Mon-N	.992	85	704	67	6	77	**6**
1970	Mon-N	.991	18	98	13	1	12	1
1971	Mon-N	.964	9	50	3	2	2	-1
1972	Mon-N	1.000	3	5	0	0	0	0
1977	Cin-N	.975	19	107	10	3	11	0
Total	6	.988	138	981	94	3	103	6
SS								
1963	Pit-N	.909	3	5	5	1	2	0
1964	Pit-N	.000	2	0	0	1	0	-1
1967	LA-N	.500	1	0	1	1	0	0
1968	LA-N	1.000	1	0	1	0	0	-1
Total	4	.733	7	5	6	4	2	-2

■ Bob Bailor OF

YEAR	TM/L	PCT	G	PO	A	E	DP	FR
1977	Tor-A	.988	63	156	10	2	2	11
1978	Tor-A	.964	125	303	15	12	**7**	15
1979	Tor-A	.987	118	210	16	3	2	1
1980	Tor-A	.991	98	205	16	2	5	10
1981	NY-N	1.000	13	13	0	0	0	0
1983	NY-N	1.000	3	5	0	0	0	0
1985	LA-N	—	1	0	0	0	0	0
Total	7	.980	421	892	57	9	16	37
SS								
1975	Bal-A	1.000	2	3	5	0	0	1
1976	Bal-A	—	1	0	0	0	0	0
1977	Tor-A	.959	53	79	155	10	25	-8
1978	Tor-A	1.000	4	1	3	0	0	-1
1980	Tor-A	1.000	12	24	29	0	7	4
1981	NY-N	.955	22	18	46	3	6	-1
1982	NY-N	.984	60	64	116	3	18	-11
1983	NY-N	.969	75	84	162	8	35	-7
1984	LA-N	1.000	16	15	51	0	10	7
1985	LA-N	1.000	5	3	10	0	1	1
Total	10	.973	250	291	577	4	102	-15
2B								
1975	Bal-A	1.000	1	2	4	0	1	1
1980	Tor-A	—	1	0	0	0	0	0
1981	NY-N	.963	13	12	14	1	3	-1
1982	NY-N	.982	56	86	129	4	23	-5
1983	NY-N	.960	50	73	120	8	25	0
1984	LA-N	.944	23	38	47	5	8	1
1985	LA-N	1.000	16	18	30	0	5	4
Total	7	.970	160	229	344	8	65	0
3B								
1978	Tor-A	.967	28	25	64	3	8	3
1979	Tor-A	1.000	9	7	16	0	0	-2
1980	Tor-A	1.000	11	4	16	0	2	1
1981	NY-N	—	1	0	0	0	0	0
1982	NY-N	.907	21	13	26	4	1	-5
1983	NY-N	1.000	11	9	14	0	5	2
1984	LA-N	.962	17	6	19	1	1	1
1985	LA-N	.962	45	14	63	3	6	10
Total	8	.964	143	78	218	1	23	10

■ Harold Baines OF

YEAR	TM/L	PCT	G	PO	A	E	DP	FR
1980	Chi-A	.963	137	229	6	9	1	-15
1981	Chi-A	.985	80	120	10	2	1	-5
1982	Chi-A	.980	**161**	326	10	7	4	-2
1983	Chi-A	.973	155	312	10	9	3	-1
1984	Chi-A	.981	147	307	8	6	1	-1
1985	Chi-A	.994	159	318	8	2	2	2
1986	Chi-A	.984	141	295	15	5	5	1
1987	Chi-A	1.000	8	13	0	0	0	-1
1988	Chi-A	.882	9	14	1	2	0	-1
1989	Chi-A	.981	25	52	0	0	1	-2
	Tex-A	.667	1	2	0	1	0	-2
	Yr	.964	26	54	0	2	0	-2

YEAR	TM/L	PCT	G	PO	A	E	DP	FR
1990	Tex-A	.833	2	5	0	1	0	0
Total	11	.979	1025	1993	68	5	17	-20

■ Doug Baird 3B

YEAR	TM/L	PCT	G	PO	A	E	DP	FR
1915	Pit-N	.939	120	142	226	24	13	-4
1916	Pit-N	.933	80	90	145	17	12	1
1917	Pit-N	.935	41	56	73	9	3	-4
	StL-N	.941	103	110	259	23	24	14
	Yr	.940	144	166	332	32	27	10
1918	StL-N	.967	81	99	219	11	12	16
1919	Phi-N	.950	66	100	147	13	17	11
	StL-N	.773	8	6	11	5	0	-3
	Bro-N	1.000	17	16	37	0	2	1
	Yr	.946	91	122	195	18	19	9
1920	Bro-N	.800	2	1	3	1	0	0
	NY-N	1.000	4	4	5	0	1	1
	Yr	.929	6	5	8	1	1	1
Total	6	.944	522	624	1125	103	84	33
OF								
1915	Pit-N	.982	20	49	5	1	0	4
1916	Pit-N	.943	16	31	2	2	0	1
1917	StL-N	—	2	0	0	0	0	0
1918	StL-N	1.000	1	2	0	0	0	0
1919	StL-N	—	1	0	0	0	0	0
Total	5	.967	40	82	7	3	0	5
2B								
1915	Pit-N	1.000	3	5	4	0	0	-1
1916	Pit-N	.942	29	62	68	8	10	-6
1917	Pit-N	.750	2	1	2	1	0	-1
1919	StL-N	.000	1	0	0	1	0	-1
Total	4	.934	35	68	74	0	10	-9
SS								
1918	StL-N	—	1	0	0	0	0	0

■ Del Baker C

YEAR	TM/L	PCT	G	PO	A	E	DP	FR
1914	Det-A	.920	38	79	25	9	3	-5
1915	Det-A	.940	61	184	53	15	8	-4
1916	Det-A	.975	59	164	29	5	4	-2
Total	3	.948	158	427	107	9	15	-11

■ Gene Baker 2B

YEAR	TM/L	PCT	G	PO	A	E	DP	FR
1953	Chi-N	.917	6	11	11	2	3	-3
1954	Chi-N	.967	134	355	385	25	102	-3
1955	Chi-N	.967	154	432	444	30	114	7
1956	Chi-N	.969	140	362	426	25	99	17
1957	Pit-N	.966	13	30	26	2	6	-3
1958	Pit-N	1.000	3	8	11	0	2	1
1960	Pit-N	1.000	1	1	0	0	0	0
Total	7	.968	451	1199	1303	4	326	16
3B								
1957	Chi-N	.867	12	11	15	4	1	-4
	Pit-N	.955	60	61	108	8	12	0
	Yr	.942	72	72	123	12	13	-4
1958	Pit-N	1.000	11	11	17	0	0	-1
1960	Pit-N	1.000	7	6	9	0	2	2
1961	Pit-N	1.000	3	0	6	0	0	1
Total	4	.953	93	89	155	2	15	-2
SS								
1957	Pit-N	.925	28	38	85	10	17	-1

■ Floyd Baker 3B

YEAR	TM/L	PCT	G	PO	A	E	DP	FR
1943	StL-A	1.000	1	1	1	0	0	0
1945	Chi-A	.971	58	36	99	4	6	1
1946	Chi-A	.962	6	10	15	1	1	1
1947	Chi-A	.980	101	84	253	7	28	18
1948	Chi-A	.961	71	78	171	10	17	13
1949	Chi-A	.977	122	106	269	9	31	12
1950	Chi-A	.987	53	50	102	2	7	3
1951	Chi-A	.924	44	27	46	6	4	0
1952	Was-A	1.000	1	0	1	0	0	0
1953	Was-A	.000	1	0	0	1	0	0
	Bos-A	.963	37	22	57	3	6	0
	Yr	.952	38	22	57	4	6	0
1954	Bos-A	.889	7	4	4	1	1	1
	Phi-N	1.000	7	6	11	0	0	3
1955	Phi-N	1.000	1	5	3	0	0	1
Total	12	.971	510	429	1032	4	101	53
2B								
1944	StL-A	.979	17	24	22	1	3	-1
1945	Chi-A	.977	11	15	28	1	4	1
1947	Chi-A	1.000	1	3	2	0	1	0
1948	Chi-A	.972	18	51	55	3	17	0
1949	Chi-A	—	1	0	0	0	0	0
1950	Chi-A	1.000	3	2	3	0	2	0
1951	Chi-A	1.000	5	11	9	0	3	-1
1952	Was-A	.994	68	151	176	2	36	-15
1953	Bos-A	.988	16	45	36	1	12	1
1954	Bos-A	1.000	1	2	0	0	0	0
	Phi-N	1.000	2	3	3	0	1	1
Total	10	.988	143	307	334	8	79	-14
SS								
1943	StL-A	.961	10	23	26	2	7	0
1944	StL-A	.940	16	17	46	4	6	-2
1947	Chi-A	1.000	1	1	3	0	0	0
1948	Chi-A	1.000	1	2	1	0	0	0
1949	Chi-A	1.000	3	5	11	0	1	0
1951	Chi-A	1.000	3	2	3	0	1	0
1952	Was-A	.895	7	15	19	4	6	-1
Total	7	.946	41	65	109	0	21	-3
OF								
1950	Chi-A	1.000	2	1	0	0	0	0

■ Frank Baker SS

YEAR	TM/L	PCT	G	PO	A	E	DP	FR
1970	NY-A	.973	35	62	118	5	22	4
1971	NY-A	.949	38	53	97	8	28	11
1973	Bal-A	.964	32	30	51	3	16	3
1974	Bal-A	.842	17	7	25	6	4	1
Total	4	.953	122	152	291	2	70	19
2B								
1973	Bal-A	.926	7	11	14	2	1	1
1974	Bal-A	.824	3	9	5	3	1	0
Total	2	.886	10	20	19	5	2	1
3B								
1973	Bal-A	—	1	0	0	0	0	0
1974	Bal-A	1.000	1	0	1	0	0	0
Total	2	1.000	2	0	1	0	0	0
1B								
1973	Bal-A	1.000	1	3	0	0	0	0

■ George Baker C

YEAR	TM/L	PCT	G	PO	A	E	DP	FR
1883	Bal-a	.800	3	10	2	3	1	-1
1884	StL-U	.897	68	435	113	63	11	4
1885	StL-N	.865	32	148	31	28	1	-8
1886	KC-N	.889	1	5	3	1	0	1
Total	4	.887	104	598	149	5	13	-4
OF								
1883	Bal-a	.500	1	1	0	1	0	0
1884	StL-U	.667	4	2	2	2	0	0
1885	StL-N	.750	2	3	0	1	0	0
Total	3	.667	7	6	2	4	0	0
SS								
1883	Bal-a	.667	4	2	4	3	1	-1
1884	StL-U	.889	2	2	6	1	1	0
Total	2	.778	6	4	10	4	2	-1
3B								
1885	StL-U	.667	3	1	3	2	1	0
1885	StL-N	.667	3	1	3	2	1	0
Total	2	.667	6	2	6	4	2	0
2B								
1884	StL-U	.833	4	11	14	5	1	1
1885	StL-N	.750	1	3	0	1	0	-1
Total	2	.824	5	14	14	6	1	0

■ Frank Baker 3B

YEAR	TM/L	PCT	G	PO	A	E	DP	FR
1908	Phi-A	1.000	9	12	22	0	0	2
1909	Phi-A	.920	146	209	277	42	16	-8
1910	Phi-A	.920	146	207	313	45	35	6
1911	Phi-A	.942	148	217	274	30	26	0
1912	Phi-A	.941	149	217	321	34	25	10
1913	Phi-A	.921	149	233	280	44	19	8
1914	Phi-A	.955	149	221	292	24	20	10
1916	NY-A	.940	96	133	210	22	16	2
1917	NY-A	.949	146	202	317	28	21	11
1918	NY-A	.972	126	175	282	13	30	11
1919	NY-A	.955	141	176	286	22	28	-2
1921	NY-A	.959	83	84	173	11	16	-2
1922	NY-A	.962	60	68	108	7	7	-10
Total	13	.943	1548	2154	3155	322	259	38

■ Dusty Baker OF

YEAR	TM/L	PCT	G	PO	A	E	DP	FR
1968	Atl-N	—	3	0	0	0	0	0
1969	Atl-N	1.000	3	2	0	0	0	0
1970	Atl-N	.800	11	11	1	3	0	0
1971	Atl-N	1.000	18	29	1	0	1	1
1972	Atl-N	.989	123	344	8	4	1	9
1973	Atl-N	.983	156	390	10	7	1	4
1974	Atl-N	.981	148	359	10	7	2	14
1975	Atl-N	.990	136	287	10	3	0	5
1976	LA-N	.986	106	254	3	1	1	-7
1977	LA-N	.987	152	227	8	3	2	-14
1978	LA-N	.985	145	250	13	4	1	-4
1979	LA-N	.990	150	289	14	3	4	5
1980	LA-N	.991	151	308	5	3	3	-2
1981	LA-N	.990	101	181	8	2	1	-2
1982	LA-N	.975	144	226	7	6	1	-11
1983	LA-N	.981	143	249	4	5	2	-6
1984	SF-N	.974	62	112	1	3	0	-5
1985	Oak-A	.971	35	65	3	2	0	0
1986	Oak-A	1.000	55	80	4	0	1	-3
Total	19	.985	1842	3663	110	6	21	-16
1B								
1985	Oak-A	.993	58	400	26	3	33	-5
1986	Oak-A	1.000	3	10	0	0	0	0
Total	2	.993	61	410	26	3	33	-5

■ Bill Baker C

YEAR	TM/L	PCT	G	PO	A	E	DP	FR
1940	Cin-N	1.000	24	87	9	0	1	4
1941	Cin-N	1.000	1	2	0	0	0	0
	Pit-N	.967	33	73	14	3	1	0
	Yr	.967	34	75	14	3	1	0
1942	Pit-N	1.000	11	19	1	0	0	1
1943	Pit-N	.979	56	157	29	4	3	0
1946	Pit-N	.965	41	95	14	4	2	-5
1948	StL-N	.994	36	152	15	1	2	-1
1949	StL-N	1.000	10	16	1	0	1	-2
Total	7	.983	212	601	83	2	10	-3
1B								
1946	Pit-N	1.000	1	2	0	0	1	0

■ Steve Balboni 1B

YEAR	TM/L	PCT	G	PO	A	E	DP	FR
1981	NY-A	1.000	3	14	1	0	2	0
1982	NY-A	.990	26	194	13	2	23	-1
1983	NY-A	.984	23	178	9	3	19	-1
1984	KC-A	.987	125	1102	79	15	102	-6
1985	KC-A	.993	160	1573	101	12	138	-8
1986	KC-A	.987	137	1236	98	18	115	-6
1987	KC-A	.989	55	521	41	6	39	2
1988	KC-A	.980	13	94	5	2	11	-1
	Sea-A	.994	40	334	25	2	34	-1
	Yr	.991	53	428	30	4	45	-2
1989	NY-A	.994	20	150	7	1	15	-2
1990	NY-A	.984	28	183	7	3	23	-3
Total	10	.989	630	5579	386	4	521	-27

■ Kid Baldwin C

YEAR	TM/L	PCT	G	PO	A	E	DP	FR
1884	KC-U	.885	44	199	86	37	4	-6
	CP-U	1.000	1	1	0	0	0	0
	Yr	.885	45	200	86	37	4	-6
1885	Cin-a	.891	25	121	30	24	3	-2
1886	Cin-a	.891	71	355	102	56	13	-7
1887	Cin-a	.874	96	381	165	79	9	-3
1888	Cin-a	.918	65	350	107	41	6	-3
1889	Cin-a	.912	55	274	89	35	5	5
1890	Cin-N	.902	20	92	27	13	3	3
	Phi-a	.887	19	100	33	17	3	0
Total	7	.893	396	1873	639	302	46	-13
OF								
1884	KC-U	.917	10	19	3	2	0	2
1885	Cin-a	.789	6	14	1	4	0	0
1886	Cin-a	1.000	6	9	1	0	0	0
1887	Cin-a	—	2	0	0	0	0	-1
1888	Cin-a	—	2	0	0	0	0	-1
1889	Cin-a	.750	4	3	0	1	0	-1
1890	Cin-N	1.000	2	3	1	0	0	1
Total	7	.885	32	48	6	7	0	0
3B								
1884	KC-U	.500	1	0	0	2	0	-1
1885	Cin-a	.500	1	1	1	2	0	-1
1886	Cin-a	.769	13	5	15	6	0	-2
1889	Cin-a	.667	1	0	4	2	0	0
1890	Phi-a	.800	5	6	14	5	1	1
Total	5	.730	21	12	34	7	1	-3
2B								
1884	KC-U	1.000	1	1	3	0	0	1
1885	Cin-a	.909	2	6	4	1	1	-1
Total	2	.933	3	7	7	1	1	0
1B								
1888	Cin-a	1.000	1	5	1	0	0	0
1889	Cin-a	1.000	1	11	0	0	0	0
Total	2	1.000	2	16	1	0	0	0

■ Neal Ball SS

YEAR	TM/L	PCT	G	PO	A	E	DP	FR
1907	NY-A	.817	11	22	27	11	2	-1
1908	NY-A	.898	130	268	438	80	28	-6
1909	Cle-A	.914	95	198	289	46	42	-11
1910	Cle-A	.927	27	48	66	9	9	-4
1911	Cle-A	1.000	1	2	3	0	0	0
1913	Bos-A	.857	7	16	26	7	1	1
Total	6	.902	271	554	849	153	82	-21
2B								
1907	NY-A	.889	5	7	9	2	1	-2
1908	NY-A	.667	1	2	0	1	0	-1
1909	NY-A	.917	8	15	18	3	1	-3
1910	Cle-A	.976	6	17	24	1	1	4
1911	Cle-A	.945	94	206	289	29	38	6
1912	Cle-A	.938	37	93	88	12	12	0
	Bos-A	.927	17	13	25	3	1	-3
	Yr	.936	54	106	113	15	13	-3
1913	Bos-A	.902	10	14	23	4	4	-2
Total	7	.939	178	367	476	5	58	-1
3B								
1910	Cle-A	1.000	3	2	5	0	0	1
1911	Cle-A	.891	17	20	37	7	3	-1
1913	Bos-A	—	1	0	0	0	0	0
Total	3	.901	21	22	42	7	3	0
OF								
1910	Cle-A	.857	6	6	0	1	0	-2

■ Dave Bancroft SS

YEAR	TM/L	PCT	G	PO	A	E	DP	FR
1915	Phi-N	.928	153	336	492	64	60	5
1916	Phi-N	.933	142	326	510	60	64	25
1917	Phi-N	.936	120	274	439	49	56	29
1918	Phi-N	.928	125	371	457	64	57	18
1919	Phi-N	.951	88	242	306	28	43	10
1920	Phi-N	.981	42	106	153	5	28	9
	NY-N	.946	108	256	445	40	67	30
	Yr	.955	150	362	598	45	95	39
1921	NY-N	.960	153	396	546	39	105	17
1922	NY-N	.941	156	405	579	62	93	22
1923	NY-N	.936	96	246	381	43	54	21
1924	Bos-N	.961	79	186	259	18	57	-5
1925	Bos-N	.945	125	300	459	44	81	10
1926	Bos-N	.956	123	317	398	33	75	-3
1927	Bos-N	.939	104	275	329	39	66	7
1928	Bro-N	.948	149	350	484	46	66	4
1929	Bro-N	.955	102	224	309	25	45	0
1930	NY-N	.966	8	13	15	1	0	1
Total	16	.944	1873	4623	6561	660	1017	200
2B								
1917	Phi-N	.850	3	11	6	3	2	-1
1923	NY-N	.958	11	34	35	3	8	1
Total	2	.935	14	45	41	6	10	0
3B								
1926	Bos-N	1.000	2	1	2	0	0	0
1927	Bos-N	—	1	0	0	0	0	0
Total	2	1.000	3	1	2	0	0	0
OF								
1917	Phi-N	1.000	2	4	0	0	0	0

■ Chris Bando C

YEAR	TM/L	PCT	G	PO	A	E	DP	FR
1981	Cle-A	.967	15	53	5	2	0	-2
1982	Cle-A	.990	63	268	23	3	1	-6
1983	Cle-A	.995	43	170	19	1	2	-1
1984	Cle-A	.982	63	305	30	6	4	-4
1985	Cle-A	.986	67	251	28	4	3	-4
1986	Cle-A	.990	86	359	30	4	3	-10
1987	Cle-A	.990	86	351	34	4	8	-2
1988	Cle-A	.979	32	123	14	3	2	0
	Det-A	—	1	0	0	0	0	0
	Yr	.979	33	123	14	3	2	0
1989	Oak-A	1.000	1	8	0	0	0	1
Total	9	.987	457	1888	183	7	23	-28

YEAR	TM/L	PCT	G	PO	A	E	DP	FR
		3B						
1982	Cle-A	—	2	0	0	0	0	0
1984	Cle-A	—	1	0	0	0	0	0
Total	2	—	3	0	0	0	0	0
		1B						
1984	Cle-A	1.000	1	2	0	0	0	0

■ Sal Bando 3B

YEAR	TM/L	PCT	G	PO	A	E	DP	FR
1966	KC-A	.933	7	5	23	2	1	4
1967	KC-A	.959	44	43	96	6	7	8
1968	Oak-A	.964	162	188	272	17	27	-11
1969	Oak-A	.954	162	178	321	24	36	-13
1970	Oak-A	.954	152	158	258	20	22	-22
1971	Oak-A	.971	153	141	267	12	22	-17
1972	Oak-A	.960	151	123	337	19	29	7
1973	Oak-A	.949	159	126	281	22	24	-23
1974	Oak-A	.946	141	113	287	23	28	-13
1975	Oak-A	.967	160	122	314	15	36	-16
1976	Oak-A	.962	155	125	304	17	26	-5
1977	Mil-A	.966	135	96	277	13	31	-2
1978	Mil-A	.968	134	89	329	14	25	12
1979	Mil-A	.963	109	87	222	12	16	-9
1980	Mil-A	.934	57	46	110	11	12	-4
1981	Mil-A	.967	15	7	22	1	3	1
Total	16	.959	1896	1647	3720	228	345	103
		1B						
1978	Mil-A	.979	5	43	3	1	4	0
1979	Mil-A	1.000	4	18	2	0	3	0
1980	Mil-A	.947	7	16	2	1	2	0
1981	Mil-A	1.000	9	58	3	0	6	0
Total	4	.986	25	135	10	2	15	0
		SS						
1976	Oak-A	1.000	5	2	6	0	1	0
1977	Mil-A	1.000	1	1	3	0	0	0
Total	2	1.000	6	3	9	0	1	0
		2B						
1972	Oak-A	.500	1	1	0	1	0	-1
1977	Mil-A	1.000	1	1	3	0	1	0
1979	Mil-A	1.000	1	1	1	0	0	0
Total	3	.875	3	3	4	1	1	-1
		OF						
1968	Oak-A	—	1	0	0	0	0	0

■ Ernie Banks 1B

YEAR	TM/L	PCT	G	PO	A	E	DP	FR
1961	Chi-N	.987	7	68	6	1	8	0
1962	Chi-N	.993	149	**1458**	106	11	**134**	1
1963	Chi-N	.993	125	1178	78	9	97	-1
1964	Chi-N	.994	157	**1565**	132	10	122	**12**
1965	Chi-N	.992	162	**1682**	93	15	143	-4
1966	Chi-N	.992	130	1178	81	10	88	0
1967	Chi-N	.993	147	**1383**	91	10	111	1
1968	Chi-N	.996	147	1379	88	6	118	-1
1969	Chi-N	**.997**	153	**1419**	87	4	116	1
1970	Chi-N	.993	62	528	35	4	53	-2
1971	Chi-N	1.000	20	167	12	0	15	1
Total	11	.994	1259	12005	809	0	1005	8
		SS						
1953	Chi-N	.981	10	19	33	1	9	3
1954	Chi-N	.959	154	312	475	34	105	-1
1955	Chi-N	**.972**	154	290	482	22	102	5
1956	Chi-N	.962	139	279	357	25	92	-16
1957	Chi-N	.975	100	168	261	11	59	-13
1958	Chi-N	.960	154	292	468	**32**	100	-2
1959	Chi-N	**.985**	154	271	**519**	12	95	6
1960	Chi-N	**.977**	156	**283**	**488**	18	**94**	11
1961	Chi-N	.965	104	173	358	19	68	10
Total	9	.969	1125	2087	3441	174	724	3
		3B						
1957	Chi-N	.982	58	73	87	3	12	-4
1962	Chi-N	1.000	3	4	1	0	1	0
1966	Chi-N	.842	8	5	11	3	0	0
Total	3	.968	69	82	99	6	13	-4
		OF						
1961	Chi-N	.974	23	32	6	1	0	2

■ Alan Bannister OF

YEAR	TM/L	PCT	G	PO	A	E	DP	FR
1974	Phi-N	1.000	8	10	0	0	0	1
1975	Phi-N	1.000	18	51	0	0	0	4
1976	Chi-A	.988	43	80	1	1	0	3
1977	Chi-A	1.000	3	3	1	0	0	1
1978	Chi-A	1.000	15	22	0	0	0	1
1979	Chi-A	.968	47	88	3	3	0	-3
1980	Chi-A	1.000	23	35	0	0	0	-1
	Cle-A	.971	40	66	2	2	1	-1
	Yr	.981	63	101	2	2	1	-2
1981	Cle-A	.986	35	70	2	1	0	0
1982	Cle-A	.991	55	115	1	1	0	-2
1983	Cle-A	.969	91	148	7	5	2	-7
1984	Hou-N	1.000	1	1	0	0	0	0
	Tex-A	1.000	3	7	0	0	0	0
1985	Tex-A	1.000	14	19	0	0	0	0
Total	12	.983	396	715	17	3	3	-5
		2B						
1975	Phi-N	1.000	1	1	0	0	0	0
1976	Chi-A	1.000	4	4	12	0	2	1
1977	Chi-A	1.000	3	3	5	0	1	-1
1978	Chi-A	.833	2	3	2	1	0	-1
1979	Chi-A	.963	65	150	160	12	32	-21
1980	Cle-A	.968	41	77	106	6	20	-13
1981	Cle-A	.992	30	51	74	1	14	-11
1982	Cle-A	.960	48	91	123	9	22	-4
1983	Cle-A	.979	27	35	59	2	12	-4
1984	Tex-A	.959	25	40	30	3	4	-11
1985	Tex-A	.970	10	16	16	1	2	-2
Total	11	.968	256	471	587	5	109	-68
		SS						
1974	Phi-N	—	2	0	0	0	0	0

YEAR	TM/L	PCT	G	PO	A	E	DP	FR
1975	Phi-N	.750	1	2	4	2	0	0
1976	Chi-N	.886	14	8	23	4	5	1
1977	Chi-N	.936	133	259	325	**40**	51	-33
1978	Chi-N	.958	8	9	14	1	3	0
1980	Cle-A	1.000	2	0	1	0	1	0
1981	Cle-A	1.000	1	3	0	0	0	-1
1982	Cle-A	1.000	2	1	0	0	0	0
1984	Hou-N	.947	4	10	8	1	1	-1
Total	9	.933	167	292	375	8	61	-34
		3B						
1976	Chi-A	—	1	0	0	0	0	0
1979	Chi-A	.850	12	10	24	6	4	-2
1980	Chi-A	.893	17	8	42	6	5	1
	Cle-A	1.000	3	3	2	0	0	0
	Yr	.902	20	11	44	6	5	1
1982	Cle-A	—	1	0	0	0	0	0
1984	Tex-A	.500	1	1	0	1	0	-1
1985	Tex-A	1.000	5	0	1	0	0	0
Total	6	.875	40	22	69	3	9	-2
		1B						
1979	Chi-A	1.000	1	2	0	0	1	0
1981	Cle-A	.833	2	5	0	1	0	0
1983	Cle-A	1.000	3	3	0	0	0	0
1984	Tex-A	1.000	1	12	0	0	0	0
1985	Tex-A	1.000	4	11	1	0	2	0
Total	5	.971	11	33	1	1	3	0

■ Jimmy Bannon OF

YEAR	TM/L	PCT	G	PO	A	E	DP	FR
1893	StL-N	.795	24	29	2	8	0	-5
1894	Bos-N	.873	128	240	**43**	**41**	**12**	**18**
1895	Bos-N	.879	122	209	30	33	3	10
1896	Bos-N	.901	76	132	13	16	2	1
Total	4	.877	350	610	88	8	17	24
		SS						
1893	StL-N	.588	2	2	8	7	2	-1
1896	Bos-N	.861	5	13	18	5	4	1
Total	2	.774	7	15	26	2	6	0
		2B						
1896	Bos-N	.878	6	16	20	5	1	0
		3B						
1896	Bos-N	.750	3	3	6	3	0	-1

■ Walter Barbare 3B

YEAR	TM/L	PCT	G	PO	A	E	DP	FR
1914	Cle-A	.933	14	12	30	3	3	1
1915	Cle-A	.960	68	99	141	10	12	7
1916	Cle-A	.977	12	12	30	1	2	1
1918	Bos-A	.826	11	6	13	4	1	-4
1919	Pit-N	.961	80	109	136	10	11	-7
1920	Pit-N	1.000	5	4	10	0	1	1
1921	Bos-N	1.000	2	2	2	0	1	0
1922	Bos-N	.975	38	44	72	3	5	0
Total	8	.959	230	288	434	1	36	-1
		SS						
1914	Cle-A	.667	1	1	1	1	1	-1
1918	Bos-A	1.000	1	0	1	0	0	0
1920	Pit-N	.923	34	54	102	13	14	-10
1921	Bos-N	.957	121	294	393	31	58	-16
Total	4	.949	157	349	497	5	73	-27
		2B						
1919	Pit-N	1.000	1	2	1	0	0	0
1920	Pit-N	1.000	12	21	49	0	6	4
1921	Bos-N	.976	8	15	26	1	4	1
1922	Bos-N	.966	45	95	157	9	27	1
Total	4	.973	66	133	233	0	37	4
		1B						
1915	Cle-A	1.000	1	2	0	0	0	0
1922	Bos-N	.982	14	102	9	2	12	1
Total	2	.983	15	104	9	2	12	1

■ Jap Barbeau 3B

YEAR	TM/L	PCT	G	PO	A	E	DP	FR
1906	Cle-A	.830	32	29	49	16	5	-6
1909	Pit-N	.891	85	99	139	29	8	-20
	StL-N	.901	47	56	72	14	7	-11
	Yr	.895	132	155	211	43	15	-31
1910	StL-N	.917	6	4	18	2	0	2
Total	3	.884	170	188	278	1	20	-35
		2B						
1905	Cle-A	.905	11	24	33	6	6	1
1910	StL-N	1.000	1	2	1	0	1	0
Total	2	.909	12	26	34	6	7	1
		SS						
1906	Cle-A	.861	6	12	19	5	0	-1

■ Turner Barber OF

YEAR	TM/L	PCT	G	PO	A	E	DP	FR
1915	Was-A	.952	19	17	3	1	1	-2
1916	Was-A	.833	10	10	0	2	0	-3
1917	Chi-N	1.000	7	13	2	0	0	1
1918	Chi-N	.940	27	45	2	3	0	-2
1919	Chi-N	.949	68	123	7	7	1	-2
1920	Chi-N	.966	17	27	1	1	0	-1
1921	Chi-N	.970	123	234	23	8	4	3
1922	Chi-N	.953	47	78	4	4	1	-3
1923	Bro-N	1.000	12	20	1	0	1	-1
Total	9	.959	330	567	43	6	8	-10
		1B						
1918	Chi-N	.976	4	37	3	1	3	0
1920	Chi-N	.988	69	739	30	9	40	-5
1922	Chi-N	1.000	16	164	4	0	11	-1
Total	3	.990	89	940	37	0	54	-6
		2B						
1920	Chi-N	1.000	2	1	1	0	0	0

■ George Barclay OF

YEAR	TM/L	PCT	G	PO	A	E	DP	FR
1902	StL-N	.904	137	247	16	28	5	-7
1903	StL-N	.901	107	187	13	22	0	-8
1904	StL-N	.947	103	170	7	10	2	-6
	Bos-N	.935	24	27	2	2	1	-3
	Yr	.945	127	197	9	12	3	-9
1905	Bos-N	.854	28	39	2	7	1	-4
Total	4	.911	399	670	40	9	9	-28

■ Jesse Barfield OF

YEAR	TM/L	PCT	G	PO	A	E	DP	FR
1981	Tor-A	1.000	25	71	2	0	1	2
1982	Tor-A	.963	137	217	15	9	4	-9
1983	Tor-A	.966	120	213	16	8	4	-1
1984	Tor-A	.952	88	190	9	10	5	4
1985	Tor-A	.989	154	349	**22**	4	**8**	**17**
1986	Tor-A	.992	157	368	**20**	3	**8**	**20**
1987	Tor-A	.992	158	341	**17**	3	4	14
1988	Tor-A	.988	136	325	12	4	4	**14**
1989	Tor-A	.979	21	43	4	1	1	1
	NY-A	.972	129	297	16	9	3	12
	Yr	.973	150	340	**20**	10	4	13
1990	NY-A	.973	151	305	16	9	3	5
Total	10	.980	1276	2719	149	0	45	79

■ Ray Barker 1B

YEAR	TM/L	PCT	G	PO	A	E	DP	FR
1965	Cle-A	1.000	3	2	0	0	0	0
	NY-A	.991	61	398	45	4	41	-17
	Yr	.991	64	400	45	4	41	-17
1966	NY-A	.987	47	196	25	3	11	5
1967	NY-A	.961	13	66	8	3	5	-1
Total	3	.987	124	662	78	0	57	-13
		3B						
1965	NY-A	1.000	3	0	4	0	0	1
		OF						
1960	Bal-A	—	1	0	0	0	0	0

■ Sam Barkley 2B

YEAR	TM/L	PCT	G	PO	A	E	DP	FR
1884	Tol-a	.930	103	318	358	51	46	26
1885	StL-a	.921	96	286	328	53	38	14
1886	Pit-a	.936	112	362	328	47	52	-3
1887	Pit-N	.900	36	112	114	25	14	-3
1888	KC-a	.938	116	341	314	43	44	-7
1889	KC-a	.923	41	90	103	16	20	-12
Total	6	.929	504	1509	1545	235	214	15
		1B						
1885	StL-a	.985	11	125	3	2	8	0
1886	Pit-a	1.000	2	20	1	0	1	0
1887	Pit-N	.979	53	552	15	12	24	-1
1889	KC-a	.964	4	26	1	1	1	0
Total	4	.980	70	723	20	5	34	-1
		OF						
1886	Pit-a	1.000	8	9	0	0	0	-1
		C						
1884	Tol-a	.800	2	8	0	2	0	-1

■ Babe Barna OF

YEAR	TM/L	PCT	G	PO	A	E	DP	FR
1937	Phi-A	.800	9	8	0	2	0	-2
1938	Phi-A	.917	7	10	1	1	0	-1
1941	NY-N	1.000	10	16	2	0	1	0
1942	NY-N	.983	89	169	4	3	0	-4
1943	NY-N	.984	31	58	2	1	0	-2
	Bos-A	.940	29	44	3	3	1	-5
Total	5	.969	175	305	12	0	2	-14
		1B						
1937	Phi-A	1.000	1	9	2	0	3	1

■ Red Barnes OF

YEAR	TM/L	PCT	G	PO	A	E	DP	FR
1927	Was-A	1.000	3	3	1	0	1	0
1928	Was-A	.978	104	255	16	6	2	4
1929	Was-A	.877	30	48	2	7	0	-6
1930	Chi-A	.939	72	179	6	12	3	0
Total	4	.953	209	485	25	5	6	-2

■ Ross Barnes SS

YEAR	TM/L	PCT	G	PO	A	E	DP	FR
1879	Cin-N	.864	61	93	211	48	14	6
1881	Bos-N	.854	63	91	214	**52**	17	1
Total	2	.859	124	184	425	100	31	7
		2B						
1876	Chi-N	**.910**	66	167	199	36	22	5
1877	Chi-N	.838	22	49	70	23	5	-8
1879	Cin-N	.853	16	44	43	15	5	-8
1881	Bos-N	.851	7	19	21	7	3	-1
Total	4	.883	111	279	333	1	35	-12

■ Clyde Barnhart OF

YEAR	TM/L	PCT	G	PO	A	E	DP	FR
1922	Pit-N	.956	26	41	2	2	0	-2
1923	Pit-N	.985	92	179	14	3	1	2
1924	Pit-N	.970	88	186	8	6	3	0
1925	Pit-N	.962	138	295	11	12	2	-8
1926	Pit-N	.991	61	101	5	1	1	-3
1927	Pit-N	.978	94	222	5	5	2	1
1928	Pit-N	.971	48	96	3	3	0	-4
Total	7	.973	547	1120	48	2	9	-14
		3B						
1920	Pit-N	.971	12	10	23	1	3	0
1921	Pit-N	.956	118	101	204	14	19	-19
1922	Pit-N	.918	30	35	32	6	4	-9
1928	Pit-N	—	1	0	0	0	0	0
Total	4	.951	161	146	259	1	26	-28

■ Jimmy Barrett OF

YEAR	TM/L	PCT	G	PO	A	E	DP	FR
1899	Cin-N	.936	26	42	2	3	0	-2
1900	Cin-N	.929	137	287	25	24	6	4
1901	Det-A	.940	135	300	**31**	21	7	15
1902	Det-A	.961	136	**326**	22	14	6	8
1903	Det-A	.955	136	303	**19**	15	7	7
1904	Det-A	.971	162	**339**	29	11	6	**12**
1905	Det-A	1.000	18	29	0	0	0	-3
1906	Cin-N	1.000	4	3	1	0	1	0
1907	Bos-A	.966	99	183	14	7	5	4
1908	Bos-A	1.000	1	2	0	0	0	-1
Total	10	.954	855	1814	143	5	38	44

■ Johnny Barrett OF

YEAR	TM/L	PCT	G	PO	A	E	DP	FR
1942	Pit-N	.973	94	202	11	6	4	5
1943	Pit-N	.988	99	165	6	2	0	-12
1944	Pit-N	.972	147	373	12	**11**	4	9
1945	Pit-N	.976	132	318	8	8	0	4
1946	Pit-N	.919	21	33	1	3	1	-2
	Bos-N	.962	17	24	1	1	0	0

YEAR	TM/L	PCT	G	PO	A	E	DP	FR
Yr		.937	38	57	2	4	1	-2
Total	5	.974	510	1115	39	1	9	4

■ Marty Barrett 2B

YEAR	TM/L	PCT	G	PO	A	E	DP	FR
1982	Bos-A	1.000	7	11	21	0	4	5
1983	Bos-A	.984	23	32	28	1	8	4
1984	Bos-A	.987	136	245	417	9	67	0
1985	Bos-A	.987	155	355	479	11	110	15
1986	Bos-A	.982	158	303	450	14	104	-3
1987	Bos-A	.988	137	320	438	9	108	32
1988	Bos-A	.990	150	312	402	7	97	2
1989	Bos-A	.975	80	152	245	10	53	1
1990	Bos-A	.992	60	90	147	2	27	10
Total	9	.986	906	1820	2627	3	578	66
3B								
1990	Bos-A	1.000	1	0	1	0	1	0

■ Bob Barrett 3B

YEAR	TM/L	PCT	G	PO	A	E	DP	FR
1924	Chi-N	.875	8	6	8	2	0	-1
1925	Chi-N	1.000	6	6	2	0	2	-1
1927	Bro-N	.920	96	76	167	21	12	-8
1929	Bos-A	.938	34	28	62	6	3	6
Total	4	.924	144	116	239	9	17	-4
2B								
1924	Chi-N	.943	25	48	68	7	11	0
1925	Chi-N	1.000	4	7	7	0	1	-2
1929	Bos-A	—	2	0	0	0	0	0
Total	3	.949	31	55	75	7	12	-2
1B								
1924	Chi-N	.949	10	69	5	4	8	0
1929	Bos-A	1.000	4	24	2	0	2	0
Total	2	.962	14	93	7	4	10	0
OF								
1929	Bos-A	1.000	1	1	0	0	0	0

■ Bill Barrett OF

YEAR	TM/L	PCT	G	PO	A	E	DP	FR
1923	Chi-A	.940	40	89	5	6	1	0
1924	Chi-A	.927	28	45	6	4	4	-1
1925	Chi-A	.956	27	42	1	2	0	-4
1926	Chi-A	.969	102	179	8	6	2	-5
1927	Chi-A	.963	147	289	22	12	6	7
1928	Chi-A	.988	37	72	7	1	0	3
1929	Bos-A	.974	109	204	17	6	4	4
1930	Bos-A	1.000	5	5	0	0	0	-1
	Was-A	1.000	1	1	0	0	0	0
	Yr	1.000	6	6	0	0	0	-1
Total	8	.964	496	926	66	7	17	3
SS								
1921	Phi-A	.925	8	12	25	3	1	2
1924	Chi-A	.904	77	167	199	39	36	-14
1925	Chi-A	.875	4	4	10	2	0	0
Total	3	.905	89	183	234	4	37	-12
2B								
1925	Chi-A	.943	41	83	115	12	23	-3
1928	Chi-A	.963	25	50	55	4	7	-8
Total	2	.950	66	133	170	6	30	-11
3B								
1921	Phi-A	1.000	2	0	5	0	0	1
1923	Chi-A	1.000	1	2	3	0	0	0
1924	Chi-A	.929	8	11	15	2	2	0
1925	Chi-A	1.000	4	3	5	0	1	0
1929	Bos-A	1.000	1	0	1	0	0	0
Total	5	.957	16	16	29	2	3	1
1B								
1921	Phi-A	1.000	1	1	0	0	0	0
1926	Chi-A	.857	2	11	1	2	1	0
Total	2	.867	3	12	1	2	1	0

■ Shad Barry OF

YEAR	TM/L	PCT	G	PO	A	E	DP	FR
1899	Was-N	.946	23	33	2	2	0	-4
1900	Bos-N	.956	24	39	4	2	2	-1
1901	Bos-N	.926	11	24	1	2	0	0
	Phi-N	1.000	13	29	0	0	0	-1
	Yr	.964	24	53	1	2	0	-1
1902	Phi-N	.939	137	185	15	13	3	-5
1903	Phi-N	.970	107	211	14	7	2	1
1904	Phi-N	.979	32	79	14	2	5	14
	Chi-N	.917	30	52	3	5	0	-1
	Yr	.955	62	131	17	7	5	13
1905	Cin-N	1.000	2	1	0	0	0	-1
1906	Cin-N	.917	30	48	7	5	0	1
	StL-N	.930	35	37	3	3	1	-5
	Yr	.922	65	85	10	8	1	-4
1907	StL-N	.963	81	93	11	4	0	-6
1908	StL-N	.967	69	109	10	4	0	1
	NY-N	.971	31	34	0	1	0	-6
	Yr	.968	100	143	10	5	0	-5
Total	10	.955	625	974	84	0	13	-13
1B								
1899	Was-N	.994	22	164	4	1	8	-1
1900	Bos-N	.963	10	103	2	4	5	-2
1902	Phi-N	1.000	1	8	0	0	0	-2
1903	Phi-N	.974	30	291	13	8	10	-2
1904	Chi-N	.974	18	181	8	5	11	-2
1905	Chi-N	.982	26	256	18	5	10	0
	Cin-N	.982	124	1216	61	23	77	-7
	Yr	.982	150	1472	79	28	87	-7
1906	Cin-N	.993	43	433	25	3	24	0
	StL-N	.967	21	224	13	8	8	-1
	Yr	.984	64	657	38	11	32	-1
Total	7	.981	295	2876	144	7	153	-15
2B								
1899	Was-N	.921	7	19	16	3	3	-3
1900	Bos-N	.857	16	32	22	9	5	-8
1901	Phi-N	.903	35	65	93	17	7	-8
1904	Chi-N	1.000	2	3	2	0	1	0
Total	4	.897	60	119	133	9	16	-19
3B								
1899	Was-N	.833	13	11	14	5	0	-2

YEAR	TM/L	PCT	G	PO	A	E	DP	FR
1900	Bos-N	.667	1	0	2	1	0	0
1901	Phi-N	.791	16	23	30	14	1	-3
1903	Phi-N	.667	1	1	1	1	0	-1
1904	Phi-N	.600	1	1	2	2	0	-1
	Chi-N	.943	16	21	29	3	0	2
	Yr	.914	17	22	31	5	0	1
1906	StL-N	.944	6	4	13	1	0	-1
Total	6	.849	54	61	91	7	1	-6
SS								
1899	Was-N	.875	13	27	29	8	2	-5
1900	Bos-N	.917	18	25	52	7	1	-5
1901	Phi-N	1.000	1	1	0	0	0	0
1904	Chi-N	.843	8	13	30	8	4	0
1908	StL-N	.625	2	3	2	3	1	-2
Total	5	.875	42	69	113	6	8	-12

■ Jack Barry SS

YEAR	TM/L	PCT	G	PO	A	E	DP	FR
1908	Phi-A	.889	14	20	28	6	0	-6
1909	Phi-A	.927	124	196	351	43	40	-31
1910	Phi-A	.916	145	279	406	63	54	-22
1911	Phi-A	.944	127	268	384	39	49	-7
1912	Phi-A	.925	139	238	438	55	55	-6
1913	Phi-A	.953	134	248	403	32	60	-8
1914	Phi-A	.947	140	244	447	39	61	5
1915	Phi-A	.952	54	106	150	13	21	-4
Total	8	.935	877	1599	2607	290	340	-79
2B								
1908	Phi-A	.966	20	29	56	3	3	-3
1915	Bos-A	.962	78	143	216	14	19	-4
1916	Bos-A	.974	94	200	282	13	30	2
1917	Bos-A	.974	116	196	339	14	40	-11
1919	Bos-A	.922	31	54	88	12	13	-7
Total	5	.966	339	622	981	6	105	-23
3B								
1908	Phi-A	.875	3	5	2	1	0	-2

■ Dick Bartell SS

YEAR	TM/L	PCT	G	PO	A	E	DP	FR
1927	Pit-N	1.000	1	3	2	0	1	0
1928	Pit-N	.930	27	52	81	10	14	-3
1929	Pit-N	.953	74	179	246	21	42	-3
1930	Pit-N	.941	126	304	458	48	111	5
1931	Phi-N	.948	133	315	432	41	96	3
1932	Phi-N	.963	154	359	529	34	83	10
1933	Phi-N	.951	152	381	493	45	100	9
1934	Phi-N	.954	146	350	483	40	93	14
1935	NY-N	.954	137	339	424	37	71	10
1936	NY-N	.956	144	317	559	40	106	45
1937	NY-N	.958	128	281	476	33	96	38
1938	NY-N	.952	127	288	447	37	85	22
1939	Chi-N	.943	101	241	307	33	62	-5
1940	Det-A	.953	139	295	394	34	74	12
1941	Det-A	.920	5	12	11	2	2	1
	NY-N	.974	21	31	45	2	5	-5
1942	NY-N	.951	31	59	76	7	14	-8
1943	NY-N	.965	33	66	127	7	17	8
Total	17	.953	1679	3872	5590	471	1072	153
3B								
1928	Pit-N	—	1	0	0	0	0	0
1939	Chi-N	—	1	0	0	0	0	0
1941	NY-N	.959	84	91	169	11	16	-6
1942	NY-N	.965	52	76	115	7	13	9
1943	NY-N	.980	54	62	131	4	9	11
1946	NY-N	1.000	4	0	3	0	0	1
Total	6	.967	196	229	418	2	38	15
2B								
1928	Pit-N	.974	39	106	118	6	26	5
1929	Pit-N	.973	70	213	212	12	45	7
1931	Phi-N	.933	3	4	10	1	2	0
1946	NY-N	1.000	2	1	0	0	0	0
Total	4	.972	114	324	340	9	73	12

■ Bob Barton C

YEAR	TM/L	PCT	G	PO	A	E	DP	FR
1965	SF-N	1.000	2	13	0	0	0	0
1966	SF-N	.994	39	161	19	1	4	7
1967	SF-N	1.000	7	33	3	0	0	1
1968	SF-N	.995	45	194	23	1	4	12
1969	SF-N	.985	49	186	9	3	3	0
1970	SD-N	.995	59	347	28	2	5	6
1971	SD-N	.981	119	698	67	15	10	12
1972	SD-N	.989	29	170	13	2	1	1
1973	Cin-N	1.000	2	5	0	0	0	1
1974	SD-N	.981	29	179	23	4	3	9
Total	10	.987	380	1986	185	8	30	49

■ Monty Basgall 2B

YEAR	TM/L	PCT	G	PO	A	E	DP	FR
1948	Pit-N	1.000	22	37	35	0	4	6
1949	Pit-N	.972	98	224	224	13	58	-8
1951	Pit-N	.969	55	140	144	9	39	11
Total	3	.973	175	401	403	2	101	9
3B								
1949	Pit-N	1.000	3	0	1	0	0	0

■ Eddie Basinski SS

YEAR	TM/L	PCT	G	PO	A	E	DP	FR
1944	Bro-N	.857	3	1	5	1	0	0
1945	Bro-N	.926	101	166	262	34	59	-10
Total	2	.925	104	167	267	5	59	-10
2B								
1944	Bro-N	.960	37	85	82	7	15	-2
1945	Bro-N	.941	6	11	5	1	3	0
1947	Pit-N	.972	56	116	130	7	34	-1
Total	3	.966	99	212	217	5	52	-3

■ Kevin Bass OF

YEAR	TM/L	PCT	G	PO	A	E	DP	FR
1982	Mil-A	1.000	14	7	0	0	0	1
	Hou-N	.917	7	11	0	1	0	0
1983	Hou-N	.945	52	68	1	4	1	-5
1984	Hou-N	.975	81	149	4	4	2	-1
1985	Hou-N	.997	141	328	10	1	1	2
1986	Hou-N	.984	155	303	12	5	4	9
1987	Hou-N	.987	155	287	11	4	2	6

YEAR	TM/L	PCT	G	PO	A	E	DP	FR
1988	Hou-N	.979	147	267	7	6	2	-3
1989	Hou-N	.985	84	186	6	3	0	2
1990	SF-N	.968	55	88	2	3	0	-8
Total	9	.983	891	1694	53	1	12	3

■ Charley Bassett 2B

YEAR	TM/L	PCT	G	PO	A	E	DP	FR
1884	Pro-N	.800	1	1	3	1	0	0
1885	Pro-N	.900	39	84	123	23	18	-1
1887	Ind-N	.931	119	273	444	53	62	16
1888	Ind-N	.922	128	250	423	57	44	-16
1889	Ind-N	.937	127	322	451	52	67	10
1890	NY-N	.952	100	201	332	27	43	10
1891	NY-N	.924	9	23	38	5	5	4
1892	NY-N	.938	30	76	105	12	10	9
	Lou-N	.920	6	6	17	2	0	0
	Yr	.936	36	82	122	14	10	9
Total	8	.932	559	1236	1936	232	249	32
3B								
1884	Pro-N	.815	13	17	27	10	1	1
1885	Pro-N	.928	20	27	50	6	1	5
1886	KC-N	.857	8	11	13	4	0	-1
1891	NY-N	.908	121	143	270	42	18	5
1892	NY-N	.800	5	4	12	4	1	0
	Lou-N	.861	73	76	179	41	13	0
	Yr	.858	78	80	191	45	14	0
Total	5	.886	240	278	551	107	34	10
SS								
1884	Pro-N	.826	7	2	17	4	0	0
1885	Pro-N	.912	23	29	75	10	5	1
1886	KC-N	.886	82	120	277	51	25	8
Total	3	.889	112	151	369	5	30	9
OF								
1884	Pro-N	1.000	2	3	0	0	0	0
C								
1885	Pro-N	1.000	1	1	0	0	0	0

■ Johnny Bassler C

YEAR	TM/L	PCT	G	PO	A	E	DP	FR
1913	Cle-A	.500	1	1	0	1	0	-1
1914	Cle-A	.946	25	99	42	8	3	0
1921	Det-A	.975	114	433	113	14	7	3
1922	Det-A	.980	118	421	113	11	12	-3
1923	Det-A	.988	128	447	133	7	8	12
1924	Det-A	.979	122	402	103	11	11	-5
1925	Det-A	.983	118	375	87	8	14	-9
1926	Det-A	1.000	63	223	61	0	6	1
1927	Det-A	.974	67	206	56	7	8	-2
Total	9	.980	756	2607	708	7	69	-4
3B								
1914	Cle-A	—	1	0	0	0	0	0
OF								
1914	Cle-A	—	1	0	0	0	0	0

■ Charlie Bastian SS

YEAR	TM/L	PCT	G	PO	A	E	DP	FR
1884	Wil-U	.875	1	2	5	1	3	2
1885	Phi-N	.890	103	164	337	62	34	5
1886	Phi-N	.875	10	14	28	6	4	0
1887	Phi-N	.895	18	23	45	8	4	-5
1888	Phi-N	.800	1	3	1	1	0	-1
1889	Chi-N	.919	45	63	153	19	9	3
1890	Chi-P	.880	64	85	202	39	24	-6
1891	Cin-a	1.000	1	0	1	0	0	0
Total	8	.892	243	354	772	136	78	-2
2B								
1884	Wil-U	.907	16	37	61	10	3	9
	KC-U	.950	11	28	29	3	3	-1
	Yr	.923	27	65	90	13	6	8
1886	Phi-N	.945	87	157	286	26	19	-5
1887	Phi-N	.921	39	78	120	17	15	-7
1888	Phi-N	.945	65	145	253	23	14	13
1889	Chi-N	1.000	1	4	10	0	1	3
1890	Chi-P	.950	12	36	21	3	4	-4
1891	Cin-a	1.000	1	4	4	0	1	1
Total	7	.939	232	489	784	2	60	9
3B								
1886	Phi-N	.889	8	4	12	2	0	-1
1887	Phi-N	1.000	4	9	5	0	2	-1
1888	Phi-N	.925	14	14	23	3	2	0
1890	Chi-P	.889	4	8	8	2	0	0
Total	4	.922	30	35	48	7	4	-2

■ Emil Batch 3B

YEAR	TM/L	PCT	G	PO	A	E	DP	FR
1904	Bro-N	.880	28	26	55	11	3	-2
1905	Bro-N	.887	145	203	246	57	22	-8
1906	Bro-N	.833	2	3	2	1	0	-1
1907	Bro-N	1.000	2	2	1	0	0	0
Total	4	.886	177	234	304	9	25	-11
OF								
1906	Bro-N	.964	50	101	5	4	0	2
1907	Bro-N	.937	102	180	14	13	4	-1
Total	2	.946	152	281	19	7	4	1
2B								
1907	Bro-N	.000	1	0	0	1	0	-1
SS								
1907	Bro-N	.800	1	2	2	1	0	-1

■ John Bateman C

YEAR	TM/L	PCT	G	PO	A	E	DP	FR
1963	Hou-N	.971	115	690	81	23	7	3
1964	Hou-N	.987	72	400	43	6	4	7
1965	Hou-N	.985	39	234	26	4	3	0
1966	Hou-N	.981	121	731	63	15	14	3
1967	Hou-N	.989	71	483	46	6	5	2
1968	Hou-N	.985	108	690	49	11	6	-2
1969	Mon-N	.966	66	433	26	7	5	1
1970	Mon-N	.983	137	824	62	15	19	-2
1971	Mon-N	.985	137	726	56	12	12	-10
1972	Mon-N	1.000	7	28	1	0	0	0
	Phi-N	.972	80	447	38	14	6	1
	Yr	.973	87	475	39	14	6	-1
Total	10	.982	953	5686	491	113	81	1

■ Johnny Bates OF

YEAR	TM/L	PCT	G	PO	A	E	DP	FR
1906	Bos-N	.958	140	238	12	11	4	-10
1907	Bos-N	.979	120	171	18	4	5	-2
1908	Bos-N	.948	117	205	15	12	2	-4
1909	Bos-N	.945	60	123	15	8	0	5
	Phi-N	.959	73	128	12	6	3	-2
	Yr	.952	133	251	27	14	3	3
1910	Phi-N	.954	131	308	24	16	8	7
1911	Cin-N	.966	147	352	21	13	4	0
1912	Cin-N	.950	65	157	15	9	4	9
1913	Cin-N	.946	111	192	19	12	6	0
1914	Cin-N	.913	54	91	4	9	1	-3
	Chi-N	1.000	3	5	0	0	0	1
	Bal-F	.950	59	108	7	6	0	-1
	Yr	.933	113	199	11	15	1	-4
Total	9	.955	1080	2078	162	106	37	0

■ Ray Bates 3B

YEAR	TM/L	PCT	G	PO	A	E	DP	FR
1913	Cle-A	.905	12	6	13	2	2	1
1917	Phi-A	.933	124	168	267	31	17	6
Total	2	.932	136	174	280	3	19	7
	OF							
1913	Cle-A	—	2	0	0	0	0	-1

■ Earl Battey C

YEAR	TM/L	PCT	G	PO	A	E	DP	FR
1955	Chi-A	1.000	5	19	2	0	0	2
1956	Chi-A	.800	3	4	0	1	0	0
1957	Chi-A	.989	43	165	19	2	2	6
1958	Chi-A	.988	49	220	27	3	6	2
1959	Chi-A	.990	20	92	10	1	1	3
1960	Was-A	.982	136	749	65	15	10	6
1961	Min-A	.993	131	812	60	6	9	7
1962	Min-A	.991	147	872	82	9	9	6
1963	Min-A	.994	146	861	66	6	11	1
1964	Min-A	.990	125	813	52	9	4	-5
1965	Min-A	.986	128	652	56	10	10	-8
1966	Min-A	.995	113	705	45	4	9	4
1967	Min-A	.987	41	212	17	3	2	-2
Total	13	.990	1087	6176	501	9	73	22

■ Joe Battin 3B

YEAR	TM/L	PCT	G	PO	A	E	DP	FR
1876	StL-N	.867	63	115	145	40	8	14
1877	StL-N	.823	32	58	77	29	6	5
1882	Pit-a	.876	34	62	108	24	5	21
1883	Pit-a	.891	98	151	258	50	12	29
1884	Pit-a	.919	43	53	95	13	4	8
	CP-U	.908	18	31	48	8	3	11
	Bal-U	.813	17	17	35	12	1	2
	Yr	.868	35	48	83	20	4	13
1890	Syr-a	.794	29	44	60	27	2	-4
Total	6	.870	334	501	826	203	41	86
	2B							
1876	StL-N	1.000	1	3	1	0	0	0
1877	StL-N	.825	21	54	59	24	4	-6
Total	2	.830	22	57	60	4	4	-6
	OF							
1877	StL-N	.667	5	4	0	2	0	-1

■ Matt Batts C

YEAR	TM/L	PCT	G	PO	A	E	DP	FR
1947	Bos-A	1.000	6	15	2	0	1	0
1948	Bos-A	.986	41	118	18	2	3	-1
1949	Bos-A	.977	50	193	23	5	2	2
1950	Bos-A	.994	73	306	29	2	3	3
1951	Bos-A	.975	11	32	7	1	0	0
	StL-A	.960	64	259	30	12	6	-7
	Yr	.962	75	291	37	13	6	-7
1952	Det-A	.983	55	262	36	5	4	3
1953	Det-A	.986	103	463	44	7	7	-13
1954	Det-A	.967	8	24	5	1	1	1
	Chi-A	.992	42	225	19	2	3	6
	Yr	.989	50	249	24	3	4	7
1955	Cin-N	.986	21	65	8	1	2	-2
Total	9	.983	474	1962	221	8	32	-8

■ Hank Bauer OF

YEAR	TM/L	PCT	G	PO	A	E	DP	FR
1948	NY-A	.964	14	26	1	1	0	0
1949	NY-A	.977	95	156	11	4	3	0
1950	NY-A	.987	110	228	8	3	3	1
1951	NY-A	.990	107	188	7	2	1	-4
1952	NY-A	.984	139	233	16	4	2	-2
1953	NY-A	.992	126	230	13	2	3	0
1954	NY-A	.989	108	179	6	2	1	-9
1955	NY-A	.981	133	248	13	5	3	2
1956	NY-A	.969	146	242	10	8	2	-10
1957	NY-A	.986	135	200	7	3	1	-11
1958	NY-A	.980	123	186	7	4	0	0
1959	NY-A	.972	111	139	2	4	0	-17
1960	KC-A	.978	67	85	4	2	1	-9
1961	KC-A	.958	35	44	2	2	0	-3
Total	14	.982	1449	2384	107	6	20	-71
	C							
1955	NY-A	—	1	0	0	0	0	0

■ Paddy Baumann 2B

YEAR	TM/L	PCT	G	PO	A	E	DP	FR
1911	Det-A	.956	23	58	71	6	6	5
1912	Det-A	.838	5	16	15	6	1	0
1913	Det-A	.943	49	97	136	14	15	-7
1914	Det-A	1.000	3	5	8	0	1	1
1915	NY-A	.978	43	103	116	5	17	-1
1916	NY-A	1.000	9	10	17	0	2	-1
1917	NY-A	.941	18	32	32	4	8	-9
Total	7	.953	150	321	395	5	50	-14
	3B							
1912	Det-A	.786	6	3	8	3	0	-1
1915	NY-A	.980	19	26	24	1	3	-1
1916	NY-A	.933	26	38	46	6	5	-3
1917	NY-A	—	1	0	0	0	0	0
Total	4	.935	52	67	78	0	8	-5
	OF							
1911	Det-A	1.000	3	10	0	0	0	1
1912	Det-A	—	2	0	0	0	0	-1
1915	NY-A	1.000	1	2	0	0	0	0
1916	NY-A	.958	28	45	1	2	1	-3
1917	NY-A	1.000	7	5	0	0	0	-2
Total	5	.969	41	62	1	2	1	-5

■ Frank Baumholtz OF

YEAR	TM/L	PCT	G	PO	A	E	DP	FR
1947	Cin-N	.977	150	282	18	7	2	-2
1948	Cin-N	.987	110	216	11	3	2	1
1949	Cin-N	.964	20	53	1	2	0	0
	Chi-N	.986	43	67	3	1	3	-5
	Yr	.976	63	120	4	3	3	-5
1951	Chi-N	.975	140	307	6	8	2	-21
1952	Chi-N	.974	101	248	10	7	3	12
1953	Chi-N	.980	130	290	6	6	0	-15
1954	Chi-N	.988	71	168	2	2	0	-1
1955	Chi-N	.993	63	131	3	1	1	1
1956	Phi-N	.962	15	23	2	1	0	0
Total	9	.980	843	1785	62	8	13	-30

■ Harry Bay OF

YEAR	TM/L	PCT	G	PO	A	E	DP	FR
1901	Cin-N	.953	40	78	3	4	3	-1
1902	Cin-N	.778	3	6	1	2	0	0
	Cle-A	.973	107	242	13	7	3	4
1903	Cle-A	.950	140	293	13	16	3	-3
1904	Cle-A	.987	132	281	15	4	6	7
1905	Cle-A	.970	144	305	14	10	4	0
1906	Cle-A	.979	68	131	8	3	2	-2
1907	Cle-A	.968	31	55	5	2	1	0
Total	7	.968	665	1391	72	8	22	5

■ Don Baylor OF

YEAR	TM/L	PCT	G	PO	A	E	DP	FR
1970	Bal-A	1.000	6	15	0	0	0	1
1971	Bal-A	1.000	1	4	0	0	0	0
1972	Bal-A	.975	84	152	2	4	0	-6
1973	Bal-A	.981	110	204	5	4	0	-6
1974	Bal-A	.989	129	218	1	5	0	-19
1975	Bal-A	.982	135	268	8	5	0	-6
1976	Oak-A	.981	76	152	1	3	0	-7
1977	Cal-A	.966	77	139	3	5	0	-3
1978	Cal-A	.974	39	76	0	2	0	-2
1979	Cal-A	.976	97	198	3	5	0	-2
1980	Cal-A	.969	54	119	4	4	0	-1
1981	Cal-A	1.000	1	6	0	0	0	1
1983	NY-A	1.000	5	10	0	0	0	0
1984	NY-A	.889	5	8	0	1	0	-1
1986	Bos-A	1.000	3	6	0	0	0	0
Total	15	.977	822	1575	27	8	0	-51
	1B							
1972	Bal-A	.982	9	54	2	1	5	-1
1973	Bal-A	.935	6	24	5	2	2	1
1974	Bal-A	1.000	8	42	1	0	2	-1
1975	Bal-A	1.000	2	18	0	0	1	0
1976	Oak-A	.987	69	629	44	9	40	-3
1977	Cal-A	.987	18	141	13	2	14	0
1978	Cal-A	.969	17	118	9	4	6	-1
1979	Cal-A	1.000	1	5	0	0	1	0
1981	Cal-A	1.000	4	32	3	0	2	0
1983	NY-A	.938	1	13	2	1	0	0
1986	Bos-A	.986	13	65	4	1	7	-1
Total	11	.984	148	1141	83	0	80	-6

■ Billy Beane OF

YEAR	TM/L	PCT	G	PO	A	E	DP	FR
1984	NY-N	1.000	5	2	0	0	0	-1
1985	NY-N	1.000	2	1	0	0	0	0
1986	Min-A	1.000	67	118	0	0	0	3
1987	Min-A	1.000	7	8	0	0	0	0
1988	Det-A	1.000	6	5	0	0	0	0
1989	Oak-A	1.000	25	44	0	0	0	2
Total	6	1.000	112	178	0	0	0	4
	1B							
1989	Oak-A	.938	4	13	2	1	1	0
	C							
1989	Oak-A	1.000	1	1	0	0	0	0
	3B							
1989	Oak-A	1.000	1	0	1	0	0	0

■ Ted Beard OF

YEAR	TM/L	PCT	G	PO	A	E	DP	FR
1948	Pit-N	1.000	22	66	0	0	0	2
1949	Pit-N	.900	10	9	0	1	0	-1
1950	Pit-N	.983	49	112	4	2	0	2
1951	Pit-N	1.000	15	23	2	0	0	0
1952	Pit-N	1.000	13	27	1	0	0	0
1957	Chi-A	.974	28	33	5	1	0	0
1958	Chi-A	1.000	15	15	0	0	0	0
Total	7	.987	152	285	12	4	0	3

■ Ollie Beard SS

YEAR	TM/L	PCT	G	PO	A	E	DP	FR
1889	Cin-a	.896	141	214	537	87	63	20
1890	Cin-N	.897	113	145	419	65	43	0
1891	Lou-a	.882	7	7	23	4	1	1
Total	3	.896	261	366	979	156	107	21
	3B							
1890	Cin-N	.857	9	10	26	6	2	2
1891	Lou-a	.879	61	84	149	32	16	6
Total	2	.876	70	94	175	8	18	8

■ Jim Beauchamp 1B

YEAR	TM/L	PCT	G	PO	A	E	DP	FR
1964	Hou-N	1.000	2	6	1	0	1	0
1965	Hou-N	.969	3	25	6	1	1	0
	Mil-N	1.000	2	13	0	0	1	0
	Yr	.978	5	38	6	1	2	1
1968	Cin-N	1.000	1	7	1	0	1	0
1969	Cin-N	.968	3	28	2	1	2	0
1970	StL-N	1.000	5	26	3	0	1	1
1971	StL-N	.982	44	311	19	6	27	-2
1972	NY-N	.979	35	180	9	4	16	-2
1973	NY-N	.969	11	59	3	2	7	-1
Total	8	.980	106	655	44	4	57	-3
	OF							
1964	Hou-N	.913	15	21	0	2	0	-2
1965	Hou-N	1.000	9	11	1	0	0	0
1968	Cin-N	1.000	13	27	0	0	0	1
1969	Cin-N	1.000	9	10	0	0	0	0
1970	Cin-N	1.000	16	7	0	0	0	0
	StL-N	1.000	10	16	1	0	0	1
	Yr	1.000	26	23	1	0	0	1
1971	StL-N	—	1	0	0	0	0	0
1972	NY-N	.889	5	8	0	1	0	-1
Total	7	.971	78	100	2	3	0	-1

■ Ginger Beaumont OF

YEAR	TM/L	PCT	G	PO	A	E	DP	FR
1899	Pit-N	.924	100	235	20	21	6	6
1900	Pit-N	.944	138	274	10	17	3	-12
1901	Pit-N	.943	133	289	8	18	2	-5
1902	Pit-N	.975	130	260	15	7	8	0
1903	Pit-N	.948	141	258	15	15	2	-7
1904	Pit-N	.968	153	287	14	10	6	-4
1905	Pit-N	.972	97	200	12	6	5	0
1906	Pit-N	.945	78	148	6	9	2	-5
1907	Bos-N	.962	149	296	30	13	12	5
1908	Bos-N	.965	121	257	17	10	3	-1
1909	Bos-N	.969	111	234	15	8	3	1
1910	Chi-N	.957	56	107	5	5	0	2
Total	12	.956	1407	2845	167	139	52	-20
	1B							
1899	Pit-N	.889	2	15	1	2	1	0

■ Clyde Beck 3B

YEAR	TM/L	PCT	G	PO	A	E	DP	FR
1927	Chi-N	.933	17	27	43	5	5	6
1928	Chi-N	.958	87	74	156	10	24	-6
1929	Chi-N	.978	33	18	70	2	5	3
1930	Chi-N	1.000	2	0	3	0	1	1
1931	Chi-N	.960	38	34	62	4	12	0
Total	5	.959	177	153	334	1	47	4
	2B							
1926	Chi-N	.993	30	68	80	1	19	12
1927	Chi-N	.969	99	238	358	19	62	16
1928	Chi-N	1.000	1	5	4	0	1	0
1930	Chi-N	.945	24	52	68	7	17	4
Total	4	.970	154	363	510	7	99	32
	SS							
1927	Chi-N	1.000	1	2	1	0	0	0
1928	Chi-N	.966	47	88	139	8	28	5
1929	Chi-N	.947	14	24	48	4	15	2
1930	Chi-N	.953	57	97	165	13	36	-5
1931	Chi-N	.909	6	7	3	1	0	-2
Total	5	.957	125	218	356	6	79	0

■ Erve Beck 2B

YEAR	TM/L	PCT	G	PO	A	E	DP	FR
1899	Bro-N	.931	6	7	20	2	1	-1
1901	Cle-A	.927	132	310	404	56	44	-11
1902	Cle-A	.936	32	70	92	11	11	-5
Total	3	.929	170	387	516	9	56	-17
	1B							
1902	Cin-N	1.000	6	64	5	0	5	1
	Det-A	.971	36	343	26	11	24	2
	OF							
1902	Cin-N	.900	6	9	0	1	0	-1
	Det-A	.857	5	5	1	1	0	0
	SS							
1899	Bro-N	.600	2	1	2	2	0	-1

■ Fred Beck 1B

YEAR	TM/L	PCT	G	PO	A	E	DP	FR
1909	Bos-N	.975	33	330	18	9	13	-1
1910	Bos-N	.975	19	186	9	5	14	-1
1911	Cin-N	.960	6	23	1	1	2	0
1914	Chi-F	.982	157	1614	55	31	86	-13
1915	Chi-F	.992	117	1073	42	9	57	-6
Total	5	.984	332	3226	125	5	172	-21
	OF							
1909	Bos-N	.966	57	134	8	5	5	5
1910	Bos-N	.963	134	293	19	12	6	-2
1911	Cin-N	1.000	16	25	2	0	0	0
	Phi-N	.957	61	81	7	4	4	-6
	Yr	.966	77	106	9	4	4	-6
Total	3	.964	268	533	36	1	15	-3

■ Zinn Beck 3B

YEAR	TM/L	PCT	G	PO	A	E	DP	FR
1913	StL-N	1.000	5	4	11	0	0	1
1914	StL-N	.935	122	141	264	28	24	8
1915	StL-N	.935	62	59	127	13	10	2
1916	StL-N	.910	52	45	86	13	7	-6
1918	NY-A	—	1	0	0	0	0	0
Total	5	.932	242	249	488	4	41	5
	SS							
1913	StL-N	.833	5	7	18	5	2	-1
1914	StL-N	.931	16	41	54	7	6	2
1915	StL-N	.846	4	3	8	2	0	-1
Total	3	.903	25	51	80	4	8	0
	1B							
1916	StL-N	1.000	1	1	0	0	1	0
1918	NY-A	1.000	5	16	2	0	2	0
Total	2	1.000	6	17	2	0	3	0
	2B							
1915	StL-N	.750	2	1	2	1	0	0
1916	StL-N	—	1	0	0	0	0	0
Total	2	.750	3	1	2	1	0	0

■ Beals Becker OF

YEAR	TM/L	PCT	G	PO	A	E	DP	FR
1908	Pit-N	1.000	17	17	4	0	0	-1
	Bos-N	.941	43	40	8	3	1	-4
	Yr	.958	60	57	12	3	1	-5
1909	Bos-N	.932	152	222	26	18	8	-2
1910	NY-N	.972	45	63	7	2	0	6
1911	NY-N	.975	55	72	7	2	0	1
1912	NY-N	.958	117	230	20	11	4	3
1913	Cin-N	.971	28	64	3	2	2	2
	Phi-N	.977	77	172	6	3	1	1
	Yr	.980	105	236	9	5	3	3
1914	Phi-N	.947	126	270	17	16	3	6

YEAR	TM/L	PCT	G	PO	A	E	DP	FR
1915	Phi-N	.943	98	177	5	11	0	-5
Total	8	.955	758	1327	103	8	19	7
1B								
1910	NY-N	1.000	1	5	0	0	0	0
1913	Phi-N	.900	1	7	2	1	0	0
Total	2	.933	2	12	2	1	0	0

■ Glenn Beckert 2B

YEAR	TM/L	PCT	G	PO	A	E	DP	FR
1965	Chi-N	.973	153	326	494	23	101	9
1966	Chi-N	.970	152	373	402	24	89	-20
1967	Chi-N	.968	144	327	422	25	89	4
1968	Chi-N	.977	155	356	461	19	107	6
1969	Chi-N	.965	129	262	401	24	71	6
1970	Chi-N	.970	138	302	412	22	88	10
1971	Chi-N	.986	129	275	382	9	76	-3
1972	Chi-N	.976	118	256	396	16	71	11
1973	Chi-N	.984	88	163	262	7	50	-12
1974	SD-N	.938	36	70	80	10	16	-16
Total	10	.973	1242	2710	3712	179	758	-5
3B								
1974	SD-N	1.000	1	1	0	0	0	0
1975	SD-N	1.000	4	0	6	0	0	-1
Total	2	1.000	5	1	6	0	0	-1
SS								
1966	Chi-N	1.000	1	0	1	0	0	0
OF								
1970	Chi-N	1.000	1	1	0	0	0	0

■ Jake Beckley 1B

YEAR	TM/L	PCT	G	PO	A	E	DP	FR
1888	Pit-N	.979	71	744	19	16	38	-3
1889	Pit-N	.982	122	1236	53	24	73	2
1890	Pit-P	.976	121	1256	58	32	61	0
1891	Pit-N	.982	133	1250	87	24	63	12
1892	Pit-N	.978	151	1523	132	38	88	21
1893	Pit-N	.986	131	1360	95	21	83	11
1894	Pit-N	.978	131	1227	84	30	80	5
1895	Pit-N	.978	129	1340	54	31	76	-7
1896	Pit-N	.982	56	558	31	11	42	0
	NY-N	.982	45	418	22	8	18	0
	Yr	.982	101	976	53	19	60	0
1897	NY-N	.973	17	166	15	5	12	2
	Cin-N	.979	97	830	45	19	56	-3
	Yr	.978	114	996	60	24	68	-1
1898	Cin-N	.983	118	1167	53	21	76	-1
1899	Cin-N	.986	134	1291	72	19	74	5
1900	Cin-N	.980	140	1389	63	30	91	6
1901	Cin-N	.977	140	1366	71	34	79	-4
1902	Cin-N	.983	129	1262	64	23	84	-3
1903	Cin-N	.979	119	1127	78	30	56	4
1904	StL-N	.988	142	1526	64	20	65	-11
1905	StL-N	.982	134	1442	69	28	56	-9
1906	StL-N	.987	85	928	43	13	38	-4
1907	StL-N	.988	32	303	13	4	17	-2
Total	20	.981	2377	23709	1315	481	1326	21
OF								
1889	Pit-N	1.000	1	0	1	0	0	1
1896	Pit-N	1.000	3	2	0	0	0	-1
	NY-N	.750	2	3	0	1	0	-1
	Yr	.833	5	5	0	1	0	-2
Total	2	.857	6	5	1	1	0	-1
2B								
1896	Pit-N	—	1	0	0	0	0	0

■ Julio Becquer 1B

YEAR	TM/L	PCT	G	PO	A	E	DP	FR
1955	Was-A	1.000	2	15	2	0	2	0
1957	Was-A	1.000	43	300	19	0	29	0
1958	Was-A	.994	42	319	34	2	26	6
1959	Was-A	.990	53	454	32	5	38	2
1960	Was-A	.989	77	611	38	7	59	-3
1961	LA-A	1.000	5	11	1	0	0	0
	Min-A	1.000	18	55	3	0	8	-1
	Yr	1.000	23	66	4	0	8	-1
Total	6	.993	240	1765	129	4	162	4
OF								
1958	Was-A	1.000	1	1	0	0	0	0
1961	Min-A	1.000	5	7	1	0	0	0
Total	2	1.000	6	8	1	0	0	0

■ Ed Beecher OF

YEAR	TM/L	PCT	G	PO	A	E	DP	FR
1887	Pit-N	.915	41	85	12	9	1	7
1889	Was-N	.861	39	61	7	11	1	-1
1890	Buf-P	.810	126	211	24	55	4	-4
1891	Was-a	.824	58	109	13	26	4	3
	Phi-a	1.000	16	18	2	0	0	-1
	Yr	.845	74	127	15	26	4	2
Total	4	.843	280	484	58	101	10	4
1B								
1889	Was-N	.931	3	27	0	2	2	-1

■ Ollie Bejma 2B

YEAR	TM/L	PCT	G	PO	A	E	DP	FR
1934	StL-A	.960	14	39	33	3	5	-6
1935	StL-A	.952	47	105	153	13	32	-4
1936	StL-A	.963	32	60	71	5	8	-11
1939	Chi-A	.981	81	170	199	7	36	-13
Total	4	.967	174	374	456	8	81	-34
SS								
1934	StL-A	.952	32	66	93	8	22	-3
1935	StL-A	.952	8	16	24	2	2	0
1936	StL-A	—	1	0	0	0	0	0
1939	Chi-A	1.000	1	3	1	0	0	-1
Total	4	.953	42	85	118	0	24	-4
3B								
1934	StL-A	1.000	13	8	19	0	0	-2
1935	StL-A	1.000	2	1	1	0	0	0
1936	StL-A	.893	7	14	11	3	1	0
1939	Chi-A	1.000	1	1	1	0	0	0
Total	4	.949	23	24	32	3	1	-2
OF								
1934	StL-A	1.000	9	16	0	0	0	-1

■ Mark Belanger SS

YEAR	TM/L	PCT	G	PO	A	E	DP	FR
1965	Bal-A	1.000	4	1	1	0	2	3
1966	Bal-A	1.000	6	9	20	0	3	4
1967	Bal-A	.952	38	65	94	8	17	3
1968	Bal-A	.969	145	248	444	22	73	12
1969	Bal-A	.968	148	251	449	23	79	-10
1970	Bal-A	.970	143	212	412	19	78	8
1971	Bal-A	.978	149	280	443	16	77	0
1972	Bal-A	.975	105	180	285	12	53	21
1973	Bal-A	.971	154	241	530	23	100	3
1974	Bal-A	.984	155	243	552	13	100	9
1975	Bal-A	.978	152	259	508	17	105	28
1976	Bal-A	.982	153	239	545	14	97	16
1977	Bal-A	.985	142	244	417	10	82	21
1978	Bal-A	.985	134	184	409	9	76	34
1979	Bal-A	.990	98	110	195	3	38	3
1980	Bal-A	.975	109	133	258	10	49	-1
1981	Bal-A	.973	63	86	162	7	21	4
1982	LA-N	.953	44	20	62	4	4	8
Total	18	.977	1942	3005	5786	210	1054	166
2B								
1967	Bal-A	.986	26	33	40	1	6	2
1982	LA-N	1.000	1	0	1	0	0	0
Total	2	.987	27	33	41	1	6	2
3B								
1967	Bal-A	1.000	2	2	4	0	1	1

■ Wayne Belardi 1B

YEAR	TM/L	PCT	G	PO	A	E	DP	FR
1950	Bro-N	1.000	1	2	0	0	0	0
1953	Bro-N	.984	38	283	23	5	34	0
1954	Det-A	.988	79	636	51	8	54	2
1956	Det-A	.988	31	240	17	3	21	0
Total	4	.987	149	1161	91	6	109	2
OF								
1956	Det-A	.600	2	3	0	2	0	-1

■ Buddy Bell 3B

YEAR	TM/L	PCT	G	PO	A	E	DP	FR
1972	Cle-A	1.000	6	10	13	0	2	1
1973	Cle-A	.958	154	144	363	22	44	25
1974	Cle-A	.963	115	112	274	15	31	4
1975	Cle-A	.950	153	146	330	25	29	-3
1976	Cle-A	.956	158	104	330	20	23	5
1977	Cle-A	.960	118	111	253	15	23	13
1978	Cle-A	.970	139	112	355	15	30	28
1979	Tex-A	.969	147	112	364	15	22	23
1980	Tex-A	.981	120	123	282	8	26	22
1981	Tex-A	.961	96	96	281	14	18	30
1982	Tex-A	.976	145	131	396	13	35	35
1983	Tex-A	.967	154	123	383	17	29	16
1984	Tex-A	.958	147	129	323	20	28	20
1985	Tex-A	.942	83	70	192	16	22	13
	Cin-N	.946	67	54	105	9	13	-9
1986	Cin-N	.975	151	105	290	10	28	1
1987	Cin-N	.979	142	93	241	7	17	-17
	Hou-N	.924	66	31	114	12	8	-10
	Yr	.931	79	37	138	13	10	-10
1988	Tex-A	1.000	9	3	12	0	0	1
Total	18	.964	2183	1798	4925	254	430	198
OF								
1972	Cle-A	.990	123	274	10	3	4	11
1973	Cle-A	1.000	2	2	0	0	0	0
1977	Cle-A	.958	11	23	0	1	0	-1
Total	3	.987	136	299	10	4	4	10
SS								
1979	Tex-A	.980	33	35	65	2	9	-12
1980	Tex-A	—	3	0	0	0	0	-1
1981	Tex-A	1.000	1	1	3	0	1	0
1982	Tex-A	1.000	4	0	1	0	0	0
Total	4	.981	41	36	69	2	10	-13
1B								
1976	Cle-A	1.000	2	5	1	0	0	0
1988	Cin-N	.909	2	8	2	1	0	0
	Hou-N	.977	7	43	0	1	4	-2
	Yr	.964	9	51	2	2	4	-2
1989	Tex-A	1.000	1	7	1	0	0	0
Total	3	.971	12	63	4	2	4	-2
2B								
1986	Cin-N	1.000	1	0	1	0	0	0

■ Gus Bell OF

YEAR	TM/L	PCT	G	PO	A	E	DP	FR
1950	Pit-N	.977	104	203	10	5	3	2
1951	Pit-N	.986	145	267	18	4	4	0
1952	Pit-N	.972	123	202	8	6	2	-9
1953	Cin-N	.977	151	447	16	11	5	9
1954	Cin-N	.986	153	406	12	6	2	-3
1955	Cin-N	.987	154	364	4	5	0	-14
1956	Cin-N	.986	149	330	12	5	4	-12
1957	Cin-N	.988	121	311	7	4	1	-5
1958	Cin-N	.996	107	235	7	1	2	-11
1959	Cin-N	.996	145	269	15	1	1	5
1960	Cin-N	.988	131	239	13	3	1	0
1961	Cin-N	.991	75	112	1	1	0	-3
1962	NY-N	.979	26	40	7	1	3	2
	Mil-N	.987	58	75	3	1	0	-5
	Yr	.984	84	115	10	2	3	-3
Total	13	.985	1642	3500	133	4	28	-44

■ Jay Bell SS

YEAR	TM/L	PCT	G	PO	A	E	DP	FR
1987	Cle-A	.947	38	67	93	9	22	3
1988	Cle-A	.965	72	103	170	10	37	-12
1989	Pit-N	.968	78	109	197	10	41	-15
1990	Pit-N	.970	159	260	459	22	85	-3
Total	4	.966	347	539	919	1	185	-27
2B								
1986	Cle-A	.778	2	1	6	2	1	1

■ George Bell OF

YEAR	TM/L	PCT	G	PO	A	E	DP	FR
1981	Tor-A	.969	44	92	3	3	2	2
1983	Tor-A	.954	34	61	1	3	0	-1
1984	Tor-A	.971	147	289	11	9	1	-2
1985	Tor-A	.968	157	320	13	11	3	0
1986	Tor-A	.966	147	269	17	10	1	0
1987	Tor-A	.960	148	248	14	11	1	-5
1988	Tor-A	.946	149	253	8	15	1	-12
1989	Tor-A	.963	134	258	4	10	1	-10
1990	Tor-A	.979	106	226	4	5	1	0
Total	9	.964	1066	2016	75	7	11	-28
3B								
1984	Tor-A	1.000	3	0	2	0	0	0
1985	Tor-A	1.000	2	0	1	0	0	0
1986	Tor-A	1.000	2	1	0	0	0	0
1987	Tor-A	—	1	0	0	0	0	0
Total	4	1.000	8	1	3	0	0	0
2B								
1987	Tor-A	1.000	1	1	0	0	0	0

■ Kevin Bell 3B

YEAR	TM/L	PCT	G	PO	A	E	DP	FR
1976	Chi-A	.970	67	70	124	6	10	3
1977	Chi-A	1.000	4	4	8	0	2	1
1978	Chi-A	.946	52	23	64	5	6	11
1979	Chi-A	.923	68	51	153	17	11	12
1980	Chi-A	.925	83	35	151	15	12	7
1982	Oak-A	.857	3	3	3	1	1	0
Total	6	.940	277	186	503	4	42	34
SS								
1977	Chi-A	.909	5	7	13	2	5	-1
1979	Chi-A	1.000	2	0	1	0	0	0
1980	Chi-A	.750	3	1	2	1	1	0
Total	3	.889	10	8	16	3	6	-1
OF								
1977	Chi-A	1.000	1	1	0	0	0	0

■ Les Bell 3B

YEAR	TM/L	PCT	G	PO	A	E	DP	FR
1925	StL-N	.924	153	151	284	36	39	-1
1926	StL-N	.950	155	165	254	22	25	-22
1927	StL-N	.904	100	85	142	24	13	-16
1928	Bos-N	.948	153	177	314	27	37	5
1929	Bos-N	.953	127	107	198	15	15	-19
1930	Chi-N	.948	70	63	102	9	14	-1
1931	Chi-N	.944	70	66	118	11	18	4
Total	7	.939	828	814	1412	144	161	-50
SS								
1923	StL-N	.917	15	35	53	8	9	-1
1924	StL-N	.905	17	44	42	9	8	-4
1925	StL-N	1.000	1	0	1	0	0	0
1927	StL-N	.905	10	16	41	6	8	2
1929	Bos-N	.714	1	4	1	2	0	-1
Total	5	.905	44	99	138	5	25	-4
1B								
1930	Chi-N	1.000	2	18	3	0	1	1
2B								
1929	Bos-N	1.000	1	0	2	0	0	0

■ Beau Bell OF

YEAR	TM/L	PCT	G	PO	A	E	DP	FR
1935	StL-A	.918	37	65	2	6	0	-4
1936	StL-A	.974	142	291	11	8	6	-2
1937	StL-A	.984	131	222	22	4	6	0
1938	StL-A	.979	132	266	12	6	3	4
1939	StL-A	1.000	9	20	0	0	0	0
	Det-A	1.000	37	73	4	0	1	1
	Yr	1.000	46	93	4	0	1	1
1940	Cle-A	1.000	97	193	5	6	1	-4
1941	Cle-A	1.000	14	22	0	0	0	-1
Total	7	.976	599	1152	56	0	17	-6
1B								
1935	StL-A	.977	15	122	6	3	11	-1
1936	StL-A	.966	17	134	8	5	14	-1
1937	StL-A	.977	26	238	17	6	18	0
1938	StL-A	1.000	4	24	0	0	4	-1
1940	Cle-A	.984	14	116	8	2	16	0
Total	6	.979	86	718	43	6	72	-4
3B								
1935	StL-A	.500	3	0	1	1	0	0
1937	StL-A	1.000	2	2	3	0	0	0
Total	2	.857	5	2	4	1	0	0

■ Rafael Belliard SS

YEAR	TM/L	PCT	G	PO	A	E	DP	FR
1982	Pit-N	1.000	4	2	2	0	0	3
1983	Pit-N	1.000	3	1	3	0	1	1
1984	Pit-N	.889	12	11	13	3	4	1
1985	Pit-N	.947	12	13	23	2	3	6
1986	Pit-N	.970	96	117	269	12	42	8
1987	Pit-N	.979	71	104	176	6	29	4
1988	Pit-N	.977	117	131	258	9	50	-12
1989	Pit-N	.978	40	46	90	3	13	2
1990	Pit-N	.933	10	11	17	2	3	2
Total	9	.972	365	436	851	7	145	15
2B								
1984	Pit-N	1.000	1	1	0	0	0	0
1986	Pit-N	1.000	23	30	48	0	8	4
1987	Pit-N	1.000	7	9	15	0	2	2
1988	Pit-N	1.000	3	3	3	0	1	0
1989	Pit-N	1.000	20	23	46	0	7	4
1990	Pit-N	1.000	21	23	16	0	5	2
Total	6	1.000	75	89	128	0	23	12
3B								
1989	Pit-N	1.000	6	2	2	0	0	0
1990	Pit-N	1.000	5	3	3	0	0	1
Total	2	1.000	11	5	5	0	0	1

■ Harry Bemis C

YEAR	TM/L	PCT	G	PO	A	E	DP	FR
1902	Cle-A	.964	87	333	120	17	2	9
1903	Cle-A	.988	74	315	82	5	6	-7
1904	Cle-A	.958	79	393	86	21	8	-2
1905	Cle-A	.972	58	259	53	9	4	-6
1906	Cle-A	.963	81	340	73	16	7	-10
1907	Cle-A	.957	51	180	42	10	3	-7
1908	Cle-A	.964	76	326	74	15	5	-6

YEAR	TM/L	PCT	G	PO	A	E	DP	FR
1909	Cle-A	.971	36	167	33	6	0	-1
1910	Cle-A	.961	46	186	63	10	4	-3
Total	9	.966	588	2499	626	109	39	-33
1B								
1903	Cle-A	.990	10	99	3	1	3	-1
1904	Cle-A	.955	13	103	4	5	6	-2
1905	Cle-A	1.000	1	1	0	0	0	0
1907	Cle-A	1.000	2	26	0	0	3	-1
1908	Cle-A	1.000	2	11	1	0	0	0
Total	5	.976	28	240	8	6	12	-4
2B								
1902	Cle-A	1.000	1	0	1	0	0	0
1903	Cle-A	1.000	1	0	1	0	0	0
1904	Cle-A	1.000	1	1	0	0	0	0
1905	Cle-A	1.000	4	7	15	0	0	1
Total	4	1.000	7	8	17	0	0	1
OF								
1902	Cle-A	1.000	2	1	0	0	0	-1
3B								
1905	Cle-A	1.000	2	4	5	0	0	0

■ Johnny Bench C

YEAR	TM/L	PCT	G	PO	A	E	DP	FR
1967	Cin-N	.995	26	175	16	1	0	5
1968	Cin-N	.991	154	**942**	**102**	9	10	**7**
1969	Cin-N	.992	147	793	76	7	10	-3
1970	Cin-N	.986	**140**	759	73	12	12	8
1971	Cin-N	.988	**141**	687	59	9	9	-3
1972	Cin-N	.993	130	742	56	6	9	-3
1973	Cin-N	.995	134	693	61	4	7	0
1974	Cin-N	.993	137	757	68	6	**16**	-1
1975	Cin-N	.989	121	568	51	7	9	3
1976	Cin-N	**.997**	128	**651**	60	2	11	-3
1977	Cin-N	.987	135	705	66	10	10	-13
1978	Cin-N	.989	107	605	48	7	6	-7
1979	Cin-N	.986	126	619	68	10	11	-8
1980	Cin-N	.991	105	505	39	5	7	-17
1981	Cin-N	.979	7	41	5	1	0	0
1982	Cin-N	1.000	1	1	0	0	0	0
1983	Cin-N	.950	5	17	2	1	0	-1
Total	17	.990	1744	9260	850	7	127	-36
3B								
1970	Cin-N	1.000	1	1	0	0	0	0
1971	Cin-N	1.000	3	2	6	0	0	0
1972	Cin-N	.900	4	2	7	1	0	-1
1973	Cin-N	1.000	1	0	2	0	0	0
1974	Cin-N	.962	36	22	55	3	2	-5
1977	Cin-N	.500	1	0	1	1	0	0
1982	Cin-N	.917	107	54	155	19	10	-17
1983	Cin-N	.933	42	26	58	6	5	-7
Total	8	.929	195	107	284	0	17	-30
1B								
1970	Cin-N	.987	12	74	4	1	7	-1
1971	Cin-N	.972	12	34	1	1	7	-1
1972	Cin-N	.944	6	17	0	1	1	-1
1973	Cin-N	1.000	4	29	0	0	3	-1
1974	Cin-N	1.000	5	15	0	0	0	0
1975	Cin-N	.978	9	45	0	1	2	-1
1976	Cin-N	—	1	0	0	0	0	0
1977	Cin-N	.958	4	21	2	1	3	0
1978	Cin-N	.976	11	75	5	2	7	0
1979	Cin-N	1.000	2	13	1	0	1	0
1981	Cin-N	.983	38	334	23	6	35	-2
1982	Cin-N	1.000	8	53	4	0	7	0
1983	Cin-N	.989	32	249	14	3	21	-3
Total	13	.984	144	959	54	6	94	-10
OF								
1970	Cin-N	.913	23	20	1	2	0	-1
1971	Cin-N	1.000	12	12	1	0	0	0
1972	Cin-N	.938	17	30	0	2	0	-1
1973	Cin-N	.946	23	35	0	2	0	-2
1975	Cin-N	1.000	19	33	1	0	0	0
1976	Cin-N	.667	5	4	0	2	0	-1
1977	Cin-N	1.000	8	9	0	0	0	0
1978	Cin-N	—	2	0	0	0	0	0
1983	Cin-N	—	1	0	0	0	0	0
Total	9	.948	110	143	3	8	0	-5

■ Bruce Benedict C

YEAR	TM/L	PCT	G	PO	A	E	DP	FR
1978	Atl-N	.990	22	81	14	1	1	2
1979	Atl-N	.984	76	344	35	6	3	1
1980	Atl-N	.988	120	502	76	7	6	4
1981	Atl-N	.986	90	404	**73**	7	7	**7**
1982	Atl-N	**.993**	118	602	73	5	9	2
1983	Atl-N	.992	134	738	91	7	12	1
1984	Atl-N	.991	95	504	37	5	2	0
1985	Atl-N	.989	70	314	35	4	1	-3
1986	Atl-N	.993	57	252	28	2	1	-4
1987	Atl-N	.989	35	165	21	2	3	4
1988	Atl-N	.989	89	384	54	5	3	7
1989	Atl-N	.995	65	361	40	2	2	16
Total	12	.990	971	4651	577	3	50	43

■ Benny Bengough C

YEAR	TM/L	PCT	G	PO	A	E	DP	FR
1923	NY-A	.973	19	58	14	2	2	0
1924	NY-A	1.000	11	34	3	0	3	3
1925	NY-A	**.993**	94	325	83	3	12	5
1926	NY-A	.973	35	107	36	4	2	8
1927	NY-A	.986	30	114	31	2	0	11
1928	NY-A	.992	58	206	37	2	7	6
1929	NY-A	.982	23	47	8	1	1	-5
1930	NY-A	.990	44	171	18	2	2	9
1931	StL-A	.986	37	119	26	2	6	-1
1932	StL-A	.989	47	153	30	2	7	7
Total	10	.988	398	1334	286	0	42	43

■ Juan Beniquez OF

YEAR	TM/L	PCT	G	PO	A	E	DP	FR
1974	Bos-A	.978	97	264	4	6	2	10
1975	Bos-A	.991	44	104	3	1	2	2
1976	Tex-A	.986	141	**410**	**18**	6	3	14
1977	Tex-A	.988	123	311	10	4	1	0
1978	Tex-A	.972	126	309	8	9	1	-5
1979	NY-A	.981	60	99	4	2	0	4
1980	Sea-A	.957	65	176	3	8	0	2
1981	Cal-A	.959	55	117	0	5	0	-4
1982	Cal-A	.983	107	113	4	2	1	-10
1983	Cal-A	.968	84	174	8	6	1	-2
1984	Cal-A	.971	98	197	5	6	1	-4
1985	Cal-A	1.000	71	119	1	0	0	-5
1986	Bal-A	.963	54	102	1	4	0	-1
1987	KC-A	1.000	22	33	0	0	0	-2
	Tor-A	.875	7	7	0	1	0	-1
	Yr	.976	29	40	0	1	0	-3
1988	Tor-A	—	1	0	0	0	0	0
Total	15	.977	1155	2535	69	0	12	-2
1B								
1985	Cal-A	.988	46	319	24	4	42	-2
1986	Bal-A	.990	14	96	8	1	14	0
1987	KC-A	1.000	6	50	1	0	6	-1
	Tor-A	1.000	2	7	0	0	0	0
	Yr	1.000	8	57	1	0	6	-1
Total	3	.990	68	472	33	5	62	-3
3B								
1975	Bos-A	1.000	14	6	14	0	0	-1
1979	NY-A	1.000	3	1	11	0	0	2
1985	Cal-A	1.000	1	1	0	0	0	0
1986	Bal-A	.882	25	13	47	8	1	-3
1987	KC-A	.800	6	0	4	1	0	0
Total	5	.915	49	21	76	9	1	-2
SS								
1971	Bos-A	.895	15	24	27	6	5	-8
1972	Bos-A	.900	27	38	88	14	19	4
1985	Cal-A	1.000	1	0	1	0	0	0
Total	3	.899	43	62	116	0	24	-4
2B								
1976	Tex-A	.500	1	1	0	1	0	0

■ Stan Benjamin OF

YEAR	TM/L	PCT	G	PO	A	E	DP	FR
1939	Phi-N	.867	7	12	1	2	0	0
1940	Phi-N	.980	2	3	1	0	0	1
1941	Phi-N	.980	110	185	11	4	3	-6
1942	Phi-N	.976	45	75	7	2	1	1
1945	Cle-A	1.000	4	9	2	0	0	2
Total	5	.975	168	284	22	8	4	-2
1B								
1941	Phi-N	.987	8	69	7	1	2	1
1942	Phi-N	.972	15	99	6	3	11	-1
Total	2	.978	23	168	13	4	13	0
3B								
1939	Phi-N	.895	5	6	11	2	1	0
1941	Phi-N	—	1	0	0	0	0	0
Total	2	.895	6	6	11	2	1	0
2B								
1941	Phi-N	—	2	0	0	0	0	0

■ Charlie Bennett C

YEAR	TM/L	PCT	G	PO	A	E	DP	FR
1878	Mil-N	.831	35	176	31	42	4	-11
1880	Wor-N	.913	46	280	45	31	3	-5
1881	Det-N	**.962**	70	**418**	85	20	6	10
1882	Det-N	.945	65	**446**	70	30	8	2
1883	Det-N	**.944**	72	333	88	25	**11**	0
1884	Det-N	.917	80	454	97	50	9	-8
1885	Det-N	.919	62	347	87	38	10	-4
1886	Det-N	**.955**	69	**425**	84	24	**13**	5
1887	Det-N	.951	45	197	57	13	9	-4
1888	Det-N	**.966**	73	424	94	18	10	0
1889	Bos-N	**.955**	82	419	74	23	9	8
1890	Bos-N	**.959**	85	448	90	23	8	3
1891	Bos-N	**.960**	75	383	75	19	**10**	11
1892	Bos-N	.948	35	169	31	11	3	0
1893	Bos-N	.953	60	204	40	12	1	-5
Total	15	.942	954	5123	1048	379	114	2
OF								
1878	Mil-N	.719	20	21	2	9	0	-5
1880	Wor-N	.929	6	11	2	1	1	1
1881	Det-N	1.000	3	5	0	0	0	0
1883	Det-N	.857	12	12	0	2	0	-1
1884	Det-N	.800	5	3	1	1	0	0
1885	Det-N	.857	19	10	2	2	0	-1
1886	Det-N	1.000	4	5	0	0	0	0
1887	Det-N	—	1	0	0	0	0	0
Total	8	.831	70	67	7	5	1	-6
3B								
1881	Det-N	.839	5	9	17	5	2	3
1882	Det-N	.870	11	24	23	7	2	1
1884	Det-N	.500	1	1	0	1	0	-1
1885	Det-N	.813	10	22	17	9	3	0
Total	4	.892	27	56	57	2	7	3
2B								
1882	Det-N	.947	7	18	18	2	2	-1
1883	Det-N	.869	15	37	36	11	6	-7
1884	Det-N	.875	1	2	5	1	1	0
Total	3	.892	23	57	59	4	9	-8
SS								
1882	Det-N	—	1	0	0	0	0	0
1884	Det-N	.667	4	4	10	7	0	-2
1886	Det-N	1.000	1	2	2	0	1	0
Total	3	.720	6	6	12	7	1	-2
1B								
1882	Det-N	1.000	1	5	0	0	0	0
1884	Det-N	.714	1	4	1	2	0	0
1887	Det-N	1.000	1	4	0	0	2	0
1888	Det-N	1.000	1	4	0	0	0	0
Total	4	.905	4	17	2	2	2	0

■ Herschel Bennett OF

YEAR	TM/L	PCT	G	PO	A	E	DP	FR
1923	StL-A	1.000	1	1	0	0	0	0
1924	StL-A	.966	21	26	2	1	0	-4
1925	StL-A	.916	73	140	12	14	1	-2
1926	StL-A	.950	50	106	9	6	3	3
1927	StL-A	.946	55	118	5	7	1	1
Total	5	.937	200	391	28	8	5	-2

■ Pug Bennett 2B

YEAR	TM/L	PCT	G	PO	A	E	DP	FR
1906	StL-N	.948	**153**	295	447	41	43	-7
1907	StL-N	.939	83	175	208	25	26	-17
Total	2	.945	236	470	655	6	69	-24
3B								
1907	StL-N	1.000	3	3	6	0	1	1

■ Todd Benzinger 1B

YEAR	TM/L	PCT	G	PO	A	E	DP	FR
1987	Bos-A	1.000	2	9	1	0	0	0
1988	Bos-A	.991	85	520	38	5	47	-2
1989	Cin-N	.995	158	1417	73	7	96	-13
1990	Cin-N	.992	95	707	52	6	58	-3
Total	4	.994	340	2653	164	8	201	-18
OF								
1987	Bos-A	.987	61	146	6	2	2	2
1988	Bos-A	.988	48	82	6	1	0	-2
1990	Cin-N	1.000	10	26	0	0	0	0
Total	3	.989	119	254	6	3	2	0

■ Johnny Berardino 2B

YEAR	TM/L	PCT	G	PO	A	E	DP	FR
1939	StL-A	.958	114	315	339	**29**	67	3
1940	StL-A	.986	13	35	35	1	11	2
1942	StL-A	1.000	4	7	13	0	3	2
1946	StL-A	.972	143	374	414	23	96	-2
1947	StL-A	.977	86	242	221	11	61	-9
1948	Cle-A	.988	20	39	46	1	11	1
1949	Cle-A	.959	8	19	28	2	4	1
1950	Cle-A	1.000	1	7	3	0	1	1
	Pit-N	.964	36	84	106	7	28	2
1951	StL-A	.800	2	1	3	1	0	0
1952	Cle-A	.960	8	6	18	1	2	1
	Pit-N	.960	18	37	58	4	13	6
Total	10	.968	453	1166	1284	0	297	8
SS								
1939	StL-A	.733	2	3	8	4	2	0
1940	StL-A	.939	112	250	336	**38**	83	8
1941	StL-A	.954	123	261	305	27	81	-14
1942	StL-A	.950	6	10	9	1	2	-2
1948	Cle-A	.949	12	15	22	2	3	0
1949	Cle-A	1.000	3	0	1	0	0	0
1952	Cle-A	1.000	8	1	3	0	0	0
Total	7	.944	266	540	684	2	171	-8
3B								
1939	StL-A	1.000	8	7	16	0	2	1
1940	StL-A	.930	9	12	28	3	2	4
1941	StL-A	1.000	1	1	0	0	0	0
1942	StL-A	.889	6	8	8	2	5	1
1948	Cle-A	1.000	3	1	3	0	1	0
1949	Cle-A	.935	25	19	39	4	3	-2
1950	Cle-A	—	1	0	0	0	0	0
	Pit-N	1.000	3	3	9	0	0	1
1951	StL-A	.917	31	44	44	8	6	-5
1952	Cle-A	1.000	4	1	4	0	0	0
Total	9	.936	91	96	151	7	19	0
1B								
1942	StL-A	.977	5	40	2	1	3	0
1948	Cle-A	1.000	18	144	14	0	19	2
1951	StL-A	1.000	1	2	0	0	0	0
1952	Cle-A	1.000	2	14	0	0	0	0
Total	4	.995	26	191	16	1	22	2
OF								
1951	StL-A	—	1	0	0	0	0	0

■ Lou Berberet C

YEAR	TM/L	PCT	G	PO	A	E	DP	FR
1954	NY-A	1.000	3	12	0	0	0	1
1955	NY-A	1.000	1	10	0	0	0	0
1956	Was-A	.997	59	266	28	1	6	0
1957	Was-A	**1.000**	77	349	48	0	8	-3
1958	Was-A	.917	2	8	3	1	1	1
	Bos-A	.984	49	234	18	4	2	-6
	Yr	.981	51	242	21	5	3	-5
1959	Det-A	.989	95	511	39	6	4	-11
1960	Det-A	.993	81	396	36	3	4	-1
Total	7	.992	367	1786	172	5	25	-18

■ Moe Berg C

YEAR	TM/L	PCT	G	PO	A	E	DP	FR
1927	Chi-A	.966	10	23	5	1	0	-1
1928	Chi-A	.990	73	256	52	3	8	5
1929	Chi-A	.982	106	290	86	7	12	-3
1930	Chi-A	.986	20	55	14	1	1	0
1931	Cle-A	.889	8	12	4	2	0	1
1932	Was-A	1.000	75	229	35	0	9	7
1933	Was-A	1.000	35	76	10	0	3	3
1934	Was-A	.988	31	77	8	1	1	-4
	Cle-A	.980	28	137	13	3	1	5
	Yr	.983	59	214	21	4	2	1
1935	Bos-A	.991	37	99	15	1	2	2
1936	Bos-A	.986	39	175	29	3	3	12
1937	Bos-A	.979	47	208	24	5	2	3
1938	Bos-A	1.000	7	11	1	0	1	1
1939	Bos-A	.965	13	45	10	2	1	4
Total	13	.986	529	1693	306	9	44	35
SS								
1923	Bro-N	.906	47	86	126	22	20	-6
1926	Chi-A	.948	31	59	86	8	21	6
1927	Chi-A	.793	6	10	13	6	3	-2
Total	3	.913	84	155	225	6	43	-2
2B								
1923	Bro-N	—	1	0	0	0	0	0
1926	Chi-A	1.000	2	1	3	0	0	0
1927	Chi-A	.952	11	4	16	1	2	0
Total	3	.960	14	5	19	1	2	0
3B								
1926	Chi-A	—	1	0	0	0	0	0
1927	Chi-A	.833	3	2	3	1	0	0

YEAR	TM/L	PCT	G	PO	A	E	DP	FR
Total	2	.833	4	2	3	1	0	0
1B								
1938	Bos-A	1.000	1	3	0	0	1	0

■ Augie Bergamo OF

YEAR	TM/L	PCT	G	PO	A	E	DP	FR
1944	StL-N	.988	50	83	0	1	0	-7
1945	StL-N	.969	77	146	9	5	3	-3
Total	2	.975	127	229	9	6	3	-10
1B								
1944	StL-N	1.000	2	4	0	0	0	0
1945	StL-N	1.000	2	14	0	0	1	0
Total	2	1.000	4	18	0	0	1	0

■ Marty Bergen C

YEAR	TM/L	PCT	G	PO	A	E	DP	FR
1896	Bos-N	.920	63	207	70	24	6	9
1897	Bos-N	.963	85	351	66	16	4	4
1898	Bos-N	.962	117	496	109	24	4	5
1899	Bos-N	.955	72	253	89	16	4	2
Total	4	.954	337	1307	334	0	18	20
1B								
1896	Bos-N	.857	1	6	0	1	0	0
1898	Bos-N	1.000	2	15	0	0	2	0
Total	2	.955	3	21	0	1	2	0
OF								
1897	Bos-N	.667	1	2	0	1	0	0

■ Bill Bergen C

YEAR	TM/L	PCT	G	PO	A	E	DP	FR
1901	Cin-N	.970	87	406	117	16	8	-7
1902	Cin-N	.959	89	406	137	23	13	15
1903	Cin-N	.980	58	251	85	7	3	2
1904	Bro-N	.959	93	414	151	24	10	13
1905	Bro-N	.954	76	371	127	24	8	12
1906	Bro-N	.977	103	485	149	15	9	4
1907	Bro-N	.968	51	175	67	8	3	2
1908	Bro-N	.989	99	470	137	7	9	15
1909	Bro-N	.976	112	536	202	18	18	21
1910	Bro-N	.981	89	373	151	10	15	18
1911	Bro-N	.981	84	346	121	9	10	15
Total	11	.972	941	4233	1444	161	106	110
1B								
1904	Bro-N	1.000	1	1	0	0	0	0

■ Boze Berger 2B

YEAR	TM/L	PCT	G	PO	A	E	DP	FR
1935	Cle-A	.964	120	309	419	27	91	14
1936	Cle-A	.893	8	12	13	3	5	3
1937	Chi-A	.500	1	0	1	1	0	0
1938	Chi-A	.931	42	86	117	15	23	-12
1939	Bos-A	1.000	2	0	1	0	0	0
Total	5	.954	173	407	551	6	119	5
SS								
1932	Cle-A	1.000	1	3	2	0	0	1
1935	Cle-A	.875	3	2	5	1	1	0
1936	Cle-A	.833	2	5	5	2	2	0
1937	Chi-A	.750	1	1	2	1	1	0
1938	Chi-A	.946	67	144	224	21	55	5
1939	Bos-A	.947	10	8	10	1	1	0
Total	6	.941	84	163	248	6	60	6
3B								
1935	Cle-A	—	1	0	0	0	0	0
1936	Cle-A	.900	7	5	13	2	2	2
1937	Chi-A	.931	40	35	73	8	8	0
1938	Chi-A	.875	9	9	12	3	1	-2
1939	Bos-A	1.000	5	4	10	0	1	1
Total	5	.925	62	53	108	3	12	1
1B								
1935	Cle-A	.938	2	14	1	1	1	0
1936	Cle-A	.959	8	45	2	2	2	0
Total	2	.954	10	59	3	3	3	0

■ Wally Berger OF

YEAR	TM/L	PCT	G	PO	A	E	DP	FR
1930	Bos-N	.966	145	307	10	11	3	-4
1931	Bos-N	.977	156	457	16	11	5	4
1932	Bos-N	.993	134	396	10	3	3	-1
1933	Bos-N	.977	136	382	6	9	4	1
1934	Bos-N	.978	150	385	9	9	2	-3
1935	Bos-N	.965	149	458	8	17	1	7
1936	Bos-N	.966	133	384	10	14	1	2
1937	Bos-N	1.000	28	51	1	0	0	-4
	NY-N	.965	52	107	4	4	0	0
	Yr	.976	80	158	5	4	0	-4
1938	NY-N	1.000	9	29	0	0	0	3
	Cin-N	.966	98	192	7	7	2	-2
	Yr	.970	107	221	7	7	2	1
1939	Cin-N	.970	95	158	6	5	0	-8
1940	Phi-N	.947	11	18	0	1	0	-1
Total	11	.974	1296	3324	87	1	21	-6
1B								
1931	Bos-N	1.000	1	2	0	0	0	0
1932	Bos-N	1.000	11	102	4	0	7	-1
1940	Phi-N	1.000	1	2	0	0	0	0
Total	3	1.000	13	106	4	0	7	-1

■ Marty Berghammer SS

YEAR	TM/L	PCT	G	PO	A	E	DP	FR
1913	Cin-N	.909	54	97	143	24	16	4
1914	Cin-N	.906	33	33	63	10	4	4
1915	Pit-F	.943	132	286	359	39	55	-16
Total	3	.931	219	416	565	3	75	-8
2B								
1911	Chi-A	1.000	2	5	2	0	0	0
1913	Cin-N	.896	13	14	29	5	4	0
1914	Cin-N	1.000	13	12	25	0	5	3
Total	3	.946	28	31	56	5	9	3

■ Dave Bergman 1B

YEAR	TM/L	PCT	G	PO	A	E	DP	FR
1977	NY-A	1.000	2	5	0	0	0	0
1978	Hou-N	.993	66	280	16	2	26	-1
1979	Hou-N	1.000	4	8	0	0	1	0
1980	Hou-N	.995	59	183	16	1	23	3
1981	Hou-N	1.000	1	3	1	0	0	0
	SF-N	.992	33	232	24	2	21	3
	Yr	.992	34	235	25	2	21	3
1982	SF-N	.991	69	308	20	3	18	1
1983	SF-N	.994	50	291	27	2	20	2
1984	Det-A	.989	114	657	75	8	63	9
1985	Det-A	.991	44	306	25	3	25	1
1986	Det-A	.986	41	255	29	4	30	3
1987	Det-A	.992	65	353	29	3	33	1
1988	Det-A	.990	64	367	37	4	31	1
1989	Det-A	.993	123	912	85	7	88	5
1990	Det-A	.995	27	203	13	1	19	-1
Total	14	.992	762	4363	397	0	398	27
OF								
1975	NY-A	.917	6	10	1	1	1	1
1977	NY-A	1.000	3	3	0	0	0	0
1978	Hou-N	.960	29	48	0	2	0	-1
1980	Hou-N	1.000	5	4	0	0	0	0
1981	SF-N	.952	15	20	0	1	0	-1
1982	SF-N	.929	6	13	0	1	0	0
1983	SF-N	1.000	6	8	0	0	0	0
1984	Det-A	1.000	2	1	0	0	0	0
1985	Det-A	—	1	0	0	0	0	0
1986	Det-A	—	2	0	0	0	0	0
1987	Det-A	1.000	7	4	0	0	0	0
1988	Det-A	1.000	13	19	0	0	0	0
1989	Det-A	—	1	0	0	0	0	0
1990	Det-A	—	5	0	0	0	0	0
Total	14	.963	101	130	1	5	1	-1

■ Tony Bernazard 2B

YEAR	TM/L	PCT	G	PO	A	E	DP	FR
1979	Mon-N	.982	14	22	34	1	4	-1
1980	Mon-N	.976	39	63	103	4	18	4
1981	Chi-A	.987	104	228	320	7	66	-2
1982	Chi-A	.985	137	353	443	12	116	25
1983	Chi-A	.976	59	96	189	7	38	-2
	Sea-A	.979	79	166	233	12	51	1
	Yr	.973	138	262	422	19	89	-1
1984	Cle-A	.971	136	264	397	20	85	-11
1985	Cle-A	.979	147	311	399	16	86	-31
1986	Cle-A	.979	146	351	442	17	95	-1
1987	Cle-A	.983	78	153	200	6	39	-16
	Oak-A	.953	59	90	135	11	22	-18
	Yr	.971	137	243	335	17	61	-34
Total	9	.978	998	2097	2895	113	620	-52
SS								
1980	Mon-N	.931	22	19	48	5	7	-2
1981	Chi-A	1.000	1	0	1	0	0	0
1985	Cle-A	1.000	1	2	0	0	1	0
Total	3	.933	24	21	49	5	8	-2

■ Dale Berra SS

YEAR	TM/L	PCT	G	PO	A	E	DP	FR
1978	Pit-N	1.000	2	3	4	0	0	0
1979	Pit-N	.940	22	25	53	5	11	2
1980	Pit-N	.952	45	59	98	8	16	1
1981	Pit-N	.945	30	42	62	6	12	-1
1982	Pit-N	.961	153	238	498	30	77	-3
1983	Pit-N	.963	161	286	505	30	103	16
1984	Pit-N	.955	135	186	449	30	65	-2
1985	NY-A	.889	6	2	6	1	0	0
1986	NY-A	.972	19	29	40	2	8	-2
1987	Hou-N	.963	18	13	39	2	4	-3
Total	10	.959	591	883	1754	114	296	8
3B								
1977	Pit-N	.973	14	14	22	1	1	3
1978	Pit-N	.908	55	28	80	11	11	1
1979	Pit-N	.879	22	18	33	7	3	-1
1980	Pit-N	.968	48	23	69	3	7	1
1981	Pit-N	.976	42	21	62	2	6	2
1982	Pit-N	1.000	6	3	7	0	0	0
1984	Pit-N	—	1	0	0	0	0	0
1985	NY-A	.917	41	20	68	8	9	4
1986	NY-A	.950	18	11	27	2	3	1
Total	9	.937	247	138	368	4	40	11
2B								
1980	Pit-N	1.000	4	6	4	0	0	0
1981	Pit-N	1.000	18	26	43	0	9	2
1987	Hou-N	1.000	3	1	1	0	0	0
Total	3	1.000	25	33	48	0	9	2

■ Yogi Berra C

YEAR	TM/L	PCT	G	PO	A	E	DP	FR
1946	NY-A	1.000	6	28	6	0	2	2
1947	NY-A	.972	51	259	18	8	5	-5
1948	NY-A	.979	71	297	36	7	5	-9
1949	NY-A	.989	109	544	60	7	18	11
1950	NY-A	.985	148	777	64	13	16	1
1951	NY-A	.984	141	693	82	13	25	7
1952	NY-A	.992	140	700	73	6	10	1
1953	NY-A	.986	133	566	64	9	9	3
1954	NY-A	.990	149	717	63	8	14	-1
1955	NY-A	.984	145	748	54	13	10	-2
1956	NY-A	.995	135	732	55	11	15	6
1957	NY-A	.995	121	704	61	4	12	17
1958	NY-A	1.000	88	509	41	0	8	4
1959	NY-A	.997	116	698	61	2	9	6
1960	NY-A	.989	63	256	22	3	6	-9
1961	NY-A	1.000	15	76	8	0	0	0
1962	NY-A	.990	31	175	16	2	6	6
1963	NY-A	.988	35	244	13	3	5	8
1965	NY-N	.941	2	15	1	1	0	1
Total	19	.989	1699	8738	798	110	175	47
OF								
1947	NY-A	.980	24	48	0	1	0	-1
1948	NY-A	.980	50	93	4	2	2	-1
1956	NY-A	1.000	1	1	2	0	0	1
1957	NY-A	1.000	6	3	0	0	0	0
1958	NY-A	.955	21	39	3	2	1	1
1959	NY-A	.818	7	8	1	2	1	0
1960	NY-A	.967	36	56	2	2	0	-3
1961	NY-A	.988	87	161	7	2	2	0
1962	NY-A	.941	28	63	1	4	0	0
Total	9	.970	260	472	20	5	6	-3
1B								
1958	NY-A	1.000	2	10	0	0	2	0
3B								
1954	NY-A	1.000	1	1	1	0	0	0

■ Ray Berres C

YEAR	TM/L	PCT	G	PO	A	E	DP	FR
1934	Bro-N	.969	37	79	14	3	0	-1
1936	Bro-N	.988	105	436	59	6	7	24
1937	Pit-N	1.000	2	9	2	0	0	1
1938	Pit-N	.993	40	128	21	1	0	4
1939	Pit-N	.993	80	269	36	2	4	-3
1940	Pit-N	.980	21	40	9	1	2	3
	Bos-N	.981	85	254	56	6	6	0
	Yr	.981	106	294	65	7	8	3
1941	Bos-N	.995	120	356	64	2	13	9
1942	NY-N	.973	12	34	2	1	1	-2
1943	NY-N	.981	17	43	9	1	1	4
1944	NY-N	1.000	12	13	4	0	1	0
1945	NY-N	1.000	20	43	2	0	0	1
Total	11	.989	551	1704	278	3	35	40

■ Ken Berry OF

YEAR	TM/L	PCT	G	PO	A	E	DP	FR
1962	Chi-A	1.000	2	4	1	0	1	1
1963	Chi-A	.857	2	6	0	1	0	0
1964	Chi-A	1.000	12	15	0	0	0	-1
1965	Chi-A	.980	156	331	6	7	1	-3
1966	Chi-A	.991	141	208	10	2	1	-8
1967	Chi-A	.992	143	233	9	2	1	-4
1968	Chi-A	.981	151	352	11	7	2	-3
1969	Chi-A	1.000	120	215	7	0	1	-11
1970	Chi-A	.988	138	331	9	4	2	3
1971	Cal-A	.988	101	237	5	3	0	1
1972	Cal-A	1.000	116	272	13	0	5	10
1973	Cal-A	.997	129	307	5	1	0	0
1974	Mil-A	.995	82	187	8	1	1	10
1975	Cle-A	.926	18	24	1	2	0	2
Total	14	.989	1311	2722	85	0	15	-3
2B								
1963	Chi-A	—	1	0	0	0	0	0

■ Charlie Berry C

YEAR	TM/L	PCT	G	PO	A	E	DP	FR
1925	Phi-A	.900	4	9	0	1	0	-1
1928	Bos-A	.959	63	153	34	8	2	-10
1929	Bos-A	.983	72	236	51	5	8	3
1930	Bos-A	.988	85	279	56	4	4	7
1931	Bos-A	.985	102	312	78	6	8	-3
1932	Bos-A	.944	10	28	6	2	3	-1
	Chi-A	.981	70	212	52	5	5	-1
	Yr	.977	80	240	58	7	8	-2
1933	Chi-A	.987	83	260	39	4	1	-8
1934	Phi-A	.987	99	339	48	5	9	0
1935	Phi-A	.987	56	189	37	3	7	-1
1936	Phi-A	.971	12	29	4	1	0	1
1938	Phi-A	1.000	1	1	1	0	1	0
Total	11	.982	657	2047	406	4	48	-14

■ Claude Berry C

YEAR	TM/L	PCT	G	PO	A	E	DP	FR
1904	Chi-A	1.000	3	5	1	0	0	1
1906	Phi-A	.938	10	52	24	5	0	5
1907	Phi-A	.944	8	29	5	2	0	-2
1914	Pit-F	.970	122	550	202	23	18	1
1915	Pit-F	.980	99	384	144	11	8	-1
Total	5	.971	242	1020	376	1	26	4

■ Neil Berry SS

YEAR	TM/L	PCT	G	PO	A	E	DP	FR
1948	Det-A	.930	41	67	120	14	31	1
1949	Det-A	1.000	4	2	3	0	0	0
1950	Det-A	.944	12	20	31	3	13	1
1951	Det-A	.944	38	63	106	10	19	7
1952	Det-A	.965	66	90	158	9	26	3
1953	StL-A	.947	6	4	14	1	1	1
1954	Bal-A	1.000	5	6	7	0	2	0
Total	7	.949	172	252	439	7	92	13
2B								
1948	Det-A	.980	26	71	79	3	15	2
1949	Det-A	.970	95	225	234	14	56	0
1950	Det-A	1.000	2	2	4	0	1	1
1951	Det-A	1.000	10	9	9	0	2	1
1953	StL-A	.964	15	26	27	2	8	0
	Chi-A	1.000	3	5	10	0	1	2
	Yr	.971	18	31	37	2	9	2
Total	5	.974	151	338	363	9	83	6
3B								
1950	Det-A	1.000	1	0	1	0	0	0
1951	Det-A	.900	7	6	12	2	1	0
1952	Det-A	1.000	2	1	2	0	0	0
1953	StL-A	.825	18	15	18	7	1	-2
Total	4	.859	28	22	33	9	2	-2

■ Damon Berryhill C

YEAR	TM/L	PCT	G	PO	A	E	DP	FR
1987	Chi-N	.909	11	37	3	4	0	-4
1988	Chi-N	.982	90	448	54	9	5	-3
1989	Chi-N	.992	89	473	41	4	4	-12
1990	Chi-N	.978	15	87	3	2	0	-2
Total	4	.984	205	1045	101	9	9	-21

■ Dick Bertell C

YEAR	TM/L	PCT	G	PO	A	E	DP	FR
1960	Chi-N	1.000	5	18	6	0	0	-1
1961	Chi-N	.982	90	396	49	8	10	7
1962	Chi-N	.986	76	306	36	5	0	-12
1963	Chi-N	.988	99	549	84	8	15	16
1964	Chi-N	.981	110	531	52	11	3	-5
1965	Chi-N	.981	34	128	29	3	2	3
	SF-N	.992	22	113	6	1	2	3
	Yr	.986	56	241	35	4	4	6
1967	Chi-N	1.000	2	12	1	0	0	0
Total	7	.985	438	2053	263	6	32	11

■ Reno Bertoia 3B

YEAR	TM/L	PCT	G	PO	A	E	DP	FR
1954	Det-A	1.000	8	1	2	0	0	1

YEAR	TM/L	PCT	G	PO	A	E	DP	FR
1955	Det-A	.923	14	12	24	3	4	3
1956	Det-A	1.000	2	3	4	0	1	1
1957	Det-A	.953	83	76	125	10	8	-18
1958	Det-A	.950	68	70	139	11	13	5
1959	Was-A	1.000	5	6	8	0	1	0
1960	Was-A	.961	112	94	227	13	19	0
1961	Min-A	.900	32	22	59	9	3	-5
	KC-A	.942	29	27	70	6	6	3
	Det-A	.931	13	10	17	2	2	-1
	Yr	.923	74	59	146	17	11	-3
1962	Det-A	1.000	1	0	1	0	0	1
Total	9	.949	367	321	676	4	57	-10

2B

YEAR	TM/L	PCT	G	PO	A	E	DP	FR
1953	Det-A	.500	1	1	0	1	0	0
1954	Det-A	.969	15	26	36	2	6	15
1955	Det-A	.967	6	7	22	1	4	3
1956	Det-A	.982	18	51	57	2	18	9
1957	Det-A	1.000	2	2	1	0	0	0
1959	Was-A	.971	71	139	198	10	40	-10
1960	Was-A	.979	21	26	20	1	8	0
1961	KC-A	1.000	6	12	13	0	5	1
	Det-A	1.000	7	7	7	0	3	1
	Yr	1.000	13	19	20	0	8	2
1962	Det-A	1.000	1	0	1	0	0	1
Total	9	.974	148	271	355	7	84	20

SS

YEAR	TM/L	PCT	G	PO	A	E	DP	FR
1954	Det-A	.750	3	0	3	1	1	1
1955	Det-A	1.000	5	4	6	0	0	1
1957	Det-A	1.000	7	1	2	0	0	0
1958	Det-A	.833	5	2	3	1	0	-1
1959	Was-A	1.000	1	0	1	0	0	0
1961	Det-A	—	1	0	0	0	0	0
1962	Det-A	—	1	0	0	0	0	0
Total	7	.917	23	7	15	2	1	1

OF

YEAR	TM/L	PCT	G	PO	A	E	DP	FR
1958	Det-A	—	1	0	0	0	0	0

■ Bob Bescher OF

YEAR	TM/L	PCT	G	PO	A	E	DP	FR
1908	Cin-N	1.000	32	82	2	0	2	4
1909	Cin-N	.953	117	247	14	13	4	0
1910	Cin-N	.947	150	339	16	20	4	7
1911	Cin-N	.954	153	267	21	14	2	-6
1912	Cin-N	.963	143	347	15	14	4	8
1913	Cin-N	.968	138	283	22	10	2	7
1914	NY-N	.960	126	298	14	13	7	2
1915	StL-N	.971	129	257	12	8	1	3
1916	StL-N	.953	151	284	18	15	2	1
1917	StL-N	.984	32	61	0	1	0	-3
1918	Cle-A	.969	17	28	3	1	0	0
Total	11	.960	1188	2493	137	109	28	23

■ Bruno Betzel 2B

YEAR	TM/L	PCT	G	PO	A	E	DP	FR
1914	StL-N	1.000	4	4	11	0	0	2
1915	StL-N	.667	3	1	1	1	0	0
1916	StL-N	.960	113	275	366	27	64	**28**
1917	StL-N	.962	75	159	217	15	40	13
1918	StL-N	.900	10	26	37	7	6	1
Total	5	.956	205	465	632	0	110	44

3B

YEAR	TM/L	PCT	G	PO	A	E	DP	FR
1914	StL-N	—	1	0	0	0	0	0
1915	StL-N	.937	105	105	221	22	10	6
1916	StL-N	.888	33	34	69	13	3	2
1917	StL-N	.875	4	2	5	1	1	0
1918	StL-N	.914	34	32	64	9	3	-2
Total	5	.922	177	173	359	5	17	6

OF

YEAR	TM/L	PCT	G	PO	A	E	DP	FR
1916	StL-N	1.000	7	10	0	0	0	0
1917	StL-N	.972	23	32	3	1	1	-1
1918	StL-N	.978	21	42	2	1	1	-1
Total	3	.978	51	84	5	2	2	-2

SS

YEAR	TM/L	PCT	G	PO	A	E	DP	FR
1915	StL-N	.818	2	3	6	2	1	-1

■ Kurt Bevacqua 3B

YEAR	TM/L	PCT	G	PO	A	E	DP	FR
1971	Cle-A	1.000	3	2	2	0	1	0
1972	Cle-A	1.000	1	2	5	0	1	2
1973	KC-A	.935	40	26	60	6	7	-8
1974	Pit-N	.955	8	8	13	1	0	0
	KC-A	.931	13	8	19	2	5	-1
1975	Mil-A	.948	60	50	96	8	12	-1
1977	Tex-A	1.000	11	4	13	0	3	-2
1978	Tex-A	.877	49	20	87	15	7	-5
1979	SD-N	.954	64	45	120	8	13	2
1980	SD-N	.929	13	1	12	1	1	-2
	Pit-N	.958	9	5	18	1	1	1
	Yr	.947	22	6	30	2	2	-1
1981	Pit-N	1.000	2	0	1	0	0	0
1982	SD-N	1.000	1	1	0	0	0	0
1983	SD-N	.950	12	5	14	1	1	0
1984	SD-N	.933	10	4	10	1	2	-1
1985	SD-N	.946	33	32	56	5	7	-2
Total	14	.938	329	213	526	9	61	-17

2B

YEAR	TM/L	PCT	G	PO	A	E	DP	FR
1971	Cle-A	.971	36	70	64	4	10	-6
1973	KC-A	.952	16	19	21	2	3	-2
1974	KC-A	.929	7	8	5	1	3	-1
1975	Mil-A	.975	32	95	63	4	20	1
1976	Mil-A	1.000	2	0	6	0	0	2
1977	Tex-A	.947	5	2	16	1	0	-1
1978	Tex-A	.952	13	31	29	3	4	1
1979	SD-N	.967	16	27	32	2	4	-6
1980	SD-N	.929	2	2	1	0	0	-1
1981	Pit-N	.941	4	7	9	1	3	1
Total	10	.966	133	261	246	8	47	-12

1B

YEAR	TM/L	PCT	G	PO	A	E	DP	FR
1973	KC-A	.987	9	68	7	1	10	1
1974	KC-A	.987	14	74	3	1	12	-1
1975	Mil-A	1.000	3	4	2	0	0	1

YEAR	TM/L	PCT	G	PO	A	E	DP	FR
1977	Tex-A	1.000	5	26	2	0	1	0
1978	Tex-A	1.000	1	11	0	0	1	0
1979	SD-N	.977	8	38	4	1	4	0
1980	SD-N	—	1	0	0	0	0	0
	Pit-N	1.000	2	20	0	0	0	0
	Yr	1.000	3	20	0	0	0	0
1982	SD-N	.989	30	253	16	3	13	-2
1983	SD-N	.995	27	185	12	1	14	-2
1984	SD-N	1.000	20	66	5	0	8	0
1985	SD-N	.909	9	16	4	2	1	1
Total	11	.989	129	761	55	9	64	-2

OF

YEAR	TM/L	PCT	G	PO	A	E	DP	FR
1971	Cle-A	.800	5	4	0	1	0	0
1972	Cle-A	.900	11	9	0	1	0	-1
1973	KC-A	1.000	10	7	2	0	0	1
1974	Pit-N	—	1	0	0	0	0	0
1977	Tex-A	1.000	14	10	0	0	0	-1
1979	SD-N	1.000	8	5	0	0	0	0
1980	SD-N	1.000	4	4	0	0	0	0
1982	SD-N	1.000	3	2	0	0	0	0
1983	SD-N	1.000	12	17	2	0	1	1
1984	SD-N	1.000	3	3	0	0	0	0
1985	SD-N	1.000	1	1	0	0	0	0
Total	11	.971	72	62	4	2	1	0

SS

YEAR	TM/L	PCT	G	PO	A	E	DP	FR
1971	Cle-A	1.000	2	1	6	0	0	-1
1974	KC-A	.667	2	0	2	1	0	0
1975	Mil-A	.938	5	8	7	1	3	0
Total	3	.923	9	9	15	2	3	-1

■ Monte Beville C

YEAR	TM/L	PCT	G	PO	A	E	DP	FR
1903	NY-A	.960	75	296	66	15	4	-12
1904	NY-A	.882	3	12	3	2	0	-1
	Det-A	.957	30	129	27	7	2	-1
	Yr	.950	33	141	30	9	2	-2
Total	2	.957	108	437	96	4	6	-14

1B

YEAR	TM/L	PCT	G	PO	A	E	DP	FR
1903	NY-A	1.000	3	18	3	0	3	1
1904	NY-A	.906	4	28	1	3	0	-1
	Det-A	.964	24	225	14	9	9	-1
	Yr	.957	28	253	15	12	9	-2
Total	2	.960	31	271	18	2	12	-1

■ Buddy Biancalana SS

YEAR	TM/L	PCT	G	PO	A	E	DP	FR
1982	KC-A	1.000	3	2	8	0	1	2
1983	KC-A	.914	6	11	21	3	3	3
1984	KC-A	.946	33	28	94	7	13	3
1985	KC-A	.961	74	80	168	10	31	23
1986	KC-A	.946	89	102	177	16	40	0
1987	KC-A	.886	22	12	27	5	4	1
	Hou-N	.889	16	8	16	3	2	-1
Total	6	.945	243	243	511	4	94	31

2B

YEAR	TM/L	PCT	G	PO	A	E	DP	FR
1984	KC-A	.988	29	34	50	1	15	4
1985	KC-A	1.000	4	3	1	0	1	0
1986	KC-A	1.000	12	6	13	0	1	2
1987	KC-A	1.000	12	9	18	0	6	4
	Hou-N	1.000	3	1	2	0	1	0
Total	4	.993	60	53	84	1	24	10

■ Dante Bichette OF

YEAR	TM/L	PCT	G	PO	A	E	DP	FR
1988	Cal-A	.979	21	44	2	1	0	3
1989	Cal-A	.990	40	95	6	1	2	4
1990	Cal-A	.965	105	183	12	7	5	-1
Total	3	.974	166	322	20	9	7	6

■ Lou Bierbauer 2B

YEAR	TM/L	PCT	G	PO	A	E	DP	FR
1886	Phi-a	.910	133	380	429	80	54	0
1887	Phi-a	.921	126	332	378	61	45	-8
1888	Phi-a	.916	121	342	**399**	**68**	39	21
1889	Phi-a	.941	130	**472**	406	55	80	37
1890	Bro-P	.931	**133**	372	**468**	62	**77**	**25**
1891	Pit-N	.929	121	331	384	55	42	-2
1892	Pit-N	.950	**152**	385	**555**	49	66	**32**
1893	Pit-N	**.959**	128	352	441	34	71	16
1894	Pit-N	.938	130	309	**453**	50	58	9
1895	Pit-N	.946	117	284	**400**	39	52	14
1896	Pit-N	.966	59	140	206	12	32	12
1897	StL-N	.921	12	25	33	5	4	-2
1898	StL-N	.429	2	0	3	4	0	-2
Total	13	.935	1364	3724	4555	574	620	152

3B

YEAR	TM/L	PCT	G	PO	A	E	DP	FR
1888	Phi-a	.958	13	22	24	2	2	1
1898	StL-N	—	1	0	0	0	0	0
Total	2	.958	14	22	24	2	2	1

C

YEAR	TM/L	PCT	G	PO	A	E	DP	FR
1886	Phi-a	.897	4	24	2	3	0	-1
1889	Phi-a	—	1	0	0	0	0	0
Total	2	.897	5	24	2	3	0	-1

SS

YEAR	TM/L	PCT	G	PO	A	E	DP	FR
1886	Phi-a	.500	2	2	4	6	1	-3
1898	StL-N	1.000	1	3	7	0	0	1
Total	2	.727	3	5	11	6	1	-2

■ Carson Bigbee OF

YEAR	TM/L	PCT	G	PO	A	E	DP	FR
1916	Pit-N	.923	19	45	3	4	0	1
1917	Pit-N	.961	107	235	9	10	2	2
1918	Pit-N	.958	92	168	13	8	4	-1
1919	Pit-N	.971	124	343	21	11	5	11
1920	Pit-N	.971	133	289	16	9	4	5
1921	Pit-N	.977	146	351	27	9	**6**	**17**
1922	Pit-N	.956	150	345	27	17	5	15
1923	Pit-N	.990	122	283	12	3	3	7
1924	Pit-N	.943	75	155	9	10	2	-1
1925	Pit-N	.942	42	66	3	4	1	0
1926	Pit-N	.966	21	26	2	1	0	0
Total	13	.966	1031	2302	142	6	32	56

2B

YEAR	TM/L	PCT	G	PO	A	E	DP	FR
1916	Pit-N	.946	23	36	51	5	7	-6
1917	Pit-N	.936	16	34	39	5	7	-5

YEAR	TM/L	PCT	G	PO	A	E	DP	FR
Total	2	.941	39	70	90	0	14	-11

SS

YEAR	TM/L	PCT	G	PO	A	E	DP	FR
1917	Pit-N	1.000	2	3	8	0	1	0

3B

YEAR	TM/L	PCT	G	PO	A	E	DP	FR
1916	Pit-N	.500	1	0	1	1	0	-1

■ Craig Biggio C

YEAR	TM/L	PCT	G	PO	A	E	DP	FR
1988	Hou-N	.991	50	292	28	3	0	16
1989	Hou-N	.990	125	728	56	8	6	-6
1990	Hou-N	.985	113	546	54	9	4	-9
Total	3	.988	288	1566	138	0	10	1

OF

YEAR	TM/L	PCT	G	PO	A	E	DP	FR
1989	Hou-N	.933	5	14	0	1	0	0
1990	Hou-N	.967	50	111	6	4	0	1
Total	2	.963	55	125	6	5	0	1

■ Larry Biittner OF

YEAR	TM/L	PCT	G	PO	A	E	DP	FR
1971	Was-A	.940	41	72	6	5	0	-1
1972	Tex-A	.961	65	93	5	4	1	-2
1973	Tex-A	.980	57	91	6	2	1	-1
1974	Mon-N	1.000	4	7	1	0	0	1
1975	Mon-N	.972	93	166	8	5	0	-2
1976	Mon-N	.947	7	17	1	1	0	1
	Chi-N	1.000	24	34	1	0	0	0
	Yr	.981	31	51	2	1	0	1
1977	Chi-N	.988	52	79	1	1	1	-6
1978	Chi-N	.980	29	47	1	1	0	-2
1979	Chi-N	.925	44	46	3	4	0	-4
1980	Chi-N	.983	38	55	4	1	2	-1
1981	Cin-N	1.000	3	4	2	0	1	1
1982	Cin-N	.978	31	42	2	1	0	0
1983	Tex-A	1.000	2	4	0	0	0	0
Total	13	.970	490	757	41	5	6	-16

1B

YEAR	TM/L	PCT	G	PO	A	E	DP	FR
1971	Was-A	.923	3	11	1	1	1	0
1972	Tex-A	.991	65	410	36	4	36	4
1973	Tex-A	1.000	20	143	14	0	16	1
1976	Chi-N	.985	33	232	33	4	20	6
1977	Chi-N	.987	80	713	64	10	50	8
1978	Chi-N	.987	62	554	52	8	53	7
1979	Chi-N	.992	32	236	20	2	24	1
1980	Chi-N	.996	41	250	19	1	14	1
1981	Cin-N	1.000	8	53	3	0	2	0
1982	Cin-N	.993	15	128	12	1	13	1
1983	Tex-A	.987	22	136	15	2	13	2
Total	11	.990	381	2866	269	3	242	31

■ Dann Bilardello C

YEAR	TM/L	PCT	G	PO	A	E	DP	FR
1983	Cin-N	.991	105	494	72	5	4	-1
1984	Cin-N	.992	68	323	34	3	2	2
1985	Cin-N	.986	42	198	20	3	1	8
1986	Mon-N	.982	77	391	38	8	3	2
1989	Pit-N	.970	33	150	14	5	1	6
1990	Pit-N	1.000	19	69	9	0	0	3
Total	6	.987	344	1625	187	4	12	20

■ Steve Bilko 1B

YEAR	TM/L	PCT	G	PO	A	E	DP	FR
1949	StL-N	1.000	5	42	3	0	1	0
1950	StL-N	.989	9	81	7	1	8	0
1951	StL-N	.984	19	170	13	3	18	0
1952	StL-N	.995	20	177	24	1	14	4
1953	StL-N	.991	154	**1446**	**124**	15	145	7
1954	StL-N	1.000	6	21	7	0	3	2
	Chi-N	1.000	22	182	28	0	17	6
	Yr	1.000	28	203	35	0	20	8
1958	Cin-N	.995	21	172	11	1	19	-1
	LA-N	.995	25	173	17	1	20	2
	Yr	.995	46	345	28	2	39	1
1960	Det-A	.991	62	501	36	5	47	0
1961	LA-A	.989	86	577	61	7	56	4
1962	LA-A	.995	50	371	28	2	36	-1
Total	10	.992	479	3913	359	6	384	23

OF

YEAR	TM/L	PCT	G	PO	A	E	DP	FR
1961	LA-A	1.000	3	2	0	0	0	0

■ Josh Billings C

YEAR	TM/L	PCT	G	PO	A	E	DP	FR
1913	Cle-A	.857	1	4	2	1	0	0
1914	Cle-A	.813	3	10	3	3	0	2
1915	Cle-A	1.000	7	29	6	0	0	-1
1916	Cle-A	.981	12	38	13	1	3	3
1917	Cle-A	.974	48	134	51	5	2	2
1918	Cle-A	1.000	1	2	0	0	0	0
1919	StL-A	.982	26	76	33	2	2	5
1920	StL-A	.967	40	138	36	6	1	-5
1921	StL-A	.982	12	45	9	1	0	2
1922	StL-A	1.000	3	5	1	0	0	0
1923	StL-A	.917	4	8	3	1	1	0
Total	11	.970	157	489	157	0	9	8

OF

YEAR	TM/L	PCT	G	PO	A	E	DP	FR
1915	Cle-A	1.000	1	1	0	0	0	0

1B

YEAR	TM/L	PCT	G	PO	A	E	DP	FR
1919	StL-A	.500	1	0	1	1	0	0

■ Dick Billings C

YEAR	TM/L	PCT	G	PO	A	E	DP	FR
1970	Was-A	.929	8	25	3	0	0	-1
1971	Was-A	.992	62	337	35	3	5	3
1972	Tex-A	.981	92	478	45	10	**13**	-5
1973	Tex-A	.975	72	356	32	10	3	-18
1974	Tex-A	1.000	13	55	2	0	1	1
	StL-N	1.000	1	0	0	0	0	0
Total	5	.984	248	1259	117	3	22	-20

OF

YEAR	TM/L	PCT	G	PO	A	E	DP	FR
1968	Was-A	.929	8	12	1	1	0	0
1969	Was-A	1.000	6	9	0	0	0	0
1971	Was-A	1.000	4	31	2	1	0	0
1972	Tex-A	.959	41	66	5	3	0	0
1973	Tex-A	1.000	4	3	0	0	0	0
1974	Tex-A	1.000	1	1	0	0	0	0
Total	6	.966	92	132	8	5	0	0

YEAR	TM/L	PCT	G	PO	A	E	DP	FR
3B								
1968	Was-A	1.000	4	2	5	0	0	0
1969	Was-A	1.000	1	0	4	0	1	0
1971	Was-A	1.000	2	1	0	0	0	0
1972	Tex-A	.850	5	3	14	3	0	0
Total	4	.906	12	6	23	3	1	0
1B								
1972	Tex-A	—	1	0	0	0	0	0
1973	Tex-A	.864	3	17	2	3	1	0
Total	2	.864	4	17	2	3	1	0

■ George Binks OF
YEAR	TM/L	PCT	G	PO	A	E	DP	FR
1944	Was-A	1.000	3	4	0	0	0	0
1945	Was-A	.977	128	321	13	8	4	0
1946	Was-A	1.000	28	68	1	0	0	2
1947	Phi-A	.965	75	157	8	6	1	-1
1948	Phi-A	1.000	14	18	1	0	0	-1
	StL-A	1.000	5	7	0	0	0	0
	Yr	1.000	19	25	1	0	0	-1
Total	5	.977	253	575	23	4	5	0
1B								
1945	Was-A	.994	20	164	12	1	13	0
1947	Phi-A	.989	13	82	7	1	4	0
1948	StL-A	1.000	4	10	0	0	1	0
Total	3	.993	37	256	19	2	18	0

■ Jud Birchall OF
YEAR	TM/L	PCT	G	PO	A	E	DP	FR
1882	Phi-a	.860	74	134	14	24	0	0
1883	Phi-a	.809	**96**	168	22	**45**	0	6
1884	Phi-a	.838	52	81	7	17	1	2
Total	3	.832	222	383	43	6	1	8
3B								
1884	Phi-a	1.000	2	1	8	0	0	1
2B								
1882	Phi-a	1.000	1	4	4	0	0	0

■ Joe Birmingham OF
YEAR	TM/L	PCT	G	PO	A	E	DP	FR
1906	Cle-A	1.000	9	16	3	0	0	2
1907	Cle-A	.949	130	268	28	16	8	13
1908	Cle-A	.957	121	250	20	12	6	6
1909	Cle-A	.948	98	203	15	12	2	4
1910	Cle-A	.961	103	223	24	10	8	13
1911	Cle-A	.973	102	231	19	7	6	7
1912	Cle-A	.952	96	198	18	11	8	3
1913	Cle-A	.974	36	73	2	2	0	-3
1914	Cle-A	1.000	14	14	1	0	0	-2
Total	9	.958	709	1476	130	0	38	43
3B								
1906	Cle-A	—	1	0	0	0	0	0
1910	Cle-A	1.000	1	1	5	0	0	1
1911	Cle-A	.905	16	22	35	6	4	1
Total	3	.913	18	23	40	6	4	2
1B								
1912	Cle-A	.962	9	66	9	3	3	2
SS								
1907	Cle-A	.941	5	9	7	1	3	0
1908	Cle-A	1.000	1	0	3	0	0	0
Total	2	.950	6	9	10	1	3	0

■ Max Bishop 2B
YEAR	TM/L	PCT	G	PO	A	E	DP	FR
1924	Phi-A	.969	80	189	273	15	50	6
1925	Phi-A	.957	104	229	352	26	53	5
1926	Phi-A	**.987**	119	235	365	8	55	0
1927	Phi-A	.967	106	211	342	19	48	3
1928	Phi-A	**.978**	125	284	371	15	62	-11
1929	Phi-A	.970	129	301	371	21	58	-26
1930	Phi-A	.976	127	267	418	17	61	-6
1931	Phi-A	.984	130	314	414	12	84	0
1932	Phi-A	**.988**	106	232	340	7	68	-10
1933	Phi-A	.975	113	254	359	16	52	-13
1934	Bos-A	.990	57	147	155	3	37	0
1935	Bos-A	.978	34	89	90	4	11	-5
Total	12	.976	1230	2752	3850	163	639	-57
1B								
1934	Bos-A	.994	15	146	9	1	11	0
1935	Bos-A	1.000	11	19	1	0	0	0
Total	2	.994	26	165	10	1	11	0
SS								
1935	Bos-A	1.000	2	6	3	0	1	-1

■ Del Bissonette 1B
YEAR	TM/L	PCT	G	PO	A	E	DP	FR
1928	Bro-N	.987	**155**	1482	77	**20**	95	-3
1929	Bro-N	.987	113	1093	47	15	70	-9
1930	Bro-N	.987	146	1427	72	**20**	**142**	-9
1931	Bro-N	.990	152	**1460**	66	16	136	-7
1933	Bro-N	.988	32	298	19	4	25	0
Total	5	.988	598	5760	281	5	468	-28

■ Lena Blackburne SS
YEAR	TM/L	PCT	G	PO	A	E	DP	FR
1910	Chi-A	.911	74	173	265	43	29	19
1912	Chi-A	.800	4	3	1	1	1	1
1915	Chi-A	.909	9	11	19	3	3	1
1918	Cin-N	.938	125	319	413	48	**69**	10
1919	Bos-N	1.000	1	5	2	0	0	0
Total	5	.927	213	511	700	5	102	29
3B								
1912	Chi-A	1.000	1	0	1	0	0	0
1915	Chi-A	.949	83	88	134	12	12	-9
1919	Bos-N	.948	24	34	39	4	3	3
	Phi-N	.933	72	85	167	18	11	6
	Yr	.937	96	119	206	22	14	9
Total	3	.942	180	207	341	4	26	0
2B								
1914	Chi-A	.963	143	239	**433**	26	28	1
1919	Bos-N	1.000	1	2	4	0	1	1
Total	2	.963	144	241	437	6	29	2
1B								
1919	Bos-N	1.000	1	2	0	0	0	0
	Phi-N	1.000	1	1	1	0	0	0
	Yr	1.000	2	3	1	0	0	0

■ Tim Blackwell C
YEAR	TM/L	PCT	G	PO	A	E	DP	FR
1974	Bos-A	.971	44	182	21	6	5	2
1975	Bos-A	.984	57	230	23	4	3	7
1976	Phi-N	1.000	4	17	0	0	0	1
1977	Phi-N	1.000	1	2	0	0	0	0
	Mon-N	.925	14	35	2	3	1	0
	Yr	.929	15	37	2	3	1	0
1978	Chi-N	.987	49	213	20	3	3	7
1979	Chi-N	.975	63	245	28	7	3	1
1980	Chi-N	.982	103	572	93	12	**16**	**17**
1981	Chi-N	.993	56	268	28	2	1	2
1982	Mon-N	.985	18	58	9	1	1	2
1983	Mon-N	.935	5	28	1	2	0	0
Total	10	.981	414	1850	225	0	33	39

■ Ray Blades OF
YEAR	TM/L	PCT	G	PO	A	E	DP	FR
1922	StL-N	.931	29	61	6	5	0	0
1923	StL-N	.967	83	194	11	7	2	4
1924	StL-N	.956	109	256	6	12	1	2
1925	StL-N	.979	114	266	13	6	4	4
1926	StL-N	.980	105	229	10	5	1	-2
1927	StL-N	.914	50	64	0	6	0	-15
1928	StL-N	.972	19	34	1	1	1	-3
1930	StL-N	.957	32	66	1	3	0	0
1931	StL-N	.871	20	26	1	4	0	-3
1932	StL-N	.975	62	117	2	3	0	-3
Total	10	.963	623	1313	51	2	9	-16
3B								
1922	StL-N	.750	1	1	2	1	0	-1
1923	StL-N	1.000	4	0	1	0	0	0
1924	StL-N	.938	7	7	8	1	0	-2
1925	StL-N	1.000	1	1	0	0	0	0
1932	StL-N	—	1	0	0	0	0	0
Total	5	.909	14	9	11	2	0	-3
2B								
1924	StL-N	1.000	7	12	16	0	2	-3
SS								
1922	StL-N	.773	4	5	12	5	2	-3

■ Footsie Blair 2B
YEAR	TM/L	PCT	G	PO	A	E	DP	FR
1929	Chi-N	1.000	2	6	6	0	3	1
1930	Chi-N	.958	115	257	429	30	83	8
1931	Chi-N	.956	44	103	115	10	18	-4
Total	3	.958	161	366	550	0	104	5
1B								
1929	Chi-N	1.000	7	64	3	0	3	0
1931	Chi-N	.987	23	142	5	2	10	-1
Total	2	.991	30	206	8	2	13	-1
3B								
1929	Chi-N	.897	8	12	14	3	0	0
1930	Chi-N	.900	13	9	27	4	2	0
1931	Chi-N	.000	1	0	0	1	0	0
Total	3	.886	22	21	41	8	2	0

■ Paul Blair OF
YEAR	TM/L	PCT	G	PO	A	E	DP	FR
1964	Bal-A	1.000	6	2	0	0	0	1
1965	Bal-A	.992	116	241	5	2	0	-2
1966	Bal-A	.990	127	204	4	2	2	-15
1967	Bal-A	.985	146	**369**	13	6	3	**16**
1968	Bal-A	.993	132	271	10	2	2	-4
1969	Bal-A	.988	150	**407**	14	5	5	**17**
1970	Bal-A	.990	128	368	10	4	3	**17**
1971	Bal-A	.991	138	331	4	3	1	0
1972	Bal-A	.991	139	337	10	3	1	4
1973	Bal-A	.990	144	369	**14**	4	4	5
1974	Bal-A	.985	151	447	7	7	2	5
1975	Bal-A	.988	138	327	8	3	1	-6
1976	Bal-A	.979	139	327	6	7	1	-13
1977	NY-A	.969	79	125	1	4	0	4
1978	NY-A	.989	64	87	2	1	1	3
1979	NY-A	1.000	2	6	0	0	0	1
	Cin-N	.992	67	117	3	1	0	8
1980	NY-A	1.000	12	8	0	0	0	1
Total	17	.988	1878	4343	111	4	26	42
3B								
1968	Bal-A	.667	1	1	1	1	1	0
1970	Bal-A	.000	1	0	0	1	0	0
1978	NY-A	—	3	0	0	0	0	0
Total	3	.500	5	1	1	2	1	0
2B								
1978	NY-A	.833	5	2	3	1	0	-1
SS								
1978	NY-A	1.000	4	1	0	0	0	0
1975	Bal-A	—	1	0	0	0	0	0

■ Walter Blair C
YEAR	TM/L	PCT	G	PO	A	E	DP	FR
1907	NY-A	.922	7	36	11	4	0	1
1908	NY-A	.956	60	225	58	13	4	-12
1909	NY-A	.964	42	151	37	7	2	-8
1910	NY-A	.970	6	22	10	1	2	-2
1911	NY-A	.970	84	379	101	15	12	4
1914	Buf-F	.984	128	604	194	13	17	4
1915	Buf-F	**.981**	97	404	150	11	15	4
Total	7	.974	424	1821	561	4	52	-9
OF								
1908	NY-A	.800	9	12	0	3	0	-1
1B								
1908	NY-A	1.000	3	9	1	0	0	0
1911	NY-A	.889	1	7	1	1	0	0
Total	2	.947	4	16	2	1	0	0

■ Harry Blake OF
YEAR	TM/L	PCT	G	PO	A	E	DP	FR
1894	Cle-N	.932	73	120	16	10	4	2
1895	Cle-N	.898	83	119	13	15	3	-2
1896	Cle-N	.944	103	184	17	12	5	3
1897	Cle-N	.989	32	87	3	1	2	4
1898	Cle-N	.952	136	234	25	13	3	8
1899	StL-N	.979	87	176	10	4	3	-2
Total	6	.948	514	920	84	5	20	13

YEAR	TM/L	PCT	G	PO	A	E	DP	FR
2B								
1899	StL-N	.844	4	13	14	5	2	0
1B								
1898	Cle-N	1.000	2	5	0	0	1	0
1899	StL-N	.917	1	10	1	1	1	0
Total	2	.941	3	15	1	1	2	0
SS								
1896	Cle-N	.667	1	2	4	3	0	-1
1899	StL-N	1.000	1	1	0	0	0	0
Total	2	.700	2	3	4	3	0	-1
C								
1899	StL-N	1.000	1	3	2	0	0	0

■ Bob Blakiston OF
YEAR	TM/L	PCT	G	PO	A	E	DP	FR
1882	Phi-a	.855	38	52	13	11	0	3
1883	Phi-a	.857	37	43	5	8	0	-3
1884	Phi-a	.902	28	48	7	6	1	4
	Ind-a	1.000	1	2	0	0	0	0
	Yr	.905	29	50	7	6	1	4
Total	3	.872	104	145	25	5	1	4
3B								
1882	Phi-a	.774	34	32	81	33	3	-2
1883	Phi-a	.786	5	2	9	3	0	-1
1884	Phi-a	.800	2	1	3	1	0	0
Total	3	.776	41	35	93	7	3	-3
1B								
1883	Phi-a	.897	6	32	3	4	0	0
1884	Phi-a	.917	1	11	0	1	0	0
	Ind-a	.884	5	36	2	5	0	0
	Yr	.891	6	47	2	6	0	0
Total	2	.894	12	79	5	0	0	0
2B								
1882	Phi-a	.000	1	0	0	1	0	-1
1884	Phi-a	.571	1	3	1	3	0	-2
Total	2	.500	2	3	1	4	0	-3
SS								
1884	Phi-a	.800	1	0	4	1	0	0

■ Johnny Blanchard OF
YEAR	TM/L	PCT	G	PO	A	E	DP	FR
1959	NY-A	.889	8	8	0	1	0	-1
1961	NY-A	1.000	15	24	0	0	0	0
1962	NY-A	.987	47	76	2	1	0	-3
1963	NY-A	.987	64	76	2	1	0	-9
1964	NY-A	1.000	14	21	1	0	0	0
1965	KC-A	1.000	20	22	0	0	0	-2
	Mil-N	—	1	0	0	0	0	0
Total	6	.987	169	227	5	3	0	-17
C								
1955	NY-A	1.000	1	7	0	0	0	0
1959	NY-A	.963	12	25	1	1	1	0
1960	NY-A	.988	28	151	7	2	0	10
1961	NY-A	.990	48	268	18	3	2	-2
1962	NY-A	.952	15	59	1	3	0	-4
1964	NY-A	.984	25	118	7	2	1	-3
1965	NY-A	.961	12	67	7	3	0	-1
	KC-A	.984	14	55	5	1	1	-7
	Yr	.971	26	122	12	4	1	-8
Total	7	.982	155	750	46	5	5	-7
1B								
1959	NY-A	1.000	1	3	0	0	0	0
1962	NY-A	.923	2	24	0	2	0	-1
1964	NY-A	1.000	3	27	3	0	5	0
Total	3	.966	6	54	3	2	5	-1

■ Larvell Blanks SS
YEAR	TM/L	PCT	G	PO	A	E	DP	FR
1972	Atl-N	1.000	4	8	13	0	0	0
1973	Atl-N	1.000	2	0	1	0	0	0
1974	Atl-N	.889	2	1	7	1	1	0
1975	Atl-N	.960	129	183	414	25	68	-13
1976	Cle-A	.977	56	59	109	4	28	-15
1977	Cle-A	.960	66	74	116	8	21	-26
1978	Cle-A	.926	43	56	107	13	22	-8
1979	Tex-A	.972	49	39	65	3	16	-9
1980	Atl-N	.947	56	43	100	8	21	-3
Total	9	.957	407	463	932	2	176	-74
2B								
1972	Atl-N	1.000	18	38	55	0	12	5
1973	Atl-N	1.000	2	1	2	0	0	-2
1975	Atl-N	.964	12	29	24	2	7	1
1976	Cle-A	.966	46	93	104	7	25	-4
1977	Cle-A	1.000	12	15	23	0	3	0
1978	Cle-A	1.000	17	25	31	0	3	-2
1979	Tex-A	1.000	16	26	25	0	6	0
1980	Atl-N	1.000	1	1	0	0	0	0
Total	8	.982	124	228	264	9	56	-2
3B								
1972	Atl-N	1.000	2	3	6	0	0	1
1973	Atl-N	—	3	0	0	0	0	0
1976	Cle-A	1.000	2	0	1	0	0	0
1977	Cle-A	.946	18	11	42	3	3	1
1978	Cle-A	1.000	3	2	6	0	0	1
1980	Atl-N	.924	43	21	89	9	10	10
Total	6	.938	71	37	144	2	13	13

■ Don Blasingame 2B
YEAR	TM/L	PCT	G	PO	A	E	DP	FR
1955	StL-N	.955	3	8	13	1	1	2
1956	StL-N	.986	98	280	303	8	89	**23**
1957	StL-N	.984	**154**	372	**512**	14	**128**	**26**
1958	StL-N	.964	137	312	380	**26**	97	-1
1959	StL-N	.979	150	362	439	17	104	**20**
1960	SF-N	.979	133	318	329	14	66	-13
1961	Cin-N	.972	116	277	304	17	53	-19
1962	Cin-N	.976	137	334	352	17	66	-9
1963	Cin-N	.974	11	22	16	1	6	0
	Was-A	.991	64	162	177	3	52	1
1964	Was-A	.977	135	259	336	14	70	-30
1965	Was-A	.984	110	235	248	8	68	1
1966	Was-A	.984	58	119	132	4	32	-1
	KC-A	1.000	4	5	9	0	2	-1

YEAR	TM/L	PCT	G	PO	A	E	DP	FR
	Yr	.985	62	124	141	4	34	-2
Total	12	.979	1310	3065	3550	144	834	-1
SS								
1955	StL-N	.889	2	2	6	1	1	0
1956	StL-N	.946	49	93	135	13	31	-1
1966	Was-A	—	1	0	0	0	0	0
Total	3	.944	52	95	141	4	32	-1
3B								
1956	StL-N	1.000	2	0	4	0	0	0
1963	Cin-N	1.000	2	0	1	0	0	0
Total	2	1.000	4	0	5	0	0	0

■ Johnny Blatnik OF

YEAR	TM/L	PCT	G	PO	A	E	DP	FR
1948	Phi-N	.946	105	220	9	13	1	-1
1949	Phi-N	1.000	2	3	0	0	0	0
1950	Phi-N	1.000	1	2	0	0	0	0
	StL-N	.875	7	6	1	1	0	-1
	Yr	.900	8	8	1	1	0	-1
Total	3	.945	115	231	10	4	1	-2

■ Buddy Blattner 2B

YEAR	TM/L	PCT	G	PO	A	E	DP	FR
1942	StL-N	1.000	3	3	2	0	1	0
1946	NY-N	.976	114	285	315	15	62	1
1947	NY-N	.947	34	79	100	10	14	-2
1948	NY-N	1.000	7	8	22	0	4	2
1949	Phi-N	.981	15	24	27	1	5	-6
Total	5	.971	173	399	466	6	86	-5
3B								
1947	NY-N	.929	11	7	6	1	1	-1
1949	Phi-N	.957	12	11	11	1	2	-3
Total	2	.946	23	18	17	2	3	-4
SS								
1942	StL-N	.900	13	11	16	3	2	-1
1949	Phi-N	—	1	0	0	0	0	0
Total	2	.900	14	11	16	3	2	-1
1B								
1946	NY-N	1.000	1	1	0	0	0	0

■ Jeff Blauser SS

YEAR	TM/L	PCT	G	PO	A	E	DP	FR
1987	Atl-N	.962	50	65	166	9	28	10
1988	Atl-N	.947	8	15	21	2	4	-1
1989	Atl-N	.958	30	37	55	4	5	-5
1990	Atl-N	.961	93	141	257	16	47	-4
Total	4	.961	181	258	499	31	84	0
3B								
1989	Atl-N	.929	78	42	128	13	9	-6
1990	Atl-N	1.000	9	5	6	0	1	0
Total	2	.933	87	47	134	3	10	-6
2B								
1988	Atl-N	.967	9	20	38	2	4	3
1989	Atl-N	.970	39	58	71	4	14	-5
1990	Atl-N	1.000	14	23	25	0	6	2
Total	3	.975	62	101	134	6	24	0
OF								
1989	Atl-N	—	2	0	0	0	0	0
1990	Atl-N	—	1	0	0	0	0	0
Total	2	—	3	0	0	0	0	0

■ Marv Blaylock 1B

YEAR	TM/L	PCT	G	PO	A	E	DP	FR
1955	Phi-N	.991	77	528	44	5	35	1
1956	Phi-N	.992	124	949	72	8	86	-5
1957	Phi-N	1.000	12	19	1	0	0	0
Total	3	.992	213	1496	117	3	121	-4
OF								
1955	Phi-N	1.000	6	9	4	0	1	3
1956	Phi-N	1.000	1	1	0	0	0	0
1957	Phi-N	1.000	1	3	0	0	0	0
Total	3	1.000	8	13	4	0	1	3

■ Curt Blefary OF

YEAR	TM/L	PCT	G	PO	A	E	DP	FR
1965	Bal-A	.979	136	227	10	5	3	0
1966	Bal-A	.976	109	159	5	4	0	-9
1967	Bal-A	.968	103	170	13	6	5	5
1968	Bal-A	.962	92	144	9	6	1	1
1969	Hou-N	1.000	1	3	0	0	0	0
1970	NY-A	.972	79	103	1	3	0	-12
1971	NY-A	.875	6	6	1	1	0	0
	Oak-A	1.000	14	15	1	0	0	0
	Yr	.958	20	21	2	1	0	0
1972	Oak-A	1.000	1	3	0	0	0	0
	SD-N	1.000	3	1	0	0	0	0
Total	8	.972	544	831	40	5	9	-15
1B								
1966	Bal-A	.992	20	115	12	1	9	1
1967	Bal-A	.989	52	413	50	5	34	6
1968	Bal-A	.988	12	78	4	1	9	-1
1969	Hou-N	.987	152	1235	103	17	117	5
1970	NY-A	1.000	6	56	2	0	9	-1
1971	NY-A	1.000	4	41	2	0	1	0
1972	Oak-A	—	1	0	0	0	0	0
	SD-N	.974	6	34	4	1	3	0
Total	7	.989	253	1972	177	5	182	10
C								
1968	Bal-A	.983	40	215	22	4	1	-9
1971	NY-A	.975	14	70	7	2	0	-1
1972	SD-N	.982	12	51	3	1	0	-7
Total	3	.981	66	336	32	7	1	-17
3B								
1971	Oak-A	.929	5	2	11	1	0	-1
1972	SD-N	1.000	3	0	1	0	0	0
Total	2	.933	8	2	12	1	0	-1
2B								
1971	Oak-A	1.000	1	0	1	0	0	0
1972	Oak-A	—	1	1	0	0	0	-1
Total	2	1.000	3	1	1	0	0	-1

■ Jack Bliss C

YEAR	TM/L	PCT	G	PO	A	E	DP	FR
1908	StL-N	.992	43	194	59	2	6	5
1909	StL-N	.951	32	138	37	9	10	1
1910	StL-N	.980	13	39	10	1	0	-1

YEAR	TM/L	PCT	G	PO	A	E	DP	FR
1911	StL-N	.952	84	332	103	22	9	-10
1912	StL-N	.973	41	140	42	5	7	-6
Total	5	.966	213	843	251	9	32	-11
SS								
1911	StL-N	1.000	1	0	1	0	0	0

■ Bruno Block C

YEAR	TM/L	PCT	G	PO	A	E	DP	FR
1907	Was-A	.949	21	59	16	4	1	-5
1910	Chi-A	.964	47	244	77	12	8	1
1911	Chi-A	.972	38	201	40	7	2	-3
1912	Chi-A	.980	46	222	65	6	4	2
1914	Chi-F	.966	34	132	39	6	7	0
Total	5	.969	186	858	237	5	22	-5

■ Ron Blomberg 1B

YEAR	TM/L	PCT	G	PO	A	E	DP	FR
1972	NY-A	.985	95	813	32	13	88	-8
1973	NY-A	.980	41	359	28	8	38	3
1978	Chi-A	.986	7	70	3	1	2	-1
Total	3	.983	143	1242	63	2	128	-6
OF								
1969	NY-A	1.000	2	2	0	0	0	0
1971	NY-A	.970	57	96	1	3	1	-5
1974	NY-A	1.000	19	32	2	0	0	1
1975	NY-A	1.000	1	2	0	0	0	0
Total	4	.978	79	132	3	3	1	-4

■ Joe Blong OF

YEAR	TM/L	PCT	G	PO	A	E	DP	FR
1876	StL-N	.895	62	64	13	9	2	0
1877	StL-N	.835	40	60	6	13	0	-1
Total	2	.867	102	124	19	2	2	-1

■ Jimmy Bloodworth 2B

YEAR	TM/L	PCT	G	PO	A	E	DP	FR
1937	Was-A	.946	14	28	42	4	9	-1
1939	Was-A	.972	73	226	219	13	66	13
1940	Was-A	.978	96	260	274	12	74	9
1941	Was-A	.971	132	**380**	**436**	24	107	**35**
1942	Det-A	.972	134	334	431	22	66	10
1943	Det-A	.972	129	349	393	21	74	17
1946	Det-A	.974	71	157	184	9	46	-1
1947	Pit-N	.979	87	222	206	9	56	-14
1949	Cin-N	.981	92	229	234	9	56	-4
1950	Cin-N	1.000	4	7	5	0	0	-3
	Phi-N	1.000	27	46	50	0	13	-3
	Yr	1.000	31	53	55	0	13	-6
1951	Phi-N	1.000	8	19	24	0	4	-1
Total	11	.975	867	2257	2498	123	571	57
1B								
1940	Was-A	.986	17	191	21	3	17	4
1949	Cin-N	.996	23	208	18	1	19	2
1950	Phi-N	1.000	7	26	3	0	1	0
1951	Phi-N	1.000	6	19	2	0	0	0
Total	4	.992	53	444	44	4	37	6
3B								
1940	Was-A	1.000	6	5	9	0	3	1
1941	Was-A	.933	6	6	8	1	1	0
1949	Cin-N	.952	8	10	10	1	0	-1
1950	Phi-N	1.000	2	0	1	0	0	0
Total	4	.961	22	21	28	2	4	0
OF								
1939	Was-A	1.000	5	11	1	0	1	1
SS								
1941	Was-A	1.000	1	0	2	0	0	0
1942	Det-A	1.000	2	2	0	0	0	0
Total	2	1.000	3	2	2	0	0	0

■ Lu Blue 1B

YEAR	TM/L	PCT	G	PO	A	E	DP	FR
1921	Det-A	.990	152	1478	85	16	75	-7
1922	Det-A	.991	144	1506	95	15	107	0
1923	Det-A	.992	129	1347	93	12	74	5
1924	Det-A	.986	108	1099	85	17	72	3
1925	Det-A	.988	148	1480	101	19	115	0
1926	Det-A	.985	109	1153	57	19	95	-6
1927	Det-A	.984	104	1040	68	18	99	-1
1928	StL-A	.989	**154**	1472	**107**	17	**121**	2
1929	StL-A	.994	151	**1491**	88	10	127	-3
1930	StL-A	.987	111	1110	68	16	91	0
1931	Chi-A	.990	**155**	**1452**	81	16	105	-3
1932	Chi-A	.986	105	1014	88	16	106	**9**
1933	Bro-N	1.000	1	2	0	0	0	0
Total	13	.989	1571	15644	1016	191	1187	-1
OF								
1926	Det-A	.667	1	3	1	2	0	0

■ Ossie Bluege 3B

YEAR	TM/L	PCT	G	PO	A	E	DP	FR
1922	Was-A	.925	17	17	32	4	3	-2
1923	Was-A	.936	106	125	243	25	**29**	5
1924	Was-A	.943	102	102	194	18	10	-7
1925	Was-A	.953	144	158	285	22	29	1
1926	Was-A	.952	134	139	256	20	15	-19
1927	Was-A	.961	146	185	**337**	21	20	**15**
1928	Was-A	.960	144	150	**330**	20	34	**12**
1929	Was-A	.967	35	34	82	4	9	5
1930	Was-A	.964	**134**	138	**258**	15	20	-1
1931	Was-A	**.960**	152	151	**286**	18	24	-5
1932	Was-A	.970	149	158	295	14	**28**	6
1933	Was-A	.965	138	116	247	13	25	-8
1934	Was-A	.950	41	41	92	7	10	8
1935	Was-A	.940	25	25	54	5	5	5
1936	Was-A	.979	15	8	39	1	4	4
1937	Was-A	1.000	2	1	4	0	0	0
1938	Was-A	1.000	1	0	2	0	1	0
1939	Was-A	.875	2	3	4	1	0	0
Total	18	.957	1487	1551	3040	208	266	19
SS								
1922	Was-A	1.000	2	2	2	0	0	-1
1924	Was-A	.938	4	6	9	1	0	0
1925	Was-A	1.000	4	2	5	0	0	0
1926	Was-A	.913	8	7	14	2	3	0
1929	Was-A	1.000	10	13	27	0	3	0
1931	Was-A	—	1	0	0	0	0	0

YEAR	TM/L	PCT	G	PO	A	E	DP	FR
1934	Was-A	.979	30	48	95	3	16	1
1935	Was-A	.967	58	117	177	10	32	-3
1936	Was-A	.981	23	41	61	2	7	-1
1937	Was-A	.952	28	67	91	8	19	3
1938	Was-A	.936	10	12	32	3	6	0
1939	Was-A	.929	2	7	6	1	4	0
Total	12	.965	180	321	518	0	90	-1
2B								
1923	Was-A	1.000	4	6	8	0	2	-2
1924	Was-A	.939	10	24	22	3	4	-4
1928	Was-A	—	1	0	0	0	0	0
1929	Was-A	.969	14	27	36	2	12	-2
1934	Was-A	1000	5	17	15	0	2	0
1935	Was-A	.867	4	6	7	2	2	-1
1936	Was-A	.993	52	128	158	2	35	-3
1938	Was-A	.990	38	85	110	2	26	0
1939	Was-A	1.000	2	7	5	0	0	0
Total	9	.984	130	300	361	1	83	-12
1B								
1937	Was-A	1.000	2	10	0	0	0	0
1938	Was-A	1.000	1	2	0	0	0	0
1939	Was-A	.989	11	86	7	1	9	1
Total	3	.991	14	98	7	1	9	1
OF								
1934	Was-A	1.000	5	8	0	0	0	0

■ John Boccabella C

YEAR	TM/L	PCT	G	PO	A	E	DP	FR
1966	Chi-N	1.000	5	25	2	0	0	-1
1967	Chi-N	1.000	1	2	0	0	0	0
1968	Chi-N	1.000	4	27	0	0	0	0
1969	Mon-N	1.000	32	137	19	0	0	1
1970	Mon-N	.989	24	79	10	1	2	5
1971	Mon-N	.979	37	127	11	3	2	-3
1972	Mon-N	.983	73	316	33	6	6	6
1973	Mon-N	.980	117	610	65	**14**	10	1
1974	SF-N	.991	26	110	6	1	1	-2
Total	9	.984	319	1433	146	5	21	5
1B								
1963	Chi-N	.996	24	234	12	1	29	-1
1964	Chi-N	1.000	5	41	3	0	3	0
1965	Chi-N	1.000	2	11	1	0	0	0
1966	Chi-N	1.000	30	182	15	0	12	1
1967	Chi-N	1.000	3	22	1	0	3	0
1970	Mon-N	.993	33	234	33	2	25	7
1971	Mon-N	.996	37	207	22	1	26	3
1972	Mon-N	1.000	7	51	5	0	6	1
1973	Mon-N	—	1	0	0	0	0	0
Total	9	.996	142	982	92	4	104	11
OF								
1964	Chi-N	—	2	0	0	0	0	0
1965	Chi-N	.500	1	1	0	1	0	0
1966	Chi-N	.981	33	48	3	1	1	0
1967	Chi-N	1.000	9	11	0	0	0	0
1968	Chi-N	—	1	0	0	0	0	0
Total	5	.969	46	60	3	2	1	0
3B								
1970	Mon-N	1.000	1	1	1	0	0	0
1971	Mon-N	1.000	2	1	0	0	0	0
1972	Mon-N	1.000	1	0	1	0	0	0
Total	3	1.000	4	2	2	0	0	0

■ Bruce Bochte 1B

YEAR	TM/L	PCT	G	PO	A	E	DP	FR
1974	Cal-A	.979	24	183	7	4	16	-3
1975	Cal-A	.987	105	850	51	12	90	-7
1976	Cal-A	.991	59	489	39	5	37	0
1977	Cle-A	.990	36	277	21	3	17	0
1978	Sea-A	1.000	1	3	0	0	1	0
1979	Sea-A	.991	147	1361	114	**14**	140	5
1980	Sea-A	.996	133	1273	98	6	143	**5**
1981	Sea-A	.995	82	745	49	4	70	-4
1982	Sea-A	.997	34	267	21	1	38	0
1984	Oak-A	.993	144	1048	66	8	119	-13
1985	Oak-A	.990	128	942	60	10	83	-9
1986	Oak-A	.991	115	912	88	9	79	2
Total	12	.992	1008	8355	614	6	833	-24
OF								
1974	Cal-A	.985	39	65	2	1	0	-1
1976	Cal-A	.988	86	162	3	2	1	-4
1977	Cal-A	1.000	24	48	5	0	1	2
	Cle-A	.966	76	161	7	6	1	0
	Yr	.974	100	209	12	6	2	2
1978	Sea-A	.984	91	172	7	3	2	-3
1981	Sea-A	1.000	14	21	0	0	0	-1
1982	Sea-A	.988	99	161	5	2	1	-6
Total	6	.983	429	790	29	4	6	-13

■ Bruce Bochy C

YEAR	TM/L	PCT	G	PO	A	E	DP	FR
1978	Hou-N	.974	53	268	35	8	5	3
1979	Hou-N	.970	55	198	29	7	4	-1
1980	Hou-N	1.000	10	19	1	0	0	-2
1982	NY-N	.961	16	90	8	4	1	4
1983	SD-N	1.000	11	51	5	0	0	2
1984	SD-N	.988	36	147	12	2	2	4
1985	SD-N	.988	46	148	11	2	2	1
1986	SD-N	.991	48	202	22	2	3	3
1987	SD-N	.962	23	95	7	4	0	-4
Total	9	.979	298	1218	130	9	17	10
1B								
1980	Hou-N	—	1	0	0	0	0	0
1982	NY-N	1.000	2	2	0	0	0	0
Total	2	1.000	2	2	0	0	0	0

■ Eddie Bockman 3B

YEAR	TM/L	PCT	G	PO	A	E	DP	FR
1946	NY-A	.933	4	8	6	1	3	1
1947	Cle-A	.946	12	10	25	2	4	5
1948	Pit-N	.962	51	50	100	6	9	8
1949	Pit-N	.958	68	59	127	8	14	6
Total	4	.958	135	127	258	7	30	20

YEAR	TM/L	PCT	G	PO	A	E	DP	FR
2B								
1947	Cle-A	.929	4	7	6	1	2	1
1948	Pit-N	1.000	1	1	0	0	0	0
1949	Pit-N	1.000	5	3	1	0	0	0
Total	3	.947	10	11	7	1	2	1
SS								
1947	Cle-A	—	1	0	0	0	0	0
OF								
1947	Cle-A	1.000	1	5	2	0	2	3
■ Ping Bodie OF								
1911	Chi-A	.969	128	256	24	9	9	5
1912	Chi-A	.969	130	208	11	7	3	-13
1913	Chi-A	.968	119	226	14	8	1	-4
1914	Chi-A	.959	95	175	14	8	2	-2
1917	Phi-A	.963	145	258	32	11	7	5
1918	NY-A	.971	90	181	17	6	3	4
1919	NY-A	.959	134	293	13	13	6	-8
1920	NY-A	.968	129	264	12	9	2	-10
1921	NY-A	.944	25	32	2	2	0	-6
Total	9	.965	995	1893	139	73	33	-29
2B								
1911	Chi-A	.910	16	31	40	7	4	2
1B								
1917	Phi-A	1.000	1	9	0	0	1	0
■ Tony Boeckel 3B								
1917	Pit-N	.935	62	71	116	13	9	-4
1919	Pit-N	.930	45	43	77	9	2	-8
	Bos-N	.960	93	98	188	12	11	-4
	Yr	.951	138	141	265	21	13	-12
1920	Bos-N	.936	149	219	266	33	30	-6
1921	Bos-N	.933	153	184	276	33	19	-12
1922	Bos-N	.952	106	128	168	15	13	-11
1923	Bos-N	.939	147	169	265	28	27	-10
Total	6	.941	755	912	1356	143	111	-55
SS								
1920	Bos-N	1.000	3	10	7	0	1	0
1923	Bos-N	1.000	1	1	2	0	0	0
Total	2	1.000	4	11	9	0	1	0
2B								
1920	Bos-N	—	1	0	0	0	0	0
■ Wade Boggs 3B								
1982	Bos-A	.967	44	28	119	5	11	10
1983	Bos-A	.947	153	118	368	27	40	8
1984	Bos-A	.959	156	141	330	20	30	21
1985	Bos-A	.965	161	134	335	17	30	8
1986	Bos-A	.953	149	121	267	19	30	-1
1987	Bos-A	.965	145	111	277	14	37	3
1988	Bos-A	.971	151	122	250	11	17	-5
1989	Bos-A	.958	152	123	264	17	29	-4
1990	Bos-A	.946	152	108	241	20	18	-22
Total	9	.958	1263	1006	2451	150	242	18
1B								
1982	Bos-A	.994	49	460	49	3	40	8
1987	Bos-A	1.000	1	1	0	0	0	0
Total	2	.994	50	461	49	3	40	8
OF								
1982	Bos-A	1.000	1	1	0	0	0	0
■ Sam Bohne 2B								
1921	Cin-N	.973	102	256	327	16	56	0
1922	Cin-N	.958	85	183	320	22	50	12
1923	Cin-N	.975	96	243	333	15	46	4
1924	Cin-N	.941	48	98	140	15	18	-7
1925	Cin-N	1.000	10	21	24	0	3	0
1926	Bro-N	.965	31	53	84	5	8	8
Total	6	.966	372	854	1228	73	181	17
SS								
1916	StL-N	.870	14	15	32	7	3	-4
1922	Cin-N	.927	20	43	71	9	10	-1
1923	Cin-N	.942	9	17	32	3	3	-1
1924	Cin-N	.965	40	86	135	8	21	-3
1925	Cin-N	.933	49	84	138	16	24	-6
1926	Cin-N	.931	20	29	52	6	8	-3
Total	6	.937	152	274	460	9	69	-18
3B								
1921	Cin-N	.947	53	57	123	10	17	8
1923	Cin-N	.940	35	33	77	7	6	2
1924	Cin-N	1.000	12	10	19	0	1	1
1925	Cin-N	1.000	2	1	1	0	0	0
1926	Bro-N	.981	15	22	31	1	3	3
Total	5	.954	117	123	251	8	27	14
OF								
1925	Cin-N	1.000	4	7	0	0	0	0
1B								
1923	Cin-N	1.000	1	6	0	0	0	0
1925	Cin-N	1.000	2	18	0	0	0	0
Total	2	1.000	3	24	0	0	0	0
■ Bruce Boisclair OF								
1974	NY-N	.923	5	10	2	1	0	2
1976	NY-N	.981	87	156	3	3	1	0
1977	NY-N	.959	91	140	1	6	0	-7
1978	NY-N	.983	69	114	3	2	0	1
1979	NY-N	1.000	24	34	2	0	0	0
Total	5	.975	276	454	11	2	1	-4
1B								
1977	NY-N	1.000	9	19	1	0	1	0
1978	NY-N	1.000	1	1	0	0	0	0
1979	NY-N	1.000	1	2	0	0	0	0
Total	3	1.000	11	22	1	0	1	0
■ Joe Boley SS								
1927	Phi-A	.951	114	182	318	26	49	-11
1928	Phi-A	.949	132	244	320	30	51	-17
1929	Phi-A	.963	88	161	229	15	50	-10
1930	Phi-A	.970	120	221	296	16	62	-7
1931	Phi-A	.954	62	102	149	12	31	-13
1932	Phi-A	.897	10	8	18	3	2	-7
	Cle-A	—	1	0	0	0	0	0
	Yr	.897	11	8	18	3	2	-7
Total	6	.957	527	918	1330	102	245	-65
3B								
1929	Phi-A	1.000	1	1	0	0	0	0
2B								
1931	Phi-A	1.000	1	0	1	0	0	0
■ Jim Bolger OF								
1950	Cin-N	—	2	0	0	0	0	0
1954	Cin-N	—	2	0	0	0	0	0
1955	Chi-N	.955	51	125	1	6	0	5
1957	Chi-N	.987	63	152	4	2	1	7
1958	Chi-N	.940	37	46	1	3	0	0
1959	Phi-N	.938	9	15	0	1	0	0
Total	6	.966	164	338	6	2	1	12
3B								
1957	Chi-N	.714	3	2	3	2	0	-1
■ Frank Bolling 2B								
1954	Det-A	.974	113	248	232	13	54	-29
1956	Det-A	.978	102	223	260	11	72	-15
1957	Det-A	.980	146	394	401	16	112	-3
1958	Det-A	.985	154	342	445	12	109	8
1959	Det-A	.987	126	281	340	8	81	-1
1960	Det-A	.978	138	375	377	17	93	-5
1961	Mil-N	.988	148	326	489	10	112	1
1962	Mil-N	.989	119	252	298	6	70	-9
1963	Mil-N	.981	141	326	379	14	107	-2
1964	Mil-N	.985	117	212	255	7	68	-9
1965	Mil-N	.976	147	310	393	17	90	-16
1966	Atl-N	.983	67	134	150	5	35	-15
Total	12	.982	1518	3423	4019	136	1003	-95
■ Milt Bolling SS								
1952	Bos-A	.984	11	22	41	1	6	6
1953	Bos-A	.956	109	174	321	23	71	5
1954	Bos-A	.946	107	186	370	32	73	15
1955	Bos-A	.800	2	1	3	1	0	0
1956	Bos-A	.947	26	31	59	5	11	-7
1957	Was-A	.956	37	42	89	6	17	0
1958	Det-A	.946	13	14	21	2	7	2
Total	7	.952	305	470	904	70	185	21
2B								
1956	Bos-A	.750	1	1	2	1	0	-1
1957	Was-A	.982	53	126	143	5	36	9
1958	Det-A	1.000	1	1	2	0	0	0
Total	3	.979	55	128	147	6	36	8
3B								
1954	Bos-A	.923	5	5	7	1	0	0
1956	Bos-A	.897	11	6	20	3	2	0
1957	Was-A	.000	1	0	0	1	0	0
1958	Det-A	1.000	1	0	1	0	0	0
Total	4	.886	18	11	28	5	2	0
■ Don Bollweg 1B								
1950	StL-N	1.000	4	26	0	0	3	-1
1951	StL-N	.941	2	16	0	1	2	0
1953	NY-A	.983	43	323	15	6	37	-4
1954	Phi-A	.978	71	530	51	13	55	2
1955	KC-A	1.000	3	8	0	0	3	0
Total	5	.980	123	903	66	0	100	-3
■ Cliff Bolton C								
1931	Was-A	.947	13	15	3	1	0	-5
1933	Was-A	.889	9	14	2	2	1	-1
1934	Was-A	.981	39	134	20	3	4	-4
1935	Was-A	.971	106	356	52	12	8	-23
1936	Was-A	.979	83	287	44	7	4	-3
1937	Det-A	.982	13	47	9	1	2	0
1941	Was-A	1.000	3	2	0	0	0	0
Total	7	.974	266	855	130	6	19	-36
OF								
1933	Was-A	1.000	1	2	0	0	0	0
■ Walt Bond OF								
1960	Cle-A	1.000	36	76	2	0	1	1
1961	Cle-A	1.000	12	17	1	0	0	1
1962	Cle-A	1.000	12	25	0	0	0	-1
1964	Hou-N	.957	71	111	4	5	0	-6
1965	Hou-N	.964	38	54	0	2	0	-2
1967	Min-A	.875	3	7	0	1	0	0
Total	6	.974	172	290	4	8	1	-7
1B								
1964	Hou-N	.989	76	685	40	8	46	-5
1965	Hou-N	.983	74	650	49	12	52	0
Total	2	.986	150	1335	89	20	98	-5
■ Barry Bonds OF								
1986	Pit-N	.983	110	280	9	5	2	10
1987	Pit-N	.986	145	330	15	5	3	17
1988	Pit-N	.980	136	292	5	6	0	1
1989	Pit-N	.984	156	365	14	6	1	14
1990	Pit-N	.983	150	338	14	6	2	11
Total	5	.983	697	1605	57	8	8	53
■ Bobby Bonds OF								
1968	SF-N	.978	80	169	6	4	1	6
1969	SF-N	.978	155	339	9	8	2	11
1970	SF-N	.969	157	326	14	11	7	11
1971	SF-N	.994	154	329	10	2	1	7
1972	SF-N	.978	153	345	8	8	3	10
1973	SF-N	.970	158	346	12	11	5	8
1974	SF-N	.966	148	305	11	11	3	4
1975	NY-A	.987	129	287	12	4	6	9
1976	Cal-A	.977	98	199	9	5	3	-7
1977	Cal-A	.986	140	272	5	4	0	-1
1978	Chi-A	.956	22	40	3	2	1	-1
	Tex-A	.970	111	213	13	7	5	2
	Yr	.968	133	253	16	9	6	1
1979	Cle-A	.979	116	267	9	6	1	8
1980	StL-N	.967	70	114	5	4	2	-5
1981	Chi-A	.982	45	108	2	2	0	0
Total	14	.977	1736	3659	128	89	40	62
■ Juan Bonilla 2B								
1981	SD-N	.976	97	229	290	13	72	-11
1982	SD-N	.975	45	99	134	6	26	-8
1983	SD-N	.986	149	335	414	11	95	-15
1985	NY-A	.955	7	7	14	1	3	1
1986	Bal-A	.981	70	122	140	5	38	-8
1987	NY-A	.965	22	40	43	3	10	0
Total	6	.980	390	832	1035	9	244	-41
3B								
1986	Bal-A	.918	33	21	35	5	10	-1
1987	NY-A	1.000	1	0	1	0	0	0
Total	2	.919	34	21	36	5	10	-1
■ Bobby Bonilla 3B								
1986	Pit-N	1.000	4	3	9	0	1	1
1987	Pit-N	.932	89	53	138	14	12	-14
1988	Pit-N	.935	159	121	336	32	17	-1
1989	Pit-N	.929	156	125	330	35	31	6
1990	Pit-N	.923	14	10	26	3	1	-1
Total	5	.932	422	312	839	4	62	-9
OF								
1986	Chi-A	.989	43	91	2	1	1	2
	Pit-N	.974	51	73	3	2	0	-4
1987	Pit-N	.972	46	70	0	2	0	-2
1989	Pit-N	—	1	0	0	0	0	0
1990	Pit-N	.961	149	289	8	12	1	-5
Total	4	.969	290	523	13	7	2	-9
1B								
1986	Chi-A	.997	30	270	20	1	25	-1
	Pit-N	.947	4	14	4	1	2	1
1987	Pit-N	1.000	6	19	1	0	1	0
1989	Pit-N	1.000	8	65	4	0	6	0
1990	Pit-N	1.000	3	16	1	0	0	0
Total	4	.995	51	384	30	2	34	0
■ Barry Bonnell OF								
1977	Atl-N	.989	75	181	3	2	1	6
1978	Atl-N	.984	105	172	7	3	1	8
1979	Atl-N	.983	124	220	8	4	2	-18
1980	Tor-A	.973	122	271	15	8	3	-7
1981	Tor-A	.975	66	148	5	4	1	1
1982	Tor-A	.979	125	232	3	5	0	-10
1983	Tor-A	.986	117	212	7	3	0	-2
1984	Sea-A	.994	94	153	8	1	0	-2
1985	Sea-A	.976	22	38	2	1	0	1
1986	Sea-A	.941	9	16	0	1	0	-1
Total	10	.982	859	1643	58	2	8	-24
3B								
1977	Atl-N	.933	32	22	62	6	0	4
1978	Atl-N	.935	15	15	28	3	2	1
1979	Atl-N	1.000	1	1	0	0	0	0
1982	Tor-A	1.000	9	2	4	0	1	0
1983	Tor-A	1.000	4	1	6	0	1	0
1984	Sea-A	.762	10	3	13	5	0	-4
Total	6	.918	71	44	113	4	4	1
1B								
1984	Sea-A	1.000	5	15	2	0	1	0
1985	Sea-A	1.000	5	23	0	0	3	-1
1986	Sea-A	.973	8	30	6	1	1	1
Total	3	.987	18	68	8	1	5	0
■ Frank Bonner 2B								
1894	Bal-N	.904	27	60	62	13	8	-12
1896	Bro-N	.915	9	8	35	4	3	-1
1899	Was-N	.940	85	192	264	29	34	2
1902	Cle-A	.907	34	67	89	16	5	-10
	Phi-A	.933	11	31	39	5	8	3
	Yr	.915	45	98	128	21	13	-7
1903	Bos-N	.957	24	64	68	6	12	3
Total	5	.931	190	422	557	3	70	-15
3B								
1894	Bal-N	.833	2	4	1	1	1	-1
1895	Bal-N	.742	11	8	15	8	2	-5
	StL-N	.656	10	8	13	11	0	-5
	Yr	.698	21	16	28	19	2	-10
Total	2	.710	23	20	29	0	3	-11
SS								
1894	Bal-N	1.000	1	1	2	0	0	-1
1903	Bos-N	.907	22	40	48	9	7	-7
Total	2	.910	23	41	50	9	7	-8
OF								
1894	Bal-N	1.000	4	2	0	0	0	-2
1895	StL-N	1.000	5	10	0	0	0	0
Total	2	1.000	9	12	0	0	0	-2
C								
1895	StL-N	1.000	1	0	0	0	0	0
■ Zeke Bonura 1B								
1934	Chi-A	.996	127	1239	77	5	94	5
1935	Chi-A	.994	138	1421	83	9	102	2
1936	Chi-A	.996	146	1500	107	7	150	12
1937	Chi-A	.989	115	1114	63	13	123	-1
1938	Was-A	.993	129	1209	93	9	132	3
1939	NY-N	.992	122	1205	90	11	110	5
1940	Was-A	.982	79	712	42	14	70	-4
	Chi-N	.991	44	408	40	4	34	5
Total	7	.992	900	8808	595	2	815	27
■ Al Bool C								
1928	Pit-N	1.000	2	8	2	0	0	0
1930	Pit-N	.967	65	190	42	8	4	0
1931	Bos-N	.989	37	73	14	1	4	-2
Total	3	.973	104	271	58	9	8	-3
■ Ike Boone OF								
1923	Bos-A	.929	4	13	0	1	0	0

YEAR	TM/L	PCT	G	PO	A	E	DP	FR
1924	Bos-A	.976	124	189	17	5	3	-7
1925	Bos-A	.941	118	198	9	13	1	-7
1927	Chi-A	1.000	11	15	0	0	0	-2
1930	Bro-N	.960	27	47	1	2	0	-2
1932	Bro-N	1.000	8	8	1	0	1	0
Total 6		.960	292	470	28	1	5	-18

■ Luke Boone 2B

YEAR	TM/L	PCT	G	PO	A	E	DP	FR
1914	NY-A	.960	90	238	294	22	32	**23**
1915	NY-A	.965	115	249	392	23	59	**29**
1916	NY-A	1.000	8	12	21	0	3	2
1918	Pit-N	1.000	1	0	1	0	0	0
Total 4		.964	214	499	708	5	94	54

SS

YEAR	TM/L	PCT	G	PO	A	E	DP	FR
1913	NY-A	.857	4	8	10	3	0	-1
1915	NY-A	.972	11	15	20	1	2	-9
1916	NY-A	.847	12	22	39	11	3	0
1918	Pit-N	.921	26	56	84	12	6	0
Total 4		.904	53	101	153	7	11	-10

3B

YEAR	TM/L	PCT	G	PO	A	E	DP	FR
1914	NY-A	.900	9	11	16	3	1	0
1915	NY-A	1.000	4	7	7	0	0	0
1916	NY-A	.973	25	24	48	2	5	5
Total 3		.958	38	42	71	5	6	5

OF

YEAR	TM/L	PCT	G	PO	A	E	DP	FR
1914	NY-A	—	1	0	0	0	0	0

■ Ray Boone 3B

YEAR	TM/L	PCT	G	PO	A	E	DP	FR
1952	Cle-A	.800	2	2	2	1	2	0
1953	Det-A	.958	97	111	211	14	32	1
1954	Det-A	.964	148	**170**	332	19	22	2
1955	Det-A	.953	126	135	252	19	33	-5
1956	Det-A	.959	130	151	243	17	23	-6
1957	Det-A	.895	4	5	12	2	0	1
1959	KC-A	1.000	3	2	6	0	0	0
Total 7		.958	510	576	1058	2	112	-7

SS

YEAR	TM/L	PCT	G	PO	A	E	DP	FR
1948	Cle-A	.889	4	3	5	1	0	1
1949	Cle-A	.947	76	162	210	21	58	0
1950	Cle-A	.945	102	178	267	26	64	-9
1951	Cle-A	.957	**151**	311	425	**33**	108	-7
1952	Cle-A	.941	96	177	251	27	55	-10
1953	Cle-A	.952	31	64	94	8	24	-1
	Det-A	.923	3	4	8	1	2	0
	Yr	.950	34	68	102	9	26	-1
1954	Det-A	—	1	0	0	0	0	0
Total 7		.949	464	899	1260	117	311	-24

1B

YEAR	TM/L	PCT	G	PO	A	E	DP	FR
1957	Det-A	.990	117	972	45	10	103	-11
1958	Det-A	.988	32	236	15	3	26	-1
	Chi-A	.986	63	511	34	8	45	-2
	Yr	.986	95	747	49	11	71	-3
1959	Chi-A	.955	6	37	5	2	2	0
	KC-A	.983	38	275	23	5	20	1
	Mil-N	1.000	3	19	1	0	4	0
	Yr	.969	9	56	6	2	6	0
1960	Mil-N	1.000	4	33	3	0	3	0
	Bos-A	.994	22	166	11	1	19	0
Total 4		.988	285	2249	137	9	222	-13

2B

YEAR	TM/L	PCT	G	PO	A	E	DP	FR
1952	Cle-A	1.000	1	1	1	0	0	0

■ Bob Boone C

YEAR	TM/L	PCT	G	PO	A	E	DP	FR
1972	Phi-N	.936	14	66	7	5	1	-6
1973	Phi-N	.990	145	868	**89**	10	16	7
1974	Phi-N	.976	146	**825**	77	**22**	7	-7
1975	Phi-N	.990	92	456	44	5	7	0
1976	Phi-N	.993	108	557	36	4	5	-10
1977	Phi-N	.989	131	653	80	8	9	1
1978	Phi-N	**.991**	129	619	55	6	6	-9
1979	Phi-N	.988	117	527	65	7	8	-13
1980	Phi-N	.979	138	741	88	**18**	7	4
1981	Phi-N	.985	75	365	32	6	1	-3
1982	Cal-A	.989	**143**	**650**	87	8	6	6
1983	Cal-A	.980	**142**	606	83	**14**	12	4
1984	Cal-A	.984	**137**	660	**71**	12	10	7
1985	Cal-A	.987	**147**	670	71	10	**15**	4
1986	Cal-A	.988	**144**	812	**84**	11	**16**	11
1987	Cal-A	.983	127	684	56	**13**	11	-1
1988	Cal-A	.986	121	506	**66**	8	9	-10
1989	KC-A	.991	**129**	**752**	64	7	6	3
1990	KC-A	.985	40	243	19	4	0	2
Total 19		.986	2225	11260	1174	178	154	-10

3B

YEAR	TM/L	PCT	G	PO	A	E	DP	FR
1975	Phi-N	1.000	3	3	4	0	0	0
1977	Phi-N	1.000	2	1	3	0	0	0
1979	Phi-N	.500	2	0	1	1	0	0
Total 3		.923	7	4	8	1	0	0

1B

YEAR	TM/L	PCT	G	PO	A	E	DP	FR
1976	Phi-N	.943	4	30	3	2	0	0
1978	Phi-N	.939	3	31	0	2	1	-1
Total 2		.941	7	61	3	4	1	-1

OF

YEAR	TM/L	PCT	G	PO	A	E	DP	FR
1978	Phi-N	1.000	1	0	0	0	0	0

■ Frenchy Bordagaray OF

YEAR	TM/L	PCT	G	PO	A	E	DP	FR
1934	Chi-A	.938	17	28	2	2	0	-2
1935	Bro-N	.980	105	227	14	5	2	5
1936	Bro-N	.991	92	207	8	2	0	5
1937	StL-N	.979	28	46	1	1	0	0
1938	StL-N	.959	29	67	3	3	0	3
1939	Cin-N	1.000	43	60	1	0	1	0
1941	NY-A	.967	19	28	1	1	1	-1
1942	Bro-N	1.000	17	22	0	0	0	1
1943	Bro-N	.989	53	87	6	1	2	1
1944	Bro-N	.974	25	73	1	2	0	2
1945	Bro-N	1.000	22	32	0	0	0	0
Total 11		.982	450	877	37	7	6	14

3B

YEAR	TM/L	PCT	G	PO	A	E	DP	FR
1936	Bro-N	.750	6	3	3	2	0	-1
1937	StL-N	.942	50	59	71	8	2	-7
1938	StL-N	.786	4	5	6	3	0	-1
1943	Bro-N	.885	25	28	26	7	0	-12
1944	Bro-N	.945	98	107	150	15	14	-20
1945	Bro-N	.886	57	54	93	19	7	-6
Total 6		.918	240	256	349	4	23	-47

2B

YEAR	TM/L	PCT	G	PO	A	E	DP	FR
1936	Bro-N	.923	11	20	28	4	3	-1
1939	Cin-N	.929	2	7	6	1	1	0
Total 2		.924	13	27	34	5	4	-1

■ Pat Borders C

YEAR	TM/L	PCT	G	PO	A	E	DP	FR
1988	Tor-A	.973	43	205	14	6	0	2
1989	Tor-A	.980	68	261	27	6	1	0
1990	Tor-A	.993	115	515	46	4	6	-2
Total 3		.985	226	981	87	6	7	0

2B

YEAR	TM/L	PCT	G	PO	A	E	DP	FR
1988	Tor-A	1.000	1	0	3	0	0	0

3B

YEAR	TM/L	PCT	G	PO	A	E	DP	FR
1988	Tor-A	.667	1	0	2	1	0	0

■ Glenn Borgmann C

YEAR	TM/L	PCT	G	PO	A	E	DP	FR
1972	Min-A	.965	56	304	31	12	4	-2
1973	Min-A	1.000	12	55	2	0	0	-3
1974	Min-A	**.997**	128	652	52	2	7	-2
1975	Min-A	.989	125	618	81	8	6	-5
1976	Min-A	.976	24	110	13	3	1	1
1977	Min-A	1.000	17	70	8	0	1	2
1978	Min-A	.990	46	185	20	2	6	5
1979	Min-A	.993	31	129	11	1	0	7
1980	Chi-A	1.000	32	134	18	0	1	1
Total 9		.989	471	2257	236	8	26	4

■ Bob Borkowski OF

YEAR	TM/L	PCT	G	PO	A	E	DP	FR
1950	Chi-N	.97	65	150	3	4	1	3
1951	Chi-N	.933	25	41	1	3	0	1
1952	Cin-N	.991	103	219	5	2	1	-12
1953	Cin-N	.982	67	104	3	2	0	-7
1954	Cin-N	1.000	36	69	3	0	0	0
1955	Cin-N	1.000	11	5	0	0	0	0
	Bro-N	1.000	9	7	0	0	0	0
	Yr	1.000	20	12	0	0	0	-1
Total 6		.982	316	595	15	1	2	-16

1B

YEAR	TM/L	PCT	G	PO	A	E	DP	FR
1950	Chi-N	1.000	1	5	1	0	0	0
1952	Cin-N	.977	5	39	3	1	3	0
1953	Cin-N	.909	2	10	0	1	1	-1
1954	Cin-N	1.000	3	13	0	0	1	0
1955	Cin-N	.875	1	6	1	1	1	0
Total 5		.963	12	73	5	3	6	-1

■ Steve Boros 3B

YEAR	TM/L	PCT	G	PO	A	E	DP	FR
1957	Det-A	.906	9	7	22	3	1	2
1961	Det-A	.953	116	115	192	15	15	-21
1962	Det-A	.931	105	105	151	19	15	-13
1964	Cin-N	.961	114	95	204	12	18	4
1965	Cin-N	1.000	2	0	1	0	0	0
Total 5		.948	346	322	570	9	49	-28

1B

YEAR	TM/L	PCT	G	PO	A	E	DP	FR
1963	Chi-N	.975	14	111	7	3	7	-1

OF

YEAR	TM/L	PCT	G	PO	A	E	DP	FR
1963	Chi-N	.938	11	15	0	1	0	-1

2B

YEAR	TM/L	PCT	G	PO	A	E	DP	FR
1958	Det-A	1.000	1	2	0	0	0	2
1962	Det-A	.926	6	13	12	2	4	-2
Total 2		.931	7	15	12	2	4	0

SS

YEAR	TM/L	PCT	G	PO	A	E	DP	FR
1957	Det-A	1.000	5	1	5	0	0	1

■ Babe Borton 1B

YEAR	TM/L	PCT	G	PO	A	E	DP	FR
1912	Chi-A	.997	30	312	16	1	14	0
1913	Chi-A	.991	26	301	12	3	19	-1
	NY-A	.978	33	331	32	8	16	4
	Yr	.984	**59**	**632**	44	11	**35**	3
1915	StL-F	.993	159	1571	58	12	91	-10
1916	StL-A	.991	22	205	8	2	7	-1
Total 4		.991	270	2720	126	6	147	-8

■ Don Bosch OF

YEAR	TM/L	PCT	G	PO	A	E	DP	FR
1966	Pit-N	—	1	0	0	0	0	0
1967	NY-N	1.000	39	55	2	0	0	3
1968	NY-N	.974	33	73	3	2	1	6
1969	Mon-N	.964	32	52	1	2	0	1
Total 4		.979	105	180	6	4	1	10

■ Rick Bosetti OF

YEAR	TM/L	PCT	G	PO	A	E	DP	FR
1976	Phi-N	1.000	6	9	0	0	0	1
1977	StL-N	.986	35	42	3	0	0	3
1978	Tor-A	.986	135	417	17	6	1	20
1979	Tor-A	.974	**162**	**466**	**18**	**13**	4	11
1980	Tor-A	.985	51	124	4	2	0	0
1981	Tor-A	1.000	19	40	0	0	0	2
	Oak-A	1.000	5	12	0	0	0	1
	Yr	1.000	24	52	0	0	0	3
1982	Oak-A	1.000	6	14	2	0	0	2
Total 7		.982	419	1124	45	1	5	40

■ Thad Bosley OF

YEAR	TM/L	PCT	G	PO	A	E	DP	FR
1977	Cal-A	.963	55	130	1	5	0	0
1978	Chi-A	.975	64	155	3	4	0	3
1979	Chi-A	.967	28	57	2	2	1	3
1980	Chi-A	.958	52	91	1	4	0	0
1981	Mil-A	.966	37	55	1	2	0	-2
1982	Sea-A	.991	19	12	1	0	0	-3
1983	Chi-N	1.000	20	27	1	0	1	0
1984	Chi-N	.976	33	39	2	1	0	-1
1985	Chi-N	.988	55	84	0	1	0	1
1986	Chi-N	.969	41	31	0	1	0	-4
1987	KC-A	.966	28	28	0	1	0	-1
1988	KC-A	1.000	6	4	0	0	0	0
	Cal-A	.965	26	55	0	2	0	2
	Yr	.967	32	59	0	2	0	2
1989	Tex-A	1.000	8	12	1	0	1	2
1990	Tex-A	1.000	9	4	0	0	0	0
Total 4		.972	481	784	13	3	3	0

■ Harley Boss 1B

YEAR	TM/L	PCT	G	PO	A	E	DP	FR
1928	Was-A	.970	5	32	0	1	2	-1
1929	Was-A	.977	18	119	9	3	13	0
1930	Was-A	1.000	1	2	0	0	0	0
1933	Cle-A	.994	110	1062	71	7	89	**6**
Total 4		.992	134	1215	80	1	104	5

■ Lyman Bostock OF

YEAR	TM/L	PCT	G	PO	A	E	DP	FR
1975	Min-A	.985	92	188	3	3	0	-2
1976	Min-A	.988	124	320	10	4	2	0
1977	Min-A	.989	149	349	10	4	0	10
1978	Cal-A	.989	146	366	7	4	2	-2
Total 4		.988	511	1223	30	5	4	6

■ Daryl Boston OF

YEAR	TM/L	PCT	G	PO	A	E	DP	FR
1984	Chi-A	.910	34	59	2	6	1	2
1985	Chi-A	.989	93	179	7	2	1	-11
1986	Chi-A	.969	53	152	3	5	1	2
1987	Chi-A	.991	92	207	3	2	3	1
1988	Chi-A	.951	85	190	4	10	2	0
1989	Chi-A	.971	75	134	2	4	0	3
1990	Chi-A	—	1	0	0	0	0	0
	NY-N	.986	109	203	3	3	1	-10
Total 7		.973	542	1124	24	2	9	-13

■ Ken Boswell 2B

YEAR	TM/L	PCT	G	PO	A	E	DP	FR
1967	NY-N	.971	6	10	24	1	3	1
1968	NY-N	.965	69	154	203	13	37	-1
1969	NY-N	.959	96	190	229	18	51	-15
1970	NY-N	.996	101	204	244	2	49	-15
1971	NY-N	.973	109	191	234	12	56	-29
1972	NY-N	.990	94	208	183	4	53	-31
1973	NY-N	.923	9	8	4	1	0	-1
1974	NY-N	1.000	28	69	63	0	11	2
1975	Hou-N	.991	31	40	65	1	11	-5
1976	Hou-N	1.000	3	1	0	0	0	0
1977	Hou-N	1.000	26	33	31	0	9	-3
Total 11		.979	566	1108	1280	2	280	-97

3B

YEAR	TM/L	PCT	G	PO	A	E	DP	FR
1967	NY-N	1.000	4	2	10	0	2	1
1973	NY-N	.973	17	7	29	1	3	1
1974	NY-N	.922	20	11	48	5	6	3
1975	Hou-N	.912	23	14	38	5	2	-4
1976	Hou-N	.933	16	7	21	2	4	-5
1977	Hou-N	1.000	2	0	4	0	0	0
Total 6		.936	82	41	150	3	17	-4

OF

YEAR	TM/L	PCT	G	PO	A	E	DP	FR
1974	NY-N	.941	7	14	2	1	1	1
1976	Hou-N	—	1	0	0	0	0	0
Total 2		.941	8	14	2	1	1	1

■ Jim Bottomley 1B

YEAR	TM/L	PCT	G	PO	A	E	DP	FR
1922	StL-N	.986	34	346	12	5	22	-3
1923	StL-N	.986	130	1264	43	18	95	-12
1924	StL-N	.982	133	1297	48	**24**	110	-12
1925	StL-N	.987	**153**	**1466**	74	**21**	**133**	-4
1926	StL-N	.989	154	1607	54	**19**	118	-15
1927	StL-N	.985	**152**	**1656**	70	**20**	**149**	-11
1928	StL-N	.987	148	1454	52	**20**	113	-14
1929	StL-N	.991	145	1347	75	13	122	-6
1930	StL-N	.987	124	1164	41	12	127	-13
1931	StL-N	.987	93	897	43	12	95	-3
1932	StL-N	.986	74	662	41	10	67	-3
1933	Cin-N	.991	145	1511	72	15	112	-9
1934	Cin-N	.989	139	1303	77	15	106	-3
1935	Cin-N	.992	97	934	53	8	74	-2
1936	StL-A	.992	140	1250	47	10	103	-10
1937	StL-A	.995	24	179	12	1	16	1
Total 16		.988	1885	18337	814	223	1562	119

2B

YEAR	TM/L	PCT	G	PO	A	E	DP	FR
1924	StL-N	1.000	1	0	1	0	0	0

■ Ed Bouchee 1B

YEAR	TM/L	PCT	G	PO	A	E	DP	FR
1956	Phi-N	1.000	6	54	3	0	6	0
1957	Phi-N	.986	**154**	1182	**125**	**16**	93	**4**
1958	Phi-N	.993	89	690	58	5	59	0
1959	Phi-N	.986	**134**	**1127**	**95**	17	96	0
1960	Phi-N	.994	22	158	15	1	12	1
	Chi-N	.991	80	709	56	7	56	0
	Yr	.992	102	867	71	8	68	1
1961	Chi-N	.983	107	852	76	16	97	1
1962	NY-N	.976	19	137	23	4	16	4
Total 7		.988	611	4909	451	6	435	10

■ Lou Boudreau SS

YEAR	TM/L	PCT	G	PO	A	E	DP	FR
1939	Cle-A	.953	53	103	184	14	31	8
1940	Cle-A	**.968**	155	277	**454**	24	**116**	**12**
1941	Cle-A	**.966**	147	**296**	444	26	97	13
1942	Cle-A	**.965**	146	281	426	25	107	0
1943	Cle-A	**.970**	152	**328**	488	25	**122**	**28**
1944	Cle-A	**.978**	**149**	**339**	**516**	19	**134**	**26**
1945	Cle-A	.983	97	217	289	9	73	1
1946	Cle-A	**.970**	139	**315**	405	22	94	**16**
1947	Cle-A	**.982**	148	305	475	14	**120**	**17**
1948	Cle-A	**.975**	151	297	483	20	**119**	9
1949	Cle-A	.982	88	176	272	8	78	7
1950	Cle-A	.986	61	118	170	4	44	6
1951	Bos-A	.951	52	80	153	12	45	-1
1952	Bos-A	1.000	1	0	1	0	0	0
Total 14		.973	1539	3132	4760	223	1180	136

3B

YEAR	TM/L	PCT	G	PO	A	E	DP	FR
1938	Cle-A	—	1	1	0	0	0	0
1949	Cle-A	.965	38	34	76	4	13	-1

YEAR	TM/L	PCT	G	PO	A	E	DP	FR
1950	Cle-A	1.000	2	3	1	0	0	0
1951	Bos-A	.949	15	10	27	2	5	0
1952	Bos-A	—	1	0	0	0	0	0
Total	5	.962	57	47	104	6	18	-1
		1B						
1949	Cle-A	1.000	6	41	3	0	3	0
1950	Cle-A	1.000	8	34	5	0	2	1
1951	Bos-A	.833	2	4	1	1	1	0
Total	3	.989	16	79	9	1	6	1
		C						
1943	Cle-A	1.000	1	3	1	0	0	0
1944	Cle-A	1.000	1	1	1	0	0	0
1948	Cle-A	—	1	0	0	0	0	0
Total	3	1.000	3	4	2	0	0	0
		2B						
1949	Cle-A	1.000	1	2	2	0	1	0
1950	Cle-A	1.000	2	1	0	0	0	0
Total	2	1.000	3	3	2	0	1	0

■ Pat Bourque 1B

YEAR	TM/L	PCT	G	PO	A	E	DP	FR
1971	Chi-N	.957	11	75	13	4	6	2
1972	Chi-N	1.000	7	57	6	0	8	1
1973	Chi-N	.986	38	327	35	5	32	5
	Oak-A	1.000	5	21	0	0	2	0
1974	Oak-A	.988	39	158	8	2	18	-1
	Min-A	.987	21	133	18	2	15	3
	Yr	.988	60	291	26	4	33	2
Total	4	.985	121	771	80	3	81	10

■ Larry Bowa SS

YEAR	TM/L	PCT	G	PO	A	E	DP	FR
1970	Phi-N	.979	143	202	418	13	69	-21
1971	Phi-N	**.987**	157	272	**560**	11	**97**	10
1972	Phi-N	**.987**	150	212	494	9	88	5
1973	Phi-N	.979	122	191	361	12	87	0
1974	Phi-N	**.984**	162	256	462	12	104	-16
1975	Phi-N	.962	135	227	403	25	82	-12
1976	Phi-N	.975	156	180	492	17	90	-14
1977	Phi-N	.983	154	222	518	13	94	1
1978	Phi-N	**.986**	156	224	502	10	87	2
1979	Phi-N	**.991**	146	229	448	6	80	-13
1980	Phi-N	.975	147	225	449	17	70	-13
1981	Phi-N	.975	102	117	309	11	50	-10
1982	Chi-N	.973	140	210	396	17	64	-30
1983	Chi-N	**.984**	145	230	464	11	102	15
1984	Chi-N	.974	132	217	378	16	64	7
1985	Chi-N	.970	66	91	197	9	34	12
	NY-N	.882	9	9	6	2	3	0
	Yr	.965	75	100	203	11	37	12
Total	16	.980	2222	3314	6857	211	1265	-77
		2B						
1970	Phi-N	—	1	0	0	0	0	0
1985	NY-N	1.000	4	9	7	0	2	1
Total	2	1.000	5	9	7	0	2	1

■ Sam Bowens OF

YEAR	TM/L	PCT	G	PO	A	E	DP	FR
1963	Bal-A	.952	13	20	0	1	0	-2
1964	Bal-A	.981	135	249	8	5	1	3
1965	Bal-A	.982	68	108	3	2	1	2
1966	Bal-A	.960	68	114	7	5	2	2
1967	Bal-A	.977	32	41	2	1	0	-1
1968	Was-A	.957	27	42	2	2	0	-1
1969	Was-A	.971	30	32	1	1	0	1
Total	7	.974	373	606	23	7	4	4

■ Frank Bowerman C

YEAR	TM/L	PCT	G	PO	A	E	DP	FR
1895	Bal-N	1.000	1	2	0	0	0	0
1896	Bal-N	.900	3	12	6	2	0	1
1897	Bal-N	.948	36	155	29	10	1	6
1898	Bal-N	.950	4	12	7	1	1	1
	Pit-N	.946	59	204	76	16	8	4
	Yr	.946	63	216	83	17	9	5
1899	Pit-N	.948	79	276	128	22	7	12
1900	NY-N	.929	75	232	136	28	15	15
1901	NY-N	.950	46	256	67	17	6	13
1902	NY-N	.956	98	428	143	26	10	2
1903	NY-N	.977	55	316	66	9	9	1
1904	NY-N	.976	79	413	79	12	11	-2
1905	NY-N	.982	72	383	66	8	4	-4
1906	NY-N	.984	67	300	80	6	8	3
1907	NY-N	.990	62	320	70	4	5	-2
1908	Bos-N	.971	63	228	69	9	12	-4
1909	Bos-N	.928	27	122	33	12	6	1
Total	15	.963	826	3659	1055	182	103	47
		1B						
1896	Bal-N	1.000	1	9	0	0	1	0
1898	Pit-N	.989	9	84	3	1	5	0
1899	Pit-N	.965	28	259	16	10	14	0
1901	NY-N	1.000	1	10	0	0	0	0
1902	NY-N	1.000	3	17	1	0	0	0
1903	NY-N	1.000	4	32	1	0	0	0
1904	NY-N	1.000	9	80	3	0	3	0
1905	NY-N	.968	17	142	10	5	8	0
1906	NY-N	.990	20	177	12	2	2	1
1907	NY-N	.993	29	286	9	2	9	-3
1908	Bos-N	.973	11	101	8	3	2	1
Total	11	.982	132	1197	63	3	44	-1
		2B						
1901	NY-N	.917	3	8	14	2	0	2
1904	NY-N	.857	2	2	4	1	0	0
1905	NY-N	1.000	1	3	0	0	0	0
Total	3	.912	6	13	18	3	0	2
		SS						
1900	NY-N	.688	2	3	8	5	2	0
1901	NY-N	.750	3	2	7	3	0	0
Total	2	.714	5	5	15	8	2	0
		3B						
1901	NY-N	.857	3	5	7	2	0	1
		OF						
1903	NY-N	—	1	0	0	0	0	0

■ Steve Bowling OF

YEAR	TM/L	PCT	G	PO	A	E	DP	FR
1976	Mil-A	.975	13	38	1	1	1	3
1977	Tor-A	.987	87	139	14	2	0	10
Total	2	.985	100	177	15	3	1	13

■ Bob Bowman OF

YEAR	TM/L	PCT	G	PO	A	E	DP	FR
1955	Phi-N	1.000	2	3	0	0	0	0
1956	Phi-N	.833	5	5	0	1	0	-1
1957	Phi-N	.929	81	123	8	10	2	-1
1958	Phi-N	.988	57	82	1	1	0	-3
1959	Phi-N	1.000	20	29	1	0	1	1
Total	5	.955	165	242	10	2	3	-4

■ Bob Boyd 1B

YEAR	TM/L	PCT	G	PO	A	E	DP	FR
1951	Chi-A	1.000	6	36	1	0	8	-1
1953	Chi-A	1.000	29	275	16	0	25	0
1954	Chi-A	.981	12	51	2	1	3	-1
1956	Bal-A	.990	60	469	24	5	46	-5
1957	Bal-A	.991	132	**1073**	70	10	107	-3
1958	Bal-A	.994	99	757	53	5	85	-2
1959	Bal-A	.985	109	927	46	**15**	88	-9
1960	Bal-A	1.000	17	64	4	0	9	0
1961	KC-A	1.000	8	44	2	0	4	-1
	Mil-N	1.000	3	20	5	0	3	1
Total	9	.991	475	3716	223	6	378	-21
		OF						
1953	Chi-A	.963	16	26	0	1	0	-1
1954	Chi-A	.955	13	20	1	1	0	0
1956	Bal-A	1.000	8	5	0	0	0	0
1957	Bal-A	—	1	0	0	0	0	0
Total	4	.963	38	51	1	2	0	-1

■ Clete Boyer 3B

YEAR	TM/L	PCT	G	PO	A	E	DP	FR
1955	KC-A	1.000	11	7	17	0	1	3
1956	KC-A	1.000	7	6	14	0	3	3
1957	KC-A	—	1	0	0	0	0	0
1959	NY-A	.973	16	9	27	1	0	2
1960	NY-A	.967	99	102	219	11	24	**21**
1961	NY-A	.967	141	151	**353**	17	36	**32**
1962	NY-A	.964	151	**187**	396	22	**41**	**36**
1963	NY-A	.954	141	165	309	23	32	**19**
1964	NY-A	.968	123	118	278	13	28	**15**
1965	NY-A	.968	147	134	**354**	16	**46**	**25**
1966	NY-A	.966	85	87	226	11	12	**20**
1967	Atl-N	**.970**	150	166	291	14	30	5
1968	Atl-N	.981	69	74	135	4	17	0
1969	Atl-N	**.965**	141	139	275	15	18	3
1970	Atl-N	.954	126	107	268	18	21	13
1971	Atl-N	.961	25	18	56	3	6	3
Total	16	.965	1439	1470	3218	168	315	200
		SS						
1955	KC-A	.963	12	13	13	1	4	2
1959	NY-A	.990	26	40	63	1	14	4
1960	NY-A	.957	33	55	78	6	20	7
1961	NY-A	1.000	12	19	20	0	5	-1
1963	NY-A	.963	9	18	34	2	8	3
1964	NY-A	.973	21	46	61	3	13	5
1965	NY-A	1.000	2	3	0	0	0	0
1966	NY-A	.976	59	114	170	7	26	0
1967	Atl-N	.967	6	11	18	1	5	0
1970	Atl-N	.947	5	6	12	1	1	0
1971	Atl-N	1.000	1	0	1	0	0	0
Total	11	.973	186	325	470	2	96	20
		2B						
1955	KC-A	.920	10	12	11	2	1	1
1956	KC-A	.971	51	94	110	6	31	15
1957	KC-A	—	1	0	1	0	0	0
1963	NY-A	1.000	1	1	1	0	0	0
Total	4	.966	63	107	122	8	32	16
		OF						
1961	NY-A	—	1	0	0	0	0	0

■ Ken Boyer 3B

YEAR	TM/L	PCT	G	PO	A	E	DP	FR
1955	StL-N	.952	139	124	253	19	24	7
1956	StL-N	.961	149	130	**309**	18	**37**	9
1957	StL-N	.912	41	41	93	13	7	6
1958	StL-N	.962	144	**156**	350	20	**41**	**25**
1959	StL-N	.956	143	134	300	20	**32**	**16**
1960	StL-N	.959	146	140	300	19	**37**	13
1961	StL-N	.951	**153**	117	**346**	24	23	**13**
1962	StL-N	.956	**160**	158	318	22	**34**	4
1963	StL-N	.925	159	129	293	**34**	23	-13
1964	StL-N	.951	**162**	131	337	24	30	3
1965	StL-N	**.968**	143	113	250	12	18	-11
1966	NY-N	.951	130	113	292	21	33	10
1967	NY-N	.949	44	27	84	6	7	-2
	Chi-A	.957	33	22	67	4	4	1
1968	Chi-A	.900	5	2	7	1	1	-1
	LA-N	.922	34	30	53	7	4	-1
Total	14	.952	1785	1567	3652	264	355	79
		OF						
1957	StL-N	**.996**	105	275	2	1	1	-6
1958	StL-N	1.000	6	11	0	0	0	0
Total	2	.997	111	286	2	1	1	-6
		1B						
1966	NY-N	1.000	2	12	2	0	1	0
1967	NY-N	.988	18	52	3	0	5	0
	Chi-A	.993	18	132	12	1	12	1
1968	Chi-A	1.000	1	10	1	0	1	0
	LA-N	.988	32	245	11	3	25	-2
1969	LA-N	.971	4	31	2	1	6	0
Total	4	.990	65	482	31	5	50	-1
		SS						
1955	StL-N	.973	18	31	42	2	10	-4
1958	StL-N	1.000	1	1	0	0	0	0
1959	StL-N	.905	12	9	10	2	1	-3
Total	3	.959	31	41	52	4	11	-7

■ Jack Boyle C

YEAR	TM/L	PCT	G	PO	A	E	DP	FR
1886	Cin-a	.769	1	8	2	3	0	0
1887	StL-a	**.897**	86	339	114	52	7	-14
1888	StL-a	**.932**	70	381	123	37	11	12
1889	StL-a	.947	80	378	108	27	11	3
1890	Chi-P	.940	50	218	49	17	5	7
1891	StL-a	.936	91	428	88	35	11	-12
1892	NY-N	.922	79	418	126	**46**	9	20
1893	Phi-N	1.000	6	13	1	0	0	0
1896	Phi-N	.920	28	83	21	9	3	-4
1897	Phi-N	.962	50	156	45	8	3	-7
1898	Phi-N	.800	3	8	4	3	1	0
Total	11	.929	544	2430	681	237	61	5
		1B						
1887	StL-a	.933	2	12	2	1	1	1
1889	StL-a	.938	4	14	1	1	0	0
1890	Chi-P	.957	7	64	2	3	4	-1
1891	StL-a	1.000	3	16	0	0	0	0
1892	NY-N	.967	40	360	23	13	23	1
1893	Phi-N	.988	112	1066	74	14	71	7
1894	Phi-N	.983	114	950	61	18	76	1
1895	Phi-N	.973	**133**	1245	61	**36**	69	-6
1896	Phi-N	.974	12	113	1	3	7	-2
1897	Phi-N	.982	24	215	4	4	7	-3
1898	Phi-N	.919	4	32	2	3	2	0
Total	11	.978	455	4087	231	6	260	-2
		3B						
1887	StL-a	—	1	0	0	0	0	0
1889	StL-a	.929	12	15	24	3	2	2
1890	Chi-P	.793	30	38	58	25	1	-6
1891	StL-a	.923	8	12	12	2	0	-1
1894	Phi-N	.500	1	0	1	1	0	0
Total	5	.838	52	65	95	3	3	-5
		SS						
1890	Chi-P	.778	16	13	43	16	6	-6
1891	StL-a	.849	26	34	56	16	6	-2
1892	NY-N	.800	2	3	1	1	1	0
Total	3	.820	44	50	100	3	13	-8
		OF						
1887	StL-a	1.000	2	1	0	0	0	-1
1888	StL-a	1.000	1	1	0	0	0	0
1889	StL-a	.750	5	2	1	1	1	-1
1890	Chi-P	1.000	2	2	2	0	0	-1
1891	StL-a	1.000	3	2	0	0	0	-1
1892	NY-N	1.000	2	6	2	0	1	2
Total	6	.950	15	14	5	1	2	0
		2B						
1889	StL-a	.500	1	0	1	1	0	-1
1891	StL-a	.929	3	6	7	1	0	0
1893	Phi-N	.929	2	6	7	1	0	0
1894	Phi-N	1.000	1	2	1	0	0	0
Total	4	.909	7	14	16	3	0	-1

■ Buzz Boyle OF

YEAR	TM/L	PCT	G	PO	A	E	DP	FR
1929	Bos-N	1.000	17	32	1	0	0	-1
1930	Bos-N	—	1	0	0	0	0	0
1933	Bro-N	.975	90	195	2	5	0	-5
1934	Bro-N	.970	121	275	**20**	9	1	11
1935	Bro-N	.963	124	244	18	10	5	2
Total	5	.970	353	746	41	4	6	7

■ Gibby Brack OF

YEAR	TM/L	PCT	G	PO	A	E	DP	FR
1937	Bro-N	.969	101	208	10	7	0	3
1938	Bro-N	1.000	13	26	3	0	1	4
	Phi-N	.964	68	156	5	6	2	0
	Yr	.969	81	182	8	6	3	4
1939	Phi-N	.959	48	89	4	4	1	-2
Total	3	.967	230	479	22	7	4	5
		1B						
1939	Phi-N	.976	19	158	7	4	11	-3

■ Buddy Bradford OF

YEAR	TM/L	PCT	G	PO	A	E	DP	FR
1966	Chi-A	.833	9	5	0	1	0	-2
1967	Chi-A	.900	14	9	0	1	0	0
1968	Chi-A	.965	99	162	4	6	0	-5
1969	Chi-A	.961	88	141	5	6	1	-5
1970	Chi-A	.979	27	46	1	1	0	0
	Cle-A	.984	64	119	1	2	0	6
	Yr	.982	91	165	2	3	0	5
1971	Cle-A	.930	18	39	1	3	0	3
	Cin-N	.986	66	67	2	1	1	3
1972	Chi-A	1.000	28	32	1	0	0	2
1973	Chi-A	.992	51	114	9	1	2	9
1974	Chi-A	.980	32	47	2	1	0	-2
1975	Chi-A	.966	18	27	1	1	0	-1
	StL-N	.935	25	42	1	3	0	1
1976	Chi-A	.978	48	91	0	2	0	-3
Total	11	.971	587	941	28	9	4	5
		3B						
1970	Cle-A	—	1	0	0	0	0	0

■ Hugh Bradley 1B

YEAR	TM/L	PCT	G	PO	A	E	DP	FR
1910	Bos-A	.995	21	181	7	1	9	-1
1911	Bos-A	.993	12	128	8	1	7	1
1912	Bos-A	.989	40	354	21	4	13	0
1914	Pit-F	.990	118	1132	60	12	52	0
1915	Bro-F	.996	26	246	22	1	7	3
	New-F	.986	8	69	1	1	4	-1
	Yr	.994	34	315	23	2	11	2
Total	5	.991	225	2110	119	0	92	2
		OF						
1910	Bos-A	—	1	0	0	0	0	0
1915	Pit-F	.952	15	20	0	1	0	-2
	Bro-F	1.000	7	12	0	0	0	-1
	Yr	.970	22	32	0	1	0	-3
Total	2	.970	23	32	0	1	0	-3
		C						
1910	Bos-A	1.000	3	9	0	0	0	-1
1915	Bro-F	1.000	1	0	0	0	0	0
Total	2	1.000	4	9	0	0	0	-1

Phil Bradley — OF

YEAR	TM/L	PCT	G	PO	A	E	DP	FR
1983	Sea-A	.974	21	36	1	1	0	-2
1984	Sea-A	.992	117	235	3	2	1	-2
1985	Sea-A	.986	159	336	10	5	3	4
1986	Sea-A	.996	140	250	11	1	0	-3
1987	Sea-A	.983	158	273	13	5	1	-5
1988	Phi-N	.990	153	298	14	3	2	6
1989	Bal-A	.990	140	284	4	3	0	-8
1990	Bal-A	.987	70	149	3	2	0	-5
	Chi-A	.973	38	70	1	2	0	-2
	Yr	.982	108	219	4	4	0	-7
Total	8	.988	996	1931	60	4	7	-17

Scott Bradley — C

YEAR	TM/L	PCT	G	PO	A	E	DP	FR
1984	NY-A	1.000	3	2	0	0	0	0
1985	NY-A	.923	3	12	0	1	0	1
1986	Sea-A	.990	59	281	21	3	5	-12
1987	Sea-A	.983	82	433	29	8	4	-8
1988	Sea-A	.991	85	524	37	5	6	5
1989	Sea-A	.993	70	388	25	3	4	2
1990	Sea-A	.995	63	349	24	2	4	1
Total	7	.990	365	1989	136	2	23	-11

3B
1987	Sea-A	1.000	8	5	10	0	0	0
1988	Sea-A	1.000	3	0	5	0	0	0
1990	Sea-A	1.000	5	3	6	0	0	1
Total	3	1.000	16	8	21	0	0	1

OF
1984	NY-A	1.000	5	8	0	0	0	-1
1986	Chi-A	—	1	0	0	0	0	0
1987	Sea-A	—	2	0	0	0	0	0
1988	Sea-A	1.000	4	10	0	0	0	0
1989	Sea-A	1.000	1	2	0	0	0	0
Total	5	1.000	13	20	0	0	0	-1

1B
1988	Sea-A	.900	2	9	0	1	1	0
1989	Sea-A	.917	2	10	1	1	2	0
1990	Sea-A	1.000	1	2	0	0	0	0
Total	3	.917	5	21	1	2	3	0

Bill Bradley — 3B

YEAR	TM/L	PCT	G	PO	A	E	DP	FR
1899	Chi-N	.884	30	46	68	15	7	-1
1900	Chi-N	.882	106	164	291	61	11	14
1901	Cle-A	.930	133	192	298	37	25	10
1902	Cle-A	.923	137	188	324	43	21	11
1903	Cle-A	.924	136	151	299	37	18	11
1904	Cle-A	.955	154	178	308	23	18	9
1905	Cle-A	.945	146	188	313	29	17	13
1906	Cle-A	.966	82	107	177	10	6	5
1907	Cle-A	.938	139	164	278	29	18	4
1908	Cle-A	.939	118	142	209	23	13	-17
1909	Cle-A	.957	87	89	157	11	16	-9
1910	Cle-A	.956	61	89	126	10	8	-1
1915	KC-F	.949	61	55	95	8	4	-6
Total	13	.933	1390	1753	2943	336	182	43

SS
1899	Chi-N	.784	5	15	14	8	1	-3
1908	Cle-A	.951	30	50	87	7	3	-15
Total	2	.917	35	65	101	5	4	-18

1B
1900	Chi-N	.986	15	128	13	2	10	3
1909	Cle-A	1.000	3	33	0	0	1	-1
Total	2	.989	18	161	13	2	11	2

2B
| 1909 | Cle-A | .818 | 3 | 4 | 5 | 2 | 0 | -1 |

Steve Brady — OF

YEAR	TM/L	PCT	G	PO	A	E	DP	FR
1883	NY-a	.917	16	20	2	2	1	-1
1884	NY-a	.918	110	154	26	16	1	2
1885	NY-a	.879	105	178	10	26	3	-6
1886	NY-a	.830	123	160	25	38	1	-5
Total	4	.875	354	512	63	2	6	-10

1B
1883	NY-a	.961	81	824	29	35	31	4
1884	NY-a	.947	5	35	1	2	1	0
1885	NY-a	1.000	4	12	0	0	1	0
1886	NY-a	1.000	1	8	1	0	1	0
Total	4	.961	91	879	31	7	34	4

2B
1884	NY-a	—	1	0	0	0	0	0
1885	NY-a	.833	2	8	7	3	1	0
Total	2	.833	3	8	7	3	1	0

3B
| 1885 | NY-a | 1.000 | 1 | 0 | 1 | 0 | 0 | 0 |

Bobby Bragan — SS

YEAR	TM/L	PCT	G	PO	A	E	DP	FR
1940	Phi-N	.936	132	268	443	49	83	1
1941	Phi-N	.944	154	322	437	45	86	-7
1942	Phi-N	.939	78	161	238	26	49	9
1944	Bro-N	.954	51	77	109	9	16	-4
Total	4	.941	415	828	1227	129	234	-1

C
1942	Phi-N	.988	22	68	15	1	4	-1
1943	Bro-N	.973	57	253	34	8	6	4
1944	Bro-N	.980	35	130	20	3	5	3
1947	Bro-N	1.000	21	56	5	0	1	3
1948	Bro-N	1.000	5	11	1	0	0	0
Total	5	.980	140	518	75	2	16	9

3B
1940	Phi-N	—	2	0	0	0	0	0
1941	Phi-N	1.000	1	1	1	0	0	0
1942	Phi-N	—	3	0	0	0	0	0
1943	Bro-N	.962	12	9	16	1	0	0
1944	Bro-N	.952	6	4	16	1	0	1
Total	5	.959	24	14	33	2	0	1

2B
1941	Phi-N	1.000	2	1	0	0	0	0
1942	Phi-N	1.000	4	13	10	0	2	1
1944	Bro-N	1.000	1	0	1	0	0	0
Total	3	1.000	7	14	11	0	2	1

Glenn Braggs — OF

YEAR	TM/L	PCT	G	PO	A	E	DP	FR
1986	Mil-A	.910	56	116	5	12	0	-2
1987	Mil-A	.972	123	301	6	9	1	10
1988	Mil-A	.978	54	134	1	3	0	-2
1989	Mil-A	.972	132	267	6	8	1	-4
1990	Mil-A	.965	32	81	1	3	0	1
	Cin-N	.968	60	110	10	4	3	5
Total	5	.964	457	1009	29	9	5	8

Dave Brain — 3B

YEAR	TM/L	PCT	G	PO	A	E	DP	FR
1903	StL-N	.889	46	70	106	22	9	5
1904	StL-N	.885	30	40	68	14	1	2
1905	StL-N	1.000	6	8	15	0	0	1
	Pit-N	.923	78	82	170	21	13	5
	Yr	.929	84	90	185	21	13	6
1906	Bos-N	.917	139	208	321	48	26	26
1907	Bos-N	.916	130	191	323	47	27	23
1908	NY-N	1.000	2	1	0	0	0	0
Total	6	.913	431	600	1003	152	76	62

SS
1903	StL-N	.908	72	163	244	41	34	5
1904	StL-N	.927	59	109	182	23	21	-3
1905	StL-N	.910	29	58	74	13	4	-12
	Pit-N	.958	4	11	12	1	2	1
	Yr	.917	33	69	86	14	6	-11
1908	NY-N	.667	1	2	2	2	0	-1
Total	4	.915	165	343	514	0	61	-10

OF
1904	StL-N	1.000	19	35	0	0	0	-2
1905	StL-N	1.000	6	11	3	0	0	2
1907	Bos-N	1.000	3	7	2	0	0	2
1908	Cin-N	.947	16	36	0	2	0	-1
	NY-N	—	3	0	0	0	0	-1
	Yr	.947	19	36	0	2	0	-2
Total	4	.979	47	89	5	2	0	0

2B
1901	Chi-A	.909	5	14	16	3	4	1
1904	StL-N	.938	13	35	55	6	3	6
1908	NY-N	.867	3	5	8	2	0	-1
Total	3	.924	21	54	79	1	7	6

1B
| 1904 | StL-N | .956 | 4 | 40 | 3 | 2 | 1 | 0 |

Al Brancato — SS

YEAR	TM/L	PCT	G	PO	A	E	DP	FR
1939	Phi-A	—	1	0	0	0	0	0
1940	Phi-A	.949	80	136	180	17	35	-2
1941	Phi-A	.915	139	263	395	61	80	-19
1945	Phi-A	.959	10	22	25	2	5	-1
Total	4	.927	230	421	600	0	120	-22

3B
1939	Phi-A	.939	20	20	42	4	2	-1
1940	Phi-A	.926	25	24	51	6	4	2
1941	Phi-A	1.000	7	4	8	0	2	0
Total	3	.937	52	48	101	0	8	1

Ron Brand — C

YEAR	TM/L	PCT	G	PO	A	E	DP	FR
1963	Pit-N	.968	33	138	13	5	3	8
1965	Hou-N	.988	102	585	54	8	8	-6
1966	Hou-N	.986	25	132	6	2	1	-2
1967	Hou-N	.998	67	397	36	1	3	-2
1968	Hou-N	1.000	29	153	14	0	3	3
1969	Mon-N	.985	84	492	44	8	7	-8
1970	Mon-N	.969	9	30	1	1	0	-1
1971	Mon-N	1.000	1	1	0	0	0	0
Total	8	.988	350	1928	168	5	25	-8

SS
1970	Mon-N	.952	19	22	37	3	8	-3
1971	Mon-N	.957	22	25	42	3	10	4
Total	2	.955	41	47	79	6	18	1

3B
1963	Pit-N	1.000	2	1	0	0	1	0
1965	Hou-N	1.000	6	7	5	0	2	0
1966	Hou-N	—	1	0	0	0	0	0
1968	Hou-N	—	1	0	0	0	0	0
1970	Mon-N	.889	12	6	18	3	0	-1
1971	Mon-N	1.000	4	0	2	0	0	0
Total	6	.929	26	14	25	3	3	-1

OF
1965	Hou-N	1.000	5	6	1	0	1	1
1966	Hou-N	1.000	3	3	0	0	0	0
1967	Hou-N	—	1	0	0	0	0	0
1968	Hou-N	1.000	1	1	0	0	0	0
1969	Mon-N	—	2	0	0	0	0	0
1970	Mon-N	1.000	5	1	0	0	0	0
1971	Mon-N	1.000	4	2	0	0	0	0
Total	7	1.000	21	13	1	0	1	1

2B
1963	Pit-N	1.000	2	2	0	0	0	0
1966	Hou-N	.974	9	15	23	1	5	-3
1967	Hou-N	1.000	1	0	1	0	0	0
1970	Mon-N	1.000	3	1	1	0	0	0
1971	Mon-N	—	1	0	0	0	0	0
Total	5	.977	16	18	25	1	5	-3

Jackie Brandt — OF

YEAR	TM/L	PCT	G	PO	A	E	DP	FR
1956	StL-N	1.000	26	33	1	0	1	2
	NY-N	.989	96	165	8	2	0	-1
	Yr	.990	122	198	9	2	1	1
1958	SF-N	1.000	14	28	0	0	0	1
1959	SF-N	.984	116	176	10	3	2	-4
1960	Bal-A	.983	142	284	10	5	2	-9
1961	Bal-A	.974	136	293	6	8	2	-7
1962	Bal-A	.976	138	293	9	8	2	1
1963	Bal-A	.984	134	272	9	4	1	-8
1964	Bal-A	.981	134	345	14	7	2	11
1965	Bal-A	.961	84	143	6	6	0	5
1966	Phi-N	.988	71	78	3	1	0	0
1967	Phi-N	1.000	3	1	0	0	0	0
	Hou-N	1.000	6	3	0	0	0	0
	Yr	1.000	9	4	0	0	0	0
Total	11	.980	1100	2131	76	4	12	-10

3B
1959	SF-N	.818	18	9	27	8	1	-3
1960	Bal-A	—	2	0	0	0	0	0
1961	Bal-A	—	1	0	0	0	0	0
1962	Bal-A	1.000	2	0	1	0	0	0
1963	Bal-A	1.000	1	0	2	0	0	0
1967	Hou-N	1.000	1	0	1	0	0	0
Total	6	.833	25	9	31	8	1	-3

1B
1959	SF-N	.947	3	17	1	1	1	0
1960	Bal-A	.500	1	1	0	1	0	0
1967	Hou-N	.991	14	102	6	1	5	-1
Total	3	.977	18	120	7	3	6	-1

2B
| 1959 | SF-N | 1.000 | 1 | 2 | 1 | 0 | 0 | -1 |

Otis Brannan — 2B

YEAR	TM/L	PCT	G	PO	A	E	DP	FR
1928	StL-A	.964	135	272	434	26	74	-8
1929	StL-A	.975	19	31	47	2	6	-1
Total	2	.966	154	303	481	8	80	-9

Kitty Bransfield — 1B

YEAR	TM/L	PCT	G	PO	A	E	DP	FR
1898	Bos-N	1.000	1	4	0	0	0	0
1901	Pit-N	.981	139	1374	52	28	72	-10
1902	Pit-N	.984	101	1064	41	18	40	-6
1903	Pit-N	.981	127	1347	88	28	82	6
1904	Pit-N	.981	139	1454	89	30	70	-3
1905	Phi-N	.985	151	1398	92	23	75	-2
1906	Phi-N	.980	139	1318	88	29	57	-2
1907	Phi-N	.978	92	862	53	21	46	-2
1908	Phi-N	.986	143	1472	89	22	67	-1
1909	Phi-N	.989	138	1377	89	16	71	7
1910	Phi-N	.982	110	1026	51	20	82	-4
1911	Phi-N	.987	8	74	4	1	2	0
	Chi-N	1.000	3	27	1	0	6	0
	Yr	.991	11	101	5	1	8	0
Total	12	.983	1291	12797	737	236	670	-17

C
| 1898 | Bos-N | .889 | 4 | 8 | 0 | 1 | 0 | -1 |

Mickey Brantley — OF

YEAR	TM/L	PCT	G	PO	A	E	DP	FR
1986	Sea-A	.983	25	54	3	1	1	1
1987	Sea-A	.982	82	163	3	3	1	-6
1988	Sea-A	.982	147	327	5	6	1	5
1989	Sea-A	1.000	23	50	1	0	0	0
Total	4	.984	277	594	12	0	3	0

Steve Braun — OF

YEAR	TM/L	PCT	G	PO	A	E	DP	FR
1971	Min-A	—	2	0	0	0	0	0
1972	Min-A	.955	9	19	2	1	0	1
1973	Min-A	1.000	6	7	0	0	0	0
1974	Min-A	.964	108	180	10	7	2	-5
1975	Min-A	.971	106	195	6	6	1	-5
1976	Min-A	.971	32	64	4	2	0	-1
1977	Sea-A	.975	100	186	11	5	3	2
1978	Sea-A	1.000	4	5	0	0	0	0
	KC-A	.964	33	52	1	2	0	-4
	Yr	.967	37	57	1	2	0	-4
1979	KC-A	1.000	18	26	4	0	1	4
1980	KC-A	1.000	5	2	0	0	0	-1
1981	StL-N	1.000	12	15	2	0	1	1
1982	StL-N	1.000	8	4	0	0	0	-1
1983	StL-N	1.000	22	23	0	0	0	-1
1984	StL-N	1.000	19	10	1	0	0	-3
1985	StL-N	1.000	14	14	1	0	0	0
Total	15	.973	498	802	42	3	8	-13

3B
1971	Min-A	.933	73	48	106	11	7	-12
1972	Min-A	.970	74	49	146	6	14	-8
1973	Min-A	.941	102	79	175	16	21	-11
1974	Min-A	.912	17	15	37	5	6	0
1975	Min-A	—	2	0	0	0	0	0
1976	Min-A	.897	16	7	28	4	3	-3
1977	Sea-A	—	1	0	0	0	0	0
1978	KC-A	.905	11	11	8	2	2	-3
1979	KC-A	—	2	0	0	0	0	0
1980	Tor-A	1.000	1	0	1	0	0	0
1981	StL-N	—	1	0	0	0	0	0
1982	StL-N	.875	5	2	5	1	0	-2
1983	StL-N	1.000	1	3	4	0	1	0
1984	StL-N	—	1	0	0	0	0	0
Total	14	.941	310	214	510	5	54	-39

2B
1971	Min-A	.990	28	41	58	1	11	0
1972	Min-A	.974	20	36	39	2	12	-1
1975	Min-A	.800	1	1	3	1	0	0
Total	3	.978	49	78	100	4	23	-1

SS
1971	Min-A	.979	10	18	29	1	6	-1
1972	Min-A	.867	11	6	20	4	0	-5
Total	2	.936	21	24	49	5	6	-6

1B
| 1975 | Min-A | .964 | 9 | 75 | 5 | 3 | 3 | -1 |

Sid Bream — 1B

YEAR	TM/L	PCT	G	PO	A	E	DP	FR
1983	LA-N	1.000	4	8	0	0	1	0
1984	LA-N	1.000	14	95	11	0	9	2
1985	LA-N	.994	16	148	14	1	8	2
	Pit-N	.992	25	219	21	2	21	2
	Yr	.993	41	367	35	3	29	4
1986	Pit-N	.989	153	1320	166	17	107	24
1987	Pit-N	.988	144	1236	127	17	109	11
1988	Pit-N	.995	138	1118	140	6	88	21
1989	Pit-N	.992	13	111	7	1	5	0
1990	Pit-N	.993	142	971	104	8	80	10
Total	8	.991	649	5226	590	52	428	72

OF
YEAR	TM/L	PCT	G	PO	A	E	DP	FR
1986	Pit-N	—	2	0	0	0	0	0

■ Hal Breeden 1B
YEAR	TM/L	PCT	G	PO	A	E	DP	FR
1971	Chi-N	.982	8	48	7	1	2	1
1972	Mon-N	.994	26	159	10	1	12	-1
1973	Mon-N	.991	66	515	45	5	50	3
1974	Mon-N	.987	56	422	31	6	43	1
1975	Mon-N	.989	12	84	4	1	5	0
Total	5	.990	168	1228	97	4	112	4

OF
1972	Mon-N	—	1	0	0	0	0	0

■ Marv Breeding 2B
YEAR	TM/L	PCT	G	PO	A	E	DP	FR
1960	Bal-A	.977	152	359	422	18	116	5
1961	Bal-A	.970	80	179	179	11	53	7
1962	Bal-A	.977	73	146	196	8	47	22
1963	Was-A	.966	22	52	60	4	14	-3
	LA-N	.972	17	15	20	1	0	-4
Total	4	.975	344	751	877	2	230	27

3B
1962	Bal-A	.000	1	0	0	1	0	0
1963	Was-A	.914	29	24	50	7	1	-6
	LA-N	—	1	0	0	0	0	0
Total	2	.902	31	24	50	8	1	-6

SS
1962	Bal-A	—	1	0	0	0	0	0
1963	Was-A	.800	2	1	3	1	0	-1
	LA-N	1.000	1	0	1	0	0	0
Total	2	.833	4	1	4	1	0	-1

■ Bob Brenly C
YEAR	TM/L	PCT	G	PO	A	E	DP	FR
1981	SF-N	.964	14	50	3	2	2	-2
1982	SF-N	.961	61	265	32	12	2	0
1983	SF-N	.983	90	403	70	8	9	3
1984	SF-N	.986	127	635	69	10	4	-14
1985	SF-N	.984	110	662	62	12	8	-3
1986	SF-N	.995	101	518	55	3	4	2
1987	SF-N	.988	108	642	83	9	10	10
1988	SF-N	.984	69	334	27	6	2	-3
1989	Tor-A	.975	13	37	2	1	0	1
	SF-N	1.000	12	31	5	0	0	1
Total	9	.984	705	3577	408	3	41	-5

1B
1983	SF-N	.985	10	61	3	1	6	-1
1984	SF-N	.983	22	171	7	3	17	-2
1985	SF-N	.978	10	42	3	1	4	0
1986	SF-N	.979	19	133	4	3	7	-2
1987	SF-N	1.000	6	43	2	0	4	0
1989	Tor-A	1.000	5	24	3	0	1	1
Total	6	.984	72	474	22	8	39	-4

3B
1981	SF-N	.714	3	2	3	2	0	-1
1982	SF-N	—	1	0	0	0	0	0
1985	SF-N	.897	17	15	20	4	4	-2
1986	SF-N	.906	45	37	59	10	9	-6
1987	SF-N	1.000	2	0	1	0	0	0
Total	5	.895	68	54	83	6	13	-9

OF
1981	SF-N	—	1	0	0	0	0	0
1983	SF-N	1.000	2	1	0	0	0	0
1984	SF-N	1.000	3	1	0	0	0	0
Total	3	1.000	6	2	0	0	0	0

■ Jack Brennan C
YEAR	TM/L	PCT	G	PO	A	E	DP	FR
1884	StL-U	.891	33	147	74	27	2	-3
1888	KC-a	.884	25	104	49	20	4	-1
1889	Phi-a	.818	13	27	18	10	2	-3
1890	Cle-P	.845	42	136	49	34	6	-5
Total	4	.869	113	414	190	1	14	-12

OF
1884	StL-U	.947	16	16	2	1	1	-2
1885	StL-N	.500	2	1	0	1	0	-1
1888	KC-a	1.000	5	4	0	0	0	-1
1889	Phi-a	1.000	7	9	3	0	1	1
1890	Cle-P	.667	6	6	4	5	1	1
Total	5	.865	36	36	9	7	3	-2

3B
1884	StL-U	.656	7	6	15	11	1	-1
1885	StL-N	.333	1	0	1	2	0	-1
1888	KC-a	.696	5	3	13	7	1	-1
1889	Phi-a	.700	4	2	12	6	0	0
1890	Cle-P	.814	14	11	24	8	1	0
Total	5	.719	31	22	65	4	3	-3

2B
1889	Phi-a	.860	7	15	22	6	2	-1

SS
1884	StL-U	.750	1	2	1	1	0	-1

■ Roger Bresnahan C
YEAR	TM/L	PCT	G	PO	A	E	DP	FR
1900	Chi-N	—	1	0	0	0	0	0
1901	Bal-A	.919	69	199	63	23	3	-16
1902	Bal-A	.947	22	67	22	5	0	-3
	NY-N	.955	16	85	22	5	4	2
1903	NY-N	.919	11	46	11	5	1	-3
1905	NY-N	.970	87	492	114	19	15	-1
1906	NY-N	.974	82	407	125	14	6	6
1907	NY-N	.986	95	483	94	8	11	-7
1908	NY-N	.985	139	657	140	12	12	-17
1909	StL-N	.960	59	211	78	12	3	-6
1910	StL-N	.961	77	295	100	16	11	-8
1911	StL-N	.968	77	325	102	14	9	-1
1912	StL-N	.974	28	138	49	5	4	7
1913	Chi-N	.963	58	194	67	10	2	-3
1914	Chi-N	.978	85	365	113	11	6	-3
1915	Chi-N	.982	68	345	95	8	9	2
Total	15	.971	974	4309	1195	167	96	-51

OF
1897	Was-N	—	1	0	0	0	0	-1
1901	Bal-A	.833	8	9	1	2	0	-1
1902	Bal-A	.853	15	26	3	5	0	-1
	NY-N	.946	27	29	6	2	1	0
1903	NY-N	.965	84	150	14	6	6	3
1904	NY-N	.954	93	151	14	8	9	0
1905	NY-N	1.000	8	11	1	0	0	1
1906	NY-N	.962	40	71	6	3	2	0
1907	NY-N	1.000	2	5	2	0	0	2
1910	StL-N	1.000	2	1	0	0	0	0
1914	Chi-N	1.000	1	1	0	0	0	0
Total	10	.951	281	454	47	6	18	3

3B
1901	Bal-A	1.000	4	2	3	0	0	0
1902	Bal-A	.880	30	33	55	12	4	-4
	NY-N	—	1	0	0	0	0	0
1903	NY-N	.833	4	3	12	3	0	1
1904	NY-N	.000	1	0	0	2	0	-1
1907	NY-N	.667	1	1	3	2	0	0
1909	StL-N	.667	1	2	2	2	0	0
Total	6	.847	42	41	75	1	4	-4

1B
1902	NY-N	.957	4	41	3	2	1	0
1903	NY-N	.940	13	101	9	7	4	0
1904	NY-N	.948	10	83	8	5	0	0
1907	NY-N	.952	6	58	2	3	1	-1
Total	4	.947	33	283	22	7	6	-1

2B
1901	Bal-A	.917	2	9	2	1	1	-2
1904	NY-N	1.000	1	0	1	0	0	0
1909	NY-N	.947	9	11	25	2	6	-1
1911	StL-N	.833	2	2	3	1	0	0
1914	Chi-N	.967	14	11	18	1	0	0
Total	5	.943	28	33	49	5	7	-3

SS
1902	NY-N	.818	4	9	9	4	2	-2
1904	NY-N	1.000	4	7	7	0	4	1
Total	2	.889	8	16	16	4	6	-1

■ Rube Bressler OF
YEAR	TM/L	PCT	G	PO	A	E	DP	FR
1918	Cin-N	1.000	3	6	0	0	0	0
1919	Cin-N	.965	48	105	4	4	1	0
1920	Cin-N	.800	3	8	0	2	0	0
1921	Cin-N	.953	85	155	6	8	2	-8
1922	Cin-N	.000	2	0	0	1	0	0
1923	Cin-N	1.000	6	8	0	0	0	0
1924	Cin-N	.966	49	106	6	4	1	-1
1925	Cin-N	.978	38	86	2	2	0	-1
1926	Cin-N	.970	80	155	4	5	1	-8
1927	Cin-N	.972	120	261	15	8	5	3
1928	Bro-N	.985	137	254	7	4	0	-8
1929	Bro-N	.954	122	263	7	13	0	-1
1930	Bro-N	.995	90	200	5	1	1	0
1931	Bro-N	.982	35	54	1	1	0	-4
1932	Phi-N	1.000	18	43	4	0	1	2
	StL-N	1.000	4	8	0	0	0	0
	Yr	1.000	22	51	4	0	1	2
Total	15	.971	840	1712	61	3	12	-27

1B
1920	Cin-N	.895	2	16	1	2	1	0
1921	Cin-N	1.000	6	47	1	0	3	-1
1922	Cin-N	1.000	3	16	0	0	0	0
1923	Cin-N	.983	22	219	9	4	12	-1
1924	Cin-N	.990	50	455	29	5	35	2
1925	Cin-N	.982	52	516	21	10	46	-3
1926	Cin-N	1.000	4	28	1	0	1	0
1930	Bro-N	1.000	7	62	6	0	7	1
1931	Bro-N	1.000	1	12	1	0	0	0
Total	9	.986	147	1371	69	1	105	-2

■ Eddie Bressoud SS
YEAR	TM/L	PCT	G	PO	A	E	DP	FR
1956	NY-N	.950	48	67	125	10	26	-9
1957	NY-N	.940	33	55	87	9	16	2
1958	SF-N	.917	4	5	6	1	1	0
1959	SF-N	.974	92	151	267	11	37	-6
1960	SF-N	.960	115	191	339	22	53	6
1961	SF-N	.964	34	46	60	4	12	-9
1962	Bos-A	.965	153	291	482	28	107	25
1963	Bos-A	.962	137	260	351	24	76	-9
1964	Bos-A	.972	158	248	411	19	78	-14
1965	Bos-A	.963	86	147	195	13	45	-5
1966	Bos-A	.960	94	135	252	16	52	2
1967	StL-N	.929	48	34	58	7	12	-4
Total	12	.963	1002	1630	2633	164	515	-21

2B
1958	SF-N	.966	57	100	98	7	24	-2
1959	SF-N	1.000	1	0	1	0	0	0
1961	SF-N	1.000	1	1	1	0	0	0
1966	NY-N	.971	7	16	17	1	3	1
Total	4	.967	66	117	117	8	27	-1

3B
1957	NY-N	.846	12	12	10	4	0	-1
1958	SF-N	1.000	6	0	2	0	0	0
1959	SF-N	.500	1	0	2	2	0	-1
1961	SF-N	1.000	3	4	0	0	0	-1
1965	Bos-A	1.000	2	0	1	0	1	0
1966	NY-N	.932	32	20	68	5	9	4
1967	StL-N	—	1	0	0	0	0	0
Total	7	.915	57	36	83	1	10	1

1B
1959	SF-N	1.000	1	2	0	0	1	0
1966	NY-N	.980	9	42	6	1	3	1
Total	2	.980	10	44	6	1	4	1

OF
1965	Bos-A	—	1	0	0	0	0	0

■ George Brett 3B
YEAR	TM/L	PCT	G	PO	A	E	DP	FR
1973	KC-A	.974	13	9	28	1	2	3
1974	KC-A	.948	132	102	279	21	16	-9
1975	KC-A	.949	159	131	355	26	27	-6
1976	KC-A	.948	157	140	335	26	22	3
1977	KC-A	.957	135	115	325	20	33	18
1978	KC-A	.961	128	104	289	16	25	6
1979	KC-A	.944	149	129	373	30	28	13
1980	KC-A	.955	112	103	256	17	28	4
1981	KC-A	.946	88	74	170	14	7	-9
1982	KC-A	.959	134	107	294	17	22	-6
1983	KC-A	.919	102	85	188	24	25	-22
1984	KC-A	.949	101	59	201	14	18	-5
1985	KC-A	.967	152	107	339	15	33	10
1986	KC-A	.952	115	97	218	16	17	-2
1987	KC-A	.897	11	7	19	3	3	0
1990	KC-A	1.000	1	1	0	0	0	0
Total	16	.951	1689	1370	3669	260	306	-2

1B
1979	KC-A	.981	8	47	5	1	6	0
1980	KC-A	1.000	1	4	0	0	1	0
1983	KC-A	.991	14	104	3	1	9	-3
1987	KC-A	.993	83	798	50	6	69	-4
1988	KC-A	.992	124	1126	70	10	105	-9
1989	KC-A	.998	104	896	80	2	71	4
1990	KC-A	.993	102	865	66	7	89	-1
Total	7	.993	436	3840	274	7	350	-13

OF
1982	KC-A	1.000	12	23	1	0	1	0
1983	KC-A	1.000	13	21	1	0	0	0
1989	KC-A	1.000	2	2	0	0	0	0
1990	KC-A	1.000	9	14	1	0	0	0
Total	4	1.000	36	60	3	0	1	0

SS
1974	KC-A	—	1	0	0	0	0	0
1975	KC-A	1.000	1	1	1	0	0	0
1976	KC-A	1.000	4	6	15	0	1	0
1977	KC-A	.000	1	0	0	1	0	-1
1978	KC-A	—	1	0	0	0	0	0
1986	KC-A	—	2	0	0	0	0	-1
1988	KC-A	—	1	0	0	0	0	0
Total	7	.958	11	7	16	1	1	-2

■ Fred Brickell OF
YEAR	TM/L	PCT	G	PO	A	E	DP	FR
1926	Pit-N	.920	14	20	3	2	1	0
1927	Pit-N	1.000	3	5	0	0	0	2
1928	Pit-N	.958	50	107	6	5	1	1
1929	Pit-N	1.000	27	54	3	0	0	2
1930	Pit-N	.951	61	134	3	7	1	1
	Phi-N	.963	53	151	6	6	0	5
	Yr	.958	114	285	9	13	1	6
1931	Phi-N	.978	122	341	8	8	2	-2
1932	Phi-N	.935	12	27	2	2	1	2
1933	Phi-N	1.000	4	10	1	0	0	2
Total	8	.967	346	849	32	0	6	13

■ Jim Brideweser SS
YEAR	TM/L	PCT	G	PO	A	E	DP	FR
1951	NY-A	.818	2	4	5	2	3	0
1952	NY-A	.935	22	9	20	2	3	3
1953	NY-A	.833	3	5	0	1	0	0
1954	Bal-A	.944	48	67	103	10	22	-6
1955	Chi-A	.949	26	27	48	4	12	5
1956	Chi-A	.938	10	4	11	1	1	0
	Det-A	.987	32	27	51	1	12	7
	Yr	.979	42	31	62	2	13	7
1957	Bal-A	.943	74	88	144	14	33	5
Total	7	.946	217	231	382	5	86	14

2B
1952	NY-A	.875	4	4	3	1	1	0
1954	Bal-A	.927	19	39	37	6	8	-5
1955	Chi-A	1.000	2	3	2	0	1	0
1956	Det-A	.977	31	84	83	4	20	5
1957	Bal-A	1.000	1	2	2	0	0	0
Total	5	.959	57	132	127	1	30	0

3B
1952	NY-A	.000	1	0	0	1	0	0
1955	Chi-A	1.000	3	0	1	0	0	0
1956	Det-A	1.000	4	2	5	0	1	1
1957	Bal-A	1.000	3	3	0	0	0	0
Total	4	.917	11	5	6	1	1	1

■ Rocky Bridges SS
YEAR	TM/L	PCT	G	PO	A	E	DP	FR
1951	Bro-N	.939	9	11	20	2	4	3
1952	Bro-N	.941	13	5	11	1	1	2
1953	Cin-N	1.000	6	4	1	0	1	0
1954	Cin-N	1.000	20	11	15	0	2	3
1955	Cin-N	.968	26	11	19	1	4	1
1956	Cin-N	1.000	7	3	7	0	0	2
1957	Cin-N	—	1	0	0	0	0	0
	Was-A	.971	108	226	382	18	77	25
1958	Was-A	.976	112	191	331	13	73	6
1959	Det-A	.952	110	179	293	24	66	-7
1960	Cle-A	1.000	3	2	3	0	1	1
	Cle-N	1.000	7	11	22	0	3	3
	Yr	1.000	10	13	25	0	4	3
1961	LA-A	.967	25	32	57	3	12	2
Total	11	.968	447	686	1161	2	244	39

2B
1951	Bro-N	1.000	10	11	12	0	1	2
1952	Bro-N	.986	24	35	34	1	11	9
1953	Cin-N	.976	115	329	320	16	94	11
1954	Cin-N	.971	19	29	38	2	10	6
1955	Cin-N	1.000	9	10	10	0	3	2
1956	Cin-N	1.000	8	7	4	0	0	2
1957	Cin-N	1.000	2	2	0	0	0	0
	Was-A	.973	14	33	40	2	7	5
1958	Was-A	1.000	3	3	1	0	0	0
1959	Det-A	1.000	5	16	15	0	4	2
1960	Cle-N	1.000	3	1	1	0	1	1
Total	11	.980	270	592	614	4	154	48

YEAR	TM/L	PCT	G	PO	A	E	DP	FR
3B								
1951	Bro-N	.871	40	26	62	13	10	-1
1952	Bro-N	.923	6	4	8	1	0	1
1953	Cin-N	1.000	3	2	7	0	0	1
1954	Cin-N	1.000	13	5	7	0	1	2
1955	Cin-N	.965	59	48	88	5	7	4
1956	Cin-N	.966	51	15	13	1	1	5
1957	Cin-N	—	1	0	0	0	0	0
	Was-A	—	1	0	0	0	0	0
1958	Was-A	1.000	3	0	1	0	0	0
1960	Det-A	1.000	7	2	5	0	0	1
	Cle-A	.667	3	1	5	3	1	-1
	Yr	.813	10	3	10	3	1	0
1961	LA-A	1.000	4	0	1	0	0	0
Total	10	.929	191	103	197	3	20	12
OF								
1956	Cin-N	—	1	0	0	0	0	0

■ Al Bridwell   SS

YEAR	TM/L	PCT	G	PO	A	E	DP	FR
1905	Cin-N	.923	5	12	12	2	4	0
1906	Bos-N	.930	119	322	390	54	43	18
1907	Bos-N	.942	140	325	437	47	57	7
1908	NY-N	.933	147	277	486	55	39	11
1909	NY-N	.940	145	269	441	45	55	0
1911	NY-N	.917	76	129	249	34	26	6
	Bos-N	.950	51	78	149	12	19	-11
	Yr	.929	127	207	398	46	45	-5
1912	Bos-N	.936	31	52	80	9	14	-6
1913	Chi-N	.948	136	282	399	37	46	2
1914	StL-F	.944	103	217	291	30	36	-9
Total	10	.939	1094	2267	3351	366	391	24
2B								
1905	Cin-N	.886	7	14	25	5	5	1
1914	StL-F	.980	11	23	25	1	1	-2
1915	StL-F	.952	42	60	98	8	9	1
Total	3	.946	60	97	148	4	15	0
3B								
1905	Cin-N	.944	43	55	79	8	6	1
1915	StL-F	.925	15	17	32	4	1	0
Total	2	.938	58	72	111	2	7	1
OF								
1905	Cin-N	.926	18	23	2	2	0	-2
1906	Bos-N	—	1	0	0	0	0	0
Total	2	.926	19	23	2	2	0	-2
1B								
1905	Cin-N	—	1	0	0	0	0	0
1915	StL-F	—	1	0	0	0	0	0
Total	2	—	2	0	0	0	0	0

■ Bunny Brief   1B

YEAR	TM/L	PCT	G	PO	A	E	DP	FR
1912	StL-A	1.000	4	29	2	0	3	0
1913	StL-A	.986	62	622	34	9	41	-1
1915	Chi-A	.986	46	458	23	7	21	-2
1917	Pit-N	.988	34	309	22	4	23	1
Total	4	.987	146	1418	81	0	88	-2
OF								
1912	StL-A	.826	9	19	0	4	0	-1
1913	StL-A	.950	8	18	1	1	0	0
Total	2	.884	17	37	1	5	0	-1

■ Dan Briggs   1B

YEAR	TM/L	PCT	G	PO	A	E	DP	FR
1975	Cal-A	.953	6	40	1	2	4	-1
1976	Cal-A	.993	44	274	23	2	32	2
1977	Cal-A	.993	45	136	12	1	10	1
1979	SD-N	.986	50	326	28	5	20	3
1981	Mon-N	1.000	3	13	2	0	1	1
1982	Chi-N	1.000	4	9	0	0	1	0
Total	6	.989	152	798	66	0	68	6
OF								
1975	Cal-A	1.000	5	9	0	0	0	0
1976	Cal-A	.967	40	84	3	3	1	0
1977	Cal-A	.952	13	18	2	1	0	1
1978	Cle-A	1.000	15	38	1	0	1	2
1979	SD-N	.972	44	67	3	2	1	2
1981	Mon-N	1.000	3	3	0	0	0	0
1982	Chi-N	.875	10	5	2	1	0	1
Total	7	.971	130	224	11	7	3	6

■ John Briggs   OF

YEAR	TM/L	PCT	G	PO	A	E	DP	FR
1964	Phi-N	.957	19	21	1	1	0	1
1965	Phi-N	.982	66	110	2	2	0	-2
1966	Phi-N	.977	69	126	3	3	0	-7
1967	Phi-N	.979	94	182	2	4	0	-5
1968	Phi-N	.968	65	120	1	4	0	-3
1969	Phi-N	.971	108	197	6	6	0	1
1970	Phi-N	.980	95	188	7	4	1	5
1971	Phi-N	.846	8	10	1	2	0	-1
	Mil-A	.958	65	110	4	5	1	-1
1972	Mil-A	.980	106	194	6	4	1	-2
1973	Mil-A	.968	137	294	9	10	1	2
1974	Mil-A	.973	149	309	10	9	2	-4
1975	Mil-A	.962	21	47	3	2	0	0
	Min-A	1.000	35	63	2	0	0	-1
	Yr	.983	56	110	5	2	0	-1
Total	12	.973	1037	1971	57	6	6	-17
1B								
1964	Phi-N	1.000	1	1	0	0	0	0
1968	Phi-N	.991	36	303	22	3	33	0
1969	Phi-N	1.000	2	16	0	0	2	0
1971	Mil-A	.990	60	458	40	5	53	2
1972	Mil-A	.996	28	220	12	1	20	-1
1975	Min-A	.983	49	420	53	8	38	8
Total	6	.989	176	1418	127	7	146	9

■ Harry Bright   1B

YEAR	TM/L	PCT	G	PO	A	E	DP	FR
1962	Was-A	.989	99	800	70	10	83	0
1963	Cin-N	1.000	1	2	0	0	0	0
	NY-A	.985	35	263	8	4	32	-5
1964	NY-A	1.000	2	9	0	0	0	0

YEAR	TM/L	PCT	G	PO	A	E	DP	FR
Total	3	.988	137	1074	78	4	115	-5
3B								
1958	Pit-N	1.000	7	4	11	0	0	0
1959	Pit-N	1.000	3	1	5	0	0	-1
1961	Was-A	.928	40	47	95	11	14	6
1962	Was-A	.667	1	0	2	1	0	0
1963	NY-A	.952	12	19	21	2	1	0
Total	5	.936	63	71	134	4	15	5
C								
1961	Was-A	1.000	8	24	4	0	1	0
1962	Was-A	1.000	3	2	0	0	0	0
Total	2	1.000	11	26	4	0	1	0
OF								
1959	Pit-N	1.000	4	3	0	0	0	0
2B								
1959	Pit-N	1.000	1	2	0	0	0	0
1961	Was-A	1.000	1	0	2	0	0	0
Total	2	1.000	2	2	2	0	0	0

■ Greg Briley   OF

YEAR	TM/L	PCT	G	PO	A	E	DP	FR
1988	Sea-A	.929	11	13	0	1	0	-2
1989	Sea-A	.958	105	179	5	8	1	-9
1990	Sea-A	.989	107	177	4	2	1	-7
Total	3	.972	223	369	9	1	2	-18
2B								
1989	Sea-A	.981	10	18	33	1	6	1

■ Chuck Brinkman   C

YEAR	TM/L	PCT	G	PO	A	E	DP	FR
1969	Chi-A	1.000	14	28	2	0	0	1
1970	Chi-A	.974	9	32	5	1	1	1
1971	Chi-A	1.000	14	45	4	0	0	2
1972	Chi-A	.985	33	118	11	2	3	8
1973	Chi-A	.987	63	262	36	4	5	11
1974	Chi-A	1.000	8	19	1	0	0	-1
	Pit-N	1.000	4	9	0	0	0	0
Total	6	.988	145	513	59	7	9	22

■ Ed Brinkman   SS

YEAR	TM/L	PCT	G	PO	A	E	DP	FR
1962	Was-A	.942	38	64	81	9	20	0
1963	Was-A	.950	143	241	462	37	97	7
1964	Was-A	.969	125	234	364	19	75	-3
1965	Was-A	.964	150	292	369	25	76	4
1966	Was-A	.965	158	263	501	28	83	12
1967	Was-A	.979	109	160	309	10	54	14
1968	Was-A	.967	74	97	197	10	28	3
1969	Was-A	.976	150	248	511	19	92	15
1970	Was-A	.974	157	301	569	23	103	31
1971	Det-A	.980	159	235	513	15	91	12
1972	Det-A	.990	156	233	495	7	81	2
1973	Det-A	.968	162	249	480	24	89	-13
1974	Det-A	.972	151	237	493	21	88	13
1975	StL-N	.948	24	40	69	6	15	0
	NY-A	.933	39	30	53	6	13	-3
Total	14	.970	1795	2924	5466	259	1005	94
3B								
1961	Was-A	.889	3	2	6	1	1	0
1962	Was-A	1.000	10	7	15	0	2	2
1974	Det-A	1.000	2	2	5	0	1	1
1975	Tex-A	1.000	1	0	1	0	0	0
	NY-A	1.000	3	1	2	0	0	0
	Yr	1.000	4	1	3	0	0	0
Total	4	.976	19	12	29	1	4	3
2B								
1968	Was-A	.500	2	0	1	1	0	0
1975	NY-A	1.000	3	0	4	0	0	0
Total	2	.833	5	0	5	1	0	0
OF								
1968	Was-A	—	1	0	0	0	0	0

■ Fatty Briody   C

YEAR	TM/L	PCT	G	PO	A	E	DP	FR
1880	Tro-N	.700	1	4	3	3	0	1
1882	Cle-N	.902	53	251	89	37	6	5
1883	Cle-N	.900	33	171	46	24	5	2
1884	Cle-N	.922	42	243	74	27	5	6
	Cin-U	.943	22	194	38	14	1	11
1885	StL-N	.893	60	243	83	39	3	-11
1886	KC-N	.919	54	258	95	31	4	-3
1887	Det-N	.907	33	144	61	21	4	3
1888	KC-a	.896	13	52	17	8	3	-2
Total	8	.910	311	1560	506	204	31	12
2B								
1883	Cle-N	1.000	4	7	9	0	2	1
1885	StL-N	1.000	1	0	3	0	0	0
Total	2	1.000	5	7	12	0	2	1
OF								
1884	Cle-N	1.000	1	1	0	0	0	0
1885	StL-N	1.000	1	2	0	0	0	0
1886	KC-N	1.000	2	3	0	0	0	0
Total	3	1.000	4	6	0	0	0	0
1B								
1883	Cle-N	1.000	2	11	0	0	1	0
1886	KC-N	.889	1	8	0	1	0	0
Total	2	.950	3	19	0	1	1	0
3B								
1883	Cle-N	.750	1	2	1	1	0	0
1885	StL-N	1.000	1	0	1	0	0	0
Total	2	.800	2	2	2	1	0	0

■ Greg Brock   1B

YEAR	TM/L	PCT	G	PO	A	E	DP	FR
1982	LA-N	1.000	3	9	0	0	0	0
1983	LA-N	.991	140	1162	106	12	94	5
1984	LA-N	.995	83	703	65	4	61	7
1985	LA-N	.994	122	1113	84	7	86	2
1986	LA-N	.996	99	726	87	3	46	12
1987	Mil-A	.993	141	1065	109	8	111	3
1988	Mil-A	.993	114	915	102	7	89	9
1989	Mil-A	.995	100	850	58	5	86	-5
1990	Mil-A	.995	115	885	63	5	89	-4
Total	9	.994	917	7428	674	1	662	29

■ Lou Brock   OF

YEAR	TM/L	PCT	G	PO	A	E	DP	FR
1961	Chi-N	.750	3	6	0	2	0	0
1962	Chi-N	.965	106	243	7	9	2	-4
1963	Chi-N	.973	140	269	17	8	7	11
1964	Chi-N	.959	52	86	8	4	1	0
	StL-N	.949	102	180	7	10	0	0
	Yr	.953	154	266	15	14	1	0
1965	StL-N	.959	153	272	11	12	1	1
1966	StL-N	.936	154	269	9	19	1	-2
1967	StL-N	.956	157	272	12	13	2	0
1968	StL-N	.952	156	269	9	14	1	-5
1969	StL-N	.949	157	255	7	14	2	-7
1970	StL-N	.962	152	247	9	10	2	-8
1971	StL-N	.951	157	262	7	14	3	-11
1972	StL-N	.952	149	253	6	13	1	-7
1973	StL-N	.963	159	310	3	12	1	-6
1974	StL-N	.967	152	283	8	10	2	-6
1975	StL-N	.966	128	247	5	9	0	-3
1976	StL-N	.983	123	221	6	4	0	-7
1977	StL-N	.954	130	184	2	9	1	-20
1978	StL-N	.975	79	114	2	3	0	-11
1979	StL-N	.958	98	152	7	7	2	-14
Total	19	.959	2507	4394	142	196	29	-99

■ Steve Brodie   OF

YEAR	TM/L	PCT	G	PO	A	E	DP	FR
1890	Bos-N	.953	132	225	19	12	6	6
1891	Bos-N	.951	133	268	25	15	9	10
1892	StL-N	.943	137	296	21	19	4	7
1893	StL-N	.951	107	273	21	15	7	9
	Bal-N	.963	25	50	2	2	0	-3
	Yr	.953	132	323	23	17	7	6
1894	Bal-N	.950	129	310	14	17	4	-5
1895	Bal-N	.965	131	307	23	12	2	5
1896	Bal-N	.972	132	320	22	10	6	11
1897	Pit-N	.983	100	218	11	4	1	0
1898	Pit-N	.958	42	110	4	5	1	3
	Bal-N	.923	23	55	5	5	0	3
	Yr	.946	65	165	9	10	1	6
1899	Bal-N	.979	137	310	15	7	5	1
1901	Bal-A	.963	83	178	4	7	0	-3
1902	NY-N	.953	109	219	22	12	7	7
Total	12	.959	1420	3139	208	142	52	51
2B								
1892	StL-N	.903	16	29	36	7	8	1
3B								
1892	StL-N	1.000	2	1	2	0	0	0

■ Jack Brohamer   2B

YEAR	TM/L	PCT	G	PO	A	E	DP	FR
1972	Cle-A	.977	132	285	393	16	87	5
1973	Cle-A	.971	97	215	279	15	67	17
1974	Cle-A	.987	99	203	269	6	67	-4
1975	Cle-A	.976	66	166	162	8	52	4
1976	Chi-A	.984	117	263	334	10	74	17
1977	Chi-A	1.000	18	29	29	0	6	-1
1978	Bos-A	.969	23	39	54	3	13	-1
1979	Bos-A	.982	36	65	98	3	21	-1
1980	Bos-A	1.000	4	2	12	0	0	-1
	Cle-A	.979	47	77	113	4	27	-3
	Yr	.981	51	79	125	4	27	-2
Total	9	.979	639	1344	1743	5	414	34
3B								
1972	Cle-A	1.000	1	0	0	0	0	0
1976	Chi-A	1.000	1	2	4	0	1	1
1977	Chi-A	.923	38	25	71	8	9	3
1978	Bos-A	.974	30	25	49	2	5	-2
1979	Bos-A	.962	22	9	42	2	6	1
1980	Bos-A	.900	13	10	17	3	3	-2
Total	6	.945	105	71	185	5	24	1

■ Tom Brookens   3B

YEAR	TM/L	PCT	G	PO	A	E	DP	FR
1979	Det-A	.945	42	39	99	8	11	7
1980	Det-A	.931	138	112	279	29	27	1
1981	Det-A	.952	71	58	139	10	13	-4
1982	Det-A	.939	113	72	206	18	20	5
1983	Det-A	.928	103	54	164	17	21	-4
1984	Det-A	.969	68	32	63	3	10	5
1985	Det-A	.943	151	123	261	23	26	2
1986	Det-A	.955	35	26	59	4	4	1
1987	Det-A	.954	122	85	208	14	15	3
1988	Det-A	.952	136	101	234	17	16	-3
1989	NY-A	.926	51	17	70	7	4	-5
1990	Cle-A	.923	35	9	51	5	4	1
Total	12	.943	1065	728	1833	155	171	9
2B								
1979	Det-A	.963	19	37	42	3	10	4
1980	Det-A	1.000	9	13	26	0	10	3
1982	Det-A	.979	26	37	57	2	7	4
1983	Det-A	.973	10	8	28	1	4	4
1984	Det-A	.950	26	28	48	4	14	9
1985	Det-A	1.000	3	2	6	0	1	1
1986	Det-A	.985	31	67	61	2	18	2
1987	Det-A	.930	11	20	20	3	10	0
1988	Det-A	1.000	1	0	1	0	0	0
1989	NY-A	1.000	5	4	7	0	1	0
1990	Cle-A	.989	21	40	48	1	14	4
Total	11	.974	162	256	344	6	89	31
SS								
1980	Det-A	1.000	1	2	2	0	1	0
1982	Det-A	1.000	9	7	13	0	0	0
1983	Det-A	.960	30	35	62	4	9	4
1984	Det-A	.958	28	38	76	5	11	7
1985	Det-A	.923	8	3	9	1	1	0
1986	Det-A	.974	14	13	24	1	4	1
1987	Det-A	.955	16	14	28	2	8	0
1988	Det-A	—	3	0	0	0	0	0
1989	NY-A	1.000	7	2	7	0	2	1
1990	Cle-A	1.000	3	5	4	0	1	0
Total	10	.964	119	119	225	3	37	13

YEAR	TM/L	PCT	G	PO	A	E	DP	FR
		OF						
1982	Det-A	1.000	1	3	0	0	0	0
1986	Det-A	—	3	0	0	0	0	0
1989	NY-A	1.000	3	4	1	0	0	1
Total	3	1.000	7	7	1	0	0	1
		1B						
1990	Cle-A	1.000	2	3	1	0	1	0
		C						
1985	Det-A	1.000	1	7	1	0	0	0

■ Hubie Brooks 3B

YEAR	TM/L	PCT	G	PO	A	E	DP	FR
1980	NY-N	.966	23	16	40	2	2	-1
1981	NY-N	.924	93	65	192	21	14	-2
1982	NY-N	.931	126	89	237	24	17	-8
1983	NY-N	.950	145	107	289	21	25	3
1984	NY-N	.929	129	79	211	22	22	-16
Total	5	.936	516	356	969	0	80	-24
		OF						
1981	NY-N	1.000	3	2	0	0	0	0
1988	Mon-N	.968	149	261	8	9	1	-8
1989	Mon-N	.964	140	234	6	9	2	-8
1990	LA-N	.964	150	255	9	10	2	-7
Total	4	.965	442	752	23	8	5	-23
		SS						
1981	NY-N	1.000	1	0	1	0	0	0
1984	NY-N	.938	26	33	-73	7	19	-2
1985	Mon-N	.958	155	203	441	28	81	-34
1986	Mon-N	.958	80	116	222	15	37	-14
1987	Mon-N	.953	109	131	271	20	53	-26
Total	5	.955	371	483	1008	0	190	-76
		2B						
1983	NY-N	1.000	7	9	14	0	3	0

■ Mandy Brooks OF

YEAR	TM/L	PCT	G	PO	A	E	DP	FR
1925	Chi-N	.977	89	249	9	6	2	3
1926	Chi-N	1.000	18	23	2	0	2	1
Total	2	.979	107	272	11	6	4	4

■ Mark Brouhard OF

YEAR	TM/L	PCT	G	PO	A	E	DP	FR
1980	Mil-A	.964	12	27	0	1	0	0
1981	Mil-A	.990	51	92	7	1	2	2
1982	Mil-A	.986	30	69	2	1	0	2
1983	Mil-A	.991	42	112	1	1	0	0
1984	Mil-A	.983	52	107	6	2	2	2
1985	Mil-A	.964	29	53	0	2	0	-3
Total	6	.983	216	460	16	8	4	3
		1B						
1980	Mil-A	1.000	10	50	4	0	3	1

■ Dan Brouthers 1B

YEAR	TM/L	PCT	G	PO	A	E	DP	FR
1879	Tro-N	.926	37	406	6	33	11	-4
1880	Tro-N	.893	3	25	0	3	1	-1
1881	Buf-N	.952	30	329	11	17	17	-1
1882	Buf-N	.974	84	882	19	24	35	1
1883	Buf-N	.961	97	1040	35	44	40	1
1884	Buf-N	.964	93	958	30	37	38	-1
1885	Buf-N	.975	98	996	25	26	54	-2
1886	Det-N	.968	121	1256	27	42	64	-8
1887	Det-N	.969	123	1141	35	38	67	-5
1888	Det-N	.971	129	1345	48	42	56	-2
1889	Bos-N	.974	126	1243	58	35	78	1
1890	Bos-P	.963	123	1187	73	49	78	2
1891	Bos-a	.978	130	1313	34	30	82	-7
1892	Bro-N	.982	152	1498	105	29	69	12
1893	Bro-N	.986	77	736	47	11	51	3
1894	Bal-N	.976	123	1184	65	31	83	-1
1895	Bal-N	1.000	5	40	3	0	8	0
	Lou-N	.953	24	214	10	11	14	-2
	Yr	.960	29	254	13	11	22	-2
1896	Phi-N	.983	57	566	23	10	44	-3
1904	NY-N	1.000	1	6	0	0	0	0
Total	19	.971	1633	16365	654	512	890	-15
		OF						
1881	Buf-N	.797	35	56	7	16	1	-3
		3B						
1883	Buf-N	1.000	1	1	5	0	0	1
1884	Buf-N	.000	1	0	0	2	0	-1
Total	2	.750	2	1	5	2	0	0

■ Frank Brower OF

YEAR	TM/L	PCT	G	PO	A	E	DP	FR
1920	Was-A	.900	20	32	4	4	2	0
1921	Was-A	.917	46	90	9	9	3	3
1922	Was-A	.978	121	210	9	5	1	-4
1923	Cle-A	1.000	4	3	0	0	0	-1
1924	Cle-A	1.000	3	1	0	0	0	-1
Total	5	.952	194	336	22	8	6	-3
		1B						
1920	Was-A	1.000	9	97	5	0	3	0
1921	Was-A	1.000	4	20	1	0	1	0
1922	Was-A	1.000	7	61	5	0	0	0
1923	Cle-A	.988	112	1047	66	13	87	-1
1924	Cle-A	.990	26	187	17	2	11	0
Total	5	.990	158	1412	94	5	102	-1
		3B						
1920	Was-A	.750	1	2	1	1	2	0

■ Bob Brower OF

YEAR	TM/L	PCT	G	PO	A	E	DP	FR
1986	Tex-A	1.000	17	9	0	0	0	1
1987	Tex-A	.964	106	183	2	7	0	2
1988	Tex-A	.972	59	104	2	3	1	1
1989	NY-A	.970	25	62	2	2	1	4
Total	4	.968	207	358	6	2	2	8

■ Darrell Brown OF

YEAR	TM/L	PCT	G	PO	A	E	DP	FR
1981	Det-A	1.000	6	2	0	0	0	0
1982	Oak-A	1.000	7	9	0	0	0	0
1983	Min-A	.995	81	188	2	1	0	-7
1984	Min-A	.993	55	144	4	1	0	5
Total	4	.994	149	343	6	2	0	-2

■ Drummond Brown C

YEAR	TM/L	PCT	G	PO	A	E	DP	FR
1913	Bos-N	.960	12	41	7	2	0	-4
1914	KC-F	.954	23	92	33	6	5	5
1915	KC-F	.961	65	270	104	15	4	-2
Total	3	.960	100	403	144	3	9	-1
		1B						
1914	KC-F	1.000	2	2	0	0	0	0
1915	KC-F	1.000	1	6	0	0	0	0
Total	2	1.000	3	8	0	0	0	0

■ Eddie Brown OF

YEAR	TM/L	PCT	G	PO	A	E	DP	FR
1920	NY-N	1.000	2	6	0	0	0	0
1921	NY-N	.956	30	63	2	3	0	1
1924	Bro-N	.975	114	311	3	8	0	0
1925	Bro-N	.972	153	449	7	13	3	5
1926	Bos-N	.965	153	401	10	15	2	7
1927	Bos-N	.980	150	335	10	7	1	-2
1928	Bos-N	.960	129	302	6	13	3	1
Total	7	.970	731	1867	38	9	9	12
		1B						
1927	Bos-N	1.000	1	12	0	0	0	0
1928	Bos-N	1.000	1	7	0	0	0	0
Total	2	1.000	2	19	0	0	0	0

■ Jimmy Brown 2B

YEAR	TM/L	PCT	G	PO	A	E	DP	FR
1937	StL-N	.964	112	235	360	22	57	-6
1938	StL-N	.968	49	121	151	9	37	4
1939	StL-N	.963	50	120	143	10	25	-6
1940	StL-N	.977	48	115	135	6	32	-4
1941	StL-N	.962	11	22	28	2	9	-1
1942	StL-N	.970	82	211	215	13	56	-3
1943	StL-N	.978	19	44	45	2	9	2
1946	Pit-N	.969	21	55	69	4	12	3
Total	8	.968	392	923	1146	8	237	-16
		3B						
1937	StL-N	1.000	1	1	2	0	0	0
1938	StL-N	.963	24	25	54	3	5	3
1940	StL-N	.921	41	47	58	9	5	-9
1941	StL-N	.965	123	135	276	15	22	3
1942	StL-N	.947	66	85	111	11	9	-3
1943	StL-N	1.000	9	12	15	0	4	1
Total	7	.951	273	320	527	4	46	-7
		SS						
1937	StL-N	.913	25	41	53	9	10	-9
1938	StL-N	.923	30	49	59	9	13	-6
1939	StL-N	.957	104	208	349	25	67	0
1940	StL-N	.925	28	36	50	7	5	-9
1942	StL-N	.750	12	3	3	2	1	-1
1943	StL-N	1.000	6	9	16	0	1	0
1946	Pit-N	.960	30	57	88	6	15	-3
Total	7	.946	235	403	618	8	112	-28

■ Chris Brown 3B

YEAR	TM/L	PCT	G	PO	A	E	DP	FR
1984	SF-N	.900	23	23	40	7	3	-2
1985	SF-N	.971	120	94	243	10	15	5
1986	SF-N	.933	111	73	177	18	17	-14
1987	SF-N	.905	37	33	62	10	5	-2
	SD-N	.942	43	27	70	6	12	-4
	Yr	.923	80	60	132	16	17	-6
1988	SD-N	.949	72	54	131	10	15	5
1989	Det-A	.909	17	15	25	4	4	-1
Total	6	.943	423	319	748	5	71	-13
		SS						
1986	SF-N	1.000	2	0	4	0	0	0
1987	SF-N	—	1	0	0	0	0	0
Total	2	1.000	3	0	4	0	0	0

■ Larry Brown SS

YEAR	TM/L	PCT	G	PO	A	E	DP	FR
1963	Cle-A	.938	46	71	126	13	17	-8
1964	Cle-A	1.000	4	4	5	0	0	0
1965	Cle-A	.977	95	167	262	10	55	5
1966	Cle-A	.961	90	131	238	15	45	-2
1967	Cle-A	.967	150	233	414	22	90	1
1968	Cle-A	.966	154	255	371	22	70	-14
1969	Cle-A	.959	101	172	276	19	59	-12
1970	Cle-A	.950	27	34	62	5	15	-3
1971	Cle-A	.980	13	24	25	1	4	-6
	Oak-A	.959	31	40	76	5	19	4
	Yr	.965	44	64	101	6	23	-2
1974	Tex-A	—	1	0	0	0	0	0
Total	10	.964	712	1131	1855	112	374	-35
		2B						
1963	Cle-A	.989	27	42	50	1	8	0
1964	Cle-A	.981	103	185	270	9	56	11
1965	Cle-A	.938	22	28	48	5	11	-2
1966	Cle-A	.923	10	22	26	4	7	-1
1969	Cle-A	1.000	5	6	6	0	0	-1
1970	Cle-A	.981	16	28	25	1	6	0
1971	Oak-A	.989	23	38	55	1	11	0
1972	Oak-A	.974	46	110	111	6	30	-9
1973	Bal-A	1.000	1	1	0	0	0	0
1974	Tex-A	1.000	8	15	11	0	4	2
Total	10	.976	265	475	602	7	133	0
		3B						
1969	Cle-A	.982	29	22	33	1	4	-4
1970	Cle-A	.933	17	10	18	2	2	1
1971	Oak-A	1.000	10	4	10	0	1	0
1972	Oak-A	1.000	1	0	1	0	1	0
1973	Bal-A	.880	15	9	13	3	2	-2
1974	Tex-A	.931	47	14	53	5	8	6
Total	6	.944	119	59	128	1	18	1

■ Lew Brown C

YEAR	TM/L	PCT	G	PO	A	E	DP	FR
1876	Bos-N	.856	45	192	45	40	4	-2
1877	Bos-N	.897	55	360	67	49	5	13
1878	Pro-N	.880	45	232	84	43	11	4
1879	Pro-N	.847	48	286	63	63	5	-5
1883	Lou-a	1.000	1	1	0	0	0	0
1884	Bos-U	.914	54	414	117	50	6	11

YEAR	TM/L	PCT	G	PO	A	E	DP	FR
Total	6	.884	248	1485	376	245	31	21
		1B						
1877	Bos-N	1.000	4	27	0	0	0	0
1878	Pro-N	.943	15	178	3	11	7	-1
1879	Chi-N	.974	6	72	2	2	5	0
1881	Det-N	.959	27	252	8	11	20	-1
	Pro-N	.964	5	52	1	2	4	0
	Yr	.960	32	304	9	13	24	-1
1883	Bos-N	.943	14	146	2	9	7	-2
	Lou-a	.891	14	134	5	17	6	-1
1884	Bos-U	.941	33	322	11	21	9	0
Total	6	.943	118	1183	32	3	58	-5
		OF						
1876	Bos-N	1.000	1	1	0	0	0	0
1878	Pro-N	—	1	0	0	0	0	0
1879	Pro-N	.625	6	4	1	3	0	-1
1881	Pro-N	.833	13	9	1	2	0	-4
1884	Bos-U	.500	2	1	0	1	0	-1
Total	5	.739	23	15	2	6	0	-6

■ Mike Brown OF

YEAR	TM/L	PCT	G	PO	A	E	DP	FR
1983	Cal-A	.949	31	52	4	3	1	-1
1984	Cal-A	.968	44	57	4	2	0	-2
1985	Cal-A	1.000	48	78	3	0	1	1
	Pit-N	.938	56	87	3	6	1	-6
1986	Pit-N	.973	71	107	3	3	2	-4
1988	Cal-A	.946	18	33	2	2	0	0
Total	5	.964	268	414	19	6	5	-12

■ Ollie Brown OF

YEAR	TM/L	PCT	G	PO	A	E	DP	FR
1965	SF-N	1.000	4	4	0	0	0	0
1966	SF-N	.978	114	163	12	4	1	-2
1967	SF-N	.985	115	190	5	3	0	-4
1968	SF-N	1.000	35	32	1	0	0	-3
1969	SD-N	.976	148	269	14	7	4	5
1970	SD-N	.964	137	258	12	10	3	4
1971	SD-N	.982	134	263	9	5	2	3
1972	SD-N	1.000	17	34	1	0	0	0
	Oak-A	1.000	16	31	0	0	0	0
	Mil-A	.992	56	116	8	1	3	7
	Yr	.994	72	147	8	1	3	7
1973	Mil-A	1.000	4	1	0	0	0	0
1974	Hou-N	1.000	20	39	0	0	0	0
	Phi-N	.921	33	34	1	3	0	-4
	Yr	.961	53	73	1	3	0	-4
1975	Phi-N	1.000	63	67	0	0	0	-2
1976	Phi-N	.949	75	105	7	6	2	0
1977	Phi-N	1.000	21	16	1	0	0	-1
Total	13	.977	992	1622	71	9	15	3
		3B						
1972	Mil-A	—	1	0	0	0	0	0

■ Oscar Brown OF

YEAR	TM/L	PCT	G	PO	A	E	DP	FR
1969	Atl-N	1.000	3	2	0	0	0	0
1970	Atl-N	.960	25	24	0	1	0	-1
1971	Atl-N	1.000	15	20	1	0	0	1
1972	Atl-N	.899	59	82	7	10	2	3
1973	Atl-N	1.000	13	32	1	0	0	1
Total	5	.939	115	160	9	1	2	4

■ Dick Brown C

YEAR	TM/L	PCT	G	PO	A	E	DP	FR
1957	Cle-A	.986	33	190	18	3	4	1
1958	Cle-A	.987	62	281	24	4	6	8
1959	Cle-A	.996	48	245	20	1	5	3
1960	Chi-A	.986	14	66	7	1	1	3
1961	Det-A	.990	91	460	38	5	7	-1
1962	Det-A	.994	132	742	42	5	8	1
1963	Bal-A	.986	58	317	23	5	7	6
1964	Bal-A	.988	84	380	29	5	4	4
1965	Bal-A	.983	92	466	40	9	6	9
Total	9	.989	614	3147	241	8	48	34

■ Bobby Brown 3B

YEAR	TM/L	PCT	G	PO	A	E	DP	FR
1946	NY-A	1.000	2	1	3	0	0	0
1947	NY-A	.932	27	21	34	4	3	-8
1948	NY-A	.946	41	43	62	6	7	-6
1949	NY-A	.949	86	84	158	13	17	-4
1950	NY-A	.958	82	63	140	9	13	-4
1951	NY-A	.955	90	80	151	11	14	-5
1952	NY-A	.894	24	23	61	10	4	3
1954	NY-A	1.000	17	15	31	0	2	0
Total	8	.948	369	330	640	3	60	-24
		SS						
1946	NY-A	1.000	5	8	9	0	1	-3
1947	NY-A	.917	11	13	20	3	5	-2
1948	NY-A	.931	26	40	68	8	20	-7
Total	3	.935	42	61	97	1	26	-12
		2B						
1948	NY-A	.955	17	42	43	4	6	-5
		OF						
1947	NY-A	1.000	3	1	0	0	0	0
1948	NY-A	1.000	4	5	0	0	0	0
1949	NY-A	1.000	3	5	0	0	0	0
Total	3	1.000	10	11	0	0	0	0

■ Bobby Brown OF

YEAR	TM/L	PCT	G	PO	A	E	DP	FR
1979	Tor-A	1.000	4	8	0	0	0	0
	NY-A	.949	27	56	0	3	0	2
	Yr	.955	31	64	0	3	0	2
1980	NY-A	.972	131	303	7	9	0	4
1981	NY-A	.949	29	54	2	3	0	4
1982	Sea-A	.968	68	148	5	5	1	3
1983	SD-N	.963	54	103	1	4	0	-6
1984	SD-N	.971	53	100	2	3	0	2
1985	SD-N	1.000	28	20	2	0	2	0
Total	7	.968	394	792	19	7	3	10

■ Tommy Brown SS

YEAR	TM/L	PCT	G	PO	A	E	DP	FR
1944	Bro-N	.925	46	89	109	16	24	-9
1945	Bro-N	.918	55	93	164	23	27	-4
1947	Bro-N	.909	1	3	7	1	2	2

YEAR	TM/L	PCT	G	PO	A	E	DP	FR
1952	Chi-N	.911	39	58	85	14	17	-16
1953	Chi-N	.903	25	44	68	12	13	-6
Total	5	.916	166	287	433	6	83	-33
OF								
1945	Bro-N	—	1	0	0	0	0	0
1947	Bro-N	.800	3	4	0	1	0	0
1949	Bro-N	.931	27	53	1	4	0	1
1950	Bro-N	.917	16	31	2	3	0	0
1951	Bro-N	.909	5	9	1	1	0	0
	Phi-N	.966	32	56	0	2	0	-1
	Yr	.957	37	65	1	3	0	-1
1952	Phi-N	1.000	3	1	0	0	0	0
1953	Chi-N	.857	6	4	2	1	0	1
Total	7	.932	93	158	6	2	0	1
3B								
1947	Bro-N	1.000	6	5	8	0	0	1
1948	Bro-N	.936	43	43	60	7	7	-1
1951	Phi-N	.750	1	2	1	1	0	-1
Total	3	.937	50	50	69	8	7	-1
2B								
1951	Phi-N	.952	14	33	26	3	7	-7
1952	Chi-N	.962	10	27	23	2	4	-3
Total	2	.956	24	60	49	5	11	-10
1B								
1948	Bro-N	1.000	1	1	0	0	0	0
1951	Phi-N	.979	12	83	9	2	7	1
1952	Phi-N	1.000	3	21	3	0	0	0
	Chi-N	.974	5	37	1	1	3	-1
	Yr	.984	8	58	4	1	3	-1
Total	3	.981	21	142	13	3	10	0
■ Tom Brown OF								
1882	Bal-a	.728	45	59	16	28	1	0
1883	Col-a	.805	96	151	22	42	3	-1
1884	Col-a	.847	107	164	18	33	5	-5
1885	Pit-a	.828	108	186	21	**43**	2	-2
1886	Pit-a	.837	115	185	30	42	**12**	6
1887	Pit-N	.870	47	130	10	21	0	3
	Ind-N	.813	36	58	7	15	2	-1
	Yr	.851	83	188	17	36	2	2
1888	Bos-N	.896	107	172	18	22	3	-4
1889	Bos-N	.901	90	169	13	20	1	2
1890	Bos-P	.911	128	276	32	30	8	4
1891	Bos-a	.878	137	228	23	35	7	-10
1892	Lou-N	.919	**153**	351	37	34	**8**	**19**
1893	Lou-N	.929	122	**339**	39	29	**13**	**27**
1894	Lou-N	.912	129	331	21	34	8	3
1895	StL-N	.950	83	215	15	12	5	8
	Was-N	.909	34	59	1	6	0	-7
	Yr	.942	117	274	16	18	5	1
1896	Was-N	.928	116	262	7	21	2	-5
1897	Was-N	.928	115	252	17	21	5	1
1898	Was-N	.925	15	36	1	3	0	0
Total	17	.890	1783	3623	348	491	85	38
■ Willard Brown 1B								
1890	NY-P	.953	9	97	4	5	4	-1
1891	Phi-N	**.989**	97	997	48	12	60	4
1893	Bal-N	.985	7	63	3	1	3	0
	Lou-N	.989	111	1082	51	13	76	-2
	Yr	.988	118	1145	54	14	79	-2
1894	Lou-N	.977	13	113	17	3	6	4
	StL-N	1.000	3	28	2	0	2	0
	Yr	.982	16	141	19	3	8	4
Total	4	.987	240	2380	125	4	151	5
C								
1887	NY-N	.914	46	229	69	28	5	5
1888	NY-N	.893	20	134	24	19	0	7
1889	NY-N	.846	37	138	38	32	3	-5
1890	NY-P	.900	34	124	38	18	1	0
1891	Phi-N	.930	19	60	20	6	2	2
1893	Lou-N	—	1	0	0	0	0	0
Total	6	.895	157	685	189	103	11	9
OF								
1887	NY-N	.000	2	0	0	1	0	0
1889	NY-N	1.000	3	8	1	0	0	1
1890	NY-P	.938	13	15	0	1	0	-3
1891	Phi-N	1.000	2	2	1	0	0	0
Total	4	.931	20	25	2	2	0	-2
3B								
1887	NY-N	.667	3	2	2	2	0	-1
1890	NY-P	.900	3	3	6	1	0	0
Total	2	.813	6	5	8	3	0	-1
2B								
1890	NY-P	.750	2	2	1	1	0	-1
■ Gates Brown OF								
1963	Det-A	1.000	16	35	3	0	1	4
1964	Det-A	.981	106	205	4	4	0	3
1965	Det-A	.973	56	108	1	3	0	1
1966	Det-A	.980	43	46	4	1	1	-3
1967	Det-A	1.000	20	22	1	0	0	-2
1968	Det-A	1.000	17	18	1	0	0	-1
1969	Det-A	.906	14	28	1	3	0	0
1970	Det-A	.950	26	37	1	2	0	-2
1971	Det-A	.986	56	68	2	1	0	-6
1972	Det-A	.977	72	122	5	3	1	0
1973	Det-A	1.000	2	1	0	0	0	0
Total	11	.977	428	690	23	7	3	-6
1B								
1968	Det-A	1.000	1	3	0	0	0	0
■ Byron Browne OF								
1965	Chi-N	.667	4	2	0	1	0	0
1966	Chi-N	.967	114	200	3	7	0	-3
1967	Chi-N	1.000	8	12	0	0	0	0
1968	Hou-N	1.000	2	7	1	0	1	1
1969	StL-N	1.000	16	35	3	0	1	4
1970	Phi-N	.975	88	150	4	4	1	-3
1971	Phi-N	1.000	30	21	0	0	0	-1
1972	Phi-N	1.000	9	2	0	0	0	-1
Total	8	.973	271	429	11	2	3	-3
■ George Browne OF								
1901	Phi-N	1.000	8	13	0	0	0	-1
1902	Phi-N	.910	70	158	14	17	1	8
	NY-N	.895	53	104	7	13	1	0
	Yr	.904	123	262	21	30	2	8
1903	NY-N	.918	141	212	13	20	4	-4
1904	NY-N	.925	149	201	20	18	7	-5
1905	NY-N	.915	127	175	9	17	1	-9
1906	NY-N	.934	121	153	17	12	3	-5
1907	NY-N	.941	121	146	14	10	5	-9
1908	Bos-N	.950	138	248	20	14	8	4
1909	Chi-N	.944	12	16	1	1	0	-2
	Was-A	.935	101	147	12	11	3	-2
1910	Was-A	.667	5	4	0	2	0	-2
	Chi-A	.952	29	38	2	2	1	-3
	Yr	.917	34	42	2	4	1	-5
1911	Bro-N	1.000	2	4	0	0	0	0
Total	11	.927	1077	1619	129	137	34	-30
■ Jerry Browne 2B								
1986	Tex-A	.923	8	9	15	2	4	-1
1987	Tex-A	.980	130	258	338	12	66	-17
1988	Tex-A	.958	70	112	139	11	27	-25
1989	Cle-A	.979	151	305	380	15	67	-48
1990	Cle-A	.985	139	286	382	10	69	-21
Total	5	.978	498	970	1254	0	233	112
■ Pete Browning OF								
1883	Lou-a	.861	48	94	5	16	1	1
1884	Lou-a	.964	24	49	4	2	2	4
1885	Lou-a	.900	**112**	214	20	26	4	5
1886	Lou-a	.791	112	153	14	**44**	1	-10
1887	Lou-a	.868	134	281	21	**46**	7	-2
1888	Lou-a	.888	99	174	16	24	8	-1
1889	Lou-a	.882	83	152	12	22	4	-3
1890	Cle-P	.893	118	248	18	32	4	4
1891	Pit-N	.904	50	115	8	13	0	5
	Cin-N	.924	55	103	6	9	2	-1
	Yr	.913	105	218	14	22	2	4
1892	Lou-N	.911	21	40	1	4	2	-1
	Cin-N	.917	82	152	13	15	0	-2
	Yr	.916	103	192	14	19	2	-3
1893	Lou-N	.881	57	114	5	16	1	-3
1894	StL-N	1.000	2	2	0	0	0	-1
	Bro-N	1.000	1	1	0	0	0	0
	Yr	1.000	3	3	0	0	0	-1
Total	12	.883	998	1892	143	269	36	-5
3B								
1882	Lou-a	.778	13	17	32	14	3	1
1883	Lou-a	.879	10	14	15	4	1	-2
1884	Lou-a	.806	52	79	66	35	4	-11
Total	3	.808	75	110	113	3	8	-12
2B								
1882	Lou-a	.890	42	157	127	35	19	10
1883	Lou-a	.833	3	9	11	4	0	0
1884	Lou-a	.818	4	9	9	4	0	-2
Total	3	.882	49	175	147	3	19	8
SS								
1882	Lou-a	.863	18	26	62	14	9	1
1883	Lou-a	.768	26	15	61	23	7	-7
Total	2	.816	44	41	123	7	16	-6
1B								
1883	Lou-a	.875	1	5	2	1	0	1
1884	Lou-a	.963	23	255	6	10	17	-1
1892	Cin-N	1.000	2	11	0	0	0	0
Total	3	.962	26	271	8	1	17	0
■ Bill Brubaker 3B								
1932	Pit-N	.909	7	7	13	2	2	0
1933	Pit-N	1.000	1	0	1	0	0	0
1934	Pit-N	1.000	3	1	5	0	1	1
1935	Pit-N	.889	5	3	5	1	0	0
1936	Pit-N	.940	**145**	**134**	209	**22**	8	-15
1937	Pit-N	.952	115	98	216	16	16	2
1938	Pit-N	.875	18	27	29	8	4	0
1939	Pit-N	.938	32	21	84	7	4	6
1940	Pit-N	.955	19	23	40	3	4	5
1943	Bos-N	.778	5	2	5	2	0	-1
Total	10	.938	350	316	607	1	39	-2
2B								
1939	Pit-N	.950	65	162	202	19	43	4
1B								
1937	Pit-N	1.000	1	2	0	0	0	0
1938	Pit-N	1.000	9	76	2	0	4	-1
1940	Pit-N	1.000	4	25	2	0	1	0
1943	Bos-N	1.000	3	7	1	0	2	0
Total	4	1.000	17	110	5	0	7	-1
SS								
1937	Pit-N	.944	3	8	9	1	1	0
1938	Pit-N	.923	3	7	5	1	2	0
1939	Pit-N	.800	1	0	4	1	0	0
1940	Pit-N	1.000	8	4	4	0	0	0
Total	4	.932	15	19	22	3	3	0
OF								
1938	Pit-N	1.000	1	1	0	0	0	0
■ Earle Brucker C								
1937	Phi-A	.971	92	323	48	11	**13**	-7
1938	Phi-A	.986	44	188	20	3	1	-2
1939	Phi-A	1.000	47	150	18	0	5	-5
1940	Phi-A	.966	13	47	9	2	1	2
Total	4	.980	196	708	95	6	20	-12
1B								
1938	Phi-A	—	1	1	0	0	0	0
■ Frank Bruggy C								
1921	Phi-N	.953	86	231	73	15	14	-8
1922	Phi-A	.925	31	73	25	8	2	-1
1923	Phi-A	.950	34	72	23	5	1	1
1924	Phi-A	.928	44	91	25	9	0	-7
1925	Cin-N	.870	6	17	3	3	0	0
Total	5	.941	201	484	149	0	17	-15
1B								
1921	Phi-N	1.000	2	5	0	0	2	0
1923	Phi-A	1.000	5	16	1	0	1	0
Total	2	1.000	7	21	1	0	3	0
■ Mike Brumley SS								
1987	Chi-N	.965	34	43	93	5	24	4
1989	Det-A	.980	42	48	96	3	13	-8
1990	Sea-A	.983	47	58	111	3	23	-2
Total	3	.976	123	149	300	1	60	-6
2B								
1987	Chi-N	—	1	0	0	0	0	0
1989	Det-A	.932	24	31	51	6	10	2
1990	Sea-A	1.000	6	3	7	0	3	1
Total	3	.939	31	34	58	6	13	3
3B								
1989	Det-A	.813	11	0	13	3	1	0
1990	Sea-A	.750	3	1	5	2	0	0
Total	2	.792	14	1	18	5	1	0
OF								
1989	Det-A	1.000	4	1	0	0	0	0
1990	Sea-A	1.000	2	1	0	0	0	0
Total	2	1.000	6	2	0	0	0	0
■ Mike Brumley C								
1964	Was-A	.991	132	628	44	6	4	-13
1965	Was-A	.990	66	376	25	4	2	1
1966	Was-A	1.000	7	19	4	0	0	0
Total	3	.991	205	1023	73	0	6	-12
■ Glenn Brummer C								
1981	StL-N	1.000	19	43	3	0	1	2
1982	StL-N	.970	32	88	8	3	1	3
1983	StL-N	.978	41	122	11	3	2	0
1984	StL-N	.973	26	101	9	3	0	4
1985	Tex-A	.989	47	182	5	2	2	-2
Total	5	.981	165	536	36	1	6	7
OF								
1985	Tex-A	1.000	1	1	0	0	0	0
■ Tom Brunansky OF								
1981	Cal-A	.938	11	27	3	2	1	2
1982	Min-A	.986	127	343	8	5	0	**16**
1983	Min-A	.985	146	375	16	6	**8**	19
1984	Min-A	.984	153	304	13	5	**6**	0
1985	Min-A	.984	155	300	14	5	2	0
1986	Min-A	.982	152	315	10	6	1	3
1987	Min-A	.990	138	273	10	3	1	3
1988	Min-A	.864	13	19	0	3	0	-3
	StL-N	**.996**	143	267	10	1	0	-1
1989	StL-N	.977	155	291	9	7	2	-3
1990	StL-N	.950	17	37	1	2	1	0
	Bos-A	.982	121	267	7	5	1	6
Total	10	.983	1331	2818	101	0	23	42
1B								
1989	StL-N	—	1	0	1	0	0	0
■ Bill Bruton OF								
1953	Mil-N	.979	150	397	15	9	**5**	4
1954	Mil-N	.981	141	350	**14**	7	3	-3
1955	Mil-N	.968	149	**412**	17	**14**	6	9
1956	Mil-N	.969	145	391	10	**13**	1	-2
1957	Mil-N	.981	79	206	5	4	2	-3
1958	Mil-N	.977	96	203	6	5	0	-11
1959	Mil-N	.991	133	309	6	3	2	-3
1960	Mil-N	.986	149	351	10	5	3	-2
1961	Det-A	.988	155	**410**	4	5	2	4
1962	Det-A	.983	145	**394**	5	7	2	12
1963	Det-A	.991	138	339	6	3	3	3
1964	Det-A	.987	81	143	7	2	3	4
Total	12	.983	1561	3905	105	7	32	12
■ Billy Bryan C								
1961	KC-A	1.000	4	16	1	0	0	-1
1962	KC-A	.976	22	117	4	3	0	-2
1963	KC-A	.981	24	147	4	3	0	5
1964	KC-A	.991	65	317	22	3	5	-9
1965	KC-A	.984	95	527	44	9	6	-5
1966	KC-A	.965	21	99	11	4	2	0
	NY-A	.988	14	73	11	1	2	0
	Yr	.975	35	172	22	5	4	0
1967	NY-A	1.000	1	5	1	0	1	1
1968	Was-A	.983	28	155	15	3	1	-3
Total	8	.984	274	1456	113	6	17	-14
1B								
1966	KC-A	1.000	3	26	0	0	1	-1
	NY-A	.944	3	16	1	1	3	0
	Yr	.977	6	42	1	1	4	-1
■ Steve Brye OF								
1970	Min-A	1.000	6	4	0	0	0	0
1971	Min-A	.966	28	53	4	2	0	1
1972	Min-A	.994	93	170	9	1	1	2
1973	Min-A	.986	87	209	4	3	1	8
1974	Min-A	**.997**	129	301	10	1	2	12
1975	Min-A	.983	72	112	7	2	0	0
1976	Min-A	.987	78	147	1	2	0	-2
1977	Min-A	1.000	83	166	8	0	1	10
1978	Pit-N	.983	47	57	2	1	0	0
Total	9	.991	623	1219	45	2	5	31
■ Jerry Buchek 2B								
1964	StL-N	.917	9	16	17	3	3	3
1965	StL-N	.994	33	65	91	1	22	4

YEAR	TM/L	PCT	G	PO	A	E	DP	FR
1966	StL-N	.974	49	79	107	5	30	-1
1967	NY-N	.977	95	203	255	11	54	3
1968	NY-N	1.000	12	19	20	0	4	0
Total	5	.978	198	382	490	0	113	9

SS

YEAR	TM/L	PCT	G	PO	A	E	DP	FR
1961	StL-N	.912	31	42	62	10	20	-6
1963	StL-N	1.000	1	1	1	0	1	0
1964	StL-N	.929	20	8	18	2	2	4
1965	StL-N	.957	18	27	63	4	16	6
1966	StL-N	.933	48	69	113	13	22	-10
1967	NY-N	.957	9	6	16	1	2	1
Total	6	.934	127	153	273	0	63	-5

3B

YEAR	TM/L	PCT	G	PO	A	E	DP	FR
1964	StL-N	—	1	0	0	0	0	0
1965	StL-N	1.000	1	1	0	0	0	0
1966	StL-N	.917	4	3	8	1	0	-1
1967	NY-N	1.000	17	17	29	0	3	1
1968	NY-N	.935	37	30	70	7	7	-1
Total	5	.952	60	51	107	8	10	-1

OF

YEAR	TM/L	PCT	G	PO	A	E	DP	FR
1968	NY-N	1.000	9	8	1	0	0	1

■ **Jim Bucher** 3B

YEAR	TM/L	PCT	G	PO	A	E	DP	FR
1934	Bro-N	.750	6	1	5	2	0	-1
1935	Bro-N	.982	39	43	64	2	4	-1
1936	Bro-N	.910	39	32	69	10	4	0
1937	Bro-N	.915	43	37	70	10	6	-1
1938	StL-N	1.000	1	1	0	0	0	0
1944	Bos-A	.958	44	48	89	6	10	-3
1945	Bos-A	.940	32	26	68	6	8	-1
Total	7	.939	204	188	365	6	32	-7

2B

YEAR	TM/L	PCT	G	PO	A	E	DP	FR
1934	Bro-N	.920	20	37	43	7	10	0
1935	Bro-N	.950	41	90	121	11	24	-7
1936	Bro-N	.944	32	49	68	7	11	-8
1937	Bro-N	.951	49	128	122	13	29	-11
1938	StL-N	.955	14	32	31	3	9	-3
1944	Bos-A	.952	21	51	49	5	15	-6
1945	Bos-A	1.000	2	1	1	0	0	0
Total	7	.947	179	388	435	6	98	-35

OF

YEAR	TM/L	PCT	G	PO	A	E	DP	FR
1935	Bro-N	.928	37	61	3	5	1	-3
1936	Bro-N	.970	30	64	1	2	0	-1
1937	Bro-N	1.000	6	8	0	0	0	0
Total	3	.951	73	133	4	7	1	-4

■ **Dick Buckley** C

YEAR	TM/L	PCT	G	PO	A	E	DP	FR
1888	Ind-N	.898	51	213	60	31	5	-13
1889	Ind-N	.877	55	182	53	33	2	-24
1890	NY-N	.931	62	365	93	34	4	13
1891	NY-N	.958	74	446	83	23	7	16
1892	StL-N	.937	119	513	123	43	14	-12
1893	StL-N	.914	9	26	6	3	2	2
1894	StL-N	.936	27	88	29	8	2	2
	Phi-N	.966	42	157	39	7	2	4
	Yr	.954	69	245	68	15	4	6
1895	Phi-N	.919	38	152	29	16	5	6
Total	8	.931	477	2142	515	198	43	-6

3B

YEAR	TM/L	PCT	G	PO	A	E	DP	FR
1888	Ind-N	.789	22	17	28	12	4	-9
1889	Ind-N	.881	12	9	28	5	1	0
1890	NY-N	.737	8	3	11	5	0	-1
1891	NY-N	1.000	1	1	2	0	0	0
Total	4	.818	43	30	69	2	5	-10

1B

YEAR	TM/L	PCT	G	PO	A	E	DP	FR
1888	Ind-N	1.000	1	8	1	0	0	0
1889	Ind-N	1.000	1	3	0	0	1	0
1892	StL-N	1.000	2	22	1	0	0	0
1894	StL-N	—	1	0	0	0	0	0
	Phi-N	1.000	1	13	1	0	0	0
	Yr	1.000	2	13	1	0	0	0
Total	4	1.000	6	46	3	0	2	0

OF

YEAR	TM/L	PCT	G	PO	A	E	DP	FR
1888	Ind-N	—	1	0	0	0	0	0
1889	Ind-N	1.000	1	0	1	0	0	1
Total	2	1.000	2	0	1	0	0	1

■ **Bill Buckner** 1B

YEAR	TM/L	PCT	G	PO	A	E	DP	FR
1970	LA-N	1.000	1	1	0	0	0	0
1971	LA-N	1.000	11	70	6	0	4	0
1972	LA-N	.991	35	311	21	3	28	0
1973	LA-N	.998	93	888	50	2	93	-3
1974	LA-N	.980	6	49	1	1	2	-1
1976	LA-N	—	1	0	0	0	0	0
1977	Chi-N	.990	99	966	58	10	75	0
1978	Chi-N	.995	105	1075	83	6	85	8
1979	Chi-N	.995	140	1258	124	7	118	17
1980	Chi-N	.993	94	826	73	6	67	7
1981	Chi-N	.984	105	996	81	17	92	1
1982	Chi-N	.993	161	1547	159	12	89	16
1983	Chi-N	.992	144	1366	161	13	132	22
1984	Chi-N	1.000	7	66	5	0	5	1
	Bos-A	.986	113	974	96	15	75	5
1985	Bos-A	.992	162	1384	184	12	140	25
1986	Bos-A	.989	138	1067	157	14	104	20
1987	Bos-A	.991	74	605	58	6	53	2
	Cal-A	1.000	5	35	2	0	1	0
	Yr	.992	79	640	60	6	54	2
1988	Cal-A	1.000	1	1	1	0	1	0
	KC-A	.994	21	160	12	1	11	0
	Yr	.994	22	161	13	1	12	0
1989	KC-A	.985	24	181	13	3	19	0
1990	Chi-N	1.000	15	75	6	0	6	0
Total	20	.992	1555	13901	1351	128	1200	120

OF

YEAR	TM/L	PCT	G	PO	A	E	DP	FR
1970	LA-N	1.000	20	36	1	0	1	2
1971	LA-N	.994	86	165	5	1	0	0
1972	LA-N	.992	61	123	1	1	0	-2
1973	LA-N	.989	48	93	0	1	0	-4
1974	LA-N	.976	137	235	4	6	0	-8
1975	LA-N	.986	72	138	4	2	0	0
1976	LA-N	.985	153	315	7	5	0	-1
1980	Chi-N	.979	50	90	5	2	2	-3
1983	Chi-N	1.000	15	25	0	0	0	-1
1984	Chi-N	1.000	2	5	1	0	0	1
Total	10	.986	644	1225	28	8	3	-16

■ **Don Buddin** SS

YEAR	TM/L	PCT	G	PO	A	E	DP	FR
1956	Bos-A	.953	113	213	370	29	98	14
1958	Bos-A	.958	136	269	445	31	102	15
1959	Bos-A	.949	150	235	412	35	89	-17
1960	Bos-A	.951	124	230	356	30	79	-5
1961	Bos-A	.956	109	204	294	23	70	-1
1962	Hou-N	.952	27	38	62	5	13	3
	Det-N	.978	19	40	49	2	13	-1
Total	6	.954	678	1229	1988	155	464	8

3B

YEAR	TM/L	PCT	G	PO	A	E	DP	FR
1962	Hou-N	.850	9	6	11	3	1	0
	Det-A	—	2	0	0	0	0	0

2B

YEAR	TM/L	PCT	G	PO	A	E	DP	FR
1962	Det-A	1.000	5	8	6	0	1	-1

■ **Steve Buechele** 3B

YEAR	TM/L	PCT	G	PO	A	E	DP	FR
1985	Tex-A	.969	69	52	137	6	17	5
1986	Tex-A	.968	137	111	226	11	17	16
1987	Tex-A	.964	123	68	175	9	13	0
1988	Tex-A	.962	153	110	297	16	25	8
1989	Tex-A	.969	145	106	264	12	22	14
1990	Tex-A	.966	88	70	157	8	7	6
Total	6	.966	715	517	1256	2	101	49

2B

YEAR	TM/L	PCT	G	PO	A	E	DP	FR
1985	Tex-A	1.000	1	0	1	0	0	0
1986	Tex-A	.992	33	59	66	1	25	2
1987	Tex-A	1.000	18	20	36	0	7	3
1988	Tex-A	1.000	2	4	3	0	0	-1
1989	Tex-A	1.000	18	21	23	0	6	2
1990	Tex-A	1.000	4	2	3	0	0	0
Total	6	.996	76	106	132	1	38	6

OF

YEAR	TM/L	PCT	G	PO	A	E	DP	FR
1986	Tex-A	1.000	2	4	0	0	0	0
1987	Tex-A	1.000	2	1	0	0	0	0
Total	2	1.000	4	5	0	0	0	0

SS

YEAR	TM/L	PCT	G	PO	A	E	DP	FR
1989	Tex-A	1.000	1	1	1	0	1	0

■ **Fritz Buelow** C

YEAR	TM/L	PCT	G	PO	A	E	DP	FR
1899	StL-N	1.000	4	11	1	0	0	-1
1900	StL-N	.864	4	13	6	3	0	-1
1901	Det-A	.967	69	213	84	10	4	5
1902	Det-A	.927	63	174	81	20	5	-1
1903	Det-A	.961	60	254	66	13	6	1
1904	Det-A	.975	42	179	52	6	1	2
	Cle-A	.979	42	199	36	5	4	2
	Yr	.977	84	378	88	11	5	4
1905	Cle-A	.963	60	262	72	13	4	-6
1906	Cle-A	.938	33	114	39	10	5	4
1907	StL-A	.983	25	77	36	2	4	0
Total	9	.960	402	1494	473	2	33	5

OF

YEAR	TM/L	PCT	G	PO	A	E	DP	FR
1899	StL-N	.500	2	1	0	1	0	-1
1900	StL-N	—	1	0	0	0	0	-1
1905	Cle-A	1.000	8	5	0	0	0	-2
Total	3	.857	11	6	0	1	0	-4

1B

YEAR	TM/L	PCT	G	PO	A	E	DP	FR
1902	Det-A	1.000	2	16	0	0	2	0
1903	Det-A	1.000	2	24	1	0	1	0
1905	Cle-A	1.000	3	6	1	0	1	0
1906	Cle-A	1.000	1	10	0	0	0	0
Total	4	1.000	8	56	2	0	4	0

3B

YEAR	TM/L	PCT	G	PO	A	E	DP	FR
1905	Cle-A	1.000	2	1	3	0	0	0

■ **Don Buford** OF

YEAR	TM/L	PCT	G	PO	A	E	DP	FR
1966	Chi-A	1.000	11	13	1	0	0	0
1967	Chi-A	1.000	1	1	0	0	0	0
1968	Bal-A	1.000	65	130	4	0	0	1
1969	Bal-A	.983	128	228	7	4	1	-2
1970	Bal-A	.987	130	221	13	3	3	1
1971	Bal-A	.987	115	217	6	3	0	-3
1972	Bal-A	.989	105	173	6	2	1	-5
Total	7	.988	555	983	37	2	5	-8

2B

YEAR	TM/L	PCT	G	PO	A	E	DP	FR
1963	Chi-A	.800	2	3	1	1	0	-1
1964	Chi-A	.968	92	196	198	13	60	-17
1965	Chi-A	.981	139	326	357	13	93	-1
1966	Chi-A	.955	37	88	81	8	18	-11
1967	Chi-A	.962	51	102	99	8	30	-4
1968	Bal-A	.964	58	109	107	8	22	-7
1969	Bal-A	.956	10	22	21	2	2	-5
1970	Bal-A	.857	3	2	4	1	0	-2
Total	8	.969	392	848	868	4	225	-48

3B

YEAR	TM/L	PCT	G	PO	A	E	DP	FR
1963	Chi-A	.955	9	10	11	1	1	-3
1964	Chi-A	.969	37	30	63	3	5	1
1965	Chi-A	.986	41	13	59	1	9	3
1966	Chi-A	.939	133	98	301	26	24	12
1967	Chi-A	.948	121	95	250	19	16	8
1968	Bal-A	—	2	0	0	0	0	0
1969	Bal-A	1.000	6	5	10	0	2	0
1970	Bal-A	1.000	3	1	2	0	0	0
Total	8	.950	352	252	696	0	57	21

■ **Jay Buhner** OF

YEAR	TM/L	PCT	G	PO	A	E	DP	FR
1987	NY-A	1.000	7	11	1	0	1	1
1988	NY-A	.964	22	52	2	2	0	3
	Sea-A	.993	59	134	7	1	3	6
	Yr	.985	81	186	9	3	3	9
1989	Sea-A	.966	57	106	6	4	3	-2
1990	Sea-A	.966	40	55	1	2	0	-5
Total	4	.977	185	358	17	9	7	3

■ **Bud Bulling** C

YEAR	TM/L	PCT	G	PO	A	E	DP	FR
1977	Min-A	.952	10	37	3	2	0	0
1981	Sea-A	.977	62	239	21	6	2	-2
1982	Sea-A	.991	56	304	24	3	5	7
1983	Sea-A	1.000	5	17	0	0	0	2
Total	4	.983	133	597	48	1	7	7

■ **Al Bumbry** OF

YEAR	TM/L	PCT	G	PO	A	E	DP	FR
1972	Bal-A	1.000	2	4	0	0	0	0
1973	Bal-A	.978	86	134	2	3	0	-11
1974	Bal-A	.953	67	115	7	6	0	8
1975	Bal-A	1.000	39	70	2	0	1	5
1976	Bal-A	.989	116	251	9	3	2	-2
1977	Bal-A	.991	130	329	7	3	0	-5
1978	Bal-A	.985	28	62	2	1	0	-1
1979	Bal-A	.982	146	367	7	7	1	-6
1980	Bal-A	.990	160	488	7	5	1	11
1981	Bal-A	.992	100	255	6	2	2	0
1982	Bal-A	.986	147	404	9	6	1	2
1983	Bal-A	.988	104	235	3	3	1	-10
1984	Bal-A	.988	99	230	7	3	1	-9
1985	SD-N	.939	17	31	0	2	0	0
Total	14	.986	1241	2975	68	4	10	-18

3B

YEAR	TM/L	PCT	G	PO	A	E	DP	FR
1975	Bal-A	—	1	0	0	0	0	0

■ **Al Burch** OF

YEAR	TM/L	PCT	G	PO	A	E	DP	FR
1906	StL-N	.934	91	155	15	12	6	1
1907	StL-N	.922	43	85	10	8	4	0
	Bro-N	.890	36	64	9	9	0	1
	Yr	.908	84	149	19	17	4	1
1908	Bro-N	.971	116	242	24	8	6	-13
1909	Bro-N	.955	151	320	23	16	4	6
1910	Bro-N	.957	70	124	11	6	6	-3
1911	Bro-N	.972	43	98	6	3	3	4
Total	6	.950	555	1088	98	2	29	22

1B

YEAR	TM/L	PCT	G	PO	A	E	DP	FR
1909	Bro-N	1.000	1	15	0	0	1	0
1910	Bro-N	.970	13	122	7	4	9	-1
Total	2	.973	14	137	7	4	10	-1

2B

YEAR	TM/L	PCT	G	PO	A	E	DP	FR
1907	Bro-N	1.000	1	1	5	0	0	1
1911	Bro-N	1.000	3	6	8	0	0	1
Total	2	1.000	4	7	13	0	0	2

■ **Ernie Burch** OF

YEAR	TM/L	PCT	G	PO	A	E	DP	FR
1884	Cle-N	.899	32	52	10	7	1	5
1886	Bro-a	.884	113	142	10	20	3	-13
1887	Bro-a	.899	49	90	8	11	1	1
Total	3	.891	194	284	28	8	5	-7

■ **Bob Burda** 1B

YEAR	TM/L	PCT	G	PO	A	E	DP	FR
1965	SF-N	.969	11	31	0	1	1	-1
1966	SF-N	1.000	7	26	2	0	0	0
1969	SF-N	.995	45	206	12	1	15	0
1970	SF-N	.933	8	14	0	1	1	-1
	Mil-A	1.000	7	24	1	0	2	-1
1971	StL-N	1.000	13	62	6	0	4	1
1972	Bos-A	.992	15	122	7	1	13	0
Total	6	.992	106	485	28	4	36	-2

OF

YEAR	TM/L	PCT	G	PO	A	E	DP	FR
1962	StL-N	.917	6	11	0	1	0	0
1965	SF-N	1.000	1	3	0	0	0	0
1966	SF-N	1.000	4	2	0	0	0	0
1969	SF-N	.938	19	28	2	2	0	0
1970	SF-N	1.000	1	2	0	0	0	0
	Mil-A	.987	64	71	3	1	1	-7
1971	StL-N	—	1	0	0	0	0	0
1972	Bos-A	1.000	1	2	0	0	0	0
Total	7	.969	97	119	5	4	1	-7

■ **Jack Burdock** 2B

YEAR	TM/L	PCT	G	PO	A	E	DP	FR
1876	Har-N	.895	69	211	174	45	18	0
1877	Har-N	.903	55	185	189	40	25	5
1878	Bos-N	.918	60	245	212	41	34	21
1879	Bos-N	.911	84	303	300	59	43	10
1880	Bos-N	.923	86	328	275	50	39	12
1881	Bos-N	.911	72	202	207	40	35	-11
1882	Bos-N	.932	83	223	256	35	28	4
1883	Bos-N	.921	96	224	290	44	39	-1
1884	Bos-N	.922	87	183	278	39	23	2
1885	Bos-N	.917	45	99	134	21	16	-5
1886	Bos-N	.904	59	145	165	33	22	-8
1887	Bos-N	.882	65	117	188	41	34	-18
1888	Bos-N	.903	22	53	68	13	9	0
	Bro-a	.904	70	172	223	42	23	2
1891	Bro-N	1.000	3	4	9	0	1	-1
Total	14	.912	956	2694	2968	543	389	12

3B

YEAR	TM/L	PCT	G	PO	A	E	DP	FR
1876	Har-N	1.000	1	0	1	0	1	0
1877	Har-N	.810	3	5	12	4	0	2
1884	Bos-N	—	1	0	0	0	0	0
Total	3	.818	5	5	13	4	1	2

SS

YEAR	TM/L	PCT	G	PO	A	E	DP	FR
1881	Bos-N	1.000	1	1	0	1	0	0

■ **Smoky Burgess** C

YEAR	TM/L	PCT	G	PO	A	E	DP	FR
1949	Chi-N	1.000	8	21	6	0	2	1
1951	Chi-N	.980	64	210	35	5	6	-3
1952	Phi-N	.978	104	439	47	11	6	-7
1953	Phi-N	.993	95	395	23	3	8	-8
1954	Phi-N	.975	91	356	30	10	4	-8
1955	Phi-N	1.000	6	35	1	0	0	1
	Cin-N	.986	107	457	35	7	6	-10
	Yr	.987	113	492	36	7	6	-9
1956	Cin-N	1.000	55	257	18	0	2	-2
1957	Cin-N	.988	45	223	15	3	0	-5
1958	Cin-N	.988	58	297	21	4	2	4

YEAR	TM/L	PCT	G	PO	A	E	DP	FR
1959	Pit-N	.984	101	441	39	8	4	-17
1960	Pit-N	.994	89	485	38	3	7	-0
1961	Pit-N	.991	92	426	27	4	4	-14
1962	Pit-N	.988	101	550	45	7	5	-12
1963	Pit-N	.990	72	364	40	4	4	-11
1964	Pit-N	.992	44	237	18	2	3	-9
1965	Chi-A	1.000	5	17	3	0	0	0
1966	Chi-A	1.000	2	4	0	0	0	0
								-
Total	17	.988	1139	5214	441	1	63	100

■ Eddie Burke OF

YEAR	TM/L	PCT	G	PO	A	E	DP	FR
1890	Phi-N	.904	96	202	23	24	4	5
	Pit-N	.911	31	80	2	8	1	0
	Yr	.906	127	282	25	32	5	5
1891	Mil-a	.918	35	70	8	7	3	3
1892	Cin-N	1.000	14	12	2	0	1	-2
	NY-N	.909	30	45	5	5	0	0
	Yr	.928	44	57	7	5	1	-2
1893	NY-N	.912	135	278	22	29	2	2
1894	NY-N	.933	136	260	17	20	3	-4
1895	NY-N	.914	39	77	8	8	2	2
	Cin-N	.899	56	135	8	16	2	2
	Yr	.905	95	212	16	24	4	4
1896	Cin-N	.935	122	290	13	21	3	3
1897	Cin-N	.940	95	224	11	15	4	7
Total	8	.921	789	1673	119	153	25	18
2B								
1890	Phi-N	.840	4	12	9	4	1	-2
1892	NY-N	.857	59	149	181	55	19	-3
Total	2	.856	63	161	190	9	20	-5
3B								
1892	Cin-N	.000	1	0	0	1	0	-1

■ Glenn Burke OF

YEAR	TM/L	PCT	G	PO	A	E	DP	FR
1976	LA-N	.971	20	33	0	1	0	1
1977	LA-N	.971	74	98	1	3	0	1
1978	LA-N	1.000	15	10	0	0	0	0
	Oak-A	.987	67	152	1	2	0	3
1979	Oak-A	1.000	23	46	2	0	0	-1
Total	4	.983	199	339	4	6	0	4
1B								
1978	Oak-A	1.000	1	1	0	0	0	0

■ Jimmy Burke 3B

YEAR	TM/L	PCT	G	PO	A	E	DP	FR
1898	Cle-N	.853	13	8	21	5	0	-4
1901	Mil-A	.860	64	83	132	35	5	-7
	Chi-A	.857	11	17	31	8	0	2
	Pit-N	.877	14	16	34	7	3	3
	Yr	.863	78	99	166	42	8	-4
1902	Pit-N	.902	9	14	23	4	0	2
1903	StL-N	.911	93	139	199	33	14	5
1904	StL-N	.897	118	148	217	42	10	-7
1905	StL-N	.924	122	174	238	34	13	3
Total	6	.899	444	599	895	168	45	-3
2B								
1899	StL-N	.923	2	4	8	1	2	1
1902	Pit-N	.895	27	52	84	16	8	-3
1903	StL-N	.933	15	25	58	6	0	2
Total	3	.909	44	81	150	3	10	0
SS								
1901	Chi-A	.867	31	56	94	23	10	-4
1902	Pit-N	.905	4	8	11	2	0	-1
Total	2	.871	35	64	105	5	10	-5
OF								
1902	Pit-N	.947	18	16	2	1	0	-3
1903	StL-N	.857	5	6	0	1	0	-1
Total	2	.923	23	22	2	2	0	-4

■ Les Burke 2B

YEAR	TM/L	PCT	G	PO	A	E	DP	FR
1923	Det-A	1.000	1	0	2	0	0	0
1924	Det-A	.957	58	125	167	13	30	-5
1925	Det-A	.962	52	100	130	9	27	2
1926	Det-A	.942	15	27	38	4	8	3
Total	4	.958	126	252	337	6	65	0
3B								
1923	Det-A	.500	2	1	1	2	0	-1
1926	Det-A	.920	7	7	16	2	0	1
Total	2	.862	9	8	17	4	0	0
SS								
1924	Det-A	.913	6	6	15	2	2	-1
1926	Det-A	1.000	1	1	0	0	0	0
Total	2	.917	7	7	15	2	2	-1

■ Jesse Burkett OF

YEAR	TM/L	PCT	G	PO	A	E	DP	FR
1890	NY-N	.824	90	108	23	28	4	1
1891	Cle-N	.892	40	53	5	7	1	-3
1892	Cle-N	.904	145	271	20	31	7	3
1893	Cle-N	.849	125	239	19	46	5	-8
1894	Cle-N	.915	125	242	17	24	5	-4
1895	Cle-N	.884	131	273	17	38	4	-3
1896	Cle-N	.926	133	269	18	23	4	-2
1897	Cle-N	.949	127	226	18	13	3	-2
1898	Cle-N	.938	150	268	17	19	3	-8
1899	StL-N	.938	140	296	20	21	3	-2
1900	StL-N	.934	141	337	17	25	6	4
1901	StL-N	.923	142	307	17	27	4	-1
1902	StL-A	.924	137	300	17	26	5	6
1903	StL-A	.941	132	230	10	15	4	-4
1904	StL-A	.942	147	266	24	18	4	5
1905	Bos-A	.929	148	276	11	22	0	-1
Total	16	.917	2053	3961	270	383	62	-19
2B								
1899	StL-N	.714	1	2	3	2	0	-1
SS								
1902	StL-A	1.000	1	1	0	1	0	0
3B								
1902	StL-A	1.000	1	1	2	0	1	0

■ Ellis Burks OF

YEAR	TM/L	PCT	G	PO	A	E	DP	FR
1987	Bos-A	.988	132	320	15	4	2	10
1988	Bos-A	.977	142	370	9	9	0	6
1989	Bos-A	.977	95	245	7	6	3	5
1990	Bos-A	.994	143	324	7	2	0	-4
Total	4	.984	512	1259	38	1	5	17

■ Rick Burleson SS

YEAR	TM/L	PCT	G	PO	A	E	DP	FR
1974	Bos-A	.957	88	143	256	18	42	-6
1975	Bos-A	.963	158	267	498	29	102	-1
1976	Bos-A	.957	152	274	478	34	88	-7
1977	Bos-A	.970	154	285	482	24	111	12
1978	Bos-A	.981	144	285	482	15	100	19
1979	Bos-A	.980	153	272	523	16	109	22
1980	Bos-A	.974	155	301	528	22	147	25
1981	Cal-A	.979	109	208	394	13	88	21
1982	Cal-A	.986	11	19	51	1	12	7
1983	Cal-A	.969	31	54	102	5	16	0
1986	Cal-A	.984	37	43	77	2	12	-4
Total	11	.971	1192	2151	3871	179	827	88
2B								
1974	Bos-A	.980	31	65	79	3	24	1
1986	Cal-A	1.000	6	15	11	0	3	-2
1987	Bal-A	.977	55	112	145	6	39	-1
Total	3	.979	92	192	235	9	66	-2
3B								
1974	Bos-A	1.000	2	2	1	0	0	0
1986	Cal-A	.857	4	4	2	1	0	-1
Total	2	.900	6	6	3	1	0	-1

■ Johnny Burnett SS

YEAR	TM/L	PCT	G	PO	A	E	DP	FR
1928	Cle-A	.867	2	6	7	2	3	0
1929	Cle-A	.923	10	18	30	4	3	5
1930	Cle-A	.895	19	22	55	9	12	-3
1931	Cle-A	.938	63	115	157	18	35	-7
1932	Cle-A	.946	103	184	304	28	52	-17
1933	Cle-A	.938	41	84	127	14	21	-2
1934	Cle-A	.918	9	18	27	4	5	-1
1935	StL-A	.914	18	26	38	6	9	-3
Total	8	.935	265	473	745	5	140	-28
3B								
1930	Cle-A	.973	27	22	50	2	2	-2
1931	Cle-A	.911	21	17	34	5	3	-3
1933	Cle-A	.840	12	10	11	4	2	-3
1934	Cle-A	.981	42	43	59	2	6	-5
1935	StL-A	.939	31	25	52	5	5	-2
Total	5	.947	133	117	206	8	18	-15
2B								
1927	Cle-A	.833	2	2	3	1	1	5
1929	Cle-A	.909	8	12	8	2	0	1
1931	Cle-A	.937	35	59	105	11	14	-6
1932	Cle-A	.929	26	48	69	9	10	-5
1933	Cle-A	.949	17	30	63	5	8	0
1934	Cle-a	.842	3	9	7	3	1	-2
1935	StL-A	.971	12	20	46	2	4	-1
Total	7	.936	103	180	301	3	38	-8
OF								
1931	Cle-A	1.000	1	3	0	0	0	0
1934	Cle-A	1.000	2	3	0	0	0	0
Total	2	1.000	3	6	0	0	0	0

■ Ed Burns C

YEAR	TM/L	PCT	G	PO	A	E	DP	FR
1912	StL-N	—	1	0	0	0	0	0
1913	Phi-N	.980	15	38	10	1	2	-4
1914	Phi-N	.947	55	180	72	14	5	-2
1915	Phi-N	.981	62	241	61	6	6	-6
1916	Phi-N	.981	75	283	87	7	5	-9
1917	Phi-N	.971	15	47	20	2	0	-1
1918	Phi-N	.981	68	184	77	5	3	-4
Total	7	.974	291	973	327	5	21	-26
SS								
1916	Phi-N	.667	1	2	0	1	0	-1
OF								
1916	Phi-N	—	1	0	0	0	0	0

■ George Burns 1B

YEAR	TM/L	PCT	G	PO	A	E	DP	FR
1914	Det-A	.982	137	1579	79	30	72	-5
1915	Det-A	.986	104	1155	57	17	65	-4
1916	Det-A	.985	124	1355	54	22	71	-10
1917	Det-A	.990	104	1127	57	12	44	-4
1918	Phi-A	.983	128	1384	104	26	109	6
1919	Phi-A	.980	86	918	71	20	44	3
1920	Cle-A	.979	12	84	9	2	1	1
1921	Cle-A	.990	73	534	41	6	40	2
1922	Bos-A	.987	140	1412	94	20	103	-1
1923	Bos-A	.990	146	1485	92	16	103	-1
1924	Cle-A	.987	127	1227	110	18	85	8
1925	Cle-A	.989	126	1195	82	14	94	-1
1926	Cle-A	.988	151	1499	99	19	122	1
1927	Cle-A	.990	139	1362	102	15	111	3
1928	Cle-A	.984	53	470	38	8	44	2
	NY-A	1.000	2	7	0	0	0	0
	Yr	.985	55	477	38	8	44	2
1929	Phi-A	1.000	19	99	5	0	9	0
Total	16	.987	1671	16892	1094	245	1117	0
OF								
1918	Phi-A	.833	2	5	0	1	0	0
1919	Phi-A	.934	34	53	4	4	2	-2
1920	Phi-A	.958	13	20	3	1	0	1
	Cle-A	—	1	0	0	0	0	0
	Yr	.958	14	20	3	1	0	1
Total	3	.934	50	78	7	6	2	-1

■ George Burns OF

YEAR	TM/L	PCT	G	PO	A	E	DP	FR
1911	NY-N	1.000	6	6	7	0	0	-1
1912	NY-N	1.000	23	24	3	0	1	1
1913	NY-N	.963	150	321	22	13	1	7
1914	NY-N	.950	154	326	19	18	5	4
1915	NY-N	.960	155	278	13	12	4	-2
1916	NY-N	.962	155	289	19	12	3	2

YEAR	TM/L	PCT	G	PO	A	E	DP	FR
1917	NY-N	.974	152	325	16	9	4	6
1918	NY-N	.965	119	292	10	11	1	7
1919	NY-N	.990	139	290	15	3	4	1
1920	NY-N	.983	154	336	11	6	5	0
1921	NY-N	.972	149	360	16	11	2	-9
1922	Cin-N	.976	156	386	20	10	3	-3
1923	Cin-N	.960	154	327	11	14	3	-3
1924	Cin-N	.963	90	168	13	7	4	1
1925	Phi-N	.990	88	189	9	2	2	-2
Total	15	.970	1844	3918	197	128	42	9
3B								
1921	NY-N	1.000	1	0	1	0	0	0

■ Jim Burns OF

YEAR	TM/L	PCT	G	PO	A	E	DP	FR
1888	KC-a	.853	15	25	4	5	2	2
1889	KC-a	.913	134	323	11	32	4	-7
1891	Was-a	.771	20	26	1	8	0	-4
Total	3	.897	169	374	16	5	6	-9
3B								
1889	KC-a	.500	1	0	1	1	0	0
SS								
1891	Was-a	.667	1	1	5	3	0	0

■ Jack Burns 1B

YEAR	TM/L	PCT	G	PO	A	E	DP	FR
1930	StL-A	1.000	8	70	6	0	10	1
1931	StL-A	.993	143	1346	125	11	131	18
1932	StL-A	.992	150	1399	101	12	130	4
1933	StL-A	.992	143	1336	81	12	129	2
1934	StL-A	.992	154	1365	81	12	132	0
1935	StL-A	.992	141	1239	57	11	115	-8
1936	StL-A	1.000	2	28	1	0	3	0
	Det-A	.994	138	1280	73	8	126	1
	Yr	.994	140	1308	74	8	129	1
Total	7	.992	879	8063	525	6	776	18

■ Tom Burns 3B

YEAR	TM/L	PCT	G	PO	A	E	DP	FR
1880	Chi-N	.815	9	8	14	5	0	0
1881	Chi-N	.700	3	6	1	3	1	-1
1884	Chi-N	.889	3	3	5	1	0	0
1886	Chi-N	.890	112	149	247	49	12	14
1887	Chi-N	.872	107	168	246	61	23	19
1888	Chi-N	.905	134	194	273	49	16	18
1889	Chi-N	.880	136	225	301	72	30	3
1890	Chi-N	.898	139	188	290	54	25	0
1891	Chi-N	.892	53	92	107	24	11	-1
1892	Pit-N	.690	8	10	10	9	0	-5
Total	10	.886	704	1043	1494	327	118	47
SS								
1880	Chi-N	.864	79	62	186	39	9	-24
1881	Chi-N	.870	80	100	249	52	20	-5
1882	Chi-N	.827	41	60	131	40	9	2
1883	Chi-N	.872	79	121	260	56	25	5
1884	Chi-N	.838	80	99	254	68	21	-2
1885	Chi-N	.844	111	151	370	96	35	-2
1891	Chi-N	.818	4	7	11	4	1	-1
Total	7	.853	474	600	1461	355	120	-27
2B								
1881	Chi-N	.958	3	10	13	1	1	1
1882	Chi-N	.911	43	129	127	25	21	-3
1883	Chi-N	.806	19	59	57	28	5	-6
1885	Chi-N	—	1	0	0	0	0	0
Total	4	.880	66	198	197	4	27	-8
OF								
1883	Chi-N	—	1	0	0	0	0	0
1887	Chi-N	1.000	8	16	2	0	2	2
1891	Chi-N	1.000	2	7	0	0	0	1
1892	Pit-N	.667	3	1	1	1	0	0
Total	4	.964	14	24	3	1	2	3
C								
1880	Chi-N	.714	2	3	2	2	0	-1

■ Oyster Burns OF

YEAR	TM/L	PCT	G	PO	A	E	DP	FR
1884	Bal-a	.826	24	17	2	4	1	-6
1885	Bal-a	.908	45	74	15	9	4	6
1888	Bal-a	.855	56	97	3	17	1	-3
	Bro-a	.815	14	22	0	5	0	-4
	Yr	.847	70	119	3	22	1	-7
1889	Bro-a	.920	113	139	21	14	5	-4
1890	Bro-N	.941	116	137	23	10	4	-3
1891	Bro-N	.922	113	173	16	16	5	4
1892	Bro-N	.937	129	162	16	12	4	-6
1893	Bro-N	.932	108	159	19	13	5	-1
1894	Bro-N	.949	125	208	15	12	4	-4
1895	Bro-N	.918	19	41	4	4	1	1
	NY-N	.870	32	42	5	7	0	-4
	Yr	.893	51	83	9	11	1	-3
Total	10	.920	894	1271	139	123	34	-24
SS								
1884	Wil-U	.778	2	1	6	2	0	0
1885	Bal-a	.830	10	14	25	8	4	-4
1887	Bal-a	.841	98	136	245	72	20	-19
1888	Bal-a	.839	23	43	61	20	8	-3
	Bro-a	.851	36	50	98	26	5	-8
	Yr	.846	59	93	159	46	13	-11
1889	Bro-a	.892	19	21	62	10	4	-4
1891	Bro-N	.780	6	11	21	9	1	-1
1892	Bro-N	.762	5	9	7	5	0	-5
1893	Bro-N	.500	1	0	1	1	0	-1
Total	8	.841	200	285	526	153	42	-45
3B								
1884	Bal-a	1.000	1	1	0	0	0	0
1885	Bal-a	.870	6	9	13	3	0	0
1887	Bal-a	.838	42	69	81	29	3	1
1888	Bal-a	.909	2	3	7	1	0	1
1890	Bro-N	1.000	1	1	6	0	2	1
1891	Bro-N	.750	5	3	12	5	0	-1
1892	Bro-N	.793	7	12	11	6	2	-2
Total	7	.839	66	102	127	4	6	-1

YEAR	TM/L	PCT	G	PO	A	E	DP	FR
2B								
1884	Bal-a	.877	10	32	32	9	1	1
1885	Bal-a	.853	6	10	19	5	3	-2
1887	Bal-a	—	1	0	0	0	0	0
1888	Bal-a	1.000	1	2	4	0	0	0
	Bro-a	1.000	3	9	6	0	1	-1
	Yr	1.000	4	11	10	0	1	-1
Total	4	.891	21	53	61	4	5	-2
1B								
1885	Bal-a	.889	1	8	0	1	1	0
1895	NY-N	1.000	1	11	0	0	2	0
Total	2	.950	2	19	0	1	3	0
■ Buster Burrell C								
1891	NY-N	.856	15	67	16	14	1	-3
1895	Bro-N	.838	12	24	7	6	1	-2
1896	Bro-N	.928	60	176	42	17	3	-11
1897	Bro-N	.884	27	77	22	13	0	-5
Total	4	.896	114	344	87	0	5	-21
1B								
1897	Bro-N	1.000	4	40	3	0	1	1
OF								
1891	NY-N	.000	1	0	0	1	0	-1
■ Larry Burright 2B								
1962	LA-N	.962	109	176	206	15	35	14
1963	NY-N	.961	15	29	44	3	11	6
1964	NY-N	1.000	3	10	12	0	3	4
Total	3	.964	127	215	262	8	49	24
SS								
1962	LA-N	1.000	1	0	1	0	0	0
1963	NY-N	.946	19	40	66	6	10	6
Total	2	.947	20	40	67	6	10	6
3B								
1963	NY-N	1.000	1	1	1	0	0	0
■ Jeff Burroughs OF								
1970	Was-A	1.000	3	5	0	0	0	0
1971	Was-A	.966	50	82	3	3	0	-5
1972	Tex-A	.935	19	27	2	2	0	-1
1973	Tex-A	.975	148	304	13	8	2	7
1974	Tex-A	.972	150	231	10	7	5	-13
1975	Tex-A	.966	148	249	10	9	2	-13
1976	Tex-A	.987	155	289	12	4	3	-7
1977	Atl-N	.974	154	249	9	7	3	-8
1978	Atl-N	.975	146	224	13	6	2	-9
1979	Atl-N	.963	110	175	8	7	1	-6
1980	Atl-N	.977	73	129	0	3	0	-8
1981	Sea-A	.985	87	127	4	2	1	-14
1982	Oak-A	.981	34	52	0	1	0	0
1984	Oak-A	1.000	4	1	0	0	0	0
Total	14	.974	1281	2144	84	9	19	-77
1B								
1972	Tex-A	1.000	1	6	0	0	1	0
1973	Tex-A	1.000	3	16	1	0	1	0
1974	Tex-A	.923	2	11	1	1	1	0
Total	3	.972	6	33	2	1	3	0
■ Dick Burrus 1B								
1919	Phi-A	.986	38	337	21	5	15	-2
1920	Phi-A	.989	31	252	16	3	22	0
1925	Bos-N	.990	151	1416	85	15	110	1
1926	Bos-N	.991	128	1153	103	12	97	12
1927	Bos-N	.972	61	505	44	16	51	1
1928	Bos-N	.977	32	286	15	7	29	-2
Total	6	.986	441	3949	284	8	324	10
OF								
1919	Phi-A	.688	10	10	1	5	2	-2
1920	Phi-A	.000	2	0	0	1	0	-1
Total	2	.647	12	10	1	6	2	-3
■ Ellis Burton OF								
1958	StL-N	1.000	7	12	0	0	0	-1
1960	StL-N	1.000	23	8	0	0	0	-2
1963	StL-N	1.000	16	8	1	0	1	0
	Chi-N	.975	90	151	6	4	1	-10
1964	Chi-N	.981	29	51	0	1	0	-2
1965	Chi-N	1.000	12	19	1	0	0	1
Total	5	.981	177	249	8	5	2	-14
■ Jim Busby OF								
1950	Chi-A	.964	12	25	2	1	1	1
1951	Chi-A	.982	139	360	16	7	4	-3
1952	Chi-A	1.000	16	42	0	0	0	3
	Was-A	.993	128	430	4	3	0	6
	Yr	.994	144	472	4	3	0	9
1953	Was-A	.988	150	482	15	6	4	14
1954	Was-A	.988	155	491	6	6	1	8
1955	Was-A	.993	47	132	1	1	0	2
	Chi-A	.984	99	243	6	4	3	-1
	Yr	.987	146	375	7	5	3	1
1956	Cle-A	.989	133	344	3	4	0	-1
1957	Cle-A	.978	26	44	1	1	1	2
	Bal-A	.984	85	233	8	4	1	5
	Yr	.983	111	277	9	5	2	7
1958	Bal-A	.995	103	196	1	1	0	-11
1959	Bos-A	.980	34	49	1	1	0	1
1960	Bos-A	—	1	0	0	0	0	0
	Bal-A	.985	71	133	2	2	1	-1
	Yr	.985	72	133	2	2	1	-1
1961	Bal-A	.987	71	76	2	1	0	6
1962	Hou-N	1.000	10	4	0	0	0	0
Total	13	.988	1280	3284	68	2	16	31
3B								
1958	Bal-A	—	1	0	0	0	0	0
C								
1962	Hou-N	—	1	0	0	0	0	0

YEAR	TM/L	PCT	G	PO	A	E	DP	FR
■ Ed Busch SS								
1943	Phi-A	.941	4	10	6	1	1	-3
1944	Phi-A	.940	111	204	330	34	50	-24
1945	Phi-A	.952	116	209	370	29	67	2
Total	3	.946	231	423	706	4	118	-25
2B								
1944	Phi-A	.942	27	51	62	7	12	-5
1945	Phi-A	.889	2	4	4	1	2	-1
Total	2	.938	29	55	66	8	14	-6
3B								
1944	Phi-A	1.000	4	2	1	0	0	0
1945	Phi-A	.889	2	4	4	1	2	0
Total	2	.917	6	6	5	1	2	0
1B								
1945	Phi-A	1.000	1	3	0	0	1	0
■ Donie Bush SS								
1908	Det-A	.938	20	42	63	7	9	-3
1909	Det-A	.925	157	308	567	71	38	4
1910	Det-A	.940	141	310	487	51	31	9
1911	Det-A	.925	150	372	556	75	42	17
1912	Det-A	.929	144	317	547	66	45	29
1913	Det-A	.938	153	331	510	56	61	2
1914	Det-A	.944	157	425	544	58	64	34
1915	Det-A	.937	155	340	504	57	61	9
1916	Det-A	.954	144	278	435	34	41	-15
1917	Det-A	.932	147	281	423	51	41	-18
1918	Det-A	.931	128	280	364	48	29	-21
1919	Det-A	.943	129	290	376	40	38	-12
1920	Det-A	.938	140	258	421	45	39	-17
1921	Det-A	.949	81	172	260	23	35	0
	Was-A	.932	21	34	62	7	11	-4
	Yr	.946	102	206	322	30	46	-4
Total	14	.936	1867	4038	6119	689	585	14
3B								
1910	Det-A	1.000	1	0	2	0	0	0
1922	Was-A	.957	37	31	79	5	12	-2
1923	Was-A	.813	5	4	9	3	0	-1
Total	3	.940	43	35	90	8	12	-3
2B								
1921	Det-A	.942	23	45	69	7	0	-5
1922	Was-A	1.000	1	0	2	0	0	0
1923	Was-A	1.000	2	1	6	0	0	-1
Total	3	.946	26	46	77	7	0	-6
■ Randy Bush OF								
1982	Min-A	1.000	6	7	0	0	0	0
1985	Min-A	.969	41	63	0	2	0	-3
1986	Min-A	.977	102	167	2	4	0	-11
1987	Min-A	.982	75	107	1	2	0	-6
1988	Min-A	.979	109	187	3	4	0	-9
1989	Min-A	.986	109	200	7	3	1	-4
1990	Min-A	1.000	32	52	1	0	0	-1
Total	7	.982	474	783	14	5	1	-34
1B								
1983	Min-A	1.000	3	21	3	0	1	1
1984	Min-A	1.000	2	5	0	0	1	0
1985	Min-A	1.000	1	16	0	0	1	0
1986	Min-A	1.000	3	15	0	0	2	-1
1987	Min-A	.968	9	57	4	2	4	-1
1988	Min-A	1.000	6	19	2	0	1	0
1989	Min-A	1.000	25	139	7	0	13	-1
1990	Min-A	1.000	6	12	2	0	1	0
Total	8	.993	55	284	18	2	24	-2
■ Doc Bushong C								
1876	Phi-N	.769	5	24	6	9	0	1
1880	Wor-N	.918	40	261	76	30	6	15
1881	Wor-N	.918	76	368	124	44	10	6
1882	Wor-N	.897	69	308	101	47	8	-5
1883	Cle-N	.909	63	370	88	46	5	10
1884	Cle-N	.886	62	355	98	58	11	6
1885	StL-a	.932	85	429	122	40	10	8
1886	StL-a	.942	106	647	134	48	14	5
1887	StL-a	.927	52	201	93	23	3	6
1888	Bro-a	.915	69	347	105	42	8	-9
1889	Bro-a	.894	25	85	41	15	5	-1
1890	Bro-N	.913	15	82	13	9	1	0
Total	12	.916	667	3477	1001	411	81	42
OF								
1880	Wor-N	—	1	0	0	0	0	0
1884	Cle-N	—	1	0	0	0	0	0
1887	StL-a	1.000	2	3	0	0	0	0
1890	Bro-N	—	2	0	0	0	0	0
Total	4	1.000	6	3	0	0	0	0
3B								
1880	Wor-N	—	1	0	0	0	0	0
1885	StL-a	—	1	0	0	0	0	0
1887	StL-a	—	2	0	0	0	0	0
Total	3	—	4	0	0	0	0	0
1B								
1886	StL-a	1.000	1	6	0	0	0	0
■ Sal Butera C								
1980	Min-A	.950	32	106	9	6	0	-1
1981	Min-A	.970	59	254	41	9	0	1
1982	Min-A	.988	53	230	26	3	5	6
1983	Det-A	.929	4	12	1	1	0	1
1984	Mon-N	.982	9	40	0	0	0	1
1985	Mon-N	.984	66	227	20	4	5	0
1986	Cin-N	.979	53	215	17	5	2	1
1987	Cin-N	.920	5	19	4	2	0	1
	Min-A	.983	51	213	21	4	3	1
1988	Tor-A	.991	23	97	10	1	1	3
Total	9	.978	348	1382	149	5	16	14
1B								
1981	Min-A	1.000	1	2	0	0	0	0

YEAR	TM/L	PCT	G	PO	A	E	DP	FR
■ Art Butler SS								
1911	Bos-N	.500	1	0	1	1	0	-1
1913	Pit-N	.912	26	64	70	13	5	-5
1914	StL-N	.927	83	155	228	30	24	-18
1915	StL-N	.916	125	232	346	53	43	-34
1916	StL-N	—	1	0	0	0	0	0
Total	5	.919	236	451	645	7	72	-58
2B								
1911	Bos-N	.769	4	5	5	3	0	-2
1912	Pit-N	.960	43	71	99	7	12	-22
1913	Pit-N	.919	28	62	74	12	9	-6
1915	StL-N	1.000	2	3	5	0	0	0
1916	StL-N	.947	8	8	10	1	3	-1
Total	5	.937	85	149	193	3	24	-31
OF								
1913	Pit-N	.000	2	0	0	1	0	0
1914	StL-N	—	1	0	0	0	0	0
1916	StL-N	.882	15	15	0	2	0	-2
Total	3	.833	18	15	0	3	0	-2
3B								
1911	Bos-N	.930	14	14	26	3	1	-1
1913	Pit-N	1.000	2	1	0	0	0	0
1916	StL-N	—	1	0	0	0	0	0
Total	3	.932	17	15	26	3	1	-1
■ Brett Butler OF								
1981	Atl-N	.987	37	76	2	1	0	0
1982	Atl-N	1.000	77	129	2	0	0	-6
1983	Atl-N	.987	143	284	13	4	4	8
1984	Cle-A	.991	156	448	13	4	3	5
1985	Cle-A	.998	150	437	19	1	5	14
1986	Cle-A	.993	159	434	9	3	3	1
1987	Cle-A	.990	136	393	4	4	2	11
1988	SF-N	.988	155	395	3	5	1	0
1989	SF-N	.986	152	407	11	6	3	6
1990	SF-N	.986	159	420	4	6	0	-3
Total	10	.990	1324	3423	80	4	21	36
■ Johnny Butler SS								
1926	Bro-N	.949	102	243	317	30	43	-5
1927	Bro-N	.959	90	214	251	20	49	-2
1928	Chi-N	.857	2	2	4	1	1	0
1929	StL-N	.973	8	17	19	1	2	1
Total	4	.954	202	476	591	6	95	-6
3B								
1926	Bro-N	.981	42	38	67	2	3	-1
1927	Bro-N	.960	60	65	105	7	7	1
1928	Chi-N	.950	59	51	120	9	9	10
1929	StL-N	.964	9	13	14	1	0	0
Total	4	.961	170	167	306	9	19	10
2B								
1926	Bro-N	.952	8	17	23	2	2	-1
■ Sammy Byrd OF								
1929	NY-A	.950	54	108	6	6	2	0
1930	NY-A	.992	85	119	2	1	0	-12
1931	NY-A	.974	88	148	3	4	1	-13
1932	NY-A	.964	91	129	4	5	1	4
1933	NY-A	.987	71	75	1	1	0	4
1934	NY-A	.988	104	156	2	2	1	-13
1935	Cin-N	.970	115	284	10	9	1	-3
1936	Cin-N	.989	37	86	1	1	1	3
Total	8	.975	645	1105	29	9	7	-30
■ Bobby Byrne 3B								
1907	StL-N	.920	148	212	348	49	24	21
1908	StL-N	.925	122	183	248	35	14	11
1909	StL-N	.922	105	164	252	35	11	16
	Pit-N	.987	46	50	107	2	3	5
	Yr	.939	151	214	359	37	14	21
1910	Pit-N	.929	148	167	289	35	11	-7
1911	Pit-N	.930	152	181	282	35	21	-3
1912	Pit-N	.948	130	144	187	18	14	-23
1913	Pit-N	.940	110	154	176	21	14	-11
	Phi-N	.963	15	20	32	2	0	3
	Yr	.943	125	174	208	23	14	-8
1914	Phi-N	.900	22	35	37	8	4	-1
1915	Phi-N	.969	105	98	183	9	9	-7
1916	Phi-N	.933	40	46	79	9	8	3
1917	Phi-N	1.000	4	2	1	0	0	-1
Total	11	.934	1147	1456	2221	258	133	6
2B								
1914	Phi-N	.934	101	187	312	35	19	-2
1917	Chi-A	1.000	1	0	1	0	0	0
Total	2	.935	102	187	313	5	19	-2
SS								
1907	StL-N	.889	1	3	5	1	0	0
1908	StL-N	.737	4	4	10	5	1	-2
Total	2	.786	5	7	15	6	1	-2
■ Milt Byrnes OF								
1943	StL-A	.997	114	289	13	1	3	3
1944	StL-A	.976	122	282	7	7	1	-15
1945	StL-A	.988	125	319	12	4	0	11
Total	3	.987	361	890	32	2	4	-1
1B								
1945	StL-A	1.000	2	14	1	0	0	0
■ Putsy Caballero 2B								
1947	Phi-N	1.000	2	3	5	0	1	0
1948	Phi-N	.921	23	40	53	8	9	-1
1949	Phi-N	.981	21	58	44	2	12	4
1950	Phi-N	.950	5	12	7	1	2	9
1951	Phi-N	.985	54	133	124	4	37	10
1952	Phi-N	.923	7	9	3	1	2	0
Total	6	.968	112	255	236	6	63	22
3B								
1944	Phi-N	.889	2	4	4	1	0	2

YEAR	TM/L	PCT	G	PO	A	E	DP	FR
1945	Phi-N	.857	5	4	2	1	1	2
1947	Phi-N	1.000	1	0	1	0	0	0
1948	Phi-N	.962	79	105	147	10	14	7
1950	Phi-N	1.000	4	1	1	0	0	1
1951	Phi-N	—	3	0	0	0	0	0
1952	Phi-N	1.000	7	8	9	0	0	1
Total	7	.960	101	122	164	2	15	13

SS

1949	Phi-N	1.000	1	2	4	0	1	1
1950	Phi-N	1.000	2	1	0	0	0	0
1951	Phi-N	—	1	0	0	0	0	0
1952	Phi-N	.857	8	7	11	3	3	1
Total	4	.893	12	10	15	3	4	2

■ Enos Cabell   3B

1973	Bal-A	—	1	0	0	0	0	0
1974	Bal-A	.929	19	5	34	3	1	4
1975	Hou-N	.985	22	23	43	1	5	0
1976	Hou-N	.958	143	128	263	17	24	-9
1977	Hou-N	.948	144	140	280	23	17	-7
1978	Hou-N	.958	153	136	274	18	15	-15
1979	Hou-N	.957	132	109	178	13	11	-24
1980	Hou-N	.927	150	118	250	29	15	-19
1981	SF-N	.854	22	14	27	7	2	-5
1982	Det-A	.925	59	44	91	11	7	-11
1983	Det-A	—	4	0	0	0	0	0
1985	LA-N	.920	32	21	71	8	6	1
1986	LA-N	.846	7	6	16	4	2	1
Total	13	.944	888	744	1527	134	105	-84

1B

1972	Bal-A	1.000	1	7	0	0	1	0
1973	Bal-A	.991	23	111	4	1	14	-1
1974	Bal-A	.995	28	173	10	1	17	0
1975	Hou-N	.976	25	75	5	2	12	0
1976	Hou-N	1.000	3	3	0	0	0	0
1977	Hou-N	.973	8	34	2	1	2	0
1978	Hou-N	1.000	14	75	3	0	4	-1
1979	Hou-N	.997	51	287	21	1	20	1
1980	Hou-N	—	1	0	0	0	0	0
1981	SF-N	.987	69	620	63	9	56	5
1982	Det-A	.992	83	548	52	5	62	3
1983	Det-A	.997	106	830	79	3	76	8
1984	Hou-N	.993	112	971	66	7	97	0
1985	Hou-N	.994	49	311	22	2	30	-1
	LA-N	.992	21	119	4	1	5	-2
	Yr	.993	70	430	26	3	35	-3
1986	LA-N	.987	61	360	32	5	29	0
Total	15	.992	655	4524	363	8	425	12

OF

1974	Bal-A	1.000	22	45	0	0	0	1
1975	Hou-N	.973	67	99	10	3	0	1
1982	Det-A	—	3	0	0	0	0	0
1985	LA-N	1.000	4	5	0	0	0	0
1986	LA-N	1.000	16	23	1	0	0	-1
Total	5	.984	112	172	11	3	0	1

SS

1977	Hou-N	1.000	1	2	6	0	0	1
1978	Hou-N	—	1	0	0	0	0	0
1983	Det-A	—	1	0	0	0	0	0
Total	3	1.000	3	2	6	0	0	1

2B

1974	Bal-A	1.000	1	0	1	0	0	0

■ Hick Cady   C

1912	Bos-A	.990	43	249	56	3	4	11
1913	Bos-A	.992	39	198	44	2	3	9
1914	Bos-A	.971	58	217	80	9	1	-3
1915	Bos-A	.980	77	313	79	8	12	-1
1916	Bos-A	.967	63	188	49	8	4	-14
1917	Bos-A	.959	14	54	17	3	2	1
1919	Phi-N	.984	29	85	35	2	2	-6
Total	7	.979	323	1304	360	5	28	-3

1B

1912	Bos-A	1.000	4	31	1	0	2	0
1916	Bos-A	1.000	3	7	2	0	0	1
Total	2	1.000	7	38	3	0	2	1

■ John Cahill   OF

1884	Col-a	.843	56	62	8	13	0	-1
1886	StL-N	.866	124	166	34	31	5	4
1887	Ind-N	.826	56	84	11	20	1	-3
Total	3	.851	236	312	53	4	6	0

3B

1886	StL-N	.000	1	0	0	2	0	-1
1887	Ind-N	.800	9	6	14	5	2	-3
Total	2	.741	10	6	14	7	2	-4

SS

1884	Col-a	.862	5	8	17	4	2	1
1886	StL-N	.333	1	0	1	2	0	-1
1887	Ind-N	1.000	1	0	1	0	0	0
Total	3	.818	7	8	19	6	2	0

■ Ivan Calderon   OF

1984	Sea-A	1.000	11	22	0	0	0	1
1985	Sea-A	.981	53	100	5	2	2	1
1986	Sea-A	.937	32	55	4	4	1	-2
	Chi-A	.900	5	9	0	1	0	0
	Yr	.932	37	64	4	5	1	-2
1987	Chi-A	.984	139	295	8	5	3	1
1988	Chi-A	.954	67	141	5	7	1	-5
1989	Chi-A	.978	103	217	8	5	3	2
1990	Chi-A	.975	130	268	7	7	1	0
Total	7	.974	540	1107	37	1	11	-2

1B

1985	Sea-A	1.000	2	8	0	0	1	0
1989	Chi-A	.978	26	167	9	4	21	-3

YEAR	TM/L	PCT	G	PO	A	E	DP	FR
1990	Chi-A	1.000	2	1	0	0	0	0
Total	3	.979	30	176	9	4	22	-3

■ Marty Callaghan   OF

1922	Chi-N	.946	53	85	2	5	0	-4
1923	Chi-N	.969	38	60	3	2	0	-1
1928	Cin-N	.980	69	140	5	3	3	-4
1930	Cin-N	.986	54	142	3	2	1	3
Total	4	.973	214	427	13	2	4	-6

■ Nixey Callahan   OF

1897	Chi-N	.889	21	40	8	6	1	3
1898	Chi-N	.800	9	10	2	3	0	-1
1899	Chi-N	1.000	9	15	0	0	0	-2
1902	Chi-A	.971	23	33	1	1	0	-3
1903	Chi-A	1.000	8	15	1	0	0	0
1904	Chi-A	.977	104	158	9	4	0	-7
1905	Chi-A	.956	93	120	10	6	0	-8
1911	Chi-A	.963	114	173	10	7	2	-9
1912	Chi-A	.939	107	166	3	11	0	-16
1913	Chi-A	1.000	1	2	0	0	0	0
Total	10	.953	489	732	44	8	3	-43

3B

1897	Chi-N	.833	2	2	3	1	1	0
1901	Chi-N	.850	6	7	10	3	2	-1
1903	Chi-A	.895	102	113	203	37	5	-7
Total	3	.892	110	122	216	1	8	-8

2B

1897	Chi-N	.918	30	65	92	14	10	-1
1898	Chi-N	.500	1	1	0	1	0	0
1899	Chi-N	1.000	1	3	4	0	1	0
1901	Chi-N	.500	2	1	0	1	0	-1
1904	Chi-A	.922	28	49	70	10	5	-10
Total	5	.916	62	119	166	6	16	-12

SS

1897	Chi-N	.849	18	26	53	14	9	2
1898	Chi-N	.714	1	3	2	2	0	-1
1899	Chi-N	.800	2	4	4	2	1	-1
1902	Chi-A	1.000	1	3	1	0	0	0
Total	4	.842	22	36	60	8	10	0

1B

1898	Chi-N	1.000	1	1	0	0	0	0

■ Johnny Callison   OF

1958	Chi-A	.976	18	39	2	1	1	1
1959	Chi-A	.983	41	54	3	1	0	0
1960	Phi-N	.989	86	176	7	2	4	4
1961	Phi-N	.967	124	227	10	8	2	1
1962	Phi-N	.980	152	327	24	7	7	25
1963	Phi-N	.994	157	298	26	2	4	21
1964	Phi-N	.988	162	319	19	4	3	18
1965	Phi-N	.982	159	313	21	6	2	18
1966	Phi-N	.990	154	275	12	3	2	5
1967	Phi-N	.977	147	286	12	7	1	8
1968	Phi-N	1.000	109	187	10	0	1	2
1969	Phi-N	.990	129	273	12	3	3	14
1970	Chi-N	.973	144	244	8	7	3	-2
1971	Chi-N	.982	89	158	3	3	0	-4
1972	NY-A	.992	74	127	4	1	1	-4
1973	NY-A	.960	32	46	2	2	0	1
Total	16	.984	1777	3349	175	7	34	108

■ Hank Camelli   C

1943	Pit-N	1.000	1	4	1	0	0	0
1944	Pit-N	.959	61	170	16	8	0	3
1945	Pit-N	1.000	1	4	0	0	0	0
1946	Pit-N	.971	39	117	18	4	2	4
1947	Bos-N	.977	51	194	20	5	3	6
Total	5	.970	153	489	55	7	5	13

■ Dolph Camilli   1B

1933	Chi-N	.994	16	163	14	1	21	2
1934	Chi-N	.988	32	294	24	4	25	2
	Phi-N	.985	102	882	55	14	77	-4
	Yr	.986	134	1176	79	18	102	-2
1935	Phi-N	.987	156	1442	96	20	118	-1
1936	Phi-N	.988	150	1446	79	18	122	-10
1937	Phi-N	.994	131	1256	99	8	104	4
1938	Bro-N	.995	145	1356	95	8	129	-1
1939	Bro-N	.990	157	1515	129	17	138	10
1940	Bro-N	.992	140	1299	79	11	85	-4
1941	Bro-N	.989	148	1379	98	16	107	3
1942	Bro-N	.992	150	1334	85	12	123	-1
1943	Bro-N	.992	95	853	60	7	78	0
1945	Bos-A	.991	54	505	44	5	62	2
Total	12	.990	1476	13724	957	141	1189	2

■ Doug Camilli   C

1960	LA-N	.980	6	46	3	1	1	0
1961	LA-N	.986	12	64	5	1	1	2
1962	LA-N	.983	39	162	8	3	1	-5
1963	LA-N	.977	47	285	15	7	1	8
1964	LA-N	.990	46	266	19	3	0	8
1965	Was-A	.980	59	319	23	7	2	1
1966	Was-A	.990	39	180	21	2	2	4
1967	Was-A	.993	24	128	10	1	2	0
1969	Was-A	1.000	1	2	1	0	0	0
Total	9	.984	273	1452	105	5	10	18

■ Ken Caminiti   3B

1987	Hou-N	.949	61	50	98	8	11	3
1988	Hou-N	.948	28	12	43	3	2	0
1989	Hou-N	.954	160	126	335	22	27	13
1990	Hou-N	.945	149	118	243	21	22	-11
Total	4	.950	398	306	719	4	62	5

■ Roy Campanella   C

1948	Bro-N	.981	78	413	45	9	12	9
1949	Bro-N	.985	127	684	55	11	5	4

YEAR	TM/L	PCT	G	PO	A	E	DP	FR
1950	Bro-N	.985	123	683	54	11	14	-5
1951	Bro-N	.986	140	722	72	11	12	7
1952	Bro-N	.994	122	662	55	4	7	-7
1953	Bro-N	.989	140	807	57	10	9	1
1954	Bro-N	.989	111	600	58	7	7	-3
1955	Bro-N	.992	121	672	54	6	8	0
1956	Bro-N	.985	121	659	49	11	3	3
1957	Bro-N	.993	100	618	51	5	5	16
Total	10	.988	1183	6520	550	5	82	25

■ Bert Campaneris   SS

1964	KC-A	.981	38	58	94	3	14	-5
1965	KC-A	.938	109	187	269	30	50	-16
1966	KC-A	.971	138	283	350	19	80	-16
1967	KC-A	.954	145	259	365	30	75	-19
1968	Oak-A	.956	155	279	458	34	86	2
1969	Oak-A	.967	125	220	391	21	72	-5
1970	Oak-A	.973	143	267	414	19	92	-9
1971	Oak-A	.960	133	231	399	26	85	-5
1972	Oak-A	.977	148	283	494	18	93	7
1973	Oak-A	.969	149	228	496	23	87	-7
1974	Oak-A	.966	133	207	423	22	76	-9
1975	Oak-A	.962	137	199	378	23	58	-31
1976	Oak-A	.969	149	231	490	23	66	-6
1977	Tex-A	.968	149	269	483	25	91	18
1978	Tex-A	.954	89	151	263	20	44	4
1979	Tex-A	.962	8	12	13	1	5	4
	Cal-A	.957	82	136	220	16	69	-5
	Yr	.957	90	148	233	17	74	8
1980	Cal-A	.957	64	108	157	12	41	-5
1981	Cal-A	1.000	3	0	3	0	2	1
Total	18	.964	2097	3608	6160	365	1186	-93

3B

1964	KC-A	.850	6	5	12	3	2	0
1965	KC-A	—	1	0	0	0	0	0
1981	Cal-A	.900	45	10	44	6	5	-3
1983	NY-A	.932	24	12	29	3	1	-2
Total	4	.903	76	27	85	2	8	-5

OF

1964	KC-A	.953	27	39	2	2	0	-2
1965	KC-A	.936	39	68	5	5	3	0
1968	Oak-A	1.000	3	4	0	0	0	0
Total	3	.944	69	111	7	7	3	-2

2B

1965	KC-A	1.000	1	0	1	0	0	0
1980	Cal-A	—	1	0	0	0	0	0
1981	Cal-A	1.000	2	0	2	0	0	0
1983	NY-A	.964	32	40	67	4	18	-1
Total	4	.965	36	40	70	4	18	-1

1B

1965	KC-A	1.000	1	1	0	0	0	0

C

1965	KC-A	1.000	1	2	1	0	0	0

■ Count Campau   OF

1888	Det-N	.933	70	101	10	8	3	-4
1890	StL-a	.934	74	113	14	9	1	3
1894	Was-N	1.000	2	4	0	0	0	0
Total	3	.934	146	218	24	7	4	-1

3B

1890	StL-a	1.000	1	0	2	0	0	0

1B

1890	StL-a	1.000	1	5	0	0	0	0

■ Vin Campbell   OF

1910	Pit-N	.895	74	145	8	18	2	-5
1911	Pit-N	.923	21	35	1	3	0	-2
1912	Bos-N	.938	144	340	20	24	6	-1
1914	Ind-F	.925	132	218	18	19	6	-5
1915	New-F	.947	126	200	15	12	3	-5
Total	5	.929	497	938	62	6	17	-18

■ Bruce Campbell   OF

1930	Chi-A	1.000	4	8	0	0	0	0
1931	Chi-A	.900	4	9	0	1	0	0
1932	Chi-A	1.000	4	5	0	0	0	-1
	StL-A	.935	139	301	13	22	4	1
	Yr	.935	143	306	13	22	4	0
1933	StL-A	.950	144	250	18	14	4	-7
1934	StL-A	.935	123	230	14	17	3	-1
1935	Cle-A	.992	75	129	2	1	1	-11
1936	Cle-A	.960	47	68	4	3	2	-2
1937	Cle-A	.978	123	204	14	5	5	-4
1938	Cle-A	.967	122	220	13	8	3	0
1939	Cle-A	.942	115	200	12	13	3	-6
1940	Det-A	.959	74	133	6	6	0	-4
1941	Det-A	.976	133	241	5	6	1	-11
1942	Was-A	.955	87	188	4	9	1	-1
Total	13	.956	1194	2186	105	105	27	-47

■ Dave Campbell   2B

1968	Det-A	1.000	5	4	3	0	1	0
1969	Det-A	.944	5	10	7	1	1	-1
1970	SD-N	.974	153	359	455	22	96	12
1971	SD-N	.968	69	136	200	11	42	0
1972	SD-N	1.000	1	4	3	0	0	0
1973	SD-N	.979	27	68	73	3	18	-1
	StL-N	.933	6	6	8	1	1	-3
	Yr	.975	33	74	81	4	19	-4
1974	Hou-N	.895	9	8	9	2	4	4
Total	7	.971	275	595	758	0	163	11

3B

1969	Det-A	1.000	1	0	1	0	0	0
1971	SD-N	.935	40	33	54	6	6	-2
1972	SD-N	.988	31	21	64	1	3	4
1973	SD-N	.800	2	1	3	1	1	0
	Hou-N	1.000	5	2	12	0	1	2

YEAR	TM/L	PCT	G	PO	A	E	DP	FR
	Yr	.947	7	3	15	1	2	2
1974	Hou-N	1.000	2	0	8	0	0	2
Total	5	.961	81	57	142	8	11	6
1B								
1967	Det-A	.500	1	1	0	1	0	0
1969	Det-A	.967	13	28	1	1	4	-1
1971	SD-N	1.000	2	7	2	0	2	1
1973	SD-N	1.000	3	10	0	0	0	0
	Hou-N	1.000	2	1	0	0	1	0
	Yr	1.000	5	11	0	0	1	0
1974	Hou-N	1.000	6	12	0	0	1	0
Total	5	.969	27	59	3	2	8	0
SS								
1971	SD-N	.900	4	1	8	1	0	0
OF								
1971	SD-N	1.000	2	2	0	0	0	0
1973	Hou-N	—	1	0	0	0	0	0
1974	Hou-N	—	1	0	0	0	0	0
Total	3	1.000	4	2	0	0	0	0

■ Paul Campbell 1B

YEAR	TM/L	PCT	G	PO	A	E	DP	FR
1946	Bos-A	1.000	5	34	1	0	2	0
1948	Det-A	.969	27	172	18	6	11	3
1949	Det-A	.988	74	561	38	7	67	-3
Total	3	.984	106	767	57	3	80	0
OF								
1942	Bos-A	1.000	4	1	0	0	0	1

■ Gilly Campbell C

YEAR	TM/L	PCT	G	PO	A	E	DP	FR
1933	Chi-N	.949	20	66	9	4	1	-2
1935	Cin-N	.986	66	238	36	4	1	1
1936	Cin-N	.984	71	257	49	5	9	6
1937	Cin-N	.967	17	51	7	2	0	0
1938	Bro-N	.958	44	139	22	7	2	0
Total	5	.975	218	751	123	2	13	5
1B								
1935	Cin-N	1.000	5	37	1	0	3	0
1936	Cin-N	1.000	1	3	0	0	2	0
Total	2	1.000	6	40	1	0	5	0
OF								
1935	Cin-N	1.000	1	3	0	0	0	0

■ Sil Campusano OF

YEAR	TM/L	PCT	G	PO	A	E	DP	FR
1988	Tor-A	.934	69	111	2	8	0	3
1990	Phi-N	.976	47	40	1	1	0	-1
Total	2	.945	116	151	3	9	0	2

■ Jim Canavan OF

YEAR	TM/L	PCT	G	PO	A	E	DP	FR
1892	Chi-N	1.000	4	6	1	0	0	0
1893	Cin-N	.931	117	243	15	19	0	-2
1894	Cin-N	.904	95	188	9	21	6	-3
Total	3	.920	216	437	25	0	6	-5
2B								
1891	Mil-a	.864	24	51	76	20	4	-1
1892	Chi-N	.923	112	282	349	53	40	-2
1893	Cin-N	.938	5	12	18	2	0	1
1894	Cin-N	.714	1	4	6	4	1	1
1897	Bro-N	.909	63	157	162	32	18	-21
Total	5	.910	205	506	611	111	63	-22
SS								
1891	Cin-a	.860	101	217	304	85	31	-11
	Mil-a	.860	11	14	35	8	1	-1
	Yr	.860	112	231	339	93	32	-12
1892	Chi-N	.917	2	6	5	1	1	0
1894	Cin-N	1.000	3	2	13	0	0	1
Total	3	.864	117	239	357	4	33	-11
3B								
1893	Cin-N	—	1	0	0	0	0	0
1894	Cin-N	1.000	2	2	1	0	0	0
Total	2	1.000	3	2	1	0	0	0
1B								
1894	Cin-N	.818	1	9	0	2	1	-1

■ Casey Candaele 2B

YEAR	TM/L	PCT	G	PO	A	E	DP	FR
1986	Mon-N	.983	24	44	73	2	13	-1
1987	Mon-N	.985	68	76	125	3	18	0
1988	Mon-N	.988	35	62	102	2	17	1
	Hou-N	1.000	10	16	24	0	4	3
	Yr	.990	45	78	126	2	21	4
1990	Hou-N	.989	49	75	107	2	18	-1
Total	6	.987	186	273	431	9	70	2
OF								
1987	Mon-N	.985	67	132	3	2	0	2
1988	Hou-N	1.000	5	1	0	0	0	0
1990	Hou-N	1.000	58	66	1	0	0	1
Total	3	.990	130	199	4	2	0	3
SS								
1987	Mon-N	.962	25	28	48	3	10	-1
1990	Hou-N	.944	13	6	11	1	2	-1
Total	2	.959	38	34	59	4	12	-2
3B								
1986	Mon-N	1.000	4	1	1	0	0	0
1988	Hou-N	—	1	0	0	0	0	0
1990	Hou-N	1.000	1	0	1	0	0	0
Total	3	1.000	6	1	2	0	0	0
1B								
1987	Mon-N	1.000	1	1	0	0	0	0

■ John Cangelosi OF

YEAR	TM/L	PCT	G	PO	A	E	DP	FR
1985	Chi-A	1.000	3	1	0	0	0	0
1986	Chi-A	.969	129	276	7	9	1	1
1987	Pit-N	.962	47	74	3	3	0	-2
1988	Pit-N	.963	24	52	0	2	0	0
1989	Pit-N	.973	46	71	1	2	0	-1
1990	Pit-N	1.000	12	24	0	0	0	-1
Total	6	.970	261	498	11	6	1	-3

■ Rip Cannell OF

YEAR	TM/L	PCT	G	PO	A	E	DP	FR
1904	Bos-N	.897	93	135	5	16	1	-11
1905	Bos-N	.935	154	315	14	23	6	-8
Total	2	.923	247	450	19	9	7	-19

■ Chris Cannizzaro C

YEAR	TM/L	PCT	G	PO	A	E	DP	FR
1960	StL-N	1.000	6	19	3	0	1	1
1961	StL-N	1.000	5	5	0	0	0	1
1962	NY-N	.973	56	218	34	7	3	3
1963	NY-N	1.000	15	49	6	0	0	-1
1964	NY-N	.988	53	225	28	3	6	2
1965	NY-N	.977	112	435	69	12	8	11
1968	Pit-N	.976	25	111	10	3	1	-1
1969	SD-N	.988	132	644	69	9	8	-14
1970	SD-N	.980	110	559	44	12	5	-18
1971	SD-N	.992	19	114	6	1	2	-2
	Chi-N	.983	70	311	26	6	2	-11
	Yr	.985	89	425	32	7	4	-13
1972	LA-N	.983	72	312	26	6	4	-8
1973	LA-N	1.000	13	33	0	0	0	0
1974	SD-N	.979	26	126	12	3	2	5
Total	13	.983	714	3161	333	2	42	-32
OF								
1962	NY-N	1.000	1	1	0	0	0	0

■ Jose Canseco OF

YEAR	TM/L	PCT	G	PO	A	E	DP	FR
1985	Oak-A	.951	26	56	2	3	1	0
1986	Oak-A	.958	155	319	4	14	1	-4
1987	Oak-A	.975	130	263	12	7	3	6
1988	Oak-A	.975	144	304	11	7	3	4
1989	Oak-A	.956	56	119	5	3	2	-1
1990	Oak-A	.995	88	182	7	1	2	-2
Total	6	.973	599	1243	41	5	12	3

■ Bernie Carbo OF

YEAR	TM/L	PCT	G	PO	A	E	DP	FR
1970	Cin-N	.979	119	177	8	4	2	-8
1971	Cin-N	.982	90	154	7	3	0	-6
1972	Cin-N	1.000	4	9	0	0	0	0
	StL-N	.967	92	162	15	6	3	3
	Yr	.969	96	171	15	6	3	3
1973	StL-N	.978	94	171	11	4	3	2
1974	Bos-A	.994	87	164	5	1	1	-4
1975	Bos-A	.976	85	157	7	4	1	-5
1976	Bos-A	1.000	1	1	0	0	0	0
	Mil-A	1.000	33	71	5	0	1	2
	Yr	1.000	34	72	5	0	1	2
1977	Bos-A	.951	67	131	5	7	1	-1
1978	Bos-A	1.000	9	26	0	0	0	1
	Cle-A	1.000	4	1	0	0	0	0
	Yr	1.000	13	27	0	0	0	1
1979	StL-N	1.000	17	10	0	0	0	-3
Total	10	.978	702	1234	63	9	12	-19
3B								
1972	StL-N	1.000	1	0	1	0	0	0

■ Jose Cardenal OF

YEAR	TM/L	PCT	G	PO	A	E	DP	FR
1963	SF-N	—	2	0	0	0	0	0
1964	SF-N	.909	16	8	2	1	0	2
1965	Cal-A	.964	129	286	12	11	2	6
1966	Cal-A	.992	146	351	10	3	4	8
1967	Cal-A	.986	101	195	10	3	0	-1
1968	Cle-A	.974	153	367	12	10	7	8
1969	Cle-A	.982	142	327	9	6	2	4
1970	StL-N	.969	134	276	6	9	0	-5
1971	StL-N	.969	83	181	9	6	1	7
	Mil-A	.979	52	133	6	3	0	6
1972	Chi-N	.971	137	223	11	7	1	-5
1973	Chi-N	.980	142	234	13	5	2	-4
1974	Chi-N	.965	137	262	15	10	4	5
1975	Chi-N	.975	151	313	14	8	3	10
1976	Chi-N	.981	128	246	10	5	1	0
1977	Chi-N	.989	62	85	1	1	0	-7
1978	Phi-N	.833	13	5	0	1	0	-1
1979	Phi-N	1.000	12	14	0	0	0	-2
	NY-N	1.000	9	17	0	0	0	-1
	Yr	1.000	21	31	0	0	0	-3
1980	NY-N	1.000	6	12	1	0	0	0
	KC-A	.970	23	30	2	1	0	-1
Total	18	.976	1778	3565	143	0	27	29
1B								
1978	Phi-N	.990	50	360	17	4	39	-4
1979	Phi-N	1.000	2	2	0	0	0	0
	NY-N	1.000	2	16	0	0	3	-1
	Yr	1.000	3	18	0	0	3	-1
1980	NY-N	1.000	5	18	0	0	1	-1
Total	3	.990	58	396	17	4	43	-6
3B								
1965	Cal-A	1.000	2	1	1	0	0	0
1969	Cle-A	1.000	5	2	3	0	0	0
Total	2	1.000	7	3	4	0	0	0
2B								
1965	Cal-A	—	1	0	0	0	0	0
1977	Chi-N	.000	1	0	0	1	0	-1
Total	2	.000	2	0	0	1	0	-1
SS								
1977	Chi-N	—	1	0	0	0	0	0

■ Leo Cardenas SS

YEAR	TM/L	PCT	G	PO	A	E	DP	FR
1960	Cin-N	.958	47	76	128	9	32	7
1961	Cin-N	.973	63	83	133	6	21	-5
1962	Cin-N	.972	149	273	443	21	84	-7
1963	Cin-N	.972	157	270	420	20	84	4
1964	Cin-N	.960	163	336	436	32	87	-10
1965	Cin-N	.975	155	292	440	19	92	-1
1966	Cin-N	.980	160	279	446	15	87	-15
1967	Cin-N	.971	108	190	316	15	57	-10
1968	Cin-N	.955	136	221	388	29	66	-23
1969	Min-A	.965	160	310	570	32	126	33
1970	Min-A	.978	160	280	487	17	91	0
1971	Min-A	.985	153	266	445	11	89	0
1972	Cal-A	.970	150	241	471	22	82	3
1973	Cle-A	.964	67	87	154	9	33	-10
1974	Tex-A	.933	10	9	19	2	2	0
1975	Tex-A	1.000	5	5	7	0	3	2

YEAR	TM/L	PCT	G	PO	A	E	DP	FR
Total	16	.971	1843	3218	5303	259	1036	-36
3B								
1973	Cle-A	.889	5	3	13	2	4	2
1974	Tex-A	1.000	21	17	35	0	1	2
1975	Tex-A	.956	43	32	76	5	9	9
Total	3	.962	69	52	124	7	14	13
2B								
1975	Tex-A	1.000	3	1	2	0	0	0

■ Rod Carew 1B

YEAR	TM/L	PCT	G	PO	A	E	DP	FR
1974	Min-A	1.000	1	6	0	0	0	0
1975	Min-A	.978	14	123	8	3	10	-1
1976	Min-A	.989	152	1394	108	16	149	-1
1977	Min-A	.994	151	1459	121	10	161	7
1978	Min-A	.989	148	1362	105	16	134	2
1979	Cal-A	.988	103	804	55	10	101	-7
1980	Cal-A	.994	103	897	76	6	82	-4
1981	Cal-A	.995	90	877	60	5	90	-1
1982	Cal-A	.992	134	1339	94	12	115	1
1983	Cal-A	.994	89	890	42	6	94	-9
1984	Cal-A	.981	83	724	59	15	73	-4
1985	Cal-A	.994	116	1055	65	7	121	-8
Total	12	.991	1184	10930	774	106	1130	-25
2B								
1967	Min-A	.976	134	289	314	15	60	-10
1968	Min-A	.968	117	262	280	18	48	-13
1969	Min-A	.970	118	244	302	17	80	-17
1970	Min-A	.961	45	73	122	8	26	-11
1971	Min-A	.976	142	321	329	16	76	-25
1972	Min-A	.984	139	331	378	16	85	0
1973	Min-A	.984	147	383	413	13	96	7
1974	Min-A	.967	148	375	416	33	114	9
1975	Min-A	.973	123	285	369	18	79	2
1976	Min-A	1.000	7	4	2	0	0	-1
1977	Min-A	1.000	4	4	3	0	0	-1
1978	Min-A	1.000	4	1	0	0	0	0
1983	Cal-A	1.000	2	1	0	0	0	0
Total	13	.973	1130	2573	2928	154	664	-60
SS								
1968	Min-A	1.000	4	4	5	0	2	-1
3B								
1971	Min-A	1.000	2	3	2	0	0	-1
OF								
1978	Min-A	—	1	0	0	0	0	0

■ Andy Carey 3B

YEAR	TM/L	PCT	G	PO	A	E	DP	FR
1952	NY-A	.889	14	11	21	4	4	0
1953	NY-A	.988	40	29	55	1	8	9
1954	NY-A	.967	120	154	283	15	32	17
1955	NY-A	.954	135	154	301	22	37	14
1956	NY-A	.947	131	114	265	21	26	-3
1957	NY-A	.977	81	66	147	5	9	3
1958	NY-A	.961	99	99	195	12	22	10
1959	NY-A	.916	34	39	48	8	10	2
1960	NY-A	1.000	2	0	1	0	0	0
	KC-A	.975	91	95	179	7	26	0
	Yr	.975	93	95	180	7	26	0
1961	KC-A	.944	39	32	70	6	12	-1
	Chi-A	.961	54	26	73	4	4	-5
	Yr	.953	93	58	143	10	16	-6
1962	LA-N	.932	42	28	54	6	4	1
Total	11	.958	882	847	1692	111	194	47
SS								
1952	NY-A	.667	1	2	2	0	0	-1
1953	NY-A	.500	2	0	1	1	0	0
Total	2	.625	3	2	3	3	0	-1
2B								
1953	NY-A	1.000	1	5	0	0	0	0
OF								
1960	NY-A	—	1	0	0	0	0	0

■ Scoops Carey 1B

YEAR	TM/L	PCT	G	PO	A	E	DP	FR
1895	Bal-N	.987	123	1132	43	15	73	-7
1898	Lou-N	.961	8	94	5	4	5	0
1902	Was-A	.989	120	1190	69	14	54	0
1903	Was-A	.977	47	435	23	11	18	-3
Total	4	.986	298	2851	140	4	150	-6
OF								
1895	Bal-N	1.000	1	4	0	0	0	0
SS								
1895	Bal-N	1.000	1	1	2	0	0	0
3B								
1895	Bal-N	1.000	1	0	1	0	0	0

■ Max Carey OF

YEAR	TM/L	PCT	G	PO	A	E	DP	FR
1910	Pit-N	1.000	2	10	1	0	0	2
1911	Pit-N	.975	122	304	11	8	5	0
1912	Pit-N	.968	150	369	19	13	10	14
1913	Pit-N	.961	154	363	28	16	6	20
1914	Pit-N	.966	154	318	23	12	3	5
1915	Pit-N	.982	139	307	21	6	5	18
1916	Pit-N	.983	154	419	32	8	10	23
1917	Pit-N	.979	153	440	28	10	8	20
1918	Pit-N	.958	126	359	25	17	9	13
1919	Pit-N	.947	63	173	5	10	1	4
1920	Pit-N	.967	129	345	10	12	0	-3
1921	Pit-N	.957	139	431	15	20	6	10
1922	Pit-N	.969	155	449	22	15	4	15
1923	Pit-N	.962	153	450	28	19	4	15
1924	Pit-N	.965	149	428	16	16	3	0
1925	Pit-N	.950	130	363	20	20	2	7
1926	Pit-N	.943	82	225	8	14	3	3
	Bro-N	.933	27	70	0	5	0	-1
	Yr	.941	109	295	8	19	3	2
1927	Bro-N	.970	141	331	19	11	6	12
1928	Bro-N	.986	95	202	8	3	1	-9
1929	Bro-N	1.000	1	7	0	0	0	0
Total	20	.966	2421	6363	339	235	86	174

Tom Carey 2B

YEAR	TM/L	PCT	G	PO	A	E	DP	FR
1935	StL-A	.961	76	189	253	18	52	-1
1936	StL-A	.967	128	308	434	25	82	-1
1937	StL-A	.983	87	202	253	8	58	-3
1939	Bos-A	1.000	35	75	87	0	19	6
1940	Bos-A	1.000	4	3	8	0	2	-1
1941	Bos-A	1.000	9	10	8	0	3	2
1942	Bos-A	1.000	1	1	0	0	0	0
1946	Bos-A	.900	3	3	6	1	2	1
Total	8	.973	343	791	1049	2	218	3

SS

YEAR	TM/L	PCT	G	PO	A	E	DP	FR
1936	StL-A	1.000	1	0	1	0	0	0
1937	StL-A	.971	44	91	144	7	25	6
1939	Bos-A	.959	10	18	29	2	3	0
1940	Bos-A	.953	20	21	40	3	12	6
1941	Bos-A	1.000	8	4	6	0	0	1
Total	5	.967	83	134	220	2	40	13

3B

YEAR	TM/L	PCT	G	PO	A	E	DP	FR
1937	StL-A	—	1	0	0	0	0	0
1940	Bos-A	1.000	4	0	1	0	0	0
1941	Bos-A	1.000	1	1	1	0	0	0
Total	3	1.000	6	1	2	0	0	0

Tom Carey SS

YEAR	TM/L	PCT	G	PO	A	E	DP	FR
1876	Har-N	.882	68	74	218	39	9	-1
1877	Har-N	.826	60	49	203	53	11	-6
1878	Pro-N	.874	61	56	207	38	8	1
1879	Cle-N	.864	80	79	263	54	13	-3
Total	4	.862	269	258	891	184	41	-9

Fred Carisch C

YEAR	TM/L	PCT	G	PO	A	E	DP	FR
1903	Pit-N	.969	4	24	7	1	0	1
1904	Pit-N	.984	22	89	32	2	4	1
1905	Pit-N	.973	30	137	42	5	3	1
1906	Pit-N	.909	4	15	5	2	0	0
1912	Cle-A	.952	23	100	40	7	5	6
1913	Cle-A	.971	79	391	114	15	10	13
1914	Cle-A	.962	38	183	44	9	5	0
1923	Det-A	1.000	2	1	0	0	0	0
Total	8	.968	202	940	284	1	27	22

1B

YEAR	TM/L	PCT	G	PO	A	E	DP	FR
1904	Pit-N	.982	14	148	12	3	2	1

Roy Carlyle OF

YEAR	TM/L	PCT	G	PO	A	E	DP	FR
1925	Bos-A	.909	67	125	5	13	0	-6
1926	Bos-A	.904	38	62	4	7	0	-4
	NY-A	.941	15	15	1	1	0	-3
	Yr	.911	53	77	5	8	0	-7
Total	2	.910	120	202	10	1	0	-13

Eddie Carnett OF

YEAR	TM/L	PCT	G	PO	A	E	DP	FR
1944	Chi-A	.949	88	197	7	11	0	1
1945	Cle-A	.971	16	33	1	1	1	0
Total	2	.952	104	230	8	2	1	1

1B

YEAR	TM/L	PCT	G	PO	A	E	DP	FR
1944	Chi-A	.996	25	226	9	1	16	-2

John Carney 1B

YEAR	TM/L	PCT	G	PO	A	E	DP	FR
1889	Was-N	.957	53	521	16	24	29	-5
1890	Buf-P	.972	24	232	9	7	17	-1
	Cle-P	.956	6	42	1	2	5	-1
	Yr	.969	30	274	10	9	22	-2
1891	Cin-a	.974	99	984	45	28	42	1
	Mil-a	.986	31	324	20	5	16	4
	Yr	.977	130	1308	65	33	58	5
Total	3	.971	213	2103	91	6	109	-2

OF

YEAR	TM/L	PCT	G	PO	A	E	DP	FR
1889	Was-N	.786	16	20	2	6	1	-2
1890	Buf-P	.500	4	1	1	2	0	-1
	Cle-P	.857	19	21	3	4	0	-3
	Yr	.813	23	22	4	6	0	-4
Total	2	.800	39	42	6	2	1	-6

Pat Carney OF

YEAR	TM/L	PCT	G	PO	A	E	DP	FR
1901	Bos-N	.933	13	14	0	1	0	-3
1902	Bos-N	.930	137	153	19	13	7	-8
1903	Bos-N	.953	92	112	10	6	4	-6
1904	Bos-N	.953	71	89	12	5	5	-2
Total	4	.942	313	368	41	5	16	-19

1B

YEAR	TM/L	PCT	G	PO	A	E	DP	FR
1903	Bos-N	—	1	0	0	0	0	0
1904	Bos-N	1.000	1	3	0	0	0	0
Total	2	1.000	2	3	0	0	0	0

Hick Carpenter 3B

YEAR	TM/L	PCT	G	PO	A	E	DP	FR
1879	Syr-N	.861	18	35	27	10	0	-4
1880	Cin-N	.853	67	136	126	45	9	1
1881	Wor-N	.848	83	141	172	56	14	3
1882	Cin-a	.835	80	137	167	60	7	-1
1883	Cin-a	.870	95	133	181	47	6	-6
1884	Cin-a	.881	108	157	168	44	16	-9
1885	Cin-a	.860	112	153	191	56	17	-6
1886	Cin-a	.841	111	127	221	66	23	-6
1887	Cin-a	.846	127	144	242	70	17	-13
1888	Cin-a	.866	136	142	286	66	15	-12
1889	Cin-a	.835	121	143	207	69	18	-25
1892	StL-N	.714	1	2	3	2	0	0
Total	12	.853	1059	1450	1991	591	142	-78

1B

YEAR	TM/L	PCT	G	PO	A	E	DP	FR
1879	Syr-N	.948	34	298	10	17	12	1
1880	Cin-N	.936	9	72	1	5	0	-1
1889	Cin-a	1.000	2	18	1	0	1	0
Total	3	.948	45	388	12	2	13	0

OF

YEAR	TM/L	PCT	G	PO	A	E	DP	FR
1879	Syr-N	.781	11	19	6	7	0	2
1884	Cin-a	—	1	0	0	0	0	0
Total	2	.781	12	19	6	7	0	2

2B

YEAR	TM/L	PCT	G	PO	A	E	DP	FR
1879	Syr-N	.643	3	3	6	5	0	-3

SS

YEAR	TM/L	PCT	G	PO	A	E	DP	FR
1880	Cin-N	1.000	1	5	1	0	0	-1

Charlie Carr 1B

YEAR	TM/L	PCT	G	PO	A	E	DP	FR
1898	Was-N	.950	20	200	8	11	15	-2
1901	Phi-N	.926	2	23	2	2	0	0
1903	Det-N	.982	135	1276	111	25	60	12
1904	Det-N	.983	92	901	99	17	46	16
	Cle-N	.973	32	332	22	10	13	0
	Yr	.980	124	1233	121	27	59	16
1905	Cle-N	.991	87	940	50	9	33	-2
1906	Cin-N	.983	22	221	16	4	16	1
1914	Ind-F	.991	115	1088	59	11	67	1
Total	7	.984	505	4981	367	9	250	26

Chico Carrasquel SS

YEAR	TM/L	PCT	G	PO	A	E	DP	FR
1950	Chi-A	.961	141	234	458	28	113	11
1951	Chi-A	.975	147	300	477	20	107	12
1952	Chi-A	.964	99	176	248	16	50	-16
1953	Chi-A	.976	149	278	462	18	87	3
1954	Chi-A	.975	155	280	492	20	102	11
1955	Chi-A	.973	144	222	424	18	81	0
1956	Cle-A	.967	141	240	352	20	70	-25
1957	Cle-A	.960	122	212	357	24	75	-5
1958	Cle-A	.931	32	41	67	8	16	-18
	KC-A	.972	22	24	45	2	6	-5
	Yr	.947	54	65	112	10	22	-23
1959	Bal-N	.970	89	124	237	11	63	-10
Total	10	.969	1241	2131	3619	185	770	-42

3B

YEAR	TM/L	PCT	G	PO	A	E	DP	FR
1956	Cle-A	1.000	1	0	2	0	0	0
1958	Cle-A	1.000	14	13	17	0	1	-1
	KC-A	.976	32	29	52	2	10	-1
	Yr	.982	46	42	69	2	11	-2
1959	Bal-N	1.000	2	1	1	0	0	0
Total	3	.983	49	43	72	2	11	-2

2B

YEAR	TM/L	PCT	G	PO	A	E	DP	FR
1959	Bal-N	.984	22	29	33	1	4	-3

1B

YEAR	TM/L	PCT	G	PO	A	E	DP	FR
1959	Bal-N	.750	1	3	0	1	1	0

Cam Carreon C

YEAR	TM/L	PCT	G	PO	A	E	DP	FR
1959	Chi-A	1.000	1	3	0	0	0	0
1960	Chi-A	1.000	7	22	2	0	0	0
1961	Chi-A	.995	71	395	25	2	6	8
1962	Chi-A	.995	93	519	30	3	5	8
1963	Chi-A	.987	92	429	36	6	7	0
1964	Cle-A	.987	34	134	13	2	2	-4
1965	Cle-A	1.000	19	122	9	0	1	1
1966	Bal-A	1.000	3	24	0	0	0	0
Total	8	.993	320	1648	115	3	21	13

Mark Carreon OF

YEAR	TM/L	PCT	G	PO	A	E	DP	FR
1987	NY-N	.800	5	4	0	1	0	0
1988	NY-N	1.000	4	1	0	0	0	-1
1989	NY-N	.983	39	57	0	1	0	-1
1990	NY-N	1.000	60	87	1	0	0	-1
Total	4	.987	108	149	1	2	0	-3

Bill Carrigan C

YEAR	TM/L	PCT	G	PO	A	E	DP	FR
1906	Bos-A	.940	35	139	48	12	2	-1
1908	Bos-A	.955	47	203	74	13	5	6
1909	Bos-A	.972	77	347	110	13	9	1
1910	Bos-A	.962	110	495	134	25	12	-19
1911	Bos-A	.972	62	326	94	12	11	-1
1912	Bos-A	.970	87	413	102	16	7	-12
1913	Bos-A	.979	82	383	127	11	8	-8
1914	Bos-A	.984	78	350	84	7	8	3
1915	Bos-A	.945	44	183	54	6	3	9
1916	Bos-A	1.000	27	122	27	0	1	6
Total	10	.971	649	2961	854	115	66	-18

1B

YEAR	TM/L	PCT	G	PO	A	E	DP	FR
1908	Bos-A	1.000	3	20	1	0	1	0
1909	Bos-A	1.000	8	64	8	0	5	2
1911	Bos-A	.980	6	48	0	1	2	-1
Total	3	.993	17	132	9	1	8	1

Fred Carroll C

YEAR	TM/L	PCT	G	PO	A	E	DP	FR
1884	Col-a	.944	54	379	89	28	3	14
1885	Pit-a	.926	60	328	99	34	3	4
1886	Pit-a	.921	70	435	87	45	8	10
1887	Pit-N	.886	40	176	33	27	3	-10
1888	Pit-N	.897	54	269	61	38	9	-2
1889	Pit-N	.930	43	161	51	16	2	-6
1890	Pit-P	.856	56	206	50	43	1	-14
Total	7	.913	377	1954	470	231	29	-4

OF

YEAR	TM/L	PCT	G	PO	A	E	DP	FR
1884	Col-a	.769	15	27	3	9	0	1
1885	Pit-a	.821	12	20	3	5	0	1
1886	Pit-a	.838	27	52	5	11	1	1
1887	Pit-N	.833	40	96	9	21	0	-4
1888	Pit-N	.825	38	45	2	10	1	-7
1889	Pit-N	.867	41	67	5	11	2	-2
1890	Pit-P	.912	49	103	1	10	0	4
1891	Pit-N	.915	91	160	12	16	2	6
Total	8	.868	319	570	40	3	6	-8

1B

YEAR	TM/L	PCT	G	PO	A	E	DP	FR
1886	Pit-a	.961	25	259	12	11	16	1
1887	Pit-N	.930	17	177	10	14	6	0
1888	Pit-N	.965	5	52	3	2	0	0
1889	Pit-N	.986	7	70	2	1	1	0
1890	Pit-P	.962	7	71	4	3	6	0
Total	5	.955	61	629	31	1	29	1

SS

YEAR	TM/L	PCT	G	PO	A	E	DP	FR
1886	Pit-a	.900	1	7	2	1	1	1
1887	Pit-N	1.000	1	2	4	0	0	0
Total	2	.938	2	9	6	1	1	1

3B

YEAR	TM/L	PCT	G	PO	A	E	DP	FR
1888	Pit-N	1.000	1	2	0	0	0	0
1889	Pit-N	1.000	1	1	3	0	0	0
Total	2	1.000	2	1	5	0	0	0

Cliff Carroll OF

YEAR	TM/L	PCT	G	PO	A	E	DP	FR
1882	Pro-N	1.000	10	17	2	0	2	1
1883	Pro-N	.902	58	109	11	13	4	4
1884	Pro-N	.904	113	206	11	23	1	2
1885	Pro-N	.886	104	207	10	28	2	3
1886	Was-N	.862	111	153	22	28	4	-2
1887	Was-N	.902	103	146	19	18	6	0
1888	Pit-N	.667	5	5	1	3	0	-1
1890	Chi-N	.936	136	265	28	20	7	11
1891	Chi-N	.915	130	168	15	17	5	-5
1892	StL-N	.901	101	181	19	22	1	4
1893	Bos-N	.917	120	226	18	22	5	1
Total	11	.905	991	1683	156	194	37	18

Gary Carter C

YEAR	TM/L	PCT	G	PO	A	E	DP	FR
1974	Mon-N	1.000	6	26	4	0	1	0
1975	Mon-N	.984	66	280	37	5	6	-9
1976	Mon-N	.994	60	311	36	2	7	2
1977	Mon-N	.990	146	811	101	9	14	2
1978	Mon-N	.989	152	781	83	10	9	8
1979	Mon-N	.989	138	751	88	9	12	11
1980	Mon-N	.993	149	822	108	7	8	13
1981	Mon-N	.993	100	509	58	4	11	2
1982	Mon-N	.991	153	954	104	10	6	13
1983	Mon-N	.995	144	847	107	5	14	8
1984	Mon-N	.993	143	772	65	6	6	-5
1985	NY-N	.992	143	956	67	8	11	3
1986	NY-N	.991	122	869	62	8	13	5
1987	NY-N	.991	135	874	70	9	13	-1
1988	NY-N	.990	119	797	54	9	5	-3
1989	NY-N	.980	47	266	31	6	6	-2
1990	SF-N	.992	80	323	31	3	2	-3
Total	17	.991	1903	10949	1106	110	144	44

OF

YEAR	TM/L	PCT	G	PO	A	E	DP	FR
1974	Mon-N	1.000	2	2	0	0	0	0
1975	Mon-N	.974	92	150	1	4	1	-10
1976	Mon-N	1.000	36	53	6	0	1	2
1977	Mon-N	1.000	1	2	0	0	0	0
1985	NY-N	—	1	0	0	0	0	0
1986	NY-N	.833	4	5	0	1	0	0
1987	NY-N	1.000	1	2	0	0	0	0
Total	7	.978	137	214	7	5	2	-8

1B

YEAR	TM/L	PCT	G	PO	A	E	DP	FR
1978	Mon-N	1.000	1	6	0	0	0	0
1981	Mon-N	1.000	1	6	0	0	1	0
1983	Mon-N	1.000	1	8	1	0	1	0
1984	Mon-N	.996	25	218	13	1	19	-1
1985	NY-N	1.000	6	31	3	0	2	0
1986	NY-N	1.000	9	68	5	0	4	0
1987	NY-N	1.000	4	10	0	0	1	0
1988	NY-N	.980	10	45	3	1	3	0
1989	NY-N	—	1	0	0	0	0	0
1990	SF-N	1.000	3	25	0	0	3	-1
Total	10	.995	61	417	25	2	34	-2

3B

YEAR	TM/L	PCT	G	PO	A	E	DP	FR
1975	Mon-N	—	1	0	0	0	0	0
1986	NY-N	1.000	1	1	3	0	1	0
1988	NY-N	1.000	1	0	1	0	0	0
Total	3	1.000	3	1	4	0	1	0

Joe Carter OF

YEAR	TM/L	PCT	G	PO	A	E	DP	FR
1983	Chi-N	1.000	16	26	0	0	0	0
1984	Cle-A	.956	59	122	9	6	0	0
1985	Cle-A	.983	135	278	11	5	2	1
1986	Cle-A	.976	104	241	8	6	2	5
1987	Cle-A	.965	62	138	1	5	0	-5
1988	Cle-A	.985	156	444	8	7	3	6
1989	Cle-A	.978	146	350	6	8	3	-6
1990	SD-N	.988	150	385	13	5	4	6
Total	8	.980	828	1984	56	2	14	7

1B

YEAR	TM/L	PCT	G	PO	A	E	DP	FR
1984	Cle-A	1.000	7	47	2	0	4	-1
1985	Cle-A	.974	11	33	5	1	2	1
1986	Cle-A	.993	70	559	47	4	50	-4
1987	Cle-A	.983	84	644	45	12	61	-7
1989	Cle-A	.991	11	93	14	1	4	0
1990	SD-N	.948	14	107	3	6	15	-3
Total	6	.985	197	1483	116	4	136	-12

2B

YEAR	TM/L	PCT	G	PO	A	E	DP	FR
1985	Cle-A	1.000	1	1	1	0	0	0

3B

YEAR	TM/L	PCT	G	PO	A	E	DP	FR
1985	Cle-A	—	1	0	0	0	0	0

Ed Cartwright 1B

YEAR	TM/L	PCT	G	PO	A	E	DP	FR
1890	StL-a	.976	75	706	25	18	37	-1
1894	Was-N	.973	132	1219	71	36	63	-2
1895	Was-N	.984	122	1102	95	19	69	14
1896	Was-N	.978	133	1276	71	30	76	0
1897	Was-N	.963	33	285	26	12	17	2
Total	5	.977	495	4588	288	115	262	13

Rico Carty OF

YEAR	TM/L	PCT	G	PO	A	E	DP	FR
1964	Mil-N	.978	121	176	5	4	1	-8
1965	Mil-N	.958	73	112	3	5	1	-4
1966	Atl-N	.971	126	226	8	7	0	1
1967	Atl-N	.959	112	203	7	9	3	0
1969	Atl-N	.952	79	118	0	6	0	-9
1970	Atl-N	.974	133	219	5	6	0	-6
1972	Atl-N	.979	78	139	3	3	1	-5
1973	Tex-N	1.000	53	87	2	0	0	0
	Chi-N	.947	19	36	0	2	0	-1
1975	Cle-A	.952	12	20	0	1	0	0
1976	Cle-A	1.000	1	2	0	0	0	0
Total	10	.970	807	1338	33	3	6	-38

1B

YEAR	TM/L	PCT	G	PO	A	E	DP	FR
1966	Atl-N	1.000	2	4	0	0	0	0
1967	Atl-N	.971	9	64	2	2	3	-1
1974	Cle-A	.985	8	64	1	1	9	-1
1975	Cle-A	.990	26	189	15	2	21	0

YEAR	TM/L	PCT	G	PO	A	E	DP	FR
1976	Cle-A	1.000	12	79	3	0	8	-2
1977	Cle-A	1.000	2	20	3	0	4	1
Total	6	.989	59	420	24	5	45	-3
C								
1966	Atl-N	.970	17	88	8	3	1	-2
3B								
1966	Atl-N	—	1	0	0	0	0	0
■ Bob Caruthers OF								
1884	StL-a	.750	16	11	1	4	0	-5
1885	StL-a	.733	7	9	2	4	0	0
1886	StL-a	.852	43	42	10	9	3	-3
1887	StL-a	.903	54	91	11	11	1	1
1888	Bro-a	.899	51	93	5	11	3	-1
1889	Bro-a	—	3	0	0	0	0	-1
1890	Bro-N	.860	39	45	4	8	0	-8
1891	Bro-N	.783	17	16	2	5	0	-3
1892	StL-N	.892	122	159	14	21	2	-9
1893	Chi-N	1.000	1	1	0	0	0	0
	Cin-N	.857	13	23	1	4	0	-1
	Yr	.862	14	24	1	4	0	-1
Total	10	.875	366	490	50	7	9	-30
1B								
1887	StL-a	.946	7	51	2	3	3	0
1889	Bro-a	.667	2	4	0	2	0	0
1892	StL-N	.923	4	35	1	3	4	-1
Total	3	.921	13	90	3	8	7	-1
2B								
1886	StL-a	.857	2	5	1	1	0	-1
1891	Bro-N	.500	1	0	1	1	0	-1
1892	StL-N	.868	6	11	22	5	4	-1
Total	3	.851	9	16	24	7	4	-3
■ Paul Casanova C								
1965	Was-A	.938	4	15	0	1	0	-2
1966	Was-A	.981	119	674	53	14	12	-11
1967	Was-A	.984	137	827	70	15	19	-5
1968	Was-A	.989	92	472	46	6	3	-9
1969	Was-A	.992	122	583	59	5	5	-6
1970	Was-A	.988	100	461	48	6	12	-2
1971	Was-A	.985	83	416	40	7	4	-5
1972	Atl-N	.975	43	139	16	4	3	-6
1973	Atl-N	.977	78	330	48	9	3	7
1974	Atl-N	.986	33	123	15	2	4	-1
Total	10	.985	811	4040	395	9	65	-40
■ George Case OF								
1937	Was-A	.945	22	51	1	3	0	0
1938	Was-A	.964	101	207	7	8	2	-2
1939	Was-A	.955	123	332	7	16	2	10
1940	Was-A	.970	154	384	10	12	0	-3
1941	Was-A	.975	151	362	21	10	3	13
1942	Was-A	.951	120	270	4	14	1	-2
1943	Was-A	.985	140	318	8	5	2	-3
1944	Was-A	.970	114	288	7	9	2	8
1945	Was-A	.979	123	316	17	7	3	14
1946	Cle-A	.983	118	226	5	4	0	-5
1947	Was-A	.963	21	51	1	2	0	1
Total	11	.970	1187	2805	88	0	15	31
■ Dennis Casey OF								
1884	Wil-U	1.000	2	3	0	0	0	0
	Bal-a	.898	37	48	5	6	2	0
1885	Bal-a	.821	63	100	10	24	0	-5
Total	2	.847	102	151	15	0	2	-5
■ Doc Casey 3B								
1898	Was-N	.893	22	22	45	8	4	-1
1899	Was-N	.853	9	12	17	5	3	0
	Bro-N	.892	134	162	258	51	20	-19
	Yr	.889	143	174	275	56	23	-19
1900	Bro-N	1.000	1	1	2	0	0	0
1901	Det-A	.887	127	133	324	58	25	5
1902	Det-A	.904	132	174	309	51	17	1
1903	Chi-N	.915	112	143	190	31	5	-19
1904	Chi-N	.911	134	157	241	39	11	-10
1905	Chi-N	.949	142	160	252	22	7	-9
1906	Bro-N	.919	149	172	272	39	11	-17
1907	Bro-N	.955	138	176	274	21	16	-6
Total	10	.915	1100	1312	2184	325	119	-75
SS								
1898	Was-N	.800	4	7	13	5	1	-1
1905	Chi-N	1.000	1	2	2	0	0	0
Total	2	.828	5	9	15	5	1	-1
C								
1898	Was-N	.929	3	9	4	1	0	0
1904	Chi-N	1.000	2	6	3	0	0	0
Total	2	.957	5	15	7	1	0	0
■ Dave Cash 2B								
1969	Pit-N	.990	17	37	60	1	9	5
1970	Pit-N	.974	55	147	156	8	46	5
1971	Pit-N	.987	105	228	304	7	80	11
1972	Pit-N	.992	97	260	342	5	81	28
1973	Pit-N	.979	92	227	276	11	46	5
1974	Phi-N	.977	162	396	519	22	141	29
1975	Phi-N	.981	162	400	481	17	126	9
1976	Phi-N	.988	158	407	424	10	118	-2
1977	Mon-N	.986	153	343	443	11	73	-11
1978	Mon-N	.986	159	362	400	11	91	-30
1979	Mon-N	.971	47	88	110	6	18	-6
1980	SD-N	.987	123	290	326	8	72	4
Total	12	.984	1330	3185	3841	117	901	47
3B								
1971	Pit-N	.964	24	25	29	2	2	-4
1973	Pit-N	.981	17	17	35	1	3	1
Total	2	.972	41	42	64	3	5	-3
SS								
1971	Pit-N	.500	3	1	0	1	0	-1

YEAR	TM/L	PCT	G	PO	A	E	DP	FR
■ Norm Cash 1B								
1959	Chi-A	.984	31	231	14	4	19	-1
1960	Det-A	.991	99	739	59	7	68	-1
1961	Det-A	.992	157	1231	127	11	121	6
1962	Det-A	.992	146	1081	116	10	94	6
1963	Det-A	.994	142	1161	99	7	93	2
1964	Det-A	.997	137	1105	92	4	97	4
1965	Det-A	.992	139	1091	97	9	96	7
1966	Det-A	.988	158	1271	114	17	118	6
1967	Det-A	.995	146	1135	112	6	89	10
1968	Det-A	.992	117	924	88	8	66	10
1969	Det-A	.994	134	1016	96	7	99	6
1970	Det-A	.989	114	868	70	10	76	2
1971	Det-A	.992	131	1020	75	9	105	0
1972	Det-A	.993	134	1060	70	8	102	0
1973	Det-A	.991	114	856	64	8	72	2
1974	Det-A	.985	44	368	24	6	32	-2
Total	16	.992	1943	15157	1317	131	1347	57
OF								
1958	Chi-A	1.000	4	2	0	0	0	1
1960	Det-A	1.000	4	4	0	0	0	0
1962	Det-A	1.000	3	10	0	0	0	1
Total	3	1.000	11	16	0	0	0	2
■ Ed Caskin SS								
1879	Tro-N	.902	42	42	169	23	10	9
1880	Tro-N	.885	82	97	297	51	16	7
1881	Tro-N	.906	63	85	205	30	18	1
1883	NY-N	.855	81	146	250	67	14	-1
1884	NY-N	.883	96	121	278	53	28	2
1885	StL-N	.714	1	0	5	2	0	0
1886	NY-N	1.000	1	3	0	0	0	-1
Total	7	.883	366	494	1204	226	86	17
3B								
1885	StL-N	.884	69	82	139	29	5	-2
C								
1879	Tro-N	.875	22	105	35	20	1	2
1880	Tro-N	—	2	0	0	0	0	0
1883	NY-N	.857	1	6	0	1	0	0
1884	NY-N	.878	6	28	15	6	0	3
1885	StL-N	.667	2	6	2	4	0	-2
Total	5	.864	33	145	52	1	1	3
2B								
1879	Tro-N	.863	6	23	21	7	1	-1
1883	NY-N	.852	13	42	27	12	5	-7
Total	2	.856	19	65	48	9	6	-8
■ John Cassidy OF								
1876	Har-N	1.000	8	7	2	0	0	0
1877	Har-N	.722	58	41	16	22	2	-5
1878	Chi-N	.810	60	89	30	28	6	6
1879	Tro-N	.889	8	7	1	1	0	-1
1880	Tro-N	.880	82	128	18	20	1	-4
1881	Tro-N	.872	84	143	20	24	0	-9
1882	Tro-N	.778	16	19	2	6	1	-3
1883	Pro-N	.864	88	120	26	23	2	1
1884	Bro-a	.847	101	125	25	27	5	-6
1885	Bro-a	.852	54	62	7	12	3	-7
Total	10	.845	559	741	147	163	20	-28
3B								
1882	Tro-N	.661	13	16	21	19	0	-6
1884	Bro-a	.667	4	5	5	5	0	-2
Total	2	.662	17	21	26	4	0	-8
1B								
1876	Har-N	.947	4	34	2	2	3	1
1879	Tro-N	.857	2	17	1	3	2	0
1883	Pro-N	.857	1	11	1	2	0	0
Total	3	.904	7	62	4	7	5	1
2B								
1880	Tro-N	.500	1	2	0	2	0	-1
1883	Pro-N	.750	1	1	2	1	0	0
Total	2	.625	2	3	2	3	0	-1
SS								
1881	Tro-N	.833	1	1	4	1	1	0
1884	Bro-a	.500	1	1	1	2	0	-1
Total	2	.700	2	2	5	3	1	-1
C								
1878	Chi-N	1.000	1	2	1	0	0	1
■ Joe Cassidy SS								
1904	Was-A	.937	99	249	301	37	38	8
1905	Was-A	.934	151	408	520	66	50	33
Total	2	.935	250	657	821	103	88	41
OF								
1904	Was-A	.931	32	65	2	5	2	0
3B								
1904	Was-A	.900	23	22	59	9	2	4
■ Pete Castiglione 3B								
1949	Pit-N	.957	98	100	213	14	26	3
1950	Pit-N	.970	35	40	58	3	8	-4
1951	Pit-N	.957	99	103	228	15	25	11
1952	Pit-N	.951	57	67	129	10	7	6
1953	Pit-N	.978	44	44	88	3	6	4
	StL-N	.967	51	7	22	1	4	4
	Yr	.976	94	51	110	4	10	8
1954	StL-N	1.000	5	0	1	0	0	0
Total	6	.960	388	361	739	6	76	24
SS								
1947	Pit-N	.970	13	26	39	2	6	1
1948	Pit-N	1.000	1	0	1	0	0	1
1949	Pit-N	1.000	17	13	23	0	6	4
1950	Pit-N	.956	29	38	49	4	11	-9
1951	Pit-N	.948	28	45	64	6	11	-7
1953	StL-N	.909	3	3	7	1	1	1
Total	6	.960	91	125	183	3	35	-17
2B								
1950	Pit-N	.944	9	18	16	2	3	-4
1953	StL-N	.935	9	14	15	2	3	3

YEAR	TM/L	PCT	G	PO	A	E	DP	FR
Total	2	.940	18	32	31	4	6	-1
1B								
1950	Pit-N	.957	3	20	2	1	1	0
1952	Pit-N	1.000	1	2	0	0	0	0
Total	2	.960	4	22	2	1	1	0
OF								
1949	Pit-N	1.000	2	2	0	0	0	0
1952	Pit-N	—	1	0	0	0	0	0
Total	2	1.000	3	2	0	0	0	0
■ Manny Castillo 3B								
1980	KC-A	1.000	3	0	3	0	0	1
1982	Sea-A	.938	130	96	209	20	18	-27
1983	Sea-A	.971	55	35	101	4	9	7
Total	3	.949	188	131	313	4	27	-19
2B								
1980	KC-A	1.000	1	2	5	0	0	1
1982	Sea-A	.960	9	13	11	1	6	-1
1983	Sea-A	.952	5	6	14	1	4	1
Total	3	.962	15	21	30	2	10	1
1B								
1983	Sea-A	.976	11	37	3	1	4	0
■ Juan Castillo 2B								
1986	Mil-A	1.000	17	32	32	0	7	5
1987	Mil-A	.973	97	181	219	11	54	-9
1988	Mil-A	.932	18	14	41	4	7	4
1989	Mil-A	1.000	3	6	5	0	1	1
Total	4	.972	135	233	297	5	69	1
SS								
1986	Mil-A	.846	4	8	14	4	3	0
1987	Mil-A	1.000	13	7	25	0	4	1
1988	Mil-A	.971	13	9	24	1	4	2
Total	3	.946	30	24	63	5	11	3
3B								
1986	Mil-A	1.000	2	1	0	0	0	0
1987	Mil-A	.900	7	2	7	1	1	0
1988	Mil-A	.900	17	1	17	2	2	2
Total	3	.903	26	4	24	3	3	2
OF								
1986	Mil-A	—	1	0	0	0	0	0
1988	Mil-A	—	1	0	0	0	0	0
Total	2	—	2	0	0	0	0	0
■ Marty Castillo 3B								
1981	Det-A	1.000	4	3	8	0	3	2
1983	Det-A	.990	58	35	68	1	6	2
1984	Det-A	.950	33	12	26	2	1	-1
1985	Det-A	.962	25	6	19	1	1	2
Total	4	.978	120	56	121	4	11	5
C								
1981	Det-A	1.000	1	1	0	0	0	0
1982	Det-A	1.000	1	1	0	0	0	0
1983	Det-A	1.000	10	38	1	0	0	2
1984	Det-A	.970	36	149	11	5	2	4
1985	Det-A	.977	32	117	12	3	1	5
Total	5	.976	80	306	24	8	3	11
OF								
1981	Det-A	1.000	1	1	0	0	0	0
■ Carmelo Castillo OF								
1982	Cle-A	.978	43	91	0	2	0	3
1983	Cle-A	.929	19	23	3	2	1	2
1984	Cle-A	.933	70	123	2	9	0	-3
1985	Cle-A	.953	51	101	0	5	0	1
1986	Cle-A	.939	37	58	4	4	1	7
1987	Cle-A	1.000	23	29	3	0	0	2
1988	Cle-A	.933	45	69	1	5	0	-2
1989	Min-A	.976	67	119	3	3	1	4
1990	Min-A	.923	21	24	0	2	0	0
Total	9	.953	376	637	16	32	3	14
■ John Castino 3B								
1979	Min-A	.963	143	85	277	14	31	17
1980	Min-A	.961	138	105	340	18	34	23
1981	Min-A	.975	98	86	224	8	24	11
1982	Min-A	.974	21	25	50	2	6	4
1983	Min-A	.975	8	15	24	1	1	4
1984	Min-A	1.000	8	8	12	0	1	-1
Total	6	.967	416	324	927	3	97	58
2B								
1981	Min-A	.957	4	10	12	1	5	0
1982	Min-A	.995	96	193	228	2	63	1
1983	Min-A	.990	132	301	406	7	94	3
Total	3	.991	232	504	646	0	162	4
SS								
1979	Min-A	.938	5	6	9	1	3	1
1980	Min-A	.951	18	23	55	4	14	5
Total	2	.949	23	29	64	5	17	6
OF								
1982	Min-A	1.000	6	12	0	0	0	0
■ Foster Castleman 3B								
1954	NY-N	—	2	0	0	0	0	0
1955	NY-N	—	1	0	0	0	0	0
1956	NY-N	.947	107	90	213	17	10	7
1957	NY-N	.867	7	3	10	2	1	-1
1958	Bal-A	1.000	4	1	1	0	0	0
Total	5	.944	121	94	224	9	11	6
SS								
1956	NY-N	—	2	0	0	0	0	0
1957	NY-N	1.000	1	2	1	0	0	0
1958	Bal-A	.964	91	102	165	10	37	-19
Total	3	.964	94	104	166	0	37	-20
2B								
1955	NY-N	1.000	6	14	10	0	2	-2
1956	NY-N	1.000	1	1	0	0	0	0
1957	NY-N	1.000	1	1	0	0	0	0
1958	Bal-A	.944	4	9	8	1	3	0
Total	4	.978	12	25	19	1	5	-2

YEAR	TM/L	PCT	G	PO	A	E	DP	FR
		OF						
1958	Bal-A	1.000	1	1	0	0	0	0

■ Danny Cater 1B

YEAR	TM/L	PCT	G	PO	A	E	DP	FR
1964	Phi-N	.970	7	62	3	2	5	-1
1965	Chi-A	.933	3	14	0	1	0	-1
1966	KC-A	.994	53	459	36	3	48	1
1967	KC-A	.997	44	297	30	1	32	2
1968	Oak-A	**.995**	121	985	68	5	89	0
1969	Oak-A	.992	132	1087	97	9	112	6
1970	NY-A	.992	131	981	70	8	79	0
1971	NY-A	.995	78	564	62	3	54	**9**
1972	Bos-A	.993	90	656	61	5	65	6
1973	Bos-A	.997	37	287	17	1	37	0
1974	Bos-A	1.000	23	126	10	0	9	1
1975	StL-N	.981	12	49	4	1	4	0
Total	12	.994	731	5567	458	9	534	23
		OF						
1964	Phi-N	.981	39	48	4	1	2	2
1965	Chi-A	.978	127	174	6	4	2	-10
1966	Chi-A	.909	18	20	0	2	0	-4
	KC-A	.976	22	40	1	1	1	0
	Yr	.953	40	60	1	3	1	-4
1967	KC-A	.989	55	84	2	1	0	-2
1968	Oak-A	1.000	20	21	0	0	0	-1
1969	Oak-A	1.000	20	30	2	0	0	1
1970	NY-A	1.000	7	11	0	0	0	-1
Total	7	.980	308	428	15	9	5	-15
		3B						
1964	Phi-N	—	1	0	0	0	0	0
1965	Chi-A	.941	11	1	15	1	1	-1
1966	KC-A	.958	42	46	67	5	6	-6
1967	KC-A	.916	56	43	77	11	3	-16
1970	NY-A	.930	42	24	83	8	10	-3
1971	NY-A	.938	52	41	111	10	7	-2
1973	Bos-A	.917	21	16	39	5	8	1
Total	7	.934	225	171	392	0	35	-27
		2B						
1968	Oak-A	1.000	1	1	1	0	0	0
1969	Oak-A	1.000	4	8	9	0	1	0
Total	2	1.000	5	9	10	0	1	0

■ Ted Cather OF

YEAR	TM/L	PCT	G	PO	A	E	DP	FR
1912	StL-N	.944	5	15	2	1	0	2
1913	StL-N	.915	57	67	8	7	0	-5
1914	StL-N	.981	28	49	4	1	1	1
	Bos-N	.953	48	57	4	3	1	4
	Yr	.966	76	106	8	4	2	-3
1915	Bos-N	.902	32	35	2	4	0	-5
Total	4	.938	170	223	20	6	2	-11
		1B						
1913	StL-N	1.000	1	4	0	0	0	0

■ Howdy Caton SS

YEAR	TM/L	PCT	G	PO	A	E	DP	FR
1917	Pit-N	.895	14	21	47	8	5	-2
1918	Pit-N	.928	79	136	276	32	35	-7
1919	Pit-N	.927	17	24	27	4	3	-8
1920	Pit-N	.929	96	191	296	37	40	-22
Total	4	.926	206	372	646	1	83	-39
		3B						
1919	Pit-N	.949	14	12	25	2	1	-3
		OF						
1919	Pit-N	1.000	1	2	0	0	0	0

■ Wayne Causey SS

YEAR	TM/L	PCT	G	PO	A	E	DP	FR
1955	Bal-A	1.000	1	0	1	0	1	0
1961	KC-A	.975	11	14	25	1	3	2
1962	KC-A	.953	51	108	137	12	22	-1
1963	KC-A	.978	135	266	402	15	81	5
1964	KC-A	.967	131	266	352	21	75	-5
1965	KC-A	.972	62	111	162	8	34	-5
1966	KC-A	.951	10	14	25	2	3	-1
	Chi-A	.500	1	0	1	1	0	-1
	Yr	.930	11	14	26	3	3	-2
1967	Chi-A	1.000	2	0	1	0	0	0
1968	Atl-N	1.000	2	0	1	0	1	0
Total	9	.969	406	779	1107	0	220	-6
		2B						
1955	Bal-A	.833	7	5	5	2	0	-2
1956	Bal-A	.967	7	13	16	1	0	-1
1957	Bal-A	.960	6	12	12	1	2	3
1961	KC-A	.964	9	17	10	1	2	0
1962	KC-A	.966	9	13	15	1	0	0
1964	KC-A	.981	17	48	58	2	13	6
1965	KC-A	.994	45	75	89	1	21	-8
1966	Chi-A	.980	60	86	110	4	15	-15
1967	Chi-A	.978	96	153	199	8	36	-8
1968	Chi-A	.971	41	47	54	3	11	-13
	Cal-A	1.000	4	4	10	0	3	1
	Atl-N	1.000	6	11	11	0	2	-4
	Yr	.976	47	58	65	3	13	-17
Total	10	.978	307	484	589	4	105	-41
		3B						
1955	Bal-A	.912	55	25	79	10	10	-6
1956	Bal-A	.980	30	13	36	1	4	3
1957	Bal-A	1.000	5	2	1	0	0	0
1961	KC-A	.955	88	102	193	14	20	18
1962	KC-A	.986	26	22	48	1	3	3
1963	KC-A	1.000	2	1	3	0	0	0
1964	KC-A	.917	9	9	13	2	3	-1
1965	KC-A	.942	35	35	62	6	5	-6
1966	KC-A	.871	15	15	12	4	3	-4
	Chi-A	1.000	1	0	2	0	0	0
	Yr	.879	16	15	14	4	3	-4
1968	Atl-N	.000	2	0	0	1	0	-1
Total	10	.945	268	224	449	9	48	6

■ Phil Cavarretta 1B

YEAR	TM/L	PCT	G	PO	A	E	DP	FR
1934	Chi-N	1.000	5	53	5	0	6	1
1935	Chi-N	.986	145	1347	98	**20**	**129**	2

YEAR	TM/L	PCT	G	PO	A	E	DP	FR
1936	Chi-N	.987	115	980	71	14	93	-2
1937	Chi-N	.982	43	355	33	7	27	1
1938	Chi-N	.996	28	206	16	1	14	0
1939	Chi-N	.991	13	106	6	1	10	-1
1940	Chi-N	.991	52	524	30	5	57	-1
1941	Chi-N	.989	33	335	12	4	18	-3
1942	Chi-N	.992	61	567	44	5	48	3
1943	Chi-N	.987	134	1290	67	**18**	103	-10
1944	Chi-N	.992	139	1337	77	11	121	-5
1945	Chi-N	.993	120	1149	77	9	83	-2
1946	Chi-N	.992	51	450	40	4	26	2
1947	Chi-N	.987	24	217	13	3	23	-1
1948	Chi-N	.998	41	374	28	1	46	1
1949	Chi-N	.993	70	673	63	5	58	8
1950	Chi-N	.986	67	606	47	9	55	0
1951	Chi-N	.994	53	444	42	3	53	3
1952	Chi-N	.991	13	98	10	1	13	1
1954	Chi-A	.993	44	261	17	2	29	-2
1955	Chi-A	1.000	3	3	0	0	0	0
Total	21	.990	1254	11375	796	123	1012	-5
		OF						
1937	Chi-N	.972	55	99	7	3	1	2
1938	Chi-N	.962	52	71	5	3	0	-3
1939	Chi-N	—	1	0	0	0	0	0
1941	Chi-N	.992	66	128	3	1	2	-7
1942	Chi-N	.989	70	177	5	2	1	0
1943	Chi-N	1.000	7	15	0	0	0	0
1944	Chi-N	.931	13	26	1	2	0	-1
1945	Chi-N	1.000	11	23	1	0	0	0
1946	Chi-N	.967	86	196	7	7	2	3
1947	Chi-N	.977	100	203	11	5	3	0
1948	Chi-N	.974	40	72	4	2	0	-1
1949	Chi-N	1.000	25	39	4	0	1	1
1950	Chi-N	1.000	3	3	0	0	0	0
1954	Chi-A	.889	9	8	0	1	0	-1
Total	14	.977	538	1060	48	6	10	-7

■ Ike Caveney SS

YEAR	TM/L	PCT	G	PO	A	E	DP	FR
1922	Cin-N	.934	118	256	404	47	74	-6
1923	Cin-N	.942	138	313	477	**49**	86	0
1924	Cin-N	.924	90	200	310	42	60	3
1925	Cin-N	.941	111	209	349	35	72	9
Total	4	.936	457	978	1540	173	292	6
		2B						
1924	Cin-N	.929	5	10	16	2	1	0

■ Cesar Cedeno OF

YEAR	TM/L	PCT	G	PO	A	E	DP	FR
1970	Hou-N	.968	90	211	1	7	0	0
1971	Hou-N	.989	157	345	6	4	0	-7
1972	Hou-N	.981	137	345	9	7	1	5
1973	Hou-N	.981	136	357	10	7	2	10
1974	Hou-N	.993	157	**446**	11	3	4	16
1975	Hou-N	.982	131	322	8	6	2	1
1976	Hou-N	.980	146	377	11	8	5	3
1977	Hou-N	**.997**	137	335	14	1	2	5
1978	Hou-N	.987	50	149	2	2	1	6
1979	Hou-N	1.000	40	116	2	0	0	5
1980	Hou-N	.977	136	338	9	8	3	0
1981	Hou-N	.988	34	82	1	1	0	0
1982	Cin-N	.990	131	301	4	3	2	-3
1983	Cin-N	.993	73	138	5	1	1	-1
1984	Cin-N	.980	77	140	7	3	0	2
1985	Cin-N	.990	53	96	1	1	0	0
	StL-N	—	2	0	0	0	0	0
	Yr	.990	55	96	1	1	0	0
1986	LA-N	.944	31	33	1	2	0	-2
Total	17	.985	1718	4131	102	4	23	40
		1B						
1971	Hou-N	1.000	2	3	0	0	0	0
1979	Hou-N	.981	91	832	33	**17**	79	-10
1981	Hou-N	.991	46	428	27	4	27	-1
1982	Cin-N	1.000	1	0	1	0	0	0
1983	Cin-N	1.000	17	120	5	0	7	-3
1984	Cin-N	.983	44	215	14	4	16	-2
1985	Cin-N	.992	34	110	8	1	10	0
	StL-N	.993	23	145	5	1	16	-3
	Yr	.993	57	255	13	2	27	-3
Total	7	.986	258	1853	93	7	156	-19

■ Orlando Cepeda 1B

YEAR	TM/L	PCT	G	PO	A	E	DP	FR
1958	SF-N	.989	**147**	**1322**	97	**16**	131	-3
1959	SF-N	.984	122	929	70	16	74	-3
1960	SF-N	.982	63	518	27	10	37	-8
1961	SF-N	.997	81	644	47	2	50	-2
1962	SF-N	.991	**160**	1353	88	13	125	-7
1963	SF-N	.985	150	1262	83	**21**	91	-7
1964	SF-N	.986	139	1211	80	**18**	89	-3
1965	SF-N	1.000	4	27	2	0	1	0
1966	SF-N	1.000	6	55	1	0	5	-1
	StL-N	.989	120	1109	62	13	111	-6
	Yr	.990	**126**	1164	63	13	116	-7
1967	StL-N	.993	151	1304	90	10	103	3
1968	StL-N	.988	154	1362	90	17	109	-5
1969	Atl-N	.994	153	1318	101	9	91	3
1970	Atl-N	.992	148	1288	112	12	100	3
1971	Atl-N	.992	63	586	49	5	60	2
1972	Atl-N	1.000	22	171	13	0	15	1
Total	15	.990	1683	14459	1012	162	1192	-36
		OF						
1959	SF-N	.956	44	64	1	3	0	-2
1960	SF-N	.983	91	163	10	3	3	3
1961	SF-N	.978	80	130	4	3	0	-3
1962	SF-N	.750	3	2	1	1	0	0
1963	SF-N	—	3	0	0	0	0	0
1964	SF-N	—	1	0	0	0	0	0
1965	SF-N	1.000	2	1	0	0	0	0
1966	SF-N	.778	8	7	0	2	0	-1
Total	8	.970	231	368	15	2	3	-3

YEAR	TM/L	PCT	G	PO	A	E	DP	FR
		3B						
1959	SF-N	.625	4	2	3	3	0	-2

■ Rick Cerone C

YEAR	TM/L	PCT	G	PO	A	E	DP	FR
1975	Cle-A	1.000	7	18	1	0	0	-1
1976	Cle-A	.963	6	25	1	1	1	1
1977	Tor-A	.994	31	146	15	1	1	-2
1978	Tor-A	.992	84	426	44	4	7	3
1979	Tor-A	.980	136	560	68	13	10	-9
1980	NY-A	.990	147	800	73	9	9	6
1981	NY-A	.992	69	353	26	3	1	-6
1982	NY-A	.989	89	509	25	6	5	-7
1983	NY-A	.991	78	412	18	4	2	0
1984	NY-A	.996	38	230	9	1	1	3
1985	Atl-N	.986	91	384	48	6	4	-8
1986	Mil-A	.991	68	391	44	4	2	7
1987	NY-A	**.998**	111	538	38	1	6	5
1988	Bos-A	**1.000**	83	471	28	0	4	-4
1989	Bos-A	.984	97	578	41	10	5	2
1990	NY-A	.995	35	177	14	1	1	-2
Total	16	.990	1170	6018	493	4	59	-12
		1B						
1987	NY-A	1.000	2	4	0	0	0	0
		3B						
1983	NY-A	—	1	0	0	0	0	0
		OF						
1989	Bos-A	1.000	1	1	0	0	0	0
		2B						
1990	NY-A	1.000	1	2	0	0	0	-1

■ Bob Cerv OF

YEAR	TM/L	PCT	G	PO	A	E	DP	FR
1951	NY-A	.875	9	14	0	2	0	-1
1952	NY-A	1.000	27	52	1	0	0	1
1954	NY-A	.897	24	25	1	3	0	-4
1955	NY-A	1.000	20	25	1	0	0	-1
1956	NY-A	.984	44	59	4	1	2	1
1957	KC-A	.964	89	157	6	6	1	-3
1958	KC-A	.985	136	311	13	5	3	13
1959	KC-A	.980	119	231	8	5	2	2
1960	KC-A	.977	21	39	4	1	1	1
	NY-A	.982	51	101	6	2	0	2
	Yr	.980	72	140	10	3	1	3
1961	LA-A	.944	15	17	0	1	0	-3
	NY-A	.983	30	55	2	1	0	2
	Yr	.974	45	72	2	2	0	-1
1962	NY-A	1.000	3	4	0	0	0	0
	Hou-N	.833	6	4	1	1	0	-1
Total	11	.976	594	1094	47	8	9	9
		1B						
1960	NY-A	.960	3	22	2	1	3	0
1961	NY-A	1.000	3	24	3	0	2	1
Total	2	.981	6	46	5	1	5	1

■ Ron Cey 3B

YEAR	TM/L	PCT	G	PO	A	E	DP	FR
1972	LA-N	.900	11	7	20	3	1	-2
1973	LA-N	.961	146	111	**328**	13	**39**	16
1974	LA-N	.959	158	155	365	22	25	17
1975	LA-N	.960	158	144	309	19	23	-4
1976	LA-N	.965	144	111	334	16	22	11
1977	LA-N	.964	153	138	346	18	29	17
1978	LA-N	.966	**158**	116	336	16	26	5
1979	LA-N	**.977**	150	123	265	9	25	-1
1980	LA-N	.972	157	**127**	317	13	24	7
1981	LA-N	.941	84	71	184	16	15	7
1982	LA-N	.963	149	93	320	16	23	11
1983	Chi-N	.955	157	90	270	17	12	-20
1984	Chi-N	**.967**	144	97	230	11	22	-20
1985	Chi-N	.943	140	75	273	**21**	21	-7
1986	Chi-N	.952	77	41	118	8	7	-6
1987	Oak-A	1.000	3	1	3	0	1	0
Total	16	.961	1989	1500	4018	223	315	31
		1B						
1987	Oak-A	.982	7	55	1	1	3	-1

■ Chet Chadbourne OF

YEAR	TM/L	PCT	G	PO	A	E	DP	FR
1907	Bos-A	1.000	10	16	1	0	0	0
1914	KC-F	.965	146	238	**34**	10	6	9
1915	KC-F	**.979**	152	308	24	7	7	1
1918	Bos-N	.925	27	60	2	5	1	-2
Total	4	.969	335	622	61	2	14	9
		2B						
1906	Bos-A	.926	11	20	43	5	3	2
		SS						
1906	Bos-A	.889	1	3	5	1	1	1

■ Dave Chalk 3B

YEAR	TM/L	PCT	G	PO	A	E	DP	FR
1974	Cal-A	.958	38	32	81	5	16	3
1975	Cal-A	.976	149	108	333	11	30	6
1976	Cal-A	.970	49	35	94	4	9	5
1977	Cal-A	.948	114	114	266	21	21	-2
1978	Cal-A	.977	22	9	33	1	4	-2
1979	Oak-A	.930	16	15	25	3	1	-2
1980	KC-A	.964	33	24	56	3	3	0
1981	KC-A	.955	14	9	12	1	3	0
Total	8	.962	462	346	900	9	87	8
		SS						
1973	Cal-A	.962	22	36	66	4	20	2
1974	Cal-A	.938	99	168	269	**29**	55	-4
1976	Cal-A	.971	102	141	293	13	45	-1
1977	Cal-A	.917	4	18	4	2	2	-1
1978	Cal-A	.955	97	168	237	19	46	-20
1979	Tex-A	1.000	3	0	3	0	0	0
	Oak-A	.913	16	30	33	6	8	-7
	Yr	.917	19	30	36	6	8	-7
1980	KC-A	1.000	1	0	1	0	0	0
1981	KC-A	—	1	0	0	0	0	0
Total	8	.953	345	561	906	3	176	-31
		2B						
1977	Cal-A	.941	7	15	17	2	4	0
1978	Cal-A	.973	29	39	69	3	12	2

YEAR	TM/L	PCT	G	PO	A	E	DP	FR
1979	Tex-A	1.000	1	1	0	0	0	0
	Oak-A	.988	37	77	93	2	22	-8
	Yr	.988	38	78	93	2	22	-8
1980	KC-A	.955	17	33	31	3	7	-3
1981	KC-A	1.000	10	10	19	0	2	-1
Total	5	.976	101	175	229	0	47	-10

■ Chris Chambliss 1B

YEAR	TM/L	PCT	G	PO	A	E	DP	FR
1971	Cle-A	.992	108	943	55	8	85	-5
1972	Cle-A	.993	119	1109	56	8	109	-6
1973	Cle-A	.991	154	1437	114	14	153	7
1974	Cle-A	.982	17	162	6	3	14	-2
	NY-A	.992	106	873	78	8	93	7
	Yr	.990	123	1035	84	11	107	5
1975	NY-A	.991	147	1222	106	12	113	3
1976	NY-A	.994	155	1440	109	9	123	-2
1977	NY-A	.989	157	1368	98	16	129	-5
1978	NY-A	**.997**	155	1366	111	4	119	4
1979	NY-A	.995	134	1299	95	7	135	0
1980	Atl-N	.993	158	**1626**	101	12	140	-2
1981	Atl-N	.997	107	1046	**94**	4	83	7
1982	Atl-N	.993	151	1352	138	10	**144**	14
1983	Atl-N	.996	126	1092	89	5	117	0
1984	Atl-N	.993	109	996	70	8	84	2
1985	Atl-N	.997	39	299	25	1	31	2
1986	Atl-N	.993	20	141	6	1	15	-2
Total	16	.993	1962	17771	1351	130	1687	22

■ Mike Champion 2B

YEAR	TM/L	PCT	G	PO	A	E	DP	FR
1976	SD-N	.940	11	23	24	3	2	-4
1977	SD-N	.974	149	301	348	17	82	-26
1978	SD-N	.932	20	24	44	5	12	2
Total	3	.968	180	348	416	5	96	-28

3B

1978	SD-N	1.000	4	0	1	0	0	0

■ Frank Chance 1B

YEAR	TM/L	PCT	G	PO	A	E	DP	FR
1898	Chi-N	.900	3	18	0	2	0	-1
1899	Chi-N	1.000	1	2	0	0	0	0
1900	Chi-N	.857	1	5	1	1	0	0
1901	Chi-N	.882	6	27	3	4	1	0
1902	Chi-N	.969	38	391	20	13	21	-2
1903	Chi-N	.972	121	1204	68	**36**	49	-2
1904	Chi-N	.990	123	1205	106	13	48	12
1905	Chi-N	.990	115	1165	75	13	54	2
1906	Chi-N	.989	136	1376	82	16	71	0
1907	Chi-N	**.992**	109	1129	80	10	64	7
1908	Chi-N	.989	126	1291	86	15	56	4
1909	Chi-N	.994	92	901	40	6	43	-2
1910	Chi-N	.996	87	773	38	3	48	-2
1911	Chi-N	.990	29	289	11	3	12	-2
1912	Chi-N	1.000	2	22	0	0	1	0
1913	NY-A	1.000	7	86	5	0	2	0
1914	NY-A	1.000	1	1	0	0	0	0
Total	17	.987	997	9885	615	135	470	14

C

1898	Chi-N	.950	33	62	14	4	3	-4
1899	Chi-N	.950	57	166	64	12	6	-3
1900	Chi-N	.932	51	155	65	16	2	2
1901	Chi-N	.987	13	55	20	1	2	-1
1902	Chi-N	.972	29	113	27	4	2	-1
1903	Chi-N	.889	2	8	0	1	0	-1
1904	Chi-N	1.000	1	8	1	0	0	0
Total	7	.952	186	567	191	8	15	-8

OF

1898	Chi-N	.800	17	23	5	7	1	0
1899	Chi-N	—	1	0	0	0	0	-1
1901	Chi-N	.932	51	61	7	5	0	-4
1902	Chi-N	1.000	4	4	0	0	0	-1
Total	4	.893	73	88	12	2	1	-6

■ Bob Chance 1B

YEAR	TM/L	PCT	G	PO	A	E	DP	FR
1964	Cle-A	.988	81	567	24	7	47	-9
1965	Was-A	.988	48	391	25	5	39	-1
1966	Was-A	.974	13	73	3	2	6	-1
1967	Was-A	1.000	10	75	5	0	6	0
1969	Cal-A	.909	1	10	0	1	0	0
Total	5	.987	153	1116	57	5	98	-11

OF

1963	Cle-A	.909	14	20	0	2	0	-2
1964	Cle-A	1.000	31	39	0	0	0	-2
1965	Was-A	1.000	3	5	0	0	0	0
Total	3	.970	48	64	0	2	0	-4

■ Darrel Chaney SS

YEAR	TM/L	PCT	G	PO	A	E	DP	FR
1969	Cin-N	.947	91	115	191	17	44	-12
1970	Cin-N	.941	30	28	52	5	5	0
1971	Cin-N	1.000	7	14	18	0	1	-1
1972	Cin-N	.963	64	83	149	9	24	-9
1973	Cin-N	.964	75	103	216	12	44	9
1974	Cin-N	.958	12	15	31	2	7	5
1975	Cin-N	.961	34	43	106	6	18	10
1976	Atl-N	.950	151	243	466	**37**	88	0
1977	Atl-N	.979	41	73	116	4	17	-1
1978	Atl-N	.976	77	97	189	7	30	-7
1979	Atl-N	.945	39	40	80	7	15	-4
Total	11	.959	621	854	1614	106	293	-10

2B

1970	Cin-N	.943	18	28	38	4	10	5
1971	Cin-N	1.000	1	2	2	0	0	0
1972	Cin-N	1.000	12	14	19	0	6	2
1973	Cin-N	.957	14	17	28	2	8	3
1974	Cin-N	.968	38	58	62	4	12	8
1975	Cin-N	1.000	23	28	44	0	9	6
1976	Atl-N	1.000	1	1	0	0	0	0
1977	Atl-N	.964	24	40	66	4	13	5
1978	Atl-N	1.000	1	1	2	0	1	0
1979	Atl-N	1.000	5	2	5	0	1	0
Total	10	.970	137	190	267	4	60	29

3B

YEAR	TM/L	PCT	G	PO	A	E	DP	FR
1970	Cin-N	—	3	0	0	0	0	0
1971	Cin-N	1.000	1	0	1	0	0	0
1972	Cin-N	.929	10	3	10	1	0	0
1973	Cin-N	1.000	12	3	2	0	0	0
1974	Cin-N	.952	81	17	42	3	2	4
1975	Cin-N	.952	13	6	14	1	0	0
1976	Atl-N	1.000	1	0	1	0	0	0
1978	Atl-N	1.000	8	2	8	0	1	0
1979	Atl-N	.929	4	3	10	1	0	0
Total	9	.953	133	34	88	6	3	4

C

1979	Atl-N	—	1	0	0	0	0	0

■ Harry Chapman C

YEAR	TM/L	PCT	G	PO	A	E	DP	FR
1912	Chi-N	1.000	1	7	3	0	0	1
1914	StL-F	.973	51	247	77	9	8	-3
1915	StL-F	.989	53	293	79	4	6	8
1916	StL-A	.981	14	37	15	1	2	2
Total	4	.982	119	584	174	4	16	8

1B

1914	StL-F	1.000	1	1	0	0	0	0

2B

1914	StL-F	1.000	1	0	1	0	0	0

OF

1914	StL-F	—	1	0	0	0	0	0

■ Kelvin Chapman 2B

YEAR	TM/L	PCT	G	PO	A	E	DP	FR
1979	NY-N	.980	22	50	46	2	15	-4
1984	NY-N	.979	57	104	131	5	32	2
1985	NY-N	.970	48	70	89	5	17	-6
Total	3	.976	127	224	266	2	64	-8

3B

1979	NY-N	1.000	1	1	0	0	0	0
1984	NY-N	.800	3	1	3	1	1	-1
1985	NY-N	—	1	0	0	0	0	0
Total	3	.833	5	2	3	1	1	-1

■ Ray Chapman SS

YEAR	TM/L	PCT	G	PO	A	E	DP	FR
1912	Cle-A	.904	31	70	72	15	10	-10
1913	Cle-A	.936	138	299	408	48	59	-9
1914	Cle-A	.913	72	161	187	33	24	-12
1915	Cle-A	.944	154	**378**	469	50	38	9
1916	Cle-A	.935	52	117	170	20	19	4
1917	Cle-A	.938	156	**360**	**528**	59	71	**24**
1918	Cle-A	.938	**128**	321	398	49	42	6
1919	Cle-A	.944	115	255	347	36	44	0
1920	Cle-A	.959	111	243	371	26	43	12
Total	9	.939	957	2204	2950	336	350	24

2B

1914	Cle-A	.945	33	62	92	9	1	-2
1916	Cle-A	.930	16	37	43	6	3	-2
Total	2	.940	49	99	135	5	4	-4

3B

1916	Cle-A	.962	36	53	97	6	13	11

OF

1913	Cle-A	—	1	0	0	0	0	0
1918	Cle-A	.667	1	2	0	1	0	0
Total	2	.667	2	2	0	1	0	0

■ Sam Chapman OF

YEAR	TM/L	PCT	G	PO	A	E	DP	FR
1938	Phi-A	.952	110	229	8	12	0	-1
1939	Phi-A	.955	117	350	11	17	2	2
1940	Phi-A	.963	129	348	13	14	2	3
1941	Phi-A	.967	141	**416**	**21**	**15**	**5**	11
1945	Phi-A	1.000	8	18	0	0	0	2
1946	Phi-A	.970	145	369	13	**12**	4	**15**
1947	Phi-A	.987	146	**428**	16	6	2	5
1948	Phi-A	.982	118	368	8	7	2	3
1949	Phi-A	.979	154	**450**	11	10	3	8
1950	Phi-A	.978	140	**428**	11	10	4	7
1951	Phi-A	.957	17	43	1	2	0	0
	Cle-A	.985	84	132	2	2	1	-4
	Yr	.978	101	175	3	4	1	-4
Total	11	.972	1309	3579	115	107	25	49

1B

1939	Phi-A	.974	19	147	5	4	6	-2
1951	Cle-A	1.000	1	1	0	0	1	0
Total	2	.975	20	148	5	4	7	-2

■ Ben Chapman OF

YEAR	TM/L	PCT	G	PO	A	E	DP	FR
1931	NY-A	.963	137	300	14	12	1	8
1932	NY-A	.949	150	303	13	17	2	1
1933	NY-A	.975	147	288	**24**	8	4	11
1934	NY-A	.967	149	368	12	13	2	1
1935	NY-A	.964	138	372	**25**	15	**7**	13
1936	NY-A	.965	36	106	3	4	0	5
	Was-A	.959	97	271	10	12	4	1
	Yr	.961	133	377	13	16	4	6
1937	Was-A	.957	32	87	1	4	0	0
	Bos-A	.985	112	262	9	4	1	8
	Yr	.978	144	349	10	8	**1**	**8**
1938	Bos-A	.966	126	267	15	10	5	6
1939	Cle-A	.971	146	356	12	11	0	-9
1940	Cle-A	.964	140	307	10	12	3	2
1941	Was-A	.983	26	54	3	1	1	-1
	Chi-A	.992	49	122	4	1	1	2
	Yr	.989	75	176	7	2	2	1
1945	Phi-N	.933	10	13	1	1	0	-1
Total	12	.967	1495	3476	156	125	31	47

3B

1930	NY-A	.912	91	100	149	**24**	11	-8
1938	Bos-A	1.000	1	0	1	0	0	0
1945	Phi-N	.800	4	2	6	2	1	-1
Total	3	.908	96	102	156	6	12	-9

2B

1930	NY-A	.939	45	132	146	18	36	2
1931	NY-A	.967	11	25	33	2	4	0
Total	2	.944	56	157	179	0	40	2

SS

YEAR	TM/L	PCT	G	PO	A	E	DP	FR
1937	Bos-A	.750	1	2	1	1	0	-1

■ Joe Charboneau OF

1980	Cle-A	.963	67	125	6	5	1	0
1981	Cle-A	.963	27	51	1	2	0	0
1982	Cle-A	.955	18	21	0	1	0	-3
Total	3	.962	112	197	7	8	1	-3

■ Ed Charles 3B

1962	KC-A	.964	140	145	285	16	27	4
1963	KC-A	.949	158	153	310	25	19	-8
1964	KC-A	.954	147	138	259	19	25	-15
1965	KC-A	.971	128	150	251	12	28	-1
1966	KC-A	.963	104	85	201	11	21	-5
1967	KC-A	.966	18	17	40	2	1	0
	NY-N	.944	89	85	201	17	16	9
1968	NY-N	.954	106	69	200	13	19	1
1969	NY-N	.946	52	37	86	7	9	0
Total	8	.957	942	879	1833	122	165	-15

2B

1962	KC-A	1.000	2	3	1	0	1	0
1965	KC-A	1.000	1	1	3	0	1	0
Total	2	1.000	3	4	4	0	2	0

1B

1966	KC-A	1.000	1	1	0	0	0	0
1968	NY-N	1.000	2	10	1	0	0	0
Total	2	1.000	3	11	1	0	0	0

SS

1965	KC-A	—	1	0	0	0	0	0

OF

1966	KC-A	—	1	0	0	0	0	0

■ Chappy Charles 2B

1908	StL-N	.921	65	123	182	26	5	-10
1909	StL-N	.918	71	162	186	31	28	0
	Cin-N	.932	10	16	25	3	1	-2
	Yr	.920	81	178	211	34	29	-2
Total	2	.920	146	301	393	0	34	-12

SS

1908	StL-N	.910	31	57	95	15	20	-2
1909	StL-N	.923	26	62	81	12	5	-2
	Cin-N	.933	3	6	8	1	0	-1
	Yr	.924	29	68	89	13	5	-3
1910	Cin-N	.818	4	8	10	4	2	-2
Total	3	.911	64	133	194	2	27	-7

3B

1908	StL-N	.909	23	35	45	8	0	0
1909	StL-N	.923	2	6	6	1	0	1
Total	2	.911	25	41	51	9	0	1

■ Mike Chartak OF

1940	NY-A	1.000	3	4	0	0	0	-1
1942	Was-A	.926	24	48	2	4	1	-1
	StL-A	.974	64	142	10	4	3	4
	Yr	.962	88	190	12	8	4	3
1943	StL-A	.970	77	160	4	5	2	-4
1944	StL-A	1.000	7	16	0	0	0	0
Total	4	.967	175	370	16	3	6	-2

1B

1943	StL-A	.977	18	161	9	4	8	-2
1944	StL-A	1.000	12	89	5	0	5	0
Total	2	.985	30	250	14	4	13	-2

■ Hal Chase 1B

1905	NY-A	.976	124	1174	61	**31**	63	-9
1906	NY-A	.980	150	1507	89	33	54	-2
1907	NY-A	.973	121	1144	77	34	50	-1
1908	NY-A	.980	98	1020	54	22	35	-3
1909	NY-A	.978	118	1202	71	**28**	53	-2
1910	NY-A	.981	130	1373	65	28	68	-4
1911	NY-A	.974	124	**1257**	82	**36**	**62**	-1
1912	NY-A	.979	122	1162	79	**27**	49	3
1913	NY-A	.982	29	312	16	6	16	-1
	Chi-A	.976	102	1009	71	27	53	1
	Yr	.977	131	1321	87	33	69	0
1914	Chi-A	.981	58	632	43	13	27	2
	Buf-F	.980	73	690	38	15	33	-1
1915	Buf-F	.983	143	1460	83	**26**	84	0
1916	Cin-N	.986	98	932	37	14	66	-5
1917	Cin-N	.983	151	1499	80	**28**	100	-3
1918	Cin-N	.980	67	607	38	13	59	-2
1919	NY-N	.984	107	1205	65	21	62	-1
Total	15	.980	1815	18185	1049	402	934	-29

OF

1907	NY-A	1.000	4	8	2	0	0	2
1908	NY-A	.500	3	2	0	2	0	-1
1911	NY-A	.917	5	11	0	1	1	-2
1913	NY-A	1.000	5	9	0	0	0	-1
1915	Buf-F	1.000	1	3	0	0	0	0
1916	Cin-N	1.000	25	51	0	0	0	-1
1918	Cin-N	1.000	2	3	0	0	0	0
Total	7	.967	47	87	2	3	1	-3

2B

1905	NY-A	.667	1	1	1	1	0	0
1906	NY-A	1.000	1	2	3	0	0	0
1908	NY-A	.818	3	2	7	2	0	-1
1911	NY-A	1.000	2	3	3	0	1	0
1912	NY-A	.808	7	11	10	5	1	-5
1913	NY-A	.765	5	10	3	4	0	-3
1916	Cin-N	.937	16	40	49	6	7	1
Total	7	.890	35	69	76	8	9	-8

SS

1905	NY-A	1.000	2	3	0	0	0	0
1909	NY-A	—	1	1	0	0	0	0
1910	NY-A	1.000	3	3	0	0	0	0

3B

1908	NY-A	1.000	1	2	4	0	1	1

■ Cupid Childs 2B

YEAR	TM/L	PCT	G	PO	A	E	DP	FR
1888	Phi-N	.857	2	2	4	1	1	0
1890	Syr-a	.928	125	372	367	57	59	13
1891	Cle-N	.910	141	371	455	82	54	-12
1892	Cle-N	.938	145	357	441	53	51	-6
1893	Cle-N	.926	123	348	424	62	56	10
1894	Cle-N	.916	118	313	374	63	51	-3
1895	Cle-N	.921	119	337	394	63	42	10
1896	Cle-N	.942	132	375	487	53	73	42
1897	Cle-N	.944	114	319	384	42	42	17
1898	Cle-N	.931	110	273	370	48	37	9
1899	StL-N	.934	125	323	355	48	45	-12
1900	Chi-N	.935	137	323	431	52	57	16
1901	Chi-N	.939	63	146	192	22	34	9
Total	13	.930	1454	3859	4678	646	602	93
	SS							
1890	Syr-a	.833	1	3	2	1	0	-1

■ Pete Childs 2B

YEAR	TM/L	PCT	G	PO	A	E	DP	FR
1901	StL-N	.907	19	39	49	9	4	-4
	Chi-N	.959	60	128	198	14	19	13
	Yr	.947	79	167	247	23	23	9
1902	Phi-N	.945	123	271	349	36	26	-9
Total	2	.946	202	438	596	9	49	0
	OF							
1901	StL-N	1.000	2	2	0	0	0	-1
	SS							
1901	StL-N	.333	1	0	1	2	0	-1

■ Rich Chiles OF

YEAR	TM/L	PCT	G	PO	A	E	DP	FR
1971	Hou-N	1.000	27	35	0	0	0	-3
1972	Hou-N	1.000	2	4	0	0	0	0
1973	NY-N	1.000	8	22	1	0	1	3
1976	Hou-N	1.000	1	1	0	0	0	0
1977	Min-A	.946	22	35	0	2	0	-2
1978	Min-A	.965	61	108	3	4	0	0
Total	6	.972	121	205	4	6	1	-2

■ Lou Chiozza 2B

YEAR	TM/L	PCT	G	PO	A	E	DP	FR
1934	Phi-N	.938	85	215	257	31	37	-17
1935	Phi-N	.947	120	296	405	39	54	3
1936	Phi-N	.938	33	63	103	11	13	-1
1937	NY-N	1.000	2	1	0	0	0	0
1938	NY-N	.944	34	59	109	10	9	-6
Total	5	.943	274	634	874	1	113	-21
	3B							
1934	Phi-N	.844	26	13	41	10	2	-7
1935	Phi-N	1.000	2	1	0	0	0	0
1936	Phi-N	.882	26	26	34	8	2	-1
1937	NY-N	.939	93	90	171	17	9	1
1938	NY-N	1.000	1	0	1	0	0	0
1939	NY-N	.915	30	20	55	7	7	-3
Total	6	.915	178	150	302	2	20	-10
	OF							
1934	Phi-N	1.000	17	38	0	0	0	0
1936	Phi-N	.972	90	235	7	7	1	-2
1937	NY-N	1.000	12	30	1	0	0	1
1938	NY-N	.958	16	21	2	1	0	-1
Total	4	.977	135	324	10	8	1	-2
	SS							
1939	NY-N	.976	8	19	21	1	4	0

■ Harry Chiti C

YEAR	TM/L	PCT	G	PO	A	E	DP	FR
1950	Chi-N	1.000	1	1	1	0	0	-1
1951	Chi-N	.913	8	34	8	4	1	0
1952	Chi-N	.984	32	170	13	3	6	6
1955	Chi-N	.984	113	495	69	9	10	2
1956	Chi-N	.981	67	327	35	7	2	3
1958	KC-A	.987	83	425	41	6	9	5
1959	KC-A	.988	47	228	25	3	5	2
1960	KC-A	.983	52	263	24	5	1	-1
	Det-A	.984	36	173	17	3	0	1
	Yr	.984	88	436	41	8	1	0
1961	Det-A	1.000	5	19	3	0	0	1
1962	NY-N	.971	14	62	4	2	1	-1
Total	10	.983	458	2197	240	2	35	17

■ Neil Chrisley OF

YEAR	TM/L	PCT	G	PO	A	E	DP	FR
1957	Was-A	.810	11	16	1	4	0	-2
1958	Was-A	.992	69	117	6	1	2	3
1959	Det-A	1.000	21	28	0	0	0	-2
1960	Det-A	.981	47	101	2	2	0	0
Total	4	.975	148	262	9	7	2	-1
	1B							
1960	Det-A	.889	2	8	0	1	0	0
	3B							
1958	Was-A	—	1	0	0	0	0	0

■ John Christensen OF

YEAR	TM/L	PCT	G	PO	A	E	DP	FR
1984	NY-N	.500	5	1	0	1	0	-1
1985	NY-N	.956	38	41	2	2	0	-4
1987	Sea-A	1.000	43	60	3	0	1	1
1988	Min-A	1.000	17	20	0	0	0	0
Total	4	.977	103	122	5	3	1	-4

■ Cuckoo Christensen OF

YEAR	TM/L	PCT	G	PO	A	E	DP	FR
1926	Cin-N	.978	93	170	6	4	2	-10
1927	Cin-N	.957	50	106	6	5	3	-1
Total	2	.970	143	276	12	9	5	-11

■ Mark Christman 3B

YEAR	TM/L	PCT	G	PO	A	E	DP	FR
1938	Det-A	.983	69	86	140	4	14	8
1939	Det-A	.900	5	4	5	1	1	-1
1943	StL-A	.991	37	41	74	1	5	2
1944	StL-A	.972	145	172	316	14	34	4
1945	StL-A	.973	77	79	137	6	12	-3
1946	StL-A	.975	77	61	171	6	21	9
1948	Was-A	.962	9	12	13	1	1	-1
1949	Was-A	.967	23	18	41	2	7	3
Total	8	.975	442	473	897	5	95	21

YEAR	TM/L	PCT	G	PO	A	E	DP	FR
	SS							
1938	Det-A	.949	21	46	66	6	17	1
1939	Det-A	.960	64	151	209	15	45	22
1943	StL-A	.990	24	48	52	1	15	-3
1946	StL-A	.968	47	77	137	7	23	1
1947	Was-A	.978	106	203	291	11	75	-10
1948	Was-A	.969	102	207	259	15	59	-30
1949	Was-A	.923	4	7	5	1	1	-1
Total	7	.969	368	739	1019	6	235	-20
	1B							
1943	StL-A	1.000	20	161	11	0	11	0
1944	StL-A	.971	3	33	1	1	2	-1
1949	Was-A	.979	6	42	5	1	2	1
Total	3	.992	29	236	17	2	15	0
	2B							
1939	StL-A	—	1	0	0	0	0	0
1943	StL-A	.985	14	29	35	1	10	0
1947	Was-A	1.000	1	2	2	0	0	0
1948	Was-A	.917	3	6	5	1	0	-1
1949	Was-A	1.000	1	2	2	0	0	0
Total	5	.976	20	39	44	2	10	-1

■ Joe Christopher OF

YEAR	TM/L	PCT	G	PO	A	E	DP	FR
1959	Pit-N	1.000	9	5	0	0	0	0
1960	Pit-N	1.000	17	24	0	0	0	2
1961	Pit-N	.978	55	86	2	2	1	-2
1962	NY-N	.972	94	133	5	4	4	0
1963	NY-N	.983	45	58	1	1	1	-3
1964	NY-N	.974	145	251	10	7	2	-1
1965	NY-N	.989	112	180	3	2	0	-7
1966	Bos-A	1.000	2	1	0	0	0	0
Total	8	.979	479	738	21	6	8	-11

■ Gino Cimoli OF

YEAR	TM/L	PCT	G	PO	A	E	DP	FR
1956	Bro-N	.946	62	35	0	2	0	3
1957	Bro-N	.979	138	265	11	6	2	4
1958	LA-N	.974	104	180	10	5	2	0
1959	StL-N	.979	141	267	12	6	2	-9
1960	Pit-N	.964	91	181	5	7	1	1
1961	Pit-N	.971	19	33	1	1	0	0
	Mil-N	.985	31	66	0	1	0	-2
	Yr	.980	50	99	1	2	0	-2
1962	KC-A	.968	147	231	8	8	2	-8
1963	KC-A	.985	136	256	14	4	3	4
1964	KC-A	1.000	4	6	0	0	0	0
	Bal-A	.893	35	25	0	3	0	-2
	Yr	.912	39	31	0	3	0	-2
1965	Cal-A	1.000	1	2	0	0	0	0
Total	10	.974	909	1547	61	3	12	-9

■ Bill Cissell 2B

YEAR	TM/L	PCT	G	PO	A	E	DP	FR
1930	Chi-A	.948	107	251	336	32	60	-14
1931	Chi-A	.962	23	57	69	5	11	-4
1932	Cle-A	.964	129	329	475	30	82	11
1933	Cle-A	.947	62	151	205	20	24	-10
1934	Bos-A	.959	96	280	281	24	62	-2
1937	Phi-A	.962	33	87	115	8	17	3
1938	NY-A	.977	33	87	127	5	20	9
Total	7	.958	483	1242	1608	124	276	-9
	SS							
1928	Chi-A	.938	123	255	360	41	77	-2
1929	Chi-A	.937	152	357	459	55	90	-3
1930	Chi-A	.867	10	15	24	6	2	-3
1931	Chi-A	.944	83	168	233	24	47	-7
1932	Chi-A	.928	12	40	24	5	9	0
	Cle-A	.929	6	3	10	1	1	0
	Yr	.928	18	43	34	6	10	0
1933	Cle-A	.967	46	87	146	8	23	3
1934	Bos-A	.833	7	6	9	3	3	-2
Total	7	.939	439	931	1265	143	252	-14
	3B							
1930	Chi-A	.966	24	24	62	3	7	7
1931	Chi-A	—	1	0	0	0	0	0
1933	Cle-A	—	1	0	0	0	0	0
1934	Bos-A	1.000	2	1	2	0	0	0
1938	NY-N	.875	6	3	11	2	0	0
Total	5	.954	34	28	75	5	7	7

■ Bud Clancy 1B

YEAR	TM/L	PCT	G	PO	A	E	DP	FR
1924	Chi-A	.947	8	69	3	4	4	-2
1926	Chi-A	.991	10	104	6	1	11	0
1927	Chi-A	.991	123	1184	81	11	76	0
1928	Chi-A	.991	128	1175	93	12	104	5
1929	Chi-A	.991	74	647	49	6	47	2
1930	Chi-A	.995	60	583	24	3	38	-3
1932	Bro-N	.996	53	524	40	2	55	3
1934	Phi-N	1.000	10	99	4	0	11	-1
Total	8	.992	466	4385	300	9	346	4

■ John Clapp C

YEAR	TM/L	PCT	G	PO	A	E	DP	FR
1876	StL-N	.874	61	333	56	56	5	11
1877	StL-N	.887	53	269	44	40	2	-4
1878	Ind-N	.930	9	29	11	3	0	-2
1879	Buf-N	.906	63	286	60	36	4	-11
1880	Cin-N	.897	73	420	121	62	5	14
1881	Cle-N	.890	48	211	73	35	8	3
1883	NY-N	.895	16	80	31	13	1	7
Total	7	.892	323	1628	396	245	25	12
	OF							
1876	StL-N	.667	4	2	0	1	0	-1
1877	StL-N	.778	10	7	0	2	0	-1
1878	Ind-N	.890	44	60	5	8	0	-3
1879	Buf-N	.733	7	11	0	4	0	-2
1880	Cin-N	.941	10	16	0	1	0	-1
1881	Cle-N	.827	21	37	6	9	2	0
1883	NY-N	.800	5	7	1	2	0	0
Total	7	.849	101	140	12	7	2	-8
	1B							
1877	StL-N	1.000	1	9	1	0	0	0
1878	Ind-N	.967	12	143	2	5	6	0

YEAR	TM/L	PCT	G	PO	A	E	DP	FR
Total	2	.969	13	152	3	5	6	0
	SS							
1878	Ind-N	.750	3	1	8	3	0	-2
	2B							
1876	StL-N	.000	1	0	0	1	0	-1
1878	Ind-N	.800	1	1	7	2	0	0
Total	2	.727	2	1	7	3	0	-1

■ Allie Clark OF

YEAR	TM/L	PCT	G	PO	A	E	DP	FR
1947	NY-A	1.000	16	36	0	0	0	0
1948	Cle-A	.982	65	108	4	2	1	-7
1949	Cle-A	1.000	17	14	1	0	0	-4
1950	Cle-A	.987	41	75	2	1	0	-2
1951	Cle-A	1.000	3	3	0	0	0	-1
	Phi-A	.984	32	60	2	1	1	-1
	Yr	.985	35	63	2	1	1	-2
1952	Phi-A	.988	48	78	2	1	0	-4
1953	Phi-A	1.000	19	33	2	0	0	-1
	Chi-A	1.000	1	1	0	0	0	0
	Yr	1.000	20	34	2	0	0	-1
Total	7	.988	242	408	13	5	2	-20
	3B							
1948	Cle-A	.875	5	2	5	1	2	-1
1951	Phi-A	.906	10	9	20	3	3	-1
Total	2	.900	15	11	25	4	5	-2
	1B							
1948	Cle-A	1.000	1	5	0	0	0	0
1949	Cle-A	1.000	1	1	0	0	0	0
1952	Phi-A	1.000	2	4	0	0	0	0
1953	Chi-A	1.000	1	5	0	0	2	0
Total	4	1.000	5	15	0	0	2	0

■ Earl Clark OF

YEAR	TM/L	PCT	G	PO	A	E	DP	FR
1927	Bos-N	1.000	13	30	0	0	0	0
1928	Bos-N	.987	27	77	0	1	0	0
1929	Bos-N	.978	74	216	7	5	3	1
1930	Bos-N	.977	63	165	3	4	1	7
1931	Bos-N	.970	14	30	2	1	0	0
1932	Bos-N	1.000	16	19	2	0	1	4
1933	Bos-N	1.000	6	10	0	0	0	-1
1934	StL-A	1.000	9	22	0	0	0	0
Total	8	.981	222	569	14	1	5	11

■ Dave Clark OF

YEAR	TM/L	PCT	G	PO	A	E	DP	FR
1986	Cle-A	1.000	10	26	0	0	0	1
1987	Cle-A	1.000	13	24	1	0	0	1
1988	Cle-A	.947	23	36	0	2	0	1
1989	Cle-A	.964	21	27	0	1	0	-1
1990	Chi-N	1.000	39	60	2	0	0	-3
Total	5	.983	106	173	3	3	0	-1

■ Jack Clark OF

YEAR	TM/L	PCT	G	PO	A	E	DP	FR
1975	SF-N	1.000	3	7	0	0	0	0
1976	SF-N	.987	26	71	3	1	1	3
1977	SF-N	.975	114	226	11	6	2	4
1978	SF-N	.982	152	320	16	6	5	10
1979	SF-N	.982	140	261	13	5	7	5
1980	SF-N	.967	120	229	7	8	1	-4
1981	SF-N	.981	98	193	14	4	4	5
1982	SF-N	.980	155	281	10	6	2	-3
1983	SF-N	.967	133	249	17	9	3	7
1984	SF-N	.990	54	94	3	1	0	-5
1985	StL-N	1.000	12	12	0	0	0	0
1987	StL-N	1.000	1	1	0	0	0	0
1988	NY-A	.951	19	38	1	2	0	-1
1989	SD-N	1.000	12	22	1	0	0	0
Total	14	.978	1039	2004	96	8	25	21
	1B							
1983	SF-N	1.000	2	13	3	0	2	1
1984	SF-N	.970	4	26	6	1	3	1
1985	StL-N	.988	121	1116	66	14	102	-8
1986	StL-N	.995	64	623	35	3	66	-6
1987	StL-N	.989	126	1151	77	14	116	-8
1988	NY-A	.970	10	91	7	3	8	-1
1989	SD-N	.988	131	1135	88	15	99	0
1990	SD-N	.994	110	855	69	6	72	-3
Total	8	.990	568	5010	351	6	468	-24
	3B							
1975	SF-N	1.000	2	1	1	0	0	0
1979	SF-N	1.000	2	1	0	0	0	0
Total	2	1.000	4	2	1	0	0	0

■ Mel Clark OF

YEAR	TM/L	PCT	G	PO	A	E	DP	FR
1951	Phi-N	1.000	7	13	0	0	0	-1
1952	Phi-N	.988	38	81	5	0	1	1
1953	Phi-N	.991	51	104	2	1	0	-2
1954	Phi-N	.961	63	114	9	5	2	1
1955	Phi-N	1.000	8	19	3	0	1	3
1957	Det-A	1.000	2	4	0	0	0	0
Total	6	.983	169	335	19	6	4	2
	3B							
1952	Phi-N	1.000	1	0	1	0	0	0

■ Bob Clark OF

YEAR	TM/L	PCT	G	PO	A	E	DP	FR
1979	Cal-A	.978	19	41	4	1	0	4
1980	Cal-A	.982	77	213	6	4	2	13
1981	Cal-A	1.000	34	66	5	0	0	4
1982	Cal-A	1.000	102	88	2	0	0	4
1983	Cal-A	1.000	72	122	0	0	0	-4
1984	Mil-A	.981	56	106	0	2	0	-4
1985	Mil-A	1.000	27	72	1	0	0	2
Total	7	.990	387	708	18	7	2	19
	3B							
1983	Cal-A	—	1	0	0	0	0	0

■ Bob Clark C

YEAR	TM/L	PCT	G	PO	A	E	DP	FR
1886	Bro-a	.864	44	219	67	45	7	-7
1887	Bro-a	.871	45	197	66	39	7	-1
1888	Bro-a	.884	36	197	61	34	6	-1
1889	Bro-a	.870	53	275	86	54	4	5
1890	Bro-N	.836	42	164	40	40	5	-12

YEAR	TM/L	PCT	G	PO	A	E	DP	FR
1891	Cin-N	.868	16	50	16	10	1	-5
1893	Lou-N	.947	10	9	9	1	1	-2
Total	7	.867	246	1111	345	223	31	-23
	OF							
1886	Bro-a	.808	17	20	1	5	1	-3
1887	Bro-a	.571	3	4	0	3	0	-1
1888	Bro-a	.923	8	11	1	1	0	0
1890	Bro-N	1.000	1	1	0	0	0	0
1893	Lou-N	1.000	1	1	0	0	0	0
Total	5	.813	30	37	2	9	1	-4
	SS							
1886	Bro-a	.776	12	7	38	13	3	-2
1893	Lou-N	1.000	1	0	2	0	0	0
Total	2	.783	13	7	40	3	3	-2
	1B							
1888	Bro-a	1.000	1	3	0	0	0	0

■ Will Clark　1B

YEAR	TM/L	PCT	G	PO	A	E	DP	FR
1986	SF-N	.989	102	942	72	11	76	-1
1987	SF-N	.991	139	1253	103	13	130	2
1988	SF-N	.993	158	1492	104	12	126	-3
1989	SF-N	.994	158	1445	111	10	117	0
1990	SF-N	.992	153	1456	119	12	118	1
Total	5	.992	710	6588	509	8	567	-1

■ Willie Clark　1B

YEAR	TM/L	PCT	G	PO	A	E	DP	FR
1895	NY-N	.974	23	213	14	6	16	1
1896	NY-N	.975	65	634	25	17	40	-4
1897	NY-N	.984	107	1038	64	18	69	3
1898	Pit-N	.984	57	601	27	10	29	0
1899	Pit-N	.989	78	837	36	10	37	1
Total	5	.983	330	3323	166	1	191	1
	OF							
1897	NY-N	1.000	7	9	0	0	0	-1
	3B							
1897	NY-N	1.000	1	0	3	0	0	0

■ Fred Clarke　OF

YEAR	TM/L	PCT	G	PO	A	E	DP	FR
1894	Lou-N	.885	75	162	15	23	2	4
1895	Lou-N	.881	132	344	20	49	4	11
1896	Lou-N	.908	131	277	18	30	2	0
1897	Lou-N	.926	127	282	18	24	0	6
1898	Lou-N	.940	149	344	19	23	3	6
1899	Lou-N	.964	144	327	20	13	2	2
1900	Pit-N	.944	104	263	8	16	2	3
1901	Pit-N	.970	127	282	13	9	0	3
1902	Pit-N	.958	113	215	13	10	2	-1
1903	Pit-N	.962	101	168	10	7	3	-8
1904	Pit-N	.979	70	135	4	3	2	0
1905	Pit-N	.976	137	270	16	7	4	4
1906	Pit-N	.974	110	209	15	6	3	6
1907	Pit-N	.987	144	298	15	4	2	6
1908	Pit-N	.973	151	350	15	10	2	10
1909	Pit-N	.987	152	362	17	5	2	7
1910	Pit-N	.967	118	284	10	10	4	7
1911	Pit-N	.970	101	216	8	7	3	2
1913	Pit-N	1.000	2	2	0	0	0	0
1915	Pit-N	—	1	0	0	0	0	0
Total	20	.952	2189	4790	254	256	42	68
	SS							
1899	Lou-N	.759	3	13	9	7	0	-1
1901	Pit-N	.500	1	1	2	3	1	-1
1903	Pit-N	1.000	2	3	1	0	0	0
Total	3	.744	6	17	12	0	1	-2
	3B							
1901	Pit-N	—	1	0	0	0	0	0

■ Horace Clarke　2B

YEAR	TM/L	PCT	G	PO	A	E	DP	FR
1965	NY-A	1.000	7	5	10	0	1	0
1966	NY-A	.964	16	42	38	3	9	-2
1967	NY-A	.990	140	348	410	8	79	15
1968	NY-A	.984	139	357	444	13	80	30
1969	NY-A	.982	156	373	429	15	112	-4
1970	NY-A	.979	157	379	478	18	95	-7
1971	NY-A	.981	156	386	455	16	97	-3
1972	NY-A	.985	143	347	399	11	104	6
1973	NY-A	.979	147	378	442	18	107	6
1974	NY-A	1.000	20	27	27	0	5	-5
	SD-N	.978	21	40	47	2	6	-4
Total	10	.983	1102	2682	3179	104	695	32
	SS							
1965	NY-A	1.000	1	1	1	0	0	0
1966	NY-A	.970	63	102	154	8	37	-17
Total	2	.970	64	103	155	8	37	-17
	3B							
1965	NY-A	.923	17	15	45	5	4	3
1966	NY-A	.857	4	2	4	1	2	0
Total	2	.917	21	17	49	6	6	3

■ Nig Clarke　C

YEAR	TM/L	PCT	G	PO	A	E	DP	FR
1905	Cle-A	1.000	5	7	2	0	0	-1
	Det-A	1.000	2	12	2	0	0	1
	Cle-A	.961	37	159	37	8	3	0
	Yr	.965	44	178	41	8	3	0
1906	Cle-A	.982	54	211	58	5	4	-1
1907	Cle-A	.961	115	470	119	24	9	-10
1908	Cle-A	.969	90	327	108	14	6	-7
1909	Cle-A	.952	44	192	65	13	2	-2
1910	Cle-A	.974	17	82	32	3	0	3
1911	StL-A	.926	73	251	111	29	15	-4
1919	Phi-N	.969	22	63	30	3	1	1
1920	Pit-N	1.000	3	12	4	0	0	1
Total	9	.960	462	1786	568	9	40	-19
	1B							
1911	StL-A	.927	4	37	1	3	2	-1

■ Josh Clarke　OF

YEAR	TM/L	PCT	G	PO	A	E	DP	FR
1898	Lou-N	.917	5	11	0	1	0	-1
1905	StL-N	.942	26	48	1	3	0	-2
1908	Cle-A	.963	131	220	13	9	1	-3

YEAR	TM/L	PCT	G	PO	A	E	DP	FR
1909	Cle-A	.600	4	3	0	2	0	-1
1911	Bos-N	.938	30	68	7	5	1	3
Total	5	.949	196	350	21	0	2	-4
	2B							
1905	StL-N	.892	16	2648		9	0	-5
	SS							
1905	StL-N	.933	4	7	7	1	0	-2

■ Tommy Clarke　C

YEAR	TM/L	PCT	G	PO	A	E	DP	FR
1909	Cin-N	.965	17	85	26	4	1	4
1910	Cin-N	.971	56	217	52	8	3	0
1911	Cin-N	.970	81	313	74	12	10	2
1912	Cin-N	.983	63	239	58	5	7	5
1913	Cin-N	.979	100	378	131	11	5	-9
1914	Cin-N	.973	106	448	132	16	12	-3
1915	Cin-N	.981	72	294	71	7	7	-5
1916	Cin-N	.965	51	187	58	9	3	-11
1917	Cin-N	.991	29	93	23	1	2	-6
1918	Chi-N	—	1	0	0	0	0	0
Total	10	.975	576	2254	625	3	50	-23
	1B							
1911	Cin-N	.833	1	5	0	1	1	0

■ Boileryard Clarke　C

YEAR	TM/L	PCT	G	PO	A	E	DP	FR
1893	Bal-N	.909	38	135	45	18	3	-1
1894	Bal-N	.903	23	80	22	11	1	-2
1895	Bal-N	.938	60	176	67	16	8	5
1896	Bal-N	.948	67	203	53	14	5	-9
1897	Bal-N	.939	59	191	38	15	2	-16
1898	Bal-N	.962	70	289	69	14	6	5
1899	Bos-N	.940	60	213	69	18	4	-2
1900	Bos-N	.928	67	246	104	27	8	8
1901	Was-A	.952	107	358	122	24	11	-10
1902	Was-A	.972	87	288	97	11	8	-4
1903	Was-A	.933	37	148	46	14	1	-7
1904	Was-A	.977	52	229	72	7	9	2
1905	NY-N	.971	12	31	2	1	0	0
Total	13	.947	739	2587	806	190	66	-31
	1B							
1893	Bal-N	.980	11	97	3	2	5	-1
1894	Bal-N	.976	5	40	0	1	5	-1
1895	Bal-N	.978	6	43	2	1	5	0
1896	Bal-N	.959	14	116	2	5	11	-2
1897	Bal-N	1.000	4	35	2	0	4	0
1898	Bal-N	.967	10	87	2	3	4	-1
1900	Bos-N	1.000	8	60	4	0	1	1
1901	Was-A	.960	3	24	0	1	1	-1
1903	Was-A	.981	88	891	44	18	44	-5
1904	Was-A	.981	29	288	14	6	15	-2
1905	NY-N	.973	15	106	4	3	4	-1
Total	11	.979	193	1787	77	0	99	-13

■ Ellis Clary　3B

YEAR	TM/L	PCT	G	PO	A	E	DP	FR
1942	StL-A	1.000	2	1	0	0	0	0
1943	Was-A	.945	68	86	119	12	6	-8
	StL-A	.972	14	10	25	1	3	-1
	Yr	.949	82	96	144	13	9	-9
1944	StL-A	1.000	1	10	19	0	2	-1
1945	StL-A	.947	16	15	21	2	3	4
Total	4	.953	111	122	184	5	14	-6
	2B							
1942	Was-A	.969	69	162	181	11	37	-17
1943	StL-A	.950	3	8	11	1	1	0
1944	StL-A	.938	6	6	9	1	2	0
1945	StL-A	.250	3	1	0	3	0	-1
Total	4	.959	81	177	201	6	40	-18
	SS							
1943	Was-A	1.000	1	0	1	0	0	0

■ Dain Clay　OF

YEAR	TM/L	PCT	G	PO	A	E	DP	FR
1943	Cin-N	.936	33	42	2	3	0	-2
1944	Cin-N	.993	98	272	4	2	0	-4
1945	Cin-N	.989	152	446	10	5	3	1
1946	Cin-N	.988	120	312	10	4	3	2
Total	4	.987	403	1072	26	4	6	-3

■ Doug Clemens　OF

YEAR	TM/L	PCT	G	PO	A	E	DP	FR
1960	StL-N	1.000	1	2	0	0	0	0
1961	StL-N	.667	3	2	0	1	0	-1
1962	StL-N	.974	34	38	0	1	0	-3
1963	StL-N	1.000	3	3	1	0	0	1
1964	StL-N	.970	22	30	2	1	0	0
	Chi-N	.923	40	67	5	6	1	1
	Yr	.937	62	97	7	7	1	1
1965	Chi-N	.981	105	145	7	3	0	-8
1966	Chi-N	1.000	28	41	1	0	1	0
1967	Phi-N	1.000	10	5	0	0	0	-2
1968	Phi-N	1.000	17	25	1	0	0	0
Total	9	.969	263	358	17	2	2	-12
	1B							
1966	Phi-N	1.000	1	2	1	0	0	0

■ Roberto Clemente　OF

YEAR	TM/L	PCT	G	PO	A	E	DP	FR
1955	Pit-N	.978	118	253	18	6	5	12
1956	Pit-N	.957	139	274	17	13	2	7
1957	Pit-N	.979	109	272	9	6	1	13
1958	Pit-N	.982	135	312	22	6	3	21
1959	Pit-N	.948	104	229	10	13	1	7
1960	Pit-N	.971	142	246	19	8	2	1
1961	Pit-N	.969	144	256	27	9	5	13
1962	Pit-N	.973	142	269	19	8	1	13
1963	Pit-N	.958	151	239	11	11	2	-5
1964	Pit-N	.968	154	289	13	10	2	8
1965	Pit-N	.968	145	288	16	10	1	10
1966	Pit-N	.965	154	318	17	12	3	16
1967	Pit-N	.970	145	273	17	9	4	8
1968	Pit-N	.984	131	297	9	5	1	11
1969	Pit-N	.980	135	226	14	5	1	6
1970	Pit-N	.966	104	189	12	7	2	5
1971	Pit-N	.993	124	267	11	2	4	8

YEAR	TM/L	PCT	G	PO	A	E	DP	FR
1972	Pit-N	1.000	94	199	5	0	2	5
Total	18	.973	2370	4696	266	140	42	160
	2B							
1956	Pit-N	.667	2	1	1	1	0	-1
	3B							
1956	Pit-N	.667	1	0	2	1	0	0

■ Jack Clements　C

YEAR	TM/L	PCT	G	PO	A	E	DP	FR
1884	Phi-U	.890	20	114	32	18	0	-2
	Phi-N	.827	9	51	16	14	1	1
1885	Phi-N	.891	41	181	47	28	2	-5
1886	Phi-N	.930	47	318	52	28	3	7
1887	Phi-N	.940	59	328	79	26	8	8
1888	Phi-N	.927	85	494	104	47	6	-3
1889	Phi-N	.916	78	380	77	42	7	-8
1890	Phi-N	.944	91	503	92	35	12	0
1891	Phi-N	.927	107	415	108	41	10	-7
1892	Phi-N	.950	109	557	107	35	12	3
1893	Phi-N	.942	92	329	75	25	5	-15
1894	Phi-N	.946	45	178	32	12	4	-3
1895	Phi-N	.969	88	280	69	11	7	-12
1896	Phi-N	.966	53	149	51	7	3	-3
1897	Phi-N	.962	49	163	40	8	3	-3
1898	StL-N	.971	86	287	81	11	8	-6
1899	Cle-N	.938	4	8	7	1	0	0
1900	Bos-N	.948	10	45	10	3	2	0
Total	17	.937	1073	4780	1079	392	93	-48
	OF							
1884	Phi-U	.764	22	28	14	13	2	6
1885	Phi-N	.810	11	15	2	4	1	0
1886	Phi-N	.900	7	16	2	2	0	1
1888	Phi-N	1.000	1	2	0	0	0	0
Total	4	.806	41	61	18	9	3	7
	1B							
1890	Phi-N	1.000	5	46	3	0	2	1
1891	Phi-N	—	2	0	0	0	0	0
1893	Phi-N	.667	1	1	1	1	1	0
Total	3	.981	8	47	4	1	3	1
	SS							
1884	Phi-U	—	1	0	0	0	0	0
1887	Phi-N	1.000	3	7	10	0	2	0
Total	2	1.000	4	7	10	0	2	0
	3B							
1887	Phi-N	1.000	4	3	2	0	0	0

■ Verne Clemons　C

YEAR	TM/L	PCT	G	PO	A	E	DP	FR
1916	StL-A	.889	2	5	3	1	0	0
1919	StL-N	.982	75	289	89	7	8	2
1920	StL-N	.977	103	408	111	12	11	-6
1921	StL-N	.985	107	357	101	7	12	-4
1922	StL-N	.996	63	172	50	1	2	2
1923	StL-N	.981	41	124	34	3	1	5
1924	StL-N	.983	17	46	11	1	1	-1
Total	7	.983	408	1401	399	2	35	-2

■ Donn Clendenon　1B

YEAR	TM/L	PCT	G	PO	A	E	DP	FR
1962	Pit-N	.990	52	382	24	4	44	-2
1963	Pit-N	.991	151	1450	118	15	154	7
1964	Pit-N	.989	119	1153	75	14	116	0
1965	Pit-N	.984	158	1572	119	28	161	6
1966	Pit-N	.985	152	1452	96	24	182	-1
1967	Pit-N	.988	123	1199	89	15	122	5
1968	Pit-N	.990	155	1587	128	11	134	10
1969	Mon-N	.987	24	214	20	3	22	2
	NY-N	.984	58	418	25	7	46	-3
	Yr	.985	82	632	45	10	68	-1
1970	NY-N	.991	100	722	62	7	72	-2
1971	NY-N	.985	72	505	37	8	49	-2
1972	StL-N	.986	36	259	26	4	34	3
Total	11	.988	1200	10913	819	146	1136	23
	OF							
1961	Pit-N	1.000	8	15	1	0	0	0
1962	Pit-N	.943	19	32	1	2	0	0
1969	Mon-N	.900	11	16	2	2	2	1
	NY-N	—	1	0	0	0	0	0
	Yr	.900	12	16	2	2	2	1
Total	3	.944	39	63	4	4	2	1
	3B							
1965	Pit-N	1.000	1	0	2	0	0	0

■ Harlond Clift　3B

YEAR	TM/L	PCT	G	PO	A	E	DP	FR
1934	StL-A	.929	141	150	245	30	28	-16
1935	StL-A	.934	127	130	240	26	12	-6
1936	StL-A	.951	152	158	310	24	27	3
1937	StL-A	.947	155	198	405	34	50	41
1938	StL-A	.962	149	176	306	19	31	14
1939	StL-A	.953	149	184	324	25	34	12
1940	StL-A	.959	147	161	329	21	32	4
1941	StL-A	.959	154	195	316	22	27	7
1942	StL-A	.941	141	160	287	28	28	-1
1943	StL-A	.950	104	126	252	20	20	19
	Was-A	.968	8	18	12	1	0	0
	Yr	.951	112	144	264	21	20	19
1944	Was-A	.842	12	10	22	6	2	-2
1945	Was-A	.934	111	111	214	23	18	-3
Total	12	.948	1550	1777	3262	279	309	66
	2B							
1935	StL-A	.971	6	14	19	1	2	-1
	SS							
1942	StL-A	—	1	0	0	0	0	0

■ Monk Cline　OF

YEAR	TM/L	PCT	G	PO	A	E	DP	FR
1882	Bal-a	.825	39	78	16	20	1	7
1884	Lou-a	.875	90	143	25	24	1	8
1885	Lou-a	1.000	1	1	0	0	0	0
1888	KC-a	.883	70	91	22	15	4	6
1891	Lou-a	.906	21	27	2	3	0	-3
Total	5	.867	221	340	65	2	6	18
	SS							
1882	Bal-a	.680	8	4	13	8	3	-1

YEAR	TM/L	PCT	G	PO	A	E	DP	FR
1884	Lou-a	.750	6	3	12	5	0	-2
Total	2	.711	14	7	25	3	3	-3
2B								
1882	Bal-a	—	2	0	0	0	0	0
1888	KC-a	.875	3	3	4	1	1	-1
Total	2	.875	5	3	4	1	1	-1
3B								
1882	Bal-a	1.000	1	3	4	0	0	1
1885	Lou-a	1.000	1	1	1	0	0	-1
1888	KC-a	1.000	1	1	1	0	0	0
Total	3	1.000	3	5	6	0	0	0

■ Ty Cline OF

YEAR	TM/L	PCT	G	PO	A	E	DP	FR
1960	Cle-A	1.000	6	22	0	0	0	2
1961	Cle-A	1.000	12	19	0	0	0	-2
1962	Cle-A	.992	107	238	3	2	1	-3
1963	Mil-N	.992	62	116	5	1	3	9
1964	Mil-N	.982	54	50	4	1	0	5
1965	Mil-N	.969	86	119	5	4	1	8
1966	Chi-N	1.000	5	7	0	0	0	0
	Atl-N	1.000	19	21	1	0	0	1
	Yr	1.000	24	28	1	0	0	1
1967	Atl-N	1.000	1	1	0	0	0	0
	SF-N	1.000	37	51	0	0	0	-1
	Yr	1.000	38	52	0	0	0	-1
1968	SF-N	.971	70	93	6	3	1	1
1969	Mon-N	.988	41	77	2	1	1	2
1970	Cin-N	.966	20	27	1	1	1	1
1971	Cin-N	1.000	28	39	0	0	0	-1
Total	12	.986	548	880	27	3	8	22
1B								
1964	Mil-N	1.000	6	33	1	0	1	0
1965	Mil-N	1.000	5	23	2	0	1	0
1966	Atl-N	.984	6	61	1	1	9	-1
1968	SF-N	.995	24	179	8	1	12	-1
1969	Mon-N	.991	17	99	6	1	6	0
1970	Cin-N	1.000	2	6	0	0	0	0
1971	Cin-N	1.000	2	1	0	0	0	0
Total	7	.993	62	402	18	3	29	-2

■ Gene Clines OF

YEAR	TM/L	PCT	G	PO	A	E	DP	FR
1970	Pit-N	1.000	7	4	0	0	0	-1
1971	Pit-N	.981	74	146	8	3	2	6
1972	Pit-N	.958	83	131	7	6	0	-3
1973	Pit-N	.968	77	145	6	5	0	0
1974	Pit-N	.989	78	177	6	2	1	7
1975	NY-N	.982	60	98	9	2	2	6
1976	Tex-A	.987	103	215	9	3	1	0
1977	Chi-N	.986	63	68	3	1	0	-9
1978	Chi-N	.978	66	84	6	2	0	-3
Total	9	.979	611	1068	54	4	6	3

■ Billy Clingman 3B

YEAR	TM/L	PCT	G	PO	A	E	DP	FR
1895	Pit-N	.887	106	137	256	50	16	13
1896	Lou-N	.925	121	188	281	38	21	24
1897	Lou-N	.947	113	176	269	25	16	29
1898	Lou-N	.914	79	119	191	29	12	12
1903	Cle-A	.750	3	2	4	2	0	-1
Total	5	.919	422	622	1001	144	65	77
SS								
1890	Cin-N	.892	6	8	25	4	4	0
1898	Lou-N	.913	74	169	259	41	34	2
1899	Lou-N	.916	109	195	381	53	43	-4
1900	Chi-N	.872	47	81	150	34	19	-14
1901	Was-A	.932	137	290	462	55	56	18
1903	Cle-A	.943	7	13	20	2	5	-1
Total	6	.916	380	756	1297	189	161	1
2B								
1890	Cin-N	1.000	1	0	1	0	0	-1
1891	Cin-a	.667	1	0	2	1	0	-1
1898	Lou-N	1.000	1	1	8	0	0	1
1903	Cle-A	.932	11	24	31	4	2	1
Total	4	.931	14	25	42	5	2	0
OF								
1898	Lou-N	1.000	1	3	0	0	0	0

■ Jim Clinton OF

YEAR	TM/L	PCT	G	PO	A	E	DP	FR
1876	Lou-N	.783	14	14	4	5	1	-1
1882	Wor-N	.734	26	43	4	17	1	-4
1883	Bal-a	.842	92	158	18	33	2	5
1884	Bal-a	.807	104	134	17	36	5	-1
1885	Cin-a	.877	105	215	14	32	4	0
1886	Bal-a	.894	23	41	1	5	1	0
Total	6	.838	364	605	58	128	14	-1
2B								
1883	Bal-a	.739	2	9	8	6	1	1
1884	Bal-a	.800	1	1	3	1	0	0
Total	2	.750	3	10	11	7	1	1
1B								
1876	Lou-N	1.000	1	6	0	0	0	0

■ Lou Clinton OF

YEAR	TM/L	PCT	G	PO	A	E	DP	FR
1960	Bos-A	.966	89	165	4	6	2	0
1961	Bos-A	1.000	13	30	3	0	0	3
1962	Bos-A	.979	103	185	6	4	1	-3
1963	Bos-A	.982	146	319	7	6	0	8
1964	Bos-A	1.000	35	59	6	0	1	4
	LA-A	.985	86	123	12	2	3	2
	Yr	.990	121	182	18	2	4	6
1965	Cal-A	.983	73	107	6	2	1	2
	KC-A	—	1	0	0	0	0	0
	Cle-A	.941	9	15	1	1	0	0
	Yr	.977	83	122	7	3	1	2
1966	NY-A	.976	63	80	2	2	0	0
1967	NY-A	—	1	0	0	0	0	0
Total	8	.980	619	1083	47	23	8	16

■ Otis Clymer OF

YEAR	TM/L	PCT	G	PO	A	E	DP	FR
1905	Pit-N	.986	89	137	7	2	5	-3
1906	Pit-N	.900	11	17	1	2	0	-1
1907	Pit-N	.923	15	24	0	2	0	-2
	Was-A	.912	51	79	4	8	0	-4
1908	Was-A	.933	82	81	16	7	7	0
1909	Was-A	.922	41	44	3	4	1	-4
1913	Chi-N	.933	26	54	2	4	0	-2
	Bos-N	.880	11	22	0	3	0	-1
	Yr	.918	37	76	2	7	0	-3
Total	6	.939	326	458	33	2	13	-17
2B								
1908	Was-A	.941	13	14	18	2	1	-6
1B								
1905	Pit-N	1.000	1	2	1	0	0	0
1907	Pit-N	.813	1	13	0	3	1	-1
	Was-A	—	1	0	0	0	0	0
Total	2	.842	3	15	1	3	1	-1
3B								
1908	Was-A	.667	2	2	0	1	0	-1

■ Gil Coan OF

YEAR	TM/L	PCT	G	PO	A	E	DP	FR
1946	Was-A	.969	29	62	0	2	0	-2
1947	Was-A	1.000	11	22	1	0	1	0
1948	Was-A	.970	131	341	11	11	3	11
1949	Was-A	.975	97	225	8	6	3	2
1950	Was-A	.970	98	220	4	7	1	-3
1951	Was-A	.965	132	374	17	14	2	24
1952	Was-A	.984	86	185	4	3	1	0
1953	Was-A	1.000	46	105	2	0	1	1
1954	Bal-A	.968	67	148	1	5	0	-1
1955	Bal-A	.983	43	53	5	1	0	-1
	Chi-A	1.000	3	2	0	0	0	0
	NY-N	1.000	6	4	0	0	0	0
	Yr	.984	49	57	5	1	0	-1
Total	10	.973	749	1741	53	9	12	31

■ Ty Cobb OF

YEAR	TM/L	PCT	G	PO	A	E	DP	FR
1905	Det-A	.958	41	85	6	4	1	2
1906	Det-A	.961	96	208	14	9	4	6
1907	Det-A	.961	150	238	30	11	12	11
1908	Det-A	.944	150	212	23	14	5	4
1909	Det-A	.946	156	222	24	14	7	3
1910	Det-A	.958	137	305	18	14	4	9
1911	Det-A	.957	146	376	24	18	10	11
1912	Det-A	.940	140	324	21	22	5	0
1913	Det-A	.947	119	262	22	16	8	3
1914	Det-A	.949	96	177	8	10	0	-10
1915	Det-A	.951	156	328	22	18	7	-3
1916	Det-A	.953	143	325	18	17	9	-1
1917	Det-A	.973	152	373	27	11	9	13
1918	Det-A	.975	95	225	12	6	1	1
1919	Det-A	.973	123	272	19	8	3	-2
1920	Det-A	.966	112	246	8	9	2	-7
1921	Det-A	.970	121	301	27	10	2	13
1922	Det-A	.980	134	330	14	7	3	4
1923	Det-A	.969	141	362	14	12	2	5
1924	Det-A	.986	155	417	12	6	8	5
1925	Det-A	.948	105	267	9	15	1	-2
1926	Det-A	.950	55	109	4	6	2	-5
1927	Phi-A	.969	127	243	9	8	2	-5
1928	Phi-A	.964	85	154	7	6	0	-1
Total	24	.961	2935	6361	392	271	107	54
1B								
1916	Det-A	1.000	1	10	0	0	0	0
1918	Det-A	.980	13	133	12	3	6	1
Total	2	.981	14	143	12	3	6	1
2B								
1918	Det-A	.800	1	1	3	1	0	-1
3B								
1918	Det-A	1.000	1	1	1	0	0	0

■ Mickey Cochrane C

YEAR	TM/L	PCT	G	PO	A	E	DP	FR
1925	Phi-A	.984	133	419	79	8	9	-9
1926	Phi-A	.975	115	502	90	15	9	12
1927	Phi-A	.986	123	559	85	9	11	3
1928	Phi-A	.966	130	645	71	25	8	2
1929	Phi-A	.983	135	659	77	13	9	8
1930	Phi-A	.993	130	654	69	5	11	6
1931	Phi-A	.986	117	560	63	9	9	10
1932	Phi-A	.993	137	652	94	5	15	12
1933	Phi-A	.989	128	476	67	6	8	-7
1934	Det-A	.988	124	517	69	7	7	-5
1935	Det-A	.989	110	504	50	6	6	-5
1936	Det-A	.983	42	159	13	3	1	-8
1937	Det-A	1.000	27	108	13	0	1	-2
Total	13	.985	1451	6414	840	111	104	17
OF								
1932	Phi-A	—	1	0	0	0	0	0

■ Rich Coggins OF

YEAR	TM/L	PCT	G	PO	A	E	DP	FR
1972	Bal-A	1.000	13	39	1	0	1	4
1973	Bal-A	.987	101	220	6	3	3	3
1974	Bal-A	.984	105	238	3	4	1	-1
1975	Mon-N	1.000	10	16	0	0	0	-1
	NY-A	.970	36	62	2	2	2	3
1976	NY-A	1.000	2	3	0	0	0	1
	Chi-A	1.000	26	45	1	0	0	-2
	Yr	1.000	28	48	1	0	0	-1
Total	5	.986	293	623	13	9	7	7

■ Ed Cogswell 1B

YEAR	TM/L	PCT	G	PO	A	E	DP	FR
1879	Bos-N	.967	49	539	10	19	24	1
1880	Tro-N	.961	47	475	15	20	18	1
1882	Wor-N	.937	13	145	3	10	11	-1
Total	3	.960	109	1159	28	9	53	1

■ Andy Cohen 2B

YEAR	TM/L	PCT	G	PO	A	E	DP	FR
1926	NY-N	.792	10	4	15	5	0	0
1928	NY-N	.969	126	304	434	24	90	3
1929	NY-N	.964	94	227	315	20	52	12
Total	3	.964	230	535	764	9	142	15
SS								
1926	NY-N	1.000	10	6	12	0	1	1
1928	NY-N	.947	3	6	12	1	1	0
1929	NY-N	1.000	1	0	1	0	0	0
Total	3	.974	14	12	25	1	2	1
3B								
1926	NY-N	1.000	2	1	2	0	0	0
1928	NY-N	—	1	0	0	0	0	0
1929	NY-N	1.000	1	0	2	0	0	0
Total	3	1.000	4	1	4	0	0	0

■ Jimmie Coker C

YEAR	TM/L	PCT	G	PO	A	E	DP	FR
1958	Phi-N	1.000	2	11	0	0	0	1
1960	Phi-N	.982	76	394	43	8	5	2
1961	Phi-N	.984	11	59	1	1	0	1
1963	SF-N	1.000	2	4	0	0	0	-1
1964	Cin-N	1.000	11	63	10	0	0	3
1965	Cin-N	.993	19	145	7	1	2	6
1966	Cin-N	.979	39	205	25	5	2	4
1967	Cin-N	.976	34	146	14	4	4	-1
Total	8	.983	194	1027	100	9	13	15
OF								
1966	Cin-N	—	2	0	0	0	0	0

■ Rocky Colavito OF

YEAR	TM/L	PCT	G	PO	A	E	DP	FR
1955	Cle-A	1.000	2	7	1	0	1	2
1956	Cle-A	.968	98	177	6	6	0	-3
1957	Cle-A	.962	130	268	12	11	2	7
1958	Cle-A	.981	129	243	14	5	6	5
1959	Cle-A	.985	154	319	7	5	1	5
1960	Det-A	.976	144	271	11	7	5	3
1961	Det-A	.975	161	329	16	9	4	7
1962	Det-A	.992	161	359	10	3	1	14
1963	Det-A	.988	159	319	10	4	0	4
1964	KC-A	.973	159	275	10	8	1	1
1965	Cle-A	1.000	162	265	9	0	1	2
1966	Cle-A	.982	146	261	10	5	0	3
1967	Cle-A	.962	50	75	2	3	1	-3
	Chi-A	.977	58	83	2	2	2	-6
	Yr	.970	108	158	4	5	3	-9
1968	LA-N	1.000	33	45	2	0	1	-2
	NY-A	.933	28	27	1	2	0	-5
Total	14	.980	1774	3323	123	0	26	34
1B								
1958	Cle-A	.955	11	84	0	4	5	-3

■ Nate Colbert 1B

YEAR	TM/L	PCT	G	PO	A	E	DP	FR
1968	Hou-N	.977	5	43	0	1	2	-1
1969	SD-N	.990	134	1217	87	13	96	1
1970	SD-N	.991	153	1406	90	14	126	-8
1971	SD-N	.993	153	1372	106	10	125	1
1972	SD-N	.996	150	1290	103	6	119	7
1973	SD-N	.992	144	1300	98	11	124	3
1974	SD-N	.988	79	510	49	7	43	0
1975	Det-A	.982	44	407	22	8	31	-3
	Mon-N	.988	22	151	9	2	18	-1
1976	Mon-N	.969	6	58	4	2	2	0
Total	9	.991	890	7754	568	4	686	3
OF								
1968	Hou-N	.952	11	19	1	1	0	1
1974	SD-N	.980	48	95	3	2	0	1
1976	Mon-N	1.000	7	8	2	0	1	1
Total	3	.977	66	122	6	3	1	3
3B								
1970	SD-N	—	1	0	0	0	0	0

■ Dick Cole SS

YEAR	TM/L	PCT	G	PO	A	E	DP	FR
1951	Pit-N	1.000	8	12	14	0	1	0
1953	Pit-N	.965	77	139	192	12	40	-4
1954	Pit-N	.949	66	101	178	15	29	-10
1955	Pit-N	1.000	12	18	30	0	5	2
1956	Pit-N	.900	6	2	7	1	4	-3
Total	5	.961	169	272	421	8	79	-15
2B								
1951	StL-N	.969	14	21	41	2	10	5
	Pit-N	.981	34	85	74	3	18	-2
	Yr	.978	48	106	115	5	28	3
1953	Pit-N	1.000	7	16	11	0	2	0
1954	Pit-N	.967	17	43	46	3	5	-2
1955	Pit-N	.969	24	60	67	4	13	1
1956	Pit-N	1.000	12	14	17	0	3	1
1957	Mil-N	.952	10	11	9	1	5	1
Total	6	.975	118	250	265	3	56	-1
3B								
1954	Pit-N	.941	55	48	112	10	7	0
1955	Pit-N	.935	33	25	61	6	7	-1
1956	Pit-N	.947	18	4	14	1	2	-1
1957	Mil-N	1.000	1	1	0	0	0	0
Total	4	.940	107	78	187	7	16	-2
1B								
1953	Pit-N	1.000	1	1	0	0	0	0
1957	Mil-N	—	1	0	0	0	0	0
Total	2	1.000	2	1	0	0	0	0

■ Choo Choo Coleman C

YEAR	TM/L	PCT	G	PO	A	E	DP	FR
1961	Phi-N	.977	14	38	4	1	1	-1
1962	NY-N	.995	44	187	22	1	2	-9
1963	NY-N	.969	91	418	54	15	9	4
1966	NY-N	.963	5	24	2	1	0	0
Total	4	.977	154	667	82	8	12	-6
OF								
1963	NY-N	—	1	0	0	0	0	0

■ Jerry Coleman 2B

YEAR	TM/L	PCT	G	PO	A	E	DP	FR
1949	NY-A	.981	122	298	315	12	102	0
1950	NY-A	.977	152	384	384	18	137	-15
1951	NY-A	.968	120	245	268	17	84	1
1952	NY-A	.971	11	33	34	2	17	2
1953	NY-A	1.000	7	11	8	0	4	2
1954	NY-A	.977	79	183	198	9	62	19

YEAR	TM/L	PCT	G	PO	A	E	DP	FR
1955	NY-A	1.000	13	32	23	0	7	2
1956	NY-A	.979	41	89	94	4	32	12
1957	NY-A	.969	45	74	84	5	32	5
Total	9	.976	572	1349	1408	7	477	28
SS								
1949	NY-A	.957	4	6	16	1	4	1
1950	NY-A	.909	6	4	6	1	1	0
1951	NY-A	.982	18	27	27	1	8	2
1953	NY-A	.500	1	0	1	1	0	0
1954	NY-A	.941	30	26	54	5	9	-1
1955	NY-A	.966	29	33	51	3	17	-4
1956	NY-A	.967	24	40	48	3	14	5
1957	NY-A	.750	4	1	5	2	1	0
Total	8	.953	116	137	208	7	54	3
3B								
1954	NY-A	—	1	0	0	0	0	0
1955	NY-A	.500	1	1	0	1	0	-1
1956	NY-A	.905	18	9	10	2	0	-1
1957	NY-A	.958	21	15	31	2	1	0
Total	4	.930	41	25	41	5	1	-2

■ **Gordy Coleman** 1B

YEAR	TM/L	PCT	G	PO	A	E	DP	FR
1959	Cle-A	.955	3	18	3	1	1	0
1960	Cin-N	.998	66	559	63	1	69	7
1961	Cin-N	.991	150	1162	121	11	93	7
1962	Cin-N	.989	128	1021	83	12	100	-2
1963	Cin-N	.987	107	752	65	11	66	1
1964	Cin-N	.990	49	352	35	4	28	4
1965	Cin-N	.991	89	621	48	6	52	1
1966	Cin-N	.986	65	399	29	6	33	-1
1967	Cin-N	1.000	2	9	1	0	0	0
Total	9	.990	659	4893	448	2	442	17

■ **John Coleman** OF

YEAR	TM/L	PCT	G	PO	A	E	DP	FR
1883	Phi-N	.865	31	69	14	13	4	9
1884	Phi-N	.844	27	48	6	10	2	2
	Phi-a	.743	24	20	6	9	1	-1
1885	Phi-a	.844	93	128	23	28	5	-1
1886	Phi-a	.862	115	183	23	33	6	1
	Pit-a	.786	11	10	1	3	0	-2
	Yr	.858	126	193	24	36	6	-1
1887	Pit-N	.899	115	214	17	26	3	-1
1888	Pit-N	.928	91	160	20	14	2	4
1889	Phi-a	.000	1	0	0	1	0	-1
1890	Pit-N	1.000	2	1	0	0	0	0
Total	8	.873	510	833	110	137	23	10
1B								
1884	Phi-N	1.000	2	9	0	0	0	0
	Phi-a	.882	2	15	0	2	0	0
1886	Phi-a	1.000	6	42	1	0	3	0
1887	Phi-N	.857	2	12	0	2	0	-1
1888	Pit-N	.976	25	235	4	6	12	-2
Total	4	.970	37	313	5	0	15	-3
2B								
1883	Phi-N	—	1	0	0	0	0	-1
1886	Phi-a	1.000	1	0	2	0	0	0
Total	2	1.000	2	0	2	0	0	-1

■ **Ed Coleman** OF

YEAR	TM/L	PCT	G	PO	A	E	DP	FR
1932	Phi-A	1.000	16	24	3	0	1	0
1933	Phi-A	.948	89	178	5	10	2	-5
1934	Phi-A	.980	86	140	8	3	2	-4
1935	Phi-A	—	1	0	0	0	0	0
	StL-A	.974	102	173	11	5	1	-6
	Yr	.974	103	173	11	5	1	-6
1936	StL-A	.939	18	31	0	2	0	-4
Total	5	.966	312	546	27	0	6	-19

■ **Ray Coleman** OF

YEAR	TM/L	PCT	G	PO	A	E	DP	FR
1947	StL-A	.984	93	174	7	3	4	-3
1948	StL-A	.889	5	8	0	1	0	-1
	Phi-A	.978	53	126	7	3	3	2
	Yr	.972	58	134	7	4	3	1
1950	StL-A	.985	98	253	7	4	1	6
1951	StL-A	.975	87	185	9	5	1	3
	Chi-A	.980	51	141	3	3	1	6
	Yr	.977	138	326	12	8	2	9
1952	Chi-A	.978	73	130	5	3	0	6
	StL-A	1.000	16	27	0	0	0	0
	Yr	.982	89	157	5	3	0	6
Total	5	.980	476	1044	38	2	10	19

■ **Bob Coleman** C

YEAR	TM/L	PCT	G	PO	A	E	DP	FR
1913	Pit-N	.978	24	68	21	2	2	-3
1914	Pit-N	.977	72	223	68	7	4	2
1916	Cle-A	.972	12	24	11	1	1	-3
Total	3	.976	108	315	100	0	7	-4

■ **Vince Coleman** OF

YEAR	TM/L	PCT	G	PO	A	E	DP	FR
1985	StL-N	.979	150	305	16	7	1	7
1986	StL-N	.972	149	300	12	9	2	1
1987	StL-N	.970	150	274	16	9	3	2
1988	StL-N	.971	150	290	14	9	1	2
1989	StL-N	.962	142	247	5	10	1	-10
1990	StL-N	.981	120	244	12	5	2	4
Total	6	.973	861	1660	75	9	10	6

■ **Darnell Coles** 3B

YEAR	TM/L	PCT	G	PO	A	E	DP	FR
1983	Sea-A	.941	26	17	47	4	8	-4
1984	Sea-A	.918	42	28	62	8	10	-3
1985	Sea-A	.900	7	2	7	1	0	1
1986	Det-A	.938	133	107	242	23	23	-5
1987	Det-A	.847	36	31	63	17	5	-3
	Pit-N	.903	10	9	19	3	0	-1
1988	Pit-N	—	1	0	0	0	0	0
1989	Sea-A	.949	26	15	59	4	6	3
1990	Sea-A	.815	6	2	20	5	0	2
	Det-A	.926	8	6	19	2	2	2
	Yr	.870	14	8	39	7	2	4
Total	8	.918	295	217	538	7	54	-8

YEAR	TM/L	PCT	G	PO	A	E	DP	FR
OF								
1984	Sea-A	1.000	3	3	1	0	0	1
1985	Sea-A	1.000	2	4	0	0	0	0
1986	Det-A	1.000	2	3	0	0	0	0
1987	Det-A	1.000	8	3	0	0	0	0
	Pit-N	1.000	26	28	1	0	0	-2
1988	Pit-N	.990	55	98	0	1	0	-6
	Sea-A	.986	47	66	3	1	0	-7
1989	Sea-A	.975	89	184	9	5	3	4
1990	Sea-A	.970	20	32	0	1	0	-1
	Det-A	1.000	11	11	0	0	0	0
	Yr	.977	31	43	0	1	0	-1
Total	7	.982	263	432	14	8	3	-11
1B								
1987	Det-A	1.000	9	50	3	0	1	0
	Pit-N	1.000	1	2	0	0	0	0
1988	Pit-N	.667	1	2	0	1	0	0
	Sea-A	—	1	0	0	0	0	0
1989	Sea-A	.977	18	118	8	3	11	-1
1990	Sea-A	.955	4	18	3	1	1	1
Total	4	.976	34	190	14	5	13	0
SS								
1985	Sea-A	.918	15	19	37	5	10	6
1986	Det-A	1.000	2	1	0	0	0	0
1987	Det-A	1.000	1	0	1	0	0	0
Total	3	.921	18	20	38	5	10	6

■ **Dave Collins** OF

YEAR	TM/L	PCT	G	PO	A	E	DP	FR
1975	Cal-A	.988	75	159	3	2	2	-2
1976	Cal-A	.994	71	160	3	1	0	-3
1977	Sea-A	.983	73	124	6	2	2	-2
1978	Cin-N	.969	24	30	1	1	3	2
1979	Cin-N	.976	91	159	2	4	2	-12
1980	Cin-N	.986	141	337	5	5	1	-7
1981	Cin-N	.977	94	167	4	4	2	-5
1982	NY-A	.992	60	114	5	1	0	2
1983	Tor-A	.989	112	251	8	3	1	4
1984	Tor-A	.991	108	203	8	2	3	-2
1985	Oak-A	.978	91	221	1	5	0	2
1986	Det-A	.995	94	211	2	1	1	1
1987	Cin-N	1.000	21	36	0	0	0	0
1988	Cin-N	.965	35	53	2	2	0	-2
1989	Cin-N	1.000	16	41	0	0	0	2
1990	StL-N	.900	12	9	0	1	0	0
Total	16	.986	1118	2275	50	4	17	-22
1B								
1979	Cin-N	1.000	10	64	1	0	6	-2
1982	NY-A	.985	52	384	23	6	30	-3
1983	Tor-A	1.000	5	19	1	0	2	0
1984	Tor-A	1.000	6	34	3	0	4	0
1988	Cin-N	.867	3	13	0	2	2	-1
1990	StL-N	1.000	49	80	0	0	5	-2
Total	6	.987	125	594	28	8	49	-8

■ **Eddie Collins** 2B

YEAR	TM/L	PCT	G	PO	A	E	DP	FR
1906	Phi-A	—	1	0	0	0	0	0
1908	Phi-A	.944	47	111	127	14	5	-3
1909	Phi-A	.967	152	373	406	27	55	8
1910	Phi-A	.972	153	402	451	25	67	35
1911	Phi-A	.967	132	348	349	24	49	3
1912	Phi-A	.955	153	387	426	38	63	15
1913	Phi-A	.965	148	314	449	28	54	16
1914	Phi-A	.970	152	354	387	23	55	0
1915	Chi-A	.974	155	344	487	22	54	13
1916	Chi-A	.976	155	346	415	19	75	-6
1917	Chi-A	.969	156	353	388	24	68	-25
1918	Chi-A	.974	96	231	285	14	53	-1
1919	Chi-A	.974	140	347	401	20	66	3
1920	Chi-A	.976	153	449	471	23	76	10
1921	Chi-A	.968	136	376	458	28	84	27
1922	Chi-A	.976	154	406	451	21	73	-10
1923	Chi-A	.975	142	347	430	20	77	-4
1924	Chi-A	.977	150	396	446	20	83	-7
1925	Chi-A	.970	116	290	346	20	74	-9
1926	Chi-A	.973	101	228	307	15	53	-6
1927	Phi-A	.965	56	124	150	10	31	-7
1928	Phi-A	—	1	0	0	0	0	0
Total	22	.970	2650	6526	7630	435	1215	52
SS								
1906	Phi-A	.900	3	8	10	2	0	0
1907	Phi-A	.833	6	11	9	4	1	1
1908	Phi-A	.924	28	60	61	10	7	-7
1909	Phi-A	1.000	1	2	4	0	0	0
1927	Phi-A	—	1	0	0	0	0	0
1928	Phi-A	1.000	1	0	1	0	0	0
Total	6	.912	40	81	85	6	8	-7
OF								
1908	Phi-A	.929	10	13	0	1	0	-1
3B								
1906	Phi-A	1.000	1	1	1	0	0	0

■ **Hub Collins** 2B

YEAR	TM/L	PCT	G	PO	A	E	DP	FR
1886	Lou-a	.833	1	4	1	1	0	0
1887	Lou-a	.891	10	19	22	5	2	-4
1888	Lou-a	.928	19	52	51	8	4	2
	Bro-a	.897	12	30	31	7	4	-3
	Yr	.916	31	82	82	15	8	-1
1889	Bro-a	.929	138	385	410	61	56	-2
1890	Bro-N	.945	129	298	420	42	56	4
1891	Bro-N	.910	72	180	222	40	19	-15
Total	6	.928	381	968	1157	164	141	-16
OF								
1886	Lou-a	.885	24	44	2	6	0	0
1887	Lou-a	.887	109	192	19	27	1	2
1888	Lou-a	.890	82	175	20	24	6	13
1891	Bro-N	.855	35	46	1	8	0	-7
1892	Bro-N	.925	21	37	0	3	0	-2
Total	5	.887	271	494	42	8	7	6

YEAR	TM/L	PCT	G	PO	A	E	DP	FR
SS								
1886	Lou-a	—	1	0	0	0	0	0
1887	Lou-a	.615	4	5	3	5	0	-5
1888	Lou-a	.811	15	41	32	17	4	-3
Total	3	.786	20	46	35	2	4	-8
1B								
1886	Lou-a	—	1	0	0	0	0	0
1887	Lou-a	.947	8	87	2	5	3	-1
Total	2	.947	9	87	2	5	3	-1
3B								
1886	Lou-a	1.000	2	1	1	0	0	-1
1887	Lou-a	.750	1	2	1	1	0	-1
Total	2	.833	3	3	2	1	0	-2

■ **Ripper Collins** 1B

YEAR	TM/L	PCT	G	PO	A	E	DP	FR
1931	StL-N	.995	68	563	42	3	54	4
1932	StL-N	.999	81	701	46	1	72	-1
1933	StL-N	.994	123	1054	79	7	82	3
1934	StL-N	.991	154	1289	110	13	115	8
1935	StL-N	.987	150	1269	95	18	107	1
1936	StL-N	.990	61	475	37	5	48	-1
1937	Chi-N	.991	111	1068	80	11	94	1
1938	Chi-N	.996	135	1264	111	6	118	10
1941	Pit-N	.947	11	64	8	4	5	1
Total	9	.992	894	7747	608	8	695	26
OF								
1931	StL-N	.900	3	9	0	1	0	0
1932	StL-N	.954	60	96	7	5	2	-3
1936	StL-N	.933	9	13	1	1	0	0
1941	Pit-N	1.000	3	2	0	0	0	0
Total	4	.948	75	120	8	7	2	-3

■ **Jimmy Collins** 3B

YEAR	TM/L	PCT	G	PO	A	E	DP	FR
1895	Lou-N	.926	77	131	181	25	12	18
1896	Bos-N	.909	80	134	207	34	16	21
1897	Bos-N	.917	134	214	303	47	20	21
1898	Bos-N	.932	152	243	332	42	20	15
1899	Bos-N	.943	151	217	376	36	23	21
1900	Bos-N	.935	141	251	329	40	21	10
1901	Bos-A	.914	138	203	328	50	24	14
1902	Bos-A	.954	107	143	255	19	14	9
1903	Bos-A	.952	130	178	260	22	19	12
1904	Bos-A	.945	156	191	320	30	15	6
1905	Bos-A	.923	131	164	268	36	12	6
1906	Bos-A	.911	32	43	70	11	2	2
1907	Bos-A	.874	41	46	72	17	2	-7
	Phi-A	.904	98	97	185	30	11	-2
	Yr	.895	139	143	257	47	13	-9
1908	Phi-A	.928	115	117	216	26	14	-7
Total	14	.929	1683	2372	3702	465	225	139
OF								
1895	Bos-N	.714	10	9	1	4	0	-2
	Lou-N	.956	18	40	3	2	1	2
	Yr	.898	28	49	4	6	1	0
SS								
1895	Lou-N	.833	1	2	3	1	1	0
1896	Bos-N	.750	4	7	11	6	2	-1
1900	Bos-N	1.000	1	1	2	0	0	0
Total	3	.788	6	10	16	7	3	-1
2B								
1895	Lou-N	1.000	2	3	12	0	0	2

■ **Zip Collins** OF

YEAR	TM/L	PCT	G	PO	A	E	DP	FR
1914	Pit-N	.962	49	92	8	4	2	0
1915	Pit-N	.942	89	217	11	14	3	1
	Bos-N	1.000	4	6	1	0	0	0
	Yr	.944	93	223	12	14	3	1
1916	Bos-N	.947	78	114	10	7	3	-3
1917	Bos-N	1.000	5	13	0	0	0	0
1921	Phi-A	.915	20	51	3	5	0	0
Total	5	.946	245	493	33	0	8	-2

■ **Shano Collins** OF

YEAR	TM/L	PCT	G	PO	A	E	DP	FR
1910	Chi-A	.949	66	101	11	6	6	3
1911	Chi-A	1.000	3	3	0	0	0	0
1912	Chi-A	.969	105	177	11	6	0	-2
1913	Chi-A	.949	147	244	19	14	3	1
1914	Chi-A	.970	154	268	21	9	5	9
1915	Chi-A	.963	104	197	13	8	2	3
1916	Chi-A	.959	137	238	20	11	6	7
1917	Chi-A	.992	73	125	6	1	4	-2
1918	Chi-A	.973	93	230	20	7	1	14
1919	Chi-A	.957	46	82	7	4	5	1
1920	Chi-A	.950	13	19	0	1	0	-2
1921	Bos-A	.966	139	264	22	10	8	4
1922	Bos-A	.951	117	245	6	13	1	-7
1923	Bos-A	.953	89	164	17	9	2	-2
1924	Bos-A	.957	56	85	4	4	0	-8
1925	Bos-A	—	1	0	0	0	0	-1
Total	16	.962	1343	2442	177	103	43	18
1B								
1910	Chi-A	.955	28	255	19	13	11	1
1911	Chi-A	.978	98	878	72	21	46	5
1912	Chi-A	.992	46	455	35	4	24	4
1915	Chi-A	.978	47	516	28	12	26	-1
1916	Chi-A	1.000	4	34	4	0	2	1
1918	Chi-A	.944	5	32	2	2	1	0
1919	Chi-A	1.000	8	76	4	0	1	0
1920	Chi-A	.988	116	1146	63	15	69	-6
1921	Bos-A	1.000	3	21	0	0	2	0
1922	Bos-A	1.000	1	3	0	0	0	0
1924	Bos-A	.954	12	98	6	5	6	-1
Total	11	.981	368	3514	235	2	188	3
2B								
1911	Chi-A	.818	3	3	6	2	0	-1

■ **Joe Collins** 1B

YEAR	TM/L	PCT	G	PO	A	E	DP	FR
1949	NY-A	.920	5	23	0	2	2	-1
1950	NY-A	.987	99	480	36	7	62	1
1951	NY-A	.987	114	556	56	8	65	5

YEAR	TM/L	PCT	G	PO	A	E	DP	FR
1952	NY-A	.990	119	1047	73	11	123	-3
1953	NY-A	.989	113	826	65	10	100	0
1954	NY-A	.992	117	759	60	7	105	1
1955	NY-A	.998	73	395	42	1	63	1
1956	NY-A	1.000	43	251	30	0	37	5
1957	NY-A	.987	32	218	14	3	23	-1
Total	9	.990	715	4555	376	9	580	11

OF

YEAR	TM/L	PCT	G	PO	A	E	DP	FR
1950	NY-A	1.000	2	1	0	0	0	0
1951	NY-A	.952	15	19	1	1	0	0
1953	NY-A	.917	4	11	0	1	0	0
1955	NY-A	.981	27	50	3	1	0	0
1956	NY-A	.990	51	95	2	1	0	1
1957	NY-A	1.000	15	16	1	0	0	0
Total	6	.980	114	192	7	4	0	1

■ Pat Collins C

YEAR	TM/L	PCT	G	PO	A	E	DP	FR
1919	StL-A	.929	5	20	6	2	0	-1
1920	StL-A	1.000	7	8	2	0	0	-2
1921	StL-A	.961	31	105	19	5	3	-1
1922	StL-A	.980	28	129	19	3	4	6
1923	StL-A	.980	47	161	31	4	4	-1
1924	StL-A	.969	20	52	10	2	0	-1
1926	NY-A	.971	100	401	74	14	**14**	2
1927	NY-A	.976	89	267	56	8	1	-7
1928	NY-A	.977	70	182	30	5	1	-5
1929	Bos-N	1.000	6	14	2	0	0	0
Total	10	.974	403	1339	249	3	27	-9

1B

YEAR	TM/L	PCT	G	PO	A	E	DP	FR
1922	StL-A	.982	5	53	3	1	0	0

■ Bill Collins OF

YEAR	TM/L	PCT	G	PO	A	E	DP	FR
1910	Bos-N	**.977**	151	**355**	23	9	2	**18**
1911	Bos-N	1.000	13	31	1	0	0	2
	Chi-N	1.000	4	1	0	0	0	0
	Yr	1.000	17	32	1	0	0	2
1913	Bro-N	.921	27	57	1	5	0	-1
1914	Buf-F	.864	15	14	5	3	0	-1
Total	4	.966	210	458	30	7	2	18

3B

YEAR	TM/L	PCT	G	PO	A	E	DP	FR
1911	Bos-N	1.000	1	2	1	0	0	0

■ Frank Colman OF

YEAR	TM/L	PCT	G	PO	A	E	DP	FR
1942	Pit-N	1.000	8	14	2	0	0	0
1943	Pit-N	1.000	11	27	0	0	0	-1
1944	Pit-N	.964	53	102	4	4	0	-3
1945	Pit-N	1.000	12	17	0	0	0	-1
1946	Pit-N	1.000	8	15	1	0	0	0
	NY-A	1.000	5	9	0	0	0	0
1947	NY-A	1.000	6	7	1	0	0	1
Total	6	.980	103	191	8	4	0	-4

1B

YEAR	TM/L	PCT	G	PO	A	E	DP	FR
1944	Pit-N	1.000	6	7	0	0	0	0
1945	Pit-N	.993	22	126	14	1	10	1
1946	Pit-N	.947	2	16	2	1	2	0
Total	3	.988	30	149	16	2	12	1

■ Bob Coluccio OF

YEAR	TM/L	PCT	G	PO	A	E	DP	FR
1973	Mil-A	.992	108	236	12	2	3	8
1974	Mil-A	.989	131	346	10	4	2	13
1975	Mil-A	1.000	22	57	1	0	0	1
	Chi-A	.980	59	92	4	2	0	0
	Yr	.987	81	149	5	2	0	1
1977	Chi-A	1.000	19	28	1	0	1	1
1978	StL-N	1.000	2	1	0	0	0	0
Total	5	.990	341	760	28	8	6	23

■ Earle Combs OF

YEAR	TM/L	PCT	G	PO	A	E	DP	FR
1924	NY-A	1.000	11	12	0	0	0	-3
1925	NY-A	.979	150	401	12	9	2	4
1926	NY-A	.970	145	375	8	12	2	1
1927	NY-A	.968	**152**	411	6	14	0	2
1928	NY-A	.980	149	**424**	11	9	7	8
1929	NY-A	.966	141	358	10	13	5	-3
1930	NY-A	.969	135	275	5	9	1	-4
1931	NY-A	.974	129	335	5	9	2	0
1932	NY-A	.967	139	343	6	12	3	-6
1933	NY-A	.975	104	227	3	6	1	-6
1934	NY-A	.993	62	145	1	1	0	-1
1935	NY-A	.993	70	143	2	1	0	-5
Total	12	.974	1387	3449	69	95	23	-13

■ Wayne Comer OF

YEAR	TM/L	PCT	G	PO	A	E	DP	FR
1967	Det-A	—	1	0	0	0	0	0
1968	Det-A	1.000	27	20	0	0	0	1
1969	Sea-A	.980	139	287	14	6	**6**	1
1970	Mil-A	1.000	5	5	0	0	0	0
	Was-A	.960	58	70	2	3	0	0
	Yr	.962	63	75	2	3	0	0
1972	Det-A	1.000	17	5	0	0	0	1
Total	5	.978	247	387	16	9	6	3

C

YEAR	TM/L	PCT	G	PO	A	E	DP	FR
1968	Det-A	1.000	1	2	0	0	0	0
1969	Sea-A	—	1	0	0	0	0	0
Total	2	1.000	2	2	0	0	0	0

3B

YEAR	TM/L	PCT	G	PO	A	E	DP	FR
1969	Sea-A	—	1	0	0	0	0	0
1970	Was-A	.000	1	0	0	1	0	0
Total	2	.000	2	0	0	1	0	0

■ Charlie Comiskey 1B

YEAR	TM/L	PCT	G	PO	A	E	DP	FR
1882	StL-a	.967	**77**	**860**	14	30	25	-1
1883	StL-a	.963	96	**1085**	20	43	49	-1
1884	StL-a	.969	108	**1193**	38	40	56	2
1885	StL-a	.969	83	879	24	29	34	1
1886	StL-a	.975	122	1156	49	31	67	6
1887	StL-a	.976	116	1135	51	29	60	6
1888	StL-a	.970	**133**	1293	46	42	52	-2
1889	StL-a	.970	134	1225	45	39	71	-1
1890	Chi-P	.965	88	882	41	33	52	-2
1891	StL-a	.980	**141**	**1433**	62	31	78	3

YEAR	TM/L	PCT	G	PO	A	E	DP	FR
1892	Cin-N	.984	141	1469	73	25	**103**	1
1893	Cin-N	.979	64	675	21	15	57	-6
1894	Cin-N	.972	60	536	24	16	36	-4
Total	13	.973	1363	13821	508	403	740	2

2B

YEAR	TM/L	PCT	G	PO	A	E	DP	FR
1884	StL-a	—	1	0	0	0	0	0
1886	StL-a	.912	9	29	23	5	4	-1
1887	StL-a	.870	9	23	24	7	2	-3
1888	StL-a	.800	3	4	4	2	0	-1
1889	StL-a	1.000	3	1	7	0	0	0
Total	5	.891	25	57	58	4	6	-5

OF

YEAR	TM/L	PCT	G	PO	A	E	DP	FR
1883	StL-a	—	1	0	0	0	0	0
1886	StL-a	1.000	2	1	0	0	0	-1
1887	StL-a	1.000	3	4	0	0	0	0
1888	StL-a	1.000	5	1	0	0	0	-2
1889	StL-a	1.000	3	1	0	0	0	0
1891	StL-a	1.000	2	3	0	0	0	0
1894	Cin-N	—	1	0	0	0	0	0
Total	7	1.000	17	10	0	0	0	-4

■ Adam Comorosky OF

YEAR	TM/L	PCT	G	PO	A	E	DP	FR
1926	Pit-N	1.000	6	7	0	0	0	0
1927	Pit-N	.978	16	43	1	1	0	1
1928	Pit-N	.968	49	118	2	4	1	1
1929	Pit-N	.963	121	256	6	10	3	-6
1930	Pit-N	.969	152	337	12	11	2	-1
1931	Pit-N	.978	90	214	4	5	2	-1
1932	Pit-N	.981	92	255	4	5	2	6
1933	Pit-N	1.000	30	66	1	0	0	-2
1934	Cin-N	.970	122	285	5	9	1	-1
1935	Cin-N	.953	40	79	3	4	0	1
Total	10	.972	718	1660	38	9	11	-2

■ Pete Compton OF

YEAR	TM/L	PCT	G	PO	A	E	DP	FR
1911	StL-A	.917	28	37	7	4	3	1
1912	StL-A	.925	72	139	9	12	1	0
1913	StL-A	.862	21	23	2	4	1	-4
1915	StL-F	1.000	2	2	0	0	0	-1
	Bos-N	.971	31	66	2	2	1	1
1916	StL-A	.939	30	60	2	4	1	1
	Pit-N	.917	5	11	0	1	0	0
	Yr	.936	35	71	2	5	1	1
1918	NY-N	.971	19	30	3	1	0	1
Total	6	.933	208	368	25	8	7	-1

■ Clint Conatser OF

YEAR	TM/L	PCT	G	PO	A	E	DP	FR
1948	Bos-N	.974	76	146	3	4	1	2
1949	Bos-N	.951	44	93	5	5	0	2
Total	2	.965	120	239	8	9	1	4

■ Dave Concepcion SS

YEAR	TM/L	PCT	G	PO	A	E	DP	FR
1970	Cin-N	.945	93	137	244	22	51	-8
1971	Cin-N	.974	112	160	294	12	62	-6
1972	Cin-N	.969	114	194	365	18	75	3
1973	Cin-N	.974	88	165	292	12	56	2
1974	Cin-N	.963	160	239	**536**	30	99	9
1975	Cin-N	.977	130	238	445	16	102	9
1976	Cin-N	.968	150	304	**506**	27	93	**17**
1977	Cin-N	**.986**	**156**	280	490	11	101	8
1978	Cin-N	.969	152	255	459	23	72	-5
1979	Cin-N	.967	148	284	495	27	**102**	14
1980	Cin-N	.978	155	265	451	16	98	-13
1981	Cin-N	.960	106	200	322	22	71	4
1982	Cin-N	.977	145	262	459	17	94	13
1983	Cin-N	.979	139	225	376	13	67	-21
1984	Cin-N	.978	104	156	247	9	41	-30
1985	Cin-N	.962	151	212	404	24	64	-31
1986	Cin-N	.965	60	74	174	9	32	-2
1987	Cin-N	.727	2	2	6	3	2	-1
1988	Cin-N	1.000	13	10	29	0	8	3
Total	19	.971	2178	3670	6594	311	1290	-35

2B

YEAR	TM/L	PCT	G	PO	A	E	DP	FR
1970	Cin-N	1.000	3	7	3	0	0	0
1971	Cin-N	.955	10	8	13	1	3	1
1972	Cin-N	1.000	1	0	1	0	1	0
1980	Cin-N	—	1	0	0	0	0	0
1986	Cin-N	.981	10	25	28	1	12	0
1987	Cin-N	.992	59	125	133	2	36	1
1988	Cin-N	.994	46	80	92	1	24	-3
Total	7	.990	130	245	270	5	76	-1

3B

YEAR	TM/L	PCT	G	PO	A	E	DP	FR
1971	Cin-N	1.000	7	0	3	0	0	1
1972	Cin-N	.900	9	3	6	1	0	0
1975	Cin-N	1.000	6	3	1	0	0	0
1982	Cin-N	—	1	0	0	0	0	0
1983	Cin-N	.944	54	28	74	6	3	-4
1985	Cin-N	1.000	5	2	1	0	0	0
1986	Cin-N	1.000	10	9	17	0	3	0
1987	Cin-N	1.000	13	5	20	0	2	0
1988	Cin-N	1.000	9	8	5	0	0	0
Total	10	.966	120	60	138	7	8	-3

1B

YEAR	TM/L	PCT	G	PO	A	E	DP	FR
1982	Cin-N	1.000	1	9	0	0	1	0
1983	Cin-N	—	1	0	0	0	0	0
1984	Cin-N	.941	6	29	3	2	2	0
1986	Cin-N	1.000	12	45	4	0	6	0
1987	Cin-N	1.000	26	118	10	0	3	0
1988	Cin-N	.983	16	53	5	1	4	0
Total	6	.989	62	254	22	3	16	0

OF

YEAR	TM/L	PCT	G	PO	A	E	DP	FR
1971	Cin-N	1.000	5	14	0	0	0	0
1973	Cin-N	1.000	2	2	0	0	0	0
1974	Cin-N	—	1	0	0	0	0	0
Total	3	1.000	8	16	0	0	0	0

■ Onix Concepcion SS

YEAR	TM/L	PCT	G	PO	A	E	DP	FR
1980	KC-A	.833	6	5	10	3	1	1
1981	KC-A	—	1	0	0	0	0	0

YEAR	TM/L	PCT	G	PO	A	E	DP	FR
1982	KC-A	.948	46	63	138	11	25	0
1983	KC-A	.958	21	40	52	4	11	-2
1984	KC-A	.972	85	105	280	11	53	2
1985	KC-A	.959	128	127	367	21	63	-9
Total	6	.960	287	340	847	50	153	-8

2B

YEAR	TM/L	PCT	G	PO	A	E	DP	FR
1982	KC-A	1.000	24	29	30	0	3	-1
1983	KC-A	.962	28	33	69	4	16	6
1984	KC-A	1.000	6	11	15	0	6	1
1985	KC-A	1.000	2	0	3	0	0	0
Total	4	.979	60	73	117	4	25	6

3B

YEAR	TM/L	PCT	G	PO	A	E	DP	FR
1983	KC-A	.913	31	19	54	7	8	1
1984	KC-A	—	1	0	0	0	0	0
Total	2	.913	32	19	54	7	8	1

■ Bunk Congalton OF

YEAR	TM/L	PCT	G	PO	A	E	DP	FR
1902	Chi-N	.987	45	71	6	1	1	0
1905	Cle-A	.923	12	10	2	1	0	-1
1906	Cle-A	.957	114	174	6	8	0	-9
1907	Cle-A	1.000	6	10	1	0	0	0
	Bos-A	.969	123	169	18	6	4	-2
	Yr	.971	129	179	19	6	4	-2
Total	4	.967	300	434	33	6	5	-12

■ Tony Conigliaro OF

YEAR	TM/L	PCT	G	PO	A	E	DP	FR
1964	Bos-A	.973	106	176	7	5	0	2
1965	Bos-A	.976	137	277	11	7	1	**12**
1966	Bos-A	.973	146	244	8	7	1	-4
1967	Bos-A	.983	95	172	5	3	1	2
1969	Bos-A	.981	137	207	4	4	2	-12
1970	Bos-A	.977	146	252	7	6	1	-2
1971	Cal-A	.994	72	155	6	1	1	2
Total	7	.979	839	1483	48	3	7	0

■ Billy Conigliaro OF

YEAR	TM/L	PCT	G	PO	A	E	DP	FR
1969	Bos-A	.926	24	25	0	2	0	-4
1970	Bos-A	.968	108	201	8	7	0	3
1971	Bos-A	.983	100	232	5	4	2	1
1972	Mil-A	.992	50	120	5	1	2	4
1973	Oak-A	1.000	40	70	5	0	0	4
Total	5	.980	322	648	23	4	4	8

2B

YEAR	TM/L	PCT	G	PO	A	E	DP	FR
1973	Oak-A	—	1	0	0	0	0	-1

■ Ed Connolly C

YEAR	TM/L	PCT	G	PO	A	E	DP	FR
1929	Bos-A	.889	5	7	1	1	0	-1
1930	Bos-A	1.000	26	39	12	0	1	-1
1931	Bos-A	.981	41	87	18	2	1	-1
1932	Bos-A	.957	75	233	55	13	0	3
Total	4	.966	147	366	86	6	2	0

■ Joe Connolly OF

YEAR	TM/L	PCT	G	PO	A	E	DP	FR
1913	Bos-N	.954	124	214	16	11	2	-4
1914	Bos-N	.974	118	168	19	5	1	-9
1915	Bos-N	.971	93	158	10	5	2	-1
1916	Bos-N	.980	31	46	4	1	1	1
Total	4	.967	366	586	49	2	6	-13

■ Jim Connor 2B

YEAR	TM/L	PCT	G	PO	A	E	DP	FR
1892	Chi-N	.917	9	14	19	3	0	-6
1897	Chi-N	.936	76	176	293	32	40	**22**
1898	Chi-N	.946	138	330	437	44	**75**	-4
1899	Chi-N	.942	44	82	147	14	20	4
Total	4	.942	267	602	896	3	135	16

3B

YEAR	TM/L	PCT	G	PO	A	E	DP	FR
1899	Chi-N	.874	25	19	64	12	5	2

■ Roger Connor 1B

YEAR	TM/L	PCT	G	PO	A	E	DP	FR
1881	Tro-N	.950	**85**	836	40	**46**	**51**	2
1882	Tro-N	.951	43	443	22	24	31	**3**
1883	NY-N	.958	98	958	40	44	37	3
1885	NY-N	.975	110	1178	**42**	31	**66**	3
1886	NY-N	.973	118	1164	65	34	55	**10**
1887	NY-N	**.993**	**127**	**1325**	44	10	67	5
1888	NY-N	.982	133	1337	43	26	57	0
1889	NY-N	.977	131	1265	32	30	68	-8
1890	NY-P	**.985**	123	**1335**	80	21	**79**	11
1891	NY-N	.983	129	1362	56	25	77	1
1892	Phi-N	**.985**	155	1483	59	23	99	-6
1893	NY-N	.974	**135**	**1423**	83	40	70	2
1894	NY-N	.976	21	192	14	5	12	1
	StL-N	.974	99	897	68	26	72	5
	Yr	.974	120	1089	82	31	84	6
1895	StL-N	.986	103	953	62	14	60	4
1896	StL-N	**.988**	126	1217	**94**	16	48	**12**
1897	StL-N	.984	22	237	12	4	6	0
Total	16	.978	1758	17605	856	419	955	48

3B

YEAR	TM/L	PCT	G	PO	A	E	DP	FR
1880	Tro-N	.821	**83**	116	159	**60**	**10**	-10
1882	Tro-N	.862	14	23	33	9	0	2
1884	NY-N	.733	12	11	22	12	2	-2
1889	NY-N	1.000	1	1	1	0	0	0
1893	NY-N	—	1	0	0	0	0	0
Total	5	.819	111	151	215	81	12	-10

2B

YEAR	TM/L	PCT	G	PO	A	E	DP	FR
1884	NY-N	.860	67	230	205	71	30	6
1888	NY-N	1.000	1	9	2	0	2	2
Total	2	.863	68	239	207	71	32	8

OF

YEAR	TM/L	PCT	G	PO	A	E	DP	FR
1882	Tro-N	.831	24	52	2	11	0	-2
1884	NY-N	.833	37	58	7	13	0	-3
1894	NY-N	.800	1	3	1	1	0	1
Total	3	.831	62	113	10	25	0	-4

■ Wid Conroy 3B

YEAR	TM/L	PCT	G	PO	A	E	DP	FR
1901	Mil-A	.868	12	14	19	5	2	?
1903	NY-A	.919	123	164	243	36	11	
1904	NY-A	.944	110	137	231	22		
1905	NY-A	.928	48	80	87	13		
1906	NY-A	—	2	0	0	0		

YEAR	TM/L	PCT	G	PO	A	E	DP	FR
1908	NY-A	.939	119	179	249	28	12	10
1909	Was-A	.938	120	136	239	25	14	0
1910	Was-A	.961	46	61	87	6	6	2
1911	Was-A	.930	85	87	177	20	11	6
Total	9	.934	665	858	1332	155	65	29
SS								
1901	Mil-A	.922	118	285	408	59	46	22
1902	Pit-N	.925	95	192	327	42	39	9
1903	NY-A	1.000	4	3	4	0	0	0
1904	NY-A	.947	27	61	64	7	5	-6
1905	NY-A	.940	17	42	36	5	9	2
1906	NY-A	.944	49	95	142	14	14	-2
1907	NY-A	.931	38	95	94	14	15	6
1909	Was-A	1.000	1	0	4	0	1	1
Total	8	.929	349	773	1079	141	129	32
OF								
1902	Pit-N	1.000	3	2	0	0	0	-1
1904	NY-A	1.000	3	6	0	0	0	0
1905	NY-A	.986	25	67	1	1	0	4
1906	NY-A	.968	97	200	12	7	1	1
1907	NY-A	.955	100	204	10	10	2	6
1908	NY-A	.963	10	24	2	1	0	2
1909	Was-A	.909	5	10	0	1	0	0
1910	Was-A	.959	46	90	4	4	0	2
1911	Was-A	.912	15	30	1	3	0	0
Total	9	.961	304	633	30	7	3	14
2B								
1905	NY-A	.955	3	7	14	1	0	2
1908	NY-A	.957	12	33	34	3	3	1
1909	Was-A	.950	13	24	33	3	3	-1
1910	Was-A	.870	5	12	8	3	0	-2
1911	Was-A	1.000	1	1	0	0	0	0
Total	5	.943	34	77	89	10	6	0
1B								
1905	NY-A	.960	10	91	4	4	4	-1

■ Bill Conroy C

YEAR	TM/L	PCT	G	PO	A	E	DP	FR
1935	Phi-A	1.000	1	11	0	0	0	1
1936	Phi-A	1.000	1	3	0	0	0	0
1937	Phi-A	1.000	18	57	6	0	2	-1
1942	Bos-A	.971	83	324	40	11	6	0
1943	Bos-A	.969	38	135	19	5	3	2
1944	Bos-A	.972	19	60	9	2	2	0
Total	6	.974	160	590	74	8	13	2
1B								
1937	Phi-A	1.000	1	1	0	0	0	0

■ Billy Consolo SS

YEAR	TM/L	PCT	G	PO	A	E	DP	FR
1954	Bos-A	.953	50	79	123	10	24	-4
1957	Bos-A	.933	42	61	149	15	30	11
1958	Bos-A	.965	11	17	38	2	9	7
1959	Bos-A	.818	2	6	3	2	1	-2
	Was-A	.952	75	111	229	17	44	9
	Yr	.948	77	117	232	19	45	7
1960	Was-A	.938	82	83	158	16	36	-4
1961	Min-A	—	3	0	0	0	0	0
1962	LA-A	.846	4	1	10	2	0	1
	KC-A	.950	48	72	120	10	25	-1
	Yr	.944	52	73	130	12	25	0
Total	7	.945	317	430	830	4	169	17
2B								
1953	Bos-A	.981	11	23	29	1	10	8
1954	Bos-A	.957	12	24	20	2	4	0
1955	Bos-A	.889	4	11	5	2	1	-3
1956	Bos-A	.920	25	9	14	2	4	12
1957	Bos-A	.985	16	29	37	1	11	1
1958	Bos-A	.925	13	20	17	3	7	0
1959	Was-A	1.000	4	9	10	0	3	2
1960	Was-A	.950	12	14	24	2	3	2
1961	Min-A	1.000	3	5	1	0	0	1
1962	LA-A	1.000	1	1	3	0	1	1
Total	10	.959	101	145	160	3	44	24
3B								
1953	Bos-A	.808	16	3	18	5	3	2
1954	Bos-A	.944	18	10	41	3	2	2
1957	Bos-A	1.000	2	2	3	0	0	0
1958	Bos-A	—	1	0	0	0	0	0
1960	Was-A	1.000	2	0	1	0	0	0
1961	Min-A	—	1	0	0	0	0	0
1962	Phi-N	—	1	0	0	0	0	0
	LA-A	.917	20	4	7	1	2	1
Total	7	.908	61	19	70	9	7	5

■ Doc Cook OF

YEAR	TM/L	PCT	G	PO	A	E	DP	FR
1913	NY-A	.939	20	43	3	3	1	1
1914	NY-A	.949	127	171	15	10	2	-5
1915	NY-A	.959	131	188	20	9	4	1
1916	NY-A	1.000	3	3	0	0	0	-1
Total	4	.953	281	405	38	2	7	-4

■ Paul Cook C

YEAR	TM/L	PCT	G	PO	A	E	DP	FR
1884	Phi-N	.818	3	16	2	4	1	-1
1886	Lou-a	.869	21	110	36	22	1	-4
1887	Lou-a	.916	55	220	95	29	4	-8
1888	Lou-a	.901	53	221	81	33	7	-9
1889	Lou-a	.925	74	293	138	35	6	7
1890	Bro-P	.890	36	129	49	22	4	2
1891	Lou-a	.909	35	120	39	16	0	-8
	StL-a	.921	7	49	9	5	0	3
	Yr	.912	42	169	48	21	0	-5
Total	7	.906	284	1158	449	166	23	-18
1B								
1886	Lou-a	.945	43	420	13	25	21	-2
1887	Lou-a	.909	6	50	0	5	1	-1
1889	Lou-a	1.000	1	10	2	0	1	1
1890	Bro-P	.961	21	190	8	8	16	-1
1891	Lou-a	.969	10	90	3	3	6	-1
Total	5	.950	81	760	26	1	45	-4

YEAR	TM/L	PCT	G	PO	A	E	DP	FR
OF								
1886	Lou-a	1.000	2	2	0	0	0	0
1888	Lou-a	.500	4	1	0	1	0	-2
1889	Lou-a	.917	7	20	2	2	1	2
1890	Bro-P	1.000	1	1	0	0	0	0
Total	4	.897	14	24	2	3	1	0
SS								
1888	Lou-a	.667	1	2	0	1	0	-1
1889	Lou-a	—	1	0	0	0	0	0
Total	2	.667	2	2	0	1	0	-1

■ Dusty Cooke OF

YEAR	TM/L	PCT	G	PO	A	E	DP	FR
1930	NY-A	.978	73	133	2	3	1	-6
1931	NY-A	1.000	11	23	0	0	0	-1
1933	Bos-A	.956	118	257	6	12	5	-10
1934	Bos-A	.976	44	79	1	2	0	-4
1935	Bos-A	.972	82	172	4	5	1	-2
1936	Bos-A	.972	91	207	3	6	2	0
1938	Cin-N	.963	51	126	4	5	1	1
Total	7	.969	470	997	20	3	10	-22

■ Duff Cooley OF

YEAR	TM/L	PCT	G	PO	A	E	DP	FR
1893	StL-N	.947	15	17	1	1	0	-2
1894	StL-N	.833	39	74	1	15	1	-6
1895	StL-N	.936	124	320	17	23	1	12
1896	StL-N	.959	40	91	2	4	0	-1
	Phi-N	.901	64	130	6	15	2	-5
	Yr	.923	104	221	8	19	2	-6
1897	Phi-N	.960	131	322	16	14	6	7
1898	Phi-N	.943	149	352	15	22	2	4
1899	Phi-N	.946	14	35	0	2	0	-1
1901	Bos-N	.943	53	127	5	8	1	2
1902	Bos-N	.952	127	250	7	13	2	-7
1903	Bos-N	.952	126	246	11	13	4	-3
1904	Bos-N	.976	116	201	3	5	4	-6
1905	Det-A	.959	96	223	12	10	5	7
Total	12	.945	1094	2388	96	145	28	1
1B								
1894	StL-N	1.000	1	7	0	0	1	0
1897	StL-N	1.000	2	19	0	0	1	0
1899	Phi-N	.971	79	756	34	24	56	-3
1900	Pit-N	.989	66	683	20	8	39	-5
1901	Bos-N	.990	10	91	4	1	3	0
1902	Bos-N	.985	7	60	6	1	1	1
1903	Bos-N	.947	13	105	3	6	2	-2
1904	Bos-N	.975	6	39	0	1	0	1
Total	8	.978	184	1760	67	1	103	-10
3B								
1894	StL-N	.721	13	10	21	12	1	-4
1895	StL-N	.952	5	10	10	1	2	1
Total	2	.797	18	20	31	3	3	-3
C								
1893	StL-N	.967	10	23	6	1	0	-3
1895	StL-N	.667	1	1	1	1	0	0
Total	2	.939	11	24	7	2	0	-3
SS								
1893	StL-N	.846	5	6	5	2	2	-3
1894	StL-N	—	1	0	0	0	0	0
1895	StL-N	.789	3	5	10	4	0	-2
Total	3	.813	9	11	15	6	2	-5
1899	Phi-N	.000	1	0	0	2	0	-1

■ Jimmy Cooney SS

YEAR	TM/L	PCT	G	PO	A	E	DP	FR
1917	Bos-A	1.000	1	4	5	0	0	1
1919	NY-N	1.000	4	6	10	0	2	-1
1924	StL-N	.969	99	242	322	18	68	1
1925	StL-N	.976	37	70	94	4	22	-8
1926	Chi-N	.972	141	344	492	24	107	19
1927	Chi-N	.973	33	75	102	5	13	-2
	Phi-N	.980	74	155	238	8	51	17
	Yr	.978	107	230	340	13	64	15
1928	Bos-N	.982	11	23	31	1	10	1
Total	7	.974	400	919	1294	0	273	28
2B								
1917	Bos-A	1.000	10	26	34	0	7	4
1919	NY-N	1.000	1	1	1	0	0	0
1924	StL-N	1.000	1	1	1	0	0	0
1925	StL-N	.972	15	27	43	2	9	-2
1928	Bos-N	.941	4	4	12	1	1	0
Total	5	.980	31	59	90	3	17	2
3B								
1924	StL-N	1.000	7	3	9	0	0	0
OF								
1925	StL-N	—	1	0	0	0	0	0

■ Jimmy Cooney SS

YEAR	TM/L	PCT	G	PO	A	E	DP	FR
1890	Chi-N	.936	135	237	452	47	50	-2
1891	Chi-N	.917	118	145	433	52	39	8
1892	Chi-N	.912	65	101	211	30	15	-8
	Was-N	.862	6	12	13	4	1	-3
	Yr	.908	71	113	224	34	16	-11
Total	3	.923	324	495	1109	133	105	-5
C								
1890	Chi-N	1.000	1	1	0	0	0	0

■ Johnny Cooney OF

YEAR	TM/L	PCT	G	PO	A	E	DP	FR
1923	Bos-N	1.000	11	27	3	0	0	3
1924	Bos-N	.944	16	50	1	3	0	2
1925	Bos-N	—	1	0	0	0	0	0
1926	Bos-N	1.000	1	3	0	0	0	0
1928	Bos-N	1.000	2	2	0	0	0	0
1929	Bos-N	1.000	16	45	0	0	0	2
1935	Bro-N	1.000	10	23	0	0	0	1
1936	Bro-N	.994	130	336	11	2	3	3
1937	Bro-N	.976	111	279	9	7	2	2
1938	Bro-N	.982	110	209	6	4	2	-6
1939	Bos-N	.996	116	236	10	2	2	-9
1940	Bos-N	.992	99	238	5	2	0	-3
1941	Bos-N	.996	111	274	9	1	3	1
1942	Bos-N	.984	54	59	2	1	0	-3
1943	Bro-N	1.000	2	4	0	0	0	0
1944	Bro-N	1.000	2	3	0	0	0	0
	NY-A	1.000	2	3	0	0	0	0
Total	16	.988	794	1791	56	2	12	-7
1B								
1923	Bos-N	1.000	1	2	0	0	0	0
1924	Bos-N	1.000	1	2	0	0	0	0
1925	Bos-N	.950	3	18	1	1	4	0
1926	Bos-N	.996	31	241	24	1	27	4
1928	Bos-N	.941	3	16	0	1	2	-1
1937	Bro-N	1.000	2	2	0	0	0	0
1938	Bos-N	1.000	13	87	4	0	7	-1
1939	Bos-N	1.000	2	5	0	0	0	0
1940	Bos-N	1.000	7	56	4	0	5	0
1941	Bos-N	1.000	4	41	2	0	4	0
1942	Bos-N	.995	23	195	10	1	10	-2
1943	Bro-N	1.000	3	16	0	0	1	0
Total	12	.995	93	681	45	4	60	0

■ Cecil Cooper 1B

YEAR	TM/L	PCT	G	PO	A	E	DP	FR
1971	Bos-A	.988	11	82	3	1	6	-2
1972	Bos-A	1.000	3	19	0	0	2	-1
1973	Bos-A	.984	29	227	17	4	25	-1
1974	Bos-A	.983	74	637	40	12	66	-1
1975	Bos-A	.995	35	197	20	1	20	2
1976	Bos-A	.994	66	600	42	4	49	-1
1977	Mil-A	.992	148	1386	118	12	134	5
1978	Mil-A	.988	84	842	66	11	71	2
1979	Mil-A	.993	135	1323	78	10	119	-8
1980	Mil-A	.997	142	1336	106	5	160	4
1981	Mil-A	.992	101	987	72	9	111	0
1982	Mil-A	.997	154	1428	98	5	156	-1
1983	Mil-A	.993	158	1452	87	11	144	-10
1984	Mil-A	.991	122	1061	98	10	106	3
1985	Mil-A	.986	123	1087	94	17	101	-2
1986	Mil-A	.988	90	697	61	9	78	-4
Total	16	.992	1475	13361	1000	121	1348	-15

■ Claude Cooper OF

YEAR	TM/L	PCT	G	PO	A	E	DP	FR
1913	NY-N	.895	15	16	1	2	0	1
1914	Bro-F	.926	101	188	12	16	4	-1
1915	Bro-F	.958	121	274	26	13	3	17
1916	Phi-N	.945	29	51	3	3	0	0
1917	Phi-N	.923	12	12	0	1	0	-1
Total	5	.943	278	541	40	5	7	16
1B								
1915	Bro-F	.979	32	262	18	6	11	1
1916	Phi-N	1.000	1	1	1	0	0	0
Total	2	.979	33	263	19	6	11	1

■ Walker Cooper C

YEAR	TM/L	PCT	G	PO	A	E	DP	FR
1940	StL-N	1.000	6	19	4	0	0	0
1941	StL-N	.966	63	247	39	10	11	4
1942	StL-N	.972	115	519	62	17	6	3
1943	StL-N	.975	112	504	49	14	5	-2
1944	StL-N	.980	97	442	40	10	7	3
1945	StL-N	.966	4	27	1	1	0	1
1946	NY-N	.972	73	277	38	9	3	-12
1947	NY-N	.979	132	561	51	13	8	-10
1948	NY-N	.979	79	307	21	7	3	-13
1949	NY-N	.982	40	148	18	3	2	-2
	Cin-N	.978	77	316	43	8	3	-2
	Yr	.979	117	464	61	11	5	-4
1950	Cin-N	.972	13	62	7	2	0	1
	Bos-N	.973	88	386	47	12	9	-5
	Yr	.973	101	448	54	14	9	-4
1951	Bos-N	.981	90	367	57	8	9	-1
1952	Bos-N	.983	89	417	55	8	8	-4
1953	Mil-N	.983	35	165	6	3	1	-5
1954	Pit-N	1.000	2	6	0	0	0	0
	Chi-N	.978	48	190	31	5	4	-2
	Yr	.978	50	196	31	5	4	-2
1955	Chi-N	.961	31	88	11	4	1	-11
1956	StL-N	.984	16	56	4	1	0	-3
1957	StL-N	.957	13	62	5	3	0	-2
Total	18	.977	1223	5166	589	138	80	-62

■ Claude Corbitt SS

YEAR	TM/L	PCT	G	PO	A	E	DP	FR
1946	Cin-N	.947	77	126	229	20	45	-13
1948	Cin-N	1.000	11	17	19	0	2	-2
1949	Cin-N	.984	18	29	31	1	10	-3
Total	3	.956	106	172	279	1	57	-18
2B								
1948	Cin-N	.973	52	101	112	6	18	-8
1949	Cin-N	.953	17	37	24	3	7	-2
Total	2	.968	69	138	136	9	25	-10
3B								
1945	Bro-N	1.000	2	1	3	0	1	0
1948	Cin-N	.980	16	20	29	1	4	2
1949	Cin-N	.000	1	0	0	1	0	0
Total	3	.964	19	21	32	2	5	2

■ Tommy Corcoran SS

YEAR	TM/L	PCT	G	PO	A	E	DP	FR
1890	Pit-P	.884	123	210	431	84	36	4
1891	Phi-a	.911	133	300	434	72	5	12
1892	Bro-N	.925	151	291	495	64	49	-2
1893	Bro-N	.907	115	218	444	68	44	14
1894	Bro-N	.904	129	280	439	76	45	-4
1895	Bro-N	.924	127	293	488	64	49	18
1896	Bro-N	.926	132	323	477	64	69	24
1897	Cin-N	.913	63	155	213	35	34	2
1898	Cin-N	.932	153	353	561	67	76	14
1899	Cin-N	.931	123	281	416	52	52	3
1900	Cin-N	.921	124	262	436	60	56	-4
1901	Cin-N	.919	30	69	112	16	20	4
1902	Cin-N	.926	137	292	412	56	49	-13
1903	Cin-N	.943	115	263	367	38	42	6
1904	Cin-N	.936	150	353	471	56	54	2
1905	Cin-N	.952	151	344	531	44	67	20

YEAR	TM/L	PCT	G	PO	A	E	DP	FR
1906	Cin-N	.941	117	263	379	40	51	8
Total	17	.924	2073	4550	7106	956	798	108

2B

YEAR	TM/L	PCT	G	PO	A	E	DP	FR
1897	Cin-N	.955	47	131	147	13	17	3
1899	Cin-N	.973	14	21	52	2	3	1
1900	Cin-N	.958	5	11	12	1	3	0
1902	Cin-N	1.000	1	2	5	0	0	0
1907	NY-N	.939	62	108	183	19	15	-5
Total	5	.950	129	273	399	5	38	-1

■ Tim Corcoran 1B

YEAR	TM/L	PCT	G	PO	A	E	DP	FR
1979	Det-A	1.000	5	35	1	0	2	0
1980	Det-A	.985	48	249	18	4	32	0
1981	Min-A	1.000	16	108	9	0	10	1
1983	Phi-N	1.000	3	4	0	0	0	0
1984	Phi-N	.997	51	318	21	1	20	-2
1985	Phi-N	.993	59	386	25	3	27	-1
1986	NY-N	1.000	1	8	1	0	1	0
Total	7	.993	183	1108	75	8	92	-2

OF

YEAR	TM/L	PCT	G	PO	A	E	DP	FR
1977	Det-A	1.000	18	38	0	0	0	4
1978	Det-A	.985	109	186	6	3	4	-13
1979	Det-A	1.000	9	10	1	0	0	1
1980	Det-A	.963	18	25	1	1	0	0
1984	Phi-N	1.000	17	20	0	0	0	-1
1985	Phi-N	1.000	3	3	0	0	0	0
Total	6	.986	174	282	8	4	4	-9

■ Fred Corey 3B

YEAR	TM/L	PCT	G	PO	A	E	DP	FR
1880	Wor-N	.750	1	3	0	1	0	-1
1882	Wor-N	.773	6	8	9	5	0	-2
1883	Phi-a	.799	34	36	83	30	4	2
1884	Phi-a	.887	104	121	209	42	10	13
1885	Phi-a	.872	92	102	184	42	14	8
Total	5	.863	237	270	485	120	28	20

OF

YEAR	TM/L	PCT	G	PO	A	E	DP	FR
1880	Wor-N	.759	29	19	3	7	1	-8
1881	Wor-N	.827	25	37	6	9	1	-1
1882	Wor-N	.600	15	5	1	4	0	-2
1883	Phi-a	.720	14	16	2	7	0	-2
Total	4	.767	83	77	12	7	2	-13

SS

YEAR	TM/L	PCT	G	PO	A	E	DP	FR
1880	Wor-N	.857	3	1	5	1	0	0
1881	Wor-N	.907	7	5	34	4	1	3
1882	Wor-N	.847	26	29	76	19	5	-5
1883	Phi-a	.667	1	0	4	2	0	0
1885	Phi-a	.833	1	2	3	1	1	0
Total	5	.855	38	37	122	7	7	-2

2B

YEAR	TM/L	PCT	G	PO	A	E	DP	FR
1878	Pro-N	.917	2	2	9	1	0	1
1883	Phi-a	.855	9	25	22	8	3	-3
Total	2	.866	11	27	31	9	3	-2

1B

YEAR	TM/L	PCT	G	PO	A	E	DP	FR
1878	Pro-N	1.000	1	8	0	0	1	0
1880	Wor-N	—	1	0	0	0	0	0
1882	Wor-N	.962	5	50	0	2	1	0
Total	3	.967	7	58	0	2	2	0

C

YEAR	TM/L	PCT	G	PO	A	E	DP	FR
1883	Phi-a	1.000	1	0	1	0	0	0

■ Roy Corhan SS

YEAR	TM/L	PCT	G	PO	A	E	DP	FR
1911	Chi-A	.924	43	98	146	20	18	11
1916	StL-N	.917	84	153	278	39	35	1
Total	2	.920	127	251	424	9	53	12

■ Pop Corkhill OF

YEAR	TM/L	PCT	G	PO	A	E	DP	FR
1883	Cin-a	.930	85	162	10	13	0	1
1884	Cin-a	.934	92	169	29	14	5	11
1885	Cin-a	.938	110	205	35	16	5	16
1886	Cin-a	.919	112	156	25	16	6	1
1887	Cin-a	.952	128	310	29	17	7	15
1888	Cin-a	.958	116	255	17	12	5	5
	Bro-a	.980	19	48	2	1	0	2
	Yr	.961	135	303	19	13	5	7
1889	Bro-a	.949	138	317	35	19	8	12
1890	Bro-N	.977	48	122	6	3	1	7
1891	Phi-a	.956	83	182	14	9	3	7
	Cin-N	1.000	1	7	0	0	0	1
	Pit-N	.935	41	77	9	6	3	2
	Yr	.939	42	84	9	6	3	3
1892	Pit-N	.953	68	148	13	8	4	7
Total	10	.947	1041	2158	224	134	47	87

1B

YEAR	TM/L	PCT	G	PO	A	E	DP	FR
1883	Cin-a	1.000	2	4	0	0	0	0
1884	Cin-a	.985	6	62	2	1	4	0
1885	Cin-a	1.000	3	28	2	0	1	1
1886	Cin-a	.966	7	50	7	2	2	2
1888	Cin-a	1.000	1	11	0	0	0	0
1889	Bro-a	—	1	0	0	0	0	0
1890	Bro-N	1.000	6	35	0	0	0	0
Total	7	.985	26	190	11	3	7	3

SS

YEAR	TM/L	PCT	G	PO	A	E	DP	FR
1883	Cin-a	1.000	2	1	5	0	0	0
1884	Cin-a	.870	11	18	29	7	0	-3
1886	Cin-a	.813	3	3	10	3	0	-1
1889	Bro-a	1.000	1	1	1	0	1	0
Total	4	.872	17	23	45	0	1	-4

3B

YEAR	TM/L	PCT	G	PO	A	E	DP	FR
1884	Cin-a	1.000	3	4	6	0	0	1
1886	Cin-a	.837	12	21	20	8	0	-3
Total	2	.864	15	25	26	8	0	-2

2B

YEAR	TM/L	PCT	G	PO	A	E	DP	FR
1883	Cin-a	.917	2	5	6	1	0	0
1888	Cin-a	1.000	1	2	6	0	0	1
Total	2	.950	3	7	12	1	0	1

■ Pat Corrales C

YEAR	TM/L	PCT	G	PO	A	E	DP	FR
1965	Phi-N	.982	62	358	24	7	2	-4
1966	StL-N	.975	27	133	23	4	2	9
1968	Cin-N	.991	20	101	8	1	0	0
1969	Cin-N	.986	29	133	7	2	3	3
1970	Cin-N	.983	42	167	11	3	3	4
1971	Cin-N	.980	39	145	4	3	3	1
1972	Cin-N	1.000	2	6	2	0	0	1
	SD-N	.993	43	245	21	2	3	3
	Yr	.993	45	251	23	2	3	4
1973	SD-N	.986	28	130	6	2	1	-1
Total	8	.984	292	1418	106	4	17	16

■ Vic Correll C

YEAR	TM/L	PCT	G	PO	A	E	DP	FR
1972	Bos-A	1.000	1	9	1	0	0	1
1974	Atl-N	.988	59	282	40	4	4	7
1975	Atl-N	.973	97	413	63	13	2	-1
1976	Atl-N	.981	65	319	36	7	1	4
1977	Atl-N	.973	49	247	38	8	2	4
1978	Cin-N	.980	52	180	18	4	0	2
1979	Cin-N	.992	47	221	19	2	1	7
1980	Cin-N	.919	10	33	1	3	0	0
Total	8	.979	380	1704	216	1	10	24

■ Red Corriden SS

YEAR	TM/L	PCT	G	PO	A	E	DP	FR
1910	StL-A	.902	14	37	55	10	3	4
1912	Det-A	.842	3	6	10	3	0	-1
1913	Chi-N	.907	37	47	80	13	12	-1
1914	Chi-N	.894	91	174	212	46	29	-32
Total	4	.896	145	264	357	2	44	-30

3B

YEAR	TM/L	PCT	G	PO	A	E	DP	FR
1910	StL-A	.943	12	24	26	3	0	0
1912	Det-A	.929	25	28	50	6	5	-2
1913	Chi-N	1.000	1	1	0	0	0	0
1914	Chi-N	.889	8	5	11	2	1	0
1915	Chi-N	.667	1	1	1	1	0	0
Total	5	.925	47	59	88	2	6	-2

2B

YEAR	TM/L	PCT	G	PO	A	E	DP	FR
1912	Det-A	.881	7	16	21	5	0	-1
1913	Chi-N	.875	2	4	3	1	0	0
1914	Chi-N	—	3	0	0	0	0	0
Total	3	.880	12	20	24	6	0	-1

OF

YEAR	TM/L	PCT	G	PO	A	E	DP	FR
1915	Chi-N	—	1	0	0	0	0	0

■ Joe Coscarart 3B

YEAR	TM/L	PCT	G	PO	A	E	DP	FR
1935	Bos-N	.962	41	28	74	4	5	2
1936	Bos-N	.935	97	91	168	18	16	2
Total	2	.943	138	119	242	2	21	4

SS

YEAR	TM/L	PCT	G	PO	A	E	DP	FR
1935	Bos-N	.941	27	61	66	8	10	-5
1936	Bos-N	.864	6	10	9	3	2	-1
Total	2	.930	33	71	75	1	12	-6

2B

YEAR	TM/L	PCT	G	PO	A	E	DP	FR
1935	Bos-N	.969	15	26	37	2	5	-1
1936	Bos-N	1.000	1	2	4	0	0	0
Total	2	.972	16	28	41	2	5	-1

■ Pete Coscarart 2B

YEAR	TM/L	PCT	G	PO	A	E	DP	FR
1938	Bro-N	.955	27	58	69	6	16	1
1939	Bro-N	.960	107	256	338	25	69	-8
1940	Bro-N	.958	140	326	379	31	58	-31
1941	Bro-N	.948	19	30	43	4	5	5
1942	Pit-N	.940	25	42	52	6	10	-6
1943	Pit-N	.961	85	186	263	18	54	-6
1944	Pit-N	.967	136	371	389	26	71	-5
1945	Pit-N	.978	122	257	361	14	74	21
Total	8	.963	661	1526	1894	130	357	-29

SS

YEAR	TM/L	PCT	G	PO	A	E	DP	FR
1939	Bro-N	1.000	2	1	6	0	0	0
1941	Bro-N	1.000	1	0	2	0	0	0
1942	Pit-N	.952	108	203	315	26	50	-12
1943	Pit-N	.961	47	96	151	10	30	2
1944	Pit-N	1.000	4	6	2	0	0	-1
1945	Pit-N	1.000	1	0	1	0	0	0
1946	Pit-N	—	1	0	0	0	0	0
Total	7	.956	164	306	477	6	80	-11

3B

YEAR	TM/L	PCT	G	PO	A	E	DP	FR
1939	Bro-N	1.000	4	2	4	0	0	0
1943	Pit-N	1.000	1	0	1	0	0	0
Total	2	1.000	5	2	5	0	0	0

OF

YEAR	TM/L	PCT	G	PO	A	E	DP	FR
1944	Pit-N	—	1	0	0	0	0	0

■ Chuck Cottier 2B

YEAR	TM/L	PCT	G	PO	A	E	DP	FR
1959	Mil-N	.976	10	18	22	1	2	1
1960	Mil-N	.968	92	180	214	13	40	17
1961	Det-A	1.000	2	2	6	0	2	2
	Was-A	.982	100	233	316	10	73	15
	Yr	.982	102	235	322	10	75	17
1962	Was-A	.981	134	368	354	14	100	21
1963	Was-A	.963	85	200	221	16	49	9
1964	Was-A	.982	53	109	110	4	31	13
1968	Cal-A	1.000	4	2	6	0	0	1
1969	Cal-A	1.000	2	1	1	0	0	0
Total	8	.976	482	1113	1250	8	297	79

SS

YEAR	TM/L	PCT	G	PO	A	E	DP	FR
1961	Det-A	.889	8	7	1	1	1	0
1963	Was-A	.916	24	33	65	9	16	2
1964	Was-A	1.000	2	1	1	0	0	0
Total	3	.915	34	41	67	0	17	2

3B

YEAR	TM/L	PCT	G	PO	A	E	DP	FR
1963	Was-A	—	1	0	0	0	0	0
1964	Was-A	.800	3	0	4	1	0	0
1968	Cal-A	.963	27	13	39	2	2	1
Total	3	.949	31	13	43	3	2	1

■ Henry Cotto OF

YEAR	TM/L	PCT	G	PO	A	E	DP	FR
1984	Chi-N	.984	88	117	3	2	1	10
1985	NY-A	.977	30	41	2	1	0	2
1986	NY-A	1.000	29	59	1	0	0	4
1987	NY-A	.989	57	89	2	1	0	2
1988	Sea-A	.992	120	253	6	2	0	-10
1989	Sea-A	.988	90	153	9	2	3	2
1990	Sea-A	.990	118	194	4	2	1	-9
Total	7	.989	532	906	27	0	5	1

■ Bill Coughlin 3B

YEAR	TM/L	PCT	G	PO	A	E	DP	FR
1899	Was-N	.818	6	7	11	4	0	-1
1901	Was-A	.922	137	232	275	43	16	0
1902	Was-A	.926	66	104	157	21	6	7
1903	Was-A	.952	119	170	224	20	13	4
1904	Was-A	.939	64	95	121	14	7	2
	Det-A	.929	56	53	104	12	2	-3
	Yr	.935	120	148	225	26	9	-1
1905	Det-A	.914	136	137	255	37	12	-9
1906	Det-A	.940	147	188	265	29	16	-10
1907	Det-A	.930	133	163	233	30	9	-10
1908	Det-A	.941	119	120	214	21	12	-15
Total	9	.931	983	1269	1859	231	93	-35

SS

YEAR	TM/L	PCT	G	PO	A	E	DP	FR
1902	Was-A	.926	31	75	114	15	7	2
1903	Was-A	.929	4	12	14	2	1	0
Total	2	.927	35	87	128	7	8	2

2B

YEAR	TM/L	PCT	G	PO	A	E	DP	FR
1902	Was-A	.952	26	67	73	7	8	3
1903	Was-A	1.000	2	5	1	0	0	0
Total	2	.954	28	72	74	7	8	3

■ Bob Coulson OF

YEAR	TM/L	PCT	G	PO	A	E	DP	FR
1908	Cin-N	1.000	6	15	1	0	0	1
1910	Bro-N	.922	25	43	4	4	2	0
1911	Bro-N	.968	145	253	21	9	5	-3
1914	Pit-F	.931	18	26	1	2	1	-2
Total	4	.960	194	337	27	5	8	-4

■ Clint Courtney C

YEAR	TM/L	PCT	G	PO	A	E	DP	FR
1951	NY-A	.800	1	3	1	1	0	0
1952	StL-A	.996	113	487	69	2	7	4
1953	StL-A	.980	103	436	47	10	7	-5
1954	Bal-A	.990	111	539	53	6	8	-2
1955	Chi-A	1.000	17	49	4	0	2	-1
	Was-A	.983	67	252	29	5	4	-14
	Yr	.985	84	301	33	5	6	-15
1956	Was-A	.979	76	290	35	7	7	-15
1957	Was-A	.994	59	288	35	2	6	0
1958	Was-A	.991	128	682	64	7	17	-4
1959	Was-A	.987	53	213	11	3	2	-13
1960	Bal-A	.975	58	246	23	7	2	4
1961	Bal-A	1.000	16	71	8	0	1	2
Total	11	.987	802	3556	379	0	63	-44

■ Ernie Courtney 3B

YEAR	TM/L	PCT	G	PO	A	E	DP	FR
1902	Bal-A	1.000	1	4	2	0	0	0
1903	Det-A	.938	13	17	13	2	1	-3
1905	Phi-N	.923	155	229	249	40	13	-17
1906	Phi-N	.923	96	113	163	23	9	-10
1907	Phi-N	.907	75	90	143	24	11	-7
1908	Phi-N	.915	22	18	36	5	1	-5
Total	6	.920	362	471	606	4	35	-42

1B

YEAR	TM/L	PCT	G	PO	A	E	DP	FR
1903	NY-A	1.000	1	9	1	0	0	0
1906	Phi-N	.978	13	123	9	3	5	0
1907	Phi-N	.978	48	426	29	10	23	0
1908	Phi-N	.992	13	126	6	1	6	-1
Total	4	.981	75	684	45	4	34	-1

OF

YEAR	TM/L	PCT	G	PO	A	E	DP	FR
1902	Bos-N	.974	39	71	5	2	0	-1
1906	Phi-N	1.000	3	4	0	0	0	0
1907	Phi-N	1.000	4	9	0	0	0	0
Total	3	.978	46	84	5	2	0	-1

SS

YEAR	TM/L	PCT	G	PO	A	E	DP	FR
1902	Bos-N	.923	3	6	6	1	1	0
1903	NY-A	.916	19	24	63	8	7	-2
	Det-A	.932	9	11	30	3	1	0
	Yr	.921	28	35	93	11	8	-2
1906	Phi-N	—	1	0	0	0	0	0
1907	Phi-N	.857	2	0	6	1	0	0
1908	Phi-N	1.000	2	5	4	0	0	-1
Total	5	.923	36	46	109	3	9	-3

2B

YEAR	TM/L	PCT	G	PO	A	E	DP	FR
1903	NY-A	.929	4	6	7	1	0	-1
1907	Phi-N	1.000	2	4	3	0	0	0
1908	Phi-N	1.000	5	8	15	0	0	0
Total	3	.977	11	18	25	1	0	-1

■ Wes Covington OF

YEAR	TM/L	PCT	G	PO	A	E	DP	FR
1956	Mil-N	.979	35	44	2	1	1	-4
1957	Mil-N	.981	89	150	9	3	1	-2
1958	Mil-N	.953	82	118	3	6	2	-10
1959	Mil-N	.962	94	148	6	6	2	-6
1960	Mil-N	.964	72	106	2	4	1	-9
1961	Mil-N	1.000	5	3	0	0	0	-2
	Chi-A	.900	14	16	2	2	0	-2
	KC-A	1.000	12	14	0	0	0	-3
	Phi-N	.950	45	53	4	3	1	-5
	Yr	.938	59	69	6	5	1	-7
1962	Phi-N	.944	88	98	3	6	2	-10
1963	Phi-N	.937	101	114	4	8	0	-11
1964	Phi-N	.972	108	99	4	0	0	-12
1965	Phi-N	.968	64	88	2	3	0	-3
1966	Chi-N	1.000	1	2	0	0	0	0
	LA-N	1.000	2	1	0	0	0	0
	Yr	1.000	3	3	0	0	0	0
Total	11	.961	812	1054	41	5	10	-79

■ Billy Cowan OF

YEAR	TM/L	PCT	G	PO	A	E	DP	FR
1963	Chi-N	.917	10	10	1	1	1	-1
1964	Chi-N	.968	134	297	8	10	0	-8
1965	NY-N	1.000	61	80	2	0	2	3
	Mil-N	1.000	10	8	0	0	0	
	Yr	1.000	71	88	2	0	2	
1967	Phi-N	1.000	20	19	0	0	0	
1969	NY-A	1.000	14	16	1	0		

YEAR	TM/L	PCT	G	PO	A	E	DP	FR
	Cal-A	1.000	13	15	3	0	0	1
	Yr	1.000	27	31	4	0	0	1
1970	Cal-A	.929	27	26	0	2	0	-3
1971	Cal-A	1.000	40	69	1	0	0	-1
Total	7	.977	329	540	10	3	3	-11

1B

YEAR	TM/L	PCT	G	PO	A	E	DP	FR
1969	Cal-A	1.000	6	32	1	0	3	-1
1970	Cal-A	1.000	14	69	6	0	7	0
1971	Cal-A	.971	5	32	1	1	8	-1
Total	3	.993	25	133	8	1	18	-2

2B

YEAR	TM/L	PCT	G	PO	A	E	DP	FR
1965	NY-N	1.000	2	1	1	0	0	0
1967	Phi-N	—	1	0	0	0	0	0
Total	2	1.000	3	1	1	0	0	0

3B

YEAR	TM/L	PCT	G	PO	A	E	DP	FR
1967	Phi-N	—	1	0	0	0	0	0
1970	Cal-A	1.000	2	1	0	0	0	0
Total	2	1.000	3	1	0	0	0	0

SS

YEAR	TM/L	PCT	G	PO	A	E	DP	FR
1965	NY-N	1.000	1	2	0	0	0	0

■ **Al Cowens OF**

YEAR	TM/L	PCT	G	PO	A	E	DP	FR
1974	KC-A	.988	102	151	13	2	2	6
1975	KC-A	.978	113	214	4	5	2	-6
1976	KC-A	.986	148	329	13	5	3	4
1977	KC-A	.982	159	307	14	6	1	2
1978	KC-A	.990	127	275	10	3	5	4
1979	KC-A	.986	134	288	3	4	0	-3
1980	Cal-A	1.000	30	64	0	0	0	0
	Det-A	.986	107	199	8	3	2	-5
	Yr	.989	137	263	11	3	2	-5
1981	Det-A	.994	83	166	3	1	0	-11
1982	Sea-A	.987	145	280	14	4	1	2
1983	Sea-A	.985	70	124	7	2	1	1
1984	Sea-A	.987	130	228	8	3	0	-5
1985	Sea-A	.967	110	198	10	7	2	-2
1986	Sea-A	.971	19	31	2	1	0	-1
Total	13	.985	1477	2854	112	6	19	-14

3B

YEAR	TM/L	PCT	G	PO	A	E	DP	FR
1974	KC-A	.500	2	0	1	1	0	-1
1978	KC-A	.938	5	5	10	1	1	0
Total	2	.889	7	5	11	2	1	-1

■ **Dick Cox OF**

YEAR	TM/L	PCT	G	PO	A	E	DP	FR
1925	Bro-N	.968	111	197	14	7	4	-7
1926	Bro-N	.964	117	201	12	8	2	-9
Total	2	.966	228	398	26	5	6	-16

■ **Larry Cox C**

YEAR	TM/L	PCT	G	PO	A	E	DP	FR
1973	Phi-N	1.000	1	1	0	0	0	0
1974	Phi-N	.990	29	90	9	1	0	0
1975	Phi-N	1.000	10	10	0	0	0	0
1977	Sea-A	.970	35	138	26	5	2	0
1978	Chi-N	.967	58	178	26	7	3	1
1979	Sea-A	.981	99	408	49	9	6	-3
1980	Sea-A	.993	104	412	45	3	5	11
1981	Tex-A	1.000	5	33	2	0	0	4
1982	Chi-N	1.000	2	9	2	0	1	1
Total	9	.983	343	1279	159	5	17	14

■ **Bobby Cox 3B**

YEAR	TM/L	PCT	G	PO	A	E	DP	FR
1968	NY-A	.957	132	98	279	17	22	-5
1969	NY-A	.935	56	37	122	11	14	9
Total	2	.950	188	135	401	8	36	4

2B

YEAR	TM/L	PCT	G	PO	A	E	DP	FR
1969	NY-A	1.000	6	13	23	0	3	2

■ **Billy Cox 3B**

YEAR	TM/L	PCT	G	PO	A	E	DP	FR
1948	Bro-N	.958	70	51	107	7	7	-4
1949	Bro-N	.964	100	104	213	12	28	9
1950	Bro-N	.957	107	102	233	15	35	12
1951	Bro-N	.967	139	140	264	14	26	-8
1952	Bro-N	.970	100	100	157	8	26	-6
1953	Bro-N	.974	89	86	142	6	20	-2
1954	Bro-N	.961	58	57	90	6	7	3
1955	Bal-A	.969	37	28	67	3	5	-4
Total	8	.965	700	668	1273	1	154	0

SS

YEAR	TM/L	PCT	G	PO	A	E	DP	FR
1941	Pit-N	.943	10	15	35	3	8	2
1946	Pit-N	.935	114	235	323	39	59	-16
1947	Pit-N	.968	129	220	388	20	63	-12
1948	Bro-N	.955	6	8	13	1	4	1
1950	Bro-N	.952	9	10	10	1	1	-2
1951	Bro-N	1.000	1	1	0	0	0	0
1952	Bro-N	.979	10	27	20	1	4	-3
1953	Bro-N	1.000	6	5	3	0	1	0
1954	Bro-N	.980	8	14	13	0	3	-2
1955	Bal-A	.917	6	2	9	1	1	-1
Total	10	.953	299	537	814	6	144	-33

2B

YEAR	TM/L	PCT	G	PO	A	E	DP	FR
1948	Bro-N	—	1	0	0	0	0	0
1950	Bro-N	1.000	13	31	31	0	7	1
1952	Bro-N	1.000	9	13	11	0	4	0
1953	Bro-N	.750	1	1	2	1	0	0
1954	Bro-N	.980	11	22	27	1	5	1
1955	Bal-A	1.000	18	25	28	0	4	-5
Total	6	.990	53	92	99	2	20	-3

■ **Ted Cox 3B**

YEAR	TM/L	PCT	G	PO	A	E	DP	FR
1978	Cle-A	.944	20	15	36	3	3	-1
1979	Cle-A	.964	52	29	78	4	11	1
1980	Sea-A	.945	80	47	142	11	20	-4
1981	Tor-A	.897	14	7	19	3	1	-4
Total	4	.947	166	98	275	1	35	-8

OF

YEAR	TM/L	PCT	G	PO	A	E	DP	FR
1978	Cle-A	.980	38	45	3	1	1	-1
1979	Cle-A	.933	16	26	2	2	0	2
Total	2	.962	54	71	5	3	1	1

1B

YEAR	TM/L	PCT	G	PO	A	E	DP	FR
1978	Cle-A	1.000	7	40	2	0	2	0

YEAR	TM/L	PCT	G	PO	A	E	DP	FR
1981	Tor-A	1.000	1	10	0	0	1	0
Total	2	1.000	8	50	2	0	3	0

2B

YEAR	TM/L	PCT	G	PO	A	E	DP	FR
1979	Cle-A	1.000	4	2	1	0	0	0

SS

YEAR	TM/L	PCT	G	PO	A	E	DP	FR
1978	Cle-A	1.000	1	0	1	0	0	0

■ **Estel Crabtree OF**

YEAR	TM/L	PCT	G	PO	A	E	DP	FR
1931	Cin-N	.974	101	240	19	7	6	12
1932	Cin-N	.990	95	288	9	3	3	2
1933	StL-N	.947	7	18	0	1	0	1
1941	StL-N	1.000	50	71	2	0	0	-3
1943	Cin-N	.939	65	135	4	9	2	-3
1944	Cin-N	1.000	19	26	1	0	0	-4
Total	6	.976	337	778	35	0	11	5

3B

YEAR	TM/L	PCT	G	PO	A	E	DP	FR
1931	Cin-N	.800	4	6	10	4	1	1
1941	StL-N	1.000	1	0	2	0	0	0
Total	2	.818	5	6	12	4	1	1

1B

YEAR	TM/L	PCT	G	PO	A	E	DP	FR
1931	Cin-N	1.000	2	19	1	0	2	0
1944	Cin-N	1.000	2	3	0	0	1	0
Total	2	1.000	4	22	1	0	3	0

■ **Harry Craft OF**

YEAR	TM/L	PCT	G	PO	A	E	DP	FR
1937	Cin-N	1.000	10	22	1	0	0	0
1938	Cin-N	.983	151	436	15	8	3	11
1939	Cin-N	.981	134	300	13	6	4	-1
1940	Cin-N	.997	109	284	7	1	2	3
1941	Cin-N	.983	115	280	6	5	1	-1
1942	Cin-N	.987	33	72	4	1	3	4
Total	6	.986	552	1394	46	1	13	16

1B

YEAR	TM/L	PCT	G	PO	A	E	DP	FR
1940	Cin-N	1.000	2	16	1	0	1	0

■ **Rod Craig OF**

YEAR	TM/L	PCT	G	PO	A	E	DP	FR
1979	Sea-A	.923	15	24	0	2	0	-2
1980	Sea-A	.987	63	155	2	2	1	-1
1982	Cle-A	.966	22	28	0	1	0	1
1986	Chi-A	—	2	0	0	0	0	0
Total	4	.977	102	207	2	5	1	-2

■ **Doc Cramer OF**

YEAR	TM/L	PCT	G	PO	A	E	DP	FR
1929	Phi-A	1.000	1	6	0	0	0	1
1930	Phi-A	.927	21	37	1	3	0	-2
1931	Phi-A	.979	55	133	5	3	1	1
1932	Phi-A	.976	86	233	7	6	2	11
1933	Phi-A	.971	152	387	13	12	2	2
1934	Phi-A	.985	152	385	12	6	0	2
1935	Phi-A	.975	149	429	6	11	1	-1
1936	Bos-A	.975	154	443	20	12	6	11
1937	Bos-A	.969	133	365	12	12	4	1
1938	Bos-A	.986	148	417	15	6	3	5
1939	Bos-A	.984	135	356	12	6	0	-4
1940	Bos-A	.969	149	333	11	11	2	-12
1941	Was-A	.984	152	369	9	6	1	-10
1942	Det-A	.981	150	352	15	7	6	-3
1943	Det-A	.980	138	346	9	4	3	-1
1944	Det-A	.980	141	337	13	7	2	-10
1945	Det-A	.991	140	314	7	3	4	-11
1946	Det-A	1.000	50	89	2	0	0	-4
1947	Det-A	.965	35	79	3	3	0	1
1948	Det-A	1.000	1	2	0	0	0	0
Total	20	.979	2142	5412	172	118	37	-23

SS

YEAR	TM/L	PCT	G	PO	A	E	DP	FR
1930	Phi-A	1.000	1	1	1	0	1	0

■ **Del Crandall C**

YEAR	TM/L	PCT	G	PO	A	E	DP	FR
1949	Bos-N	.982	63	287	39	6	5	6
1950	Bos-N	.967	75	311	41	12	7	3
1953	Mil-N	.986	108	566	62	9	13	14
1954	Mil-N	.989	136	665	79	8	11	13
1955	Mil-N	.985	131	611	67	10	8	-3
1956	Mil-N	.996	109	448	44	2	9	2
1957	Mil-N	.987	102	414	59	6	11	-7
1958	Mil-N	.990	124	659	64	7	6	5
1959	Mil-N	.994	146	783	71	5	15	5
1960	Mil-N	.988	141	764	70	10	9	-15
1961	Mil-N	1.000	5	17	3	0	0	-2
1962	Mil-N	.994	90	460	54	3	7	-5
1963	Mil-N	.991	75	413	38	4	2	2
1964	SF-N	.993	65	402	30	3	7	12
1965	Pit-N	.996	60	248	23	1	4	4
1966	Cle-A	.991	49	304	15	3	2	15
Total	16	.989	1479	7352	759	9	116	49

1B

YEAR	TM/L	PCT	G	PO	A	E	DP	FR
1950	Bos-N	1.000	1	8	0	0	0	0
1957	Mil-N	1.000	1	2	1	0	0	0
1962	Mil-N	1.000	5	28	1	0	2	0
1963	Mil-N	1.000	7	46	5	0	7	1
Total	4	1.000	14	84	7	0	9	1

OF

YEAR	TM/L	PCT	G	PO	A	E	DP	FR
1957	Mil-N	.929	9	13	0	1	0	-1

■ **Sam Crane SS**

YEAR	TM/L	PCT	G	PO	A	E	DP	FR
1914	Phi-A	.929	2	5	8	1	0	1
1915	Phi-A	.900	6	15	21	4	2	2
1916	Phi-A	1.000	2	1	5	0	0	0
1917	Was-A	.889	32	53	75	16	13	-4
1920	Cin-N	.945	25	43	61	6	11	-8
1921	Cin-N	.953	63	129	173	15	32	-16
1922	Bro-N	.875	3	8	13	3	2	2
Total	7	.931	133	254	356	5	60	-23

3B

YEAR	TM/L	PCT	G	PO	A	E	DP	FR
1920	Cin-N	.872	10	15	19	5	1	0
1921	Cin-N	.833	2	1	4	1	0	0
Total	2	.867	12	16	23	6	1	0

2B

YEAR	TM/L	PCT	G	PO	A	E	DP	FR
1915	Phi-A	1.000	1	1	0	0	0	0
1920	Cin-N	1.000	4	7	11	0	2	1
Total	2	1.000	5	8	11	0	2	1

OF

YEAR	TM/L	PCT	G	PO	A	E	DP	FR
1920	Cin-N	—	3	0	0	0	0	0
1921	Cin-N	—	1	0	0	0	0	0
Total	2	—	4	0	0	0	0	0

■ **Sam Crane 2B**

YEAR	TM/L	PCT	G	PO	A	E	DP	FR
1880	Buf-N	.866	10	31	27	9	5	-2
1883	NY-a	.859	96	283	249	87	26	-10
1884	Cin-U	.858	80	224	217	73	27	-9
1885	Det-N	.908	68	179	197	38	21	-4
1886	Det-N	.903	38	104	111	23	19	1
	StL-N	.897	39	91	100	22	14	-7
	Yr	.900	77	195	211	45	33	-6
1890	Pit-N	.880	15	35	53	12	4	3
	NY-N	1.000	2	1	2	0	1	0
	Yr	.883	17	36	55	12	5	3
Total	6	.878	348	948	956	264	117	-28

SS

YEAR	TM/L	PCT	G	PO	A	E	DP	FR
1886	Det-N	.931	8	8	19	2	1	0
1887	Was-N	.865	7	10	22	5	3	-1
1890	Pit-N	.947	7	14	22	2	2	1
Total	3	.913	22	32	63	9	6	0

OF

YEAR	TM/L	PCT	G	PO	A	E	DP	FR
1880	Buf-N	—	1	0	0	0	0	0
1883	NY-a	—	1	0	0	0	0	0
1886	Det-N	.667	4	1	1	1	0	0
1890	NY-N	—	1	0	0	0	0	0
	Pit-N	—	1	0	0	0	0	0
	Yr	—	2	0	0	0	0	0
Total	4	.667	8	1	1	1	0	0

1B

YEAR	TM/L	PCT	G	PO	A	E	DP	FR
1890	NY-N	.778	1	7	0	2	0	0

■ **Gavvy Cravath OF**

YEAR	TM/L	PCT	G	PO	A	E	DP	FR
1908	Bos-A	.925	77	128	7	11	3	-1
1909	Chi-A	.944	18	34	0	2	0	-2
	Was-A	1.000	1	1	0	0	0	1
	Yr	.947	19	35	1	2	0	-1
1912	Phi-N	.966	113	200	26	8	5	5
1913	Phi-N	.958	141	208	20	10	1	-11
1914	Phi-N	.930	143	205	34	18	7	-1
1915	Phi-N	.946	149	233	28	15	2	2
1916	Phi-N	.966	130	182	17	7	2	-9
1917	Phi-N	.946	139	209	17	13	3	-10
1918	Phi-N	.931	118	184	19	15	3	-9
1919	Phi-N	.914	56	89	7	9	2	-6
1920	Phi-N	.667	5	2	0	1	0	-1
Total	11	.944	1090	1675	176	109	28	-42

1B

YEAR	TM/L	PCT	G	PO	A	E	DP	FR
1908	Bos-A	.750	5	6	0	2	0	-1

■ **Sam Crawford OF**

YEAR	TM/L	PCT	G	PO	A	E	DP	FR
1899	Cin-N	.970	31	56	9	2	2	2
1900	Cin-N	.948	95	237	18	14	2	12
1901	Cin-N	.923	127	209	20	19	6	3
1902	Cin-N	.932	140	208	24	17	5	4
1903	Det-A	.960	137	225	16	10	3	4
1904	Det-A	.973	150	230	18	7	8	4
1905	Det-A	.988	103	152	18	2	3	8
1906	Det-A	.984	116	171	19	3	2	2
1907	Det-A	.965	144	311	22	12	2	8
1908	Det-A	.970	134	252	9	8	2	-9
1909	Det-A	.965	139	297	7	11	2	-7
1910	Det-A	.963	153	223	10	9	2	-10
1911	Det-A	.975	146	181	16	5	3	-12
1912	Det-A	.984	149	169	16	3	5	-18
1913	Det-A	.964	140	201	14	8	5	-9
1914	Det-A	.977	157	193	18	5	4	-8
1915	Det-A	.974	156	219	8	6	1	-14
1916	Det-A	.978	79	85	6	2	2	-10
1917	Det-A	1.000	3	7	0	0	0	0
Total	19	.965	2299	3626	268	143	59	-50

1B

YEAR	TM/L	PCT	G	PO	A	E	DP	FR
1905	Det-A	.979	51	478	41	11	22	3
1906	Det-A	.993	32	287	17	2	10	-1
1907	Det-A		2	2	0	0	0	0
1908	Det-A	.969	17	176	13	6	12	0
1909	Det-A	.971	18	189	10	6	2	-1
1910	Det-A	1.000	1	11	1	0	0	0
1913	Det-A	.964	13	156	7	6	6	-1
1916	Det-A	1.000	2	19	0	0	1	0
1917	Det-A	.988	15	158	2	2	5	-3
Total	9	.979	151	1476	91	3	58	-3

■ **Willie Crawford OF**

YEAR	TM/L	PCT	G	PO	A	E	DP	FR
1964	LA-N	1.000	4	7	0	0	0	0
1965	LA-N	1.000	8	7	0	0	0	4
1967	LA-N	.000	1	0	0	1	0	0
1968	LA-N	.966	48	78	6	3	1	1
1969	LA-N	.973	113	177	5	5	0	-6
1970	LA-N	.960	94	160	9	7	1	4
1971	LA-N	.981	97	146	5	3	1	-9
1972	LA-N	.983	74	111	2	2	0	-5
1973	LA-N	.978	138	250	13	6	4	0
1974	LA-N	.966	133	225	3	8	1	-10
1975	LA-N	.990	113	201	2	2	0	-6
1976	StL-N	.982	107	209	6	4	1	-2
1977	Hou-N	.959	30	47	0	2	0	-5
	Oak-A	.978	22	41	3	1	2	1
Total	13	.975	982	1659	54	4	11	-33

■ **George Creamer 2B**

YEAR	TM/L	PCT	G	PO	A	E	DP	FR
1878	Mil-N	.839	28	53	103	30	5	-2
1879	Syr-N	.825	10	21	31	11	1	-8
1880	Wor-N	.883	85	238	274	68	34	-7
1881	Wor-N	.904	80	230	248	51	39	-9
1882	Wor-N	.907	81	241	283	54	50	12
1883	Pit-a	.897	91	310	274	67	42	9
1884	Pit-a	.937	98	308	336	43	47	16

YEAR	TM/L	PCT	G	PO	A	E	DP	FR
Total	7	.901	473	1401	1549	324	218	11
	OF							
1878	Mil-N	.833	17	21	4	5	0	-1
1879	Syr-N	.600	2	3	0	2	0	-1
Total	2	.800	19	24	4	7	0	-2
	3B							
1878	Mil-N	.900	6	8	10	2	2	0
	SS							
1879	Syr-N	.824	3	4	10	3	1	-1

■ Birdie Cree OF

YEAR	TM/L	PCT	G	PO	A	E	DP	FR
1908	NY-A	1.000	21	35	4	0	2	1
1909	NY-A	.949	79	121	9	7	2	-4
1910	NY-A	.955	134	202	11	10	3	-12
1911	NY-A	.964	132	245	19	10	2	3
1912	NY-A	.948	50	123	5	7	1	6
1913	NY-A	.988	144	239	17	3	5	-4
1914	NY-A	.976	76	190	10	5	4	7
1915	NY-A	.945	53	97	6	6	1	-3
Total	8	.965	689	1252	81	8	20	-6
	SS							
1909	NY-A	.933	6	7	21	2	2	-1
1911	NY-A	.833	4	7	13	4	1	-2
Total	2	.889	10	14	34	6	3	-3
	2B							
1909	NY-A	1.000	4	6	7	0	0	-2
1911	NY-A	.500	2	0	1	1	0	-1
Total	2	.933	6	6	8	1	0	-3
	3B							
1909	NY-A	—	1	0	0	0	0	0

■ Creepy Crespi 2B

YEAR	TM/L	PCT	G	PO	A	E	DP	FR
1939	StL-N	.962	6	9	16	1	1	0
1941	StL-N	.962	145	382	421	32	94	0
1942	StL-N	.967	83	219	190	14	42	-4
Total	3	.963	234	610	627	7	137	-4
	SS							
1938	StL-N	.813	7	14	12	6	4	-2
1939	StL-N	.900	4	0	9	1	0	0
1940	StL-N	.833	1	2	3	1	1	0
1942	StL-N	.905	5	8	11	2	1	-1
Total	4	.855	17	24	35	0	6	-3
	3B							
1940	StL-N	1.000	2	4	1	0	0	-1

■ Lou Criger C

YEAR	TM/L	PCT	G	PO	A	E	DP	FR
1896	Cle-N	1.000	1	5	2	0	0	1
1897	Cle-N	.937	37	129	35	11	1	-1
1898	Cle-N	.957	82	322	105	19	9	15
1899	StL-N	.949	75	228	91	17	6	1
1900	StL-N	.953	75	282	105	19	8	4
1901	Bos-A	.967	68	300	109	14	11	22
1902	Bos-A	.965	80	330	117	16	6	14
1903	Bos-A	.979	96	491	156	14	10	22
1904	Bos-A	.981	95	502	112	12	7	18
1905	Bos-A	.972	109	539	147	20	5	6
1906	Bos-A	.981	6	46	7	1	0	4
1907	Bos-A	.978	75	288	109	9	12	8
1908	Bos-A	.980	84	380	120	10	11	14
1909	StL-A	.986	73	387	98	7	16	8
1910	NY-A	.993	27	120	28	1	0	1
1912	StL-A	1.000	1	5	1	0	0	1
Total	16	.971	984	4354	1342	170	102	128
	1B							
1897	Cle-N	.815	2	20	2	5	3	-1
1901	Bos-A	.976	8	80	1	2	5	-1
Total	2	.936	10	100	3	7	8	-2
	3B							
1900	StL-N	.800	1	1	3	1	0	0
	OF							
1902	Bos-A	.500	1	1	0	1	0	0

■ Tony Criscola OF

YEAR	TM/L	PCT	G	PO	A	E	DP	FR
1942	StL-A	.955	52	64	0	3	0	-3
1943	StL-A	.960	13	24	0	1	0	-1
1944	Cin-N	.977	35	80	4	2	0	-1
Total	3	.966	100	168	4	6	0	-5

■ Hughie Critz 2B

YEAR	TM/L	PCT	G	PO	A	E	DP	FR
1924	Cin-N	.956	96	229	357	27	58	3
1925	Cin-N	.970	144	340	542	27	96	22
1926	Cin-N	.981	155	357	588	18	107	24
1927	Cin-N	.969	113	239	388	20	69	-2
1928	Cin-N	.971	153	333	497	25	124	-17
1929	Cin-N	.974	106	210	395	16	72	3
1930	Cin-N	.987	28	52	97	2	17	-3
	NY-N	.972	124	346	413	22	88	5
	Yr	.974	152	398	510	24	105	2
1931	NY-N	.984	54	139	164	5	27	0
1932	NY-N	.974	151	392	471	23	94	1
1933	NY-N	.982	133	316	541	16	87	46
1934	NY-N	.978	137	353	510	19	90	25
1935	NY-N	.966	59	140	175	11	31	3
Total	12	.974	1453	3446	5138	231	960	110
	SS							
1924	Cin-N	.833	1	4	1	1	2	-1
1929	Cin-N	.875	1	1	6	1	0	0
Total	2	.857	2	5	7	2	2	-1

■ Warren Cromartie OF

YEAR	TM/L	PCT	G	PO	A	E	DP	FR
1974	Mon-N	1.000	6	8	0	0	0	0
1976	Mon-N	.943	20	32	1	2	0	-2
1977	Mon-N	.976	155	319	10	8	1	2
1978	Mon-N	.978	158	340	24	8	5	16
1979	Mon-N	.976	158	343	16	9	4	12
1980	Mon-N	1.000	2	2	0	0	0	0
1981	Mon-N	1.000	38	82	1	0	0	0
1982	Mon-N	.979	136	275	10	6	1	6
1983	Mon-N	.973	101	208	12	6	1	6
Total	9	.977	774	1609	74	9	13	42

YEAR	TM/L	PCT	G	PO	A	E	DP	FR
	1B							
1978	Mon-N	.917	4	11	0	1	0	-1
1980	Mon-N	.991	158	1457	93	14	104	-4
1981	Mon-N	.992	62	488	32	4	38	-4
1982	Mon-N	1.000	9	33	3	0	2	0
1983	Mon-N	1.000	1	1	0	0	0	0
Total	5	.991	234	1990	128	9	144	-9

■ Joe Cronin SS

YEAR	TM/L	PCT	G	PO	A	E	DP	FR
1926	Pit-N	1.000	7	1	8	0	1	1
1927	Pit-N	.692	4	2	7	4	0	-3
1928	Was-A	.953	63	133	190	16	42	8
1929	Was-A	.923	143	285	459	62	92	6
1930	Was-A	.960	154	336	509	35	95	26
1931	Was-A	.950	155	323	488	43	94	13
1932	Was-A	.959	141	306	448	32	95	6
1933	Was-A	.960	152	297	528	34	95	10
1934	Was-A	.951	127	246	486	38	86	18
1935	Bos-A	.949	139	264	431	37	86	-14
1936	Bos-A	.930	60	115	191	23	34	-3
1937	Bos-A	.958	148	300	414	31	89	-12
1938	Bos-A	.942	142	304	449	36	110	7
1939	Bos-A	.959	142	306	437	32	93	6
1940	Bos-A	.948	146	252	443	38	89	2
1941	Bos-A	.958	119	225	324	24	64	-5
1942	Bos-A	1.000	1	1	2	0	0	0
Total	17	.951	1843	3696	5814	485	1165	66
	3B							
1936	Bos-A	.949	21	18	38	3	3	1
1940	Bos-A	1.000	2	1	2	0	0	0
1941	Bos-A	.952	22	22	38	3	3	-2
1942	Bos-A	.865	11	9	23	5	4	-1
1943	Bos-A	.968	10	12	18	1	1	0
1945	Bos-A	1.000	3	2	8	0	2	1
Total	6	.941	69	64	127	2	13	-1
	1B							
1927	Pit-N	1.000	1	7	1	0	0	0
1935	Bos-A	1.000	2	13	4	0	3	1
1942	Bos-A	.976	5	37	3	1	3	0
1944	Bos-A	.981	49	428	27	9	39	-2
Total	4	.981	57	485	35	0	45	-1
	2B							
1926	Pit-N	.977	27	54	74	3	18	5
1927	Pit-N	1.000	7	3	2	0	0	-1
1929	Was-A	1.000	1	1	0	0	0	0
Total	3	.978	35	58	76	3	18	4
	OF							
1941	Bos-A	—	1	0	0	0	0	0

■ Bill Cronin C

YEAR	TM/L	PCT	G	PO	A	E	DP	FR
1928	Bos-N	1.000	3	2	0	0	1	0
1929	Bos-N	1.000	6	11	2	0	0	1
1930	Bos-N	.983	64	203	31	4	5	8
1931	Bos-N	.941	50	122	21	9	5	1
Total	4	.968	123	338	54	3	11	10

■ Jack Crooks 2B

YEAR	TM/L	PCT	G	PO	A	E	DP	FR
1889	Col-a	.987	12	31	44	1	4	5
1890	Col-a	.937	134	352	349	47	59	-2
1891	Col-a	.957	138	399	404	36	72	20
1892	StL-N	.929	101	280	296	44	43	-1
1895	Was-N	.956	117	327	364	32	43	12
1896	Was-N	.916	20	49	49	9	5	-4
	Lou-N	.925	39	112	111	18	24	4
	Yr	.922	59	161	160	27	29	0
1898	StL-N	.959	66	192	209	17	23	7
Total	7	.946	627	1742	1826	204	273	41
	3B							
1890	Col-a	.750	1	2	1	1	0	0
1892	StL-N	.876	25	30	48	11	1	-5
1893	StL-N	.908	123	210	286	50	19	5
1896	Was-N	.900	4	8	10	2	1	1
1898	StL-N	1.000	3	1	7	0	0	1
Total	5	.904	156	251	352	4	21	2
	SS							
1893	StL-N	.875	4	9	12	3	2	-1
1898	StL-N	.867	2	5	8	2	1	0
Total	2	.872	6	14	20	5	3	-1
	OF							
1890	Col-a	.000	1	0	0	1	0	-1
1892	StL-N	—	2	0	0	0	0	-1
1898	StL-N	1.000	1	5	0	0	0	0
Total	3	.833	4	5	0	1	0	-2
	C							
1893	StL-N	1.000	1	4	2	0	0	1

■ Ed Crosby SS

YEAR	TM/L	PCT	G	PO	A	E	DP	FR
1970	StL-N	.954	35	37	87	6	15	-1
1972	StL-N	.979	43	51	86	3	20	-6
1973	StL-N	.938	7	6	9	1	2	-2
	Cin-N	.953	29	21	60	4	8	4
	Yr	.950	36	27	69	5	10	2
1974	Cle-A	.943	13	9	24	2	1	-6
1975	Cle-A	.974	30	40	72	3	12	3
Total	5	.964	157	164	338	9	58	-8
	2B							
1970	StL-N	.833	2	4	1	1	1	-1
1972	StL-N	.964	38	68	92	6	21	2
1973	StL-N	.913	5	5	16	2	2	0
	Cin-N	.889	5	4	4	1	2	1
	Yr	.906	10	9	20	3	4	1
1974	Cle-A	.900	3	1	8	1	1	-1
1975	Cle-A	.961	19	25	49	3	5	1
Total	5	.952	72	107	170	4	32	2
	3B							
1970	StL-N	1.000	3	3	3	0	1	0
1972	StL-N	.968	14	11	19	1	1	-1
1973	StL-N	.500	4	0	1	1	0	-1
1974	Cle-A	.926	18	4	21	2	3	-3

YEAR	TM/L	PCT	G	PO	A	E	DP	FR
1975	Cle-A	.900	13	4	5	1	1	0
1976	Cle-A	1.000	1	0	2	0	0	1
Total	6	.936	53	22	51	5	6	-4

■ Frankie Crosetti SS

YEAR	TM/L	PCT	G	PO	A	E	DP	FR
1932	NY-A	.937	84	155	216	25	49	-4
1933	NY-A	.936	133	245	384	43	58	-8
1934	NY-A	.945	119	242	356	35	77	-8
1935	NY-A	.963	87	153	261	16	42	-7
1936	NY-A	.948	151	320	463	43	95	-8
1937	NY-A	.948	147	313	467	43	86	2
1938	NY-A	.948	157	352	506	47	120	18
1939	NY-A	.968	152	323	460	26	118	8
1940	NY-A	.954	145	246	396	31	73	-14
1941	NY-A	.944	32	80	89	10	20	7
1942	NY-A	.945	8	22	30	3	11	5
1943	NY-A	.946	90	194	260	26	58	3
1944	NY-A	.960	55	115	150	11	33	-9
1945	NY-A	.946	126	264	380	37	86	-8
1946	NY-A	.940	24	32	62	6	15	-7
1947	NY-A	—	1	0	0	0	0	0
1948	NY-A	1.000	5	5	4	0	3	0
Total	17	.949	1516	3061	4484	402	944	-16
	3B							
1932	NY-A	.949	33	31	44	4	2	-1
1934	NY-A	.930	23	20	33	4	2	-2
1941	NY-A	.950	13	14	24	2	5	3
1942	NY-A	.951	62	70	105	9	14	-7
Total	4	.947	131	135	206	9	23	-7
	2B							
1932	NY-A	1.000	1	1	0	0	0	0
1934	NY-A	1.000	1	1	0	0	0	0
1942	NY-A	1.000	2	3	4	0	0	0
1947	NY-A	—	1	0	0	0	0	0
1948	NY-A	1.000	6	1	2	0	1	0
Total	5	1.000	11	6	6	0	1	0

■ Lave Cross 3B

YEAR	TM/L	PCT	G	PO	A	E	DP	FR
1891	Phi-a	.895	24	28	49	9	2	-2
1892	Phi-N	.921	65	97	148	21	5	6
1893	Phi-N	.922	30	44	98	12	10	12
1894	Phi-N	.919	100	177	234	36	24	25
1895	Phi-N	.940	125	191	308	32	23	33
1896	Phi-N	.937	61	88	136	15	9	9
1897	Phi-N	.912	47	71	94	16	5	1
1898	StL-N	.945	149	215	351	33	20	19
1899	Cle-N	.955	38	66	81	7	7	4
	StL-N	.960	103	157	277	18	25	29
	Yr	.959	141	223	358	25	32	33
1900	StL-N	.962	16	11	39	2	1	1
	Bro-N	.943	117	162	282	27	10	2
	Yr	.945	133	173	321	29	11	3
1901	Phi-A	.919	100	140	236	33	7	5
1902	Phi-A	.942	137	185	306	30	18	7
1903	Phi-A	.950	136	152	228	20	14	-3
1904	Phi-A	.936	155	164	247	28	15	-10
1905	Phi-A	.928	147	163	252	32	6	-9
1906	Was-A	.952	130	157	242	20	9	-4
1907	Was-A	.978	41	38	98	3	2	7
Total	17	.938	1721	2306	3706	394	212	132
	C							
1887	Lou-a	.916	44	251	66	29	7	1
1888	Lou-a	.929	37	202	60	20	3	-1
1889	Phi-a	.934	55	278	102	27	7	16
1890	Phi-P	.885	49	191	70	34	7	3
1891	Phi-a	.940	43	212	38	16	5	-6
1892	Phi-N	.969	39	158	32	6	5	-2
1893	Phi-N	.974	40	144	46	5	4	1
1894	Phi-N	.976	16	36	5	1	0	-2
1896	Phi-N	1.000	2	7	0	0	0	0
Total	9	.932	324	1473	419	138	38	10
	OF							
1887	Lou-a	.850	10	16	1	3	1	-1
1888	Lou-a	.842	12	14	2	3	1	-1
1890	Phi-P	.862	15	25	0	4	0	-3
1891	Phi-a	.971	43	56	10	2	4	3
1892	Phi-N	.894	25	39	3	5	0	-3
1893	Phi-N	.931	10	27	0	2	0	-1
1896	Phi-N	1.000	2	7	0	0	0	0
1897	Phi-N	1.000	2	2	0	0	0	0
Total	8	.914	119	186	16	9	6	-6
	SS							
1888	Lou-a	1.000	2	3	5	0	0	0
1891	Phi-a	1.000	1	0	2	0	0	0
1892	Phi-N	.952	5	4	16	1	2	1
1893	Phi-N	.907	10	16	33	5	6	1
1894	Phi-N	.935	7	10	19	2	4	-1
1896	Phi-N	.942	37	77	134	13	17	4
1897	Phi-N	1.000	1	2	3	0	0	0
1898	StL-N	.833	2	3	7	2	2	-1
Total	8	.936	65	115	219	3	31	4
	2B							
1891	Phi-a	.833	1	1	4	1	1	0
1892	Phi-N	.971	14	29	37	2	5	-4
1894	Phi-N	1.000	1	3	1	0	1	0
1896	Phi-N	.964	6	10	17	1	4	1
1897	Phi-N	.964	38	68	120	7	10	1
Total	5	.963	60	111	179	1	21	-2
	1B							
1893	Phi-N	.956	6	60	5	3	7	0
1903	Phi-A	1.000	1	7	0	0	0	0
Total	2	.960	7	67	5	3	7	0

■ Monte Cross SS

YEAR	TM/L	PCT	G	PO	A	E	DP	FR
1892	Bal-N	.864	15	18	39	9	2	-3
1894	Pit-N	.924	13	34	39	6	7	2
1895	Pit-N	.883	107	254	327	77	42	-13
1896	StL-N	.892	125	298	394	84	31	-11

YEAR	TM/L	PCT	G	PO	A	E	DP	FR
1897	StL-N	.920	131	327	513	73	47	28
1898	Phi-N	.907	149	404	506	93	65	14
1899	Phi-N	.909	154	370	529	90	55	2
1900	Phi-N	.928	131	339	459	62	68	-3
1901	Phi-N	.924	139	343	445	65	31	-16
1902	Phi-A	.927	137	373	466	66	37	11
1903	Phi-A	.940	137	305	396	45	36	8
1904	Phi-A	.937	153	276	424	47	26	-16
1905	Phi-A	.929	77	160	195	27	22	-4
1906	Phi-A	.938	134	305	411	47	48	4
1907	Phi-A	.954	74	169	226	19	17	13
Total	15	.920	1676	3975	5369	810	534	16
2B								
1895	Pit-N	1.000	1	2	0	0	0	0
1903	Phi-A	1.000	1	1	0	0	0	0
1905	Phi-A	.857	2	3	3	1	0	0
Total	3	.900	4	6	3	1	0	0

■ Frank Croucher SS

YEAR	TM/L	PCT	G	PO	A	E	DP	FR
1939	Det-A	.934	93	139	256	28	47	-9
1940	Det-A	.936	26	17	27	3	2	-1
1941	Det-A	.935	136	270	361	44	85	-3
Total	3	.934	255	426	644	5	134	-13
2B								
1939	Det-A	.929	3	5	8	1	3	1
1940	Det-A	1.000	7	4	2	0	1	0
1942	Was-A	.950	18	35	60	5	9	5
Total	3	.950	28	44	70	6	13	6
3B								
1940	Det-A	.600	1	2	1	2	0	-1

■ Buck Crouse C

YEAR	TM/L	PCT	G	PO	A	E	DP	FR
1923	Chi-A	.955	22	66	18	4	1	-2
1924	Chi-A	.945	90	298	97	23	9	1
1925	Chi-A	.952	48	104	36	7	5	-3
1926	Chi-A	.985	45	164	34	3	1	3
1927	Chi-A	.972	81	202	79	8	10	7
1928	Chi-A	.959	76	196	61	11	3	-2
1929	Chi-A	.979	40	111	29	3	5	6
1930	Chi-A	.979	38	155	31	4	3	7
Total	8	.964	440	1296	385	3	37	17

■ George Crowe 1B

YEAR	TM/L	PCT	G	PO	A	E	DP	FR
1952	Bos-N	.985	55	476	42	8	40	2
1953	Mil-N	1.000	9	17	2	0	1	0
1955	Mil-N	.989	79	677	61	8	62	1
1956	Cin-N	.988	32	225	25	3	15	2
1957	Cin-N	.989	120	932	86	11	86	-2
1958	Cin-N	.992	93	713	53	6	65	-2
1959	StL-N	1.000	14	82	12	0	9	2
1960	StL-N	1.000	5	21	2	0	1	0
Total	8	.990	407	3143	283	6	279	3
2B								
1958	Cin-N	1.000	1	1	0	0	1	0

■ Terry Crowley OF

YEAR	TM/L	PCT	G	PO	A	E	DP	FR
1969	Bal-A	1.000	2	3	0	0	0	0
1970	Bal-A	.973	27	36	0	1	0	-2
1971	Bal-A	1.000	6	4	0	0	0	-1
1972	Bal-A	.990	68	95	2	1	1	-5
1973	Bal-A	.867	10	12	1	2	0	0
1974	Cin-N	1.000	22	29	1	0	0	-1
1975	Cin-N	1.000	4	8	1	0	0	1
1978	Bal-A	1.000	2	1	1	0	0	1
Total	8	.980	141	188	6	4	1	-7
1B								
1969	Bal-A	1.000	3	20	2	0	3	0
1970	Bal-A	.991	23	102	6	1	9	-2
1971	Bal-A	1.000	2	3	0	0	0	0
1972	Bal-A	1.000	15	75	6	0	6	0
1973	Bal-A	.962	7	21	4	1	3	1
1974	Cin-N	.939	7	27	4	2	0	0
1975	Cin-N	1.000	4	35	3	0	4	1
1976	Bal-A	1.000	1	13	2	0	1	0
1977	Bal-A	1.000	1	3	0	0	0	0
1978	Bal-A	—	1	0	0	0	0	0
1979	Bal-A	1.000	2	5	0	0	1	0
1980	Bal-A	1.000	3	19	5	0	1	1
1981	Bal-A	1.000	4	30	2	0	2	0
1982	Bal-A	.988	10	74	6	1	12	0
1983	Mon-N	1.000	4	19	0	0	2	-1
Total	15	.990	87	446	40	5	44	0

■ Bill Crowley OF

YEAR	TM/L	PCT	G	PO	A	E	DP	FR
1877	Lou-N	.849	58	109	20	23	2	6
1879	Buf-N	.809	43	62	14	18	4	0
1880	Buf-N	.824	74	131	23	33	3	3
1881	Bos-N	.880	72	130	17	20	5	-4
1883	Phi-a	.810	22	31	3	8	0	-2
	Cle-N	.923	11	12	0	1	0	-3
1884	Bos-N	.870	108	125	22	22	5	-5
1885	Buf-N	.874	92	152	8	23	1	-4
Total	7	.853	480	752	107	148	20	-9
C								
1877	Lou-N	1.000	2	8	1	0	0	1
1879	Buf-N	.857	10	34	8	7	0	-4
1880	Buf-N	.850	22	73	23	17	0	-2
Total	3	.860	34	115	32	4	0	-5
1B								
1879	Buf-N	.930	7	76	4	6	6	0
1883	Phi-a	.889	1	16	0	2	0	0
Total	2	.923	8	92	4	8	6	0
2B								
1877	Lou-N	1.000	1	1	1	0	0	0
1879	Buf-N	.913	3	10	11	2	2	1
Total	2	.920	4	11	12	2	2	1
SS								
1877	Lou-N	1.000	2	4	4	0	0	0
3B								
1877	Lou-N	.500	1	1	1	2	0	-1

■ Walton Cruise OF

YEAR	TM/L	PCT	G	PO	A	E	DP	FR
1914	StL-N	.976	81	158	6	4	1	1
1916	StL-N	1.000	2	2	0	0	0	0
1917	StL-N	.965	152	285	15	11	6	-4
1918	StL-N	.964	65	103	4	4	0	-9
1919	StL-N	.833	5	5	0	1	0	-1
	Bos-N	.978	66	124	7	3	1	-3
	Yr	.971	71	129	7	4	1	-4
1920	Bos-N	.950	82	122	10	7	3	-9
1921	Bos-N	.963	102	232	2	9	3	-6
1922	Bos-N	.948	100	212	9	12	3	-2
1923	Bos-N	.952	9	20	0	1	0	0
Total	9	.962	664	1263	53	2	17	-33
1B								
1919	StL-N	1.000	2	6	1	0	0	0
1921	Bos-N	1.000	2	20	2	0	1	0
1922	Bos-N	1.000	2	25	2	0	1	0
Total	3	1.000	6	51	5	0	2	0

■ Hector Cruz OF

YEAR	TM/L	PCT	G	PO	A	E	DP	FR
1973	StL-N	1.000	5	7	0	0	0	1
1975	StL-N	.941	6	16	0	1	0	0
1977	StL-N	.964	106	154	9	6	1	-6
1978	Chi-N	1.000	14	30	0	0	0	0
	SF-N	.978	53	82	5	2	3	-1
	Yr	.983	67	112	5	2	3	-1
1979	SF-N	1.000	6	5	0	0	0	0
	Cin-N	.984	69	119	8	2	4	6
	Yr	.985	75	124	8	2	4	6
1980	Cin-N	.955	29	42	0	2	0	1
1981	Chi-N	1.000	16	21	1	0	0	0
1982	Chi-N	1.000	4	1	0	0	0	-1
Total	8	.975	308	477	23	3	8	0
3B								
1975	StL-N	.800	12	4	4	2	0	-2
1976	StL-N	.934	148	100	270	26	19	-21
1977	StL-N	.500	2	0	1	1	1	-1
1978	Chi-N	1.000	7	2	14	0	0	2
	SF-N	1.000	14	3	13	0	0	0
	Yr	1.000	21	5	27	0	0	2
1979	SF-N	.833	2	3	2	1	0	-1
1981	Chi-N	.925	18	12	25	3	0	-3
Total	6	.932	203	124	329	3	20	-26

■ Henry Cruz OF

YEAR	TM/L	PCT	G	PO	A	E	DP	FR
1975	LA-N	.960	41	48	0	2	0	-1
1976	LA-N	.976	23	39	1	1	1	0
1977	Chi-A	.833	9	5	0	1	0	-1
1978	Chi-A	1.000	40	55	4	0	2	5
Total	4	.974	113	147	5	4	3	3

■ Jose Cruz OF

YEAR	TM/L	PCT	G	PO	A	E	DP	FR
1970	StL-N	1.000	4	16	0	0	0	1
1971	StL-N	.975	83	197	2	5	1	-1
1972	StL-N	.979	102	220	9	5	5	-1
1973	StL-N	.979	118	276	2	6	1	-4
1974	StL-N	.975	53	76	2	2	1	2
1975	Hou-N	.980	94	187	6	4	0	2
1976	Hou-N	.972	125	265	10	8	4	6
1977	Hou-N	.955	151	311	11	9	1	2
1978	Hou-N	.975	152	311	4	8	0	-1
1979	Hou-N	.959	156	320	7	14	0	1
1980	Hou-N	.958	158	323	16	11	1	6
1981	Hou-N	.984	105	237	5	4	2	5
1982	Hou-N	.964	155	340	9	13	3	9
1983	Hou-N	.979	160	322	9	7	1	3
1984	Hou-N	.976	160	310	11	8	1	4
1985	Hou-N	.971	137	257	12	8	3	2
1986	Hou-N	.984	134	237	5	4	1	-2
1987	Hou-N	.984	97	178	5	3	3	2
1988	NY-A	.889	8	8	0	1	0	-1
Total	19	.974	2156	4391	125	120	28	35
1B								
1974	StL-N	1.000	1	5	0	0	2	0
1978	Hou-N	1.000	2	17	1	0	1	0
Total	2	1.000	3	22	1	0	3	0

■ Julio Cruz 2B

YEAR	TM/L	PCT	G	PO	A	E	DP	FR
1977	Sea-A	.983	54	114	171	5	29	2
1978	Sea-A	.987	141	286	472	10	101	9
1979	Sea-A	.979	107	258	361	13	87	17
1980	Sea-A	.983	115	269	355	11	85	-3
1981	Sea-A	.982	92	239	294	10	72	9
1982	Sea-A	.987	151	320	434	10	98	3
1983	Sea-A	.984	60	131	173	5	41	7
	Chi-A	.983	97	213	298	9	71	10
	Yr	.983	157	344	471	14	112	17
1984	Chi-A	.976	141	273	452	18	92	-22
1985	Chi-A	.982	87	158	220	7	59	13
1986	Chi-A	.985	78	132	205	5	45	-2
Total	10	.983	1123	2393	3435	103	780	91
SS								
1978	Sea-A	.950	5	9	10	1	3	-1
1981	Sea-A	.800	1	1	3	1	0	-1
1982	Sea-A	1.000	2	1	1	0	0	0
Total	3	.926	8	11	14	2	3	-2
3B								
1982	Sea-A	1.000	1	1	3	0	0	0

■ Todd Cruz SS

YEAR	TM/L	PCT	G	PO	A	E	DP	FR
1978	Phi-N	1.000	2	1	6	0	0	1
1979	KC-A	.974	48	47	102	4	13	1
1980	Cal-A	.860	12	15	22	6	6	-4
	Chi-A	.956	90	138	298	20	52	5
	Yr	.948	102	153	320	26	58	1
1982	Sea-A	.963	136	215	439	25	98	17
1983	Sea-A	.964	63	97	224	12	42	20
Total	5	.960	351	513	1091	7	211	40
3B								
1979	KC-A	.885	9	7	16	3	3	2
1980	Cal-A	.750	4	1	2	1	0	-1
1983	Bal-A	.942	79	49	162	13	19	5
1984	Bal-A	.955	89	23	104	6	10	12
Total	4	.941	181	80	284	3	32	18
2B								
1980	Cal-A	.750	1	2	1	1	0	-1
1983	Bal-A	—	2	0	0	0	0	0
Total	2	.750	3	2	1	1	0	-1
OF								
1980	Cal-A	—	1	0	0	0	0	0

■ Mike Cubbage 3B

YEAR	TM/L	PCT	G	PO	A	E	DP	FR
1974	Tex-A	1.000	3	1	3	0	0	0
1975	Tex-A	.833	3	1	4	1	1	0
1976	Tex-A	—	1	0	0	0	0	0
	Min-A	.940	99	71	209	18	22	2
	Yr	.940	100	71	209	18	22	2
1977	Min-A	.952	126	90	266	18	29	9
1978	Min-A	.971	115	65	233	9	24	2
1979	Min-A	.928	63	34	94	10	9	-11
1980	Min-A	.976	32	29	54	2	6	3
1981	NY-N	.963	12	5	21	1	0	1
Total	8	.952	454	296	884	9	91	6
1B								
1979	Min-A	1.000	1	4	0	0	0	0
1980	Min-A	.996	72	512	44	2	56	4
Total	2	.996	73	516	44	2	56	4
2B								
1974	Tex-A	.923	2	6	6	1	4	2
1975	Tex-A	.962	37	67	111	7	24	2
1976	Tex-A	1.000	5	8	9	0	3	0
	Min-A	.500	2	1	0	1	0	0
	Yr	.947	7	9	9	1	3	0
1978	Min-A	1.000	5	4	4	0	1	-1
1979	Min-A	—	1	0	0	0	0	0
1980	Min-A	1.000	4	2	0	0	2	0
Total	6	.961	53	90	132	9	34	3

■ Tony Cuccinello 2B

YEAR	TM/L	PCT	G	PO	A	E	DP	FR
1930	Cin-N	.964	15	24	29	2	8	-4
1931	Cin-N	.969	154	376	499	28	128	5
1932	Bro-N	.973	154	385	525	25	113	19
1933	Bro-N	.977	120	311	334	15	64	-19
1934	Bro-N	.974	101	246	347	16	54	12
1935	Bro-N	.977	64	158	186	8	48	4
1936	Bos-N	.971	150	383	559	28	128	22
1937	Bos-N	.967	151	330	524	29	92	-9
1938	Bos-N	.974	147	323	458	21	84	-26
1939	Bos-N	.970	80	208	246	14	66	-3
1940	NY-N	.987	47	106	130	3	17	2
1942	Bos-N	1.000	14	20	42	0	8	-1
1943	Bos-N	1.000	2	2	2	0	0	0
1944	Chi-A	.955	6	11	10	1	8	-1
Total	14	.973	1205	2883	3891	190	812	-1
3B								
1930	Cin-N	.920	109	85	181	23	15	-14
1933	Bro-N	.956	14	18	25	2	3	1
1934	Bro-N	.961	43	54	70	5	6	0
1935	Bro-N	.951	36	34	64	5	9	2
1940	Bos-N	.978	33	30	61	2	8	1
	NY-N	.964	37	30	77	4	7	3
	Yr	.971	70	60	138	6	15	4
1942	Bos-N	.907	20	14	25	4	5	-3
1943	Bos-N	.929	4	5	8	1	2	1
	Chi-A	.965	30	33	50	3	5	-1
1944	Chi-A	.959	30	31	63	4	5	-1
1945	Chi-A	.936	112	73	221	20	22	-5
Total	9	.945	468	407	845	3	87	-16
SS								
1930	Cin-N	.750	4	2	1	1	0	-1
1943	Bos-N	—	1	0	0	0	0	0
Total	2	.750	5	2	1	1	0	-1

■ Leon Culberson OF

YEAR	TM/L	PCT	G	PO	A	E	DP	FR
1943	Bos-A	.978	79	211	10	5	2	8
1944	Bos-A	.979	72	182	6	4	2	5
1945	Bos-A	.967	91	219	14	8	6	2
1946	Bos-A	.967	49	87	1	3	0	-3
1947	Bos-A	.974	25	35	2	1	0	0
1948	Was-A	1.000	11	16	1	0	0	-1
Total	6	.974	327	750	34	1	10	11
3B								
1946	Bos-A	.846	4	2	9	2	0	0
1947	Bos-A	.833	4	1	4	1	1	-1
Total	2	.842	8	3	13	3	3	-1

■ Tim Cullen 2B

YEAR	TM/L	PCT	G	PO	A	E	DP	FR
1966	Was-A	1.000	5	7	10	0	3	2
1967	Was-A	.958	46	98	107	9	24	5
1968	Chi-A	.966	71	104	150	9	34	6
	Was-A	.961	16	34	40	3	7	1
	Yr	.965	87	138	190	12	41	7
1969	Was-A	.981	105	166	188	7	44	11
1970	Was-A	.994	112	211	262	3	65	26
1971	Was-A	.997	78	165	213	1	47	15
1972	Oak-A	.952	65	103	117	11	24	-1
Total	7	.979	498	888	1087	3	248	65
SS								
1967	Was-A	.951	69	105	224	17	40	7
1968	Was-A	.968	33	35	56	3	10	-2
1969	Was-A	.906	9	7	22	3	3	1
1970	Was-A	1.000	6	1	3	0	0	0
1971	Was-A	.963	62	97	166	10	39	5
1972	Oak-A	1.000	1	0	1	0	0	0
Total	6	.956	180	245	472	3	92	11
3B								
1966	Was-A	.889	8	7	9	2	1	0
1967	Was-A	.979	15	16	30	1	3	3
1968	Was-A	.500	3	0	1	1	0	0

YEAR	TM/L	PCT	G	PO	A	E	DP	FR
1969	Was-A	1.000	1	0	1	0	0	0
1972	Oak-A	1.000	4	4	3	0	0	0
Total	5	.947	31	27	44	4	4	3
		OF						
1967	Was-A	—	1	0	0	0	0	0

■ Roy Cullenbine OF

YEAR	TM/L	PCT	G	PO	A	E	DP	FR
1938	Det-A	1.000	17	34	1	0	0	-1
1939	Det-A	.902	46	81	2	9	1	-4
1940	Bro-N	1.000	19	33	3	0	0	0
	StL-A	.975	57	114	5	3	2	-4
1941	StL-A	.964	120	258	12	10	3	0
1942	StL-A	.930	27	48	5	4	1	0
	Was-A	.966	35	80	6	3	1	4
	NY-A	.980	19	47	2	1	0	1
	Yr	.959	81	175	13	8	2	5
1943	Cle-A	.981	121	245	14	5	6	-1
1944	Cle-A	.967	151	275	15	10	6	-6
1945	Cle-A	1.000	4	5	0	0	0	0
	Det-A	.980	146	321	23	7	3	10
	Yr	.980	150	326	23	7	3	10
1946	Det-A	.965	81	125	12	5	1	-2
Total	9	.969	843	1666	100	7	24	-3
		1B						
1939	Det-A	1.000	2	23	2	0	4	0
1940	StL-A	1.000	6	44	2	0	4	0
1941	StL-A	.982	22	193	20	4	21	1
1942	StL-A	.981	5	45	6	1	4	1
	NY-A	1.000	1	6	0	0	0	0
	Yr	.983	6	51	6	1	4	1
1943	Cle-A	.986	13	131	9	2	9	0
1946	Det-A	.984	21	168	18	3	14	2
1947	Det-A	.989	138	1184	139	15	111	16
Total	7	.988	208	1794	196	5	167	20
		3B						
1942	Was-A	.931	28	45	63	8	4	4
1945	Cle-A	.857	3	3	3	1	0	-2
Total	2	.927	31	48	66	9	4	2

■ Dick Culler SS

YEAR	TM/L	PCT	G	PO	A	E	DP	FR
1936	Phi-A	1.000	2	0	4	0	0	0
1943	Chi-A	1.000	3	4	5	0	0	0
1944	Bos-N	.904	8	14	33	5	6	2
1945	Bos-N	.954	126	252	386	31	71	-8
1946	Bos-N	.948	132	279	380	36	68	-8
1947	Bos-N	.967	77	106	212	11	31	3
1948	Chi-N	.968	43	65	114	6	18	15
1949	NY-N	.889	7	3	5	1	2	2
Total	8	.954	398	723	1139	0	196	6
		3B						
1943	Chi-A	.950	26	31	45	4	8	3
1945	Bos-N	.885	6	9	14	3	1	1
Total	2	.934	32	40	59	7	9	4
		2B						
1936	Phi-A	.946	7	20	15	2	4	-3
1943	Chi-A	.949	19	36	71	4	16	7
1948	Chi-N	1.000	2	3	1	0	0	0
Total	3	.961	28	59	87	6	20	4

■ Nick Cullop OF

YEAR	TM/L	PCT	G	PO	A	E	DP	FR
1927	Was-A	1.000	5	6	0	0	0	-1
	Cle-A	.982	20	50	4	1	0	3
	Yr	.984	25	56	4	1	0	2
1929	Bro-N	1.000	11	23	2	0	0	0
1930	Cin-N	1.000	5	7	2	0	0	1
1931	Cin-N	.968	83	177	5	6	3	-4
Total	4	.975	124	263	13	7	3	-1
		1B						
1927	Was-A	1.000	1	3	0	0	0	0
1929	Bro-N	1.000	1	3	0	0	0	0
Total	2	1.000	2	6	0	0	0	0

■ Joe Cunningham 1B

YEAR	TM/L	PCT	G	PO	A	E	DP	FR
1954	StL-N	.989	85	814	68	10	96	2
1956	StL-N	1.000	1	2	0	0	0	0
1957	StL-N	1.000	57	279	17	0	17	-1
1958	StL-N	.997	67	328	23	1	19	-2
1959	StL-N	.994	35	158	9	1	22	-1
1960	StL-N	1.000	15	114	10	0	7	0
1961	StL-N	1.000	10	69	1	0	8	-2
1962	Chi-A	.994	143	1282	90	8	118	-5
1963	Chi-A	.989	58	535	24	6	39	-7
1964	Chi-A	.996	33	264	16	1	25	0
	Was-A	.997	41	316	13	1	28	-4
	Yr	.997	74	580	29	2	53	-4
1965	Was-A	.986	59	393	24	6	44	-3
1966	Was-A	1.000	3	10	4	0	1	1
Total	12	.993	607	4564	299	4	424	-22
		OF						
1957	StL-N	.965	46	81	1	3	0	-4
1958	StL-N	.979	66	90	3	2	2	-6
1959	StL-N	.972	121	201	5	6	1	-5
1960	StL-N	.950	116	184	6	10	1	-8
1961	StL-N	.964	86	131	2	5	1	-10
1962	Chi-A	1.000	5	5	0	0	0	0
Total	6	.965	440	692	17	6	5	-33

■ Bill Cunningham OF

YEAR	TM/L	PCT	G	PO	A	E	DP	FR
1921	NY-N	1.000	20	35	1	0	0	0
1922	NY-N	.988	71	155	7	2	3	6
1923	NY-N	.992	68	123	8	1	2	5
1924	Bos-N	.970	109	243	16	8	3	8
Total	4	.982	268	556	32	1	8	19
		2B						
1923	NY-N	1.000	4	4	8	0	0	1
		3B						
1922	NY-N	—	1	0	0	0	0	0

■ Bill Cunningham 2B

YEAR	TM/L	PCT	G	PO	A	E	DP	FR
1910	Was-A	.957	21	36	52	4	7	-4
1911	Was-A	.932	93	168	244	30	18	-13
1912	Was-A	.962	7	8	17	1	1	-3
Total	3	.938	121	212	313	5	26	-20
		SS						
1912	Was-A	—	1	0	0	0	0	0

■ Guy Curtright OF

YEAR	TM/L	PCT	G	PO	A	E	DP	FR
1943	Chi-A	.972	128	301	7	9	1	-2
1944	Chi-A	.948	51	101	8	6	3	1
1945	Chi-A	.986	84	196	8	3	0	2
1946	Chi-A	1.000	15	30	2	0	1	1
Total	4	.973	278	628	25	8	5	2

■ Ned Cuthbert OF

YEAR	TM/L	PCT	G	PO	A	E	DP	FR
1876	StL-N	.843	63	95	7	19	2	-9
1877	Cin-N	.830	12	34	5	8	2	5
1882	StL-a	.896	60	74	12	10	0	-4
1883	StL-a	.794	20	22	5	7	0	-1
1884	Bal-U	.750	44	41	10	17	0	-5
Total	5	.833	199	266	39	1	4	-14
		1B						
1883	StL-a	1.000	1	15	0	0	0	0

■ George Cutshaw 2B

YEAR	TM/L	PCT	G	PO	A	E	DP	FR
1912	Bro-N	.958	91	192	290	21	31	9
1913	Bro-N	.957	147	402	448	38	79	18
1914	Bro-N	.959	153	455	444	38	74	28
1915	Bro-N	.971	154	397	473	26	53	17
1916	Bro-N	.958	154	361	467	36	51	8
1917	Bro-N	.963	134	319	377	27	43	-9
1918	Pit-N	.964	126	323	366	26	60	-3
1919	Pit-N	.980	139	344	392	15	56	-11
1920	Pit-N	.968	129	336	423	25	62	1
1921	Pit-N	.951	84	196	253	23	36	-15
1922	Det-A	.972	132	334	390	21	69	9
1923	Det-A	.988	43	103	150	3	21	12
Total	12	.965	1486	3762	4473	299	635	64
		3B						
1912	Bro-N	.889	5	4	4	1	0	0
1923	Det-A	1.000	2	0	1	0	0	0
Total	2	.900	7	4	5	1	0	0
		SS						
1912	Bro-N	—	1	0	0	0	0	0

■ Kiki Cuyler OF

YEAR	TM/L	PCT	G	PO	A	E	DP	FR
1921	Pit-N	1.000	1	1	0	0	0	0
1923	Pit-N	.931	11	26	1	2	0	0
1924	Pit-N	.943	114	246	19	16	4	6
1925	Pit-N	.967	153	362	21	13	4	6
1926	Pit-N	.968	157	405	19	14	4	14
1927	Pit-N	.980	73	195	6	4	0	4
1928	Chi-N	.982	127	257	18	5	3	7
1929	Chi-N	.974	129	288	15	8	6	7
1930	Chi-N	.980	156	377	21	8	7	16
1931	Chi-N	.970	153	347	11	11	4	3
1932	Chi-N	.969	109	239	7	8	1	-4
1933	Chi-N	.978	69	130	2	3	0	-8
1934	Chi-N	.971	142	319	15	10	3	-3
1935	Chi-N	.981	42	98	5	2	1	3
	Cin-N	.985	57	123	5	2	2	-2
	Yr	.983	99	221	10	4	3	1
1936	Cin-N	.974	140	322	9	9	3	-12
1937	Cin-N	.973	106	174	8	5	1	-7
1938	Cin-N	.993	68	125	9	1	1	0
Total	17	.972	1807	4034	191	121	44	30

■ Paul Dade OF

YEAR	TM/L	PCT	G	PO	A	E	DP	FR
1975	Cal-A	1.000	3	8	0	0	0	0
1976	Cal-A	.750	4	2	1	1	0	1
1977	Cle-A	.989	99	167	10	2	2	-2
1978	Cle-A	.962	81	171	6	7	2	1
1979	Cle-A	.962	37	73	4	3	1	-2
	SD-N	1.000	4	3	1	0	0	1
1980	SD-N	.909	8	9	1	1	0	1
Total	6	.970	236	433	23	4	5	-1
		3B						
1975	Cal-A	1.000	1	0	1	0	0	0
1976	Cal-A	—	1	0	0	0	0	0
1977	Cle-A	.928	26	23	41	5	1	-3
1979	Cle-A	—	2	0	0	0	0	0
	SD-N	.949	70	44	162	11	12	6
1980	SD-N	.846	21	5	17	4	1	3
Total	5	.936	121	72	221	0	14	6
		2B						
1976	Cal-A	1.000	2	3	3	0	0	1
1977	Cle-A	1.000	1	2	0	0	0	0
1980	SD-N	1.000	1	0	1	0	0	0
Total	3	1.000	4	5	4	0	0	1

■ Bill Dahlen SS

YEAR	TM/L	PCT	G	PO	A	E	DP	FR
1891	Chi-N	.822	15	28	46	16	4	-3
1892	Chi-N	.909	72	178	232	41	29	4
1893	Chi-N	.892	88	229	306	65	33	10
1894	Chi-N	.898	66	186	253	50	43	20
1895	Chi-N	.904	129	281	527	86	70	24
1896	Chi-N	.915	125	310	456	71	66	25
1897	Chi-N	.930	75	215	291	38	48	28
1898	Chi-N	.921	142	369	511	76	77	25
1899	Bro-N	.941	110	256	377	40	48	10
1900	Bro-N	.938	133	321	517	55	59	19
1901	Bro-N	.929	129	301	450	57	49	13
1902	Bro-N	.916	138	278	440	66	34	-6
1903	Bro-N	.948	138	296	477	42	48	18
1904	NY-N	.930	145	316	494	61	61	28
1905	NY-N	.948	147	313	501	45	58	20
1906	NY-N	.938	143	287	454	49	36	0
1907	NY-N	.941	143	292	426	45	39	7
1908	Bos-N	.952	144	291	553	43	58	38
1909	Bos-N	.908	49	101	184	29	20	9
1911	Bro-N	1.000	1	2	5	0	1	1
Total	20	.927	2132	4850	7500	975	881	302
		3B						
1891	Chi-N	.887	84	120	211	42	13	9
1892	Chi-N	.941	68	113	189	19	14	23
1893	Chi-N	.889	3	3	5	1	0	0
1894	Chi-N	.900	55	96	129	25	10	11
1899	Bro-N	.968	11	19	41	2	5	9
1909	Bos-N	1.000	2	4	5	0	0	0
Total	6	.913	223	355	580	9	42	52
		OF						
1891	Chi-N	.927	37	69	7	6	4	3
1892	Chi-N	1.000	2	3	0	0	0	0
1893	Chi-N	.935	17	27	2	2	1	-2
1895	Chi-N	1.000	1	1	0	0	0	0
1905	NY-N	1.000	1	1	0	0	0	0
Total	5	.932	58	101	9	8	5	1
		2B						
1892	Chi-N	.833	1	3	2	1	0	-1
1893	Chi-N	.927	10	27	24	4	1	0
1901	Bro-N	1.000	2	3	7	0	0	1
1909	Bos-N	.893	6	14	11	3	1	0
Total	4	.919	19	47	44	8	2	-4

■ Babe Dahlgren 1B

YEAR	TM/L	PCT	G	PO	A	E	DP	FR
1935	Bos-A	.988	149	1433	69	18	109	-7
1936	Bos-A	.980	16	136	8	3	10	0
1938	NY-A	1.000	6	26	2	0	2	0
1939	NY-A	.991	144	1303	68	13	140	-7
1940	NY-A	.990	155	1488	75	15	143	-10
1941	Bos-N	.993	39	379	28	3	45	2
	Chi-N	.991	98	957	38	9	84	-8
	Yr	.992	137	1336	66	12	129	-6
1942	Chi-N	.986	14	136	10	2	7	1
	Bro-N	1.000	10	47	4	0	6	1
	Yr	.990	24	183	14	2	13	2
1943	Phi-N	.988	73	714	46	9	66	-2
1944	Pit-N	.987	158	1440	128	20	105	8
1945	Pit-N	.996	144	1373	93	6	115	1
1946	StL-A	.981	24	187	18	4	16	1
Total	11	.990	1030	9619	587	102	848	-20
		3B						
1938	NY-A	.826	8	11	8	4	0	-2
1941	Bos-N	.944	5	5	12	1	0	0
1943	Phi-N	.904	35	33	52	9	4	-8
Total	3	.896	48	49	72	4	4	-10
		SS						
1943	Phi-N	.946	25	53	53	6	11	-13
		C						
1943	Phi-N	—	1	0	0	0	0	0

■ Con Daily C

YEAR	TM/L	PCT	G	PO	A	E	DP	FR
1884	Phi-U	.857	2	15	3	3	0	0
1885	Pro-N	.876	48	220	70	41	8	-2
1886	Bos-N	.911	49	264	55	31	5	-12
1887	Bos-N	.889	36	125	44	21	3	-2
1888	Ind-N	.893	42	215	69	34	6	4
1889	Ind-N	.887	51	225	49	35	1	-10
1890	Bro-P	.879	40	141	34	24	5	-6
1891	Bro-N	.925	55	230	65	24	2	-2
1892	Bro-N	.943	68	342	85	26	9	-2
1893	Bro-N	.935	51	215	46	18	2	-1
1894	Bro-N	.930	60	218	61	21	7	-4
1895	Bro-N	.956	39	127	25	7	7	-4
1896	Chi-N	.969	9	24	7	1	0	-1
Total	13	.912	550	2361	613	286	55	-40
		OF						
1885	Pro-N	.909	6	8	2	1	1	1
1888	Ind-N	.667	5	5	1	3	1	0
1889	Ind-N	1.000	6	8	0	0	0	0
1890	Bro-P	—	1	0	0	0	0	0
1891	Bro-N	1.000	3	6	0	0	0	0
1892	Bro-N	.944	13	14	3	1	0	0
1893	Bro-N	.800	9	11	1	3	0	-2
1895	Bro-N	1.000	1	3	0	0	0	0
Total	8	.886	44	55	7	8	2	-1
		1B						
1885	Pro-N	.972	7	68	2	2	5	0
1888	Ind-N	.982	5	55	0	1	2	-1
1889	Ind-N	.900	6	59	4	7	7	0
1890	Bro-P	.983	6	56	2	1	5	0
1891	Bro-N	1.000	1	0	1	0	0	0
1894	Bro-N	.948	7	53	2	3	5	-1
Total	6	.956	32	291	11	4	24	-2
		3B						
1888	Ind-N	.800	5	2	6	2	1	0
1889	Ind-N	1.000	1	2	4	0	1	1
Total	2	.875	6	4	10	2	2	1
		SS						
1891	Bro-N	.778	2	5	2	2	0	-1
1888	Ind-N	1.000	1	2	1	0	0	0

■ Ed Daily OF

YEAR	TM/L	PCT	G	PO	A	E	DP	FR
1886	Phi-N	.827	56	88	17	22	2	3
1887	Phi-N	.659	22	25	2	14	0	-5
	Was-N	.855	77	116	8	21	1	-7
	Yr	.812	99	141	10	35	1	-12
1888	Was-N	.912	100	179	19	19	4	3
1889	Col-N	.854	136	212	27	41	4	-3
1890	Bro-a	.892	64	107	17	15	3	4
	NY-N	.500	3	0	1	1	0	0
	Lou-a	1.000	11	13	1	0	0	-1
1891	Lou-a	.813	7	12	1	3	1	0
	Was-a	.719	21	21	2	9	1	-4
	Yr	.750	28	33	3	12	2	-4
Total	6	.857	497	773	95	145	16	-10
		1B						
1888	Was-N	1.000	1	13	0	0	0	0

YEAR	TM/L	PCT	G	PO	A	E	DP	FR
■ Pete Daley C
1955	Bos-A	1.000	14	75	4	0	0	3
1956	Bos-A	.992	57	228	14	2	1	-9
1957	Bos-A	1.000	77	289	20	0	5	-3
1958	Bos-A	.990	27	88	10	1	1	2
1959	Bos-A	.996	58	245	28	1	5	3
1960	KC-A	.990	61	263	33	3	3	-4
1961	Was-A	.988	72	285	35	4	6	7
Total	7	.993	366	1473	144	1	21	-1
OF
1960	KC-A	—	1	0	0	0	0	0
■ Tom Daley OF
1908	Cin-N	1.000	13	17	2	0	1	0
1913	Phi-A	.963	39	73	5	3	2	-1
1914	Phi-A	1.000	24	48	4	0	0	1
	NY-A	.958	58	126	12	6	2	6
	Yr	.969	82	174	16	6	2	7
1915	NY-A	1.000	2	2	0	0	1	0
Total	4	.970	136	266	23	9	6	6
■ Dom Dallessandro OF
1937	Bos-A	.965	35	54	1	2	0	-5
1940	Chi-N	.969	74	156	1	5	0	-2
1941	Chi-N	.987	131	292	4	4	0	0
1942	Chi-N	.986	66	134	6	2	1	-1
1943	Chi-N	.967	45	87	2	3	0	-3
1944	Chi-N	.982	106	212	9	4	2	-3
1946	Chi-N	.971	20	33	0	1	0	-2
1947	Chi-N	1.000	28	50	1	0	1	-1
Total	8	.980	505	1018	24	1	4	-17
■ Abner Dalrymple OF
1878	Mil-N	.832	61	128	11	28	3	6
1879	Chi-N	.728	71	103	4	40	1	-13
1880	Chi-N	.859	86	157	19	29	4	4
1881	Chi-N	.835	82	143	14	31	1	-8
1882	Chi-N	.877	84	185	8	27	4	-1
1883	Chi-N	.826	80	149	12	34	3	-2
1884	Chi-N	.882	111	176	18	26	5	1
1885	Chi-N	.879	113	180	16	27	2	-1
1886	Chi-N	.952	82	125	15	7	1	3
1887	Pit-N	.900	92	184	14	22	1	3
1888	Pit-N	.909	57	81	9	9	0	-2
1891	Mil-a	.909	32	44	6	5	1	-1
Total	12	.863	951	1655	146	285	26	-11
■ Clay Dalrymple C
1960	Phi-N	.966	48	172	25	7	3	-5
1961	Phi-N	.978	122	551	86	14	10	0
1962	Phi-N	.987	119	635	61	9	11	-12
1963	Phi-N	.981	142	881	90	19	16	0
1964	Phi-N	.991	124	737	61	7	11	3
1965	Phi-N	.993	102	657	70	5	10	18
1966	Phi-N	.993	110	615	48	5	5	-4
1967	Phi-N	.994	97	558	59	4	7	20
1968	Phi-N	.990	80	463	34	5	3	-3
1969	Bal-A	1.000	30	116	17	0	2	1
1970	Bal-A	1.000	11	78	8	0	0	6
1971	Bal-A	.971	18	94	7	3	1	2
Total	12	.987	1003	5557	566	8	79	26
■ Jack Dalton OF
1910	Bro-N	.966	72	129	12	5	3	1
1914	Bro-N	.965	116	240	7	9	2	-9
1915	Buf-F	.966	119	218	11	8	4	-5
1916	Det-A	1.000	4	3	0	0	0	-1
Total	4	.966	311	590	30	2	9	-14
■ Tom Daly C
1913	Chi-A	1.000	1	6	1	0	1	1
1914	Chi-A	1.000	4	13	2	0	1	-2
1915	Chi-A	.958	19	59	9	3	0	-2
1916	Cle-A	.982	25	86	24	2	3	-1
1918	Chi-N	.667	1	2	0	1	0	0
1919	Chi-N	.956	18	55	10	3	2	-2
1920	Chi-N	.981	29	88	18	2	0	-3
1921	Chi-N	.973	47	171	48	6	10	4
Total	8	.972	144	480	112	7	17	-5
OF
1914	Chi-A	.909	23	19	1	2	0	-6
1916	Cle-A	—	1	0	0	0	0	0
Total	2	.909	24	19	1	2	0	-6
3B
1914	Chi-A	.833	5	3	2	1	0	-2
1B
1914	Chi-A	.963	2	25	1	1	2	0
1915	Chi-A	1.000	1	2	0	0	0	0
Total	2	.966	3	27	1	1	2	0
■ Tom Daly 2B
1887	Chi-N	.933	2	5	9	1	1	1
1889	Was-N	.897	4	15	11	3	0	-2
1892	Bro-N	.960	10	21	27	2	3	-2
1893	Bro-N	.915	82	207	265	44	22	-8
1894	Bro-N	.908	123	317	354	68	52	-19
1895	Bro-N	.930	120	318	346	50	42	-19
1896	Bro-N	.909	66	168	190	36	31	-3
1898	Bro-N	.993	23	56	77	1	12	3
1899	Bro-N	.929	141	377	453	63	69	16
1900	Bro-N	.921	93	233	234	40	39	-12
1901	Bro-N	.944	133	370	357	43	46	11
1902	Chi-A	.957	137	312	370	31	70	-15
1903	Chi-A	.948	43	96	103	11	12	-13
	Cin-N	.937	79	151	221	25	22	-10
Total	13	.931	1056	2646	3017	418	421	-72
C
1887	Chi-N	.935	64	354	148	35	12	33
1888	Chi-N	.939	62	400	107	33	10	19
1889	Was-N	.917	57	268	86	32	5	4
1890	Bro-N	.953	69	332	72	20	7	2
1891	Bro-N	.881	26	133	15	20	0	-6
1892	Bro-N	.974	27	114	34	4	3	0
1896	Bro-N	.800	1	2	2	1	0	0
Total	7	.934	306	1603	464	145	37	52
3B
1892	Bro-N	.897	57	76	106	21	8	-5
1893	Bro-N	.832	45	80	83	33	5	-10
Total	2	.865	102	156	189	4	13	-15
OF
1887	Chi-N	.846	8	9	2	2	1	1
1888	Chi-N	.917	4	11	0	1	0	0
1889	Was-N	.750	3	2	1	1	0	0
1890	Bro-N	1.000	1	4	1	0	0	1
1891	Bro-N	1.000	7	9	1	0	1	0
1892	Bro-N	.897	30	49	3	6	2	-2
1900	Bro-N	1.000	2	9	1	0	1	2
Total	7	.911	55	93	9	0	5	2
1B
1887	Chi-N	1.000	2	20	0	0	3	0
1889	Was-N	.933	8	67	3	5	3	-1
1890	Bro-N	.994	12	155	5	1	7	1
1891	Bro-N	.979	15	131	9	3	5	1
1900	Bro-N	1.000	3	19	3	0	1	1
Total	5	.979	40	392	20	9	19	2
SS
1887	Chi-N	.800	2	2	2	1	1	0
1889	Was-N	.600	1	2	1	2	0	-1
1891	Bro-N	.766	11	16	33	15	2	-3
Total	3	.757	14	20	36	8	3	-4
■ Bert Daniels OF
1910	NY-A	.957	85	170	9	8	2	4
1911	NY-A	.941	120	256	15	17	6	1
1912	NY-A	.945	131	277	13	17	1	8
1913	NY-A	.966	87	128	15	5	3	1
1914	Cin-N	.974	71	144	7	4	2	-3
Total	5	.953	494	975	59	1	14	11
3B
1910	NY-A	.917	6	11	11	2	0	-1
1B
1910	NY-A	.933	4	27	1	2	2	0
■ Kal Daniels OF
1986	Cin-N	.967	47	88	0	3	0	-3
1987	Cin-N	.968	94	178	5	6	0	-6
1988	Cin-N	.982	137	256	10	5	2	0
1989	Cin-N	1.000	38	67	4	0	1	-2
	LA-N	1.000	11	21	0	0	0	-1
	Yr	1.000	49	88	4	0	1	-3
1990	LA-N	.987	127	207	13	3	2	-2
Total	5	.980	454	817	32	7	5	-14
■ Harry Danning C
1933	NY-N	1.000	1	2	0	0	0	0
1934	NY-N	.989	37	78	13	1	1	-1
1935	NY-N	.978	44	153	22	4	6	2
1936	NY-N	.988	24	70	10	1	2	2
1937	NY-N	.982	86	332	57	7	7	-5
1938	NY-N	.984	114	449	50	8	7	-8
1939	NY-N	.991	132	550	80	6	13	7
1940	NY-N	.980	131	634	91	15	13	7
1941	NY-N	.993	116	530	77	4	8	7
1942	NY-N	.979	116	459	55	11	7	-6
Total	10	.985	801	3257	455	7	64	5
1B
1941	NY-N	1.000	1	2	0	0	0	0
■ Al Dark SS
1946	Bos-N	.905	12	5	14	2	2	3
1948	Bos-N	.963	133	253	393	25	66	-12
1949	Bos-N	.961	125	232	387	25	76	-3
1950	NY-N	.962	154	288	465	30	101	-14
1951	NY-N	.944	156	295	465	45	114	1
1952	NY-N	.965	150	324	423	27	116	3
1953	NY-N	.967	110	219	343	19	79	8
1954	NY-N	.956	154	289	487	36	105	4
1955	NY-N	.962	115	213	324	21	70	-14
1956	NY-N	.961	48	89	132	9	27	-5
	StL-N	.959	99	178	292	20	66	-2
	Yr	.960	147	267	424	29	93	-7
1957	StL-N	.965	139	276	419	25	105	6
1958	StL-N	.943	8	10	23	2	6	-2
1959	Chi-N	1.000	1	1	1	0	0	0
Total	13	.960	1404	2672	4168	286	933	-27
3B
1949	Bos-N	.900	4	1	8	1	0	0
1953	NY-N	.906	8	12	17	3	5	2
1957	StL-N	1.000	1	0	2	0	0	0
1958	StL-N	.941	8	4	12	1	0	-1
	Chi-N	.949	111	107	225	18	24	-3
	Yr	.948	119	111	237	19	24	-4
1959	Chi-N	.948	131	111	255	20	20	-2
1960	Phi-N	.953	53	57	84	7	7	-8
	Mil-N	1.000	4	2	2	0	0	0
	Yr	.954	57	59	86	7	7	-8
Total	6	.947	320	294	605	0	56	-12
OF
1946	Bos-N	1.000	1	1	0	0	0	0
1953	NY-N	1.000	17	26	1	0	1	0
1960	Mil-N	.960	25	46	2	2	0	-2
Total	3	.974	43	73	3	2	1	-2
2B
1953	NY-N	.986	26	68	72	2	17	0
1960	Mil-N	—	3	0	0	0	0	0
Total	2	.986	29	68	72	2	17	0
1B
1959	Chi-N	.968	4	26	4	1	1	1
1960	Phi-N	1.000	1	1	0	0	0	0
	Mil-N	.977	10	40	2	1	4	-1
	Yr	.977	11	41	2	1	4	-1
Total	2	.973	15	67	6	2	5	0
■ Dell Darling C
1883	Chi-N	.875	6	16	5	3	1	0
1887	Chi-N	.901	20	114	41	17	2	7
1888	Chi-N	.932	20	139	26	12	5	4
1889	Chi-N	.960	36	172	45	9	2	5
1890	Chi-P	.840	9	16	5	4	0	-1
1891	StL-a	.894	17	78	23	12	0	4
Total	6	.923	108	535	145	7	10	19
1B
1890	Chi-P	.957	29	252	12	12	15	-2
OF
1887	Chi-N	.786	20	18	4	6	1	-1
1890	Chi-P	.833	7	9	1	2	0	-1
Total	2	.800	27	27	5	8	1	-2
SS
1890	Chi-P	.779	15	14	46	17	9	-5
1891	StL-a	—	1	0	0	0	0	0
Total	2	.779	16	14	46	7	9	-5
2B
1890	Chi-P	.857	3	4	8	2	0	-1
1891	StL-a	.824	2	9	5	3	1	0
Total	2	.839	5	13	13	5	1	-1
3B
1890	Chi-P	1.000	2	1	0	0	0	0
■ Bobby Darwin OF
1971	LA-N	1.000	4	9	0	0	0	0
1972	Min-A	.980	142	289	8	6	1	-10
1973	Min-A	.980	140	233	13	5	1	-18
1974	Min-A	.970	142	254	8	8	1	-21
1975	Min-A	.969	27	28	3	1	0	1
	Mil-A	.978	43	82	5	2	1	-2
	Yr	.975	70	110	8	3	1	-1
1976	Mil-A	.977	21	42	1	1	0	-1
	Bos-A	.964	17	26	1	1	0	0
	Yr	.972	38	68	2	2	0	-1
1977	Bos-A	.500	1	1	0	1	0	0
	Chi-N	—	1	0	0	0	0	0
Total	7	.976	538	964	39	5	4	-51
■ Doug Dascenzo OF
1988	Chi-N	1.000	20	55	1	0	0	3
1989	Chi-N	1.000	45	96	0	0	0	2
1990	Chi-N	1.000	107	174	2	0	1	-11
Total	3	1.000	172	325	3	0	1	-6
■ Jake Daubert 1B
1910	Bro-N	.989	144	1418	72	16	81	-3
1911	Bro-N	.989	149	1485	88	18	91	2
1912	Bro-N	.993	143	1373	76	10	68	0
1913	Bro-N	.991	139	1279	80	13	91	3
1914	Bro-N	.993	126	1097	48	8	68	-6
1915	Bro-N	.993	150	1441	102	11	73	9
1916	Bro-N	.993	126	1195	66	9	56	4
1917	Bro-N	.991	125	1188	82	12	59	6
1918	Bro-N	.991	105	1069	63	10	43	0
1919	Cin-N	.989	140	1437	80	17	75	-1
1920	Cin-N	.990	140	1358	63	15	90	-9
1921	Cin-N	.993	136	1290	78	10	98	2
1922	Cin-N	.994	156	1652	79	11	127	0
1923	Cin-N	.993	121	1224	77	9	95	6
1924	Cin-N	.990	102	1128	74	12	84	7
Total	15	.991	2002	19634	1128	181	1199	20
■ Rich Dauer 2B
1976	Bal-A	1.000	10	22	22	0	7	-3
1977	Bal-A	.982	83	179	213	7	55	5
1978	Bal-A	.998	87	193	239	1	60	0
1979	Bal-A	.979	103	213	260	10	68	-7
1980	Bal-A	.991	137	320	368	6	110	-6
1981	Bal-A	.989	94	201	253	5	71	-15
1982	Bal-A	.987	123	261	268	7	67	-37
1983	Bal-A	.988	131	273	322	7	78	-31
1984	Bal-A	.980	123	225	325	11	76	-20
1985	Bal-A	.990	73	117	181	3	44	3
Total	10	.987	964	2004	2451	7	636	111
3B
1977	Bal-A	1.000	9	3	20	0	1	1
1978	Bal-A	.949	52	29	82	6	9	3
1979	Bal-A	.943	44	21	95	7	4	1
1980	Bal-A	.970	35	14	50	2	5	2
1981	Bal-A	1.000	4	0	3	0	0	0
1982	Bal-A	.991	61	28	86	1	8	1
1983	Bal-A	.947	17	7	11	1	1	-1
1984	Bal-A	1.000	3	0	4	0	0	0
1985	Bal-A	.966	17	7	21	1	0	2
Total	9	.964	242	109	372	8	28	9
1B
1985	Bal-A	1.000	1	2	0	0	0	0
■ Darren Daulton C
1983	Phi-N	1.000	2	8	0	0	0	0
1985	Phi-N	.994	28	160	15	1	1	1
1986	Phi-N	.985	48	244	21	4	6	-4
1987	Phi-N	.991	40	200	12	2	4	1
1988	Phi-N	.977	44	195	15	5	1	-5
1989	Phi-N	.984	126	627	56	11	8	-12
1990	Phi-N	.989	139	683	70	8	10	-10
Total	7	.987	427	2117	189	1	30	-29
1B
1987	Phi-N	1.000	1	10	0	0	2	0
1988	Phi-N	.909	1	10	0	1	0	-1
Total	2	.955	2	20	1	1	2	-1
■ Vic Davalillo OF
1963	Cle-A	.988	89	247	10	3	0	12
1964	Cle-A	.986	143	346	11	5	5	8

YEAR	TM/L	PCT	G	PO	A	E	DP	FR
1965	Cle-A	.988	134	320	5	4	0	10
1966	Cle-A	.986	108	208	6	3	1	-3
1967	Cle-A	.986	125	202	5	3	1	-12
1968	Cle-A	.967	49	84	4	3	1	1
	Cal-A	.995	86	212	4	1	2	1
	Yr	.987	135	296	8	4	3	2
1969	Cal-A	1.000	22	30	0	0	0	-1
	StL-N	1.000	23	37	0	0	0	1
1970	StL-N	.972	54	67	3	2	1	1
1971	Pit-N	.983	61	112	5	2	0	2
1972	Pit-N	.979	97	181	4	4	0	-2
1973	Pit-N	1.000	10	12	0	0	0	1
	Oak-A	.967	19	28	1	1	0	1
1974	Oak-A	1.000	6	3	0	0	0	0
1977	LA-N	1.000	12	13	0	0	0	-2
1978	LA-N	1.000	25	17	0	0	0	0
1979	LA-N	1.000	3	2	0	0	0	0
Total	15	.986	1066	2121	58	1	11	18
	1B							
1969	Cal-A	1.000	3	6	1	0	1	0
1971	Pit-N	.981	16	144	10	3	18	-1
1972	Pit-N	1.000	8	19	2	0	2	0
1973	Pit-N	.977	10	77	9	2	8	2
	Oak-A	1.000	8	16	1	0	3	0
1978	LA-N	1.000	1	4	1	0	0	0
1980	LA-N	1.000	1	2	0	0	1	0
Total	6	.983	47	268	24	5	34	1

■ Jerry DaVanon SS

YEAR	TM/L	PCT	G	PO	A	E	DP	FR
1969	SD-N	.963	7	7	19	1	3	1
	StL-N	.958	16	29	39	3	6	1
	Yr	.959	23	36	58	4	9	2
1971	Bal-A	.950	11	10	28	2	6	0
1973	Cal-A	.927	14	13	25	3	5	3
1974	StL-N	.840	14	8	13	4	3	-3
1975	Hou-N	.944	21	37	65	6	13	1
1976	Hou-N	.911	17	20	21	4	8	-3
Total	6	.936	100	124	210	3	44	0
	2B							
1969	SD-N	.932	15	27	28	4	4	0
1970	StL-N	1.000	3	2	8	0	0	1
1971	Bal-A	.970	20	34	31	2	6	-3
1973	Cal-A	.941	12	12	20	2	1	3
1974	StL-N	1.000	7	9	19	0	5	2
1975	Hou-N	.976	9	16	24	1	3	1
1976	Hou-N	.980	17	30	67	2	7	6
1977	StL-N	.923	5	4	8	1	0	1
Total	8	.966	88	134	205	2	26	11
	3B							
1969	StL-N	1.000	5	6	6	0	3	2
1971	Bal-A	1.000	3	1	0	0	0	0
1973	Cal-A	.800	7	4	0	1	0	-1
1974	StL-N	.833	8	2	3	1	0	-1
1975	Hou-N	1.000	3	1	5	0	0	1
1976	Hou-N	.900	9	3	6	1	1	0
Total	6	.925	35	17	20	3	4	1
	1B							
1971	Bal-A	—	1	0	0	0	0	0
	OF							
1974	StL-N	—	1	0	0	0	0	0

■ Jim Davenport 3B

YEAR	TM/L	PCT	G	PO	A	E	DP	FR
1958	SF-N	.960	130	92	221	13	19	-3
1959	SF-N	.978	121	91	221	7	15	-3
1960	SF-N	.961	103	77	171	10	12	0
1961	SF-N	.965	132	119	235	13	25	8
1962	SF-N	.952	141	125	256	19	28	4
1963	SF-N	.962	127	122	183	12	9	0
1964	SF-N	.963	41	26	53	3	4	5
1965	SF-N	.949	39	26	48	4	3	-1
1966	SF-N	.935	36	15	43	4	5	-4
1967	SF-N	1.000	64	37	100	0	8	4
1968	SF-N	.960	82	49	120	7	12	-5
1969	SF-N	.967	104	77	158	8	15	1
1970	SF-N	1.000	10	7	7	0	0	-3
Total	13	.964	1130	863	1816	100	155	3
	SS							
1958	SF-N	.938	5	4	11	1	0	-1
1959	SF-N	1.000	1	0	1	0	0	0
1960	SF-N	1.000	7	6	7	0	2	-1
1963	SF-N	—	1	0	0	0	0	0
1964	SF-N	.979	64	65	119	4	15	-11
1965	SF-N	.959	37	50	66	5	13	-14
1966	SF-N	.961	58	62	135	8	19	-10
1967	SF-N	.963	28	24	79	4	12	-1
1968	SF-N	.963	17	9	17	1	5	-2
1969	SF-N	—	1	0	0	0	0	0
Total	10	.966	219	220	435	3	66	-40
	2B							
1963	SF-N	.987	22	30	47	1	7	2
1964	SF-N	.966	30	47	65	4	10	3
1965	SF-N	.915	26	21	33	5	5	-6
1966	SF-N	.953	21	18	23	2	2	-3
1967	SF-N	1.000	12	22	13	0	4	-2
1968	SF-N	—	1	0	0	0	0	0
Total	6	.964	112	138	181	2	28	-6
	1B							
1966	SF-N	1.000	2	12	0	0	1	0
1969	SF-N	1.000	1	7	0	0	1	0
Total	2	1.000	3	19	0	0	2	0
	OF							
1969	SF-N	1.000	1	0	1	0	0	1

■ Mark Davidson OF

YEAR	TM/L	PCT	G	PO	A	E	DP	FR
1986	Min-A	.980	31	48	0	1	0	2
1987	Min-A	1.000	86	102	3	0	0	7
1988	Min-A	.955	91	103	3	5	1	10
1989	Hou-N	1.000	23	36	0	0	0	0
1990	Hou-N	.981	51	103	1	2	0	4
Total	5	.980	282	392	7	8	1	23
	3B							
1988	Min-A	—	1	0	0	0	0	0

■ Bill Davidson OF

YEAR	TM/L	PCT	G	PO	A	E	DP	FR
1909	Chi-N	1.000	2	3	0	0	0	0
1910	Bro-N	.961	131	283	11	12	3	-11
1911	Bro-N	.956	74	168	4	8	1	-7
Total	3	.959	207	454	15	0	4	-18

■ Lefty Davis OF

YEAR	TM/L	PCT	G	PO	A	E	DP	FR
1901	Bro-N	.822	24	37	0	8	0	-5
	Pit-N	.975	86	140	18	4	7	7
	Yr	.942	110	177	18	12	7	2
1902	Pit-N	.945	59	80	6	5	1	-2
1903	NY-A	.906	102	176	7	19	1	-7
1907	Cin-N	.972	70	160	11	5	3	5
Total	4	.939	341	593	42	1	12	-2
	2B							
1901	Bro-N	1.000	1	3	0	0	0	0
	SS							
1903	NY-A	—	1	0	0	0	0	0

■ Alvin Davis 1B

YEAR	TM/L	PCT	G	PO	A	E	DP	FR
1984	Sea-A	.992	147	1271	94	11	108	-4
1985	Sea-A	.992	154	1438	103	13	131	-5
1986	Sea-A	.986	101	880	82	14	112	0
1987	Sea-A	.994	157	1386	96	9	133	-7
1988	Sea-A	.994	115	980	65	6	111	-6
1989	Sea-A	.992	125	1106	81	10	119	-3
1990	Sea-A	.994	52	435	31	3	41	-1
Total	7	.992	851	7496	552	6	755	-26

■ Brock Davis OF

YEAR	TM/L	PCT	G	PO	A	E	DP	FR
1963	Hou-N	.864	14	18	1	3	0	0
1964	Hou-N	1.000	1	2	0	0	0	0
1966	Hou-N	1.000	7	15	0	0	0	0
1970	Chi-N	—	1	0	0	0	0	0
1971	Chi-N	.982	93	213	5	4	1	0
1972	Mil-A	.970	43	63	2	2	0	-1
Total	6	.973	159	311	8	9	1	-1

■ Chili Davis OF

YEAR	TM/L	PCT	G	PO	A	E	DP	FR
1981	SF-N	1.000	6	7	0	0	0	0
1982	SF-N	.972	153	404	16	12	4	10
1983	SF-N	.976	133	357	7	9	1	5
1984	SF-N	.971	123	292	9	9	2	12
1985	SF-N	.980	126	279	10	6	2	11
1986	SF-N	.972	148	303	9	9	2	5
1987	SF-N	.975	135	265	6	7	2	-8
1988	Cal-A	.942	153	299	10	19	1	-6
1989	Cal-A	.979	147	270	5	6	0	-10
1990	Cal-A	.965	52	77	5	3	1	5
Total	10	.970	1176	2553	77	0	15	24

■ Eric Davis OF

YEAR	TM/L	PCT	G	PO	A	E	DP	FR
1984	Cin-N	.992	51	125	4	1	2	8
1985	Cin-N	.987	47	75	3	1	1	4
1986	Cin-N	.975	121	274	2	7	0	3
1987	Cin-N	.990	128	380	10	4	4	22
1988	Cin-N	.981	130	300	2	6	0	-6
1989	Cin-N	.984	125	298	2	5	1	-5
1990	Cin-N	.993	122	257	11	2	1	8
Total	7	.985	724	1709	34	6	9	34

■ George Davis SS

YEAR	TM/L	PCT	G	PO	A	E	DP	FR
1890	Cle-N	1.000	1	1	1	0	0	0
1892	Cle-N	.910	20	37	54	9	5	-6
1893	NY-N	1.000	1	0	2	0	0	0
1896	NY-N	.925	45	107	141	20	11	-1
1897	NY-N	.926	129	337	434	62	67	22
1898	NY-N	.933	121	349	421	55	61	36
1899	NY-N	.945	108	311	412	42	57	46
1900	NY-N	.944	114	279	450	43	53	29
1901	NY-N	.939	113	296	396	45	42	16
1902	Chi-A	.951	129	289	427	37	72	-2
1903	NY-N	.870	4	11	9	3	0	-1
1904	Chi-A	.937	152	347	514	58	62	17
1905	Chi-A	.948	151	330	501	46	56	16
1906	Chi-A	.946	129	263	475	42	44	10
1907	Chi-A	.949	132	223	485	38	53	9
1908	Chi-A	.913	23	51	65	11	6	-4
Total	16	.940	1372	3231	4787	511	589	187
	3B							
1891	Cle-N	.875	22	35	49	12	5	4
1892	Cle-N	.914	79	100	166	25	8	-4
1893	NY-N	.884	133	181	305	64	27	0
1894	NY-N	.908	122	150	247	40	18	-1
1895	NY-N	.881	80	122	175	40	18	9
1896	NY-N	.917	74	117	169	26	11	11
1901	NY-N	.960	17	25	47	3	2	8
Total	7	.900	527	730	1158	210	89	27
	OF							
1890	Cle-N	.946	133	282	35	18	9	12
1891	Cle-N	.931	116	257	27	21	1	10
1892	Cle-N	.903	44	55	10	7	3	1
1895	NY-N	.944	7	15	2	1	0	1
1896	NY-N	1.000	3	2	0	0	0	-1
Total	5	.936	303	611	74	7	13	23
	2B							
1890	Cle-N	1.000	2	5	2	0	1	0
1892	Cle-N	.895	3	6	11	2	1	0
1895	NY-N	.944	10	33	34	4	4	3
1906	Chi-A	1.000	1	3	0	0	1	0
1908	Chi-A	.960	95	191	314	21	25	7
1909	Chi-A	.667	2	1	3	2	0	-1
Total	6	.954	113	239	364	9	32	9
	1B							
1895	NY-N	.993	14	126	9	1	5	1
1896	NY-N	.972	3	31	4	1	0	1
1902	Chi-A	1.000	3	13	1	0	2	0
1908	Chi-A	1.000	4	49	5	0	0	1
1909	Chi-A	.986	17	189	15	3	7	2
Total	5	.989	41	408	34	5	14	5

■ Kiddo Davis OF

YEAR	TM/L	PCT	G	PO	A	E	DP	FR
1926	NY-A	—	1	0	0	0	0	0
1932	Phi-N	.975	133	411	15	11	6	8
1933	NY-N	.988	120	248	7	3	3	-12
1934	StL-N	.960	9	23	1	1	0	2
	Phi-N	.991	100	304	13	3	3	15
	Yr	.988	109	327	14	4	3	17
1935	NY-N	.977	21	42	1	1	0	-1
1936	NY-N	1.000	22	40	3	0	0	5
1937	NY-N	.932	37	41	0	3	0	0
	Cin-N	.959	35	93	1	4	0	2
	Yr	.951	72	134	1	7	0	2
1938	Cin-N	1.000	5	8	1	0	0	0
Total	8	.980	483	1210	42	6	12	19

■ Glenn Davis 1B

YEAR	TM/L	PCT	G	PO	A	E	DP	FR
1984	Hou-N	.988	16	151	15	2	13	2
1985	Hou-N	.985	89	749	57	12	76	-2
1986	Hou-N	.992	156	1253	111	11	90	1
1987	Hou-N	.991	151	1283	112	12	89	3
1988	Hou-N	.996	151	1355	103	6	104	0
1989	Hou-N	.992	156	1347	113	12	101	3
1990	Hou-N	.995	91	796	55	4	56	-3
Total	7	.992	810	6934	566	9	529	4
	OF							
1985	Hou-N	1.000	9	17	0	0	0	0

■ Harry Davis 1B

YEAR	TM/L	PCT	G	PO	A	E	DP	FR
1932	Det-A	.989	141	1327	75	16	123	-5
1933	Det-A	.978	44	433	13	10	33	-5
1937	StL-A	.991	112	1065	54	10	108	-4
Total	3	.988	297	2825	142	6	264	-14
	OF							
1937	StL-A	—	1	0	0	0	0	0

■ Harry Davis 1B

YEAR	TM/L	PCT	G	PO	A	E	DP	FR
1895	NY-N	.957	7	62	4	3	4	0
1896	NY-N	.983	23	226	11	4	14	0
	Pit-N	.966	35	325	18	12	17	-1
	Yr	.973	58	551	29	16	31	-1
1897	Pit-N	.965	64	570	29	22	26	-4
1898	Pit-N	.980	53	556	22	12	30	-1
	Lou-N	.967	34	336	20	12	23	1
	Was-N	.875	1	7	0	1	0	0
	Yr	.974	88	899	42	25	53	0
1899	Was-N	.988	18	161	4	2	6	-1
1901	Phi-N	.976	117	1265	83	33	67	8
1902	Phi-N	.984	128	1247	87	22	58	8
1903	Phi-N	.972	104	942	63	29	38	-1
1904	Phi-N	.983	102	1011	57	19	33	-1
1905	Phi-N	.985	150	1447	92	24	43	1
1906	Phi-N	.975	145	1352	91	37	66	0
1907	Phi-N	.977	149	1478	103	38	50	4
1908	Phi-A	.986	147	1410	86	22	44	1
1909	Phi-A	.988	149	1432	74	19	65	-5
1910	Phi-A	.986	139	1353	64	20	74	-4
1911	Phi-A	.977	53	427	36	11	21	2
1912	Cle-A	.941	2	14	2	1	1	0
1913	Phi-A	1.000	6	33	4	0	2	1
1914	Phi-A	1.000	1	12	0	0	0	0
1915	Phi-A	—	1	0	0	0	0	0
Total	20	.980	1628	15666	950	343	682	8
	OF							
1896	NY-N	.883	40	81	2	11	0	-4
	Pit-N	.958	10	20	3	1	2	2
	Yr	.898	50	101	5	12	2	-2
1897	Pit-N	.964	14	26	1	1	0	-2
1898	Pit-N	1.000	6	9	1	0	0	0
	Lou-N	.500	1	1	0	1	0	0
	Yr	.917	7	10	1	1	0	0
1902	Phi-A	1.000	5	8	0	0	0	-1
1903	Phi-A	.667	2	2	0	1	0	-1
Total	5	.911	78	147	7	5	2	-6
	3B							
1897	Pit-N	.810	32	47	55	24	2	-5
	SS							
1896	Pit-N	.800	1	1	3	1	0	0
1897	Pit-N	.500	1	1	0	1	0	-2
Total	2	.714	2	2	3	2	0	-2
	2B							
1898	Lou-N	.900	2	4	5	1	0	0

■ Tommy Davis OF

YEAR	TM/L	PCT	G	PO	A	E	DP	FR
1960	LA-N	.975	87	151	7	4	2	-7
1961	LA-N	.973	86	143	3	4	2	-1
1962	LA-N	.961	146	240	9	10	0	-1
1963	LA-N	.969	129	181	7	6	3	-8
1964	LA-N	.982	148	264	9	5	1	4
1965	LA-N	1.000	16	21	1	0	1	-3
1966	LA-N	.972	79	98	5	3	1	-6
1967	NY-N	.975	149	231	5	6	0	-9
1968	Chi-A	.962	116	171	8	7	2	-7
1969	Sea-A	.967	112	174	3	6	0	-9
	Hou-N	1.000	21	27	1	0	0	-2
1970	Hou-N	.949	53	71	4	4	1	-5
	Chi-N	.938	10	15	0	1	0	0
	Oak-A	.963	45	51	1	2	0	-7
	Yr	.955	98	122	5	6	1	-12
1971	Oak-A	.931	16	27	0	2	0	-1
1972	Chi-A	.800	2	4	0	1	0	0
	Bal-A	1.000	5	8	0	0	0	0
Total	13	.970	1233	1900	63	1	13	-66
	3B							
1960	LA-N	1.000	5	2	10	0	0	1
1961	LA-N	.901	59	30	88	13	6	0

YEAR	TM/L	PCT	G	PO	A	E	DP	FR
1962	LA-N	.889	39	29	51	10	7	-4
1963	LA-N	.902	40	23	60	9	7	-3
1966	LA-N	1.000	2	1	4	0	0	-1
1971	Oak-A	1.000	2	1	4	0	0	0
Total	6	.904	147	86	217	2	20	-7

1B

YEAR	TM/L	PCT	G	PO	A	E	DP	FR
1967	NY-N	.875	1	5	2	1	0	0
1968	Chi-A	.976	6	40	1	1	3	-3
1969	Sea-A	.900	1	9	0	1	0	-1
1970	Oak-A	.969	8	59	3	2	9	-1
1971	Chi-A	.989	35	247	30	3	24	3
1972	Chi-N	1.000	3	27	1	0	0	0
	Bal-A	1.000	3	20	4	0	0	1
1973	Bal-A	.971	4	32	2	1	3	0
1976	Cal-A	1.000	1	4	0	0	0	0
Total	8	.982	62	443	43	9	39	-1

2B

YEAR	TM/L	PCT	G	PO	A	E	DP	FR
1971	Oak-A	1.000	3	0	3	0	0	0

■ Ike Davis SS

YEAR	TM/L	PCT	G	PO	A	E	DP	FR
1919	Was-A	.857	4	10	2	2	1	-2
1924	Chi-A	.940	10	14	33	3	3	1
1925	Chi-A	.937	144	313	472	53	97	8
Total	3	.936	158	337	507	8	101	7

■ Jumbo Davis 3B

YEAR	TM/L	PCT	G	PO	A	E	DP	FR
1884	KC-U	.633	7	5	14	11	0	-2
1886	Bal-a	.848	60	82	114	35	6	5
1887	Bal-a	.826	87	91	199	61	7	4
1888	KC-a	.843	113	155	334	91	27	31
1889	KC-a	.803	62	93	140	57	14	0
1890	StL-a	.731	21	23	53	28	2	-1
	Bro-a	.845	38	49	87	25	9	-5
	Yr	.800	59	72	140	53	11	-6
1891	Was-a	.820	12	19	22	9	2	-2
Total	7	.824	400	517	963	317	67	30

SS

YEAR	TM/L	PCT	G	PO	A	E	DP	FR
1887	Bal-a	.836	43	57	132	37	5	-1
1888	KC-a	.813	8	12	27	9	0	-1
1889	StL-a	1.000	1	1	0	0	0	0
Total	3	.833	52	70	159	6	5	-2

OF

YEAR	TM/L	PCT	G	PO	A	E	DP	FR
1889	StL-a	1.000	1	1	0	0	0	0

■ Jody Davis C

YEAR	TM/L	PCT	G	PO	A	E	DP	FR
1981	Chi-N	.972	56	274	44	9	4	-1
1982	Chi-N	.984	129	598	89	11	11	8
1983	Chi-N	.984	150	730	75	13	7	-12
1984	Chi-N	.984	146	811	89	15	9	4
1985	Chi-N	.990	138	694	84	8	7	0
1986	Chi-N	.992	145	885	105	8	14	4
1987	Chi-N	.989	123	749	79	9	11	-2
1988	Chi-N	.995	74	383	32	2	1	-4
	Atl-N	1.000	2	13	2	0	0	0
	Yr	.995	76	396	34	2	1	-4
1989	Atl-N	.985	72	364	40	6	1	-9
1990	Atl-N	1.000	4	19	1	0	0	0
Total	10	.987	1039	5520	640	1	65	-12

1B

YEAR	TM/L	PCT	G	PO	A	E	DP	FR
1986	Chi-N	—	1	0	0	0	0	0
1989	Atl-N	1.000	2	12	0	0	3	0
1990	Atl-N	1.000	6	45	5	0	4	1
Total	3	1.000	9	57	5	0	7	1

■ Mike Davis OF

YEAR	TM/L	PCT	G	PO	A	E	DP	FR
1980	Oak-A	1.000	18	31	2	0	0	4
1981	Oak-A	1.000	2	3	0	0	0	0
1982	Oak-A	.946	13	35	0	2	0	-1
1983	Oak-A	.974	121	278	16	8	4	9
1984	Oak-A	.961	127	287	6	12	4	1
1985	Oak-A	.979	151	370	6	8	1	7
1986	Oak-A	.973	139	310	9	9	2	6
1987	Oak-A	.942	124	210	3	13	1	-11
1988	LA-N	.961	76	121	3	5	2	-6
1989	LA-N	.987	48	74	1	1	1	-4
Total	10	.968	819	1719	46	8	15	5

1B

YEAR	TM/L	PCT	G	PO	A	E	DP	FR
1980	Oak-A	.980	7	45	5	1	6	1
1981	Oak-A	—	1	0	0	0	0	0
1982	Oak-A	.919	7	30	4	3	5	0
Total	3	.955	15	75	9	4	11	1

■ Dick Davis OF

YEAR	TM/L	PCT	G	PO	A	E	DP	FR
1977	Mil-A	1.000	12	13	0	0	0	-1
1978	Mil-A	1.000	28	54	2	0	0	0
1979	Mil-A	.973	35	72	1	2	0	-2
1980	Mil-A	.971	38	63	3	2	2	1
1981	Phi-N	.974	32	37	1	1	0	-2
1982	Phi-N	1.000	16	29	0	0	0	-1
	Tor-A	1.000	1	2	0	0	0	0
	Pit-N	.971	28	33	0	1	0	-2
Total	6	.981	190	303	7	6	2	-7

■ Bob Davis C

YEAR	TM/L	PCT	G	PO	A	E	DP	FR
1973	SD-N	.941	5	32	0	2	0	2
1975	SD-N	.986	43	195	18	3	4	3
1976	SD-N	.965	47	120	19	5	1	4
1977	SD-N	.975	46	136	19	4	2	-2
1978	SD-N	.960	16	43	5	2	0	-2
1979	Tor-A	.984	32	114	11	2	1	-2
1980	Tor-A	.983	89	317	28	6	6	-3
1981	Cal-A	1.000	1	2	0	0	0	0
Total	8	.978	279	959	100	4	14	0

■ Ron Davis OF

YEAR	TM/L	PCT	G	PO	A	E	DP	FR
1962	Hou-N	1.000	5	9	0	0	0	0
1966	Hou-N	.982	48	98	9	2	1	6
1967	Hou-N	.976	80	114	9	3	2	-2
1968	Hou-N	.971	52	131	4	4	0	5
	StL-N	.979	25	44	3	1	1	3
	Yr	.973	77	175	7	5	1	8

YEAR	TM/L	PCT	G	PO	A	E	DP	FR
1969	Pit-N	.933	51	27	1	2	0	0
Total	5	.974	261	423	24	2	4	12

■ Spud Davis C

YEAR	TM/L	PCT	G	PO	A	E	DP	FR
1928	StL-N	.750	2	6	0	2	0	-1
	Phi-N	.980	49	149	46	4	7	3
	Yr	.971	51	155	46	6	7	2
1929	Phi-N	.961	89	198	47	10	7	-12
1930	Phi-N	.986	96	307	50	5	6	-3
1931	Phi-N	.994	114	420	78	3	10	1
1932	Phi-N	.987	120	408	54	6	15	-4
1933	Phi-N	.983	132	395	69	8	9	-11
1934	StL-N	.988	94	459	42	6	7	0
1935	StL-N	.992	81	335	34	3	2	-3
1936	StL-N	.985	103	390	59	7	7	-14
1937	Cin-N	.980	59	300	40	7	3	11
1938	Cin-N	.962	11	43	7	2	1	1
	Phi-N	.980	63	217	27	5	5	-12
	Yr	.977	74	260	34	7	6	-11
1939	Phi-N	1.000	85	260	40	0	1	-2
1940	Pit-N	.967	87	288	61	12	11	-7
1941	Pit-N	1.000	49	97	16	0	3	-2
1944	Pit-N	.966	35	76	10	3	3	-1
1945	Pit-N	.968	13	26	4	1	0	0
Total	16	.984	1282	4374	684	4	97	-56

1B

YEAR	TM/L	PCT	G	PO	A	E	DP	FR
1935	StL-N	1.000	5	48	0	0	4	-1

3B

YEAR	TM/L	PCT	G	PO	A	E	DP	FR
1936	StL-N	1.000	2	1	4	0	0	0

■ Willie Davis OF

YEAR	TM/L	PCT	G	PO	A	E	DP	FR
1960	LA-N	.981	22	52	1	1	0	1
1961	LA-N	.983	114	224	4	4	1	-7
1962	LA-N	.963	156	379	13	15	0	6
1963	LA-N	.978	153	337	16	8	3	9
1964	LA-N	.983	155	400	16	7	2	19
1965	LA-N	.967	141	318	6	11	1	3
1966	LA-N	.970	152	347	9	11	0	3
1967	LA-N	.971	138	300	6	9	2	0
1968	LA-N	.973	158	345	9	10	2	-2
1969	LA-N	.979	125	271	8	6	1	0
1970	LA-N	.992	143	342	12	3	4	10
1971	LA-N	.981	157	404	7	8	0	5
1972	LA-N	.987	146	373	10	5	1	4
1973	LA-N	.980	146	344	6	7	0	-2
1974	Mon-N	.969	151	369	8	12	1	1
1975	Tex-A	.990	42	100	1	1	1	1
	StL-N	.970	89	187	5	6	2	-6
1976	SD-N	.992	128	349	6	3	2	2
1979	Cal-A	1.000	7	8	0	0	0	0
Total	18	.978	2323	5449	143	127	23	51

■ Andre Dawson OF

YEAR	TM/L	PCT	G	PO	A	E	DP	FR
1976	Mon-N	.969	24	61	1	2	1	2
1977	Mon-N	.989	136	352	9	4	1	3
1978	Mon-N	.988	153	411	17	5	2	15
1979	Mon-N	.988	153	394	7	5	1	-2
1980	Mon-N	.986	147	410	14	6	3	11
1981	Mon-N	.980	103	327	10	7	1	13
1982	Mon-N	.982	147	419	8	8	2	14
1983	Mon-N	.980	157	435	6	9	2	6
1984	Mon-N	.975	134	297	11	8	2	11
1985	Mon-N	.973	131	248	9	7	1	-1
1986	Mon-N	.986	127	200	11	3	2	-4
1987	Chi-N	.986	152	271	12	4	0	2
1988	Chi-N	.989	147	267	7	3	1	-5
1989	Chi-N	.987	112	227	4	3	0	0
1990	Chi-N	.981	139	250	10	5	4	-4
Total	15	.983	1962	4569	136	9	23	61

■ Boots Day OF

YEAR	TM/L	PCT	G	PO	A	E	DP	FR
1969	StL-N	—	1	0	0	0	0	0
1970	Phi-N	.875	7	6	1	1	0	1
	Mon-N	.987	35	75	1	1	0	4
	Yr	.976	42	81	2	2	0	5
1971	Mon-N	.982	120	262	10	5	1	-1
1972	Mon-N	.979	117	225	7	5	3	-11
1973	Mon-N	1.000	51	86	2	0	0	-1
1974	Mon-N	1.000	16	18	0	0	0	0
Total	6	.983	347	672	21	2	4	-8

■ Brian Dayett OF

YEAR	TM/L	PCT	G	PO	A	E	DP	FR
1983	NY-A	1.000	9	22	1	0	1	1
1984	NY-A	.988	62	80	3	1	0	1
1985	Chi-N	1.000	10	8	0	0	0	0
1986	Chi-N	1.000	24	31	1	0	0	-1
1987	Chi-N	1.000	78	72	2	0	0	-3
Total	5	.995	183	213	7	1	0	-2

■ Charlie Deal 3B

YEAR	TM/L	PCT	G	PO	A	E	DP	FR
1912	Det-A	.942	41	48	113	10	3	10
1913	Det-A	.862	15	15	35	8	3	2
1914	Bos-N	.948	74	86	133	12	8	-5
1915	StL-F	.951	65	76	136	11	9	5
1916	StL-N	.970	22	26	39	2	5	-1
	Chi-N	1.000	2	2	8	0	1	2
1917	Chi-N	.957	130	151	254	18	21	7
1918	Chi-N	.942	118	144	247	24	21	-2
1919	Chi-N	.973	116	157	233	11	14	7
1920	Chi-N	.973	128	229	268	11	22	10
1921	Chi-N	.973	112	122	239	10	19	14
Total	10	.958	823	956	1705	117	126	49

2B

YEAR	TM/L	PCT	G	PO	A	E	DP	FR
1913	Bos-N	.935	10	11	18	2	1	-6
1916	StL-N	—	1	0	0	0	0	0
Total	2	.935	11	11	18	2	1	-6

SS

YEAR	TM/L	PCT	G	PO	A	E	DP	FR
1914	Bos-N	.667	1	0	2	1	0	0

■ Tommy Dean SS

YEAR	TM/L	PCT	G	PO	A	E	DP	FR
1967	LA-N	.981	12	19	33	1	10	6

YEAR	TM/L	PCT	G	PO	A	E	DP	FR
1969	SD-N	.978	97	139	255	9	41	4
1970	SD-N	.974	55	84	143	6	30	6
1971	SD-N	.969	28	34	60	3	12	6
Total	4	.976	192	276	491	9	93	22

3B

YEAR	TM/L	PCT	G	PO	A	E	DP	FR
1971	SD-N	.882	11	4	11	2	1	1

2B

YEAR	TM/L	PCT	G	PO	A	E	DP	FR
1969	SD-N	1.000	2	2	0	0	0	0
1971	SD-N	—	1	0	0	0	0	0
Total	2	1.000	3	2	0	0	0	0

■ Pat Deasley C

YEAR	TM/L	PCT	G	PO	A	E	DP	FR
1881	Bos-N	.914	28	133	27	15	2	-1
1882	Bos-N	.958	56	357	54	18	0	4
1883	StL-a	.930	56	301	59	27	6	1
1884	StL-a	.919	75	425	120	48	3	7
1885	NY-N	.935	54	281	80	25	4	8
1886	NY-N	.925	30	147	38	15	4	8
1887	NY-N	.867	24	86	31	18	0	-10
1888	Was-N	.922	31	177	60	20	3	9
Total	8	.927	354	1907	469	186	22	26

OF

YEAR	TM/L	PCT	G	PO	A	E	DP	FR
1881	Bos-N	.929	7	12	1	1	1	0
1882	Bos-N	.714	14	14	1	6	1	-3
1883	StL-a	1.000	2	1	0	0	0	-1
1884	StL-a	1.000	2	1	0	0	0	-1
1885	NY-N	1.000	2	2	0	0	0	-1
1886	NY-N	.800	15	20	4	6	0	0
1888	Was-N	1.000	1	1	0	0	0	0
Total	7	.814	43	51	6	3	2	-6

SS

YEAR	TM/L	PCT	G	PO	A	E	DP	FR
1881	Bos-N	.852	7	5	18	4	1	-2
1882	Bos-N	.667	1	1	1	1	0	-1
1885	NY-N	1.000	1	0	1	0	0	0
1887	NY-N	—	1	0	0	0	0	0
1888	Was-N	.800	1	1	3	1	0	0
Total	5	.833	11	7	23	6	1	-3

3B

YEAR	TM/L	PCT	G	PO	A	E	DP	FR
1887	NY-N	.750	7	12	6	6	0	-4

1B

YEAR	TM/L	PCT	G	PO	A	E	DP	FR
1881	Bos-N	.917	2	9	2	1	2	1
1884	StL-a	1.000	1	3	0	0	0	0
Total	2	.933	3	12	2	1	2	1

2B

YEAR	TM/L	PCT	G	PO	A	E	DP	FR
1888	Was-N	1.000	1	1	2	0	0	-1

■ Hank DeBerry C

YEAR	TM/L	PCT	G	PO	A	E	DP	FR
1916	Cle-A	1.000	14	34	13	0	1	-3
1917	Cle-A	.968	9	22	8	1	1	1
1922	Bro-N	.971	81	309	64	11	5	-1
1923	Bro-N	.971	60	273	65	10	8	8
1924	Bro-N	.993	63	394	57	3	8	23
1925	Bro-N	.981	55	309	50	7	4	20
1926	Bro-N	.976	37	180	22	5	3	8
1927	Bro-N	.988	67	339	59	5	8	23
1928	Bro-N	.977	80	377	56	10	5	18
1929	Bro-N	.991	68	304	36	3	6	6
1930	Bro-N	.978	35	160	14	4	2	13
Total	11	.982	569	2701	444	9	48	116

■ Doug DeCinces 3B

YEAR	TM/L	PCT	G	PO	A	E	DP	FR
1973	Bal-A	.895	8	3	14	2	2	2
1974	Bal-A	1.000	1	0	2	0	0	0
1975	Bal-A	.947	34	19	71	5	7	2
1976	Bal-A	.941	109	96	208	19	9	-5
1977	Bal-A	.958	148	124	330	20	34	10
1978	Bal-A	.975	130	111	280	10	27	12
1979	Bal-A	.964	120	99	247	13	21	-3
1980	Bal-A	.960	142	120	340	19	41	25
1981	Bal-A	.942	100	86	191	17	31	-1
1982	Cal-A	.961	153	142	399	21	41	19
1983	Cal-A	.955	84	79	216	14	26	9
1984	Cal-A	.964	140	107	266	14	22	-6
1985	Cal-A	.958	111	95	202	13	27	-10
1986	Cal-A	.965	132	119	216	12	19	-8
1987	Cal-A	.948	128	83	226	17	24	-2
	StL-N	.833	3	3	7	2	0	1
Total	15	.958	1543	1256	3215	198	331	45

2B

YEAR	TM/L	PCT	G	PO	A	E	DP	FR
1973	Bal-A	1.000	2	1	2	0	0	1
1975	Bal-A	1.000	11	41	25	0	10	3
1976	Bal-A	.989	17	49	44	1	11	4
1977	Bal-A	1.000	1	0	1	0	0	0
1978	Bal-A	.932	12	27	28	4	11	-2
Total	5	.978	43	118	100	5	32	6

SS

YEAR	TM/L	PCT	G	PO	A	E	DP	FR
1973	Bal-A	1.000	1	0	3	0	0	0
1975	Bal-A	.939	13	13	18	2	3	-1
1976	Bal-A	1.000	2	1	0	0	0	0
1982	Cal-A	.667	2	1	1	1	0	-1
1986	Cal-A	—	1	0	0	0	0	0
1987	Cal-A	—	1	0	0	0	0	0
Total	6	.925	20	15	22	3	3	-2

1B

YEAR	TM/L	PCT	G	PO	A	E	DP	FR
1975	Bal-A	1.000	2	19	1	0	0	0
1976	Bal-A	1.000	11	45	5	0	1	1
1977	Bal-A	1.000	1	1	0	0	0	0
1980	Bal-A	1.000	1	2	0	0	0	0
1981	Bal-A	1.000	1	4	0	0	0	0
1987	Cal-A	1.000	4	22	1	0	3	0
Total	6	1.000	20	93	7	0	4	1

OF

YEAR	TM/L	PCT	G	PO	A	E	DP	FR
1981	Bal-A	1.000	1	1	0	0	0	0

■ Harry Decker C

YEAR	TM/L	PCT	G	PO	A	E	DP	FR
1884	Ind-a	.870	4	17	3	3	1	-3
	KC-U	.942	11	53	12	4	2	1
1886	Det-N	.871	14	89	32	18	1	5
	Was-N	.946	4	25	10	2	0	2

YEAR	TM/L	PCT	G	PO	A	E	DP	FR
	Yr	.886	18	114	42	20	1	7
1889	Phi-N	.833	3	12	3	3	1	0
1890	Phi-N	1.000	1	2	0	0	0	0
	Pit-N	.909	70	267	72	34	5	-26
	Yr	.909	71	269	72	34	5	-26
Total	4	.903	107	465	132	4	10	-21

OF

YEAR	TM/L	PCT	G	PO	A	E	DP	FR
1884	KC-U	.813	16	20	6	6	1	2
1886	Det-N	—	1	0	0	0	0	0
1889	Phi-N	1.000	1	1	0	0	0	0
1890	Phi-N	.429	2	3	0	4	0	-1
	Pit-N	.857	4	12	0	2	0	0
	Yr	.714	6	15	0	6	0	-1
Total	4	.778	24	36	6	2	1	1

1B

YEAR	TM/L	PCT	G	PO	A	E	DP	FR
1890	Phi-N	.938	2	14	1	1	2	0
	Pit-N	.976	16	159	6	4	13	0
	Yr	.973	18	173	7	5	15	0

2B

YEAR	TM/L	PCT	G	PO	A	E	DP	FR
1889	Phi-N	.857	7	13	17	5	3	-1
1890	Pit-N	.600	1	1	2	2	0	-1
Total	2	.825	8	14	19	7	3	-2

3B

YEAR	TM/L	PCT	G	PO	A	E	DP	FR
1886	Was-N	1.000	2	4	3	0	0	1

SS

YEAR	TM/L	PCT	G	PO	A	E	DP	FR
1886	Was-N	.250	1	0	1	3	0	-1
1890	Pit-N	.778	1	1	6	2	2	1
Total	2	.615	2	1	7	5	2	0

■ George Decker OF

YEAR	TM/L	PCT	G	PO	A	E	DP	FR
1892	Chi-N	.876	62	73	12	12	3	-2
1893	Chi-N	.878	33	55	10	9	2	2
1894	Chi-N	.840	29	54	9	12	0	0
1895	Chi-N	.910	57	98	3	10	0	-6
1896	Chi-N	.928	71	131	10	11	0	-3
1897	Chi-N	.925	75	112	12	10	1	-4
1898	Lou-N	.833	6	4	1	1	0	-1
1899	Was-N	—	1	0	0	0	0	0
Total	8	.900	334	527	57	5	6	-14

1B

YEAR	TM/L	PCT	G	PO	A	E	DP	FR
1893	Chi-N	.981	27	245	10	5	18	-2
1894	Chi-N	.974	48	429	15	12	29	-5
1895	Chi-N	1.000	11	110	3	0	10	-1
1896	Chi-N	.984	36	351	19	6	25	0
1897	Chi-N	.988	38	394	23	5	22	1
1898	Chi-N	.980	75	772	17	16	31	-7
	StL-N	.993	32	279	12	2	18	0
	Yr	.984	107	1051	29	18	49	-7
1899	Lou-N	.968	38	406	15	14	21	-2
	Was-N	.955	2	20	1	1	0	0
	Yr	.967	40	426	16	15	22	-2
Total	7	.981	307	3006	115	1	175	-16

2B

YEAR	TM/L	PCT	G	PO	A	E	DP	FR
1892	Chi-N	.855	16	22	37	10	3	-10
1893	Chi-N	.837	20	32	55	17	5	-9
1894	Chi-N	1.000	2	4	7	0	0	0
1895	Chi-N	—	1	0	0	0	0	0
1897	Chi-N	.500	1	1	0	1	0	0
Total	5	.849	40	59	99	8	8	-19

3B

YEAR	TM/L	PCT	G	PO	A	E	DP	FR
1894	Chi-N	.667	7	7	7	7	1	-3
1895	Chi-N	.833	3	2	8	2	0	0
Total	2	.727	10	9	15	9	1	-3

SS

YEAR	TM/L	PCT	G	PO	A	E	DP	FR
1893	Chi-N	.714	2	1	4	2	0	-1
1894	Chi-N	.800	1	3	1	1	2	0
1895	Chi-N	1.000	1	2	2	0	0	0
Total	3	.813	4	6	7	3	2	0

■ Rob Deer OF

YEAR	TM/L	PCT	G	PO	A	E	DP	FR
1984	SF-N	.905	9	19	0	2	0	0
1985	SF-N	.982	37	54	1	1	0	-1
1986	Mil-A	.974	131	286	8	8	1	4
1987	Mil-A	.974	123	256	10	7	1	4
1988	Mil-A	.990	133	284	10	3	3	4
1989	Mil-A	.972	125	267	10	8	1	3
1990	Mil-A	.970	117	243	14	8	7	5
Total	7	.975	675	1409	53	7	13	19

1B

YEAR	TM/L	PCT	G	PO	A	E	DP	FR
1985	SF-N	.987	10	73	1	1	4	-2
1986	Mil-A	1.000	4	26	0	0	2	-1
1987	Mil-A	.982	12	48	6	1	6	0
1990	Mil-A	.986	21	130	11	2	12	-1
Total	4	.987	47	277	18	4	24	-4

■ Ivan DeJesus SS

YEAR	TM/L	PCT	G	PO	A	E	DP	FR
1974	LA-N	1.000	2	1	0	0	0	-1
1975	LA-N	.974	63	45	107	4	18	7
1976	LA-N	.950	13	18	39	3	7	4
1977	Chi-N	.962	154	234	595	33	94	36
1978	Chi-N	.967	160	232	558	27	96	13
1979	Chi-N	.959	160	235	507	32	97	0
1980	Chi-N	.969	156	229	529	24	99	8
1981	Chi-N	.959	106	221	343	24	81	10
1982	Phi-N	.973	154	216	469	19	80	-9
1983	Phi-N	.966	158	214	438	23	64	-14
1984	Phi-N	.951	141	166	400	29	57	-21
1985	StL-N	.923	13	8	16	2	1	-1
1986	NY-A	.900	7	5	4	1	0	0
1987	SF-N	.840	9	7	14	4	2	2
1988	Det-A	.893	7	8	17	3	4	1
Total	15	.963	1303	1839	4036	228	700	35

3B

YEAR	TM/L	PCT	G	PO	A	E	DP	FR
1976	LA-N	1.000	7	2	6	0	0	1
1982	Phi-N	.926	7	6	19	2	1	2
1985	StL-N	1.000	20	7	24	0	2	3
Total	3	.971	34	15	51	2	3	6

■ Ed Delahanty OF

YEAR	TM/L	PCT	G	PO	A	E	DP	FR
1888	Phi-N	.912	17	28	3	3	0	0
1889	Phi-N	.956	31	60	5	3	0	2
1890	Cle-P	1.000	18	38	5	0	2	3
1891	Phi-N	.909	99	199	22	22	3	2
1892	Phi-N	.944	121	261	25	17	6	10
1893	Phi-N	.948	117	318	31	19	8	26
1894	Phi-N	.925	88	212	23	19	4	14
1895	Phi-N	.944	103	237	16	15	4	7
1896	Phi-N	.952	99	262	18	14	4	16
1897	Phi-N	.970	129	266	23	9	2	9
1898	Phi-N	.964	144	302	20	12	5	5
1899	Phi-N	.969	143	284	26	10	4	0
1901	Phi-N	.949	84	179	9	10	2	-1
1902	Was-A	.961	111	236	11	10	0	3
1903	Was-A	.962	40	69	6	3	1	2
Total	15	.951	1344	2951	243	166	45	98

1B

YEAR	TM/L	PCT	G	PO	A	E	DP	FR
1890	Cle-P	1.000	1	1	0	0	0	0
1891	Phi-N	.946	27	265	14	16	17	-1
1893	Phi-N	.950	6	33	5	2	6	1
1894	Phi-N	.937	12	63	11	5	8	2
1896	Phi-N	.970	22	217	9	7	10	-2
1897	Phi-N	1.000	1	10	0	0	2	0
1900	Phi-N	.981	130	1299	66	27	86	-3
1901	Phi-N	.980	58	553	22	12	20	-4
1902	Was-A	.962	13	143	7	6	5	-1
1903	Was-A	1.000	1	5	0	0	0	0
Total	10	.973	271	2589	134	5	154	-8

2B

YEAR	TM/L	PCT	G	PO	A	E	DP	FR
1888	Phi-N	.872	56	129	170	44	20	-10
1889	Phi-N	.889	24	56	56	14	11	-15
1890	Cle-P	.881	20	54	50	14	7	-5
1891	Phi-N	1.000	3	2	7	0	0	1
1893	Phi-N	.943	15	40	42	5	9	4
1894	Phi-N	.970	6	12	20	1	2	2
1895	Phi-N	.829	6	20	14	7	2	-2
1896	Phi-N	1.000	1	3	2	0	1	0
Total	8	.888	131	316	361	5	52	-25

SS

YEAR	TM/L	PCT	G	PO	A	E	DP	FR
1889	Phi-N	.000	1	0	0	1	0	-1
1890	Cle-P	.830	76	143	244	79	33	-5
1894	Phi-N	.854	8	21	20	7	4	-3
1895	Phi-N	.852	9	23	23	8	2	-3
Total	4	.833	94	187	287	5	39	-12

3B

YEAR	TM/L	PCT	G	PO	A	E	DP	FR
1890	Cle-P	.929	3	7	6	1	2	0
1892	Phi-N	.833	4	2	3	1	0	0
1894	Phi-N	.796	9	17	22	10	1	1
1895	Phi-N	.800	1	2	2	1	0	0
Total	4	.824	17	28	33	3	3	1

■ Frank Delahanty OF

YEAR	TM/L	PCT	G	PO	A	E	DP	FR
1905	NY-A	1.000	3	4	0	0	0	0
1906	NY-A	.954	86	180	7	9	1	3
1907	Cle-A	.917	15	19	3	2	0	0
1908	NY-A	.957	36	64	2	3	0	-1
1914	Buf-F	.976	78	116	8	3	1	-6
	Pit-F	.984	36	57	5	1	0	-1
	Yr	.979	114	173	13	4	1	-7
1915	Pit-F	1.000	11	20	2	0	0	1
Total	6	.964	265	460	27	8	2	-4

1B

YEAR	TM/L	PCT	G	PO	A	E	DP	FR
1905	NY-A	.932	5	39	2	3	0	0

2B

YEAR	TM/L	PCT	G	PO	A	E	DP	FR
1914	Pit-F	.810	4	6	11	4	1	-2

■ Jim Delahanty 2B

YEAR	TM/L	PCT	G	PO	A	E	DP	FR
1901	Chi-N	—	1	0	0	0	0	0
1904	Bos-N	.929	18	38	41	6	1	-5
1907	StL-A	1.000	2	1	5	0	0	1
	Was-A	.941	68	172	180	22	18	-8
	Yr	.942	70	173	185	22	18	-7
1908	Was-A	.963	80	181	232	16	25	3
1909	Was-A	.956	85	177	211	18	26	-3
	Det-A	.943	46	88	127	13	13	-7
	Yr	.951	131	265	338	31	39	-10
1910	Det-A	.940	106	246	267	33	36	-14
1911	Det-A	.947	59	158	182	19	19	5
1912	Det-A	.930	44	95	117	16	19	-1
1914	Bro-F	.957	55	104	117	10	15	-18
1915	Bro-F	.857	4	7	11	3	0	-1
Total	10	.946	568	1267	1490	156	172	-48

3B

YEAR	TM/L	PCT	G	PO	A	E	DP	FR
1901	Chi-N	.877	17	21	29	7	2	-1
1904	Bos-N	.888	113	158	223	48	12	5
1906	Cin-N	.903	105	136	170	33	4	-16
1907	StL-A	.889	21	30	34	8	1	-2
	Was-A	.888	27	40	39	10	4	-5
	Yr	.888	48	70	73	18	5	-7
1911	Det-A	.755	13	15	22	12	5	-4
Total	5	.886	296	400	517	118	28	-23

OF

YEAR	TM/L	PCT	G	PO	A	E	DP	FR
1902	NY-A	.917	7	11	0	1	0	-1
1904	Bos-N	.905	9	18	1	2	0	1
1905	Bos-N	.962	124	186	16	8	1	-7
1906	Cin-N	1.000	2	1	0	0	0	-1
1907	StL-A	1.000	4	9	0	0	0	1
	Was-A	1.000	9	13	1	0	0	-1
	Yr	1.000	13	22	1	0	0	0
1912	Det-A	.889	33	53	3	7	0	-4
Total	6	.945	188	291	21	8	1	-13

1B

YEAR	TM/L	PCT	G	PO	A	E	DP	FR
1907	Was-A	.979	4	42	4	1	1	0
1911	Det-A	.978	71	744	21	17	17	-11
1914	Bro-F	.946	5	33	2	2	3	0
Total	3	.977	80	819	27	0	21	-11

SS

YEAR	TM/L	PCT	G	PO	A	E	DP	FR
1906	Cin-N	.900	5	9	9	2	0	-2

■ Joe Delahanty OF

YEAR	TM/L	PCT	G	PO	A	E	DP	FR
1907	StL-N	.933	7	14	0	1	0	-1
1908	StL-N	.977	138	243	11	6	1	-5
1909	StL-N	.985	63	126	8	2	2	-2
Total	3	.978	208	383	19	9	3	-8

2B

YEAR	TM/L	PCT	G	PO	A	E	DP	FR
1909	StL-N	.905	48	77	113	20	11	-14

■ Mike DeLa Hoz 3B

YEAR	TM/L	PCT	G	PO	A	E	DP	FR
1960	Cle-A	.895	8	7	10	2	1	-2
1961	Cle-A	.969	16	13	18	1	2	-2
1963	Cle-A	.923	6	3	9	1	0	0
1964	Mil-N	.922	25	16	43	5	6	1
1965	Mil-N	.904	22	12	35	5	3	-1
1966	Atl-N	.950	30	22	35	3	3	-1
1967	Atl-N	.964	22	20	33	2	1	-2
Total	7	.936	129	93	183	9	16	-7

2B

YEAR	TM/L	PCT	G	PO	A	E	DP	FR
1961	Cle-A	.969	17	25	38	2	2	1
1962	Cle-A	1.000	2	0	2	0	0	0
1963	Cle-A	.962	34	63	89	6	20	6
1964	Mil-N	.968	25	39	53	3	8	-4
1965	Mil-N	1.000	10	11	13	0	4	-1
1966	Atl-N	1.000	8	3	0	0	0	-1
1967	Atl-N	1.000	23	27	26	0	9	-2
Total	7	.973	119	168	221	1	43	-1

SS

YEAR	TM/L	PCT	G	PO	A	E	DP	FR
1960	Cle-A	.950	38	58	94	8	13	-12
1961	Cle-A	.943	17	39	60	6	6	4
1963	Cle-A	.750	2	2	4	2	0	-1
1964	Mil-N	.920	8	10	13	2	3	-1
1965	Mil-N	.963	41	29	50	3	12	-8
1966	Atl-N	—	1	0	0	0	0	0
1967	Atl-N	1.000	1	1	0	0	0	0
Total	7	.945	108	139	221	1	34	-18

OF

YEAR	TM/L	PCT	G	PO	A	E	DP	FR
1963	Cle-A	1.000	2	1	0	0	0	0

1B

YEAR	TM/L	PCT	G	PO	A	E	DP	FR
1965	Mil-N	1.000	1	9	1	0	1	0

■ Bill DeLancey C

YEAR	TM/L	PCT	G	PO	A	E	DP	FR
1932	StL-N	.930	8	32	8	3	3	1
1934	StL-N	.980	77	363	35	8	5	5
1935	StL-N	.971	83	372	29	12	6	-1
1940	StL-N	.929	12	24	2	2	0	1
Total	4	.972	180	791	74	5	14	6

■ Bobby DelGreco OF

YEAR	TM/L	PCT	G	PO	A	E	DP	FR
1952	Pit-N	.977	93	246	11	6	3	4
1956	Pit-N	1.000	7	9	0	0	0	0
	StL-N	.987	99	217	3	3	0	-11
	Yr	.987	106	226	3	3	0	-11
1957	StL-N	.967	16	27	2	1	0	2
	NY-A	1.000	6	5	0	0	0	0
1958	NY-A	1.000	12	5	0	0	0	0
1960	Phi-N	.970	89	247	10	8	1	8
1961	Phi-N	1.000	32	80	1	0	0	3
	KC-A	.983	73	168	8	3	2	2
1962	KC-A	.984	124	245	9	4	0	-5
1963	KC-A	.981	110	207	5	4	0	-12
1965	Phi-N	—	4	0	0	0	0	0
Total	9	.981	665	1456	49	9	6	-9

3B

YEAR	TM/L	PCT	G	PO	A	E	DP	FR
1956	Pit-N	1.000	3	2	3	0	0	0
1961	Phi-N	—	1	0	0	0	0	0
1963	KC-A	1.000	2	2	0	0	0	0
Total	3	1.000	6	4	3	0	0	0

2B

YEAR	TM/L	PCT	G	PO	A	E	DP	FR
1961	Phi-N	—	1	0	0	0	0	0

■ Jim Delsing OF

YEAR	TM/L	PCT	G	PO	A	E	DP	FR
1948	Chi-A	1.000	15	36	1	0	0	-1
1949	NY-A	1.000	5	6	0	0	0	-1
1950	StL-A	.994	53	150	4	1	3	6
1951	StL-A	.983	124	340	15	6	5	4
1952	StL-A	.986	85	206	4	3	2	5
	Det-A	.958	32	67	1	3	0	-1
	Yr	.979	117	273	5	6	2	4
1953	Det-A	.992	133	354	7	3	2	-6
1954	Det-A	.996	108	221	5	1	0	-2
1955	Det-A	.995	101	178	3	1	1	-7
1956	Det-A	1.000	3	3	0	0	0	0
	Chi-A	.957	29	21	1	1	0	2
	Yr	.962	32	24	1	1	0	2
1960	KC-A	1.000	10	24	0	0	0	1
Total	10	.990	698	1606	41	9	13	0

■ Joe DeMaestri SS

YEAR	TM/L	PCT	G	PO	A	E	DP	FR
1951	Chi-A	.959	27	26	45	3	12	5
1952	StL-A	.939	77	105	156	17	29	1
1953	Phi-A	.964	108	191	297	18	53	-16
1954	Phi-A	.965	142	285	406	25	90	-6
1955	KC-A	.964	122	206	358	21	78	-12
1956	KC-A	.964	132	210	407	23	95	6
1957	KC-A	.980	134	248	387	13	87	-7
1958	KC-A	.980	137	226	417	13	95	11
1959	KC-A	.957	115	167	320	22	63	5
1960	NY-A	1.000	17	10	21	0	1	5
1961	NY-A	.981	18	15	38	1	9	6
Total	11	.967	1029	1689	2852	156	612	-2

2B

YEAR	TM/L	PCT	G	PO	A	E	DP	FR
1951	Chi-A	.968	11	16	14	1	2	1
1952	StL-A	1.000	1	1	0	1	0	0
1954	Phi-A	1.000	1	0	1	0	0	0
1956	KC-A	—	2	0	0	0	0	0
1960	NY-A	.952	19	12	8	1	3	2
1961	NY-A	1.000	5	9	6	0	2	2

YEAR	TM/L	PCT	G	PO	A	E	DP	FR
Total	6	.971	39	38	30	2	8	5
3B								
1951	Chi-A	.750	8	1	2	1	0	0
1952	StL-A	1.000	1	0	2	0	1	1
1954	Phi-A	1.000	1	0	1	0	0	0
1961	NY-A	—	4	0	0	0	0	0
Total	4	.857	14	1	5	1	1	1

■ Frank Demaree OF

YEAR	TM/L	PCT	G	PO	A	E	DP	FR
1932	Chi-N	1.000	17	31	2	0	1	1
1933	Chi-N	.965	133	321	12	12	1	-3
1935	Chi-N	.973	98	204	13	6	3	-6
1936	Chi-N	.968	154	285	16	10	1	-4
1937	Chi-N	.980	154	283	17	6	6	-1
1938	Chi-N	.972	125	199	12	6	1	-9
1939	NY-N	.986	150	329	11	5	2	-5
1940	NY-N	.980	119	233	6	5	5	-11
1941	NY-N	1.000	10	19	1	0	0	1
	Bos-N	1.000	28	41	1	0	0	-3
	Yr	1.000	38	60	2	0	0	-2
1942	Bos-N	1.000	49	114	4	0	1	2
1943	StL-N	1.000	23	35	1	0	0	-2
1944	StL-A	.969	16	30	1	1	0	0
Total	12	.978	1076	2124	97	1	21	-40

■ Don Demeter OF

YEAR	TM/L	PCT	G	PO	A	E	DP	FR
1956	Bro-N	1.000	1	1	0	0	0	0
1958	LA-N	1.000	39	70	0	0	0	2
1959	LA-N	.983	124	223	5	4	1	-12
1960	LA-N	.989	62	92	2	1	1	1
1961	LA-N	.950	14	18	1	1	1	1
	Phi-N	.995	79	173	9	1	3	10
	Yr	.990	93	191	10	2	4	11
1962	Phi-N	.991	63	107	0	1	0	0
1963	Phi-N	1.000	119	166	6	0	1	-7
1964	Det-A	1.000	88	164	3	0	1	-9
1965	Det-A	.988	81	158	1	2	1	-3
1966	Det-A	.985	27	65	2	1	2	5
	Bos-A	.982	57	109	3	2	0	-3
	Yr	.984	84	174	5	3	2	2
1967	Bos-A	1.000	12	15	1	0	1	0
	Cle-A	.985	35	63	2	1	0	3
	Yr	.988	47	78	3	1	1	3
Total	11	.990	801	1424	35	4	12	-12
3B								
1962	Phi-N	.937	105	91	177	18	18	-5
1963	Phi-N	.927	43	28	61	7	3	1
1967	Bos-A	1.000	1	0	1	0	0	0
	Cle-A	1.000	1	2	2	0	1	0
	Yr	1.000	2	2	3	0	1	0
Total	3	.935	150	121	241	5	22	-4
1B								
1961	Phi-N	.988	22	148	15	2	22	1
1962	Phi-N	.667	1	2	0	1	1	0
1963	Phi-N	.966	26	181	19	7	11	1
1964	Det-A	.991	23	202	12	2	12	-1
1965	Det-A	.991	34	219	10	2	19	-2
1966	Det-A	1.000	4	16	4	0	1	1
	Bos-A	1.000	2	13	1	0	1	0
	Yr	1.000	6	29	5	0	2	1
Total	6	.984	112	781	61	4	67	0

■ Ray Demmitt OF

YEAR	TM/L	PCT	G	PO	A	E	DP	FR
1909	NY-A	.908	109	185	22	21	7	5
1910	StL-A	1.000	8	11	2	0	0	1
1914	Chi-A	.953	142	217	24	12	3	-5
1915	Chi-A	1.000	3	1	0	0	0	-1
1917	StL-A	1.000	14	15	0	0	0	-3
1918	StL-A	.951	114	206	25	12	8	7
1919	StL-A	.868	49	60	6	10	0	-7
Total	7	.934	439	695	79	5	18	-3

■ Gene DeMontreville 2B

YEAR	TM/L	PCT	G	PO	A	E	DP	FR
1897	Was-N	.936	33	86	103	13	6	0
1898	Bal-N	.944	123	303	386	41	35	2
1899	Bal-N	.961	60	174	197	15	16	9
1900	Bro-N	.952	48	127	130	13	16	2
1901	Bos-N	.954	120	272	344	30	35	-1
1902	Bos-N	.940	112	271	294	36	24	-19
1903	Was-A	.931	11	28	26	4	1	-4
1904	StL-A	1.000	3	5	7	0	0	-1
Total	8	.948	510	1266	1487	152	133	-12
SS								
1894	Pit-N	.889	2	1	7	1	0	-1
1895	Was-N	.929	12	33	45	6	8	4
1896	Was-N	.890	133	305	479	97	53	16
1897	Was-N	.886	99	254	352	78	47	10
1898	Bal-N	.897	28	66	100	19	11	-2
1899	Chi-N	.902	82	192	306	54	38	9
1900	Bro-N	.869	12	21	32	8	3	1
1902	Bos-N	.897	10	22	39	7	4	2
1903	Was-A	1.000	1	2	0	0	1	0
Total	9	.893	379	896	1360	270	164	39
3B								
1900	Bro-N	.862	7	11	14	4	0	-1
1901	Bos-N	.862	20	22	59	13	2	6
Total	2	.862	27	33	73	7	2	5
OF								
1900	Bro-N	—	1	0	0	0	0	-1
1B								
1900	Bro-N	—	1	0	0	0	0	0

■ Rick Dempsey C

YEAR	TM/L	PCT	G	PO	A	E	DP	FR
1969	Min-A	.833	3	5	0	1	0	-1
1970	Min-A	.923	3	12	0	1	0	0
1971	Min-A	.944	6	30	4	2	0	2
1972	Min-A	.986	23	67	5	1	0	-1
1973	NY-A	.818	5	9	0	2	0	-2
1974	NY-A	.978	31	152	22	4	0	5
1975	NY-A	.977	19	76	8	2	0	2
1976	NY-A	1.000	9	39	5	0	0	2
	Bal-A	.987	58	263	34	4	8	6
	Yr	.988	67	302	39	4	8	8
1977	Bal-A	.977	91	416	52	11	10	-3
1978	Bal-A	.985	135	636	79	11	14	-5
1979	Bal-A	.990	124	615	81	7	13	18
1980	Bal-A	.987	112	531	54	8	8	11
1981	Bal-A	.998	90	384	35	1	6	3
1982	Bal-A	.991	124	491	46	5	8	0
1983	Bal-A	.997	128	591	65	2	7	20
1984	Bal-A	.992	108	453	43	4	5	-6
1985	Bal-A	.987	131	575	49	8	5	-12
1986	Bal-A	.990	121	659	53	7	9	3
1987	Cle-A	.984	59	293	18	5	3	0
1988	LA-N	.989	74	333	29	4	4	5
1989	LA-N	.984	62	265	35	5	4	3
1990	LA-N	.992	53	213	27	2	3	0
Total	22	.988	1569	7108	744	7	107	50
OF								
1974	NY-A	—	2	0	0	0	0	0
1975	NY-A	.944	8	16	1	1	1	0
1976	NY-A	1.000	4	6	1	0	0	1
	Bal-A	—	3	0	0	0	0	0
	Yr	1.000	7	6	1	0	0	1
1980	Bal-A	1.000	6	3	0	0	0	0
Total	4	.964	23	25	2	1	1	1
1B								
1980	Bal-A	1.000	2	10	1	0	2	0
3B								
1975	NY-A	—	1	0	0	0	0	0

■ Jerry Denny 3B

YEAR	TM/L	PCT	G	PO	A	E	DP	FR
1881	Pro-N	.840	85	144	181	62	12	6
1882	Pro-N	.861	84	136	206	55	7	14
1883	Pro-N	.876	98	178	188	52	13	10
1884	Pro-N	.874	99	144	168	45	5	-3
1885	Pro-N	.869	83	128	157	43	10	0
1886	StL-N	.895	117	182	270	53	22	27
1887	Ind-N	.889	116	201	262	58	21	18
1888	Ind-N	.894	96	158	214	44	14	17
1889	Ind-N	.913	123	199	276	45	12	11
1890	NY-N	.889	106	165	210	47	16	3
1891	NY-N	.700	4	5	2	3	1	-3
	Cle-N	.884	29	39	60	13	1	-2
	Phi-N	.913	7	7	14	2	1	0
	Yr	.876	40	51	76	18	3	-5
1893	Lou-N	1.000	2	6	6	0	0	1
1894	Lou-N	.874	60	85	124	30	12	3
Total	13	.882	1109	1777	2338	552	147	102
SS								
1886	StL-N	.889	3	4	12	2	2	1
1887	Ind-N	1.000	4	12	21	0	2	5
1888	Ind-N	.916	25	65	88	14	9	11
1889	Ind-N	1.000	5	16	14	0	3	2
1890	NY-N	.957	7	19	26	2	3	1
1893	Lou-N	.920	42	91	139	20	16	-1
Total	6	.930	86	207	300	8	35	19
1B								
1884	Pro-N	.979	9	90	4	2	6	1
1891	Phi-N	.977	12	123	2	3	5	-2
Total	2	.978	21	213	6	5	11	-1
2B								
1884	Pro-N	.941	3	3	13	1	0	1
1887	Ind-N	1.000	1	5	5	0	1	1
1888	Ind-N	.778	5	12	9	6	0	-3
1889	Ind-N	.911	7	22	19	4	2	-2
1890	NY-N	1.000	1	0	1	0	0	0
Total	5	.890	17	42	47	1	3	-3
OF								
1887	Ind-N	.500	1	1	0	1	0	0
1888	Ind-N	1.000	1	1	0	0	0	0
1891	Cle-N	.846	7	10	1	2	0	-1
Total	3	.813	9	12	1	3	0	-1
C								
1884	Pro-N	—	1	0	0	0	0	0

■ Bucky Dent SS

YEAR	TM/L	PCT	G	PO	A	E	DP	FR
1973	Chi-A	.963	36	51	132	7	22	6
1974	Chi-A	.972	154	251	499	22	108	9
1975	Chi-A	.981	157	279	543	16	105	27
1976	Chi-A	.976	158	279	468	18	96	-5
1977	NY-A	.974	158	250	434	18	90	-11
1978	NY-A	.981	123	178	341	10	57	-8
1979	NY-A	.977	141	219	512	17	107	32
1980	NY-A	.982	141	224	489	13	77	13
1981	NY-A	.970	73	104	217	10	49	-2
1982	NY-A	.962	58	74	177	10	27	17
	Tex-A	.980	45	55	146	4	30	-2
	Yr	.970	103	129	323	14	57	15
1983	Tex-A	.979	129	150	369	11	71	-8
1984	KC-A	1.000	9	2	5	0	0	0
Total	12	.976	1382	2116	4332	156	839	68
2B								
1973	Chi-A	1.000	3	4	2	0	1	0
3B								
1973	Chi-A	—	1	0	0	0	0	0
1984	KC-A	1.000	2	2	1	0	0	0
Total	2	1.000	3	2	1	0	0	0

■ Sam Dente SS

YEAR	TM/L	PCT	G	PO	A	E	DP	FR
1948	StL-A	.958	76	138	207	15	46	-3
1949	Was-A	.957	153	314	462	35	106	-9
1950	Was-A	.952	128	225	406	32	88	-3
1951	Was-A	.962	65	128	173	12	43	1
1952	Chi-A	.942	27	42	56	6	14	-1
1953	Chi-A	—	1	0	0	0	0	0
1954	Cle-A	.971	60	66	133	6	33	-4
1955	Cle-A	.976	53	33	87	3	15	5
Total	8	.958	563	946	1524	109	345	-14
3B								
1947	Bos-A	.939	46	40	83	8	11	-3
1948	StL-A	.923	6	3	9	1	1	0
1951	Was-A	1.000	5	1	7	0	0	1
1952	Chi-A	1.000	18	7	17	0	2	1
1955	Cle-A	1.000	13	4	12	0	0	1
Total	5	.953	88	55	128	9	14	0
2B								
1950	Was-A	.989	29	91	91	2	23	4
1951	Was-A	.969	10	32	30	2	9	1
1952	Chi-A	1.000	6	24	20	0	6	2
1954	Cle-A	.923	7	10	14	2	3	1
1955	Cle-A	1.000	4	5	6	0	2	1
Total	5	.982	56	162	161	6	43	9
OF								
1952	Chi-A	1.000	6	4	0	0	0	0
1B								
1952	Chi-A	1.000	2	8	2	0	1	1

■ Bob Dernier OF

YEAR	TM/L	PCT	G	PO	A	E	DP	FR
1980	Phi-N	1.000	3	9	0	0	0	2
1981	Phi-N	1.000	5	2	0	0	0	1
1982	Phi-N	.981	119	255	5	5	0	6
1983	Phi-N	.988	107	164	3	2	1	10
1984	Chi-N	.986	140	355	5	5	1	0
1985	Chi-N	.972	116	310	4	9	1	4
1986	Chi-N	.987	105	222	3	3	2	-3
1987	Chi-N	.989	71	86	2	1	1	-2
1988	Phi-N	.980	54	98	2	2	0	3
1989	Phi-N	.970	74	95	1	3	0	0
Total	10	.982	794	1596	25	0	6	21

■ Russ Derry OF

YEAR	TM/L	PCT	G	PO	A	E	DP	FR
1944	NY-A	.949	28	54	2	3	0	-3
1945	NY-A	.978	68	170	4	4	2	3
1946	Phi-A	.985	50	127	3	2	2	5
Total	3	.976	146	351	9	9	4	5

■ Gene Desautels C

YEAR	TM/L	PCT	G	PO	A	E	DP	FR
1930	Det-A	.996	42	207	23	1	3	9
1931	Det-A	1.000	3	7	3	0	0	-1
1932	Det-A	.984	24	109	13	2	0	4
1933	Det-A	.976	30	75	5	2	0	2
1937	Bos-A	.993	94	491	44	4	4	3
1938	Bos-A	.985	108	423	52	7	7	5
1939	Bos-A	.994	73	310	48	2	5	9
1940	Bos-A	.992	70	325	27	3	8	-4
1941	Cle-A	.997	66	300	32	1	5	5
1942	Cle-A	.975	61	180	16	5	0	-9
1943	Cle-A	.982	66	251	28	5	4	1
1945	Cle-A	1.000	10	8	3	0	1	0
1946	Phi-A	.989	52	151	31	2	4	1
Total	13	.989	699	2837	325	4	41	25

■ Mike Devereaux OF

YEAR	TM/L	PCT	G	PO	A	E	DP	FR
1987	LA-N	1.000	18	21	1	0	0	-1
1988	LA-N	1.000	26	29	0	0	0	1
1989	Bal-A	.983	112	288	1	5	0	-7
1990	Bal-A	.983	104	281	4	5	1	1
Total	4	.984	260	619	6	0	1	-6

■ Art Devlin 3B

YEAR	TM/L	PCT	G	PO	A	E	DP	FR
1904	NY-N	.907	130	126	285	42	10	7
1905	NY-N	.932	153	156	299	33	14	5
1906	NY-N	.944	148	171	355	31	22	28
1907	NY-N	.940	140	174	282	29	12	0
1908	NY-N	.947	157	203	331	30	19	13
1909	NY-N	.934	143	191	317	36	21	14
1910	NY-N	.933	147	179	284	33	20	5
1911	NY-N	.944	79	75	144	13	3	3
1912	Bos-N	.958	26	41	50	4	7	4
1913	Bos-N	.973	69	83	134	6	4	8
Total	10	.938	1192	1399	2481	257	132	87
1B								
1911	NY-N	.953	6	40	1	2	1	-1
1912	Bos-N	.992	69	694	37	6	33	0
Total	2	.990	75	734	38	8	34	-1
SS								
1907	NY-N	.895	3	7	10	2	0	0
1911	NY-N	.875	6	3	4	1	0	0
1912	Bos-N	.945	26	33	53	5	12	-3
Total	3	.932	35	43	67	8	12	-3
2B								
1911	NY-N	1.000	6	10	5	0	1	0
OF								
1912	Bos-N	—	1	0	0	0	0	0

■ Josh Devore OF

YEAR	TM/L	PCT	G	PO	A	E	DP	FR
1908	NY-N	1.000	2	1	0	0	0	-1
1909	NY-N	.824	12	13	1	3	0	-4
1910	NY-N	.929	130	191	18	16	3	-9
1911	NY-N	.934	149	241	29	19	5	2
1912	NY-N	.918	96	155	14	15	3	-5
1913	NY-N	1.000	8	5	1	0	0	0
	Cin-N	.920	57	106	9	10	3	0
	Phi-N	.889	14	14	2	2	0	0
	Yr	.919	79	125	12	12	3	0
1914	Phi-N	.947	9	14	4	1	3	2
	Bos-N	.915	42	51	3	5	0	-5
	Yr	.923	51	65	7	6	3	-3
Total	7	.925	519	791	81	1	17	-20

■ Al DeVormer C

YEAR	TM/L	PCT	G	PO	A	E	DP	FR
1918	Chi-A	1.000	6	11	4	0	0	-2
1921	NY-A	.950	17	48	9	3	1	-1
1922	NY-A	.968	17	50	11	2	0	0
1923	Bos-A	.979	55	181	48	5	3	1
1927	NY-N	.953	54	115	27	7	0	-4
Total	5	.967	149	405	99	7	4	-6

YEAR	TM/L	PCT	G	PO	A	E	DP	FR
	1B							
1922	NY-A	1.000	1	16	0	0	0	0
1923	Bos-A	1.000	2	2	0	0	0	0
1927	NY-N	1.000	3	36	2	0	4	0
Total	3	1.000	6	54	2	0	4	0
	OF							
1918	Chi-A	1.000	1	1	0	0	0	0
■ Charlie Dexter OF								
1896	Lou-N	.896	47	87	8	11	3	-2
1897	Lou-N	.907	32	40	9	5	3	-1
1898	Lou-N	.958	95	148	13	7	2	-1
1899	Lou-N	.942	71	131	16	9	2	6
1900	Chi-N	1.000	13	31	3	0	2	4
1901	Chi-N	.950	21	38	0	2	0	-2
1902	Chi-N	1.000	10	18	1	0	0	0
	Bos-N	1.000	7	12	1	0	1	0
	Yr	1.000	17	30	2	0	1	0
1903	Bos-N	.941	106	177	13	12	6	-2
Total	8	.942	402	682	64	6	19	2
	C							
1896	Lou-N	.903	55	179	63	26	9	-1
1897	Lou-N	.898	23	65	23	10	2	-4
1898	Lou-N	.979	7	37	9	1	0	3
1900	Chi-N	.943	22	67	33	6	2	2
1901	Chi-N	1.000	3	8	5	0	1	1
1903	Bos-N	.976	6	33	7	1	3	0
Total	6	.923	116	389	140	4	17	1
	3B							
1897	Lou-N	.828	14	22	31	11	1	1
1901	Chi-N	.888	25	39	48	11	0	1
1902	Chi-N	.853	39	62	60	21	5	-12
	Bos-N	1.000	1	1	0	0	0	0
	Yr	.854	40	63	60	21	5	-12
Total	3	.859	79	124	139	3	6	-10
	1B							
1901	Chi-N	.982	54	499	39	10	28	4
1902	Chi-N	.975	22	223	10	6	15	-1
Total	2	.980	76	722	49	6	43	3
	2B							
1898	Lou-N	.911	8	22	19	4	3	-3
1900	Lou-N	1.000	1	0	1	0	0	0
1901	Chi-N	.944	13	34	33	4	3	-1
1902	Bos-N	.943	19	44	39	5	5	-4
Total	4	.937	41	100	92	3	11	-8
	SS							
1897	Lou-N	.909	2	5	5	1	2	0
1899	Lou-N	.781	6	6	19	7	0	-3
1902	Bos-N	.901	22	54	73	14	6	1
1903	Bos-N	.814	9	21	14	8	1	-7
Total	4	.868	39	86	111	0	9	-9
■ Bo Diaz C								
1977	Bos-A	1.000	2	5	0	0	0	1
1978	Cle-A	.971	44	183	18	6	4	-1
1979	Cle-A	.958	15	63	6	3	1	4
1980	Cle-A	.989	75	317	35	4	4	2
1981	Cle-A	.975	51	247	27	7	0	-3
1982	Phi-N	.989	144	850	80	10	7	-9
1983	Phi-N	.986	134	903	97	**14**	7	**14**
1984	Phi-N	.992	23	114	9	1	1	0
1985	Phi-N	.972	24	127	10	4	2	2
	Cin-N	.988	51	301	32	4	8	8
	Yr	.983	75	428	42	8	10	10
1986	Cin-N	.984	134	732	83	13	10	-6
1987	Cin-N	.992	137	747	70	7	6	-6
1988	Cin-N	.990	88	468	44	5	9	-3
1989	Cin-N	.984	43	237	14	4	1	0
Total	13	.986	965	5294	525	2	60	3
■ Buttercup Dickerson OF								
1878	Cin-N	.877	29	56	1	8	0	-2
1879	Cin-N	.801	81	144	9	38	1	-4
1880	Tro-N	.903	30	77	7	9	3	5
	Wor-N	.852	31	48	4	9	2	-3
	Yr	.883	61	125	11	18	**5**	2
1881	Wor-N	.892	80	153	28	22	6	9
1883	Pit-a	.798	78	106	28	34	2	5
1884	StL-U	.895	42	65	12	9	2	5
	Bal-a	.941	12	15	1	1	0	-1
	Lou-a	.813	8	11	2	3	0	0
	Yr	.879	20	26	3	4	0	-1
1885	Buf-N	1.000	5	6	2	0	0	0
Total	7	.854	396	681	94	133	16	14
	SS							
1880	Tro-N	1.000	1	1	1	0	0	0
1883	Pit-a	.697	8	9	14	10	1	-4
Total	2	.714	9	10	15	0	0	-4
	3B							
1884	StL-U	.824	4	8	6	3	0	0
	Bal-a	.000	1	0	0	1	0	-1
	2B							
1883	Pit-a	.750	2	3	3	2	1	-1
■ George Dickey C								
1935	Bos-A	1.000	4	7	0	0	0	-1
1936	Bos-A	.912	10	25	6	3	1	1
1941	Chi-A	1.000	17	56	5	0	1	1
1942	Chi-A	.918	29	90	11	9	5	4
1946	Chi-A	1.000	30	97	14	0	3	2
1947	Chi-A	.985	80	285	35	5	5	3
Total	6	.974	170	560	71	7	15	2
■ Bill Dickey C								
1928	NY-A	1.000	6	6	2	0	0	-1
1929	NY-A	.979	127	476	**95**	12	**13**	1
1930	NY-A	.977	101	418	51	**11**	5	-12
1931	NY-A	**.996**	125	**670**	78	3	6	3
1932	NY-A	.987	108	639	53	9	6	-2
1933	NY-A	.993	127	**721**	82	6	15	1

YEAR	TM/L	PCT	G	PO	A	E	DP	FR
1934	NY-A	.986	104	527	49	8	13	-2
1935	NY-A	**.995**	118	**536**	62	3	7	-1
1936	NY-A	.976	107	499	61	14	10	0
1937	NY-A	.991	**137**	**692**	**80**	7	11	**11**
1938	NY-A	.987	126	**518**	**74**	8	7	3
1939	NY-A	**.989**	**126**	**571**	57	7	8	7
1940	NY-A	.994	102	425	55	3	9	-1
1941	NY-A	**.994**	104	422	45	3	11	0
1942	NY-A	.976	80	322	44	9	7	2
1943	NY-A	.994	71	322	37	2	5	-2
1946	NY-A	.987	39	201	29	3	4	9
Total	17	.988	1708	7965	954	108	137	16
■ Johnny Dickshot OF								
1936	Pit-N	—	1	0	0	0	0	0
1937	Pit-N	.950	64	109	5	6	2	-5
1938	Pit-N	1.000	10	16	0	0	0	0
1939	NY-N	1.000	10	13	1	0	1	-1
1944	Chi-A	.974	40	72	3	2	1	-3
1945	Chi-A	.971	124	253	13	8	3	-1
Total	6	.968	249	463	22	6	7	-10
■ Bob Didier C								
1969	Atl-N	.994	114	633	52	4	3	1
1970	Atl-N	.988	57	297	25	4	3	2
1971	Atl-N	1.000	50	230	24	0	2	4
1972	Atl-N	1.000	11	50	11	0	1	2
1973	Det-N	1.000	7	38	5	0	3	2
1974	Bos-A	.968	5	28	2	1	0	1
Total	6	.994	244	1276	119	9	12	12
■ Chuck Diering OF								
1947	StL-N	1.000	75	55	3	0	1	6
1948	StL-N	1.000	5	4	1	0	0	1
1949	StL-N	.987	124	300	7	4	1	-7
1950	StL-N	.989	81	178	8	2	2	-3
1951	StL-N	1.000	44	67	3	0	0	7
1952	NY-N	1.000	36	25	1	0	0	3
1954	Bal-A	.983	119	330	17	6	6	10
1955	Bal-A	.976	107	242	6	6	2	-9
1956	Bal-A	1.000	40	73	4	0	0	5
Total	9	.987	631	1274	50	8	12	13
	3B							
1955	Bal-A	.965	34	31	52	3	4	6
1956	Bal-A	.500	2	1	1	2	0	-1
Total	2	.944	36	32	53	5	4	5
	SS							
1955	Bal-A	1.000	12	9	16	0	2	2
■ Dick Dietz C								
1966	SF-N	1.000	6	22	3	0	0	-1
1967	SF-N	.983	43	206	19	4	1	0
1968	SF-N	.976	90	497	37	**13**	10	-6
1969	SF-N	.973	73	432	31	**13**	5	-4
1970	SF-N	.984	139	820	58	14	9	-16
1971	SF-N	.982	135	712	37	14	4	-11
1972	LA-N	1.000	22	104	12	0	1	4
1973	Atl-N	.960	20	67	5	3	0	-1
Total	8	.980	528	2860	202	1	30	-35
	1B							
1973	Atl-N	.989	36	258	24	3	19	2
■ Don Dillard OF								
1960	Cle-A	—	1	0	0	0	0	0
1961	Cle-A	1.000	39	68	0	0	0	0
1962	Cle-A	.965	50	54	1	2	0	-4
1963	Mil-N	.951	30	34	5	2	0	1
1965	Mil-N	—	1	0	0	0	0	0
Total	5	.976	121	156	6	4	0	-3
■ Steve Dillard 2B								
1975	Bos-A	1.000	1	5	4	0	1	1
1976	Bos-A	.976	17	32	48	2	10	-2
1977	Bos-A	.967	45	74	102	6	20	8
1978	Det-A	.958	41	88	118	9	31	39
1979	Chi-N	.988	60	111	132	3	31	9
1980	Chi-N	.980	38	64	85	3	13	-2
1981	Chi-N	.974	32	54	96	4	21	4
1982	Chi-N	.959	16	29	42	3	5	-1
Total	8	.973	250	457	627	0	132	56
	3B							
1976	Bos-A	.918	18	16	29	4	4	-2
1979	Chi-N	.900	9	3	6	1	1	0
1980	Chi-N	.908	51	25	84	11	6	4
1981	Chi-N	.600	7	3	0	2	0	-2
Total	4	.902	85	47	119	8	11	0
	SS							
1976	Bos-A	.875	12	10	25	5	7	0
1977	Bos-A	1.000	9	16	20	0	3	0
1980	Chi-N	1.000	2	3	2	0	0	0
1981	Chi-N	1.000	2	2	0	0	1	0
Total	4	.940	25	31	47	5	11	0
■ Pickles Dillhoefer C								
1917	Chi-N	.985	37	146	49	3	2	9
1918	Phi-N	.923	6	9	3	1	0	-1
1919	StL-N	.967	39	111	35	5	6	-3
1920	StL-N	.953	74	291	72	18	6	0
1921	StL-N	.953	69	170	53	11	8	2
Total	5	.961	225	727	212	8	22	7
■ Bob Dillinger 3B								
1946	StL-A	.922	54	56	98	13	11	-3
1947	StL-A	.958	137	**169**	265	19	21	2
1948	StL-A	.955	**153**	**187**	242	20	30	-16
1949	StL-A	.938	133	166	209	**25**	22	-25
1950	Phi-N	.957	84	92	173	12	18	-2
	Pit-N	.957	51	60	116	8	13	-2
1951	Pit-N	.963	10	11	15	1	0	-2
	Chi-A	.930	70	70	116	14	10	-6
Total	6	.948	692	811	1234	112	125	-50

YEAR	TM/L	PCT	G	PO	A	E	DP	FR
	SS							
1946	StL-A	1.000	1	1	5	0	0	0
■ Pop Dillon 1B								
1899	Pit-N	.988	30	301	17	4	16	1
1900	Pit-N	.981	5	47	5	1	2	1
1901	Det-A	.979	74	777	44	18	57	2
1902	Det-A	.976	66	709	52	19	45	5
	Bal-A	.960	2	22	2	1	0	0
	Yr	.975	68	731	54	20	45	5
1904	Bro-N	.982	134	1304	99	25	56	3
Total	5	.980	311	3160	219	8	176	12
■ Miguel Dilone OF								
1974	Pit-N	1.000	2	1	0	0	0	1
1975	Pit-N	1.000	2	3	0	0	0	2
1976	Pit-N	1.000	3	11	0	0	0	2
1977	Pit-N	1.000	17	21	1	0	0	1
1978	Oak-A	.985	99	195	3	3	1	-11
1979	Oak-A	.959	25	47	0	2	0	-3
	Chi-N	1.000	22	27	0	0	0	3
	Yr	1.000	21	47	0	0	0	1
1980	Cle-A	.973	118	249	7	7	2	1
1981	Cle-A	.971	56	126	7	4	1	5
1982	Cle-A	.964	97	187	3	7	1	-6
1983	Cle-A	1.000	19	46	0	0	0	0
	Chi-A	1.000	2	1	0	0	0	0
	Yr	1.000	21	47	0	0	0	1
1984	Mon-N	.987	41	76	1	1	0	0
1985	Mon-N	.974	22	36	1	1	0	1
	SD-N	.917	14	21	1	2	0	0
	Yr	.952	36	57	2	3	0	1
Total	12	.975	539	1047	24	7	5	-3
	3B							
1978	Oak-A	.500	3	1	1	2	0	-1
■ Dom DiMaggio OF								
1940	Bos-A	.977	94	239	**16**	6	5	**15**
1941	Bos-A	.964	144	386	16	**15**	2	3
1942	Bos-A	.987	151	**439**	**19**	6	**7**	**14**
1946	Bos-A	.985	142	390	9	6	2	4
1947	Bos-A	.977	134	413	**19**	10	4	**14**
1948	Bos-A	.981	**155**	**503**	13	10	4	10
1949	Bos-A	.977	144	420	13	**10**	1	11
1950	Bos-A	.983	140	390	15	7	2	6
1951	Bos-A	.973	146	376	15	11	1	-3
1952	Bos-A	.975	123	303	12	8	4	-6
Total	10	.978	1373	3859	147	9	32	68
■ Joe DiMaggio OF								
1936	NY-A	.978	138	339	**22**	8	2	1
1937	NY-A	.962	150	**413**	21	**17**	4	6
1938	NY-A	.963	145	366	20	15	4	0
1939	NY-A	.986	117	328	13	5	2	4
1940	NY-A	.978	130	359	5	8	2	0
1941	NY-A	.978	139	385	16	9	**5**	7
1942	NY-A	.981	**154**	409	10	8	3	0
1946	NY-A	.982	131	314	15	6	3	1
1947	NY-A	**.997**	139	316	2	1	0	2
1948	NY-A	.972	152	441	8	13	1	-1
1949	NY-A	.985	76	195	1	3	0	-3
1950	NY-A	.976	137	363	9	9	1	-1
1951	NY-A	.990	113	288	11	3	3	0
Total	13	.978	1721	4516	153	105	30	16
	1B							
1950	NY-A	1.000	1	13	0	0	0	0
■ Vince DiMaggio OF								
1937	Bos-N	.982	130	351	**21**	7	2	10
1938	Bos-N	.973	149	415	**19**	12	**10**	9
1939	Cin-N	1.000	7	11	1	0	0	0
1940	Cin-N	1.000	1	2	0	0	0	0
	Pit-N	.979	108	220	13	5	3	-4
	Yr	.979	**109**	222	13	5	3	-4
1941	Pit-N	.976	151	391	11	10	3	2
1942	Pit-N	.988	138	**383**	**20**	9	**5**	**14**
1943	Pit-N	.985	**156**	**457**	16	7	3	9
1944	Pit-N	.984	101	234	8	4	4	-8
1945	Phi-N	.994	121	337	16	2	4	7
1946	Phi-N	1.000	6	10	0	0	0	0
	NY-N	.967	13	29	0	1	0	2
	Yr	.975	19	39	0	1	0	2
Total	10	.981	1081	2840	125	7	35	42
	2B							
1938	Bos-N	1.000	1	4	0	0	0	-1
	SS							
1943	Pit-N	.833	1	1	4	1	0	0
	3B							
1944	Pit-N	1.000	1	1	2	0	0	0
■ Jack Dittmer 2B								
1952	Bos-N	.982	90	228	267	9	60	6
1953	Mil-N	.965	138	290	343	**23**	95	-29
1954	Mil-N	.977	55	119	141	6	31	-3
1955	Mil-N	.977	28	44	42	2	9	-1
1956	Mil-N	.979	42	64	78	3	15	3
1957	Det-A	1.000	1	1	1	0	0	0
Total	6	.974	354	746	872	3	210	-24
	3B							
1957	Det-A	1.000	3	3	3	0	0	-1
■ Leo Dixon C								
1925	StL-A	.981	75	233	70	6	8	9
1926	StL-A	.977	33	101	29	3	3	4
1927	StL-A	.937	35	116	32	10	1	3
1929	Cin-N	1.000	14	42	8	0	0	4
Total	4	.971	157	492	139	9	12	20
■ Dan Dobbek OF								
1959	Was-A	1.000	16	29	1	0	0	-1
1960	Was-A	.973	78	141	5	4	1	4
1961	Min-A	.985	48	64	1	1	0	1

YEAR	TM/L	PCT	G	PO	A	E	DP	FR
Total	3	.980	142	234	7	5	1	4

■ John Dobbs OF

YEAR	TM/L	PCT	G	PO	A	E	DP	FR
1901	Cin-N	.948	100	189	11	11	4	-4
1902	Cin-N	.963	63	146	11	6	2	8
	Chi-N	.977	59	122	8	3	6	1
	Yr	.970	122	268	19	9	8	9
1903	Chi-N	1.000	16	37	1	0	0	1
	Bro-N	.966	110	241	11	9	4	4
	Yr	.970	126	278	12	9	4	5
1904	Bro-N	.936	92	200	6	14	0	-1
1905	Bro-N	.938	123	246	11	17	1	-6
Total	5	.954	563	1181	59	0	17	3
	3B							
1901	Cin-N	.750	8	7	11	6	1	-2
	2B							
1904	Bro-N	.867	2	5	8	2	1	1
	SS							
1904	Bro-N	1.000	2	2	5	0	0	0

■ Larry Doby OF

YEAR	TM/L	PCT	G	PO	A	E	DP	FR
1948	Cle-A	.955	114	287	12	14	3	9
1949	Cle-A	.976	147	355	7	9	2	-9
1950	Cle-A	.987	140	367	2	5	1	-9
1951	Cle-A	.977	132	321	12	8	3	-6
1952	Cle-A	.986	136	398	11	6	3	3
1953	Cle-A	.984	146	354	10	6	3	-12
1954	Cle-A	.995	153	411	14	2	6	2
1955	Cle-A	.994	129	313	6	2	1	-2
1956	Chi-A	.987	137	371	4	5	2	0
1957	Chi-A	.985	110	255	3	4	0	-10
1958	Cle-A	1.000	68	141	5	0	0	-2
1959	Det-A	.960	16	23	1	1	1	-1
	Chi-A	.955	12	20	1	1	1	-1
	Yr	.957	28	43	2	2	2	-2
Total	12	.983	1440	3616	88	3	26	-38
	2B							
1947	Cle-A	1.000	4	1	3	0	0	0
	1B							
1947	Cle-A	1.000	1	8	0	0	1	0
1959	Chi-A	.933	2	13	1	1	3	0
Total	2	.957	3	21	1	1	4	0
	SS							
1947	Cle-A	1.000	1	2	1	0	0	0

■ John Dodge 3B

YEAR	TM/L	PCT	G	PO	A	E	DP	FR
1912	Phi-N	1.000	23	26	48	0	5	7
1913	Cin-N	.908	91	96	170	27	10	0
Total	2	.926	114	122	218	7	15	7
	2B							
1912	Phi-N	.941	5	20	12	2	0	1
	SS							
1912	Phi-N	.833	1	2	3	1	0	0
1913	Phi-N	1.000	3	2	3	0	0	-1
Total	2	.909	4	4	6	1	0	-1

■ Bobby Doerr 2B

YEAR	TM/L	PCT	G	PO	A	E	DP	FR
1937	Bos-A	.973	47	94	124	6	29	4
1938	Bos-A	.968	145	372	420	26	118	6
1939	Bos-A	.976	126	336	431	19	95	27
1940	Bos-A	.977	151	401	480	21	118	18
1941	Bos-A	.971	132	290	389	20	85	-6
1942	Bos-A	.975	142	376	453	21	105	11
1943	Bos-A	.990	155	415	490	9	132	14
1944	Bos-A	.976	125	341	363	17	96	4
1946	Bos-A	.986	151	420	483	13	129	27
1947	Bos-A	.981	146	376	466	16	118	24
1948	Bos-A	.993	138	366	430	6	119	8
1949	Bos-A	.980	139	395	439	17	134	28
1950	Bos-A	.988	149	443	431	11	130	9
1951	Bos-A	.981	106	303	311	12	99	6
Total	14	.980	1852	4928	5710	214	1507	180

■ Cozy Dolan OF

YEAR	TM/L	PCT	G	PO	A	E	DP	FR
1913	Phi-N	.905	12	19	0	2	0	-1
1914	StL-N	.955	96	182	10	9	2	-4
1915	StL-N	.929	98	179	4	14	0	-7
Total	3	.940	206	380	14	5	2	-12
	3B							
1909	Cin-N	.750	3	2	4	2	1	-1
1911	NY-A	.947	19	21	33	3	4	-1
1912	NY-A	.768	17	15	28	13	1	-5
	Phi-N	.872	11	13	21	5	1	-1
1913	Phi-N	.857	4	2	4	1	0	0
	Pit-N	.937	35	38	66	7	8	-2
	Yr	.932	39	40	70	8	8	-2
1914	StL-N	.837	27	23	49	14	1	-1
Total	5	.876	116	114	205	5	16	-17
	SS							
1913	Phi-N	.854	10	15	26	7	2	-3
	2B							
1913	Phi-N	.875	9	13	15	4	2	-1
	1B							
1913	Phi-N	.500	1	1	0	1	0	0

■ Joe Dolan SS

YEAR	TM/L	PCT	G	PO	A	E	DP	FR
1896	Lou-N	.940	44	92	159	16	25	9
1897	Lou-N	.849	18	42	48	16	5	-5
1900	Phi-N	.939	12	27	35	4	5	0
1901	Phi-A	.881	61	88	223	42	30	7
Total	4	.902	135	249	465	8	65	11
	2B							
1897	Lou-N	.915	18	42	65	10	9	1
1899	Phi-N	.915	61	113	190	28	10	-11
1900	Phi-N	.920	29	64	74	12	8	-3
1901	Phi-N	.973	10	13	23	1	4	-3
	Phi-A	1.000	1	1	1	0	1	0
Total	4	.920	119	233	353	1	32	-16
	3B							
1900	Phi-N	.931	31	45	89	10	4	5

YEAR	TM/L	PCT	G	PO	A	E	DP	FR
1901	Phi-A	.912	35	42	103	14	5	9
Total	2	.921	66	87	192	4	9	14
	OF							
1901	Phi-A	—	1	0	0	0	0	0

■ Cozy Dolan OF

YEAR	TM/L	PCT	G	PO	A	E	DP	FR
1895	Bos-N	.500	1	1	0	1	0	-1
1900	Chi-N	.826	13	18	1	4	0	-2
1901	Chi-N	.878	41	63	9	10	3	2
	Bro-N	.967	64	108	9	4	2	-2
	Yr	.931	105	171	18	14	5	0
1902	Bro-N	.936	141	283	10	20	2	-9
1903	Cin-N	.941	4	16	0	1	0	1
	Cin-N	.937	93	107	11	8	2	-7
1904	Cin-N	.939	102	157	13	11	0	-4
1905	Cin-N	.692	9	9	0	4	0	-3
	Bos-N	.946	111	175	19	11	2	3
	Yr	.931	120	184	19	15	2	0
1906	Bos-N	.928	144	207	26	18	4	2
Total	8	.931	723	1144	98	2	15	-20
	1B							
1903	Chi-A	.971	19	218	16	7	7	1
1904	Cin-N	.977	24	199	16	5	10	0
1905	Cin-N	.965	13	131	7	5	6	-1
	Bos-N	.923	2	10	2	1	1	0
	Yr	.962	15	141	9	6	7	-1
1906	Bos-N	1.000	1	6	0	0	0	0
Total	4	.971	59	564	41	8	24	0
	2B							
1906	Bos-N	.862	7	8	17	4	1	-3

■ Tom Dolan C

YEAR	TM/L	PCT	G	PO	A	E	DP	FR
1879	Chi-N	1.000	1	6	2	0	0	1
1882	Buf-N	.941	18	70	26	6	1	-4
1883	StL-a	.957	42	214	51	12	4	8
1884	StL-a	.873	34	188	45	34	2	-8
	StL-U	.897	14	99	23	14	1	7
1885	StL-N	.928	15	77	39	9	1	8
	Bal-a	.918	35	190	67	23	1	-4
1886	StL-N	.914	11	50	14	6	0	0
Total	7	.916	173	904	274	108	10	8
	OF							
1882	Buf-N	1.000	4	1	0	0	0	0
1883	StL-a	.857	40	55	11	11	2	2
1884	StL-a	.750	2	3	0	1	0	0
	StL-U	.667	2	2	2	2	0	1
1886	Bal-a	—	3	0	0	0	0	-1
Total	4	.841	51	61	13	4	2	2
	3B							
1882	Buf-N	.600	2	1	2	2	0	-1
1884	StL-U	.850	3	6	11	3	1	2
Total	2	.800	5	7	13	5	1	0

■ Frank Doljack OF

YEAR	TM/L	PCT	G	PO	A	E	DP	FR
1930	Det-A	.930	20	38	2	3	1	0
1931	Det-A	.925	54	140	8	12	1	3
1932	Det-A	1.000	6	6	0	0	0	-2
1933	Det-A	.941	37	74	6	5	3	1
1934	Det-A	.943	30	47	3	3	0	1
1943	Cle-A	1.000	2	2	0	0	0	0
Total	6	.934	149	307	19	3	5	4
	1B							
1934	Det-A	.955	3	20	1	1	0	0

■ Jim Donahue C

YEAR	TM/L	PCT	G	PO	A	E	DP	FR
1886	NY-a	.933	19	91	34	9	1	3
1887	NY-a	.890	51	208	90	37	3	-5
1888	KC-a	.902	67	282	106	42	9	-12
1889	KC-a	.887	46	158	77	30	4	-4
1891	Col-a	.942	75	343	108	28	11	1
Total	5	.911	258	1082	415	146	28	-17
	OF							
1886	NY-a	.803	32	50	3	13	0	-4
1887	NY-a	.778	5	6	1	2	0	-1
1888	KC-a	.944	18	29	5	2	1	2
1889	KC-a	.724	14	20	1	8	0	-3
1891	Col-a	1.000	1	3	0	0	0	0
Total	5	.825	70	108	10	5	1	-6
	3B							
1887	NY-a	.750	1	2	1	1	0	0
1888	KC-a	.750	5	6	9	5	0	-1
1889	KC-a	.795	10	9	22	8	3	-1
Total	3	.778	16	17	32	4	3	-2
	1B							
1887	NY-a	.955	4	40	2	2	0	0
1891	Col-a	1.000	1	6	0	0	0	0
Total	2	.960	5	46	2	2	0	0
	2B							
1887	NY-a	.429	1	2	1	4	0	-2
1888	KC-a	.714	1	3	2	2	0	-1
Total	2	.571	2	5	3	6	0	-3

■ Jiggs Donahue 1B

YEAR	TM/L	PCT	G	PO	A	E	DP	FR
1901	Mil-a	.922	13	113	6	10	8	-2
1902	StL-A	.927	5	38	0	3	4	-1
1904	Chi-A	.979	101	1067	85	25	49	7
1905	Chi-A	.988	149	1645	114	21	77	8
1906	Chi-A	.988	154	1697	118	22	62	9
1907	Chi-A	.994	157	1846	140	12	78	21
1908	Chi-A	.994	83	968	57	6	30	5
1909	Chi-A	1.000	2	11	0	0	0	0
	Was-A	.984	81	766	36	13	28	-4
	Yr	.984	83	777	36	13	28	-4
Total	8	.987	745	8151	556	112	336	43
	C							
1900	Pit-N	.889	2	7	1	1	0	-1
1901	Pit-N	—	1	0	0	0	0	0
	Mil-a	.933	19	73	24	7	0	-1
1902	StL-A	.956	23	80	29	5	2	1

YEAR	TM/L	PCT	G	PO	A	E	DP	FR
Total	3	.943	45	160	54	3	2	-1
	OF							
1900	Pit-N	1.000	1	1	0	0	0	0
1901	Pit-N	—	1	0	0	0	0	0
Total	2	1.000	2	1	0	0	0	0

■ Pat Donahue C

YEAR	TM/L	PCT	G	PO	A	E	DP	FR
1908	Bos-A	.959	32	128	35	7	2	-1
1909	Bos-A	.982	58	249	71	6	3	-1
1910	Bos-A	1.000	1	7	0	0	0	0
	Phi-A	1.000	13	65	23	0	3	3
	Cle-A	1.000	2	5	2	0	0	-1
	Phi-A	1.000	1	3	1	0	0	1
	Yr	1.000	17	80	26	0	3	3
Total	3	.978	107	457	132	3	8	1
	1B							
1908	Bos-A	1.000	3	15	2	0	0	0
1910	Cle-A	—	1	0	0	0	0	0
Total	2	1.000	4	15	2	0	0	0

■ Tim Donahue C

YEAR	TM/L	PCT	G	PO	A	E	DP	FR
1891	Bos-a	.833	4	4	1	1	0	-1
1895	Chi-N	.915	63	234	45	26	8	-2
1896	Chi-N	.937	57	235	60	20	7	5
1897	Chi-N	.947	55	219	67	16	2	7
1898	Chi-N	.962	122	450	107	22	16	4
1899	Chi-N	.951	91	304	100	21	13	3
1900	Chi-N	.928	66	232	63	23	6	-9
1902	Was-A	1.000	3	8	3	0	0	0
Total	8	.943	461	1686	446	129	52	7
	SS							
1897	Chi-N	.833	2	1	4	1	0	0
	1B							
1897	Chi-N	.750	1	3	0	1	0	0
1899	Chi-N	1.000	1	1	0	0	0	0
Total	2	.800	2	4	0	1	0	0
	2B							
1900	Chi-N	.750	1	2	1	1	0	-1

■ John Donaldson 2B

YEAR	TM/L	PCT	G	PO	A	E	DP	FR
1966	KC-A	1.000	9	22	12	0	2	-2
1967	KC-A	.982	101	210	230	8	40	-18
1968	Oak-A	.971	98	169	263	13	48	-3
1969	Oak-A	.857	1	2	4	1	1	0
	Sea-A	.974	90	209	242	12	56	-1
	Yr	.972	91	211	246	13	57	-1
1970	Oak-A	.986	21	24	48	1	7	-3
1974	Oak-A	.962	7	11	14	1	5	1
Total	6	.976	327	647	813	6	159	-26
	3B							
1968	Oak-A	1.000	5	9	7	0	1	-1
1969	Sea-A	1.000	2	0	1	0	0	0
1970	Oak-A	1.000	1	0	3	0	1	0
1974	Oak-A	—	3	0	0	0	0	0
Total	4	1.000	9	9	11	0	2	-1
	SS							
1967	KC-A	—	1	0	0	0	0	0
1968	Oak-A	1.000	1	0	1	0	0	0
1969	Sea-A	1.000	1	1	0	0	0	0
1970	Oak-A	1.000	6	7	15	0	1	0
Total	4	1.000	9	8	16	0	1	0

■ Mike Donlin OF

YEAR	TM/L	PCT	G	PO	A	E	DP	FR
1899	StL-N	.873	51	96	7	15	2	-5
1900	StL-N	.922	47	99	7	9	5	1
1901	Bal-A	.918	74	179	12	17	2	9
1902	Cin-N	.877	32	59	5	9	1	-1
1903	Cin-N	.900	118	209	15	25	4	-2
1904	Cin-N	.872	53	87	8	14	1	-2
	NY-N	.918	37	44	1	4	1	-7
	Yr	.886	90	131	9	18	2	-9
1905	NY-N	.934	150	250	17	19	4	-12
1906	NY-N	.929	29	39	0	3	0	-6
1908	NY-N	.977	155	239	21	6	1	0
1911	NY-N	1.000	3	1	0	0	0	0
	Bos-N	.912	56	117	8	12	2	1
	Yr	.913	59	118	8	12	2	1
1912	Pit-N	.982	62	102	8	2	1	-4
Total	11	.924	867	1521	109	135	24	-28
	1B							
1899	StL-N	.931	13	116	5	9	3	-2
1900	StL-N	.947	21	209	4	12	9	-5
1901	Bal-A	.981	47	435	24	9	19	1
1903	Cin-N	.959	7	66	5	3	3	0
1904	Cin-N	.951	6	55	5	3	0	-1
1906	NY-N	1.000	1	10	1	0	0	0
Total	6	.963	95	891	42	6	34	-7
	SS							
1899	StL-N	.545	3	2	4	5	1	-2
1902	Cin-N	1.000	1	1	1	0	0	0
Total	2	.615	4	3	5	5	1	-2

■ Jim Donnelly 3B

YEAR	TM/L	PCT	G	PO	A	E	DP	FR
1884	KC-U	.536	5	8	7	13	0	-2
	Ind-a	.850	24	23	28	9	2	-5
1885	Det-N	.850	55	73	102	31	3	-3
1886	KC-N	.845	113	153	245	73	13	0
1887	Was-N	.867	115	136	275	63	21	16
1888	Was-N	.875	117	126	230	51	15	-5
1889	Was-N	.667	4	2	6	4	1	-2
1890	StL-a	.795	11	15	16	8	4	-3
1891	Col-a	.855	17	19	46	11	5	3
1896	Bal-N	.884	106	140	217	47	15	-2
1897	Pit-N	.920	44	51	87	12	1	2
	NY-N	.869	23	18	35	8	2	-6
	Yr	.905	67	69	122	20	3	-4
1898	StL-N	.500	1	0	1	1	0	0
Total	11	.862	635	764	1295	331	82	-7
	SS							
1884	Ind-a	.763	8	2	27	9	0	-2

YEAR	TM/L	PCT	G	PO	A	E	DP	FR
1887	Was-N	.909	2	3	7	1	0	0
1888	Was-N	.800	5	7	13	5	1	-1
Total	3	.797	15	12	47	5	1	-3

OF

| 1884 | Ind-a | .909 | 6 | 7 | 3 | 1 | 9 | 3 |

2B

| 1884 | Ind-a | .714 | 2 | 1 | 4 | 2 | 0 | -1 |

C

| 1884 | KC-U | .750 | 1 | 5 | 1 | 2 | 0 | -1 |

1B

| 1885 | Det-N | .933 | 1 | 13 | 1 | 1 | 1 | 0 |

■ Tom Donohue C

1979	Cal-A	.981	38	136	16	3	4	-2
1980	Cal-A	.986	84	330	29	5	5	-10
Total	2	.985	122	466	45	8	9	-12

■ Patsy Donovan OF

1890	Bos-N	.891	32	45	4	6	1	-5
	Bro-N	1.000	28	66	3	0	1	1
	Yr	.952	60	111	7	6	2	-4
1891	Lou-a	.912	105	214	15	22	0	5
	Was-a	.857	17	22	2	4	1	-2
	Yr	.907	122	236	17	26	1	3
1892	Was-N	.844	40	56	9	12	3	1
	Pit-N	.872	90	111	18	19	4	-3
	Yr	.862	130	167	27	31	7	-2
1893	Pit-N	.937	112	178	16	13	5	-1
1894	Pit-N	.932	132	267	22	21	5	8
1895	Pit-N	.961	125	187	11	8	2	-5
1896	Pit-N	.954	131	224	24	12	8	7
1897	Pit-N	.949	120	186	17	11	5	0
1898	Pit-N	.928	147	238	21	20	4	0
1899	Pit-N	.941	121	184	9	12	3	-12
1900	StL-N	.951	124	180	13	10	4	-5
1901	StL-N	.979	129	215	19	5	8	4
1902	StL-N	.959	126	179	30	9	6	10
1903	StL-N	.952	105	142	16	8	5	-1
1904	Was-A	.963	122	217	15	9	4	9
1906	Bro-N	1.000	6	9	0	0	0	-1
1907	Bro-N	1.000	1	4	0	0	0	0
Total	17	.941	1813	2924	264	201	69	10

■ Red Dooin C

1902	Phi-N	.950	84	433	117	29	10	5
1903	Phi-N	.940	51	186	82	17	1	-3
1904	Phi-N	.938	96	411	149	37	12	7
1905	Phi-N	.965	107	505	152	24	9	7
1906	Phi-N	.948	107	475	111	32	9	-12
1907	Phi-N	.959	94	436	123	24	14	3
1908	Phi-N	.966	132	554	191	26	17	12
1909	Phi-N	.958	140	717	199	40	14	4
1910	Phi-N	.956	91	472	131	28	14	-2
1911	Phi-N	.967	74	436	97	18	5	4
1912	Phi-N	.958	58	254	69	14	2	1
1913	Phi-N	.962	50	194	57	10	7	5
1914	Phi-N	.967	40	150	52	7	4	0
1915	Cin-N	.915	10	37	6	4	0	-3
	NY-N	.964	46	190	49	9	4	1
	Yr	.956	56	227	55	13	4	-2
1916	NY-N	.972	15	30	5	1	0	0
Total	15	.957	1195	5480	1590	320	122	29

OF

1902	Phi-N	.909	6	10	0	1	0	-1
1903	Phi-N	1.000	1	1	0	0	0	0
1904	Phi-N	1.000	3	4	1	0	0	0
1907	Phi-N	—	1	0	0	0	0	0
1910	Phi-N	1.000	3	1	0	0	0	0
1914	Phi-N	1.000	2	1	0	0	0	0
Total	6	.947	16	17	1	1	0	-1

1B

1903	Phi-N	1.000	1	3	0	0	1	0
1904	Phi-N	1.000	4	32	3	0	0	1
Total	2	1.000	5	35	3	0	1	1

3B

1904	Phi-N	.500	1	0	1	1	0	0
1905	Phi-N	—	1	0	0	0	0	0
Total	2	.500	2	0	1	1	0	0

2B

| 1907 | Phi-N | 1.000 | 1 | 3 | 2 | 0 | 0 | 0 |

■ Mickey Doolan SS

1905	Phi-N	.935	135	299	432	51	45	-9
1906	Phi-N	.930	154	395	480	66	51	6
1907	Phi-N	.929	145	327	463	60	59	14
1908	Phi-N	.939	129	269	419	45	32	0
1909	Phi-N	.939	147	352	484	54	58	25
1910	Phi-N	.948	148	283	500	43	71	21
1911	Phi-N	.936	145	295	474	53	68	20
1912	Phi-N	.950	146	289	476	40	49	8
1913	Phi-N	.941	148	338	482	51	63	16
1914	Bal-F	.949	145	305	476	42	55	29
1915	Bal-F	.946	119	303	400	40	67	32
	Chi-F	.914	24	46	81	12	5	0
	Yr	.941	143	349	481	52	72	32
1916	Chi-N	.918	24	46	77	11	8	3
	NY-N	.975	16	31	46	2	6	2
	Yr	.939	40	77	123	13	14	5
Total	12	.940	1625	3578	5290	570	637	167

2B

1913	Phi-N	.955	3	9	12	1	0	1
1916	NY-N	.500	2	1	0	1	0	0
1918	Bro-N	.968	91	230	283	17	37	10
Total	3	.966	96	240	295	9	37	11

■ Bill Doran 2B

1982	Hou-N	.975	26	41	78	3	17	-3
1983	Hou-N	.979	153	347	461	17	109	5
1984	Hou-N	.986	139	261	419	10	83	7
1985	Hou-N	.980	147	345	440	16	108	7

YEAR	TM/L	PCT	G	PO	A	E	DP	FR
1986	Hou-N	.974	144	262	329	16	62	-41
1987	Hou-N	.992	162	300	431	6	70	-16
1988	Hou-N	.987	130	260	371	8	73	-3
1989	Hou-N	.980	138	254	345	12	64	-27
1990	Hou-N	.989	99	170	265	5	43	-11
	Cin-N	.985	12	28	37	1	6	2
	Yr	.988	111	198	302	6	49	-9
Total	9	.983	1150	2268	3176	4	635	-80

SS

1984	Hou-N	.944	13	13	21	2	7	-1
1987	Hou-N	.500	3	0	1	1	0	-1
Total	2	.921	16	13	22	3	7	-2

3B

| 1990 | Cin-N | .667 | 4 | 0 | 4 | 2 | 0 | -1 |

■ Mike Dorgan OF

1877	StL-N	.824	50	70	5	16	3	-7
1879	StL-N	.767	16	27	6	10	2	1
1880	Pro-N	.858	77	96	25	20	4	1
1881	Wor-N	.873	23	41	7	7	1	2
	Det-N	1.000	5	12	1	0	0	1
	Yr	.897	28	53	8	7	1	3
1883	NY-N	.847	59	104	7	20	1	-5
1884	NY-N	.851	64	101	13	20	3	0
1885	NY-N	.905	88	142	11	16	4	-3
1886	NY-N	.888	116	153	13	21	4	-11
1887	NY-N	.870	69	128	6	20	0	-3
1890	Syr-a	.900	33	40	5	5	1	-2
Total	10	.867	600	914	99	155	23	-26

1B

1879	Syr-N	.954	21	200	8	10	5	1
1881	Wor-N	.953	26	298	8	15	12	-1
	Det-N	1.000	1	10	0	0	0	0
	Yr	.955	27	308	8	15	12	-1
1885	NY-N	1.000	1	11	0	0	2	0
1886	NY-N	.957	3	21	1	1	1	0
1887	NY-N	1.000	2	12	0	0	1	0
Total	5	.956	54	552	17	6	21	0

C

1877	StL-N	.826	12	44	13	12	0	-2
1879	Syr-N	.806	4	24	5	7	0	0
1883	NY-N	.778	6	4	3	2	0	1
1884	NY-N	.865	6	36	9	7	0	0
Total	4	.831	28	108	30	8	0	-1

3B

1877	StL-N	.800	2	2	2	1	0	0
1879	Syr-N	.829	11	14	20	7	2	-2
1880	Pro-N	.333	2	1	1	4	0	-2
1881	Det-N	.700	2	4	3	3	0	-1
Total	4	.758	17	21	26	5	2	-5

2B

1877	StL-N	—	1	0	0	0	0	0
1879	Syr-N	.667	1	3	3	3	0	-2
1884	NY-N	.636	3	2	5	4	0	-1
Total	3	.650	10	5	8	7	0	-3

SS

1877	StL-N	1.000	1	2	1	0	0	0
1879	Syr-N	.733	6	7	15	8	1	-4
1881	Wor-N	.889	2	2	6	1	0	0
Total	3	.786	9	11	22	9	1	-4

■ Dutch Dotterer C

1957	Cin-N	1.000	4	17	0	0	0	-1
1958	Cin-N	.981	8	48	4	1	2	4
1959	Cin-N	.992	51	230	20	2	3	0
1960	Cin-N	.979	31	122	15	3	1	1
1961	Was-A	1.000	7	26	8	0	0	2
Total	5	.988	101	443	47	6	6	6

■ Patsy Dougherty OF

1902	Bos-A	.899	102	170	8	20	1	-10
1903	Bos-A	.952	139	259	16	14	3	4
1904	Bos-A	.925	49	95	4	8	3	0
	NY-A	.925	106	135	14	12	1	-8
	Yr	.925	155	230	18	20	4	-8
1905	NY-A	.898	108	173	11	21	2	-5
1906	NY-A	1.000	12	23	3	0	1	2
	Chi-A	.985	74	118	10	2	1	-1
	Yr	.987	86	141	13	2	2	1
1907	Chi-A	.946	148	209	19	13	4	-7
1908	Chi-A	.947	128	173	7	10	1	-15
1909	Chi-A	.942	138	184	10	12	0	-15
1910	Chi-A	.923	121	158	9	14	2	-13
1911	Chi-A	.933	56	78	6	6	1	-6
Total	10	.935	1181	1775	117	132	20	-74

3B

1902	Bos-A	.857	1	5	1	1	0	0
1905	NY-A	—	1	0	0	0	0	0
Total	2	.857	2	5	1	1	0	0

■ Klondike Douglass 1B

1897	StL-N	.986	17	140	6	2	5	-1
1898	Phi-N	.976	146	1236	73	32	74	2
1899	Phi-N	.966	4	25	3	1	1	1
1901	Phi-N	1.000	6	45	0	0	2	-1
1902	Phi-N	.986	69	663	33	10	27	-2
1903	Phi-N	.985	97	902	51	15	41	-1
1904	Phi-N	.970	3	31	1	1	1	0
Total	7	.981	342	3042	167	1	151	-2

C

1896	StL-N	.958	6	18	5	1	2	-1
1897	StL-N	.948	61	171	64	13	4	-13
1899	Phi-N	.970	66	179	76	8	7	-5
1900	Phi-N	.934	47	138	59	14	4	1
1901	Phi-N	.979	41	201	29	5	2	2
1902	Phi-N	.952	29	129	30	8	1	-6
Total	6	.957	250	836	263	9	20	-24

OF

| 1896 | StL-N | .894 | 74 | 105 | 13 | 14 | 3 | -5 |

YEAR	TM/L	PCT	G	PO	A	E	DP	FR
1897	StL-N	.946	43	81	7	5	1	1
1899	Phi-N	—	1	0	0	0	0	-1
1901	Phi-N	1.000	2	6	1	0	0	1
1902	Phi-N	.923	10	10	2	1	0	-1
Total	5	.918	130	202	23	0	4	-5

3B

1897	StL-N	.400	7	1	3	6	0	-4
1899	Phi-N	1.000	4	3	4	0	0	0
1900	Phi-N	—	2	0	0	0	0	0
Total	3	.647	13	4	7	6	0	-4

SS

1896	StL-N	1.000	2	0	4	0	0	0
1897	StL-N	.000	1	0	0	1	0	-1
Total	2	.800	3	0	4	1	0	-1

■ Taylor Douthit OF

1923	StL-N	1.000	7	12	1	0	0	0
1924	StL-N	.976	50	118	5	3	2	4
1925	StL-N	.981	21	50	1	1	0	2
1926	StL-N	.958	138	440	14	20	2	15
1927	StL-N	.964	125	396	8	15	4	3
1928	StL-N	.984	154	547	10	9	4	21
1929	StL-N	.974	150	442	8	12	1	-1
1930	StL-N	.964	154	425	8	16	3	6
1931	StL-N	.972	36	105	0	3	0	2
	Cin-N	.983	95	286	6	5	3	1
	Yr	.980	131	391	6	8	3	3
1932	Cin-N	.985	88	251	6	4	2	8
1933	Chi-N	.930	18	37	3	3	0	0
Total	11	.972	1036	3109	70	1	21	61

■ Tommy Dowd OF

1891	Bos-a	—	4	0	0	0	0	-2
	Was-a	.909	5	10	0	1	0	0
	Yr	.909	9	10	0	1	0	-2
1892	Was-N	.864	23	35	3	6	2	0
1893	StL-N	.944	132	225	27	15	9	4
1894	StL-N	.930	117	199	14	16	4	4
1895	StL-N	.927	115	218	11	18	3	-3
1896	StL-N	.935	48	111	4	8	2	-1
1897	StL-N	.915	30	65	0	6	0	-4
	Phi-N	.919	73	116	9	11	3	-5
	Yr	.918	103	181	9	17	3	-9
1898	StL-N	.920	129	208	11	19	3	-12
1899	Cle-N	.954	147	341	10	17	2	-2
1901	Bos-A	.937	137	288	11	20	3	1
Total	10	.933	960	1816	100	137	31	-30

2B

1891	Was-a	.885	107	230	287	67	38	-17
1892	Was-N	.891	98	208	264	58	33	-25
1893	StL-N	.000	1	0	0	1	0	-1
1894	StL-N	.907	7	20	19	4	2	-1
1895	StL-N	1.000	2	5	3	0	0	0
1896	StL-N	.920	78	182	220	35	22	-13
1897	StL-N	.818	5	9	9	4	0	-2
	Phi-N	.908	19	47	62	11	5	-1
	Yr	.894	24	56	71	15	5	-3
1898	StL-N	.895	11	23	28	6	3	-4
Total	8	.897	328	724	892	186	103	-64

3B

1892	Was-N	.808	18	24	35	14	1	-5
1894	StL-N	—	1	0	0	0	0	0
1895	StL-N	.820	17	15	26	9	0	-4
1901	Bos-A	1.000	1	1	0	0	0	0
Total	4	.815	37	40	61	3	1	-9

SS

| 1892 | Was-N | .829 | 6 | 16 | 13 | 6 | 3 | -2 |

1B

| 1901 | Bos-A | 1.000 | 2 | 13 | 1 | 0 | 0 | 0 |

■ Tom Downey SS

1909	Cin-N	.909	119	260	363	62	54	-6
1910	Cin-N	.879	68	136	192	45	18	-13
1911	Cin-N	.906	93	198	267	48	26	-13
1912	Phi-N	.846	3	10	12	4	2	1
	Chi-N	.792	5	8	11	5	0	0
	Yr	.820	8	18	23	9	2	1
1914	Buf-F	.957	16	31	35	3	3	-3
1915	Buf-F	.923	2	5	7	1	1	1
Total	6	.901	306	648	887	168	104	-33

2B

1911	Cin-N	.902	6	15	22	4	2	1
1912	Chi-N	1.000	1	0	3	0	0	0
1914	Buf-F	.962	129	265	388	26	49	12
1915	Buf-F	.930	48	124	130	19	22	-3
Total	4	.951	184	404	543	9	73	10

3B

1910	Cin-N	.911	41	65	89	15	8	6
1911	Cin-N	.929	5	3	10	1	0	0
1912	Phi-N	.893	46	57	76	16	3	-4
	Chi-N	.875	3	3	4	1	0	0
	Yr	.892	49	60	80	17	3	-4
1914	Buf-F	1.000	5	8	15	0	2	3
1915	Buf-F	.972	35	41	63	3	3	5
Total	5	.923	135	177	257	6	16	10

1B

1911	Cin-N	1.000	2	1	0	0	0	0
1915	Buf-F	.833	1	5	0	1	0	0
Total	2	.857	3	6	0	1	0	0

C

| 1909 | Cin-N | — | 1 | 0 | 0 | 0 | 0 | 0 |

OF

| 1911 | Cin-N | 1.000 | 1 | 1 | 0 | 0 | 0 | 0 |

■ Brian Downing OF

1973	Chi-A	1.000	13	19	1	0	0	1
1974	Chi-A	1.000	39	59	2	0	2	0
1977	Chi-A	1.000	3	5	0	0	0	0
1981	Cal-A	.990	56	97	1	1	0	-6

YEAR	TM/L	PCT	G	PO	A	E	DP	FR
1982	Cal-A	**1.000**	158	321	9	0	0	-4
1983	Cal-A	.994	84	160	9	1	0	-3
1984	Cal-A	**1.000**	131	272	5	0	0	-3
1985	Cal-A	.992	121	244	5	2	0	-4
1986	Cal-A	.989	138	267	5	3	0	-5
1987	Cal-A	1.000	34	47	2	0	0	-2
Total	10	.995	777	1491	39	7	2	-26
		C						
1973	Chi-A	.981	11	46	7	1	1	2
1974	Chi-A	.994	63	278	28	2	3	-4
1975	Chi-A	.990	137	730	84	8	5	3
1976	Chi-A	.988	93	450	38	6	4	-13
1977	Chi-A	.983	61	320	28	6	5	3
1978	Cal-A	.993	128	681	82	5	6	-8
1979	Cal-A	.985	129	669	35	11	5	-22
1980	Cal-A	1.000	16	69	6	0	0	-4
1981	Cal-A	.994	37	140	17	1	2	-3
Total	9	.989	675	3383	325	0	31	-46
		3B						
1973	Chi-A	.800	8	7	9	4	0	-1
■ Red Downs	**2B**							
1907	Det-A	.930	80	149	207	27	10	-25
1908	Det-A	.925	82	180	265	36	24	1
1912	Bro-N	.881	9	14	23	5	2	-1
	Chi-N	.907	16	19	30	5	6	-1
	Yr	.896	25	33	53	10	8	-2
Total	3	.924	187	362	525	3	42	-26
		OF						
1907	Det-A	.933	20	39	3	3	1	1
		SS						
1907	Det-A	—	1	0	0	0	0	0
1912	Chi-N	.927	9	12	26	3	3	2
Total	2	.927	10	12	26	3	3	2
		3B						
1907	Det-A	—	1	0	0	0	0	0
1908	Det-A	1.000	1	1	1	0	1	0
1912	Chi-N	.900	5	3	15	2	1	1
Total	3	.909	7	4	16	2	2	1
■ Tom Dowse	**C**							
1890	Cle-N	.813	3	11	2	3	0	-2
1891	Col-a	.919	51	254	52	27	6	-4
1892	Lou-N	.918	29	105	40	13	1	1
	Cin-N	1.000	1	3	0	0	0	-1
	Phi-N	.973	15	59	13	2	4	-1
	Was-N	.885	3	17	6	3	1	1
	Yr	.931	48	184	59	18	6	0
Total	3	.921	102	449	113	8	12	-6
		OF						
1890	Cle-N	.870	26	33	7	6	2	0
1891	Col-a	.667	5	4	0	2	0	-2
1892	Lou-N	1.000	3	4	1	0	0	0
	Was-N	.800	4	4	0	1	0	-1
	Yr	.900	7	8	1	1	0	-1
Total	3	.855	38	45	8	9	2	-3
		1B						
1890	Cle-N	.982	10	107	3	2	8	0
1892	Lou-N	.991	11	105	7	1	7	1
Total	2	.987	21	212	10	3	15	1
		2B						
1892	Lou-N	.833	1	4	1	1	0	0
■ Jim Doyle	**3B**							
1910	Cin-N	.875	3	5	2	1	0	-1
1911	Chi-N	.922	127	134	278	**35**	**25**	10
Total	2	.921	130	139	280	6	25	9
		OF						
1910	Cin-N	—	1	0	0	0	0	0
■ Jack Doyle	**1B**							
1892	Cle-N	.923	1	11	1	1	0	0
1893	NY-N	1.000	1	11	1	0	4	0
1894	NY-N	.965	99	981	59	**38**	51	-1
1895	NY-N	.968	58	599	34	21	27	0
1896	Bal-N	.974	118	1173	42	**32**	85	-11
1897	Bal-N	.979	114	1105	75	25	72	4
1898	Was-N	.963	38	344	17	14	23	-1
	NY-N	.982	24	212	11	4	9	1
	Yr	.970	62	556	28	18	32	0
1899	NY-N	.976	113	1110	69	29	76	6
1900	NY-N	.971	133	1269	**96**	**41**	**92**	6
1901	Chi-N	.973	75	698	60	21	32	7
1902	NY-N	.991	49	490	34	5	28	3
	Was-A	1.000	7	67	4	0	2	0
1903	Bro-N	.981	**139**	**1418**	83	29	74	2
1904	Bro-N	1.000	8	82	7	0	1	1
	Phi-N	.977	65	585	52	15	27	3
	Yr	.980	73	667	59	15	28	4
1905	NY-A	.833	1	10	0	2	0	-1
Total	14	.975	1043	10165	645	277	603	19
		C						
1889	Col-a	.897	7	26	8	4	0	-3
1890	Col-a	.887	38	177	51	29	7	-3
1891	Cle-N	.897	29	99	31	15	1	0
1892	Cle-N	.885	9	37	9	6	2	-1
	NY-N	.892	26	110	47	19	5	2
	Yr	.890	35	147	56	25	7	1
1893	NY-N	.919	48	186	62	22	7	4
1894	NY-N	.882	6	23	7	4	0	0
1895	NY-N	.846	4	20	2	4	0	-1
1898	NY-N	1.000	2	1	3	0	0	1
1899	NY-N	.958	5	19	4	1	1	0
1902	Was-A	—	2	0	0	0	0	0
Total	10	.899	176	699	224	104	23	-1
		OF						
1889	Col-a	1.000	3	3	1	0	1	0
1890	Col-a	.706	9	11	1	5	0	-2
1891	Cle-N	.827	21	39	4	9	0	-1

YEAR	TM/L	PCT	G	PO	A	E	DP	FR
1892	Cle-N	.875	12	18	3	3	1	1
	NY-N	.897	17	26	0	3	0	-3
	Yr	.887	29	44	3	6	1	-2
1893	NY-N	.938	29	55	5	4	0	-1
1898	NY-N	.860	38	39	10	8	2	-1
1902	Was-A	1.000	4	5	0	0	0	-1
Total	7	.873	133	196	24	2	4	-7
		2B						
1889	Col-a	.875	2	4	3	1	0	-1
1890	Col-a	.900	6	15	12	3	2	-1
1892	NY-N	.864	31	59	74	21	7	-7
1895	NY-N	.904	13	28	47	8	3	1
1896	Bal-N	.000	1	0	0	1	0	-1
1898	Was-N	.960	5	12	12	1	1	-1
1902	Was-A	.929	68	145	197	26	17	-11
1904	Phi-N	1.000	1	1	3	0	0	0
Total	8	.909	127	264	348	1	30	-21
		SS						
1890	Col-a	.872	25	25	84	16	5	-1
1891	Cle-N	—	1	0	0	0	0	0
1892	Cle-N	.500	1	0	2	2	0	-1
	NY-N	.918	7	27	18	4	1	1
	Yr	.887	8	27	20	6	1	0
1893	NY-N	.800	4	12	16	7	2	1
1898	NY-N	.917	15	25	41	6	3	-1
Total	5	.877	53	89	161	5	11	-1
		3B						
1890	Col-a	.889	3	3	5	1	0	0
1891	Cle-N	.848	20	40	38	14	4	0
1892	NY-N	.723	13	19	15	13	0	-6
1893	NY-N	.875	3	2	5	1	0	0
1895	NY-N	.769	6	7	13	6	1	-1
1898	NY-N	.909	5	9	11	2	0	1
Total	6	.819	50	80	87	7	5	-6
■ Larry Doyle	**2B**							
1907	NY-N	.917	69	128	158	26	7	-22
1908	NY-N	.935	102	180	291	**33**	28	-10
1909	NY-N	.940	144	**292**	323	39	**51**	-20
1910	NY-N	.930	151	313	388	**53**	62	-17
1911	NY-N	.944	141	272	340	36	46	-24
1912	NY-N	.948	143	313	379	38	68	-8
1913	NY-N	.955	130	315	345	31	55	-14
1914	NY-N	.959	145	307	379	29	61	-19
1915	NY-N	.947	147	313	396	40	**66**	-7
1916	NY-N	.960	113	270	352	26	53	16
	Chi-N	.982	9	19	35	1	10	4
	Yr	.962	122	289	387	**27**	63	20
1917	Chi-N	.952	128	300	348	33	54	-2
1918	NY-N	.969	73	121	221	11	24	-12
1919	NY-N	.956	100	214	311	24	48	2
1920	NY-N	.967	133	278	389	23	61	-26
Total	14	.949	1728	3635	4655	443	694	159
■ Denny Doyle	**2B**							
1970	Phi-N	.978	103	251	228	11	55	-16
1971	Phi-N	.967	91	241	264	17	62	4
1972	Phi-N	.982	119	265	288	10	66	-9
1973	Phi-N	.974	114	231	296	14	71	9
1974	Cal-A	.983	146	311	404	12	99	**16**
1975	Cal-A	.926	6	12	13	2	2	2
	Bos-A	.974	84	141	193	9	35	-30
	Yr	.970	90	153	206	11	37	-28
1976	Bos-A	.977	112	209	311	12	67	-25
1977	Bos-A	.979	137	230	412	14	90	-10
Total	8	.977	912	1891	2409	101	547	-59
		3B						
1975	Cal-A	—	1	0	0	0	0	0
	Bos-A	.917	6	2	9	1	0	-1
	Yr	.917	7	2	9	1	0	-1
		SS						
1974	Cal-A	1.000	2	0	1	0	0	0
1975	Bos-A	1.000	2	0	5	0	0	0
Total	2	1.000	4	0	6	0	0	0
■ Delos Drake	**OF**							
1911	Det-A	.942	83	141	4	9	1	-10
1914	StL-F	.957	116	207	16	10	2	1
1915	StL-F	.974	97	180	10	5	2	-5
Total	3	.959	296	528	30	4	5	-14
		1B						
1911	Det-A	.882	2	14	1	2	0	0
1914	StL-F	.981	18	146	5	3	12	-2
1915	StL-F	1.000	1	1	0	0	0	0
Total	3	.971	21	161	6	5	12	-2
■ Chuck Dressen	**3B**							
1925	Cin-N	.951	47	40	95	7	8	3
1926	Cin-N	.966	123	108	**284**	14	19	**18**
1927	Cin-N	**.967**	142	131	**315**	15	20	15
1928	Cin-N	.938	135	122	283	**27**	27	-2
1929	Cin-N	.932	98	77	157	17	9	-20
1930	Cin-N	1.000	10	2	5	0	2	2
1931	Cin-N	.846	4	4	7	2	1	0
1933	NY-N	.972	16	14	21	1	2	0
Total	8	.953	575	498	1167	3	86	16
		2B						
1925	Cin-N	.958	5	9	14	1	1	-1
1929	Cin-N	1.000	8	9	34	0	2	0
1930	Cin-N	1.000	3	1	2	0	0	1
Total	3	.986	16	19	50	1	3	0
		OF						
1925	Cin-N	1.000	4	5	0	0	0	0
1926	Cin-N	1.000	1	1	0	0	0	0
Total	2	1.000	5	6	0	0	0	0
		SS						
1926	Cin-N	.667	1	2	0	1	0	-1
1927	Cin-N	.556	2	1	4	4	0	-2

YEAR	TM/L	PCT	G	PO	A	E	DP	FR
Total	2	.583	3	3	4	5	0	-3
■ Dan Driessen	**1B**							
1973	Cin-N	1.000	35	97	7	0	11	0
1974	Cin-N	.985	47	118	14	2	18	2
1975	Cin-N	.986	41	268	20	4	34	-1
1976	Cin-N	.997	40	291	21	1	33	-1
1977	Cin-N	.994	148	1182	75	7	116	-3
1978	Cin-N	**.996**	151	1264	93	6	92	3
1979	Cin-N	.993	143	1289	79	9	112	-3
1980	Cin-N	.995	151	1349	67	7	115	-4
1981	Cin-N	.995	74	558	30	3	54	-5
1982	Cin-N	**.998**	144	1239	78	3	123	-7
1983	Cin-N	**.996**	112	917	71	4	73	-2
1984	Cin-N	.991	70	507	29	5	31	-4
	Mon-N	.995	45	363	23	2	38	-1
	Yr	.992	115	870	52	7	69	-5
1985	Mon-N	.997	88	804	64	3	79	3
	SF-N	.998	49	399	27	1	32	-2
	Yr	.997	137	1203	91	4	111	1
1986	SF-N	1.000	4	25	3	0	0	1
	Hou-N	1.000	12	52	3	0	5	0
	Yr	1.000	16	77	6	0	5	1
1987	StL-N	.993	21	141	10	1	13	0
Total	15	.995	1375	10863	732	8	979	-24
		3B						
1973	Cin-N	.946	87	62	150	12	19	-10
1974	Cin-N	.915	126	67	192	24	19	-22
Total	2	.929	213	129	342	6	38	-32
		OF						
1973	Cin-N	1.000	1	1	0	0	0	0
1974	Cin-N	1.000	3	1	0	0	0	0
1975	Cin-N	.976	29	41	0	1	0	-2
1976	Cin-N	.962	20	23	2	1	0	-1
Total	4	.971	53	66	2	2	0	-3
■ Lew Drill	**C**							
1902	Was-A	.919	28	89	25	10	1	-8
	Bal-A	1.000	1	2	2	0	0	0
	Was-A	.926	25	86	26	9	1	-4
	Yr	.924	54	177	53	19	2	-12
1903	Was-A	.966	47	208	47	9	5	-4
1904	Was-A	.934	29	124	32	11	5	-5
	Det-A	.950	49	195	51	13	6	-8
	Yr	.944	78	319	83	24	11	-13
1905	Det-A	.970	71	345	73	13	10	-3
Total	4	.953	250	1049	256	5	28	-32
		OF						
1902	Was-A	.857	4	5	1	1	1	0
	Was-A	.857	4	5	1	1	1	0
	Yr	.857	8	10	2	2	2	0
1904	Was-A	.857	14	11	1	2	0	-3
Total	2	.857	22	21	3	4	2	-3
		1B						
1902	Bal-A	1.000	1	14	1	0	1	0
1903	Was-A	1.000	3	18	1	0	4	0
1904	Det-A	1.000	2	14	0	0	1	0
Total	3	1.000	6	46	2	0	6	0
		2B						
1902	Was-A	.700	4	5	9	6	1	-2
	Was-A	—	1	0	0	0	0	0
	Yr	.700	5	5	9	6	1	-2
		3B						
1902	Was-A	—	1	0	0	0	0	0
■ Walt Dropo	**1B**							
1949	Bos-A	1.000	11	103	4	0	13	-1
1950	Bos-A	.988	134	1142	77	15	147	-4
1951	Bos-A	.987	93	878	63	12	91	-1
1952	Bos-A	.994	35	319	21	2	31	-1
	Det-A	.989	115	1005	78	12	104	-1
	Yr	.990	150	1324	**99**	14	135	**-2**
1953	Det-A	.990	150	1260	127	14	121	12
1954	Det-A	.996	95	681	54	3	60	1
1955	Chi-A	.995	140	1101	62	6	95	-3
1956	Chi-A	**.993**	117	855	50	6	95	-3
1957	Chi-A	.987	69	483	39	7	49	2
1958	Chi-A	1.000	16	98	8	0	8	1
	Cin-N	1.000	43	300	27	0	31	1
1959	Cin-N	1.000	23	103	11	0	11	2
	Bal-A	.990	54	386	18	4	42	-2
1960	Bal-A	.993	67	397	27	3	50	-1
1961	Bal-A	1.000	12	62	6	0	11	1
Total	13	.992	1174	9173	672	4	968	1
		3B						
1959	Bal-A	1.000	2	0	2	0	1	1
1960	Bal-A	—	1	0	0	0	0	0
Total	2	1.000	3	0	2	0	1	1
■ Rob Ducey	**OF**							
1987	Tor-A	1.000	28	31	0	0	0	1
1988	Tor-A	1.000	26	35	1	0	0	0
1989	Tor-A	1.000	35	56	3	0	2	4
1990	Tor-A	1.000	19	37	0	0	0	-1
Total	4	1.000	108	159	4	0	2	4
■ Charlie Duffee	**OF**							
1889	StL-a	.936	132	296	**43**	23	7	**19**
1890	StL-a	.951	66	120	17	7	8	9
1891	Col-a	.927	128	235	**33**	21	7	11
1892	Was-N	.913	125	230	34	25	**8**	18
1893	Cin-N	.400	4	2	0	3	0	-2
Total	5	.927	455	883	127	9	30	55
		3B						
1889	StL-a	.680	5	5	12	8	0	-1
1890	StL-a	.880	33	41	62	14	2	1
1891	Col-a	.879	7	13	16	4	3	1
1892	Was-N	.889	6	7	9	2	1	1
Total	4	.855	51	66	99	8	6	2

YEAR	TM/L	PCT	G	PO	A	E	DP	FR
1B								
1892	Was-N	.936	4	41	3	3	2	0
SS								
1890	StL-a	1.000	1	2	0	0	0	0
1891	Col-a	1.000	2	2	4	0	0	-1
Total	2	1.000	3	4	4	0	0	-1
2B								
1889	StL-a	1.000	2	6	1	0	1	0
■ Frank Duffy SS								
1970	Cin-N	1.000	5	4	12	0	4	1
1971	Cin-N	.944	10	10	24	2	5	5
	SF-N	.968	6	13	17	1	5	4
	Yr	.955	16	23	41	3	10	9
1972	Cle-A	.977	126	197	360	13	75	3
1973	Cle-A	**.986**	115	198	377	8	82	12
1974	Cle-A	.980	**158**	242	491	15	83	-8
1975	Cle-A	.977	145	225	464	16	85	14
1976	Cle-A	**.983**	132	222	344	10	83	11
1977	Cle-A	.967	121	145	301	15	62	3
1978	Bos-A	.929	21	36	55	7	13	-1
Total	9	.977	839	1292	2445	7	497	44
3B								
1971	SF-N	1.000	1	0	1	0	0	0
1978	Bos-A	.960	22	10	14	1	1	2
Total	2	.962	23	10	15	1	1	2
2B								
1971	SF-N	1.000	1	1	1	0	0	0
1978	Bos-A	1.000	12	17	29	0	5	6
1979	Bos-A	1.000	3	3	2	0	0	1
Total	3	1.000	16	21	32	0	5	7
1B								
1979	Bos-A	—	1	0	0	0	0	0
■ Hugh Duffy OF								
1888	Chi-N	.910	67	103	19	12	5	6
1889	Chi-N	.894	126	184	19	24	2	-9
1890	Chi-P	.917	137	255	34	26	5	13
1891	Bos-a	.917	124	166	23	17	3	0
1892	Bos-N	.942	146	259	17	17	4	-8
1893	Bos-N	.953	131	313	15	16	6	-2
1894	Bos-N	.927	124	315	27	27	5	5
1895	Bos-N	.945	130	322	20	20	7	6
1896	Bos-N	.957	120	250	15	12	2	0
1897	Bos-N	.975	129	266	12	7	2	1
1898	Bos-N	.956	152	332	18	16	2	3
1899	Bos-N	.970	147	344	9	11	1	-4
1900	Bos-N	.957	49	107	5	5	2	-1
1901	Mil-A	.967	77	141	5	5	0	-6
1904	Phi-N	.850	14	16	1	3	0	-3
1905	Phi-N	.909	8	19	1	2	0	1
Total	16	.943	1681	3392	240	220	46	2
SS								
1888	Chi-N	.769	3	1	9	3	0	-1
1889	Chi-N	.789	10	3	27	8	2	-7
1891	Bos-a	—	1	0	0	0	0	0
1894	Bos-N	.714	2	4	6	4	0	-1
1896	Bos-N	.929	2	2	11	1	2	1
1897	Bos-N	1.000	2	2	4	0	1	1
Total	6	.812	20	12	57	6	5	-7
2B								
1896	Bos-N	.894	9	15	27	5	1	0
1897	Bos-N	.950	6	9	10	1	0	-2
1900	Bos-N	1.000	1	2	2	0	0	0
Total	3	.915	16	26	39	6	1	-2
3B								
1888	Chi-N	.714	1	3	2	2	0	0
1891	Bos-a	1.000	3	10	5	0	0	1
1892	Bos-N	.400	2	0	2	3	0	-1
1898	Bos-N	—	1	0	0	0	0	0
Total	4	.815	7	13	9	5	0	0
1B								
1898	Bos-N	1.000	1	2	0	0	0	0
C								
1898	Bos-N	—	1	0	0	0	0	0
■ Joe Dugan 3B								
1919	Phi-A	.889	2	5	3	1	0	-1
1920	Phi-A	.948	60	76	126	11	13	-4
1921	Phi-A	.953	119	118	208	16	19	-25
1922	Bos-A	.943	64	72	143	13	13	-3
	NY-A	.967	60	59	117	6	10	-9
	Yr	**.954**	124	131	260	19	23	-12
1923	NY-A	.974	146	155	300	12	28	-12
1924	NY-A	.962	**148**	177	250	17	22	-13
1925	NY-A	.970	96	118	202	10	19	**7**
1926	NY-A	.955	122	122	221	16	10	-16
1927	NY-A	.938	111	93	196	19	15	-19
1928	NY-A	.952	91	87	129	11	13	-18
1929	Bos-N	.918	24	13	32	4	3	-6
1931	Det-A	.900	5	4	5	1	0	-1
Total	12	.957	1048	1099	1932	137	165	120
SS								
1917	Phi-A	.917	39	58	108	15	12	1
1918	Phi-A	.930	86	212	282	37	46	10
1919	Phi-A	.929	98	228	295	40	39	1
1920	Phi-A	.918	32	79	99	16	13	0
1922	Bos-A	.938	21	45	46	6	11	-6
1929	Bos-A	.813	5	5	8	3	0	-2
Total	6	.926	281	627	838	117	121	4
2B								
1917	Phi-A	.857	2	3	3	1	1	-1
1918	Phi-A	.950	34	92	115	11	23	7
1919	Phi-A	.950	4	10	9	1	4	0
1920	Phi-A	.956	31	70	103	8	22	3
1924	NY-A	.857	2	2	4	1	0	-1
1928	NY-A	—	1	0	0	0	0	0

YEAR	TM/L	PCT	G	PO	A	E	DP	FR
1929	Bos-N	1.000	2	3	3	0	2	0
Total	7	.950	76	180	237	2	52	8
OF								
1929	Bos-N	—	2	0	0	0	0	0
■ Dave Duncan C								
1964	KC-A	.981	22	99	7	2	6	4
1967	KC-A	.979	32	176	13	4	2	-6
1968	Oak-A	.987	79	474	41	7	5	1
1969	Oak-A	.982	56	209	15	4	1	-11
1970	Oak-A	.978	73	373	28	9	9	3
1971	Oak-A	.984	102	678	41	**12**	3	3
1972	Oak-A	.993	113	661	43	5	9	2
1973	Cle-A	.988	86	533	41	7	8	1
1974	Cle-A	.976	134	557	47	15	7	-9
1975	Bal-A	.982	95	397	41	8	5	-8
1976	Bal-A	.985	93	371	35	6	9	-12
Total	11	.984	885	4528	352	9	64	-32
1B								
1974	Cle-A	1.000	3	7	1	0	3	0
■ Pat Duncan OF								
1915	Pit-N	1.000	1	1	0	0	0	0
1919	Cin-N	.982	27	51	3	1	1	0
1920	Cin-N	.964	**154**	334	15	13	4	3
1921	Cin-N	.971	145	349	19	11	2	10
1922	Cin-N	.971	151	316	19	10	4	0
1923	Cin-N	**.993**	146	291	11	2	2	-4
1924	Cin-N	.927	83	124	3	10	0	-16
Total	7	.970	707	1466	70	7	13	-7
■ Mariano Duncan SS								
1985	LA-N	.954	123	174	386	27	57	-2
1986	LA-N	.951	106	172	317	25	46	-2
1987	LA-N	.930	67	90	191	**21**	37	-2
1989	LA-N	.943	16	19	31	3	8	2
	Cin-N	.955	44	65	103	8	17	-7
	Yr	.952	60	84	134	11	25	-5
1990	Cin-N	.914	12	16	16	3	4	0
Total	5	.948	368	536	1044	7	169	-11
2B								
1985	LA-N	.969	19	50	44	3	7	-6
1987	LA-N	1.000	7	11	22	0	3	2
1989	LA-N	.917	8	9	13	2	3	0
	Cin-N	1.000	5	4	8	0	2	0
	Yr	.944	13	13	21	2	5	0
1990	Cin-N	.973	115	245	287	15	51	0
Total	4	.972	154	319	374	0	66	-4
OF								
1987	LA-N	—	2	0	0	0	0	0
1989	LA-N	.800	7	4	0	1	0	0
1990	Cin-N	1.000	1	4	0	0	0	0
Total	3	.889	10	8	0	1	0	0
■ Vern Duncan OF								
1913	Phi-N	1.000	3	2	1	0	0	0
1914	Bal-F	.914	148	255	20	**26**	**8**	-3
1915	Bal-F	.965	124	257	19	10	6	6
Total	3	.939	275	514	40	6	14	3
3B								
1914	Bal-F	.958	8	11	12	1	0	0
1915	Bal-F	.757	21	26	27	17	6	-6
Total	2	.809	29	37	39	8	6	-6
2B								
1914	Bal-F	—	1	0	0	0	0	0
1915	Bal-F	1.000	1	2	5	0	0	0
Total	2	1.000	2	2	5	0	0	0
■ Gus Dundon 2B								
1904	Chi-A	**.973**	103	186	282	13	25	-13
1905	Chi-A	.983	100	211	303	9	22	10
1906	Chi-A	.921	18	53	52	9	5	3
Total	3	.972	221	450	637	1	52	0
SS								
1904	Chi-A	1.000	2	4	6	0	1	1
1905	Chi-A	.925	6	12	25	3	3	3
1906	Chi-A	.931	14	28	39	5	3	4
Total	3	.934	22	44	70	8	7	8
3B								
1904	Chi-A	1.000	3	4	1	0	0	-2
■ Sam Dungan OF								
1892	Chi-N	.905	113	183	8	20	2	-6
1893	Chi-N	.920	107	175	20	17	3	4
1894	Chi-N	1.000	10	15	2	0	1	0
	Lou-N	.941	8	15	1	1	1	0
	Yr	.971	18	30	3	1	2	0
1900	Chi-N	.800	3	4	0	1	0	-1
1901	Was-N	.947	104	145	15	9	4	-3
Total	5	.924	345	537	46	8	11	-6
1B								
1901	Was-N	.981	35	349	11	7	15	-2
■ Fred Dunlap 2B								
1880	Cle-N	.911	85	252	**290**	53	**44**	8
1881	Cle-N	.909	79	258	254	51	41	7
1882	Cle-N	.900	**84**	268	**297**	63	**62**	18
1883	Cle-N	.911	93	**304**	290	58	49	9
1884	StL-U	**.926**	100	**341**	**300**	51	**54**	29
1885	StL-N	**.934**	106	314	374	49	53	25
1886	StL-N	.931	71	215	231	33	42	22
	Det-N	.918	51	118	162	25	22	3
	Yr	.926	122	333	393	58	64	25
1887	Det-N	.948	65	212	225	24	44	12
1888	Pit-N	.940	82	240	279	33	44	12
1889	Pit-N	**.950**	121	342	393	39	51	1
1890	Pit-N	.874	17	36	54	13	4	-3
	NY-P	1.000	1	1	1	0	0	-1
1891	Was-a	.818	7	14	8	19	6	-3
Total	12	.924	963	2909	3169	498	513	149

YEAR	TM/L	PCT	G	PO	A	E	DP	FR
OF								
1883	Cle-N	1.000	1	1	0	0	0	0
1884	StL-U	1.000	1	2	2	0	0	2
1886	Det-N	—	1	0	0	0	0	0
Total	3	1.000	3	3	2	0	0	2
3B								
1881	Cle-N	.500	1	0	1	1	0	-1
■ Jack Dunleavy OF								
1903	StL-N	.972	38	58	11	2	5	6
1904	StL-N	.987	44	68	6	1	2	0
1905	StL-N	.962	118	177	25	8	7	2
Total	3	.969	200	303	42	1	14	8
2B								
1905	StL-N	1.000	1	0	3	0	0	0
■ Jack Dunn 3B								
1897	Bro-N	.800	3	2	6	2	1	0
1898	Bro-N	.714	2	1	4	2	1	-1
1901	Bal-A	.872	67	98	133	34	6	-6
1902	NY-N	.915	18	27	27	5	2	-3
1903	NY-N	.935	25	25	47	5	1	-1
1904	NY-N	.914	28	25	49	7	7	-1
Total	6	.890	143	178	266	5	18	-12
SS								
1897	Bro-N	.700	1	3	4	3	0	0
1898	Bro-N	.867	4	11	15	4	1	0
1899	Bro-N	—	1	0	0	0	0	0
1901	Bal-A	.857	19	52	50	17	7	-3
1902	NY-N	.924	36	74	109	15	13	-3
1903	NY-N	.907	27	47	80	13	18	-2
1904	NY-N	.918	10	21	24	4	0	-2
Total	7	.897	98	208	282	6	39	-10
OF								
1897	Bro-N	1.000	3	2	0	0	0	-1
1898	Bro-N	1.000	4	8	2	0	2	2
1901	Bal-A	1.000	1	1	0	0	0	0
1902	NY-N	.962	43	47	4	2	2	-4
1903	NY-N	1.000	1	1	0	0	0	0
1904	NY-N	1.000	7	6	0	0	0	-2
Total	6	.973	59	65	6	2	4	-5
2B								
1897	Bro-N	.889	4	7	9	2	0	-1
1901	Bal-A	1.000	1	2	3	0	0	0
1902	NY-N	1.000	2	2	4	0	0	0
1903	NY-N	.902	19	28	46	8	5	-3
1904	NY-N	.852	9	7	16	4	0	-3
Total	5	.899	35	46	78	4	5	-7
■ Shawon Dunston SS								
1985	Chi-N	.958	73	144	248	17	39	13
1986	Chi-N	.961	149	**320**	**465**	**32**	**96**	20
1987	Chi-N	.969	94	160	271	14	54	5
1988	Chi-N	.973	151	**257**	455	20	76	6
1989	Chi-N	.972	138	213	379	17	76	7
1990	Chi-N	.970	144	255	392	20	77	6
Total	6	.967	749	1349	2210	120	418	57
■ Leon Durham 1B								
1980	StL-N	.981	8	44	8	1	6	2
1981	Chi-N	1.000	3	16	0	0	1	0
1982	Chi-N	1.000	1	10	1	0	0	0
1983	Chi-N	1.000	6	35	2	0	2	0
1984	Chi-N	.994	130	1162	96	7	96	6
1985	Chi-N	.995	151	1421	107	7	121	2
1986	Chi-N	.995	141	1231	80	7	101	-7
1987	Chi-N	.990	123	1049	57	11	90	-9
1988	Chi-N	.995	20	167	15	1	16	1
	Chi-N	.993	17	129	6	1	8	-1
	Yr	.994	37	296	21	2	24	0
1989	StL-N	.961	18	44	5	2	7	1
Total	10	.994	618	5308	377	7	448	-5
OF								
1980	StL-N	.987	78	136	14	2	2	2
1981	Chi-N	.970	83	159	4	5	1	-3
1982	Chi-N	.963	143	301	11	12	1	-9
1983	Chi-N	.966	95	168	2	6	0	-6
Total	4	.970	399	764	31	5	4	-16
■ Leo Durocher SS								
1928	NY-A	.940	29	46	96	9	11	3
1929	NY-A	.958	93	197	299	22	59	**25**
1930	Cin-N	.959	103	216	350	24	77	9
1931	Cin-N	.965	120	212	344	20	86	-4
1932	Cin-N	.960	142	283	429	30	76	-14
1933	Cin-N	.953	16	37	64	5	10	6
	StL-N	.961	123	238	358	24	64	-1
	Yr	.960	139	275	422	29	74	5
1934	StL-N	.957	146	320	407	33	86	1
1935	StL-N	.963	142	313	420	28	81	9
1936	StL-N	**.971**	136	300	392	21	80	-11
1937	StL-N	.959	134	279	381	28	72	-11
1938	Bro-N	**.966**	141	287	399	24	90	-5
1939	Bro-N	.957	113	228	322	25	73	-7
1940	Bro-N	.959	53	102	131	10	22	1
1941	Bro-N	.917	12	16	28	4	3	0
1943	Bro-N	1.000	6	23	11	0	5	2
Total	15	.961	1509	3097	4431	307	895	3
2B								
1928	NY-A	.948	66	112	178	16	31	9
1929	NY-A	.984	12	32	28	1	7	2
1930	Cin-N	1.000	13	24	30	0	5	1
1940	Bro-N	.929	4	6	7	1	2	0
1941	Bro-N	1.000	1	1	0	0	0	0
1945	Bro-N	1.000	2	3	4	0	1	0
Total	6	.959	98	178	247	8	46	13
3B								
1939	Bro-N	1.000	1	0	2	0	0	0

YEAR	TM/L	PCT	G	PO	A	E	DP	FR
■ Cedric Durst	**OF**							
1922	StL-A	.857	6	6	0	1	0	-2
1923	StL-A	1.000	10	22	0	0	0	-1
1926	StL-A	.980	57	143	5	3	0	1
1927	NY-A	.980	36	47	1	1	0	-7
1928	NY-A	.983	33	55	2	1	1	-3
1929	NY-A	.987	72	151	5	2	1	0
1930	NY-A	1.000	6	11	0	0	0	0
	Bos-A	.968	75	145	4	5	1	-2
	Yr	.970	81	156	4	5	1	-2
Total	7	.979	295	580	17	3	3	-14
	1B							
1923	StL-A	.955	8	62	2	3	6	-2
1926	StL-A	.964	4	24	3	1	0	0
1927	NY-A	1.000	2	1	1	0	0	0
1928	NY-A	1.000	3	20	2	0	0	0
1929	NY-A	1.000	1	2	0	0	0	0
Total	5	.967	18	109	8	4	6	-2
■ Erv Dusak	**OF**							
1941	StL-N	1.000	4	16	0	0	0	2
1942	StL-N	1.000	8	14	0	0	0	0
1946	StL-N	.993	77	139	12	1	1	5
1947	StL-N	.970	89	178	13	6	2	2
1948	StL-N	.992	68	128	3	1	2	1
1950	StL-N	1.000	2	5	0	0	0	1
1951	Pit-N	1.000	12	11	0	0	0	-2
1952	Pit-N	.818	11	7	2	2	1	0
Total	8	.981	271	498	30	0	6	9
	2B							
1946	StL-N	1.000	2	1	1	0	1	0
1948	StL-N	.975	29	56	63	3	11	2
1951	Pit-N	.750	2	2	1	1	1	-1
Total	3	.969	33	59	65	4	13	1
	3B							
1942	StL-N	1.000	1	0	5	0	1	1
1946	StL-N	.962	11	6	19	1	3	2
1947	StL-N	1.000	7	3	11	0	1	1
1948	StL-N	.947	9	6	12	1	0	0
1951	Pit-N	—	2	0	0	0	0	0
Total	5	.969	30	15	47	2	5	4
	SS							
1948	StL-N	1.000	1	1	2	0	0	0
■ Jim Dwyer	**OF**							
1973	StL-N	1.000	20	32	0	0	0	1
1974	StL-N	1.000	25	27	1	0	0	0
1975	StL-N	1.000	9	18	0	0	0	1
	Mon-N	.959	52	86	8	4	1	-1
	Yr	.966	61	104	8	4	1	0
1976	Mon-N	.970	19	32	0	1	0	-3
	NY-N	1.000	2	3	0	0	0	0
	Yr	.972	21	35	0	1	0	-3
1977	StL-N	1.000	12	16	0	0	0	-1
1978	StL-N	.952	22	19	1	1	0	-3
	SF-N	.987	36	68	6	1	1	3
	Yr	.979	58	87	7	2	1	0
1979	Bos-A	.964	19	26	1	1	0	0
1980	Bos-A	.975	65	111	7	3	2	-2
1981	Bal-A	.977	59	84	2	2	0	0
1982	Bal-A	.976	49	81	0	2	0	-3
1983	Bal-A	.966	56	85	1	3	1	4
1984	Bal-A	.966	52	83	3	3	1	-2
1985	Bal-A	.993	78	131	4	1	0	-1
1986	Bal-A	1.000	24	33	3	0	1	2
1987	Bal-A	1.000	30	57	1	0	0	-1
1988	Bal-A	1.000	2	3	0	0	0	0
1989	Min-A	—	1	0	0	0	0	0
1990	Min-A	1.000	2	2	0	0	0	0
Total	18	.979	634	997	38	2	7	-6
	1B							
1974	StL-N	1.000	3	4	2	0	2	1
1978	SF-N	.993	29	129	8	1	13	0
1979	Bos-A	.981	25	141	15	3	15	2
1980	Bos-A	.976	9	32	8	1	7	2
1981	Bal-A	1.000	3	13	0	0	2	0
1982	Bal-A	1.000	1	6	0	0	0	0
1983	Bal-A	.975	4	38	1	1	3	0
1986	Bal-A	1.000	1	0	1	0	0	0
Total	8	.985	75	363	35	6	42	5
■ Jerry Dybzinski	**SS**							
1980	Cle-A	.971	73	107	198	9	37	16
1981	Cle-A	.970	34	33	64	3	10	8
1982	Cle-A	.957	77	118	239	16	39	17
1983	Cle-A	.966	118	140	252	14	47	1
1984	Chi-A	.974	76	68	154	6	32	20
1985	Pit-N	.900	5	4	5	1	0	1
Total	6	.966	383	470	912	9	165	63
	2B							
1980	Cle-A	.961	29	35	63	4	8	4
1981	Cle-A	.800	3	0	4	1	0	0
1984	Chi-A	—	1	0	0	0	0	0
Total	3	.953	33	35	67	5	8	4
	3B							
1980	Cle-A	1.000	4	4	2	0	2	1
1981	Cle-A	.800	3	2	2	1	1	0
1982	Cle-A	.875	3	2	5	1	1	0
1983	Cle-A	1.000	9	1	6	0	0	1
1984	Chi-A	.875	14	1	6	1	0	0
Total	5	.912	33	10	21	3	4	2
■ Jim Dyck	**OF**							
1952	StL-A	.984	48	118	2	2	0	2
1953	StL-A	.981	55	100	5	2	1	3
1955	Bal-A	.989	45	86	4	1	1	2
1956	Bal-A	.923	9	10	2	1	0	0
Total	4	.982	157	314	13	6	2	7

YEAR	TM/L	PCT	G	PO	A	E	DP	FR
	3B							
1951	StL-A	1.000	4	7	6	0	1	0
1952	StL-A	.962	74	79	152	9	14	7
1953	StL-A	.926	51	62	101	13	12	-2
1955	Bal-A	.927	17	18	33	4	1	-1
1956	Cin-N	1.000	1	0	1	0	0	0
Total	5	.946	147	166	293	6	28	4
	1B							
1956	Cin-N	1.000	1	4	0	0	0	0
■ Duffy Dyer	**C**							
1968	NY-N	1.000	1	8	0	0	0	0
1969	NY-N	.991	19	105	10	1	0	-1
1970	NY-N	.991	57	294	20	3	6	1
1971	NY-N	.992	53	336	21	3	3	0
1972	NY-N	.993	91	690	61	5	**12**	**17**
1973	NY-N	.994	60	308	26	2	7	-1
1974	NY-N	.982	45	196	19	4	4	-4
1975	Pit-N	.990	36	187	14	2	0	6
1976	Pit-N	.994	58	279	37	2	4	7
1977	Pit-N	**.996**	93	502	41	2	10	4
1978	Pit-N	.991	55	326	22	3	3	5
1979	Mon-N	.992	27	141	10	1	1	6
1980	Det-A	.986	37	129	10	2	2	3
1981	Det-A	—	2	0	0	0	0	0
Total	14	.992	634	3501	291	0	52	43
	OF							
1972	NY-N	.000	1	0	0	1	0	0
■ Jimmy Dykes	**3B**							
1918	Phi-A	1.000	1	0	1	0	0	0
1920	Phi-A	.902	34	49	80	14	15	2
1922	Phi-A	.945	**141**	**186**	**295**	**28**	21	-7
1923	Phi-A	1.000	2	2	3	0	0	0
1924	Phi-A	.933	27	32	65	7	5	3
1925	Phi-A	.944	64	93	127	13	8	1
1926	Phi-A	.950	82	95	188	15	16	13
1927	Phi-A	.951	25	25	52	4	4	1
1928	Phi-A	.981	20	21	30	1	4	1
1929	Phi-A	.927	48	60	79	11	9	-1
1930	Phi-A	.960	123	124	191	13	18	-12
1931	Phi-A	.974	87	105	153	7	19	3
1932	Phi-A	**.980**	141	142	251	8	20	-4
1933	Chi-A	.953	151	132	**296**	21	22	-1
1934	Chi-A	.944	74	74	160	14	9	3
1935	Chi-A	.953	98	100	166	13	12	-5
1936	Chi-A	.951	125	108	240	18	14	-6
1937	Chi-A	1.000	11	11	22	0	3	1
1938	Chi-A	1.000	1	0	4	0	0	1
1939	Chi-A	.667	2	2	0	1	0	0
Total	20	.952	1257	1361	2403	188	199	-7
	2B							
1918	Phi-A	.940	56	139	189	21	33	10
1919	Phi-A	.945	16	28	58	5	5	6
1920	Phi-A	.957	108	304	378	31	38	15
1921	Phi-A	.954	**155**	**434**	**522**	**46**	88	25
1922	Phi-A	.905	5	7	12	2	0	-1
1923	Phi-A	.964	102	245	315	21	55	5
1924	Phi-A	.961	77	217	253	19	46	**15**
1925	Phi-A	.975	58	132	175	8	37	9
1926	Phi-A	.979	44	100	136	5	26	14
1927	Phi-A	.882	3	7	8	2	0	-1
1928	Phi-A	.982	32	76	92	3	15	3
1929	Phi-A	.985	12	24	43	1	4	4
1932	Phi-A	.833	1	3	2	1	0	-1
1934	Chi-A	.948	27	65	81	8	13	-6
1935	Chi-A	.955	3	10	11	1	2	0
1938	Chi-A	.941	23	75	68	9	13	1
Total	16	.958	722	1866	2343	183	376	99
	1B							
1927	Phi-A	.989	82	814	49	10	59	-2
1928	Phi-A	.977	8	38	4	1	0	0
1934	Chi-A	.981	27	244	11	5	18	-2
1935	Chi-A	.995	16	180	8	1	15	0
1937	Chi-A	.993	15	141	5	1	12	-1
Total	5	.988	148	1417	77	8	104	-5
	SS							
1923	Phi-A	.956	20	38	48	4	9	-1
1924	Phi-A	.952	4	12	8	1	0	-2
1925	Phi-A	—	2	0	0	0	0	0
1926	Phi-A	1.000	1	1	0	0	1	0
1927	Phi-A	1.000	5	3	3	0	0	0
1928	Phi-A	.949	22	33	42	4	2	-6
1929	Phi-A	.928	60	119	151	21	27	-14
1931	Phi-A	.892	15	31	35	8	8	-5
1932	Phi-A	.951	10	10	29	2	5	-1
1938	Chi-A	—	1	0	0	0	0	0
Total	10	.934	140	247	316	0	52	-29
	OF							
1927	Phi-A	1.000	5	9	0	0	0	-1
1928	Phi-A	—	1	0	0	0	0	0
1930	Phi-A	1.000	1	1	0	0	0	0
Total	3	1.000	7	10	0	0	0	-1
■ Lenny Dykstra	**OF**							
1985	NY-N	.994	74	165	6	1	2	10
1986	NY-N	.990	139	283	8	3	2	-2
1987	NY-N	.988	118	239	4	3	1	-5
1988	NY-N	.996	112	270	3	1	0	2
1989	NY-N	.984	51	124	1	2	0	5
	Phi-N	.991	88	208	9	2	0	3
	Yr	.988	139	**332**	10	4	0	8
1990	Phi-N	.987	149	439	7	6	5	11
Total	6	.990	731	1728	38	8	10	24
■ Bill Eagan	**2B**							
1891	StL-A	.929	83	177	278	35	29	20
1893	Chi-N	.912	6	12	19	3	4	0
1898	Pit-N	.914	17	46	60	10	10	3

YEAR	TM/L	PCT	G	PO	A	E	DP	FR
Total	3	.925	106	235	357	8	43	23
■ Billy Earle	**C**							
1889	Cin-a	.872	23	119	24	21	3	-1
1890	Cin-a	.955	18	119	29	7	1	6
1892	Pit-N	.909	5	15	5	2	0	-1
1893	Pit-N	.959	27	99	19	5	2	1
1894	Lou-N	.954	18	52	31	4	1	4
	Bro-N	.930	12	36	17	4	0	-1
	Yr	.944	30	88	48	8	1	3
Total	5	.929	103	440	125	3	7	8
	OF							
1889	Cin-a	.776	26	38	7	13	2	0
1890	StL-a	.667	3	2	0	1	0	-1
1894	Lou-N	.000	1	0	0	1	0	-1
Total	3	.758	30	40	7	5	2	-2
	1B							
1889	Cin-a	.958	5	43	3	2	1	0
1894	Lou-N	1.000	1	6	0	0	0	0
Total	2	.963	6	49	3	2	1	0
	2B							
1890	StL-a	1.000	1	1	2	0	0	0
1894	Lou-N	—	1	0	0	0	0	0
	Bro-N	.600	1	0	3	2	0	-1
	Yr	.600	2	0	3	2	0	-1
Total	2	.750	3	1	5	2	0	-1
	3B							
1890	StL-a	.000	1	0	0	1	0	0
1894	Lou-N	1.000	1	0	1	0	0	0
Total	2	.500	2	0	1	1	0	0
	SS							
1890	StL-a	1.000	1	2	2	0	0	0
■ Jake Early	**C**							
1939	Was-A	.963	24	95	9	4	1	-1
1940	Was-A	.969	56	276	41	10	5	6
1941	Was-A	.965	100	385	52	**16**	**13**	-9
1942	Was-A	.981	**98**	392	**71**	9	**11**	-2
1943	Was-A	.980	**122**	443	83	**11**	10	-7
1946	Was-A	.960	64	246	45	12	7	4
1947	StL-A	.989	85	301	43	4	5	-3
1948	Was-A	.991	92	268	51	3	7	3
1949	Was-A	.973	53	160	22	5	6	-3
Total	9	.976	694	2566	417	4	65	-12
■ Mike Easler	**OF**							
1973	Hou-N	.500	2	1	0	1	0	-1
1977	Pit-N	1.000	4	7	0	0	0	0
1979	Pit-N	—	4	0	0	0	0	0
1980	Pit-N	.986	119	201	6	3	1	-8
1981	Pit-N	.980	90	188	13	4	2	6
1982	Pit-N	.973	138	243	8	7	2	-3
1983	Pit-N	.965	105	158	6	6	1	-7
1985	Bos-A	.914	20	32	0	3	0	-3
1986	NY-A	.958	11	23	0	1	0	-1
1987	Phi-N	.981	30	49	4	1	2	1
	NY-A	1.000	15	24	1	0	0	0
Total	10	.974	538	926	38	6	8	-16
	1B							
1984	Bos-A	.976	29	256	29	7	21	2
■ Luke Easter	**1B**							
1950	Cle-A	.991	128	1100	82	11	114	0
1951	Cle-A	.988	125	1043	68	14	108	-7
1952	Cle-A	.983	118	940	90	18	87	4
1953	Cle-A	.981	56	442	30	9	54	-2
Total	4	.986	427	3525	270	2	363	-5
	OF							
1949	Cle-A	1.000	12	9	0	0	0	-4
1950	Cle-A	1.000	13	14	0	0	0	0
Total	2	1.000	25	23	0	0	0	-4
■ Henry Easterday	**SS**							
1884	Phi-U	.875	28	35	98	19	6	6
1888	KC-a	**.888**	115	120	459	73	30	**26**
1889	Col-a	.890	89	134	326	57	27	12
1890	Col-a	.879	58	82	202	39	20	6
	Phi-a	.860	19	33	59	15	7	-2
	Lou-a	.886	6	7	24	4	1	1
	Yr	.875	83	122	285	58	28	5
Total	4	.884	315	411	1168	207	91	49
	2B							
1889	Col-a	.870	5	6	14	3	3	0
	3B							
1889	Col-a	—	1	0	0	0	0	0
1890	Lou-a	.500	1	0	2	2	0	-1
Total	2	.500	2	0	2	2	0	-1
■ Ted Easterly	**C**							
1909	Cle-A	.965	76	335	110	16	9	0
1910	Cle-A	.953	66	200	104	15	7	-27
1911	Cle-A	.940	22	101	25	8	0	-8
1912	Cle-A	.958	51	226	69	13	11	-4
	Chi-A	.964	10	40	13	2	3	-4
	Yr	.959	61	266	82	15	14	-8
1913	Chi-A	.976	19	96	24	3	0	2
1914	KC-F	.969	128	570	173	**24**	16	-18
1915	KC-F	.969	88	398	132	17	11	4
Total	7	.964	460	1966	650	8	57	-55
	OF							
1910	Cle-A	1.000	30	39	5	0	1	0
1911	Cle-A	.910	54	64	7	7	3	-4
1912	Chi-A	—	1	0	0	0	0	0
Total	3	.943	85	103	12	7	4	-4
■ Charlie Eden	**OF**							
1877	Chi-N	.679	15	17	2	9	1	-2
1879	Cle-N	.808	80	101	21	29	3	-5
1884	Pit-a	.759	31	40	4	14	0	-4
1885	Pit-a	.814	96	111	7	27	2	-14
Total	4	.793	222	269	34	9	6	-25

YEAR	TM/L	PCT	G	PO	A	E	DP	FR
		1B						
1879	Cle-N	.813	3	12	1	3	0	0
		3B						
1885	Pit-a	.625	2	2	3	3	0	-1
		C						
1879	Cle-N	1.000	1	1	0	0	0	0

■ Bruce Edwards C

YEAR	TM/L	PCT	G	PO	A	E	DP	FR
1946	Bro-N	.982	91	431	53	9	9	6
1947	Bro-N	.983	128	**592**	58	11	**11**	6
1948	Bro-N	.984	48	223	21	4	1	-3
1949	Bro-N	.990	41	184	13	2	0	-2
1950	Bro-N	.980	38	176	19	4	3	-3
1951	Bro-N	1.000	9	37	3	0	0	0
	Chi-N	.962	28	113	14	5	4	-3
	Yr	.971	37	150	17	5	4	-3
1952	Chi-N	.989	22	82	8	1	2	-2
1955	Was-A	.980	22	88	11	2	2	5
1956	Cin-N	.000	2	0	0	1	0	0
Total	9	.982	429	1926	200	9	32	4
		OF						
1948	Bro-N	.892	21	31	2	4	1	-1
1949	Bro-N	.857	4	6	0	1	0	0
Total	2	.886	25	37	2	5	1	-1
		3B						
1948	Bro-N	.875	14	8	20	4	0	-2
1949	Bro-N	—	1	0	0	0	0	0
1955	Was-A	.929	5	5	8	1	3	2
1956	Cin-N	—	1	0	0	0	0	0
Total	4	.891	21	13	28	5	3	0
		1B						
1948	Bro-N	1.000	1	2	0	0	0	0
1950	Bro-N	1.000	2	18	0	0	3	-1
1951	Chi-N	.951	9	69	8	4	5	0
Total	3	.960	12	89	8	4	8	-1
		2B						
1952	Chi-N	—	1	0	0	0	0	0
1956	Cin-N	1.000	1	0	1	0	0	0
Total	2	1.000	2	0	1	0	0	0

■ Dave Edwards OF

YEAR	TM/L	PCT	G	PO	A	E	DP	FR
1978	Min-A	.950	15	35	3	2	1	3
1979	Min-A	.983	86	165	7	3	0	-1
1980	Min-A	.932	72	144	7	**11**	1	6
1981	SD-N	.970	49	59	6	2	2	2
1982	SD-N	.944	45	34	0	2	0	3
Total	5	.958	267	437	23	0	4	13
		1B						
1982	SD-N	—	1	0	0	0	0	0

■ Hank Edwards OF

YEAR	TM/L	PCT	G	PO	A	E	DP	FR
1941	Cle-A	.929	16	23	3	2	0	-2
1942	Cle-A	.968	12	30	0	1	0	0
1943	Cle-A	.983	74	173	4	3	0	0
1946	Cle-A	.968	123	226	13	8	1	-1
1947	Cle-A	.990	100	199	3	2	0	-5
1948	Cle-A	.987	41	76	1	1	0	-4
1949	Cle-A	1.000	5	6	0	0	0	-1
	Chi-N	.988	51	80	4	1	2	-5
1950	Chi-N	.976	29	38	2	1	0	-4
1951	Cin-N	.985	34	64	0	1	0	-4
1952	Cin-N	.988	51	80	2	1	0	-4
	Chi-N	1.000	3	8	0	0	0	0
1953	StL-A	1.000	21	36	2	0	0	0
Total	11	.981	560	1039	34	1	3	-30

■ Doc Edwards C

YEAR	TM/L	PCT	G	PO	A	E	DP	FR
1962	Cle-A	.992	39	223	16	2	2	8
1963	Cle-A	.988	10	80	3	1	1	5
	KC-A	.987	63	341	30	5	4	-6
	Yr	.987	73	421	33	6	5	-1
1964	KC-A	.986	79	469	31	7	5	1
1965	KC-A	1.000	6	32	2	0	1	0
	NY-A	.986	43	198	16	3	5	3
	Yr	.988	49	230	18	3	6	3
1970	Phi-N	.970	34	177	19	6	6	6
Total	5	.986	274	1520	117	4	24	17
		1B						
1964	KC-A	.983	7	53	6	1	2	0

■ Johnny Edwards C

YEAR	TM/L	PCT	G	PO	A	E	DP	FR
1961	Cin-N	.982	52	257	15	5	2	-2
1962	Cin-N	.987	130	807	**92**	12	**11**	14
1963	Cin-N	**.995**	148	**1008**	87	6	**16**	12
1964	Cin-N	.992	120	**890**	73	8	**17**	**22**
1965	Cin-N	.990	110	761	61	8	9	4
1966	Cin-N	.992	98	617	40	5	3	8
1967	Cin-N	.990	73	454	30	5	4	15
1968	StL-N	.992	54	350	25	3	2	1
1969	Hou-N	**.994**	151	**1135**	79	7	9	5
1970	Hou-N	**.995**	139	854	**74**	5	11	11
1971	Hou-N	**.995**	104	555	48	3	7	8
1972	Hou-N	.988	105	645	41	8	8	-8
1973	Hou-N	.989	76	435	22	5	3	-2
1974	Hou-N	.989	32	157	16	2	3	5
Total	14	.992	1392	8925	703	2	105	93

■ Marshall Edwards OF

YEAR	TM/L	PCT	G	PO	A	E	DP	FR
1981	Mil-A	.979	36	46	1	1	0	3
1982	Mil-A	.984	54	119	2	2	1	3
1983	Mil-A	1.000	35	57	4	0	1	7
Total	3	.987	125	222	7	3	2	13

■ Mike Edwards 2B

YEAR	TM/L	PCT	G	PO	A	E	DP	FR
1977	Pit-N	1.000	4	7	8	0	2	3
1978	Oak-A	.964	133	228	309	**20**	71	-27
1979	Oak-A	.962	113	244	314	**22**	54	-14
1980	Oak-A	.971	23	19	48	2	7	9
Total	4	.964	273	498	679	4	134	-29
		SS						
1978	Oak-A	.875	9	5	9	2	1	-3
1979	Oak-A	1.000	3	2	4	0	0	0
Total	2	.909	12	7	13	2	1	-3
		OF						
1980	Oak-A	—	1	0	0	0	0	0

■ Ben Egan C

YEAR	TM/L	PCT	G	PO	A	E	DP	FR
1908	Phi-A	.933	2	11	3	1	0	0
1912	Phi-A	.958	46	175	75	11	5	4
1914	Cle-A	.975	27	146	48	5	3	5
1915	Cle-A	.970	40	199	59	8	5	9
Total	4	.966	115	531	185	5	13	18

■ Dick Egan 2B

YEAR	TM/L	PCT	G	PO	A	E	DP	FR
1908	Cin-N	.891	18	35	47	10	10	-3
1909	Cin-N	.950	116	271	376	34	45	**27**
1910	Cin-N	.961	131	264	381	26	49	-10
1911	Cin-N	.949	**152**	341	**480**	44	**67**	10
1912	Cin-N	**.973**	149	345	452	22	55	3
1913	Cin-N	.972	37	80	96	5	16	-2
1914	Bro-N	.833	2	4	6	2	0	0
1915	Bos-N	.942	22	39	59	6	15	2
1916	Bos-N	.949	59	81	125	11	11	-18
Total	9	.956	686	1460	2022	160	268	9
		SS						
1909	Cin-N	.907	10	23	26	5	4	-2
1910	Cin-N	.917	3	4	7	1	1	0
1913	Cin-N	.927	17	35	54	7	4	-1
1914	Bro-N	.914	83	150	232	36	21	-9
1915	Bos-N	.896	10	18	25	5	0	-2
1916	Bos-N	.826	12	5	14	4	1	-1
Total	6	.911	135	235	358	8	31	-15
		OF						
1914	Bro-N	1.000	3	4	0	0	0	0
1915	Bos-N	.974	24	36	2	1	0	0
Total	2	.977	27	40	2	1	0	0
		3B						
1913	Cin-N	.250	2	0	1	3	0	-1
1914	Bro-N	.972	10	17	18	1	3	2
1915	Bos-N	.500	4	1	0	1	1	-1
1916	Bos-N	.947	8	8	10	1	1	-3
Total	4	.902	24	26	29	6	5	-3
		1B						
1914	Bro-N	1.000	1	2	0	0	1	0
1915	Bos-N	.968	9	85	6	3	4	0
Total	2	.969	10	87	6	3	5	0

■ Tom Egan C

YEAR	TM/L	PCT	G	PO	A	E	DP	FR
1965	Cal-A	1.000	16	61	3	0	0	1
1966	Cal-A	1.000	6	24	2	0	0	2
1967	Cal-A	1.000	1	3	0	0	0	0
1968	Cal-A	1.000	14	72	7	0	2	2
1969	Cal-A	.985	46	240	28	4	4	7
1970	Cal-A	.988	79	367	31	5	4	0
1971	Chi-A	.986	77	443	41	7	2	5
1972	Chi-A	.986	46	257	19	4	2	3
1974	Cal-A	.996	41	249	21	1	5	15
1975	Cal-A	.965	28	145	19	6	4	4
Total	10	.987	354	1861	171	7	23	39
		1B						
1971	Chi-A	1.000	1	2	0	0	1	0

■ Dave Eggler OF

YEAR	TM/L	PCT	G	PO	A	E	DP	FR
1876	Phi-N	.913	39	109	6	11	1	4
1877	Chi-N	.861	33	60	8	11	3	1
1879	Buf-N	.919	78	114	11	11	2	-7
1883	Bal-a	.916	53	92	6	9	1	1
	Buf-N	.845	38	83	4	16	1	-2
1884	Buf-N	.887	63	104	14	15	1	-1
1885	Buf-N	.938	6	14	1	1	0	0
Total	5	.894	310	576	50	4	9	-4

■ Ike Eichrodt OF

YEAR	TM/L	PCT	G	PO	A	E	DP	FR
1925	Cle-A	.938	13	30	0	2	0	-2
1926	Cle-A	.976	27	38	3	1	1	-4
1927	Cle-A	.979	81	170	13	4	6	1
1931	Chi-A	1.000	32	70	0	0	0	-4
Total	4	.979	153	308	16	7	7	-9

■ Jim Eisenreich OF

YEAR	TM/L	PCT	G	PO	A	E	DP	FR
1982	Min-A	.973	30	72	0	2	0	1
1983	Min-A	1.000	2	6	1	0	0	1
1984	Min-A	1.000	3	5	0	0	0	0
1988	KC-A	.965	64	109	0	4	0	0
1989	KC-A	.989	123	273	4	3	0	3
1990	KC-A	**.996**	138	261	6	1	3	-2
Total	6	.987	360	726	11	0	3	3

■ Kid Elberfeld SS

YEAR	TM/L	PCT	G	PO	A	E	DP	FR
1899	Cin-N	.878	24	48	67	16	6	-4
1901	Det-A	.907	121	**332**	411	76	**62**	**23**
1902	Det-A	.921	130	326	459	67	63	9
1903	Det-A	.932	34	73	119	14	11	6
	NY-A	.914	90	222	291	48	40	7
	Yr	.919	124	295	410	62	51	13
1904	NY-A	.933	122	237	432	48	44	15
1905	NY-A	.925	108	244	317	57	35	-5
1906	NY-A	.925	98	200	317	42	18	-3
1907	NY-A	.930	118	295	400	52	31	11
1908	NY-A	.916	17	36	51	8	2	-3
1909	NY-A	.943	61	134	178	19	24	-4
1910	Was-A	.733	3	6	5	4	1	-2
1914	Bro-N	.901	18	31	33	7	6	-4
Total	12	.920	944	2184	3080	458	343	46
		3B						
1898	Phi-N	.795	14	13	18	8	1	-5
1899	Cin-N	.882	18	26	41	9	3	0
1903	Det-A	1.000	1	1	0	0	0	0
1909	NY-A	.956	44	62	91	7	6	2
1910	Was-A	.913	113	139	223	22	15	-5
1911	Was-A	.927	52	87	116	16	11	9
Total	6	.929	242	328	489	2	36	1
		2B						
1910	Was-A	.927	10	21	17	3	1	-2
1911	Was-A	.957	68	146	186	15	23	1
1914	Bro-N	1.000	1	2	2	0	0	0
Total	3	.954	79	169	205	8	24	-1

■ Frank Ellerbe 3B

YEAR	TM/L	PCT	G	PO	A	E	DP	FR
1920	Was-A	.934	75	101	167	19	8	2
1921	StL-A	.953	105	158	226	19	9	2
1922	StL-A	.955	91	137	224	17	20	**16**
1923	StL-A	.967	14	11	18	1	2	-3
1924	StL-A	.953	21	27	34	3	7	3
	Cle-A	.975	39	42	75	3	2	5
	Yr	.967	60	69	109	6	9	8
Total	5	.952	345	476	744	2	48	25
		SS						
1919	Was-A	.945	28	63	74	8	5	-4
1920	Was-A	.883	19	25	43	9	2	-7
Total	2	.923	47	88	117	7	7	-11
		2B						
1924	Cle-A	.750	2	2	1	1	0	-1
		OF						
1920	Was-A	1.000	1	1	0	0	0	0

■ Larry Elliot OF

YEAR	TM/L	PCT	G	PO	A	E	DP	FR
1962	Pit-N	1.000	3	3	0	0	0	0
1964	NY-N	.985	63	130	2	2	1	1
1966	NY-N	.912	54	73	10	8	0	-1
Total	3	.956	120	206	12	0	1	0

■ Rowdy Elliott C

YEAR	TM/L	PCT	G	PO	A	E	DP	FR
1910	Bos-N	1.000	1	1	0	0	0	0
1916	Chi-N	.969	18	77	17	3	1	-1
1917	Chi-N	.969	73	307	93	13	9	4
1918	Chi-N	.952	5	15	5	1	0	0
1920	Bro-N	.964	39	144	44	7	1	4
Total	5	.967	136	544	159	4	11	7

■ Bob Elliott 3B

YEAR	TM/L	PCT	G	PO	A	E	DP	FR
1942	Pit-N	.927	142	**173**	**285**	**36**	22	-3
1943	Pit-N	.949	151	149	**294**	24	34	-6
1944	Pit-N	.944	140	169	**285**	**27**	22	0
1945	Pit-N	.928	81	94	178	21	18	6
1946	Pit-N	**.955**	43	44	82	6	5	0
1947	Bos-N	**.956**	148	129	302	20	25	-2
1948	Bos-N	.945	**150**	**146**	298	26	18	-10
1949	Bos-N	.963	130	141	300	17	27	11
1950	Bos-N	.952	137	141	256	20	26	-17
1951	Bos-N	.941	127	138	242	**24**	31	-7
1952	NY-N	.957	13	19	25	2	3	1
1953	StL-A	.954	45	51	93	7	12	-2
	Chi-A	.963	58	54	104	6	9	-10
	Yr	.959	103	105	197	13	21	-12
Total	12	.947	1365	1448	2744	236	252	-39
		OF						
1939	Pit-N	.978	30	88	1	2	0	3
1940	Pit-N	.978	147	302	12	7	0	1
1941	Pit-N	.970	139	281	9	9	2	-6
1942	Pit-N	1.000	1	3	1	0	0	1
1945	Pit-N	.985	61	125	7	2	0	0
1946	Pit-N	.995	92	188	8	1	5	0
1952	NY-N	.978	65	83	6	2	0	-6
1953	Chi-A	.000	2	0	0	1	0	0
Total	8	.979	537	1070	44	4	7	-7
		2B						
1943	Pit-N	—	2	0	0	0	0	0
		SS						
1943	Pit-N	.750	1	1	2	1	0	0
1944	Pit-N	—	1	0	0	0	0	0
Total	2	.750	2	1	2	1	0	0

■ Rube Ellis OF

YEAR	TM/L	PCT	G	PO	A	E	DP	FR
1909	StL-N	.955	145	332	28	17	9	**13**
1910	StL-N	.942	141	268	25	18	4	5
1911	StL-N	.938	148	297	21	**21**	3	3
1912	StL-N	.929	76	173	10	14	5	0
Total	4	.943	510	1070	84	0	21	21

■ John Ellis 1B

YEAR	TM/L	PCT	G	PO	A	E	DP	FR
1970	NY-A	.992	53	449	37	4	35	1
1971	NY-A	.990	65	625	35	7	66	-2
1972	NY-A	.985	8	63	1	1	4	-1
1973	Cle-A	.984	12	117	4	2	6	-2
1974	Cle-A	.992	69	667	37	6	57	-3
1975	Cle-A	.900	2	17	1	2	1	0
1977	Tex-A	1.000	8	49	3	0	0	0
1979	Tex-A	.978	30	216	11	5	17	-3
1980	Tex-A	.992	39	240	12	2	22	-2
1981	Tex-A	.993	18	140	8	1	16	-1
Total	10	.989	304	2583	149	0	224	-13
		C						
1969	NY-A	.978	15	83	7	2	1	0
1970	NY-A	1.000	2	12	1	0	0	0
1971	NY-A	—	2	0	0	0	0	0
1972	NY-A	.965	25	127	11	5	1	2
1973	Cle-A	.980	72	370	27	8	5	-15
1974	Cle-A	.983	42	156	18	3	4	-5
1975	Cle-A	.976	84	396	44	11	3	-7
1976	Tex-A	1.000	7	21	2	0	0	-1
1977	Tex-A	1.000	16	40	2	0	1	-2
1978	Tex-A	.958	22	81	10	4	1	-2
1979	Tex-A	1.000	7	16	1	0	1	0
1980	Tex-A	1.000	3	4	0	0	0	0
Total	12	.977	297	1306	123	3	17	-30
		3B						
1970	NY-A	.750	5	0	3	1	0	0

■ Roy Elsh OF

YEAR	TM/L	PCT	G	PO	A	E	DP	FR
1923	Chi-A	.957	57	127	7	6	1	1
1924	Chi-A	.953	38	58	3	3	0	-5
1925	Chi-A	.964	16	25	2	1	2	-1

YEAR	TM/L	PCT	G	PO	A	E	DP	FR
Total	3	.957	111	210	12	0	3	-5
1B								
1924	Chi-A	.778	2	7	0	2	0	-1
1925	Chi-A	1.000	3	12	0	0	2	0
Total	2	.905	5	19	0	2	2	-1

■ Kevin Elster SS

YEAR	TM/L	PCT	G	PO	A	E	DP	FR
1986	NY-N	.962	19	16	35	2	6	4
1987	NY-N	.909	3	4	6	1	0	0
1988	NY-N	.977	148	196	345	13	61	5
1989	NY-N	.976	150	**235**	374	15	63	7
1990	NY-N	.960	92	159	251	17	42	15
Total	5	.971	412	610	1011	8	172	31

■ Bones Ely SS

YEAR	TM/L	PCT	G	PO	A	E	DP	FR
1890	Syr-a	.944	36	81	123	12	14	9
1891	Bro-N	.870	28	54	106	24	9	7
1893	StL-N	.905	44	98	139	25	16	-3
1894	StL-N	.901	126	273	442	**79**	51	2
1895	StL-N	.925	117	247	407	53	52	6
1896	Pit-N	.918	128	258	432	62	52	-2
1897	Pit-N	.927	**133**	308	451	60	41	3
1898	Pit-N	**.943**	148	311	527	51	58	8
1899	Pit-N	.928	132	274	472	58	45	1
1900	Pit-N	.935	130	242	503	52	62	13
1901	Pit-N	.916	64	112	215	30	23	-9
	Phi-A	.913	45	85	156	23	19	1
1902	Was-A	.923	105	238	350	49	31	-9
Total	12	.923	1236	2581	4323	578	473	27
OF								
1884	Buf-N	.000	1	0	0	1	0	-1
1886	Lou-a	.875	5	7	0	1	0	-1
1890	Syr-a	.915	78	179	14	18	1	10
Total	3	.909	84	186	14	0	1	8
2B								
1890	Syr-a	.800	2	2	2	1	0	0
1891	Bro-N	1.000	1	1	4	0	0	1
1894	StL-N	.778	1	3	4	2	0	-1
1899	Pit-N	.977	6	15	28	1	2	3
Total	4	.937	10	21	38	4	2	3
1B								
1890	Syr-a	.944	4	34	0	2	5	-1
3B								
1890	Syr-a	1.000	1	2	4	0	0	1
1891	Bro-N	.833	2	3	7	2	0	1
1901	Pit-N	1.000	1	0	1	0	0	0
Total	3	.895	4	5	12	2	0	2

■ Frank Emmer SS

YEAR	TM/L	PCT	G	PO	A	E	DP	FR
1916	Cin-N	.899	29	55	87	16	7	6
1926	Cin-N	.918	79	141	242	34	40	-7
Total	2	.913	108	196	329	0	47	-1
OF								
1916	Cin-N	.500	2	1	0	1	0	0
2B								
1916	Cin-N	—	1	0	0	0	0	0
3B								
1916	Cin-N	1.000	1	0	1	0	0	0

■ Clyde Engle OF

YEAR	TM/L	PCT	G	PO	A	E	DP	FR
1909	NY-A	.946	134	299	17	18	5	14
1910	NY-A	.857	3	6	0	1	0	0
	Bos-A	1.000	15	26	2	0	1	0
	Yr	.971	18	32	2	1	1	0
1911	Bos-A	1.000	10	20	1	0	0	0
1912	Bos-A	1.000	1	0	1	0	0	0
1913	Bos-A	1.000	2	2	2	0	1	1
1914	Bos-A	—	1	0	0	0	0	0
	Buf-F	1.000	9	12	3	0	0	1
1915	Buf-F	.969	100	211	8	7	2	-2
1916	Cle-A	—	1	0	0	0	0	0
Total	8	.959	276	576	34	6	9	14
1B								
1911	Bos-A	.975	65	550	43	15	24	1
1912	Bos-A	.977	25	209	8	5	11	-2
1913	Bos-A	.987	133	1239	57	17	55	-9
1914	Bos-A	.976	29	280	10	7	13	-4
1915	Buf-F	1.000	1	3	0	0	0	0
1916	Cle-A	1.000	2	5	0	0	0	0
Total	6	.982	255	2286	118	4	103	-14
3B								
1910	Bos-A	.915	51	53	119	16	7	2
1911	Bos-A	.849	51	50	108	28	7	-3
1912	Bos-A	.900	11	9	18	3	1	-3
1914	Bos-A	1.000	3	1	2	0	0	0
	Buf-F	.889	23	31	25	7	2	-8
1915	Buf-F	.938	17	16	29	3	3	1
1916	Cle-A	.810	7	5	12	4	0	-2
Total	6	.887	163	165	313	1	20	-13
2B								
1910	Bos-A	.954	27	41	83	6	7	1
1911	Bos-A	.895	13	16	35	6	3	-2
1912	Bos-A	.912	15	25	27	5	3	-3
1914	Bos-A	1.000	5	6	6	0	1	0
1915	Buf-F	.970	21	31	34	2	6	-1
Total	5	.941	81	119	185	9	20	-5
SS								
1910	Bos-A	.800	7	9	19	7	2	-3
1912	Bos-A	1.000	2	5	6	0	0	0
Total	2	.848	9	14	25	7	2	-3

■ Dave Engle C

YEAR	TM/L	PCT	G	PO	A	E	DP	FR
1983	Min-A	.973	73	299	26	9	3	18
1984	Min-A	.981	86	376	34	8	3	-8
1985	Min-A	.984	17	58	3	1	1	-2
1986	Det-A	1.000	3	11	1	0	0	0
1987	Mon-N	1.000	6	11	1	0	0	-1
1988	Mon-N	1.000	9	21	1	0	0	0
1989	Mil-A	1.000	3	1	0	0	0	0
Total	7	.979	197	777	66	8	7	-29
OF								
1981	Min-A	.980	76	144	4	3	0	-4
1982	Min-A	.985	34	63	3	1	1	1
1983	Min-A	1.000	4	7	0	0	0	0
1985	Min-A	1.000	3	8	1	0	0	1
1986	Det-A	1.000	4	1	0	0	0	0
1987	Mon-N	1.000	11	19	1	0	0	0
1988	Mon-N	1.000	4	4	0	0	0	0
Total	7	.985	136	246	9	4	1	-2
1B								
1986	Det-A	1.000	23	173	13	0	20	0
1987	Mon-N	1.000	2	3	0	0	0	0
1989	Mil-A	.973	18	133	12	4	11	0
Total	3	.988	43	309	25	4	31	0
3B								
1981	Min-A	—	1	0	0	0	0	0
1987	Mon-N	1.000	1	0	1	0	0	0
1988	Mon-N	—	1	0	0	0	0	0
Total	3	1.000	3	0	1	0	0	0

■ Woody English SS

YEAR	TM/L	PCT	G	PO	A	E	DP	FR
1927	Chi-N	.940	84	177	281	29	47	6
1928	Chi-N	.946	114	245	382	36	85	6
1929	Chi-N	.955	144	332	497	39	107	15
1930	Chi-N	.964	78	173	251	16	57	-7
1931	Chi-N	.965	138	**322**	441	28	75	-2
1932	Chi-N	.955	38	66	102	8	17	-1
1933	Chi-N	1.000	1	0	1	0	0	0
1934	Chi-N	.971	56	61	109	5	22	-33
1935	Chi-N	.980	12	21	29	1	4	-1
1936	Chi-N	.976	42	75	127	5	27	1
1937	Bro-N	.956	116	220	303	24	51	-17
1938	Bro-N	1.000	3	1	0	0	0	0
Total	12	.957	826	1693	2523	191	492	-33
3B								
1927	Chi-N	1.000	1	2	4	0	0	1
1928	Chi-N	—	2	0	0	0	0	0
1930	Chi-N	.973	83	83	135	6	19	-6
1931	Chi-N	.983	18	18	41	1	3	4
1932	Chi-N	.957	93	96	173	12	13	-1
1933	Chi-N	**.973**	103	80	173	7	9	-15
1934	Chi-N	.976	46	74	132	5	5	24
1935	Chi-N	.868	16	8	25	5	2	-4
1936	Chi-N	1.000	17	14	21	0	3	0
1938	Bro-N	.958	21	16	30	2	4	0
Total	10	.967	400	391	734	8	58	3
2B								
1934	Chi-N	.879	7	10	19	4	4	-1
1936	Chi-N	1.000	1	3	4	0	0	0
1937	Bro-N	.952	11	19	21	2	3	0
1938	Bro-N	1.000	3	7	7	0	1	1
Total	4	.938	22	39	51	6	8	0

■ Gil English 3B

YEAR	TM/L	PCT	G	PO	A	E	DP	FR
1931	NY-N	1.000	3	1	3	0	0	-1
1932	NY-N	.931	39	40	81	9	11	4
1936	Det-A	1.000	1	1	1	0	0	0
1937	Det-A	1.000	6	3	6	0	0	-1
	Bos-N	.958	71	61	121	8	9	-7
1938	Bos-N	.956	43	33	75	5	3	-3
1944	Bro-N	.944	11	16	18	2	2	-1
Total	6	.950	174	155	305	4	25	-9
SS								
1932	NY-N	.947	23	37	52	5	7	0
1938	Bos-N	1.000	2	1	0	0	0	0
1944	Bro-N	.918	13	12	33	4	6	-1
Total	3	.938	38	50	85	9	13	-1
2B								
1937	Det-A	.962	12	23	28	2	5	-6
1938	Bos-N	.667	2	1	1	1	0	-1
1944	Bro-N	—	2	0	0	0	0	0
Total	3	.946	16	24	29	3	5	-7
OF								
1938	Bos-N	1.000	3	4	1	0	0	0

■ Del Ennis OF

YEAR	TM/L	PCT	G	PO	A	E	DP	FR
1946	Phi-N	.975	138	332	16	9	4	12
1947	Phi-N	.979	135	320	12	7	2	6
1948	Phi-N	.957	151	297	15	**14**	4	-2
1949	Phi-N	.966	154	359	**16**	**13**	1	3
1950	Phi-N	.970	149	279	10	9	3	-4
1951	Phi-N	.969	135	268	14	9	3	-1
1952	Phi-N	.970	149	277	11	9	1	-5
1953	Phi-N	.980	150	284	14	6	4	2
1954	Phi-N	.957	142	303	9	**14**	1	2
1955	Phi-N	.987	145	298	9	4	2	3
1956	Phi-N	.962	153	269	8	11	0	-7
1957	StL-N	.943	127	180	3	11	0	-19
1958	StL-N	.993	84	122	11	1	2	-2
1959	Cin-N	1.000	3	5	0	0	0	0
	Chi-A	.909	25	28	2	3	0	-5
Total	14	.969	1840	3621	150	120	27	-17
1B								
1954	Phi-N	.889	1	8	0	1	0	-1

■ Mike Epstein 1B

YEAR	TM/L	PCT	G	PO	A	E	DP	FR
1966	Bal-A	1.000	4	36	2	0	3	0
1967	Bal-A	1.000	3	25	1	0	2	0
	Was-A	.987	80	718	54	10	72	-1
	Yr	.988	83	743	55	10	74	-1
1968	Was-A	.987	110	947	70	13	83	2
1969	Was-A	.990	118	1035	69	11	99	-1
1970	Was-A	.992	122	1100	70	10	104	-3
1971	Was-A	.992	24	224	12	2	30	-1
	Oak-A	.995	96	714	52	4	93	-2
	Yr	.994	120	938	64	6	123	-3
1972	Oak-A	.990	137	1111	73	12	101	-2
1973	Tex-A	.991	25	200	12	2	19	-1
	Cal-A	.993	86	710	50	5	61	0
	Yr	.993	111	910	62	7	80	-1
1974	Cal-A	.993	18	137	12	1	14	1
Total	9	.991	823	6957	477	0	681	-8

■ Tex Erwin C

YEAR	TM/L	PCT	G	PO	A	E	DP	FR
1907	Det-A	.909	4	7	3	1	0	0
1910	Bro-N	.949	68	259	114	20	10	-1
1911	Bro-N	.971	74	273	98	11	6	-6
1912	Bro-N	.949	41	176	46	12	3	-1
1913	Bro-N	.950	13	32	6	2	0	-3
1914	Bro-N	1.000	4	6	3	0	0	-1
	Cin-N	.962	12	63	12	3	0	2
	Yr	.966	16	69	15	3	0	1
Total	6	.957	216	816	282	9	19	-10

■ Nick Esasky 1B

YEAR	TM/L	PCT	G	PO	A	E	DP	FR
1984	Cin-N	1.000	25	169	7	0	11	-2
1985	Cin-N	1.000	12	37	3	0	3	0
1986	Cin-N	.991	70	512	30	5	42	-5
1987	Cin-N	.994	93	772	40	5	72	-11
1988	Cin-N	.994	116	982	52	6	70	-9
1989	Bos-A	.996	153	1317	107	6	129	4
1990	Atl-N	.944	9	79	5	5	7	-2
Total	7	.993	478	3868	244	7	334	-25
3B								
1983	Cin-N	.935	84	53	133	13	11	-10
1984	Cin-N	.910	82	51	130	18	8	-6
1985	Cin-N	.946	62	41	99	8	13	-8
1986	Cin-N	—	1	0	0	0	0	0
1987	Cin-N	.500	1	0	1	1	0	0
Total	5	.927	230	145	363	0	32	-24
OF								
1985	Cin-N	1.000	54	91	4	0	0	2
1986	Cin-N	1.000	42	73	3	0	2	2
1987	Cin-N	1.000	1	1	0	0	0	0
1989	Bos-A	1.000	1	2	0	0	0	0
Total	4	1.000	98	167	7	0	2	4

■ Jimmy Esmond SS

YEAR	TM/L	PCT	G	PO	A	E	DP	FR
1911	Cin-N	.918	44	110	104	19	19	0
1912	Cin-N	.930	74	154	180	25	22	-7
1914	Ind-F	.919	**151**	**317**	448	**67**	54	-7
1915	New-F	.939	**155**	**353**	**482**	54	67	6
Total	4	.929	424	934	1214	165	162	-8
3B								
1911	Cin-N	.939	14	26	20	3	2	0
2B								
1911	Cin-N	1.000	2	2	2	0	0	0

■ Alvaro Espinoza SS

YEAR	TM/L	PCT	G	PO	A	E	DP	FR
1984	Min-A	—	1	0	0	0	0	0
1985	Min-A	.949	31	25	69	5	15	7
1986	Min-A	.964	18	11	16	1	4	1
1988	NY-A	1.000	1	1	1	0	1	0
1989	NY-A	.970	146	237	471	22	114	16
1990	NY-A	.977	150	268	447	17	100	**21**
Total	6	.972	347	542	1004	5	234	45
2B								
1986	Min-A	.941	19	12	36	3	7	5
1988	NY-A	1.000	2	4	1	0	0	0
Total	2	.946	21	16	37	3	7	5

■ Sammy Esposito 3B

YEAR	TM/L	PCT	G	PO	A	E	DP	FR
1955	Chi-A	1.000	2	1	0	0	0	-1
1956	Chi-A	.962	61	41	109	6	17	4
1957	Chi-A	.960	53	52	92	6	10	7
1958	Chi-A	.979	63	11	35	1	2	5
1959	Chi-A	.979	45	22	25	1	1	3
1960	Chi-A	.929	37	12	40	4	4	0
1961	Chi-A	.976	28	10	30	1	5	5
1962	Chi-A	.846	41	6	16	4	1	-1
1963	KC-A	1.000	3	1	3	0	0	0
Total	9	.957	333	156	350	3	40	22
SS								
1952	Chi-A	.500	1	1	1	2	0	-1
1956	Chi-A	1.000	19	9	21	0	1	0
1957	Chi-A	.971	22	28	73	3	12	10
1958	Chi-A	.944	22	24	43	4	7	7
1959	Chi-A	.980	14	17	32	1	5	6
1960	Chi-A	1.000	11	2	7	0	1	1
1961	Chi-A	.966	20	18	39	2	3	5
1962	Chi-A	.971	20	20	47	2	5	4
1963	KC-A	.833	4	4	6	2	1	-2
Total	9	.961	133	123	269	6	35	30
2B								
1956	Chi-A	1.000	3	2	2	0	1	0
1957	Chi-A	.875	4	4	3	1	1	0
1958	Chi-A	1.000	2	1	0	0	0	0
1959	Chi-A	—	2	0	0	0	0	0
1960	Chi-A	.875	5	3	4	1	0	0
1961	Chi-A	1.000	11	23	16	0	3	2
1962	Chi-A	.923	7	3	9	1	1	1
1963	KC-A	1.000	7	2	6	0	1	0
Total	8	.963	41	38	40	3	7	3
OF								
1957	Chi-A	—	1	0	0	0	0	0
1958	Chi-A	—	1	0	0	0	0	0
Total	2	—	2	0	0	0	0	0

■ Cecil Espy OF

YEAR	TM/L	PCT	G	PO	A	E	DP	FR
1983	LA-N	1.000	15	11	0	0	0	1
1987	Tex-A	.888	8	8	1	0	1	2
1988	Tex-A	.972	98	196	10	6	0	3
1989	Tex-A	.990	133	281	5	3	2	-6
1990	Tex-A	1.000	39	56	1	0	0	4
Total	5	.984	293	552	17	9	3	4
SS								
1988	Tex-A	.750	3	2	1	1	0	0
C								
1988	Tex-A	—	2	0	0	0	0	0

YEAR	TM/L	PCT	G	PO	A	E	DP	FR
2B								
1988	Tex-A	—	1	0	0	0	0	0
1990	Tex-A	—	1	0	0	0	0	0
Total	2	—	2	0	0	0	0	0
1B								
1988	Tex-A	1.000	1	2	0	0	0	0

■ Chuck Essegian OF

YEAR	TM/L	PCT	G	PO	A	E	DP	FR
1958	Phi-N	.952	30	59	1	3	0	-2
1959	StL-N	1.000	9	8	1	0	0	-1
	LA-N	1.000	10	11	0	0	0	-2
	Yr	1.000	19	19	1	0	0	-3
1960	LA-N	.968	18	29	1	1	0	1
1961	KC-A	1.000	1	4	0	0	0	0
	Cle-A	.968	49	85	5	3	1	2
	Yr	.969	50	89	5	3	1	2
1962	Cle-A	.994	90	154	1	1	0	-8
1963	KC-A	.990	53	95	2	1	0	-3
Total	6	.981	260	445	11	9	1	-13

■ Jim Essian C

YEAR	TM/L	PCT	G	PO	A	E	DP	FR
1973	Phi-N	—	1	0	0	0	0	0
1974	Phi-N	.976	15	37	3	1	1	1
1975	Phi-N	1.000	2	1	1	0	0	0
1976	Chi-A	.974	77	319	53	10	10	3
1977	Chi-A	.986	111	592	62	9	8	5
1978	Oak-A	.981	119	431	78	10	12	14
1979	Oak-A	.981	70	348	57	8	5	11
1980	Oak-A	.987	68	333	46	5	5	4
1981	Chi-A	.990	25	92	9	1	0	5
1982	Sea-A	.994	48	282	26	2	1	6
1983	Cle-A	.989	47	170	14	2	3	4
1984	Oak-A	.985	59	229	28	4	6	11
Total	12	.984	642	2834	377	2	51	64
3B								
1974	Phi-N	1.000	1	0	1	0	1	0
1976	Chi-A	—	1	0	0	0	0	0
1977	Chi-A	1.000	2	1	0	0	0	0
1979	Oak-A	.972	10	15	20	1	2	1
1981	Chi-A	.000	2	0	0	1	0	-1
1983	Cle-A	—	1	0	0	0	0	0
1984	Oak-A	.667	1	0	2	1	0	0
Total	7	.929	18	16	23	3	3	0
1B								
1974	Phi-N	1.000	1	1	0	0	0	0
1976	Chi-A	1.000	2	1	0	0	0	0
1978	Oak-A	1.000	3	20	1	0	2	0
1979	Oak-A	1.000	4	35	2	0	4	0
1980	Oak-A	1.000	1	6	0	0	0	0
Total	5	1.000	11	63	3	0	6	0
OF								
1979	Oak-A	1.000	4	2	0	0	0	0
2B								
1978	Oak-A	1.000	1	1	0	0	0	0

■ Bobby Estalella OF

YEAR	TM/L	PCT	G	PO	A	E	DP	FR
1939	Was-A	.964	74	157	3	6	1	-4
1941	StL-A	1.000	17	23	0	0	0	-4
1942	Was-A	.986	36	69	2	1	1	-1
1943	Phi-A	.975	97	225	5	6	1	-1
1944	Phi-A	.988	128	318	12	4	4	-7
1945	Phi-A	.988	124	314	10	4	3	-1
1949	Phi-A	1.000	6	9	1	0	1	1
Total	7	.982	482	1115	33	1	11	-17
3B								
1935	Was-A	.895	15	14	37	6	1	2
1942	Was-A	.941	78	89	134	14	4	-12
Total	2	.932	93	103	171	0	5	-10
1B								
1944	Phi-A	1.000	6	28	4	0	1	1

■ Dude Esterbrook 3B

YEAR	TM/L	PCT	G	PO	A	E	DP	FR
1883	NY-a	.871	97	110	173	42	8	-5
1884	NY-a	.886	112	126	208	43	11	9
1885	NY-N	.885	84	111	159	35	14	2
1886	NY-N	.895	123	148	219	43	9	-8
1888	Ind-N	.778	3	5	2	2	0	-2
Total	5	.884	419	500	761	165	42	-4
1B								
1880	Buf-N	.939	47	463	17	31	20	0
1882	Cle-N	1.000	1	5	0	0	1	0
1887	NY-a	.950	9	73	3	4	4	0
1888	Ind-N	.976	61	628	20	16	32	-1
	Lou-a	.962	23	218	10	9	8	0
1889	Lou-a	.931	8	77	4	6	3	0
1890	NY-N	.984	45	430	13	7	24	0
Total	6	.964	194	1894	67	3	92	-1
OF								
1880	Buf-N	.781	15	19	6	7	1	1
1882	Cle-N	.893	45	102	15	14	6	9
1885	NY-N	.875	4	5	2	1	0	1
1887	NY-a	.750	7	9	0	3	0	-2
1889	Lou-a	1.000	2	1	1	0	0	0
1891	Bro-N	1.000	2	4	0	0	0	0
Total	6	.868	75	140	24	5	7	9
2B								
1880	Buf-N	.821	6	10	13	5	0	-2
1887	NY-a	.857	5	14	10	4	2	-2
1891	Bro-N	.000	1	0	0	1	0	-1
Total	3	.825	12	24	23	0	2	-5
SS								
1880	Buf-N	.500	1	1	1	2	0	-1
1887	NY-a	.676	5	9	14	11	0	-2
1889	Lou-a	.667	1	1	1	1	0	-1
Total	3	.659	7	11	16	4	0	-4
C								
1880	Buf-N	1.000	1	1	0	0	0	0

■ Andy Etchebarren C

YEAR	TM/L	PCT	G	PO	A	E	DP	FR
1962	Bal-A	.875	2	7	0	1	0	-1
1965	Bal-A	1.000	5	21	2	0	0	3
1966	Bal-A	.989	121	799	65	10	7	-3
1967	Bal-A	.989	110	673	57	8	10	0
1968	Bal-A	.998	70	414	29	1	3	9
1969	Bal-A	.990	72	380	27	4	1	1
1970	Bal-A	.984	76	392	29	7	3	1
1971	Bal-A	.986	70	337	24	5	2	1
1972	Bal-A	.992	70	334	22	3	2	6
1973	Bal-A	.991	51	201	14	2	5	1
1974	Bal-A	.976	60	269	19	7	3	1
1975	Bal-A	1.000	7	28	2	0	0	0
	Cal-A	.981	31	188	15	4	2	-3
	Yr	.983	38	216	17	4	2	-3
1976	Cal-A	.980	102	539	46	12	7	5
1977	Cal-A	.987	80	289	12	4	0	0
1978	Mil-A	1.000	4	13	2	0	0	2
Total	15	.987	931	4884	365	8	45	23

■ Nick Etten 1B

YEAR	TM/L	PCT	G	PO	A	E	DP	FR
1938	Phi-A	.987	22	212	10	3	20	-2
1939	Phi-A	.990	41	376	19	4	29	-3
1941	Phi-N	.984	150	1286	89	23	124	-3
1942	Phi-N	.985	135	1152	83	19	99	0
1943	NY-A	.989	154	1410	79	17	148	-11
1944	NY-A	.989	154	1382	106	16	144	4
1945	NY-A	.989	152	1401	94	17	149	-9
1946	NY-A	.991	84	717	55	7	80	0
1947	Phi-N	.990	11	94	10	1	4	1
Total	9	.988	903	8030	545	107	797	-23

■ Al Evans C

YEAR	TM/L	PCT	G	PO	A	E	DP	FR
1939	Was-A	.964	6	21	6	1	0	-1
1940	Was-A	1.000	9	34	2	0	0	0
1941	Was-A	.969	51	195	24	7	6	2
1942	Was-A	.961	67	254	42	12	5	-2
1944	Was-A	.933	8	10	4	1	1	-1
1945	Was-A	.973	41	160	19	5	4	-5
1946	Was-A	.966	81	336	30	13	5	-10
1947	Was-A	.989	94	389	48	5	14	-2
1948	Was-A	.983	85	245	38	5	6	-3
1949	Was-A	.992	107	322	47	3	2	-16
1950	Was-A	.987	88	289	23	4	8	-13
1951	Bos-A	1.000	10	40	1	0	0	1
Total	12	.979	647	2295	284	6	51	-50

■ Barry Evans 3B

YEAR	TM/L	PCT	G	PO	A	E	DP	FR
1978	SD-N	.947	24	13	59	4	4	1
1979	SD-N	.952	53	30	108	7	12	11
1980	SD-N	.983	43	16	41	1	2	-2
1981	SD-N	.969	24	10	21	1	1	-1
1982	NY-A	1.000	6	2	10	0	0	1
Total	5	.960	150	71	239	3	19	10
2B								
1979	SD-N	1.000	1	0	1	0	0	0
1980	SD-N	.987	19	33	42	1	9	-1
1981	SD-N	1.000	6	13	9	0	2	-1
1982	NY-A	1.000	8	11	14	0	3	1
Total	4	.992	34	57	66	1	14	-1
SS								
1979	SD-N	1.000	2	0	1	0	0	0
1980	SD-N	1.000	4	1	4	0	1	0
1981	SD-N	1.000	2	0	1	0	0	0
1982	NY-A	1.000	4	1	2	0	0	0
Total	4	1.000	12	2	8	0	1	0
1B								
1980	SD-N	1.000	1	2	0	0	1	0
1981	SD-N	.987	10	75	2	1	7	-1
Total	2	.988	11	77	2	1	8	-1

■ Darrell Evans 3B

YEAR	TM/L	PCT	G	PO	A	E	DP	FR
1969	Atl-N	.917	6	4	7	1	0	-2
1970	Atl-N	.941	12	6	26	2	0	-1
1971	Atl-N	.937	72	71	138	14	13	4
1972	Atl-N	.941	123	126	273	25	20	9
1973	Atl-N	.953	146	124	325	22	33	8
1974	Atl-N	.955	160	185	367	26	45	16
1975	Atl-N	.938	156	161	381	36	41	23
1976	Atl-N	.938	7	5	10	1	1	0
	SF-N	1.000	5	7	9	0	1	0
	Yr	.969	12	12	19	1	2	0
1977	SF-N	.988	35	18	67	1	4	-2
1978	SF-N	.952	155	147	348	25	25	10
1979	SF-N	.943	159	129	369	30	30	22
1980	SF-N	.946	140	113	328	25	26	16
1981	SF-N	.953	87	74	187	13	10	4
1982	SF-N	.933	84	59	150	15	12	-7
1983	SF-N	.924	32	14	59	6	4	0
1984	Det-A	.962	19	7	18	1	1	-3
1985	Det-A	.750	7	4	11	5	1	-2
1986	Det-A	1.000	2	1	1	0	0	0
1987	Det-A	.929	7	5	8	1	0	-1
1989	Atl-N	.931	28	13	41	4	5	-2
Total	20	.946	1442	1273	3123	253	270	92
1B								
1973	Atl-N	.987	20	142	10	2	11	0
1975	Atl-N	1.000	3	3	1	0	0	0
1976	Atl-N	.994	36	285	23	2	25	1
	SF-N	.991	83	681	68	7	53	8
	Yr	.992	119	966	91	9	78	9
1977	SF-N	.989	41	160	13	2	11	0
1980	SF-N	.985	14	119	12	2	9	1
1981	SF-N	.992	12	114	15	1	12	3
1982	SF-N	.993	49	396	49	3	31	7
1983	SF-N	.993	113	979	88	7	60	13
1984	Det-A	.997	47	324	44	1	33	5
1985	Det-A	.984	113	827	114	15	80	13
1986	Det-A	.998	105	808	108	2	85	11
1987	Det-A	.997	105	810	100	3	86	12
1988	Det-A	.993	65	509	58	4	43	5
1989	Atl-N	.985	50	358	49	6	32	7
Total	14	.992	856	6515	752	7	571	76
OF								
1971	Atl-N	1.000	3	6	0	0	0	0
1977	SF-N	.937	81	146	3	10	0	-4
Total	2	.939	84	152	3	0	0	-4
SS								
1982	SF-N	.943	13	16	34	3	2	-2
1983	SF-N	.806	9	8	17	6	3	-3
Total	2	.893	22	24	51	9	5	-5

■ Dwight Evans OF

YEAR	TM/L	PCT	G	PO	A	E	DP	FR
1972	Bos-A	1.000	17	25	3	0	0	0
1973	Bos-A	.995	113	178	4	1	0	0
1974	Bos-A	.990	122	294	8	3	2	8
1975	Bos-A	.987	115	281	15	4	8	15
1976	Bos-A	.994	145	324	15	2	4	7
1977	Bos-A	.992	63	126	2	1	0	-3
1978	Bos-A	.982	142	305	14	6	2	4
1979	Bos-A	.988	149	307	15	4	5	6
1980	Bos-A	.982	144	268	11	5	7	-6
1981	Bos-A	.993	108	259	9	2	1	7
1982	Bos-A	.973	161	346	9	10	3	0
1983	Bos-A	.987	99	222	6	3	1	2
1984	Bos-A	.994	161	311	7	2	2	-4
1985	Bos-A	.990	152	291	9	3	1	-3
1986	Bos-A	.983	149	280	10	5	3	-1
1987	Bos-A	.993	77	134	5	1	0	-7
1988	Bos-A	.987	85	151	4	2	0	-2
1989	Bos-A	.981	77	153	5	3	1	-1
Total	18	.987	2079	4255	151	7	40	22
1B								
1987	Bos-A	.982	79	619	41	12	72	-7
1988	Bos-A	.986	64	460	30	7	39	-6
Total	2	.984	143	1079	71	9	111	-13

■ Jake Evans OF

YEAR	TM/L	PCT	G	PO	A	E	DP	FR
1879	Tro-N	.884	72	153	30	24	4	16
1880	Tro-N	.906	47	68	9	8	4	-1
1881	Tro-N	.926	83	145	31	14	5	12
1882	Wor-N	.910	68	131	31	16	2	16
1883	Cle-N	.902	86	119	29	16	1	6
1884	Cle-N	.917	76	136	19	14	3	6
1885	Bal-a	.894	20	37	5	5	2	2
Total	7	.907	452	789	154	7	21	57
SS								
1882	Wor-N	.841	11	10	43	10	6	3
1883	Cle-N	1.000	3	9	6	0	1	0
1884	Cle-N	.875	2	3	4	1	0	0
Total	3	.872	16	22	53	1	7	3
2B								
1882	Wor-N	1.000	1	1	3	0	0	0
1883	Cle-N	1.000	1	2	0	0	0	0
1884	Cle-N	.920	4	11	12	2	3	-1
Total	3	.935	6	14	15	2	3	-1
3B								
1882	Wor-N	1.000	1	0	1	0	0	0
1883	Cle-N	.700	3	3	4	3	0	-1
Total	2	.727	4	3	5	3	0	-1

■ Joe Evans OF

YEAR	TM/L	PCT	G	PO	A	E	DP	FR
1920	Cle-A	.966	43	79	6	3	0	-1
1921	Cle-A	.933	47	90	8	7	2	-1
1922	Cle-A	.969	49	92	1	3	0	-7
1923	Was-A	.982	72	159	5	3	2	-3
1924	StL-A	.969	49	120	3	4	1	2
1925	StL-A	1.000	47	96	3	0	2	4
Total	6	.971	307	636	26	0	7	-6
3B								
1915	Cle-A	.885	30	25	67	12	1	0
1916	Cle-A	.915	28	27	59	8	3	4
1917	Cle-A	.939	127	138	279	27	20	3
1918	Cle-A	.932	74	91	155	18	17	4
1923	Was-A	.932	21	27	41	5	6	0
Total	5	.928	280	308	601	0	47	11
SS								
1919	Cle-A	.923	6	3	9	1	0	4
1920	Cle-A	.868	6	14	19	5	0	-1
Total	2	.882	12	17	28	6	0	3
1B								
1923	Was-A	1.000	5	49	2	0	3	0
2B								
1915	Cle-A	.833	2	1	4	1	1	0

■ Steve Evans OF

YEAR	TM/L	PCT	G	PO	A	E	DP	FR
1908	NY-N	—	1	0	0	0	0	-1
1909	StL-N	.947	141	212	19	13	10	-3
1910	StL-N	.968	141	226	16	8	3	-9
1911	StL-N	.972	150	258	17	8	5	-9
1912	StL-N	.942	134	219	24	15	2	-8
1913	StL-N	.983	74	111	5	2	0	-10
1914	Bro-F	.941	112	163	13	11	2	-2
1915	Bro-F	.960	61	89	8	4	2	-2
	Bal-F	.925	88	111	12	10	4	-5
	Yr	.940	149	200	20	14	6	-7
Total	8	.955	902	1389	114	1	28	-51
1B								
1909	StL-N	.958	2	23	0	1	1	-1
1910	StL-N	.972	10	104	2	3	4	-2
1913	StL-N	.500	1	2	0	2	0	0
1914	Bro-F	.968	27	279	22	10	17	2
1915	Bro-F	1.000	1	1	0	0	0	0
	Bal-F	.857	4	5	1	1	0	0
	Yr	.875	5	6	1	1	0	0
Total	5	.963	45	414	25	7	22	-1

■ Bill Everett 1B

YEAR	TM/L	PCT	G	PO	A	E	DP	FR
1898	Chi-N	.974	149	1519	70	42	123	-2
1899	Chi-N	.971	136	1491	95	47	103	8
1900	Chi-N	.979	23	264	10	6	14	-1

YEAR	TM/L	PCT	G	PO	A	E	DP	FR
1901	Was-A	.967	33	319	8	11	12	-4
Total	4	.973	341	3593	183	106	252	1
3B								
1895	Chi-N	.854	130	174	263	75	12	-8
1896	Chi-N	.882	97	148	180	44	10	-7
1897	Chi-N	.864	83	119	147	42	9	-4
Total	3	.865	310	441	590	161	31	-19
OF								
1896	Chi-N	.885	35	65	4	9	0	-3
1897	Chi-N	.947	8	18	0	1	0	-1
Total	2	.897	43	83	4	0	0	-4
2B								
1895	Chi-N	.929	3	4	9	1	0	0

■ Johnny Evers   2B

YEAR	TM/L	PCT	G	PO	A	E	DP	FR
1902	Chi-N	.990	18	38	58	1	5	0
1903	Chi-N	.937	110	245	306	37	39	-9
1904	Chi-N	.943	152	**381**	**518**	**54**	53	**31**
1905	Chi-N	.937	99	249	290	36	38	3
1906	Chi-N	.947	**153**	**344**	441	**44**	51	6
1907	Chi-N	.964	151	346	**500**	32	58	**28**
1908	Chi-N	.960	122	237	361	25	39	0
1909	Chi-N	.942	126	262	354	38	29	2
1910	Chi-N	.950	125	282	347	33	55	-4
1911	Chi-N	.975	33	66	90	4	17	-4
1912	Chi-N	.959	143	319	439	32	71	6
1913	Chi-N	.960	136	303	426	30	70	**30**
1914	Bos-N	**.976**	139	301	397	17	73	5
1915	Bos-N	.959	82	170	209	16	33	-1
1916	Bos-N	.951	71	98	175	14	29	-18
1917	Bos-N	.950	24	31	65	5	13	-7
	Phi-N	.983	49	83	145	4	15	-4
	Yr	.973	73	114	210	9	28	-11
1922	Chi-N	1.000	1	3	3	0	0	0
1929	Bos-N	.000	1	0	0	1	0	-1
Total	18	.955	1735	3758	5124	423	688	63
3B								
1903	Chi-N	.750	2	2	4	2	0	-1
1906	Chi-N	—	1	0	0	0	0	0
1911	Chi-N	.903	11	13	15	3	2	-2
1917	Phi-N	.864	7	2	17	3	0	-1
Total	4	.869	21	17	36	8	2	-4
SS								
1902	Chi-N	.907	8	10	29	4	1	0
1903	Chi-N	.797	11	21	26	12	1	-4
Total	2	.843	19	31	55	6	2	-4
OF								
1908	Chi-N	—	1	0	0	0	0	0

■ Tom Evers   2B

YEAR	TM/L	PCT	G	PO	A	E	DP	FR
1882	Bal-a	.500	1	3	0	3	0	-2
1884	Was-U	.869	**109**	326	296	**94**	28	11
Total	2	.866	110	329	296	7	28	9

■ Hoot Evers   OF

YEAR	TM/L	PCT	G	PO	A	E	DP	FR
1941	Det-A	—	1	0	0	0	0	0
1946	Det-A	.975	76	196	2	5	0	-1
1947	Det-A	.978	123	354	10	8	2	3
1948	Det-A	.973	138	392	8	11	0	-3
1949	Det-A	.994	123	319	12	2	2	**13**
1950	Det-A	**.997**	139	325	15	1	3	9
1951	Det-A	.976	108	234	9	6	1	-4
1952	Bos-A	.974	105	219	8	6	3	3
1953	Bos-A	.988	93	161	3	2	0	-7
1954	Bos-A	1.000	1	1	0	0	0	0
	NY-N	1.000	4	4	0	0	0	0
	Det-A	1.000	24	33	1	0	0	0
1955	Bal-A	.991	55	106	1	1	0	-3
	Cle-A	1.000	25	33	1	0	1	2
	Yr	.993	80	139	2	1	1	-1
1956	Bal-A	.985	36	63	1	1	1	-1
Total	12	.983	1051	2440	71	3	13	19

■ Buck Ewing   C

YEAR	TM/L	PCT	G	PO	A	E	DP	FR
1880	Tro-N	.864	10	44	7	8	0	-4
1881	Tro-N	.915	44	211	89	28	9	**13**
1882	Tro-N	.881	25	103	45	20	5	0
1883	NY-N	.922	63	270	96	31	8	-1
1884	NY-N	.933	80	445	**127**	41	10	-1
1885	NY-N	.918	63	337	102	39	8	10
1886	NY-N	.921	50	270	91	31	4	0
1887	NY-N	1.000	8	38	10	0	2	0
1888	NY-N	.947	78	480	143	35	**12**	13
1889	NY-N	.937	**97**	**524**	**149**	45	**10**	**15**
1890	NY-P	**.949**	81	372	107	26	7	16
1891	NY-N	.861	6	24	7	5	1	-2
1892	NY-N	.950	30	182	44	12	2	6
1893	Cle-N	.500	1	1	0	1	0	-1
Total	14	.931	636	3301	1017	322	78	64
1B								
1882	Tro-N	.857	1	6	0	1	0	0
1885	NY-N	.875	1	7	0	1	0	0
1886	NY-N	.842	2	14	2	3	0	0
1892	NY-N	.974	73	669	49	19	35	5
1893	Cle-N	1.000	1	5	1	0	0	0
1895	Cin-N	.976	105	957	79	26	69	8
1896	Cin-N	.980	69	669	49	15	41	4
1897	Cin-N	.800	1	4	0	1	0	0
Total	8	.974	253	2331	180	6	145	17
OF								
1880	Tro-N	.571	4	4	0	3	0	-1
1881	Tro-N	1.000	2	1	1	0	1	1
1882	Tro-N	1.000	1	1	0	0	0	0
1883	NY-N	.750	14	14	1	5	1	-2
1884	NY-N	1.000	12	8	1	0	0	0
1886	NY-N	.960	14	21	3	1	0	0
1889	NY-N	1.000	1	1	0	0	0	0
1893	Cle-N	.927	112	201	14	17	3	0

YEAR	TM/L	PCT	G	PO	A	E	DP	FR
1894	Cle-N	.912	52	86	7	9	2	-2
Total	10	.914	235	364	31	7	7	-6
3B								
1881	Tro-N	1.000	1	2	5	0	1	2
1882	Tro-N	.887	44	76	112	24	11	10
1883	NY-N	.667	1	3	3	3	0	0
1884	NY-N	.333	1	0	1	2	0	-1
1885	NY-N	.857	8	11	13	4	1	-2
1887	NY-N	.863	51	76	101	28	6	1
1888	NY-N	.803	21	32	29	15	3	-3
Total	7	.859	127	200	264	6	22	7
2B								
1882	Tro-N	.941	4	18	14	2	3	2
1883	NY-N	.900	11	22	41	7	2	-1
1887	NY-N	.835	19	39	62	20	9	-3
1890	NY-P	1.000	1	2	4	0	0	0
1891	NY-N	.881	8	11	26	5	3	0
1892	NY-N	.800	2	4	4	2	1	-1
1893	Cle-N	.889	5	10	14	3	1	-1
1894	Cle-N	.667	1	1	1	1	1	0
Total	8	.872	51	107	166	0	20	-4
SS								
1881	Tro-N	.898	22	42	90	15	7	8
1883	NY-N	.556	1	4	4	4	1	-2
1884	NY-N	.824	3	5	9	3	1	0
1885	NY-N	.500	1	1	1	2	0	-1
1888	NY-N	.842	4	3	13	3	1	0
Total	5	.862	34	52	117	7	10	5

■ Homer Ezzell   3B

YEAR	TM/L	PCT	G	PO	A	E	DP	FR
1923	Cle-A	.961	73	88	159	10	13	5
1924	Bos-A	.984	64	59	129	3	6	12
1925	Bos-A	.916	47	53	89	13	6	-3
Total	3	.957	184	200	377	6	25	14
SS								
1924	Bos-A	.881	21	30	59	12	9	-4
2B								
1923	StL-A	1.000	8	8	16	0	3	2
1925	Bos-A	.720	9	10	8	7	1	-4
Total	2	.857	17	18	24	7	4	-2
C								
1924	Bos-A	1.000	1	6	2	0	0	1

■ Jay Faatz   1B

YEAR	TM/L	PCT	G	PO	A	E	DP	FR
1884	Pit-a	.963	29	283	6	11	16	-1
1888	Cle-a	**.989**	120	1171	39	13	50	2
1889	Cle-N	.981	117	1145	62	24	67	6
1890	Buf-P	.982	32	312	7	6	18	-2
Total	4	.982	298	2911	114	4	151	5

■ Lenny Faedo   SS

YEAR	TM/L	PCT	G	PO	A	E	DP	FR
1980	Min-A	.818	5	4	5	2	0	-1
1981	Min-A	.971	12	24	42	2	10	3
1982	Min-A	.967	88	129	218	12	52	3
1983	Min-A	.954	51	53	133	9	22	-15
1984	Min-A	.968	15	22	39	2	4	-5
Total	5	.961	171	232	437	7	88	-15

■ Bill Fahey   C

YEAR	TM/L	PCT	G	PO	A	E	DP	FR
1971	Was-A	.909	2	8	2	1	0	0
1972	Tex-A	.992	39	236	26	2	4	10
1974	Tex-A	1.000	6	21	2	0	0	-1
1975	Tex-A	.983	21	54	5	1	1	-1
1976	Tex-A	.993	38	126	19	1	3	2
1977	Tex-A	1.000	34	104	5	0	0	-1
1979	SD-N	.994	68	277	33	2	5	-3
1980	SD-N	.977	85	309	34	8	6	-4
1981	Det-A	.981	27	96	9	2	3	3
1982	Det-A	1.000	28	85	16	0	2	5
1983	Det-A	1.000	18	39	2	0	0	1
Total	11	.989	366	1355	153	7	24	11

■ Ferris Fain   1B

YEAR	TM/L	PCT	G	PO	A	E	DP	FR
1947	Phi-A	.985	132	1141	101	**19**	118	1
1948	Phi-A	.989	145	1284	**120**	**16**	148	**9**
1949	Phi-A	.984	150	1275	122	**22**	**194**	3
1950	Phi-A	.987	151	1286	**124**	**19**	**192**	**8**
1951	Phi-A	.990	108	931	**113**	11	124	**14**
1952	Phi-A	.984	144	1245	**150**	**22**	124	**16**
1953	Chi-A	.989	127	1108	106	13	98	9
1954	Chi-A	.987	64	565	31	8	54	-4
1955	Det-A	.988	44	370	29	5	42	0
	Cle-A	.992	51	325	31	3	30	3
	Yr	.990	95	695	60	8	72	3
Total	9	.987	1116	9530	927	138	1124	59
OF								
1951	Phi-A	.813	11	11	2	3	1	0

■ Jim Fairey   OF

YEAR	TM/L	PCT	G	PO	A	E	DP	FR
1968	LA-N	.944	63	65	3	4	1	1
1969	Mon-N	.913	13	20	1	2	0	0
1970	Mon-N	.978	59	86	1	2	0	-2
1971	Mon-N	.968	58	85	7	3	1	2
1972	Mon-N	.932	37	40	1	3	0	-4
Total	5	.957	230	296	13	4	2	-3

■ Ron Fairly   1B

YEAR	TM/L	PCT	G	PO	A	E	DP	FR
1961	LA-N	.988	23	157	11	2	16	-1
1962	LA-N	.989	120	968	43	11	76	-13
1963	LA-N	**.995**	119	884	45	5	74	-7
1964	LA-N	.987	141	1081	82	15	89	-1
1965	LA-N	.991	13	99	6	1	6	2
1966	LA-N	.994	25	154	12	1	20	0
1967	LA-N	.986	68	598	47	9	54	3
1968	LA-N	.996	36	247	13	1	20	-2
1969	LA-N	.981	12	92	9	2	5	1
	Mon-N	.991	52	409	36	4	53	3
	Yr	.989	64	501	45	6	58	4
1970	Mon-N	.995	118	944	90	5	112	6
1971	Mon-N	.992	135	1108	104	10	110	7
1972	Mon-N	.993	68	521	38	4	37	2

YEAR	TM/L	PCT	G	PO	A	E	DP	FR
1973	Mon-N	1.000	5	20	1	0	4	0
1974	Mon-N	.989	67	572	42	7	41	1
1975	StL-N	.980	56	351	33	8	33	1
1976	StL-N	.995	27	174	21	1	19	5
	Oak-A	1.000	15	121	10	0	10	1
1977	Tor-A	.986	40	312	30	5	28	1
1978	Cal-A	.998	78	482	31	1	47	-2
Total	18	.991	1218	9294	704	2	854	5
OF								
1958	LA-N	.971	15	33	0	1	0	0
1959	LA-N	.963	88	97	8	4	1	-1
1960	LA-N	1.000	13	15	1	0	0	-1
1961	LA-N	.989	71	85	7	1	1	3
1962	LA-N	1.000	48	39	2	0	0	1
1963	LA-N	.970	45	62	3	2	0	0
1965	LA-N	.982	148	262	7	5	1	1
1966	LA-N	.974	98	110	2	3	0	-13
1967	LA-N	.986	97	129	8	2	1	2
1968	LA-N	.989	105	159	13	2	7	2
1969	LA-N	1.000	10	10	0	0	0	0
	Mon-N	.971	21	32	1	1	0	0
	Yr	.977	31	42	1	1	0	0
1970	Mon-N	1.000	4	1	0	0	0	0
1971	Mon-N	1.000	10	8	0	0	0	0
1972	Mon-N	.985	70	125	8	2	2	3
1973	Mon-N	.974	121	182	4	5	0	-13
1974	Mon-N	1.000	20	31	1	0	0	-1
1975	StL-N	1.000	20	32	0	0	0	0
1977	Tor-A	.971	33	63	4	2	0	-1
Total	18	.981	1037	1475	69	0	13	-18

■ Bibb Falk   OF

YEAR	TM/L	PCT	G	PO	A	E	DP	FR
1920	Chi-A	1.000	4	5	0	0	0	-1
1921	Chi-A	.958	149	288	9	13	5	-14
1922	Chi-A	.963	129	253	10	10	2	-9
1923	Chi-A	.951	80	148	6	8	3	-7
1924	Chi-A	.970	134	292	26	10	4	10
1925	Chi-A	.959	**153**	306	18	14	4	-4
1926	Chi-A	**.992**	**155**	338	16	3	4	8
1927	Chi-A	.978	145	372	22	9	**9**	**18**
1928	Chi-A	.972	78	164	9	5	0	2
1929	Cle-A	.943	120	215	15	14	4	-4
1930	Cle-A	.967	42	84	4	3	3	1
1931	Cle-A	.949	33	55	1	3	0	-3
Total	12	.967	1222	2520	136	2	38	-3

■ Carmen Fanzone   3B

YEAR	TM/L	PCT	G	PO	A	E	DP	FR
1970	Bos-A	.750	5	4	8	4	1	0
1971	Chi-N	.833	3	2	8	2	0	0
1972	Chi-N	.923	36	29	67	8	7	2
1973	Chi-N	.922	25	17	30	4	0	3
1974	Chi-N	.885	35	26	59	11	8	-1
Total	5	.896	104	78	172	9	16	-2
1B								
1971	Chi-N	1.000	2	11	1	0	2	0
1972	Chi-N	.995	21	187	5	1	12	-2
1973	Chi-N	.978	24	164	11	4	13	0
1974	Chi-N	1.000	7	50	7	0	4	2
Total	4	.989	54	412	24	5	31	0
2B								
1972	Chi-N	1.000	13	26	43	0	2	3
1974	Chi-N	.867	10	10	16	4	2	-1
Total	2	.960	23	36	59	4	4	2
OF								
1971	Chi-N	1.000	6	9	0	0	0	0
1972	Chi-N	1.000	1	1	0	0	0	0
1973	Chi-N	1.000	6	12	0	0	0	0
1974	Chi-N	1.000	1	1	0	0	0	0
Total	4	1.000	14	23	0	0	0	0
SS								
1972	Chi-N	—	1	0	0	0	0	0

■ Sid Farrar   1B

YEAR	TM/L	PCT	G	PO	A	E	DP	FR
1883	Phi-N	.965	99	1038	31	39	55	0
1884	Phi-N	.966	111	1142	**42**	42	41	4
1885	Phi-N	.975	111	1153	41	31	50	2
1886	Phi-N	**.980**	118	1220	45	26	38	3
1887	Phi-N	.977	116	1149	46	28	55	3
1888	Phi-N	.979	131	1345	53	30	47	2
1889	Phi-N	.978	130	1265	42	30	66	-5
1890	Phi-P	.973	**127**	1238	58	36	**79**	-2
Total	8	.974	943	9550	358	262	431	7

■ Duke Farrell   C

YEAR	TM/L	PCT	G	PO	A	E	DP	FR
1888	Chi-N	.874	33	171	50	32	3	-7
1889	Chi-N	.910	76	344	119	46	3	5
1890	Chi-P	.929	90	428	132	43	12	**21**
1891	Bos-a	.921	37	152	69	19	5	10
1893	Was-N	.923	81	304	**140**	**37**	5	**14**
1894	NY-N	.926	104	**460**	**140**	48	9	**32**
1895	NY-N	.941	62	269	67	21	**11**	4
1896	NY-N	.954	34	110	34	7	3	-3
	Was-N	1.000	18	59	22	0	1	2
	Yr	.970	52	169	56	7	4	-1
1897	Was-N	.945	63	220	91	18	10	9
1898	Was-N	.929	61	192	84	21	4	-7
1899	Was-N	1.000	4	9	5	0	0	0
	Bro-N	.948	78	251	111	20	9	9
	Yr	.949	82	260	116	20	9	9
1900	Bro-N	.944	74	252	88	20	8	-5
1901	Bro-N	.979	59	285	90	8	8	8
1902	Bro-N	.976	49	253	78	8	4	7
1903	Bos-A	.960	17	71	25	4	1	0
1904	Bos-A	.958	56	234	62	13	6	-6
1905	Bos-A	1.000	7	37	10	0	0	2
Total	17	.938	1003	4101	1417	365	102	95
3B								
1891	Bos-a	.918	66	87	160	22	8	10
1892	Pit-N	.879	133	180	286	64	20	-5

YEAR	TM/L	PCT	G	PO	A	E	DP	FR
1893	Was-N	.889	41	70	90	20	5	-1
1894	NY-N	.765	5	8	5	4	0	-1
1895	NY-N	.867	24	31	47	12	4	1
1896	NY-N	.800	7	8	8	4	1	-1
	Was-N	.891	14	16	25	5	0	-2
	Yr	.864	21	24	33	9	1	-3
Total	6	.886	290	400	621	131	38	1

OF

YEAR	TM/L	PCT	G	PO	A	E	DP	FR
1888	Chi-N	.883	31	50	3	7	1	-2
1889	Chi-N	.892	25	54	4	7	0	1
1890	Chi-P	.864	10	18	1	3	1	-1
1891	Bos-a	.978	23	40	4	1	0	1
1892	Pit-N	.852	20	41	5	8	1	2
Total	5	.894	109	203	17	6	2	1

1B

YEAR	TM/L	PCT	G	PO	A	E	DP	FR
1888	Chi-N	1.000	1	10	0	0	0	0
1890	Chi-P	.981	22	141	14	3	8	3
1891	Bos-a	.903	4	26	2	3	2	0
1893	Was-N	1.000	3	37	2	0	2	0
1894	NY-N	1.000	4	42	3	0	5	1
1895	NY-N	1.000	2	15	1	0	0	0
1897	Was-N	.875	1	6	1	1	1	0
1898	Was-N	.977	28	242	12	6	18	0
1901	Bro-N	.960	17	158	8	7	8	-1
1902	Bro-N	.983	24	216	12	4	4	0
Total	10	.975	106	893	55	4	48	3

SS

YEAR	TM/L	PCT	G	PO	A	E	DP	FR
1896	NY-N	.817	13	26	41	15	9	-2

■ Doc Farrell SS

YEAR	TM/L	PCT	G	PO	A	E	DP	FR
1925	NY-N	.900	13	7	29	4	2	0
1926	NY-N	.950	53	106	124	12	22	-11
1927	NY-N	.919	36	77	116	17	19	0
	Bos-N	.931	57	134	175	23	24	1
	Yr	.926	93	211	291	40	43	1
1928	Bos-N	.933	132	289	418	51	73	-17
1929	Bos-N	1.000	1	1	4	0	1	0
	NY-N	.909	4	7	13	2	1	0
	Yr	.926	5	8	17	2	2	0
1930	StL-N	.944	15	31	36	4	10	0
	Chi-N	.937	38	67	110	12	20	3
	Yr	.938	53	98	146	16	30	3
1932	NY-A	.950	5	10	9	1	2	-1
1933	NY-A	.947	22	35	36	4	8	-1
Total	8	.934	376	764	1070	130	182	-26

2B

YEAR	TM/L	PCT	G	PO	A	E	DP	FR
1925	NY-N	1.000	1	1	3	0	1	0
1926	NY-N	1.000	3	5	6	0	1	0
1927	Bos-N	.952	40	96	140	12	21	-1
1928	Bos-N	1.000	1	0	1	0	0	0
1929	Bos-N	—	1	0	0	0	0	0
	NY-N	.948	25	62	65	7	12	3
	Yr	.948	26	62	65	7	12	3
1930	StL-N	1.000	6	11	14	0	2	1
	Chi-N	1.000	1	2	0	0	0	0
	Yr	1.000	7	13	14	0	2	1
1932	NY-A	.963	16	24	28	2	7	0
1933	NY-A	.936	20	32	41	5	4	-3
1935	Bos-A	.917	4	6	5	1	1	0
Total	9	.953	118	239	303	7	48	0

3B

YEAR	TM/L	PCT	G	PO	A	E	DP	FR
1925	NY-N	1.000	7	6	14	0	2	1
1927	NY-N	.556	2	2	3	4	1	-1
	Bos-N	.955	18	22	20	2	2	-3
	Yr	.887	20	24	23	6	3	-4
1929	NY-N	.925	28	25	49	6	6	4
1932	NY-A	1.000	1	1	2	0	0	0
Total	4	.923	56	56	88	2	11	1

1B

YEAR	TM/L	PCT	G	PO	A	E	DP	FR
1930	StL-N	1.000	1	3	0	0	0	0
1932	NY-A	1.000	2	4	0	0	0	0
Total	2	1.000	3	7	0	0	0	0

■ Jack Farrell 2B

YEAR	TM/L	PCT	G	PO	A	E	DP	FR
1879	Syr-N	.870	54	162	186	52	16	-15
	Pro-N	.915	12	42	55	9	8	7
	Yr	.879	66	204	241	61	24	-8
1880	Pro-N	.887	80	207	274	61	26	-9
1881	Pro-N	.881	82	204	271	64	40	-5
1882	Pro-N	.875	84	212	283	71	41	-2
1883	Pro-N	.924	95	258	365	51	51	24
1884	Pro-N	.922	109	249	351	51	36	-1
1885	Pro-N	.900	68	158	194	39	16	-16
1886	Phi-N	.825	17	22	58	17	2	-3
	Was-N	.913	47	99	131	22	12	-13
	Yr	.888	64	121	189	39	14	-16
1887	Was-N	.910	40	70	131	20	5	-7
1888	Bal-a	.932	52	95	181	20	25	7
Total	10	.899	740	1778	2480	477	278	-33

SS

YEAR	TM/L	PCT	G	PO	A	E	DP	FR
1887	Was-N	.876	48	91	156	35	14	0
1888	Bal-a	.902	54	75	173	27	11	4
1889	Bal-a	.891	42	65	131	24	13	-6
Total	3	.889	144	231	460	6	38	-2

OF

YEAR	TM/L	PCT	G	PO	A	E	DP	FR
1881	Pro-N	.500	3	2	2	4	0	0

3B

YEAR	TM/L	PCT	G	PO	A	E	DP	FR
1884	Pro-N	.571	3	2	2	3	0	-1

■ Jack Farrell

YEAR	TM/L	PCT	G	PO	A	E	DP	FR
1914	Chi-F	.954	155	354	457	39	54	0
1915	Chi-F	.941	70	138	182	20	26	-4
Total	2	.950	225	492	639	9	80	-4

SS

YEAR	TM/L	PCT	G	PO	A	E	DP	FR
1914	Chi-F	.929	3	7	6	1	0	0
1915	Chi-F	—	1	0	0	0	0	0
Total	2	.929	4	7	6	1	0	0

■ John Farrell 2B

YEAR	TM/L	PCT	G	PO	A	E	DP	FR
1901	Was-A	.915	72	176	246	39	43	7
1902	StL-N	.947	118	297	422	40	72	31
1903	StL-N	.927	118	281	394	53	52	22
1904	StL-N	.934	130	297	450	53	55	16
1905	StL-N	.892	7	19	14	4	0	-3
Total	5	.932	445	1070	1526	189	222	73

OF

YEAR	TM/L	PCT	G	PO	A	E	DP	FR
1901	Was-A	.923	62	154	14	14	2	9
1903	StL-N	.978	12	39	5	1	0	6
Total	2	.934	74	193	19	5	2	15

SS

YEAR	TM/L	PCT	G	PO	A	E	DP	FR
1902	StL-N	.930	21	40	79	9	4	2

3B

YEAR	TM/L	PCT	G	PO	A	E	DP	FR
1901	Was-A	.800	1	2	2	1	1	0

■ Joe Farrell 3B

YEAR	TM/L	PCT	G	PO	A	E	DP	FR
1882	Det-N	.816	42	50	65	26	8	-11
1883	Det-N	.845	101	111	248	66	13	13
1884	Det-N	.842	110	126	198	61	12	-7
1886	Bal-a	.853	27	28	53	14	2	1
Total	4	.840	280	315	564	167	35	-4

2B

YEAR	TM/L	PCT	G	PO	A	E	DP	FR
1882	Det-N	.882	18	67	53	16	3	0
1886	Bal-a	.870	45	81	127	31	7	-16
Total	2	.875	63	148	180	7	10	-16

SS

YEAR	TM/L	PCT	G	PO	A	E	DP	FR
1882	Det-N	.863	9	12	32	7	0	0

OF

YEAR	TM/L	PCT	G	PO	A	E	DP	FR
1884	Det-N	—	1	0	0	0	0	0
1886	Bal-a	.500	1	2	0	2	0	0
Total	2	.500	2	2	0	2	0	0

■ Kerby Farrell 1B

YEAR	TM/L	PCT	G	PO	A	E	DP	FR
1943	Bos-N	.996	69	740	50	3	61	2
1945	Chi-A	.989	97	913	74	11	76	0
Total	2	.992	166	1653	124	4	137	2

■ Mike Felder OF

YEAR	TM/L	PCT	G	PO	A	E	DP	FR
1985	Mil-A	1.000	14	32	1	0	0	0
1986	Mil-A	1.000	42	98	0	0	0	-1
1987	Mil-A	.975	99	188	7	5	3	9
1988	Mil-A	.976	28	40	0	1	0	2
1989	Mil-A	.985	93	191	8	3	3	9
1990	Mil-A	.972	109	165	8	5	6	7
Total	6	.981	385	714	24	4	12	26

2B

YEAR	TM/L	PCT	G	PO	A	E	DP	FR
1987	Mil-A	1.000	1	2	3	0	0	0
1988	Mil-A	1.000	0	1	0	0	0	0
1989	Mil-A	.966	10	12	16	1	4	1
1990	Mil-A	1.000	1	2	0	0	0	0
Total	4	.973	13	16	20	1	4	1

3B

YEAR	TM/L	PCT	G	PO	A	E	DP	FR
1990	Mil-A	1.000	1	0	1	0	0	0

■ Gus Felix OF

YEAR	TM/L	PCT	G	PO	A	E	DP	FR
1923	Bos-N	.950	123	276	11	15	2	0
1924	Bos-N	.950	51	147	6	8	1	2
1925	Bos-N	.972	114	328	15	10	3	6
1926	Bro-N	.956	125	270	11	13	2	-8
1927	Bro-N	.947	119	221	13	13	1	-5
Total	5	.957	532	1242	56	9	9	-5

2B

YEAR	TM/L	PCT	G	PO	A	E	DP	FR
1923	Bos-N	.969	5	16	15	1	2	0

3B

YEAR	TM/L	PCT	G	PO	A	E	DP	FR
1923	Bos-N	.750	4	1	2	1	0	-1

■ Junior Felix OF

YEAR	TM/L	PCT	G	PO	A	E	DP	FR
1989	Tor-A	.966	107	243	9	9	0	4
1990	Tor-A	.966	125	244	11	9	3	0
Total	2	.966	232	487	20	8	3	4

■ Happy Felsch OF

YEAR	TM/L	PCT	G	PO	A	E	DP	FR
1915	Chi-A	.959	118	247	9	11	1	-3
1916	Chi-A	.981	141	340	19	7	5	7
1917	Chi-A	.985	152	440	24	7	5	19
1918	Chi-A	.957	53	149	7	7	5	5
1919	Chi-A	.968	135	360	32	13	15	21
1920	Chi-A	.981	142	385	25	8	10	18
Total	6	.975	741	1921	116	3	41	67

■ Frank Fennelly SS

YEAR	TM/L	PCT	G	PO	A	E	DP	FR
1884	Was-a	.863	60	88	215	48	14	13
	Cin-a	.813	28	25	84	25	12	-6
	Yr	.849	88	113	299	73	26	7
1885	Cin-a	.873	112	151	359	74	46	-11
1886	Cin-a	.848	132	169	485	117	54	14
1887	Cin-a	.855	134	161	421	99	31	-9
1888	Cin-a	.858	112	150	419	94	37	18
	Phi-a	.912	15	18	44	6	4	-1
	Yr	.863	127	169	463	100	41	17
1889	Phi-a	.872	138	181	453	93	53	-20
1890	Bro-a	.858	38	70	135	34	8	-2
Total	7	.860	769	1013	2615	590	259	-4

2B

YEAR	TM/L	PCT	G	PO	A	E	DP	FR
1884	Was-a	.917	4	11	11	2	1	0
1888	Cin-a	.897	4	13	13	3	0	0
Total	2	.906	8	24	24	5	1	0

3B

YEAR	TM/L	PCT	G	PO	A	E	DP	FR
1890	Bro-a	.886	7	10	21	4	4	2

OF

YEAR	TM/L	PCT	G	PO	A	E	DP	FR
1888	Cin-a	.500	4	3	0	3	0	-2

■ Joe Ferguson C

YEAR	TM/L	PCT	G	PO	A	E	DP	FR
1970	LA-N	1.000	3	9	0	0	0	0
1971	LA-N	.983	35	167	9	3	0	-2
1972	LA-N	1.000	7	37	1	0	1	1
1973	LA-N	.996	122	757	57	3	17	4
1974	LA-N	.988	82	436	40	6	2	-7
1975	LA-N	.994	35	158	16	1	1	-2
1976	LA-N	.966	17	74	10	3	2	-1

YEAR	TM/L	PCT	G	PO	A	E	DP	FR
	StL-N	.978	48	238	32	6	6	7
	Yr	.975	65	312	42	9	8	6
1977	Hou-N	.985	122	634	80	11	10	-8
1978	Hou-N	.994	51	288	29	2	0	-5
	LA-N	.984	62	284	23	5	2	-9
	Yr	.989	113	572	52	7	2	-14
1979	LA-N	.981	67	326	35	7	6	-9
1980	LA-N	.982	66	297	23	6	4	-3
1981	Cal-A	.976	8	35	5	1	1	1
1982	Cal-A	.993	32	138	13	1	2	6
1983	Cal-A	.968	9	27	3	1	0	-1
Total	14	.987	766	3905	376	6	54	-28

OF

YEAR	TM/L	PCT	G	PO	A	E	DP	FR
1972	LA-N	1.000	1	2	5	0	0	0
1973	LA-N	.935	20	29	0	2	0	-2
1974	LA-N	.980	32	50	0	1	0	-2
1975	LA-N	.984	34	57	4	1	3	2
1976	LA-N	.966	39	82	2	3	0	-1
	StL-N	.882	14	15	0	2	0	0
	Yr	.952	53	97	2	5	0	-1
1978	LA-N	1.000	3	1	0	0	0	0
1979	LA-N	.978	52	88	2	2	2	-2
1980	LA-N	.000	1	0	0	1	0	0
1981	LA-N	—	1	0	0	0	0	0
	Cal-A	1.000	4	6	0	0	0	0
1982	Cal-A	1.000	2	1	0	0	0	0
1983	Cal-A	1.000	3	4	0	0	0	0
Total	11	.966	207	338	8	2	5	-5

1B

YEAR	TM/L	PCT	G	PO	A	E	DP	FR
1977	Hou-N	1.000	1	10	0	0	0	0

■ Bob Ferguson 2B

YEAR	TM/L	PCT	G	PO	A	E	DP	FR
1878	Chi-N	.852	4	13	10	4	0	-2
1879	Tro-N	.909	6	24	26	5	4	2
1880	Tro-N	.904	82	294	255	58	38	-3
1881	Tro-N	.904	85	263	254	55	47	-10
1882	Tro-N	.914	79	247	221	44	38	-11
1883	Phi-N	.862	86	261	287	88	38	-7
Total	6	.895	342	1102	1053	254	165	-31

3B

YEAR	TM/L	PCT	G	PO	A	E	DP	FR
1876	Har-N	.826	69	124	133	54	5	2
1877	Har-N	.841	56	109	155	50	6	17
1879	Tro-N	.808	24	29	55	20	5	1
1884	Pit-a	1.000	1	2	0	0	0	0
Total	4	.830	150	264	343	124	16	20

SS

YEAR	TM/L	PCT	G	PO	A	E	DP	FR
1878	Chi-N	.881	57	71	226	40	17	19
1882	Tro-N	.538	2	1	6	6	0	-2
Total	2	.869	59	72	232	6	17	17

OF

YEAR	TM/L	PCT	G	PO	A	E	DP	FR
1884	Pit-a	.714	6	5	0	2	0	-2

1B

YEAR	TM/L	PCT	G	PO	A	E	DP	FR
1884	Pit-a	.895	3	34	0	4	0	-1

C

YEAR	TM/L	PCT	G	PO	A	E	DP	FR
1878	Chi-N	.818	1	7	2	2	0	0

■ Felix Fermin SS

YEAR	TM/L	PCT	G	PO	A	E	DP	FR
1987	Pit-N	.980	23	36	62	2	13	1
1988	Pit-N	.955	43	51	76	6	14	-5
1989	Cle-A	.967	153	247	512	26	84	18
1990	Cle-A	.975	147	213	421	16	81	4
Total	4	.970	366	547	1071	0	192	18

2B

YEAR	TM/L	PCT	G	PO	A	E	DP	FR
1989	Cle-A	1.000	2	6	5	0	0	0
1990	Cle-A	1.000	1	1	2	0	0	0
Total	2	1.000	3	7	7	0	0	0

■ Frank Fernandez C

YEAR	TM/L	PCT	G	PO	A	E	DP	FR
1967	NY-A	1.000	7	42	3	0	0	0
1968	NY-A	.989	45	240	27	3	2	5
1969	NY-A	.994	65	321	29	2	2	-6
1970	Oak-A	.993	76	405	25	3	6	-1
1971	Oak-A	1.000	2	6	1	0	0	2
	Was-A	1.000	1	5	0	0	0	-1
	Oak-A	1.000	1	5	0	0	0	0
	Chi-N	.980	16	91	6	2	0	0
	Yr	.982	19	102	7	2	0	1
1972	Chi-N	1.000	1	1	0	0	0	0
Total	6	.992	214	1116	91	0	10	-1

OF

YEAR	TM/L	PCT	G	PO	A	E	DP	FR
1967	NY-A	1.000	2	1	1	0	0	1
1968	NY-A	1.000	4	5	1	0	0	1
1969	NY-A	.941	14	15	1	1	0	-1
1970	Oak-A	1.000	1	2	0	0	0	0
1971	Was-A	1.000	6	7	1	0	0	0
Total	5	.971	27	30	4	1	0	1

■ Nanny Fernandez 3B

YEAR	TM/L	PCT	G	PO	A	E	DP	FR
1942	Bos-N	.914	98	123	206	31	16	0
1946	Bos-N	.940	81	83	150	15	10	-2
1947	Bos-N	.929	6	7	6	1	0	-1
1950	Pit-N	.925	52	48	101	12	6	-3
Total	4	.925	237	261	463	9	32	-6

SS

YEAR	TM/L	PCT	G	PO	A	E	DP	FR
1946	Bos-N	.923	18	25	35	5	8	0
1947	Bos-N	.933	62	89	146	17	22	-10
Total	2	.931	80	114	181	2	30	-10

OF

YEAR	TM/L	PCT	G	PO	A	E	DP	FR
1942	Bos-N	.992	44	117	4	1	0	3
1946	Bos-N	.963	14	25	1	1	1	1
1947	Bos-N	1.000	8	9	0	0	0	0
Total	3	.987	66	151	5	2	1	4

■ Chico Fernandez SS

YEAR	TM/L	PCT	G	PO	A	E	DP	FR
1956	Bro-N	.978	25	34	56	2	11	7
1957	Phi-N	.960	149	241	377	26	69	-25
1958	Phi-N	.975	148	296	415	18	88	-12
1959	Phi-N	.958	40	77	84	7	23	-2
1960	Det-A	.947	130	226	381	34	67	-4
1961	Det-A	.958	121	207	312	23	59	-7

YEAR	TM/L	PCT	G	PO	A	E	DP	FR
1962	Det-A	.960	138	235	336	24	53	-27
1963	Det-A	.947	14	30	42	4	8	2
	NY-N	.944	45	57	79	8	16	-13
Total	8	.960	810	1403	2082	146	394	-81
3B								
1961	Det-A	1.000	8	10	10	0	0	-1
1962	Det-A	1.000	2	3	2	0	0	0
1963	NY-N	.800	5	6	6	3	1	-2
Total	3	.925	15	19	18	3	1	-3
2B								
1959	Phi-N	1.000	2	0	2	0	0	0
1963	NY-N	1.000	3	6	4	0	0	-1
Total	2	1.000	5	6	6	0	0	-1
1B								
1962	Det-A	1.000	1	1	0	0	0	0
■ Tony Fernandez	**SS**							
1983	Tor-A	1.000	13	16	17	0	6	-3
1984	Tor-A	.974	73	116	178	8	40	1
1985	Tor-A	.962	160	283	**478**	30	109	5
1986	Tor-A	**.983**	163	294	445	13	103	3
1987	Tor-A	.979	146	**270**	396	14	88	6
1988	Tor-A	.981	154	247	470	14	106	10
1989	Tor-A	**.992**	140	260	475	6	93	**18**
1990	Tor-A	.989	161	**297**	480	9	93	9
Total	8	.980	1010	1783	2939	4	638	49
3B								
1984	Tor-A	.952	10	3	17	1	1	1
■ Al Ferrara	**OF**							
1963	LA-N	.950	11	18	1	1	0	0
1965	LA-N	.927	27	38	0	3	0	-4
1966	LA-N	.956	32	43	0	2	0	-1
1967	LA-N	.978	94	135	1	3	0	-10
1968	LA-N	.500	2	1	0	1	0	-1
1969	SD-N	.958	96	131	5	6	2	-13
1970	SD-N	.968	96	119	2	4	0	-16
1971	SD-N	1.000	2	1	0	0	0	-1
	Cin-N	1.000	5	7	0	0	0	0
	Yr	1.000	7	8	0	0	0	-1
Total	8	.962	365	493	9	0	2	-46
■ Mike Ferraro	**3B**							
1966	NY-A	.926	10	4	21	2	3	1
1968	NY-A	.975	22	16	61	2	3	4
1972	Mil-A	.950	115	93	174	14	16	-15
Total	3	.953	147	113	256	8	22	-10
SS								
1972	Mil-A	1.000	1	1	0	0	0	0
■ Rick Ferrell	**C**							
1929	StL-A	.962	45	140	35	7	3	0
1930	StL-A	.983	101	336	66	7	5	-10
1931	StL-A	.973	108	412	**86**	**14**	**11**	4
1932	StL-A	.986	120	486	78	8	9	-2
1933	StL-A	.991	21	91	16	1	1	2
	Bos-A	.990	116	500	76	6	9	4
	Yr	**.990**	**137**	**591**	92	7	10	6
1934	Bos-A	.990	128	531	72	6	7	3
1935	Bos-A	.979	131	520	79	**13**	**12**	**13**
1936	Bos-A	.987	121	**556**	55	8	5	7
1937	Bos-A	.990	18	93	10	1	1	0
	Was-A	.987	84	341	42	5	5	-6
	Yr	.988	**102**	434	52	**6**	**6**	**-6**
1938	Was-A	.981	131	512	69	11	15	-5
1939	Was-A	.976	83	327	46	9	9	-4
1940	Was-A	.980	99	427	67	10	5	-4
1941	Was-A	.980	21	85	13	2	1	-1
	StL-A	.995	98	340	51	2	11	-5
	Yr	.992	119	425	64	4	12	**-6**
1942	StL-A	.986	95	356	57	6	7	9
1943	StL-A	.987	70	327	52	5	7	12
1944	Was-A	.981	96	403	71	9	8	6
1945	Was-A	.990	83	331	64	4	3	0
1947	Was-A	.994	37	134	22	1	5	3
Total	18	.984	1806	7248	1127	135	139	26
■ Hobe Ferris	**2B**							
1901	Bos-A	.930	**138**	359	450	61	**68**	9
1902	Bos-A	.952	134	312	**461**	39	59	27
1903	Bos-A	.950	**139**	313	434	**39**	50	15
1904	Bos-A	.962	**156**	**366**	460	33	42	2
1905	Bos-A	.960	142	321	**421**	31	38	**15**
1906	Bos-A	.960	126	316	375	29	41	7
1907	Bos-A	.967	**150**	**424**	459	30	42	15
1909	StL-A	.952	34	92	88	9	13	2
Total	8	.954	1019	2503	3148	271	353	92
3B								
1906	Bos-A	.900	4	7	11	2	1	1
1908	StL-A	**.952**	148	**222**	316	27	**27**	16
1909	StL-A	.937	114	157	242	27	15	6
Total	3	.945	266	386	569	6	43	23
SS								
1901	Bos-A	—	1	0	0	0	0	0
1903	Bos-A	.929	2	6	7	1	1	0
Total	2	.929	3	6	7	1	1	0
■ Chick Fewster	**2B**							
1917	NY-A	.919	11	26	31	5	5	2
1918	NY-A	—	2	0	0	0	0	0
1919	NY-A	.929	4	7	6	1	1	0
1920	NY-A	1.000	3	0	1	0	0	0
1921	NY-A	.898	15	34	54	10	10	2
1922	NY-A	1.000	2	0	2	0	0	0
1923	Bos-A	.938	49	103	140	16	21	-6
1924	Cle-A	.961	94	194	229	17	36	-22
1925	Cle-A	.939	83	222	237	30	41	-10
1926	Bro-N	.953	103	225	297	26	38	-15
Total	10	.945	366	811	997	105	152	-49

YEAR	TM/L	PCT	G	PO	A	E	DP	FR
OF								
1919	NY-A	.946	41	73	15	5	2	6
1921	NY-A	.974	43	71	5	2	1	-5
1922	NY-A	.975	38	70	9	2	2	1
1925	Cle-A	—	1	0	0	0	0	0
Total	4	.964	123	214	29	9	5	2
SS								
1919	NY-A	.901	24	45	64	12	6	2
1920	NY-A	.840	6	9	12	4	1	0
1923	Bos-A	.912	37	76	100	17	10	-3
Total	3	.903	67	130	176	3	17	-1
3B								
1919	NY-A	1.000	2	1	0	0	1	0
1922	Bos-A	.959	23	30	63	4	4	4
1923	Bos-A	1.000	3	1	1	0	0	0
1924	Cle-A	.909	5	6	4	1	0	0
1925	Cle-A	1.000	10	5	13	0	2	1
Total	5	.961	43	43	81	5	7	5
■ Jim Field	**1B**							
1883	Col-a	.938	76	781	10	52	44	-7
1884	Col-a	.958	105	1150	27	52	58	-4
1885	Pit-a	.965	56	622	15	23	33	0
	Bal-a	.963	38	373	13	15	15	1
	Yr	.964	94	995	28	38	48	1
1890	Roc-a	.964	51	476	12	18	24	-4
1898	Was-N	.979	5	45	2	1	0	0
Total	5	.956	331	3447	79	161	174	-14
■ Cecil Fielder	**1B**							
1985	Tor-A	.979	25	171	17	4	21	1
1986	Tor-A	1.000	7	37	3	0	3	0
1987	Tor-A	1.000	16	98	6	0	12	0
1988	Tor-A	.991	17	99	10	1	10	1
1990	Det-A	.989	143	1190	111	14	**137**	3
Total	5	.989	208	1595	147	9	183	5
3B								
1986	Tor-A	.500	2	0	1	1	0	0
1987	Tor-A	—	2	0	0	0	0	0
1988	Tor-A	1.000	3	1	1	0	0	0
Total	3	.750	7	1	2	1	0	0
2B								
1988	Tor-A	1.000	2	1	1	0	0	0
OF								
1986	Tor-A	—	1	0	0	0	0	0
■ Jocko Fields	**OF**							
1887	Pit-N	.933	27	52	4	4	0	3
1888	Pit-N	.887	29	49	6	7	0	1
1889	Pit-N	.860	60	97	7	17	2	-4
1890	Pit-P	.879	80	153	21	24	3	6
1892	NY-N	.917	11	8	3	1	0	0
Total	5	.883	207	359	41	3	5	6
C								
1887	Pit-N	.901	14	67	24	10	2	3
1888	Pit-N	.814	14	54	16	16	2	-7
1889	Pit-N	.885	16	62	23	11	1	-1
1890	Pit-P	.859	15	49	12	10	1	-3
1891	Pit-N	.897	15	62	16	9	0	0
	Phi-N	.769	8	23	7	9	0	-3
	Yr	.857	23	85	23	18	0	-3
1892	NY-N	.852	10	53	16	12	2	0
Total	6	.863	92	370	114	7	8	-11
2B								
1890	Pit-P	.878	30	75	62	19	6	-14
SS								
1890	Pit-P	.750	4	9	12	7	3	-1
1891	Pit-N	.829	8	11	18	6	0	-3
Total	2	.794	12	20	30	3	3	-4
3B								
1887	Pit-N	—	1	0	0	0	0	0
1888	Pit-N	.750	3	0	3	1	0	0
Total	2	.750	4	0	3	1	0	0
1B								
1887	Pit-N	.885	3	22	1	3	0	0
■ Jim Finigan	**3B**							
1954	Phi-A	.948	136	151	305	**25**	**34**	2
1955	KC-A	.960	59	55	135	8	13	4
1956	KC-A	.917	32	29	70	9	7	3
1957	Det-A	.954	59	58	108	8	9	4
1958	SF-N	.750	4	0	3	1	0	-1
1959	Bal-A	.959	42	30	64	4	4	0
Total	6	.948	332	323	685	5	67	12
2B								
1955	KC-A	.975	90	236	228	12	72	-11
1956	KC-A	.969	52	114	105	7	35	-3
1957	Det-A	.923	3	8	4	1	2	0
1958	SF-N	.917	8	4	7	1	2	-1
1959	Bal-A	1.000	6	6	11	0	2	0
Total	5	.972	159	368	355	1	113	-15
SS								
1959	Bal-A	—	2	0	0	0	0	0
■ Steve Finley	**OF**							
1989	Bal-A	.986	76	144	1	2	0	0
1990	Bal-A	.977	133	298	4	7	1	0
Total	2	.980	209	442	5	9	1	0
■ Neal Finn	**2B**							
1930	Bro-N	.948	81	182	235	23	63	-6
1931	Bro-N	.975	112	260	331	15	65	0
1932	Bro-N	1.000	2	2	4	0	1	0
1933	Phi-N	.964	51	107	164	10	34	-1
Total	4	.964	246	551	734	8	163	-7
3B								
1932	Bro-N	.933	50	34	92	9	7	4
SS								
1932	Bro-N	—	1	0	0	0	0	0

YEAR	TM/L	PCT	G	PO	A	E	DP	FR
■ Lou Finney	**OF**							
1931	Phi-A	1.000	8	19	1	0	1	1
1933	Phi-A	.947	63	136	6	8	1	2
1934	Phi-A	.943	54	112	3	7	1	-1
1935	Phi-A	.943	76	145	5	9	1	-5
1936	Phi-A	.973	73	179	3	5	1	-2
1937	Phi-A	.930	39	91	2	7	1	-2
1938	Phi-A	.977	46	124	4	3	0	3
1939	Phi-A	1.000	4	12	0	0	0	0
	Bos-A	.961	24	48	1	2	1	-1
	Yr	.968	28	60	1	2	1	-1
1940	Bos-A	.975	69	148	10	4	0	1
1941	Bos-A	.945	92	181	7	11	2	-5
1942	Bos-A	.976	95	199	8	5	1	1
1944	Bos-A	1.000	2	7	1	0	0	1
1945	StL-A	.986	36	68	4	1	1	0
1946	StL-A	.938	7	14	1	1	0	1
Total	14	.961	688	1483	56	3	11	-6
1B								
1934	Phi-A	.985	15	120	9	2	16	1
1935	Phi-A	1.000	18	171	10	0	17	0
1936	Phi-A	.990	78	782	34	8	70	-4
1937	Phi-A	.989	50	428	28	5	38	0
1938	Phi-A	.990	64	574	24	6	35	-7
1939	Bos-A	.986	32	280	11	4	27	-3
1940	Bos-A	.994	51	504	23	3	41	-4
1941	Bos-A	.987	24	214	15	3	8	-1
1942	Bos-A	1.000	2	22	0	0	2	-1
1944	Bos-A	.987	59	521	23	7	53	-6
1945	StL-A	.994	22	165	14	1	13	-1
Total	11	.990	415	3781	191	9	320	-26
2B								
1937	Phi-A	1.000	1	0	1	0	0	0
3B								
1945	StL-A	.500	1	1	0	1	0	-1
■ Mike Fiore	**1B**							
1968	Bal-A	.943	5	30	3	2	7	0
1969	KC-A	.988	91	696	94	10	54	**13**
1970	KC-A	.986	20	131	15	2	11	1
	Bos-A	1.000	17	60	7	0	3	1
	Yr	.991	37	191	22	2	14	2
1971	Bos-A	1.000	12	74	5	0	8	0
1972	StL-N	1.000	6	7	0	0	2	0
Total	5	.988	151	998	124	4	85	15
OF								
1968	Bal-A	1.000	1	1	0	0	0	0
1969	KC-A	.929	13	13	0	1	0	0
1970	Bos-A	.000	2	0	0	1	0	0
1972	StL-N	—	1	0	0	0	0	0
Total	4	.875	17	14	0	2	0	0
■ William Fischer	**C**							
1913	Bro-N	.974	51	193	65	7	2	-1
1914	Bro-N	.958	30	136	45	8	6	3
1915	Chi-F	.972	80	324	100	12	9	-6
1916	Chi-N	.973	56	246	73	9	3	4
	Pit-N	.974	35	183	46	6	5	4
	Yr	.973	91	429	119	15	8	8
1917	Pit-N	.961	69	272	77	14	8	-9
Total	5	.969	321	1354	406	6	33	-5
1B								
1917	Pit-N	1.000	2	7	0	0	0	0
■ Mike Fischlin	**SS**							
1977	Hou-N	1.000	12	3	17	0	1	1
1978	Hou-N	.928	41	49	67	9	11	-4
1980	Hou-N	1.000	1	1	0	0	0	0
1981	Cle-A	.955	19	29	35	3	7	0
1982	Cle-A	.970	101	136	253	12	42	-6
1983	Cle-A	.983	15	16	41	1	12	0
1984	Cle-A	.912	15	11	20	3	5	3
1985	Cle-A	.941	22	20	28	3	5	8
1986	NY-A	.955	42	33	73	5	13	5
Total	9	.959	268	298	534	6	96	7
2B								
1981	Cle-A	.889	1	4	4	1	1	0
1982	Cle-A	1.000	6	3	3	0	1	0
1983	Cle-A	.965	71	151	179	12	46	**20**
1984	Cle-A	.981	55	90	115	4	25	14
1985	Cle-A	.990	31	44	59	1	15	22
1986	NY-A	.970	27	30	34	2	5	2
Total	6	.973	191	322	394	0	93	58
3B								
1982	Cle-A	.750	8	2	1	1	0	-1
1983	Cle-A	.889	4	2	6	1	1	0
1984	Cle-A	.933	17	3	11	1	0	1
1985	Cle-A	1.000	3	1	2	0	0	1
Total	4	.903	32	8	20	3	1	1
1B								
1985	Cle-A	1.000	6	8	0	0	0	0
C								
1982	Cle-A	1.000	1	1	0	0	0	0
■ Tom Fisher	**SS**							
1912	Bro-N	.917	74	121	200	29	23	-14
1913	Bro-N	.923	131	263	364	**52**	60	-19
1914	Chi-N	.943	15	20	46	4	3	-1
1915	Chi-N	.933	145	277	434	51	35	-20
1916	Cin-N	.905	29	52	81	14	9	-10
Total	5	.925	394	733	1125	150	130	-64
2B								
1912	Bro-N	.667	1	2	0	1	0	-1
1916	Cin-N	.909	6	7	3	1	0	-1
1918	StL-N	.979	63	147	232	8	34	**19**
1919	StL-N	.900	3	9	9	2	2	0
Total	4	.971	73	165	244	2	36	17
3B								
1912	Bro-N	—	1	0	0	0	0	0

YEAR	TM/L	PCT	G	PO	A	E	DP	FR
		OF						
1916	Cin-N	—	1	0	0	0	0	0
■ Carlton Fisk	C							
1969	Bos-A	1.000	1	2	0	0	0	-1
1971	Bos-A	.975	14	72	6	2	1	-1
1972	Bos-A	.984	131	846	72	15	10	1
1973	Bos-A	.983	131	739	50	14	8	5
1974	Bos-A	.980	50	267	26	6	2	2
1975	Bos-A	.979	71	347	30	8	2	-5
1976	Bos-A	.984	133	649	73	12	9	9
1977	Bos-A	.987	151	779	69	11	7	-1
1978	Bos-A	.980	154	733	90	17	13	11
1979	Bos-A	.982	39	155	8	3	1	-11
1980	Bos-A	.983	115	522	56	10	8	-8
1981	Chi-A	.990	95	470	44	5	10	-3
1982	Chi-A	.994	133	639	62	4	7	-3
1983	Chi-A	.991	133	709	46	7	5	-1
1984	Chi-A	.987	90	421	38	6	4	-13
1985	Chi-A	.989	130	801	60	10	13	-2
1986	Chi-A	.991	71	389	39	4	3	-1
1987	Chi-A	.990	122	550	57	6	15	-1
1988	Chi-A	.995	74	338	36	2	7	-6
1989	Chi-A	.993	90	419	37	3	1	-15
1990	Chi-A	.994	116	660	63	4	14	5
Total	21	.987	2044	10507	962	149	140	-39
		OF						
1978	Bos-A	1.000	1	1	0	0	0	0
1979	Bos-A	—	1	0	0	0	0	0
1980	Bos-A	1.000	5	13	0	0	0	0
1981	Chi-A	1.000	1	1	0	0	0	0
1986	Chi-A	.947	31	66	5	4	0	1
1987	Chi-A	1.000	2	3	0	0	0	0
Total	6	.957	41	84	5	4	0	1
		1B						
1980	Bos-A	.889	3	8	0	1	0	0
1981	Chi-A	.900	1	7	2	1	4	0
1982	Chi-A	.909	2	9	1	1	1	0
1987	Chi-A	.981	9	44	9	1	7	2
Total	4	.952	15	68	12	4	12	2
		3B						
1980	Bos-A	—	3	0	0	0	0	0
1981	Chi-A	1.000	1	1	0	0	0	0
Total	2	1.000	4	1	0	0	0	0
■ Ed Fitzgerald	C							
1948	Pit-N	.961	96	338	36	15	4	0
1949	Pit-N	.974	56	163	22	5	5	-4
1950	Pit-N	.950	5	16	3	1	0	0
1951	Pit-N	.965	38	98	13	4	2	-2
1952	Pit-N	1.000	18	49	4	0	0	0
1953	Pit-N	1.000	5	13	3	0	0	-1
	Was-A	.989	85	319	33	4	3	-2
1954	Was-A	.973	107	396	38	12	5	-17
1955	Was-A	.982	72	304	30	6	5	-6
1956	Was-A	.974	50	206	19	6	5	2
1957	Was-A	.963	37	142	16	6	3	-8
1958	Was-A	.970	21	94	4	3	0	-5
1959	Was-A	1.000	16	68	13	0	2	-1
	Cle-A	.978	45	192	26	5	3	0
	Yr	.984	61	260	39	5	5	-1
Total	12	.975	651	2398	260	7	37	-44
		1B						
1958	Was-A	1.000	5	31	1	0	5	0
		3B						
1952	Pit-N	.875	2	6	1	1	0	-1
■ Mike Fitzgerald	C							
1983	NY-N	.957	8	37	8	2	0	2
1984	NY-N	.995	107	715	47	4	6	7
1985	Mon-N	.987	108	542	46	8	7	-6
1986	Mon-N	.993	71	415	35	3	5	-7
1987	Mon-N	.981	104	602	27	12	2	-1
1988	Mon-N	.979	47	258	21	6	2	5
1989	Mon-N	.984	77	459	35	8	5	-7
1990	Mon-N	.990	98	560	41	6	10	-3
Total	8	.987	620	3588	260	9	37	-10
		OF						
1988	Mon-N	1.000	4	4	0	0	0	0
1989	Mon-N	1.000	6	6	2	0	0	1
1990	Mon-N	1.000	6	5	1	0	0	1
Total	3	1.000	16	15	3	0	0	2
		3B						
1989	Mon-N	1.000	8	0	7	0	0	0
		1B						
1987	Mon-N	1.000	1	1	0	0	0	0
		2B						
1987	Mon-N	—	1	0	0	0	0	0
■ Ed Fitzpatrick	2B							
1915	Bos-N	.967	71	135	160	10	23	-3
1916	Bos-N	.950	46	76	96	9	14	-8
1917	Bos-N	.929	22	33	46	6	2	-8
Total	3	.956	139	244	302	5	39	-19
		OF						
1915	Bos-N	1.000	29	43	1	0	0	-1
1916	Bos-N	1.000	28	38	0	0	0	-1
1917	Bos-N	.946	19	33	2	2	1	0
Total	3	.983	76	114	3	2	1	-2
		3B						
1917	Bos-N	.774	15	5	19	7	2	-5
■ Max Flack	OF							
1914	Chi-F	.973	133	232	18	7	3	0
1915	Chi-F	.969	138	226	24	8	5	2
1916	Chi-N	.991	136	193	22	2	4	-5
1917	Chi-N	.947	117	199	14	12	3	-3
1918	Chi-N	.978	121	199	20	5	5	-2
1919	Chi-N	.986	116	194	18	3	1	-2
1920	Chi-N	.967	132	216	16	8	2	-7

YEAR	TM/L	PCT	G	PO	A	E	DP	FR
1921	Chi-N	.989	130	244	19	3	2	-1
1922	Chi-N	.933	15	28	0	2	0	-2
	StL-N	.968	66	116	5	4	3	-8
	Yr	.961	81	144	5	6	3	-10
1923	StL-N	.951	121	242	8	13	4	-8
1924	StL-N	.971	52	90	9	3	0	-1
1925	StL-N	.991	59	103	8	1	1	-3
Total	12	.972	1336	2282	181	1	33	-40
■ Ira Flagstead	OF							
1917	Det-A	—	2	0	0	0	0	-1
1919	Det-A	.951	83	140	15	8	4	2
1920	Det-A	.967	82	164	13	6	4	7
1921	Det-A	1.000	12	22	4	0	1	1
1922	Det-A	.967	32	54	4	2	1	-2
1923	Bos-A	.962	102	218	33	10	8	20
1924	Bos-A	.975	144	374	9	10	2	-2
1925	Bos-A	.976	144	429	24	11	6	20
1926	Bos-A	.982	98	264	14	5	4	9
1927	Bos-A	.986	129	326	19	5	4	10
1928	Bos-A	.973	135	346	18	10	4	5
1929	Bos-A	.955	13	21	0	1	0	-3
	Was-A	.971	11	30	4	1	1	3
	Pit-N	1.000	9	24	0	0	0	0
	Yr	.978	22	45	0	1	0	-3
1930	Pit-N	.961	40	70	4	3	1	-3
Total	13	.973	1036	2482	161	2	40	66
		SS						
1921	Det-A	.903	55	111	139	27	8	-10
		2B						
1921	Det-A	.972	8	17	18	1	13	2
		3B						
1921	Det-A	1.000	1	0	4	0	0	1
■ Tim Flannery	2B							
1979	SD-N	.991	21	45	60	1	16	2
1980	SD-N	.988	53	115	131	3	31	0
1981	SD-N	.950	7	7	12	1	1	-1
1982	SD-N	.974	104	221	260	13	46	-25
1983	SD-N	1.000	21	31	49	0	6	0
1984	SD-N	.944	22	17	34	3	4	-1
1985	SD-N	.977	121	261	287	13	72	-18
1986	SD-N	.993	108	209	246	3	52	-5
1987	SD-N	.986	84	139	207	5	40	3
1988	SD-N	1.000	2	1	0	0	0	0
1989	SD-N	1.000	1	0	1	0	0	0
Total	11	.982	544	1046	1287	2	268	-45
		3B						
1980	SD-N	.951	41	25	73	5	3	-4
1981	SD-N	.967	15	9	20	1	4	0
1982	SD-N	.947	5	4	14	1	0	1
1983	SD-N	.969	52	27	99	4	13	10
1984	SD-N	.947	14	6	12	1	2	-1
1985	SD-N	—	1	0	0	0	0	0
1986	SD-N	.938	23	12	18	2	1	-1
1987	SD-N	.913	8	2	19	2	2	1
1988	SD-N	.972	51	27	76	3	8	-3
1989	SD-N	.920	33	14	55	6	3	2
Total	10	.953	243	126	386	5	36	5
		SS						
1982	SD-N	1.000	2	1	4	0	1	0
1983	SD-N	1.000	7	5	8	0	0	-1
1984	SD-N	.973	14	13	23	1	6	-4
1986	SD-N	1.000	8	5	11	0	3	0
1987	SD-N	1.000	2	1	0	0	0	0
1988	SD-N	—	1	0	0	0	0	0
Total	6	.986	34	25	46	1	10	-5
■ Les Fleming	1B							
1941	Cle-A	1.000	2	20	1	0	3	0
1942	Cle-A	.993	156	1503	90	12	152	-9
1945	Cle-A	.973	5	32	4	1	2	0
1946	Cle-A	.984	80	607	62	11	60	3
1947	Cle-A	.989	77	662	63	8	78	3
1949	Pit-N	1.000	5	43	0	0	4	-1
Total	6	.990	325	2867	220	2	299	-4
		OF						
1939	Det-A	1.000	3	6	0	0	0	0
1945	Cle-A	.938	33	59	2	4	2	-3
1946	Cle-A	.500	1	1	0	1	0	0
Total	3	.932	37	66	2	5	2	-3
■ Art Fletcher	SS							
1909	NY-N	.893	22	40	52	11	7	1
1910	NY-N	.895	22	31	37	8	5	-3
1911	NY-N	.926	74	116	224	27	22	1
1912	NY-N	.927	126	237	428	52	60	16
1913	NY-N	.932	136	245	435	50	42	-7
1914	NY-N	.922	135	299	446	63	46	6
1915	NY-N	.936	149	302	544	58	76	34
1916	NY-N	.940	133	253	497	48	56	20
1917	NY-N	.956	151	276	565	39	71	27
1918	NY-N	.959	124	268	484	32	54	22
1919	NY-N	.944	127	265	521	47	49	24
1920	NY-N	.914	41	79	154	22	16	-2
	Phi-N	.958	102	223	368	26	47	12
	Yr	.945	143	302	522	48	63	10
1922	Phi-N	.939	106	202	379	38	63	7
Total	13	.939	1448	2836	5134	521	614	158
		3B						
1909	NY-N	1.000	6	6	9	0	1	1
1910	NY-N	.955	11	8	13	1	0	0
1911	NY-N	.944	21	17	34	3	5	3
1912	NY-N	1.000	1	1	0	0	0	0
Total	4	.957	39	32	56	4	6	4
		2B						
1909	NY-N	.806	7	6	19	6	2	1
1910	NY-N	.925	11	20	17	3	3	-2
1911	NY-N	.959	13	20	27	2	0	0

YEAR	TM/L	PCT	G	PO	A	E	DP	FR
1912	NY-N	.800	2	3	1	1	0	0
Total	4	.904	33	49	64	2	5	-1
■ Elbie Fletcher	1B							
1934	Bos-N	.875	1	7	0	1	1	0
1935	Bos-N	.997	39	353	27	1	22	2
1937	Bos-N	.993	148	1587	108	12	117	1
1938	Bos-N	.990	146	1424	126	15	108	10
1939	Bos-N	.986	31	335	8	5	34	-5
	Pit-N	.993	101	1010	56	8	97	-4
	Yr	.991	132	1345	64	13	131	-9
1940	Pit-N	.993	147	1512	104	11	128	4
1941	Pit-N	.991	151	1444	118	14	113	9
1942	Pit-N	.992	144	1379	118	12	104	11
1943	Pit-N	.996	154	1541	108	6	141	3
1946	Pit-N	.995	147	1356	106	8	97	1
1947	Pit-N	.986	50	324	25	5	28	0
1949	Bos-N	.991	121	965	71	9	96	0
Total	12	.993	1380	13237	975	107	1086	32
■ Scott Fletcher	SS							
1981	Chi-N	.857	4	2	4	1	0	0
1982	Chi-N	1.000	11	11	23	0	3	0
1983	Chi-A	.965	100	107	275	14	52	14
1984	Chi-A	.973	134	193	381	16	75	-2
1985	Chi-A	.993	44	56	83	1	18	0
1986	Tex-A	.973	136	196	354	15	86	-5
1987	Tex-A	.966	155	249	413	23	98	5
1988	Tex-A	.983	139	215	414	11	90	1
1989	Tex-A	.960	81	124	190	13	45	-18
	Chi-A	.909	8	9	11	2	5	-2
	Yr	.957	89	133	201	15	50	-20
Total	9	.972	812	1162	2148	6	472	-7
		2B						
1981	Chi-N	.972	13	31	39	2	10	5
1983	Chi-A	.978	12	18	26	1	12	4
1984	Chi-A	.969	28	39	56	3	13	0
1985	Chi-A	1.000	37	38	55	0	11	-1
1986	Tex-A	.975	11	15	24	1	5	-2
1989	Chi-A	1.000	53	108	161	0	38	-2
1990	Chi-A	.988	151	305	436	9	115	-6
Total	7	.988	305	554	797	6	204	-2
		3B						
1981	Chi-N	1.000	1	1	1	0	0	0
1983	Chi-A	.889	7	1	7	1	0	0
1984	Chi-A	1.000	3	2	2	0	1	0
1985	Chi-A	.934	55	29	70	7	7	-1
1986	Tex-A	1.000	12	5	10	0	2	0
Total	5	.941	78	38	90	8	10	-1
■ Elmer Flick	OF							
1898	Phi-N	.931	133	237	21	19	4	7
1899	Phi-N	.931	125	234	24	19	7	9
1900	Phi-N	.914	138	232	23	24	6	3
1901	Phi-N	.962	138	278	23	12	7	15
1902	Phi-A	.947	11	17	1	1	0	0
	Cle-A	.929	110	156	13	13	2	-4
	Yr	.930	121	173	14	14	2	-4
1903	Cle-A	.955	140	219	15	11	3	1
1904	Cle-A	.955	145	234	19	12	5	7
1905	Cle-A	.938	131	178	18	13	3	0
1906	Cle-A	.981	150	248	13	5	4	-10
1907	Cle-A	.956	147	219	22	11	7	1
1908	Cle-A	1.000	9	10	1	0	1	0
1909	Cle-A	.958	61	87	4	4	1	-2
1910	Cle-A	.955	18	21	0	1	0	-3
Total	13	.947	1456	2370	197	145	50	24
		2B						
1904	Cle-A	1.000	6	14	23	0	1	3
1905	Cle-A	.857	1	4	2	1	0	0
1906	Cle-A	.952	8	15	25	2	3	-1
Total	3	.965	15	33	50	3	4	2
■ Silver Flint	C							
1878	Ind-N	.908	59	285	102	39	7	-1
1879	Chi-N	.915	78	341	109	42	6	-4
1880	Chi-N	.934	67	408	117	37	4	11
1881	Chi-N	.938	80	319	92	27	6	-7
1882	Chi-N	.935	81	440	91	37	3	-3
1883	Chi-N	.877	83	301	104	57	4	-3
1884	Chi-N	.884	73	354	110	61	9	0
1885	Chi-N	.927	68	356	100	36	2	11
1886	Chi-N	.893	54	300	93	47	2	15
1887	Chi-N	.909	47	255	73	33	3	2
1888	Chi-N	.926	22	96	42	11	7	-2
1889	Chi-N	.903	15	65	19	9	0	1
Total	12	.913	727	3520	1052	436	53	20
		OF						
1878	Ind-N	.688	9	11	0	5	0	-2
1879	Chi-N	1.000	1	2	0	0	0	0
1880	Chi-N	.800	13	6	2	2	1	1
1881	Chi-N	1.000	8	3	0	0	0	-3
1882	Chi-N	.857	10	6	0	1	0	-4
1883	Chi-N	.750	3	10	2	4	0	-8
1885	Chi-N	—	1	0	0	0	0	0
Total	7	.778	65	38	4	2	1	-16
		1B						
1881	Chi-N	1.000	1	4	0	0	0	0
1886	Chi-N	1.000	3	13	1	0	1	0
1887	Chi-N	.963	2	25	1	1	1	0
Total	3	.978	6	42	2	1	2	0
■ Curt Flood	OF							
1958	StL-N	.978	120	346	18	8	3	14
1959	StL-N	.967	106	147	1	5	1	6
1960	StL-N	.993	134	290	7	2	0	-5
1961	StL-N	.984	119	241	13	4	4	-3
1962	StL-N	.990	151	387	12	4	5	9
1963	StL-N	.988	158	401	12	5	2	14
1964	StL-N	.988	162	391	10	5	2	7

YEAR	TM/L	PCT	G	PO	A	E	DP	FR
1965	StL-N	.986	151	349	7	5	3	5
1966	StL-N	**1.000**	159	**391**	5	0	1	3
1967	StL-N	.988	126	314	4	4	1	8
1968	StL-N	.983	149	**386**	11	7	4	14
1969	StL-N	.989	152	**362**	14	4	2	11
1971	Was-A	.941	10	16	0	1	0	-1
Total	13	.987	1697	4021	114	4	28	82
	3B							
1957	Cin-N	—	2	0	0	0	0	0
1958	StL-N	—	1	0	0	0	0	0
1960	StL-N	1.000	1	1	0	0	0	0
Total	3	1.000	4	1	0	0	0	0
	2B							
1957	Cin-N	1.000	1	1	0	0	0	-1
1959	StL-N	—	1	0	0	0	0	0
Total	2	1.000	2	1	0	0	0	-1

■ Tim Flood   2B

YEAR	TM/L	PCT	G	PO	A	E	DP	FR
1899	StL-N	.878	10	15	28	6	3	-1
1902	Bro-N	.942	132	297	374	41	33	-15
1903	Bro-N	.924	84	195	216	34	37	-9
Total	3	.933	226	507	618	1	73	-25
	OF							
1902	Bro-N	1.000	1	1	0	0	0	0
1903	Bro-N	1.000	1	1	1	0	0	1
Total	2	1.000	2	2	1	0	0	1
	SS							
1903	Bro-N	.875	2	4	10	2	0	0

■ Gil Flores   OF

YEAR	TM/L	PCT	G	PO	A	E	DP	FR
1977	Cal-A	.978	85	177	5	4	2	-7
1978	NY-N	.944	8	17	0	1	0	0
1979	NY-N	.976	32	39	1	1	0	0
Total	3	.976	125	233	6	6	2	-7

■ Jake Flowers   2B

YEAR	TM/L	PCT	G	PO	A	E	DP	FR
1923	StL-N	1.000	2	2	3	0	0	0
1926	StL-N	.984	11	17	43	1	4	1
1927	Bro-N	1.000	1	2	5	0	0	0
1928	Bro-N	.971	94	260	270	16	46	-6
1929	Bro-N	.962	39	96	109	8	17	-5
1930	Bro-N	.949	65	153	200	19	42	-7
1931	Bro-N	1.000	6	17	13	0	2	1
	StL-N	.988	21	34	51	1	13	3
	Yr	.991	27	51	64	1	15	4
1932	StL-N	1.000	2	6	7	0	2	1
1933	Bro-N	.980	19	44	56	2	5	-3
Total	9	.967	260	631	757	7	131	-15
	SS							
1923	StL-N	.971	7	10	24	1	1	0
1926	StL-N	.500	1	1	0	1	0	0
1927	Bro-N	.944	65	137	184	19	29	-8
1928	Bro-N	1.000	6	3	3	0	0	1
1931	Bro-N	1.000	1	2	5	0	0	1
	StL-N	.971	24	35	66	3	14	0
	Yr	.973	25	37	71	3	14	1
1932	StL-N	.947	7	10	8	1	2	-2
1933	Bro-N	.955	36	79	90	8	13	-8
Total	7	.952	147	277	380	3	59	-17
	3B							
1923	StL-N	.800	2	3	1	1	0	-1
1931	StL-N	1.000	1	1	0	0	0	0
1932	StL-N	.980	54	59	91	3	10	1
1933	Bro-N	.950	8	7	12	1	1	0
Total	4	.972	65	70	104	5	11	0
	1B							
1926	StL-N	.957	3	20	2	1	1	0
	OF							
1930	Bro-N	1.000	1	1	0	0	0	0
1933	Bro-N	—	1	0	0	0	0	0
Total	2	1.000	2	1	0	0	0	0

■ John Flynn   1B

YEAR	TM/L	PCT	G	PO	A	E	DP	FR
1910	Pit-N	.977	93	869	49	22	54	-3
1911	Pit-N	1.000	13	101	8	0	7	1
1912	Was-A	.974	20	176	15	5	9	1
Total	3	.978	126	1146	72	7	70	-1
	OF							
1911	Pit-N	—	1	0	0	0	0	0

■ Doug Flynn   2B

YEAR	TM/L	PCT	G	PO	A	E	DP	FR
1975	Cin-N	1.000	30	33	59	0	10	6
1976	Cin-N	.988	55	68	90	2	21	-4
1977	Cin-N	1.000	9	5	9	0	2	2
	NY-N	.991	29	54	57	1	14	1
	Yr	.992	38	59	66	1	16	3
1978	NY-N	.986	128	249	299	8	70	5
1979	NY-N	.983	148	**369**	380	13	**98**	-1
1980	NY-N	**.991**	128	283	370	6	70	2
1981	NY-N	.987	100	220	301	7	58	**11**
1982	Tex-A	.989	55	117	146	3	31	5
	Mon-N	.983	58	135	157	5	40	5
1983	Mon-N	.986	107	205	290	7	57	6
1984	Mon-N	.979	88	148	223	8	47	-1
1985	Mon-N	1.000	6	3	2	0	0	0
	Det-A	.984	20	31	32	1	14	6
Total	11	.986	961	1920	2415	1	532	43
	SS							
1975	Cin-N	.983	17	18	40	1	9	3
1976	Cin-N	.978	20	34	54	2	11	0
1977	Cin-N	1.000	4	4	11	0	2	2
	NY-N	.954	65	101	146	12	24	-13
	Yr	.956	69	105	157	12	26	-11
1978	NY-N	.968	60	83	127	7	21	-4
1979	NY-N	.961	20	33	41	3	9	2
1980	NY-N	1.000	3	1	4	0	0	0
1981	NY-N	1.000	5	9	18	0	3	1
1982	Tex-A	.962	35	44	108	6	17	-3
1983	Mon-N	.970	37	44	85	4	20	1
1984	Mon-N	.956	34	41	68	5	19	-7

YEAR	TM/L	PCT	G	PO	A	E	DP	FR
1985	Mon-N	—	1	0	0	0	0	0
	Det-A	1.000	8	8	11	0	3	1
Total	11	.966	309	420	713	0	138	-17
	3B							
1975	Cin-N	.962	40	6	19	1	1	0
1976	Cin-N	1.000	23	5	8	0	1	0
1977	Cin-N	1.000	25	5	12	0	0	2
	NY-N	.667	2	2	0	1	0	-1
	Yr	.950	27	7	12	1	0	1
1985	Det-A	1.000	4	0	1	0	0	0
Total	4	.967	94	18	40	2	2	1

■ Jim Fogarty   OF

YEAR	TM/L	PCT	G	PO	A	E	DP	FR
1884	Phi-N	.915	78	193	12	19	3	6
1885	Phi-N	.941	88	**227**	26	16	5	**20**
1886	Phi-N	.953	60	114	9	6	3	3
1887	Phi-N	.920	123	273	**39**	27	**9**	**29**
1888	Phi-N	.930	117	239	26	20	**9**	14
1889	Phi-N	**.961**	128	**302**	42	14	6	**18**
1890	Phi-P	.963	91	192	17	8	3	9
Total	7	.940	685	1540	171	110	38	99
	3B							
1884	Phi-N	.786	14	22	22	12	1	-1
1885	Phi-N	.789	5	4	11	4	1	1
1886	Phi-N	.667	3	3	3	3	0	-2
1887	Phi-N	.000	2	0	0	1	0	0
1888	Phi-N	.750	5	8	7	5	1	-1
1890	Phi-P	—	1	0	0	0	0	0
Total	6	.762	30	37	43	5	3	-3
	2B							
1884	Phi-N	.889	4	10	6	2	1	-3
1885	Phi-N	.897	10	25	27	6	2	-1
1886	Phi-N	.843	13	30	29	11	6	-6
1887	Phi-N	1.000	1	0	2	0	0	0
Total	4	.872	28	65	64	9	9	-10
	SS							
1884	Phi-N	.875	3	4	3	1	0	-1
1885	Phi-N	.938	8	17	28	3	4	3
1886	Phi-N	.867	3	5	8	2	1	0
1887	Phi-N	.875	2	1	6	1	1	0
1888	Phi-N	1.000	1	4	2	0	1	0
Total	5	.918	17	31	47	7	7	2

■ Hank Foiles   C

YEAR	TM/L	PCT	G	PO	A	E	DP	FR
1953	Cin-N	.909	3	7	3	1	0	-1
	Cle-A	.933	7	10	4	1	1	2
1955	Cle-A	.988	41	222	23	3	7	15
1956	Cle-A	—	1	0	0	0	0	0
	Pit-N	.988	73	291	30	4	8	-1
1957	Pit-N	.981	109	436	32	**9**	2	-5
1958	Pit-N	.990	103	456	41	5	5	8
1959	Pit-N	1.000	51	153	8	0	3	9
1960	KC-A	.900	2	9	0	1	0	0
	Cle-A	.982	22	99	12	2	4	0
	Det-A	1.000	22	96	11	0	1	4
	Yr	.987	46	204	23	3	5	4
1961	Bal-A	.995	38	194	17	1	4	3
1962	Cin-N	.981	41	249	14	5	1	2
1963	Cin-N	1.000	1	5	1	0	0	0
	LA-A	.974	30	135	13	4	4	3
Total	10	.986	544	2362	209	6	40	39

■ Curry Foley   OF

YEAR	TM/L	PCT	G	PO	A	E	DP	FR
1879	Bos-N	.611	17	9	2	7	0	-3
1880	Bos-N	.837	35	35	6	8	1	-5
1881	Buf-N	.795	55	79	14	24	5	-3
1882	Buf-N	.833	**84**	118	22	28	7	-1
1883	Buf-N	.885	23	44	2	6	0	-1
Total	5	.819	214	285	46	3	13	-13
	1B							
1879	Bos-N	.944	2	16	1	1	0	0
1880	Bos-N	.942	25	220	8	14	9	0
1881	Buf-N	.959	27	292	10	13	9	0
Total	3	.951	54	528	19	8	18	0

■ Marv Foley   C

YEAR	TM/L	PCT	G	PO	A	E	DP	FR
1978	Chi-A	.938	10	41	4	3	0	-3
1979	Chi-A	.993	33	128	11	1	1	-1
1980	Chi-A	.991	64	216	17	2	3	2
1982	Chi-A	.980	15	45	4	1	0	5
1984	Tex-A	.988	36	147	13	2	3	1
Total	5	.986	158	577	49	9	7	4
	1B							
1980	Chi-A	1.000	3	4	0	0	0	0
1982	Chi-A	1.000	1	2	0	0	0	0
1984	Tex-A	—	1	0	0	0	0	0
Total	3	1.000	5	6	0	0	0	0
	3B							
1982	Chi-A	—	2	0	0	0	0	0
1984	Tex-A	1.000	1	1	1	0	0	0
Total	2	1.000	3	1	1	0	0	0

■ Tom Foley   SS

YEAR	TM/L	PCT	G	PO	A	E	DP	FR
1983	Cin-N	.983	37	48	69	2	15	8
1984	Cin-N	.965	83	104	197	11	31	-2
1985	Cin-N	.971	15	29	38	2	11	2
	Phi-N	.981	45	75	128	4	26	-5
	Yr	.978	60	104	166	6	37	-3
1986	Phi-N	.975	24	36	41	2	10	0
	Mon-N	.965	29	30	53	3	8	-6
	Yr	.970	53	66	94	5	18	-6
1987	Mon-N	.963	49	64	93	6	21	-1
1988	Mon-N	.973	32	39	68	3	15	4
1989	Mon-N	1.000	14	10	6	0	4	-1
1990	Mon-N	.987	45	52	89	2	22	3
Total	8	.973	373	497	782	5	163	-6
	2B							
1983	Cin-N	1.000	5	6	7	0	1	1
1984	Cin-N	1.000	10	15	31	0	5	3
1985	Cin-N	.983	18	23	36	1	10	0

YEAR	TM/L	PCT	G	PO	A	E	DP	FR
1986	Phi-N	1.000	1	0	2	0	1	1
	Mon-N	.991	25	44	71	1	9	0
	Yr	.992	26	44	73	1	10	1
1987	Mon-N	.982	39	69	93	3	22	2
1988	Mon-N	.972	89	164	255	12	46	7
1989	Mon-N	.988	108	188	295	6	53	**21**
1990	Mon-N	.940	20	18	29	3	4	-1
Total	8	.981	315	527	819	6	151	34
	3B							
1984	Cin-N	—	1	0	0	0	0	0
1985	Cin-N	—	1	0	0	0	0	0
1986	Phi-N	—	1	0	0	0	0	0
	Mon-N	1.000	15	7	23	0	1	2
	Yr	1.000	16	7	23	0	1	2
1987	Mon-N	1.000	9	1	4	0	0	0
1988	Mon-N	1.000	9	1	1	0	0	0
1989	Mon-N	.913	16	5	16	2	1	0
1990	Mon-N	1.000	7	0	5	0	0	1
Total	7	.969	59	14	49	2	2	3
	1B							
1990	Mon-N	—	1	0	0	0	0	0

■ Will Foley   3B

YEAR	TM/L	PCT	G	PO	A	E	DP	FR
1876	Cin-N	.804	46	67	101	41	4	4
1877	Cin-N	.836	56	94	130	44	**9**	6
1878	Mil-N	.812	53	68	87	36	8	-9
1879	Cin-N	.820	29	46	54	22	8	2
1881	Det-N	.769	5	5	5	3	3	-1
1884	CP-U	.804	19	18	23	10	2	-3
Total	6	.817	208	298	400	156	34	-1
	C							
1876	Cin-N	.784	20	70	10	22	1	0
1878	Mil-N	.942	7	33	16	3	0	2
Total	2	.838	27	103	26	5	1	2
	OF							
1879	Cin-N	.855	25	38	9	8	0	2
	2B							
1879	Cin-N	.789	3	6	9	4	0	-1

■ Tim Foli   SS

YEAR	TM/L	PCT	G	PO	A	E	DP	FR
1970	NY-N	1.000	2	1	7	0	0	1
1971	NY-N	1.000	12	12	20	0	5	3
1972	Mon-N	.966	148	**281**	487	27	94	10
1973	Mon-N	.960	123	245	396	27	84	9
1974	Mon-N	.971	120	220	412	19	85	**20**
1975	Mon-N	.973	151	**260**	**497**	21	**104**	6
1976	Mon-N	.975	146	247	469	18	**102**	7
1977	Mon-N	1.000	13	33	42	0	6	1
	SF-N	.974	102	184	302	13	72	3
	Yr	.977	115	217	344	13	78	4
1978	NY-N	.966	112	190	314	18	78	-15
1979	NY-N	1.000	3	4	6	0	1	1
	Pit-N	.978	132	255	404	15	97	-1
	Yr	**.978**	135	259	410	15	98	0
1980	Pit-N	.981	125	212	402	12	87	0
1981	Pit-N	.965	81	140	247	14	52	-9
1982	Cal-A	**.985**	139	235	432	10	87	5
1983	Cal-A	.975	74	115	274	10	51	10
1984	NY-A	.950	28	37	59	5	17	1
1985	Pit-N	.980	13	16	34	1	6	3
Total	16	.973	1524	2687	4804	210	1028	55
	2B							
1971	NY-N	.964	58	115	125	9	33	5
1972	Mon-N	—	1	0	0	0	0	0
1973	Mon-N	1.000	2	3	3	0	1	0
1975	Mon-N	1.000	1	1	0	0	0	0
1977	SF-N	1.000	1	0	1	0	0	0
1982	Cal-A	.947	8	12	24	2	6	-1
1984	NY-A	1.000	21	39	43	0	12	4
Total	7	.971	92	170	196	1	52	8
	3B							
1970	NY-N	1.000	2	3	3	0	1	1
1971	NY-N	.959	36	17	54	3	5	5
1974	Mon-N	—	1	0	0	0	0	0
1976	Mon-N	1.000	1	2	1	0	0	0
1977	SF-N	—	1	0	0	0	0	0
1982	Cal-A	1.000	2	0	6	0	0	1
1983	Cal-A	.930	13	16	24	3	3	0
1984	NY-A	.968	10	10	20	1	3	2
Total	8	.957	66	48	108	7	12	9
	OF							
1971	NY-N	1.000	1	6	0	0	0	1
1973	Mon-N	—	1	0	0	0	0	0
1977	SF-N	—	1	0	0	0	0	0
Total	3	1.000	3	6	0	0	0	1
	1B							
1984	NY-A	1.000	2	2	0	0	0	0

■ Dee Fondy   1B

YEAR	TM/L	PCT	G	PO	A	E	DP	FR
1951	Chi-N	.976	44	387	27	10	40	-3
1952	Chi-N	.990	143	1257	103	14	92	2
1953	Chi-N	.987	149	1274	115	18	105	4
1954	Chi-N	.993	138	1228	119	9	129	7
1955	Chi-N	.991	147	1304	**107**	**13**	135	1
1956	Chi-N	.985	133	1048	94	17	101	-3
1957	Chi-N	.991	11	103	6	1	10	-1
	Pit-N	.982	73	698	54	14	63	-3
	Yr	.983	84	801	60	15	73	-4
1958	Cin-N	.987	36	135	16	2	15	2
Total	8	.988	874	7434	641	8	690	6
	OF							
1958	Cin-N	1.000	22	25	0	0	0	0

■ Lew Fonseca   1B

YEAR	TM/L	PCT	G	PO	A	E	DP	FR
1921	Cin-N	.994	16	150	6	1	11	-1
1923	Cin-N	.986	14	129	7	2	10	0
1924	Cin-N	.982	6	51	3	1	1	0
1925	Phi-N	.994	55	498	26	3	37	0
1927	Cle-A	.992	13	118	1	1	9	-3

YEAR	TM/L	PCT	G	PO	A	E	DP	FR
1928	Cle-A	1.000	56	541	41	0	65	4
1929	Cle-A	.995	147	1486	107	8	141	6
1930	Cle-A	.980	28	274	24	6	15	3
1931	Cle-A	.993	26	284	15	2	18	0
	Chi-A	1.000	2	5	0	0	1	0
	Yr	.993	28	289	15	2	19	0
1933	Chi-A	1.000	12	138	12	0	15	2
Total	10	.994	375	3674	242	4	323	11
2B								
1921	Cin-N	.961	50	125	149	11	20	0
1922	Cin-N	.970	71	197	251	14	40	8
1923	Cin-N	.957	45	123	169	13	27	8
1924	Cin-N	1.000	10	11	27	0	3	-2
1925	Phi-N	.956	69	150	219	17	31	-8
1927	Cle-A	.973	96	229	304	15	51	-3
1928	Cle-A	1.000	1	1	4	0	0	0
1931	Chi-A	.979	21	46	49	2	8	-10
Total	8	.966	363	882	1172	2	180	-7
OF								
1921	Cin-N	.941	16	32	0	2	0	-1
1931	Chi-A	.974	95	183	4	5	1	-6
1932	Chi-A	1.000	8	14	2	0	1	1
Total	3	.971	119	229	6	7	2	-6
3B								
1928	Cle-A	.935	15	11	32	3	1	1
1930	Cle-A	.750	6	3	6	3	0	-1
1931	Chi-A	—	1	0	0	0	0	0
Total	3	.897	22	14	38	6	1	0
SS								
1928	Cle-A	1.000	4	0	1	0	1	0

■ Barry Foote C

YEAR	TM/L	PCT	G	PO	A	E	DP	FR
1974	Mon-N	.984	122	640	83	12	12	9
1975	Mon-N	.985	115	590	50	10	10	11
1976	Mon-N	.989	96	476	59	6	13	7
1977	Mon-N	.988	13	76	7	1	1	0
	Phi-N	.980	17	45	4	1	1	-1
	Yr	.985	30	121	11	2	2	-1
1978	Phi-N	1.000	31	78	5	0	0	2
1979	Chi-N	.979	129	713	63	17	9	-4
1980	Chi-N	.992	55	317	36	3	5	1
1981	Chi-N	1.000	8	30	3	0	2	1
	NY-A	.996	34	227	14	1	3	9
1982	NY-A	.973	17	71	2	2	0	-3
Total	9	.985	637	3263	326		56	30
3B								
1976	Mon-N	1.000	2	0	2	0	0	0
1B								
1976	Mon-N	1.000	1	11	0	0	0	0
1981	NY-A	1.000	1	4	0	0	1	0
Total	2	1.000	2	15	0	0	1	0

■ Davy Force SS

YEAR	TM/L	PCT	G	PO	A	E	DP	FR
1876	Phi-N	.898	60	108	237	39	11	21
	NY-N	—	1	0	0	0	0	0
	Yr	.898	61	108	237	39	11	21
1877	StL-N	.914	50	75	160	22	9	5
1879	Buf-N	.929	78	74	264	26	26	2
1880	Buf-N	.927	30	59	118	14	10	13
1881	Buf-N	.945	21	25	78	6	6	2
1882	Buf-N	.908	61	66	209	28	13	8
1883	Buf-N	.884	78	79	240	42	22	-3
1884	Buf-N	.898	105	110	312	48	21	-3
1885	Buf-N	.913	24	28	66	9	5	-1
1886	Was-N	.909	56	58	211	27	21	15
Total	10	.908	564	682	1895	261	144	59
2B								
1880	Buf-N	.939	53	163	206	24	27	17
1881	Buf-N	.937	51	168	218	26	19	22
1882	Buf-N	1.000	1	1	3	0	0	0
1883	Buf-N	.850	7	19	15	6	4	-1
1884	Buf-N	.857	1	3	3	1	0	0
1885	Buf-N	.882	42	113	134	33	23	0
1886	Was-N	.870	8	18	22	6	3	0
Total	7	.919	163	485	601	6	76	38
3B								
1876	Phi-N	.714	2	2	3	2	0	0
1877	StL-N	.929	8	11	15	2	0	1
1879	Buf-N	1.000	1	1	1	0	0	0
1881	Buf-N	1.000	1	0	2	0	0	0
1882	Buf-N	.900	11	18	18	4	0	-1
1883	Buf-N	.894	13	17	25	5	2	1
1885	Buf-N	.800	6	7	13	5	1	-2
1886	Was-N	.933	4	1	13	1	0	1
Total	8	.886	46	57	90	9	3	0
OF								
1881	Buf-N	1.000	3	2	1	0	0	0

■ Curt Ford OF

YEAR	TM/L	PCT	G	PO	A	E	DP	FR
1985	StL-N	.750	4	3	0	1	0	-1
1986	StL-N	.975	64	109	7	3	3	2
1987	StL-N	.981	75	157	2	3	0	0
1988	StL-N	.965	40	54	1	2	1	2
1989	Phi-N	1.000	52	46	3	0	0	0
1990	Phi-N	1.000	3	2	0	0	0	0
Total	6	.977	238	371	13	9	4	3
1B								
1988	StL-N	1.000	7	41	5	0	4	1
1989	Phi-N	1.000	1	0	1	0	0	0
Total	2	1.000	8	41	6	0	4	1
2B								
1989	Phi-N	1.000	1	0	1	0	0	0

■ Dan Ford OF

YEAR	TM/L	PCT	G	PO	A	E	DP	FR
1975	Min-A	.988	120	246	3	3	2	-12
1976	Min-A	.968	139	267	6	9	1	-10
1977	Min-A	.964	137	205	9	8	2	-15
1978	Min-A	.977	149	376	6	9	2	8
1979	Cal-A	.977	141	332	10	8	2	11
1980	Cal-A	.940	45	75	3	5	0	-4
1981	Cal-A	.960	97	188	3	8	0	-8
1982	Bal-A	.975	119	263	6	7	2	0
1983	Bal-A	.987	103	218	2	3	0	-5
1984	Bal-A	1.000	15	36	1	0	0	1
Total	10	.974	1065	2206	49	0	11	-34

■ Hod Ford SS

YEAR	TM/L	PCT	G	PO	A	E	DP	FR
1919	Bos-N	.946	8	10	25	2	3	2
1920	Bos-N	.912	18	28	65	9	3	4
1921	Bos-N	.972	33	96	109	6	17	3
1922	Bos-N	.953	115	267	387	32	58	-5
1923	Bos-N	.938	19	39	52	6	6	-2
1925	Bro-N	.966	66	126	185	11	33	0
1926	Cin-N	.963	57	152	190	13	57	4
1927	Cin-N	.952	104	218	323	27	75	-7
1928	Cin-N	.972	149	355	508	25	128	12
1929	Cin-N	.953	108	239	368	30	86	-1
1930	Cin-N	.974	74	139	198	9	45	-3
1931	Cin-N	.954	73	107	162	13	41	0
1932	StL-N	.750	1	2	1	1	1	0
	Bos-N	.987	16	26	48	1	8	-3
	Yr	.975	17	28	49	2	9	-3
1933	Bos-N	1.000	5	17	23	0	4	5
Total	14	.960	846	1821	2644	185	565	9
2B								
1920	Bos-N	.972	59	122	219	10	21	12
1921	Bos-N	.973	119	297	417	20	48	13
1922	Bos-N	.982	28	68	94	3	13	1
1923	Bos-N	.970	95	213	300	16	61	-7
1924	Phi-N	.970	145	337	543	27	96	12
1927	Cin-N	1.000	12	21	31	0	5	0
1929	Cin-N	.980	42	94	152	5	30	9
1930	Cin-N	.984	66	152	217	6	45	4
1931	Cin-N	1.000	3	4	6	0	2	1
1932	Bos-N	.984	20	30	30	1	7	0
Total	10	.974	589	1338	2009	8	328	45
3B								
1919	Bos-N	1.000	2	3	6	0	0	1
1931	Cin-N	1.000	1	0	1	0	0	0
1932	Bos-N	1.000	2	1	3	0	0	0
Total	3	1.000	5	4	10	0	0	1
1B								
1920	Bos-N	1.000	4	24	1	0	2	0

■ Ted Ford OF

YEAR	TM/L	PCT	G	PO	A	E	DP	FR
1970	Cle-A	1.000	12	24	1	0	0	2
1971	Cle-A	1.000	55	107	4	0	0	4
1972	Tex-A	.977	119	242	11	6	2	8
1973	Cle-A	1.000	10	6	0	0	0	-4
Total	4	.985	196	379	16	6	2	10

■ Tom Forster 2B

YEAR	TM/L	PCT	G	PO	A	E	DP	FR
1882	Det-N	.830	21	58	54	23	5	-7
1884	Pit-a	.857	1	2	4	1	0	0
1885	NY-a	.903	52	127	143	29	21	-10
1886	NY-a	.891	62	152	193	42	26	-9
Total	4	.885	136	339	394	5	52	-26
SS								
1884	Pit-a	.897	28	45	103	17	8	7
1886	NY-a	.714	1	2	8	4	2	2
Total	2	.883	29	47	111	1	10	9
OF								
1885	NY-a	.571	5	4	0	6	0	-2
1886	NY-a	.800	4	3	1	1	1	0
Total	2	.632	9	11	1	7	1	-2
3B								
1884	Pit-a	.818	6	9	9	4	0	0

■ Ray Fosse C

YEAR	TM/L	PCT	G	PO	A	E	DP	FR
1967	Cle-A	1.000	7	46	7	0	0	5
1968	Cle-A	1.000	1	1	0	0	0	0
1969	Cle-A	.977	37	237	18	6	2	4
1970	Cle-A	.989	120	854	70	10	7	8
1971	Cle-A	.988	126	748	73	10	16	-3
1972	Cle-A	.985	124	713	70	12	9	6
1973	Oak-A	.987	141	713	63	10	5	1
1974	Oak-A	.973	68	299	28	9	6	-2
1975	Oak-A	.981	82	250	15	5	1	6
1976	Cle-A	.987	85	483	42	7	9	6
1977	Cle-A	.983	77	426	48	8	4	9
	Sea-A	.968	8	29	1	1	1	-3
	Yr	.982	85	455	49	9	5	6
1979	Mil-A	1.000	13	32	3	0	1	-1
Total	12	.985	889	4831	438	8	61	30
1B								
1971	Cle-A	1.000	4	19	0	0	6	-1
1972	Cle-A	1.000	3	27	1	0	3	0
1975	Oak-A	1.000	1	3	0	0	0	0
1976	Cle-A	1.000	3	10	1	0	1	0
1977	Cle-A	1.000	1	1	0	0	0	0
1979	Mil-A	1.000	1	9	0	0	0	0
Total	6	1.000	13	69	2	0	10	-1
2B								
1975	Oak-A	—	1	0	0	0	0	-1

■ Pop Foster OF

YEAR	TM/L	PCT	G	PO	A	E	DP	FR
1898	NY-N	.967	21	28	1	1	0	-3
1899	NY-N	.949	84	103	8	6	3	-9
1900	NY-N	1.000	12	16	1	0	1	-1
1901	Was-A	.925	102	200	9	17	1	-2
	Chi-A	.909	9	9	1	1	0	-1
	Yr	.924	111	209	10	18	1	-3
Total	4	.938	228	356	20	5	5	-16
SS								
1898	NY-N	.727	2	2	6	3	0	-1
1899	NY-N	1.000	1	1	0	0	0	0
1900	NY-N	.867	7	11	28	6	3	-1
1901	Was-A	1.000	2	0	4	0	0	1
Total	4	.862	12	14	42	9	3	-1
3B								
1898	NY-N	.781	10	7	18	7	1	-1
1899	NY-N	.750	1	2	1	1	0	-1
Total	2	.778	11	9	19	8	1	-2
2B								
1900	NY-N	.889	5	6	18	3	0	-1

■ Eddie Foster 3B

YEAR	TM/L	PCT	G	PO	A	E	DP	FR
1912	Was-A	.920	154	168	348	45	22	12
1913	Was-A	.901	105	112	217	36	20	4
1914	Was-A	.929	157	200	247	34	25	-18
1915	Was-A	.919	79	92	147	21	14	-1
1916	Was-A	.929	84	104	143	19	14	-15
1917	Was-A	.935	86	95	178	19	15	-1
1918	Was-A	.936	127	156	281	30	31	3
1919	Was-A	.946	115	120	267	22	16	7
1920	Bos-A	.957	88	99	233	15	20	12
1921	Bos-A	.943	94	74	189	16	18	-8
1922	Bos-A	.886	28	21	41	8	2	-10
	StL-A	.916	37	41	79	11	12	-2
	Yr	.905	65	62	120	19	14	-12
1923	StL-A	.913	7	7	14	2	4	-1
Total	12	.930	1161	1289	2384	278	213	-18
2B								
1915	Was-A	.953	75	161	206	18	31	-4
1916	Was-A	.960	72	126	213	14	27	-1
1917	Was-A	.952	57	122	153	14	19	-5
1918	Was-A	.818	2	3	6	2	0	-1
1920	Bos-A	.949	21	28	47	4	9	2
1921	Bos-A	.954	22	42	61	5	0	-5
1923	StL-A	.961	20	35	38	3	11	-8
Total	7	.954	269	517	724	0	97	-22
SS								
1910	Was-A	.909	22	37	63	10	6	-2
1922	Bos-A	1.000	3	2	0	0	0	-1
Total	2	.913	25	39	66	0	6	-3

■ George Foster OF

YEAR	TM/L	PCT	G	PO	A	E	DP	FR
1969	SF-N	1.000	8	3	0	0	0	0
1970	SF-N	1.000	7	10	0	0	0	0
1971	SF-N	.980	30	48	1	1	0	-1
	Cin-N	.986	102	267	8	4	3	7
	Yr	.985	132	315	9	5	3	6
1972	Cin-N	.973	47	71	1	2	1	-2
1973	Cin-N	1.000	13	19	0	0	1	0
1974	Cin-N	.989	98	172	2	2	1	-14
1975	Cin-N	.990	125	299	11	3	3	13
1976	Cin-N	.994	142	322	9	2	3	8
1977	Cin-N	.992	158	352	12	3	1	13
1978	Cin-N	.971	157	319	10	10	1	2
1979	Cin-N	.982	116	214	7	4	1	-2
1980	Cin-N	.997	141	295	6	1	1	2
1981	Cin-N	.991	108	224	8	2	1	4
1982	NY-N	.974	138	289	12	8	4	7
1983	NY-N	.988	153	314	12	4	3	5
1984	Cin-N	.976	141	278	6	7	1	3
1985	NY-N	.976	123	198	7	5	2	-7
1986	NY-N	.962	62	96	4	4	1	-4
	Chi-A	1.000	11	19	2	0	0	0
Total	18	.984	1880	3809	119	2	28	34
1B								
1975	Cin-N	—	1	0	0	0	0	0
1976	Cin-N	—	1	0	0	0	0	0
Total	2	.	2	0	0	0	0	0

■ Roy Foster OF

YEAR	TM/L	PCT	G	PO	A	E	DP	FR
1970	Cle-A	.965	131	188	6	7	0	-9
1971	Cle-A	.968	107	174	9	6	2	-4
1972	Cle-A	.966	45	54	2	2	0	-4
Total	3	.967	283	416	17	5	2	-17

■ Bob Fothergill OF

YEAR	TM/L	PCT	G	PO	A	E	DP	FR
1922	Det-A	.945	38	50	2	3	1	-7
1923	Det-A	.977	68	121	4	3	0	-8
1924	Det-A	.968	45	89	2	3	1	-3
1925	Det-A	.977	59	120	6	3	2	-2
1926	Det-A	.961	103	245	3	10	0	-1
1927	Det-A	.961	137	315	3	13	1	-6
1928	Det-A	.959	90	179	6	8	0	-4
1929	Det-A	.967	59	116	2	4	1	-4
1930	Det-A	.947	38	53	1	3	0	-5
	Chi-A	.879	31	49	2	7	0	-3
	Yr	.913	69	102	3	10	0	-8
1931	Chi-A	.972	74	169	2	5	0	1
1932	Chi-A	.952	86	136	4	7	0	-12
1933	Bos-A	1.000	4	4	0	0	0	0
Total	12	.961	832	1646	37	9	6	-53

■ Jack Fournier 1B

YEAR	TM/L	PCT	G	PO	A	E	DP	FR
1912	Chi-A	.988	17	154	16	2	4	3
1913	Chi-A	.990	29	267	16	3	9	1
1914	Chi-A	.978	97	1025	78	25	30	5
1915	Chi-A	.986	65	674	41	10	31	1
1916	Chi-A	.976	85	855	49	22	47	-3
1918	NY-A	.976	27	274	13	7	23	-2
1920	StL-N	.983	138	1373	88	25	100	1
1921	StL-N	.987	149	1416	73	19	91	-4
1922	StL-N	.982	109	902	60	18	63	2
1923	Bro-N	.985	133	1281	82	21	90	4
1924	Bro-N	.985	153	1388	99	22	102	7
1925	Bro-N	.989	145	1317	82	15	105	3
1926	Bro-N	.986	64	548	28	8	19	-2
1927	Bos-N	.989	102	901	63	11	63	0
Total	14	.984	1313	12375	788	208	777	16
OF								
1913	Chi-A	.958	23	39	7	2	1	3
1914	Chi-A	.833	6	9	1	2	1	0
1915	Chi-A	.945	57	110	10	7	3	3
1916	Chi-A	1.000	1	22	0	0	0	0
Total	4	.942	87	160	18	1	5	6

Dave Foutz 1B

YEAR	TM/L	PCT	G	PO	A	E	DP	FR
1885	StL-a	.965	15	160	5	6	12	0
1886	StL-a	.953	11	97	5	5	5	0
1887	StL-a	.981	15	153	2	3	11	-1
1888	Bro-a	.983	42	455	13	8	21	0
1889	Bro-N	.979	134	1371	33	30	65	-4
1890	Bro-N	.978	113	1192	39	28	63	0
1891	Bro-N	.976	124	1235	47	31	50	-4
1892	Bro-N	.968	6	59	2	2	3	-1
1893	Bro-N	.982	54	578	19	11	19	-4
1894	Bro-N	.976	72	658	33	17	37	-3
1895	Bro-N	.943	8	83	0	5	3	-2
1896	Bro-N	.889	1	7	1	1	0	0
Total	12	.977	595	6048	199	147	289	-19

OF

1884	StL-a	.800	14	8	0	2	0	-5
1885	StL-a	.625	4	5	0	3	0	-1
1886	StL-a	.901	34	57	7	7	0	2
1887	StL-a	.899	50	85	4	10	0	-3
1888	Bro-a	.895	78	115	13	15	3	1
1890	Bro-N	.938	13	28	2	2	1	0
1892	Bro-N	.850	29	29	5	6	0	-4
1893	Bro-N	.913	77	157	10	16	1	-3
1895	Bro-N	.879	20	26	3	4	1	-2
1896	Bro-N	1.000	1	0	1	0	0	0
Total	10	.895	320	510	45	5	6	-15

SS

1891	Bro-N	1.000	1	4	6	0	0	2

Pete Fox OF

YEAR	TM/L	PCT	G	PO	A	E	DP	FR
1933	Det-A	.978	124	313	5	7	0	-2
1934	Det-A	.974	121	245	13	7	4	6
1935	Det-A	.988	125	244	9	3	1	-2
1936	Det-A	.968	55	118	3	4	0	-3
1937	Det-A	.976	143	321	6	8	0	-2
1938	Det-A	.994	155	301	13	2	2	-2
1939	Det-A	.970	126	275	12	9	3	5
1940	Det-A	.967	85	169	6	6	0	-2
1941	Bos-A	.977	62	123	5	3	2	-3
1942	Bos-A	.966	71	111	2	4	0	-9
1943	Bos-A	.961	125	261	10	11	2	-7
1944	Bos-A	.987	119	228	7	3	1	-5
1945	Bos-A	.989	57	84	5	1	1	-6
Total	13	.977	1368	2793	96	8	16	-32

Nellie Fox 2B

YEAR	TM/L	PCT	G	PO	A	E	DP	FR
1947	Phi-A	1.000	1	1	0	0	0	1
1948	Phi-A	.950	3	13	6	1	1	-2
1949	Phi-A	.982	77	191	196	7	68	-1
1950	Chi-A	.974	121	340	344	18	100	0
1951	Chi-A	.981	147	413	449	17	112	-3
1952	Chi-A	.985	151	406	433	13	111	7
1953	Chi-A	.983	154	451	426	15	101	3
1954	Chi-A	.989	155	400	392	9	103	-6
1955	Chi-A	.974	154	399	483	24	110	27
1956	Chi-A	.986	154	478	396	12	124	3
1957	Chi-A	.986	155	453	453	13	141	21
1958	Chi-A	.985	155	444	399	13	117	2
1959	Chi-A	.988	156	364	453	10	93	-3
1960	Chi-A	.985	149	412	447	13	126	12
1961	Chi-A	.982	159	413	407	15	97	-6
1962	Chi-A	.990	154	376	428	8	93	1
1963	Chi-A	.988	134	305	342	8	71	-8
1964	Hou-N	.977	115	231	317	13	51	-6
1965	Hou-N	1.000	1	0	2	0	0	0
Total	19	.984	2295	6090	6373	209	1619	42

3B

1965	Hou-N	1.000	6	4	11	0	1	0

1B

1965	Hou-N	1.000	2	8	1	0	1	0

Jimmie Foxx 1B

YEAR	TM/L	PCT	G	PO	A	E	DP	FR
1927	Phi-A	.975	32	258	15	7	10	-2
1928	Phi-A	.993	30	273	6	2	19	-5
1929	Phi-A	.995	142	1226	74	6	98	-4
1930	Phi-A	.990	153	1362	79	14	101	-2
1931	Phi-A	.993	112	964	49	7	89	-3
1932	Phi-A	.994	141	1328	79	9	115	-1
1933	Phi-A	.990	149	1402	93	15	98	6
1934	Phi-A	.993	140	1378	85	10	133	5
1935	Phi-A	.997	121	1109	77	3	107	5
1936	Bos-A	.991	149	1226	76	12	108	1
1937	Bos-A	.994	150	1287	106	8	122	10
1938	Bos-A	.987	149	1282	116	19	137	6
1939	Bos-A	.992	123	1101	91	10	104	7
1940	Bos-A	.990	95	844	79	9	87	8
1941	Bos-A	.992	124	1155	112	10	105	9
1942	Bos-A	.996	27	231	34	1	28	6
	Chi-N	.983	52	489	24	9	32	-4
	Phi-N	.988	40	292	27	4	19	1
Total	17	.992	1919	17207	1222	155	1528	43

3B

1928	Phi-A	.940	60	59	129	12	9	0
1929	Phi-A	.960	8	7	17	1	2	0
1931	Phi-A	.908	26	24	55	8	4	0
1932	Phi-A	.933	13	10	18	2	1	-3
1934	Phi-A	1.000	9	10	17	0	1	0
1935	Phi-A	1.000	2	1	0	0	0	0
1936	Bos-A	1.000	1	1	1	0	0	0
1940	Bos-A	1.000	1	1	3	0	0	0
1941	Bos-A	.765	5	7	6	4	1	-2
1944	Chi-N	1.000	2	2	6	0	0	1
1945	Phi-N	.900	14	10	26	4	0	-3
Total	11	.930	141	132	278	1	18	-7

C

1925	Phi-A	—	1	0	0	0	0	0
1926	Phi-A	1.000	12	19	5	0	0	2
1927	Phi-A	1.000	5	14	1	0	0	0
1928	Phi-A	.972	19	84	20	3	4	3
1935	Phi-A	.992	26	116	16	1	1	1
1937	Bos-A	—	1	0	0	0	0	0
1940	Bos-A	.995	42	178	18	1	2	-9
1942	Chi-N	1.000	1	2	0	0	0	0
1944	Chi-N	1.000	1	7	0	0	0	0
Total	9	.990	108	420	60	5	7	-3

OF

1926	Phi-A	1.000	3	7	0	0	0	0
1931	Phi-A	1.000	1	2	0	0	0	0
1936	Bos-A	.964	16	27	0	1	0	-1
1941	Bos-A	—	1	0	0	0	0	0
Total	4	.973	21	36	0	1	0	-1

SS

1933	Phi-A	1.000	1	0	1	0	0	0

Joe Foy 3B

YEAR	TM/L	PCT	G	PO	A	E	DP	FR
1966	Bos-A	.953	139	150	279	21	28	1
1967	Bos-A	.921	118	109	204	27	13	-10
1968	Bos-A	.935	147	116	313	30	36	3
1969	KC-A	.964	113	117	209	12	20	-8
1970	NY-N	.937	97	90	179	18	20	-1
1971	Was-A	.960	37	44	77	5	12	4
Total	6	.943	651	626	1261	113	129	-11

OF

1967	Bos-A	1.000	1	1	0	0	0	0
1968	Bos-A	1.000	3	2	0	0	0	0
1969	KC-A	.971	16	32	2	1	1	1
Total	3	.974	20	35	2	1	1	1

SS

1966	Bos-A	.893	13	19	31	6	7	-2
1969	KC-A	.800	5	3	5	2	2	-1
1971	Was-A	1.000	1	0	1	0	0	0
Total	3	.881	19	22	37	8	9	-3

1B

1969	KC-A	.986	16	131	11	2	6	0

2B

1969	KC-A	.833	3	2	3	1	0	-1
1971	Was-A	1.000	3	0	2	0	0	0
Total	2	.875	6	2	5	1	0	-1

Julio Franco SS

YEAR	TM/L	PCT	G	PO	A	E	DP	FR
1982	Phi-N	1.000	11	8	23	0	2	-1
1983	Cle-A	.961	149	247	438	28	92	-7
1984	Cle-A	.955	159	280	481	36	116	-1
1985	Cle-A	.949	151	238	419	35	95	-19
1986	Cle-A	.971	134	231	374	18	81	-7
1987	Cle-A	.963	111	157	285	17	53	-23
Total	6	.960	715	1161	2020	134	439	-58

2B

1985	Cle-A	.970	8	14	18	1	4	-3
1986	Cle-A	.982	13	17	39	1	9	2
1987	Cle-A	.979	9	18	28	1	3	0
1988	Cle-A	.982	151	310	434	14	87	-10
1989	Tex-A	.980	140	256	386	13	70	-6
1990	Tex-A	.975	152	310	444	19	101	-2
Total	6	.979	473	925	1349	9	274	-19

3B

1982	Phi-N	1.000	2	0	2	0	0	0

Tito Francona OF

YEAR	TM/L	PCT	G	PO	A	E	DP	FR
1956	Bal-A	.977	122	240	10	6	1	1
1957	Bal-A	.992	73	119	0	1	0	-9
1958	Chi-A	1.000	35	50	3	0	1	-3
	Det-A	1.000	18	22	0	0	0	-2
	Yr	1.000	53	72	3	0	1	-5
1959	Cle-A	.972	64	136	2	4	0	-1
1960	Cle-A	.989	138	278	4	3	0	2
1961	Cle-A	.987	138	289	5	4	1	0
1963	Cle-A	.986	122	215	2	3	0	-6
1964	Cle-A	.985	69	65	2	1	0	-8
1965	StL-N	.972	34	35	0	1	0	-3
1966	StL-N	1.000	9	14	0	0	0	0
1967	Phi-N	1.000	1	1	0	0	0	0
	Atl-N	1.000	6	4	2	0	0	1
	Yr	1.000	7	5	2	0	0	1
1968	Atl-N	.978	65	89	2	2	1	-4
1969	Atl-N	.957	15	21	1	1	0	0
	Oak-A	1.000	1	0	1	0	0	1
1970	Oak-A	1.000	1	3	0	0	0	0
Total	14	.984	911	1581	34	6	4	-31

1B

1956	Bal-A	.989	21	86	3	1	7	-1
1957	Bal-A	1.000	4	11	1	0	2	0
1958	Det-A	1.000	1	1	0	0	0	0
1959	Cle-A	.997	35	296	19	1	21	0
1960	Cle-A	.987	13	68	8	1	6	1
1961	Cle-A	.966	14	106	6	4	9	-2
1962	Cle-A	.986	158	1402	127	22	157	3
1963	Cle-A	1.000	11	77	6	0	3	0
1964	Cle-A	.990	17	92	5	1	10	-2
1965	StL-N	.991	13	102	3	1	8	-2
1966	StL-N	.987	30	210	18	3	20	1
1967	Phi-N	1.000	24	167	14	0	15	1
	Atl-N	.991	56	503	32	5	36	-1
	Yr	.993	80	670	46	5	51	0
1968	Atl-N	.993	33	293	10	2	17	-5
1969	Atl-N	.979	7	43	3	1	4	0
	Oak-A	.988	19	158	6	2	11	-3
1970	Oak-A	1.000	6	24	3	0	3	1
	Mil-A	1.000	13	76	7	0	10	1
	Yr	1.000	19	100	10	0	13	2
Total	15	.989	475	3715	271	4	339	-8

Terry Francona 1B

YEAR	TM/L	PCT	G	PO	A	E	DP	FR
1981	Mon-N	1.000	1	1	0	0	0	0
1982	Mon-N	1.000	16	21	0	2	0	-1
1983	Mon-N	.990	47	88	7	1	9	0
1984	Mon-N	.994	50	427	49	3	43	7
1985	Mon-N	.988	57	382	35	5	32	2
1986	Chi-N	1.000	23	98	7	0	9	0
1987	Cin-N	.995	57	373	45	2	38	5
1988	Cle-A	.977	5	40	3	1	3	0
1989	Mil-A	.989	46	320	25	4	32	0
1990	Mil-A	1.000	2	6	0	0	1	0
Total	10	.992	304	1756	171	6	169	13

OF

1981	Mon-N	1.000	26	40	5	0	0	0
1982	Mon-N	.936	33	44	0	3	0	-6
1983	Mon-N	.978	51	84	3	2	1	0
1984	Mon-N	1.000	6	4	1	0	0	1
1985	Mon-N	.981	28	49	2	1	0	0
1986	Chi-N	1.000	30	25	0	0	0	-1
1987	Cin-N	1.000	8	4	0	0	0	0
1988	Cle-A	1.000	5	7	2	0	0	1
1989	Mil-A	1.000	16	19	1	0	0	1
Total	9	.980	203	276	14	6	1	-4

3B

1985	Mon-N	1.000	1	0	3	0	0	1

Charlie Frank OF

YEAR	TM/L	PCT	G	PO	A	E	DP	FR
1893	StL-N	.930	40	84	9	7	1	3
1894	StL-N	.869	77	161	11	26	4	-2
Total	2	.889	117	245	20	3	5	1

1B

1894	StL-N	1.000	3	30	1	0	0	0

Herman Franks C

YEAR	TM/L	PCT	G	PO	A	E	DP	FR
1939	StL-N	.973	13	34	2	1	0	3
1940	Bro-N	.990	43	183	22	2	3	9
1941	Bro-N	.986	54	191	21	3	6	3
1947	Phi-A	1.000	4	12	1	0	0	-1
1948	Phi-A	.977	27	113	17	3	2	2
1949	NY-N	1.000	1	4	1	0	0	0
Total	6	.985	142	537	64	9	11	16

OF

1941	Bro-N	—	1	0	0	0	0	0

Johnny Frederick OF

YEAR	TM/L	PCT	G	PO	A	E	DP	FR
1929	Bro-N	.975	143	410	13	11	1	3
1930	Bro-N	.990	142	394	12	4	3	10
1931	Bro-N	.965	145	398	10	15	2	-4
1932	Bro-N	.976	88	201	6	5	2	-2
1933	Bro-N	.971	138	289	8	9	1	-6
1934	Bro-N	.957	77	121	11	6	3	-3
Total	6	.974	733	1813	60	0	12	-2

1B

1934	Bro-N	1.000	1	2	2	0	0	1

Roger Freed OF

YEAR	TM/L	PCT	G	PO	A	E	DP	FR
1970	Bal-A	1.000	1	4	0	0	0	0
1971	Phi-N	.989	106	184	4	2	1	-7
1972	Phi-N	.971	46	64	4	2	2	2
1976	Mon-N	1.000	1	1	0	0	0	0
1977	StL-N	.833	6	5	0	1	0	-1
1978	StL-N	1.000	6	3	0	0	0	0
Total	6	.982	166	261	8	5	3	-6

1B

1970	Bal-A	1.000	3	21	1	0	6	0
1974	Cin-N	1.000	1	2	0	0	0	0
1976	Mon-N	1.000	3	24	1	0	1	0
1977	StL-N	1.000	18	102	7	0	13	0
1978	StL-N	.992	15	110	10	1	13	0
1979	StL-N	.889	1	7	1	1	0	0
Total	6	.993	41	266	20	2	33	0

C

1971	Phi-N	1.000	1	1	0	0	0	0

Bill Freehan C

YEAR	TM/L	PCT	G	PO	A	E	DP	FR
1961	Det-A	1.000	3	14	4	0	0	1
1963	Det-A	.995	73	407	22	2	5	-2
1964	Det-A	.993	141	923	61	7	7	-3
1965	Det-A	.996	129	865	57	4	4	-1
1966	Det-A	.996	132	898	56	4	11	-1
1967	Det-A	.992	147	950	63	8	9	-8
1968	Det-A	.994	138	971	73	6	15	5
1969	Det-A	.992	120	821	49	7	7	5
1970	Det-A	.997	114	742	42	2	6	-16
1971	Det-A	.996	144	912	50	4	6	-13
1972	Det-A	.989	105	648	57	8	9	-1
1973	Det-A	.995	98	584	50	3	3	8
1974	Det-A	.986	63	312	45	5	6	-3
1975	Det-A	.991	113	582	64	6	8	-8
1976	Det-A	.983	61	312	28	6	2	-4
Total	15	.993	1581	9941	721	2	98	-41

1B

1963	Det-A	.994	19	147	16	1	14	2
1964	Det-A	1.000	1	7	0	0	0	0
1966	Det-A	1.000	5	44	4	0	3	0
1967	Det-A	1.000	11	77	5	0	6	0
1968	Det-A	.994	21	162	10	1	11	0
1969	Det-A	.980	20	138	7	3	7	-2
1972	Det-A	1.000	1	6	0	0	0	-1
1973	Det-A	1.000	7	54	3	0	2	0
1974	Det-A	.994	65	590	36	4	49	-1
1975	Det-A	1.000	5	53	0	0	4	0
1976	Det-A	1.000	2	16	6	0	2	2
Total	11	.994	157	1294	92	9	98	2

OF

1968	Det-A	—	1	0	0	0	0	0
1971	Det-A	—	1	0	0	0	0	0
Total	2	—	2	0	0	0	0	0

Jerry Freeman 1B

YEAR	TM/L	PCT	G	PO	A	E	DP	FR
1908	Was-A	.975	154	1548	66	41	69	-13
1909	Was-A	.956	14	146	7	7	11	-1
Total	2	.974	168	1694	73	8	80	-14

OF

1909	Was-A	.000	1	0	0	1	0	-1

Buck Freeman OF

YEAR	TM/L	PCT	G	PO	A	E	DP	FR
1898	Was-N	.978	29	39	5	1	2	1
1899	Was-N	.944	**155**	220	14	14	3	-12
1900	Bos-N	.950	91	130	3	7	1	-12
1901	Bos-A	1.000	1	1	0	0	0	0
1902	Bos-A	.944	**138**	222	15	14	3	-1
1903	Bos-A	.933	141	195	13	15	2	-6
1904	Bos-A	.954	157	216	14	11	4	-6
1905	Bos-A	.955	57	64	0	3	0	-8
1906	Bos-A	.989	65	74	12	1	2	-1
1907	Bos-A	1.000	3	6	0	0	0	0
Total	10	.950	837	1167	76	66	17	-45

1B
YEAR	TM/L	PCT	G	PO	A	E	DP	FR
1900	Bos-N	.970	19	148	13	5	5	1
1901	Bos-A	.974	128	1278	55	**36**	71	-4
1905	Bos-A	.972	66	585	29	18	20	-7
1906	Bos-A	.984	43	393	35	7	0	3
Total	4	.975	256	2404	132	66	96	-7

3B
YEAR	TM/L	PCT	G	PO	A	E	DP	FR
1905	Bos-A	.750	2	2	4	2	0	0
1906	Bos-A	.889	4	5	3	1	1	-1
Total	2	.824	6	7	7	3	1	-1

2B
YEAR	TM/L	PCT	G	PO	A	E	DP	FR
1901	Bos-A	—	1	0	0	0	0	0

Gene Freese 3B

YEAR	TM/L	PCT	G	PO	A	E	DP	FR
1955	Pit-N	.943	65	55	127	11	16	-4
1956	Pit-N	.963	47	38	65	4	2	-3
1957	Pit-N	.924	74	62	132	**16**	16	-2
1958	Pit-N	.800	1	0	4	1	0	1
	StL-N	1.000	3	5	6	0	0	0
	Yr	.938	4	5	10	**1**	0	1
1959	Phi-N	.916	109	83	156	22	15	-22
1960	Chi-A	.946	122	88	263	20	29	0
1961	Cin-N	.950	151	123	254	20	23	-17
1962	Cin-N	1.000	10	11	10	0	1	-2
1963	Cin-N	.930	62	44	103	11	8	-6
1964	Pit-N	.920	72	48	112	14	12	-6
1965	Pit-N	.951	19	12	27	2	1	-1
	Chi-A	.824	8	4	10	3	1	-3
1966	Chi-A	.894	34	12	64	9	5	3
	Hou-N	.800	4	4	8	3	0	0
Total	12	.934	781	589	1341	136	129	-62

2B
YEAR	TM/L	PCT	G	PO	A	E	DP	FR
1955	Pit-N	.965	57	128	173	11	41	2
1956	Pit-N	1.000	26	31	50	0	7	-4
1957	Pit-N	1.000	10	13	16	0	4	0
1958	StL-N	.934	14	32	25	4	4	-5
1959	Phi-N	.923	6	8	4	1	1	-1
1961	Cin-N	1.000	1	2	0	0	0	0
1966	Hou-N	1.000	3	2	7	0	0	0
Total	7	.968	117	216	275	16	57	-8

SS
YEAR	TM/L	PCT	G	PO	A	E	DP	FR
1958	StL-N	.924	28	45	52	8	10	-19

OF
YEAR	TM/L	PCT	G	PO	A	E	DP	FR
1957	Pit-N	.909	10	19	1	2	0	0
1963	Cin-N	—	1	0	0	0	0	0
1966	Hou-N	1.000	1	2	0	0	0	0
Total	3	.917	12	21	1	2	0	0

Jim Fregosi SS

YEAR	TM/L	PCT	G	PO	A	E	DP	FR
1961	LA-A	.944	11	12	22	2	3	0
1962	LA-A	.943	52	96	150	15	35	4
1963	LA-A	.964	151	271	446	27	90	1
1964	LA-A	.966	137	225	421	23	89	1
1965	Cal-A	.968	160	**312**	481	26	93	6
1966	Cal-A	.959	**162**	297	**531**	**35**	**125**	**15**
1967	Cal-A	.965	151	258	435	25	73	-7
1968	Cal-A	.962	**159**	273	454	29	**92**	-14
1969	Cal-A	.972	**160**	255	465	21	88	-16
1970	Cal-A	.973	150	264	468	20	99	2
1971	Cal-A	.938	74	93	237	22	31	-11
1972	NY-N	1.000	6	13	17	0	6	0
1973	NY-N	.906	17	20	38	6	10	-6
	Tex-A	1.000	6	8	4	0	2	-1
Total	13	.963	1396	2397	4169	251	836	-26

1B
YEAR	TM/L	PCT	G	PO	A	E	DP	FR
1966	Cal-A	1.000	1	2	0	0	0	0
1970	Cal-A	1.000	6	49	7	0	4	1
1971	Cal-A	1.000	18	141	13	0	13	1
1972	NY-N	1.000	3	7	1	0	0	0
1973	NY-N	1.000	3	12	3	0	1	1
	Tex-A	1.000	10	61	4	0	4	0
1974	Tex-A	1.000	47	315	24	0	32	1
1975	Tex-A	.985	54	355	34	6	31	3
1976	Tex-A	.995	26	183	14	1	20	0
1977	Tex-A	1.000	5	31	4	0	2	1
	Pit-N	.981	15	99	5	2	9	-1
1978	Pit-N	1.000	2	13	1	0	1	0
Total	10	.994	190	1268	110	9	117	7

3B
YEAR	TM/L	PCT	G	PO	A	E	DP	FR
1972	NY-N	.935	85	71	144	15	9	-7
1973	NY-N	.936	17	15	29	3	2	-1
	Tex-A	.937	34	29	45	5	7	-7
1974	Tex-A	.929	32	16	49	5	3	-3
1975	Tex-A	1.000	4	1	1	0	0	0
1976	Tex-A	.800	5	0	4	1	0	0
1977	Pit-N	—	1	0	0	0	0	0
1978	Pit-N	.667	5	1	3	2	0	-1
Total	7	.929	183	133	275	31	21	-19

OF
YEAR	TM/L	PCT	G	PO	A	E	DP	FR
1971	Cal-A	1.000	7	7	1	0	0	0
1973	NY-N	—	1	0	0	0	0	0
Total	2	1.000	8	7	1	0	0	0

2B
YEAR	TM/L	PCT	G	PO	A	E	DP	FR
1978	Pit-N	—	1	0	0	0	0	0

Howard Freigau 3B

YEAR	TM/L	PCT	G	PO	A	E	DP	FR
1922	StL-N	—	1	0	0	0	0	0
1923	StL-N	.500	1	0	1	1	0	0
1924	StL-N	.958	98	127	171	13	24	3
1925	Chi-N	.913	96	98	185	27	20	0
1926	Chi-N	**.966**	135	133	242	13	22	-2
1927	Chi-N	.883	30	22	46	9	3	1
1928	Bro-N	.810	10	8	9	4	0	-3
Total	7	.940	371	388	654	67	69	-1

SS
YEAR	TM/L	PCT	G	PO	A	E	DP	FR
1922	StL-N	1.000	2	2	3	0	1	1
1923	StL-N	.929	87	193	290	37	42	-1
1924	StL-N	1.000	2	1	1	0	0	0
1925	StL-N	.936	7	17	27	3	6	3
	Chi-N	.916	17	31	56	8	8	-4
	Yr	.923	24	48	83	11	14	-1
1926	Chi-N	1.000	2	1	2	0	0	0
1928	Bro-N	—	1	0	0	0	0	0
	Bos-N	.938	14	28	33	4	5	-6
	Yr	.938	15	28	33	4	5	-6
Total	6	.929	132	273	412	52	62	-7

2B
YEAR	TM/L	PCT	G	PO	A	E	DP	FR
1923	StL-N	.949	16	33	41	4	10	2
1925	StL-N	1.000	1	2	1	0	0	0
1928	Bos-N	.922	11	20	27	4	4	-4
Total	3	.939	28	55	69	8	14	-2

1B
YEAR	TM/L	PCT	G	PO	A	E	DP	FR
1923	StL-N	.932	9	47	8	4	5	1
1925	Chi-N	.980	7	47	1	1	3	-1
Total	2	.954	16	94	9	5	8	0

OF
YEAR	TM/L	PCT	G	PO	A	E	DP	FR
1923	StL-N	—	1	0	0	0	0	0
1926	Chi-N	1.000	1	2	0	0	0	0
Total	2	1.000	2	2	0	0	0	0

Jim French C

YEAR	TM/L	PCT	G	PO	A	E	DP	FR
1965	Was-A	.974	13	68	8	2	0	-1
1966	Was-A	.979	10	45	2	1	0	-1
1967	Was-A	.968	6	28	2	1	0	-1
1968	Was-A	.984	53	268	42	5	2	2
1969	Was-A	.989	63	316	44	4	8	8
1970	Was-A	.973	62	267	23	8	4	-6
1971	Was-A	.985	14	60	7	1	2	-1
Total	7	.982	221	1052	128	22	16	0

OF
YEAR	TM/L	PCT	G	PO	A	E	DP	FR
1970	Was-A	—	1	0	0	0	0	0

Walt French OF

YEAR	TM/L	PCT	G	PO	A	E	DP	FR
1923	Phi-A	1.000	10	17	1	0	0	-1
1925	Phi-A	.971	19	31	3	1	0	0
1926	Phi-A	.971	99	186	12	6	7	3
1927	Phi-A	.956	94	190	6	9	2	0
1928	Phi-A	1.000	19	33	1	0	0	-1
1929	Phi-A	1.000	10	8	0	0	0	-3
Total	6	.968	251	465	23	16	9	-2

Lonny Frey 2B

YEAR	TM/L	PCT	G	PO	A	E	DP	FR
1935	Bro-N	1.000	4	10	13	0	3	0
1936	Bro-N	.926	30	64	74	11	12	-9
1937	Chi-N	.982	13	24	32	1	5	-1
1938	Cin-N	.964	121	278	390	25	80	-7
1939	Cin-N	.976	124	324	412	18	83	15
1940	Cin-N	.977	150	**366**	**512**	21	**111**	18
1941	Cin-N	**.970**	**145**	340	432	24	93	-2
1942	Cin-N	.977	140	340	424	18	95	5
1943	Cin-N	**.985**	144	399	461	13	**112**	12
1946	Cin-N	.963	65	169	172	13	33	0
1947	Chi-N	1.000	9	17	20	0	4	-2
	NY-N	.923	8	14	22	3	7	3
1948	NY-N	.920	13	24	22	4	4	-1
Total	12	.973	966	2369	2986	151	642	31

SS
YEAR	TM/L	PCT	G	PO	A	E	DP	FR
1933	Bro-N	.896	34	66	89	18	11	-14
1934	Bro-N	.945	109	232	375	35	81	14
1935	Bro-N	.937	127	264	388	**44**	72	-4
1936	Bro-N	.918	117	238	331	**51**	52	-22
1937	Chi-N	.938	30	53	67	8	11	-15
1938	Cin-N	.875	3	3	11	2	1	-1
Total	6	.931	420	856	1261	158	228	-42

OF
YEAR	TM/L	PCT	G	PO	A	E	DP	FR
1936	Bro-N	1.000	1	1	0	0	0	0
1937	Chi-N	1.000	5	7	0	0	0	0
1946	Cin-N	.957	28	41	4	2	0	-3
Total	3	.964	34	49	4	2	0	-3

3B
YEAR	TM/L	PCT	G	PO	A	E	DP	FR
1934	Bro-N	.884	13	13	25	5	1	-1
1937	Chi-N	.889	9	6	2	1	2	-2
Total	2	.885	22	19	27	6	3	-3

Pepe Frias SS

YEAR	TM/L	PCT	G	PO	A	E	DP	FR
1973	Mon-N	.950	46	64	126	10	24	10
1974	Mon-N	.962	30	38	64	4	11	9
1975	Mon-N	.938	29	46	59	7	14	12
1976	Mon-N	.935	35	54	72	7	16	9
1977	Mon-N	1.000	14	10	21	0	2	3
1978	Mon-N	1.000	3	0	4	0	0	1
1979	Atl-N	.954	137	229	432	32	79	0
1980	Tex-A	.947	106	117	167	16	38	-17
	LA-N	.933	11	5	9	1	2	2
1981	LA-N	.906	15	11	18	3	2	-4
Total	9	.951	426	574	972	80	188	25

2B
YEAR	TM/L	PCT	G	PO	A	E	DP	FR
1973	Mon-N	.966	44	56	85	5	22	6
1974	Mon-N	.982	15	21	34	1	6	6
1975	Mon-N	1.000	7	2	2	0	0	0
1976	Mon-N	.957	35	26	41	3	11	6
1977	Mon-N	.917	16	17	28	1	7	5
1978	Mon-N	1.000	61	17	24	0	6	11
1980	Tex-A	.667	2	0	2	1	1	0
1981	LA-N	.875	6	4	3	1	1	-1
Total	8	.968	186	143	219	12	54	33

3B
YEAR	TM/L	PCT	G	PO	A	E	DP	FR
1973	Mon-N	1.000	6	2	4	0	1	0
1974	Mon-N	1.000	27	3	17	0	1	3
1975	Mon-N	1.000	11	7	6	0	2	2
1976	Mon-N	.667	4	1	3	2	1	0
1977	Mon-N	1.000	1	0	1	0	0	0
1980	Mon-N	1.000	7	7	13	0	1	1
1981	LA-N	—	1	0	0	0	0	0
Total	7	.970	57	20	44	2	6	6

OF
YEAR	TM/L	PCT	G	PO	A	E	DP	FR
1973	Mon-N	—	1	0	0	0	0	0
1974	Mon-N	1.000	3	2	0	0	0	0
1976	Mon-N	—	1	0	0	0	0	0
Total	3	1.000	5	2	0	0	0	0

Bernie Friberg 3B

YEAR	TM/L	PCT	G	PO	A	E	DP	FR
1922	Chi-N	1.000	5	3	3	0	0	0
1923	Chi-N	.955	146	168	294	22	**33**	7
1924	Chi-N	.954	142	163	268	21	21	4
1925	Chi-N	.889	26	24	40	8	5	-4
	Phi-N	1.000	14	15	17	0	4	0
	Yr	.923	40	39	57	8	9	**-4**
1927	Phi-N	.959	103	124	226	15	23	24
1928	Phi-N	1.000	5	4	11	0	1	1
1930	Phi-N	.935	8	9	20	2	0	1
1931	Phi-N	.957	25	21	46	3	0	-1
1933	Bos-A	.875	5	2	5	1	0	0
Total	9	.953	479	533	930	72	87	32

2B
YEAR	TM/L	PCT	G	PO	A	E	DP	FR
1920	Chi-N	.963	24	57	74	5	9	6
1922	Chi-N	1.000	3	2	4	0	2	0
1925	Chi-N	.965	77	181	257	16	36	4
1926	Phi-N	.976	144	**381**	512	22	89	22
1927	Phi-N	1.000	5	10	12	0	1	2
1928	Phi-N	1.000	3	2	4	0	1	0
1929	Phi-N	1.000	8	10	19	0	2	-2
1930	Phi-N	.953	44	104	141	12	26	-3
1931	Phi-N	.955	64	159	206	17	43	5
1932	Phi-N	.957	56	107	137	11	22	-1
1933	Bos-A	.950	6	14	24	2	5	1
Total	11	.966	434	1027	1390	85	236	34

OF
YEAR	TM/L	PCT	G	PO	A	E	DP	FR
1919	Chi-N	1.000	7	13	0	0	0	0
1920	Chi-N	.968	24	28	2	1	0	1
1922	Chi-N	.972	74	126	13	4	4	-2
1925	Chi-N	1.000	12	18	1	0	0	0
1928	Phi-N	1.000	3	2	0	0	0	0
1929	Phi-N	.991	40	102	5	1	1	3
1930	Phi-N	.933	35	66	4	5	1	0
Total	7	.972	195	355	25	11	6	2

SS
YEAR	TM/L	PCT	G	PO	A	E	DP	FR
1925	Chi-N	.000	2	0	0	1	0	-1
1928	Phi-N	.908	31	45	63	11	17	0
1929	Phi-N	.923	73	132	190	27	32	-27
1930	Phi-N	.889	12	6	10	2	2	-2
1931	Phi-N	1.000	3	6	11	0	3	1
1933	Bos-A	1.000	2	1	3	0	1	0
Total	6	.919	123	190	277	41	55	-29

1B
YEAR	TM/L	PCT	G	PO	A	E	DP	FR
1922	Chi-N	1.000	6	44	1	0	4	0
1925	Chi-N	1.000	6	46	3	0	2	0
1928	Phi-N	1.000	2	9	1	0	1	0
1929	Phi-N	1.000	2	8	0	0	0	0
1931	Phi-N	.975	5	34	5	1	2	1
Total	5	.993	21	141	10	1	9	1

C
YEAR	TM/L	PCT	G	PO	A	E	DP	FR
1925	Phi-N	—	1	0	0	0	0	0

Jim Fridley OF

YEAR	TM/L	PCT	G	PO	A	E	DP	FR
1952	Cle-A	.978	54	87	3	2	0	-3
1954	Bal-A	.985	67	132	1	2	0	-3
1958	Cin-N	1.000	2	1	0	0	0	0
Total	3	.982	123	220	4	4	0	-6

Owen Friend 2B

YEAR	TM/L	PCT	G	PO	A	E	DP	FR
1949	StL-A	1.000	2	4	8	0	1	1
1950	StL-A	.961	93	244	302	22	62	13
1953	Det-A	.947	26	74	69	8	22	4
	Cle-A	1.000	19	32	42	0	14	5
	Yr	.964	45	106	111	8	36	9
1955	Bos-A	—	1	0	0	0	0	0
Total	4	.963	141	354	421	30	99	23

3B
YEAR	TM/L	PCT	G	PO	A	E	DP	FR
1950	StL-A	.889	24	24	32	7	4	-3
1953	Cle-A	1.000	2	1	0	0	0	0
1955	Chi-N	1.000	2	2	2	0	0	0
Total	3	.896	27	26	34	7	4	-3

SS
YEAR	TM/L	PCT	G	PO	A	E	DP	FR
1950	StL-A	.900	3	3	6	1	2	0
1953	Cle-A	1.000	8	6	15	0	2	1
1955	Bos-A	.951	14	20	38	3	5	3
	Chi-N	1.000	1	1	0	0	0	0
Total	3	.957	26	30	59	4	9	4

Frankie Frisch 2B

YEAR	TM/L	PCT	G	PO	A	E	DP	FR
1919	NY-N	.972	29	82	92	5	7	3
1921	NY-N	.963	61	147	218	14	36	5
1922	NY-N	.975	85	176	288	12	40	5
1923	NY-N	**.973**	135	307	451	21	80	-12
1924	NY-N	.972	143	**391**	537	27	**103**	**23**
1925	NY-N	.957	42	105	162	12	20	6
1926	NY-N	.957	127	261	471	19	69	10
1927	StL-N	**.979**	153	396	**641**	22	**104**	**49**
1928	StL-N	**.976**	139	383	474	21	80	3
1929	StL-N	.970	121	295	374	21	66	-6
1930	StL-N	.969	123	307	473	25	93	**27**
1931	StL-N	.974	129	290	424	19	93	**16**

YEAR	TM/L	PCT	G	PO	A	E	DP	FR
1932	StL-N	.971	75	214	250	14	53	18
1933	StL-N	.982	132	371	378	14	71	3
1934	StL-N	.977	115	294	351	15	74	5
1935	StL-N	.982	88	193	252	8	48	-7
1936	StL-N	.965	60	124	176	11	27	-8
1937	StL-N	1.000	5	12	14	0	0	-1
Total	18	.974	1762	4348	6026	280	1064	139
3B								
1919	NY-N	.982	20	18	38	1	0	1
1920	NY-N	.967	109	104	251	12	23	9
1921	NY-N	.936	93	79	200	19	16	-1
1922	NY-N	.944	53	52	117	10	12	8
1923	NY-N	.984	17	20	42	1	3	4
1924	NY-N	1.000	2	7	6	0	3	2
1925	NY-N	.931	46	37	97	10	4	0
1926	NY-N	.923	7	9	15	2	2	1
1929	NY-N	.977	13	9	33	1	1	2
1930	StL-N	.933	10	8	20	2	3	1
1932	StL-N	1.000	37	38	59	0	5	0
1934	StL-N	.932	25	31	37	5	6	-1
1935	StL-N	.857	5	6	6	2	0	-1
1936	StL-N	.944	22	35	16	3	5	-4
Total	14	.953	459	453	937	8	83	21
SS								
1919	NY-N	.857	1	2	4	1	0	0
1920	NY-N	1.000	2	2	5	0	0	0
1922	NY-N	1.000	1	0	1	0	0	0
1924	NY-N	1.000	10	10	14	0	1	0
1925	NY-N	.932	39	73	134	15	21	-2
1927	StL-N	1.000	1	0	2	0	0	0
1929	StL-N	1.000	1	1	0	0	0	0
1932	StL-N	.882	4	5	10	2	2	-1
1933	StL-N	.937	15	24	35	4	5	-6
1936	StL-N	.667	1	0	2	1	0	-1
Total	10	.934	75	117	207	3	29	-10

■ Emil Frisk OF

YEAR	TM/L	PCT	G	PO	A	E	DP	FR
1901	Det-A	.750	2	3	0	1	0	-1
1905	StL-A	.923	115	117	15	11	2	-8
Total	2	.918	117	120	15	2	2	-9

■ Harry Fritz 3B

YEAR	TM/L	PCT	G	PO	A	E	DP	FR
1913	Phi-A	.846	5	6	5	2	0	-1
1914	Chi-F	.912	46	34	59	9	7	-8
1915	Chi-F	.964	70	79	106	7	8	-7
Total	3	.941	121	119	170	8	15	-16
SS								
1914	Chi-F	.967	9	13	16	1	4	-1
1915	Chi-F	—	1	0	0	0	0	0
Total	2	.967	10	13	16	1	4	-1
2B								
1914	Chi-F	1.000	1	1	1	0	0	0
1915	Chi-F	1.000	6	6	3	0	0	-1
Total	2	1.000	7	7	4	0	0	-1

■ Doug Frobel OF

YEAR	TM/L	PCT	G	PO	A	E	DP	FR
1982	Pit-N	1.000	12	18	0	0	0	0
1983	Pit-N	.964	24	27	0	1	0	-1
1984	Pit-N	.956	112	188	9	9	3	-2
1985	Pit-N	.941	36	46	2	3	1	-2
	Mon-N	.923	6	12	0	1	0	0
	Yr	.938	42	58	2	4	1	-2
1987	Cle-A	1.000	12	6	0	0	0	0
Total	5	.957	202	297	11	4	4	-5

■ Tito Fuentes 2B

YEAR	TM/L	PCT	G	PO	A	E	DP	FR
1965	SF-N	1.000	7	11	8	0	3	-1
1966	SF-N	.960	60	138	170	13	24	-8
1967	SF-N	.980	130	274	313	12	79	25
1970	SF-N	.966	78	141	205	12	41	0
1971	SF-N	.973	152	373	465	23	109	1
1972	SF-N	.964	152	361	417	29	89	-21
1973	SF-N	.993	160	386	478	6	102	-5
1974	SF-N	.979	103	238	287	11	70	-4
1975	SD-N	.970	142	389	448	26	105	4
1976	SD-N	.971	127	339	387	22	91	2
1977	Det-A	.970	151	379	459	26	115	4
1978	Oak-A	.944	13	17	17	2	4	-12
Total	12	.974	1275	3046	3654	182	832	-15
SS								
1965	SF-N	.919	18	16	41	5	5	-6
1966	SF-N	.957	76	145	233	17	44	-5
1967	SF-N	1.000	5	2	2	0	0	0
1969	SF-N	.931	30	28	53	6	11	-5
1970	SF-N	.975	36	41	74	3	12	-1
Total	5	.953	165	232	403	1	72	-18
3B								
1965	SF-N	—	1	0	0	0	0	0
1969	SF-N	.925	36	22	64	7	7	-2
1970	SF-N	.942	24	20	45	4	4	-1
1973	SF-N	1.000	1	0	1	0	0	0
Total	4	.933	62	42	110	1	11	-3

■ Vern Fuller 2B

YEAR	TM/L	PCT	G	PO	A	E	DP	FR
1966	Cle-A	1.000	16	29	27	0	12	-4
1967	Cle-A	.986	64	133	144	4	39	0
1968	Cle-A	.988	73	112	129	3	24	-7
1969	Cle-A	.978	102	217	192	9	53	8
1970	Cle-A	.919	16	18	16	3	4	1
Total	5	.982	271	509	508	9	132	-2
3B								
1968	Cle-A	.933	23	21	21	3	1	-4
1969	Cle-A	1.000	7	5	4	0	2	0
1970	Cle-A	1.000	4	0	6	0	0	1
Total	3	.950	34	26	31	3	3	-3
SS								
1967	Cle-A	—	2	0	0	0	0	0
1968	Cle-A	.000	4	0	0	1	0	-1
Total	2	.000	6	0	0	1	0	-1

YEAR	TM/L	PCT	G	PO	A	E	DP	FR
1B								
1970	Cle-A	1.000	1	0	1	0	0	0

■ Shorty Fuller SS

YEAR	TM/L	PCT	G	PO	A	E	DP	FR
1888	Was-N	.845	47	67	140	38	14	-5
1889	StL-a	.913	140	240	459	67	46	0
1890	StL-a	.870	130	222	389	91	39	-1
1891	StL-a	.856	103	168	309	80	36	-11
1892	NY-N	.888	141	294	434	92	44	1
1893	NY-N	.911	130	260	464	71	48	10
1894	NY-N	.884	89	205	291	65	39	-3
1895	NY-N	.913	126	270	499	73	59	34
1896	NY-N	.874	18	42	62	15	8	1
Total	9	.891	924	1768	3047	592	333	26
2B								
1888	Was-N	1.000	2	2	3	0	0	-2
1891	StL-a	.916	39	83	113	18	21	1
1894	NY-N	.875	1	2	5	1	0	0
Total	3	.916	42	87	121	9	21	-1
OF								
1894	NY-N	1.000	2	4	0	0	0	0
3B								
1894	NY-N	.667	2	2	4	3	1	-1

■ Chick Fullis OF

YEAR	TM/L	PCT	G	PO	A	E	DP	FR
1929	NY-N	.962	78	151	3	6	0	-7
1930	NY-N	—	2	0	0	0	0	0
1931	NY-N	.988	68	154	5	2	2	2
1932	NY-N	.990	55	97	1	1	0	-5
1933	Phi-N	.977	151	410	15	10	3	5
1934	Phi-N	.956	27	42	1	2	0	-4
	StL-N	.969	56	124	2	4	1	2
	Yr	.966	83	166	3	6	1	-2
1936	StL-N	1.000	26	53	2	0	2	4
Total	7	.977	463	1031	29	5	8	-3
2B								
1931	NY-N	.947	9	12	24	2	2	-1
1932	NY-N	1.000	1	0	1	0	0	0
Total	2	.949	10	12	25	2	2	-1
3B								
1933	Phi-N	—	1	0	0	0	0	0

■ Chick Fulmer SS

YEAR	TM/L	PCT	G	PO	A	E	DP	FR
1876	Lou-N	.861	66	83	209	47	13	-3
1882	Cin-a	.897	79	130	243	43	14	-13
1883	Cin-a	.863	92	134	243	60	26	-2
1884	Cin-a	.786	29	22	66	24	7	-12
Total	4	.867	266	369	761	174	60	-30
2B								
1879	Buf-N	.905	76	273	301	60	46	17
1880	Buf-N	.882	11	34	33	9	2	-2
1884	StL-a	.778	1	4	3	2	0	-1
Total	3	.901	88	311	337	1	48	14
OF								
1884	Cin-a	.833	2	1	4	1	0	2
3B								
1884	Cin-a	—	1	0	0	0	0	0

■ Chris Fulmer C

YEAR	TM/L	PCT	G	PO	A	E	DP	FR
1884	Was-U	.937	34	213	41	17	4	-5
1886	Bal-a	.949	68	465	113	31	5	2
1887	Bal-a	.913	48	201	73	26	5	-8
1888	Bal-a	.903	45	237	42	30	5	-14
1889	Bal-a	.857	2	10	2	2	0	-1
Total	5	.929	197	1126	271	106	19	-26
OF								
1884	Was-U	.971	16	31	3	1	0	3
1886	Bal-a	.905	12	15	4	2	0	1
1887	Bal-a	.824	8	14	0	3	0	-1
1888	Bal-a	.818	7	7	2	2	0	0
1889	Bal-a	.938	14	15	0	1	0	-4
Total	5	.910	57	82	9	9	0	-1
1B								
1884	Was-U	1.000	5	23	1	0	0	0

■ Dave Fultz OF

YEAR	TM/L	PCT	G	PO	A	E	DP	FR
1898	Phi-N	.871	14	26	1	4	1	-1
1899	Bal-N	.940	31	78	0	5	0	-2
1901	Phi-A	.935	106	216	13	16	0	-1
1902	Phi-A	.961	114	231	18	10	1	0
1903	NY-A	.933	77	156	11	12	2	-1
1904	NY-A	.976	90	194	8	5	2	3
1905	NY-A	.966	122	252	4	9	2	-6
Total	7	.952	554	1153	55	1	8	-8
2B								
1898	Phi-N	.875	3	3	4	1	0	0
1899	Phi-N	.750	1	1	2	1	0	-1
	Bal-N	.833	2	4	1	1	1	-1
	Yr	.800	3	5	3	2	1	-2
1901	Phi-A	.942	18	32	49	5	1	-6
1902	Phi-A	.911	16	16	25	4	5	-5
Total	4	.919	40	56	81	2	7	-13
3B								
1899	Bal-N	.838	20	16	41	11	1	-4
1903	NY-A	.727	2	3	5	3	0	0
Total	2	.823	22	19	46	4	1	-4
SS								
1898	Phi-N	.900	1	3	6	1	0	0
1899	Phi-N	.667	1	1	1	1	0	0
1901	Phi-A	.818	9	16	38	12	1	1
Total	3	.823	11	23	42	4	2	1
1B								
1899	Bal-N	1.000	1	4	0	0	0	0

■ Liz Funk OF

YEAR	TM/L	PCT	G	PO	A	E	DP	FR
1930	Det-A	.965	129	354	8	13	4	8
1932	Chi-A	.979	120	318	15	7	4	2
1933	Chi-a	—	2	0	0	0	0	0
Total	3	.972	251	672	23	0	8	10

■ Carl Furillo OF

YEAR	TM/L	PCT	G	PO	A	E	DP	FR
1946	Bro-N	.984	112	292	9	5	4	4
1947	Bro-N	.977	121	287	9	7	3	-1
1948	Bro-N	.983	104	274	13	5	2	6
1949	Bro-N	.965	142	286	13	11	2	-3
1950	Bro-N	.971	153	246	18	8	2	-3
1951	Bro-N	.986	157	330	24	5	6	13
1952	Bro-N	.988	131	225	12	3	2	-2
1953	Bro-N	.988	131	232	11	3	3	0
1954	Bro-N	.972	149	306	10	9	3	4
1955	Bro-N	.981	140	249	10	5	4	-3
1956	Bro-N	.984	146	230	10	4	2	-7
1957	Bro-N	.988	107	153	7	2	1	-8
1958	LA-N	.975	119	187	5	5	0	-9
1959	LA-N	.920	25	23	0	2	0	-4
1960	LA-N	1.000	2	2	0	0	0	0
Total	15	.979	1739	3322	151	4	34	-13

■ Len Gabrielson OF

YEAR	TM/L	PCT	G	PO	A	E	DP	FR
1960	Mil-N	—	1	0	0	0	0	0
1963	Mil-N	1.000	22	32	0	0	0	-1
1964	Mil-N	1.000	2	2	0	0	0	0
	Chi-N	.984	68	116	5	2	0	-1
	Yr	.984	70	118	5	2	0	-1
1965	Chi-N	1.000	14	14	0	0	0	-1
	SF-N	.975	77	112	3	3	1	-3
	Yr	.977	91	126	3	3	1	-4
1966	SF-N	.948	67	72	1	4	0	-9
1967	Cal-A	1.000	1	0	0	0	0	0
	LA-N	.980	68	92	7	2	0	-1
1968	LA-N	.976	86	114	6	3	1	-7
1969	LA-N	.981	47	50	1	1	0	-5
1970	LA-N	1.000	2	1	0	0	0	0
Total	9	.977	455	605	23	5	2	-28
1B								
1963	Mil-N	.968	16	111	9	4	5	-1
1964	Mil-N	1.000	12	59	2	0	9	-1
	Chi-N	1.000	8	63	5	0	7	0
	Yr	1.000	20	122	7	0	16	-1
1965	Chi-N	1.000	1	1	0	0	0	0
	SF-N	1.000	5	30	6	0	4	2
	Yr	1.000	6	31	6	0	4	2
1966	SF-N	1.000	6	44	4	0	5	0
1969	LA-N	1.000	2	11	0	0	0	0
1970	LA-N	1.000	1	2	1	0	1	0
Total	6	.989	51	321	27	4	31	0
3B								
1963	Mil-N	—	3	0	0	0	0	0

■ Gary Gaetti 3B

YEAR	TM/L	PCT	G	PO	A	E	DP	FR
1981	Min-A	1.000	8	5	17	0	1	1
1982	Min-A	.963	142	106	286	15	35	-2
1983	Min-A	.967	154	131	360	17	46	13
1984	Min-A	.960	154	142	334	20	26	16
1985	Min-A	.962	156	146	316	18	31	16
1986	Min-A	.956	156	118	334	21	36	20
1987	Min-A	.973	150	134	261	11	28	-4
1988	Min-A	.977	115	105	189	7	24	-5
1989	Min-A	.973	125	104	251	10	23	11
1990	Min-A	.959	151	102	318	18	36	15
Total	10	.965	1311	1093	2666	137	286	81
SS								
1982	Min-A	.714	2	0	5	2	1	-1
1983	Min-A	1.000	3	0	1	0	0	0
1984	Min-A	.750	2	2	1	1	1	-1
1986	Min-A	1.000	2	1	0	0	0	0
1988	Min-A	1.000	2	0	0	0	0	0
1990	Min-A	1.000	2	0	1	0	0	0
Total	6	.813	13	2	11	3	2	-2
OF								
1984	Min-A	1.000	8	19	0	0	0	0
1985	Min-A	1.000	4	10	0	0	0	0
1986	Min-A	1.000	1	2	0	0	0	0
Total	3	1.000	13	31	0	0	0	0
1B								
1985	Min-A	1.000	1	6	0	0	0	0
1989	Min-A	1.000	2	11	2	0	1	0
1990	Min-A	1.000	2	23	0	0	0	0
Total	3	1.000	5	40	2	0	1	-1
2B								
1986	Min-A	—	1	0	0	0	0	-1

■ Phil Gagliano 2B

YEAR	TM/L	PCT	G	PO	A	E	DP	FR
1963	StL-N	1.000	3	5	2	0	0	1
1964	StL-N	.918	12	17	28	4	5	2
1965	StL-N	.960	57	130	134	11	31	-10
1966	StL-N	—	1	0	0	0	0	0
1967	StL-N	.972	27	55	51	3	9	-8
1968	StL-N	.982	17	24	32	1	6	-2
1969	StL-N	.989	20	50	41	1	11	-2
1970	StL-N	.900	2	5	4	1	1	1
	Chi-N	1.000	16	14	25	0	2	2
	Yr	.980	18	19	29	1	3	1
1971	Bos-A	1.000	7	10	12	0	2	-2
1972	Bos-A	1.000	4	5	9	0	0	1
1973	Cin-N	1.000	4	2	5	0	0	0
1974	Cin-N	1.000	2	1	0	0	0	0
Total	12	.969	172	318	343	1	67	-19
3B								
1963	StL-N	1.000	1	0	1	0	0	0
1964	StL-N	—	1	0	0	0	0	0
1965	StL-N	.948	19	20	35	3	3	1
1966	StL-N	.982	41	30	77	2	7	-5
1967	StL-N	.930	25	20	46	5	4	-3
1968	StL-N	1.000	10	5	19	0	2	0
1969	StL-N	.900	9	10	8	2	0	0
1970	StL-N	1.000	6	3	4	0	1	0
	Chi-N	.000	1	0	0	1	0	0

YEAR	TM/L	PCT	G	PO	A	E	DP	FR
	Yr	.875	7	3	4	1	1	0
1971	Bos-A	1.000	4	1	2	0	0	-1
1972	Bos-A	.800	5	1	3	1	0	-1
1973	Cin-N	.824	7	5	9	3	1	-2
1974	Cin-N	1.000	1	0	2	0	0	0
Total	12	.953	130	95	206	5	18	-14
OF								
1964	StL-N	1.000	2	4	0	0	0	0
1965	StL-N	.962	25	51	0	2	0	-1
1966	StL-N	1.000	5	6	0	0	0	0
1968	StL-N	1.000	5	2	1	0	0	1
1969	StL-N	1.000	2	1	1	0	0	1
1971	Bos-A	1.000	11	11	0	0	0	-1
1972	Bos-A	.962	12	22	3	1	0	1
1973	Cin-N	1.000	1	2	0	0	0	0
Total	8	.972	63	99	5	3	0	1
1B								
1964	StL-N	1.000	1	5	0	0	1	0
1966	StL-N	1.000	8	59	9	0	9	2
1967	StL-N	1.000	4	39	1	0	3	-1
1969	StL-N	.981	9	47	5	1	5	1
1970	StL-N	1.000	3	16	0	0	2	0
	Chi-N	1.000	1	11	0	0	0	0
	Yr	1.000	4	27	0	0	2	0
1972	Bos-A	1.000	2	3	0	0	0	0
1973	Cin-N	—	1	0	0	0	0	0
1974	Cin-N	1.000	1	4	0	0	1	0
Total	8	.995	30	184	15	1	21	2
SS								
1967	StL-N	1.000	2	1	1	0	0	0

■ Greg Gagne SS

YEAR	TM/L	PCT	G	PO	A	E	DP	FR
1983	Min-A	.923	10	10	14	2	2	-5
1985	Min-A	.968	106	149	269	14	48	4
1986	Min-A	.959	155	228	377	**26**	96	-17
1987	Min-A	.970	136	194	391	18	75	18
1988	Min-A	.970	146	200	373	18	79	-14
1989	Min-A	.971	146	218	389	18	66	-3
1990	Min-A	.976	135	184	377	14	62	2
Total	7	.968	834	1183	2190	110	428	-15
OF								
1987	Min-A	1.000	4	2	0	0	0	0
1988	Min-A	1.000	2	2	0	0	0	0
1989	Min-A	—	1	0	0	0	0	0
1990	Min-A	—	1	0	0	0	0	0
Total	4	1.000	8	4	0	0	0	0
2B								
1986	Min-A	1.000	4	0	4	0	0	0
1987	Min-A	—	1	0	0	0	0	0
1988	Min-A	—	1	0	0	0	0	0
Total	3	1.000	6	0	4	0	0	0
3B								
1988	Min-A	—	1	0	0	0	0	0

■ Ed Gagnier SS

YEAR	TM/L	PCT	G	PO	A	E	DP	FR
1914	Bro-F	.933	88	219	244	33	37	-1
1915	Bro-F	.930	13	21	45	5	6	1
Total	2	.933	101	240	289	8	43	0
2B								
1915	Bro-F	1.000	6	12	10	0	1	1
	Buf-F	.800	1	3	1	1	0	0
	Yr	.963	7	15	11	1	1	1
3B								
1914	Bro-F	.913	6	11	10	2	2	0

■ Del Gainer 1B

YEAR	TM/L	PCT	G	PO	A	E	DP	FR
1909	Det-A	.929	2	12	1	1	0	0
1911	Det-A	.975	69	671	38	18	36	-4
1912	Det-A	.986	50	547	22	8	25	-3
1913	Det-A	.988	103	1118	50	14	55	-5
1914	Det-A	1.000	1	4	0	0	0	0
	Bos-A	.981	18	100	6	2	2	0
	Yr	.982	19	104	6	2	2	0
1915	Bos-A	.988	56	457	33	6	22	2
1916	Bos-A	.997	48	362	23	1	18	1
1917	Bos-A	.989	50	490	27	6	29	-1
1919	Bos-A	.978	21	163	11	4	6	-1
1922	StL-N	.979	26	175	9	4	7	-1
Total	10	.985	444	4099	220	4	200	-12
OF								
1912	Det-A	—	1	0	0	0	0	0
1914	Bos-A	—	1	0	0	0	0	-1
1915	Bos-A	1.000	6	5	1	0	0	-1
1919	Bos-A	.966	18	27	1	1	0	-3
1922	StL-N	.941	10	14	2	1	1	1
Total	5	.962	36	46	4	2	1	-4
2B								
1914	Bos-A	.962	11	23	27	2	4	-2
1916	Bos-A	1.000	2	0	1	0	0	0
Total	2	.962	13	23	28	2	4	-2

■ Joe Gaines OF

YEAR	TM/L	PCT	G	PO	A	E	DP	FR
1960	Cin-N	1.000	3	6	0	0	0	0
1961	Cin-N	.500	3	1	0	1	0	0
1962	Cin-N	1.000	13	8	0	0	0	1
1963	Bal-A	.945	39	52	0	3	0	-3
1964	Bal-A	.846	5	11	0	2	0	0
	Hou-N	.957	81	130	4	6	1	-3
1965	Hou-N	.913	65	83	1	8	0	-7
1966	Hou-N	.500	3	1	0	1	0	-1
Total	7	.934	212	292	5	1	1	-13

■ Augie Galan OF

YEAR	TM/L	PCT	G	PO	A	E	DP	FR
1935	Chi-N	.978	154	351	12	8	4	4
1936	Chi-N	.987	145	381	9	5	3	0
1937	Chi-N	.980	140	328	9	7	3	7
1938	Chi-N	.987	103	211	10	3	3	3
1939	Chi-N	.970	145	290	6	9	0	-6
1940	Chi-N	.984	54	114	6	2	2	1
1941	Chi-N	.959	31	45	2	2	0	-2

YEAR	TM/L	PCT	G	PO	A	E	DP	FR
	Bro-N	1.000	6	11	1	0	0	1
	Yr	.967	37	56	3	2	0	-1
1942	Bro-N	.990	55	101	2	1	0	-2
1943	Bro-N	.981	124	347	12	7	1	6
1944	Bro-N	.988	147	323	10	4	3	1
1945	Bro-N	.982	49	106	3	2	1	-2
1946	Bro-N	.935	60	97	4	7	1	-3
1947	Cin-N	.988	118	246	2	3	0	-6
1948	Cin-N	.967	18	29	0	1	0	-3
1949	NY-N	—	1	0	0	0	0	0
	Phi-A	1.000	9	16	0	0	0	-1
Total	15	.981	1359	2996	88	1	21	-2
1B								
1942	Bro-N	1.000	4	29	2	0	0	0
1943	Bro-N	1.000	13	131	17	0	8	4
1945	Bro-N	.988	66	558	34	7	53	-5
1946	Bro-N	.951	12	91	6	5	7	-2
1949	NY-N	1.000	3	7	0	0	1	0
Total	5	.986	98	816	59	2	69	-3
3B								
1934	Chi-N	1.000	3	1	8	0	2	1
1945	Bro-N	.931	40	29	79	8	5	-4
1946	Bro-N	.934	19	23	34	4	1	-2
Total	3	.935	62	53	121	2	8	-5
2B								
1934	Chi-N	.961	43	90	106	8	16	-9
1937	Chi-N	.956	8	10	33	2	4	3
1940	Chi-N	.833	2	5	5	2	0	-1
1942	Bro-N	1.000	3	6	4	0	2	0
1944	Bro-N	—	2	0	0	0	0	0
Total	5	.956	58	111	148	2	22	-7
SS								
1934	Chi-N	1.000	1	1	1	0	0	-1
1937	Chi-N	1.000	2	0	2	0	0	0
Total	2	1.000	3	1	3	0	0	-1

■ Andres Galarraga 1B

YEAR	TM/L	PCT	G	PO	A	E	DP	FR
1985	Mon-N	.995	23	173	22	1	14	4
1986	Mon-N	.995	102	805	40	4	59	-8
1987	Mon-N	.993	146	**1300**	103	10	96	0
1988	Mon-N	.991	156	1464	103	15	124	-4
1989	Mon-N	.992	147	1335	91	11	97	-2
1990	Mon-N	.993	**154**	1300	94	10	93	-5
Total	6	.993	728	6377	453	1	483	-15

■ Milt Galatzer OF

YEAR	TM/L	PCT	G	PO	A	E	DP	FR
1933	Cle-A	.975	40	74	4	2	0	-1
1934	Cle-A	.980	49	91	7	2	0	0
1935	Cle-A	.934	81	134	7	10	0	-8
1936	Cle-A	.964	42	51	2	2	2	-1
Total	4	.959	212	350	20	6	2	-10
1B								
1933	Cle-A	1.000	5	30	3	0	2	1
1936	Cle-A	1.000	1	1	0	0	0	0
1939	Cin-N	1.000	2	11	0	0	0	0
Total	3	1.000	8	42	3	0	2	1

■ Al Gallagher 3B

YEAR	TM/L	PCT	G	PO	A	E	DP	FR
1970	SF-N	.971	91	70	128	6	12	1
1971	SF-N	.951	128	88	204	15	18	-16
1972	SF-N	.974	69	64	120	5	7	-4
1973	SF-N	.833	5	4	1	1	0	-1
	Cal-A	.961	98	59	186	10	13	4
Total	4	.961	391	285	639	7	50	-16
2B								
1973	Cal-A	1.000	1	1	0	0	0	0
SS								
1973	Cal-A	1.000	1	0	1	0	0	0

■ Dave Gallagher OF

YEAR	TM/L	PCT	G	PO	A	E	DP	FR
1987	Cle-A	.972	14	34	1	1	1	3
1988	Chi-A	1.000	95	228	5	0	2	-5
1989	Chi-A	.993	160	390	8	3	4	-3
1990	Chi-A	.981	37	50	1	1	1	3
	Bal-A	.980	20	46	2	1	1	4
	Yr	.980	57	96	3	2	2	7
Total	4	.992	326	748	17	6	9	2

■ Joe Gallagher OF

YEAR	TM/L	PCT	G	PO	A	E	DP	FR
1939	NY-A	1.000	12	18	1	0	0	-1
	StL-A	.944	67	143	8	9	1	1
	Yr	.950	79	161	9	9	1	0
1940	StL-A	.966	15	27	1	1	1	-2
	Bro-N	.941	20	31	1	2	0	-2
Total	2	.950	114	219	11	2	2	-4

■ Bob Gallagher OF

YEAR	TM/L	PCT	G	PO	A	E	DP	FR
1973	Hou-N	1.000	42	77	1	0	0	3
1974	Hou-N	.978	62	44	0	1	0	1
1975	NY-N	.900	16	9	0	1	0	2
Total	3	.985	120	130	1	2	0	6
1B								
1973	Hou-N	1.000	1	1	0	0	0	0
1974	Hou-N	1.000	4	7	1	0	0	0
Total	2	1.000	5	8	1	0	0	0

■ Mike Gallego 2B

YEAR	TM/L	PCT	G	PO	A	E	DP	FR
1985	Oak-A	.991	42	46	66	1	22	8
1986	Oak-A	.986	19	23	50	1	6	9
1987	Oak-A	.968	31	49	73	4	22	13
1988	Oak-A	.993	83	119	166	2	33	1
1989	Oak-A	.970	41	58	106	5	18	8
1990	Oak-A	.990	83	153	258	4	48	12
Total	6	.986	299	448	719	7	149	51
SS								
1985	Oak-A	1.000	21	8	17	0	2	3
1986	Oak-A	1.000	1	1	0	0	0	0
1987	Oak-A	.920	17	21	25	4	6	1
1988	Oak-A	.946	42	34	72	6	14	0
1989	Oak-A	.967	94	152	255	14	68	9
1990	Oak-A	.977	38	43	86	3	26	1

YEAR	TM/L	PCT	G	PO	A	E	DP	FR
Total	6	.964	213	259	455	7	116	14
3B								
1985	Oak-A	1.000	12	3	11	0	1	2
1986	Oak-A	1.000	2	0	1	0	0	0
1987	Oak-A	1.000	24	5	24	0	1	4
1988	Oak-A	1.000	16	2	16	0	2	2
1989	Oak-A	1.000	3	1	2	0	0	0
1990	Oak-A	.882	27	10	35	6	4	0
Total	6	.948	84	21	89	6	8	8
OF								
1990	Oak-A	1.000	1	1	0	0	0	0

■ Chick Galloway SS

YEAR	TM/L	PCT	G	PO	A	E	DP	FR
1919	Phi-A	.969	17	45	49	3	11	1
1920	Phi-A	.928	84	184	252	34	52	2
1921	Phi-A	.922	110	205	305	43	52	-22
1922	Phi-A	.952	**155**	321	493	41	76	3
1923	Phi-A	.944	134	285	408	41	73	2
1924	Phi-A	.952	129	285	389	34	71	2
1925	Phi-A	.954	148	296	431	35	89	-3
1926	Phi-A	.935	133	274	315	41	49	-13
1927	Phi-A	.946	61	114	150	15	20	4
1928	Det-A	.914	22	49	47	9	11	-4
Total	10	.943	993	2058	2839	296	474	-28
3B								
1920	Phi-A	1.000	3	5	6	0	2	1
1921	Phi-A	.932	20	21	48	5	0	-1
1927	Phi-A	1.000	7	5	7	0	0	1
1928	Det-A	.969	21	26	37	2	3	0
Total	4	.957	51	57	98	7	5	1
2B								
1920	Phi-A	.947	4	11	7	1	5	1
1921	Phi-A	1.000	1	0	2	0	0	0
Total	2	.952	5	11	9	1	5	1
1B								
1928	Det-A	1.000	1	1	0	0	0	0
OF								
1928	Det-A	1.000	1	1	0	0	0	0

■ Oscar Gamble OF

YEAR	TM/L	PCT	G	PO	A	E	DP	FR
1969	Phi-N	.913	24	41	1	4	0	-1
1970	Phi-N	.956	74	148	4	7	0	1
1971	Phi-N	.970	80	125	4	4	1	-8
1972	Phi-N	1.000	35	54	2	0	1	0
1973	Cle-A	.971	37	67	1	2	0	-4
1974	Cle-A	1.000	13	19	1	0	0	0
1975	Cle-A	.987	82	146	8	2	2	0
1976	NY-A	.981	104	199	10	4	3	-4
1977	Chi-A	.987	49	73	1	1	0	-2
1978	SD-N	.979	107	172	12	4	3	-4
1979	Tex-A	1.000	21	41	2	0	2	2
	NY-A	.943	27	47	3	3	2	-1
	Yr	.969	48	88	5	3	4	1
1980	NY-A	1.000	49	65	2	0	1	-2
1981	NY-A	1.000	43	77	0	0	0	1
1982	NY-A	1.000	29	59	6	0	1	4
1983	NY-A	.942	32	64	1	4	1	0
1984	NY-A	1.000	12	15	1	0	0	0
Total	16	.977	818	1412	59	5	17	-18
1B								
1972	Phi-N	—	1	0	0	0	0	0

■ Chick Gandil 1B

YEAR	TM/L	PCT	G	PO	A	E	DP	FR
1910	Chi-A	.989	74	854	57	10	34	7
1912	Was-A	**.990**	117	1106	68	12	49	2
1913	Was-A	.990	145	1436	103	15	**89**	**8**
1914	Was-A	.991	145	1284	**143**	13	**84**	**24**
1915	Was-A	.986	134	1237	77	**19**	65	-1
1916	Cle-A	**.995**	145	**1557**	**105**	9	84	**8**
1917	Chi-A	**.995**	149	1405	77	8	84	-5
1918	Chi-A	.992	114	1123	64	10	70	-3
1919	Chi-A	**.997**	115	1116	60	3	-71	-4
Total	9	.992	1138	11118	754	9	630	36
OF								
1910	Chi-A	1.000	2	3	0	0	0	0

■ Bob Ganley OF

YEAR	TM/L	PCT	G	PO	A	E	DP	FR
1905	Pit-N	1.000	32	46	3	0	0	-3
1906	Pit-N	.965	134	207	16	8	5	-2
1907	Was-A	.940	154	276	23	**19**	5	9
1908	Was-A	.964	150	280	13	11	1	4
1909	Was-A	1.000	17	19	0	0	0	-3
	Phi-A	.980	77	185	9	4	2	7
	Yr	.982	94	204	9	4	2	4
Total	5	.962	564	1013	64	2	13	12

■ Ron Gant OF

YEAR	TM/L	PCT	G	PO	A	E	DP	FR
1989	Atl-N	.979	14	47	0	1	0	2
1990	Atl-N	.978	146	357	7	8	2	-1
Total	2	.979	160	404	7	9	2	1
2B								
1987	Atl-N	.972	20	45	59	3	17	0
1988	Atl-N	.963	122	295	378	**26**	82	1
Total	2	.964	142	340	437	9	99	1
3B								
1988	Atl-N	.923	22	21	39	5	6	-2
1989	Atl-N	.887	53	23	103	16	8	1
Total	2	.899	75	44	142	1	14	-1

■ Jim Gantner 2B

YEAR	TM/L	PCT	G	PO	A	E	DP	FR
1978	Mil-A	.980	21	41	55	2	10	3
1979	Mil-A	.984	22	50	76	2	16	2
1980	Mil-A	.988	66	118	203	4	53	-3
1981	Mil-A	.984	107	251	352	10	**95**	**15**
1982	Mil-A	.982	131	307	398	13	104	9
1983	Mil-A	.984	158	374	**512**	14	**128**	10
1984	Mil-A	.985	153	**362**	469	13	111	10
1985	Mil-A	.988	124	262	402	8	89	4
1986	Mil-A	.985	135	304	347	10	87	-11
1987	Mil-A	.984	57	95	153	4	36	4

YEAR	TM/L	PCT	G	PO	A	E	DP	FR
1988	Mil-A	.986	154	**325**	428	11	92	-9
1989	Mil-A	.987	114	241	362	8	88	9
1990	Mil-A	.982	80	164	220	7	54	-7
Total	13	.985	1322	2894	3977	106	963	36
3B								
1976	Mil-A	.982	24	17	37	1	3	-3
1977	Mil-A	.902	14	8	29	4	3	1
1978	Mil-A	.931	15	2	25	2	2	2
1979	Mil-A	.952	42	28	71	5	8	1
1980	Mil-A	.938	69	41	126	11	15	1
1985	Mil-A	.943	24	16	34	3	5	-2
1986	Mil-A	1.000	3	5	6	0	0	0
1987	Mil-A	.970	38	24	40	2	8	-1
1988	Mil-A	1.000	1	0	2	0	0	0
1990	Mil-A	.920	9	3	20	2	2	0
Total	10	.947	239	144	390	0	46	-1
SS								
1978	Mil-A	.800	1	2	2	1	0	0
1979	Mil-A	1.000	3	2	13	0	2	1
1980	Mil-A	1.000	1	0	6	0	2	1
1985	Mil-A	—	1	0	0	0	0	0
1986	Mil-A	—	1	0	0	0	0	0
Total	5	.962	7	4	21	1	4	2
1B								
1978	Mil-A	1.000	1	1	0	0	1	0

■ Charlie Ganzel   C

YEAR	TM/L	PCT	G	PO	A	E	DP	FR
1884	StP-U	.956	6	36	7	2	0	-3
1885	Phi-N	.888	33	175	39	27	3	0
1886	Phi-N	.600	1	5	1	4	0	-1
	Det-N	.911	45	274	63	33	9	1
	Yr	.903	46	279	64	37	9	0
1887	Det-N	.913	51	275	71	33	5	6
1888	Det-N	.956	28	156	41	9	11	2
1889	Bos-N	.927	39	188	55	19	9	3
1890	Bos-N	.958	22	131	27	7	4	6
1891	Bos-N	.956	59	288	59	16	3	4
1892	Bos-N	.933	51	202	50	18	1	-6
1893	Bos-N	.952	40	117	43	8	6	-1
1894	Bos-N	.897	59	184	52	27	4	-4
1895	Bos-N	.962	76	345	65	16	9	15
1896	Bos-N	.989	41	139	47	2	4	8
1897	Bos-N	.942	27	103	26	8	1	2
Total	14	.934	578	2618	646	229	71	32
OF								
1884	StP-U	—	1	0	0	0	0	0
1885	Phi-N	1.000	1	1	0	0	0	0
1886	Det-N	.800	7	7	1	2	0	0
1887	Det-N	1.000	4	5	0	0	0	0
1888	Det-N	.818	5	6	3	2	0	1
1889	Bos-N	.943	26	27	6	2	2	-1
1890	Bos-N	1.000	15	13	1	0	0	0
1891	Bos-N	1.000	13	16	2	0	0	0
1892	Bos-N	1.000	2	4	0	0	0	0
1893	Bos-N	.906	23	46	2	5	0	-1
1894	Bos-N	1.000	3	1	0	0	0	-1
Total	11	.928	100	126	15	1	2	-2
2B								
1888	Det-N	.900	49	110	168	31	11	-5
1890	Bos-N	1.000	1	3	3	0	0	-1
1894	Bos-N	1.000	1	1	0	0	0	0
Total	3	.902	51	114	171	1	11	-6
1B								
1886	Det-N	1.000	5	47	2	0	3	0
1887	Det-N	1.000	2	20	2	0	3	1
1888	Det-N	1.000	1	3	0	0	1	0
1889	Bos-N	—	7	0	0	0	0	-1
1892	Bos-N	1.000	1	16	0	0	0	0
1893	Bos-N	.983	10	115	4	2	8	-1
1894	Bos-N	.985	7	65	0	1	5	-1
1895	Bos-N	1.000	2	11	4	0	0	1
1896	Bos-N	.912	3	31	0	3	2	-1
1897	Bos-N	.917	2	10	1	1	1	0
Total	10	.979	40	318	13	7	23	-2
SS								
1888	Det-N	.750	3	1	8	3	0	-1
1889	Bos-N	.818	6	10	17	6	2	-2
1890	Bos-N	.938	3	4	11	1	1	0
1894	Bos-N	.923	2	6	6	1	0	0
1895	Bos-N	.875	2	2	5	1	1	0
1896	Bos-N	.500	2	0	3	3	0	-1
Total	6	.830	18	23	50	5	4	-4
3B								
1887	Det-N	.667	1	1	3	2	0	0
1888	Det-N	.825	9	12	21	7	1	1
1889	Bos-N	.500	1	1	0	1	0	0
Total	3	.792	11	14	24	0	1	1

■ John Ganzel   1B

YEAR	TM/L	PCT	G	PO	A	E	DP	FR
1898	Pit-N	.963	12	102	3	4	5	-1
1900	Chi-N	.980	78	817	34	17	40	-4
1901	NY-N	**.986**	138	**1421**	77	21	59	2
1903	NY-A	**.988**	129	1385	94	18	68	7
1904	NY-A	.988	118	1243	63	16	49	-2
1907	Cin-N	.990	143	1346	84	14	**89**	1
1908	Cin-N	**.990**	108	1116	61	12	52	-2
Total	7	.987	726	7430	416	102	362	1
2B								
1904	NY-A	.952	9	10	30	2	4	0
SS								
1904	NY-A	1.000	1	1	3	0	0	0

■ Joe Garagiola   C

YEAR	TM/L	PCT	G	PO	A	E	DP	FR
1946	StL-N	.990	70	260	25	3	6	-1
1947	StL-N	.987	74	281	23	4	2	0
1948	StL-N	.990	23	83	14	1	1	2
1949	StL-N	.984	80	332	35	6	1	7
1950	StL-N	1.000	30	99	8	0	2	-4
1951	StL-N	1.000	23	81	6	0	2	-2
	Pit-N	.986	61	255	30	4	4	-8
	Yr	.989	84	336	36	4	6	-10
1952	Pit-N	.978	105	418	63	11	9	-4
1953	Pit-N	.989	22	82	10	1	0	-4
	Chi-N	.988	68	296	34	4	2	1
	Yr	.988	90	378	44	5	2	-3
1954	Chi-N	.982	55	191	23	4	0	-7
	NY-N	1.000	3	17	0	0	0	0
	Yr	.983	58	208	23	4	0	-7
Total	9		614	2395	271	8	29	-24

■ Mike Garbark   C

YEAR	TM/L	PCT	G	PO	A	E	DP	FR
1944	NY-A	.988	85	372	47	5	9	8
1945	NY-A	.972	59	202	41	7	10	3
Total	2	.982	144	574	88	2	19	11

■ Bob Garbark   C

YEAR	TM/L	PCT	G	PO	A	E	DP	FR
1934	Cle-A	1.000	5	8	0	0	0	-2
1935	Cle-A	1.000	6	33	3	0	0	2
1938	Chi-N	1.000	20	64	7	0	0	2
1939	Chi-N	1.000	21	22	3	0	0	1
1944	Phi-A	1.000	15	23	1	0	0	0
1945	Bos-A	.993	67	249	31	2	9	-3
Total	6	.996	134	399	45	2	9	0
1B								
1938	Chi-N	1.000	1	2	0	0	0	0

■ Barbaro Garbey   1B

YEAR	TM/L	PCT	G	PO	A	E	DP	FR
1984	Det-A	.989	65	391	42	5	50	2
1985	Det-A	.991	37	190	20	2	24	1
1988	Tex-A	1.000	7	34	7	0	3	2
Total	3	.990	109	615	69	7	77	5
OF								
1984	Det-A	1.000	10	11	0	0	0	0
1985	Det-A	.974	24	38	0	1	0	-2
1988	Tex-A	.900	8	9	0	1	0	0
Total	3	.967	42	58	0	2	0	-2
3B								
1984	Det-A	.750	20	7	14	7	1	-6
1985	Det-A	—	1	0	0	0	0	0
1988	Tex-A	1.000	3	2	1	0	0	0
Total	3	.774	24	9	15	7	1	-6
2B								
1984	Det-A	1.000	3	2	2	0	2	0

■ Kiko Garcia   SS

YEAR	TM/L	PCT	G	PO	A	E	DP	FR
1976	Bal-A	1.000	11	15	27	0	7	1
1977	Bal-A	.966	61	78	152	8	43	21
1978	Bal-A	.945	74	86	173	15	35	5
1979	Bal-A	.955	113	173	271	21	66	-15
1980	Bal-A	.974	96	135	240	10	52	-3
1981	Hou-N	.950	28	38	76	6	11	4
1982	Hou-N	.946	21	28	60	5	13	4
1983	Phi-N	1.000	22	13	22	0	2	1
1984	Phi-N	.965	30	17	38	2	2	1
1985	Phi-N	1.000	3	0	2	0	0	-1
Total	10	.961	459	583	1061	7	231	18
2B								
1977	Bal-A	—	2	0	0	0	0	0
1978	Bal-A	.750	3	1	2	1	0	0
1979	Bal-A	.933	25	34	49	6	12	-3
1980	Bal-A	.989	27	41	52	1	13	5
1981	Hou-N	.977	9	16	26	1	2	0
1982	Hou-N	1.000	1	0	2	0	0	0
1983	Phi-N	.970	52	78	84	5	15	16
1984	Phi-N	1.000	1	2	1	0	0	0
Total	8	.965	120	172	216	4	42	18
3B								
1979	Bal-A	—	2	0	0	0	0	0
1981	Hou-N	.840	13	4	17	4	1	0
1982	Hou-N	1.000	2	1	0	0	0	0
1983	Phi-N	.923	10	3	9	1	1	1
1984	Phi-N	1.000	23	6	15	0	4	3
1985	Phi-N	—	1	0	0	0	0	0
Total	6	.917	51	14	41	5	6	4
OF								
1979	Bal-A	1.000	2	2	1	0	0	1
1980	Bal-A	1.000	1	1	0	0	0	0
Total	2	1.000	3	3	1	0	0	1

■ Damaso Garcia   2B

YEAR	TM/L	PCT	G	PO	A	E	DP	FR
1978	NY-A	.959	16	36	35	3	10	2
1980	Tor-A	.980	138	316	471	16	112	16
1981	Tor-A	.972	62	132	181	9	32	-15
1982	Tor-A	.980	141	273	461	15	94	10
1983	Tor-A	.981	130	266	360	12	75	-16
1984	Tor-A	.980	149	267	427	14	95	-14
1985	Tor-A	.981	143	302	371	13	88	-35
1986	Tor-A	.985	106	224	286	8	66	-7
1988	Atl-N	.984	13	26	35	1	5	-4
1989	Mon-N	.972	62	86	157	7	25	6
Total	10	.980	960	1928	2784	8	602	-57
SS								
1978	NY-A	.000	3	0	0	1	0	-1
1979	NY-A	.902	10	9	28	4	4	-5
Total	2	.881	13	9	28	5	4	-6
3B								
1979	NY-A	—	1	0	0	0	0	0
1989	Mon-N	—	1	0	0	0	0	0
Total	2	—	2	0	0	0	0	0
1B								
1986	Tor-A	1.000	1	1	0	0	0	0

■ Pedro Garcia   2B

YEAR	TM/L	PCT	G	PO	A	E	DP	FR
1973	Mil-A	.970	160	406	470	**27**	111	-12
1974	Mil-A	.970	140	382	365	23	102	-11
1975	Mil-A	.985	94	230	293	8	67	19
1976	Mil-A	.971	39	74	95	5	26	-3
	Det-A	.958	77	168	219	17	53	-1
	Yr	.962	116	242	314	22	79	-4
1977	Tor-A	.971	34	73	97	5	22	-2
Total	5	.971	544	1333	1539	5	381	-10

■ Danny Gardella   OF

YEAR	TM/L	PCT	G	PO	A	E	DP	FR
1944	NY-N	.912	25	58	4	6	1	1
1945	NY-N	.954	94	182	6	9	1	-6
Total	2	.943	119	240	10	5	2	-5
1B								
1945	NY-N	.981	15	137	16	3	8	2

■ Ron Gardenhire   SS

YEAR	TM/L	PCT	G	PO	A	E	DP	FR
1981	NY-N	.969	18	20	42	2	7	4
1982	NY-N	.956	135	234	398	29	68	16
1983	NY-N	1.000	15	13	30	0	4	0
1984	NY-N	.947	49	78	100	10	15	-6
1985	NY-N	.911	13	15	26	4	3	-1
Total	5	.955	230	360	596	5	97	13
2B								
1981	NY-N	1.000	6	7	7	0	0	0
1982	NY-N	1.000	1	1	1	0	0	0
1984	NY-N	1.000	18	18	43	0	5	4
1985	NY-N	1.000	5	5	5	0	0	0
Total	4	1.000	30	31	56	0	5	4
3B								
1981	NY-N	1.000	1	1	1	0	0	0
1982	NY-N	—	1	0	0	0	0	0
1984	NY-N	.867	7	2	11	2	0	-1
1985	NY-N	1.000	2	1	1	0	0	0
Total	4	.895	11	4	13	2	0	-1

■ Earle Gardner   2B

YEAR	TM/L	PCT	G	PO	A	E	DP	FR
1908	NY-A	.947	20	49	59	6	13	4
1909	NY-A	.945	22	35	51	5	3	-7
1910	NY-A	.936	70	169	199	25	36	6
1911	NY-A	.959	101	181	290	20	44	-3
1912	NY-A	.922	43	93	107	17	11	-1
Total	5	.944	256	527	706	3	107	-1

■ Gid Gardner   OF

YEAR	TM/L	PCT	G	PO	A	E	DP	FR
1880	Cle-N	—	1	0	0	0	0	0
1883	Bal-a	.837	35	62	5	13	0	0
1884	Bal-a	.860	40	62	12	12	0	3
	CP-U	.872	29	32	2	5	0	-3
1885	Bal-a	.733	5	10	1	4	0	0
1887	Ind-N	1.000	11	13	1	0	0	-1
Total	5	.855	121	179	21	4	0	-1
2B								
1883	Bal-a	.808	4	8	13	5	0	-1
1884	CP-U	.875	1	4	3	1	1	1
1885	Bal-a	.891	39	113	132	30	16	3
1887	Bal-a	.875	7	13	22	5	1	-2
1888	Phi-N	1.000	1	2	1	0	0	-1
	Was-N	1.000	1	2	0	0	0	0
	Yr	1.000	2	4	1	0	0	-1
Total	5	.884	53	142	171	1	18	0
3B								
1883	Bal-a	.818	3	4	5	2	0	0
1884	CP-U	.952	8	10	10	1	2	1
Total	2	.906	11	14	15	3	2	1
1B								
1884	Bal-a	1.000	2	13	2	0	2	1
1885	Bal-a	1.000	1	4	1	0	0	0
Total	2	1.000	3	17	3	0	3	1
SS								
1884	Bal-U	.714	1	3	2	2	1	0
1888	Was-N	.750	1	2	4	2	1	0
Total	2	.733	2	5	6	4	2	0

■ Ray Gardner   SS

YEAR	TM/L	PCT	G	PO	A	E	DP	FR
1929	Cle-A	.952	82	175	240	21	50	8
1930	Cle-A	.861	22	12	19	5	1	6
Total	2	.945	104	187	259	6	51	14
2B								
1930	Cle-A	1.000	5	3	3	0	0	0
3B								
1930	Cle-A	1.000	1	1	1	0	0	0

■ Billy Gardner   2B

YEAR	TM/L	PCT	G	PO	A	E	DP	FR
1954	NY-N	.971	13	17	17	1	1	2
1955	NY-N	.889	4	4	4	1	0	-1
1956	Bal-A	.974	132	274	331	16	76	-9
1957	Bal-A	**.987**	148	393	424	11	96	7
1958	Bal-A	.985	151	349	350	11	113	-20
1959	Bal-A	.976	139	333	392	**18**	**104**	31
1960	Was-A	.973	145	355	407	**21**	101	-1
1961	Min-A	.973	41	86	96	5	32	-3
	NY-A	1.000	6	9	7	0	0	2
	Yr	.975	47	95	103	5	34	-3
1962	NY-A	1.000	1	1	0	0	0	0
	Bos-A	.963	38	66	91	6	21	-9
	Yr	.963	39	67	91	6	21	-9
1963	Bos-A	.989	21	36	54	1	13	6
Total	10	.978	839	1923	2173	1	559	3
SS								
1954	NY-N	1.000	5	7	9	0	1	2
1955	NY-N	.940	38	65	122	12	28	0
1956	Bal-A	.972	25	24	46	2	1	-3
1957	Bal-A	.975	9	13	26	1	7	-2
1958	Bal-A	1.000	13	5	6	0	0	-2
1959	Bal-A	1.000	1	0	1	0	0	0
1960	Was-A	1.000	13	5	11	0	2	-1
1962	Bos-A	.955	4	6	15	1	1	0
Total	8	.958	108	125	236	6	40	-6
3B								
1954	NY-N	.987	30	18	56	1	2	6
1955	NY-N	1.000	10	7	13	0	1	0
1956	Bal-A	1.000	6	3	9	0	0	0
1959	Bal-A	1.000	1	1	0	0	0	0
1961	Min-A	.600	2	0	3	2	0	-1

YEAR	TM/L	PCT	G	PO	A	E	DP	FR
	NY-A	.952	33	26	54	4	6	3
	Yr	.933	35	26	57	6	6	2
1962	NY-A	1.000	1	0	2	0	0	1
	Bos-A	.889	7	7	17	3	1	1
	Yr	.897	8	7	19	3	1	2
1963	Bos-A	1.000	2	1	5	0	0	1
Total	7	.957	92	63	159	0	10	11

■ Larry Gardner 3B

YEAR	TM/L	PCT	G	PO	A	E	DP	FR
1908	Bos-A	.333	3	1	0	2	0	-3
1909	Bos-A	.800	8	4	12	4	0	-2
1911	Bos-A	.962	72	92	161	10	3	9
1912	Bos-A	.930	143	167	296	35	16	0
1913	Bos-A	.943	130	126	220	21	13	-16
1914	Bos-A	.942	153	187	312	31	18	0
1915	Bos-A	.933	127	134	227	26	16	-6
1916	Bos-A	.953	147	149	278	21	24	-14
1917	Bos-A	.937	146	148	315	31	18	-7
1918	Phi-A	.964	127	158	291	17	33	10
1919	Cle-A	.946	139	143	291	25	23	-6
1920	Cle-A	.976	154	156	362	13	32	-2
1921	Cle-A	.950	152	179	335	27	23	-1
1922	Cle-A	.951	128	133	259	20	24	-5
1923	Cle-A	.962	19	10	41	2	2	3
1924	Cle-A	.875	8	1	6	1	1	0
Total	16	.948	1656	1788	3406	286	246	-40

2B

YEAR	TM/L	PCT	G	PO	A	E	DP	FR
1910	Bos-A	.944	113	222	320	32	28	-7
1911	Bos-A	.964	62	152	195	13	31	15
1924	Cle-A	.909	6	8	12	2	1	-3
Total	3	.951	181	382	527	7	60	5

SS

YEAR	TM/L	PCT	G	PO	A	E	DP	FR
1909	Bos-A	.909	5	6	4	1	1	-1

■ Debs Garms OF

YEAR	TM/L	PCT	G	PO	A	E	DP	FR
1932	StL-A	.953	33	79	3	4	1	1
1933	StL-A	.960	47	91	5	4	1	-1
1934	StL-A	.942	56	111	2	7	0	-4
1935	StL-A	.800	2	4	0	1	0	0
1937	Bos-N	.977	81	168	1	4	0	-6
1938	Bos-N	.985	63	126	6	2	2	0
1939	Bos-N	.964	96	183	6	7	2	-6
1940	Pit-N	.946	19	32	3	2	0	-1
1941	Pit-N	.957	24	45	0	2	0	-3
1943	StL-N	.980	47	93	3	2	0	-1
1944	StL-N	1.000	23	34	0	0	0	-3
1945	StL-N	1.000	10	7	1	0	0	0
Total	12	.966	501	973	30	5	6	-24

3B

YEAR	TM/L	PCT	G	PO	A	E	DP	FR
1937	Bos-N	.971	36	32	68	3	2	-2
1938	Bos-N	.942	54	48	98	9	6	-5
1939	Bos-N	.958	37	31	83	5	5	2
1940	Pit-N	.964	64	65	123	7	15	0
1941	Pit-N	.911	29	28	44	7	1	-7
1943	StL-N	.851	23	18	22	7	5	-4
1944	StL-N	.968	21	14	16	1	1	-4
1945	StL-N	.956	32	23	42	3	4	-8
Total	8	.947	296	259	496	2	39	-28

2B

YEAR	TM/L	PCT	G	PO	A	E	DP	FR
1938	Bos-N	—	1	0	0	0	0	0

SS

YEAR	TM/L	PCT	G	PO	A	E	DP	FR
1943	StL-N	1.000	1	1	0	0	0	0

■ Phil Garner 2B

YEAR	TM/L	PCT	G	PO	A	E	DP	FR
1974	Oak-A	1.000	3	3	1	0	0	0
1975	Oak-A	.968	160	354	426	26	93	-16
1976	Oak-A	.975	159	378	465	22	91	-14
1977	Pit-N	.972	50	114	95	6	20	-12
1978	Pit-N	.976	81	190	213	10	50	6
1979	Pit-N	.981	83	175	234	8	58	2
1980	Pit-N	.976	151	349	499	21	116	16
1981	Pit-N	.968	50	121	148	9	31	-6
	Hou-N	.982	31	62	102	3	17	0
	Yr	.973	81	183	250	12	48	-6
1982	Hou-N	.980	136	273	429	14	90	0
1984	Hou-N	.956	35	65	88	7	26	8
1985	Hou-N	.983	15	26	32	1	10	1
1986	Hou-N	1.000	7	8	11	0	2	0
1987	Hou-N	1.000	2	0	1	0	0	0
	LA-N	.917	12	6	16	2	2	1
	Yr	.920	14	6	17	2	2	1
Total	13	.974	975	2124	2760	129	606	-14

3B

YEAR	TM/L	PCT	G	PO	A	E	DP	FR
1973	Oak-A	1.000	9	2	3	0	1	1
1974	Oak-A	.955	19	6	15	1	1	3
1977	Pit-N	.971	107	98	240	10	28	14
1978	Pit-N	.930	81	67	172	18	12	4
1979	Pit-N	.936	78	47	144	13	16	3
1982	Hou-N	.940	18	12	35	3	4	1
1983	Hou-N	.945	154	100	314	24	22	4
1984	Hou-N	.979	82	71	163	5	16	16
1985	Hou-N	.932	123	75	197	20	14	-10
1986	Hou-N	.984	84	58	141	23	13	1
1987	Hou-N	.976	36	28	54	2	3	2
	LA-N	.923	46	29	67	8	5	5
	Yr	.947	82	57	121	10	8	7
1988	SF-N	—	2	0	0	0	0	0
Total	12	.944	839	593	1542	127	135	44

SS

YEAR	TM/L	PCT	G	PO	A	E	DP	FR
1974	Oak-A	1.000	8	2	8	0	0	1
1975	Oak-A	1.000	1	1	1	0	1	0
1977	Pit-N	.964	12	11	16	1	1	-1
1978	Pit-N	1.000	4	1	4	0	1	1
1979	Pit-N	.968	14	12	18	1	8	1
1980	Pit-N	1.000	1	0	1	0	0	0
1987	LA-N	.889	2	2	6	1	0	0
Total	7	.965	42	29	54	3	11	2

■ Ralph Garr OF

YEAR	TM/L	PCT	G	PO	A	E	DP	FR
1969	Atl-N	.857	7	6	0	1	0	0
1970	Atl-N	1.000	21	43	0	0	0	0
1971	Atl-N	.968	153	315	15	11	3	6
1972	Atl-N	.962	131	246	8	10	1	-1
1973	Atl-N	.968	148	293	9	10	2	-1
1974	Atl-N	.967	139	255	8	9	2	-5
1975	Atl-N	.966	148	298	12	11	2	3
1976	Chi-A	.978	125	254	7	6	2	-3
1977	Chi-A	.987	126	225	10	3	2	-2
1978	Chi-A	.959	109	205	5	9	2	-6
1979	Chi-A	.951	67	94	3	5	1	-8
1980	Cal-A	.750	2	3	0	1	0	0
Total	12	.968	1176	2237	77	6	17	-17

■ Wayne Garrett 3B

YEAR	TM/L	PCT	G	PO	A	E	DP	FR
1969	NY-N	.951	72	40	115	8	10	-8
1970	NY-N	.944	70	57	113	10	6	-7
1971	NY-N	.967	53	30	89	4	7	-2
1972	NY-N	.960	82	66	150	9	13	8
1973	NY-N	.942	130	80	280	22	36	13
1974	NY-N	.955	144	111	318	20	31	12
1975	NY-N	.966	94	64	160	8	24	11
1976	NY-N	.948	64	47	137	10	12	5
	Mon-N	1.000	2	1	0	0	0	0
	Yr	.949	66	48	138	10	12	5
1977	Mon-N	.969	49	34	101	0	2	3
1978	Mon-N	.969	13	6	25	1	2	1
	StL-N	.927	19	12	26	3	5	-2
	Yr	.945	32	18	51	4	7	-1
Total	10	.956	792	548	1515	5	148	34

2B

YEAR	TM/L	PCT	G	PO	A	E	DP	FR
1969	NY-N	.985	47	102	97	3	27	-4
1970	NY-N	.989	45	94	92	2	28	-11
1971	NY-N	1.000	9	18	11	0	4	-2
1972	NY-N	.945	22	48	38	5	6	-6
1973	NY-N	.970	6	14	18	1	6	1
1975	NY-N	1.000	1	0	1	0	0	0
1976	NY-N	1.000	10	25	18	0	3	-2
	Mon-N	.982	54	121	157	5	32	1
	Yr	.985	64	146	175	5	35	-1
1977	Mon-N	—	1	0	0	0	0	0
Total	8	.982	195	422	432	6	106	-23

SS

YEAR	TM/L	PCT	G	PO	A	E	DP	FR
1969	NY-N	1.000	9	5	6	0	0	-1
1970	NY-N	1.000	1	1	0	0	0	0
1973	NY-N	.885	9	8	15	3	4	-2
1974	NY-N	1.000	9	12	31	0	2	2
1975	NY-N	1.000	3	1	1	0	0	0
1976	NY-N	1.000	1	1	1	0	1	0
Total	6	.965	32	28	54	3	7	-1

■ Gil Garrido SS

YEAR	TM/L	PCT	G	PO	A	E	DP	FR
1964	SF-N	.969	14	5	26	1	3	-1
1968	Atl-N	.987	17	26	51	1	12	3
1969	Atl-N	.973	81	99	192	8	32	-11
1970	Atl-N	.975	80	119	233	9	36	-1
1971	Atl-N	.961	32	32	67	4	17	-1
1972	Atl-N	1.000	10	4	5	0	2	0
Total	6	.974	234	285	574	3	102	-11

2B

YEAR	TM/L	PCT	G	PO	A	E	DP	FR
1970	Atl-N	.990	26	43	59	1	10	0
1971	Atl-N	.986	18	25	46	1	9	4
1972	Atl-N	.989	21	38	53	1	9	1
Total	3	.989	65	106	158	3	28	5

3B

YEAR	TM/L	PCT	G	PO	A	E	DP	FR
1971	Atl-N	.950	28	4	15	1	3	2
1972	Atl-N	1.000	3	1	4	0	0	0
Total	2	.960	31	5	19	1	3	2

■ Ford Garrison OF

YEAR	TM/L	PCT	G	PO	A	E	DP	FR
1943	Bos-A	.988	32	77	2	1	0	0
1944	Bos-A	.969	12	31	0	1	0	6
	Phi-A	.987	119	289	6	4	0	6
	Yr	.985	131	320	6	5	0	6
1945	Phi-A	1.000	5	11	1	0	0	0
1946	Phi-A	1.000	8	8	0	0	0	-3
Total	4	.986	176	416	9	6	0	3

■ Steve Garvey 1B

YEAR	TM/L	PCT	G	PO	A	E	DP	FR
1972	LA-N	1.000	3	33	2	0	3	0
1973	LA-N	.993	76	718	26	5	58	-7
1974	LA-N	.995	156	1536	62	8	108	-13
1975	LA-N	.995	160	1500	77	8	96	-10
1976	LA-N	.998	162	1583	67	3	138	-15
1977	LA-N	.995	160	1606	55	8	137	-16
1978	LA-N	.994	161	1546	74	9	121	-9
1979	LA-N	.995	162	1402	93	7	101	-2
1980	LA-N	.996	162	1502	112	6	122	3
1981	LA-N	.999	110	1019	55	1	84	-6
1982	LA-N	.995	158	1539	111	8	102	1
1983	SD-N	.994	100	888	49	6	69	-11
1984	SD-N	1.000	159	1232	87	0	117	-4
1985	SD-N	.997	162	1442	92	5	138	-8
1986	SD-N	.994	148	1160	53	7	94	-18
1987	SD-N	1.000	20	138	11	0	10	0
Total	16	.996	2059	18844	1026	1	1498	115

3B

YEAR	TM/L	PCT	G	PO	A	E	DP	FR
1970	LA-N	.943	27	23	59	5	4	7
1971	LA-N	.939	79	53	161	14	11	19
1972	LA-N	.902	85	71	187	28	18	13
Total	3	.922	191	147	407	7	33	39

OF

YEAR	TM/L	PCT	G	PO	A	E	DP	FR
1973	LA-N	.875	10	13	1	2	0	-1

2B

YEAR	TM/L	PCT	G	PO	A	E	DP	FR
1970	LA-N	—	1	0	0	0	0	0

■ Rod Gaspar OF

YEAR	TM/L	PCT	G	PO	A	E	DP	FR
1969	NY-N	.983	91	104	12	2	6	9

YEAR	TM/L	PCT	G	PO	A	E	DP	FR
1970	NY-N	1.000	8	13	0	0	0	1
1971	SD-N	1.000	2	4	0	0	0	0
1974	SD-N	1.000	8	4	0	0	0	1
Total	4	.986	109	125	12	2	6	11

1B

YEAR	TM/L	PCT	G	PO	A	E	DP	FR
1974	SD-N	1.000	2	2	1	0	0	0

■ Alex Gaston C

YEAR	TM/L	PCT	G	PO	A	E	DP	FR
1920	NY-N	.917	3	10	1	1	0	-1
1921	NY-N	.950	11	19	0	1	0	0
1922	NY-N	1.000	13	24	3	0	0	0
1923	NY-N	.957	21	34	11	2	0	0
1926	Bos-A	.981	98	284	69	7	5	-10
1929	Bos-A	.986	49	116	25	2	6	-2
Total	6	.979	195	487	109	3	11	-13

■ Cito Gaston OF

YEAR	TM/L	PCT	G	PO	A	E	DP	FR
1967	Atl-N	.800	7	7	1	2	0	-1
1969	SD-N	.959	113	243	12	11	4	1
1970	SD-N	.975	142	310	7	8	0	0
1971	SD-N	.982	133	271	8	5	1	-6
1972	SD-N	.977	94	158	10	4	3	-3
1973	SD-N	.947	119	198	16	12	4	0
1974	SD-N	.992	63	119	7	1	1	2
1975	Atl-N	.974	35	72	2	2	0	0
1976	Atl-N	.977	28	42	1	1	0	-3
1977	Atl-N	1.000	9	14	0	0	0	-1
1978	Atl-N	.957	29	45	0	2	0	-1
	Pit-N	—	1	0	0	0	0	0
	Yr	.957	30	45	0	2	0	-1
Total	11	.970	773	1479	64	8	13	-12

1B

YEAR	TM/L	PCT	G	PO	A	E	DP	FR
1975	Atl-N	.889	1	8	0	1	1	0
1976	Atl-N	1.000	2	16	1	0	2	0
1977	Atl-N	.971	5	30	4	1	2	0
1978	Atl-N	.958	4	21	2	1	1	0
Total	4	.965	12	75	7	3	6	0

■ Doc Gautreau 2B

YEAR	TM/L	PCT	G	PO	A	E	DP	FR
1925	Phi-A	.933	4	7	7	1	1	1
	Bos-N	.976	68	171	231	10	39	-4
1926	Bos-N	.942	74	170	205	23	42	-20
1927	Bos-N	.965	57	136	196	12	22	-2
1928	Bos-N	.750	4	1	2	1	0	0
Total	4	.960	207	485	641	7	105	-25

SS

YEAR	TM/L	PCT	G	PO	A	E	DP	FR
1928	Bos-N	1.000	1	1	0	0	0	0

■ Mike Gazella 3B

YEAR	TM/L	PCT	G	PO	A	E	DP	FR
1923	NY-A	1.000	2	1	4	0	0	0
1926	NY-A	.913	45	37	78	11	5	-4
1927	NY-A	.961	44	40	59	4	6	-6
1928	NY-A	.969	16	10	21	1	1	-1
Total	4	.940	107	88	162	6	12	-11

SS

YEAR	TM/L	PCT	G	PO	A	E	DP	FR
1923	NY-A	1.000	4	1	5	0	0	0
1926	NY-A	.904	11	22	25	5	4	0
1927	NY-A	.750	6	1	2	1	0	0
1928	NY-A	.909	3	2	8	1	0	0
Total	4	.904	24	26	40	7	4	0

2B

YEAR	TM/L	PCT	G	PO	A	E	DP	FR
1923	NY-A	1.000	2	2	0	0	0	0
1928	NY-A	.667	4	0	2	1	0	0
Total	2	.800	6	2	2	1	0	0

■ Joe Gedeon 2B

YEAR	TM/L	PCT	G	PO	A	E	DP	FR
1913	Was-A	1.000	2	1	3	0	0	0
1916	NY-A	.955	122	235	341	27	55	-10
1917	NY-A	.983	31	83	86	3	12	4
1918	StL-A	.977	123	309	409	17	45	16
1919	StL-A	.975	118	290	345	16	44	-3
1920	StL-A	.964	153	365	421	29	75	-26
Total	6	.969	549	1283	1605	2	231	-19

OF

YEAR	TM/L	PCT	G	PO	A	E	DP	FR
1913	Was-A	.929	15	23	3	2	1	1
1914	Was-A	.667	4	2	0	1	0	-1
Total	2	.903	19	25	3	3	1	0

3B

YEAR	TM/L	PCT	G	PO	A	E	DP	FR
1913	Was-A	.941	7	7	9	1	1	1

SS

YEAR	TM/L	PCT	G	PO	A	E	DP	FR
1913	Was-A	1.000	2	1	1	0	0	0

■ Rich Gedman C

YEAR	TM/L	PCT	G	PO	A	E	DP	FR
1980	Bos-A	.867	2	13	0	2	0	0
1981	Bos-A	.990	59	275	30	3	1	-2
1982	Bos-A	.977	86	397	29	10	5	-6
1983	Bos-A	.980	68	274	26	6	5	-2
1984	Bos-A	.977	125	693	58	18	5	-7
1985	Bos-A	.983	139	768	78	15	13	4
1986	Bos-A	.994	134	866	65	6	10	11
1987	Bos-A	.976	51	306	14	8	1	-3
1988	Bos-A	.992	93	570	40	5	4	2
1989	Bos-A	.981	91	486	36	10	6	-1
1990	Bos-A	.970	9	27	5	1	0	0
	Hou-N	1.000	39	180	25	0	5	7
Total	11	.984	896	4855	406	4	56	3

■ Billy Geer SS

YEAR	TM/L	PCT	G	PO	A	E	DP	FR
1878	Cin-N	.867	60	58	177	36	15	-4
1880	Wor-N	.800	9	0	4	1	0	-1
1884	Phi-U	.772	9	10	34	13	1	1
	Bro-a	.870	107	177	364	81	34	18
1885	Lou-a	.872	14	26	49	11	2	2
Total	4	.864	191	271	628	142	52	16

2B

YEAR	TM/L	PCT	G	PO	A	E	DP	FR
1878	Cin-N	.818	2	4	5	2	0	0
1884	Bro-a	—	2	0	0	0	0	0
Total	2	.818	4	4	5	2	0	0

OF

YEAR	TM/L	PCT	G	PO	A	E	DP	FR
1880	Wor-N	1.000	1	1	0	0	0	0

■ Lou Gehrig 1B

YEAR	TM/L	PCT	G	PO	A	E	DP	FR
1923	NY-A	.933	9	53	3	4	4	-1
1924	NY-A	1.000	2	9	1	0	0	0
1925	NY-A	.989	114	1126	53	13	72	-8
1926	NY-A	.991	155	1566	73	15	87	-8
1927	NY-A	.992	155	1662	88	15	108	-6
1928	NY-A	.989	154	1488	79	18	112	-8
1929	NY-A	.994	154	1458	82	9	134	-5
1930	NY-A	.989	153	1298	89	15	109	1
1931	NY-A	.991	154	1352	58	13	120	-10
1932	NY-A	.987	156	1293	75	18	101	-6
1933	NY-A	.993	152	1290	64	9	102	-3
1934	NY-A	.994	153	1284	80	8	126	2
1935	NY-A	.990	149	1337	82	15	96	0
1936	NY-A	.994	155	1377	82	9	128	1
1937	NY-A	.989	157	1370	74	16	113	-6
1938	NY-A	.991	157	1483	100	14	157	-1
1939	NY-A	.971	8	64	4	2	5	-1
Total	17	.991	2137	19510	1087	193	1574	-59

OF
1924	NY-A	1.000	1	1	0	0	0	0
1925	NY-A	.818	6	9	0	2	0	-1
1930	NY-A	1.000	1	2	0	0	0	0
1931	NY-A	.750	1	3	0	1	0	0
Total	4	.833	9	15	0	3	0	-1

SS
1934	NY-A	—	1	0	0	0	0	0

■ Charlie Gehringer 2B

1924	Det-A	.967	5	12	17	1	2	4
1925	Det-A	1.000	6	8	20	0	5	4
1926	Det-A	.973	112	255	323	16	56	-12
1927	Det-A	.965	121	304	438	27	84	20
1928	Det-A	.962	154	377	507	35	101	2
1929	Det-A	.975	154	404	501	23	93	-3
1930	Det-A	.979	154	399	501	19	97	2
1931	Det-A	.979	78	224	236	10	54	-2
1932	Det-A	.967	152	396	495	30	110	-1
1933	Det-A	.981	155	358	542	17	111	7
1934	Det-A	.981	154	355	516	17	100	7
1935	Det-A	.985	149	349	489	13	99	3
1936	Det-A	.974	154	397	524	25	116	16
1937	Det-A	.986	142	331	485	12	102	6
1938	Det-A	.976	152	393	455	21	115	-1
1939	Det-A	.977	107	245	312	13	67	-3
1940	Det-A	.972	138	276	374	19	72	-20
1941	Det-A	.982	116	279	324	11	59	-3
1942	Det-A	1.000	3	7	9	0	1	1
Total	19	.976	2206	5369	7068	309	1444	31

1B
1931	Det-A	.987	9	68	6	1	3	1

3B
1926	Det-A	1.000	6	9	17	0	0	2

■ Phil Geier OF

1896	Phi-N	.813	12	12	1	3	0	-3
1897	Phi-N	.932	45	71	11	6	1	2
1900	Cin-N	.941	27	59	5	4	0	3
1901	Phi-A	.934	50	80	5	6	1	-3
	Mil-A	1.000	8	8	2	0	1	-1
	Yr	.941	58	88	7	6	2	-4
1904	Bos-N	.933	137	243	20	19	11	0
Total	5	.932	279	473	44	8	14	-2

2B
1896	Phi-N	.941	3	6	10	1	3	0
1897	Phi-N	.945	37	87	118	12	5	-7
1904	Bos-N	.882	5	4	11	2	0	-1
Total	3	.940	45	97	139	5	8	-8

3B
1897	Phi-N	1.000	2	0	4	0	1	0
1900	Cin-N	.500	2	2	2	4	1	-2
1901	Phi-A	—	1	0	0	0	0	0
	Mil-A	.800	3	1	7	2	0	-1
	Yr	.800	4	1	7	2	0	-1
1904	Bos-N	.682	7	5	10	7	0	-2
Total	4	.705	15	8	23	3	2	-5

SS
1897	Phi-N	.882	6	16	14	4	1	-3
1901	Phi-A	.600	2	2	1	2	0	-1
1904	Bos-N	1.000	1	4	3	0	0	0
Total	3	.870	9	22	18	6	1	-4

C
1896	Phi-N	—	2	0	0	0	0	0

■ Gary Geiger OF

1958	Cle-A	.986	53	133	3	2	2	8
1959	Bos-A	.989	95	173	5	2	1	-1
1960	Bos-A	1.000	66	121	9	0	1	3
1961	Bos-A	.988	137	324	12	4	1	4
1962	Bos-A	.987	129	287	8	4	1	2
1963	Bos-A	.984	95	234	11	4	1	8
1964	Bos-A	1.000	4	6	0	0	0	1
1965	Bos-A	.970	16	32	0	1	0	1
1966	Atl-N	.982	49	49	5	1	1	2
1967	Atl-N	.980	38	47	2	1	0	-1
1969	Hou-N	.968	65	57	3	2	0	1
1970	Hou-N	1.000	2	1	0	0	0	0
Total	12	.986	749	1464	58	1	8	27

1B
1963	Bos-A	.933	6	12	2	1	1	0

3B
1958	Cle-A	.600	2	0	3	2	0	0

■ Charlie Gelbert SS

1929	StL-N	.948	146	338	499	46	95	7
1930	StL-N	.947	139	322	472	44	104	9
1931	StL-N	.959	130	281	435	31	91	13
1932	StL-N	.945	122	246	389	37	69	0
1935	StL-N	.959	21	31	39	3	8	0
1936	StL-N	.958	28	38	53	4	10	0
1937	Cin-N	.968	37	66	87	5	16	-2
	Det-A	.934	16	22	35	4	7	0
1939	Was-A	.970	28	41	90	4	17	-2
1940	Was-A	.920	12	20	26	4	3	-5
	Bos-A	—	1	0	0	0	0	0
	Yr	.920	13	20	26	4	3	-5
Total	9	.951	680	1405	2125	182	420	20

3B
1935	StL-N	.978	37	34	56	2	8	5
1936	StL-N	.965	60	60	104	6	11	8
1937	Cin-N	1.000	1	3	1	0	0	0
1939	Was-A	.944	20	19	32	3	3	-1
1940	Bos-A	.926	29	23	65	7	5	5
Total	5	.957	147	139	258	8	27	17

2B
1935	StL-N	1.000	3	3	3	0	0	0
1936	StL-N	1.000	8	9	5	0	1	0
1937	Was-A	1.000	9	19	12	0	4	0
1939	Was-A	1.000	1	1	1	0	1	0
1940	Was-A	.875	1	4	3	1	0	-1
Total	5	.984	22	36	24	1	6	-1

■ Jim Gentile 1B

1957	Bro-N	1.000	2	14	0	0	3	0
1958	LA-N	.981	8	50	2	1	9	-1
1960	Bal-A	.993	124	885	52	7	98	-6
1961	Bal-A	.989	144	1209	100	14	129	2
1962	Bal-A	.988	150	1214	121	16	121	1
1963	Bal-A	.995	143	1185	110	6	122	8
1964	KC-A	.988	128	1018	84	13	92	-1
1965	KC-A	.981	35	239	17	5	24	-1
	Hou-N	.993	68	544	43	4	41	3
1966	Hou-N	.989	43	321	30	4	28	2
	Cle-A	.944	9	46	5	3	4	0
Total	9	.990	854	6725	564	3	671	7

■ Wally Gerber SS

1914	Pit-N	.921	17	31	62	8	7	1
1915	Pit-N	.934	21	56	58	8	9	4
1917	StL-A	.939	12	13	33	3	2	-2
1918	StL-A	.922	56	109	174	24	20	-9
1919	StL-A	.940	140	284	422	45	42	-8
1920	StL-A	.939	154	288	513	52	65	7
1921	StL-A	.943	113	269	331	36	60	-3
1922	StL-A	.944	153	322	470	47	93	2
1923	StL-A	.950	154	334	461	42	86	7
1924	StL-A	.946	147	317	425	42	78	-7
1925	StL-A	.949	71	144	206	19	39	5
1926	StL-A	.944	129	261	358	37	92	3
1927	StL-A	.946	141	290	427	41	91	9
1928	StL-A	.783	6	6	12	5	4	-2
	Bos-A	.955	103	201	328	25	50	34
	Yr	.948	109	207	340	30	54	32
1929	Bos-A	.937	30	35	39	5	3	4
Total	15	.943	1447	2960	4319	439	741	45

2B
1915	Pit-N	1.000	2	2	5	0	0	0
1917	StL-A	.889	2	3	5	1	2	0
1929	Bos-A	.957	22	35	76	5	10	10
Total	3	.955	26	40	86	6	12	10

3B
1915	Pit-N	.930	23	25	41	5	2	-1
1927	StL-A	—	1	0	0	0	0	0
Total	2	.930	24	25	41	5	2	-1

■ Bob Geren C

1988	NY-A	1.000	10	18	3	0	0	1
1989	NY-A	.991	60	308	24	3	4	0
1990	NY-A	.993	107	487	55	4	5	13
Total	3	.992	177	813	82	7	9	14

■ Joe Gerhardt 2B

1876	Lou-N	.941	5	16	16	2	1	2
1877	Lou-N	.888	57	167	244	52	30	19
1878	Cin-N	.906	60	159	206	38	26	5
1879	Cin-N	.908	55	191	192	39	23	2
1881	Det-N	.908	79	259	242	51	62	8
1883	Lou-a	.906	78	278	263	56	42	20
1884	Lou-a	.920	106	341	391	64	64	27
1885	NY-N	.911	112	314	352	65	59	13
1886	NY-N	.924	123	340	355	57	50	4
1887	NY-a	.896	84	288	271	65	48	14
1890	Bro-a	.938	99	359	348	47	67	36
	StL-a	.955	20	50	55	5	5	3
	Yr	.940	119	409	403	52	72	39
1891	Lou-a	.833	2	4	6	2	0	0
Total	12	.913	880	2766	2941	543	477	153

1B
1876	Lou-N	.944	54	664	13	40	13	0
1877	Lou-N	1.000	1	11	0	0	0	0
1879	Cin-N	.946	8	82	5	5	4	1
Total	3	.945	63	757	18	5	17	1

3B
1876	Lou-N	.692	2	5	4	4	0	0
1879	Cin-N	.851	16	29	34	11	3	4
1881	Det-N	1.000	1	2	0	0	0	0
1887	NY-N	1.000	1	1	0	0	0	0
	NY-a	1.000	1	0	2	0	0	0
1890	StL-a	.932	17	18	37	4	3	2
Total	5	.876	38	55	79	9	6	6

SS
1876	Lou-N	.917	3	3	8	1	1	0
1877	Lou-N	1.000	1	1	0	0	0	0
1879	Cin-N	1.000	1	2	0	0	0	0
Total	3	.958	5	10	13	1	2	0

OF
1876	Lou-N	1.000	2	7	3	0	0	0
1877	Lou-N	1.000	1	3	0	0	0	0
Total	2	1.000	3	10	3	0	0	3

■ Ken Gerhart OF

1986	Bal-A	.971	20	34	0	1	0	-2
1987	Bal-A	.973	91	174	3	5	0	-5
1988	Bal-A	.975	93	192	3	5	1	-3
Total	3	.974	204	400	6	1	1	-10

■ Dick Gernert 1B

1952	Bos-A	.987	99	877	67	12	104	-1
1953	Bos-A	.986	136	1223	84	19	139	-3
1954	Bos-A	1.000	6	47	1	0	5	-1
1955	Bos-A	.974	5	35	3	1	2	0
1956	Bos-A	.991	37	307	37	3	36	5
1957	Bos-A	.989	71	681	50	8	82	1
1958	Bos-A	.991	114	1101	93	11	118	8
1959	Bos-A	.995	75	552	49	3	54	5
1960	Chi-N	.987	18	132	16	2	13	2
	Det-A	1.000	13	93	4	0	13	-1
1961	Cin-N	.993	21	125	17	1	9	3
1962	Hou-N	1.000	9	62	2	0	9	-1
Total	11	.990	604	5235	423	0	584	17

OF
1956	Bos-A	.985	50	60	4	1	2	-2
1957	Bos-A	.889	16	16	0	2	0	-1
1959	Bos-A	.974	25	36	2	1	0	1
1960	Chi-N	1.000	5	10	1	0	0	1
	Det-A	.875	6	7	0	1	0	0
Total	4	.965	102	129	7	5	2	-1

■ Cesar Geronimo OF

1969	Hou-N	1.000	9	1	0	0	0	1
1970	Hou-N	.920	26	23	0	2	0	2
1971	Hou-N	.977	64	42	1	1	0	3
1972	Cin-N	.982	106	150	10	3	1	-8
1973	Cin-N	.992	130	243	9	2	2	-2
1974	Cin-N	.987	145	355	13	5	2	19
1975	Cin-N	.993	148	408	12	3	5	9
1976	Cin-N	.985	146	386	4	6	2	-3
1977	Cin-N	.992	147	375	9	3	2	5
1978	Cin-N	.981	115	259	4	5	1	-4
1979	Cin-N	.993	118	291	11	2	2	1
1980	Cin-N	1.000	86	110	2	0	1	8
1981	KC-A	.980	57	96	1	2	0	-8
1982	KC-A	1.000	44	93	3	0	0	5
1983	KC-A	.986	35	69	2	1	0	2
Total	15	.988	1376	2901	81	5	18	30

■ Doc Gessler OF

1903	Det-A	.974	28	36	1	1	1	-2
	Bro-N	.984	43	56	4	1	1	-3
1904	Bro-N	.920	88	170	15	16	2	3
1905	Bro-N	.875	12	19	2	3	0	0
1906	Chi-N	1.000	21	27	4	0	0	-1
1908	Bos-A	.950	126	162	8	9	4	-7
1909	Bos-A	.933	109	135	18	11	1	-1
	Was-A	1.000	16	19	1	0	1	-1
	Yr	.940	125	154	19	11	2	-2
1910	Was-A	.953	144	161	23	9	3	-3
1911	Was-A	.943	126	130	19	9	2	-10
Total	8	.945	713	915	95	9	15	-25

1B
1904	Bro-N	.917	1	10	1	1	0	0
1905	Bro-N	.973	107	998	77	30	54	2
1906	Bro-N	.946	9	79	9	5	4	0
	Chi-N	1.000	1	4	0	0	0	0
	Yr	.948	10	83	9	5	4	0
1909	Was-A	1.000	1	11	1	0	0	0
1911	Was-A	1.000	1	5	1	0	0	0
Total	5	.971	120	1107	89	6	58	2

2B
1904	Bro-N	1.000	1	1	1	0	0	0

■ Tom Gettinger OF

1889	StL-a	.750	4	6	0	2	0	-1
1890	StL-a	.886	58	62	8	9	1	-6
1895	Lou-N	.910	63	127	5	13	1	-3
Total	3	.897	125	195	13	4	2	-10

■ Jake Gettman OF

1897	Was-N	.981	36	49	3	1	0	-3
1898	Was-N	.926	139	234	18	20	4	1
1899	Was-N	1.000	16	31	0	1	0	-1
Total	3	.941	191	314	22	1	4	-3

1B
1898	Was-N	.969	3	27	4	1	3	1
1899	Was-N	1.000	2	19	0	0	0	0
Total	2	.980	5	46	4	1	3	1

■ Gus Getz 3B

1909	Bos-N	.934	36	32	81	8	3	0
1910	Bos-N	.915	22	23	42	6	4	2
1914	Bro-N	.949	55	69	134	11	12	12
1915	Bro-N	.951	128	140	290	22	14	9
1916	Bro-N	.913	20	18	24	4	0	-3
1917	Cin-N	.833	3	3	2	1	0	-1
1918	Cle-A	.941	5	6	10	1	0	0
	Pit-N	.875	2	3	4	1	1	1
Total	7	.942	271	294	587	4	34	20

2B
1909	Bos-N	.750	2	1	2	1	0	0
1910	Bos-N	.980	13	20	30	1	1	2
1917	Cin-N	.875	4	5	2	1	1	-1
Total	3	.952	19	26	34	3	2	1

SS
1909	Bos-N	.923	2	3	9	1	0	1
1910	Bos-N	.938	4	5	10	1	1	0
1915	Bro-N	.600	2	3	0	2	0	-1
1916	Bro-N	.970	7	12	20	1	2	0
Total	4	.925	15	23	39	5	3	0

YEAR	TM/L	PCT	G	PO	A	E	DP	FR
				OF				
1910	Bos-N	.909	8	9	1	1	0	0
				1B				
1916	Bro-N	.960	3	23	1	1	1	0
■ Patsy Gharrity C								
1916	Was-A	1.000	16	58	12	0	1	0
1917	Was-A	.800	5	3	1	1	0	0
1919	Was-A	.969	60	276	68	11	7	-1
1920	Was-A	.965	121	409	148	20	13	-1
1921	Was-A	.977	115	408	110	12	14	-1
1922	Was-A	.981	87	285	86	7	9	3
1923	Was-A	.986	35	108	29	2	5	2
Total	7	.974	439	1547	454	3	49	2
				1B				
1916	Was-A	.973	16	140	4	4	4	-2
1917	Was-A	.980	46	371	29	8	19	-2
1919	Was-A	.971	7	65	1	2	2	-2
1920	Was-A	.957	7	65	2	3	1	-1
1923	Was-A	.982	33	309	18	6	22	-2
1930	Was-A	1.000	1	2	0	0	0	0
Total	6	.978	110	952	54	3	48	-5
				OF				
1917	Was-A	—	1	0	0	0	0	0
1919	Was-A	.934	33	53	4	4	1	-2
1920	Was-A	1.000	1	2	0	0	0	0
Total	3	.937	35	55	4	4	1	-2
■ Jake Gibbs C								
1963	NY-A	1.000	1	5	0	0	0	-1
1964	NY-A	1.000	2	10	0	0	0	0
1965	NY-A	.991	21	106	10	1	1	2
1966	NY-A	.988	54	295	27	4	4	4
1967	NY-A	.975	99	582	55	16	7	-1
1968	NY-A	.991	121	642	55	6	7	-6
1969	NY-A	.990	66	364	31	4	6	8
1970	NY-A	.987	44	208	19	3	1	2
1971	NY-A	.988	51	229	12	3	1	-6
Total	9	.986	459	2441	209	7	27	2
				3B				
1962	NY-A	—	1	0	0	0	0	0
■ Frank Gibson C								
1913	Det-A	.914	19	57	17	7	1	-6
1921	Bos-N	.979	41	111	31	3	4	1
1922	Bos-N	.981	29	83	19	2	5	-1
1923	Bos-N	.923	20	31	5	3	1	-2
1924	Bos-N	.972	46	159	52	6	4	4
1925	Bos-N	.968	86	271	60	11	7	-3
1926	Bos-N	1.000	13	37	12	0	2	1
1927	Bos-N	.965	47	130	35	6	3	-3
Total	8	.967	301	879	231	8	27	-9
				1B				
1922	Bos-N	.983	20	162	9	3	9	0
1924	Bos-N	.965	10	106	3	4	9	-1
1925	Bos-N	1.000	2	5	1	0	0	0
Total	3	.976	32	273	13	7	18	-1
				OF				
1913	Det-A	.000	2	0	0	1	0	-1
				3B				
1924	Bos-N	.857	2	3	3	1	0	-1
■ George Gibson C								
1905	Pit-N	.966	44	200	54	9	4	3
1906	Pit-N	.971	81	336	97	13	10	-5
1907	Pit-N	.972	109	499	125	18	12	-3
1908	Pit-N	.973	140	607	136	21	10	-16
1909	Pit-N	.983	150	655	192	15	9	1
1910	Pit-N	.984	143	633	203	14	8	1
1911	Pit-N	.979	98	452	117	12	16	0
1912	Pit-N	.990	94	484	101	6	11	0
1913	Pit-N	.986	48	182	34	3	4	-8
1914	Pit-N	.974	101	358	126	13	8	-9
1915	Pit-N	.965	118	551	134	25	14	8
1916	Pit-N	.989	29	140	39	2	2	7
1917	NY-N	.986	35	116	27	2	4	0
1918	NY-N	1.000	4	1	1	0	0	0
Total	14	.977	1194	5214	1386	153	112	-21
				1B				
1907	Pit-N	1.000	1	2	0	0	0	0
■ Russ Gibson C								
1967	Bos-A	1.000	48	254	16	0	3	-7
1968	Bos-A	.983	74	428	36	8	7	2
1969	Bos-A	.979	83	466	41	11	2	-6
1970	SF-N	.971	23	126	7	4	1	2
1971	SF-N	.965	22	79	4	3	0	0
1972	SF-N	1.000	5	16	1	0	1	-1
Total	6	.983	255	1369	105	6	14	-10
				1B				
1968	Bos-A	1.000	1	3	0	0	0	0
■ Kirk Gibson OF								
1979	Det-A	1.000	10	15	0	0	0	-2
1980	Det-A	.992	49	122	1	1	0	2
1981	Det-A	.973	67	142	1	4	0	-3
1982	Det-A	.994	64	167	4	1	3	3
1983	Det-A	.975	54	116	2	3	0	-3
1984	Det-A	.954	139	245	4	12	2	-13
1985	Det-A	.963	144	286	1	11	0	-9
1986	Det-A	.990	114	190	2	2	1	-12
1987	Det-A	.974	121	253	6	7	0	1
1988	LA-N	.964	148	311	6	12	3	4
1989	LA-N	.980	70	146	3	3	2	-2
1990	LA-N	.995	81	191	4	1	1	2
Total	12	.975	1061	2184	34	7	12	-32
■ Gus Gil 2B								
1967	Cle-A	1.000	49	79	67	0	13	2
1969	Sea-A	.983	18	18	40	1	7	1
1970	Mil-A	.978	38	70	61	3	13	-1

YEAR	TM/L	PCT	G	PO	A	E	DP	FR
1971	Mil-A	.977	8	19	24	1	3	0
Total	4	.987	113	186	192	5	36	2
				3B				
1969	Sea-A	.942	38	38	75	7	8	2
1970	Mil-A	1.000	14	9	31	0	1	4
1971	Mil-A	1.000	6	1	3	0	0	0
Total	3	.957	58	48	109	7	9	6
				SS				
1969	Sea-A	.960	12	9	15	1	1	-2
				1B				
1967	Cle-A	—	1	0	0	0	0	0
■ Charlie Gilbert OF								
1940	Bro-N	.960	43	91	4	4	1	5
1941	Chi-N	1.000	22	51	0	0	0	1
1942	Chi-N	.981	47	99	6	2	2	3
1943	Chi-N	1.000	6	9	1	0	0	1
1946	Chi-N	1.000	2	1	1	0	0	1
	Phi-N	1.000	69	154	9	0	4	5
	Yr	1.000	71	155	10	0	4	6
1947	Phi-N	.961	37	70	4	3	2	2
Total	6	.982	226	475	25	9	9	17
■ Tookie Gilbert 1B								
1950	NY-N	.988	111	784	65	10	80	1
1953	NY-N	.995	44	381	26	2	34	1
Total	2	.991	155	1165	91	12	114	2
■ Pete Gilbert 3B								
1890	Bal-a	.899	29	34	55	10	5	-3
1891	Bal-a	.862	139	201	324	84	34	2
1892	Bal-N	.889	4	4	12	2	0	1
1894	Bro-N	.941	3	8	8	1	2	2
	Lou-N	.742	28	45	50	33	5	-6
	Yr	.766	31	53	58	34	7	-4
Total	4	.851	203	292	449	130	46	-4
				2B				
1894	Bro-N	.938	3	4	11	1	0	0
■ Wally Gilbert 3B								
1928	Bro-N	.965	39	30	81	4	7	-1
1929	Bro-N	.956	142	137	271	19	16	7
1930	Bro-N	.944	150	130	312	26	27	9
1931	Bro-N	.948	145	125	295	23	24	8
1932	Cin-N	.929	111	90	198	22	16	-6
Total	5	.947	587	512	1157	4	90	17
■ Billy Gilbert 2B								
1901	Mil-A	.936	127	319	395	49	66	0
1903	NY-N	.935	128	314	366	47	42	11
1904	NY-N	.946	146	305	466	44	48	8
1905	NY-N	.947	115	245	367	34	41	26
1906	NY-N	.940	98	223	324	35	32	23
1908	StL-N	.952	89	222	254	24	23	6
1909	StL-N	.922	12	19	28	4	1	0
Total	7	.942	715	1647	2200	237	253	74
				SS				
1902	Bal-A	.907	129	349	410	78	72	-5
■ Rod Gilbreath 2B								
1972	Atl-N	1.000	7	13	13	0	3	1
1974	Atl-N	1.000	2	5	6	0	1	0
1975	Atl-N	.980	52	121	125	5	29	2
1976	Atl-N	.975	104	239	311	14	76	9
1977	Atl-N	.978	122	277	305	13	61	2
1978	Atl-N	.976	39	74	87	4	13	-4
Total	6	.978	326	729	847	6	183	10
				3B				
1972	Atl-N	.941	4	3	13	1	1	2
1973	Atl-N	.960	22	16	32	2	4	0
1975	Atl-N	.952	10	5	15	1	0	1
1976	Atl-N	.750	7	6	3	3	1	-2
1977	Atl-N	1.000	1	0	3	0	0	0
1978	Atl-N	.968	62	34	117	5	9	1
Total	6	.954	106	64	183	2	15	2
				SS				
1975	Atl-N	1.000	1	1	1	0	0	0
1976	Atl-N	—	1	0	0	0	0	0
Total	2	1.000	2	1	1	0	0	0
■ Brian Giles 2B								
1981	NY-N	1.000	2	1	2	0	1	1
1982	NY-N	.992	45	121	129	2	27	14
1983	NY-N	.980	140	299	380	14	87	15
1985	Mil-A	1.000	13	27	27	0	5	5
1986	Chi-A	1.000	7	15	11	0	6	4
1990	Sea-A	1.000	2	6	5	0	2	1
Total	6	.985	209	469	554	6	128	40
				SS				
1981	NY-N	1.000	2	4	6	0	1	2
1982	NY-N	1.000	2	1	4	0	1	1
1983	NY-N	1.000	12	10	10	0	3	0
1985	Mil-A	.963	20	21	31	2	5	3
1986	Chi-A	—	1	0	0	0	0	0
1990	Sea-A	.978	37	51	80	3	25	5
Total	6	.978	74	87	131	5	35	11
				3B				
1990	Sea-A	1.000	1	0	3	0	1	1
■ Frank Gilhooley OF								
1911	StL-N	—	1	0	0	0	0	0
1912	StL-N	1.000	11	16	1	0	0	-2
1913	NY-A	.977	24	40	2	1	0	-1
1914	NY-A	—	1	0	0	0	0	0
1915	NY-A	1.000	1	1	0	0	0	0
1916	NY-A	.971	57	93	9	3	3	3
1917	NY-A	.933	46	78	5	6	1	-1
1918	NY-A	.961	111	206	15	9	8	0
1919	Bos-A	.922	33	44	3	4	0	-5
Total	9	.957	285	478	35	3	12	-6

YEAR	TM/L	PCT	G	PO	A	E	DP	FR
■ Bob Gilks OF								
1887	Cle-a	1.000	3	4	1	0	1	0
1888	Cle-a	.899	87	133	10	16	2	-4
1889	Cle-N	1.000	29	53	5	0	0	-2
1890	Cle-N	.941	123	237	20	16	2	3
1893	Bal-N	.969	15	26	5	1	1	3
Total	5	.937	257	453	41	3	6	0
				3B				
1888	Cle-a	.833	28	31	69	20	9	3
				SS				
1888	Cle-a	.882	4	5	10	2	1	0
1889	Cle-N	.914	13	21	43	6	2	1
1890	Cle-N	.800	3	4	8	3	2	-1
Total	3	.892	20	30	61	1	5	0
				1B				
1887	Cle-a	.981	6	50	2	1	2	0
1889	Cle-N	.971	10	96	6	3	7	1
Total	2	.975	16	146	8	4	9	1
				2B				
1887	Cle-a	.800	1	3	1	1	0	0
1888	Cle-a	1.000	1	1	2	0	0	0
1889	Cle-N	1.000	1	2	0	0	0	0
1890	Cle-N	.909	2	6	4	1	1	-1
Total	4	.905	5	12	7	2	2	-1
■ Carden Gillenwater OF								
1940	StL-N	1.000	7	12	0	0	0	0
1943	Bro-N	1.000	4	5	1	0	0	0
1945	Bos-N	.979	140	451	24	10	5	19
1946	Bos-N	.979	78	180	6	4	2	-3
1948	Was-A	.974	67	186	4	5	0	-4
Total	5	.979	296	834	35	9	7	12
■ Pete Gillespie OF								
1880	Tro-N	.905	82	185	14	21	5	6
1881	Tro-N	.933	84	180	16	14	5	3
1882	Tro-N	.827	74	144	9	32	1	-6
1883	NY-N	.897	98	216	11	26	6	5
1884	NY-N	.893	101	159	8	20	1	-4
1885	NY-N	.942	102	133	12	9	2	-4
1886	NY-N	.901	97	121	6	14	0	-13
1887	NY-N	.946	76	91	14	6	1	-2
Total	8	.903	714	1229	90	142	21	-15
				3B				
1887	NY-N	—	1	0	0	0	0	0
■ Jim Gilliam 2B								
1953	Bro-N	.976	149	332	426	19	102	3
1954	Bro-N	.977	143	340	388	17	99	-10
1955	Bro-N	.968	99	213	269	16	64	-7
1956	Bro-N	.981	102	233	326	11	64	14
1957	Bro-N	.986	148	407	390	11	90	2
1958	LA-N	.993	32	65	68	1	19	-2
1959	LA-N	.967	8	16	13	1	2	-1
1960	LA-N	.992	30	51	69	1	12	-7
1961	LA-N	.981	71	133	179	6	45	0
1962	LA-N	.981	113	192	262	9	60	-12
1963	LA-N	.985	119	242	277	8	61	-9
1964	LA-N	.942	25	47	50	6	8	-11
1965	LA-N	.929	5	6	7	1	2	-2
1966	LA-N	1.000	2	2	0	0	0	-1
Total	14	.979	1046	2279	2724	107	628	-43
				3B				
1958	LA-N	.940	44	38	103	9	16	5
1959	LA-N	.958	132	121	245	16	18	3
1960	LA-N	.960	130	101	262	15	21	16
1961	LA-N	.956	74	48	104	7	9	2
1962	LA-N	.941	90	51	126	11	12	-1
1963	LA-N	.948	55	25	66	5	6	0
1964	LA-N	.936	86	54	121	12	7	-8
1965	LA-N	.960	80	55	135	8	13	-9
1966	LA-N	.953	70	40	103	7	8	-12
Total	9	.952	761	533	1265	0	110	-4
				OF				
1954	Bro-N	1.000	4	9	0	0	0	0
1955	Bro-N	.970	46	96	2	3	0	-2
1956	Bro-N	.991	56	107	6	1	1	-1
1957	Bro-N	1.000	2	9	0	0	0	1
1958	LA-N	.987	75	142	5	2	3	-3
1959	LA-N	1.000	3	6	0	0	0	0
1961	LA-N	1.000	11	14	0	0	0	0
1962	LA-N	—	1	0	0	0	0	0
1964	LA-N	—	2	0	0	0	0	0
1965	LA-N	.960	22	24	0	1	0	-5
Total	10	.984	222	407	13	7	3	-10
				1B				
1966	LA-N	1.000	2	1	0	0	0	0
■ Barney Gilligan C								
1879	Cle-N	.870	27	147	41	28	0	1
1880	Cle-N	.969	23	124	33	5	4	7
1881	Pro-N	.930	36	184	41	17	9	-3
1882	Pro-N	.932	54	287	82	27	8	8
1883	Pro-N	.900	74	379	108	54	10	8
1884	Pro-N	.928	81	605	94	54	7	10
1885	Pro-N	.872	65	305	84	57	13	-4
1886	Was-N	.925	71	358	101	37	7	-16
1887	Was-N	.874	26	94	38	19	3	-1
1888	Det-N	.875	1	5	2	1	0	1
Total	10	.912	458	2488	624	299	62	10
				OF				
1879	Cle-N	.826	23	32	6	8	0	-1
1880	Cle-N	1.000	4	5	1	0	1	1
1881	Pro-N	.500	1	1	0	1	0	0
1885	Pro-N	1.000	1	1	0	0	0	0
1886	Was-N	.806	14	20	5	6	1	1
1887	Was-N	—	1	0	0	0	0	0
Total	6	.826	44	59	12	5	2	1

YEAR	TM/L	PCT	G	PO	A	E	DP	FR
SS								
1879	Cle-N	.909	2	3	7	1	0	0
1880	Cle-N	.944	4	3	14	1	2	-1
1881	Pro-N	.851	10	8	32	7	0	-1
1882	Pro-N	.714	2	0	5	2	1	0
1885	Pro-N	.852	5	7	16	4	0	-1
1886	Was-N	—	1	0	0	0	0	0
1887	Was-N	.857	3	4	8	2	1	0
Total	7	.863	27	25	82	7	4	-3
3B								
1884	Pro-N	—	1	0	0	0	0	0
1886	Was-N	.600	1	1	2	2	0	0
Total	2	.600	2	1	2	2	0	0
1B								
1884	Pro-N	.889	1	8	0	1	0	0
2B								
1885	Pro-N	.667	1	2	2	2	0	-1

■ Grover Gilmore OF

YEAR	TM/L	PCT	G	PO	A	E	DP	FR
1914	KC-F	.973	132	196	24	6	7	3
1915	KC-F	.979	119	215	17	5	4	7
Total	2	.976	251	411	41	1	11	10

■ Joe Ginsberg C

YEAR	TM/L	PCT	G	PO	A	E	DP	FR
1948	Det-A	.943	11	46	4	3	3	-2
1950	Det-A	.981	31	97	8	2	3	-4
1951	Det-A	.978	95	388	56	10	7	-1
1952	Det-A	.984	101	442	41	8	7	-13
1953	Det-A	.988	15	71	12	1	2	0
	Cle-A	.966	39	130	10	5	2	-5
	Yr	.974	54	201	22	6	4	-5
1954	Cle-A	1.000	1	1	0	0	0	0
1956	KC-A	.989	57	238	28	3	3	-2
	Bal-A	1.000	8	31	3	0	0	0
	Yr	.990	65	269	31	3	3	-2
1957	Bal-A	.986	66	252	20	4	6	1
1958	Bal-A	.994	39	156	8	1	2	3
1959	Bal-A	.993	62	241	29	2	4	6
1960	Bal-A	.940	14	59	4	4	0	2
	Chi-A	.993	25	129	8	1	0	4
	Yr	.976	39	188	12	5	0	6
1961	Chi-A	1.000	2	3	0	0	0	0
	Bos-A	1.000	6	11	1	0	0	-1
	Yr	1.000	8	14	1	0	0	-1
1962	NY-N	1.000	2	9	2	0	1	1
Total	13	.983	574	2304	234	4	40	-11

■ Al Gionfriddo OF

YEAR	TM/L	PCT	G	PO	A	E	DP	FR
1944	Pit-N	1.000	1	3	0	0	0	0
1945	Pit-N	.964	106	235	6	9	2	-14
1946	Pit-N	.944	33	49	2	3	0	0
1947	Bro-N	.938	17	29	1	2	0	-1
Total	4	.959	157	316	9	4	2	-15

■ Joe Girardi C

YEAR	TM/L	PCT	G	PO	A	E	DP	FR
1989	Chi-N	.981	59	332	28	7	1	13
1990	Chi-N	.985	133	653	61	11	5	-7
Total	2	.984	192	985	89	8	6	6

■ Tony Giuliani C

YEAR	TM/L	PCT	G	PO	A	E	DP	FR
1936	StL-A	.966	66	226	29	9	7	5
1937	StL-A	.986	19	61	10	1	1	0
1938	Was-A	1.000	46	138	17	0	4	0
1939	Was-A	.979	50	201	28	5	3	2
1940	Bro-N	1.000	1	1	0	0	0	0
1941	Bro-N	1.000	3	5	1	0	0	1
1943	Was-A	.962	49	154	24	7	1	-1
Total	7	.976	234	786	109	2	16	7

■ Dan Gladden OF

YEAR	TM/L	PCT	G	PO	A	E	DP	FR
1983	SF-N	1.000	18	53	0	0	0	2
1984	SF-N	.988	85	232	8	3	1	6
1985	SF-N	.975	124	273	3	7	0	-6
1986	SF-N	.987	89	226	7	3	2	9
1987	Min-A	.987	111	223	9	3	2	4
1988	Min-A	.991	140	319	12	3	5	12
1989	Min-A	.966	117	245	8	9	3	1
1990	Min-A	.980	133	286	12	6	3	7
Total	8	.983	817	1857	59	4	16	35
2B								
1988	Min-A	—	1	0	0	0	0	0
3B								
1988	Min-A	—	1	0	0	0	0	0

■ Jack Glasscock SS

YEAR	TM/L	PCT	G	PO	A	E	DP	FR
1880	Cle-N	.891	77	107	252	44	21	7
1881	Cle-N	**.911**	79	**105**	**274**	37	29	**9**
1882	Cle-N	.900	**83**	111	**311**	47	**40**	**24**
1883	Cle-N	**.922**	93	134	313	38	28	**18**
1884	Cle-N	.893	69	118	267	46	16	**26**
	Cin-U	.889	36	45	107	19	4	2
1885	StL-N	**.917**	110	156	**397**	50	33	**19**
1886	StL-N	**.906**	120	156	**392**	57	**43**	**22**
1887	Ind-N	.906	122	211	**493**	**73**	**58**	**35**
1888	Ind-N	**.901**	110	201	334	59	36	10
1889	Ind-N	**.915**	132	246	**478**	67	**60**	**35**
1890	NY-N	.910	124	275	421	69	46	20
1891	NY-N	.913	97	164	274	42	39	-2
1892	StL-N	.916	139	280	472	69	46	5
1893	StL-N	.907	48	85	159	25	19	-7
	Pit-N	.934	66	155	239	28	40	12
	Yr	.923	114	240	398	53	59	5
1894	Pit-N	.933	85	189	295	35	46	8
1895	Lou-N	.900	13	32	49	9	6	2
	Was-N	.895	25	51	103	18	10	6
	Yr	.897	38	83	152	27	16	8
Total	16	.910	1628	2821	5630	832	620	251
2B								
1879	Cle-N	.919	66	201	208	36	18	-9
1881	Cle-N	.833	6	23	22	9	3	0
1883	Cle-N	.920	3	11	12	2	3	0

YEAR	TM/L	PCT	G	PO	A	E	DP	FR
1884	Cle-N	.880	3	13	9	3	4	1
	Cin-U	.889	2	6	2	1	0	-1
1885	StL-N	1.000	1	2	7	0	0	0
1888	Ind-N	.913	3	8	13	2	3	2
1889	Ind-N	.909	2	3	7	1	1	0
Total	7	.910	86	267	280	4	32	-7
3B								
1879	Cle-N	.899	14	32	30	7	0	4
1882	Cle-N	1.000	1	1	2	0	1	0
Total	2	.903	15	33	32	7	1	4
1B								
1895	Lou-N	.957	5	41	3	2	3	0
OF								
1886	StL-N	1.000	1	1	0	0	0	0

■ Tommy Glaviano 3B

YEAR	TM/L	PCT	G	PO	A	E	DP	FR
1949	StL-N	.929	73	67	181	19	15	**13**
1950	StL-N	.935	106	103	255	25	16	6
1952	StL-N	.934	52	46	95	10	5	4
1953	Phi-N	.892	14	14	19	4	2	-2
Total	4	.931	245	230	550	8	38	21
2B								
1949	StL-N	.958	7	14	9	1	3	1
1950	StL-N	1.000	5	15	13	0	4	0
1951	StL-N	.977	9	18	25	1	6	0
1952	StL-N	1.000	1	1	0	0	0	0
1953	Phi-N	.947	12	17	19	2	3	0
Total	5	.970	34	65	66	4	16	1
OF								
1951	StL-N	.972	17	35	0	1	0	-2
SS								
1950	StL-N	1.000	1	1	1	0	1	0
1953	Phi-N	1.000	1	0	1	0	0	0
Total	2	1.000	2	1	2	0	1	0

■ Harry Gleason 3B

YEAR	TM/L	PCT	G	PO	A	E	DP	FR
1901	Bos-A	.667	1	0	2	1	1	1
1902	Bos-A	.930	35	41	66	8	7	2
1903	Bos-A	.750	2	0	3	1	0	-1
1904	StL-A	.928	20	26	38	5	4	-1
1905	StL-A	.911	144	118	271	38	8	-17
Total	5	.914	202	185	380	3	20	-16
OF								
1902	Bos-A	.944	23	50	1	3	0	-1
1904	StL-A	—	1	0	0	0	0	0
Total	2	.944	24	50	1	3	0	-1
SS								
1904	StL-A	.908	20	29	60	9	7	0
2B								
1902	Bos-A	.750	4	4	8	4	1	-1
1904	StL-A	.955	5	11	10	1	0	-1
1905	StL-A	.979	7	26	21	1	1	3
Total	3	.930	16	41	39	6	2	1

■ Jack Gleason 3B

YEAR	TM/L	PCT	G	PO	A	E	DP	FR
1882	StL-a	.768	73	107	**168**	**83**	**11**	1
1883	StL-a	1.000	1	0	4	0	0	1
	Lou-a	.795	83	83	107	49	6	-32
	Yr	.798	84	83	111	49	6	-31
1884	StL-U	.768	92	95	170	80	11	-6
1885	StL-N	.857	2	3	3	1	0	0
1886	Phi-a	.797	77	85	150	60	19	-6
Total	5	.781	328	373	602	273	47	-42
OF								
1877	StL-N	—	1	0	0	0	0	0
1882	StL-a	.889	6	5	3	1	0	1
1883	StL-a	.833	9	7	3	2	0	0
Total	3	.857	16	12	6	3	0	1
2B								
1882	StL-a	—	1	0	0	0	0	-1
SS								
1883	Lou-a	.800	1	2	2	1	0	-1

■ Bill Gleason SS

YEAR	TM/L	PCT	G	PO	A	E	DP	FR
1882	StL-a	.833	**79**	**131**	**294**	**85**	**23**	**9**
1883	StL-a	.871	**98**	120	257	56	22	-1
1884	StL-a	.867	**110**	119	316	67	23	-17
1885	StL-a	.869	**112**	115	303	63	18	-41
1886	StL-a	.853	125	128	352	83	37	-29
1887	StL-a	.875	135	169	411	83	27	-10
1888	Phi-a	.858	121	112	370	80	32	-13
1889	Lou-a	.822	16	26	57	18	4	-3
Total	8	.860	796	920	2360	535	186	105
3B								
1884	StL-a	—	1	0	0	0	0	0
1888	Phi-a	1.000	1	1	0	0	0	0
Total	2	1.000	2	1	0	0	0	0
1B								
1888	Phi-a	.750	1	5	1	2	0	0

■ Kid Gleason 2B

YEAR	TM/L	PCT	G	PO	A	E	DP	FR
1889	Phi-N	.889	2	5	3	1	0	-1
1890	Phi-N	.750	2	2	7	3	0	-1
1892	StL-N	.978	9	20	24	1	0	-1
1895	Bal-N	.899	85	205	250	51	32	-14
1896	NY-N	.938	130	329	397	48	38	3
1897	NY-N	.930	129	309	395	**53**	43	1
1898	NY-N	.938	144	366	**468**	**55**	**57**	**20**
1899	NY-N	.946	146	**403**	**465**	50	60	**26**
1900	NY-N	.931	111	321	326	48	51	15
1901	Det-A	.925	135	334	**457**	**64**	67	6
1902	Det-A	.941	118	**320**	349	**42**	66	6
1903	Phi-N	.959	102	236	280	22	30	-4
1904	Phi-N	.942	152	379	463	52	44	1
1905	Phi-N	.947	**155**	**365**	457	46	49	-8
1906	Phi-N	.947	135	215	358	32	39	-29
1907	Phi-N	.979	26	72	67	3	8	-1
1908	Phi-N	1.000	1	1	1	0	0	0
1912	Chi-A	1.000	1	1	1	0	0	0

YEAR	TM/L	PCT	G	PO	A	E	DP	FR
Total	18	.938	1583	3883	4768	571	584	19
OF								
1888	Phi-N	—	1	0	0	0	0	0
1889	Phi-N	1.000	3	2	0	0	0	0
1891	Phi-N	1.000	9	17	0	0	0	-1
1892	StL-N	.842	10	14	2	3	0	-1
1893	StL-N	.957	11	21	1	1	0	0
1895	Bal-N	1.000	4	2	0	0	0	-2
1896	NY-N	1.000	1	1	0	0	0	0
1903	Phi-N	.857	4	6	0	1	0	0
1907	Phi-N	1.000	1	2	0	0	0	0
1908	Phi-N	1.000	1	2	0	0	0	0
Total	10	.933	45	67	3	5	0	-4
SS								
1891	Phi-N	.765	4	8	5	4	1	-2
1893	StL-N	.625	1	2	3	3	0	-1
1897	NY-N	.813	3	5	8	3	1	0
1898	NY-N	.881	6	17	20	5	1	-1
1900	NY-N	.500	1	2	1	3	0	-1
1907	Phi-N	.889	4	4	4	1	1	-1
Total	6	.806	19	38	41	9	4	-6
3B								
1895	Bal-N	.833	12	22	18	8	1	-3
1896	NY-N	.846	3	4	7	2	0	0
1904	Phi-N	1.000	1	1	1	0	0	0
Total	3	.841	16	27	26	0	1	-3
1B								
1892	StL-N	1.000	1	4	0	0	0	0
1894	StL-N	1.000	1	13	1	0	0	0
	Bal-N	1.000	1	6	0	0	1	0
	Yr	1.000	2	19	1	0	1	0
1907	Phi-N	.972	4	34	1	1	2	-1
Total	3	.983	7	57	2	1	3	-1

■ Jim Gleeson OF

YEAR	TM/L	PCT	G	PO	A	E	DP	FR
1936	Cle-A	.958	33	67	1	3	0	-3
1939	Chi-N	.957	91	175	5	8	1	-4
1940	Chi-N	.983	123	273	14	5	3	-1
1941	Cin-N	.981	84	153	1	3	0	-9
1942	Cin-N	.889	5	7	1	1	0	0
Total	5	.972	336	675	22	0	4	-17

■ Ed Glenn OF

YEAR	TM/L	PCT	G	PO	A	E	DP	FR
1884	Ric-a	.833	43	85	5	18	2	5
1886	Pit-a	.865	71	124	10	21	2	0
1888	KC-a	.857	3	6	0	1	0	0
	Bos-N	.957	19	42	2	2	2	2
Total	3	.867	136	257	17	2	6	7
3B								
1888	Bos-N	1.000	1	1	0	0	0	0

■ Joe Glenn C

YEAR	TM/L	PCT	G	PO	A	E	DP	FR
1932	NY-A	1.000	5	17	1	0	0	-2
1933	NY-A	1.000	5	24	0	0	1	-2
1935	NY-A	.984	16	54	7	1	0	0
1936	NY-A	.970	44	167	24	6	2	3
1937	NY-A	.978	24	79	12	2	1	4
1938	NY-A	.974	40	134	15	4	3	0
1939	StL-A	.968	82	280	48	11	4	-14
1940	Bos-A	.961	19	67	6	3	0	0
Total	8	.972	235	822	113	7	11	-11

■ Al Glossop 2B

YEAR	TM/L	PCT	G	PO	A	E	DP	FR
1939	NY-N	.980	10	15	34	1	7	0
1940	NY-N	.952	24	54	86	7	8	0
	Bos-N	.938	18	31	59	6	12	4
	Yr	.947	42	85	145	13	20	**4**
1942	Phi-N	.961	118	322	351	27	79	7
1943	Bro-N	.897	24	39	39	9	5	-5
1946	Chi-N	1.000	2	4	2	0	0	0
Total	5	.954	196	465	571	0	111	6
3B								
1940	Bos-N	.951	18	17	41	3	4	3
1942	Phi-N	—	1	0	0	0	0	0
1943	Bro-N	.917	17	13	20	3	1	-2
Total	3	.938	36	30	61	6	5	1
SS								
1940	Bos-N	1.000	1	2	2	0	0	0
1943	Bro-N	.927	33	50	102	12	18	1
1946	Chi-N	.909	2	5	5	1	0	-1
Total	3	.927	36	57	109	3	18	0
OF								
1943	Bro-N	—	1	0	0	0	0	0

■ Bill Glynn 1B

YEAR	TM/L	PCT	G	PO	A	E	DP	FR
1949	Phi-N	1.000	1	10	1	0	0	0
1952	Cle-A	.973	32	167	16	5	18	0
1953	Cle-A	**.993**	135	1036	81	8	133	5
1954	Cle-A	.987	96	424	35	6	38	3
Total	4	.989	264	1637	133	9	189	8
OF								
1953	Cle-A	1.000	2	6	0	0	0	0
1954	Cle-A	—	1	0	0	0	0	0
Total	2	1.000	3	6	0	0	0	0

■ John Gochnauer SS

YEAR	TM/L	PCT	G	PO	A	E	DP	FR
1901	Bro-N	1.000	3	4	9	0	0	-1
1902	Cle-A	.933	127	223	447	48	59	-3
1903	Cle-A	.867	134	226	414	**98**	45	-22
Total	3	.901	264	453	870	146	104	-26

■ Jonah Goldman SS

YEAR	TM/L	PCT	G	PO	A	E	DP	FR
1928	Cle-A	.878	7	13	23	5	2	0
1930	Cle-A	.945	93	203	246	26	51	18
1931	Cle-A	.947	30	42	82	7	12	14
Total	3	.941	130	258	351	8	65	32
3B								
1930	Cle-A	.980	20	19	29	1	4	3

■ Gordon Goldsberry 1B

YEAR	TM/L	PCT	G	PO	A	E	DP	FR
1949	Chi-A	.990	38	359	24	4	37	-1

YEAR	TM/L	PCT	G	PO	A	E	DP	FR
1950	Chi-A	.989	40	235	29	3	37	5
1951	Chi-A	1.000	8	28	5	0	4	1
1952	StL-A	.983	72	524	40	10	56	-2
Total	4	.987	158	1146	98	7	134	3
		OF						
1950	Chi-A	1.000	3	1	0	0	0	0
1952	StL-A	1.000	2	4	0	0	0	0
Total	2	1.000	5	5	0	0	0	0

■ Mike Goliat 2B

YEAR	TM/L	PCT	G	PO	A	E	DP	FR
1949	Phi-N	.969	50	140	143	9	31	-2
1950	Phi-N	.972	145	345	393	21	89	-18
1951	Phi-N	.968	37	88	95	6	24	-8
	StL-A	1.000	2	6	7	0	2	0
1952	StL-A	1.000	3	4	4	0	3	1
Total	4	.971	237	583	642	6	149	-27
		1B						
1949	Phi-N	1.000	5	47	2	0	2	0
		3B						
1951	Phi-N	.909	2	3	7	1	0	1

■ Chile Gomez 2B

YEAR	TM/L	PCT	G	PO	A	E	DP	FR
1935	Phi-N	.954	32	72	113	9	27	12
1936	Phi-N	.948	71	137	229	20	33	12
1942	Was-A	.973	23	46	61	3	13	-1
Total	3	.954	126	255	403	2	73	23
		SS						
1935	Phi-N	.948	36	78	103	10	9	0
1936	Phi-N	.921	40	80	118	17	23	6
Total	2	.933	76	158	221	7	32	6
		3B						
1942	Was-A	—	1	0	0	0	0	0

■ Luis Gomez SS

YEAR	TM/L	PCT	G	PO	A	E	DP	FR
1974	Min-A	.960	74	97	190	12	37	18
1975	Min-A	.975	70	50	65	3	17	19
1976	Min-A	.988	24	32	51	1	16	6
1977	Min-A	.975	7	19	20	1	10	4
1978	Tor-A	.976	153	247	400	16	97	-10
1979	Tor-A	.984	15	20	41	1	6	3
1980	Atl-N	.968	119	135	319	15	55	12
1981	Atl-N	.895	21	15	19	4	2	-2
Total	8	.970	483	615	1105	3	240	50
		2B						
1974	Min-A	1.000	2	0	4	0	0	0
1975	Min-A	1.000	6	5	15	0	3	5
1976	Min-A	1.000	8	4	5	0	1	1
1977	Min-A	.983	19	26	33	1	5	1
1979	Tor-A	.971	20	29	38	2	10	-2
1981	Atl-N	1.000	3	5	3	0	0	0
Total	6	.982	58	69	98	3	19	5
		3B						
1976	Min-A	1.000	4	0	2	0	0	0
1977	Min-A	1.000	4	1	2	0	0	0
1979	Tor-A	1.000	22	21	37	0	9	1
1981	Atl-N	1.000	9	3	3	0	0	0
Total	4	1.000	39	25	44	0	9	1
		OF						
1976	Min-A	—	1	0	0	0	0	0
1977	Min-A	—	1	0	0	0	0	0
Total	2	—	2	0	0	0	0	0

■ Jesse Gonder C

YEAR	TM/L	PCT	G	PO	A	E	DP	FR
1960	NY-A	1.000	1	7	0	0	0	1
1963	Cin-N	1.000	7	21	2	0	0	2
	NY-N	.978	31	120	16	3	3	-13
	Yr	.981	38	141	18	3	3	-11
1964	NY-N	.979	97	397	70	10	7	1
1965	NY-N	.992	31	103	20	1	5	-5
	Mil-N	.989	13	78	8	1	1	5
	Yr	.991	44	181	28	2	6	0
1966	Pit-N	.978	52	238	27	6	4	-1
1967	Pit-N	.971	18	56	10	2	0	0
Total	6	.981	250	1020	153	3	20	-10

■ Rene Gonzales 3B

YEAR	TM/L	PCT	G	PO	A	E	DP	FR
1986	Mon-N	1.000	5	5	8	0	1	1
1987	Bal-A	.963	29	18	34	2	2	4
1988	Bal-A	.966	80	45	153	7	19	12
1989	Bal-A	.923	17	8	16	2	1	-1
1990	Bal-A	.929	16	3	10	1	1	1
Total	5	.962	147	79	221	2	24	17
		2B						
1987	Bal-A	1.000	6	0	4	0	1	1
1988	Bal-A	.979	14	17	29	1	6	3
1989	Bal-A	.978	54	93	125	5	35	0
1990	Bal-A	.994	43	61	94	1	19	8
Total	4	.984	117	171	252	7	61	12
		SS						
1984	Mon-N	.957	27	17	28	2	5	1
1986	Mon-N	1.000	6	2	11	0	2	0
1987	Bal-A	1.000	1	4	5	0	2	1
1988	Bal-A	1.000	2	1	3	0	1	0
1989	Bal-A	1.000	1	2	5	0	1	1
1990	Bal-A	1.000	9	4	10	0	3	1
Total	6	.979	46	30	62	2	14	4
		OF						
1988	Bal-A	1.000	1	1	0	0	0	0
1990	Bal-A	—	1	0	0	0	0	0
Total	2	1.000	2	1	0	0	0	0
		1B						
1988	Bal-A	1.000	1	2	0	0	0	0

■ Tony Gonzalez OF

YEAR	TM/L	PCT	G	PO	A	E	DP	FR
1960	Cin-N	.957	31	43	2	2	0	-1
	Phi-N	.981	67	146	6	3	0	5
	Yr	.975	98	189	8	5	0	4
1961	Phi-N	.984	118	246	7	4	4	-8
1962	Phi-N	1.000	114	268	8	0	2	1
1963	Phi-N	.986	151	263	11	4	2	-9

YEAR	TM/L	PCT	G	PO	A	E	DP	FR
1964	Phi-N	.996	119	243	5	1	2	-3
1965	Phi-N	.983	104	167	3	3	1	-11
1966	Phi-N	.986	121	206	7	3	1	0
1967	Phi-N	.993	143	260	10	2	1	4
1968	Phi-N	.979	117	227	4	5	1	-7
1969	SD-N	.975	49	114	2	3	0	2
	Atl-N	.989	82	173	1	2	0	3
	Yr	.983	131	287	3	5	0	5
1970	Atl-N	.987	119	235	1	3	0	-6
	Cal-A	.960	24	46	2	2	0	0
1971	Cal-A	.987	88	146	4	2	1	-6
Total	12	.987	1447	2783	73	9	15	-36

■ Fernando Gonzalez 2B

YEAR	TM/L	PCT	G	PO	A	E	DP	FR
1974	NY-A	.982	42	86	82	3	22	1
1977	Pit-N	1.000	6	9	9	0	2	-2
1978	Pit-N	.923	4	6	6	1	0	-3
	SD-N	.982	94	190	256	8	68	0
	Yr	.981	98	196	262	9	68	-3
1979	SD-N	.976	103	217	225	11	52	-14
Total	4	.979	249	508	578	3	144	-18
		3B						
1972	Pit-N	.500	1	0	1	1	0	0
1973	Pit-N	.923	5	5	7	1	0	-1
1974	KC-A	1.000	8	10	7	0	1	0
	NY-A	.952	7	4	16	1	1	2
	Yr	.974	15	14	23	1	2	2
1977	Pit-N	.972	37	15	54	2	3	-3
1978	Pit-N	.500	3	1	0	1	0	-1
1979	SD-N	1.000	3	1	1	0	0	0
Total	6	.953	64	36	86	6	5	-3
		OF						
1977	Pit-N	1.000	16	17	0	0	0	-1
		SS						
1974	NY-A	.800	3	4	0	1	0	-1
1977	Pit-N	1.000	2	2	3	0	1	0
Total	2	.900	5	6	3	1	1	-1

■ Jose Gonzalez OF

YEAR	TM/L	PCT	G	PO	A	E	DP	FR
1985	LA-N	1.000	18	10	0	0	0	1
1986	LA-N	.924	57	73	0	6	0	2
1987	LA-N	1.000	16	19	1	0	0	3
1988	LA-N	.938	24	15	0	1	0	1
1989	LA-N	.968	87	171	8	6	2	3
1990	LA-N	1.000	81	62	1	0	0	4
Total	6	.965	283	350	10	3	2	14

■ Julio Gonzalez 2B

YEAR	TM/L	PCT	G	PO	A	E	DP	FR
1977	Hou-N	.968	45	73	142	7	28	2
1978	Hou-N	.983	54	62	112	3	21	-10
1979	Hou-N	.987	32	59	89	2	16	0
1980	Hou-N	1.000	2	1	0	0	0	0
1981	StL-N	.889	4	3	5	1	0	0
1982	StL-N	1.000	9	10	13	0	4	1
1983	Det-A	.923	5	5	7	1	2	1
Total	7	.976	151	213	368	4	71	-6
		SS						
1977	Hou-N	.921	63	81	151	20	28	-28
1978	Hou-N	.917	17	19	25	4	7	-10
1979	Hou-N	.966	21	31	54	3	11	1
1980	Hou-N	1.000	16	18	23	0	7	3
1981	StL-N	1.000	5	3	7	0	1	1
1982	StL-N	1.000	1	1	2	0	0	0
1983	Det-A	.889	6	5	19	3	1	2
Total	7	.936	129	158	281	0	55	-31
		3B						
1978	Hou-N	1.000	4	2	2	0	0	0
1979	Hou-N	1.000	9	2	3	0	0	0
1980	Hou-N	.917	11	3	8	1	1	1
1981	StL-N	1.000	2	1	1	0	0	0
1982	StL-N	.907	21	10	29	4	1	-2
1983	Det-A	—	1	0	0	0	0	0
Total	6	.924	48	18	43	5	2	-1

■ Mike Gonzalez C

YEAR	TM/L	PCT	G	PO	A	E	DP	FR
1912	Bos-N	.875	1	3	4	1	0	1
1914	Cin-N	.954	83	252	101	17	5	12
1915	StL-N	.992	32	93	24	1	3	2
1916	StL-N	.981	93	367	136	10	8	8
1917	StL-N	.977	68	241	97	8	8	0
1918	StL-N	.978	100	362	124	11	17	0
1919	NY-N	.962	52	179	49	9	3	-4
1920	NY-N	1.000	8	9	4	0	0	-1
1921	NY-N	1.000	2	5	0	0	0	0
1924	StL-N	.986	119	413	96	7	15	-7
1925	StL-N	.982	22	92	16	2	3	4
	Chi-N	.989	50	155	31	2	7	0
	Yr	.987	72	247	47	4	10	4
1926	Chi-N	.989	78	306	53	4	5	6
1927	Chi-N	.994	36	136	29	1	6	9
1928	Chi-N	.983	45	198	35	4	8	8
1929	Chi-N	.992	60	212	34	2	7	5
1931	StL-N	1.000	12	15	4	0	0	0
1932	StL-N	1.000	7	12	1	0	0	2
Total	17	.980	868	3050	838	9	95	45
		1B						
1915	StL-N	.989	8	82	7	1	6	1
1916	StL-N	1.000	13	116	2	0	7	-1
1917	StL-N	.982	18	203	13	4	11	1
1918	StL-N	1.000	4	43	0	0	1	0
1919	NY-N	.967	4	26	3	1	2	1
1921	NY-N	.981	6	50	2	1	5	0
1925	Chi-N	1.000	9	91	6	0	6	1
Total	7	.989	60	572	33	7	38	3
		OF						
1917	StL-N	—	1	0	0	0	0	0
1918	StL-N	1.000	5	4	0	0	0	0
Total	2	1.000	6	4	0	0	0	0

■ Pedro Gonzalez 2B

YEAR	TM/L	PCT	G	PO	A	E	DP	FR
1963	NY-A	.963	7	17	9	1	2	-1
1964	NY-A	1.000	6	17	8	0	2	0
1965	Cle-A	.980	112	265	287	11	59	9
1966	Cle-A	.984	104	237	257	8	62	11
1967	Cle-A	.971	64	114	120	7	29	-4
Total	5	.980	293	650	681	7	154	15
		1B						
1964	NY-A	.992	31	114	11	1	10	2
1967	Cle-A	1.000	4	10	0	0	0	0
Total	2	.993	35	124	11	1	10	2
		OF						
1964	NY-A	1.000	20	23	0	0	0	1
1965	Cle-A	1.000	3	1	0	0	0	0
1966	Cle-A	—	1	0	0	0	0	0
Total	3	1.000	24	24	0	0	0	1
		3B						
1964	NY-A	.926	9	7	18	2	1	2
1965	Cle-A	—	2	0	0	0	0	0
1966	Cle-A	1.000	1	0	3	0	0	0
1967	Cle-A	1.000	4	0	1	0	0	0
Total	4	.935	16	7	22	2	1	2
		SS						
1967	Cle-A	.500	3	0	1	1	0	-1

■ Johnny Gooch C

YEAR	TM/L	PCT	G	PO	A	E	DP	FR
1921	Pit-N	.985	13	49	15	1	2	3
1922	Pit-N	.970	103	382	102	15	10	-1
1923	Pit-N	.975	66	217	56	7	7	4
1924	Pit-N	.988	69	198	47	3	12	-6
1925	Pit-N	.968	76	172	39	7	8	-5
1926	Pit-N	.980	80	202	38	5	6	-5
1927	Pit-N	.974	91	285	57	9	7	2
1928	Pit-N	.957	31	92	20	5	3	5
	Bro-N	.969	38	112	15	4	3	-2
	Yr	.964	69	204	35	9	6	3
1929	Cin-N	.975	86	251	61	8	7	4
1930	Cin-N	.955	79	233	42	13	4	-5
1933	Bos-A	.991	26	86	19	1	1	4
Total	11	.973	758	2279	511	8	70	-2

■ Wilbur Good OF

YEAR	TM/L	PCT	G	PO	A	E	DP	FR
1908	Cle-A	.845	42	60	0	11	0	-8
1909	Cle-A	.953	80	110	12	6	2	2
1910	Bos-N	.969	23	56	7	2	1	5
1911	Bos-N	.945	43	108	13	7	1	6
	Chi-N	.928	40	74	3	6	1	-1
	Yr	.938	83	182	16	13	2	5
1912	Chi-N	1.000	10	7	1	0	0	1
1913	Chi-N	.974	26	37	1	1	0	-2
1914	Chi-N	.930	154	242	25	20	10	-5
1915	Chi-N	.936	125	192	13	14	4	-7
1916	Phi-N	.983	46	55	4	1	1	-1
1918	Chi-A	.982	35	103	4	2	1	4
Total	10	.942	624	1044	83	0	21	-6

■ Ival Goodman OF

YEAR	TM/L	PCT	G	PO	A	E	DP	FR
1935	Cin-N	.960	146	322	17	14	4	5
1936	Cin-N	.972	120	274	6	8	2	1
1937	Cin-N	.974	141	291	13	8	0	3
1938	Cin-N	.988	142	306	10	4	1	3
1939	Cin-N	.981	123	246	16	5	4	5
1940	Cin-N	.970	135	252	6	8	0	-9
1941	Cin-N	.966	40	84	1	3	0	-3
1942	Cin-N	.991	57	101	7	1	2	-2
1943	Cin-N	.968	61	120	2	4	1	-5
1944	Chi-N	1.000	35	65	0	0	0	5
Total	10	.975	1000	2061	78	5	14	-7

■ Billy Goodman 2B

YEAR	TM/L	PCT	G	PO	A	E	DP	FR
1948	Bos-A	—	2	0	0	0	0	-1
1950	Bos-A	.967	5	16	13	1	7	0
1951	Bos-A	.965	44	117	129	9	32	-3
1952	Bos-A	.975	103	284	340	16	95	21
1953	Bos-A	.974	112	267	306	15	88	-10
1954	Bos-A	.979	72	173	208	8	59	4
1955	Bos-A	.973	143	348	373	23	93	-18
1956	Bos-A	.966	95	215	266	17	69	-11
1957	Bal-A	.929	5	14	12	2	4	-1
1958	Chi-A	1.000	1	2	2	0	0	0
1959	Chi-A	1.000	3	4	5	0	1	0
1960	Chi-A	1.000	7	9	14	0	5	2
1961	Chi-A	1.000	1	1	1	0	0	0
1962	Hou-N	.972	31	25	45	2	6	-4
Total	14	.972	624	1475	1714	3	459	-21
		1B						
1948	Bos-A	.993	117	1101	69	8	118	-3
1949	Bos-A	.992	117	1069	79	9	148	-1
1950	Bos-A	.995	21	193	12	1	15	0
1951	Bos-A	.995	62	554	29	3	61	-5
1952	Bos-A	.985	23	184	17	3	17	0
1953	Bos-A	.965	20	151	13	6	18	-1
1954	Bos-A	.986	27	195	16	3	26	0
1955	Bos-A	.981	5	47	5	1	3	1
1957	Bal-A	.967	8	56	3	2	7	-1
1958	Chi-A	1.000	3	19	2	0	2	0
1961	Chi-A	1.000	2	6	0	0	0	0
1962	Hou-N	—	1	0	0	0	0	0
Total	12	.991	406	3575	245	6	415	-10
		3B						
1948	Bos-A	.800	2	0	4	1	2	0
1950	Bos-A	.935	27	29	58	6	4	-3
1951	Bos-A	1.000	1	1	3	0	1	0
1952	Bos-A	.929	5	3	10	1	0	0
1954	Bos-A	.944	12	11	23	2	5	-1
1957	Bal-A	.961	54	54	93	6	9	-6
1958	Chi-A	.954	111	67	204	13	16	-18
1959	Chi-A	.950	74	57	135	10	10	-2
1960	Chi-A	.982	20	17	38	1	2	1

YEAR	TM/L	PCT	G	PO	A	E	DP	FR
1961	Chi-A	.944	7	4	13	1	1	0
1962	Hou-N	.825	17	11	22	7	2	-5
Total	11	.947	330	254	603	8	52	-34

OF

YEAR	TM/L	PCT	G	PO	A	E	DP	FR
1947	Bos-A	1.000	1	2	0	0	0	0
1950	Bos-A	.991	45	104	2	1	1	-2
1951	Bos-A	.975	38	70	9	2	2	2
1952	Bos-A	1.000	4	4	0	0	0	0
1954	Bos-A	.938	13	14	1	1	0	-1
1955	Bos-A	—	1	0	0	0	0	0
1957	Bal-A	.900	9	9	0	1	0	-1
Total	7	.977	111	203	12	5	3	-2

SS

YEAR	TM/L	PCT	G	PO	A	E	DP	FR
1950	Bos-A	1.000	1	2	4	0	1	0
1957	Bal-A	1.000	5	1	2	0	0	-1
1958	Chi-A	1.000	1	1	2	0	0	0
Total	3	1.000	7	4	8	0	1	-1

■ Ed Goodson   1B

YEAR	TM/L	PCT	G	PO	A	E	DP	FR
1970	SF-N	.941	2	14	2	1	1	0
1971	SF-N	1.000	14	81	7	0	3	1
1972	SF-N	.991	42	299	27	3	9	2
1974	SF-N	.997	73	593	30	2	52	-4
1975	SF-N	.993	16	139	13	1	13	1
	Atl-N	.990	13	91	7	1	8	0
	Yr	.992	29	230	20	2	21	1
1976	LA-N	1.000	3	7	0	0	0	0
1977	LA-N	1.000	13	32	2	0	5	0
Total	7	.994	176	1256	88	8	91	0

3B

YEAR	TM/L	PCT	G	PO	A	E	DP	FR
1973	SF-N	.911	93	64	171	23	13	-14
1974	SF-N	1.000	8	7	16	0	1	0
1975	SF-N	.907	13	9	30	4	2	1
	Atl-N	1.000	1	1	2	0	0	0
	Yr	.913	14	10	32	4	2	1
1976	LA-N	.833	16	8	27	7	2	-3
1977	LA-N	1.000	4	6	7	0	0	1
Total	5	.911	135	95	253	4	18	-15

OF

YEAR	TM/L	PCT	G	PO	A	E	DP	FR
1976	LA-N	1.000	2	2	0	0	0	0

2B

YEAR	TM/L	PCT	G	PO	A	E	DP	FR
1976	LA-N	—	1	0	0	0	0	0

■ Pep Goodwin   SS

YEAR	TM/L	PCT	G	PO	A	E	DP	FR
1914	KC-F	.907	67	85	208	30	21	-10
1915	KC-F	.906	42	64	109	18	11	-8
Total	2	.907	109	149	317	8	32	-18

3B

YEAR	TM/L	PCT	G	PO	A	E	DP	FR
1914	KC-F	.899	40	49	67	13	4	-3

2B

YEAR	TM/L	PCT	G	PO	A	E	DP	FR
1915	KC-F	.950	23	42	71	6	6	0

1B

YEAR	TM/L	PCT	G	PO	A	E	DP	FR
1914	KC-F	1.000	1	2	0	0	0	0

■ Joe Gordon   2B

YEAR	TM/L	PCT	G	PO	A	E	DP	FR
1938	NY-A	.960	126	290	450	**31**	98	**24**
1939	NY-A	.967	**151**	370	**461**	28	116	6
1940	NY-A	.975	**155**	374	**505**	23	116	14
1941	NY-A	.958	131	332	397	**32**	**109**	7
1942	NY-A	.966	**147**	354	442	**28**	**121**	4
1943	NY-A	.969	152	407	**490**	**29**	114	**26**
1946	NY-A	.974	108	281	346	17	87	21
1947	Cle-A	.978	**155**	341	**466**	18	110	-4
1948	Cle-A	.971	144	330	436	23	97	-7
1949	Cle-A	.980	145	297	430	15	123	-18
1950	Cle-A	.969	105	224	283	16	69	-18
Total	11	.970	1519	3600	4706	260	1160	55

1B

YEAR	TM/L	PCT	G	PO	A	E	DP	FR
1941	NY-A	.984	30	224	17	4	35	-1

SS

YEAR	TM/L	PCT	G	PO	A	E	DP	FR
1948	Cle-A	1.000	2	2	3	0	1	0

■ Sid Gordon   OF

YEAR	TM/L	PCT	G	PO	A	E	DP	FR
1941	NY-N	1.000	9	18	0	0	0	-1
1943	NY-N	.969	28	60	2	2	0	-1
1946	NY-N	.995	101	197	8	1	0	-1
1947	NY-N	.971	124	254	13	8	0	-1
1948	NY-N	1.000	23	40	3	0	0	0
1949	NY-N	1.000	15	29	0	0	0	-1
1950	Bos-N	.990	123	278	8	3	1	7
1951	Bos-N	.984	122	249	4	4	1	-5
1952	Bos-N	.996	142	263	9	1	0	-3
1953	Mil-N	.977	137	245	10	6	2	-3
1954	Pit-N	.977	73	121	9	3	1	-3
1955	Pit-N	.875	4	7	0	1	0	0
	NY-N	1.000	17	27	3	0	0	2
	Yr	.974	21	34	3	1	0	2
Total	12	.985	918	1788	69	9	5	-10

3B

YEAR	TM/L	PCT	G	PO	A	E	DP	FR
1942	NY-N	.913	6	9	12	2	0	1
1943	NY-N	.941	53	62	115	11	12	5
1946	NY-N	.947	30	18	54	4	3	1
1947	NY-N	.000	2	0	0	4	0	-2
1948	NY-N	.948	115	126	220	19	19	-6
1949	NY-N	.958	123	112	206	14	18	-22
1950	Bos-N	.967	10	5	24	1	0	0
1951	Bos-N	.961	34	51	71	5	8	1
1952	Bos-N	1.000	2	3	4	0	0	0
1954	Pit-N	.925	40	28	71	8	5	-6
1955	Pit-N	1.000	8	5	21	0	4	2
	NY-N	1.000	31	30	58	0	6	5
	Yr	1.000	39	35	79	0	10	7
Total	11	.950	454	449	856	8	75	-21

1B

YEAR	TM/L	PCT	G	PO	A	E	DP	FR
1943	NY-N	.991	41	423	25	4	46	-1
1949	NY-N	1.000	1	10	0	0	0	0
Total	2	.991	42	433	25	4	46	-1

2B

YEAR	TM/L	PCT	G	PO	A	E	DP	FR
1943	NY-N	1.000	3	6	6	0	1	-2

■ George Gore   OF

YEAR	TM/L	PCT	G	PO	A	E	DP	FR
1879	Chi-N	.872	54	93	9	15	0	-3
1880	Chi-N	.879	74	134	18	21	4	4
1881	Chi-N	.874	72	146	21	24	3	2
1882	Chi-N	.842	84	153	23	33	5	3
1883	Chi-N	.867	92	195	27	34	4	7
1884	Chi-N	.868	103	185	25	32	5	0
1885	Chi-N	.884	109	204	17	29	2	-6
1886	Chi-N	.876	118	184	20	29	4	-5
1887	NY-N	.889	111	221	20	30	7	-2
1888	NY-N	.836	64	88	4	18	0	-7
1889	NY-N	.864	120	239	21	41	5	-10
1890	NY-P	.877	93	146	11	22	3	-12
1891	NY-N	.909	130	234	16	25	3	-6
1892	NY-N	.932	53	102	8	8	2	-1
	StL-N	.844	20	35	3	7	0	-2
	Yr	.908	73	137	11	15	2	-1
Total	14	.876	1297	2359	243	368	47	-36

1B

YEAR	TM/L	PCT	G	PO	A	E	DP	FR
1879	Chi-N	.957	9	108	2	5	3	0
1880	Chi-N	.971	7	66	0	2	2	0
1881	Chi-N	1.000	1	8	1	0	1	0
Total	3	.964	17	182	3	7	6	0

3B

YEAR	TM/L	PCT	G	PO	A	E	DP	FR
1881	Chi-N	.000	1	0	0	1	0	0

■ Johnny Goryl   2B

YEAR	TM/L	PCT	G	PO	A	E	DP	FR
1958	Chi-N	.948	35	45	65	6	13	5
1959	Chi-N	.973	11	11	25	1	1	0
1962	Min-A	.923	4	2	10	1	1	13
1963	Min-A	.958	34	63	73	6	16	-9
1964	Min-A	.975	28	60	56	3	8	1
Total	5	.960	112	181	229	7	39	10

3B

YEAR	TM/L	PCT	G	PO	A	E	DP	FR
1957	Chi-N	.952	9	6	14	1	4	-1
1958	Chi-N	.931	44	46	88	10	13	6
1959	Chi-N	1.000	4	0	6	0	1	0
1963	Min-A	.900	11	2	7	1	0	0
1964	Min-A	1.000	13	13	14	0	1	2
Total	5	.942	81	67	129	2	19	7

SS

YEAR	TM/L	PCT	G	PO	A	E	DP	FR
1962	Min-A	—	1	0	0	0	0	-5
1963	Min-A	1.000	7	10	12	0	2	0
Total	2	1.000	8	10	12	0	2	-5

■ Jim Gosger   OF

YEAR	TM/L	PCT	G	PO	A	E	DP	FR
1963	Bos-A	.818	4	9	0	2	0	1
1965	Bos-A	.975	81	195	4	5	2	7
1966	Bos-A	.985	32	66	0	1	0	-1
	KC-A	.994	77	158	3	1	0	2
	Yr	.991	109	224	3	2	0	1
1967	KC-A	.981	113	201	6	4	1	2
1968	Oak-A	1.000	64	99	5	0	3	9
1969	Sea-A	1.000	26	36	1	0	0	3
	NY-N	1.000	5	5	0	0	0	0
1970	Mon-N	1.000	71	124	5	0	1	0
1971	Mon-N	.952	23	39	1	2	0	0
1973	NY-N	1.000	35	45	0	0	0	-2
1974	NY-N	1.000	24	17	0	0	0	-1
Total	10	.985	555	994	25	5	7	20

1B

YEAR	TM/L	PCT	G	PO	A	E	DP	FR
1970	Mon-N	.978	19	128	7	3	14	-1
1971	Mon-N	1.000	6	40	4	0	2	0
Total	2	.984	25	168	11	3	16	-1

■ Goose Goslin   OF

YEAR	TM/L	PCT	G	PO	A	E	DP	FR
1921	Was-A	1.000	14	30	1	0	0	0
1922	Was-A	.932	93	198	9	15	1	-3
1923	Was-A	.957	149	310	26	15	5	7
1924	Was-A	.960	154	369	12	16	4	5
1925	Was-A	.971	150	385	24	12	1	14
1926	Was-A	.964	147	373	25	15	8	19
1927	Was-A	.955	148	356	8	17	3	2
1928	Was-A	.962	125	266	14	11	4	3
1929	Was-A	.968	142	299	7	10	1	-4
1930	Was-A	.937	47	72	2	5	1	-5
	StL-N	.973	101	237	13	7	0	12
	Yr	.964	148	309	15	12	1	7
1931	StL-N	.960	151	319	14	14	1	5
1932	StL-N	.951	149	330	16	18	5	6
1933	Was-A	.965	128	261	17	10	7	2
1934	Det-A	.953	149	290	15	15	2	2
1935	Det-A	.965	144	326	6	12	2	2
1936	Det-A	.955	144	266	11	13	1	-9
1937	Det-A	.954	40	81	2	4	1	-3
1938	Was-A	1.000	13	25	0	0	0	0
Total	18	.960	2188	4793	222	209	47	55

3B

YEAR	TM/L	PCT	G	PO	A	E	DP	FR
1932	StL-A	1.000	1	1	3	0	0	0

1B

YEAR	TM/L	PCT	G	PO	A	E	DP	FR
1937	Det-A	.929	1	12	1	1	0	0

■ Howie Goss   OF

YEAR	TM/L	PCT	G	PO	A	E	DP	FR
1962	Pit-N	.985	66	62	2	1	1	4
1963	Hou-N	.993	123	276	7	2	2	2
Total	2	.991	189	338	9	3	3	6

■ Julio Gotay   SS

YEAR	TM/L	PCT	G	PO	A	E	DP	FR
1960	StL-N	.750	2	1	2	1	0	-1
1961	StL-N	.804	10	16	25	10	6	-4
1962	StL-N	.956	120	179	339	24	65	3
1965	Cal-N	1.000	1	0	4	0	1	1
1967	Hou-N	.960	20	33	63	4	9	-1
Total	5	.944	153	229	433	9	81	-2

2B

YEAR	TM/L	PCT	G	PO	A	E	DP	FR
1962	StL-N	.970	8	11	21	1	5	3
1963	Pit-N	.667	1	2	0	1	0	1
1965	Cal-N	.961	23	27	47	3	8	3
1967	Hou-N	.971	30	58	74	4	18	-3
1968	Hou-N	.982	48	116	103	4	28	10

YEAR	TM/L	PCT	G	PO	A	E	DP	FR
1969	Hou-N	.987	16	34	41	1	12	6
Total	6	.974	126	248	286	4	71	20

3B

YEAR	TM/L	PCT	G	PO	A	E	DP	FR
1960	StL-N	1.000	1	0	1	0	0	0
1962	StL-N	—	1	0	0	0	0	0
1965	Cal-N	1.000	9	7	12	0	0	0
1966	Hou-N	1.000	1	1	1	0	0	0
1967	Hou-N	1.000	3	2	6	0	0	0
1968	Hou-N	—	1	0	0	0	0	0
1969	Hou-N	—	1	0	0	0	0	0
Total	7	1.000	17	10	20	0	0	0

OF

YEAR	TM/L	PCT	G	PO	A	E	DP	FR
1962	StL-N	—	2	0	0	0	0	0

■ Hank Gowdy   C

YEAR	TM/L	PCT	G	PO	A	E	DP	FR
1911	Bos-N	1.000	1	6	3	0	0	0
1912	Bos-N	.926	22	82	30	9	5	-2
1913	Bos-N	1.000	2	9	0	0	0	-1
1914	Bos-N	.968	115	475	151	21	11	-7
1915	Bos-N	.974	114	460	148	16	11	0
1916	Bos-N	.980	116	533	158	14	19	2
1917	Bos-N	.969	49	204	75	9	3	-2
1919	Bos-N	.977	74	230	105	8	11	5
1920	Bos-N	.980	74	231	104	7	12	10
1921	Bos-N	.981	53	162	50	4	3	-1
1922	Bos-N	.971	72	204	63	8	7	0
1923	Bos-N	.982	15	43	12	1	0	-2
	NY-N	.986	43	121	18	2	1	-8
	Yr	.985	58	164	30	3	1	-10
1924	NY-N	.982	78	223	51	5	8	5
1925	NY-N	1.000	41	124	26	0	1	1
1929	Bos-N	1.000	9	11	2	0	1	0
1930	Bos-N	.972	15	31	4	1	0	1
Total	16	.975	893	3149	1000	105	93	0

1B

YEAR	TM/L	PCT	G	PO	A	E	DP	FR
1910	NY-N	.943	5	30	3	2	1	0
1911	NY-N	1.000	2	22	0	0	0	0
	Bos-N	.966	26	245	12	9	9	-2
	Yr	.969	28	267	12	9	9	-2
1912	Bos-N	1.000	7	56	4	0	2	1
1914	Bos-N	.985	9	59	5	1	5	1
1919	Bos-N	1.000	1	10	0	0	0	0
1922	Bos-N	1.000	1	6	0	0	0	0
Total	6	.974	51	428	24	2	17	0

■ Billy Grabarkewitz   3B

YEAR	TM/L	PCT	G	PO	A	E	DP	FR
1969	LA-N	1.000	6	1	6	0	0	0
1970	LA-N	.959	97	88	190	12	19	7
1971	LA-N	1.000	10	6	21	0	2	3
1972	Cal-N	.902	24	15	40	6	1	-2
1973	Phi-N	1.000	3	0	1	0	0	0
1974	Phi-N	—	1	0	0	0	0	0
	Chi-N	1.000	6	2	4	0	0	0
	Yr	1.000	7	2	4	0	0	0
Total	6	.952	159	119	278	0	25	-1

2B

YEAR	TM/L	PCT	G	PO	A	E	DP	FR
1969	LA-N	1.000	3	1	1	0	0	0
1970	LA-N	.988	20	43	42	1	10	-5
1971	LA-N	1.000	13	26	31	0	8	1
1972	LA-N	.957	19	45	43	4	12	-2
1973	Cal-N	.965	18	41	42	3	11	-4
	Phi-N	.960	20	45	51	4	16	0
1974	Chi-N	.954	45	67	100	8	8	0
1975	Oak-A	.833	4	4	1	1	0	0
Total	7	.965	142	272	311	1	65	-10

SS

YEAR	TM/L	PCT	G	PO	A	E	DP	FR
1969	LA-N	.954	18	18	44	3	4	-2
1970	LA-N	.958	50	47	135	8	16	-3
1971	LA-N	1.000	1	1	0	0	0	0
1972	LA-N	.667	2	1	1	1	1	0
1973	Cal-A	—	1	0	0	0	0	0
1974	Chi-N	1.000	7	6	18	0	2	0
Total	6	.958	79	73	198	2	23	-3

OF

YEAR	TM/L	PCT	G	PO	A	E	DP	FR
1973	Cal-A	—	1	0	0	0	0	0
	Phi-N	—	1	0	0	0	0	0
1974	Phi-N	1.000	5	8	0	0	0	1
Total	2	1.000	7	8	0	0	0	1

■ Johnny Grabowski   C

YEAR	TM/L	PCT	G	PO	A	E	DP	FR
1924	Chi-A	.972	19	48	22	2	0	1
1925	Chi-A	.983	21	48	9	1	0	0
1926	Chi-A	.973	38	121	22	4	0	-2
1927	NY-A	.984	68	197	47	4	3	0
1928	NY-A	.987	75	265	32	4	8	2
1929	NY-A	.943	22	70	12	5	1	0
1931	Det-A	.984	39	160	28	3	5	2
Total	7	.979	282	909	172	3	17	3

1B

YEAR	TM/L	PCT	G	PO	A	E	DP	FR
1926	Chi-A	1.000	1	7	0	0	0	0

■ Joe Grace   OF

YEAR	TM/L	PCT	G	PO	A	E	DP	FR
1938	StL-A	.933	12	13	1	1	0	-2
1939	StL-A	.968	53	83	9	3	0	-1
1940	StL-A	.958	51	86	6	4	0	-5
1941	StL-A	.983	88	164	13	3	1	-2
1946	StL-A	.967	43	82	6	3	1	-1
	Was-A	.959	74	185	4	8	2	3
	Yr	.962	117	267	10	11	3	2
1947	Was-A	.976	67	162	4	4	0	-5
Total	6	.969	388	775	43	6	4	-5

C

YEAR	TM/L	PCT	G	PO	A	E	DP	FR
1940	StL-A	1.000	12	16	1	0	1	-2
1941	StL-A	.917	9	20	2	2	0	-3
Total	2	.951	21	36	3	2	1	-5

■ Mark Grace   1B

YEAR	TM/L	PCT	G	PO	A	E	DP	FR
1988	Chi-N	.987	133	1182	87	17	91	-4
1989	Chi-N	.996	142	1230	126	6	93	13

YEAR	TM/L	PCT	G	PO	A	E	DP	FR
1990	Chi-N	.992	153	1324	**180**	12	116	**27**
Total	3	.992	428	3736	393	5	300	36

■ Earl Grace C

YEAR	TM/L	PCT	G	PO	A	E	DP	FR
1929	Chi-N	1.000	27	106	18	0	1	3
1931	Chi-N	1.000	2	9	1	0	0	0
	Pit-N	.974	45	128	23	4	5	-1
	Yr	**.976**	47	137	24	4	5	-1
1932	Pit-N	.998	114	364	48	1	10	-7
1933	Pit-N	.980	88	305	37	7	7	0
1934	Pit-N	.982	83	304	26	6	4	-9
1935	Pit-N	.990	69	269	35	3	9	2
1936	Phi-N	.976	65	217	29	6	3	-5
1937	Phi-N	.990	64	275	30	3	10	-3
Total	8	.987	557	1977	247	0	49	-20
	1B							
1934	Pit-N	1.000	1	8	1	0	1	0

■ Mike Grady C

YEAR	TM/L	PCT	G	PO	A	E	DP	FR
1894	Phi-N	.878	44	101	29	18	7	-10
1895	Phi-N	.926	38	103	10	9	2	-8
1896	Phi-N	.942	61	167	60	14	12	-6
1897	Phi-N	1.000	3	11	4	0	0	0
1898	NY-N	.944	57	214	57	16	4	2
1899	NY-N	.939	43	127	57	12	5	-7
1900	NY-N	.932	41	120	45	12	3	-9
1901	Was-A	.933	30	110	30	10	4	-3
1904	StL-N	.955	77	323	77	19	7	-20
1905	StL-N	.956	71	288	79	17	7	-12
1906	StL-N	.983	60	218	67	5	9	-9
Total	11	.946	525	1782	515	132	60	-82
	1B							
1894	Phi-N	.949	11	71	3	4	4	-1
1895	Phi-N	—	1	0	0	0	0	0
1897	StL-N	.974	83	797	48	23	54	-1
1898	NY-N	.897	7	60	1	7	1	-2
1899	NY-N	.947	4	34	2	2	5	0
1900	NY-N	.936	12	94	9	7	6	0
1901	Was-A	.975	59	575	52	16	34	9
1904	StL-N	1.000	11	93	5	0	4	0
1905	StL-N	.956	20	180	17	9	5	1
1906	StL-N	.981	38	299	18	6	7	-1
Total	10	.970	246	2203	155	4	120	5
	3B							
1895	Phi-N	.000	1	0	0	2	0	-1
1896	Phi-N	.700	7	6	8	6	0	-2
1899	NY-N	.877	35	20	80	14	4	-4
1900	NY-N	.750	7	6	9	5	2	-1
1904	StL-N	.800	1	0	4	1	0	0
Total	5	.826	51	32	101	8	6	-8
	OF							
1894	Phi-N	.800	2	3	1	1	0	0
1895	Phi-N	.875	5	6	1	1	0	0
1897	StL-N	1.000	1	1	0	0	0	0
1898	NY-N	.875	30	43	6	7	1	-1
1899	NY-N	.750	4	2	1	1	0	0
1900	NY-N	.600	5	3	0	2	0	-2
1901	Was-A	1.000	3	3	1	0	0	0
Total	7	.855	50	61	10	2	2	-3
	SS							
1898	NY-N	.778	3	4	10	4	1	-1
1900	NY-N	.859	11	21	40	10	7	-1
Total	2	.843	14	25	50	4	8	-2
	2B							
1900	NY-N	.833	2	3	2	1	0	0
1904	StL-N	1.000	3	5	7	0	0	1
Total	2	.944	5	8	9	1	0	1

■ Dan Graham C

YEAR	TM/L	PCT	G	PO	A	E	DP	FR
1980	Bal-A	.981	73	328	35	7	3	1
1981	Bal-A	.975	40	138	20	4	1	-2
Total	2	.979	113	466	55	1	4	-1
	3B							
1980	Bal-A	1.000	9	5	7	0	2	0
1981	Bal-A	.875	4	3	4	1	1	-1
Total	2	.950	13	8	11	1	3	-1
	OF							
1980	Bal-A	—	1	0	0	0	0	0

■ Peaches Graham C

YEAR	TM/L	PCT	G	PO	A	E	DP	FR
1908	Bos-N	.955	62	242	75	15	6	-2
1909	Bos-N	.948	76	293	111	22	14	-3
1910	Bos-N	.966	87	318	132	16	11	-8
1911	Bos-N	.912	26	104	31	13	4	-5
	Chi-N	.972	28	78	25	3	3	-5
	Yr	.937	54	182	56	16	7	-10
1912	Bos-N	.944	19	77	25	6	0	1
Total	5	.953	298	1112	399	5	38	-24
	OF							
1909	Bos-N	1.000	6	4	1	0	0	0
1910	Bos-N	—	1	0	0	0	0	0
Total	2	1.000	7	4	1	0	0	0
	2B							
1902	Cle-N	1.000	1	2	5	0	0	0
1908	Bos-N	.900	5	7	11	2	0	-1
Total	2	.926	6	9	16	2	0	-1
	3B							
1909	Bos-N	.667	1	1	1	1	1	0
1910	Bos-N	.833	2	2	3	1	0	0
Total	2	.778	3	3	4	2	1	0
	SS							
1909	Bos-N	1.000	1	2	6	0	0	1
	1B							
1910	Bos-N	1.000	1	2	0	0	0	0

■ Jack Graham 1B

YEAR	TM/L	PCT	G	PO	A	E	DP	FR
1946	Bro-N	1.000	2	13	1	0	0	0
	NY-N	1.000	7	63	4	0	3	0
	Yr	1.000	9	76	5	0	3	0
1949	StL-A	.984	136	1118	87	19	120	-6

YEAR	TM/L	PCT	G	PO	A	E	DP	FR
Total	2	.985	145	1194	92	9	123	-6
	OF							
1946	NY-N	.949	62	105	7	6	0	-4

■ Alex Grammas SS

YEAR	TM/L	PCT	G	PO	A	E	DP	FR
1954	StL-N	.966	142	252	432	24	100	**30**
1955	StL-N	.968	126	235	340	19	76	7
1956	StL-N	1.000	5	3	9	0	1	0
	Cin-N	.955	12	12	9	1	2	-1
	Yr	.971	17	15	18	1	3	-1
1957	Cin-N	.966	42	23	33	2	3	-2
1958	Cin-N	.993	61	55	84	1	21	-1
1959	StL-N	.964	130	216	373	22	80	**12**
1960	StL-N	.972	46	56	81	4	12	6
1961	StL-N	.960	65	81	136	9	29	10
1962	StL-N	.933	16	11	17	2	2	2
	Chi-N	1.000	13	20	42	0	11	1
	Yr	.978	29	31	59	2	13	3
1963	Cin-N	.955	13	8	13	1	1	-3
Total	10	.968	671	972	1569	5	338	61
	3B							
1954	StL-N	1.000	1	1	0	0	0	0
1956	Cin-N	.968	58	41	79	4	8	3
1957	Cin-N	1.000	9	6	15	0	1	2
1958	Cin-N	.960	38	35	60	4	4	-3
1960	StL-N	.972	13	8	27	1	5	5
1961	StL-N	1.000	3	0	3	0	0	-1
1962	Chi-N	—	1	0	0	0	0	0
Total	7	.968	123	91	184	9	18	6
	2B							
1956	Cin-N	1.000	5	4	8	0	1	2
1957	Cin-N	.983	20	31	27	1	6	3
1958	Cin-N	.985	14	36	30	1	7	2
1960	StL-N	.962	38	38	63	4	16	9
1961	StL-N	.987	18	31	43	1	11	7
1962	StL-N	—	2	0	0	0	0	0
	Chi-N	1.000	3	3	7	0	1	0
	Yr	1.000	5	3	7	0	1	0
Total	6	.979	100	143	178	7	42	23

■ Jack Graney OF

YEAR	TM/L	PCT	G	PO	A	E	DP	FR
1910	Cle-A	.949	114	209	14	12	5	1
1911	Cle-A	.927	142	258	22	22	5	2
1912	Cle-A	.958	75	148	11	7	5	4
1913	Cle-A	.970	148	275	16	9	5	2
1914	Cle-A	.935	127	274	15	20	0	5
1915	Cle-A	.972	115	227	17	7	1	5
1916	Cle-A	.959	154	309	22	14	5	3
1917	Cle-A	.959	145	288	14	13	6	-8
1918	Cle-A	.975	45	77	2	2	0	-6
1919	Cle-A	.961	125	281	13	12	2	6
1920	Cle-A	.941	47	76	4	5	0	-6
1921	Cle-A	.933	32	42	0	3	0	-9
1922	Cle-A	.862	13	24	1	4	0	-1
Total	13	.953	1282	2488	151	130	34	-2

■ Eddie Grant 3B

YEAR	TM/L	PCT	G	PO	A	E	DP	FR
1907	Phi-N	.916	74	106	145	23	6	-2
1908	Phi-N	.930	134	197	271	**35**	**22**	3
1909	Phi-N	.957	**154**	184	310	22	18	1
1910	Phi-N	.935	**152**	**193**	256	31	22	-10
1911	Cin-N	.953	122	158	208	18	21	-2
1912	Cin-N	.927	15	17	21	3	2	0
1913	Cin-N	.929	26	23	42	5	4	-5
	NY-N	1.000	5	1	12	0	0	4
	Yr	.940	31	24	54	5	4	-1
1914	NY-N	.948	52	44	101	8	7	-2
1915	NY-N	.970	35	39	57	3	3	2
Total	9	.942	769	962	1423	148	105	-15
	SS							
1908	Phi-N	.909	13	31	39	7	2	-1
1911	Cin-N	.836	11	20	26	9	2	-4
1912	Cin-N	.948	56	102	171	15	20	1
1913	NY-N	1.000	1	1	0	0	0	0
1914	NY-N	.892	21	29	62	11	5	-2
1915	NY-N	.889	1	1	7	1	0	0
Total	6	.919	103	184	305	3	29	-6
	2B							
1905	Cle-A	.833	2	1	4	1	0	-2
1913	NY-N	.875	3	2	5	1	1	2
1914	NY-N	.929	16	24	28	4	4	-2
1915	NY-N	1.000	9	13	15	0	0	-4
Total	4	.939	30	40	52	6	5	-6
	1B							
1915	NY-N	1.000	1	1	0	0	0	0

■ George Grantham 2B

YEAR	TM/L	PCT	G	PO	A	E	DP	FR
1923	Chi-N	.942	**150**	**374**	**518**	**55**	90	1
1924	Chi-N	.941	118	273	426	**44**	78	0
1927	Pit-N	.953	124	279	363	32	65	-21
1928	Pit-N	—	1	0	0	0	0	0
1929	Pit-N	.967	76	205	239	15	54	-2
1930	Pit-N	.958	141	324	488	**36**	84	-14
1931	Pit-N	.918	51	114	142	23	34	-14
1932	Cin-N	.959	115	258	347	26	45	-28
1933	Cin-N	.948	72	160	189	19	33	-11
Total	9	.949	848	1987	2712	250	483	-89
	1B							
1925	Pit-N	.989	102	925	44	11	96	-4
1926	Pit-N	.990	132	1203	66	13	106	-2
1927	Pit-N	.989	29	247	12	3	22	-2
1928	Pit-N	.986	119	1117	71	17	83	2
1929	Pit-N	.986	12	71	1	1	5	2
1930	Pit-N	1.000	4	33	4	0	4	1
1931	Pit-N	.985	78	742	27	12	67	-8
1932	Cin-N	.984	10	115	5	2	7	-1
1933	Cin-N	1.000	12	114	7	0	9	0
1934	NY-N	1.000	4	21	1	0	1	0
Total	10	.988	502	4588	238	9	400	-16

YEAR	TM/L	PCT	G	PO	A	E	DP	FR
	OF							
1929	Pit-N	.967	19	25	4	1	1	1
	3B							
1922	Chi-N	1.000	5	5	4	0	1	-2
1924	Chi-N	.833	6	4	16	4	0	1
1928	Pit-N	1.000	1	1	2	0	1	0
1934	NY-N	1.000	2	1	1	0	0	0
Total	4	.895	14	11	23	4	2	-1

■ Mickey Grasso C

YEAR	TM/L	PCT	G	PO	A	E	DP	FR
1946	NY-N	.967	7	24	5	1	0	0
1950	Was-A	.942	69	238	38	**17**	6	6
1951	Was-A	.967	49	182	26	7	6	-2
1952	Was-A	.970	114	485	64	**17**	4	6
1953	Was-A	.984	59	219	24	4	4	1
1954	Cle-A	.833	4	9	1	2	0	0
1955	NY-N	.900	8	9	1	1	0	0
Total	7	.964	310	1166	158	9	20	11

■ Gary Gray 1B

YEAR	TM/L	PCT	G	PO	A	E	DP	FR
1980	Cle-A	1.000	6	14	2	0	1	0
1981	Sea-A	.993	34	275	16	2	34	0
1982	Sea-A	.984	60	476	31	8	36	-1
Total	3	.988	100	765	49	0	71	-1
	OF							
1977	Tex-A	—	1	0	0	0	0	0
1980	Cle-A	1.000	6	2	0	0	0	0
1981	Sea-A	1.000	4	6	0	0	0	1
Total	3	1.000	11	8	0	0	0	1

■ David Green OF

YEAR	TM/L	PCT	G	PO	A	E	DP	FR
1981	StL-N	.970	18	31	1	1	0	2
1982	StL-N	.991	68	111	4	1	5	1
1983	StL-N	.970	136	214	10	7	2	-10
1984	StL-N	1.000	14	15	1	0	1	0
1985	SF-N	.944	12	17	0	1	0	0
1987	StL-N	.882	10	14	1	2	0	0
Total	6	.972	258	402	17	2	4	-3
	1B							
1984	StL-N	.991	117	1088	69	10	98	-2
1985	SF-N	.987	78	628	42	9	54	-2
1987	StL-N	1.000	3	4	0	0	1	0
Total	3	.990	198	1720	111	9	153	-4

■ Danny Green OF

YEAR	TM/L	PCT	G	PO	A	E	DP	FR
1898	Chi-N	.970	47	87	10	3	5	5
1899	Chi-N	.947	115	175	22	11	12	1
1900	Chi-N	.938	102	218	10	15	2	0
1901	Chi-N	.932	133	**312**	16	24	7	8
1902	Chi-A	.942	129	217	11	14	4	-3
1903	Chi-A	.933	133	219	16	17	**8**	2
1904	Chi-A	.964	146	231	13	9	5	1
1905	Chi-A	.914	107	119	9	12	3	-11
Total	8	.941	912	1578	107	105	46	3

■ Pumpsie Green 2B

YEAR	TM/L	PCT	G	PO	A	E	DP	FR
1959	Bos-A	.972	45	109	132	7	38	4
1960	Bos-A	.982	69	82	83	3	17	-3
1961	Bos-A	1.000	7	7	6	0	1	0
1962	Bos-A	.953	18	16	25	2	6	-7
Total	4	.975	139	214	246	2	62	-6
	SS							
1959	Bos-A	—	1	0	0	0	0	0
1960	Bos-A	.951	41	68	86	8	16	-10
1961	Bos-A	.940	57	84	166	16	35	-5
1962	Bos-A	.842	5	6	10	3	2	-3
Total	4	.940	104	158	262	7	53	-18
	3B							
1963	NY-N	.857	16	12	36	8	2	-1

■ Gene Green OF

YEAR	TM/L	PCT	G	PO	A	E	DP	FR
1957	StL-N	1.000	3	2	0	0	0	-1
1958	StL-N	.956	75	141	12	7	3	5
1959	StL-N	.944	19	28	6	2	2	4
1960	Bal-A	1.000	1	0	1	0	0	0
1961	Was-A	1.000	21	28	0	0	0	-1
1962	Cle-A	.964	33	51	2	2	1	-1
1963	Cle-A	1.000	18	16	1	0	0	-2
Total	7	.963	170	266	22	1	6	4
	C							
1958	StL-N	.994	48	287	23	2	2	2
1959	StL-N	1.000	11	34	3	0	0	1
1961	Was-A	.986	79	326	22	5	3	-17
1963	Cin-N	.932	8	37	4	3	0	-2
Total	4	.987	146	684	52	0	5	-16
	1B							
1962	Cle-A	1.000	2	5	0	0	0	0

■ Lenny Green OF

YEAR	TM/L	PCT	G	PO	A	E	DP	FR
1957	Bal-A	.950	15	19	0	1	0	0
1958	Bal-A	.965	53	81	1	3	0	7
1959	Bal-A	1.000	23	9	2	0	0	1
	Was-A	.979	58	89	4	2	0	0
	Yr	.981	81	98	6	2	0	1
1960	Was-A	.991	100	219	4	2	0	-6
1961	Min-A	.978	153	356	3	8	0	-5
1962	Min-A	.995	156	361	8	2	2	4
1963	Min-A	.988	119	165	1	2	0	3
1964	Min-A	1.000	7	1	0	0	0	0
	LA-A	.977	23	41	1	1	0	0
	Bal-A	1.000	8	22	0	0	0	2
	Yr	.985	38	64	1	1	0	2
1965	Bos-A	.980	95	198	2	4	1	-1
1966	Bos-A	.978	27	41	3	1	0	1
1967	Det-A	.983	44	57	0	1	0	-3
1968	Det-A	—	2	0	0	0	0	0
Total	12	.984	883	1659	29	7	3	3

■ Dick Green 2B

YEAR	TM/L	PCT	G	PO	A	E	DP	FR
1963	KC-A	.950	4	5	14	1	2	1
1964	KC-A	.990	120	262	361	6	69	17

YEAR	TM/L	PCT	G	PO	A	E	DP	FR
1965	KC-A	.980	126	252	341	12	73	-6
1966	KC-A	.979	137	300	389	15	86	0
1967	KC-A	.991	50	116	108	2	28	1
1968	Oak-A	.974	61	124	170	8	35	13
1969	Oak-A	**.986**	131	302	379	10	93	10
1970	Oak-A	.978	127	259	332	13	66	0
1971	Oak-A	.986	143	366	384	11	98	8
1972	Oak-A	.964	26	35	45	3	9	2
1973	Oak-A	.988	133	264	297	7	86	-8
1974	Oak-A	.983	100	233	243	8	67	-5
Total	12	.983	1158	2518	3063	6	712	33

3B

YEAR	TM/L	PCT	G	PO	A	E	DP	FR
1966	KC-A	.750	2	2	1	1	0	-1
1967	KC-A	.946	59	54	86	8	5	-4
1968	Oak-A	1.000	1	1	0	0	0	0
1970	Oak-A	1.000	5	2	4	0	1	0
1973	Oak-A	1.000	1	0	1	0	0	0
Total	5	.944	68	59	92	9	6	-5

SS

YEAR	TM/L	PCT	G	PO	A	E	DP	FR
1963	KC-A	.941	6	9	23	2	3	1
1967	KC-A	1.000	1	2	4	0	1	0
1971	Oak-A	—	1	0	0	0	0	0
1973	Oak-A	1.000	1	1	0	0	0	0
Total	4	.951	9	12	27	2	4	1

C

YEAR	TM/L	PCT	G	PO	A	E	DP	FR
1968	Oak-A	—	1	0	0	0	0	0
1970	Oak-A	—	1	0	0	0	0	0
Total	2	—	2	0	0	0	0	0

1B

YEAR	TM/L	PCT	G	PO	A	E	DP	FR
1967	KC-A	1.000	1	5	0	0	0	0

■ Hank Greenberg 1B

YEAR	TM/L	PCT	G	PO	A	E	DP	FR
1933	Det-A	.988	117	1133	63	14	111	1
1934	Det-A	.990	153	1454	84	16	124	1
1935	Det-A	.992	152	1437	**99**	13	142	**6**
1936	Det-A	.992	12	119	9	1	14	1
1937	Det-A	.992	154	**1477**	102	13	133	5
1938	Det-A	.991	155	**1484**	120	14	146	7
1939	Det-A	**.993**	136	1205	75	9	108	-1
1946	Det-A	.990	140	1272	93	**15**	110	2
1947	Pit-N	.992	119	983	79	9	85	2
Total	9	.991	1138	10564	724	104	973	24

OF

YEAR	TM/L	PCT	G	PO	A	E	DP	FR
1940	Det-A	.954	148	298	14	**15**	1	0
1941	Det-A	.914	19	32	0	3	0	-4
1945	Det-A	1.000	72	129	3	0	0	-10
Total	3	.964	239	459	17	8	1	-14

■ Jim Greengrass OF

YEAR	TM/L	PCT	G	PO	A	E	DP	FR
1952	Cin-N	.965	17	55	0	2	0	2
1953	Cin-N	.983	153	341	11	6	0	6
1954	Cin-N	.968	137	298	9	10	0	4
1955	Cin-N	1.000	11	30	1	0	0	2
	Phi-N	.988	83	159	10	2	0	3
	Yr	.990	94	189	11	2	0	5
1956	Phi-N	.991	62	104	3	1	1	-2
Total	5	.980	463	987	34	1	1	15

3B

YEAR	TM/L	PCT	G	PO	A	E	DP	FR
1955	Phi-N	.500	2	2	1	3	0	-2

■ Mike Greenwell OF

YEAR	TM/L	PCT	G	PO	A	E	DP	FR
1985	Bos-A	.929	17	14	0	0	0	-1
1986	Bos-A	1.000	15	18	1	0	1	2
1987	Bos-A	.971	91	162	8	5	0	-1
1988	Bos-A	.981	147	302	6	6	2	4
1989	Bos-A	.967	139	220	11	8	1	-9
1990	Bos-A	.977	159	287	13	7	1	-3
Total	6	.976	568	1003	39	6	5	-8

C

YEAR	TM/L	PCT	G	PO	A	E	DP	FR
1987	Bos-A	.750	1	3	0	1	0	-1

■ Bill Greenwood 2B

YEAR	TM/L	PCT	G	PO	A	E	DP	FR
1882	Phi-a	.667	2	0	2	1	0	0
1884	Bro-a	.900	92	230	300	59	40	-7
1887	Bal-a	**.928**	117	357	360	56	33	7
1888	Bal-a	.913	86	158	243	38	17	-14
1889	Col-a	.914	118	313	322	60	50	-3
1890	Roc-a	.921	123	341	343	**59**	59	2
Total	6	.916	538	1399	1570	273	199	-15

SS

YEAR	TM/L	PCT	G	PO	A	E	DP	FR
1884	Bro-a	—	1	0	0	0	0	0
1888	Bal-a	.828	28	45	56	21	8	-8
1890	Roc-a	.833	1	2	3	1	1	0
Total	3	.828	30	47	59	2	9	-8

OF

YEAR	TM/L	PCT	G	PO	A	E	DP	FR
1882	Phi-a	.909	7	10	0	1	0	-1
1887	Bal-a	—	1	0	0	0	0	0
1888	Bal-a	—	1	0	0	0	0	0
Total	3	.909	9	10	0	1	0	-1

■ Ed Greer OF

YEAR	TM/L	PCT	G	PO	A	E	DP	FR
1885	Bal-a	.908	47	93	6	10	1	1
1886	Bal-a	.875	9	5	2	1	0	-1
	Phi-a	.921	70	143	9	13	3	5
	Yr	.919	79	148	11	14	3	4
1887	Phi-a	.857	3	5	1	1	0	0
	Bro-a	.921	76	155	8	14	1	1
	Yr	.918	79	160	9	15	1	1
Total	3	.916	205	401	26	9	5	6

C

YEAR	TM/L	PCT	G	PO	A	E	DP	FR
1885	Bal-a	.887	12	34	13	6	0	0
1886	Bal-a	.786	2	7	4	3	2	-1
	Phi-a	1.000	1	2	4	0	0	1
	Yr	.850	3	9	8	3	2	0
1887	Bro-a	.929	16	70	22	7	3	3
Total	3	.907	31	113	43	6	5	3

■ Ed Gremminger 3B

YEAR	TM/L	PCT	G	PO	A	E	DP	FR
1895	Cle-N	.873	20	24	38	9	3	-2
1902	Bos-N	**.951**	140	**222**	282	26	15	3
1903	Bos-N	.935	**140**	**217**	**300**	36	**20**	**16**
1904	Det-A	.950	83	103	123	12	3	-16
Total	4	.940	383	566	743	83	41	1

■ Bill Grey 3B

YEAR	TM/L	PCT	G	PO	A	E	DP	FR
1890	Phi-N	.852	8	15	8	4	1	-3
1891	Phi-N	.333	1	1	0	2	0	-1
1895	Cin-N	.906	27	47	59	11	7	4
1896	Cin-N	.667	1	1	1	1	0	0
1898	Pit-N	.879	137	172	258	59	16	-20
Total	5	.879	174	236	326	77	24	-20

2B

YEAR	TM/L	PCT	G	PO	A	E	DP	FR
1890	Phi-N	.850	8	11	23	6	2	-4
1895	Cin-N	.896	16	27	33	7	5	-4
1896	Cin-N	.927	12	25	51	6	6	4
Total	3	.899	36	63	107	19	13	-4

C

YEAR	TM/L	PCT	G	PO	A	E	DP	FR
1890	Phi-N	.860	7	28	9	6	1	-2
1891	Phi-N	.804	11	30	7	9	1	-3
1895	Cin-N	.857	5	10	2	2	0	-1
1896	Cin-N	.921	11	26	9	3	1	0
Total	4	.858	34	94	27	20	3	-6

OF

YEAR	TM/L	PCT	G	PO	A	E	DP	FR
1890	Phi-N	1.000	10	13	2	0	0	1
1891	Phi-N	.882	10	13	2	2	0	-1
1895	Cin-N	—	1	0	0	0	0	-1
1896	Cin-N	—	3	0	0	0	0	-1
Total	4	.938	24	26	4	2	0	-2

SS

YEAR	TM/L	PCT	G	PO	A	E	DP	FR
1891	Phi-N	.875	3	3	4	1	0	-1
1895	Cin-N	.826	5	5	14	4	1	-3
1896	Cin-N	.902	8	9	28	4	1	0
Total	3	.875	16	17	46	9	2	-4

1B

YEAR	TM/L	PCT	G	PO	A	E	DP	FR
1890	Phi-N	.500	1	2	0	2	0	0
1896	Cin-N	.913	2	20	1	2	1	0
Total	2	.852	3	22	1	4	1	0

■ Bobby Grich 2B

YEAR	TM/L	PCT	G	PO	A	E	DP	FR
1970	Bal-A	1.000	9	28	31	0	5	3
1971	Bal-A	1.000	2	5	7	0	2	0
1972	Bal-A	.986	45	95	113	3	27	-7
1973	Bal-A	**.995**	162	**431**	509	5	**130**	21
1974	Bal-A	.979	160	484	453	20	132	8
1975	Bal-A	.977	150	**423**	484	21	**122**	24
1976	Bal-A	.985	140	**389**	400	12	91	0
1978	Cal-A	.983	144	325	419	13	77	0
1979	Cal-A	.984	**153**	340	438	13	111	2
1980	Cal-A	.989	146	326	463	9	101	3
1981	Cal-A	.983	100	230	349	10	85	10
1982	Cal-A	.986	142	338	450	11	112	8
1983	Cal-A	.969	118	270	415	**22**	94	16
1984	Cal-A	.982	91	182	249	8	65	4
1985	Cal-A	**.997**	116	224	380	2	99	16
1986	Cal-A	.980	87	127	221	7	49	-11
Total	16	.984	1765	4217	5381	156	1302	97

SS

YEAR	TM/L	PCT	G	PO	A	E	DP	FR
1970	Bal-A	.915	20	28	47	7	4	-1
1971	Bal-A	1.000	5	6	24	0	2	2
1972	Bal-A	.950	81	106	215	17	46	-19
1977	Cal-A	.983	52	88	141	4	23	-4
1983	Cal-A	1.000	1	1	0	0	0	0
Total	5	.959	159	229	427	28	75	-22

1B

YEAR	TM/L	PCT	G	PO	A	E	DP	FR
1972	Bal-A	1.000	16	97	9	0	8	1
1980	Cal-A	1.000	3	27	1	0	3	0
1984	Cal-A	.977	25	120	10	3	18	0
1985	Cal-A	1.000	16	98	9	0	14	1
1986	Cal-A	1.000	11	75	8	0	5	1
Total	5	.993	71	417	37	3	48	3

3B

YEAR	TM/L	PCT	G	PO	A	E	DP	FR
1970	Bal-A	1.000	1	0	1	0	0	0
1972	Bal-A	1.000	8	1	1	0	0	0
1976	Bal-A	—	2	0	0	0	0	0
1984	Cal-A	.970	21	9	23	1	1	0
1985	Cal-A	.966	15	9	19	1	2	-1
1986	Cal-A	1.000	2	0	2	0	0	0
Total	6	.970	49	19	46	2	3	-1

■ Tom Grieve OF

YEAR	TM/L	PCT	G	PO	A	E	DP	FR
1970	Was-A	.939	39	46	0	3	0	-5
1972	Tex-A	.985	49	60	6	1	0	0
1973	Tex-A	1.000	59	68	0	0	0	-2
1974	Tex-A	1.000	38	62	5	0	1	2
1975	Tex-A	.969	63	93	3	1	0	-3
1976	Tex-A	.983	52	112	4	2	2	-1
1977	Tex-A	.976	60	77	5	2	1	-5
1978	NY-N	.979	26	43	3	1	0	2
1979	StL-N	.875	5	7	0	1	0	-1
Total	9	.982	391	568	26	1	4	-13

1B

YEAR	TM/L	PCT	G	PO	A	E	DP	FR
1974	Tex-A	1.000	1	2	0	0	1	0
1978	NY-N	1.000	2	9	2	0	1	1
Total	2	1.000	3	11	2	0	2	1

■ Ken Griffey OF

YEAR	TM/L	PCT	G	PO	A	E	DP	FR
1989	Sea-A	.969	127	302	12	**10**	**6**	2
1990	Sea-A	.980	151	330	8	7	1	-6
Total	2	.975	278	632	20	7	7	-4

■ Ken Griffey OF

YEAR	TM/L	PCT	G	PO	A	E	DP	FR
1973	Cin-N	1.000	21	25	1	0	0	-5
1974	Cin-N	1.000	70	115	5	0	1	0
1975	Cin-N	.967	119	202	6	7	0	-9
1976	Cin-N	.979	144	270	10	6	2	-3
1977	Cin-N	.990	147	298	10	3	5	5
1978	Cin-N	.969	154	296	13	10	2	1
1979	Cin-N	.984	93	175	8	3	1	1
1980	Cin-N	.978	138	266	5	6	3	-4
1981	Cin-N	.989	99	268	8	3	1	5
1982	NY-A	.983	125	282	8	5	2	6
1983	NY-A	.976	14	40	0	1	0	0
1984	NY-A	.974	82	181	6	5	0	4
1985	NY-A	.970	110	222	8	7	3	1
1986	NY-A	.971	51	96	5	3	2	-1
	Atl-N	.986	77	136	1	2	0	-4
1987	Atl-N	.995	107	181	7	1	1	-3
1988	Atl-N	.969	42	61	2	2	0	-5
1989	Cin-N	.987	58	76	2	1	1	-5
1990	Cin-N	1.000	6	12	0	0	0	0
	Sea-A	.963	20	25	1	1	0	-4
Total	18	.981	1677	3227	106	6	22	-20

1B

YEAR	TM/L	PCT	G	PO	A	E	DP	FR
1983	NY-A	.992	101	830	57	7	82	-2
1984	NY-A	.959	27	241	16	11	23	-3
1985	NY-A	1.000	1	5	0	0	0	0
1986	Atl-N	1.000	1	0	1	0	0	0
1987	Atl-N	.962	3	24	1	1	2	-1
1988	Atl-N	.987	11	68	8	1	8	0
	Cin-N	.986	10	64	6	1	1	0
	Yr	.986	21	132	14	2	9	0
1989	Cin-N	.979	9	46	0	1	3	-2
1990	Cin-N	.979	9	42	4	1	2	0
Total	8	.984	172	1320	93	3	121	-8

■ Alfredo Griffin SS

YEAR	TM/L	PCT	G	PO	A	E	DP	FR
1976	Cle-A	.750	6	1	2	1	0	0
1977	Cle-A	.940	13	17	30	3	6	-1
1978	Cle-A	.917	2	4	7	1	5	3
1979	Tor-A	.956	153	272	501	**36**	124	6
1980	Tor-A	.955	155	295	489	**37**	126	2
1981	Tor-A	.937	97	186	275	**31**	64	-18
1982	Tor-A	.968	**162**	**319**	479	**26**	92	6
1983	Tor-A	.957	157	**280**	413	25	84	-4
1984	Tor-A	.962	115	189	269	18	65	-8
1985	Oak-A	.960	162	278	440	30	87	-15
1986	Oak-A	.966	162	282	421	25	85	-11
1987	Oak-A	.963	137	245	386	24	72	0
1988	LA-N	.965	93	145	264	15	44	2
1989	LA-N	.975	131	208	333	14	69	-5
1990	LA-N	.959	139	221	382	**26**	63	10
Total	15	.961	1684	2942	4691	312	986	-35

2B

YEAR	TM/L	PCT	G	PO	A	E	DP	FR
1981	Tor-A	1.000	1	1	1	0	1	0
1983	Tor-A	1.000	5	7	9	0	2	1
1984	Tor-A	.968	2	41	51	3	7	3
1987	Oak-A	1.000	1	5	3	0	1	0
Total	4	.975	28	54	64	3	11	4

3B

YEAR	TM/L	PCT	G	PO	A	E	DP	FR
1981	Tor-A	1.000	4	4	3	0	0	-1

■ Doug Griffin 2B

YEAR	TM/L	PCT	G	PO	A	E	DP	FR
1970	Cal-A	.964	11	21	33	2	9	1
1971	Bos-A	.986	124	311	344	9	90	7
1972	Bos-A	.978	129	321	331	15	81	2
1973	Bos-A	.990	113	294	284	6	77	-14
1974	Bos-A	.979	91	178	242	9	53	-13
1975	Bos-A	.967	99	195	215	14	45	-10
1976	Bos-A	.989	44	77	98	2	15	-1
1977	Bos-A	1.000	3	2	4	0	1	0
Total	8	.981	614	1399	1551	7	371	-28

3B

YEAR	TM/L	PCT	G	PO	A	E	DP	FR
1970	Cal-A	1.000	8	3	9	0	0	0

SS

YEAR	TM/L	PCT	G	PO	A	E	DP	FR
1974	Bos-A	1.000	1	2	1	0	1	0
1975	Bos-A	—	1	0	0	0	0	0
Total	2	1.000	2	2	1	0	1	0

■ Ivy Griffin 1B

YEAR	TM/L	PCT	G	PO	A	E	DP	FR
1919	Phi-A	.989	17	162	21	2	11	4
1920	Phi-A	.990	127	1252	96	13	77	6
1921	Phi-A	.973	27	236	13	7	12	-2
Total	3	.988	171	1650	130	2	100	8

2B

YEAR	TM/L	PCT	G	PO	A	E	DP	FR
1920	Phi-A	.867	2	7	6	2	0	-1

■ Mike Griffin OF

YEAR	TM/L	PCT	G	PO	A	E	DP	FR
1887	Bal-a	.924	136	256	13	22	1	-12
1888	Bal-a	.938	**137**	274	27	20	6	7
1889	Bal-a	.910	109	246	17	26	5	1
1890	Phi-P	**.954**	115	278	33	15	**10**	**17**
1891	Bro-N	**.960**	134	**353**	31	16	7	**26**
1892	Bro-N	**.986**	127	267	25	4	7	13
1893	Bro-N	.965	93	232	19	9	8	9
1894	Bro-N	.969	106	297	14	10	5	7
1895	Bro-N	.969	131	**349**	23	12	**12**	**14**
1896	Bro-N	.961	122	316	8	13	1	3
1897	Bro-N	.956	134	353	13	17	6	5
1898	Bro-N	.974	134	314	20	9	7	9
Total	12	.956	1478	3535	243	173	75	99

SS

YEAR	TM/L	PCT	G	PO	A	E	DP	FR
1889	Bal-a	.828	25	38	68	22	7	-9
1892	Bro-N	.769	2	1	9	3	1	0
1895	Bro-N	.750	1	0	6	2	0	0
Total	3	.819	28	39	83	7	8	-9

2B

YEAR	TM/L	PCT	G	PO	A	E	DP	FR
1889	Bal-a	.833	5	14	6	4	0	-2
1893	Bro-N	.889	2	2	6	1	0	0
Total	2	.848	7	16	12	5	0	-2

■ Sandy Griffin OF

YEAR	TM/L	PCT	G	PO	A	E	DP	FR
1884	NY-N	.842	16	14	2	3	1	-3
1890	Roc-a	.856	107	159	7	28	1	-18
1891	Was-a	.939	20	30	1	2	1	-3
1893	StL-N	.906	23	46	2	5	0	-2
Total	4	.873	166	249	12	8	3	-26

2B

YEAR	TM/L	PCT	G	PO	A	E	DP	FR
1890	Roc-a	.667	1	1	1	1	0	0

Bert Griffith OF

YEAR	TM/L	PCT	G	PO	A	E	DP	FR
1922	Bro-N	.981	77	148	7	3	3	-2
1923	Bro-N	.949	62	111	1	6	0	-7
1924	Was-A	1.000	2	7	0	0	0	0
Total	3	.968	141	266	8	9	3	-9
1B								
1922	Bro-N	.980	6	44	4	1	2	0

Tommy Griffith OF

YEAR	TM/L	PCT	G	PO	A	E	DP	FR
1913	Bos-N	.886	35	55	7	8	1	-1
1914	Bos-N	.931	14	20	7	2	2	4
1915	Cin-N	.952	160	225	11	12	1	-20
1916	Cin-N	.967	155	238	28	9	5	-2
1917	Cin-N	.974	100	165	19	5	3	1
1918	Cin-N	.969	118	201	18	7	3	-3
1919	Bro-N	.954	125	210	20	11	3	-4
1920	Bro-N	.972	92	132	7	4	1	-12
1921	Bro-N	.972	124	215	27	7	5	2
1922	Bro-N	.952	82	167	13	9	4	2
1923	Bro-N	.927	127	215	14	18	4	-9
1924	Bro-N	.965	139	210	9	8	3	-14
1925	Bro-N	1.000	2	2	0	0	0	0
	Chi-N	.937	60	109	9	8	1	-4
	Yr	.938	62	111	9	8	1	-4
Total	13	.956	1333	2164	189	108	36	-60

Art Griggs 1B

YEAR	TM/L	PCT	G	PO	A	E	DP	FR
1909	StL-A	.982	49	454	32	9	20	1
1910	StL-A	.968	17	170	10	6	9	-1
1911	Cle-A	1.000	1	13	0	0	0	0
1912	Cle-A	.986	71	661	43	10	33	1
1914	Bro-F	.980	27	238	8	5	10	-2
1915	Bro-F	1.000	5	54	4	0	3	1
1918	Det-A	.986	25	263	9	4	10	-3
Total	7	.983	195	1853	106	4	85	-3
OF								
1909	StL-A	.918	41	50	6	5	2	-3
1910	StL-A	.878	49	68	4	10	1	-4
1911	Cle-A	1.000	4	2	0	0	0	-1
1914	Bro-F	.000	1	0	0	1	0	-1
1915	Bro-F	1.000	1	2	0	0	0	0
Total	5	.892	96	122	10	6	3	-9
2B								
1909	StL-A	.842	8	11	21	6	0	-3
1910	StL-A	.930	41	78	94	13	19	-5
1911	Cle-A	.949	11	23	33	3	3	0
Total	3	.922	60	112	148	2	22	-8
3B								
1910	StL-A	.889	3	4	4	1	0	-1
1911	Cle-A	1.000	3	1	3	0	0	0
Total	2	.923	6	5	7	1	0	-1
SS								
1909	StL-A	.600	1	2	1	2	1	-1
1910	StL-A	.833	3	2	8	2	0	0
Total	2	.765	4	4	9	4	1	-1

Denver Grigsby OF

YEAR	TM/L	PCT	G	PO	A	E	DP	FR
1923	Chi-N	1.000	22	41	1	0	0	-2
1924	Chi-N	.974	121	244	16	7	4	3
1925	Chi-N	.966	39	81	4	3	2	-1
Total	3	.975	182	366	21	0	6	0

John Grim C

YEAR	TM/L	PCT	G	PO	A	E	DP	FR
1890	Roc-a	.947	15	69	20	5	2	1
1891	Mil-a	.926	16	94	18	9	2	4
1892	Lou-N	.940	69	262	85	22	7	-7
1893	Lou-N	.952	92	281	112	20	15	-4
1894	Lou-N	.931	77	262	100	27	9	9
1895	Bro-N	.947	91	253	103	20	10	-1
1896	Bro-N	.939	77	242	82	21	7	0
1897	Bro-N	.947	77	241	98	19	8	5
1898	Bro-N	.950	52	155	56	11	6	-4
1899	Bro-N	.966	12	39	17	2	3	2
Total	10	.943	578	1898	691	156	69	5
2B								
1888	Phi-N	.750	1	2	4	2	0	0
1890	Roc-a	.913	4	13	8	2	3	0
1891	Mil-a	.864	3	6	13	3	1	1
1892	Lou-N	.955	10	19	23	2	4	-1
1893	Lou-N	1.000	2	5	3	0	0	0
1894	Lou-N	.916	24	58	73	12	10	1
Total	6	.915	44	103	124	1	18	1
1B								
1890	Roc-a	1.000	2	13	0	0	2	0
1892	Lou-N	.982	11	106	5	2	6	0
1893	Lou-N	.966	3	26	2	1	3	0
1894	Lou-N	.972	7	67	2	2	6	-1
1895	Bro-N	1.000	1	8	0	0	0	0
1896	Bro-N	.972	5	35	0	1	1	0
Total	6	.978	29	255	9	6	18	-2
SS								
1890	Roc-a	.851	21	42	55	17	8	-7
1892	Lou-N	.750	1	1	2	1	0	-1
1893	Lou-N	.333	1	1	0	2	0	-1
Total	3	.835	23	44	57	0	8	-9
3B								
1890	Roc-a	.900	8	11	16	3	0	0
1891	Mil-a	.897	10	11	15	3	1	-1
1892	Lou-N	.667	1	0	4	2	0	-1
1894	Lou-N	1.000	1	0	2	0	0	0
Total	4	.881	20	22	37	8	1	-2
OF								
1888	Phi-N	—	1	0	0	0	0	0
1890	Roc-a	1.000	3	3	0	0	0	-1
1892	Lou-N	1.000	8	17	1	0	0	1
1893	Lou-N	—	1	0	0	0	0	0
1895	Bro-N	—	1	0	0	0	0	0
Total	5	1.000	14	20	1	0	0	0

Oscar Grimes 3B

YEAR	TM/L	PCT	G	PO	A	E	DP	FR
1939	Cle-A	1.000	3	3	1	0	0	0
1940	Cle-A	1.000	1	0	4	0	0	1
1941	Cle-A	—	1	0	0	0	0	0
1942	Cle-A	.944	8	5	12	1	1	1
1944	NY-A	.945	97	105	189	17	14	-10
1945	NY-A	.937	141	162	296	31	35	2
1946	Phi-A	.926	6	6	19	2	0	2
Total	7	.940	257	281	521	1	50	-4
2B								
1938	Cle-A	1.000	2	3	2	0	1	-1
1939	Cle-A	.968	48	102	109	7	21	-4
1941	Cle-A	.967	13	28	31	2	7	-1
1942	Cle-A	.944	24	46	39	5	10	-4
1946	NY-A	.957	5	11	11	1	2	1
	Phi-A	.958	43	98	105	9	30	-10
	Yr	.957	48	109	116	10	32	-9
Total	5	.961	135	288	297	4	71	-19
1B								
1938	Cle-A	1.000	1	7	0	0	1	0
1939	Cle-A	.989	43	341	17	4	36	-2
1940	Cle-A	.958	4	21	2	1	2	0
1941	Cle-A	.995	62	544	31	3	53	-4
1942	Cle-A	1.000	1	4	0	0	0	0
1943	NY-A	1.000	1	8	1	0	3	0
1945	NY-A	1.000	1	4	1	0	0	0
Total	7	.992	113	929	52	8	95	-6
SS								
1939	Cle-A	.919	37	58	66	11	18	-5
1942	Cle-A	.333	1	0	1	2	0	-1
1943	NY-A	1.000	3	2	7	0	3	-1
1944	NY-A	.929	20	35	57	7	10	-1
1946	NY-A	.895	7	20	14	4	3	-1
	Phi-A	.765	4	7	6	4	1	-3
	Yr	.855	11	27	20	8	4	-4
Total	5	.907	72	122	151	8	35	-12

Ray Grimes 1B

YEAR	TM/L	PCT	G	PO	A	E	DP	FR
1920	Bos-A	1.000	1	13	0	0	2	0
1921	Chi-N	.993	147	1544	68	12	93	-5
1922	Chi-N	.987	138	1378	68	19	106	-2
1923	Chi-N	.991	62	629	30	6	46	-1
1924	Chi-N	.982	50	530	12	10	40	-7
1926	Phi-N	.981	28	241	16	5	28	0
Total	6	.989	426	4335	194	2	315	-15

Charlie Grimm 1B

YEAR	TM/L	PCT	G	PO	A	E	DP	FR
1918	StL-N	.971	42	385	14	12	24	-5
1919	Pit-N	.968	13	118	2	4	1	-2
1920	Pit-N	.995	148	1496	95	8	95	-4
1921	Pit-N	.994	150	1517	67	9	93	-6
1922	Pit-N	.994	154	1478	68	10	104	-3
1923	Pit-N	.995	152	1453	81	8	130	2
1924	Pit-N	.995	151	1596	72	8	139	-3
1925	Chi-N	.989	139	1317	73	15	125	0
1926	Chi-N	.988	147	1416	68	18	139	-6
1927	Chi-N	.990	147	1437	99	15	117	3
1928	Chi-N	.993	147	1458	70	10	147	-2
1929	Chi-N	.992	120	1228	74	10	114	0
1930	Chi-N	.995	113	1040	68	6	103	1
1931	Chi-N	.993	144	1357	79	10	107	2
1932	Chi-N	.993	149	1429	123	11	127	10
1933	Chi-N	.996	104	979	84	4	94	9
1934	Chi-N	.995	74	683	43	4	39	1
1935	Chi-N	1.000	2	27	1	0	4	0
1936	Chi-N	1.000	35	297	33	0	31	5
Total	19	.993	2131	20711	1214	162	1733	10
OF								
1916	Phi-A	.875	7	7	0	1	0	-2
1918	StL-N	1.000	2	4	2	0	0	1
Total	2	.929	9	11	2	1	0	-1
3B								
1918	StL-N	1.000	1	0	1	0	0	0

Moose Grimshaw 1B

YEAR	TM/L	PCT	G	PO	A	E	DP	FR
1905	Bos-A	.980	74	768	35	16	35	-5
1906	Bos-A	.987	110	1165	64	16	39	-1
1907	Bos-A	.973	15	136	7	4	10	-1
Total	3	.984	199	2069	106	6	84	-7
OF								
1907	Bos-A	.966	23	27	1	1	0	-3
SS								
1907	Bos-A	.889	2	5	3	1	0	-2

Marquis Grissom OF

YEAR	TM/L	PCT	G	PO	A	E	DP	FR
1989	Mon-N	.943	23	32	1	2	0	-2
1990	Mon-N	.988	87	165	5	2	0	0
Total	2	.981	110	197	6	4	0	-2

Dick Groat SS

YEAR	TM/L	PCT	G	PO	A	E	DP	FR
1952	Pit-N	.952	94	229	272	25	61	1
1955	Pit-N	.961	149	330	450	32	107	15
1956	Pit-N	.954	141	287	420	34	74	0
1957	Pit-N	.968	123	226	380	20	74	-1
1958	Pit-N	.975	149	307	461	20	127	3
1959	Pit-N	.964	145	301	473	29	97	3
1960	Pit-N	.966	136	237	443	24	92	11
1961	Pit-N	.957	144	235	473	32	117	9
1962	Pit-N	.965	161	314	521	38	126	14
1963	StL-N	.964	158	257	448	26	91	-13
1964	StL-N	.949	160	249	499	40	91	-12
1965	StL-N	.962	148	242	450	27	86	-9
1966	Phi-N	.974	139	260	454	19	79	10
1967	Phi-N	.947	6	13	23	2	5	2
	SF-N	.912	24	18	44	6	10	-8
	Yr	.925	30	31	67	8	15	-6
Total	14	.961	1877	3505	5811	374	1237	25
3B								
1956	Pit-N	1.000	2	1	4	0	1	0
1957	Pit-N	.833	2	0	5	1	0	0
1961	Pit-N	1.000	1	2	1	0	0	0
1965	StL-N	1.000	2	0	5	0	1	0
1966	Phi-N	.982	20	18	37	1	2	1
Total	5	.973	27	21	52	2	4	1
1B								
1966	Phi-N	—	1	0	0	0	0	0
2B								
1967	SF-N	1.000	1	0	1	0	0	0

Heinie Groh 3B

YEAR	TM/L	PCT	G	PO	A	E	DP	FR
1912	NY-N	1.000	6	6	3	0	0	0
1913	NY-N	1.000	2	2	0	0	0	0
1915	Cin-N	.969	131	153	280	14	34	12
1916	Cin-N	.957	110	123	252	17	32	13
1917	Cin-N	.966	154	178	331	18	28	6
1918	Cin-N	.969	126	180	253	14	37	2
1919	Cin-N	.971	121	171	226	12	22	-2
1920	Cin-N	.969	144	179	252	14	30	-6
1921	Cin-N	.950	97	97	188	15	27	1
1922	NY-N	.965	110	100	207	11	25	1
1923	NY-N	.975	118	117	233	9	18	4
1924	NY-N	.983	145	121	286	7	13	3
1925	NY-N	.909	16	14	16	3	1	-5
1926	NY-N	.950	7	6	13	1	1	-1
1927	Pit-N	.958	12	9	14	1	0	-1
Total	15	.967	1299	1456	2554	136	268	27
2B								
1912	NY-N	.887	12	21	26	6	4	2
1913	Cin-N	.963	113	249	358	23	43	10
1914	Cin-N	.936	134	252	394	44	56	-8
1915	Cin-N	.973	29	63	80	4	12	-1
1916	Cin-N	.980	33	93	108	4	9	7
1917	Cin-N	1.000	2	8	9	0	2	2
1925	NY-N	1.000	2	2	2	0	0	-1
Total	7	.954	325	688	977	1	126	11
SS								
1912	NY-N	.905	7	7	12	2	0	0
1913	NY-N	1.000	1	1	1	0	1	0
	Cin-N	.917	4	4	7	1	0	0
	Yr	.929	5	5	8	1	1	0
1914	Cin-N	.909	2	5	5	1	1	0
1916	Cin-N	.905	5	10	9	2	2	-1
1920	Cin-N	1.000	1	1	3	0	0	0
Total	5	.915	20	28	37	6	4	-1

Emil Gross C

YEAR	TM/L	PCT	G	PO	A	E	DP	FR
1879	Pro-N	.897	30	152	39	22	1	-6
1880	Pro-N	.866	87	429	126	86	5	-19
1881	Pro-N	.893	50	240	70	37	5	-2
1883	Phi-N	.789	55	207	70	74	1	-23
1884	CP-U	.860	15	98	43	23	1	2
Total	5	.859	237	1126	348	242	13	-48
OF								
1881	Pro-N	.667	1	2	0	1	0	0
1883	Phi-N	.500	2	3	0	3	0	-1
1884	CP-U	.545	9	5	1	5	0	-2
Total	3	.550	12	10	1	9	0	-3

Greg Gross OF

YEAR	TM/L	PCT	G	PO	A	E	DP	FR
1973	Hou-N	1.000	9	13	2	0	0	0
1974	Hou-N	.994	151	296	15	2	4	5
1975	Hou-N	.958	121	216	14	10	2	1
1976	Hou-N	.978	115	208	13	5	4	1
1977	Chi-N	.991	71	109	3	1	0	-6
1978	Phi-N	.979	111	182	6	4	1	-18
1979	Phi-N	.978	73	82	5	2	2	1
1980	Phi-N	.973	91	68	5	2	2	1
1981	Phi-N	.982	55	48	7	1	2	5
1982	Phi-N	.983	71	55	3	1	0	2
1983	Phi-N	.991	110	104	1	1	0	-6
1984	Phi-N	.986	48	67	2	1	0	0
1985	Phi-N	1.000	52	48	4	0	0	-4
1986	Phi-N	1.000	27	32	1	0	0	-3
1987	Phi-N	1.000	50	33	1	0	0	0
1988	Phi-N	1.000	37	22	1	0	0	0
1989	Hou-N	.929	12	13	0	1	0	-1
Total	17	.982	1204	1596	83	1	17	-22
1B								
1980	Phi-N	1.000	1	1	0	0	0	0
1983	Phi-N	1.000	1	0	0	0	0	0
1984	Phi-N	.993	28	128	11	1	9	1
1985	Phi-N	1.000	8	18	4	0	1	1
1986	Phi-N	1.000	5	8	2	0	0	0
1987	Phi-N	1.000	11	20	1	0	1	-1
1988	Phi-N	.989	14	86	6	1	13	-1
1989	Hou-N	1.000	6	24	1	0	2	-1
Total	8	.994	74	286	25	2	26	-1

Wayne Gross 3B

YEAR	TM/L	PCT	G	PO	A	E	DP	FR
1977	Oak-A	.932	145	126	242	27	26	-23
1978	Oak-A	.917	106	72	150	20	22	-7
1979	Oak-A	.943	120	120	211	20	19	-11
1980	Oak-A	.948	99	69	130	11	13	-28
1981	Oak-A	.946	73	65	127	11	7	-9
1982	Oak-A	.970	108	113	182	9	25	-6
1983	Oak-A	.952	67	47	92	7	10	-1
1984	Bal-A	.937	117	64	205	18	13	-5
1985	Bal-A	.933	67	41	98	10	14	0
1986	Oak-A	.000	1	0	0	1	0	0
Total	10	.941	903	717	1437	134	149	-90
1B								
1976	Oak-A	.966	3	27	1	1	2	0
1977	Oak-A	1.000	1	1	0	0	0	0
1978	Oak-A	.960	15	48	0	2	3	-2
1979	Oak-A	.993	18	129	14	1	8	1
1980	Oak-A	1.000	10	56	6	0	3	0
1981	Oak-A	.750	2	3	0	1	0	0
1982	Oak-A	.980	16	90	7	2	6	-1
1983	Oak-A	.996	74	426	21	2	41	-5

YEAR	TM/L	PCT	G	PO	A	E	DP	FR
1984	Bal-A	1.000	3	5	0	0	0	0
1985	Bal-A	1.000	9	40	4	0	1	0
Total	10	.990	151	825	53	9	64	-7

OF

YEAR	TM/L	PCT	G	PO	A	E	DP	FR
1976	Oak-A	1.000	2	3	0	0	0	0
1979	Oak-A	1.000	2	3	0	0	0	0
Total	2	1.000	4	6	0	0	0	0

■ Jerry Grote C

YEAR	TM/L	PCT	G	PO	A	E	DP	FR
1963	Hou-N	1.000	3	10	0	0	0	-1
1964	Hou-N	.985	98	522	52	9	5	2
1966	NY-N	.981	115	516	55	11	7	0
1967	NY-N	.990	119	609	62	7	8	2
1968	NY-N	.994	115	754	60	5	8	6
1969	NY-N	.991	112	718	63	7	11	18
1970	NY-N	.991	125	855	46	8	12	8
1971	NY-N	.990	122	892	41	9	4	5
1972	NY-N	.998	59	405	42	1	5	3
1973	NY-N	.995	81	545	34	3	0	8
1974	NY-N	.988	94	549	36	7	1	-4
1975	NY-N	.995	111	706	55	4	8	5
1976	NY-N	.993	95	617	49	5	6	11
1977	NY-N	1.000	28	124	15	0	0	-2
	LA-N	1.000	16	47	7	0	1	3
	Yr	1.000	44	171	22	0	1	1
1978	LA-N	.985	32	123	12	2	0	7
1981	KC-A	1.000	22	87	6	0	0	4
	LA-N	1.000	1	2	0	0	0	0
Total	16	.991	1348	8081	635	8	76	75

3B

YEAR	TM/L	PCT	G	PO	A	E	DP	FR
1966	NY-N	1.000	2	3	0	0	1	0
1972	NY-N	1.000	3	1	1	0	0	0
1973	NY-N	.800	2	1	3	1	1	0
1977	NY-N	.913	11	7	14	2	2	0
	LA-N	1.000	2	2	4	0	1	1
	Yr	.931	13	9	18	2	3	1
1978	LA-N	.917	7	2	9	1	0	1
Total	5	.922	27	16	31	4	5	2

OF

YEAR	TM/L	PCT	G	PO	A	E	DP	FR
1972	NY-N	1.000	1	1	0	0	0	0
1976	NY-N	1.000	2	5	0	0	0	0
Total	2	1.000	3	6	0	0	0	0

■ Johnny Groth OF

YEAR	TM/L	PCT	G	PO	A	E	DP	FR
1946	Det-A	1.000	4	6	0	0	0	0
1947	Det-A	1.000	1	5	0	0	0	0
1948	Det-A	.900	4	8	1	1	1	0
1949	Det-A	.966	99	247	8	9	3	-2
1950	Det-A	.985	157	374	9	6	0	-16
1951	Det-A	.993	112	266	12	2	3	-5
1952	Det-A	.986	139	329	14	5	3	-7
1953	StL-A	.991	141	425	18	4	5	12
1954	Chi-A	.988	125	314	7	4	3	-5
1955	Chi-A	1.000	26	61	1	0	0	3
	Was-A	.984	48	122	2	2	1	2
	Yr	.989	74	183	3	2	1	5
1956	KC-A	1.000	84	140	8	0	3	3
1957	KC-A	.974	50	37	0	1	0	0
	Det-A	1.000	36	73	0	0	0	2
	Yr	.991	86	110	0	1	0	2
1958	Det-A	.990	80	95	2	1	1	3
1959	Det-A	.983	41	58	0	1	0	1
1960	Det-A	1.000	8	6	0	0	0	1
Total	15	.987	1155	2566	82	6	23	-8

■ Roy Grover 2B

YEAR	TM/L	PCT	G	PO	A	E	DP	FR
1916	Phi-A	.952	20	40	40	4	7	-7
1917	Phi-A	.960	139	279	425	29	51	5
1919	Phi-A	.915	12	26	28	5	3	-4
	Was-A	.947	24	58	50	6	6	-4
	Yr	.936	36	84	78	11	9	-8
Total	3	.956	195	403	543	4	67	-10

3B

YEAR	TM/L	PCT	G	PO	A	E	DP	FR
1919	Phi-A	.700	3	4	3	3	0	-2

■ John Grubb OF

YEAR	TM/L	PCT	G	PO	A	E	DP	FR
1972	SD-N	1.000	6	16	0	0	0	1
1973	SD-N	.988	102	229	11	3	1	4
1974	SD-N	.976	122	321	8	8	1	7
1975	SD-N	.991	139	334	3	3	0	-8
1976	SD-N	.974	98	183	3	5	0	-6
1977	Cle-A	1.000	28	47	2	0	0	0
1978	Cle-A	.973	110	199	14	6	4	1
	Tex-A	1.000	13	14	2	0	1	1
	Yr	.974	123	213	16	6	5	2
1979	Tex-A	.986	82	135	8	2	4	-3
1980	Tex-A	.952	77	112	6	6	1	-8
1981	Tex-A	.990	58	95	2	1	0	-7
1982	Tex-A	.965	77	135	4	5	1	-5
1983	Det-A	1.000	26	34	1	0	0	-2
1984	Det-A	1.000	36	47	0	0	0	-1
1985	Det-A	1.000	18	23	0	0	0	-1
1986	Det-A	1.000	19	26	1	0	0	-1
1987	Det-A	1.000	31	42	1	0	0	1
Total	16	.981	1042	1992	66	9	13	-27

1B

YEAR	TM/L	PCT	G	PO	A	E	DP	FR
1976	SD-N	1.000	9	64	3	0	7	-1

3B

YEAR	TM/L	PCT	G	PO	A	E	DP	FR
1973	SD-N	—	2	0	0	0	0	0
1974	SD-N	—	2	0	0	0	0	0
1976	SD-N	.667	3	1	1	1	0	-1
1987	Det-A	—	1	0	0	0	0	0
Total	4	.667	8	1	1	1	0	-1

■ Frank Grube C

YEAR	TM/L	PCT	G	PO	A	E	DP	FR
1931	Chi-A	.977	81	248	50	7	3	-11
1932	Chi-A	.957	92	303	55	16	5	-2
1933	Chi-A	.984	83	266	44	5	5	-7
1934	StL-A	.963	55	186	21	8	4	-1
1935	StL-A	1.000	3	8	0	0	0	0

YEAR	TM/L	PCT	G	PO	A	E	DP	FR
	Chi-A	.944	9	28	6	2	0	2
	Yr	.955	12	36	6	2	0	2
1936	Chi-A	.991	32	89	19	1	2	2
1941	StL-A	.951	18	45	13	3	1	3
Total	7	.970	373	1173	208	2	20	-14

■ Kelly Gruber 3B

YEAR	TM/L	PCT	G	PO	A	E	DP	FR
1984	Tor-A	.933	12	4	10	1	0	2
1985	Tor-A	1.000	5	2	6	0	0	0
1986	Tor-A	.940	42	19	59	5	3	8
1987	Tor-A	.948	119	52	168	12	11	5
1988	Tor-A	.971	156	114	349	14	31	26
1989	Tor-A	.945	119	86	291	22	15	18
1990	Tor-A	.955	145	123	280	19	21	-2
Total	7	.955	598	400	1163	3	81	57

OF

YEAR	TM/L	PCT	G	PO	A	E	DP	FR
1984	Tor-A	1.000	2	2	0	0	0	0
1986	Tor-A	.857	9	6	0	1	0	0
1987	Tor-A	1.000	2	1	0	0	0	0
1988	Tor-A	1.000	2	3	0	0	0	0
1989	Tor-A	1.000	16	35	2	0	1	1
1990	Tor-A	1.000	6	6	0	0	0	1
Total	6	.982	37	53	2	1	1	1

SS

YEAR	TM/L	PCT	G	PO	A	E	DP	FR
1984	Tor-A	.667	1	0	2	1	0	0
1986	Tor-A	1.000	5	3	2	0	0	0
1987	Tor-A	.980	21	20	28	1	7	3
1988	Tor-A	—	1	0	0	0	0	0
1989	Tor-A	1.000	1	0	2	0	0	0
Total	5	.966	29	23	34	2	7	3

2B

YEAR	TM/L	PCT	G	PO	A	E	DP	FR
1985	Tor-A	—	1	0	0	0	0	0
1986	Tor-A	.969	14	15	16	1	5	2
1987	Tor-A	1.000	7	3	4	0	1	0
1988	Tor-A	.909	7	4	16	2	4	0
Total	4	.951	29	22	36	3	10	2

■ Mike Guerra C

YEAR	TM/L	PCT	G	PO	A	E	DP	FR
1937	Was-A	.750	1	3	0	1	0	-1
1944	Was-A	.960	58	211	32	10	8	-3
1945	Was-A	.990	38	163	28	2	3	6
1946	Was-A	.938	27	75	16	6	4	-2
1947	Phi-A	.964	62	203	36	9	5	2
1948	Phi-A	.973	47	163	20	5	1	0
1949	Phi-A	.982	95	328	48	7	3	-2
1950	Phi-A	.990	78	253	33	3	8	-6
1951	Bos-A	1.000	10	46	4	0	1	-1
	Was-A	.977	66	192	25	5	0	-11
	Yr	.982	76	238	29	5	1	-12
Total	9	.975	482	1637	242	8	33	-18

OF

YEAR	TM/L	PCT	G	PO	A	E	DP	FR
1944	Was-A	—	1	0	0	0	0	0

■ Mario Guerrero SS

YEAR	TM/L	PCT	G	PO	A	E	DP	FR
1973	Bos-A	.974	46	59	129	5	30	7
1974	Bos-A	.969	93	136	266	13	50	0
1975	StL-N	.955	64	76	198	13	29	6
1976	Cal-A	.932	41	49	75	9	13	-12
1977	Cal-A	.985	31	48	85	2	16	0
1978	Oak-A	.958	142	258	330	26	67	-30
1979	Oak-A	.952	43	68	129	10	33	-4
1980	Oak-A	.962	116	184	276	18	50	-42
Total	8	.961	576	878	1488	6	288	-75

2B

YEAR	TM/L	PCT	G	PO	A	E	DP	FR
1973	Bos-A	.971	24	47	54	3	19	-15
1976	Cal-A	.973	41	80	97	5	19	1
1977	Cal-A	1.000	12	13	20	0	2	1
Total	3	.975	77	140	171	8	40	-13

■ Pedro Guerrero OF

YEAR	TM/L	PCT	G	PO	A	E	DP	FR
1979	LA-N	1.000	12	19	0	0	0	-1
1980	LA-N	.987	40	74	1	1	0	1
1981	LA-N	.974	75	145	4	4	0	-2
1982	LA-N	.976	137	269	11	7	6	5
1984	LA-N	1.000	58	106	4	0	0	-3
1985	LA-N	.974	81	141	7	4	2	0
1986	LA-N	1.000	10	9	1	0	0	-1
1987	LA-N	.971	109	163	6	5	0	-7
1988	LA-N	1.000	2	1	0	0	0	0
	StL-N	.909	7	10	0	1	0	-1
	Yr	.917	9	11	0	1	0	-1
Total	9	.978	531	937	34	2	8	-9

1B

YEAR	TM/L	PCT	G	PO	A	E	DP	FR
1978	LA-N	1.000	4	25	1	0	0	0
1979	LA-N	.972	8	33	2	1	0	0
1980	LA-N	1.000	2	14	2	0	1	0
1981	LA-N	1.000	1	6	0	0	0	0
1983	LA-N	.909	2	7	3	1	0	1
1984	LA-N	.957	16	129	6	6	12	-2
1985	LA-N	1.000	12	89	5	0	7	-1
1986	LA-N	1.000	4	30	0	0	4	-1
1987	LA-N	.981	40	319	38	7	30	3
1988	LA-N	.990	15	86	13	1	6	2
	StL-N	1.000	37	348	22	0	18	-1
	Yr	.998	52	434	35	1	24	1
1989	StL-N	.990	160	1445	72	15	99	-14
1990	StL-N	.989	132	1083	73	13	74	-10
Total	12	.989	433	3614	237	4	251	-23

3B

YEAR	TM/L	PCT	G	PO	A	E	DP	FR
1979	LA-N	1.000	3	1	2	0	1	0
1980	LA-N	1.000	3	3	9	0	1	1
1981	LA-N	.903	21	14	51	7	5	2
1982	LA-N	.917	24	13	42	5	3	1
1983	LA-N	.934	157	123	305	30	22	6
1984	LA-N	.917	76	36	141	16	12	-6
1985	LA-N	.936	44	21	111	9	9	6
1988	LA-N	.895	45	21	64	10	2	-14
Total	8	.926	373	232	725	7	55	-4

YEAR	TM/L	PCT	G	PO	A	E	DP	FR

2B

YEAR	TM/L	PCT	G	PO	A	E	DP	FR
1980	LA-N	.949	12	12	25	2	3	0

■ Ozzie Guillen SS

YEAR	TM/L	PCT	G	PO	A	E	DP	FR
1985	Chi-A	.980	150	220	382	12	80	11
1986	Chi-A	.970	157	261	459	22	93	14
1987	Chi-A	.975	149	266	475	19	105	13
1988	Chi-A	.977	156	273	570	20	115	43
1989	Chi-A	.973	155	272	512	22	106	14
1990	Chi-A	.977	159	252	474	17	100	3
Total	6	.975	926	1544	2872	112	599	98

■ Lou Guisto 1B

YEAR	TM/L	PCT	G	PO	A	E	DP	FR
1916	Cle-A	1.000	6	66	3	0	3	0
1917	Cle-A	.989	59	611	33	7	45	-1
1921	Cle-A	1.000	1	5	1	0	0	0
1922	Cle-A	.995	24	202	14	1	15	1
1923	Cle-A	.988	40	389	28	5	30	1
Total	5	.990	130	1273	79	3	93	1

■ Brad Gulden C

YEAR	TM/L	PCT	G	PO	A	E	DP	FR
1978	LA-N	1.000	3	8	1	0	1	1
1979	NY-A	.995	40	178	24	1	4	11
1980	NY-A	1.000	2	3	0	0	0	0
1981	Sea-A	1.000	6	24	3	0	0	2
1982	Mon-N	1.000	2	6	2	0	0	1
1984	Cin-N	.975	100	485	53	14	8	-4
1986	SF-N	1.000	10	26	1	0	0	-1
Total	7	.982	163	730	84	5	13	10

■ Ted Gullic OF

YEAR	TM/L	PCT	G	PO	A	E	DP	FR
1930	StL-A	.967	82	136	12	5	3	1
1933	StL-A	.988	36	75	7	1	3	5
Total	2	.975	118	211	19	6	6	6

3B

YEAR	TM/L	PCT	G	PO	A	E	DP	FR
1933	StL-A	.980	33	41	58	2	2	6

1B

YEAR	TM/L	PCT	G	PO	A	E	DP	FR
1930	StL-A	1.000	3	29	5	0	0	1
1933	StL-A	.984	14	113	9	2	3	1
Total	2	.987	17	142	14	2	3	2

■ Tom Gunning C

YEAR	TM/L	PCT	G	PO	A	E	DP	FR
1884	Bos-N	.914	12	60	14	7	1	-6
1885	Bos-N	.877	48	252	68	45	4	-6
1886	Bos-N	.892	27	162	27	23	4	-4
1887	Phi-N	.895	28	133	55	22	6	5
1888	Phi-a	.894	23	130	38	20	4	0
1889	Phi-a	.838	8	24	7	6	2	-2
Total	6	.887	146	761	209	123	21	-13

■ Joe Gunson C

YEAR	TM/L	PCT	G	PO	A	E	DP	FR
1884	Was-U	.915	33	210	49	24	0	7
1889	KC-a	.862	32	118	44	26	2	-7
1892	Bal-N	.921	67	281	92	32	3	0
1893	StL-N	.927	35	130	36	13	4	2
	Cle-N	.942	20	60	21	5	1	2
	Yr	.932	55	190	57	18	5	4
Total	4	.912	187	799	242	100	10	4

OF

YEAR	TM/L	PCT	G	PO	A	E	DP	FR
1884	Was-U	.804	18	27	10	9	0	5
1889	KC-a	—	1	0	0	0	0	0
1892	Bal-N	.865	20	30	2	5	1	-2
1893	StL-N	1.000	5	8	1	0	1	0
Total	4	.848	44	65	13	4	2	3

1B

YEAR	TM/L	PCT	G	PO	A	E	DP	FR
1892	Bal-N	1.000	2	13	0	0	1	0

3B

YEAR	TM/L	PCT	G	PO	A	E	DP	FR
1889	KC-a	.000	1	0	0	1	0	0

2B

YEAR	TM/L	PCT	G	PO	A	E	DP	FR
1892	Bal-N	1.000	1	0	4	0	1	1

■ Frankie Gustine 2B

YEAR	TM/L	PCT	G	PO	A	E	DP	FR
1940	Pit-N	.941	130	288	402	43	92	-8
1941	Pit-N	.954	104	269	317	28	45	-2
1942	Pit-N	.954	108	227	312	26	53	-9
1943	Pit-N	.969	40	75	115	6	23	-2
1944	Pit-N	.957	11	23	21	2	3	1
1945	Pit-N	.960	29	69	75	6	11	-1
1946	Pit-N	.967	113	290	328	21	61	6
1949	Chi-N	.961	16	52	47	4	15	4
Total	8	.955	551	1293	1617	136	303	-11

3B

YEAR	TM/L	PCT	G	PO	A	E	DP	FR
1939	Pit-N	.896	22	17	52	8	3	4
1941	Pit-N	.882	15	24	36	8	2	1
1942	Pit-N	.800	2	2	2	1	1	0
1944	Pit-N	—	1	0	0	0	0	0
1946	Pit-N	.966	7	9	19	1	1	2
1947	Pit-N	.944	156	193	330	31	35	15
1948	Pit-N	.947	118	119	256	21	21	6
1949	Chi-N	.931	55	52	110	12	13	-3
1950	StL-A	.857	6	10	8	3	3	0
Total	9	.936	382	426	813	5	79	28

SS

YEAR	TM/L	PCT	G	PO	A	E	DP	FR
1942	Pit-N	1.000	2	2	2	0	0	0
1943	Pit-N	.938	68	135	230	24	41	-2
1944	Pit-N	.938	116	183	330	34	52	-27
1945	Pit-N	.930	104	177	291	35	52	-18
1946	Pit-N	.968	13	20	40	2	8	0
Total	5	.937	303	517	893	5	153	-47

C

YEAR	TM/L	PCT	G	PO	A	E	DP	FR
1942	Pit-N	1.000	1	2	0	0	0	0
1945	Pit-N	1.000	1	2	0	0	0	0
Total	2	1.000	2	4	0	0	0	0

1B

YEAR	TM/L	PCT	G	PO	A	E	DP	FR
1943	Pit-N	.500	1	3	0	3	1	-1

■ Cesar Gutierrez SS

YEAR	TM/L	PCT	G	PO	A	E	DP	FR
1967	SF-N	.946	15	15	20	2	4	3
1969	SF-N	.800	4	0	4	1	0	0
	Det-A	.946	16	25	45	4	6	1
1970	Det-A	.957	135	183	326	23	60	-18

YEAR	TM/L	PCT	G	PO	A	E	DP	FR
1971	Det-A	.971	14	11	22	1	2	3
Total	4	.955	184	234	417	1	72	-11
3B								
1969	SF-N	.882	7	3	12	2	0	0
1971	Det-A	1.000	5	1	3	0	1	1
Total	2	.905	12	4	15	2	1	1
2B								
1967	SF-N	1.000	1	2	0	0	0	0
1971	Det-A	1.000	2	2	1	0	1	1
Total	2	1.000	3	4	1	0	1	1

■ Jackie Gutierrez SS

YEAR	TM/L	PCT	G	PO	A	E	DP	FR
1983	Bos-A	.938	4	9	6	1	1	0
1984	Bos-A	.949	150	228	347	31	60	-33
1985	Bos-A	.943	99	143	238	23	47	5
1988	Phi-N	.919	22	22	46	6	7	-2
Total	4	.945	275	402	637	1	115	-30
2B								
1986	Bal-A	.990	53	93	102	2	29	7
1987	Bal-A	—	1	0	0	0	0	0
Total	2	.990	54	93	102	2	29	7
3B								
1986	Bal-A	.818	6	3	6	2	0	0
1987	Bal-A	—	1	0	0	0	0	0
1988	Phi-N	.905	13	6	13	2	0	0
Total	3	.875	20	9	19	4	0	0

■ Don Gutteridge 2B

YEAR	TM/L	PCT	G	PO	A	E	DP	FR
1942	StL-A	.973	145	377	454	23	94	3
1943	StL-A	.958	132	328	331	29	64	-31
1944	StL-A	.957	146	368	407	35	95	-8
1945	StL-A	.970	128	334	334	21	66	-18
1946	Bos-A	1.000	9	8	12	0	3	1
1947	Bos-A	.938	20	38	37	5	8	0
Total	6	.964	580	1453	1575	113	330	-53
3B								
1936	StL-N	.967	23	25	34	2	3	0
1937	StL-N	.978	105	133	176	7	18	3
1938	StL-N	.945	73	94	148	14	17	9
1939	StL-N	.934	143	136	203	24	24	-18
1940	StL-N	.877	39	24	33	8	3	-2
1942	StL-A	1.000	2	0	1	0	0	0
1946	Bos-A	.833	8	7	13	4	0	-2
1947	Bos-A	.947	19	18	36	3	3	-1
Total	8	.946	412	437	644	2	68	-11
SS								
1937	StL-N	.933	8	12	16	2	2	-2
1938	StL-N	.918	68	150	196	31	39	-9
1939	StL-N	1.000	2	0	1	0	0	0
Total	3	.919	78	162	213	3	41	-11
OF								
1945	StL-A	.958	14	23	0	1	0	0

■ Tony Gwynn OF

YEAR	TM/L	PCT	G	PO	A	E	DP	FR
1982	SD-N	.991	52	110	1	1	0	-1
1983	SD-N	.994	81	163	9	1	1	2
1984	SD-N	.989	156	345	11	4	4	11
1985	SD-N	.989	152	337	14	4	2	11
1986	SD-N	.989	160	337	19	4	3	16
1987	SD-N	.981	156	298	13	6	1	4
1988	SD-N	.982	133	264	8	5	1	1
1989	SD-N	.984	157	353	13	6	1	-3
1990	SD-N	.985	141	327	11	5	2	11
Total	9	.987	1188	2534	99	6	15	52

■ Bert Haas 1B

YEAR	TM/L	PCT	G	PO	A	E	DP	FR
1937	Bro-N	1.000	3	12	0	0	1	0
1942	Cin-N	.986	6	67	3	1	5	0
1943	Cin-N	.993	44	364	42	3	46	7
1946	Cin-N	.994	140	1346	91	9	140	-1
1947	Cin-N	.985	53	510	23	8	49	-5
1948	Phi-N	.987	35	290	18	4	17	-2
1949	NY-N	.983	23	160	10	3	13	0
1951	Chi-A	1.000	7	41	4	0	4	0
Total	8	.991	311	2790	191	8	275	-1
3B								
1942	Cin-N	.925	146	160	273	35	33	-10
1943	Cin-N	.940	23	25	54	5	6	3
1946	Cin-N	1.000	6	9	14	0	2	1
1948	Phi-N	.892	54	76	89	20	9	-6
1949	NY-N	.833	11	6	9	3	1	-1
1951	Chi-A	1.000	1	0	1	0	0	0
Total	6	.919	241	276	440	3	51	-13
OF								
1937	Bro-N	1.000	4	6	0	0	0	0
1942	Cin-N	1.000	2	8	0	0	0	1
1943	Cin-N	.978	18	43	1	1	0	0
1947	Cin-N	.956	69	170	2	8	0	-3
1951	Chi-A	1.000	4	3	0	0	0	0
Total	5	.963	97	230	3	9	0	-2

■ Mule Haas OF

YEAR	TM/L	PCT	G	PO	A	E	DP	FR
1925	Pit-N	1.000	2	2	0	0	0	0
1928	Phi-A	.974	82	175	9	5	1	-3
1929	Phi-A	.982	139	373	10	7	2	2
1930	Phi-A	.976	131	360	11	9	5	12
1931	Phi-A	.989	102	272	6	3	4	4
1932	Phi-A	.987	137	372	6	5	2	-2
1933	Chi-A	.983	146	347	9	6	2	-7
1934	Chi-A	.991	89	204	5	2	1	-5
1935	Chi-A	.989	84	183	4	2	1	0
1936	Chi-A	.989	96	176	7	2	2	-8
1937	Chi-A	.750	2	3	0	1	0	0
1938	Phi-A	1.000	12	19	1	0	1	0
Total	12	.984	1022	2486	68	2	21	-7
1B								
1936	Chi-A	.964	7	77	4	3	6	0
1937	Chi-A	.975	32	251	19	7	22	1
1938	Phi-A	1.000	6	48	1	0	2	-1
Total	3	.976	45	376	24	0	30	0

■ Stan Hack 3B

YEAR	TM/L	PCT	G	PO	A	E	DP	FR
1932	Chi-N	.913	51	36	90	12	5	-5
1933	Chi-N	.983	17	19	40	1	8	6
1934	Chi-N	.949	109	102	198	16	10	0
1935	Chi-N	.942	111	87	237	20	21	10
1936	Chi-N	.950	140	121	202	17	13	-12
1937	Chi-N	.968	150	151	247	13	25	-10
1938	Chi-N	.954	152	178	300	23	26	7
1939	Chi-N	.956	156	177	278	21	15	-7
1940	Chi-N	.954	148	175	302	23	27	13
1941	Chi-N	.954	150	138	295	21	22	-16
1942	Chi-N	.965	139	154	261	15	21	-10
1943	Chi-N	.960	136	149	264	17	11	-7
1944	Chi-N	.939	75	96	164	17	7	3
1945	Chi-N	.975	146	195	312	13	27	18
1946	Chi-N	.968	90	102	168	9	6	-3
1947	Chi-N	.962	66	64	136	8	11	7
Total	16	.957	1836	1944	3494	246	255	-6
1B								
1935	Chi-N	.986	7	66	7	1	5	1
1936	Chi-N	1.000	11	104	8	0	15	0
1937	Chi-N	.962	4	21	4	1	5	1
1940	Chi-N	1.000	1	7	2	0	0	1
1941	Chi-N	1.000	1	1	0	0	0	0
1944	Chi-N	.986	18	130	10	2	16	-1
1945	Chi-N	.976	5	38	2	1	2	0
Total	7	.988	47	367	33	5	43	2

■ Mert Hackett C

YEAR	TM/L	PCT	G	PO	A	E	DP	FR
1883	Bos-N	.909	44	254	57	31	2	0
1884	Bos-N	.928	71	512	104	48	2	5
1885	Bos-N	.901	34	194	53	27	6	6
1886	KC-N	.926	53	252	63	25	6	-10
1887	Ind-N	.938	40	128	52	12	4	-7
Total	5	.921	242	1340	329	143	20	-6
OF								
1883	Bos-N	.400	4	1	1	3	0	-1
1886	KC-N	.769	13	10	0	3	0	-2
1887	Ind-N	1.000	2	1	0	0	0	0
Total	3	.684	19	12	1	6	0	-3
3B								
1884	Bos-N	.714	1	1	4	2	0	1
1B								
1887	Ind-N	.500	1	1	0	1	0	0

■ Walter Hackett SS

YEAR	TM/L	PCT	G	PO	A	E	DP	FR
1884	Bos-U	.855	103	126	294	71	12	12
1885	Bos-N	.828	15	17	36	11	4	-5
Total	2	.852	118	143	330	2	16	7
2B								
1885	Bos-N	.893	20	42	50	11	5	-7

■ Kent Hadley 1B

YEAR	TM/L	PCT	G	PO	A	E	DP	FR
1958	KC-A	1.000	2	21	0	0	1	-1
1959	KC-A	.989	95	656	42	8	66	-2
1960	NY-A	.991	24	99	6	1	10	0
Total	3	.989	121	776	48	9	77	-3

■ Chick Hafey OF

YEAR	TM/L	PCT	G	PO	A	E	DP	FR
1924	StL-N	.927	24	48	3	4	1	0
1925	StL-N	.955	88	180	9	9	2	-4
1926	StL-N	.974	64	106	6	3	1	-2
1927	StL-N	.980	94	179	19	4	7	4
1928	StL-N	.965	133	287	13	11	3	1
1929	StL-N	.966	130	278	8	10	1	-3
1930	StL-N	.976	116	189	11	5	1	-9
1931	StL-N	.983	118	226	4	4	1	-9
1932	Cin-N	.965	65	131	5	5	0	-4
1933	Cin-N	.987	144	364	16	5	5	1
1934	Cin-N	.967	140	380	7	13	1	-1
1935	Cin-N	.912	15	31	0	3	0	-2
1937	Cin-N	.971	64	128	5	4	0	0
Total	13	.971	1195	2527	106	0	23	-28

■ Joe Hague 1B

YEAR	TM/L	PCT	G	PO	A	E	DP	FR
1968	StL-N	1.000	2	15	1	0	1	0
1969	StL-N	1.000	9	73	5	0	3	0
1970	StL-N	.994	82	672	48	4	65	-2
1971	StL-N	.996	91	618	50	3	63	1
1972	StL-N	1.000	22	188	10	0	16	0
	Cin-N	1.000	22	167	7	0	12	-1
Yr		1.000	44	355	17	0	28	-1
1973	Cin-N	1.000	4	21	2	0	3	0
Total	6	.996	232	1754	123	7	163	-2
OF								
1968	StL-N	.800	3	4	0	1	0	0
1969	StL-N	.939	17	31	0	2	0	-1
1970	StL-N	.988	52	77	3	1	1	-1
1971	StL-N	.967	36	58	0	2	0	-2
1972	StL-N	1.000	3	2	1	0	0	1
	Cin-N	1.000	19	29	2	0	1	1
Yr		1.000	22	31	3	0	1	2
1973	StL-N	1.000	5	5	0	0	0	-1
Total	6	.972	135	206	6	6	2	-3

■ Bill Hague 3B

YEAR	TM/L	PCT	G	PO	A	E	DP	FR
1876	Lou-N	.754	67	67	89	51	5	-26
1877	Lou-N	.843	59	78	78	29	4	-19
1878	Pro-N	.925	62	81	177	21	5	19
1879	Pro-N	.822	51	54	122	38	2	4
Total	4	.843	239	280	466	139	16	-22
SS								
1876	Lou-N	.500	1	0	1	1	0	0

■ Don Hahn OF

YEAR	TM/L	PCT	G	PO	A	E	DP	FR
1969	Mon-N	1.000	3	3	1	0	0	1
1970	Mon-N	.986	61	65	5	1	1	0
1971	NY-N	.973	80	140	2	4	1	10
1972	NY-N	1.000	10	8	0	0	0	-2
1973	NY-N	.989	87	176	2	2	0	-6
1974	NY-N	.987	106	217	8	3	0	-5
1975	Phi-N	1.000	7	4	1	0	0	1
	StL-N	1.000	4	4	0	0	0	0
	SD-N	1.000	26	24	1	0	0	2
Yr		1.000	37	32	2	0	0	3
Total	7	.985	384	641	20	0	2	1

■ Ed Hahn OF

YEAR	TM/L	PCT	G	PO	A	E	DP	FR
1905	NY-A	.957	43	83	5	4	1	2
1906	NY-A	1.000	7	13	0	0	0	-1
	Chi-A	.949	130	164	21	10	3	-6
Yr		.952	137	177	21	10	3	-7
1907	Chi-A	.990	156	182	24	2	6	-5
1908	Chi-A	.965	118	160	4	6	2	-11
1909	Chi-A	.990	76	93	3	1	1	-7
1910	Chi-A	.933	15	14	0	1	0	-3
Total	6	.970	545	709	57	4	13	-31

■ Jerry Hairston OF

YEAR	TM/L	PCT	G	PO	A	E	DP	FR
1973	Chi-A	.944	33	64	3	4	0	-2
1974	Chi-A	.926	22	24	1	2	0	-3
1975	Chi-A	.951	59	111	6	6	1	-3
1976	Chi-A	.973	40	71	1	2	0	-3
1977	Chi-A	1.000	11	15	1	0	0	0
	Pit-N	.923	14	12	0	1	0	0
1981	Chi-A	.933	7	14	0	1	0	-1
1982	Chi-A	1.000	36	34	2	0	1	5
1983	Chi-A	.968	32	29	1	1	0	2
1984	Chi-A	.967	37	57	2	2	0	3
1985	Chi-A	1.000	5	5	0	0	0	0
1986	Chi-A	1.000	11	11	1	0	0	0
1987	Chi-A	1.000	13	27	0	0	0	0
Total	12	.963	320	474	18	9	2	-6
1B								
1973	Chi-A	.993	19	130	10	1	11	0
1986	Chi-A	1.000	19	121	8	0	11	-2
1987	Chi-A	.984	7	55	5	1	7	0
Total	3	.994	45	306	23	2	29	-2
2B								
1977	Pit-N	1.000	1	1	0	0	0	0

■ Odell Hale 2B

YEAR	TM/L	PCT	G	PO	A	E	DP	FR
1931	Cle-A	.851	10	14	26	7	3	-2
1933	Cle-A	.954	73	213	259	23	45	6
1934	Cle-A	.956	137	408	480	41	107	26
1935	Cle-A	1.000	1	0	0	0	0	0
1936	Cle-A	1.000	3	3	15	0	2	1
1937	Cle-A	.972	64	180	207	11	37	16
1938	Cle-A	.963	127	304	343	25	72	-13
1939	Cle-A	.966	73	141	146	10	31	-15
1941	Bos-A	.667	1	2	0	1	0	-1
	NY-N	.964	29	89	72	6	16	1
Total	9	.959	518	1354	1549	124	313	19
3B								
1931	Cle-A	.918	15	20	25	4	1	-2
1933	Cle-A	.897	21	24	28	6	2	-2
1934	Cle-A	1.000	5	4	8	0	1	0
1935	Cle-A	.938	149	160	312	31	17	7
1936	Cle-A	.946	148	169	323	28	26	15
1937	Cle-A	.964	90	96	199	11	24	10
1939	Cle-A	.667	2	1	1	1	0	-1
1940	Cle-A	.700	3	2	5	3	0	-1
1941	Bos-A	.857	6	8	4	2	0	-2
Total	9	.942	439	484	905	6	71	24
SS								
1931	Cle-A	.000	1	0	0	1	0	-1

■ John Hale OF

YEAR	TM/L	PCT	G	PO	A	E	DP	FR
1974	LA-N	—	3	0	0	0	0	0
1975	LA-N	.977	68	128	2	3	0	1
1976	LA-N	.983	37	55	3	1	0	0
1977	LA-N	.986	73	68	1	1	0	1
1978	Sea-A	.988	98	160	1	2	0	2
1979	Sea-A	1.000	42	34	0	0	0	-2
Total	6	.985	321	445	7	7	0	2

■ Bob Hale 1B

YEAR	TM/L	PCT	G	PO	A	E	DP	FR
1955	Bal-A	.974	44	300	33	9	25	2
1956	Bal-A	.975	51	366	29	10	33	0
1957	Bal-A	1.000	5	22	1	0	1	0
1958	Bal-A	1.000	2	11	3	0	3	1
1959	Bal-A	1.000	8	48	2	0	5	-1
1960	Cle-A	.944	5	14	3	1	1	0
1961	NY-A	1.000	5	15	1	0	1	0
Total	7	.977	120	776	72	0	69	2

■ Sammy Hale 3B

YEAR	TM/L	PCT	G	PO	A	E	DP	FR
1920	Det-A	.886	16	8	31	5	2	-2
1923	Phi-A	.916	107	85	222	28	17	-19
1924	Phi-A	.948	55	39	108	8	10	-8
1925	Phi-A	.919	96	98	173	24	19	-4
1926	Phi-A	.947	77	82	152	13	16	-2
1927	Phi-A	.961	128	152	247	16	46	1
1928	Phi-A	.932	79	86	189	20	17	12
1929	Phi-A	.956	99	90	171	12	13	-7
1930	StL-A	.947	47	46	80	7	5	-3
Total	9	.939	704	686	1373	133	145	-32
OF								
1920	Det-A	1.000	4	6	1	0	0	0
1924	Phi-A	.857	5	3	3	1	0	0
1926	Phi-A	—	1	0	0	0	0	0
Total	3	.929	10	9	4	1	0	0
2B								
1920	Det-A	—	1	0	0	0	0	0
1925	Phi-A	1.000	1	0	1	0	0	0
1929	Phi-A	1.000	1	4	1	0	1	0
Total	3	1.000	3	4	2	0	1	0
SS								
1924	Phi-A	1.000	1	0	0	0	0	0

■ Albert Hall OF

YEAR	TM/L	PCT	G	PO	A	E	DP	FR
1981	Atl-N	—	2	0	0	0	0	0

YEAR	TM/L	PCT	G	PO	A	E	DP	FR
1983	Atl-N	.750	4	3	0	1	0	0
1984	Atl-N	.932	66	64	4	5	1	0
1985	Atl-N	.900	13	7	2	1	0	1
1986	Atl-N	.900	14	26	1	3	0	0
1987	Atl-N	.981	69	148	5	3	1	0
1988	Atl-N	.973	63	137	7	4	1	5
1989	Pit-N	.909	12	10	0	1	0	-1
Total	8	.958	243	395	19	8	3	5

■ George Hall　OF

YEAR	TM/L	PCT	G	PO	A	E	DP	FR
1876	Phi-N	.801	60	150	7	**39**	3	-2
1877	Lou-N	**.900**	**61**	92	7	11	1	-6
Total	2	.837	121	242	14	0	4	-8

■ Irv Hall　2B

YEAR	TM/L	PCT	G	PO	A	E	DP	FR
1943	Phi-A	.857	1	2	4	1	2	0
1944	Phi-A	.980	97	248	286	11	40	-6
1945	Phi-A	.978	151	422	**498**	21	108	**26**
1946	Phi-A	.973	40	105	113	6	20	-3
Total	4	.977	289	777	901	9	170	17
	SS							
1943	Phi-A	.948	148	298	435	40	91	-11
1944	Phi-A	.936	40	86	132	15	29	1
1946	Phi-A	.950	7	10	9	1	3	-1
Total	3	.945	195	394	576	6	123	-11
	1B							
1944	Phi-A	1.000	4	32	1	0	2	0
	3B							
1943	Phi-A	1.000	1	0	1	0	0	0

■ Jimmie Hall　OF

YEAR	TM/L	PCT	G	PO	A	E	DP	FR
1963	Min-A	.982	143	306	13	6	5	-1
1964	Min-A	.985	137	323	13	5	0	6
1965	Min-A	.976	141	282	7	7	2	-3
1966	Min-A	.978	103	175	6	4	1	0
1967	Cal-A	.990	120	197	6	2	1	-3
1968	Cal-A	.981	39	52	0	1	0	-4
	Cle-A	.983	29	57	1	1	1	2
	Yr	.982	68	109	1	2	1	-2
1969	Cle-A	1.000	3	5	0	0	0	0
	NY-A	.963	50	78	1	3	0	-6
	Chi-N	1.000	5	5	0	0	0	-1
	Yr	1.000	8	10	0	0	0	-1
1970	Chi-N	1.000	8	10	0	0	0	0
	Atl-N	1.000	28	17	1	0	0	0
	Yr	1.000	36	27	1	0	0	0
Total	8	.982	806	1507	48	9	10	-10
	1B							
1969	NY-A	.968	7	56	5	2	4	0

■ Mel Hall　OF

YEAR	TM/L	PCT	G	PO	A	E	DP	FR
1981	Chi-N	—	3	0	0	0	0	0
1982	Chi-N	.939	22	42	4	3	1	1
1983	Chi-N	.988	112	239	8	3	2	-6
1984	Chi-N	.961	46	69	5	3	2	0
	Cle-A	.993	69	143	3	1	0	-1
1985	Cle-A	1.000	15	18	0	0	0	0
1986	Cle-A	.972	126	233	7	7	1	-8
1987	Cle-A	.989	122	264	3	3	2	1
1988	Cle-A	.967	141	288	3	10	1	-6
1989	NY-A	.993	75	141	3	1	2	-4
1990	NY-A	.973	50	70	2	2	0	-5
Total	10	.979	781	1507	38	3	11	-28

■ Tom Haller　C

YEAR	TM/L	PCT	G	PO	A	E	DP	FR
1961	SF-N	1.000	25	117	7	0	4	2
1962	SF-N	.992	91	472	38	4	6	-2
1963	SF-N	.994	85	499	38	3	7	-4
1964	SF-N	.989	113	739	50	9	12	-1
1965	SF-N	.987	**133**	**864**	50	**12**	9	-4
1966	SF-N	.991	136	797	57	8	5	-6
1967	SF-N	.997	136	797	64	3	5	0
1968	LA-N	.994	139	863	81	6	**23**	3
1969	LA-N	.992	132	800	48	7	4	-9
1970	LA-N	.993	106	524	26	4	7	-8
1971	LA-N	.978	67	320	34	8	3	4
1972	Det-A	1.000	36	220	15	0	1	8
Total	12	.992	1199	7012	508	4	86	-17
	OF							
1963	SF-N	.889	7	7	1	1	0	0
1964	SF-N	—	3	0	0	0	0	0
1967	SF-N	—	1	0	0	0	0	0
Total	3	.889	11	7	1	1	0	0
	1B							
1966	SF-N	1.000	4	33	2	0	3	0

■ Jocko Halligan　OF

YEAR	TM/L	PCT	G	PO	A	E	DP	FR
1890	Buf-P	.824	43	73	11	18	1	1
1891	Cin-N	.856	61	89	6	16	1	-3
1892	Chi-N	.875	26	38	4	6	1	-1
	Bal-N	.861	22	27	4	5	1	-1
	Yr	.869	48	65	8	11	2	-2
Total	3	.848	152	227	25	5	4	-4
	C							
1890	Buf-P	.723	16	31	16	18	2	-4
1892	Bal-N	.762	5	11	5	5	1	-3
Total	2	.733	21	42	21	3	3	-7
	1B							
1892	Bal-N	.954	19	182	4	9	8	-3

■ Bill Hallman　OF

YEAR	TM/L	PCT	G	PO	A	E	DP	FR
1901	Mil-A	.905	139	226	21	**26**	6	-2
1903	Chi-N	.953	57	114	7	6	0	2
1906	Pit-N	.935	23	40	3	3	0	0
1907	Pit-N	.966	84	134	9	5	1	-6
Total	4	.933	303	514	40	0	7	-6

■ Bill Hallman　2B

YEAR	TM/L	PCT	G	PO	A	E	DP	FR
1888	Phi-N	.857	4	7	11	3	1	-1
1889	Phi-N	.867	13	40	32	11	7	-4
1890	Phi-P	.908	14	23	46	7	7	-2

YEAR	TM/L	PCT	G	PO	A	E	DP	FR
1891	Phi-a	.930	**141**	327	399	55	53	-5
1892	Phi-N	.936	138	335	379	49	60	-24
1893	Phi-N	.950	120	281	370	34	54	-14
1894	Phi-N	.930	119	318	320	48	62	-19
1895	Phi-N	.943	122	299	392	42	57	6
1896	Phi-N	.945	120	304	368	39	62	3
1897	Phi-N	.958	31	79	80	7	10	-10
	StL-N	.939	77	189	244	28	35	2
	Yr	.944	108	268	324	35	45	-8
1898	Bro-N	.944	124	268	419	41	46	0
1901	Phi-N	.971	90	177	261	13	20	-6
1903	Phi-N	.932	22	45	65	8	5	-1
Total	13	.940	1135	2692	3386	385	479	-75
	3B							
1888	Phi-N	.500	1	1	1	2	0	-1
1890	Phi-P	.781	10	9	16	7	1	-4
1898	Bro-N	.818	10	5	13	4	1	-3
1901	Phi-N	.959	33	33	61	4	2	1
1902	Phi-N	.932	72	71	147	16	3	-6
1903	Phi-N	.884	19	13	25	5	0	-3
Total	6	.912	145	132	263	8	7	-16
	SS							
1888	Phi-N	.800	1	1	3	1	0	0
1889	Phi-N	.895	106	237	337	67	39	10
1890	Phi-P	.923	2	3	9	1	0	0
1895	Phi-N	.769	3	1	9	3	0	-1
1901	Cle-A	.815	5	11	11	5	1	-3
1903	Phi-N	.750	3	2	4	2	0	-1
Total	6	.888	120	255	373	9	40	5
	OF							
1888	Phi-N	1.000	3	1	0	0	0	0
1890	Phi-P	.885	34	41	5	6	4	-4
1903	Phi-N	1.000	4	5	2	0	1	2
Total	3	.900	41	47	7	6	5	-2
	C							
1888	Phi-N	.898	10	44	9	6	1	-4
1889	Phi-N	.667	1	1	1	1	0	0
1890	Phi-P	.906	26	118	27	15	3	1
Total	3	.901	37	163	37	2	4	-3
	1B							
1893	Phi-N	.982	12	107	5	2	7	0
1897	StL-N	.960	3	21	3	1	0	1
1903	Phi-N	.989	9	83	5	1	0	0
Total	3	.982	24	211	13	4	7	1

■ Al Halt　3B

YEAR	TM/L	PCT	G	PO	A	E	DP	FR
1915	Bro-F	.930	111	174	224	**30**	**23**	8
1918	Cle-A	.971	14	11	22	1	1	-2
Total	2	.933	125	185	246	1	24	6
	SS							
1914	Bro-F	.890	71	164	184	43	30	-10
1915	Bro-F	.914	40	66	125	18	10	-6
1918	Cle-A	.929	4	5	8	1	1	0
Total	3	.899	115	235	317	2	41	-16
	2B							
1914	Bro-F	1.000	3	3	2	0	0	0
1918	Cle-A	1.000	4	4	10	0	1	0
Total	2	1.000	7	7	12	0	1	0
	1B							
1918	Cle-A	1.000	2	13	3	0	1	1
	OF							
1914	Bro-F	1.000	1	1	0	0	0	0

■ Darryl Hamilton　OF

YEAR	TM/L	PCT	G	PO	A	E	DP	FR
1988	Mil-A	1.000	37	75	1	0	0	3
1990	Mil-A	.992	72	120	1	1	0	7
Total	2	.995	109	195	2	1	0	10

■ Jeff Hamilton　3B

YEAR	TM/L	PCT	G	PO	A	E	DP	FR
1986	LA-N	.968	66	37	85	4	6	11
1987	LA-N	.935	31	27	60	6	5	9
1988	LA-N	.941	105	67	157	14	8	-1
1989	LA-N	.951	147	**139**	233	19	29	-5
1990	LA-N	1.000	7	3	12	0	2	1
Total	5	.950	356	273	547	3	50	15
	SS							
1986	LA-N	1.000	2	3	2	0	0	0
1987	LA-N	—	1	0	0	0	0	0
1988	LA-N	1.000	2	0	3	0	1	1
1989	LA-N	—	1	0	0	0	0	0
Total	4	1.000	6	3	5	0	1	1
	1B							
1988	LA-N	—	1	0	0	0	0	0
	2B							
1989	LA-N	—	1	0	0	0	0	0

■ Billy Hamilton　OF

YEAR	TM/L	PCT	G	PO	A	E	DP	FR
1888	KC-a	.961	35	45	4	2	0	-2
1889	KC-a	.857	137	202	20	37	6	-7
1890	Phi-N	.882	123	232	23	**34**	4	3
1891	Phi-N	.907	133	287	17	31	7	5
1892	Phi-N	.919	139	291	26	28	7	14
1893	Phi-N	.937	82	228	8	16	6	4
1894	Phi-N	.964	129	**361**	15	14	4	5
1895	Phi-N	.913	123	313	11	31	5	-1
1896	Bos-N	.934	131	276	8	20	2	-11
1897	Bos-N	.962	126	296	10	12	0	-3
1898	Bos-N	.904	110	189	8	21	2	-15
1899	Bos-N	.952	81	166	11	9	2	-2
1900	Bos-N	.947	136	326	14	19	6	2
1901	Bos-N	.945	99	232	7	14	4	1
Total	14	.926	1584	3444	182	288	55	-7

■ Ken Hamlin　SS

YEAR	TM/L	PCT	G	PO	A	E	DP	FR
1957	Pit-N	1.000	1	2	0	0	0	0
1959	Pit-N	1.000	3	4	6	0	2	1
1960	KC-A	.955	139	195	341	25	61	-40
1961	LA-A	.963	39	63	93	6	25	13
1962	Was-A	.963	87	126	210	13	47	-11
1965	Was-A	.957	47	40	72	5	14	-12

YEAR	TM/L	PCT	G	PO	A	E	DP	FR
Total	6	.959	316	430	722	9	149	-51
	2B							
1962	Was-A	—	2	0	0	0	0	0
1965	Was-A	.976	77	145	138	7	31	-16
1966	Was-A	.963	50	90	118	8	28	6
Total	3	.970	129	235	256	5	59	-10
	3B							
1965	Was-A	—	1	0	0	0	0	0
1966	Was-A	1.000	1	1	2	0	0	0
Total	2	1.000	2	1	2	0	0	0

■ Granny Hamner　SS

YEAR	TM/L	PCT	G	PO	A	E	DP	FR
1944	Phi-N	.933	21	27	98	9	17	6
1945	Phi-N	.861	13	31	37	11	7	3
1946	Phi-N	.857	2	1	5	1	1	-1
1947	Phi-N	1.000	2	5	6	0	1	0
1948	Phi-N	.928	37	60	94	12	20	-7
1949	Phi-N	.961	154	280	**506**	32	**101**	0
1950	Phi-N	**.944**	**157**	293	513	48	100	-5
1951	Phi-N	.958	150	255	458	31	93	-2
1952	Phi-N	.951	151	267	470	**38**	102	-4
1953	Phi-N	.922	71	91	169	22	40	-14
1954	Phi-N	.833	1	1	4	1	1	0
1955	Phi-N	.948	32	49	78	7	12	-15
1956	Phi-N	.937	110	177	302	32	69	-12
1957	Phi-N	1.000	5	4	9	0	1	-1
1958	Phi-N	1.000	3	7	8	0	0	-1
1959	Phi-N	.947	15	13	41	3	4	-7
	Cle-A	.960	10	11	13	1	2	-1
Total	16	.946	934	1572	2811	248	571	-61
	2B							
1948	Phi-N	.967	87	210	224	15	46	-1
1953	Phi-N	.970	93	194	290	15	65	6
1954	Phi-N	.978	**152**	361	412	17	97	-22
1955	Phi-N	.960	82	152	183	14	39	-21
1956	Phi-N	1.000	11	6	4	0	1	0
1957	Phi-N	.963	125	260	282	**21**	54	-38
1958	Phi-N	.958	11	20	26	2	4	-1
1959	Cle-A	1.000	7	12	19	0	4	0
Total	8	.969	568	1215	1440	4	310	-77
	3B							
1948	Phi-N	—	3	0	0	0	0	0
1958	Phi-N	.984	22	17	45	1	7	0
1959	Phi-N	—	1	0	0	0	0	0
	Cle-A	.929	5	7	6	1	0	-1
Total	3	.974	31	24	51	2	7	-1

■ Garry Hancock　OF

YEAR	TM/L	PCT	G	PO	A	E	DP	FR
1978	Bos-A	1.000	19	29	3	0	1	3
1980	Bos-A	.963	27	49	3	2	0	2
1981	Bos-A	1.000	8	11	2	0	0	1
1982	Bos-A	1.000	7	4	0	0	0	0
1983	Oak-A	.981	67	100	4	2	3	4
1984	Oak-A	1.000	18	19	0	0	0	1
Total	6	.982	146	212	12	4	4	10
	1B							
1983	Oak-A	.987	27	149	6	2	14	-3
1984	Oak-A	1.000	4	5	0	0	1	0
Total	2	.988	31	154	6	2	15	-3

■ Lee Handley　3B

YEAR	TM/L	PCT	G	PO	A	E	DP	FR
1936	Cin-N	.952	7	7	13	1	2	1
1937	Pit-N	—	1	0	0	0	0	0
1938	Pit-N	.948	136	119	**304**	23	**26**	9
1939	Pit-N	.936	100	83	180	18	14	-10
1940	Pit-N	.925	80	84	139	18	12	1
1941	Pit-N	.947	114	125	247	21	19	-1
1944	Pit-N	1.000	11	6	17	0	0	2
1945	Pit-N	.947	79	85	183	15	13	15
1946	Pit-N	.958	102	107	237	15	13	**15**
1947	Phi-N	.975	83	87	144	6	8	4
Total	10	.949	713	703	1464	117	107	36
	2B							
1936	Cin-N	.926	16	42	45	7	6	-2
1937	Pit-N	.950	126	296	375	35	67	-14
1940	Pit-N	.900	2	5	4	1	3	0
1944	Pit-N	.947	19	39	32	4	7	1
1946	Pit-N	.846	3	9	2	2	0	-2
1947	Phi-N	.833	3	4	1	1	0	-1
Total	6	.945	169	395	459	0	83	-18
	SS							
1944	Pit-N	1.000	3	6	7	0	3	0
1947	Phi-N	.750	1	2	4	2	0	-1
Total	2	.905	4	8	11	2	3	-1

■ Fred Haney　3B

YEAR	TM/L	PCT	G	PO	A	E	DP	FR
1922	Det-A	.937	53	43	105	10	11	3
1923	Det-A	.954	55	68	119	9	12	5
1924	Det-A	.933	59	48	146	14	9	5
1925	Det-A	.953	106	115	207	16	22	-2
1926	Bos-A	.957	137	149	322	**21**	**30**	6
1927	Bos-A	.936	34	61	56	8	5	-2
1929	StL-N	.958	6	8	15	1	2	3
Total	7	.949	450	492	970	9	91	18
	2B							
1923	Det-A	.955	69	159	183	16	27	-10
1924	Det-A	1.000	3	4	7	0	0	0
Total	2	.957	72	163	190	6	27	-10
	SS							
1922	Det-A	—	2	0	0	0	0	0
1923	Det-A	.967	16	33	54	3	6	2
1924	Det-A	.789	4	5	10	4	1	-1
Total	3	.936	22	38	64	7	7	1
	1B							
1922	Det-A	.984	11	115	7	2	6	0
	OF							
1927	Bos-A	—	1	0	0	0	0	-1

■ Larry Haney　C

YEAR	TM/L	PCT	G	PO	A	E	DP	FR
1966	Bal-A	.985	20	123	6	2	1	3

YEAR	TM/L	PCT	G	PO	A	E	DP	FR
1967	Bal-A	.991	57	311	31	3	3	2
1968	Bal-A	.994	32	149	18	1	3	3
1969	Sea-A	.956	20	98	10	5	1	-1
	Oak-A	.994	53	157	14	1	4	0
	Yr	.979	73	255	24	6	5	-1
1970	Oak-A	1.000	1	6	0	0	0	0
1972	Oak-A	.800	4	4	0	1	0	-1
1973	Oak-A	1.000	2	3	0	0	0	0
	StL-N	1.000	2	2	0	0	0	0
1974	Oak-A	.992	73	218	18	2	1	**10**
1975	Oak-A	1.000	43	69	4	0	1	7
1976	Oak-A	.974	87	290	45	9	2	10
1977	Mil-A	.985	63	223	32	4	3	8
1978	Mil-A	1.000	4	6	0	0	0	0
Total	12	.985	461	1659	178	8	19	41
			3B					
1974	Oak-A	.750	3	0	3	1	1	0
1975	Oak-A	1.000	4	1	0	0	0	0
Total	2	.800	7	1	3	1	1	0
			1B					
1974	Oak-A	1.000	2	1	0	0	0	0
1972	Oak-A	—	1	0	0	0	0	-1

■ Charlie Hanford OF

YEAR	TM/L	PCT	G	PO	A	E	DP	FR
1914	Buf-F	.973	155	331	24	10	5	10
1915	Chi-F	.971	43	66	2	2	0	-4
Total	2	.972	198	397	26	2	5	6

■ Frank Hankinson 3B

YEAR	TM/L	PCT	G	PO	A	E	DP	FR
1878	Chi-N	.875	57	**94**	138	33	**9**	8
1879	Chi-N	.786	5	5	17	6	0	2
1880	Cle-N	.844	56	68	89	29	7	-11
1881	Tro-N	.907	84	**151**	169	33	**21**	7
1883	NY-N	.870	93	122	166	43	9	-5
1884	NY-N	.871	105	135	182	47	8	-2
1885	NY-a	**.906**	94	106	212	33	9	**18**
1886	NY-a	.873	136	181	**316**	72	**26**	**25**
1887	NY-a	.864	127	161	276	69	26	8
1888	KC-a	.714	7	6	14	8	1	-3
Total	10	.875	764	1029	1579	373	116	47
			OF					
1879	Chi-N	.923	14	21	3	2	0	1
1880	Cle-N	1.000	12	9	2	0	0	-2
1883	NY-N	.500	1	1	0	1	0	-1
1884	NY-N	—	1	0	0	0	0	0
1888	KC-a	.900	7	8	1	1	0	-1
Total	5	.918	35	39	6	4	0	-3
			2B					
1888	KC-a	.947	13	32	40	4	3	-1
			SS					
1881	Tro-N	.667	1	1	1	1	1	0
1888	KC-a	.881	9	8	29	5	6	0
Total	2	.867	10	9	30	6	7	0
			1B					
1888	KC-a	1.000	2	18	0	0	2	0

■ Ned Hanlon OF

YEAR	TM/L	PCT	G	PO	A	E	DP	FR
1880	Cle-N	.804	69	135	9	**35**	4	-3
1881	Det-N	.897	74	141	15	18	4	-3
1882	Det-N	.887	82	**194**	19	27	**8**	11
1883	Det-N	.884	90	216	13	30	**6**	2
1884	Det-N	.874	114	241	30	39	5	10
1885	Det-N	.863	105	220	19	**38**	2	1
1886	Det-N	.929	**126**	205	18	17	4	-5
1887	Det-N	.904	118	264	18	30	4	-2
1888	Det-N	.919	109	230	7	21	3	-7
1889	Pit-N	.919	116	277	18	26	2	-1
1890	Pit-P	.911	118	**291**	15	30	4	-2
1891	Pit-N	.881	119	219	25	**33**	1	1
1892	Bal-N	.786	11	20	2	6	0	0
Total	13	.891	1251	2653	208	350	47	2
			2B					
1882	Det-N	1.000	1	3	1	0	0	0
1883	Det-N	.808	11	31	28	14	4	-4
1886	Det-N	—	1	0	0	0	0	0
Total	3	.818	13	34	29	4	4	-4
			SS					
1880	Cle-N	1.000	4	5	9	0	1	0
1881	Det-N	.538	2	2	5	6	0	-2
1891	Pit-N	—	1	0	0	0	0	0
Total	3	.778	7	7	14	6	1	-2

■ Truck Hannah C

YEAR	TM/L	PCT	G	PO	A	E	DP	FR
1918	NY-A	.974	88	343	111	12	**16**	3
1919	NY-A	**.984**	73	298	66	6	12	-8
1920	NY-A	.961	78	308	64	15	1	-5
Total	3	.973	239	949	241	3	29	-10
			1B					
1919	NY-A	.500	1	1	0	1	0	0

■ Ron Hansen SS

YEAR	TM/L	PCT	G	PO	A	E	DP	FR
1958	Bal-A	.943	12	10	23	2	4	0
1959	Bal-A	.889	2	2	6	1	1	1
1960	Bal-A	.964	**153**	**325**	456	29	110	6
1961	Bal-A	.959	149	256	437	30	**110**	10
1962	Bal-A	.965	64	114	159	10	37	4
1963	Chi-A	.983	144	247	**483**	13	95	**27**
1964	Chi-A	.975	158	**292**	514	21	**105**	16
1965	Chi-A	.969	**161**	287	**527**	26	97	**17**
1966	Chi-A	.946	23	49	73	7	17	2
1967	Chi-A	.964	157	243	**482**	27	**91**	2
1968	Was-A	.963	81	137	256	15	45	1
	Chi-A	.952	7	3	17	1	2	2
	Yr	.963	88	140	273	16	47	3
1969	Chi-A	.966	8	14	14	1	1	0
1970	NY-A	.983	15	20	39	1	6	-2
1971	NY-A	1.000	3	8	4	0	0	-1
1972	KC-A	.944	6	4	13	1	1	1
Total	15	.968	1143	2011	3503	185	722	86
			3B					
1968	Was-A	.905	5	8	11	2	3	1
	Chi-A	.959	29	20	51	3	4	5
	Yr	.947	34	28	62	5	7	6
1969	Chi-A	.913	7	7	14	2	1	0
1970	NY-A	1.000	1	5	16	0	1	0
1971	NY-A	.918	30	16	51	6	9	-1
1972	KC-A	1.000	4	1	15	0	2	2
Total	5	.943	86	57	158	3	20	7
			2B					
1961	Bal-A	.975	7	16	23	1	8	2
1965	Chi-A	—	1	0	0	0	0	0
1968	Chi-A	1.000	2	2	1	0	0	0
1969	Chi-A	.967	26	44	44	3	12	-1
1970	NY-A	1.000	1	0	2	0	0	0
1971	NY-A	.957	9	28	17	2	7	-1
1972	KC-A	—	0	0	0	0	0	0
Total	7	.967	47	90	87	6	27	0
			1B					
1969	Chi-A	.988	21	151	11	2	14	0

■ Bill Harbidge OF

YEAR	TM/L	PCT	G	PO	A	E	DP	FR
1876	Har-N	.750	6	5	1	2	1	0
1877	Har-N	1.000	5	12	1	0	0	1
1878	Chi-N	.889	8	7	1	1	0	0
1879	Chi-N	.571	4	3	1	3	0	-1
1880	Tro-N	.500	1	1	0	1	0	0
1882	Tro-N	.836	23	43	3	9	1	-2
1883	Phi-N	.796	44	83	7	23	1	-5
1884	Cin-U	.906	80	101	24	13	2	5
Total	8	.849	171	255	38	2	5	-2
			C					
1876	Har-N	.799	24	97	30	32	0	1
1877	Har-N	.881	32	143	27	23	2	-5
1878	Chi-N	.878	53	257	66	**45**	1	-7
1880	Tro-N	.887	9	37	10	6	2	2
1882	Tro-N	.846	3	9	2	2	0	0
1883	Phi-N	.676	7	18	5	11	1	-3
Total	6	.855	128	561	140	119	6	-12
			SS					
1883	Phi-N	.747	11	17	39	19	1	-1
1884	Cin-U	.625	3	0	5	3	0	-1
Total	2	.735	14	17	44	2	1	-2
			2B					
1877	Har-N	.677	4	8	13	10	0	-2
1883	Phi-N	.850	9	16	18	6	0	-3
Total	2	.775	13	24	31	6	0	-5
			1B					
1876	Har-N	.818	2	9	0	2	0	0
1882	Tro-N	.902	6	55	0	6	3	-1
1884	Cin-U	.957	2	20	2	1	1	1
Total	3	.905	10	84	2	9	4	0
			3B					
1877	Har-N	—	1	0	0	0	0	0
1883	Phi-N	.824	5	4	10	3	0	0
Total	2	.824	6	4	10	3	0	0

■ Carroll Hardy OF

YEAR	TM/L	PCT	G	PO	A	E	DP	FR
1958	Cle-A	1.000	17	35	2	0	0	3
1959	Cle-A	1.000	15	41	0	0	0	4
1960	Cle-A	1.000	17	17	0	0	0	2
	Bos-A	.968	59	88	3	3	1	3
	Yr	.973	76	105	3	3	1	5
1961	Bos-A	.961	76	142	7	6	3	1
1962	Bos-A	.991	105	205	7	2	1	4
1963	Hou-N	.947	10	17	1	1	0	0
1964	Hou-N	.990	41	100	3	1	0	5
1967	Min-A	—	4	0	0	0	0	0
Total	8	.981	344	645	23	3	5	22

■ Bubbles Hargrave C

YEAR	TM/L	PCT	G	PO	A	E	DP	FR
1913	Chi-N	1.000	2	3	1	0	0	0
1914	Chi-N	.930	16	34	6	3	0	-4
1915	Chi-N	1.000	9	13	7	0	0	-1
1921	Cin-N	.973	73	270	50	9	2	-7
1922	Cin-N	.982	87	261	60	6	5	-9
1923	Cin-N	.988	109	404	90	6	**12**	2
1924	Cin-N	.983	91	322	80	7	7	-1
1925	Cin-N	.979	84	283	42	7	1	6
1926	Cin-N	.988	93	276	50	4	7	-12
1927	Cin-N	**.988**	92	261	57	4	10	-10
1928	Cin-N	.991	57	181	37	2	2	2
1930	NY-A	.992	34	112	13	1	0	-5
Total	10	.983	747	2420	493	9	46	-51

■ Pinky Hargrave C

YEAR	TM/L	PCT	G	PO	A	E	DP	FR
1923	Was-A	.941	5	12	4	1	1	-2
1924	Was-A	1.000	8	17	2	0	0	-1
1925	Was-A	1.000	1	6	1	0	0	1
	StL-A	.981	62	211	44	5	4	-5
	Yr	.981	63	217	45	5	4	-4
1926	StL-A	.977	58	165	50	5	7	-2
1928	Det-A	.977	88	301	35	8	5	-14
1929	Det-A	.973	48	175	38	6	7	0
1930	Det-A	.984	40	175	14	3	3	-4
	Was-A	1.000	9	39	4	0	3	1
	Yr	.987	49	214	18	3	6	-3
1931	Was-A	.978	25	79	8	2	1	-2
1932	Bos-N	.968	73	206	39	8	4	-4
1933	Bos-N	.957	25	59	7	3	3	1
Total	10	.976	442	1445	246	1	38	-31
			3B					
1923	Was-A	.917	8	6	5	1	1	-2
			OF					
1923	Was-A	1.000	1	1	0	0	0	0

■ Charlie Hargreaves C

YEAR	TM/L	PCT	G	PO	A	E	DP	FR
1923	Bro-N	.921	15	48	10	5	0	-3
1924	Bro-N	1.000	9	24	4	0	0	-1
1925	Bro-N	.986	18	53	19	1	1	1
1926	Bro-N	.986	70	224	65	4	6	4
1927	Bro-N	.985	44	160	32	3	6	-1
1928	Bro-N	.979	20	81	13	2	1	2
	Pit-N	.962	77	230	47	11	7	-6
	Yr	.966	97	311	60	13	8	-4
1929	Pit-N	.981	101	308	56	7	7	2
1930	Pit-N	1.000	11	50	9	0	1	6
Total	8	.977	365	1178	255	3	29	4
			1B					
1925	Bro-N	.947	2	16	2	1	1	0

■ Mike Hargrove 1B

YEAR	TM/L	PCT	G	PO	A	E	DP	FR
1974	Tex-A	.987	91	631	72	9	57	**10**
1975	Tex-A	.984	48	326	43	6	24	6
1976	Tex-A	.984	141	1222	110	**21**	103	1
1977	Tex-A	.993	152	1393	100	11	134	0
1978	Tex-A	.987	140	1221	**116**	**17**	90	7
1979	SD-N	.986	37	323	17	5	24	-2
	Cle-A	.996	28	221	13	1	23	-3
1980	Cle-A	.993	**160**	**1391**	88	10	128	-5
1981	Cle-A	.989	88	766	76	**9**	67	6
1982	Cle-A	.996	153	1293	**123**	5	110	**11**
1983	Cle-A	.994	131	1098	115	7	131	12
1984	Cle-A	.991	124	790	83	8	86	6
1985	Cle-A	.991	84	595	66	6	66	2
Total	12	.991	1377	11270	1022	115	1043	51
			OF					
1974	Tex-A	1.000	6	7	0	0	0	0
1975	Tex-A	.964	96	187	2	7	0	-7
1979	Cle-A	.993	65	135	3	1	0	-2
1985	Cle-A	1.000	1	4	0	0	0	0
Total	4	.977	168	333	5	8	0	-9

■ Tim Harkness 1B

YEAR	TM/L	PCT	G	PO	A	E	DP	FR
1961	LA-N	1.000	2	11	1	0	2	0
1962	LA-N	1.000	59	116	8	0	14	1
1963	NY-N	.986	106	898	112	14	73	**17**
1964	NY-N	.993	32	251	28	2	32	4
Total	4	.989	199	1276	149	6	121	22

■ Dick Harley OF

YEAR	TM/L	PCT	G	PO	A	E	DP	FR
1897	StL-N	.899	89	186	19	23	3	1
1898	StL-N	.926	141	311	**26**	27	3	9
1899	Cle-N	.924	142	299	27	**27**	7	5
1900	Cin-N	1.000	5	6	0	0	0	4
1901	Cin-N	.898	133	245	20	**30**	2	-5
1902	Det-A	.930	125	238	15	19	1	-2
1903	Chi-N	.923	103	162	18	15	2	3
Total	7	.918	738	1447	125	141	18	10

■ Larry Harlow OF

YEAR	TM/L	PCT	G	PO	A	E	DP	FR
1975	Bal-A	1.000	4	2	0	0	0	0
1977	Bal-A	.887	38	47	0	6	0	3
1978	Bal-A	.979	138	313	7	7	2	-10
1979	Bal-A	.970	31	32	0	1	0	1
	Cal-A	.975	58	115	4	3	1	4
	Yr	.974	89	147	4	4	1	5
1980	Cal-A	.976	94	234	11	6	5	11
1981	Cal-A	.981	39	52	1	1	0	-2
Total	6	.971	402	795	23	4	8	7
			1B					
1980	Cal-A	1.000	1	1	0	0	0	0

■ Chuck Harmon 3B

YEAR	TM/L	PCT	G	PO	A	E	DP	FR
1954	Cin-N	.961	67	70	129	8	19	3
1955	Cin-N	.935	39	38	48	6	3	2
1956	StL-N	—	1	0	0	0	0	0
1957	Phi-N	.929	5	5	8	1	1	1
Total	4	.952	112	113	185	5	23	6
			OF					
1955	Cin-N	1.000	32	76	2	0	1	4
1956	Cin-N	1.000	6	4	0	0	0	1
	StL-N	1.000	11	7	0	0	0	1
	Yr	1.000	17	11	0	0	0	1
1957	StL-N	1.000	8	4	0	0	0	0
	Phi-N	1.000	25	37	0	0	0	2
	Yr	1.000	33	41	0	0	0	3
Total	3	1.000	82	128	2	0	1	8
			1B					
1954	Cin-N	1.000	3	16	3	0	3	1
1955	Cin-N	1.000	4	12	0	0	2	0
1956	Cin-N	1.000	2	1	0	0	0	0
	StL-N	1.000	2	4	0	0	0	0
	Yr	1.000	4	5	0	0	0	0
1957	Phi-N	1.000	2	8	0	0	3	0
Total	4	1.000	13	41	3	0	9	1

■ Terry Harmon 2B

YEAR	TM/L	PCT	G	PO	A	E	DP	FR
1969	Phi-N	.988	19	37	45	1	11	4
1970	Phi-N	1.000	14	26	24	0	6	1
1971	Phi-N	.986	58	122	166	4	39	8
1972	Phi-N	.996	50	106	136	1	31	1
1973	Phi-N	.988	43	88	74	2	20	2
1974	Phi-N	1.000	5	0	3	0	0	1
1975	Phi-N	1.000	7	2	7	0	1	1
1976	Phi-N	.958	13	10	13	1	2	1
1977	Phi-N	.982	28	27	28	1	8	4
Total	9	.989	237	418	496	10	118	23
			SS					
1969	Phi-N	.968	38	57	123	6	31	4
1970	Phi-N	.989	35	37	56	1	10	-3
1971	Phi-N	.923	9	12	24	3	5	0
1972	Phi-N	.935	15	9	20	2	0	-2
1973	Phi-N	.976	19	12	29	1	6	0
1974	Phi-N	1.000	9	3	0	1	2	2
1975	Phi-N	.989	25	30	58	1	8	0
1976	Phi-N	.960	19	16	32	2	4	1
1977	Phi-N	.889	16	8	32	5	6	4
Total	9	.964	183	190	377	21	71	6

YEAR	TM/L	PCT	G	PO	A	E	DP	FR
3B								
1969	Phi-N	1.000	2	0	1	0	0	0
1970	Phi-N	.667	2	1	1	1	0	0
1971	Phi-N	1.000	3	0	1	0	0	0
1972	Phi-N	.818	5	1	8	2	1	0
1973	Phi-N	—	1	0	0	0	0	0
1975	Phi-N	—	1	0	0	0	0	0
1976	Phi-N	1.000	5	2	4	0	0	1
1977	Phi-N	.778	3	2	5	2	0	0
Total	8	.839	22	6	20	5	1	1
1B								
1971	Phi-N	1.000	2	10	0	0	0	0

■ Brian Harper C

YEAR	TM/L	PCT	G	PO	A	E	DP	FR
1984	Pit-N	1.000	2	9	0	0	0	0
1985	StL-N	—	2	0	0	0	0	0
1986	Det-A	1.000	2	5	0	0	0	0
1988	Min-A	.991	48	207	15	2	0	-6
1989	Min-A	.978	101	456	35	**11**	7	-14
1990	Min-A	.985	120	672	53	11	5	1
Total	6	.984	275	1349	103	4	12	-19
OF								
1981	Cal-A	.833	2	5	0	1	0	0
1982	Pit-N	1.000	8	10	0	0	0	0
1983	Pit-N	1.000	35	40	0	0	0	-4
1984	Pit-N	.981	37	48	3	1	0	0
1985	StL-N	1.000	13	8	0	0	0	0
1986	Det-A	.929	11	13	0	1	0	0
1987	Oak-A	—	1	0	0	0	0	0
1989	Min-A	1.000	3	3	0	0	0	0
Total	8	.977	110	127	3	3	0	-4
3B								
1985	StL-N	1.000	6	5	5	0	0	-1
1988	Min-A	1.000	2	1	0	0	0	0
1989	Min-A	1.000	2	1	1	0	0	0
1990	Min-A	1.000	3	1	2	0	0	0
Total	4	1.000	13	8	8	0	0	-1
1B								
1983	Pit-N	—	1	0	0	0	0	0
1985	StL-N	1.000	1	2	0	0	0	0
1986	Det-A	1.000	2	7	2	0	2	1
1989	Min-A	1.000	2	2	0	0	0	0
1990	Min-A	1.000	2	13	3	0	0	1
Total	5	1.000	8	24	5	0	2	2

■ George Harper OF

YEAR	TM/L	PCT	G	PO	A	E	DP	FR
1916	Det-A	.938	14	15	0	1	0	-4
1917	Det-A	.980	31	48	2	1	0	-3
1918	Det-A	.956	64	125	5	6	2	-1
1922	Cin-N	.955	109	220	15	11	2	-1
1923	Cin-N	.967	29	56	3	2	0	0
1924	Cin-N	.964	22	51	3	2	0	2
	Phi-N	.991	109	219	13	2	4	2
	Yr	.986	131	270	16	4	4	4
1925	Phi-N	.971	126	319	16	10	5	9
1926	Phi-N	.942	55	111	2	7	1	-4
1927	NY-N	.975	142	299	13	8	5	-2
1928	NY-N	.957	18	40	4	2	1	2
	StL-N	.988	84	156	13	2	2	0
	Yr	.982	102	196	17	4	3	2
1929	Bos-N	.972	130	266	7	8	2	-6
Total	11	.970	933	1925	96	2	24	-6

■ Terry Harper OF

YEAR	TM/L	PCT	G	PO	A	E	DP	FR
1980	Atl-N	.968	18	30	0	1	0	-1
1981	Atl-N	.976	27	38	2	1	1	1
1982	Atl-N	.987	41	74	4	1	1	0
1983	Atl-N	.952	60	95	5	5	0	-1
1984	Atl-N	1.000	29	60	3	0	0	3
1985	Atl-N	.978	131	215	10	5	0	-7
1986	Atl-N	.970	83	92	5	3	0	-8
1987	Det-A	.952	14	20	0	1	0	0
	Pit-N	1.000	20	25	0	0	0	-1
Total	8	.976	423	649	29	7	2	-14

■ Tommy Harper OF

YEAR	TM/L	PCT	G	PO	A	E	DP	FR
1963	Cin-N	.983	118	224	7	4	1	5
1964	Cin-N	.994	92	149	4	1	2	0
1965	Cin-N	.983	159	277	6	5	0	0
1966	Cin-N	.996	147	257	5	1	2	2
1967	Cin-N	.995	100	208	6	1	0	8
1968	Cle-A	.984	115	121	0	2	0	-18
1969	Sea-A	.980	26	49	0	1	0	-2
1970	Mil-A	1.000	13	19	1	0	0	0
1971	Mil-A	.975	90	155	2	4	0	-7
1972	Bos-A	.985	144	321	4	5	4	-4
1973	Bos-A	.985	143	251	13	4	2	-1
1974	Bos-A	.982	61	105	2	2	0	-8
1975	Cal-A	.941	9	15	1	1	0	1
	Oak-A	1.000	9	17	0	0	0	1
	Yr	.971	18	32	1	1	0	1
1976	Bal-A	—	1	0	0	0	0	0
Total	14	.986	1227	2168	51	1	11	-24
3B								
1962	Cin-N	.929	6	6	7	1	1	-1
1963	Cin-N	—	1	0	0	0	0	0
1964	Cin-N	1.000	2	0	2	0	0	0
1965	Cin-N	1.000	2	0	4	0	0	-2
1969	Sea-A	.951	59	70	123	10	9	0
1970	Mil-A	.943	128	123	275	**24**	23	3
1971	Mil-A	.935	70	71	115	13	10	-14
1975	Oak-A	—	2	0	0	0	0	0
Total	8	.943	270	270	526	8	43	-14
2B								
1965	Cin-N	1.000	1	2	0	0	0	0
1968	Cle-A	1.000	2	0	1	0	0	0
1969	Sea-A	.959	59	113	145	11	33	-14
1970	Mil-A	.963	22	50	54	4	10	-5
1971	Mil-A	.667	1	1	1	1	1	-1
Total	5	.958	85	166	201	6	44	-20
1B								
1975	Cal-A	.992	19	117	6	1	15	-2
	Oak-A	.963	16	100	3	4	8	-2
	Yr	.978	35	217	9	5	23	-4
1976	Bal-A	1.000	1	2	0	0	0	0
Total	2	.979	36	219	9	5	23	-4

■ Toby Harrah 3B

YEAR	TM/L	PCT	G	PO	A	E	DP	FR
1971	Was-A	.952	7	6	14	1	1	0
1973	Tex-A	.937	52	39	79	8	4	-9
1974	Tex-A	1.000	3	2	8	0	0	0
1975	Tex-A	.971	28	16	52	2	4	0
1976	Tex-A	.923	5	4	8	1	1	-1
1977	Tex-A	.963	**159**	108	278	15	20	-24
1978	Tex-A	.965	91	54	167	8	15	-12
1979	Cle-A	.940	127	91	160	16	19	-39
1980	Cle-A	.971	**156**	120	317	13	27	2
1981	Cle-A	.949	**101**	63	179	13	12	-11
1982	Cle-A	.971	**159**	126	279	12	25	-18
1983	Cle-A	**.971**	137	101	273	11	32	-10
1984	NY-A	.968	74	51	128	6	17	3
Total	13	.963	1099	781	1942	106	177	119
SS								
1969	Was-A	—	1	0	1	0	0	0
1971	Was-A	.955	116	181	307	23	69	-7
1972	Tex-A	.960	106	166	308	20	64	-9
1973	Tex-A	.951	76	116	253	19	41	-4
1974	Tex-A	.963	**158**	**281**	466	**29**	98	-2
1975	Tex-A	.963	118	198	375	22	68	14
1976	Tex-A	.955	146	**290**	473	**36**	81	1
1977	Tex-A	—	1	0	0	0	0	0
1978	Tex-A	.988	49	75	163	3	25	3
1979	Cle-A	.962	33	22	55	3	11	-9
1980	Cle-A	1.000	1	0	2	0	1	0
1981	Cle-A	1.000	3	1	1	0	0	0
1982	Cle-A	—	2	0	0	0	0	0
1985	Tex-A	—	2	0	0	0	0	-1
Total	14	.960	813	1331	2403	155	458	-14
2B								
1975	Tex-A	.949	21	39	54	5	10	-1
1982	Cle-A	—	3	0	0	0	0	0
1983	Cle-A	—	1	0	0	0	0	0
1984	NY-A	1.000	4	1	4	0	0	0
1985	Tex-A	.989	122	212	351	6	71	-16
1986	Tex-A	.982	93	166	211	7	49	-20
Total	6	.983	244	418	620	8	130	-37
OF								
1984	NY-A	—	1	0	0	0	0	0

■ Bud Harrelson SS

YEAR	TM/L	PCT	G	PO	A	E	DP	FR
1965	NY-N	.955	18	28	36	3	6	4
1966	NY-N	.993	29	52	91	1	26	5
1967	NY-N	.958	**149**	254	467	32	88	7
1968	NY-N	.972	106	199	317	15	58	-5
1969	NY-N	.969	119	243	347	19	70	-5
1970	NY-N	.971	156	**305**	401	21	84	-28
1971	NY-N	.978	140	257	441	16	86	11
1972	NY-N	.970	115	191	334	16	51	-11
1973	NY-N	.979	103	153	315	10	49	-3
1974	NY-N	.968	97	196	325	17	65	16
1975	NY-N	.941	34	44	67	7	18	1
1976	NY-N	.962	117	183	300	20	44	-5
1977	NY-N	.984	98	141	239	6	41	-1
1978	Phi-N	1.000	15	14	30	0	7	5
1979	Phi-N	.889	17	9	15	3	1	0
1980	Tex-A	.952	87	118	220	17	57	11
Total	16	.969	1400	2387	3975	203	751	2
2B								
1978	Phi-N	.972	43	58	79	4	24	10
1979	Phi-N	.990	25	54	47	1	11	4
1980	Tex-A	.833	2	3	2	1	1	0
Total	3	.976	70	115	128	6	36	14
3B								
1979	Phi-N	1.000	9	0	9	0	1	2
OF								
1979	Phi-N	—	1	0	0	0	0	0

■ Ken Harrelson 1B

YEAR	TM/L	PCT	G	PO	A	E	DP	FR
1963	KC-A	.980	34	283	16	6	24	-3
1964	KC-A	1.000	15	105	13	0	14	0
1965	KC-A	.992	125	1044	70	9	93	-2
1966	KC-A	.985	58	485	48	8	42	4
	Was-A	.991	70	641	38	6	53	-3
	Yr	.989	128	1126	86	14	95	1
1967	Was-A	.996	23	215	16	1	17	1
	KC-A	.992	45	333	25	3	21	-1
	Bos-A	1.000	1	3	0	0	0	0
	Yr	.993	69	551	41	4	38	0
1968	Bos-A	.980	19	135	9	3	9	-1
1969	Bos-A	.991	10	105	11	1	15	2
	Cle-A	1.000	16	40	4	0	6	0
	Yr	.994	26	145	15	1	21	2
1970	Cle-A	1.000	13	80	7	0	15	1
1971	Cle-A	.988	40	311	23	4	29	-1
Total	9	.990	469	3780	280	1	338	-3
OF								
1963	KC-A	.978	28	43	1	0	0	-1
1964	KC-A	.977	24	40	2	1	0	-1
1965	KC-A	.857	4	5	1	1	0	0
1966	KC-A	1.000	3	3	0	0	0	0
1967	Bos-A	.929	23	25	1	2	0	-3
1968	Bos-A	**1.000**	132	241	8	0	1	5
1969	Cle-A	.985	144	257	7	4	2	0
1971	Cle-A	1.000	7	9	0	0	0	0
Total	8	.986	365	623	20	9	3	0

■ Jerry Harrington C

YEAR	TM/L	PCT	G	PO	A	E	DP	FR
1890	Cin-N	.957	65	345	73	19	3	5
1891	Cin-N	.908	92	388	106	**50**	6	-3
1892	Cin-N	.989	22	73	21	1	0	1
1893	Lou-N	.853	10	23	6	5	1	-4
Total	4	.932	189	829	206	5	10	-1
3B								
1891	Cin-N	—	1	0	0	0	0	0
1B								
1892	Cin-N	.800	1	3	1	1	0	0

■ Spencer Harris OF

YEAR	TM/L	PCT	G	PO	A	E	DP	FR
1925	Chi-A	.957	27	42	3	2	0	-5
1926	Chi-A	.949	63	106	6	6	2	-6
1929	Was-A	1.000	4	7	0	0	0	-1
1930	Phi-A	.958	13	21	2	1	1	0
Total	4	.954	107	176	11	9	3	-12

■ Gail Harris 1B

YEAR	TM/L	PCT	G	PO	A	E	DP	FR
1955	NY-N	.982	75	617	50	12	65	0
1956	NY-N	.975	11	108	9	3	12	0
1957	NY-N	.985	61	502	37	8	53	-2
1958	Det-A	.986	**122**	942	79	**15**	90	3
1959	Det-A	.992	93	728	57	6	59	2
1960	Det-A	1.000	5	8	1	0	1	0
Total	6	.986	367	2905	233	4	280	3

■ Dave Harris OF

YEAR	TM/L	PCT	G	PO	A	E	DP	FR
1925	Bos-N	.962	90	217	12	9	3	3
1928	Bos-N	.833	6	10	0	2	0	-1
1930	Chi-A	1.000	23	46	1	0	0	0
	Was-A	.983	59	106	8	2	3	1
	Yr	.988	82	152	9	2	3	1
1931	Was-A	.950	60	111	4	6	1	-2
1932	Was-A	.932	34	66	3	5	0	0
1933	Was-A	.964	45	79	1	3	0	-3
1934	Was-A	.973	64	103	7	3	1	0
Total	7	.963	381	738	36	0	8	-2
3B								
1933	Was-A	1.000	2	2	1	0	0	0
1934	Was-A	.944	5	8	9	1	1	0
Total	2	.952	7	10	10	1	1	0
1B								
1933	Was-A	1.000	6	20	0	0	1	0
2B								
1930	Chi-A	—	1	0	0	0	0	0

■ Joe Harris 1B

YEAR	TM/L	PCT	G	PO	A	E	DP	FR
1914	NY-A	1.000	1	10	0	0	0	0
1917	Cle-A	.985	95	1019	86	17	58	**8**
1919	Cle-A	.988	46	454	38	6	22	3
1922	Bos-A	.984	21	173	17	3	12	2
1923	Bos-A	.974	9	71	5	2	4	0
1924	Bos-A	.993	128	1288	103	10	102	6
1925	Bos-A	1.000	6	45	1	0	2	-1
	Was-A	.989	58	393	38	5	39	2
	Yr	.990	64	438	39	5	41	1
1926	Was-A	.994	36	293	17	2	20	-2
1927	Pit-N	.990	116	1056	78	11	84	3
1928	Pit-N	1.000	6	36	5	0	7	1
Total	10	.989	522	4838	388	6	350	22
OF								
1914	NY-A	1.000	1	1	0	0	0	0
1917	Cle-A	1.000	5	10	3	0	0	2
1922	Bos-A	.953	83	186	15	10	2	5
1923	Bos-A	.968	132	288	11	10	1	-2
1924	Bos-A	1.000	3	9	0	0	0	0
1925	Was-A	.986	41	68	3	1	1	-3
1926	Was-A	.985	35	61	3	1	0	-2
1927	Pit-N	1.000	3	1	0	0	0	0
1928	Bro-N	.958	16	21	2	1	1	-2
Total	9	.967	319	645	37	3	5	-2
SS								
1919	Cle-A	1.000	4	7	6	0	1	-1
3B								
1917	Cle-A	.000	2	0	0	1	0	0

■ Lenny Harris 3B

YEAR	TM/L	PCT	G	PO	A	E	DP	FR
1988	Cin-N	1.000	10	3	21	0	0	2
1989	Cin-N	.944	16	7	27	2	1	2
	LA-N	1.000	8	4	4	0	1	-1
	Yr	.955	24	11	31	2	2	1
1990	LA-N	.959	94	77	133	9	11	2
Total	3	.962	128	91	185	11	13	5
2B								
1988	Cin-N	.958	6	11	12	1	2	-1
1989	Cin-N	.980	32	74	75	3	19	0
	LA-N	.961	14	21	28	2	8	-4
	Yr	.975	46	95	103	5	27	-4
1990	LA-N	.985	44	62	70	2	13	-9
Total	3	.978	96	168	185	8	42	-14
OF								
1989	LA-N	1.000	21	30	1	0	0	-2
1990	LA-N	1.000	2	1	0	0	0	0
Total	2	1.000	23	31	1	0	0	-2
SS								
1989	Cin-N	.843	17	11	32	8	3	0
	LA-N	1.000	1	0	1	0	0	0
	Yr	.846	18	11	33	8	3	0
1990	LA-N	1.000	1	0	2	0	0	0
Total	2	.852	19	11	35	8	3	0

■ Ned Harris OF

YEAR	TM/L	PCT	G	PO	A	E	DP	FR
1941	Det-A	1.000	12	16	0	0	0	-3
1942	Det-A	.944	104	164	5	10	2	-12
1943	Det-A	.961	96	192	6	8	2	-5
Total	3	.955	212	372	11	8	4	-20

■ Bucky Harris 2B

YEAR	TM/L	PCT	G	PO	A	E	DP	FR
1919	Was-A	.925	8	21	28	4	4	2
1920	Was-A	.958	134	345	401	33	59	-10

YEAR	TM/L	PCT	G	PO	A	E	DP	FR
1921	Was-A	.959	154	417	481	38	**91**	12
1922	Was-A	.970	**154**	**483**	483	30	**116**	**26**
1923	Was-A	.961	144	**418**	449	**35**	**120**	**20**
1924	Was-A	.968	143	393	386	26	**100**	-13
1925	Was-A	.970	144	402	429	26	**107**	3
1926	Was-A	.963	141	**356**	427	30	74	-11
1927	Was-A	**.972**	128	**316**	413	21	68	1
1928	Was-A	.970	96	251	326	18	61	11
1929	Det-A	.900	4	5	13	2	0	1
1931	Det-A	1.000	3	5	6	0	1	0
Total	12	.965	1253	3412	3842	263	801	42
SS								
1923	Was-A	.667	1	0	2	1	0	0
1929	Det-A	—	1	0	0	0	0	0
Total	2	.667	2	0	2	1	0	0
3B								
1928	Was-A	1.000	1	3	0	0	0	0
OF								
1928	Was-A	—	1	0	0	0	0	0

■ Vic Harris 2B

YEAR	TM/L	PCT	G	PO	A	E	DP	FR
1972	Tex-A	.960	58	110	132	10	29	0
1973	Tex-A	.947	18	35	37	4	8	3
1974	Chi-N	.943	56	122	144	16	20	-17
1975	Chi-N	.933	5	6	8	1	2	0
1976	StL-N	.945	37	91	97	11	24	-6
1977	SF-N	.973	27	45	63	3	16	-3
1978	SF-N	1.000	10	14	19	0	4	0
1980	Mil-N	1.000	1	1	0	0	0	0
Total	8	.954	212	424	500	5	100	-23
OF								
1973	Tex-A	.977	113	297	5	7	1	3
1975	Chi-N	.900	11	9	0	1	0	0
1976	StL-N	.976	35	81	1	2	0	2
1977	SF-N	—	3	0	0	0	0	0
1978	SF-N	.889	6	8	0	1	0	0
1980	Mil-N	.967	31	58	1	2	1	-1
Total	6	.973	199	453	7	3	2	4
3B								
1973	Tex-A	.855	25	22	37	10	7	-3
1975	Chi-N	1.000	7	0	6	0	0	1
1976	StL-N	.857	12	1	5	1	0	-1
1977	SF-N	.947	9	9	9	1	2	-1
1980	Mil-N	1.000	2	0	3	0	0	0
Total	5	.885	55	32	60	2	9	-4
SS								
1972	Tex-A	1.000	1	3	3	0	1	0
1976	StL-N	—	1	0	0	0	0	0
1977	SF-N	.907	11	15	24	4	3	-4
1978	SF-N	.934	22	18	39	4	4	-6
Total	4	.927	35	36	66	8	8	-10

■ Chuck Harrison 1B

YEAR	TM/L	PCT	G	PO	A	E	DP	FR
1965	Hou-N	.983	12	107	8	2	9	0
1966	Hou-N	.992	114	974	78	8	68	4
1967	Hou-N	.987	59	438	27	6	24	0
1969	KC-A	.993	55	415	36	3	27	2
1971	KC-A	.992	39	335	24	3	31	0
Total	5	.991	279	2269	173	2	159	6

■ Jim Ray Hart 3B

YEAR	TM/L	PCT	G	PO	A	E	DP	FR
1963	SF-N	1.000	7	10	9	0	1	0
1964	SF-N	.937	149	139	277	28	24	5
1965	SF-N	.919	144	134	231	**32**	16	-11
1966	SF-N	.941	139	100	282	24	24	-6
1967	SF-N	.937	89	60	177	16	10	-9
1968	SF-N	.925	72	63	109	14	11	-12
1969	SF-N	.833	3	0	5	1	0	-1
1970	SF-N	.908	56	39	69	11	2	-16
1971	SF-N	.833	3	2	3	1	2	-1
1972	SF-N	.886	20	17	22	5	2	-9
1973	SF-N	.600	1	0	3	2	0	0
Total	11	.929	683	564	1187	134	92	-60
OF								
1964	SF-N	1.000	6	4	1	0	1	1
1965	SF-N	.895	15	17	0	2	0	-1
1966	SF-N	.941	17	31	1	2	0	-1
1967	SF-N	.977	72	81	3	2	1	-5
1968	SF-N	.955	65	102	3	5	1	-3
1969	SF-N	.943	68	80	2	5	1	-7
1970	SF-N	.958	18	21	2	1	0	0
1971	SF-N	1.000	3	5	0	0	0	0
Total	8	.954	264	341	12	7	4	-16

■ Grover Hartley C

YEAR	TM/L	PCT	G	PO	A	E	DP	FR
1911	NY-N	.962	10	44	7	2	0	3
1912	NY-N	.960	25	63	9	3	1	2
1913	NY-N	.978	21	38	7	1	0	3
1914	StL-F	.956	32	148	46	9	2	-7
1915	StL-F	.972	113	565	151	**21**	11	-6
1916	StL-A	.968	75	263	98	12	10	1
1917	StL-A	.875	4	4	3	1	0	1
1924	NY-N	1.000	3	6	2	0	0	0
1925	NY-N	.974	37	90	24	3	7	4
1926	NY-N	1.000	13	31	4	0	1	0
1927	Bos-N	.967	86	214	51	9	5	-13
1929	Cle-A	1.000	13	16	0	0	0	-3
1930	Cle-A	.750	1	2	1	1	0	0
1934	StL-A	1.000	2	3	0	0	0	0
Total	14	.968	435	1487	403	2	37	-15
1B								
1913	NY-N	1.000	1	3	0	0	0	0
1914	StL-F	1.000	9	78	2	0	5	-1
1915	StL-F	—	1	0	0	0	0	0
1925	NY-N	.980	8	47	3	1	7	0
Total	4	.993	19	128	5	1	12	-1
2B								
1914	StL-F	.961	13	21	28	2	5	-1

YEAR	TM/L	PCT	G	PO	A	E	DP	FR
3B								
1914	StL-F	1.000	3	1	3	0	0	0
1917	StL-A	1.000	1	2	1	0	0	1
Total	2	1.000	4	3	4	0	0	1
OF								
1914	StL-F	1.000	2	1	0	0	0	-1
SS								
1917	StL-A	—	1	0	0	0	0	-1

■ Fred Hartman 3B

YEAR	TM/L	PCT	G	PO	A	E	DP	FR
1894	Pit-N	.876	49	65	97	23	6	-4
1897	StL-N	.867	124	159	253	**63**	14	-4
1898	NY-N	.882	123	146	280	57	16	9
1899	NY-N	.886	50	56	100	20	11	-4
1901	Chi-A	.894	119	151	263	49	15	-5
1902	StL-N	.908	105	138	229	37	9	-3
Total	6	.886	570	715	1222	249	71	-11
SS								
1902	StL-N	.800	4	7	9	4	1	-1
1B								
1902	StL-N	.963	3	23	3	1	1	1

■ Gabby Hartnett C

YEAR	TM/L	PCT	G	PO	A	E	DP	FR
1922	Chi-N	.982	27	79	29	2	0	5
1923	Chi-N	.994	39	143	24	1	2	3
1924	Chi-N	.963	105	369	97	**18**	12	-3
1925	Chi-N	.958	110	**409**	114	**23**	**15**	10
1926	Chi-N	.978	88	307	86	9	6	6
1927	Chi-N	.973	**126**	479	99	16	**21**	5
1928	Chi-N	**.989**	118	455	**103**	6	14	9
1929	Chi-N	1.000	1	4	0	0	0	0
1930	Chi-N	**.989**	**136**	**646**	68	8	**11**	3
1931	Chi-N	.981	105	444	68	10	**16**	2
1932	Chi-N	.982	117	484	75	10	8	7
1933	Chi-N	.989	140	550	77	7	7	6
1934	Chi-N	**.996**	129	**605**	**86**	3	**11**	**14**
1935	Chi-N	.984	110	477	**77**	9	**11**	**14**
1936	Chi-N	**.991**	114	504	75	5	8	9
1937	Chi-N	**.996**	103	436	65	2	7	1
1938	Chi-N	**.995**	83	358	40	2	8	-4
1939	Chi-N	.992	86	336	47	3	3	-7
1940	Chi-N	.951	22	69	9	4	2	1
1941	NY-N	.994	34	138	15	1	1	-3
Total	20	.984	1793	7292	1254	139	163	78
1B								
1923	Chi-N	.986	31	270	15	4	23	0
1932	Chi-N	1.000	1	14	0	0	2	0
1940	Chi-N	1.000	1	1	1	0	0	0
Total	3	.987	33	285	16	4	25	0

■ Topsy Hartsel OF

YEAR	TM/L	PCT	G	PO	A	E	DP	FR
1898	Lou-N	.931	21	25	2	2	1	-2
1899	Lou-N	.927	22	36	2	3	1	-2
1900	Cin-N	.957	18	22	0	1	0	-5
1901	Chi-N	.951	140	273	16	15	3	-1
1902	Phi-A	.955	137	238	18	12	2	-1
1903	Phi-A	.966	96	144	6	5	0	-5
1904	Phi-A	.959	147	216	15	10	2	-4
1905	Phi-A	.939	149	255	6	17	1	-7
1906	Phi-A	.969	144	238	15	8	5	0
1907	Phi-A	.967	143	191	11	7	2	-11
1908	Phi-A	.960	129	211	6	9	2	-5
1909	Phi-A	.966	74	140	5	5	0	-3
1910	Phi-A	.945	83	113	8	7	2	-7
1911	Phi-A	.941	9	13	3	1	0	1
Total	14	.956	1312	2115	108	102	21	-52

■ Roy Hartsfield 2B

YEAR	TM/L	PCT	G	PO	A	E	DP	FR
1950	Bos-N	.949	96	236	247	**26**	53	-23
1951	Bos-N	.969	114	336	293	20	87	-5
1952	Bos-N	.950	29	61	73	7	10	-6
Total	3	.959	239	633	613	3	150	-34

■ Roy Hartzell OF

YEAR	TM/L	PCT	G	PO	A	E	DP	FR
1907	StL-A	1.000	2	1	0	0	0	-1
1908	StL-A	.943	82	117	15	8	5	5
1909	StL-A	.940	85	120	21	9	5	10
1910	StL-A	.935	23	24	5	2	1	0
1911	NY-A	.938	8	13	2	1	0	0
1912	NY-A	.940	56	101	9	7	2	4
1913	NY-A	1.000	31	49	6	0	0	4
1914	NY-A	.973	128	241	15	7	2	1
1915	NY-A	.963	107	200	10	8	2	-3
1916	NY-A	1.000	28	27	1	0	0	-6
Total	10	.959	550	893	84	2	17	10
3B								
1906	StL-A	.889	103	119	209	**41**	11	-1
1907	StL-A	.911	38	49	74	12	5	-1
1908	StL-A	.833	7	6	9	3	0	-3
1910	StL-A	.929	89	123	203	25	19	4
1911	NY-A	.936	124	158	221	26	18	-11
1912	NY-A	.906	56	92	100	20	4	0
1913	NY-A	.931	21	31	23	4	1	-5
1915	NY-A	.833	2	2	3	1	0	0
Total	8	.915	440	580	842	132	58	-17
SS								
1906	StL-A	.875	6	5	16	3	2	-1
1907	StL-A	.800	2	2	6	2	0	-1
1908	StL-A	.878	18	33	53	12	6	-6
1909	StL-A	.929	65	132	196	25	15	-6
1910	StL-A	.928	38	86	108	15	14	-3
1911	NY-A	.964	12	24	30	2	4	-1
1912	NY-A	.879	10	21	30	7	0	-2
1913	NY-A	.909	4	3	7	1	6	0
Total	8	.918	155	306	446	7	47	-20
2B								
1906	StL-A	1.000	2	1	2	0	0	0
1907	StL-A	.974	12	36	40	2	1	2
1908	StL-A	.941	4	5	11	1	0	-1
1909	StL-A	1.000	1	5	2	0	0	0

YEAR	TM/L	PCT	G	PO	A	E	DP	FR
1912	NY-A	.889	2	6	2	1	0	-2
1913	NY-A	.942	81	203	234	27	29	4
1914	NY-A	.905	5	8	11	2	0	-1
1915	NY-A	1.000	5	6	8	0	0	0
Total	8	.946	112	270	310	3	30	2

■ Mickey Haslin SS

YEAR	TM/L	PCT	G	PO	A	E	DP	FR
1934	Phi-N	.833	4	6	9	3	2	0
1935	Phi-N	.931	87	212	249	34	52	-4
1937	NY-N	.920	9	10	36	4	4	5
Total	3	.927	100	228	294	1	58	1
2B								
1933	Phi-N	.956	26	52	79	6	12	-4
1934	Phi-N	.956	21	43	43	4	5	-2
1935	Phi-N	.944	9	24	27	3	1	0
1936	Phi-N	.938	12	23	37	4	7	-4
	Bos-N	1.000	7	14	28	0	3	1
	Yr	.962	19	37	65	4	10	-3
1937	NY-N	1.000	4	2	7	0	1	1
1938	NY-N	.941	13	29	35	4	8	-2
Total	6	.955	92	187	256	1	37	-10
3B								
1934	Phi-N	.941	26	18	46	4	4	-1
1935	Phi-N	.944	11	11	23	2	1	1
1936	Phi-N	.727	5	2	6	3	1	-2
	Bos-N	.892	17	18	i5	4	0	-5
	Yr	.854	22	20	21	7	1	-7
1937	NY-N	1.000	4	1	4	0	1	1
1938	NY-N	.902	15	6	31	4	0	0
Total	5	.914	78	56	125	7	7	-6

■ Bill Hassamaer OF

YEAR	TM/L	PCT	G	PO	A	E	DP	FR
1894	Was-N	.916	68	109	11	11	4	-1
1895	Was-N	.964	75	102	4	4	1	-6
Total	2	.938	143	211	15	5	5	-7
1B								
1895	Was-N	.987	9	74	4	1	5	0
	Lou-N	.980	21	181	17	4	12	2
	Yr	.982	30	255	21	5	17	2
1896	Lou-N	.976	29	292	32	8	24	6
Total	2	.979	59	547	53	3	41	8
3B								
1894	Was-N	.876	31	65	83	21	3	11
1895	Was-N	.750	1	3	3	2	1	0
Total	2	.870	32	68	86	3	4	11
2B								
1894	Was-N	.906	14	44	33	8	5	-4
1895	Lou-N	.889	1	3	5	1	2	0
Total	2	.904	15	47	38	9	7	-4
SS								
1894	Was-N	.750	4	7	8	5	2	-2
1895	Was-N	.500	1	2	2	4	1	-1
	Lou-N	1.000	1	3	5	0	0	0
	Yr	.750	2	5	7	4	1	-1
Total	2	.750	6	12	15	9	3	-3

■ Buddy Hassett 1B

YEAR	TM/L	PCT	G	PO	A	E	DP	FR
1936	Bro-N	.983	**156**	1401	**121**	**26**	89	**5**
1937	Bro-N	.984	131	1125	**116**	**20**	96	**10**
1938	Bro-N	.974	8	61	13	2	6	3
1939	Bos-N	.985	123	1143	112	**19**	**127**	**10**
1940	Bos-N	.979	98	877	91	**21**	102	**9**
1941	Bos-N	.991	99	895	78	9	92	6
1942	NY-A	.991	132	1128	118	11	130	11
Total	7	.985	747	6630	649	108	642	54
OF								
1937	Bro-N	.938	7	15	0	1	0	-1
1938	Bro-N	.945	71	154	0	9	0	-4
1939	Bos-N	.977	23	41	2	1	0	0
1940	Bos-N	1.000	13	22	0	0	0	0
Total	4	.955	114	232	2	1	0	-5

■ Ron Hassey C

YEAR	TM/L	PCT	G	PO	A	E	DP	FR
1978	Cle-A	.993	24	130	15	1	1	5
1979	Cle-A	.992	68	345	29	3	4	6
1980	Cle-A	.993	113	549	52	4	8	-7
1981	Cle-A	.991	56	296	38	3	6	7
1982	Cle-A	.993	105	562	38	4	6	8
1983	Cle-A	.985	113	514	43	3	4	-3
1984	Cle-A	1.000	44	203	15	0	1	-2
	Chi-N	1.000	6	30	1	0	0	0
1985	NY-A	.984	69	402	20	7	2	5
1986	NY-A	.985	51	251	9	4	4	-13
	Chi-N	1.000	11	67	5	0	0	1
	Yr	.988	62	318	14	4	4	-12
1987	Chi-A	1.000	24	114	12	0	4	1
1988	Oak-A	.994	91	465	31	3	7	0
1989	Oak-A	.991	78	421	25	4	4	7
1990	Oak-A	.997	59	307	18	1	2	4
Total	13	.993	912	4656	351	7	53	19
1B								
1979	Cle-A	1.000	2	23	0	0	1	-1
1980	Cle-A	1.000	3	15	0	0	0	0
1981	Cle-A	1.000	2	31	6	0	1	2
1982	Cle-A	1.000	2	4	0	0	0	0
1984	Cle-A	.889	1	7	1	1	0	0
	Chi-N	.960	4	23	1	1	2	0
1985	NY-A	1.000	2	18	0	0	2	0
1989	Oak-A	1.000	1	4	0	0	0	0
1990	Oak-A	1.000	3	5	0	0	0	0
Total	8	.986	23	130	8	2	8	1

■ Mickey Hatcher OF

YEAR	TM/L	PCT	G	PO	A	E	DP	FR
1979	LA-N	.974	19	36	1	1	0	1
1980	LA-N	1.000	25	18	1	0	0	1
1981	Min-A	.992	91	239	3	2	0	-1
1982	Min-A	.988	47	78	7	1	0	3
1983	Min-A	.979	56	137	4	3	1	2
1984	Min-A	.974	100	249	11	7	1	10
1985	Min-A	.991	97	215	6	2	2	4

YEAR	TM/L	PCT	G	PO	A	E	DP	FR
1986	Min-A	.971	46	60	6	2	4	2
1987	LA-N	1.000	7	6	0	0	0	0
1988	LA-N	1.000	29	35	2	0	1	0
1989	LA-N	.961	48	68	5	3	2	-2
1990	LA-N	1.000	10	10	0	0	0	-1
Total	12	.983	575	1151	46	1	11	19

1B

YEAR	TM/L	PCT	G	PO	A	E	DP	FR
1981	Min-A	.984	7	56	7	1	5	1
1983	Min-A	1.000	7	62	4	0	6	0
1984	Min-A	.984	17	115	9	2	9	-1
1985	Min-A	.970	4	31	1	1	2	-1
1986	Min-A	.988	22	159	9	2	12	-2
1987	LA-N	.992	37	234	24	2	29	2
1988	LA-N	.982	25	153	15	3	6	0
1989	LA-N	1.000	5	16	2	0	3	0
1990	LA-N	1.000	25	73	7	0	9	0
Total	9	.989	149	899	78	1	81	-1

3B

YEAR	TM/L	PCT	G	PO	A	E	DP	FR
1979	LA-N	.895	17	11	23	4	0	0
1980	LA-N	.921	18	13	22	3	2	0
1981	Min-A	1.000	2	1	1	0	0	0
1982	Min-A	1.000	5	3	10	0	1	0
1983	Min-A	1.000	1	0	3	0	2	1
1984	Min-A	—	1	0	0	0	0	0
1986	Min-A	1.000	3	1	1	0	0	0
1987	LA-N	.929	49	37	81	9	7	0
1988	LA-N	1.000	3	1	2	0	0	0
1989	LA-N	.950	16	5	14	1	2	-2
1990	LA-N	.813	10	3	10	3	0	-2
Total	11	.924	125	75	167	0	14	-3

Billy Hatcher   OF

YEAR	TM/L	PCT	G	PO	A	E	DP	FR
1984	Chi-N	1.000	4	2	1	0	0	1
1985	Chi-N	.988	44	77	2	1	0	-1
1986	Hou-N	.983	121	226	7	4	0	-4
1987	Hou-N	.986	140	276	16	4	6	5
1988	Hou-N	.983	142	280	7	5	2	2
1989	Hou-N	.991	104	223	1	2	1	0
	Pit-N	1.000	20	27	0	0	0	-4
	Yr	.992	124	250	1	2	1	-4
1990	Cin-N	.997	131	308	10	1	2	1
Total	7	.989	706	1419	44	7	11	0

Fred Hatfield   3B

YEAR	TM/L	PCT	G	PO	A	E	DP	FR
1950	Bos-A	1.000	3	4	9	0	2	3
1951	Bos-A	.959	49	40	124	7	15	21
1952	Bos-A	1.000	17	7	23	0	0	4
	Det-A	.968	107	114	253	12	32	15
	Yr	.971	124	121	276	12	32	19
1953	Det-A	.978	54	56	121	4	13	8
1954	Det-A	.911	15	15	26	4	4	0
1955	Det-A	.904	16	17	30	5	2	-2
1956	Chi-A	.961	100	83	189	11	21	4
1957	Chi-A	.951	44	23	74	5	10	2
1958	Cle-A	1.000	2	1	6	0	0	1
	Cin-N	—	1	0	0	0	0	0
Total	9	.962	408	360	855	8	99	56

2B

YEAR	TM/L	PCT	G	PO	A	E	DP	FR
1953	Det-A	.968	28	64	87	5	21	2
1954	Det-A	.972	54	114	126	7	29	-7
1955	Det-A	.975	92	216	251	12	74	-4
1956	Det-A	1.000	4	7	6	0	1	-1
1958	Cin-N	—	1	0	0	0	0	0
Total	5	.973	179	401	470	4	125	-10

SS

YEAR	TM/L	PCT	G	PO	A	E	DP	FR
1952	Det-A	.923	9	11	13	2	3	-1
1953	Det-A	—	1	0	0	0	0	0
1955	Det-A	.939	14	19	43	4	4	0
1956	Chi-A	1.000	3	1	2	0	0	0
Total	4	.937	27	31	58	6	7	-1

Gil Hatfield   SS

YEAR	TM/L	PCT	G	PO	A	E	DP	FR
1888	NY-N	.768	13	7	36	13	3	0
1889	NY-N	.858	24	48	73	20	6	1
1890	NY-P	.785	27	36	66	28	8	-14
1891	Was-a	.869	105	211	334	82	40	6
1895	Lou-N	1.000	2	0	1	0	0	0
Total	5	.850	171	302	510	143	57	-7

3B

YEAR	TM/L	PCT	G	PO	A	E	DP	FR
1885	Buf-N	.913	8	7	14	2	0	0
1887	NY-N	1.000	2	5	3	0	0	0
1888	NY-N	.813	14	18	21	9	0	-2
1889	NY-N	.833	2	4	1	1	1	-1
1890	NY-P	.842	42	43	90	25	5	-4
1891	Was-a	.892	27	50	57	13	3	3
1893	Bro-N	.875	34	47	65	16	2	-7
1895	Lou-N	.889	3	3	5	1	0	-1
Total	8	.866	132	177	256	7	11	-12

OF

YEAR	TM/L	PCT	G	PO	A	E	DP	FR
1888	NY-N	.800	1	2	2	1	1	2
1890	NY-P	.667	1	2	0	1	0	0
1891	Was-a	.778	3	6	1	2	0	0
Total	3	.765	5	10	3	4	1	2

2B

YEAR	TM/L	PCT	G	PO	A	E	DP	FR
1885	Buf-N	.750	3	3	9	4	0	0
1888	NY-N	.875	1	3	4	1	1	0
Total	2	.792	4	6	13	5	1	0

Grady Hatton   3B

YEAR	TM/L	PCT	G	PO	A	E	DP	FR
1946	Cin-N	.941	116	108	194	19	14	-19
1947	Cin-N	.938	136	143	248	26	18	-8
1948	Cin-N	.932	123	141	243	28	21	5
1949	Cin-N	.975	136	143	290	11	29	-1
1950	Cin-N	.954	126	145	230	18	19	-2
1951	Cin-N	.972	87	103	176	8	24	4
1953	Cin-N	1.000	5	5	4	0	1	1
1954	Chi-A	1.000	10	12	15	0	1	-1
	Bos-A	.966	93	77	204	10	20	6
	Yr	.969	103	89	219	10	21	5

YEAR	TM/L	PCT	G	PO	A	E	DP	FR
1955	Bos-A	.976	111	97	225	8	22	-2
1956	StL-N	—	1	0	0	0	0	0
	Bal-A	.952	12	5	15	1	0	-1
Total	10	.956	956	979	1844	129	169	-20

2B

YEAR	TM/L	PCT	G	PO	A	E	DP	FR
1948	Cin-N	1.000	3	1	0	0	0	0
1950	Cin-N	1.000	1	1	0	0	0	0
1952	Cin-N	.990	120	316	289	6	68	-17
1953	Cin-N	.991	35	56	49	1	15	-9
1955	Bos-A	—	1	0	0	0	0	0
1956	StL-N	.951	13	24	34	3	8	-4
	Bal-A	1.000	15	19	26	0	3	-3
1960	Chi-N	.931	8	11	16	2	2	-2
Total	7	.986	196	428	414	2	96	-35

1B

YEAR	TM/L	PCT	G	PO	A	E	DP	FR
1953	Cin-N	1.000	10	72	3	0	14	-2
1954	Chi-A	1.000	3	6	0	0	1	0
	Bos-A	1.000	1	0	0	0	0	0
	Yr	1.000	4	6	0	0	1	0
Total	2	1.000	14	78	3	0	15	-2

OF

YEAR	TM/L	PCT	G	PO	A	E	DP	FR
1946	Cin-N	.667	2	2	0	1	0	-1
1948	Cin-N	—	1	0	0	0	0	0
1951	Cin-N	1.000	2	1	0	0	0	0
Total	3	.750	5	3	0	1	0	-1

SS

YEAR	TM/L	PCT	G	PO	A	E	DP	FR
1948	Cin-N	1.000	2	3	5	0	1	0
1950	Cin-N	—	1	0	0	0	0	0
1954	Bos-A	1.000	1	1	3	0	0	0
Total	3	1.000	4	4	8	0	1	0

Arnold Hauser   SS

YEAR	TM/L	PCT	G	PO	A	E	DP	FR
1910	StL-N	.931	117	212	345	41	31	-8
1911	StL-N	.918	134	223	400	56	51	-15
1912	StL-N	.934	132	262	446	50	54	10
1913	StL-N	.848	8	11	17	5	2	-4
1915	Chi-F	.851	16	25	38	11	7	-4
Total	5	.924	407	733	1246	163	145	-21

3B

YEAR	TM/L	PCT	G	PO	A	E	DP	FR
1910	StL-N	1.000	1	0	1	0	0	0
1911	StL-N	1.000	2	2	2	0	1	0
1915	Chi-F	1.000	6	3	5	0	0	0
Total	3	1.000	9	5	8	0	1	0

2B

YEAR	TM/L	PCT	G	PO	A	E	DP	FR
1913	StL-N	1.000	4	7	8	0	2	0

Joe Hauser   1B

YEAR	TM/L	PCT	G	PO	A	E	DP	FR
1922	Phi-A	.986	94	936	55	14	61	-3
1923	Phi-A	.990	146	1475	86	15	109	-3
1924	Phi-A	.993	146	1513	94	12	131	-3
1926	Phi-A	.996	65	630	35	3	39	0
1928	Phi-A	.986	88	811	41	12	51	-6
1929	Cle-A	.986	8	65	5	1	2	1
Total	6	.990	547	5430	316	7	393	-14

George Hausmann   2B

YEAR	TM/L	PCT	G	PO	A	E	DP	FR
1944	NY-N	.960	122	301	350	27	66	-7
1945	NY-N	.968	154	376	489	29	65	5
1949	NY-N	.984	13	25	37	1	8	0
Total	3	.965	289	702	876	7	139	-2

Thorny Hawkes   2B

YEAR	TM/L	PCT	G	PO	A	E	DP	FR
1879	Tro-N	.896	64	220	264	56	26	16
1884	Was-a	.917	38	125	107	21	10	4
Total	2	.903	102	345	371	7	36	20

OF

YEAR	TM/L	PCT	G	PO	A	E	DP	FR
1884	Was-a	.750	2	3	0	1	0	0

Jack Hayden   OF

YEAR	TM/L	PCT	G	PO	A	E	DP	FR
1901	Phi-A	.841	50	63	11	14	0	-4
1906	Bos-A	.973	85	136	7	4	1	-1
1908	Chi-N	1.000	11	19	0	0	0	-1
Total	3	.929	146	218	18	8	1	-6

Charlie Hayes   3B

YEAR	TM/L	PCT	G	PO	A	E	DP	FR
1988	SF-N	—	3	0	0	0	0	0
1989	SF-N	1.000	3	2	1	0	0	0
	Phi-N	.910	82	49	173	22	15	10
	Yr	.911	85	51	174	22	15	10
1990	Phi-N	.957	146	121	324	20	30	23
Total	3	.941	234	172	498	2	45	33

OF

YEAR	TM/L	PCT	G	PO	A	E	DP	FR
1988	SF-N	1.000	4	5	0	0	0	0

1B

YEAR	TM/L	PCT	G	PO	A	E	DP	FR
1990	Phi-N	1.000	4	28	2	0	0	0

2B

YEAR	TM/L	PCT	G	PO	A	E	DP	FR
1990	Phi-N	1.000	1	2	3	0	1	0

Frankie Hayes   C

YEAR	TM/L	PCT	G	PO	A	E	DP	FR
1933	Phi-A	.889	3	7	1	1	0	1
1934	Phi-A	.955	89	279	36	15	4	-10
1936	Phi-A	.972	143	489	69	16	8	-21
1937	Phi-A	.971	56	208	23	7	4	-3
1938	Phi-A	.975	90	319	38	9	2	-16
1939	Phi-A	.978	114	380	60	10	12	-11
1940	Phi-A	.971	134	515	63	17	9	-12
1941	Phi-A	.983	123	403	65	8	11	-10
1942	Phi-A	1.000	20	66	11	0	0	-4
	StL-A	.971	51	175	25	6	2	-6
	Yr	.979	71	241	36	6	2	-10
1943	StL-A	.982	76	301	40	6	8	-9
1944	Phi-A	.983	155	636	89	13	10	3
1945	Phi-A	.994	32	131	28	1	6	2
	Cle-A	.988	119	508	63	7	23	2
	Yr	.989	151	639	91	8	29	4
1946	Cle-A	.981	50	302	16	6	2	-1
	Chi-A	.972	52	199	32	5	4	-4
	Yr	.980	102	501	48	11	6	-4
1947	Bos-A	.917	4	20	2	2	1	1
Total	14	.977	1311	4938	661	129	106	-97

1B

YEAR	TM/L	PCT	G	PO	A	E	DP	FR
1940	Phi-A	.941	2	16	0	1	0	-1
1943	StL-A	1.000	1	0	1	0	0	0
1944	Phi-A	1.000	1	1	0	0	1	0
Total	3	.947	4	17	1	1	1	-1

Jackie Hayes   C

YEAR	TM/L	PCT	G	PO	A	E	DP	FR
1882	Wor-N	.830	15	57	16	15	2	-4
1883	Pit-a	.911	62	277	70	34	2	-12
1884	Pit-a	.912	24	135	30	16	2	-2
	Bro-a	.946	14	86	20	6	1	3
	Yr	.925	38	221	50	22	3	1
1885	Bro-a	.900	42	209	53	29	4	-2
1886	Was-N	.926	14	65	22	7	1	-3
1887	Bal-a	.833	1	4	1	1	0	-1
1890	Bro-P	.500	2	1	0	1	0	0
Total	7	.906	174	834	212	109	12	-21

OF

YEAR	TM/L	PCT	G	PO	A	E	DP	FR
1882	Wor-N	.855	58	93	13	18	2	-2
1883	Pit-a	.829	18	27	2	6	0	-1
1884	Pit-a	.800	3	3	1	1	0	0
	Bro-a	.857	2	5	1	1	0	1
	Yr	.833	5	8	2	2	0	1
1886	Was-N	1.000	12	19	0	0	0	0
1887	Bal-a	.250	4	1	0	3	0	-2
1890	Bro-P	.867	6	12	1	2	0	0
Total	6	.852	103	160	18	1	2	-4

1B

YEAR	TM/L	PCT	G	PO	A	E	DP	FR
1883	Pit-a	.958	5	41	5	2	0	2
1884	Pit-a	.958	5	43	3	2	3	1
Total	2	.958	10	84	8	4	3	3

SS

YEAR	TM/L	PCT	G	PO	A	E	DP	FR
1882	Wor-N	.778	1	2	5	2	0	1
1883	Pit-a	.714	5	5	5	4	0	-2
1890	Bro-P	.769	3	8	2	3	1	-2
Total	3	.750	9	15	12	9	1	-3

3B

YEAR	TM/L	PCT	G	PO	A	E	DP	FR
1882	Wor-N	.727	5	10	6	6	0	-2
1887	Bal-a	.750	3	2	4	2	0	-1
Total	2	.733	8	12	10	8	0	-3

2B

YEAR	TM/L	PCT	G	PO	A	E	DP	FR
1883	Pit-a	.700	1	4	3	3	0	-1
1884	Pit-a	.857	1	2	4	1	1	0
1886	Was-N	.667	1	1	1	1	1	0
1890	Bro-P	1.000	1	2	1	0	0	0
Total	4	.783	4	9	9	5	2	-1

Jackie Hayes   2B

YEAR	TM/L	PCT	G	PO	A	E	DP	FR
1928	Was-A	.974	41	101	123	6	26	4
1929	Was-A	.974	57	125	176	8	40	-4
1930	Was-A	.981	29	69	88	3	20	8
1931	Was-A	.962	19	52	50	4	8	-4
1932	Chi-A	.967	97	241	346	20	78	5
1933	Chi-A	.981	138	344	497	16	89	10
1934	Chi-A	.980	61	147	188	7	35	-8
1935	Chi-A	.966	85	202	275	17	48	-6
1936	Chi-A	.979	89	216	334	12	70	15
1937	Chi-A	.984	143	353	490	14	115	20
1938	Chi-A	.976	61	146	183	8	51	-3
1939	Chi-A	.974	69	172	201	10	51	5
1940	Chi-A	.981	15	21	32	1	8	0
Total	13	.976	904	2189	2983	126	639	42

3B

YEAR	TM/L	PCT	G	PO	A	E	DP	FR
1927	Was-A	1.000	1	1	2	0	1	0
1928	Was-A	1.000	2	0	3	0	0	0
1929	Was-A	.945	63	56	132	11	19	7
1930	Was-A	1.000	9	10	17	0	3	1
1931	Was-A	1.000	8	1	5	0	0	0
1932	Chi-A	.903	10	13	15	3	0	-2
1936	Chi-A	1.000	2	4	1	0	0	0
Total	7	.949	95	85	175	4	23	6

SS

YEAR	TM/L	PCT	G	PO	A	E	DP	FR
1927	Was-A	.969	8	11	20	1	1	-1
1928	Was-A	.955	15	33	51	4	10	4
1929	Was-A	1.000	2	2	4	0	2	1
1931	Was-A	1.000	3	5	7	0	0	0
1932	Chi-A	.865	10	20	25	7	5	2
1936	Chi-A	.963	13	33	45	3	12	2
Total	6	.945	51	104	152	5	30	4

1B

YEAR	TM/L	PCT	G	PO	A	E	DP	FR
1930	Was-A	.974	8	70	5	2	10	0

Von Hayes   OF

YEAR	TM/L	PCT	G	PO	A	E	DP	FR
1981	Cle-A	.939	13	29	2	2	1	1
1982	Cle-A	.981	139	306	9	6	4	4
1983	Phi-N	.972	103	165	7	5	0	-3
1984	Phi-N	.988	148	341	2	4	1	-10
1985	Phi-N	.984	146	368	9	6	1	6
1986	Phi-N	1.000	31	65	4	0	1	3
1987	Phi-N	.982	32	52	2	1	0	1
1988	Phi-N	.977	16	42	0	1	0	0
1989	Phi-N	.980	128	236	9	5	1	0
1990	Phi-N	.979	127	272	8	6	0	3
Total	10	.982	883	1876	52	6	9	5

1B

YEAR	TM/L	PCT	G	PO	A	E	DP	FR
1982	Cle-A	1.000	4	15	0	0	2	0
1986	Phi-N	.990	134	1182	96	13	105	-2
1987	Phi-N	.990	144	1164	78	12	100	-9
1988	Phi-N	.990	85	712	55	8	66	-2
1989	Phi-N	.995	30	182	16	1	20	1
Total	5	.990	397	3255	245	4	293	-12

3B

YEAR	TM/L	PCT	G	PO	A	E	DP	FR
1981	Cle-A	.750	5	1	2	1	0	-1
1982	Cle-A	1.000	5	2	8	0	0	0
1988	Phi-N	1.000	3	2	3	0	0	0
1989	Phi-N	.909	10	8	22	3	3	1
Total	4	.923	23	13	35	4	3	0

YEAR	TM/L	PCT	G	PO	A	E	DP	FR
■ Red Hayworth C								
1944	StL-A	.967	87	339	39	13	4	0
1945	StL-A	.992	55	216	23	2	5	3
Total	2	.976	142	555	62	5	9	3
■ Ray Hayworth C								
1926	Det-A	1.000	8	9	0	0	0	-1
1929	Det-A	.951	14	46	12	3	1	0
1930	Det-A	.977	76	277	27	7	4	-11
1931	Det-A	.973	88	334	61	11	5	4
1932	Det-A	.991	106	399	59	4	8	2
1933	Det-A	.994	133	546	79	4	14	1
1934	Det-A	.984	54	226	23	4	3	6
1935	Det-A	.996	48	211	35	1	4	11
1936	Det-A	.988	81	305	28	4	5	-4
1937	Det-A	.992	28	118	14	1	2	6
1938	Det-A	.971	7	32	1	1	0	2
	Bro-N	1.000	3	4	0	0	0	0
1939	Bro-N	1.000	18	35	3	0	0	1
	NY-N	1.000	5	16	4	0	0	1
	Yr	1.000	23	51	7	0	0	2
1944	Bro-N	1.000	6	18	2	0	0	1
1945	Bro-N	1.000	2	5	0	0	0	0
Total	14	.987	677	2581	348	0	46	19
■ Fran Healy C								
1969	KC-A	1.000	5	16	1	0	0	0
1971	SF-N	.966	22	104	8	4	1	-2
1972	SF-N	.995	43	174	21	1	3	7
1973	KC-A	.979	92	429	43	10	3	-3
1974	KC-A	.977	138	620	64	16	4	-5
1975	KC-A	.982	51	258	17	5	2	-7
1976	KC-A	1.000	6	30	5	0	0	0
	NY-A	.983	31	104	15	2	0	3
	Yr	.987	37	134	20	2	0	3
1977	NY-A	.971	26	98	3	3	0	0
1978	NY-A	—	1	0	0	0	0	0
Total	9	.980	415	1833	177	1	13	-7
■ Jeff Heath OF								
1936	Cle-A	1.000	12	10	1	0	0	-2
1937	Cle-A	1.000	14	27	0	0	0	-1
1938	Cle-A	.974	122	254	5	7	2	0
1939	Cle-A	.964	108	263	7	10	2	6
1940	Cle-A	.971	90	197	6	6	1	1
1941	Cle-A	.949	151	259	20	15	1	-8
1942	Cle-A	.980	146	326	12	7	3	4
1943	Cle-A	.968	111	264	4	9	1	-2
1944	Cle-A	.952	37	76	4	4	2	0
1945	Cle-A	.973	101	214	3	6	1	-5
1946	Was-A	.969	47	92	3	3	0	-4
	StL-A	.962	83	147	5	6	1	-10
	Yr	.965	130	239	8	9	1	-14
1947	StL-A	.987	140	297	7	4	4	-1
1948	Bos-N	.991	106	223	6	2	2	-2
1949	Bos-N	.983	31	56	2	1	1	-2
Total	14	.972	1299	2705	85	0	21	-26
■ Mike Heath C								
1978	NY-A	.970	33	151	11	5	1	2
1979	Oak-A	.969	22	80	13	3	0	-3
1980	Oak-A	.986	47	268	19	4	5	14
1981	Oak-A	.978	78	391	45	10	6	5
1982	Oak-A	.973	90	350	50	11	8	-6
1983	Oak-A	.973	80	316	47	10	6	-9
1984	Oak-A	.986	108	423	54	7	7	-14
1985	Oak-A	.981	112	483	44	10	9	-9
1986	StL-N	.967	63	259	30	10	4	-6
	Det-A	.987	29	145	9	2	1	-2
1987	Det-A	.989	67	337	38	4	5	7
1988	Det-A	.984	75	357	24	6	3	2
1989	Det-A	.986	117	582	66	9	10	0
1990	Det-A	.980	117	585	54	13	7	-1
Total	13	.981	1038	4727	504	104	72	-20
OF								
1979	Oak-A	.978	46	86	5	2	2	-1
1980	Oak-A	1.000	8	24	1	0	0	3
1981	Oak-A	1.000	6	8	0	0	0	0
1982	Oak-A	.938	10	14	1	1	0	0
1983	Oak-A	.978	24	45	0	1	0	0
1984	Oak-A	.986	45	71	1	1	1	0
1985	Oak-A	.982	35	49	5	1	0	4
1986	StL-N	1.000	2	1	0	0	0	0
1987	Det-A	1.000	24	26	1	0	0	0
1988	Det-A	1.000	9	4	0	0	0	0
1989	Det-A	1.000	3	1	0	0	0	0
1990	Det-A	1.000	3	2	0	0	0	0
Total	12	.983	215	331	14	6	3	6
3B								
1979	Oak-A	1.000	7	1	14	0	0	0
1982	Oak-A	1.000	5	4	3	0	0	0
1983	Oak-A	1.000	2	1	0	0	0	0
1984	Oak-A	1.000	2	1	1	0	0	0
1985	Oak-A	.962	13	7	18	1	1	-1
1986	Det-A	.000	1	0	0	1	0	0
1987	Det-A	.750	4	1	2	1	0	0
1989	Det-A	.750	4	1	2	1	0	0
Total	8	.933	38	16	40	4	1	-1
SS								
1984	Oak-A	—	1	0	0	0	0	-1
1987	Det-A	1.000	2	0	1	0	0	0
1990	Det-A	1.000	1	1	0	0	0	0
Total	3	1.000	4	1	1	0	0	-1
1B								
1987	Det-A	1.000	4	20	1	0	3	0
2B								
1987	Det-A	—	1	0	0	0	0	0
■ Tommy Heath C								
1935	StL-A	.982	37	97	10	2	3	-1

YEAR	TM/L	PCT	G	PO	A	E	DP	FR
1937	StL-A	1.000	14	55	6	0	1	0
1938	StL-A	.986	65	315	42	5	5	7
Total	3	.987	116	467	58	7	9	6
■ Cliff Heathcote OF								
1918	StL-N	.934	87	222	6	16	0	-8
1919	StL-N	.967	101	225	10	8	3	-6
1920	StL-N	.964	129	296	26	12	3	1
1921	StL-N	.926	51	83	5	7	0	-2
1922	StL-N	.950	32	93	2	5	1	6
	Chi-N	.986	60	131	5	2	1	-1
	Yr	.971	92	224	7	7	2	5
1923	Chi-N	.980	112	231	14	5	1	2
1924	Chi-N	.979	111	228	7	5	3	-2
1925	Chi-N	.970	99	241	21	8	8	13
1926	Chi-N	.985	133	306	22	5	8	13
1927	Chi-N	.987	57	136	13	2	7	9
1928	Chi-N	.973	39	67	5	2	1	2
1929	Chi-N	.985	52	131	4	2	2	3
1930	Chi-N	.986	35	66	4	1	0	1
1931	Cin-N	.989	59	164	13	2	4	12
Total	14	.971	1157	2620	157	2	42	43
1B								
1919	StL-N	1.000	2	24	0	0	0	0
1932	Phi-N	.962	7	47	3	2	7	0
Total	2	.974	9	71	3	2	7	0
■ Richie Hebner 3B								
1969	Pit-N	.944	124	79	240	19	31	3
1970	Pit-N	.940	117	64	235	19	24	1
1971	Pit-N	.949	108	89	172	14	21	-8
1972	Pit-N	.969	121	76	210	9	17	-15
1973	Pit-N	.939	139	92	260	23	19	-14
1974	Pit-N	.937	141	115	304	28	34	-6
1975	Pit-N	.946	126	86	244	19	17	-15
1976	Pit-N	.953	126	87	236	16	16	-10
1977	Phi-N	.929	13	6	20	2	2	1
1978	Phi-N	.963	19	7	45	2	4	3
1979	NY-N	.940	134	99	246	22	26	-7
1980	Det-A	.958	32	19	49	3	10	-4
1982	Pit-N	—	1	0	0	0	0	0
1983	Pit-N	.967	40	16	43	2	1	-5
1984	Chi-N	.963	14	2	24	1	2	-1
1985	Chi-N	.870	7	2	18	3	0	0
Total	16	.946	1262	839	2346	182	224	-77
1B								
1969	Pit-N	1.000	1	2	0	0	1	0
1977	Phi-N	.991	103	927	65	9	91	2
1978	Phi-N	.994	117	987	49	6	86	-5
1979	NY-N	.966	6	26	2	1	1	0
1980	Det-A	.998	61	466	35	1	35	-1
1981	Det-A	.995	61	531	29	3	36	-3
1982	Det-A	.990	40	286	25	3	15	3
	Pit-N	1.000	4	27	1	0	1	0
1983	Pit-N	1.000	7	39	2	0	3	0
1984	Chi-N	1.000	3	35	2	0	4	0
1985	Chi-N	.991	12	108	6	1	15	0
Total	10	.993	415	3434	216	4	288	-4
OF								
1982	Pit-N	.964	21	25	2	1	0	0
1983	Pit-N	1.000	7	8	0	0	0	0
1984	Chi-N	1.000	3	2	0	0	0	0
1985	Chi-N	—	1	0	0	0	0	0
Total	4	.974	32	35	2	1	0	0
2B								
1977	Phi-N	—	1	0	0	0	0	0
1978	Phi-N	—	1	0	0	0	0	0
Total	2	—	2	0	0	0	0	0
■ Danny Heep OF								
1979	Hou-N	1.000	2	7	0	0	0	1
1981	Hou-N	—	1	0	0	0	0	0
1982	Hou-N	1.000	39	62	2	0	1	-1
1983	NY-N	1.000	61	90	4	0	1	-4
1984	NY-N	.967	48	86	1	3	1	0
1985	NY-N	.977	78	126	1	3	0	-4
1986	NY-N	.988	56	83	2	1	1	-2
1987	LA-N	.962	22	23	2	1	1	0
1988	LA-N	1.000	32	45	1	0	0	0
1989	Bos-A	.989	75	92	2	1	1	-7
1990	Bos-A	1.000	14	19	1	0	2	1
Total	11	.986	428	633	16	9	7	-15
1B								
1980	Hou-N	.990	22	188	8	2	8	-2
1981	Hou-N	.990	22	198	9	2	12	-3
1982	Hou-N	.993	16	130	4	1	9	-2
1983	NY-N	1.000	14	69	7	0	11	0
1984	NY-N	.983	10	51	6	1	3	1
1985	NY-N	.970	4	28	4	1	3	0
1987	LA-N	1.000	6	29	4	0	2	1
1988	LA-N	.969	12	84	9	3	5	1
1989	Bos-A	.986	19	124	12	2	17	0
1990	Bos-A	.963	5	23	3	1	1	1
Total	10	.987	130	924	66	3	71	-3
■ Don Heffner 2B								
1934	NY-A	.971	68	158	179	10	46	-8
1935	NY-A	.980	10	20	29	1	5	-1
1936	NY-A	1.000	5	3	10	0	2	1
1937	NY-A	.980	38	107	94	4	28	-6
1938	StL-A	.971	141	365	363	22	103	-9
1939	StL-A	.958	32	84	97	8	21	0
1940	StL-A	.977	125	311	426	17	102	19
1941	StL-A	.974	105	224	307	14	52	3
1942	StL-A	.906	6	13	16	3	1	1
1943	StL-A	.974	13	21	17	1	4	0
	Phi-A	.977	47	98	127	5	27	-10
	Yr	.978	60	119	144	6	31	-10
1944	Det-A	.962	5	12	13	1	4	-1

YEAR	TM/L	PCT	G	PO	A	E	DP	FR
Total	11	.973	595	1416	1678	6	395	-11
SS								
1936	NY-A	.917	3	5	6	1	3	-1
1937	NY-A	.960	13	16	32	2	2	-1
1939	StL-A	.944	73	138	218	21	33	-4
Total	3	.945	89	159	256	4	38	-6
3B								
1936	NY-A	.971	8	11	22	1	2	4
1937	NY-A	1.000	3	3	6	0	0	0
Total	2	.977	11	14	28	1	2	4
1B								
1937	NY-A	1.000	1	1	0	0	0	0
1942	StL-A	1.000	4	21	3	0	4	1
1943	StL-A	1.000	1	6	1	0	0	0
	Phi-A	1.000	1	1	0	0	0	0
	Yr	1.000	2	7	1	0	0	0
Total	3	1.000	7	29	4	0	4	1
OF								
1937	NY-A	—	1	0	0	0	0	0
■ Jim Hegan C								
1941	Cle-A	.973	16	63	10	2	2	0
1942	Cle-A	.977	66	227	32	6	7	8
1946	Cle-A	.991	87	486	47	5	11	9
1947	Cle-A	.989	133	566	54	7	14	7
1948	Cle-A	.990	142	637	76	7	17	21
1949	Cle-A	.990	152	651	73	7	16	10
1950	Cle-A	.993	129	656	64	5	14	23
1951	Cle-A	.991	129	597	66	6	8	11
1952	Cle-A	.987	107	498	53	7	7	6
1953	Cle-A	.976	106	399	42	11	3	2
1954	Cle-A	.994	137	661	49	4	9	12
1955	Cle-A	.997	111	583	34	2	12	7
1956	Cle-A	.985	118	648	28	10	2	15
1957	Cle-A	1.000	58	287	14	0	4	2
1958	Det-A	.996	45	211	19	1	4	1
	Phi-N	.991	25	104	8	1	1	4
1959	Phi-N	.990	25	84	11	1	2	0
	SF-N	.975	21	72	6	2	1	5
	Yr	.983	46	156	17	3	3	5
1960	Cle-A	.977	22	76	9	2	2	2
Total	17	.990	1629	7506	695	6	136	145
■ Mike Hegan 1B								
1964	NY-A	1.000	2	17	4	0	2	1
1966	NY-A	.991	13	103	8	1	6	0
1967	NY-A	1.000	54	309	20	0	29	0
1969	Sea-A	.993	19	136	13	1	14	1
1970	Mil-A	.994	139	1097	113	7	104	12
1971	Mil-A	1.000	45	307	33	0	20	4
	Oak-A	1.000	47	126	12	0	14	3
	Yr	1.000	92	433	45	0	34	7
1972	Oak-A	.988	56	160	4	2	13	-2
1973	Oak-A	.992	37	349	27	3	25	0
	NY-A	.991	93	509	31	5	38	-2
	Yr	.996	34	243	12	1	21	-1
1974	NY-A	1.000	17	137	8	0	9	0
	Mil-A	.991	17	106	4	1	12	-1
	Yr	.996	34	243	12	1	21	-1
1975	Mil-A	.995	27	182	20	1	19	2
1976	Mil-A	.969	10	57	6	2	8	0
1977	Mil-A	.980	6	46	4	1	3	0
Total	12	.995	553	3297	286	9	300	21
OF								
1967	NY-A	1.000	10	17	0	0	0	-1
1969	Sea-A	.955	64	100	7	5	1	-1
1970	Mil-A	1.000	8	7	0	0	0	0
1971	Oak-A	.667	2	2	0	1	0	0
1972	Oak-A	1.000	3	5	1	0	0	1
1973	Oak-A	1.000	3	3	0	0	0	0
1974	Mil-A	1.000	17	30	1	0	0	0
1975	Mil-A	.984	42	59	1	1	0	-2
1976	Mil-A	1.000	20	31	0	0	0	-1
1977	Mil-A	1.000	8	2	0	0	0	0
Total	10	.974	177	256	10	7	1	-4
■ Jack Heidemann SS								
1969	Cle-A	1.000	3	1	5	0	0	1
1970	Cle-A	.961	132	216	354	23	79	-2
1971	Cle-A	.977	81	113	188	7	34	-9
1972	Cle-A	.964	10	10	17	1	3	-1
1974	Cle-A	1.000	4	1	3	0	0	0
	StL-N	.967	45	42	46	3	9	-10
1975	NY-N	.951	44	70	84	8	14	-11
1976	NY-N	1.000	3	2	5	0	1	0
Total	7	.965	322	455	702	2	140	-32
3B								
1974	Cle-A	1.000	6	1	2	0	0	0
	StL-N	—	1	0	0	0	0	0
1975	NY-N	.857	4	1	5	1	0	0
1976	Mil-A	.962	40	30	45	3	2	-5
Total	3	.955	51	32	52	4	2	-5
2B								
1974	Cle-A	1.000	1	1	1	0	1	0
1975	NY-N	.500	1	1	0	1	0	-1
1976	NY-N	1.000	1	3	2	0	2	0
	Mil-A	1.000	24	44	44	0	17	-2
1977	Mil-A	1.000	1	2	1	0	1	1
Total	4	.990	28	51	48	1	21	-2
1B								
1974	Cle-A	1.000	1	2	0	0	0	0
■ Emmett Heidrick OF								
1898	StL-N	.850	19	29	5	6	1	-1
1899	StL-N	.925	145	211	34	20	6	4
1900	StL-N	.959	83	215	21	10	4	15
1901	StL-A	.945	118	258	15	16	2	1
1902	StL-A	.940	109	264	16	18	4	4
1903	StL-A	.954	119	252	17	13	5	2

YEAR	TM/L	PCT	G	PO	A	E	DP	FR
1904	StL-A	.963	130	291	22	12	6	11
1908	StL-A	.957	25	42	3	2	1	-1
Total	8	.946	748	1562	133	7	29	35

SS

1902	StL-A	.500	1	2	0	2	0	-1

3B

1902	StL-A	.667	1	2	0	1	0	-1

C

1903	StL-A	—	1	0	0	0	0	0

■ **Harry Heilmann OF**

YEAR	TM/L	PCT	G	PO	A	E	DP	FR
1914	Det-A	.870	31	35	5	6	1	-5
1916	Det-A	.952	77	110	10	6	0	-3
1917	Det-A	.960	123	200	17	9	4	-4
1918	Det-A	.957	40	60	6	3	1	-2
1920	Det-A	1.000	22	27	6	0	0	1
1921	Det-A	.962	147	241	10	10	1	-12
1922	Det-A	.948	115	175	6	10	2	-12
1923	Det-A	.960	130	272	13	12	7	1
1924	Det-A	.970	147	263	31	9	6	8
1925	Det-A	.970	148	278	9	9	1	-3
1926	Det-A	.972	134	228	18	7	4	-1
1927	Det-A	.966	135	218	11	8	5	-8
1928	Det-A	.971	125	215	17	7	2	1
1929	Det-A	.966	114	193	8	7	3	-6
1930	Cin-N	.955	106	279	16	14	5	-14
Total	15	.962	1594	2794	183	117	42	-31

1B

1914	Det-A	.978	16	165	12	4	11	0
1916	Det-A	.991	30	325	17	3	16	-1
1917	Det-A	.986	27	266	23	4	9	2
1918	Det-A	.987	37	367	18	5	11	-2
1919	Det-A	.979	140	1402	78	31	61	-10
1920	Det-A	.985	122	1207	80	19	52	-1
1921	Det-A	.950	3	16	3	1	1	0
1922	Det-A	1.000	5	25	5	0	0	1
1923	Det-A	.991	12	101	8	1	5	1
1924	Det-A	.983	4	54	4	1	4	0
1928	Det-A	.992	25	234	17	2	20	0
1929	Det-A	—	2	0	0	0	0	0
1930	Cin-N	.975	19	178	14	5	17	1
1932	Cin-N	.981	6	49	3	1	2	0
Total	14	.984	448	4389	282	7	209	-9

2B

1914	Det-A	.958	6	9	14	1	1	-1
1916	Det-A	.871	9	7	20	4	0	-6
1918	Det-A	1.000	2	0	4	0	1	0
Total	3	.915	17	16	38	5	2	-7

■ **Bob Heise SS**

1967	NY-N	.917	3	4	7	1	0	0
1968	NY-N	.929	6	6	7	1	4	-5
1969	NY-N	.915	3	4	5	0	0	-3
1970	SF-N	.915	33	25	72	9	14	-1
1971	SF-N	.833	3	2	3	1	1	0
	Mil-A	.961	51	85	138	9	36	6
1972	Mil-A	.971	9	9	25	1	3	0
1973	Mil-A	.956	29	32	55	4	8	0
1974	Cal-A	1.000	3	4	7	0	1	0
1975	Bos-A	.909	4	4	6	1	2	1
1976	Bos-A	.909	9	16	24	4	6	2
1977	KC-A	.942	21	19	30	3	8	4
Total	11	.945	174	210	379	43	83	4

2B

1967	NY-N	.973	12	39	32	2	6	1
1968	NY-N	1.000	1	0	1	0	1	0
1970	SF-N	.963	28	53	52	4	10	0
1971	SF-N	—	1	0	0	0	0	0
	Mil-A	1.000	3	9	9	0	2	1
1972	Mil-A	.990	49	98	108	2	26	0
1973	Mil-A	1.000	4	8	9	0	1	0
1974	StL-N	1.000	3	7	8	0	2	2
	Cal-A	1.000	17	29	41	0	11	2
1975	Bos-A	.955	14	11	10	1	3	1
1976	Bos-A	—	1	0	0	0	0	0
1977	KC-A	1.000	21	20	27	0	8	4
Total	10	.984	154	274	297	9	70	11

3B

1967	NY-N	1.000	2	3	4	0	0	0
1970	SF-N	—	2	0	0	0	0	0
1971	SF-N	1.000	2	0	1	0	0	0
	Mil-A	.941	11	4	12	1	1	0
1972	Mil-A	.948	24	18	37	3	2	-3
1973	Mil-A	.941	9	3	13	1	0	-1
1974	Cal-A	1.000	6	4	7	0	1	0
1975	Bos-A	.940	45	36	90	8	7	9
1976	Bos-A	.968	22	11	19	1	1	1
1977	KC-A	.813	12	3	10	3	3	2
Total	9	.942	135	82	193	7	15	8

1B

1973	Mil-A	1.000	4	7	1	0	0	0
1975	Bos-A	1.000	1	1	0	0	0	0
1977	KC-A	—	1	0	0	0	0	0
Total	3	1.000	6	8	1	0	0	0

OF

1971	Mil-A	—	1	0	0	0	0	0

■ **Al Heist OF**

1960	Chi-N	.985	33	65	2	1	0	3
1961	Chi-N	.978	99	211	9	5	0	-4
1962	Hou-N	.974	23	36	1	1	0	1
Total	3	.979	155	312	12	7	0	0

■ **Woodie Held SS**

1954	NY-A	1.000	4	2	3	0	1	0
1958	KC-A	1.000	1	1	3	0	0	0
	Cle-A	.920	14	12	34	4	5	1
	Yr	.926	15	13	37	4	5	1
1959	Cle-A	.962	103	177	277	18	43	-9

YEAR	TM/L	PCT	G	PO	A	E	DP	FR
1960	Cle-A	.967	109	208	345	19	87	9
1961	Cle-A	.960	144	258	393	27	90	-14
1962	Cle-A	.956	133	221	371	27	101	-13
1963	Cle-A	.800	5	2	2	1	1	-1
1965	Was-A	.000	2	0	0	1	0	-1
1966	Bal-A	1.000	3	1	6	0	0	0
1967	Cal-A	1.000	13	12	27	0	7	0
1968	Cal-A	.929	5	6	7	1	1	-1
1969	Chi-A	1.000	3	2	4	0	1	1
Total	12	.960	539	902	1472	8	337	-28

OF

1957	KC-A	.996	92	266	12	1	2	12
1958	KC-A	1.000	41	75	1	0	0	1
	Cle-A	.966	43	82	3	3	1	5
	Yr	.982	84	157	4	3	1	6
1959	Cle-A	1.000	6	7	0	0	0	0
1962	Cle-A	—	1	0	0	0	0	0
1963	Cle-A	.982	35	51	3	1	2	1
1964	Cle-A	.967	41	58	1	2	0	0
1965	Was-A	.963	106	175	5	7	2	-3
1966	Bal-A	1.000	10	10	1	0	0	0
1967	Bal-A	1.000	2	3	0	0	0	0
	Cal-A	.952	17	20	0	1	0	-1
	Yr	.958	19	23	0	1	0	-1
1968	Cal-A	1.000	3	2	0	0	0	0
	Chi-A	1.000	33	30	2	0	1	2
	Yr	1.000	36	32	2	0	1	2
1969	Chi-A	1.000	18	17	0	0	0	0
Total	11	.982	448	796	28	5	8	17

2B

1959	Cle-A	1.000	3	0	1	0	0	0
1963	Cle-A	.982	96	188	251	8	50	1
1964	Cle-A	.966	52	96	128	8	35	5
1965	Was-A	1.000	4	2	1	0	0	0
1966	Bal-A	.913	5	12	9	2	1	-3
1967	Bal-A	.974	9	18	19	1	6	1
	Cal-A	1.000	3	2	6	0	1	0
	Yr	.978	12	20	25	1	7	1
1968	Cal-A	1.000	5	4	5	0	0	-1
	Chi-A	1.000	1	0	1	0	0	0
	Yr	1.000	6	4	6	0	0	-1
1969	Chi-A	1.000	1	2	2	0	0	0
Total	8	.975	179	324	423	9	93	3

3B

1954	NY-A	—	1	0	0	0	0	0
1958	KC-A	1.000	4	4	9	0	1	0
	Cle-A	1.000	4	4	5	0	0	1
	Yr	1.000	8	8	14	0	1	1
1959	Cle-A	.984	40	33	87	2	8	1
1962	Cle-A	1.000	5	6	6	0	1	0
1963	Cle-A	.667	3	2	4	3	0	-2
1964	Cle-A	.953	30	29	53	4	5	-1
1965	Was-A	1.000	5	6	9	0	3	1
1966	Bal-A	1.000	3	0	2	0	0	0
1967	Bal-A	.800	5	1	3	1	0	0
	Cal-A	.979	19	10	37	1	3	-1
	Yr	.962	24	11	40	2	3	-1
1968	Cal-A	1.000	5	2	6	0	1	0
	Chi-A	.833	5	2	3	1	0	0
	Yr	.929	10	4	9	1	1	0
1969	Chi-A	1.000	3	2	9	0	0	1
Total	11	.965	132	101	233	2	22	0

■ **Tommy Helms 2B**

1965	Cin-N	1.000	1	1	1	0	1	0
1966	Cin-N	1.000	20	45	50	0	9	-3
1967	Cin-N	.978	88	185	224	9	50	1
1968	Cin-N	.979	127	322	370	15	82	8
1969	Cin-N	.975	125	320	344	17	87	-3
1970	Cin-N	.983	148	350	410	13	107	2
1971	Cin-N	.990	149	395	468	9	130	14
1972	Hou-N	.979	139	353	441	17	115	26
1973	Hou-N	.988	145	325	438	9	104	-1
1974	Hou-N	.985	133	308	360	10	99	-11
1975	Hou-N	.988	42	58	109	2	19	0
1976	Pit-N	1.000	11	22	19	0	4	2
1977	Bos-A	1.000	1	4	3	0	0	0
Total	13	.983	1129	2688	3237	101	807	35

3B

1965	Cin-N	1.000	2	1	0	0	0	-1
1966	Cin-N	.961	113	110	208	13	16	-10
1968	Cin-N	1.000	1	0	2	0	0	0
1975	Hou-N	—	3	0	0	0	0	0
1976	Pit-N	.921	22	8	27	3	4	0
1977	Bos-A	1.000	2	0	1	0	0	0
Total	6	.957	143	119	238	6	20	-13

SS

1965	Cin-N	.973	8	15	21	1	5	-1
1967	Cin-N	.944	46	79	123	12	25	-10
1968	Cin-N	—	2	0	0	0	0	0
1969	Cin-N	1.000	4	5	3	0	2	0
1970	Cin-N	1.000	12	3	2	0	0	-1
1975	Hou-N	—	1	0	0	0	0	0
1976	Pit-N	—	1	0	0	0	0	0
Total	7	.951	74	102	149	3	32	-12

■ **Charlie Hemphill OF**

1899	StL-N	.750	10	13	2	5	1	-2
	Cle-N	.859	54	61	6	11	1	-8
	Yr	.837	64	74	8	16	2	-10
1901	Bos-A	.925	136	188	22	17	4	-4
1902	Cle-A	.860	19	34	3	6	0	-1
	StL-A	.952	101	164	15	9	6	-2
	Yr	.935	120	198	18	15	6	-3
1903	StL-A	.961	104	155	11	7	4	2
1904	StL-A	.926	108	177	12	15	5	-1
1906	StL-A	.961	154	307	17	13	1	1
1907	StL-A	.957	153	320	12	15	2	-2

YEAR	TM/L	PCT	G	PO	A	E	DP	FR
1908	NY-A	.937	142	285	13	20	2	-1
1909	NY-A	.976	45	75	6	2	1	-1
1910	NY-A	.971	94	159	10	5	2	-2
1911	NY-A	.952	55	95	4	5	0	-7
Total	11	.944	1175	2033	139	130	29	-28

2B

1902	StL-A	.875	2	2	5	1	1	-1
1904	StL-A	1.000	1	2	2	0	0	0
Total	2	.917	3	4	7	1	1	-1

■ **Rollie Hemsley C**

1928	Pit-N	.962	49	127	24	6	4	1
1929	Pit-N	.954	80	240	48	14	7	8
1930	Pit-N	.979	98	325	50	8	11	3
1931	Pit-N	1.000	9	35	5	0	0	1
	Chi-N	.975	53	236	40	7	5	6
	Yr	.978	62	271	45	7	5	7
1932	Chi-N	.974	47	173	17	5	3	1
1933	Cin-N	.970	41	109	22	4	1	5
	StL-A	.965	27	98	13	4	2	-3
1934	StL-A	.973	114	487	92	16	15	24
1935	StL-A	.979	141	510	105	13	10	9
1936	StL-A	.969	114	340	68	13	16	-11
1937	StL-A	.969	94	332	70	13	13	-6
1938	Cle-A	.980	58	358	38	8	5	15
1939	Cle-A	.984	106	499	58	9	7	6
1940	Cle-A	.994	117	591	65	4	8	8
1941	Cle-A	.980	96	401	42	9	8	-3
1942	Cin-N	.982	34	199	15	4	3	11
	NY-A	.991	29	103	11	1	3	1
1943	NY-A	.981	52	234	31	5	3	2
1944	NY-A	.983	76	298	41	6	7	-3
1946	Phi-N	.977	45	170	42	5	10	11
1947	Phi-N	1.000	2	3	0	0	0	0
Total	19	.978	1482	5868	897	154	141	86

OF

1932	Chi-N	1.000	1	1	1	0	0	1
1934	StL-A	1.000	6	12	0	0	0	0
Total	2	1.000	7	13	1	0	0	1

1B

1937	StL-A	1.000	2	6	1	0	0	0

■ **Solly Hemus SS**

1951	StL-N	.965	105	181	344	19	72	14
1952	StL-N	.960	148	253	452	29	104	3
1953	StL-N	.964	150	257	476	27	90	6
1954	StL-N	.944	66	49	102	9	18	-18
1955	StL-N	1.000	2	0	1	0	0	0
Total	5	.962	471	740	1375	4	284	5

2B

1949	StL-N	.981	16	29	24	1	4	2
1951	StL-N	.973	12	40	32	2	14	0
1953	StL-N	1.000	3	0	1	0	0	0
1954	StL-N	1.000	12	27	25	0	8	-1
1955	StL-N	1.000	10	18	20	0	3	-2
1956	Phi-N	.974	49	94	93	5	18	-25
1957	Phi-N	.980	24	51	45	2	10	-3
1958	Phi-N	.969	85	188	220	13	52	-14
1959	StL-N	1.000	1	0	3	0	0	0
Total	9	.975	212	447	463	3	109	-43

3B

1950	StL-N	1.000	5	2	8	0	1	1
1952	StL-N	.909	2	3	7	1	0	1
1954	StL-N	.971	27	9	24	1	3	-1
1955	StL-N	.956	43	38	70	5	7	-2
1956	Phi-N	1.000	1	1	2	0	0	0
1958	Phi-N	—	1	1	0	0	0	0
1959	StL-N	1.000	1	0	2	0	0	0
Total	7	.960	80	53	113	7	11	-1

■ **Dave Henderson OF**

1981	Sea-A	1.000	58	105	4	0	1	5
1982	Sea-A	.985	101	249	11	4	4	4
1983	Sea-A	.982	133	304	17	6	4	3
1984	Sea-A	.988	97	242	11	3	5	2
1985	Sea-A	.986	138	335	8	5	3	-6
1986	Sea-A	.979	80	182	9	4	1	8
	Bos-A	.981	32	49	2	1	0	5
	Yr	.980	112	231	11	5	1	13
1987	Bos-A	.958	64	114	0	5	0	-4
	SF-N	1.000	9	10	1	0	0	0
1988	Oak-A	.982	143	382	5	7	2	-2
1989	Oak-A	.977	149	385	5	9	1	0
1990	Oak-A	.988	116	319	5	4	1	3
Total	10	.983	1120	2676	78	8	22	18

■ **Ken Henderson OF**

1965	SF-N	.980	48	47	2	1	2	5
1966	SF-N	.917	10	11	0	1	0	-1
1967	SF-N	.947	52	86	3	5	1	-1
1968	SF-N	1.000	2	2	0	0	0	0
1969	SF-N	.969	111	175	10	6	2	-3
1970	SF-N	.966	146	272	15	10	2	5
1971	SF-N	.966	138	277	3	10	1	-4
1972	SF-N	.974	123	247	14	7	3	8
1973	Chi-A	.972	44	102	1	3	0	-1
1974	Chi-A	.987	162	462	7	6	3	6
1975	Chi-A	.990	137	394	7	4	0	20
1976	Atl-N	.987	122	219	3	3	0	-7
1977	Tex-A	.983	65	113	0	2	0	-8
1978	NY-N	1.000	7	15	0	0	0	0
	Cin-N	1.000	38	78	0	0	0	-1
	Yr	1.000	45	93	0	0	0	-1
1979	Cin-N	1.000	2	2	0	0	0	0
	Chi-N	.950	23	19	0	1	0	-3
	Yr	.955	25	21	0	1	0	-3
1980	Chi-N	.944	22	31	3	2	1	0
Total	16	.977	1252	2552	68	1	15	15

YEAR	TM/L	PCT	G	PO	A	E	DP	FR
		3B						
1969	SF-N	1.000	3	0	2	0	0	0
		1B						
1971	SF-N	—	1	0	0	0	0	0

■ Rickey Henderson OF

YEAR	TM/L	PCT	G	PO	A	E	DP	FR
1979	Oak-A	.973	88	215	5	6	0	6
1980	Oak-A	.984	157	407	15	7	1	17
1981	Oak-A	.979	107	**327**	7	7	0	18
1982	Oak-A	.977	144	379	2	9	0	6
1983	Oak-A	.992	142	349	9	3	1	8
1984	Oak-A	.969	140	341	7	11	1	6
1985	NY-A	.980	141	439	7	9	3	11
1986	NY-A	.986	146	426	4	6	0	5
1987	NY-A	.980	69	189	3	4	1	4
1988	NY-A	.965	136	320	7	12	**5**	6
1989	NY-A	.993	65	144	3	1	0	1
	Oak-A	.985	82	191	3	3	1	3
	Yr	.988	147	335	6	4	1	4
1990	Oak-A	.983	118	289	5	5	0	6
Total	12	.980	1535	4016	77	3	13	97

■ Steve Henderson OF

YEAR	TM/L	PCT	G	PO	A	E	DP	FR
1977	NY-N	.980	97	189	4	4	1	0
1978	NY-N	.968	155	315	18	11	3	6
1979	NY-N	.990	94	201	6	2	3	4
1980	NY-N	.981	136	299	7	6	1	5
1981	Chi-N	.951	77	152	4	**8**	2	-11
1982	Chi-N	.956	70	126	5	6	0	-3
1983	Sea-A	.970	112	182	15	6	2	-2
1984	Sea-A	.936	53	84	4	6	0	-4
1985	Oak-A	.953	58	79	3	4	0	-5
1986	Oak-A	.800	7	8	0	2	0	-1
1987	Oak-A	.943	31	33	0	2	0	-3
1988	Hou-N	1.000	8	12	1	0	0	1
Total	12	.968	898	1680	67	7	12	-13
		1B						
1988	Hou-N	1.000	1	2	0	0	0	0

■ George Hendrick OF

YEAR	TM/L	PCT	G	PO	A	E	DP	FR
1971	Oak-A	.981	36	52	1	1	0	-1
1972	Oak-A	1.000	41	68	0	0	0	1
1973	Cle-A	.988	110	242	7	3	1	-5
1974	Cle-A	.989	133	355	9	4	2	0
1975	Cle-A	.983	143	338	4	6	1	4
1976	Cle-A	.987	146	288	13	4	**6**	-11
1977	SD-N	.983	142	386	11	7	2	8
1978	SD-N	.986	33	72	1	1	0	1
	StL-N	.996	101	241	5	1	0	1
	Yr	.994	134	313	**6**	**2**	**0**	2
1979	StL-N	.993	138	254	20	2	7	7
1980	StL-N	.994	149	322	10	2	2	4
1981	StL-N	.983	101	227	6	4	0	-12
1982	StL-N	.980	134	238	6	5	1	-8
1983	StL-N	.989	51	85	2	1	0	-3
1984	StL-N	.990	116	188	9	2	1	-5
1985	Pit-N	.971	65	133	2	4	0	1
	Cal-A	1.000	12	18	1	0	0	0
1986	Cal-A	.968	93	144	6	5	2	0
1987	Cal-A	.967	45	58	1	2	0	-3
1988	Cal-A	.933	24	42	0	3	0	1
Total	18	.985	1813	3751	114	7	25	-20
		1B						
1983	StL-N	.992	92	819	77	7	72	2
1984	StL-N	1.000	1	1	0	0	0	0
1986	Cal-A	1.000	7	44	3	0	3	0
1987	Cal-A	.984	9	56	4	1	7	-1
1988	Cal-A	1.000	12	87	9	0	10	2
Total	5	.993	121	1007	93	8	92	3

■ Harvey Hendrick 1B

YEAR	TM/L	PCT	G	PO	A	E	DP	FR
1925	Cle-A	1.000	3	26	2	0	1	0
1927	Bro-N	.986	53	466	32	7	36	0
1929	Bro-N	.983	39	380	33	7	28	3
1930	Bro-N	1.000	7	24	1	0	4	0
1931	Cin-N	.987	137	1348	67	**18**	**147**	-5
1932	Cin-N	.986	94	922	60	14	72	-4
1933	Chi-N	.983	38	328	23	6	31	-1
1934	Phi-N	.978	7	45	0	1	4	-1
Total	8	.986	378	3539	218	3	323	-8
		OF						
1923	NY-A	.947	13	16	2	1	0	-2
1924	NY-A	.975	17	38	1	1	0	0
1927	Bro-N	.969	64	90	5	3	1	-6
1928	Bro-N	1.000	17	36	2	0	1	1
1929	Bro-N	.975	42	75	3	2	0	-2
1930	Bro-N	.947	42	68	4	4	2	-2
1932	StL-N	1.000	5	6	1	0	0	0
1933	Chi-N	.895	8	16	1	2	0	-1
1934	Phi-N	.962	12	24	1	1	0	-1
Total	9	.965	220	369	20	4	4	-13
		3B						
1928	Bro-N	.913	91	74	200	26	19	3
1929	Bro-N	.857	7	9	15	4	0	1
1932	StL-N	.862	12	8	17	4	3	-2
1933	Chi-N	1.000	1	0	1	0	0	0
1934	Phi-N	.800	7	0	8	2	0	-2
Total	5	.902	118	91	241	6	22	0
		SS						
1929	Bro-N	.824	4	3	11	3	1	-1
		2B						
1927	Bro-N	.875	1	4	3	1	1	0

■ Ellie Hendricks C

YEAR	TM/L	PCT	G	PO	A	E	DP	FR
1968	Bal-A	.991	53	303	21	3	3	-4
1969	Bal-A	**.998**	87	479	40	1	2	5
1970	Bal-A	.986	95	509	35	8	6	-7
1971	Bal-A	.985	90	429	33	7	5	-6
1972	Bal-A	.986	28	130	15	2	3	1
	Chi-N	.978	16	83	7	2	1	1

YEAR	TM/L	PCT	G	PO	A	E	DP	FR
1973	Bal-A	.994	38	148	9	1	1	4
1974	Bal-A	1.000	54	192	13	0	3	0
1975	Bal-A	**.995**	83	332	36	2	3	-1
1976	Bal-A	.971	27	87	13	3	1	-5
	NY-A	1.000	18	60	4	0	1	1
	Yr	.982	45	147	17	3	2	-4
1977	NY-A	1.000	6	11	0	0	0	0
1978	NY-A	.955	6	19	2	1	0	0
1979	Bal-A	.500	1	1	0	1	0	0
Total	12	.990	602	2783	228	1	29	-11
		1B						
1969	Bal-A	1.000	4	9	1	0	0	0
1971	Bal-A	1.000	3	24	1	0	3	0
1974	Bal-A	1.000	1	2	0	0	1	0
Total	3	1.000	8	35	2	0	4	0

■ Tim Hendryx OF

YEAR	TM/L	PCT	G	PO	A	E	DP	FR
1912	Cle-A	1.000	22	44	1	0	0	-2
1915	NY-A	.968	12	28	2	1	0	1
1916	NY-A	1.000	15	18	1	0	0	-2
1917	NY-A	.955	107	215	17	11	1	5
1918	StL-A	.982	65	108	4	2	2	-9
1920	Bos-A	.964	98	208	6	8	1	-10
1921	Bos-A	.958	41	66	2	3	0	-4
Total	7	.966	360	687	33	5	4	-21
		3B						
1911	Cle-A	1.000	3	2	3	0	0	-1

■ Butch Henline C

YEAR	TM/L	PCT	G	PO	A	E	DP	FR
1921	Phi-N	.987	32	113	44	2	5	9
1922	Phi-N	**.983**	119	400	113	9	13	2
1923	Phi-N	.978	96	288	71	8	8	-16
1924	Phi-N	.973	83	248	76	9	12	-1
1925	Phi-N	.956	68	209	53	12	9	-3
1926	Phi-N	.970	77	217	46	8	9	-9
1927	Bro-N	.947	60	216	50	15	6	1
1928	Bro-N	.976	45	141	22	4	3	-4
1929	Bro-N	.967	21	72	15	3	2	0
1930	Chi-A	1.000	3	10	2	0	0	0
1931	Chi-A	.889	4	14	2	2	0	1
Total	11	.971	608	1928	494	2	67	-20
		OF						
1923	Phi-N	1.000	1	3	0	0	0	0
1924	Phi-N	1.000	2	1	0	0	0	0
1925	Phi-N	1.000	1	2	0	0	0	0
1926	Phi-N	1.000	2	1	0	0	0	0
Total	4	1.000	6	7	0	0	0	0
		1B						
1926	Phi-N	.966	4	26	2	1	3	0

■ Tommy Henrich OF

YEAR	TM/L	PCT	G	PO	A	E	DP	FR
1937	NY-A	.970	59	90	6	3	1	-5
1938	NY-A	.984	130	239	14	4	1	-1
1939	NY-A	.991	88	205	7	2	1	1
1940	NY-A	.969	76	147	10	5	2	-2
1941	NY-A	.980	139	280	13	6	4	-2
1942	NY-A	.987	119	219	10	3	5	-3
1946	NY-A	.992	111	224	10	2	5	2
1947	NY-A	.983	132	278	13	5	2	5
1948	NY-A	.978	102	216	8	5	4	2
1949	NY-A	.958	61	110	5	5	2	-4
Total	10	.981	1017	2008	96	0	27	-7
		1B						
1939	NY-A	1.000	1	2	0	0	0	0
1940	NY-A	1.000	2	5	0	0	0	0
1942	NY-A	1.000	7	59	3	0	9	-1
1946	NY-A	.987	41	364	22	5	35	-3
1947	NY-A	1.000	6	59	1	0	6	-1
1948	NY-A	.984	46	352	21	6	41	-4
1949	NY-A	.996	52	445	28	2	64	-3
1950	NY-A	.987	34	224	7	3	23	-5
Total	8	.990	189	1510	82	6	178	-17

■ Olaf Henriksen OF

YEAR	TM/L	PCT	G	PO	A	E	DP	FR
1911	Bos-A	.953	25	38	3	2	1	0
1912	Bos-A	.909	11	10	0	1	0	-2
1913	Bos-A	1.000	7	9	0	0	0	-1
1914	Bos-A	.947	29	35	1	2	0	-5
1915	Bos-A	.967	25	27	2	1	2	-2
1916	Bos-A	1.000	31	43	2	0	0	-4
Total	6	.966	128	162	8	6	3	-16

■ John Henry C

YEAR	TM/L	PCT	G	PO	A	E	DP	FR
1910	Was-A	.989	18	60	28	1	4	1
1911	Was-A	.969	51	248	96	11	6	9
1912	Was-A	.977	65	347	113	11	7	8
1913	Was-A	**.982**	96	476	127	11	9	4
1914	Was-A	.980	92	513	124	13	9	6
1915	Was-A	.972	94	478	122	17	4	4
1916	Was-A	.981	116	538	124	13	17	-4
1917	Was-A	.988	59	274	54	4	6	1
1918	Bos-N	.964	38	121	38	6	5	1
Total	9	.978	629	3055	826	7	67	30
		1B						
1910	Was-A	1.000	10	105	7	0	6	1
1911	Was-A	.970	30	301	27	10	9	3
Total	2	.978	40	406	34	0	15	4

■ Babe Herman OF

YEAR	TM/L	PCT	G	PO	A	E	DP	FR
1926	Bro-N	.956	35	61	4	3	0	0
1927	Bro-N	1.000	1	1	0	0	0	0
1928	Bro-N	.937	127	225	12	**16**	2	-7
1929	Bro-N	.941	141	244	10	**16**	2	-13
1930	Bro-N	.978	153	260	10	6	1	-16
1931	Bro-N	.960	150	287	24	13	7	3
1932	Cin-N	.946	146	392	18	13	**6**	**15**
1933	Chi-N	.957	131	252	12	12	1	-6
1934	Chi-N	.971	113	192	7	6	2	-10
1935	Pit-N	.958	15	22	1	1	0	-2
	Cin-N	.976	76	156	5	4	0	-2

YEAR	TM/L	PCT	G	PO	A	E	DP	FR
	Yr	.974	91	178	6	5	0	-4
1936	Cin-N	.967	92	175	3	6	0	-8
1937	Det-A	1.000	2	3	0	0	0	0
1945	Bro-N	—	3	0	0	0	0	0
Total	13	.961	1185	2270	106	6	21	-46
		1B						
1926	Bro-N	.986	101	913	60	14	55	2
1927	Bro-N	.980	105	968	68	**21**	64	1
1929	Bro-N	.944	2	16	1	1	1	0
1934	Chi-N	.984	7	59	3	1	5	-1
1935	Pit-N	.900	3	18	0	2	1	-1
	Cin-N	.985	14	123	9	2	11	0
	Yr	.974	17	141	9	4	12	-1
1936	Cin-N	1.000	4	9	1	0	1	0
Total	6	.982	236	2106	142	1	138	1

■ Billy Herman 2B

YEAR	TM/L	PCT	G	PO	A	E	DP	FR
1931	Chi-N	.939	25	76	79	10	17	3
1932	Chi-N	.961	**154**	401	**527**	**38**	102	17
1933	Chi-N	.956	153	466	512	45	114	29
1934	Chi-N	.975	111	278	385	17	64	16
1935	Chi-N	**.964**	154	416	520	35	**109**	**19**
1936	Chi-N	**.975**	153	457	492	24	110	15
1937	Chi-N	.954	137	384	468	**41**	97	19
1938	Chi-N	**.981**	151	404	517	18	111	25
1939	Chi-N	.967	**156**	377	485	29	**95**	-3
1940	Chi-N	.974	135	**366**	448	22	94	**19**
1941	Chi-N	.898	11	33	20	6	5	-5
	Bro-N	.970	133	297	354	20	64	-27
	Yr	.964	**144**	**330**	374	26	**69**	-32
1942	Bro-N	.973	153	383	402	22	97	-11
1943	Bro-N	.971	117	291	322	18	69	-15
1946	Bro-N	1.000	16	42	36	0	5	-2
	Bos-N	.956	44	95	101	9	22	-12
	Yr	.968	60	137	137	9	27	-14
1947	Pit-N	1.000	10	14	13	0	2	-9
Total	15	.967	1813	4780	5681	354	1177	78
		3B						
1943	Bro-N	.976	37	54	68	3	2	-1
1946	Bro-N	.945	29	31	55	5	8	0
	Bos-N	.933	5	5	9	1	1	-1
	Yr	.943	34	36	64	6	9	-1
Total	2	.961	71	90	132	9	11	-2
		1B						
1942	Bro-N	.969	3	29	2	1	2	0
1946	Bos-N	.995	22	179	6	1	12	-3
1947	Pit-N	1.000	2	6	2	0	0	0
Total	3	.991	27	214	10	2	14	-3

■ Gene Hermanski OF

YEAR	TM/L	PCT	G	PO	A	E	DP	FR
1943	Bro-N	.976	17	36	4	1	1	2
1946	Bro-N	.938	34	45	0	3	0	-3
1947	Bro-N	.982	66	105	5	2	0	0
1948	Bro-N	.971	119	225	13	7	1	-1
1949	Bro-N	.980	77	140	7	3	1	-4
1950	Bro-N	.989	78	172	5	2	0	0
1951	Bro-N	.977	19	41	2	1	1	1
	Chi-N	.966	63	134	9	5	1	0
	Yr	.969	82	175	11	6	2	1
1952	Chi-N	.981	76	146	7	3	3	1
1953	Chi-N	1.000	13	18	0	0	0	-1
	Pit-N	1.000	13	26	0	0	0	0
	Yr	1.000	26	44	0	0	0	-1
Total	9	.977	575	1088	52	7	8	0

■ Enzo Hernandez SS

YEAR	TM/L	PCT	G	PO	A	E	DP	FR
1971	SD-N	.955	143	260	445	**33**	82	-11
1972	SD-N	.963	107	169	319	19	59	6
1973	SD-N	.977	67	106	190	7	42	-1
1974	SD-N	.966	145	229	449	24	64	-8
1975	SD-N	.965	111	168	327	18	70	8
1976	SD-N	.964	101	132	344	18	64	4
1977	SD-N	1.000	7	4	6	0	0	2
1978	LA-N	—	2	0	0	0	0	0
Total	8	.964	683	1068	2080	119	381	0
		OF						
1972	SD-N	—	3	0	0	0	0	0

■ Jackie Hernandez SS

YEAR	TM/L	PCT	G	PO	A	E	DP	FR
1965	Cal-A	1.000	2	0	1	0	0	5
1966	Cal-A	.933	8	6	8	1	1	5
1967	Min-A	.974	15	19	19	1	2	5
1968	Min-A	.927	79	119	197	25	43	9
1969	KC-A	.954	144	306	375	**33**	60	-15
1970	KC-A	.951	77	142	187	17	38	-5
1971	Pit-N	.950	75	105	235	18	42	10
1972	Pit-N	.929	68	110	180	22	34	**16**
1973	Pit-N	.940	49	45	81	8	19	7
Total	9	.945	517	852	1283	125	239	42
		3B						
1965	Cal-A	.600	1	1	2	2	0	0
1966	Cal-A	.857	11	2	4	1	0	2
1967	Min-A	.929	13	8	5	1	2	1
1971	Pit-N	1.000	9	4	17	0	0	2
1972	Pit-N	1.000	4	0	2	0	0	0
Total	5	.918	38	15	30	4	2	5
		2B						
1966	Cal-A	.926	8	13	12	2	6	10
		OF						
1966	Cal-A	1.000	3	1	0	0	0	0
		1B						
1968	Min-A	1.000	1	3	0	0	1	0

■ Keith Hernandez 1B

YEAR	TM/L	PCT	G	PO	A	E	DP	FR
1974	StL-N	.973	9	70	1	2	8	-2
1975	StL-N	.996	56	469	36	2	34	3
1976	StL-N	.990	110	862	**107**	10	87	**16**
1977	StL-N	.992	158	1453	106	12	**146**	5
1978	StL-N	.994	158	1436	96	10	124	5
1979	StL-N	.995	160	**1489**	146	8	145	19

YEAR	TM/L	PCT	G	PO	A	E	DP	FR
1980	StL-N	.995	157	1572	115	9	146	5
1981	StL-N	.997	98	1054	86	3	99	7
1982	StL-N	.994	158	1586	135	11	140	7
1983	StL-N	.991	54	581	51	6	62	3
	NY-N	.993	90	837	96	7	85	10
	Yr	.992	144	1418	147	13	147	13
1984	NY-N	.994	153	1214	142	8	127	18
1985	NY-N	.997	157	1310	139	4	113	15
1986	NY-N	.996	149	1199	149	5	115	18
1987	NY-N	.993	154	1298	149	10	110	18
1988	NY-N	.998	93	734	77	2	63	8
1989	NY-N	.991	58	405	31	4	22	-1
1990	Cle-A	.994	42	340	20	2	28	-2
Total	17	.994	2014	17909	1682	115	1654	150
OF								
1981	StL-N	1.000	3	2	0	0	0	0
1982	StL-N	1.000	4	5	0	0	0	0
Total	2	1.000	7	7	0	0	0	0

■ Larry Herndon OF

YEAR	TM/L	PCT	G	PO	A	E	DP	FR
1974	SF-N	1.000	1	1	0	0	0	1
1976	SF-N	.967	110	226	8	8	4	-11
1977	SF-N	.957	44	87	2	4	0	6
1978	SF-N	.974	149	369	3	10	0	-3
1979	SF-N	.963	122	196	10	8	2	-5
1980	SF-N	.959	122	247	8	11	1	-1
1981	SF-N	.977	93	207	8	5	1	5
1982	Det-A	.983	155	328	11	6	3	1
1983	Det-A	.951	133	283	6	15	1	-3
1984	Det-A	.986	117	199	7	3	0	-8
1985	Det-A	.976	136	273	7	7	4	-1
1986	Det-A	.988	83	156	2	2	0	-1
1987	Det-A	.989	57	82	4	1	1	0
1988	Det-A	1.000	15	21	0	0	0	0
Total	14	.972	1337	2675	76	0	17	-20

■ Tom Herr 2B

YEAR	TM/L	PCT	G	PO	A	E	DP	FR
1979	StL-N	1.000	6	12	11	0	3	6
1980	StL-N	.984	58	107	136	4	37	-1
1981	StL-N	.992	103	211	374	5	74	4
1982	StL-N	.987	128	263	427	9	97	4
1983	StL-N	.986	86	178	245	6	60	-18
1984	StL-N	.992	144	328	452	6	106	-1
1985	StL-N	.985	158	337	448	12	120	-31
1986	StL-N	.988	152	352	414	9	121	-22
1987	StL-N	.989	137	306	350	7	103	-17
1988	StL-N	.984	15	28	35	1	9	-6
	Min-A	.988	73	140	195	4	54	-8
1989	Phi-N	.990	144	281	415	7	80	-2
1990	Phi-N	.991	114	240	290	5	79	-3
	NY-N	.979	26	35	59	2	15	-5
	Yr	.989	140	275	349	7	94	-8
Total	12	.989	1344	2818	3851	7	958	-96
SS								
1980	StL-N	.956	14	17	48	3	10	3
1988	Min-A	—	2	0	0	0	0	0
Total	2	.956	16	17	48	3	10	3

■ Pancho Herrera 1B

YEAR	TM/L	PCT	G	PO	A	E	DP	FR
1958	Phi-N	1.000	11	31	4	0	3	1
1960	Phi-N	.988	134	1017	109	14	88	8
1961	Phi-N	.993	115	1003	96	8	104	6
Total	3	.990	260	2051	209	2	195	15
2B								
1960	Phi-N	.988	17	36	46	1	11	3
3B								
1958	Phi-N	.980	16	21	27	1	3	1

■ Ed Herrmann C

YEAR	TM/L	PCT	G	PO	A	E	DP	FR
1967	Chi-A	1.000	2	12	1	0	0	1
1969	Chi-A	.983	92	420	41	8	7	-1
1970	Chi-A	.988	88	433	51	6	10	6
1971	Chi-A	.995	97	556	56	3	5	10
1972	Chi-A	.989	112	641	69	8	10	2
1973	Chi-A	.984	114	616	70	11	11	8
1974	Chi-A	.987	107	561	55	8	8	4
1975	NY-A	.979	24	121	18	3	5	7
1976	Cal-A	.954	27	74	9	4	1	-5
	Hou-N	.987	79	412	37	6	5	1
1977	Hou-N	.990	49	280	29	3	2	10
1978	Hou-N	1.000	14	65	3	0	0	0
	Mon-N	.977	12	39	3	1	1	-1
	Yr	.991	26	104	6	1	1	-1
Total	11	.987	817	4230	442	1	65	42

■ Mike Hershberger OF

YEAR	TM/L	PCT	G	PO	A	E	DP	FR
1961	Chi-A	1.000	13	29	2	0	0	1
1962	Chi-A	.984	135	236	7	4	0	-4
1963	Chi-A	.976	119	230	13	6	3	5
1964	Chi-A	.984	134	231	10	4	2	2
1965	KC-A	.988	144	238	14	3	7	5
1966	KC-A	.977	143	285	14	7	3	9
1967	KC-A	.982	130	206	17	4	2	6
1968	Oak-A	.978	90	128	5	3	0	-5
1969	Oak-A	.980	35	50	0	1	0	-4
1970	Mil-A	.946	35	34	1	2	0	-3
1971	Chi-A	.960	59	96	1	4	0	-2
Total	11	.980	1037	1763	84	8	17	10

■ Willard Hershberger C

YEAR	TM/L	PCT	G	PO	A	E	DP	FR
1938	Cin-N	.960	39	108	13	5	2	0
1939	Cin-N	.987	60	204	21	3	2	-2
1940	Cin-N	.985	37	121	11	2	0	-2
Total	3	.980	136	433	45	0	4	-4
2B								
1938	Cin-N	.000	1	0	0	1	0	-1

■ Buck Herzog 2B

YEAR	TM/L	PCT	G	PO	A	E	DP	FR
1908	NY-N	.921	42	61	125	16	19	3
1909	NY-N	.750	6	2	1	1	0	0
1911	NY-N	1.000	3	6	6	0	0	0
1913	NY-N	1.000	2	2	3	0	0	0
1916	NY-N	.978	44	90	128	5	18	4
1917	NY-N	.948	113	251	327	32	60	-9
1918	Bos-N	.961	99	240	322	23	43	7
1919	Bos-N	.953	70	130	191	16	23	-14
	Chi-N	.987	52	81	151	3	14	-11
	Yr	.967	122	211	342	19	37	-25
1920	Chi-N	.938	59	128	175	20	25	-9
Total	9	.954	490	991	1429	116	203	-30
3B								
1908	NY-N	1.000	4	0	1	0	0	0
1909	NY-N	1.000	4	1	3	0	0	0
1910	Bos-N	.915	105	110	223	31	17	4
1911	Bos-N	1.000	4	6	11	0	2	2
	NY-N	.926	65	86	138	18	7	9
	Yr	.931	69	92	149	18	9	11
1912	NY-N	.942	140	159	308	29	21	19
1913	NY-N	.947	84	95	139	13	18	1
1916	Cin-N	1.000	12	15	21	0	1	0
	NY-N	.952	27	29	70	5	4	6
	Yr	.964	39	44	91	5	5	6
1920	Chi-N	.910	28	25	66	9	7	3
Total	8	.935	473	526	980	105	77	44
SS								
1908	NY-N	.902	12	22	33	6	2	-2
1909	NY-N	1.000	1	1	1	0	1	0
1911	Bos-N	.934	74	149	249	28	31	6
	NY-N	1.000	1	2	0	0	0	0
	Yr	.935	75	151	249	28	31	6
1914	Cin-N	.939	137	324	474	52	58	31
1915	Cin-N	.945	153	391	513	53	90	30
1916	Cin-N	.931	65	162	203	27	30	-2
	NY-N	.897	9	21	40	7	6	4
	Yr	.926	74	183	243	34	36	2
1918	Bos-N	.868	7	19	14	5	1	-3
Total	7	.936	459	1091	1527	178	219	64
OF								
1908	NY-N	—	1	0	0	0	0	0
1909	NY-N	.914	29	49	4	5	1	-2
1916	Cin-N	—	1	0	0	0	0	0
Total	3	.914	31	49	4	5	1	-2
1B								
1914	Cin-N	.955	2	20	1	1	2	0
1915	Cin-N	1.000	2	9	2	0	0	1
1918	Bos-N	.984	12	115	6	2	6	-1
1919	Bos-N	1.000	1	2	0	0	0	0
1920	Chi-N	1.000	1	1	0	0	0	0
Total	5	.981	18	147	9	3	8	0

■ Whitey Herzog OF

YEAR	TM/L	PCT	G	PO	A	E	DP	FR
1956	Was-A	.980	103	240	9	5	0	8
1957	Was-A	.981	28	53	0	1	0	0
1958	Was-A	1.000	7	5	0	0	0	0
	KC-A	.968	37	30	0	1	0	1
	Yr	.972	44	35	0	1	0	1
1959	KC-A	.963	34	77	2	3	1	0
1960	KC-A	.985	69	128	4	2	1	2
1961	Bal-A	1.000	98	143	2	0	0	-12
1962	Bal-A	.978	70	132	4	3	0	-1
1963	Det-A	1.000	4	4	0	0	0	0
Total	8	.982	450	812	21	5	2	-6
1B								
1956	Was-A	.946	5	34	1	2	3	-1
1958	KC-A	.983	22	111	6	2	9	0
1959	KC-A	1.000	1	10	0	0	0	0
1960	KC-A	.846	2	9	2	2	2	0
1963	Det-A	.976	7	40	1	1	2	-1
Total	5	.968	37	204	10	7	16	-2

■ Johnny Heving C

YEAR	TM/L	PCT	G	PO	A	E	DP	FR
1924	Bos-A	.969	29	93	33	4	1	3
1925	Bos-A	.958	34	103	35	6	1	2
1928	Bos-A	.967	62	153	25	6	2	-4
1929	Bos-A	.988	55	207	40	3	4	5
1930	Bos-A	.987	71	195	35	3	7	-4
1931	Phi-A	.993	40	139	11	1	0	3
1932	Phi-A	1.000	28	85	5	0	2	-1
Total	7	.981	319	975	184	3	17	4

■ Mike Heydon C

YEAR	TM/L	PCT	G	PO	A	E	DP	FR
1898	Bal-N	.917	3	8	3	1	1	-1
1899	Was-A	.833	2	3	2	1	0	0
1901	StL-N	.941	13	54	10	4	2	-2
1904	Was-A	1.000	4	16	5	0	1	2
1905	Was-A	.955	77	368	125	23	7	11
1906	Was-A	.937	49	200	68	18	4	-1
1907	Was-A	.961	57	247	52	12	4	-7
Total	7	.952	205	896	265	9	19	2
OF								
1901	StL-N	—	1	0	0	0	0	-1

■ Jack Hiatt C

YEAR	TM/L	PCT	G	PO	A	E	DP	FR
1964	LA-A	.889	3	8	0	1	0	-2
1965	SF-N	.987	21	71	7	1	1	-1
1967	SF-N	.941	3	15	1	1	0	-1
1968	SF-N	.994	58	328	31	2	4	-2
1969	SF-N	.992	60	335	30	3	6	0
1970	Mon-N	.961	12	73	1	3	0	-3
	Chi-N	.990	63	380	22	4	1	5
	Yr	.986	75	453	23	7	1	2
1971	Hou-N	.991	65	329	20	3	6	-1
1972	Hou-N	1.000	10	36	4	0	1	-3
	Cal-A	1.000	17	48	4	0	0	-8
Total		.970	312	1623	120	8	19	-16
1B								
1964	LA-A	1.000	2	9	2	0	2	0
1965	SF-N	.962	7	48	3	2	3	0
1966	SF-N	.982	7	49	6	1	4	1
1967	SF-N	.990	36	288	17	3	25	-1
1968	SF-N	1.000	10	59	6	0	2	1
1969	SF-N	1.000	3	24	0	0	4	-1
1970	Mon-N	1.000	2	6	0	0	0	0
	Chi-N	1.000	2	7	1	0	0	0
	Yr	1.000	4	13	1	0	0	0
1971	Hou-N	—	1	0	0	0	0	0
Total	8	.989	70	490	35	6	40	0
OF								
1967	SF-N	—	2	0	0	0	0	0

■ Charlie Hickman 1B

YEAR	TM/L	PCT	G	PO	A	E	DP	FR
1898	Bos-N	.938	6	59	2	4	8	-1
1899	Bos-N	.778	1	7	0	2	2	-1
1901	NY-N	1.000	2	16	3	0	0	1
1902	Cle-A	.966	98	1079	47	40	63	-7
1903	Cle-A	.972	125	1310	66	40	67	-8
1904	Cle-A	.967	40	391	22	14	17	-3
	Det-A	.970	39	396	23	13	18	-2
	Yr	.969	79	787	45	27	35	-5
1905	Det-A	.957	12	103	8	5	4	0
	Was-A	.972	3	33	2	1	1	0
	Yr	.961	15	136	10	6	5	0
1906	Was-A	.977	18	160	9	4	8	-1
1907	Was-A	.965	30	289	16	11	12	-2
1908	Cle-A	.966	20	214	15	8	6	0
Total	10	.968	394	4057	213	142	206	-24
OF								
1898	Bos-N	1.000	7	17	1	0	0	1
1899	Bos-N	.842	7	16	0	3	0	-1
1900	NY-N	.923	7	11	1	1	0	0
1901	NY-N	.904	50	58	8	7	1	-4
1902	Bos-N	.939	27	60	2	4	0	1
1904	Cle-A	.667	1	2	0	1	0	0
1905	Det-A	.940	47	72	7	5	3	3
1906	Was-A	.955	95	137	12	7	2	0
1907	Was-A	.931	18	23	4	2	1	1
	Chi-A	.667	3	2	0	1	0	-1
	Yr	.906	21	25	4	3	1	0
1908	Cle-A	.907	28	34	5	4	1	0
Total	10	.931	290	432	40	5	8	0
2B								
1901	NY-N	.957	7	7	15	1	1	-2
1902	Cle-A	.857	3	1	5	1	0	0
1903	Cle-A	.875	7	13	22	5	2	1
1904	Cle-A	.943	45	85	147	14	7	2
1905	Was-A	.922	85	170	281	38	19	7
1906	Was-A	1.000	1	4	4	0	0	0
1907	Was-A	.714	3	4	6	4	0	-3
1908	Cle-A	.750	1	0	3	1	0	0
Total	8	.923	152	284	483	4	29	5
3B								
1900	NY-N	.842	120	183	276	86	19	-5
1901	NY-N	.839	15	20	32	10	2	1
1906	Was-A	.900	5	4	14	2	0	0
Total	3	.844	140	207	322	8	21	0
SS								
1901	NY-N	.892	23	47	77	15	4	-3

■ Jim Hickman OF

YEAR	TM/L	PCT	G	PO	A	E	DP	FR
1915	Bal-F	.963	20	45	7	2	2	4
1916	Bro-N	1.000	3	2	0	0	0	0
1917	Bro-N	.942	101	222	22	15	6	2
1918	Bro-N	.914	46	76	9	8	1	-2
1919	Bro-N	.962	29	47	3	2	1	1
Total	5	.941	199	392	41	7	10	5

■ Jim Hickman OF

YEAR	TM/L	PCT	G	PO	A	E	DP	FR
1962	NY-N	.971	124	265	7	8	0	-9
1963	NY-N	.963	82	149	6	6	2	-6
1964	NY-N	.976	113	237	8	6	1	-4
1965	NY-N	.965	91	136	3	5	0	-1
1966	NY-N	.986	45	63	5	1	2	3
1967	LA-N	1.000	37	52	2	0	1	3
1968	Chi-N	.975	66	115	4	3	0	-1
1969	Chi-N	.981	125	153	6	3	0	-13
1970	Chi-N	.974	79	143	7	4	1	-2
1971	Chi-N	.982	69	106	3	2	0	-7
1972	Chi-N	1.000	27	38	0	0	0	-3
1973	Chi-N	1.000	13	13	0	0	0	0
Total	12	.976	871	1470	51	8	7	-41
1B								
1965	NY-N	.992	30	240	20	2	20	2
1966	NY-N	.992	17	120	12	1	14	2
1967	LA-N	1.000	2	2	0	0	0	0
1970	Chi-N	.990	74	563	60	6	46	5
1971	Chi-N	.997	44	364	31	1	28	1
1972	Chi-N	.992	77	670	70	6	61	10
1973	Chi-N	.988	51	398	31	5	37	-1
1974	StL-N	.986	14	64	7	1	13	1
Total	8	.992	309	2421	231	2	219	22
3B								
1963	NY-N	.914	59	45	103	14	14	0
1964	NY-N	—	1	0	0	0	0	0
1965	NY-N	.889	14	10	6	2	2	-1
1967	LA-N	1.000	1	1	0	0	1	0
1974	StL-N	1.000	1	1	0	0	1	0
Total	5	.912	77	56	110	6	17	-1

■ Joe Hicks OF

YEAR	TM/L	PCT	G	PO	A	E	DP	FR
1959	Chi-A	1.000	4	3	1	0	0	1
1960	Chi-A	1.000	14	14	0	0	0	1
1961	Was-A	1.000	7	14	1	0	0	1
1962	Was-A	.962	42	74	1	3	1	1
1963	NY-N	.966	41	83	1	3	0	1
Total	5	.970	108	188	4	6	1	3

■ Mike Higgins 3B

YEAR	TM/L	PCT	G	PO	A	E	DP	FR
1930	Phi-A	1.000	5	2	6	0	0	-1
1933	Phi-A	.947	152	159	270	24	23	-6
1934	Phi-A	.914	144	147	247	37	34	-19

(continued)

YEAR	TM/L	PCT	G	PO	A	E	DP	FR
1935	Phi-A	.947	131	162	214	21	15	-14
1936	Phi-A	.941	145	151	266	26	24	-14
1937	Bos-A	.935	152	161	258	29	29	-17
1938	Bos-A	.914	138	140	272	39	28	-10
1939	Det-A	.914	130	140	241	36	22	-11
1940	Det-A	.928	129	133	239	29	16	-11
1941	Det-A	.946	145	153	304	26	14	1
1942	Det-A	.926	137	134	243	30	24	-13
1943	Det-A	.940	138	156	253	26	22	-7
1944	Det-A	.954	146	146	311	22	21	-7
1946	Det-A	.949	17	12	25	2	2	-2
	Bos-A	.947	59	52	109	9	14	0
	Yr	.947	76	64	134	11	16	-2
Total	14	.935	1768	1848	3258	356	288	131

2B

YEAR	TM/L	PCT	G	PO	A	E	DP	FR
1930	Phi-A	—	2	0	0	0	0	0

SS

YEAR	TM/L	PCT	G	PO	A	E	DP	FR
1930	Phi-A	1.000	1	1	1	0	0	0

■ Andy High 3B

YEAR	TM/L	PCT	G	PO	A	E	DP	FR
1922	Bro-N	.958	130	131	257	17	23	3
1923	Bro-N	.969	80	98	150	8	13	3
1924	Bro-N	1.000	1	2	5	0	1	2
1925	Bro-N	.857	11	6	12	3	2	-4
	Bos-N	.979	60	47	93	3	7	-9
	Yr	.963	71	53	105	6	9	-13
1926	Bos-N	.962	81	99	155	10	15	2
1927	Bos-N	.915	89	93	122	20	9	-21
1928	StL-N	.935	73	56	117	12	10	-15
1929	StL-N	.967	123	91	204	10	17	-16
1930	StL-N	.990	48	34	68	1	5	-6
1931	StL-N	1.000	23	13	26	0	5	-2
1932	Cin-N	.950	46	34	62	5	2	-9
1933	Cin-N	.966	11	8	20	1	1	1
1934	Phi-N	.906	14	13	16	3	3	-2
Total	13	.956	790	725	1307	93	113	-73

2B

YEAR	TM/L	PCT	G	PO	A	E	DP	FR
1922	Bro-N	1.000	1	1	3	0	0	0
1923	Bro-N	1.000	5	2	4	0	2	1
1924	Bro-N	.964	133	295	437	27	55	-11
1925	Bro-N	.938	11	27	34	4	6	-1
	Bos-N	1.000	1	0	2	0	0	0
	Yr	.940	12	27	36	4	6	-1
1926	Bos-N	.932	49	101	132	17	21	-8
1927	Bos-N	1.000	8	18	25	0	6	1
1928	StL-N	.976	19	35	47	2	10	-4
1929	StL-N	.976	22	59	61	3	16	-3
1930	StL-N	1.000	3	3	3	0	0	0
1931	StL-N	.983	19	19	38	1	4	-2
1932	Cin-N	.923	12	9	15	2	5	-1
1933	Cin-N	1.000	2	0	1	0	0	0
1934	Phi-N	1.000	2	1	1	0	0	0
Total	13	.961	287	570	803	56	125	-28

SS

YEAR	TM/L	PCT	G	PO	A	E	DP	FR
1922	Bro-N	.938	22	35	56	6	6	-8
1923	Bro-N	.935	45	94	122	15	23	-12
1924	Bro-N	.971	17	31	36	2	4	0
1925	Bro-N	1.000	3	0	2	0	1	0
1927	Bos-N	1.000	2	2	0	0	0	0
Total	5	.943	89	162	216	23	34	-20

■ Hugh High OF

YEAR	TM/L	PCT	G	PO	A	E	DP	FR
1913	Det-A	.982	52	104	8	2	0	1
1914	Det-A	.959	53	92	2	4	1	-7
1915	NY-A	.981	117	254	10	5	1	-1
1916	NY-A	.950	110	216	14	12	2	-1
1917	NY-A	.986	100	188	16	3	3	0
1918	NY-A	1.000	4	6	1	0	1	0
Total	6	.972	436	860	51	26	8	-8

■ Dick Higham OF

YEAR	TM/L	PCT	G	PO	A	E	DP	FR
1876	Har-N	.869	59	57	16	11	1	1
1878	Pro-N	.811	62	76	27	24	4	1
1880	Tro-N	—	1	0	0	0	0	0
Total	3	.834	122	133	43	35	5	2

C

YEAR	TM/L	PCT	G	PO	A	E	DP	FR
1876	Har-N	.788	13	38	14	14	0	-4
1878	Pro-N	.667	1	1	1	1	0	0
1880	Tro-N	1.000	1	1	0	0	0	-2
Total	3	.786	15	40	15	15	0	-6

SS

YEAR	TM/L	PCT	G	PO	A	E	DP	FR
1876	Har-N	.800	1	1	3	1	0	0

2B

YEAR	TM/L	PCT	G	PO	A	E	DP	FR
1876	Har-N	1.000	1	3	2	0	0	0

■ Don Hill 2B

YEAR	TM/L	PCT	G	PO	A	E	DP	FR
1984	Oak-A	1.000	4	3	3	0	0	0
1985	Oak-A	.973	122	228	320	15	56	-41
1986	Oak-A	.984	68	92	150	4	27	-9
1987	Chi-A	.987	84	153	223	5	47	-24
1988	Chi-A	.975	59	106	132	6	36	-11
1990	Cal-A	.990	60	128	173	3	48	9
Total	6	.981	397	710	1001	33	214	-76

SS

YEAR	TM/L	PCT	G	PO	A	E	DP	FR
1983	Oak-A	.961	53	87	136	9	24	0
1984	Oak-A	.949	66	99	125	12	28	-12
1986	Oak-A	—	2	0	0	0	0	0
1990	Cal-A	.965	24	35	47	3	7	-4
Total	4	.957	145	221	308	24	59	-16

3B

YEAR	TM/L	PCT	G	PO	A	E	DP	FR
1984	Oak-A	—	2	0	0	0	0	0
1986	Oak-A	.938	33	12	63	5	4	-3
1987	Chi-A	.885	32	14	55	9	8	-5
1988	Chi-A	.941	12	12	20	2	2	0
1990	Cal-A	.891	21	8	33	5	4	-1
Total	5	.912	100	46	171	21	18	-9

1B

YEAR	TM/L	PCT	G	PO	A	E	DP	FR
1990	Cal-A	1.000	3	23	2	0	5	0

■ Hunter Hill 3B

YEAR	TM/L	PCT	G	PO	A	E	DP	FR
1903	StL-A	.923	86	110	165	23	10	-1
1904	StL-A	.826	56	78	79	33	3	-16
	Was-A	.895	71	86	126	25	4	-5
	Yr	.864	127	164	205	58	7	-21
1905	Was-A	.908	103	130	206	34	10	-1
Total	3	.895	316	404	576	115	27	-23

OF

YEAR	TM/L	PCT	G	PO	A	E	DP	FR
1904	StL-A	1.000	1	1	0	0	0	0
	Was-A	.833	5	5	0	1	0	-1
	Yr	.857	6	6	0	1	0	-1

■ Jesse Hill OF

YEAR	TM/L	PCT	G	PO	A	E	DP	FR
1935	NY-A	.951	94	203	9	11	1	3
1936	Was-A	.967	60	83	5	3	1	-8
1937	Was-A	.986	21	73	0	1	0	3
	Phi-A	.954	68	163	4	8	0	-8
	Yr	.964	89	236	4	9	0	-5
Total	3	.959	243	522	18	23	2	-10

■ Marc Hill C

YEAR	TM/L	PCT	G	PO	A	E	DP	FR
1973	StL-N	1.000	1	5	0	0	0	0
1974	StL-N	1.000	9	41	5	0	0	3
1975	SF-N	.994	60	282	27	2	7	1
1976	SF-N	.995	49	185	24	1	3	0
1977	SF-N	.989	102	505	57	6	4	-4
1978	SF-N	.986	116	586	56	9	3	-1
1979	SF-N	.991	58	283	31	3	4	-6
1980	SF-N	.972	14	61	8	2	2	2
	Sea-N	.991	29	101	10	1	0	-1
1981	Chi-A	1.000	14	11	1	0	0	1
1982	Chi-A	.993	49	135	15	1	2	4
1983	Chi-A	.991	55	214	12	2	1	5
1984	Chi-A	.991	72	308	17	3	4	0
1985	Chi-A	.985	37	185	11	3	1	7
1986	Chi-A	1.000	22	59	7	0	0	7
Total	14	.990	687	2961	281	33	31	18

1B

YEAR	TM/L	PCT	G	PO	A	E	DP	FR
1976	SF-N	1.000	1	1	0	0	0	0
1978	SF-N	1.000	2	6	0	0	0	0
1979	SF-N	1.000	1	2	0	0	1	0
1981	Chi-A	—	1	0	0	0	0	0
1982	Chi-A	1.000	1	1	1	0	0	0
1983	Chi-A	1.000	1	1	0	0	0	0
1984	Chi-A	1.000	2	7	0	0	2	0
Total	7	1.000	9	18	1	0	3	0

3B

YEAR	TM/L	PCT	G	PO	A	E	DP	FR
1975	SF-N	—	1	0	0	0	0	0
1981	Chi-A	—	1	0	0	0	0	0
1982	Chi-A	—	1	0	0	0	0	0
1985	Chi-A	1.000	1	0	2	0	0	0
Total	4	1.000	4	0	2	0	0	0

■ Chuck Hiller 2B

YEAR	TM/L	PCT	G	PO	A	E	DP	FR
1961	SF-N	.973	67	133	158	8	34	-14
1962	SF-N	.964	161	367	417	29	105	-18
1963	SF-N	.963	109	224	277	19	48	-15
1964	SF-N	.977	60	111	143	6	29	2
1965	SF-N	1.000	2	0	1	0	0	-1
	NY-N	.959	80	145	182	14	39	-11
	Yr	.959	82	145	183	14	39	-12
1966	NY-N	.981	45	85	123	4	31	9
1967	NY-N	.968	14	24	37	2	9	2
	Phi-N	.947	6	9	9	1	1	-3
	Yr	.963	20	33	46	3	10	-1
1968	Pit-N	.857	2	4	2	1	0	0
Total	8	.967	546	1102	1349	84	296	-49

3B

YEAR	TM/L	PCT	G	PO	A	E	DP	FR
1964	SF-N	.800	1	2	2	1	0	0
1965	NY-N	1.000	2	3	0	0	0	0
1966	NY-N	.975	14	9	30	1	1	2
Total	3	.958	17	14	32	2	1	2

OF

YEAR	TM/L	PCT	G	PO	A	E	DP	FR
1965	NY-N	1.000	4	3	0	0	0	0
1966	NY-N	1.000	9	16	0	0	0	-1
Total	2	1.000	13	19	0	0	0	-1

■ Dave Hilton 3B

YEAR	TM/L	PCT	G	PO	A	E	DP	FR
1972	SD-N	.939	13	12	19	2	1	-3
1973	SD-N	.970	47	40	88	4	11	0
1974	SD-N	.948	55	51	94	8	13	-3
1975	SD-N	.900	4	2	7	1	0	1
Total	4	.954	119	105	208	15	25	-5

2B

YEAR	TM/L	PCT	G	PO	A	E	DP	FR
1973	SD-N	.979	23	39	53	2	8	-5
1974	SD-N	.905	15	19	19	4	4	-1
Total	2	.956	38	58	72	6	12	-6

■ Bill Hinchman OF

YEAR	TM/L	PCT	G	PO	A	E	DP	FR
1905	Cin-N	.905	12	18	1	2	1	-1
1906	Cin-N	.963	16	23	3	1	2	1
1907	Cle-A	.958	148	231	18	11	3	-5
1908	Cle-A	.975	75	106	13	3	1	2
1909	Cle-A	.918	131	241	18	23	1	2
1915	Pit-N	.969	156	261	17	9	5	-3
1916	Pit-N	.962	124	222	8	9	2	-7
1917	Pit-N	.945	48	99	5	6	0	-1
1918	Pit-N	1.000	40	28	8	0	0	-1
Total	9	.954	750	1229	91	64	15	-13

1B

YEAR	TM/L	PCT	G	PO	A	E	DP	FR
1905	Cin-N	1.000	1	10	0	0	0	0
1907	Cle-A	1.000	4	47	4	0	3	1
1908	Cle-A	1.000	4	42	3	0	0	0
1916	Pit-N	.976	31	274	12	7	10	-2
1917	Pit-N	.974	20	176	13	5	10	0
1918	Pit-N	.893	3	23	2	3	0	0
Total	6	.976	63	572	34	15	23	-1

SS

YEAR	TM/L	PCT	G	PO	A	E	DP	FR
1908	Cle-A	.892	51	88	185	33	26	-9
1909	Cle-A	.867	6	8	18	4	3	-1
Total	2	.890	57	96	203	7	29	-10

3B

YEAR	TM/L	PCT	G	PO	A	E	DP	FR
1905	Cin-N	.727	4	3	5	3	0	-1

2B

YEAR	TM/L	PCT	G	PO	A	E	DP	FR
1907	Cle-A	—	1	0	0	0	0	0

■ Paul Hines OF

YEAR	TM/L	PCT	G	PO	A	E	DP	FR
1876	Chi-N	.923	64	159	8	14	4	3
1877	Chi-N	.806	49	75	4	19	1	-4
1878	Pro-N	.849	61	109	15	22	4	2
1879	Pro-N	.867	85	146	24	26	3	5
1880	Pro-N	.927	75	148	17	13	7	6
1881	Pro-N	.897	78	178	14	22	2	0
1882	Pro-N	.861	82	151	16	27	4	-1
1883	Pro-N	.905	89	169	21	20	2	2
1884	Pro-N	.895	108	202	20	26	5	0
1885	Pro-N	.865	92	199	18	34	3	2
1886	Was-N	.899	92	167	19	21	1	2
1887	Was-N	.886	109	180	14	25	5	-14
1888	Ind-N	.912	125	255	13	26	3	-7
1889	Ind-N	1.000	12	31	4	0	0	2
1890	Pit-N	.838	14	29	2	6	1	-1
	Bos-N	.881	69	114	4	16	2	-12
	Yr	.871	83	143	6	22	3	-13
1891	Was-a	.856	47	81	8	15	4	-3
Total	16	.887	1251	2393	221	332	51	-18

1B

YEAR	TM/L	PCT	G	PO	A	E	DP	FR
1880	Pro-N	1.000	4	50	1	0	3	0
1881	Pro-N	—	1	0	0	0	0	0
1882	Pro-N	.923	2	24	0	2	3	0
1883	Pro-N	.963	9	99	6	4	8	1
1884	Pro-N	.955	7	64	0	3	4	-1
1885	Pro-N	.957	4	44	1	2	1	0
1886	Was-N	.960	10	95	1	4	3	-1
1887	Was-N	.962	7	75	1	3	0	-1
1888	Ind-N	.951	6	57	1	3	6	-1
1889	Ind-N	.964	109	1090	57	43	66	1
1890	Pit-N	.973	17	166	13	5	8	3
	Bos-N	1.000	1	9	0	0	0	0
	Yr	.974	18	175	13	5	8	3
1891	Was-a	.970	8	63	1	2	3	-1
Total	12	.964	185	1836	82	71	105	0

2B

YEAR	TM/L	PCT	G	PO	A	E	DP	FR
1876	Chi-N	—	1	0	0	0	0	0
1877	Chi-N	.788	11	27	36	17	4	-3
1880	Pro-N	.933	6	9	19	2	1	-1
1881	Pro-N	.750	4	6	9	5	2	-1
1885	Pro-N	1.000	1	1	3	0	0	0
1886	Was-N	.846	3	5	6	2	1	0
1887	Was-N	.810	5	8	9	4	0	-2
Total	7	.821	31	56	82	30	8	-7

3B

YEAR	TM/L	PCT	G	PO	A	E	DP	FR
1885	Pro-N	.750	1	1	2	1	0	0
1886	Was-N	.825	15	33	33	14	1	2
Total	2	.821	16	34	35	15	1	2

SS

YEAR	TM/L	PCT	G	PO	A	E	DP	FR
1878	Pro-N	.714	1	0	5	2	0	0
1885	Pro-N	1.000	1	0	1	0	0	0
1886	Was-N	.750	5	11	7	6	0	-2
1887	Was-N	.880	4	7	15	3	2	0
1888	Ind-N	.800	2	0	4	1	0	0
Total	5	.806	13	18	32	12	2	-2

■ Chuck Hinton OF

YEAR	TM/L	PCT	G	PO	A	E	DP	FR
1961	Was-A	.963	92	175	6	7	4	-2
1962	Was-A	.988	136	233	7	3	1	-5
1963	Was-A	.989	125	274	8	3	1	6
1964	Was-A	.985	131	258	7	4	3	5
1965	Cle-A	.966	72	110	4	4	0	-1
1966	Cle-A	.973	104	176	6	5	1	3
1967	Cle-A	.976	136	239	5	6	0	1
1968	Cal-A	1.000	37	39	0	0	0	0
1969	Cal-A	.941	40	32	0	2	0	0
1970	Cle-A	.976	35	36	4	1	0	1
1971	Cle-A	1.000	20	18	0	0	0	-2
Total	11	.979	928	1590	47	35	10	6

1B

YEAR	TM/L	PCT	G	PO	A	E	DP	FR
1963	Was-A	1.000	6	56	3	0	3	0
1965	Cle-A	.990	40	266	22	3	21	1
1966	Cle-A	1.000	6	24	0	0	2	-1
1968	Cal-A	.987	48	334	33	5	30	3
1970	Cal-A	.994	40	164	8	1	14	-2
1971	Cle-A	1.000	20	83	5	0	16	-1
Total	6	.991	160	927	71	9	86	0

2B

YEAR	TM/L	PCT	G	PO	A	E	DP	FR
1962	Was-A	.982	12	26	29	1	15	-1
1965	Cle-A	.928	23	32	45	6	9	-4
1966	Cle-A	1.000	2	3	0	0	0	0
1967	Cle-A	1.000	5	4	4	0	2	0
1968	Cal-A	.966	9	14	14	1	2	-2
1970	Cal-A	1.000	3	0	1	0	0	0
Total	6	.956	54	79	93	8	28	-7

3B

YEAR	TM/L	PCT	G	PO	A	E	DP	FR
1963	Was-A	.860	19	12	31	7	5	-4
1964	Was-A	—	2	0	0	0	0	0
1965	Cle-A	—	1	0	0	0	0	0
1968	Cal-A	.941	3	13	13	1	0	0
1969	Cle-A	.952	14	5	15	1	1	0
1970	Cle-A	1.000	2	1	0	0	0	0
Total	6	.899	51	21	59	9	6	-4

C

YEAR	TM/L	PCT	G	PO	A	E	DP	FR
1970	Cle-A	1.000	4	28	2	0	0	0
1971	Cle-A	1.000	5	22	0	0	0	-2
Total	2	1.000	9	50	2	0	0	-2

SS

YEAR	TM/L	PCT	G	PO	A	E	DP	FR
1962	Was-A	—	1	0	0	0	0	0
1963	Was-A	1.000	2	3	1	0	0	0
Total	2	1.000	3	3	1	0	0	0

Gene Hiser OF

YEAR	TM/L	PCT	G	PO	A	E	DP	FR
1971	Chi-N	1.000	9	19	0	0	0	1
1972	Chi-N	1.000	15	21	2	0	1	2
1973	Chi-N	.980	64	48	0	1	0	-1
1974	Chi-N	1.000	8	8	0	0	0	0
1975	Chi-N	1.000	18	25	0	0	0	0
Total	5	.992	114	121	2	1	1	2
		1B						
1975	Chi-N	1.000	1	3	0	0	1	0

Larry Hisle OF

YEAR	TM/L	PCT	G	PO	A	E	DP	FR
1968	Phi-N	1.000	6	8	0	0	0	0
1969	Phi-N	.977	140	324	11	8	2	6
1970	Phi-N	.978	121	262	5	6	0	0
1971	Phi-N	.962	27	48	2	2	0	2
1973	Min-A	.975	143	337	11	9	0	13
1974	Min-A	.979	137	279	4	6	1	-2
1975	Min-A	.976	58	118	2	3	0	0
1976	Min-A	.984	154	361	16	6	1	11
1977	Min-A	.974	134	287	11	8	2	-12
1978	Mil-A	.978	87	172	6	4	2	-8
1979	Mil-A	1.000	10	17	2	0	0	0
Total	11	.978	1017	2213	70	2	8	10

Billy Hitchcock 3B

YEAR	TM/L	PCT	G	PO	A	E	DP	FR
1942	Det-A	—	1	0	0	0	0	0
1946	Was-A	.921	46	53	87	12	7	-1
1947	StL-A	.931	17	25	42	5	5	5
1948	Bos-A	1.000	15	23	35	0	3	6
1951	Phi-A	.929	45	45	99	11	14	7
1952	Phi-A	.942	104	105	222	20	26	-2
1953	Det-A	.929	12	9	17	2	1	1
Total	7	.938	240	260	502	0	56	16
		2B						
1946	Det-A	1.000	1	1	2	0	0	0
1947	StL-A	.977	46	127	127	6	31	6
1948	Bos-A	.951	15	31	47	4	12	0
1949	Bos-A	.973	8	21	15	1	5	-6
1950	Phi-A	.967	107	297	319	21	105	-2
1951	Phi-A	.970	23	47	51	3	16	1
1953	Det-A	—	1	0	0	0	0	0
Total	7	.969	201	524	561	5	169	-1
		SS						
1942	Det-A	.944	80	157	199	21	39	-2
1946	Was-A	.966	53	112	142	9	27	-2
1947	StL-A	.969	7	12	19	1	5	1
1950	Phi-A	.667	1	2	0	1	0	-1
1953	Det-A	1.000	1	1	1	0	1	0
Total	5	.953	142	284	361	2	72	-4
		1B						
1947	StL-A	.959	5	45	2	2	4	-1
1949	Bos-A	.993	29	256	15	2	28	-2
1951	Phi-A	1.000	1	8	0	0	1	0
1952	Phi-A	.982	13	97	13	2	8	2
Total	4	.986	48	406	30	6	41	-1

Myril Hoag OF

YEAR	TM/L	PCT	G	PO	A	E	DP	FR
1931	NY-A	1.000	23	12	1	0	0	-7
1932	NY-A	.962	35	22	3	1	0	1
1934	NY-A	.974	86	142	7	4	2	5
1935	NY-A	.986	37	66	2	1	0	2
1936	NY-A	.955	39	82	2	4	1	-1
1937	NY-A	.955	99	181	8	9	2	-5
1938	NY-A	.965	70	132	5	5	3	-3
1939	StL-A	.971	117	218	13	7	2	-3
1940	StL-A	.971	46	64	4	2	0	-5
1941	Chi-A	.957	99	215	6	10	1	-4
1942	Chi-A	.972	112	266	12	8	4	-4
1944	Chi-A	.969	14	29	2	1	1	0
	Cle-A	.947	66	171	9	10	3	4
	Yr	.950	80	200	11	11	4	4
1945	Cle-A	.987	33	73	4	1	1	-1
Total	13	.965	876	1673	78	3	20	-19
		3B						
1931	NY-A	1.000	1	0	1	0	0	0
1935	NY-A	—	1	0	0	0	0	0
Total	2	1.000	2	0	1	0	0	0
		1B						
1932	NY-A	1.000	1	4	0	0	0	0

Don Hoak 3B

YEAR	TM/L	PCT	G	PO	A	E	DP	FR
1954	Bro-N	.950	75	71	139	11	12	4
1955	Bro-N	.960	78	82	183	11	15	17
1956	Chi-N	.949	110	122	158	15	16	-18
1957	Cin-N	.971	149	193	269	14	29	0
1958	Cin-N	.964	112	132	244	14	29	4
1959	Pit-N	.961	155	169	322	20	31	9
1960	Pit-N	.948	155	132	324	25	34	4
1961	Pit-N	.953	143	137	267	20	29	-3
1962	Phi-N	.969	116	93	220	10	19	-2
1963	Phi-N	.958	106	88	205	13	13	6
Total	10	.959	1199	1219	2331	153	227	21
		2B						
1957	Cin-N	1.000	1	1	1	0	0	0
		SS						
1958	Cin-N	1.000	1	1	1	0	0	0

Doc Hoblitzel 1B

YEAR	TM/L	PCT	G	PO	A	E	DP	FR
1908	Cin-N	.985	32	313	24	5	11	2
1909	Cin-N	.982	142	1444	74	28	80	-3
1910	Cin-N	.984	148	1454	67	24	64	-7
1911	Cin-N	.990	158	1442	91	16	81	2
1912	Cin-N	.988	147	1326	87	21	73	2
1913	Cin-N	.988	134	1373	60	17	76	-5
1914	Cin-N	.988	75	802	31	10	43	-4
	Bos-A	.979	68	627	30	14	22	-5
1915	Bos-A	.987	117	1095	63	15	51	-1
1916	Bos-A	.989	126	1225	67	15	64	-1
1917	Bos-A	.990	118	1274	52	14	58	-8
1918	Bos-A	.996	19	209	15	1	18	1
Total	11	.987	1284	12584	661	180	641	-27
		2B						
1910	Cin-N	1.000	7	7	16	0	2	-1

Butch Hobson 3B

YEAR	TM/L	PCT	G	PO	A	E	DP	FR
1975	Bos-A	1.000	1	1	3	0	0	1
1976	Bos-A	.936	76	60	146	14	11	-7
1977	Bos-A	.946	159	128	272	23	27	-28
1978	Bos-A	.899	133	122	261	43	25	-14
1979	Bos-A	.935	142	110	251	25	17	-20
1980	Bos-A	.910	57	52	109	16	5	-9
1981	Cal-A	.929	83	85	139	17	13	-11
Total	7	.926	651	558	1181	138	98	-88
		1B						
1982	NY-A	.951	11	37	2	2	3	0
		2B						
1979	Bos-A	—	1	0	0	0	0	0

Oris Hockett OF

YEAR	TM/L	PCT	G	PO	A	E	DP	FR
1938	Bro-A	.893	17	24	1	3	0	-3
1939	Bro-N	1.000	1	1	1	0	0	0
1941	Cle-A	1.000	2	2	0	0	0	-1
1942	Cle-A	.980	145	284	12	6	3	-4
1943	Cle-A	.960	139	347	13	15	3	-3
1944	Cle-A	.986	110	275	6	4	1	-11
1945	Chi-A	.982	106	273	7	5	3	-1
Total	7	.974	520	1206	40	3	10	-23

Johnny Hodapp 2B

YEAR	TM/L	PCT	G	PO	A	E	DP	FR
1929	Cle-A	.977	72	162	271	10	32	5
1930	Cle-A	.970	154	403	557	30	106	12
1931	Cle-A	.969	121	274	413	22	73	16
1932	Cle-A	1.000	7	7	12	0	0	-2
	Chi-A	.857	5	16	14	5	5	-1
	Yr	.907	12	23	26	5	5	-3
1933	Bos-A	.960	101	273	334	25	65	4
Total	5	.967	460	1135	1601	2	281	34
		3B						
1925	Cle-A	.960	37	42	79	5	7	3
1926	Cle-A	.750	3	1	2	1	0	-1
1927	Cle-A	.935	67	69	132	14	15	2
1928	Cle-A	.944	101	103	220	19	20	0
1932	Chi-A	.857	4	1	5	1	0	-1
Total	5	.942	212	216	438	0	42	3
		OF						
1932	Chi-A	.967	31	58	0	2	0	-3
		1B						
1927	Cle-A	.956	4	42	1	2	4	-1
1928	Cle-A	.993	13	130	4	1	14	-2
1933	Bos-A	.985	10	66	1	1	3	-1
Total	3	.984	27	238	6	4	21	-4

Gil Hodges 1B

YEAR	TM/L	PCT	G	PO	A	E	DP	FR
1948	Bro-N	.986	96	830	60	13	85	-2
1949	Bro-N	.995	156	1336	80	7	142	-4
1950	Bro-N	.994	153	1273	100	8	159	0
1951	Bro-N	.992	158	1365	126	12	171	7
1952	Bro-N	.992	153	1322	116	11	152	5
1953	Bro-N	.993	127	1025	99	8	105	8
1954	Bro-N	.995	154	1381	132	7	129	9
1955	Bro-N	.991	139	1274	105	12	126	4
1956	Bro-N	.992	138	1190	103	10	105	5
1957	Bro-N	.990	150	1317	115	14	115	2
1958	LA-N	.992	122	907	69	8	134	0
1959	LA-N	.992	113	891	66	8	77	-1
1960	LA-N	.995	92	403	33	2	40	1
1961	LA-N	.998	100	454	37	1	44	0
1962	NY-N	.986	47	315	32	5	23	3
1963	NY-N	1.000	10	61	8	0	7	2
Total	16	.992	1908	15344	1281	126	1614	39
		OF						
1953	Bro-N	.975	24	37	2	1	1	0
1955	Bro-N	.900	16	17	1	2	0	-1
1956	Bro-N	.955	30	42	0	2	0	-3
1958	LA-N	1.000	9	6	0	0	0	0
Total	4	.955	79	102	3	5	1	-4
		C						
1947	Bro-N	.958	24	79	12	4	2	-2
1948	Bro-N	.977	38	160	12	4	5	1
1956	Bro-N	1.000	1	2	0	0	0	0
1958	LA-N	1.000	1	1	0	0	0	0
Total	4	.971	64	242	24	8	7	-1
		3B						
1943	Bro-N	.600	1	1	2	2	1	0
1957	Bro-N	1.000	2	2	2	0	1	0
1958	LA-N	.981	15	18	34	1	3	3
1959	LA-N	1.000	4	5	8	0	3	1
1960	LA-N	.864	10	8	11	3	2	0
Total	5	.938	32	34	57	6	10	4
		2B						
1957	Bro-N	—	1	0	0	0	0	0

Ron Hodges C

YEAR	TM/L	PCT	G	PO	A	E	DP	FR
1973	NY-N	.992	40	241	13	2	6	2
1974	NY-N	.953	44	227	14	12	1	-1
1975	NY-N	1.000	9	69	1	0	0	0
1976	NY-N	.976	52	262	18	7	0	-9
1977	NY-N	.992	27	112	19	1	3	0
1978	NY-N	.982	30	145	20	3	5	7
1979	NY-N	.980	22	82	16	2	1	1
1980	NY-N	.982	9	47	1	1	0	4
1981	NY-N	1.000	7	23	1	0	0	-1
1982	NY-N	.980	74	362	35	8	4	-1
1983	NY-N	.971	96	360	45	12	4	-11
1984	NY-N	.979	35	165	20	4	2	0
Total	12	.978	445	2095	211	2	26	-9

Ralph Hodgin OF

YEAR	TM/L	PCT	G	PO	A	E	DP	FR
1939	Bos-N	1.000	9	15	0	0	0	0
1943	Chi-A	1.000	42	87	2	0	0	-1
1944	Chi-A	1.000	33	93	1	0	0	2
1946	Chi-A	.983	57	114	3	2	0	-6
1947	Chi-A	.990	41	99	2	1	0	-1
1948	Chi-A	.970	79	184	9	6	0	0
Total	6	.985	261	592	17	9	0	-6
		3B						
1943	Chi-A	.945	56	34	120	9	7	-5
1944	Chi-A	.942	82	77	215	18	22	9
Total	2	.943	138	111	335	7	29	4

Jack Hoey OF

YEAR	TM/L	PCT	G	PO	A	E	DP	FR
1906	Bos-A	.915	94	155	7	15	0	-8
1907	Bos-A	.857	21	24	0	4	0	-5
1908	Bos-A	1.000	11	11	2	0	0	0
Total	3	.913	126	190	9	9	0	-13

Stew Hofferth C

YEAR	TM/L	PCT	G	PO	A	E	DP	FR
1944	Bos-N	.984	47	158	22	3	3	0
1945	Bos-N	.980	45	168	31	4	7	6
1946	Bos-N	1.000	15	66	3	0	1	-1
Total	3	.985	107	392	56	7	11	5

Danny Hoffman OF

YEAR	TM/L	PCT	G	PO	A	E	DP	FR
1903	Phi-A	.950	62	111	4	6	0	-1
1904	Phi-A	.936	51	83	5	6	1	0
1905	Phi-A	.942	118	216	12	14	4	-2
1906	Phi-A	1.000	7	12	2	0	0	1
	NY-A	.938	98	176	7	12	1	-9
	Yr	.943	105	188	9	12	1	-8
1907	NY-A	.953	135	286	20	15	4	8
1908	StL-A	.962	99	185	19	8	8	11
1909	StL-A	.968	110	230	10	8	6	2
1910	StL-A	.960	106	202	14	9	5	0
1911	StL-A	.908	23	63	6	7	1	3
Total	9	.951	809	1564	99	5	30	15

Glenn Hoffman SS

YEAR	TM/L	PCT	G	PO	A	E	DP	FR
1980	Bos-A	.875	5	5	9	2	2	0
1981	Bos-A	.960	78	131	233	15	52	5
1982	Bos-A	.972	150	246	439	20	93	13
1983	Bos-A	.962	143	240	417	26	82	-6
1984	Bos-A	.957	56	39	71	5	17	5
1985	Bos-A	.975	93	155	231	10	61	0
1986	Bos-A	.923	11	14	10	2	3	-2
1987	Bos-A	.984	16	14	49	1	9	2
	LA-N	.966	40	70	101	6	19	1
1989	Cal-A	.982	23	18	37	1	8	2
Total	9	.966	615	932	1597	8	346	20
		3B						
1980	Bos-A	.946	110	72	193	15	17	0
1981	Bos-A	1.000	1	1	1	0	0	0
1984	Bos-A	1.000	4	1	3	0	1	1
1985	Bos-A	.500	3	0	1	1	0	-1
1986	Bos-A	1.000	1	1	1	0	0	0
1987	Bos-A	1.000	3	1	0	0	0	0
1989	Cal-A	.957	18	14	30	2	2	4
Total	7	.947	140	90	229	8	20	4
		2B						
1980	Bos-A	1.000	2	1	0	0	0	0
1984	Bos-A	1.000	2	3	0	0	0	0
1985	Bos-A	1.000	3	2	0	0	0	0
1987	Bos-A	1.000	2	0	2	0	0	0
1989	Cal-A	1.000	4	6	7	0	2	0
Total	5	1.000	13	12	9	0	2	0
		1B						
1989	Cal-A	1.000	1	7	1	0	0	0

Solly Hofman OF

YEAR	TM/L	PCT	G	PO	A	E	DP	FR
1903	Pit-N	—	2	0	0	0	0	-1
1904	Chi-N	1.000	6	7	2	0	1	1
1905	Chi-N	1.000	3	4	1	0	0	0
1906	Chi-N	.976	23	38	2	1	1	-2
1907	Chi-N	.938	69	136	14	10	4	6
1908	Chi-N	.955	50	118	9	6	1	4
1909	Chi-N	.965	153	347	16	13	5	5
1910	Chi-N	.975	110	249	19	7	4	4
1911	Chi-N	.968	107	230	11	8	5	-8
1912	Chi-N	.987	27	67	7	1	4	5
	Pit-N	1.000	15	39	3	0	0	3
	Yr	.991	42	106	10	1	4	8
1913	Pit-N	.964	24	50	3	2	1	1
1914	Bro-F	.978	21	37	7	1	2	4
1915	Buf-F	.961	82	132	16	6	5	1
1916	NY-A	1.000	6	17	2	0	0	2
	Chi-N	1.000	4	7	1	0	0	0
Total	14	.967	702	1478	113	5	33	25
		2B						
1905	Chi-N	.955	59	138	178	15	13	3
1906	Chi-N	1.000	4	4	2	0	0	0
1907	Chi-N	.947	3	10	8	1	4	0
1908	Chi-N	.941	22	41	55	6	5	2
1914	Bro-F	.951	108	232	289	27	39	-1
1915	Buf-F	1.000	2	1	2	0	0	0
Total	6	.951	198	426	534	9	61	4
		1B						
1905	Chi-N	.968	9	86	6	3	2	0
1906	Chi-N	.990	21	186	9	2	10	-1
1907	Chi-N	.990	18	204	4	2	7	-2
1908	Chi-N	.972	37	357	20	11	10	-1
1910	Chi-N	.978	24	212	8	5	10	-2
1911	Chi-N	.984	36	353	17	6	17	-1
1912	Chi-N	.975	9	77	2	2	7	-1
1914	Bro-F	.979	22	173	16	4	13	3
1915	Buf-F	.979	11	86	7	2	1	1
Total	9	.980	187	1734	89	7	77	-4
		SS						
1904	Chi-N	.750	1	1	2	1	0	-1
1905	Chi-N	.923	9	17	19	3	3	0
1906	Chi-N	.945	9	20	32	3	7	2
1907	Chi-N	.921	42	81	116	17	21	2

YEAR	TM/L	PCT	G	PO	A	E	DP	FR
1914	Bro-F	1.000	1	1	0	0	0	0
1915	Buf-F	1.000	1	4	4	0	1	0
Total	6	.925	63	124	173	4	32	3
		3B						
1905	Chi-N	.846	3	3	8	2	0	0
1906	Chi-N	.923	4	5	7	1	0	-1
1907	Chi-N	.857	4	4	2	1	0	-2
1908	Chi-N	1.000	9	16	13	0	0	0
1910	Chi-N	1.000	1	0	1	0	0	0
1915	Buf-F	1.000	4	8	0	0	0	-1
Total	6	.944	25	36	31	4	0	-4

■ Fred Hofmann   C

YEAR	TM/L	PCT	G	PO	A	E	DP	FR
1919	NY-A	1.000	1	1	1	0	0	0
1920	NY-A	.905	14	17	2	2	0	-4
1921	NY-A	.952	18	69	11	4	1	0
1922	NY-A	.962	29	91	11	4	0	-3
1923	NY-A	.979	70	292	34	7	7	-2
1924	NY-A	.991	54	179	45	2	2	3
1925	NY-A	1.000	1	0	1	0	0	0
1927	Bos-A	.943	81	241	59	18	4	-4
1928	Bos-A	.982	71	223	44	5	7	4
Total	9	.969	339	1113	208	2	21	-4
		1B						
1921	NY-A	1.000	1	7	0	0	0	0

■ Shanty Hogan   C

YEAR	TM/L	PCT	G	PO	A	E	DP	FR
1926	Bos-N	.852	4	18	5	4	0	1
1927	Bos-N	.985	61	215	54	4	3	1
1928	NY-N	.978	124	389	57	10	11	-10
1929	NY-N	.979	93	286	47	7	5	-4
1930	NY-N	.982	96	386	46	8	5	-3
1931	NY-N	.996	113	469	54	2	10	-1
1932	NY-N	.983	136	522	71	10	11	-8
1933	Bos-N	.997	95	280	56	1	11	-1
1934	Bos-N	.986	90	291	53	5	8	-3
1935	Bos-N	.990	56	175	25	2	2	-5
1936	Was-A	.989	19	83	8	1	5	2
1937	Was-A	.979	21	76	17	2	2	2
Total	12	.985	908	3190	493	6	73	-29
		OF						
1925	Bos-N	1.000	5	8	0	0	0	-1

■ Eddie Hogan   OF

YEAR	TM/L	PCT	G	PO	A	E	DP	FR
1884	Mil-U	.806	11	16	9	6	1	7
1887	NY-a	.750	29	37	5	14	1	-3
1888	Cle-a	.896	78	104	8	13	1	-5
Total	3	.844	118	157	22	3	3	-1
		SS						
1887	NY-a	.692	4	3	6	4	0	-2
		3B						
1887	NY-a	.500	1	0	2	2	0	-1

■ Willie Hogan   OF

YEAR	TM/L	PCT	G	PO	A	E	DP	FR
1911	Phi-A	.900	6	7	2	1	0	0
	StL-A	.929	117	263	26	22	3	14
	Yr	.928	123	270	28	23	3	14
1912	StL-A	.972	100	229	14	7	6	11
Total	2	.947	223	499	42	0	9	25
		1B						
1911	StL-A	.959	5	45	2	2	3	-1

■ George Hogriever   OF

YEAR	TM/L	PCT	G	PO	A	E	DP	FR
1895	Cin-N	.934	66	174	10	13	3	6
1901	Mil-A	.901	54	134	3	15	1	2
Total	2	.920	120	308	13	8	4	8
		2B						
1895	Cin-N	.667	3	10	2	6	0	-3

■ Bill Holbert   C

YEAR	TM/L	PCT	G	PO	A	E	DP	FR
1876	Lou-N	.843	12	62	24	16	3	7
1878	Mil-N	.877	21	72	28	14	1	1
1879	Syr-N	.897	56	277	64	39	4	-2
	Tro-N	.893	4	16	9	3	1	1
	Yr	.897	60	293	73	42	5	-1
1880	Tro-N	.911	58	261	107	36	6	8
1881	Tro-N	.918	43	201	69	24	10	4
1882	Tro-N	.892	58	247	124	45	13	15
1883	NY-a	.920	68	527	138	58	8	28
1884	NY-a	.920	59	374	142	45	7	14
1885	NY-a	.900	39	227	80	34	3	7
1886	NY-a	.922	45	265	100	31	6	16
1887	NY-a	.894	60	237	102	40	9	-5
1888	Bro-a	.926	15	74	26	8	2	1
Total	12	.907	538	2840	1013	393	73	95
		OF						
1878	Mil-N	.818	30	35	19	12	1	4
1879	Syr-N	1.000	4	3	0	0	0	2
1880	Tro-N	.875	3	7	0	1	0	0
1881	Tro-N	.750	3	5	1	2	0	0
1882	Tro-N	.750	3	3	0	1	0	-1
1883	NY-a	.667	5	3	1	2	0	-1
1884	NY-a	1.000	5	8	1	0	0	1
1885	NY-a	1.000	13	23	5	0	2	4
1886	NY-a	1.000	3	4	1	0	1	1
Total	9	.869	69	91	28	8	4	8
		3B						
1882	Tro-N	.783	12	19	28	13	1	1
1885	NY-a	.630	5	6	11	10	2	0
Total	2	.736	17	25	39	3	3	1
		1B						
1887	NY-a	.963	8	72	6	3	4	1
		SS						
1884	NY-a	.833	1	1	4	1	0	0
1886	NY-a	.750	1	1	5	2	1	0
1887	NY-a	1.000	2	2	6	0	1	1
Total	3	.864	4	4	15	3	2	1
		2B						
1883	NY-a	—	1	0	0	0	0	0
1887	NY-a	—	1	0	0	0	0	0

YEAR	TM/L	PCT	G	PO	A	E	DP	FR
Total	2	—	2	0	0	0	0	0

■ Jim Holdsworth   OF

YEAR	TM/L	PCT	G	PO	A	E	DP	FR
1876	NY-N	.902	49	109	10	13	1	1
1877	Har-N	.833	55	79	11	18	1	-5
1882	Tro-N	1.000	1	1	1	0	0	1
1884	Ind-a	.929	5	12	1	1	1	1
Total	4	.875	110	201	23	2	3	-2
		2B						
1876	NY-N	.875	3	10	4	2	1	-2

■ Walter Holke   1B

YEAR	TM/L	PCT	G	PO	A	E	DP	FR
1914	NY-N	.950	2	17	2	1	1	0
1916	NY-N	.997	34	331	13	1	15	0
1917	NY-N	.989	153	1635	70	19	104	-5
1918	NY-N	.990	88	938	68	10	50	5
1919	Bos-N	.993	136	1474	95	11	86	6
1920	Bos-N	.991	143	1528	81	14	92	-2
1921	Bos-N	.997	150	1471	86	4	100	3
1922	Bos-N	.993	105	1017	44	8	65	-4
1923	Phi-N	.991	146	1425	69	13	136	-1
1924	Phi-N	.993	148	1516	90	12	134	4
1925	Phi-N	.994	23	164	12	1	16	1
	Cin-N	.997	65	642	35	2	60	1
	Yr	.996	88	806	47	3	76	2
Total	11	.993	1193	12158	665	6	859	8

■ Bug Holliday   OF

YEAR	TM/L	PCT	G	PO	A	E	DP	FR
1889	Cin-a	.923	135	234	29	22	6	-7
1890	Cin-N	.948	131	253	20	15	5	-3
1891	Cin-N	.939	111	186	13	13	3	-8
1892	Cin-N	.933	152	271	20	21	6	-4
1893	Cin-N	.944	125	270	14	17	4	-10
1894	Cin-N	.914	119	243	22	25	5	0
1895	Cin-N	.940	32	60	3	4	1	-4
1896	Cin-N	.925	16	36	1	3	0	-1
1897	Cin-N	.940	42	76	2	5	0	-4
1898	Cin-N	.969	28	61	1	2	1	-2
Total	10	.935	891	1690	125	127	31	-43
		1B						
1893	Cin-N	1.000	1	15	0	0	1	0
1894	Cin-N	.889	1	8	0	1	0	0
1896	Cin-N	.967	5	27	2	1	2	0
1897	Cin-N	1.000	3	23	2	0	0	0
Total	4	.975	10	73	4	2	3	0
		SS						
1896	Cin-N	.667	1	1	3	2	0	-1
1897	Cin-N	.857	4	5	13	3	1	-2
Total	2	.815	5	6	16	5	1	-3
		2B						
1897	Cin-N	.900	3	4	5	1	1	-1

■ Charlie Hollocher   SS

YEAR	TM/L	PCT	G	PO	A	E	DP	FR
1918	Chi-N	.929	131	278	418	53	39	-19
1919	Chi-N	.941	115	219	418	40	49	6
1920	Chi-N	.954	80	196	280	23	34	8
1921	Chi-N	.963	137	282	491	30	72	3
1922	Chi-N	.965	152	332	502	30	89	-5
1923	Chi-N	.963	65	124	212	13	35	-9
1924	Chi-N	.969	71	156	248	13	42	4
Total	7	.954	751	1587	2569	202	360	-12

■ Ed Holly   SS

YEAR	TM/L	PCT	G	PO	A	E	DP	FR
1906	StL-N	.939	10	24	22	3	7	-3
1907	StL-N	.927	147	317	474	62	45	13
1914	Pit-F	.942	94	238	263	31	30	-4
1915	Pit-F	.865	11	21	24	7	4	-4
Total	4	.931	262	600	783	103	86	2
		2B						
1907	StL-N	.882	3	9	6	2	0	-1
1914	Pit-F	1.000	1	2	1	0	0	0
Total	2	.900	4	11	7	2	0	-1
		3B						
1915	Pit-F	1.000	3	3	2	0	0	1
		OF						
1914	Pit-F	1.000	2	1	3	0	0	2

■ Wattie Holm   OF

YEAR	TM/L	PCT	G	PO	A	E	DP	FR
1924	StL-N	.988	64	162	9	2	1	2
1925	StL-N	.976	13	40	1	1	1	2
1926	StL-N	.962	39	75	1	3	1	-3
1927	StL-N	.967	97	201	3	7	0	-8
1928	StL-N	1.000	7	18	0	0	0	0
1929	StL-N	.944	44	115	4	7	2	4
1932	StL-N	1.000	4	9	0	0	0	0
Total	7	.970	268	620	18	0	5	-3
		3B						
1924	StL-N	.500	4	1	0	1	0	-1
1927	StL-N	1.000	9	4	22	0	2	1
1928	StL-N	.918	83	100	145	22	9	-10
1929	StL-N	1.000	1	1	0	0	0	0
Total	4	.922	97	106	167	3	11	-10
		C						
1924	StL-N	.947	9	15	3	1	1	-1

■ Billy Holm   C

YEAR	TM/L	PCT	G	PO	A	E	DP	FR
1943	Chi-N	1.000	7	21	4	0	0	1
1944	Chi-N	.979	50	166	18	4	2	-2
1945	Bos-A	.980	57	170	30	4	3	-3
Total	3	.981	114	357	52	8	5	-4

■ Ducky Holmes   OF

YEAR	TM/L	PCT	G	PO	A	E	DP	FR
1895	Lou-N	.780	29	32	7	11	1	-2
1896	Lou-N	.790	33	43	6	13	1	-5
1897	NY-N	.904	77	113	9	13	2	-7
1898	StL-N	.900	22	39	6	5	3	2
	Bal-N	.935	113	247	13	18	4	5
	Yr	.930	135	286	19	23	7	5
1899	Bal-N	.927	138	321	24	27	5	6
1901	Det-A	.907	131	217	18	24	5	-2
1902	Det-A	.950	92	155	16	9	5	4

YEAR	TM/L	PCT	G	PO	A	E	DP	FR
1903	Was-A	.912	14	26	5	3	0	3
	Chi-A	.965	82	151	14	6	0	3
	Yr	.956	96	177	19	9	0	6
1904	Chi-A	.975	63	111	8	3	3	2
1905	Chi-A	.936	89	150	11	11	1	-1
Total	10	.924	883	1605	137	143	30	8
		SS						
1895	Lou-N	.800	8	11	17	7	1	-7
1896	Lou-N	.444	1	1	3	5	2	-1
1897	Lou-N	1.000	1	4	4	0	2	1
	NY-N	.667	1	0	6	3	0	0
	Yr	.824	2	4	10	3	2	0
Total	3	.754	11	16	30	5	5	-8
		3B						
1895	Lou-N	.750	4	5	4	3	0	-2
1903	Was-A	.909	4	3	7	1	0	-1
	Chi-A	.800	3	3	5	2	0	-1
	Yr	.857	7	6	12	3	0	-2
Total	2	.818	11	11	16	6	0	-4
		2B						
1896	Lou-N	.667	1	0	2	1	0	-1
1903	Was-A	.800	2	5	3	2	0	-1
Total	2	.769	3	5	5	3	0	-2

■ Tommy Holmes   OF

YEAR	TM/L	PCT	G	PO	A	E	DP	FR
1942	Bos-N	.990	140	373	16	4	4	9
1943	Bos-N	.993	152	408	18	3	3	2
1944	Bos-N	.991	155	426	14	4	7	3
1945	Bos-N	.983	154	334	13	6	4	-1
1946	Bos-N	.987	146	294	17	4	7	4
1947	Bos-N	.989	147	336	12	4	4	4
1948	Bos-N	.983	137	283	8	5	4	-3
1949	Bos-N	.987	103	210	10	3	4	-1
1950	Bos-N	1.000	88	151	6	0	0	-4
1951	Bos-N	1.000	3	2	0	0	0	0
1952	Bro-N	1.000	6	6	1	0	0	0
Total	11	.989	1231	2823	115	3	37	12

■ Jim Holt   OF

YEAR	TM/L	PCT	G	PO	A	E	DP	FR
1968	Min-A	.973	38	34	2	1	0	4
1969	Min-A	1.000	5	2	0	0	0	0
1970	Min-A	.995	130	201	2	1	0	-10
1971	Min-A	.986	106	209	4	3	2	-6
1972	Min-A	.917	7	10	1	1	0	0
1973	Min-A	.990	102	193	6	2	2	-4
1974	Min-A	1.000	5	5	0	0	0	0
1975	Oak-A	—	2	0	0	0	0	0
Total	8	.988	395	654	15	8	4	-20
		1B						
1968	Min-A	1.000	1	1	0	0	1	0
1969	Min-A	1.000	1	2	0	0	1	0
1970	Min-A	1.000	2	7	0	0	0	0
1971	Min-A	1.000	3	10	0	0	1	0
1972	Min-A	1.000	1	6	1	0	0	0
1973	Min-A	1.000	33	222	20	0	13	1
1974	Min-A	.996	67	449	43	2	57	5
	Oak-A	1.000	17	50	6	0	5	1
	Yr	.996	84	499	49	2	62	6
1975	Oak-A	.991	52	192	18	2	19	2
Total	8	.996	177	939	88	4	97	9
		C						
1975	Oak-A	—	1	0	0	0	0	0

■ Harry Hooper   OF

YEAR	TM/L	PCT	G	PO	A	E	DP	FR
1909	Bos-A	.952	74	124	14	7	3	4
1910	Bos-A	.938	155	241	30	18	7	11
1911	Bos-A	.954	130	181	27	10	1	6
1912	Bos-A	.964	147	220	22	9	6	1
1913	Bos-A	.968	147	248	25	9	7	9
1914	Bos-A	.973	140	231	23	7	5	11
1915	Bos-A	.972	149	255	23	8	7	11
1916	Bos-A	.966	151	266	19	10	5	8
1917	Bos-A	.971	151	245	20	8	3	-1
1918	Bos-A	.963	126	221	16	9	8	10
1919	Bos-A	.979	128	262	19	6	2	10
1920	Bos-A	.963	139	263	22	11	2	7
1921	Chi-A	.975	108	182	12	5	3	-3
1922	Chi-A	.962	149	288	19	12	7	7
1923	Chi-A	.960	143	272	15	12	3	-4
1924	Chi-A	.986	123	251	22	4	8	11
1925	Chi-A	.976	124	231	16	6	4	4
Total	17	.966	2284	3981	344	151	81	92

■ Joe Hoover   SS

YEAR	TM/L	PCT	G	PO	A	E	DP	FR
1943	Det-A	.944	144	301	393	41	84	-6
1944	Det-A	.932	119	256	405	48	102	15
1945	Det-A	.944	68	126	163	17	35	-7
Total	3	.939	331	683	961	106	221	2
		2B						
1944	Det-A	1.000	2	1	2	1	0	1

■ Buster Hoover   OF

YEAR	TM/L	PCT	G	PO	A	E	DP	FR
1884	Phi-U	.780	37	51	13	18	2	3
	Phi-N	.929	10	12	1	1	0	-2
1886	Bal-a	.839	40	70	3	14	0	-1
1892	Cin-N	.966	14	25	3	1	2	1
Total	3	.840	101	158	20	4	4	1
		SS						
1884	Phi-U	.712	15	19	33	21	4	-5
		1B						
1884	Phi-U	.958	6	41	5	2	3	2
		2B						
1884	Phi-U	.822	6	24	13	8	2	-1
		3B						
1884	Phi-U	1.000	1	0	1	0	0	0

■ Gail Hopkins   1B

YEAR	TM/L	PCT	G	PO	A	E	DP	FR
1968	Chi-A	1.000	7	45	1	0	3	-2
1969	Chi-A	.994	101	903	51	6	81	-3
1970	Chi-A	.987	77	629	42	9	67	-1

YEAR	TM/L	PCT	G	PO	A	E	DP	FR
1971	KC-A	.990	83	669	57	7	76	3
1972	KC-A	.990	13	97	2	1	7	-1
1973	KC-A	1.000	10	32	3	0	3	0
1974	LA-N	1.000	2	17	2	0	0	0
Total	7	.991	293	2392	158	3	237	-4
	C							
1970	Chi-A	1.000	8	16	0	0	0	-1
1974	LA-N	1.000	2	3	1	0	0	0
Total	2	1.000	10	19	1	0	0	-1
	3B							
1972	KC-A	1.000	1	1	0	0	0	0

■ Marty Hopkins   3B

YEAR	TM/L	PCT	G	PO	A	E	DP	FR
1934	Phi-N	1.000	9	6	13	0	2	-1
	Chi-A	.957	63	63	136	9	4	4
1935	Chi-A	.960	49	27	68	4	4	-6
Total	2	.960	121	96	217	3	10	-3
	2B							
1935	Chi-A	.846	5	8	14	4	3	-2

■ Johnny Hopp   OF

YEAR	TM/L	PCT	G	PO	A	E	DP	FR
1940	StL-N	.967	39	86	1	3	0	4
1941	StL-N	.982	91	213	4	4	1	2
1943	StL-N	.950	52	113	1	6	3	1
1944	StL-N	**.997**	131	316	2	1	1	-12
1945	StL-N	.980	104	244	5	5	2	1
1946	Bos-N	1.000	58	135	3	0	1	2
1947	Bos-N	.980	125	296	2	6	0	-9
1948	Pit-N	1.000	80	192	3	0	1	3
1949	Pit-N	.929	7	12	1	1	0	0
	Bro-N	1.000	4	6	1	0	0	1
	Pit-N	1.000	9	21	0	0	0	-1
	Yr	.976	20	39	2	1	0	0
1950	Pit-N	1.000	7	13	1	0	0	0
	NY-A	1.000	6	11	0	0	0	0
1952	Det-A	1.000	4	6	0	0	0	-1
Total	11	.985	717	1664	24	6	9	-9
	1B							
1939	StL-N	1.000	2	6	1	0	1	0
1940	StL-N	.979	10	43	3	1	4	0
1941	StL-N	.989	39	329	17	4	23	-1
1942	StL-N	.983	88	746	44	14	68	-3
1943	StL-N	.969	27	173	16	6	13	1
1944	StL-N	1.000	6	36	0	0	3	0
1945	StL-N	.986	15	131	11	2	11	0
1946	Bos-N	.981	68	535	42	11	44	-1
1948	Pit-N	.996	25	211	18	1	21	1
1949	Pit-N	.946	6	49	4	3	4	0
	Bro-N	1.000	2	1	1	0	0	0
	Pit-N	.994	71	593	40	4	65	-1
	Yr	.990	79	643	45	7	69	-1
1950	Pit-N	.990	70	534	32	6	61	-6
	NY-A	1.000	12	38	2	0	1	0
1951	NY-A	.992	25	121	5	1	10	-1
1952	NY-A	1.000	12	52	5	0	8	0
	Det-A	1.000	1	1	0	0	0	0
	Yr	1.000	13	53	5	0	8	0
Total	13	.986	479	3599	243	3	334	-11

■ Bob Horner   3B

YEAR	TM/L	PCT	G	PO	A	E	DP	FR
1978	Atl-N	.956	89	81	199	13	17	6
1979	Atl-N	.930	82	56	143	15	11	-4
1980	Atl-N	.935	121	78	251	23	20	4
1981	Atl-N	.938	79	51	129	12	6	-15
1982	Atl-N	.970	137	102	217	10	20	-17
1983	Atl-N	.958	104	76	153	10	18	-13
1984	Atl-N	.965	32	21	61	3	6	-1
1985	Atl-N	.887	40	25	61	11	6	-10
Total	8	.946	684	490	1214	7	104	-50
	1B							
1979	Atl-N	.984	45	414	24	7	32	-2
1980	Atl-N	1.000	1	2	2	0	0	1
1983	Atl-N	1.000	1	2	0	0	0	0
1985	Atl-N	1.000	87	892	58	0	105	-1
1986	Atl-N	.995	139	**1378**	102	8	**138**	2
1988	StL-N	.990	57	463	40	5	39	-1
Total	6	.994	330	3151	226	0	314	-1

■ Rogers Hornsby   2B

YEAR	TM/L	PCT	G	PO	A	E	DP	FR
1916	StL-N	.875	1	3	4	1	0	0
1919	StL-N	.967	25	46	101	5	13	8
1920	StL-N	.962	**149**	**343**	524	**34**	**76**	11
1921	StL-N	.969	142	305	477	25	59	-1
1922	StL-N	**.967**	**154**	**398**	473	30	**81**	-7
1923	StL-N	.962	96	192	283	19	48	-21
1924	StL-N	.965	143	301	517	30	102	-4
1925	StL-N	.954	136	287	416	34	95	-20
1926	StL-N	.962	134	245	433	27	73	-29
1927	NY-N	.972	**155**	299	582	25	98	3
1928	Bos-N	.973	140	295	450	21	85	-24
1929	Chi-N	.973	**156**	286	**547**	23	**106**	1
1930	Chi-N	.916	25	44	76	11	16	-3
1931	Chi-N	.951	69	107	205	16	24	-15
1933	StL-N	.967	17	24	35	2	7	-7
1935	StL-A	1.000	2	1	2	0	0	0
1937	StL-N	.947	17	30	41	4	10	-4
Total	17	.965	1561	3206	5166	307	893	112
	SS							
1915	StL-N	.922	18	48	46	8	12	1
1916	StL-N	.910	45	90	132	22	22	-6
1917	StL-N	.939	144	268	527	52	**82**	21
1918	StL-N	.933	109	208	434	46	55	11
1919	StL-N	.933	37	66	115	13	12	-7
1921	StL-N	.950	3	11	8	1	3	-1
Total	6	.932	356	691	1262	142	186	19
	3B							
1916	StL-N	.928	83	82	174	20	7	5
1919	StL-N	.933	72	73	151	16	11	1

YEAR	TM/L	PCT	G	PO	A	E	DP	FR
1921	StL-N	.800	3	2	2	1	0	-1
1931	Chi-N	.922	26	21	50	6	6	0
1932	Chi-N	.733	6	1	10	4	0	-2
1934	StL-N	1.000	1	1	3	0	1	1
1935	StL-A	1.000	1	1	2	0	0	0
Total	7	.924	192	181	392	7	25	4
	1B							
1916	StL-N	.987	15	150	5	2	6	-1
1919	StL-N	1.000	5	48	0	0	3	-1
1921	StL-N	1.000	1	8	0	0	0	0
1923	StL-N	.987	10	131	16	2	13	4
1935	StL-N	1.000	3	36	1	0	1	0
1936	StL-N	1.000	1	10	0	0	0	0
Total	6	.990	35	383	22	4	23	2
	OF							
1918	StL-N	1.000	3	3	0	0	0	0
1921	StL-N	1.000	6	14	0	0	0	0
1932	Chi-N	1.000	10	16	0	0	0	-2
1934	StL-A	1.000	1	1	0	0	0	0
Total	4	1.000	20	34	0	0	0	-2

■ Joe Hornung   OF

YEAR	TM/L	PCT	G	PO	A	E	DP	FR
1879	Buf-N	.844	77	129	12	26	1	-2
1880	Buf-N	.874	67	127	12	20	2	0
1881	Bos-N	**.948**	83	**198**	19	12	5	11
1882	Bos-N	**.932**	84	191	14	15	4	10
1883	Bos-N	**.936**	98	175	15	13	3	6
1884	Bos-N	.916	110	182	14	18	1	4
1885	Bos-N	.919	25	33	1	3	0	-3
1886	Bos-N	.948	94	187	12	11	1	6
1887	Bos-N	**.935**	98	192	23	15	3	13
1888	Bos-N	.947	107	151	10	9	0	-8
1889	Bal-a	.913	134	250	32	27	10	12
1890	NY-N	.931	77	110	12	9	3	-3
Total	12	.922	1054	1925	176	178	33	46
	1B							
1879	Buf-N	1.000	1	6	0	0	1	0
1880	Buf-N	.939	18	179	7	12	3	0
1882	Bos-N	1.000	1	5	1	0	0	0
1884	Bos-N	.944	6	51	0	3	2	-1
1890	NY-N	.977	36	363	14	9	23	1
Total	5	.963	62	604	22	4	29	0
	3B							
1883	Bos-N	—	1	0	0	0	0	0
1889	Bal-a	1.000	1	1	0	0	0	-1
1890	NY-N	.810	5	11	6	4	1	-1
Total	3	.818	7	12	6	4	1	-2
	2B							
1880	Buf-N	.879	5	13	16	4	2	-1
	SS							
1890	NY-N	.800	2	4	4	2	1	-1

■ Tony Horton   1B

YEAR	TM/L	PCT	G	PO	A	E	DP	FR
1964	Bos-A	.967	8	55	3	2	3	-1
1965	Bos-A	.980	44	311	24	7	30	0
1966	Bos-A	1.000	6	43	5	0	7	1
1967	Bos-A	.929	6	48	4	4	4	-1
	Cle-A	.991	94	763	46	7	62	-5
	Yr	.987	100	811	50	11	66	-6
1968	Cle-A	.992	128	972	63	8	80	-3
1969	Cle-A	.989	**157**	1179	**100**	**14**	**130**	0
1970	Cle-A	.994	112	898	73	6	106	3
Total	7	.990	555	4269	318	8	422	-6
	OF							
1964	Bos-A	1.000	24	39	2	0	0	0

■ Willie Horton   OF

YEAR	TM/L	PCT	G	PO	A	E	DP	FR
1963	Det-A	1.000	9	13	0	0	0	-1
1964	Det-A	.943	23	33	0	2	0	-3
1965	Det-A	.988	141	249	7	3	1	3
1966	Det-A	.979	137	233	4	5	1	-4
1967	Det-A	.971	110	165	5	5	2	-6
1968	Det-A	.973	139	212	6	6	2	-5
1969	Det-A	.972	136	272	8	8	0	6
1970	Det-A	.982	96	154	10	3	1	-2
1971	Det-A	.963	118	176	8	7	1	-13
1972	Det-A	1.000	98	131	6	0	0	-8
1973	Det-A	.942	107	160	2	**10**	0	-13
1974	Det-A	.947	64	106	2	6	0	-7
1977	Det-A	1.000	1	1	0	0	0	0
	Tex-A	.938	10	15	0	1	0	-2
	Yr	.941	11	16	0	1	0	-2
1978	Oak-A	.333	1	1	0	2	0	-1
Total	14	.972	1190	1921	58	8	8	-56
	3B							
1965	Det-A	1.000	1	0	2	0	0	0

■ Tim Hosley   C

YEAR	TM/L	PCT	G	PO	A	E	DP	FR
1970	Det-A	1.000	4	22	3	0	0	0
1971	Det-A	1.000	4	21	0	0	0	0
1973	Oak-A	.952	13	19	1	1	0	-1
1974	Oak-A	1.000	8	11	1	0	0	0
1975	Chi-N	.968	53	254	16	9	3	-2
1976	Oak-A	.968	37	79	13	3	0	-1
1977	Oak-A	.955	19	74	11	4	0	2
1978	Oak-A	.962	6	22	3	1	0	1
Total	8	.968	144	502	48	8	3	1
	1B							
1971	Det-A	1.000	1	5	0	0	0	0
1974	Oak-A	1.000	1	2	0	0	0	0
1977	Oak-A	.900	3	7	2	1	0	0
1981	Oak-A	.750	1	3	0	1	0	0
Total	4	.905	6	17	2	2	0	0

■ Dave Hostetler   1B

YEAR	TM/L	PCT	G	PO	A	E	DP	FR
1981	Mon-N	1.000	2	4	0	0	2	0
1982	Tex-A	.990	109	1099	48	12	102	-11
1983	Tex-A	1.000	2	11	0	0	0	0
1984	Tex-A	1.000	14	90	8	0	9	1
1988	Pit-N	.944	4	15	2	1	0	0

YEAR	TM/L	PCT	G	PO	A	E	DP	FR
Total	5	.990	131	1219	58	3	113	-10
	C							
1988	Pit-N	—	1	0	0	0	0	0

■ Pete Hotaling   OF

YEAR	TM/L	PCT	G	PO	A	E	DP	FR
1879	Cin-N	.843	69	118	16	25	2	0
1880	Cle-N	.896	78	115	14	15	4	-4
1881	Wor-N	.862	74	142	21	26	2	-2
1882	Bos-N	.865	**84**	150	16	26	5	1
1883	Cle-N	.829	**100**	181	23	**42**	5	-2
1884	Cle-N	.849	102	174	23	35	5	-3
1885	Bro-a	.893	94	159	17	21	3	0
1887	Cle-a	.903	126	267	23	31	5	1
1888	Cle-a	.878	98	170	10	25	7	-9
Total	9	.869	825	1476	163	246	38	-18
	C							
1879	Cin-N	.932	8	26	15	3	1	3
1880	Cle-N	.857	2	5	1	1	0	0
1881	Wor-N	.783	3	11	7	5	0	1
Total	3	.878	13	42	23	9	2	4
	2B							
1879	Cin-N	.800	6	14	18	8	5	-3
1884	Cle-N	—	1	0	0	0	0	0
Total	2	.800	7	14	18	8	5	-3
	3B							
1879	Cin-N	.750	3	0	3	1	0	0

■ Sadie Houck   SS

YEAR	TM/L	PCT	G	PO	A	E	DP	FR
1879	Bos-N	.826	33	47	86	28	9	-9
1881	Det-N	.868	75	88	241	50	**40**	1
1883	Det-N	.852	**101**	**162**	**328**	85	**36**	4
1884	Phi-a	**.893**	108	122	**379**	60	30	**23**
1885	Phi-a	.863	93	121	362	77	34	22
1886	Bal-a	.849	55	73	152	40	4	-6
	Was-N	.858	51	58	159	36	9	1
1887	NY-a	.831	10	8	41	10	3	4
Total	7	.863	526	679	1748	386	165	38
	OF							
1879	Bos-N	.814	47	62	17	18	2	1
1880	Bos-N	.786	12	21	1	6	0	-1
	Pro-N	.873	49	86	10	14	0	-1
	Yr	.855	61	107	11	20	0	-2
1886	Bal-a	.400	1	2	0	3	0	-1
Total	3	.829	109	171	28	1	2	-2
	2B							
1884	Phi-a	—	1	0	0	0	0	0
1886	Bal-a	.886	5	13	18	4	2	1
	Was-N	1.000	1	4	2	0	1	0
1887	NY-a	.750	1	2	1	1	1	0
Total	3	.889	8	19	21	5	4	1

■ Frank House   C

YEAR	TM/L	PCT	G	PO	A	E	DP	FR
1950	Det-A	1.000	5	4	1	0	0	0
1951	Det-A	.957	18	56	11	3	1	1
1954	Det-A	.992	107	434	56	4	7	-1
1955	Det-A	.987	93	423	35	6	5	1
1956	Det-A	.986	88	450	33	7	8	-7
1957	Det-A	.997	97	535	54	2	5	8
1958	KC-A	.992	55	236	22	2	4	-7
1959	KC-A	.982	95	447	43	9	7	-9
1960	Cin-N	1.000	8	21	2	0	1	1
1961	Det-A	.974	14	36	1	1	0	-1
Total	10	.988	580	2642	258	4	38	-14

■ Charlie Householder   1B

YEAR	TM/L	PCT	G	PO	A	E	DP	FR
1882	Bal-a	.971	74	749	20	23	30	**3**
1884	Bro-a	.959	40	426	18	19	17	2
Total	2	.967	114	1175	38	2	47	5
	C							
1882	Bal-a	1.000	3	13	0	0	0	1
1884	Bro-a	.888	31	140	43	23	5	-5
Total	2	.895	34	153	43	3	5	-4
	OF							
1884	Bro-a	.938	6	14	1	1	1	2
	2B							
1884	Bro-a	1.000	1	0	1	0	0	0

■ Paul Householder   OF

YEAR	TM/L	PCT	G	PO	A	E	DP	FR
1980	Cin-N	1.000	14	16	2	0	0	0
1981	Cin-N	1.000	19	32	1	0	0	-1
1982	Cin-N	.992	131	220	14	2	4	3
1983	Cin-N	**.991**	112	221	5	2	0	2
1984	Cin-N	1.000	10	6	1	0	0	1
	StL-N	1.000	8	3	0	0	0	0
	Yr	1.000	18	9	1	0	0	1
1985	Mil-A	.986	91	202	5	3	0	2
1986	Mil-A	1.000	22	35	1	0	1	-1
1987	Hou-N	1.000	7	3	0	0	0	0
Total	8	.991	414	738	29	7	5	6

■ Ben Houser   1B

YEAR	TM/L	PCT	G	PO	A	E	DP	FR
1910	Phi-A	1.000	26	160	7	0	10	0
1911	Bos-N	.988	20	160	11	2	13	0
1912	Bos-N	.986	83	759	37	11	48	-3
Total	3	.989	129	1079	55	3	71	-3

■ Steve Hovley   OF

YEAR	TM/L	PCT	G	PO	A	E	DP	FR
1969	Sea-A	.989	84	175	8	2	3	8
1970	Mil-A	.958	38	68	1	3	0	-2
	Oak-A	1.000	42	58	1	0	1	4
	Yr	.977	80	126	2	3	1	2
1971	Oak-A	1.000	11	15	1	0	0	1
1972	KC-A	.982	68	103	6	2	0	4
1973	KC-A	.975	79	114	4	3	1	1
Total	5	.982	322	533	21	0	5	16

■ Elston Howard   C

YEAR	TM/L	PCT	G	PO	A	E	DP	FR
1955	NY-A	1.000	9	23	3	0	2	0
1956	NY-A	1.000	26	108	14	0	5	1
1957	NY-A	.984	32	178	11	3	4	-3
1958	NY-A	.997	67	355	26	1	8	0

YEAR	TM/L	PCT	G	PO	A	E	DP	FR
1959	NY-A	.992	43	221	23	2	2	1
1960	NY-A	.987	91	410	40	6	9	2
1961	NY-A	.993	111	635	43	5	4	8
1962	NY-A	.995	129	713	44	4	12	-2
1963	NY-A	.994	132	786	51	5	8	-4
1964	NY-A	.998	146	939	67	2	9	9
1965	NY-A	.991	95	614	43	6	6	-5
1966	NY-A	.985	100	553	44	9	6	-4
1967	NY-A	.984	48	289	26	5	4	1
	Bos-A	.996	41	246	14	1	5	2
	Yr	.990	89	535	40	6	9	1
1968	Bos-A	.995	68	377	30	2	3	-4
Total	14	.993	1138	6447	479	1	87	0
	OF							
1955	NY-A	.978	75	124	10	3	3	2
1956	NY-A	.990	65	97	2	1	0	-3
1957	NY-A	.961	71	68	5	3	0	-6
1958	NY-A	.982	24	54	1	1	0	0
1959	NY-A	.979	28	47	0	1	0	-2
1960	NY-A	—	1	0	0	0	0	0
1965	NY-A	1.000	1	1	0	0	0	0
Total	7	.978	265	391	18	9	3	-9
	1B							
1957	NY-A	1.000	2	20	3	0	1	1
1958	NY-A	1.000	5	38	2	0	5	0
1959	NY-A	.985	50	444	26	7	39	-2
1961	NY-A	.989	9	90	4	1	12	-1
1965	NY-A	1.000	5	29	1	0	2	-2
1966	NY-A	1.000	13	112	8	0	11	0
1967	NY-A	1.000	1	1	0	0	0	0
Total	7	.990	85	734	44	8	70	-4

Frank Howard OF

YEAR	TM/L	PCT	G	PO	A	E	DP	FR
1958	LA-N	1.000	8	12	1	0	0	0
1959	LA-N	1.000	6	10	0	0	0	0
1960	LA-N	.984	115	177	8	3	1	-4
1961	LA-N	.934	65	79	6	6	0	-5
1962	LA-N	.972	131	187	19	6	4	3
1963	LA-N	.960	111	190	4	8	0	-2
1964	LA-N	.979	122	183	2	4	0	-8
1965	Was-A	.981	138	204	5	4	0	-9
1966	Was-A	.982	135	216	5	4	1	-8
1967	Was-A	.986	141	210	5	3	1	-11
1968	Was-A	.955	107	160	11	8	1	-3
1969	Was-A	.974	114	147	3	4	0	-16
1970	Was-A	.973	120	172	6	5	4	-11
1971	Was-A	.993	100	141	7	1	0	-11
1972	Tex-A	.962	21	25	0	1	0	-2
	Det-A	1.000	1	1	0	0	0	0
	Yr	.963	22	26	0	1	0	-2
Total	15	.975	1435	2114	82	7	12	-87
	1B							
1960	LA-N	.957	4	19	3	1	2	0
1961	LA-N	.959	7	43	4	2	2	-1
1967	Was-A	1.000	4	15	1	0	0	0
1968	Was-A	.976	55	416	41	11	38	1
1969	Was-A	.980	70	455	31	10	38	-5
1970	Was-A	.987	48	429	25	6	37	-4
1971	Was-A	.992	68	414	58	4	40	8
1972	Tex-A	.981	66	440	27	9	39	-3
	Det-A	.952	10	55	5	3	5	0
	Yr	.978	76	495	32	12	44	-3
1973	Det-A	.923	2	12	0	1	0	0
Total	9	.981	334	2298	195	7	201	-4

Del Howard OF

YEAR	TM/L	PCT	G	PO	A	E	DP	FR
1905	Pit-N	.974	28	35	3	1	0	-2
1906	Bos-N	.911	87	119	14	13	3	-4
1907	Bos-N	.969	45	54	8	2	2	-4
	Chi-N	.917	8	11	0	1	0	-2
	Yr	.961	53	65	8	3	2	-6
1908	Chi-N	.965	81	129	10	5	1	-5
Total	4	.946	249	348	35	2	6	-17
1905	Pit-N	.978	90	912	48	22	57	-5
1906	Bos-N	.938	2	28	2	2	0	0
1907	Chi-N	.972	33	301	16	9	17	-2
1908	Chi-N	.966	5	26	2	1	0	0
1909	Chi-N	.980	57	593	32	13	29	0
Total	5	.977	187	1860	100	7	103	-7
	2B							
1906	Bos-N	.933	45	88	121	15	10	-6
1907	Bos-N	.947	3	7	11	1	3	1
Total	2	.934	48	95	132	6	13	-5
	SS							
1906	Bos-N	.882	14	46	36	11	3	-2

Larry Howard C

YEAR	TM/L	PCT	G	PO	A	E	DP	FR
1970	Hou-N	.993	26	125	11	1	0	-5
1971	Hou-N	.992	22	106	12	1	2	3
1972	Hou-N	.980	53	323	15	7	2	1
1973	Hou-N	.989	20	79	7	1	0	-1
	Atl-N	1.000	2	8	1	0	0	0
	Yr	.990	22	87	8	1	0	-1
Total	4	.986	123	641	46	0	4	-2
	1B							
1970	Hou-N	1.000	2	5	1	0	0	0
	OF							
1970	Hou-N	—	1	0	0	0	0	0
1972	Hou-N	—	1	0	0	0	0	0
Total	2	—	2	0	0	0	0	0

Wilbur Howard OF

YEAR	TM/L	PCT	G	PO	A	E	DP	FR
1973	Mil-A	.969	12	29	2	1	0	3
1974	Hou-N	1.000	50	65	3	0	1	4
1975	Hou-N	.995	95	194	7	1	0	4
1976	Hou-N	.961	63	96	2	4	1	1
1977	Hou-N	.990	62	100	2	1	1	2
1978	Hou-N	1.000	16	39	2	0	0	2

YEAR	TM/L	PCT	G	PO	A	E	DP	FR
Total	6	.987	298	523	18	7	3	16
	2B							
1976	Hou-N	.889	2	2	6	1	1	0
1977	Hou-N	1.000	4	5	3	0	0	0
1978	Hou-N	—	1	0	0	0	0	0
Total	3	.941	7	7	9	1	1	0
	C							
1978	Hou-N	1.000	3	4	1	0	0	0

Art Howe 3B

YEAR	TM/L	PCT	G	PO	A	E	DP	FR
1974	Pit-N	.937	20	11	48	4	8	4
1975	Pit-N	.938	42	17	89	7	4	4
1976	Hou-N	.938	8	6	9	1	1	0
1977	Hou-N	.981	19	16	37	1	1	2
1978	Hou-N	1.000	11	10	13	0	0	0
1979	Hou-N	.967	59	47	70	4	6	-3
1980	Hou-N	.974	25	11	27	1	3	-1
1981	Hou-N	.966	98	52	206	9	16	6
1982	Hou-N	.972	72	53	153	6	13	7
1984	StL-N	.979	45	23	70	2	6	7
1985	StL-N	1.000	1	1	1	0	0	0
Total	11	.965	400	247	723	5	58	26
	2B							
1976	Hou-N	1.000	2	1	7	0	2	1
1977	Hou-N	.985	96	192	279	7	49	5
1978	Hou-N	.977	107	224	289	12	51	-3
1979	Hou-N	.991	68	126	188	3	33	7
1980	Hou-N	1.000	3	0	4	0	0	0
1984	StL-N	1.000	8	3	4	0	2	1
Total	6	.984	284	546	771	2	137	11
	1B							
1978	Hou-N	.857	1	6	0	1	0	0
1979	Hou-N	1.000	3	15	3	0	3	1
1980	Hou-N	.986	77	580	49	9	47	2
1981	Hou-N	1.000	2	15	0	0	3	0
1982	Hou-N	.997	35	291	21	1	34	0
1984	StL-N	.979	11	45	2	1	6	-1
1985	StL-N	1.000	1	4	0	0	1	0
Total	7	.988	130	956	75	2	94	2
	SS							
1974	Pit-N	1.000	2	0	1	0	0	0
1975	Pit-N	1.000	3	2	0	0	0	0
1977	Hou-N	1.000	11	5	17	0	2	-1
1980	Hou-N	1.000	5	7	6	0	2	0
1984	StL-N	1.000	5	0	4	0	0	-1
Total	5	1.000	26	14	28	0	4	-1

Dixie Howell C

YEAR	TM/L	PCT	G	PO	A	E	DP	FR
1947	Pit-N	.974	74	272	30	8	2	-1
1949	Cin-N	.987	56	191	35	3	2	6
1950	Cin-N	.986	81	338	26	5	4	-4
1951	Cin-N	.987	73	275	28	4	5	0
1952	Cin-N	.981	16	43	9	1	0	1
1955	Bro-N	.981	13	49	4	1	0	-1
1956	Bro-N	1.000	6	21	1	0	0	0
Total	7	.984	319	1189	133	2	13	5

Jack Howell 3B

YEAR	TM/L	PCT	G	PO	A	E	DP	FR
1985	Cal-A	.931	42	33	75	8	10	-1
1986	Cal-A	.977	39	28	56	2	4	-1
1987	Cal-A	.967	48	31	85	4	13	-2
1988	Cal-A	.953	152	96	249	17	19	-20
1989	Cal-A	.974	142	95	322	11	27	22
1990	Cal-A	.939	102	70	193	17	18	6
Total	6	.958	525	353	980	9	91	4
	OF							
1986	Cal-A	1.000	8	10	1	0	1	1
1987	Cal-A	.987	89	150	4	2	0	-7
1988	Cal-A	1.000	2	1	0	0	0	0
1989	Cal-A	1.000	4	2	0	0	0	0
Total	4	.988	103	163	5	2	1	-6
	2B							
1987	Cal-A	.909	13	4	6	1	2	-1
	1B							
1990	Cal-A	1.000	1	2	0	0	0	0
	SS							
1990	Cal-A	.875	1	4	3	1	0	0

Roy Howell 3B

YEAR	TM/L	PCT	G	PO	A	E	DP	FR
1974	Tex-A	.906	12	5	24	3	1	-2
1975	Tex-A	.933	115	80	214	21	32	-7
1976	Tex-A	.926	130	103	245	28	20	-8
1977	Tex-A	1.000	1	1	0	0	0	0
	Tor-A	.953	87	81	165	12	12	-7
	Yr	.954	88	82	165	12	12	-7
1978	Tor-A	.950	131	109	306	22	27	11
1979	Tor-A	.952	133	108	290	20	28	1
1980	Tor-A	.958	138	105	257	16	24	-18
1981	Mil-A	.958	53	38	98	6	9	-5
1984	Mil-A	.907	46	21	67	9	7	1
Total	9	.944	846	651	1666	137	160	-34
	1B							
1977	Tex-A	.875	1	7	0	1	1	0
1981	Mil-A	1.000	3	20	2	0	1	0
1982	Mil-A	.933	4	26	2	2	1	0
1983	Mil-A	.960	2	20	4	1	4	1
1984	Mil-A	1.000	4	19	2	0	4	0
Total	5	.962	14	92	10	4	11	1
	OF							
1977	Tex-A	1.000	2	5	0	0	0	0
1978	Tor-A	1.000	5	7	0	0	0	0
1981	Mil-A	—	1	0	0	0	0	0
1982	Mil-A	1.000	2	2	0	0	0	0
Total	4	1.000	10	14	0	0	0	0

Bill Howerton OF

YEAR	TM/L	PCT	G	PO	A	E	DP	FR
1949	StL-N	.900	6	9	0	1	0	0
1950	StL-N	.969	94	183	2	6	0	-4
1951	StL-N	.949	17	35	2	2	1	0
	Pit-N	.950	53	93	3	5	0	-5

YEAR	TM/L	PCT	G	PO	A	E	DP	FR
	Yr	.950	70	128	5	7	1	-5
1952	Pit-N	.900	5	9	0	1	0	-1
	NY-N	1.000	3	6	0	0	0	0
	Yr	.938	8	15	0	1	0	-1
Total	4	.958	178	335	7	5	1	-10
	3B							
1951	Pit-N	.875	4	2	5	1	0	0
1952	Pit-N	.333	1	0	1	2	0	-1
Total	2	.727	5	2	6	3	0	-1

Dick Howser SS

YEAR	TM/L	PCT	G	PO	A	E	DP	FR
1961	KC-A	.950	157	299	427	38	85	-17
1962	KC-A	.962	72	138	191	13	37	-8
1963	KC-A	.957	10	21	23	2	6	-4
	Cle-A	.950	44	80	90	9	15	-17
	Yr	.951	54	101	113	11	21	-21
1964	Cle-A	.974	162	291	463	20	100	3
1965	Cle-A	.977	73	119	173	7	33	-5
1966	Cle-A	.951	26	24	54	4	8	-4
1967	NY-A	1.000	3	2	6	0	0	-1
1968	NY-A	1.000	1	1	1	0	0	-1
Total	8	.963	548	975	1428	3	284	-54
	2B							
1965	Cle-A	1.000	17	25	38	0	8	-1
1966	Cle-A	.986	26	29	41	1	8	-3
1967	NY-A	.990	22	55	46	1	15	-4
1968	NY-A	.982	29	58	103	3	19	6
Total	4	.988	94	167	228	5	50	-2
	3B							
1967	NY-A	.939	12	7	24	2	3	-2
1968	NY-A	1.000	2	2	2	0	0	0
Total	2	.946	14	9	26	2	3	-2

Dummy Hoy OF

YEAR	TM/L	PCT	G	PO	A	E	DP	FR
1888	Was-N	.897	136	296	26	37	7	5
1889	Was-N	.890	127	255	29	35	4	-6
1890	Buf-P	.912	122	289	23	30	9	5
1891	StL-a	.909	141	255	26	28	3	-1
1892	Was-N	.884	152	275	16	38	3	-12
1893	Was-N	.892	130	281	26	37	8	-1
1894	Cin-N	.896	126	314	29	40	3	3
1895	Cin-N	.883	107	235	14	33	6	-3
1896	Cin-N	.946	120	303	14	18	3	5
1897	Cin-N	.934	128	359	10	26	5	7
1898	Lou-N	.946	148	348	19	21	6	6
1899	Lou-N	.927	154	321	21	27	8	-6
1901	Chi-A	.958	132	278	16	13	6	2
1902	Cin-N	.933	72	149	4	11	1	-5
Total	14	.915	1795	3958	273	394	72	-1
1890	Buf-P	1.000	1	1	2	0	1	0

Kent Hrbek 1B

YEAR	TM/L	PCT	G	PO	A	E	DP	FR
1981	Min-A	1.000	13	124	4	0	14	-1
1982	Min-A	.993	138	1174	88	9	125	0
1983	Min-A	.990	137	1151	89	13	125	-2
1984	Min-A	.990	148	1320	99	14	113	-6
1985	Min-A	.995	156	1339	114	8	114	1
1986	Min-A	.992	147	1218	104	10	137	-2
1987	Min-A	.996	137	1179	68	5	112	-10
1988	Min-A	.997	105	842	57	3	92	-6
1989	Min-A	.995	89	723	60	4	66	1
1990	Min-A	.997	120	1057	81	3	100	0
Total	10	.994	1190	10127	764	9	998	-25
	3B							
1990	Min-A	1.000	1	0	2	0	0	0

Glenn Hubbard 2B

YEAR	TM/L	PCT	G	PO	A	E	DP	FR
1978	Atl-N	.979	44	102	130	5	30	3
1979	Atl-N	.968	91	193	268	15	57	5
1980	Atl-N	.978	117	268	405	15	91	19
1981	Atl-N	.991	98	188	344	5	50	-4
1982	Atl-N	.983	144	312	505	14	111	20
1983	Atl-N	.985	148	313	484	12	103	21
1984	Atl-N	.988	117	237	405	8	78	20
1985	Atl-N	.989	140	339	539	10	127	62
1986	Atl-N	.976	142	282	487	19	120	41
1987	Atl-N	.986	139	284	478	11	114	28
1988	Oak-A	.987	104	195	267	6	60	4
1989	Oak-A	.968	48	82	132	7	34	10
Total	12	.983	1332	2795	4444	127	975	229

Ken Hubbs 2B

YEAR	TM/L	PCT	G	PO	A	E	DP	FR
1961	Chi-N	1.000	8	13	15	0	2	-2
1962	Chi-N	.983	159	363	489	15	103	4
1963	Chi-N	.974	152	338	493	22	96	20
Total	3	.979	319	714	997	7	201	22

Clarence Huber 3B

YEAR	TM/L	PCT	G	PO	A	E	DP	FR
1920	Det-A	.907	11	21	28	5	0	2
1921	Det-A	1.000	1	1	0	0	0	0
1925	Phi-N	.947	120	107	199	17	16	-9
1926	Phi-N	.956	115	110	214	15	22	8
Total	4	.948	247	239	441	7	38	1

Rex Hudler 2B

YEAR	TM/L	PCT	G	PO	A	E	DP	FR
1984	NY-A	1.000	9	4	7	0	1	0
1985	NY-A	.977	16	36	50	2	12	7
1986	Bal-A	.800	13	2	2	1	0	1
1988	Mon-N	.978	41	74	105	4	22	5
1989	Mon-N	.958	38	27	42	3	9	-2
1990	StL-N	.946	10	9	26	2	3	0
Total	6	.970	127	152	232	2	47	11
	OF							
1988	Mon-N	1.000	4	3	0	0	0	0
1989	Mon-N	1.000	23	16	0	0	0	-1
1990	StL-N	.979	45	89	3	2	0	2
Total	3	.982	72	108	3	2	0	2
	SS							
1985	NY-A	1.000	1	0	1	0	0	0
1988	Mon-N	.944	27	39	63	6	8	-5

YEAR	TM/L	PCT	G	PO	A	E	DP	FR
1989	Mon-N	.892	18	16	17	4	4	-6
1990	StL-N	1.000	1	1	1	0	0	0
Total	4	.932	47	56	82	0	12	-11
1B								
1985	NY-A	1.000	1	6	0	0	2	0
1990	StL-N	1.000	6	54	4	0	6	0
Total	2	1.000	7	60	4	0	8	0
3B								
1986	Bal-A	1.000	1	0	1	0	0	0
1990	StL-N	.929	6	5	8	1	0	0
Total	2	.933	7	5	9	1	0	0

■ Johnny Hudson 2B

YEAR	TM/L	PCT	G	PO	A	E	DP	FR
1936	Bro-N	.667	1	1	1	1	0	0
1937	Bro-N	1.000	1	0	2	0	0	0
1938	Bro-N	.963	132	304	395	**27**	79	-3
1939	Bro-N	.962	45	89	114	8	25	-7
1940	Bro-N	.978	27	35	53	2	9	1
1941	Chi-N	.927	13	15	23	3	3	1
1945	NY-N	1.000	2	1	1	0	0	1
Total	7	.962	221	445	589	1	116	-7
SS								
1936	Bro-N	.889	4	9	7	2	1	-1
1937	Bro-N	.867	11	9	17	4	2	-4
1938	Bro-N	1.000	3	0	3	0	0	0
1939	Bro-N	.959	50	86	145	10	31	-12
1940	Bro-N	.921	38	59	92	13	11	-1
1941	Chi-N	.907	17	22	27	5	6	-3
Total	6	.933	123	185	291	4	51	-21
3B								
1939	Bro-N	1.000	1	0	1	0	0	0
1940	Bro-N	1.000	1	0	1	0	0	0
1941	Chi-N	.957	10	4	18	1	0	1
1945	NY-N	.875	5	4	3	1	1	4
Total	4	.939	17	8	23	2	1	5

■ Frank Huelsman OF

YEAR	TM/L	PCT	G	PO	A	E	DP	FR
1897	StL-N	.000	2	0	0	1	0	-1
1904	Chi-A	.000	1	0	0	1	0	-1
	Det-A	1.000	4	5	0	0	0	-1
	StL-A	1.000	18	19	0	0	0	-3
	Was-A	.960	84	138	7	6	2	-3
	Yr	.960	107	162	7	7	2	-8
1905	Was-A	.929	116	189	7	15	2	-9
Total	3	.941	225	351	14	3	4	-18

■ Miller Huggins 2B

YEAR	TM/L	PCT	G	PO	A	E	DP	FR
1904	Cin-N	.945	140	337	448	46	32	1
1905	Cin-N	.945	149	346	**525**	**51**	55	**36**
1906	Cin-N	.948	156	341	**458**	**44**	**62**	22
1907	Cin-N	.961	**156**	**353**	443	32	**73**	0
1908	Cin-N	.959	135	302	406	30	45	3
1909	Cin-N	.933	31	70	97	12	14	4
1910	StL-N	.963	151	325	452	30	58	3
1911	StL-N	.961	136	281	439	29	62	11
1912	StL-N	.943	114	272	337	37	50	-7
1913	StL-N	**.977**	113	266	339	14	44	0
1914	StL-N	.964	147	328	428	28	58	-5
1915	StL-N	.957	105	194	315	23	44	4
1916	StL-N	1.000	7	10	10	0	0	4
Total	13	.956	1530	3425	4697	376	597	76
3B								
1909	Cin-N	.930	15	25	28	4	0	-1

■ Roy Hughes 2B

YEAR	TM/L	PCT	G	PO	A	E	DP	FR
1935	Cle-A	.987	40	97	132	3	24	2
1936	Cle-A	.973	152	**421**	466	**25**	98	5
1937	Cle-A	.995	32	94	111	1	25	10
1938	StL-A	.957	21	41	47	4	13	2
1939	StL-A	1.000	6	11	13	0	4	1
	Phi-N	.984	65	183	184	6	30	0
1940	Phi-N	1.000	1	1	0	0	0	0
1945	Chi-N	.990	21	47	48	1	6	0
1946	Phi-N	1.000	7	16	12	0	3	-2
Total	8	.980	345	911	1013	0	203	18
3B								
1935	Cle-A	.333	1	1	1	4	0	-1
1937	Cle-A	.939	58	63	122	12	7	1
1938	StL-A	1.000	5	4	13	0	3	3
1944	Chi-N	.951	66	87	146	12	18	**9**
1945	Chi-N	1.000	9	8	9	0	1	-1
1946	Phi-N	.980	31	47	49	2	6	-1
Total	6	.948	170	210	340	0	35	10
SS								
1935	Cle-A	.932	29	54	83	10	20	-2
1938	StL-A	—	2	0	0	0	0	0
1939	StL-A	1.000	1	0	1	0	0	0
1944	Chi-N	.973	52	133	157	8	36	2
1945	Chi-N	.931	36	61	100	12	21	-7
1946	Phi-N	.942	34	47	83	8	15	-8
Total	6	.950	154	295	424	8	92	-15
1B								
1945	Chi-N	1.000	2	4	0	0	0	0
1946	Phi-N	.929	1	13	0	1	3	-1
Total	2	.944	3	17	0	1	3	-1

■ Emil Huhn 1B

YEAR	TM/L	PCT	G	PO	A	E	DP	FR
1915	New-F	.985	101	1001	53	16	68	-2
1916	Cin-N	1.000	14	103	6	0	6	1
1917	Cin-N	1.000	1	3	0	0	0	0
Total	3	.986	116	1107	59	6	74	-1
C								
1915	New-F	.978	16	70	18	2	2	0
1916	Cin-N	.989	18	69	19	1	1	1
1917	Cin-N	.969	15	47	15	2	0	-2
Total	3	.979	49	186	52	5	3	-1
OF								
1916	Cin-N	—	1	0	0	0	0	0

■ Tim Hulett 3B

YEAR	TM/L	PCT	G	PO	A	E	DP	FR
1984	Chi-A	1.000	4	0	3	0	0	1
1985	Chi-A	.924	115	69	210	**23**	22	7
1986	Chi-A	.951	89	70	144	11	10	-3
1987	Chi-A	.953	61	44	118	8	15	-2
1989	Bal-A	.955	11	9	12	1	1	-1
1990	Bal-A	.961	24	17	56	3	4	3
Total	6	.942	304	209	543	6	52	5
2B								
1983	Chi-A	.875	6	8	6	2	1	2
1984	Chi-A	1.000	3	4	12	0	2	4
1985	Chi-A	.989	28	48	46	1	19	1
1986	Chi-A	.987	66	109	187	4	44	-3
1987	Chi-A	.972	8	11	24	1	4	0
1989	Bal-A	.976	23	61	59	3	12	-4
1990	Bal-A	.986	16	27	45	1	11	3
Total	7	.982	150	268	379	2	93	3
OF								
1985	Chi-A	—	1	0	0	0	0	0

■ Rudy Hulswitt SS

YEAR	TM/L	PCT	G	PO	A	E	DP	FR
1899	Lou-N	.333	1	1	1	4	0	-1
1902	Phi-N	.917	125	**318**	400	65	37	8
1903	Phi-N	.906	**138**	**354**	430	**81**	43	-3
1904	Phi-N	.912	113	273	310	56	42	-13
1908	Cin-N	.936	118	242	368	42	37	-7
1909	StL-N	.930	65	147	200	26	16	-5
1910	StL-N	.854	30	39	78	20	4	-12
Total	7	.915	590	1374	1787	294	179	-33
2B								
1908	Cin-N	1.000	1	3	2	0	0	0
1909	StL-N	.922	12	19	28	4	4	-1
1910	StL-N	.750	2	1	2	1	0	0
Total	3	.917	15	23	32	5	4	-1
3B								
1902	Phi-N	.778	3	2	5	2	1	-1

■ John Hummel 2B

YEAR	TM/L	PCT	G	PO	A	E	DP	FR
1905	Bro-N	.962	30	62	90	6	13	0
1906	Bro-N	.953	50	115	148	13	25	2
1907	Bro-N	.951	44	106	129	12	14	10
1908	Bro-N	.963	43	105	127	9	10	3
1909	Bro-N	.950	38	66	106	9	6	2
1910	Bro-N	**.965**	153	344	424	28	67	-14
1911	Bro-N	**.972**	127	296	352	19	58	-5
1912	Bro-N	.969	58	120	159	9	17	-9
1913	Bro-N	1.000	3	3	4	0	1	0
1914	Bro-N	—	1	0	0	0	0	0
1918	NY-A	1.000	1	1	2	0	0	0
Total	11	.963	548	1218	1541	105	211	-11
OF								
1906	Bro-N	.952	21	38	2	2	0	0
1907	Bro-N	1.000	33	74	6	0	0	4
1908	Bro-N	.973	95	162	20	5	8	5
1909	Bro-N	1.000	17	33	2	0	1	1
1912	Bro-N	.966	44	55	2	2	0	-4
1913	Bro-N	.938	28	39	6	3	1	1
1914	Bro-N	1.000	19	28	4	0	1	2
1915	Bro-N	1.000	21	27	0	0	0	-1
1918	NY-A	.960	15	24	0	1	0	-3
Total	9	.976	293	480	42	3	11	5
1B								
1906	Bro-N	.982	15	157	6	3	9	-2
1907	Bro-N	.985	12	129	5	2	7	-1
1908	Bro-N	.989	8	82	7	1	5	1
1909	Bro-N	.987	54	571	15	8	22	-5
1911	Bro-N	1.000	4	36	5	0	3	1
1912	Bro-N	1.000	11	122	7	0	5	1
1913	Bro-N	.983	6	53	5	1	4	1
1914	Bro-N	.982	36	310	17	6	12	-1
1915	Bro-N	1.000	11	66	2	0	5	-1
1918	NY-A	.971	3	33	1	1	3	-1
Total	10	.987	160	1559	70	2	75	-7
SS								
1907	Bro-N	.944	8	12	22	2	2	-1
1908	Bro-N	.952	9	17	28	3	2	-1
1909	Bro-N	.887	36	57	84	18	9	-14
1911	Bro-N	.833	2	5	5	2	0	-1
1913	Bro-N	.953	17	31	51	4	8	-2
1914	Bro-N	1.000	1	1	1	0	0	0
1915	Bro-N	1.000	1	2	2	0	0	0
Total	7	.916	74	125	192	9	21	-19

■ Terry Humphrey C

YEAR	TM/L	PCT	G	PO	A	E	DP	FR
1971	Mon-N	.981	9	50	3	1	0	2
1972	Mon-N	.986	65	322	37	5	4	-3
1973	Mon-N	1.000	35	159	9	0	1	5
1974	Mon-N	.990	17	85	15	1	4	6
1975	Det-A	1.000	18	61	9	0	1	1
1976	Cal-A	.980	71	397	42	9	4	1
1977	Cal-A	.989	123	661	63	8	10	-1
1978	Cal-A	.978	52	252	21	6	5	11
1979	Cal-A	.983	9	55	3	1	1	6
Total	9	.986	399	2042	202	1	30	28
2B								
1978	Cal-A	—	1	0	0	0	0	0
3B								
1978	Cal-A	1.000	1	0	1	0	0	0

■ Randy Hundley C

YEAR	TM/L	PCT	G	PO	A	E	DP	FR
1964	SF-N	—	2	0	0	0	0	0
1965	SF-N	1.000	6	34	9	0	1	4
1966	Chi-N	.986	**149**	871	**85**	14	8	-11
1967	Chi-N	.996	**152**	**865**	59	4	7	-14
1968	Chi-N	.995	**160**	885	81	5	11	-15
1969	Chi-N	.992	**151**	918	**79**	8	**17**	10
1970	Chi-N	.990	73	455	26	5	2	-1
1971	Chi-N	.979	8	43	3	1	0	3
1972	Chi-N	**.995**	113	569	53	3	7	7
1973	Chi-N	.993	122	648	59	5	7	9
1974	Min-A	.965	28	148	17	6	2	1
1975	SD-N	.970	51	237	20	8	3	0
1976	Chi-N	.923	9	22	2	2	0	0
1977	Chi-N	1.000	2	10	0	0	0	1
Total	14	.990	1026	5765	493	1	65	-6

■ Bill Hunnefield SS

YEAR	TM/L	PCT	G	PO	A	E	DP	FR
1926	Chi-A	.931	98	185	257	33	44	-8
1927	Chi-A	.933	79	153	211	26	38	-11
1928	Chi-A	1.000	3	8	10	0	1	1
1929	Chi-A	.667	2	1	1	1	0	0
1930	Chi-A	.932	22	31	37	5	9	-10
1931	Cle-A	.853	21	36	45	14	8	-9
	NY-N	.933	5	6	8	1	2	0
Total	6	.925	230	420	569	0	102	-37
2B								
1926	Chi-A	.976	15	40	41	2	8	-2
1927	Chi-A	.955	17	32	32	3	3	-9
1928	Chi-A	.967	82	167	249	14	48	-12
1929	Chi-A	.969	29	65	90	5	18	-4
1931	Cle-A	—	1	0	0	0	0	0
	Bos-N	1.000	4	1	2	0	0	1
	NY-N	.951	56	112	140	13	27	-5
	Yr	.951	60	113	142	13	27	-4
Total	5	.963	204	417	554	7	104	-31
3B								
1926	Chi-A	.969	17	25	37	2	2	1
1927	Chi-A	1.000	1	3	1	0	0	0
1928	Chi-A	—	1	0	0	0	0	0
1929	Chi-A	1.000	4	2	5	0	0	0
1931	Bos-N	.864	5	6	13	3	0	1
Total	5	.948	28	36	56	5	2	2
1B								
1930	Chi-A	1.000	1	2	0	0	0	0

■ Ken Hunt OF

YEAR	TM/L	PCT	G	PO	A	E	DP	FR
1959	NY-A	1.000	5	9	0	0	0	0
1960	NY-A	.957	24	22	0	1	0	1
1961	LA-A	.950	134	261	6	**14**	1	-12
1963	LA-A	.972	50	69	1	2	0	-3
	Was-A	1.000	5	12	0	0	0	0
	Yr	.976	55	81	1	2	0	-3
1964	Was-A	1.000	37	68	1	0	1	4
Total	5	.964	255	441	8	7	2	-10
1B								
1962	LA-A	.867	3	13	0	2	0	-1
2B								
1961	LA-A	1.000	1	0	1	0	0	0

■ Ron Hunt 2B

YEAR	TM/L	PCT	G	PO	A	E	DP	FR
1963	NY-N	.967	142	350	416	**26**	85	2
1964	NY-N	.979	109	244	317	12	73	-9
1965	NY-N	.979	46	106	128	5	17	-5
1966	NY-N	.970	123	295	384	21	81	7
1967	LA-N	.980	90	211	224	9	50	-13
1968	SF-N	.972	147	289	410	**20**	66	-17
1969	SF-N	.979	125	254	356	13	67	-9
1970	SF-N	.968	85	162	173	11	38	-26
1971	Mon-N	.979	133	270	370	14	72	-8
1972	Mon-N	.982	122	257	353	11	61	-8
1973	Mon-N	.982	102	219	280	9	54	-21
1974	Mon-N	.969	31	67	88	5	18	-3
	StL-N	1.000	5	10	13	0	3	-1
	Yr	.973	36	77	101	5	21	-4
Total	12	.976	1260	2734	3512	156	685	111
3B								
1963	NY-N	1.000	1	1	0	0	0	0
1964	NY-N	.909	12	14	26	4	3	1
1965	NY-N	.857	6	2	16	3	2	1
1966	NY-N	1.000	1	0	2	0	0	0
1967	LA-N	.833	8	4	11	3	1	-2
1969	SF-N	1.000	1	0	1	0	0	0
1970	SF-N	.915	16	10	33	4	1	-1
1971	Mon-N	.979	19	10	30	2	5	-1
1972	Mon-N	1.000	5	4	13	0	0	1
1973	Mon-N	.931	14	6	21	2	2	0
1974	Mon-N	.941	75	37	140	11	14	-11
Total	11	.929	158	88	293	9	28	-12
SS								
1966	NY-N	1.000	1	0	2	0	0	0
1974	Mon-N	—	1	0	0	0	0	0
Total	2	1.000	2	0	2	0	0	0

■ Billy Hunter SS

YEAR	TM/L	PCT	G	PO	A	E	DP	FR
1953	StL-A	.970	152	284	**512**	**25**	99	15
1954	Bal-A	.948	124	249	333	**32**	76	1
1955	NY-A	.958	98	115	249	16	60	1
1956	NY-A	1.000	32	49	58	0	20	9
1957	KC-A	.938	35	46	89	9	19	-2
1958	KC-A	.933	12	10	32	3	4	-4
	Cle-A	.948	75	124	165	16	47	1
	Yr	.946	87	134	197	19	51	-3
Total	6	.958	528	877	1438	101	325	21
2B								
1957	KC-A	.974	64	111	152	7	40	-4
1958	KC-A	1.000	8	14	18	0	6	1
Total	2	.977	72	125	170	7	46	-3
3B								
1956	NY-A	1.000	4	2	6	0	2	1
1957	KC-A	.952	17	18	22	2	2	1
1958	KC-A	—	1	0	0	0	0	0
	Cle-A	1.000	2	0	1	0	0	0
	Yr	1.000	3	0	1	0	0	0
Total	3	.961	24	20	29	2	4	2

■ Steve Huntz SS

YEAR	TM/L	PCT	G	PO	A	E	DP	FR
1969	StL-N	.945	52	65	91	9	20	-5
1970	SD-N	.958	57	86	166	11	32	-8

YEAR	TM/L	PCT	G	PO	A	E	DP	FR
1971	Chi-A	1.000	7	3	9	0	2	0
Total	3	.955	116	154	266	0	54	-13

3B

YEAR	TM/L	PCT	G	PO	A	E	DP	FR
1969	StL-N	1.000	6	2	9	0	0	0
1970	SD-N	.932	51	32	91	9	7	-5
1971	Chi-A	1.000	6	7	13	0	1	0
1975	SD-N	.939	16	13	33	3	6	1
Total	4	.943	79	54	146	2	14	-4

2B

YEAR	TM/L	PCT	G	PO	A	E	DP	FR
1967	StL-N	1.000	2	3	2	0	0	-1
1969	StL-N	1.000	12	10	21	0	2	0
1971	Chi-A	1.000	14	21	32	0	7	-1
1975	SD-N	1.000	2	2	0	0	0	0
Total	4	1.000	30	36	55	0	9	-2

■ Clint Hurdle   OF

YEAR	TM/L	PCT	G	PO	A	E	DP	FR
1977	KC-A	1.000	9	17	0	0	0	0
1978	KC-A	.958	78	132	5	6	1	-4
1979	KC-A	.968	50	88	2	3	0	-1
1980	KC-A	.960	126	233	8	10	1	-11
1981	KC-A	1.000	28	59	1	0	0	0
1982	Cin-N	.950	17	17	2	1	0	1
1983	NY-N	—	1	0	0	0	0	0
1985	NY-N	.917	10	10	1	1	0	0
1986	StL-N	1.000	10	12	0	0	0	0
Total	9	.965	329	568	19	1	2	-15

1B

YEAR	TM/L	PCT	G	PO	A	E	DP	FR
1978	KC-A	.986	52	412	25	6	47	-5
1986	StL-N	.994	39	301	22	2	31	0
1987	NY-N	1.000	1	1	0	0	0	0
Total	3	.990	92	714	47	8	78	-5

C

YEAR	TM/L	PCT	G	PO	A	E	DP	FR
1985	NY-N	1.000	17	79	6	0	0	0
1986	StL-N	1.000	5	19	1	0	0	0
Total	2	1.000	22	98	7	0	0	0

3B

YEAR	TM/L	PCT	G	PO	A	E	DP	FR
1978	KC-A	—	1	0	0	0	0	0
1979	KC-A	1.000	1	1	0	0	0	0
1983	NY-N	.800	9	1	15	4	2	-1
1986	StL-N	.909	4	2	8	1	0	0
Total	4	.844	15	4	23	5	2	-1

■ Don Hurst   1B

YEAR	TM/L	PCT	G	PO	A	E	DP	FR
1928	Phi-N	.989	104	964	68	12	92	4
1929	Phi-N	.985	154	1509	112	24	125	5
1930	Phi-N	.984	96	845	59	15	92	-1
1931	Phi-N	.986	135	1206	104	18	117	11
1932	Phi-N	.993	150	1341	94	10	105	-2
1933	Phi-N	.985	142	1355	114	23	132	7
1934	Phi-N	.994	34	317	17	2	30	-1
	Chi-N	.986	48	413	18	6	39	-2
	Yr	.990	82	730	35	8	69	-3
Total	7	.987	863	7950	586	110	732	21

OF

YEAR	TM/L	PCT	G	PO	A	E	DP	FR
1930	Phi-N	.857	7	12	0	2	0	-1

■ Jeff Huson   SS

YEAR	TM/L	PCT	G	PO	A	E	DP	FR
1988	Mon-N	.932	15	17	38	4	5	1
1989	Mon-N	.886	20	21	41	8	7	0
1990	Tex-A	.960	119	157	254	17	69	-12
Total	3	.948	154	195	333	9	81	-11

3B

YEAR	TM/L	PCT	G	PO	A	E	DP	FR
1988	Mon-N	1.000	1	0	1	0	0	0
1989	Mon-N	1.000	1	1	1	0	0	0
1990	Tex-A	.955	36	12	30	2	2	-1
Total	3	.957	38	13	32	2	2	-1

2B

YEAR	TM/L	PCT	G	PO	A	E	DP	FR
1988	Mon-N	1.000	2	1	2	0	0	0
1989	Mon-N	1.000	9	18	23	0	4	4
1990	Tex-A	1.000	12	14	20	0	5	1
Total	3	1.000	23	33	45	0	9	5

OF

YEAR	TM/L	PCT	G	PO	A	E	DP	FR
1988	Mon-N	—	1	0	0	0	0	0

■ Tom Hutton   1B

YEAR	TM/L	PCT	G	PO	A	E	DP	FR
1966	LA-N	1.000	3	2	0	0	0	0
1969	LA-N	.993	16	130	19	1	9	4
1972	Phi-N	.992	87	555	36	5	46	0
1973	Phi-N	.998	71	527	43	1	61	4
1974	Phi-N	.996	39	235	15	1	25	-1
1975	Phi-N	.994	71	307	32	2	37	5
1976	Phi-N	1.000	72	292	28	0	25	4
1977	Phi-N	.993	73	135	15	1	11	3
1978	Tor-A	.976	9	38	2	1	3	-1
	Mon-N	1.000	17	101	3	0	7	-2
1979	Mon-N	1.000	25	78	11	0	4	3
1980	Mon-N	1.000	7	19	1	0	3	0
1981	Mon-N	1.000	9	22	2	0	2	0
Total	12	.995	499	2441	207	2	233	19

OF

YEAR	TM/L	PCT	G	PO	A	E	DP	FR
1972	Phi-N	.990	48	93	2	1	1	1
1974	Phi-N	.980	33	50	0	1	0	-2
1975	Phi-N	.909	12	9	1	1	1	0
1976	Phi-N	1.000	1	2	0	0	0	0
1977	Phi-N	1.000	9	8	0	0	0	0
1978	Tor-A	1.000	55	85	2	0	0	-7
	Mon-N	1.000	5	1	0	0	0	0
1979	Mon-N	1.000	9	11	0	0	0	0
1980	Mon-N	1.000	4	1	0	0	0	0
1981	Mon-N	1.000	2	1	0	0	0	0
Total	9	.989	178	261	5	3	2	-8

■ Ham Hyatt   1B

YEAR	TM/L	PCT	G	PO	A	E	DP	FR
1909	Pit-N	1.000	2	19	1	0	2	0
1910	Pit-N	.986	38	323	19	5	19	-1
1912	Pit-N	.875	3	6	1	1	2	0
1913	Pit-N	1.000	5	37	1	0	1	-1
1914	Pit-N	.980	7	50	0	1	1	-1
1915	StL-N	.991	64	616	21	6	31	-4
1918	NY-A	1.000	5	41	3	0	5	0
Total	7	.989	124	1092	46	3	61	-7

OF

YEAR	TM/L	PCT	G	PO	A	E	DP	FR
1909	Pit-N	.933	6	9	5	1	1	3
1910	Pit-N	1.000	4	4	0	0	0	0
1912	Pit-N	.955	15	20	1	1	0	-3
1913	Pit-N	.714	5	4	1	2	2	0
1915	StL-N	.933	25	40	2	3	1	-1
1918	NY-A	1.000	25	43	3	0	1	-1
Total	6	.950	80	120	12	7	5	-2

C

YEAR	TM/L	PCT	G	PO	A	E	DP	FR
1914	Pit-N	1.000	1	1	0	0	0	0

■ Pete Incaviglia   OF

YEAR	TM/L	PCT	G	PO	A	E	DP	FR
1986	Tex-A	.921	114	157	6	14	1	-16
1987	Tex-A	.945	132	216	8	13	0	-8
1988	Tex-A	.989	93	172	12	2	1	0
1989	Tex-A	.973	125	213	7	6	2	-5
1990	Tex-A	.974	145	290	12	8	2	3
Total	5	.962	609	1048	45	3	6	-26

■ Dane Iorg   OF

YEAR	TM/L	PCT	G	PO	A	E	DP	FR
1977	StL-N	.875	7	7	0	1	0	-1
1978	StL-N	1.000	25	33	5	0	0	1
1979	StL-N	.964	39	51	2	2	0	-3
1980	StL-N	.991	63	108	2	1	0	-5
1981	StL-N	.963	57	78	0	3	0	-10
1982	StL-N	.971	63	99	2	3	0	-3
1983	StL-N	.974	22	37	0	1	0	-1
1984	StL-N	1.000	5	5	1	0	0	0
	KC-A	.977	22	42	0	1	0	-1
1985	KC-A	1.000	32	41	0	0	0	0
1986	SD-N	1.000	3	4	0	0	0	0
Total	10	.977	338	505	12	2	0	-23

1B

YEAR	TM/L	PCT	G	PO	A	E	DP	FR
1977	Phi-N	.986	9	64	4	1	6	0
1979	StL-N	1.000	10	70	5	0	2	0
1980	StL-N	1.000	5	25	0	0	2	-1
1981	StL-N	1.000	8	47	5	0	1	1
1982	StL-N	1.000	10	77	5	0	6	0
1983	StL-N	.979	11	90	5	2	11	-1
1984	StL-N	1.000	6	30	1	0	4	0
	KC-A	.995	43	357	22	2	33	-2
1985	KC-A	1.000	2	13	1	0	2	0
1986	SD-N	1.000	10	39	1	0	3	-1
Total	9	.994	114	812	49	5	70	-4

3B

YEAR	TM/L	PCT	G	PO	A	E	DP	FR
1980	StL-N	1.000	1	1	0	0	0	0
1981	StL-N	1.000	2	0	2	0	0	0
1982	StL-N	1.000	2	1	3	0	0	0
1984	KC-A	—	1	0	0	0	0	0
1985	KC-A	1.000	1	1	3	0	0	0
1986	SD-N	1.000	6	0	1	0	0	0
Total	6	1.000	13	3	9	0	0	0

■ Garth Iorg   3B

YEAR	TM/L	PCT	G	PO	A	E	DP	FR
1980	Tor-A	.983	20	13	44	1	7	2
1981	Tor-A	.927	17	12	26	3	3	0
1982	Tor-A	.946	100	57	155	12	13	-8
1983	Tor-A	.976	85	36	127	4	9	-4
1984	Tor-A	.945	112	62	110	10	15	0
1985	Tor-A	.951	104	39	137	9	13	5
1986	Tor-A	.955	90	30	98	6	6	-2
1987	Tor-A	.973	28	10	26	1	3	1
Total	8	.955	556	259	723	6	69	-6

2B

YEAR	TM/L	PCT	G	PO	A	E	DP	FR
1978	Tor-A	.966	18	34	51	3	14	3
1980	Tor-A	.988	32	67	104	2	29	8
1981	Tor-A	.963	46	82	152	9	29	0
1982	Tor-A	.986	30	57	81	2	17	3
1983	Tor-A	.971	39	69	96	5	22	1
1984	Tor-A	1.000	7	3	6	0	2	1
1985	Tor-A	1.000	23	32	55	0	11	5
1986	Tor-A	.961	52	61	87	6	10	-13
1987	Tor-A	.982	91	139	195	6	33	-14
Total	9	.976	338	544	827	3	167	-6

OF

YEAR	TM/L	PCT	G	PO	A	E	DP	FR
1980	Tor-A	1.000	14	12	0	0	0	0

1B

YEAR	TM/L	PCT	G	PO	A	E	DP	FR
1980	Tor-A	1.000	11	27	4	0	8	1
1981	Tor-A	1.000	1	4	0	0	1	0
Total	2	1.000	12	31	4	0	9	1

SS

YEAR	TM/L	PCT	G	PO	A	E	DP	FR
1980	Tor-A	1.000	1	3	3	0	1	0
1981	Tor-A	1.000	2	1	4	0	0	0
1983	Tor-A	1.000	1	1	0	0	0	0
1984	Tor-A	1.000	2	1	1	0	1	0
1986	Tor-A	1.000	2	1	0	0	0	0
Total	5	1.000	8	7	8	0	2	0

■ Monte Irvin   OF

YEAR	TM/L	PCT	G	PO	A	E	DP	FR
1949	NY-N	1.000	10	15	3	0	0	1
1950	NY-N	.991	49	109	2	1	0	0
1951	NY-N	.996	112	237	10	1	1	3
1952	NY-N	1.000	32	44	3	0	1	-4
1953	NY-N	.973	113	244	10	7	4	6
1954	NY-N	.976	128	274	7	7	0	3
1955	NY-N	.961	45	94	4	4	0	2
1956	Chi-N	.991	96	216	6	2	0	7
Total	8	.983	585	1233	45	2	6	-18

1B

YEAR	TM/L	PCT	G	PO	A	E	DP	FR
1949	NY-N	1.000	5	40	3	0	5	0
1950	NY-N	.979	59	459	48	11	62	3
1951	NY-N	.980	39	348	50	8	47	8
1954	NY-N	1.000	1	2	0	0	0	0
Total	4	.980	104	849	101	9	114	11

3B

YEAR	TM/L	PCT	G	PO	A	E	DP	FR
1949	NY-N	.923	5	1	11	1	1	-1
1950	NY-N	1.000	1	1	1	0	0	0
1954	NY-N	.000	1	0	0	1	0	0
Total	3	.875	7	2	12	2	1	-1

■ Arthur Irwin   SS

YEAR	TM/L	PCT	G	PO	A	E	DP	FR
1880	Wor-N	.895	82	95	339	51	27	32
1881	Wor-N	.851	50	50	155	36	11	-8
1882	Wor-N	.832	33	41	123	33	16	6
1883	Pro-N	.856	94	93	293	65	29	-8
1884	Pro-N	.881	102	99	307	55	20	-5
1885	Pro-N	.875	58	70	209	40	17	5
1886	Phi-N	.891	100	137	322	56	21	5
1887	Phi-N	.892	100	178	301	58	30	-9
1888	Phi-N	.900	122	204	374	64	31	10
1889	Phi-N	.845	18	25	46	13	6	-6
	Was-N	.895	85	165	279	52	36	11
	Yr	.888	103	190	325	65	42	5
1890	Bos-P	.878	96	137	331	65	44	3
1891	Bos-a	.778	6	7	14	6	5	-1
1894	Phi-N	—	1	0	0	0	0	0
Total	13	.881	947	1301	3093	594	293	35

3B

YEAR	TM/L	PCT	G	PO	A	E	DP	FR
1880	Wor-N	.818	3	3	6	2	0	0
1882	Wor-N	.837	51	84	147	45	8	15
1885	Pro-N	.667	1	0	2	1	0	0
1886	Phi-N	.333	1	0	1	2	0	-1
Total	4	.829	56	87	156	0	8	14

2B

YEAR	TM/L	PCT	G	PO	A	E	DP	FR
1883	Pro-N	.938	4	7	8	1	0	0
1885	Pro-N	.333	1	0	1	2	0	-1
1888	Phi-N	1.000	3	5	9	0	2	1
1889	Was-N	1.000	1	2	0	0	0	0
Total	4	.914	9	14	18	3	2	0

C

YEAR	TM/L	PCT	G	PO	A	E	DP	FR
1880	Wor-N	—	1	0	0	0	0	0

■ Charlie Irwin   3B

YEAR	TM/L	PCT	G	PO	A	E	DP	FR
1894	Chi-N	.822	67	89	123	46	15	-9
1896	Cin-N	.931	127	200	262	34	28	6
1897	Cin-N	.940	134	186	236	27	19	-6
1898	Cin-N	.940	136	223	305	34	20	13
1899	Cin-N	.909	78	108	142	25	5	-12
1900	Cin-N	.931	61	74	128	15	11	-7
1901	Cin-N	.893	67	87	139	27	10	4
	Bro-N	.956	65	88	106	9	5	-2
	Yr	.921	132	175	245	36	15	2
1902	Bro-N	.927	130	173	244	33	21	-10
Total	8	.921	865	1228	1685	250	134	-23

SS

YEAR	TM/L	PCT	G	PO	A	E	DP	FR
1893	Chi-N	.910	21	55	66	12	10	-1
1894	Chi-N	.887	61	118	218	43	20	-2
1895	Chi-N	.900	3	3	6	1	1	-2
1899	Cin-N	.963	6	8	18	1	2	0
1900	Cin-N	.909	16	34	56	9	2	-3
1902	Bro-N	.800	1	1	3	1	0	0
Total	6	.897	108	219	367	7	35	-8

2B

YEAR	TM/L	PCT	G	PO	A	E	DP	FR
1899	Cin-N	.900	3	4	5	1	1	-1
1900	Cin-N	.933	3	8	6	1	1	-1
Total	2	.920	6	12	11	2	2	-2

OF

YEAR	TM/L	PCT	G	PO	A	E	DP	FR
1900	Cin-N	1.000	6	9	1	0	0	0

1B

YEAR	TM/L	PCT	G	PO	A	E	DP	FR
1899	Cin-N	1.000	1	4	0	0	1	0

■ John Irwin   3B

YEAR	TM/L	PCT	G	PO	A	E	DP	FR
1884	Bos-U	.780	105	117	191	87	7	4
1886	Phi-a	1.000	1	0	4	0	0	0
1887	Was-N	.846	4	4	7	2	0	-1
1888	Was-N	.759	10	12	10	7	1	-3
1889	Was-N	.868	58	82	129	32	14	0
1890	Buf-P	.883	64	79	139	29	13	2
1891	Bos-a	.750	2	4	5	3	0	0
	Lou-a	.795	14	13	22	9	1	-7
	Yr	.786	16	17	27	12	1	-7
Total	7	.829	258	311	507	169	36	-5

SS

YEAR	TM/L	PCT	G	PO	A	E	DP	FR
1886	Phi-a	.714	2	2	3	2	0	-1
1887	Was-N	.875	5	9	12	3	1	-2
1888	Was-N	.860	27	54	87	23	5	1
1891	Bos-a	.667	1	1	1	1	0	0
Total	4	.854	35	66	103	9	6	-2

OF

YEAR	TM/L	PCT	G	PO	A	E	DP	FR
1891	Bos-a	.882	17	25	5	4	0	1

1B

YEAR	TM/L	PCT	G	PO	A	E	DP	FR
1882	Wor-N	.636	1	7	0	4	1	-1
1890	Buf-P	.991	12	103	11	1	13	3
Total	2	.960	13	110	11	5	14	2

2B

YEAR	TM/L	PCT	G	PO	A	E	DP	FR
1890	Buf-P	.778	1	2	5	2	1	0

■ Frank Isbell   1B

YEAR	TM/L	PCT	G	PO	A	E	DP	FR
1901	Chi-A	.980	137	1387	101	31	79	13
1902	Chi-A	.986	133	1401	93	21	97	9
1903	Chi-A	.984	117	1180	87	20	57	6
1904	Chi-A	.986	57	599	48	9	22	5
1905	Chi-A	.988	9	68	14	1	4	4
1908	Chi-A	.990	65	824	46	9	30	3
1909	Chi-A	.994	101	1204	66	8	48	9
Total	7	.986	619	6663	455	9	337	43

2B

YEAR	TM/L	PCT	G	PO	A	E	DP	FR
1898	Chi-N	.667	3	2	8	5	0	-3
1901	Chi-A	1.000	2	1	2	0	0	0
1903	Chi-A	1.000	2	3	3	0	0	0
1904	Chi-A	.924	27	53	80	11	6	-5
1905	Chi-A	.964	43	76	112	7	18	-7
1906	Chi-A	.949	132	292	363	35	36	-18
1907	Chi-A	.957	119	276	384	30	41	9
1908	Chi-A	.916	18	40	58	9	0	-1
1909	Chi-A	.933	5	15	13	2	3	0
Total	9	.947	351	758	1023	9	104	-25

YEAR	TM/L	PCT	G	PO	A	E	DP	FR
OF								
1898	Chi-N	.956	28	40	3	2	0	-3
1903	Chi-A	1.000	1	3	0	0	0	0
1904	Chi-A	1.000	5	5	0	0	0	-1
1905	Chi-A	.946	41	65	5	4	1	1
1906	Chi-A	.944	14	17	0	1	0	-3
1907	Chi-A	1.000	5	9	1	0	0	0
1909	Chi-A	.800	9	7	1	2	0	-3
Total	7	.945	103	146	10	9	1	-9
3B								
1898	Chi-N	.750	3	2	7	3	1	-1
1901	Chi-A	.667	1	0	2	1	0	0
1903	Chi-A	.831	19	25	49	15	1	2
Total	3	.817	23	27	58	9	2	1
SS								
1898	Chi-N	.750	2	3	6	3	2	-1
1901	Chi-A	1.000	1	1	1	0	0	0
1902	Chi-A	.917	4	4	7	1	3	0
1903	Chi-A	—	1	0	0	0	0	0
1904	Chi-A	.821	4	6	17	5	1	0
1905	Chi-A	.938	2	10	5	1	2	1
1907	Chi-A	—	1	0	0	0	0	0
Total	7	.857	15	24	36	0	8	0
C								
1902	Chi-A	1.000	1	0	2	0	0	0
1906	Chi-A	1.000	1	4	0	0	0	0
Total	2	1.000	2	4	2	0	0	0

■ Mike Ivie 1B

YEAR	TM/L	PCT	G	PO	A	E	DP	FR
1974	SD-N	.986	11	67	5	1	9	0
1975	SD-N	.989	78	490	36	6	47	2
1976	SD-N	.995	135	1020	70	5	89	1
1977	SD-N	.992	105	863	56	7	76	-1
1978	SF-N	.995	76	550	18	3	33	-7
1979	SF-N	.995	98	724	40	4	51	-4
1980	SF-N	.993	72	669	32	5	46	-6
1981	SF-N	1.000	5	37	4	0	2	1
	Hou-N	.989	10	76	11	1	5	2
	Yr	.992	15	113	15	1	7	3
1983	Det-A	1.000	12	86	6	0	6	0
Total	9	.993	602	4582	278	2	364	-12
3B								
1975	SD-N	.899	61	49	102	17	7	-7
1976	SD-N	1.000	2	1	1	0	1	0
1977	SD-N	.938	25	23	37	4	3	-4
1979	SF-N	1.000	4	3	4	0	0	0
Total	4	.913	92	76	144	1	11	-11
OF								
1978	SF-N	.935	22	29	0	2	0	-1
1979	SF-N	1.000	24	25	3	0	0	1
Total	2	.966	46	54	3	2	0	0
C								
1971	SD-N	1.000	6	22	2	0	0	-2
1975	SD-N	1.000	1	1	0	0	0	0
1976	SD-N	.846	2	11	0	2	0	0
Total	3	.947	9	34	2	2	0	-2
2B								
1979	SF-N	—	1	0	0	0	0	0

■ Ray Jablonski 3B

YEAR	TM/L	PCT	G	PO	A	E	DP	FR
1953	StL-N	.932	157	94	278	27	27	-16
1954	StL-N	.925	149	122	298	34	25	-7
1955	Cin-N	.872	28	24	44	10	3	-9
1956	Cin-N	.970	127	117	172	9	11	-25
1957	NY-N	.941	70	44	130	11	15	-3
1958	SF-N	.946	57	49	91	8	2	-8
1959	StL-N	.900	19	7	20	3	2	-3
	KC-A	.947	17	13	23	2	3	-3
1960	KC-A	.944	6	4	13	1	0	0
Total	8	.936	630	474	1069	105	88	-74
OF								
1955	Cin-N	.979	28	45	2	1	0	-2
1957	NY-N	—	1	0	0	0	0	0
Total	2	.979	29	45	2	1	0	-2
1B								
1954	StL-N	1.000	1	5	1	0	0	0
1957	NY-N	.984	6	55	6	1	5	0
Total	2	.985	7	60	7	1	5	0
2B								
1956	Cin-N	—	1	0	0	0	0	0
SS								
1959	StL-N	—	1	0	0	0	0	0

■ Fred Jacklitsch C

YEAR	TM/L	PCT	G	PO	A	E	DP	FR
1900	Phi-N	1.000	3	2	1	0	1	-2
1901	Phi-N	.971	30	126	39	5	3	0
1902	Phi-N	.927	29	121	31	12	0	-7
1903	Bro-N	.975	53	201	71	7	7	-7
1904	Bro-N	.846	5	14	8	4	0	-1
1905	NY-A	1.000	1	6	1	0	0	0
1907	Phi-N	.984	58	270	97	6	15	11
1908	Phi-N	.976	30	126	38	4	1	3
1909	Phi-N	.964	11	44	10	2	0	-1
1910	Phi-N	.989	13	72	21	1	0	5
1914	Bal-F	.988	118	580	167	9	13	3
1915	Bal-F	.992	45	206	50	2	8	-7
1917	Bos-N	1.000	1	0	0	0	0	0
Total	13	.978	397	1769	534	2	48	-3
1B								
1904	Bro-N	.957	11	106	6	5	6	-1
1907	Phi-N	.958	6	44	2	2	3	-1
1910	Phi-N	1.000	2	5	0	0	0	0
Total	3	.959	19	155	8	7	9	-2
2B								
1903	Bro-N	.600	1	2	1	2	0	-1
1904	Bro-N	.848	8	10	18	5	0	-5
1909	Phi-N	.500	1	1	0	1	0	-1
1910	Phi-N	1.000	1	2	2	0	0	0
Total	4	.818	11	15	21	8	0	-7
OF								
1902	Phi-N	.667	1	2	0	1	0	0
1903	Bro-N	—	1	0	0	0	0	0
1907	Phi-N	—	1	0	0	0	0	0
Total	3	.667	3	2	0	1	0	0
3B								
1901	Phi-N	1.000	1	0	1	0	0	0
1910	Phi-N	.667	1	1	1	1	0	0
Total	2	.750	2	1	2	1	0	0
SS								
1915	Bal-F	1.000	1	0	1	0	0	0

■ Darrin Jackson OF

YEAR	TM/L	PCT	G	PO	A	E	DP	FR
1985	Chi-N	1.000	4	7	0	0	0	0
1987	Chi-N	1.000	5	1	0	0	0	0
1988	Chi-N	.983	74	116	1	2	0	5
1989	Chi-N	.970	39	61	3	2	2	5
	SD-N	.954	24	60	2	3	2	2
	Yr	.962	63	121	5	5	4	7
1990	SD-N	.985	39	63	1	1	1	1
Total	5	.975	185	308	7	8	5	13

■ George Jackson OF

YEAR	TM/L	PCT	G	PO	A	E	DP	FR
1911	Bos-N	.929	39	74	4	6	1	-3
1912	Bos-N	.943	107	230	20	15	3	5
1913	Bos-N	.875	3	6	1	1	0	1
Total	3	.938	149	310	25	22	4	3

■ Jim Jackson OF

YEAR	TM/L	PCT	G	PO	A	E	DP	FR
1901	Bal-A	**.971**	96	234	4	7	1	3
1902	NY-N	.897	34	57	4	7	0	-2
1905	Cle-A	.950	106	193	16	11	3	5
1906	Cle-A	.975	104	189	5	5	2	-6
Total	4	.959	340	673	29	30	6	0
3B								
1905	Cle-A	.833	3	5	5	2	0	-1

■ Joe Jackson OF

YEAR	TM/L	PCT	G	PO	A	E	DP	FR
1908	Phi-A	.875	5	6	1	1	0	0
1909	Phi-A	.833	4	10	0	2	0	0
1910	Cle-A	.977	20	40	2	1	1	1
1911	Cle-A	.958	147	242	32	12	8	8
1912	Cle-A	.950	150	273	30	16	2	12
1913	Cle-A	.930	148	211	28	18	5	2
1914	Cle-A	.967	119	195	13	7	4	2
1915	Cle-A	.961	49	68	6	3	0	-2
	Chi-A	.947	46	84	6	5	1	-2
	Yr	.953	95	152	12	8	1	-4
1916	Chi-A	.975	155	290	17	8	5	-1
1917	Chi-A	.984	145	341	18	6	4	9
1918	Chi-A	1.000	17	36	1	0	0	0
1919	Chi-A	.967	139	252	15	9	4	-4
1920	Chi-A	.965	145	314	14	12	2	-1
Total	13	.962	1289	2362	183	100	36	24
1B								
1915	Cle-A	.977	30	284	15	7	12	-2

■ Randy Jackson 3B

YEAR	TM/L	PCT	G	PO	A	E	DP	FR
1950	Chi-N	.911	27	26	56	8	3	-4
1951	Chi-N	.956	143	**198**	**323**	**24**	32	8
1952	Chi-N	.958	104	91	203	13	13	-3
1953	Chi-N	.949	133	141	265	22	24	3
1954	Chi-N	.955	124	118	266	18	21	0
1955	Chi-N	.949	134	125	247	20	**26**	-13
1956	Bro-N	.993	80	84	184	2	19	**21**
1957	Bro-N	.976	34	27	53	2	7	-2
1958	LA-N	.964	17	13	41	2	6	7
	Cle-A	.901	24	25	57	9	4	5
1959	Cle-A	1.000	2	0	2	0	0	-1
	Chi-N	.941	22	20	28	3	2	-2
Total	10	.955	844	868	1725	123	157	19
OF								
1952	Chi-N	1.000	1	2	0	0	0	0
1959	Chi-N	—	1	0	0	0	0	0
Total	2	1.000	2	2	0	0	0	0

■ Reggie Jackson OF

YEAR	TM/L	PCT	G	PO	A	E	DP	FR
1967	KC-A	.933	34	55	1	4	0	-3
1968	Oak-A	.959	151	269	14	**12**	5	7
1969	Oak-A	.964	150	278	14	11	2	2
1970	Oak-A	.956	142	251	8	**12**	0	-4
1971	Oak-A	.977	145	285	15	7	3	6
1972	Oak-A	.971	135	301	5	**9**	**5**	6
1973	Oak-A	.971	145	302	4	9	0	-2
1974	Oak-A	.967	127	296	8	10	2	5
1975	Oak-A	.965	147	315	13	**12**	5	4
1976	Bal-A	.964	121	284	8	**11**	3	2
1977	NY-A	.949	127	236	7	13	0	-7
1978	NY-A	.986	104	212	6	3	1	0
1979	NY-A	.986	125	274	7	4	2	3
1980	NY-A	.962	94	174	3	7	0	-8
1981	NY-A	.974	61	111	3	3	0	-3
1982	Cal-A	.972	139	200	6	6	1	-23
1983	Cal-A	.986	47	66	4	1	1	-4
1984	Cal-A	1.000	3	7	0	0	0	0
1985	Cal-A	.944	81	112	6	7	1	-10
1986	Cal-A	.833	4	4	1	1	0	0
1987	Oak-A	1.000	20	30	0	0	0	-1
Total	21	.967	2102	4062	133	142	31	-30

■ Sonny Jackson SS

YEAR	TM/L	PCT	G	PO	A	E	DP	FR
1963	Hou-N	.833	1	0	5	1	0	1
1964	Hou-N	.870	7	8	12	3	1	-3
1965	Hou-N	.969	8	16	15	1	3	0
1966	Hou-N	.961	150	270	449	**37**	73	-13
1967	Hou-N	.943	128	204	379	**35**	63	-8
1968	Atl-N	.952	99	132	307	22	35	-17
1969	Atl-N	.961	97	161	254	17	48	-23
1970	Atl-N	.933	87	123	240	26	40	-23
1972	Atl-N	.976	17	28	52	2	9	-3
1973	Atl-N	.963	36	42	88	5	10	-2
Total	10	.949	630	984	1801	149	282	-91
OF								
1971	Atl-N	.980	145	336	8	7	0	-3
1972	Atl-N	1.000	10	6	0	0	0	0
1973	Atl-N	.981	56	51	1	1	0	0
1974	Atl-N	1.000	1	2	0	0	0	0
Total	4	.981	212	395	9	8	0	-3
3B								
1965	Hou-N	—	1	0	0	0	0	0
1972	Atl-N	.958	6	13	10	1	0	0
Total	2	.958	7	13	10	1	0	0

■ Ron Jackson 1B

YEAR	TM/L	PCT	G	PO	A	E	DP	FR
1954	Chi-A	.988	35	244	9	3	15	-2
1955	Chi-A	.988	29	162	9	2	14	-1
1956	Chi-A	1.000	19	138	11	0	16	1
1957	Chi-A	.992	13	125	5	1	10	-1
1958	Chi-A	.997	38	289	16	1	29	-2
1959	Chi-A	1.000	5	30	1	0	3	0
1960	Bos-A	.973	9	66	5	2	10	0
Total	7	.992	148	1054	56	9	97	-5

■ Ron Jackson 1B

YEAR	TM/L	PCT	G	PO	A	E	DP	FR
1977	Cal-A	.990	43	278	27	3	27	3
1978	Cal-A	.994	75	580	56	4	50	3
1979	Min-A	.994	**157**	**1447**	**137**	9	**175**	**12**
1980	Min-A	.991	119	983	74	10	105	3
1981	Min-A	.988	36	309	26	4	26	0
	Det-A	1.000	29	218	15	0	20	-1
	Yr	.993	65	527	41	4	46	-1
1982	Cal-A	.994	37	315	19	2	37	0
1983	Cal-A	.992	35	334	21	3	34	0
1984	Cal-A	.990	21	186	13	2	17	0
Total	8	.993	552	4650	388	7	491	20
3B								
1975	Cal-A	.833	3	2	3	1	0	-1
1976	Cal-A	.950	114	85	222	16	19	2
1977	Cal-A	.964	30	33	48	3	6	1
1978	Cal-A	.950	31	25	32	3	6	-6
1979	Min-A	1.000	1	1	3	0	0	0
1980	Min-A	—	2	0	0	0	0	0
1981	Min-A	.833	3	2	3	1	0	-1
1982	Cal-A	1.000	9	2	12	0	0	1
1983	Cal-A	.957	38	41	92	6	9	7
1984	Cal-A	.950	9	9	10	1	1	0
	Bal-A	.960	10	12	12	1	4	1
	Yr	.956	19	21	22	2	5	1
Total	10	.953	250	212	437	2	45	4
OF								
1975	Cal-A	.947	9	17	1	1	0	0
1976	Cal-A	1.000	4	1	0	0	0	0
1977	Cal-A	1.000	3	3	0	0	0	0
1978	Cal-A	.500	1	1	0	1	0	0
1979	Min-A	—	1	0	0	0	0	0
1980	Min-A	1.000	15	17	0	0	0	0
1981	Min-A	1.000	7	18	1	0	1	1
1983	Cal-A	.875	15	27	1	4	0	-2
1984	Cal-A	1.000	1	1	0	0	0	0
Total	9	.936	56	85	3	6	0	-1
2B								
1976	Cal-A	1.000	7	5	3	0	1	0
SS								
1977	Cal-A	—	1	0	0	0	0	0
1979	Min-A	—	1	0	0	0	0	0
Total	2	—	2	0	0	0	0	0

■ Travis Jackson SS

YEAR	TM/L	PCT	G	PO	A	E	DP	FR
1922	NY-N	.909	3	3	7	1	1	0
1923	NY-N	.943	60	86	210	18	26	-6
1924	NY-N	.937	151	332	534	**58**	101	0
1925	NY-N	.941	110	277	366	40	64	4
1926	NY-N	.962	108	256	351	24	71	0
1927	NY-N	.952	124	287	**444**	37	**85**	**27**
1928	NY-N	.952	**149**	354	**547**	45	112	**28**
1929	NY-N	**.969**	**149**	329	**552**	28	**110**	19
1930	NY-N	.956	115	218	441	30	72	**11**
1931	NY-N	**.970**	**145**	303	**496**	25	79	10
1932	NY-N	.925	52	106	166	22	31	-5
1933	NY-N	.890	21	32	41	9	13	3
1934	NY-N	.945	130	283	458	**43**	59	10
1936	NY-N	.971	9	11	22	1	2	1
Total	14	.952	1326	2877	4635	381	826	102
3B								
1923	NY-N	.928	31	17	47	5	3	0
1927	NY-N	1.000	2	5	5	0	0	1
1933	NY-N	.971	21	20	46	2	3	4
1934	NY-N	1.000	9	9	19	0	1	2
1935	NY-N	.947	128	139	220	20	13	-7
1936	NY-N	.952	116	99	196	15	8	-2
Total	6	.951	307	289	533	2	28	-2
2B								
1923	NY-N	1.000	1	4	8	0	2	3
OF								
1926	NY-N	1.000	1	3	1	0	1	1

■ Bo Jackson OF

YEAR	TM/L	PCT	G	PO	A	E	DP	FR
1986	KC-A	.886	23	29	2	4	0	-3
1987	KC-A	.955	113	180	9	9	1	-8
1988	KC-A	.973	121	246	11	7	2	3
1989	KC-A	.967	110	224	11	8	2	4
1990	KC-A	.952	97	230	8	12	2	1
Total	5	.960	464	909	41	40	7	-3

■ Spook Jacobs 2B

YEAR	TM/L	PCT	G	PO	A	E	DP	FR
1954	Phi-A	.974	131	347	300	17	98	-19
1955	KC-A	1.000	7	9	9	0	4	-3
1956	KC-A	.931	31	78	71	5	26	-3
	Pit-N	.926	11	26	24	4	5	-4
Total	3	.971	180	460	404	6	133	-29

Baby Doll Jacobson OF

YEAR	TM/L	PCT	G	PO	A	E	DP	FR
1915	Det-A	1.000	7	8	1	0	0	-2
	StL-A	.981	32	50	2	1	1	-1
	Yr	.984	39	58	3	1	1	-3
1917	StL-A	.975	131	292	18	8	6	7
1919	StL-A	.949	106	270	9	15	2	2
1920	StL-A	.979	154	394	18	9	5	11
1921	StL-A	.982	142	378	7	7	1	3
1922	StL-A	.969	137	367	9	12	3	5
1923	StL-A	.974	146	409	10	11	4	8
1924	StL-A	.986	152	488	7	7	4	16
1925	StL-A	.965	139	343	18	13	9	1
1926	StL-A	.964	50	105	2	4	0	-6
	Bos-A	.980	98	193	7	4	1	-8
	Yr	.975	148	298	9	8	1	-14
1927	Bos-A	.979	39	90	4	2	0	1
	Cle-A	.932	31	81	1	6	0	-1
	Phi-A	1.000	14	9	0	0	0	-5
	Yr	.959	84	180	5	8	0	-5
Total	11	.973	1378	3477	113	9	36	31

1B

YEAR	TM/L	PCT	G	PO	A	E	DP	FR
1915	Det-A	.983	10	114	4	2	5	-1
1917	StL-A	.947	11	119	7	7	4	-1
1919	StL-A	.987	8	75	2	1	2	-1
1920	StL-A	—	1	0	0	0	0	0
1921	StL-A	1.000	11	91	12	0	10	3
1922	StL-A	.967	7	57	2	2	0	-1
Total	6	.976	48	456	27	2	21	-1

Brook Jacoby 3B

YEAR	TM/L	PCT	G	PO	A	E	DP	FR
1981	Atl-N	1.000	3	3	4	0	1	2
1983	Atl-N	1.000	2	0	2	0	0	-1
1984	Cle-A	.951	126	86	187	14	17	-20
1985	Cle-A	.958	161	114	319	19	26	-8
1986	Cle-A	.941	158	109	292	25	24	-13
1987	Cle-A	.946	144	134	254	22	19	-8
1988	Cle-A	.975	151	99	298	10	23	1
1989	Cle-A	.955	144	92	268	17	15	-10
1990	Cle-A	.981	99	44	158	4	14	-4
Total	9	.957	988	681	1782	111	139	-61

1B

YEAR	TM/L	PCT	G	PO	A	E	DP	FR
1987	Cle-A	1.000	7	58	7	0	5	1
1990	Cle-A	.997	78	584	28	2	61	-8
Total	2	.997	85	642	35	2	66	-7

SS

YEAR	TM/L	PCT	G	PO	A	E	DP	FR
1984	Cle-A	1.000	1	0	1	0	0	0

2B

YEAR	TM/L	PCT	G	PO	A	E	DP	FR
1985	Cle-A	—	1	0	0	0	0	0

Charlie James OF

YEAR	TM/L	PCT	G	PO	A	E	DP	FR
1960	StL-N	.917	37	21	1	2	1	0
1961	StL-N	.962	90	151	3	6	1	-5
1962	StL-N	.988	116	156	7	2	1	-9
1963	StL-N	.994	101	169	4	1	1	-3
1964	StL-N	.963	60	76	3	3	0	-5
1965	Cin-N	.909	7	10	0	1	0	0
Total	6	.976	411	583	18	5	4	-22

Cleo James OF

YEAR	TM/L	PCT	G	PO	A	E	DP	FR
1968	LA-N	1.000	2	2	0	0	0	0
1970	Chi-N	1.000	90	115	5	0	1	7
1971	Chi-N	.979	48	89	4	2	2	2
1973	Chi-N	.960	22	23	1	1	0	2
Total	4	.988	162	229	10	3	3	11

3B

YEAR	TM/L	PCT	G	PO	A	E	DP	FR
1971	Chi-N	1.000	2	1	1	0	0	0

Dion James OF

YEAR	TM/L	PCT	G	PO	A	E	DP	FR
1983	Mil-A	1.000	9	12	1	0	0	1
1984	Mil-A	.989	118	252	7	3	1	1
1985	Mil-A	1.000	11	20	0	0	0	-1
1987	Atl-N	.996	126	262	4	1	1	-6
1988	Atl-N	.987	120	222	5	3	0	-5
1989	Atl-N	1.000	46	87	0	0	0	-2
	Cle-A	.976	37	82	1	2	0	-2
1990	Cle-A	.947	33	54	0	3	0	-3
Total	7	.988	500	991	18	2	2	-17

1B

YEAR	TM/L	PCT	G	PO	A	E	DP	FR
1989	Atl-N	1.000	8	39	7	0	5	2
	Cle-A	.750	2	3	0	1	0	0
1990	Cle-A	.996	35	228	17	1	21	-1
Total	2	.993	45	270	24	2	26	1

Chris James OF

YEAR	TM/L	PCT	G	PO	A	E	DP	FR
1986	Phi-N	1.000	11	19	0	0	0	-1
1987	Phi-N	.990	108	198	5	2	1	-2
1988	Phi-N	.989	116	256	7	3	3	8
1989	Phi-N	.985	37	61	3	1	0	-2
	SD-N	.987	79	145	3	2	0	-3
	Yr	.986	116	206	6	3	0	-5
1990	Cle-A	1.000	14	25	1	0	0	0
Total	5	.989	365	704	19	8	4	0

3B

YEAR	TM/L	PCT	G	PO	A	E	DP	FR
1988	Phi-N	.921	31	26	44	6	3	-6
1989	Phi-N	.900	11	5	13	2	2	-1
	SD-N	.857	6	4	8	2	2	-1
	Yr	.882	17	9	21	4	4	-2
Total	2	.909	48	35	65	10	7	-8

Charlie Jamieson OF

YEAR	TM/L	PCT	G	PO	A	E	DP	FR
1915	Was-A	1.000	17	36	5	0	0	4
1916	Was-A	.913	41	59	4	6	3	-3
1917	Was-A	.875	9	14	0	2	0	-2
	Phi-A	.937	83	121	12	9	4	-2
	Yr	.930	92	135	12	11	4	-4
1918	Phi-A	.970	102	182	15	6	4	0
1919	Cle-A	1.000	3	4	0	0	0	-1
1920	Cle-A	.966	98	185	14	7	0	-2
1921	Cle-A	.974	137	277	17	8	3	-6
1922	Cle-A	.978	144	289	18	7	5	-1
1923	Cle-A	.974	152	360	18	10	1	8
1924	Cle-A	.974	139	330	11	9	6	4
1925	Cle-A	.955	135	324	16	16	4	7
1926	Cle-A	.960	143	293	15	13	5	0
1927	Cle-A	.969	127	300	13	10	2	5
1928	Cle-A	.984	111	282	22	5	1	20
1929	Cle-A	.980	93	192	8	4	1	-2
1930	Cle-A	.955	95	162	7	8	0	-5
1931	Cle-A	.833	7	10	0	2	0	-2
1932	Cle-A	1.000	2	3	1	0	0	1
Total	18	.967	1638	3423	196	122	39	23

1B

YEAR	TM/L	PCT	G	PO	A	E	DP	FR
1916	Was-A	.939	4	29	2	2	1	0
1920	Cle-A	.909	4	9	1	1	0	0
Total	2	.932	8	38	3	3	1	0

Hal Janvrin SS

YEAR	TM/L	PCT	G	PO	A	E	DP	FR
1913	Bos-A	.923	48	80	124	17	8	-5
1914	Bos-A	.853	20	40	47	15	10	-6
1915	Bos-A	.917	64	105	160	24	14	-15
1916	Bos-A	.921	59	110	122	20	22	-11
1917	Bos-A	.900	10	2	7	1	0	-1
1919	Was-A	.615	2	6	2	5	0	-2
	StL-N	.750	1	1	2	1	0	-1
1920	StL-N	.926	27	42	46	7	10	-5
1921	Bro-N	.922	17	22	25	4	2	-1
1922	Bro-N	.400	4	0	2	3	1	-1
Total	9	.907	252	408	537	7	67	-47

2B

YEAR	TM/L	PCT	G	PO	A	E	DP	FR
1913	Bos-A	.895	8	13	21	4	0	-4
1914	Bos-A	.919	59	92	136	20	12	-19
1915	Bos-A	.963	8	13	13	1	2	-1
1916	Bos-A	.958	39	56	103	7	15	-9
1917	Bos-A	.940	38	57	101	10	17	1
1919	Was-A	.927	56	108	120	18	14	-24
	StL-N	1.000	2	7	2	0	0	-1
1920	StL-N	.977	6	10	33	1	5	5
1921	StL-N	1.000	1	1	5	0	0	0
	Bro-N	.915	10	18	25	4	6	-2
	Yr	.925	11	19	30	4	6	-2
1922	Bro-N	.889	15	13	35	6	3	-2
Total	9	.933	242	388	594	1	74	-56

1B

YEAR	TM/L	PCT	G	PO	A	E	DP	FR
1911	Bos-A	.951	4	38	1	2	1	-1
1913	Bos-A	.981	6	52	1	1	4	-1
1914	Bos-A	.990	57	531	43	6	27	3
1916	Bos-A	.976	4	36	4	1	0	1
1917	Bos-A	1.000	1	4	0	0	0	0
1920	StL-N	.987	25	218	13	3	18	0
1921	StL-N	.968	9	58	3	2	5	0
	Bro-N	.965	8	53	2	2	0	-1
	Yr	.967	17	111	5	4	5	-1
1922	Bro-N	1.000	1	7	0	0	0	0
Total	8	.984	115	997	67	7	55	1

3B

YEAR	TM/L	PCT	G	PO	A	E	DP	FR
1911	Bos-A	.733	5	5	6	4	0	-1
1913	Bos-A	.935	19	27	31	4	5	0
1914	Bos-A	.895	6	6	11	2	1	-1
1915	Bos-A	.873	20	17	31	7	2	-4
1916	Bos-A	1.000	4	1	4	0	0	0
1919	StL-N	1.000	1	0	2	0	0	0
1921	Bro-N	.800	5	2	2	1	0	0
1922	Bro-N	1.000	2	1	1	0	0	0
Total	8	.891	62	59	88	8	8	-6

OF

YEAR	TM/L	PCT	G	PO	A	E	DP	FR
1920	StL-N	.950	20	37	1	2	0	-1
1921	Bro-N	.667	1	2	0	1	0	-1
1922	Bro-N	1.000	1	1	0	0	0	0
Total	3	.932	22	40	1	3	0	-2

Julian Javier 2B

YEAR	TM/L	PCT	G	PO	A	E	DP	FR
1960	StL-N	.962	119	272	338	24	71	5
1961	StL-N	.966	113	239	332	20	82	0
1962	StL-N	.977	151	344	414	18	96	1
1963	StL-N	.969	161	377	415	25	93	-14
1964	StL-N	.966	154	360	401	27	97	-7
1965	StL-N	.975	69	128	179	8	40	-6
1966	StL-N	.981	145	306	364	13	89	2
1967	StL-N	.965	138	311	352	24	72	-19
1968	StL-N	.976	139	304	339	16	68	-24
1969	StL-N	.967	141	244	374	21	70	-18
1970	StL-N	.980	137	329	413	15	84	13
1971	StL-N	.978	80	163	186	8	45	2
1972	Cin-N	1.000	5	3	6	0	0	0
Total	13	.972	1552	3380	4113	219	907	-65

3B

YEAR	TM/L	PCT	G	PO	A	E	DP	FR
1971	StL-N	1.000	1	1	2	0	0	0
1972	Cin-N	.896	19	11	32	5	4	-3
Total	2	.902	20	12	34	5	4	-3

SS

YEAR	TM/L	PCT	G	PO	A	E	DP	FR
1962	StL-N	.667	4	0	2	1	0	-1

1B

YEAR	TM/L	PCT	G	PO	A	E	DP	FR
1972	Cin-N	1.000	1	1	0	0	0	0

Stan Javier OF

YEAR	TM/L	PCT	G	PO	A	E	DP	FR
1984	NY-A	1.000	5	3	0	0	0	0
1986	Oak-A	1.000	51	118	1	0	1	10
1987	Oak-A	.983	71	111	3	2	3	7
1988	Oak-A	.980	115	240	6	5	2	0
1989	Oak-A	.991	107	219	4	2	0	1
1990	Oak-A	1.000	13	19	0	0	0	1
	LA-N	1.000	87	204	2	0	1	-3
Total	6	.990	449	914	16	9	7	14

1B

YEAR	TM/L	PCT	G	PO	A	E	DP	FR
1987	Oak-A	.976	6	38	2	1	1	0
1988	Oak-A	1.000	4	34	1	0	3	-1
1989	Oak-A	1.000	1	1	0	0	1	0
Total	3	.987	11	73	3	1	5	-1

2B

YEAR	TM/L	PCT	G	PO	A	E	DP	FR
1989	Oak-A	1.000	1	1	4	0	1	0

Hal Jeffcoat OF

YEAR	TM/L	PCT	G	PO	A	E	DP	FR
1948	Chi-N	.976	119	307	12	8	3	4
1949	Chi-N	.963	101	250	12	10	2	8
1950	Chi-N	.967	53	83	6	3	0	0
1951	Chi-N	.989	87	166	11	2	5	1
1952	Chi-N	.996	95	218	16	1	2	2
1953	Chi-N	.973	100	175	6	5	2	15
1954	Chi-N	1.000	3	1	0	0	0	0
1958	Cin-N	1.000	1	1	0	0	0	0
Total	8	.978	559	1201	63	9	14	30

Gregg Jefferies 2B

YEAR	TM/L	PCT	G	PO	A	E	DP	FR
1988	NY-N	.970	10	16	16	1	4	-2
1989	NY-N	.975	123	223	254	12	41	-29
1990	NY-N	.976	118	219	278	12	49	-11
Total	3	.976	251	458	548	5	94	-42

3B

YEAR	TM/L	PCT	G	PO	A	E	DP	FR
1988	NY-N	.979	20	17	30	1	5	-2
1989	NY-N	.957	20	19	26	2	3	-3
1990	NY-N	.956	34	23	63	4	5	2
Total	3	.962	74	59	119	7	13	-3

Stan Jefferson OF

YEAR	TM/L	PCT	G	PO	A	E	DP	FR
1986	NY-N	1.000	7	13	0	0	0	1
1987	SD-N	.987	107	232	3	3	1	-3
1988	SD-N	1.000	38	62	0	0	0	-1
1989	NY-N	1.000	7	3	0	0	0	0
	Bal-A	.988	32	79	3	1	1	2
	Yr	.988	39	82	3	1	1	2
1990	Bal-A	1.000	5	9	0	0	0	0
	Cle-A	.985	34	61	4	1	1	5
	Yr	.987	39	70	4	1	1	5
Total	5	.989	230	459	10	5	3	4

Steve Jeltz SS

YEAR	TM/L	PCT	G	PO	A	E	DP	FR
1983	Phi-N	1.000	2	3	4	0	0	0
1984	Phi-N	.992	27	37	91	1	8	11
1985	Phi-N	.958	86	106	215	14	38	6
1986	Phi-N	.967	141	229	406	22	81	-2
1987	Phi-N	.971	114	191	271	14	55	3
1988	Phi-N	.976	148	195	368	14	73	-1
1989	Phi-N	.985	63	71	121	3	15	-4
1990	KC-A	.969	23	23	39	2	9	6
Total	8	.971	604	855	1515	0	279	19

2B

YEAR	TM/L	PCT	G	PO	A	E	DP	FR
1983	Phi-N	1.000	4	1	1	0	1	0
1989	Phi-N	1.000	23	32	40	0	12	2
1990	KC-A	.977	34	28	57	2	12	6
Total	3	.988	61	61	98	2	25	8

3B

YEAR	TM/L	PCT	G	PO	A	E	DP	FR
1983	Phi-N	—	2	0	0	0	0	0
1984	Phi-N	1.000	1	0	2	0	0	0
1989	Phi-N	.945	30	8	44	3	6	3
1990	KC-A	1.000	3	1	1	0	0	0
Total	4	.949	36	9	47	3	6	3

OF

YEAR	TM/L	PCT	G	PO	A	E	DP	FR
1987	Phi-N	1.000	1	1	0	0	0	0
1989	Phi-N	—	1	0	0	0	0	0
1990	KC-A	1.000	13	6	1	0	0	1
Total	3	1.000	15	7	1	0	0	1

Tom Jenkins OF

YEAR	TM/L	PCT	G	PO	A	E	DP	FR
1925	Bos-A	.938	15	30	0	2	0	-2
1926	Bos-A	1.000	13	25	0	0	0	-1
	Phi-A	1.000	6	14	0	0	0	0
	Yr	1.000	19	39	0	0	0	-1
1929	StL-A	1.000	3	4	0	0	0	-1
1930	StL-A	1.000	2	4	0	0	0	0
1931	StL-A	.952	58	93	6	5	1	-4
1932	StL-A	.939	12	29	2	2	0	1
Total	6	.958	109	197	8	9	1	-7

Hughie Jennings SS

YEAR	TM/L	PCT	G	PO	A	E	DP	FR
1891	Lou-a	.894	70	187	225	49	28	9
1892	Lou-N	.907	152	343	537	90	59	15
1893	Lou-N	.899	23	52	90	16	11	6
	Bal-N	.886	15	34	36	9	4	-2
	Yr	.895	38	86	126	25	15	4
1894	Bal-N	.928	128	307	499	63	69	33
1895	Bal-N	.940	131	425	457	56	71	36
1896	Bal-N	.928	130	377	476	66	70	34
1897	Bal-N	.933	116	335	425	55	54	27
1898	Bal-N	.929	115	289	368	50	41	3
1899	Bro-N	.925	11	25	22	10	3	-7
	Bro-N	.833	1	3	2	1	1	-1
	Yr	.825	12	28	24	11	4	-8
1901	Phi-N	.857	1	4	2	1	0	-1
1902	Phi-N	.882	5	8	7	2	0	-1
1907	Det-A	.500	1	1	1	2	0	-1
Total	12	.922	899	2390	3147	470	411	150

1B

YEAR	TM/L	PCT	G	PO	A	E	DP	FR
1891	Lou-a	.973	17	174	5	5	10	-1
1899	Bro-N	.962	4	22	3	1	1	1
	Bro-N	.987	46	424	22	6	23	1
	Yr	.985	50	446	25	7	24	2
1900	Bro-N	.982	112	1050	76	21	71	6
1901	Phi-N	.979	80	745	38	17	20	-3
1902	Phi-N	.983	69	659	46	12	32	4
1909	Det-A	1.000	2	9	1	0	0	2
1918	Det-A	1.000	1	2	0	0	0	0
Total	7	.981	331	3085	191	2	159	8

2B

YEAR	TM/L	PCT	G	PO	A	E	DP	FR
1898	Bal-N	.925	27	75	72	12	10	-3
1899	Bal-N	1.000	2	3	5	0	0	-1
	Bro-N	.833	1	3	2	1	0	-1
	Yr	.929	3	6	7	1	0	-2
1900	Bro-N	.846	2	3	8	2	0	0

YEAR	TM/L	PCT	G	PO	A	E	DP	FR
1901	Phi-N	1.000	1	1	6	0	1	0
1902	Phi-N	.952	4	10	10	1	1	-1
1907	Det-A	.750	1	1	2	1	0	0
Total	6	.922	38	96	105	7	12	-6
	OF							
1893	Bal-N	—	1	0	0	0	0	0
1898	Bal-N	1.000	1	1	0	0	0	0
1903	Bro-N	1.000	4	7	0	0	0	0
Total	3	1.000	6	8	0	0	0	0
	3B							
1891	Lou-a	.750	3	3	6	3	0	-1

■ Woody Jensen   OF

YEAR	TM/L	PCT	G	PO	A	E	DP	FR
1931	Pit-N	.974	67	182	2	5	1	0
1932	Pit-N	—	1	0	0	0	0	0
1933	Pit-N	.980	40	95	1	2	0	-2
1934	Pit-N	.993	66	143	1	1	0	-1
1935	Pit-N	.977	140	290	6	7	1	-6
1936	Pit-N	.975	153	338	6	9	1	-1
1937	Pit-N	.963	120	256	5	10	1	-1
1938	Pit-N	.900	38	45	0	5	0	-3
1939	Pit-N	1.000	3	0	1	0	0	0
Total	9	.972	628	1349	22	9	4	-14

■ Jackie Jensen   OF

YEAR	TM/L	PCT	G	PO	A	E	DP	FR
1950	NY-A	.947	23	36	0	2	0	0
1951	NY-A	.974	48	106	6	3	1	4
1952	NY-A	1.000	5	8	0	0	0	-1
	Was-A	.977	143	283	17	7	1	3
	Yr	.978	148	291	17	7	1	2
1953	Was-A	.983	146	274	9	5	0	-6
1954	Bos-A	.986	151	331	12	5	0	-15
1955	Bos-A	.977	150	281	11	7	3	-2
1956	Bos-A	.962	151	291	13	12	2	-2
1957	Bos-A	.960	144	251	16	11	4	0
1958	Bos-A	.981	153	293	14	6	3	3
1959	Bos-A	.982	146	311	12	6	4	11
1961	Bos-A	.986	131	274	14	4	2	9
Total	11	.977	1391	2739	124	8	20	4

■ Johnny Jeter   OF

YEAR	TM/L	PCT	G	PO	A	E	DP	FR
1969	Pit-N	1.000	20	12	1	0	0	1
1970	Pit-N	1.000	56	53	2	0	0	1
1971	SD-N	.967	17	57	1	2	1	4
1972	SD-N	.987	91	222	1	3	0	-3
1973	Chi-A	.955	72	144	3	7	0	-9
1974	Cle-A	.833	6	5	0	1	0	-2
Total	6	.975	262	493	8	3	1	-8

■ Sam Jethroe   OF

YEAR	TM/L	PCT	G	PO	A	E	DP	FR
1950	Bos-N	.969	141	355	17	12	6	4
1951	Bos-N	.974	140	356	18	10	4	0
1952	Bos-N	.970	151	413	10	13	3	2
1954	Pit-N	1.000	1	1	0	0	0	0
Total	4	.971	433	1125	45	5	13	6

■ Houston Jimenez   SS

YEAR	TM/L	PCT	G	PO	A	E	DP	FR
1983	Min-A	.969	36	43	83	4	20	4
1984	Min-A	.959	107	145	273	18	59	-5
1987	Pit-N	1.000	2	1	8	0	1	1
1988	Cle-A	1.000	2	3	2	0	2	0
Total	4	.962	147	192	366	2	82	0
	2B							
1987	Pit-N	1.000	2	2	0	0	0	0
1988	Cle-A	.973	7	10	26	1	3	5
Total	2	.974	9	12	26	1	3	5

■ Manny Jimenez   OF

YEAR	TM/L	PCT	G	PO	A	E	DP	FR
1962	KC-A	.985	122	185	7	3	0	-7
1963	KC-A	.960	40	66	6	3	0	-1
1964	KC-A	.939	49	59	3	4	1	-5
1966	KC-A	.909	12	9	1	1	0	-2
1967	Pit-N	1.000	6	4	0	0	0	-1
1968	Pit-N	.857	5	6	0	1	0	-1
Total	6	.966	234	329	17	2	1	-17

■ Alex Johnson   OF

YEAR	TM/L	PCT	G	PO	A	E	DP	FR
1964	Phi-N	.980	35	47	1	1	0	0
1965	Phi-N	.966	82	109	3	4	0	-2
1966	StL-N	.962	22	23	2	1	0	-3
1967	StL-N	.970	57	91	7	3	2	7
1968	Cin-N	.947	140	243	8	14	2	-5
1969	Cin-N	.927	132	222	5	18	1	-9
1970	Cal-A	.959	156	269	11	12	0	-3
1971	Cal-A	.926	61	84	3	7	0	-12
1972	Cle-A	.955	95	145	4	7	1	-12
1973	Tex-A	.987	41	72	4	1	0	-1
1974	Tex-A	.956	81	168	6	8	2	-4
	NY-A	—	1	0	0	0	0	0
	Yr	.956	82	168	6	8	2	-4
1975	NY-A	1.000	7	9	0	0	0	0
1976	Det-A	.954	90	159	7	8	1	-6
Total	13	.953	1000	1641	61	4	9	-50

■ Cliff Johnson   1B

YEAR	TM/L	PCT	G	PO	A	E	DP	FR
1973	Hou-N	1.000	5	47	2	0	7	0
1974	Hou-N	.994	21	147	9	1	13	0
1975	Hou-N	.991	47	407	21	4	33	-3
1976	Hou-N	1.000	16	117	1	0	8	-2
1977	Hou-N	1.000	10	64	7	0	8	1
	NY-A	.990	11	89	8	1	11	1
1978	NY-A	1.000	1	4	0	0	0	0
1980	Chi-N	.992	46	468	16	4	34	-5
1981	Oak-A	1.000	9	42	1	0	2	-1
1982	Oak-A	.987	11	66	8	1	7	1
1983	Tor-A	1.000	6	47	4	0	5	0
1984	Tor-A	1.000	2	26	0	0	0	-1
1985	Tor-A	.947	3	17	1	1	4	0
1986	Tor-A	1.000	1	8	1	0	2	0
Total	13	.993	189	1549	79	2	134	-9

YEAR	TM/L	PCT	G	PO	A	E	DP	FR
	C							
1972	Hou-N	1.000	1	6	0	0	0	0
1974	Hou-N	.978	28	123	9	3	4	-3
1975	Hou-N	.963	41	195	16	8	4	-10
1976	Hou-N	.977	66	312	34	8	2	-8
1977	NY-A	1.000	15	56	6	0	0	2
1978	NY-A	.975	22	67	10	2	1	1
1979	NY-A	1.000	4	10	1	0	0	0
	Cle-A	—	1	0	0	0	0	0
	Yr	1.000	5	10	1	0	0	0
1980	Chi-N	1.000	1	1	0	0	0	0
Total	8	.976	179	770	76	1	11	-18
	OF							
1975	Hou-N	1.000	1	2	1	0	0	1
1976	Hou-N	.975	20	39	0	1	0	-1
1977	Hou-N	.946	34	49	4	3	0	-2
1980	Chi-N	.667	3	2	0	1	0	0
Total	4	.951	58	92	5	5	0	-2

■ Darrell Johnson   C

YEAR	TM/L	PCT	G	PO	A	E	DP	FR
1952	StL-A	.990	22	86	14	1	3	1
	Chi-A	.955	21	75	9	4	1	4
	Yr	.974	43	161	23	5	4	5
1957	NY-A	1.000	20	75	6	0	1	4
1958	NY-A	1.000	4	22	3	0	1	1
1960	StL-N	1.000	8	10	1	0	0	1
1961	Phi-N	.982	21	99	13	2	2	3
	Cin-N	1.000	20	99	10	0	2	4
	Yr	.991	41	198	23	2	4	7
1962	Cin-N	1.000	2	16	2	0	0	2
	Bal-A	1.000	6	30	2	0	1	-1
Total	6	.988	124	512	62	7	11	19

■ Dave Johnson   2B

YEAR	TM/L	PCT	G	PO	A	E	DP	FR
1965	Bal-A	1.000	3	4	12	0	5	2
1966	Bal-A	.971	126	288	347	19	75	2
1967	Bal-A	.981	144	340	348	13	75	0
1968	Bal-A	.978	127	260	330	13	67	7
1969	Bal-A	.984	142	355	369	12	93	-3
1970	Bal-A	.990	149	379	390	8	101	1
1971	Bal-A	.984	140	361	367	12	103	-1
1972	Bal-A	.990	116	286	307	6	81	10
1973	Atl-N	.966	156	383	464	30	106	-3
1974	Atl-N	.982	71	148	177	6	43	3
1977	Phi-N	1.000	9	7	15	0	4	0
1978	Phi-N	.930	15	26	27	4	6	-6
Total	12	.980	1198	2837	3153	123	759	12
	1B							
1974	Atl-N	.993	73	641	54	5	57	4
1977	Phi-N	1.000	43	291	14	0	26	-2
1978	Phi-N	1.000	7	29	4	0	4	1
Total	3	.995	123	961	72	5	87	3
	SS							
1965	Bal-A	.857	2	2	4	1	1	0
1966	Bal-A	.941	3	6	10	1	2	0
1968	Bal-A	.974	34	34	40	2	7	-3
1969	Bal-A	1.000	2	3	1	0	0	0
1970	Bal-A	1.000	2	3	1	0	1	0
Total	5	.963	43	48	56	4	11	-3
	3B							
1965	Bal-A	.929	9	5	21	2	1	1
1967	Bal-A	.875	3	4	3	1	1	0
1977	Phi-N	1.000	6	1	2	0	0	0
1978	Phi-N	.857	9	2	10	2	0	-1
	Chi-N	.839	12	4	22	5	1	-3
	Yr	.844	21	6	32	7	1	-4
Total	4	.881	39	16	58	0	3	-3

■ Deron Johnson   1B

YEAR	TM/L	PCT	G	PO	A	E	DP	FR
1961	KC-A	1.000	3	11	2	0	2	0
1962	KC-A	1.000	2	3	0	0	0	0
1964	Cin-N	.990	131	940	81	10	82	3
1966	Cin-N	.990	71	186	10	2	19	-2
1967	Cin-N	.997	81	587	41	2	47	-1
1968	Atl-N	.996	97	738	46	3	66	-4
1969	Phi-N	.993	18	129	6	1	8	-2
1970	Phi-N	.995	154	1178	73	6	104	-11
1971	Phi-N	.995	136	1219	88	7	124	-2
1972	Phi-N	.982	62	479	24	9	43	-4
1973	Phi-N	.976	10	77	6	2	12	0
	Oak-A	.994	23	167	6	1	20	-3
1974	Oak-A	.991	28	211	9	2	14	-2
	Mil-A	.833	2	9	1	2	3	0
	Yr	.983	30	220	10	4	17	-2
1975	Chi-A	.994	55	456	24	3	38	-4
	Bos-A	1.000	2	19	0	0	2	0
	Yr	.994	57	475	24	3	40	-4
1976	Bos-A	1.000	5	30	1	0	3	0
Total	14	.993	880	6439	418	0	587	-32
	3B							
1960	NY-A	.750	5	0	3	1	0	0
1961	NY-A	1.000	8	2	15	0	0	2
	KC-A	.952	19	17	43	3	5	2
	Yr	.962	27	19	58	3	5	4
1962	KC-A	.500	2	0	1	1	0	-1
1964	Cin-N	1.000	1	0	3	0	0	0
1965	Cin-N	.948	159	132	266	22	26	-12
1966	Cin-N	1.000	18	12	22	0	1	-2
1967	Cin-N	.962	24	19	32	2	4	-1
1968	Atl-N	.981	21	21	32	1	0	1
1969	Phi-N	.928	50	36	92	10	4	-7
1970	Phi-N	1.000	3	2	1	0	0	0
1971	Phi-N	.907	22	14	35	5	1	-3
Total	11	.947	332	255	545	5	41	-21
	OF							
1961	KC-A	.948	59	104	6	6	0	-2
1962	KC-A	1.000	2	2	0	0	0	0
1964	Cin-N	1.000	10	12	0	0	0	0

YEAR	TM/L	PCT	G	PO	A	E	DP	FR
1966	Cin-N	.980	106	141	4	3	1	-8
1969	Phi-N	1.000	72	85	1	0	0	-6
Total	5	.975	249	344	11	9	1	-16

■ Don Johnson   2B

YEAR	TM/L	PCT	G	PO	A	E	DP	FR
1943	Chi-N	.957	10	32	35	3	8	3
1944	Chi-N	.947	154	385	462	47	85	1
1945	Chi-N	.975	138	309	440	19	74	10
1946	Chi-N	.981	83	192	228	8	34	-10
1947	Chi-N	.970	108	255	291	17	65	-6
1948	Chi-N	1.000	2	2	1	0	1	0
Total	6	.966	495	1175	1457	4	267	-2
	3B							
1947	Chi-N	1.000	6	5	11	0	4	2
1948	Chi-N	.600	2	1	2	2	1	-1
Total	2	.905	8	6	13	2	5	1

■ Ernie Johnson   SS

YEAR	TM/L	PCT	G	PO	A	E	DP	FR
1912	Chi-A	.984	16	23	37	1	3	3
1915	StL-F	.942	152	348	477	51	64	18
1916	StL-A	.936	60	115	192	21	19	-6
1917	StL-A	.924	39	77	106	15	8	2
1918	StL-A	.821	11	6	17	5	1	-2
1921	Chi-A	.947	141	291	494	44	80	18
1922	Chi-A	.952	141	259	468	37	74	3
1923	Chi-A	.922	12	24	35	5	9	0
	NY-A	.977	15	21	22	1	4	-1
	Yr	.944	27	45	57	6	13	-1
1924	NY-A	.857	9	2	4	1	1	0
1925	NY-A	.959	28	30	17	2	4	-4
Total	10	.944	624	1196	1869	183	267	31
	2B							
1917	StL-A	.904	18	34	51	9	9	3
1924	NY-A	.955	27	54	74	6	12	-1
1925	NY-A	.955	34	58	90	7	17	-5
Total	3	.943	79	146	215	2	38	-3
	3B							
1916	StL-A	.903	12	11	17	3	1	-2
1917	StL-A	.981	14	11	40	1	2	6
1918	StL-A	—	1	0	0	0	0	0
1923	NY-A	1.000	1	1	1	0	0	0
1924	NY-A	1.000	2	4	3	0	0	0
1925	NY-A	1.000	2	0	1	0	0	0
Total	6	.957	32	27	62	4	3	4

■ Howard Johnson   3B

YEAR	TM/L	PCT	G	PO	A	E	DP	FR
1982	Det-A	.901	33	25	39	7	6	-5
1983	Det-A	.851	21	10	30	7	2	-6
1984	Det-A	.944	108	58	143	12	16	-16
1985	NY-N	.941	113	67	171	15	21	-11
1986	NY-N	.903	45	22	71	10	10	0
1987	NY-N	.938	140	82	235	21	15	-11
1988	NY-N	.951	131	65	187	13	16	-6
1989	NY-N	.910	143	63	180	24	15	-26
1990	NY-N	.913	92	52	159	20	11	-2
Total	9	.928	826	444	1215	129	112	-83
	SS							
1984	Det-A	.833	9	3	7	2	4	-1
1985	NY-N	.909	7	11	19	3	6	-1
1986	NY-N	.903	34	28	65	10	14	-2
1987	NY-N	.955	38	36	70	5	12	-6
1988	NY-N	.964	52	45	87	5	21	-8
1989	NY-N	1.000	31	34	37	0	7	-7
1990	NY-N	.972	73	98	176	8	28	-2
Total	7	.956	244	255	461	3	92	-27
	OF							
1982	Det-A	1.000	9	11	1	0	0	0
1984	Det-A	1.000	1	1	0	0	0	0
1985	NY-N	—	1	0	0	0	0	0
1986	NY-N	1.000	1	2	0	0	0	0
1987	NY-N	—	2	0	0	0	0	0
Total	5	1.000	14	14	1	0	0	0
	1B							
1984	Det-A	1.000	1	1	0	0	1	0

■ Spud Johnson   OF

YEAR	TM/L	PCT	G	PO	A	E	DP	FR
1889	Col-a	.879	69	75	12	12	2	-4
1890	Col-a	.926	135	164	12	14	1	-16
1891	Cle-N	.872	79	99	10	16	1	-5
Total	3	.899	283	338	34	2	4	-25
	3B							
1889	Col-a	.835	44	62	75	27	8	-6
	1B							
1889	Col-a	.889	2	16	0	2	0	-1
1891	Cle-N	.917	1	11	0	1	0	0
Total	2	.900	3	27	0	3	0	-1
	SS							
1889	Col-a	1.000	1	3	0	0	0	-1

■ Lance Johnson   OF

YEAR	TM/L	PCT	G	PO	A	E	DP	FR
1987	StL-N	.931	25	27	0	2	0	-1
1988	Chi-A	.970	31	63	1	2	0	-4
1989	Chi-A	.983	45	113	0	2	0	-1
1990	Chi-A	.973	148	353	5	10	3	-6
Total	4	.972	249	556	6	6	3	-12

■ Lamar Johnson   1B

YEAR	TM/L	PCT	G	PO	A	E	DP	FR
1974	Chi-A	1.000	7	40	2	0	8	0
1975	Chi-A	.960	6	46	2	2	4	-1
1976	Chi-A	.983	34	210	18	4	20	0
1977	Chi-A	.990	45	346	32	4	31	1
1978	Chi-A	.992	108	887	71	8	74	2
1979	Chi-A	.987	94	748	63	11	62	-1
1980	Chi-A	.990	80	671	56	7	70	2
1981	Chi-A	.989	36	264	15	3	31	0
1982	Tex-A	.982	12	105	4	2	6	-1
Total	9	.989	422	3317	263	1	306	2
	OF							
1976	Chi-A	—	1	0	0	0	0	0

Lou Johnson OF

YEAR	TM/L	PCT	G	PO	A	E	DP	FR
1960	Chi-N	1.000	25	43	4	0	0	4
1961	LA-A	—	1	0	0	0	0	0
1962	Mil-N	1.000	55	61	1	0	1	0
1965	LA-N	.985	128	199	3	3	2	-7
1966	LA-N	.985	148	249	8	4	2	2
1967	LA-N	.976	91	153	7	4	0	-1
1968	Chi-N	.970	57	97	0	3	0	-6
	Cle-A	.989	57	87	5	1	1	0
1969	Cal-A	.935	44	56	2	4	0	-2
Total	8	.981	606	945	30	9	6	-10

Randy Johnson 3B

YEAR	TM/L	PCT	G	PO	A	E	DP	FR
1982	Atl-N	1.000	4	1	3	0	0	0
1983	Atl-N	.991	53	39	69	1	11	9
1984	Atl-N	.939	81	44	171	14	14	5
Total	3	.956	138	84	243	5	25	14
2B								
1982	Atl-N	.955	13	20	44	3	7	5
1983	Atl-N	1.000	4	5	3	0	2	0
Total	2	.960	17	25	47	3	9	5

Bob Johnson OF

YEAR	TM/L	PCT	G	PO	A	E	DP	FR
1933	Phi-A	.952	142	298	16	16	3	2
1934	Phi-A	.967	139	304	17	11	3	11
1935	Phi-A	.946	147	337	13	20	4	6
1936	Phi-A	.962	131	289	13	12	3	2
1937	Phi-A	.976	133	313	14	8	3	10
1938	Phi-A	.963	150	400	21	16	3	5
1939	Phi-A	.967	150	369	15	13	3	10
1940	Phi-A	.962	136	310	15	13	4	6
1941	Phi-A	.990	122	287	17	3	0	8
1942	Phi-A	.963	149	318	18	13	1	7
1943	Was-A	.996	88	212	11	1	1	6
1944	Bos-A	.977	142	270	23	7	3	5
1945	Bos-A	.975	140	296	15	8	4	1
Total	13	.968	1769	4003	208	141	35	79
1B								
1936	Phi-A	1.000	1	5	0	0	2	0
1941	Phi-A	.982	28	254	18	5	29	-2
1943	Was-A	1.000	10	69	9	0	8	2
Total	3	.986	39	328	27	5	39	0
2B								
1936	Phi-A	.945	22	51	69	7	20	-3
1937	Phi-A	1.000	2	1	1	0	0	0
1938	Phi-A	.857	3	6	6	2	3	-1
1939	Phi-A	—	1	0	0	0	0	0
Total	4	.937	28	58	76	9	23	-4
3B								
1938	Phi-A	—	1	0	0	0	0	0
1943	Was-A	.895	19	27	41	8	5	1
Total	2	.895	20	27	41	8	5	1

Bob Johnson SS

YEAR	TM/L	PCT	G	PO	A	E	DP	FR
1960	KC-A	.947	30	23	48	4	10	0
1961	Was-A	.956	57	110	172	13	31	-2
1962	Was-A	.961	50	81	140	9	27	-6
1963	Bal-A	.973	7	13	23	1	2	1
1964	Bal-A	.964	18	20	33	2	5	-9
1965	Bal-A	.944	23	27	57	5	7	-6
1967	NY-N	.971	14	21	13	1	2	-2
1968	Cin-N	.500	2	0	1	1	0	0
Total	8	.956	201	295	487	6	84	-24
2B								
1960	KC-A	.986	27	71	69	2	13	10
1961	Was-A	1.000	2	1	5	0	0	0
1962	Was-A	1.000	3	2	6	0	0	0
1963	Bal-A	.987	50	97	131	3	34	-2
1964	Bal-A	.981	15	21	31	1	9	-3
1965	Bal-A	.960	5	10	14	1	2	-1
1966	Bal-A	.966	20	33	52	3	11	1
1967	NY-N	.987	39	72	82	2	21	-4
1968	Atl-N	1.000	4	3	5	0	1	0
1969	Oak-A	1.000	2	1	1	0	0	0
Total	10	.983	167	311	396	2	92	1
3B								
1960	KC-A	.962	11	8	17	1	0	1
1961	Was-A	1.000	2	0	1	0	0	0
1962	Was-A	.944	72	79	142	13	12	2
1963	Bal-A	1.000	5	2	6	0	0	0
1964	Bal-A	1.000	1	0	1	0	0	0
1965	Bal-A	.938	13	9	21	2	2	-2
1966	Bal-A	1.000	3	3	7	0	0	0
1967	NY-N	1.000	1	0	1	0	0	0
1968	Atl-N	.948	48	45	101	8	9	0
1969	StL-N	.833	4	3	7	2	1	-1
1970	Oak-A	.952	6	4	16	1	1	1
Total	11	.946	166	153	320	7	25	1
1B								
1963	Bal-A	.961	8	70	3	3	5	-1
1964	Bal-A	.985	15	123	12	2	13	1
1965	Bal-A	.996	34	264	14	1	18	-1
1966	Bal-A	.992	17	119	6	1	9	-1
1967	NY-N	.972	23	129	9	4	14	-1
1968	Cin-N	.875	1	7	0	1	1	0
1969	StL-N	1.000	1	1	0	0	0	0
	Oak-A	1.000	7	59	5	0	8	0
1970	Oak-A	1.000	1	4	0	0	0	0
Total	8	.986	107	776	49	2	68	-3
OF								
1962	Was-A	1.000	1	2	0	0	0	0
1964	Bal-A	—	1	0	0	0	0	0
Total	2	1.000	2	2	0	0	0	0

Roy Johnson OF

YEAR	TM/L	PCT	G	PO	A	E	DP	FR
1929	Det-A	.928	146	377	25	31	5	14
1930	Det-A	.936	118	218	15	16	4	4
1931	Det-A	.960	150	332	25	15	8	15
1932	Det-A	.929	48	102	3	8	0	-3
	Bos-A	.930	85	167	6	13	0	-6
	Yr	.930	133	269	9	21	0	-9
1933	Bos-A	.922	125	280	14	25	3	3
1934	Bos-A	.948	137	260	12	15	1	-3
1935	Bos-A	.944	142	267	21	17	1	0
1936	NY-A	.944	33	66	2	4	0	-2
1937	NY-A	.840	12	21	0	4	0	-3
	Bos-N	.965	63	131	5	5	0	-4
1938	Bos-N	.769	7	10	0	3	0	-2
Total	10	.938	1066	2231	128	156	22	13
3B								
1937	Bos-N	.000	1	0	0	1	0	-1

Tim Johnson SS

YEAR	TM/L	PCT	G	PO	A	E	DP	FR
1973	Mil-A	.962	135	253	381	25	88	-18
1974	Mil-A	.970	64	82	178	8	30	-2
1975	Mil-A	.971	10	10	23	1	3	2
1976	Mil-A	1.000	1	2	1	0	0	0
1977	Mil-A	.944	6	5	12	1	5	2
1978	Mil-A	1.000	2	1	0	0	0	-1
	Tor-A	.975	49	23	55	2	7	0
	Yr	.975	51	24	55	2	7	-1
Total	6	.965	267	376	650	7	133	-17
2B								
1974	Mil-A	.991	26	56	52	1	21	1
1975	Mil-A	1.000	11	20	23	0	5	1
1976	Mil-A	.980	100	161	222	8	42	-17
1977	Mil-A	.929	10	11	2	1	0	0
1978	Tor-A	1.000	13	14	37	0	10	5
1979	Tor-A	.958	25	62	52	5	21	4
Total	6	.979	185	324	388	5	99	-6
3B								
1974	Mil-A	—	1	0	0	0	0	0
1975	Mil-A	.857	11	7	17	4	0	-2
1976	Mil-A	1.000	17	4	15	0	0	0
1977	Mil-A	1.000	4	1	5	0	0	1
1979	Tor-A	.900	9	2	16	2	1	1
Total	5	.918	42	14	53	6	1	0
1B								
1975	Mil-A	1.000	2	1	0	0	0	0
1976	Mil-A	—	1	0	0	0	0	0
1979	Tor-A	1.000	7	27	2	0	2	0
Total	3	1.000	10	28	2	0	2	0
OF								
1974	Mil-A	1.000	1	1	0	0	0	0
1977	Mil-A	—	1	0	0	0	0	0
Total	2	1.000	2	1	0	0	0	0

Bill Johnson 3B

YEAR	TM/L	PCT	G	PO	A	E	DP	FR
1943	NY-A	.966	155	183	326	18	32	12
1946	NY-A	.955	74	71	163	11	15	7
1947	NY-A	.952	132	136	204	17	12	-17
1948	NY-A	.947	118	147	213	20	25	6
1949	NY-A	.951	81	77	136	11	16	-1
1950	NY-A	.958	100	82	169	11	20	0
1951	NY-A	.960	13	8	16	1	0	-3
	StL-N	.976	124	99	316	10	32	11
1952	StL-N	.951	89	56	177	12	10	2
1953	StL-N	1.000	11	1	8	0	1	2
Total	9	.959	897	860	1728	111	163	19
1B								
1949	NY-A	.986	21	130	10	2	10	-1
1950	NY-A	.933	5	14	0	1	1	-1
Total	2	.981	26	144	10	3	11	-2
2B								
1949	NY-A	—	1	0	0	0	0	0

Bill Johnson OF

YEAR	TM/L	PCT	G	PO	A	E	DP	FR
1884	Phi-U	—	1	0	0	0	0	0
1887	Ind-N	.765	11	11	2	4	0	-2
1890	Bal-a	.865	24	39	6	7	3	2
1891	Bal-a	.877	129	235	28	37	5	6
1892	Bal-N	.667	4	4	0	2	0	-1
Total	5	.867	169	289	36	0	8	5

Jimmy Johnston 3B

YEAR	TM/L	PCT	G	PO	A	E	DP	FR
1917	Bro-N	—	3	0	0	0	0	0
1918	Bro-N	1.000	4	5	13	0	0	2
1920	Bro-N	.934	146	159	282	31	21	-6
1921	Bro-N	.935	150	162	312	33	34	8
1922	Bro-N	.934	26	36	35	5	1	-3
1923	Bro-N	.929	14	13	26	3	4	0
1924	Bro-N	.931	10	12	15	2	0	-1
1925	Bro-N	.886	81	76	110	24	10	-20
1926	Bos-N	.865	14	10	22	5	3	-3
Total	9	.926	448	473	815	103	73	-23
OF								
1911	Chi-A	1.000	1	1	0	0	0	0
1914	Chi-A	.929	28	58	7	5	3	7
1916	Bro-N	.964	106	224	16	9	3	8
1917	Bro-N	.958	92	150	8	7	1	0
1918	Bro-N	.956	96	178	18	9	4	4
1919	Bro-N	.960	14	24	0	1	0	-1
1920	Bro-N	.917	7	10	1	1	1	0
1924	Bro-N	1.000	1	1	0	0	0	0
1925	Bro-N	.850	20	31	3	6	1	-2
1926	Bos-N	1.000	1	1	0	0	0	0
	NY-N	1.000	14	13	0	0	0	-4
	Yr	1.000	15	14	0	0	0	-4
Total	10	.951	380	691	53	8	13	12
2B								
1914	Chi-A	.870	4	11	9	3	0	1
1917	Bro-N	.905	3	6	13	2	0	1
1918	Bro-N	—	2	1	0	1	0	0
1919	Bro-N	.960	87	157	294	19	31	-4
1922	Bro-N	.947	62	162	210	21	36	4
1923	Bro-N	.948	84	221	291	28	25	3
1926	Bos-N	1.000	2	1	2	0	0	0
Total	7	.950	243	560	820	3	93	5
SS								
1917	Bro-N	.750	4	7	2	3	1	-2
1919	Bro-N	1.000	1	2	6	0	0	0
1920	Bro-N	1.000	3	2	6	0	0	0
1921	Bro-N	.882	3	6	9	2	2	0
1922	Bro-N	.948	50	102	189	16	34	6
1923	Bro-N	.946	52	135	215	20	24	17
1924	Bro-N	.939	63	136	203	22	32	-2
1925	Bro-N	.667	2	1	1	1	0	0
Total	8	.941	178	391	631	4	93	19
1B								
1917	Bro-N	.960	14	106	14	5	3	2
1918	Bro-N	.982	21	197	16	4	8	1
1919	Bro-N	1.000	2	18	2	0	1	0
1924	Bro-N	1.000	4	22	1	0	0	0
1925	Bro-N	.966	8	81	5	3	4	0
Total	5	.975	49	424	38	2	16	3

Dick Johnston OF

YEAR	TM/L	PCT	G	PO	A	E	DP	FR
1884	Ric-a	.865	37	86	10	15	3	9
1885	Bos-N	.842	26	40	8	9	2	1
1886	Bos-N	.892	109	243	29	33	4	15
1887	Bos-N	.933	127	339	34	27	9	22
1888	Bos-N	.898	135	286	30	36	3	5
1889	Bos-N	.917	132	267	22	26	6	-8
1890	Bos-P	.800	2	3	1	1	0	0
	NY-P	.897	76	164	18	21	3	3
	Yr	.894	78	167	19	22	3	3
1891	Cin-a	.895	99	193	20	25	4	-1
Total	8	.903	743	1621	172	193	34	46
SS								
1884	Ric-a	.667	2	1	3	2	0	0
1890	NY-P	1.000	2	2	0	0	0	0
Total	2	.750	4	3	3	2	0	0

Doc Johnston 1B

YEAR	TM/L	PCT	G	PO	A	E	DP	FR
1909	Cin-N	1.000	3	25	2	0	0	0
1912	Cle-A	.991	41	330	17	3	27	-2
1913	Cle-A	.989	133	1319	76	15	76	-1
1914	Cle-A	.987	90	847	36	12	43	-7
1915	Pit-N	.991	147	1453	48	13	65	-12
1916	Pit-N	.987	110	1042	47	14	44	-2
1918	Cle-A	.989	73	738	40	9	25	-3
1919	Cle-A	.984	98	957	57	16	57	-3
1920	Cle-A	.992	147	1427	91	12	83	-1
1921	Cle-A	.988	116	960	62	12	72	-1
1922	Phi-A	.990	65	641	31	7	34	-5
Total	11	.989	1023	9739	507	113	526	-37
OF								
1914	Cle-A	1.000	2	6	0	0	0	0

Jay Johnstone OF

YEAR	TM/L	PCT	G	PO	A	E	DP	FR
1966	Cal-A	.975	61	114	2	3	1	-5
1967	Cal-A	.973	63	141	3	4	0	6
1968	Cal-A	.984	29	58	4	1	1	3
1969	Cal-A	.983	144	331	12	6	4	5
1970	Cal-A	.981	100	200	7	4	3	-5
1971	Chi-A	.968	119	232	9	8	1	-4
1972	Chi-A	.988	97	154	5	2	1	5
1973	Oak-A	1.000	7	7	0	0	0	0
1974	Phi-N	.968	59	88	4	3	1	-5
1975	Phi-N	.976	101	152	10	4	3	-4
1976	Phi-N	.982	122	266	8	5	1	7
1977	Phi-N	1.000	91	163	9	0	1	1
1978	Phi-N	1.000	7	4	0	0	0	0
	NY-A	1.000	22	31	0	0	0	0
1979	NY-A	1.000	19	32	0	0	0	1
	SD-N	.985	45	60	4	1	0	-2
1980	LA-N	.965	61	100	9	4	0	0
1981	LA-N	.957	16	19	3	1	0	1
1982	Chi-N	.982	86	154	8	3	0	1
1983	Chi-N	.935	44	55	3	4	1	-1
1984	Chi-N	1.000	15	12	0	0	0	-2
Total	19	.979	1308	2373	100	3	18	2
1B								
1976	Phi-N	.906	6	27	2	3	1	-1
1977	Phi-N	.993	19	131	6	1	16	-1
1978	Phi-N	.988	8	73	7	1	9	1
1979	SD-N	.979	22	125	14	3	10	1
1981	LA-N	1.000	2	14	1	0	2	0
Total	5	.980	57	370	30	8	38	0
2B								
1973	Oak-A	—	2	0	0	0	0	-1

Smead Jolley OF

YEAR	TM/L	PCT	G	PO	A	E	DP	FR
1930	Chi-A	.950	151	249	17	14	4	-3
1931	Chi-A	.857	23	29	1	5	1	-5
1932	Chi-A	.923	11	11	1	1	0	-3
	Bos-A	.943	126	234	12	15	3	-7
	Yr	.942	137	245	13	16	3	-10
1933	Bos-A	.955	102	178	12	9	3	-6
Total	4	.944	413	701	43	4	11	-24
C								
1932	Bos-A	1.000	5	21	2	0	0	0

Charlie Jones OF

YEAR	TM/L	PCT	G	PO	A	E	DP	FR
1901	Bos-A	.929	10	13	0	1	0	-2
1904	Chi-A	1.000	5	9	2	0	0	1
1905	Was-A	.971	142	340	24	11	6	16
1906	Was-A	.961	128	279	20	12	7	8
1907	Was-A	.967	111	226	6	8	2	-1
1908	StL-A	.963	72	116	13	5	2	-1
Total	6	.966	468	983	65	7	17	21
2B								
1906	Was-A	1.000	1	3	0	0	0	0
1907	Was-A	1.000	5	7	3	0	0	0
Total	2	1.000	6	10	3	0	0	0
1B								
1907	Was-A	1.000	4	34	4	0	2	0

YEAR	TM/L	PCT	G	PO	A	E	DP	FR
SS								
1907	Was-A	1.000	2	0	1	0	0	0
■ **Charley Jones** OF								
1876	Cin-N	.857	64	151	11	27	2	1
1877	Cin-N	.852	8	21	2	4	0	1
	Chi-N	1.000	2	5	1	0	0	1
	Cin-N	.838	38	112	12	24	2	10
	Yr	.845	48	138	15	28	2	12
1878	Cin-N	.896	61	120	9	15	1	6
1879	Bos-N	.933	83	162	20	13	1	12
1880	Bos-N	.826	66	108	11	25	3	-5
1883	Cin-a	.876	90	172	12	26	1	2
1884	Cin-a	.887	112	207	12	28	0	3
1885	Cin-a	.891	112	214	22	29	6	12
1886	Cin-a	.879	127	217	23	33	1	3
1887	Cin-a	.900	41	74	7	9	2	0
	NY-a	.917	62	114	18	12	6	4
	Yr	.910	103	188	25	21	8	4
1888	KC-a	.750	6	8	1	3	0	-1
Total	11	.882	872	1685	161	248	25	49
1B								
1877	Cin-N	.920	10	100	3	9	4	-1
1887	NY-a	.000	1	0	0	1	0	0
Total	2	.912	11	100	3	0	4	-1
■ **Cleon Jones** OF								
1963	NY-N	1.000	5	6	0	0	0	0
1965	NY-N	1.000	23	36	2	0	0	1
1966	NY-N	.979	129	275	10	6	2	-3
1967	NY-N	.977	115	210	5	5	3	-6
1968	NY-N	.963	139	226	7	9	0	-7
1969	NY-N	.991	122	223	4	2	0	0
1970	NY-N	.981	130	243	10	5	3	5
1971	NY-N	.981	132	248	4	5	1	-1
1972	NY-N	.986	84	136	8	2	1	0
1973	NY-N	.967	92	168	6	6	0	-1
1974	NY-N	.970	120	220	8	7	0	-2
1975	NY-N	1.000	12	9	0	0	0	-3
1976	Chi-A	1.000	8	7	0	0	0	-2
Total	13	.978	1111	2007	64	7	10	-19
1B								
1969	NY-N	1.000	15	99	7	0	3	0
1972	NY-N	.979	20	174	12	4	9	0
Total	2	.986	35	273	19	4	12	0
■ **Davy Jones** OF								
1901	Mil-A	.911	14	41	0	4	0	1
1902	StL-A	.973	15	31	5	1	3	5
	Chi-N	.955	64	146	3	7	1	-1
1903	Chi-N	.970	130	249	14	8	3	0
1904	Chi-N	.932	97	128	8	10	0	-10
1906	Det-A	.981	83	193	10	4	3	4
1907	Det-A	.971	125	282	15	9	2	13
1908	Det-A	.960	32	67	5	3	2	2
1909	Det-A	.982	57	103	4	2	1	-2
1910	Det-A	.956	101	181	13	9	2	1
1911	Det-A	.950	92	156	15	9	3	-1
1912	Det-A	.962	81	141	13	6	4	-1
1913	Chi-A	.867	9	11	2	2	0	-1
1914	Pit-F	.970	93	216	11	7	1	8
1915	Pit-F	.926	13	24	1	2	0	-1
Total	14	.962	1006	1969	119	3	25	17
■ **Fielder Jones** OF								
1896	Bro-N	.928	103	171	10	14	6	-4
1897	Bro-N	.941	135	233	22	16	8	4
1898	Bro-N	.946	144	229	17	14	7	-4
1899	Bro-N	.946	96	199	11	12	2	-3
1900	Bro-N	.957	136	315	15	15	3	0
1901	Chi-A	.937	133	216	20	16	5	1
1902	Chi-A	.972	135	323	25	10	11	12
1903	Chi-A	.985	136	324	11	5	3	0
1904	Chi-A	.977	149	325	15	8	4	5
1905	Chi-A	.970	153	337	21	11	5	7
1906	Chi-A	.988	144	312	23	4	5	8
1907	Chi-A	.973	154	307	18	9	6	2
1908	Chi-A	.968	149	288	17	10	5	-1
1915	StL-F	1.000	3	1	0	0	0	-1
Total	14	.964	1770	3580	225	144	70	26
SS								
1898	Bro-N	.538	2	4	3	6	0	-3
■ **Dalton Jones** 2B								
1964	Bos-A	.959	85	181	193	16	41	-8
1965	Bos-A	1.000	8	17	14	0	4	0
1966	Bos-A	.962	70	129	121	10	26	-14
1967	Bos-A	1.000	19	8	13	0	2	-1
1968	Bos-A	.986	26	32	38	1	8	-2
1969	Bos-A	.500	1	0	1	1	0	-1
1970	Det-A	.985	35	59	70	2	18	-2
1971	Det-A	1.000	1	0	1	0	0	0
1972	Tex-A	.967	17	26	32	2	8	-4
Total	9	.967	262	452	483	2	107	-32
3B								
1964	Bos-A	.667	1	0	2	1	0	-1
1965	Bos-A	.930	81	63	163	17	14	-3
1966	Bos-A	.818	3	4	5	2	2	-1
1967	Bos-A	.912	30	15	47	6	4	-4
1968	Bos-A	.862	8	10	15	4	0	-1
1969	Bos-A	1.000	9	10	9	0	0	-1
1970	Det-A	.944	18	9	25	2	4	-1
1971	Det-A	.909	13	4	16	2	2	-3
1972	Tex-A	.979	23	15	31	1	3	-2
Total	9	.927	186	130	313	5	27	-17
1B								
1967	Bos-A	1.000	1	0	1	0	0	0
1968	Bos-A	.996	56	449	27	2	47	-2
1969	Bos-A	.992	81	692	54	6	61	1
1970	Det-A	1.000	10	43	4	0	4	0

YEAR	TM/L	PCT	G	PO	A	E	DP	FR
1971	Det-A	1.000	3	4	0	0	1	0
1972	Tex-A	1.000	7	17	0	0	0	0
Total	6	.994	158	1205	86	8	113	-1
OF								
1971	Det-A	1.000	16	17	0	0	0	-2
1972	Tex-A	—	2	0	0	0	0	0
Total	2	1.000	18	17	0	0	0	-2
SS								
1964	Bos-A	1.000	1	1	1	0	0	0
■ **Jake Jones** 1B								
1941	Chi-A	1.000	3	25	0	0	0	-1
1942	Chi-A	.961	5	47	2	2	2	-1
1946	Chi-A	.986	20	201	5	3	18	-3
1947	Chi-A	.988	43	444	31	6	49	-1
	Bos-A	.991	109	1018	73	10	110	-2
	Yr	.990	152	1462	104	16	159	-3
1948	Bos-A	.993	31	275	22	2	30	2
Total	5	.989	211	2010	133	3	209	-6
■ **Lynn Jones** OF								
1979	Det-A	.980	84	142	3	3	1	1
1980	Det-A	1.000	17	31	0	0	0	1
1981	Det-A	.989	60	85	5	1	2	-1
1982	Det-A	1.000	56	86	3	0	2	1
1983	Det-A	.968	31	28	2	1	0	2
1984	KC-A	.962	45	51	0	2	0	-5
1985	KC-A	.983	100	115	2	2	1	5
1986	KC-A	.971	62	34	0	1	0	3
Total	8	.983	455	572	15	0	6	7
2B								
1986	KC-A	—	1	0	0	0	0	0
■ **Mack Jones** OF								
1961	Mil-N	1.000	26	45	2	0	1	-2
1962	Mil-N	.973	91	142	3	4	0	-6
1963	Mil-N	.978	80	135	1	3	0	-11
1965	Mil-N	.980	133	239	2	5	2	-11
1966	Atl-N	.981	112	251	1	5	0	-6
1967	Atl-N	.985	126	252	7	4	1	-3
1968	Cin-N	.988	60	82	1	1	0	-5
1969	Mon-N	.959	129	226	6	10	0	-1
1970	Mon-N	.968	87	118	3	4	1	-7
1971	Mon-N	.952	27	39	1	2	0	-2
Total	10	.976	871	1529	27	8	5	-54
1B								
1966	Atl-N	—	1	0	0	0	0	0
■ **Bob Jones** OF								
1974	Tex-A	1.000	2	5	0	0	0	0
1975	Tex-A	1.000	5	6	0	0	0	0
1976	Cal-A	.990	62	98	6	1	0	3
1981	Tex-A	1.000	10	20	4	0	0	3
1983	Tex-A	1.000	11	24	0	0	0	1
1984	Tex-A	1.000	22	42	2	0	1	1
1985	Tex-A	1.000	30	30	0	0	0	-1
1986	Tex-A	.909	9	10	0	1	0	0
Total	8	.992	151	235	12	2	1	7
1B								
1983	Tex-A	—	1	0	0	0	0	0
1984	Tex-A	.990	15	97	5	1	7	-1
1985	Tex-A	1.000	4	14	0	0	1	0
1986	Tex-A	1.000	2	19	1	0	2	0
Total	4	.993	22	130	6	1	10	-1
■ **Bob Jones** 3B								
1917	Det-A	.920	8	7	16	2	1	1
1918	Det-A	.947	63	81	117	11	6	-7
1919	Det-A	.944	127	134	219	21	14	-24
1920	Det-A	.942	67	80	146	14	7	-5
1921	Det-A	.950	141	194	324	27	12	10
1922	Det-A	.962	119	161	267	17	22	11
1923	Det-A	.954	97	109	224	16	17	5
1924	Det-A	.956	106	108	196	14	12	2
1925	Det-A	.985	46	43	91	2	5	9
Total	9	.953	774	917	1600	124	96	-2
2B								
1917	Det-A	.938	18	19	41	4	1	-1
1920	Det-A	.952	5	10	10	1	2	0
Total	2	.941	23	29	51	5	3	-1
1B								
1918	Det-A	1.000	6	62	0	0	2	-1
OF								
1918	Det-A	—	1	0	0	0	0	0
SS								
1920	Det-A	1.000	1	0	2	0	0	0
■ **Ruppert Jones** OF								
1976	KC-A	1.000	17	21	0	0	0	0
1977	Sea-A	.981	155	465	11	9	3	13
1978	Sea-A	.985	128	393	10	6	2	12
1979	Sea-A	.989	161	453	13	5	4	8
1980	NY-A	.988	82	246	4	3	1	6
1981	SD-N	.993	104	295	9	2	3	5
1982	SD-N	.984	114	314	3	5	1	2
1983	SD-N	.981	111	249	3	5	2	-8
1984	Det-A	1.000	73	150	4	0	1	5
1985	Cal-A	.995	73	179	12	1	5	12
1986	Cal-A	.981	121	205	5	4	0	-10
1987	Cal-A	.965	66	81	1	3	0	-6
Total	12	.986	1205	3051	75	3	22	39
1B								
1983	SD-N	.957	5	19	3	1	1	0
■ **Tom Jones** 1B								
1902	Bal-A	.955	37	341	22	17	23	-1
1904	StL-A	.988	134	1443	92	19	51	3
1905	StL-A	.985	135	1502	105	25	52	7
1906	StL-A	.983	143	1476	116	25	55	11
1907	StL-A	.983	155	1687	103	31	69	-2
1908	StL-A	.986	155	1616	90	24	79	-2

YEAR	TM/L	PCT	G	PO	A	E	DP	FR
1909	StL-A	.989	95	950	70	11	57	6
	Det-A	.984	44	452	33	8	20	2
	Yr	.988	139	1402	103	19	77	8
1910	Det-A	.985	135	1405	67	23	50	-4
Total	8	.984	1033	10872	698	183	456	24
2B								
1902	Bal-A	—	1	0	0	0	0	0
1904	StL-A	.979	23	37	56	2	3	-3
Total	2	.979	24	37	56	2	3	-3
OF								
1904	StL-A	1.000	4	5	1	0	0	0
3B								
1909	StL-A	1.000	2	6	5	0	0	1
■ **Tracy Jones** OF								
1986	Cin-N	1.000	24	43	1	0	0	1
1987	Cin-N	.990	95	189	2	2	0	-1
1988	Cin-N	.955	25	42	0	2	0	-1
	Mon-N	1.000	43	54	2	0	0	-4
	Yr	.980	68	96	2	2	0	-5
1989	SF-N	1.000	30	35	0	0	0	-4
	Det-A	.986	36	72	0	1	0	-4
1990	Det-A	.952	27	37	3	2	0	0
	Sea-A	1.000	18	31	0	0	0	-2
	Yr	.973	45	68	3	2	0	-2
Total	5	.986	298	503	8	7	0	-15
1B								
1986	Cin-N	1.000	2	3	0	0	0	0
■ **Nippy Jones** 1B								
1948	StL-N	.986	128	1148	63	17	98	-9
1949	StL-N	.984	98	876	40	15	85	-8
1950	StL-N	.983	8	54	3	1	8	0
1951	StL-N	.991	71	698	48	7	78	-1
1952	Phi-N	.976	8	73	7	2	8	0
1957	Mil-N	.994	20	143	12	1	12	0
Total	6	.987	333	2992	173	3	289	-18
2B								
1946	StL-N	.800	3	2	2	1	1	1
1947	StL-N	.935	13	32	40	5	5	-1
Total	2	.927	16	34	42	6	6	0
OF								
1947	StL-N	1.000	2	2	0	0	0	0
1957	Mil-N	1.000	1	1	0	0	0	0
Total	2	1.000	3	3	0	0	0	0
■ **Puddin' Head Jones** 3B								
1947	Phi-N	.909	17	19	41	6	3	2
1948	Phi-N	.926	17	30	33	5	1	2
1949	Phi-N	.948	145	181	308	27	19	-4
1950	Phi-N	.954	157	190	323	25	30	-5
1951	Phi-N	.966	147	190	286	17	33	-9
1952	Phi-N	.969	147	216	281	16	31	4
1953	Phi-N	.975	147	176	253	11	36	-3
1954	Phi-N	.968	141	184	277	15	23	-2
1955	Phi-N	.960	146	202	235	18	22	-13
1956	Phi-N	.973	149	202	264	13	23	1
1957	Phi-N	.966	126	140	197	12	18	-7
1958	Phi-N	.967	110	137	186	11	13	-13
1959	Phi-N	.975	46	40	76	3	5	-3
	Cle-A	.929	4	3	10	1	2	2
	Cin-N	.966	68	92	105	7	9	-3
1960	Cin-N	.962	46	43	59	4	5	-3
1961	Cin-N	.000	1	0	0	1	0	0
Total	15	.963	1614	2045	2934	192	273	-55
1B								
1958	Phi-N	1.000	1	4	0	0	0	0
2B								
1960	Cin-N	1.000	1	1	0	0	0	0
■ **Eddie Joost** SS								
1936	Cin-N	.947	7	5	13	1	3	0
1939	Cin-N	.818	6	6	12	4	3	-3
1940	Cin-N	.960	78	145	240	16	48	-3
1941	Cin-N	.942	147	310	415	45	85	-6
1942	Cin-N	.933	130	248	380	45	79	-17
1943	Bos-N	1.000	1	2	3	0	1	0
1947	Phi-A	.956	151	370	452	38	100	-3
1948	Phi-A	.973	135	325	409	20	115	4
1949	Phi-A	.969	144	352	442	25	126	8
1950	Phi-A	.956	131	241	389	29	117	-7
1951	Phi-A	.974	140	325	422	20	115	-7
1952	Phi-A	.962	146	278	431	28	81	-7
1953	Phi-A	.958	51	102	147	11	33	-6
1954	Phi-A	.963	9	9	17	1	3	-3
1955	Bos-A	.932	20	37	72	8	19	5
Total	15	.958	1296	2755	3844	291	928	-34
2B								
1936	Cin-N	1.000	5	10	9	0	1	-1
1937	Cin-N	.875	6	8	13	3	2	0
1939	Cin-N	.957	32	88	89	8	20	0
1940	Cin-N	1.000	7	12	16	0	3	0
1941	Cin-N	.950	4	6	13	1	2	0
1942	Cin-N	.955	15	51	54	5	14	6
1943	Bos-N	.948	60	141	167	17	37	-4
1945	Bos-N	.945	19	45	41	5	9	-7
1954	Phi-A	1.000	1	1	4	0	1	0
1955	Bos-A	.902	17	18	19	4	4	0
Total	10	.949	166	380	425	3	93	-6
3B								
1940	Cin-N	1.000	4	4	14	0	0	2
1941	Cin-N	1.000	1	1	0	0	0	0
1943	Bos-N	.945	67	104	171	16	15	16
1945	Bos-N	.885	16	19	35	7	4	0
1954	Phi-A	1.000	5	4	11	0	1	0
1955	Bos-A	1.000	2	0	1	0	0	0
Total	6	.941	95	131	233	3	20	18
1B								
1941	Cin-N	1.000	2	10	0	0	1	0

■ Dutch Jordan 2B

YEAR	TM/L	PCT	G	PO	A	E	DP	FR
1903	Bro-N	.928	54	101	132	18	12	-11
1904	Bro-N	.958	70	142	176	14	17	-17
Total	2	.945	124	243	308	2	29	-28

3B

YEAR	TM/L	PCT	G	PO	A	E	DP	FR
1903	Bro-N	.868	18	30	29	9	2	-2
1904	Bro-N	.914	11	14	18	3	0	-1
Total	2	.883	29	44	47	2	2	-3

1B

YEAR	TM/L	PCT	G	PO	A	E	DP	FR
1903	Bro-N	1.000	1	7	0	0	1	0
1904	Bro-N	1.000	4	11	2	0	0	1
Total	2	1.000	5	18	2	0	1	1

OF

YEAR	TM/L	PCT	G	PO	A	E	DP	FR
1903	Bro-N	1.000	4	7	0	0	0	0

■ Buck Jordan 1B

YEAR	TM/L	PCT	G	PO	A	E	DP	FR
1929	NY-N	1.000	1	1	0	0	1	0
1931	Was-A	.978	7	45	0	1	3	-1
1932	Bos-N	.991	49	514	31	5	48	-1
1933	Bos-N	.991	150	**1513**	88	14	117	-3
1934	Bos-N	.989	117	1165	66	14	85	-3
1935	Bos-N	.983	95	857	66	16	59	1
1936	Bos-N	.993	136	1307	96	10	**137**	1
1937	Cin-N	.989	76	669	46	8	55	-2
1938	Phi-N	1.000	17	134	12	0	11	0
Total	9	.990	648	6205	405	8	516	-8

3B

YEAR	TM/L	PCT	G	PO	A	E	DP	FR
1935	Bos-N	.963	8	13	13	1	1	0
1938	Phi-N	.973	58	42	103	4	13	-4
Total	2	.972	66	55	116	5	14	-4

OF

YEAR	TM/L	PCT	G	PO	A	E	DP	FR
1935	Bos-N	1.000	2	6	0	0	0	0

■ Jimmy Jordan 2B

YEAR	TM/L	PCT	G	PO	A	E	DP	FR
1933	Bro-N	.929	11	18	21	3	2	0
1934	Bro-N	.954	41	77	111	9	27	-4
1935	Bro-N	.983	46	119	175	5	26	20
1936	Bro-N	.970	98	209	247	14	41	-17
Total	4	.969	196	423	554	1	96	-1

SS

YEAR	TM/L	PCT	G	PO	A	E	DP	FR
1933	Bro-N	.969	51	104	182	9	25	12
1934	Bro-N	.956	51	80	135	10	13	-6
1935	Bro-N	.956	28	55	98	7	13	7
1936	Bro-N	1.000	9	18	17	0	2	-1
Total	4	.964	139	257	432	6	53	12

3B

YEAR	TM/L	PCT	G	PO	A	E	DP	FR
1934	Bro-N	.923	9	14	10	2	1	-2
1935	Bro-N	.818	5	3	6	2	0	0
1936	Bro-N	.950	6	8	11	1	1	1
Total	3	.912	20	25	27	5	2	-1

■ Ricky Jordan 1B

YEAR	TM/L	PCT	G	PO	A	E	DP	FR
1988	Phi-N	.992	69	579	35	5	41	-5
1989	Phi-N	.993	140	1271	61	9	99	-11
1990	Phi-N	.995	84	743	37	4	65	-8
Total	3	.993	293	2593	133	8	205	-24

■ Tim Jordan 1B

YEAR	TM/L	PCT	G	PO	A	E	DP	FR
1901	Was-A	.941	6	62	2	4	2	-1
1903	NY-A	.889	2	16	0	2	3	-1
1906	Bro-N	.978	126	1240	64	**30**	44	-9
1907	Bro-N	.980	143	1417	78	**31**	71	-6
1908	Bro-N	.982	146	1462	55	**28**	52	-15
1909	Bro-N	.983	95	937	29	17	36	-9
Total	6	.980	518	5134	228	112	208	-41

■ Art Jorgens C

YEAR	TM/L	PCT	G	PO	A	E	DP	FR
1929	NY-A	.979	15	41	6	1	1	0
1930	NY-A	.960	16	43	5	2	1	0
1931	NY-A	.962	40	144	10	6	0	-1
1932	NY-A	.967	56	240	20	9	3	0
1933	NY-A	.982	19	108	2	2	2	2
1934	NY-A	.984	56	288	20	5	7	6
1935	NY-A	1.000	33	130	12	0	5	6
1936	NY-A	.990	30	87	9	1	0	3
1937	NY-A	1.000	11	27	2	0	0	0
1938	NY-A	.923	8	18	6	2	0	1
1939	NY-A	1.000	2	2	0	0	0	1
Total	11	.978	286	1128	92	8	19	18

■ Spider Jorgensen 3B

YEAR	TM/L	PCT	G	PO	A	E	DP	FR
1947	Bro-N	.949	128	116	235	19	26	-5
1948	Bro-N	.887	24	22	33	7	3	-6
1949	Bro-N	.946	36	28	59	5	5	-5
1950	Bro-N	1.000	1	0	1	0	0	0
	NY-N	.913	5	7	14	2	1	1
	Yr	.917	6	7	15	2	1	1
1951	NY-N	1.000	1	0	1	0	0	0
Total	5	.940	195	173	343	3	35	-15

OF

YEAR	TM/L	PCT	G	PO	A	E	DP	FR
1951	NY-N	1.000	11	14	0	0	0	-2

■ Mike Jorgensen 1B

YEAR	TM/L	PCT	G	PO	A	E	DP	FR
1968	NY-N	1.000	4	32	1	0	3	0
1970	NY-N	.992	50	116	12	1	9	2
1971	NY-N	1.000	1	6	2	0	1	1
1972	Mon-N	.995	76	757	56	4	66	4
1973	Mon-N	**.995**	123	990	80	5	88	**6**
1974	Mon-N	.998	91	606	51	1	47	6
1975	Mon-N	.994	133	1150	91	7	123	**5**
1976	Mon-N	.989	81	599	57	7	59	6
1977	Mon-N	1.000	5	23	4	0	1	1
	Oak-A	.989	48	330	32	4	26	2
1978	Tex-A	.994	78	299	31	2	23	7
1979	Tex-A	.988	60	287	30	4	28	3
1980	NY-N	.995	72	511	35	3	32	-1
1981	NY-N	.991	40	108	8	1	8	0
1982	NY-N	.991	56	106	5	1	14	-1
1983	NY-N	1.000	19	36	3	0	5	1
	Atl-N	1.000	19	36	3	0	6	0
	Yr	1.000	38	72	6	0	11	1
1984	Atl-N	1.000	8	25	0	0	0	0
	StL-N	.991	39	194	19	2	30	2
	Yr	.992	47	219	19	2	30	2
1985	StL-N	.994	49	318	17	2	32	-1
Total	17	.994	1052	6529	537	4	601	43

OF

YEAR	TM/L	PCT	G	PO	A	E	DP	FR
1970	NY-N	.935	10	29	0	2	0	2
1971	NY-N	.951	31	58	0	3	0	-1
1972	Mon-N	.957	28	44	1	2	0	-2
1973	Mon-N	1.000	11	12	0	0	0	0
1974	Mon-N	1.000	29	47	3	0	0	0
1975	Mon-N	1.000	6	3	0	0	0	0
1976	Mon-N	.981	41	52	1	1	0	-2
1977	Oak-A	1.000	20	35	0	0	0	-1
1978	Tex-A	1.000	9	18	0	0	0	1
1979	Tex-A	1.000	20	33	1	0	0	1
1980	NY-N	.981	31	51	2	1	1	1
1981	NY-N	1.000	19	35	1	0	0	0
1982	NY-N	.962	16	25	0	1	0	0
1983	Atl-N	1.000	6	9	0	0	0	0
1984	Atl-N	1.000	4	3	0	0	0	0
1985	StL-N	—	2	0	0	0	0	0
Total	16	.979	283	454	9	0	1	-1

■ Felix Jose OF

YEAR	TM/L	PCT	G	PO	A	E	DP	FR
1988	Oak-A	1.000	6	8	0	0	0	1
1989	Oak-A	.974	19	35	2	1	0	1
1990	Oak-A	.977	92	212	5	5	1	3
	StL-N	1.000	23	42	0	0	0	-3
Total	3	.981	140	297	7	6	1	2

■ Duane Josephson C

YEAR	TM/L	PCT	G	PO	A	E	DP	FR
1965	Chi-A	1.000	4	21	1	0	0	1
1966	Chi-A	.974	11	66	8	2	1	2
1967	Chi-A	1.000	59	292	24	0	3	-5
1968	Chi-A	.990	122	641	**86**	7	**15**	11
1969	Chi-A	.984	47	227	27	4	1	0
1970	Chi-A	.985	84	353	38	6	7	-10
1971	Bos-A	.989	87	491	32	6	5	-5
1972	Bos-A	1.000	6	18	0	0	0	0
Total	8	.989	420	2109	216	5	32	-6

1B

YEAR	TM/L	PCT	G	PO	A	E	DP	FR
1972	Bos-A	.980	16	137	9	3	8	0

■ Von Joshua OF

YEAR	TM/L	PCT	G	PO	A	E	DP	FR
1969	LA-N	.800	8	4	0	1	0	0
1970	LA-N	.941	41	47	1	3	1	1
1971	LA-N	1.000	5	7	0	0	0	0
1973	LA-N	.984	46	61	2	1	0	-2
1974	LA-N	.943	35	33	0	2	0	-3
1975	SF-N	**.993**	117	279	10	2	3	3
1976	SF-N	.948	35	70	3	4	1	-2
	Mil-A	.982	105	268	10	5	4	0
1977	Mil-A	.970	140	311	8	10	0	-14
1979	LA-N	.967	46	56	2	2	0	0
1980	SD-N	1.000	12	18	0	0	0	1
Total	10	.975	590	1154	36	0	9	-15

1B

YEAR	TM/L	PCT	G	PO	A	E	DP	FR
1980	SD-N	1.000	2	8	1	0	1	0

■ Bill Joyce 3B

YEAR	TM/L	PCT	G	PO	A	E	DP	FR
1890	Bro-P	.811	**133**	176	284	107	22	-11
1891	Bro-a	.849	64	82	149	41	12	-1
1892	Bro-N	.862	94	141	164	49	8	-19
1894	Was-N	.866	99	152	183	52	20	-3
1895	Was-N	.844	126	186	232	**77**	16	-8
1896	Was-N	.888	48	50	108	20	6	0
	NY-N	.883	49	71	103	23	4	0
	Yr	.885	97	121	211	**43**	10	0
1897	NY-N	.852	106	165	199	63	17	0
1898	NY-N	.891	14	18	31	6	0	0
Total	8	.851	733	1041	1453	438	105	-42

1B

YEAR	TM/L	PCT	G	PO	A	E	DP	FR
1891	Bos-a	1.000	1	8	0	0	0	0
1897	NY-N	.880	2	22	0	3	2	-1
1898	NY-N	.966	130	1252	87	47	73	8
Total	3	.965	133	1282	87	0	75	7

2B

YEAR	TM/L	PCT	G	PO	A	E	DP	FR
1896	Was-N	.899	33	84	85	19	12	-7
1898	NY-N	.800	2	1	3	1	0	0
Total	2	.896	35	85	88	0	12	-7

OF

YEAR	TM/L	PCT	G	PO	A	E	DP	FR
1892	Bro-N	.875	3	7	0	1	0	0

■ Wally Joyner 1B

YEAR	TM/L	PCT	G	PO	A	E	DP	FR
1986	Cal-A	.989	152	1222	139	15	128	9
1987	Cal-A	.993	149	1276	92	10	133	-7
1988	Cal-A	.995	**156**	**1369**	**143**	8	**148**	11
1989	Cal-A	**.997**	**159**	**1487**	99	4	146	-4
1990	Cal-A	.995	83	727	62	4	78	2
Total	5	.994	699	6081	535	1	633	11

■ Joe Judge 1B

YEAR	TM/L	PCT	G	PO	A	E	DP	FR
1915	Was-A	.990	10	96	5	1	7	0
1916	Was-A	.986	103	935	69	14	53	4
1917	Was-A	.988	100	906	60	12	59	-1
1918	Was-A	.985	**130**	1304	92	21	71	2
1919	Was-A	.988	133	1177	78	15	66	-4
1920	Was-A	.992	124	1194	62	10	67	-8
1921	Was-A	.996	152	1417	89	6	109	-3
1922	Was-A	.996	147	1392	101	6	**131**	3
1923	Was-A	**.993**	112	1070	88	8	**113**	**8**
1924	Was-A	.994	140	1276	86	8	108	-2
1925	Was-A	**.993**	109	901	71	7	92	3
1926	Was-A	.994	128	1145	95	8	90	10
1927	Was-A	**.996**	136	1309	71	6	79	-6
1928	Was-A	.996	149	1412	92	6	118	1
1929	Was-A	**.996**	112	1323	88	6	116	3
1930	Was-A	**.998**	117	1050	67	2	95	2
1931	Was-A	.994	15	155	10	1	9	1
1932	Was-A	.997	78	668	46	2	71	1
1933	Bro-N	.989	28	243	17	3	24	0
	Bos-A	.989	29	267	13	0	21	0
1934	Bos-A	1.000	2	24	1	0	1	0
Total	20	.993	2084	19264	1301	142	1500	14

OF

YEAR	TM/L	PCT	G	PO	A	E	DP	FR
1915	Was-A	1.000	2	1	0	0	0	-1

■ Wally Judnich OF

YEAR	TM/L	PCT	G	PO	A	E	DP	FR
1940	StL-A	**.989**	133	356	7	4	4	-2
1941	StL-A	.980	140	383	11	8	3	0
1942	StL-A	**.991**	122	330	4	3	0	-4
1946	StL-A	**.995**	137	409	6	2	2	8
1947	StL-A	1.000	15	38	1	0	0	0
1948	Cle-A	.970	49	93	4	3	0	-2
1949	Pit-N	1.000	8	27	0	0	0	1
Total	7	.988	604	1636	33	0	9	1

1B

YEAR	TM/L	PCT	G	PO	A	E	DP	FR
1947	StL-A	.989	129	1067	76	13	118	-6
1948	Cle-A	.994	20	147	7	1	19	-2
Total	2	.989	149	1214	83	4	137	-8

■ Billy Jurges SS

YEAR	TM/L	PCT	G	PO	A	E	DP	FR
1931	Chi-N	1.000	3	5	4	0	0	0
1932	Chi-N	.964	108	223	394	23	69	**32**
1933	Chi-N	.958	143	298	476	34	95	**20**
1934	Chi-N	.966	98	205	334	19	63	**14**
1935	Chi-N	.964	146	348	484	31	**99**	**30**
1936	Chi-N	.960	116	249	379	26	80	17
1937	Chi-N	**.975**	128	258	370	16	74	-7
1938	Chi-N	.953	136	277	417	34	82	0
1939	NY-N	**.965**	137	295	482	28	95	**15**
1940	NY-N	.967	63	123	196	11	36	-1
1941	NY-N	.957	134	230	432	30	82	7
1942	NY-N	.978	124	251	401	15	67	7
1943	NY-N	.955	99	209	303	24	44	-3
1944	NY-N	.976	10	15	25	1	6	0
1945	NY-N	.974	8	15	22	1	1	1
1946	NY-N	.976	73	119	204	8	26	-3
1947	Chi-N	.925	14	13	36	4	10	-4
Total	17	.964	1540	3133	4959	305	929	125

3B

YEAR	TM/L	PCT	G	PO	A	E	DP	FR
1931	Chi-N	.963	54	42	115	6	11	9
1932	Chi-N	1.000	5	4	7	0	1	0
1943	NY-N	.988	28	27	56	1	10	3
1944	NY-N	.961	61	48	124	7	7	0
1945	NY-N	.937	44	40	94	9	3	1
1946	Chi-N	1.000	7	8	8	0	0	0
Total	6	.961	199	169	404	3	32	13

2B

YEAR	TM/L	PCT	G	PO	A	E	DP	FR
1931	Chi-N	.968	33	66	83	5	21	2
1944	NY-N	1.000	1	1	0	0	0	0
1946	Chi-N	—	2	0	0	0	0	0
Total	3	.968	36	67	83	5	21	2

■ Skip Jutze C

YEAR	TM/L	PCT	G	PO	A	E	DP	FR
1972	StL-N	.964	17	93	15	4	1	0
1973	Hou-N	.984	86	450	31	8	4	-6
1974	Hou-N	1.000	7	16	2	0	0	0
1975	Hou-N	.988	47	147	15	2	3	4
1976	Hou-N	.986	42	125	21	2	5	3
1977	Sea-A	.984	40	170	15	3	3	-2
Total	6	.983	239	1001	99	9	16	-1

■ Mike Kahoe C

YEAR	TM/L	PCT	G	PO	A	E	DP	FR
1895	Cin-N	1.000	3	2	0	0	0	-1
1899	Cin-N	.957	13	48	18	3	3	5
1900	Cin-N	.963	51	207	79	11	5	8
1901	Cin-N	1.000	4	13	3	0	1	-1
	Chi-N	.974	63	368	74	12	8	11
	Yr	.974	67	381	77	12	9	10
1902	Chi-N	.875	4	17	4	3	0	0
	StL-A	.967	53	214	52	9	4	0
1903	StL-A	.971	71	333	64	12	8	-3
1904	StL-A	.968	69	307	91	13	3	2
1905	Phi-N	.975	15	58	20	2	2	0
1907	Chi-N	1.000	3	5	1	0	0	-1
	Was-A	.976	15	61	19	2	0	1
1908	Was-A	.983	11	51	7	1	1	5
1909	Was-A	.867	3	9	4	2	0	0
Total	11	.968	378	1693	436	0	35	26

1B

YEAR	TM/L	PCT	G	PO	A	E	DP	FR
1901	Chi-N	.891	6	37	4	5	2	0
1907	Chi-N	1.000	1	4	0	0	0	0
Total	2	.900	7	41	4	5	2	0

SS

YEAR	TM/L	PCT	G	PO	A	E	DP	FR
1900	Cin-N	.200	1	0	1	4	1	-1
1902	Chi-N	1.000	1	0	1	0	0	0
Total	2	.333	2	0	2	4	1	-1

3B

YEAR	TM/L	PCT	G	PO	A	E	DP	FR
1902	Chi-N	.667	2	0	2	1	1	0

OF

YEAR	TM/L	PCT	G	PO	A	E	DP	FR
1903	StL-A	—	2	0	0	0	0	-1

■ Al Kaiser OF

YEAR	TM/L	PCT	G	PO	A	E	DP	FR
1911	Chi-N	.905	22	35	3	4	0	-2
	Bos-N	.922	58	101	6	9	3	-1
	Yr	.918	80	136	9	13	3	-3
1912	Bos-N	.900	4	8	1	1	0	0
1914	Ind-F	.918	50	98	3	9	0	-2
Total	3	.917	134	242	13	3	3	-5

1B

YEAR	TM/L	PCT	G	PO	A	E	DP	FR
1914	Ind-F	.714	1	9	1	4	0	-1

■ Al Kaline OF

YEAR	TM/L	PCT	G	PO	A	E	DP	FR
1953	Det-A	1.000	20	11	1	0	0	0
1954	Det-A	.971	135	283	16	9	0	5
1955	Det-A	.979	152	306	14	7	4	4
1956	Det-A	.984	153	343	**18**	6	4	**16**
1957	Det-A	.985	145	319	13	5	2	11

YEAR	TM/L	PCT	G	PO	A	E	DP	FR
1958	Det-A	.994	145	316	23	2	4	22
1959	Det-A	.989	136	364	4	4	0	4
1960	Det-A	.987	142	367	5	5	1	3
1961	Det-A	.990	147	378	9	4	3	18
1962	Det-A	.983	100	225	8	4	1	10
1963	Det-A	.992	140	257	5	2	0	-4
1964	Det-A	.990	136	278	6	3	2	9
1965	Det-A	.985	112	193	2	3	0	-2
1966	Det-A	.993	136	279	7	2	1	-1
1967	Det-A	.983	130	217	14	4	2	6
1968	Det-A	.978	74	131	1	3	0	-3
1969	Det-A	.966	118	192	9	7	4	-1
1970	Det-A	.988	91	156	3	2	1	-2
1971	Det-A	1.000	129	207	6	0	0	-9
1972	Det-A	.991	84	111	5	1	0	-6
1973	Det-A	1.000	63	102	1	0	0	-3
Total	21	.986	2488	5035	170	3	29	77
1B								
1968	Det-A	.976	22	152	13	4	15	0
1969	Det-A	1.000	9	65	2	0	3	-1
1970	Det-A	.990	52	374	31	4	39	0
1971	Det-A	1.000	5	27	1	0	3	0
1972	Det-A	1.000	11	37	4	0	5	0
1973	Det-A	.996	36	245	12	1	32	-3
Total	6	.991	135	900	63	9	97	-4
3B								
1961	Det-A	1.000	1	1	1	0	0	0
1965	Det-A	1.000	1	2	1	0	0	0
Total	2	1.000	2	3	2	0	0	0

■ **Willie Kamm 3B**

YEAR	TM/L	PCT	G	PO	A	E	DP	FR
1923	Chi-A	.960	149	173	352	22	29	7
1924	Chi-A	.971	146	190	312	15	31	8
1925	Chi-A	.957	152	182	310	22	32	0
1926	Chi-A	.978	142	177	323	11	16	14
1927	Chi-A	.972	146	236	279	15	21	1
1928	Chi-A	.977	155	243	278	12	33	-3
1929	Chi-A	.978	145	221	270	11	27	4
1930	Chi-A	.939	106	142	209	23	17	15
1931	Chi-A	.938	18	29	32	4	4	2
	Cle-A	.947	114	129	208	19	29	1
	Yr	.945	132	158	240	23	33	3
1932	Cle-A	.967	148	164	299	16	20	7
1933	Cle-A	.984	131	153	221	6	16	0
1934	Cle-A	.978	118	109	248	8	24	11
1935	Cle-A	.875	4	3	4	1	0	-2
Total	13	.967	1674	2151	3345	185	299	65

■ **Alex Kampouris 2B**

YEAR	TM/L	PCT	G	PO	A	E	DP	FR
1934	Cin-N	.946	16	35	53	5	7	-1
1935	Cin-N	.957	141	367	411	35	88	1
1936	Cin-N	.969	119	270	376	21	71	28
1937	Cin-N	.961	146	367	439	33	87	3
1938	Cin-N	.973	21	43	66	3	11	0
	NY-N	.972	79	198	255	13	52	13
	Yr	.972	100	241	321	16	63	13
1939	NY-N	.973	62	146	179	9	34	10
1941	Bro-N	.987	15	31	45	1	7	0
1942	Bro-N	.970	9	16	16	1	5	2
1943	Bro-N	.946	18	43	44	5	8	-1
	Was-A	.957	10	19	25	2	1	-4
Total	9	.964	636	1535	1909	128	371	51
3B								
1939	NY-N	.917	11	8	14	2	1	-1
1943	Was-A	.936	33	44	58	7	12	1
Total	2	.932	44	52	72	9	13	0
SS								
1935	Cin-N	.829	6	14	15	6	0	-2
OF								
1936	Cin-N	1.000	1	1	0	0	0	0
1943	Was-A	1.000	1	3	0	0	0	0
Total	2	1.000	2	4	0	0	0	0

■ **John Kane OF**

YEAR	TM/L	PCT	G	PO	A	E	DP	FR
1907	Cin-N	.959	42	87	6	4	0	3
1908	Cin-N	.981	127	292	15	6	2	4
1909	Chi-N	.917	8	9	2	1	0	-1
1910	Chi-N	1.000	18	21	0	0	0	-1
Total	4	.975	195	409	23	1	2	5
3B								
1907	Cin-N	.878	25	20	59	11	2	-1
1909	Chi-N	.778	3	3	4	2	1	0
1910	Chi-N	.846	4	4	7	2	0	-1
Total	3	.866	32	27	70	5	3	-2
SS								
1907	Cin-N	.885	6	11	12	3	0	-2
1909	Chi-N	1.000	3	7	9	0	1	1
1910	Chi-N	1.000	2	2	3	0	0	0
Total	3	.936	11	20	24	3	1	-1
2B								
1907	Cin-N	.833	2	2	3	1	0	0
1908	Cin-N	1.000	1	6	2	0	0	0
1909	Chi-N	1.000	2	7	9	0	1	2
1910	Chi-N	.889	6	4	4	1	1	0
Total	4	.949	11	19	18	2	2	2

■ **Rod Kanehl 2B**

YEAR	TM/L	PCT	G	PO	A	E	DP	FR
1962	NY-N	.944	62	183	187	22	53	16
1963	NY-N	.857	12	22	14	6	3	-2
1964	NY-N	.988	34	78	84	2	15	11
Total	3	.950	108	283	285	0	71	25
OF								
1962	NY-N	.957	20	21	1	1	0	1
1963	NY-N	.974	58	69	5	2	2	5
1964	NY-N	1.000	25	54	4	0	3	5
Total	3	.981	103	144	10	3	5	11
3B								
1962	NY-N	.873	30	15	40	8	4	2
1963	NY-N	.846	13	7	15	4	0	1
1964	NY-N	.932	19	20	35	4	7	5
Total	3	.892	62	42	90	6	11	8
1B								
1962	NY-N	.947	3	16	2	1	0	0
1963	NY-N	1.000	3	30	1	0	2	0
1964	NY-N	1.000	2	9	2	0	1	1
Total	3	.984	8	55	5	1	3	1
SS								
1962	NY-N	—	2	0	0	0	0	0

■ **Ron Karkovice C**

YEAR	TM/L	PCT	G	PO	A	E	DP	FR
1986	Chi-A	.996	37	227	19	1	4	14
1987	Chi-A	.982	37	147	20	3	3	10
1988	Chi-A	.995	46	190	24	1	4	8
1989	Chi-A	.986	68	299	47	5	6	17
1990	Chi-A	.994	64	296	31	2	4	6
Total	5	.991	252	1159	141	2	21	55

■ **Eddie Kasko SS**

YEAR	TM/L	PCT	G	PO	A	E	DP	FR
1957	StL-N	.955	13	18	24	2	5	-2
1958	StL-N	.961	77	111	186	12	47	1
1959	Cin-N	.976	84	182	271	11	61	10
1960	Cin-N	.974	15	19	19	1	4	-3
1961	Cin-N	.964	112	201	286	18	59	-17
1962	Cin-N	.944	21	19	49	4	13	-1
1963	Cin-N	.960	15	15	33	2	8	1
1964	Hou-N	.978	128	228	388	14	72	11
1965	Hou-N	.976	59	96	152	6	27	-10
1966	Bos-A	.976	20	29	53	2	7	4
Total	10	.971	544	918	1461	2	303	-6
3B								
1957	StL-N	.961	120	100	224	13	21	-5
1958	StL-N	1.000	1	0	1	0	0	0
1959	Cin-N	.943	31	10	23	2	2	1
1960	Cin-N	.976	86	98	186	10	20	9
1961	Cin-N	1.000	12	6	7	0	0	-1
1962	Cin-N	.941	114	101	204	19	18	-7
1963	Cin-N	.958	48	41	75	5	5	-1
1964	Hou-N	.500	2	1	0	1	0	-1
1965	Hou-N	1.000	2	2	3	0	0	0
1966	Bos-A	1.000	10	11	23	0	5	3
Total	10	.957	426	370	746	0	71	-2
2B								
1957	StL-N	—	1	0	0	0	0	0
1958	StL-N	.982	12	25	31	1	7	5
1959	Cin-N	1.000	2	0	1	0	0	0
1960	Cin-N	.975	33	77	82	4	23	-6
1961	Cin-N	1.000	6	7	8	0	1	0
1963	Cin-N	1.000	1	1	0	0	0	0
1966	Bos-A	.946	8	15	20	2	4	0
Total	7	.974	63	125	142	7	35	-1

■ **Ray Katt C**

YEAR	TM/L	PCT	G	PO	A	E	DP	FR
1952	NY-N	1.000	8	39	4	0	0	1
1953	NY-N	.975	8	33	6	1	0	-1
1954	NY-N	.973	82	265	23	8	4	-5
1955	NY-N	.987	122	482	45	7	7	-6
1956	NY-N	.978	37	164	18	4	1	0
	StL-N	.984	47	231	16	4	3	-2
	Yr	.982	84	395	34	8	4	-2
1957	StL-N	.981	68	238	25	5	4	-6
1958	StL-N	.971	14	63	4	2	2	0
1959	StL-N	.976	14	38	2	1	0	-1
Total	8	.981	400	1553	143	2	21	-20

■ **Benny Kauff OF**

YEAR	TM/L	PCT	G	PO	A	E	DP	FR
1912	NY-A	1.000	4	4	0	0	0	-1
1914	Ind-F	.953	154	310	31	17	5	16
1915	Bro-F	.959	136	317	32	15	7	15
1916	NY-N	.962	154	329	22	14	6	-4
1917	NY-N	.976	153	357	12	9	4	-9
1918	NY-N	.952	67	147	11	8	4	-3
1919	NY-N	.950	134	306	18	17	3	-8
1920	NY-N	.960	51	111	10	5	0	6
Total	8	.960	853	1881	136	5	29	12

■ **Marty Kavanagh 2B**

YEAR	TM/L	PCT	G	PO	A	E	DP	FR
1914	Det-A	.929	115	228	333	43	30	-6
1915	Det-A	.928	42	59	95	12	7	-13
1916	Det-A	1.000	2	0	1	0	0	0
	Cle-A	.894	9	11	31	5	2	1
	Yr	.896	11	11	32	5	2	1
1918	StL-N	.920	4	11	12	2	0	-1
Total	4	.926	172	309	472	2	39	-19
1B								
1914	Det-A	.949	4	36	1	2	0	-1
1915	Det-A	.987	44	500	24	7	16	-2
1916	Cle-A	1.000	1	3	0	0	0	0
1918	Cle-A	.967	12	113	5	4	7	-1
	Det-A	.964	12	129	6	5	6	-1
	Yr	.966	24	242	11	9	13	-2
Total	4	.978	73	781	36	8	29	-5
OF								
1915	Det-A	1.000	2	4	0	0	0	0
1916	Det-A	1.000	11	19	1	0	0	0
1917	Cle-A	1.000	2	2	1	0	1	0
1918	StL-N	1.000	8	14	0	0	0	-1
Total	4	1.000	23	39	2	0	1	-1
3B								
1915	Det-A	—	1	0	0	0	0	0
1916	Det-A	1.000	1	1	0	0	1	0
	Cle-A	.500	1	0	2	1	0	-1
	Yr	.600	2	1	2	1	1	-1
Total	2	.600	3	1	2	2	1	-1
SS								
1915	Det-A	1.000	2	0	2	0	1	0

■ **Eddie Kazak 3B**

YEAR	TM/L	PCT	G	PO	A	E	DP	FR
1948	StL-N	.900	6	7	11	2	2	1
1949	StL-N	.926	80	64	175	19	20	-2
1950	StL-N	.936	48	36	95	9	7	1
1951	StL-N	.933	10	11	17	2	1	-1
1952	StL-N	1.000	1	0	1	0	0	0
	Cin-N	.667	3	1	1	1	0	-1
	Yr	.750	4	1	2	1	0	-1
Total	5	.927	148	119	300	3	30	-2
2B								
1949	StL-N	.846	5	10	12	4	2	-2
1B								
1952	Cin-N	1.000	1	4	0	0	0	0

■ **Ted Kazanski 2B**

YEAR	TM/L	PCT	G	PO	A	E	DP	FR
1956	Phi-N	.979	116	246	261	11	68	-10
1957	Phi-N	.971	22	28	38	2	10	-2
1958	Phi-N	.988	59	117	130	3	37	-6
Total	3	.981	197	391	429	6	115	-18
SS								
1953	Phi-N	.949	95	185	239	23	53	-19
1954	Phi-N	.945	38	43	77	7	18	-7
1955	Phi-N	1.000	4	4	6	0	1	0
1956	Phi-N	—	1	0	0	0	0	0
1957	Phi-N	1.000	3	1	0	0	0	0
1958	Phi-N	.946	22	8	27	2	3	-2
Total	6	.949	163	241	349	2	75	-28
3B								
1955	Phi-N	1.000	4	1	3	0	0	0
1957	Phi-N	.968	36	35	57	3	11	0
1958	Phi-N	.917	16	15	18	3	1	-4
Total	3	.956	56	51	78	6	12	-4

■ **Bob Kearney C**

YEAR	TM/L	PCT	G	PO	A	E	DP	FR
1979	SF-N	—	1	0	0	0	0	0
1981	Oak-A	—	1	0	0	0	0	0
1982	Oak-A	.970	22	114	14	4	1	4
1983	Oak-A	.982	101	437	41	9	5	6
1984	Sea-A	.988	133	823	63	11	9	5
1985	Sea-A	.995	108	529	50	3	7	7
1986	Sea-A	.989	79	419	46	5	3	13
1987	Sea-A	.981	24	94	10	2	0	5
Total	8	.987	469	2416	224	4	25	40

■ **Willie Keeler OF**

YEAR	TM/L	PCT	G	PO	A	E	DP	FR
1893	NY-N	.667	3	2	0	1	0	-1
	Bro-N	.786	8	9	2	3	0	-1
	Yr	.765	11	11	2	4	0	-2
1894	Bal-N	.938	128	215	25	16	4	3
1895	Bal-N	.946	131	260	20	16	5	12
1896	Bal-N	.969	126	227	20	8	6	6
1897	Bal-N	.970	129	217	12	7	2	-2
1898	Bal-N	.961	128	210	14	9	2	1
1899	Bro-N	.979	141	208	21	5	4	-2
1900	Bro-N	.940	136	227	22	16	4	5
1901	Bro-N	.985	125	181	17	3	4	0
1902	Bro-N	.978	133	208	14	5	5	2
1903	NY-A	.935	128	177	10	13	4	-8
1904	NY-A	.935	142	186	16	14	7	-3
1905	NY-A	.968	137	194	17	7	1	2
1906	NY-A	.987	152	213	16	3	3	-2
1907	NY-A	.969	107	144	13	5	5	-2
1908	NY-A	.936	88	123	9	9	2	-1
1909	NY-A	.968	95	111	9	4	2	-5
1910	NY-A	1.000	2	1	0	0	0	1
Total	18	.959	2039	3113	257	144	60	5
3B								
1892	NY-N	.878	14	15	21	5	1	-3
1893	Bro-N	.833	12	20	30	10	2	0
1898	Bal-N	1.000	1	1	0	0	0	0
1901	Bro-N	.760	10	8	11	6	2	-4
1903	NY-A	.846	4	6	5	2	0	-1
1905	NY-A	.750	3	4	2	2	0	-2
Total	6	.831	44	54	69	5	5	-10
2B								
1893	NY-N	1.000	2	2	2	0	0	-2
1894	Bal-N	1.000	1	2	1	0	0	0
1900	Bro-N	1.000	1	1	0	0	0	0
1901	Bro-N	1.000	3	5	8	0	0	-1
1905	NY-A	.933	12	9	19	2	1	-4
Total	5	.961	19	18	31	2	1	-7
SS								
1893	NY-N	.750	2	1	5	2	0	-1

■ **Jim Keenan C**

YEAR	TM/L	PCT	G	PO	A	E	DP	FR
1880	Buf-N	.947	2	11	7	1	0	3
1882	Pit-a	.906	22	142	21	17	3	3
1884	Ind-a	.923	59	399	71	39	5	-5
1885	Cin-a	.926	33	164	37	16	1	-4
1886	Cin-a	.915	30	170	45	20	2	0
1887	Cin-a	.934	38	161	67	16	8	7
1888	Cin-a	.946	69	356	114	27	7	-2
1889	Cin-a	.962	66	319	91	16	11	-1
1890	Cin-N	.950	50	244	63	16	5	4
1891	Cin-N	.903	34	131	27	17	3	-4
Total	10	.935	403	2097	543	185	45	1
1B								
1884	Ind-a	.971	6	62	4	2	1	1
1885	Cin-a	.897	4	26	0	3	1	-1
1886	Cin-a	.975	4	38	1	1	2	0
1887	Cin-a	.989	11	91	1	1	7	0
1888	Cin-a	.994	16	150	6	1	6	1
1889	Cin-a	.979	21	183	7	4	14	0
1890	Cin-N	1.000	2	26	1	0	1	0
1891	Cin-N	.974	41	456	24	13	19	2
Total	8	.977	105	1032	44	5	51	3
OF								
1882	Pit-a	1.000	3	3	0	0	0	-1
1884	Ind-a	.500	2	1	1	2	0	-2
1886	Cin-a	.875	7	6	1	1	1	-1
1890	Cin-N	—	1	0	0	0	0	0
Total	4	.800	13	10	2	3	1	-4

YEAR	TM/L	PCT	G	PO	A	E	DP	FR
3B								
1886	Cin-a	.846	5	6	5	2	1	-1
1889	Cin-a	.500	1	1	1	2	0	-1
1890	Cin-N	1.000	1	1	0	0	0	0
1891	Cin-N	.833	1	3	2	1	0	0
Total	4	.792	8	11	8	5	1	-2
SS								
1882	Pit-a	.333	1	0	1	2	0	-1
1884	Ind-a	.667	2	0	4	2	0	0
Total	2	.556	3	0	5	4	0	-1

■ Bill Keister SS

YEAR	TM/L	PCT	G	PO	A	E	DP	FR
1898	Bos-N	1.000	4	3	6	0	1	0
1899	Bal-N	.895	90	169	283	53	25	-20
1900	StL-N	.814	7	14	21	8	1	-2
1901	Bal-A	.851	112	231	322	97	30	-23
1902	Was-A	.917	2	3	8	1	1	0
Total	5	.870	215	420	640	159	58	-45
2B								
1896	Bal-N	.923	8	10	14	2	1	-4
1898	Bos-N	1.000	4	4	9	0	1	0
1899	Bal-N	.942	46	94	117	13	11	-11
1900	StL-N	.927	116	206	315	41	26	-22
1902	Was-A	.952	40	97	121	11	9	-1
Total	5	.936	214	411	576	7	48	-38
OF								
1898	Bos-N	1.000	1	3	1	0	0	1
1899	Bal-N	1.000	1	2	1	0	0	1
1902	Was-A	.912	65	115	9	12	3	1
1903	Phi-N	.940	100	136	22	10	1	3
Total	4	.929	167	256	33	2	4	6
3B								
1896	Bal-N	.760	6	6	13	6	1	-1
1900	StL-N	.929	3	4	9	1	0	0
1902	Was-A	.808	14	14	28	10	1	-3
Total	3	.813	23	24	50	7	2	-4

■ George Kell 3B

YEAR	TM/L	PCT	G	PO	A	E	DP	FR
1943	Phi-A	1.000	1	1	3	0	0	0
1944	Phi-A	.958	139	167	289	20	25	-5
1945	Phi-A	**.964**	147	**186**	**345**	20	32	**22**
1946	Phi-A	.979	26	36	57	2	5	3
	Det-A	.984	105	105	210	5	22	5
	Yr	.983	**131**	141	**267**	**7**	27	8
1947	Det-A	.962	152	167	333	20	25	18
1948	Det-A	.969	92	108	146	8	15	-8
1949	Det-A	.975	134	154	271	11	23	1
1950	Det-A	**.982**	157	186	315	9	30	-3
1951	Det-A	**.960**	147	175	**310**	20	**34**	9
1952	Det-A	.959	39	38	78	5	7	-2
	Bos-A	.959	73	75	138	9	14	-7
	Yr	**.959**	112	113	216	14	21	-9
1953	Bos-A	.972	124	114	231	10	23	-12
1954	Bos-A	.920	25	31	49	7	5	-3
	Chi-A	.957	31	19	48	3	4	-6
	Yr	**.936**	56	50	97	10	9	-9
1955	Chi-A	.976	105	83	165	6	8	-16
1956	Chi-A	1.000	18	17	28	0	6	-4
	Bal-A	.974	97	97	165	7	19	-7
	Yr	.978	115	114	193	7	19	-11
1957	Bal-A	.979	80	66	122	4	15	-2
Total	15	.969	1692	1825	3303	166	306	-17
1B								
1946	Det-A	1.000	1	2	0	0	0	0
1954	Chi-A	.996	32	253	8	1	27	-5
1955	Chi-A	.993	24	133	5	1	12	-2
1956	Chi-A	1.000	4	19	3	0	4	0
	Bal-A	1.000	2	4	1	0	0	0
	Yr	1.000	6	23	4	0	4	0
1957	Bal-A	1.000	22	146	5	0	10	-2
Total	5	.997	85	557	22	2	53	-9
OF								
1953	Bos-A	1.000	7	4	0	0	0	0
1954	Chi-A	1.000	2	3	0	0	0	0
1955	Chi-A	—	1	0	0	0	0	0
Total	3	1.000	10	7	0	0	0	0
2B								
1956	Bal-A	1.000	1	1	1	0	1	0

■ Mick Kelleher SS

YEAR	TM/L	PCT	G	PO	A	E	DP	FR
1972	StL-N	.984	23	60	61	2	14	5
1973	StL-N	.955	42	30	55	4	10	9
1974	Hou-N	.944	18	23	62	5	10	4
1975	StL-N	.909	7	3	7	1	1	1
1976	Chi-N	.980	101	147	289	9	52	11
1977	Chi-N	1.000	14	13	27	0	5	5
1978	Chi-N	1.000	10	8	11	0	1	2
1979	Chi-N	.971	14	9	24	1	4	4
1980	Chi-N	1.000	17	12	33	0	4	8
1981	Det-A	1.000	9	9	31	0	5	5
1982	Cal-A	.965	28	31	52	3	8	5
Total	11	.976	283	345	652	5	114	59
3B								
1976	Chi-N	.943	22	12	21	2	1	0
1977	Chi-N	—	1	0	0	0	0	0
1978	Chi-N	1.000	37	11	41	0	3	6
1979	Chi-N	.966	32	17	40	2	4	5
1980	Chi-N	.850	31	8	9	3	2	2
1981	Det-A	.930	39	12	28	3	2	0
1982	Cal-A	—	1	0	0	0	0	0
	Cal-A	1.000	6	3	8	0	0	1
	Yr	1.000	7	3	8	0	0	1
Total	7	.955	169	63	147	0	12	14
2B								
1976	Chi-N	.957	5	8	14	1	4	2
1977	Chi-N	.976	40	65	99	4	16	14
1978	Chi-N	1.000	17	33	48	0	6	9
1979	Chi-N	.978	29	52	84	3	16	13

YEAR	TM/L	PCT	G	PO	A	E	DP	FR
1980	Chi-N	.974	57	62	87	4	17	16
1981	Det-A	.962	11	9	16	1	5	1
1982	Det-A	1.000	1	0	1	0	0	0
Total	7	.978	160	229	349	3	64	55

■ Charlie Keller OF

YEAR	TM/L	PCT	G	PO	A	E	DP	FR
1939	NY-A	.969	105	213	5	7	1	-5
1940	NY-A	.967	136	317	5	11	2	0
1941	NY-A	.980	137	328	7	7	2	3
1942	NY-A	.985	152	321	10	5	1	1
1943	NY-A	.994	141	338	8	2	0	4
1945	NY-A	1.000	44	110	4	0	0	2
1946	NY-A	.979	149	324	4	7	0	-2
1947	NY-A	.967	43	85	2	3	0	-4
1948	NY-A	.977	66	126	1	3	0	-7
1949	NY-A	.976	31	41	0	1	0	-6
1950	Det-A	1.000	6	10	0	0	0	0
1951	Det-A	1.000	8	22	0	0	0	1
1952	NY-A	—	1	0	0	0	0	0
Total	13	.980	1019	2235	46	6	6	-13

■ Joe Kelley OF

YEAR	TM/L	PCT	G	PO	A	E	DP	FR
1891	Bos-N	.852	12	21	2	4	0	-1
1892	Pit-N	.919	56	101	13	10	4	2
	Bal-N	.824	10	14	0	3	0	-3
	Yr	.908	66	115	13	13	4	-1
1893	Bal-N	.940	125	307	22	21	4	7
1894	Bal-N	.951	129	276	16	15	3	2
1895	Bal-N	.964	131	244	21	10	5	-1
1896	Bal-N	.958	131	280	20	13	3	4
1897	Bal-N	.959	130	240	15	11	3	-2
1898	Bal-N	.969	122	235	18	8	4	1
1899	Bro-N	.977	143	307	26	8	7	8
1900	Bro-N	.959	77	174	12	8	2	3
1902	Bal-A	.973	48	101	7	3	2	0
	Cin-N	.971	20	30	4	1	1	0
1903	Cin-N	.947	67	117	8	7	0	-3
1904	Cin-N	1.000	6	9	0	0	0	-1
1905	Cin-N	.974	85	137	11	4	0	-2
1906	Cin-N	.966	122	184	13	7	5	-5
1908	Bos-N	.938	51	71	5	5	1	-7
Total	16	.957	1465	2848	213	138	44	2
1B								
1900	Bro-N	.978	32	259	12	6	13	-2
1901	Bro-N	.975	115	984	82	27	63	7
1902	Bal-A	1.000	5	37	4	0	4	1
1903	Cin-N	.987	6	68	8	1	2	0
1904	Cin-N	.988	117	1049	76	14	48	1
1905	Cin-N	1.000	2	14	0	0	2	0
1906	Cin-N	1.000	3	25	1	0	2	0
1908	Bos-N	.978	11	118	15	3	2	3
Total	8	.982	291	2554	198	1	136	12
3B								
1897	Bal-N	1.000	2	0	1	0	0	0
1898	Bal-N	.500	2	0	1	1	0	0
1900	Bro-N	.913	13	17	25	4	3	-1
1901	Bro-N	.875	5	4	10	2	0	-1
1902	Bal-A	.906	8	15	14	3	1	-1
	Cin-N	.914	9	12	20	3	0	0
1903	Cin-N	.963	8	12	14	1	0	0
1906	Cin-N	.833	1	2	3	1	0	0
Total	7	.909	48	62	88	5	4	-3
2B								
1902	Cin-N	.971	10	35	31	2	7	3
1903	Cin-N	.927	11	25	26	4	4	-2
1904	Cin-N	1.000	1	1	2	0	0	0
Total	3	.952	22	61	59	6	11	1
SS								
1897	Bal-N	.900	3	2	7	1	0	0
1902	Cin-N	1.000	2	1	4	0	1	0
1903	Cin-N	.839	12	17	30	9	5	-3
1906	Cin-N	1.000	1	1	3	0	0	0
Total	4	.867	18	21	44	0	6	-3

■ George Kelly 1B

YEAR	TM/L	PCT	G	PO	A	E	DP	FR
1915	NY-N	.983	9	55	3	1	1	0
1916	NY-N	.981	13	100	2	2	4	-2
1917	NY-N	1.000	1	2	0	0	1	0
	Pit-N	.971	8	66	2	2	3	-1
	Yr	.972	9	68	2	2	4	-1
1919	NY-N	.994	32	341	11	2	17	-3
1920	NY-N	.994	**155**	**1759**	**103**	11	**115**	4
1921	NY-N	.990	149	1552	**115**	17	**132**	12
1922	NY-N	.993	151	1642	**103**	13	**123**	10
1923	NY-N	.993	145	**1568**	60	12	111	-6
1924	NY-N	.993	125	1309	60	10	107	-2
1925	NY-N	.989	25	263	16	3	13	1
1926	NY-N	**.993**	114	1196	79	9	89	6
1927	Cin-N	.992	49	456	32	4	46	2
1928	Cin-N	.991	99	894	69	9	99	**8**
1929	Cin-N	.993	147	1537	103	11	127	4
1930	Cin-N	.993	50	503	35	4	44	2
	Chi-N	.998	39	414	32	1	31	4
	Yr	.995	89	917	67	5	75	6
1932	Bro-N	.984	62	575	36	10	48	-2
Total	16	.992	1373	14232	861	121	1111	37
2B								
1917	NY-N	—	1	0	0	0	0	0
1924	NY-N	.931	5	9	18	2	2	1
1925	NY-N	.981	108	273	394	13	68	19
1926	NY-N	.944	18	37	65	6	12	2
1927	Cin-N	.927	13	19	32	4	2	-4
Total	5	.971	145	338	509	5	84	18
OF								
1915	NY-N	.889	4	7	1	1	0	0
1916	NY-N	1.000	12	6	0	0	1	0
1917	NY-N	1.000	4	2	2	0	0	1
1924	NY-N	.976	14	39	1	1	0	1

YEAR	TM/L	PCT	G	PO	A	E	DP	FR
1925	NY-N	.941	17	31	1	2	0	-2
1927	Cin-N	1.000	2	1	0	0	0	0
1928	Cin-N	.944	13	33	1	2	1	0
1932	Bro-N	1.000	1	1	0	0	0	0
Total	8	.955	67	120	6	6	2	0
3B								
1916	NY-N	1.000	1	1	0	0	0	0
1924	NY-N	—	1	0	0	0	0	0
Total	2	1.000	2	1	0	0	0	0

■ Pat Kelly OF

YEAR	TM/L	PCT	G	PO	A	E	DP	FR
1968	Min-A	.955	10	20	1	1	0	1
1969	KC-A	.980	107	237	12	5	3	4
1970	KC-A	.963	118	254	8	10	2	7
1971	Chi-A	.991	61	100	7	1	0	0
1972	Chi-A	.968	109	173	8	6	3	-4
1973	Chi-A	.978	141	254	9	6	2	-4
1974	Chi-A	.976	53	79	2	2	2	-5
1975	Chi-A	**.991**	115	222	4	2	1	-6
1976	Chi-A	.950	26	37	1	2	0	-2
1977	Bal-A	.984	109	181	2	3	1	-12
1978	Bal-A	.969	80	123	3	4	1	-9
1979	Bal-A	1.000	24	36	0	0	0	-2
1980	Bal-A	1.000	36	48	4	0	0	0
1981	Cle-A	1.000	8	6	0	0	0	0
Total	14	.978	997	1770	61	2	15	-32

■ Jim Kelly OF

YEAR	TM/L	PCT	G	PO	A	E	DP	FR
1914	Pit-N	1.000	7	12	1	0	0	0
1915	Pit-F	.952	148	292	27	**16**	5	14
1918	Bos-N	.955	35	82	2	4	0	-1
Total	3	.954	190	386	30	0	5	13

■ John Kelly C

YEAR	TM/L	PCT	G	PO	A	E	DP	FR
1882	Cle-N	.800	30	113	35	37	2	-9
1883	Bal-a	.803	38	169	35	50	3	-10
1884	Cin-U	.865	37	210	60	42	3	0
	Was-U	.967	3	22	7	1	0	0
	Yr	.874	40	232	67	43	3	0
Total	3	.834	108	514	137	130	8	-19
OF								
1883	Bal-a	.733	13	19	3	8	0	-1
	Phi-N	1.000	1	1	1	0	0	0
1884	Cin-U	.857	2	6	0	1	0	0
	Was-U	1.000	1	1	0	0	0	0
	Yr	.875	3	7	0	1	0	0
Total	2	.775	17	27	4	9	0	-1

■ Joe Kelly OF

YEAR	TM/L	PCT	G	PO	A	E	DP	FR
1914	Pit-N	.946	139	319	15	19	3	-4
1916	Chi-N	.953	46	98	4	5	0	2
1917	Bos-N	.946	116	284	16	**17**	8	14
1918	Bos-N	.933	45	93	4	7	0	0
1919	Bos-N	.943	16	30	3	2	0	0
Total	5	.945	362	824	42	0	11	12

■ King Kelly OF

YEAR	TM/L	PCT	G	PO	A	E	DP	FR
1878	Cin-N	.765	47	51	24	23	2	2
1879	Cin-N	.747	29	46	13	20	0	2
1880	Chi-N	.779	64	49	32	23	1	4
1881	Chi-N	.841	72	85	31	22	2	4
1882	Chi-N	.887	38	50	21	9	3	8
1883	Chi-N	.813	82	101	38	32	5	7
1884	Chi-N	.794	63	69	31	26	1	5
1885	Chi-N	.867	69	95	**29**	19	2	8
1886	Chi-N	.811	56	62	24	20	1	4
1887	Bos-N	.856	61	78	11	15	2	-6
1888	Bos-N	.727	34	28	4	12	2	-9
1889	Bos-N	.848	113	155	24	32	4	-3
1890	Bos-P	1.000	6	13	2	0	1	2
1891	Cin-a	.900	7	8	1	1	0	-1
	Bos-N	.500	6	2	0	2	0	-2
1892	Bos-N	.000	2	0	0	2	0	-1
1893	NY-N	.000	1	0	0	1	0	-1
Total	16	.820	750	892	285	259	26	23
C								
1878	Cin-N	.873	17	99	39	20	3	7
1879	Cin-N	.908	21	82	36	12	1	7
1880	Chi-N	.821	17	40	15	12	2	-4
1881	Chi-N	.787	11	28	9	10	1	-7
1882	Chi-N	.800	12	13	3	4	0	-2
1883	Chi-N	.840	38	73	37	21	2	-4
1884	Chi-N	.833	28	105	55	32	3	-6
1885	Chi-N	.875	37	146	64	30	2	4
1886	Chi-N	.927	53	259	94	28	3	1
1887	Bos-N	.885	24	80	35	15	3	-4
1888	Bos-N	.905	76	367	146	**54**	8	6
1889	Bos-N	.876	23	56	29	12	2	-7
1890	Bos-P	.915	56	198	60	24	2	3
1891	Cin-a	.904	66	217	102	34	11	12
	Bos-a	.950	4	16	3	1	0	1
	Bos-N	.844	11	44	10	10	2	-3
	Yr	.894	77	261	112	44	13	9
1892	Bos-N	.912	72	319	98	40	11	4
1893	NY-N	.895	17	55	22	9	1	-1
Total	16	.892	583	2197	857	368	57	-3
3B								
1878	Cin-N	1.000	2	0	2	0	0	0
1879	Cin-N	.832	33	36	88	25	3	6
1880	Chi-N	.857	14	22	20	7	0	-2
1881	Chi-N	.952	8	8	12	1	0	1
1882	Chi-N	.875	3	1	6	1	0	0
1883	Chi-N	.778	3	3	4	2	0	0
1884	Chi-N	.778	10	12	16	8	2	-1
1885	Chi-N	.625	2	2	3	3	0	-1
1886	Chi-N	.824	8	6	8	3	2	-3
1887	Bos-N	.500	2	1	1	2	0	-1
1890	Bos-P	.833	2	2	3	1	0	0
1891	Cin-a	.879	8	11	18	4	2	0
1892	Bos-N	.714	2	2	4	2	0	0

YEAR	TM/L	PCT	G	PO	A	E	DP	FR
Total	13	.831	96	108	182	9	9	-1
SS								
1880	Chi-N	—	1	0	0	0	0	0
1882	Chi-N	.810	42	66	117	43	9	-8
1884	Chi-N	.710	12	7	37	18	3	-4
1886	Chi-N	.800	5	3	1	1	1	-1
1887	Bos-N	.800	2	5	7	3	0	-1
1890	Bos-P	.814	27	43	75	27	6	-10
1891	Cin-a	1.000	1	4	6	0	0	1
Total	7	.801	94	128	243	2	19	-23
2B								
1879	Cin-N	.667	1	0	2	1	0	-1
1880	Chi-N	1.000	1	0	1	0	0	0
1883	Chi-N	.680	3	6	11	8	0	-1
1885	Chi-N	.880	6	7	15	3	1	1
1886	Chi-N	.839	6	14	12	5	4	-1
1887	Bos-N	.846	30	88	105	35	19	1
1891	Cin-a	1.000	6	7	12	0	3	1
Total	7	.843	53	122	158	2	27	0
1B								
1882	Chi-N	.714	1	3	2	2	0	0
1884	Chi-N	.833	2	8	2	2	1	0
1885	Chi-N	.769	2	9	1	3	0	0
1886	Chi-N	.957	9	41	4	2	0	1
1890	Bos-P	.885	4	18	5	3	3	1
1891	Cin-a	.871	5	27	0	4	1	-1
1892	Bos-N	.864	2	19	0	3	2	-1
Total	7	.880	25	125	14	9	7	0

■ Roberto Kelly OF

YEAR	TM/L	PCT	G	PO	A	E	DP	FR
1987	NY-A	.955	17	42	0	2	0	2
1988	NY-A	.986	30	70	1	1	0	6
1989	NY-A	.984	137	353	9	6	2	3
1990	NY-A	.988	160	420	5	5	0	1
Total	4	.985	344	885	15	4	2	12

■ Ken Keltner 3B

YEAR	TM/L	PCT	G	PO	A	E	DP	FR
1937	Cle-A	1.000	1	0	1	0	0	0
1938	Cle-A	.956	149	141	271	19	19	-10
1939	Cle-A	**.974**	**154**	**187**	297	13	**40**	6
1940	Cle-A	.953	148	170	277	22	27	-6
1941	Cle-A	**.971**	149	181	**346**	16	**36**	22
1942	Cle-A	**.945**	**151**	166	**353**	30	**38**	16
1943	Cle-A	.969	107	113	228	11	24	6
1944	Cle-A	.968	**149**	168	**369**	18	**37**	15
1946	Cle-A	.965	112	112	195	11	18	-2
1947	Cle-A	.972	150	156	266	12	**29**	-9
1948	Cle-A	.969	**153**	123	**312**	14	27	0
1949	Cle-A	.980	69	51	145	4	11	-1
1950	Bos-A	.947	8	8	10	1	0	-1
Total	13	.965	1500	1576	3070	171	306	36
1B								
1950	Bos-A	1.000	1	1	0	0	0	0

■ Rudy Kemmler C

YEAR	TM/L	PCT	G	PO	A	E	DP	FR
1879	Pro-N	.833	2	13	7	4	0	2
1881	Cle-N	1.000	1	5	2	0	1	1
1882	Cin-a	.909	3	8	2	1	0	-1
	Pit-a	.920	23	123	37	14	1	0
	Yr	.919	**26**	131	39	**15**	**1**	-1
1883	Col-a	.872	82	388	97	71	10	-8
1884	Col-a	.906	58	268	77	36	3	-21
1885	Pit-a	.870	18	86	28	17	0	-2
1886	StL-a	.914	32	159	63	21	3	3
1889	Col-a	.930	8	35	18	4	1	2
Total	8	.894	227	1085	331	168	19	-24
OF								
1882	Cin-a	—	1	0	0	0	0	0
	Pit-a	—	1	0	0	0	0	0
	Yr	—	2	0	0	0	0	0
1883	Col-a	.667	2	2	2	2	1	1
1884	Col-a	1.000	1	3	0	0	0	0
Total	3	.778	5	5	2	2	1	1
1B								
1884	Col-a	.957	2	22	0	1	1	0
1886	StL-a	.926	3	23	2	2	1	0
Total	2	.940	5	45	2	3	2	0

■ Steve Kemp OF

YEAR	TM/L	PCT	G	PO	A	E	DP	FR
1977	Det-A	.981	148	252	10	5	1	-9
1978	Det-A	.977	**157**	325	11	8	2	-6
1979	Det-A	.976	120	229	12	6	2	2
1980	Det-A	.995	85	197	4	1	3	3
1981	Det-A	.986	92	207	4	3	0	0
1982	Chi-A	.976	154	280	6	7	1	-12
1983	NY-A	.987	101	215	5	3	3	0
1984	NY-A	.972	75	138	2	4	0	-9
1985	Pit-N	1.000	63	105	1	0	0	-4
1986	Pit-N	1.000	4	9	0	0	0	0
1988	Tex-A	1.000	5	5	0	0	0	0
Total	11	.982	1004	1962	55	7	12	-34
1B								
1988	Tex-A	1.000	1	1	0	0	0	0

■ Fred Kendall C

YEAR	TM/L	PCT	G	PO	A	E	DP	FR
1969	SD-N	1.000	9	37	5	0	0	0
1970	SD-N	1.000	2	5	1	0	0	-1
1971	SD-N	1.000	39	176	13	0	1	1
1972	SD-N	.995	82	504	41	3	11	2
1973	SD-N	.984	138	749	64	13	7	-18
1974	SD-N	.983	133	631	64	12	12	-25
1975	SD-N	.977	85	337	38	9	6	-9
1976	SD-N	.994	**146**	582	54	4	6	-21
1977	Cle-A	.991	102	506	35	5	5	-13
1978	Bos-A	.926	5	22	3	2	0	2
1979	SD-N	.977	40	154	18	4	3	4
1980	SD-N	.938	14	30	0	2	0	0
Total	12	.987	795	3733	336	4	51	-78
1B								
1970	SD-N	1.000	1	1	0	0	0	0
1971	SD-N	1.000	1	7	0	0	0	0
1972	SD-N	1.000	1	2	0	0	0	0
1978	Bos-A	1.000	13	85	8	0	7	1
1979	SD-N	1.000	2	8	1	0	0	0
1980	SD-N	1.000	1	1	1	0	0	0
Total	6	1.000	19	104	10	0	7	1
OF								
1970	SD-N	1.000	1	1	0	0	0	0
3B								
1971	SD-N	1.000	1	1	1	0	0	0

■ Ed Kennedy OF

YEAR	TM/L	PCT	G	PO	A	E	DP	FR
1883	NY-a	.884	94	112	10	16	0	-7
1884	NY-a	.915	100	138	13	14	4	6
1885	NY-a	.841	96	154	15	32	1	1
1886	Bro-a	.909	6	10	0	1	0	-1
Total	4	.878	296	414	38	3	5	-1
SS								
1884	NY-a	1.000	1	0	1	0	0	0
2B								
1884	NY-a	1.000	1	2	3	0	1	0
C								
1884	NY-a	1.000	1	2	1	0	0	0

■ John Kennedy 3B

YEAR	TM/L	PCT	G	PO	A	E	DP	FR
1962	Was-A	.778	2	2	5	2	0	0
1963	Was-A	.954	26	16	46	3	4	6
1964	Was-A	.941	106	97	191	18	14	7
1965	LA-N	.971	95	35	64	3	5	10
1966	LA-N	.965	87	39	127	6	10	13
1967	NY-A	.960	34	31	64	4	5	6
1969	Sea-A	.967	23	21	37	2	2	3
1970	Mil-A	1.000	5	3	3	0	2	1
	Bos-A	.960	33	31	65	4	4	2
	Yr	.962	38	34	68	4	6	3
1971	Bos-A	1.000	5	2	13	0	1	1
1972	Bos-A	.824	11	4	10	3	0	-3
1973	Bos-A	.946	24	17	36	3	5	7
1974	Bos-A	1.000	4	1	4	0	0	0
Total	12	.953	455	299	665	8	52	53
SS								
1962	Was-A	.974	9	13	25	1	4	0
1963	Was-A	.857	2	3	3	1	1	0
1964	Was-A	.966	49	71	130	7	27	1
1965	LA-N	.938	5	5	10	1	1	1
1966	LA-N	.979	28	37	57	2	15	2
1967	NY-A	.915	36	43	87	12	16	2
1969	Sea-A	.916	33	42	45	8	11	-7
1970	Mil-A	1.000	4	5	7	0	0	0
1971	Bos-A	.927	33	41	74	9	18	-10
1972	Bos-A	.956	27	44	65	5	13	-3
Total	10	.946	226	304	503	6	106	-18
2B								
1964	Was-A	1.000	2	1	3	0	1	0
1966	LA-N	1.000	15	26	26	0	7	2
1967	NY-A	1.000	2	9	1	0	0	0
1970	Mil-A	.921	16	26	32	5	7	-2
	Bos-A	1.000	2	3	5	0	1	1
	Yr	.930	18	29	37	5	8	-1
1971	Bos-A	.974	37	71	76	4	16	-8
1972	Bos-A	.962	32	62	66	5	21	-1
1973	Bos-A	.980	31	75	72	3	25	11
1974	Bos-A	.778	6	7	7	4	3	-1
Total	8	.964	143	280	288	1	81	2
1B								
1970	Mil-A	1.000	1	3	0	0	0	0

■ Junior Kennedy 2B

YEAR	TM/L	PCT	G	PO	A	E	DP	FR
1974	Cin-N	.909	17	10	10	2	1	-1
1978	Cin-N	.979	71	94	138	5	27	12
1979	Cin-N	.980	59	95	144	5	28	-1
1980	Cin-N	.988	103	200	303	6	53	2
1981	Cin-N	.980	16	21	27	1	8	2
1982	Chi-N	.978	71	109	160	6	25	17
1983	Chi-N	1.000	7	11	17	0	3	2
Total	7	.982	344	540	799	5	145	33
SS								
1979	Cin-N	1.000	5	10	16	0	2	1
1982	Chi-N	.936	28	28	60	6	10	-4
1983	Chi-N	1.000	1	1	0	0	0	0
Total	3	.950	34	39	76	6	12	-3
3B								
1974	Cin-N	1.000	5	5	3	0	0	0
1978	Cin-N	1.000	4	0	4	0	1	1
1979	Cin-N	1.000	4	0	2	0	0	0
1981	Cin-N	1.000	5	1	5	0	0	0
1982	Cin-N	1.000	7	1	8	0	0	0
1983	Chi-N	—	4	0	0	0	0	0
Total	6	1.000	29	7	22	0	1	1

■ Doc Kennedy C

YEAR	TM/L	PCT	G	PO	A	E	DP	FR
1879	Cle-N	.891	46	277	50	40	2	-1
1880	Cle-N	.899	65	397	68	52	**9**	-5
1881	Cle-N	.920	35	207	36	21	4	4
1882	Cle-N	.857	1	9	9	3	0	3
Total	4	.901	147	890	163	116	15	1
OF								
1880	Cle-N	1.000	2	1	0	0	0	0
1881	Cle-N	.800	3	7	1	2	0	0
1883	Buf-N	.583	4	7	0	5	0	-1
Total	3	.696	9	15	1	7	0	-1
1B								
1879	Cle-N	.956	4	41	2	2	2	0
1883	Buf-N	1.000	1	14	0	0	2	0
Total	2	.966	5	55	2	2	4	0
3B								
1881	Cle-N	1.000	1	1	1	0	0	0

■ Bob Kennedy OF

YEAR	TM/L	PCT	G	PO	A	E	DP	FR
1942	Chi-A	.971	16	31	2	1	0	0
1946	Chi-A	.965	75	157	10	6	1	2
1947	Chi-A	.968	106	204	8	7	3	-5
1948	Chi-A	.970	30	61	3	2	0	-1
	Cle-A	1.000	50	35	0		1	2
	Yr	.981	80	96	5	2	1	1
1949	Cle-A	.990	98	190	12	2	4	-1
1950	Cle-A	.987	144	294	13	4	3	1
1951	Cle-A	.968	106	174	9	6	2	-7
1952	Cle-A	1.000	13	24	0	0	0	1
1953	Cle-A	.989	89	91	2	0	0	-1
1954	Cle-A	—	1	0	0	0	0	0
	Bal-A	.976	21	40	0	1	0	0
	Yr	.976	22	40	0	1	0	0
1955	Bal-A	1.000	14	27	0	0	0	-1
	Chi-A	1.000	20	16	0	0	0	-1
	Yr	1.000	34	43	0	0	0	-2
1956	Det-A	.931	29	52	2	4	0	1
1957	Bro-N	1.000	9	4	0	0	0	-1
Total	13	.978	821	1400	63	3	14	-11
3B								
1939	Chi-A	.750	2	0	3	1	0	-1
1940	Chi-A	.938	**154**	**178**	322	**33**	25	-3
1941	Chi-A	.934	71	88	153	17	12	3
1942	Chi-A	.956	96	99	207	14	17	4
1946	Chi-A	.906	29	19	77	10	6	2
1947	Chi-A	1.000	1	1	2	0	0	0
1949	Cle-A	.983	21	13	44	1	4	-1
1952	Cle-A	1.000	3	1	12	0	1	2
1954	Bal-A	.938	71	81	131	14	10	-5
1955	Bal-A	—	1	0	0	0	0	0
	Chi-A	.938	55	32	73	7	10	-7
	Yr	.938	56	32	73	7	10	-7
1956	Chi-A	1.000	6	4	3	0	2	-1
	Det-A	.901	27	35	38	8	3	-3
	Yr	.909	33	39	41	8	5	-4
1957	Bro-N	1.000	3	4	2	0	0	-1
Total	12	.939	540	555	1067	105	90	-11
1B								
1948	Cle-A	1.000	1	3	0	0	1	0
1955	Bal-A	1.000	6	47	4	0	6	0
	Chi-A	1.000	3	7	0	0	1	0
	Yr	1.000	9	54	4	0	7	0
Total	2	1.000	10	57	4	0	8	0
2B								
1948	Cle-A	1.000	2	4	5	0	1	1

■ Terry Kennedy C

YEAR	TM/L	PCT	G	PO	A	E	DP	FR
1978	StL-N	.980	10	46	4	1	1	0
1979	StL-N	.993	32	135	7	1	1	-4
1980	StL-N	.967	41	182	21	7	3	-3
1981	SD-N	.964	**100**	465	63	**20**	**12**	-8
1982	SD-N	.990	139	666	56	7	**11**	-19
1983	SD-N	.986	143	782	79	12	8	-10
1984	SD-N	.982	**147**	708	54	14	6	-15
1985	SD-N	.986	140	654	67	10	**12**	-2
1986	SD-N	.990	123	692	70	8	13	0
1987	Bal-A	.993	**142**	750	**58**	6	11	-19
1988	Bal-A	.994	79	332	23	2	3	-8
1989	SF-N	.986	121	516	47	8	6	-4
1990	SF-N	.991	103	390	38	4	3	-12
Total	13	.986	1320	6318	587	100	90	104
OF								
1980	StL-N	1.000	28	49	1	0	0	-1
1B								
1982	SD-N	.984	12	111	10	2	7	0
1983	SD-N	1.000	4	25	3	0	4	0
1985	SD-N	1.000	5	8	1	0	0	0
1989	SF-N	1.000	2	3	0	0	0	0
Total	4	.988	23	147	14	2	11	0

■ Jerry Kenney 3B

YEAR	TM/L	PCT	G	PO	A	E	DP	FR
1969	NY-A	.975	83	63	207	7	20	10
1970	NY-A	.960	135	111	300	17	18	15
1971	NY-A	.953	109	69	237	15	20	10
1972	NY-A	1.000	1	0	1	0	0	0
Total	4	.962	328	243	745	9	58	35
SS								
1967	NY-A	.952	18	29	50	4	5	-4
1969	NY-A	1.000	10	17	27	0	8	0
1971	NY-A	1.000	5	5	12	0	4	1
1972	NY-A	.969	45	57	131	6	30	4
Total	4	.970	78	108	220	0	47	1
OF								
1969	NY-A	1.000	31	66	2	0	1	0
2B								
1970	NY-A	1.000	2	3	7	0	1	0
1973	Cle-A	1.000	5	9	12	0	1	-2
Total	2	1.000	7	12	19	0	2	-2
1B								
1971	NY-A	—	1	0	0	0	0	0

■ Duke Kenworthy 2B

YEAR	TM/L	PCT	G	PO	A	E	DP	FR
1914	KC-F	.952	145	**437**	407	**43**	**79**	21
1915	KC-F	.936	108	230	283	35	35	-7
1917	StL-A	.889	4	6	10	2	3	1
Total	3	.945	257	673	700	0	117	15
OF								
1912	Was-A	1.000	12	14	3	0	0	0
1915	KC-F	1.000	7	7	2	0	0	0
Total	2	1.000	19	21	5	0	0	0

■ Joe Keough OF

YEAR	TM/L	PCT	G	PO	A	E	DP	FR
1968	Oak-A	.962	29	48	2	2	0	-1
1969	KC-A	1.000	49	82	2	0	1	0
1970	KC-A	.985	34	63	2	1	0	-1
1971	KC-A	.982	100	164	4	3	1	-8
1972	KC-A	1.000	16	12	1	0	1	-1
Total	5	.984	228	369	11	6	3	-11

YEAR	TM/L	PCT	G	PO	A	E	DP	FR
		1B						
1968	Oak-A	1.000	1	3	0	0	0	0
1969	KC-A	1.000	1	1	0	0	0	0
1970	KC-A	.976	18	113	11	3	13	0
Total	3	.977	20	117	11	3	13	0
■ **Marty Keough** OF								
1957	Bos-A	1.000	7	16	0	0	0	1
1958	Bos-A	.974	25	38	0	1	0	-2
1959	Bos-A	.993	69	147	5	1	1	-4
1960	Bos-A	1.000	29	58	3	0	0	2
	Cle-A	.986	42	67	2	1	0	-1
	Yr	.992	71	125	5	1	0	1
1961	Was-A	.978	100	213	7	5	2	2
1962	Cin-N	.968	71	88	2	3	1	1
1963	Cin-N	1.000	28	27	0	0	0	0
1964	Cin-N	.991	81	105	4	1	1	-1
1965	Cin-N	1.000	4	1	0	0	0	0
1966	Atl-N	.000	3	0	0	1	0	0
	Chi-N	1.000	5	2	0	0	0	0
	Yr	.667	8	2	0	1	0	0
Total	10	.984	464	762	23	3	5	-2
		1B						
1958	Bos-A	.941	2	16	0	1	1	-1
1959	Bos-A	1.000	3	17	0	0	1	0
1961	Was-A	.990	10	95	6	1	8	-1
1962	Cin-N	.988	29	148	20	2	11	1
1963	Cin-N	.992	46	223	24	2	25	2
1964	Cin-N	1.000	4	14	1	0	3	0
1965	Cin-N	.988	32	74	5	1	4	1
1966	Atl-N	1.000	4	27	0	0	0	0
Total	8	.990	130	614	56	7	53	2
■ **John Kerins** 1B								
1884	Ind-a	**.972**	87	887	41	27	20	**7**
1885	Lou-a	.947	96	966	**28**	**56**	47	-3
1886	Lou-a	.970	47	495	19	16	25	2
1887	Lou-a	.970	74	695	18	22	26	-2
1888	Lou-a	.886	4	31	0	4	0	-1
1889	Bal-a	.981	9	50	3	1	1	0
1890	StL-a	.968	17	170	10	6	12	1
Total	7	.963	334	3294	119	132	131	4
		C						
1884	Ind-a	.750	5	3	0	1	0	0
1885	Lou-a	.943	19	104	44	9	5	8
1886	Lou-a	.933	65	487	**157**	46	12	**39**
1887	Lou-a	.917	35	261	93	32	7	27
1888	Lou-a	.898	33	245	63	35	4	11
1889	Lou-a	1.000	1	0	1	0	0	0
	Bal-a	.852	4	18	5	4	0	-1
	Yr	.857	5	18	6	4	0	-1
1890	StL-a	1.000	2	2	0	0	0	0
Total	7	.921	163	1120	363	127	28	84
		OF						
1884	Ind-a	.875	5	5	2	1	0	0
1885	Lou-a	—	3	0	0	0	0	-1
1886	Lou-a	.667	7	8	2	5	0	-1
1887	Lou-a	.889	5	8	0	1	0	-1
1888	Lou-a	.844	47	63	2	12	1	-6
1889	Lou-a	.500	2	1	0	1	0	-1
	Bal-a	1.000	2	3	0	0	0	0
	Yr	.800	4	4	0	1	0	-1
Total	6	.825	71	88	6	0	1	-10
		3B						
1884	Ind-a	.333	1	1	0	2	0	-1
1885	Lou-a	1.000	1	1	2	0	0	0
1888	Lou-a	.857	2	3	3	1	1	0
Total	3	.769	4	5	5	3	1	-1
		SS						
1886	Lou-a	1.000	1	1	5	0	0	1
1889	Bal-a	1.000	1	2	2	0	0	0
Total	2	1.000	2	3	7	0	0	1
		2B						
1888	Lou-a	.571	1	2	2	3	0	-1
■ **John Kerr** 2B								
1929	Chi-A	.971	122	307	459	23	84	**23**
1930	Chi-A	.980	52	130	166	6	33	1
1931	Chi-A	.968	117	297	366	22	78	8
1932	Was-A	.954	17	46	57	5	9	0
1933	Was-A	.966	16	25	31	2	4	3
1934	Was-A	.973	13	42	29	2	6	2
Total	6	.970	337	847	1108	0	214	37
		SS						
1923	Det-A	.877	15	19	45	9	5	4
1929	Chi-A	1.000	1	3	5	0	0	1
1930	Chi-A	.969	20	42	52	3	7	-1
1931	Chi-A	1.000	1	1	4	0	0	0
1932	Was-A	.939	14	25	37	4	7	-1
Total	5	.936	51	90	143	6	19	3
		3B						
1924	Det-A	—	3	0	0	0	0	0
1931	Chi-A	.880	7	9	13	3	1	-1
1932	Was-A	1.000	8	2	3	0	1	0
1933	Was-A	—	1	0	0	0	0	0
1934	Was-A	.971	17	21	47	2	4	7
Total	5	.950	36	32	63	5	6	6
		OF						
1924	Det-A	1.000	2	1	0	0	0	0
■ **Buddy Kerr** SS								
1943	NY-N	.955	27	60	90	7	10	5
1944	NY-N	.954	149	328	507	**40**	81	17
1945	NY-N	.964	**148**	**333**	**515**	32	**81**	**28**
1946	NY-N	**.982**	126	240	400	12	66	6
1947	NY-N	.977	138	270	**461**	17	77	12
1948	NY-N	.967	143	269	456	25	72	3
1949	NY-N	.959	89	125	224	15	33	6
1950	Bos-N	.965	155	310	471	28	97	2

YEAR	TM/L	PCT	G	PO	A	E	DP	FR
1951	Bos-N	.969	63	110	173	9	31	12
Total	9	.967	1038	2045	3297	185	548	91
		3B						
1946	NY-N	.963	18	24	28	2	2	1
		2B						
1951	Bos-N	1.000	5	5	4	0	3	1
■ **Don Kessinger** SS								
1964	Chi-N	1.000	4	3	7	0	1	-1
1965	Chi-N	.948	105	176	338	**28**	69	21
1966	Chi-N	.951	148	202	**474**	35	68	-10
1967	Chi-N	.973	143	215	457	19	77	-3
1968	Chi-N	.962	**159**	263	**573**	**33**	**97**	18
1969	Chi-N	**.976**	**157**	**266**	542	20	**101**	25
1970	Chi-N	.972	154	257	**501**	22	86	9
1971	Chi-N	.966	154	263	512	27	**97**	4
1972	Chi-N	.965	146	259	504	28	90	4
1973	Chi-N	.964	158	**274**	526	30	**109**	**17**
1974	Chi-N	.958	150	**259**	476	32	87	2
1975	Chi-N	.967	140	205	436	22	100	-2
1976	StL-N	.969	113	212	350	18	84	4
1977	StL-N	.978	26	37	54	2	15	4
	Chi-A	.959	21	32	38	3	12	-4
1978	Chi-A	.974	123	171	321	13	60	-16
1979	Chi-A	.988	54	57	103	2	17	-1
Total	16	.966	1955	3151	6212	334	1170	75
		2B						
1976	StL-N	.958	31	53	85	6	21	-8
1977	StL-N	.950	24	32	63	5	9	-2
	Chi-A	1.000	13	27	27	0	10	0
1978	Chi-A	1.000	9	12	14	0	2	-3
1979	Chi-A	1.000	1	2	6	0	0	0
Total	4	.967	78	126	195	1	42	-13
		3B						
1975	Chi-N	.943	13	5	28	2	3	-1
1976	StL-N	1.000	2	1	0	0	0	0
1977	Chi-A	.667	4	0	2	1	0	0
	Chi-A	.920	9	7	16	2	0	0
Total	3	.922	28	13	46	5	3	-1
		1B						
1979	Chi-A	1.000	1	2	0	0	0	0
■ **Sam Khalifa** SS								
1985	Pit-N	.967	95	156	316	16	45	13
1986	Pit-N	.961	60	85	163	10	25	14
1987	Pit-N	.917	5	5	6	1	1	-5
Total	3	.964	160	246	485	7	71	22
		2B						
1986	Pit-N	1.000	6	9	5	0	4	1
■ **Pete Kilduff** 2B								
1917	NY-N	.954	21	34	49	4	11	-2
	Chi-N	1.000	5	11	17	0	2	2
	Yr	.965	26	45	66	4	13	0
1918	Chi-N	.935	30	72	72	10	18	-3
1919	Chi-N	.966	8	8	20	1	3	0
	Bro-N	1.000	1	0	2	0	0	0
	Yr	.968	9	8	22	1	3	0
1920	Bro-N	.967	134	316	454	26	69	8
1921	Bro-N	.963	105	243	379	24	57	12
Total	5	.963	304	684	993	5	160	17
		SS						
1917	NY-N	.857	5	4	8	2	0	-1
	Chi-N	.920	51	91	128	19	19	-16
	Yr	.917	56	95	136	21	19	-17
1919	Chi-N	.838	7	16	15	6	2	-4
Total	2	.907	63	111	151	7	21	-21
		3B						
1917	NY-N	1.000	1	1	1	0	1	0
1919	Chi-N	.974	14	11	26	1	2	0
	Bro-N	.862	26	16	40	9	4	-4
	Yr	.903	40	27	66	10	6	-4
1920	Bro-N	.882	5	6	9	2	2	0
1921	Bro-N	1.000	1	0	4	0	1	1
Total	4	.905	47	34	80	2	10	-3
■ **Harmon Killebrew** 1B								
1960	Was-A	.987	71	584	32	8	69	-6
1961	Min-A	.987	119	972	67	14	91	-5
1962	Min-A	.933	4	14	0	1	4	-1
1965	Min-A	.988	72	636	35	8	64	-4
1966	Min-A	.989	42	330	15	4	30	-5
1967	Min-A	.992	**160**	1283	86	11	100	-6
1968	Min-A	.994	77	594	56	4	50	5
1969	Min-A	.997	80	574	34	2	55	-4
1970	Min-A	.986	28	204	9	3	14	-3
1971	Min-A	.997	90	658	56	2	52	2
1972	Min-A	.992	130	995	**99**	9	82	**11**
1973	Min-A	.998	57	431	45	1	42	**8**
1974	Min-A	.992	33	218	21	2	21	5
1975	KC-A	1.000	6	28	0	0	4	-1
Total	14	.992	969	7521	555	9	678	-4
		3B						
1955	Was-A	.935	23	23	49	5	3	6
1956	Was-A	.951	20	18	40	3	3	0
1957	Was-A	.947	7	2	16	1	2	-1
1958	Was-A	1.000	9	8	13	0	1	0
1959	Was-A	.938	150	129	325	**30**	18	-7
1960	Was-A	.943	65	45	103	9	7	-3
1961	Min-A	.920	45	28	75	9	10	-5
1965	Min-A	.966	44	37	78	4	3	-3
1966	Min-A	.951	107	83	190	14	11	-10
1967	Min-A	.833	3	2	3	1	0	-1
1968	Min-A	.880	11	7	15	3	1	-1
1969	Min-A	.929	105	75	185	20	12	-18
1970	Min-A	.948	138	108	203	17	14	-25
1971	Min-A	.925	64	42	93	11	3	-17
Total	14	.940	791	607	1388	127	88	-85

YEAR	TM/L	PCT	G	PO	A	E	DP	FR
		OF						
1959	Was-A	1.000	4	6	0	0	0	0
1961	Min-A	1.000	2	3	1	0	0	1
1962	Min-A	.967	151	227	5	8	0	-12
1963	Min-A	.987	137	219	7	3	0	-8
1964	Min-A	.971	157	232	1	7	0	-13
1965	Min-A	—	1	0	0	0	0	0
1966	Min-A	1.000	18	22	0	0	0	0
Total	7	.976	470	709	14	8	0	-32
		2B						
1954	Was-A	1.000	3	5	2	0	0	-2
1955	Was-A	1.000	3	1	0	0	0	0
1956	Was-A	.909	4	6	4	1	1	-1
1957	Was-A	—	1	0	0	0	0	0
Total	4	.947	11	12	6	1	1	-3
■ **Red Killefer** OF								
1907	Det-A	1.000	1	2	0	0	0	0
1909	Det-A	—	1	0	0	0	0	0
	Was-A	.957	24	44	1	2	0	-2
	Yr	.957	25	44	1	2	0	-2
1910	Was-A	.870	12	17	3	3	0	-1
1914	Cin-N	.968	37	55	5	2	0	-4
1915	Cin-N	.970	150	339	17	11	**5**	-4
1916	Cin-N	.966	68	138	6	5	2	0
Total	6	.965	293	595	32	3	7	-9
		2B						
1908	Det-A	.956	16	30	35	3	7	-1
1909	Det-A	.912	17	28	55	8	3	-1
	Was-A	.722	3	1	12	5	0	0
	Yr	.881	20	29	67	13	3	-1
1910	Was-A	.940	88	173	231	26	27	-4
1914	Cin-N	.923	5	5	7	1	0	-2
Total	4	.931	129	237	340	3	37	-8
		3B						
1908	Det-A	.636	4	1	6	4	1	-2
1909	Was-A	.806	6	12	13	6	2	0
1914	Cin-N	.000	1	0	0	1	0	0
Total	3	.744	11	13	19	1	3	-2
		SS						
1908	Det-A	.857	7	17	13	5	1	-3
1909	Was-A	1.000	1	4	2	0	0	0
Total	2	.878	8	21	15	5	1	-3
		C						
1909	Was-A	.846	3	10	1	2	1	-1
		1B						
1915	Cin-N	.714	2	5	0	2	1	-1
■ **Bill Killefer** C								
1909	StL-A	.905	11	36	21	6	2	2
1910	StL-A	.938	73	311	124	**29**	16	**12**
1911	Phi-N	.975	6	29	10	1	1	2
1912	Phi-N	.973	85	407	134	15	17	**17**
1913	Phi-N	.988	**118**	570	**166**	**9**	16	17
1914	Phi-N	.978	90	464	**154**	14	11	**16**
1915	Phi-N	.972	104	539	126	19	6	**14**
1916	Phi-N	**.985**	91	443	89	8	15	0
1917	Phi-N	**.984**	**120**	**615**	138	12	**14**	9
1918	Chi-N	.982	**104**	**487**	110	11	12	9
1919	Chi-N	**.987**	**100**	**478**	124	8	7	**16**
1920	Chi-N	.977	61	304	80	9	6	**18**
1921	Chi-N	.964	42	147	43	7	6	-1
Total	13	.976	1005	4830	1319	148	129	131
		1B						
1913	Phi-N	1.000	1	1	0	0	0	0
		OF						
1917	Phi-N	1.000	1	2	0	0	0	0
■ **Bruce Kimm** C								
1976	Det-A	.970	61	256	33	9	5	6
1977	Det-A	.958	12	43	3	2	0	6
1979	Chi-N	.969	9	30	1	1	0	2
1980	Chi-A	.985	98	375	26	6	2	-2
Total	4	.977	180	704	63	8	7	12
■ **Jerry Kindall** 2B								
1957	Chi-N	.920	28	52	63	10	7	-2
1958	Chi-N	1.000	3	6	5	0	2	1
1960	Chi-N	.966	82	147	218	13	44	13
1961	Chi-N	.950	50	124	122	13	34	4
1962	Cle-A	.978	154	358	**494**	19	114	21
1963	Cle-A	.987	37	68	86	2	16	5
1964	Min-A	.969	51	68	87	5	16	3
1965	Min-A	.963	106	242	252	19	62	-1
Total	8	.967	511	1065	1327	1	295	44
		SS						
1956	Chi-N	.956	18	33	53	4	12	2
1957	Chi-N	.857	9	8	16	4	2	-3
1960	Chi-N	1.000	2	0	4	0	1	1
1961	Chi-N	.937	47	82	111	13	27	3
1963	Cle-A	.958	46	63	97	7	15	-2
1964	Min-A	.968	7	12	18	1	5	2
1965	Min-A	.875	7	4	10	2	0	0
Total	7	.943	136	202	309	1	62	3
		3B						
1957	Chi-N	.977	19	13	30	1	1	1
1965	Min-A	.667	10	0	4	2	1	0
Total	2	.940	29	13	34	3	2	1
		1B						
1963	Cle-A	1.000	4	3	0	0	0	0
1964	Cle-A	.989	23	80	11	1	7	3
	Min-A	1.000	1	0	0	0	0	0
	Yr	.989	24	81	11	1	7	3
Total	2	.990	28	84	11	1	7	3
■ **Ralph Kiner** OF								
1946	Pit-N	.969	140	339	6	**11**	2	3
1947	Pit-N	.983	152	**390**	8	7	1	9
1948	Pit-N	.975	154	382	6	10	1	-9
1949	Pit-N	.979	152	311	12	7	3	-4

YEAR	TM/L	PCT	G	PO	A	E	DP	FR
1950	Pit-N	.965	150	287	13	11	2	-1
1951	Pit-N	.967	94	195	7	7	1	-1
1952	Pit-N	.970	149	250	9	8	0	-11
1953	Pit-N	1.000	41	71	5	0	1	-2
	Chi-N	.964	116	211	6	8	2	-5
	Yr	.973	157	282	11	8	3	-7
1954	Chi-N	.971	147	298	6	9	1	-2
1955	Cle-A	.986	87	141	2	2	0	-7
Total	10	.974	1382	2875	80	0	14	-30
1B								
1951	Pit-N	.982	58	556	29	11	59	-6

■ Hal King C

YEAR	TM/L	PCT	G	PO	A	E	DP	FR
1967	Hou-N	1.000	11	62	8	0	1	-2
1968	Hou-N	.968	19	83	8	3	0	-3
1970	Atl-N	.985	62	316	14	5	1	-10
1971	Atl-N	.983	60	274	23	5	0	-1
1972	Tex-A	.970	38	181	16	6	3	-7
1973	Cin-N	1.000	9	26	1	0	1	-1
1974	Cin-N	1.000	5	6	1	0	0	0
Total	7	.982	204	948	71	9	6	-24

■ Jim King OF

YEAR	TM/L	PCT	G	PO	A	E	DP	FR
1955	Chi-N	.990	93	184	10	2	2	4
1956	Chi-N	.990	82	187	10	2	2	8
1957	StL-N	1.000	8	7	0	0	0	-2
1958	SF-N	1.000	15	18	0	0	0	-2
1961	Was-A	.980	91	138	7	3	2	-1
1962	Was-A	.979	101	178	9	4	**4**	1
1963	Was-A	.987	123	213	13	3	2	-1
1964	Was-A	.973	121	240	10	7	0	7
1965	Was-A	.993	88	127	7	1	1	2
1966	Was-A	.987	85	147	4	2	0	-2
1967	Was-A	.962	31	50	0	2	0	-1
	Chi-A	1.000	12	15	0	0	0	-2
	Cle-A	1.000	1	1	0	0	0	0
	Yr	.971	44	66	0	2	0	-3
Total	11	.984	851	1505	70	6	13	11
C								
1961	Was-A	1.000	1	1	0	0	0	0
1967	Was-A	—	1	0	0	0	0	0
Total	2	1.000	2	1	0	0	0	0

■ Jeff King 3B

YEAR	TM/L	PCT	G	PO	A	E	DP	FR
1989	Pit-N	.941	13	9	23	2	2	1
1990	Pit-N	.938	115	58	215	18	15	16
Total	2	.938	128	67	238	0	17	17
1B								
1989	Pit-N	.995	46	384	22	2	32	-2
1990	Pit-N	1.000	1	3	0	0	0	0
Total	2	.995	47	387	22	2	32	-2
2B								
1989	Pit-N	1.000	7	10	14	0	2	0
SS								
1989	Pit-N	—	1	0	0	0	0	0

■ Lee King OF

YEAR	TM/L	PCT	G	PO	A	E	DP	FR
1916	Pit-N	.714	8	4	1	2	0	-1
1917	Pit-N	.968	102	198	16	7	6	4
1918	Pit-N	.909	36	50	0	5	0	-6
1919	NY-N	.667	7	2	0	1	0	-1
1920	NY-N	.951	84	167	8	9	1	-13
1921	NY-N	.921	35	52	6	5	0	0
	Phi-N	.911	57	115	8	12	0	-2
	Yr	.914	92	167	14	17	0	-2
1922	Phi-N	.946	15	34	1	2	1	0
	NY-N	1.000	5	14	0	0	0	1
	Yr	.961	20	48	1	2	1	1
Total	7	.940	349	636	40	3	8	-18
1B								
1921	NY-N	1.000	1	0	1	0	0	0
1922	NY-N	1.000	5	54	2	0	2	0
Total	2	1.000	6	54	3	0	2	0

■ Mike Kingery OF

YEAR	TM/L	PCT	G	PO	A	E	DP	FR
1986	KC-A	.973	59	102	6	3	2	-6
1987	Sea-A	.992	114	226	15	2	3	7
1988	Sea-A	.989	44	85	3	1	0	3
1989	Sea-A	1.000	23	70	0	0	0	5
1990	SF-N	.978	95	126	7	3	2	-13
Total	5	.986	335	609	31	9	7	-4
1B								
1988	Sea-A	.952	10	17	3	1	1	1

■ Dave Kingman OF

YEAR	TM/L	PCT	G	PO	A	E	DP	FR
1971	SF-N	.950	14	19	0	1	0	-1
1972	SF-N	.932	22	40	1	3	0	-1
1974	SF-N	1.000	2	7	0	0	0	0
1975	NY-N	.958	71	134	3	6	0	-1
1976	NY-N	.959	111	202	10	9	0	1
1977	NY-N	.974	45	76	0	2	0	-3
	SD-N	.964	28	50	3	2	1	0
	Cal-A	1.000	2	3	0	0	0	0
	Yr	.975	47	79	0	2	0	-3
1978	Chi-N	.978	100	170	8	4	2	-5
1979	Chi-N	.954	139	240	11	12	3	-2
1980	Chi-N	.941	61	103	8	7	0	-1
1981	NY-N	.927	48	86	3	7	0	-3
1983	NY-N	1.000	5	7	0	0	0	0
Total	11	.957	648	1137	47	3	6	-16
1B								
1971	SF-N	.981	20	149	9	3	9	-2
1972	SF-N	.988	56	402	20	5	39	-3
1973	SF-N	.986	46	259	17	4	23	0
1974	SF-N	.983	91	680	60	**13**	66	4
1975	NY-N	.988	58	386	38	5	36	3
1976	NY-N	1.000	16	91	8	0	11	1
1977	NY-N	.992	17	112	8	1	6	0
	SD-N	.990	13	92	11	1	4	1
	Cal-A	.974	8	70	5	2	5	0

YEAR	TM/L	PCT	G	PO	A	E	DP	FR
	Yr	.985	25	182	13	3	11	0
1978	Chi-N	.967	6	56	2	2	4	-1
1980	Chi-N	.947	2	16	2	1	0	0
1981	NY-N	.974	56	462	31	13	39	-4
1982	NY-N	.986	143	1232	69	18	88	-14
1983	NY-N	.994	50	443	28	3	43	-4
1984	Oak-A	1.000	9	55	2	0	3	-2
1985	Oak-A	1.000	9	50	1	0	3	-1
1986	Oak-A	.895	3	17	0	2	2	-1
Total	15	.985	603	4572	311	3	381	-23
3B								
1972	SF-N	.932	59	54	138	14	10	6
1973	SF-N	.910	60	54	129	18	7	3
1974	SF-N	.797	21	9	38	12	3	-3
1975	NY-N	.919	12	6	28	3	1	0
1977	SD-N	.833	2	3	2	1	0	-1
Total	5	.906	154	126	335	8	21	5

■ Tom Kinslow C

YEAR	TM/L	PCT	G	PO	A	E	DP	FR
1886	Was-N	1.000	3	11	4	0	0	0
1887	NY-a	1.000	2	6	3	0	0	0
1890	Bro-P	.909	64	298	72	37	7	10
1891	Bro-N	.922	61	252	54	26	6	-9
1892	Bro-N	.933	66	355	89	32	6	5
1893	Bro-N	.932	76	290	80	27	11	-1
1894	Bro-N	.907	61	217	47	27	4	-8
1895	Pit-N	.962	18	67	10	3	1	-1
1896	Lou-N	.810	5	14	3	4	2	-1
1898	Was-N	.800	3	5	3	2	0	-1
	StL-N	.925	14	44	18	5	4	1
	Yr	.909	17	49	21	7	4	0
Total	10	.923	373	1559	383	163	41	-5
1B								
1894	Bro-N	1.000	1	2	0	0	0	0
1896	Lou-N	1.000	1	9	1	0	0	0
1898	Was-N	—	1	0	0	0	0	0
Total	3	1.000	3	11	1	0	0	0
OF								
1893	Bro-N	1.000	2	1	0	0	0	-1

■ La Rue Kirby OF

YEAR	TM/L	PCT	G	PO	A	E	DP	FR
1914	StL-F	.973	50	100	7	3	2	2
1915	StL-F	.969	52	87	8	3	2	-2
Total	2	.971	102	187	15	6	4	0

■ Jay Kirke OF

YEAR	TM/L	PCT	G	PO	A	E	DP	FR
1910	Det-A	—	1	0	0	0	0	0
1911	Bos-N	.929	14	24	2	2	0	-1
1912	Bos-N	.903	72	118	22	15	2	4
1913	Bos-N	.923	13	19	5	2	0	3
1914	Cle-A	.974	42	73	3	2	1	0
Total	5	.927	142	234	32	1	3	6
1B								
1911	Bos-N	.944	3	34	0	2	1	-1
1912	Bos-N	1.000	1	9	0	0	2	0
1914	Cle-A	.989	18	162	12	2	9	1
1915	Cle-A	.986	87	886	52	13	37	-1
1918	NY-N	.978	16	165	12	4	7	1
Total	5	.984	125	1256	76	1	56	0
3B								
1911	Bos-N	1.000	1	3	1	0	0	0
1912	Bos-N	.895	14	28	23	6	2	0
Total	2	.902	15	31	24	6	2	0
2B								
1910	Det-A	.917	7	16	17	3	1	-2
1911	Bos-N	1.000	1	2	3	0	1	0
Total	2	.927	8	18	20	3	2	-2
SS								
1911	Bos-N	1.000	1	5	5	0	0	2
1912	Bos-N	.667	2	4	0	2	0	-2
Total	2	.875	3	9	5	2	0	0

■ Willie Kirkland OF

YEAR	TM/L	PCT	G	PO	A	E	DP	FR
1958	SF-N	.961	115	187	12	8	4	-4
1959	SF-N	.969	117	212	8	7	0	0
1960	SF-N	.978	143	252	16	6	5	3
1961	Cle-A	.974	138	290	12	8	5	6
1962	Cle-A	.972	125	233	11	7	0	2
1963	Cle-A	.984	112	234	11	4	2	9
1964	Bal-A	.989	58	86	7	1	3	6
	Was-A	.907	27	39	0	4	0	-5
	Yr	.964	85	125	7	5	3	1
1965	Was-A	.987	92	151	3	2	0	0
1966	Was-A	.983	68	56	3	1	0	0
Total	9	.974	995	1740	83	8	19	17

■ Ed Kirkpatrick OF

YEAR	TM/L	PCT	G	PO	A	E	DP	FR
1963	LA-A	1.000	10	18	0	0	0	0
1964	LA-A	.969	63	90	3	3	0	-5
1965	Cal-A	.969	19	28	3	1	0	0
1966	Cal-A	.994	102	151	4	1	1	-9
1967	Cal-A	—	1	0	0	0	0	0
1968	Cal-A	.982	45	53	2	1	1	3
1969	KC-A	.995	82	180	8	1	1	7
1970	KC-A	1.000	19	24	0	0	0	0
1971	KC-A	.962	61	118	2	1	1	1
1973	KC-A	.990	108	198	3	2	0	-6
1974	Pit-N	1.000	14	27	0	0	0	0
1975	Pit-N	1.000	14	26	0	0	0	-1
1976	Pit-N	1.000	9	15	1	0	0	1
1977	Pit-N	1.000	2	3	0	0	0	0
	Tex-A	1.000	6	14	0	0	0	0
	Mil-A	.973	22	36	0	1	0	-2
	Yr	.980	28	50	0	1	0	-2
Total	14	.989	577	981	26	1	4	-17
C								
1962	LA-A	1.000	1	10	0	0	0	1
1963	LA-A	.986	14	64	5	1	1	0
1967	Cal-A	1.000	2	4	0	0	0	-2
1968	Cal-A	.800	4	3	1	1	0	0

YEAR	TM/L	PCT	G	PO	A	E	DP	FR
1969	KC-A	1.000	8	17	1	0	0	0
1970	KC-A	.978	89	463	61	**12**	**12**	-6
1971	KC-A	.979	59	294	28	7	5	0
1972	KC-A	.991	108	590	49	6	5	-4
1973	KC-A	.974	14	66	8	2	0	-2
1974	Pit-N	.920	6	22	1	2	0	-1
1977	Tex-A	1.000	1	1	0	0	0	0
Total	11	.982	306	1534	154	1	23	-14
1B								
1966	Cal-A	1.000	3	18	1	0	0	0
1968	Cal-A	.889	2	6	2	1	0	0
1969	Cal-A	1.000	2	5	0	0	0	0
1970	KC-A	1.000	16	139	9	0	13	-1
1972	Cal-A	—	1	0	0	0	0	0
1974	Pit-N	.993	59	512	31	4	55	-2
1975	Pit-N	1.000	28	141	9	0	10	0
1976	Pit-N	.990	25	190	15	2	15	1
1977	Pit-N	.972	10	66	4	2	7	0
	Tex-A	.963	3	23	3	1	1	0
Total	9	.992	149	1100	74	0	101	-2
3B								
1969	KC-A	1.000	2	1	3	0	0	0
1976	Pit-N	.333	1	0	1	2	0	-1
1977	Pit-N	—	1	0	0	0	0	0
	Mil-A	1.000	1	2	0	0	0	0
Total	3	.778	5	3	4	2	0	-1
2B								
1969	KC-A	1.000	1	1	1	0	0	0

■ Ron Kittle OF

YEAR	TM/L	PCT	G	PO	A	E	DP	FR
1982	Chi-A	1.000	5	3	0	0	0	0
1983	Chi-A	.964	139	234	7	9	0	-14
1984	Chi-A	.972	124	226	14	7	2	-2
1985	Chi-A	.989	57	88	2	1	1	-2
1986	Chi-A	1.000	20	37	3	0	1	0
	NY-A	1.000	1	2	0	0	0	0
	Yr	1.000	21	39	3	0	1	1
1987	NY-A	1.000	2	4	1	0	0	1
1989	Chi-A	1.000	5	8	1	0	0	0
Total	7	.974	353	602	28	7	3	-16
1B								
1989	Chi-A	.982	27	208	11	4	28	-3
1990	Chi-A	.987	25	150	5	2	18	-4
	Bal-A	1.000	5	26	1	0	1	0
	Yr	.989	30	176	6	2	19	-4
Total	2	.985	57	384	17	6	47	-7

■ Malachi Kittridge C

YEAR	TM/L	PCT	G	PO	A	E	DP	FR
1890	Chi-N	.944	96	458	113	34	9	0
1891	Chi-N	.940	79	384	87	30	5	-2
1892	Chi-N	.946	69	369	87	26	5	13
1893	Chi-N	.939	70	260	81	22	4	4
1894	Chi-N	.925	51	209	36	20	4	3
1895	Chi-N	.976	59	197	48	6	4	-2
1896	Chi-N	.962	64	251	56	12	12	0
1897	Chi-N	.952	79	324	75	20	5	2
1898	Lou-N	.944	86	258	80	20	10	-11
1899	Lou-N	.974	43	132	59	5	6	8
	Was-N	.943	43	148	58	11	3	5
	Yr	**.961**	86	**280**	**117**	16	9	13
1901	Bos-N	.984	113	581	136	12	7	10
1902	Bos-N	.981	72	363	99	9	5	4
1903	Bos-N	.981	30	160	42	4	5	5
1904	Was-A	.982	79	346	99	8	4	-4
1905	Was-A	.978	76	323	113	10	8	3
1906	Was-A	.946	22	106	17	7	1	-2
	Cle-A	.938	5	14	1	1	0	0
	Yr	.945	27	120	18	8	1	-2
Total	16	.961	1196	5121	1363	264	99	36

■ Bobby Klaus 2B

YEAR	TM/L	PCT	G	PO	A	E	DP	FR
1964	Cin-N	.972	18	33	36	2	7	3
	NY-N	.986	25	58	80	2	11	1
	Yr	.981	43	91	116	4	18	4
1965	NY-N	.968	72	146	188	11	46	11
Total	2	.973	115	237	304	5	64	15
3B								
1964	Cin-N	1.000	11	8	18	0	1	1
	NY-N	.947	28	23	48	4	3	-2
	Yr	.960	39	31	66	4	4	-1
1965	NY-N	1.000	25	18	41	0	3	3
Total	2	.975	64	49	107	4	7	2
SS								
1964	Cin-N	.833	3	2	3	1	0	0
	NY-N	.800	5	3	1	1	0	-2
	Yr	.818	8	5	4	2	0	-2
1965	NY-N	1.000	28	15	25	0	5	1
Total	2	.961	36	20	29	2	5	-1

■ Billy Klaus SS

YEAR	TM/L	PCT	G	PO	A	E	DP	FR
1952	Bos-N	.500	4	1	0	1	0	-1
1955	Bos-A	.955	126	207	391	28	55	-8
1956	Bos-A	.943	26	35	64	6	8	-9
1957	Bos-A	.961	118	204	417	25	93	11
1958	Bos-A	.883	27	18	35	7	2	-6
1959	Bal-A	.970	59	77	147	7	21	-9
1960	Bal-A	1.000	12	10	17	0	5	3
1961	Was-A	.973	18	24	47	2	8	-2
1962	Phi-N	.918	30	29	49	7	11	-5
1963	Phi-N	1.000	5	1	2	0	0	-1
Total	10	.955	425	606	1169	3	203	-27
3B								
1955	Bos-A	.900	8	7	20	3	0	0
1956	Bos-A	.945	106	120	242	21	18	5
1959	Bal-A	.955	49	43	84	6	7	-2
1960	Bal-A	1.000	2	0	6	0	0	1
1961	Was-A	.961	51	40	107	6	3	-3
1962	Phi-N	.983	53	43	72	2	4	-2

YEAR	TM/L	PCT	G	PO	A	E	DP	FR
1963	Phi-N	1.000	3	0	5	0	1	-1
Total	7	.954	272	253	536	8	33	-2
2B								
1959	Bal-A	—	1	0	0	0	0	0
1960	Bal-A	.960	30	19	29	2	9	4
1961	Was-A	1.000	1	0	1	0	1	0
1962	Phi-N	1.000	11	21	21	0	6	1
Total	4	.978	43	40	51	2	16	5
OF								
1961	Was-A	—	1	0	0	0	0	0

■ **Chuck Klein** OF

YEAR	TM/L	PCT	G	PO	A	E	DP	FR
1928	Phi-N	.978	63	128	7	3	0	1
1929	Phi-N	.966	149	321	18	12	3	4
1930	Phi-N	.960	156	362	44	17	10	28
1931	Phi-N	.971	148	292	13	9	0	-5
1932	Phi-N	.960	154	331	29	15	3	8
1933	Phi-N	.986	152	339	21	5	5	8
1934	Chi-N	.962	110	222	6	9	2	-4
1935	Chi-N	.958	111	215	11	10	7	-3
1936	Phi-N	.917	29	63	3	6	0	-1
	Phi-N	.930	117	213	13	17	2	-10
	Yr	.927	146	276	16	23	2	-11
1937	Phi-N	.949	102	175	11	10	3	-5
1938	Phi-N	.960	119	229	8	10	1	-4
1939	Phi-N	1.000	11	20	1	0	1	0
	Pit-N	.951	66	133	4	7	0	-4
	Yr	.958	77	153	5	7	1	-4
1940	Phi-N	.984	96	180	4	3	2	-5
1941	Phi-N	.958	14	22	1	1	0	-1
1943	Phi-N	.000	2	0	0	1	0	-1
1944	Phi-N	1.000	1	5	0	0	0	1
Total	16	.962	1600	3250	194	135	39	7
1B								
1939	Phi-N	—	1	0	0	0	0	0

■ **Lou Klein** 2B

YEAR	TM/L	PCT	G	PO	A	E	DP	FR
1943	StL-N	.973	126	301	356	18	99	-6
1945	StL-N	1.000	2	2	0	0	0	0
1946	StL-N	.975	23	58	60	3	18	-3
1949	StL-N	1.000	9	14	13	0	3	0
1951	Phi-A	.975	42	85	107	5	32	-4
Total	5	.975	202	460	536	6	152	-13
SS								
1943	StL-N	.941	51	55	88	9	19	-12
1945	StL-N	.929	7	12	14	2	3	-1
1949	StL-N	.890	21	17	64	10	7	-4
Total	3	.923	79	84	166	1	29	-17
3B								
1945	StL-N	.929	4	5	8	1	0	0
1949	StL-N	.909	7	2	8	1	0	0
Total	2	.920	11	7	16	2	0	0
OF								
1945	StL-N	1.000	7	19	1	0	1	1

■ **Red Kleinow** C

YEAR	TM/L	PCT	G	PO	A	E	DP	FR
1904	NY-A	.966	62	276	66	12	5	-7
1905	NY-A	.978	83	361	82	10	4	-8
1906	NY-A	.972	95	381	102	14	8	0
1907	NY-A	.967	86	318	97	14	5	-13
1908	NY-A	.973	89	381	116	14	5	-5
1909	NY-A	.966	77	343	83	15	6	-3
1910	NY-A	1.000	5	19	5	0	0	0
	Bos-A	.968	49	266	64	11	12	5
	Yr	.970	54	285	69	11	12	5
1911	Bos-A	1.000	8	21	8	0	0	0
	Phi-N	1.000	4	11	3	0	0	0
Total	8	.971	558	2377	626	0	45	-31
1B								
1905	NY-A	.969	3	28	3	1	0	0
1906	NY-A	.500	1	1	0	1	0	0
1907	NY-A	1.000	1	8	0	0	0	0
Total	3	.952	5	37	3	2	0	0
3B								
1904	NY-A	1.000	2	2	5	0	0	0
2B								
1908	NY-A	.800	2	2	2	1	0	-1
OF								
1904	NY-A	—	1	0	0	0	0	0

■ **Johnny Kling** C

YEAR	TM/L	PCT	G	PO	A	E	DP	FR
1900	Chi-N	.901	15	49	15	7	2	-3
1901	Chi-N	.952	69	319	75	20	7	-10
1902	Chi-N	.974	112	471	158	17	16	6
1903	Chi-N	.969	132	565	189	24	13	0
1904	Chi-N	.974	104	499	135	17	6	-6
1905	Chi-N	.969	106	538	136	24	12	0
1906	Chi-N	.982	96	520	126	12	7	4
1907	Chi-N	.987	98	499	109	8	11	3
1908	Chi-N	.979	117	596	149	16	11	-2
1910	Chi-N	.979	86	407	118	11	10	-5
1911	Chi-N	.969	25	122	34	5	2	5
	Bos-N	.951	71	302	106	21	6	-4
	Yr	.956	96	424	140	26	8	1
1912	Bos-N	.958	74	322	108	19	20	5
1913	Cin-N	.975	63	259	94	9	3	10
Total	13	.971	1168	5468	1552	210	126	3
OF								
1901	Chi-N	1.000	1	3	0	0	0	0
1904	Chi-N	.909	10	10	0	1	0	-2
1905	Chi-N	1.000	4	4	0	0	0	-1
1906	Chi-N	1.000	3	0	1	0	0	0
1908	Chi-N	.909	6	6	4	1	1	2
Total	5	.933	24	23	5	2	1	-1
1B								
1901	Chi-N	.857	1	6	0	1	0	0
1904	Chi-N	.962	6	51	0	2	2	-2
1905	Chi-N	1.000	1	7	1	0	0	0
1907	Chi-N	1.000	2	10	2	0	1	1

YEAR	TM/L	PCT	G	PO	A	E	DP	FR
1908	Chi-N	1.000	2	5	0	0	0	0
Total	5	.965	12	79	3	3	3	-1
SS								
1902	Chi-N	.600	1	1	2	2	1	-1
3B								
1911	Bos-N	—	1	0	0	0	0	0

■ **Ted Kluszewski** 1B

YEAR	TM/L	PCT	G	PO	A	E	DP	FR
1947	Cin-N	1.000	2	10	0	0	1	0
1948	Cin-N	.990	98	833	65	9	60	1
1949	Cin-N	.989	134	1140	65	14	109	-6
1950	Cin-N	.987	131	1123	61	15	101	-11
1951	Cin-N	.997	154	1381	88	5	115	-6
1952	Cin-N	.993	133	1121	66	8	116	-10
1953	Cin-N	.995	147	1285	58	7	149	-17
1954	Cin-N	.996	149	1237	101	5	166	-4
1955	Cin-N	.995	153	1388	86	8	153	-9
1956	Cin-N	.990	131	1166	89	13	110	-5
1957	Cin-N	.989	23	161	15	2	11	0
1958	Pit-N	.994	72	591	36	4	62	-5
1959	Pit-N	1.000	20	151	12	0	14	-1
	Chi-A	1.000	29	220	10	0	13	-2
1960	Chi-A	.997	39	325	19	1	38	-2
1961	LA-A	.996	66	520	28	6	51	-5
Total	15	.993	1481	12652	799	7	1269	-82

■ **Mickey Klutts** 3B

YEAR	TM/L	PCT	G	PO	A	E	DP	FR
1977	NY-A	1.000	4	2	13	0	1	2
1978	NY-A	.750	1	1	2	1	1	0
1979	Oak-A	.913	6	7	14	2	0	0
1980	Oak-A	.947	62	46	80	7	3	-3
1981	Oak-A	.957	14	7	15	1	1	-5
1982	Oak-A	.946	49	41	82	7	6	-3
1983	Tor-A	1.000	17	4	11	0	2	-3
Total	7	.948	153	108	217	8	14	-12
SS								
1976	NY-A	.875	2	4	3	1	0	0
1977	NY-A	1.000	1	3	2	0	0	0
1979	Oak-A	.882	10	9	21	4	3	-2
1980	Oak-A	.957	8	8	14	1	3	-1
Total	4	.914	21	24	40	6	6	-3
2B								
1979	Oak-A	.971	8	19	15	1	3	-2
1980	Oak-A	.950	7	9	10	1	2	-2
Total	2	.964	15	28	25	2	5	-4

■ **Clyde Kluttz** C

YEAR	TM/L	PCT	G	PO	A	E	DP	FR
1942	Bos-N	.979	57	200	29	5	5	0
1943	Bos-N	.973	55	176	43	6	5	2
1944	Bos-N	.980	58	199	40	5	5	4
1945	Bos-N	.987	19	64	11	1	1	0
	NY-N	.978	57	195	32	5	5	-6
	Yr	.981	76	259	43	6	6	-6
1946	NY-N	.857	2	6	0	1	0	-1
	StL-N	.980	49	177	24	4	4	2
	Yr	.976	51	183	24	5	4	1
1947	Pit-N	.987	69	247	55	4	7	3
1948	Pit-N	.978	91	298	54	8	8	0
1951	StL-A	1.000	1	3	2	0	0	1
	Was-A	.968	46	165	14	6	2	-7
	Yr	.968	47	168	16	6	2	-6
1952	Was-N	.979	52	163	27	4	4	-1
Total	9	.978	556	1893	331	9	46	-3

■ **Otto Knabe** 2B

YEAR	TM/L	PCT	G	PO	A	E	DP	FR
1907	Phi-N	.960	121	293	336	26	53	-1
1908	Phi-N	.969	151	344	470	26	42	11
1909	Phi-N	.938	110	237	312	36	38	8
1910	Phi-N	.954	136	383	381	37	72	14
1911	Phi-N	.950	142	310	412	38	54	4
1912	Phi-N	.952	123	258	342	30	45	1
1913	Phi-N	.959	148	311	466	33	58	11
1914	Bal-F	.956	144	289	389	31	49	1
1915	Bal-F	.975	94	203	264	12	52	7
1916	Pit-N	.962	28	43	83	5	3	0
	Chi-N	.939	42	72	128	13	17	6
	Yr	.948	70	115	211	18	20	6
Total	10	.957	1239	2743	3583	287	483	62
OF								
1907	Phi-N	1.000	5	8	2	0	1	2
1909	Phi-N	—	1	0	0	0	0	0
1915	Bal-F	—	1	0	0	0	0	0
1916	Chi-N	1.000	1	2	0	0	0	0
Total	4	1.000	8	10	2	0	1	2
3B								
1905	Pit-N	.786	3	2	9	3	1	0
1916	Chi-N	—	1	0	0	0	0	0
Total	2	.786	4	2	9	3	1	0
SS								
1916	Chi-N	1.000	1	0	1	0	0	0

■ **Alan Knicely** C

YEAR	TM/L	PCT	G	PO	A	E	DP	FR
1979	Hou-N	1.000	3	2	0	0	0	-1
1981	Hou-N	1.000	2	11	2	0	0	1
1982	Hou-N	.977	23	112	15	3	2	-5
1983	Cin-N	1.000	31	108	11	0	1	-2
1984	Cin-N	1.000	1	2	0	0	0	0
1985	Cin-N	.968	46	231	13	8	1	-14
1986	StL-N	1.000	2	2	0	0	0	0
Total	7	.979	108	468	41	1	4	-21
1B								
1983	Cin-N	1.000	2	2	1	0	1	0
1984	Cin-N	.984	8	58	5	1	5	0
1985	Cin-N	1.000	1	6	1	0	0	0
1986	StL-N	.995	29	185	16	1	20	-1
Total	4	.993	40	249	22	2	27	-1
OF								
1981	Hou-N	—	1	0	0	0	0	0
1982	Hou-N	.941	16	16	0	1	0	-1
1983	Cin-N	1.000	8	14	1	0	1	1

YEAR	TM/L	PCT	G	PO	A	E	DP	FR
Total	3	.969	25	30	1	1	1	0
3B								
1979	Hou-N	—	1	0	0	0	0	0
1982	Hou-N	—	1	0	0	0	0	0
Total	2	—	2	0	0	0	0	0

■ **Bill Knickerbocker** SS

YEAR	TM/L	PCT	G	PO	A	E	DP	FR
1933	Cle-A	.939	80	151	233	25	37	2
1934	Cle-A	.962	146	262	451	28	106	-7
1935	Cle-A	.956	128	247	453	32	82	9
1936	Cle-A	.952	155	313	486	40	97	-1
1937	StL-A	.958	115	205	368	25	59	-11
1938	NY-A	1.000	3	4	3	0	2	0
1939	NY-A	1.000	2	1	6	0	0	1
1940	NY-A	.985	19	22	43	1	12	0
1942	Phi-A	.000	1	0	0	1	0	-1
Total	9	.955	649	1205	2043	152	395	-8
2B								
1937	StL-A	.963	6	15	11	1	5	-2
1938	NY-A	.982	34	78	86	3	23	-2
1939	NY-A	1.000	2	5	6	0	1	1
1941	Chi-A	.970	88	204	221	13	58	-17
1942	Phi-A	.964	81	178	220	15	45	-11
Total	5	.970	211	480	544	2	132	-31
3B								
1940	NY-A	.900	17	11	34	5	6	-2

■ **Lon Knight** OF

YEAR	TM/L	PCT	G	PO	A	E	DP	FR
1876	Phi-N	.833	9	15	0	3	0	-1
1880	Wor-N	.863	49	47	22	11	1	4
1881	Det-N	.890	82	116	21	17	6	0
1882	Det-N	.867	84	112	25	21	2	0
1883	Phi-a	.858	93	123	22	24	5	0
1884	Phi-a	.911	108	158	36	19	6	11
1885	Phi-a	.921	29	49	9	5	3	4
	Pro-N	.957	25	39	6	2	2	3
Total	7	.887	479	659	141	102	25	21
1B								
1876	Phi-N	.922	13	91	3	8	6	0
1881	Det-N	1.000	1	2	0	0	0	0
1882	Det-N	.850	2	17	0	3	0	-1
1884	Phi-a	1.000	1	7	0	0	0	0
Total	4	.916	17	117	3	1	6	-1
2B								
1876	Phi-N	.656	6	17	4	11	3	-5
1881	Det-N	.800	1	1	3	1	0	-1
1883	Phi-a	.900	2	4	5	1	0	-1
Total	3	.723	9	22	12	3	3	-7
3B								
1883	Phi-a	.800	3	2	10	3	0	1

■ **Ray Knight** 3B

YEAR	TM/L	PCT	G	PO	A	E	DP	FR
1974	Cin-N	1.000	14	2	8	0	0	1
1977	Cin-N	.941	37	11	21	2	2	2
1978	Cin-N	.868	60	8	38	7	1	5
1979	Cin-N	.962	149	120	262	15	26	-16
1980	Cin-N	.969	162	120	291	13	19	-15
1981	Cin-N	.957	105	69	176	11	18	-13
1982	Hou-N	.964	67	57	131	7	18	4
1984	Hou-N	.946	54	37	86	7	6	0
	NY-N	.962	27	14	36	2	4	-4
	Yr	.951	81	51	122	9	10	-4
1985	NY-N	.958	73	52	109	7	5	-11
1986	NY-N	.948	132	88	204	16	17	-11
1987	Bal-A	.956	130	110	282	18	28	11
1988	Det-A	1.000	11	6	9	0	0	-1
Total	12	.957	1021	694	1653	105	144	-48
1B								
1978	Cin-N	1.000	1	2	0	0	0	0
1982	Hou-N	.990	96	945	55	10	76	-6
1983	Hou-N	.993	143	1285	73	9	131	-10
1984	Hou-N	1.000	24	199	9	0	16	-2
	NY-N	1.000	3	6	1	0	1	0
	Yr	1.000	27	205	10	0	17	-2
1985	NY-N	1.000	1	2	1	0	0	0
1986	NY-N	1.000	1	6	0	0	0	0
1987	Bal-A	.984	6	59	2	1	7	-1
1988	Det-A	.991	64	432	33	4	40	-2
Total	8	.992	339	2936	174	4	271	-21
2B								
1977	Cin-N	.962	17	28	23	2	5	2
1978	Cin-N	1.000	4	1	2	0	0	0
1985	NY-N	1.000	2	2	3	0	0	0
Total	3	.967	23	31	28	2	5	2
OF								
1977	Cin-N	1.000	5	6	0	0	0	0
1978	Cin-N	1.000	3	2	1	0	0	1
1988	Det-A	—	2	0	0	0	0	0
Total	3	1.000	10	8	1	0	0	1
SS								
1977	Cin-N	1.000	3	0	2	0	1	1
1978	Cin-N	1.000	1	0	0	0	0	0
Total	2	1.000	4	0	2	0	1	1

■ **John Knight** SS

YEAR	TM/L	PCT	G	PO	A	E	DP	FR
1905	Phi-A	.895	79	139	185	38	9	-27
1909	NY-A	.901	77	141	204	38	19	0
1910	NY-A	.929	79	169	247	32	39	1
1911	NY-A	.907	82	200	247	46	30	-8
Total	4	.909	317	649	883	154	97	-34
3B								
1905	Phi-A	.833	4	6	4	2	0	-1
1906	Phi-A	.922	67	71	130	17	6	2
1907	Phi-A	.862	40	49	82	21	5	0
	Bos-A	.922	92	129	211	28	13	8
	Yr	.906	132	178	293	49	18	8
1910	NY-A	1.000	4	8	9	0	0	1
1911	NY-A	1.000	1	1	1	0	1	0
Total	5	.912	208	264	437	8	25	10

1B

YEAR	TM/L	PCT	G	PO	A	E	DP	FR
1909	NY-A	.986	19	190	17	3	11	2
1910	NY-A	.988	23	247	8	3	9	-2
1911	NY-A	.981	27	236	26	5	14	4
1912	Was-A	1.000	5	40	4	0	2	1
1913	NY-A	.980	50	494	45	11	26	5
Total	5	.983	124	1207	100	2	62	10

2B

YEAR	TM/L	PCT	G	PO	A	E	DP	FR
1906	Phi-A	.938	7	11	19	2	0	-2
1907	Bos-A	.846	4	11	11	4	3	0
1909	NY-A	.923	17	38	46	7	4	-1
1910	NY-A	.938	7	13	17	2	0	-1
1911	NY-A	.887	21	54	80	17	8	7
1912	Was-A	.926	27	55	45	8	8	-6
1913	NY-A	.952	21	50	70	6	6	3
Total	7	.919	104	232	288	6	29	0

OF

YEAR	TM/L	PCT	G	PO	A	E	DP	FR
1910	NY-A	1.000	1	2	0	0	0	0

■ Bobby Knoop 2B

YEAR	TM/L	PCT	G	PO	A	E	DP	FR
1964	LA-A	.978	161	357	522	20	123	37
1965	Cal-A	.971	142	331	402	22	89	13
1966	Cal-A	.981	161	381	488	17	135	16
1967	Cal-A	.986	159	386	392	11	91	1
1968	Cal-A	.981	151	350	425	15	94	16
1969	Cal-A	.977	27	64	66	3	14	2
	Chi-A	.985	104	271	320	9	76	23
	Yr	.984	131	335	386	12	90	25
1970	Chi-A	.984	126	276	403	11	102	35
1971	KC-A	.968	52	89	120	7	31	-1
1972	KC-A	.972	33	61	80	4	24	8
Total	9	.980	1116	2566	3218	119	779	150

3B

YEAR	TM/L	PCT	G	PO	A	E	DP	FR
1971	KC-A	—	1	0	0	0	0	0
1972	KC-A	—	4	0	0	0	0	0
Total	2	—	5	0	0	0	0	0

■ Fritz Knothe 3B

YEAR	TM/L	PCT	G	PO	A	E	DP	FR
1932	Bos-N	.947	87	81	168	14	7	-3
1933	Bos-N	.978	33	34	56	2	6	-4
	Phi-N	.949	32	45	85	7	8	15
	Yr	.961	65	79	141	9	14	11
Total	2	.953	152	160	309	3	21	8

SS

YEAR	TM/L	PCT	G	PO	A	E	DP	FR
1933	Bos-N	.974	9	15	22	1	4	-3

2B

YEAR	TM/L	PCT	G	PO	A	E	DP	FR
1933	Phi-N	.857	4	4	2	1	0	0

■ Jimmy Knowles 3B

YEAR	TM/L	PCT	G	PO	A	E	DP	FR
1884	Bro-a	.771	11	9	18	8	0	-2
1886	Was-a	.848	53	68	122	34	10	5
1887	NY-a	.500	1	0	1	1	0	0
1890	Roc-a	.881	123	162	303	63	19	7
1892	NY-N	.792	15	13	25	10	2	-4
Total	5	.861	203	252	469	116	31	6

2B

YEAR	TM/L	PCT	G	PO	A	E	DP	FR
1886	Was-a	.899	62	196	224	47	32	21
1887	NY-a	.934	16	49	36	6	4	-3
Total	2	.905	78	245	260	3	36	18

1B

YEAR	TM/L	PCT	G	PO	A	E	DP	FR
1884	Pit-a	.961	46	499	15	21	20	0
	Bro-a	.953	30	310	18	16	18	3
	Yr	.958	76	809	33	37	38	3

SS

YEAR	TM/L	PCT	G	PO	A	E	DP	FR
1892	NY-N	1.000	1	1	1	0	0	0

■ Ben Koehler OF

YEAR	TM/L	PCT	G	PO	A	E	DP	FR
1905	StL-A	.969	124	227	24	8	11	5
1906	StL-A	.957	52	81	8	4	4	-1
Total	2	.966	176	308	32	2	15	4

2B

YEAR	TM/L	PCT	G	PO	A	E	DP	FR
1905	StL-A	.955	6	9	12	1	1	1
1906	StL-A	.900	7	12	15	3	3	-3
Total	2	.923	13	21	27	4	4	-2

1B

YEAR	TM/L	PCT	G	PO	A	E	DP	FR
1905	StL-A	.991	12	111	5	1	6	-1

SS

YEAR	TM/L	PCT	G	PO	A	E	DP	FR
1906	StL-A	.800	1	1	3	1	0	0

3B

YEAR	TM/L	PCT	G	PO	A	E	DP	FR
1906	StL-A	1.000	1	1	1	0	0	0

■ Len Koenecke OF

YEAR	TM/L	PCT	G	PO	A	E	DP	FR
1932	NY-N	.924	35	61	0	5	0	-7
1934	Bro-N	.994	121	310	6	2	0	-1
1935	Bro-N	.966	91	222	3	8	0	-8
Total	3	.976	247	593	9	5	0	-16

■ Mark Koenig SS

YEAR	TM/L	PCT	G	PO	A	E	DP	FR
1925	NY-A	.944	28	53	81	8	16	-3
1926	NY-A	.931	141	281	422	52	66	0
1927	NY-A	.936	122	262	423	47	76	14
1928	NY-A	.923	125	260	328	49	69	-20
1929	NY-A	.911	61	107	160	26	30	-9
1930	NY-A	.905	19	36	59	10	14	2
	Det-A	.922	70	115	181	25	40	-14
	Yr	.918	89	151	240	35	54	-12
1931	Det-A	.909	35	59	90	15	13	-12
1932	Chi-N	.932	31	58	106	12	21	10
1933	Chi-N	.948	26	33	58	5	15	3
1934	Cin-N	.921	58	137	189	28	34	3
1935	NY-N	.958	21	45	69	5	17	2
1936	NY-N	.905	10	11	27	4	4	0
Total	12	.927	747	1457	2193	286	415	-24

3B

YEAR	TM/L	PCT	G	PO	A	E	DP	FR
1929	NY-A	.916	37	26	61	8	7	-4
1930	Det-A	1.000	2	2	3	0	0	0
1933	Chi-N	.922	37	32	74	9	9	2
1934	Cin-N	.930	64	57	130	14	9	0
1935	NY-N	.935	15	10	19	2	2	-1
1936	NY-N	.667	3	2	0	1	0	-1

YEAR	TM/L	PCT	G	PO	A	E	DP	FR
Total	6	.924	158	129	287	4	27	-4

2B

YEAR	TM/L	PCT	G	PO	A	E	DP	FR
1929	NY-A	—	1	0	0	0	0	0
1931	Det-A	.955	55	132	146	13	28	-11
1933	Chi-N	1.000	2	7	2	0	1	0
1934	Cin-N	.966	26	85	85	6	22	3
1935	NY-N	.968	64	123	206	11	20	-11
1936	NY-N	.905	8	8	11	2	1	0
Total	6	.962	156	355	450	2	72	-19

1B

YEAR	TM/L	PCT	G	PO	A	E	DP	FR
1934	Cin-N	1.000	4	42	1	0	2	-1

OF

YEAR	TM/L	PCT	G	PO	A	E	DP	FR
1930	Det-A	—	1	0	0	0	0	0

■ Dick Kokos OF

YEAR	TM/L	PCT	G	PO	A	E	DP	FR
1948	StL-A	.964	71	126	8	5	2	-5
1949	StL-A	.981	138	290	16	6	5	2
1950	StL-A	.970	127	342	8	11	2	9
1953	StL-A	.963	83	152	5	6	1	-4
1954	Bal-A	1.000	1	3	0	0	0	0
Total	5	.971	420	913	37	8	10	2

■ Gary Kolb OF

YEAR	TM/L	PCT	G	PO	A	E	DP	FR
1960	StL-N	1.000	2	4	0	0	0	1
1962	StL-N	1.000	6	9	0	0	0	0
1963	StL-N	.981	58	50	1	1	1	0
1964	Mil-N	1.000	14	12	0	0	0	0
1965	Mil-N	1.000	13	11	0	0	0	1
	NY-N	.976	29	37	4	1	0	2
	Yr	.981	42	48	4	1	0	3
1968	Pit-N	.900	25	34	2	4	1	0
Total	6	.965	147	157	7	6	2	4

C

YEAR	TM/L	PCT	G	PO	A	E	DP	FR
1963	StL-N	1.000	1	2	0	0	0	0
1964	Mil-N	1.000	2	6	0	0	0	0
1968	Pit-N	1.000	10	17	3	0	1	0
1969	Pit-N	1.000	7	29	4	0	0	1
Total	4	1.000	20	54	7	0	1	1

3B

YEAR	TM/L	PCT	G	PO	A	E	DP	FR
1963	StL-N	—	1	0	0	0	0	0
1964	Mil-N	.846	7	3	8	2	1	-1
1965	NY-N	.500	1	0	1	1	1	0
1968	Pit-N	.889	4	3	5	1	1	0
Total	4	.833	13	6	14	4	3	-1

2B

YEAR	TM/L	PCT	G	PO	A	E	DP	FR
1964	Mil-N	.875	6	5	9	2	1	-2
1968	Pit-N	1.000	1	2	1	0	0	0
Total	2	.895	7	7	10	2	1	-2

1B

YEAR	TM/L	PCT	G	PO	A	E	DP	FR
1965	NY-N	1.000	1	3	0	0	1	0

■ Don Kolloway 2B

YEAR	TM/L	PCT	G	PO	A	E	DP	FR
1940	Chi-A	.922	10	19	28	4	7	-2
1941	Chi-A	.955	62	118	181	14	23	-7
1942	Chi-A	.966	116	308	345	23	80	-5
1943	Chi-A	.968	85	246	240	16	71	-1
1946	Chi-A	.972	90	235	281	15	74	2
1947	Chi-A	.962	99	274	306	23	76	5
1948	Chi-A	.966	83	241	276	18	62	10
1949	Det-A	.956	62	135	149	13	44	-18
1950	Det-A	1.000	1	1	3	0	0	0
1952	Det-A	.968	8	14	16	1	4	-2
Total	10	.964	616	1591	1825	127	441	-18

1B

YEAR	TM/L	PCT	G	PO	A	E	DP	FR
1941	Chi-A	.905	4	34	4	4	6	0
1942	Chi-A	.986	33	328	15	5	28	-4
1947	Chi-A	.991	11	99	8	1	9	0
1949	Det-A	.990	57	472	35	5	49	-2
1950	Det-A	.989	118	1087	85	13	133	3
1951	Det-A	.992	59	452	49	4	53	6
1952	Det-A	.979	32	252	28	6	15	2
Total	7	.987	314	2724	224	8	293	5

3B

YEAR	TM/L	PCT	G	PO	A	E	DP	FR
1946	Chi-A	.920	31	32	72	9	8	1
1947	Chi-A	.880	8	5	17	3	1	-1
1948	Chi-A	.926	18	23	27	4	1	1
1949	Chi-A	—	2	0	0	0	0	0
	Det-A	1.000	7	6	12	0	1	-1
	Yr	1.000	9	6	12	0	1	-1
1953	Phi-A	—	1	0	0	0	0	0
Total	5	.924	67	66	128	6	11	0

■ Fred Kommers OF

YEAR	TM/L	PCT	G	PO	A	E	DP	FR
1913	Pit-N	.979	40	94	1	2	0	-2
1914	StL-F	.908	67	107	11	12	1	-2
	Bal-F	.938	12	15	0	1	0	-2
	Yr	.911	79	122	11	13	1	-4
Total	2	.938	119	216	12	5	1	-6

■ Brad Komminsk OF

YEAR	TM/L	PCT	G	PO	A	E	DP	FR
1983	Atl-N	.944	13	16	1	1	0	0
1984	Atl-N	.993	80	135	2	1	0	-5
1985	Atl-N	.959	92	161	2	7	0	-8
1986	Atl-N	1.000	2	1	0	0	0	0
1987	Mil-A	1.000	5	10	0	0	0	1
1989	Cle-A	.995	68	181	3	1	1	7
1990	SF-N	1.000	7	3	0	0	0	0
	Bal-A	1.000	40	67	2	0	0	2
Total	7	.983	307	574	10	0	1	-3

3B

YEAR	TM/L	PCT	G	PO	A	E	DP	FR
1986	Atl-N	1.000	2	0	2	0	0	0

■ Ed Konetchy 1B

YEAR	TM/L	PCT	G	PO	A	E	DP	FR
1907	StL-N	.975	91	922	71	25	46	4
1908	StL-N	.986	154	1610	122	24	61	11
1909	StL-N	.985	152	1584	97	26	71	5
1910	StL-N	.991	144	1499	98	15	81	8
1911	StL-N	.991	158	1652	71	16	85	-6
1912	StL-N	.991	142	1392	90	13	77	5
1913	StL-N	.995	140	1432	91	7	71	8
1914	Pit-N	.995	154	1576	93	8	70	5
1915	Pit-F	.994	152	1536	81	10	83	0
1916	Bos-N	.990	158	1626	96	18	96	9
1917	Bos-N	.994	129	1351	70	8	65	2
1918	Bos-N	.992	112	1226	61	11	69	-3
1919	Bro-N	.994	132	1288	89	9	62	7
1920	Bro-N	.990	130	1332	79	14	70	1
1921	Bro-N	.987	54	564	28	8	41	-1
	Phi-N	.986	71	771	55	12	38	5
	Yr	.986	125	1335	83	20	79	4
Total	15	.990	2073	21361	1292	224	1086	60

OF

YEAR	TM/L	PCT	G	PO	A	E	DP	FR
1912	StL-N	1.000	1	4	1	0	0	1
1918	Bos-N	1.000	6	13	3	0	1	2
Total	2	1.000	7	17	4	0	1	3

■ Larry Kopf SS

YEAR	TM/L	PCT	G	PO	A	E	DP	FR
1914	Phi-A	.899	13	37	34	8	3	1
1915	Phi-A	.920	74	152	205	31	24	-8
1916	Cin-N	.942	11	16	33	3	4	-2
1917	Cin-N	.916	145	276	470	68	59	-11
1919	Cin-N	.943	135	273	407	41	39	-34
1920	Cin-N	.929	123	249	363	47	50	-33
1921	Cin-N	.947	93	195	304	28	39	-15
1922	Bos-N	.910	33	77	115	19	22	0
1923	Bos-N	.905	37	76	123	21	25	-6
Total	9	.928	664	1351	2054	266	265	108

2B

YEAR	TM/L	PCT	G	PO	A	E	DP	FR
1913	Cle-A	.917	3	4	7	1	1	2
1914	Phi-A	.833	5	7	8	3	0	0
1915	Phi-A	1.000	2	4	3	0	0	0
1920	Cin-N	1.000	2	2	7	0	0	1
1921	Cin-N	.885	4	9	14	3	3	0
1922	Bos-N	.944	78	175	243	25	35	-14
1923	Bos-N	.909	4	10	10	2	1	-2
Total	7	.937	98	211	292	4	40	-13

3B

YEAR	TM/L	PCT	G	PO	A	E	DP	FR
1913	Cle-A	1.000	1	1	3	0	0	1
1914	Phi-A	.895	8	8	9	2	0	0
1915	Phi-A	.876	42	49	71	17	6	0
1920	Cin-N	1.000	2	0	1	0	0	0
1921	Cin-N	1.000	3	2	4	0	0	0
1922	Bos-N	.969	13	7	24	1	1	0
Total	6	.899	69	67	112	0	7	1

OF

YEAR	TM/L	PCT	G	PO	A	E	DP	FR
1920	Cin-N	—	1	0	0	0	0	0
1921	Cin-N	1.000	1	1	0	0	0	0
Total	2	1.000	2	1	0	0	0	0

■ Merlin Kopp OF

YEAR	TM/L	PCT	G	PO	A	E	DP	FR
1915	Was-A	.933	9	14	0	1	0	-1
1918	Phi-A	.972	96	221	20	7	6	12
1919	Phi-A	.924	65	127	7	11	0	-2
Total	3	.953	170	362	27	9	6	9

■ Joe Koppe SS

YEAR	TM/L	PCT	G	PO	A	E	DP	FR
1958	Mil-N	.833	3	5	10	3	3	6
1959	Phi-N	.954	113	218	347	27	67	6
1960	Phi-N	.956	55	107	133	11	23	-12
1961	Phi-N	.800	5	2	2	1	1	0
	LA-A	.947	88	127	250	21	51	-6
1962	LA-A	.957	118	197	356	25	63	3
1963	LA-A	.962	19	27	50	3	6	4
1964	LA-A	.945	31	51	103	9	19	14
1965	Cal-A	1.000	4	3	11	0	2	3
Total	8	.952	436	737	1262	100	235	18

2B

YEAR	TM/L	PCT	G	PO	A	E	DP	FR
1959	Phi-N	1.000	11	7	15	0	0	0
1961	LA-A	1.000	3	6	2	0	0	-1
1962	LA-A	1.000	5	6	10	0	3	2
1963	LA-A	.984	14	30	32	1	10	4
1964	LA-A	.933	13	4	10	1	1	1
1965	Cal-A	.979	10	17	29	1	4	6
Total	6	.982	56	70	98	3	18	12

3B

YEAR	TM/L	PCT	G	PO	A	E	DP	FR
1960	Phi-N	.600	2	0	3	2	1	0
1961	LA-A	1.000	1	2	4	0	0	1
1962	LA-A	.600	4	0	3	2	0	-1
1963	LA-A	.905	18	7	12	2	1	0
1964	LA-A	.846	3	6	5	2	2	0
1965	Cal-A	1.000	4	3	0	0	0	0
Total	6	.849	32	18	27	8	4	0

OF

YEAR	TM/L	PCT	G	PO	A	E	DP	FR
1963	LA-A	1.000	3	5	0	0	0	0

■ Andy Kosco OF

YEAR	TM/L	PCT	G	PO	A	E	DP	FR
1965	Min-A	1.000	14	17	3	0	1	2
1966	Min-A	.986	40	70	2	1	0	0
1967	Min-A	.923	7	12	0	1	0	-1
1968	NY-A	.960	95	160	9	7	0	-6
1969	LA-N	.981	109	153	6	3	2	-7
1970	LA-N	.981	58	101	2	2	0	-1
1971	Mil-A	.988	45	81	2	1	1	0
1972	Cal-A	.985	36	62	2	1	0	-2
	Bos-A	1.000	12	19	1	0	0	0
	Yr	.988	48	81	3	1	0	-2
1973	Cin-N	1.000	36	50	1	0	0	-4
1974	Cin-N	—	1	0	0	0	0	0
Total	10	.979	453	725	28	6	4	-19

1B

YEAR	TM/L	PCT	G	PO	A	E	DP	FR
1965	Min-A	1.000	2	18	0	0	0	0
1966	Min-A	.967	5	29	0	1	3	-1
1968	NY-A	.992	28	243	15	2	18	0
1969	LA-N	1.000	3	8	0	0	0	0
1970	LA-N	1.000	1	1	0	0	0	0
1971	Mil-A	.995	29	175	11	1	22	-1
1973	Cin-N	1.000	9	0	0	0	0	0
Total	7	.992	69	483	26	4	44	-2

YEAR	TM/L	PCT	G	PO	A	E	DP	FR
	3B							
1971	Mil-A	.952	12	8	12	1	0	-2
1974	Cin-N	.846	8	4	7	2	0	-2
Total	2	.912	20	12	19	3	0	-4

■ Ernie Koy OF

YEAR	TM/L	PCT	G	PO	A	E	DP	FR
1938	Bro-N	.984	135	306	7	5	4	-11
1939	Bro-N	.962	114	252	4	10	1	-2
1940	Bro-N	1.000	19	25	0	0	0	0
	StL-N	.970	91	192	2	6	0	-3
	Yr	.973	110	217	2	6	0	-3
1941	StL-N	1.000	12	18	0	0	0	-1
	Cin-N	.990	49	92	3	1	1	-3
	Yr	.991	61	110	3	1	1	-4
1942	Phi-N	.981	78	149	4	3	1	1
Total	5	.977	498	1034	20	5	7	-19
	3B							
1938	Bro-N	—	1	0	0	0	0	0

■ Al Kozar 2B

YEAR	TM/L	PCT	G	PO	A	E	DP	FR
1948	Was-A	.967	**149**	348	444	27	89	-21
1949	Was-A	.977	102	232	235	11	57	-7
1950	Was-A	.962	15	33	43	3	8	0
	Chi-A	1.000	4	6	8	0	3	3
	Yr	.968	19	39	51	3	11	3
Total	3	.971	270	619	730	1	157	-25
	3B							
1950	Chi-A	—	1	0	0	0	0	0

■ Ed Kranepool 1B

YEAR	TM/L	PCT	G	PO	A	E	DP	FR
1962	NY-N	1.000	3	9	3	0	0	1
1963	NY-N	1.000	20	150	13	0	16	1
1964	NY-N	.991	104	975	80	10	78	4
1965	NY-N	.992	147	1375	93	12	116	2
1966	NY-N	.992	132	1161	85	10	100	5
1967	NY-N	.992	139	1137	87	10	103	4
1968	NY-N	.994	113	921	75	6	76	5
1969	NY-N	.993	106	809	64	6	76	3
1970	NY-N	1.000	8	47	3	0	5	0
1971	NY-N	**.998**	108	786	61	2	67	-1
1972	NY-N	.996	108	705	48	3	65	0
1973	NY-N	.998	51	395	27	1	39	0
1974	NY-N	.977	24	165	8	4	18	-3
1975	NY-N	.997	82	666	46	2	51	0
1976	NY-N	.996	86	675	33	3	48	-6
1977	NY-N	.991	41	286	30	3	21	3
1978	NY-N	1.000	3	27	4	0	3	1
1979	NY-N	1.000	29	203	19	0	18	1
Total	18	.994	1304	10492	779	2	900	20
	OF							
1963	NY-N	.954	55	78	5	4	1	-3
1964	NY-N	1.000	6	8	0	0	0	0
1966	NY-N	.909	11	19	1	2	0	-1
1968	NY-N	1.000	2	3	0	0	0	0
1969	NY-N	1.000	2	3	0	0	0	0
1971	NY-N	1.000	11	9	0	0	0	0
1972	NY-N	—	1	0	0	0	0	0
1973	NY-N	.982	32	53	1	1	0	-1
1974	NY-N	.977	33	42	1	1	0	-3
1975	NY-N	1.000	4	5	0	0	0	0
1976	NY-N	1.000	31	46	2	0	0	0
1977	NY-N	.984	42	61	0	1	0	-2
1978	NY-N	1.000	12	9	0	0	0	-1
1979	NY-N	1.000	8	12	0	0	0	0
Total	14	.975	250	348	10	9	1	-11

■ Danny Kravitz C

YEAR	TM/L	PCT	G	PO	A	E	DP	FR
1956	Pit-N	.944	26	93	8	6	1	1
1957	Pit-N	1.000	15	45	9	0	1	0
1958	Pit-N	.967	37	103	16	4	3	-6
1959	Pit-N	.986	45	198	19	3	3	-1
1960	Pit-N	1.000	1	1	0	0	0	0
	KC-A	.971	47	216	16	7	3	-3
Total	5	.973	171	656	68	0	11	-9
	3B							
1956	Pit-N	1.000	2	0	2	0	1	1

■ Mike Kreevich OF

YEAR	TM/L	PCT	G	PO	A	E	DP	FR
1931	Chi-N	1.000	4	5	1	0	0	1
1936	Chi-A	.964	133	300	17	12	5	6
1937	Chi-A	**.988**	138	401	13	5	4	5
1938	Chi-A	.975	127	379	7	10	2	1
1939	Chi-A	.975	139	419	**18**	11	4	**11**
1940	Chi-A	.982	144	**428**	12	8	3	11
1941	Chi-A	**.994**	113	302	7	2	2	-2
1942	Phi-A	.981	107	314	4	6	0	3
1943	StL-A	.993	51	146	5	1	1	10
1944	StL-A	.986	100	282	4	4	0	12
1945	StL-A	.991	81	230	3	2	0	2
	Was-A	.971	40	98	2	3	0	-1
	Yr	.985	121	328	5	5	0	1
Total	11	.982	1177	3304	93	4	21	59
	3B							
1935	Chi-A	1.000	6	8	4	0	0	-2
1939	Chi-A	.933	4	6	8	1	0	0
Total	2	.966	10	14	12	1	0	-2

■ Wayne Krenchicki 3B

YEAR	TM/L	PCT	G	PO	A	E	DP	FR
1979	Bal-A	.875	7	9	5	2	0	0
1981	Bal-A	.875	6	2	5	1	0	0
1982	Cin-N	.955	70	35	93	6	7	6
1983	Cin-N	.980	39	7	41	1	3	2
	Det-A	.934	48	29	56	6	8	-8
1984	Cin-N	.967	62	25	91	4	5	3
1985	Cin-N	.967	52	34	84	4	9	5
1986	Mon-N	.947	24	20	34	3	4	1
Total	7	.955	308	161	409	7	36	9
	1B							
1983	Det-A	1.000	3	7	1	0	0	0
1984	Cin-N	.900	3	9	0	1	1	0

YEAR	TM/L	PCT	G	PO	A	E	DP	FR
1986	Mon-N	.991	41	305	24	3	22	0
Total	3	.989	47	321	25	4	23	0
	2B							
1979	Bal-A	1.000	6	3	7	0	1	1
1980	Bal-A	1.000	1	0	1	0	0	0
1981	Bal-A	1.000	7	5	14	0	5	3
1982	Cin-N	1.000	9	5	10	0	3	2
1983	Cin-N	—	1	0	0	0	0	0
	Det-A	.938	6	5	10	1	2	0
1984	Cin-N	1.000	3	1	1	0	0	0
1985	Cin-N	1.000	3	1	3	0	0	0
1986	Mon-N	1.000	1	0	1	0	0	0
Total	8	.985	37	20	47	1	11	6
	SS							
1980	Bal-A	1.000	6	9	8	0	2	0
1981	Bal-A	.964	16	16	37	2	7	2
1983	Det-A	.909	6	2	8	1	1	0
Total	3	.964	28	27	53	3	10	2
	OF							
1986	Mon-N	—	1	0	0	0	0	0

■ Chuck Kress 1B

YEAR	TM/L	PCT	G	PO	A	E	DP	FR
1947	Cin-N	.983	8	52	7	1	5	1
1949	Cin-N	.974	16	72	4	2	6	0
	Chi-A	.994	95	907	66	6	103	6
1950	Chi-A	1.000	2	19	1	0	2	0
1954	Det-A	.971	7	63	5	2	4	0
	Bro-N	.500	1	1	0	1	1	0
Total	4	.990	129	1114	83	2	121	1
	OF							
1954	Det-A	—	1	0	0	0	0	0

■ Red Kress SS

YEAR	TM/L	PCT	G	PO	A	E	DP	FR
1927	StL-A	.974	7	12	25	1	4	1
1928	StL-A	.929	**150**	**318**	400	**55**	99	-17
1929	StL-A	**.946**	146	312	441	43	**94**	-2
1930	StL-A	.938	123	271	349	**41**	83	-9
1931	StL-A	.933	38	37	47	6	7	-7
1932	Chi-A	.936	53	125	155	19	35	5
1934	Was-A	1.000	1	4	5	0	1	1
1935	Was-A	.964	53	118	204	12	53	16
1936	Was-A	.927	64	143	212	28	52	6
1938	StL-A	**.965**	150	321	388	26	100	-15
1939	StL-A	.933	13	27	29	4	10	-3
	Det-A	.959	25	48	69	5	15	-1
	Yr	.951	38	75	98	9	25	-4
1940	Det-A	.951	12	25	33	3	5	5
Total	12	.944	835	1761	2357	243	558	-20
	3B							
1930	StL-A	.902	31	35	57	10	4	-3
1931	StL-A	.936	84	92	141	16	12	-8
1932	Chi-A	.909	14	23	27	5	5	2
	Chi-A	.895	19	17	34	6	4	-1
	Yr	.902	33	40	61	11	9	1
1934	Was-A	—	1	0	0	0	0	0
1939	Det-A	.933	4	7	7	1	1	0
1940	Det-A	.924	17	20	41	5	1	3
Total	6	.921	170	194	307	3	27	-7
	1B							
1931	StL-A	.963	10	94	10	4	8	1
1932	Chi-A	1.000	1	10	2	0	4	1
1933	Chi-A	.978	111	1169	60	**28**	83	-3
1934	Was-A	.993	30	291	11	2	16	-2
1935	Was-A	.974	5	35	2	1	8	0
1936	Was-A	.976	5	37	3	1	2	0
Total	6	.980	162	1636	88	6	121	-3
	OF							
1931	StL-A	.947	40	82	8	5	1	4
1932	Chi-A	.956	64	139	12	7	2	5
1933	Chi-A	.941	8	16	0	1	0	-1
1934	Was-A	.941	10	15	1	1	0	0
1935	Was-A	.800	2	4	0	1	0	0
Total	5	.952	124	256	21	4	3	9
	2B							
1934	Chi-A	1.000	3	5	2	0	0	-4
	Was-A	1.000	6	18	15	0	4	0
	Yr	1.000	9	23	17	0	4	-4
1935	Was-A	1.000	1	0	2	0	0	0
1936	Was-A	.995	33	86	100	1	21	4
1939	Det-A	.927	16	29	47	6	13	4
Total	4	.977	59	138	166	7	38	4

■ Chad Kreuter C

YEAR	TM/L	PCT	G	PO	A	E	DP	FR
1988	Tex-A	.990	16	93	8	1	0	2
1989	Tex-A	.992	85	453	26	4	4	15
1990	Tex-A	.977	20	39	4	1	0	-2
Total	3	.990	121	585	38	6	4	15

■ John Kroner 2B

YEAR	TM/L	PCT	G	PO	A	E	DP	FR
1936	Bos-A	.964	38	76	109	7	17	-2
1937	Cle-A	.969	64	155	189	11	45	-2
1938	Cle-A	.974	31	70	77	4	23	10
Total	3	.968	133	301	375	2	85	6
	3B							
1935	Bos-A	1.000	2	0	1	0	0	-1
1936	Bos-A	.966	28	29	56	3	8	3
1937	Cle-A	.842	11	2	14	3	1	-1
1938	Cle-A	.923	3	3	9	1	1	1
Total	4	.942	44	34	80	7	10	2
	SS							
1936	Bos-A	.916	18	41	46	8	11	-2
1938	Cle-A	1.000	1	0	1	0	0	0
Total	2	.917	19	41	47	8	11	-2
	1B							
1938	Cle-A	.950	3	34	4	2	1	0
	OF							
1936	Bos-A	—	1	0	0	0	0	0

■ Rocky Krsnich 3B

YEAR	TM/L	PCT	G	PO	A	E	DP	FR
1949	Chi-A	.935	16	18	40	4	4	4

YEAR	TM/L	PCT	G	PO	A	E	DP	FR
1952	Chi-A	.959	37	45	72	5	6	10
1953	Chi-A	.929	57	31	100	10	7	**9**
Total	3	.942	110	94	212	9	17	23

■ Otto Krueger 3B

YEAR	TM/L	PCT	G	PO	A	E	DP	FR
1899	Cle-N	.763	9	12	17	9	2	-2
1901	StL-N	.881	**142**	171	**275**	**60**	11	-9
1902	StL-N	.866	18	22	36	9	1	-2
1903	Pit-N	.976	13	11	29	1	2	2
1904	Pit-N	.893	10	9	16	3	1	-2
1905	Phi-N	—	1	0	0	0	0	0
Total	6	.879	193	225	373	2	17	-13
	SS							
1899	Cle-N	1.000	2	4	4	0	1	0
1902	StL-N	.897	107	184	390	66	47	3
1903	Pit-N	.884	29	42	72	15	13	-7
1904	Pit-N	.915	32	54	96	14	8	-3
1905	Phi-N	.930	23	40	66	8	10	-7
Total	5	.902	193	324	628	103	79	-14
	OF							
1903	Pit-N	.948	28	48	7	3	0	1
1904	Pit-N	.905	33	52	5	6	1	-1
1905	Phi-N	1.000	6	4	0	0	0	-2
Total	3	.928	67	104	12	9	1	-2
	2B							
1899	Cle-N	.923	2	6	6	1	1	0
1900	StL-N	.852	12	20	26	8	2	-4
1903	Pit-N	.929	3	8	5	1	2	-1
Total	3	.877	17	34	37	0	5	-5

■ Ernie Krueger C

YEAR	TM/L	PCT	G	PO	A	E	DP	FR
1913	Cle-A	1.000	4	4	3	0	0	0
1915	Cle-A	.905	8	30	8	4	1	-4
1917	NY-N	.857	5	6	0	1	0	2
	Bro-N	.979	23	115	25	3	4	1
1918	Bro-N	.986	23	104	38	2	3	6
1919	Bro-N	.963	66	305	88	**15**	2	-4
1920	Bro-N	.959	46	165	46	9	4	-4
1921	Bro-N	.969	52	179	39	7	4	-2
1925	Cin-N	.946	30	75	12	5	3	-4
Total	8	.964	257	983	259	6	21	-3

■ Art Kruger OF

YEAR	TM/L	PCT	G	PO	A	E	DP	FR
1907	Cin-N	.972	96	199	11	6	3	0
1910	Cle-A	.947	47	81	8	5	2	2
	Cle-A	.974	15	35	2	1	1	2
	Yr	.955	62	116	10	6	3	4
1914	KC-F	.963	120	249	14	10	1	-1
1915	KC-F	.984	66	116	8	2	2	0
Total	4	.968	344	680	43	4	9	-3

■ John Kruk OF

YEAR	TM/L	PCT	G	PO	A	E	DP	FR
1986	SD-N	.981	74	102	4	2	0	-5
1987	SD-N	.978	29	41	3	1	0	1
1988	SD-N	1.000	55	99	4	0	0	-1
1989	SD-N	.962	27	48	3	2	0	1
	Phi-N	.983	72	111	5	2	2	-5
	Yr	.977	99	159	8	4	2	-4
1990	Phi-N	.986	87	141	2	2	0	-10
Total	5	.984	344	542	21	9	2	-19
	1B							
1986	SD-N	.975	9	37	2	1	3	-1
1987	SD-N	.996	101	870	75	4	74	3
1988	SD-N	.995	63	535	33	3	45	-3
1989	Phi-N	1.000	7	53	1	0	2	1
1990	Phi-N	.996	61	402	43	2	34	3
Total	5	.995	241	1897	154	0	158	1

■ Dick Kryhoski 1B

YEAR	TM/L	PCT	G	PO	A	E	DP	FR
1949	NY-A	.983	51	363	31	7	39	-1
1950	Det-A	.991	47	409	27	4	44	0
1951	Det-A	.991	112	964	81	9	95	3
1952	StL-A	.989	86	680	49	8	80	-5
1953	StL-A	.992	88	685	66	6	77	5
1954	Bal-A	.992	69	591	52	5	52	3
1955	KC-A	.988	14	76	6	1	7	0
Total	7	.990	467	3768	312	0	394	5

■ Tony Kubek SS

YEAR	TM/L	PCT	G	PO	A	E	DP	FR
1957	NY-A	.968	41	74	108	6	26	6
1958	NY-A	.961	134	242	453	28	98	**21**
1959	NY-A	.968	67	121	217	11	42	6
1960	NY-A	.968	136	228	443	22	84	3
1961	NY-A	.959	145	261	449	30	107	**13**
1962	NY-A	.954	35	71	117	9	27	4
1963	NY-A	.980	132	227	403	13	80	10
1964	NY-A	.978	99	186	307	11	52	4
1965	NY-A	.964	93	134	237	14	53	-9
Total	9	.967	882	1544	2734	144	569	58
	OF							
1957	NY-A	.938	50	88	2	6	0	-4
1958	NY-A	1.000	3	5	0	0	0	0
1959	NY-A	.976	53	78	3	2	2	-1
1960	NY-A	1.000	29	23	1	0	0	0
1962	NY-A	1.000	6	17	0	0	0	0
1963	NY-A	—	1	0	0	0	0	0
1965	NY-A	1.000	3	2	0	0	0	0
Total	7	.965	145	213	6	8	2	-5
	3B							
1957	NY-A	.925	38	26	72	8	7	-1
1959	NY-A	.966	17	20	36	2	5	1
Total	2	.939	55	46	108	0	12	0
	2B							
1957	NY-A	1.000	1	1	1	0	0	0
1958	NY-A	1.000	1	0	1	0	0	0
1959	NY-A	—	1	0	0	0	0	0
Total	3	1.000	3	1	1	0	0	0
	1B							
1958	NY-A	1.000	1	2	0	0	0	0

YEAR	TM/L	PCT	G	PO	A	E	DP	FR
1965	NY-A	1.000	1	2	1	0	0	0
Total	2	1.000	2	4	1	0	0	0

■ Ted Kubiak 2B

YEAR	TM/L	PCT	G	PO	A	E	DP	FR
1967	KC-A	1.000	10	11	11	0	1	-1
1968	Oak-A	.929	24	43	49	7	9	-3
1969	Oak-A	.971	33	75	91	5	17	-3
1970	Mil-A	.989	91	233	238	5	63	-8
1971	Mil-A	.971	48	119	115	7	23	0
	StL-N	.967	14	25	33	2	4	-1
1972	Tex-A	.990	25	55	49	1	12	-1
	Oak-A	.988	49	80	88	2	21	2
	Yr	.989	74	135	137	3	33	1
1973	Oak-A	.973	83	89	129	6	28	-3
1974	Oak-A	.995	71	101	117	1	32	-6
1975	Oak-A	1.000	6	3	5	0	1	0
	SD-N	1.000	11	14	15	0	3	0
1976	SD-N	.992	25	56	61	1	16	-6
Total	10	.981	490	904	1001	7	230	-30

SS

YEAR	TM/L	PCT	G	PO	A	E	DP	FR
1967	KC-A	.984	20	23	40	1	5	0
1968	Oak-A	.920	12	17	29	4	4	0
1969	Oak-A	.976	42	78	124	5	24	2
1970	Mil-A	.956	73	128	174	14	35	-10
1971	Mil-A	.958	39	52	107	7	21	-2
	StL-N	.959	17	24	23	2	4	-2
1972	Tex-A	.980	15	21	27	1	4	-2
1973	Oak-A	.977	26	28	56	2	13	9
1974	Oak-A	.951	19	18	40	3	4	-3
1975	Oak-A	1.000	7	8	18	0	4	1
1976	SD-N	.667	6	0	2	1	0	-1
Total	10	.963	276	397	640	0	118	-8

3B

YEAR	TM/L	PCT	G	PO	A	E	DP	FR
1967	KC-A	.833	5	3	7	2	1	-1
1972	Tex-A	1.000	1	0	1	0	1	0
	Oak-A	—	1	0	0	0	0	0
	Yr	1.000	2	0	1	0	1	0
1973	Oak-A	1.000	2	0	1	0	0	0
1974	Oak-A	.933	14	10	18	2	2	0
1975	Oak-A	1.000	7	1	8	0	0	1
	SD-N	.954	64	36	110	7	9	1
1976	SD-N	.971	27	20	47	2	5	-3
Total	6	.953	121	70	192	3	18	-2

1B

YEAR	TM/L	PCT	G	PO	A	E	DP	FR
1975	SD-N	1.000	1	1	1	0	0	0
1976	SD-N	1.000	1	1	0	0	0	0
Total	2	1.000	2	2	1	0	0	0

■ Bill Kuehne 3B

YEAR	TM/L	PCT	G	PO	A	E	DP	FR
1883	Col-a	.833	69	61	133	39	11	-6
1884	Col-a	.881	110	120	219	46	13	11
1885	Pit-a	.865	97	102	187	45	14	-2
1886	Pit-a	.892	47	44	88	16	5	-2
1887	Pit-N	1.000	4	4	11	0	0	-1
1888	Pit-N	.910	75	96	168	26	10	8
1889	Pit-N	.885	75	89	157	32	14	-2
1890	Pit-P	.850	126	159	304	82	18	6
1891	Col-a	.885	68	85	146	30	15	-2
	Lou-a	.904	41	56	95	16	8	2
	Yr	.893	109	141	241	46	23	0
1892	Lou-N	.874	76	104	160	38	16	-3
	StL-N	.895	5	5	12	2	0	0
	Cin-N	.941	4	7	9	1	2	2
	StL-N	1.000	1	0	5	0	2	1
	Yr	.880	86	116	186	41	20	0
Total	10	.876	798	932	1694	373	128	12

SS

YEAR	TM/L	PCT	G	PO	A	E	DP	FR
1883	Col-a	.909	7	10	20	3	5	3
1885	Pit-a	.850	7	7	27	6	2	0
1887	Pit-N	.883	91	136	310	59	29	-10
1888	Pit-N	.916	63	112	159	25	19	-8
1889	Pit-N	.905	2	5	14	2	1	3
1892	StL-N	1.000	1	0	3	0	0	0
Total	6	.894	171	270	533	5	56	-12

OF

YEAR	TM/L	PCT	G	PO	A	E	DP	FR
1883	Col-a	1.000	3	5	1	0	0	1
1886	Pit-N	.899	54	87	11	11	0	2
1887	Pit-N	.600	3	3	0	2	0	-1
1889	Pit-N	1.000	13	27	1	0	1	1
Total	4	.912	73	122	13	3	1	3

2B

YEAR	TM/L	PCT	G	PO	A	E	DP	FR
1883	Col-a	.792	18	56	58	30	5	-3
1889	Pit-N	1.000	5	8	13	0	0	0
1892	Cin-N	.783	2	12	6	5	3	0
Total	3	.814	25	76	77	5	8	-3

1B

YEAR	TM/L	PCT	G	PO	A	E	DP	FR
1886	Pit-a	.989	18	172	0	2	7	-2
1887	Pit-N	.958	4	23	0	1	2	0
1889	Pit-N	1.000	2	18	2	0	1	1
Total	3	.986	24	213	2	3	10	-1

■ Harvey Kuenn OF

YEAR	TM/L	PCT	G	PO	A	E	DP	FR
1956	Det-A	—	1	0	0	0	0	0
1958	Det-A	.984	138	358	9	6	1	11
1959	Det-A	.988	137	247	6	3	0	-1
1960	Cle-A	.966	119	222	7	8	3	0
1961	SF-N	.988	93	157	9	2	0	1
1962	SF-N	.970	105	160	3	5	1	-7
1963	SF-N	.975	64	74	4	2	2	-5
1964	SF-N	.952	88	97	2	5	0	-14
1965	SF-N	1.000	14	14	0	0	0	-2
	Chi-N	.975	35	36	3	1	1	-3
	Yr	.981	49	50	3	1	1	-5
1966	Chi-N	—	1	0	0	0	0	0
	Phi-N	1.000	31	31	0	0	0	-2
	Yr	1.000	32	31	0	0	0	-2
Total	10	.978	826	1396	43	2	8	-22

SS

YEAR	TM/L	PCT	G	PO	A	E	DP	FR
1952	Det-A	.962	19	44	57	4	12	2
1953	Det-A	.973	155	308	441	21	78	-21
1954	Det-A	.966	155	294	496	28	85	3
1955	Det-A	.956	141	253	378	29	83	-28
1956	Det-A	.968	141	219	388	20	86	-19
1957	Det-A	.955	136	225	354	27	86	-48
1961	SF-N	1.000	1	0	2	0	1	0
Total	7	.964	748	1343	2116	129	431	111

3B

YEAR	TM/L	PCT	G	PO	A	E	DP	FR
1957	Det-A	.950	17	24	33	3	4	-1
1960	Cle-A	.857	5	0	6	1	0	-1
1961	SF-N	.890	32	33	32	8	4	-10
1962	SF-N	.930	30	20	44	3	4	-7
1963	SF-N	.898	53	41	56	11	1	-23
1964	SF-N	1.000	2	1	0	0	0	0
1966	Phi-N	—	1	0	0	0	0	0
Total	7	.918	140	119	171	6	13	-42

1B

YEAR	TM/L	PCT	G	PO	A	E	DP	FR
1957	Det-A	1.000	1	2	0	0	1	0
1964	SF-N	.978	11	38	7	1	4	1
1965	SF-N	1.000	7	27	5	0	0	1
	Chi-N	.667	1	4	0	2	0	-1
	Yr	.947	8	31	5	2	0	0
1966	Phi-N	.990	13	99	3	1	11	-2
Total	4	.979	33	170	15	4	16	-1

■ Joe Kuhel 1B

YEAR	TM/L	PCT	G	PO	A	E	DP	FR
1930	Was-A	.981	16	149	8	3	10	-1
1931	Was-A	.991	139	1255	57	12	119	-7
1932	Was-A	.994	85	761	45	5	64	-2
1933	Was-A	.996	153	1498	61	7	126	-7
1934	Was-A	.994	63	618	23	4	62	-4
1935	Was-A	.991	151	1425	87	14	150	0
1936	Chi-A	.993	149	1452	73	10	138	-2
1937	Was-A	.993	136	1242	85	9	141	3
1938	Chi-A	.988	111	1136	59	14	97	-7
1939	Chi-A	.992	136	1256	72	11	113	-4
1940	Chi-A	.988	155	1395	91	18	112	-5
1941	Chi-A	.994	151	1444	108	10	113	-1
1942	Chi-A	.991	112	1085	70	11	94	-4
1943	Chi-A	.995	153	1471	106	8	143	1
1944	Was-A	.987	138	1251	83	17	119	-2
1945	Was-A	.989	141	1323	94	16	101	-6
1946	Was-A	1.000	5	29	3	0	2	0
	Chi-A	.994	63	596	38	4	65	-2
	Yr	.994	68	625	41	4	67	-2
Total	17	.992	2057	19386	1163	173	1769	-50

■ Walt Kuhn C

YEAR	TM/L	PCT	G	PO	A	E	DP	FR
1912	Chi-A	.966	75	318	104	15	8	9
1913	Chi-A	.980	24	75	22	2	1	-2
1914	Chi-A	.987	16	60	17	1	3	-1
Total	3	.971	115	453	143	8	12	6

2B

YEAR	TM/L	PCT	G	PO	A	E	DP	FR
1912	Chi-A	—	1	0	0	0	0	0

■ Duane Kuiper 2B

YEAR	TM/L	PCT	G	PO	A	E	DP	FR
1974	Cle-A	1.000	8	16	19	0	3	1
1975	Cle-A	.972	87	192	230	12	65	-14
1976	Cle-A	.987	128	300	365	9	92	20
1977	Cle-A	.985	148	334	449	12	104	2
1978	Cle-A	.979	149	341	408	16	91	-19
1979	Cle-A	.988	140	345	380	9	89	-4
1980	Cle-A	.995	42	87	111	1	28	-8
1981	Cle-A	.983	72	118	174	5	24	-6
1982	SF-N	.978	51	101	124	5	24	-7
1983	SF-N	.988	64	107	140	3	17	-8
1984	SF-N	.969	31	59	66	4	14	6
Total	11	.983	920	2000	2466	6	551	-37

1B

YEAR	TM/L	PCT	G	PO	A	E	DP	FR
1976	Cle-A	.920	5	21	2	2	3	0
1984	SF-N	1.000	1	3	0	0	0	0
Total	2	.929	6	24	2	2	3	0

■ Jeff Kunkel SS

YEAR	TM/L	PCT	G	PO	A	E	DP	FR
1984	Tex-A	.922	48	81	120	17	22	-1
1985	Tex-A	1.000	2	2	5	0	1	1
1986	Tex-A	.769	5	4	6	3	0	0
1987	Tex-A	—	1	0	0	0	0	0
1988	Tex-A	.969	19	28	34	2	8	5
1989	Tex-A	.936	59	68	150	15	21	4
1990	Tex-A	.958	67	77	126	9	28	6
Total	7	.938	201	260	441	6	80	15

2B

YEAR	TM/L	PCT	G	PO	A	E	DP	FR
1987	Tex-A	.955	10	17	25	2	8	3
1988	Tex-A	.949	28	42	70	6	15	3
1989	Tex-A	1.000	8	14	12	0	6	2
1990	Tex-A	1.000	13	12	18	0	3	2
Total	4	.963	59	85	125	8	32	10

OF

YEAR	TM/L	PCT	G	PO	A	E	DP	FR
1987	Tex-A	—	3	0	0	0	0	0
1988	Tex-A	1.000	6	4	0	0	0	0
1989	Tex-A	.952	30	59	1	3	0	1
1990	Tex-A	1.000	5	2	0	0	0	0
Total	4	.957	44	65	1	3	0	1

3B

YEAR	TM/L	PCT	G	PO	A	E	DP	FR
1987	Tex-A	1.000	3	1	2	0	0	0
1988	Tex-A	1.000	10	4	15	0	0	2
1989	Tex-A	.600	4	1	5	4	0	-1
1990	Tex-A	.950	15	10	28	2	3	2
Total	4	.917	32	16	50	6	3	3

1B

YEAR	TM/L	PCT	G	PO	A	E	DP	FR
1987	Tex-A	.500	1	1	0	1	0	0

■ Rusty Kuntz OF

YEAR	TM/L	PCT	G	PO	A	E	DP	FR
1979	Chi-A	1.000	5	12	1	0	1	2
1980	Chi-A	.979	34	45	2	1	1	2
1981	Chi-A	1.000	51	54	0	0	0	8
1982	Chi-A	1.000	21	21	0	0	0	0
1983	Chi-A	.976	27	40	0	1	0	2
	Min-A	.986	30	66	3	1	1	1
	Yr	.982	57	106	3	2	1	3
1984	Det-A	.987	67	74	2	1	1	0
Total	6	.988	235	312	8	4	4	15

1B

YEAR	TM/L	PCT	G	PO	A	E	DP	FR
1985	Det-A	.000	1	0	0	1	0	0

■ Whitey Kurowski 3B

YEAR	TM/L	PCT	G	PO	A	E	DP	FR
1941	StL-N	1.000	4	2	3	0	0	-1
1942	StL-N	.944	104	124	194	19	19	10
1943	StL-N	.952	137	166	255	21	29	1
1944	StL-N	.965	146	188	281	17	20	4
1945	StL-N	.964	131	172	235	15	28	3
1946	StL-N	.966	138	175	249	15	17	0
1947	StL-N	.954	141	140	250	19	17	-14
1948	StL-N	.939	65	55	100	10	7	-11
1949	StL-N	1.000	2	3	2	0	0	0
Total	9	.957	868	1025	1569	116	137	-8

SS

YEAR	TM/L	PCT	G	PO	A	E	DP	FR
1942	StL-N	—	1	0	0	0	0	0
1943	StL-N	1.000	2	1	2	0	0	0
1944	StL-N	1.000	1	0	2	0	0	0
1945	StL-N	.833	6	2	3	1	0	-1
Total	4	.909	10	3	7	1	0	-1

2B

YEAR	TM/L	PCT	G	PO	A	E	DP	FR
1944	StL-N	1.000	9	4	7	0	1	0

OF

YEAR	TM/L	PCT	G	PO	A	E	DP	FR
1942	StL-N	—	1	0	0	0	0	0

■ Craig Kusick 1B

YEAR	TM/L	PCT	G	PO	A	E	DP	FR
1973	Min-A	.989	11	86	5	1	7	0
1974	Min-A	.996	75	479	42	2	45	2
1975	Min-A	.990	51	372	31	4	45	1
1976	Min-A	.977	23	109	17	3	16	3
1977	Min-A	.972	23	133	7	4	9	-1
1978	Min-A	.987	27	213	22	3	14	3
1979	Min-A	1.000	8	46	3	0	6	0
	Tor-A	.978	20	163	15	4	14	1
	Yr	.983	28	209	18	4	20	1
Total	7	.988	238	1601	142	1	156	0

OF

YEAR	TM/L	PCT	G	PO	A	E	DP	FR
1973	Min-A	1.000	2	3	0	0	0	0
1978	Min-A	.938	9	15	0	1	0	-1
Total	2	.947	11	18	0	1	0	-1

■ Art Kusnyer C

YEAR	TM/L	PCT	G	PO	A	E	DP	FR
1970	Chi-A	.941	3	12	4	1	0	1
1971	Cal-A	.958	6	19	4	1	0	0
1972	Cal-A	.975	63	362	33	10	3	-1
1973	Cal-A	.979	41	130	13	3	2	1
1976	Mil-A	.938	14	41	4	3	2	0
1978	KC-A	.946	9	32	3	2	0	3
Total	6	.970	136	596	61	0	7	4

■ Randy Kutcher OF

YEAR	TM/L	PCT	G	PO	A	E	DP	FR
1986	SF-N	.990	51	99	3	1	1	3
1987	SF-N	1.000	6	8	0	0	0	1
1988	Bos-A	1.000	7	6	1	0	0	2
1989	Bos-A	.982	57	108	0	2	0	4
1990	Bos-A	1.000	34	41	0	0	0	4
Total	5	.989	155	262	4	3	1	14

3B

YEAR	TM/L	PCT	G	PO	A	E	DP	FR
1986	SF-N	—	4	0	0	0	0	0
1987	SF-N	1.000	2	2	1	0	0	0
1988	Bos-A	.800	2	0	4	1	0	1
1989	Bos-A	.917	6	3	8	1	0	1
1990	Bos-A	1.000	11	6	15	0	0	3
Total	5	.951	25	11	28	2	0	5

SS

YEAR	TM/L	PCT	G	PO	A	E	DP	FR
1986	SF-N	1.000	13	11	6	0	2	-1
1987	SF-N	1.000	1	0	1	0	0	0
Total	2	1.000	14	11	7	0	2	-1

2B

YEAR	TM/L	PCT	G	PO	A	E	DP	FR
1986	SF-N	1.000	3	1	2	0	0	0
1987	SF-N	1.000	2	4	3	0	1	1
1990	Bos-A	1.000	5	8	11	0	2	4
Total	3	1.000	10	13	16	0	3	5

C

YEAR	TM/L	PCT	G	PO	A	E	DP	FR
1989	Bos-A	1.000	1	1	0	0	0	0

■ Chet Laabs OF

YEAR	TM/L	PCT	G	PO	A	E	DP	FR
1937	Det-A	.971	62	133	2	4	0	-2
1938	Det-A	.971	53	128	4	4	1	3
1939	Det-A	.933	5	13	1	1	0	1
	StL-A	.972	79	199	7	6	0	-4
	Yr	.969	84	212	8	7	0	-3
1940	StL-A	.969	63	124	3	4	1	-5
1941	StL-A	.982	100	217	6	4	2	-2
1942	StL-A	.970	139	276	13	9	3	-2
1943	StL-A	.976	150	346	16	9	4	6
1944	StL-A	1.000	55	108	3	0	2	-3
1945	StL-A	.986	35	68	1	1	0	-2
1946	StL-A	.987	72	151	5	2	2	0
1947	Phi-A	.977	7	11	1	0	0	1
Total	11	.977	820	1780	62	4	15	-9

■ Coco Laboy 3B

YEAR	TM/L	PCT	G	PO	A	E	DP	FR
1969	Mon-N	.944	156	115	307	25	28	4
1970	Mon-N	.946	132	105	194	17	19	-5
1971	Mon-N	.937	65	37	67	7	4	2
1972	Mon-N	.889	24	16	33	4	2	1
1973	Mon-N	.889	20	13	19	4	2	1
Total	5	.944	397	286	620	57	55	0

2B

YEAR	TM/L	PCT	G	PO	A	E	DP	FR
1970	Mon-N	1.000	3	2	6	0	1	1
1971	Mon-N	1.000	2	3	1	0	0	0
1972	Mon-N	1.000	3	1	1	0	0	0
1973	Mon-N	—	1	0	0	0	0	0

YEAR	TM/L	PCT	G	PO	A	E	DP	FR
Total	4	1.000	9	6	8	0	1	1

SS

YEAR	TM/L	PCT	G	PO	A	E	DP	FR
1972	Mon-N	1.000	2	1	0	0	0	0

■ Candy LaChance 1B

YEAR	TM/L	PCT	G	PO	A	E	DP	FR
1894	Bro-N	.979	56	508	16	11	26	-6
1895	Bro-N	.983	125	1286	53	23	68	-5
1896	Bro-N	.986	89	956	37	14	62	-3
1897	Bro-N	.978	126	1289	64	30	76	-4
1898	Bro-N	.988	74	807	20	10	53	-5
1899	Bal-N	.984	125	1272	40	21	72	-7
1901	Cle-A	.979	133	1342	58	30	73	-3
1902	Bos-A	.983	138	1544	46	27	80	-11
1903	Bos-A	.984	141	1471	57	25	68	-11
1904	Bos-A	.992	157	1691	59	14	65	-14
1905	Bos-A	.988	12	154	7	2	6	0
Total	11	.984	1176	12320	457	207	649	-69

SS

YEAR	TM/L	PCT	G	PO	A	E	DP	FR
1898	Bro-N	.868	48	107	143	38	20	-12

OF

YEAR	TM/L	PCT	G	PO	A	E	DP	FR
1893	Bro-N	.833	5	5	0	1	0	-2
1894	Bro-N	1.000	3	2	0	0	0	-1
1895	Bro-N	.800	3	4	0	1	0	-1
1898	Bro-N	.952	13	20	0	1	0	-3
Total	4	.912	24	31	0	3	0	-7

C

YEAR	TM/L	PCT	G	PO	A	E	DP	FR
1893	Bro-N	.654	6	13	4	9	0	-4
1894	Bro-N	.818	10	15	3	4	0	-2
Total	2	.729	16	28	7	3	0	-6

■ Pete LaCock 1B

YEAR	TM/L	PCT	G	PO	A	E	DP	FR
1974	Chi-N	.991	11	98	10	1	5	1
1975	Chi-N	.988	53	453	43	6	39	4
1976	Chi-N	.975	54	435	30	12	47	-2
1977	KC-A	.990	29	186	17	2	16	1
1978	KC-A	.993	106	700	39	5	67	-6
1979	KC-A	.997	108	829	68	3	79	2
1980	KC-A	.997	86	267	21	1	27	2
Total	7	.991	447	2968	228	0	280	2

OF

YEAR	TM/L	PCT	G	PO	A	E	DP	FR
1972	Chi-N	1.000	3	2	0	0	0	0
1973	Chi-N	1.000	5	5	1	0	0	1
1974	Chi-N	.974	22	36	2	1	0	0
1975	Chi-N	1.000	26	26	2	0	0	1
1976	Chi-N	.957	19	19	3	1	0	1
1977	KC-A	1.000	12	17	2	0	0	1
1980	KC-A	.978	29	44	1	1	1	0
Total	7	.982	116	149	11	3	1	4

■ Leon Lacy OF

YEAR	TM/L	PCT	G	PO	A	E	DP	FR
1975	LA-N	.960	43	89	7	4	1	2
1976	Atl-N	1.000	5	6	0	0	0	0
	LA-N	.979	37	91	1	2	0	0
	Yr	.980	42	97	1	2	0	0
1977	LA-N	1.000	32	18	0	0	0	-2
1978	LA-N	.971	44	66	2	2	1	-2
1979	Pit-N	.973	41	70	3	2	0	-3
1980	Pit-N	.984	88	173	7	3	1	5
1981	Pit-N	.977	63	121	7	3	1	0
1982	Pit-N	.965	113	186	7	7	1	-5
1983	Pit-N	1.000	98	167	2	0	0	-4
1984	Pit-N	.996	127	268	15	1	4	14
1985	Bal-A	.984	115	231	9	4	0	0
1986	Bal-A	.992	120	239	8	2	4	2
1987	Bal-A	.973	80	135	11	4	2	2
Total	13	.983	1006	1860	79	4	15	9

2B

YEAR	TM/L	PCT	G	PO	A	E	DP	FR
1972	LA-N	.973	58	125	161	8	38	-8
1973	LA-N	.965	41	80	85	6	22	-1
1974	LA-N	.968	34	38	53	3	8	3
1975	LA-N	.935	43	62	68	9	10	-7
1976	Atl-N	.969	44	88	101	6	25	-8
	LA-N	1.000	2	5	2	0	0	0
	Yr	.970	46	93	103	6	25	-8
1977	LA-N	.978	22	33	57	2	11	-1
1978	LA-N	.938	24	46	45	6	5	-3
1979	Pit-N	.923	5	7	5	1	1	-2
1984	Pit-N	.875	2	4	3	1	0	-1
Total	9	.962	275	488	580	2	120	-28

3B

YEAR	TM/L	PCT	G	PO	A	E	DP	FR
1974	LA-N	—	1	0	0	0	0	0
1976	Atl-N	.500	1	0	1	1	0	0
	LA-N	1.000	3	3	6	0	3	1
	Yr	.909	4	3	7	1	3	1
1977	LA-N	.895	12	5	12	2	0	-1
1978	LA-N	.950	9	2	17	1	1	1
1980	Pit-N	1.000	3	2	4	0	0	0
1981	Pit-N	1.000	1	0	1	0	0	0
1982	Pit-N	1.000	2	0	2	0	0	0
Total	7	.932	32	12	43	4	4	1

SS

YEAR	TM/L	PCT	G	PO	A	E	DP	FR
1975	LA-N	1.000	1	1	0	0	0	0
1978	LA-N	—	1	0	0	0	0	0
Total	2	1.000	2	1	0	0	0	0

■ Mike Laga 1B

YEAR	TM/L	PCT	G	PO	A	E	DP	FR
1982	Det-A	.994	19	163	4	1	18	-2
1983	Det-A	1.000	5	9	1	0	2	0
1984	Det-A	1.000	4	12	1	0	1	0
1985	Det-A	.974	9	33	5	1	4	1
1986	Det-A	1.000	12	98	7	0	10	0
	StL-N	1.000	16	109	14	0	9	2
1987	StL-N	.973	12	66	7	2	10	1
1988	StL-N	1.000	37	293	17	0	26	1
1989	SF-N	—	4	16	1	0	0	0
1990	SF-N	1.000	10	33	5	0	4	1
Total	9	.996	123	832	62	4	84	4

■ Joe Lahoud OF

YEAR	TM/L	PCT	G	PO	A	E	DP	FR
1968	Bos-A	.926	25	23	2	2	0	-4
1969	Bos-A	.979	66	91	3	2	0	-3
1970	Bos-A	.963	13	23	3	1	0	2
1971	Bos-A	.993	69	139	4	1	3	2
1972	Mil-A	.974	97	189	2	5	0	-3
1973	Mil-A	1.000	40	85	2	0	1	4
1974	Cal-A	.976	106	156	6	4	2	-10
1975	Cal-A	1.000	29	41	1	0	0	-1
1976	Cal-A	.962	26	51	0	2	0	-2
	Tex-A	1.000	5	3	0	0	0	0
	Yr	.964	31	54	0	2	0	-2
1977	KC-A	.952	15	18	2	1	0	0
1978	KC-A	—	1	0	0	0	0	0
Total	11	.979	492	819	25	8	6	-15

1B

YEAR	TM/L	PCT	G	PO	A	E	DP	FR
1969	Bos-A	—	1	0	0	0	0	0

■ Nap Lajoie 2B

YEAR	TM/L	PCT	G	PO	A	E	DP	FR
1898	Phi-N	.949	146	442	406	46	59	-1
1899	Phi-N	.954	67	224	231	22	39	23
1900	Phi-N	.954	102	287	341	30	69	30
1901	Phi-A	.960	119	395	381	32	60	24
1902	Phi-A	1.000	1	2	3	0	0	0
	Cle-A	.974	86	270	283	15	49	30
	Yr	.974	87	272	286	15	49	30
1903	Cle-A	.955	122	366	402	36	61	39
1904	Cle-A	.962	95	272	255	21	42	6
1905	Cle-A	.991	59	148	177	3	25	9
1906	Cle-A	.973	130	354	415	21	76	26
1907	Cle-A	.969	128	314	461	25	86	43
1908	Cle-A	.964	156	450	538	37	78	48
1909	Cle-A	.959	120	282	373	28	55	19
1910	Cle-A	.966	149	387	419	28	60	16
1911	Cle-A	.948	37	91	93	10	16	-4
1912	Cle-A	.959	97	241	249	21	49	4
1913	Cle-A	.970	126	279	363	20	59	9
1914	Cle-A	.959	80	187	215	17	45	7
1915	Phi-A	.962	110	251	332	23	61	12
1916	Phi-A	.973	105	254	325	16	61	30
Total	19	.963	2035	5496	6262	451	1050	370

1B

YEAR	TM/L	PCT	G	PO	A	E	DP	FR
1896	Phi-N	.995	39	363	11	2	27	-3
1897	Phi-N	.984	108	1079	37	18	45	-9
1898	Phi-N	1.000	1	7	1	0	1	0
1903	Cle-A	1.000	1	11	0	0	0	0
1904	Cle-A	1.000	2	20	1	0	0	0
1905	Cle-A	1.000	5	50	2	0	0	0
1907	Cle-A	.991	9	95	11	1	1	2
1908	Cle-A	1.000	1	10	5	0	0	2
1909	Cle-A	1.000	8	89	3	0	5	0
1910	Cle-A	.984	10	114	8	2	3	1
1911	Cle-A	.990	41	388	16	4	17	-3
1912	Cle-A	.984	20	171	12	3	13	0
1914	Cle-A	.985	31	300	18	5	22	0
1915	Phi-A	.981	5	49	3	1	0	0
1916	Phi-A	.983	5	52	7	1	1	1
Total	15	.988	286	2798	135	7	137	-9

SS

YEAR	TM/L	PCT	G	PO	A	E	DP	FR
1901	Phi-A	.975	12	35	43	2	3	4
1904	Cle-A	.927	44	86	130	17	10	-6
1906	Cle-A	.951	7	15	24	2	2	1
1915	Phi-A	.958	10	14	32	2	5	1
Total	4	.943	73	150	229	3	20	0

OF

YEAR	TM/L	PCT	G	PO	A	E	DP	FR
1897	Phi-N	.956	19	37	6	2	0	3
1899	Phi-N	1.000	5	12	1	0	0	1
1916	Phi-A	1.000	2	1	0	0	0	0
Total	3	.966	26	50	7	2	0	3

3B

YEAR	TM/L	PCT	G	PO	A	E	DP	FR
1897	Phi-N	1.000	2	1	2	0	0	0
1900	Phi-N	—	1	0	1	0	0	0
1903	Cle-A	1.000	1	1	5	0	0	1
1906	Cle-A	.923	15	20	40	5	3	4
1915	Phi-A	1.000	2	4	6	0	1	1
Total	5	.940	21	26	53	5	4	6

■ Eddie Lake SS

YEAR	TM/L	PCT	G	PO	A	E	DP	FR
1939	StL-N	.857	2	3	3	1	1	-1
1940	StL-N	1.000	6	5	3	0	0	-1
1941	StL-N	.903	15	15	13	3	4	0
1943	Bos-A	.961	63	128	195	13	43	3
1944	Bos-A	.927	41	53	100	12	28	-6
1945	Bos-A	.948	130	265	459	40	112	20
1946	Det-A	.947	155	232	391	35	85	-21
1947	Det-A	.943	158	268	441	43	94	-29
1949	Det-A	.959	38	71	114	8	28	-3
1950	Det-A	—	1	0	0	0	0	0
Total	10	.947	609	1040	1719	155	395	-38

2B

YEAR	TM/L	PCT	G	PO	A	E	DP	FR
1940	StL-N	.957	17	30	36	3	4	-6
1941	StL-N	.786	5	5	6	3	1	0
1944	Bos-A	1.000	3	0	10	0	1	1
1945	Bos-A	—	1	0	0	0	0	0
1948	Det-A	.972	45	110	132	7	31	-1
1949	Det-A	.966	19	25	31	2	6	-4
Total	6	.962	90	170	215	5	43	-10

3B

YEAR	TM/L	PCT	G	PO	A	E	DP	FR
1941	StL-N	.950	15	20	37	3	6	6
1944	Bos-A	1.000	1	1	1	0	0	0
1948	Det-A	.964	17	12	15	1	0	-2
1949	Det-A	1.000	18	17	22	0	3	-2
1950	Det-A	—	1	0	0	0	0	0
Total	5	.969	52	50	75	4	9	2

■ Steve Lake C

YEAR	TM/L	PCT	G	PO	A	E	DP	FR
1983	Chi-N	1.000	32	115	22	0	3	4
1984	Chi-N	.955	24	72	13	4	0	0
1985	Chi-N	.995	55	182	25	1	1	6
1986	Chi-N	1.000	10	30	3	0	2	0
	StL-N	.976	26	75	6	2	1	1
	Yr	.983	36	105	9	2	3	1
1987	StL-N	.996	59	253	21	1	2	-2
1988	StL-N	.983	19	51	8	1	1	-1
1989	Phi-N	.990	55	262	33	3	3	2
1990	Phi-N	.993	28	115	19	1	1	4
Total	8	.990	308	1155	150	3	14	14

■ Al Lakeman C

YEAR	TM/L	PCT	G	PO	A	E	DP	FR
1942	Cin-N	.970	17	57	7	2	2	2
1943	Cin-N	1.000	21	55	8	0	2	-1
1945	Cin-N	.963	74	226	31	10	4	-10
1946	Cin-N	1.000	6	12	2	0	1	0
1947	Phi-N	.966	23	80	5	3	1	-3
1948	Phi-N	1.000	22	73	4	0	0	-2
1954	Det-A	1.000	4	10	0	0	0	1
Total	7	.974	167	513	57	5	10	-13

1B

YEAR	TM/L	PCT	G	PO	A	E	DP	FR
1947	Phi-N	.995	29	206	13	1	15	-1
1949	Bos-N	1.000	2	19	2	0	2	1
Total	2	.996	31	225	15	1	17	0

■ Dan Lally OF

YEAR	TM/L	PCT	G	PO	A	E	DP	FR
1891	Pit-N	.839	41	45	2	9	0	-7
1897	StL-N	.897	84	192	9	23	2	2
Total	2	.886	125	237	11	2	2	-5

1B

YEAR	TM/L	PCT	G	PO	A	E	DP	FR
1897	StL-N	.944	3	31	3	2	1	0

■ Ray Lamanno C

YEAR	TM/L	PCT	G	PO	A	E	DP	FR
1941	Cin-N	1.000	1	1	0	0	0	0
1942	Cin-N	.978	104	421	59	11	7	-10
1946	Cin-N	.974	61	222	37	7	6	2
1947	Cin-N	.986	109	556	62	9	6	8
1948	Cin-N	.978	125	537	49	13	11	-12
Total	5	.980	400	1737	207	0	30	-12

■ Bill Lamar OF

YEAR	TM/L	PCT	G	PO	A	E	DP	FR
1917	NY-A	1.000	11	26	1	0	0	0
1918	NY-A	.884	27	58	3	8	2	-2
1919	NY-A	1.000	3	4	0	0	0	-1
	Bos-A	.922	36	64	7	6	1	-2
	Yr	.926	39	68	7	6	1	-3
1920	Bro-N	1.000	12	12	1	0	0	-1
1921	Bro-N	—	1	0	0	0	0	0
1924	Phi-A	.971	87	187	13	6	4	4
1925	Phi-A	.953	131	283	18	15	4	4
1926	Phi-A	.954	107	199	10	10	2	-3
1927	Phi-A	.952	79	148	9	8	1	-3
Total	9	.952	494	981	62	3	14	-4

1B

YEAR	TM/L	PCT	G	PO	A	E	DP	FR
1919	NY-A	1.000	1	1	0	0	0	0

■ Bobby LaMotte SS

YEAR	TM/L	PCT	G	PO	A	E	DP	FR
1920	Was-A	.750	1	0	3	1	0	0
1921	Was-A	.940	12	20	43	4	1	1
1922	Was-A	1.000	6	11	9	0	0	-5
1925	StL-A	.926	93	220	270	39	67	-2
1926	StL-A	.919	30	47	66	10	15	-2
Total	5	.927	142	298	391	4	83	-4

3B

YEAR	TM/L	PCT	G	PO	A	E	DP	FR
1920	Was-A	1.000	1	0	1	0	0	0
1922	Was-A	.954	62	91	139	11	10	13
1925	StL-A	1.000	3	5	0	0	0	0
1926	StL-A	—	1	0	0	0	0	0
Total	4	.956	67	94	145	1	10	13

■ Grover Land C

YEAR	TM/L	PCT	G	PO	A	E	DP	FR
1908	Cle-A	.955	8	18	3	1	0	-1
1910	Cle-A	.982	33	169	47	4	3	6
1911	Cle-A	.961	34	146	50	8	5	1
1913	Cle-A	.924	17	83	26	9	3	0
1914	Bro-F	.970	97	490	147	20	11	0
1915	Bro-F	.960	81	314	114	18	13	-5
Total	6	.964	270	1220	387	0	35	1

1B

YEAR	TM/L	PCT	G	PO	A	E	DP	FR
1911	Cle-A	1.000	1	2	0	0	0	0

■ Rafael Landestoy 2B

YEAR	TM/L	PCT	G	PO	A	E	DP	FR
1977	LA-N	1.000	8	5	12	0	2	2
1978	Hou-N	1.000	2	1	0	0	1	0
1979	Hou-N	.971	114	166	234	12	53	-2
1980	Hou-N	.991	94	97	134	2	33	0
1981	Hou-N	.966	31	52	63	4	11	-4
	Cin-N	1.000	3	3	1	0	0	0
	Yr	.967	34	55	64	4	11	-4
1982	Cin-N	1.000	16	27	23	0	4	2
1983	LA-N	1.000	14	15	21	0	6	3
1984	LA-N	.886	14	15	16	4	4	2
Total	8	.976	296	381	504	2	114	3

SS

YEAR	TM/L	PCT	G	PO	A	E	DP	FR
1977	LA-N	1.000	3	3	6	0	0	0
1978	Hou-N	.980	50	65	132	4	18	-13
1979	Hou-N	—	3	2	3	0	1	0
1980	Hou-N	.972	65	87	157	7	34	-6
1982	Cin-N	—	2	0	0	0	0	0
1983	LA-N	1.000	2	0	0	0	0	0
Total	6	.976	124	157	300	1	53	-19

3B

YEAR	TM/L	PCT	G	PO	A	E	DP	FR
1980	Hou-N	1.000	3	1	4	0	0	0
1982	Cin-N	1.000	21	12	31	0	7	3
1983	Cin-N	—	1	0	0	0	0	0
	LA-N	.909	10	5	5	1	0	1
	Yr	.909	11	5	5	1	0	1
1984	LA-N	.833	12	3	8	2	1	1
Total	4	.958	46	20	48	3	8	5

OF

YEAR	TM/L	PCT	G	PO	A	E	DP	FR
1978	Hou-N	1.000	3	4	0	0	0	0
1982	Cin-N	1.000	3	2	0	0	0	0
1983	Cin-N	.000	1	0	0	1	0	0
	LA-N	.889	10	8	0	1	0	0

YEAR	TM/L	PCT	G	PO	A	E	DP	FR
	Yr	.800	11	8	0	2	0	0
1984	LA-N	1.000	5	5	0	0	0	0
Total	4	.905	22	19	0	2	0	0
	1B							
1983	Cin-N	1.000	2	6	0	0	1	0

■ Jim Landis OF

YEAR	TM/L	PCT	G	PO	A	E	DP	FR
1957	Chi-A	.985	90	192	8	3	**4**	6
1958	Chi-A	.986	142	331	9	5	1	1
1959	Chi-A	.993	148	**420**	10	3	2	9
1960	Chi-A	.985	147	372	13	6	3	6
1961	Chi-A	.988	139	389	9	5	3	13
1962	Chi-A	.995	144	360	2	2	1	3
1963	Chi-A	**.993**	124	264	6	2	0	-6
1964	Chi-A	.995	101	183	7	1	2	-10
1965	KC-A	.985	108	258	0	4	0	2
1966	Cle-A	1.000	61	86	0	0	0	2
1967	Det-A	.952	12	18	2	1	0	1
	Bos-A	1.000	5	4	0	0	0	0
	Hou-N	1.000	44	50	6	0	1	-1
	Yr	.987	56	68	8	1	1	0
Total	11	.989	1265	2927	72	2	17	26

■ Ken Landreaux OF

YEAR	TM/L	PCT	G	PO	A	E	DP	FR
1977	Cal-A	.970	22	59	5	2	2	6
1978	Cal-A	.986	83	138	6	2	0	0
1979	Min-A	.981	147	292	10	6	1	-20
1980	Min-A	.976	120	231	8	6	0	-18
1981	LA-N	**1.000**	95	210	4	0	0	-8
1982	LA-N	.986	117	281	3	4	1	-4
1983	LA-N	.990	137	299	4	3	1	-8
1984	LA-N	.986	129	212	3	3	2	-22
1985	LA-N	.975	140	267	4	7	1	-15
1986	LA-N	.955	85	145	5	7	0	-2
1987	LA-N	.951	63	72	5	4	3	1
Total	11	.981	1138	2206	57	4	11	-90

■ Hobie Landrith C

YEAR	TM/L	PCT	G	PO	A	E	DP	FR
1950	Cin-N	1.000	4	15	2	0	0	-1
1951	Cin-N	1.000	4	23	2	0	0	1
1952	Cin-N	1.000	14	56	7	0	0	0
1953	Cin-N	.985	47	179	13	3	4	0
1954	Cin-N	.986	42	123	15	2	1	4
1955	Cin-N	1.000	27	86	14	0	3	3
1956	Chi-N	.975	99	483	55	**14**	9	-2
1957	StL-N	.987	67	339	29	5	3	5
1958	StL-N	.992	45	227	16	2	3	2
1959	SF-N	.992	109	576	45	5	5	6
1960	SF-N	.966	70	346	23	**13**	5	-5
1961	SF-N	.985	30	126	9	2	2	1
1962	NY-N	.968	21	87	3	3	0	0
	Bal-A	.982	60	289	34	6	5	5
1963	Bal-A	1.000	1	1	0	0	0	0
	Was-A	.978	37	160	17	4	3	2
	Yr	.978	38	161	17	4	3	2
Total	14	.983	677	3116	284	9	43	21

■ Don Landrum OF

YEAR	TM/L	PCT	G	PO	A	E	DP	FR
1957	Phi-N	1.000	2	9	0	0	0	1
1960	StL-N	1.000	13	34	1	0	0	1
1961	StL-N	1.000	25	42	3	0	1	3
1962	StL-N	1.000	26	19	0	0	0	0
	Chi-N	.969	59	122	3	4	3	1
	Yr	.973	85	141	3	4	3	1
1963	Chi-N	.972	57	100	3	3	0	-1
1964	Chi-N	1.000	1	1	1	0	0	1
1965	Chi-N	.988	115	241	3	3	0	-4
1966	SF-N	.968	54	55	6	2	0	5
Total	8	.982	352	623	20	2	4	7
	2B							
1961	StL-N	—	1	0	0	0	0	0

■ Tito Landrum OF

YEAR	TM/L	PCT	G	PO	A	E	DP	FR
1980	StL-N	.976	29	40	1	1	0	-1
1981	StL-N	1.000	67	72	6	0	1	4
1982	StL-N	1.000	56	50	2	0	1	5
1983	StL-N	1.000	5	1	0	0	0	0
	Bal-A	1.000	26	39	0	0	0	1
1984	StL-N	.979	88	93	1	2	0	0
1985	StL-N	1.000	73	91	2	0	1	3
1986	StL-N	.993	78	131	6	1	1	7
1987	StL-N	1.000	23	41	1	0	0	3
	LA-N	.971	31	32	1	1	0	1
	Yr	.987	54	73	2	1	0	4
1988	Bal-A	1.000	12	15	0	0	0	0
Total	9	.992	488	605	20	5	4	21
	1B							
1987	StL-N	1.000	1	4	0	0	0	0

■ Don Lang 3B

YEAR	TM/L	PCT	G	PO	A	E	DP	FR
1938	Cin-N	.976	15	15	25	1	3	3
1948	StL-N	.964	95	81	188	10	13	9
Total	2	.966	110	96	213	1	16	12
	2B							
1938	Cin-N	1.000	1	1	0	0	0	0
1948	StL-N	.889	2	5	3	1	2	0
Total	2	.900	3	6	3	1	2	0
	SS							
1938	Cin-N	.667	1	1	1	1	0	-1

■ Bill Lange OF

YEAR	TM/L	PCT	G	PO	A	E	DP	FR
1893	Chi-N	.954	40	97	7	5	1	2
1894	Chi-N	.910	109	267	25	29	10	6
1895	Chi-N	.924	123	298	28	27	6	10
1896	Chi-N	.932	121	313	18	24	3	10
1897	Chi-N	.946	118	264	17	16	4	2
1898	Chi-N	.970	111	269	19	9	4	10
1899	Chi-N	.976	94	224	22	6	11	13
Total	7	.942	716	1732	136	116	39	53
	2B							
1893	Chi-N	.888	57	151	181	42	21	-6

YEAR	TM/L	PCT	G	PO	A	E	DP	FR
	1B							
1898	Chi-N	1.000	2	17	0	0	1	0
1899	Chi-N	.968	14	149	4	5	9	-1
Total	2	.971	16	166	4	5	10	-1
	3B							
1893	Chi-N	.907	8	14	25	4	3	3
1894	Chi-N	.500	1	2	1	3	0	-1
Total	2	.857	9	16	26	7	3	2
	SS							
1893	Chi-N	.878	7	18	25	6	2	1
1894	Chi-N	.500	2	1	3	4	0	-1
Total	2	.825	9	19	28	0	2	0
	C							
1893	Chi-N	.921	7	23	12	3	1	2
1896	Chi-N	1.000	1	1	0	0	0	0
Total	2	.923	8	24	12	3	1	2

■ Sam Langford OF

YEAR	TM/L	PCT	G	PO	A	E	DP	FR
1927	Cle-A	1.000	20	39	1	0	0	-2
1928	Cle-A	.972	107	239	5	7	2	-8
Total	2	.976	127	278	6	7	2	-10

■ Hal Lanier SS

YEAR	TM/L	PCT	G	PO	A	E	DP	FR
1964	SF-N	1.000	3	2	4	0	0	0
1965	SF-N	—	1	0	0	0	0	0
1966	SF-N	.952	41	49	110	8	14	6
1967	SF-N	.974	137	197	440	17	73	24
1968	SF-N	**.979**	150	**282**	496	17	72	14
1969	SF-N	.969	150	252	530	25	98	**29**
1970	SF-N	.967	130	256	397	22	83	12
1971	SF-N	.968	8	11	19	1	6	2
1972	NY-A	.943	9	10	23	2	5	1
1973	NY-A	.960	26	32	64	4	13	-1
Total	10	.971	655	1091	2083	6	364	87
	2B							
1964	SF-N	.979	98	224	294	11	48	10
1965	SF-N	.976	158	294	445	18	75	-5
1966	SF-N	.991	112	254	313	5	66	22
1967	SF-N	.978	34	56	79	3	19	5
1970	SF-N	1.000	4	3	1	0	1	0
1971	SF-N	1.000	13	30	31	0	6	4
1972	NY-A	1.000	3	7	8	0	1	1
1973	NY-A	1.000	8	13	17	0	3	2
Total	8	.982	430	881	1188	7	219	39
	3B							
1971	SF-N	.957	83	33	79	5	6	-1
1972	NY-A	.973	47	15	56	2	7	6
1973	NY-A	—	1	0	0	0	0	0
Total	3	.963	131	48	135	7	13	5
	1B							
1970	SF-N	1.000	2	4	1	0	1	0
1971	SF-N	1.000	3	17	1	0	1	0
Total	2	1.000	5	21	2	0	2	0

■ Carney Lansford 3B

YEAR	TM/L	PCT	G	PO	A	E	DP	FR
1978	Cal-A	.942	117	93	182	17	18	-25
1979	Cal-A	**.983**	**157**	**135**	263	7	29	-24
1980	Cal-A	.955	150	**151**	250	19	29	-24
1981	Bos-A	.951	86	70	180	13	17	0
1982	Bos-A	.968	114	83	216	10	19	-13
1983	Oak-A	.957	78	60	163	10	19	-6
1984	Oak-A	.957	151	137	268	18	27	-8
1985	Oak-A	.976	97	85	119	5	11	-31
1986	Oak-A	.982	100	67	147	4	13	-12
1987	Oak-A	**.980**	142	98	249	7	15	-5
1988	Oak-A	**.979**	143	113	220	7	16	-12
1989	Oak-A	.957	136	104	183	13	11	-25
1990	Oak-A	**.970**	126	100	194	9	22	-20
Total	13	.966	1597	1296	2634	139	246	205
	1B							
1986	Oak-A	.995	60	413	22	2	24	-7
1987	Oak-A	1.000	17	58	9	0	5	2
1988	Oak-A	1.000	9	12	1	0	2	0
1989	Oak-A	1.000	15	91	5	0	9	-1
1990	Oak-A	1.000	5	28	1	0	2	-1
Total	5	.997	106	602	38	2	42	-7
	SS							
1978	Cal-A	.833	2	1	4	1	0	-1
1983	Oak-A	—	1	0	0	0	0	0
Total	2	.833	3	1	4	1	0	-1
	2B							
1986	Oak-A	1.000	1	0	1	0	0	0
1988	Oak-A	—	1	0	0	0	0	0
Total	2	1.000	2	0	1	0	0	0

■ Frank LaPorte 2B

YEAR	TM/L	PCT	G	PO	A	E	DP	FR
1905	NY-A	.918	11	19	26	4	4	-3
1906	NY-A	1.000	5	10	18	0	5	3
1908	Bos-A	.950	27	39	94	7	6	8
	NY-A	.934	26	51	77	9	10	-2
	Yr	.942	53	90	171	16	16	6
1909	NY-A	.938	83	142	208	23	30	-15
1910	NY-A	.959	79	127	220	15	21	-8
1911	StL-A	.950	**133**	287	**398**	**36**	**59**	-7
1912	StL-A	.944	39	83	102	11	20	-1
	Was-A	.939	37	60	108	11	10	3
	Yr	.941	76	143	210	22	30	2
1913	Was-A	.976	13	20	20	1	4	-1
1914	Ind-F	.956	132	300	373	31	61	6
1915	New-F	.960	**146**	**330**	**431**	32	**69**	5
Total	10	.952	731	1468	2075	180	299	-12
	3B							
1906	NY-A	.904	114	118	210	35	11	-9
1907	NY-A	.896	64	65	115	21	4	-7
1908	Bos-A	.977	12	22	20	1	1	2
1910	NY-A	.974	15	15	22	1	0	-2
1911	StL-A	1.000	3	2	11	0	0	2
1913	Was-A	.952	46	47	91	7	8	3

YEAR	TM/L	PCT	G	PO	A	E	DP	FR
Total	6	.919	254	269	469	5	24	-11
	OF							
1906	NY-A	1.000	1	5	1	0	0	1
1907	NY-A	.913	63	84	10	9	0	-3
1908	Bos-A	.857	5	5	1	1	0	0
	NY-A	.923	11	12	0	1	0	-2
	Yr	.900	16	17	1	2	0	-2
1910	NY-A	.881	23	33	4	5	0	-1
1912	StL-A	.900	32	40	5	5	4	-2
1913	Was-A	.950	12	16	3	1	1	1
Total	6	.909	147	195	24	2	5	-6
	1B							
1907	NY-A	1.000	1	8	0	0	2	0

■ Jack Lapp C

YEAR	TM/L	PCT	G	PO	A	E	DP	FR
1908	Phi-A	.947	13	55	16	4	0	-1
1909	Phi-A	.938	19	95	26	8	2	2
1910	Phi-A	.980	63	361	88	9	6	7
1911	Phi-A	.972	57	270	47	9	8	-8
1912	Phi-A	.958	83	354	105	20	10	-14
1913	Phi-A	.968	78	313	110	14	3	-14
1914	Phi-A	.977	67	330	88	10	4	-7
1915	Phi-A	.967	89	376	115	17	**23**	-3
1916	Chi-A	.989	34	131	41	2	2	0
Total	9	.969	503	2285	636	3	58	-38
	1B							
1911	Phi-A	1.000	4	26	4	0	0	1
1913	Phi-A	1.000	1	2	0	0	2	0
1915	Phi-A	.980	12	94	3	2	0	-1
Total	3	.985	17	122	7	2	2	0

■ Norm Larker 1B

YEAR	TM/L	PCT	G	PO	A	E	DP	FR
1958	LA-N	.980	35	178	14	4	18	-1
1959	LA-N	.990	55	456	42	5	53	3
1960	LA-N	.993	119	914	80	7	81	4
1961	LA-N	.995	86	589	52	3	68	2
1962	Hou-N	.991	135	1148	103	11	103	**7**
1963	Mil-N	.992	42	320	33	3	23	3
	SF-N	.929	11	24	2	2	3	0
	Yr	.987	53	344	35	5	26	3
Total	6	.991	483	3629	326	5	349	18
	OF							
1958	LA-N	.985	43	61	3	1	0	-4
1959	LA-N	1.000	30	35	6	0	0	2
1960	LA-N	1.000	2	3	0	0	0	0
1961	LA-N	—	1	0	0	0	0	0
1962	Hou-N	1.000	6	5	0	0	0	0
Total	5	.991	82	104	9	1	0	-2

■ Barry Larkin SS

YEAR	TM/L	PCT	G	PO	A	E	DP	FR
1986	Cin-N	.976	36	47	119	4	21	0
1987	Cin-N	.965	119	168	358	19	72	0
1988	Cin-N	.960	148	231	470	**29**	67	10
1989	Cin-N	.976	82	142	267	10	31	**16**
1990	Cin-N	.977	156	254	**469**	17	**86**	**20**
Total	5	.970	541	842	1683	9	277	46
	2B							
1986	Cin-N	1.000	3	4	6	0	1	0

■ Gene Larkin 1B

YEAR	TM/L	PCT	G	PO	A	E	DP	FR
1987	Min-A	.989	26	165	10	2	12	-2
1988	Min-A	.994	60	466	28	3	46	-5
1989	Min-A	.992	67	463	28	4	45	-5
1990	Min-A	.992	28	222	13	2	28	-3
Total	4	.992	181	1316	79	1	131	-15
	OF							
1989	Min-A	1.000	32	61	0	0	0	-1
1990	Min-A	1.000	47	77	5	0	1	-1
Total	2	1.000	79	138	5	0	1	-2

■ Henry Larkin 1B

YEAR	TM/L	PCT	G	PO	A	E	DP	FR
1887	Phi-a	.976	23	195	6	5	12	0
1888	Phi-a	.967	122	1222	36	**43**	44	-5
1889	Phi-a	.973	131	1230	37	35	**88**	-3
1890	Cle-P	.978	125	1268	40	30	63	-8
1891	Phi-a	.974	111	987	33	27	56	-5
1892	Was-N	.969	117	1121	69	38	77	2
1893	Was-N	.963	81	781	29	31	48	-9
Total	7	.971	710	6804	250	209	388	-28
	OF							
1884	Phi-a	.856	85	106	7	19	0	-7
1885	Phi-a	.882	108	208	23	31	**9**	12
1886	Phi-a	.866	**139**	264	21	44	2	-5
1887	Phi-a	.895	93	183	14	23	0	2
1890	Cle-P	—	1	0	0	0	0	-1
1891	Phi-a	.915	23	42	1	4	0	-1
1892	Was-N	.500	2	1	1	1	0	-1
Total	7	.877	451	804	66	122	11	-3
	2B							
1884	Phi-a	.833	2	1	4	1	1	0
1887	Phi-a	.890	10	38	27	8	11	1
1888	Phi-a	.851	14	41	33	13	7	-3
1889	Phi-a	.667	1	3	1	2	1	-1
Total	4	.860	27	83	65	4	20	-3
	3B							
1889	Phi-a	.500	1	0	1	0	1	0

■ Lyn Lary SS

YEAR	TM/L	PCT	G	PO	A	E	DP	FR
1929	NY-A	.962	14	26	51	3	9	3
1930	NY-A	.940	113	224	324	35	58	-8
1931	NY-A	.946	**155**	321	484	46	85	9
1932	NY-A	.941	80	152	218	23	39	3
1933	NY-A	.952	16	12	28	2	4	0
1934	Bos-A	**.965**	129	260	396	24	66	-5
1935	Was-A	.953	30	63	78	7	13	-4
	StL-A	.962	93	258	306	22	66	13
	Yr	.960	**123**	**321**	**384**	29	79	9
1936	StL-A	.956	155	339	495	38	88	-3
1937	Cle-A	.963	**156**	325	489	31	95	6
1938	Cle-A	.964	141	296	399	26	88	0

YEAR	TM/L	PCT	G	PO	A	E	DP	FR
1939	Cle-A	.000	2	0	0	1	0	-1
	Bro-N	.947	12	19	17	2	5	2
	StL-N	.961	30	51	71	5	9	-5
	Yr	.958	42	70	88	7	14	-3
1940	StL-A	.952	12	27	32	3	7	1
Total	12	.956	1138	2373	3388	268	632	11
3B								
1929	NY-A	.943	55	38	95	8	10	2
1932	NY-A	.714	2	2	3	2	1	-1
1933	NY-A	.938	28	32	44	5	5	2
1939	Bro-N	.867	7	6	7	2	0	0
	StL-N	1.000	3	1	0	0	0	0
	Yr	.875	10	7	7	2	0	0
Total	4	.931	95	79	149	7	16	3
1B								
1932	NY-A	1.000	5	26	1	0	2	0
1933	NY-A	1.000	3	11	0	0	1	0
1934	NY-A	.800	1	4	0	1	1	0
Total	3	.977	9	41	1	1	4	0
2B								
1929	NY-A	1.000	2	1	0	0	0	0
1932	NY-A	1.000	2	0	1	0	0	0
1940	StL-A	1.000	1	2	1	0	0	0
Total	3	1.000	5	3	2	0	0	0
OF								
1932	NY-A	—	1	0	0	0	0	0
1933	NY-A	—	1	0	0	0	0	0
Total	2	—	2	0	0	0	0	0

■ Juice Latham 1B

YEAR	TM/L	PCT	G	PO	A	E	DP	FR
1877	Lou-N	.950	59	659	**24**	**36**	**28**	1
1882	Phi-a	**.972**	74	792	12	23	28	0
1883	Lou-a	.956	67	625	21	30	40	2
1884	Lou-a	.961	76	788	32	33	48	3
Total	4	.960	276	2864	89	122	144	6
2B								
1883	Lou-a	.854	14	39	43	14	7	-1
SS								
1883	Lou-a	.688	9	4	18	10	2	-4
3B								
1884	Lou-a	1.000	1	2	0	0	0	0

■ Arlie Latham 3B

YEAR	TM/L	PCT	G	PO	A	E	DP	FR
1883	StL-a	.866	**98**	120	256	58	**14**	22
1884	StL-a	.864	110	142	**302**	**70**	**16**	**40**
1885	StL-a	.875	109	112	**217**	47	16	1
1886	StL-a	.827	133	138	284	**88**	22	0
1887	StL-a	.877	132	155	288	62	17	3
1888	StL-a	.882	133	178	287	62	19	3
1889	StL-a	.883	116	197	249	59	22	11
1890	Chi-P	.880	52	65	119	25	9	3
	Cin-N	.853	41	54	103	27	10	6
1891	Cin-N	.879	135	177	**370**	**75**	**24**	**21**
1892	Cin-N	.883	**142**	167	329	66	26	-4
1893	Cin-N	.892	127	172	281	55	23	-11
1894	Cin-N	.860	127	158	248	**66**	20	-11
1895	Cin-N	.861	108	126	197	52	13	-15
1896	StL-N	.744	8	14	15	10	2	-1
Total	14	.870	1571	1975	3545	822	253	68
2B								
1886	StL-a	1.000	1	1	6	0	0	0
1887	StL-a	.867	5	12	14	4	2	-2
1889	StL-a	1.000	3	7	7	0	1	0
1892	Cin-N	.909	9	25	25	5	3	0
1894	Cin-N	.923	2	5	7	1	3	1
1895	Cin-N	.000	1	0	0	1	0	-1
1899	Was-N	1.000	1	1	0	0	1	0
1909	NY-N	1.000	2	0	2	0	0	0
Total	8	.911	24	51	61	1	10	-2
SS								
1880	Buf-N	.887	12	12	35	6	1	-1
1888	StL-a	—	1	0	0	0	0	0
Total	2	.887	13	12	35	6	1	-1
OF								
1880	Buf-N	.944	10	17	0	1	0	-1
1892	Cin-N	—	1	0	0	0	0	0
1899	Was-N	1.000	1	1	0	0	0	0
Total	3	.947	12	18	0	1	0	-1
C								
1880	Buf-N	1.000	1	2	1	0	0	0
1883	StL-a	—	1	0	0	0	0	0
1884	StL-a	—	1	0	0	0	0	0
1885	StL-a	.846	2	4	7	2	0	1
1887	StL-a	1.000	2	2	3	0	0	1
1891	Cin-N	—	1	0	0	0	0	0
Total	6	.905	8	8	11	2	0	2
1B								
1895	Cin-N	.900	3	15	3	2	3	0

■ Charlie Lau C

YEAR	TM/L	PCT	G	PO	A	E	DP	FR
1956	Det-A	1.000	3	17	0	0	0	1
1958	Det-A	.985	27	120	10	2	3	1
1959	Det-A	1.000	2	11	1	0	1	1
1960	Mil-N	1.000	16	94	11	0	2	5
1961	Mil-N	.968	25	114	7	4	2	-3
	Bal-A	.990	17	90	6	1	2	5
1962	Bal-A	.996	56	269	15	1	1	-4
1963	Bal-A	.964	8	48	5	2	1	1
	KC-A	.982	50	258	15	5	2	-10
	Yr	.979	58	306	20	7	3	-9
1964	KC-A	.990	35	179	12	2	0	-7
	Bal-A	.992	47	243	13	2	2	-3
	Yr	.991	82	422	25	4	2	-10
1965	Bal-A	.989	35	165	9	2	1	-7
Total	9	.988	321	1608	104	1	17	-20

■ Billy Lauder 3B

YEAR	TM/L	PCT	G	PO	A	E	DP	FR
1898	Phi-N	.866	97	132	171	47	6	-16
1899	Phi-N	.893	151	210	307	62	22	-14

YEAR	TM/L	PCT	G	PO	A	E	DP	FR
1901	Phi-A	.833	2	4	6	2	0	1
1902	NY-N	.907	121	189	251	45	17	3
1903	NY-N	.908	108	140	194	34	10	-6
Total	5	.894	479	675	929	190	55	-32
OF								
1902	NY-N	1.000	4	6	1	0	0	0

■ Tim Laudner C

YEAR	TM/L	PCT	G	PO	A	E	DP	FR
1981	Min-A	1.000	12	49	5	0	0	0
1982	Min-A	.976	93	454	41	**12**	5	-15
1983	Min-A	.986	57	259	22	4	5	5
1984	Min-A	.978	81	362	38	9	2	8
1985	Min-A	.969	68	233	19	8	3	-5
1986	Min-A	.984	68	299	13	5	3	-15
1987	Min-A	.987	101	517	28	7	2	-7
1988	Min-A	.992	109	621	35	5	8	0
1989	Min-A	.991	68	328	16	3	3	0
Total	9	.984	657	3122	217	3	31	-29
1B								
1985	Min-A	1.000	1	3	0	0	0	0
1987	Min-A	1.000	7	30	1	0	3	0
1988	Min-A	1.000	3	3	0	0	0	0
1989	Min-A	1.000	11	19	0	0	2	0
Total	4	1.000	22	55	1	0	5	0

■ Cookie Lavagetto 3B

YEAR	TM/L	PCT	G	PO	A	E	DP	FR
1935	Pit-N	.886	15	8	23	4	0	-2
1936	Pit-N	.913	15	15	21	4	0	0
1937	Bro-N	.955	45	52	74	6	8	2
1938	Bro-N	.929	132	136	229	**28**	**26**	-12
1939	Bro-N	.948	149	163	278	24	28	-5
1940	Bro-N	.932	116	137	191	**24**	12	-14
1941	Bro-N	.938	120	117	215	22	17	-20
1946	Bro-N	.927	67	70	108	14	11	-5
1947	Bro-N	.961	18	20	29	2	3	3
Total	9	.936	675	718	1168	128	105	-53
2B								
1934	Pit-N	.961	83	214	234	18	39	-14
1935	Pit-N	.951	42	92	120	11	10	-10
1936	Pit-N	.951	37	85	110	10	24	0
1937	Pit-N	.949	100	229	294	28	56	-9
1938	Bro-N	1.000	4	6	11	0	2	1
Total	5	.954	266	626	769	7	131	-32
1B								
1947	Bro-N	1.000	3	20	2	0	0	0
SS								
1936	Pit-N	.333	1	0	1	2	1	-1

■ Mike LaValliere C

YEAR	TM/L	PCT	G	PO	A	E	DP	FR
1984	Phi-N	1.000	6	20	2	0	0	2
1985	StL-N	1.000	12	48	5	0	3	-2
1986	StL-N	.988	108	468	47	6	8	1
1987	Pit-N	.992	112	584	70	5	11	6
1988	Pit-N	.987	114	565	55	8	6	-1
1989	Pit-N	.991	65	306	24	3	3	-7
1990	Pit-N	.990	95	478	36	5	6	1
Total	7	.990	512	2469	239	7	37	0

■ Doc Lavan SS

YEAR	TM/L	PCT	G	PO	A	E	DP	FR
1913	StL-A	.899	46	82	141	25	24	-5
	Phi-A	1.000	5	6	12	0	0	0
	Yr	.906	51	88	153	25	24	-5
1914	StL-A	.916	74	178	193	34	17	-12
1915	StL-A	.913	**157**	313	475	**75**	**81**	5
1916	StL-A	.950	106	217	386	32	52	**34**
1917	StL-A	.923	110	229	338	47	67	12
1918	Was-A	.917	117	275	354	**57**	43	-10
1919	StL-N	.929	99	207	352	43	49	9
1920	StL-N	.942	138	327	489	**50**	77	16
1921	StL-N	.950	150	382	540	**49**	88	**19**
1922	StL-N	.937	82	169	246	28	39	14
1923	StL-N	.924	40	64	95	13	20	1
1924	StL-N	.818	2	2	7	2	2	1
Total	12	.930	1126	2451	3628	455	559	84
2B								
1917	StL-A	.912	7	15	16	3	3	0
1923	StL-N	—	1	0	0	0	0	0
1924	StL-N	1.000	2	1	3	0	0	0
Total	3	.921	10	16	19	3	3	0
3B								
1922	StL-N	.882	5	3	12	2	1	1
1923	StL-N	1.000	4	5	8	0	0	1
Total	2	.933	9	8	20	2	1	2
1B								
1923	StL-N	.938	3	14	1	1	1	0
OF								
1918	Was-A	—	1	0	0	0	0	-1

■ Rudy Law OF

YEAR	TM/L	PCT	G	PO	A	E	DP	FR
1978	LA-N	1.000	6	3	0	0	0	0
1980	LA-N	.988	106	233	6	3	3	-8
1982	Chi-A	.973	94	215	2	6	0	-10
1983	Chi-A	**.994**	132	302	5	2	2	-8
1984	Chi-A	.985	130	322	5	5	2	-10
1985	Chi-A	.987	120	226	7	3	3	-1
1986	KC-A	.987	77	145	2	2	0	-5
Total	7	.986	665	1446	27	1	10	-42

■ Vance Law 3B

YEAR	TM/L	PCT	G	PO	A	E	DP	FR
1980	Pit-N	—	1	0	0	0	0	0
1981	Pit-N	1.000	2	2	0	0	0	0
1982	Chi-A	.937	39	19	55	5	3	-6
1983	Chi-A	.966	139	91	309	14	28	9
1984	Chi-A	.955	137	79	199	13	24	-15
1985	Mon-N	.969	11	8	23	1	2	2
1986	Mon-N	1.000	13	9	5	0	1	0
1987	Chi-N	.971	22	11	22	1	2	0
1988	Chi-N	.953	150	111	272	19	22	-11
1989	Chi-N	.949	119	76	168	13	13	-18
Total	10	.957	633	406	1053	6	95	-42

YEAR	TM/L	PCT	G	PO	A	E	DP	FR
2B								
1980	Pit-N	.964	11	23	30	2	5	-2
1981	Pit-N	1.000	19	40	45	0	9	3
1982	Chi-A	.909	10	11	19	3	5	-2
1983	Chi-A	1.000	3	3	2	0	0	0
1984	Chi-A	.973	22	29	42	2	6	0
1985	Mon-N	.985	126	276	367	10	86	-2
1986	Mon-N	.993	94	170	284	3	50	17
1987	Mon-N	.980	106	158	276	9	47	-10
Total	8	.984	391	710	1065	9	208	4
SS								
1980	Pit-N	.970	8	8	24	1	3	-1
1981	Pit-N	1.000	7	8	13	0	1	1
1982	Chi-A	.953	85	126	239	18	44	-4
1983	Chi-A	—	2	0	0	0	0	-1
1984	Chi-A	1.000	4	0	4	0	1	1
Total	5	.957	106	142	280	9	49	-4
1B								
1985	Mon-N	.993	20	136	12	1	10	1
1986	Mon-N	.990	20	94	9	1	8	1
1987	Mon-N	.990	17	89	9	1	5	1
Total	3	.991	57	319	30	3	23	3
OF								
1982	Chi-A	—	1	0	0	0	0	0
1983	Chi-A	—	1	0	0	0	0	0
1984	Chi-A	.923	5	11	1	1	1	0
1985	Mon-N	—	1	0	0	0	0	0
1986	Mon-N	—	1	0	0	0	0	0
1988	Chi-N	1.000	1	1	0	0	0	0
1989	Chi-N	—	1	0	0	0	0	0
Total	7	.929	11	12	1	1	1	0

■ Tom Lawless 2B

YEAR	TM/L	PCT	G	PO	A	E	DP	FR
1982	Cin-N	.978	47	87	136	5	35	7
1984	Cin-N	1.000	23	34	35	0	5	-2
	Mon-N	1.000	9	9	12	0	2	0
	Yr	1.000	32	43	47	0	7	-2
1985	StL-N	1.000	11	10	20	0	2	3
1986	StL-N	1.000	7	4	6	0	0	1
1987	StL-N	1.000	7	5	14	0	3	-1
1988	StL-N	1.000	5	3	7	0	2	1
1989	Tor-A	1.000	7	17	13	0	5	3
1990	Tor-A	1.000	1	4	1	0	1	1
Total	8	.988	117	173	244	5	55	13
3B								
1984	Cin-N	.923	6	7	5	1	1	-1
1985	StL-N	.971	13	9	24	1	2	5
1986	StL-N	.875	12	5	9	2	1	2
1987	StL-N	1.000	3	0	1	0	0	0
1988	StL-N	1.000	24	9	22	0	1	2
1989	Tor-A	.842	12	4	12	3	1	1
1990	Tor-A	.800	4	1	3	1	0	1
Total	7	.933	74	35	76	8	6	10
OF								
1986	StL-N	1.000	1	2	0	0	0	0
1987	StL-N	—	1	0	0	0	0	0
1988	StL-N	1.000	6	9	0	0	0	0
1989	Tor-A	1.000	16	17	0	0	0	1
1990	Tor-A	1.000	2	6	0	0	0	1
Total	5	1.000	26	34	0	0	0	2
1B								
1988	StL-N	1.000	1	2	0	0	0	0
C								
1989	Tor-A	1.000	1	1	1	0	0	0

■ Johnny Lazor OF

YEAR	TM/L	PCT	G	PO	A	E	DP	FR
1943	Bos-A	.979	63	135	7	3	0	6
1944	Bos-A	1.000	6	7	2	0	0	1
1945	Bos-A	.961	81	141	6	6	0	-10
1946	Bos-A	1.000	7	6	0	0	0	-1
Total	4	.971	157	289	15	9	0	-4
C								
1944	Bos-A	1.000	1	1	0	0	0	0

■ Tony Lazzeri 2B

YEAR	TM/L	PCT	G	PO	A	E	DP	FR
1926	NY-A	.961	**149**	298	461	31	72	-19
1927	NY-A	.971	113	213	398	18	60	6
1928	NY-A	.956	110	236	331	26	56	-11
1929	NY-A	.969	147	368	467	**27**	**101**	-4
1930	NY-A	.971	77	184	245	13	39	-1
1931	NY-A	.958	90	216	288	22	52	1
1932	NY-A	.978	134	362	405	17	70	6
1933	NY-A	.968	138	338	407	**25**	71	-14
1934	NY-A	.976	92	218	265	12	52	-13
1935	NY-A	.970	118	285	329	19	72	-18
1936	NY-A	.968	148	346	414	**25**	88	-31
1937	NY-A	.966	125	251	382	22	64	-8
1938	Chi-N	1.000	4	8	17	0	1	0
1939	Bro-N	.914	11	28	36	6	9	0
Total	14	.967	1456	3351	4445	263	807	106
3B								
1926	NY-A	—	1	0	0	0	0	0
1927	NY-A	.957	9	10	12	1	0	-3
1930	NY-A	.949	60	90	113	11	12	5
1931	NY-A	.958	39	39	53	4	4	-4
1932	NY-A	1.000	5	2	7	0	0	0
1934	NY-A	.935	30	36	51	6	7	0
1938	Chi-N	.833	7	6	4	2	0	-1
1939	Bro-N	1.000	1	2	0	0	0	0
	NY-N	.889	13	11	21	4	1	-2
	Yr	.897	15	12	23	4	1	-2
Total	8	.942	166	195	263	8	24	-5
SS								
1926	NY-A	.885	5	9	14	3	2	-1
1927	NY-A	.945	38	58	115	10	15	2
1930	NY-A	.952	8	16	24	2	8	2
1935	NY-A	.935	9	18	25	3	4	-2

YEAR	TM/L	PCT	G	PO	A	E	DP	FR
1936	NY-A	1.000	2	2	4	0	0	-1
1938	Chi-N	.946	25	33	54	5	11	-7
Total	6	.942	87	136	236	3	40	-7
OF								
1930	NY-A	1.000	1	1	0	0	0	0
1938	Chi-N	1.000	1	2	0	0	0	0
Total	2	1.000	2	3	0	0	0	0
1B								
1930	NY-A	1.000	1	3	0	0	1	0
■ Freddy Leach OF								
1923	Phi-N	.950	26	38	0	2	0	-3
1924	Phi-N	1.000	7	8	1	0	0	-1
1925	Phi-N	.952	65	178	2	9	1	-4
1926	Phi-N	.979	123	313	15	7	2	3
1927	Phi-N	.981	140	385	26	8	10	10
1928	Phi-N	.978	120	296	11	7	5	11
1929	NY-N	.974	95	149	2	4	0	-21
1930	NY-N	.978	124	208	11	5	4	-10
1931	NY-N	.976	125	239	6	6	1	-8
1932	Bos-N	.977	50	126	2	3	0	-1
Total	10	.975	875	1940	76	1	23	-24
1B								
1928	Phi-N	.996	25	249	18	1	28	2
■ Rick Leach OF								
1981	Det-A	1.000	15	16	0	0	0	0
1982	Det-A	1.000	14	20	1	0	0	0
1983	Det-A	.947	13	18	0	1	0	-1
1984	Tor-A	1.000	23	23	1	0	0	1
1985	Tor-A	1.000	4	6	0	0	0	0
1986	Tor-A	.978	39	44	0	1	0	-1
1987	Tor-A	.981	43	51	1	1	0	-1
1988	Tor-A	1.000	49	74	1	0	0	0
1989	Tex-A	.951	41	57	1	3	0	-1
1990	SF-N	.989	52	86	3	1	0	0
Total	10	.983	293	395	8	7	0	-3
1B								
1981	Det-A	1.000	32	133	14	0	15	2
1982	Det-A	.995	56	410	28	2	36	5
1983	Det-A	.994	73	447	45	3	37	5
1984	Tor-A	1.000	15	69	13	0	9	3
1985	Tor-A	.987	10	72	6	1	8	0
1986	Tor-A	.971	7	63	5	2	11	-1
1987	Tor-A	1.000	5	6	0	0	0	0
1988	Tor-A	1.000	4	19	4	0	1	1
1989	Tex-A	1.000	4	17	1	0	2	0
1990	SF-N	1.000	7	37	2	0	4	0
Total	10	.994	213	1273	118	8	123	10
■ Tommy Leach OF								
1900	Pit-N	1.000	4	1	0	0	0	-2
1905	Pit-N	.988	71	158	11	2	2	4
1906	Pit-N	.972	60	131	6	4	0	2
1907	Pit-N	.980	111	284	15	6	5	12
1908	Pit-N	1.000	2	6	2	0	0	2
1909	Pit-N	.969	138	333	12	11	3	2
1910	Pit-N	.966	131	352	14	13	4	5
1911	Pit-N	.987	89	208	15	3	3	8
1912	Pit-N	.986	24	65	4	1	3	4
	Chi-N	.975	73	181	11	5	4	4
	Yr	.978	97	246	15	6	7	8
1913	Chi-N	.990	121	271	15	3	5	0
1914	Chi-N	.968	136	321	16	11	5	5
1915	Cin-N	.959	96	200	9	9	2	3
1918	Pit-N	.952	23	37	3	2	1	0
Total	13	.975	1079	2548	133	0	37	49
3B								
1898	Lou-N	.727	3	2	6	3	0	0
1899	Lou-N	.908	80	135	200	34	13	11
1900	Pit-N	.864	31	45	69	18	4	1
1901	Pit-N	.903	92	122	196	34	9	9
1902	Pit-N	.926	134	170	316	39	10	13
1903	Pit-N	.879	127	178	292	65	16	7
1904	Pit-N	.907	146	212	371	60	18	36
1905	Pit-N	.935	58	80	123	14	13	7
1906	Pit-N	.929	65	73	135	16	4	0
1907	Pit-N	.880	33	45	65	15	5	-1
1908	Pit-N	.937	150	199	293	33	19	-6
1909	Pit-N	.960	13	22	26	2	2	0
1911	Pit-N	—	1	0	0	0	0	0
1912	Chi-N	.941	4	9	7	1	0	0
1913	Chi-N	.727	2	6	2	3	0	-1
1914	Chi-N	.879	16	25	26	7	0	-2
Total	16	.909	955	1323	2127	344	113	74
SS								
1899	Lou-N	.840	25	56	75	25	3	-10
1900	Pit-N	.889	8	12	20	4	2	-2
1901	Pit-N	.952	4	8	12	1	2	0
1905	Pit-N	1.000	2	5	4	0	0	0
1906	Pit-N	1.000	1	5	2	0	0	0
1907	Pit-N	.857	6	3	15	3	2	0
1910	Pit-N	.889	2	5	3	1	1	0
1911	Pit-N	.918	13	18	27	4	3	-3
1918	Pit-N	.769	3	3	7	3	1	-2
Total	9	.872	64	115	165	1	14	-17
2B								
1898	Lou-N	1.000	1	0	1	0	0	0
1899	Lou-N	.750	2	3	3	2	1	-1
1900	Pit-N	.957	7	16	28	2	3	3
1905	Pit-N	1.000	2	2	3	0	0	-1
1907	Pit-N	—	1	0	0	0	0	0
1910	Pit-N	1.000	1	1	0	0	0	0
Total	6	.934	14	22	35	4	4	1
■ John Leary 1B								
1914	StL-A	.987	130	1256	75	17	64	-2
1915	StL-A	.985	53	433	32	7	41	2
Total	2	.987	183	1689	107	4	105	0

YEAR	TM/L	PCT	G	PO	A	E	DP	FR
C								
1914	StL-A	.965	15	67	16	3	4	-3
1915	StL-A	.882	11	36	9	6	1	-4
Total	2	.934	26	103	25	9	5	-7
■ Bevo LeBourveau OF								
1919	Phi-N	1.000	15	27	6	0	0	2
1920	Phi-N	.949	72	133	16	8	1	3
1921	Phi-N	.911	76	126	7	13	2	-10
1922	Phi-N	.920	42	77	4	7	1	-3
1929	Phi-N	1.000	3	8	0	0	0	0
Total	5	.935	208	371	33	8	4	-8
■ Cliff Lee OF								
1919	Pit-N	.917	6	11	0	1	0	-1
1920	Pit-N	1.000	2	4	0	0	0	0
1921	Phi-N	.933	27	40	2	3	0	-2
1922	Phi-N	.967	89	167	10	6	3	-5
1923	Phi-N	.959	83	136	4	6	1	-8
1924	Phi-N	1.000	13	23	1	0	0	1
	Cin-N	—	1	0	0	0	0	0
	Yr	1.000	14	23	1	0	0	1
1925	Cle-A	.951	70	129	7	7	2	-3
1926	Cle-A	1.000	9	23	0	0	0	0
Total	8	.960	300	533	24	3	6	-18
1B								
1921	Phi-N	.987	48	502	20	7	35	-3
1922	Phi-N	.984	18	173	7	3	16	-1
1923	Phi-N	.986	16	131	9	2	10	0
1924	Phi-N	1.000	4	41	2	0	4	0
Total	4	.987	86	847	38	2	65	-4
C								
1919	Pit-N	.962	28	85	17	4	0	-10
1920	Pit-N	.974	19	51	24	2	3	1
1921	Phi-N	1.000	2	4	3	0	0	0
1926	Cle-A	1.000	3	2	0	0	0	0
Total	4	.969	52	142	44	6	3	-9
3B								
1922	Phi-N	1.000	1	0	0	1	0	-1
■ Dud Lee SS								
1920	StL-A	.333	1	0	1	2	0	-1
1921	StL-A	.922	31	78	87	14	9	2
1924	Bos-A	.937	90	198	246	30	43	-8
1925	Bos-A	.924	84	188	260	37	64	17
1926	Bos-A	1.000	2	4	3	0	1	-1
Total	5	.928	208	468	597	3	117	9
2B								
1921	StL-A	.961	30	60	64	5	21	3
3B								
1921	StL-A	1.000	3	0	1	0	0	0
■ Hal Lee OF								
1930	Bro-N	1.000	12	17	0	0	0	0
1931	Phi-N	.967	38	86	1	3	1	1
1932	Phi-N	.965	148	380	11	14	3	7
1933	Phi-N	.981	45	97	5	2	0	0
	Bos-N	.977	87	207	6	5	2	1
	Yr	.978	132	304	11	7	2	1
1934	Bos-N	.985	128	317	5	5	1	3
1935	Bos-N	.962	110	273	7	11	0	3
1936	Bos-N	.973	150	319	5	9	1	-7
Total	7	.973	718	1696	40	9	8	8
2B								
1934	Bos-N	.792	4	10	9	5	4	-3
■ Leron Lee OF								
1969	StL-N	1.000	7	7	1	0	0	0
1970	StL-N	.969	77	120	3	4	0	-6
1971	StL-N	.800	8	4	0	1	0	-1
	SD-N	.920	68	86	6	8	1	-9
	Yr	.914	76	90	6	9	1	-10
1972	SD-N	.975	96	186	6	5	2	2
1973	SD-N	.970	84	154	7	5	0	-2
1974	Cle-A	.958	62	131	5	6	1	0
1975	Cle-A	1.000	5	7	0	0	0	0
	LA-N	1.000	4	1	0	0	0	0
1976	LA-N	1.000	10	12	0	0	0	-2
Total	8	.962	421	708	28	9	4	-18
■ Manny Lee 2B								
1985	Tor-A	.971	38	27	40	2	8	15
1986	Tor-A	.990	29	32	72	1	10	4
1987	Tor-A	.966	27	51	61	4	16	2
1988	Tor-A	.988	98	221	261	6	64	6
1989	Tor-A	.985	40	103	96	3	29	-6
1990	Tor-A	.993	112	259	286	4	65	-12
Total	6	.987	344	693	816	0	192	9
SS								
1985	Tor-A	.952	8	7	13	1	3	4
1986	Tor-A	.857	5	3	3	1	1	0
1987	Tor-A	.987	26	26	49	1	10	10
1988	Tor-A	.940	23	28	35	4	6	3
1989	Tor-A	.974	28	40	73	3	18	5
1990	Tor-A	1.000	9	6	15	0	1	2
Total	6	.968	99	110	188	0	39	24
3B								
1985	Tor-A	1.000	5	0	3	0	0	1
1986	Tor-A	1.000	2	1	1	0	0	0
1988	Tor-A	.867	8	1	12	2	1	1
1989	Tor-A	.891	17	9	32	5	4	0
Total	4	.894	32	11	48	7	5	2
OF								
1989	Tor-A	—	1	0	0	0	0	0
■ Watty Lee OF								
1901	Was-A	.750	7	5	1	2	0	-2
1902	Was-A	.916	96	171	14	17	1	0
1903	Was-A	.930	47	100	6	8	2	4
Total	3	.917	150	276	21	7	3	2

YEAR	TM/L	PCT	G	PO	A	E	DP	FR
■ Jim Lefebvre 2B								
1965	LA-N	.970	156	349	429	24	91	-12
1966	LA-N	.980	119	246	332	12	59	-8
1967	LA-N	.968	34	70	112	6	23	6
1968	LA-N	.978	62	126	137	6	29	-9
1969	LA-N	.973	37	62	83	4	16	-4
1970	LA-N	.988	70	142	177	4	34	-6
1971	LA-N	.988	102	244	260	6	69	-17
1972	LA-N	.987	33	66	82	2	21	-1
Total	8	.979	613	1305	1612	4	342	-51
3B								
1966	LA-N	.952	40	22	57	4	4	-2
1967	LA-N	.955	92	49	205	12	12	0
1968	LA-N	.949	16	15	22	2	4	-1
1969	LA-N	.985	44	34	98	2	7	6
1970	LA-N	.964	21	20	34	2	4	2
1971	LA-N	.850	7	3	14	3	2	0
1972	LA-N	.913	11	4	17	2	3	0
Total	7	.957	231	147	447	7	36	5
1B								
1967	LA-N	1.000	5	54	4	0	4	0
1968	LA-N	1.000	3	29	2	0	0	0
1969	LA-N	1.000	6	58	4	0	3	0
1970	LA-N	1.000	1	6	1	0	3	0
Total	4	1.000	15	147	11	0	10	0
OF								
1968	LA-N	1.000	5	9	0	0	0	0
■ Joe Lefebvre OF								
1980	NY-A	.975	71	75	3	2	1	-4
1981	SD-N	.994	84	167	6	1	2	-1
1982	SD-N	1.000	36	38	1	0	0	-1
1983	SD-N	1.000	6	1	1	0	0	0
	Phi-N	.990	74	92	4	1	0	-4
	Yr	.990	80	93	5	1	0	-4
1984	Phi-N	.966	47	82	4	3	1	-1
1986	Phi-N	1.000	3	4	0	0	0	0
Total	6	.986	321	459	19	7	4	-11
3B								
1982	SD-N	.972	39	32	73	3	6	-1
1983	SD-N	1.000	4	1	4	0	0	0
	Phi-N	.800	9	3	13	4	0	-2
	Yr	.840	13	4	17	4	0	-2
1984	Phi-N	1.000	1	1	0	0	0	0
Total	3	.948	53	37	90	7	6	-3
C								
1982	SD-N	1.000	3	2	0	0	0	0
1983	SD-N	1.000	2	3	0	0	0	0
	Phi-N	1.000	3	5	0	0	0	0
	Yr	1.000	5	8	0	0	1	0
Total	2	1.000	8	10	0	0	1	0
■ Ron LeFlore OF								
1974	Det-A	.935	59	151	8	11	3	8
1975	Det-A	.973	134	317	13	9	3	2
1976	Det-A	.973	132	381	14	11	1	10
1977	Det-A	.972	152	365	12	11	0	-7
1978	Det-A	.976	155	440	9	11	4	-2
1979	Det-A	.990	113	293	6	3	3	0
1980	Mon-N	.957	130	233	14	11	1	-2
1981	Chi-A	.960	82	162	6	7	2	-1
1982	Chi-A	.939	83	179	7	12	1	-2
Total	9	.968	1040	2521	89	6	18	6
■ Mike Lehane 1B								
1890	Col-a	.982	140	1430	73	27	80	10
1891	Col-a	.981	137	1362	71	28	98	7
Total	2	.982	277	2792	144	5	178	17
SS								
1884	Was-U	.688	3	1	10	5	0	0
OF								
1884	Was-U	—	1	0	0	0	0	0
3B								
1884	Was-U	—	1	0	0	0	0	0
■ Paul Lehner OF								
1946	StL-A	.941	12	15	1	1	0	-1
1947	StL-A	.980	127	344	1	7	0	-11
1948	StL-A	.974	89	223	4	6	2	-10
1949	StL-A	.987	55	153	1	2	0	3
1950	Phi-A	.981	101	247	10	5	1	7
1951	Phi-A	1.000	6	16	1	0	0	1
	Chi-A	.980	20	47	3	1	0	1
	StL-A	1.000	18	44	0	0	0	0
	Cle-A	1.000	1	1	0	0	0	0
	Yr	.991	45	108	4	1	0	2
1952	Bos-A	1.000	2	3	0	0	0	0
Total	7	.981	431	1093	21	2	3	-10
1B								
1948	StL-A	1.000	2	12	1	0	1	0
1949	StL-A	.989	18	161	13	2	13	0
Total	2	.989	20	173	14	2	14	0
■ Hank Leiber OF								
1933	NY-N	1.000	1	3	1	0	0	1
1934	NY-N	.971	51	99	3	3	1	0
1935	NY-N	.965	154	357	5	13	2	-17
1936	NY-N	.961	86	165	9	7	3	-4
1937	NY-N	.988	46	78	1	1	0	-5
1938	NY-N	.974	89	181	6	5	3	-10
1939	Chi-N	.977	98	249	5	6	0	0
1940	Chi-N	.985	103	187	8	3	0	-4
1941	Chi-N	.964	29	52	1	2	0	-2
1942	NY-N	.990	41	93	2	1	1	1
Total	10	.973	698	1464	41	1	10	-40
1B								
1936	NY-N	—	1	0	0	0	0	0
1940	Chi-N	.984	12	115	11	2	10	1
1941	Chi-N	.980	15	140	7	3	13	-1
Total	3	.982	28	255	18	5	23	0

Nemo Leibold — OF

YEAR	TM/L	PCT	G	PO	A	E	DP	FR
1913	Cle-A	.945	74	142	12	9	1	0
1914	Cle-A	.931	107	221	22	18	4	9
1915	Cle-A	.969	52	147	10	5	0	9
	Chi-A	1.000	22	57	5	0	0	4
	Yr	.978	74	204	15	5	0	13
1916	Chi-A	1.000	24	31	1	0	2	-5
1917	Chi-A	.961	122	204	18	9	3	0
1918	Chi-A	.979	114	259	16	6	5	8
1919	Chi-A	.928	122	218	26	**19**	4	7
1920	Chi-A	.977	105	190	18	5	5	5
1921	Bos-A	.949	117	283	15	16	**9**	4
1922	Bos-A	.966	71	190	10	7	3	6
1923	Bos-A	.909	10	9	1	1	1	-3
	Was-A	.980	84	186	13	4	2	1
	Yr	.977	94	195	14	5	3	-2
1924	Was-A	.994	70	148	7	1	0	-3
1925	Was-A	.972	26	33	2	1	0	-6
Total	13	.961	1120	2318	176	101	39	36

3B

YEAR	TM/L	PCT	G	PO	A	E	DP	FR
1925	Was-A	1.000	1	1	1	0	1	0

Jack Lelivelt — OF

YEAR	TM/L	PCT	G	PO	A	E	DP	FR
1909	Was-A	.970	91	179	14	6	3	8
1910	Was-A	.964	86	149	13	6	5	5
1911	Was-A	.939	49	82	11	6	1	3
1912	NY-A	.963	36	75	4	3	2	0
1913	NY-A	1.000	5	12	1	0	0	1
	Cle-A	—	1	0	0	0	0	-1
	Yr	1.000	6	12	1	0	0	0
1914	Cle-A	.933	13	14	0	1	0	-3
Total	6	.962	281	511	43	2	11	13

1B

YEAR	TM/L	PCT	G	PO	A	E	DP	FR
1910	Was-A	.947	7	68	4	4	2	-1
1911	Was-A	.957	7	60	7	3	1	1
1914	Cle-A	1.000	1	1	0	0	0	0
Total	3	.952	15	129	11	7	3	0

Johnnie LeMaster — SS

YEAR	TM/L	PCT	G	PO	A	E	DP	FR
1975	SF-N	.967	22	26	62	3	12	-1
1976	SF-N	.937	31	54	109	11	17	10
1977	SF-N	.934	54	66	133	14	16	7
1978	SF-N	.966	96	135	260	14	40	2
1979	SF-N	.959	106	160	303	20	52	0
1980	SF-N	.957	134	200	372	26	54	-14
1981	SF-N	.964	103	166	294	17	57	-8
1982	SF-N	.963	130	223	382	23	63	-8
1983	SF-N	.964	139	215	402	23	58	-22
1984	SF-N	.964	129	222	391	23	70	4
1985	SF-N	.955	10	12	9	1	1	-1
	Cle-A	.949	10	19	18	2	7	2
	Pit-N	.983	21	43	71	2	12	13
1987	Oak-A	1.000	7	4	5	0	2	1
Total	12	.961	992	1545	2811	179	461	-15

3B

YEAR	TM/L	PCT	G	PO	A	E	DP	FR
1977	SF-N	1.000	2	0	1	0	0	0
1987	Oak-A	1.000	8	2	6	0	2	2
Total	2	1.000	10	2	7	0	2	2

2B

YEAR	TM/L	PCT	G	PO	A	E	DP	FR
1978	SF-N	1.000	2	0	1	0	0	0
1987	Oak-A	.955	5	8	13	1	1	3
Total	2	.957	7	8	14	1	1	3

Chet Lemon — OF

YEAR	TM/L	PCT	G	PO	A	E	DP	FR
1975	Chi-A	—	1	0	0	0	0	0
1976	Chi-A	.992	131	353	12	3	1	6
1977	Chi-A	.978	149	**512**	12	12	2	**27**
1978	Chi-A	.983	95	284	8	5	2	9
1979	Chi-A	.977	147	411	10	10	2	3
1980	Chi-A	.981	139	347	11	7	2	-2
1981	Chi-A	.984	93	240	2	4	1	-1
1982	Det-A	.984	121	242	11	4	2	0
1983	Det-A	.988	145	406	6	5	3	5
1984	Det-A	.995	140	427	6	2	1	7
1985	Det-A	.990	144	411	6	4	3	3
1986	Det-A	.985	124	316	6	5	1	-3
1987	Det-A	.992	145	350	4	3	1	-1
1988	Det-A	.974	144	296	8	8	3	0
1989	Det-A	.985	111	189	6	3	0	-8
1990	Det-A	.973	96	209	7	6	1	3
Total	16	.984	1925	4993	115	1	25	48

3B

YEAR	TM/L	PCT	G	PO	A	E	DP	FR
1975	Chi-A	.923	6	5	7	1	0	-3

2B

YEAR	TM/L	PCT	G	PO	A	E	DP	FR
1980	Chi-A	—	1	0	0	0	0	0

Jim Lemon — OF

YEAR	TM/L	PCT	G	PO	A	E	DP	FR
1950	Cle-A	.824	10	13	1	3	1	-1
1953	Was-A	.913	11	20	1	2	0	-1
1954	Was-A	.951	33	58	0	3	0	-5
1955	Was-A	.923	6	12	0	1	0	-1
1956	Was-A	.963	141	301	11	**12**	**6**	5
1957	Was-A	.971	131	227	4	7	2	-8
1958	Was-A	.978	137	255	8	6	2	-1
1959	Was-A	.969	142	281	4	9	0	-2
1960	Was-A	.960	145	251	11	**11**	1	-3
1961	Min-A	.940	120	182	7	12	0	-11
1962	Min-A	1.000	3	1	0	0	0	-1
1963	Min-A	.800	4	4	0	1	0	-1
	Phi-N	.963	18	26	0	1	0	0
Total	12	.961	901	1631	47	8	12	-30

1B

YEAR	TM/L	PCT	G	PO	A	E	DP	FR
1953	Cle-A	.750	2	6	0	2	0	-1
1957	Was-A	.909	3	26	4	3	0	0
1963	Chi-A	.979	25	136	7	3	18	-3
Total	3	.957	30	168	11	8	18	-4

Don Lenhardt — OF

YEAR	TM/L	PCT	G	PO	A	E	DP	FR
1950	StL-A	.975	39	78	1	2	1	-3
1951	StL-A	.982	27	54	0	1	0	-2
	Chi-A	.983	53	116	2	2	0	-3
	Yr	.983	80	170	2	3	0	-5
1952	Bos-A	.981	27	52	0	1	0	-4
	Det-A	.989	43	89	5	1	1	1
	StL-A	1.000	11	25	0	0	0	0
	Yr	.988	81	166	5	2	1	-3
1953	StL-A	.969	77	148	8	5	1	-2
1954	Bal-A	1.000	7	9	0	0	0	-1
	Bos-A	1.000	13	13	0	0	0	-2
	Yr	1.000	20	22	0	0	0	-3
Total	5	.980	297	584	16	2	3	-16

1B

YEAR	TM/L	PCT	G	PO	A	E	DP	FR
1950	StL-A	.988	86	618	39	8	77	-7
1951	StL-A	1.000	1	3	0	0	0	0
	Chi-A	1.000	2	6	0	0	0	0
	Yr	1.000	3	9	0	0	0	0
1952	StL-A	1.000	2	11	2	0	5	0
1954	Bal-A	1.000	2	13	3	0	0	1
Total	4	.989	93	651	44	8	82	-6

3B

YEAR	TM/L	PCT	G	PO	A	E	DP	FR
1950	StL-A	.969	10	13	18	1	1	-1
1953	StL-A	.929	6	5	8	1	0	-1
1954	Bos-A	1.000	1	0	3	0	0	0
Total	3	.959	17	18	29	2	1	-2

Ed Lennox — 3B

YEAR	TM/L	PCT	G	PO	A	E	DP	FR
1906	Phi-A	.909	6	9	21	3	0	5
1909	Bro-N	**.959**	121	167	210	16	18	-4
1910	Bro-N	.950	100	135	149	15	14	-15
1912	Chi-N	.934	24	25	32	4	1	-5
1914	Pit-F	.954	123	136	193	16	12	-15
1915	Pit-F	1.000	3	5	10	0	0	2
Total	6	.953	377	477	615	4	45	-32

Eddie Leon — SS

YEAR	TM/L	PCT	G	PO	A	E	DP	FR
1968	Cle-A	1.000	6	3	5	0	3	3
1969	Cle-A	.952	64	114	185	15	43	9
1970	Cle-A	.930	23	26	40	5	10	-3
1971	Cle-A	.968	24	36	54	3	13	-5
1972	Cle-A	.967	35	52	95	5	22	-6
1973	Chi-A	.972	122	198	382	17	78	-3
1974	Chi-A	.962	21	17	33	2	8	4
1975	NY-A	—	1	0	0	0	0	0
Total	8	.963	296	446	794	7	177	-1

2B

YEAR	TM/L	PCT	G	PO	A	E	DP	FR
1970	Cle-A	.982	141	342	378	13	102	11
1971	Cle-A	.983	107	235	271	9	71	5
1972	Cle-A	.993	36	51	84	1	17	5
1973	Cle-A	1.000	3	4	10	0	2	0
1974	Chi-A	.971	7	20	14	1	10	4
Total	5	.983	294	652	757	4	202	25

3B

YEAR	TM/L	PCT	G	PO	A	E	DP	FR
1970	Cle-A	1.000	1	0	1	0	0	0
1974	Chi-A	1.000	2	0	2	0	0	0
Total	2	1.000	3	0	3	0	0	0

Andy Leonard — OF

YEAR	TM/L	PCT	G	PO	A	E	DP	FR
1876	Bos-N	.925	35	68	6	6	2	1
1877	Bos-N	.875	37	79	5	12	2	2
1878	Bos-N	.777	60	65	8	21	1	-7
Total	3	.856	132	212	19	9	5	-4

SS

YEAR	TM/L	PCT	G	PO	A	E	DP	FR
1877	Bos-N	.864	21	28	48	12	3	-6
1880	Cin-N	.833	23	11	59	14	4	-10
Total	2	.849	44	39	107	6	7	-16

2B

YEAR	TM/L	PCT	G	PO	A	E	DP	FR
1876	Bos-N	.854	30	89	81	29	10	-1

3B

YEAR	TM/L	PCT	G	PO	A	E	DP	FR
1880	Cin-N	.829	10	18	16	7	0	-1

Jeffrey Leonard — OF

YEAR	TM/L	PCT	G	PO	A	E	DP	FR
1977	LA-N	1.000	10	7	0	0	0	0
1978	Hou-N	1.000	8	16	1	0	1	1
1979	Hou-N	.959	123	227	6	10	1	-4
1980	Hou-N	.979	56	87	6	2	0	1
1981	Hou-N	1.000	2	3	0	0	0	0
	SF-N	1.000	28	79	2	0	0	3
	Yr	1.000	30	82	2	0	0	3
1982	SF-N	.958	74	135	2	6	0	-4
1983	SF-N	.975	136	253	17	7	2	6
1984	SF-N	.970	131	247	14	8	4	4
1985	SF-N	.977	126	203	10	5	0	-4
1986	SF-N	.970	87	158	4	5	1	-4
1987	SF-N	.966	127	193	7	7	2	-9
1988	SF-N	.987	43	74	0	1	0	-4
	Mil-A	.985	91	191	4	3	1	0
1989	Sea-A	.982	26	54	2	1	0	0
1990	Sea-A	.983	79	118	0	2	0	-11
Total	14	.974	1147	2045	75	7	12	-25

1B

YEAR	TM/L	PCT	G	PO	A	E	DP	FR
1980	Hou-N	.987	11	74	3	1	7	-1
1981	Hou-N	1.000	2	23	1	0	0	0
	SF-N	.980	5	47	2	1	5	0
	Yr	.986	7	70	3	1	5	0
1982	SF-N	.400	1	2	0	3	0	-1
Total	3	.968	19	146	6	5	12	-2

Joe Leonard — 3B

YEAR	TM/L	PCT	G	PO	A	E	DP	FR
1914	Pit-N	.909	38	29	51	8	2	-8
1916	Was-A	.952	42	54	66	6	6	-7
1917	Was-A	.925	68	78	119	16	15	-4
1919	Was-A	.975	25	34	43	2	5	-1
Total	4	.937	173	195	279	2	28	-20

2B

YEAR	TM/L	PCT	G	PO	A	E	DP	FR
1916	Cle-A	1.000	1	1	1	0	0	0
1919	Was-A	.944	28	47	55	6	9	-8
Total	2	.945	29	48	56	6	9	-8

1B

YEAR	TM/L	PCT	G	PO	A	E	DP	FR
1917	Was-A	1.000	19	174	14	0	17	2
1919	Was-A	1.000	4	31	1	0	0	0
Total	2	1.000	23	205	15	0	17	2

SS

YEAR	TM/L	PCT	G	PO	A	E	DP	FR
1914	Pit-N	1.000	1	0	1	0	0	0
1917	Was-A	1.000	1	0	1	0	0	0
Total	2	1.000	2	0	2	0	0	0

OF

YEAR	TM/L	PCT	G	PO	A	E	DP	FR
1917	Was-A	—	1	0	0	0	0	0
1919	Was-A	—	1	0	0	0	0	0
Total	2	—	2	0	0	0	0	0

Ted Lepcio — 2B

YEAR	TM/L	PCT	G	PO	A	E	DP	FR
1952	Bos-A	.972	57	139	169	9	39	9
1953	Bos-A	.981	34	71	85	3	25	12
1954	Bos-A	.971	80	233	230	14	58	17
1956	Bos-A	.966	57	143	166	11	47	**4**
1957	Bos-A	.976	68	136	194	8	58	9
1958	Bos-A	.980	40	93	99	4	27	-3
1959	Bos-A	1.000	1	0	1	0	0	0
	Det-A	.959	24	59	58	5	18	-2
	Yr	.959	25	59	59	5	18	-2
1960	Phi-A	.846	5	5	6	2	1	-1
1961	Min-A	.989	22	39	51	1	18	4
Total	9	.972	388	918	1059	7	291	49

3B

YEAR	TM/L	PCT	G	PO	A	E	DP	FR
1952	Bos-A	.932	25	25	43	5	7	0
1953	Bos-A	.933	11	10	18	2	2	1
1954	Bos-A	.933	24	28	42	5	3	0
1955	Bos-A	.943	45	48	84	8	6	6
1956	Bos-A	.971	22	27	40	2	4	4
1959	Det-A	.962	11	5	20	1	0	1
1960	Phi-N	.942	50	39	58	6	2	-3
1961	Chi-A	.000	1	0	0	1	0	0
	Min-A	.919	35	13	21	3	2	-1
	Yr	.895	36	13	21	4	2	-1
Total	8	.940	224	195	326	3	26	8

SS

YEAR	TM/L	PCT	G	PO	A	E	DP	FR
1952	Bos-A	—	1	0	0	0	0	0
1953	Bos-A	.985	20	15	52	1	10	4
1954	Bos-A	.952	14	15	25	2	3	0
1959	Det-A	.951	35	32	65	5	12	-4
1960	Phi-N	.941	14	6	10	1	3	-1
1961	Min-A	.714	6	0	5	2	0	-1
Total	6	.953	90	68	157	1	28	-2

Don Leppert — C

YEAR	TM/L	PCT	G	PO	A	E	DP	FR
1961	Pit-N	.968	21	80	11	3	1	1
1962	Pit-N	.989	44	243	23	3	2	4
1963	Was-A	.984	60	281	20	5	4	-7
1964	Was-A	.990	43	191	14	2	2	1
Total	4	.985	168	795	68	3	9	-1

Walt Lerian — C

YEAR	TM/L	PCT	G	PO	A	E	DP	FR
1928	Phi-N	.977	74	239	61	7	12	-3
1929	Phi-N	**.986**	103	271	69	5	13	1
Total	2	.982	177	510	130	2	25	-2

Roy Leslie — 1B

YEAR	TM/L	PCT	G	PO	A	E	DP	FR
1917	Chi-N	.969	6	59	3	2	3	0
1919	StL-N	.957	9	62	4	3	5	0
1922	Phi-N	.990	139	1517	63	16	110	-4
Total	3	.988	154	1638	70	1	118	-4

Sam Leslie — 1B

YEAR	TM/L	PCT	G	PO	A	E	DP	FR
1931	NY-N	1.000	6	16	1	0	0	0
1932	NY-N	1.000	2	7	0	0	0	0
1933	NY-N	.990	35	371	21	4	28	0
	Bro-N	.982	95	855	49	17	44	-6
	Yr	.984	130	1226	70	21	72	-6
1934	Bro-N	.993	138	1262	93	9	104	5
1935	Bro-N	.989	138	1233	81	14	106	0
1936	NY-N	.991	99	1030	68	10	81	0
1937	NY-N	.990	44	444	38	5	45	3
1938	NY-N	.988	32	304	15	4	21	-3
Total	8	.989	589	5522	366	3	429	-1

OF

YEAR	TM/L	PCT	G	PO	A	E	DP	FR
1929	NY-N	1.000	1	1	0	0	0	0

Jim Levey — SS

YEAR	TM/L	PCT	G	PO	A	E	DP	FR
1930	StL-A	.958	8	20	26	2	6	1
1931	StL-A	.920	139	269	398	**58**	92	-10
1932	StL-A	.939	**152**	284	439	**47**	83	-18
1933	StL-A	.945	138	298	428	42	73	-6
Total	4	.936	437	871	1291	149	254	-33

Fred Lewis — OF

YEAR	TM/L	PCT	G	PO	A	E	DP	FR
1881	Bos-N	.837	27	35	6	8	1	-2
1883	Phi-N	.814	38	84	8	21	1	-1
	StL-a	.848	49	89	6	17	0	0
1884	StL-a	.853	73	118	15	23	1	3
	StL-U	.909	8	10	0	1	0	-1
1885	StL-A	.957	45	71	18	4	2	5
1886	Cin-a	.884	76	126	11	18	1	-2
Total	5	.866	316	533	64	2	6	2

3B

YEAR	TM/L	PCT	G	PO	A	E	DP	FR
1886	Cin-a	.500	1	0	1	1	0	0

Duffy Lewis — OF

YEAR	TM/L	PCT	G	PO	A	E	DP	FR
1910	Bos-A	.944	149	261	28	17	9	10
1911	Bos-A	.939	125	203	27	15	4	5
1912	Bos-A	.947	**154**	301	23	18	4	6
1913	Bos-A	.960	142	262	29	12	3	11
1914	Bos-A	.952	142	254	22	14	2	-2
1915	Bos-A	.952	152	263	15	14	3	-7
1916	Bos-A	.970	151	306	16	10	4	-1
1917	Bos-A	.972	150	324	20	10	6	4
1919	NY-A	.985	**141**	254	13	4	4	-6
1920	NY-A	.961	99	182	14	8	1	-2
1921	Was-A	.980	27	47	3	1	0	-2
Total	11	.959	1432	2657	210	123	40	16

3B

YEAR	TM/L	PCT	G	PO	A	E	DP	FR
1913	Bos-A	—	1	0	0	0	0	0

YEAR	TM/L	PCT	G	PO	A	E	DP	FR
Jack Lewis	**2B**							
1911	Bos-A	.931	18	30	51	6	5	-2
1914	Pit-F	.949	115	304	332	34	33	10
1915	Pit-F	.962	45	97	132	9	18	0
Total	3	.951	178	431	515	9	56	8
	SS							
1914	Pit-F	—	1	0	0	0	0	0
1915	Pit-F	.971	11	17	17	1	0	-2
Total	2	.971	12	17	17	1	0	-2
	OF							
1915	Pit-F	1.000	6	6	1	0	0	-1
	1B							
1915	Pit-F	.970	5	30	2	1	1	0
	3B							
1915	Pit-F	—	1	0	0	0	0	0
Buddy Lewis	**3B**							
1935	Was-A	.941	6	5	11	1	1	0
1936	Was-A	.933	139	152	297	**32**	24	5
1937	Was-A	.938	**156**	146	293	29	32	-19
1938	Was-A	.912	151	161	**329**	**47**	**32**	0
1939	Was-A	.933	134	122	326	32	31	**14**
1940	Was-A	.950	36	42	72	6	11	1
1941	Was-A	.890	49	51	87	17	10	-10
Total	7	.927	671	679	1415	164	141	-9
	OF							
1940	Was-A	.960	112	206	11	9	1	-4
1941	Was-A	.972	96	229	16	7	3	11
1945	Was-A	.981	69	151	8	3	3	2
1946	Was-A	.970	145	304	**16**	10	5	2
1947	Was-A	.968	130	259	11	9	2	-2
1949	Was-A	.979	67	136	4	3	1	-4
Total	6	.971	619	1285	66	1	15	5
Johnny Lewis	**OF**							
1964	StL-N	.966	36	53	3	2	1	2
1965	NY-N	.975	142	257	14	7	3	-6
1966	NY-N	.988	49	77	2	1	1	-2
1967	NY-N	1.000	10	15	1	0	0	0
Total	4	.977	237	402	20	0	5	-6
Phil Lewis	**SS**							
1905	Bro-N	.904	118	253	371	66	63	-6
1906	Bro-N	.922	135	244	393	54	35	-22
1907	Bro-N	.938	136	277	372	43	37	-20
1908	Bro-N	.943	116	227	352	35	33	-7
Total	4	.926	505	1001	1488	198	168	-55
Sixto Lezcano	**OF**							
1974	Mil-A	.972	15	32	3	1	1	1
1975	Mil-A	.977	129	240	10	6	1	-17
1976	Mil-A	.973	142	345	10	10	3	7
1977	Mil-A	.988	108	238	11	3	2	8
1978	Mil-A	.979	127	262	**18**	6	5	6
1979	Mil-A	.986	135	281	10	4	2	0
1980	Mil-A	.983	108	228	8	4	4	-1
1981	StL-N	.973	65	103	5	3	1	-7
1982	SD-N	.990	134	275	**16**	3	**8**	10
1983	SD-N	.968	91	171	8	6	1	1
	Phi-N	1.000	15	18	2	0	0	1
	Yr	.971	106	189	10	6	1	2
1984	Pit-N	.981	87	151	3	3	0	-4
1985	Pit-N	.967	40	57	2	2	0	-1
Total	12	.980	1196	2401	106	1	28	4
Al Libke	**OF**							
1945	Cin-N	.963	108	223	13	9	**6**	0
1946	Cin-N	.972	115	191	14	6	4	-8
Total	2	.967	223	414	27	5	10	-8
	1B							
1945	Cin-N	1.000	2	13	0	0	1	0
Jim Lillie	**OF**							
1883	Buf-N	.835	47	73	8	16	2	-5
1884	Buf-N	.852	114	190	**41**	**40**	**7**	**14**
1885	Buf-N	.862	112	183	23	33	4	0
1886	KC-N	.884	114	199	30	30	3	9
Total	4	.863	387	645	102	119	16	18
	SS							
1883	Buf-N	—	1	0	0	0	0	0
1885	Buf-N	.857	3	5	7	2	1	-1
Total	2	.857	4	5	7	2	1	-1
	C							
1883	Buf-N	.733	2	8	3	4	0	0
	3B							
1883	Buf-N	.600	1	3	0	2	0	-1
	2B							
1883	Buf-N	—	1	0	0	0	0	0
	1B							
1885	Buf-N	1.000	1	8	1	0	0	0
Bob Lillis	**SS**							
1958	LA-N	.964	19	29	52	3	10	-3
1959	LA-N	.919	20	27	52	7	10	8
1960	LA-N	.982	23	24	30	1	8	8
1961	LA-N	.000	1	0	0	1	0	-1
	StL-N	.928	56	73	134	16	19	-5
	Yr	.924	57	73	134	17	19	-6
1962	Hou-N	.972	99	169	290	13	54	3
1963	Hou-N	.957	124	223	336	25	52	-7
1964	Hou-N	.959	43	75	114	8	21	-2
1965	Hou-N	.968	104	188	273	15	49	-13
1966	Hou-N	.957	18	26	41	3	8	2
1967	Hou-N	.947	23	25	64	5	8	4
Total	10	.959	530	859	1386	7	239	-6
	2B							
1960	LA-N	1.000	1	2	1	0	1	0
1961	LA-N	1.000	1	6	3	0	1	1
	StL-N	.981	24	43	62	2	13	6
	Yr	.983	25	49	65	2	14	7
1962	Hou-N	.983	33	46	71	2	14	4

YEAR	TM/L	PCT	G	PO	A	E	DP	FR
1963	Hou-N	.983	19	24	34	1	7	2
1964	Hou-N	.995	52	86	107	1	18	4
1965	Hou-N	.962	6	7	18	1	1	1
1966	Hou-N	.951	35	70	65	7	15	-11
1967	Hou-N	.667	3	2	2	2	1	-1
Total	8	.976	174	286	363	6	71	6
	3B							
1960	LA-N	1.000	14	14	21	0	2	6
1961	LA-N	1.000	12	1	2	0	0	1
1962	Hou-N	1.000	9	8	17	0	4	2
1963	Hou-N	1.000	6	2	5	0	0	0
1964	Hou-N	.958	12	8	15	1	1	-1
1965	Hou-N	1.000	9	11	13	0	2	0
1966	Hou-N	1.000	6	3	3	0	1	0
1967	Hou-N	—	2	0	0	0	0	0
Total	8	.992	70	47	76	1	10	8
Lou Limmer	**1B**							
1951	Phi-A	.988	58	450	40	6	54	2
1954	Phi-A	.988	79	597	56	8	63	2
Total	2	.988	137	1047	96	4	117	4
Rufino Linares	**OF**							
1981	Atl-N	.963	60	124	6	5	1	1
1982	Atl-N	1.000	53	92	4	0	1	2
1984	Atl-N	.958	13	21	2	1	0	0
1985	Cal-A	1.000	2	1	0	0	0	0
Total	4	.977	128	238	12	6	2	3
Carl Lind	**2B**							
1927	Cle-A	.969	11	21	41	2	6	2
1928	Cle-A	.960	154	390	505	37	116	4
1929	Cle-A	.957	64	192	209	18	66	16
1930	Cle-A	1.000	2	0	1	0	0	0
Total	4	.960	231	603	756	7	188	22
	SS							
1927	Cle-A	—	1	0	0	0	0	0
1930	Cle-A	.940	22	48	77	8	19	11
Total	2	.940	23	48	77	8	19	11
	3B							
1929	Cle-A	1.000	1	0	2	0	0	0
Jose Lind	**2B**							
1987	Pit-N	.995	35	53	139	1	12	6
1988	Pit-N	.987	153	333	473	11	73	3
1989	Pit-N	.976	151	309	438	18	81	-14
1990	Pit-N	.991	152	330	449	7	74	17
Total	4	.986	491	1025	1499	7	240	12
Johnny Lindell	**OF**							
1943	NY-A	.966	122	269	11	10	1	0
1944	NY-A	.986	149	468	9	7	3	7
1945	NY-A	.982	41	108	2	2	0	1
1946	NY-A	.982	74	159	8	3	3	3
1947	NY-A	.978	118	308	6	7	1	-5
1948	NY-A	.994	79	165	7	1	1	2
1949	NY-A	.983	65	114	4	2	1	-2
1950	NY-A	.857	6	6	0	1	0	-2
	StL-N	.984	33	61	1	1	1	-2
1953	Phi-N	.667	2	2	0	1	0	-1
Total	9	.980	689	1660	48	5	11	1
	1B							
1946	NY-A	.976	14	116	4	3	15	-2
1953	Pit-N	.923	2	12	0	1	0	-1
Total	2	.971	16	128	4	4	15	-3
Chris Lindsay	**1B**							
1905	Det-A	.978	88	761	57	18	40	0
1906	Det-A	.977	122	1122	66	28	55	-5
Total	2	.978	210	1883	123	6	95	-5
	2B							
1906	Det-A	.907	17	40	38	8	4	-2
	3B							
1906	Det-A	—	1	0	0	0	0	0
Freddy Lindstrom	**3B**							
1924	NY-N	.973	11	15	21	1	1	2
1925	NY-N	.957	96	123	147	12	9	0
1926	NY-N	.962	138	151	251	16	23	-3
1927	NY-N	.968	87	93	178	9	12	5
1928	NY-N	**.958**	**153**	145	**340**	21	34	**15**
1929	NY-N	.966	128	134	258	14	24	7
1930	NY-N	.953	148	132	291	21	24	6
1932	NY-N	.867	15	11	15	4	1	-2
1935	Chi-N	.943	33	31	35	4	7	-4
Total	9	.959	809	835	1536	102	135	26
	OF							
1926	NY-N	1.000	1	1	0	0	0	0
1927	NY-N	.968	51	89	3	3	0	-5
1931	NY-N	.975	73	150	4	4	1	-5
1932	NY-N	.982	128	315	18	6	2	-4
1933	Pit-N	.988	130	388	7	5	2	7
1934	Pit-N	.990	92	181	8	2	1	-2
1935	Chi-N	.979	50	136	5	3	0	4
1936	Bro-N	.982	26	51	4	1	0	0
Total	8	.983	551	1311	49	4	6	-5
	2B							
1924	NY-N	.911	23	19	32	5	6	4
1931	NY-N	1.000	1	2	5	0	1	1
1931	NY-N	.800	4	8	4	3	2	-2
Total	3	.897	28	29	41	8	9	3
	SS							
1925	NY-N	.667	1	2	2	2	0	-1
Larry Lintz	**2B**							
1973	Mon-N	.945	34	49	89	8	16	1
1974	Mon-N	.961	67	117	178	12	28	-9
1975	Mon-N	.970	39	88	105	6	18	-6
	StL-N	.889	6	5	11	2	0	4
	Yr	.963	45	93	116	8	18	-2
1976	Oak-A	1.000	5	2	2	0	0	2

YEAR	TM/L	PCT	G	PO	A	E	DP	FR
1977	Oak-A	1.000	28	28	35	0	9	11
Total	5	.962	179	289	420	8	71	3
1973	Mon-N	.975	15	14	25	1	3	1
1974	Mon-N	.953	31	51	72	6	20	-4
1975	Mon-N	1.000	2	3	4	0	0	0
	StL-N	.944	6	5	12	1	3	5
	Yr	.960	8	8	16	1	3	5
1977	Oak-A	.667	2	0	2	1	0	0
Total	4	.954	56	73	115	9	26	2
	OF							
1976	Oak-A	—	3	0	0	0	0	0
	3B							
1974	Mon-N	1.000	1	1	2	0	0	0
1977	Oak-A	1.000	1	1	0	0	0	0
Total	2	1.000	2	2	2	0	0	0
Phil Linz	**SS**							
1962	NY-A	.937	21	33	41	5	7	-2
1963	NY-A	.963	22	34	69	4	13	2
1964	NY-A	.952	55	80	176	13	35	10
1965	NY-A	.954	71	126	205	16	29	7
1966	Phi-N	.875	6	2	5	1	1	0
1967	Phi-N	.833	7	3	2	1	0	-1
	NY-N	1.000	8	10	11	0	1	0
	Yr	.963	15	13	13	1	1	-1
Total	6	.952	190	288	509	0	86	16
	2B							
1962	NY-A	.875	5	8	6	2	1	-1
1963	NY-A	1.000	6	11	13	0	2	-1
1964	NY-A	1.000	5	5	7	0	1	-1
1965	NY-A	1.000	1	0	1	0	0	0
1966	Phi-N	1.000	3	3	3	0	1	0
1967	NY-N	.964	11	27	26	2	7	-2
1968	NY-N	.968	71	136	162	10	36	-12
Total	7	.967	102	190	218	4	48	-17
	3B							
1962	NY-A	.923	8	12	12	2	2	0
1963	NY-A	1.000	13	7	21	0	2	1
1964	NY-A	.952	41	41	99	7	7	4
1965	NY-A	.958	4	8	15	1	1	3
1966	Phi-N	.971	14	13	21	1	2	1
1967	Phi-N	—	1	0	0	0	0	0
	NY-N	—	1	0	0	0	0	0
	Yr	—	2	0	0	0	0	0
Total	6	.958	82	81	168	1	14	9
	OF							
1962	NY-A	—	2	0	0	0	0	0
1963	NY-A	1.000	12	17	0	0	0	-1
1964	NY-A	—	3	0	0	0	0	0
1965	NY-A	1.000	4	10	0	0	0	0
1967	NY-N	—	1	0	0	0	0	0
Total	5	1.000	22	27	0	0	0	-1
Johnny Lipon	**SS**							
1942	Det-A	.945	34	85	103	11	24	7
1946	Det-A	.933	8	14	14	2	5	3
1948	Det-A	.970	117	211	346	17	63	-11
1949	Det-A	.965	120	240	364	22	92	3
1950	Det-A	.958	147	273	**483**	**33**	**126**	9
1951	Det-A	.949	125	244	364	38	80	-13
1952	Det-A	.978	39	80	101	4	12	-2
	Bos-A	.982	69	118	218	6	53	14
	Yr	.981	108	198	319	10	65	12
1953	Bos-A	.951	58	85	150	12	26	4
Total	8	.961	717	1350	2143	140	481	14
	3B							
1946	Det-A	1.000	1	0	1	0	0	0
1948	Det-A	1.000	1	1	0	0	0	0
1952	Bos-A	.938	7	4	11	1	2	1
1953	StL-A	1.000	6	0	4	0	0	0
Total	4	.957	15	5	17	1	2	1
	2B							
1948	Det-A	—	1	0	0	0	0	0
1953	StL-A	1.000	1	4	0	0	0	0
Total	2	1.000	2	4	0	0	0	-1
Nelson Liriano	**2B**							
1987	Tor-A	.995	37	83	107	1	28	3
1988	Tor-A	.961	80	121	177	12	48	-13
1989	Tor-A	.980	122	267	330	12	76	-18
1990	Tor-A	.983	49	93	132	4	26	-12
	Min-A	.968	50	83	128	7	27	-15
	Yr	.975	99	176	260	11	53	-27
Total	4	.977	338	647	874	6	205	-55
	3B							
1988	Tor-A	—	1	0	0	0	0	0
	SS							
1990	Min-A	—	1	0	0	0	0	-1
Joe Lis	**1B**							
1972	Phi-N	.996	30	221	13	1	18	-1
1973	Min-A	.987	96	626	48	9	59	0
1974	Min-A	.992	18	114	6	1	9	0
	Cle-A	1.000	31	175	10	0	14	0
	Yr	.997	49	289	16	1	23	0
1975	Cle-A	1.000	8	39	2	0	2	0
1976	Cle-A	1.000	17	107	8	0	10	0
1977	Sea-A	1.000	4	24	1	0	3	0
Total	6	.992	204	1306	88	1	115	-1
	OF							
1970	Phi-N	.947	9	18	0	1	0	-1
1971	Phi-N	.978	35	42	2	1	0	-4
1972	Phi-N	.960	14	21	3	1	1	1
1974	Cle-A	.000	1	0	0	2	0	-1
Total	4	.945	59	81	5	5	1	-5
	3B							
1974	Cle-A	.950	9	8	11	1	1	0

YEAR	TM/L	PCT	G	PO	A	E	DP	FR
C								
1977	Sea-A	—	1	0	0	0	0	0

■ Bryan Little 2B

YEAR	TM/L	PCT	G	PO	A	E	DP	FR
1982	Mon-N	1.000	16	11	18	0	1	-1
1983	Mon-N	.995	51	77	111	1	17	-9
1984	Mon-N	.982	77	137	197	6	44	-21
1985	Chi-A	.989	68	100	164	3	33	-5
1986	Chi-A	1.000	12	17	21	0	3	-1
	NY-A	.975	14	37	40	2	9	5
	Yr	.983	26	54	61	2	12	4
Total	5	.987	238	379	551	2	107	-32
SS								
1982	Mon-N	.960	10	10	14	1	1	-1
1983	Mon-N	.968	66	104	131	8	27	-22
1984	Mon-N	1.000	2	0	2	0	0	0
1985	Chi-A	1.000	1	1	1	0	1	0
1986	Chi-A	1.000	7	4	8	0	3	1
Total	5	.969	86	119	162	9	32	-22
3B								
1985	Chi-A	.000	2	0	0	2	0	-1
1986	Chi-A	1.000	1	1	0	0	0	0
Total	2	.333	3	1	0	2	0	-1

■ Danny Litwhiler OF

YEAR	TM/L	PCT	G	PO	A	E	DP	FR
1940	Phi-N	.986	34	68	4	1	1	0
1941	Phi-N	.964	150	**393**	12	**15**	3	**15**
1942	Phi-N	**1.000**	151	308	9	0	0	1
1943	Phi-N	.989	34	86	5	1	1	3
	StL-N	1.000	70	139	7	0	1	0
	Yr	.996	104	225	12	1	2	3
1944	StL-N	.974	136	294	6	8	1	-4
1946	Bos-N	.985	65	128	2	2	0	-4
1947	Bos-N	.976	66	119	2	3	0	-2
1948	Bos-N	1.000	8	24	1	0	0	1
	Cin-N	.988	83	165	3	2	1	-3
	Yr	.990	91	189	4	2	1	-2
1949	Cin-N	.987	82	143	6	2	1	-4
1950	Cin-N	.958	29	46	0	2	0	-3
1951	Cin-N	.933	7	14	0	1	0	-1
Total	11	.982	915	1927	57	7	9	-1
3B								
1946	Bos-N	1.000	2	0	2	0	0	0
1948	Cin-N	.978	15	11	34	1	1	2
1949	Cin-N	.909	3	4	6	1	1	0
Total	3	.966	20	15	42	2	2	2

■ Paddy Livingston C

YEAR	TM/L	PCT	G	PO	A	E	DP	FR
1901	Cle-A	1.000	1	0	1	0	0	0
1906	Cin-N	.960	47	202	62	11	5	2
1909	Phi-A	.969	64	306	106	13	6	9
1910	Phi-A	.968	37	205	68	9	5	4
1911	Phi-A	.977	26	133	36	4	1	4
1912	Cle-A	.976	14	63	18	2	0	0
1917	StL-N	1.000	6	26	6	0	0	1
Total	7	.969	195	935	297	9	17	20

■ Mickey Livingston C

YEAR	TM/L	PCT	G	PO	A	E	DP	FR
1938	Was-A	.667	2	2	0	1	0	-1
1941	Phi-N	.974	71	263	31	8	5	0
1942	Phi-N	.987	78	275	36	4	8	-5
1943	Phi-N	.988	84	268	49	4	5	-2
	Chi-A	1.000	31	114	13	0	0	-5
	Yr	.991	115	382	62	4	5	-7
1945	Chi-A	.990	68	263	27	3	2	-1
1946	Chi-A	.981	56	239	25	5	3	2
1947	Chi-A	1.000	7	27	1	0	0	0
	NY-A	.800	1	3	1	1	0	0
	Yr	.970	8	30	2	1	0	0
1948	NY-N	.980	42	135	10	3	2	-1
1949	NY-N	.985	19	60	5	1	0	-1
	Bos-N	.977	22	76	9	2	0	0
	Yr	.980	41	136	14	3	0	-1
1951	Bro-N	1.000	2	3	2	0	1	0
Total	10	.984	483	1728	209	2	26	-14
1B								
1941	Phi-N	—	1	0	0	0	0	0
1942	Phi-N	.984	6	59	1	1	5	-1
1943	Phi-N	—	2	0	0	0	0	0
	Chi-A	—	4	0	0	0	0	0
	Yr	—	6	0	0	0	0	0
1945	Chi-A	1.000	1	1	0	0	0	0
Total	4	.984	14	60	1	1	5	-1

■ Hans Lobert 3B

YEAR	TM/L	PCT	G	PO	A	E	DP	FR
1903	Pit-N	.778	3	3	4	2	0	-1
1905	Cin-N	.918	13	20	25	4	2	1
1906	Cin-N	.959	35	47	69	5	4	1
1907	Cin-N	.880	5	12	10	3	0	0
1908	Cin-N	.921	99	121	181	26	11	-10
1909	Cin-N	.921	122	182	204	33	16	-15
1910	Cin-N	.932	90	123	164	21	11	-2
1911	Phi-N	.954	147	**202**	213	20	13	-17
1912	Phi-N	.976	64	80	86	4	3	-13
1913	Phi-N	**.974**	145	**181**	221	11	13	-17
1914	Phi-N	**.943**	133	188	174	22	10	-25
1915	NY-N	.950	103	109	192	16	9	-5
1916	NY-N	.961	20	14	35	2	2	2
1917	NY-N	.906	21	10	19	3	2	2
Total	14	.944	1000	1292	1601	172	96	-99
SS								
1903	Pit-N	1.000	1	0	1	0	0	0
1906	Cin-N	.908	31	49	80	13	4	-14
1907	Cin-N	.941	142	299	382	43	53	-18
1908	Cin-N	.921	35	64	87	13	5	-14
1913	Phi-N	1.000	3	1	3	0	0	0
1914	Phi-N	1.000	2	6	4	0	0	-1
Total	6	.934	214	419	557	9	62	-47
OF								
1905	Chi-N	—	1	0	0	0	0	-1
1906	Cin-N	1.000	1	1	0	0	0	0
1908	Cin-N	.929	21	37	2	3	0	-1
Total	3	.930	23	38	2	3	0	-2
2B								
1903	Pit-N	.857	1	3	3	1	1	0
1906	Cin-N	.962	10	21	29	2	0	2
1913	Phi-N	1.000	1	2	0	0	0	0
Total	3	.951	12	26	32	3	1	2

■ Harry Lochhead SS

YEAR	TM/L	PCT	G	PO	A	E	DP	FR
1899	Cle-N	.909	146	319	490	81	54	2
1901	Det-A	.857	1	2	4	1	0	0
	Phi-A	.757	9	10	18	9	1	-8
	Yr	.773	10	12	22	10	1	-8
Total	2	.903	156	331	512	1	55	-6
2B								
1899	Cle-N	1.000	1	1	3	0	0	0

■ Don Lock OF

YEAR	TM/L	PCT	G	PO	A	E	DP	FR
1962	Was-A	.973	67	144	2	4	0	1
1963	Was-A	.980	146	**377**	14	8	**6**	9
1964	Was-A	.987	149	354	**19**	5	3	7
1965	Was-A	.969	136	278	6	9	3	-3
1966	Was-A	.977	129	295	8	7	1	3
1967	Phi-N	.973	97	172	8	5	2	5
1968	Phi-N	.955	78	145	2	7	1	3
1969	Phi-N	—	1	0	0	0	0	0
	Bos-A	1.000	28	24	0	0	0	1
Total	8	.976	831	1789	59	5	16	25
1B								
1969	Bos-A	1.000	4	10	2	0	0	1

■ Gene Locklear OF

YEAR	TM/L	PCT	G	PO	A	E	DP	FR
1973	Cin-N	1.000	5	4	0	0	0	0
	SD-N	.952	37	77	2	4	0	0
	Yr	.954	42	81	2	4	0	0
1974	SD-N	1.000	12	22	1	0	0	-1
1975	SD-N	.970	51	92	4	3	1	-4
1976	SD-N	.952	11	20	0	1	0	-1
	NY-A	1.000	3	4	0	0	0	0
1977	NY-A	.667	1	1	0	1	0	0
Total	5	.962	120	221	7	9	1	-6

■ Whitey Lockman 1B

YEAR	TM/L	PCT	G	PO	A	E	DP	FR
1951	NY-N	.986	119	1045	89	16	113	2
1952	NY-N	.992	**154**	**1435**	111	13	**155**	2
1953	NY-N	.989	120	1042	100	13	96	6
1954	NY-N	.987	145	1261	88	**18**	122	-8
1955	NY-N	.995	68	613	34	3	61	-5
1956	NY-N	.980	7	48	2	1	1	-1
	StL-N	.875	2	14	0	2	1	-1
	Yr	.955	9	62	2	3	2	-2
1957	NY-N	.991	102	981	71	10	94	-2
1958	SF-N	1.000	7	59	2	0	5	-1
1959	Bal-A	.992	22	116	3	1	13	-2
	Cin-N	.971	20	92	10	3	9	1
1960	Cin-N	1.000	5	10	0	0	2	0
Total	10	.989	771	6716	510	0	672	-9
OF								
1945	NY-N	.961	32	72	1	3	1	-2
1948	NY-N	.987	144	**388**	6	5	0	-2
1949	NY-N	.973	151	353	10	10	1	1
1950	NY-N	.978	128	305	11	7	3	12
1951	NY-N	.987	34	75	3	1	2	-1
1953	NY-N	1.000	30	64	2	0	0	1
1954	NY-N	1.000	2	4	0	0	0	0
1955	NY-N	.983	81	167	4	3	1	0
1956	NY-N	.960	39	69	3	3	1	-3
	StL-N	.955	57	103	2	5	0	-3
	Yr	.957	96	172	5	8	1	-6
1957	NY-N	.913	27	41	1	4	0	-2
1958	SF-N	1.000	25	17	0	0	0	0
1959	Bal-A	—	1	0	0	0	0	0
	Cin-N	1.000	1	2	0	0	0	-1
Total	12	.976	752	1660	43	1	9	-1
2B								
1958	SF-N	.956	15	24	19	2	5	-3
1959	Bal-A	.933	5	8	6	1	4	-1
	Cin-N	1.000	6	9	13	0	4	-1
Total	2	.963	26	41	38	3	13	-5
3B								
1959	Cin-N	1.000	1	0	1	0	0	0

■ Dario Lodigiani 3B

YEAR	TM/L	PCT	G	PO	A	E	DP	FR
1938	Phi-A	.915	13	17	26	4	3	0
1939	Phi-A	.944	89	103	181	17	8	1
1941	Chi-A	.962	86	120	187	12	22	6
1942	Chi-A	.944	43	40	96	8	4	5
1946	Chi-A	.935	44	41	88	9	4	-5
Total	5	.947	275	321	578	0	41	7
2B								
1938	Phi-A	.953	80	193	233	21	45	-6
1939	Phi-A	.932	28	56	82	10	16	1
1942	Chi-A	.974	7	15	22	1	5	0
Total	3	.949	115	264	337	2	66	-5

■ Johnny Logan SS

YEAR	TM/L	PCT	G	PO	A	E	DP	FR
1951	Bos-N	.958	58	98	155	11	31	4
1952	Bos-N	**.972**	117	247	385	18	81	**18**
1953	Mil-N	**.975**	150	**295**	481	20	104	**21**
1954	Mil-N	**.969**	**154**	324	**489**	26	104	14
1955	Mil-N	.963	**154**	268	**511**	30	100	8
1956	Mil-N	.968	148	266	467	24	94	3
1957	Mil-N	.962	129	263	**440**	**29**	94	**24**
1958	Mil-N	.959	144	273	**481**	32	99	10
1959	Mil-N	.975	138	260	431	18	78	-3
1960	Mil-N	.956	136	235	417	30	77	2
1961	Mil-N	1.000	2	0	3	0	1	0
	Pit-N	.960	6	9	15	1	3	0
	Yr	.964	8	9	18	1	4	0
1963	Pit-N	.920	44	74	122	17	28	2
Total	12	.965	1380	2612	4397	256	894	103
3B								
1961	Pit-N	1.000	7	3	11	0	2	1
1962	Pit-N	.980	19	13	35	1	5	2
1963	Pit-N	1.000	4	3	4	0	1	0
Total	3	.986	30	19	50	1	8	3

■ Jack Lohrke 3B

YEAR	TM/L	PCT	G	PO	A	E	DP	FR
1947	NY-N	.939	111	118	188	20	20	-2
1948	NY-N	.898	50	37	69	12	4	-5
1949	NY-N	.929	19	22	30	4	2	-2
1950	NY-N	.958	16	8	15	1	2	0
1951	NY-N	.943	17	10	23	2	2	0
1952	Phi-N	.857	3	1	5	1	1	0
1953	Phi-N	.500	1	0	1	1	0	0
Total	7	.928	217	196	331	1	31	-9
2B								
1948	NY-N	.950	36	88	101	10	17	3
1949	NY-N	.969	23	44	80	4	5	5
1950	NY-N	1.000	1	2	3	0	1	0
1952	Phi-N	1.000	1	0	1	0	0	0
1953	Phi-N	.750	2	0	3	1	0	0
Total	5	.955	63	134	188	5	23	8
SS								
1949	NY-N	.981	15	20	33	1	6	0
1951	NY-N	1.000	1	1	0	0	0	0
1952	Phi-N	1.000	5	6	9	0	2	1
1953	Phi-N	1.000	2	2	4	0	1	1
Total	4	.987	23	29	46	1	9	2

■ Sherm Lollar C

YEAR	TM/L	PCT	G	PO	A	E	DP	FR
1946	Cle-A	.990	24	89	9	1	1	-3
1947	NY-A	1.000	9	44	3	0	0	1
1948	NY-A	.976	10	36	4	1	1	1
1949	StL-A	.988	93	279	39	4	3	-4
1950	StL-A	.981	109	367	48	8	9	-5
1951	StL-A	**.995**	85	361	48	2	8	-2
1952	Chi-A	.989	120	590	53	7	4	-3
1953	Chi-A	**.994**	107	470	51	3	2	-3
1954	Chi-A	.993	93	395	38	3	8	-3
1955	Chi-A	.995	136	664	62	4	**12**	**9**
1956	Chi-A	**.993**	132	679	40	5	6	3
1957	Chi-A	.998	96	454	45	1	5	-2
1958	Chi-A	.987	116	597	63	9	8	0
1959	Chi-A	.993	122	623	51	5	**14**	**7**
1960	Chi-A	**.995**	123	555	54	3	**12**	-4
1961	Chi-A	**.998**	107	464	48	1	6	-11
1962	Chi-A	.991	66	298	23	3	0	-9
1963	Chi-A	.981	23	94	9	2	2	-2
Total	18	.992	1571	7059	688	2	101	-30
1B								
1953	Chi-A	1.000	1	3	0	0	0	0
1959	Chi-A	.995	24	177	17	1	19	2
1963	Chi-A	1.000	2	4	0	0	0	0
Total	3	.995	27	184	17	1	19	2
3B								
1951	StL-A	—	1	0	0	0	0	0

■ Ernie Lombardi C

YEAR	TM/L	PCT	G	PO	A	E	DP	FR
1931	Bro-N	.984	50	218	23	4	5	3
1932	Cin-N	.963	110	288	76	**14**	6	-9
1933	Cin-N	.972	95	223	52	8	3	-15
1934	Cin-N	.989	111	383	61	5	8	-3
1935	Cin-N	.983	82	298	49	6	4	-5
1936	Cin-N	.962	105	330	54	**15**	10	-13
1937	Cin-N	.973	90	333	58	11	3	-16
1938	Cin-N	.985	123	512	73	9	8	-3
1939	Cin-N	.984	120	536	63	**10**	7	5
1940	Cin-N	.989	101	397	46	5	5	-4
1941	Cin-N	.983	116	496	70	10	9	1
1942	Bos-N	.980	85	251	41	6	3	-15
1943	NY-N	.971	73	296	36	10	8	-13
1944	NY-N	.968	100	350	47	**13**	**11**	-15
1945	NY-N	.983	**96**	**425**	49	8	8	3
1946	NY-N	.978	63	272	36	7	7	1
1947	NY-N	.980	24	86	11	2	2	-3
Total	17	.979	1544	5694	845	143	107	101

■ Steve Lombardozzi 2B

YEAR	TM/L	PCT	G	PO	A	E	DP	FR
1985	Min-A	.982	26	31	80	2	16	11
1986	Min-A	**.991**	155	289	407	6	102	-3
1987	Min-A	.977	133	245	356	14	91	-1
1988	Min-A	.986	90	140	211	5	47	-7
1989	Hou-N	.922	18	20	27	4	5	0
Total	5	.983	422	725	1081	1	247	0
SS								
1988	Min-A	1.000	12	12	23	0	6	0
3B								
1988	Min-A	1.000	5	0	3	0	1	0
1989	Hou-N	1.000	1	0	1	0	0	0
Total	2	1.000	6	0	4	0	1	0

■ Herman Long SS

YEAR	TM/L	PCT	G	PO	A	E	DP	FR
1889	KC-a	.874	128	**335**	479	117	55	**32**
1890	Bos-N	.898	101	230	352	66	40	11
1891	Bos-N	.902	139	**345**	441	85	**60**	**15**
1892	Bos-N	.889	141	297	497	**99**	65	13
1893	Bos-N	.883	123	271	469	98	**67**	17
1894	Bos-N	.885	98	217	359	75	52	5
1895	Bos-N	.891	122	280	409	84	48	-7
1896	Bos-N	.897	120	311	415	83	52	10
1897	Bos-N	.905	107	274	353	66	40	-2
1898	Bos-N	.923	142	351	472	67	65	-2
1899	Bos-N	.929	135	351	435	60	**68**	-10
1900	Bos-N	.937	125	257	454	48	34	-6
1901	Bos-N	.946	138	304	468	44	55	1
1902	Bos-N	.946	107	285	366	37	46	**23**
1903	NY-A	.889	22	52	60	14	6	-4

YEAR	TM/L	PCT	G	PO	A	E	DP	FR
	Det-A	.879	38	90	107	27	12	-2
	Yr	.883	60	142	167	41	18	-6
Total	15	.906	1794	4225	6136	1070	765	94
2B								
1889	KC-a	.904	8	20	27	5	4	1
1893	Bos-N	.935	5	11	18	2	1	0
1894	Bos-N	.920	3	17	6	2	1	0
1895	Bos-N	1.000	2	9	3	0	1	-1
1898	Bos-N	1.000	2	7	7	0	0	0
1902	Bos-N	.916	13	41	35	7	6	0
1903	Det-A	.970	31	71	91	5	6	4
1904	Phi-N	.889	1	4	4	1	0	1
Total	8	.944	65	180	191	2	19	5
OF								
1889	KC-a	—	1	0	0	0	0	0
1892	Bos-N	.875	12	16	5	3	0	1
1894	Bos-N	.833	5	5	0	1	0	-2
1897	Bos-N	—	1	0	0	0	0	0
Total	4	.867	19	21	5	4	0	-1
1B								
1899	Bos-N	1.000	2	20	2	0	1	1
3B								
1892	Bos-N	—	1	0	0	0	0	0

■ Dale Long 1B

YEAR	TM/L	PCT	G	PO	A	E	DP	FR
1951	Pit-N	1.000	1	8	0	0	0	0
	StL-A	.988	28	227	19	3	23	0
1955	Pit-N	.988	119	968	97	**13**	114	6
1956	Pit-N	.982	**138**	1201	99	**24**	92	-3
1957	Pit-N	1.000	7	54	5	0	6	0
	Chi-N	.995	104	908	72	5	81	-1
	Yr	.995	111	962	77	5	87	-1
1958	Chi-N	.992	137	1173	84	10	130	-2
1959	Chi-N	.985	85	731	49	12	63	-2
1960	SF-N	1.000	10	73	6	0	5	0
	NY-A	.988	11	78	4	1	3	0
1961	Was-A	.983	95	827	62	**15**	87	-7
1962	Was-A	.996	51	459	32	2	46	0
	NY-A	.992	31	242	21	2	21	1
	Yr	.995	82	701	53	4	67	1
1963	NY-A	.917	2	11	0	1	1	0
Total	10	.988	819	6960	550	8	672	-8
C								
1958	Chi-N	1.000	2	0	1	0	0	0
OF								
1951	StL-A	—	1	0	0	0	0	0

■ Tom Long OF

YEAR	TM/L	PCT	G	PO	A	E	DP	FR
1911	Was-A	.875	13	13	1	2	0	-2
1915	StL-N	.927	136	236	18	**20**	1	-2
1916	StL-N	.945	106	143	13	9	2	-12
1917	StL-N	.919	137	173	9	16	2	-26
Total	4	.928	392	565	41	7	5	-42

■ Joe Lonnett C

YEAR	TM/L	PCT	G	PO	A	E	DP	FR
1956	Phi-N	1.000	7	24	2	0	1	0
1957	Phi-N	.997	65	305	16	1	3	5
1958	Phi-N	.988	15	78	7	1	3	2
1959	Phi-N	.983	43	171	4	3	0	-6
Total	4	.992	130	578	29	5	7	1

■ Stan Lopata C

YEAR	TM/L	PCT	G	PO	A	E	DP	FR
1948	Phi-N	1.000	4	17	1	0	1	0
1949	Phi-N	.973	58	236	19	7	2	-3
1950	Phi-N	.974	51	176	13	5	3	0
1951	Phi-N	1.000	1	6	0	0	0	0
1952	Phi-N	.987	55	274	21	4	6	6
1953	Phi-N	.987	80	344	27	5	2	4
1954	Phi-N	.989	75	336	26	4	1	8
1955	Phi-N	.995	66	332	37	2	9	4
1956	Phi-N	.982	102	573	24	11	**10**	-14
1957	Phi-N	.988	108	634	36	8	9	-9
1958	Phi-N	.987	80	418	28	6	6	-7
1959	Mil-N	1.000	11	43	0	0	1	-2
1960	Mil-N	.944	4	17	0	1	0	1
Total	13	.986	695	3406	232	3	50	-12
1B								
1954	Phi-N	1.000	1	0	1	0	0	0
1955	Phi-N	.994	24	148	13	1	7	0
1956	Phi-N	.984	39	300	16	5	31	-5
1959	Mil-N	1.000	2	6	0	0	0	0
Total	4	.988	66	454	30	6	38	-5

■ Davey Lopes 2B

YEAR	TM/L	PCT	G	PO	A	E	DP	FR
1972	LA-N	.964	11	27	27	2	5	-2
1973	LA-N	.984	135	319	379	11	90	-12
1974	LA-N	.965	143	309	360	**24**	71	-22
1975	LA-N	.979	137	307	375	15	58	-19
1976	LA-N	.964	100	218	266	18	56	-19
1977	LA-N	.979	130	287	380	14	74	8
1978	LA-N	.974	147	337	424	**20**	88	4
1979	LA-N	.981	152	341	**384**	14	82	-34
1980	LA-N	.980	140	304	416	15	85	-16
1981	LA-N	.993	55	129	161	2	30	-4
1982	Oak-A	.977	125	289	338	15	82	-17
1983	Oak-A	.983	123	254	278	9	81	-33
1984	Oak-A	.948	17	20	35	3	8	-7
	Chi-N	1.000	0	2	0	0	0	0
1985	Chi-N	1.000	1	1	2	0	1	0
Total	14	.977	1418	3142	3829	162	811	173
OF								
1973	LA-N	1.000	5	3	0	0	0	0
1975	LA-N	1.000	24	45	3	0	1	1
1976	LA-N	.974	19	36	2	1	0	-1
1978	LA-N	1.000	2	3	0	0	0	0
1982	Oak-A	1.000	6	6	0	0	0	0
1983	Oak-A	1.000	7	8	0	0	0	0
1984	Oak-A	.965	42	78	4	3	2	-2
	Chi-N	1.000	9	6	0	0	0	-1

YEAR	TM/L	PCT	G	PO	A	E	DP	FR
1985	Chi-N	.991	79	113	2	1	0	-8
1986	Chi-N	1.000	22	31	0	0	0	0
	Hou-N	1.000	19	44	3	0	1	3
	Yr	1.000	41	75	3	0	1	3
1987	Hou-N	.857	5	6	0	1	0	0
Total	10	.985	239	379	14	6	4	-8
3B								
1973	LA-N	1.000	1	0	1	0	0	0
1983	Oak-A	1.000	5	5	9	0	2	0
1984	Oak-A	1.000	5	1	8	0	0	0
1985	Chi-N	1.000	4	1	2	0	0	0
1986	Chi-N	.902	32	20	54	8	3	-2
	Hou-N	1.000	5	1	8	0	1	1
	Yr	.912	37	21	62	8	4	-1
Total	5	.932	52	28	82	8	6	-1
SS								
1973	LA-N	1.000	2	1	0	0	0	0
1975	LA-N	.933	14	8	6	1	1	-4
Total	2	.938	16	9	6	1	1	-4

■ Al Lopez C

YEAR	TM/L	PCT	G	PO	A	E	DP	FR
1928	Bro-N	1.000	3	9	0	0	0	-2
1930	Bro-N	.983	126	465	66	9	9	4
1931	Bro-N	.977	105	390	69	11	6	-8
1932	Bro-N	.976	125	456	**82**	13	10	-3
1933	Bro-N	.991	124	449	**84**	5	14	**17**
1934	Bro-N	.982	**137**	542	62	11	4	-7
1935	Bro-N	.980	**126**	472	65	11	8	5
1936	Bos-N	.975	127	447	**107**	14	9	9
1937	Bos-N	.984	102	342	83	7	5	7
1938	Bos-N	.989	71	240	42	3	4	3
1939	Bos-N	.986	129	424	72	7	11	2
1940	Bos-N	.987	36	119	33	2	4	2
	Pit-N	.992	59	224	29	2	7	3
	Yr	.990	95	343	62	4	11	5
1941	Pit-N	.980	114	345	54	8	5	-1
1942	Pit-N	**.995**	99	327	53	2	**14**	**5**
1943	Pit-N	**.991**	116	378	66	4	9	8
1944	Pit-N	**.984**	115	372	52	7	6	5
1945	Pit-N	.992	91	326	38	3	7	8
1946	Pit-N	.985	56	173	30	3	4	0
1947	Cle-A	1.000	57	144	28	0	1	0
Total	19	.985	1918	6644	1115	122	137	57
2B								
1933	Bro-N	1.000	1	3	4	0	1	1
1934	Bro-N	1.000	2	4	2	0	1	0
Total	2	1.000	3	7	6	0	2	1
3B								
1934	Bro-N	1.000	2	2	4	0	1	0
1943	Pit-N	.500	1	0	1	1	0	0
Total	2	.875	3	2	5	1	1	0
1B								
1936	Bos-N	1.000	1	1	0	0	0	0

■ Carlos Lopez OF

YEAR	TM/L	PCT	G	PO	A	E	DP	FR
1976	Cal-A	1.000	4	4	0	0	0	0
1977	Sea-A	.972	90	160	11	5	3	3
1978	Bal-A	.988	114	151	7	2	2	-16
Total	3	.979	208	315	18	7	5	-13

■ Hector Lopez OF

YEAR	TM/L	PCT	G	PO	A	E	DP	FR
1956	KC-A	.959	20	44	3	2	0	1
1957	KC-A	1.000	3	3	0	0	0	0
1958	KC-A	1.000	1	2	0	0	0	0
1959	KC-A	.955	35	62	1	3	1	-3
1960	NY-A	.976	106	199	8	5	2	1
1961	NY-A	.977	72	123	7	3	0	2
1962	NY-A	.984	84	176	3	3	0	2
1963	NY-A	.957	124	187	11	9	2	-7
1964	NY-A	.971	103	130	2	4	1	-2
1965	NY-A	.942	75	94	5	6	0	-7
1966	NY-A	.936	29	43	1	3	0	-2
Total	11	.967	652	1063	39	8	6	-15
3B								
1955	KC-A	.936	93	104	233	**23**	26	13
1956	KC-A	.940	121	152	254	**26**	23	3
1957	KC-A	.937	111	117	227	23	20	5
1958	KC-A	.956	55	56	95	7	8	-6
1959	NY-A	.926	76	66	147	17	15	-5
1960	NY-A	.000	1	0	0	2	0	-1
1962	NY-A	1.000	1	0	1	0	0	0
1964	NY-A	1.000	1	1	2	0	0	0
Total	8	.937	459	496	959	8	92	9
2B								
1955	KC-A	.970	36	93	98	6	32	2
1956	KC-A	.947	8	18	18	2	7	-1
1957	KC-A	1.000	4	5	2	0	1	-1
1958	KC-A	.974	96	251	282	**14**	78	13
1959	KC-A	.933	33	81	71	11	15	-12
1960	NY-A	1.000	5	5	1	0	0	0
1962	NY-A	1.000	1	1	0	0	0	0
1963	NY-A	1.000	1	1	1	0	0	0
Total	8	.966	184	455	473	3	133	0
SS								
1956	KC-A	1.000	4	4	7	0	2	0
1958	KC-A	—	1	0	0	0	0	0
Total	2	1.000	5	4	7	0	2	0
1B								
1965	NY-A	.857	2	6	0	1	0	0

■ Bris Lord OF

YEAR	TM/L	PCT	G	PO	A	E	DP	FR
1905	Phi-A	.963	61	94	9	4	3	0
1906	Phi-A	.941	115	212	13	14	4	-2
1907	Phi-A	.951	53	91	6	5	0	-2
1909	Cle-A	.992	67	110	13	1	4	5
1910	Cle-A	.956	56	77	14	4	4	4
	Phi-A	.980	70	142	6	3	2	4
	Yr	.972	126	219	20	7	6	8
1911	Phi-A	.963	132	271	17	11	5	8

YEAR	TM/L	PCT	G	PO	A	E	DP	FR
1912	Phi-A	.942	97	148	15	10	5	-1
1913	Bos-N	.914	62	81	4	8	0	-10
Total	8	.957	713	1226	97	0	27	6

■ Harry Lord 3B

YEAR	TM/L	PCT	G	PO	A	E	DP	FR
1907	Bos-A	.919	10	12	22	3	0	0
1908	Bos-A	.902	144	181	271	**49**	13	-9
1909	Bos-A	.929	134	180	268	34	10	-7
1910	Bos-A	.927	70	90	138	18	10	-6
	Chi-A	.952	44	44	75	6	4	-11
	Yr	.935	114	134	213	24	14	-17
1911	Chi-A	.941	138	175	226	25	21	-17
1912	Chi-A	.895	106	127	172	35	11	-23
1913	Chi-A	.924	**150**	142	221	30	13	-31
1914	Chi-A	.933	19	10	32	3	0	-5
1915	Buf-F	.946	92	85	158	14	13	-14
Total	9	.924	907	1046	1583	217	95	123
OF								
1912	Chi-A	.957	45	61	5	3	3	-4
1914	Chi-A	—	1	0	0	0	0	0
1915	Buf-F	1.000	1	1	0	0	0	0
Total	3	.957	47	62	5	3	3	-4
SS								
1910	Phi-A	.727	1	2	6	3	1	1

■ Baldy Louden 2B

YEAR	TM/L	PCT	G	PO	A	E	DP	FR
1912	Det-A	.951	87	200	288	25	25	**22**
1913	Det-A	.906	30	43	72	12	6	-3
1915	Buf-F	.978	88	191	262	10	36	**8**
1916	Cin-N	**.968**	108	238	345	19	48	18
Total	4	.961	313	672	967	6	115	45
SS								
1912	Det-A	.912	5	10	21	3	0	2
1913	Det-A	1.000	6	5	14	0	1	2
1914	Buf-F	.931	115	299	285	43	34	-18
1915	Buf-F	.910	27	65	87	15	9	2
1916	Cin-N	.950	23	41	72	6	3	-1
Total	5	.931	176	420	479	7	47	-13
3B								
1907	NY-A	.750	3	4	8	4	0	1
1912	Det-A	.894	26	32	61	11	0	-1
1913	Det-A	.943	26	23	59	5	4	1
1915	Buf-F	.972	19	27	42	2	6	3
Total	4	.921	74	86	170	2	10	4
OF								
1913	Det-A	1.000	5	5	1	0	0	0

■ Joe Lovitto OF

YEAR	TM/L	PCT	G	PO	A	E	DP	FR
1972	Tex-A	.976	103	233	7	6	2	9
1973	Tex-A	1.000	3	3	0	0	0	0
1974	Tex-A	.972	107	201	7	6	1	-14
1975	Tex-A	.985	38	62	5	1	1	2
Total	4	.975	251	499	17	3	4	-3
3B								
1973	Tex-A	.898	20	23	21	5	3	2
1B								
1974	Tex-A	1.000	5	23	0	0	0	0
1975	Tex-A	1.000	2	9	0	0	0	0
Total	2	1.000	7	32	0	0	3	0
C								
1975	Tex-A	—	1	0	0	0	0	0

■ Bobby Lowe 2B

YEAR	TM/L	PCT	G	PO	A	E	DP	FR
1891	Bos-N	.923	17	23	49	6	2	-5
1892	Bos-N	.915	10	36	29	6	4	1
1893	Bos-N	.936	121	308	409	49	58	1
1894	Bos-N	.927	130	345	402	59	62	-6
1895	Bos-N	.954	99	265	336	29	50	**15**
1896	Bos-N	.965	73	193	280	17	31	24
1897	Bos-N	.952	123	270	404	34	33	-4
1898	Bos-N	.958	145	397	457	37	63	15
1899	Bos-N	.954	**148**	361	461	40	66	3
1900	Bos-N	.951	127	**323**	335	34	38	-7
1901	Bos-N	.954	18	52	52	5	9	3
1902	Chi-N	.957	117	326	406	33	59	26
1903	Chi-N	.948	22	37	72	6	8	3
1904	Det-A	.964	140	328	402	27	44	0
1905	Det-A	.742	6	6	17	8	1	-2
1906	Det-A	.959	17	56	60	5	2	5
Total	16	.950	1313	3326	4171	395	530	72
OF								
1890	Bos-N	.971	15	34	0	1	0	0
1891	Bos-N	.927	107	186	16	16	2	-1
1892	Bos-N	.928	90	175	17	15	2	7
1905	Det-A	.980	24	45	5	1	0	3
1907	Det-A	1.000	4	1	0	0	0	-2
Total	5	.936	240	441	38	3	4	7
3B								
1890	Bos-N	.897	12	19	16	4	1	-3
1891	Bos-N	.333	1	1	0	2	0	-1
1892	Bos-N	.900	14	24	39	7	3	4
1894	Bos-N	1.000	1	0	1	0	0	0
1901	Bos-N	.912	111	149	192	33	12	-8
1902	Chi-N	1.000	2	3	4	0	0	0
1903	Chi-N	.667	1	2	4	3	0	0
1905	Det-A	.981	22	16	36	1	4	0
1906	Det-A	1.000	5	3	5	0	0	0
1907	Det-A	.870	10	4	16	3	0	-2
Total	10	.910	179	221	313	3	17	-11
SS								
1890	Bos-N	.951	24	50	66	6	1	-5
1891	Bos-N	1.000	2	4	5	0	1	1
1892	Bos-N	.875	13	29	34	9	9	1
1893	Bos-N	.903	5	12	16	3	1	0
1894	Bos-N	1.000	2	3	5	0	1	1
1898	Bos-N	.947	2	8	10	1	1	2
1899	Bos-N	1.000	4	5	12	0	0	0
1905	Det-A	.933	4	9	5	1	0	-2

YEAR	TM/L	PCT	G	PO	A	E	DP	FR
1906	Det-A	.915	19	43	76	11	1	2
1907	Det-A	1.000	2	2	1	0	0	-1
Total	10	.927	77	165	230	1	15	-1
1B								
1903	Chi-N	.967	6	54	4	2	5	0
1905	Det-A	1.000	1	9	0	0	0	0
Total	2	.971	7	63	4	2	5	0

■ John Lowenstein OF

YEAR	TM/L	PCT	G	PO	A	E	DP	FR
1970	Cle-A	1.000	2	2	0	0	0	0
1971	Cle-A	.947	18	17	1	1	0	0
1972	Cle-A	1.000	58	77	7	0	3	3
1973	Cle-A	.931	51	62	5	5	1	-4
1974	Cle-A	.986	100	200	6	3	1	-3
1975	Cle-A	.983	36	56	2	1	1	-2
1976	Cle-A	.972	61	97	7	3	1	3
1977	Cle-A	1.000	39	62	1	0	0	2
1978	Tex-A	.929	16	12	1	1	0	0
1979	Bal-A	.992	72	120	4	1	2	4
1980	Bal-A	.992	91	128	3	1	0	2
1981	Bal-A	.990	73	100	3	1	0	-2
1982	Bal-A	1.000	111	202	2	0	0	-4
1983	Bal-A	.982	107	155	8	3	1	-11
1984	Bal-A	.971	67	94	5	3	0	2
1985	Bal-A	1.000	4	7	0	0	0	0
Total	16	.984	906	1391	55	3	10	-10
3B								
1970	Cle-A	.778	2	1	6	2	1	0
1973	Cle-A	.960	8	9	15	1	2	0
1974	Cle-A	.966	28	23	63	3	4	-1
1975	Cle-A	.941	8	5	11	1	0	-1
1978	Tex-A	.926	25	22	41	5	2	-5
1979	Bal-A	1.000	1	0	2	0	0	0
Total	6	.943	72	60	138	2	9	-7
2B								
1970	Cle-A	1.000	10	12	31	0	5	4
1971	Cle-A	.986	29	81	59	2	17	-1
1973	Cle-A	.991	25	49	64	1	19	-4
1974	Cle-A	1.000	4	3	7	0	0	0
1975	Cle-A	1.000	2	0	3	0	0	0
1983	Bal-A	—	1	0	0	0	0	0
Total	6	.990	71	145	164	3	41	-1
1B								
1972	Cle-A	1.000	2	5	0	0	0	0
1973	Cle-A	1.000	1	4	1	0	0	0
1974	Cle-A	1.000	12	88	8	0	6	1
1976	Cle-A	.955	9	81	3	4	8	-2
1977	Cle-A	1.000	1	1	0	0	0	0
1979	Bal-A	1.000	1	4	1	0	1	0
1984	Bal-A	1.000	2	19	0	0	2	-1
Total	7	.982	28	202	13	4	17	-2
SS								
1970	Cle-A	—	1	0	0	0	0	0
1971	Cle-A	.917	3	5	6	1	1	-1
Total	2	.917	4	5	6	1	1	-1

■ Peanuts Lowrey OF

YEAR	TM/L	PCT	G	PO	A	E	DP	FR
1942	Chi-N	.978	19	43	2	1	1	4
1943	Chi-N	.982	113	315	13	6	4	6
1945	Chi-N	.987	138	280	17	4	1	4
1946	Chi-N	.979	126	308	15	7	3	3
1947	Chi-N	.981	25	50	2	1	0	-1
1948	Chi-N	.983	103	225	9	4	2	5
1949	Chi-N	.966	31	56	1	2	0	-3
	Cin-N	.995	78	202	7	1	2	7
	Yr	.989	109	258	8	3	2	4
1950	Cin-N	.987	72	153	4	2	1	2
	StL-N	.833	4	5	0	1	0	0
	Yr	.982	76	158	4	3	1	2
1951	StL-N	.983	85	220	6	4	3	-4
1952	StL-N	.978	106	174	3	4	1	-9
1953	StL-N	1.000	38	42	1	0	0	-3
1954	StL-N	1.000	12	5	0	0	0	0
1955	Phi-N	.973	28	35	1	1	0	-2
Total	13	.983	978	2113	81	8	18	9
3B								
1946	Chi-N	.918	20	22	34	5	2	0
1947	Chi-N	.945	91	83	194	16	21	10
1948	Chi-N	.960	9	9	15	1	2	-2
1949	Chi-N	.667	1	1	1	1	0	-1
1950	StL-N	.952	5	5	15	1	2	1
1951	StL-N	.821	11	5	18	5	2	-1
1952	StL-N	.864	6	2	17	3	1	1
1953	StL-N	—	1	0	0	0	0	0
Total	8	.929	144	127	294	2	30	8
2B								
1943	Chi-N	.941	3	6	10	1	3	2
1947	Chi-N	1.000	6	5	4	0	0	-1
1948	Chi-N	1.000	2	4	5	0	0	0
1950	Cin-N	1.000	1	0	1	0	0	0
	StL-N	1.000	6	21	16	0	4	1
	Yr	1.000	7	21	17	0	4	1
1951	StL-N	1.000	3	5	1	0	0	0
1953	StL-N	.932	10	22	19	3	6	-2
1955	Phi-N	1.000	2	2	4	0	1	0
Total	7	.969	33	65	60	4	14	0
SS								
1943	Chi-N	.952	16	20	39	3	4	2
1945	Chi-N	.750	2	1	2	1	0	-1
1948	Chi-N	—	1	0	0	0	0	-1
Total	3	.939	19	21	41	4	4	0
1B								
1955	Phi-N	1.000	1	7	1	0	1	0

■ Dwight Lowry C

YEAR	TM/L	PCT	G	PO	A	E	DP	FR
1984	Det-A	1.000	31	87	8	0	2	4
1986	Det-A	.992	55	246	16	2	2	-1
1987	Det-A	1.000	12	38	1	0	0	0

YEAR	TM/L	PCT	G	PO	A	E	DP	FR
1988	Min-A	1.000	5	12	1	0	0	2
Total	4	.995	103	383	26	2	4	5
1B								
1986	Det-A	1.000	1	2	1	0	0	0
1987	Det-A	1.000	1	2	1	0	0	0
Total	2	1.000	2	4	2	0	0	0
OF								
1986	Det-A	1.000	1	2	0	0	0	0

■ Johnny Lucadello 2B

YEAR	TM/L	PCT	G	PO	A	E	DP	FR
1939	StL-A	.912	7	16	15	3	3	-4
1940	StL-A	.968	16	37	53	3	14	0
1941	StL-A	.962	70	147	185	13	36	-6
1946	StL-A	.989	19	53	36	1	10	-3
1947	NY-A	1.000	5	3	0	0	0	-2
Total	5	.965	117	256	289	0	63	-15
3B								
1938	StL-A	.909	6	5	5	1	0	-1
1941	StL-A	.952	6	10	10	1	0	-1
1946	StL-A	.942	37	31	66	6	4	-4
Total	3	.941	49	46	81	8	4	-6
SS								
1941	StL-A	.855	12	33	14	8	4	-9
OF								
1941	StL-A	1.000	1	5	0	0	0	0

■ Fred Luderus 1B

YEAR	TM/L	PCT	G	PO	A	E	DP	FR
1909	Chi-N	.950	11	110	4	6	4	-2
1910	Chi-N	.975	17	151	7	4	7	0
	Phi-N	.985	19	184	12	3	15	1
	Yr	.981	36	335	19	7	22	1
1911	Phi-N	.985	146	1373	77	22	85	-2
1912	Phi-N	.990	146	1421	104	15	77	10
1913	Phi-N	.984	155	1533	92	26	76	1
1914	Phi-N	.975	121	1102	76	30	49	1
1915	Phi-N	.993	141	1409	99	11	76	10
1916	Phi-N	.982	146	1499	71	28	83	-2
1917	Phi-N	.991	154	1597	91	16	91	4
1918	Phi-N	.988	125	1307	98	17	74	7
1919	Phi-N	.985	138	1385	108	22	82	9
1920	Phi-N	.983	7	55	4	1	6	0
Total	12	.986	1326	13126	843	201	725	37

■ Eddie Lukon OF

YEAR	TM/L	PCT	G	PO	A	E	DP	FR
1941	Cin-N	.980	22	47	2	1	1	0
1945	Cin-N	1.000	2	6	0	0	0	0
1946	Cin-N	.985	83	190	5	3	1	1
1947	Cin-N	1.000	55	103	4	0	2	0
Total	4	.989	162	346	11	4	4	1

■ Mike Lum OF

YEAR	TM/L	PCT	G	PO	A	E	DP	FR
1967	Atl-N	.944	6	16	1	1	0	1
1968	Atl-N	.976	95	115	7	3	0	-11
1969	Atl-N	.992	89	119	2	1	1	10
1970	Atl-N	.988	98	168	3	2	0	6
1971	Atl-N	.990	125	286	10	3	2	10
1972	Atl-N	.976	109	241	4	6	1	4
1973	Atl-N	.985	64	126	3	2	0	1
1974	Atl-N	.989	50	91	0	1	0	-3
1975	Atl-N	1.000	38	95	0	0	0	-3
1976	Cin-N	1.000	38	48	0	0	0	-4
1977	Cin-N	1.000	24	36	0	0	0	0
1978	Cin-N	.987	43	69	6	1	2	5
1979	Atl-N	1.000	3	6	0	0	0	0
1980	Atl-N	1.000	19	19	0	0	0	0
1981	Atl-N	1.000	1	3	0	0	0	0
	Chi-N	.923	14	12	0	1	0	-2
	Yr	.938	15	15	0	1	0	-2
Total	15	.986	816	1450	36	1	6	17
1B								
1971	Atl-N	1.000	1	1	1	0	0	0
1972	Atl-N	1.000	2	6	2	0	0	1
1973	Atl-N	.991	84	707	42	7	64	-4
1974	Atl-N	.994	60	463	26	3	44	-3
1975	Atl-N	.992	60	562	34	5	41	-1
1977	Cin-N	.980	8	47	2	1	4	-1
1978	Cin-N	.971	7	31	2	1	0	0
1979	Atl-N	.998	51	414	30	1	36	2
1980	Atl-N	1.000	10	39	4	0	1	1
1981	Chi-N	1.000	1	0	0	0	0	0
Total	10	.993	284	2271	143	8	190	-5

■ Harry Lumley OF

YEAR	TM/L	PCT	G	PO	A	E	DP	FR
1904	Bro-N	.955	150	228	26	12	8	4
1905	Bro-N	.912	129	177	21	19	4	-1
1906	Bro-N	.949	131	231	13	13	5	1
1907	Bro-N	.959	118	171	15	8	7	-4
1908	Bro-N	.955	116	157	13	8	6	-5
1909	Bro-N	.948	52	83	9	5	1	2
1910	Bro-N	.833	4	5	0	1	0	-1
Total	7	.946	700	1052	97	6	31	-4

■ Jerry Lumpe 2B

YEAR	TM/L	PCT	G	PO	A	E	DP	FR
1959	NY-A	1.000	1	2	1	0	1	0
	KC-A	.986	61	133	158	4	41	-1
	Yr	.987	62	135	159	4	42	-1
1960	KC-A	.982	134	355	364	13	99	-6
1961	KC-A	.979	147	403	426	18	105	16
1962	KC-A	.986	156	343	435	11	97	-4
1963	KC-A	.988	155	341	451	10	92	2
1964	Det-A	.983	158	339	394	13	95	-21
1965	Det-A	.985	139	281	308	9	69	-18
1966	Det-A	.991	95	202	223	4	51	-6
1967	Det-A	.963	54	70	85	6	12	-2
Total	9	.984	1100	2469	2845	8	662	-40
3B								
1956	NY-A	1.000	1	1	1	0	0	0
1957	NY-A	.956	30	20	45	3	6	-2
1958	NY-A	.943	65	57	126	11	13	3
1959	NY-A	1.000	12	5	24	0	3	2

YEAR	TM/L	PCT	G	PO	A	E	DP	FR
	KC-A	.750	4	2	1	1	0	-1
	Yr	.970	16	7	25	1	3	1
1967	Det-A	.917	6	3	8	1	0	-1
Total	5	.948	118	88	205	6	22	1
SS								
1956	NY-A	.916	17	32	55	8	15	3
1957	NY-A	.933	6	2	12	1	2	1
1958	NY-A	1.000	5	6	9	0	2	1
1959	NY-A	1.000	4	4	11	0	2	0
	KC-A	.967	56	85	148	8	39	-9
	Yr	.969	60	89	159	8	41	-9
1960	KC-A	.960	15	28	44	3	13	-1
1962	KC-A	1.000	2	1	0	0	0	0
Total	6	.956	105	158	279	0	73	-5

■ Don Lund OF

YEAR	TM/L	PCT	G	PO	A	E	DP	FR
1947	Bro-N	1.000	5	11	0	0	0	0
1948	Bro-N	.977	25	41	2	1	0	1
	StL-N	1.000	45	72	3	0	0	-3
1952	Det-A	1.000	7	10	1	0	0	0
1953	Det-A	.980	123	275	12	6	0	8
1954	Det-A	.971	31	32	1	1	0	0
Total	5	.983	236	441	19	8	0	6

■ Tony Lupien 1B

YEAR	TM/L	PCT	G	PO	A	E	DP	FR
1940	Bos-A	1.000	8	37	2	0	4	0
1942	Bos-A	.992	121	1091	68	9	99	-7
1943	Bos-A	.993	153	1487	118	12	149	4
1944	Phi-N	.992	151	1453	103	13	114	1
1945	Phi-N	1.000	15	129	16	0	11	3
1948	Chi-A	.993	154	1436	92	11	155	-4
Total	6	.993	602	5633	399	5	532	-3

■ Al Luplow OF

YEAR	TM/L	PCT	G	PO	A	E	DP	FR
1961	Cle-A	1.000	5	9	2	0	1	1
1962	Cle-A	.960	86	162	4	7	0	-1
1963	Cle-A	.994	85	157	7	1	1	3
1964	Cle-A	1.000	5	5	0	0	0	0
1965	Cle-A	1.000	6	3	0	0	0	1
1966	NY-N	.987	101	147	4	2	1	-7
1967	NY-N	.966	33	55	1	2	0	-1
	Pit-N	.961	25	45	4	2	1	3
	Yr	.963	58	100	5	4	1	2
Total	7	.977	346	583	22	4	4	-1

■ Scott Lusader OF

YEAR	TM/L	PCT	G	PO	A	E	DP	FR
1987	Det-A	.967	22	29	0	1	0	-1
1988	Det-A	1.000	4	7	0	0	0	1
1989	Det-A	.933	33	56	0	4	0	-2
1990	Det-A	.982	42	53	1	1	0	-2
Total	4	.961	101	145	1	6	0	-4

■ Billy Lush OF

YEAR	TM/L	PCT	G	PO	A	E	DP	FR
1895	Was-N	.692	5	9	0	4	0	-1
1896	Was-N	.885	91	142	19	21	4	-1
1897	Was-N	1.000	3	5	1	0	0	1
1901	Bos-N	.960	7	22	2	1	1	3
1902	Bos-N	.952	116	251	24	14	5	10
1903	Det-A	.968	101	227	17	8	4	17
1904	Cle-A	.959	138	269	11	12	4	3
Total	7	.943	461	925	74	0	18	32
3B								
1902	Bos-N	1.000	1	0	2	0	0	0
1903	Det-A	.941	12	15	17	2	0	-3
Total	2	.944	13	15	19	2	0	-3
2B								
1896	Was-N	.778	3	3	4	2	0	-1
1903	Det-A	.857	3	9	3	2	1	-2
Total	2	.826	6	12	7	4	1	-3
SS								
1903	Det-A	.800	3	6	3	1	1	-1

■ Rube Lutzke 3B

YEAR	TM/L	PCT	G	PO	A	E	DP	FR
1923	Cle-A	.940	143	186	358	35	23	20
1924	Cle-A	.947	103	154	238	22	25	20
1925	Cle-A	.936	69	61	129	13	9	0
1926	Cle-A	.960	142	160	302	19	27	-1
1927	Cle-A	.938	98	120	199	21	24	6
Total	5	.945	555	681	1226	110	108	45
2B								
1924	Cle-A	1.000	3	7	3	0	1	0
1925	Cle-A	.980	10	22	27	1	5	-1
Total	2	.983	13	29	30	1	6	-1

■ Greg Luzinski OF

YEAR	TM/L	PCT	G	PO	A	E	DP	FR
1972	Phi-N	.960	145	255	9	11	2	-2
1973	Phi-N	.993	159	262	7	2	1	-9
1974	Phi-N	.981	82	146	10	3	0	-2
1975	Phi-N	.966	159	248	10	9	0	-11
1976	Phi-N	.964	144	204	8	8	0	-16
1977	Phi-N	.964	148	205	11	8	2	-15
1978	Phi-N	.984	154	232	7	4	2	-16
1979	Phi-N	.946	125	156	3	9	1	-21
1980	Phi-N	.993	105	137	2	1	0	-18
Total	9	.972	1221	1845	67	5	8	110
1B								
1970	Phi-N	1.000	3	20	3	0	1	1
1971	Phi-N	.996	28	247	34	1	16	6
1972	Phi-N	.667	2	2	0	1	0	0
1983	Cal-A	1.000	2	6	1	0	1	0
Total	4	.994	35	275	38	2	18	7

■ Jerry Lynch OF

YEAR	TM/L	PCT	G	PO	A	E	DP	FR
1954	Pit-N	.965	83	127	10	5	2	-4
1955	Pit-N	.950	71	104	11	6	3	-4
1956	Pit-N	1.000	1	3	0	0	0	0
1957	Cin-N	1.000	24	38	0	0	0	-2
1958	Cin-N	.970	101	154	5	5	2	-10
1959	Cin-N	.979	98	180	5	4	3	-1
1960	Cin-N	.913	32	41	1	4	1	-4

YEAR	TM/L	PCT	G	PO	A	E	DP	FR
1961	Cin-N	.948	44	53	2	3	0	-6
1962	Cin-N	.970	73	89	7	3	1	-5
1963	Cin-N	1.000	7	5	0	0	0	-1
	Pit-N	.960	64	70	2	3	0	-9
	Yr	.962	71	75	2	3	0	-10
1964	Pit-N	.983	78	59	0	1	0	-17
1965	Pit-N	.903	26	27	.1	3	0	-3
1966	Pit-N	1.000	4	5	0	0	0	1
Total	13	.964	706	955	44	7	12	-65

C

YEAR	TM/L	PCT	G	PO	A	E	DP	FR
1955	Pit-N	1.000	2	8	2	0	0	-1
1957	Cin-N	1.000	2	2	0	0	0	0
Total	2	1.000	4	10	2	0	0	-1

■ Fred Lynn   OF

YEAR	TM/L	PCT	G	PO	A	E	DP	FR
1974	Bos-A	1.000	12	18	2	0	0	0
1975	Bos-A	.983	144	404	11	7	1	9
1976	Bos-A	.984	128	367	13	6	4	8
1977	Bos-A	.994	125	333	7	2	1	1
1978	Bos-A	.984	149	408	11	7	2	3
1979	Bos-A	.987	143	381	10	5	4	1
1980	Bos-A	.994	110	302	11	2	4	5
1981	Cal-A	.978	69	176	4	4	1	-1
1982	Cal-A	.991	133	317	6	3	3	-9
1983	Cal-A	.993	113	274	8	2	4	-6
1984	Cal-A	.982	140	321	12	6	5	8
1985	Bal-A	.994	123	314	6	2	2	-5
1986	Bal-A	.984	107	244	2	4	1	-9
1987	Bal-A	.991	101	229	2	2	1	-5
1988	Bal-A	.991	83	216	1	2	0	-4
	Det-A	1.000	22	41	2	0	0	-1
	Yr	.992	105	257	3	2	0	-5
1989	Det-A	.992	68	119	5	1	0	-3
1990	SD-N	1.000	55	92	1	0	0	-3
Total	17	.988	1825	4556	114	5	33	-11

■ Barry Lyons   C

YEAR	TM/L	PCT	G	PO	A	E	DP	FR
1986	NY-N	.941	3	16	0	1	0	0
1987	NY-N	.984	49	223	17	4	0	1
1988	NY-N	.979	32	129	8	3	0	-2
1989	NY-N	.980	76	463	29	10	4	1
1990	NY-N	.980	23	180	12	4	1	3
	LA-N	1.000	2	3	0	0	0	-1
	Yr	.980	25	183	12	4	1	2
Total	5	.980	185	1014	66	2	5	2

1B

YEAR	TM/L	PCT	G	PO	A	E	DP	FR
1988	NY-N	1.000	1	1	1	0	0	0

■ Denny Lyons   3B

YEAR	TM/L	PCT	G	PO	A	E	DP	FR
1885	Pro-N	.824	4	6	8	3	0	0
1886	Phi-a	.807	32	35	53	21	1	-7
1887	Phi-a	.866	137	255	215	73	29	-6
1888	Phi-a	.878	111	159	193	49	11	-13
1889	Phi-a	.860	130	202	291	80	29	9
1890	Phi-a	.909	88	147	203	35	14	9
1891	StL-a	.871	120	151	246	59	16	-6
1892	NY-N	.871	108	152	206	53	13	-5
1893	Pit-N	.918	131	214	303	46	23	5
1894	Pit-N	.898	71	119	155	31	11	7
1895	StL-N	.894	33	61	49	13	2	-4
1896	Pit-N	.893	116	165	201	44	15	-15
1897	Pit-N	1.000	2	6	4	0	0	1
Total	13	.882	1083	1672	2127	507	164	-25

1B

YEAR	TM/L	PCT	G	PO	A	E	DP	FR
1889	Phi-a	.875	1	7	0	1	0	0
1897	Pit-N	.989	35	339	15	4	15	-1
Total	2	.986	36	346	15	5	15	-1

■ Harry Lyons   OF

YEAR	TM/L	PCT	G	PO	A	E	DP	FR
1887	Phi-a	.500	1	1	0	1	0	0
	StL-a	1.000	1	2	0	0	0	0
1888	StL-a	.891	122	237	32	33	4	8
1889	NY-N	1.000	5	5	0	0	0	-1
1890	Roc-a	.920	132	264	25	25	4	11
1892	NY-N	.910	96	186	16	20	2	3
1893	NY-N	.917	47	113	9	11	3	2
Total	6	.908	404	808	82	0	13	23

3B

YEAR	TM/L	PCT	G	PO	A	E	DP	FR
1888	StL-a	1.000	2	0	1	0	0	0
1890	Roc-a	.800	2	1	3	1	0	0
Total	2	.833	4	1	4	1	0	0

2B

YEAR	TM/L	PCT	G	PO	A	E	DP	FR
1887	StL-a	1.000	1	1	5	0	1	1
1888	StL-a	—	1	0	0	0	0	0
Total	2	1.000	2	1	5	0	1	1

SS

YEAR	TM/L	PCT	G	PO	A	E	DP	FR
1888	StL-a	.400	1	0	2	3	0	-1
1890	Roc-a	.000	1	0	0	1	0	0

■ Steve Lyons   OF

YEAR	TM/L	PCT	G	PO	A	E	DP	FR
1985	Bos-A	.973	114	253	4	7	0	-14
1986	Bos-A	.972	55	100	3	3	1	6
	Chi-A	.987	35	73	2	1	0	1
	Yr	.978	90	173	5	4	1	7
1987	Chi-A	1.000	15	33	2	0	1	3
1988	Chi-A	.932	14	40	1	3	1	1
1989	Chi-A	1.000	20	24	0	0	0	0
1990	Chi-A	1.000	7	9	0	0	0	0
Total	6	.975	260	532	12	4	3	-3

3B

YEAR	TM/L	PCT	G	PO	A	E	DP	FR
1985	Bos-A	1.000	1	0	2	0	0	0
1986	Chi-A	1.000	3	1	6	0	0	0
1987	Chi-A	.971	51	35	99	4	11	10
1988	Chi-A	.927	128	81	238	25	36	10
1989	Chi-A	.895	28	16	35	6	3	-3
1990	Chi-A	1.000	5	0	4	0	1	1
Total	6	.937	216	133	384	5	51	18

1B

YEAR	TM/L	PCT	G	PO	A	E	DP	FR
1986	Chi-A	1.000	1	1	0	0	0	0

YEAR	TM/L	PCT	G	PO	A	E	DP	FR
1988	Chi-A	1.000	1	2	0	0	0	0
1989	Chi-A	.988	40	230	24	3	24	2
1990	Chi-A	.991	61	206	19	2	26	1
Total	4	.990	103	439	43	5	50	3

2B

YEAR	TM/L	PCT	G	PO	A	E	DP	FR
1987	Chi-A	1.000	1	1	0	0	0	0
1988	Chi-A	.900	4	5	4	1	1	-1
1989	Chi-A	.982	70	142	185	6	46	-3
1990	Chi-A	.951	15	29	29	3	6	-1
Total	4	.975	90	177	218	0	53	-5

SS

YEAR	TM/L	PCT	G	PO	A	E	DP	FR
1985	Bos-A	—	1	0	0	0	0	0
1989	Chi-A	1.000	3	2	1	0	0	0
1990	Chi-A	1.000	1	0	1	0	0	0
Total	3	1.000	5	2	2	0	0	0

C

YEAR	TM/L	PCT	G	PO	A	E	DP	FR
1988	Chi-A	—	2	0	0	0	0	0
1989	Chi-A	—	1	0	0	0	0	0
Total	2	—	3	0	0	0	0	0

■ Jim Lyttle   OF

YEAR	TM/L	PCT	G	PO	A	E	DP	FR
1969	NY-A	.983	28	55	3	1	1	3
1970	NY-A	.989	70	84	2	1	0	4
1971	NY-A	1.000	29	47	1	0	0	1
1972	Chi-A	.971	21	32	1	1	0	1
1973	Mon-N	.974	36	73	3	2	1	4
1974	Mon-N	1.000	18	6	1	0	0	2
1975	Mon-N	1.000	16	17	1	0	0	-1
1976	Mon-N	.977	29	39	3	1	2	1
	LA-N	1.000	18	48	5	0	2	5
	Yr	.990	47	87	8	1	4	6
Total	8	.988	265	401	20	5	7	20

■ Mike Macfarlane   C

YEAR	TM/L	PCT	G	PO	A	E	DP	FR
1987	KC-A	1.000	8	29	2	0	0	-1
1988	KC-A	.994	68	309	18	2	3	-14
1989	KC-A	.996	59	249	17	1	4	4
1990	KC-A	.991	112	660	23	6	9	-20
Total	4	.993	247	1247	60	9	16	-31

■ Ken Macha   3B

YEAR	TM/L	PCT	G	PO	A	E	DP	FR
1977	Pit-N	.964	17	5	22	1	0	-3
1978	Pit-N	.970	21	11	21	1	3	-3
1979	Mon-N	.913	13	12	18	0	1	3
1980	Mon-N	.910	33	18	43	6	3	-5
1981	Tor-A	.892	19	5	28	4	2	-1
Total	5	.938	103	51	132	2	9	-9

1B

YEAR	TM/L	PCT	G	PO	A	E	DP	FR
1977	Pit-N	1.000	11	66	3	0	5	-1
1979	Mon-N	1.000	2	12	0	0	1	0
1980	Mon-N	1.000	2	12	0	0	2	0
1981	Tor-A	.990	16	94	8	1	8	0
Total	4	.995	31	184	11	1	16	-1

OF

YEAR	TM/L	PCT	G	PO	A	E	DP	FR
1977	Pit-N	1.000	4	1	0	0	0	0
1979	Mon-N	—	2	0	0	0	0	0
1980	Mon-N	—	1	0	0	0	0	0
Total	3	1.000	7	1	0	0	0	0

C

YEAR	TM/L	PCT	G	PO	A	E	DP	FR
1974	Mon-N	1.000	1	1	0	0	0	0
1979	Mon-N	—	1	0	0	0	0	0
1980	Mon-N	1.000	1	1	0	0	0	0
1981	Tor-A	—	1	0	0	0	0	0
Total	4	1.000	4	2	0	0	0	0

■ Connie Mack   C

YEAR	TM/L	PCT	G	PO	A	E	DP	FR
1886	Was-N	.957	10	88	22	5	2	9
1887	Was-N	.906	76	391	119	53	15	7
1888	Was-N	.916	79	361	152	47	8	4
1889	Was-N	.891	45	189	81	33	9	5
1890	Buf-P	.925	112	449	140	48	13	-13
1891	Pit-N	.926	72	359	79	35	1	11
1892	Pit-N	.951	92	404	143	28	11	25
1893	Pit-N	.941	37	128	47	11	5	5
1894	Pit-N	.947	69	274	67	19	6	6
1895	Pit-N	.962	12	41	10	2	1	-2
1896	Pit-N	1.000	5	14	3	0	0	0
Total	11	.927	609	2698	863	281	71	57

1B

YEAR	TM/L	PCT	G	PO	A	E	DP	FR
1888	Was-N	1.000	1	16	0	0	0	0
1889	Was-N	.920	22	188	7	17	10	-3
1890	Buf-P	1.000	5	36	6	0	1	2
1891	Pit-N	1.000	3	26	0	0	0	0
1892	Pit-N	.909	1	10	0	1	0	0
1895	Pit-N	1.000	1	7	0	0	1	0
1896	Pit-N	.974	28	247	16	7	14	0
Total	7	.957	61	530	29	5	26	-1

OF

YEAR	TM/L	PCT	G	PO	A	E	DP	FR
1887	Was-N	1.000	5	11	0	0	0	0
1888	Was-N	1.000	4	7	1	0	0	1
1889	Was-N	.905	34	55	12	7	3	5
1890	Buf-P	.889	9	15	1	2	0	-1
1892	Pit-N	1.000	3	1	0	0	0	-1
Total	5	.920	55	89	14	9	3	4

2B

YEAR	TM/L	PCT	G	PO	A	E	DP	FR
1887	Was-N	.818	2	1	8	2	1	0

SS

YEAR	TM/L	PCT	G	PO	A	E	DP	FR
1888	Was-N	.667	1	0	2	1	0	0

■ Denny Mack   SS

YEAR	TM/L	PCT	G	PO	A	E	DP	FR
1876	StL-N	.886	41	42	114	20	6	-7
1880	Buf-N	.940	16	18	45	4	3	-1
1882	Lou-a	.898	49	51	161	24	9	1
1883	Pit-a	.844	38	29	106	25	7	1
Total	4	.886	144	140	426	3	25	-6

2B

YEAR	TM/L	PCT	G	PO	A	E	DP	FR
1876	StL-N	.857	5	14	10	4	2	0
1880	Buf-N	1.000	1	1	1	0	0	0
1882	Lou-a	.820	24	55	59	25	11	-2
1883	Pit-a	1.000	1	1	7	0	0	1

YEAR	TM/L	PCT	G	PO	A	E	DP	FR
Total	4	.836	31	71	77	9	13	-1

1B

YEAR	TM/L	PCT	G	PO	A	E	DP	FR
1883	Pit-a	.963	25	226	10	9	11	2

OF

YEAR	TM/L	PCT	G	PO	A	E	DP	FR
1876	StL-N	.600	2	3	0	2	0	-1
1882	Lou-a	1.000	5	2	0	0	0	-2
Total	2	.714	7	5	0	2	0	-3

■ Reddy Mack   2B

YEAR	TM/L	PCT	G	PO	A	E	DP	FR
1885	Lou-a	.885	11	33	36	9	9	0
1886	Lou-a	.900	137	350	446	88	60	6
1887	Lou-a	.912	128	366	395	73	48	5
1888	Lou-a	.907	112	307	344	67	35	4
1889	Bal-a	.897	135	367	358	83	70	-11
1890	Bal-a	.932	26	62	76	10	7	1
Total	6	.905	549	1485	1655	330	229	5

OF

YEAR	TM/L	PCT	G	PO	A	E	DP	FR
1889	Bal-a	1.000	1	5	0	0	0	0

■ Ray Mack   2B

YEAR	TM/L	PCT	G	PO	A	E	DP	FR
1938	Cle-A	1.000	2	8	6	0	0	2
1939	Cle-A	.976	34	80	86	4	26	2
1940	Cle-A	.965	146	323	417	27	109	-9
1941	Cle-A	.970	145	363	386	23	109	-5
1942	Cle-A	.969	143	340	434	25	105	-4
1943	Cle-A	.967	153	381	444	28	123	-2
1944	Cle-A	.951	83	226	243	24	73	10
1946	Cle-A	.970	61	118	142	8	37	1
1947	Chi-N	.965	21	58	78	5	15	7
Total	9	.966	788	1897	2236	144	597	2

3B

YEAR	TM/L	PCT	G	PO	A	E	DP	FR
1939	Cle-A	1.000	1	0	1	0	0	0

■ Shane Mack   OF

YEAR	TM/L	PCT	G	PO	A	E	DP	FR
1987	SD-N	.982	91	159	1	3	0	-6
1988	SD-N	.983	55	110	4	2	1	9
1990	Min-A	.988	109	230	8	3	1	3
Total	3	.985	255	499	13	8	2	6

■ Pete Mackanin   2B

YEAR	TM/L	PCT	G	PO	A	E	DP	FR
1975	Mon-N	.966	127	300	410	25	100	19
1976	Mon-N	.965	100	201	289	18	60	-3
1977	Mon-N	1.000	9	11	14	0	3	2
1979	Phi-N	1.000	2	1	3	0	0	1
1980	Min-A	.968	71	114	191	9	47	6
1981	Min-A	.980	31	62	87	3	15	6
Total	6	.968	340	689	994	6	225	31

SS

YEAR	TM/L	PCT	G	PO	A	E	DP	FR
1973	Tex-A	.947	33	39	85	7	15	1
1974	Tex-A	1.000	2	3	8	0	3	2
1975	Mon-N	—	1	0	0	0	0	0
1976	Mon-N	1.000	3	0	1	0	0	0
1977	Mon-N	.933	8	19	23	3	8	2
1979	Phi-N	1.000	2	0	3	0	0	1
1980	Min-A	.949	30	42	88	7	27	10
1981	Min-A	.935	28	34	53	6	11	-9
Total	8	.945	107	137	261	3	64	7

3B

YEAR	TM/L	PCT	G	PO	A	E	DP	FR
1973	Tex-A	1.000	10	0	3	0	0	0
1975	Mon-N	.500	1	0	1	1	0	0
1976	Mon-N	.950	8	2	17	1	4	1
1977	Mon-N	.909	5	3	7	1	0	0
1978	Phi-N	1.000	1	0	1	0	0	0
1979	Phi-N	1.000	2	0	3	0	0	1
1980	Min-A	.800	3	0	4	1	0	0
1981	Min-A	1.000	4	1	3	0	1	0
Total	8	.918	34	6	39	4	5	2

1B

YEAR	TM/L	PCT	G	PO	A	E	DP	FR
1978	Phi-N	1.000	1	6	1	0	0	0
1980	Min-A	1.000	4	12	2	0	1	0
1981	Min-A	.964	10	74	6	3	13	-1
Total	3	.971	15	92	9	3	14	-1

OF

YEAR	TM/L	PCT	G	PO	A	E	DP	FR
1976	Mon-N	—	1	0	0	0	0	0
1977	Mon-N	1.000	4	1	0	0	0	0
Total	2	1.000	5	1	0	0	0	0

■ Felix Mackiewicz   OF

YEAR	TM/L	PCT	G	PO	A	E	DP	FR
1941	Phi-A	1.000	3	5	0	0	0	-1
1942	Phi-A	1.000	3	6	1	0	0	1
1943	Phi-A	1.000	3	9	0	0	0	0
1945	Cle-A	.987	112	288	11	4	4	3
1946	Cle-A	.983	72	172	2	3	1	4
1947	Cle-A	1.000	2	5	0	0	0	0
	Was-A	1.000	3	3	0	0	0	0
	Yr	1.000	5	8	0	0	0	0
Total	6	.986	198	488	14	7	5	7

■ Jimmy Macullar   SS

YEAR	TM/L	PCT	G	PO	A	E	DP	FR
1879	Syr-N	.864	37	61	111	27	9	1
1883	Cin-a	.333	1	0	1	2	0	-1
1884	Bal-a	.866	107	120	318	68	23	1
1885	Bal-a	.877	98	175	311	68	28	1
1886	Bal-a	.852	82	115	208	56	19	-9
Total	5	.865	325	471	949	221	79	-7

OF

YEAR	TM/L	PCT	G	PO	A	E	DP	FR
1879	Syr-N	.881	26	69	5	10	0	3
1882	Cin-a	.922	79	141	13	13	2	0
1883	Cin-a	.900	14	17	1	2	0	-2
1885	Bal-a	1.000	2	3	0	0	0	0
1886	Bal-a	—	2	0	0	0	0	-1
Total	5	.909	123	230	19	5	2	0

2B

YEAR	TM/L	PCT	G	PO	A	E	DP	FR
1879	Syr-N	.706	4	8	4	5	0	-3
1886	Bal-a	.750	1	1	5	2	0	0
Total	2	.720	5	9	9	7	0	-3

3B

YEAR	TM/L	PCT	G	PO	A	E	DP	FR
1879	Syr-N	1.000	1	1	0	0	0	0

■ Elliott Maddox   OF

YEAR	TM/L	PCT	G	PO	A	E	DP	FR
1970	Det-A	.983	37	55	2	1	1	3

YEAR	TM/L	PCT	G	PO	A	E	DP	FR
1971	Was-A	.990	103	197	7	2	1	-7
1972	Tex-A	.990	94	199	7	2	4	-1
1973	Tex-A	.981	89	144	7	3	1	-4
1974	NY-A	.986	135	334	18	5	4	5
1975	NY-A	1.000	55	157	5	0	3	7
1976	NY-A	1.000	13	21	2	0	1	1
1977	Bal-A	.990	45	99	0	1	0	5
1978	NY-N	.988	79	155	8	2	3	2
1979	NY-N	.985	65	129	5	2	1	4
1980	NY-N	1.000	4	3	0	0	0	0
Total	11	.989	719	1493	61	8	19	15
	3B							
1970	Det-A	.919	40	41	83	11	8	2
1971	Was-A	.947	12	4	14	1	3	2
1973	Tex-A	1.000	7	4	7	0	1	1
1974	NY-A	—	1	0	0	0	0	0
1977	Bal-A	—	1	0	0	0	0	0
1978	NY-N	.949	43	40	72	6	5	-4
1979	NY-N	.950	11	2	17	1	0	1
1980	NY-N	.956	115	96	209	14	18	-2
Total	8	.947	230	187	402	3	35	0
	SS							
1970	Det-A	.909	19	6	14	2	0	-1
	2B							
1970	Det-A	1.000	1	2	1	0	1	0
1974	NY-A	1.000	2	2	1	0	0	0
1975	NY-A	1.000	1	1	0	0	0	0
Total	3	1.000	4	5	2	0	1	0
	1B							
1978	NY-N	.500	1	1	0	1	0	0
1980	NY-N	1.000	2	12	2	0	1	0
Total	2	.938	3	13	2	1	1	0

■ Garry Maddox OF

YEAR	TM/L	PCT	G	PO	A	E	DP	FR
1972	SF-N	.979	121	279	7	6	3	-4
1973	SF-N	.969	140	370	4	**12**	0	3
1974	SF-N	.986	131	345	3	5	0	3
1975	SF-N	1.000	13	37	3	0	0	4
	Phi-N	.983	97	288	10	5	4	15
	Yr	.985	110	**325**	13	5	4	**19**
1976	Phi-N	.989	144	441	10	5	0	18
1977	Phi-N	.977	138	383	7	9	2	7
1978	Phi-N	.983	154	**444**	7	8	1	14
1979	Phi-N	.996	140	433	13	2	2	**20**
1980	Phi-N	.976	143	405	7	10	0	5
1981	Phi-N	.977	94	251	8	6	4	4
1982	Phi-N	**.992**	111	253	8	2	4	2
1983	Phi-N	.977	95	216	1	5	0	-5
1984	Phi-N	1.000	69	160	3	0	1	6
1985	Phi-N	.980	94	143	3	3	0	-9
1986	Phi-N	1.000	3	1	0	0	0	0
Total	15	.983	1687	4449	94	8	21	83

■ Ed Madjeski C

YEAR	TM/L	PCT	G	PO	A	E	DP	FR
1932	Phi-A	1.000	8	30	7	0	3	2
1933	Phi-A	.958	41	122	14	6	3	-4
1934	Phi-A	.000	1	0	0	1	0	-1
	Chi-A	.973	79	348	49	11	11	3
	Yr	.971	80	348	49	12	11	2
1937	NY-N	1.000	5	8	2	0	1	-2
Total	4	.970	134	508	72	8	18	-2

■ Bill Madlock 3B

YEAR	TM/L	PCT	G	PO	A	E	DP	FR
1973	Tex-A	.918	21	13	32	4	2	-6
1974	Chi-N	.946	121	84	229	18	14	-12
1975	Chi-N	.943	128	79	250	20	14	-11
1976	Chi-N	.961	136	107	234	14	21	-20
1977	SF-N	.949	126	96	220	17	16	-17
1979	Pit-N	.969	85	63	153	7	12	-6
1980	Pit-N	.955	127	86	214	14	18	-16
1981	Pit-N	.956	78	50	147	9	17	-4
1982	Pit-N	.952	146	92	266	18	23	-6
1983	Pit-N	.958	126	59	193	11	20	-13
1984	Pit-N	.942	98	66	176	15	17	-8
1985	Pit-N	.940	98	46	175	14	10	-15
	LA-N	.948	32	28	63	5	7	3
	Yr	.943	130	74	238	**19**	17	-12
1986	LA-N	.910	101	72	170	24	7	-8
1987	LA-N	.912	16	8	23	3	2	-4
	Det-A	1.000	1	0	1	0	0	0
Total	14	.948	1440	949	2546	193	200	143
	2B							
1977	SF-N	.950	6	5	14	1	2	0
1978	SF-N	.974	114	223	299	14	48	-24
1979	SF-N	.976	63	137	144	7	32	-13
Total	3	.974	183	365	457	2	82	-37
	1B							
1978	SF-N	1.000	3	11	1	0	1	0
1979	SF-N	1.000	5	9	0	0	3	0
1980	Pit-N	.962	12	73	3	3	7	-1
1982	Pit-N	1.000	3	22	1	0	2	0
1984	Pit-N	1.000	1	10	0	0	0	0
1985	Pit-N	1.000	12	81	5	0	3	0
1986	LA-N	.800	2	7	1	2	1	0
1987	LA-N	—	1	0	0	0	0	0
	Det-A	.989	22	167	11	2	14	-2
Total	8	.983	61	380	22	7	31	-3

■ Dave Magadan 1B

YEAR	TM/L	PCT	G	PO	A	E	DP	FR
1986	NY-N	1.000	9	48	5	0	5	1
1987	NY-N	.975	13	71	7	2	4	0
1988	NY-N	.988	71	441	38	6	36	0
1989	NY-N	.991	87	574	59	6	50	3
1990	NY-N	**.998**	113	830	71	2	52	2
Total	5	.993	293	1964	180	6	147	6
	3B							
1987	NY-N	.981	50	17	85	2	5	3
1988	NY-N	.952	48	18	61	4	6	-1

YEAR	TM/L	PCT	G	PO	A	E	DP	FR
1989	NY-N	.977	28	13	30	1	4	-1
1990	NY-N	.972	19	7	28	1	1	1
Total	4	.970	145	55	204	8	16	2

■ Lee Magee OF

YEAR	TM/L	PCT	G	PO	A	E	DP	FR
1912	StL-N	.956	85	198	18	10	2	9
1913	StL-N	.982	108	250	21	5	5	14
1914	StL-N	.970	102	210	14	7	4	-4
1916	NY-A	.975	128	301	17	8	3	4
1917	NY-A	.938	50	84	6	6	1	-8
	StL-A	—	1	0	0	0	0	0
	Yr	.938	51	84	6	6	1	-8
1919	Chi-N	.978	45	80	7	2	1	-1
Total	6	.969	519	1123	83	8	16	14
	2B							
1911	StL-N	.975	18	42	35	2	6	-1
1912	StL-N	.942	23	52	79	8	9	1
1913	StL-N	.963	22	49	56	4	8	2
1914	StL-N	1.000	6	4	9	0	1	1
1915	Bro-F	.937	115	271	321	**40**	46	-1
1916	NY-A	1.000	2	4	9	0	0	0
1917	StL-A	1.000	6	18	23	0	1	2
1918	Cin-N	.956	114	275	361	**29**	**73**	10
1919	Bro-N	.938	36	74	124	13	10	1
	Chi-N	.941	7	13	19	2	0	-1
	Yr	.939	43	87	143	15	10	0
Total	9	.949	349	802	1036	8	154	14
	1B							
1912	StL-N	1.000	6	48	3	0	6	0
1913	StL-N	1.000	6	72	8	0	4	2
1914	StL-N	.998	39	412	28	1	20	3
1915	Bro-F	.952	2	19	1	1	1	0
1917	StL-A	1.000	5	42	4	0	3	1
Total	5	.997	58	593	44	2	34	6
	3B							
1917	StL-A	.971	20	20	47	2	4	4
1918	Cin-N	1.000	3	6	3	0	1	-1
1919	Bro-N	.958	9	9	14	1	0	-2
	Chi-N	.900	10	11	16	3	0	-2
	Yr	.926	19	20	30	4	0	-4
Total	3	.955	42	46	80	6	5	-1
	SS							
1911	StL-N	.800	3	3	9	3	0	-1
1912	StL-N	.500	1	1	1	2	0	-1
1913	StL-N	1.000	2	3	1	0	0	0
1919	Cin-N	.923	13	26	46	6	4	-2
Total	4	.891	19	33	57	1	4	-4

■ Sherry Magee OF

YEAR	TM/L	PCT	G	PO	A	E	DP	FR
1904	Phi-N	.921	94	156	19	15	2	5
1905	Phi-N	.963	**155**	341	19	14	6	11
1906	Phi-N	.982	154	316	18	6	2	11
1907	Phi-N	.978	139	297	13	7	7	7
1908	Phi-N	.970	142	279	15	9	5	2
1909	Phi-N	.970	143	283	11	9	0	-6
1910	Phi-N	.974	154	285	9	8	2	-8
1911	Phi-N	**.981**	120	248	14	5	3	5
1912	Phi-N	.963	124	251	8	10	2	-6
1913	Phi-N	.968	123	236	7	8	2	-7
1914	Phi-N	.940	67	137	3	9	0	-3
1915	Bos-N	.981	135	346	16	7	4	8
1916	Bos-N	.978	120	220	6	5	0	-6
1917	Bos-N	.954	65	137	7	7	3	2
	Cin-N	.989	41	83	7	1	1	3
	Yr	.967	106	220	14	8	4	5
1918	Cin-N	.978	38	87	3	2	0	0
1919	Cin-N	.990	47	98	1	1	0	-4
Total	16	.970	1861	3800	176	123	39	14
	1B							
1904	Phi-N	.909	1	10	0	1	0	0
1912	Phi-N	.968	6	61	0	2	2	-2
1913	Phi-N	1.000	4	21	0	0	2	0
1914	Phi-N	.970	32	296	32	10	7	5
1915	Bos-N	1.000	21	178	10	0	7	1
1916	Bos-N	1.000	2	11	3	0	0	1
1917	Bos-N	1.000	2	14	0	0	2	0
	Cin-N	.957	2	19	3	1	1	1
	Yr	.973	4	33	3	1	3	1
1918	Cin-N	.981	66	598	38	12	40	-2
Total	8	.980	136	1208	87	6	61	4
	SS							
1914	Phi-N	.934	39	95	119	15	9	1
1916	Bos-N	—	1	0	0	0	0	0
Total	2	.934	40	95	119	5	9	1
	2B							
1914	Phi-N	.947	8	21	33	3	4	5
1918	Cin-N	.957	6	7	15	1	1	-3
1919	Cin-N	1.000	1	4	2	0	1	0
Total	3	.953	15	32	50	4	6	2
	3B							
1919	Cin-N	1.000	1	0	1	0	0	0

■ George Magoon SS

YEAR	TM/L	PCT	G	PO	A	E	DP	FR
1898	Bro-N	.925	93	199	357	45	38	13
1899	Bal-N	.923	62	143	215	30	19	6
	Chi-N	.896	59	138	216	41	34	7
	Yr	.909	121	281	431	71	53	13
1901	Cin-N	.919	112	253	345	53	36	-18
1902	Cin-N	.850	3	9	8	3	3	-1
Total	4	.916	329	742	1141	172	130	7
	2B							
1901	Cin-N	.944	15	31	37	4	6	-2
1902	Cin-N	.930	41	83	144	17	16	4
1903	Cin-N	.971	32	79	91	5	8	3
	Chi-N	.936	94	198	253	31	28	-21
Total	3	.941	182	391	525	7	58	-16
	3B							
1903	Cin-N	.889	9	10	22	4	1	1

■ Freddie Maguire 2B

YEAR	TM/L	PCT	G	PO	A	E	DP	FR
1922	NY-N	.944	3	4	13	1	1	2
1923	NY-N	.881	16	21	31	7	7	12
1928	Chi-N	.976	138	**410**	**524**	23	**126**	**50**
1929	Bos-N	.971	138	334	437	23	94	8
1930	Bos-N	.969	146	387	476	28	104	-4
1931	Bos-N	**.976**	148	372	478	21	94	9
Total	6	.971	589	1528	1959	103	426	77
	3B							
1923	NY-N	—	1	1	0	0	0	0
	SS							
1929	Bos-N	1.000	1	1	1	0	0	0

■ Fritz Maisel 3B

YEAR	TM/L	PCT	G	PO	A	E	DP	FR
1913	NY-A	.950	51	70	83	8	3	-5
1914	NY-A	.928	148	206	245	**35**	17	-18
1915	NY-A	.940	134	184	223	26	20	-9
1916	NY-A	.925	11	12	25	3	3	0
1917	NY-A	.931	7	12	15	2	0	0
1918	StL-A	.949	79	108	154	14	10	-4
Total	6	.938	430	592	745	8	53	-36
	2B							
1916	NY-A	1.000	4	11	6	0	0	-2
1917	NY-A	.967	100	219	280	17	37	-2
Total	2	.968	104	230	286	7	37	-4
	OF							
1916	NY-A	.980	26	48	1	1	1	-4
1918	StL-A	—	1	0	0	0	0	0
Total	2	.980	27	48	1	1	1	-4

■ George Maisel OF

YEAR	TM/L	PCT	G	PO	A	E	DP	FR
1913	StL-A	.833	5	5	0	1	0	-2
1921	Chi-N	.978	108	259	12	6	2	-4
1922	Chi-N	1.000	26	50	2	0	0	1
Total	3	.979	139	314	14	7	2	-5
	3B							
1916	Det-A	.857	3	1	5	1	1	2

■ Hank Majeski 3B

YEAR	TM/L	PCT	G	PO	A	E	DP	FR
1939	Bos-N	.945	99	111	196	18	19	12
1941	Bos-N	.911	11	15	26	4	2	1
1946	NY-A	.750	2	1	2	1	0	-1
	Phi-A	.967	72	78	159	8	22	8
	Yr	**.964**	74	79	161	9	22	7
1947	Phi-A	.988	134	160	263	5	28	5
1948	Phi-A	**.975**	142	163	268	11	19	1
1949	Phi-A	.957	113	117	219	15	37	-4
1950	Chi-A	.970	112	115	246	11	31	10
1951	Chi-A	.950	9	4	15	1	2	0
	Phi-A	.974	88	82	217	8	17	14
	Yr	.972	97	86	232	9	19	14
1952	Phi-A	.976	34	33	87	3	9	4
	Cle-A	.913	11	9	12	2	3	-1
	Yr	.966	45	42	99	5	12	3
1953	Cle-A	1.000	7	1	3	0	0	0
1954	Cle-A	.943	10	13	20	2	1	-1
1955	Cle-A	1.000	9	4	6	0	1	-1
	Bal-A	1.000	8	5	11	0	1	-1
	Yr	1.000	17	9	17	0	2	-2
Total	12	.968	861	911	1750	9	192	46
	2B							
1947	Phi-A	—	1	0	0	0	0	-1
1952	Cle-A	1.000	3	6	6	0	4	1
1953	Cle-A	1.000	10	8	8	0	2	-1
1954	Cle-A	.990	25	54	44	1	10	5
1955	Cle-A	1.000	4	7	8	0	1	-1
	Bal-A	1.000	5	6	4	0	1	-2
	Yr	1.000	9	13	12	0	2	-3
Total	5	.993	48	81	70	1	18	1
	SS							
1947	Phi-A	1.000	4	10	20	0	4	3
1948	Phi-A	.974	8	13	24	1	4	1
Total	2	.985	12	23	44	1	8	4
	OF							
1953	Cle-A	—	1	0	0	0	0	0

■ Candy Maldonado OF

YEAR	TM/L	PCT	G	PO	A	E	DP	FR
1981	LA-N	1.000	9	8	0	0	0	0
1982	LA-N	1.000	3	5	0	0	0	1
1983	LA-N	1.000	33	26	0	0	0	-1
1984	LA-N	.955	102	124	4	6	0	-14
1985	LA-N	.984	113	121	6	2	0	4
1986	SF-N	.983	101	161	10	3	0	-2
1987	SF-N	.973	116	176	7	5	0	-8
1988	SF-N	.962	139	251	5	10	1	-8
1989	SF-N	.974	116	181	6	5	1	-11
1990	Cle-A	.993	134	293	9	2	1	6
Total	10	.977	866	1346	47	3	3	-33
	3B							
1984	LA-N	.333	1	0	1	2	0	-1
1986	SF-N	1.000	1	1	1	0	0	0
Total	2	.500	5	0	2	2	0	-1

■ Bobby Malkmus 2B

YEAR	TM/L	PCT	G	PO	A	E	DP	FR
1957	Mil-N	.972	7	16	19	1	4	4
1958	Was-A	.964	26	55	53	4	14	8
1960	Phi-N	.989	23	43	49	1	9	5
1961	Phi-N	.988	58	146	180	4	52	12
Total	4	.982	114	260	301	0	79	29
	SS							
1958	Was-A	—	1	0	0	0	0	0
1960	Phi-N	1.000	29	18	37	0	11	1
1961	Phi-N	.949	34	48	81	7	12	0
1962	Phi-N	1.000	1	1	4	0	1	3
Total	4	.964	65	67	122	7	24	4
	3B							
1958	Was-A	1.000	2	0	1	0	0	0
1960	Phi-N	.957	12	7	15	1	0	1
1961	Phi-N	.982	25	16	38	1	3	4
Total	3	.975	39	23	54	2	3	5

Les Mallon 2B

YEAR	TM/L	PCT	G	PO	A	E	DP	FR
1931	Phi-N	.956	97	231	290	24	57	7
1932	Phi-N	.955	88	199	228	20	42	-30
1934	Bos-N	.967	42	92	145	8	17	-4
1935	Bos-N	.975	73	166	219	10	31	-10
Total	4	.962	300	688	882	2	147	-37

3B
1931	Phi-N	1.000	3	1	4	0	0	0
1932	Phi-N	.800	5	3	5	2	0	-1
1935	Bos-N	.923	36	34	62	8	3	-3
Total	3	.916	44	38	71	0	3	-4

1B
1931	Phi-N	.971	5	31	2	1	4	0

SS
1931	Phi-N	.864	3	7	12	3	1	-1

OF
1935	Bos-N	1.000	1	1	0	0	0	0

Billy Maloney OF

YEAR	TM/L	PCT	G	PO	A	E	DP	FR
1901	Mil-A	.857	8	18	0	3	0	-1
1902	StL-A	.906	23	26	3	3	1	-2
	Cin-N	.848	18	24	4	5	0	-2
1905	Chi-N	.954	145	251	18	13	4	2
1906	Bro-N	.966	151	355	19	13	6	11
1907	Bro-N	.967	144	336	18	12	5	5
1908	Bro-N	.947	107	238	11	14	4	3
Total	6	.954	596	1248	73	3	20	16

C
1901	Mil-A	.952	72	284	111	20	6	10
1902	StL-A	.933	7	22	6	2	1	-2
	Cin-N	.925	7	31	6	3	1	-1
1908	Bro-N	1.000	4	17	8	0	0	2
Total	3	.951	90	354	131	5	8	9

Frank Malzone 3B

YEAR	TM/L	PCT	G	PO	A	E	DP	FR
1955	Bos-A	1.000	4	2	15	0	1	2
1956	Bos-A	.931	26	24	57	6	4	1
1957	Bos-A	.954	153	151	370	25	31	14
1958	Bos-A	.950	155	139	378	27	36	17
1959	Bos-A	.953	154	134	357	24	40	8
1960	Bos-A	.948	151	159	318	26	36	8
1961	Bos-A	.950	149	136	304	23	45	-5
1962	Bos-A	.967	156	154	313	16	32	5
1963	Bos-A	.964	148	151	283	16	18	4
1964	Bos-A	.959	143	141	259	17	24	0
1965	Bos-A	.969	96	79	170	8	19	-3
1966	Cal-A	.925	35	38	60	8	3	-1
Total	12	.955	1370	1308	2884	196	289	50

Gus Mancuso C

YEAR	TM/L	PCT	G	PO	A	E	DP	FR
1928	StL-N	.984	11	54	7	1	0	4
1930	StL-N	.969	61	277	33	10	2	1
1931	StL-N	.972	56	239	40	8	6	6
1932	StL-N	.977	82	454	53	12	7	7
1933	NY-N	.972	142	580	83	19	15	3
1934	NY-N	.977	122	448	67	12	7	7
1935	NY-N	.972	126	484	71	16	4	-5
1936	NY-N	.977	138	524	104	15	15	5
1937	NY-N	.982	81	410	69	9	4	15
1938	NY-N	.977	44	184	24	5	5	4
1939	Chi-N	.981	76	333	36	7	6	5
1940	Bro-N	.982	56	193	26	4	6	6
1941	StL-N	.989	105	482	58	6	6	10
1942	StL-N	.917	3	11	0	1	0	-1
	NY-N	.982	38	140	21	3	1	3
	Yr	.977	41	151	21	4	1	2
1943	NY-N	.974	77	336	40	10	8	0
1944	NY-N	.976	72	249	37	7	4	4
1945	Phi-N	.988	70	215	34	3	4	1
Total	17	.977	1360	5613	803	148	100	75

Frank Mancuso C

YEAR	TM/L	PCT	G	PO	A	E	DP	FR
1944	StL-A	.953	87	311	35	17	9	-7
1945	StL-A	.989	115	467	55	6	10	-7
1946	StL-A	.973	85	298	31	9	3	-17
1947	Was-A	.958	35	144	15	7	1	-4
Total	4	.972	322	1220	136	9	23	-35

Angel Mangual OF

YEAR	TM/L	PCT	G	PO	A	E	DP	FR
1969	Pit-N	.000	3	0	0	1	0	0
1971	Oak-A	.988	81	163	3	2	1	3
1972	Oak-A	.971	74	166	4	5	2	-3
1973	Oak-A	.947	50	88	2	5	0	1
1974	Oak-A	.961	74	142	5	6	0	1
1975	Oak-A	.978	39	44	1	1	0	2
1976	Oak-A	1.000	7	4	1	0	0	0
Total	7	.969	328	607	16	0	3	4

1B
1973	Oak-A	—	2	0	0	0	0	0

2B
1973	Oak-A	—	1	0	0	0	0	-1

3B
1974	Oak-A	—	1	0	0	0	0	0

Pepe Mangual OF

YEAR	TM/L	PCT	G	PO	A	E	DP	FR
1972	Mon-N	1.000	3	2	0	0	0	0
1973	Mon-N	.966	22	28	0	1	0	-1
1974	Mon-N	1.000	22	22	0	0	0	-3
1975	Mon-N	.972	138	308	8	9	2	-8
1976	Mon-N	.968	62	146	3	5	1	-3
	NY-N	.985	38	64	2	1	1	2
	Yr	.973	100	210	5	6	2	-1
1977	NY-N	.833	4	5	0	1	0	0
Total	6	.972	289	575	13	7	4	-13

Clyde Manion C

YEAR	TM/L	PCT	G	PO	A	E	DP	FR
1920	Det-A	.940	30	83	27	7	3	-2
1921	Det-A	1.000	3	5	3	0	0	1
1922	Det-A	.932	22	61	7	5	0	-3
1923	Det-A	.857	3	5	1	1	0	0
1924	Det-A	.750	3	3	0	1	0	-1
1926	Det-A	.972	74	227	48	8	2	0
1928	StL-A	.980	71	302	49	7	10	11
1929	StL-A	.976	34	141	22	4	2	4
1930	StL-A	.985	56	214	44	4	4	11
1932	Cin-N	.970	47	137	23	5	3	4
1933	Cin-N	.981	34	84	19	2	2	4
1934	Cin-N	1.000	24	57	13	0	2	3
Total	12	.973	401	1319	256	4	28	32

1B
1922	Det-A	1.000	1	0	1	0	0	0
1923	Det-A	—	1	0	0	0	0	0
1924	Det-A	1.000	1	1	0	0	0	0
Total	3	1.000	3	1	1	0	0	0

Phil Mankowski 3B

YEAR	TM/L	PCT	G	PO	A	E	DP	FR
1976	Det-A	.971	23	20	47	2	8	2
1977	Det-A	.964	85	73	196	10	15	13
1978	Det-A	.972	80	42	129	5	17	8
1979	Det-A	.963	36	22	56	3	6	-1
1980	NY-N	.571	3	0	4	3	0	-1
1982	NY-N	.957	13	2	20	1	2	0
Total	6	.962	240	159	452	4	48	21

2B
1977	Det-A	—	1	0	0	0	0	0

Fred Mann OF

YEAR	TM/L	PCT	G	PO	A	E	DP	FR
1883	Col-a	.854	82	124	16	24	4	1
1884	Col-a	.857	97	120	12	22	2	-7
1885	Pit-a	.908	97	157	10	17	2	-7
1886	Pit-a	.878	116	203	13	30	2	-3
1887	Cle-a	.879	64	112	11	17	4	1
	Phi-a	.916	55	102	7	10	2	-4
	Yr	.896	119	214	18	27	6	-3
Total	5	.881	511	818	69	120	16	-19

3B
1882	Wor-N	.703	18	24	28	22	2	-7
	Phi-a	.798	29	32	39	18	3	-10
1883	Col-a	.762	6	7	9	5	1	-2
1885	Pit-a	.833	3	2	3	1	0	0
Total	3	.758	56	65	79	6	6	-19

1B
1882	Wor-N	1.000	1	11	1	0	0	0
1883	Col-a	.917	9	86	2	8	0	-1
Total	2	.926	10	97	3	8	0	-1

2B
1884	Col-a	.923	2	6	6	1	1	0

SS
1883	Col-a	.667	1	0	2	1	0	0

Les Mann OF

YEAR	TM/L	PCT	G	PO	A	E	DP	FR
1913	Bos-N	.960	120	250	14	11	2	-6
1914	Bos-N	.952	123	273	24	15	8	6
1915	Chi-F	.969	130	269	17	9	3	6
1916	Chi-N	.972	115	200	9	6	1	-6
1917	Chi-N	.953	116	203	20	11	2	3
1918	Chi-N	.961	129	229	15	10	3	-5
1919	Chi-N	.982	78	155	10	3	2	2
	Bos-N	.929	40	82	9	7	1	2
	Yr	.962	118	237	19	10	3	4
1920	Bos-N	.980	110	228	13	5	1	1
1921	Bos-N	.969	79	174	11	6	2	-4
1922	StL-N	.978	57	87	3	2	1	3
1923	StL-N	.979	26	44	3	1	0	0
1924	Bos-N	1.000	28	59	4	0	0	2
1925	Bos-N	.992	57	116	7	1	1	3
1926	Bos-N	.966	46	79	5	3	0	2
1927	Bos-N	.955	24	38	4	2	1	1
	NY-N	1.000	22	27	2	0	0	-2
	Yr	.973	46	65	6	2	1	-1
1928	NY-N	.952	68	97	3	5	1	-5
Total	16	.966	1368	2610	173	7	29	3

SS
1915	Chi-F	—	1	0	0	0	0	0

Jim Manning OF

YEAR	TM/L	PCT	G	PO	A	E	DP	FR
1884	Bos-N	.878	73	115	15	18	2	-1
1885	Bos-N	.898	83	164	21	21	3	6
1886	Det-N	.947	26	32	4	2	1	-1
1887	Det-N	.867	10	13	0	2	0	-2
1889	KC-a	.927	69	119	20	11	2	6
Total	5	.903	261	443	60	4	8	8

2B
1884	Bos-N	.833	9	13	17	6	1	0
1889	KC-a	.907	63	119	184	31	23	-15
Total	2	.900	72	132	201	7	24	-15

SS
1884	Bos-N	.881	9	11	26	5	4	1
1885	Bos-N	.500	1	0	1	1	0	0
	Det-N	.802	20	20	53	18	7	-6
	Yr	.796	21	20	54	19	7	-6
1886	Det-N	1.000	1	0	1	0	0	0
1887	Det-N	.625	3	3	7	6	0	-3
1889	KC-a	—	1	0	0	0	0	0
Total	5	.803	35	34	88	0	11	-8

3B
1884	Bos-N	1.000	3	0	3	0	0	0
1889	KC-a	.500	1	0	2	2	0	-1
Total	2	.714	4	0	5	2	0	-1

Jack Manning OF

YEAR	TM/L	PCT	G	PO	A	E	DP	FR
1876	Bos-N	.777	56	73	7	23	0	-5
1877	Cin-N	.815	12	20	2	5	0	0
1878	Bos-N	.753	59	61	9	23	1	-15
1880	Cin-N	.798	47	59	12	18	1	-2
1881	Buf-N	1.000	1	0	1	0	0	0
1883	Phi-N	.853	98	155	37	33	5	9
1884	Phi-N	.847	104	140	26	30	7	-3
1885	Phi-N	.896	107	134	21	18	3	-7
1886	Bal-a	.887	137	165	16	23	3	-10
Total	9	.844	621	807	131	173	20	-33

SS
YEAR	TM/L	PCT	G	PO	A	E	DP	FR
1876	Bos-N	—	1	0	0	0	0	0
1877	Cin-N	.742	26	30	62	32	2	-11
Total	2	.742	27	30	62	2	2	-11

1B
1877	Cin-N	.962	17	173	5	7	4	0
1880	Cin-N	.714	1	5	0	2	0	0
Total	2	.953	18	178	5	9	4	0

2B
1876	Bos-N	.400	1	2	0	3	0	-1
1877	Cin-N	.765	2	9	4	4	1	-2
Total	2	.682	3	11	4	7	1	-3

Rick Manning OF

YEAR	TM/L	PCT	G	PO	A	E	DP	FR
1975	Cle-A	.974	118	331	12	9	2	10
1976	Cle-A	.987	136	359	8	5	1	16
1977	Cle-A	.990	68	191	2	2	0	1
1978	Cle-A	.995	144	377	7	2	1	0
1979	Cle-A	.986	141	417	9	6	2	10
1980	Cle-A	.990	139	379	7	4	1	4
1981	Cle-A	.987	103	305	6	4	3	10
1982	Cle-A	.978	152	387	10	9	1	-1
1983	Cle-A	.987	50	146	1	2	0	3
	Mil-A	.991	108	325	1	3	0	2
	Yr	.990	158	471	2	5	0	5
1984	Mil-A	.987	114	231	2	3	2	-21
1985	Mil-A	.976	74	160	2	4	0	4
1986	Mil-A	.988	83	155	3	2	0	-4
1987	Mil-A	.958	78	68	1	3	0	2
Total	13	.985	1508	3831	71	8	13	36

Tim Manning 2B

YEAR	TM/L	PCT	G	PO	A	E	DP	FR
1883	Bal-a	.913	35	105	106	20	8	3
1884	Bal-a	.907	91	228	277	52	28	-2
1885	Bal-a	.919	41	118	132	22	19	2
Total	3	.911	167	451	515	4	55	3

SS
1882	Pro-N	.787	17	17	42	16	3	-7
1885	Pro-N	.854	10	18	23	7	2	-3
Total	2	.813	27	35	65	3	5	-10

C
1882	Pro-N	.789	4	15	0	4	0	-2

3B
1885	Bal-a	1.000	3	3	4	0	0	0

Fred Manrique 2B

YEAR	TM/L	PCT	G	PO	A	E	DP	FR
1984	Tor-A	.938	9	5	10	1	3	3
1985	Mon-N	1.000	2	2	4	0	0	1
1986	StL-N	—	1	0	0	0	0	0
1987	Chi-A	.984	92	147	234	6	58	13
1988	Chi-A	.985	129	228	308	8	77	10
1989	Chi-A	.961	57	94	127	9	30	-6
	Tex-A	.919	17	24	33	5	6	-3
	Yr	.952	74	118	160	14	36	-9
1990	Min-A	.974	67	104	155	7	40	-10
Total	7	.976	374	604	871	6	214	8

SS
1981	Tor-A	.949	11	10	27	2	7	3
1985	Mon-N	1.000	2	2	3	0	0	0
1987	Chi-A	.988	23	29	52	1	6	5
1988	Chi-A	.906	12	13	35	5	6	3
1989	Chi-A	1.000	2	2	2	0	2	0
	Tex-A	.963	37	52	79	5	22	-8
	Yr	.964	39	54	81	5	24	-8
Total	5	.959	87	108	198	3	43	3

3B
1981	Tor-A	.000	2	0	0	1	0	0
1985	Mon-N	1.000	1	1	3	0	1	1
1986	StL-N	1.000	4	1	3	0	0	-1
1989	Chi-A	.833	1	3	2	1	0	0
	Tex-A	.900	6	2	7	1	1	0
	Yr	.875	7	5	9	2	1	0
Total	4	.880	14	7	15	3	2	0

Mike Mansell OF

YEAR	TM/L	PCT	G	PO	A	E	DP	FR
1879	Syr-N	.881	67	204	11	29	2	15
1880	Cin-N	.865	53	147	13	25	5	12
1882	Pit-a	.829	79	159	16	36	1	3
1883	Pit-a	.883	96	186	11	26	1	4
1884	Pit-a	.796	27	36	3	10	1	-1
	Phi-a	.762	20	30	2	10	0	-1
	Ric-a	.763	29	24	5	9	1	-5
	Yr	.775	76	90	10	29	2	-7
Total	5	.854	371	786	61	145	11	27

Tom Mansell OF

YEAR	TM/L	PCT	G	PO	A	E	DP	FR
1879	Tro-N	.742	40	63	3	23	1	-6
	Syr-N	1.000	1	2	0	0	0	0
	Yr	.747	41	65	3	23	1	-6
1883	Det-N	.758	34	35	12	15	1	-2
	StL-a	.786	28	32	1	9	0	-6
1884	Cin-a	.752	65	88	3	30	0	-11
	Col-a	.667	23	11	3	7	0	-4
	Yr	.739	88	99	6	37	0	-15
Total	3	.751	191	231	22	4	2	-29

Felix Mantilla 2B

YEAR	TM/L	PCT	G	PO	A	E	DP	FR
1957	Mil-N	.980	13	20	29	1	6	2
1958	Mil-N	.967	21	41	47	3	12	0
1959	Mil-N	.970	60	97	126	7	26	3
1960	Mil-N	.956	26	38	27	3	6	-6
1961	Mil-N	.981	10	25	27	1	4	-2
1962	NY-N	.967	14	35	24	2	4	-3
1963	Bos-A	1.000	5	13	11	0	3	0
1964	Bos-A	.995	45	97	119	1	25	0
1965	Bos-A	.976	123	251	286	13	64	-20
1966	Hou-N	1.000	6	13	0	2	0	
Total	10	.977	326	623	709	1	152	-26

SS
1956	Mil-N	1.000	15	19	41	0	8	9

YEAR	TM/L	PCT	G	PO	A	E	DP	FR
1957	Mil-N	.931	35	58	90	11	21	3
1958	Mil-N	1.000	5	8	11	0	3	0
1959	Mil-N	.929	23	29	76	8	13	3
1960	Mil-N	.939	25	35	58	6	9	-4
1961	Mil-N	.933	19	5	9	1	2	-1
1962	NY-N	.950	25	28	48	4	10	-4
1963	Bos-A	.965	27	49	62	4	16	-5
1964	Bos-A	1.000	6	11	16	0	4	0
Total	9	.951	180	242	411	4	86	1
OF								
1957	Mil-N	—	1	0	0	0	0	0
1958	Mil-N	.987	43	73	2	1	0	-1
1959	Mil-N	1.000	7	6	0	0	0	0
1960	Mil-N	1.000	8	7	0	0	0	0
1961	Mil-N	1.000	10	12	1	0	0	0
1963	Bos-A	1.000	11	21	1	0	0	0
1964	Bos-A	.984	48	60	2	1	0	-2
1965	Bos-A	.927	27	37	1	3	0	-1
1966	Hou-N	1.000	1	3	0	0	0	0
Total	9	.978	156	219	7	5	0	-4
3B								
1956	Mil-N	.857	3	2	4	1	0	0
1957	Mil-N	1.000	7	9	17	0	1	2
1958	Mil-N	1.000	2	0	1	0	0	0
1959	Mil-N	.867	9	4	9	2	1	0
1961	Mil-N	.941	6	5	11	1	1	0
1962	NY-N	.948	95	76	179	14	22	-1
1964	Bos-A	.824	7	5	9	3	0	-3
1966	Hou-N	.938	14	15	30	3	1	0
Total	8	.940	143	116	260	4	26	-2
1B								
1965	Bos-A	1.000	2	8	1	0	0	0
1966	Hou-N	.990	14	100	3	1	8	-1
Total	2	.991	16	108	4	1	8	-1
■ Mickey Mantle OF								
1951	NY-A	.959	86	135	4	6	1	-15
1952	NY-A	.968	141	347	15	12	5	-6
1953	NY-A	.982	121	322	10	6	2	-4
1954	NY-A	.975	144	327	20	9	5	-4
1955	NY-A	.995	145	372	11	2	2	3
1956	NY-A	.990	144	370	10	4	3	2
1957	NY-A	.979	139	324	6	7	1	-7
1958	NY-A	.977	150	331	5	8	2	-5
1959	NY-A	.995	143	366	7	2	3	2
1960	NY-A	.991	150	326	9	3	1	-8
1961	NY-A	.983	150	351	6	6	0	-3
1962	NY-A	.978	117	214	4	5	1	-13
1963	NY-A	.990	52	99	2	1	0	-1
1964	NY-A	.978	132	217	3	5	1	-24
1965	NY-A	.966	108	165	3	6	0	-6
1966	NY-A	1.000	97	172	2	0	0	-10
Total	16	.982	2019	4438	117	2	27	-99
1B								
1967	NY-A	.993	131	1089	91	8	82	0
1968	NY-A	.988	131	1195	76	15	91	-3
Total	2	.991	262	2284	167	3	173	-3
SS								
1953	NY-A	—	1	0	0	0	0	0
1954	NY-A	1.000	4	5	5	0	1	-1
1955	NY-A	1.000	2	4	0	0	1	-1
Total	3	1.000	7	9	5	0	1	-2
3B								
1952	NY-A	.500	1	1	1	2	0	-1
2B								
1954	NY-A	1.000	1	2	0	0	0	0
■ Heinie Manush OF								
1923	Det-A	.953	79	158	6	8	0	-4
1924	Det-A	.979	106	224	4	5	1	-6
1925	Det-A	.982	73	153	7	3	0	-5
1926	Det-A	.967	120	283	7	10	3	-4
1927	Det-A	.971	149	361	9	11	3	-3
1928	StL-A	.992	154	355	6	3	2	2
1929	StL-A	.987	141	293	11	4	3	-2
1930	StL-A	.990	48	96	5	1	0	2
	Was-A	.988	86	159	5	2	0	-2
	Yr	.989	134	255	10	3	0	0
1931	Was-A	.977	143	245	5	6	1	-11
1932	Was-A	.988	146	318	6	4	3	-3
1933	Was-A	.982	150	325	10	6	1	-2
1934	Was-A	.980	131	293	5	6	2	1
1935	Was-A	.985	111	251	8	4	5	4
1936	Bos-A	.966	72	110	3	4	1	-13
1937	Bro-N	.970	123	187	7	6	1	-15
1938	Bro-N	1.000	12	29	1	0	0	1
1939	Pit-N	1.000	1	1	0	0	0	0
Total	17	.979	1845	3841	105	3	26	-60
1B								
1924	Det-A	1.000	1	1	0	0	0	0
■ Kirt Manwaring C								
1987	SF-N	.909	6	9	1	1	0	-1
1988	SF-N	.979	40	162	24	4	2	-1
1989	SF-N	.982	81	289	32	6	3	0
1990	SF-N	1.000	8	22	3	0	1	2
Total	4	.980	135	482	60	1	6	0
■ Cliff Mapes OF								
1948	NY-A	.958	21	42	4	2	1	4
1949	NY-A	.976	108	228	14	6	4	5
1950	NY-A	.950	102	183	8	10	4	-5
1951	NY-A	1.000	34	25	0	0	0	0
	StL-A	.983	53	111	4	2	1	-3
	Yr	.986	87	136	4	2	1	-3
1952	Det-A	.967	62	86	3	3	1	-4
Total	5	.969	380	675	33	3	11	-3
■ Rabbit Maranville SS								
1912	Bos-N	.929	26	46	97	11	11	5

YEAR	TM/L	PCT	G	PO	A	E	DP	FR
1913	Bos-N	.949	143	317	475	43	49	15
1914	Bos-N	.938	156	407	574	65	92	52
1915	Bos-N	.941	149	391	486	55	63	21
1916	Bos-N	.947	155	386	515	50	79	22
1917	Bos-N	.947	142	341	474	46	67	14
1918	Bos-N	.932	11	34	34	5	2	2
1919	Bos-N	.941	131	361	488	53	74	29
1920	Bos-N	.948	133	354	462	45	62	14
1921	Pit-N	.962	153	325	529	34	72	-11
1922	Pit-N	.961	138	359	453	33	81	7
1923	Pit-N	.965	141	332	505	30	94	12
1925	Chi-N	.955	74	162	261	20	51	4
1926	Bro-N	.948	60	138	192	18	28	7
1927	StL-N	.962	9	17	34	2	6	3
1928	StL-N	.969	112	236	362	19	57	-6
1929	Bos-N	.961	145	319	536	35	104	20
1930	Bos-N	.965	138	343	445	29	98	-12
1931	Bos-N	.949	137	271	432	38	93	-21
Total	19	.952	2153	5139	7354	631	1183	177
2B								
1922	Pit-N	.975	18	60	59	3	11	4
1924	Pit-N	.973	152	365	568	26	109	4
1926	Bro-N	.987	18	23	54	1	2	3
1928	StL-N	1.000	2	1	2	0	1	0
1929	Bos-N	1.000	1	5	1	0	0	0
1931	Bos-N	.929	11	18	21	3	5	-3
1932	Bos-N	.975	149	402	473	22	91	6
1933	Bos-N	.971	142	362	384	22	82	-26
1935	Bos-N	.963	20	32	46	3	10	-5
Total	9	.973	513	1268	1608	0	311	-17
3B								
1930	Bos-N	1.000	4	6	5	0	1	0
■ Marty Marion SS								
1940	StL-N	.949	125	245	366	33	76	-6
1941	StL-N	.954	155	299	489	38	85	7
1942	StL-N	.960	147	296	448	31	87	7
1943	StL-N	.970	128	232	424	20	93	25
1944	StL-N	.972	144	268	461	21	90	5
1945	StL-N	.967	122	237	372	21	70	-2
1946	StL-N	.973	145	290	480	21	105	19
1947	StL-N	.981	141	329	452	15	104	20
1948	StL-N	.974	142	263	445	19	80	9
1949	StL-N	.976	134	242	441	17	74	17
1950	StL-N	.978	101	180	313	11	73	-1
1952	StL-N	.980	63	105	138	5	41	-7
Total	12	.969	1547	2986	4829	252	978	93
3B								
1953	StL-A	1.000	2	1	0	0	0	-1
■ Roger Maris OF								
1957	Cle-A	.975	112	266	10	7	2	0
1958	Cle-A	.967	47	113	6	4	1	4
	KC-A	.975	99	190	9	5	3	2
	Yr	.972	146	303	15	9	4	6
1959	KC-A	.975	117	231	7	6	4	3
1960	NY-A	.985	131	263	6	4	1	2
1961	NY-A	.968	160	266	9	9	1	-10
1962	NY-A	.991	154	316	4	3	0	2
1963	NY-A	.988	86	162	6	2	1	1
1964	NY-A	.996	137	250	6	1	0	1
1965	NY-A	.971	43	66	1	2	0	-5
1966	NY-A	.993	95	133	3	1	0	-10
1967	StL-N	.991	118	224	5	2	1	2
1968	StL-N	.983	84	169	4	3	1	2
Total	12	.982	1383	2649	76	9	15	-6
■ Lefty Marr OF								
1886	Cin-a	.696	8	15	1	7	0	-1
1889	Col-a	.824	47	81	8	19	1	0
1890	Cin-N	.930	64	68	12	6	3	-3
1891	Cin-N	.835	72	75	6	16	2	-10
	Cin-a	.923	14	23	1	2	0	-1
Total	4	.853	205	262	28	0	6	-15
3B								
1889	Col-a	.856	66	111	151	44	13	9
1890	Cin-N	.856	63	71	125	33	5	-8
Total	2	.856	129	182	276	7	18	1
SS								
1889	Col-a	.844	26	52	94	27	8	3
1890	Cin-N	1.000	3	1	7	0	0	0
Total	2	.851	29	53	101	7	8	3
1B								
1889	Col-a	1.000	2	10	0	0	0	0
C								
1889	Col-a	—	1	0	0	0	0	0
■ William Marriott 3B								
1921	Chi-N	.667	1	1	1	1	1	0
1925	Bos-N	.928	89	96	187	22	13	3
1926	Bro-N	.927	104	80	173	20	6	-8
1927	Bro-N	.889	2	3	5	1	0	1
Total	4	.925	196	180	366	4	20	-4
2B								
1920	Chi-N	.892	14	26	40	8	2	-4
1921	Chi-N	.826	6	9	10	4	1	-1
Total	2	.876	20	35	50	2	3	-5
OF								
1917	Chi-N	.667	1	2	0	1	0	0
1921	Chi-N	1.000	1	0	1	0	0	1
1925	Bos-N	1.000	1	4	0	0	0	0
Total	3	.875	3	6	1	1	0	1
SS								
1921	Chi-N	1.000	1	1	1	0	0	0
■ Armando Marsans OF								
1911	Cin-N	.968	34	58	2	2	0	-3
1912	Cin-N	.975	98	222	11	6	2	-2
1913	Cin-N	.963	94	170	12	7	2	-9
1914	Cin-N	.916	36	72	4	7	1	-1

YEAR	TM/L	PCT	G	PO	A	E	DP	FR
1915	StL-F	.975	35	71	8	2	3	3
1916	StL-A	.977	150	351	25	9	7	5
1917	StL-A	.963	67	155	3	6	1	-6
	NY-A	.974	25	71	4	2	3	2
	Yr	.967	92	226	7	8	3	-3
1918	NY-A	.943	36	64	2	4	0	-6
Total	8	.967	575	1234	71	5	18	-16
1B								
1911	Cin-N	1.000	1	4	0	0	0	0
1912	Cin-N	.957	6	43	1	2	0	-1
1913	Cin-N	.967	22	229	9	8	18	-2
Total	3	.966	29	276	10	0	18	-3
3B								
1911	Cin-N	.667	1	2	0	1	0	-1
1913	Cin-N	1.000	2	2	5	0	1	0
1917	StL-A	1.000	5	4	16	0	0	2
Total	3	.967	8	8	21	1	1	1
1914	StL-F	.927	7	19	19	3	7	1
1917	StL-A	.750	1	2	1	1	0	0
Total	2	.911	8	21	20	4	7	1
SS								
1913	Cin-N	1.000	1	1	0	0	0	0
1914	StL-F	.857	2	7	5	2	1	-1
Total	2	.867	3	8	5	2	1	-1
■ Fred Marsh 3B								
1951	StL-A	.928	117	137	225	28	31	3
1952	StL-A	.909	21	15	45	6	7	0
1953	Chi-A	.940	32	17	30	3	5	2
1954	Chi-A	.975	36	36	83	3	8	18
1955	Bal-A	.793	18	7	16	6	0	-3
1956	Bal-A	.778	8	3	4	2	0	0
Total	6	.928	232	215	403	8	51	20
SS								
1951	StL-A	1.000	3	1	0	0	0	0
1952	StL-A	.944	3	7	10	1	5	1
	StL-A	.945	57	65	107	10	27	-15
	Yr	.945	60	72	117	11	32	-14
1953	Chi-A	.964	17	17	36	2	5	4
1954	Chi-A	1.000	3	1	3	0	0	1
1955	Bal-A	.939	16	12	19	2	4	0
1956	Bal-A	.929	8	5	8	1	2	0
Total	6	.948	107	108	183	6	43	-9
2B								
1951	StL-A	.900	2	3	6	1	2	0
1952	StL-A	.963	9	12	14	1	3	1
	Was-A	1.000	5	12	7	0	3	-2
	Yr	.978	14	24	21	1	6	-1
1953	Chi-A	1.000	2	4	3	0	1	0
1955	Bal-A	.983	76	197	158	6	51	-12
1956	Bal-A	1.000	5	9	6	0	3	1
Total	5	.982	99	237	194	8	64	-11
1B								
1953	Chi-A	.962	5	23	2	1	0	0
1954	Chi-A	1.000	2	2	0	0	0	0
Total	2	.964	7	25	2	1	0	0
OF								
1952	Was-A	.750	2	3	0	1	0	0
1954	Chi-A	.667	1	2	0	1	0	0
Total	2	.714	3	5	0	2	0	0
■ Dave Marshall OF								
1968	SF-N	.924	50	58	3	5	3	-4
1969	SF-N	.956	87	106	3	5	0	-7
1970	NY-N	.973	43	71	2	2	0	0
1971	NY-N	.989	64	92	2	1	0	-2
1972	NY-N	.972	42	70	0	2	0	-2
1973	SD-N	1.000	8	14	0	0	0	0
Total	6	.966	294	411	10	5	3	-15
■ Ed Marshall SS								
1930	NY-N	.947	45	73	123	11	23	-5
1931	NY-N	.933	11	22	20	3	5	0
1932	NY-N	.922	63	119	199	27	37	-3
Total	3	.931	119	214	342	1	65	-8
2B								
1929	NY-N	1.000	5	7	11	0	0	-2
1930	NY-N	.988	17	33	52	1	5	2
1931	NY-N	.956	47	102	135	11	26	3
Total	3	.966	69	142	198	2	31	3
3B								
1930	NY-N	.875	3	4	4	1	1	0
1931	NY-N	1.000	3	0	5	0	0	1
Total	2	.923	8	3	9	1	1	1
■ Mike Marshall OF								
1981	LA-N	1.000	2	3	0	0	0	0
1982	LA-N	1.000	19	22	0	0	0	-1
1983	LA-N	.976	109	160	3	4	1	-11
1984	LA-N	.981	118	200	9	4	1	-1
1985	LA-N	.991	125	206	9	2	2	-4
1986	LA-N	.963	97	149	8	6	1	-4
1987	LA-N	.987	102	147	4	2	0	-8
1988	LA-N	.966	90	137	4	5	0	-8
1989	LA-N	.978	102	179	2	4	0	-6
1990	NY-N	—	1	0	0	0	0	0
	Bos-A	.929	8	13	0	1	0	1
Total	10	.978	773	1216	39	8	5	-42
1B								
1981	LA-N	1.000	3	9	0	0	0	0
1982	LA-N	.981	13	100	5	2	6	-1
1983	LA-N	.992	33	235	18	2	15	-2
1984	LA-N	.993	15	131	8	1	11	-1
1985	LA-N	.969	7	59	3	2	7	-1
1988	LA-N	.996	53	468	45	2	31	4
1990	NY-N	.993	42	277	24	2	19	0
	Bos-A	1.000	8	42	7	0	5	2
Total	7	.992	174	1321	110	1	96	1

YEAR	TM/L	PCT	G	PO	A	E	DP	FR
3B								
1981	LA-N	1.000	3	2	2	0	0	0

■ Max Marshall OF

YEAR	TM/L	PCT	G	PO	A	E	DP	FR
1942	Cin-N	.976	129	245	3	6	2	-8
1943	Cin-N	.981	129	240	12	5	4	-7
1944	Cin-N	.965	59	131	6	5	3	-2
Total	3	.975	317	616	21	6	9	-17

■ Jim Marshall 1B

YEAR	TM/L	PCT	G	PO	A	E	DP	FR
1958	Bal-A	1.000	52	382	19	0	37	-2
	Chi-N	.992	15	114	7	1	11	-1
1959	Chi-N	.997	72	558	51	2	52	2
1960	SF-N	.968	28	170	9	6	13	-3
1961	SF-N	1.000	4	8	1	0	1	0
1962	NY-N	1.000	5	47	4	0	6	0
	Pit-N	1.000	26	182	16	0	21	1
	Yr	1.000	31	229	20	0	27	1
Total	5	.994	202	1461	107	9	141	-3
OF								
1958	Bal-A	1.000	8	3	0	0	0	0
	Chi-N	1.000	11	5	1	0	0	0
1959	Chi-N	1.000	8	7	1	0	0	0
1960	SF-N	1.000	6	7	0	0	0	0
1961	SF-N	1.000	2	1	0	0	0	0
1962	NY-N	—	1	0	0	0	0	0
Total	5	1.000	36	23	2	0	0	0

■ Willard Marshall OF

YEAR	TM/L	PCT	G	PO	A	E	DP	FR
1942	NY-N	.975	107	222	13	6	4	-4
1946	NY-N	.978	125	253	14	6	2	-7
1947	NY-N	.972	**155**	334	**19**	10	**6**	6
1948	NY-N	.983	142	266	**16**	5	2	-3
1949	NY-N	.974	138	292	13	8	3	-1
1950	Bos-N	.958	85	150	11	7	2	-1
1951	Bos-N	**1.000**	136	220	11	0	3	-11
1952	Bos-N	.938	16	27	3	2	3	0
	Cin-N	.985	105	188	13	3	2	1
	Yr	.979	121	215	16	5	5	1
1953	Cin-N	.995	95	187	11	1	1	3
1954	Chi-A	.960	29	23	1	1	0	-3
1955	Chi-A	.957	12	22	0	1	0	-1
Total	11	.979	1145	2184	125	0	28	-19

■ Doc Marshall C

YEAR	TM/L	PCT	G	PO	A	E	DP	FR
1904	Phi-N	.944	7	20	14	2	0	2
	NY-N	—	1	0	0	0	0	0
	Bos-N	.955	10	45	19	3	3	2
	NY-N	.917	2	16	6	2	1	2
	Yr	.945	20	81	39	7	4	6
1906	NY-N	1.000	13	47	13	0	0	-2
	StL-N	.961	38	193	56	10	4	10
	Yr	.969	51	240	**69**	**10**	4	8
1907	NY-N	.952	83	374	142	26	9	6
1908	StL-N	1.000	6	26	6	0	1	2
	Chi-N	1.000	4	9	2	0	1	2
	Yr	1.000	10	35	8	0	2	4
1909	Bro-N	.968	49	210	61	9	2	-5
Total	5	.960	213	940	319	2	21	19
OF								
1904	Bos-N	—	1	0	0	0	0	0
	NY-N	.500	2	0	1	1	0	0
	Yr	.500	3	0	1	1	0	0
1906	NY-N	1.000	16	19	3	0	0	-1
1908	Chi-N	.938	3	13	2	1	0	3
1909	Bro-N	—	1	0	0	0	0	0
Total	4	.950	23	32	6	2	0	2
1B								
1906	NY-N	1.000	2	11	1	0	1	0
2B								
1904	NY-N	.800	1	1	3	1	0	0

■ Billy Martin 2B

YEAR	TM/L	PCT	G	PO	A	E	DP	FR
1950	NY-A	.976	22	24	16	1	5	-1
1951	NY-A	.988	23	36	49	1	15	14
1952	NY-A	.984	107	244	323	9	92	18
1953	NY-A	.985	146	376	390	12	**121**	1
1955	NY-A	.977	17	42	44	2	19	2
1956	NY-A	.980	105	241	260	10	84	-10
1957	NY-A	.947	26	58	67	7	18	-3
	KC-A	.987	52	121	111	3	28	-19
	Yr	.973	78	179	178	10	46	-22
1959	Cle-A	.997	67	147	149	1	37	-11
1960	Cin-N	.975	97	228	207	11	52	-13
1961	Min-A	.963	105	217	224	17	61	-15
Total	10	.980	767	1734	1840	4	532	-37
SS								
1951	NY-A	.895	6	7	10	2	2	2
1953	NY-A	.941	18	13	19	2	5	-2
1955	NY-A	.909	3	4	6	1	1	-1
1957	KC-A	1.000	2	1	5	0	1	0
1958	Det-A	.958	88	159	229	17	58	-14
1961	Min-A	—	1	0	0	0	0	0
Total	6	.954	118	184	269	2	67	-15
3B								
1950	NY-A	—	1	0	0	0	0	0
1951	NY-A	.833	2	2	3	1	0	0
1956	NY-A	.889	16	12	28	5	3	-5
1957	NY-A	.973	13	11	25	1	2	0
	KC-A	.964	20	29	24	2	4	-2
	Yr	.967	33	40	49	3	6	-2
1958	Det-A	.972	41	47	59	3	5	-4
1959	Cle-A	.875	4	3	4	1	0	-1
Total	6	.950	97	104	143	3	14	-12
OF								
1951	NY-A	—	1	0	0	0	0	0

■ Hersh Martin OF

YEAR	TM/L	PCT	G	PO	A	E	DP	FR
1937	Phi-N	.978	139	**353**	9	8	1	-1
1938	Phi-N	.965	116	298	7	11	2	-3
1939	Phi-N	.976	95	276	5	7	1	7
1940	Phi-N	.979	23	42	4	1	0	1
1944	NY-A	.964	80	177	8	7	4	3
1945	NY-A	.984	102	233	8	4	1	1
Total	6	.974	555	1379	41	8	9	8

■ Jerry Martin OF

YEAR	TM/L	PCT	G	PO	A	E	DP	FR
1974	Phi-N	1.000	11	5	0	0	0	0
1975	Phi-N	.979	49	90	3	2	1	7
1976	Phi-N	.975	110	78	0	2	0	3
1977	Phi-N	.984	106	117	4	2	1	1
1978	Phi-N	.987	112	148	8	2	1	4
1979	Chi-N	.981	144	297	11	6	4	-9
1980	Chi-N	.978	129	262	8	6	0	-13
1981	SF-N	.993	64	138	4	1	1	-6
1982	KC-A	.980	142	333	4	7	2	1
1983	KC-A	.957	13	22	0	1	0	-3
1984	NY-N	.980	30	40	2	0	1	2
Total	11	.982	910	1530	44	9	11	-13
1B								
1976	Phi-N	1.000	1	7	0	0	2	0
1977	Phi-N	—	1	0	0	0	0	0
1984	NY-N	1.000	3	16	1	0	4	0
Total	3	1.000	5	23	1	0	6	0

■ Jack Martin SS

YEAR	TM/L	PCT	G	PO	A	E	DP	FR
1912	NY-A	.898	65	127	217	39	18	3
1914	Bos-N	.930	83	185	251	33	24	-3
Total	2	.915	148	312	468	2	42	0
3B								
1912	NY-A	.842	4	3	13	3	0	1
1914	Bos-N	.949	26	31	43	4	5	1
Total	2	.928	30	34	56	7	5	2
2B								
1912	NY-A	1.000	1	1	3	0	0	0
1914	Bos-N	—	1	0	0	0	0	0
Total	2	1.000	2	1	3	0	0	0
1B								
1914	Bos-N	.500	1	1	0	1	0	0

■ Pepper Martin OF

YEAR	TM/L	PCT	G	PO	A	E	DP	FR
1928	StL-N	1.000	4	2	0	0	0	3
1931	StL-N	.967	110	282	10	10	2	-4
1932	StL-N	.976	69	151	10	4	3	-4
1935	StL-N	.941	16	32	0	2	0	-1
1936	StL-N	.976	127	226	13	6	5	-5
1937	StL-N	.973	82	204	12	6	3	11
1938	StL-N	.986	62	138	1	2	1	-1
1939	StL-N	.975	51	113	4	3	0	1
1940	StL-N	.974	63	103	8	3	0	2
1944	StL-N	.980	29	48	1	1	0	0
Total	10	.973	613	1299	59	7	14	2
3B								
1932	StL-N	.973	15	18	18	1	1	-1
1933	StL-N	.943	145	139	273	25	14	-3
1934	StL-N	.936	107	85	195	**19**	7	-5
1935	StL-N	.904	114	113	171	30	17	-13
1936	StL-N	.781	15	13	12	7	1	-7
1937	StL-N	.933	5	6	8	1	2	1
1938	StL-N	1.000	4	1	3	0	0	0
1939	StL-N	.918	22	15	30	4	2	-4
1940	StL-N	1.000	2	3	5	0	0	1
Total	9	.927	429	393	715	7	44	-31

■ J.C. Martin C

YEAR	TM/L	PCT	G	PO	A	E	DP	FR
1962	Chi-A	1.000	6	18	0	0	0	0
1963	Chi-A	.983	98	468	48	9	9	15
1964	Chi-A	.986	120	530	43	8	6	11
1965	Chi-A	.982	112	348	41	7	4	7
1966	Chi-A	.982	63	243	23	5	3	0
1967	Chi-A	.987	96	478	39	7	3	5
1968	NY-N	.994	53	334	24	2	4	0
1969	NY-N	.996	48	275	9	1	2	-6
1970	Chi-N	.983	36	163	15	3	2	2
1971	Chi-N	.996	43	218	21	1	2	3
1972	Chi-N	.970	17	60	4	2	1	-3
Total	11	.987	692	3135	267	5	36	34
1B								
1960	Chi-A	1.000	1	3	0	0	0	0
1961	Chi-A	.988	60	314	29	4	27	2
1962	Chi-A	1.000	1	1	0	0	0	0
1963	Chi-A	1.000	3	8	1	0	0	0
1965	Chi-A	1.000	4	36	0	0	3	-1
1967	Chi-A	1.000	1	1	0	0	0	0
1968	NY-N	.970	14	124	7	4	7	-1
1969	NY-N	1.000	2	4	0	0	0	0
1970	Chi-N	.500	3	1	1	2	0	0
Total	9	.981	89	492	38	0	37	0
3B								
1959	Chi-A	.667	2	0	2	1	0	0
1960	Chi-A	1.000	5	5	8	0	0	0
1961	Chi-A	.955	36	39	89	6	11	7
1962	Chi-A	1.000	1	0	2	0	0	0
1963	Chi-A	—	1	0	0	0	0	0
1965	Chi-A	1.000	2	1	2	0	0	0
Total	6	.955	47	45	103	7	11	7
OF								
1971	Chi-N	—	1	0	0	0	0	0

■ Joe Martin 2B

YEAR	TM/L	PCT	G	PO	A	E	DP	FR
1936	StL-N	.949	83	169	242	22	50	-13
1937	StL-N	.946	48	93	134	13	27	-5
1938	StL-N	.967	99	225	301	18	59	-9
1939	StL-N	**.977**	107	242	304	13	62	-3
1940	StL-N	.975	33	47	71	3	12	-8
1941	Pit-N	.972	53	127	154	8	26	-4
1942	Pit-N	.979	30	68	70	3	14	-10
1943	Chi-N	.980	22	37	63	2	10	3
Total	8	.966	475	1008	1339	2	260	-49

YEAR	TM/L	PCT	G	PO	A	E	DP	FR
3B								
1940	StL-N	.972	73	52	89	4	2	-18
1941	Pit-N	.800	2	1	3	1	0	0
1943	Chi-N	1.000	8	4	5	0	0	-1
Total	3	.969	83	57	97	5	2	-19
1B								
1937	StL-N	.988	9	75	4	1	3	-1
1939	StL-N	1.000	1	7	1	0	0	0
1941	Pit-N	1.000	1	6	0	0	0	0
1942	Pit-N	1.000	1	1	0	0	0	0
1943	Chi-N	1.000	2	23	1	0	1	0
Total	5	.992	14	112	6	1	4	-1
SS								
1936	StL-N	1.000	3	4	8	0	2	0
1937	StL-N	—	1	0	0	0	0	0
1942	Pit-N	—	1	0	0	0	0	0
Total	3	1.000	5	4	8	0	2	0

■ Carlos Martinez 1B

YEAR	TM/L	PCT	G	PO	A	E	DP	FR
1989	Chi-A	.991	34	217	13	2	13	-1
1990	Chi-A	.988	82	632	38	8	50	-5
Total	2	.989	116	849	51	0	63	-6
3B								
1988	Chi-A	.909	15	7	33	4	1	3
1989	Chi-A	.912	68	45	121	16	12	-4
Total	2	.912	83	52	154	0	13	-1
OF								
1989	Chi-A	.913	10	21	0	2	0	-1
1990	Chi-A	—	1	0	0	0	0	0
Total	2	.913	11	21	0	2	0	-1

■ Carmelo Martinez OF

YEAR	TM/L	PCT	G	PO	A	E	DP	FR
1983	Chi-N	1.000	1	1	0	0	0	0
1984	SD-N	.976	142	312	15	8	4	13
1985	SD-N	.978	150	298	13	7	3	3
1986	SD-N	.978	60	83	5	2	0	-3
1987	SD-N	.968	78	116	6	4	0	-2
1988	SD-N	.993	64	143	6	1	2	6
1989	SD-N	.982	65	103	5	2	1	-1
1990	Phi-N	1.000	20	32	1	0	0	0
	Pit-N	1.000	2	2	0	0	0	0
	Yr	1.000	22	34	1	0	0	0
Total	8	.979	582	1090	51	4	10	16
1B								
1983	Chi-N	.992	26	231	15	2	18	0
1984	SD-N	1.000	2	5	0	0	0	0
1985	SD-N	1.000	3	4	1	0	2	0
1986	SD-N	1.000	26	59	9	0	4	1
1987	SD-N	.990	65	475	36	6	41	-2
1988	SD-N	.991	41	287	26	3	29	2
1989	SD-N	1.000	32	122	13	0	10	1
1990	Phi-N	1.000	43	318	24	2	31	-1
	Pit-N	1.000	5	22	4	0	4	1
	Yr	.995	48	340	28	2	35	0
Total	8	.993	243	1523	128	2	139	2
3B								
1983	Chi-N	1.000	1	1	2	0	0	0
1986	SD-N	1.000	1	0	0	0	0	0
Total	2	1.000	2	1	2	0	0	0

■ Dave Martinez OF

YEAR	TM/L	PCT	G	PO	A	E	DP	FR
1986	Chi-N	.988	46	77	2	1	1	5
1987	Chi-N	.980	139	283	10	6	1	-1
1988	Chi-N	.970	72	162	2	5	0	2
	Mon-N	.992	60	119	2	1	1	2
	Yr	.979	132	281	4	6	1	4
1989	Mon-N	.967	118	199	7	7	1	-17
1990	Mon-N	.989	108	257	6	3	1	-2
Total	5	.980	543	1097	29	3	5	-11

■ Edgar Martinez 3B

YEAR	TM/L	PCT	G	PO	A	E	DP	FR
1987	Sea-A	1.000	12	13	19	0	1	1
1988	Sea-A	.929	13	5	8	1	1	-4
1989	Sea-A	.949	61	40	72	6	9	-6
1990	Sea-A	.928	143	89	259	**27**	16	-1
Total	4	.937	229	147	358	4	27	-10

■ Buck Martinez C

YEAR	TM/L	PCT	G	PO	A	E	DP	FR
1969	KC-A	.972	55	290	25	9	7	-2
1970	KC-A	.958	5	20	3	1	0	1
1971	KC-A	.968	21	84	6	3	0	2
1973	KC-A	.966	14	52	4	2	1	-1
1974	KC-A	.977	38	151	16	4	1	1
1975	KC-A	.980	79	361	39	8	4	1
1976	KC-A	.991	94	420	40	4	4	5
1977	KC-A	.993	28	133	8	1	0	3
1978	Mil-A	.989	89	327	32	8	7	-3
1979	Mil-A	.967	68	198	39	8	2	-2
1980	Mil-A	.985	76	293	33	5	3	10
1981	Mil-A	.991	45	192	22	2	3	1
1982	Tor-A	.988	93	382	35	5	8	5
1983	Tor-A	.989	85	331	25	4	3	-3
1984	Tor-A	.995	98	360	34	2	5	4
1985	Tor-A	.988	42	155	16	2	5	4
1986	Tor-A	.994	78	289	19	2	6	-2
Total	17	.984	1008	4038	396	0	59	16
OF								
1969	KC-A	1.000	1	2	1	0	1	1

■ Marty Martinez SS

YEAR	TM/L	PCT	G	PO	A	E	DP	FR
1962	Min-A	.920	11	6	17	2	2	13
1967	Atl-N	.920	25	36	68	9	14	3
1968	Atl-N	.955	54	85	151	11	32	-6
1969	Hou-N	.925	17	23	39	5	5	-6
1970	Hou-N	.929	29	34	64	1	9	-4
1971	Hou-N	1.000	7	7	15	0	2	0
1972	StL-N	1.000	3	1	0	0	0	0
	Oak-A	.941	6	8	24	2	5	4
	Tex-A	.944	5	10	7	1	1	-1
	Yr	.942	11	18	31	3	6	3

YEAR	TM/L	PCT	G	PO	A	E	DP	FR
Total	7	.950	157	209	386	1	70	3
3B								
1962	Min-A	1.000	1	0	1	0	0	0
1967	Atl-N	1.000	2	0	2	0	2	1
1968	Atl-N	.943	37	23	60	5	8	-1
1969	Hou-N	.909	15	7	23	3	2	0
1970	Hou-N	1.000	10	6	11	0	0	0
1971	Hou-N	1.000	3	0	2	0	0	0
1972	StL-N	1.000	1	1	0	0	0	0
	Oak-A	1.000	1	0	2	0	0	0
	Tex-A	.818	4	2	7	2	1	0
	Yr	.846	5	2	9	2	1	0
Total	7	.936	74	39	108	0	13	0
2B								
1967	Atl-N	1.000	9	5	3	0	0	0
1968	Atl-N	.985	16	21	46	1	4	2
1969	Hou-N	1.000	1	2	0	0	0	0
1970	Hou-N	1.000	4	5	3	0	1	0
1971	Hou-N	.968	9	12	18	1	3	0
1972	StL-N	1.000	2	2	1	0	1	0
	Oak-A	.944	17	20	14	2	3	-1
	Tex-A	1.000	1	1	0	0	0	0
	Yr	.946	18	21	14	2	3	-1
Total	6	.975	59	68	85	4	12	1
C								
1967	Atl-N	1.000	3	2	0	0	0	0
1968	Atl-N	.979	14	40	7	1	0	1
1969	Hou-N	.900	7	24	3	3	0	-2
1970	Hou-N	.923	6	12	0	1	0	-1
Total	4	.946	30	78	10	5	0	-2
OF								
1969	Hou-N	1.000	21	21	1	0	0	0
1B								
1967	Atl-N	1.000	1	2	0	0	0	0
1971	Hou-N	1.000	4	22	2	0	2	0
Total	2	1.000	5	24	2	0	2	0

■ Ted Martinez SS

YEAR	TM/L	PCT	G	PO	A	E	DP	FR
1970	NY-N	1.000	1	1	4	0	1	0
1971	NY-N	.976	23	26	54	2	14	-2
1972	NY-N	.983	42	62	110	3	21	5
1973	NY-N	.941	44	66	110	11	12	-6
1974	NY-N	.952	75	123	212	17	32	12
1975	StL-N	.500	1	0	1	1	0	0
	Oak-A	.955	45	32	53	4	9	1
1977	LA-N	.973	13	18	18	1	5	1
1978	LA-N	.912	17	21	31	5	4	5
1979	LA-N	.962	21	16	34	2	4	0
Total	9	.956	282	365	627	6	102	16
2B								
1970	NY-N	1.000	4	8	7	0	3	0
1971	NY-N	.977	13	17	25	1	3	-5
1972	NY-N	.994	47	81	77	1	9	-6
1973	NY-N	1.000	5	5	4	0	1	0
1974	NY-N	1.000	11	14	22	0	4	2
1975	StL-N	1.000	2	1	0	0	0	0
	Oak-A	1.000	31	23	21	0	7	2
1977	LA-N	.992	27	59	67	1	23	12
1978	LA-N	1.000	10	12	10	0	3	3
1979	LA-N	1.000	18	25	29	0	2	1
Total	9	.994	168	245	262	3	55	9
3B								
1971	NY-N	1.000	3	2	1	0	0	0
1972	NY-N	1.000	2	0	6	0	0	1
1973	NY-N	1.000	14	12	23	0	2	3
1974	NY-N	.917	12	11	22	3	2	1
1975	StL-N	1.000	1	1	2	0	0	0
	Oak-A	1.000	14	6	7	0	0	1
1977	LA-N	.933	12	3	11	1	1	1
1978	LA-N	1.000	16	6	10	0	0	2
1979	LA-N	.769	23	4	6	3	1	-1
Total	8	.950	97	45	88	7	6	8
OF								
1971	NY-N	—	1	0	0	0	0	0
1972	NY-N	.971	15	32	1	1	0	1
1973	NY-N	.974	21	36	2	1	0	1
1974	NY-N	1.000	10	16	1	0	0	1
1975	StL-N	1.000	7	9	0	0	0	0
Total	5	.980	54	93	4	2	0	3

■ Joe Marty OF

YEAR	TM/L	PCT	G	PO	A	E	DP	FR
1937	Chi-N	.976	84	196	4	5	0	-5
1938	Chi-N	.987	68	143	6	2	1	3
1939	Chi-N	.933	21	24	4	2	0	-1
	Phi-N	.974	79	176	9	5	3	5
	Yr	.968	100	200	13	7	3	4
1940	Phi-N	.974	118	296	7	8	0	0
1941	Phi-N	.964	132	286	7	11	0	-10
Total	5	.972	502	1121	37	3	4	-8

■ Bob Martyn OF

YEAR	TM/L	PCT	G	PO	A	E	DP	FR
1957	KC-A	.976	49	77	3	2	0	1
1958	KC-A	.967	63	112	4	4	2	0
Total	2	.970	112	189	7	6	2	1

■ John Marzano C

YEAR	TM/L	PCT	G	PO	A	E	DP	FR
1987	Bos-A	.986	52	337	24	5	7	1
1988	Bos-A	1.000	10	77	4	0	0	5
1989	Bos-A	1.000	7	29	4	0	0	4
1990	Bos-A	1.000	32	153	14	0	3	4
Total	4	.992	101	596	46	5	10	10

■ Clyde Mashore OF

YEAR	TM/L	PCT	G	PO	A	E	DP	FR
1970	Mon-N	1.000	10	12	0	0	0	0
1971	Mon-N	.967	47	59	0	2	0	0
1972	Mon-N	.988	74	80	3	1	0	-2
1973	Mon-N	.958	44	65	4	3	0	4
Total	4	.970	175	216	7	6	0	2
3B								
1971	Mon-N	1.000	1	1	0	0	0	0

YEAR	TM/L	PCT	G	PO	A	E	DP	FR
2B								
1973	Mon-N	—	1	0	0	0	0	0

■ Phil Masi C

YEAR	TM/L	PCT	G	PO	A	E	DP	FR
1939	Bos-N	.960	42	104	15	5	4	-2
1940	Bos-N	.966	52	137	32	6	2	-1
1941	Bos-N	.978	83	194	31	5	3	-7
1942	Bos-N	.961	39	78	21	4	1	4
1943	Bos-N	.991	73	192	40	2	2	-7
1944	Bos-N	.977	63	180	34	5	3	-2
1945	Bos-N	.980	95	335	**52**	8	7	1
1946	Bos-N	.981	**124**	**470**	56	10	5	-5
1947	Bos-N	**.989**	123	411	58	5	1	-7
1948	Bos-N	.988	109	458	39	6	5	0
1949	Bos-N	.993	37	134	13	1	1	-2
	Pit-N	.994	44	157	21	1	7	-3
	Yr	**.994**	81	291	34	2	8	-5
1950	Chi-A	.996	114	440	52	2	9	-1
1951	Chi-A	.979	78	299	24	7	7	0
1952	Chi-A	.956	25	101	7	5	2	0
Total	14	.983	1101	3690	495	2	59	-32
1B								
1944	Bos-N	.985	12	118	11	2	9	1
1945	Bos-N	.966	7	55	2	2	1	-1
1949	Pit-N	1.000	2	17	3	0	3	1
Total	3	.981	21	190	16	4	13	1
OF								
1942	Bos-N	1.000	4	4	0	0	0	0
3B								
1944	Bos-N	1.000	2	0	1	0	0	0

■ Leech Maskrey OF

YEAR	TM/L	PCT	G	PO	A	E	DP	FR
1882	Lou-a	.902	76	136	11	16	1	0
1883	Lou-a	.914	**96**	**193**	19	20	1	10
1884	Lou-a	.896	103	138	17	18	2	3
1885	Lou-a	.899	108	169	9	20	2	-3
1886	Lou-a	.800	5	4	0	1	0	-1
	Cin-a	.926	26	46	4	4	1	1
	Yr	.915	31	50	4	5	1	0
Total	5	.904	414	686	60	9	7	10
3B								
1884	Lou-a	1.000	3	1	2	0	0	0
1885	Lou-a	.750	3	0	3	1	0	0
1886	Cin-a	.750	2	4	5	3	0	0
Total	3	.789	8	5	10	4	0	0
SS								
1883	Lou-a	—	1	0	0	0	0	0
1884	Lou-a	.750	1	2	1	1	0	-1
Total	2	.750	2	2	1	1	0	-1
2B								
1882	Lou-a	.600	1	1	2	2	0	0

■ Don Mason 2B

YEAR	TM/L	PCT	G	PO	A	E	DP	FR
1966	SF-N	.905	9	10	9	2	1	9
1967	SF-N	1.000	2	0	3	0	0	1
1968	SF-N	1.000	5	6	5	0	0	-1
1969	SF-N	.956	51	122	139	12	36	11
1970	SF-N	.950	14	11	8	1	1	2
1971	SD-N	.965	90	188	231	15	47	-11
1972	SD-N	.692	3	3	6	4	0	0
1973	SD-N	.750	1	1	2	1	1	1
Total	8	.955	175	341	403	5	86	12
3B								
1968	SF-N	1.000	2	2	3	0	0	0
1969	SF-N	.882	21	10	35	6	0	-1
1971	SD-N	.750	3	1	2	1	0	-1
Total	3	.883	26	13	40	7	0	-2
SS								
1968	SF-N	1.000	4	1	1	0	0	0
1969	SF-N	.800	7	3	5	2	1	0
Total	2	.833	11	4	6	2	1	-1

■ Jim Mason SS

YEAR	TM/L	PCT	G	PO	A	E	DP	FR
1971	Was-A	.955	3	8	13	1	1	2
1972	Tex-A	.948	32	52	93	8	14	-5
1973	Tex-A	.947	74	113	206	18	43	7
1974	NY-A	.964	152	241	430	25	87	-4
1975	NY-A	.955	93	134	209	16	45	-10
1976	NY-A	.966	93	128	245	13	47	7
1977	Tor-A	.971	22	49	51	3	9	-5
	Tex-A	.976	32	26	57	2	11	8
	Yr	.973	54	75	108	5	20	3
1978	Tex-A	.938	42	41	79	8	12	2
1979	Mon-N	.966	33	31	53	3	9	0
Total	9	.959	576	823	1436	7	278	2
3B								
1972	Tex-A	.905	10	6	13	2	0	-1
1973	Tex-A	—	1	0	0	0	0	0
1977	Tex-A	1.000	1	0	1	0	0	0
1978	Tex-A	.955	11	6	13	2	2	0
1979	Mon-N	1.000	6	4	9	0	1	1
Total	5	.911	29	16	35	5	3	0
2B								
1973	Tex-A	.964	19	30	24	2	8	2
1975	NY-A	—	1	0	0	0	0	0
1978	Tex-A	—	1	0	0	0	0	0
Total	3	.964	21	30	24	2	8	2

■ Tommy Matchick SS

YEAR	TM/L	PCT	G	PO	A	E	DP	FR
1967	Det-A	1.000	1	1	0	0	0	1
1968	Det-A	.950	59	53	118	9	20	-13
1969	Det-A	.933	6	6	8	1	2	-1
1970	Bos-A	—	1	0	0	0	0	0
	KC-A	.985	43	64	130	3	32	11
	Yr	.985	44	64	130	3	32	11
Total	4	.967	110	124	256	3	54	-2
3B								
1969	Det-A	.984	27	15	45	1	2	-3
1970	Bos-A	1.000	2	1	2	0	0	0
	KC-A	—	1	0	0	0	0	0

YEAR	TM/L	PCT	G	PO	A	E	DP	FR
	Yr	1.000	3	1	2	0	0	0
1971	Mil-A	.979	41	31	62	2	6	2
1972	Bal-A	.857	3	2	4	1	0	-1
Total	4	.976	74	49	113	4	8	-2
2B								
1968	Det-A	.983	13	25	34	1	7	0
1969	Det-A	.972	47	89	122	6	32	-2
1970	Bos-A	1.000	1	1	2	0	1	0
	KC-A	1.000	10	21	21	0	6	2
	Yr	1.000	11	22	23	0	7	2
1971	Mil-A	—	1	0	0	0	0	0
Total	4	.978	72	136	179	7	46	0
1B								
1968	Det-A	1.000	6	28	2	0	4	0
1969	Det-A	1.000	2	11	1	0	0	0
Total	2	1.000	8	39	3	0	4	0

■ Eddie Mathews 3B

YEAR	TM/L	PCT	G	PO	A	E	DP	FR
1952	Bos-N	.957	142	160	259	19	21	-10
1953	Mil-N	.939	**157**	154	311	**30**	33	3
1954	Mil-N	.966	127	112	254	13	**28**	-1
1955	Mil-N	.952	137	140	**280**	21	23	-4
1956	Mil-N	.944	**150**	133	287	**25**	22	-12
1957	Mil-N	.964	147	131	**299**	**16**	27	-2
1958	Mil-N	.955	**149**	116	**351**	22	24	5
1959	Mil-N	.961	148	144	305	18	21	3
1960	Mil-N	.950	153	**141**	280	22	23	-13
1961	Mil-N	.961	151	**168**	281	18	30	-6
1962	Mil-N	.964	140	141	283	16	22	3
1963	Mil-N	**.968**	121	113	276	13	23	**17**
1964	Mil-N	.962	128	130	247	15	19	2
1965	Mil-N	.956	153	113	301	19	19	9
1966	Atl-N	.946	127	114	237	20	31	-2
1967	Hou-N	.948	24	22	33	3	3	-3
	Det-A	.933	21	14	28	3	0	-3
1968	Det-A	1.000	6	3	10	0	0	-1
Total	17	.956	2181	2049	4322	293	369	-15
1B								
1962	Mil-N	1.000	7	67	2	0	7	-1
1964	Mil-N	.967	7	54	5	2	4	0
1967	Hou-N	.987	79	572	40	8	50	-1
	Det-A	.992	13	106	12	1	9	1
1968	Det-A	.974	6	34	3	1	5	0
Total	4	.987	112	833	62	2	75	-1
OF								
1954	Mil-N	.913	10	21	0	2	0	-1
1963	Mil-N	.914	42	63	1	6	0	-4
Total	2	.914	52	84	1	8	0	-5

■ Nelson Mathews OF

YEAR	TM/L	PCT	G	PO	A	E	DP	FR
1960	Chi-N	1.000	2	5	0	0	0	0
1961	Chi-N	1.000	2	5	0	0	0	0
1962	Chi-N	.962	14	25	0	1	0	-1
1963	Chi-N	.979	46	91	1	2	1	2
1964	KC-A	.968	154	**384**	5	**13**	2	1
1965	KC-A	.981	57	103	1	2	0	0
Total	6	.972	275	613	7	8	3	2

■ Gary Matthews OF

YEAR	TM/L	PCT	G	PO	A	E	DP	FR
1972	SF-N	.971	19	34	0	1	0	-2
1973	SF-N	.983	145	277	11	5	0	0
1974	SF-N	.970	151	281	9	9	2	-3
1975	SF-N	.967	113	225	11	8	2	6
1976	SF-N	.975	**156**	265	8	7	0	-12
1977	Atl-N	.965	145	262	11	10	1	-1
1978	Atl-N	.969	127	238	10	8	0	-1
1979	Atl-N	.974	156	292	12	8	4	1
1980	Atl-N	.960	143	258	8	**11**	0	-9
1981	Phi-N	.963	100	170	11	7	1	-2
1982	Phi-N	.966	**162**	268	14	10	2	-2
1983	Phi-N	.972	122	174	11	5	2	-5
1984	Chi-N	.955	145	224	7	**11**	0	-12
1985	Chi-N	.975	85	119	7	3	2	-7
1986	Chi-N	.940	105	137	5	**9**	1	-15
1987	Chi-N	1.000	2	2	0	0	0	0
Total	16	.968	1876	3226	135	112	17	-64

■ Wid Matthews OF

YEAR	TM/L	PCT	G	PO	A	E	DP	FR
1923	Phi-A	.947	127	316	3	**18**	0	-8
1924	Was-A	.985	44	121	7	2	2	5
1925	Was-A	1.000	1	1	0	0	0	0
Total	3	.957	172	438	10	0	2	-3

■ Bobby Mattick SS

YEAR	TM/L	PCT	G	PO	A	E	DP	FR
1938	Chi-N	—	1	0	0	0	0	0
1939	Chi-N	.927	48	102	179	22	28	7
1940	Cin-N	.946	126	233	431	38	76	10
1941	Cin-N	.982	12	24	31	1	6	-1
1942	Cin-N	1.000	3	7	6	0	1	1
Total	5	.943	190	366	647	1	111	17
3B								
1940	Chi-N	—	1	0	0	0	0	0
1941	Cin-N	1.000	5	4	11	0	0	0
Total	2	1.000	6	4	11	0	0	0
2B								
1941	Cin-N	—	1	0	0	0	0	0

■ Wally Mattick OF

YEAR	TM/L	PCT	G	PO	A	E	DP	FR
1912	Chi-A	.982	79	154	8	3	1	-3
1913	Chi-A	.977	64	116	14	3	2	2
1918	StL-N	1.000	3	5	1	0	0	0
Total	3	.980	146	275	23	6	3	-1

■ Don Mattingly 1B

YEAR	TM/L	PCT	G	PO	A	E	DP	FR
1982	NY-A	1.000	7	4	0	0	0	0
1983	NY-A	.992	42	278	12	1	30	-4
1984	NY-A	**.996**	133	1107	124	5	135	**12**
1985	NY-A	**.995**	159	1318	87	7	**154**	-11
1986	NY-A	**.996**	160	**1377**	100	6	132	-9
1987	NY-A	**.996**	140	1239	91	5	122	-4
1988	NY-A	.993	143	1250	99	9	131	-3

YEAR	TM/L	PCT	G	PO	A	E	DP	FR
1989	NY-A	.995	145	1274	87	7	143	-5
1990	NY-A	.997	89	800	78	3	81	6
Total	9	.995	1012	8647	678	3	928	-18
	OF							
1982	NY-A	1.000	6	11	1	0	0	2
1983	NY-A	.974	48	72	3	2	1	-3
1984	NY-A	.974	19	36	2	1	1	0
1988	NY-A	—	1	0	0	0	0	0
1989	NY-A	1.000	1	2	0	0	0	0
1990	NY-A	—	1	0	0	0	0	0
Total	6	.977	76	121	6	3	2	-1
	3B							
1986	NY-A	.923	3	1	11	1	2	2
	2B							
1983	NY-A	—	1	0	0	0	0	0

■ Len Matuszek 1B

YEAR	TM/L	PCT	G	PO	A	E	DP	FR
1981	Phi-N	1.000	1	2	0	0	1	0
1982	Phi-N	1.000	3	11	0	0	1	0
1983	Phi-N	1.000	21	144	9	0	8	-1
1984	Phi-N	.990	81	643	55	7	40	4
1985	Tor-A	1.000	5	19	2	0	1	0
	LA-N	1.000	10	23	1	0	2	0
1986	LA-N	.977	31	197	20	5	18	0
1987	LA-N	1.000	3	4	1	0	0	0
Total	7	.990	155	1043	88	2	71	3
	OF							
1984	Phi-N	.500	1	1	0	1	0	0
1985	LA-N	1.000	17	24	0	0	0	-1
1986	LA-N	1.000	37	38	2	0	0	-1
Total	3	.985	55	63	2	1	0	-2
	3B							
1981	Phi-N	1.000	1	3	4	0	0	2
1982	Phi-N	.750	8	1	8	3	0	-2
1985	LA-N	1.000	1	0	1	0	0	0
Total	3	.850	10	4	13	3	0	0

■ Gene Mauch 2B

YEAR	TM/L	PCT	G	PO	A	E	DP	FR
1947	Pit-N	.963	6	13	13	1	0	-1
1948	Bro-N	.950	7	12	7	1	2	1
	Chi-A	.925	26	56	55	9	18	-3
	Yr	.929	33	68	62	10	20	-2
1949	Chi-A	.971	25	58	74	4	17	9
1950	Bos-N	.968	28	77	72	5	17	0
1951	Bos-N	1.000	2	1	0	0	0	0
1956	Bos-A	.935	6	12	17	2	4	-2
1957	Bos-A	.962	58	127	153	11	41	-10
Total	7	.958	158	356	391	3	99	-6
	SS							
1944	Pit-N	1.000	5	7	9	0	3	-2
1947	Pit-N	.857	4	5	7	2	1	-1
1948	Bro-N	1.000	1	1	0	0	0	0
	Chi-A	.970	19	21	43	2	6	-3
	Yr	.970	20	22	43	2	6	-3
1949	Chi-A	.939	19	35	42	5	9	2
1950	Bos-N	1.000	5	4	8	0	1	0
1951	Bos-N	1.000	10	15	16	0	2	0
1952	StL-N	.500	2	1	0	1	0	0
Total	7	.955	65	89	125	3	22	-4
	3B							
1949	Chi-A	1.000	7	5	9	0	1	1
1950	Bos-N	.778	7	2	5	2	0	-1
1951	Bos-N	.000	3	0	0	1	0	0
Total	3	.875	17	7	14	3	1	0

■ Carmen Mauro OF

YEAR	TM/L	PCT	G	PO	A	E	DP	FR
1948	Chi-N	1.000	2	7	0	0	0	1
1950	Chi-N	.946	49	86	2	5	0	-5
1951	Chi-N	.900	6	17	1	2	0	1
1953	Bro-N	1.000	1	1	0	0	0	0
	Was-A	1.000	6	10	1	0	0	1
	Phi-A	.969	49	119	5	4	0	6
	Yr	.971	55	129	6	4	0	7
Total	4	.958	113	240	9	1	0	4
	3B							
1953	Phi-A	—	1	0	0	0	0	0

■ Dal Maxvill SS

YEAR	TM/L	PCT	G	PO	A	E	DP	FR
1962	StL-N	.962	76	111	169	11	41	-1
1963	StL-N	.974	24	17	21	1	5	4
1964	StL-N	1.000	13	5	4	0	0	1
1965	StL-N	.952	12	10	10	1	1	1
1966	StL-N	.967	128	219	428	22	88	23
1967	StL-N	.974	148	236	470	19	74	1
1968	StL-N	.969	151	232	458	22	81	-9
1969	StL-N	.969	131	216	408	20	78	21
1970	StL-N	.982	136	216	426	12	80	31
1971	StL-N	.979	140	188	413	13	71	29
1972	StL-N	.980	95	145	243	8	56	7
	Oak-A	1.000	4	3	8	0	1	2
1973	Oak-A	.966	18	13	15	1	4	3
	Pit-N	.971	74	105	234	10	46	4
1974	Pit-N	.946	8	12	23	2	8	1
	Oak-A	.977	29	23	62	2	14	7
1975	Oak-A	.955	20	8	13	1	1	3
Total	14	.973	1207	1759	3405	145	649	128
	2B							
1963	StL-N	.964	9	8	19	1	5	3
1964	StL-N	.972	15	21	14	1	5	4
1965	StL-N	.993	49	64	76	1	22	11
1966	StL-N	1.000	5	4	6	0	3	1
1967	StL-N	1.000	7	5	16	0	4	2
1970	StL-N	.990	22	44	59	1	11	7
1972	StL-N	.967	11	28	30	2	4	2
	Oak-A	.983	24	25	32	1	8	2
1973	Oak-A	.900	11	1	8	1	1	1
1974	Oak-A	1.000	30	12	18	0	2	2
1975	Oak-A	1.000	2	2	0	0	0	0
Total	10	.984	185	214	278	8	65	35

YEAR	TM/L	PCT	G	PO	A	E	DP	FR
	3B							
1962	StL-N	—	1	0	0	0	0	0
1963	StL-N	—	3	0	0	0	0	0
1964	StL-N	1.000	1	0	1	0	0	0
1973	Oak-A	—	1	0	0	0	0	0
1974	Oak-A	—	1	0	0	0	0	0
Total	5	1.000	7	0	1	0	0	0
	OF							
1964	StL-N	1.000	1	1	0	0	0	0
1966	StL-N	—	1	0	0	0	0	0
Total	2	1.000	2	1	0	0	0	0

■ Charlie Maxwell OF

YEAR	TM/L	PCT	G	PO	A	E	DP	FR
1950	Bos-A	1.000	2	6	0	0	0	0
1951	Bos-A	.926	13	25	0	2	0	-2
1952	Bos-A	1.000	3	6	1	0	0	1
1954	Bos-A	1.000	27	25	1	0	0	-2
1955	Det-A	.967	26	55	3	2	0	3
1956	Det-A	.987	136	281	12	4	1	6
1957	Det-A	.997	137	317	6	1	1	9
1958	Det-A	.986	114	201	4	3	0	-4
1959	Det-A	.986	136	285	6	4	1	7
1960	Det-A	.996	120	254	5	1	0	5
1961	Det-A	.965	25	53	2	2	0	1
1962	Det-A	.966	15	28	0	1	0	-1
	Chi-A	.990	56	100	2	1	1	-1
	Yr	.985	71	128	2	2	1	-2
1963	Chi-A	.924	24	29	2	0	1	-4
Total	13	.988	834	1665	44	1	5	18
	1B							
1952	Bos-A	.966	3	24	4	1	1	1
1955	Det-A	.958	2	21	2	1	0	0
1958	Det-A	.989	14	89	4	1	9	-1
1962	Det-A	1.000	1	1	0	0	0	0
	Chi-A	.980	6	47	3	1	6	0
	Yr	.981	7	48	3	1	6	0
1963	Chi-A	1.000	17	107	5	0	14	0
Total	5	.987	43	289	18	4	30	0

■ Carlos May OF

YEAR	TM/L	PCT	G	PO	A	E	DP	FR
1968	Chi-A	.960	17	24	0	1	0	-3
1969	Chi-A	.982	100	154	10	3	0	-3
1970	Chi-A	.991	141	203	12	2	2	-8
1971	Chi-A	.947	9	17	1	1	0	0
1972	Chi-A	.983	145	215	13	4	2	-6
1973	Chi-A	.992	70	118	7	1	0	-2
1974	Chi-A	.988	129	245	11	3	1	-2
1975	Chi-A	.975	46	72	6	2	1	-1
1976	Chi-A	1.000	9	13	0	0	0	-1
	NY-A	.950	7	19	0	1	0	-1
	Yr	.970	16	32	0	1	0	-2
1977	NY-A	1.000	4	3	0	0	0	0
Total	10	.984	677	1083	60	8	6	-27
	1B							
1970	Chi-A	.977	7	73	11	2	6	2
1971	Chi-A	.986	130	1189	71	18	90	-5
1972	Chi-A	.971	5	32	2	1	0	0
1973	Chi-A	1.000	2	11	1	0	0	0
1975	Chi-A	.989	63	508	46	6	54	1
1976	NY-A	1.000	1	9	0	0	0	0
1977	Cal-A	.986	3	15	2	0	1	0
Total	7	.986	211	1837	133	7	151	-2

■ Dave May OF

YEAR	TM/L	PCT	G	PO	A	E	DP	FR
1967	Bal-A	.969	19	30	1	1	0	-1
1968	Bal-A	.984	61	62	1	1	0	-2
1969	Bal-A	.940	40	43	4	3	0	1
1970	Bal-A	1.000	9	5	0	0	0	-1
	Mil-A	.989	99	255	6	3	0	15
	Yr	.989	108	260	6	3	0	14
1971	Mil-A	.975	142	342	10	9	3	6
1972	Mil-A	.985	138	376	9	6	3	10
1973	Mil-A	.979	152	401	9	9	3	1
1974	Mil-A	.989	121	249	10	3	2	-14
1975	Atl-N	.964	53	103	3	4	2	-1
1976	Atl-N	.972	60	98	5	3	1	0
1977	Tex-A	.969	111	181	8	6	2	-7
1978	Mil-A	.944	16	32	2	2	1	1
Total	12	.978	1021	2177	68	0	17	8

■ Jerry May C

YEAR	TM/L	PCT	G	PO	A	E	DP	FR
1964	Pit-N	.988	11	80	5	1	0	5
1965	Pit-N	1.000	4	2	0	0	0	0
1966	Pit-N	.984	41	114	12	2	3	9
1967	Pit-N	.993	110	550	52	4	9	-1
1968	Pit-N	.988	135	752	70	10	10	3
1969	Pit-N	.994	52	325	22	2	3	-5
1970	Pit-N	.994	45	280	32	2	2	13
1971	KC-A	.997	71	314	38	1	6	0
1972	KC-A	.979	41	175	13	4	1	-1
1973	KC-A	.940	11	43	4	3	2	-1
	NY-N	1.000	4	14	0	0	0	-1
Total	10	.990	525	2649	248	9	36	21

■ Lee May 1B

YEAR	TM/L	PCT	G	PO	A	E	DP	FR
1966	Cin-N	.972	16	132	9	4	15	-1
1967	Cin-N	.994	81	621	43	4	49	-2
1968	Cin-N	.996	122	1040	70	5	86	0
1969	Cin-N	.993	156	1387	102	11	128	0
1970	Cin-N	.993	153	1362	109	10	143	0
1971	Cin-N	.994	143	1261	78	8	118	-7
1972	Hou-N	.996	146	1318	76	6	133	-3
1973	Hou-N	.993	144	1220	78	9	112	-3
1974	Hou-N	.994	145	1253	88	8	116	1
1975	Bal-A	.993	144	1312	106	10	138	3
1976	Bal-A	.996	94	722	62	3	61	0
1977	Bal-A	.995	110	907	56	5	101	-7
1978	Bal-A	.973	4	34	2	1	3	0
1979	Bal-A	.913	2	21	0	2	2	-1
1980	Bal-A	1.000	7	57	3	0	4	0

YEAR	TM/L	PCT	G	PO	A	E	DP	FR
1981	KC-A	1.000	8	63	2	0	8	-1
1982	KC-A	.989	32	175	10	2	18	-2
Total	17	.994	1507	12885	894	8	1235	-23
	OF							
1967	Cin-N	.977	48	82	3	2	1	2
1968	Cin-N	1.000	33	54	3	0	0	1
1969	Cin-N	1.000	7	8	0	0	0	0
Total	3	.987	88	144	6	2	1	3

■ Pinky May 3B

YEAR	TM/L	PCT	G	PO	A	E	DP	FR
1939	Phi-N	.956	132	153	263	19	28	8
1940	Phi-N	.954	135	139	297	21	12	12
1941	Phi-N	.972	140	194	324	15	31	25
1942	Phi-N	.963	107	109	227	13	23	17
1943	Phi-N	.963	132	142	280	16	20	11
Total	5	.962	646	737	1391	4	114	73
	SS							
1940	Phi-N	.875	1	1	6	1	1	1

■ Milt May C

YEAR	TM/L	PCT	G	PO	A	E	DP	FR
1971	Pit-N	1.000	31	168	12	0	3	3
1972	Pit-N	.985	33	179	21	3	2	4
1973	Pit-N	.973	79	402	36	12	4	-7
1974	Hou-N	.993	116	525	63	4	10	2
1975	Hou-N	.986	102	568	70	9	8	2
1976	Det-A	1.000	6	33	5	0	0	1
1977	Det-A	.986	111	551	78	9	12	-6
1978	Det-A	.979	94	406	58	10	5	1
1979	Det-A	1.000	5	19	1	0	0	1
	Chi-A	.981	65	277	27	6	1	2
	Yr	.982	70	296	28	6	1	3
1980	SF-N	.986	103	500	59	8	12	-5
1981	SF-N	.989	93	468	48	6	4	-1
1982	SF-N	.987	110	552	61	8	5	-3
1983	SF-N	.981	56	285	32	6	5	-3
	Pit-N	1.000	4	23	3	0	0	2
	Yr	.983	60	308	35	6	5	-1
1984	Pit-N	.993	26	135	15	1	2	4
Total	14	.986	1034	5091	589	2	73	-2

■ John Mayberry 1B

YEAR	TM/L	PCT	G	PO	A	E	DP	FR
1968	Hou-N	1.000	2	25	0	0	1	0
1970	Hou-N	.995	45	371	35	2	29	3
1971	Hou-N	.997	37	317	15	1	20	-3
1972	KC-A	.995	146	1338	82	7	141	0
1973	KC-A	.994	149	1457	81	9	156	-5
1974	KC-A	.990	106	963	61	10	101	-2
1975	KC-A	.988	131	1199	100	16	105	3
1976	KC-A	.996	160	1484	105	7	132	-3
1977	KC-A	.995	145	1296	81	7	118	-6
1978	Tor-A	.993	139	1143	52	8	120	-15
1979	Tor-A	.995	135	1192	74	6	129	-9
1980	Tor-A	.994	136	1243	79	8	138	-4
1981	Tor-A	1.000	4	39	1	0	3	0
	NY-A	.996	63	455	25	2	49	-4
	Yr	.996	67	494	26	2	52	-4
Total	14	.994	1478	13169	827	8	1307	-51

■ Lee Maye OF

YEAR	TM/L	PCT	G	PO	A	E	DP	FR
1959	Mil-N	.976	44	80	3	2	1	2
1960	Mil-N	.968	19	29	1	1	0	-2
1961	Mil-N	.972	96	169	6	5	0	-4
1962	Mil-N	.977	94	209	2	5	1	5
1963	Mil-N	.983	111	231	4	4	1	5
1964	Mil-N	.961	135	264	7	11	1	5
1965	Mil-N	.962	13	23	2	1	0	1
	Hou-N	.953	103	177	6	9	1	-2
	Yr	.954	116	200	8	10	1	-1
1966	Hou-N	.949	97	145	4	8	0	-6
1967	Cle-A	.981	77	102	2	2	0	-6
1968	Cle-A	.984	80	123	4	2	0	-1
1969	Cle-A	.982	28	55	0	1	0	0
	Was-A	.944	65	100	1	6	1	-7
	Yr	.957	93	155	1	7	1	-7
1970	Was-A	1.000	68	75	4	0	1	-8
1971	Chi-A	1.000	10	11	1	0	0	0
Total	13	.970	1040	1793	47	7	7	-18
	3B							
1964	Mil-N	1.000	5	4	2	0	0	0
1970	Was-A	1.000	1	0	1	0	0	0
Total	2	1.000	6	4	3	0	0	0
	2B							
1967	Cle-A	—	1	0	0	0	0	0
	1B							
1968	Cle-A	.000	1	0	0	1	0	0

■ Ed Mayer 3B

YEAR	TM/L	PCT	G	PO	A	E	DP	FR
1890	Phi-N	.878	117	173	224	55	22	-7
1891	Phi-N	.895	31	47	72	14	3	0
Total	2	.882	148	220	296	9	25	-7
	OF							
1891	Phi-N	.855	29	39	8	8	0	-2
	SS							
1891	Phi-N	.825	7	10	23	7	0	-3
	2B							
1891	Phi-N	1.000	1	4	2	0	1	0

■ Wally Mayer C

YEAR	TM/L	PCT	G	PO	A	E	DP	FR
1911	Chi-A	.900	1	7	2	1	0	0
1912	Chi-A	1.000	6	13	1	0	0	0
1914	Chi-A	.968	33	137	47	6	3	6
1915	Chi-A	.990	20	89	15	1	0	-1
1917	Bos-A	.964	4	19	8	1	1	2
1918	Bos-A	.964	23	63	18	3	0	0
1919	StL-A	.959	25	84	33	5	1	6
Total	7	.969	112	412	124	7	5	13
	3B							
1914	Chi-A	.500	1	1	0	1	0	-1

Buster Maynard OF

YEAR	TM/L	PCT	G	PO	A	E	DP	FR
1940	NY-N	.929	7	13	0	1	0	-1
1942	NY-N	.982	58	103	6	2	2	6
1943	NY-N	.965	74	130	9	5	2	-4
1946	NY-N	.750	3	3	0	1	0	0
Total	4	.967	142	249	15	9	4	1

3B

YEAR	TM/L	PCT	G	PO	A	E	DP	FR
1942	NY-N	.943	10	13	20	2	3	4
1943	NY-N	.931	22	20	47	5	2	0
Total	2	.935	32	33	67	7	5	4

2B

YEAR	TM/L	PCT	G	PO	A	E	DP	FR
1942	NY-N	.667	1	0	2	1	0	0

Eddie Mayo 2B

YEAR	TM/L	PCT	G	PO	A	E	DP	FR
1944	Det-A	.978	143	384	458	19	**120**	**28**
1945	Det-A	**.980**	124	326	393	15	91	18
1946	Det-A	.965	49	96	125	8	28	-11
1947	Det-A	.983	142	326	365	12	80	-23
1948	Det-A	.975	86	202	223	11	48	-10
Total	5	.978	544	1334	1564	5	367	2

3B

YEAR	TM/L	PCT	G	PO	A	E	DP	FR
1936	NY-N	.981	40	32	69	2	8	5
1937	Bos-N	.956	50	57	73	6	2	-4
1938	Bos-N	.923	6	4	8	1	2	1
1943	Phi-A	**.976**	123	176	223	10	18	-3
1948	Det-A	1.000	10	9	19	0	1	0
Total	5	.972	229	278	392	9	31	-1

SS

YEAR	TM/L	PCT	G	PO	A	E	DP	FR
1938	Bos-N	1.000	2	2	2	0	1	0
1944	Det-A	.966	11	17	40	2	5	1
Total	2	.968	13	19	42	2	6	1

Willie Mays OF

YEAR	TM/L	PCT	G	PO	A	E	DP	FR
1951	NY-N	.976	121	353	12	9	2	5
1952	NY-N	.991	34	109	6	1	2	9
1954	NY-N	.985	151	448	13	7	9	11
1955	NY-N	.982	152	407	23	8	8	14
1956	NY-N	.979	152	415	14	9	6	8
1957	NY-N	.980	150	422	14	9	5	5
1958	SF-N	.980	151	429	17	9	2	10
1959	SF-N	.984	147	353	6	6	2	0
1960	SF-N	.981	152	392	12	8	2	8
1961	SF-N	.980	153	385	7	8	3	4
1962	SF-N	.991	161	429	6	4	1	7
1963	SF-N	.981	157	397	7	8	1	8
1964	SF-N	.984	155	370	10	6	4	8
1965	SF-N	.983	151	337	13	6	4	10
1966	SF-N	.982	150	370	8	7	2	5
1967	SF-N	.976	134	277	3	7	0	-5
1968	SF-N	.978	142	301	7	7	2	-2
1969	SF-N	.976	109	199	4	5	0	-12
1970	SF-N	.975	129	269	6	7	3	-2
1971	SF-N	.970	84	192	2	6	1	-4
1972	SF-N	1.000	14	29	0	0	0	-1
	NY-N	.974	49	109	3	3	1	3
	Yr	.979	63	138	3	3	1	2
1973	NY-N	.991	45	103	2	1	0	2
Total	22	.981	2843	7095	195	141	60	91

1B

YEAR	TM/L	PCT	G	PO	A	E	DP	FR
1964	SF-N	1.000	1	6	1	0	1	0
1968	SF-N	1.000	1	9	0	0	1	0
1969	SF-N	1.000	1	6	0	0	1	0
1970	SF-N	1.000	5	34	3	0	3	0
1971	SF-N	.974	48	384	27	11	43	2
1972	NY-N	.987	11	75	2	1	3	-1
1973	NY-N	.980	17	143	4	3	9	-2
Total	7	.979	84	657	37	15	61	-5

SS

YEAR	TM/L	PCT	G	PO	A	E	DP	FR
1963	SF-N	—	1	0	0	0	0	0
1964	SF-N	—	1	0	0	0	0	0
Total	2	—	2	0	0	0	0	0

3B

YEAR	TM/L	PCT	G	PO	A	E	DP	FR
1964	SF-N	1.000	1	0	1	0	0	0

Bill Mazeroski 2B

YEAR	TM/L	PCT	G	PO	A	E	DP	FR
1956	Pit-N	.981	81	163	242	8	56	11
1957	Pit-N	.978	144	308	443	17	96	4
1958	Pit-N	.980	**152**	344	**496**	17	118	**19**
1959	Pit-N	.981	133	303	373	13	100	-9
1960	Pit-N	**.989**	151	413	449	10	**127**	**25**
1961	Pit-N	.975	**152**	**410**	**505**	23	**144**	**31**
1962	Pit-N	.985	159	425	509	14	**138**	**41**
1963	Pit-N	.984	138	340	**506**	14	**131**	57
1964	Pit-N	.975	**162**	346	**543**	23	**122**	**34**
1965	Pit-N	**.988**	127	290	439	9	113	26
1966	Pit-N	**.992**	**162**	411	538	8	**161**	**41**
1967	Pit-N	.981	**163**	417	498	18	**131**	17
1968	Pit-N	.981	142	319	467	15	107	26
1969	Pit-N	.988	65	134	192	4	46	14
1970	Pit-N	.987	102	227	325	7	87	24
1971	Pit-N	.986	46	95	121	3	22	-1
1972	Pit-N	.986	15	29	39	1	7	3
Total	17	.983	2094	4974	6685	204	1706	363

3B

YEAR	TM/L	PCT	G	PO	A	E	DP	FR
1971	Pit-N	1.000	7	2	5	0	0	0
1972	Pit-N	1.000	3	0	4	0	0	0
Total	2	1.000	10	2	9	0	0	0

Mel Mazzera OF

YEAR	TM/L	PCT	G	PO	A	E	DP	FR
1935	StL-A	.950	10	18	1	1	0	0
1938	StL-A	.976	47	74	7	2	1	0
1939	StL-A	.983	25	56	1	1	0	0
1940	Phi-N	.985	42	62	5	1	2	-1
Total	4	.978	124	210	14	5	3	-1

1B

YEAR	TM/L	PCT	G	PO	A	E	DP	FR
1940	Phi-N	1.000	11	28	1	0	1	0

Lee Mazzilli OF

YEAR	TM/L	PCT	G	PO	A	E	DP	FR
1976	NY-N	.983	23	55	2	1	2	3
1977	NY-N	.992	156	386	9	3	1	3
1978	NY-N	.987	144	386	8	5	3	8
1979	NY-N	.989	143	358	12	4	1	0
1980	NY-N	.994	66	166	4	1	1	1
1981	NY-N	.970	89	192	5	6	1	2
1982	Tex-A	.945	26	51	1	3	1	-3
	NY-N	1.000	2	4	0	0	0	0
	Yr	.949	28	55	1	3	1	-3
1983	Pit-N	.985	57	130	3	2	1	3
1984	Pit-N	.989	74	92	2	1	0	-11
1985	Pit-N	.929	5	13	0	1	0	0
1986	Pit-N	1.000	18	26	0	0	0	-2
	NY-N	1.000	10	16	0	0	0	0
	Yr	1.000	28	42	0	0	0	-2
1987	NY-N	1.000	25	24	1	0	0	-1
1988	NY-N	1.000	18	23	1	0	0	0
1989	NY-N	.889	10	8	0	1	0	-1
	Tor-A	1.000	2	3	0	0	0	0
Total	14	.986	868	1933	48	8	11	2

1B

YEAR	TM/L	PCT	G	PO	A	E	DP	FR
1979	NY-N	.993	15	122	12	1	15	1
1980	NY-N	.983	92	708	49	13	67	-3
1982	NY-A	.995	23	179	7	1	26	-3
1983	Pit-N	.956	7	43	0	2	5	-2
1984	Pit-N	1.000	5	11	0	0	0	0
1985	Pit-N	.986	19	139	6	2	15	-1
1986	Pit-N	1.000	7	35	1	0	1	-1
	NY-N	1.000	8	51	1	0	2	-1
	Yr	1.000	15	86	2	0	3	-2
1987	NY-N	1.000	13	58	2	0	1	-1
1988	NY-N	.969	16	91	3	3	5	-2
1989	NY-N	1.000	8	39	1	0	2	-1
	Tor-A	.944	2	16	1	1	1	0
Total	10	.986	215	1492	83	3	140	-14

Jimmy McAleer OF

YEAR	TM/L	PCT	G	PO	A	E	DP	FR
1889	Cle-N	.955	110	247	29	13	9	8
1890	Cle-P	.940	86	249	15	17	4	11
1891	Cle-N	.924	**136**	284	19	25	1	5
1892	Cle-N	.948	149	**367**	18	21	6	12
1893	Cle-N	.928	91	230	16	19	3	4
1894	Cle-N	.953	64	175	9	9	3	3
1895	Cle-N	.934	131	341	14	25	1	3
1896	Cle-N	.958	116	278	18	13	5	7
1897	Cle-N	.947	24	51	3	3	0	-1
1898	Cle-N	.965	104	239	10	9	4	3
1901	Cle-A	1.000	2	3	0	0	0	0
1902	StL-A	—	2	0	0	0	0	-1
Total	12	.944	1015	2464	151	154	36	54

2B

YEAR	TM/L	PCT	G	PO	A	E	DP	FR
1898	Cle-N	.889	2	4	4	1	0	0

3B

YEAR	TM/L	PCT	G	PO	A	E	DP	FR
1901	Cle-A	—	1	0	0	0	0	0

Sport McAllister OF

YEAR	TM/L	PCT	G	PO	A	E	DP	FR
1896	Cle-N	.500	4	1	0	1	0	-6
1897	Cle-N	.894	38	40	2	5	0	-3
1898	Cle-N	.941	8	13	3	1	0	1
1899	Cle-N	.943	79	106	10	7	4	-7
1901	Det-A	.722	11	13	0	5	0	-3
1902	Det-A	1.000	1	4	0	0	0	0
	Det-A	1.000	11	17	1	0	1	0
	Yr	1.000	12	21	1	0	1	0
1903	Det-A	.667	5	2	0	1	0	-2
Total	7	.914	147	196	16	0	5	-20

C

YEAR	TM/L	PCT	G	PO	A	E	DP	FR
1896	Cle-N	1.000	2	5	0	0	0	-1
1897	Cle-N	.833	2	5	0	1	0	-1
1899	Cle-N	.862	17	36	20	9	2	-7
1901	Det-A	.898	35	95	37	15	1	-8
1902	Det-A	.833	2	4	1	1	0	-1
	Det-A	.970	7	21	11	1	1	2
	Yr	.949	9	25	12	2	1	1
1903	Det-A	.975	18	85	32	3	2	4
Total	6	.921	83	251	101	0	6	-12

1B

YEAR	TM/L	PCT	G	PO	A	E	DP	FR
1897	Cle-N	1.000	3	18	0	0	0	0
1899	Cle-N	.938	6	43	2	3	2	-1
1901	Det-A	.944	28	261	10	16	16	-4
1902	Det-A	1.000	5	31	6	0	2	2
	Bal-A	1.000	1	7	0	0	1	0
	Det-A	.991	21	206	8	2	11	-1
	Yr	.992	27	244	14	2	14	1
1903	Det-A	1.000	1	3	0	0	0	0
Total	5	.966	65	569	26	1	32	-4

SS

YEAR	TM/L	PCT	G	PO	A	E	DP	FR
1897	Cle-N	.833	4	6	9	3	1	-2
1899	Cle-N	.960	3	16	8	1	0	1
1901	Det-A	.882	3	5	10	2	1	0
1902	Det-A	.903	5	14	14	3	2	0
	Det-A	.714	1	0	5	2	0	-1
	Yr	.868	6	14	19	5	2	-1
1903	Det-A	.888	46	77	129	26	12	-9
Total	5	.888	62	118	175	7	16	-11

3B

YEAR	TM/L	PCT	G	PO	A	E	DP	FR
1899	Cle-N	.806	7	15	14	7	3	0
1901	Det-A	.800	10	7	9	4	1	-4
1902	Det-A	1.000	2	0	8	0	1	1
	Det-A	.778	4	1	6	2	0	0
	Yr	.882	6	1	14	2	1	1
1903	Det-A	.786	4	3	8	3	0	-1
Total	4	.816	27	26	45	6	5	-4

2B

YEAR	TM/L	PCT	G	PO	A	E	DP	FR
1897	Cle-N	1.000	1	2	2	0	0	0
1899	Cle-N	.800	1	2	2	1	0	-1
1902	Det-A	.769	3	3	7	3	1	-2
	Bal-A	.923	2	4	8	1	0	0
	Yr	.846	5	7	15	4	1	-2
Total	3	.857	13	11	19	5	1	-3

Dick McAuliffe 2B

YEAR	TM/L	PCT	G	PO	A	E	DP	FR
1962	Det-A	.965	70	186	146	12	32	-12
1963	Det-A	.971	15	36	32	2	8	-4
1967	Det-A	.965	145	270	307	**21**	74	-3
1968	Det-A	.986	148	288	348	9	79	-19
1969	Det-A	.976	72	167	196	9	40	0
1970	Det-A	.975	127	280	333	16	75	-1
1971	Det-A	.987	123	322	308	8	86	8
1972	Det-A	.975	116	266	249	13	63	-7
1973	Det-A	.986	102	217	265	7	62	5
1974	Bos-A	.971	53	123	115	7	33	-6
Total	10	.977	971	2155	2299	104	552	-39

SS

YEAR	TM/L	PCT	G	PO	A	E	DP	FR
1960	Det-A	.884	7	12	26	5	7	1
1961	Det-A	.933	55	79	115	14	29	-22
1962	Det-A	.918	16	13	32	4	3	-2
1963	Det-A	.963	133	220	356	22	68	-20
1964	Det-A	.958	160	262	467	**32**	84	-8
1965	Det-A	.956	112	190	286	22	58	-15
1966	Det-A	.964	105	160	292	17	49	-10
1967	Det-A	.933	43	30	67	7	8	-11
1968	Det-A	1.000	5	4	0	0	1	-1
1970	Det-A	.943	15	16	34	3	3	-5
1971	Det-A	1.000	7	4	2	0	1	-1
1972	Det-A	1.000	3	1	2	0	0	0
1973	Det-A	1.000	2	0	1	0	1	0
1974	Bos-A	1.000	3	1	1	0	1	0
Total	14	.955	666	992	1685	126	313	-94

3B

YEAR	TM/L	PCT	G	PO	A	E	DP	FR
1961	Det-A	.912	22	13	39	5	3	-6
1962	Det-A	.909	49	61	79	14	10	-6
1966	Det-A	.956	15	14	29	2	3	0
1970	Det-A	.931	12	3	24	2	5	1
1972	Det-A	—	1	0	0	0	0	0
1974	Bos-A	.957	40	27	62	4	4	-2
1975	Bos-A	.769	7	2	8	3	1	-2
Total	7	.923	146	120	241	0	26	-15

Wickey McAvoy C

YEAR	TM/L	PCT	G	PO	A	E	DP	FR
1913	Phi-A	1.000	4	14	7	0	0	1
1914	Phi-A	.971	8	25	8	1	1	1
1915	Phi-A	.931	64	235	100	25	8	5
1917	Phi-A	.955	8	27	15	2	0	3
1918	Phi-A	.960	74	236	123	**15**	15	5
1919	Phi-A	.973	57	182	73	7	6	-3
Total	6	.954	215	719	326	0	30	12

1B

YEAR	TM/L	PCT	G	PO	A	E	DP	FR
1918	Phi-A	1.000	1	6	0	0	0	0

OF

YEAR	TM/L	PCT	G	PO	A	E	DP	FR
1918	Phi-A	1.000	1	1	0	0	0	0

Algie McBride OF

YEAR	TM/L	PCT	G	PO	A	E	DP	FR
1896	Chi-N	.917	9	21	1	2	0	0
1898	Cin-N	.959	120	288	18	13	3	7
1899	Cin-N	.950	64	124	8	7	2	-2
1900	Cin-N	.915	110	163	10	16	5	-9
1901	Cin-N	.968	28	59	1	2	0	-2
	NY-N	.948	65	84	8	5	3	-3
	Yr	.956	93	143	9	7	3	-5
Total	5	.946	396	739	46	5	13	-9

Bake McBride OF

YEAR	TM/L	PCT	G	PO	A	E	DP	FR
1973	StL-N	.976	17	39	1	1	0	3
1974	StL-N	.990	144	395	9	4	1	9
1975	StL-N	.990	107	289	4	3	1	15
1976	StL-N	.981	66	201	5	4	0	9
1977	StL-N	1.000	33	48	2	0	0	-3
	Phi-N	.986	73	140	6	2	1	0
	Yr	**.990**	106	188	8	2	1	-3
1978	Phi-N	.996	119	234	8	1	3	2
1979	Phi-N	.989	147	341	12	4	3	15
1980	Phi-N	.990	133	282	6	3	1	2
1981	Phi-N	.987	56	76	2	1	1	-9
1982	Cle-A	1.000	22	37	0	0	0	-3
1983	Cle-A	.977	46	81	4	2	1	-2
Total	11	.989	963	2163	59	5	12	38

George McBride SS

YEAR	TM/L	PCT	G	PO	A	E	DP	FR
1901	Mil-A	1.000	3	5	7	0	2	-1
1905	Pit-N	.906	8	9	20	3	2	-1
	StL-N	.938	80	147	273	28	29	-2
	Yr	.935	88	156	293	31	31	-3
1906	StL-N	.944	90	194	310	30	33	9
1908	Was-A	.948	**155**	372	568	52	**58**	**33**
1909	Was-A	**.935**	156	341	499	58	56	11
1910	Was-A	.939	154	370	518	58	57	27
1911	Was-A	.941	**154**	353	546	56	**60**	23
1912	Was-A	**.941**	**152**	349	498	53	**55**	**31**
1913	Was-A	**.960**	150	316	490	34	62	11
1914	Was-A	**.958**	156	367	460	36	**72**	12
1915	Was-A	**.968**	146	326	422	25	47	9
1916	Was-A	.957	139	282	438	32	53	13
1917	Was-A	.943	41	73	109	11	15	-2
1918	Was-A	.986	14	28	44	1	4	2
1919	Was-A	.932	15	29	40	5	2	1
1920	Was-A	.966	13	24	32	2	3	0
Total	16	.948	1626	3585	5274	484	610	173

3B

YEAR	TM/L	PCT	G	PO	A	E	DP	FR
1905	Pit-N	.902	17	18	28	5	3	-3
1917	Was-A	1.000	6	4	11	0	0	1
Total	2	.924	23	22	39	5	3	-2

2B

YEAR	TM/L	PCT	G	PO	A	E	DP	FR
1917	Was-A	1.000	2	1	2	0	0	0
1918	Was-A	1.000	2	1	1	0	0	0
Total	2	1.000	4	2	3	0	0	0

1B

YEAR	TM/L	PCT	G	PO	A	E	DP	FR
1905	StL-N	1.000	1	2	0	0	1	0

Tom McBride OF

YEAR	TM/L	PCT	G	PO	A	E	DP	FR
1943	Bos-A	.984	24	60	2	1	1	1

YEAR	TM/L	PCT	G	PO	A	E	DP	FR
1944	Bos-A	.992	57	113	8	1	1	5
1945	Bos-A	.984	81	180	10	3	4	4
1946	Bos-A	1.000	43	61	1	0	0	-4
1947	Bos-A	1.000	1	2	1	0	0	1
	Was-A	.972	51	103	2	3	0	-1
	Yr	.973	52	105	3	3	0	0
1948	Was-A	.983	55	108	7	2	3	2
Total	6	.985	312	627	31	0	9	8
1B								
1944	Bos-A	.980	5	46	2	1	6	0
1945	Bos-A	1.000	11	101	8	0	11	1
Total	2	.994	16	147	10	1	17	1
3B								
1947	Was-A	—	1	0	0	0	0	0

■ Jack McCandless OF

YEAR	TM/L	PCT	G	PO	A	E	DP	FR
1914	Bal-F	1.000	8	10	1	0	0	0
1915	Bal-F	.945	105	209	16	13	8	3
Total	2	.948	113	219	17	3	8	3

■ Alex McCarthy 2B

YEAR	TM/L	PCT	G	PO	A	E	DP	FR
1911	Pit-N	.969	11	24	39	2	8	3
1912	Pit-N	.962	105	237	320	22	52	3
1913	Pit-N	1.000	6	6	8	0	1	0
1914	Pit-N	.910	10	17	44	6	3	3
1915	Pit-N	.950	9	18	20	2	2	-1
	Chi-N	.972	12	34	35	2	8	6
	Yr	.964	21	52	55	4	10	5
1916	Chi-N	.931	34	54	95	11	9	-1
	Pit-N	1.000	7	6	7	0	2	0
	Yr	.936	41	60	102	11	11	-1
1917	Pit-N	.985	13	28	36	1	3	2
Total	7	.957	207	424	604	6	88	15
SS								
1910	Pit-N	.875	3	4	10	2	2	0
1911	Pit-N	.981	33	70	88	3	12	-3
1913	Pit-N	.902	12	19	27	5	3	-2
1914	Pit-N	.909	6	7	13	2	1	0
1915	Pit-N	.969	5	14	17	1	2	1
	Chi-N	—	1	0	0	0	0	0
	Yr	.969	6	14	17	1	2	1
1916	Chi-N	.800	3	2	2	1	0	-1
	Pit-N	.955	39	92	100	9	15	-5
	Yr	.951	42	94	102	10	15	-6
1917	Pit-N	.965	9	15	40	2	6	3
Total	7	.954	111	223	297	5	41	-7
3B								
1911	Pit-N	—	1	0	0	0	0	0
1912	Pit-N	1.000	4	5	5	0	1	0
1913	Pit-N	1.000	12	8	20	0	0	1
1914	Pit-N	.975	36	39	79	3	6	8
1915	Pit-N	1.000	4	4	4	0	2	0
	Chi-N	1.000	12	13	33	0	3	6
	Yr	1.000	16	17	37	0	5	6
1916	Pit-N	1.000	5	2	8	0	1	0
1917	Pit-N	.964	26	42	39	3	9	2
Total	7	.980	100	113	188	6	22	17
OF								
1911	Pit-N	—	1	0	0	0	0	0
1B								
1915	Pit-N	—	1	0	0	0	0	0

■ Jack McCarthy OF

YEAR	TM/L	PCT	G	PO	A	E	DP	FR
1893	Cin-N	.887	47	87	7	12	0	-1
1894	Cin-N	.895	25	45	6	6	0	1
1898	Pit-N	.935	137	296	19	22	4	4
1899	Pit-N	.961	138	281	18	12	5	-5
1900	Chi-N	.944	123	233	20	15	4	-1
1901	Cle-A	.949	86	157	9	9	5	-1
1902	Cle-A	.944	95	178	6	11	0	-5
1903	Cle-A	.964	108	178	10	7	5	-3
1904	Chi-N	.961	115	213	8	9	0	-5
1905	Chi-N	.986	37	63	9	1	4	3
1906	Bro-N	.924	86	158	13	14	1	2
1907	Bro-N	1.000	25	38	0	0	0	4
Total	12	.946	1046	1960	128	120	29	-18
1B								
1893	Cin-N	.963	2	24	2	1	1	0
1894	Cin-N	.958	15	148	13	7	12	1
1905	Chi-N	.940	6	44	3	3	5	0
Total	3	.955	23	216	18	1	18	1

■ Johnny McCarthy 1B

YEAR	TM/L	PCT	G	PO	A	E	DP	FR
1934	Bro-N	.961	13	89	9	4	13	1
1935	Bro-N	.982	19	110	0	2	11	-3
1936	NY-N	.981	4	45	6	1	5	1
1937	NY-N	.987	110	1123	82	16	89	2
1938	NY-N	.993	125	1315	77	10	111	-3
1939	NY-N	1.000	12	114	2	0	13	-2
1940	NY-N	1.000	6	57	5	0	6	1
1941	NY-N	.987	8	67	7	1	4	1
1943	Bos-N	.996	78	839	53	4	51	1
1946	Bos-N	1.000	2	18	0	0	3	-1
1948	NY-N	.966	6	27	1	1	2	0
Total	11	.990	383	3804	242	9	308	-2
OF								
1939	NY-N	—	4	0	0	0	0	0
1941	NY-N	1.000	1	1	0	0	0	0
Total	2	1.000	5	1	0	0	0	0

■ Tommy McCarthy OF

YEAR	TM/L	PCT	G	PO	A	E	DP	FR
1884	Bos-U	.794	48	39	11	13	1	-3
1885	Bos-N	.865	40	69	8	12	0	3
1886	Phi-N	.818	8	8	1	2	0	-1
1887	Phi-N	.897	8	24	2	3	0	3
1888	StL-a	.932	131	243	**44**	21	**12**	**30**
1889	StL-a	.893	**140**	229	38	32	**11**	15
1890	StL-a	.893	102	157	19	21	5	4
1891	StL-a	.895	113	164	24	22	5	3
1892	Bos-N	.883	152	219	29	33	4	2
1893	Bos-N	.902	108	202	28	25	4	5
1894	Bos-N	.904	127	291	28	34	10	11
1895	Bos-N	.909	109	199	16	28	2	-7
1896	Bro-N	.920	103	175	20	17	6	-2
Total	13	.897	1189	2019	268	263	60	63
2B								
1887	Phi-N	.789	5	8	7	4	1	-1
1889	StL-a	.667	2	1	1	1	0	-1
1890	StL-a	1.000	1	0	1	0	0	0
1891	StL-a	.842	14	34	30	12	2	-4
1893	Bos-N	.882	7	15	15	4	3	-1
1894	Bos-N	1.000	1	0	2	0	0	0
1895	Bos-N	.865	9	13	19	5	1	-3
Total	7	.849	39	71	75	6	7	-10
3B								
1887	Phi-N	.250	2	1	0	3	0	-2
1890	StL-a	.848	32	48	75	22	6	3
1891	StL-a	.600	3	0	3	2	0	-1
Total	3	.825	37	49	78	7	6	0
SS								
1887	Phi-N	.563	3	7	2	7	0	-4
1891	StL-a	.846	12	30	36	12	7	1
1893	Bos-N	.850	3	11	6	3	2	-1
1894	Bos-N	1.000	2	0	3	0	0	0
Total	4	.812	20	48	47	2	9	-4

■ Lew McCarty C

YEAR	TM/L	PCT	G	PO	A	E	DP	FR
1913	Bro-N	1.000	9	37	10	0	1	1
1914	Bro-N	.970	84	398	117	16	9	0
1915	Bro-N	.969	81	310	101	13	5	-9
1916	Bro-N	.985	27	97	33	2	2	-5
	NY-N	.993	24	112	26	1	2	0
	Yr	.989	51	209	59	3	4	-5
1917	NY-N	.979	54	235	43	6	0	-4
1918	NY-N	.975	75	288	67	9	3	-7
1919	NY-N	.970	59	203	56	8	1	-8
1920	NY-N	1.000	5	16	6	0	0	2
	StL-N	1.000	3	5	4	0	1	0
	Yr	1.000	8	21	10	0	1	2
Total	8	.975	421	1701	463	5	24	-30
1B								
1916	Bro-N	.981	17	148	9	3	9	0

■ Tim McCarver C

YEAR	TM/L	PCT	G	PO	A	E	DP	FR
1959	StL-N	.971	6	32	2	1	0	-1
1960	StL-N	1.000	5	9	0	0	0	0
1961	StL-N	.969	20	86	9	3	0	-2
1963	StL-N	.994	126	722	55	5	7	1
1964	StL-N	.987	**137**	762	43	**11**	9	-9
1965	StL-N	**.995**	111	687	43	4	4	-3
1966	StL-N	.992	148	841	62	7	7	-5
1967	StL-N	**.997**	130	819	**67**	3	10	2
1968	StL-N	.986	109	708	54	11	6	3
1969	StL-N	.986	136	925	66	14	10	8
1970	Phi-N	.991	44	314	18	3	2	0
1971	Phi-N	.985	125	673	51	11	8	-7
1972	Phi-N	.989	40	245	20	3	0	-3
	Mon-N	.990	45	285	24	3	2	2
	Yr	.990	85	530	44	6	2	-1
1973	StL-N	.985	11	63	4	1	1	-1
1974	StL-N	.969	21	86	9	3	0	0
	Bos-A	1.000	8	37	5	0	0	1
1975	Bos-A	.957	7	18	4	1	1	0
	Phi-N	.984	10	58	5	1	1	1
1976	Phi-N	1.000	41	254	9	0	1	5
1977	Phi-N	.988	42	233	14	3	3	1
1978	Phi-N	.995	34	175	12	1	1	2
1979	Phi-N	.989	31	174	12	2	0	3
Total	20	.990	1387	8206	588	1	73	-2
1B								
1973	StL-N	.986	77	545	30	8	47	-5
1974	StL-N	.977	6	40	2	1	1	0
1975	Bos-A	1.000	1	3	0	0	0	0
	Phi-N	1.000	1	4	0	0	0	0
1976	Phi-N	1.000	2	11	0	0	0	0
1977	Phi-N	1.000	3	5	0	0	2	0
1978	Phi-N	.977	11	40	2	1	4	0
1980	Phi-N	1.000	2	8	0	0	0	0
Total	7	.986	103	656	34	0	54	-5
OF								
1972	Mon-N	.964	14	27	0	1	0	-1
1979	Phi-N	—	1	0	0	0	0	0
Total	2	.964	15	27	0	1	0	-1
3B								
1972	Mon-N	.875	6	4	3	1	1	-1

■ Al McCauley 1B

YEAR	TM/L	PCT	G	PO	A	E	DP	FR
1884	Ind-a	.947	5	35	1	2	3	0
1890	Phi-N	.973	116	1053	26	30	68	-6
1891	Was-a	.969	59	541	22	18	27	-2
Total	3	.971	180	1629	49	0	98	-8
OF								
1884	Ind-a	.000	3	0	0	2	0	-2

■ Harvey McClellan SS

YEAR	TM/L	PCT	G	PO	A	E	DP	FR
1919	Chi-A	.833	2	4	1	1	0	-1
1920	Chi-A	.917	4	6	5	1	0	-3
1921	Chi-A	.977	15	24	60	2	12	9
1922	Chi-A	.878	8	16	20	5	0	-4
1923	Chi-A	.958	139	217	394	27	64	-18
1924	Chi-A	.938	21	26	65	6	6	2
Total	6	.952	189	293	545	2	82	-15
3B								
1919	Chi-A	1.000	3	2	6	0	1	1
1920	Chi-A	1.000	2	1	1	0	0	0
1921	Chi-A	.929	5	4	9	1	5	1
1922	Chi-A	.971	71	77	159	7	15	0
1924	Chi-A	1.000	1	1	1	0	0	0
Total	5	.970	82	85	176	8	21	2
2B								
1921	Chi-A	.968	21	52	69	4	4	6
1922	Chi-A	1.000	2	1	2	0	0	0
1923	Chi-A	1.000	2	5	7	0	2	0
1924	Chi-A	.967	7	8	21	1	1	1
Total	4	.971	32	66	99	5	7	7
OF								
1921	Chi-A	.972	15	32	3	1	0	2
1922	Chi-A	—	1	0	0	0	0	-1
1924	Chi-A	1.000	1	1	0	0	0	0
Total	3	.973	17	33	3	1	0	1

■ Bill McClellan 2B

YEAR	TM/L	PCT	G	PO	A	E	DP	FR
1878	Chi-N	.866	42	87	139	35	15	-9
1881	Pro-N	1.000	1	2	3	0	0	0
1885	Bro-a	.902	55	172	177	38	20	4
1886	Bro-a	.907	**141**	423	435	88	64	-7
1887	Bro-a	.879	**136**	366	397	105	52	-22
1888	Bro-a	.905	56	145	149	31	23	-10
	Cle-a	.792	5	7	12	5	3	-2
	Yr	.897	61	152	161	36	26	-12
Total	6	.893	436	1202	1312	302	177	-46
SS								
1878	Chi-N	.815	5	2	20	5	0	1
1881	Pro-N	.855	50	59	147	35	18	-6
1883	Phi-N	.849	78	152	254	72	25	6
1884	Phi-N	.852	**111**	**165**	313	**83**	20	-12
1888	Cle-a	.667	2	3	7	5	0	0
Total	5	.849	246	381	741	200	63	-11
3B								
1883	Phi-N	1.000	1	0	2	0	0	0
1885	Bro-a	.837	57	65	84	29	9	-9
Total	2	.839	58	65	86	9	9	-9
OF								
1878	Chi-N	—	1	0	0	0	0	0
1881	Pro-N	.857	17	21	3	4	0	-1
1883	Phi-N	.625	2	5	0	3	0	-1
1884	Phi-N	.000	1	0	0	1	0	-1
1888	Bro-a	.976	18	36	4	1	0	3
	Cle-a	.875	15	11	3	2	0	-2
	Yr	.947	33	47	7	3	0	1
Total	5	.883	54	73	10	1	0	-2

■ Amby McConnell 2B

YEAR	TM/L	PCT	G	PO	A	E	DP	FR
1908	Bos-A	.939	126	237	349	**38**	32	-18
1909	Bos-A	.954	121	251	389	**31**	43	14
1910	Bos-A	.959	10	17	30	2	0	-1
	Chi-A	.952	32	61	78	7	10	-1
	Yr	**.954**	42	78	108	9	10	-2
1911	Chi-A	.973	103	189	280	13	31	-7
Total	4	.954	392	755	1126	1	116	-13
SS								
1908	Bos-A	.700	3	1	6	3	1	-1

■ Frank McCormick 1B

YEAR	TM/L	PCT	G	PO	A	E	DP	FR
1934	Cin-N	.941	2	16	0	1	1	-1
1937	Cin-N	1.000	20	194	16	0	20	2
1938	Cin-N	.995	**151**	1441	95	7	127	-3
1939	Cin-N	**.996**	156	**1518**	100	7	**153**	1
1940	Cin-N	**.995**	155	**1587**	98	8	**146**	0
1941	Cin-N	.995	154	1464	92	8	**130**	1
1942	Cin-N	.993	144	**1403**	101	10	**132**	6
1943	Cin-N	.995	120	1156	85	6	116	3
1944	Cin-N	.992	153	**1508**	**135**	13	130	**12**
1945	Cin-N	.994	151	**1469**	**118**	9	104	**5**
1946	Phi-N	**.999**	134	1185	98	1	92	4
1947	Phi-N	.989	12	86	4	1	9	-1
	Bos-N	.996	46	428	26	2	31	-1
	Yr	.995	58	514	30	3	40	-2
1948	Bos-N	.987	50	343	33	5	30	3
Total	13	.995	1448	13798	1001	8	1221	31
2B								
1937	Cin-N	.857	4	4	2	1	0	-1
OF								
1937	Cin-N	1.000	1	1	0	0	0	0

■ Moose McCormick OF

YEAR	TM/L	PCT	G	PO	A	E	DP	FR
1904	NY-N	.916	55	95	3	9	2	-5
	Pit-N	.940	66	87	7	6	0	-6
	Yr	.928	121	182	10	15	2	-11
1908	Phi-N	1.000	5	11	0	0	0	0
	NY-N	.901	65	97	3	11	2	-11
	Yr	.910	70	108	3	11	2	-11
1909	NY-N	.924	110	144	13	13	6	-14
1912	NY-N	.667	6	2	0	1	0	-1
1913	NY-N	.909	15	19	1	2	1	-1
Total	5	.920	322	455	27	2	11	-38
1B								
1912	NY-N	1.000	1	1	0	0	0	0

■ Jerry McCormick 3B

YEAR	TM/L	PCT	G	PO	A	E	DP	FR
1883	Bal-a	.799	93	138	196	**84**	10	0
1884	Phi-U	.811	54	90	116	48	8	9
	Was-U	.792	38	42	42	22	5	-6
	Yr	.806	92	132	158	70	13	3
Total	2	.802	185	270	354	154	23	3
SS								
1884	Phi-U	.952	3	3	17	1	0	3
	Was-U	.833	4	2	13	3	2	0
	Yr	.897	7	5	30	4	2	3
2B								
1884	Phi-U	.884	5	18	20	5	3	3
OF								
1884	Phi-U	.667	5	6	0	3	0	-2

Mike McCormick OF

YEAR	TM/L	PCT	G	PO	A	E	DP	FR
1940	Cin-N	.986	107	266	9	4	2	10
1941	Cin-N	.976	101	240	9	6	2	7
1942	Cin-N	.990	38	93	2	1	1	2
1943	Cin-N	.909	4	10	0	1	0	-1
1946	Cin-N	1.000	21	56	1	0	0	1
	Bos-N	.973	48	109	1	3	0	2
	Yr	.982	69	165	2	3	0	3
1947	Bos-N	.981	79	155	4	3	0	-2
1948	Bos-N	.975	100	187	7	5	3	-1
1949	Bro-N	1.000	49	75	3	0	0	-1
1950	Chi-A	.982	44	105	4	2	2	6
1951	Was-A	.966	62	134	7	5	0	0
Total	10	.980	653	1430	47	0	10	23

Barry McCormick 3B

YEAR	TM/L	PCT	G	PO	A	E	DP	FR
1896	Chi-N	.835	35	34	72	21	5	-4
1897	Chi-N	.851	56	62	115	31	10	0
1898	Chi-N	.888	136	152	322	60	31	5
1900	Chi-N	.869	21	29	57	13	1	2
1901	Chi-N	.909	3	4	6	1	0	0
1902	StL-A	.905	132	147	271	44	26	-13
1903	StL-A	.933	28	29	54	6	6	1
Total	7	.885	411	457	897	176	79	-9

2B

1895	Lou-N	.800	1	2	2	1	0	-1
1896	Chi-N	.846	3	8	3	2	3	-1
1897	Chi-N	1.000	1	0	1	0	0	0
1898	Chi-N	.833	1	2	3	1	0	0
1899	Chi-N	.941	99	200	344	34	47	5
1900	Chi-N	.880	5	8	14	3	1	-2
1903	StL-A	.969	28	50	77	4	8	-5
	Was-A	.960	63	130	205	14	27	8
	Yr	.962	91	180	282	18	35	3
1904	Was-A	.938	113	204	355	37	39	-1
Total	8	.944	314	604	1004	6	125	3

SS

1895	Lou-N	1.000	2	2	5	0	1	0
1896	Chi-N	.795	6	8	23	8	4	0
1897	Chi-N	.903	46	109	153	28	16	-3
1898	Chi-N	.500	1	1	1	2	0	-1
1899	Chi-N	.800	3	5	7	3	2	-1
1900	Chi-N	.907	84	161	307	48	32	-8
1901	Chi-N	.911	112	202	405	59	46	0
1902	StL-A	.974	7	10	27	1	2	2
1903	StL-A	.950	4	8	11	1	2	0
Total	9	.906	265	506	939	150	105	-11

OF

1896	Chi-N	1.000	1	1	0	0	0	0
1902	StL-A	1.000	1	2	0	0	0	0
Total	2	1.000	2	3	0	0	0	0

Barney McCosky OF

YEAR	TM/L	PCT	G	PO	A	E	DP	FR
1939	Det-A	.986	145	428	7	6	2	4
1940	Det-A	.983	141	349	7	6	2	-2
1941	Det-A	.985	122	328	6	5	2	0
1942	Det-A	.981	154	351	7	7	2	5
1946	Det-A	.966	24	56	1	2	0	0
	Phi-A	.981	85	207	2	4	0	-6
	Yr	.978	109	263	3	6	0	-6
1947	Phi-A	.983	136	346	8	6	2	9
1948	Phi-A	.990	134	277	9	3	1	-4
1950	Phi-A	.987	42	73	1	1	1	-7
1951	Phi-A	1.000	7	13	0	0	0	0
	Cin-N	1.000	11	17	0	0	0	-2
	Cle-A	1.000	16	28	0	0	0	-1
1952	Cle-A	.944	19	17	0	1	0	-3
Total	10	.984	1036	2490	48	1	12	-7

Willie McCovey 1B

YEAR	TM/L	PCT	G	PO	A	E	DP	FR
1959	SF-N	.989	51	424	29	5	29	-2
1960	SF-N	.985	71	557	39	9	42	-3
1961	SF-N	.985	84	669	55	11	55	-1
1962	SF-N	.991	17	105	7	1	12	-1
1963	SF-N	.994	23	143	14	1	5	1
1964	SF-N	.965	26	177	14	7	19	-2
1965	SF-N	.991	156	1310	87	13	93	0
1966	SF-N	.984	145	1287	81	22	91	-3
1967	SF-N	.989	127	1221	81	15	102	1
1968	SF-N	.985	146	1305	103	21	91	3
1969	SF-N	.992	148	1392	79	12	116	-6
1970	SF-N	.989	146	1217	134	15	117	13
1971	SF-N	.983	95	828	63	15	80	-2
1972	SF-N	.986	74	617	32	9	52	-5
1973	SF-N	.988	117	930	76	12	89	1
1974	SD-N	.987	104	815	47	11	59	-6
1975	SD-N	.986	115	979	73	15	94	0
1976	SD-N	.991	51	420	44	4	39	5
1977	SF-N	.989	136	1072	60	13	93	-7
1978	SF-N	.987	97	721	44	10	49	-4
1979	SF-N	.987	89	740	48	10	60	-1
1980	SF-N	.992	27	241	12	2	18	-2
Total	22	.987	2045	17170	1222	233	1405	-21

OF

1962	SF-N	.976	57	81	2	2	1	-1
1963	SF-N	.942	135	220	7	14	0	-7
1964	SF-N	.935	83	96	5	7	1	-7
Total	3	.947	275	397	14	3	2	-15

Benny McCoy 2B

YEAR	TM/L	PCT	G	PO	A	E	DP	FR
1938	Det-A	.963	6	10	16	1	4	3
1939	Det-A	.958	34	79	104	8	19	0
1940	Phi-A	.951	130	261	392	34	82	-15
1941	Phi-A	.963	135	285	423	27	87	-13
Total	4	.957	305	635	935	0	192	-25

SS

1939	Det-A	.962	16	29	46	3	6	-2

3B

1938	Det-A	.000	1	0	0	2	0	-1
1940	Phi-A	.667	1	1	1	1	0	-1
Total	2	.400	2	1	1	3	0	-2

Tommy McCraw 1B

YEAR	TM/L	PCT	G	PO	A	E	DP	FR
1963	Chi-A	.993	97	673	47	5	65	-3
1964	Chi-A	.992	84	601	37	5	57	-3
1965	Chi-A	.993	72	251	22	2	18	3
1966	Chi-A	.990	121	843	67	9	56	-12
1967	Chi-A	.991	123	1167	110	11	92	13
1968	Chi-A	.986	135	1285	93	20	103	0
1969	Chi-A	.989	44	254	14	3	21	-2
1970	Chi-A	.987	59	357	33	5	34	3
1971	Was-A	.978	30	44	1	1	3	-1
1972	Cle-A	.992	38	345	26	3	29	2
1973	Cal-A	.996	25	219	22	1	27	3
1974	Cal-A	1.000	29	147	11	0	10	1
	Cle-A	.990	38	285	24	3	28	2
	Yr	.994	67	432	35	3	38	3
1975	Cle-A	1.000	16	110	6	0	9	-1
Total	13	.991	911	6581	513	8	552	5

OF

1964	Chi-A	.952	36	36	4	2	0	0
1965	Chi-A	.978	64	85	2	2	0	-3
1966	Chi-A	1.000	41	50	1	0	0	4
1967	Chi-A	1.000	6	10	0	0	0	0
1969	Chi-A	1.000	41	48	1	0	0	-4
1970	Chi-A	.947	49	70	2	4	0	-5
1971	Was-A	.958	60	90	1	4	0	-3
1972	Cle-A	1.000	84	159	2	0	0	-2
1973	Cal-A	1.000	34	49	3	0	1	0
1974	Cal-A	1.000	12	15	3	0	1	2
	Cle-A	1.000	1	1	0	0	0	0
	Yr	1.000	13	16	3	0	1	2
1975	Cle-A	.667	3	2	0	1	0	0
Total	11	.980	431	615	19	3	2	-11

Tom McCreery OF

YEAR	TM/L	PCT	G	PO	A	E	DP	FR
1895	Lou-N	.875	18	20	1	3	0	-3
1896	Lou-N	.916	111	177	20	18	4	1
1897	Lou-N	.856	89	130	13	24	2	-5
	NY-N	.900	45	53	10	7	1	-1
	Yr	.869	134	183	23	31	3	-6
1898	NY-N	.820	35	37	4	9	0	-5
	Pit-N	.934	51	107	6	8	1	-1
	Yr	.901	86	144	10	17	1	-6
1899	Pit-N	.911	97	198	16	21	2	-1
1900	Pit-N	.887	35	62	9	9	2	-2
1901	Bro-N	.947	82	189	9	11	2	4
1902	Bro-N	1.000	4	4	1	0	1	0
1903	Bro-N	.892	38	54	4	7	2	-2
	Bos-N	.900	23	52	2	6	1	0
	Yr	.896	61	106	6	13	3	-2
Total	9	.905	628	1083	95	123	18	-11

1B

1895	Lou-N	.500	1	1	0	1	0	0
1901	Bro-N	.958	4	22	1	1	2	0
1902	Bro-N	.979	108	1032	59	23	53	-1
Total	3	.978	113	1055	60	5	55	-1

SS

1895	Lou-N	.737	4	6	8	5	1	-4
1899	Pit-N	.840	9	21	21	8	1	-5
1901	Bro-N	.846	2	6	5	2	2	0
Total	3	.817	15	33	34	5	4	-9

2B

1896	Lou-N	1.000	1	3	1	0	1	-1
1897	NY-N	.857	3	3	9	2	1	-1
1899	Pit-N	.868	7	15	18	5	2	-2
Total	3	.875	11	21	28	7	4	-4

3B

1895	Lou-N	.000	1	0	0	1	0	0

Clyde McCullough C

YEAR	TM/L	PCT	G	PO	A	E	DP	FR
1940	Chi-N	1.000	7	44	4	0	1	2
1941	Chi-N	.982	119	481	64	10	6	-8
1942	Chi-N	.980	97	386	61	9	10	-2
1943	Chi-N	.977	81	271	25	7	2	-14
1946	Chi-N	.989	89	390	40	4	4	-2
1947	Chi-N	.984	64	280	35	5	3	6
1948	Chi-N	.973	51	225	25	7	5	5
1949	Pit-N	.985	90	363	39	6	8	7
1950	Pit-N	.985	100	362	45	6	3	-9
1951	Pit-N	.988	87	364	52	5	10	9
1952	Pit-N	.981	61	227	38	5	4	6
1953	Chi-N	.987	73	273	31	4	7	-4
1954	Chi-N	.989	26	103	3	2	1	-2
1955	Chi-N	.989	37	160	12	2	0	7
1956	Chi-N	1.000	7	24	3	0	0	1
Total	15	.984	989	3953	477	2	64	2

3B

1954	Chi-N	.833	3	2	4	0	3	1

1B

1952	Pit-N	—	1	0	0	0	0	0

Harry McCurdy C

YEAR	TM/L	PCT	G	PO	A	E	DP	FR
1922	StL-N	.967	9	24	5	1	2	-1
1923	StL-N	.969	58	157	30	6	4	-7
1926	Chi-A	.975	25	64	10	2	1	-4
1927	Chi-A	.972	82	261	55	9	8	-3
1928	Chi-A	.964	34	95	11	4	2	-3
1930	Phi-N	.966	41	97	16	4	1	-6
1931	Phi-N	.968	45	157	27	6	1	-1
1932	Phi-N	.974	42	132	17	4	3	-1
1933	Phi-N	—	2	0	0	0	0	0
Total	9	.970	338	987	171	6	22	-26

1B

1922	StL-N	—	2	0	0	0	0	0
1926	Chi-A	.958	8	20	3	1	2	1
1934	Cin-N	1.000	1	11	2	0	2	1
Total	3	.973	11	31	5	1	4	2

Tex McDonald OF

YEAR	TM/L	PCT	G	PO	A	E	DP	FR
1913	Bos-N	1.000	1	2	0	0	0	0
1914	Pit-F	.925	29	36	13	4	3	5
	Buf-F	.953	61	94	7	5	2	-2
	Yr	.943	90	130	20	9	5	3
1915	Buf-F	.924	65	93	4	8	1	-7
Total	3	.936	156	225	24	7	6	-4

SS

1912	Cin-N	.915	42	84	89	16	7	-9
1913	Cin-N	—	1	0	0	0	0	0
1914	Pit-F	.889	5	5	11	2	1	-1
Total	3	.913	48	89	100	8	8	-10

2B

1913	Bos-N	.900	6	12	15	3	2	0
1914	Pit-F	.925	27	41	70	9	7	-7
	Buf-F	.962	10	25	25	2	2	-1
	Yr	.936	37	66	95	11	9	-8
Total	2	.931	43	78	110	4	11	-8

3B

1913	Bos-N	.869	31	25	61	13	7	-2

Ed McDonald 3B

YEAR	TM/L	PCT	G	PO	A	E	DP	FR
1911	Bos-N	.955	53	63	86	7	10	-5
1912	Bos-N	.940	118	147	216	23	18	-1
Total	2	.945	171	210	302	0	28	-6

SS

1911	Bos-N	1.000	1	2	0	0	0	0

Gil McDougald 2B

YEAR	TM/L	PCT	G	PO	A	E	DP	FR
1951	NY-A	.981	55	120	137	5	26	-12
1952	NY-A	.977	38	109	99	5	31	-2
1953	NY-A	.982	26	23	33	1	9	0
1954	NY-A	.989	92	224	233	5	84	1
1955	NY-A	.985	126	352	348	11	119	19
1956	NY-A	.985	31	57	77	2	28	3
1957	NY-A	.991	21	59	48	1	18	-2
1958	NY-A	.977	115	265	298	13	97	-6
1959	NY-A	.989	53	119	146	3	40	5
1960	NY-A	.994	42	57	99	1	16	-2
Total	10	.984	599	1385	1518	7	468	3

3B

1951	NY-A	.949	82	54	112	9	20	-4
1952	NY-A	.968	117	124	273	13	38	14
1953	NY-A	.953	136	147	299	22	36	5
1954	NY-A	.958	35	16	53	3	4	0
1955	NY-A	.961	17	15	34	2	4	0
1956	NY-A	.947	5	5	13	1	4	2
1957	NY-A	1.000	7	7	12	0	1	0
1959	NY-A	.973	25	13	59	2	5	3
1960	NY-A	.945	84	70	137	12	15	0
Total	9	.958	508	451	992	4	127	20

SS

1956	NY-A	.970	92	177	273	14	77	-1
1957	NY-A	.976	121	247	391	16	104	17
1958	NY-A	.969	19	34	59	3	14	3
1959	NY-A	.975	52	58	140	5	25	0
Total	4	.973	284	516	863	8	220	19

Oddibe McDowell OF

YEAR	TM/L	PCT	G	PO	A	E	DP	FR
1985	Tex-A	.993	103	282	9	2	2	5
1986	Tex-A	.991	148	325	13	3	3	-5
1987	Tex-A	.989	125	263	5	3	1	-5
1988	Tex-A	.989	113	267	2	3	1	-8
1989	Cle-A	.992	64	124	5	1	1	-4
	Atl-N	.978	68	179	2	4	0	1
1990	Atl-N	.971	72	134	2	4	0	-5
Total	6	.988	693	1574	38	0	8	-21

Ed McFarland C

YEAR	TM/L	PCT	G	PO	A	E	DP	FR
1893	Cle-N	—	1	0	0	0	0	0
1896	StL-N	.961	80	276	117	16	6	9
1897	StL-N	.965	23	80	31	4	3	3
	Phi-N	.951	37	117	38	8	1	0
	Yr	.957	60	197	69	12	4	3
1898	Phi-N	.960	121	420	136	23	7	-1
1899	Phi-N	.968	94	305	125	14	14	17
1900	Phi-N	.963	93	278	137	16	9	-2
1901	Phi-N	.970	74	316	102	13	9	2
1902	Chi-A	.967	69	282	71	12	7	3
1903	Chi-A	.968	56	240	65	10	7	0
1904	Chi-A	.975	49	195	39	6	2	-11
1905	Chi-A	.973	70	343	88	12	8	6
1906	Chi-A	.973	7	32	4	1	0	-1
1907	Chi-A	.972	43	192	47	7	4	-1
1908	Bos-A	.978	13	63	24	2	3	3
Total	14	.967	830	3139	1024	144	73	27

OF

1893	Cle-N	1.000	5	4	0	0	0	-2
1896	StL-N	—	2	0	0	0	0	-1
1897	StL-N	.857	3	6	0	1	0	-1
1902	Chi-A	—	2	0	0	0	0	-1
Total	4	.909	12	10	0	1	0	-4

1B

1897	StL-N	.897	3	21	5	3	0	1
1902	Chi-A	1.000	1	9	0	0	0	0
1903	Chi-A	1.000	1	4	0	0	0	0
Total	3	.929	5	34	5	3	0	1

3B

1893	Cle-N	.800	2	0	4	1	0	-1
1900	Phi-N	1.000	1	2	0	0	0	0
Total	2	.857	3	2	4	1	0	-1

2B

1897	StL-N	.778	1	4	3	2	0	-1

Herm McFarland OF

YEAR	TM/L	PCT	G	PO	A	E	DP	FR
1896	Lou-N	.833	28	51	4	11	3	-9
1898	Cin-N	.968	17	29	1	1	0	-2
1901	Chi-A	.946	132	283	14	17	3	5
1902	Chi-A	1.000	7	13	0	0	0	0
	Bal-A	.965	61	152	12	6	1	6

(continued)

YEAR	TM/L	PCT	G	PO	A	E	DP	FR
	Yr	.967	68	165	12	6	1	6
1903	NY-A	.939	103	207	9	14	2	-3
Total	5	.941	348	735	40	9	9	3
C								
1896	Lou-N	.556	1	3	2	4	0	0

■ Dan McGann

YEAR	TM/L	PCT	G	PO	A	E	DP	FR
1B								
1898	Bal-N	.983	145	1416	68	26	78	2
1899	Bro-N	.985	61	645	31	10	49	2
	Was-N	.990	76	667	36	7	37	2
	Yr	.988	137	1312	67	17	86	4
1900	StL-N	.990	121	1212	58	13	41	-1
1901	StL-N	.984	103	1030	50	18	64	-3
1902	Bal-A	.987	68	658	41	9	52	3
	NY-N	.981	61	634	39	13	38	2
1903	NY-N	.988	129	1188	64	15	58	0
1904	NY-N	.991	141	1481	94	15	62	3
1905	NY-N	.991	136	1350	86	13	59	4
1906	NY-N	.995	133	1391	83	8	61	3
1907	NY-N	.994	81	781	55	5	36	5
1908	Bos-N	.988	121	1229	93	16	66	7
Total	11	.989	1376	13682	798	168	701	29
2B								
1896	Bos-N	.905	43	88	111	21	10	-17
1900	StL-N	1.000	1	3	1	0	0	0
1908	Bos-N	.955	9	18	24	2	0	-2
Total	3	.914	53	109	136	3	10	-19
SS								
1895	Lou-N	.852	8	21	25	8	1	-2
3B								
1895	Lou-N	.852	6	9	14	4	0	0
OF								
1895	Lou-N	1.000	5	5	0	0	0	-1

■ Chippy McGarr

YEAR	TM/L	PCT	G	PO	A	E	DP	FR
3B								
1889	KC-a	.857	11	18	18	6	6	-2
1890	Bos-N	.933	115	151	228	27	13	-2
1893	Cle-N	.886	63	93	147	31	7	0
1894	Cle-N	.902	128	170	242	45	17	-7
1895	Cle-N	.870	108	125	217	51	13	-5
1896	Cle-N	.924	113	123	228	29	20	-6
Total	6	.903	538	680	1080	189	76	-22
SS								
1886	Phi-a	.850	71	109	231	60	25	1
1887	Phi-a	.875	137	198	402	86	42	-1
1888	StL-a	.500	1	0	2	2	0	-1
1889	KC-a	.667	3	3	9	6	1	-2
	Bal-a	.583	3	3	4	5	0	-2
	Yr	.633	6	6	13	11	1	-4
1890	Bos-N	.880	5	7	15	3	2	0
Total	5	.859	220	320	663	162	70	-5
2B								
1884	CP-U	.905	13	32	25	6	2	-4
1888	StL-a	.895	33	70	100	20	11	-2
1889	KC-a	.941	5	18	14	2	5	1
1895	Cle-N	.944	4	12	5	1	1	0
Total	4	.905	55	132	144	9	19	-5
OF								
1884	CP-U	.600	6	3	0	2	0	-2
1889	KC-a	.917	6	9	2	1	0	1
1890	Bos-N	1.000	1	2	0	0	0	0
Total	3	.842	13	14	2	3	0	-1
C								
1896	Cle-N	—	1	0	0	0	0	0

■ Jack McGeachey

YEAR	TM/L	PCT	G	PO	A	E	DP	FR
OF								
1886	Det-N	.875	6	6	1	1	0	-1
	StL-N	.880	55	88	15	14	3	3
	Yr	.880	61	94	16	15	3	2
1887	Ind-N	.894	98	231	22	30	3	5
1888	Ind-N	.932	117	194	27	16	5	5
1889	Ind-N	.918	131	189	36	20	8	8
1890	Bro-P	.906	104	206	16	23	1	-1
1891	Phi-a	.920	50	82	10	8	0	2
	Bos-a	.910	41	57	4	6	0	-4
	Yr	.916	91	139	14	14	0	-2
Total	6	.909	602	1053	131	118	20	17
3B								
1886	StL-N	.583	2	3	4	5	1	-1
1887	Ind-N	.400	1	0	2	3	0	-1
Total	2	.529	3	3	6	8	1	-2
2B								
1886	StL-N	.867	2	5	8	2	1	0
SS								
1888	Ind-N	—	1	0	0	0	0	0

■ Mike McGeary

YEAR	TM/L	PCT	G	PO	A	E	DP	FR
2B								
1876	StL-N	.889	56	132	180	39	16	6
1877	StL-N	.883	39	125	140	35	12	5
1879	Pro-N	.884	73	218	255	62	21	-5
1880	Pro-N	.909	2	3	7	1	1	0
1882	Det-N	.842	3	8	8	3	0	0
Total	5	.885	173	486	590	140	50	6
3B								
1876	StL-N	1.000	1	0	4	0	0	1
1877	StL-N	.920	19	39	41	7	0	2
1879	Pro-N	.917	12	20	35	5	4	6
1880	Pro-N	.887	17	13	34	6	1	3
	Cle-N	.887	29	37	49	11	4	-3
	Yr	.887	46	50	83	17	5	0
1881	Cle-N	.724	11	8	13	8	1	-7
Total	5	.888	89	117	176	7	10	2
SS								
1880	Pro-N	1.000	1	1	5	0	0	0
1882	Det-N	.928	33	56	112	13	5	8
Total	2	.930	34	57	117	3	5	8
C								
1876	StL-N	.750	5	14	1	5	1	0
OF								
1876	StL-N	—	1	0	0	0	0	0
1880	Cle-N	.429	2	3	0	4	0	-1
Total	2	.429	3	3	0	4	0	-1

■ Willie McGee

YEAR	TM/L	PCT	G	PO	A	E	DP	FR
OF								
1982	StL-N	.958	117	245	3	11	0	-15
1983	StL-N	.987	145	385	7	5	1	0
1984	StL-N	.985	141	374	10	6	4	5
1985	StL-N	.978	149	382	11	9	2	5
1986	StL-N	.991	121	325	9	3	0	10
1987	StL-N	.981	152	353	9	7	1	1
1988	StL-N	.975	135	348	9	9	0	4
1989	StL-N	.976	47	118	2	3	0	1
1990	StL-N	.957	124	341	13	16	4	8
	Oak-A	.986	28	72	1	1	1	1
Total	9	.977	1159	2943	74	70	13	20
SS								
1987	StL-N	1.000	1	1	1	0	0	0

■ Ed McGhee

YEAR	TM/L	PCT	G	PO	A	E	DP	FR
OF								
1950	Chi-A	1.000	1	1	0	0	0	0
1953	Phi-A	.982	99	319	4	6	0	3
1954	Phi-A	.933	13	42	0	3	0	2
	Chi-A	.982	34	51	4	1	1	3
	Yr	.960	47	93	4	4	1	5
1955	Chi-A	.923	17	12	0	1	0	1
Total	4	.975	164	425	8	1	1	9

■ Beauty McGowan

YEAR	TM/L	PCT	G	PO	A	E	DP	FR
OF								
1922	Phi-A	.965	82	210	13	8	2	8
1923	Phi-A	.971	79	154	12	5	1	0
1928	StL-A	.962	47	99	3	4	1	-1
1929	StL-A	.975	117	257	16	7	5	7
1937	Bos-N	1.000	2	2	0	0	0	0
Total	5	.970	327	722	44	4	9	14

■ John McGraw

YEAR	TM/L	PCT	G	PO	A	E	DP	FR
3B								
1892	Bal-N	.813	3	5	8	3	0	0
1894	Bal-N	.892	118	131	247	46	17	0
1895	Bal-N	.878	95	100	239	47	19	10
1896	Bal-N	.833	18	22	38	12	4	-2
1897	Bal-N	.886	105	112	182	38	16	-13
1898	Bal-N	.900	137	142	271	46	16	-11
1899	Bal-N	.945	117	142	270	24	14	2
1900	StL-N	.909	99	106	213	32	7	-8
1901	Bal-A	.890	69	80	107	23	5	-18
1902	Bal-A	.864	19	26	25	8	6	-8
1903	NY-N	.667	1	2	0	1	0	-1
1906	NY-N	—	1	0	0	0	0	0
Total	12	.898	782	868	1600	280	104	-49
SS								
1891	Bal-a	.811	21	32	41	17	6	-13
1892	Bal-N	.940	8	19	28	3	3	1
1893	Bal-N	.894	117	218	350	67	40	-21
1902	NY-N	.926	34	59	115	14	12	-2
1903	NY-N	1.000	1	0	1	0	0	0
1904	NY-N	.917	2	6	5	1	0	1
Total	6	.895	183	334	540	102	61	-34
OF								
1891	Bal-a	.700	9	7	0	3	0	-3
1892	Bal-N	.897	34	45	7	6	1	0
1893	Bal-N	.941	11	16	0	1	0	-2
1898	Bal-N	.857	3	6	0	1	0	0
1903	NY-N	—	2	0	0	0	0	-1
1905	NY-N	—	1	0	0	0	0	0
Total	6	.880	60	74	7	1	1	-6
2B								
1891	Bal-a	.947	3	8	10	1	1	1
1892	Bal-N	.925	34	96	101	16	12	0
1894	Bal-N	.938	6	12	18	2	0	-2
1895	Bal-N	—	1	0	0	0	0	0
1903	NY-N	—	2	0	0	0	0	0
1904	NY-N	.947	2	6	12	1	3	2
Total	6	.929	48	122	141	0	16	1
1B								
1896	Bal-N	1.000	1	10	0	0	0	0

■ Fred McGriff

YEAR	TM/L	PCT	G	PO	A	E	DP	FR
1B								
1986	Tor-A	1.000	1	3	0	0	0	0
1987	Tor-A	.983	14	108	7	2	5	-1
1988	Tor-A	.997	153	1344	93	5	143	-5
1989	Tor-A	.989	159	1460	115	17	148	-1
1990	Tor-A	.996	147	1246	126	6	119	-9
Total	5	.993	474	4161	341	0	415	-2

■ Deacon McGuire

YEAR	TM/L	PCT	G	PO	A	E	DP	FR
C								
1884	Tol-a	.906	41	224	56	29	1	-3
1885	Det-N	.920	31	249	52	26	2	13
1886	Phi-N	.899	49	298	50	39	3	-7
1887	Phi-N	.884	41	214	52	35	6	0
1888	Phi-N	.800	10	49	11	15	1	-4
	Det-N	.810	3	13	4	4	0	-2
	Cle-a	.891	17	102	29	16	3	1
	Yr	.860	27	151	40	31	4	-3
1890	Roc-a	.938	71	386	99	32	9	6
1891	Was-a	.911	98	442	130	56	8	-9
1892	Was-N	.936	89	381	100	33	8	-1
1893	Was-N	.889	50	172	45	27	3	-6
1894	Was-N	.918	104	288	114	36	8	-1
1895	Was-N	.936	132	408	179	40	11	11
1896	Was-N	.936	98	349	87	30	14	-3
1897	Was-N	.947	73	290	88	21	6	8
1898	Was-N	.967	93	371	93	16	11	0
1899	Was-N	.973	56	178	71	7	3	-5
	Bro-N	.967	46	144	58	6	2	2
	Yr	.972	102	322	129	13	5	-3
1900	Bro-N	.952	69	218	77	15	7	-8
1901	Bro-N	.960	81	415	94	21	4	-4
1902	Det-A	.952	70	210	65	14	6	-6
1903	Det-A	.960	69	330	73	17	9	-6
1904	NY-A	.970	97	530	120	20	11	14
1905	NY-A	.975	71	366	69	11	4	-6
1906	NY-A	.962	49	218	38	10	2	-1
1907	NY-A	1.000	1	3	1	0	0	1
1910	Cle-A	1.000	1	2	1	0	0	-1
1912	Det-A	.714	1	2	3	2	0	0
Total	25	.938	1611	6852	1859	578	142	-17
1B								
1888	Cle-a	.983	6	56	1	1	0	0
1890	Roc-a	.987	15	152	3	2	6	-1
1891	Was-N	1.000	1	5	0	0	0	0
1892	Was-N	1.000	8	71	0	0	2	-1
1893	Was-N	.947	12	115	11	7	11	1
1896	Was-N	1.000	1	2	1	0	0	0
1897	Was-N	.985	6	65	0	1	2	-1
1898	Was-N	.965	37	336	27	13	26	3
1899	Was-N	.923	1	12	0	1	0	0
1901	Bro-N	1.000	3	24	0	0	2	0
1903	Det-N	.500	1	1	0	1	0	0
1904	NY-A	1.000	1	6	0	0	0	0
1906	NY-A	.889	1	8	0	1	0	0
1908	Cle-A	1.000	1	10	0	0	0	0
Total	14	.971	94	863	43	7	49	1
OF								
1884	Tol-a	.800	4	4	0	1	0	-1
1885	Det-N	1.000	3	3	0	0	0	-1
1886	Phi-N	.500	1	1	1	2	0	0
1888	Cle-a	.750	3	3	0	1	0	-1
1890	Roc-a	1.000	3	2	0	0	0	-1
1891	Was-a	.833	18	12	3	3	0	-2
1892	Was-N	1.000	1	1	1	0	0	1
Total	7	.816	33	26	5	7	0	-5
3B								
1888	Phi-N	.667	2	0	2	1	0	-1
1891	Was-N	.647	3	4	7	6	0	-1
Total	2	.650	5	4	9	7	0	-2
SS								
1884	Tol-a	.800	3	3	5	2	0	-1
1895	Was-N	.667	1	0	2	1	0	0
Total	2	.769	4	3	7	3	0	-1

■ Mark McGwire

YEAR	TM/L	PCT	G	PO	A	E	DP	FR
1B								
1987	Oak-A	.992	145	1173	90	10	91	-4
1988	Oak-A	.993	154	1228	88	9	118	-8
1989	Oak-A	.995	141	1170	114	6	122	7
1990	Oak-A	.997	154	1329	95	5	126	-5
Total	4	.994	594	4900	387	0	457	-10
3B								
1986	Oak-A	.833	16	10	20	6	1	-3
1987	Oak-A	.813	8	2	11	3	0	-1
Total	2	.827	24	12	31	9	1	-4
OF								
1987	Oak-A	1.000	3	1	0	0	0	0
1988	Oak-A	—	1	0	0	0	0	0
Total	2	1.000	4	1	0	0	0	0

■ Austin McHenry

YEAR	TM/L	PCT	G	PO	A	E	DP	FR
OF								
1918	StL-N	.952	80	145	14	8	3	0
1919	StL-N	.985	103	183	20	3	3	4
1920	StL-N	.952	133	297	21	16	1	10
1921	StL-N	.965	152	371	13	14	3	7
1922	StL-N	.935	61	132	13	10	3	5
Total	5	.960	529	1128	81	1	13	26

■ Stuffy McInnis

YEAR	TM/L	PCT	G	PO	A	E	DP	FR
1B								
1911	Phi-A	.982	97	891	55	17	55	-2
1912	Phi-A	.984	153	1533	100	27	88	3
1913	Phi-A	.992	148	1504	80	12	85	-2
1914	Phi-A	.995	149	1423	85	7	78	0
1915	Phi-A	.989	119	1123	83	13	63	5
1916	Phi-A	.992	140	1404	96	12	87	7
1917	Phi-A	.993	150	1658	95	12	81	1
1918	Bos-A	.992	94	1066	71	9	45	5
1919	Bos-A	.995	118	1236	82	7	84	3
1920	Bos-A	.996	148	1586	91	7	101	-1
1921	Bos-A	.999	152	1549	102	1	109	4
1922	Cle-A	.997	140	1376	73	5	96	-5
1923	Bos-N	.991	154	1500	89	14	136	4
1924	Bos-N	.994	146	1435	95	10	129	7
1925	Pit-N	.993	46	377	24	3	40	1
1926	Pit-N	.988	40	300	17	4	32	-1
1927	Phi-N	1.000	1	1	0	0	0	0
Total	17	.993	1995	19962	1238	160	1309	29
SS								
1909	Phi-A	.886	14	34	44	10	5	4
1910	Phi-A	.927	17	20	31	4	3	-4
1911	Phi-A	.851	24	57	46	18	3	-13
Total	3	.879	55	111	121	2	11	-13
3B								
1910	Phi-A	1.000	4	5	3	0	0	0
1918	Bos-A	.987	23	34	42	1	8	-1
Total	2	.988	27	39	45	1	8	-1
2B								
1910	Phi-A	.923	5	7	5	1	0	0
OF								
1910	Phi-A	1.000	1	1	0	0	0	0

■ Matty McIntyre

YEAR	TM/L	PCT	G	PO	A	E	DP	FR
OF								
1901	Phi-a	.921	82	155	8	14	0	-3
1904	Det-A	.959	152	334	16	15	4	12
1905	Det-A	.968	131	286	18	10	6	16
1906	Det-A	.982	133	254	25	5	8	12
1907	Det-A	1.000	20	43	3	0	1	3
1908	Det-A	.977	151	329	17	8	4	15
1909	Det-A	.975	122	217	14	6	1	0
1910	Det-A	.946	77	147	12	9	2	4
1911	Chi-A	.948	146	235	18	14	5	-2
1912	Chi-A	1.000	25	37	2	0	0	-1

YEAR	TM/L	PCT	G	PO	A	E	DP	FR
Total	10	.964	1039	2037	133	1	31	56
■ Dave McKay 2B								
1977	Tor-A	.968	40	75	107	6	21	4
1978	Tor-A	.984	140	310	408	12	96	-6
1979	Tor-A	.974	46	119	148	7	37	6
1980	Oak-A	.977	62	99	151	6	24	-10
1981	Oak-A	.970	38	83	108	6	23	-3
1982	Oak-A	.968	59	99	116	7	22	-3
Total	6	.976	385	785	1038	4	223	-12
3B								
1975	Min-A	.923	33	38	70	9	12	1
1976	Min-A	.911	41	25	77	10	13	-1
1977	Tor-A	.951	32	32	65	5	7	5
1978	Tor-A	1.000	2	0	5	0	0	1
1979	Tor-A	1.000	2	0	2	0	0	0
1980	Oak-A	.963	54	39	66	4	5	2
1981	Oak-A	.926	43	29	59	7	3	-1
1982	Oak-A	.931	16	19	35	4	1	0
Total	8	.935	223	182	379	9	41	7
SS								
1976	Min-A	1.000	2	2	0	0	0	-1
1977	Tor-A	.957	20	34	33	3	8	-2
1978	Tor-A	1.000	3	0	1	0	0	0
1980	Oak-A	1.000	10	17	25	0	4	0
1981	Oak-A	1.000	7	6	5	0	0	-2
1982	Oak-A	1.000	3	2	2	0	1	0
Total	6	.977	45	61	66	3	13	-5
■ Ed McKean SS								
1887	Cle-a	.847	123	195	351	**99**	32	-6
1888	Cle-a	.909	78	120	240	36	13	4
1889	Cle-N	.907	122	206	398	62	42	5
1890	Cle-N	.903	134	266	433	**75**	46	-15
1891	Cle-N	.887	**141**	248	463	**91**	42	-12
1892	Cle-N	.862	129	207	369	92	29	-45
1893	Cle-N	.902	125	247	431	74	55	-4
1894	Cle-N	.905	**130**	269	411	71	43	-21
1895	Cle-N	.909	**131**	246	424	67	42	-19
1896	Cle-N	.915	**133**	214	400	57	57	-33
1897	Cle-N	.920	125	226	385	53	36	-30
1898	Cle-N	.932	151	304	425	53	47	-36
1899	StL-N	.886	42	72	123	25	13	-13
Total	13	.900	1564	2820	4853	855	497	225
OF								
1887	Cle-a	1.000	4	5	0	0	0	-1
1888	Cle-a	.885	48	79	6	11	2	0
Total	2	.891	52	84	6	1	2	-1
2B								
1887	Cle-a	.864	8	20	18	6	2	-1
1888	Cle-a	.850	9	27	24	9	4	-1
1889	Cle-N	1.000	1	3	3	0	0	0
1890	Cle-N	1.000	3	2	6	0	1	0
1899	StL-N	.915	10	20	23	4	4	-4
Total	5	.885	31	72	74	9	11	-6
1B								
1899	StL-N	.972	15	162	10	5	8	1
3B								
1888	Cle-a	1.000	1	0	1	0	0	0
■ Bill McKechnie 3B								
1907	Pit-N	1.000	2	1	3	0	0	0
1910	Pit-N	1.000	8	5	10	0	0	-1
1911	Pit-N	.900	6	5	4	1	0	0
1912	Pit-N	.978	13	15	30	1	0	2
1913	NY-N	.750	2	1	2	1	0	0
1914	Ind-F	.939	**149**	195	**327**	34	**28**	23
1915	New-F	.956	117	**184**	226	19	17	2
1916	NY-N	.940	71	70	134	13	8	-3
	Cin-N	.960	35	38	59	4	6	-4
	Yr	.947	106	108	193	17	14	-7
1917	Cin-N	1.000	4	3	1	0	0	0
1918	Pit-N	.966	**126**	162	261	15	26	-1
1920	Pit-N	.943	20	21	29	3	2	-1
Total	11	.952	553	700	1086	1	87	17
2B								
1907	Pit-N	1.000	1	0	1	0	0	0
1910	Pit-N	.971	36	89	112	6	15	5
1911	Pit-N	.970	17	49	48	3	16	3
1912	Pit-N	1.000	3	1	4	0	2	1
1913	NY-N	.950	28	57	76	7	12	7
1917	Cin-N	.943	26	49	51	6	11	-4
1920	Pit-N	.938	6	12	18	2	2	0
Total	7	.959	117	257	310	4	58	12
1B								
1910	Pit-N	.970	4	28	4	1	1	0
1911	Pit-N	.975	57	524	32	14	28	-1
1912	Pit-N	.800	2	4	0	1	0	0
1920	Pit-N	1.000	1	4	0	0	0	0
Total	4	.974	64	560	36	6	29	0
SS								
1910	Pit-N	.928	14	24	40	5	4	3
1911	Pit-N	.938	12	20	25	3	5	-2
1912	Pit-N	.917	4	3	8	1	2	0
1913	NY-A	.889	7	16	16	4	1	-1
1917	Cin-N	.880	13	24	42	9	4	-2
1920	Pit-N	.949	10	19	37	3	7	0
Total	6	.916	60	106	168	5	23	-2
OF								
1913	Bos-N	1.000	1	3	0	0	0	0
1915	New-F	—	1	0	0	0	0	0
Total	2	1.000	2	3	0	0	0	0
■ Red McKee C								
1913	Det-A	.950	62	237	84	17	5	-4
1914	Det-A	.964	27	87	20	4	2	-6
1915	Det-A	.954	35	116	30	7	4	-6
1916	Det-A	.955	26	76	31	5	2	-5
Total	4	.954	150	516	165	3	14	-21
■ Alex McKinnon 1B								
1884	NY-N	.955	**116**	1097	31	53	57	-2
1885	StL-N	**.978**	100	1102	26	25	50	-2
1886	StL-N	.963	119	1170	35	46	61	-5
1887	Pit-N	.977	48	483	25	12	27	3
Total	4	.967	383	3852	117	136	195	-6
■ Tom McLaughlin SS								
1883	Lou-a	.844	19	17	59	14	5	4
1884	Lou-a	.892	94	122	331	55	**34**	18
1885	Lou-a	.905	19	31	64	10	7	2
1886	NY-a	.886	63	93	203	38	11	5
1891	Was-a	.871	14	25	36	9	6	0
Total	5	.886	209	288	693	126	63	29
2B								
1883	Lou-a	.818	2	5	4	2	0	0
1884	Lou-a	1.000	1	0	1	0	0	0
1885	Lou-a	.883	93	320	266	78	43	-1
1886	NY-a	.938	10	32	29	4	6	2
Total	4	.887	106	357	300	4	49	1
OF								
1883	Lou-a	.825	17	30	3	7	0	0
1886	NY-a	.667	1	1	1	1	0	0
Total	2	.814	18	31	4	8	0	0
3B								
1883	Lou-a	.667	2	2	4	3	0	-1
1884	Lou-a	.875	4	4	10	2	2	1
Total	2	.800	6	6	14	5	2	0
1B								
1883	Lou-a	.981	5	51	2	1	3	1
■ Larry McLean C								
1903	Chi-N	.889	1	7	1	1	0	0
1904	StL-N	.954	24	126	20	7	1	-2
1906	Cin-N	.954	12	49	13	3	0	-1
1907	Cin-N	.975	89	365	110	12	12	-1
1908	Cin-N	.963	69	280	82	14	9	-3
1909	Cin-N	.978	95	379	119	11	16	-5
1910	Cin-N	.983	119	485	158	11	**18**	-4
1911	Cin-N	.968	98	414	138	18	**16**	7
1912	Cin-N	.973	98	425	124	15	16	-3
1913	StL-N	.981	42	143	60	4	8	-6
	NY-N	.953	28	101	20	6	1	-3
	Yr	.970	70	244	80	10	9	-9
1914	NY-N	.973	74	211	42	7	8	-4
1915	NY-N	.985	12	47	18	1	0	2
Total	12	.973	761	3032	905	110	105	-23
1B								
1901	Bos-A	1.000	5	38	2	0	2	0
1907	Cin-N	.974	13	111	3	3	10	-2
1908	Cin-N	.955	19	165	5	8	2	-3
Total	3	.967	37	314	10	1	14	-5
■ Mark McLemore 2B								
1986	Cal-A	1.000	2	3	10	0	1	4
1987	Cal-A	.974	132	291	358	17	96	-5
1988	Cal-A	.979	63	107	171	6	52	4
1989	Cal-A	.966	27	55	88	5	24	4
1990	Cal-A	1.000	8	14	15	0	3	1
	Cle-A	1.000	3	7	7	0	3	2
	Yr	1.000	11	21	22	0	6	3
Total	5	.976	235	477	649	8	179	10
SS								
1987	Cal-A	1.000	6	2	5	0	2	0
1990	Cal-A	.882	8	15	15	4	3	-3
Total	2	.902	14	17	20	4	5	-3
3B								
1988	Cal-A	1.000	5	1	7	0	1	0
1990	Cle-A	1.000	4	1	2	0	1	0
Total	2	1.000	9	2	9	0	2	0
■ Marty McManus 2B								
1921	StL-A	.952	96	212	269	24	44	-16
1922	StL-A	.964	153	398	467	**32**	103	3
1923	StL-A	.960	133	386	373	32	86	-1
1924	StL-A	.972	119	329	369	20	68	7
1925	StL-A	.967	**154**	**440**	**479**	**31**	93	4
1926	StL-A	.966	61	173	199	13	45	7
1927	Det-A	.972	35	102	106	6	29	2
1931	Det-A	.974	21	46	66	3	11	3
	Bos-A	.918	7	12	33	4	2	3
	Yr	.957	28	58	99	7	13	6
1932	Bos-A	.969	49	123	161	9	26	6
1933	Bos-A	.965	26	53	84	5	11	-4
1934	Bos-N	.964	73	156	247	15	39	-6
Total	11	.965	927	2430	2853	194	557	8
3B								
1920	StL-A	.667	1	0	2	1	0	0
1921	StL-A	.894	13	16	26	5	7	2
1926	StL-A	.958	84	119	197	14	18	8
1927	Det-A	.953	22	21	40	3	2	0
1928	Det-A	.955	92	114	183	14	12	-1
1929	Det-A	.972	150	206	289	14	29	8
1930	Det-A	**.966**	130	**152**	241	14	**23**	5
1931	Det-A	.950	79	92	172	14	18	10
	Bos-A	1.000	11	11	32	0	6	6
	Yr	.956	90	103	204	14	24	16
1932	Bos-A	.918	30	24	66	8	2	0
1933	Bos-A	.957	76	79	123	9	9	-1
1934	Bos-N	.941	37	32	79	7	6	1
Total	11	.957	725	866	1450	103	132	38
1B								
1921	StL-A	.961	9	58	15	3	3	4
1922	StL-A	.875	1	6	1	1	0	0
1923	StL-A	1.000	20	169	12	0	16	0
1926	StL-A	1.000	4	40	3	0	5	0
1927	Det-A	1.000	6	40	5	0	2	1
1928	Det-A	.988	45	376	28	5	33	1
1930	Det-A	1.000	1	1	0	0	1	0
1931	Det-A	—	1	0	0	0	0	0
1932	Bos-A	1.000	1	3	1	0	0	0
1933	Bos-A	1.000	4	11	0	0	0	0
Total	10	.988	92	704	65	9	60	6
SS								
1921	StL-A	1.000	2	4	2	0	0	0
1927	Det-A	.960	39	82	112	8	21	-4
1928	Det-A	1.000	2	1	2	0	0	0
1929	Det-A	1.000	8	9	20	0	2	-1
1930	Det-A	1.000	3	3	8	0	2	1
1932	Bos-A	.500	2	1	0	1	0	0
Total	6	.964	56	100	144	9	25	-4
OF								
1925	StL-A	—	1	0	0	0	0	0
■ Norm McMillan 3B								
1922	NY-A	1.000	5	2	1	0	0	-1
1923	Bos-A	.942	67	119	139	16	13	1
1924	StL-A	.972	19	17	18	1	0	-2
1928	Chi-N	.935	18	12	31	3	1	-3
1929	Chi-N	.944	120	131	226	**21**	19	6
Total	5	.944	229	281	415	1	33	1
2B								
1923	Bos-A	.937	34	78	101	12	15	1
1924	StL-A	.966	37	100	100	7	18	0
1928	Chi-N	.977	19	32	53	2	12	2
Total	3	.957	90	210	254	1	45	3
SS								
1923	Bos-A	.956	28	60	92	7	21	9
1924	StL-A	.909	7	2	8	1	0	-1
Total	2	.953	35	62	100	8	21	8
OF								
1922	NY-A	.921	26	35	0	3	0	-7
1B								
1924	StL-A	.944	2	16	1	1	1	0
■ Roy McMillan SS								
1951	Cin-N	.963	54	78	132	8	23	1
1952	Cin-N	.971	154	297	**495**	24	101	11
1953	Cin-N	.972	155	288	519	23	**114**	14
1954	Cin-N	.959	154	341	464	34	129	6
1955	Cin-N	.969	150	290	495	25	**111**	17
1956	Cin-N	**.975**	150	319	511	21	**105**	30
1957	Cin-N	**.977**	151	253	418	16	86	-8
1958	Cin-N	**.980**	145	278	394	14	81	4
1959	Cin-N	.974	73	163	205	10	50	-7
1960	Cin-N	.964	116	171	315	18	68	-13
1961	Mil-N	**.975**	154	**257**	**496**	19	110	0
1962	Mil-N	.972	135	243	424	19	85	1
1963	Mil-N	.979	94	143	283	9	60	7
1964	Mil-N	.933	8	7	7	1	2	-1
	NY-N	.976	111	217	353	14	64	1
	Yr	.975	119	224	360	15	66	0
1965	NY-N	.964	153	248	477	27	80	-4
1966	NY-N	.975	71	112	203	8	35	5
Total	16	.972	2028	3705	6191	290	1304	64
3B								
1951	Cin-N	.976	12	13	28	1	5	4
2B								
1951	Cin-N	1.000	1	1	0	0	0	0
1960	Cin-N	.944	10	3	14	1	2	0
Total	2	.947	11	4	14	1	2	0
■ Tommy McMillan SS								
1908	Bro-N	.873	29	52	86	20	10	-3
1909	Bro-N	.914	105	190	310	47	32	-9
1910	Bro-N	.898	23	48	66	13	7	-1
	Cin-N	.927	82	162	270	34	32	10
	Yr	.921	105	210	336	47	39	9
1912	NY-A	.948	41	74	109	10	12	-4
Total	4	.917	280	526	841	124	93	-7
OF								
1908	Bro-N	.938	14	30	0	2	0	-2
2B								
1909	Bro-N	.909	2	7	3	1	1	0
3B								
1909	Bro-N	.000	1	0	0	1	0	0
■ Ken McMullen 3B								
1963	LA-N	.933	71	47	133	13	8	6
1964	LA-N	.750	4	4	2	2	0	-2
1965	Was-A	.954	142	155	299	**22**	29	5
1966	Was-A	.951	141	125	280	21	26	-1
1967	Was-A	.965	145	153	348	18	**38**	12
1968	Was-A	.962	145	185	296	19	26	7
1969	Was-A	.976	154	**185**	347	13	35	13
1970	Was-A	.971	15	26	40	2	7	6
	Cal-A	.959	122	128	266	17	32	9
	Yr	.960	137	154	306	19	39	15
1971	Cal-A	.966	158	137	344	17	27	-1
1972	Cal-A	.970	137	89	267	11	26	2
1973	LA-N	.922	24	5	54	5	2	4
1974	LA-N	1.000	7	5	11	0	0	0
1975	LA-N	1.000	7	8	0	0	0	0
1976	Oak-A	.952	35	10	30	2	1	1
1977	Mil-A	1.000	7	1	6	0	1	1
Total	15	.961	1318	1259	2731	162	258	62
1B								
1964	LA-N	.991	13	101	7	1	7	-1
1965	Was-A	—	1	0	0	0	0	0
1966	Was-A	1.000	8	62	4	0	7	0
1975	LA-N	1.000	3	19	4	0	1	1
1976	Oak-A	1.000	26	204	8	0	19	-1
1977	Mil-A	.978	11	79	9	2	9	1
Total	6	.994	62	465	32	3	43	1

OF

YEAR	TM/L	PCT	G	PO	A	E	DP	FR
1962	LA-N	1.000	2	1	0	0	0	0
1963	LA-N	1.000	1	0	1	0	0	1
1964	LA-N	1.000	3	1	0	0	0	0
1965	Was-A	1.000	8	14	1	0	0	0
1966	Was-A	1.000	1	3	0	0	0	0
1976	Oak-A	1.000	5	8	0	0	0	0
Total	6	1.000	20	27	2	0	0	1

SS

YEAR	TM/L	PCT	G	PO	A	E	DP	FR
1968	Was-A	1.000	11	9	6	0	0	-2

2B

YEAR	TM/L	PCT	G	PO	A	E	DP	FR
1963	LA-N	1.000	1	1	0	0	0	0
1974	LA-N	1.000	3	8	3	0	1	-1
1976	Oak-A	1.000	1	0	1	0	0	0
Total	3	1.000	5	9	4	0	1	-1

■ Fred McMullin 3B

YEAR	TM/L	PCT	G	PO	A	E	DP	FR
1916	Chi-A	.950	63	74	115	10	11	-4
1917	Chi-A	.932	52	61	90	11	4	-10
1918	Chi-A	.941	69	74	151	14	9	-1
1919	Chi-A	.931	46	45	90	10	10	0
1920	Chi-A	.962	29	23	53	3	3	-4
Total	5	.942	259	277	499	8	37	-19

2B

YEAR	TM/L	PCT	G	PO	A	E	DP	FR
1916	Chi-A	1.000	1	3	1	0	0	0
1918	Chi-A	—	1	0	0	0	0	0
1919	Chi-A	.938	5	9	6	1	1	0
1920	Chi-A	1.000	3	8	3	0	2	0
Total	4	.968	10	20	10	1	3	0

SS

YEAR	TM/L	PCT	G	PO	A	E	DP	FR
1914	Det-A	.667	1	1	1	1	0	0
1916	Chi-A	1.000	2	1	0	0	0	0
1917	Chi-A	.500	2	2	2	4	0	-3
1920	Chi-A	—	1	0	0	0	0	0
Total	4	.583	6	4	3	5	0	-3

■ Eric McNair SS

YEAR	TM/L	PCT	G	PO	A	E	DP	FR
1929	Phi-A	1.000	4	6	5	0	0	0
1930	Phi-A	.915	31	57	61	11	10	-5
1931	Phi-A	.918	13	19	26	4	6	-2
1932	Phi-A	.953	133	242	391	31	89	-7
1933	Phi-A	.966	46	113	143	9	29	2
1934	Phi-A	.951	151	305	489	41	109	4
1935	Phi-A	.955	121	232	346	27	78	-21
1936	Bos-A	.966	84	171	230	14	47	-5
1937	Bos-A	.842	9	13	19	6	4	-2
1938	Bos-A	.870	15	12	28	6	3	1
1939	Chi-A	.934	9	20	37	4	7	4
1941	Det-A	.857	3	2	4	1	1	-1
1942	Det-A	.881	21	27	32	8	6	-7
	Phi-A	.952	29	50	68	6	10	-5
	Yr	.927	50	77	100	14	16	-12
Total	13	.949	669	1269	1879	168	399	-44

2B

YEAR	TM/L	PCT	G	PO	A	E	DP	FR
1930	Phi-A	1.000	5	6	6	0	1	1
1931	Phi-A	.963	16	35	43	3	15	-3
1933	Phi-A	.942	27	56	73	8	10	-4
1936	Bos-A	.973	35	92	89	5	19	-8
1937	Bos-A	.969	106	242	316	18	67	-3
1938	Bos-A	.957	14	27	40	3	12	3
1939	Chi-A	.982	19	41	68	2	13	5
1940	Chi-A	.958	65	128	170	13	27	-16
1942	Phi-A	.500	1	0	1	1	0	-1
Total	9	.964	288	627	806	3	164	-26

3B

YEAR	TM/L	PCT	G	PO	A	E	DP	FR
1930	Phi-A	.929	29	36	43	6	2	-3
1931	Phi-A	.915	47	43	86	12	15	0
1935	Phi-A	.974	11	20	18	1	1	0
1936	Bos-A	.900	11	9	27	4	1	1
1937	Bos-A	.769	4	1	9	3	1	-1
1938	Bos-A	.833	3	4	1	1	0	-1
1939	Chi-A	.937	103	90	194	19	23	-5
1940	Chi-A	.429	1	2	1	4	0	-1
1941	Det-A	.970	11	12	20	1	0	-1
Total	9	.924	220	217	399	1	43	-11

1B

YEAR	TM/L	PCT	G	PO	A	E	DP	FR
1935	Phi-A	1.000	2	18	0	0	1	0
1937	Bos-A	—	1	0	0	0	0	0
Total	2	1.000	3	18	0	0	1	0

OF

YEAR	TM/L	PCT	G	PO	A	E	DP	FR
1930	Phi-A	1.000	1	1	0	0	0	0

■ Mike McNally 2B

YEAR	TM/L	PCT	G	PO	A	E	DP	FR
1915	Bos-A	1.000	5	3	4	0	1	0
1916	Bos-A	.964	35	49	84	5	10	7
1917	Bos-A	1.000	6	5	12	0	2	3
1919	Bos-A	.930	3	4	7	0	0	2
1920	Bos-A	.930	76	168	233	30	38	-9
1921	NY-A	.941	16	26	38	4	7	2
1922	NY-A	.943	9	11	22	2	0	1
1923	NY-A	1.000	5	2	5	0	0	0
1924	NY-A	.985	25	29	38	1	7	6
1925	Was-A	—	1	0	0	0	0	0
Total	10	.946	181	297	443	2	65	12

3B

YEAR	TM/L	PCT	G	PO	A	E	DP	FR
1915	Bos-A	.891	18	17	24	5	3	0
1916	Bos-A	.842	14	12	20	6	0	0
1917	Bos-A	.935	14	12	31	3	1	2
1919	Bos-A	.943	11	10	23	2	5	6
1921	NY-A	.974	49	54	131	5	5	10
1922	NY-A	.983	34	41	74	2	6	-1
1923	NY-A	.895	7	5	12	2	0	0
1924	NY-A	.970	13	14	18	1	3	4
1925	Was-A	1.000	7	11	10	0	1	2
Total	9	.952	167	176	343	6	21	28

SS

YEAR	TM/L	PCT	G	PO	A	E	DP	FR
1916	Bos-A	1.000	7	2	8	0	0	1
1917	Bos-A	1.000	9	4	5	0	0	1
1919	Bos-A	.950	11	7	12	1	1	2
1920	Bos-A	.944	8	8	9	1	0	-1
1922	NY-A	1.000	4	0	1	0	0	0
1923	NY-A	1.000	13	3	10	0	1	0
1924	NY-A	1.000	6	5	6	0	0	1
1925	Was-A	.000	2	0	0	2	0	-1
Total	8	.952	60	29	51	4	2	3

1B

YEAR	TM/L	PCT	G	PO	A	E	DP	FR
1920	Bos-A	.983	6	54	4	1	2	0
1922	NY-A	1.000	1	9	0	0	0	0
Total	2	.985	7	63	4	1	2	0

OF

YEAR	TM/L	PCT	G	PO	A	E	DP	FR
1916	Bos-A	—	1	0	0	0	0	-1

■ Earl McNeely OF

YEAR	TM/L	PCT	G	PO	A	E	DP	FR
1924	Was-A	.973	42	105	3	3	1	-2
1925	Was-A	.975	112	259	13	7	3	-2
1926	Was-A	.969	118	274	9	9	3	0
1927	Was-A	.977	47	81	3	2	1	-6
1928	StL-A	.984	120	229	19	4	2	7
1929	StL-A	.980	62	96	4	2	0	-7
1930	StL-A	.939	38	60	2	4	0	-7
1931	StL-A	.969	37	59	3	2	1	-5
Total	8	.974	576	1163	56	3	11	-22

1B

YEAR	TM/L	PCT	G	PO	A	E	DP	FR
1925	Was-A	1.000	1	3	0	0	0	0
1927	Was-A	.951	4	37	2	2	3	-1
1930	StL-A	.985	27	242	16	4	30	0
1931	StL-A	—	1	0	0	0	0	0
Total	4	.980	33	282	18	6	33	-1

■ Jerry McNertney C

YEAR	TM/L	PCT	G	PO	A	E	DP	FR
1964	Chi-A	.987	69	360	30	5	5	8
1966	Chi-A	.969	37	112	14	4	0	6
1967	Chi-A	.996	52	229	41	1	4	14
1968	Chi-A	.955	64	299	39	5	8	14
1969	Sea-A	.988	122	697	67	9	13	1
1970	Mil-A	.984	94	387	46	7	3	-10
1971	StL-N	.955	36	192	7	3	1	-2
1972	StL-N	.982	10	50	4	1	0	2
1973	Pit-N	1.000	9	11	0	0	0	1
Total	7	.987	493	2337	248	5	34	34

1B

YEAR	TM/L	PCT	G	PO	A	E	DP	FR
1968	Chi-A	1.000	1	2	0	0	1	0
1970	Mil-A	.988	13	74	7	1	3	0
Total	2	.988	14	76	7	1	4	0

■ Pat McNulty OF

YEAR	TM/L	PCT	G	PO	A	E	DP	FR
1922	Cle-A	.956	22	43	0	2	0	-3
1924	Cle-A	.961	75	137	9	6	2	-4
1925	Cle-A	.965	111	206	16	8	2	-2
1926	Cle-A	.909	9	8	2	1	0	-2
1927	Cle-A	.906	12	28	1	3	1	0
Total	5	.957	229	422	28	0	5	-11

■ Bid McPhee 2B

YEAR	TM/L	PCT	G	PO	A	E	DP	FR
1882	Cin-a	.920	78	274	207	42	36	-1
1883	Cin-a	.928	96	314	277	46	48	3
1884	Cin-a	.924	112	415	365	64	74	16
1885	Cin-a	.936	110	339	354	47	57	6
1886	Cin-a	.939	140	529	464	65	90	31
1887	Cin-a	.924	129	442	434	72	76	26
1888	Cin-a	.940	111	369	365	47	65	31
1889	Cin-a	.946	135	429	446	50	85	41
1890	Cin-N	.942	132	404	431	51	62	30
1891	Cin-N	.954	138	389	492	42	72	23
1892	Cin-N	.948	144	451	471	51	86	25
1893	Cin-N	.954	127	396	455	41	101	34
1894	Cin-N	.945	126	389	446	49	72	31
1895	Cin-N	.955	115	355	366	34	57	15
1896	Cin-N	.978	117	297	357	15	56	5
1897	Cin-N	.966	81	209	267	17	34	13
1898	Cin-N	.956	130	299	396	32	74	-11
1899	Cin-N	.955	105	245	312	26	41	-3
Total	18	.944	2126	6545	6905	791	1186	315

OF

YEAR	TM/L	PCT	G	PO	A	E	DP	FR
1898	Cin-N	.600	3	3	0	2	0	-1
1899	Cin-N	—	1	0	0	0	0	-1
Total	2	.600	4	3	0	2	0	-2

3B

YEAR	TM/L	PCT	G	PO	A	E	DP	FR
1889	Cin-a	.714	1	1	4	2	0	0

■ Mox McQuery 1B

YEAR	TM/L	PCT	G	PO	A	E	DP	FR
1884	Cin-U	.978	35	340	8	8	9	1
1885	Det-N	.976	69	707	28	18	32	3
1886	KC-N	.969	122	1295	50	43	61	1
1890	Syr-a	.972	122	1146	45	34	63	-1
1891	Was-a	.977	68	701	30	17	39	1
Total	5	.973	416	4189	161	120	204	5

OF

YEAR	TM/L	PCT	G	PO	A	E	DP	FR
1885	Det-N	1.000	1	7	1	0	1	2

■ Glenn McQuillen OF

YEAR	TM/L	PCT	G	PO	A	E	DP	FR
1938	StL-A	.971	30	66	0	2	0	1
1941	StL-A	.933	6	14	0	1	0	0
1942	StL-A	.969	77	156	2	5	0	-5
1946	StL-A	.977	48	77	8	2	0	0
Total	4	.970	161	313	10	0	0	-4

■ George McQuinn 1B

YEAR	TM/L	PCT	G	PO	A	E	DP	FR
1936	Cin-N	.992	38	336	27	3	30	1
1938	StL-A	.992	148	1207	90	10	134	0
1939	StL-A	.993	154	1377	116	11	122	10
1940	StL-A	.992	150	1436	124	13	157	10
1941	StL-A	.995	125	1138	109	6	109	8
1942	StL-A	.991	144	1384	105	13	116	1
1943	StL-A	.992	122	1072	86	9	88	2
1944	StL-A	.994	146	1332	72	9	116	-5
1945	StL-A	.991	136	1143	105	11	87	4
1946	Phi-A	.988	134	1098	99	15	107	3
1947	NY-A	.994	142	1198	93	8	120	-1
1948	NY-A	.993	90	693	48	5	79	-1
Total	12	.992	1529	13414	1074	113	1265	32

■ Hal McRae OF

YEAR	TM/L	PCT	G	PO	A	E	DP	FR
1970	Cin-N	.981	46	52	1	1	0	-5
1971	Cin-N	.966	91	167	6	6	1	-3
1972	Cin-N	.867	12	13	0	2	0	-1
1973	KC-A	.963	64	101	4	4	2	-4
1974	KC-A	.950	56	132	2	7	1	-1
1975	KC-A	.986	114	207	7	3	2	-6
1976	KC-A	.970	31	63	2	2	0	-3
1977	KC-A	.958	47	84	8	4	1	-1
1978	KC-A	1.000	3	3	1	0	0	0
1980	KC-A	1.000	9	17	0	0	0	-1
1981	KC-A	.909	4	10	1	1	0	-1
1982	KC-A	.500	1	1	0	1	0	0
Total	12	.966	478	850	31	1	7	-26

3B

YEAR	TM/L	PCT	G	PO	A	E	DP	FR
1970	Cin-N	1.000	6	1	5	0	1	0
1972	Cin-N	.810	11	3	14	4	1	-3
1973	KC-A	.667	2	0	2	1	0	-1
1974	KC-A	1.000	1	0	1	0	1	0
1975	KC-A	—	1	0	0	0	0	0
Total	5	.839	21	4	22	5	3	-4

2B

YEAR	TM/L	PCT	G	PO	A	E	DP	FR
1968	Cin-N	.926	16	33	30	5	8	-4
1970	Cin-N	1.000	1	0	1	0	0	0
Total	2	.928	17	33	31	5	8	-4

■ Kevin McReynolds OF

YEAR	TM/L	PCT	G	PO	A	E	DP	FR
1983	SD-N	.989	38	87	4	1	1	3
1984	SD-N	.991	143	422	10	4	1	13
1985	SD-N	.993	150	430	12	3	3	16
1986	SD-N	.977	154	332	9	8	4	0
1987	NY-N	.987	150	286	8	4	0	2
1988	NY-N	.985	147	252	18	4	5	6
1989	NY-N	.969	145	307	10	10	3	9
1990	NY-N	.988	144	237	14	3	2	1
Total	8	.985	1071	2353	85	7	19	50

■ Jim McTamany OF

YEAR	TM/L	PCT	G	PO	A	E	DP	FR
1885	Bro-a	.896	35	43	0	5	0	-5
1886	Bro-a	.893	111	215	27	29	5	14
1887	Bro-a	.918	134	281	32	28	8	7
1888	KC-a	.913	130	245	27	26	5	6
1889	Col-a	.902	139	247	28	30	8	5
1890	Col-a	.940	125	232	17	16	8	2
1891	Col-a	.929	81	161	10	13	4	-2
	Phi-a	.901	58	118	10	14	1	0
	Yr	.917	139	279	20	27	5	-2
Total	7	.913	813	1542	151	161	39	17

■ Cal McVey 1B

YEAR	TM/L	PCT	G	PO	A	E	DP	FR
1876	Chi-N	.959	55	485	10	21	21	3
1877	Chi-N	.944	1	17	0	1	0	0
1879	Cin-N	.946	72	736	5	42	33	-6
Total	3	.951	128	1238	15	4	54	-3

3B

YEAR	TM/L	PCT	G	PO	A	E	DP	FR
1876	Chi-N	1.000	1	2	0	0	0	0
1877	Chi-N	.837	17	18	23	8	0	-2
1878	Cin-N	.814	61	78	106	42	6	-11
1879	Cin-N	1.000	1	2	0	0	0	0
Total	4	.821	80	100	129	0	6	-13

C

YEAR	TM/L	PCT	G	PO	A	E	DP	FR
1876	Chi-N	.923	6	23	1	2	0	0
1877	Chi-N	.859	40	137	34	28	3	-8
1878	Cin-N	1.000	3	5	1	0	0	0
1879	Cin-N	—	1	0	0	0	0	0
Total	4	.870	50	165	36	0	3	-8

OF

YEAR	TM/L	PCT	G	PO	A	E	DP	FR
1876	Chi-N	—	1	0	0	0	0	0
1879	Cin-N	.875	7	14	0	2	0	-1
Total	2	.875	8	14	0	2	0	-1

2B

YEAR	TM/L	PCT	G	PO	A	E	DP	FR
1877	Chi-N	1.000	1	1	4	0	1	0

■ Bob Meacham SS

YEAR	TM/L	PCT	G	PO	A	E	DP	FR
1983	NY-A	.929	18	13	52	5	8	7
1984	NY-A	.955	96	136	269	19	52	-11
1985	NY-A	.963	155	236	390	24	103	-17
1986	NY-A	.948	56	70	149	12	31	-5
1987	NY-A	.961	56	70	127	8	25	-4
1988	NY-A	.959	24	14	33	2	9	-4
Total	6	.957	405	539	1020	0	228	-34

2B

YEAR	TM/L	PCT	G	PO	A	E	DP	FR
1984	NY-A	1.000	2	4	3	0	0	0
1987	NY-A	.980	25	40	57	2	11	3
1988	NY-A	.976	21	39	44	2	8	-3
Total	3	.979	48	83	104	4	19	0

3B

YEAR	TM/L	PCT	G	PO	A	E	DP	FR
1983	NY-A	.938	4	3	12	1	1	2
1988	NY-A	.786	5	3	8	3	2	-1
Total	2	.867	9	6	20	4	3	1

■ Joe Medwick OF

YEAR	TM/L	PCT	G	PO	A	E	DP	FR
1932	StL-N	.970	26	63	2	2	1	1
1933	StL-N	.980	147	318	17	7	2	6
1934	StL-N	.965	149	322	10	14	1	0
1935	StL-N	.965	154	352	8	13	0	0
1936	StL-N	.985	155	367	16	6	4	13
1937	StL-N	.988	156	329	9	4	1	0
1938	StL-N	.974	144	330	12	9	6	9
1939	StL-N	.976	149	313	10	8	1	1
1940	StL-N	.988	37	81	1	1	0	-2
	Bro-N	.980	103	240	7	5	0	5
	Yr	.982	140	321	8	6	0	3
1941	Bro-N	.983	131	270	11	5	2	0
1942	Bro-N	.990	140	287	5	3	1	-1
1943	Bro-N	.971	42	65	2	2	0	-6
	NY-N	.988	74	157	10	2	2	4

YEAR	TM/L	PCT	G	PO	A	E	DP	FR
	Yr	.983	116	222	12	4	2	-2
1944	NY-N	.993	122	290	8	2	2	5
1945	NY-N	.979	23	46	1	1	0	-1
	Bos-N	1.000	38	78	7	0	2	2
	Yr	.992	61	124	8	1	2	1
1946	Bro-N	1.000	18	30	0	0	0	-1
1947	StL-N	1.000	43	56	3	0	2	-2
1948	StL-N	—	1	0	0	0	0	0
Total	17	.980	1852	3994	139	4	27	33

1B

YEAR	TM/L	PCT	G	PO	A	E	DP	FR
1943	NY-N	1.000	3	26	1	0	1	0
1945	Bos-N	1.000	15	124	3	0	6	-3
1946	Bro-N	.800	1	8	0	2	2	-1
Total	3	.988	19	158	4	2	9	-4

■ Dave Meier OF

YEAR	TM/L	PCT	G	PO	A	E	DP	FR
1984	Min-A	.978	50	87	2	2	0	0
1985	Min-A	.987	63	77	1	1	1	2
1987	Tex-A	.917	8	11	0	1	0	0
Total	3	.978	121	175	3	4	1	2

3B

YEAR	TM/L	PCT	G	PO	A	E	DP	FR
1984	Min-A	—	1	0	0	0	0	0
1988	Chi-N	1.000	1	1	0	0	0	-1
Total	2	1.000	2	1	0	0	0	-1

■ Roman Mejias OF

YEAR	TM/L	PCT	G	PO	A	E	DP	FR
1955	Pit-N	.926	44	67	8	6	2	2
1957	Pit-N	1.000	42	60	6	0	0	1
1958	Pit-N	.973	57	104	3	3	0	5
1959	Pit-N	.970	85	155	8	5	2	2
1961	Pit-N	1.000	2	1	0	0	0	0
1962	Hou-N	.946	142	217	10	13	2	-4
1963	Bos-A	.973	86	177	6	5	1	2
1964	Bos-A	.962	37	49	2	2	0	3
Total	8	.963	495	830	43	4	7	11

■ Sam Mejias OF

YEAR	TM/L	PCT	G	PO	A	E	DP	FR
1976	StL-N	1.000	17	19	1	0	0	2
1977	Mon-N	.966	56	55	2	2	1	3
1978	Mon-N	.949	52	35	2	2	0	3
1979	Chi-N	.875	23	7	0	1	0	0
	Cin-N	1.000	5	1	0	0	0	0
	Yr	.889	28	8	0	1	0	0
1980	Cin-N	.989	67	89	4	1	1	8
1981	Cin-N	.972	58	34	1	1	0	2
Total	6	.973	278	240	10	7	2	18

■ Sam Mele OF

YEAR	TM/L	PCT	G	PO	A	E	DP	FR
1947	Bos-A	.992	115	233	10	2	1	1
1948	Bos-A	.971	55	99	2	3	0	2
1949	Bos-A	.955	11	20	1	1	0	-1
	Was-A	.966	63	108	5	4	3	-3
	Yr	.964	74	128	6	5	3	-3
1950	Was-A	.990	99	192	8	2	0	-5
1951	Was-A	.993	124	263	8	2	1	1
1952	Was-A	.917	7	11	0	1	0	-1
	Chi-A	1.000	112	157	8	0	1	-11
	Yr	.994	119	168	8	1	1	-12
1953	Chi-A	.996	138	213	14	1	1	-7
1954	Bal-A	.962	62	97	5	4	1	-7
	Bos-A	.955	13	20	1	1	1	-1
	Yr	.961	75	117	6	5	2	-8
1955	Bos-A	1.000	7	14	3	0	0	2
	Cin-N	.960	13	24	0	1	0	-1
1956	Cle-A	.969	20	29	2	1	0	0
Total	10	.985	839	1480	67	3	9	-35

1B

YEAR	TM/L	PCT	G	PO	A	E	DP	FR
1947	Bos-A	1.000	1	5	0	0	0	0
1949	Was-A	.989	11	79	7	1	9	0
1950	Was-A	.988	16	149	18	2	13	3
1951	Was-A	1.000	15	122	7	0	11	-1
1952	Chi-A	1.000	3	10	0	0	0	0
1953	Chi-A	1.000	2	4	0	0	0	0
1954	Bos-A	.994	22	168	8	1	17	-2
1955	Cin-N	—	1	0	0	0	0	0
1956	Cle-A	1.000	8	59	5	0	5	0
Total	9	.994	79	596	45	4	55	0

■ Luis Melendez OF

YEAR	TM/L	PCT	G	PO	A	E	DP	FR
1970	StL-N	1.000	18	31	2	0	0	1
1971	StL-N	.959	66	90	3	4	0	1
1972	StL-N	.959	105	206	5	9	0	1
1973	StL-N	.990	95	196	8	2	4	5
1974	StL-N	.977	46	84	0	2	0	5
1975	StL-N	.983	89	169	3	3	1	3
1976	StL-N	1.000	8	14	0	0	0	1
	SD-N	.988	60	85	0	1	0	4
	Yr	.990	68	99	0	1	0	5
1977	SD-N	1.000	2	1	0	0	0	0
Total	8	.977	489	876	21	1	5	21

SS

YEAR	TM/L	PCT	G	PO	A	E	DP	FR
1974	StL-N	1.000	1	0	1	0	0	0

■ Ski Melillo 2B

YEAR	TM/L	PCT	G	PO	A	E	DP	FR
1926	StL-A	.965	88	225	297	19	65	6
1927	StL-A	.935	101	229	293	**36**	72	-2
1928	StL-A	.961	28	66	82	6	15	3
1929	StL-A	.973	141	342	**519**	24	98	23
1930	StL-A	.979	148	384	**572**	21	**107**	27
1931	StL-A	.968	**151**	**428**	**543**	**32**	**118**	33
1932	StL-A	.981	**153**	393	**526**	18	**110**	11
1933	StL-A	**.991**	130	**362**	451	7	**110**	**23**
1934	StL-A	**.981**	141	**412**	462	17	**110**	18
1935	StL-A	.970	18	38	60	3	9	0
	Bos-A	.973	105	286	372	18	85	18
	Yr	.973	123	324	432	21	94	18
1936	Bos-A	.980	93	239	242	10	59	-8
1937	Bos-A	.939	19	33	29	4	9	-4
Total	12	.973	1316	3437	4448	215	965	148

3B

YEAR	TM/L	PCT	G	PO	A	E	DP	FR
1926	StL-A	.930	11	13	27	3	6	2
1928	StL-A	1.000	19	13	22	0	0	0
1937	Bos-A	1.000	2	0	1	0	0	0
Total	3	.962	32	26	50	3	6	2

SS

YEAR	TM/L	PCT	G	PO	A	E	DP	FR
1937	Bos-A	1.000	2	0	5	0	1	1

■ Paul Meloan OF

YEAR	TM/L	PCT	G	PO	A	E	DP	FR
1910	Chi-A	.948	65	76	16	5	1	4
1911	Chi-A	.000	1	0	0	1	0	-1
	StL-A	.904	54	69	6	8	1	-6
	Yr	.893	55	69	6	9	1	-7
Total	2	.923	120	145	22	4	2	-3

■ Bill Melton 3B

YEAR	TM/L	PCT	G	PO	A	E	DP	FR
1968	Chi-A	.968	33	17	75	3	5	4
1969	Chi-A	.952	148	112	322	22	36	6
1970	Chi-A	.926	70	47	179	18	19	6
1971	Chi-A	.968	148	116	371	16	26	27
1972	Chi-A	.935	56	47	125	12	12	3
1973	Chi-A	.953	151	115	347	23	31	14
1974	Chi-A	.939	123	100	272	**24**	29	-3
1975	Chi-A	.945	138	131	313	**26**	23	1
1976	Cal-A	.966	21	7	21	1	2	-1
1977	Cle-A	.933	13	8	20	2	1	1
Total	10	.949	901	700	2045	147	184	58

OF

YEAR	TM/L	PCT	G	PO	A	E	DP	FR
1969	Chi-A	1.000	11	13	3	0	0	1
1970	Chi-A	1.000	71	111	8	0	3	-1
Total	2	1.000	82	124	11	0	3	0

1B

YEAR	TM/L	PCT	G	PO	A	E	DP	FR
1976	Cal-A	.992	30	220	15	2	20	-1
1977	Cle-A	1.000	15	134	8	0	10	-1
Total	2	.995	45	354	23	2	30	-2

■ Bob Melvin C

YEAR	TM/L	PCT	G	PO	A	E	DP	FR
1985	Det-A	.989	41	175	13	2	1	7
1986	SF-N	.988	84	442	59	6	7	6
1987	SF-N	.998	78	407	43	1	7	4
1988	SF-N	.984	89	403	31	7	4	-8
1989	Bal-A	.991	75	303	20	3	1	-13
1990	Bal-A	.997	76	364	25	1	2	0
Total	6	.991	443	2094	191	0	22	-4

1B

YEAR	TM/L	PCT	G	PO	A	E	DP	FR
1987	SF-N	1.000	1	7	1	0	1	0
1988	SF-N	1.000	1	3	0	0	0	0
1990	Bal-A	1.000	1	1	1	0	0	0
Total	3	1.000	3	11	2	0	1	0

3B

YEAR	TM/L	PCT	G	PO	A	E	DP	FR
1986	SF-N	1.000	1	1	1	0	0	0

■ Mario Mendoza SS

YEAR	TM/L	PCT	G	PO	A	E	DP	FR
1974	Pit-N	.964	87	77	187	10	21	5
1975	Pit-N	.952	53	29	70	5	10	8
1976	Pit-N	.967	45	42	103	5	19	12
1977	Pit-N	.928	45	36	80	9	13	11
1978	Pit-N	.955	14	7	14	1	0	2
1979	Sea-A	.968	148	177	422	20	91	28
1980	Sea-A	.959	114	149	290	19	68	7
1981	Tex-A	.970	88	114	270	12	47	-2
1982	Tex-A	.882	12	14	16	4	6	2
Total	9	.961	606	645	1452	5	275	73

3B

YEAR	TM/L	PCT	G	PO	A	E	DP	FR
1975	Pit-N	—	1	0	0	0	0	0
1976	Pit-N	1.000	2	0	2	0	0	0
1977	Pit-N	.917	19	5	6	1	0	1
1978	Pit-N	.870	18	4	16	3	1	2
Total	4	.892	40	9	24	4	1	3

2B

YEAR	TM/L	PCT	G	PO	A	E	DP	FR
1976	Pit-N	—	1	0	0	0	0	0
1978	Pit-N	.980	21	17	31	1	3	6
Total	2	.980	22	17	31	1	3	6

■ Denis Menke SS

YEAR	TM/L	PCT	G	PO	A	E	DP	FR
1962	Mil-N	.911	9	16	25	4	6	0
1963	Mil-N	.976	82	120	250	9	45	5
1964	Mil-N	.964	141	253	422	25	76	5
1965	Mil-N	.967	54	65	140	7	22	-6
1966	Atl-N	.955	106	165	282	21	50	-22
1967	Atl-N	.965	124	181	349	19	65	-22
1968	Hou-N	.965	35	45	92	5	21	-2
1969	Hou-N	.956	131	161	356	24	63	-13
1970	Hou-N	.954	133	192	394	**28**	66	-20
1971	Hou-N	.966	17	16	40	2	5	0
1973	Cin-N	1.000	7	4	3	0	0	0
1974	Hou-N	1.000	2	0	2	0	0	0
Total	12	.961	841	1218	2355	144	419	-75

3B

YEAR	TM/L	PCT	G	PO	A	E	DP	FR
1962	Mil-N	.958	15	9	37	2	4	4
1963	Mil-N	.928	51	58	96	12	9	6
1964	Mil-N	1.000	6	1	2	0	0	0
1965	Mil-N	.800	4	3	5	2	1	0
1966	Atl-N	.970	39	38	58	3	4	0
1967	Atl-N	1.000	3	2	1	0	0	0
1968	Hou-N	1.000	4	3	6	0	1	0
1969	Hou-N	1.000	1	2	2	0	0	0
1970	Hou-N	.833	5	1	4	1	1	0
1971	Hou-N	.942	32	24	41	4	4	-3
1972	Cin-N	.955	130	85	258	16	20	1
1973	Cin-N	.966	123	68	189	9	19	16
1974	Hou-N	.991	7	2	16	0	1	0
Total	13	.954	420	296	715	9	64	26

2B

YEAR	TM/L	PCT	G	PO	A	E	DP	FR
1962	Mil-N	.980	20	49	47	2	10	0
1963	Mil-N	.971	22	51	51	3	12	1
1964	Mil-N	.968	15	29	31	2	8	1
1968	Hou-N	.982	119	269	285	10	47	-15
1969	Hou-N	.978	23	42	47	2	9	3
1970	Hou-N	.991	21	51	62	1	14	5
1971	Hou-N	.947	5	7	11	1	2	0
1973	Cin-N	1.000	5	7	5	0	1	0
1974	Hou-N	1.000	3	1	4	0	0	0
Total	9	.980	233	506	543	1	103	-9

1B

YEAR	TM/L	PCT	G	PO	A	E	DP	FR
1962	Mil-N	1.000	2	11	0	0	3	0
1963	Mil-N	1.000	1	3	1	0	1	0
1965	Mil-N	1.000	8	42	1	0	4	0
1966	Atl-N	1.000	7	25	1	0	2	0
1968	Hou-N	1.000	5	29	1	0	2	0
1969	Hou-N	.984	9	52	9	1	3	2
1970	Hou-N	1.000	5	14	0	0	0	0
1971	Hou-N	.997	101	845	59	3	77	0
1972	Cin-N	1.000	11	40	2	0	5	0
1973	Cin-N	1.000	1	1	0	0	0	0
1974	Hou-N	1.000	12	18	1	0	4	0
Total	11	.997	162	1080	75	4	101	2

OF

YEAR	TM/L	PCT	G	PO	A	E	DP	FR
1962	Mil-N	1.000	1	2	0	0	0	0
1963	Mil-N	1.000	1	2	0	0	0	0
1970	Hou-N	1.000	3	4	0	0	0	0
Total	3	1.000	5	8	0	0	0	0

■ Mike Menosky OF

YEAR	TM/L	PCT	G	PO	A	E	DP	FR
1914	Pit-F	.942	41	60	5	4	0	-3
1915	Pit-F	.917	9	11	0	1	0	-2
1916	Was-A	.952	9	17	3	1	2	1
1917	Was-A	.982	94	208	15	4	3	7
1919	Was-A	.979	103	222	7	5	1	0
1920	Bos-A	.961	141	281	17	12	2	-3
1921	Bos-A	.970	133	278	12	9	3	-4
1922	Bos-A	.977	103	240	14	6	3	6
1923	Bos-A	.920	49	103	12	10	1	3
Total	9	.967	682	1420	85	2	15	5

■ Rudy Meoli SS

YEAR	TM/L	PCT	G	PO	A	E	DP	FR
1973	Cal-A	.933	95	122	252	**27**	52	-3
1974	Cal-A	.935	8	9	20	2	6	1
1975	Cal-A	.976	28	19	61	2	15	1
1979	Phi-N	.984	16	23	37	1	5	1
Total	4	.944	147	173	370	2	71	-1

3B

YEAR	TM/L	PCT	G	PO	A	E	DP	FR
1973	Cal-A	.864	13	5	14	3	2	0
1974	Cal-A	.946	20	6	47	3	0	1
1975	Cal-A	.824	15	9	19	6	2	-1
1978	Chi-N	1.000	5	2	9	0	0	4
1979	Phi-N	1.000	1	0	1	0	0	0
Total	5	.903	54	22	90	2	4	4

2B

YEAR	TM/L	PCT	G	PO	A	E	DP	FR
1973	Cal-A	1.000	8	15	18	0	3	2
1974	Cal-A	—	1	0	0	0	0	0
1975	Cal-A	.933	11	11	17	2	3	1
1978	Chi-N	.900	6	4	5	1	0	2
1979	Phi-N	.981	15	14	37	1	7	3
Total	5	.968	41	44	77	4	13	8

1B

YEAR	TM/L	PCT	G	PO	A	E	DP	FR
1974	Cal-A	—	1	0	0	0	0	0

■ Orlando Mercado C

YEAR	TM/L	PCT	G	PO	A	E	DP	FR
1982	Sea-A	1.000	8	31	1	0	0	1
1983	Sea-A	.995	65	342	27	2	2	4
1984	Sea-A	.992	29	118	10	1	0	-5
1986	Tex-A	.996	45	240	25	1	5	16
1987	Det-A	.980	10	40	8	1	1	3
	LA-N	1.000	7	13	0	0	0	0
1988	Oak-A	.959	16	45	2	2	0	0
1989	Min-A	1.000	19	73	9	0	2	4
1990	NY-N	.991	40	213	8	2	2	2
	Mon-N	1.000	8	26	1	0	0	3
	Yr	.992	48	239	9	2	2	5
Total	8	.993	247	1141	91	9	12	28

■ Fred Merkle 1B

YEAR	TM/L	PCT	G	PO	A	E	DP	FR
1907	NY-N	.949	15	122	7	7	4	-1
1908	NY-N	1.000	11	60	1	0	2	-1
1909	NY-N	.976	70	625	27	16	29	-3
1910	NY-N	.981	144	1390	84	**29**	**87**	1
1911	NY-N	.985	148	1375	**117**	22	73	**15**
1912	NY-N	.980	129	1229	72	**27**	77	-1
1913	NY-N	.986	153	1463	76	22	86	-4
1914	NY-N	.990	146	1463	88	16	80	3
1915	NY-N	.989	110	1123	53	13	62	-3
1916	NY-N	.984	112	1183	58	20	61	0
	Bro-N	.992	15	126	4	1	3	-1
	Yr	.985	127	1309	62	21	64	-1
1917	Bro-N	1.000	2	23	1	0	1	0
	Chi-N	.983	140	1415	66	26	84	-5
	Yr	.983	**142**	**1438**	67	26	85	-5
1918	Chi-N	.990	129	1388	82	15	69	-1
1919	Chi-N	.985	132	**1494**	56	**23**	66	-10
1920	Chi-N	.985	85	906	54	15	52	0
1925	NY-A	1.000	5	28	1	0	3	0
1926	NY-A	1.000	1	6	0	0	0	0
Total	16	.985	1547	15419	847	252	839	-9

OF

YEAR	TM/L	PCT	G	PO	A	E	DP	FR
1908	NY-N	1.000	5	3	0	0	0	-1
1915	NY-N	.973	30	68	5	2	1	3
1916	Bro-N	1.000	4	5	1	0	0	2
1917	Chi-N	1.000	6	15	2	0	1	2
1920	Chi-N	—	1	0	0	0	0	0
Total	5	.980	46	91	8	2	2	4

2B

YEAR	TM/L	PCT	G	PO	A	E	DP	FR
1908	NY-N	1.000	1	2	2	0	1	0
1909	NY-N	1.000	1	3	0	0	0	0
1919	Chi-N	—	1	0	0	0	0	0
Total	3	1.000	3	5	2	0	1	0

3B

YEAR	TM/L	PCT	G	PO	A	E	DP	FR
1908	NY-N	—	1	0	0	0	0	0

YEAR	TM/L	PCT	G	PO	A	E	DP	FR
■ Lloyd Merriman OF								
1949	Cin-N	.969	86	214	7	7	1	-4
1950	Cin-N	.989	84	181	4	2	1	-7
1951	Cin-N	.997	102	309	5	1	2	4
1954	Cin-N	.981	25	51	0	1	0	-1
1955	Cin-N	.977	47	82	2	2	2	1
Total	5	.985	344	837	18	3	6	-7
■ Bill Merritt C								
1891	Chi-N	.955	11	31	11	2	1	-3
1892	Lou-N	.940	46	175	58	15	6	-2
1893	Bos-N	.945	37	129	25	9	6	-3
1894	Bos-N	.881	8	30	7	5	1	1
	Pit-N	.952	28	85	35	6	5	-1
	Cin-N	.953	24	55	26	4	0	-4
	Yr	.941	60	170	68	15	6	-4
1895	Cin-N	.955	20	65	19	4	3	1
	Pit-N	.935	63	245	58	21	7	-2
	Yr	.939	83	310	77	25	10	-1
1896	Pit-N	.941	62	242	75	20	5	4
1897	Pit-N	.946	53	202	43	14	6	-5
1899	Bos-N	1.000	1	2	2	0	0	0
Total	8	.942	353	1261	359	100	40	-14
1B								
1891	Chi-N	.909	1	10	0	1	1	0
1894	Pit-N	1.000	4	18	0	0	0	0
	Cin-N	.875	1	7	0	1	0	0
	Yr	.962	5	25	0	1	0	0
1895	Pit-N	.966	2	27	1	1	2	0
1896	Pit-N	1.000	3	33	2	0	2	0
1897	Pit-N	.986	7	68	4	1	4	0
Total	5	.977	18	163	7	4	9	0
3B								
1894	Cin-N	.923	3	2	10	1	2	1
1896	Pit-N	.750	5	3	9	4	0	-2
Total	2	.828	8	5	19	5	2	-1
OF								
1893	Bos-N	1.000	2	1	0	0	0	-1
1894	Bos-N	1.000	1	3	0	0	0	0
	Pit-N	1.000	2	2	0	0	0	-1
	Cin-N	—	1	0	0	0	0	0
	Yr	1.000	4	5	0	0	0	-1
Total	2	1.000	6	6	0	0	0	-2
2B								
1895	Cin-N	.857	1	5	1	1	0	-1
1896	Pit-N	1.000	3	4	8	0	1	0
Total	2	.947	4	9	9	1	1	-1
SS								
1896	Pit-N	.833	2	4	1	1	0	-1
■ Sam Mertes OF								
1896	Phi-N	.907	35	85	3	9	0	-1
1898	Chi-N	.880	60	97	13	15	6	1
1899	Chi-N	.923	108	197	20	18	4	-1
1900	Chi-N	.923	88	180	13	16	4	-2
1901	Chi-A	1.000	5	20	0	0	0	2
1902	Chi-A	.922	120	223	26	21	5	8
1903	NY-N	.973	137	265	24	8	5	8
1904	NY-N	.956	147	244	17	12	1	-1
1905	NY-N	.960	150	230	10	10	3	-11
1906	NY-N	.970	71	119	10	4	0	1
	StL-N	.890	53	77	4	10	0	-6
	Yr	.938	124	196	14	14	0	-5
Total	10	.938	974	1737	140	123	28	-2
2B								
1896	Phi-N	—	1	0	0	0	0	0
1898	Chi-N	.848	4	11	17	5	6	2
1901	Chi-A	.940	132	337	396	47	54	-8
1902	Chi-A	.778	1	1	6	2	1	1
Total	4	.934	138	349	419	4	61	-5
1B								
1898	Chi-N	1.000	2	1	0	0	0	0
1899	Chi-N	.933	3	24	4	2	4	1
1900	Chi-N	.973	33	340	17	10	16	-1
1902	Chi-A	1.000	1	10	1	0	1	0
1903	NY-N	.900	1	9	0	1	0	0
Total	5	.969	40	384	22	3	21	0
SS								
1896	Phi-N	1.000	1	1	2	0	1	0
1898	Chi-N	.857	14	19	23	7	4	-1
1899	Chi-N	.833	1	2	3	1	1	0
1900	Chi-N	.939	7	12	19	2	2	-1
1902	Chi-A	1.000	5	17	15	0	2	-1
1904	NY-N	1.000	1	4	2	0	0	0
Total	6	.922	29	55	64	10	10	-3
3B								
1902	Chi-A	.833	1	4	1	1	0	-1
C								
1902	Chi-A	.750	2	3	0	1	0	-1
1903	NY-N	1.000	1	0	1	0	0	0
Total	2	.800	3	3	1	1	0	-1
3B								
1902	Chi-A	.833	1	4	1	1	0	-1
■ Lennie Merullo SS								
1941	Chi-N	.968	7	12	18	1	5	2
1942	Chi-N	.946	143	299	438	42	80	-1
1943	Chi-N	.940	125	218	396	39	68	-12
1944	Chi-N	.937	56	115	167	19	26	2
1945	Chi-N	.948	118	209	336	30	49	-4
1946	Chi-N	.946	44	78	131	12	23	18
1947	Chi-N	.949	108	219	322	29	77	7
Total	7	.945	601	1150	1808	172	328	12
1B								
1944	Chi-N	1.000	1	1	0	0	0	0
■ Steve Mesner 3B								
1939	Chi-N	1.000	1	1	0	0	0	0
1941	StL-N	.958	22	23	45	3	8	5
1943	Cin-N	.944	130	132	274	24	29	1
1944	Cin-N	.951	120	120	246	19	21	-7
1945	Cin-N	.971	148	170	326	15	35	11
Total	5	.956	421	446	891	1	93	10
SS								
1938	Chi-N	.667	1	0	2	1	0	-1
1939	Chi-N	.927	12	12	39	4	7	1
Total	2	.914	13	12	41	5	7	0
2B								
1939	Chi-N	1.000	1	3	4	0	1	0
1945	Cin-N	1.000	3	3	3	0	1	0
Total	2	1.000	4	6	7	0	2	0
■ Bud Metheny OF								
1943	NY-A	.963	91	156	1	6	0	-16
1944	NY-A	.956	132	232	8	11	2	-11
1945	NY-A	.984	128	227	12	4	2	-9
Total	3	.968	351	615	21	1	4	-36
■ Catfish Metkovich OF								
1943	Bos-A	.955	76	183	6	9	3	-5
1944	Bos-A	.962	82	242	8	10	2	2
1945	Bos-A	.989	42	87	2	1	0	-2
1946	Bos-A	.948	81	125	3	7	0	-12
1947	Cle-A	.989	119	349	2	4	2	-3
1949	Chi-A	.968	87	212	1	7	0	-8
1951	Pit-N	.994	69	171	4	1	0	-5
1952	Pit-N	1.000	33	72	1	0	0	-2
1953	Pit-N	1.000	4	7	1	0	0	1
	Chi-N	1.000	38	67	1	0	0	1
	Yr	1.000	42	74	2	0	0	2
1954	Mil-N	1.000	13	17	2	0	0	1
Total	10	.976	644	1532	31	9	7	-32
1B								
1943	Bos-A	1.000	2	23	3	0	2	1
1944	Bos-A	.986	50	469	33	7	38	2
1945	Bos-A	.985	97	935	76	15	96	0
1947	Cle-A	1.000	1	1	1	0	0	0
1951	Pit-N	.991	37	306	27	3	32	2
1952	Pit-N	.988	72	530	33	7	59	-4
1953	Pit-N	1.000	5	47	0	0	2	-1
	Chi-N	.950	7	37	1	2	2	-1
	Yr	.977	12	84	1	2	4	-2
1954	Mil-N	1.000	18	143	15	0	15	2
Total	8	.987	289	2491	189	4	246	1
■ Charlie Metro OF								
1943	Det-A	.966	14	28	0	1	0	4
1944	Det-A	1.000	20	44	1	0	0	2
	Phi-A	1.000	11	16	1	0	0	1
	Yr	1.000	31	60	2	0	0	3
1945	Phi-A	.972	57	100	5	3	0	-3
Total	3	.980	102	188	7	4	0	4
3B								
1944	Phi-A	.923	5	5	7	1	1	0
2B								
1944	Phi-A	1.000	2	0	2	0	0	1
■ Roger Metzger SS								
1970	Chi-N	.833	1	1	4	1	1	1
1971	Hou-N	.977	148	275	459	17	91	-5
1972	Hou-N	.971	153	238	504	22	101	5
1973	Hou-N	.982	149	231	429	12	83	-19
1974	Hou-N	.976	143	238	451	17	85	-10
1975	Hou-N	.977	126	186	441	15	83	11
1976	Hou-N	.986	150	253	462	10	93	-4
1977	Hou-N	.973	96	130	260	11	45	-3
1978	Hou-N	.964	42	59	103	6	21	-5
	SF-N	.974	74	112	184	8	30	-12
	Yr	.970	116	171	287	14	51	-17
1979	SF-N	.956	78	108	219	15	34	1
1980	SF-N	.971	13	14	19	1	4	3
Total	11	.976	1173	1845	3535	135	671	-37
2B								
1976	Hou-N	1.000	2	5	6	0	0	0
1977	Hou-N	—	1	0	0	0	0	0
1978	Hou-N	1.000	1	0	2	0	0	0
1979	SF-N	1.000	10	14	18	0	4	2
1980	SF-N	—	1	0	0	0	0	0
Total	5	1.000	15	19	26	0	4	2
3B								
1979	SF-N	—	1	0	0	0	0	0
■ Alex Metzler OF								
1925	Chi-A	1.000	9	24	3	0	0	2
1926	Phi-A	1.000	17	34	3	0	1	2
1927	Chi-A	.965	134	397	16	15	6	16
1928	Chi-A	.968	134	288	11	10	3	-4
1929	Chi-A	.960	142	316	16	14	3	1
1930	Chi-A	.969	27	30	1	1	0	-5
	StL-A	.951	56	114	2	6	0	-5
	Yr	.955	83	144	3	7	0	-10
Total	6	.965	519	1203	52	6	13	7
■ Irish Meusel OF								
1914	Was-A	1.000	1	1	0	0	0	0
1918	Phi-N	.972	120	296	14	9	2	10
1919	Phi-N	.968	128	256	14	9	4	-2
1920	Phi-N	.929	129	260	16	21	6	0
1921	Phi-N	.929	84	153	18	13	4	1
	NY-N	.971	62	122	10	4	0	0
	Yr	.947	146	275	28	17	4	1
1922	NY-N	.980	154	291	15	6	1	-12
1923	NY-N	.949	145	268	15	15	2	-12
1924	NY-N	.967	138	287	4	10	0	-7
1925	NY-N	.959	126	244	16	11	2	-6
1926	NY-N	.958	112	197	10	9	1	-12
1927	Bro-N	1.000	2	2	0	0	0	-1
Total	11	.959	1216	2391	129	107	23	-41
1918	Phi-N	.857	4	7	11	3	2	-1
1B								
1920	Phi-N	1.000	3	23	1	0	2	0
■ Bob Meusel OF								
1920	NY-A	.947	64	116	10	7	3	2
1921	NY-A	.934	147	253	28	20	8	5
1922	NY-A	.950	121	202	24	12	0	0
1923	NY-A	.953	121	206	17	11	2	-7
1924	NY-A	.951	143	252	17	14	4	-7
1925	NY-A	.985	131	249	9	4	6	-4
1926	NY-A	.960	107	211	4	9	1	-5
1927	NY-A	.975	131	249	15	14	1	-4
1928	NY-A	.975	131	259	16	7	6	4
1929	NY-A	.968	96	206	9	7	2	3
1930	Cin-N	.962	112	223	8	9	3	-13
Total	11	.958	1304	2426	157	114	36	-26
3B								
1920	NY-A	.893	45	34	75	13	3	-12
1924	NY-A	1.000	2	2	0	0	0	0
1925	NY-A	.970	27	22	42	2	2	-5
Total	3	.921	74	58	117	5	5	-17
1B								
1920	NY-A	1.000	2	12	0	0	3	0
■ Benny Meyer OF								
1913	Bro-N	.943	26	47	3	3	0	0
1914	Bal-F	.916	132	172	14	17	6	-9
1915	Bal-F	.931	34	53	1	4	0	-3
	Buf-F	.947	88	134	9	8	1	-6
	Yr	.943	122	187	10	12	1	-9
Total	3	.931	280	406	27	2	7	-18
SS								
1914	Bal-F	.938	4	7	8	1	0	-1
C								
1913	Bro-N	—	1	0	0	0	0	0
2B								
1925	Phi-N	—	1	0	0	0	0	0
■ Dan Meyer 1B								
1975	Det-A	.990	46	441	37	5	39	1
1976	Det-A	.994	19	168	10	1	15	-1
1977	Sea-A	.992	159	1407	109	12	134	-1
1978	Sea-A	.989	121	1104	79	13	119	-1
1979	Sea-A	1.000	15	73	9	0	5	0
1980	Sea-A	1.000	4	27	0	0	4	-1
1981	Sea-A	1.000	3	17	0	0	3	-1
1982	Oak-A	.990	58	373	31	4	38	-1
1983	Oak-A	.987	41	293	16	4	28	-2
1984	Oak-A	.944	3	15	2	1	1	0
Total	10	.991	469	3918	288	0	386	-5
OF								
1974	Det-A	.967	12	29	0	1	0	-1
1975	Det-A	.950	74	130	4	7	0	-13
1976	Det-A	.988	47	76	4	1	1	-9
1978	Sea-A	1.000	2	3	0	0	0	0
1979	Sea-A	.942	31	49	0	3	0	-3
1980	Sea-A	.961	123	189	10	8	2	-14
1981	Sea-A	.931	14	26	1	2	0	0
1982	Oak-A	.938	11	14	1	1	0	0
1983	Oak-A	1.000	11	12	0	0	0	1
1985	Oak-A	1.000	1	1	0	0	0	0
Total	10	.960	326	529	20	3	3	-39
3B								
1979	Sea-A	.936	101	76	201	19	22	-9
1980	Sea-A	.882	5	3	12	2	1	0
1981	Sea-A	.961	49	36	87	5	12	4
1983	Oak-A	—	1	0	0	0	0	0
1985	Oak-A	—	1	0	0	0	0	0
Total	5	.941	157	115	300	6	35	-5
■ Dutch Meyer 2B								
1940	Det-A	.960	21	28	44	3	6	0
1941	Det-A	.972	40	107	101	6	19	6
1942	Det-A	.989	14	31	56	1	14	6
1945	Cle-A	.978	130	317	313	14	66	-32
1946	Cle-A	.977	64	110	150	6	26	-13
Total	5	.977	269	593	664	0	131	-33
■ Billy Meyer C								
1913	Chi-A	.857	1	5	1	1	0	1
1916	Phi-A	.961	48	217	79	12	5	7
1917	Phi-A	.962	55	235	66	12	2	10
Total	3	.960	104	457	146	5	7	18
■ Chief Meyers C								
1909	NY-N	.963	64	376	71	17	4	5
1910	NY-N	.969	117	638	154	25	16	6
1911	NY-N	.979	128	729	108	18	11	-3
1912	NY-N	.973	122	576	111	19	10	-10
1913	NY-N	.967	116	579	143	25	12	5
1914	NY-N	.970	126	487	150	20	16	-14
1915	NY-N	.986	96	464	90	8	15	-3
1916	Bro-N	.984	74	389	95	8	9	7
1917	Bro-N	.974	44	186	37	6	3	-6
	Bos-N	1.000	24	113	37	0	3	7
	Yr	.984	68	299	74	6	6	1
Total	9	.974	911	4537	996	146	99	-6
■ Gene Michael SS								
1966	Pit-N	.903	8	9	19	3	7	5
1967	LA-N	.950	83	117	204	17	30	5
1968	NY-A	.939	43	67	103	11	15	-1
1969	NY-A	.968	118	205	365	19	64	-1
1970	NY-A	.957	123	248	379	28	78	2
1971	NY-A	.973	136	243	474	20	88	17
1972	NY-A	.969	121	218	437	21	89	24
1973	NY-A	.965	129	208	433	23	84	4
1974	NY-A	.970	39	35	63	3	11	2
1975	Det-A	.938	44	52	99	10	23	-5

YEAR	TM/L	PCT	G	PO	A	E	DP	FR
Total	10	.962	844	1402	2576	155	489	52
2B								
1966	Pit-N	1.000	2	1	1	0	0	0
1970	NY-A	1.000	3	11	9	0	1	-1
1974	NY-A	.970	45	86	106	6	29	3
1975	Det-A	1.000	7	9	23	0	5	-8
Total	4	.976	57	107	139	6	35	-6
3B								
1966	Pit-N	—	1	0	0	0	0	0
1970	NY-A	1.000	4	0	2	0	0	0
1974	NY-A	1.000	2	1	1	0	0	0
1975	Det-A	1.000	4	2	3	0	0	0
Total	4	1.000	11	3	6	0	0	0

■ Cass Michaels 2B

YEAR	TM/L	PCT	G	PO	A	E	DP	FR
1945	Chi-A	1.000	1	1	2	0	0	0
1946	Chi-A	.957	66	185	195	17	51	1
1947	Chi-A	.982	60	160	175	6	52	9
1948	Chi-A	.976	55	148	171	8	50	8
1949	Chi-A	.976	**154**	392	**484**	22	**135**	12
1950	Chi-A	.964	35	111	78	7	36	-6
	Was-A	.975	104	298	323	16	91	8
	Yr	.972	139	409	401	**23**	127	2
1951	Was-A	.964	128	258	391	24	86	-23
1952	Was-A	.977	22	50	75	3	16	1
	StL-A	1.000	8	14	12	0	4	-1
	Phi-A	.993	55	151	133	2	30	-13
	Yr	.989	85	215	220	**5**	50	-13
1953	Chi-A	.970	110	304	302	19	81	-11
1954	Chi-A	1.000	2	1	2	0	1	0
Total	10	.973	800	2073	2343	124	633	-15
SS								
1944	Chi-A	.930	21	36	70	8	12	5
1945	Chi-A	.936	126	259	426	**47**	74	10
1946	Chi-A	.938	6	14	16	2	8	1
1947	Chi-A	1.000	2	2	3	0	0	0
1948	Chi-A	.957	85	164	285	20	65	5
Total	5	.943	240	475	800	7	159	21
3B								
1943	Chi-A	1.000	2	1	1	0	0	-1
1944	Chi-A	1.000	3	1	1	0	0	0
1946	Chi-A	.927	13	14	24	3	3	1
1947	Chi-A	.938	44	48	89	9	9	2
1952	StL-A	.916	42	43	88	12	12	0
1954	Chi-A	.958	91	95	180	12	10	-4
Total	6	.942	195	202	383	6	34	-2
OF								
1948	Chi-A	1.000	1	1	0	0	0	0

■ Eddie Miksis 2B

YEAR	TM/L	PCT	G	PO	A	E	DP	FR
1946	Bro-N	1.000	1	0	1	0	0	0
1947	Bro-N	1.000	13	23	24	0	4	4
1948	Bro-N	.967	54	106	101	7	15	1
1949	Bro-N	—	3	0	0	0	0	0
1950	Bro-N	.964	15	34	20	2	4	2
1951	Bro-N	—	1	0	0	0	0	0
	Chi-N	.969	102	279	317	19	71	3
	Yr	.969	103	279	317	19	71	3
1952	Chi-N	.950	54	126	140	14	22	-11
1953	Chi-N	.954	92	210	262	**23**	65	-7
1954	Chi-N	.961	21	62	61	5	16	5
1956	Chi-N	.976	19	30	52	2	9	0
1958	Cin-N	.909	7	10	10	2	1	2
Total	11	.962	382	880	988	4	207	-1
OF								
1947	Bro-N	1.000	11	25	0	0	0	1
1954	Chi-N	—	1	0	0	0	0	0
1955	Chi-N	**.989**	111	267	6	3	1	-5
1956	Chi-N	.982	33	54	1	1	0	0
1957	StL-N	1.000	31	13	0	0	0	-1
1958	Cin-N	1.000	32	21	0	0	0	2
Total	6	.990	219	380	7	4	1	-3
3B								
1944	Bro-N	.896	15	19	24	5	8	-1
1946	Bro-N	.970	13	13	19	1	0	0
1947	Bro-N	.900	5	5	4	1	0	-1
1948	Bro-N	.967	22	16	42	2	4	2
1949	Bro-N	.978	29	26	62	2	4	5
1950	Bro-N	1.000	7	5	4	0	0	2
1951	Bro-N	1.000	6	3	4	0	2	2
1954	Chi-N	1.000	2	2	2	0	0	0
1955	Chi-N	.958	18	23	46	3	5	5
1956	Chi-N	.975	48	59	96	4	5	3
1958	Cin-N	.958	14	6	17	1	0	3
Total	11	.963	179	177	320	9	28	19
SS								
1944	Bro-N	.933	10	22	20	3	5	-3
1947	Bro-N	1.000	2	1	1	0	0	0
1948	Bro-N	1.000	5	3	5	0	1	1
1949	Bro-N	1.000	4	3	4	0	3	1
1950	Bro-N	.925	15	18	31	4	6	2
1952	Chi-N	.980	40	81	114	4	21	-2
1953	Chi-N	.954	53	105	144	12	31	-6
1956	Chi-N	1.000	2	1	2	0	0	-1
1958	Bal-A	—	1	0	0	0	0	0
	Cin-N	.900	5	4	5	1	1	-1
Total	9	.959	137	238	326	4	68	-7
1B								
1949	Bro-N	1.000	1	4	0	0	1	0
1958	Cin-N	—	1	0	0	0	0	0
Total	2	1.000	2	4	0	0	1	0

■ Clyde Milan OF

YEAR	TM/L	PCT	G	PO	A	E	DP	FR
1907	Was-A	.929	47	80	12	7	1	4
1908	Was-A	.959	122	265	18	12	6	9
1909	Was-A	.972	120	222	19	7	3	5
1910	Was-A	.946	142	267	**30**	17	**10**	11
1911	Was-A	.957	**154**	347	33	17	2	11
1912	Was-A	.935	**154**	326	31	**25**	6	8
1913	Was-A	.932	**154**	296	20	23	7	-7
1914	Was-A	.949	113	230	10	13	0	-4
1915	Was-A	.946	151	352	13	21	3	0
1916	Was-A	.961	149	**372**	**27**	16	8	**17**
1917	Was-A	.962	153	339	18	14	3	-5
1918	Was-A	.972	124	299	17	9	3	2
1919	Was-A	.953	86	195	9	10	2	-3
1920	Was-A	.971	123	291	15	9	1	8
1921	Was-A	.931	99	196	19	16	2	2
1922	Was-A	1.000	12	18	3	0	1	1
Total	16	.953	1903	4095	294	216	58	59

■ Larry Milbourne 2B

YEAR	TM/L	PCT	G	PO	A	E	DP	FR
1974	Hou-N	.974	87	92	131	6	23	16
1975	Hou-N	.968	43	67	85	5	27	7
1976	Hou-N	.965	32	67	100	6	19	-1
1977	Sea-A	.982	41	78	135	4	29	9
1978	Sea-A	.958	15	38	53	4	12	8
1979	Sea-A	.967	49	90	141	8	37	-2
1980	Sea-A	.976	38	55	111	4	28	9
1981	NY-A	.970	14	35	29	2	10	-1
1982	NY-A	.944	3	9	8	1	4	1
	Min-A	.981	26	49	52	2	14	-10
	Cle-A	.981	63	128	178	6	34	-1
	Yr	.979	92	186	238	9	52	-10
1983	Phi-N	.963	27	38	40	3	4	1
	NY-A	1.000	19	40	44	0	9	2
1984	Sea-A	.964	14	25	29	2	8	0
Total	11	.974	471	811	1136	3	258	38
SS								
1974	Hou-N	.963	8	9	17	1	1	2
1975	Hou-N	.940	22	28	51	5	8	3
1977	Sea-A	.943	40	42	74	7	17	-4
1978	Sea-A	.955	23	26	58	4	11	7
1979	Sea-A	.981	65	46	109	3	20	-14
1980	Sea-A	.976	34	45	79	3	21	0
1981	NY-A	.955	39	37	91	6	15	-6
1982	NY-A	.917	9	3	8	1	0	-1
	Cle-A	.879	21	17	34	7	6	-5
	Yr	.886	30	20	42	8	6	-6
1983	Phi-N	1.000	8	2	6	0	0	-1
	NY-A	.941	6	5	11	1	3	1
1984	Sea-A	.867	5	6	7	2	0	-1
Total	10	.953	280	266	545	0	102	-19
3B								
1977	Sea-A	.000	1	0	0	1	0	0
1978	Sea-A	.989	32	28	58	1	4	0
1979	Sea-A	.958	11	8	15	1	0	-1
1980	Sea-A	.889	6	3	5	1	1	0
1981	NY-A	1.000	3	2	1	0	1	0
1982	NY-A	1.000	3	0	5	0	0	1
	Cle-A	.941	9	4	12	1	1	0
	Yr	.955	12	4	17	1	1	1
1983	Phi-N	1.000	3	0	2	0	0	0
	NY-A	1.000	4	1	2	0	1	0
1984	Sea-A	.900	4	0	9	1	0	0
Total	8	.944	112	68	150	3	14	-8
OF								
1974	Hou-N	1.000	4	1	0	0	0	0

■ Dee Miles OF

YEAR	TM/L	PCT	G	PO	A	E	DP	FR
1935	Was-A	.970	45	92	5	3	1	-2
1936	Was-A	.958	10	22	1	1	0	0
1939	Phi-A	.968	77	146	4	5	1	-6
1940	Phi-A	.945	50	117	3	7	0	0
1941	Phi-A	1.000	35	79	2	0	1	1
1942	Phi-A	.984	81	177	6	3	0	0
1943	Bos-A	.968	25	58	3	2	1	0
Total	7	.971	323	691	24	1	4	-7

■ Felix Millan 2B

YEAR	TM/L	PCT	G	PO	A	E	DP	FR
1966	Atl-N	.973	25	54	56	3	12	-2
1967	Atl-N	.972	41	84	125	6	24	3
1968	Atl-N	.980	145	330	438	16	91	3
1969	Atl-N	**.980**	**162**	373	**444**	17	72	-16
1970	Atl-N	.979	142	337	359	15	83	-19
1971	Atl-N	.982	141	373	437	15	120	6
1972	Atl-N	.987	120	273	339	8	67	-16
1973	NY-N	.989	153	410	411	9	99	-4
1974	NY-N	.979	134	374	315	15	81	-20
1975	NY-N	.972	**162**	379	419	23	95	-25
1976	NY-N	.977	136	311	315	15	68	-24
1977	NY-N	.977	89	197	188	9	43	-16
Total	12	.980	1450	3495	3846	151	855	130
SS								
1966	Atl-N	1.000	1	3	0	0	1	0
3B								
1966	Atl-N	—	1	0	0	0	0	0

■ Dusty Miller OF

YEAR	TM/L	PCT	G	PO	A	E	DP	FR
1889	Bal-a	1.000	3	4	0	0	0	-1
1890	StL-a	.872	24	33	8	6	3	2
1895	Cin-N	.937	**132**	243	25	18	8	11
1896	Cin-N	.902	125	199	21	24	7	-2
1897	Cin-N	.929	119	203	18	17	2	2
1898	Cin-N	.929	152	292	23	24	4	8
1899	Cin-N	.927	80	148	18	13	4	7
	StL-N	.875	10	20	1	3	1	-1
	Yr	.921	90	168	19	16	5	6
Total	7	.923	645	1142	114	105	29	26
SS								
1889	Bal-a	.636	3	7	21	16	0	-7
1890	StL-a	.909	3	2	8	1	0	0
Total	2	.691	11	9	29	7	0	-7

■ Bruce Miller 3B

YEAR	TM/L	PCT	G	PO	A	E	DP	FR
1973	SF-N	.900	4	1	8	1	0	1
1974	SF-N	.938	41	26	96	8	3	7
1975	SF-N	.949	68	66	120	10	11	5
1976	SF-N	1.000	2	1	1	0	0	0
Total	4	.944	115	94	225	9	14	13
2B								
1973	SF-N	.909	3	4	6	1	0	0
1974	SF-N	.968	9	7	23	1	3	3
1975	SF-N	.963	21	44	59	4	17	5
1976	SF-N	.920	8	8	15	2	3	-1
Total	4	.954	41	63	103	8	23	7
SS								
1973	SF-N	1.000	1	2	0	0	0	0
1974	SF-N	.955	13	22	42	3	5	3
1975	SF-N	.917	6	4	7	1	3	0
Total	3	.951	20	28	49	4	8	3

■ Bing Miller OF

YEAR	TM/L	PCT	G	PO	A	E	DP	FR
1921	Was-A	.945	109	247	13	15	4	2
1922	Phi-A	.977	139	314	19	8	3	5
1923	Phi-A	.978	119	262	10	6	0	-1
1924	Phi-A	.973	94	172	11	5	4	-2
1925	Phi-A	.975	115	190	7	5	1	-9
1926	Phi-A	1.000	34	53	1	0	0	-5
	StL-A	.939	94	219	12	15	2	4
	Yr	.950	128	272	13	15	2	-1
1927	StL-A	.970	126	309	9	10	3	4
1928	Phi-A	.968	133	298	8	10	2	0
1929	Phi-A	.970	145	311	10	10	4	6
1930	Phi-A	.976	**154**	309	10	8	3	5
1931	Phi-A	.987	137	305	7	4	1	6
1932	Phi-A	.979	84	180	3	4	0	3
1933	Phi-A	1.000	30	39	1	0	0	-2
1934	Phi-A	1.000	46	72	2	0	1	-2
1935	Bos-A	.962	29	48	2	2	0	-1
1936	Bos-A	1.000	13	14	1	0	1	0
Total	16	.971	1601	3342	126	102	29	13
1B								
1924	Phi-A	.973	7	66	7	2	7	1
1925	Phi-A	.979	12	87	6	2	6	-1
1926	Phi-A	1.000	1	1	0	0	1	0
1933	Phi-A	.960	6	23	1	1	2	0
Total	4	.974	26	177	14	5	16	0

■ Eddie Miller SS

YEAR	TM/L	PCT	G	PO	A	E	DP	FR
1936	Cin-N	.938	4	5	10	1	1	0
1937	Cin-N	.926	30	45	68	9	16	7
1939	Bos-N	.970	77	183	275	14	76	12
1940	Bos-N	**.970**	151	**405**	487	28	**122**	**15**
1941	Bos-N	**.966**	154	336	485	29	**112**	12
1942	Bos-N	**.983**	142	285	450	13	78	4
1943	Cin-N	**.979**	**154**	**335**	543	19	**121**	**27**
1944	Cin-N	.971	**155**	**357**	**544**	27	**100**	12
1945	Cin-N	**.975**	115	245	382	16	61	5
1946	Cin-N	.970	88	184	297	15	79	**23**
1947	Cin-N	.972	**151**	295	445	21	88	-5
1948	Cin-N	.966	122	229	341	20	63	-14
1949	Phi-N	—	1	0	0	0	0	0
1950	StL-N	.980	51	72	173	5	29	13
Total	14	.972	1395	2976	4500	217	946	111
2B								
1936	Cin-N	—	1	0	0	0	0	0
1949	Phi-N	.986	82	240	189	6	54	-10
1950	StL-N	1.000	1	3	3	0	2	1
Total	3	.986	84	243	192	6	56	-9
3B								
1937	Cin-N	1.000	4	1	1	0	0	0

■ Elmer Miller OF

YEAR	TM/L	PCT	G	PO	A	E	DP	FR
1912	StL-N	1.000	11	24	1	0	1	1
1915	NY-A	.955	26	41	1	2	0	-4
1916	NY-A	.969	42	84	9	3	5	5
1917	NY-A	.961	112	204	16	9	2	-6
1918	NY-A	.947	62	149	13	9	0	4
1921	NY-A	.947	56	134	10	8	2	3
1922	NY-A	.982	51	101	7	2	0	-2
	Bos-A	.957	35	85	3	4	2	0
	Yr	.970	86	186	10	6	2	-2
Total	7	.960	395	822	60	7	12	1

■ Doggie Miller C

YEAR	TM/L	PCT	G	PO	A	E	DP	FR
1884	Pit-a	.902	36	173	47	24	3	-10
1885	Pit-a	.893	33	177	49	27	4	-3
1886	Pit-a	.918	61	247	56	27	0	-25
1887	Pit-N	.928	73	266	58	25	1	-24
1888	Pit-N	.908	68	268	76	35	6	-18
1889	Pit-N	.889	76	299	87	**48**	8	-6
1890	Pit-N	.917	10	38	17	5	1	-2
1891	Pit-N	.938	41	190	51	16	2	4
1892	Pit-N	.943	63	265	80	21	10	-1
1893	Pit-N	.916	40	141	45	17	3	0
1894	StL-N	.941	41	140	36	11	3	-2
1895	StL-N	.932	46	137	41	13	5	-7
1896	Lou-N	.922	48	138	50	16	4	-7
Total	13	.918	636	2479	693	285	50	101
OF								
1884	Pit-a	.798	49	74	13	22	1	5
1885	Pit-a	.857	6	6	0	1	0	-2
1886	Pit-a	.889	23	37	3	5	0	-1
1888	Pit-N	.838	14	28	3	6	1	-1
1889	Pit-N	.915	32	58	7	6	0	3
1890	Pit-N	.934	27	52	5	4	0	2
1891	Pit-N	.952	25	34	6	2	1	1
1892	Pit-N	.906	76	96	10	11	2	-9
1894	StL-N	.857	4	5	1	1	0	0
1895	StL-N	.762	21	28	4	10	1	-1
1896	Lou-N	1.000	8	10	1	0	1	-1

YEAR	TM/L	PCT	G	PO	A	E	DP	FR
Total	12	.872	309	464	55	6	6	-11
3B								
1884	Pit-a	.714	3	3	2	2	0	-1
1885	Pit-a	.500	2	0	1	1	0	-1
1887	Pit-N	—	1	0	0	0	0	0
1888	Pit-N	.824	4	5	9	3	2	1
1889	Pit-N	.938	3	6	9	1	1	1
1890	Pit-N	.850	88	127	213	60	18	10
1891	Pit-N	.853	34	33	83	20	1	-2
1892	Pit-N	.667	2	1	1	1	0	-1
1894	StL-N	.832	52	68	96	33	6	-7
1895	StL-N	.829	46	54	72	26	5	-12
1896	Lou-N	.786	8	3	19	6	3	-1
Total	11	.840	243	300	505	153	36	-13
SS								
1885	Pit-a	.750	2	2	10	4	0	0
1890	Pit-N	.839	13	16	36	10	1	-6
1891	Pit-N	.823	37	66	101	36	10	-16
1892	Pit-N	.905	19	51	54	11	10	-1
1894	StL-N	.600	1	2	1	2	0	-1
1895	StL-N	.881	9	10	27	5	1	-3
1896	Lou-N	.600	2	2	1	2	1	-1
Total	7	.844	83	149	230	0	23	-28
2B								
1884	Pit-a	.667	1	2	0	1	0	-1
1886	Pit-a	.750	1	2	4	2	1	-1
1890	Pit-N	.872	6	21	13	5	0	-2
1894	StL-N	.880	18	31	50	11	3	-4
1896	Lou-N	.921	25	28	54	7	6	-8
Total	5	.887	51	84	121	6	10	-16
1B								
1891	Pit-N	1.000	1	14	1	0	0	0
1894	StL-N	.984	12	115	7	2	5	0
1895	StL-N	.980	6	47	1	1	4	-1
1896	Lou-N	1.000	3	21	5	0	0	2
Total	4	.986	22	197	14	3	9	1

■ Hughie Miller 1B

YEAR	TM/L	PCT	G	PO	A	E	DP	FR
1914	StL-F	.990	130	1256	65	14	48	0
1915	StL-F	1.000	6	13	0	0	0	0
Total	2	.990	136	1269	65	4	48	0

■ Dots Miller 1B

YEAR	TM/L	PCT	G	PO	A	E	DP	FR
1910	Pit-N	—	1	0	0	0	0	0
1912	Pit-N	.985	147	1385	85	23	93	1
1913	Pit-N	.985	150	1400	78	22	67	-2
1914	StL-N	.993	91	1019	57	8	46	2
1915	StL-N	.991	94	1000	50	10	54	-1
1916	StL-N	.993	93	948	43	7	60	1
1917	StL-N	.998	46	518	26	1	36	1
1919	StL-N	.981	68	687	40	14	34	0
1920	Phi-N	.988	9	80	5	1	7	0
1921	Phi-N	.974	38	396	23	11	26	-1
Total	10	.988	737	7433	407	7	423	1
2B								
1909	Pit-N	.953	150	260	426	34	50	-11
1910	Pit-N	.946	119	263	318	33	45	-19
1911	Pit-N	.943	129	273	357	38	65	-6
1914	StL-N	.867	5	5	8	2	2	0
1915	StL-N	.970	55	136	156	9	28	6
1916	StL-N	.971	38	72	98	5	14	3
1917	StL-N	.960	92	219	308	22	56	17
1919	StL-N	.951	28	69	87	8	13	2
1920	Phi-N	.948	59	134	160	16	34	-10
1921	Phi-N	.962	6	8	17	1	1	0
Total	10	.953	681	1439	1935	168	308	-18
SS								
1910	Pit-N	1.000	1	3	3	0	0	0
1913	Pit-N	.769	3	6	4	3	1	-2
1914	StL-N	.944	60	152	182	20	19	-2
1915	StL-N	.933	3	6	8	1	1	-1
1916	StL-N	.931	21	36	58	7	10	-1
1917	StL-N	.902	11	18	28	5	8	0
1920	Phi-N	.889	12	20	28	6	5	-1
Total	7	.929	111	241	311	2	44	-7
3B								
1915	StL-N	1.000	9	0	1	0	0	0
1916	StL-N	1.000	1	0	1	0	0	0
1920	Phi-N	.938	17	20	41	4	2	2
1921	Phi-N	.940	41	37	73	7	9	2
Total	4	.940	68	57	116	1	11	4
OF								
1920	Phi-N	—	1	0	0	0	0	0

■ Joe Miller SS

YEAR	TM/L	PCT	G	PO	A	E	DP	FR
1884	Tol-a	.864	105	125	320	70	26	1
1885	Lou-a	.891	79	94	266	44	23	0
Total	2	.876	184	219	586	114	49	1
3B								
1885	Lou-a	.698	11	12	25	16	1	0
2B								
1885	Lou-a	.873	8	17	38	8	2	3

■ Hack Miller OF

YEAR	TM/L	PCT	G	PO	A	E	DP	FR
1916	Bro-N	1.000	3	1	0	0	0	0
1918	Bos-A	1.000	10	10	0	0	0	-3
1922	Chi-N	.959	116	219	15	10	3	-5
1923	Chi-N	.978	129	256	17	6	4	2
1924	Chi-N	.948	32	54	1	3	0	-5
1925	Chi-N	.878	21	35	1	5	1	-4
Total	6	.962	311	575	34	4	8	-15

■ Otto Miller C

YEAR	TM/L	PCT	G	PO	A	E	DP	FR
1910	Bro-N	.987	28	116	37	2	2	9
1911	Bro-N	.927	22	61	28	7	0	-3
1912	Bro-N	.975	94	455	141	15	11	12
1913	Bro-N	.962	103	448	12	18	13	-37
1914	Bro-N	.964	50	233	65	11	5	0
1915	Bro-N	.981	83	363	91	9	8	8
1916	Bro-N	.968	69	311	85	13	6	4

YEAR	TM/L	PCT	G	PO	A	E	DP	FR
1917	Bro-N	.979	91	412	95	11	8	1
1918	Bro-N	.972	62	276	77	10	6	4
1919	Bro-N	.966	51	223	58	10	5	2
1920	Bro-N	.986	89	418	65	7	8	-1
1921	Bro-N	.972	91	338	107	13	10	10
1922	Bro-N	.968	57	216	56	9	3	4
Total	13	.973	890	3870	917	135	85	13
1B								
1913	Bro-N	1.000	1	12	0	0	1	0
1914	Bro-N	1.000	1	3	1	0	0	0
1918	Bro-N	1.000	1	13	1	0	1	0
Total	3	1.000	3	28	2	0	2	0

■ Norm Miller OF

YEAR	TM/L	PCT	G	PO	A	E	DP	FR
1965	Hou-N	1.000	2	2	0	0	0	0
1966	Hou-N	1.000	8	12	0	0	0	0
1967	Hou-N	.967	53	84	3	3	1	-1
1968	Hou-N	.971	74	131	1	4	1	-2
1969	Hou-N	.984	114	172	7	3	3	0
1970	Hou-N	.947	72	101	6	6	1	-1
1971	Hou-N	1.000	20	23	0	0	0	-2
1972	Hou-N	1.000	29	35	1	0	1	-1
1973	Hou-N	—	1	0	0	0	0	0
	Atl-N	.667	1	2	0	1	0	0
	Yr	.667	2	2	0	1	0	0
1974	Atl-N	1.000	4	3	1	0	0	0
Total	10	.972	378	565	19	7	7	-7
3B								
1966	Hou-N	.875	2	3	4	1	2	0
C								
1970	Hou-N	1.000	1	2	0	0	0	0
1971	Hou-N	—	1	0	0	0	0	0
Total	2	1.000	2	2	0	0	0	0

■ Otto Miller 3B

YEAR	TM/L	PCT	G	PO	A	E	DP	FR
1927	StL-A	.917	11	8	14	2	2	0
1930	Bos-A	.948	83	78	160	13	13	-4
1931	Bos-A	.953	75	75	147	11	12	1
Total	3	.949	169	161	321	6	27	-3
2B								
1930	Bos-A	.938	15	19	41	4	7	-2
1931	Bos-A	.966	25	60	83	5	15	-1
Total	2	.958	40	79	124	9	22	-3
SS								
1927	StL-A	.938	35	21	40	4	7	-4

■ Ralph Miller 3B

YEAR	TM/L	PCT	G	PO	A	E	DP	FR
1920	Phi-N	.940	91	89	179	17	15	1
1921	Phi-N	.857	10	16	32	8	4	5
Total	2	.927	101	105	211	5	19	6
SS								
1920	Phi-N	1.000	2	3	4	0	1	0
1921	Phi-N	.910	46	91	132	22	20	-5
Total	2	.913	48	94	136	2	21	-5
1B								
1920	Phi-N	.929	3	13	0	1	0	0
2B								
1924	Was-A	.941	3	5	11	1	1	0
OF								
1920	Phi-N	—	1	0	0	0	0	0

■ Rick Miller OF

YEAR	TM/L	PCT	G	PO	A	E	DP	FR
1971	Bos-A	.969	14	30	1	1	0	2
1972	Bos-A	.967	75	80	7	3	0	10
1973	Bos-A	.978	137	301	4	7	1	-11
1974	Bos-A	.989	105	253	7	3	3	-4
1975	Bos-A	.981	65	101	2	2	1	7
1976	Bos-A	.991	82	220	4	2	1	7
1977	Bos-A	.992	79	118	5	1	3	2
1978	Cal-A	.989	129	353	9	4	5	21
1979	Cal-A	.989	117	349	3	4	1	6
1980	Cal-A	.984	118	299	11	5	3	0
1981	Bos-A	.987	95	219	5	3	0	-6
1982	Bos-A	.983	127	277	6	5	2	-12
1983	Bos-A	.993	66	141	4	1	1	1
1984	Bos-A	.974	31	36	1	1	0	0
1985	Bos-A	1.000	8	9	0	0	0	0
Total	15	.986	1248	2786	69	2	21	23
1B								
1983	Bos-A	1.000	2	10	1	0	1	0
1984	Bos-A	1.000	8	44	4	0	1	0
Total	2	1.000	10	54	5	0	2	0

■ Doc Miller OF

YEAR	TM/L	PCT	G	PO	A	E	DP	FR
1910	Bos-N	.951	130	203	9	11	3	-14
1911	Bos-N	.961	146	243	26	11	4	-2
1912	Bos-N	.948	50	79	12	5	4	-2
	Phi-N	.986	40	61	9	1	1	0
	Yr	.964	90	140	21	6	5	-2
1913	Phi-N	.800	12	8	0	2	0	-3
1914	Cin-N	.976	47	79	2	2	1	-3
Total	5	.958	425	673	58	2	13	-24

■ Ward Miller OF

YEAR	TM/L	PCT	G	PO	A	E	DP	FR
1909	Pit-N	.967	14	28	1	1	0	-1
	Cin-N	.981	26	51	2	1	0	-7
	Yr	.976	40	79	3	2	0	-8
1910	Cin-N	.944	26	44	7	3	1	2
1912	Chi-N	.943	64	109	6	7	2	-5
1913	Chi-N	.980	63	136	9	3	5	8
1914	StL-F	.953	111	248	15	13	3	10
1915	StL-F	.963	154	299	16	12	3	3
1916	StL-A	.943	136	218	12	14	0	-5
1917	StL-A	.966	25	24	4	1	1	-4
Total	8	.957	619	1157	72	5	15	1

■ Wally Millies C

YEAR	TM/L	PCT	G	PO	A	E	DP	FR
1934	Bro-N	1.000	2	10	1	0	1	1
1936	Was-A	.968	72	205	40	8	3	0
1937	Was-A	.971	56	199	33	7	7	2
1939	Phi-N	.964	84	229	37	10	3	-8

YEAR	TM/L	PCT	G	PO	A	E	DP	FR
1940	Phi-N	.958	24	59	9	3	0	2
1941	Phi-N	.800	1	2	2	1	0	0
Total	6	.966	239	704	122	9	14	-3

■ Jocko Milligan C

YEAR	TM/L	PCT	G	PO	A	E	DP	FR
1884	Phi-a	.939	65	474	100	37	5	11
1885	Phi-a	.935	61	419	84	35	11	8
1886	Phi-a	.919	40	231	51	25	5	-1
1887	Phi-a	.907	47	262	79	35	10	7
1888	StL-a	.941	58	317	85	25	11	6
1889	StL-a	.933	66	367	105	34	7	16
1890	Phi-P	.893	59	260	66	39	13	6
1891	Phi-a	.939	87	470	101	37	9	0
1892	Was-N	.947	59	237	87	18	10	5
1893	Bal-N	.833	1	5	0	1	0	-1
	NY-N	.934	42	188	67	18	5	15
	Yr	.932	43	193	67	19	5	14
Total	10	.930	585	3230	825	304	86	72
1B								
1885	Phi-a	.968	6	59	1	2	3	0
1886	Phi-a	.981	29	291	12	6	8	2
1887	Phi-a	.966	50	436	13	16	21	-1
1888	StL-a	1.000	5	38	1	0	1	0
1889	StL-a	.968	9	58	2	2	3	0
1890	Phi-P	.963	3	26	0	1	1	-1
1891	Phi-a	.981	32	293	11	6	18	0
1892	Was-N	.980	28	285	12	6	12	-1
1893	Bal-N	.981	22	187	17	4	10	2
Total	9	.976	184	1673	69	3	77	1
OF								
1884	Phi-a	1.000	1	3	1	0	0	1
1885	Phi-a	—	2	0	0	0	0	-1
1886	Phi-a	.857	5	12	0	2	0	0
1887	Phi-a	—	1	0	0	0	0	-1
Total	4	.889	9	15	1	2	0	-1
3B								
1886	Phi-a	.750	2	4	5	3	0	0

■ Randy Milligan 1B

YEAR	TM/L	PCT	G	PO	A	E	DP	FR
1988	Pit-N	.987	25	213	15	3	19	-1
1989	Bal-A	.995	117	914	83	5	92	1
1990	Bal-A	.990	98	846	87	9	94	5
Total	3	.992	240	1973	185	7	205	5
OF								
1988	Pit-N	—	2	0	0	0	0	0

■ Buster Mills OF

YEAR	TM/L	PCT	G	PO	A	E	DP	FR
1934	StL-N	1.000	18	45	0	0	0	1
1935	Bro-N	.971	17	33	0	1	0	-1
1937	Bos-A	.946	120	239	8	14	0	-4
1938	StL-A	.964	113	235	9	9	2	3
1940	NY-A	1.000	14	22	0	0	0	-2
1942	Cle-A	.973	53	142	4	4	2	8
1946	Cle-A	1.000	6	11	0	0	0	0
Total	7	.964	341	727	21	8	4	5

■ Eddie Milner OF

YEAR	TM/L	PCT	G	PO	A	E	DP	FR
1981	Cin-N	1.000	4	2	0	0	0	0
1982	Cin-N	.987	107	215	8	3	1	6
1983	Cin-N	.990	139	392	9	4	0	13
1984	Cin-N	.983	108	285	8	5	4	6
1985	Cin-N	.983	135	340	12	6	3	9
1986	Cin-N	.990	127	292	6	3	0	1
1987	SF-N	.993	84	135	2	1	0	4
1988	Cin-N	.968	15	29	1	1	0	1
Total	8	.987	719	1690	44	3	8	40

■ John Milner 1B

YEAR	TM/L	PCT	G	PO	A	E	DP	FR
1972	NY-N	1.000	10	73	6	0	9	0
1973	NY-N	.989	95	771	47	9	66	-5
1974	NY-N	.994	133	1147	77	7	103	-1
1975	NY-N	.991	29	204	25	2	21	4
1976	NY-N	1.000	12	44	2	0	4	1
1977	NY-N	.994	87	672	48	4	64	0
1978	Pit-N	.984	28	169	13	3	15	0
1979	Pit-N	.989	48	255	18	3	27	-1
1980	Pit-N	.991	70	502	32	5	48	-2
1981	Pit-N	.980	8	48	1	1	2	-1
	Mon-N	.978	21	165	16	4	14	1
	Yr	.979	29	213	17	5	16	0
1982	Mon-N	1.000	5	23	2	0	4	0
	Pit-N	1.000	1	1	0	0	1	0
	Yr	1.000	6	24	2	0	5	0
Total	11	.991	547	4074	287	8	378	-6
OF								
1971	NY-N	1.000	3	8	1	0	0	1
1972	NY-N	.965	91	160	7	6	0	1
1973	NY-N	.949	29	33	4	2	0	0
1975	NY-N	.985	31	63	2	1	0	1
1976	NY-N	.985	112	195	7	3	2	-1
1977	NY-N	.968	22	28	2	1	1	0
1978	Pit-N	1.000	69	118	1	0	0	-2
1979	Pit-N	.958	64	112	2	5	1	-5
1980	Pit-N	.889	11	8	0	1	0	-1
1981	Pit-N	1.000	8	12	0	0	0	0
Total	10	.976	440	737	26	9	4	-6

■ Mike Milosevich SS

YEAR	TM/L	PCT	G	PO	A	E	DP	FR
1944	NY-A	.954	91	176	281	22	68	7
1945	NY-A	.957	22	36	52	4	11	0
Total	2	.954	113	212	333	6	79	7
2B								
1945	NY-A	1.000	1	1	3	0	0	1

■ Don Mincher 1B

YEAR	TM/L	PCT	G	PO	A	E	DP	FR
1960	Was-A	.977	20	209	5	5	14	-4
1961	Was-A	.969	29	234	18	8	28	-1
1962	Min-A	.978	25	211	13	5	17	-1
1963	Min-A	.983	60	446	27	8	34	-5
1964	Min-A	.992	76	549	43	5	50	0
1965	Min-A	.992	99	818	45	7	64	-3

YEAR	TM/L	PCT	G	PO	A	E	DP	FR
1966	Min-A	.992	130	995	85	9	62	5
1967	Cal-A	.994	142	1177	88	8	92	-1
1968	Cal-A	.991	113	949	59	9	90	-3
1969	Sea-A	.995	122	1033	93	6	98	8
1970	Oak-A	.990	137	1109	91	12	107	2
1971	Oak-A	.996	27	202	23	1	11	3
	Was-A	.990	88	705	59	8	80	3
	Yr	.991	115	907	82	9	91	6
1972	Tex-A	.994	59	467	44	3	45	6
	Oak-A	.988	11	77	3	1	4	-1
	Yr	.993	70	544	47	4	49	5
Total	13	.990	1138	9181	696	5	796	8
OF								
1965	Min-A	—	1	0	0	0	0	0
1967	Cal-A	1.000	1	1	0	0	0	0
Total	2	1.000	2	1	0	0	0	0

■ Minnie Minoso OF

YEAR	TM/L	PCT	G	PO	A	E	DP	FR
1949	Cle-A	1.000	7	11	0	0	0	0
1951	Chi-A	.961	82	145	4	6	0	-8
1952	Chi-A	.979	143	322	11	7	3	10
1953	Chi-A	.967	147	279	15	10	3	1
1954	Chi-A	.978	146	340	14	8	3	12
1955	Chi-A	.971	138	287	19	9	3	12
1956	Chi-A	.974	148	284	10	8	1	-3
1957	Chi-A	.984	152	293	9	5	2	-1
1958	Cle-A	.975	147	301	13	8	1	7
1959	Cle-A	.985	148	314	14	5	1	12
1960	Chi-A	.980	154	282	14	6	3	3
1961	Chi-A	.956	147	273	10	13	2	-4
1962	StL-N	.972	27	33	2	1	0	-2
1963	Was-A	.955	74	103	4	5	0	-10
1964	Chi-A	1.000	5	9	0	0	0	0
Total	15	.974	1665	3276	139	1	22	29
3B								
1951	Chi-A	.936	68	82	122	14	10	-3
1952	Chi-A	1.000	9	1	11	0	0	1
1953	Chi-A	.895	10	3	14	2	0	-1
1954	Chi-A	.947	9	7	11	1	1	-1
1955	Chi-A	1.000	2	2	2	0	1	0
1956	Chi-A	.800	8	2	6	2	0	-1
1957	Cle-A	—	1	0	0	0	0	0
1958	Cle-A	—	1	0	0	0	0	0
1963	Was-A	1.000	8	5	22	0	1	1
Total	9	.939	116	102	188	9	13	-4
1B								
1951	Cle-A	.952	7	37	3	2	1	0
1956	Chi-A	1.000	1	1	0	0	0	0
Total	2	.953	8	38	3	2	1	0
SS								
1951	Chi-A	1.000	1	0	1	0	0	0
1952	Chi-A	—	1	0	0	0	0	0
Total	2	1.000	2	0	1	0	0	0

■ Willie Miranda SS

YEAR	TM/L	PCT	G	PO	A	E	DP	FR
1951	Was-A	.818	2	7	2	2	0	0
1952	Chi-A	1.000	4	4	9	0	2	2
	StL-A	.900	7	6	12	2	1	-1
	Chi-A	.975	50	68	129	5	26	10
	Yr	.970	61	78	150	7	29	11
1953	StL-A	.933	8	8	6	1	1	3
	NY-A	.984	45	52	74	2	19	17
	Yr	.979	53	60	80	3	20	20
1954	NY-A	.948	89	89	129	12	36	16
1955	Bal-A	.958	153	300	481	34	101	19
1956	Bal-A	.962	147	229	436	26	91	2
1957	Bal-A	.966	115	166	324	17	59	-3
1958	Bal-A	.962	102	137	216	14	53	-2
1959	Bal-A	.974	47	51	98	4	23	20
Total	9	.962	768	1117	1916	119	412	83
3B								
1952	Chi-A	1.000	4	0	4	0	1	1
	Chi-A	1.000	1	1	0	0	0	0
	Yr	1.000	5	1	4	0	1	1
1953	StL-A	1.000	6	1	2	0	0	1
1954	NY-A	1.000	1	1	4	0	0	1
1959	Bal-A	.933	11	6	8	1	1	1
Total	4	.964	23	9	18	1	2	4
2B								
1952	Chi-A	1.000	1	0	4	0	0	2
	Chi-A	1.000	1	0	4	0	0	2
	Yr	1.000	2	0	8	0	0	4
1954	NY-A	1.000	4	1	0	0	0	0
1955	Bal-A	1.000	1	0	1	0	0	0
1959	Bal-A	1.000	5	3	2	0	1	1
Total	4	1.000	12	4	11	0	1	5
1B								
1951	Was-A	1.000	1	2	0	0	0	0

■ Johnny Mitchell SS

YEAR	TM/L	PCT	G	PO	A	E	DP	FR
1921	NY-A	.958	7	6	17	1	1	-1
1922	NY-A	1.000	1	2	0	0	1	-1
	Bos-A	.962	58	98	184	11	31	-4
	Yr	.963	62	99	186	11	31	-5
1923	Bos-A	.961	87	184	264	18	40	1
1924	Bro-N	.951	64	131	216	18	30	-1
1925	Bro-N	.947	90	184	266	25	49	-4
Total	5	.955	310	604	949	3	151	-10
2B								
1921	NY-A	.762	5	7	9	5	0	-5
1923	Bos-A	1.000	5	10	7	0	0	-1
Total		.868	10	17	16	5	0	-6

■ Kevin Mitchell OF

YEAR	TM/L	PCT	G	PO	A	E	DP	FR
1986	NY-N	.983	68	114	3	2	1	0
1987	SD-N	1.000	3	3	0	0	0	0
	SF-N	—	3	0	0	0	0	0
	Yr	1.000	6	3	0	0	0	0
1988	SF-N	.908	40	57	2	6	0	-3
1989	SF-N	.978	147	305	8	7	0	1
1990	SF-N	.971	138	295	9	9	3	2
Total	5	.971	399	774	22	4	4	0
3B								
1984	NY-N	.833	5	1	4	1	2	-1
1986	NY-N	.941	7	7	9	1	0	-1
1987	SD-N	.945	51	29	108	8	9	4
	SF-N	.962	68	44	131	7	10	-4
	Yr	.954	119	73	239	15	19	0
1988	SF-N	.943	102	61	203	16	18	-1
1989	SF-N	1.000	2	0	2	0	0	0
Total	5	.948	235	142	457	3	39	-3
SS								
1986	NY-N	.935	24	31	56	6	7	-6
1987	SF-N	1.000	1	0	1	0	0	0
Total	2	.936	25	31	57	6	7	-6
1B								
1986	NY-N	.875	2	6	1	1	2	0

■ Dale Mitchell OF

YEAR	TM/L	PCT	G	PO	A	E	DP	FR
1946	Cle-A	1.000	11	28	0	0	0	0
1947	Cle-A	.977	115	252	8	6	1	1
1948	Cle-A	.991	140	307	12	3	3	3
1949	Cle-A	.994	149	337	10	2	2	1
1950	Cle-A	.972	127	236	3	7	1	-12
1951	Cle-A	.992	124	253	3	2	0	-4
1952	Cle-A	.992	128	258	2	2	0	-5
1953	Cle-A	.970	125	224	2	7	1	-11
1954	Cle-A	.889	6	7	1	1	0	-1
1955	Cle-A	1.000	3	1	0	0	0	0
1956	Cle-A	—	1	0	0	0	0	0
	Bro-N	1.000	2	3	0	0	0	0
Total	11	.985	931	1906	41	0	8	-28
1B								
1954	Cle-A	1.000	1	2	0	0	0	0
1955	Cle-A	1.000	8	26	0	0	5	0
Total	2	1.000	9	28	2	0	5	0

■ Mike Mitchell OF

YEAR	TM/L	PCT	G	PO	A	E	DP	FR
1907	Cin-N	.962	146	265	39	12	9	23
1908	Cin-N	.959	118	193	16	9	2	1
1909	Cin-N	.962	145	262	20	11	3	6
1910	Cin-N	.958	149	257	19	12	4	-5
1911	Cin-N	.971	140	280	23	9	8	7
1912	Cin-N	.947	144	251	18	15	8	-9
1913	Cin-N	.941	82	176	14	12	0	5
	Pit-N	.946	54	150	9	9	0	6
	Yr	.943	136	326	23	21	0	11
1914	Pit-N	.984	76	174	11	3	6	7
	Was-A	.957	53	99	11	5	0	4
Total	8	.959	1107	2107	180	7	40	45

■ Bobby Mitchell OF

YEAR	TM/L	PCT	G	PO	A	E	DP	FR
1980	LA-N	1.000	8	5	0	0	0	1
1981	LA-N	1.000	7	6	0	0	0	0
1982	Min-A	.997	121	350	8	1	3	10
1983	Min-A	.990	44	94	2	1	1	-1
Total	4	.996	180	455	10	2	4	10

■ Bobby Mitchell OF

YEAR	TM/L	PCT	G	PO	A	E	DP	FR
1970	NY-A	1.000	7	20	0	0	0	1
1971	Mil-A	.974	19	35	2	1	1	3
1973	Mil-A	.960	20	24	0	1	0	-2
1974	Mil-A	.969	26	30	1	1	0	1
1975	Mil-A	.992	72	128	2	1	1	-2
Total	5	.984	144	237	5	4	2	1

■ George Mitterwald C

YEAR	TM/L	PCT	G	PO	A	E	DP	FR
1966	Min-A	1.000	3	13	0	0	0	1
1968	Min-A	.961	10	69	4	3	0	0
1969	Min-A	.987	63	340	33	5	6	11
1970	Min-A	.996	117	740	62	3	8	24
1971	Min-A	.986	120	656	53	10	7	-11
1972	Min-A	.984	61	272	33	5	4	6
1973	Min-A	.992	122	676	59	6	6	4
1974	Chi-N	.974	68	335	40	10	4	-3
1975	Chi-N	.976	59	247	32	7	4	-2
1976	Chi-N	.981	64	320	40	7	2	1
1977	Chi-N	.989	109	621	78	8	13	12
Total	11	.987	796	4289	434	4	54	43
1B								
1975	Chi-N	.987	10	68	6	1	6	1
1976	Chi-N	.995	25	192	10	1	11	-1
1977	Chi-N	1.000	1	2	0	0	0	0
Total	3	.993	36	262	16	2	17	0
OF								
1969	Min-A	—	1	0	0	0	0	0

■ Johnny Mize 1B

YEAR	TM/L	PCT	G	PO	A	E	DP	FR
1936	StL-N	.994	97	897	66	6	63	1
1937	StL-N	.988	144	1308	67	17	104	-13
1938	StL-N	.989	140	1297	93	15	117	-2
1939	StL-N	.987	152	1348	90	19	123	-4
1940	StL-N	.990	153	1376	80	14	105	-7
1941	StL-N	.994	122	1157	82	8	104	3
1942	NY-N	.995	138	1393	74	8	98	-3
1946	NY-N	.989	101	928	83	11	80	5
1947	NY-N	.996	154	1381	118	6	120	9
1948	NY-N	.991	152	1359	111	13	114	4
1949	NY-N	.994	101	906	65	6	77	2
	NY-A	.980	6	47	3	1	5	0
1950	NY-A	.996	72	490	31	2	73	-3
1951	NY-A	.994	93	632	44	4	86	-4
1952	NY-A	.987	27	218	18	3	32	1
1953	NY-A	1.000	15	113	7	0	19	0
Total	15	.992	1667	14850	1032	133	1320	-11
OF								
1936	StL-N	1.000	8	12	1	0	0	1

■ John Mizerock C

YEAR	TM/L	PCT	G	PO	A	E	DP	FR
1983	Hou-N	.967	33	154	24	6	5	2
1985	Hou-N	.966	15	77	8	3	1	4
1986	Hou-N	.987	42	221	12	3	0	4
1989	Atl-N	1.000	11	48	4	0	0	1
Total	4	.979	101	500	48	2	6	11

■ Dave Moates OF

YEAR	TM/L	PCT	G	PO	A	E	DP	FR
1975	Tex-A	.984	51	114	6	2	1	6
1976	Tex-A	.991	66	106	4	1	2	9
Total	2	.987	117	220	10	3	3	15

■ Danny Moeller OF

YEAR	TM/L	PCT	G	PO	A	E	DP	FR
1907	Pit-N	.800	11	11	1	3	1	-2
1908	Pit-N	.950	27	38	0	2	0	-4
1912	Was-A	.944	132	227	25	15	5	10
1913	Was-A	.926	153	249	27	22	4	6
1914	Was-A	.930	150	208	19	17	4	-1
1915	Was-A	.952	116	167	13	9	6	-2
1916	Was-A	.963	63	94	11	4	3	2
	Cle-A	1.000	8	8	0	0	0	-2
	Yr	.966	71	102	11	4	3	0
Total	7	.938	660	1002	96	2	23	7
2B								
1916	Cle-A	1.000	1	3	2	0	1	0

■ Johnny Mokan OF

YEAR	TM/L	PCT	G	PO	A	E	DP	FR
1921	Pit-N	.946	15	35	0	2	0	0
1922	Pit-N	.903	23	25	3	3	1	-4
	Phi-N	.905	37	62	5	7	1	-4
	Yr	.905	60	87	8	10	2	-8
1923	Phi-N	.969	105	235	16	8	1	7
1924	Phi-N	.986	94	195	9	3	1	0
1925	Phi-N	.984	68	120	1	2	0	-5
1926	Phi-N	.967	123	221	16	8	4	-7
1927	Phi-N	.962	63	97	5	4	0	-6
Total	7	.966	528	990	55	7	8	-19
3B								
1922	Phi-N	.800	2	3	1	1	1	-1
1923	Phi-N	1.000	1	2	3	0	0	1
Total	2	.900	3	5	4	1	1	0

■ Bob Molinaro OF

YEAR	TM/L	PCT	G	PO	A	E	DP	FR
1975	Det-A	1.000	6	8	1	0	0	-1
1977	Chi-A	1.000	1	1	0	0	0	0
1978	Chi-A	1.000	62	88	2	0	0	-3
1979	Bal-A	1.000	5	7	0	0	0	1
1980	Chi-A	.957	49	85	3	4	0	-3
1981	Chi-A	1.000	2	3	0	0	0	0
1982	Chi-N	1.000	4	2	0	0	0	-1
Total	7	.980	129	194	6	4	0	-7

■ Paul Molitor 3B

YEAR	TM/L	PCT	G	PO	A	E	DP	FR
1978	Mil-A	1.000	1	2	0	0	0	0
1980	Mil-A	1.000	1	1	1	0	0	0
1982	Mil-A	.942	150	128	340	29	48	1
1983	Mil-A	.966	146	105	343	16	37	2
1984	Mil-A	.933	7	7	21	2	3	3
1985	Mil-A	.953	135	126	263	19	30	-2
1986	Mil-A	.944	91	82	170	15	25	2
1987	Mil-A	.947	41	25	64	5	8	-1
1988	Mil-A	.941	105	86	187	17	15	-8
1989	Mil-A	.950	112	78	243	17	18	7
1990	Mil-A	.900	2	2	7	1	1	1
Total	11	.950	791	642	1639	121	185	5
2B								
1978	Mil-A	.976	91	197	283	12	57	-10
1979	Mil-A	.979	122	289	413	15	81	3
1980	Mil-A	.971	91	240	294	16	80	-1
1987	Mil-A	1.000	19	35	49	0	16	2
1988	Mil-A	1.000	1	1	0	0	0	0
1989	Mil-A	.986	16	28	44	1	9	-3
1990	Mil-A	.988	60	136	190	4	36	-1
Total	7	.979	400	926	1274	8	279	-10
SS								
1978	Mil-A	.945	31	54	118	10	17	5
1979	Mil-A	.979	10	20	27	1	3	-2
1980	Mil-A	.938	12	19	41	4	10	-1
1982	Mil-A	.842	4	6	10	3	0	-2
Total	4	.942	57	99	196	8	30	0
OF								
1981	Mil-A	.976	46	119	4	3	1	4
1986	Mil-A	1.000	4	4	1	0	0	1
Total	2	.977	50	123	5	3	1	5
1B								
1990	Mil-A	.986	37	325	25	5	28	-1

■ Fritz Mollwitz 1B

YEAR	TM/L	PCT	G	PO	A	E	DP	FR
1913	Chi-N	1.000	2	19	0	0	0	0
1914	Chi-N	.962	4	24	1	1	0	0
	Cin-N	.991	32	315	20	3	18	1
	Yr	.989	36	339	21	4	18	1
1915	Cin-N	.996	153	1545	79	7	107	0
1916	Cin-N	.981	54	482	23	10	29	0
	Chi-N	.976	19	116	7	3	6	0
	Yr	.980	73	598	30	13	35	0
1917	Pit-N	.994	36	341	17	2	16	-1
1918	Pit-N	.990	119	1252	73	13	67	0
1919	Pit-N	.994	53	478	19	3	21	-3
	StL-N	.994	25	299	15	2	20	1
	Yr	.994	78	777	34	5	41	-2
Total	7	.991	497	4871	254	4	284	-2
OF								
1914	Chi-N	—	1	0	0	0	0	0
1916	Chi-N	.889	6	8	0	1	0	-1
1919	Pit-N	1.000	1	1	0	0	0	0
Total	3	.900	8	9	0	1	0	-1
2B								
1917	Pit-N	1.000	1	0	1	0	0	0

■ Rick Monday OF

YEAR	TM/L	PCT	G	PO	A	E	DP	FR
1966	KC-A	.964	15	26	1	1	0	1
1967	KC-A	.972	113	260	14	8	6	11

YEAR	TM/L	PCT	G	PO	A	E	DP	FR
1968	Oak-A	.978	144	299	11	7	3	-5
1969	Oak-A	.964	119	262	3	10	0	-7
1970	Oak-A	.981	109	257	3	5	2	-2
1971	Oak-A	.984	111	238	6	4	1	-2
1972	Chi-N	**.996**	134	268	6	1	2	-12
1973	Chi-N	.973	148	317	9	9	2	-4
1974	Chi-N	.984	139	302	10	5	**5**	-2
1975	Chi-N	.973	131	315	6	9	0	-2
1976	Chi-N	.993	103	278	4	2	0	1
1977	LA-N	.991	115	208	3	2	0	-18
1978	LA-N	.995	103	209	3	1	0	0
1979	LA-N	.964	10	27	0	1	0	1
1980	LA-N	.969	50	92	1	3	0	-2
1981	LA-N	.962	41	50	1	2	0	-5
1982	LA-N	.943	57	62	4	4	0	-7
1983	LA-N	.969	44	62	1	2	0	-3
1984	LA-N	1.000	2	2	0	0	0	0
Total	19	.979	1688	3534	86	6	21	-57
	1B							
1976	Chi-N	.991	32	309	22	3	17	1
1977	LA-N	1.000	3	13	2	0	0	0
1978	LA-N	1.000	1	8	0	0	1	0
1982	LA-N	1.000	4	24	3	0	2	0
1983	LA-N	.950	4	18	1	1	1	0
1984	LA-N	.987	10	72	4	1	3	-1
Total	6	.990	54	444	32	5	24	0

■ **Don Money** 3B

YEAR	TM/L	PCT	G	PO	A	E	DP	FR
1970	Phi-N	.961	119	131	236	15	27	11
1971	Phi-N	.953	68	52	130	9	13	1
1972	Phi-N	**.978**	151	**139**	316	10	31	**20**
1973	Mil-A	**.971**	124	112	224	10	24	-19
1974	Mil-A	**.989**	157	131	336	5	42	-9
1975	Mil-A	.951	99	95	179	14	22	-19
1976	Mil-A	.958	103	96	202	13	21	-4
1977	Mil-A	.952	15	9	31	2	1	0
1978	Mil-A	.987	25	21	55	1	9	2
1979	Mil-A	1.000	26	18	64	0	6	2
1980	Mil-A	.940	55	41	117	10	18	1
1981	Mil-A	.977	56	27	100	3	8	-5
1982	Mil-A	.923	16	10	38	4	2	3
1983	Mil-A	.980	11	15	33	1	0	5
Total	14	.968	1025	897	2061	7	224	-11
	2B							
1971	Phi-N	.981	20	41	64	2	6	1
1974	Mil-A	—	1	0	0	0	0	0
1977	Mil-A	.981	116	256	357	12	82	-3
1978	Mil-A	.984	36	66	116	3	30	-2
1979	Mil-A	.971	16	26	42	2	7	-2
1980	Mil-A	1.000	2	3	3	0	2	0
1982	Mil-A	—	1	0	0	0	0	0
Total	7	.981	192	392	582	9	127	-6
	SS							
1968	Phi-N	1.000	4	6	8	0	3	-1
1969	Phi-N	.969	126	212	443	21	82	17
1970	Phi-N	1.000	2	2	0	0	1	0
1972	Phi-N	1.000	2	1	0	0	0	0
1973	Mil-A	.966	21	34	52	3	17	-4
1975	Mil-A	.967	7	14	15	1	2	-2
1976	Mil-A	—	1	0	0	0	0	0
1978	Mil-A	.917	2	3	8	1	0	0
Total	8	.968	165	272	526	6	105	10
	1B							
1978	Mil-A	.994	61	615	37	4	49	-2
1979	Mil-A	1.000	19	196	11	0	20	-1
1980	Mil-A	.986	14	132	9	2	15	0
1981	Mil-A	1.000	1	6	0	0	1	0
1982	Mil-A	1.000	11	62	11	0	9	3
1983	Mil-A	1.000	2	10	0	0	2	0
Total	6	.995	108	1021	68	6	96	0
	OF							
1971	Phi-N	1.000	40	74	3	0	2	0
1977	Mil-A	.956	23	41	2	2	0	-1
Total	2	.984	63	115	5	2	2	-1

■ **Ed Montague** SS

YEAR	TM/L	PCT	G	PO	A	E	DP	FR
1928	Cle-A	.914	15	22	31	5	7	4
1930	Cle-A	.917	46	84	104	17	19	-14
1931	Cle-A	.924	64	127	202	27	30	16
1932	Cle-A	.891	57	91	129	27	22	-13
Total	4	.912	182	324	466	6	78	-7
	3B							
1928	Cle-A	.800	9	10	14	6	3	1
1930	Cle-A	1.000	13	13	21	0	1	-1
1932	Cle-A	.900	11	5	13	2	2	0
Total	3	.905	33	28	48	8	6	0

■ **Willie Montanez** 1B

YEAR	TM/L	PCT	G	PO	A	E	DP	FR
1966	Cal-A	1.000	2	1	0	0	1	0
1970	Phi-N	1.000	5	7	2	0	3	1
1971	Phi-N	1.000	9	13	1	0	1	0
1972	Phi-N	.992	14	111	7	1	16	0
1973	Phi-N	.994	99	785	52	5	87	-3
1974	Phi-N	.992	137	1216	79	10	126	-1
1975	Phi-N	.990	21	183	17	2	20	2
	SF-N	.994	134	1150	81	8	114	-1
	Yr	.993	155	1333	98	10	134	1
1976	SF-N	.989	58	583	51	7	54	4
	Atl-N	.986	103	986	56	15	87	-6
	Yr	.987	161	1569	107	22	141	-2
1977	Atl-N	.992	134	1129	70	10	88	-4
1978	NY-N	.995	158	1350	**104**	8	**138**	5
1979	NY-N	.989	108	905	76	11	95	3
	Tex-A	.995	19	191	16	1	14	1
1980	SD-N	.994	124	1185	84	8	105	1
	Mon-N	1.000	4	29	2	0	0	0
	Yr	.994	128	1214	86	8	105	1
1981	Mon-N	.992	16	117	12	1	8	1
	Pit-N	1.000	11	56	1	0	4	-1
	Yr	.995	27	173	13	1	12	0
1982	Pit-N	1.000	2	5	1	0	1	0
	Phi-N	1.000	6	4	2	0	0	1
	Yr	1.000	8	9	3	0	1	1
Total	14	.992	1164	10006	714	7	962	1
	OF							
1970	Phi-N	1.000	10	8	1	0	0	1
1971	Phi-N	.972	158	364	11	11	3	-2
1972	Phi-N	.985	130	318	**15**	5	2	8
1973	Phi-N	.986	51	67	6	1	2	1
1974	Phi-N	1.000	1	1	0	0	0	0
1982	Pit-N	—	2	0	0	0	0	0
Total	6	.979	352	758	33	7	7	8

■ **Bob Montgomery** C

YEAR	TM/L	PCT	G	PO	A	E	DP	FR
1970	Bos-A	.981	22	143	13	3	3	0
1971	Bos-A	.989	66	361	15	4	3	-2
1972	Bos-A	.985	22	120	10	2	2	-2
1973	Bos-A	.974	33	168	19	5	2	0
1974	Bos-A	.977	79	318	28	8	3	-6
1975	Bos-A	.987	53	210	23	3	6	-5
1976	Bos-A	.983	30	106	12	2	2	-1
1977	Bos-A	.982	15	50	6	1	0	1
1978	Bos-A	.976	10	35	5	1	0	1
1979	Bos-A	.984	31	121	5	2	0	-4
Total	10	.983	361	1632	136	1	21	-20
	1B							
1975	Bos-A	.939	6	29	2	2	1	0

■ **Wally Moon** OF

YEAR	TM/L	PCT	G	PO	A	E	DP	FR
1954	StL-N	.978	148	387	11	9	2	-3
1955	StL-N	.975	100	188	5	5	1	-3
1956	StL-N	.988	97	159	8	2	2	-3
1957	StL-N	.966	133	245	8	9	1	-4
1958	StL-N	.984	82	122	5	2	0	-9
1959	LA-N	.983	143	224	13	4	2	0
1960	LA-N	.986	127	194	15	3	3	1
1961	LA-N	.970	133	186	5	6	1	-9
1962	LA-N	.981	36	51	2	1	1	0
1963	LA-N	.962	96	125	2	5	0	-12
1964	LA-N	1.000	23	33	0	0	0	-2
1965	LA-N	1.000	23	25	1	0	0	-5
Total	12	.978	1141	1939	75	6	13	-49
	1B							
1955	StL-N	.986	51	445	34	7	40	-1
1956	StL-N	.984	52	498	47	9	52	2
1959	LA-N	1.000	1	2	0	0	0	0
1962	LA-N	.978	32	249	18	6	28	-2
Total	4	.983	136	1194	99	2	120	-1

■ **Junior Moore** 3B

YEAR	TM/L	PCT	G	PO	A	E	DP	FR
1976	Atl-N	.929	6	5	8	1	1	0
1977	Atl-N	.942	104	86	189	17	10	-3
1978	Chi-A	.857	6	4	8	2	0	-1
1980	Chi-A	.929	34	28	64	7	6	-2
Total	4	.936	150	123	269	7	17	-6
	OF							
1976	Atl-N	1.000	1	1	0	0	0	0
1978	Chi-A	1.000	5	8	1	0	0	1
1979	Chi-A	.966	61	83	3	3	0	-2
1980	Chi-A	1.000	3	2	0	0	0	0
Total	4	.970	70	94	4	3	0	-1
	2B							
1976	Atl-N	1.000	1	1	2	0	0	0
1977	Atl-N	—	1	0	0	0	0	0
1979	Chi-A	1.000	2	0	2	0	0	0
Total	3	1.000	4	1	4	0	0	0
	1B							
1980	Chi-A	1.000	1	0	1	0	0	0

■ **Charlie Moore** C

YEAR	TM/L	PCT	G	PO	A	E	DP	FR
1973	Mil-A	.981	8	48	5	1	0	3
1974	Mil-A	.985	61	229	28	4	5	3
1975	Mil-A	.960	47	194	21	9	2	-5
1976	Mil-A	.969	49	207	42	8	1	0
1977	Mil-A	.980	137	566	78	**13**	10	-5
1978	Mil-A	.983	95	314	41	6	2	-3
1979	Mil-A	.979	106	414	58	10	7	9
1980	Mil-A	.989	105	319	28	4	3	-15
1981	Mil-A	.970	34	147	16	5	0	-1
1982	Mil-A	.960	20	86	29	4	2	-1
1983	Mil-A	1.000	7	8	1	0	0	-1
1984	Mil-A	.964	7	26	1	1	0	0
1985	Mil-A	.977	102	504	54	13	7	5
1986	Mil-A	.992	72	425	43	4	6	12
1987	Tor-A	.984	44	236	10	4	0	8
Total	15	.980	894	3723	435	6	45	9
	OF							
1975	Mil-A	.977	22	40	2	1	0	-1
1976	Mil-A	.978	28	42	2	1	0	0
1981	Mil-A	1.000	8	13	1	0	0	1
1982	Mil-A	.988	115	231	13	3	**6**	2
1983	Mil-A	.978	150	301	9	7	1	-7
1984	Mil-A	.984	61	119	2	2	0	0
1985	Mil-A	1.000	3	7	0	0	0	0
1986	Mil-A	1.000	4	4	1	0	1	1
1987	Tor-A	.667	5	1	1	1	0	0
Total	9	.981	396	758	31	5	8	-4
	2B							
1982	Mil-A	1.000	1	0	1	0	0	0
1986	Mil-A	1.000	1	0	1	0	0	0
Total	2	1.000	2	0	2	0	0	0
	3B							
1976	Mil-A	1.000	1	0	1	0	0	0

■ **Gene Moore** OF

YEAR	TM/L	PCT	G	PO	A	E	DP	FR
1931	Cin-N	1.000	3	8	0	0	0	0
1933	StL-N	.967	10	29	0	0	0	1
1934	StL-N	.923	3	12	0	1	0	1
1936	Bos-N	.977	151	314	**32**	8	2	13
1937	Bos-N	.978	148	340	**21**	8	1	**11**
1938	Bos-N	.981	47	97	4	2	0	-1
1939	Bro-N	.961	86	140	8	6	3	-7
1940	Bro-N	1.000	6	8	0	0	0	-1
	Bos-N	.986	94	198	11	3	3	2
	Yr	.986	100	206	11	3	3	1
1941	Bos-N	.968	110	229	13	8	2	1
1942	Was-N	—	1	0	0	0	0	0
1943	Was-N	.985	57	125	5	2	0	-1
1944	StL-A	.968	98	208	5	7	2	-1
1945	StL-A	.970	100	184	10	6	0	-6
Total	13	.975	914	1892	109	2	13	12
	1B							
1939	Bro-N	1.000	1	1	0	0	0	0
1943	Was-N	—	1	0	0	0	0	0
1944	StL-A	.667	1	2	0	1	1	0
Total	3	.750	3	3	0	1	1	0

■ **Eddie Moore** 2B

YEAR	TM/L	PCT	G	PO	A	E	DP	FR
1924	Pit-N	1.000	4	1	4	0	0	0
1925	Pit-N	.952	122	307	401	**36**	82	-6
1926	Pit-N	.911	29	49	63	11	15	-9
	Bos-N	.973	39	90	123	6	27	-3
	Yr	.950	63	139	186	17	42	-12
1927	Bos-N	.966	39	101	125	8	26	1
1928	Bos-N	1.000	1	0	1	0	0	0
1929	Bro-N	.955	74	135	228	17	31	-18
1930	Bro-N	.991	23	42	72	1	13	4
1932	NY-N	1.000	5	7	13	0	2	2
1934	Cle-A	.932	18	51	45	7	11	-1
Total	9	.956	349	783	1075	6	207	-28
	OF							
1924	Pit-N	.988	35	78	6	1	1	1
1925	Pit-N	.972	15	32	3	1	0	1
1927	Bos-N	1.000	16	47	1	0	1	1
1928	Bos-N	.958	54	131	7	6	3	3
1929	Bro-N	.875	2	7	0	1	0	0
1930	Bro-N	.981	23	51	0	1	0	0
Total	6	.973	145	346	17	0	5	6
	SS							
1923	Pit-N	.923	6	12	12	2	2	-5
1926	Pit-N	.714	1	2	3	2	1	-1
	Bos-N	.921	14	24	34	5	5	-1
	Yr	.900	15	26	37	7	6	-2
1927	Bos-N	1.000	1	3	4	0	3	1
1929	Bro-N	.948	36	63	120	10	21	0
1930	Bro-N	.893	17	24	43	8	10	0
1932	NY-N	.930	21	44	63	8	11	0
1934	Cle-A	1.000	2	1	1	0	0	0
Total	7	.928	98	173	280	5	53	-6
	3B							
1924	Pit-N	1.000	13	14	24	0	1	0
1925	Pit-N	.667	3	1	3	2	0	-2
1926	Pit-N	.962	9	5	20	1	0	0
	Bos-N	1.000	1	0	2	0	1	0
	Yr	.964	10	5	22	1	1	0
1927	Bos-N	.947	52	49	93	8	6	-5
1929	Bro-N	—	1	1	0	0	0	0
1930	Bro-N	—	1	0	0	0	0	0
1932	NY-N	.857	6	1	5	1	0	0
1934	Cle-A	1.000	3	4	1	0	0	0
Total	8	.949	89	74	148	2	8	-7

■ **Johnny Moore** OF

YEAR	TM/L	PCT	G	PO	A	E	DP	FR
1929	Chi-N	.971	15	32	1	1	0	1
1931	Chi-N	.964	22	51	3	2	0	0
1932	Chi-N	.983	109	272	12	5	2	-6
1933	Cin-N	.974	132	329	12	9	4	7
1934	Cin-N	1.000	10	23	0	0	0	0
	Phi-N	.981	115	244	18	5	2	7
	Yr	.983	125	267	18	5	2	7
1935	Phi-N	.973	150	233	18	7	6	-13
1936	Phi-N	.948	112	214	5	12	1	-9
1937	Phi-N	.943	72	124	9	8	1	-4
Total	8	.970	737	1522	78	9	16	-17

■ **Jo-Jo Moore** OF

YEAR	TM/L	PCT	G	PO	A	E	DP	FR
1930	NY-N	1.000	1	2	0	0	0	0
1931	NY-N	1.000	1	2	0	0	0	0
1932	NY-N	.982	86	160	6	3	1	-7
1933	NY-N	.966	132	266	19	10	6	3
1934	NY-N	.954	131	242	8	12	1	-12
1935	NY-N	.972	155	342	11	10	2	-1
1936	NY-N	.981	149	291	25	6	3	6
1937	NY-N	.975	140	226	12	6	0	-10
1938	NY-N	.978	114	214	8	5	1	-4
1939	NY-N	.986	136	260	13	4	2	0
1940	NY-N	.982	133	259	9	5	1	-2
1941	NY-N	.972	116	237	5	7	0	-5
Total	12	.975	1294	2501	116	8	17	-32

■ **Randy Moore** OF

YEAR	TM/L	PCT	G	PO	A	E	DP	FR
1927	Chi-A	1.000	4	8	1	0	1	0
1928	Chi-A	.946	16	34	1	2	0	0
1930	Bos-N	.986	34	70	3	1	0	2
1931	Bos-N	.952	29	55	4	3	1	0
1932	Bos-N	.987	41	75	2	1	0	-4
1933	Bos-N	.979	122	275	11	6	1	1
1934	Bos-N	.965	72	157	7	6	1	0
1935	Bos-N	.950	78	161	10	9	3	1
1936	Bro-N	.964	21	27	0	1	0	-3
1937	StL-N	—	1	0	0	0	0	0
Total	10	.969	418	862	39	9	6	-2
	1B							
1932	Bos-N	.984	22	167	16	3	20	0
1933	Bos-N	.988	10	80	1	1	4	-2
1934	Bos-N	.983	37	339	16	6	23	-3
1935	Bos-N	.982	21	209	10	4	11	-2

YEAR	TM/L	PCT	G	PO	A	E	DP	FR
Total	4	.984	90	795	43	4	58	-7
3B								
1930	Bos-N	.868	13	9	24	5	3	-1
1931	Bos-N	.944	22	16	35	3	2	1
1932	Bos-N	.985	31	16	49	1	8	-3
Total	3	.943	66	41	108	9	13	-3
C								
1932	Bos-N	—	1	0	0	0	0	0
1937	Bro-N	.889	10	27	5	4	0	0
Total	2	.889	11	27	5	4	0	0
2B								
1931	Bos-N	—	1	0	0	0	0	0

■ Terry Moore OF

YEAR	TM/L	PCT	G	PO	A	E	DP	FR
1935	StL-N	.984	117	354	11	6	3	12
1936	StL-N	.977	133	**418**	14	10	**7**	17
1937	StL-N	.988	106	307	9	4	2	9
1938	StL-N	.987	75	219	5	3	1	5
1939	StL-N	**.994**	121	291	16	2	1	7
1940	StL-N	.987	133	**383**	11	5	4	**14**
1941	StL-N	.984	121	293	14	5	3	4
1942	StL-N	.986	126	271	9	4	0	-7
1946	StL-N	.982	66	158	5	3	0	-1
1947	StL-N	.983	120	292	6	5	2	-2
1948	StL-N	.993	71	131	2	1	0	-5
Total	11	.985	1189	3117	102	8	23	53
3B								
1938	StL-N	.893	6	9	16	3	1	2
1942	StL-N	.000	1	0	0	1	0	0
Total	2	.862	7	9	16	4	1	2

■ Andres Mora OF

YEAR	TM/L	PCT	G	PO	A	E	DP	FR
1976	Bal-A	.951	31	55	3	3	0	-1
1977	Bal-A	1.000	57	66	2	0	0	-8
1978	Bal-A	.978	69	129	4	3	0	-1
1980	Cle-A	1.000	3	6	0	0	0	0
Total	4	.978	160	256	9	6	0	-10
3B								
1977	Bal-A	—	1	0	0	0	0	0

■ Jerry Morales OF

YEAR	TM/L	PCT	G	PO	A	E	DP	FR
1969	SD-N	1.000	19	27	2	0	1	2
1970	SD-N	.926	26	25	0	2	0	-2
1971	SD-N	1.000	7	8	0	0	0	0
1972	SD-N	.987	96	214	8	3	2	10
1973	SD-N	.991	100	214	5	2	1	4
1974	Chi-N	.975	143	266	5	7	2	-5
1975	Chi-N	.979	151	273	11	6	1	-1
1976	Chi-N	.983	136	273	12	5	**6**	5
1977	Chi-N	.985	128	247	8	4	3	-12
1978	StL-N	.977	126	254	5	6	0	-1
1979	Det-A	.986	119	206	6	3	2	-7
1980	NY-N	.973	63	107	3	3	1	3
1981	Chi-N	.986	72	142	2	2	1	-3
1982	Chi-N	1.000	41	72	5	0	1	7
1983	Chi-N	1.000	29	29	1	0	0	0
Total	15	.983	1256	2357	73	3	21	0
3B								
1972	SD-N	.000	4	0	0	1	0	0

■ Rich Morales SS

YEAR	TM/L	PCT	G	PO	A	E	DP	FR
1967	Chi-A	.944	7	6	11	1	1	2
1968	Chi-A	.966	7	12	16	1	4	2
1969	Chi-A	1.000	13	9	23	0	4	3
1970	Chi-A	.967	24	14	45	2	8	5
1971	Chi-A	.976	57	66	138	5	14	-1
1972	Chi-A	.968	86	120	213	11	32	-5
1973	SD-N	1.000	10	15	24	0	4	3
1974	SD-N	.933	29	16	26	3	4	2
Total	8	.970	233	258	496	3	71	11
2B								
1968	Chi-A	1.000	5	5	10	0	1	0
1969	Chi-A	.976	38	68	95	4	18	7
1970	Chi-A	.980	12	24	25	1	2	0
1971	Chi-A	.875	3	2	5	1	1	0
1972	Chi-A	1.000	16	10	14	0	4	1
1973	Chi-A	1.000	2	2	2	0	0	0
	SD-N	.988	79	176	239	5	45	19
	SD-N	.948	18	31	24	3	7	3
Total	7	.981	173	318	414	4	78	30
3B								
1969	Chi-A	—	1	0	0	0	0	0
1970	Chi-A	.889	20	11	21	4	4	0
1971	Chi-A	.885	18	7	16	3	3	0
1972	Chi-A	1.000	14	3	21	0	2	2
1973	Chi-A	1.000	5	1	3	0	0	1
1974	SD-N	1.000	6	2	11	0	1	1
Total	6	.932	64	24	72	7	9	4
OF								
1971	Chi-A	—	1	0	0	0	0	0
1B								
1974	SD-N	1.000	1	5	0	0	0	0

■ Charles Moran SS

YEAR	TM/L	PCT	G	PO	A	E	DP	FR
1903	Was-A	**.943**	96	216	300	31	37	3
1904	Was-A	.919	61	114	171	25	17	-14
Total	2	.935	157	330	471	6	54	-11
3B								
1904	Was-A	1.000	1	2	3	0	0	1
	StL-A	.937	81	69	169	16	2	-3
	Yr	.938	82	71	172	16	2	-2
1905	StL-A	.706	5	7	5	5	1	-3
Total	2	.924	87	78	177	1	3	-5
2B								
1903	Was-A	.933	2	4	10	1	2	2
1905	StL-A	.954	20	36	47	4	6	1
Total	2	.951	22	40	57	5	8	1
OF								
1904	StL-A	—	1	0	0	0	0	0

■ Herbie Moran OF

YEAR	TM/L	PCT	G	PO	A	E	DP	FR
1908	Phi-A	.952	19	39	1	2	0	1
	Bos-N	1.000	8	19	2	0	3	2
1909	Bos-N	1.000	8	14	1	0	0	0
1910	Bos-N	.958	20	39	7	2	3	4
1912	Bro-N	.961	129	273	24	12	5	1
1913	Bro-N	.950	129	231	15	13	7	-5
1914	Cin-N	.954	107	175	11	9	4	-7
	Bos-N	.940	41	59	4	4	0	-6
	Yr	.950	148	234	15	13	4	-13
1915	Bos-N	.964	123	168	17	7	3	-7
Total	7	.957	584	1017	82	9	25	-17

■ Pat Moran C

YEAR	TM/L	PCT	G	PO	A	E	DP	FR
1901	Bos-N	.973	28	159	20	5	4	-1
1902	Bos-N	**.982**	71	333	95	8	5	2
1903	Bos-N	.967	107	500	**214**	24	**17**	**21**
1904	Bos-N	.957	72	326	114	20	**12**	0
1905	Bos-N	**.986**	78	389	113	7	5	14
1906	Chi-N	.979	61	335	78	9	6	2
1907	Chi-N	.973	59	258	72	9	9	-1
1908	Chi-N	.968	45	242	56	10	5	2
1909	Chi-N	.984	74	381	97	8	3	0
1910	Phi-N	.989	56	278	83	4	5	0
1911	Phi-N	.984	32	148	41	3	4	-1
1912	Phi-N	.955	13	35	7	2	1	-1
1914	Phi-N	—	1	0	0	0	0	0
Total	13	.976	697	3384	990	109	76	37
3B								
1901	Bos-N	.667	4	1	3	2	0	-1
1904	Bos-N	.890	39	47	83	16	4	3
Total	2	.882	43	48	86	8	4	2
1B								
1901	Bos-N	.958	13	133	5	6	4	-2
1902	Bos-N	1.000	3	6	0	0	0	0
1903	Bos-N	1.000	1	8	0	0	0	0
1904	Bos-N	.955	2	18	3	1	0	1
Total	4	.961	19	165	8	7	4	-1
OF								
1901	Bos-N	1.000	3	4	0	0	0	0
1902	Bos-N	1.000	1	1	0	0	0	0
Total	2	1.000	4	5	0	0	0	0
SS								
1901	Bos-N	.857	3	1	5	1	0	-2
2B								
1901	Bos-N	1.000	1	1	4	0	0	0

■ Al Moran SS

YEAR	TM/L	PCT	G	PO	A	E	DP	FR
1963	NY-N	.951	116	189	332	27	57	6
1964	NY-N	.957	15	14	31	2	5	4
Total	2	.951	131	203	363	9	62	10
3B								
1963	NY-N	1.000	1	1	0	0	0	0
1964	NY-N	1.000	1	1	0	0	0	0
Total	2	1.000	2	2	0	0	0	0

■ Billy Moran 2B

YEAR	TM/L	PCT	G	PO	A	E	DP	FR
1958	Cle-A	.960	74	136	154	12	38	**13**
1959	Cle-A	1.000	6	6	8	0	1	0
1961	LA-A	.966	51	108	116	8	31	-4
1962	LA-A	.986	160	**422**	477	13	103	19
1963	LA-A	.973	151	**352**	**455**	**22**	98	**15**
1964	LA-A	1.000	3	1	3	0	1	0
	Cle-A	.978	15	23	21	1	3	1
	Yr	.980	18	24	24	1	4	1
1965	Cle-A	1.000	7	4	6	0	2	1
Total	7	.976	467	1052	1240	6	277	45
3B								
1964	LA-A	.929	47	47	84	10	5	-6
	Cle-A	.972	42	34	69	3	4	2
	Yr	.947	89	81	153	13	9	-4
SS								
1958	Cle-A	.969	38	38	56	3	18	0
1959	Cle-A	.889	5	7	1	1	1	-1
1961	LA-A	.833	2	1	4	1	0	0
1964	LA-A	—	1	0	0	0	0	0
1965	Cle-A	1.000	1	2	5	0	0	0
Total	5	.958	47	48	66	5	19	-1
1B								
1964	Cle-A	—	2	0	0	0	0	0

■ Ray Morehart 2B

YEAR	TM/L	PCT	G	PO	A	E	DP	FR
1924	Chi-A	.857	2	4	2	1	0	-1
1926	Chi-A	.950	48	71	136	11	13	-5
1927	NY-A	.945	53	101	175	16	27	4
Total	3	.946	103	176	313	8	40	-2
SS								
1924	Chi-A	.873	27	35	68	15	12	-11

■ Keith Moreland OF

YEAR	TM/L	PCT	G	PO	A	E	DP	FR
1980	Phi-N	1.000	2	3	1	0	0	1
1981		—	2	0	0	0	0	0
1982	Chi-N	.989	86	169	9	2	0	4
1983	Chi-N	.976	151	236	7	6	1	-12
1984	Chi-N	.976	103	154	6	4	0	-8
1985	Chi-N	.976	148	233	10	6	2	-9
1986	Chi-N	.980	121	181	13	4	3	-4
1988	SD-N	.982	64	107	2	2	0	-4
Total	8	.979	677	1083	48	4	6	-32
3B								
1980	Phi-N	.800	4	2	2	1	0	0
1981	Phi-N	.810	7	7	10	4	1	-1
1982	Chi-N	1.000	2	4	2	0	0	-1
1984	Chi-N	1.000	8	5	4	0	1	-2
1985	Chi-N	.886	11	8	13	4	1	-4
1986	Chi-N	.917	24	10	34	4	3	-4
1987	Chi-N	.934	150	99	300	**28**	27	4
1988	SD-N	.875	2	3	4	1	0	0
1989	Det-A	.846	12	2	20	4	2	-2
Total	9	.920	220	140	389	6	35	-10

YEAR	TM/L	PCT	G	PO	A	E	DP	FR
C								
1978	Phi-N	1.000	1	4	0	0	0	0
1979	Phi-N	1.000	13	71	3	0	1	0
1980	Phi-N	.967	39	183	21	7	7	-2
1981	Phi-N	.982	50	256	20	5	2	-7
1982	Chi-N	.975	44	211	27	6	2	-5
1983	Chi-N	1.000	3	8	0	0	0	-1
1984	Chi-N	1.000	3	4	0	0	0	0
1985	Chi-N	1.000	2	2	0	0	0	0
1986	Chi-N	.984	13	57	6	1	0	-3
1989	Det-A	—	1	0	0	0	0	0
Total	10	.979	169	796	77	9	12	-18
1B								
1981	Phi-N	1.000	2	4	1	0	1	0
1984	Chi-N	.977	29	230	20	6	18	-1
1985	Chi-N	.962	12	70	6	3	4	-1
1986	Chi-N	1.000	12	92	5	0	10	-1
1987	Chi-N	—	1	0	0	0	0	0
1988	SD-N	.994	73	637	52	4	55	0
1989	Det-A	1.000	31	241	12	0	21	-4
Total	7	.991	160	1274	96	3	109	-7

■ Omar Moreno OF

YEAR	TM/L	PCT	G	PO	A	E	DP	FR
1975	Pit-N	.000	1	0	0	1	0	0
1976	Pit-N	.960	42	93	3	4	1	4
1977	Pit-N	.977	147	366	10	9	4	1
1978	Pit-N	.984	152	409	9	7	2	11
1979	Pit-N	.975	**162**	**490**	11	13	3	15
1980	Pit-N	.990	**162**	**479**	15	5	2	18
1981	Pit-N	.997	103	302	6	1	1	5
1982	Pit-N	.983	157	396	10	7	3	5
1983	Hou-N	.977	97	251	8	6	3	4
	NY-A	.992	48	120	1	1	1	4
1984	NY-A	.985	108	262	9	4	2	-3
1985	NY-A	1.000	26	56	2	0	0	6
	KC-A	1.000	21	30	1	0	1	1
	Yr	1.000	47	86	3	0	1	1
1986	Atl-N	.977	97	151	8	5	3	-4
Total	12	.982	1323	3405	93	3	26	61

■ Ed Morgan 1B

YEAR	TM/L	PCT	G	PO	A	E	DP	FR
1928	Cle-A	.968	36	335	27	12	36	0
1930	Cle-A	.987	129	1275	80	18	116	1
1931	Cle-A	.984	117	1114	72	**19**	102	2
1932	Cle-A	.985	142	**1430**	74	**23**	100	-7
1933	Cle-A	.997	32	302	21	1	14	3
1934	Bos-A	.988	137	1283	56	16	111	-7
Total	6	.986	593	5739	330	9	479	-8
OF								
1928	Cle-A	.974	21	34	3	1	0	-3
1929	Cle-A	.908	80	100	8	11	1	-11
1930	Cle-A	1.000	19	23	0	0	0	-4
1933	Cle-A	—	1	0	0	0	0	0
Total	4	.933	121	157	11	2	1	-18
3B								
1928	Cle-A	.919	14	18	39	5	5	3
1931	Cle-A	.917	3	3	8	1	0	1
1932	Cle-A	.000	1	0	0	1	0	0
Total	3	.907	18	21	47	7	5	4

■ Joe Morgan 2B

YEAR	TM/L	PCT	G	PO	A	E	DP	FR
1963	Hou-N	.909	7	15	15	3	2	-3
1964	Hou-N	.949	10	31	25	3	4	0
1965	Hou-N	.969	157	348	492	**27**	82	-2
1966	Hou-N	.965	117	256	316	21	61	-16
1967	Hou-N	.979	130	297	344	14	67	-5
1968	Hou-N	.882	5	9	6	2	2	-4
1969	Hou-N	.972	132	303	328	18	79	-2
1970	Hou-N	.979	142	349	430	17	98	11
1971	Hou-N	.986	**157**	336	**482**	12	93	-3
1972	Cin-N	**.990**	149	**370**	436	8	92	-7
1973	Cin-N	.990	154	**417**	440	9	**106**	-8
1974	Cin-N	.982	142	344	385	13	92	-13
1975	Cin-N	**.986**	142	356	425	11	96	-7
1976	Cin-N	.981	133	342	335	13	85	-23
1977	Cin-N	**.993**	151	**351**	359	5	100	-18
1978	Cin-N	.980	124	252	290	11	49	-31
1979	Cin-N	.980	121	259	329	12	74	-13
1980	Hou-N	.988	130	244	348	7	68	-12
1981	SF-N	.991	87	177	258	4	61	-11
1982	SF-N	.989	120	254	364	7	69	-5
1983	Phi-N	.971	117	231	331	17	63	-2
1984	Oak-A	.977	100	201	229	10	62	-31
Total	22	.981	2527	5742	6967	244	1505	205
OF								
1967	Hou-N	1.000	1	2	0	0	0	0
1968	Hou-N	1.000	1	1	0	0	0	0
1969	Hou-N	1.000	14	12	0	0	0	-1
Total	3	1.000	16	15	0	0	0	-1
3B								
1982	SF-N	.750	3	1	2	1	0	-1

■ Ray Morgan 2B

YEAR	TM/L	PCT	G	PO	A	E	DP	FR
1912	Was-A	.939	76	150	173	21	21	-7
1913	Was-A	.950	134	254	359	32	**61**	-5
1914	Was-A	.948	146	290	379	37	**58**	-9
1915	Was-A	.965	57	102	175	10	23	-2
1916	Was-A	.957	82	133	222	16	34	-12
1917	Was-A	.961	95	206	243	18	45	-7
1918	Was-A	.959	80	172	251	19	29	-4
Total	7	.953	670	1307	1802	152	271	-46
3B								
1911	Was-A	.900	25	29	43	8	1	-3
1912	Was-A	1.000	1	0	1	0	0	0
1915	Was-A	1.000	1	0	1	0	0	0
1916	Was-A	—	1	0	0	0	0	0
1917	Was-A	.833	3	4	6	2	0	-1
Total	5	.894	32	33	51	0	1	-4

SS

YEAR	TM/L	PCT	G	PO	A	E	DP	FR
1912	Was-A	.875	4	7	7	2	2	0
1913	Was-A	.952	4	7	13	1	0	-1
1915	Was-A	.667	2	3	3	3	1	-2
1916	Was-A	.878	9	12	24	5	1	-3
Total	4	.874	19	29	47	1	4	-6

1B

YEAR	TM/L	PCT	G	PO	A	E	DP	FR
1916	Was-A	.975	3	39	0	1	2	-1

OF

YEAR	TM/L	PCT	G	PO	A	E	DP	FR
1918	Was-A	1.000	2	3	0	0	1	0

■ Bobby Morgan 2B

YEAR	TM/L	PCT	G	PO	A	E	DP	FR
1952	Bro-N	1.000	5	6	3	0	0	0
1954	Phi-N	.933	5	6	8	1	1	0
1955	Phi-N	.980	88	192	204	8	46	-11
1956	Phi-N	1.000	3	7	7	0	1	0
	StL-N	.980	13	25	25	1	3	1
	Yr	.985	16	32	32	1	4	1
1957	Phi-N	1.000	1	1	0	0	0	1
	Chi-N	.976	116	220	343	14	58	9
	Yr	.976	117	221	343	14	58	10
Total	5	.978	231	457	590	4	109	0

SS

YEAR	TM/L	PCT	G	PO	A	E	DP	FR
1950	Bro-N	.919	10	10	24	3	5	-2
1952	Bro-N	.882	4	10	5	2	1	-2
1953	Bro-N	.970	21	49	47	3	13	0
1954	Phi-N	.954	129	237	361	29	71	-23
1955	Phi-N	.958	41	89	117	9	23	-2
1956	StL-N	.941	6	8	8	1	2	0
Total	6	.954	211	403	562	7	115	-29

3B

YEAR	TM/L	PCT	G	PO	A	E	DP	FR
1950	Bro-N	.969	52	33	121	5	15	8
1952	Bro-N	.968	60	45	107	5	10	5
1953	Bro-N	.920	36	22	58	7	6	-2
1954	Phi-N	1.000	8	8	12	0	1	1
1955	Phi-N	.938	6	4	11	1	1	0
1956	Phi-N	.857	5	7	11	3	1	0
	StL-N	.889	11	9	23	4	1	0
	Yr	.877	16	16	34	7	2	0
1957	Chi-N	.971	12	15	18	1	1	-1
Total	7	.951	190	143	361	6	36	11

1B

YEAR	TM/L	PCT	G	PO	A	E	DP	FR
1955	Phi-N	1.000	1	6	0	0	0	0

■ George Moriarty 3B

YEAR	TM/L	PCT	G	PO	A	E	DP	FR
1903	Chi-N	1.000	1	3	1	0	0	0
1904	Chi-N	.778	2	4	3	2	0	0
1906	NY-A	.912	39	47	77	12	3	1
1907	NY-A	.899	91	115	160	31	8	-1
1908	NY-A	.933	28	47	78	9	2	10
1909	Det-A	**.939**	106	117	253	24	11	3
1910	Det-A	.927	134	165	302	37	17	-1
1911	Det-A	.929	129	157	273	33	11	-4
1912	Det-A	.933	33	42	70	8	6	-1
1913	Det-A	.938	94	122	183	20	9	-2
1914	Det-A	.956	126	125	**312**	20	16	**17**
1915	Det-A	.875	12	7	14	3	1	1
1916	Chi-A	1.000	1	0	1	0	0	0
Total	13	.931	796	951	1727	199	84	23

1B

YEAR	TM/L	PCT	G	PO	A	E	DP	FR
1906	NY-A	.964	5	51	3	2	2	0
1907	NY-A	.975	22	225	7	6	8	-3
1908	NY-A	.976	52	544	26	14	27	-3
1909	Det-A	.990	24	283	12	3	12	-1
1911	Det-A	1.000	1	5	1	0	0	0
1912	Det-A	.987	71	800	27	11	19	-6
1914	Det-A	1.000	3	26	1	0	0	0
1915	Det-A	1.000	1	3	0	0	0	0
1916	Chi-A	1.000	1	2	1	0	0	0
Total	9	.982	180	1939	78	6	68	-13

OF

YEAR	TM/L	PCT	G	PO	A	E	DP	FR
1904	Chi-N	.800	2	4	0	1	0	0
1906	NY-A	.917	15	31	2	3	0	0
1907	NY-A	.769	9	8	2	3	0	-1
1908	NY-A	.938	10	14	1	1	0	-1
1913	Det-A	.933	7	14	0	1	0	-1
1915	Det-A	1.000	1	1	0	0	0	0
Total	6	.895	44	72	5	9	0	-3

2B

YEAR	TM/L	PCT	G	PO	A	E	DP	FR
1906	NY-A	1.000	1	0	2	0	0	0
1907	NY-A	.950	8	22	16	2	3	-4
1908	NY-A	1.000	4	4	12	0	1	1
1915	Det-A	—	1	0	0	0	0	0
Total	4	.966	14	26	30	2	4	-3

SS

YEAR	TM/L	PCT	G	PO	A	E	DP	FR
1907	NY-A	.667	1	1	1	1	1	0

■ Russ Morman 1B

YEAR	TM/L	PCT	G	PO	A	E	DP	FR
1986	Chi-A	.989	47	342	26	4	31	-3
1988	Chi-A	.981	22	101	5	2	8	-1
1989	Chi-A	.988	35	157	13	2	21	1
1990	KC-A	1.000	3	19	3	0	1	0
Total	4	.988	107	619	47	8	61	-3

OF

YEAR	TM/L	PCT	G	PO	A	E	DP	FR
1988	Chi-A	1.000	10	13	0	0	0	0
1990	KC-A	1.000	8	8	1	0	0	0
Total	2	1.000	18	21	1	0	0	0

■ John Morrill 1B

YEAR	TM/L	PCT	G	PO	A	E	DP	FR
1876	Bos-N	.881	3	37	0	5	0	-1
1877	Bos-N	.932	18	170	8	13	11	0
1878	Bos-N	.957	59	606	22	28	**36**	3
1879	Bos-N	.968	33	313	16	11	23	**4**
1880	Bos-N	.966	46	434	**26**	16	26	**6**
1881	Bos-N	.969	74	743	37	25	32	6
1882	Bos-N	.964	76	741	19	28	22	-1
1883	Bos-N	**.974**	81	794	20	22	33	0
1884	Bos-N	.971	91	953	34	30	33	**5**
1885	Bos-N	.969	92	952	32	31	53	0

YEAR	TM/L	PCT	G	PO	A	E	DP	FR
1886	Bos-N	.963	42	396	24	16	23	3
1887	Bos-N	.984	**127**	1231	50	21	**76**	4
1888	Bos-N	.979	133	**1398**	**72**	31	67	9
1889	Was-N	.980	40	369	18	8	15	1
1890	Bos-P	1.000	1	15	0	0	0	0
Total	15	.971	916	9152	375	285	450	39

3B

YEAR	TM/L	PCT	G	PO	A	E	DP	FR
1877	Bos-N	.864	30	33	43	12	1	-7
1878	Bos-N	.667	1	1	3	2	0	-1
1879	Bos-N	.878	51	70	96	23	2	-2
1880	Bos-N	.837	40	44	69	22	4	-7
1881	Bos-N	1.000	2	6	10	0	1	3
1882	Bos-N	.750	1	2	1	1	1	-1
1883	Bos-N	.789	6	6	9	4	0	-1
1884	Bos-N	.600	2	0	3	2	0	-1
1885	Bos-N	.900	2	2	7	1	0	0
1889	Was-N	.500	3	2	2	4	1	-1
Total	10	.852	138	166	243	1	10	-18

2B

YEAR	TM/L	PCT	G	PO	A	E	DP	FR
1876	Bos-N	.857	37	105	117	37	18	6
1877	Bos-N	.760	3	10	9	6	2	0
1881	Bos-N	.967	4	15	14	1	0	0
1882	Bos-N	.933	2	7	7	1	0	1
1883	Bos-N	1.000	2	5	5	0	1	0
1884	Bos-N	.914	17	52	44	9	4	0
1885	Bos-N	.920	17	56	48	9	8	1
1886	Bos-N	.873	20	47	63	16	8	-2
1888	Bos-N	.833	2	3	7	2	0	-1
1889	Was-N	.833	1	2	3	1	0	0
Total	10	.883	105	302	317	2	41	5

SS

YEAR	TM/L	PCT	G	PO	A	E	DP	FR
1882	Bos-N	.733	3	2	9	4	0	-1
1883	Bos-N	.929	2	5	8	1	0	1
1886	Bos-N	.895	55	92	156	29	13	-2
1890	Bos-P	.750	1	1	2	1	0	0
Total	4	.887	61	100	175	5	13	-2

OF

YEAR	TM/L	PCT	G	PO	A	E	DP	FR
1876	Bos-N	.545	5	6	0	5	0	-2
1877	Bos-N	.611	11	10	1	7	0	-2
1878	Bos-N	1.000	1	1	0	0	0	0
1882	Bos-N	—	1	0	0	0	0	0
1883	Bos-N	.750	7	9	0	3	0	-2
1884	Bos-N	—	1	0	0	0	0	0
Total	6	.643	26	26	1	5	0	-6

C

YEAR	TM/L	PCT	G	PO	A	E	DP	FR
1876	Bos-N	.811	23	90	43	31	3	5

■ John Morris OF

YEAR	TM/L	PCT	G	PO	A	E	DP	FR
1986	StL-N	.986	31	68	0	1	0	2
1987	StL-N	.989	74	86	0	1	0	1
1988	StL-N	.857	16	12	0	2	0	-2
1989	StL-N	1.000	51	45	0	0	0	0
1990	StL-N	1.000	6	4	0	0	0	0
Total	5	.982	178	215	0	4	0	1

■ Jim Morrison 3B

YEAR	TM/L	PCT	G	PO	A	E	DP	FR
1977	Phi-N	.875	5	0	7	1	0	1
1978	Phi-N	1.000	3	2	1	0	0	0
1979	Chi-A	.943	29	17	65	5	5	5
1981	Chi-A	.956	87	64	199	12	14	8
1982	Chi-A	.914	50	19	87	10	10	-7
	Pit-N	.964	26	15	39	2	2	2
1983	Pit-N	.911	26	12	29	4	3	-2
1984	Pit-N	.938	61	32	119	10	8	1
1985	Pit-N	.961	59	39	84	5	9	-1
1986	Pit-N	.946	151	92	257	20	12	-13
1987	Pit-N	.975	82	46	151	5	11	0
	Det-A	.962	16	10	41	2	1	3
1988	Det-A	1.000	4	3	2	0	0	0
	Atl-N	.933	20	14	28	3	1	-1
Total	11	.949	619	365	1109	9	76	-4

2B

YEAR	TM/L	PCT	G	PO	A	E	DP	FR
1978	Phi-N	.968	31	86	96	6	22	13
1979	Chi-A	.982	48	104	120	4	33	-5
1980	Chi-A	.969	**161**	**422**	481	**29**	**117**	-3
1981	Chi-A	1.000	1	0	1	0	1	0
1982	Pit-N	1.000	1	2	4	0	0	0
1983	Pit-N	.973	28	42	65	3	16	5
1984	Pit-N	1.000	26	49	44	0	13	-1
1985	Pit-N	1.000	15	34	37	0	5	2
1986	Pit-N	1.000	1	0	1	0	0	0
1987	Pit-N	1.000	9	19	29	0	8	2
	Det-A	1.000	3	9	5	0	2	0
Total	10	.975	324	767	883	2	217	13

SS

YEAR	TM/L	PCT	G	PO	A	E	DP	FR
1980	Chi-A	1.000	1	0	1	0	0	0
1982	Pit-N	—	1	0	0	0	0	0
1983	Pit-N	1.000	7	2	5	0	2	0
1984	Pit-N	1.000	2	2	3	0	0	0
1986	Pit-N	—	1	0	0	0	0	0
1987	Pit-N	.931	17	7	20	2	5	-1
	Det-A	1.000	3	1	5	0	1	0
1988	Det-A	1.000	1	1	0	0	0	0
Total	7	.959	33	13	34	2	8	-1

OF

YEAR	TM/L	PCT	G	PO	A	E	DP	FR
1978	Phi-N	—	1	0	0	0	0	0
1982	Pit-N	—	2	0	0	0	0	0
1985	Pit-N	—	1	0	0	0	0	0
1987	Det-A	1.000	3	5	0	0	0	0
1988	Det-A	.889	2	8	0	1	0	0
	Atl-N	1.000	4	12	0	0	1	0
Total	5	.962	13	25	0	1	0	0

1B

YEAR	TM/L	PCT	G	PO	A	E	DP	FR
1984	Pit-N	1.000	1	6	0	0	0	0
1987	Det-A	1.000	1	2	0	0	1	0
1988	Det-A	1.000	4	19	0	0	2	-1
Total	3	1.000	6	24	0	0	3	-1

■ Jo-Jo Morrissey 2B

YEAR	TM/L	PCT	G	PO	A	E	DP	FR
1932	Cin-N	.987	42	93	138	3	24	9
1933	Cin-N	.979	88	187	295	18	46	6
1936	Chi-A	1.000	1	1	0	0	0	0
Total	3	.971	131	281	433	1	70	15

SS

YEAR	TM/L	PCT	G	PO	A	E	DP	FR
1932	Cin-N	.967	45	43	76	4	10	-2
1933	Cin-N	.933	63	101	148	18	30	-14
1936	Chi-A	.955	4	10	11	1	1	1
Total	3	.944	112	154	235	3	41	-15

3B

YEAR	TM/L	PCT	G	PO	A	E	DP	FR
1932	Cin-N	.971	12	8	26	1	4	2
1933	Cin-N	.882	15	12	18	4	0	-1
1936	Chi-A	.895	9	6	11	2	1	0
Total	3	.920	36	26	55	7	5	1

OF

YEAR	TM/L	PCT	G	PO	A	E	DP	FR
1932	Cin-N	—	1	0	0	0	0	0

■ Bubba Morton OF

YEAR	TM/L	PCT	G	PO	A	E	DP	FR
1961	Det-A	.952	30	39	1	2	1	1
1962	Det-A	.991	62	110	4	1	1	5
1963	Det-A	.875	3	7	0	1	0	0
	Mil-N	1.000	9	14	0	0	0	0
1966	Cal-A	1.000	14	25	1	0	0	0
1967	Cal-A	1.000	61	83	1	0	0	-5
1968	Cal-A	.985	50	64	1	1	1	-3
1969	Cal-A	1.000	49	70	5	0	1	0
Total	7	.988	278	412	13	5	4	-2

1B

YEAR	TM/L	PCT	G	PO	A	E	DP	FR
1962	Det-A	1.000	3	14	0	0	0	0
1969	Cal-A	1.000	1	2	0	0	0	0
Total	2	1.000	4	16	0	0	0	0

3B

YEAR	TM/L	PCT	G	PO	A	E	DP	FR
1968	Cal-A	—	1	0	0	0	0	0

■ Walt Moryn OF

YEAR	TM/L	PCT	G	PO	A	E	DP	FR
1954	Bro-N	.881	20	34	3	5	1	0
1955	Bro-N	.833	7	5	0	1	0	-1
1956	Chi-N	.983	141	268	**18**	5	2	8
1957	Chi-N	.960	147	276	13	**12**	3	3
1958	Chi-N	.978	141	265	4	6	1	-4
1959	Chi-N	.989	104	175	9	2	1	-7
1960	Chi-N	.964	30	52	2	2	1	-1
	StL-N	.990	62	100	4	1	0	-2
	Yr	.981	92	152	6	3	1	-3
1961	StL-N	.889	7	8	0	1	0	-1
	Pit-N	.950	11	17	2	1	1	1
	Yr	.931	18	25	2	2	1	0
Total	8	.972	670	1200	55	6	10	-4

■ Lloyd Moseby OF

YEAR	TM/L	PCT	G	PO	A	E	DP	FR
1980	Tor-A	.982	104	208	12	4	1	0
1981	Tor-A	.989	100	259	4	3	0	-3
1982	Tor-A	.992	145	361	4	3	0	-7
1983	Tor-A	.983	147	399	10	7	1	5
1984	Tor-A	.990	156	473	8	5	2	8
1985	Tor-A	.980	152	394	7	8	1	-7
1986	Tor-A	.984	147	371	6	6	1	-4
1987	Tor-A	.980	153	294	5	6	1	-13
1988	Tor-A	.984	125	304	2	5	1	-8
1989	Tor-A	.986	120	288	3	4	1	-7
1990	Det-A	.983	116	288	9	5	5	3
Total	11	.985	1465	3639	72	6	14	-33

■ Jerry Moses C

YEAR	TM/L	PCT	G	PO	A	E	DP	FR
1968	Bos-A	.963	6	26	0	1	0	-3
1969	Bos-A	.981	36	191	11	4	1	-5
1970	Bos-A	.990	88	578	45	6	3	2
1971	Cal-A	.977	63	299	38	8	3	6
1972	Cle-A	.982	39	201	16	4	7	1
1973	NY-A	1.000	17	93	9	0	0	4
1974	Det-A	.985	74	377	26	6	6	-3
1975	SD-N	.900	5	17	1	2	0	-1
Total	8	.984	328	1782	146	1	20	-1

1B

YEAR	TM/L	PCT	G	PO	A	E	DP	FR
1972	Cle-A	.952	3	19	1	1	1	0
1975	Chi-A	1.000	1	1	0	0	0	0
Total	2	.955	4	20	1	1	1	0

OF

YEAR	TM/L	PCT	G	PO	A	E	DP	FR
1970	Bos-A	—	1	0	0	0	0	0
1971	Cal-A	—	1	0	0	0	0	0
Total	2	—	2	0	0	0	0	0

■ John Moses OF

YEAR	TM/L	PCT	G	PO	A	E	DP	FR
1982	Sea-A	.947	19	16	2	1	0	-1
1983	Sea-A	.979	71	87	8	2	1	10
1984	Sea-A	1.000	19	26	1	0	0	1
1985	Sea-A	1.000	29	35	1	0	0	0
1986	Sea-A	.987	93	211	9	3	1	-2
1987	Sea-A	.987	100	220	5	3	0	-3
1988	Min-A	1.000	82	123	1	0	0	2
1989	Min-A	.988	108	156	3	2	0	5
1990	Min-A	1.000	85	103	2	0	0	4
Total	9	.989	606	977	32	1	2	16

1B

YEAR	TM/L	PCT	G	PO	A	E	DP	FR
1986	Sea-A	.952	7	38	2	2	3	-1
1987	Sea-A	.981	16	51	2	1	3	-1
1989	Min-A	1.000	2	12	0	0	0	0
1990	Min-A	1.000	6	5	0	0	0	0
Total	4	.973	31	106	4	3	6	-2

■ Wally Moses OF

YEAR	TM/L	PCT	G	PO	A	E	DP	FR
1935	Phi-A	.943	80	157	7	10	1	-2
1936	Phi-A	.974	144	396	12	11	3	-2
1937	Phi-A	.958	154	323	16	15	4	2
1938	Phi-A	.966	139	304	11	11	3	4
1939	Phi-A	.965	103	209	10	8	2	2
1940	Phi-A	.974	133	295	10	8	1	1
1941	Phi-A	.975	109	263	12	7	**5**	6
1942	Chi-A	.980	145	323	14	7	3	6

YEAR	TM/L	PCT	G	PO	A	E	DP	FR
1943	Chi-A	.979	148	370	12	8	2	6
1944	Chi-A	.975	134	267	7	7	2	-6
1945	Chi-A	.977	139	329	12	8	1	5
1946	Chi-A	1.000	36	84	2	0	0	-1
	Bos-A	.979	44	92	3	2	1	0
	Yr	.989	80	176	5	2	1	-1
1947	Bos-A	.974	58	109	2	3	0	-7
1948	Bos-A	.981	45	101	2	2	1	0
1949	Phi-A	.983	92	169	7	3	3	-7
1950	Phi-A	.987	62	147	7	2	2	1
1951	Phi-A	.984	27	62	1	1	1	-1
Total	17	.973	1792	4000	147	113	35	3

■ Les Moss C

YEAR	TM/L	PCT	G	PO	A	E	DP	FR
1946	StL-A	.968	12	55	5	2	1	1
1947	StL-A	.983	96	362	43	7	6	-5
1948	StL-A	.988	103	357	52	5	8	-9
1949	StL-A	.970	83	283	41	10	9	-5
1950	StL-A	.957	60	204	20	10	4	0
1951	StL-A	.967	12	50	8	2	1	0
	Bos-A	.984	69	285	28	5	4	0
	Yr	.981	81	335	36	7	5	0
1952	StL-A	.957	39	118	17	6	3	-3
1953	StL-A	.978	71	296	21	7	4	-6
1954	Bal-A	.972	38	159	16	5	4	-2
1955	Bal-A	1.000	17	66	5	0	4	2
	Chi-A	.990	32	90	5	1	1	0
	Yr	.994	49	156	10	1	5	2
1956	Chi-A	.994	49	149	10	1	1	-6
1957	Chi-A	.980	39	138	8	3	2	-7
Total	12	.978	720	2612	279	4	52	-40

■ Johnny Mostil OF

YEAR	TM/L	PCT	G	PO	A	E	DP	FR
1921	Chi-A	.946	91	215	12	13	1	0
1922	Chi-A	.966	123	333	9	12	2	5
1923	Chi-A	.974	143	422	21	12	7	22
1924	Chi-A	.974	102	281	13	8	2	7
1925	Chi-A	.985	153	446	11	7	5	7
1926	Chi-A	.968	147	440	15	15	4	17
1927	Chi-A	.857	6	5	1	1	0	-2
1928	Chi-A	.976	131	394	18	10	3	18
1929	Chi-A	.963	11	25	1	1	1	-1
Total	9	.971	907	2561	101	9	25	73

2B

1918	Chi-A	.923	9	15	21	3	4	-2
1921	Chi-A	1.000	1	0	2	0	0	0
Total	2	.927	10	15	23	3	4	-2

3B

1923	Chi-A	.913	5	10	11	2	1	0

SS

1923	Chi-A	.800	1	2	2	1	1	0

■ Manny Mota OF

YEAR	TM/L	PCT	G	PO	A	E	DP	FR
1962	SF-N	1.000	27	24	3	0	0	3
1963	Pit-N	.953	37	40	1	2	0	-3
1964	Pit-N	.961	93	120	4	5	1	-9
1965	Pit-N	.985	95	127	5	2	1	-1
1966	Pit-N	.994	96	150	3	1	0	-2
1967	Pit-N	.988	99	153	9	2	2	-2
1968	Pit-N	.981	92	149	5	3	1	-5
1969	Mon-N	.907	22	39	0	4	0	-2
	LA-N	.969	80	118	8	4	2	-3
	Yr	.954	102	157	8	8	2	-5
1970	LA-N	.973	111	172	8	5	3	-6
1971	LA-N	.965	80	108	3	4	1	-9
1972	LA-N	.993	99	141	3	1	1	-11
1973	LA-N	1.000	74	96	4	0	0	-10
1974	LA-N	1.000	3	1	0	0	0	-1
1975	LA-N	1.000	5	9	0	0	0	1
1976	LA-N	1.000	6	11	1	0	0	1
1977	LA-N	1.000	1	1	0	0	0	0
1979	LA-N	—	1	0	0	0	0	0
Total	17	.979	1021	1459	57	3	12	-59

3B

1962	SF-N	.913	7	9	12	2	2	1
1966	Pit-N	1.000	4	2	1	0	0	0
1967	Pit-N	1.000	2	3	5	0	1	0
1968	Pit-N	—	1	0	0	0	0	0
1970	LA-N	1.000	1	0	1	0	0	0
Total	5	.943	15	14	19	2	3	1

2B

1962	SF-N	1.000	3	5	3	0	0	0
1963	Pit-N	—	1	0	0	0	0	0
1964	Pit-N	1.000	1	0	1	0	0	0
1968	Pit-N	1.000	1	1	3	0	1	0
Total	4	1.000	6	6	7	0	1	0

C

1964	Pit-N	1.000	1	2	0	0	0	0

■ Darryl Motley OF

YEAR	TM/L	PCT	G	PO	A	E	DP	FR
1981	KC-A	.968	39	88	3	3	1	1
1983	KC-A	.978	18	42	2	1	0	3
1984	KC-A	.984	138	301	7	5	2	0
1985	KC-A	.967	114	198	4	7	1	-11
1986	KC-A	.979	66	92	2	2	1	-6
	Atl-N	1.000	3	5	0	0	0	0
1987	Atl-N	1.000	2	2	0	0	0	0
Total	6	.976	380	728	18	8	5	-13

■ Curt Motton OF

YEAR	TM/L	PCT	G	PO	A	E	DP	FR
1967	Bal-A	.973	18	36	0	1	0	0
1968	Bal-A	.989	54	91	2	1	0	-3
1969	Bal-A	1.000	20	26	0	0	0	-2
1970	Bal-A	1.000	21	32	1	0	0	0
1971	Bal-A	1.000	16	20	1	0	0	0
1972	Mil-A	—	3	0	0	0	0	0
	Cal-A	1.000	9	15	0	0	0	2
	Yr	1.000	12	15	0	0	0	2
1973	Bal-A	—	1	0	0	0	0	0
1974	Bal-A	1.000	2	4	0	0	0	1
Total	8	.991	144	224	4	2	0	-2

■ Mike Mowrey 3B

YEAR	TM/L	PCT	G	PO	A	E	DP	FR
1905	Cin-N	.759	7	6	16	7	1	0
1906	Cin-N	.930	15	20	33	4	1	4
1907	Cin-N	.929	127	167	214	29	14	-18
1908	Cin-N	.936	56	51	110	11	6	-6
1909	Cin-N	.947	22	16	38	3	3	-1
	StL-N	1.000	2	0	1	0	0	0
	Yr	.948	24	16	39	3	3	-1
1910	StL-N	.927	141	171	301	37	30	12
1911	StL-N	.944	134	174	267	26	19	7
1912	StL-N	.931	108	131	220	26	22	3
1913	StL-N	.953	131	143	284	21	23	14
1914	Pit-N	.960	78	83	156	10	8	-2
1915	Pit-F	.959	151	174	268	19	15	-19
1916	Bro-N	.965	144	154	291	16	17	0
1917	Bro-N	.952	80	73	164	12	13	-3
Total	13	.944	1196	1363	2363	221	172	-9

SS

1906	Cin-N	1.000	1	1	4	0	0	0
1907	Cin-N	.875	11	11	31	6	0	-1
1908	Cin-N	.769	3	3	7	3	0	-1
1909	Cin-N	.893	13	32	43	9	8	1
1911	StL-N	1.000	1	1	0	0	0	0
Total	5	.881	29	48	85	8	8	-1

2B

1906	Cin-N	—	1	0	0	0	0	0
1908	Cin-N	—	1	0	0	0	0	0
1909	StL-N	.921	7	18	17	3	0	-1
1917	Bro-N	1.000	2	4	6	0	1	0
Total	4	.938	11	22	23	3	1	-1

OF

1908	Cin-N	.909	3	10	0	1	0	0

■ Joe Mowry OF

YEAR	TM/L	PCT	G	PO	A	E	DP	FR
1933	Bos-N	.994	64	155	2	1	2	0
1934	Bos-N	.976	20	40	1	1	1	0
1935	Bos-N	.970	45	62	3	2	0	0
Total	3	.985	129	257	6	4	3	0

2B

1934	Bos-N	1.000	1	5	4	0	1	1

■ Mike Moynahan SS

YEAR	TM/L	PCT	G	PO	A	E	DP	FR
1880	Buf-N	.862	27	30	70	16	7	-6
1883	Phi-a	.833	95	105	268	75	14	0
1884	Cle-N	.769	3	1	9	3	1	0
Total	3	.837	125	136	347	4	22	-6

OF

1881	Phi-a	.883	32	65	3	9	2	-2
1884	Phi-a	.500	1	1	0	1	0	0
	Cle-N	.750	3	7	2	3	0	1
Total	2	.857	36	73	5	3	2	-1

2B

1884	Cle-N	.852	6	7	16	4	0	-2

3B

1881	Cle-N	.000	1	0	0	1	0	-1
	Det-N	.857	1	3	3	1	0	1
	Yr	.750	2	3	3	2	0	0

■ Heinie Mueller OF

YEAR	TM/L	PCT	G	PO	A	E	DP	FR
1920	StL-N	1.000	4	12	0	0	0	0
1921	StL-N	.976	54	117	5	3	1	3
1922	StL-N	.947	44	83	6	5	2	1
1923	StL-N	.963	74	197	9	8	3	11
1924	StL-N	.962	53	122	4	5	2	2
1925	StL-N	.955	72	165	6	8	3	-5
1926	StL-N	.950	51	106	7	6	3	0
	NY-N	.950	82	194	13	11	2	5
	Yr	.950	133	300	20	17	5	5
1927	NY-N	.944	56	100	1	6	0	-9
1928	Bos-N	.985	41	127	6	2	1	7
1929	Bos-N	1.000	24	45	1	0	0	-1
1935	StL-A	.500	2	1	0	1	0	0
Total	11	.960	557	1269	58	5	17	14

1B

1924	StL-N	.982	27	213	11	4	17	-1
1927	NY-N	1.000	1	17	1	0	3	0
1935	StL-A	.955	3	18	3	1	3	0
Total	3	.981	31	248	15	5	23	-1

■ Don Mueller OF

YEAR	TM/L	PCT	G	PO	A	E	DP	FR
1948	NY-N	.973	22	33	3	1	0	0
1949	NY-N	1.000	6	8	0	0	0	0
1950	NY-N	.986	125	205	7	3	2	-9
1951	NY-N	.983	115	233	5	4	1	-4
1952	NY-N	.987	120	221	8	3	4	-2
1953	NY-N	.972	122	203	7	6	0	-9
1954	NY-N	.979	153	263	14	6	5	-3
1955	NY-N	.976	146	239	5	6	1	-14
1956	NY-N	.989	117	180	4	2	2	-10
1957	NY-N	.989	115	174	13	2	4	-5
1958	Chi-A	.968	43	57	3	2	1	-4
Total	11	.982	1084	1816	69	5	20	-60

■ Heinie Mueller 2B

YEAR	TM/L	PCT	G	PO	A	E	DP	FR
1938	Phi-N	.967	111	229	266	17	44	-25
1939	Phi-N	.964	51	132	137	10	37	-9
1940	Phi-N	.966	34	68	76	5	12	-7
1941	Phi-N	.980	29	74	71	3	18	-2
Total	4	.968	225	503	550	5	111	-43

3B

1938	Phi-N	.909	21	20	40	6	4	-1
1939	Phi-N	.973	17	12	24	1	0	-2
1940	Phi-N	1.000	13	14	19	0	1	0
1941	Phi-N	.980	19	14	36	1	3	1
Total	4	.957	70	60	119	8	8	-2

OF

1939	Phi-N	1.000	17	19	2	0	0	1
1940	Phi-N	1.000	31	59	1	0	0	-1
1941	Phi-N	.929	21	26	0	2	0	-2
Total	3	.982	69	104	3	2	0	-2

1B

1940	Phi-N	1.000	2	5	0	0	0	0

SS

1939	Phi-N	1.000	1	0	3	0	1	0

■ Ray Mueller C

YEAR	TM/L	PCT	G	PO	A	E	DP	FR
1935	Bos-N	.978	40	64	27	2	6	-2
1936	Bos-N	.986	23	66	7	1	2	-3
1937	Bos-N	.995	57	169	44	1	6	2
1938	Bos-N	.993	75	239	47	2	4	-3
1939	Bos-N	.971	81	203	32	7	5	-4
1940	Pit-N	1.000	4	7	2	0	0	1
1943	Cin-N	.988	140	579	100	8	17	20
1944	Cin-N	.983	155	471	65	9	5	-6
1946	Cin-N	.994	100	405	65	3	12	9
1947	Cin-N	.984	55	221	28	4	2	-2
1948	Cin-N	.982	10	51	5	1	0	1
1949	Cin-N	1.000	31	110	15	0	1	-3
	NY-N	.982	56	197	21	4	1	0
	Yr	.988	87	307	36	4	2	-3
1950	NY-N	1.000	4	24	0	0	0	2
	Pit-N	.996	63	204	30	1	3	2
	Yr	.996	67	228	30	1	3	4
1951	Bos-N	1.000	23	85	15	0	2	3
Total	14	.988	917	3095	503	3	66	17

■ Mike Muldoon 3B

YEAR	TM/L	PCT	G	PO	A	E	DP	FR
1882	Cle-N	.880	61	86	133	30	12	3
1883	Cle-N	.825	98	122	170	62	9	-8
1884	Cle-N	.833	109	126	204	66	15	-6
1885	Bal-a	.870	101	103	184	43	16	-2
1886	Bal-a	.825	44	41	86	27	4	0
Total	5	.846	413	478	777	228	56	-13

2B

1884	Cle-N	.875	1	4	3	1	1	0
1885	Bal-a	.750	1	3	0	1	1	-1
1886	Bal-a	.912	57	136	184	31	18	2
Total	3	.909	59	143	187	3	20	1

OF

1882	Cle-N	.877	23	46	4	7	0	0
1883	Cle-N	1.000	2	1	0	0	0	-1
1884	Cle-N	—	1	0	0	0	0	0
Total	3	.879	26	47	4	7	0	-1

■ Charlie Mullen 1B

YEAR	TM/L	PCT	G	PO	A	E	DP	FR
1910	Chi-A	.982	37	364	23	7	21	1
1911	Chi-A	.969	20	176	12	6	2	0
1914	NY-A	.994	93	898	62	6	54	3
1915	NY-A	.982	27	201	15	4	0	1
1916	NY-A	1.000	17	135	7	0	1	0
Total	5	.988	194	1774	119	3	78	5

2B

1916	NY-A	.943	20	45	38	5	5	-5

OF

1910	Chi-A	1.000	2	1	0	0	0	-1
1916	NY-A	.923	6	11	1	1	1	0
Total	2	.929	8	12	1	1	1	-1

■ Joe Mulligan 3B

YEAR	TM/L	PCT	G	PO	A	E	DP	FR
1915	Chi-N	—	1	0	0	0	0	0
1921	Chi-A	.955	151	162	307	22	28	-13
1922	Chi-A	.971	84	94	205	9	14	6
1928	Pit-N	.929	6	5	8	1	2	0
Total	4	.961	242	261	520	2	44	-7

SS

1915	Chi-N	.907	10	23	26	5	9	3
1916	Chi-N	.888	58	116	200	40	27	3
1921	Chi-A	1.000	1	0	1	0	0	0
1922	Chi-A	.929	7	10	16	2	0	-2
Total	4	.893	76	149	243	7	36	4

2B

1928	Pit-N	.958	4	13	10	1	5	0

■ Pat Mullin OF

YEAR	TM/L	PCT	G	PO	A	E	DP	FR
1940	Det-A	—	1	0	0	0	0	0
1941	Det-A	.944	51	117	2	7	0	-2
1946	Det-A	.949	75	121	8	7	1	-3
1947	Det-A	.988	106	229	10	3	2	5
1948	Det-A	.972	131	274	7	8	0	-3
1949	Det-A	.989	79	169	4	2	0	-3
1950	Det-A	1.000	32	62	4	0	1	0
1951	Det-A	.939	83	151	4	10	1	-6
1952	Det-A	.979	65	131	6	3	2	3
1953	Det-A	.944	14	16	1	1	0	-2
Total	10	.970	637	1270	46	1	7	-11

■ Rance Mulliniks 3B

YEAR	TM/L	PCT	G	PO	A	E	DP	FR
1981	KC-A	.900	5	4	5	1	1	0
1982	Tor-A	.938	102	60	137	13	13	-14
1983	Tor-A	.971	116	70	161	7	12	-18
1984	Tor-A	.968	119	65	148	7	13	-12
1985	Tor-A	.971	119	75	162	7	16	-16
1986	Tor-A	.975	110	60	176	6	13	-1
1987	Tor-A	.927	96	29	137	13	14	-6
1988	Tor-A	1.000	7	3	5	0	0	0
1989	Tor-A	.985	29	15	50	1	9	2
1990	Tor-A	.949	22	12	25	2	4	0
Total	10	.961	725	393	1006	7	95	-65

SS

1977	Cal-A	.963	77	112	229	13	37	0
1978	Cal-A	.953	47	68	93	8	22	2
1979	Cal-A	.957	22	46	43	4	13	-7
1980	Cal-A	.966	18	19	34	1	6	0
1981	KC-A	.966	7	7	21	1	4	2
1982	Tor-A	.963	16	9	17	1	3	-1
1983	Tor-A	1.000	5	7	23	0	7	0
1984	Tor-A	.857	3	2	4	1	2	-1
1987	Tor-A	—	1	0	0	0	0	0

YEAR	TM/L	PCT	G	PO	A	E	DP	FR
Total	9	.962	206	270	464	9	93	-5
2B								
1980	KC-A	1.000	14	11	19	0	4	2
1981	KC-A	.900	10	14	13	3	4	1
1983	Tor-A	1.000	2	0	1	0	0	0
1984	Tor-A	—	1	0	0	0	0	0
1986	Tor-A	—	1	0	0	0	0	0
Total	5	.951	28	25	33	3	8	3
1B								
1990	Tor-A	1.000	3	11	0	0	1	0

■ Joe Mulvey 3B

YEAR	TM/L	PCT	G	PO	A	E	DP	FR
1883	Phi-N	.750	3	9	3	4	1	-1
1884	Phi-N	.834	100	**151**	216	**73**	20	11
1885	Phi-N	.848	107	**144**	201	62	12	-7
1886	Phi-N	.879	107	99	191	40	2	-18
1887	Phi-N	.865	111	123	197	50	18	-15
1888	Phi-N	.891	100	87	174	32	9	-14
1889	Phi-N	.893	129	165	284	54	20	0
1890	Phi-P	.857	120	144	227	62	15	-16
1891	Phi-a	.894	113	172	241	49	18	2
1892	Phi-N	.883	25	40	58	13	5	3
1893	Was-N	.874	55	76	140	31	10	5
1895	Bro-N	.917	13	25	30	5	1	2
Total	12	.871	983	1235	1962	475	131	-48
SS								
1883	Pro-N	.692	4	1	8	4	0	-3
OF								
1886	Phi-N	—	1	0	0	0	0	0

■ Jerry Mumphrey OF

YEAR	TM/L	PCT	G	PO	A	E	DP	FR
1974	StL-N	—	1	0	0	0	0	0
1975	StL-N	1.000	3	9	0	0	0	0
1976	StL-N	.993	94	261	6	2	1	4
1977	StL-N	.971	133	291	8	9	1	-9
1978	StL-N	.995	116	178	10	1	1	-6
1979	StL-N	.984	114	180	3	3	0	-13
1980	SD-N	.974	153	398	10	11	1	-2
1981	NY-A	.966	79	219	5	**8**	0	5
1982	NY-A	.986	123	336	5	5	2	3
1983	NY-A	.983	83	227	7	4	1	5
	Hou-N	.990	43	103	1	1	0	3
1984	Hou-N	.988	137	317	5	4	2	-5
1985	Hou-N	.969	126	248	6	8	1	0
1986	Chi-N	.982	92	161	3	3	3	-4
1987	Chi-N	.992	85	124	5	1	0	-6
1988	Chi-N	1.000	4	5	0	0	0	-1
Total	15	.981	1386	3057	74	0	13	-26

■ Thurman Munson C

YEAR	TM/L	PCT	G	PO	A	E	DP	FR
1969	NY-A	.986	25	119	18	2	0	0
1970	NY-A	.989	**125**	631	**80**	8	11	6
1971	NY-A	**.998**	117	547	67	1	4	-2
1972	NY-A	.977	**132**	575	71	**15**	11	-5
1973	NY-A	.984	**142**	673	**80**	12	11	6
1974	NY-A	.974	137	743	**75**	**22**	10	1
1975	NY-A	.972	130	700	95	**23**	**14**	9
1976	NY-A	.981	121	537	78	12	8	-2
1977	NY-A	.984	136	657	73	12	4	-5
1978	NY-A	.986	125	666	61	10	4	1
1979	NY-A	.978	88	405	44	10	5	-6
Total	11	.982	1278	6253	742	127	82	1
OF								
1971	NY-A	—	1	0	0	0	0	0
1975	NY-A	1.000	2	5	0	0	0	0
1976	NY-A	.818	11	9	0	2	0	-1
1978	NY-A	.970	13	32	0	1	0	-1
Total	4	.939	27	46	0	3	0	-2
1B								
1975	NY-A	1.000	2	20	0	0	1	-1
1979	NY-A	1.000	3	23	0	0	2	-1
Total	2	1.000	5	43	0	0	3	-2
3B								
1975	NY-A	—	1	0	0	0	0	0

■ John Munyan C

YEAR	TM/L	PCT	G	PO	A	E	DP	FR
1887	Cle-a	.862	3	15	10	4	2	2
1890	StL-a	.939	83	452	115	37	8	-2
1891	StL-a	.943	45	180	37	13	1	-2
Total	3	.937	131	647	162	4	11	-2
OF								
1887	Cle-a	.762	12	15	1	5	0	-3
1890	Col-a	.667	2	3	1	2	0	0
	StL-a	1.000	7	9	1	0	0	0
	Yr	.875	9	12	2	2	0	0
1891	StL-a	.680	12	15	2	8	0	-2
Total	3	.758	33	42	5	5	0	-5
3B								
1887	Cle-a	.333	2	0	1	2	0	-1
1890	StL-a	.700	3	5	2	3	1	-2
1891	StL-a	.714	3	3	2	2	1	-1
Total	3	.650	8	8	5	7	2	-4
SS								
1890	StL-a	1.000	1	2	1	0	0	0
1891	StL-a	.920	5	9	14	2	2	1
Total	2	.929	6	11	15	2	2	1
2B								
1890	StL-a	.880	5	6	16	3	1	0

■ Bobby Murcer OF

YEAR	TM/L	PCT	G	PO	A	E	DP	FR
1969	NY-A	.964	118	212	4	8	0	-5
1970	NY-A	.992	155	375	**15**	3	3	6
1971	NY-A	.985	143	317	10	5	1	-3
1972	NY-A	.992	151	**382**	11	3	1	4
1973	NY-A	.985	160	380	**14**	6	2	0
1974	NY-A	.978	156	297	**21**	7	2	4
1975	SF-N	.981	144	201	10	4	3	-12
1976	SF-N	.961	146	282	11	12	2	-2
1977	Chi-N	.980	150	237	11	5	5	-8
1978	Chi-N	.979	138	225	8	5	0	-12
1979	Chi-N	1.000	54	110	4	0	0	-1
	NY-A	.983	70	169	4	3	0	-4
1980	NY-A	.955	59	82	2	4	0	-7
Total	12	.981	1644	3269	125	5	19	-40
3B								
1969	NY-A	.877	31	23	77	14	11	1
SS								
1965	NY-A	.932	11	28	41	5	14	7
1966	NY-A	.931	18	31	50	6	4	-4
1977	Chi-N	—	1	0	0	0	0	0
Total	3	.932	30	59	91	1	18	3
2B								
1977	Chi-N	1.000	1	1	0	0	0	0

■ Tim Murnane 1B

YEAR	TM/L	PCT	G	PO	A	E	DP	FR
1876	Bos-N	.927	**65**	689	5	**55**	**30**	-5
1877	Bos-N	.935	5	39	4	3	1	1
1878	Pro-N	.940	48	543	22	36	25	1
1884	Bos-U	.950	63	588	7	31	8	-4
Total	4	.938	181	1859	38	125	64	-7
OF								
1876	Bos-N	.900	3	7	2	1	0	1
1877	Bos-N	.815	30	39	5	10	2	-3
1878	Pro-N	.500	1	2	0	2	0	0
1884	Bos-U	.818	16	15	3	4	0	-1
Total	4	.811	50	63	10	7	2	-3
2B								
1876	Bos-N	1.000	1	1	2	0	0	0

■ Dale Murphy OF

YEAR	TM/L	PCT	G	PO	A	E	DP	FR
1980	Atl-N	.985	154	374	14	6	4	-1
1981	Atl-N	.981	103	254	11	5	**4**	-1
1982	Atl-N	.979	**162**	407	6	9	2	-2
1983	Atl-N	.987	**160**	373	10	6	0	-3
1984	Atl-N	.987	**160**	369	10	5	1	-5
1985	Atl-N	.980	**161**	334	8	7	4	-13
1986	Atl-N	.981	159	303	6	6	1	-10
1987	Atl-N	.977	**159**	325	14	8	1	8
1988	Atl-N	.992	**156**	340	15	3	4	**11**
1989	Atl-N	.985	151	331	5	5	0	5
1990	Atl-N	.981	97	208	3	4	0	2
	Phi-N	.992	55	113	4	1	1	-3
	Yr	.985	152	321	7	5	1	-1
Total	11	.983	1677	3731	106	5	22	-12
1B								
1978	Atl-N	.984	129	1137	92	**20**	84	5
1979	Atl-N	.980	76	685	42	15	61	-4
1980	Atl-N	1.000	1	10	1	0	0	0
1981	Atl-N	1.000	3	10	0	0	1	0
Total	4	.983	209	1842	135	5	146	1
C								
1976	Atl-N	.974	19	100	13	3	0	1
1977	Atl-N	.954	18	114	11	6	2	-1
1978	Atl-N	.970	21	83	13	3	0	0
1979	Atl-N	.966	27	127	15	5	2	-3
Total	4	.966	85	424	52	7	4	-3

■ Danny Murphy 2B

YEAR	TM/L	PCT	G	PO	A	E	DP	FR
1900	NY-N	.888	22	46	49	12	9	-6
1901	NY-N	.895	5	6	11	2	0	-3
1902	Phi-A	.963	76	167	197	14	22	-12
1903	Phi-A	.949	133	241	349	32	34	-13
1904	Phi-A	.941	150	280	455	**46**	35	13
1905	Phi-A	.955	**151**	290	390	32	29	-9
1906	Phi-A	.955	119	239	308	26	38	-11
1907	Phi-A	.965	122	271	386	24	28	13
1908	Phi-A	.965	56	144	162	11	13	4
1911	Phi-A	1.000	4	2	12	0	2	0
1915	Bro-F	1.000	1	0	1	0	0	-1
Total	11	.953	839	1686	2320	199	210	-25
OF								
1908	Phi-A	.963	84	145	11	6	4	7
1909	Phi-A	**.977**	149	191	17	5	5	-2
1910	Phi-A	.974	151	209	15	6	5	-3
1911	Phi-A	.961	136	162	**34**	8	6	6
1912	Phi-A	.891	36	39	2	5	2	-6
1913	Phi-A	1.000	9	5	0	0	1	-2
1914	Bro-F	.986	46	65	8	1	2	1
1915	Bro-F	1.000	1	0	0	0	0	0
Total	8	.967	612	816	87	1	25	1
1B								
1908	Phi-A	.950	2	19	0	1	1	-1

■ Dwayne Murphy OF

YEAR	TM/L	PCT	G	PO	A	E	DP	FR
1978	Oak-A	1.000	45	49	1	0	1	5
1979	Oak-A	.988	118	322	10	4	0	4
1980	Oak-A	.990	158	**507**	13	5	0	19
1981	Oak-A	.985	106	326	6	5	0	9
1982	Oak-A	.983	147	**452**	14	8	3	15
1983	Oak-A	.979	124	365	7	8	0	5
1984	Oak-A	.988	153	**474**	14	6	2	12
1985	Oak-A	.980	150	432	6	5	1	0
1986	Oak-A	.993	97	276	6	2	3	7
1987	Oak-A	.984	79	185	1	3	0	5
1988	Det-A	1.000	43	122	1	0	0	5
1989	Phi-N	.986	52	69	1	1	1	-1
Total	12	.987	1272	3579	80	7	11	85
SS								
1982	Oak-A	1.000	1	0	4	0	0	2
1B								
1987	Oak-A	1.000	1	2	0	0	0	0
2B								
1987	Oak-A	1.000	1	0	1	0	0	0

■ Eddie Murphy OF

YEAR	TM/L	PCT	G	PO	A	E	DP	FR
1912	Phi-A	.947	33	48	6	3	1	0
1913	Phi-A	.942	135	166	14	11	2	-12
1914	Phi-A	.941	148	194	15	13	4	-5
1915	Phi-A	.899	58	55	7	7	0	-7
	Chi-A	.952	70	113	7	6	0	-1
	Yr	.933	128	168	14	13	0	-8
1916	Chi-A	1.000	24	28	2	0	0	-2
1917	Chi-A	1.000	9	2	0	0	0	-4
1918	Chi-A	.958	63	111	3	5	1	-5
1919	Chi-A	.917	6	10	1	1	0	0
1920	Chi-A	.886	19	23	8	4	0	2
1926	Pit-N	1.000	3	5	0	0	0	0
Total	10	.942	568	755	63	0	8	-34
3B								
1915	Phi-A	.893	6	9	16	3	0	2
1916	Chi-A	.000	1	0	0	1	0	-1
1920	Chi-A	.900	3	4	5	1	2	-1
Total	3	.872	10	13	21	5	2	0
2B								
1918	Chi-A	.933	8	13	15	2	1	-5

■ Morgan Murphy C

YEAR	TM/L	PCT	G	PO	A	E	DP	FR
1890	Bos-P	.903	67	257	59	34	8	3
1891	Bos-a	**.954**	104	**532**	118	31	8	9
1892	Cin-N	.955	74	315	67	18	6	-1
1893	Cin-N	.932	56	162	45	15	6	-7
1894	Cin-N	.901	74	194	70	29	5	-6
1895	Cin-N	.907	25	70	18	9	1	-4
1896	StL-N	.926	48	178	48	18	5	-2
1897	StL-N	.950	53	145	62	11	3	-5
1898	Pit-N	.957	5	14	8	1	1	1
	Phi-N	.964	25	77	30	4	2	0
	Yr	.963	30	91	38	5	3	1
1900	Phi-N	.980	11	33	15	1	1	2
1901	Phi-A	.929	8	32	7	3	1	1
Total	11	.936	550	2009	547	174	47	-9
1B								
1893	Cin-N	1.000	1	7	2	0	0	1
1897	StL-N	1.000	8	46	4	0	3	1
1901	Phi-A	.778	2	7	0	2	0	0
Total	3	.971	10	60	6	2	3	2
OF								
1890	Bos-P	—	1	0	0	0	0	-1
1891	Bos-a	1.000	4	1	0	0	0	-2
Total	2	1.000	5	1	0	0	0	-3
SS								
1890	Bos-P	1.000	2	0	3	0	0	0
1894	Cin-N	.857	1	1	5	1	0	0
Total	2	.900	3	1	8	1	0	0
3B								
1890	Bos-P	—	1	0	0	0	0	0
1894	Cin-N	1.000	1	1	1	0	0	0
Total	2	1.000	2	1	1	0	0	0

■ Eddie Murray 1B

YEAR	TM/L	PCT	G	PO	A	E	DP	FR
1977	Bal-A	.992	42	368	17	3	34	-5
1978	Bal-A	.997	**157**	**1504**	106	5	143	1
1979	Bal-A	.994	**157**	**1456**	107	10	135	1
1980	Bal-A	.994	154	1369	77	9	158	-9
1981	Bal-A	**.999**	99	899	**91**	1	98	**10**
1982	Bal-A	**.997**	149	1269	97	4	106	1
1983	Bal-A	.993	153	1393	114	10	136	3
1984	Bal-A	.992	**159**	**1538**	**143**	13	**152**	8
1985	Bal-A	.987	154	1338	152	**19**	**154**	13
1986	Bal-A	.989	119	1045	88	13	100	-3
1987	Bal-A	.993	156	1371	145	10	**146**	12
1988	Bal-A	.989	103	867	106	11	101	10
1989	LA-N	**.996**	159	1316	**137**	6	**122**	13
1990	LA-N	.992	150	1180	113	10	88	4
Total	14	.993	1911	16913	1493	124	1673	57
3B								
1978	Bal-A	.900	3	3	6	1	1	0
1989	LA-N	—	2	0	0	0	0	0
Total	2	.900	5	3	6	1	1	0
OF								
1977	Bal-A	1.000	3	7	0	0	0	0

■ Red Murray OF

YEAR	TM/L	PCT	G	PO	A	E	DP	FR
1906	StL-N	.962	34	43	7	2	0	-1
1907	StL-N	.935	131	232	25	**18**	4	5
1908	StL-N	.914	154	274	22	**28**	4	-4
1909	NY-N	.947	149	222	**30**	14	1	2
1910	NY-N	.948	148	246	**26**	15	3	1
1911	NY-N	.954	131	196	12	10	4	-11
1912	NY-N	**.968**	143	255	20	9	7	-3
1913	NY-N	.965	147	279	24	11	3	2
1914	NY-N	1.000	49	56	2	0	0	-2
1915	NY-N	.959	34	66	4	3	1	2
	Chi-N	.966	40	82	4	3	1	3
	Yr	.963	74	148	8	6	2	5
1917	NY-N	1.000	11	11	0	0	0	0
Total	11	.950	1171	1962	176	113	28	-6
C								
1906	StL-N	.930	7	30	10	3	2	-1
1917	NY-N	1.000	1	2	0	0	0	0
Total	2	.933	8	32	10	3	2	-1
2B								
1915	Chi-N	1.000	1	0	4	0	0	0

■ Larry Murray OF

YEAR	TM/L	PCT	G	PO	A	E	DP	FR
1974	NY-A	—	3	0	0	0	0	0
1975	NY-A	1.000	4	1	0	0	0	0
1976	NY-A	1.000	7	9	1	0	0	1
1977	Oak-A	.992	78	114	3	1	3	4
1978	Oak-A	1.000	6	6	0	0	0	0
1979	Oak-A	.963	90	173	7	7	2	7
Total	6	.975	188	303	11	8	5	12

2B

YEAR	TM/L	PCT	G	PO	A	E	DP	FR
1979	Oak-A	1.000	3	1	1	0	0	0

SS

YEAR	TM/L	PCT	G	PO	A	E	DP	FR
1977	Oak-A	—	1	0	0	0	0	0

■ Ray Murray C

YEAR	TM/L	PCT	G	PO	A	E	DP	FR
1950	Cle-A	.972	45	156	15	5	2	-5
1951	Cle-A	1.000	1	4	1	0	0	1
	Phi-A	.985	39	107	24	2	5	-2
	Yr	.986	40	111	25	2	5	-1
1952	Phi-A	.995	42	175	35	1	3	8
1953	Phi-A	.989	78	330	45	4	8	4
1954	Bal-A	.989	21	83	9	1	3	1
Total	5	.987	226	855	129	3	21	7

■ Ivan Murrell OF

YEAR	TM/L	PCT	G	PO	A	E	DP	FR
1963	Hou-N	1.000	2	3	0	0	0	0
1964	Hou-N	1.000	5	2	0	0	0	-1
1967	Hou-N	.846	6	11	0	2	0	-1
1968	Hou-N	.931	15	24	3	2	2	3
1969	SD-N	.959	72	137	3	6	0	0
1970	SD-N	.970	101	183	8	6	2	1
1971	SD-N	.978	72	133	2	3	0	1
1972	SD-N	1.000	1	2	0	0	0	0
1973	SD-N	.959	37	69	2	3	0	2
1974	Atl-N	.983	32	56	2	1	1	4
Total	10	.965	343	620	20	3	5	9

1B

YEAR	TM/L	PCT	G	PO	A	E	DP	FR
1969	SD-N	1.000	2	15	1	0	3	0
1970	SD-N	1.000	1	1	0	0	1	0
1973	SD-N	.990	24	180	14	2	14	1
1974	Atl-N	1.000	13	105	7	0	10	1
Total	4	.994	40	301	22	2	28	2

■ Danny Murtaugh 2B

YEAR	TM/L	PCT	G	PO	A	E	DP	FR
1941	Phi-N	.978	85	233	247	11	49	3
1942	Phi-N	.958	32	86	98	8	15	5
1943	Phi-N	.974	113	321	345	18	76	0
1946	Phi-N	.958	6	13	10	1	0	-4
1947	Bos-N	1.000	2	7	6	0	1	0
1948	Pit-N	.979	146	375	412	17	95	1
1949	Pit-N	.975	74	202	182	10	58	3
1950	Pit-N	.976	108	273	292	14	84	3
1951	Pit-N	.970	65	110	113	7	35	-3
Total	9	.975	631	1620	1705	6	413	8

SS

YEAR	TM/L	PCT	G	PO	A	E	DP	FR
1941	Phi-N	1.000	1	1	0	0	0	0
1942	Phi-N	.939	60	132	176	20	32	-2
Total	2	.939	61	133	176	0	32	-2

3B

YEAR	TM/L	PCT	G	PO	A	E	DP	FR
1942	Phi-N	.926	53	84	103	15	14	4
1947	Bos-N	—	2	0	0	0	0	0
1951	Pit-N	.800	3	0	4	1	0	0
Total	3	.923	58	84	107	6	14	4

■ Tony Muser 1B

YEAR	TM/L	PCT	G	PO	A	E	DP	FR
1969	Bos-A	1.000	2	17	3	0	3	1
1971	Chi-A	.963	4	23	3	1	1	0
1972	Chi-A	.986	29	135	7	2	12	0
1973	Chi-A	.992	89	680	38	6	70	-2
1974	Chi-A	.998	80	419	13	1	46	-4
1975	Chi-A	.993	41	263	22	2	35	2
	Bal-A	.996	62	213	15	1	23	1
	Yr	.994	103	476	37	3	58	3
1976	Bal-A	.991	109	683	62	7	65	4
1977	Bal-A	.992	77	215	19	2	36	3
1978	Mil-A	.988	12	79	5	1	4	0
Total	9	.992	505	2727	187	3	295	5

OF

YEAR	TM/L	PCT	G	PO	A	E	DP	FR
1972	Chi-A	—	1	0	0	0	0	0
1973	Chi-A	1.000	2	1	0	0	0	0
1976	Bal-A	1.000	12	10	1	0	0	1
1977	Bal-A	.947	11	17	1	1	0	1
Total	4	.968	26	28	2	1	0	2

■ Stan Musial OF

YEAR	TM/L	PCT	G	PO	A	E	DP	FR
1941	StL-N	1.000	11	20	1	0	0	0
1942	StL-N	.984	135	296	6	5	0	3
1943	StL-N	.982	155	376	15	7	4	12
1944	StL-N	.987	146	353	16	5	2	12
1946	StL-N	.983	42	110	4	2	0	3
1948	StL-N	.981	155	347	10	7	3	5
1949	StL-N	.991	156	326	10	3	5	-4
1950	StL-N	.964	77	132	2	5	1	-9
1951	StL-N	.974	91	216	13	6	4	10
1952	StL-N	.987	129	298	6	4	2	-8
1953	StL-N	.984	157	294	9	5	1	-3
1954	StL-N	.990	152	271	13	3	4	-2
1955	StL-N	.987	51	75	2	1	0	-2
1956	StL-N	.989	53	84	5	1	0	-6
1959	StL-N	1.000	3	1	0	0	0	0
1960	StL-N	.990	59	97	2	1	0	-5
1961	StL-N	.994	103	149	9	1	0	-5
1962	StL-N	.977	119	164	6	4	1	-10
1963	StL-N	.968	96	121	1	4	0	-12
Total	19	.984	1890	3730	130	4	27	-21

1B

YEAR	TM/L	PCT	G	PO	A	E	DP	FR
1946	StL-N	.989	114	1056	65	13	119	-7
1947	StL-N	.994	149	1360	77	8	138	-7
1948	StL-N	1.000	2	7	1	0	0	0
1949	StL-N	1.000	1	11	1	0	0	0
1950	StL-N	.996	69	628	37	3	66	-4
1951	StL-N	.994	60	600	32	4	60	-4
1952	StL-N	.995	25	204	12	1	13	-1
1954	StL-N	.950	10	36	2	2	4	-1
1955	StL-N	.992	110	925	90	8	93	8
1956	StL-N	.993	103	870	90	7	96	7
1957	StL-N	.992	130	1167	99	10	131	2
1958	StL-N	.989	124	1019	100	13	127	8
1959	StL-N	.990	90	623	63	7	72	3
1960	StL-N	.991	29	203	17	2	16	-1
Total	14	.992	1016	8709	688	8	935	3

■ George Myatt 2B

YEAR	TM/L	PCT	G	PO	A	E	DP	FR
1943	Was-A	.930	11	21	32	4	4	-1
1944	Was-A	.957	121	341	299	29	81	-17
1945	Was-A	.972	94	228	231	13	48	-21
1946	Was-A	1.000	2	3	1	0	0	0
1947	Was-A	1.000	1	0	1	0	0	0
Total	5	.962	229	593	564	6	133	-39

3B

YEAR	TM/L	PCT	G	PO	A	E	DP	FR
1938	NY-N	.935	19	16	42	4	5	2
1939	NY-N	.907	14	10	29	4	3	1
1943	Was-A	.875	2	4	3	1	0	0
1945	Was-A	.885	6	5	18	3	2	2
1946	Was-A	.900	7	7	11	2	1	-2
Total	5	.912	48	42	103	4	11	3

SS

YEAR	TM/L	PCT	G	PO	A	E	DP	FR
1938	NY-N	.919	24	61	86	13	19	6
1943	Was-A	1.000	2	2	0	0	0	0
1944	Was-A	.862	15	35	40	12	9	-5
1945	Was-A	—	1	0	0	0	0	0
Total	4	.900	42	98	126	5	28	1

OF

YEAR	TM/L	PCT	G	PO	A	E	DP	FR
1944	Was-A	1.000	3	8	0	0	0	0
1945	Was-A	.971	32	60	6	2	0	1
Total	2	.974	35	68	6	2	0	1

■ Glenn Myatt C

YEAR	TM/L	PCT	G	PO	A	E	DP	FR
1920	Phi-A	.927	22	36	15	4	1	-3
1921	Phi-A	.939	27	59	18	5	2	2
1923	Cle-A	.934	69	188	37	16	3	-8
1924	Cle-A	.978	95	248	63	7	7	-15
1925	Cle-A	.973	98	273	53	9	6	-18
1926	Cle-A	1.000	35	94	18	0	0	-1
1927	Cle-A	.978	26	67	20	2	4	2
1928	Cle-A	.967	30	72	15	3	2	-9
1929	Cle-A	.976	41	99	24	3	3	-1
1930	Cle-A	.977	71	214	43	6	8	-7
1931	Cle-A	.991	53	176	34	2	2	-4
1932	Cle-A	.988	65	211	32	3	3	-8
1933	Cle-A	.965	27	65	17	3	2	-1
1934	Cle-A	.980	34	132	14	3	3	-1
1935	Cle-A	1.000	10	41	4	0	0	-1
	NY-N	1.000	4	7	0	0	0	-1
1936	Det-A	1.000	27	79	12	0	1	-2
Total	16	.974	734	2061	419	6	47	-76

OF

YEAR	TM/L	PCT	G	PO	A	E	DP	FR
1920	Phi-A	.900	37	47	7	6	2	-2
1925	Cle-A	—	1	0	0	0	0	-1
Total	2	.900	38	47	7	6	2	-3

■ Buddy Myer 2B

YEAR	TM/L	PCT	G	PO	A	E	DP	FR
1927	Bos-A	1.000	1	1	4	0	2	1
1929	Was-A	.958	88	205	271	21	51	-13
1930	Was-A	.965	134	330	405	27	89	-18
1931	Was-A	.984	137	333	398	12	87	-16
1932	Was-A	.975	139	352	426	20	97	-18
1933	Was-A	.978	129	356	417	17	92	-1
1934	Was-A	.975	135	367	420	20	101	-13
1935	Was-A	.984	151	460	473	20	138	8
1936	Was-A	.985	43	120	143	4	31	3
1937	Was-A	.966	119	308	338	23	90	-17
1938	Was-A	.982	121	308	355	12	91	2
1939	Was-A	.968	65	175	188	12	48	-1
1940	Was-A	.967	54	119	176	10	34	4
1941	Was-A	.982	24	53	54	2	12	-8
Total	14	.974	1340	3487	4068	200	963	-87

SS

YEAR	TM/L	PCT	G	PO	A	E	DP	FR
1925	Was-A	1.000	4	1	3	0	0	-2
1926	Was-A	.928	118	215	297	40	47	-15
1927	Was-A	.933	15	29	41	5	9	-3
	Bos-A	.940	101	238	311	35	64	7
	Yr	.939	116	267	352	40	73	4
Total	3	.934	238	483	652	0	120	-13

3B

YEAR	TM/L	PCT	G	PO	A	E	DP	FR
1926	Was-A	.900	8	11	7	2	0	-2
1927	Bos-A	.935	14	17	26	3	3	-1
1928	Bos-A	.967	144	137	306	15	35	4
1929	Was-A	.936	53	69	91	11	13	-2
Total	4	.955	219	234	430	1	51	-1

OF

YEAR	TM/L	PCT	G	PO	A	E	DP	FR
1927	Bos-A	.957	10	20	2	1	0	0
1930	Was-A	—	2	0	0	0	0	-1
1937	Was-A	—	1	0	0	0	0	0
Total	3	.957	13	20	2	1	0	-1

■ George Myers C

YEAR	TM/L	PCT	G	PO	A	E	DP	FR
1884	Buf-N	.837	49	271	58	64	4	-4
1885	Buf-N	.899	69	305	95	45	4	-2
1886	StL-N	.928	72	368	80	35	8	-11
1887	Ind-N	.929	50	176	58	18	8	-12
1888	Ind-N	.929	47	211	63	21	4	-6
1889	Ind-N	.872	18	54	28	12	0	1
Total	6	.901	305	1385	382	195	28	-34

OF

YEAR	TM/L	PCT	G	PO	A	E	DP	FR
1884	Buf-N	.788	34	49	3	14	1	-7
1885	Buf-N	.822	23	36	1	8	0	-3
1886	Ind-N	.875	6	7	0	1	0	-1
1887	Ind-N	.957	15	21	1	1	1	0
1888	Ind-N	.913	10	15	6	2	0	3
1889	Ind-N	.909	23	52	8	6	1	6
Total	6	.861	111	180	19	2	3	-2

3B

YEAR	TM/L	PCT	G	PO	A	E	DP	FR
1886	StL-N	.714	1	3	2	2	0	0
1887	Ind-N	1.000	1	1	1	0	0	0
1888	Ind-N	.733	14	6	16	8	2	-5
Total	3	.744	16	10	19	0	2	-5

1B

YEAR	TM/L	PCT	G	PO	A	E	DP	FR
1887	Ind-N	1.000	6	38	3	0	4	1
1888	Ind-N	.750	1	3	0	1	0	0
1889	Ind-N	1.000	1	0	1	0	0	0
Total	3	.978	8	41	4	1	4	1

■ Greg Myers C

YEAR	TM/L	PCT	G	PO	A	E	DP	FR
1987	Tor-A	1.000	7	24	1	0	0	2
1989	Tor-A	1.000	11	46	6	0	1	2
1990	Tor-A	.993	87	411	30	3	4	-1
Total	3	.994	105	481	37	3	5	3

■ Hi Myers OF

YEAR	TM/L	PCT	G	PO	A	E	DP	FR
1909	Bro-N	1.000	6	9	0	0	0	-1
1911	Bro-N	.889	13	22	2	3	0	0
1914	Bro-N	.964	60	102	4	4	0	-5
1915	Bro-N	.964	153	352	23	14	5	-1
1916	Bro-N	.969	106	242	11	8	5	-3
1917	Bro-N	.982	66	162	6	3	1	3
1918	Bro-N	.975	107	294	17	8	7	8
1919	Bro-N	.979	131	358	13	8	5	5
1920	Bro-N	.978	152	386	17	9	5	0
1921	Bro-N	.968	124	278	25	10	5	5
1922	Bro-N	.974	152	399	16	11	2	1
1923	StL-N	.977	87	239	15	6	0	4
1924	StL-N	.945	22	50	2	3	1	1
1925	Cin-N	1.000	3	5	0	0	0	0
Total	14	.972	1182	2898	151	7	36	12

2B

YEAR	TM/L	PCT	G	PO	A	E	DP	FR
1917	Bro-N	.925	19	46	52	8	5	-4
1921	Bro-N	.958	21	40	51	4	11	1
1922	Bro-N	.833	1	0	5	1	0	0
1924	StL-N	1.000	3	3	11	0	0	0
Total	4	.941	44	89	119	3	16	-3

3B

YEAR	TM/L	PCT	G	PO	A	E	DP	FR
1917	Bro-N	.957	15	14	31	2	1	-1
1920	Bro-N	1.000	2	2	2	0	0	0
1921	Bro-N	1.000	1	1	2	0	0	0
1924	StL-N	.870	12	8	12	3	0	-2
Total	4	.934	30	24	47	5	1	-3

1B

YEAR	TM/L	PCT	G	PO	A	E	DP	FR
1917	Bro-N	.971	22	188	13	6	8	0

■ Bert Myers 3B

YEAR	TM/L	PCT	G	PO	A	E	DP	FR
1896	StL-N	.867	121	162	242	62	16	-9
1898	Was-N	.835	31	35	61	19	6	-3
1900	Phi-N	.909	7	6	24	3	3	2
Total	3	.863	159	203	327	4	25	-10

SS

YEAR	TM/L	PCT	G	PO	A	E	DP	FR
1896	StL-N	1.000	1	3	1	0	0	0

■ Al Myers 2B

YEAR	TM/L	PCT	G	PO	A	E	DP	FR
1884	Mil-U	.848	12	26	30	10	1	2
1885	Phi-N	.884	93	201	287	64	31	-18
1886	KC-N	.913	118	298	384	65	50	1
1887	Was-N	.909	78	193	248	44	23	-2
1888	Was-N	.918	132	271	399	60	37	-26
1889	Was-N	.942	46	147	148	18	26	3
	Phi-N	.853	75	192	261	78	33	-9
	Yr	.886	121	339	409	96	59	-6
1890	Phi-N	.948	117	347	352	38	62	14
1891	Phi-N	.937	135	354	438	53	67	-10
Total	8	.914	806	2029	2547	430	330	-45

SS

YEAR	TM/L	PCT	G	PO	A	E	DP	FR
1887	Was-N	.814	27	51	93	33	6	-2

■ Lynn Myers SS

YEAR	TM/L	PCT	G	PO	A	E	DP	FR
1938	StL-N	.944	69	110	195	18	36	-1
1939	StL-N	.897	36	55	76	15	21	3
Total	2	.930	105	165	271	3	57	2

3B

YEAR	TM/L	PCT	G	PO	A	E	DP	FR
1939	StL-N	.957	13	7	15	1	4	2

2B

YEAR	TM/L	PCT	G	PO	A	E	DP	FR
1939	StL-N	.857	5	3	3	1	0	0

■ Hap Myers 1B

YEAR	TM/L	PCT	G	PO	A	E	DP	FR
1911	StL-A	.976	11	121	3	3	5	-2
	Bos-A	.947	12	102	6	6	5	-1
	Yr	.963	23	223	9	9	10	-3
1913	Bos-N	.987	135	1344	85	19	57	5
1914	Bro-F	.989	88	784	44	9	47	1
1915	Bro-F	.990	107	961	56	10	52	1
Total	4	.987	353	3312	194	7	166	4

OF

YEAR	TM/L	PCT	G	PO	A	E	DP	FR
1910	Bos-A	1.000	2	1	0	0	0	0

■ Billy Myers SS

YEAR	TM/L	PCT	G	PO	A	E	DP	FR
1935	Cin-N	.939	112	230	335	37	77	3
1936	Cin-N	.938	98	225	304	35	73	8
1937	Cin-N	.948	121	190	360	30	67	4
1938	Cin-N	.939	123	255	380	41	74	3
1939	Cin-N	.951	151	309	512	42	110	6
1940	Cin-N	.961	88	155	269	17	62	-5
1941	Cin-N	.939	19	33	60	6	12	3
Total	7	.946	712	1397	2220	208	475	22

2B

YEAR	TM/L	PCT	G	PO	A	E	DP	FR
1937	Cin-N	1.000	6	8	8	0	1	0
1938	Cin-N	.908	11	28	31	6	1	-1
1941	Cin-N	1.000	1	4	6	0	1	1
Total	3	.934	18	40	45	6	3	0

■ Bill Nahorodny C

YEAR	TM/L	PCT	G	PO	A	E	DP	FR
1976	Phi-N	1.000	2	7	0	0	0	0
1977	Chi-A	1.000	7	26	6	0	1	0
1978	Chi-A	.980	104	486	53	11	6	-4
1979	Chi-A	.973	60	223	25	7	3	0
1980	Atl-N	.940	54	174	24	2	2	-7
1981	Atl-N	1.000	9	38	3	0	0	0
1982	Cle-A	1.000	35	111	11	0	2	0
1984	Sea-A	.976	10	38	2	1	0	-2
Total	8	.983	275	1072	121	1	15	-18

YEAR	TM/L	PCT	G	PO	A	E	DP	FR
1B								
1978	Chi-A	1.000	4	23	2	0	0	0
1980	Atl-N	1.000	1	6	0	0	0	0
1981	Atl-N	1.000	1	1	0	0	0	0
1984	Sea-A	1.000	1	3	0	0	2	0
Total	4	1.000	7	33	2	0	2	0
■ Doc Nance OF								
1897	Lou-N	.986	35	60	8	1	4	4
1898	Lou-N	.946	22	28	7	2	2	2
1901	Det-A	.932	132	240	20	19	6	1
Total	3	.943	189	328	35	2	12	7
■ Hal Naragon C								
1951	Cle-A	.929	2	12	1	1	1	0
1954	Cle-A	1.000	45	132	14	0	1	-1
1955	Cle-A	.991	52	199	15	2	3	-4
1956	Cle-A	.988	48	162	7	2	0	-11
1957	Cle-A	.990	39	179	14	2	2	-2
1959	Cle-A	1.000	10	51	3	0	1	-1
	Was-A	.993	54	262	13	2	0	-1
	Yr	.994	64	313	16	2	1	-2
1960	Was-A	.978	29	119	14	3	1	-3
1961	Min-A	.994	36	168	12	1	4	-5
1962	Min-A	1.000	9	41	0	0	1	0
Total	9	.991	324	1325	93	3	14	-28
■ Jerry Narron C								
1979	NY-A	.973	56	167	15	5	2	-4
1980	Sea-A	.992	39	115	11	1	0	-8
1981	Sea-A	.996	65	248	11	1	3	-14
1983	Cal-A	.895	6	14	3	2	0	-1
1984	Cal-A	.994	46	146	10	1	1	-8
1985	Cal-A	1.000	45	144	14	0	4	2
1986	Cal-A	.988	51	155	14	2	3	2
1987	Sea-A	1.000	3	9	0	0	0	0
Total	8	.989	311	998	78	2	13	-31
1B								
1984	Cal-A	1.000	7	38	2	0	5	0
1985	Cal-A	1.000	1	2	0	0	0	0
Total	2	1.000	8	40	2	0	5	0
■ Billy Nash 3B								
1884	Ric-a	.828	45	77	87	34	8	7
1885	Bos-N	.864	19	24	27	8	3	-2
1886	Bos-N	.863	90	137	177	50	9	0
1887	Bos-N	.884	117	207	242	59	19	8
1888	Bos-N	.913	105	139	250	37	20	22
1889	Bos-N	.905	128	205	274	50	25	12
1890	Bos-P	.866	129	198	307	78	37	18
1891	Bos-N	.900	140	213	264	53	20	-12
1892	Bos-N	.898	135	197	351	62	23	25
1893	Bos-N	.923	128	189	300	41	23	3
1894	Bos-N	.933	132	204	267	34	24	6
1895	Bos-N	.882	132	193	246	59	26	-8
1896	Phi-N	.911	65	87	148	23	12	7
1897	Phi-N	.919	79	114	146	23	10	-3
1898	Phi-N	.958	20	35	33	3	6	-1
Total	15	.897	1464	2219	3119	614	265	82
2B								
1885	Bos-N	.867	8	10	16	4	3	-2
1888	Bos-N	.904	31	90	108	21	11	3
1897	Phi-N	.889	4	7	9	2	1	-1
Total	3	.899	43	107	133	7	15	0
SS								
1886	Bos-N	.851	17	23	40	11	5	-3
1897	Phi-N	.887	19	51	51	13	6	-4
Total	2	.873	36	74	91	4	11	-7
OF								
1887	Bos-N	.933	5	13	1	1	0	1
1892	Bos-N	—	1	0	0	0	0	0
Total	2	.933	6	13	1	1	0	1
■ Charlie Neal 2B								
1956	Bro-N	.972	51	70	103	5	24	2
1957	Bro-N	1.000	3	8	8	0	1	1
1958	LA-N	.976	132	334	343	17	121	12
1959	LA-N	.989	151	386	413	9	110	20
1960	LA-N	.977	136	250	291	13	78	-16
1961	LA-N	.976	104	211	246	11	63	2
1962	NY-N	.970	85	187	240	13	54	-3
1963	Cin-N	1.000	1	0	1	0	1	0
Total	8	.978	663	1446	1645	8	452	18
SS								
1956	Bro-N	1.000	1	0	1	0	0	0
1957	Bro-N	.949	100	151	298	24	60	-4
1958	LA-N	.933	9	10	18	2	2	0
1959	LA-N	1.000	1	0	2	0	0	0
1960	LA-N	1.000	3	1	5	0	1	1
1962	NY-N	.938	39	63	118	12	30	-6
1963	NY-N	.967	8	15	14	1	6	-2
	Cin-N	1.000	1	1	0	1	0	0
	Yr	.968	9	16	14	1	6	-2
Total	7	.947	162	241	456	9	99	-11
3B								
1957	Bro-N	.950	23	23	34	3	5	0
1962	NY-N	.925	12	6	31	3	1	1
1963	NY-N	.961	66	61	135	8	10	2
	Cin-N	.927	19	21	17	3	0	-2
	Yr	.955	85	82	152	11	10	0
Total	3	.951	120	111	217	7	16	1
■ Greasy Neale OF								
1916	Cin-N	.973	133	307	20	9	6	16
1917	Cin-N	.979	119	216	13	5	3	9
1918	Cin-N	.981	102	249	11	5	2	9
1919	Cin-N	.959	138	285	16	13	4	0
1920	Cin-N	.987	150	347	19	5	7	13
1921	Phi-N	.842	16	16	0	3	0	-6
	Cin-N	.964	60	128	7	5	2	-2
	Yr	.950	76	144	7	8	2	-8
1922	Cin-N	.864	16	18	1	3	0	-2
1924	Cin-N	1.000	2	3	0	0	0	0
Total	8	.972	736	1569	87	8	22	25
■ Jim Nealon 1B								
1906	Pit-N	.987	154	1592	102	23	90	1
1907	Pit-N	.978	104	998	68	24	35	0
Total	2	.983	258	2590	170	7	125	1
■ Tom Needham C								
1904	Bos-N	.945	77	326	140	27	8	6
1905	Bos-N	.949	77	292	134	23	6	-7
1906	Bos-N	.959	76	317	130	19	9	0
1907	Bos-N	.967	78	281	101	13	9	-10
1908	NY-N	.975	47	168	30	5	2	8
1909	Chi-N	.980	7	43	5	1	0	1
1910	Chi-N	.982	27	131	31	3	0	3
1911	Chi-N	.984	23	94	32	2	2	5
1912	Chi-N	.994	32	116	39	1	3	-1
1913	Chi-N	.962	14	51	24	3	4	5
1914	Chi-N	.943	7	22	11	2	0	2
Total	11	.962	465	1841	677	9	43	12
1B								
1905	Bos-N	1.000	2	18	1	0	1	0
1906	Bos-N	1.000	2	19	0	0	1	0
1907	Bos-N	1.000	1	7	0	0	0	0
1910	Chi-N	1.000	1	2	0	0	0	0
1913	Chi-N	1.000	1	2	0	0	0	0
Total	5	1.000	7	48	1	0	2	0
OF								
1904	Bos-N	—	1	0	0	0	0	0
1905	Bos-N	.500	3	1	0	1	0	-2
1906	Bos-N	—	1	0	0	0	0	0
Total	3	.500	5	1	0	1	0	-2
2B								
1906	Bos-N	.917	5	6	16	2	0	-1
3B								
1906	Bos-N	.500	1	0	1	1	1	0
■ Cal Neeman C								
1957	Chi-N	.990	118	703	56	8	13	1
1958	Chi-N	.992	71	340	25	3	6	2
1959	Chi-N	.994	38	158	9	1	1	-1
1960	Chi-N	1.000	9	34	4	0	1	4
	Phi-N	.979	52	252	31	6	2	5
	Yr	.982	61	286	35	6	3	9
1961	Phi-N	.986	19	63	5	1	0	2
1962	Pit-N	.983	24	103	15	2	1	8
1963	Cle-A	1.000	9	32	2	0	1	3
	Was-A	.970	12	29	3	1	3	2
	Yr	.985	21	61	5	1	4	5
Total	7	.988	352	1714	150	2	28	26
■ Bernie Neis OF								
1920	Bro-N	.957	83	145	11	7	4	-2
1921	Bro-N	.946	77	126	13	8	1	4
1922	Bro-N	.897	27	32	3	4	0	2
1923	Bro-N	.941	111	268	20	18	3	0
1924	Bro-N	.937	62	114	5	8	1	-1
1925	Bos-N	.970	87	282	8	9	1	14
1926	Bos-N	.925	23	60	2	5	1	1
1927	Cle-A	.978	29	83	5	2	0	5
	Chi-A	.927	21	36	2	3	1	-3
	Yr	.962	50	119	7	5	1	2
Total	8	.950	520	1146	69	4	12	20
2B								
1921	Bro-N	1.000	1	0	1	0	0	0
■ Dave Nelson 2B								
1968	Cle-A	.987	59	115	114	3	26	-1
1969	Cle-A	.966	33	78	94	6	28	5
1970	Was-A	.986	33	64	79	2	19	1
1971	Was-A	1.000	1	0	1	0	0	0
1973	Tex-A	.984	140	327	364	11	98	-12
1974	Tex-A	.969	120	295	337	20	74	1
1975	Tex-A	.959	23	56	60	5	16	1
1976	KC-A	.975	46	70	88	4	14	2
1977	KC-A	.926	11	11	14	2	3	-2
Total	9	.976	466	1016	1151	3	278	-5
3B								
1971	Was-A	.938	84	63	149	14	15	-13
1972	Tex-A	.945	119	107	222	19	25	-9
Total	2	.943	203	170	371	3	40	-22
OF								
1969	Cle-A	1.000	2	1	0	0	0	0
1972	Tex-A	.889	15	24	0	3	0	-2
Total	2	.893	17	25	0	3	0	-2
SS								
1968	Cle-A	.957	14	9	13	1	1	0
1B								
1976	KC-A	1.000	3	9	2	0	3	1
■ Rocky Nelson 1B								
1949	StL-N	1.000	70	564	24	0	48	-4
1950	StL-N	.992	70	596	51	5	66	3
1951	StL-N	1.000	4	29	1	0	5	-1
	Pit-N	.990	32	275	24	3	32	1
	Yr	.991	36	304	25	3	37	0
1952	Bro-N	1.000	5	16	0	0	2	-1
1954	Cle-A	1.000	2	6	0	0	1	0
1956	Bro-N	.991	25	189	20	2	20	1
	StL-N	1.000	14	54	7	0	6	1
	Yr	.993	39	243	27	2	26	2
1959	Pit-N	.994	56	337	18	2	45	-3
1960	Pit-N	.996	73	463	37	2	48	1
1961	Pit-N	.996	35	231	15	1	26	-1
Total	9	.995	386	2760	197	5	299	-3
OF								
1951	StL-N	—	1	0	0	0	0	0
	Pit-N	1.000	12	22	1	0	0	0
	Yr	1.000	13	22	1	0	0	0
1956	StL-N	1.000	8	11	0	0	0	0
1959	Pit-N	.667	2	2	0	1	0	0
Total	3	.973	23	35	1	1	0	0
■ Candy Nelson SS								
1878	Ind-N	.841	19	19	50	13	1	-6
1879	Tro-N	.834	24	37	89	25	8	3
1881	Wor-N	.898	24	20	94	13	6	2
1883	NY-a	.875	97	98	232	47	18	-6
1884	NY-a	.879	110	113	292	56	16	-16
1885	NY-a	.892	107	153	370	63	33	14
1886	NY-a	.855	73	103	216	54	17	-6
1887	NY-a	.896	32	46	100	17	12	3
1890	Bro-a	.866	57	60	198	40	20	-7
Total	9	.875	543	649	1641	328	131	-19
1879	Tro-N	1.000	4	5	1	0	0	1
1886	NY-a	.908	36	56	3	6	2	-2
1887	NY-a	.895	37	74	11	10	6	7
1890	Bro-a	1.000	4	7	0	0	0	0
Total	4	.908	81	142	15	6	8	6
2B								
1884	NY-a	1.000	1	7	0	0	0	-1
1887	NY-a	1.000	1	1	0	0	0	0
Total	2	1.000	2	8	0	0	0	-1
3B								
1885	NY-a	—	1	0	0	0	0	0
1887	NY-N	—	1	0	0	0	0	0
Total	2	—	2	0	0	0	0	0
■ Dick Nen 1B								
1963	LA-N	1.000	5	22	0	0	0	-1
1965	Was-A	.993	65	519	61	4	48	9
1966	Was-A	.990	76	566	38	6	44	-1
1967	Was-A	.995	65	516	42	3	49	2
1968	Chi-N	.987	52	219	11	3	12	-1
1970	Was-A	1.000	1	4	1	0	0	0
Total	6	.992	264	1846	153	6	153	8
OF								
1967	Was-A	—	1	0	0	0	0	0
■ Graig Nettles 3B								
1968	Min-A	.923	5	5	7	1	1	0
1969	Min-A	.982	21	12	42	1	3	0
1970	Cle-A	.967	154	134	358	17	40	29
1971	Cle-A	.973	158	159	412	16	54	42
1972	Cle-A	.956	150	114	338	21	27	5
1973	NY-A	.953	157	117	410	26	39	26
1974	NY-A	.961	154	147	377	21	29	17
1975	NY-A	.964	157	135	379	19	31	11
1976	NY-A	.965	158	137	383	19	30	17
1977	NY-A	.974	156	132	321	12	31	-3
1978	NY-A	.975	159	109	326	11	30	-6
1979	NY-A	.966	144	110	339	16	30	9
1980	NY-A	.960	88	58	182	10	18	-3
1981	NY-A	.972	97	63	214	8	14	8
1982	NY-A	.934	113	73	255	23	23	8
1983	NY-A	.956	126	78	273	16	18	1
1984	SD-N	.936	119	93	201	20	14	-10
1985	SD-N	.959	130	122	229	15	16	-9
1986	SD-N	.941	114	83	174	16	14	-2
1987	Atl-N	.951	40	12	46	3	6	-3
1988	Mon-N	.818	12	5	13	4	2	-1
Total	21	.961	2412	1898	5279	295	470	136
OF								
1968	Min-A	.968	16	28	2	1	0	1
1969	Min-A	.987	54	76	2	1	0	0
1970	Cle-A	1.000	3	1	0	0	0	0
Total	3	.982	73	105	4	2	0	1
1B								
1968	Min-A	1.000	3	17	0	0	1	0
1987	Atl-N	1.000	6	49	10	0	7	2
1988	Mon-N	.966	5	27	1	1	2	-1
Total	3	.990	14	93	11	1	10	1
SS								
1974	NY-A	—	1	0	0	0	0	-1
1976	NY-A	1.000	1	0	1	0	0	0
1978	NY-A	1.000	2	1	0	0	0	0
1980	NY-A	1.000	1	1	0	0	0	0
Total	4	1.000	5	2	1	0	0	-1
■ Jim Nettles OF								
1970	Min-A	1.000	11	8	0	0	0	0
1971	Min-A	.986	62	139	3	2	1	10
1972	Min-A	.982	78	156	5	3	1	6
1974	Det-A	1.000	41	80	1	0	0	-7
1979	KC-A	1.000	8	19	0	0	0	1
1981	Oak-A	—	1	0	0	0	0	0
Total	6	.988	201	402	9	5	2	10
1B								
1972	Min-A	1.000	1	1	0	0	0	0
1979	KC-A	1.000	1	2	0	0	0	0
Total	2	1.000	2	3	0	0	0	0
■ Morris Nettles OF								
1974	Cal-A	.990	54	99	0	1	0	-3
1975	Cal-A	.974	90	186	4	5	0	0
Total	2	.980	144	285	4	6	0	-3
■ Johnny Neun 1B								
1925	Det-A	.990	13	99	4	1	5	-1
1926	Det-A	.993	49	433	22	3	34	-3
1927	Det-A	.980	53	548	30	12	45	-3
1928	Det-A	.975	25	180	16	5	16	0
1930	Bos-N	.991	55	431	31	4	46	0
1931	Bos-N	.994	36	159	9	1	15	0
Total	6	.987	231	1850	112	6	161	-7

Al Newman 2B

YEAR	TM/L	PCT	G	PO	A	E	DP	FR
1985	Mon-N	1.000	15	18	33	0	6	9
1986	Mon-N	.967	59	76	127	7	25	10
1987	Min-A	.988	47	54	111	2	20	-5
1988	Min-A	.985	23	29	35	1	9	-1
1989	Min-A	.980	84	116	171	6	37	-14
1990	Min-A	.993	89	118	173	2	48	2
Total	6	.983	317	411	650	8	145	1

SS

1985	Mon-N	1.000	2	1	3	0	1	1
1986	Mon-N	.933	22	22	34	4	10	-1
1987	Min-A	.982	55	62	103	3	24	-4
1988	Min-A	.987	28	31	44	1	12	-2
1989	Min-A	.940	31	35	59	6	16	-7
1990	Min-A	.949	48	57	92	8	25	-7
Total	6	.961	186	208	335	2	88	-20

3B

1987	Min-A	1.000	12	4	11	0	0	0
1988	Min-A	.966	60	37	76	4	12	-1
1989	Min-A	.954	37	32	51	4	5	0
1990	Min-A	.945	28	13	39	3	8	4
Total	4	.960	137	86	177	1	25	3

OF

1987	Min-A	—	2	0	0	0	0	0
1989	Min-A	1.000	4	8	1	0	0	1
1990	Min-A	1.000	3	2	0	0	0	0
Total	3	1.000	9	10	1	0	0	1

Jeff Newman C

1976	Oak-A	.981	43	140	18	3	1	6
1977	Oak-A	.970	94	251	36	9	5	10
1978	Oak-A	.969	61	222	27	8	3	-4
1979	Oak-A	.977	81	378	53	10	7	0
1980	Oak-A	.976	55	229	19	6	0	-13
1981	Oak-A	.995	37	182	15	1	2	3
1982	Oak-A	.989	67	320	27	4	5	1
1983	Bos-A	.990	51	171	19	2	3	1
1984	Bos-A	.992	24	118	8	1	0	2
Total	9	.981	513	2011	222	4	26	6

1B

1978	Oak-A	.979	36	177	14	4	17	-1
1979	Oak-A	.982	46	350	30	7	29	-1
1980	Oak-A	.982	60	446	35	9	28	-1
1981	Oak-A	.995	30	185	13	1	12	-1
1982	Oak-A	.960	3	23	1	1	1	0
Total	5	.983	175	1181	93	2	87	-4

3B

1979	Oak-A	.933	7	2	12	1	2	0
1980	Oak-A	—	2	0	0	0	0	0
1982	Oak-A	1.000	1	4	0	0	0	-1
Total	3	.947	10	6	12	1	2	-1

2B

1980	Oak-A	—	1	0	0	0	0	-1

Patrick Newnam 1B

1910	StL-A	.972	103	1041	56	**32**	53	-4
1911	StL-A	.986	20	200	14	3	11	1
Total	2	.974	123	1241	70	5	64	-3

Skeeter Newsome SS

1935	Phi-A	.956	24	56	75	6	20	5
1936	Phi-A	.957	123	273	417	31	87	7
1937	Phi-A	.954	122	256	408	32	76	7
1938	Phi-A	.971	15	24	43	2	7	1
1939	Phi-A	.950	93	176	221	21	44	1
1941	Bos-A	.958	69	95	133	10	28	13
1942	Bos-A	.933	7	14	14	2	4	1
1943	Bos-A	.962	98	222	310	21	69	10
1944	Bos-A	.963	126	249	421	26	79	10
1945	Bos-A	.978	33	61	114	4	21	13
1946	Phi-N	.955	107	179	310	23	53	-12
1947	Phi-N	.969	85	131	247	12	60	2
Total	12	.959	902	1736	2713	190	548	58

2B

1935	Phi-A	.938	13	16	29	3	5	2
1936	Phi-A	1.000	2	1	0	0	0	0
1939	Phi-A	1.000	2	2	0	0	0	0
1941	Bos-A	.975	23	46	71	3	8	2
1942	Bos-A	.967	10	32	26	2	5	-1
1944	Bos-A	.940	8	21	26	3	4	1
1945	Bos-A	.963	82	206	231	17	54	6
1946	Phi-N	.923	3	1	11	1	0	0
1947	Phi-N	1.000	6	5	3	0	0	-1
Total	9	.962	149	330	397	9	80	9

3B

1935	Phi-A	1.000	4	5	6	0	0	0
1936	Phi-A	1.000	1	0	1	0	0	0
1942	Bos-A	.925	12	10	27	3	4	2
1943	Bos-A	1.000	15	23	36	0	2	3
1944	Bos-A	.000	1	0	0	0	0	0
1945	Bos-A	.976	11	9	31	1	3	3
1946	Phi-N	1.000	2	1	0	0	0	0
1947	Phi-N	1.000	3	0	2	0	0	0
Total	8	.968	49	48	103	5	9	8

OF

1935	Phi-A	1.000	1	2	0	0	0	0
1936	Phi-A	—	1	0	0	0	0	0
Total	2	1.000	2	2	0	0	0	0

Gus Niarhos C

1946	NY-A	.989	29	76	10	1	1	6
1948	NY-A	.990	82	376	33	4	7	11
1949	NY-A	1.000	30	84	7	0	2	4
1950	Chi-A	.978	36	167	14	4	2	8
1951	Chi-A	.985	59	240	31	4	5	3
1952	Bos-A	.992	25	107	12	1	2	6
1953	Bos-A	.985	16	61	5	1	2	4
1954	Phi-N	1.000	3	9	1	0	0	1
1955	Phi-N	1.000	7	13	2	0	0	1
Total	9	.988	287	1133	115	5	21	44

Simon Nicholls SS

1903	Det-A	.600	2	3	3	4	0	-2
1906	Phi-A	.965	12	22	33	2	4	-2
1907	Phi-A	.930	82	178	258	33	12	-5
1908	Phi-A	.913	120	221	370	56	26	-17
1909	Phi-A	.889	14	24	32	7	3	-2
1910	Cle-A	.000	3	0	0	0	1	-1
Total	6	.917	233	448	696	103	45	-29

2B

1907	Phi-A	.917	28	41	69	10	3	-10
1908	Phi-A	.948	23	51	58	6	6	-2
Total	2	.932	51	92	127	6	9	-12

3B

1907	Phi-A	.783	13	8	10	5	2	-4
1908	Phi-A	.933	7	8	6	1	1	-1
1909	Phi-A	.926	5	8	17	2	1	3
Total	3	.877	25	24	33	8	4	-2

1B

1909	Phi-A	1.000	1	7	0	0	1	0

Reid Nichols OF

1980	Bos-A	.962	9	24	1	1	0	1
1981	Bos-A	1.000	27	35	3	0	1	5
1982	Bos-A	.989	82	169	9	2	4	10
1983	Bos-A	.994	72	168	4	1	1	6
1984	Bos-A	.988	48	79	3	1	0	5
1985	Bos-A	.933	10	14	0	1	0	4
	Chi-A	1.000	48	70	1	0	0	-2
	Yr	.988	58	84	1	1	0	-2
1986	Chi-A	.989	53	90	3	1	0	5
1987	Mon-N	.990	58	97	4	1	0	7
Total	8	.990	408	746	28	8	6	37

2B

1985	Chi-A	1.000	3	1	1	0	1	0
1986	Chi-A	1.000	2	0	1	0	0	0
Total	2	1.000	5	1	2	0	1	0

3B

1981	Bos-A	1.000	1	0	1	0	0	0
1987	Mon-N	.667	3	1	1	1	0	0
Total	2	.750	4	1	2	1	0	0

SS

1983	Bos-A	1.000	1	0	1	0	0	0

Dave Nicholson OF

1960	Bal-A	.982	44	51	3	1	1	-1
1962	Bal-A	.983	80	111	4	2	0	5
1963	Chi-A	.970	123	213	10	7	1	-4
1964	Chi-A	.972	92	136	4	4	0	-6
1965	Chi-A	1.000	36	30	0	0	0	2
1966	Hou-A	.968	90	139	11	5	0	2
1967	Atl-N	1.000	7	10	1	0	0	0
Total	7	.974	472	690	33	9	2	-6

Fred Nicholson OF

1917	Det-A	1.000	3	3	0	0	0	-1
1919	Pit-N	.939	17	29	2	2	1	0
1920	Pit-N	.957	58	125	9	6	2	3
1921	Bos-N	.983	59	112	4	2	0	-3
1922	Bos-N	.915	63	125	5	12	0	-4
Total	5	.950	200	394	20	2	3	-5

1B

1919	Pit-N	1.000	1	14	1	0	1	0
1921	Bos-N	.958	4	21	2	1	2	0
Total	2	.974	5	35	3	1	3	0

2B

1921	Bos-N	.769	2	5	5	3	2	-1

Parson Nicholson 2B

1888	Det-N	.935	24	44	71	8	5	-2
1890	Tol-a	.929	**134**	294	385	52	45	-7
Total	2	.930	158	338	456	0	50	-9

SS

1895	Was-N	.797	10	17	34	13	4	-2

C

1890	Tol-a	—	1	0	0	0	0	0

Bill Nicholson OF

1936	Phi-A	1.000	1	1	0	0	0	0
1939	Chi-N	.955	58	123	5	6	0	0
1940	Chi-N	.950	123	235	10	13	2	-4
1941	Chi-N	.971	143	293	10	9	2	-2
1942	Chi-N	.986	151	327	18	5	2	10
1943	Chi-N	.978	154	340	16	8	2	4
1944	Chi-N	.979	**156**	305	18	7	4	-1
1945	Chi-N	.990	151	300	12	3	4	-2
1946	Chi-N	.973	80	179	4	5	1	-1
1947	Chi-N	**.990**	140	281	7	3	1	-7
1948	Chi-N	.980	136	244	7	5	1	-9
1949	Chi-N	.995	91	185	10	1	1	-2
1950	Phi-N	.952	15	20	0	1	0	-1
1951	Phi-N	.987	41	75	1	1	0	-3
1952	Phi-N	1.000	19	33	0	0	0	-2
1953	Phi-N	1.000	12	13	0	0	0	-1
Total	16	.979	1471	2954	118	7	20	-23

Hugh Nicol OF

1881	Chi-N	.932	26	44	11	4	1	5
1882	Chi-N	.887	47	59	27	11	1	9
1883	StL-a	.916	84	133	**31**	15	4	13
1884	StL-a	.873	87	144	**48**	28	3	**22**
1885	StL-a	.888	111	213	33	31	2	13
1886	StL-a	.942	57	86	11	6	0	1
1887	Cin-a	.918	125	194	20	19	1	-3
1888	Cin-a	.957	125	187	15	9	3	-1
1889	Cin-a	.918	115	168	22	17	4	3
1890	Cin-N	.921	46	62	8	6	3	0
Total	10	.912	823	1290	226	146	22	61

2B

1883	StL-a	.836	11	29	32	12	3	-1
1884	StL-a	.889	23	61	75	17	12	2
1886	StL-a	.789	4	10	5	4	2	2
1888	Cin-a	.966	12	29	27	2	6	-1
1889	Cin-a	.951	7	24	15	2	3	-1
1890	Cin-N	1.000	1	0	1	0	0	-1
Total	6	.893	58	153	155	7	26	-4

SS

1881	Chi-N	.667	1	1	1	1	0	-1
1882	Chi-N	.733	3	3	8	4	1	-1
1884	StL-a	—	1	0	0	0	0	0
1886	StL-a	.775	8	7	24	9	0	-3
1888	Cin-a	.667	1	1	1	1	0	-1
1890	Cin-N	.588	3	4	6	7	0	-1
Total	6	.718	22	16	40	2	1	-10

3B

1884	StL-a	—	1	0	0	0	0	0
1885	StL-a	1.000	1	1	2	0	0	0
1889	Cin-a	1.000	3	1	2	0	0	0
Total	3	1.000	5	2	4	0	0	0

Steve Nicosia C

1978	Pit-N	1.000	1	8	1	0	0	1
1979	Pit-N	.991	65	320	25	3	4	4
1980	Pit-N	.984	58	284	25	5	4	-1
1981	Pit-N	.982	52	257	23	5	2	0
1982	Pit-N	.990	35	182	22	2	1	4
1983	Pit-N	.988	15	76	3	1	0	-1
	SF-N	.984	9	55	6	1	0	2
	Yr	.986	24	131	9	2	0	1
1984	SF-N	.985	41	190	11	3	1	-5
1985	Mon-N	.988	23	80	5	1	1	-6
	Tor-A	1.000	6	23	2	0	1	1
Total	8	.987	305	1475	123	1	14	-1

OF

1982	Pit-N	1.000	3	1	0	0	0	0

1B

1985	Mon-N	1.000	2	6	0	0	0	0

Bert Niehoff 2B

1914	Cin-N	1.000	3	3	9	0	0	1
1915	Phi-N	.946	148	307	411	**41**	55	-7
1916	Phi-N	.936	144	285	437	**49**	**65**	-1
1917	Phi-N	.945	96	203	326	31	37	15
1918	Phi-N	.975	22	54	65	3	11	2
	NY-N	.871	7	14	13	4	2	-2
	Yr	.954	29	68	78	7	13	0
Total	5	.943	420	866	1261	128	170	8

3B

1913	Cin-N	.917	2	2	9	1	0	2
1914	Cin-N	.924	134	154	272	35	15	7
1916	Phi-N	.857	2	2	4	1	0	0
1917	Phi-N	1.000	6	5	19	0	5	3
Total	4	.927	144	163	304	7	20	12

1B

1917	Phi-N	1.000	7	11	0	0	0	0

Butch Nieman OF

1943	Bos-N	.963	93	195	12	8	1	-1
1944	Bos-N	.975	126	261	13	7	2	-2
1945	Bos-N	.932	57	132	4	10	1	-1
Total	3	.961	276	588	29	5	4	-4

Bob Nieman OF

1951	StL-A	.962	11	24	1	1	0	0
1952	StL-A	.976	125	230	10	6	**5**	-3
1953	Det-A	.979	135	271	10	6	1	1
1954	Det-A	.984	62	119	2	2	0	-6
1955	Chi-A	.976	78	118	4	3	2	-9
1956	Chi-A	1.000	10	24	0	0	0	0
	Bal-A	.980	114	243	4	5	1	1
	Yr	.982	124	267	4	5	1	1
1957	Bal-A	.980	120	237	6	5	0	0
1958	Bal-A	.961	100	145	3	6	0	-15
1959	Bal-A	.973	97	171	6	5	0	-3
1960	StL-N	.940	55	63	0	4	0	-9
1961	StL-N	1.000	4	2	0	0	0	-1
	Cle-A	.960	12	23	1	1	0	0
1962	SF-N	1.000	3	2	0	0	0	0
Total	12	.975	926	1672	47	9	9	-44

Tom Nieto C

1984	StL-N	.994	32	135	18	1	0	4
1985	StL-N	.990	95	384	28	4	3	-3
1986	Mon-N	.978	30	123	11	3	1	-2
1987	Min-A	.996	40	210	17	1	5	1
1988	Min-A	.991	24	108	6	1	1	3
1989	Phi-N	1.000	11	63	2	0	0	3
1990	Phi-N	.984	17	57	5	1	1	2
Total	7	.991	249	1080	87	1	11	8

Harry Niles OF

1906	StL-A	.967	108	140	**34**	6	5	**13**
1907	StL-A	1.000	1	2	0	0	0	0
1908	NY-A	1.000	7	11	1	0	0	0
1909	Bos-A	.952	117	197	20	11	3	5
1910	Bos-A	.920	15	21	2	2	1	0
	Cle-A	.975	50	70	7	2	1	-1
	Yr	.962	65	91	9	4	2	-1
Total	5	.960	298	441	64	1	10	17

2B

1907	StL-A	.949	116	280	352	**34**	41	-6
1908	NY-A	.928	85	166	220	30	15	-24
	Bos-A	1.000	8	17	20	0	2	-1
	Yr	.934	93	183	240	30	17	-25
1909	Bos-A	.957	5	9	13	1	1	1
Total	3	.943	214	472	605	5	59	-32

3B

1906	StL-A	.912	34	44	49	9	3	-7
1909	Bos-A	.896	13	18	25	5	0	-2
1910	Cle-A	1.000	5	8	10	0	1	0

YEAR	TM/L	PCT	G	PO	A	E	DP	FR
Total	3	.917	52	70	84	4	4	-9
SS								
1908	Bos-A	1.000	2	1	2	0	0	0
1909	Bos-A	.804	9	16	29	11	5	-2
1910	Cle-A	.829	7	10	19	6	2	-3
Total	3	.819	18	27	50	7	7	-5
■ **Rabbit Nill**	**2B**							
1904	Was-A	.878	15	29	36	9	3	-4
1905	Was-A	.944	33	78	91	10	9	0
1906	Was-A	.949	25	37	74	6	6	4
1907	Was-A	.962	39	76	102	7	9	-3
1908	Cle-A	1.000	1	3	3	0	0	1
Total	5	.943	113	223	306	2	27	-2
3B								
1905	Was-A	.897	52	60	97	18	6	-3
1906	Was-A	.861	15	5	26	5	1	-3
1907	Was-A	1.000	1	1	2	0	0	0
	Cle-A	.815	7	6	16	5	1	-1
	Yr	.833	8	7	18	5	1	-1
Total	3	.884	75	72	141	8	8	-7
SS								
1905	Was-A	.952	6	8	12	1	0	1
1906	Was-A	.882	31	67	105	23	13	-1
1907	Cle-A	.850	4	7	10	3	0	-3
1908	Cle-A	.833	6	8	22	6	2	1
Total	4	.879	47	90	149	3	15	-2
OF								
1906	Was-A	.957	15	39	6	2	1	5
1907	Was-A	.975	18	37	2	1	0	1
1908	Cle-A	1.000	3	2	0	0	0	-1
Total	3	.966	36	78	8	3	1	5
■ **Al Nixon**	**OF**							
1915	Bro-N	1.000	14	11	1	0	1	0
1916	Bro-N	—	1	0	0	0	0	0
1918	Bro-N	1.000	4	6	0	0	0	0
1921	Bos-N	.980	43	92	4	2	1	4
1922	Bos-N	.975	79	189	6	5	0	2
1923	Bos-N	.987	80	214	14	3	4	12
1926	Phi-N	.977	88	206	7	5	3	1
1927	Phi-N	.969	44	121	3	4	0	6
1928	Phi-N	1.000	20	40	1	0	0	1
Total	9	.980	373	879	36	9	9	26
■ **Otis Nixon**	**OF**							
1983	NY-A	.938	9	14	1	1	0	2
1984	Cle-A	1.000	46	81	3	0	0	6
1985	Cle-A	.971	80	129	5	4	1	13
1986	Cle-A	.969	95	90	3	3	0	8
1987	Cle-A	1.000	17	21	0	0	0	2
1988	Mon-N	.994	82	176	2	1	1	-6
1989	Mon-N	.988	98	160	2	2	0	4
1990	Mon-N	.994	88	149	5	1	0	6
Total	8	.986	515	820	21	2	2	35
SS								
1990	Mon-N	1.000	1	0	1	0	1	0
■ **Donell Nixon**	**OF**							
1987	Sea-A	1.000	32	76	1	0	0	2
1988	SF-N	.983	46	59	0	1	0	3
1989	SF-N	.967	64	87	0	3	0	0
1990	Bal-A	1.000	4	5	0	0	0	0
Total	4	.983	146	227	1	4	0	5
■ **Russ Nixon**	**C**							
1957	Cle-A	.984	57	268	31	5	5	-5
1958	Cle-A	.991	101	499	31	5	4	-10
1959	Cle-A	.985	74	374	31	6	8	-8
1960	Cle-A	.993	25	134	8	1	2	0
	Bos-A	.987	74	354	26	5	3	-17
	Yr	.989	99	488	34	6	5	-17
1961	Bos-A	.975	66	330	24	9	2	-2
1962	Bos-A	1.000	38	201	7	0	1	-2
1963	Bos-A	.992	76	483	22	4	1	-10
1964	Bos-A	.990	45	273	11	3	3	-4
1965	Bos-A	.981	38	200	10	4	0	-6
1966	Min-A	.986	32	137	5	2	0	-4
1967	Min-A	.994	69	308	26	2	1	-11
1968	Bos-A	.994	27	147	6	1	1	-5
Total	12	.988	722	3708	238	7	31	-84
■ **Matt Nokes**	**C**							
1985	SF-N	.977	14	84	2	2	0	-1
1986	Det-A	1.000	7	43	2	0	2	1
1987	Det-A	.992	109	595	32	5	2	-9
1988	Det-A	.989	110	574	45	7	8	-3
1989	Det-A	.978	51	235	26	6	3	-5
1990	Det-A	.984	19	55	7	1	1	-3
	NY-A	.995	46	181	27	1	5	-5
	Yr	.993	65	236	34	2	6	-8
Total	6	.989	356	1767	141	2	21	-25
OF								
1987	Det-A	1.000	3	5	0	0	0	0
1990	NY-A	1.000	2	1	0	0	0	0
Total	2	1.000	5	6	0	0	0	0
3B								
1987	Det-A	—	2	0	0	0	0	0
■ **Joe Nolan**	**C**							
1972	NY-N	.938	3	12	3	1	0	-1
1975	Atl-N	1.000	1	2	0	0	0	0
1977	Atl-N	1.000	19	80	7	0	2	0
1978	Atl-N	.979	61	295	24	7	3	-4
1979	Atl-N	.983	74	328	27	6	2	-7
1980	Atl-N	1.000	6	20	3	0	1	1
	Cin-N	.982	51	251	23	5	6	1
	Yr	.983	57	271	26	5	7	2
1981	Cin-N	.995	81	393	18	2	2	-11
1982	Bal-A	.978	72	292	22	7	2	-4
1983	Bal-A	.980	65	223	16	5	2	-10
1984	Bal-A	.962	6	22	3	1	0	2
1985	Bal-A	1.000	5	22	2	0	0	1
Total	11	.984	444	1940	148	4	20	-32
■ **Pete Noonan**	**C**							
1904	Phi-A	.969	22	103	22	4	2	-3
1906	StL-N	.957	23	118	37	7	0	4
1907	StL-N	.951	70	369	98	24	12	3
Total	3	.955	115	590	157	5	14	4
1B								
1904	Phi-A	.991	10	102	5	1	4	0
1906	Chi-N	1.000	1	1	0	0	1	0
	StL-N	.959	16	152	11	7	5	0
	Yr	.959	17	153	11	7	6	0
Total	2	.971	27	255	16	8	10	0
■ **Tim Nordbrook**	**SS**							
1974	Bal-A	1.000	5	4	13	0	3	0
1975	Bal-A	.970	37	15	50	2	7	5
1976	Bal-A	1.000	12	9	20	0	5	2
	Cal-A	.941	4	7	9	1	0	2
	Yr	.978	16	16	29	1	5	4
1977	Chi-A	.850	11	17	17	6	3	-2
	Tor-A	.989	24	35	57	1	10	1
	Yr	.947	35	52	74	7	13	-1
1978	Tor-A	1.000	7	1	5	0	1	2
	Mil-A	.909	2	1	9	1	0	0
	Yr	.941	9	2	14	1	1	2
1979	Mil-A	1.000	2	1	0	0	0	-1
Total	6	.961	104	90	180	1	29	9
2B								
1974	Bal-A	1.000	1	2	4	0	2	1
1975	Bal-A	1.000	3	4	1	0	0	0
1976	Bal-A	1.000	14	5	4	0	1	1
	Cal-A	1.000	1	2	0	0	0	0
	Yr	1.000	15	7	4	0	1	1
Total	3	1.000	19	13	9	0	3	2
3B								
1977	Chi-A	—	1	0	0	0	0	0
■ **Wayne Nordhagen**	**OF**							
1976	Chi-A	1.000	10	20	1	0	0	1
1977	Chi-A	.944	46	50	1	3	0	-3
1978	Chi-A	.941	36	46	2	3	1	-2
1979	Chi-A	1.000	12	19	4	0	0	3
1980	Chi-A	.969	74	120	6	4	1	-6
1981	Chi-A	.947	60	85	4	5	1	-9
1982	Tor-A	1.000	10	15	1	0	1	1
	Pit-N	1.000	1	2	0	0	0	1
1983	Chi-N	1.000	7	7	0	0	0	-1
Total	8	.962	256	364	19	5	4	-16
C								
1976	Chi-A	.944	5	15	2	1	0	0
1977	Chi-A	.500	3	2	0	2	2	-1
1978	Chi-A	.944	12	41	10	3	1	-2
1979	Chi-A	.750	5	9	0	3	0	-1
Total	4	.898	25	67	12	9	3	-4
■ **Irv Noren**	**OF**							
1950	Was-A	.984	121	357	20	6	5	13
1951	Was-A	.978	126	420	15	10	1	16
1952	Was-A	1.000	12	42	2	0	0	3
	NY-A	1.000	60	95	3	0	1	-4
	Yr	1.000	72	137	5	0	1	-1
1953	NY-A	.991	96	208	11	2	1	5
1954	NY-A	.980	116	242	9	5	2	2
1955	NY-A	.980	126	238	9	5	0	-1
1956	NY-A	.875	10	6	1	1	0	-1
1957	KC-A	1.000	6	7	1	0	0	0
	StL-N	1.000	8	6	0	0	0	0
1958	StL-N	.974	77	75	1	2	0	-3
1959	StL-N	—	2	0	0	0	0	0
	Chi-N	1.000	40	81	4	0	1	3
	Yr	1.000	42	81	4	0	1	3
1960	Chi-N	1.000	1	1	0	0	0	0
Total	11	.984	801	1778	76	1	11	31
1B								
1950	Was-A	.957	17	143	14	7	16	1
1952	NY-A	.986	19	135	10	2	14	-1
1954	NY-A	1.000	1	1	0	0	0	0
1956	NY-A	1.000	1	4	1	0	0	0
1957	KC-A	.990	25	191	12	2	24	-1
1959	StL-N	1.000	1	1	0	0	1	0
	Chi-N	1.000	1	3	0	0	0	0
	Yr	1.000	2	4	0	0	1	0
1960	Chi-N	.833	1	5	0	1	1	0
Total	7	.977	66	483	38	2	56	-1
■ **Dan Norman**	**OF**							
1977	NY-N	1.000	6	8	0	0	0	-1
1978	NY-N	1.000	18	33	1	0	0	0
1979	NY-N	.967	33	54	4	2	0	0
1980	NY-N	1.000	19	19	1	0	0	-1
1982	Mon-N	.969	31	30	1	1	0	1
Total	5	.981	107	144	7	3	0	-1
■ **Nelson Norman**	**SS**							
1978	Tex-A	.984	18	14	46	1	7	9
1979	Tex-A	.952	142	177	302	24	64	-15
1980	Tex-A	.943	17	21	45	4	12	7
1981	Tex-A	.963	5	5	21	1	5	3
1982	Pit-N	1.000	1	1	2	0	0	0
1987	Mon-N	.667	1	1	1	1	1	0
Total	6	.954	184	219	417	1	88	3
3B								
1978	Tex-A	1.000	6	2	4	0	1	1
2B								
1979	Tex-A	—	1	0	0	0	0	0
1982	Pit-N	—	2	0	0	0	0	0
Total	2	—	3	0	0	0	0	0
■ **Jim Norris**	**OF**							
1977	Cle-A	.982	124	320	9	6	1	16
1978	Cle-A	.988	78	153	6	2	2	-2
1979	Cle-A	.982	93	214	2	4	0	2
1980	Tex-A	1.000	82	73	3	0	0	-3
Total	4	.985	377	760	20	2	3	17
1B								
1977	Cle-A	1.000	3	6	0	0	1	0
1978	Cle-A	1.000	6	43	2	0	4	0
1980	Tex-A	1.000	10	23	1	0	1	0
Total	3	1.000	19	72	3	0	6	0
■ **Leo Norris**	**SS**							
1936	Phi-N	.936	121	317	345	45	70	-9
1937	Phi-N	.972	20	28	42	2	7	-1
Total	2	.940	141	345	387	7	77	-10
2B								
1936	Phi-N	.966	38	97	130	8	28	0
1937	Phi-N	.949	74	160	193	19	35	-8
Total	2	.956	112	257	323	7	63	-8
3B								
1937	Phi-N	.981	24	24	29	1	1	-2
■ **Bill North**	**OF**							
1971	Chi-N	1.000	6	4	0	0	0	-1
1972	Chi-N	.955	48	61	3	3	1	0
1973	Oak-A	.980	138	**429**	14	9	**5**	21
1974	Oak-A	.991	138	437	9	4	2	16
1975	Oak-A	.975	138	**420**	10	11	1	15
1976	Oak-A	.978	144	397	8	9	1	0
1977	Oak-A	.983	52	112	1	2	0	-4
1978	Oak-A	1.000	17	31	1	0	0	-1
	LA-N	.975	103	232	2	6	1	-6
1979	SF-N	.987	130	300	8	4	2	-4
1980	SF-N	.982	115	313	6	6	1	3
1981	SF-N	.966	37	84	1	3	1	-1
Total	11	.981	1066	2820	63	7	15	38
■ **Hub Northen**	**OF**							
1910	StL-A	.926	26	48	2	4	0	-2
1911	Bro-N	.911	19	46	5	5	0	2
1912	Bro-N	.950	102	178	11	10	3	-8
Total	3	.939	147	272	18	9	3	-8
■ **Ron Northey**	**OF**							
1942	Phi-N	.952	109	206	12	**11**	2	0
1943	Phi-N	.978	145	292	19	7	6	1
1944	Phi-N	.981	151	286	**24**	6	**7**	-1
1946	Phi-N	.971	111	194	7	6	3	-10
1947	Phi-N	1.000	13	19	1	0	1	-2
	StL-N	.949	94	122	8	7	1	-10
	Yr	.955	107	141	9	7	2	-12
1948	StL-N	.989	67	85	2	1	0	-11
1949	StL-N	.980	73	93	4	2	2	-12
1950	Cin-N	.955	24	21	0	1	0	-6
	Chi-N	.976	27	38	3	1	2	-2
	Yr	.969	51	59	3	2	2	-8
1955	Chi-A	1.000	2	1	0	0	0	0
1956	Chi-A	1.000	4	4	1	0	0	0
Total	10	.972	820	1361	81	2	24	-51
3B								
1947	StL-N	.900	2	2	7	1	0	1
■ **Jim Northrup**	**OF**							
1964	Det-A	1.000	2	4	0	0	0	0
1965	Det-A	.976	54	82	0	2	0	-5
1966	Det-A	.980	113	241	8	5	1	10
1967	Det-A	.972	143	271	3	8	1	-10
1968	Det-A	.979	151	321	7	7	1	13
1969	Det-A	.985	143	323	8	5	2	2
1970	Det-A	.993	136	284	4	2	1	7
1971	Det-A	.981	108	205	4	4	0	-2
1972	Det-A	.978	127	215	8	5	2	-2
1973	Det-A	.982	116	207	6	4	2	-3
1974	Det-A	.973	97	209	5	6	0	1
	Mon-N	1.000	13	13	0	0	0	-3
	Bal-A	1.000	6	4	1	0	0	1
Total	12	.981	1267	2470	56	0	10	5
1B								
1971	Det-A	.981	32	236	16	5	23	-1
1972	Det-A	1.000	2	9	1	0	0	0
Total	2	.981	34	245	17	5	23	-1
■ **Willie Norwood**	**OF**							
1977	Min-A	.952	28	59	0	3	0	2
1978	Min-A	.944	115	227	7	**14**	1	-6
1979	Min-A	.974	71	147	4	4	0	1
1980	Min-A	1.000	17	42	0	0	0	0
Total	4	.959	231	475	11	1	1	-1
■ **Joe Nossek**	**OF**							
1964	Min-A	—	2	0	0	0	0	0
1965	Min-A	.970	48	64	1	2	1	2
1966	Min-A	—	2	0	0	0	0	0
	KC-A	.983	78	161	8	3	1	1
	Yr	.983	80	161	8	3	1	1
1967	KC-A	.982	63	105	2	2	0	6
1969	Oak-A	1.000	12	7	0	0	0	0
	StL-N	1.000	1	2	0	0	0	1
Total	5	.980	206	339	11	7	2	11
3B								
1965	Min-A	.943	9	8	25	2	0	2
1966	KC-A	—	1	0	0	0	0	0
Total	2	.943	10	8	25	2	0	2
■ **Lou Novikoff**	**OF**							
1941	Chi-N	1.000	54	92	3	0	0	-3
1942	Chi-N	.964	120	232	11	9	2	-1
1943	Chi-N	.980	61	96	2	2	1	-8
1944	Chi-N	.976	29	39	1	1	0	-5

YEAR	TM/L	PCT	G	PO	A	E	DP	FR
1946	Phi-N	1.000	3	9	0	0	0	1
Total	5	.976	267	468	17	2	3	-16

■ Les Nunamaker C

YEAR	TM/L	PCT	G	PO	A	E	DP	FR
1911	Bos-A	.972	59	309	79	11	8	7
1912	Bos-A	.971	35	166	33	6	3	-3
1913	Bos-A	.977	27	147	23	4	1	3
1914	Bos-A	1.000	3	1	4	0	0	0
	NY-A	.971	70	304	126	13	12	4
	Yr	.971	73	305	130	13	12	4
1915	NY-A	.964	77	324	99	16	9	-4
1916	NY-A	.983	79	353	102	8	13	-7
1917	NY-A	.976	91	372	113	12	12	-4
1918	StL-A	.979	81	315	108	9	10	1
1919	Cle-A	.927	16	39	12	4	0	-4
1920	Cle-A	.963	17	42	10	2	1	1
1921	Cle-A	.970	46	166	31	6	3	4
1922	Cle-A	.936	13	39	5	3	0	-2
Total	12	.972	614	2577	745	4	72	-4

1B

YEAR	TM/L	PCT	G	PO	A	E	DP	FR
1914	Bos-A	1.000	1	4	0	0	0	0
	NY-A	.913	5	20	1	2	1	0
	Yr	.926	6	24	1	2	1	0
1915	NY-A	1.000	2	26	1	0	0	0
1918	StL-A	.714	1	5	0	2	0	-1
1920	Cle-A	.938	6	27	3	2	0	0
Total	4	.935	15	82	5	6	1	-1

OF

YEAR	TM/L	PCT	G	PO	A	E	DP	FR
1918	StL-A	.667	1	2	0	1	0	0

■ Nyls Nyman OF

YEAR	TM/L	PCT	G	PO	A	E	DP	FR
1974	Chi-A	1.000	3	6	1	0	1	1
1975	Chi-A	.958	94	177	6	8	0	-13
1976	Chi-A	1.000	7	13	0	0	0	1
Total	3	.962	104	196	7	8	1	-11

■ Rebel Oakes OF

YEAR	TM/L	PCT	G	PO	A	E	DP	FR
1909	Cin-N	.979	113	218	15	5	3	-2
1910	StL-N	.939	127	266	12	18	3	-11
1911	StL-N	.961	151	**364**	26	16	8	6
1912	StL-N	.947	136	324	15	19	5	-3
1913	StL-N	.968	145	321	16	11	2	-6
1914	Pit-F	.960	145	313	23	14	2	6
1915	Pit-F	.973	153	348	12	10	2	-3
Total	7	.961	970	2154	119	3	25	-13

■ Johnny Oates C

YEAR	TM/L	PCT	G	PO	A	E	DP	FR
1970	Bal-A	.939	4	30	1	2	1	1
1972	Bal-A	**.995**	82	391	31	2	4	-3
1973	Atl-N	.981	86	409	57	9	6	-5
1974	Atl-N	.992	91	434	55	4	4	13
1975	Atl-N	1.000	6	21	1	0	0	0
	Phi-N	.990	82	429	44	5	10	1
	Yr	.990	88	450	45	5	10	1
1976	Phi-N	.994	33	155	15	1	1	1
1977	LA-N	.987	56	258	37	4	3	5
1978	LA-N	.956	24	77	10	4	1	-2
1979	LA-N	.975	20	64	13	2	2	3
1980	NY-A	.991	39	99	10	1	1	2
1981	NY-A	.963	10	49	3	2	0	1
Total	11	.987	533	2416	277	6	33	17

■ Ken Oberkfell 3B

YEAR	TM/L	PCT	G	PO	A	E	DP	FR
1978	StL-N	—	4	0	0	0	0	0
1979	StL-N	.967	17	10	19	1	2	-1
1980	StL-N	.971	16	4	30	1	2	-1
1981	StL-N	.956	102	77	246	15	**23**	11
1982	StL-N	**.972**	135	78	304	11	23	11
1983	StL-N	**.960**	127	79	231	13	27	7
1984	StL-N	.967	46	29	90	4	7	5
	Atl-N	.964	45	31	77	4	8	-5
	Yr	.966	91	60	167	8	15	0
1985	Atl-N	.963	117	70	220	11	19	-4
1986	Atl-N	.976	130	65	258	8	24	11
1987	Atl-N	.979	126	76	248	7	20	-3
1988	Atl-N	.951	113	83	207	15	21	-6
	Pit-N	1.000	2	1	5	0	0	0
	Yr	.952	115	84	212	15	21	-6
1989	SF-N	.971	38	8	25	1	1	2
1990	Hou-N	.935	24	12	31	3	3	-2
Total	13	.965	1042	623	1991	4	180	21

2B

YEAR	TM/L	PCT	G	PO	A	E	DP	FR
1977	StL-N	1.000	6	3	4	0	1	-1
1978	StL-N	.987	17	30	48	1	8	3
1979	StL-N	**.985**	117	213	323	8	65	-3
1980	StL-N	.989	101	223	310	6	62	-7
1982	StL-N	1.000	1	2	1	0	0	0
1983	StL-N	.960	32	51	69	5	16	-4
1984	StL-N	1.000	2	1	1	0	0	0
	Atl-N	1.000	4	3	5	0	0	0
	Yr	1.000	6	4	6	0	0	0
1985	Atl-N	.982	16	18	37	1	7	3
1986	Atl-N	.977	41	51	77	3	15	-2
1987	Atl-N	1.000	11	13	17	0	3	-1
1988	Atl-N	1.000	1	1	0	0	0	0
	Pit-N	1.000	11	15	24	0	3	-3
	Yr	1.000	12	16	24	0	3	-3
1989	Pit-N	1.000	3	5	5	0	1	0
	SF-N	.900	7	8	10	2	1	-2
	Yr	.933	10	13	15	2	2	-2
1990	Hou-N	1.000	11	12	14	0	6	0
Total	13	.984	381	649	945	6	188	-17

1B

YEAR	TM/L	PCT	G	PO	A	E	DP	FR
1988	Pit-N	1.000	1	7	0	0	0	0
1989	Pit-N	.988	9	75	5	1	4	0
	SF-N	1.000	7	35	0	0	4	0
	Yr	.992	16	110	7	1	8	0
1990	Hou-N	.987	11	69	7	1	7	0
Total	3	.990	28	186	14	2	15	0

SS

YEAR	TM/L	PCT	G	PO	A	E	DP	FR
1979	StL-N	1.000	2	0	1	0	0	0
1981	StL-N	1.000	1	0	1	0	0	0
1983	StL-N	1.000	1	2	3	0	1	0
1984	StL-N	—	1	0	0	0	0	0
1988	Pit-N	1.000	3	0	1	0	0	0
Total	5	1.000	8	2	6	0	1	0

■ Mike O'Berry C

YEAR	TM/L	PCT	G	PO	A	E	DP	FR
1979	Bos-A	.957	43	103	7	5	1	0
1980	Chi-N	.982	19	94	16	2	2	4
1981	Cin-N	.983	55	208	22	4	2	3
1982	Cin-N	.990	21	84	12	1	2	-1
1983	Cal-A	1.000	26	77	8	0	0	-1
1984	NY-A	1.000	12	53	5	0	1	1
1985	Mon-N	1.000	20	53	6	0	2	4
Total	7	.984	196	672	76	2	10	10

3B

YEAR	TM/L	PCT	G	PO	A	E	DP	FR
1984	NY-A	—	1	0	0	0	0	0

■ Charlie O'Brien C

YEAR	TM/L	PCT	G	PO	A	E	DP	FR
1985	Oak-A	.958	16	23	0	1	0	0
1987	Mil-A	1.000	10	78	11	0	0	5
1988	Mil-A	.991	40	210	20	2	4	12
1989	Mil-A	.986	62	314	36	5	5	6
1990	Mil-A	.992	46	217	24	2	5	4
	NY-N	.986	28	191	21	3	1	9
Total	5	.989	202	1033	112	3	15	36

■ Eddie O'Brien SS

YEAR	TM/L	PCT	G	PO	A	E	DP	FR
1953	Pit-N	.935	81	122	207	23	39	-14
1955	Pit-N	.889	4	4	4	1	0	0
1956	Pit-N	.978	23	35	53	2	14	11
Total	3	.942	108	161	264	6	53	-3

OF

YEAR	TM/L	PCT	G	PO	A	E	DP	FR
1955	Pit-N	.993	56	132	8	1	1	1
1956	Pit-N	1.000	6	2	0	0	0	0
Total	2	.993	62	134	8	1	1	1

3B

YEAR	TM/L	PCT	G	PO	A	E	DP	FR
1955	Pit-N	.882	7	8	7	2	0	-1
1956	Pit-N	1.000	4	0	1	0	0	0
Total	2	.889	11	8	8	2	0	-1

2B

YEAR	TM/L	PCT	G	PO	A	E	DP	FR
1956	Pit-N	1.000	2	1	0	0	0	0

■ John O'Brien 2B

YEAR	TM/L	PCT	G	PO	A	E	DP	FR
1891	Bro-N	.854	43	85	102	32	13	-22
1893	Chi-N	.900	4	10	8	2	1	-2
1895	Lou-N	.938	125	304	396	46	56	3
1896	Lou-N	.919	49	125	147	24	19	-1
	Was-N	.952	73	166	228	20	33	2
	Yr	.938	122	291	375	44	52	1
1897	Was-N	.942	86	223	260	30	43	3
1899	Bal-N	.966	39	98	132	8	21	7
	Pit-N	.946	79	211	243	26	32	3
	Yr	.953	118	309	375	34	53	10
Total	6	.936	498	1222	1516	188	218	-7

1B

YEAR	TM/L	PCT	G	PO	A	E	DP	FR
1895	Lou-N	.973	3	35	1	1	2	0

■ Jack O'Brien OF

YEAR	TM/L	PCT	G	PO	A	E	DP	FR
1899	Was-N	.926	121	266	21	23	5	5
1901	Was-A	.929	11	26	0	2	0	0
	Cle-A	.941	92	150	9	10	4	-3
	Yr	.939	103	176	9	12	4	-3
1903	Bos-A	.958	71	128	9	6	2	-3
Total	3	.937	295	570	39	1	11	-1

3B

YEAR	TM/L	PCT	G	PO	A	E	DP	FR
1899	Was-N	.714	4	5	10	6	1	0
1901	Cle-A	1.000	1	1	2	0	0	0
1903	Bos-A	.893	11	10	15	3	3	0
Total	3	.827	16	16	27	9	4	0

2B

YEAR	TM/L	PCT	G	PO	A	E	DP	FR
1903	Bos-A	.733	4	4	7	4	0	-2

SS

YEAR	TM/L	PCT	G	PO	A	E	DP	FR
1903	Bos-A	—	1	0	0	0	0	0

■ Jack O'Brien C

YEAR	TM/L	PCT	G	PO	A	E	DP	FR
1882	Phi-a	**.925**	45	205	66	22	1	0
1883	Phi-a	.876	58	301	58	51	3	-4
1884	Phi-a	.930	30	169	43	16	6	-2
1885	Phi-a	.903	43	193	58	27	3	-6
1886	Phi-a	.918	36	172	52	20	3	-5
1887	Bro-a	.839	25	95	40	26	4	-5
1888	Bal-a	.925	37	205	43	20	4	-9
1890	Phi-a	.800	1	2	2	1	1	0
Total	8	.903	275	1342	362	183	25	-31

1B

YEAR	TM/L	PCT	G	PO	A	E	DP	FR
1882	Phi-a	1.000	1	7	0	0	0	0
1884	Phi-a	1.000	1	15	1	0	1	0
1885	Phi-a	1.000	7	66	2	0	4	1
1886	Phi-a	.947	24	209	4	12	15	-2
1888	Bal-a	.987	7	76	0	1	5	-1
1890	Phi-a	.976	109	1018	52	26	61	4
Total	6	.974	149	1391	59	9	86	2

OF

YEAR	TM/L	PCT	G	PO	A	E	DP	FR
1882	Phi-a	.846	18	21	12	6	0	5
1883	Phi-a	.882	25	54	6	8	2	5
1884	Phi-a	.800	5	11	1	3	1	1
1885	Phi-a	.667	3	6	0	3	0	-1
1886	Phi-a	.750	3	2	1	1	0	0
1887	Bro-a	.750	4	3	0	1	0	-1
1888	Bal-a	.500	13	5	0	5	0	-5
1890	Phi-a	1.000	1	1	0	0	0	0
Total	8	.820	72	103	20	7	3	4

3B

YEAR	TM/L	PCT	G	PO	A	E	DP	FR
1882	Phi-a	1.000	1	1	3	0	0	0
1883	Phi-a	.714	19	16	24	16	3	-3
1885	Phi-a	1.000	2	3	6	0	1	1
1886	Phi-a	.818	27	21	69	20	3	2

YEAR	TM/L	PCT	G	PO	A	E	DP	FR
Total	4	.799	49	41	102	6	7	0

SS

YEAR	TM/L	PCT	G	PO	A	E	DP	FR
1883	Phi-a	.667	1	1	1	1	0	0
1885	Phi-a	.822	9	8	29	8	2	-3
1886	Phi-a	.756	10	8	26	11	2	-4
Total	3	.785	20	17	56	0	4	-7

2B

YEAR	TM/L	PCT	G	PO	A	E	DP	FR
1886	Phi-a	.842	7	14	18	6	3	-3
1887	Bro-a	1.000	1	0	2	0	0	0
Total	2	.850	8	14	20	6	3	-3

■ Johnny O'Brien 2B

YEAR	TM/L	PCT	G	PO	A	E	DP	FR
1953	Pit-N	.982	77	172	210	7	48	-4
1955	Pit-N	.969	78	185	220	13	53	5
1956	Pit-N	.959	53	67	98	7	17	6
1957	Pit-N	1.000	2	1	0	0	0	0
1958	StL-N	1.000	1	2	0	0	0	0
1959	Mil-N	.987	37	70	83	2	24	-2
Total	6	.974	248	497	611	9	142	5

SS

YEAR	TM/L	PCT	G	PO	A	E	DP	FR
1953	Pit-N	—	1	0	0	0	0	0
1956	Pit-N	1.000	1	0	1	0	0	0
1957	Pit-N	.885	8	11	12	3	2	-1
1958	StL-N	1.000	5	1	1	0	0	0
Total	4	.897	15	12	14	3	2	-1

■ Pete O'Brien 2B

YEAR	TM/L	PCT	G	PO	A	E	DP	FR
1901	Cin-N	.889	15	35	37	9	6	-2
1906	StL-A	.933	120	254	274	**38**	31	-38
1907	Cle-A	.943	17	28	55	5	4	-1
	Was-A	—	1	0	0	0	0	0
	Yr	.943	18	28	55	5	4	-1
Total	3	.929	153	317	366	2	41	-41

3B

YEAR	TM/L	PCT	G	PO	A	E	DP	FR
1906	StL-A	1.000	20	25	35	0	0	2
1907	Cle-A	.879	12	9	20	4	2	-2
	Was-A	.912	26	37	67	10	0	6
	Yr	.905	38	46	87	14	2	6
Total	2	.932	58	71	122	4	2	6

SS

YEAR	TM/L	PCT	G	PO	A	E	DP	FR
1906	StL-A	.922	11	18	29	4	1	-4
1907	Cle-A	.891	11	16	25	5	4	-8
	Was-A	.885	13	14	32	6	3	-2
	Yr	.888	24	30	57	11	7	-10
Total	2	.899	35	48	86	5	8	-14

■ Pete O'Brien 1B

YEAR	TM/L	PCT	G	PO	A	E	DP	FR
1982	Tex-A	1.000	3	22	2	0	4	0
1983	Tex-A	.993	133	1144	**120**	9	104	**14**
1984	Tex-A	.992	141	1270	105	11	103	1
1985	Tex-A	.995	159	1457	98	8	125	-6
1986	Tex-A	.992	155	1224	115	11	123	2
1987	Tex-A	.992	158	1233	**146**	11	118	**17**
1988	Tex-A	.995	155	1346	140	8	124	**13**
1989	Cle-A	.994	154	1359	114	9	111	3
1990	Sea-A	.995	97	850	76	5	68	6
Total	9	.993	1155	9905	916	2	880	50

OF

YEAR	TM/L	PCT	G	PO	A	E	DP	FR
1982	Tex-A	1.000	11	17	1	0	1	-1
1983	Tex-A	.960	27	47	1	2	1	-1
1984	Tex-A	1.000	1	1	0	0	0	0
1987	Tex-A	—	2	0	0	0	0	0
1990	Sea-A	1.000	6	2	0	0	0	0
Total	5	.972	47	67	2	2	2	-2

■ Syd O'Brien 3B

YEAR	TM/L	PCT	G	PO	A	E	DP	FR
1969	Bos-A	.939	53	34	105	9	12	-2
1970	Chi-A	.938	68	59	137	13	18	-2
1971	Cal-A	1.000	6	5	12	0	0	0
1972	Cal-A	.889	8	0	8	1	1	0
	Mil-A	.852	9	6	17	4	3	-1
	Yr	.861	17	6	25	5	4	-1
Total	4	.934	144	104	279	7	34	-5

SS

YEAR	TM/L	PCT	G	PO	A	E	DP	FR
1969	Bos-A	.882	15	13	17	4	6	-2
1970	Chi-A	.833	5	3	7	2	1	-1
1971	Cal-A	.961	52	87	136	9	30	-2
1972	Cal-A	.909	4	1	9	1	0	0
Total	4	.945	76	104	169	6	37	-5

2B

YEAR	TM/L	PCT	G	PO	A	E	DP	FR
1969	Bos-A	.951	12	18	21	2	12	2
1970	Chi-A	.957	43	96	127	10	31	-3
1971	Cal-A	.951	7	14	25	2	7	1
1972	Cal-A	1.000	3	3	3	0	1	1
	Mil-A	.913	7	10	11	2	3	0
	Yr	.931	10	13	14	2	4	1
Total	4	.953	72	141	187	6	54	1

1B

YEAR	TM/L	PCT	G	PO	A	E	DP	FR
1971	Cal-A	1.000	1	1	0	0	1	0
1972	Cal-A	1.000	1	9	0	0	1	0
Total	2	1.000	2	9	0	0	1	0

OF

YEAR	TM/L	PCT	G	PO	A	E	DP	FR
1971	Cal-A	1.000	1	1	0	0	0	0

■ Tommy O'Brien OF

YEAR	TM/L	PCT	G	PO	A	E	DP	FR
1943	Pit-N	.964	48	76	4	3	0	-3
1944	Pit-N	.965	48	50	5	2	1	-4
1945	Pit-N	.961	45	72	2	3	0	-4
1949	Bos-A	.984	32	58	2	1	0	-2
1950	Bos-A	1.000	9	14	1	0	0	0
	Was-A	1.000	3	7	1	0	0	1
	Yr	1.000	12	21	2	0	0	1
Total	5	.970	185	277	15	9	1	-12

3B

YEAR	TM/L	PCT	G	PO	A	E	DP	FR
1943	Pit-N	.909	9	11	19	3	0	0
1944	Pit-N	1.000	1	0	1	0	0	0
Total	2	.912	10	11	20	3	0	0

■ Tom O'Brien 2B

YEAR	TM/L	PCT	G	PO	A	E	DP	FR
1882	Wor-N	.786	2	6	5	3	2	-1

YEAR	TM/L	PCT	G	PO	A	E	DP	FR
1883	Bal-a	.825	29	77	93	36	8	-4
1884	Bos-U	.853	99	257	267	90	23	1
1885	Bal-a	.929	2	3	10	1	0	1
1887	NY-a	.900	2	5	4	1	1	0
1890	Roc-a	.825	8	12	21	7	3	-1
Total	6	.846	142	360	400	138	37	-4
1B								
1884	Bos-U	1.000	2	21	0	0	0	0
1885	Bal-a	.932	6	38	3	3	1	0
1887	NY-a	.963	20	177	5	7	9	-1
1890	Roc-a	.971	68	677	20	21	40	-3
Total	4	.968	96	913	28	1	50	-4
OF								
1882	Wor-N	.789	20	41	4	12	0	-1
1883	Bal-a	1.000	4	6	0	0	0	0
1884	Bos-U	.875	3	7	0	1	0	0
1887	NY-a	.905	8	19	0	2	0	0
Total	4	.837	35	73	4	5	0	-1
3B								
1882	Wor-N	.000	1	0	0	2	0	-1
1887	NY-a	.750	2	2	1	1	0	0
Total	2	.500	3	2	1	3	0	-1
C								
1884	Bos-U	1.000	1	5	0	0	0	0

■ Tom O'Brien OF

YEAR	TM/L	PCT	G	PO	A	E	DP	FR
1897	Bal-N	.957	24	38	6	2	2	2
1898	Bal-N	.833	16	22	3	5	4	0
	Pit-N	.924	69	144	15	13	4	4
	Yr	.911	85	166	18	18	8	4
1899	NY-N	.933	127	243	21	19	7	-1
1900	Pit-N	.942	25	48	1	3	0	-3
Total	4	.928	261	495	46	2	17	2
1B								
1897	Bal-N	.968	25	205	9	7	7	-1
1898	Pit-N	.971	21	198	4	6	12	-2
1899	NY-N	—	0	0	0	0	0	0
1900	Pit-N	.961	65	670	26	28	37	-7
Total	4	.964	112	1073	39	1	56	-10
3B								
1898	Pit-N	.778	8	4	10	4	1	-2
1899	NY-N	.859	21	18	37	9	2	-1
Total	2	.841	29	22	47	3	3	-3
2B								
1898	Pit-N	.891	7	18	23	5	1	0
1899	NY-N	1.000	1	4	3	0	2	0
1900	Pit-N	1.000	4	4	4	0	1	0
Total	3	.918	12	26	30	5	4	0
SS								
1898	Pit-N	.767	4	12	11	7	1	-2
1899	NY-N	.800	2	3	5	2	1	0
1900	Pit-N	.818	2	4	5	2	1	-1
Total	3	.784	8	19	21	1	3	-3

■ Darby O'Brien OF

YEAR	TM/L	PCT	G	PO	A	E	DP	FR
1887	NY-a	.913	121	244	20	25	4	6
1888	Bro-a	.932	136	231	15	18	1	2
1889	Bro-a	.906	136	255	14	28	5	-7
1890	Bro-N	.960	85	176	14	8	2	1
1891	Bro-N	.951	103	203	11	11	1	2
1892	Bro-N	.956	122	222	16	11	4	4
Total	6	.934	703	1331	90	101	17	8
1B								
1887	NY-a	.934	10	67	4	5	5	0
SS								
1887	NY-a	.750	2	0	3	1	0	0
3B								
1887	NY-a	1.000	1	1	1	0	0	0

■ Billy O'Brien 1B

YEAR	TM/L	PCT	G	PO	A	E	DP	FR
1884	KC-U	1.000	1	17	1	0	0	0
1887	Was-N	.974	104	1159	26	32	53	-5
1888	Was-N	.975	132	1272	38	33	55	-4
1889	Was-N	1.000	2	19	0	0	0	0
1890	Bro-a	.973	96	1015	35	29	66	-2
Total	5	.974	335	3482	100	4	174	-11
3B								
1884	StP-U	.840	8	7	14	4	0	1
	KC-U	.714	3	1	9	4	0	1
	Yr	.795	11	8	23	8	0	2
1887	Was-N	.867	4	8	5	2	0	-1
1888	Was-N	1.000	1	1	1	0	0	0
Total	3	.821	16	17	29	0	0	1
OF								
1887	Was-N	1.000	4	7	3	0	0	2
2B								
1887	Was-N	1.000	2	1	5	0	0	0

■ Danny O'Connell 2B

YEAR	TM/L	PCT	G	PO	A	E	DP	FR
1953	Pit-N	.970	47	107	149	8	27	1
1954	Mil-N	.979	103	244	314	12	83	7
1955	Mil-N	.981	114	309	357	13	76	17
1956	Mil-N	.985	138	295	381	10	98	-5
1957	Mil-N	.982	48	128	145	5	43	6
	NY-N	.980	68	156	194	7	50	1
	Yr	.981	116	284	339	12	93	7
1958	SF-N	.986	104	222	278	7	70	3
1959	SF-N	1.000	8	16	9	0	1	1
1961	Was-A	.978	61	144	170	7	52	-2
1962	Was-A	.946	22	36	52	5	8	-2
Total	9	.980	713	1657	2049	4	508	27
3B								
1950	Pit-N	.964	12	15	39	2	2	5
1953	Pit-N	.958	104	119	221	15	16	7
1954	Mil-N	1.000	1	0	4	0	0	0
1955	Mil-N	.923	7	8	4	1	2	-1
1956	Mil-N	.833	4	3	2	1	0	-1
1957	NY-N	.962	30	33	69	4	6	5
1958	SF-N	—	3	0	0	0	0	0
1959	SF-N	.927	26	15	36	4	3	6
1961	Was-A	.939	73	75	173	16	14	3
1962	Was-A	.961	41	34	89	5	13	1
Total	10	.956	335	346	700	8	63	28
SS								
1950	Pit-N	.977	65	147	228	9	47	12
1954	Mil-N	—	1	0	0	0	0	0
1955	Mil-N	1.000	1	0	1	0	0	0
1956	Mil-N	1.000	1	1	1	0	1	0
Total	4	.977	68	148	230	9	48	12
1B								
1954	Mil-N	1.000	8	63	5	0	7	0

■ Jack O'Connor C

YEAR	TM/L	PCT	G	PO	A	E	DP	FR
1887	Cin-a	.813	5	13	13	6	0	2
1888	Cin-a	.852	2	14	9	4	0	3
1889	Col-a	.955	84	420	127	26	6	-1
1890	Col-a	.962	106	539	146	27	13	11
1891	Col-a	.982	21	78	29	2	2	2
1892	Cle-N	.966	34	158	40	7	4	4
1893	Cle-N	.949	56	182	62	13	2	2
1894	Cle-N	.942	45	161	35	12	1	5
1895	Cle-N	.923	47	128	41	14	2	-5
1896	Cle-N	.966	37	109	31	5	3	-5
1897	Cle-N	.940	13	35	12	3	0	-2
1898	Cle-N	.963	48	156	53	8	2	-1
1899	StL-N	.943	57	185	63	15	3	0
1900	StL-N	.957	10	33	11	2	0	0
	Pit-N	.940	40	108	44	9	2	-10
	Yr	.947	50	141	55	11	2	-10
1901	Pit-N	.978	59	256	59	7	5	-1
1902	Pit-N	.979	42	187	49	5	2	-2
1903	NY-A	.988	63	282	56	4	6	0
1904	StL-A	.943	14	55	11	4	0	4
1906	StL-A	.990	51	248	64	3	2	10
1907	StL-A	.991	25	87	29	1	4	-2
1910	StL-A	1.000	1	1	0	0	0	0
Total	21	.961	860	3435	984	177	59	6
OF								
1887	Cin-a	.947	7	16	2	1	1	2
1888	Cin-a	.795	34	54	8	16	0	-2
1889	Col-a	.851	19	38	2	7	1	0
1890	Col-a	.826	9	18	1	4	1	0
1891	Col-a	.878	40	57	8	9	3	1
1892	Cle-N	.935	106	152	21	12	4	4
1893	Cle-N	.929	44	70	8	6	0	-4
1894	Cle-N	.923	33	88	8	8	3	4
1896	Cle-N	.933	12	13	1	1	0	-2
1897	Cle-N	.941	52	93	3	6	0	-5
1898	Cle-N	.957	15	19	3	1	1	0
1902	Pit-N	—	1	0	0	0	0	0
Total	12	.906	372	618	65	1	14	-2
1B								
1889	Col-a	.964	3	27	0	1	3	0
1894	Cle-N	.983	7	55	3	1	4	0
1895	Cle-N	.995	41	392	25	2	22	2
1896	Cle-N	.992	17	120	8	1	10	0
1897	Cle-N	.981	36	349	8	7	10	-5
1898	Cle-N	.983	69	586	36	11	33	3
1899	StL-N	.988	26	242	13	3	17	1
1900	Pit-N	1.000	2	20	1	0	3	0
1902	Pit-N	.983	6	56	1	1	3	-1
1903	NY-A	1.000	1	5	0	0	0	0
Total	10	.986	208	1852	95	7	105	0
SS								
1890	Col-a	.857	8	9	9	3	1	-1
2B								
1889	Col-a	.929	4	7	6	1	1	0
1890	Col-a	.929	2	6	7	1	3	1
Total	2	.929	6	13	13	2	4	1
3B								
1890	Col-a	1.000	1	0	1	0	0	0
1895	Cle-N	1.000	1	2	0	0	0	0
Total	2	1.000	2	2	1	0	0	0

■ Ken O'Dea C

YEAR	TM/L	PCT	G	PO	A	E	DP	FR
1935	Chi-N	.964	63	213	27	9	3	-1
1936	Chi-N	.979	55	211	27	5	1	-2
1937	Chi-N	.985	64	234	29	4	4	-7
1938	Chi-N	.970	71	294	32	10	3	4
1939	NY-N	.947	30	78	11	5	1	-2
1940	NY-N	.992	31	89	29	1	1	2
1941	NY-N	1.000	14	62	9	0	0	2
1942	StL-N	.979	49	247	37	6	6	10
1943	StL-N	.989	56	237	32	3	6	6
1944	StL-N	.994	69	326	34	2	4	8
1945	StL-N	.995	91	321	50	2	14	3
1946	StL-N	.991	22	99	14	1	0	5
	Bos-N	1.000	12	39	5	0	1	-1
	Yr	.994	34	138	19	1	1	4
Total	12	.983	627	2450	336	8	44	27

■ Lefty O'Doul OF

YEAR	TM/L	PCT	G	PO	A	E	DP	FR
1919	NY-A	—	1	0	0	0	0	0
1920	NY-A	—	1	0	0	0	0	-1
1923	Bos-A	1.000	1	1	0	0	0	0
1928	NY-N	.962	94	149	4	6	0	-14
1929	Phi-N	.971	154	320	14	10	5	-1
1930	Phi-N	.953	131	262	3	13	1	-13
1931	Bro-N	.954	132	285	4	14	0	-6
1932	Bro-N	.979	148	317	4	7	0	-10
1933	Bro-N	.947	41	88	1	5	0	-3
	NY-N	.974	63	109	4	3	0	-5
	Yr	.962	104	197	5	8	0	-8
1934	NY-N	.968	38	60	1	2	0	-6
Total	10	.964	804	1591	35	0	6	-59

■ Fred Odwell OF

YEAR	TM/L	PCT	G	PO	A	E	DP	FR
1904	Cin-N	.956	126	284	18	14	6	15
1905	Cin-N	.967	126	216	18	8	5	4
1906	Cin-N	.963	57	94	10	4	0	3
1907	Cin-N	.975	84	186	9	5	2	6
Total	4	.964	393	780	55	1	13	28
2B								
1904	Cin-N	1.000	1	1	0	0	0	0
1907	Cin-N	.500	1	1	0	1	0	0
Total	2	.667	2	2	0	1	0	0

■ Ron Oester 2B

YEAR	TM/L	PCT	G	PO	A	E	DP	FR
1980	Cin-N	.980	79	144	194	7	42	-12
1981	Cin-N	.980	103	202	328	11	61	4
1982	Cin-N	.972	118	258	325	17	72	4
1983	Cin-N	.977	154	315	413	17	80	-25
1984	Cin-N	.980	147	357	388	15	75	-16
1985	Cin-N	.989	149	366	457	9	100	5
1986	Cin-N	.978	151	367	475	19	100	18
1987	Cin-N	.974	69	183	186	10	37	6
1988	Cin-N	.995	49	108	104	1	24	1
1989	Cin-N	.985	102	211	239	7	42	6
1990	Cin-N	.982	50	80	88	3	14	-7
Total	11	.980	1171	2591	3197	116	647	-16
SS								
1978	Cin-N	1.000	6	3	9	0	2	1
1979	Cin-N	1.000	2	1	2	0	0	1
1980	Cin-N	.956	17	16	27	2	4	-1
1981	Cin-N	1.000	9	11	13	0	3	1
1982	Cin-N	.980	29	37	60	2	11	1
1984	Cin-N	—	1	0	0	0	0	0
1988	Cin-N	1.000	5	2	9	0	2	2
1989	Cin-N	1.000	2	4	10	0	2	2
Total	8	.981	71	74	130	4	24	7
3B								
1980	Cin-N	.800	3	1	3	1	0	-1
1982	Cin-N	.900	13	9	18	3	4	-1
1990	Cin-N	.667	3	0	2	1	0	0
Total	3	.868	19	10	23	5	4	-2

■ Bob O'Farrell C

YEAR	TM/L	PCT	G	PO	A	E	DP	FR
1915	Chi-N	.667	2	1	1	1	0	-1
1916	Chi-N	—	1	0	0	0	0	0
1917	Chi-N	1.000	3	9	1	0	1	-1
1918	Chi-N	.974	45	115	36	4	3	-6
1919	Chi-N	.965	38	119	48	6	5	-4
1920	Chi-N	.956	86	317	100	19	6	-6
1921	Chi-N	.967	90	269	87	12	8	-5
1922	Chi-N	.977	125	446	143	14	22	15
1923	Chi-N	.976	124	418	118	13	11	1
1924	Chi-N	.984	57	204	40	4	5	-2
1925	Chi-N	1.000	3	6	0	0	0	-1
	StL-N	.975	92	324	67	10	5	-5
	Yr	.975	95	330	67	10	5	-6
1926	StL-N	.983	146	466	117	10	12	8
1927	StL-N	.979	53	141	45	4	5	-1
1928	StL-N	.985	14	61	4	1	1	0
	NY-N	.988	63	138	27	2	1	-1
	Yr	.987	77	199	31	3	2	-1
1929	NY-N	.979	84	254	22	6	6	0
1930	NY-N	.973	69	259	34	8	6	0
1931	NY-N	.980	80	223	27	5	1	1
1932	NY-N	.969	41	85	9	3	2	1
1933	StL-N	.970	50	211	19	7	1	-5
1934	Cin-N	.993	42	124	25	1	2	0
	Chi-N	1.000	22	93	10	0	2	3
	Yr	.996	64	217	35	1	4	3
1935	StL-N	1.000	8	12	0	0	0	1
Total	21	.976	1338	4295	980	130	101	-13

■ Rowland Office OF

YEAR	TM/L	PCT	G	PO	A	E	DP	FR
1972	Atl-N	1.000	1	3	0	0	0	0
1974	Atl-N	.994	119	171	0	1	0	-29
1975	Atl-N	.967	107	229	6	8	0	-9
1976	Atl-N	.986	92	204	3	3	2	-7
1977	Atl-N	.988	104	249	8	3	3	2
1978	Atl-N	.990	136	291	4	3	2	-8
1979	Atl-N	.988	97	164	4	2	0	3
1980	Mon-N	.987	97	150	2	2	1	-5
1981	Mon-N	.938	15	15	0	1	0	-1
1982	Mon-N	1.000	1	2	0	0	0	0
1983	NY-A	1.000	2	2	0	0	0	0
Total	11	.985	771	1480	27	3	8	-54
1B								
1977	Atl-N	1.000	1	1	0	0	0	0

■ Ben Oglivie OF

YEAR	TM/L	PCT	G	PO	A	E	DP	FR
1971	Bos-A	.958	11	22	1	1	1	1
1972	Bos-A	.981	65	98	5	2	2	-3
1973	Bos-A	.983	32	56	2	1	0	6
1974	Det-A	.947	63	87	3	5	0	4
1975	Det-A	.975	86	192	4	5	1	2
1976	Det-A	.986	64	136	7	2	0	-4
1977	Det-A	.988	118	236	10	6	3	2
1978	Mil-A	.980	89	187	5	4	0	-2
1979	Mil-A	.985	120	252	7	4	0	-2
1980	Mil-A	.978	152	384	18	9	3	15
1981	Mil-A	.982	101	211	3	4	1	-5
1982	Mil-A	.982	159	359	15	7	3	7
1983	Mil-A	.985	113	259	8	4	1	2
1984	Mil-A	.970	125	256	6	8	1	-3
1985	Mil-A	.965	91	190	4	7	0	-2
1986	Mil-A	.991	50	105	4	1	1	0
Total	16	.978	1439	3030	102	0	17	18
1B								
1974	Det-A	1.000	10	75	8	0	13	2
1975	Det-A	1.000	5	40	4	0	4	1
1976	Det-A	.990	9	98	1	1	13	-2
1978	Mil-A	.978	11	88	3	2	4	-2
1979	Mil-A	.986	9	68	3	1	3	-1
Total	5	.990	44	369	19	4	37	-2

■ Bruce Ogrodowski C

YEAR	TM/L	PCT	G	PO	A	E	DP	FR
1936	StL-N	.989	85	314	32	4	6	5
1937	StL-N	.984	87	387	50	7	2	3
Total	2	.986	172	701	82	1	8	8

■ Bill O'Hara OF

YEAR	TM/L	PCT	G	PO	A	E	DP	FR
1909	NY-N	.978	111	202	19	5	4	1
1910	StL-N	1.000	4	7	1	0	0	0
Total	2	.979	115	209	20	5	4	1
1B								
1910	StL-N	1.000	1	7	0	0	0	0

■ Bob Oldis C

YEAR	TM/L	PCT	G	PO	A	E	DP	FR
1953	Was-A	1.000	7	23	3	0	1	2
1954	Was-A	.941	8	30	2	2	0	-1
1955	Was-A	1.000	6	12	1	0	0	0
1960	Pit-N	1.000	22	42	2	0	0	2
1961	Pit-N	1.000	4	11	3	0	3	2
1962	Phi-N	.987	30	134	14	2	4	1
1963	Phi-N	.979	43	170	15	4	4	5
Total	7	.983	120	422	40	8	12	11
3B								
1954	Was-A	—	2	0	0	0	0	0

■ Rube Oldring OF

YEAR	TM/L	PCT	G	PO	A	E	DP	FR
1907	Phi-A	.974	117	180	10	5	0	-10
1908	Phi-A	.941	116	246	9	16	3	3
1909	Phi-A	.963	89	174	7	7	1	-1
1910	Phi-A	**.978**	134	249	14	6	6	-2
1911	Phi-A	**.979**	119	225	13	5	2	-9
1912	Phi-A	.974	98	214	8	6	1	-3
1913	Phi-A	.968	131	236	9	8	3	-5
1914	Phi-A	.965	117	215	7	8	5	-6
1915	Phi-A	.982	96	212	9	4	3	6
1916	Phi-A	.897	40	64	6	8	2	-2
	NY-A	.957	43	66	1	3	3	-3
	Yr	.926	83	130	7	11	5	-5
1918	Phi-A	.949	30	35	2	2	0	-7
Total	11	.966	1130	2116	95	8	29	-39
3B								
1906	Phi-A	.897	49	53	87	16	5	3
1915	Phi-A	.839	8	12	14	5	3	-1
1918	Phi-A	1.000	2	2	4	0	1	0
Total	3	.891	59	67	105	1	9	2
SS								
1905	NY-A	.967	8	24	34	2	4	5
1906	Phi-A	.800	3	1	3	1	0	0
1913	Phi-A	.958	5	12	11	1	0	-2
Total	3	.955	16	37	48	4	4	3
2B								
1906	Phi-A	1.000	2	1	0	0	0	0
1918	Phi-A	.833	2	2	3	1	2	-1
Total	2	.857	4	3	3	1	2	-1
1B								
1906	Phi-A	1.000	1	10	0	0	0	0
1909	Phi-A	.500	1	1	0	1	0	0
Total	2	.917	2	11	0	1	0	0

■ Charley O'Leary SS

YEAR	TM/L	PCT	G	PO	A	E	DP	FR
1904	Det-A	.933	135	308	439	54	48	6
1905	Det-A	.933	148	358	411	55	40	-8
1906	Det-A	.926	127	**326**	398	**58**	37	-8
1907	Det-A	.943	138	**353**	448	48	35	-4
1908	Det-A	.920	64	130	179	27	15	-12
1909	Det-A	.882	4	6	9	2	1	0
1910	Det-A	.960	18	35	60	4	2	4
1913	StL-N	.951	103	193	297	25	22	-11
Total	8	.935	737	1709	2241	273	200	-33
2B								
1908	Det-A	1.000	1	1	0	0	0	0
1909	Det-A	.986	15	36	34	1	3	-1
1910	Det-A	.935	38	81	93	12	10	-4
1911	Det-A	.966	67	169	201	13	19	4
1912	Det-A	1.000	3	5	11	0	0	2
1913	StL-N	.957	15	25	41	3	11	3
Total	6	.960	139	317	380	9	43	4
3B								
1909	Det-A	.922	54	59	118	15	4	-2
1910	Det-A	1.000	6	5	14	0	3	2
1911	Det-A	.952	6	9	11	1	3	0
Total	3	.931	66	73	143	6	10	0
OF								
1909	Det-A	1.000	2	3	0	0	0	0

■ Tony Oliva OF

YEAR	TM/L	PCT	G	PO	A	E	DP	FR
1962	Min-A	1.000	2	3	0	0	0	0
1964	Min-A	.981	159	313	5	6	0	6
1965	Min-A	.964	147	284	10	**11**	3	7
1966	Min-A	.972	**159**	335	9	**10**	3	12
1967	Min-A	.987	146	286	8	4	2	9
1968	Min-A	.983	126	227	7	4	1	4
1969	Min-A	.982	**152**	311	14	6	3	9
1970	Min-A	.968	157	351	12	**12**	4	15
1971	Min-A	.969	121	216	6	7	3	-4
1972	Min-A	.857	9	6	0	1	0	-2
Total	10	.975	1178	2332	71	1	19	56

■ Al Oliver OF

YEAR	TM/L	PCT	G	PO	A	E	DP	FR
1968	Pit-N	1.000	1	3	0	0	0	0
1969	Pit-N	.977	21	42	1	1	0	0
1970	Pit-N	.986	80	136	4	2	1	-3
1971	Pit-N	.981	116	305	4	6	2	3
1972	Pit-N	.985	138	332	4	5	1	-5
1973	Pit-N	.964	109	238	5	9	0	-5
1974	Pit-N	.986	98	284	3	4	1	6
1975	Pit-N	.987	153	380	5	5	3	-2
1976	Pit-N	.984	106	301	4	5	0	2
1977	Pit-N	.981	148	305	6	6	1	0
1978	Tex-A	.987	107	219	8	3	1	1
1979	Tex-A	.975	119	260	9	7	2	-10
1980	Tex-A	.973	157	314	9	9	2	-2
1983	Mon-N	—	1	0	0	0	0	0
1984	Phi-N	1.000	5	4	1	0	0	0
1985	LA-N	.882	17	13	2	2	0	-3
Total	16	.980	1376	3136	65	4	14	-18
1B								
1969	Pit-N	.991	106	869	49	8	87	-3
1970	Pit-N	.989	77	582	48	7	68	1
1971	Pit-N	1.000	25	192	11	0	16	0
1972	Pit-N	1.000	3	21	0	0	3	0
1973	Pit-N	.992	50	454	31	4	42	-1
1974	Pit-N	.993	49	418	23	3	28	-2
1975	Pit-N	1.000	4	29	1	0	3	0
1976	Pit-N	1.000	3	26	0	0	5	-1
1980	Tex-A	1.000	1	1	0	0	0	0
1981	Tex-A	1.000	1	2	0	0	0	0
1982	Mon-N	.986	159	1286	92	**19**	96	-9
1983	Mon-N	.990	**153**	1207	118	**13**	93	3
1984	SF-N	.985	82	665	55	11	50	-1
	Phi-N	.987	19	149	5	2	8	-3
	Yr	.985	101	814	60	13	58	-4
1985	Tor-N	1.000	1	3	0	0	0	0
Total	14	.990	733	5904	433	7	499	-16

■ Gene Oliver C

YEAR	TM/L	PCT	G	PO	A	E	DP	FR
1959	StL-N	.963	9	24	2	1	0	-1
1961	StL-N	1.000	15	75	6	0	4	2
1962	StL-N	.991	98	494	46	5	7	-3
1963	StL-N	.981	35	197	14	4	1	2
	Mil-N	.667	2	2	0	1	0	-1
	Yr	.977	37	199	14	5	1	1
1964	Mil-N	1.000	1	3	1	0	0	0
1965	Mil-N	.976	64	376	34	10	7	0
1966	Atl-N	.990	48	286	22	3	3	11
1967	Atl-N	.968	14	79	11	3	4	2
	Phi-N	.987	79	425	30	6	3	-12
1968	Bos-A	.984	10	58	3	1	0	-2
	Chi-N	1.000	1	10	1	0	0	1
1969	Chi-N	1.000	6	28	2	0	1	2
Total	10	.985	382	2057	172	4	30	1
1B								
1959	StL-N	1.000	5	39	2	0	1	0
1962	StL-N	1.000	3	14	1	0	2	0
1963	Mil-N	.985	55	440	19	7	39	-8
1964	Mil-N	.982	76	622	34	12	50	-5
1965	Mil-N	.983	52	374	37	7	30	4
1966	Atl-N	1.000	5	19	4	0	3	1
1967	Atl-N	1.000	2	11	0	0	1	0
1968	Chi-N	1.000	2	14	0	0	0	0
Total	8	.984	200	1533	97	6	126	-8
OF								
1959	StL-N	.955	42	62	1	3	0	-2
1961	StL-N	.667	1	2	0	1	0	0
1962	StL-N	1.000	8	6	0	0	0	0
1963	Mil-N	.967	35	29	0	1	0	-2
1965	Mil-N	—	1	0	0	0	0	0
1966	Atl-N	1.000	2	3	0	0	0	0
1968	Bos-A	—	1	0	0	0	0	0
	Chi-N	1.000	1	1	0	0	0	0
Total	7	.954	91	103	1	5	0	-4

■ Joe Oliver C

YEAR	TM/L	PCT	G	PO	A	E	DP	FR
1989	Cin-N	.986	47	260	21	4	1	-1
1990	Cin-N	**.992**	118	686	59	6	8	2
Total	2	.990	165	946	80	0	9	1

■ Nate Oliver 2B

YEAR	TM/L	PCT	G	PO	A	E	DP	FR
1963	LA-N	.961	57	109	112	9	26	5
1964	LA-N	.967	98	194	247	15	44	-10
1965	LA-N	1.000	2	2	1	0	0	3
1966	LA-N	.977	68	99	114	5	22	12
1967	SF-N	.973	39	73	72	4	13	-2
1968	SF-N	.950	14	18	39	3	10	4
1969	Chi-N	1.000	13	22	31	0	9	11
Total	7	.969	291	517	616	6	124	23
SS								
1963	LA-N	1.000	2	2	2	0	0	0
1964	LA-N	—	1	0	0	0	0	0
1966	LA-N	—	2	0	0	0	0	-1
1967	LA-N	.944	32	51	85	8	22	-7
1968	SF-N	.774	13	7	17	7	1	-3
Total	5	.916	50	60	104	5	23	-11
3B								
1966	LA-N	.000	1	0	0	1	0	0
1968	SF-N	1.000	1	0	2	0	0	0
Total	2	.667	2	0	2	1	0	0
OF								
1967	LA-N	1.000	1	1	0	0	0	0

■ Bob Oliver 1B

YEAR	TM/L	PCT	G	PO	A	E	DP	FR
1969	KC-A	1.000	12	72	6	0	6	0
1970	KC-A	.993	115	1020	65	8	100	-4
1971	KC-A	.988	68	470	31	6	53	-1
1972	Cal-A	.994	127	1079	54	7	93	-5
1973	Cal-A	.987	32	282	14	4	21	-3
1974	Cal-A	.985	57	373	18	6	40	-4
	Bal-A	.974	4	32	5	1	1	1
	Yr	.984	61	405	23	7	41	-3
1975	NY-A	1.000	4	39	2	0	9	0
Total	7	.991	423	3367	195	2	323	-16
OF								
1965	Pit-N	1.000	3	3	0	0	0	0
1969	KC-A	.977	98	199	11	5	4	8
1971	KC-A	.990	48	94	3	1	0	1
1972	KC-A	.979	16	45	1	1	0	2
	Cal-A	.857	8	12	0	2	0	-1
	Yr	.951	24	57	1	3	0	1
1973	Cal-A	1.000	47	77	4	0	0	1
1974	Cal-A	.889	4	6	2	1	0	1
Total	6	.979	224	436	21	0	4	11
3B								
1969	KC-A	.813	8	5	8	3	0	-2
1970	KC-A	.958	46	57	80	6	11	-4
1971	KC-A	.833	2	2	3	1	0	-1
1973	Cal-A	.952	49	37	103	7	5	0
1974	Cal-A	.939	46	27	65	6	6	-9
1975	NY-A	1.000	1	0	2	0	0	0
Total	6	.944	152	128	261	3	22	-16

■ Tom Oliver OF

YEAR	TM/L	PCT	G	PO	A	E	DP	FR
1930	Bos-A	.982	**154**	**477**	9	9	3	**15**
1931	Bos-A	**.993**	148	**433**	15	3	4	13
1932	Bos-A	.983	116	328	12	6	4	4
1933	Bos-A	.985	86	187	9	3	3	4
Total	4	.986	504	1425	45	1	14	36

■ Luis Olmo OF

YEAR	TM/L	PCT	G	PO	A	E	DP	FR
1943	Bro-N	.957	57	128	6	6	0	2
1944	Bro-N	.971	64	194	5	6	2	8
1945	Bro-N	.971	106	225	8	7	2	-1
1949	Bro-N	.950	34	54	3	3	0	0
1950	Bos-N	.974	55	74	1	2	0	-3
1951	Bos-N	1.000	16	23	2	0	0	-1
Total	6	.968	332	698	25	4	4	5
3B								
1944	Bro-N	.900	31	39	42	9	3	-5
1945	Bro-N	.838	31	28	34	12	5	-10
1950	Bos-N	1.000	1	0	1	0	0	0
Total	3	.873	63	67	77	1	8	-15
2B								
1944	Bro-N	.935	42	83	91	12	13	-8
1945	Bro-N	1.000	1	0	1	0	0	0
Total	2	.936	43	83	92	2	13	-8

■ Greg Olson C

YEAR	TM/L	PCT	G	PO	A	E	DP	FR
1989	Min-A	1.000	3	4	0	0	0	0
1990	Atl-N	.987	97	501	43	7	3	0
Total	2	.987	100	505	43	7	3	-8
3B								
1990	Atl-N	—	1	0	0	0	0	0

■ Ivy Olson SS

YEAR	TM/L	PCT	G	PO	A	E	DP	FR
1911	Cle-A	.909	139	293	428	72	51	-16
1912	Cle-A	.917	56	118	180	27	10	1
1914	Cle-A	.942	31	58	89	9	14	4
1915	Bro-N	.909	7	16	14	3	2	0
1916	Bro-N	.920	103	234	303	47	28	-12
1917	Bro-N	.941	133	283	431	45	53	-2
1918	Bro-N	.918	126	265	388	58	42	-25
1919	Bro-N	.947	**140**	349	445	44	57	-2
1920	Bro-N	.935	125	275	404	47	48	-12
1921	Bro-N	.943	133	343	465	**49**	71	8
1922	Bro-N	.957	51	139	149	13	43	-9
1923	Bro-N	.500	2	1	0	1	0	-1
1924	Bro-N	.941	8	15	17	2	6	-2
Total	13	.932	1054	2389	3313	417	425	-68
2B								
1912	Cle-A	.925	21	47	64	9	6	3
1913	Cle-A	.889	1	5	3	1	1	1
1914	Cle-A	.985	23	62	72	2	5	6
1915	Cin-N	.938	39	88	125	14	17	9
	Bro-N	—	1	0	0	0	0	0
	Yr	.938	40	88	125	14	17	9
1916	Bro-N	.917	3	7	4	1	0	0
1920	Bro-N	.949	21	51	78	7	20	5
1921	Bro-N	.935	20	36	65	7	12	-2
1922	Bro-N	.960	85	193	283	20	39	3
1923	Bro-N	.974	72	161	244	11	36	6
1924	Bro-N	1.000	2	1	0	0	0	0
Total	10	.957	288	651	938	2	136	31
3B								
1911	Cle-A	.667	1	0	2	1	0	-1
1912	Cle-A	.944	36	62	74	8	2	3
1913	Cle-A	.953	73	97	145	12	7	5
1914	Cle-A	.937	19	42	32	5	1	1
1915	Cin-N	.927	15	17	34	4	0	3
	Bro-N	1.000	1	0	1	0	0	0
	Yr	.929	16	17	35	4	0	3
1917	Bro-N	.647	6	4	7	6	0	-4
1923	Bro-N	1.000	4	1	1	0	0	0
Total	7	.935	155	223	296	6	10	7
1B								
1913	Cle-A	.964	21	206	10	8	17	-2
1914	Cle-A	1.000	3	17	1	0	0	0
1915	Cin-N	.986	7	65	7	1	3	1
1916	Bro-N	1.000	1	2	0	0	0	0
1923	Bro-N	1.000	2	5	0	0	0	0
Total	5	.972	34	295	18	9	20	-1
OF								
1912	Cle-A	1.000	3	3	0	0	0	-1
1914	Cle-A	1.000	6	14	1	0	0	-1
1915	Bro-N	—	1	0	0	0	0	0
Total	3	1.000	10	17	1	0	0	-2

■ Karl Olson OF

YEAR	TM/L	PCT	G	PO	A	E	DP	FR
1951	Bos-A	1.000	5	8	0	0	0	0
1953	Bos-A	.970	24	31	1	1	0	0
1954	Bos-A	.957	78	122	10	6	1	6
1955	Bos-A	1.000	21	27	1	0	0	1
1956	Was-A	.990	101	192	4	2	0	-15
1957	Was-A	1.000	6	10	0	0	0	1
	Det-A	1.000	5	6	0	0	0	0
	Yr	1.000	11	16	0	0	0	1
Total	6	.979	240	396	16	9	1	-7

■ Marv Olson 2B

YEAR	TM/L	PCT	G	PO	A	E	DP	FR
1931	Bos-A	.963	15	49	55	4	9	3
1932	Bos-A	.955	106	266	324	28	68	-15

YEAR	TM/L	PCT	G	PO	A	E	DP	FR
1933	Bos-A	—	1	0	0	0	0	0
Total	3	.956	122	315	379	2	77	-12

3B

YEAR	TM/L	PCT	G	PO	A	E	DP	FR
1932	Bos-A	1.000	1	0	3	0	0	0

■ Tom O'Malley 3B

YEAR	TM/L	PCT	G	PO	A	E	DP	FR
1982	SF-N	.965	83	59	160	8	9	1
1983	SF-N	.940	117	70	213	18	12	1
1984	SF-N	1.000	7	5	8	0	1	0
	Chi-A	1.000	6	2	1	0	0	-2
1985	Bal-A	.833	3	2	3	1	0	-1
1986	Bal-A	.938	55	37	98	9	8	-1
1987	Tex-A	.962	40	21	56	3	3	-4
1988	Mon-N	.905	7	4	15	2	0	1
1989	NY-N	1.000	3	2	1	0	0	0
1990	NY-N	.983	38	26	33	1	4	3
Total	9	.951	359	228	588	2	37	-2

1B

YEAR	TM/L	PCT	G	PO	A	E	DP	FR
1990	NY-N	.938	3	15	0	1	0	-1

2B

YEAR	TM/L	PCT	G	PO	A	E	DP	FR
1982	SF-N	—	1	0	0	0	0	0
1987	Tex-A	—	1	0	0	0	0	0
Total	2	—	2	0	0	0	0	0

SS

YEAR	TM/L	PCT	G	PO	A	E	DP	FR
1982	SF-N	1.000	1	1	1	0	1	0

■ Ollie O'Mara SS

YEAR	TM/L	PCT	G	PO	A	E	DP	FR
1912	Det-A	.857	1	2	4	1	0	0
1914	Bro-N	.918	63	110	183	26	17	-12
1915	Bro-N	.906	149	319	431	78	44	-34
1916	Bro-N	.898	51	117	148	30	30	-5
Total	4	.907	264	548	766	135	91	-51

3B

YEAR	TM/L	PCT	G	PO	A	E	DP	FR
1918	Bro-N	.951	121	126	262	20	15	-2
1919	Bro-N	.875	2	4	3	1	0	0
Total	2	.950	123	130	265	1	15	-2

■ Mickey O'Neil C

YEAR	TM/L	PCT	G	PO	A	E	DP	FR
1919	Bos-N	.981	11	33	19	1	3	3
1920	Bos-N	.962	105	304	153	18	10	7
1921	Bos-N	.978	95	276	117	13	8	7
1922	Bos-N	.978	79	239	70	7	3	1
1923	Bos-N	.973	95	298	104	11	5	14
1924	Bos-N	.985	106	362	108	7	8	2
1925	Bos-N	.972	69	208	31	7	3	-9
1926	Bro-N	.965	74	247	53	11	5	-3
1927	Was-A	1.000	4	5	1	0	0	0
	NY-N	.969	16	48	14	2	2	3
Total	9	.972	654	2020	670	7	47	25

2B

YEAR	TM/L	PCT	G	PO	A	E	DP	FR
1920	Bos-N	—	1	0	0	0	0	0

■ Tip O'Neill OF

YEAR	TM/L	PCT	G	PO	A	E	DP	FR
1883	NY-N	.800	7	7	1	2	0	-1
1884	StL-a	.811	64	67	6	17	1	-6
1885	StL-a	.881	52	83	6	12	1	-1
1886	StL-a	.927	138	279	14	23	4	8
1887	StL-a	.895	124	247	8	30	2	-6
1888	StL-a	.937	130	231	8	16	1	-1
1889	StL-a	.936	134	264	12	19	3	-2
1890	Chi-P	.926	137	231	8	19	1	-12
1891	StL-a	.935	129	197	5	14	0	-13
1892	Cin-N	.922	109	188	13	17	3	-3
Total	10	.917	1024	1794	81	169	16	-37

1B

YEAR	TM/L	PCT	G	PO	A	E	DP	FR
1884	StL-a	1.000	1	2	0	0	0	0

■ Jack O'Neill C

YEAR	TM/L	PCT	G	PO	A	E	DP	FR
1902	StL-N	.973	59	246	79	9	5	1
1903	StL-N	.972	74	348	135	14	8	16
1904	Chi-N	.981	49	256	62	6	5	5
1905	Chi-N	.974	50	276	63	9	8	7
1906	Bos-N	.971	48	259	72	10	6	11
Total	5	.974	280	1385	411	8	32	40

1B

YEAR	TM/L	PCT	G	PO	A	E	DP	FR
1906	Bos-N	1.000	2	20	3	0	1	1

OF

YEAR	TM/L	PCT	G	PO	A	E	DP	FR
1906	Bos-N	.000	1	0	0	1	0	-1

■ Paul O'Neill OF

YEAR	TM/L	PCT	G	PO	A	E	DP	FR
1985	Cin-N	1.000	2	3	1	0	0	0
1987	Cin-N	.949	42	73	2	4	0	1
1988	Cin-N	.984	118	237	5	4	0	0
1989	Cin-N	.983	115	223	7	4	1	1
1990	Cin-N	.993	141	271	12	2	0	3
Total	5	.983	418	807	27	4	1	5

1B

YEAR	TM/L	PCT	G	PO	A	E	DP	FR
1987	Cin-N	1.000	2	17	0	0	2	-1
1988	Cin-N	.989	21	173	8	2	14	-2
Total	2	.990	23	190	8	2	16	-3

■ Steve O'Neill C

YEAR	TM/L	PCT	G	PO	A	E	DP	FR
1911	Cle-A	.986	9	55	17	1	1	4
1912	Cle-A	.961	68	316	108	17	9	9
1913	Cle-A	.973	80	353	119	13	9	3
1914	Cle-A	.956	82	393	134	24	22	1
1915	Cle-A	.968	115	556	175	24	17	5
1916	Cle-A	.971	128	540	154	21	36	5
1917	Cle-A	.980	127	446	145	12	19	1
1918	Cle-A	.983	113	409	154	10	10	1
1919	Cle-A	.977	123	472	125	14	13	-7
1920	Cle-A	.976	148	576	128	17	1	-8
1921	Cle-A	.982	105	393	92	9	8	3
1922	Cle-A	.974	130	450	116	15	9	-13
1923	Cle-A	.968	111	354	68	14	3	-11
1924	Bos-A	.970	92	342	75	13	2	1
1925	NY-A	.946	31	113	27	8	8	3
1927	StL-A	.983	60	180	57	4	8	1
1928	StL-A	.958	10	19	4	1	0	-4
Total	17	.972	1532	5967	1698	217	175	-6

YEAR	TM/L	PCT	G	PO	A	E	DP	FR
1914	Cle-A	1.000	1	1	0	0	1	0

■ Bill O'Neill OF

YEAR	TM/L	PCT	G	PO	A	E	DP	FR
1904	Bos-A	.933	9	14	0	1	0	-1
	Was-A	.899	93	151	9	18	1	-9
	Yr	.902	102	165	9	19	1	-10
1906	Chi-A	.949	93	118	12	7	1	-6
Total	2	.921	195	283	21	6	2	-16

2B

YEAR	TM/L	PCT	G	PO	A	E	DP	FR
1904	Was-A	.857	3	3	9	2	0	-1

SS

YEAR	TM/L	PCT	G	PO	A	E	DP	FR
1904	Bos-A	.643	2	2	7	5	0	-1

■ Steve Ontiveros 3B

YEAR	TM/L	PCT	G	PO	A	E	DP	FR
1974	SF-N	.929	75	64	144	16	16	-6
1975	SF-N	.923	89	64	188	21	14	0
1976	SF-N	1.000	7	4	6	0	1	-2
1977	Chi-N	.955	155	100	324	20	24	-2
1978	Chi-N	.965	77	57	194	9	16	10
1979	Chi-N	.941	142	98	268	23	27	-5
1980	Chi-N	.929	24	13	39	4	1	-1
Total	7	.944	569	400	1163	3	99	-6

1B

YEAR	TM/L	PCT	G	PO	A	E	DP	FR
1973	SF-N	1.000	5	35	6	0	2	1
1974	SF-N	.983	19	160	14	3	14	1
1975	SF-N	1.000	4	9	1	0	1	0
1976	SF-N	.867	4	12	1	2	1	-1
1978	Chi-N	1.000	1	7	0	0	0	0
1979	Chi-N	1.000	1	7	1	0	0	0
Total	6	.981	34	230	23	5	19	1

OF

YEAR	TM/L	PCT	G	PO	A	E	DP	FR
1973	SF-N	1.000	1	1	0	0	0	0
1974	SF-N	1.000	2	1	0	0	0	0
1975	SF-N	1.000	8	7	0	0	0	0
1976	SF-N	1.000	7	2	1	0	0	0
Total	4	1.000	18	11	1	0	0	0

■ Jose Oquendo 2B

YEAR	TM/L	PCT	G	PO	A	E	DP	FR
1986	StL-N	.935	21	22	36	4	11	-2
1987	StL-N	1.000	32	50	65	0	20	2
1988	StL-N	.997	69	149	184	1	41	5
1989	StL-N	.994	156	346	500	5	106	20
1990	StL-N	.996	150	285	393	3	65	0
Total	5	.994	428	852	1178	3	243	25

SS

YEAR	TM/L	PCT	G	PO	A	E	DP	FR
1983	NY-N	.960	116	182	326	21	65	6
1984	NY-N	.972	67	95	152	7	33	2
1986	StL-N	.956	29	30	56	4	12	-3
1987	StL-N	.968	23	11	50	2	7	4
1988	StL-N	.952	17	23	37	3	8	2
1989	StL-N	.970	7	9	23	1	2	1
1990	StL-N	.950	4	9	10	1	2	-1
Total	7	.963	263	359	654	9	129	11

OF

YEAR	TM/L	PCT	G	PO	A	E	DP	FR
1986	StL-N	—	1	0	0	0	0	0
1987	StL-N	1.000	46	65	4	0	1	2
1988	StL-N	1.000	15	22	0	0	0	0
Total	3	1.000	62	87	4	0	1	2

3B

YEAR	TM/L	PCT	G	PO	A	E	DP	FR
1986	StL-N	1.000	1	0	2	0	0	0
1987	StL-N	.909	8	6	14	2	1	0
1988	StL-N	.957	47	22	88	5	8	3
Total	3	.950	56	28	104	7	9	3

1B

YEAR	TM/L	PCT	G	PO	A	E	DP	FR
1987	StL-N	1.000	3	17	0	0	2	0
1988	StL-N	.966	16	51	6	2	4	0
1989	StL-N	1.000	1	1	0	0	0	0
Total	3	.974	20	69	6	2	6	0

C

YEAR	TM/L	PCT	G	PO	A	E	DP	FR
1988	StL-N	1.000	1	1	0	0	0	0

■ Joe Orengo 3B

YEAR	TM/L	PCT	G	PO	A	E	DP	FR
1940	StL-N	.976	34	39	43	2	5	-1
1941	NY-N	.958	59	74	132	9	12	10
1943	Bro-N	1.000	6	4	9	0	0	0
1944	Det-A	.911	11	11	30	4	1	2
1945	Chi-A	.923	7	5	7	1	0	1
Total	5	.957	117	133	221	6	18	12

1B

YEAR	TM/L	PCT	G	PO	A	E	DP	FR
1943	NY-N	.992	82	730	61	6	49	4
1944	Det-A	.983	5	55	3	1	2	0
Total	2	.992	87	785	64	7	51	4

2B

YEAR	TM/L	PCT	G	PO	A	E	DP	FR
1940	StL-N	.952	77	204	216	21	45	7
1941	NY-N	1.000	6	18	20	0	3	3
1944	Det-A	1.000	2	4	5	0	1	1
1945	Chi-A	—	1	0	0	0	0	0
Total	4	.957	86	226	241	1	49	11

SS

YEAR	TM/L	PCT	G	PO	A	E	DP	FR
1939	StL-N	.667	7	3	3	3	0	0
1940	StL-N	.942	19	38	59	6	10	-1
1941	NY-N	.984	9	25	37	1	7	5
1944	Det-A	.903	29	54	86	15	20	4
Total	4	.924	64	120	185	5	37	8

■ Frank O'Rourke 3B

YEAR	TM/L	PCT	G	PO	A	E	DP	FR
1912	Bos-N	.667	1	1	1	1	0	0
1917	Bro-N	.954	58	72	134	10	6	7
1920	Was-A	1.000	1	3	2	0	0	0
1922	Bos-A	.960	20	12	36	2	1	0
1925	Det-A	.941	6	7	9	1	0	-1
1926	Det-A	.936	60	83	121	14	18	4
1927	StL-A	.955	121	183	244	20	27	6
1928	StL-A	.954	96	150	162	15	13	-9
1929	StL-A	.943	151	171	242	25	30	-19
1930	StL-A	.950	84	116	150	14	16	4
Total	10	.949	598	798	1101	102	111	-8

SS

YEAR	TM/L	PCT	G	PO	A	E	DP	FR
1912	Bos-N	.915	59	92	167	24	16	-7

YEAR	TM/L	PCT	G	PO	A	E	DP	FR
1920	Was-A	.952	13	35	45	4	12	4
1921	Was-A	.922	122	272	377	55	52	-7
1922	Bos-A	.909	49	86	134	22	17	-11
1924	Det-A	.925	7	12	25	3	1	1
1926	Det-A	.941	10	9	7	1	0	-1
1928	StL-A	1.000	2	1	2	0	0	0
1929	StL-A	1.000	2	7	9	0	1	2
1930	StL-A	.968	23	40	82	4	13	6
1931	StL-A	1.000	2	1	3	0	0	1
Total	10	.926	289	555	851	113	112	-12

2B

YEAR	TM/L	PCT	G	PO	A	E	DP	FR
1918	Bro-N	.857	2	2	10	2	1	0
1924	Det-A	.970	40	115	140	8	27	10
1925	Det-A	.971	118	309	382	21	67	15
1926	Det-A	.967	41	98	135	8	25	6
1927	StL-A	.972	16	53	51	3	18	2
1929	StL-A	1.000	3	6	4	0	1	-1
Total	6	.969	220	583	722	2	139	34

1B

YEAR	TM/L	PCT	G	PO	A	E	DP	FR
1927	StL-A	1.000	3	10	4	0	2	1
1930	StL-A	.933	3	11	3	1	2	1
1931	StL-A	1.000	1	14	0	0	0	0
Total	3	.977	7	35	7	1	4	2

OF

YEAR	TM/L	PCT	G	PO	A	E	DP	FR
1918	Bro-N	1.000	1	1	1	0	0	0

■ Jim O'Rourke OF

YEAR	TM/L	PCT	G	PO	A	E	DP	FR
1876	Bos-N	.856	68	154	7	27	1	-3
1877	Bos-N	.846	60	112	9	22	0	-2
1878	Bos-N	.860	57	102	15	19	4	3
1879	Pro-N	.785	56	51	11	17	2	-10
1880	Bos-N	.907	37	57	11	7	1	3
1881	Buf-N	.914	18	27	5	3	0	-2
1882	Buf-N	.866	81	140	15	24	3	-2
1883	Buf-N	.866	61	89	8	15	0	-5
1884	Buf-N	.894	86	112	6	14	2	-9
1885	NY-N	.940	112	162	10	11	0	-16
1886	NY-N	.926	63	101	11	9	1	-1
1887	NY-N	.931	28	60	7	5	1	2
1888	NY-N	.960	87	130	13	6	1	3
1889	NY-N	.893	128	165	18	22	2	-11
1890	NY-P	.930	111	175	25	15	3	5
1891	NY-N	.906	126	195	18	22	1	-3
1892	NY-N	.913	111	146	11	15	1	-10
1893	Was-N	.927	87	174	16	15	2	3
Total	18	.898	1377	2152	216	268	25	-55

C

YEAR	TM/L	PCT	G	PO	A	E	DP	FR
1876	Bos-N	—	1	0	0	0	0	0
1878	Bos-N	.824	2	12	2	3	1	0
1879	Pro-N	.891	5	32	9	5	0	1
1880	Bos-N	.827	9	32	11	9	0	-3
1881	Buf-N	.822	8	30	7	8	0	-4
1882	Buf-N	1.000	2	6	1	0	0	0
1883	Buf-N	.926	33	128	34	13	0	-4
1884	Buf-N	1.000	10	27	11	0	1	1
1885	NY-N	.852	8	20	3	4	0	-1
1886	NY-N	.946	47	250	83	19	3	7
1887	NY-N	.890	40	137	66	25	4	-5
1888	NY-N	.952	15	77	22	5	0	-1
1889	NY-N	1.000	1	1	2	0	0	0
1891	NY-N	.949	14	49	26	4	2	4
1892	NY-N	.952	4	14	6	1	0	0
1893	Was-N	.946	9	36	17	3	2	3
1904	NY-N	.800	1	4	0	1	0	-1
Total	17	.920	209	855	300	100	13	-3

3B

YEAR	TM/L	PCT	G	PO	A	E	DP	FR
1879	Pro-N	.889	3	0	8	1	0	1
1880	Bos-N	.914	10	17	15	3	2	-1
1881	Buf-N	.821	56	85	80	36	8	-15
1882	Buf-N	.600	1	3	0	2	0	-1
1883	Buf-N	.667	8	6	6	6	2	-3
1884	Buf-N	.750	1	3	3	2	1	1
1887	NY-N	.842	38	46	50	18	2	-7
1888	NY-N	.667	2	1	3	2	0	-1
Total	8	.823	119	161	165	0	15	-26

1B

YEAR	TM/L	PCT	G	PO	A	E	DP	FR
1876	Bos-N	.941	2	16	0	1	0	0
1877	Bos-N	.857	1	6	0	1	2	0
1878	Bos-N	1.000	2	10	0	0	0	0
1879	Pro-N	.952	20	219	1	11	4	-2
1880	Bos-N	.929	19	141	4	11	11	-1
1881	Buf-N	1.000	1	5	0	0	0	0
1884	Buf-N	.937	18	208	1	14	8	-3
1886	NY-N	1.000	2	18	2	0	1	1
1888	NY-N	.978	4	43	2	1	3	0
1892	NY-N	.889	1	8	0	1	1	0
1893	Was-N	.970	33	277	19	9	15	0
Total	11	.952	103	951	29	9	45	-5

SS

YEAR	TM/L	PCT	G	PO	A	E	DP	FR
1880	Bos-N	.844	17	20	56	14	4	0
1881	Buf-N	1.000	3	1	5	0	0	0
1882	Buf-N	1.000	2	0	1	0	0	0
1883	Buf-N	.762	3	3	13	5	0	1
Total	4	.839	25	24	75	9	4	0

2B

YEAR	TM/L	PCT	G	PO	A	E	DP	FR
1887	NY-N	1.000	2	5	4	0	1	0

■ John O'Rourke OF

YEAR	TM/L	PCT	G	PO	A	E	DP	FR
1879	Bos-N	.882	71	147	10	21	2	4
1880	Bos-N	.871	81	156	19	26	0	3
1883	NY-a	.856	76	95	12	18	2	-3
Total	3	.871	228	398	41	5	4	0

1B

YEAR	TM/L	PCT	G	PO	A	E	DP	FR
1883	NY-N	.750	1	9	0	3	0	-1

■ Tim O'Rourke 3B

YEAR	TM/L	PCT	G	PO	A	E	DP	FR
1890	Syr-a	.866	87	117	168	44	9	-11
1891	Col-a	.879	34	48	76	17	7	0

(O'Rourke, continued)

YEAR	TM/L	PCT	G	PO	A	E	DP	FR
1892	Bal-N	.333	1	1	0	1	2	0	-1
1893	Bal-N	.933	5	6	8	1	2	0	-1
	Lou-N	.842	6	4	12	3	0	-2
	Yr	.882	11	10	20	4	2	-3
1894	Lou-N	.615	3	2	6	5	0	-1
	StL-N	.861	18	29	33	10	3	-2
	Yr	.824	21	31	39	15	3	-3
Total	5	.861	154	206	304	2	21	-18

SS

YEAR	TM/L	PCT	G	PO	A	E	DP	FR
1892	Bal-N	.869	58	104	180	43	17	-11
1893	Bal-N	.667	1	2	2	2	0	-1
	Lou-N	.865	60	118	176	46	26	-15
	Yr	.861	61	120	178	48	26	-16
1894	Lou-N	.800	3	4	8	3	3	-1
	Was-N	.923	3	15	9	2	0	1
	Yr	.878	6	19	17	5	3	0
Total	3	.866	125	243	375	6	46	-27

OF

YEAR	TM/L	PCT	G	PO	A	E	DP	FR
1892	Bal-N	1.000	4	1	0	0	0	-2
1893	Bal-N	.980	25	48	1	1	0	-2
	Lou-N	.933	26	25	3	2	0	-4
	Yr	.962	51	73	4	3	0	-6
1894	Lou-N	.854	18	34	1	6	0	-2
Total	3	.926	73	108	5	9	0	-10

1B

YEAR	TM/L	PCT	G	PO	A	E	DP	FR
1894	Lou-N	.977	30	270	24	7	29	3

2B

YEAR	TM/L	PCT	G	PO	A	E	DP	FR
1894	Lou-N	.889	1	6	2	1	4	0
	Was-N	.909	4	9	11	2	0	0
	Yr	.903	5	15	13	3	4	0

■ Dave Orr 1B

YEAR	TM/L	PCT	G	PO	A	E	DP	FR
1883	NY-a	1.000	1	10	0	0	0	0
	NY-N	.938	12	136	1	9	4	-1
	Yr	.942	13	146	1	9	4	-1
1884	NY-a	.960	110	1161	24	49	29	-5
1885	NY-a	.966	107	1089	20	39	48	-3
1886	NY-a	.981	136	1445	34	28	62	0
1887	NY-a	.969	81	806	28	27	41	0
1888	Bro-a	.979	99	976	44	22	41	4
1889	Col-a	.983	134	1291	61	23	64	9
1890	Bro-P	.972	107	1009	42	30	67	-4
Total	8	.973	787	7923	254	227	356	0

OF

YEAR	TM/L	PCT	G	PO	A	E	DP	FR
1883	NY-N	1.000	1	2	0	0	0	0
1884	NY-a	1.000	3	2	0	0	1	-1
1887	NY-a	.800	3	4	0	1	0	-1
Total	3	.889	7	8	0	1	1	-2

■ Ernie Orsatti OF

YEAR	TM/L	PCT	G	PO	A	E	DP	FR
1927	StL-N	.922	26	56	3	5	2	0
1928	StL-N	1.000	17	29	2	0	0	0
1929	StL-N	.974	77	176	12	5	5	8
1930	StL-N	1.000	11	22	4	0	2	3
1931	StL-N	.988	45	83	0	1	0	-1
1932	StL-N	.976	96	197	3	5	0	-5
1933	StL-N	.986	107	274	5	4	1	0
1934	StL-N	.986	90	207	5	3	0	-4
1935	StL-N	.975	60	115	3	3	2	-1
Total	9	.979	529	1159	37	6	12	0

1B

YEAR	TM/L	PCT	G	PO	A	E	DP	FR
1928	StL-N	.977	5	41	1	1	2	-1
1929	StL-N	.988	10	83	2	1	4	-1
1930	StL-N	.985	22	188	15	3	17	1
1931	StL-N	.923	1	11	1	1	0	0
1932	StL-N	.909	1	10	0	1	1	0
1933	StL-N	.962	3	25	0	1	2	-1
Total	6	.979	42	358	19	8	26	-2

■ John Orsino C

YEAR	TM/L	PCT	G	PO	A	E	DP	FR
1961	SF-N	.959	25	130	9	6	4	-2
1962	SF-N	.963	16	72	6	3	1	-2
1963	Bal-A	.990	109	636	37	7	8	-7
1964	Bal-A	.976	66	384	31	10	3	1
1965	Bal-A	.987	62	342	25	5	3	-8
1966	Was-A	1.000	2	3	0	0	0	0
Total	6	.982	280	1567	108	1	19	-18

1B

YEAR	TM/L	PCT	G	PO	A	E	DP	FR
1963	Bal-A	1.000	3	20	1	0	2	0
1964	Bal-A	1.000	5	42	1	0	4	-1
1965	Bal-A	.969	5	30	1	1	1	-1
1966	Was-A	1.000	5	25	2	0	3	0
Total	4	.992	18	117	5	1	10	-2

■ Joe Orsulak OF

YEAR	TM/L	PCT	G	PO	A	E	DP	FR
1983	Pit-N	1.000	4	2	2	0	0	1
1984	Pit-N	1.000	25	41	1	0	0	2
1985	Pit-N	.976	115	229	10	6	1	5
1986	Pit-N	.981	120	193	11	4	2	-4
1988	Bal-A	.979	117	228	6	5	2	-4
1989	Bal-A	.985	109	250	10	4	2	5
1990	Bal-A	.989	109	267	5	3	2	7
Total	7	.983	599	1210	45	2	9	12

■ Jorge Orta 2B

YEAR	TM/L	PCT	G	PO	A	E	DP	FR
1972	Chi-A	.958	14	20	26	2	8	1
1973	Chi-A	.969	122	254	300	18	75	-26
1974	Chi-A	.971	123	297	313	18	93	-13
1975	Chi-A	.978	135	354	354	16	95	-12
1977	Chi-A	.970	139	287	335	19	64	-47
1978	Chi-A	.984	114	275	290	9	62	-22
1979	Chi-A	.978	41	57	75	3	17	-10
1984	KC-A	—	1	0	0	0	0	0
Total	8	.974	689	1544	1693	5	414	130

OF

YEAR	TM/L	PCT	G	PO	A	E	DP	FR
1976	Chi-A	.971	77	156	9	5	1	2
1980	Cle-A	.982	120	269	10	5	1	6
1981	Cle-A	.994	86	150	11	1	2	0
1982	LA-N	.947	17	35	1	2	1	1
1983	Tor-A	1.000	17	16	1	0	1	1
1984	KC-A	.980	26	48	0	1	0	2
Total	6	.981	343	674	32	4	6	12

3B

YEAR	TM/L	PCT	G	PO	A	E	DP	FR
1972	Chi-A	.870	9	2	18	3	2	0
1976	Chi-A	.930	49	31	102	10	9	-2
Total	2	.922	58	33	120	3	11	-2

SS

YEAR	TM/L	PCT	G	PO	A	E	DP	FR
1972	Chi-A	.958	18	28	41	3	13	-2
1973	Chi-A	1.000	1	1	1	0	0	0
1974	Chi-A	—	3	0	0	0	0	0
Total	3	.959	22	29	42	3	13	-2

■ Junior Ortiz C

YEAR	TM/L	PCT	G	PO	A	E	DP	FR
1982	Pit-N	1.000	7	27	3	0	0	1
1983	Pit-N	1.000	4	20	0	0	0	0
	NY-N	.965	67	273	31	11	2	1
	Yr	.967	71	293	31	11	2	1
1984	NY-N	.980	32	136	13	3	3	-3
1985	Pit-N	.985	23	115	14	2	3	0
1986	Pit-N	.983	36	165	13	3	2	0
1987	Pit-N	.975	72	313	39	9	2	0
1988	Pit-N	.983	40	152	23	3	2	-2
1989	Pit-N	.995	84	334	32	2	2	-9
1990	Min-A	1.000	68	247	25	0	6	2
Total	9	.984	433	1782	193	3	22	-10

■ Roberto Ortiz OF

YEAR	TM/L	PCT	G	PO	A	E	DP	FR
1941	Was-A	.860	21	34	3	6	0	-1
1942	Was-A	.941	9	15	1	1	0	-1
1943	Was-A	1.000	1	3	0	0	0	0
1944	Was-A	.949	80	165	2	9	1	-8
1949	Was-A	.946	32	48	5	3	1	-3
1950	Was-A	1.000	19	24	2	0	0	-2
	Phi-A	1.000	3	5	0	0	0	0
	Yr	1.000	22	29	2	0	0	-2
Total	6	.942	165	294	13	9	2	-15

■ Fred Osborn OF

YEAR	TM/L	PCT	G	PO	A	E	DP	FR
1907	Phi-N	1.000	36	60	2	0	0	-4
1908	Phi-N	.969	152	359	14	12	3	2
1909	Phi-N	.979	54	126	14	3	3	10
Total	3	.975	242	545	30	5	6	8

1B

YEAR	TM/L	PCT	G	PO	A	E	DP	FR
1907	Phi-N	1.000	1	8	0	0	1	0

■ Bobo Osborne 1B

YEAR	TM/L	PCT	G	PO	A	E	DP	FR
1957	Det-A	1.000	4	20	1	0	1	0
1959	Det-A	.983	56	377	27	7	36	-1
1961	Det-A	1.000	11	50	3	0	4	-1
1962	Det-A	1.000	7	11	2	0	0	0
1963	Was-A	.988	81	713	55	9	68	-1
Total	5	.987	159	1171	88	6	109	-3

3B

YEAR	TM/L	PCT	G	PO	A	E	DP	FR
1961	Det-A	.957	8	10	12	1	2	-2
1962	Det-A	.857	13	11	19	5	0	-2
1963	Was-A	.889	16	6	26	4	1	-2
Total	3	.894	37	27	57	0	3	-6

OF

YEAR	TM/L	PCT	G	PO	A	E	DP	FR
1957	Det-A	1.000	5	8	0	0	0	0
1959	Det-A	.500	1	1	0	1	0	0
Total	2	.900	6	9	0	1	0	0

C

YEAR	TM/L	PCT	G	PO	A	E	DP	FR
1962	Det-A	—	1	0	0	0	0	0

■ Johnny Ostrowski OF

YEAR	TM/L	PCT	G	PO	A	E	DP	FR
1943	Chi-N	1.000	5	8	0	0	1	0
1944	Chi-N	.500	2	1	0	1	0	-1
1949	Chi-A	.944	41	81	3	5	0	-1
1950	Chi-A	1.000	14	26	1	0	0	0
	Was-A	.947	45	105	3	6	1	0
	Chi-A	1.000	1	1	0	0	0	0
	Yr	.958	60	132	4	6	1	3
Total	4	.950	108	222	7	2	2	1

3B

YEAR	TM/L	PCT	G	PO	A	E	DP	FR
1943	Chi-N	.800	4	3	5	2	1	-2
1945	Chi-N	.750	4	1	2	1	0	-1
1946	Chi-N	.934	50	33	80	8	5	1
1949	Chi-A	.929	8	4	9	1	0	0
Total	4	.919	66	41	96	2	6	-2

2B

YEAR	TM/L	PCT	G	PO	A	E	DP	FR
1946	Chi-N	1.000	1	2	2	0	0	0

■ Amos Otis OF

YEAR	TM/L	PCT	G	PO	A	E	DP	FR
1967	NY-N	1.000	16	22	2	0	1	0
1969	NY-N	1.000	35	46	3	0	0	3
1970	KC-A	.990	159	388	15	4	6	10
1971	KC-A	.990	144	404	10	4	4	18
1972	KC-A	.992	137	351	6	3	3	4
1973	KC-A	.986	135	330	10	5	4	1
1974	KC-A	.986	143	425	8	6	3	7
1975	KC-A	.988	130	310	9	4	3	-1
1976	KC-A	.992	152	373	5	3	1	-11
1977	KC-A	.991	140	326	10	3	0	-7
1978	KC-A	.995	136	382	9	2	1	5
1979	KC-A	.992	146	385	11	3	5	-1
1980	KC-A	.988	105	310	6	4	1	3
1981	KC-A	.993	97	294	6	2	1	8
1982	KC-A	.997	125	308	5	1	1	-7
1983	KC-A	.996	96	233	6	1	1	4
1984	Pit-N	.964	32	49	5	2	0	2
Total	17	.991	1928	4936	126	7	35	38

3B

YEAR	TM/L	PCT	G	PO	A	E	DP	FR
1967	NY-N	1.000	1	1	0	0	0	0
1969	NY-N	.857	3	3	3	1	0	-1
Total	2	.875	4	4	3	1	0	-1

■ Mel Ott OF

YEAR	TM/L	PCT	G	PO	A	E	DP	FR
1926	NY-N	.913	10	18	3	2	0	1
1927	NY-N	.982	32	52	2	1	1	-4
1928	NY-N	.970	115	214	14	7	4	-2
1929	NY-N	.973	149	335	26	10	12	14
1930	NY-N	.969	146	320	23	11	6	11
1931	NY-N	.981	137	332	20	7	4	-2
1932	NY-N	.984	154	347	11	6	5	1
1933	NY-N	.983	152	283	12	5	3	-9
1934	NY-N	.974	153	286	12	8	1	-10
1935	NY-N	.990	137	285	17	3	7	4
1936	NY-N	.985	148	250	20	4	3	-5
1937	NY-N	1.000	91	156	13	0	1	1
1938	NY-N	1.000	37	65	3	0	0	-2
1939	NY-N	.973	96	175	6	5	2	-5
1940	NY-N	.982	111	210	9	4	2	-1
1941	NY-N	.968	145	256	19	9	3	-3
1942	NY-N	.990	152	269	15	3	3	-3
1943	NY-N	.975	111	219	12	6	1	-1
1944	NY-N	.986	103	199	6	3	0	-6
1945	NY-N	.983	118	217	11	4	1	-5
1946	NY-N	1.000	16	23	2	0	1	-1
Total	21	.980	2313	4511	256	8	60	-27

3B

YEAR	TM/L	PCT	G	PO	A	E	DP	FR
1928	NY-N	1.000	1	0	2	0	0	0
1935	NY-N	.936	15	19	25	3	3	0
1937	NY-N	.939	60	42	113	10	5	-2
1938	NY-N	.957	113	98	238	15	14	2
1939	NY-N	.900	20	15	39	6	4	-1
1940	NY-N	.934	42	30	83	8	8	0
1943	NY-N	—	1	0	0	0	0	0
1944	NY-N	.778	4	1	13	4	0	0
Total	8	.940	256	205	513	6	34	-1

2B

YEAR	TM/L	PCT	G	PO	A	E	DP	FR
1928	NY-N	.964	5	14	13	1	4	-1
1929	NY-N	.833	1	4	1	1	0	-1
Total	2	.941	6	18	14	2	4	-2

■ Ed Ott C

YEAR	TM/L	PCT	G	PO	A	E	DP	FR
1975	Pit-N	1.000	2	2	0	0	0	0
1976	Pit-N	1.000	8	20	6	0	1	-1
1977	Pit-N	.982	90	455	49	9	6	-5
1978	Pit-N	.975	97	537	42	15	7	-9
1979	Pit-N	.994	116	612	53	4	6	-3
1980	Pit-N	.983	117	569	73	11	5	-3
1981	Cal-A	.979	72	287	36	7	1	0
Total	7	.983	502	2482	259	6	26	-21

OF

YEAR	TM/L	PCT	G	PO	A	E	DP	FR
1974	Pit-N	1.000	2	1	0	0	0	0
1978	Pit-N	.917	4	10	1	1	0	1
1980	Pit-N	1.000	3	2	0	0	0	0
Total	3	.933	9	13	1	1	0	1

■ Jimmy Outlaw OF

YEAR	TM/L	PCT	G	PO	A	E	DP	FR
1939	Bos-N	.964	39	80	1	3	0	2
1943	Det-A	1.000	16	32	2	0	0	-1
1944	Det-A	.964	137	254	14	10	2	-3
1945	Det-A	.967	105	192	13	7	6	-3
1946	Det-A	1.000	43	71	5	0	0	-1
1947	Det-A	.983	37	58	0	1	0	-1
1948	Det-A	1.000	13	19	1	0	0	1
Total	7	.972	390	706	36	1	8	-6

3B

YEAR	TM/L	PCT	G	PO	A	E	DP	FR
1937	Cin-N	.914	41	41	87	12	4	4
1939	Bos-N	1.000	2	3	0	0	0	0
1945	Det-A	.938	21	18	42	4	5	-1
1946	Det-A	.927	38	30	59	7	4	-6
1947	Det-A	.947	9	11	7	1	0	-1
1948	Det-A	.920	47	39	87	11	8	2
Total	6	.924	158	142	282	5	21	-2

■ Mickey Owen C

YEAR	TM/L	PCT	G	PO	A	E	DP	FR
1937	StL-N	.974	78	287	49	9	6	-3
1938	StL-N	.980	116	463	67	11	8	1
1939	StL-N	.982	126	452	52	9	8	5
1940	StL-N	.980	113	378	56	9	8	2
1941	Bro-N	.995	128	530	64	3	7	6
1942	Bro-N	.987	133	595	66	9	12	4
1943	Bro-N	.987	100	414	47	6	11	-5
1944	Bro-N	.979	125	506	57	12	8	-10
1945	Bro-N	.963	24	92	13	4	2	-3
1949	Chi-N	.969	59	219	35	8	5	-1
1950	Chi-N	.978	86	318	39	8	4	3
1951	Chi-N	.969	57	188	28	7	6	8
1954	Bos-A	.989	30	85	8	1	4	-2
Total	13	.982	1175	4527	581	6	93	5

3B

YEAR	TM/L	PCT	G	PO	A	E	DP	FR
1943	Bro-N	.917	3	3	8	1	0	1

SS

YEAR	TM/L	PCT	G	PO	A	E	DP	FR
1943	Bro-N	1.000	1	4	0	0	0	0

2B

YEAR	TM/L	PCT	G	PO	A	E	DP	FR
1944	Bro-N	1.000	1	1	0	0	0	0

■ Larry Owen C

YEAR	TM/L	PCT	G	PO	A	E	DP	FR
1981	Atl-N	.964	10	23	4	1	2	2
1982	Atl-N	1.000	2	2	1	0	0	0
1983	Atl-N	.970	16	30	2	1	1	1
1985	Atl-N	.966	25	129	11	5	1	2
1987	KC-A	.983	75	370	38	7	4	19
1988	KC-A	.989	37	168	13	2	1	5
Total	6	.980	165	722	69	6	9	29

■ Marv Owen 3B

YEAR	TM/L	PCT	G	PO	A	E	DP	FR
1931	Det-A	.927	37	33	81	9	9	2
1933	Det-A	.944	136	143	226	22	19	-11
1934	Det-A	.956	154	202	253	21	33	-7
1935	Det-A	.958	131	148	215	16	19	-10
1936	Det-A	.952	153	190	281	24	28	-3
1937	Det-A	.970	106	108	219	10	17	0
1938	Chi-A	.948	140	136	305	24	29	0
1939	Chi-A	.953	55	63	99	8	11	-2
1940	Bos-A	.962	9	9	16	1	3	0
Total	9	.953	921	1032	1695	135	168	-31

YEAR	TM/L	PCT	G	PO	A	E	DP	FR
			SS					
1931	Det-A	.937	37	81	113	13	22	-2
			1B					
1931	Det-A	.990	27	185	12	2	14	0
1936	Det-A	1.000	2	12	0	0	1	0
1940	Bos-A	.984	8	53	8	1	9	2
Total	3	.989	37	250	20	3	24	2
			2B					
1931	Det-A	1.000	4	9	14	0	0	0

■ Spike Owen SS

YEAR	TM/L	PCT	G	PO	A	E	DP	FR
1983	Sea-A	.970	80	122	233	11	45	0
1984	Sea-A	.977	151	245	463	17	86	16
1985	Sea-A	.975	117	196	361	14	76	27
1986	Sea-A	.972	112	209	372	17	99	34
	Bos-A	.976	42	70	95	4	34	-2
	Yr	.973	154	279	467	21	133	32
1987	Bos-A	.975	130	176	336	13	69	-14
1988	Bos-A	.967	76	102	192	10	34	0
1989	Mon-N	**.979**	142	232	388	13	65	11
1990	Mon-N	**.989**	148	216	340	6	52	-13
Total	8	.976	998	1568	2780	105	560	59

■ Frank Owens C

YEAR	TM/L	PCT	G	PO	A	E	DP	FR
1905	Bos-A	1.000	1	2	1	0	0	0
1909	Chi-A	.959	57	266	62	14	2	-5
1914	Bro-F	.967	58	228	67	10	10	-15
1915	Bal-F	.976	99	462	146	15	**19**	1
Total	4	.969	215	958	276	9	31	-19

■ Ray Oyler SS

YEAR	TM/L	PCT	G	PO	A	E	DP	FR
1965	Det-A	.955	57	79	156	11	17	5
1966	Det-A	.965	69	107	194	11	42	15
1967	Det-A	.964	146	185	374	21	61	**15**
1968	Det-A	.977	111	139	207	8	31	9
1969	Sea-A	.965	106	143	266	15	47	9
1970	Cal-A	1.000	13	6	10	0	1	-1
Total	6	.966	502	659	1207	6	199	52
			2B					
1965	Det-A	1.000	11	12	6	0	1	0
			3B					
1965	Det-A	1.000	1	0	3	0	0	1
1970	Cal-A	1.000	2	1	2	0	0	0
Total	2	1.000	3	1	5	0	0	1
			1B					
1965	Det-A	1.000	1	1	1	0	0	0

■ Tom Paciorek OF

YEAR	TM/L	PCT	G	PO	A	E	DP	FR
1970	LA-N	1.000	3	1	0	0	0	0
1971	LA-N	1.000	1	1	0	0	0	0
1972	LA-N	1.000	6	9	2	0	0	1
1973	LA-N	.979	77	92	2	2	0	-1
1974	LA-N	.944	77	83	1	5	1	-3
1975	LA-N	.972	54	69	0	2	0	-3
1976	Atl-N	.983	84	115	3	2	0	-7
1977	Atl-N	.923	9	12	0	1	0	0
1978	Sea-A	.980	54	95	3	2	0	-6
1979	Sea-A	1.000	75	137	2	0	0	-7
1980	Sea-A	1.000	60	105	3	0	1	1
1981	Sea-A	.974	103	253	10	7	1	7
1982	Chi-A	1.000	6	2	0	0	0	0
1983	Chi-A	.987	55	74	2	1	0	-4
1984	Chi-A	.971	41	64	2	2	0	-4
1985	Chi-A	.970	23	31	1	1	0	0
	NY-N	1.000	29	35	0	0	0	-3
1986	Tex-A	.967	25	26	3	1	1	1
1987	Tex-A	.950	12	19	0	1	0	0
Total	18	.979	794	1223	34	7	4	-28
			1B					
1972	LA-N	.979	6	44	3	1	4	0
1973	LA-N	1.000	4	25	1	0	3	0
1974	LA-N	1.000	1	2	0	0	0	0
1976	Atl-N	1.000	12	101	6	0	8	-1
1977	Atl-N	.984	32	236	16	4	20	0
1978	Atl-N	1.000	2	21	0	0	1	0
	Sea-A	1.000	3	20	2	0	1	0
1979	Sea-A	.991	15	100	10	1	12	1
1980	Sea-A	.982	36	255	19	5	24	0
1982	Chi-A	.993	102	833	66	6	85	1
1983	Chi-A	1.000	67	555	36	0	42	-3
1984	Chi-A	.993	67	532	23	4	50	-11
1985	Chi-A	1.000	6	45	5	0	3	1
	NY-N	1.000	8	41	3	0	3	0
1986	Tex-A	1.000	23	141	14	0	13	1
1987	Tex-A	1.000	12	63	7	0	9	1
Total	14	.994	396	3014	211	1	278	-10
			3B					
1976	Atl-N	.500	1	0	1	1	0	0
1977	Atl-N	—	1	0	0	0	0	0
1986	Tex-A	.927	21	11	27	3	2	0
Total	3	.907	23	11	28	4	2	0
			SS					
1986	Tex-A	1.000	1	0	1	0	0	0

■ Dick Padden 2B

YEAR	TM/L	PCT	G	PO	A	E	DP	FR
1896	Pit-N	.931	61	176	149	24	14	-12
1897	Pit-N	.941	**134**	**369**	402	48	36	2
1898	Pit-N	.947	128	301	407	40	46	-3
1899	Was-N	.936	48	140	124	18	12	-5
1901	StL-N	.950	115	286	336	33	47	2
1902	StL-A	**.967**	117	288	363	22	64	18
1903	StL-A	.955	29	57	93	7	17	6
1904	StL-A	.959	132	288	373	28	31	-9
1905	StL-A	.950	16	52	44	4	2	0
Total	9	.950	780	1937	2291	224	269	-1
			SS					
1899	Was-N	.913	85	201	281	46	33	14
1901	StL-N	.848	8	15	24	7	2	-2
Total	2	.908	93	216	305	3	35	12

■ Tom Padden C

YEAR	TM/L	PCT	G	PO	A	E	DP	FR
1932	Pit-N	.985	43	111	19	2	1	-1
1933	Pit-N	.984	27	100	22	2	1	6
1934	Pit-N	.978	76	297	20	7	3	-5
1935	Pit-N	.966	94	425	64	**17**	2	14
1936	Pit-N	.976	87	342	62	10	6	2
1937	Pit-N	.983	34	143	28	3	4	7
1943	Phi-N	1.000	16	61	6	0	2	4
	Was-A	1.000	2	3	1	0	0	0
Total	7	.977	379	1482	222	1	19	27

■ Don Padgett C

YEAR	TM/L	PCT	G	PO	A	E	DP	FR
1938	StL-N	.864	6	17	2	3	0	-2
1939	StL-N	.978	61	249	18	6	5	-2
1940	StL-N	.962	72	243	34	11	5	-8
1941	StL-N	.944	18	62	5	4	0	-4
1946	Bro-N	1.000	10	24	3	0	1	-1
	Bos-N	.939	26	65	12	5	1	-6
	Yr	.954	36	89	15	5	2	-7
1947	Phi-N	.962	39	111	16	5	1	-7
1948	Phi-N	.957	19	64	2	3	0	-4
Total	7	.962	251	835	92	7	13	-34
			OF					
1937	StL-N	.955	109	225	9	**11**	5	1
1938	StL-N	.962	71	140	14	6	3	5
1941	StL-N	.959	62	115	1	5	0	-5
Total	3	.958	242	480	24	2	8	1
			1B					
1938	StL-N	1.000	16	138	11	0	12	0
1939	StL-N	.964	6	27	0	1	1	-1
1940	StL-N	1.000	2	1	0	0	0	0
1941	StL-N	1.000	2	12	1	0	1	0
Total	4	.995	26	178	12	1	14	-1

■ Ernie Padgett 3B

YEAR	TM/L	PCT	G	PO	A	E	DP	FR
1924	Bos-N	.967	113	95	194	10	26	-4
1925	Bos-N	.895	7	9	8	2	1	-2
1926	Cle-A	.930	29	12	41	4	4	1
Total	3	.957	149	116	243	6	31	-5
			2B					
1923	Bos-N	1.000	1	4	4	0	1	1
1924	Bos-N	.957	29	60	94	7	15	-6
1925	Bos-N	.964	47	91	124	8	19	-18
1927	Cle-A	1.000	4	4	2	0	0	0
Total	4	.962	81	159	224	5	35	-23
			SS					
1923	Bos-N	.947	2	10	8	1	3	2
1925	Bos-N	.948	18	27	28	3	10	0
1926	Cle-A	1.000	2	1	5	0	0	1
Total	3	.952	22	38	41	4	13	3

■ Andy Pafko OF

YEAR	TM/L	PCT	G	PO	A	E	DP	FR
1943	Chi-N	1.000	13	25	0	0	0	-2
1944	Chi-N	.983	123	333	**24**	6	4	**13**
1945	Chi-N	**.995**	140	371	11	2	0	-1
1946	Chi-N	.978	64	165	13	4	4	10
1947	Chi-N	.985	127	327	9	5	3	4
1949	Chi-N	.987	98	217	8	3	2	-7
1950	Chi-N	.978	144	342	12	8	1	-6
1951	Chi-N	.992	48	119	6	1	3	4
	Bro-N	.993	76	144	8	1	0	0
	Yr	.993	124	263	14	2	3	4
1952	Bro-N	.988	139	229	18	3	2	0
1953	Mil-N	.976	139	241	5	6	1	-9
1954	Mil-N	.969	138	245	9	8	3	-5
1955	Mil-N	.980	58	96	1	2	0	-4
1956	Mil-N	.978	37	43	2	1	0	-2
1957	Mil-N	.982	69	108	1	2	1	-4
1958	Mil-N	1.000	93	107	2	0	0	2
1959	Mil-N	.978	64	87	1	2	0	1
Total	16	.984	1570	3199	130	4	24	-6
			3B					
1948	Chi-N	.938	139	125	**314**	**29**	**29**	13
1949	Chi-N	.934	49	40	101	10	10	-4
1952	Bro-N	.919	13	15	19	3	3	-3
1955	Mil-N	.972	12	9	26	1	1	-1
Total	4	.938	213	189	460	3	43	5

■ Jose Pagan SS

YEAR	TM/L	PCT	G	PO	A	E	DP	FR
1959	SF-N	1.000	5	0	1	0	0	0
1960	SF-N	.917	11	16	17	3	2	-8
1961	SF-N	.964	132	227	334	21	55	-17
1962	SF-N	**.973**	164	286	461	21	84	-25
1963	SF-N	.970	143	262	375	20	69	-17
1964	SF-N	.958	132	204	302	22	52	-17
1965	SF-N	.941	26	28	67	6	7	-5
	Pit-N	.881	7	16	21	5	4	6
	Yr	.923	33	44	88	11	11	1
1966	Pit-N	.924	18	23	50	6	8	1
1967	Pit-N	.973	16	18	55	2	8	3
1968	Pit-N	.960	8	5	19	1	4	0
Total	10	.963	662	1085	1702	107	293	-79
			3B					
1959	SF-N	.900	18	13	23	4	2	3
1960	SF-N	—	1	0	0	0	0	0
1965	SF-N	.923	15	3	9	1	1	3
1966	Pit-N	.949	83	57	166	12	18	1
1967	Pit-N	.938	25	11	49	4	3	5
1968	Pit-N	.924	30	16	45	5	3	-2
1969	Pit-N	.954	44	27	76	5	7	-2
1970	Pit-N	.957	53	43	91	6	14	-1
1971	Pit-N	.980	41	34	62	2	8	-1
1972	Pit-N	.899	32	25	37	7	3	-8
1973	Phi-N	.958	16	7	16	1	1	-2
Total	11	.945	358	236	574	7	60	-4
			OF					
1961	SF-N	1.000	4	3	0	0	0	0
1963	SF-N	—	1	0	0	0	0	0
1964	SF-N	1.000	8	6	1	0	0	1
1966	Pit-N	1.000	3	5	1	0	0	1
1967	Pit-N	.977	23	41	2	1	1	1
1968	Pit-N	1.000	19	17	1	0	0	0
1969	Pit-N	1.000	23	29	0	0	0	-1
1970	Pit-N	1.000	4	2	0	0	0	0
1971	Pit-N	1.000	3	4	0	0	0	0
1972	Pit-N	1.000	2	2	0	0	0	0
1973	Phi-N	1.000	2	4	1	0	0	1
Total	11	.992	92	113	6	1	1	3
			2B					
1959	SF-N	1.000	3	4	2	0	1	0
1963	SF-N	—	1	0	0	0	0	0
1966	Pit-N	1.000	3	1	2	0	0	0
1967	Pit-N	1.000	2	3	3	0	2	0
1968	Pit-N	.500	2	1	0	1	0	-1
1969	Pit-N	1.000	1	0	2	0	0	0
1970	Pit-N	—	1	0	0	0	0	0
1973	Phi-N	—	1	0	0	0	0	0
Total	8	.947	14	9	9	1	3	-1
			1B					
1968	Pit-N	1.000	1	1	0	0	0	0
1970	Pit-N	1.000	1	1	0	0	0	0
1971	Pit-N	1.000	2	15	0	0	1	0
1973	Phi-N	1.000	5	10	1	0	1	0
Total	4	1.000	9	27	1	0	2	0
			C					
1967	Pit-N	—	1	0	0	0	0	0

■ Mitchell Page OF

YEAR	TM/L	PCT	G	PO	A	E	DP	FR
1977	Oak-A	.954	133	279	11	**14**	0	3
1978	Oak-A	.973	114	211	4	6	0	-5
1979	Oak-A	1.000	4	6	0	0	0	0
1983	Oak-A	1.000	10	12	0	0	0	2
Total	4	.963	261	508	15	0	0	0

■ Jim Pagliaroni C

YEAR	TM/L	PCT	G	PO	A	E	DP	FR
1955	Bos-A	—	1	0	0	0	0	0
1960	Bos-A	.990	18	91	5	1	0	-3
1961	Bos-A	.984	108	586	39	**10**	5	-4
1962	Bos-A	.987	73	411	33	6	4	-3
1963	Pit-N	.988	85	435	56	6	4	4
1964	Pit-N	.992	96	584	42	5	5	0
1965	Pit-N	.994	131	669	42	4	**14**	-6
1966	Pit-N	**.997**	118	613	37	2	6	-16
1967	Pit-N	.984	38	172	13	3	6	-1
1968	Oak-A	.997	63	375	16	1	3	-9
1969	Oak-A	.981	7	43	8	1	2	2
	Sea-A	.988	29	160	11	2	1	-5
	Yr	.987	36	203	19	3	3	-3
Total	11	.991	767	4139	302	1	50	-41
			1B					
1969	Sea-A	1.000	2	12	0	0	0	0
			OF					
1969	Sea-A	1.000	1	1	0	0	0	0

■ Mike Pagliarulo 3B

YEAR	TM/L	PCT	G	PO	A	E	DP	FR
1984	NY-A	.955	67	44	106	7	16	6
1985	NY-A	.951	134	67	187	13	15	-17
1986	NY-A	.953	143	103	283	19	25	7
1987	NY-A	.959	147	96	297	17	35	4
1988	NY-A	.943	124	82	232	19	16	0
1989	NY-A	.936	69	25	122	10	6	-4
	SD-N	.936	49	19	83	7	3	0
1990	SD-N	.955	116	79	200	13	16	1
Total	7	.951	849	515	1510	105	132	-3
			SS					
1986	NY-A	1.000	2	1	0	0	0	0
			1B					
1987	NY-A	1.000	1	1	0	0	0	0

■ Tom Pagnozzi C

YEAR	TM/L	PCT	G	PO	A	E	DP	FR
1987	StL-N	1.000	25	53	4	0	0	-4
1988	StL-N	.971	28	119	13	4	0	-2
1989	StL-N	.982	38	99	9	2	1	-3
1990	StL-N	.989	63	334	39	4	4	**10**
Total	4	.985	154	605	65	0	5	1
			1B					
1987	StL-N	1.000	1	8	1	0	2	0
1988	StL-N	1.000	28	221	15	0	11	0
1989	StL-N	1.000	2	1	0	0	0	0
1990	StL-N	1.000	2	11	0	0	0	0
Total	4	1.000	33	241	16	0	13	0
			3B					
1988	StL-N	1.000	5	0	2	0	0	0
1989	StL-N	—	1	0	0	0	0	0
Total	2	1.000	6	0	2	0	0	0

■ Rafael Palmeiro 1B

YEAR	TM/L	PCT	G	PO	A	E	DP	FR
1987	Chi-N	.992	18	112	8	1	15	-1
1988	Chi-N	1.000	5	30	5	0	1	1
1989	Tex-A	.991	147	1167	**119**	12	106	**10**
1990	Tex-A	.995	146	1215	91	7	123	-1
Total	4	.993	316	2524	223	0	245	9
			OF					
1986	Chi-N	.900	20	34	2	4	1	0
1987	Chi-N	1.000	45	64	1	0	1	-3
1988	Chi-N	.983	147	292	6	5	1	-1
Total	3	.978	212	390	9	9	3	-4

■ Jim Pankovits 2B

YEAR	TM/L	PCT	G	PO	A	E	DP	FR
1984	Hou-N	.925	15	17	20	3	7	-4
1985	Hou-N	1.000	21	24	35	0	7	1
1986	Hou-N	.969	26	38	57	3	10	4
1987	Hou-N	1.000	9	8	10	0	3	2
1988	Hou-N	.939	31	40	68	7	18	-1
1990	Bos-A	—	2	0	0	0	0	0
Total	6	.961	104	127	190	3	45	2
			OF					
1984	Hou-N	1.000	3	3	0	0	0	0
1985	Hou-N	.983	33	56	2	1	1	0

YEAR	TM/L	PCT	G	PO	A	E	DP	FR
1986	Hou-N	.833	5	4	1	1	0	0
1987	Hou-N	1.000	6	11	3	0	0	2
Total	4	.976	47	74	6	2	1	2
3B								
1985	Hou-N	—	1	0	0	0	0	0
1987	Hou-N	1.000	4	0	2	0	0	0
1988	Hou-N	.850	11	5	12	3	2	-1
Total	3	.864	16	5	14	3	2	-1
SS								
1984	Hou-N	1.000	4	2	2	0	0	0
1985	Hou-N	.667	1	1	1	1	0	-1
Total	2	.857	5	3	3	1	0	-1
1B								
1988	Hou-N	.750	2	3	0	1	0	0
C								
1986	Hou-N	—	1	0	0	0	0	0

■ Freddy Parent SS

YEAR	TM/L	PCT	G	PO	A	E	DP	FR
1901	Bos-A	.918	**138**	260	446	63	52	0
1902	Bos-A	.932	**138**	287	**492**	57	60	3
1903	Bos-A	.930	**139**	296	456	57	36	9
1904	Bos-A	.929	**155**	327	493	**63**	44	-8
1905	Bos-A	.920	153	294	461	**66**	48	-7
1906	Bos-A	.933	143	312	472	56	48	-4
1907	Bos-A	.922	43	80	155	20	16	-2
1908	Chi-A	.930	118	212	442	49	33	5
1909	Chi-A	.929	98	182	357	41	34	**16**
1910	Chi-A	.944	4	3	14	1	1	1
Total	10	.927	1129	2253	3788	473	372	13
OF								
1907	Bos-A	.978	47	78	12	2	1	4
1909	Chi-A	1.000	38	70	6	0	0	1
1910	Chi-A	.970	62	92	5	3	1	-6
Total	3	.981	147	240	23	5	2	-1
2B								
1899	StL-N	.889	2	3	5	1	1	-1
1906	Bos-A	.842	6	8	8	3	1	-2
1907	Bos-A	1.000	5	10	17	0	1	0
1909	Chi-A	—	1	0	0	0	0	0
1910	Chi-A	.952	11	24	35	3	3	3
1911	Chi-A	1.000	3	5	10	0	0	1
Total	6	.947	28	50	75	7	6	1
3B								
1907	Bos-A	.824	7	7	7	3	2	-2
1910	Chi-A	1.000	1	0	1	0	0	0
Total	2	.833	8	7	8	3	2	-2

■ Mark Parent C

YEAR	TM/L	PCT	G	PO	A	E	DP	FR
1986	SD-N	.889	3	16	0	2	0	-1
1987	SD-N	1.000	10	36	3	0	0	0
1988	SD-N	.986	36	203	15	3	3	5
1989	SD-N	1.000	41	241	17	0	2	5
1990	SD-N	.992	60	324	31	3	6	7
Total	5	.991	150	820	66	8	11	16
1B								
1989	SD-N	1.000	1	5	0	0	0	0

■ Dave Parker OF

YEAR	TM/L	PCT	G	PO	A	E	DP	FR
1973	Pit-N	.964	39	77	3	3	1	3
1974	Pit-N	.964	49	101	5	4	1	2
1975	Pit-N	.972	141	311	7	9	2	6
1976	Pit-N	.956	134	294	12	**14**	0	6
1977	Pit-N	.965	**158**	**389**	26	15	9	**28**
1978	Pit-N	.960	147	302	12	**13**	3	4
1979	Pit-N	.960	158	341	15	**15**	1	9
1980	Pit-N	.965	130	235	14	9	0	-1
1981	Pit-N	.941	60	110	1	7	0	-8
1982	Pit-N	.957	63	108	2	5	1	-6
1983	Pit-N	.973	142	282	3	8	2	1
1984	Cin-N	.974	151	296	6	8	1	0
1985	Cin-N	.972	159	329	12	10	1	7
1986	Cin-N	.970	159	278	9	**9**	2	-7
1987	Cin-N	.967	142	278	13	10	3	5
1988	Oak-A	.953	34	58	3	3	0	3
1989	Oak-A	1.000	1	2	0	0	0	0
Total	17	.965	1867	3791	143	142	27	52
1B								
1974	Pit-N	1.000	6	53	3	0	9	0
1987	Cin-N	.988	9	76	4	1	7	-1
1988	Oak-A	1.000	1	5	2	0	0	1
1990	Mil-A	.960	3	24	0	1	4	-1
Total	4	.988	19	158	9	2	20	-1
2B								
1977	Pit-N	—	1	0	0	0	0	0

■ Wes Parker 1B

YEAR	TM/L	PCT	G	PO	A	E	DP	FR
1964	LA-N	.986	31	260	24	4	18	3
1965	LA-N	.997	154	1434	95	5	112	0
1966	LA-N	.992	140	1118	70	9	74	0
1967	LA-N	**.996**	112	913	68	4	72	4
1968	LA-N	**.999**	114	939	69	1	74	2
1969	LA-N	.995	128	1189	79	6	87	1
1970	LA-N	**.996**	161	1498	125	7	116	4
1971	LA-N	.996	148	1215	97	5	113	4
1972	LA-N	**.997**	120	1074	68	4	91	1
Total	9	.996	1108	9640	695	5	757	19
OF								
1964	LA-N	.971	69	66	2	2	0	3
1965	LA-N	—	1	0	0	0	0	0
1966	LA-N	1.000	14	31	0	0	0	0
1967	LA-N	.974	18	36	2	1	0	1
1968	LA-N	.977	28	41	1	1	0	0
1969	LA-N	1.000	2	1	0	0	0	0
1971	LA-N	1.000	18	25	1	0	1	0
1972	LA-N	1.000	5	11	0	0	0	0
Total	8	.982	155	211	6	4	1	4

■ Frank Parkinson 2B

YEAR	TM/L	PCT	G	PO	A	E	DP	FR
1922	Phi-N	.963	139	323	**562**	**34**	78	**31**
1923	Phi-N	.950	37	84	123	11	24	3
1924	Phi-N	1.000	10	12	24	0	5	1
Total	3	.962	186	419	709	5	107	35
SS								
1921	Phi-N	.931	105	233	404	47	55	9
1923	Phi-N	.928	15	23	41	5	10	1
1924	Phi-N	.959	21	32	62	4	13	5
Total	3	.934	141	288	507	6	78	15
3B								
1921	Phi-N	1.000	1	1	1	0	0	0
1923	Phi-N	.917	11	11	11	2	2	-1
1924	Phi-N	.952	28	19	41	3	5	0
Total	3	.944	40	31	53	5	7	-1

■ Lance Parrish C

YEAR	TM/L	PCT	G	PO	A	E	DP	FR
1977	Det-A	1.000	12	76	6	0	0	2
1978	Det-A	.987	79	353	39	5	5	5
1979	Det-A	.989	142	707	79	9	10	3
1980	Det-A	.990	121	557	66	6	8	-1
1981	Det-A	.993	90	407	40	3	6	-2
1982	Det-A	.989	132	627	76	8	8	7
1983	Det-A	.995	131	695	73	4	8	1
1984	Det-A	.991	127	720	67	7	**11**	2
1985	Det-A	.993	120	695	53	5	9	-6
1986	Det-A	.989	85	483	48	6	5	2
1987	Phi-N	.989	127	724	66	9	1	-2
1988	Phi-N	.988	117	639	73	9	**11**	-3
1989	Cal-A	.993	122	638	63	5	7	2
1990	Cal-A	.993	131	760	**88**	6	**15**	12
Total	14	.991	1536	8081	837	2	104	22
1B								
1980	Det-A	.977	5	42	1	1	7	-1
1988	Phi-N	1.000	1	1	0	0	1	0
1990	Cal-A	1.000	4	34	2	0	6	0
Total	3	.988	10	77	3	1	14	-1
OF								
1980	Det-A	1.000	5	8	0	0	0	0
1982	Det-A	—	1	0	0	0	0	0
Total	2	1.000	6	8	0	0	0	0

■ Larry Parrish 3B

YEAR	TM/L	PCT	G	PO	A	E	DP	FR
1974	Mon-N	.986	24	20	51	1	3	8
1975	Mon-N	.919	143	105	291	35	33	-2
1976	Mon-N	.945	153	122	310	25	**35**	4
1977	Mon-N	.936	115	81	225	21	11	-9
1978	Mon-N	.947	139	122	288	23	20	-5
1979	Mon-N	.947	153	119	290	23	25	-9
1980	Mon-N	.949	124	106	231	18	15	-8
1981	Mon-N	.935	95	**91**	141	16	7	-17
1982	Tex-A	—	3	0	0	0	0	0
1984	Tex-A	.967	12	2	27	1	3	2
1985	Tex-A	1.000	2	0	3	0	0	0
1986	Tex-A	.935	30	23	35	4	2	-5
1987	Tex-A	.918	28	19	26	4	6	-8
Total	13	.941	1021	810	1918	171	160	-49
OF								
1982	Tex-A	.962	124	190	12	8	4	-12
1983	Tex-A	.962	132	215	11	9	1	-12
1984	Tex-A	.982	81	153	8	3	3	-4
1985	Tex-A	.991	69	111	4	1	0	-7
1987	Tex-A	—	1	0	0	0	0	0
Total	5	.971	407	669	35	1	8	-35
1B								
1988	Bos-A	.988	36	221	25	3	18	3
2B								
1975	Mon-N	—	1	0	0	0	0	0
SS								
1975	Mon-N	—	1	0	0	0	0	0

■ Tom Parrott OF

YEAR	TM/L	PCT	G	PO	A	E	DP	FR
1893	Cin-N	—	1	0	0	0	0	-1
1894	Cin-N	.872	13	29	5	5	1	2
1895	Cin-N	.905	9	18	1	2	0	-1
1896	StL-N	.951	108	276	16	15	7	13
Total	4	.940	131	323	22	2	8	13
1B								
1894	Cin-N	.939	12	84	8	6	7	0
1895	Cin-N	.973	14	103	5	3	10	-1
1896	StL-N	.966	6	51	5	2	0	1
Total	3	.959	32	238	18	1	17	0
3B								
1893	Chi-N	1.000	2	2	2	0	0	0
1894	Chi-N	1.000	1	1	2	0	0	0
Total	2	1.000	3	3	4	0	0	0
2B								
1893	Chi-N	1.000	1	1	4	0	0	0
1894	Chi-N	.889	1	3	5	1	0	0
Total	2	.929	2	4	9	1	0	0
SS								
1894	Cin-N	.400	1	1	1	3	0	-1

■ Jiggs Parrott 3B

YEAR	TM/L	PCT	G	PO	A	E	DP	FR
1892	Chi-N	.891	78	115	164	34	7	-2
1893	Chi-N	.904	99	145	251	42	21	**10**
1894	Chi-N	1.000	1	2	1	0	0	0
Total	3	.899	178	262	416	6	28	8
2B								
1893	Chi-N	.947	7	13	23	2	2	0
1894	Chi-N	.931	123	285	379	49	56	-6
Total	2	.932	130	298	402	1	58	-6
OF								
1893	Chi-N	.833	4	5	0	1	0	-1
1895	Chi-N	—	1	0	0	0	0	0
Total	2	.833	5	5	0	1	0	-1
SS								
1895	Chi-N	1.000	1	2	1	0	0	-1
1B								
1895	Chi-N	—	1	0	0	0	0	0

■ Dixie Parsons C

YEAR	TM/L	PCT	G	PO	A	E	DP	FR
1939	Det-A	1.000	4	2	0	0	0	0
1942	Det-A	.981	62	274	44	6	6	9
1943	Det-A	.975	40	167	31	5	2	5
Total	3	.979	106	443	75	1	8	14

■ Roy Partee C

YEAR	TM/L	PCT	G	PO	A	E	DP	FR
1943	Bos-A	.983	91	349	57	7	11	-6
1944	Bos-A	.989	85	326	40	4	5	-6
1946	Bos-A	.974	38	139	12	4	1	-6
1947	Bos-A	.975	54	207	26	6	4	-1
1948	StL-A	.982	76	297	22	6	7	1
Total	5	.982	344	1318	157	7	28	-18

■ Jay Partridge 2B

YEAR	TM/L	PCT	G	PO	A	E	DP	FR
1927	Bro-N	.938	140	330	454	**52**	63	-16
1928	Bro-N	.908	18	38	41	8	7	-4
Total	2	.935	158	368	495	0	70	-20
3B								
1928	Bro-N	.833	2	2	3	1	0	-1

■ Ben Paschal OF

YEAR	TM/L	PCT	G	PO	A	E	DP	FR
1920	Bos-A	1.000	7	10	1	0	0	0
1924	NY-A	1.000	4	4	1	0	1	0
1925	NY-A	.953	66	117	6	6	0	-4
1926	NY-A	.935	74	134	10	10	0	-3
1927	NY-A	.976	27	39	1	1	0	-5
1928	NY-A	1.000	25	26	1	0	0	-6
1929	NY-A	.951	20	37	2	2	0	-1
Total	7	.953	223	367	22	9	1	-19

■ Dode Paskert OF

YEAR	TM/L	PCT	G	PO	A	E	DP	FR
1907	Cin-N	.973	16	33	3	1	0	1
1908	Cin-N	.953	116	250	15	13	3	5
1909	Cin-N	.968	82	172	11	6	3	0
1910	Cin-N	.957	139	**355**	25	17	4	10
1911	Phi-N	.979	153	361	20	8	6	3
1912	Phi-N	.967	141	336	19	12	4	4
1913	Phi-N	.972	120	330	19	10	**8**	15
1914	Phi-N	.958	128	303	19	14	4	7
1915	Phi-N	.970	92	181	10	6	2	4
1916	Phi-N	.983	146	332	14	6	4	-4
1917	Phi-N	**.984**	138	286	19	5	4	-6
1918	Phi-N	.980	121	283	12	6	1	-7
1919	Chi-N	.969	80	146	12	5	1	-8
1920	Chi-N	.956	137	306	23	15	3	-3
1921	Cin-N	.984	24	60	2	1	2	1
Total	15	.969	1633	3734	223	125	49	22
1B								
1909	Cin-N	1.000	6	35	1	0	6	0
1910	Cin-N	.857	2	12	0	2	0	-1
1915	Phi-N	.982	5	50	4	1	1	0
Total	3	.971	13	97	5	3	7	-1
3B								
1912	Phi-N	.667	1	2	0	1	0	-1
1918	Phi-N	.870	6	6	14	3	2	-1
Total	2	.846	7	8	14	4	2	-2
SS								
1914	Phi-N	.765	4	6	7	4	1	0
1916	Phi-N	1.000	1	2	2	0	0	0
Total	2	.810	5	8	9	4	1	-1
2B								
1912	Phi-N	1.000	2	4	6	0	0	0

■ Dan Pasqua OF

YEAR	TM/L	PCT	G	PO	A	E	DP	FR
1985	NY-A	1.000	37	72	2	0	0	9
1986	NY-A	.987	81	148	4	2	1	-4
1987	NY-A	.985	74	132	2	2	0	-1
1988	Chi-A	**.996**	112	258	6	1	2	5
1989	Chi-A	.993	66	149	3	1	2	2
1990	Chi-A	.962	43	71	5	3	1	1
Total	6	.990	413	830	22	9	6	12
1B								
1986	NY-A	1.000	5	24	0	0	5	0
1987	NY-A	1.000	12	82	8	0	2	1
1988	Chi-A	.985	7	58	8	1	11	1
Total	3	.994	24	164	16	1	18	1

■ Freddie Patek SS

YEAR	TM/L	PCT	G	PO	A	E	DP	FR
1968	Pit-N	.938	52	80	164	6	23	-1
1969	Pit-N	.954	146	227	399	30	81	-2
1970	Pit-N	.971	65	122	212	10	42	11
1971	KC-A	.968	147	**301**	459	25	**107**	10
1972	KC-A	.971	136	230	**510**	22	**113**	**29**
1973	KC-A	.966	135	242	503	26	**115**	**35**
1974	KC-A	.967	149	250	493	25	**108**	4
1975	KC-A	.959	136	231	405	27	78	-7
1976	KC-A	.962	143	233	426	26	87	-6
1977	KC-A	.958	154	252	413	29	70	-19
1978	KC-A	.949	137	240	350	**32**	84	-25
1979	KC-A	.955	104	153	249	19	54	-28
1980	Cal-A	.953	81	129	199	16	42	-18
1981	Cal-A	1.000	3	0	4	0	0	1
Total	14	.962	1588	2690	4786	293	1004	-16
2B								
1981	Cal-A	.983	16	27	31	1	8	1
3B								
1968	Pit-N	1.000	1	1	2	0	0	0
1981	Cal-A	.875	7	0	7	1	0	0
Total	2	.909	8	1	9	1	0	0
OF								
1968	Pit-N	1.000	5	9	0	0	0	0

■ Carlos Paula OF

YEAR	TM/L	PCT	G	PO	A	E	DP	FR
1954	Was-A	1.000	6	14	1	0	0	1
1955	Was-A	.941	85	154	5	**10**	3	-4
1956	Was-A	.974	20	37	0	1	0	-2
Total	3	.950	111	205	6	1	3	-5

■ Gene Paulette 1B

YEAR	TM/L	PCT	G	PO	A	E	DP	FR
1911	NY-N	.938	7	29	1	2	0	-1
1917	StL-A	.982	5	51	3	1	1	0
	StL-N	.993	93	1130	45	8	82	-1

YEAR	TM/L	PCT	G	PO	A	E	DP	FR
1918	StL-N	.983	97	1093	59	**20**	64	-2
1919	StL-N	.990	35	392	24	4	23	2
	Phi-N	—	1	0	0	0	0	0
	Yr	.990	36	392	24	4	23	**2**
1920	Phi-N	.988	139	1428	99	18	94	6
Total	5	.988	377	4123	231	3	264	4
2B								
1917	StL-A	.857	3	5	7	2	2	0
1918	StL-N	.979	7	24	23	1	1	1
1919	Phi-N	.957	58	141	173	14	28	1
Total	3	.956	68	170	203	7	31	2
SS								
1911	NY-N	—	1	0	0	0	0	0
1918	StL-N	.943	12	40	42	5	10	3
1919	StL-N	.895	3	6	11	2	3	0
1920	Phi-N	1.000	2	4	4	0	1	0
Total	4	.939	18	50	57	7	14	3
OF								
1918	StL-N	1.000	6	14	2	0	2	2
1919	Phi-N	1.000	10	15	1	0	0	0
Total	2	1.000	16	29	3	0	2	2
3B								
1911	NY-N	—	1	0	0	0	0	0
1917	StL-A	1.000	1	0	0	1	0	0
1918	StL-N	1.000	2	0	2	0	0	0
Total	3	.667	4	0	2	1	0	0

■ Don Pavletich C

YEAR	TM/L	PCT	G	PO	A	E	DP	FR
1962	Cin-N	1.000	2	5	0	0	0	-2
1963	Cin-N	1.000	13	92	4	0	1	0
1964	Cin-N	.983	27	161	8	3	1	-3
1965	Cin-N	.986	54	335	16	5	5	-1
1966	Cin-N	.975	55	323	30	9	2	-10
1967	Cin-N	.986	66	383	31	6	5	-4
1968	Cin-N	1.000	5	21	3	0	1	0
1969	Chi-A	.974	51	195	26	6	3	-4
1970	Bos-A	1.000	10	43	4	0	1	0
1971	Bos-A	.973	8	35	1	1	1	-2
Total	10	.983	291	1593	123	0	20	-26
1B								
1962	Cin-N	1.000	25	162	11	0	12	0
1963	Cin-N	.991	57	317	16	3	20	-3
1964	Cin-N	1.000	1	7	0	0	1	0
1965	Cin-N	.983	9	56	2	1	9	-1
1966	Cin-N	1.000	10	56	2	0	8	-1
1967	Cin-N	1.000	6	31	3	0	3	0
1968	Cin-N	1.000	22	164	10	0	13	0
1969	Chi-A	.989	13	90	2	1	13	-2
1970	Bos-A	1.000	16	80	8	0	10	1
Total	9	.995	159	963	54	5	89	-6
3B								
1967	Cin-N	.000	1	0	0	1	0	-1

■ Fred Payne C

YEAR	TM/L	PCT	G	PO	A	E	DP	FR
1906	Det-A	.966	47	177	49	8	3	-4
1907	Det-A	.981	46	205	55	5	4	2
1908	Det-A	.954	17	52	10	3	1	-3
1909	Chi-A	.987	27	110	38	2	5	-1
1910	Chi-A	.974	78	409	106	14	11	-3
1911	Chi-A	.963	56	213	48	10	10	-4
Total	6	.972	271	1166	306	2	34	-13
OF								
1906	Det-A	.976	17	36	5	1	3	3
1907	Det-A	1.000	5	8	1	0	1	0
1908	Det-A	1.000	1	2	0	0	0	0
1909	Chi-A	1.000	3	1	0	0	0	-1
1910	Chi-A	1.000	2	1	0	0	0	-1
Total	5	.982	28	48	6	1	4	1

■ Johnny Peacock C

YEAR	TM/L	PCT	G	PO	A	E	DP	FR
1937	Bos-A	.980	9	42	8	1	1	1
1938	Bos-A	.984	57	177	12	3	2	-8
1939	Bos-A	.972	84	314	33	10	6	-8
1940	Bos-A	.994	48	159	13	1	0	-7
1941	Bos-A	.988	70	298	33	4	7	-4
1942	Bos-A	.988	82	280	44	4	8	-6
1943	Bos-A	.972	32	121	18	4	2	-1
1944	Bos-A	1.000	2	1	1	0	0	0
	Phi-N	.990	73	274	38	3	4	1
1945	Phi-N	.969	23	55	7	2	2	-5
	Bro-N	.975	38	142	13	4	5	0
	Yr	.973	61	197	20	6	7	-5
Total	9	.983	518	1863	220	6	37	-37
1B								
1938	Bos-A	.900	1	9	0	1	2	0
OF								
1938	Bos-A	1.000	1	1	0	0	0	0
2B								
1944	Phi-N	1.000	1	0	1	0	0	0

■ Albie Pearson OF

YEAR	TM/L	PCT	G	PO	A	E	DP	FR
1958	Was-A	.980	141	338	6	7	1	2
1959	Was-A	.974	21	37	0	1	0	-3
	Bal-A	.987	50	75	2	1	0	3
	Yr	.983	71	112	2	2	0	0
1960	Bal-A	.975	32	38	1	1	0	-1
1961	LA-A	.956	113	233	7	11	2	3
1962	LA-A	.989	160	366	8	4	0	0
1963	LA-A	.983	148	340	10	6	5	0
1964	LA-A	.978	66	132	1	3	1	-7
1965	Cal-A	.988	101	166	5	2	1	-2
1966	Cal-A	—	1	0	0	0	0	0
Total	9	.980	833	1725	40	6	10	-5

■ Hal Peck OF

YEAR	TM/L	PCT	G	PO	A	E	DP	FR
1944	Phi-A	1.000	2	3	0	0	0	0
1945	Phi-A	.943	110	190	9	**12**	3	-12
1946	Phi-A	.981	35	47	4	1	1	-5
1947	Cle-A	.983	97	166	5	3	3	-11
1948	Cle-A	1.000	9	13	0	0	0	-1
1949	Cle-A	1.000	2	1	0	0	0	0
Total	6	.965	255	420	18	6	7	-29

■ Roger Peckinpaugh SS

YEAR	TM/L	PCT	G	PO	A	E	DP	FR
1910	Cle-A	.906	14	20	38	6	3	-6
1912	Cle-A	.924	68	127	188	26	16	-2
1913	NY-A	.931	93	184	303	36	30	-6
1914	NY-A	.956	**157**	356	500	39	45	3
1915	NY-A	.942	142	291	468	47	60	**11**
1916	NY-A	.946	**145**	285	**468**	43	50	1
1917	NY-A	.934	148	292	467	54	**84**	10
1918	NY-A	.961	122	260	**439**	28	**75**	**25**
1919	NY-A	.943	121	271	**434**	43	57	**28**
1920	NY-A	.962	137	263	441	28	56	3
1921	NY-A	.948	149	318	443	42	75	-5
1922	Was-A	.951	147	265	527	41	**93**	**22**
1923	Was-A	.948	**154**	311	**510**	45	**105**	**23**
1924	Was-A	.963	**155**	278	487	29	**81**	9
1925	Was-A	.952	124	215	345	28	71	-16
1926	Was-A	.960	46	82	109	8	21	-1
1927	Chi-A	.964	60	101	170	10	30	-1
Total	17	.949	1982	3919	6337	553	952	98
1B								
1925	Was-A	1.000	1	4	1	0	0	0
1926	Was-A	.875	1	7	0	1	0	0
Total	2	.923	2	11	1	1	0	0

■ Bill Pecota SS

YEAR	TM/L	PCT	G	PO	A	E	DP	FR
1986	KC-A	1.000	2	0	1	0	0	0
1987	KC-A	.977	36	40	85	3	20	3
1988	KC-A	.976	41	59	107	4	20	8
1989	KC-A	.988	29	27	54	1	8	5
1990	KC-A	.981	21	44	57	2	19	5
Total	5	.979	129	170	304	0	67	21
2B								
1987	KC-A	1.000	15	20	27	0	6	3
1988	KC-A	1.000	3	4	2	0	1	0
1989	KC-A	1.000	12	8	19	0	3	3
1990	KC-A	.986	50	82	122	3	21	1
Total	4	.990	80	114	170	3	31	7
3B								
1986	KC-A	.974	12	7	30	1	1	10
1987	KC-A	.909	17	7	23	3	2	1
1988	KC-A	.979	21	10	36	1	2	5
1989	KC-A	.889	7	2	6	1	2	1
1990	KC-A	1.000	11	5	15	0	2	2
Total	5	.959	68	31	110	6	9	19
OF								
1988	KC-A	.889	9	8	0	1	0	0
1989	KC-A	1.000	15	5	0	0	0	0
1990	KC-A	1.000	6	10	0	0	0	0
Total	3	.958	30	23	0	1	0	0
1B								
1988	KC-A	1.000	11	17	0	0	2	0
1989	KC-A	1.000	4	8	0	0	1	0
1990	KC-A	1.000	4	19	1	0	2	0
Total	3	1.000	19	44	1	0	5	0
C								
1988	KC-A	—	1	0	0	0	0	0

■ Al Pedrique SS

YEAR	TM/L	PCT	G	PO	A	E	DP	FR
1987	NY-N	1.000	4	2	7	0	0	1
	Pit-N	.968	76	115	185	10	43	-11
	Yr	.969	80	117	192	10	43	-10
1988	Pit-N	.974	46	64	122	5	23	2
1989	Det-A	.974	12	13	24	1	6	1
Total	3	.971	138	194	338	6	72	-7
3B								
1987	Pit-N	1.000	3	0	1	0	0	0
1988	Pit-N	1.000	5	1	2	0	0	0
1989	Det-A	.960	12	7	17	1	1	2
Total	3	.966	20	8	20	1	1	2
2B								
1987	NY-N	1.000	1	1	2	0	0	0
	Pit-N	.500	2	0	1	1	0	0
	Yr	.800	3	1	3	1	0	0
1989	Det-A	.973	8	15	21	1	7	4
Total	2	.952	11	16	24	2	7	4

■ Homer Peel OF

YEAR	TM/L	PCT	G	PO	A	E	DP	FR
1927	StL-N	—	1	0	0	0	0	0
1929	Phi-N	.990	39	94	2	1	1	2
1930	StL-N	.968	21	30	0	1	0	-2
1933	NY-N	.962	45	49	1	2	0	-5
1934	NY-N	.929	10	13	0	1	0	-1
Total	5	.974	116	186	3	5	1	-6
1B								
1929	Phi-N	.818	1	6	3	2	1	1

■ Heinie Peitz C

YEAR	TM/L	PCT	G	PO	A	E	DP	FR
1892	StL-N	1.000	1	3	0	0	0	0
1893	StL-N	.948	74	296	86	21	7	13
1894	StL-N	.938	39	146	51	13	3	5
1895	StL-N	.937	71	260	80	23	10	1
1896	Cin-N	.968	67	201	42	8	6	0
1897	Cin-N	**.979**	71	260	67	7	8	5
1898	Cin-N	.945	101	323	90	**24**	12	-5
1899	Cin-N	.977	91	**329**	89	10	4	-2
1900	Cin-N	.958	80	310	125	19	13	6
1901	Cin-N	.982	49	260	60	6	4	-2
1902	Cin-N	.966	47	189	70	9	12	4
1903	Cin-N	.970	78	365	93	14	7	-3
1904	Cin-N	.975	64	255	89	9	10	4
1905	Pit-N	.965	87	337	105	16	14	-11
1906	Pit-N	.979	38	176	45	5	2	0
1913	StL-N	.625	2	3	2	3	0	-1
Total	16	.963	960	3723	1094	187	112	14
3B								
1894	StL-N	.897	47	67	73	16	4	-3
1895	StL-N	.783	10	12	6	5	1	-2
1901	Cin-N	.950	6	7	12	1	2	1
1902	Cin-N	1.000	6	4	12	0	0	1
1903	Cin-N	.927	9	17	21	3	0	2
1904	Cin-N	1.000	1	1	0	0	0	0
Total	6	.903	79	108	124	5	7	-1
1B								
1893	StL-N	.981	5	50	1	1	4	-1
1894	StL-N	.967	14	107	12	4	11	2
1895	StL-N	.954	11	76	7	4	6	0
1900	Cin-N	.985	8	63	2	1	1	0
1901	Cin-N	1.000	2	9	1	0	0	0
1902	Cin-N	.968	6	59	1	2	5	-1
1903	Cin-N	1.000	11	106	6	0	9	1
1904	Cin-N	1.000	18	169	11	0	7	1
Total	8	.983	75	639	41	2	43	2
2B								
1901	Cin-N	.980	21	45	54	2	8	2
1902	Cin-N	.919	48	124	126	22	23	-5
1903	Cin-N	.944	4	8	9	1	1	0
1905	Pit-N	1.000	1	1	0	0	0	-1
Total	4	.936	74	178	189	5	32	-4
SS								
1893	StL-N	.855	11	25	28	9	5	-3
OF								
1893	StL-N	.900	10	17	1	2	0	-1
1913	StL-N	—	1	0	0	0	0	0
Total	2	.900	11	17	1	2	0	-1

■ Eddie Pellagrini SS

YEAR	TM/L	PCT	G	PO	A	E	DP	FR
1946	Bos-A	.848	9	13	15	5	4	0
1947	Bos-A	.950	26	39	76	6	10	-3
1948	StL-A	.964	98	194	292	18	85	**24**
1949	StL-A	.961	76	164	227	16	52	7
1951	Phi-N	.893	8	15	10	3	3	-3
1952	Cin-N	1.000	1	3	2	0	1	0
1953	Pit-N	1.000	3	1	3	0	0	0
1954	Pit-N	—	1	0	0	0	0	0
Total	8	.956	222	429	625	8	155	25
2B								
1951	Phi-N	.990	53	80	110	2	19	-14
1952	Phi-N	.983	22	57	62	2	14	10
1953	Pit-N	.972	31	69	72	4	12	-5
1954	Pit-N	1.000	7	24	17	0	5	0
Total	4	.984	113	230	261	8	50	-9
3B								
1946	Bos-A	.891	14	16	25	5	4	0
1947	Bos-A	.926	42	34	66	8	7	-4
1951	Phi-N	1.000	6	9	12	0	1	0
1952	Cin-N	1.000	1	1	1	0	0	0
1953	Pit-N	.935	12	6	23	2	1	0
1954	Pit-N	.968	31	18	43	2	5	2
Total	6	.937	106	84	170	7	18	-2
1B								
1952	Cin-N	1.000	8	58	2	0	5	0

■ John Peltz OF

YEAR	TM/L	PCT	G	PO	A	E	DP	FR
1884	Ind-a	.818	106	155	16	**38**	1	4
1888	Bal-a	.500	1	1	0	1	0	0
1890	Bro-a	.904	98	207	18	24	6	3
	Syr-a	.857	5	4	2	1	1	0
	Tol-a	.886	20	28	3	4	1	-2
	Yr	.900	123	239	23	29	8	1
Total	3	.865	230	395	39	8	9	5

■ Tony Pena C

YEAR	TM/L	PCT	G	PO	A	E	DP	FR
1980	Pit-N	.952	6	38	2	2	0	1
1981	Pit-N	.985	64	286	41	5	10	2
1982	Pit-N	.982	137	763	89	16	6	-7
1983	Pit-N	.992	149	**976**	90	9	9	-1
1984	Pit-N	.991	146	**895**	**95**	9	**15**	12
1985	Pit-N	.988	**146**	922	**100**	12	9	7
1986	Pit-N	.981	139	810	99	**18**	13	5
1987	StL-N	.988	112	615	51	8	8	1
1988	StL-N	**.994**	**142**	777	70	5	8	5
1989	StL-N	**.997**	134	674	70	2	**13**	10
1990	Bos-A	.995	**142**	**864**	74	5	13	10
Total	11	.989	1317	7620	781	1	104	43
1B								
1985	Pit-N	1.000	1	3	2	0	0	1
1986	Pit-N	1.000	4	14	0	0	0	0
1987	StL-N	1.000	4	7	0	0	0	0
1988	StL-N	.955	3	19	2	1	1	0
1990	Bos-A	1.000	1	2	0	0	0	0
Total	5	.980	13	45	4	1	1	1
OF								
1987	StL-N	1.000	2	2	0	0	0	0
1989	StL-N	1.000	1	1	0	0	0	0
Total	2	1.000	3	3	0	0	0	0

■ Roberto Pena SS

YEAR	TM/L	PCT	G	PO	A	E	DP	FR
1965	Chi-N	.930	50	74	151	17	29	-10
1966	Chi-N	.957	5	10	12	1	2	0
1968	Phi-N	.954	133	230	434	32	93	6
1969	SD-N	.977	65	91	161	6	29	-15
1970	Oak-A	.961	12	20	29	2	3	0
	Mil-A	.981	99	149	274	8	58	-12
	Yr	.979	111	169	303	10	61	-12
1971	Mil-A	.985	23	22	45	1	9	-2
Total	6	.962	387	596	1106	7	223	-33
3B								
1969	SD-N	.929	27	15	37	4	2	-3
1970	Oak-A	.769	5	3	7	3	3	-1
1971	Mil-A	.972	37	21	49	2	7	-2
Total	3	.936	69	39	93	9	12	-6
1B								
1969	SD-N	1.000	12	111	11	0	5	1
1970	Mil-A	1.000	7	24	0	0	0	-1
1971	Mil-A	.996	50	247	18	1	22	0
Total	3	.998	69	382	29	1	27	0

YEAR	TM/L	PCT	G	PO	A	E	DP	FR
2B								
1969	SD-N	.980	33	72	76	3	18	-7
1970	Mil-A	.982	15	26	29	1	4	-3
1971	Mil-A	—	1	0	0	0	0	0
Total	3	.981	49	98	105	4	22	-10

■ Jim Pendleton   OF

YEAR	TM/L	PCT	G	PO	A	E	DP	FR
1953	Mil-N	.961	105	141	7	6	1	6
1954	Mil-N	.950	50	90	5	5	0	3
1955	Mil-N	1.000	1	3	0	0	0	0
1957	Pit-N	.917	9	10	1	1	0	-1
1959	Cin-N	.971	24	31	2	1	0	2
1962	Hou-N	.963	90	126	4	5	0	-3
Total	6	.959	279	401	19	8	1	7
3B								
1955	Mil-N	—	1	0	0	0	0	0
1956	Mil-N	—	2	0	0	0	0	0
1957	Pit-N	.800	2	2	2	1	0	-1
1959	Cin-N	.953	16	13	28	2	0	2
1962	Hou-N	1.000	3	1	0	0	0	0
Total	5	.939	24	16	30	3	0	1
SS								
1953	Mil-N	1.000	7	11	28	0	3	3
1955	Mil-N	1.000	1	3	0	0	0	0
1956	Mil-N	1.000	3	1	2	0	0	0
1957	Pit-N	—	1	0	0	0	0	0
1959	Cin-N	1.000	3	1	1	0	1	0
1962	Hou-N	—	2	0	0	0	0	0
Total	6	1.000	17	16	31	0	4	3
1B								
1956	Mil-N	1.000	1	2	0	0	0	0
1962	Hou-N	.965	8	54	1	2	5	-1
Total	2	.966	9	56	1	2	5	-1
2B								
1956	Mil-N	1.000	1	0	1	0	0	0

■ Terry Pendleton   3B

YEAR	TM/L	PCT	G	PO	A	E	DP	FR
1984	StL-N	.943	66	59	155	13	10	9
1985	StL-N	.965	149	129	361	18	26	23
1986	StL-N	.962	**156**	**133**	371	20	**36**	**25**
1987	StL-N	.949	**158**	117	**369**	26	27	**16**
1988	StL-N	.963	101	75	239	12	13	11
1989	StL-N	**.971**	**161**	113	**392**	15	25	**30**
1990	StL-N	.947	117	91	248	19	18	7
Total	7	.959	908	717	2135	123	155	121
OF								
1986	StL-N	—	1	0	0	0	0	0

■ Jimmy Peoples   C

YEAR	TM/L	PCT	G	PO	A	E	DP	FR
1884	Cin-a	.955	14	61	24	4	1	5
1885	Cin-a	.826	5	15	4	4	0	-1
	Bro-a	.895	37	173	57	27	3	-8
	Yr	.889	42	188	61	**31**	3	-9
1886	Bro-a	.879	76	384	145	73	6	10
1887	Bro-a	.853	57	226	106	57	3	-7
1888	Bro-a	.904	25	169	38	22	6	6
1889	Col-a	.922	22	109	33	12	1	-1
Total	6	.886	236	1137	407	199	20	4
SS								
1884	Cin-a	.829	47	54	140	40	19	-8
1885	Bro-a	.923	2	2	10	1	1	1
1886	Bro-a	.859	14	19	42	10	8	3
1887	Bro-a	.950	4	5	14	1	0	1
1888	Bro-a	.871	5	9	18	4	1	2
1889	Col-a	1.000	1	0	1	0	0	0
Total	6	.849	73	89	225	6	29	-1
OF								
1884	Cin-a	.917	10	18	4	2	0	2
1885	Cin-a	1.000	1	1	0	0	0	0
	Bro-a	1.000	1	1	0	0	0	0
	Yr	1.000	2	2	0	0	0	0
1886	Bro-a	.842	8	14	2	3	0	1
1887	Bro-a	.786	8	11	0	3	0	-2
1888	Bro-a	1.000	2	3	0	0	0	0
1889	Col-a	.875	5	7	0	1	0	-1
Total	6	.871	35	55	6	9	0	0
1B								
1884	Cin-a	1.000	1	9	0	0	1	0
1885	Bro-a	1.000	1	5	1	0	1	0
1887	Bro-a	.957	4	21	1	1	2	0
Total	3	.974	6	35	2	1	4	0
3B								
1884	Cin-a	—	1	0	0	0	0	0
1885	Bro-a	1.000	1	0	2	0	2	1
1886	Bro-a	.750	1	2	1	1	0	0
Total	3	.833	3	2	3	1	2	1
2B								
1887	Bro-a	.600	1	2	1	2	0	-1
1889	Col-a	.700	2	4	3	3	0	-1
Total	2	.667	3	6	4	5	0	-2

■ Joe Pepitone   1B

YEAR	TM/L	PCT	G	PO	A	E	DP	FR
1962	NY-A	.982	16	100	11	2	9	0
1963	NY-A	.995	143	1140	103	6	111	5
1964	NY-A	.988	**155**	**1333**	121	18	**128**	**6**
1965	NY-A	.997	115	1036	71	3	104	0
1966	NY-A	**.995**	119	1044	92	6	92	**8**
1967	NY-A	.980	6	44	6	1	5	-1
1968	NY-A	1.000	12	128	4	0	10	-1
1969	NY-A	**.995**	132	**1254**	74	7	118	-6
1970	Hou-N	.995	50	376	29	2	45	0
	Chi-N	1.000	13	27	2	0	0	1
	Yr	.995	63	403	31	2	45	0
1971	Chi-N	.990	95	872	64	9	75	1
1972	Chi-N	.997	66	552	31	2	51	0
1973	Chi-N	.985	28	240	19	4	28	0
	Atl-N	.963	3	26	0	1	5	-1
	Yr	.983	31	266	19	5	33	-1
Total	12	.993	953	8172	627	1	781	11

YEAR	TM/L	PCT	G	PO	A	E	DP	FR
OF								
1962	NY-A	1.000	32	26	0	0	0	-2
1963	NY-A	.931	16	26	1	2	0	-1
1964	NY-A	1.000	30	13	0	0	0	0
1965	NY-A	.980	41	45	4	1	0	-6
1966	NY-A	.967	55	82	5	3	2	1
1967	NY-A	.976	123	277	7	7	1	0
1968	NY-A	.980	92	190	4	4	1	-8
1970	Hou-N	.981	28	52	1	1	0	0
	Chi-N	.992	56	121	1	1	0	2
	Yr	.989	84	173	2	2	0	2
1971	Chi-N	.970	23	32	0	1	0	-2
Total	9	.978	496	864	23	0	4	-16

■ Roy Pepper   OF

YEAR	TM/L	PCT	G	PO	A	E	DP	FR
1932	StL-N	.971	17	33	1	1	0	0
1933	StL-N	1.000	2	3	0	0	0	0
1934	StL-N	.963	136	299	15	12	**4**	9
1935	StL-N	.982	57	103	5	2	1	-5
1936	StL-N	.941	18	31	1	2	0	-2
Total	5	.967	230	469	22	7	5	2

■ Jack Perconte   2B

YEAR	TM/L	PCT	G	PO	A	E	DP	FR
1980	LA-N	1.000	9	13	18	0	3	3
1981	LA-N	1.000	2	4	13	0	3	5
1982	Cle-A	.976	82	131	199	8	23	8
1983	Cle-A	.950	13	20	37	3	12	8
1984	Sea-A	.981	150	303	438	14	90	0
1985	Sea-A	.986	125	244	381	9	91	0
1986	Cle-A	.990	24	46	54	1	12	-7
Total	7	.982	405	761	1140	5	234	17

■ Tony Perez   1B

YEAR	TM/L	PCT	G	PO	A	E	DP	FR
1964	Cin-N	.981	6	51	0	1	2	-1
1965	Cin-N	.989	93	525	40	6	55	-1
1966	Cin-N	.989	75	530	23	6	46	-5
1967	Cin-N	1.000	18	134	5	0	12	0
1970	Cin-N	1.000	8	36	6	0	4	1
1971	Cin-N	.989	44	168	4	2	16	-3
1972	Cin-N	.993	136	1207	68	9	111	-6
1973	Cin-N	.991	**151**	**1318**	85	**13**	**131**	-4
1974	Cin-N	**.996**	**157**	1292	75	6	111	-5
1975	Cin-N	.993	132	1192	72	9	113	-5
1976	Cin-N	.996	136	1158	73	5	110	-4
1977	Mon-N	.992	148	1312	110	11	88	8
1978	Mon-N	.991	145	1181	82	11	116	-1
1979	Mon-N	.991	129	1114	65	11	81	-6
1980	Bos-A	.993	137	1301	87	10	150	-1
1981	Bos-A	.993	56	519	37	4	63	0
1982	Bos-A	.857	2	5	1	1	0	0
1983	Phi-N	.998	69	514	40	1	36	1
1984	Cin-N	.990	31	186	12	2	17	-2
1985	Cin-N	.995	50	340	22	2	34	-2
1986	Cin-N	.984	55	398	29	7	46	-3
Total	21	.992	1778	14481	936	117	1342	-39
3B								
1967	Cin-N	.963	139	113	221	13	13	-26
1968	Cin-N	.952	160	**151**	343	**25**	**33**	5
1969	Cin-N	.937	**160**	136	**342**	32	35	1
1970	Cin-N	.923	153	131	286	**35**	34	-8
1971	Cin-N	.959	148	113	**304**	18	26	10
Total	5	.946	760	644	1496	123	141	-18
2B								
1967	Cin-N	1.000	1	2	8	0	1	2

■ Marty Perez   SS

YEAR	TM/L	PCT	G	PO	A	E	DP	FR
1969	Cal-A	1.000	7	11	17	0	6	6
1970	Cal-A	.833	2	3	2	1	1	1
1971	Atl-N	.955	126	195	382	27	91	-14
1972	Atl-N	.957	141	220	378	27	73	-34
1973	Atl-N	.962	139	215	416	25	78	-9
1974	Atl-N	.923	14	8	16	2	4	-2
1975	Atl-N	.917	7	3	8	1	1	-1
1976	Atl-N	.959	17	22	25	2	6	-3
	SF-N	1.000	5	7	13	0	4	0
	Yr	.971	22	29	38	2	10	-3
1977	Oak-A	1.000	4	1	3	0	0	0
1978	Oak-A	.300	3	1	3	1	0	0
Total	10	.958	465	686	1263	6	264	-56
2B								
1969	Cal-A	1.000	2	1	1	0	0	0
1971	Atl-N	.000	1	0	0	1	0	-1
1974	Atl-N	.985	102	225	311	8	64	-7
1975	Atl-N	.985	116	259	341	9	74	-6
1976	Atl-N	.976	18	38	44	2	10	0
	SF-N	.979	89	189	273	10	51	7
	Yr	.978	107	227	317	12	61	7
1977	Oak-A	.974	105	192	287	13	48	0
1978	Oak-A	1.000	1	1	0	0	0	0
Total	7	.980	434	905	1257	3	247	-7
3B								
1969	Cal-A	1.000	2	0	1	0	0	0
1974	Atl-N	1.000	6	3	6	0	1	1
1976	Atl-N	1.000	2	0	2	0	1	1
1977	NY-A	1.000	1	0	4	0	1	1
	Oak-A	.927	12	14	24	3	5	1
	Yr	.933	13	14	28	3	6	2
1978	Oak-A	1.000	11	2	9	0	1	2
Total	5	.956	34	19	46	3	8	5

■ Broderick Perkins   1B

YEAR	TM/L	PCT	G	PO	A	E	DP	FR
1978	SD-N	.993	59	538	41	4	56	3
1979	SD-N	.982	28	155	10	3	16	-1
1980	SD-N	.988	20	149	9	2	14	-1
1981	SD-N	.997	80	598	38	2	56	-2
1982	SD-N	.990	98	817	64	5	61	1
1983	Cle-A	.991	19	112	6	1	12	-2
1984	Cle-A	1.000	2	8	0	0	2	0
Total	7	.993	306	2377	165	7	217	-2

YEAR	TM/L	PCT	G	PO	A	E	DP	FR
OF								
1980	SD-N	.909	10	10	0	1	0	-1
1981	SD-N	.800	3	4	0	1	0	0
1982	SD-N	.933	11	14	0	1	0	0
1983	Cle-A	.975	17	36	3	1	0	2
Total		.944	41	64	3	4	0	1

■ Cy Perkins   C

YEAR	TM/L	PCT	G	PO	A	E	DP	FR
1915	Phi-A	.920	6	38	8	4	0	1
1917	Phi-A	.978	6	31	14	1	1	4
1918	Phi-A	.990	60	201	103	3	11	**12**
1919	Phi-A	.971	87	340	**134**	14	**15**	7
1920	Phi-A	.979	146	524	179	15	15	**23**
1921	Phi-A	.971	**141**	**540**	137	**20**	16	5
1922	Phi-A	.984	141	432	130	9	10	-3
1923	Phi-A	.971	**137**	475	102	**17**	12	-6
1924	Phi-A	.983	128	415	102	9	9	-1
1925	Phi-A	.980	58	213	36	5	3	**11**
1926	Phi-A	.984	55	205	38	4	5	9
1927	Phi-A	.979	54	162	29	4	2	1
1929	Phi-A	.982	19	47	7	1	0	4
1930	Phi-A	.990	38	85	15	1	1	2
1931	NY-A	1.000	16	51	0	0	0	-5
Total	16	.978	1111	3809	1037	109	100	64
SS								
1919	Phi-A	.935	8	12	17	2	1	0
1B								
1927	Phi-A	1.000	1	1	0	0	0	0
1930	Phi-A	1.000	1	2	0	0	1	0
Total	2	1.000	2	3	0	0	1	0
2B								
1920	Phi-A	1.000	1	4	3	0	1	0
3B								
1925	Phi-A	—	1	0	0	0	0	0

■ George Perring   3B

YEAR	TM/L	PCT	G	PO	A	E	DP	FR
1908	Cle-A	.925	41	59	77	11	1	-1
1909	Cle-A	.932	67	83	151	17	6	6
1910	Cle-A	.931	33	32	63	7	4	0
1914	KC-F	.934	101	100	223	23	20	10
1915	KC-F	.958	102	135	226	16	14	10
Total	5	.939	344	409	740	4	45	25
1B								
1910	Cle-A	.968	4	55	6	2	3	1
1914	KC-F	.990	41	386	18	4	26	0
1915	KC-F	.993	31	259	14	2	13	1
Total	3	.989	76	700	38	8	42	2
SS								
1908	Cle-A	.928	48	74	159	18	15	-5
1909	Cle-A	.929	11	15	24	3	3	0
1914	KC-F	.500	1	0	1	1	0	-1
1915	KC-F	—	1	0	0	0	0	0
Total	4	.925	61	89	184	2	18	-6
2B								
1909	Cle-A	.909	4	7	13	2	2	1
1915	KC-F	.962	31	60	94	6	11	5
Total	2	.956	35	67	107	8	13	6

■ Gerald Perry   1B

YEAR	TM/L	PCT	G	PO	A	E	DP	FR
1983	Atl-N	.982	7	55	0	1	5	-2
1984	Atl-N	.988	64	476	26	6	41	-4
1985	Atl-N	.985	55	541	37	9	48	0
1986	Atl-N	1.000	1	8	1	0	2	0
1987	Atl-N	.990	136	1288	72	14	118	-9
1988	Atl-N	.988	141	1282	106	**17**	102	1
1989	Atl-N	.987	72	618	51	9	49	1
1990	KC-A	.986	51	394	40	6	41	2
Total	8	.988	527	4662	333	2	406	-11
OF								
1983	Atl-N	—	1	0	0	0	0	0
1984	Atl-N	.927	53	74	2	6	0	-7
1985	Atl-N	—	1	0	0	0	0	0
1986	Atl-N	.889	21	16	0	2	0	-4
1987	Atl-N	1.000	7	9	0	0	0	0
Total	5	.927	83	99	2	8	0	-11

■ Bob Perry   OF

YEAR	TM/L	PCT	G	PO	A	E	DP	FR
1963	LA-A	.946	55	86	1	5	0	-7
1964	LA-A	.975	62	115	2	3	0	0
Total	2	.962	117	201	3	8	0	-7

■ Johnny Pesky   SS

YEAR	TM/L	PCT	G	PO	A	E	DP	FR
1942	Bos-A	.955	**147**	320	**465**	37	94	18
1946	Bos-A	.969	153	296	479	25	96	12
1947	Bos-A	.976	133	251	391	16	90	-11
1950	Bos-A	.965	8	23	32	2	7	5
1951	Bos-A	.961	106	204	340	22	74	10
1952	Bos-A	1.000	2	3	2	0	1	0
	Det-A	.952	41	78	101	9	25	-4
	Yr	.953	43	81	103	9	26	-4
1954	Was-A	—	1	0	0	0	0	0
Total	7	.964	591	1175	1810	111	387	30
3B								
1947	Bos-A	.984	22	25	38	1	7	-1
1948	Bos-A	.951	141	121	303	**22**	**35**	6
1949	Bos-A	.970	**148**	**184**	**333**	16	**48**	**21**
1950	Bos-A	.974	116	160	257	11	29	**17**
1951	Bos-A	.892	11	14	19	4	2	-2
1952	Bos-A	.917	19	16	28	4	0	-5
	Det-A	1.000	3	2	5	0	0	0
	Yr	.927	22	18	33	4	0	-5
Total	6	.963	460	522	983	8	121	36
2B								
1951	Bos-A	1.000	5	5	11	0	3	0
1952	Bos-A	.969	22	27	36	2	12	-2
1953	Det-A	.991	73	166	183	3	49	-13
1954	Was-A	.979	37	92	91	4	22	-8
Total	4	.985	137	290	321	9	86	-23

John Peters SS

YEAR	TM/L	PCT	G	PO	A	E	DP	FR
1876	Chi-N	**.932**	66	95	193	21	**16**	-1
1877	Chi-N	.883	**60**	**124**	**215**	45	**23**	**19**
1878	Mil-N	.887	22	33	69	13	4	1
1879	Chi-N	.837	83	94	271	**71**	14	-9
1880	Pro-N	**.900**	**86**	**111**	268	42	26	-2
1881	Buf-N	.869	53	102	183	43	17	6
1882	Pit-a	.883	77	90	280	49	21	6
1883	Pit-a	.818	8	9	27	8	3	3
1884	Pit-a	.667	1	1	1	1	0	-1
Total	9	.881	456	659	1507	293	124	22
2B								
1878	Mil-N	.853	34	97	136	40	14	4
1882	Pit-a	.667	1	2	2	2	0	-1
Total	2	.849	35	99	138	2	14	3
OF								
1881	Buf-N	.556	1	3	2	4	0	1

Rick Peters OF

YEAR	TM/L	PCT	G	PO	A	E	DP	FR
1979	Det-A	1.000	1	3	0	0	0	0
1980	Det-A	.977	109	296	1	7	1	-4
1981	Det-A	.991	38	103	3	1	1	3
1983	Oak-A	.986	47	141	3	2	1	9
1986	Oak-A	1.000	27	28	0	0	0	2
Total	5	.983	222	571	7	0	3	10
3B								
1979	Det-A	.000	3	0	0	2	0	-1
2B								
1979	Det-A	1.000	2	1	0	0	0	0
1986	Oak-A	1.000	1	1	1	0	1	0
Total	2	1.000	3	2	1	0	1	0

Rusty Peters 2B

YEAR	TM/L	PCT	G	PO	A	E	DP	FR
1936	Phi-A	—	1	0	0	0	0	0
1937	Phi-A	.966	70	138	170	11	34	-11
1940	Cle-A	.922	9	24	23	4	7	-1
1941	Cle-A	.857	3	4	2	1	2	0
1942	Cle-A	—	1	0	0	0	0	0
1943	Cle-A	1.000	6	5	6	0	1	0
1944	Cle-A	.976	63	151	181	8	45	-4
1947	StL-A	.955	13	34	29	3	8	7
Total	8	.966	166	356	411	7	97	-9
SS								
1936	Phi-A	.898	25	44	53	11	12	-1
1937	Phi-A	.921	13	16	42	5	3	-1
1938	Phi-A	.714	2	3	2	2	0	-2
1940	Cle-A	1.000	6	4	5	0	0	0
1941	Cle-A	.891	11	13	28	5	5	2
1942	Cle-A	.944	24	21	46	4	8	2
1943	Cle-A	1.000	14	17	16	0	7	1
1944	Cle-A	.976	13	25	16	1	5	-1
1946	Cle-A	1.000	7	11	13	0	3	0
1947	StL-A	1.000	2	0	2	0	0	0
Total	10	.931	117	154	223	8	43	0
3B								
1936	Phi-A	.923	10	7	29	3	3	3
1937	Phi-A	.875	31	37	54	13	2	-2
1940	Cle-A	.826	6	3	16	4	1	0
1941	Cle-A	.857	9	9	15	4	2	1
1942	Cle-A	—	1	0	0	0	0	0
1943	Cle-A	.913	46	39	76	11	9	-6
1944	Cle-A	1.000	8	4	12	0	2	1
Total	7	.896	111	99	202	5	19	-3
OF								
1936	Phi-A	—	2	0	0	0	0	0
1943	Cle-A	1.000	2	5	0	0	0	0
Total	2	1.000	4	5	0	0	0	0
1B								
1940	Cle-A	1.000	1	1	0	0	0	0

Cap Peterson OF

YEAR	TM/L	PCT	G	PO	A	E	DP	FR
1963	SF-N	1.000	3	1	0	0	0	0
1964	SF-N	1.000	10	8	0	0	0	0
1965	SF-N	1.000	27	22	1	0	0	-3
1966	SF-N	1.000	51	62	2	0	1	-3
1967	Was-A	.970	101	190	5	6	1	0
1968	Was-A	1.000	52	82	2	0	0	-5
1969	Cle-A	.977	30	40	2	1	1	0
Total	7	.983	274	405	12	7	3	-11
3B								
1963	SF-N	.714	5	1	4	2	0	-1
1964	SF-N	1.000	1	2	1	0	0	0
1969	Cle-A	—	4	0	0	0	0	0
Total	3	.800	10	3	5	2	0	-1
2B								
1963	SF-N	.917	8	14	19	3	0	-4
1964	SF-N	—	1	0	0	0	0	0
Total	2	.917	9	14	19	3	0	-4
1B								
1964	SF-N	1.000	2	1	0	0	0	0
1966	SF-N	.929	2	11	2	1	2	0
Total	2	.933	4	12	2	1	2	0
SS								
1962	SF-N	1.000	2	1	2	0	1	-1
1963	SF-N	1.000	1	0	1	0	0	0
Total	2	1.000	3	1	3	0	1	-1

Geno Petralli C

YEAR	TM/L	PCT	G	PO	A	E	DP	FR
1982	Tor-A	.981	12	49	3	1	0	-2
1983	Tor-A	1.000	5	7	0	0	0	0
1984	Tor-A	1.000	1	1	1	0	0	0
1985	Tex-A	.990	41	179	16	2	6	1
1986	Tex-A	.988	41	159	7	2	2	-6
1987	Tex-A	.995	63	349	26	2	2	8
1988	Tex-A	.981	85	409	45	9	7	5
1989	Tex-A	.989	49	258	15	3	3	-11
1990	Tex-A	.991	118	599	43	6	5	-1
Total	9	.989	415	2010	156	5	25	-6
3B								
1982	Tor-A	1.000	3	2	1	0	0	0
1986	Tex-A	.846	15	4	7	2	0	-2
1987	Tex-A	.882	17	8	7	2	2	-1
1988	Tex-A	.857	9	0	6	1	0	0
1990	Tex-A	1.000	7	1	1	0	0	0
Total	5	.881	51	15	22	5	2	-3
2B								
1986	Tex-A	—	2	0	0	0	0	0
1987	Tex-A	1.000	4	1	1	0	0	0
1988	Tex-A	1.000	2	1	3	0	0	0
1990	Tex-A	1.000	3	2	0	0	2	0
Total	4	1.000	11	4	6	0	2	0
1B								
1987	Tex-A	1.000	5	10	0	0	0	0
1988	Tex-A	1.000	2	11	0	0	1	0
Total	2	1.000	7	21	0	0	1	0
OF								
1987	Tex-A	.667	3	2	0	1	0	0

Rico Petrocelli SS

YEAR	TM/L	PCT	G	PO	A	E	DP	FR
1963	Bos-A	.833	1	3	2	1	0	0
1965	Bos-A	.958	93	151	278	19	45	10
1966	Bos-A	.954	127	206	381	28	69	0
1967	Bos-A	.970	141	223	402	19	73	3
1968	Bos-A	**.978**	117	169	360	12	66	11
1969	Bos-A	**.981**	153	269	466	14	103	5
1970	Bos-A	.970	141	262	393	20	77	-10
1976	Bos-A	1.000	1	0	1	0	0	0
Total	8	.969	774	1283	2283	113	433	19
3B								
1966	Bos-A	1.000	5	5	9	0	3	1
1969	Bos-A	.750	1	0	3	1	0	0
1970	Bos-A	.981	18	14	37	1	3	1
1971	Bos-A	**.976**	156	118	334	11	37	-1
1972	Bos-A	.970	146	146	278	13	**38**	-1
1973	Bos-A	.980	99	73	224	6	22	6
1974	Bos-A	.962	116	83	219	12	23	-19
1975	Bos-A	.960	113	85	229	13	13	-18
1976	Bos-A	.967	73	57	120	6	11	-4
Total	9	.970	727	581	1453	3	150	-35
2B								
1976	Bos-A	1.000	5	9	13	0	4	0
1B								
1968	Bos-A	1.000	1	9	1	0	2	0
1976	Bos-A	1.000	1	4	0	0	0	0
Total	2	1.000	2	13	1	0	2	0

Joe Pettini SS

YEAR	TM/L	PCT	G	PO	A	E	DP	FR
1980	SF-N	.955	42	48	99	7	16	-15
1981	SF-N	.870	12	6	14	3	3	1
1982	SF-N	.934	26	24	33	4	5	0
1983	SF-N	.949	26	29	46	4	12	7
Total	4	.943	106	107	192	8	36	-7
3B								
1980	SF-N	.978	18	10	35	1	5	3
1981	SF-N	.875	9	0	7	1	0	1
1982	SF-N	—	1	0	0	0	0	0
1983	SF-N	.846	12	3	8	2	0	0
Total	4	.940	40	13	50	4	5	4
2B								
1980	SF-N	1.000	8	5	13	0	3	0
1981	SF-N	.920	12	7	16	2	1	2
1983	SF-N	1.000	14	12	28	0	4	4
Total	3	.977	34	27	57	2	8	6

Gary Pettis OF

YEAR	TM/L	PCT	G	PO	A	E	DP	FR
1982	Cal-A	1.000	8	5	1	0	0	1
1983	Cal-A	.982	21	49	5	1	2	2
1984	Cal-A	.983	134	337	11	6	4	-7
1985	Cal-A	.990	122	368	13	4	5	10
1986	Cal-A	.985	153	**462**	9	7	3	13
1987	Cal-A	.980	131	344	2	7	2	2
1988	Det-A	.987	126	361	5	5	0	5
1989	Det-A	.988	119	325	1	4	0	1
1990	Tex-A	.993	128	285	10	2	4	-1
Total	9	.986	942	2536	57	6	20	26

Fred Pfeffer 2B

YEAR	TM/L	PCT	G	PO	A	E	DP	FR
1882	Tro-N	.824	2	8	6	3	0	-1
1883	Chi-N	.887	79	264	264	67	49	15
1884	Chi-N	.903	**112**	**395**	**422**	**88**	**85**	**46**
1885	Chi-N	.893	109	**325**	**391**	**86**	**66**	25
1886	Chi-N	.903	118	**343**	340	73	66	8
1887	Chi-N	.917	**123**	**393**	402	**72**	**68**	**25**
1888	Chi-N	.931	**135**	421	457	65	**78**	39
1889	Chi-N	.943	134	**452**	**483**	56	**69**	21
1890	Chi-P	.916	124	**441**	387	**76**	73	24
1891	Chi-N	.921	137	**429**	474	77	**78**	25
1892	Lou-N	.933	116	315	377	50	72	12
1893	Lou-N	.939	125	355	398	49	74	6
1894	Lou-N	.937	90	255	284	36	58	12
1895	Lou-N	.944	3	8	9	1	2	1
1896	NY-N	.760	4	9	10	6	0	-2
	Chi-N	.947	94	227	307	30	43	9
	Yr	.939	98	236	317	36	43	7
1897	Chi-N	.883	32	73	93	22	12	-6
Total	16	.920	1537	4713	5104	857	893	259
SS								
1882	Tro-N	.857	**83**	**161**	276	**73**	35	12
1883	Chi-N	.804	18	15	63	19	6	1
1894	Lou-N	.872	15	26	56	12	9	1
1895	Lou-N	.742	5	11	12	8	3	-3
Total	4	.847	121	213	407	112	53	10
1B								
1883	Chi-N	.957	2	2	0	0	1	0
1886	Chi-N	1.000	1	1	0	0	0	0
1892	Lou-N	.933	10	79	4	6	3	-1
1895	Lou-N	.921	3	34	1	3	1	-1
Total	4	.931	15	116	5	9	5	-2
OF								
1885	Chi-N	1.000	1	2	0	0	0	0
1887	Chi-N	1.000	2	1	0	0	0	0
Total	2	1.000	3	3	0	0	0	0
3B								
1883	Chi-N	1.000	1	0	1	0	0	0

Art Phelan 3B

YEAR	TM/L	PCT	G	PO	A	E	DP	FR
1910	Cin-N	1.000	8	8	13	0	0	0
1912	Cin-N	.924	127	153	250	33	18	0
1913	Cin-N	.927	38	47	68	9	3	-3
1914	Chi-N	.905	7	5	14	2	0	0
1915	Chi-N	.939	110	136	203	22	14	-1
Total	5	.931	290	349	548	6	35	-4
2B								
1910	Cin-N	1.000	5	8	7	0	1	-1
1912	Cin-N	1.000	3	2	5	0	0	-2
1913	Chi-N	.931	46	56	79	10	9	-5
1914	Cin-N	1.000	3	1	2	0	0	0
1915	Chi-N	.954	24	61	64	6	5	0
Total	5	.947	81	128	157	6	15	-8
SS								
1910	Cin-N	—	1	0	0	0	0	0
1913	Chi-N	1.000	1	0	1	0	0	0
1914	Chi-N	.917	2	6	5	1	1	0
Total	3	.923	4	6	6	1	1	0
OF								
1910	Cin-N	1.000	3	3	0	0	0	0

Dick Phelan 2B

YEAR	TM/L	PCT	G	PO	A	E	DP	FR
1884	Bal-U	.872	100	272	251	77	33	-7
1885	Buf-N	.808	4	6	15	5	2	-1
Total	2	.869	104	278	266	2	35	-8
3B								
1884	Bal-U	.769	5	5	5	3	1	0
1885	StL-N	1.000	2	2	0	0	0	-1
Total	2	.800	7	7	5	3	1	-1
OF								
1884	Bal-U	—	1	0	0	0	0	0

Ed Phelps C

YEAR	TM/L	PCT	G	PO	A	E	DP	FR
1902	Pit-N	.968	13	52	9	2	1	-5
1903	Pit-N	.980	76	315	81	8	7	-8
1904	Pit-N	.964	91	360	97	17	8	-10
1905	Cin-N	.949	44	189	55	13	5	-6
1906	Cin-N	.987	12	61	14	1	0	-1
	Pit-N	.971	40	170	31	6	4	-3
	Yr	.975	52	231	45	7	4	-4
1907	Pit-N	.979	35	145	38	4	1	-4
1908	Pit-N	.977	20	69	15	2	0	0
1909	StL-N	.954	83	330	87	20	11	-10
1910	StL-N	.976	80	320	84	10	10	-15
1912	Bro-N	.976	32	130	35	4	4	-5
1913	Bro-N	.875	4	6	1	1	0	-2
Total	11	.968	530	2147	547	8	51	-69
1B								
1902	Pit-N	.975	5	37	2	1	2	0
1903	Pit-N	1.000	3	30	2	0	0	0
1904	Pit-N	1.000	1	12	0	0	0	0
1907	Pit-N	1.000	1	11	1	0	2	0
Total	4	.990	10	90	5	1	4	0

Babe Phelps C

YEAR	TM/L	PCT	G	PO	A	E	DP	FR
1933	Chi-N	1.000	2	6	2	0	1	1
1934	Chi-N	.981	18	44	7	1	0	-2
1935	Bro-N	.957	34	118	16	6	4	-2
1936	Bro-N	.977	98	334	49	9	6	-15
1937	Bro-N	.971	111	465	76	16	10	-6
1938	Bro-N	.980	55	218	25	5	5	-4
1939	Bro-N	.980	92	361	40	8	9	1
1940	Bro-N	.977	99	428	35	11	3	-9
1941	Bro-N	.971	11	33	1	1	0	-1
1942	Pit-N	.959	72	244	40	12	5	-3
Total	10	.974	592	2251	291	9	43	-40
OF								
1936	Bro-N	1.000	1	3	0	0	0	0
1B								
1940	Bro-N	1.000	1	8	0	0	0	0

Ken Phelps 1B

YEAR	TM/L	PCT	G	PO	A	E	DP	FR
1980	KC-A	1.000	2	14	0	0	2	0
1981	KC-A	1.000	2	4	1	0	0	0
1983	Sea-A	1.000	22	164	16	0	11	3
1984	Sea-A	.987	9	72	4	1	7	-1
1985	Sea-A	1.000	8	31	2	0	5	0
1986	Sea-A	.983	55	487	34	9	58	-3
1987	Sea-A	1.000	1	8	0	0	0	0
1988	Sea-A	.952	3	18	2	1	2	0
	NY-A	—	1	0	0	0	0	0
	Yr	.952	4	18	2	1	2	0
1989	NY-A	.980	8	47	1	1	4	-1
	Oak-A	—	1	0	0	0	0	0
	Yr	.980	9	47	1	1	4	-1
1990	Oak-A	.964	5	24	3	1	3	0
	Cle-A	1.000	14	87	7	0	4	0
	Yr	.992	19	111	10	1	7	0
Total	10	.987	131	956	70	3	96	-2

Dave Philley OF

YEAR	TM/L	PCT	G	PO	A	E	DP	FR
1941	Chi-A	—	2	0	0	0	0	0
1946	Chi-A	.983	17	55	3	1	0	4
1947	Chi-A	.986	133	355	9	5	2	-7
1948	Chi-A	.978	128	381	**22**	9	**6**	10
1949	Chi-A	.987	145	282	**16**	7	3	-5
1950	Chi-A	.980	154	367	19	8	**8**	-4
1951	Chi-A	.938	6	15	0	1	0	0
	Phi-A	.978	120	299	15	7	4	-3
	Yr	.976	**126**	314	15	8	4	-3
1952	Phi-A	.991	149	442	13	4	3	5

YEAR	TM/L	PCT	G	PO	A	E	DP	FR
1953	Phi-A	.981	157	296	**18**	6	0	0
1954	Cle-A	.984	129	237	6	4	0	-9
1955	Cle-A	1.000	34	44	2	0	2	-1
	Bal-A	.970	82	154	6	5	2	-2
	Yr	.976	116	198	8	5	4	-3
1956	Bal-A	.935	31	56	2	4	2	-2
	Chi-A	1.000	30	50	2	0	0	-1
	Yr	.965	61	106	4	4	2	-3
1957	Chi-A	.975	17	39	0	1	0	0
	Det-A	.941	12	16	0	1	0	-1
	Yr	.965	29	55	0	2	0	-1
1958	Phi-N	1.000	24	32	0	0	0	-2
1959	Phi-N	1.000	34	64	4	0	1	0
1960	Phi-N	—	3	0	0	0	0	0
	SF-N	.941	10	16	0	1	0	-2
	Bal-A	1.000	8	15	0	0	0	0
	Yr	1.000	11	15	0	0	0	-1
1961	Bal-A	1.000	25	21	0	0	0	-5
1962	Bos-A	1.000	4	6	0	0	0	0
Total	18	.981	1454	3242	137	4	33	-26
1B								
1956	Chi-A	.978	51	299	17	7	31	-5
1957	Chi-A	1.000	2	15	0	0	2	0
	Det-A	.996	27	203	25	1	19	3
	Yr	.996	29	218	25	1	21	3
1958	Phi-N	.994	18	151	12	1	12	0
1959	Phi-N	.979	24	174	11	4	17	-2
1960	Phi-N	1.000	2	1	0	0	1	-1
1961	Bal-A	1.000	1	3	0	0	0	0
Total	6	.986	125	846	65	3	82	-5
3B								
1947	Chi-A	1.000	4	1	6	0	1	1
1951	Phi-A	—	2	0	0	0	0	0
1952	Phi-A	1.000	2	3	3	0	0	0
1953	Phi-A	—	1	0	0	0	0	0
1955	Bal-A	.500	2	0	1	1	0	-1
1956	Bal-A	.857	5	2	4	1	1	-1
1957	Det-A	—	1	0	0	0	0	0
1960	SF-N	—	3	0	0	0	0	0
	Bal-A	—	1	0	0	0	0	0
Total	8	.909	21	6	14	2	2	-1

■ Adolfo Phillips OF

YEAR	TM/L	PCT	G	PO	A	E	DP	FR
1964	Phi-N	1.000	4	5	1	0	0	1
1965	Phi-N	1.000	32	46	0	0	0	1
1966	Phi-N	1.000	1	2	0	0	0	0
	Chi-N	.978	111	258	14	6	2	7
	Yr	.979	112	260	14	6	2	7
1967	Chi-N	.981	141	340	13	7	0	12
1968	Chi-N	.979	141	311	11	7	3	3
1969	Chi-N	.956	25	43	0	2	0	1
	Mon-N	.981	53	99	3	2	0	-3
	Yr	.973	78	142	3	4	0	-2
1970	Mon-N	.985	75	130	1	2	0	-8
1972	Cle-A	1.000	10	7	0	0	0	1
Total	8	.980	593	1241	43	6	5	15

■ Eddie Phillips C

YEAR	TM/L	PCT	G	PO	A	E	DP	FR
1924	Bos-N	1.000	1	0	1	0	0	0
1929	Det-A	.967	63	255	34	10	4	-5
1931	Pit-N	.986	103	293	49	5	12	-8
1932	NY-A	.990	9	46	6	0	0	1
1934	Was-A	.984	53	162	21	3	4	-7
1935	Cle-N	.980	69	233	18	5	3	-9
Total	6	.980	298	989	129	3	23	-28

■ Jack Phillips 1B

YEAR	TM/L	PCT	G	PO	A	E	DP	FR
1947	NY-A	.986	10	71	1	1	8	-2
1948	NY-A	.889	1	8	0	1	0	0
1949	NY-A	.977	38	245	14	6	31	-2
	Pit-N	1.000	16	135	8	0	11	0
1950	Pit-N	.986	54	450	39	7	46	2
1951	Pit-N	.991	53	322	21	3	37	-1
1952	Pit-N	1.000	1	2	0	0	1	0
1955	Det-A	.992	35	236	13	2	16	-1
1956	Det-A	.981	56	422	32	9	49	-1
Total	8	.986	264	1891	128	9	199	-5
3B								
1949	Pit-N	—	1	0	0	0	0	0
1950	Pit-N	.846	3	5	6	2	1	-1
1951	Pit-N	.900	4	2	7	1	1	0
1955	Det-A	1.000	3	3	2	0	0	0
Total	4	.893	11	10	15	3	2	-1
2B								
1956	Det-A	.500	1	1	0	1	0	-1
OF								
1956	Det-A	1.000	1	2	0	0	0	0

■ Bubba Phillips 3B

YEAR	TM/L	PCT	G	PO	A	E	DP	FR
1955	Det-A	.857	4	3	9	2	1	1
1956	Chi-A	1.000	2	2	2	0	1	0
1957	Chi-A	.958	97	91	227	14	18	12
1958	Chi-A	.954	47	38	86	6	12	6
1959	Chi-A	.951	100	90	202	15	13	6
1960	Cle-A	.953	85	87	135	11	18	-2
1961	Cle-A	.958	143	**188**	246	19	23	-18
1962	Cle-A	.977	145	175	243	10	16	-15
1963	Det-A	.961	117	116	226	14	26	2
1964	Det-A	.983	22	18	40	1	5	2
Total	10	.960	762	808	1416	2	133	-6
OF								
1955	Det-A	.992	65	128	2	1	0	7
1956	Chi-A	1.000	35	59	2	0	1	5
1957	Chi-A	1.000	20	56	3	0	0	4
1958	Chi-A	.977	37	84	1	2	1	2
1959	Chi-A	1.000	23	37	0	0	0	0
1960	Cle-A	.917	25	22	0	2	0	0
1962	Cle-A	.889	3	8	0	1	0	0
1963	Det-A	.900	5	9	0	1	0	0
1964	Det-A	—	1	0	0	0	0	0
Total	9	.983	214	403	8	7	2	18
SS								
1960	Cle-A	—	1	0	0	0	0	0
2B								
1962	Cle-A	—	1	0	0	0	0	0

■ Tony Phillips 2B

YEAR	TM/L	PCT	G	PO	A	E	DP	FR
1983	Oak-A	.970	63	103	124	7	26	-5
1984	Oak-A	.982	90	121	156	5	36	3
1985	Oak-A	.984	24	18	43	1	7	-1
1986	Oak-A	.976	88	160	290	11	40	4
1987	Oak-A	.974	87	160	260	11	40	-1
1988	Oak-A	.974	27	29	47	2	12	-6
1989	Oak-A	.985	84	140	252	6	46	-10
1990	Det-A	.996	47	91	135	1	37	7
Total	8	.980	510	822	1307	4	244	-9
SS								
1982	Oak-A	.953	39	46	95	7	17	-5
1983	Oak-A	.941	101	112	257	23	59	2
1984	Oak-A	.941	91	133	235	23	54	-14
1986	Oak-A	1.000	1	0	3	0	0	0
1987	Oak-A	.971	9	14	19	1	3	-2
1988	Oak-A	.875	10	3	4	1	1	-1
1989	Oak-A	.947	17	11	25	2	5	-3
1990	Det-A	.978	11	12	33	1	9	1
Total	8	.945	279	331	671	8	148	-22
3B								
1983	Oak-A	1.000	4	3	2	0	0	0
1985	Oak-A	.980	31	36	60	2	6	1
1986	Oak-A	.964	30	20	33	2	3	-4
1987	Oak-A	.920	11	3	20	2	4	1
1988	Oak-A	.913	32	15	27	4	3	-4
1989	Oak-A	.900	49	19	44	7	3	-7
1990	Det-A	.931	104	69	200	20	16	0
Total	7	.937	261	165	386	7	35	-13
OF								
1984	Oak-A	1.000	1	1	0	0	0	0
1986	Oak-A	1.000	4	11	0	0	0	0
1987	Oak-A	1.000	2	2	0	0	0	0
1988	Oak-A	.923	31	34	2	3	0	-1
1989	Oak-A	1.000	16	14	0	0	0	0
1990	Det-A	.889	8	8	0	1	0	-1
Total	6	.947	62	70	2	4	0	-2
1B								
1988	Oak-A	1.000	3	3	0	0	2	0
1989	Oak-A	1.000	1	9	1	0	1	0
Total	2	1.000	4	12	1	0	3	0

■ Marr Phillips SS

YEAR	TM/L	PCT	G	PO	A	E	DP	FR
1884	Ind-a	.862	97	108	335	71	16	14
1885	Det-N	.881	33	35	120	21	6	3
	Pit-a	.875	4	2	12	2	2	-1
1890	Roc-a	.918	64	101	222	29	24	6
Total	3	.884	198	246	689	123	48	22

■ Mike Phillips SS

YEAR	TM/L	PCT	G	PO	A	E	DP	FR
1973	SF-N	.941	20	21	43	4	5	-1
1974	SF-N	.953	23	33	69	5	12	3
1975	NY-N	.944	115	185	334	**31**	52	1
1976	NY-N	.955	53	67	125	9	16	-9
1977	NY-N	1.000	24	22	31	0	4	-4
	StL-N	.957	5	11	11	1	6	2
	Yr	.987	29	33	42	1	10	-2
1978	StL-N	.975	10	14	25	1	7	1
1979	StL-N	.973	25	33	76	3	11	12
1980	StL-N	.971	37	49	117	5	26	15
1981	SD-N	1.000	1	0	1	0	1	0
	Mon-N	.974	26	31	43	2	8	0
	Yr	.974	27	31	44	2	9	0
1982	Mon-N	1.000	2	2	1	0	0	0
1983	Mon-N	.000	3	0	0	1	0	-1
Total	11	.956	344	468	876	2	148	19
2B								
1973	SF-N	1.000	7	11	9	0	3	1
1974	SF-N	.962	30	67	61	5	16	0
1975	SF-N	.969	6	14	17	1	4	2
	NY-N	1.000	1	1	1	0	0	0
	Yr	.971	7	15	18	1	4	2
1976	NY-N	.989	19	44	48	1	9	-1
1977	NY-N	1.000	4	7	4	0	0	-1
	StL-N	.971	31	42	57	3	15	4
	Yr	.973	35	49	61	3	15	3
1978	StL-N	.971	55	93	110	6	24	-2
1979	StL-N	.981	16	21	30	1	5	1
1980	StL-N	.950	9	13	6	1	0	-1
1981	SD-N	.979	9	23	23	1	6	3
	Mon-N	1.000	6	3	7	0	1	1
	Yr	.982	15	26	30	1	7	4
1982	Mon-N	1.000	10	6	9	0	1	2
Total	10	.975	203	345	382	9	84	9
3B								
1973	SF-N	.931	28	10	17	2	1	0
1974	SF-N	.909	34	25	65	9	5	1
1975	SF-N	1.000	6	3	12	0	0	2
1976	NY-N	.957	10	4	18	1	1	1
1977	NY-N	.913	9	4	17	2	1	0
	StL-N	.909	5	4	6	1	0	0
	Yr	.912	14	8	23	3	1	0
1978	StL-N	—	1	0	0	0	0	0
1979	StL-N	1.000	1	1	0	0	0	0
1980	StL-N	.727	8	1	7	3	1	-1
1983	Mon-N	—	2	0	0	0	0	0
Total	9	.915	104	51	143	8	9	3

■ Dick Phillips 1B

YEAR	TM/L	PCT	G	PO	A	E	DP	FR
1962	SF-N	1.000	1	1	0	0	0	0
1963	Was-A	.994	68	655	59	4	73	4
1964	Was-A	.994	61	473	39	3	50	2
1966	Was-A	1.000	5	46	2	0	2	0
Total	4	.995	135	1175	100	7	125	6
3B								
1963	Was-A	1.000	4	0	3	0	0	0
1964	Was-A	1.000	4	2	4	0	0	0
Total	2	1.000	8	2	7	0	0	0
2B								
1963	Was-A	1.000	5	2	2	0	0	0

■ Bill Phillips 1B

YEAR	TM/L	PCT	G	PO	A	E	DP	FR
1879	Cle-N	.954	75	726	22	36	23	2
1880	Cle-N	.963	85	842	25	33	**37**	2
1881	Cle-N	.966	85	806	24	29	**51**	-1
1882	Cle-N	.971	78	827	24	25	**55**	3
1883	Cle-N	.967	97	953	22	33	53	-2
1884	Cle-N	.959	111	1107	30	48	59	-2
1885	Bro-a	**.973**	99	**1109**	24	32	40	0
1886	Bro-a	.978	**141**	1395	33	32	65	-2
1887	Bro-a	**.982**	132	1299	46	24	62	4
1888	KC-a	.980	129	**1476**	55	32	66	3
Total	10	.971	1032	10540	305	324	511	7
C								
1879	Cle-N	.763	11	48	10	18	2	-4
1882	Cle-N	1.000	1	3	1	0	0	0
Total	2	.775	12	51	11	8	2	-4
OF								
1879	Cle-N	1.000	2	1	0	0	0	0

■ Rob Picciolo SS

YEAR	TM/L	PCT	G	PO	A	E	DP	FR
1977	Oak-A	.966	148	213	381	21	70	7
1978	Oak-A	.958	41	51	63	5	17	2
1979	Oak-A	.964	105	191	265	17	51	4
1980	Oak-A	.977	49	76	94	4	20	-10
1981	Oak-A	.981	82	99	157	5	30	-15
1982	Oak-A	.979	18	34	58	2	11	3
	Mil-A	.947	6	7	11	1	2	2
	Yr	.973	24	41	69	3	13	5
1983	Mil-A	1.000	7	11	14	0	6	2
1984	Cal-A	.974	66	51	99	4	17	8
1985	Cal-A	1.000	9	4	5	0	1	1
Total	9	.970	531	737	1147	9	225	-4
2B								
1978	Oak-A	.957	19	20	25	2	2	2
1979	Oak-A	1.000	6	11	16	0	4	1
1980	Oak-A	.990	47	87	114	2	19	-14
1982	Mil-A	1.000	11	6	3	0	1	0
1983	Mil-A	1.000	2	6	2	0	1	0
1984	Cal-A	.975	9	14	25	1	5	4
1985	Oak-A	.971	17	27	39	2	7	3
Total	7	.983	111	171	224	7	38	-4
3B								
1978	Oak-A	1.000	13	3	2	0	0	0
1979	Oak-A	1.000	4	1	7	0	0	1
1983	Mil-A	1.000	2	0	2	0	0	0
1984	Cal-A	.933	13	3	11	1	0	1
1985	Oak-A	.889	19	6	18	3	2	2
Total	5	.930	51	13	40	4	2	4
1B								
1983	Mil-A	.923	1	10	2	1	1	0
1985	Oak-A	1.000	13	19	4	0	2	1
Total	2	.972	14	29	6	1	3	1
OF								
1979	Oak-A	—	1	0	0	0	0	0
1980	Oak-A	1.000	1	1	0	0	0	0
1984	Cal-A	1.000	1	1	0	0	0	0
1985	Oak-A	—	2	0	0	0	0	0
Total	4	1.000	5	2	0	0	0	0

■ Val Picinich C

YEAR	TM/L	PCT	G	PO	A	E	DP	FR
1916	Phi-A	.967	37	179	52	8	6	0
1917	Phi-A	.786	2	10	1	3	0	-1
1918	Was-A	.960	46	216	48	11	5	-2
1919	Was-A	.978	69	303	92	9	5	**15**
1920	Was-A	.978	45	185	41	5	6	9
1921	Was-A	.966	45	197	29	8	1	3
1922	Was-A	.976	76	276	55	8	4	7
1923	Bos-A	.957	81	247	89	15	7	-2
1924	Bos-A	.951	52	157	36	10	2	-3
1925	Bos-A	.968	74	222	53	9	3	-7
1926	Cin-N	.967	86	240	52	10	6	0
1927	Cin-N	.980	61	218	31	5	8	5
1928	Cin-N	.983	93	279	65	6	6	-3
1929	Bro-N	.979	85	311	62	8	8	-3
1930	Bro-N	.944	22	43	8	3	0	-1
1931	Bro-N	.967	15	55	4	2	1	1
1932	Bro-N	.985	24	59	6	1	1	-2
1933	Bro-N	.889	6	6	2	1	0	0
	Pit-N	.982	16	48	6	1	0	-3
	Yr	.969	22	54	8	2	0	-3
Total	18	.970	935	3251	732	123	69	13
1B								
1925	Bos-A	.955	2	20	1	1	1	0

■ Charlie Pick 2B

YEAR	TM/L	PCT	G	PO	A	E	DP	FR
1918	Chi-N	.964	20	42	66	4	6	1
1919	Chi-N	.946	71	135	253	22	31	12
	Bos-N	.924	21	44	53	8	11	-2
	Yr	.942	92	179	306	30	42	10
1920	Bos-N	.952	94	219	333	28	45	0
Total	3	.949	206	440	705	2	93	11
3B								
1916	Phi-A	.899	108	143	230	**42**	25	4
1918	Chi-N	.824	8	3	11	3	6	-1
1919	Chi-N	.889	3	2	6	1	0	0
	Bos-N	.895	5	5	12	2	0	0
	Yr	.893	8	7	18	3	0	0
Total	3	.896	124	153	259	8	31	3
OF								
1914	Was-A	.833	7	8	2	2	0	0

YEAR	TM/L	PCT	G	PO	A	E	DP	FR
1916	Phi-A	.882	8	13	2	2	0	0
1919	Bos-N	1.000	3	8	0	0	0	0
Total	3	.892	18	29	4	4	0	0
1B								
1919	Bos-N	1.000	2	15	0	0	0	0

■ Ollie Pickering OF

YEAR	TM/L	PCT	G	PO	A	E	DP	FR
1896	Lou-N	.901	45	97	12	12	4	3
1897	Lou-N	.937	62	134	15	10	2	5
	Cle-N	.950	46	110	5	6	1	0
	Yr	.943	108	**244**	20	16	**3**	**5**
1901	Cle-A	.949	137	315	22	18	9	15
1902	Cle-A	.979	64	138	5	3	1	-2
1903	Phi-A	.970	135	272	17	9	5	4
1904	Phi-A	.939	121	217	13	15	2	-1
1907	StL-A	.949	151	210	14	12	5	-11
1908	Was-A	.940	98	135	6	9	1	-7
Total	8	.949	859	1628	109	4	30	6
1B								
1902	Cle-A	.944	2	17	0	1	1	0
2B								
1897	Cle-N	—	1	0	0	0	0	0

■ Urbane Pickering 3B

YEAR	TM/L	PCT	G	PO	A	E	DP	FR
1931	Bos-A	.967	74	90	143	8	8	2
1932	Bos-A	.941	126	110	222	**21**	22	-6
Total	2	.951	200	200	365	9	30	-4
2B								
1931	Bos-A	.914	16	39	46	8	4	-4
C								
1932	Bos-A	.500	1	1	0	1	0	0

■ John Pickett 2B

YEAR	TM/L	PCT	G	PO	A	E	DP	FR
1889	KC-a	.909	11	21	19	4	2	-5
1890	Phi-P	.893	100	236	284	62	46	-21
1892	Bal-N	.915	36	86	109	18	9	-5
Total	3	.900	147	343	412	4	57	-31
OF								
1889	KC-a	.900	28	43	2	5	1	-4
3B								
1889	KC-a	.720	14	13	23	14	1	-7

■ Jim Piersall OF

YEAR	TM/L	PCT	G	PO	A	E	DP	FR
1950	Bos-A	1.000	2	9	0	0	0	1
1952	Bos-A	1.000	22	38	3	0	0	1
1953	Bos-A	.987	151	352	15	5	7	15
1954	Bos-A	.985	126	249	10	4	2	0
1955	Bos-A	.993	147	425	7	3	2	7
1956	Bos-A	**.991**	**155**	**455**	10	4	1	11
1957	Bos-A	.990	151	**397**	12	4	0	5
1958	Bos-A	.985	125	314	8	5	2	5
1959	Cle-A	.982	91	216	3	4	2	-4
1960	Cle-A	.992	134	355	5	3	0	5
1961	Cle-A	**.991**	120	328	9	3	3	10
1962	Was-A	**.997**	132	308	5	1	0	0
1963	Was-A	1.000	25	65	0	0	0	2
	NY-N	1.000	38	65	3	0	0	1
	LA-A	1.000	18	28	0	0	0	-1
1964	LA-A	1.000	72	115	2	0	2	-2
1965	Cal-A	.984	41	62	0	1	0	1
1966	Cal-A	.973	63	69	3	2	0	1
1967	Cal-A	1.000	1	1	0	0	0	0
Total	17	.990	1614	3851	95	9	21	58
SS								
1952	Bos-A	.928	30	41	75	9	13	-7
3B								
1952	Bos-A	.500	1	0	1	1	0	-1
1959	Cle-A	1.000	1	0	1	0	0	0
Total	2	.667	2	0	2	1	0	-1

■ Tony Piet 2B

YEAR	TM/L	PCT	G	PO	A	E	DP	FR
1931	Pit-N	.987	44	103	133	3	17	-4
1932	Pit-N	.970	**154**	378	454	26	80	-28
1933	Pit-N	.955	97	241	305	26	61	-5
1934	Cin-N	.948	49	126	149	15	27	-6
1935	Chi-A	.975	59	129	216	9	32	5
1936	Chi-A	.966	68	135	261	14	47	9
1937	Chi-A	1.000	13	36	44	0	12	6
1938	Det-A	—	1	0	0	0	0	0
Total	8	.967	485	1148	1562	3	276	-23
3B								
1934	Cin-N	.934	51	45	96	10	7	-4
1935	Chi-A	.943	17	21	29	3	1	-2
1936	Chi-A	.957	32	32	56	4	2	-4
1937	Chi-A	.939	86	83	163	16	12	-4
1938	Det-A	.919	18	12	45	5	3	1
Total	5	.939	204	193	389	8	25	-13
SS								
1931	Pit-N	1.000	1	0	1	0	0	0
OF								
1935	Cin-N	1.000	1	1	0	0	0	0

■ Joe Pignatano C

YEAR	TM/L	PCT	G	PO	A	E	DP	FR
1957	Bro-N	1.000	6	36	1	0	0	3
1958	LA-N	1.000	57	286	18	0	3	**9**
1959	LA-N	.997	49	322	17	1	8	7
1960	LA-N	.984	40	231	21	4	2	15
1961	KC-A	.979	83	379	35	9	7	1
1962	SF-N	1.000	7	7	3	0	0	-1
	NY-N	.991	25	100	10	1	2	4
	Yr	.992	32	107	13	1	2	3
Total	6	.990	267	1361	105	5	22	38
3B								
1961	KC-A	1.000	2	1	0	0	0	0

■ Lip Pike OF

YEAR	TM/L	PCT	G	PO	A	E	DP	FR
1876	StL-N	.896	62	82	13	11	**5**	-5
1877	Cin-N	.802	38	79	10	22	1	2
1878	Cin-N	.824	31	38	4	9	1	4
1881	Wor-N	.647	5	10	1	6	1	-1
1887	NY-a	1.000	1	2	0	0	0	0

YEAR	TM/L	PCT	G	PO	A	E	DP	FR
Total	5	.833	137	211	28	8	8	-8
2B								
1876	StL-N	.846	2	8	3	2	2	0
1877	Cin-N	.838	22	62	57	23	5	-6
1878	Pro-N	.788	5	13	13	7	0	-3
Total	3	.830	29	83	73	2	7	-9
SS								
1877	Cin-N	.647	2	3	8	6	1	0

■ Al Pilarcik OF

YEAR	TM/L	PCT	G	PO	A	E	DP	FR
1956	KC-A	.976	67	154	9	4	1	0
1957	Bal-A	.996	126	234	15	1	2	5
1958	Bal-A	.986	118	213	5	3	0	-4
1959	Bal-A	.978	106	133	3	3	1	-4
1960	Bal-A	1.000	75	75	4	0	0	-2
1961	KC-A	1.000	21	31	2	0	1	1
	Chi-A	.944	17	32	2	2	0	3
	Yr	.971	38	63	4	2	1	4
Total	6	.986	530	872	40	3	5	-1

■ Babe Pinelli 3B

YEAR	TM/L	PCT	G	PO	A	E	DP	FR
1918	Chi-A	.847	24	28	33	11	4	-7
1920	Det-A	.954	74	110	183	14	20	**21**
1922	Cin-N	.945	**156**	**204**	**350**	**32**	19	**21**
1923	Cin-N	.938	116	131	250	25	17	**9**
1924	Cin-N	.956	143	**182**	**318**	23	21	**27**
1925	Cin-N	.945	109	113	265	22	21	22
1926	Cin-N	.978	40	35	96	3	5	8
1927	Cin-N	.968	15	11	19	1	1	1
Total	8	.947	677	814	1514	131	108	102
SS								
1920	Det-A	.900	18	32	40	8	0	-1
1925	Cin-N	.922	17	38	56	8	15	-1
1926	Cin-N	.886	27	17	45	8	4	-6
1927	Cin-N	.971	9	13	21	1	2	-1
Total	4	.913	71	100	162	5	21	-9
2B								
1920	Det-A	.833	1	2	3	1	0	0
1926	Cin-N	.938	3	6	9	1	0	0
1927	Cin-N	1.000	5	9	14	0	2	-1
Total	3	.956	9	17	26	2	2	-1

■ Lou Piniella OF

YEAR	TM/L	PCT	G	PO	A	E	DP	FR
1968	Cle-A	1.000	2	1	0	0	0	0
1969	KC-A	.977	129	278	13	7	1	12
1970	KC-A	.984	139	247	6	4	2	-3
1971	KC-A	.986	115	201	6	3	2	-6
1972	KC-A	.986	150	275	8	7	2	-3
1973	KC-A	.986	128	196	9	3	3	-9
1974	NY-A	.989	130	265	16	3	0	6
1975	NY-A	.986	46	65	5	1	0	-2
1976	NY-A	.982	49	106	4	2	0	0
1977	NY-A	.975	51	77	2	2	0	-3
1978	NY-A	.969	103	213	4	7	0	-2
1979	NY-A	.982	112	204	13	4	1	0
1980	NY-A	.971	104	157	8	5	1	-3
1981	NY-A	.986	36	69	2	1	1	2
1982	NY-A	1.000	40	68	2	0	1	3
1983	NY-A	.959	43	67	4	3	2	-2
1984	NY-A	1.000	24	40	3	0	0	0
Total	17	.981	1401	2529	105	2	16	-10
1B								
1970	KC-A	1.000	1	3	0	0	0	0
1974	NY-A	1.000	1	5	0	0	0	0
1977	NY-A	1.000	1	9	1	0	0	0
Total	3	1.000	3	17	1	0	0	0

■ George Pinkney 3B

YEAR	TM/L	PCT	G	PO	A	E	DP	FR
1885	Bro-a	.874	51	56	83	20	4	-5
1886	Bro-a	.858	141	**184**	234	69	17	-16
1887	Bro-a	**.890**	136	196	**290**	60	26	**13**
1888	Bro-a	.898	143	189	234	48	14	-25
1889	Bro-a	**.897**	138	183	278	53	19	-8
1890	Bro-N	.933	126	179	222	29	15	-14
1891	Bro-N	.904	130	146	261	43	10	-20
1892	StL-N	.888	78	84	161	31	12	-8
1893	Lou-N	.923	18	126	279	34	26	-2
Total	9	.897	1061	1343	2042	387	143	-85
2B								
1884	Cle-a	.848	25	56	67	22	10	-12
1885	Bro-a	.904	57	147	173	34	15	-6
Total	2	.888	82	203	240	6	25	-18
SS								
1884	Cle-N	.857	11	17	43	10	1	4
1885	Bro-a	.882	3	4	11	2	1	0
1887	Bro-a	1.000	2	1	4	0	0	0
1891	Bro-N	.875	5	6	15	3	0	0
Total	4	.871	21	28	73	5	2	4

■ Vada Pinson OF

YEAR	TM/L	PCT	G	PO	A	E	DP	FR
1958	Cin-N	1.000	27	50	4	0	1	1
1959	Cin-N	.984	**154**	**423**	11	7	4	12
1960	Cin-N	.981	**154**	401	11	8	1	3
1961	Cin-N	.976	153	**391**	19	10	4	13
1962	Cin-N	.989	152	344	13	4	1	0
1963	Cin-N	.979	**162**	357	9	8	0	3
1964	Cin-N	.972	156	299	14	9	1	-2
1965	Cin-N	**.992**	159	354	9	3	1	8
1966	Cin-N	.964	154	344	9	13	1	1
1967	Cin-N	.986	157	341	4	5	1	1
1968	Cin-N	.978	123	258	7	6	0	-3
1969	StL-N	**.996**	124	218	6	1	2	1
1970	Cle-A	.982	141	265	8	5	3	5
1971	Cle-A	.978	141	305	11	7	2	9
1972	Cal-A	.991	134	205	11	2	3	-2
1973	Cal-A	.965	120	210	11	8	2	0
1974	KC-A	.980	110	188	9	4	2	-8
1975	KC-A	.993	82	144	6	1	0	2
Total	18	.981	2403	5097	172	101	29	40

YEAR	TM/L	PCT	G	PO	A	E	DP	FR
1B								
1970	Cle-A	1.000	7	19	1	0	2	0
1971	Cle-A	1.000	3	10	0	0	2	0
1972	Cal-A	1.000	1	2	0	0	0	0
1974	KC-A	1.000	1	10	0	0	0	0
1975	KC-A	1.000	4	7	0	0	0	0
Total	5	1.000	16	48	1	0	4	0

■ Wally Pipp 1B

YEAR	TM/L	PCT	G	PO	A	E	DP	FR
1913	Det-A	.977	10	80	4	2	6	-1
1915	NY-A	**.992**	134	**1396**	85	12	**85**	3
1916	NY-A	.992	148	1513	99	13	**89**	5
1917	NY-A	.990	155	1609	**109**	17	97	4
1918	NY-A	.988	91	918	61	12	75	0
1919	NY-A	.991	138	**1488**	94	15	77	1
1920	NY-A	.991	153	**1649**	100	15	**101**	0
1921	NY-A	.991	153	1624	89	16	116	-4
1922	NY-A	.993	**152**	**1667**	88	13	106	-5
1923	NY-A	.992	144	1461	81	12	97	-4
1924	NY-A	**.994**	**153**	1447	106	9	106	2
1925	NY-A	.991	47	399	38	4	40	4
1926	Cin-N	.992	**155**	**1710**	92	15	**140**	2
1927	Cin-N	**.996**	114	1145	66	5	86	0
1928	Cin-N	.989	72	673	40	8	69	1
Total	15	.992	1819	18779	1152	168	1290	8

■ Jake Pitler 2B

YEAR	TM/L	PCT	G	PO	A	E	DP	FR
1917	Pit-N	**.966**	106	283	277	20	46	-11
1918	Pit-N	.667	1	2	2	2	0	0
Total	2	.962	107	285	279	2	46	-11
OF								
1917	Pit-N	1.000	3	3	0	0	0	0

■ Pinky Pittinger SS

YEAR	TM/L	PCT	G	PO	A	E	DP	FR
1921	Bos-A	1.000	2	5	1	0	0	0
1922	Bos-A	.911	29	47	86	13	11	4
1923	Bos-A	.970	10	12	20	1	1	-1
1925	Chi-N	.940	24	48	77	8	10	-1
1927	Cin-N	.919	9	17	17	3	4	-1
1928	Cin-N	.892	12	9	24	4	7	5
1929	Cin-N	.956	50	107	153	12	37	1
Total	7	.938	136	245	378	1	70	7
3B								
1921	Bos-A	1.000	3	3	8	0	1	2
1922	Bos-A	.920	33	41	62	9	8	2
1923	Bos-A	1.000	3	8	6	0	0	1
1925	Chi-N	.961	24	23	50	3	4	5
1927	Cin-N	.500	2	1	0	1	0	0
1928	Cin-N	1.000	4	4	4	0	0	1
1929	Cin-N	.957	9	6	16	1	1	1
Total	7	.943	77	84	146	4	14	12
2B								
1921	Bos-A	—	1	0	0	0	0	0
1923	Bos-A	.959	42	77	86	7	12	-11
1927	Cin-N	.963	20	37	66	4	15	4
1928	Cin-N	1.000	4	2	5	0	0	2
1929	Cin-N	.933	4	4	10	1	2	1
Total	5	.960	71	120	167	2	29	-4
OF								
1921	Bos-A	.985	27	60	4	1	0	0

■ Whitey Platt OF

YEAR	TM/L	PCT	G	PO	A	E	DP	FR
1942	Chi-N	1.000	4	7	1	0	0	0
1943	Chi-N	.952	14	20	0	1	0	-1
1946	Chi-A	.971	61	130	4	4	1	0
1948	StL-A	.948	114	230	5	13	2	-8
1949	StL-A	.986	59	135	3	2	0	1
Total	5	.964	252	522	13	0	3	-9
1B								
1949	StL-A	.958	2	21	2	1	1	0

■ Herb Plews 2B

YEAR	TM/L	PCT	G	PO	A	E	DP	FR
1956	Was-A	.947	66	137	166	**17**	38	-3
1957	Was-A	.979	79	199	175	8	42	-12
1958	Was-A	.976	64	133	153	7	41	-13
1959	Was-A	.971	6	18	16	1	2	1
	Bos-A	.833	2	3	2	1	1	1
	Yr	.951	8	21	18	2	3	2
Total	4	.967	217	490	512	4	124	-26
3B								
1956	Was-A	1.000	2	2	6	0	0	0
1957	Was-A	.833	1	4	11	3	1	-2
1958	Was-A	.897	36	23	55	9	4	-7
Total	3	.894	49	29	72	2	5	-9
SS								
1956	Was-A	.800	5	1	3	1	1	0
1957	Was-A	1.000	4	0	2	0	0	0
Total	2	.857	9	1	5	1	1	0

■ Bill Plummer C

YEAR	TM/L	PCT	G	PO	A	E	DP	FR
1968	Chi-N	1.000	1	2	0	0	0	0
1970	Cin-N	.857	4	6	0	1	0	-2
1971	Cin-N	1.000	4	7	2	0	0	0
1972	Cin-N	.994	35	148	9	1	2	1
1973	Cin-N	.994	42	170	9	1	3	0
1974	Cin-N	.974	49	208	13	6	1	5
1975	Cin-N	.990	63	186	14	2	5	-3
1976	Cin-N	.977	54	235	21	6	1	5
1977	Cin-N	.986	50	194	15	3	3	-1
1978	Sea-A	.978	40	127	9	3	1	-5
Total	10	.984	342	1283	92	3	16	0
3B								
1971	Cin-N	1.000	2	1	4	0	0	0
1972	Cin-N	—	1	0	0	0	0	0
1973	Cin-N	.750	5	2	1	1	0	0
1974	Cin-N	1.000	1	0	1	0	0	0
Total	4	.900	9	3	6	1	0	-1
1B								
1972	Cin-N	1.000	1	8	0	0	0	0

YEAR	TM/L	PCT	G	PO	A	E	DP	FR
■ Biff Pocoroba C								
1975	Atl-N	.970	62	237	25	8	2	-3
1976	Atl-N	.978	54	273	39	7	5	5
1977	Atl-N	.989	100	542	78	7	8	4
1978	Atl-N	.990	79	454	43	5	1	2
1979	Atl-N	.933	7	39	3	3	0	0
1980	Atl-N	.934	10	56	1	4	0	-1
1981	Atl-N	1.000	9	28	4	0	2	-1
1982	Atl-N	.988	36	143	16	2	2	-4
1983	Atl-N	.983	34	166	12	3	1	-3
Total	9	.982	391	1938	221	9	21	-1
3B								
1981	Atl-N	.938	21	15	30	3	4	-4
1982	Atl-N	1.000	2	1	0	0	0	0
Total	2	.939	23	16	30	3	4	-4
■ Jimmy Pofahl SS								
1940	Was-A	.952	112	191	302	25	69	-11
1941	Was-A	.934	21	30	55	6	8	-4
1942	Was-A	.956	49	108	130	11	35	0
Total	3	.951	182	329	487	2	112	-11
2B								
1940	Was-A	1.000	4	9	15	0	4	1
1942	Was-A	.943	15	36	46	5	9	-1
Total	2	.955	19	45	61	5	13	0
3B								
1942	Was-A	.962	14	22	28	2	1	2
■ Luis Polonia OF								
1987	Oak-A	.979	104	235	2	5	1	-4
1988	Oak-A	.988	76	155	3	2	1	-2
1989	Oak-A	.985	55	126	3	2	1	1
	NY-A	.982	53	105	6	2	1	-2
	Yr	.984	108	231	9	4	2	-1
1990	Cal-A	.980	85	142	3	3	2	-7
Total	4	.982	373	763	17	4	6	-14
■ Harlin Pool OF								
1934	Cin-N	.953	94	196	8	10	1	-3
1935	Cin-N	.962	18	24	1	1	0	-2
Total	2	.954	112	220	9	1	1	-5
■ Jim Poole 1B								
1925	Phi-A	.982	123	1166	65	23	102	-7
1926	Phi-A	.992	101	881	55	8	71	0
1927	Phi-A	.993	31	264	17	2	14	0
Total	3	.987	255	2311	137	3	187	-7
OF								
1926	Phi-A	1.000	1	1	0	0	0	0
■ Tom Poorman OF								
1880	Buf-N	.727	10	8	0	3	0	-2
	Chi-N	.778	7	6	1	2	0	0
	Yr	.750	17	14	1	5	0	-2
1884	Tol-a	.845	93	129	29	29	5	4
1885	Bos-N	.867	56	82	9	14	1	-3
1886	Bos-N	.902	88	145	21	18	6	5
1887	Phi-a	.911	135	237	18	25	6	3
1888	Phi-a	.898	97	115	8	14	1	-10
Total	6	.885	486	722	86	105	19	-3
2B								
1887	Phi-a	—	2	0	0	0	0	0
■ Dave Pope OF								
1952	Cle-A	1.000	10	13	0	0	0	-1
1954	Cle-A	1.000	29	45	1	0	0	0
1955	Cle-A	.954	31	62	0	3	0	-1
	Bal-A	1.000	73	150	3	0	1	5
	Yr	.986	104	212	3	3	1	4
1956	Bal-A	1.000	4	3	0	0	0	-1
	Cle-A	1.000	18	34	1	0	0	0
	Yr	1.000	22	37	1	0	0	-1
Total	4	.990	165	307	5	3	1	2
■ Paul Popovich 2B								
1966	Chi-N	.889	2	5	3	1	1	-1
1967	Chi-N	.985	17	26	39	1	11	1
1968	LA-N	.983	89	172	229	7	48	3
1969	LA-N	.985	23	27	38	1	9	1
	Chi-N	.974	25	50	64	3	13	-8
	Yr	.978	48	77	102	4	22	-7
1970	Chi-N	.990	22	42	58	1	18	0
1971	Chi-N	.985	40	74	119	3	26	4
1972	Chi-N	.981	36	59	98	3	22	14
1973	Chi-N	.981	84	171	247	8	53	24
1974	Pit-N	.962	12	21	30	2	5	0
1975	Pit-N	1.000	8	16	14	0	2	-2
Total	10	.982	358	663	939	0	208	36
SS								
1967	Chi-N	.967	31	40	77	4	12	-4
1968	LA-N	.978	45	59	119	4	20	1
1969	LA-N	.667	3	0	2	1	0	0
	Chi-N	1.000	7	13	23	0	7	2
	Yr	.974	10	13	25	1	7	2
1970	Chi-N	.962	17	24	27	2	7	-2
1971	Chi-N	—	1	0	0	0	0	0
1972	Chi-N	.979	8	18	29	1	8	4
1973	Chi-N	1.000	9	8	14	0	5	2
1974	Pit-N	1.000	10	3	8	0	4	0
1975	Pit-N	.889	8	1	7	1	1	-1
Total	9	.973	139	166	306	3	64	2
3B								
1967	Chi-N	—	2	0	0	0	0	0
1968	LA-N	1.000	7	1	1	0	0	0
1969	Chi-N	.917	6	2	9	1	1	0
1970	Chi-N	.955	16	9	12	1	1	-3
1971	Chi-N	.969	16	4	27	1	1	0
1972	Chi-N	—	1	0	0	0	0	0
1973	Chi-N	1.000	1	0	1	0	0	0
Total	7	.957	49	16	50	3	3	-3

YEAR	TM/L	PCT	G	PO	A	E	DP	FR
OF								
1969	Chi-N	1.000	1	1	0	0	0	0
■ Tom Poquette OF								
1973	KC-A	.870	20	19	1	3	0	0
1976	KC-A	.979	98	188	1	4	0	-8
1977	KC-A	1.000	96	177	4	0	1	-3
1978	KC-A	.955	63	144	5	7	0	4
1979	KC-A	1.000	10	7	1	0	1	0
	Bos-A	.949	43	73	2	4	1	-2
	Yr	.954	53	80	3	4	2	-2
1981	Bos-A	—	2	0	0	0	0	0
	Tex-A	.963	18	26	0	1	0	-3
	Yr	.963	20	26	0	1	0	-3
1982	KC-A	.957	23	44	1	2	0	0
Total	7	.971	373	678	15	15	3	-12
■ Darrell Porter C								
1971	Mil-A	.977	22	108	18	3	2	2
1972	Mil-A	.976	18	113	8	3	3	5
1973	Mil-A	.977	90	373	47	10	9	-4
1974	Mil-A	.978	117	484	60	12	8	-3
1975	Mil-A	.979	124	532	82	13	10	0
1976	Mil-A	.975	111	491	52	14	7	-4
1977	KC-A	.982	125	663	61	13	4	1
1978	KC-A	.988	145	608	62	8	10	-5
1979	KC-A	.982	141	628	68	13	15	-1
1980	KC-A	.978	81	322	37	8	6	3
1981	StL-N	.979	52	206	31	5	2	-3
1982	StL-N	.983	111	469	64	9	8	-6
1983	StL-N	.989	133	578	70	7	8	-7
1984	StL-N	.984	122	620	58	11	6	-12
1985	StL-N	.990	82	386	26	4	4	-2
1986	Tex-A	.994	25	165	9	1	2	3
1987	Tex-A	1.000	7	10	1	0	0	0
Total	17	.982	1506	6756	754	134	104	-33
1B								
1987	Tex-A	1.000	5	11	1	0	2	0
■ Dick Porter OF								
1929	Cle-A	.941	28	44	4	3	1	-1
1930	Cle-A	.962	118	189	12	8	4	-4
1931	Cle-A	.970	109	184	7	6	0	-7
1932	Cle-A	.982	145	269	2	5	0	-16
1933	Cle-A	.996	124	236	9	1	3	-5
1934	Cle-A	1.000	10	14	0	0	0	-2
	Bos-A	.940	65	109	1	7	1	-10
	Yr	.947	75	123	1	7	1	-12
Total	6	.973	599	1045	35	0	9	-45
2B								
1929	Cle-A	.958	20	54	60	5	9	-4
1931	Cle-A	1.000	1	3	5	0	0	1
Total	2	.961	21	57	65	5	9	-3
■ Leo Posada OF								
1960	KC-A	1.000	9	11	1	0	0	-1
1961	KC-A	.973	102	205	8	6	0	1
1962	KC-A	1.000	11	15	1	0	1	0
Total	3	.976	122	231	10	6	1	0
■ Wally Post OF								
1949	Cin-N	.750	3	3	0	1	0	0
1951	Cin-N	.963	9	25	1	1	0	1
1952	Cin-N	1.000	16	38	1	0	0	1
1953	Cin-N	.960	11	22	2	1	0	1
1954	Cin-N	.957	116	231	13	11	2	3
1955	Cin-N	.978	154	298	13	7	2	-1
1956	Cin-N	.969	136	292	16	10	1	10
1957	Cin-N	.985	124	252	12	4	4	6
1958	Phi-N	.952	91	185	12	10	0	5
1959	Phi-N	.992	120	226	12	2	3	6
1960	Phi-N	1.000	22	43	1	0	0	0
	Cin-N	.985	67	125	8	2	0	1
	Yr	.989	89	168	9	2	0	1
1961	Cin-N	.959	81	133	7	6	3	-1
1962	Cin-N	.935	90	110	5	8	0	-10
1963	Cin-N	1.000	1	3	0	0	0	0
	Min-A	1.000	12	14	0	0	0	-1
1964	Min-A	.667	2	2	0	1	0	-1
Total	15	.970	1055	2002	103	4	15	20
■ Jake Powell OF								
1930	Was-A	1.000	2	3	0	0	0	0
1934	Was-A	.955	9	18	3	1	0	1
1935	Was-A	.976	136	361	10	9	4	-4
1936	Was-A	.951	53	115	2	6	1	-3
	NY-A	.976	84	196	6	5	2	4
	Yr	.967	137	311	8	11	3	1
1937	NY-A	.981	94	201	5	4	2	0
1938	NY-A	.978	43	86	1	2	0	-3
1939	NY-A	.983	23	56	1	1	0	2
1940	NY-A	1.000	7	15	1	0	0	1
1943	Was-A	.978	33	83	4	2	0	3
1944	Was-A	.980	92	196	5	4	0	-1
1945	Was-A	.950	27	56	1	3	1	-1
	Phi-N	.986	44	67	1	1	2	-5
Total	11	.975	647	1453	44	8	12	-6
2B								
1935	Was-A	1.000	2	2	2	0	0	1
3B								
1944	Was-A	—	1	0	0	0	0	0
■ Hosken Powell OF								
1978	Min-A	.983	117	219	9	4	2	-17
1979	Min-A	.977	93	165	6	4	3	-8
1980	Min-A	.968	129	265	11	9	1	-1
1981	Min-A	.970	64	122	6	4	1	-1
1982	Tor-A	.974	75	111	2	3	0	-3
1983	Tor-A	.981	33	52	0	1	0	0
Total	6	.975	511	934	34	5	7	-30

YEAR	TM/L	PCT	G	PO	A	E	DP	FR
1B								
1983	Tor-A	1.000	1	0	1	0	1	0
■ Boog Powell 1B								
1962	Bal-A	1.000	1	10	0	0	0	0
1963	Bal-A	.980	23	135	12	3	10	-1
1964	Bal-A	1.000	5	45	6	0	5	1
1965	Bal-A	.992	78	538	52	5	50	5
1966	Bal-A	.989	136	1094	68	13	96	-5
1967	Bal-A	.986	114	903	64	14	82	-4
1968	Bal-A	.990	149	1293	79	14	102	-4
1969	Bal-A	.995	144	1192	84	7	105	-2
1970	Bal-A	.992	145	1209	89	10	107	-2
1971	Bal-A	.995	124	1031	67	5	97	-3
1972	Bal-A	.988	133	1116	70	15	111	-3
1973	Bal-A	.989	111	988	77	12	95	2
1974	Bal-A	.996	102	866	61	4	102	1
1975	Cle-A	.997	121	997	69	3	92	-2
1976	Cle-A	.987	89	698	61	10	76	1
1977	LA-N	.938	4	15	0	1	1	-1
Total	16	.991	1479	12130	859	116	1131	-17
OF								
1961	Bal-A	1.000	3	3	0	0	0	-1
1962	Bal-A	.969	112	184	1	6	0	-9
1963	Bal-A	.969	121	181	6	6	1	-11
1964	Bal-A	.974	124	178	13	5	1	-3
1965	Bal-A	1.000	71	120	1	0	0	-3
Total	5	.976	431	666	21	7	2	-27
■ Martin Powell 1B								
1881	Det-N	.947	55	537	17	31	47	-2
1882	Det-N	.940	80	680	14	44	27	-5
1883	Det-N	.950	101	995	32	54	62	-3
1884	Cin-U	.940	43	463	11	30	19	-2
1885	Phi-a	.973	19	178	3	5	6	0
Total	5	.947	298	2853	77	164	161	-12
C								
1881	Det-N	—	1	0	0	0	0	0
■ Ray Powell OF								
1913	Det-A	—	1	0	0	0	0	0
1917	Bos-N	.976	88	231	14	6	2	6
1918	Bos-N	.949	53	121	8	7	2	-3
1919	Bos-N	.951	122	213	21	12	7	-2
1920	Bos-N	.956	147	370	25	18	5	1
1921	Bos-N	.954	149	377	21	19	3	-3
1922	Bos-N	.980	136	377	18	8	2	7
1923	Bos-N	.941	84	214	8	14	0	-6
1924	Bos-N	.947	46	117	9	7	3	7
Total	9	.959	826	2020	124	1	24	7
■ Vic Power 1B								
1954	Phi-A	.988	21	150	12	2	17	0
1955	KC-A	.993	144	1281	130	10	140	14
1956	KC-A	.993	76	671	62	5	73	6
1957	KC-A	.998	113	968	99	2	95	14
1958	KC-A	.992	50	439	48	4	57	6
	Cle-A	.993	41	263	29	2	37	4
	Yr	.992	91	702	77	6	94	10
1959	Cle-A	.995	121	1039	110	6	98	15
1960	Cle-A	.996	147	1177	145	5	145	21
1961	Cle-A	.994	141	1154	142	9	101	17
1962	Min-A	.993	142	1193	134	10	133	14
1963	Min-A	.992	124	896	76	8	86	2
1964	Min-A	.990	12	86	9	1	8	1
	LA-A	1.000	48	282	30	0	22	4
	Phi-N	.993	17	123	11	1	9	1
	Yr	.991	29	209	20	2	17	2
1965	Cal-A	.996	107	419	41	2	35	6
Total	12	.994	1304	10141	1078	6	1056	125
2B								
1956	KC-A	.974	47	122	138	7	40	1
1957	KC-A	1.000	4	12	7	0	0	-2
1958	KC-A	1.000	1	2	0	0	0	0
	Cle-A	.974	27	49	65	3	16	0
	Yr	.975	28	51	65	3	16	0
1959	Cle-A	.971	21	48	54	3	6	-4
1961	Cle-A	.955	7	20	22	2	7	2
1962	Min-A	1.000	2	2	0	0	0	-5
1963	Min-A	.957	18	44	45	4	9	-2
1964	Min-A	1.000	1	0	3	0	0	0
	LA-A	1.000	5	6	2	0	2	0
	Yr	1.000	6	6	5	0	2	0
1965	Cal-A	1.000	6	8	10	0	3	1
Total	9	.972	139	313	346	9	83	-9
OF								
1954	Phi-A	.985	101	256	13	4	3	15
1956	KC-A	1.000	7	14	0	0	0	-1
1957	KC-A	.923	6	12	0	1	0	-1
1958	Cle-A	1.000	1	1	0	0	0	-1
Total	4	.983	115	283	13	5	3	13
3B								
1954	Phi-A	1.000	1	0	1	0	0	0
1958	Cle-A	.977	42	51	78	3	12	2
1959	Cle-A	.944	7	7	10	1	1	-1
1960	Cle-A	1.000	4	1	3	0	0	0
1963	Min-A	1.000	5	7	8	0	0	0
1964	LA-A	.958	28	20	49	3	2	-1
1965	Cal-A	1.000	2	3	3	0	0	-1
Total	7	.972	89	89	152	7	15	-1
SS								
1954	Phi-A	—	1	0	0	0	0	0
1958	Cle-A	1.000	2	1	0	0	0	0
1960	Cle-A	1.000	5	7	3	0	1	1
Total	3	1.000	8	8	3	0	1	0
■ Mike Powers C								
1898	Lou-N	.962	22	58	17	3	2	-4
1899	Lou-N	.942	38	118	27	9	5	-8
	Was-N	.942	12	37	12	3	0	1

YEAR	TM/L	PCT	G	PO	A	E	DP	FR
Yr		.942	**50**	**155**	**39**	12	5	-7
1901	Phi-A	.952	111	400	137	27	6	-4
1902	Phi-A	.950	68	229	110	18	5	2
1903	Phi-A	.982	66	349	86	8	3	-2
1904	Phi-A	.965	56	338	52	14	6	-4
1905	Phi-A	.928	21	115	27	11	2	4
	NY-A	1.000	4	15	0	0	0	0
	Phi-A	.991	19	87	22	1	2	-5
	Yr	.957	44	217	49	12	4	-1
1906	Phi-A	.974	57	299	79	10	2	10
1907	Phi-A	.983	59	313	80	7	8	14
1908	Phi-A	.967	60	303	74	13	3	6
1909	Phi-A	1.000	1	9	1	0	0	0
Total	11	.965	594	2670	724	124	44	10

1B

YEAR	TM/L	PCT	G	PO	A	E	DP	FR
1898	Lou-N	1.000	6	51	4	0	1	1
1899	Lou-N	.918	7	43	2	4	1	-1
	Was-N	1.000	1	10	0	0	0	0
	Yr	.932	8	53	2	4	1	-1
1901	Phi-A	.938	3	30	0	2	1	-1
1902	Phi-A	1.000	3	21	2	0	1	0
1903	Phi-A	.981	7	49	2	1	3	0
1905	NY-A	.975	7	72	5	2	2	0
1906	Phi-A	1.000	1	2	0	0	0	0
1908	Phi-A	1.000	2	6	2	0	0	1
Total	8	.971	37	284	17	9	9	0

OF

YEAR	TM/L	PCT	G	PO	A	E	DP	FR
1898	Lou-N	.750	1	3	0	1	0	0
1904	Phi-A	1.000	1	1	0	0	0	0
Total	2	.800	2	4	0	1	0	0

■ Phil Powers C

YEAR	TM/L	PCT	G	PO	A	E	DP	FR
1878	Chi-N	.930	8	47	19	5	0	6
1880	Bos-N	.851	37	152	59	37	6	-2
1881	Cle-N	.955	4	17	4	1	1	0
1882	Cin-a	.921	10	49	9	5	1	1
1883	Cin-a	.893	17	58	17	9	0	-3
1884	Cin-a	.891	31	152	53	25	2	1
1885	Cin-a	.833	15	67	23	18	1	-4
	Bal-a	.844	8	31	7	7	0	-4
	Yr	.837	23	98	30	25	1	-8
Total	7	.877	130	573	191	107	11	-5

OF

YEAR	TM/L	PCT	G	PO	A	E	DP	FR
1880	Bos-N	—	2	0	0	0	0	0
1882	Cin-a	.000	1	0	0	1	0	-1
1883	Cin-a	.864	13	16	3	3	0	-1
1884	Cin-a	1.000	2	2	0	0	0	-1
1885	Bal-a	1.000	1	3	0	0	0	-1
Total	5	.857	19	21	3	4	0	-3

1B

YEAR	TM/L	PCT	G	PO	A	E	DP	FR
1882	Cin-a	.956	5	39	4	2	2	1
1884	Cin-a	.900	2	6	3	1	3	1
Total	2	.945	7	45	7	3	5	2

3B

YEAR	TM/L	PCT	G	PO	A	E	DP	FR
1881	Cle-N	1.000	1	0	1	0	0	0

■ Johnny Pramesa C

YEAR	TM/L	PCT	G	PO	A	E	DP	FR
1949	Cin-N	.966	13	27	1	1	0	-1
1950	Cin-N	.981	73	328	37	7	2	2
1951	Cin-N	.968	63	241	27	9	4	-6
1952	Chi-N	.958	17	62	6	3	3	2
Total	4	.973	166	658	71	0	9	-3

■ Del Pratt 2B

YEAR	TM/L	PCT	G	PO	A	E	DP	FR
1912	StL-A	.943	122	273	326	36	49	8
1913	StL-A	.951	146	**364**	425	**41**	56	4
1914	StL-A	.944	**152**	358	423	**46**	48	-2
1915	StL-A	.965	**158**	**417**	441	31	**82**	12
1916	StL-A	.966	**158**	**438**	491	33	74	22
1917	StL-A	.959	119	324	353	29	64	15
1918	NY-A	.969	**126**	**340**	386	23	**82**	12
1919	NY-A	.969	**140**	315	**491**	26	64	**28**
1920	NY-A	.971	**154**	354	**515**	26	**77**	12
1921	Bos-A	.961	134	283	408	28	90	-1
1922	Bos-A	.966	**154**	362	484	30	80	-13
1923	Det-A	.947	60	108	140	14	21	-11
1924	Det-A	.948	65	133	192	18	38	1
Total	13	.960	1688	4069	5075	381	825	87

1B

YEAR	TM/L	PCT	G	PO	A	E	DP	FR
1913	StL-A	.988	9	76	6	1	4	1
1917	StL-A	1.000	2	22	2	0	0	0
1923	Det-A	1.000	17	169	10	0	10	0
1924	Det-A	.990	51	496	25	5	35	-3
Total	4	.993	79	763	43	6	49	-2

SS

YEAR	TM/L	PCT	G	PO	A	E	DP	FR
1912	StL-A	.896	21	45	75	14	12	4

3B

YEAR	TM/L	PCT	G	PO	A	E	DP	FR
1912	StL-A	.875	1	2	5	1	0	1
1923	Det-A	.892	12	4	29	4	1	1
1924	Det-A	1.000	4	2	8	0	0	1
Total	3	.909	17	8	42	5	1	3

OF

YEAR	TM/L	PCT	G	PO	A	E	DP	FR
1912	StL-A	1.000	8	19	1	0	0	1
1924	Det-A	1.000	1	2	0	0	0	0
Total	2	1.000	9	21	1	0	0	1

■ Jim Presley 3B

YEAR	TM/L	PCT	G	PO	A	E	DP	FR
1984	Sea-A	.958	69	48	113	7	12	-3
1985	Sea-A	.961	154	82	335	17	24	6
1986	Sea-A	.965	155	110	308	15	31	6
1987	Sea-A	.953	148	113	**311**	21	28	11
1988	Sea-A	.940	146	112	234	22	25	-13
1989	Sea-A	.924	90	54	154	17	13	-6
1990	Atl-N	.930	133	101	231	**25**	19	-4
Total	7	.949	895	620	1686	124	152	-3

1B

YEAR	TM/L	PCT	G	PO	A	E	DP	FR
1989	Sea-A	.995	30	168	15	1	16	1
1990	Atl-N	.989	17	77	11	1	10	2
Total	2	.993	47	245	26	2	26	3

SS

YEAR	TM/L	PCT	G	PO	A	E	DP	FR
1987	Sea-A	1.000	4	0	4	0	1	0

■ Jim Price C

YEAR	TM/L	PCT	G	PO	A	E	DP	FR
1967	Det-A	.974	24	139	8	4	1	0
1968	Det-A	.996	42	223	14	1	1	2
1969	Det-A	.989	51	337	18	4	4	3
1970	Det-A	.979	38	266	8	6	2	-1
1971	Det-A	.981	25	99	7	2	2	1
Total	5	.985	180	1064	55	7	10	5

■ Jerry Priddy 2B

YEAR	TM/L	PCT	G	PO	A	E	DP	FR
1941	NY-A	.968	31	74	79	5	26	6
1942	NY-A	.964	8	15	38	2	9	5
1943	Was-A	.971	134	364	411	23	105	7
1946	Was-A	.962	138	378	428	**32**	105	2
1947	Was-A	.966	146	**382**	405	16	89	-2
1948	StL-A	.968	146	**407**	471	**29**	**132**	24
1949	StL-A	.968	145	**407**	415	**27**	96	-3
1950	Det-A	.981	**157**	440	**542**	19	**150**	31
1951	Det-A	.980	**154**	**437**	**463**	18	**118**	10
1952	Det-A	.968	75	211	209	14	48	-1
1953	Det-A	.977	45	111	106	5	28	2
Total	11	.973	1179	3226	3567	190	906	81

3B

YEAR	TM/L	PCT	G	PO	A	E	DP	FR
1941	NY-A	.941	14	15	33	3	2	3
1942	NY-A	.945	35	36	65	6	2	1
1943	Was-A	1.000	1	3	0	0	0	0
1953	Det-A	1.000	2	0	3	0	0	0
Total	4	.945	52	54	101	9	4	4

1B

YEAR	TM/L	PCT	G	PO	A	E	DP	FR
1941	NY-A	1.000	10	78	7	0	18	1
1942	NY-A	.989	11	91	2	1	15	-2
1953	Det-A	1.000	11	92	9	0	7	1
Total	3	.996	32	261	18	1	40	0

SS

YEAR	TM/L	PCT	G	PO	A	E	DP	FR
1942	NY-A	1.000	3	4	9	0	0	1
1943	Was-A	.947	15	31	40	4	6	-3
1951	Det-A	1.000	1	1	1	0	0	0
Total	3	.956	19	36	50	4	6	-2

■ Doc Prothro 3B

YEAR	TM/L	PCT	G	PO	A	E	DP	FR
1920	Was-A	1.000	2	0	2	0	2	0
1923	Was-A	1.000	6	5	11	0	0	3
1924	Was-A	.915	45	40	68	10	6	-11
1925	Bos-A	.945	108	115	211	19	16	-5
1926	Cin-N	1.000	2	0	2	0	0	0
Total	5	.940	163	160	294	9	24	-13

SS

YEAR	TM/L	PCT	G	PO	A	E	DP	FR
1920	Was-A	1.000	2	4	3	0	2	-1
1925	Bos-A	.923	3	7	5	1	1	-1
Total	2	.950	5	11	8	1	3	-2

■ Ron Pruitt OF

YEAR	TM/L	PCT	G	PO	A	E	DP	FR
1975	Tex-A	—	1	0	0	0	0	0
1976	Cle-A	1.000	26	41	3	0	1	3
1977	Cle-A	.972	69	104	2	3	0	-5
1978	Cle-A	.967	16	29	0	1	0	-1
1979	Cle-A	.957	29	43	1	2	0	-2
1980	Cle-A	1.000	6	9	0	0	1	0
	Chi-A	1.000	11	20	0	0	0	-1
	Yr	1.000	17	29	1	0	1	-1
1981	Cle-A	1.000	3	3	0	0	0	0
1982	SF-N	—	1	0	0	0	0	0
Total	8	.977	162	249	7	6	2	-6

C

YEAR	TM/L	PCT	G	PO	A	E	DP	FR
1975	Tex-A	1.000	13	21	5	0	0	0
1976	Cle-A	1.000	6	24	3	0	1	2
1977	Cle-A	1.000	4	9	4	0	0	0
1978	Cle-A	.984	48	170	15	3	4	-4
1979	Cle-A	1.000	11	22	3	0	1	-1
1980	Chi-A	.833	5	5	0	1	0	-1
1981	Cle-A	—	1	0	0	0	0	0
1982	SF-N	1.000	1	5	0	0	0	0
Total	8	.986	89	256	30	4	6	-4

3B

YEAR	TM/L	PCT	G	PO	A	E	DP	FR
1976	Cle-A	.929	6	3	10	1	0	1
1977	Cle-A	—	1	0	0	0	0	0
1978	Cle-A	—	2	0	0	0	0	0
1979	Cle-A	1.000	3	1	1	0	0	0
1980	Cle-A	—	2	0	0	0	0	0
	Chi-A	1.000	3	0	1	0	0	0
	Yr	1.000	5	0	1	0	0	0
Total	5	.941	17	4	12	1	0	1

1B

YEAR	TM/L	PCT	G	PO	A	E	DP	FR
1976	Cle-A	1.000	1	5	0	0	0	0
1980	Cle-A	—	1	0	0	0	0	0
Total	2	1.000	2	5	0	0	0	0

■ Greg Pryor 3B

YEAR	TM/L	PCT	G	PO	A	E	DP	FR
1976	Tex-A	1.000	1	0	2	0	0	0
1978	Chi-A	.968	20	12	48	2	6	6
1979	Chi-A	.929	22	15	37	4	2	3
1980	Chi-A	.942	41	28	85	7	7	3
1981	Chi-A	.931	27	12	42	4	1	1
1982	KC-A	.951	40	26	72	5	7	4
1983	KC-A	.960	60	23	91	5	7	7
1984	KC-A	.970	105	59	138	6	13	14
1985	KC-A	.946	26	5	30	2	2	4
1986	KC-A	.935	35	15	57	5	8	1
Total	10	.952	377	195	602	0	54	43

SS

YEAR	TM/L	PCT	G	PO	A	E	DP	FR
1976	Tex-A	—	1	0	0	0	0	0
1978	Chi-A	.961	28	34	64	4	9	3
1979	Chi-A	.961	119	161	362	21	54	-8
1980	Chi-A	.975	76	97	248	9	46	17
1981	Chi-A	.913	13	7	14	2	2	0
1982	KC-A	1.000	7	5	13	0	3	1
1984	KC-A	1.000	2	0	2	0	0	0
1985	KC-A	.900	13	7	11	2	3	-1
1986	KC-A	.941	17	5	11	1	1	-1
Total	9	.964	276	316	725	9	118	11

2B

YEAR	TM/L	PCT	G	PO	A	E	DP	FR
1976	Tex-A	1.000	3	4	6	0	1	0
1978	Chi-A	.966	35	54	90	5	16	-3
1979	Chi-A	.989	25	42	48	1	13	0
1980	Chi-A	1.000	5	5	11	0	2	2
1981	Chi-A	1.000	5	8	9	0	5	2
1982	KC-A	1.000	15	25	23	0	7	1
1983	KC-A	1.000	3	2	9	0	2	1
1984	KC-A	.975	22	28	49	2	14	3
1985	KC-A	.988	20	35	46	1	11	6
1986	KC-A	1.000	12	10	20	0	6	3
Total	10	.983	145	213	311	9	77	15

1B

YEAR	TM/L	PCT	G	PO	A	E	DP	FR
1982	KC-A	1.000	14	22	4	0	1	1
1983	KC-A	1.000	6	13	0	0	0	0
1984	KC-A	1.000	1	0	1	0	0	0
1985	KC-A	—	1	0	0	0	0	0
1986	KC-A	—	1	0	0	0	0	0
Total	5	1.000	23	35	5	0	1	1

■ George Puccinelli OF

YEAR	TM/L	PCT	G	PO	A	E	DP	FR
1930	StL-N	1.000	3	2	0	0	0	-1
1932	StL-N	.942	30	59	6	4	1	1
1934	StL-A	.941	6	15	1	1	0	1
1936	Phi-A	.948	117	245	11	14	1	-2
Total	4	.947	156	321	18	19	2	-1

■ Kirby Puckett OF

YEAR	TM/L	PCT	G	PO	A	E	DP	FR
1984	Min-A	.993	128	438	**16**	3	4	**22**
1985	Min-A	.984	**161**	**465**	19	8	5	13
1986	Min-A	.986	**160**	429	8	6	3	3
1987	Min-A	.986	147	341	8	5	2	1
1988	Min-A	.994	**158**	**450**	12	3	4	13
1989	Min-A	.991	157	**438**	13	4	3	14
1990	Min-A	.989	141	354	9	4	3	2
Total	7	.989	1052	2915	85	3	24	68

2B

YEAR	TM/L	PCT	G	PO	A	E	DP	FR
1990	Min-A	—	1	0	0	0	0	0

3B

YEAR	TM/L	PCT	G	PO	A	E	DP	FR
1990	Min-A	—	1	0	0	0	0	0

SS

YEAR	TM/L	PCT	G	PO	A	E	DP	FR
1990	Min-A	—	1	0	0	0	0	-1

■ Terry Puhl OF

YEAR	TM/L	PCT	G	PO	A	E	DP	FR
1977	Hou-N	.992	59	119	3	1	0	0
1978	Hou-N	.992	148	386	6	3	2	**19**
1979	Hou-N	**1.000**	152	352	7	0	3	-6
1980	Hou-N	.991	135	311	14	3	3	14
1981	Hou-N	**1.000**	88	185	5	0	1	3
1982	Hou-N	.989	138	257	4	3	3	-2
1983	Hou-N	.991	124	220	4	2	1	-5
1984	Hou-N	.986	126	213	6	3	4	-4
1985	Hou-N	1.000	53	92	3	0	1	-2
1986	Hou-N	1.000	47	65	0	0	0	-4
1987	Hou-N	.980	40	48	0	1	0	1
1988	Hou-N	.983	78	116	2	2	0	-1
1989	Hou-N	1.000	103	204	3	0	0	-1
1990	Hou-N	1.000	8	8	0	0	0	-1
Total	14	.993	1299	2576	57	8	18	11

1B

YEAR	TM/L	PCT	G	PO	A	E	DP	FR
1989	Hou-N	1.000	3	8	0	0	1	0
1990	Hou-N	1.000	1	1	0	0	0	0
Total	2	1.000	4	9	0	0	1	0

■ Luis Pujols C

YEAR	TM/L	PCT	G	PO	A	E	DP	FR
1977	Hou-N	1.000	6	18	4	0	0	0
1978	Hou-N	.981	55	271	33	6	2	2
1979	Hou-N	.993	26	136	6	1	0	1
1980	Hou-N	.990	75	348	35	4	5	-2
1981	Hou-N	.995	39	192	14	1	1	0
1982	Hou-N	.991	64	295	39	3	3	8
1983	Hou-N	.971	39	180	20	6	0	6
1984	KC-A	1.000	4	9	0	0	0	0
1985	Tex-A	1.000	1	1	0	0	0	0
Total	9	.987	309	1450	151	1	11	15

1B

YEAR	TM/L	PCT	G	PO	A	E	DP	FR
1978	Hou-N	1.000	1	1	0	0	0	0

3B

YEAR	TM/L	PCT	G	PO	A	E	DP	FR
1980	Hou-N	1.000	1	1	0	0	0	0

■ Blondie Purcell OF

YEAR	TM/L	PCT	G	PO	A	E	DP	FR
1879	Syr-N	.773	47	64	4	20	0	-11
	Cin-N	.750	10	18	3	7	0	0
	Yr	.767	57	82	7	27	0	-11
1880	Cin-N	.814	55	78	14	21	1	-3
1881	Cle-N	.786	20	40	4	12	0	-2
	Buf-N	.706	25	32	4	15	0	-6
	Yr	.748	45	72	8	**27**	0	-8
1882	Buf-N	.820	82	144	11	34	0	-7
1883	Phi-N	.841	44	60	14	14	2	1
1884	Phi-N	.874	103	182	12	28	1	-1
1885	Phi-a	.858	66	78	13	15	1	-1
	Bos-N	.840	21	19	2	4	0	-3
1886	Bal-a	.867	26	35	4	6	0	0
1887	Bal-a	.925	**140**	203	18	18	5	-4
1888	Bal-a	.906	100	145	9	16	3	-6
	Phi-a	.903	17	25	3	3	1	1
	Yr	.905	117	170	12	19	4	-5
1889	Phi-a	.903	129	172	15	20	3	-10
1890	Phi-a	.910	110	170	17	10	3	-1
Total	12	.869	995	1465	147	243	20	-53

3B

YEAR	TM/L	PCT	G	PO	A	E	DP	FR
1883	Phi-N	.777	46	60	111	49	7	3
1888	Phi-a	.667	1	1	1	1	0	0
Total	2	.776	47	61	112	0	7	3

SS

YEAR	TM/L	PCT	G	PO	A	E	DP	FR
1880	Cin-N	.750	1	0	3	1	0	-1
1886	Bal-a	—	1	0	0	0	0	-1

YEAR	TM/L	PCT	G	PO	A	E	DP	FR
1888	Bal-a	1.000	2	1	1	0	0	0
Total	3	.833	4	1	4	1	0	0
C								
1879	Syr-N	1.000	1	5	1	0	0	0
1B								
1888	Bal-a	—	1	0	0	0	0	0

■ Pid Purdy OF

YEAR	TM/L	PCT	G	PO	A	E	DP	FR
1926	Chi-A	1.000	9	17	1	0	0	0
1927	Cin-N	.946	16	35	0	2	0	-2
1928	Cin-N	.966	61	137	3	5	1	-3
1929	Cin-N	.978	42	84	3	2	0	-3
Total	4	.969	128	273	7	9	1	-8

■ Billy Purtell 3B

YEAR	TM/L	PCT	G	PO	A	E	DP	FR
1908	Chi-A	.940	25	18	60	5	5	6
1909	Chi-A	.929	71	90	158	19	11	3
1910	Chi-A	.907	102	117	233	36	16	4
	Bos-A	.908	41	41	87	13	2	-3
	Yr	.907	143	158	320	49	18	1
1911	Bos-A	.867	15	22	30	8	1	0
1914	Det-A	.946	16	19	34	3	2	0
Total	5	.915	270	307	602	4	37	10
2B								
1909	Chi-A	.970	32	72	90	5	13	2
1911	Bos-A	1.000	3	4	5	0	0	0
1914	Det-A	1.000	1	1	2	0	0	0
Total	3	.972	36	77	97	5	13	2
SS								
1910	Bos-A	.906	8	8	21	3	2	-1
1911	Bos-A	.846	3	3	8	2	0	0
1914	Det-A	.500	2	1	0	1	0	0
Total	3	.872	13	12	29	6	2	-1
OF								
1911	Bos-A	—	1	0	0	0	0	-1

■ Pat Putnam 1B

YEAR	TM/L	PCT	G	PO	A	E	DP	FR
1977	Tex-A	1.000	7	35	1	0	3	-1
1978	Tex-A	1.000	4	15	1	0	1	0
1979	Tex-A	.994	96	832	62	5	65	0
1980	Tex-A	.992	137	979	80	9	107	5
1981	Tex-A	.993	94	769	64	6	65	4
1982	Tex-A	.990	39	285	24	3	26	1
1983	Sea-A	.994	125	1067	85	7	105	3
1984	Sea-A	.974	6	32	6	1	7	1
Total	8	.993	508	4014	323	1	379	13
OF								
1981	Tex-A	.667	3	2	0	1	0	-1
1982	Tex-A	1.000	1	2	0	0	0	0
1984	Sea-A	1.000	13	14	0	0	0	-1
Total	3	.947	17	18	0	1	0	-2
3B								
1980	Tex-A	—	1	0	0	0	0	0
1982	Tex-A	—	1	0	0	0	0	0
Total	2	—	2	0	0	0	0	0

■ Jim Pyburn OF

YEAR	TM/L	PCT	G	PO	A	E	DP	FR
1955	Bal-A	1.000	1	1	0	0	0	0
1956	Bal-A	.975	77	114	5	3	3	7
1957	Bal-A	1.000	28	41	3	0	0	6
Total	3	.982	106	156	8	3	3	13
3B								
1955	Bal-A	1.000	33	26	36	0	1	-4
C								
1957	Bal-A	—	1	0	0	0	0	0

■ Frankie Pytlak C

YEAR	TM/L	PCT	G	PO	A	E	DP	FR
1932	Cle-A	1.000	12	40	7	0	0	3
1933	Cle-A	1.000	69	246	57	0	11	10
1934	Cle-A	.989	88	325	38	4	4	-11
1935	Cle-A	.984	48	166	20	3	2	-1
1936	Cle-A	.996	58	224	35	1	6	-6
1937	Cle-A	.986	115	559	80	9	13	8
1938	Cle-A	.987	99	475	56	7	11	-8
1939	Cle-A	1.000	51	227	24	0	5	2
1940	Cle-A	.996	58	235	30	1	5	7
1941	Bos-A	.991	91	416	41	4	7	0
1945	Bos-A	1.000	6	17	6	0	0	1
1946	Bos-A	1.000	4	28	1	0	0	2
Total	12	.991	699	2958	395	9	64	7
OF								
1940	Cle-A	—	1	0	0	0	0	0

■ Joe Quest 2B

YEAR	TM/L	PCT	G	PO	A	E	DP	FR
1878	Ind-N	.876	62	228	196	60	27	1
1879	Chi-N	.925	83	263	331	48	30	14
1880	Chi-N	.895	80	223	270	58	26	4
1881	Chi-N	.929	77	238	249	37	28	5
1882	Chi-N	.879	41	113	127	33	18	-5
1883	Det-N	.897	37	114	112	26	25	0
	StL-a	.890	19	48	49	12	4	-6
1884	StL-a	.894	81	232	242	56	39	-9
	Pit-a	.938	7	20	25	3	4	0
	Yr	.898	88	252	267	59	43	-9
1885	Det-N	.898	39	107	122	26	10	0
1886	Phi-a	.789	2	7	8	4	1	0
Total	9	.902	528	1593	1731	363	212	4
SS								
1880	Chi-N	.909	2	2	8	1	0	0
1881	Chi-N	1.000	1	4	3	0	0	0
1882	Chi-N	.333	1	0	1	2	0	-1
1884	Pit-a	.857	5	7	7	4	2	1
1885	Det-N	.836	15	10	46	11	3	-2
1886	Phi-a	.847	41	56	138	35	15	1
Total	6	.846	65	79	213	3	20	-1
3B								
1880	Chi-N	.500	1	1	1	0	1	0
OF								
1885	Det-N	1.000	1	0	1	0	0	0

■ Frank Quilici 2B

YEAR	TM/L	PCT	G	PO	A	E	DP	FR
1965	Min-A	.990	52	93	112	2	33	2
1967	Min-A	1.000	13	10	9	0	4	1
1968	Min-A	1.000	48	93	101	0	21	10
1969	Min-A	.994	36	84	81	1	15	17
1970	Min-A	.987	73	107	121	3	25	15
Total	5	.993	222	387	424	6	98	45
3B								
1967	Min-A	1.000	8	0	4	0	0	0
1968	Min-A	.968	40	28	64	3	9	8
1969	Min-A	.935	84	15	57	5	2	7
1970	Min-A	.864	27	7	12	3	1	1
Total	4	.944	159	50	137	1	12	16
SS								
1965	Min-A	1.000	4	3	8	0	1	1
1967	Min-A	.000	1	0	0	1	0	-1
1968	Min-A	.905	6	8	11	2	3	-1
1969	Min-A	1.000	1	0	1	0	0	0
1970	Min-A	—	1	0	0	0	0	0
Total	5	.912	13	11	20	3	4	-1
1B								
1968	Min-A	1.000	1	1	0	0	1	0

■ Joe Quinn 2B

YEAR	TM/L	PCT	G	PO	A	E	DP	FR
1886	StL-N	.823	15	33	32	14	3	-4
1888	Bos-N	.914	38	97	115	20	11	-7
1889	Bos-N	.926	47	105	144	20	17	-9
1890	Bos-P	**.942**	130	431	395	51	70	15
1891	Bos-N	.938	124	275	364	42	44	-23
1892	Bos-N	**.951**	143	356	426	40	75	2
1893	StL-N	.942	**135**	354	366	44	63	-30
1894	StL-N	.952	106	341	339	34	**74**	22
1895	StL-N	.946	**134**	**359**	390	43	**63**	-2
1896	StL-N	.956	48	92	167	12	7	3
	Bal-N	.951	8	18	21	2	3	-2
	Yr	.955	56	110	188	14	10	1
1897	Bal-N	.938	11	24	36	4	3	1
1898	Bal-N	.857	1	3	3	1	0	0
	StL-N	.962	62	139	191	13	19	-2
	Yr	**.960**	63	142	194	14	19	-2
1899	Cle-N	.962	147	350	440	31	61	3
1900	Cin-N	.933	14	26	30	4	3	-6
	Yr	.947	88	180	199	21	27	-24
1901	Was-A	.954	66	158	177	16	17	-14
Total	15	.946	1303	3315	3805	408	557	-71
SS								
1884	StL-U	.800	1	1	3	1	0	0
1886	StL-N	.333	2	0	1	2	1	0
1889	Bos-N	.860	63	67	167	38	19	-20
1896	Bal-N	1.000	1	2	2	0	0	0
1897	Bal-N	.974	21	56	57	3	10	3
1898	StL-N	.927	41	79	149	18	11	0
1900	StL-N	.909	6	17	13	3	1	-3
Total	7	.904	135	222	392	5	42	-20
OF								
1884	StL-U	.833	3	5	0	1	0	0
1885	StL-N	.875	57	83	8	13	0	-8
1886	StL-N	.895	48	89	13	12	1	5
1896	Bal-N	.875	8	7	0	1	0	-2
1897	Bal-N	1.000	6	7	1	0	0	-1
1898	Bal-N	—	1	0	0	0	0	0
	StL-N	1.000	1	2	0	0	0	0
	Yr	1.000	2	2	0	0	0	0
Total	6	.888	124	193	22	7	1	-6
1B								
1884	StL-U	.945	100	1033	33	62	55	0
1885	StL-N	.975	11	113	4	3	3	0
1886	StL-N	.948	7	72	1	4	8	-1
1897	Bal-N	.938	2	14	1	1	2	0
Total	4	.948	120	1232	39	0	68	-1
3B								
1885	StL-N	.836	31	33	64	19	1	-2
1886	StL-N	.867	4	5	8	2	0	1
1889	Bos-N	.833	2	2	3	1	0	0
1896	Bal-N	.952	5	4	16	1	0	1
1897	Bal-N	.946	37	41	81	7	6	7
1898	Bal-N	.893	8	12	13	3	1	1
1900	StL-N	1.000	1	1	3	0	0	0
Total	7	.897	88	98	188	3	8	8

■ Tom Quinn C

YEAR	TM/L	PCT	G	PO	A	E	DP	FR
1886	Pit-a	.929	3	10	3	1	0	-1
1889	Bal-a	.925	55	290	81	30	10	7
1890	Pit-P	.888	55	203	58	33	3	-5
Total	3	.910	113	503	142	4	13	1

■ Luis Quinones 3B

YEAR	TM/L	PCT	G	PO	A	E	DP	FR
1983	Oak-A	1.000	4	0	2	0	0	0
1986	SF-N	.852	31	5	18	4	2	-3
1987	Chi-N	—	1	0	0	0	0	0
1988	Cin-N	.889	4	2	6	1	0	0
1989	Cin-N	.956	50	31	99	6	5	1
1990	Cin-N	.981	22	12	41	1	0	4
Total	6	.947	112	50	166	2	7	2
2B								
1983	Oak-A	1.000	6	11	15	0	3	2
1986	SF-N	1.000	8	8	16	0	2	0
1987	Chi-N	1.000	4	3	7	0	1	0
1988	Cin-N	1.000	4	4	3	0	1	0
1989	Cin-N	.979	53	81	107	4	20	-7
1990	Cin-N	.964	13	22	31	2	12	5
Total	6	.981	88	129	179	6	39	0
SS								
1983	Oak-A	.933	3	7	7	1	4	1
1986	SF-N	.922	33	15	32	4	6	-4
1987	Chi-N	.965	28	32	51	3	9	-6
1988	Cin-N	.974	10	9	28	1	4	2
1989	Cin-N	1.000	5	0	7	0	0	1
1990	Cin-N	.875	9	8	13	3	3	1
Total	6	.946	88	71	138	2	26	-5
OF								
1983	Oak-A	1.000	4	4	0	0	0	0
1B								
1990	Cin-N	1.000	1	2	0	0	0	0

■ Rey Quinones SS

YEAR	TM/L	PCT	G	PO	A	E	DP	FR
1986	Bos-A	.940	62	86	150	15	26	-8
	Sea-A	.945	36	57	97	9	28	1
	Yr	.942	98	143	247	**24**	54	-7
1987	Sea-A	.959	135	204	384	25	76	-10
1988	Sea-A	.963	135	202	396	23	103	3
1989	Sea-A	.889	7	5	19	3	3	-2
	Pit-N	.934	69	94	174	19	24	-11
Total	4	.952	444	648	1220	4	260	-27

■ Carlos Quintana 1B

YEAR	TM/L	PCT	G	PO	A	E	DP	FR
1989	Bos-A	1.000	1	6	0	0	0	0
1990	Bos-A	.987	148	1188	**137**	17	116	**14**
Total	2	.987	149	1194	137	7	116	14
OF								
1988	Bos-A	1.000	3	4	0	0	0	0
1989	Bos-A	.926	21	25	0	2	0	-1
1990	Bos-A	1.000	3	2	0	0	0	0
Total	3	.939	27	31	0	2	0	-1

■ Jamie Quirk C

YEAR	TM/L	PCT	G	PO	A	E	DP	FR
1979	KC-A	.944	9	15	2	1	0	1
1980	KC-A	.966	15	48	9	2	1	2
1981	KC-A	.985	22	58	9	1	1	0
1982	KC-A	1.000	29	77	6	0	0	1
1983	StL-N	.929	22	68	11	6	1	-5
1984	Cle-A	—	1	0	0	0	0	0
1985	KC-A	.986	17	64	8	1	1	-4
1986	KC-A	.989	41	247	30	3	2	8
1987	KC-A	.986	108	532	40	8	3	-4
1988	KC-A	.982	79	409	31	8	5	13
1989	NY-A	1.000	6	28	4	0	2	1
	Oak-A	1.000	2	0	1	0	0	0
	Bal-A	1.000	24	96	9	0	1	3
	Yr	1.000	32	124	14	0	3	4
1990	Oak-A	.977	37	151	17	4	3	-1
Total	12	.983	412	1793	177	4	20	15
3B								
1975	KC-A	1.000	2	0	2	0	0	0
1976	KC-A	.875	11	4	10	2	0	-1
1977	Mil-A	.800	8	1	3	1	1	0
1978	KC-A	.926	10	10	15	2	1	2
1979	KC-A	1.000	3	1	4	0	0	1
1980	KC-A	.929	28	21	57	6	2	0
1981	KC-A	.857	8	5	13	3	1	-1
1982	KC-A	—	1	0	0	0	0	0
1983	StL-N	1.000	7	0	2	0	0	0
1984	Chi-A	1.000	1	1	0	0	0	0
1986	KC-A	.976	24	13	28	1	7	0
1988	KC-A	1.000	1	0	3	0	0	1
1989	Oak-A	.500	3	0	1	1	0	0
1990	Oak-A	.833	8	4	1	1	1	-1
Total	14	.921	115	60	139	7	13	1
OF								
1975	KC-A	.909	10	19	1	2	0	0
1977	Mil-A	.950	10	18	1	1	1	0
1980	KC-A	1.000	7	6	0	0	0	0
1981	KC-A	—	1	0	0	0	0	0
1982	KC-A	—	1	0	0	0	0	0
1986	KC-A	—	1	0	0	0	0	0
1989	Oak-A	1.000	1	2	0	0	0	0
1990	Oak-A	—	1	0	0	0	0	0
Total	8	.940	32	45	2	3	1	0
1B								
1976	KC-A	1.000	2	3	0	0	1	0
1980	KC-A	1.000	1	3	0	0	0	0
1982	KC-A	1.000	6	33	6	0	1	1
1985	KC-A	1.000	1	2	0	0	0	0
1986	KC-A	1.000	6	43	6	0	4	1
1988	KC-A	1.000	1	3	0	0	0	0
1989	KC-A	1.000	1	3	0	0	0	0
1990	Oak-A	1.000	8	13	0	0	0	0
Total	8	1.000	26	103	12	0	6	2
SS								
1976	KC-A	1.000	12	2	4	0	1	0
1978	KC-A	1.000	2	1	1	0	0	0
1979	KC-A	1.000	5	0	1	0	0	1
1983	StL-N	—	1	0	0	0	0	0
1987	KC-A	—	1	0	0	0	0	-1
1989	NY-A	—	1	0	0	0	0	0
Total	6	1.000	22	3	8	0	1	0
2B								
1981	KC-A	1.000	1	0	1	0	0	0

■ Marv Rackley OF

YEAR	TM/L	PCT	G	PO	A	E	DP	FR
1947	Bro-N	1.000	2	7	0	0	0	2
1948	Bro-N	.949	74	143	7	8	1	-2
1949	Bro-N	1.000	3	2	0	0	0	0
	Pit-N	1.000	8	22	0	0	0	0
	Bro-N	.986	44	72	0	1	0	-3
	Yr	.990	55	96	0	1	0	-3
Total	3	.966	131	246	7	9	1	-3

■ Rip Radcliff OF

YEAR	TM/L	PCT	G	PO	A	E	DP	FR
1934	Chi-A	.946	14	35	0	2	0	0
1935	Chi-A	.968	142	231	8	8	1	-16
1936	Chi-A	.936	132	213	6	15	2	-21
1937	Chi-A	.966	139	273	9	10	5	-5
1938	Chi-A	.979	99	230	5	5	0	2
1939	Chi-A	.970	78	130	1	4	0	-12
1940	StL-A	.973	139	282	8	8	2	-7
1941	StL-A	1.000	14	26	0	0	0	-2

(continued)

YEAR	TM/L	PCT	G	PO	A	E	DP	FR
	Det-A	.970	87	155	6	5	1	-6
	Yr	.974	101	181	6	5	1	-8
1942	Det-A	.978	24	43	1	1	1	-2
1943	Det-A	1.000	19	37	1	0	1	-2
Total	10	.967	887	1655	45	8	13	-71
1B								
1938	Chi-A	.980	23	236	10	5	25	-3
1939	Chi-A	.989	20	170	11	2	11	0
1940	StL-A	.964	4	25	2	1	2	0
1941	StL-A	1.000	3	24	1	0	2	-1
1942	Det-A	1.000	4	40	5	0	0	1
1943	Det-A	1.000	1	2	2	0	0	1
Total	6	.985	55	497	31	8	40	-2

■ Dave Rader C

YEAR	TM/L	PCT	G	PO	A	E	DP	FR
1971	SF-N	1.000	1	1	0	0	0	0
1972	SF-N	.985	127	661	45	11	7	-14
1973	SF-N	.991	148	701	48	7	5	-14
1974	SF-N	.984	109	461	38	8	4	-9
1975	SF-N	.984	94	457	37	8	7	-3
1976	SF-N	.984	81	349	32	6	4	-8
1977	StL-N	.976	38	147	13	4	2	4
1978	Chi-N	.977	114	412	51	11	7	-13
1979	Phi-N	.932	25	62	6	5	1	-4
1980	Bos-A	.981	34	140	15	3	4	3
Total	10	.983	771	3391	285	3	41	-58

■ Doug Rader 3B

YEAR	TM/L	PCT	G	PO	A	E	DP	FR
1967	Hou-N	1.000	7	7	15	0	1	1
1968	Hou-N	.930	86	83	168	19	14	2
1969	Hou-N	.945	154	126	307	25	34	**15**
1970	Hou-N	**.966**	**154**	**147**	**357**	18	**39**	**24**
1971	Hou-N	.946	135	93	275	**21**	28	2
1972	Hou-N	.958	**152**	119	**340**	20	**31**	18
1973	Hou-N	.945	**152**	**134**	296	**25**	24	-5
1974	Hou-N	.965	152	128	347	17	28	5
1975	Hou-N	**.971**	124	111	257	11	24	8
1976	SD-N	.955	137	109	318	20	22	14
1977	SD-N	.961	51	43	104	6	9	1
	Tor-A	.966	45	38	103	5	2	1
Total	11	.956	1349	1138	2887	187	256	86
1B								
1967	Hou-N	.972	36	263	18	8	26	-2
1968	Hou-N	.943	5	47	3	3	4	-1
1969	Hou-N	.933	4	14	0	1	2	-1
1970	Hou-N	1.000	1	2	0	0	0	0
1977	Tor-A	.966	7	54	3	2	1	-1
Total	5	.967	53	380	24	4	33	-5
SS								
1975	Hou-N	1.000	2	3	2	0	1	0
OF								
1977	Tor-A	1.000	1	5	0	0	0	1

■ Paul Radford OF

YEAR	TM/L	PCT	G	PO	A	E	DP	FR
1883	Bos-N	.836	72	86	16	20	2	-3
1884	Pro-N	.882	96	146	26	23	4	4
1885	Pro-N	.852	88	141	26	29	7	6
1886	KC-N	.890	92	125	29	19	5	4
1887	NY-a	.893	37	59	8	8	1	1
1888	Bro-a	.944	88	180	22	12	2	8
1889	Cle-N	.942	**136**	205	24	14	6	0
1890	Cle-P	.895	80	137	16	18	5	-2
1891	Bos-a	1.000	4	9	2	0	1	2
1892	Was-N	.933	62	86	12	7	7	3
1893	Was-N	.901	123	198	29	25	4	7
1894	Was-N	.907	24	32	7	4	0	0
Total	12	.901	902	1404	217	179	44	30
SS								
1885	Pro-N	.848	16	13	43	10	0	-4
1886	KC-N	.859	30	52	107	26	8	5
1887	NY-a	.833	76	121	229	70	28	-1
1890	Cle-P	.908	36	74	123	20	13	6
1891	Bos-a	.906	131	230	453	71	51	18
1892	Was-N	.752	20	28	51	26	7	-12
1894	Was-N	.852	47	125	181	53	15	5
Total	7	.869	356	643	1187	276	122	17
3B								
1889	Cle-N	—	1	0	0	0	0	0
1890	Cle-P	.939	7	11	20	2	1	3
1892	Was-N	.860	54	65	125	31	6	0
Total	3	.870	62	76	145	3	7	3
2B								
1885	Pro-N	.500	1	1	0	1	0	0
1886	KC-N	.667	1	2	0	1	0	-1
1887	NY-a	.904	18	46	57	11	7	-1
1888	Bro-a	1.000	2	6	6	0	1	1
1890	Cle-P	.944	4	5	12	1	0	1
1892	Was-N	.895	2	7	10	2	2	2
1893	Was-N	1.000	1	0	4	0	0	0
1894	Was-N	.883	25	62	59	16	8	-6
Total	8	.896	54	129	148	2	18	-4

■ Tim Raines OF

YEAR	TM/L	PCT	G	PO	A	E	DP	FR
1980	Mon-N	1.000	1	2	0	0	0	0
1981	Mon-N	.976	81	160	6	4	0	-1
1982	Mon-N	.992	120	232	7	2	1	2
1983	Mon-N	.988	154	307	21	4	3	13
1984	Mon-N	.988	160	420	8	5	1	4
1985	Mon-N	.993	146	284	8	2	4	1
1986	Mon-N	.979	147	270	13	6	1	3
1987	Mon-N	.988	139	297	9	4	1	9
1988	Mon-N	.988	108	235	5	3	1	4
1989	Mon-N	.996	139	253	7	1	0	-2
1990	Mon-N	.976	123	239	3	6	1	-5
Total	11	.987	1318	2699	87	7	13	28
2B								
1980	Mon-N	1.000	7	13	16	0	2	2
1981	Mon-N	1.000	1	2	2	0	0	0
1982	Mon-N	.968	36	61	119	6	11	-3
1983	Mon-N	1.000	7	7	2	0	0	-2
1984	Mon-N	.000	2	0	0	1	0	-1
Total	5	.969	53	83	139	7	13	-4

■ Bob Ramazzotti 2B

YEAR	TM/L	PCT	G	PO	A	E	DP	FR
1946	Bro-N	1.000	16	27	27	0	6	4
1948	Bro-N	1.000	1	1	1	0	0	0
1949	Chi-N	.897	4	11	15	3	5	1
1950	Chi-N	.961	31	65	81	6	17	-1
1951	Chi-N	1.000	6	10	15	0	2	3
1952	Chi-N	.979	50	90	143	5	28	-2
1953	Chi-N	.911	18	28	23	5	6	0
Total	7	.966	126	232	305	9	64	5
3B								
1946	Bro-N	.939	30	25	37	4	3	1
1948	Bro-N	1.000	2	1	0	0	0	0
1949	Bro-N	.833	3	2	3	1	0	-1
	Chi-N	.972	36	28	77	3	8	2
	Yr	.965	39	30	80	4	8	1
1950	Chi-N	.813	10	5	8	3	2	-1
1951	Chi-N	—	1	0	0	0	0	0
Total	5	.944	82	61	125	1	13	1
SS								
1949	Chi-N	1.000	12	20	35	0	7	3
1950	Chi-N	1.000	3	3	3	0	0	0
1951	Chi-N	.950	51	73	137	11	32	10
Total	3	.961	66	96	175	1	39	13

■ Mario Ramirez SS

YEAR	TM/L	PCT	G	PO	A	E	DP	FR
1980	NY-N	1.000	7	9	17	0	5	3
1981	SD-N	1.000	2	2	6	0	0	2
1982	SD-N	.963	8	9	17	1	3	1
1983	SD-N	.985	38	50	85	2	14	-2
1984	SD-N	.971	33	29	38	2	11	-1
1985	SD-N	.918	27	22	34	5	9	-4
Total	6	.970	115	121	197	0	42	-1
2B								
1980	NY-N	1.000	4	4	4	0	1	0
1982	SD-N	1.000	1	0	1	0	0	0
1984	SD-N	1.000	2	2	0	0	1	0
1985	SD-N	1.000	7	3	4	0	0	0
Total	4	1.000	14	9	9	0	2	0
3B								
1980	NY-N	—	3	0	0	0	0	0
1981	SD-N	1.000	2	3	5	0	1	2
1982	SD-N	1.000	1	1	3	0	0	1
1983	SD-N	1.000	1	0	1	0	0	0
1984	SD-N	.909	6	3	7	1	0	0
Total	5	.958	13	7	16	1	1	3

■ Orlando Ramirez SS

YEAR	TM/L	PCT	G	PO	A	E	DP	FR
1974	Cal-A	.956	31	41	90	6	20	5
1975	Cal-A	.905	40	62	90	16	27	0
1976	Cal-A	.966	30	30	82	4	11	4
1977	Cal-A	.923	3	4	8	1	1	4
1979	Cal-A	.844	10	7	20	5	3	4
Total	5	.931	114	144	290	2	62	17
2B								
1977	Cal-A	1.000	5	2	9	0	1	5

■ Rafael Ramirez SS

YEAR	TM/L	PCT	G	PO	A	E	DP	FR
1980	Atl-N	.949	46	63	140	11	25	-10
1981	Atl-N	.942	95	181	306	**30**	55	-2
1982	Atl-N	.956	**157**	**300**	528	**38**	**130**	16
1983	Atl-N	.949	152	232	490	**39**	**116**	7
1984	Atl-N	.959	145	**251**	443	**30**	**94**	-3
1985	Atl-N	.954	133	214	451	**32**	**115**	8
1986	Atl-N	.952	86	137	282	21	62	14
1987	Atl-N	.946	38	59	99	9	30	-5
1988	Hou-N	.965	**154**	232	408	23	68	-10
1989	Hou-N	.945	149	189	326	**30**	60	-41
1990	Hou-N	.953	129	190	321	25	57	-18
Total	11	.953	1284	2048	3794	288	812	-44
3B								
1986	Atl-N	.930	57	18	89	8	6	0
1987	Atl-N	.947	12	7	11	1	3	-1
Total	2	.933	69	25	100	9	9	-1
OF								
1986	Atl-N	1.000	3	1	0	0	0	0

■ Domingo Ramos SS

YEAR	TM/L	PCT	G	PO	A	E	DP	FR
1978	NY-A	—	1	0	0	0	0	0
1980	Tor-A	1.000	2	3	4	0	2	0
1982	Sea-A	.920	8	9	14	2	0	-5
1983	Sea-A	.948	28	35	75	6	19	7
1984	Sea-A	.972	13	15	20	1	2	2
1985	Sea-A	.961	36	44	73	6	15	-7
1986	Sea-A	.966	21	31	53	3	8	7
1987	Sea-A	.953	25	32	70	5	17	5
1988	Cle-A	1.000	4	2	7	0	2	1
1989	Chi-N	.959	42	43	119	7	20	5
1990	Chi-N	.949	21	39	54	5	17	-1
Total	11	.955	201	253	489	5	102	12
3B								
1983	Sea-A	.909	8	7	13	2	1	0
1984	Sea-A	.911	38	18	23	4	4	1
1985	Sea-A	.929	7	3	10	1	1	-1
1986	Sea-A	.955	8	5	16	1	2	0
1987	Sea-A	1.000	7	5	6	0	0	1
1988	Cle-A	.500	7	2	1	1	0	-1
	Cal-A	1.000	8	2	8	0	0	0
	Yr	.917	10	2	9	1	0	-1
1989	Chi-N	.879	30	6	23	4	0	-2
1990	Chi-N	.932	66	23	46	5	2	-13
Total	8	.923	174	69	146	8	10	-13
2B								
1980	Tor-A	1.000	2	2	6	0	1	0
1983	Sea-A	.909	8	9	21	0	2	2
1984	Sea-A	1.000	3	4	5	0	0	1
1985	Sea-A	.953	20	25	36	3	9	0
1986	Sea-A	.956	16	19	24	2	6	4
1987	Sea-A	1.000	6	10	12	0	2	1
1988	Cle-A	1.000	11	12	22	0	6	2
1990	Chi-N	—	1	0	0	0	0	0
Total	8	.976	67	81	126	5	26	10
1B								
1984	Sea-A	1.000	5	14	1	0	4	0
1985	Sea-A	1.000	14	15	0	0	1	-1
1988	Cle-A	1.000	5	21	5	0	0	1
Total	3	1.000	24	50	6	0	5	0
OF								
1988	Cal-A	—	1	0	0	0	0	0

■ Mike Ramsey 2B

YEAR	TM/L	PCT	G	PO	A	E	DP	FR
1980	StL-N	.960	24	36	59	4	13	1
1981	StL-N	1.000	1	2	2	0	0	0
1982	StL-N	.963	43	93	115	8	25	4
1983	StL-N	.968	66	76	106	6	29	1
1984	StL-N	1.000	7	3	12	0	1	3
	Mon-N	.952	12	10	10	1	3	1
	Yr	.972	19	13	22	1	4	4
1985	LA-N	.800	2	1	3	1	0	0
Total	6	.964	155	221	307	0	71	10
SS								
1978	StL-N	.909	4	4	6	1	3	5
1980	StL-N	.915	20	25	29	5	6	-1
1981	StL-N	.966	35	52	118	6	20	12
1982	StL-N	.991	22	37	73	1	15	4
1983	StL-N	.961	20	15	34	2	2	1
1984	StL-N	1.000	7	5	6	0	3	2
	Mon-N	.975	26	26	51	2	12	1
	Yr	.978	33	31	57	2	15	3
1985	LA-N	.923	4	4	8	1	1	0
Total	7	.965	138	168	325	8	62	24
3B								
1980	StL-N	1.000	8	1	6	0	0	0
1981	StL-N	1.000	5	2	6	0	1	1
1982	StL-N	.973	28	5	31	1	2	2
1983	StL-N	1.000	8	3	9	0	3	1
1984	StL-N	—	1	0	0	0	0	0
Total	5	.984	50	11	52	1	6	4
OF								
1981	StL-N	—	1	0	0	0	0	0
1982	StL-N	—	2	0	0	0	0	0
1983	StL-N	—	1	0	0	0	0	0
Total	3	—	4	0	0	0	0	0

■ Bob Randall 2B

YEAR	TM/L	PCT	G	PO	A	E	DP	FR
1976	Min-A	.969	153	327	423	**24**	**124**	-6
1977	Min-A	.985	101	222	297	8	74	**10**
1978	Min-A	.983	116	231	345	10	81	10
1979	Min-A	.983	71	130	166	5	48	7
1980	Min-A	1.000	1	0	1	0	0	0
Total	5	.979	442	910	1232	7	327	21
3B								
1977	Min-A	—	1	0	0	0	0	0
1978	Min-A	—	2	0	0	0	0	0
1979	Min-A	1.000	7	0	3	0	0	0
1980	Min-A	.909	4	1	9	1	1	0
Total	4	.929	14	1	12	1	1	0
1B								
1977	Min-A	—	1	0	0	0	0	0
SS								
1979	Min-A	—	1	0	0	0	0	0
OF								
1979	Min-A	—	1	0	0	0	0	0

■ Len Randle 3B

YEAR	TM/L	PCT	G	PO	A	E	DP	FR
1974	Tex-A	.935	89	92	167	18	23	-7
1975	Tex-A	.975	17	10	29	1	3	1
1976	Tex-A	1.000	2	0	1	0	0	0
1977	NY-N	.961	110	98	221	13	25	1
1978	NY-N	.967	124	108	215	11	21	-6
1980	Chi-N	.929	111	76	225	23	7	-2
1981	Sea-A	.986	59	38	105	2	8	0
1982	Sea-A	.964	9	7	20	1	1	7
Total	8	.953	521	429	983	9	88	-6
2B								
1971	Was-A	.967	66	178	178	12	50	5
1972	Tex-A	.952	65	151	166	16	38	3
1973	Tex-A	.964	5	18	9	1	3	-1
1974	Tex-A	.977	40	98	115	5	30	9
1975	Tex-A	.973	79	205	232	12	61	10
1976	Tex-A	.971	113	291	319	18	63	-6
1977	NY-N	.976	20	43	40	2	8	-7
1978	NY-N	1.000	5	3	0	0	0	-1
1980	Chi-N	.978	17	40	48	2	5	-3
1981	Sea-A	.982	21	40	72	2	14	5
1982	Sea-A	.833	6	3	7	2	3	3
Total	11	.969	437	1070	1186	2	274	17
OF								
1972	Tex-A	1.000	2	5	0	0	0	0
1973	Tex-A	.500	2	1	0	1	0	0
1974	Tex-A	1.000	21	28	3	0	0	2
1975	Tex-A	.982	66	160	8	3	4	2
1976	Tex-A	.971	30	63	4	2	0	1
1979	NY-A	1.000	6	11	0	0	0	0
1980	Chi-N	1.000	5	3	0	0	0	0
1981	Sea-A	1.000	5	10	0	0	0	0
Total	9	.981	149	300	17	6	4	6
SS								
1972	Tex-A	.800	4	5	11	4	1	-2
1974	Tex-A	—	1	0	0	0	0	0
1975	Tex-A	—	1	0	0	0	0	0
1977	NY-N	—	1	0	0	0	0	0
1981	Sea-A	.667	3	1	1	1	1	0
Total	5	.783	10	6	12	5	2	-2

YEAR	TM/L	PCT	G	PO	A	E	DP	FR
	C							
1975	Tex-A	1.000	1	1	1	0	0	0

■ Willie Randolph 2B

YEAR	TM/L	PCT	G	PO	A	E	DP	FR
1975	Pit-N	.962	14	34	42	3	8	4
1976	NY-A	.974	124	307	415	19	87	15
1977	NY-A	.980	147	350	454	16	108	6
1978	NY-A	.978	134	296	400	16	80	-8
1979	NY-A	.985	**153**	**355**	**478**	13	**128**	9
1980	NY-A	.976	138	361	401	19	97	-7
1981	NY-A	.977	93	205	268	**11**	74	-3
1982	NY-A	.981	142	352	380	14	100	-3
1983	NY-A	.979	104	265	298	12	77	3
1984	NY-A	.983	142	334	419	13	**112**	11
1985	NY-A	.985	143	303	425	11	104	-3
1986	NY-A	.972	139	313	381	**20**	94	-12
1987	NY-A	.981	119	286	338	12	89	-2
1988	NY-A	.988	110	254	339	7	83	8
1989	LA-N	.987	140	260	412	9	85	-1
1990	LA-N	.969	26	50	73	4	10	-2
	Oak-A	.982	84	148	240	7	62	-11
Total	16	.980	1952	4473	5763	206	1398	4
	3B							
1975	Pit-N	.500	1	0	3	3	0	0

■ Merritt Ranew C

YEAR	TM/L	PCT	G	PO	A	E	DP	FR
1962	Hou-N	.980	58	357	35	8	1	-4
1963	Chi-N	.980	37	138	12	3	4	-5
1964	Chi-N	1.000	9	42	8	0	0	2
	Mil-N	1.000	3	11	2	0	0	-1
	Yr	1.000	12	53	10	0	0	1
1965	Cal-A	.988	24	78	7	1	1	-10
1969	Sea-A	.969	13	60	3	2	2	-5
Total	5	.982	144	686	67	4	8	-23
	1B							
1963	Chi-N	1.000	9	75	7	0	10	1
	OF							
1969	Sea-A	1.000	3	2	0	0	0	0
	3B							
1969	Sea-A	1.000	1	0	1	0	0	0

■ Goldie Rapp 3B

YEAR	TM/L	PCT	G	PO	A	E	DP	FR
1921	NY-N	.941	56	55	135	12	12	13
	Phi-N	.950	50	62	90	8	7	-2
	Yr	.945	106	117	225	20	19	11
1922	Phi-N	.948	117	117	249	20	20	6
1923	Phi-N	.947	45	58	84	8	9	-1
Total	3	.947	268	292	558	8	48	16
	SS							
1922	Phi-N	.846	2	6	5	2	0	-1
	2B							
1921	Phi-N	1.000	1	0	1	0	0	0

■ Bill Rariden C

YEAR	TM/L	PCT	G	PO	A	E	DP	FR
1909	Bos-N	.912	13	47	15	6	2	-3
1910	Bos-N	.962	49	177	75	10	6	3
1911	Bos-N	.952	65	291	110	20	2	1
1912	Bos-N	.964	73	297	103	15	6	-5
1913	Bos-N	.976	87	377	111	12	6	3
1914	Ind-F	.981	130	**714**	**215**	18	14	**19**
1915	New-F	.978	**142**	**709**	238	21	18	**21**
1916	NY-N	.972	**119**	**576**	144	21	10	-9
1917	NY-N	.971	100	354	74	13	7	-17
1918	NY-N	**.984**	63	195	45	4	3	-9
1919	Cin-N	.983	70	283	67	6	5	3
1920	Cin-N	.972	37	107	34	4	3	0
Total	12	.973	948	4127	1231	150	82	7
	3B							
1911	Bos-N	.875	3	0	7	1	0	0
	2B							
1911	Bos-N	.833	1	2	3	1	0	0

■ Morrie Rath 2B

YEAR	TM/L	PCT	G	PO	A	E	DP	FR
1910	Phi-A	—	3	0	0	0	0	0
1912	Chi-A	**.963**	**157**	353	**463**	31	46	18
1913	Chi-A	.962	86	159	251	16	32	-1
1919	Cin-N	.974	138	**345**	**452**	21	**59**	**13**
1920	Cin-N	**.977**	126	310	399	17	60	-7
Total	5	.970	510	1167	1565	5	197	23
	3B							
1909	Phi-A	.833	2	2	3	1	0	0
1910	Phi-A	.950	11	7	12	1	0	-2
	Cle-A	.950	22	29	47	4	4	2
	Yr	.950	33	36	59	5	4	0
1920	Cin-N	1.000	1	2	1	0	0	0
Total	3	.945	36	40	63	6	4	0
	SS							
1909	Phi-A	.846	4	18	15	6	2	2
1910	Cle-A	1.000	1	0	1	0	1	0
Total	2	.850	5	18	16	6	3	2
	OF							
1920	Cin-N	—	1	0	0	0	0	0

■ Paul Ratliff C

YEAR	TM/L	PCT	G	PO	A	E	DP	FR
1963	Min-A	.976	7	37	4	1	1	2
1970	Min-A	.980	53	183	11	4	4	-16
1971	Min-A	1.000	15	73	6	0	0	1
	Mil-A	.966	13	53	3	2	1	-1
	Yr	.985	28	126	9	2	1	0
1972	Mil-A	1.000	13	38	5	0	0	-3
Total	4	.983	101	384	29	7	6	-17

■ Johnny Rawlings 2B

YEAR	TM/L	PCT	G	PO	A	E	DP	FR
1914	Cin-N	.909	7	3	17	2	1	0
1917	Bos-N	.977	96	177	290	11	40	5
1918	Bos-N	.988	20	35	45	1	5	-2
1919	Bos-N	.961	58	105	169	11	20	-10
1920	Bos-N	1.000	1	1	1	0	0	0
	Phi-N	.970	97	221	321	17	53	-2
	Yr	.970	98	222	322	17	53	-2
1921	Phi-N	.954	60	138	215	17	32	5
	NY-N	.970	86	204	280	15	61	-1
	Yr	.963	146	342	495	32	93	4
1922	NY-N	.984	77	166	252	7	45	-4
1923	Pit-N	.958	119	294	388	30	68	-8
1925	Pit-N	.981	29	60	91	3	12	3
1926	Pit-N	.970	59	126	164	9	25	-3
Total	10	.968	709	1530	2233	123	362	-17
	SS							
1914	Cin-N	.889	5	8	8	2	0	0
	KC-F	.937	61	121	222	23	25	17
1915	KC-F	.926	120	209	366	46	36	-4
1917	Bos-N	.966	17	30	56	3	6	6
1918	Bos-N	.956	71	137	256	18	27	-2
1919	Bos-N	.960	5	9	15	1	2	0
1921	NY-N	1.000	1	2	0	0	0	0
Total	6	.939	280	516	923	3	96	17
	OF							
1917	Bos-N	.000	1	0	0	1	0	0
1918	Bos-N	1.000	18	36	8	0	2	4
1919	Bos-N	1.000	10	13	1	0	0	0
Total	3	.983	29	49	9	1	2	4
	3B							
1914	Cin-N	.885	10	6	17	3	1	0
1917	Bos-N	1.000	1	0	1	0	0	0
1922	NY-N	1.000	5	3	1	0	0	0
Total	3	.903	16	9	19	3	1	0

■ Irv Ray SS

YEAR	TM/L	PCT	G	PO	A	E	DP	FR
1888	Bos-N	.879	48	58	130	26	6	-9
1889	Bos-N	.875	5	3	11	2	1	-3
	Bal-a	.784	20	24	56	22	8	-8
1890	Bal-a	.894	38	40	104	17	7	-10
1891	Bal-a	.861	40	71	103	28	9	-14
Total	4	.863	151	196	404	5	31	-44
	OF							
1889	Bal-a	.867	6	12	1	2	0	0
1891	Bal-a	.885	64	97	11	14	1	0
Total	2	.883	70	109	12	6	1	0
	3B							
1889	Bos-N	.833	4	6	4	2	1	-1
	2B							
1888	Bos-N	.600	3	3	3	4	0	-3

■ Johnny Ray 2B

YEAR	TM/L	PCT	G	PO	A	E	DP	FR
1981	Pit-N	.987	31	52	96	2	22	2
1982	Pit-N	.977	**162**	**381**	**512**	21	**89**	8
1983	Pit-N	.983	151	319	452	13	102	17
1984	Pit-N	.984	149	331	400	12	90	-9
1985	Pit-N	.976	151	305	423	18	89	-15
1986	Pit-N	.993	151	280	479	5	89	5
1987	Pit-N	.981	119	248	358	12	84	4
	Cal-A	.986	29	52	90	2	19	-1
1988	Cal-A	.972	104	194	328	15	64	1
1989	Cal-A	.984	130	279	403	11	98	4
1990	Cal-A	.987	100	241	295	7	82	12
Total	10	.982	1277	2682	3836	118	828	28
	OF							
1988	Cal-A	.938	40	75	0	5	0	-6

■ Floyd Rayford 3B

YEAR	TM/L	PCT	G	PO	A	E	DP	FR
1980	Bal-A	.900	4	2	7	1	0	0
1981	Bal-A	.898	27	11	42	6	2	5
1983	StL-N	.883	33	13	40	7	3	-4
1984	Bal-A	.942	22	17	32	3	2	2
1985	Bal-A	.972	78	62	145	6	13	2
1986	Bal-A	.912	72	40	115	15	5	5
1987	Bal-A	.800	1	2	2	1	1	0
Total	7	.931	237	147	383	9	36	10
	C							
1982	Bal-A	1.000	2	0	1	0	0	0
1984	Bal-A	.991	66	287	35	3	2	8
1985	Bal-A	.992	29	114	7	1	0	-4
1986	Bal-A	.971	10	32	2	1	0	0
1987	Bal-A	.980	17	92	8	2	3	6
Total	5	.988	124	525	53	7	5	10
	2B							
1980	Bal-A	.833	1	1	4	1	0	0
	1B							
1984	Bal-A	1.000	1	6	0	0	1	0

■ Fred Raymer 2B

YEAR	TM/L	PCT	G	PO	A	E	DP	FR
1901	Chi-N	.947	3	6	12	1	0	1
1904	Bos-N	**.958**	144	272	351	27	38	7
1905	Bos-N	.949	134	256	381	34	35	-18
Total	3	.954	251	534	744	2	73	-10
	3B							
1901	Chi-N	.881	82	79	143	30	5	-9
	SS							
1901	Chi-N	.925	29	47	76	10	9	-10
	1B							
1901	Chi-N	.983	5	54	4	1	1	0
1905	Bos-N	1.000	1	13	0	0	0	0
Total	2	.986	6	67	4	1	1	0
	OF							
1905	Bos-N	1.000	1	1	0	0	0	0

■ Harry Raymond 3B

YEAR	TM/L	PCT	G	PO	A	E	DP	FR
1888	Lou-a	.884	31	59	55	15	1	0
1889	Lou-a	.886	129	206	261	60	23	0
1890	Lou-a	.874	119	182	241	61	18	-9
1892	Pit-N	.867	12	14	25	6	1	-1
	Was-N	.783	4	4	14	5	0	1
	Yr	.838	16	18	39	11	1	0
Total	4	.878	295	465	596	147	43	-9
	SS							
1890	Lou-a	.975	4	13	26	1	4	7
1891	Lou-a	.898	14	37	51	10	9	5
Total	2	.920	18	50	77	1	13	12
	OF							
1888	Lou-a	—	1	0	0	0	0	0
1889	Lou-a	1.000	1	1	0	0	0	0
Total	2	1.000	2	1	0	0	0	0

■ Randy Ready 3B

YEAR	TM/L	PCT	G	PO	A	E	DP	FR
1983	Mil-A	1.000	4	5	8	0	1	0
1984	Mil-A	.946	36	29	76	6	4	3
1985	Mil-A	1.000	7	4	7	0	0	-1
1986	Mil-A	.900	3	2	7	1	0	0
	SD-N	.667	1	0	2	1	0	0
1987	SD-N	.912	52	30	95	12	11	-1
1988	SD-N	.952	57	42	98	7	12	-5
1989	SD-N	.963	18	16	36	2	4	2
	Phi-N	.938	14	10	20	2	3	-2
	Yr	.953	32	26	56	4	7	0
Total	7	.940	192	138	349	1	35	-4
	OF							
1985	Mil-A	.989	37	85	5	1	1	1
1986	Mil-A	.950	11	19	0	1	0	-1
1987	SD-N	1.000	16	29	1	0	0	0
1988	SD-N	.947	16	17	1	1	0	0
1989	SD-N	—	1	0	0	0	0	0
	Phi-N	.962	36	47	4	2	3	-1
	Yr	.962	37	47	4	2	3	-1
1990	Phi-N	.980	30	32	2	0	0	-1
Total	6	.980	147	229	13	5	4	-2
	2B							
1985	Mil-A	1.000	3	4	2	0	0	-1
1986	Mil-A	.966	7	14	14	1	4	-3
1987	SD-N	.984	51	65	124	3	24	-2
1988	SD-N	.973	26	53	54	3	10	-3
1989	SD-N	—	2	0	0	0	0	0
	Phi-N	.864	7	7	12	3	3	-2
	Yr	.864	9	7	12	3	3	-2
1990	Phi-N	.985	28	46	84	2	18	-2
Total	6	.976	124	189	290	2	59	-9

■ Phil Reccius 3B

YEAR	TM/L	PCT	G	PO	A	E	DP	FR
1884	Lou-a	.845	51	42	89	24	4	-3
1885	Lou-a	.829	97	105	181	**59**	**17**	-2
1887	Cle-a	.877	62	85	137	31	18	8
1888	Lou-a	.750	2	0	3	1	0	-1
Total	4	.848	212	232	410	115	39	2
	OF							
1882	Lou-a	.778	4	6	1	2	0	0
1883	Lou-a	1.000	1	1	0	0	0	0
1886	Lou-a	.889	5	6	2	1	0	1
1887	Lou-a	.926	10	23	2	2	0	2
1890	Roc-a	—	1	0	0	0	0	0
Total	5	.891	21	36	5	5	0	3
	SS							
1884	Lou-a	.864	10	4	34	6	3	1
1887	Lou-a	1.000	1	1	2	0	0	0
Total	2	.872	11	5	36	6	3	1

■ Gary Redus OF

YEAR	TM/L	PCT	G	PO	A	E	DP	FR
1982	Cin-N	.970	20	29	3	1	0	-1
1983	Cin-N	.972	120	235	11	7	0	5
1984	Cin-N	.967	114	200	6	7	3	-3
1985	Cin-N	.986	85	140	3	2	0	-6
1986	Phi-N	.980	89	185	8	4	2	5
1987	Chi-A	.979	123	262	13	6	4	6
1988	Chi-A	.987	68	140	7	2	1	-3
	Pit-N	.957	19	42	2	2	0	1
1989	Pit-N	.944	16	16	1	1	1	0
1990	Pit-N	.882	7	14	1	2	0	-1
Total	9	.975	661	1263	55	4	11	3
	1B							
1989	Pit-N	.987	72	567	54	8	42	2
1990	Pit-N	.988	72	447	35	6	29	-2
Total	2	.987	144	1014	89	4	71	0

■ Jeff Reed C

YEAR	TM/L	PCT	G	PO	A	E	DP	FR
1984	Min-A	.977	18	41	2	1	1	2
1985	Min-A	1.000	7	9	3	0	0	0
1986	Min-A	.994	64	332	19	2	5	8
1987	Mon-N	.970	74	357	36	12	6	-4
1988	Mon-N	.995	39	197	20	1	1	2
	Cin-N	.993	49	271	18	2	2	6
	Yr	.994	88	468	38	3	3	8
1989	Cin-N	.988	99	504	50	7	2	-5
1990	Cin-N	.987	70	358	26	5	1	1
Total	7	.987	420	2069	174	0	18	-10

■ Jody Reed SS

YEAR	TM/L	PCT	G	PO	A	E	DP	FR
1987	Bos-A	1.000	4	8	16	0	7	3
1988	Bos-A	.971	94	123	242	11	49	-2
1989	Bos-A	.967	77	107	213	11	42	-11
1990	Bos-A	.944	50	63	106	10	21	-11
Total	4	.965	225	301	575	2	119	-21
	2B							
1987	Bos-A	1.000	2	3	10	0	2	2
1988	Bos-A	1.000	11	20	32	0	7	3
1989	Bos-A	.978	70	143	209	8	46	12
1990	Bos-A	.990	119	215	374	6	82	4
Total	4	.986	202	381	625	4	137	21
	3B							
1987	Bos-A	—	1	0	0	0	0	0
1988	Bos-A	1.000	4	4	8	0	1	1
1989	Bos-A	1.000	4	3	1	0	0	0
Total	3	1.000	9	7	9	0	1	1
	OF							
1989	Bos-A	1.000	1	2	0	0	0	0

■ Jack Reed OF

YEAR	TM/L	PCT	G	PO	A	E	DP	FR
1961	NY-A	.933	27	14	0	1	0	1
1962	NY-A	.941	75	48	0	3	0	5
1963	NY-A	1.000	89	73	2	0	0	9
Total	3	.972	191	135	2	4	0	15

■ Randy Reese OF

YEAR	TM/L	PCT	G	PO	A	E	DP	FR
1927	NY-N	.973	16	34	2	1	1	-1

YEAR	TM/L	PCT	G	PO	A	E	DP	FR
1928	NY-N	.941	64	109	3	7	0	-6
1929	NY-N	1.000	8	12	0	0	0	0
1930	NY-N	.957	32	66	1	3	0	-3
Total	4	.954	120	221	6	1	1	-10
3B								
1927	NY-N	.912	64	50	126	17	14	-2
1928	NY-N	.950	6	6	13	1	2	0
1929	NY-N	1.000	4	1	5	0	0	0
1930	NY-N	.889	10	4	12	2	1	0
Total	4	.916	84	61	156	0	17	-2
2B								
1928	NY-N	.961	26	53	93	6	11	-3
1929	NY-N	.960	44	104	163	11	24	2
Total	2	.960	70	157	256	7	35	-1
1B								
1927	NY-N	1.000	1	8	0	0	0	0
1928	NY-N	1.000	6	54	2	0	5	0
1930	NY-N	—	1	0	0	0	0	0
Total	3	1.000	8	62	2	0	5	0
SS								
1928	NY-N	.946	6	10	25	2	3	0

■ Pee Wee Reese   SS

YEAR	TM/L	PCT	G	PO	A	E	DP	FR
1940	Bro-N	.960	83	190	238	18	41	-14
1941	Bro-N	.946	151	346	473	47	76	8
1942	Bro-N	.959	151	337	482	35	99	17
1946	Bro-N	.966	152	285	463	26	104	-3
1947	Bro-N	.966	142	266	441	25	99	-2
1948	Bro-N	.962	149	335	453	31	93	10
1949	Bro-N	.977	155	316	454	18	93	2
1950	Bro-N	.963	134	282	398	26	94	1
1951	Bro-N	.953	154	292	422	35	106	-8
1952	Bro-N	.969	145	282	376	21	89	-11
1953	Bro-N	.966	135	265	380	23	83	-1
1954	Bro-N	.965	140	270	426	25	74	-4
1955	Bro-N	.965	142	239	404	23	86	-13
1956	Bro-N	.965	136	263	367	23	79	-10
1957	Bro-N	.947	23	46	62	6	16	0
1958	LA-N	.929	22	26	52	6	14	-5
Total	16	.962	2014	4040	5891	388	1246	-33
3B								
1950	Bro-N	1.000	7	9	16	0	1	1
1956	Bro-N	.931	12	6	21	2	1	1
1957	Bro-N	.943	75	51	166	13	5	1
1958	LA-N	.932	21	18	37	4	2	-3
Total	4	.945	115	84	240	9	9	10

■ Jimmie Reese   2B

YEAR	TM/L	PCT	G	PO	A	E	DP	FR
1930	NY-A	.974	48	86	99	5	26	-8
1931	NY-A	.972	61	173	168	10	44	5
1932	StL-N	.979	77	209	220	9	48	9
Total	3	.975	186	468	487	4	118	6
3B								
1930	NY-A	1.000	5	7	6	0	0	-1

■ Rich Reese   1B

YEAR	TM/L	PCT	G	PO	A	E	DP	FR
1964	Min-A	1.000	1	3	0	0	0	0
1965	Min-A	1.000	6	14	1	0	0	0
1967	Min-A	.990	36	93	3	1	5	-1
1968	Min-A	.991	87	620	38	6	36	-1
1969	Min-A	.993	117	924	56	7	97	-4
1970	Min-A	.992	146	1118	82	10	94	-2
1971	Min-A	.994	95	673	43	4	71	-1
1972	Min-A	.988	98	392	30	5	35	3
1973	Det-A	1.000	37	106	7	0	7	0
	Min-A	1.000	17	64	6	0	8	1
	Yr	1.000	54	170	13	0	15	1
Total	9	.992	640	4007	266	3	353	-5
OF								
1965	Min-A	—	1	0	0	0	0	0
1967	Min-A	1.000	10	14	1	0	0	1
1968	Min-A	1.000	15	22	0	0	0	0
1969	Min-A	1.000	5	5	1	0	0	1
1971	Min-A	1.000	9	6	1	0	0	1
1972	Min-A	.931	13	27	0	2	0	0
1973	Det-A	.966	21	28	0	1	0	-1
Total	7	.972	74	102	3	3	0	2

■ Bobby Reeves   3B

YEAR	TM/L	PCT	G	PO	A	E	DP	FR
1926	Was-A	.940	16	21	26	3	3	1
1927	Was-A	.810	12	6	11	4	0	-1
1928	Was-A	.913	8	6	15	2	1	0
1929	Bos-A	.912	131	152	242	38	27	1
1930	Bos-A	.895	62	63	125	22	21	2
Total	5	.906	229	248	419	9	52	3
SS								
1926	Was-A	1.000	1	2	3	0	1	1
1927	Was-A	.923	96	194	296	41	36	-6
1928	Was-A	.908	66	161	194	36	32	0
1929	Bos-A	—	2	0	0	0	0	0
1930	Bos-A	.917	15	17	16	3	1	-2
Total	5	.917	180	374	509	0	70	-7
2B								
1926	Was-A	—	1	0	0	0	0	-1
1927	Was-A	.938	2	7	8	1	1	0
1928	Was-A	.932	22	57	52	8	6	-4
1929	Bos-A	—	2	0	0	0	0	0
1930	Bos-A	.977	11	43	42	2	10	5
1931	Bos-A	.912	29	63	62	12	11	-8
Total	6	.936	67	170	164	3	28	-8
OF								
1928	Was-A	—	1	0	0	0	0	0
1B								
1929	Bos-A	—	1	0	0	0	0	0

■ Bill Regan   2B

YEAR	TM/L	PCT	G	PO	A	E	DP	FR
1926	Bos-A	.965	106	264	391	24	66	17
1927	Bos-A	.960	121	283	397	28	76	3
1928	Bos-A	.963	137	293	469	29	87	15
1929	Bos-A	.962	91	193	282	19	66	-17
1930	Bos-A	.963	127	308	439	29	92	-10
1931	Pit-N	.944	28	63	90	9	14	0
Total	6	.962	610	1404	2068	138	401	8
3B								
1929	Bos-A	.917	10	8	14	2	2	1
1930	Bos-A	1.000	2	1	1	0	0	0
Total	2	.923	12	9	15	2	2	1
OF								
1928	Bos-A	—	1	0	0	0	0	0
1B								
1929	Bos-A	1.000	1	2	0	0	0	0

■ Wally Rehg   OF

YEAR	TM/L	PCT	G	PO	A	E	DP	FR
1912	Pit-N	1.000	2	2	0	0	0	0
1913	Bos-A	.943	26	30	3	2	0	-3
1914	Bos-A	.980	43	45	4	1	3	-5
1915	Bos-A	1.000	1	1	0	0	0	0
1917	Bos-A	.956	86	122	9	6	2	-13
1918	Bos-N	.988	38	75	6	1	1	3
1919	Cin-N	.875	5	5	2	1	0	1
Total	7	.965	201	280	24	1	6	-17

■ Rick Reichardt   OF

YEAR	TM/L	PCT	G	PO	A	E	DP	FR
1964	LA-A	1.000	11	26	0	0	0	1
1965	Cal-A	.975	20	38	1	1	1	0
1966	Cal-A	.976	87	153	8	4	1	1
1967	Cal-A	.974	138	254	10	7	4	5
1968	Cal-A	.989	148	267	9	3	2	4
1969	Cal-A	.981	136	244	13	5	4	4
1970	Cal-A	1.000	1	1	0	0	0	0
	Was-A	.985	79	134	0	2	0	-4
	Yr	.985	80	135	0	2	0	-4
1971	Chi-A	.981	128	203	4	4	0	-11
1972	Chi-A	.981	90	157	2	3	1	-12
1973	Chi-A	1.000	37	61	1	0	1	-2
	KC-A	1.000	7	7	1	0	0	0
	Yr	1.000	44	68	2	0	1	-2
Total	10	.982	882	1545	49	9	14	-14
1B								
1969	Cal-A	1.000	3	26	3	0	1	0
1971	Chi-A	.981	9	50	3	1	2	0
Total	2	.988	12	76	6	1	3	0
3B								
1970	Was-A	—	1	0	0	0	0	0

■ Charlie Reilly   3B

YEAR	TM/L	PCT	G	PO	A	E	DP	FR
1889	Col-a	.923	6	7	17	2	0	2
1890	Col-a	.893	137	206	354	67	26	28
1891	Pit-N	.857	99	128	232	60	8	1
1892	Phi-N	.905	70	106	169	29	13	12
1893	Phi-N	.895	104	164	235	47	21	-1
1894	Phi-N	.874	28	34	56	13	3	3
1895	Phi-N	.870	11	20	20	6	2	1
1897	Was-N	.905	101	149	224	39	17	18
Total	8	.890	556	814	1307	263	90	64
SS								
1891	Pit-N	.918	11	17	28	4	1	1
1894	Phi-N	—	1	0	0	0	0	0
1895	Phi-N	.900	34	50	103	17	12	-3
Total	3	.904	46	67	131	1	13	-2
OF								
1891	Pit-N	.800	4	11	1	3	1	1
1892	Phi-N	.964	15	26	1	1	0	-1
1894	Phi-N	.875	5	3	1	0	0	-1
1895	Phi-N	1.000	1	3	0	0	0	0
Total	4	.920	25	43	3	4	1	-1
2B								
1892	Phi-N	.923	4	4	8	1	0	-1
1894	Phi-N	.897	4	12	14	3	1	1
1895	Phi-N	1.000	3	9	10	0	1	1
Total	3	.934	11	25	32	4	2	1
1B								
1894	Phi-N	1.000	1	4	0	0	0	0

■ John Reilly   1B

YEAR	TM/L	PCT	G	PO	A	E	DP	FR
1880	Cin-N	.947	72	615	13	35	36	-3
1883	Cin-a	.961	98	959	19	40	50	-1
1884	Cin-a	.971	103	977	26	30	60	0
1885	Cin-a	.963	107	1034	22	41	59	-1
1886	Cin-a	.967	110	1120	37	40	80	0
1887	Cin-a	.980	127	1267	33	26	84	-1
1888	Cin-a	.977	117	1264	42	31	73	-1
1889	Cin-a	.984	109	1143	30	19	76	-1
1890	Cin-N	.977	132	1392	38	33	77	-3
1891	Cin-N	.982	100	1104	26	21	60	-7
Total	10	.972	1075	10875	286	316	655	-20
OF								
1880	Cin-N	.500	3	1	0	1	0	0
1883	Cin-a	1.000	1	1	0	0	0	0
1884	Cin-a	1.000	3	2	0	0	0	-1
1885	Cin-a	.889	7	8	0	1	0	-2
1886	Cin-a	.778	6	6	1	2	0	-1
1887	Cin-a	1.000	9	24	1	0	0	1
1888	Cin-a	1.000	10	11	3	0	0	0
1889	Cin-a	1.000	2	2	0	0	0	-1
1890	Cin-N	1.000	1	1	0	0	0	0
1891	Cin-N	.915	36	57	8	6	1	0
Total	10	.926	78	113	13	0	1	-4
SS								
1884	Cin-a	—	1	0	0	0	0	0

■ Charlie Reipschlager   C

YEAR	TM/L	PCT	G	PO	A	E	DP	FR
1883	NY-a	.936	29	202	46	17	1	7
1884	NY-a	.925	51	369	109	39	3	17
1885	NY-a	.879	59	262	117	52	6	-11
1886	NY-a	.880	57	268	107	51	5	-6
1887	Cle-a	.888	48	196	105	38	9	3
Total	5	.900	244	1297	484	197	24	10
OF								
1883	NY-a	1.000	8	10	0	0	0	-1
1884	NY-a	.786	8	9	2	3	1	0
1885	NY-a	1.000	6	7	0	0	0	-1
1886	NY-a	.923	9	12	0	1	0	-1
Total	4	.909	31	38	2	4	1	-3
1B								
1887	Cle-a	.983	16	118	1	2	4	-1
3B								
1885	NY-a	.952	6	7	13	1	2	1
SS								
1885	NY-a	.714	1	0	5	2	0	0
2B								
1885	NY-a	.333	1	1	0	2	0	-1

■ Pete Reiser   OF

YEAR	TM/L	PCT	G	PO	A	E	DP	FR
1940	Bro-N	.955	17	21	0	1	0	-1
1941	Bro-N	.981	133	356	14	7	0	9
1942	Bro-N	.969	125	277	9	9	2	-7
1946	Bro-N	.978	97	205	14	5	2	6
1947	Bro-N	.988	108	240	3	3	0	-3
1948	Bro-N	.981	30	52	1	1	0	-2
1949	Bos-N	.980	63	139	5	3	2	3
1950	Bos-N	.979	24	46	0	1	0	1
1951	Pit-N	.982	27	53	1	1	0	-2
1952	Cle-A	1.000	10	20	0	0	0	1
Total	10	.979	634	1409	47	1	6	5
3B								
1940	Bro-N	.960	30	38	58	4	7	2
1946	Bro-N	.960	15	16	32	2	2	1
1948	Bro-N	.917	4	4	7	1	1	-1
1949	Bos-N	.889	4	3	5	1	2	0
1950	Bos-N	—	1	0	0	0	0	0
1951	Pit-N	.909	5	3	7	1	1	0
Total	6	.951	59	64	109	9	13	2
SS								
1940	Bro-N	.926	5	13	12	2	1	-3

■ Heinie Reitz   2B

YEAR	TM/L	PCT	G	PO	A	E	DP	FR
1893	Bal-N	.939	130	315	421	48	62	-1
1894	Bal-N	.968	97	264	336	20	50	22
1895	Bal-N	.938	48	120	137	17	25	-3
1896	Bal-N	.952	118	256	335	30	54	-17
1897	Bal-N	.962	128	282	449	29	62	21
1898	Was-N	.959	132	323	401	31	56	6
1899	Pit-N	.975	34	86	110	5	8	1
Total	7	.955	687	1646	2189	180	317	29
3B								
1894	Bal-N	.911	12	14	37	5	3	4
1895	Bal-N	.913	18	18	24	4	1	0
Total	2	.912	30	32	61	9	4	4
SS								
1895	Bal-N	1.000	1	0	1	0	0	0
1896	Bal-N	.909	3	3	7	1	0	0
Total	2	.917	4	3	8	1	0	0

■ Ken Reitz   3B

YEAR	TM/L	PCT	G	PO	A	E	DP	FR
1972	StL-N	.956	20	17	26	2	3	-4
1973	StL-N	.974	135	85	211	8	19	-6
1974	StL-N	.974	151	131	278	11	29	-16
1975	StL-N	.946	160	124	279	23	21	-21
1976	SF-N	.959	155	140	303	19	32	2
1977	StL-N	.980	157	121	320	9	35	-2
1978	StL-N	.973	150	111	314	12	18	1
1979	StL-N	.972	158	124	290	12	26	-13
1980	StL-N	.979	150	86	293	8	25	-4
1981	Chi-N	.977	81	57	157	5	11	5
1982	Pit-N	1.000	4	0	6	0	0	1
Total	11	.970	1321	996	2477	109	219	-57
SS								
1973	StL-N	1.000	1	3	2	0	1	0
1974	StL-N	.750	2	0	3	1	0	-1
1976	SF-N	1.000	1	1	0	0	1	0
Total	3	.909	4	4	6	1	2	-1
2B								
1974	StL-N	—	1	0	0	0	0	0

■ Jack Remsen   OF

YEAR	TM/L	PCT	G	PO	A	E	DP	FR
1876	Har-N	.887	69	177	12	24	5	7
1877	StL-N	.906	33	73	4	8	0	1
1878	Chi-N	.944	56	103	14	7	5	6
1879	Chi-N	.862	31	52	4	9	1	-3
1881	Cle-N	.873	48	117	7	18	1	-1
1884	Phi-N	.952	12	17	3	1	0	0
	Bro-a	.914	81	152	7	15	2	4
Total	6	.900	330	691	51	2	14	14
1B								
1879	Chi-N	.915	11	135	5	13	2	-1

■ Jerry Remy   2B

YEAR	TM/L	PCT	G	PO	A	E	DP	FR
1975	Cal-A	.982	147	336	427	14	111	10
1976	Cal-A	.977	133	279	406	16	77	15
1977	Cal-A	.975	152	307	420	19	90	-12
1978	Bos-A	.983	140	327	444	13	114	2
1979	Bos-A	.970	76	147	205	11	43	-21
1980	Bos-A	.977	60	109	189	7	30	-3
1981	Bos-A	.984	87	162	272	7	58	-8
1982	Bos-A	.982	154	290	432	13	104	-16
1983	Bos-A	.990	144	295	376	7	104	-31
1984	Bos-A	.973	24	40	70	3	13	2
Total	10	.981	1117	2292	3241	110	744	-67
3B								
1977	Cal-A	—	1	0	0	0	0	0
SS								
1978	Bos-A	1.000	1	1	0	0	0	0
OF								
1980	Bos-A	—	1	0	0	0	0	0

■ Bill Renna   OF

YEAR	TM/L	PCT	G	PO	A	E	DP	FR
1953	NY-A	.983	40	57	0	1	0	-3
1954	Phi-A	.972	115	226	13	7	5	2
1955	KC-A	.992	79	118	5	1	2	-4

YEAR	TM/L	PCT	G	PO	A	E	DP	FR
1956	KC-A	.950	25	18	1	1	0	-1
1958	Bos-A	1.000	11	17	0	0	0	-1
1959	Bos-A	1.000	7	5	0	0	0	-1
Total	6	.979	277	441	19	0	7	-8

■ Tony Rensa C

YEAR	TM/L	PCT	G	PO	A	E	DP	FR
1930	Det-A	.964	18	46	7	2	1	-1
	Phi-N	.932	49	131	20	11	5	-11
1931	Phi-N	.958	17	35	11	2	2	3
1933	NY-A	.977	8	39	4	1	1	-1
1937	Chi-A	.975	23	70	9	2	3	1
1938	Chi-A	.982	57	185	36	4	4	6
1939	Chi-A	.972	13	29	6	1	0	1
Total	6	.965	185	535	93	3	16	-2

■ Roger Repoz OF

YEAR	TM/L	PCT	G	PO	A	E	DP	FR
1964	NY-A	1.000	9	1	0	0	0	0
1965	NY-A	.993	69	133	1	1	0	-4
1966	NY-A	1.000	30	21	0	0	0	0
	KC-A	.991	52	107	1	1	0	0
	Yr	.992	82	128	1	1	0	0
1967	KC-A	1.000	31	52	3	0	0	3
	Cal-A	.959	63	115	3	5	0	4
	Yr	.972	94	167	6	5	0	7
1968	Cal-A	.987	114	226	4	3	1	4
1969	Cal-A	.985	48	61	3	1	1	1
1970	Cal-A	.995	110	203	6	1	2	1
1971	Cal-A	1.000	97	172	6	0	2	-3
Total	8	.989	623	1091	27	2	6	6

1B

YEAR	TM/L	PCT	G	PO	A	E	DP	FR
1966	KC-A	.989	45	338	21	4	27	-2
1969	Cal-A	.996	31	235	19	1	25	1
1970	Cal-A	.992	18	127	3	1	9	-2
1971	Cal-A	1.000	13	55	3	0	3	0
Total	4	.993	107	755	46	6	64	-3

■ Rip Repulski OF

YEAR	TM/L	PCT	G	PO	A	E	DP	FR
1953	StL-N	.987	153	361	7	5	1	-11
1954	StL-N	.975	152	302	4	8	0	-5
1955	StL-N	.974	141	260	5	7	1	-7
1956	StL-N	.974	100	187	3	5	0	-4
1957	Phi-N	.968	130	264	6	9	2	2
1958	Phi-N	.949	56	90	3	5	0	-8
1959	LA-N	1.000	31	30	0	0	0	-3
1960	LA-N	1.000	2	1	0	0	0	0
	Bos-A	1.000	33	56	0	0	0	-1
1961	Bos-A	1.000	4	4	0	0	0	-1
Total	9	.976	802	1555	28	9	4	-38

■ Merv Rettenmund OF

YEAR	TM/L	PCT	G	PO	A	E	DP	FR
1968	Bal-A	1.000	23	29	1	0	0	-1
1969	Bal-A	.991	78	107	3	1	0	2
1970	Bal-A	.976	93	201	6	5	1	7
1971	Bal-A	.977	134	292	7	7	4	4
1972	Bal-A	.989	98	174	6	2	2	-1
1973	Bal-A	.985	90	196	4	3	1	-2
1974	Cin-N	1.000	69	103	3	0	0	-4
1975	Cin-N	1.000	61	99	1	0	1	-3
1976	SD-N	.977	43	79	6	2	1	5
1977	SD-N	1.000	27	30	0	0	0	-4
1978	Cal-A	.968	22	30	0	1	0	-1
1979	Cal-A	1.000	9	6	0	0	0	0
Total	12	.985	747	1346	37	1	10	2

3B

YEAR	TM/L	PCT	G	PO	A	E	DP	FR
1975	Cin-N	1.000	1	0	1	0	0	0
1977	SD-N	—	1	0	0	0	0	0
Total	2	1.000	2	0	1	0	0	0

■ Ken Retzer C

YEAR	TM/L	PCT	G	PO	A	E	DP	FR
1961	Was-A	.988	16	71	8	1	2	1
1962	Was-A	.985	99	488	44	8	5	0
1963	Was-A	.981	81	320	35	7	5	-11
1964	Was-A	.971	13	56	10	2	1	4
Total	4	.983	209	935	97	8	13	-6

■ Dave Revering 1B

YEAR	TM/L	PCT	G	PO	A	E	DP	FR
1978	Oak-A	.989	138	1013	110	13	98	9
1979	Oak-A	.986	104	828	80	13	77	2
1980	Oak-A	.995	95	724	67	9	56	2
1981	Oak-A	.995	29	188	13	1	12	-1
	NY-A	.994	44	276	30	2	24	3
	Yr	.994	73	464	43	3	36	2
1982	NY-A	1.000	13	113	2	0	7	-2
	Tor-A	1.000	4	36	2	0	4	0
	Sea-A	.986	27	202	11	3	22	-2
	Yr	.992	44	351	15	3	33	-4
Total	5	.989	454	3380	315	1	300	11

■ Nap Reyes 3B

YEAR	TM/L	PCT	G	PO	A	E	DP	FR
1943	NY-N	—	1	0	0	0	0	0
1944	NY-N	.956	37	36	95	6	6	7
1945	NY-N	.961	115	111	232	14	12	-3
Total	3	.960	153	147	327	0	18	4

1B

YEAR	TM/L	PCT	G	PO	A	E	DP	FR
1943	NY-N	.994	38	340	9	2	25	-5
1944	NY-N	.990	63	544	25	6	43	-5
1945	NY-N	1.000	5	59	1	0	1	-1
1950	NY-N	.667	1	2	0	1	0	0
Total	4	.991	107	945	35	9	69	-11

OF

YEAR	TM/L	PCT	G	PO	A	E	DP	FR
1944	NY-N	1.000	3	5	0	0	0	0

■ Carl Reynolds OF

YEAR	TM/L	PCT	G	PO	A	E	DP	FR
1927	Chi-A	1.000	13	37	1	0	0	2
1928	Chi-A	.979	74	135	6	3	2	-2
1929	Chi-A	.949	130	268	13	15	5	-1
1930	Chi-A	.975	132	336	11	9	1	10
1931	Chi-A	.949	109	233	10	13	3	-4
1932	Was-A	.965	95	229	3	4	0	1
1933	StL-A	.965	124	269	8	10	3	-1
1934	Bos-A	.977	100	244	6	6	3	-2
1935	Bos-A	.975	64	146	7	4	0	4
1936	Was-A	.968	72	142	8	5	0	-1
1937	Chi-N	.800	2	4	0	1	0	0
1938	Chi-N	.983	125	328	10	6	4	2
1939	Chi-N	.972	72	168	5	5	1	3
Total	13	.970	1112	2539	88	1	22	11

■ Craig Reynolds SS

YEAR	TM/L	PCT	G	PO	A	E	DP	FR
1975	Pit-N	.969	30	43	82	4	12	4
1976	Pit-N	.889	4	2	6	1	1	2
1977	Sea-A	.955	134	197	397	28	86	8
1978	Sea-A	.960	146	243	461	29	102	4
1979	Hou-N	.965	143	208	428	23	88	-16
1980	Hou-N	.969	135	162	362	17	59	12
1981	Hou-N	.973	85	139	261	11	36	-5
1982	Hou-N	.958	35	43	94	6	15	2
1983	Hou-N	1.000	8	10	11	0	6	-1
1984	Hou-N	.965	143	212	472	25	91	18
1985	Hou-N	.977	102	158	318	11	65	10
1986	Hou-N	.978	98	106	206	7	35	-11
1987	Hou-N	.970	129	160	290	14	43	-12
1988	Hou-N	.970	22	23	42	2	9	-2
1989	Hou-N	.957	26	35	54	4	10	-1
Total	15	.966	1240	1741	3484	182	658	12

2B

YEAR	TM/L	PCT	G	PO	A	E	DP	FR
1976	Pit-N	—	1	0	0	0	0	0
1983	Hou-N	.956	26	25	40	3	7	-3
1985	Hou-N	1.000	1	1	1	0	0	0
1988	Hou-N	.974	11	16	22	1	5	0
1989	Hou-N	.979	29	35	60	2	11	5
Total	5	.971	68	77	123	6	23	2

3B

YEAR	TM/L	PCT	G	PO	A	E	DP	FR
1982	Hou-N	1.000	7	2	4	0	0	0
1983	Hou-N	1.000	15	2	6	0	2	0
1984	Hou-N	1.000	1	0	1	0	0	0
1986	Hou-N	1.000	4	4	2	0	0	0
1987	Hou-N	1.000	2	0	2	0	0	0
1988	Hou-N	.818	19	6	12	4	1	-2
1989	Hou-N	.905	10	2	17	2	2	2
Total	7	.909	58	16	44	6	5	0

1B

YEAR	TM/L	PCT	G	PO	A	E	DP	FR
1986	Hou-N	1.000	5	12	1	0	0	0
1988	Hou-N	.960	10	43	5	2	5	0
1989	Hou-N	1.000	5	13	4	0	0	1
Total	3	.975	20	68	10	2	5	1

OF

YEAR	TM/L	PCT	G	PO	A	E	DP	FR
1983	Hou-N	—	1	0	0	0	0	0
1986	Hou-N	1.000	2	2	0	0	0	0
1989	Hou-N	1.000	1	1	1	0	1	1
Total	3	1.000	4	3	1	0	1	1

■ Harold Reynolds 2B

YEAR	TM/L	PCT	G	PO	A	E	DP	FR
1983	Sea-A	.975	18	30	48	2	14	-1
1984	Sea-A	1.000	6	8	12	0	3	4
1985	Sea-A	.960	61	69	123	8	22	19
1986	Sea-A	.977	126	278	415	16	111	29
1987	Sea-A	.977	160	347	507	20	111	19
1988	Sea-A	.977	158	303	471	18	111	6
1989	Sea-A	.980	151	311	506	17	109	27
1990	Sea-A	.977	160	330	499	19	110	15
Total	8	.977	840	1676	2581	100	591	118

■ R.J. Reynolds OF

YEAR	TM/L	PCT	G	PO	A	E	DP	FR
1983	LA-N	.931	18	25	2	2	1	0
1984	LA-N	.973	63	104	4	3	1	-4
1985	LA-N	.970	54	94	3	3	0	-2
	Pit-N	.958	31	65	3	3	0	0
	Yr	.965	85	159	6	6	0	-2
1986	Pit-N	.955	112	190	2	9	0	-9
1987	Pit-N	.993	99	134	7	1	2	-9
1988	Pit-N	.971	95	142	7	4	2	-8
1989	Pit-N	.990	98	200	6	2	3	1
1990	Pit-N	.972	59	102	3	3	0	-2
Total	8	.973	629	1056	37	0	9	-33

■ Ronn Reynolds C

YEAR	TM/L	PCT	G	PO	A	E	DP	FR
1982	NY-N	1.000	2	3	0	0	0	-1
1983	NY-N	.942	24	99	14	7	2	-1
1985	NY-N	.990	25	86	9	1	2	6
1986	Phi-N	.991	42	198	16	2	3	1
1987	Hou-N	.975	38	216	16	6	1	4
1990	SD-N	1.000	8	26	2	0	0	1
Total	6	.977	139	628	57	6	8	10

■ Tommie Reynolds OF

YEAR	TM/L	PCT	G	PO	A	E	DP	FR
1963	KC-A	.800	5	8	0	2	0	-1
1964	KC-A	.976	25	39	2	1	0	-1
1965	KC-A	.982	83	154	8	3	2	5
1967	NY-N	.971	72	65	3	2	1	3
1969	Oak-A	.979	89	184	5	4	2	3
1970	Cal-A	.969	32	61	1	2	0	2
1971	Cal-A	.978	26	43	2	1	1	1
1972	Mil-A	.961	41	72	2	3	0	2
Total	8	.973	373	626	23	8	6	14

3B

YEAR	TM/L	PCT	G	PO	A	E	DP	FR
1964	KC-A	.600	3	0	3	2	0	-1
1965	KC-A	—	1	0	0	0	0	0
1967	NY-N	1.000	5	3	3	0	0	0
1970	Cal-A	1.000	1	2	0	0	0	0
1971	Cal-A	1.000	1	1	1	0	0	0
1972	Mil-A	1.000	1	1	0	0	0	0
Total	6	.875	12	7	7	2	0	-1

C

YEAR	TM/L	PCT	G	PO	A	E	DP	FR
1967	NY-N	1.000	1	1	0	0	0	0

1B

YEAR	TM/L	PCT	G	PO	A	E	DP	FR
1972	Mil-A	1.000	1	4	0	0	0	0

■ Dusty Rhodes OF

YEAR	TM/L	PCT	G	PO	A	E	DP	FR
1952	NY-N	.917	56	97	3	9	0	-3
1953	NY-N	.965	47	76	6	3	4	3
1954	NY-N	.984	37	62	1	1	0	-4
1955	NY-N	.986	45	68	2	1	0	-4
1956	NY-N	.958	68	85	6	4	1	-5
1957	NY-N	1.000	44	63	0	0	0	-6
Total	6	.963	297	451	18	8	5	-19

■ Hal Rhyne SS

YEAR	TM/L	PCT	G	PO	A	E	DP	FR
1926	Pit-N	.945	44	102	123	13	28	2
1927	Pit-N	.800	7	5	7	3	2	-1
1929	Bos-A	.935	113	220	297	36	71	-3
1930	Bos-A	.944	107	188	284	28	63	4
1931	Bos-A	.963	147	295	502	31	74	17
1932	Bos-A	.966	55	92	161	9	31	0
1933	Chi-A	1.000	2	1	0	0	0	0
Total	7	.950	475	903	1374	120	269	19

2B

YEAR	TM/L	PCT	G	PO	A	E	DP	FR
1926	Pit-N	.967	66	167	220	13	46	5
1927	Pit-N	.963	45	105	101	8	19	-7
1932	Bos-A	.667	1	1	1	1	0	0
1933	Chi-A	.955	19	46	61	5	13	5
Total	4	.963	131	319	383	7	78	3

3B

YEAR	TM/L	PCT	G	PO	A	E	DP	FR
1926	Pit-N	1.000	1	2	3	0	0	0
1927	Pit-N	1.000	10	8	14	0	1	1
1929	Bos-A	1.000	1	0	1	0	0	0
1932	Bos-A	1.000	4	6	6	0	0	-1
1933	Chi-A	.857	13	1	11	2	0	0
Total	5	.963	29	17	35	2	1	0

OF

YEAR	TM/L	PCT	G	PO	A	E	DP	FR
1929	Bos-A	—	1	0	0	0	0	0

■ Del Rice C

YEAR	TM/L	PCT	G	PO	A	E	DP	FR
1945	StL-N	.994	77	284	39	2	6	9
1946	StL-N	.977	53	196	12	5	0	0
1947	StL-N	.981	94	380	33	8	7	4
1948	StL-N	.996	99	447	46	2	5	7
1949	StL-N	.992	92	355	29	3	4	-3
1950	StL-N	.984	130	572	63	10	12	6
1951	StL-N	.985	120	447	66	8	12	2
1952	StL-N	.992	147	677	81	6	8	-5
1953	StL-N	.988	135	627	60	8	6	-5
1954	StL-N	.985	52	248	20	4	2	6
1955	StL-N	.964	18	74	6	3	1	-5
	Mil-N	.981	22	90	12	2	2	0
	Yr	.973	40	164	18	5	3	-5
1956	Mil-N	.983	65	271	21	5	2	1
1957	Mil-N	.992	48	235	14	2	3	6
1958	Mil-N	.995	38	174	13	1	1	0
1959	Mil-N	.956	9	42	1	2	1	0
1960	Chi-N	.968	18	85	7	3	0	-2
	StL-N	1.000	1	4	0	0	0	0
	Bal-A	1.000	1	1	0	0	0	0
	Yr	.969	19	86	7	3	0	-2
1961	LA-N	.994	30	144	14	1	0	2
Total	17	.987	1249	5353	537	75	72	23

■ Sam Rice OF

YEAR	TM/L	PCT	G	PO	A	E	DP	FR
1916	Was-A	.957	46	83	5	4	1	2
1917	Was-A	.960	155	265	26	12	5	8
1918	Was-A	1.000	6	11	4	0	1	3
1919	Was-A	.962	141	285	18	12	3	8
1920	Was-A	.960	153	454	24	20	5	21
1921	Was-A	.964	141	380	18	15	3	10
1922	Was-A	.951	154	387	23	21	3	9
1923	Was-A	.970	147	307	21	10	8	8
1924	Was-A	.967	154	331	18	12	4	4
1925	Was-A	.962	152	339	20	12	7	9
1926	Was-A	.961	152	342	25	15	5	7
1927	Was-A	.975	139	258	12	7	2	0
1928	Was-A	.973	147	240	11	7	5	-8
1929	Was-A	.970	147	272	20	9	5	7
1930	Was-A	.963	145	297	13	12	4	4
1931	Was-A	.970	105	221	7	7	2	1
1932	Was-A	.968	42	89	3	3	0	-1
1933	Was-A	1.000	39	41	4	0	2	6
1934	Cle-A	.963	78	129	2	5	0	-8
Total	19	.965	2270	4774	278	184	67	89

■ Hal Rice OF

YEAR	TM/L	PCT	G	PO	A	E	DP	FR
1948	StL-N	1.000	8	16	0	0	0	-1
1949	StL-N	1.000	10	8	1	0	0	0
1950	StL-N	.972	37	67	3	2	0	0
1951	StL-N	.953	63	116	6	6	0	-4
1952	StL-N	.972	81	132	5	4	0	-5
1953	Pit-N	.973	70	167	14	5	2	9
1954	Pit-N	1.000	24	55	3	0	2	2
	Chi-N	.897	24	24	2	3	0	0
	Yr	.966	48	79	5	3	2	2
Total	6	.969	317	585	34	0	4	1

■ Harry Rice OF

YEAR	TM/L	PCT	G	PO	A	E	DP	FR
1924	StL-A	1.000	2	2	1	0	1	0
1925	StL-A	.984	85	175	13	3	1	7
1926	StL-A	.970	133	300	22	10	4	9
1927	StL-A	.938	130	277	26	20	7	12
1928	Det-A	.962	129	347	10	14	0	1
1929	Det-A	.960	127	345	16	15	6	5
1930	Det-A	.945	36	66	2	4	0	0
	NY-A	.969	87	244	7	8	2	8
	Yr	.964	122	310	9	12	2	8
1931	Was-A	.968	42	89	3	3	0	-1
1933	Cin-N	.991	141	315	14	3	3	2
Total	9	.966	911	2160	114	0	24	43

3B

YEAR	TM/L	PCT	G	PO	A	E	DP	FR
1924	StL-A	.917	15	16	28	4	3	0
1925	StL-A	.500	1	0	1	1	0	-1
1926	StL-A	.840	8	8	13	4	1	-2
1927	StL-A	.833	7	4	11	3	2	-1
1928	Det-A	1.000	2	1	1	0	0	0
1929	Det-A	1.000	3	2	4	0	0	0

YEAR	TM/L	PCT	G	PO	A	E	DP	FR
1930	NY-A	.667	1	1	1	1	0	0
1933	Cin-N	—	1	0	0	0	0	0
Total	8	.875	38	32	59	3	6	-4
			1B					
1924	StL-A	.750	2	2	1	1	1	0
1925	StL-A	.923	3	32	4	3	3	0
1930	NY-A	1.000	6	15	2	0	3	1
Total	3	.933	11	49	7	4	7	1
			2B					
1924	StL-A	.833	4	5	5	2	0	-1
1925	StL-A	—	1	0	0	0	0	0
1926	StL-A	.929	4	14	12	2	2	0
Total	3	.900	9	19	17	4	2	-1
			SS					
1924	StL-A	1.000	2	1	3	0	1	0
1926	StL-A	1.000	2	0	2	0	0	0
Total	2	1.000	4	1	5	0	1	0
			C					
1925	StL-A	—	1	0	0	0	0	0

■ Jim Rice OF

YEAR	TM/L	PCT	G	PO	A	E	DP	FR
1974	Bos-A	.800	3	4	0	1	0	0
1975	Bos-A	1.000	90	162	6	0	0	-5
1976	Bos-A	.967	98	199	8	7	0	-8
1977	Bos-A	.956	44	83	4	4	1	-2
1978	Bos-A	.989	114	245	13	3	1	5
1979	Bos-A	.984	125	241	8	4	1	-3
1980	Bos-A	.988	109	233	10	3	2	2
1981	Bos-A	.988	108	237	9	3	0	2
1982	Bos-A	.969	145	273	10	9	3	-6
1983	Bos-A	.984	151	339	21	6	5	12
1984	Bos-A	.989	157	336	12	4	3	7
1985	Bos-A	.964	130	236	8	9	1	-6
1986	Bos-A	.977	156	330	16	8	0	10
1987	Bos-A	.977	94	155	12	4	2	0
1988	Bos-A	.968	19	30	0	1	0	-1
Total	15	.980	1543	3103	137	6	19	7

■ Gene Richards OF

YEAR	TM/L	PCT	G	PO	A	E	DP	FR
1977	SD-N	.963	109	193	13	8	0	0
1978	SD-N	.965	124	210	8	8	0	-18
1979	SD-N	.973	132	320	7	9	2	-6
1980	SD-N	.979	156	307	21	7	4	6
1981	SD-N	.975	102	178	14	5	1	-2
1982	SD-N	.977	103	200	8	5	1	0
1983	SD-N	.980	54	96	2	2	0	-4
1984	SF-N	.940	26	46	1	3	0	-1
Total	8	.972	806	1550	74	7	8	-25
			1B					
1977	SD-N	.980	32	223	22	5	23	1
1978	SD-N	.961	26	211	12	9	23	-3
1982	SD-N	.975	25	223	12	6	17	-4
Total	3	.972	83	657	46	0	63	-6

■ Paul Richards C

YEAR	TM/L	PCT	G	PO	A	E	DP	FR
1932	Bro-N	1.000	3	21	3	0	1	3
1933	NY-N	.989	36	74	17	1	2	1
1934	NY-N	1.000	37	86	15	0	3	2
1935	NY-N	1.000	4	7	2	0	0	1
	Phi-A	.977	79	293	40	8	5	-3
1943	Det-A	.986	100	537	86	9	12	21
1944	Det-A	.979	90	413	60	10	13	16
1945	Det-A	.995	83	361	44	2	7	11
1946	Det-A	.997	54	311	35	1	6	15
Total	8	.987	486	2103	302	1	49	67

■ Hardy Richardson 2B

YEAR	TM/L	PCT	G	PO	A	E	DP	FR
1881	Buf-N	.889	5	12	12	3	0	1
1882	Buf-N	.898	83	275	280	63	28	15
1883	Buf-N	.903	92	289	344	68	33	22
1884	Buf-N	.897	71	191	243	50	18	6
1885	Buf-N	.905	50	163	169	35	17	9
1886	Det-N	.940	42	103	118	14	15	2
1887	Det-N	.941	64	219	215	27	27	12
1888	Det-N	.925	58	173	185	29	21	4
1889	Bos-N	.924	86	246	310	46	44	14
1892	Was-N	1.000	1	3	2	0	0	0
	NY-N	.931	33	82	108	14	11	2
	Yr	.933	34	85	110	14	11	2
Total	10	.915	585	1756	1986	349	214	87
			OF					
1881	Buf-N	.914	79	179	45	21	3	23
1884	Buf-N	.942	24	44	5	3	2	1
1885	Buf-N	.900	48	120	6	14	2	2
1886	Det-N	.899	80	131	21	17	1	7
1887	Det-N	.936	59	109	8	8	1	2
1889	Bos-N	.941	46	74	6	5	1	-1
1890	Bos-P	.950	124	235	13	13	3	-1
1891	Bos-a	.955	60	101	5	5	2	-2
1892	Was-N	.941	7	16	0	1	0	-3
	NY-N	.913	17	20	1	2	0	-3
	Yr	.925	24	36	1	3	0	-3
Total	9	.928	544	1029	110	9	15	28
			3B					
1879	Buf-N	.843	78	83	153	44	13	-7
1880	Buf-N	.848	81	108	154	47	6	-5
1881	Buf-N	1.000	1	2	1	0	0	1
1884	Buf-N	.864	5	9	10	3	0	1
1886	Det-N	1.000	2	1	5	0	1	1
1891	Bos-a	.929	9	12	14	2	1	0
1892	Was-N	1.000	2	0	2	0	0	0
Total	7	.852	178	215	339	6	22	-10
			SS					
1881	Buf-N	1.000	1	2	4	0	2	1
1885	Buf-N	1.000	1	1	2	0	0	0
1886	Det-N	.933	3	7	7	1	2	0
1890	Bos-P	1.000	6	12	23	0	4	3
1891	Bos-a	.923	4	7	17	2	2	2
1892	NY-N	.872	6	10	24	5	1	1

YEAR	TM/L	PCT	G	PO	A	E	DP	FR
Total	6	.935	21	39	77	8	11	7
			1B					
1884	Buf-N	.969	3	31	0	1	1	0
1890	Bos-P	1.000	1	13	1	0	1	0
1891	Bos-a	.955	3	21	0	1	0	0
1892	NY-N	.973	9	106	3	3	4	-1
Total	4	.972	16	171	4	5	6	-1
			C					
1879	Buf-N	1.000	1	11	0	0	0	1
1880	Buf-N	.828	5	15	9	5	0	0
Total	2	.875	6	26	9	5	0	1

■ Nolen Richardson 3B

YEAR	TM/L	PCT	G	PO	A	E	DP	FR
1931	Det-A	.946	38	31	75	6	2	-2
1932	Det-A	.986	65	51	92	2	8	9
Total	2	.969	103	82	167	8	10	7
			SS					
1929	Det-A	.839	13	15	11	5	2	-4
1932	Det-A	.938	4	5	10	1	1	1
1935	NY-A	.922	12	23	24	4	4	-6
1938	Cin-N	.966	35	56	87	5	13	-1
1939	Cin-N	1.000	1	4	3	0	1	1
Total	5	.941	65	103	135	5	21	-9

■ Danny Richardson 2B

YEAR	TM/L	PCT	G	PO	A	E	DP	FR
1886	NY-N	1.000	1	3	3	0	1	0
1887	NY-N	.928	108	257	384	50	46	16
1888	NY-N	.942	135	321	423	46	43	12
1889	NY-N	.934	125	332	416	53	60	9
1890	NY-P	.924	56	148	167	26	21	1
1891	NY-N	.952	114	323	429	38	60	44
1892	Was-N	.953	49	163	183	17	24	22
1893	Bro-N	.949	46	115	107	12	18	-17
1894	Lou-N	.955	10	35	28	3	5	1
Total	9	.940	644	1697	2140	245	278	88
			SS					
1884	NY-N	.827	19	33	34	14	6	-6
1886	NY-N	.857	1	1	5	1	1	0
1890	NY-P	.900	68	153	263	46	33	24
1891	NY-N	.893	9	35	32	8	4	5
1892	Was-N	.931	93	225	355	43	45	35
1893	Bro-N	.950	3	6	13	1	2	1
1894	Lou-N	.916	107	232	360	54	59	1
Total	7	.913	300	685	1062	167	150	60
			OF					
1884	NY-N	.907	55	77	20	10	3	6
1885	NY-N	.950	22	35	3	2	0	0
1886	NY-N	.953	64	94	7	5	0	-5
Total	3	.933	141	206	30	7	3	1
			3B					
1885	NY-N	.951	21	15	43	3	1	2
1886	NY-N	1.000	1	2	3	0	0	0
1887	NY-N	.833	14	16	29	9	1	-2
1892	Was-N	1.000	1	1	3	0	0	0
1893	Bro-N	.947	5	9	9	1	1	-1
Total	5	.909	42	43	87	3	3	-1

■ Bobby Richardson 2B

YEAR	TM/L	PCT	G	PO	A	E	DP	FR
1955	NY-A	.864	6	12	7	3	1	-4
1956	NY-A	1.000	5	15	4	0	2	2
1957	NY-A	.979	93	206	223	9	60	5
1958	NY-A	.973	51	104	110	6	35	4
1959	NY-A	.970	109	256	292	17	85	3
1960	NY-A	.973	141	312	337	18	103	-5
1961	NY-A	.978	161	413	376	18	136	-9
1962	NY-A	.982	161	378	451	15	116	-3
1963	NY-A	.984	150	335	424	12	105	7
1964	NY-A	.982	157	400	410	15	108	-14
1965	NY-A	.981	158	372	403	15	121	-3
1966	NY-A	.980	147	322	408	15	91	-3
Total	12	.979	1339	3125	3445	143	963	-14
			3B					
1958	NY-A	.972	13	8	27	1	3	4
1959	NY-A	1.000	12	2	3	0	0	0
1960	NY-A	1.000	11	6	13	0	1	0
1966	NY-A	1.000	2	0	2	0	0	0
Total	4	.984	38	16	45	1	3	5
			SS					
1955	NY-A	1.000	4	2	2	0	1	-1
1958	NY-A	.875	2	3	4	1	0	0
1959	NY-A	.912	14	11	41	5	9	-1
1964	NY-A	1.000	1	2	3	0	1	0
Total	4	.919	21	18	50	6	11	-2

■ Mike Richardt 2B

YEAR	TM/L	PCT	G	PO	A	E	DP	FR
1980	Tex-A	.978	20	32	55	2	11	-1
1982	Tex-A	.988	98	234	278	6	68	3
1983	Tex-A	.992	20	56	61	1	16	2
1984	Tex-A	1.000	4	5	6	0	4	1
Total	4	.988	142	327	400	9	99	5
			OF					
1982	Tex-A	1.000	6	19	1	0	0	1

■ Lance Richbourg OF

YEAR	TM/L	PCT	G	PO	A	E	DP	FR
1924	Was-A	1.000	7	11	2	0	1	1
1927	Bos-N	.953	110	233	10	12	0	-4
1928	Bos-N	.972	148	367	8	11	1	6
1929	Bos-N	.971	134	323	14	10	2	8
1930	Bos-N	.971	128	294	9	9	4	1
1931	Bos-N	.981	71	154	3	3	2	-4
1932	Chi-N	.986	33	70	2	1	1	-3
Total	7	.970	631	1452	48	6	11	5
			2B					
1921	Phi-N	1.000	4	3	4	0	0	3

■ John Richmond SS

YEAR	TM/L	PCT	G	PO	A	E	DP	FR
1879	Syr-N	.870	28	52	68	18	4	-9
1880	Bos-N	.844	31	30	73	19	14	-12
1881	Bos-N	.750	2	3	6	3	0	-1
1883	Col-a	.877	91	122	304	60	19	25

YEAR	TM/L	PCT	G	PO	A	E	DP	FR
1884	Col-a	.866	105	96	306	62	26	-9
1885	Pit-a	.849	23	14	65	14	6	-7
Total	6	.866	280	317	822	176	69	-13
			OF					
1879	Syr-N	.874	35	76	7	12	1	1
1880	Bos-N	1.000	1	1	0	0	0	0
1881	Bos-N	.969	25	59	4	2	1	1
1882	Cle-N	.917	41	65	12	7	0	1
	Phi-a	.892	18	29	4	4	0	0
1883	Col-a	1.000	2	0	2	0	0	1
1885	Pit-a	.824	11	13	1	3	0	-2
Total	6	.907	133	243	30	8	2	2
			C					
1879	Syr-N	1.000	2	4	0	0	0	0

■ Marv Rickert OF

YEAR	TM/L	PCT	G	PO	A	E	DP	FR
1942	Chi-N	1.000	6	18	1	0	0	1
1946	Chi-N	.972	104	200	5	6	1	-7
1947	Chi-N	.982	30	52	2	1	0	1
1948	Bos-N	1.000	3	9	1	0	0	1
1949	Bos-N	.981	75	149	9	3	2	0
1950	Pit-N	—	3	0	0	0	0	0
	Chi-A	.968	78	150	3	5	1	-6
Total	6	.976	299	578	21	5	4	-10
			1B					
1947	Chi-N	1.000	7	71	6	0	8	1
1949	Bos-N	.963	12	74	5	3	6	0
1950	Chi-A	1.000	1	4	0	0	0	0
Total	3	.982	20	149	11	3	14	1

■ Harry Riconda 3B

YEAR	TM/L	PCT	G	PO	A	E	DP	FR
1923	Phi-A	.911	47	45	118	16	9	4
1924	Phi-A	.927	73	95	147	19	14	2
1926	Bos-N	.818	4	6	3	2	0	-1
1928	Bro-N	.957	21	12	32	2	1	1
Total	4	.922	145	158	300	9	24	6
			2B					
1928	Bro-N	.957	53	153	160	14	21	2
			SS					
1923	Phi-A	.833	2	1	4	1	0	0
1924	Phi-A	1.000	2	2	0	0	0	-1
1928	Bro-N	.920	16	16	30	4	3	0
1929	Pit-N	.840	4	12	9	4	3	0
Total	4	.892	24	31	43	9	6	-1

■ Joe Riggert OF

YEAR	TM/L	PCT	G	PO	A	E	DP	FR
1911	Bos-A	.929	39	63	2	5	1	-4
1914	Bro-N	.972	20	32	3	1	1	-1
	StL-N	.961	30	46	3	2	0	-1
	Yr	.966	50	78	6	3	1	-2
1919	Bos-N	.950	61	165	6	9	2	0
Total	3	.950	150	306	14	7	4	-6

■ Lew Riggs 3B

YEAR	TM/L	PCT	G	PO	A	E	DP	FR
1935	Cin-N	.928	135	132	269	31	21	8
1936	Cin-N	.968	140	122	267	13	19	12
1937	Cin-N	.941	100	112	223	21	16	20
1938	Cin-N	.947	140	146	280	24	18	-1
1939	Cin-N	.957	11	6	16	1	1	-1
1940	Cin-N	.943	11	10	23	2	2	2
1941	Bro-N	.932	43	48	75	9	4	-7
1942	Bro-N	.944	46	36	65	6	7	-6
1946	Bro-N	1.000	1	2	2	0	0	0
Total	9	.945	627	614	1220	107	88	27
			2B					
1937	Cin-N	1.000	4	0	3	0	0	0
1941	Bro-N	1.000	1	4	2	0	1	0
Total	2	1.000	5	4	5	0	1	0
			1B					
1941	Bro-N	.800	1	3	1	1	1	0
1942	Bro-N	1.000	1	1	0	0	0	0
Total	2	.833	2	4	1	1	1	0
			SS					
1937	Cin-N	—	1	0	0	0	0	-1

■ Topper Rigney SS

YEAR	TM/L	PCT	G	PO	A	E	DP	FR
1922	Det-A	.938	155	262	493	50	74	-11
1923	Det-A	.944	129	209	383	35	46	-16
1924	Det-A	.967	146	273	463	25	72	10
1925	Det-A	.934	51	51	91	10	7	-14
1926	Bos-A	.969	146	286	492	25	80	20
1927	Bos-A	1.000	1	4	2	0	1	-1
	Was-A	.929	32	65	93	12	21	-3
	Yr	.932	33	69	95	12	22	-4
Total	6	.953	660	1150	2017	157	301	-15
			3B					
1925	Det-A	1.000	4	5	4	0	1	0
1927	Det-A	1.000	4	4	3	0	1	-1
	Was-A	.929	6	4	9	1	1	0
	Yr	.952	10	8	12	1	2	-1
Total	2	.967	14	13	16	1	3	-1

■ Bill Rigney 2B

YEAR	TM/L	PCT	G	PO	A	E	DP	FR
1947	NY-N	.974	72	184	229	11	41	5
1948	NY-N	.967	105	258	275	18	48	-9
1949	NY-N	.971	26	55	79	4	11	3
1950	NY-N	.966	23	29	27	2	8	4
1951	NY-N	.958	9	12	11	1	5	2
1952	NY-N	.910	9	10	17	0	3	0
1953	NY-N	1.000	1	2	0	0	0	0
Total	7	.971	245	550	638	6	116	5
			3B					
1946	NY-N	.965	73	77	143	8	8	6
1947	NY-N	.932	41	47	76	9	7	-2
1949	NY-N	.943	14	10	23	2	2	-1
1950	NY-N	.972	11	15	20	1	2	2
1951	NY-N	.953	12	13	28	2	5	3
1952	NY-N	.889	10	7	9	2	2	-1
1953	NY-N	1.000	2	3	1	0	0	0
Total	7	.952	163	172	300	4	26	7

YEAR	TM/L	PCT	G	PO	A	E	DP	FR
		SS						
1946	NY-N	.937	33	53	81	9	14	-4
1947	NY-N	.945	24	33	53	5	8	-3
1948	NY-N	.905	7	7	12	2	1	-2
1949	NY-N	.928	81	120	215	26	33	-19
1952	NY-N	.846	4	11	11	4	4	0
Total	5	.928	149	224	372	6	60	-28
		1B						
1952	NY-N	1.000	1	4	0	0	0	0

■ Culley Rikard OF

YEAR	TM/L	PCT	G	PO	A	E	DP	FR
1941	Pit-N	1.000	5	18	0	0	0	1
1942	Pit-N	.958	16	23	0	1	0	0
1947	Pit-N	.978	79	177	2	4	0	-5
Total	3	.978	100	218	2	5	0	-4

■ Ernie Riles SS

YEAR	TM/L	PCT	G	PO	A	E	DP	FR
1985	Mil-A	.957	115	183	310	22	62	-19
1986	Mil-A	.964	142	212	327	20	76	-30
1987	Mil-A	.966	21	35	49	3	14	-2
1988	Mil-A	.970	9	15	17	1	6	0
	SF-N	.979	16	10	37	1	7	1
1989	SF-N	1.000	7	1	6	0	1	0
1990	SF-N	.986	26	21	49	1	8	-2
Total	6	.964	336	477	795	8	174	-52
		3B						
1987	Mil-A	.935	65	41	103	10	11	-7
1988	Mil-A	.958	28	21	47	3	2	2
	SF-N	.975	30	15	63	2	4	6
1989	SF-N	.962	83	45	107	6	13	-5
1990	SF-N	1.000	10	4	8	0	0	0
Total	4	.956	216	126	328	1	30	-4
		2B						
1988	SF-N	1.000	17	21	33	0	6	1
1989	SF-N	.962	18	20	31	2	2	-3
1990	SF-N	.974	24	28	48	2	6	-2
Total	3	.978	59	69	112	4	14	-4
		OF						
1989	SF-N	.750	5	3	0	1	0	-1

■ Cal Ripken SS

YEAR	TM/L	PCT	G	PO	A	E	DP	FR
1981	Bal-A	.946	12	11	24	2	5	0
1982	Bal-A	.972	94	155	289	13	47	-9
1983	Bal-A	.970	**162**	272	**534**	25	**113**	16
1984	Bal-A	.971	**162**	**297**	**583**	26	**122**	39
1985	Bal-A	.967	161	**286**	474	26	**123**	7
1986	Bal-A	.982	162	240	**482**	13	105	10
1987	Bal-A	.973	**162**	240	**480**	20	103	-4
1988	Bal-A	.973	161	**284**	480	21	119	-2
1989	Bal-A	.990	**162**	**276**	**531**	8	**119**	4
1990	Bal-A	**.996**	161	242	435	3	94	-30
Total	10	.977	1399	2303	4312	157	950	31
		3B						
1981	Bal-A	.889	6	2	6	1	1	0
1982	Bal-A	.973	71	66	151	6	17	2
Total	2	.970	77	68	157	7	18	2

■ Billy Ripken 2B

YEAR	TM/L	PCT	G	PO	A	E	DP	FR
1987	Bal-A	.990	58	133	162	3	53	-3
1988	Bal-A	.984	149	309	440	12	110	2
1989	Bal-A	.985	114	255	335	9	81	12
1990	Bal-A	.987	127	250	366	8	84	-9
Total	4	.986	448	947	1303	2	328	2
		3B						
1988	Bal-A	1.000	2	1	0	0	0	0

■ Jimmy Ripple OF

YEAR	TM/L	PCT	G	PO	A	E	DP	FR
1936	NY-N	.980	76	190	5	4	1	-4
1937	NY-N	.980	111	193	6	4	1	-18
1938	NY-N	.976	131	236	13	6	2	-3
1939	NY-N	1.000	23	36	2	0	0	-2
	Bro-N	1.000	28	55	0	0	0	-3
	Yr	1.000	51	91	2	0	0	-5
1940	Bro-N	1.000	3	10	0	0	0	1
	Cin-N	1.000	30	45	0	0	0	-5
	Yr	1.000	33	55	0	0	0	-4
1941	Cin-N	1.000	25	36	1	0	1	-4
1943	Phi-A	1.000	31	55	0	0	0	-6
Total	7	.984	458	856	27	4	5	-44

■ Swede Risberg SS

YEAR	TM/L	PCT	G	PO	A	E	DP	FR
1917	Chi-A	.913	146	291	352	**61**	57	-39
1918	Chi-A	.944	30	59	76	8	12	-1
1919	Chi-A	.934	97	175	278	32	39	-13
1920	Chi-A	.934	124	238	400	45	59	-4
Total	4	.928	397	763	1106	146	167	-57
		1B						
1918	Chi-A	.976	7	79	2	2	6	-1
1919	Chi-A	.991	22	204	13	2	10	0
Total	2	.987	29	283	15	4	16	-1
		3B						
1918	Chi-A	.899	24	29	42	8	4	-5
		2B						
1918	Chi-A	.958	12	28	40	3	5	0
		OF						
1918	Chi-A	1.000	3	3	0	0	0	-1

■ Claude Ritchey 2B

YEAR	TM/L	PCT	G	PO	A	E	DP	FR
1897	Cin-N	.875	8	16	19	5	2	-2
1898	Lou-N	.952	71	208	212	21	30	1
1899	Lou-N	.938	137	352	414	51	54	-7
1900	Pit-N	.952	123	303	357	33	51	7
1901	Pit-N	.941	**139**	340	**392**	**46**	**53**	3
1902	Pit-N	**.966**	114	275	341	22	48	6
1903	Pit-N	**.961**	**137**	281	**460**	30	45	19
1904	Pit-N	.958	**156**	330	482	36	48	-2
1905	Pit-N	**.961**	153	279	478	31	**59**	-5
1906	Pit-N	**.966**	151	326	439	27	59	1
1907	Bos-N	**.971**	144	340	460	24	55	14
1908	Bos-N	.967	120	325	368	24	**46**	**16**
1909	Bos-N	.959	25	65	52	5	10	0

YEAR	TM/L	PCT	G	PO	A	E	DP	FR
Total	13	.957	1478	3440	4474	355	560	51
		SS						
1897	Cin-N	.897	70	144	204	40	21	-14
1898	Lou-N	.919	80	194	228	37	32	-17
1899	Lou-N	.941	11	13	35	3	3	0
1901	Pit-N	1.000	1	0	4	0	1	0
1904	Pit-N	1.000	2	2	2	0	0	0
1905	Pit-N	1.000	2	2	0	0	0	0
Total	6	.912	166	355	473	0	57	-31
		OF						
1897	Cin-N	.884	22	32	6	5	1	1
1902	Pit-N	—	1	0	0	0	0	0
Total	2	.884	23	32	6	5	1	1

■ Lew Ritter C

YEAR	TM/L	PCT	G	PO	A	E	DP	FR
1902	Bro-N	.973	16	91	18	3	2	3
1903	Bro-N	.940	74	309	80	**25**	6	-18
1904	Bro-N	.966	57	249	88	12	7	6
1905	Bro-N	.951	84	397	106	**26**	4	-15
1906	Bro-N	.978	53	211	61	6	4	-8
1907	Bro-N	.969	89	391	103	16	11	-1
1908	Bro-N	.961	37	132	41	7	0	-3
Total	7	.960	410	1780	497	5	34	-36
		OF						
1903	Bro-N	—	2	0	0	0	0	-1
1905	Bro-N	1.000	4	7	0	0	0	0
1906	Bro-N	.955	9	19	2	1	0	1
Total	3	.966	15	26	2	1	0	0
		2B						
1904	Bro-N	.952	5	9	11	1	6	-1
		3B						
1904	Bro-N	1.000	1	0	1	0	0	0
1905	Bro-N	1.000	2	2	3	0	0	0
1906	Bro-N	.750	2	1	5	2	0	-1
Total	3	.857	5	3	9	2	0	-1
		1B						
1906	Bro-N	.963	3	26	0	1	1	-1

■ German Rivera 3B

YEAR	TM/L	PCT	G	PO	A	E	DP	FR
1983	LA-N	.929	8	2	11	1	0	2
1984	LA-N	.937	90	55	167	15	12	16
1985	Hou-N	.941	11	7	25	2	3	3
Total	3	.937	109	64	203	8	15	21

■ Bombo Rivera OF

YEAR	TM/L	PCT	G	PO	A	E	DP	FR
1975	Mon-N	.889	5	8	0	1	0	0
1976	Mon-N	.950	56	89	7	5	3	0
1978	Min-A	.982	94	162	5	3	0	0
1979	Min-A	.989	105	169	12	2	0	-5
1980	Min-A	.922	37	58	1	5	1	-2
1982	KC-A	1.000	3	4	0	0	0	0
Total	6	.970	300	490	25	6	4	-7

■ Luis Rivera SS

YEAR	TM/L	PCT	G	PO	A	E	DP	FR
1986	Mon-N	.953	55	64	119	9	24	-9
1987	Mon-N	.923	15	9	27	3	4	2
1988	Mon-N	.962	116	160	301	18	69	-6
1989	Bos-A	.958	90	126	240	16	59	-3
1990	Bos-A	.965	112	186	310	18	69	10
Total	5	.960	388	545	997	4	225	-6
		2B						
1989	Bos-A	1.000	1	1	0	0	0	0
1990	Bos-A	1.000	3	1	0	0	0	0
Total	2	1.000	4	2	0	0	0	0
		3B						
1990	Bos-A	—	1	0	0	0	0	0

■ Jim Rivera OF

YEAR	TM/L	PCT	G	PO	A	E	DP	FR
1952	StL-A	.976	88	273	7	7	1	3
	Chi-A	.988	53	157	2	2	1	1
	Yr	.980	141	430	9	**9**	2	4
1953	Chi-A	.976	156	385	15	10	5	-7
1954	Chi-A	.959	143	255	5	**11**	0	-12
1955	Chi-A	.981	143	288	**22**	6	**7**	**13**
1956	Chi-A	.976	134	271	9	7	4	1
1957	Chi-A	.974	86	141	6	4	0	-5
1958	Chi-A	.994	99	153	7	1	3	-6
1959	Chi-A	.976	69	75	5	2	3	-2
1960	Chi-A	1.000	24	16	0	0	0	4
1961	KC-A	.981	43	51	0	1	0	-7
Total	10	.977	1038	2065	78	1	24	-17
		1B						
1957	Chi-A	.988	31	233	8	3	22	-4

■ Mickey Rivers OF

YEAR	TM/L	PCT	G	PO	A	E	DP	FR
1970	Cal-A	1.000	5	10	0	0	0	0
1971	Cal-A	.976	75	159	5	4	2	2
1972	Cal-A	.981	48	105	0	2	0	2
1973	Cal-A	.909	29	60	0	6	0	-3
1974	Cal-A	.994	116	309	9	2	3	8
1975	Cal-A	.977	152	371	13	9	3	5
1976	NY-A	.986	136	407	6	6	0	4
1977	NY-A	.982	136	380	11	7	1	5
1978	NY-A	.980	138	384	8	8	2	5
1979	NY-A	.969	69	147	4	4	0	-5
	Tex-A	.981	57	153	4	3	1	4
	Yr	.978	126	300	8	7	1	-1
1980	Tex-A	.978	141	342	19	8	4	5
1981	Tex-A	.996	97	225	12	1	3	1
1983	Tex-A	.980	23	48	1	1	0	-2
1984	Tex-A	1.000	30	49	3	0	2	0
Total	14	.982	1252	3149	95	1	21	31

■ Johnny Rizzo OF

YEAR	TM/L	PCT	G	PO	A	E	DP	FR
1938	Pit-N	.951	140	284	5	**15**	1	-7
1939	Pit-N	.974	86	186	2	5	0	-3
1940	Pit-N	.818	7	9	0	2	0	-2
	Cin-N	.974	30	68	6	2	2	4
	Phi-N	.968	91	207	6	7	4	4
	Yr	.964	128	284	12	11	6	6
1941	Phi-N	.968	62	114	8	4	2	3

YEAR	TM/L	PCT	G	PO	A	E	DP	FR
1942	Bro-N	.977	70	124	6	3	1	2
Total	5	.964	486	992	33	8	10	1
		3B						
1940	Phi-N	.914	7	6	26	3	2	5
1941	Phi-N	.600	2	1	2	2	0	-1
Total	2	.875	9	7	28	5	2	4

■ Phil Rizzuto SS

YEAR	TM/L	PCT	G	PO	A	E	DP	FR
1941	NY-A	.957	128	252	399	29	**109**	**16**
1942	NY-A	.962	144	**324**	445	30	**114**	**25**
1946	NY-A	.961	125	267	378	26	97	13
1947	NY-A	.969	151	340	450	25	111	16
1948	NY-A	.973	128	259	348	17	85	-11
1949	NY-A	.971	152	329	440	23	118	3
1950	NY-A	**.982**	155	**301**	452	14	123	9
1951	NY-A	.968	144	317	407	24	113	6
1952	NY-A	.976	**152**	308	**458**	19	**116**	19
1953	NY-A	.963	133	214	409	24	100	-3
1954	NY-A	.968	126	184	294	16	84	-1
1955	NY-A	.957	79	93	132	10	30	-9
1956	NY-A	.934	30	31	54	6	17	3
Total	13	.968	1647	3219	4666	263	1217	86
		2B						
1954	NY-A	1.000	1	1	0	0	0	0
1955	NY-A	—	1	0	0	0	0	0
Total	2	1.000	2	1	0	0	0	0

■ Roxey Roach SS

YEAR	TM/L	PCT	G	PO	A	E	DP	FR
1910	NY-A	.913	58	112	173	27	27	-5
1911	NY-A	.891	8	19	22	5	5	0
1912	Was-A	.500	2	0	1	1	0	-1
1915	Buf-F	.959	92	212	297	22	38	16
Total	4	.938	160	343	493	5	70	10
		OF						
1910	NY-A	.889	9	8	0	1	0	-2
		2B						
1911	NY-A	.880	5	7	15	3	0	-1

■ Mike Roarke C

YEAR	TM/L	PCT	G	PO	A	E	DP	FR
1961	Det-A	.988	85	383	22	5	5	4
1962	Det-A	.982	53	247	24	5	1	6
1963	Det-A	.986	16	68	5	1	1	2
1964	Det-A	.994	27	165	11	1	0	3
Total	4	.987	181	863	62	2	7	15

■ Curt Roberts 2B

YEAR	TM/L	PCT	G	PO	A	E	DP	FR
1954	Pit-N	.969	131	357	394	24	82	2
1955	Pit-N	.913	6	7	14	2	4	-1
1956	Pit-N	.988	27	39	45	1	12	-1
Total	3	.969	164	403	453	7	98	0

■ Dave Roberts 3B

YEAR	TM/L	PCT	G	PO	A	E	DP	FR
1972	SD-N	.931	84	62	166	17	20	-3
1973	SD-N	.942	111	77	245	20	25	5
1974	SD-N	.955	103	83	170	12	15	-4
1975	SD-N	.925	30	23	63	7	5	-2
1977	SD-N	1.000	1	0	1	0	0	0
1980	Tex-A	.930	37	19	47	5	2	-6
1981	Hou-N	.923	7	4	8	1	1	0
1982	Phi-N	.818	11	2	7	2	0	0
Total	9	.939	386	270	708	4	68	-10
		C						
1972	SD-N	1.000	1	1	0	0	0	0
1977	SD-N	.982	63	254	24	5	2	-3
1978	SD-N	.980	41	135	13	3	0	0
1979	Tex-A	.980	14	45	5	1	0	0
1980	Tex-A	.973	22	93	14	3	1	-3
1981	Hou-N	—	1	0	0	0	0	0
1982	Phi-N	.938	10	15	0	1	0	0
Total	7	.979	152	543	56	3	3	-6
		2B						
1972	SD-N	.966	20	29	28	2	7	-2
1973	SD-N	.920	12	15	31	4	6	-2
1975	SD-N	.950	5	14	5	1	2	-2
1977	SD-N	1.000	2	0	1	0	0	0
1979	Tex-A	1.000	8	15	23	0	9	3
1980	Tex-A	1.000	4	2	0	0	0	-1
1981	Hou-N	1.000	3	1	0	0	0	0
1982	Phi-N	1.000	7	6	13	0	4	1
Total	8	.963	61	82	101	7	28	-3
		SS						
1972	SD-N	.667	3	0	4	2	0	-1
1974	SD-N	.938	3	5	10	1	2	0
1977	SD-N	.750	1	2	4	2	2	0
1980	Tex-A	.951	33	19	39	3	8	-9
Total	4	.912	40	26	57	8	12	-10
		1B						
1978	SD-N	1.000	8	15	1	0	0	0
1979	Tex-A	1.000	6	9	0	0	1	0
1980	Tex-A	1.000	4	4	0	0	0	0
1981	Hou-N	.958	10	83	8	4	6	0
Total	4	.968	28	111	9	4	7	0
		OF						
1974	SD-N	—	0	0	0	0	0	0
1978	SD-N	—	2	0	0	0	0	0
1979	Tex-A	1.000	11	13	1	0	0	1
1980	Tex-A	1.000	5	1	0	0	0	0
Total	4	1.000	19	14	1	0	0	1

■ Bip Roberts OF

YEAR	TM/L	PCT	G	PO	A	E	DP	FR
1989	SD-N	.976	54	77	3	2	0	-2
1990	SD-N	.982	75	160	8	3	1	5
Total	2	.980	129	237	11	5	1	3
		2B						
1986	SD-N	.971	87	166	172	10	33	4
1988	SD-N	1.000	1	2	2	0	1	0
1989	SD-N	.976	9	17	23	1	7	0
1990	SD-N	.921	8	10	25	3	6	0
Total	4	.968	105	195	222	4	47	4

YEAR	TM/L	PCT	G	PO	A	E	DP	FR
	3B							
1988	SD-N	.500	2	0	1	1	0	-1
1989	SD-N	.974	37	15	59	2	3	0
1990	SD-N	.953	56	34	89	6	7	-4
Total	3	.957	95	49	149	9	10	-5
	SS							
1989	SD-N	.930	14	25	28	4	7	-5
1990	SD-N	.984	18	23	38	1	8	-4
Total	2	.958	32	48	66	5	15	-9

■ Leon Roberts OF

YEAR	TM/L	PCT	G	PO	A	E	DP	FR
1974	Det-A	.926	17	25	0	2	0	-5
1975	Det-A	.982	127	268	10	5	2	4
1976	Hou-N	.980	60	99	1	2	0	-7
1977	Hou-N	1.000	9	3	2	0	0	0
1978	Sea-A	.975	128	296	10	8	4	6
1979	Sea-A	.983	136	286	6	5	2	0
1980	Sea-A	.984	104	238	6	4	1	2
1981	Tex-A	.992	71	130	2	1	0	-6
1982	Tex-A	1.000	28	42	0	0	0	-1
	Tor-A	1.000	16	24	0	0	0	-1
	Yr	1.000	44	66	0	0	0	-2
1983	KC-A	.979	76	139	3	3	0	1
1984	KC-A	1.000	16	24	0	0	0	1
Total	11	.982	788	1574	40	0	9	-6

■ Andre Robertson SS

YEAR	TM/L	PCT	G	PO	A	E	DP	FR
1981	NY-A	1.000	8	7	17	0	2	2
1982	NY-A	.966	27	40	73	4	21	5
1983	NY-A	.960	78	91	242	14	49	18
1984	NY-A	.930	49	63	136	15	34	10
1985	NY-A	.950	14	16	22	2	8	-2
Total	5	.953	176	217	490	5	114	33
	2B							
1981	NY-A	1.000	3	2	7	0	1	1
1982	NY-A	.972	15	44	25	2	6	3
1983	NY-A	.992	29	72	60	1	15	3
1984	NY-A	.917	6	5	6	1	2	1
1985	NY-A	1.000	2	5	4	0	2	0
Total	5	.983	55	128	102	4	26	8
	3B							
1982	NY-A	—	2	0	0	0	0	0
1985	NY-A	.867	33	11	41	8	6	-4
Total	2	.867	35	11	41	8	6	-4

■ Dave Robertson OF

YEAR	TM/L	PCT	G	PO	A	E	DP	FR
1912	NY-N	—	1	0	0	0	0	0
1914	NY-N	.950	71	101	13	6	2	-3
1915	NY-N	.956	138	225	13	11	4	-5
1916	NY-N	.960	144	248	17	11	5	-2
1917	NY-N	.942	140	266	12	17	1	-6
1919	Chi-N	.932	25	53	2	4	0	-1
1920	Chi-N	.968	134	230	10	8	1	-10
1921	Chi-N	1.000	7	9	0	0	0	-1
	Pit-N	.960	58	117	2	5	0	-7
	Yr	.962	65	126	2	5	0	-8
1922	NY-N	.909	8	9	1	1	1	0
Total	9	.955	726	1258	70	3	14	-35
	1B							
1912	NY-N	1.000	1	2	0	0	0	0

■ Gene Robertson 3B

YEAR	TM/L	PCT	G	PO	A	E	DP	FR
1922	StL-A	.875	7	3	11	2	0	0
1923	StL-A	.935	74	86	117	14	6	-14
1924	StL-A	.958	111	114	203	14	22	-11
1925	StL-A	.939	154	201	288	32	41	-2
1926	StL-A	.924	55	58	112	14	9	-2
1928	NY-A	.926	70	75	112	15	5	-9
1929	NY-A	.966	77	80	116	7	6	-11
	Bos-N	.875	6	6	8	2	0	-2
1930	Bos-N	.949	17	15	22	2	3	-2
Total	8	.941	571	638	989	102	92	-53
	SS							
1919	StL-A	.750	2	2	1	1	0	-1
1922	StL-A	1.000	6	3	7	0	0	1
1925	StL-A	1.000	1	1	1	0	1	0
1926	StL-A	.898	10	13	31	5	4	-3
1929	Bos-N	1.000	1	1	4	0	0	1
Total	5	.914	20	20	44	6	5	-2
	2B							
1922	StL-A	1.000	1	2	0	0	0	-1
1923	StL-A	1.000	1	1	1	0	1	0
1924	StL-A	1.000	2	2	4	0	0	0
1926	StL-A	1.000	3	4	6	0	0	0
1928	NY-A	1.000	3	3	8	0	2	1
Total	5	1.000	10	12	19	0	3	0

■ Bob Robertson 1B

YEAR	TM/L	PCT	G	PO	A	E	DP	FR
1967	Pit-N	.990	9	91	5	1	9	0
1969	Pit-N	.996	26	214	16	1	19	1
1970	Pit-N	.995	99	907	78	5	107	5
1971	Pit-N	.993	126	1089	128	9	107	15
1972	Pit-N	.993	89	502	60	4	57	11
1973	Pit-N	.995	107	957	79	5	91	5
1974	Pit-N	.991	63	494	37	5	44	-1
1975	Pit-N	.996	27	209	18	1	10	1
1976	Pit-N	.996	29	257	17	1	28	0
1978	Sea-A	1.000	18	141	8	0	16	-1
1979	Tor-A	1.000	9	54	7	0	6	1
Total	11	.994	602	4915	453	2	494	37
	OF							
1970	Pit-N	.667	3	4	0	2	0	-1
1972	Pit-N	.974	23	35	2	1	0	1
Total	2	.932	26	39	2	3	0	0
	3B							
1970	Pit-N	.875	5	4	3	1	1	-1
1972	Pit-N	.929	11	6	20	2	2	-1
Total	2	.917	16	10	23	3	3	-2

■ Sherry Robertson OF

YEAR	TM/L	PCT	G	PO	A	E	DP	FR
1946	Was-A	1.000	1	3	0	0	0	0
1947	Was-A	.949	55	126	5	7	1	-1
1948	Was-A	.939	51	105	3	7	0	-3
1949	Was-A	.947	13	17	1	1	0	0
1950	Was-A	.952	14	19	1	1	0	-1
1951	Was-A	.949	22	54	2	3	1	2
1952	Phi-A	.938	7	15	0	1	0	-1
Total	7	.946	163	339	12	0	2	-4
	2B							
1946	Was-A	.958	14	43	48	4	10	3
1947	Was-A	1.000	4	7	7	0	1	0
1949	Was-A	.947	71	149	211	20	41	-6
1950	Was-A	.950	12	30	27	3	5	-6
1952	Phi-A	.958	8	11	12	1	2	-3
Total	5	.951	109	240	305	8	59	-12
	3B							
1941	Was-A	.750	1	1	2	1	0	0
1943	Was-A	.897	27	27	43	8	1	-4
1946	Was-A	.902	38	29	63	10	8	-5
1947	Was-A	.963	10	11	15	1	0	-1
1949	Was-A	.938	19	19	41	4	2	0
1950	Was-A	—	1	0	0	0	0	0
1952	Phi-A	—	2	0	0	0	0	0
Total	7	.913	98	87	164	4	11	-10
	SS							
1940	Was-A	.940	10	17	30	3	9	1
1943	Was-A	1.000	1	0	2	0	0	0
1946	Was-A	.872	12	13	21	5	4	-4
Total	3	.912	23	30	53	8	13	-3

■ Billy Joe Robidoux 1B

YEAR	TM/L	PCT	G	PO	A	E	DP	FR
1985	Mil-A	1.000	6	49	5	0	6	0
1986	Mil-A	.986	43	326	29	5	35	-2
1987	Mil-A	.983	10	53	4	1	9	0
1988	Mil-A	.983	30	212	25	4	21	2
1989	Chi-A	.990	15	93	7	1	17	0
1990	Bos-A	.981	11	49	4	1	4	1
Total	6	.986	115	782	74	2	92	1
	OF							
1985	Mil-A	1.000	11	15	1	0	0	0
1989	Chi-A	—	1	0	0	0	0	0
Total	2	1.000	12	15	1	0	0	0

■ Aaron Robinson C

YEAR	TM/L	PCT	G	PO	A	E	DP	FR
1945	NY-A	1.000	45	186	16	0	3	-4
1946	NY-A	.983	95	410	50	8	5	-12
1947	NY-A	.997	74	346	38	1	3	0
1948	Chi-A	.989	92	303	50	4	4	-4
1949	Det-A	.986	108	458	44	7	9	-1
1950	Det-A	.993	103	355	42	3	4	-3
1951	Det-A	1.000	35	100	17	0	0	-2
	Bos-A	.983	25	101	14	2	3	-1
	Yr	.991	60	201	31	2	3	-3
Total	7	.990	577	2259	271	5	31	-27

■ Brooks Robinson 3B

YEAR	TM/L	PCT	G	PO	A	E	DP	FR
1955	Bal-A	.833	6	2	8	2	1	-2
1956	Bal-A	.944	14	9	25	2	3	1
1957	Bal-A	.971	47	34	66	3	5	3
1958	Bal-A	.953	140	151	275	21	30	10
1959	Bal-A	.955	87	92	187	13	25	7
1960	Bal-A	.977	152	171	328	12	34	12
1961	Bal-A	.972	163	151	331	14	34	-5
1962	Bal-A	.979	162	163	339	11	32	7
1963	Bal-A	.976	160	153	330	12	43	9
1964	Bal-A	.972	163	153	327	14	40	-2
1965	Bal-A	.967	143	144	296	15	36	-6
1966	Bal-A	.976	157	174	313	12	26	4
1967	Bal-A	.980	158	147	405	11	37	31
1968	Bal-A	.970	162	168	353	16	31	17
1969	Bal-A	.976	156	163	370	13	37	19
1970	Bal-A	.966	156	157	321	17	30	-1
1971	Bal-A	.968	156	131	354	16	35	7
1972	Bal-A	.977	152	129	333	11	27	6
1973	Bal-A	.970	154	129	354	15	25	9
1974	Bal-A	.967	153	115	410	18	44	19
1975	Bal-A	.979	143	96	326	9	30	4
1976	Bal-A	.969	71	59	126	6	11	0
1977	Bal-A	1.000	15	6	28	0	2	2
Total	23	.971	2870	2697	6205	263	618	151
	2B							
1956	Bal-A	—	1	0	0	0	0	0
1958	Bal-A	.933	16	6	8	1	2	0
1959	Bal-A	—	1	0	0	0	0	0
1960	Bal-A	1.000	3	3	2	0	1	0
1961	Bal-A	1.000	2	0	1	0	0	0
1962	Bal-A	1.000	2	1	1	0	0	0
Total	6	.957	25	10	12	1	3	0
	SS							
1961	Bal-A	1.000	1	4	2	0	0	0
1962	Bal-A	1.000	3	1	0	0	0	0
1963	Bal-A	1.000	1	0	1	0	0	0
Total	3	1.000	5	5	3	0	0	0

■ Craig Robinson SS

YEAR	TM/L	PCT	G	PO	A	E	DP	FR
1972	Phi-N	1.000	4	4	16	0	4	2
1973	Phi-N	.945	42	64	109	10	25	0
1974	Atl-N	.956	142	238	395	29	73	-17
1975	Atl-N	1.000	7	14	12	0	2	1
	SF-N	.941	12	13	19	2	5	4
	Yr	.967	19	27	31	2	7	5
1976	SF-N	—	1	0	0	0	0	0
	Atl-N	.667	2	1	3	2	0	0
	Yr	.667	3	1	3	2	0	0
1977	Atl-N	1.000	23	26	27	0	6	6
Total	6	.956	233	360	581	3	115	-4
	2B							
1973	Phi-N	1.000	4	6	3	0	1	0

YEAR	TM/L	PCT	G	PO	A	E	DP	FR
1975	SF-N	.867	9	7	6	2	2	1
1976	SF-N	.952	7	2	18	1	3	4
	Atl-N	.952	5	9	11	1	1	2
	Yr	.952	12	11	29	2	4	6
Total	3	.939	25	24	38	4	7	7
	3B							
1976	SF-N	.667	2	0	2	1	0	0
	Atl-N	1.000	1	0	2	0	0	0
	Yr	.800	3	0	4	1	0	0

■ Earl Robinson OF

YEAR	TM/L	PCT	G	PO	A	E	DP	FR
1961	Bal-A	.973	82	136	6	4	3	5
1962	Bal-A	1.000	17	35	0	0	0	1
1964	Bal-A	.986	34	67	3	1	0	2
Total	3	.980	133	238	9	5	3	8
	3B							
1958	LA-N	1.000	6	4	10	0	0	1

■ Floyd Robinson OF

YEAR	TM/L	PCT	G	PO	A	E	DP	FR
1960	Chi-A	.960	17	24	0	1	0	-2
1961	Chi-A	.991	106	218	7	2	0	2
1962	Chi-A	.973	155	278	13	8	2	1
1963	Chi-A	.984	137	245	8	4	4	-3
1964	Chi-A	.987	138	225	5	3	0	-5
1965	Chi-A	.985	153	254	6	4	0	-5
1966	Chi-A	.962	113	148	2	6	0	-16
1967	Cin-N	.981	39	53	0	1	0	-3
1968	Oak-A	1.000	18	20	1	0	0	-1
	Bos-A	.833	11	5	0	1	0	-1
	Yr	.963	29	25	1	1	0	-2
Total	9	.981	887	1470	42	0	6	-33

■ Frank Robinson OF

YEAR	TM/L	PCT	G	PO	A	E	DP	FR
1956	Cin-N	.976	152	323	5	8	1	1
1957	Cin-N	.989	136	336	11	4	3	16
1958	Cin-N	.991	138	310	12	3	1	11
1959	Cin-N	.982	40	51	3	1	0	1
1960	Cin-N	.960	51	112	8	5	1	2
1961	Cin-N	.990	150	284	15	3	3	8
1962	Cin-N	.994	161	315	10	2	2	9
1963	Cin-N	.984	139	237	13	4	1	5
1964	Cin-N	.986	156	279	7	4	3	4
1965	Cin-N	.990	155	282	5	3	1	2
1966	Bal-A	.985	151	254	4	4	0	-6
1967	Bal-A	.990	126	191	7	2	2	-4
1968	Bal-A	.962	117	173	5	7	0	-6
1969	Bal-A	.987	134	226	9	3	2	-3
1970	Bal-A	.987	120	221	9	3	3	2
1971	Bal-A	.973	92	177	3	5	0	-5
1972	LA-N	.967	95	168	6	6	2	-2
1973	Cal-A	.976	17	38	3	1	1	2
1974	Cal-A	—	1	0	0	0	0	0
1976	Cle-A	1.000	2	10	0	0	1	0
Total	20	.984	2132	3978	135	8	26	37
	1B							
1957	Cin-N	.989	24	151	25	2	16	4
1959	Cin-N	.984	125	998	75	17	111	-6
1960	Cin-N	.993	78	663	54	5	60	-1
1963	Cin-N	1.000	1	1	0	0	0	0
1966	Bal-A	.968	3	28	2	1	3	0
1967	Bal-A	1.000	2	16	1	0	1	0
1968	Bal-A	1.000	3	20	0	0	1	-1
1969	Bal-A	.987	19	141	10	2	16	-1
1970	Bal-A	.977	7	41	2	1	3	-1
1971	Bal-A	.980	37	272	17	6	25	-3
1974	Cle-A	.958	4	23	0	1	1	-1
1976	Cle-A	1.000	2	10	0	0	1	0
Total	12	.986	305	2364	186	5	237	-10
	3B							
1958	Cin-N	.842	11	4	12	3	0	-2
1960	Cin-N	—	1	0	0	0	0	0
1961	Cin-N	—	1	0	0	0	0	0
Total	3	.842	13	4	12	3	0	-2

■ Jackie Robinson 2B

YEAR	TM/L	PCT	G	PO	A	E	DP	FR
1948	Bro-N	.980	116	308	315	13	80	1
1949	Bro-N	.981	156	395	421	16	119	-1
1950	Bro-N	.986	144	359	390	11	133	11
1951	Bro-N	.992	150	390	435	7	137	17
1952	Bro-N	.974	146	353	400	20	113	4
1953	Bro-N	1.000	9	16	25	0	7	2
1954	Bro-N	1.000	4	13	14	0	2	-1
1955	Bro-N	1.000	1	4	2	0	1	0
1956	Bro-N	.989	22	39	49	1	17	0
Total	9	.983	748	1877	2047	8	607	33
	3B							
1948	Bro-N	.938	6	3	12	1	1	0
1953	Bro-N	.975	44	34	84	3	14	0
1954	Bro-N	.952	50	43	95	7	6	-2
1955	Bro-N	.966	84	74	180	9	18	9
1956	Bro-N	.967	72	61	173	8	15	14
Total	5	.964	256	215	544	8	54	21
	1B							
1947	Bro-N	.989	151	1323	92	16	144	-3
1948	Bro-N	.995	30	203	15	1	16	0
1953	Bro-N	1.000	6	41	5	0	4	1
1955	Bro-N	.917	1	11	0	1	0	0
1956	Bro-N	1.000	9	67	8	0	5	1
Total	5	.990	197	1645	120	8	169	-1
	OF							
1953	Bro-N	.981	76	145	9	3	0	3
1954	Bro-N	1.000	74	110	4	0	0	-3
1955	Bro-N	1.000	10	11	0	0	0	0
1956	Bro-N	1.000	2	2	0	0	0	0
Total	4	.989	162	268	14	3	0	0
	SS							
1953	Bro-N	1.000	1	2	3	0	0	0

■ Wilbert Robinson C

YEAR	TM/L	PCT	G	PO	A	E	DP	FR
1886	Phi-a	.893	61	265	109	45	12	-6

YEAR	TM/L	PCT	G	PO	A	E	DP	FR
1887	Phi-a	.901	67	281	137	46	9	7
1888	Phi-a	.938	65	428	143	38	5	25
1889	Phi-a	.943	69	290	106	24	8	0
1890	Phi-a	.930	82	412	103	39	10	-14
	Bal-a	.989	11	83	11	1	3	6
	Yr	.938	93	495	114	40	13	-8
1891	Bal-a	.954	92	415	80	24	11	3
1892	Bal-N	.921	87	332	86	36	8	-18
1893	Bal-N	.942	93	349	70	26	8	-9
1894	Bal-N	.944	109	370	84	27	8	-6
1895	Bal-N	.979	75	243	78	7	6	13
1896	Bal-N	.948	67	260	48	17	5	2
1897	Bal-N	.965	48	186	36	8	2	-2
1898	Bal-N	.965	77	288	72	13	4	-6
1899	Bal-N	.949	105	286	83	20	2	-19
1900	StL-N	.974	54	189	72	7	3	-1
1901	Bal-A	.949	67	235	61	16	4	-3
1902	Bal-A	.949	87	262	75	18	4	-14
Total	17	.941	1316	5174	1454	412	112	-42
1B								
1886	Phi-a	.938	22	171	9	12	14	0
1887	Phi-a	.733	3	10	1	4	0	-1
1888	Phi-a	.900	1	9	0	1	2	0
1890	Bal-a	.955	3	20	1	1	1	0
1892	Bal-N	.895	2	17	0	2	3	-1
1893	Bal-N	1.000	1	1	2	0	0	1
Total	6	.923	32	228	13	0	20	-1
OF								
1886	Phi-a	.857	5	6	0	1	0	-1
1887	Phi-a	—	1	0	0	0	0	-1
1891	Bal-a	.000	1	0	0	1	0	-1
1892	Bal-N	—	1	0	0	0	0	0
Total	4	.750	8	6	0	2	0	-3

■ Eddie Robinson 1B

YEAR	TM/L	PCT	G	PO	A	E	DP	FR
1942	Cle-A	1.000	1	7	0	0	0	0
1946	Cle-A	.988	8	80	1	1	4	-2
1947	Cle-A	.994	87	800	55	5	79	-1
1948	Cle-A	.995	131	1213	79	7	123	-1
1949	Was-A	.987	143	1299	100	18	133	-2
1950	Was-A	1.000	36	324	22	0	36	0
	Chi-A	.987	119	976	60	14	105	-7
	Yr	.990	155	1300	82	14	141	-7
1951	Chi-A	.988	147	1296	91	17	143	-6
1952	Chi-A	.990	155	1329	89	14	145	-8
1953	Phi-A	.988	155	1366	71	17	135	-14
1954	NY-A	.980	29	227	19	5	21	1
1955	NY-A	.995	46	390	20	2	35	-2
1956	NY-A	1.000	14	121	6	0	13	0
	KC-A	.977	47	360	19	9	43	-4
	Yr	.983	61	481	25	9	56	-4
1957	Det-A	1.000	1	4	1	0	0	0
	Cle-A	1.000	7	40	3	0	3	0
	Yr	1.000	8	44	4	0	3	0
Total	13	.990	1126	9832	636	109	1018	-46

■ Yank Robinson 2B

YEAR	TM/L	PCT	G	PO	A	E	DP	FR
1884	Bal-U	.846	3	11	11	4	1	1
1885	StL-a	.863	19	49	52	16	6	-6
1886	StL-a	.888	125	351	406	95	66	-1
1887	StL-a	.899	117	320	355	76	52	-10
1888	StL-a	.895	102	197	256	53	18	-38
1889	StL-a	.887	132	305	333	81	53	-35
1890	Pit-P	.887	98	226	286	65	46	-19
1891	Cin-a	.867	97	222	287	78	33	-11
	StL-a	.750	1	3	0	1	0	-1
	Yr	.866	98	225	287	79	33	-12
1892	Was-N	.895	4	10	7	2	1	0
Total	9	.887	698	1694	1993	471	276	120
3B								
1884	Bal-U	.831	71	98	163	53	10	16
1885	StL-a	1.000	2	1	5	0	0	0
1886	StL-a	.708	6	9	8	7	1	-2
1887	StL-a	.727	6	3	5	3	0	-2
1892	Was-N	.852	58	70	125	34	11	-2
Total	5	.834	143	181	306	7	22	10
SS								
1882	Det-N	.800	10	10	22	8	2	-4
1884	Bal-U	.808	14	23	40	15	1	0
1886	StL-a	.750	1	0	3	1	0	0
1887	StL-a	.818	2	3	6	2	0	0
1888	StL-a	.886	34	54	94	19	6	-6
1892	Was-N	.769	5	6	14	6	1	-1
Total	6	.844	66	96	179	1	10	-11
OF								
1882	Det-N	1.000	1	1	0	0	0	0
1885	StL-a	.862	52	65	10	12	1	-1
1886	StL-a	1.000	1	2	0	0	0	0
1887	StL-a	.833	2	4	1	1	0	1
Total	4	.865	56	72	11	3	1	0
C								
1884	Bal-U	.881	11	84	20	14	2	1
1885	StL-a	.929	5	30	9	3	0	2
1887	StL-a	.750	1	2	1	1	0	0
Total	3	.890	17	116	30	8	2	3
1B								
1885	StL-a	.909	1	10	0	1	0	0

■ Bill Robinson OF

YEAR	TM/L	PCT	G	PO	A	E	DP	FR
1966	Atl-N	.800	5	4	0	1	0	0
1967	NY-A	.968	102	169	10	6	1	1
1968	NY-A	.985	98	195	3	3	1	3
1969	NY-A	.963	62	99	5	4	0	-2
1972	Phi-N	.982	72	109	2	2	1	-6
1973	Phi-N	.979	113	227	8	5	1	3
1974	Phi-N	.971	87	162	8	5	0	1
1975	Pit-N	.991	57	107	3	1	1	2

YEAR	TM/L	PCT	G	PO	A	E	DP	FR
1976	Pit-N	.993	78	140	7	1	2	1
1977	Pit-N	.949	43	56	0	3	0	-3
1978	Pit-N	.988	127	235	8	3	2	-2
1979	Pit-N	.982	125	161	6	3	0	-17
1980	Pit-N	.979	41	43	3	1	0	0
1981	Pit-N	.941	7	16	0	1	0	0
1982	Pit-N	1.000	22	39	0	0	0	0
	Phi-N	.960	19	21	3	1	0	0
	Yr	.984	41	60	3	1	0	0
1983	Phi-N	—	1	0	0	0	0	0
Total	16	.979	1059	1783	66	0	9	-19
1B								
1969	NY-A	1.000	1	4	0	0	0	0
1976	Pit-N	1.000	3	22	0	0	4	-1
1977	Pit-N	.992	86	695	34	6	62	-7
1978	Pit-N	1.000	3	14	2	0	1	0
1979	Pit-N	1.000	28	233	13	0	18	-1
1980	Pit-N	.985	49	384	19	6	30	-5
1981	Pit-N	1.000	23	131	10	0	9	0
1982	Phi-N	1.000	5	9	1	0	5	0
1983	Phi-N	1.000	3	3	0	0	0	0
Total	9	.992	201	1495	79	2	129	-14
3B								
1973	Phi-N	.850	14	7	10	3	0	-2
1976	Pit-N	.909	37	24	46	7	5	-9
1977	Pit-N	.889	17	7	25	4	1	-2
1978	Pit-N	.923	29	19	41	5	5	-3
1979	Pit-N	—	3	0	0	0	0	0
1981	Pit-N	.500	1	1	0	1	0	-1
1983	Phi-N	.000	2	0	0	1	0	-1
Total	7	.896	103	58	122	1	11	-18

■ Mike Rocco 1B

YEAR	TM/L	PCT	G	PO	A	E	DP	FR
1943	Cle-A	.995	108	1012	61	5	111	-5
1944	Cle-A	.993	155	1467	138	11	158	17
1945	Cle-A	.992	141	1203	115	10	112	4
1946	Cle-A	.996	27	201	28	1	18	5
Total	4	.994	431	3883	342	7	399	21

■ Ike Rockenfield 2B

YEAR	TM/L	PCT	G	PO	A	E	DP	FR
1905	StL-A	.926	95	210	255	37	19	-9
1906	StL-A	.956	26	67	63	6	5	-5
Total	2	.933	121	277	318	3	24	-14

■ Pat Rockett SS

YEAR	TM/L	PCT	G	PO	A	E	DP	FR
1976	Atl-N	1.000	2	0	1	0	0	-1
1977	Atl-N	.940	84	152	209	23	38	-11
1978	Atl-N	.970	51	64	97	5	16	-10
Total	3	.949	137	216	307	8	54	-22

■ Andre Rodgers SS

YEAR	TM/L	PCT	G	PO	A	E	DP	FR
1957	NY-N	.950	20	40	56	5	14	3
1958	SF-N	.972	18	26	43	2	8	-3
1959	SF-N	.933	66	110	197	22	35	-9
1960	SF-N	.953	41	51	91	7	20	-4
1961	Chi-N	.979	24	35	57	2	10	3
1962	Chi-N	.960	133	239	433	28	91	7
1963	Chi-N	.954	150	271	454	35	100	-3
1964	Chi-N	.965	126	232	428	24	68	19
1965	Pit-N	.950	33	49	85	7	22	-6
1966	Pit-N	.913	5	8	13	2	5	-1
1967	Pit-N	.895	3	4	13	2	1	0
Total	11	.956	619	1065	1870	136	374	6
1B								
1960	SF-N	.977	6	41	1	1	3	-1
1961	Chi-N	.983	42	369	26	7	34	-2
1962	Chi-N	1.000	1	11	1	0	1	0
1965	Pit-N	1.000	6	33	2	0	3	0
1966	Pit-N	1.000	2	6	0	0	1	0
1967	Pit-N	1.000	9	39	4	0	3	1
Total	6	.985	66	499	34	8	45	-2
3B								
1957	NY-N	.885	8	4	19	3	0	2
1960	SF-N	.931	21	18	36	4	2	1
1965	Pit-N	.967	15	6	23	1	2	1
1966	Pit-N	1.000	3	0	1	0	0	0
1967	Pit-N	1.000	5	4	6	0	1	1
Total	5	.936	52	32	85	8	5	5
OF								
1960	SF-N	1.000	2	2	1	0	1	1
1961	Chi-N	1.000	2	3	0	0	0	0
1966	Pit-N	1.000	3	5	0	0	0	0
Total	3	1.000	7	10	1	0	1	1
2B								
1961	Chi-N	1.000	1	1	0	0	0	0
1965	Pit-N	—	1	0	0	0	0	0
1967	Pit-N	1.000	2	0	3	0	0	0
Total	3	1.000	4	1	3	0	0	0

■ Bob Rodgers C

YEAR	TM/L	PCT	G	PO	A	E	DP	FR
1961	LA-A	.965	14	71	11	3	2	-1
1962	LA-A	.989	150	826	73	10	14	0
1963	LA-A	.979	85	416	48	10	5	-14
1964	LA-A	.987	146	884	87	13	14	12
1965	Cal-A	.991	128	682	52	7	7	4
1966	Cal-A	.992	133	662	69	6	7	-5
1967	Cal-A	.991	134	728	73	7	11	2
1968	Cal-A	.985	87	407	50	7	11	0
1969	Cal-A	1.000	18	74	9	0	3	0
Total	9	.988	895	4750	472	3	74	-2
OF								
1967	Cal-A	—	1	0	0	0	0	0

■ Aurelio Rodriguez 3B

YEAR	TM/L	PCT	G	PO	A	E	DP	FR
1967	Cal-A	.989	29	19	75	1	11	5
1968	Cal-A	.921	70	61	113	15	18	-6
1969	Cal-A	.954	159	145	352	24	42	8
1970	Cal-A	.954	17	15	41	0	7	3
	Was-A	.961	136	103	336	18	34	12
	Yr	.965	153	118	377	18	41	15

YEAR	TM/L	PCT	G	PO	A	E	DP	FR
1971	Det-A	.953	153	127	341	23	33	14
1972	Det-A	.969	153	150	348	16	33	25
1973	Det-A	.971	160	135	335	14	30	10
1974	Det-A	.961	159	132	389	21	40	22
1975	Det-A	.953	151	136	375	25	33	18
1976	Det-A	.978	128	120	280	9	21	13
1977	Det-A	.972	95	60	222	8	19	17
1978	Det-A	.987	131	79	228	4	20	-7
1979	Det-A	.956	106	72	211	13	23	6
1980	SD-N	.965	88	38	128	6	12	10
	NY-A	.954	49	26	77	5	5	-4
1981	NY-A	.951	20	11	28	2	1	3
1982	Chi-A	.969	112	78	204	9	19	13
1983	Bal-A	.969	45	18	45	2	2	2
	Chi-A	1.000	22	4	22	0	5	4
	Yr	.978	67	22	67	2	7	6
Total	17	.964	1983	1529	4150	215	408	168
SS								
1970	Was-A	1.000	7	9	21	0	1	1
1971	Det-A	1.000	1	1	3	0	2	1
1972	Det-A	.667	2	0	2	1	1	-1
1973	Det-A	1.000	1	2	3	0	1	0
1977	Det-A	—	1	0	0	0	0	-1
1980	SD-N	1.000	2	0	2	0	0	0
1982	Chi-A	1.000	2	0	1	0	0	0
Total	7	.978	16	12	32	1	5	0
2B								
1968	Cal-A	1.000	2	4	3	0	0	0
1980	NY-A	.905	6	7	12	2	4	-1
1981	NY-A	1.000	3	1	5	0	1	1
1982	Chi-A	1.000	3	1	4	0	1	1
Total	4	.949	14	13	24	2	6	1
1B								
1979	Det-A	—	1	0	0	0	0	0
1981	NY-A	1.000	1	8	1	0	2	0
Total	2	1.000	2	8	1	0	2	0

■ Ellie Rodriguez C

YEAR	TM/L	PCT	G	PO	A	E	DP	FR
1968	NY-A	1.000	9	41	3	0	0	0
1969	KC-A	.990	90	433	39	5	2	-9
1970	KC-A	.988	75	451	32	6	5	12
1971	Mil-A	.992	114	520	67	5	8	6
1972	Mil-A	.983	114	542	54	10	6	-12
1973	Mil-A	.986	75	324	40	5	5	4
1974	Cal-A	.992	137	782	75	7	7	-8
1975	Cal-A	.991	90	492	33	5	2	-8
1976	LA-N	.986	33	128	17	2	2	5
Total	9	.989	737	3713	360	5	37	-10

■ Gary Roenicke OF

YEAR	TM/L	PCT	G	PO	A	E	DP	FR
1976	Mon-N	.955	25	39	3	2	0	-1
1978	Bal-A	1.000	20	22	1	0	0	-3
1979	Bal-A	.981	130	246	10	5	1	-2
1980	Bal-A	1.000	113	197	8	0	1	-7
1981	Bal-A	.983	83	175	2	3	1	-3
1982	Bal-A	.990	125	288	7	3	0	3
1983	Bal-A	.982	100	159	7	3	0	-7
1984	Bal-A	.995	117	197	6	1	0	-9
1985	Bal-A	.993	89	134	6	1	0	5
1986	NY-A	1.000	37	39	3	0	0	0
1987	Atl-N	.968	44	60	0	2	0	-4
1988	Atl-N	1.000	35	52	0	0	0	-2
Total	12	.988	918	1608	53	0	3	-30
1B								
1982	Bal-A	1.000	10	75	6	0	7	0
1983	Bal-A	1.000	7	60	2	0	5	-1
1986	NY-A	1.000	2	6	1	0	0	0
1987	Atl-N	1.000	9	50	7	0	8	1
1988	Atl-N	1.000	1	1	0	0	0	0
Total	5	1.000	29	192	16	0	20	0
3B								
1983	Bal-A	—	2	0	0	0	0	0
1986	NY-A	1.000	3	1	2	0	0	0
Total	2	1.000	5	1	2	0	0	0

■ Ron Roenicke OF

YEAR	TM/L	PCT	G	PO	A	E	DP	FR
1981	LA-N	1.000	20	38	1	0	1	3
1982	LA-N	.984	72	59	1	1	0	-2
1983	LA-N	.987	62	75	1	1	0	0
	Sea-A	.993	54	124	12	1	3	11
1984	SD-N	1.000	10	10	0	0	0	0
1985	SF-N	.984	35	63	0	1	0	-2
1986	Phi-N	.989	83	181	3	2	0	3
1987	Phi-N	.962	26	26	1	1	0	0
1988	Cin-N	1.000	14	18	0	0	0	-1
Total	8	.989	376	594	19	7	4	12
1B								
1983	Sea-A	.978	8	44	1	1	4	-1

■ Wally Roettger OF

YEAR	TM/L	PCT	G	PO	A	E	DP	FR
1927	StL-N	.500	3	2	0	2	0	0
1928	StL-N	.981	66	152	2	3	1	-5
1929	StL-N	.993	69	137	4	1	0	-4
1930	NY-N	.992	114	233	9	2	1	-9
1931	Cin-N	.990	44	95	3	1	1	-3
	StL-N	.974	42	73	1	2	1	-5
	Yr	.983	86	168	4	3	1	-8
1932	Cin-N	.991	94	214	3	2	2	-2
1933	Cin-N	.977	55	124	4	3	2	3
1934	Pit-N	1.000	23	51	1	0	0	2
Total	7	.986	510	1081	27	6	7	-23

■ Billy Rogell SS

YEAR	TM/L	PCT	G	PO	A	E	DP	FR
1925	Bos-A	.926	6	9	16	2	5	0
1928	Bos-A	.935	67	101	159	18	26	-9
1930	Det-A	.938	33	55	95	10	16	2
1931	Det-A	.958	48	91	182	12	26	11
1932	Det-A	.944	139	275	433	42	88	8
1933	Det-A	.944	155	326	526	51	116	20
1934	Det-A	.962	154	259	518	31	99	9

YEAR	TM/L	PCT	G	PO	A	E	DP	FR
1935	Det-A	.971	150	280	512	24	104	12
1936	Det-A	.965	146	286	462	27	98	-1
1937	Det-A	.967	146	323	451	26	103	2
1938	Det-A	.959	134	291	431	31	101	8
1939	Det-A	.931	43	59	90	11	21	0
1940	Chi-N	.900	14	7	11	2	2	-2
Total	13	.956	1235	2362	3886	287	805	60
		3B						
1927	Bos-A	.966	53	49	123	6	8	6
1928	Bos-A	1.000	3	3	1	0	0	0
1930	Det-A	1.000	13	7	19	0	4	2
1932	Det-A	1.000	4	1	4	0	0	0
1936	Det-A	1.000	1	1	2	0	1	0
1939	Det-A	.934	21	17	40	4	3	2
1940	Chi-N	.818	9	8	10	4	0	-2
Total	7	.953	104	86	199	4	16	8
		2B						
1925	Bos-A	.935	49	98	145	17	29	5
1927	Bos-A	1.000	2	2	4	0	2	1
1928	Bos-A	.960	22	47	73	5	8	-2
1939	Det-A	.929	2	8	5	1	2	0
1940	Chi-N	1.000	3	4	3	0	0	-1
Total	5	.944	78	159	230	3	41	3
		OF						
1927	Bos-A	1.000	2	1	0	0	0	-1
1928	Bos-A	1.000	6	3	0	0	0	-2
1930	Det-A	—	1	0	0	0	0	0
Total	3	1.000	9	4	0	0	0	-3

■ George Rohe   3B

YEAR	TM/L	PCT	G	PO	A	E	DP	FR
1901	Bal-A	.889	6	6	2	1	2	-1
1905	Chi-A	.980	17	16	32	1	3	1
1906	Chi-A	.926	57	66	122	15	6	2
1907	Chi-A	.898	76	58	161	25	14	-1
Total	4	.917	156	146	317	2	25	1
		2B						
1905	Chi-A	.934	17	31	40	5	7	-5
1906	Chi-A	.960	5	9	15	1	2	0
1907	Chi-A	.910	39	81	111	19	16	-3
Total	3	.920	61	121	166	5	25	-8
		SS						
1907	Chi-A	.923	30	38	94	11	8	-1
		1B						
1901	Bal-A	.912	8	61	1	6	4	-2
		OF						
1906	Chi-A	.500	1	1	0	1	0	0

■ Cookie Rojas   2B

YEAR	TM/L	PCT	G	PO	A	E	DP	FR
1962	Cin-N	.949	30	60	52	6	13	-1
1963	Phi-N	.991	25	42	68	1	13	16
1964	Phi-N	.973	20	33	39	2	5	-3
1965	Phi-N	.986	84	189	230	6	57	0
1966	Phi-N	.983	106	218	288	9	68	-7
1967	Phi-N	.977	137	282	360	15	92	-3
1968	Phi-N	.987	150	365	424	10	110	11
1969	Phi-N	.980	95	259	229	10	68	-3
1970	StL-N	1.000	10	22	30	0	9	1
	KC-A	.982	97	217	283	9	69	-1
1971	KC-A	.991	111	252	293	5	76	-11
1972	KC-A	.986	131	265	360	9	82	-2
1973	KC-A	.982	137	297	429	13	114	9
1974	KC-A	.987	141	292	368	9	94	-24
1975	KC-A	.980	117	233	303	11	65	-15
1976	KC-A	1.000	40	48	45	0	11	-12
1977	KC-A	1.000	16	26	18	0	7	-2
Total	16	.984	1447	3100	3819	115	953	-47
		OF						
1963	Phi-N	1.000	1	1	0	0	0	0
1964	Phi-N	.967	70	110	7	4	1	1
1965	Phi-N	.988	55	75	6	1	0	2
1966	Phi-N	.962	56	98	3	4	1	-2
1967	Phi-N	1.000	9	13	0	0	0	0
1969	Phi-N	.500	2	1	0	1	0	0
1970	StL-N	1.000	3	1	0	0	0	0
1971	KC-A	—	1	0	0	0	0	0
Total	8	.969	197	299	16	0	2	1
		3B						
1962	Cin-N	—	1	0	0	0	0	0
1964	Phi-N	—	1	0	0	0	0	0
1967	Phi-N	—	1	0	0	0	0	0
1972	KC-A	1.000	6	0	7	0	1	0
1976	KC-A	.909	6	4	6	1	2	0
1977	KC-A	.944	31	23	62	5	6	5
Total	6	.944	46	27	75	6	9	5
		SS						
1964	Phi-N	.980	18	20	30	1	5	-3
1965	Phi-N	.920	11	6	17	2	2	-1
1966	Phi-N	1.000	2	3	4	0	0	0
1967	Phi-N	—	2	0	0	0	0	0
1970	StL-N	1.000	2	1	0	0	0	0
1971	KC-A	1.000	2	2	0	0	0	0
1972	KC-A	1.000	2	0	1	0	0	0
Total	7	.966	39	32	52	3	7	-4
		C						
1964	Phi-N	1.000	1	1	0	0	0	0
1965	Phi-N	1.000	2	4	2	0	0	0
1967	Phi-N	1.000	3	2	0	0	0	0
1968	Phi-N	—	1	0	0	0	0	0
Total	4	1.000	7	7	2	0	0	0
		1B						
1965	Phi-N	—	1	0	0	0	0	0
1976	KC-A	1.000	1	1	1	0	0	0
Total	2	1.000	2	1	1	0	0	0

■ Stan Rojek   SS

YEAR	TM/L	PCT	G	PO	A	E	DP	FR
1946	Bro-N	.974	15	14	23	1	4	4
1947	Bro-N	.971	17	23	44	2	10	3
1948	Pit-N	.962	156	262	475	29	91	-8

YEAR	TM/L	PCT	G	PO	A	E	DP	FR
1949	Pit-N	.966	144	240	461	25	92	1
1950	Pit-N	.967	68	102	160	9	39	-14
1951	Pit-N	.900	8	5	13	2	0	-1
	StL-N	.974	51	95	131	6	36	1
	Yr	.968	59	100	144	8	36	0
1952	StL-A	1.000	4	4	8	0	1	2
Total	7	.965	463	745	1315	4	273	-12
		3B						
1946	Bro-N	1.000	6	3	8	0	0	2
1947	Bro-N	1.000	7	14	18	0	4	3
1950	Pit-N	1.000	3	8	1	0	0	-1
1952	StL-N	1.000	1	1	0	0	0	0
Total	4	1.000	17	26	27	0	4	4
		3B						
1946	Bro-N	1.000	4	3	1	0	0	0
1947	Bro-N	1.000	9	4	11	0	3	1
Total	2	1.000	13	7	12	0	3	1

■ Red Rolfe   3B

YEAR	TM/L	PCT	G	PO	A	E	DP	FR
1934	NY-A	.921	26	37	56	8	5	3
1935	NY-A	.964	136	166	239	15	16	0
1936	NY-A	.957	133	162	265	19	20	3
1937	NY-A	.962	154	195	309	20	27	5
1938	NY-A	.959	151	151	294	19	26	-7
1939	NY-A	.958	152	151	282	19	22	-15
1940	NY-A	.949	138	161	288	24	24	-1
1941	NY-A	.946	134	140	263	23	28	-9
1942	NY-A	.959	60	57	132	8	16	5
Total	9	.956	1084	1220	2128	155	184	-16
		SS						
1931	NY-A	1.000	1	1	0	0	0	0
1934	NY-A	.944	46	84	103	11	26	0
1935	NY-A	.949	17	31	44	4	6	-6
Total	3	.946	64	116	147	5	32	-6

■ Rich Rollins   3B

YEAR	TM/L	PCT	G	PO	A	E	DP	FR
1961	Min-A	1.000	4	2	6	0	1	0
1962	Min-A	.943	159	137	324	28	33	-1
1963	Min-A	.935	132	121	255	26	22	-7
1964	Min-A	.947	146	134	297	24	17	-2
1965	Min-A	.958	112	112	229	15	21	1
1966	Min-A	.953	65	54	107	8	13	-4
1967	Min-A	.963	97	83	153	9	13	-10
1968	Min-A	.931	56	28	93	9	4	-2
1969	Sea-A	.948	47	42	103	8	6	2
1970	Mil-A	1.000	7	2	13	0	2	1
	Cle-A	.600	5	1	2	2	1	-1
	Yr	.900	12	3	15	2	3	0
Total	10	.947	830	716	1582	129	133	-23
		2B						
1961	Min-A	1.000	5	3	4	0	1	0
1963	Min-A	1.000	1	1	0	0	0	0
1965	Min-A	.931	16	32	35	5	4	-5
1966	Min-A	1.000	2	2	1	0	0	0
Total	4	.940	24	38	40	5	5	-5
		SS						
1962	Min-A	—	1	0	0	0	0	-5
1969	Sea-A	1.000	1	0	1	0	1	0
Total	2	1.000	2	0	1	0	1	-5
		OF						
1966	Min-A	1.000	1	1	1	0	0	-1

■ John Romano   C

YEAR	TM/L	PCT	G	PO	A	E	DP	FR
1958	Chi-A	1.000	2	13	0	0	0	1
1959	Chi-A	.979	38	169	16	4	5	1
1960	Cle-A	.988	99	470	30	6	6	-11
1961	Cle-A	.989	141	752	58	9	8	-10
1962	Cle-A	.990	130	657	63	7	6	-8
1963	Cle-A	.993	71	408	28	3	5	-10
1964	Cle-A	.991	96	714	38	7	3	-4
1965	Chi-A	.992	111	569	61	5	10	4
1966	Chi-A	.993	102	552	46	4	7	3
1967	StL-N	.983	20	111	3	2	1	0
Total	10	.990	810	4415	343	7	51	-34
		OF						
1963	Cle-A	.833	4	5	0	1	0	0
1965	Chi-A	1.000	4	6	1	0	0	0
Total	2	.923	8	11	1	1	0	0
		1B						
1964	Cle-A	1.000	1	9	0	0	0	0
1965	Chi-A	—	2	0	0	0	0	0
Total	2	1.000	3	9	0	0	0	0

■ Ed Romero   SS

YEAR	TM/L	PCT	G	PO	A	E	DP	FR
1977	Mil-A	.971	10	9	24	1	3	0
1980	Mil-A	.894	22	33	60	11	14	3
1981	Mil-A	.949	22	37	57	5	16	4
1982	Mil-A	.920	10	6	17	2	4	1
1983	Mil-A	.962	22	30	46	3	13	-6
1984	Mil-A	.955	39	60	108	8	15	-7
1985	Mil-A	.977	43	57	115	4	27	2
1986	Bos-A	.959	75	102	132	10	29	-9
1987	Bos-A	.985	24	22	44	1	9	3
1988	Bos-A	1.000	8	12	20	0	4	-1
1989	Bos-A	1.000	10	4	13	0	3	1
	Atl-N	1.000	2	1	12	0	1	2
	Mil-A	1.000	1	0	3	0	0	0
Total	11	.958	288	373	651	5	138	-13
		2B						
1980	Mil-A	.984	15	26	34	1	6	1
1981	Mil-A	.985	18	24	43	1	13	6
1982	Mil-A	.975	39	97	96	5	30	-2
1983	Mil-A	1.000	3	4	6	0	1	-2
1984	Mil-A	.981	11	19	33	1	5	2
1985	Mil-A	.979	31	80	104	4	26	9
1986	Bos-A	1.000	4	0	5	0	1	1
1987	Bos-A	.973	29	65	81	4	19	8
1988	Bos-A	1.000	5	3	11	0	0	0
1989	Bos-A	.983	22	52	67	2	17	9

YEAR	TM/L	PCT	G	PO	A	E	DP	FR
	Atl-N	.947	4	6	12	1	2	2
	Mil-A	1.000	11	16	26	0	5	1
Total	10	.980	192	392	518	9	125	35
		3B						
1980	Mil-A	1.000	3	1	8	0	0	1
1981	Mil-A	1.000	3	0	2	0	0	0
1982	Mil-A	—	2	0	0	0	0	0
1983	Mil-A	.909	5	6	4	1	0	-1
1984	Mil-A	.943	59	38	111	9	13	6
1985	Mil-A	1.000	1	1	0	0	0	0
1986	Bos-A	.935	18	7	22	2	2	1
1987	Bos-A	.974	24	13	24	1	0	-3
1988	Bos-A	1.000	15	6	11	0	1	0
1989	Bos-A	.957	14	7	15	1	4	2
	Atl-N	1.000	1	0	1	0	0	0
	Mil-A	.857	4	3	3	1	0	0
1990	Det-A	.982	27	15	41	1	9	6
Total	11	.955	176	97	242	6	29	12
		OF						
1982	Mil-A	—	1	0	0	0	0	0
1983	Mil-A	.955	15	19	2	1	0	0
1984	Mil-A	—	1	0	0	0	0	0
1985	Mil-A	1.000	14	19	0	0	0	0
1986	Bos-A	1.000	1	2	0	0	0	0
Total	5	.977	32	40	2	1	0	0
		1B						
1984	Mil-A	1.000	4	24	4	0	2	1
1987	Bos-A	1.000	8	22	2	0	0	0
1988	Bos-A	—	1	0	0	0	0	0
Total	3	1.000	13	46	6	0	2	1

■ Kevin Romine   OF

YEAR	TM/L	PCT	G	PO	A	E	DP	FR
1985	Bos-A	1.000	23	20	1	0	0	1
1986	Bos-A	1.000	33	45	1	0	1	6
1987	Bos-A	1.000	7	10	1	0	1	2
1988	Bos-A	.957	45	44	0	2	0	1
1989	Bos-A	.982	89	157	9	3	4	0
1990	Bos-A	.976	64	81	0	2	0	-2
Total	6	.981	261	357	12	7	6	8

■ Phil Roof   C

YEAR	TM/L	PCT	G	PO	A	E	DP	FR
1961	Mil-N	1.000	1	2	0	0	0	0
1964	Mil-N	1.000	1	8	0	0	0	1
1965	Cal-A	.983	9	52	6	1	1	5
	Cle-A	.994	41	162	17	1	2	13
	Yr	.992	50	214	23	2	3	18
1966	KC-A	.985	123	680	52	11	7	0
1967	KC-A	.991	113	677	55	7	6	-1
1968	Oak-A	.968	32	116	6	4	2	-1
1969	Oak-A	.983	106	493	40	9	4	-1
1970	Mil-A	.988	107	596	47	8	6	7
1971	Mil-A	.975	39	174	22	5	3	3
	Min-A	.985	29	185	16	3	2	8
	Yr	.980	68	359	38	8	5	11
1972	Min-A	.978	61	257	11	6	0	-3
1973	Min-A	.992	47	218	17	2	4	3
1974	Min-A	1.000	44	200	24	0	3	7
1975	Min-A	.989	63	245	30	3	4	6
1976	Min-A	.962	12	68	9	3	2	5
	Chi-A	1.000	4	8	3	0	1	0
	Yr	.967	16	76	12	3	3	5
1977	Tor-A	1.000	3	10	1	0	1	1
Total	15	.986	835	4151	356	3	48	53
		1B						
1966	KC-A	1.000	2	4	0	0	1	0
1970	Mil-A	—	1	0	0	0	0	0
Total	2	1.000	3	4	0	0	1	0

■ Rolando Roomes   OF

YEAR	TM/L	PCT	G	PO	A	E	DP	FR
1988	Chi-N	.833	5	5	0	1	0	0
1989	Cin-N	.981	100	201	4	4	0	0
1990	Cin-N	1.000	19	33	1	0	0	2
	Mon-N	1.000	6	6	0	0	0	1
	Yr	1.000	25	39	1	0	0	3
Total	3	.980	130	245	5	5	0	3

■ Buddy Rosar   C

YEAR	TM/L	PCT	G	PO	A	E	DP	FR
1939	NY-A	.980	35	137	10	3	1	4
1940	NY-A	.983	63	258	30	5	8	0
1941	NY-A	.996	60	246	24	1	6	0
1942	NY-A	.996	58	249	26	1	7	3
1943	Cle-A	.983	114	480	91	10	11	5
1944	Cle-A	.989	98	409	59	5	13	2
1945	Phi-A	.987	85	338	54	5	6	-1
1946	Phi-A	1.000	117	532	73	0	9	5
1947	Phi-A	.996	102	406	70	2	12	12
1948	Phi-A	.997	90	335	39	1	10	-4
1949	Phi-A	.992	31	112	9	1	2	-2
1950	Bos-A	.991	25	108	6	1	1	0
1951	Bos-A	.996	56	235	20	1	6	0
Total	13	.992	934	3845	511	6	92	24

■ Pete Rose   OF

YEAR	TM/L	PCT	G	PO	A	E	DP	FR
1963	Cin-N	—	1	0	0	0	0	0
1967	Cin-N	.982	123	211	5	4	0	-2
1968	Cin-N	.990	148	268	20	3	4	9
1969	Cin-N	.988	156	316	10	4	3	7
1970	Cin-N	.997	159	309	8	1	2	2
1971	Cin-N	.994	158	306	13	2	1	2
1972	Cin-N	.994	154	330	15	2	2	12
1973	Cin-N	.992	159	343	15	3	0	9
1974	Cin-N	.997	163	346	11	1	3	9
1975	Cin-N	.982	35	55	0	1	0	-3
1976	Cin-N	—	1	0	0	0	0	0
1978	Cin-N	1.000	7	3	0	0	0	0
1983	Phi-N	.976	35	41	0	1	0	-3
1984	Mon-N	.964	28	51	2	2	0	-1
Total	14	.991	1327	2579	99	4	15	41
		1B						
1968	Cin-N	—	1	0	0	0	0	0

YEAR	TM/L	PCT	G	PO	A	E	DP	FR
1978	Cin-N	1.000	2	15	0	0	2	0
1979	Phi-N	.995	159	1424	87	8	124	-4
1980	Phi-N	**.997**	**162**	1427	**123**	5	113	**9**
1981	Phi-N	.996	107	929	91	4	69	**9**
1982	Phi-N	.995	**162**	1428	123	8	114	5
1983	Phi-N	.990	112	786	74	9	57	3
1984	Mon-N	.988	40	298	42	4	22	6
	Cin-N	.990	23	181	9	2	14	-3
	Yr	.989	63	479	51	6	36	3
1985	Cin-N	.995	110	870	73	5	80	0
1986	Cin-N	.990	61	523	43	6	54	-1
Total	10	.994	939	7881	665	1	649	24

3B

YEAR	TM/L	PCT	G	PO	A	E	DP	FR
1966	Cin-N	.931	16	24	30	4	4	1
1975	Cin-N	.963	137	106	230	13	21	-32
1976	Cin-N	**.969**	159	115	293	13	25	-12
1977	Cin-N	.958	**161**	98	268	16	18	-24
1978	Cin-N	.961	156	117	256	15	23	-23
1979	Phi-N	.833	5	4	6	2	0	-1
Total	6	.961	634	464	1083	3	91	-91

2B

YEAR	TM/L	PCT	G	PO	A	E	DP	FR
1963	Cin-N	.971	157	360	366	22	78	-22
1964	Cin-N	.979	128	263	301	12	63	-14
1965	Cin-N	.975	**162**	**382**	403	20	93	-18
1966	Cin-N	.981	140	385	344	14	79	-8
1967	Cin-N	.959	35	76	88	7	15	-7
1968	Cin-N	1.000	3	2	0	0	0	0
1969	Cin-N	1.000	2	1	0	0	0	0
1979	Phi-N	1.000	1	1	0	0	0	0
Total	8	.975	628	1470	1502	5	328	-69

■ John Roseboro C

YEAR	TM/L	PCT	G	PO	A	E	DP	FR
1957	Bro-N	.972	19	99	4	3	0	2
1958	LA-N	.987	104	594	36	8	5	-15
1959	LA-N	.991	117	**848**	54	8	10	7
1960	LA-N	.993	87	640	48	5	**10**	4
1961	LA-N	.986	**125**	**877**	56	13	**16**	6
1962	LA-N	.985	128	**842**	57	**14**	10	-3
1963	LA-N	.992	134	908	66	8	6	-10
1964	LA-N	.993	128	809	64	6	8	0
1965	LA-N	.994	131	824	55	5	7	-3
1966	LA-N	.993	138	**904**	65	7	11	5
1967	LA-N	.984	107	550	60	10	6	-12
1968	Min-A	.991	117	689	52	7	5	-6
1969	Min-A	.980	111	585	52	**13**	**16**	0
1970	Was-A	1.000	30	122	6	0	1	-3
Total	14	.989	1476	9291	675	107	111	-28

1B

YEAR	TM/L	PCT	G	PO	A	E	DP	FR
1957	Bro-N	1.000	5	37	3	0	4	0
1960	LA-N	—	1	0	0	0	0	0
Total	2	1.000	6	37	3	0	4	0

OF

YEAR	TM/L	PCT	G	PO	A	E	DP	FR
1958	LA-N	1.000	5	4	0	0	0	0

3B

YEAR	TM/L	PCT	G	PO	A	E	DP	FR
1960	LA-N	—	1	0	0	0	0	0
1965	LA-N	—	1	0	0	0	0	0
Total	2	—	2	0	0	0	0	0

■ Dave Rosello 2B

YEAR	TM/L	PCT	G	PO	A	E	DP	FR
1973	Chi-N	.964	13	27	26	2	5	3
1974	Chi-N	.972	49	77	95	5	32	3
1976	Chi-N	1.000	1	1	0	0	0	0
1977	Chi-N	1.000	3	2	1	0	0	0
1979	Cle-A	.976	33	40	84	3	12	-3
1980	Cle-A	.980	43	69	75	3	17	2
1981	Cle-A	.979	26	46	49	2	13	3
Total	7	.975	168	262	330	5	79	8

SS

YEAR	TM/L	PCT	G	PO	A	E	DP	FR
1972	Chi-N	.846	5	11	11	4	4	1
1973	Chi-N	.857	1	3	3	1	2	0
1974	Chi-N	.929	12	20	19	3	5	0
1975	Chi-N	.952	19	27	53	4	7	1
1976	Chi-N	.966	86	128	217	12	45	-7
1977	Chi-N	.810	10	2	15	4	0	-1
1979	Cle-A	1.000	11	1	2	0	1	0
1980	Cle-A	1.000	3	0	1	0	0	0
1981	Cle-A	.900	4	5	4	1	1	-1
Total	9	.947	151	197	325	9	65	-7

3B

YEAR	TM/L	PCT	G	PO	A	E	DP	FR
1977	Chi-N	.938	21	4	26	2	2	-1
1979	Cle-A	.875	14	2	12	2	3	-1
1980	Cle-A	.957	22	7	15	1	1	1
1981	Cle-A	1.000	8	4	10	0	1	1
Total	4	.941	65	17	63	5	7	0

■ Chief Roseman OF

YEAR	TM/L	PCT	G	PO	A	E	DP	FR
1882	Tro-N	.853	82	107	21	22	6	-5
1883	NY-a	.855	91	105	19	21	3	-3
1884	NY-a	.885	107	157	12	22	0	-2
1885	NY-a	.865	101	177	9	29	1	-7
1886	NY-a	.891	134	203	18	27	6	-3
1887	Phi-a	.821	21	41	5	10	1	0
	NY-a	.868	59	99	6	16	2	-7
	Bro-a	1.000	1	3	0	0	0	-3
	Yr	.856	81	143	11	26	3	-10
1890	StL-a	.819	58	61	7	15	2	-9
Total	7	.866	654	953	97	162	21	-39

1B

YEAR	TM/L	PCT	G	PO	A	E	DP	FR
1883	NY-a	.947	2	18	0	1	2	0
1887	NY-a	.957	3	22	0	1	1	0
1890	StL-a	.974	22	216	10	6	12	1
	Lou-a	.864	2	19	0	3	3	-1
	Yr	.965	24	235	10	9	15	0
Total	3	.963	29	275	10	1	18	0

■ Al Rosen 3B

YEAR	TM/L	PCT	G	PO	A	E	DP	FR
1947	Cle-A	—	2	0	0	0	0	0
1948	Cle-A	1.000	2	1	1	0	0	0
1949	Cle-A	1.000	10	10	16	0	1	-1
1950	Cle-A	.969	154	151	**322**	15	24	0
1951	Cle-A	.958	**154**	157	277	19	20	-15
1952	Cle-A	.958	147	159	256	18	25	-21
1953	Cle-A	.964	**154**	174	**338**	19	**38**	1
1954	Cle-A	.959	87	110	149	11	14	-16
1955	Cle-A	.963	106	119	195	12	17	1
1956	Cle-A	.945	116	89	219	18	20	-7
Total	10	.961	932	970	1773	112	159	-58

1B

YEAR	TM/L	PCT	G	PO	A	E	DP	FR
1952	Cle-A	.920	4	17	6	2	3	1
1953	Cle-A	1.000	1	4	0	0	1	0
1954	Cle-A	.984	46	391	39	7	34	3
1955	Cle-A	.981	41	277	26	6	31	1
Total	4	.981	92	689	71	5	69	5

SS

YEAR	TM/L	PCT	G	PO	A	E	DP	FR
1952	Cle-A	1.000	3	1	3	0	1	0
1953	Cle-A	—	1	0	0	0	0	0
1954	Cle-A	—	1	0	0	0	0	0
Total	3	1.000	5	1	3	0	1	0

OF

YEAR	TM/L	PCT	G	PO	A	E	DP	FR
1947	Cle-A	1.000	1	1	1	0	1	1

2B

YEAR	TM/L	PCT	G	PO	A	E	DP	FR
1954	Cle-A	1.000	1	1	0	0	0	0

■ Goody Rosen OF

YEAR	TM/L	PCT	G	PO	A	E	DP	FR
1937	Bro-N	.981	21	50	1	1	1	2
1938	Bro-N	**.989**	113	263	**19**	3	4	16
1939	Bro-N	1.000	47	106	0	0	0	-3
1944	Bro-N	.991	65	199	12	2	0	11
1945	Bro-N	.993	141	392	7	3	1	-2
1946	Bro-N	—	1	0	0	0	0	0
	NY-N	.976	84	200	3	5	0	2
	Yr	.976	85	200	3	5	0	2
Total	6	.976	472	1210	42	4	6	26

■ Larry Rosenthal OF

YEAR	TM/L	PCT	G	PO	A	E	DP	FR
1936	Chi-A	.977	80	243	7	6	3	3
1937	Chi-A	.980	25	46	3	1	1	3
1938	Chi-A	.959	22	44	3	2	1	2
1939	Chi-A	.990	93	193	5	2	1	-2
1940	Chi-A	.977	92	208	4	5	0	4
1941	Chi-A	.938	18	27	3	2	0	-1
	Cle-A	1.000	14	35	1	0	0	1
	Yr	.971	32	62	4	2	0	0
1944	NY-A	.986	26	68	2	1	1	2
	Phi-A	.960	19	24	0	1	0	-1
	Yr	.979	45	92	2	2	1	1
1945	Phi-A	1.000	21	35	1	0	0	-2
Total	8	.979	410	923	29	0	7	9

1B

YEAR	TM/L	PCT	G	PO	A	E	DP	FR
1941	Cle-A	1.000	1	1	0	0	0	0

■ Chet Ross OF

YEAR	TM/L	PCT	G	PO	A	E	DP	FR
1939	Bos-N	1.000	8	19	1	0	1	1
1940	Bos-N	.962	**149**	347	12	**14**	2	6
1941	Bos-N	1.000	12	21	1	0	0	0
1942	Bos-N	.992	57	123	2	1	0	0
1943	Bos-N	.977	73	165	8	4	1	1
1944	Bos-N	1.000	38	75	8	0	2	2
Total	6	.976	337	750	32	9	6	10

■ Don Ross 3B

YEAR	TM/L	PCT	G	PO	A	E	DP	FR
1938	Det-A	.946	75	90	157	14	15	4
1940	Bro-N	.879	10	10	19	4	0	0
1942	Det-A	.915	20	17	26	4	2	-5
1943	Det-A	1.000	1	1	2	0	0	0
1945	Det-A	.960	8	6	18	1	0	0
	Cle-A	.958	106	119	175	13	14	-13
	Yr	.958	114	125	193	14	14	-13
1946	Det-A	.944	41	35	50	5	5	-11
Total	6	.946	261	278	447	1	36	-25

OF

YEAR	TM/L	PCT	G	PO	A	E	DP	FR
1942	Det-A	.964	38	77	4	3	2	0
1943	Det-A	.985	38	62	3	1	0	-3
1944	Det-A	.958	37	67	2	3	1	-4
1946	Cle-A	1.000	2	1	0	0	0	0
Total	4	.969	115	207	9	7	3	-7

SS

YEAR	TM/L	PCT	G	PO	A	E	DP	FR
1943	Det-A	.946	18	29	41	4	7	-2
1944	Det-A	1.000	2	1	4	0	0	0
Total	2	.949	20	30	45	4	7	-2

2B

YEAR	TM/L	PCT	G	PO	A	E	DP	FR
1943	Det-A	.892	7	14	19	4	2	-2

1B

YEAR	TM/L	PCT	G	PO	A	E	DP	FR
1944	Det-A	1.000	1	17	1	0	0	0

■ Claude Rossman 1B

YEAR	TM/L	PCT	G	PO	A	E	DP	FR
1906	Cle-A	.984	105	1145	45	19	47	-8
1907	Det-A	.981	153	1478	62	30	57	-14
1908	Det-A	.981	138	1429	**102**	29	70	6
1909	Det-A	.981	75	913	36	18	30	-6
Total	4	.982	471	4965	245	6	204	-22

OF

YEAR	TM/L	PCT	G	PO	A	E	DP	FR
1904	Cle-A	.933	17	14	0	1	0	-4
1906	Cle-A	1.000	1	5	0	0	0	0
1909	StL-A	1.000	2	2	0	0	0	0
Total	3	.955	20	21	0	1	0	-4

■ Frank Roth C

YEAR	TM/L	PCT	G	PO	A	E	DP	FR
1903	Phi-N	.935	60	235	82	22	9	-6
1904	Phi-N	.958	67	241	76	14	8	-10
1905	StL-A	.962	29	114	36	6	3	-6
1906	Chi-A	.990	15	76	19	1	1	3
1909	Cin-N	.967	54	188	46	8	4	-2
1910	Cin-N	.938	4	11	4	1	0	0
Total	6	.956	229	865	263	2	25	-21

3B

YEAR	TM/L	PCT	G	PO	A	E	DP	FR
1903	Phi-N	—	1	0	0	0	0	0

1B

YEAR	TM/L	PCT	G	PO	A	E	DP	FR
1904	Phi-N	.818	1	9	0	2	0	-1

2B

YEAR	TM/L	PCT	G	PO	A	E	DP	FR
1904	Phi-N	.000	1	0	0	1	0	-1

OF

YEAR	TM/L	PCT	G	PO	A	E	DP	FR
1910	Cin-N	—	1	0	0	0	0	0

■ Braggo Roth OF

YEAR	TM/L	PCT	G	PO	A	E	DP	FR
1914	Chi-A	.924	34	54	7	5	1	1
1915	Chi-A	.943	30	45	5	3	0	-1
	Cle-A	.878	39	60	5	9	1	-6
	Yr	.906	69	105	10	12	1	-7
1916	Cle-A	.954	112	166	20	9	6	3
1917	Cle-A	.957	135	228	18	11	6	0
1918	Cle-A	.936	106	175	16	13	3	-3
1919	Phi-A	.975	48	78	1	2	2	-5
	Bos-A	.943	58	125	7	8	1	-4
	Yr	.955	106	203	8	10	3	-9
1920	Was-A	.952	128	184	15	10	0	-10
1921	NY-A	.923	37	69	3	6	0	-3
Total	8	.944	727	1184	97	6	20	-28

3B

YEAR	TM/L	PCT	G	PO	A	E	DP	FR
1915	Chi-A	.837	35	34	43	15	1	-14

■ Jack Rothrock OF

YEAR	TM/L	PCT	G	PO	A	E	DP	FR
1928	Bos-A	.979	53	92	1	2	1	-8
1929	Bos-A	.970	128	342	12	11	3	2
1930	Bos-A	.947	9	17	1	1	1	0
1931	Bos-A	.982	79	153	9	3	1	1
1932	Bos-A	.973	12	35	1	1	0	1
	Chi-A	.929	19	13	0	1	0	0
	Yr	.961	**31**	48	1	2	**0**	1
1934	StL-N	.975	154	343	10	9	4	3
1935	StL-N	.980	127	283	5	6	1	-2
1937	Phi-A	.992	58	130	2	1	0	1
Total	8	.976	639	1408	41	5	11	-2

SS

YEAR	TM/L	PCT	G	PO	A	E	DP	FR
1925	Bos-A	.893	22	37	38	9	6	-4
1926	Bos-A	.692	2	3	6	4	0	-2
1927	Bos-A	.953	44	100	123	11	28	4
1928	Bos-A	.918	13	20	25	4	4	-4
1931	Bos-A	—	1	0	0	0	0	0
Total	5	.926	78	160	192	8	38	-6

2B

YEAR	TM/L	PCT	G	PO	A	E	DP	FR
1927	Bos-A	.953	36	78	104	9	19	-3
1928	Bos-A	1.000	2	2	6	0	1	0
1931	Bos-A	.953	23	64	78	7	11	-1
1934	StL-N	1.000	1	0	2	0	0	0
1937	Phi-A	1.000	1	2	1	0	0	0
Total	5	.955	63	146	191	6	31	-4

3B

YEAR	TM/L	PCT	G	PO	A	E	DP	FR
1927	Bos-A	.958	20	24	45	3	6	1
1928	Bos-A	.879	17	8	21	4	2	-3
1930	Bos-A	1.000	1	0	2	0	0	0
1931	Bos-A	.857	2	2	4	1	0	-1
1932	Chi-A	.786	8	9	13	6	1	-2
Total	5	.901	48	43	85	4	9	-5

1B

YEAR	TM/L	PCT	G	PO	A	E	DP	FR
1927	Bos-A	.978	13	121	12	3	10	1
1928	Bos-A	.984	16	120	6	2	6	-1
1931	Bos-A	1.000	8	75	6	0	3	1
1932	Chi-A	1.000	1	1	0	0	0	0
Total	4	.986	38	317	24	5	19	1

C

YEAR	TM/L	PCT	G	PO	A	E	DP	FR
1928	Bos-A	—	1	0	0	0	0	0

■ Edd Roush OF

YEAR	TM/L	PCT	G	PO	A	E	DP	FR
1913	Chi-A	1.000	2	3	0	0	0	0
1914	Ind-F	.989	43	85	5	1	1	2
1915	New-F	.972	144	331	20	10	3	4
1916	NY-N	.952	15	18	2	1	1	0
	Cin-N	.971	69	192	7	6	1	4
	Yr	.969	84	210	9	7	2	4
1917	Cin-N	.962	134	335	15	14	0	-2
1918	Cin-N	.960	113	320	13	14	2	4
1919	Cin-N	.989	133	335	22	4	5	6
1920	Cin-N	.975	139	**410**	18	11	6	12
1921	Cin-N	.980	108	286	9	6	0	-2
1922	Cin-N	.990	43	96	8	1	0	2
1923	Cin-N	.970	137	337	14	11	3	-8
1924	Cin-N	.959	119	270	13	12	4	-7
1925	Cin-N	.978	134	343	15	8	3	-1
1926	Cin-N	.955	143	304	12	15	2	-14
1927	NY-N	.975	138	327	19	9	4	-8
1928	NY-N	.955	39	100	7	5	0	4
1929	NY-N	.982	107	248	18	5	5	-5
1931	Cin-N	.981	88	197	5	4	1	-2
Total	18	.972	1848	4537	222	137	41	-11

1B

YEAR	TM/L	PCT	G	PO	A	E	DP	FR
1914	Ind-F	.947	2	17	1	1	1	0
1920	Cin-N	.985	11	127	7	2	7	0
1926	Cin-N	1.000	1	2	0	0	0	0
Total	3	.981	14	146	8	3	8	0

2B

YEAR	TM/L	PCT	G	PO	A	E	DP	FR
1920	Cin-N	—	1	0	0	0	0	0

■ Dave Rowe OF

YEAR	TM/L	PCT	G	PO	A	E	DP	FR
1877	Chi-N	.667	2	2	0	1	0	0
1882	Cle-N	.837	23	33	3	7	1	-3
1883	Bal-a	.798	50	70	5	19	0	-7
1884	StL-U	**.947**	92	146	15	9	**5**	3
1885	StL-N	.906	16	28	1	3	1	-2
1886	KC-N	.851	90	154	11	29	2	-9
1888	KC-a	.914	32	54	10	6	1	2
Total	7	.878	305	487	45	4	10	-16

SS

YEAR	TM/L	PCT	G	PO	A	E	DP	FR
1883	Bal-a	.875	7	6	15	3	1	-2
1884	StL-U	.761	14	11	40	16	1	-3
1886	KC-N	.844	11	20	34	10	5	1
Total	3	.813	32	37	89	9	7	

YEAR	TM/L	PCT	G	PO	A	E	DP	FR
2B								
1884	StL-U	.583	2	4	3	5	0	-2
1886	KC-N	.848	4	11	17	5	4	2
Total	2	.778	6	15	20	0	4	0
1B								
1883	Bal-a	.958	3	22	1	1	1	0
1884	StL-U	1.000	2	13	0	0	0	0
Total	2	.973	5	35	1	1	1	0
■ Jack Rowe SS								
1881	Buf-N	.963	7	5	21	1	2	1
1882	Buf-N	.875	22	7	70	11	3	-3
1883	Buf-N	.783	18	10	44	15	3	-8
1884	Buf-N	.850	6	3	14	3	1	-3
1885	Buf-N	.834	65	71	186	51	26	-14
1886	Det-N	.880	110	86	310	54	26	-20
1887	Det-N	.907	124	119	378	51	36	-31
1888	Det-N	.861	105	133	312	72	24	-9
1889	Pit-N	.896	75	108	228	39	26	-5
1890	Buf-P	**.901**	125	228	381	67	56	-2
Total	10	.882	657	770	1944	364	203	-94
C								
1879	Buf-N	.905	6	30	8	4	0	1
1880	Buf-N	.897	60	231	56	33	3	-16
1881	Buf-N	.900	46	187	39	25	5	-10
1882	Buf-N	.950	46	246	41	15	5	-8
1883	Buf-N	.899	49	234	50	32	3	-4
1884	Buf-N	**.943**	65	373	60	26	4	-6
1885	Buf-N	.922	23	123	30	13	0	0
1886	Det-N	1.000	3	11	1	0	0	0
Total	8	.921	298	1435	285	148	20	-43
OF								
1879	Buf-N	.778	2	6	1	2	0	1
1880	Buf-N	.787	25	32	5	10	0	3
1881	Buf-N	.857	5	14	4	3	0	3
1882	Buf-N	—	1	0	0	0	0	0
1883	Buf-N	.714	28	34	1	14	0	-7
1884	Buf-N	.848	30	38	1	7	0	-5
1885	Buf-N	.893	12	25	0	3	0	-2
Total	7	.805	103	149	12	9	0	-13
3B								
1880	Buf-N	.786	3	4	7	3	0	0
1881	Buf-N	.759	7	13	9	7	0	-3
1882	Buf-N	.722	7	7	6	5	0	-4
1883	Buf-N	.714	3	2	3	2	0	-1
Total	4	.750	20	26	25	7	0	-8
■ Bama Rowell 2B								
1940	Bos-N	.953	115	251	360	30	81	-1
1941	Bos-N	.935	112	265	312	**40**	81	-10
1947	Bos-N	.952	7	9	11	1	1	-1
1948	Phi-N	.945	12	27	25	3	4	-5
Total	4	.945	246	552	708	4	167	-17
OF								
1939	Bos-N	.853	16	27	2	5	1	-1
1940	Bos-N	.778	7	7	0	2	0	-1
1941	Bos-N	.966	14	26	2	1	1	1
1946	Bos-N	.978	85	168	8	4	2	-1
1947	Bos-N	.945	100	202	4	12	0	-9
1948	Phi-N	.944	17	34	0	2	0	-2
Total	6	.949	239	464	16	6	4	-13
3B								
1941	Bos-N	1.000	2	5	3	0	1	0
1947	Bos-N	.846	4	5	6	2	0	-1
1948	Phi-N	.821	18	15	17	7	3	-5
Total	3	.850	24	25	26	9	4	-6
■ Jerry Royster 3B								
1973	LA-N	.842	6	2	14	3	1	2
1974	LA-N	—	1	0	0	0	0	0
1975	LA-N	.714	3	1	4	2	1	-1
1976	Atl-N	.962	148	**156**	306	18	**35**	18
1977	Atl-N	.953	56	46	76	6	6	-4
1978	Atl-N	—	1	0	0	0	0	0
1979	Atl-N	.948	80	91	181	15	12	12
1980	Atl-N	1.000	48	15	37	0	1	2
1981	Atl-N	.950	24	15	23	2	2	1
1982	Atl-N	.943	62	31	51	5	3	-5
1983	Atl-N	.940	47	26	68	6	5	2
1984	Atl-N	.943	17	14	19	2	0	-2
1985	SD-N	.974	29	13	24	1	1	0
1986	SD-N	.931	59	25	83	8	9	2
1987	Chi-A	.969	30	22	41	2	4	-5
	NY-A	.909	13	4	16	2	2	0
	Yr	.954	43	26	57	4	6	-5
1988	Atl-N	.917	10	4	7	1	1	0
Total	16	.951	634	465	950	3	83	22
2B								
1973	LA-N	1.000	1	1	0	0	0	0
1974	LA-N	1.000	1	0	2	0	0	1
1975	LA-N	1.000	4	5	11	0	3	1
1977	Atl-N	.958	38	76	85	7	14	-7
1978	Atl-N	.974	75	186	193	10	39	-8
1979	Atl-N	.983	77	170	224	7	50	1
1980	Atl-N	.948	49	108	129	13	30	-10
1981	Atl-N	.960	13	20	28	2	7	2
1982	Atl-N	.948	16	21	34	3	8	1
1983	Atl-N	.989	26	42	51	1	17	4
1984	Atl-N	.973	29	51	95	4	15	4
1985	SD-N	.975	58	112	165	7	33	1
1986	SD-N	.950	21	39	37	4	7	-2
1987	Chi-A	1.000	5	12	5	0	1	-2
	NY-A	1.000	1	5	6	0	1	2
	Yr	1.000	6	17	11	0	2	0
1988	Atl-N	1.000	2	0	1	0	0	0
Total	15	.971	416	848	1066	8	225	-12
SS								
1975	LA-N	—	1	0	0	0	0	-1
1976	Atl-N	.857	2	2	4	1	0	-1
1977	Atl-N	.917	51	60	106	15	20	-17
1978	Atl-N	.956	60	98	183	13	27	-4
1982	Atl-N	.975	10	14	25	1	8	2
1983	Atl-N	.966	13	19	37	2	7	2
1984	Atl-N	.957	16	20	47	3	7	2
1985	SD-N	1.000	7	4	25	0	3	1
1986	SD-N	.970	24	19	46	2	7	-2
1987	NY-A	1.000	1	1	6	0	1	1
1988	Atl-N	1.000	2	0	1	0	0	0
Total	11	.951	187	237	480	7	80	-17
OF								
1974	LA-N	1.000	1	0	1	0	0	1
1975	LA-N	1.000	7	6	0	0	0	0
1977	Atl-N	—	1	0	0	0	0	0
1980	Atl-N	.935	41	72	0	5	1	-7
1982	Atl-N	.953	25	39	2	2	1	0
1983	Atl-N	.962	18	25	0	1	0	0
1984	Atl-N	1.000	11	14	1	0	1	0
1985	SD-N	1.000	2	1	0	0	0	0
1986	SD-N	1.000	7	4	0	0	0	0
1987	Chi-A	1.000	13	22	1	0	0	0
	NY-A	—	1	0	0	0	0	0
	Yr	1.000	14	22	1	0	0	0
1988	Atl-N	1.000	26	45	2	0	0	3
Total	11	.967	153	228	7	8	3	-3
■ Vic Roznovsky C								
1964	Chi-N	.976	26	67	14	2	2	-6
1965	Chi-N	.984	63	270	30	5	6	1
1966	Bal-A	.995	34	176	13	1	1	-2
1967	Bal-A	.993	23	133	10	1	2	-2
1969	Phi-N	1.000	2	6	0	0	0	0
Total	5	.988	148	652	67	9	11	-9
■ Al Rubeling 3B								
1940	Phi-A	.933	98	96	184	20	13	-7
1941	Phi-A	.833	6	7	8	3	1	-2
1943	Pit-N	1.000	1	2	2	0	0	0
1944	Pit-N	1.000	16	18	38	0	5	2
Total	4	.939	121	123	232	3	19	-7
2B								
1940	Phi-A	.962	10	24	27	2	6	-1
1943	Pit-N	.974	44	87	138	6	27	0
1944	Pit-N	.947	17	19	17	2	1	-2
Total	3	.969	71	130	182	0	34	-3
OF								
1944	Pit-N	1.000	18	33	1	0	1	0
■ Johnny Rucker OF								
1940	NY-N	.954	57	121	3	6	0	-3
1941	NY-N	.967	142	344	13	12	5	1
1943	NY-N	.969	117	300	9	10	3	2
1944	NY-N	.985	139	310	14	5	4	-9
1945	NY-N	.978	98	256	6	6	2	-4
1946	NY-N	.948	54	91	1	5	0	-3
Total	6	.971	607	1422	46	4	14	-20
■ Joe Rudi OF								
1967	KC-A	1.000	6	6	1	0	0	1
1968	Oak-A	.987	56	77	1	1	0	-4
1969	Oak-A	1.000	18	40	2	0	0	1
1970	Oak-A	.982	63	106	5	2	1	-3
1971	Oak-A	.996	121	249	5	1	1	2
1972	Oak-A	.992	147	247	9	2	1	-6
1973	Oak-A	.992	117	231	6	2	2	0
1974	Oak-A	.984	140	234	7	4	0	-13
1975	Oak-A	1.000	44	72	1	0	1	0
1976	Oak-A	.989	126	258	6	3	2	-5
1977	Cal-A	1.000	61	131	3	0	0	0
1978	Cal-A	.992	111	231	4	2	1	0
1979	Cal-A	.989	80	174	5	2	2	0
1980	Cal-A	.991	90	220	5	2	1	5
1981	Bos-A	—	1	0	0	0	0	0
1982	Cal-A	.947	14	18	0	1	0	0
Total	16	.991	1195	2294	60	2	12	-22
1B								
1967	KC-A	.984	9	63	0	1	1	-2
1969	Oak-A	.971	11	94	7	3	10	0
1970	Oak-A	.991	28	196	13	2	16	-2
1971	Oak-A	.971	5	31	2	1	0	0
1973	Oak-A	—	1	0	0	0	0	0
1974	Oak-A	.995	27	182	11	1	21	-2
1975	Oak-A	.991	91	732	36	7	64	-9
1976	Oak-A	1.000	2	12	1	0	2	0
1978	Cal-A	1.000	10	61	6	0	8	0
1979	Cal-A	1.000	5	33	2	0	3	0
1980	Cal-A	1.000	6	24	0	0	4	-1
1981	Bos-A	1.000	5	47	1	0	2	-1
1982	Oak-A	.991	49	398	20	4	37	-4
Total	13	.991	249	1873	99	9	168	-21
3B								
1972	Oak-A	—	1	0	0	0	0	0
■ Ken Rudolph C								
1969	Chi-N	.977	11	39	3	1	0	0
1970	Chi-N	1.000	16	67	6	0	1	1
1971	Chi-N	.989	25	153	16	0	1	7
1972	Chi-N	.966	41	178	23	7	2	6
1973	Chi-N	.970	64	259	28	9	4	-3
1974	SF-N	.996	56	253	25	1	4	3
1975	StL-N	.972	31	93	11	3	1	2
1976	StL-N	.940	14	61	2	4	1	2
1977	SF-N	.946	11	30	5	2	3	2
	Bal-A	1.000	11	36	5	0	1	5
Total	9	.980	280	1169	124	7	18	25
OF								
1969	Chi-N	1.000	3	2	0	0	0	0
■ Muddy Ruel C								
1915	StL-A	.958	6	20	3	1	0	-1
1917	NY-A	1.000	6	23	6	0	0	-1
1918	NY-A	1.000	2	8	2	0	0	0
1919	NY-A	.975	79	340	90	11	6	2
1920	NY-A	.984	80	317	62	6	2	0
1921	Bos-A	.977	109	375	86	11	7	-10
1922	Bos-A	.978	112	359	96	10	**17**	-2
1923	Was-A	.980	133	**528**	**146**	14	14	**18**
1924	Was-A	.980	**147**	**612**	112	15	**23**	**12**
1925	Was-A	.982	126	491	103	11	**18**	10
1926	Was-A	**.989**	117	452	81	6	13	0
1927	Was-A	.988	**128**	495	100	7	8	-4
1928	Was-A	**.989**	101	397	73	5	5	7
1929	Was-A	.990	62	247	52	3	6	**9**
1930	Was-A	.986	60	243	32	4	5	3
1931	Bos-A	.945	30	83	21	6	2	1
	Det-A	.975	14	60	17	2	2	3
	Yr	.958	44	143	38	8	4	4
1932	Det-A	.989	49	150	25	2	3	-2
1933	StL-A	1.000	28	72	21	0	3	2
1934	Chi-A	.976	21	75	8	2	1	-2
Total	19	.982	1410	5347	1136	116	135	45
1B								
1925	Was-A	1.000	1	2	0	0	1	0
1928	Was-A	.955	2	19	2	1	1	0
Total	2	.958	3	21	2	1	2	0
■ Chico Ruiz 2B								
1964	Cin-N	.967	30	62	84	5	19	0
1967	Cin-N	.969	56	110	142	8	27	4
1968	Cin-N	.979	34	50	93	3	18	9
1969	Cin-N	.949	39	82	87	9	25	-1
1970	Cal-A	1.000	3	1	0	0	0	0
1971	Cal-A	1.000	2	1	3	0	0	2
Total	6	.966	164	306	409	5	89	14
3B								
1964	Cin-N	.942	49	33	65	6	9	-10
1965	Cin-N	.875	4	3	4	1	0	4
1966	Cin-N	.927	27	18	33	4	2	1
1967	Cin-N	.923	13	6	6	1	1	-1
1968	Cin-N	1.000	5	5	3	0	0	0
1969	Cin-N	.667	7	2	2	2	0	-1
1970	Cal-A	.985	27	21	43	1	4	1
1971	Cal-A	1.000	3	1	1	0	0	1
Total	8	.943	135	89	157	5	16	-5
SS								
1965	Cin-N	1.000	3	0	1	0	0	0
1966	Cin-N	1.000	6	2	2	0	1	0
1967	Cin-N	.971	11	14	20	1	5	-2
1968	Cin-N	.667	3	1	1	1	1	0
1969	Cin-N	.989	29	33	58	1	11	-4
1970	Cal-A	.833	3	2	3	1	0	0
Total	6	.972	55	52	85	4	18	-6
1B								
1968	Cin-N	.977	16	40	2	1	2	0
1969	Cin-N	1.000	2	3	0	0	0	0
1970	Cal-A	1.000	2	2	0	0	1	0
Total	3	.979	20	45	2	1	3	0
OF								
1966	Cin-N	1.000	8	3	0	0	0	0
1967	Cin-N	1.000	5	1	0	0	0	0
1969	Cin-N	—	1	0	0	0	0	0
Total	3	1.000	14	4	0	0	0	0
C								
1970	Cal-A	—	1	0	0	0	0	0
■ Pete Runnels 1B								
1956	Was-A	.995	81	693	49	4	73	1
1957	Was-A	.995	72	616	44	3	59	0
1958	Bos-A	.995	42	364	15	2	41	-4
1959	Bos-A	1.000	44	387	28	0	48	1
1960	Bos-A	.994	57	142	11	1	15	0
1961	Bos-A	**.995**	113	701	50	4	92	-2
1962	Bos-A	.993	151	1309	104	10	125	-1
1963	Hou-N	.993	70	526	40	4	31	-1
1964	Hou-N	.986	14	138	5	2	8	-2
Total	9	.994	644	4876	346	0	492	-8
2B								
1952	Was-A	1.000	1	5	4	0	2	1
1953	Was-A	.944	11	24	27	3	7	-3
1954	Was-A	.968	27	90	59	5	23	-2
1955	Was-A	.976	132	349	338	17	107	-2
1956	Was-A	.973	69	179	177	10	56	0
1957	Was-A	.979	23	52	43	2	13	0
1958	Bos-A	.985	106	267	320	9	88	12
1959	Bos-A	.982	101	273	272	10	82	5
1960	Bos-A	**.986**	129	274	360	9	99	9
1961	Bos-A	1.000	7	6	11	0	5	2
1963	Hou-N	.985	36	64	64	2	18	-9
Total	11	.980	642	1583	1675	7	500	13
SS								
1951	Was-A	.949	73	159	176	18	41	-21
1952	Was-A	.966	147	**314**	406	25	97	-16
1953	Was-A	.958	121	195	324	23	87	-30
1954	Was-A	.953	107	174	313	24	69	-17
1955	Was-A	.667	2	0	2	1	0	0
1956	Was-A	1.000	3	3	3	0	2	0
1959	Bos-A	1.000	9	3	7	0	1	0
1961	Bos-A	—	1	0	0	0	0	0
Total	8	.958	463	848	1231	1	297	-84
3B								
1957	Was-A	.972	32	31	73	3	12	2
1960	Bos-A	.909	3	4	6	1	0	-1
1961	Bos-A	.949	11	8	29	2	0	1
1963	Hou-N	1.000	3	3	7	0	1	1
Total	4	.964	49	46	115	6	13	3

YEAR	TM/L	PCT	G	PO	A	E	DP	FR
		OF						
1954	Was-A	—	1	0	0	0	0	0
■ Rip Russell 1B								
1939	Chi-N	.988	143	1383	83	18	109	-5
1940	Chi-N	.982	51	518	18	10	22	-6
1941	Chi-N	.975	5	36	3	1	4	0
1942	Chi-N	.974	35	328	13	9	30	-5
Total	4	.984	234	2265	117	8	165	-16
		3B						
1940	Chi-N	1.000	3	1	4	0	0	0
1942	Chi-N	.933	10	6	8	1	0	-3
1946	Bos-A	.942	70	59	137	12	24	-1
1947	Bos-A	.923	13	7	29	3	2	1
Total	4	.940	96	73	178	6	26	-3
		2B						
1942	Chi-N	.968	24	51	69	4	10	-4
1946	Bos-A	1.000	3	2	3	0	1	0
Total	2	.969	27	53	72	4	11	-4
		OF						
1942	Chi-N	1.000	3	7	0	0	0	0
■ Jim Russell OF								
1942	Pit-N	1.000	3	12	0	0	0	1
1943	Pit-N	.990	134	285	16	3	3	2
1944	Pit-N	.986	149	345	20	5	**7**	10
1945	Pit-N	.973	140	313	9	9	1	0
1946	Pit-N	.966	134	308	7	**11**	1	-10
1947	Pit-N	.980	119	343	6	7	3	**14**
1948	Bos-N	.992	84	246	3	2	0	2
1949	Bos-N	.975	120	269	3	7	3	-14
1950	Bro-N	.993	55	131	3	1	0	4
1951	Bro-N	1.000	4	3	0	0	0	0
Total	10	.981	942	2255	67	5	18	9
		1B						
1943	Pit-N	1.000	6	38	0	0	3	-1
1946	Pit-N	.978	5	43	2	1	6	-1
Total	2	.988	11	81	2	1	9	-2
■ John Russell C								
1984	Phi-N	1.000	2	1	0	0	0	0
1986	Phi-N	.976	89	498	39	13	10	-3
1987	Phi-N	1.000	7	28	0	0	0	-1
1988	Phi-N	.945	15	77	9	5	3	3
1989	Atl-N	.990	45	178	24	2	1	-3
1990	Tex-A	.980	31	135	11	3	0	4
Total	6	.978	189	917	83	3	14	0
		OF						
1984	Phi-N	1.000	29	50	1	0	0	-1
1985	Phi-N	1.000	49	56	4	0	1	-2
1987	Phi-N	.955	10	20	1	1	0	0
1989	Atl-N	.867	14	12	1	2	0	0
1990	Tex-A	1.000	6	5	0	0	0	0
Total	5	.980	108	143	7	3	1	-3
		1B						
1985	Phi-N	.967	18	114	5	4	6	-3
1989	Atl-N	1.000	2	6	0	0	0	0
1990	Tex-A	1.000	3	8	0	0	0	0
Total	3	.971	23	128	5	4	6	-3
		3B						
1989	Atl-N	1.000	2	0	3	0	0	0
1990	Tex-A	—	1	0	0	0	0	0
Total	2	1.000	3	0	3	0	0	0
■ Bill Russell SS								
1970	LA-N	1.000	1	0	2	0	0	0
1971	LA-N	.857	6	1	5	1	2	0
1972	LA-N	.949	121	197	439	**34**	69	16
1973	LA-N	.963	**162**	243	**560**	31	106	9
1974	LA-N	.946	160	194	491	**39**	68	-19
1975	LA-N	.967	83	94	230	11	27	-21
1976	LA-N	.963	149	251	476	28	90	-14
1977	LA-N	.963	153	234	523	29	**102**	10
1978	LA-N	.962	155	245	533	31	91	12
1979	LA-N	.957	150	218	452	30	70	-27
1980	LA-N	.968	129	179	387	19	57	-22
1981	LA-N	.965	80	128	261	14	49	10
1982	LA-N	.961	150	216	502	29	64	-4
1983	LA-N	.964	127	192	392	22	61	0
1984	LA-N	.965	65	81	165	9	29	-2
1985	LA-N	.919	23	27	64	8	11	-2
1986	LA-N	.962	32	36	64	4	13	0
Total	17	.960	1746	2536	5546	339	909	-54
		OF						
1969	LA-N	.978	86	132	4	3	1	7
1970	LA-N	.983	79	167	8	3	1	6
1971	LA-N	1.000	40	49	1	0	0	3
1972	LA-N	1.000	6	5	0	0	0	0
1974	LA-N	—	1	0	0	0	0	0
1984	LA-N	1.000	18	31	1	0	0	-1
1985	LA-N	.958	21	23	0	1	0	-2
1986	LA-N	1.000	48	47	2	0	0	-1
Total	8	.985	299	454	16	7	2	11
		2B						
1971	LA-N	.964	41	81	108	7	21	2
1984	LA-N	1.000	5	3	7	0	0	0
1985	LA-N	.964	8	10	17	1	0	-1
1986	LA-N	.974	8	20	18	1	4	0
Total	4	.967	62	114	150	9	25	1
		3B						
1985	LA-N	1.000	5	0	1	0	0	0
1986	LA-N	—	1	0	0	0	0	0
Total	2	1.000	6	0	1	0	0	0
■ Babe Ruth OF								
1918	Bos-A	.949	59	121	8	7	3	1
1919	Bos-A	**.996**	111	222	14	1	6	4
1920	NY-A	.936	141	259	21	19	3	1
1921	NY-A	.966	152	348	17	13	6	4
1922	NY-A	.964	110	226	14	9	3	1
1923	NY-A	.973	148	378	20	11	2	17
1924	NY-A	.962	152	340	18	14	4	7
1925	NY-A	.974	98	207	15	6	3	9
1926	NY-A	.979	149	308	11	7	5	1
1927	NY-A	.963	151	328	14	13	4	5
1928	NY-A	.975	**154**	304	9	8	0	3
1929	NY-A	.984	133	240	5	4	2	-9
1930	NY-A	.965	144	266	10	10	0	-1
1931	NY-A	.972	142	237	5	7	2	-11
1932	NY-A	.961	128	209	10	9	1	-9
1933	NY-A	.970	132	215	9	7	4	-9
1934	NY-A	.962	111	197	3	8	0	-9
1935	Bos-N	.952	26	39	1	2	0	-3
Total	18	.968	2241	4444	204	155	48	-4
		1B						
1918	Bos-A	.965	13	130	6	5	8	-1
1919	Bos-A	.975	5	35	4	1	4	0
1920	NY-A	.909	2	10	0	1	1	0
1921	NY-A	1.000	2	8	0	0	0	0
1922	NY-A	—	1	0	0	0	0	0
1923	NY-A	.977	4	41	1	1	2	-1
1926	NY-A	1.000	2	10	0	0	2	0
1931	NY-A	1.000	1	5	0	0	0	0
1932	NY-A	1.000	1	3	0	0	0	0
1933	NY-A	.857	1	6	0	1	0	0
Total	10	.966	32	248	11	9	17	-2
■ Connie Ryan 2B								
1942	NY-N	.944	11	31	36	4	6	7
1943	Bos-N	.962	100	224	306	21	41	-24
1944	Bos-N	.974	80	210	272	13	57	14
1946	Bos-N	.968	120	285	317	20	53	-4
1947	Bos-N	.973	150	393	432	**23**	88	-7
1948	Bos-N	.966	40	89	112	7	19	5
1949	Bos-N	.958	16	40	29	3	9	1
1950	Bos-N	1.000	20	57	59	0	16	1
	Cin-N	.973	103	304	283	16	77	11
	Yr	.978	123	361	342	**16**	93	12
1951	Cin-N	.970	121	332	344	21	73	-3
1952	Phi-N	.972	**154**	348	**462**	23	95	-5
1953	Phi-N	.958	65	134	166	13	39	-6
Total	11	.970	980	2447	2818	164	573	-10
		3B						
1943	Bos-N	.971	30	33	68	3	6	5
1944	Bos-N	.979	14	23	24	1	1	-1
1946	Bos-N	.970	24	15	50	2	5	3
1948	Bos-N	.900	4	2	2	0	0	0
1949	Bos-N	.973	25	22	50	2	7	3
1951	Cin-N	.923	3	5	7	1	0	0
1953	Chi-A	.927	16	20	31	4	1	-1
Total	7	.964	116	120	232	3	20	9
		SS						
1947	Bos-N	1.000	1	1	1	0	0	0
1949	Bos-N	.965	18	33	50	3	7	1
Total	2	.966	19	34	51	3	7	1
		1B						
1949	Bos-N	1.000	3	23	2	0	1	0
1951	Cin-N	1.000	2	10	2	0	2	0
1953	Phi-N	1.000	2	4	2	0	0	1
Total	3	1.000	7	37	6	0	3	1
		OF						
1951	Cin-N	1.000	1	1	0	0	0	0
■ Jimmy Ryan OF								
1885	Chi-N	.500	1	3	0	3	0	-1
1886	Chi-N	.828	70	93	18	23	3	0
1887	Chi-N	.857	122	164	33	33	7	-9
1888	Chi-N	.878	128	217	**34**	35	5	3
1889	Chi-N	.926	106	252	36	23	**9**	12
1890	Chi-P	.919	118	257	25	25	5	2
1891	Chi-N	.905	117	231	25	27	3	5
1892	Chi-N	.921	120	241	26	23	5	7
1893	Chi-N	.908	73	162	16	18	2	0
1894	Chi-N	.910	108	221	22	24	3	9
1895	Chi-N	.937	108	161	18	12	6	2
1896	Chi-N	.912	128	207	21	22	4	0
1897	Chi-N	.945	**136**	211	28	14	7	7
1898	Chi-N	.914	144	267	20	27	2	-7
1899	Chi-N	.956	125	266	18	13	6	1
1900	Chi-N	.913	105	177	12	18	3	-11
1902	Was-A	.949	120	280	16	16	0	3
1903	Was-A	.970	114	288	7	9	1	3
Total	18	.918	1943	3698	375	365	71	24
		SS						
1885	Chi-N	.737	2	3	11	5	0	1
1886	Chi-N	.857	6	4	14	3	0	0
1889	Chi-N	.794	29	34	97	34	10	-7
1891	Chi-N	.889	2	4	4	1	0	0
1892	Chi-N	.854	9	17	24	7	2	-1
1893	Chi-N	.860	10	20	23	7	2	-1
Total	6	.817	58	82	173	7	14	-8
		2B						
1886	Chi-N	1.000	5	9	9	0	1	1
1887	Chi-N	.727	3	4	4	3	1	-1
Total	2	.897	8	13	13	3	2	0
		3B						
1886	Chi-N	.842	6	9	7	3	0	-2
■ Jack Ryan C								
1889	Lou-a	.864	15	51	25	12	1	-5
1890	Lou-a	.932	89	415	148	**41**	5	7
1891	Lou-a	.930	56	223	83	23	10	7
1894	Bos-N	.911	51	168	46	21	7	0
1895	Bos-N	.951	43	167	46	11	2	6
1896	Bos-N	.910	8	32	9	4	1	2
1898	Bro-N	.960	84	289	97	16	13	3
1899	Bal-N	1.000	2	4	4	0	1	2
1901	StL-N	.982	65	292	84	7	7	2
1902	StL-N	.966	66	258	86	12	8	-9
1903	StL-N	.971	47	168	65	7	4	-9
1913	Was-A	.000	1	1	0	0	0	0
Total	12	.947	527	2068	690	154	59	6
		1B						
1890	Lou-a	—	1	0	0	0	0	0
1891	Lou-a	.921	11	90	3	8	5	-1
1894	Bos-N	1.000	2	5	1	0	1	0
1898	Bro-N	1.000	1	3	0	0	0	0
1901	StL-N	1.000	5	50	5	0	7	1
1902	StL-N	1.000	4	37	3	0	3	1
1903	StL-N	.989	18	174	9	2	17	0
Total	7	.974	42	359	21	0	33	1
		2B						
1891	Lou-a	.846	3	8	3	2	0	-1
1895	Lou-a	.914	5	15	17	3	4	0
1901	StL-N	.882	9	17	28	6	3	1
1902	StL-N	1.000	2	5	6	0	0	0
Total	4	.900	19	45	54	1	7	0
		3B						
1889	Lou-a	.714	2	4	1	2	0	-1
1891	Lou-a	.864	6	9	10	3	0	0
1898	Bro-N	.900	4	5	4	1	1	-1
1902	StL-N	1.000	4	3	8	0	1	1
1912	Was-A	1.000	1	1	1	0	0	0
Total	5	.885	17	22	24	6	2	-1
		OF						
1889	Lou-a	1.000	4	8	0	0	0	-1
1890	Lou-a	1.000	3	5	0	0	0	0
1891	Lou-a	.600	4	3	0	2	0	-2
1895	Bos-N	1.000	1	1	0	0	0	0
1901	StL-N	.800	3	3	1	1	0	0
Total	5	.875	15	20	1	3	0	-3
		SS						
1890	Lou-a	.000	1	0	0	2	0	-1
1902	StL-N	—	1	0	0	0	0	0
1903	StL-N	.889	2	1	7	1	0	0
Total	3	.727	4	1	7	3	0	-1
■ Buddy Ryan OF								
1912	Cle-A	.963	90	167	14	7	2	4
1913	Cle-A	.986	68	138	7	2	2	-2
Total	2	.973	158	305	21	9	4	2
		1B						
1913	Cle-A	1.000	1	6	1	0	0	0
■ Blondy Ryan SS								
1930	Chi-A	1.000	2	3	3	0	1	0
1933	NY-N	.950	146	296	**494**	42	95	17
1934	NY-N	.915	30	49	70	11	14	-3
1935	Phi-N	.912	35	87	110	19	24	2
	NY-A	.908	30	48	80	13	12	-4
1937	NY-N	.941	19	40	55	6	13	1
1938	NY-N	1.000	2	1	4	0	1	0
Total	6	.936	264	524	816	1	160	13
		3B						
1930	Chi-A	.875	23	23	40	9	5	-1
1934	NY-N	.953	65	58	144	10	7	9
1935	Phi-N	1.000	1	0	1	0	0	0
1937	NY-N	1.000	1	0	1	0	0	0
1938	NY-N	.667	3	1	3	2	0	-1
Total	5	.928	93	82	189	1	12	7
		2B						
1930	Chi-A	.833	1	4	1	1	0	-1
1934	NY-N	.960	25	52	69	5	12	5
1935	Phi-N	—	1	0	0	0	0	0
1937	NY-N	1.000	1	1	1	0	0	0
1938	NY-N	1.000	5	4	9	0	1	0
Total	5	.959	33	61	80	6	13	4
■ Mike Ryan C								
1964	Bos-A	1.000	1	5	0	0	0	-1
1965	Bos-A	.981	33	194	18	4	0	1
1966	Bos-A	.992	114	685	50	6	7	1
1967	Bos-A	.988	79	473	34	6	11	0
1968	Phi-N	.991	96	501	62	5	7	-4
1969	Phi-N	.991	132	769	**79**	8	13	1
1970	Phi-N	.992	46	238	15	2	1	-13
1971	Phi-N	.990	43	222	30	0	2	12
1972	Phi-N	.992	46	216	21	2	3	6
1973	Phi-N	.992	27	121	9	1	0	0
1974	Pit-N	1.000	15	49	7	0	1	3
Total	11	.991	632	3473	325	4	45	6
■ Chris Sabo 3B								
1988	Cin-N	**.966**	135	75	318	14	**31**	**19**
1989	Cin-N	.943	76	36	145	11	12	-3
1990	Cin-N	**.966**	146	70	273	12	17	-6
Total	3	.961	357	181	736	7	60	10
		SS						
1988	Cin-N	—	2	0	0	0	0	0
■ Mike Sadek C								
1973	SF-N	.981	35	146	7	3	1	8
1975	SF-N	.995	38	207	10	1	3	6
1976	SF-N	.985	51	191	11	3	0	8
1977	SF-N	.992	57	227	32	2	3	10
1978	SF-N	.975	37	182	15	5	2	2
1979	SF-N	.993	60	246	21	2	3	3
1980	SF-N	.974	59	266	29	8	1	4
1981	SF-N	.979	19	79	15	2	2	7
Total	8	.985	356	1544	140	6	14	48
		OF						
1979	SF-N	—	1	0	0	0	0	0
■ Ed Sadowski C								
1960	Bos-A	.995	36	178	11	1	0	5
1961	LA-A	.987	56	295	17	4	4	8
1962	LA-A	.968	18	86	4	3	0	3
1963	LA-A	.997	68	340	38	1	7	**20**

YEAR	TM/L	PCT	G	PO	A	E	DP	FR
1966	Atl-N	1.000	3	15	2	0	0	1
Total	5	.991	181	914	72	9	11	37

■ Tom Saffell OF

YEAR	TM/L	PCT	G	PO	A	E	DP	FR
1949	Pit-N	.992	53	122	2	1	1	0
1950	Pit-N	.993	43	128	5	1	0	9
1951	Pit-N	.929	17	25	1	2	0	1
1955	Pit-N	.964	47	78	2	3	0	4
	KC-A	.962	9	25	0	1	0	0
Total	4	.980	169	378	10	8	1	14

■ Vic Saier 1B

YEAR	TM/L	PCT	G	PO	A	E	DP	FR
1911	Chi-N	.980	73	715	33	15	44	-4
1912	Chi-N	.992	120	1165	52	10	67	-5
1913	Chi-N	.983	149	1472	71	26	79	-5
1914	Chi-N	.986	153	1521	59	22	62	-11
1915	Chi-N	.985	139	1348	65	21	71	-5
1916	Chi-N	.984	147	1622	74	27	78	0
1917	Chi-N	1.000	6	56	7	0	3	2
1919	Pit-N	.985	51	493	17	8	18	-5
Total	8	.986	838	8392	378	129	422	-33

■ Ebba St.Claire C

YEAR	TM/L	PCT	G	PO	A	E	DP	FR
1951	Bos-N	.977	62	267	29	7	5	3
1952	Bos-N	.972	34	151	21	5	4	5
1953	Mil-N	.992	27	106	11	1	3	3
1954	NY-N	.975	16	72	7	2	3	2
Total	4	.978	139	596	68	5	15	13

■ Lenn Sakata 2B

YEAR	TM/L	PCT	G	PO	A	E	DP	FR
1977	Mil-A	.985	53	102	159	4	43	17
1978	Mil-A	.975	29	50	66	3	12	0
1979	Mil-A	1.000	4	10	13	0	5	2
1980	Bal-A	.984	34	55	72	2	18	7
1981	Bal-A	.986	20	30	42	1	10	3
1982	Bal-A	.977	83	106	145	6	34	-3
1983	Bal-A	.990	60	84	117	2	36	8
1984	Bal-A	.988	76	80	161	3	33	5
1985	Bal-A	.960	50	58	87	6	18	-1
1986	Oak-A	.984	16	21	39	1	4	5
1987	NY-A	1.000	6	5	7	0	3	0
Total	11	.982	431	601	908	8	216	43

SS

YEAR	TM/L	PCT	G	PO	A	E	DP	FR
1980	Bal-A	1.000	4	0	1	0	0	0
1981	Bal-A	.963	42	52	106	6	23	-2
1982	Bal-A	.958	56	76	154	10	27	-2
Total	3	.960	102	128	261	6	50	-4

3B

YEAR	TM/L	PCT	G	PO	A	E	DP	FR
1987	NY-A	.929	12	3	23	2	1	1

C

YEAR	TM/L	PCT	G	PO	A	E	DP	FR
1983	Bal-A	—	1	0	0	0	0	0

OF

YEAR	TM/L	PCT	G	PO	A	E	DP	FR
1984	Bal-A	—	1	0	0	0	0	0

■ Mark Salas C

YEAR	TM/L	PCT	G	PO	A	E	DP	FR
1984	StL-N	1.000	4	11	2	0	0	0
1985	Min-A	.991	115	529	39	5	10	3
1986	Min-A	.980	69	358	32	8	5	-6
1987	Min-A	.989	14	86	3	1	0	1
	NY-A	1.000	41	172	13	0	0	-1
	Yr	.996	55	258	16	1	0	0
1988	Chi-A	.979	69	251	35	6	5	0
1989	Cle-A	1.000	5	3	1	0	0	0
1990	Det-A	.988	57	227	22	3	3	-4
Total	7	.987	374	1637	147	3	23	-7

OF

YEAR	TM/L	PCT	G	PO	A	E	DP	FR
1984	StL-N	1.000	3	2	0	0	0	0
1987	NY-A	—	1	0	0	0	0	0
Total	2	1.000	4	2	0	0	0	0

3B

YEAR	TM/L	PCT	G	PO	A	E	DP	FR
1990	Det-A	1.000	1	0	1	0	0	0

■ Angel Salazar SS

YEAR	TM/L	PCT	G	PO	A	E	DP	FR
1983	Mon-N	.966	34	28	28	2	9	2
1984	Mon-N	.960	80	88	155	10	35	-3
1986	KC-A	.978	115	121	283	9	50	-5
1987	KC-A	.981	116	134	332	9	56	22
1988	Chi-N	.966	29	36	50	3	11	7
Total	5	.974	374	407	848	3	161	23

2B

YEAR	TM/L	PCT	G	PO	A	E	DP	FR
1986	KC-A	1.000	1	0	1	0	0	0
1988	Chi-N	—	2	0	0	0	0	0
Total	2	1.000	3	0	1	0	0	0

3B

YEAR	TM/L	PCT	G	PO	A	E	DP	FR
1988	Chi-N	1.000	1	2	3	0	0	0

■ Luis Salazar 3B

YEAR	TM/L	PCT	G	PO	A	E	DP	FR
1980	SD-N	.944	42	29	88	7	7	-2
1981	SD-N	.955	94	63	189	12	16	0
1982	SD-N	.938	129	104	291	26	28	20
1983	SD-N	.949	118	102	250	19	17	13
1984	SD-N	.970	58	41	90	4	5	7
1985	SD-N	.925	39	22	52	6	5	1
1987	SD-N	.957	38	17	49	3	4	0
1988	Det-A	.985	31	12	55	1	2	-1
1989	SD-N	.968	72	37	116	5	10	9
	Chi-N	.921	25	8	27	3	1	-6
	Yr	.959	97	45	143	8	11	3
1990	Chi-N	.950	91	55	136	10	12	-17
Total	10	.950	737	490	1343	6	107	24

OF

YEAR	TM/L	PCT	G	PO	A	E	DP	FR
1980	SD-N	1.000	4	10	0	0	0	0
1981	SD-N	.959	23	45	2	2	1	1
1982	SD-N	1.000	1	1	0	0	0	0
1984	SD-N	.957	24	43	2	2	0	2
1985	Chi-A	.968	84	118	3	4	2	0
1987	SD-N	1.000	10	9	0	0	0	0
1988	Det-A	.992	68	127	4	1	1	1
1989	SD-N	.947	14	18	0	1	0	0
	Chi-N	1.000	2	1	1	0	0	1
	Yr	.952	16	19	1	1	0	1
1990	Chi-N	.955	28	41	1	2	0	-1
Total	9	.973	258	413	13	2	4	4

SS

YEAR	TM/L	PCT	G	PO	A	E	DP	FR
1982	SD-N	.955	18	28	35	3	4	-3
1983	SD-N	.957	19	20	24	2	5	-3
1984	SD-N	1.000	4	3	5	0	0	0
1987	SD-N	.923	22	27	45	6	7	-6
1988	Det-A	.944	37	51	84	8	18	-7
1989	SD-N	.958	9	13	10	1	6	0
Total	6	.945	109	142	203	0	40	-19

1B

YEAR	TM/L	PCT	G	PO	A	E	DP	FR
1985	Chi-A	1.000	6	40	2	0	6	0
1987	SD-N	1.000	1	3	0	0	0	0
1988	Det-A	1.000	4	6	0	0	0	0
1989	SD-N	1.000	2	2	0	0	2	0
Total	4	1.000	13	51	2	0	8	0

2B

YEAR	TM/L	PCT	G	PO	A	E	DP	FR
1988	Det-A	1.000	5	3	8	0	1	-1

■ Bill Salkeld C

YEAR	TM/L	PCT	G	PO	A	E	DP	FR
1945	Pit-N	.973	86	279	40	9	8	-9
1946	Pit-N	.972	51	176	31	6	3	0
1947	Pit-N	.971	15	29	4	1	0	-3
1948	Bos-N	.990	59	254	32	3	5	5
1949	Bos-N	.980	63	230	21	5	3	-4
1950	Chi-A	1.000	1	4	0	0	0	0
Total	6	.979	275	972	128	4	19	-11

■ Chico Salmon 2B

YEAR	TM/L	PCT	G	PO	A	E	DP	FR
1964	Cle-A	.983	32	51	62	2	10	-3
1965	Cle-A	1.000	5	7	4	0	3	0
1966	Cle-A	.951	28	52	65	6	10	-4
1967	Cle-A	.964	24	44	64	4	10	3
1968	Cle-A	.971	45	76	92	5	18	-8
1969	Bal-A	.853	9	11	18	5	3	-2
1970	Bal-A	.932	12	19	22	3	2	-6
1971	Bal-A	.950	9	26	12	2	5	-2
Total	8	.959	164	286	339	7	61	-22

SS

YEAR	TM/L	PCT	G	PO	A	E	DP	FR
1966	Cle-A	.958	61	106	147	11	32	-9
1967	Cle-A	1.000	14	28	33	0	9	2
1968	Cle-A	.982	15	24	31	1	6	-2
1969	Bal-A	.958	9	8	15	1	0	-1
1970	Bal-A	.946	33	36	52	5	9	-12
1971	Bal-A	.750	5	1	8	3	1	-1
Total	6	.959	137	203	286	1	57	-23

1B

YEAR	TM/L	PCT	G	PO	A	E	DP	FR
1964	Cle-A	1.000	13	70	4	0	4	0
1965	Cle-A	.985	28	127	7	2	10	-1
1966	Cle-A	.987	24	141	6	2	10	-2
1967	Cle-A	.990	24	96	2	1	7	-2
1968	Cle-A	.968	11	28	2	1	3	0
1969	Bal-A	1.000	17	70	3	0	6	-1
1970	Bal-A	1.000	2	3	0	0	0	0
1971	Bal-A	1.000	9	42	2	0	4	0
1972	Bal-A	1.000	2	1	0	0	1	0
Total	9	.990	130	578	26	6	45	-6

OF

YEAR	TM/L	PCT	G	PO	A	E	DP	FR
1964	Cle-A	1.000	53	70	1	0	0	-5
1965	Cle-A	1.000	17	12	0	0	0	0
1966	Cle-A	1.000	10	7	0	0	0	0
1967	Cle-A	1.000	28	31	1	0	0	2
1968	Cle-A	1.000	13	11	0	0	0	0
1969	Bal-A	—	1	0	0	0	0	0
Total	6	1.000	122	131	2	0	0	-3

3B

YEAR	TM/L	PCT	G	PO	A	E	DP	FR
1965	Cle-A	.909	5	5	5	1	1	-2
1966	Cle-A	1.000	6	9	7	0	1	0
1967	Cle-A	1.000	4	0	3	0	0	1
1968	Cle-A	.971	18	13	20	1	2	-2
1969	Bal-A	.778	3	1	6	2	0	0
1970	Bal-A	.941	11	3	13	1	1	-2
1971	Bal-A	.933	6	6	8	1	2	0
1972	Bal-A	1.000	1	0	2	0	0	0
Total	8	.944	54	37	64	6	7	-5

■ Jack Saltzgaver 3B

YEAR	TM/L	PCT	G	PO	A	E	DP	FR
1934	NY-A	.953	84	71	130	10	10	-15
1935	NY-A	.968	18	14	16	1	2	-3
1936	NY-A	.972	16	14	21	1	1	-1
1945	Pit-N	—	1	0	0	0	0	0
Total	4	.957	119	99	167	2	13	-19

2B

YEAR	TM/L	PCT	G	PO	A	E	DP	FR
1932	NY-A	.958	16	38	30	3	5	-3
1935	NY-A	.937	25	40	64	7	8	-11
1936	NY-A	.964	6	15	12	1	2	-3
1945	Pit-N	.963	31	63	66	5	11	-3
Total	4	.953	78	156	172	6	26	-20

1B

YEAR	TM/L	PCT	G	PO	A	E	DP	FR
1934	NY-A	.923	4	22	2	2	3	0
1935	NY-A	1.000	6	16	2	0	1	0
1936	NY-A	1.000	4	15	1	0	2	0
1937	NY-A	1.000	4	31	0	0	4	0
Total	4	.978	18	84	6	2	10	0

■ Ron Samford SS

YEAR	TM/L	PCT	G	PO	A	E	DP	FR
1955	Det-A	1.000	1	0	2	0	0	0
1957	Det-A	.964	35	34	72	4	18	9
1959	Was-A	.947	64	92	177	15	33	-1
Total	3	.952	100	126	251	9	51	8

2B

YEAR	TM/L	PCT	G	PO	A	E	DP	FR
1954	NY-N	1.000	3	3	2	0	0	3
1957	Det-A	.974	11	17	21	1	5	4
1959	Was-A	.967	23	38	37	3	6	1
Total	3	.967	37	58	60	4	11	8

3B

YEAR	TM/L	PCT	G	PO	A	E	DP	FR
1957	Det-A	.800	4	2	2	1	0	0

■ Bill Sample OF

YEAR	TM/L	PCT	G	PO	A	E	DP	FR
1978	Tex-A	—	2	0	0	0	0	0
1979	Tex-A	1.000	103	173	7	0	1	-5
1980	Tex-A	.973	72	105	2	3	0	-2
1981	Tex-A	.993	64	132	4	1	1	-1
1982	Tex-A	.981	91	196	6	4	0	0
1983	Tex-A	.988	146	329	8	4	0	2
1984	Tex-A	.986	122	285	3	4	2	4
1985	NY-A	.989	55	89	1	1	0	-3
1986	Atl-N	.986	56	69	1	1	1	-5
Total	9	.987	711	1378	32	8	5	-10

2B

YEAR	TM/L	PCT	G	PO	A	E	DP	FR
1986	Atl-N	—	1	0	0	0	0	0

■ Juan Samuel 2B

YEAR	TM/L	PCT	G	PO	A	E	DP	FR
1983	Phi-N	.916	18	44	54	9	9	3
1984	Phi-N	.962	160	388	438	33	77	-22
1985	Phi-N	.983	159	389	463	15	88	-2
1986	Phi-N	.967	143	290	440	25	83	-9
1987	Phi-N	.978	160	374	434	18	99	-19
1988	Phi-N	.978	152	343	385	16	92	-27
1990	LA-N	.972	108	194	258	13	47	-9
Total	7	.972	900	2022	2472	129	495	-85

OF

YEAR	TM/L	PCT	G	PO	A	E	DP	FR
1988	Phi-N	1.000	3	8	1	0	0	1
1989	Phi-N	.993	50	133	2	1	0	7
	NY-N	.986	84	206	4	3	3	2
	Yr	.989	134	339	6	4	3	9
1990	LA-N	.965	31	79	4	3	0	3
Total	3	.984	168	426	11	7	3	13

3B

YEAR	TM/L	PCT	G	PO	A	E	DP	FR
1988	Phi-N	1.000	1	0	1	0	0	0

■ Heinie Sand SS

YEAR	TM/L	PCT	G	PO	A	E	DP	FR
1923	Phi-N	.934	120	277	411	49	91	-1
1924	Phi-N	.959	137	333	460	34	95	2
1925	Phi-N	.928	143	352	420	60	91	-6
1926	Phi-N	.939	149	358	495	55	88	-3
1927	Phi-N	.949	86	201	247	24	36	-13
1928	Phi-N	.951	137	290	410	36	94	-1
Total	6	.943	772	1811	2443	258	495	-22

3B

YEAR	TM/L	PCT	G	PO	A	E	DP	FR
1923	Phi-N	.970	11	19	13	1	1	-1
1927	Phi-N	.967	58	43	105	5	10	-2
Total	2	.968	69	62	118	6	11	-3

■ Ryne Sandberg 2B

YEAR	TM/L	PCT	G	PO	A	E	DP	FR
1981	Phi-N	1.000	1	1	2	0	1	1
1982	Chi-N	.993	24	57	95	1	9	7
1983	Chi-N	.986	157	330	571	13	126	41
1984	Chi-N	.993	156	314	550	6	102	23
1985	Chi-N	.986	153	353	500	12	99	8
1986	Chi-N	.994	153	309	492	5	86	5
1987	Chi-N	.985	131	294	375	10	84	1
1988	Chi-N	.987	153	291	522	11	79	11
1989	Chi-N	.992	155	294	466	6	80	1
1990	Chi-N	.989	154	278	469	8	81	6
Total	10	.989	1237	2521	4042	72	747	104

3B

YEAR	TM/L	PCT	G	PO	A	E	DP	FR
1982	Chi-N	.970	133	79	278	11	19	-2

SS

YEAR	TM/L	PCT	G	PO	A	E	DP	FR
1981	Phi-N	1.000	5	6	5	0	0	4
1983	Chi-N	1.000	1	0	1	0	0	0
1985	Chi-N	1.000	1	0	1	0	0	0
Total	3	1.000	7	6	7	0	0	4

■ Ray Sanders 1B

YEAR	TM/L	PCT	G	PO	A	E	DP	FR
1942	StL-N	.991	77	626	35	6	54	-4
1943	StL-N	.995	141	1302	71	7	142	-7
1944	StL-N	.994	152	1370	64	8	142	-13
1945	StL-N	.986	142	1259	90	19	113	-5
1946	Bos-N	.988	77	659	61	9	57	4
1949	Bos-N	.984	7	52	9	1	2	2
Total	6	.991	596	5268	330	50	510	-23

■ Mike Sandlock C

YEAR	TM/L	PCT	G	PO	A	E	DP	FR
1945	Bro-N	.991	47	196	20	2	3	3
1946	Bro-N	.973	17	61	11	2	1	6
1953	Pit-N	.991	64	290	49	3	4	18
Total	3	.989	128	547	80	7	8	27

SS

YEAR	TM/L	PCT	G	PO	A	E	DP	FR
1942	Bos-N	—	2	0	0	0	0	0
1944	Bos-N	.900	7	4	5	1	2	1
1945	Bro-N	.945	22	23	29	3	2	-2
Total	3	.938	31	27	34	4	4	-1

3B

YEAR	TM/L	PCT	G	PO	A	E	DP	FR
1944	Bos-N	.956	22	13	30	2	1	5
1945	Bro-N	1.000	2	1	1	0	0	0
1946	Bro-N	1.000	1	0	2	0	1	1
Total	3	.959	25	14	33	2	2	6

2B

YEAR	TM/L	PCT	G	PO	A	E	DP	FR
1945	Bro-N	.875	4	4	3	1	0	0

■ Manny Sanguillen C

YEAR	TM/L	PCT	G	PO	A	E	DP	FR
1967	Pit-N	.986	28	133	11	2	4	-5
1969	Pit-N	.981	113	825	71	17	11	3
1970	Pit-N	.988	125	775	66	10	12	1
1971	Pit-N	.994	135	712	72	5	12	4
1972	Pit-N	.988	127	721	50	9	4	-4
1973	Pit-N	.983	89	493	35	9	9	-4
1974	Pit-N	.985	151	713	76	12	8	-7
1975	Pit-N	.987	132	650	53	9	4	-5
1976	Pit-N	.978	111	518	52	13	7	-7
1977	Oak-A	.985	77	341	45	6	3	-9
1978	Pit-N	1.000	18	83	5	0	0	0
1979	Pit-N	.947	8	32	4	2	0	0
Total	12	.986	1114	5996	540	94	74	-33

OF

YEAR	TM/L	PCT	G	PO	A	E	DP	FR
1972	Pit-N	1.000	3	2	0	0	0	0
1973	Pit-N	.948	59	139	6	8	2	3
1977	Oak-A	1.000	9	17	0	0	0	-1
Total	3	.954	70	159	6	8	2	2

YEAR	TM/L	PCT	G	PO	A	E	DP	FR
1B								
1977	Oak-A	.986	7	61	9	1	4	2
1978	Pit-N	1.000	40	355	15	0	26	-2
1979	Pit-N	1.000	5	35	2	0	3	0
1980	Pit-N	.956	5	40	3	2	3	0
Total	4	.994	57	491	29	3	36	0

■ Rafael Santana SS

YEAR	TM/L	PCT	G	PO	A	E	DP	FR
1983	StL-N	.750	6	1	2	1	1	1
1984	NY-N	.970	50	92	104	6	34	-3
1985	NY-N	.965	153	301	396	25	81	-11
1986	NY-N	.973	137	203	369	16	68	17
1987	NY-N	.973	138	213	396	17	82	15
1988	NY-A	.966	148	202	421	22	96	-9
1990	Cle-A	1.000	7	2	9	0	2	-2
Total	7	.969	639	1014	1697	7	364	8
2B								
1983	StL-N	.857	9	2	4	1	1	1
1986	NY-N	—	1	0	0	0	0	0
Total	2	.857	10	2	4	1	1	1
3B								
1983	StL-N	.500	4	0	2	2	1	0

■ Benito Santiago C

YEAR	TM/L	PCT	G	PO	A	E	DP	FR
1986	SD-N	.946	17	80	7	5	2	-5
1987	SD-N	.976	146	817	80	22	12	-5
1988	SD-N	.985	136	725	75	12	11	-5
1989	SD-N	.975	127	685	81	20	10	-5
1990	SD-N	.980	98	538	51	12	6	-5
Total	5	.978	524	2845	294	1	41	-25

■ Ron Santo 3B

YEAR	TM/L	PCT	G	PO	A	E	DP	FR
1960	Chi-N	.945	94	78	144	13	6	-19
1961	Chi-N	.937	153	157	307	31	41	5
1962	Chi-N	.955	157	161	332	23	33	12
1963	Chi-N	.951	162	136	374	26	25	13
1964	Chi-N	.963	161	156	367	20	31	17
1965	Chi-N	.957	164	155	373	24	27	19
1966	Chi-N	.956	152	150	391	25	36	29
1967	Chi-N	.957	161	187	393	26	33	31
1968	Chi-N	.971	162	130	378	15	33	17
1969	Chi-N	.947	160	144	334	27	23	6
1970	Chi-N	.945	152	143	320	27	36	13
1971	Chi-N	.958	149	118	274	17	29	-3
1972	Chi-N	.948	129	108	274	21	19	6
1973	Chi-N	.950	146	107	271	20	17	-12
1974	Chi-A	.974	28	25	49	2	6	1
Total	15	.954	2130	1955	4581	317	395	135
2B								
1972	Chi-N	.944	3	9	8	1	4	0
1974	Chi-A	.970	39	97	99	6	40	5
Total	2	.968	42	106	107	7	44	5
SS								
1962	Chi-N	.944	8	6	11	1	2	-1
1966	Chi-N	.960	8	7	17	1	5	0
1972	Chi-N	1.000	1	1	0	0	0	0
1974	Chi-A	—	1	0	0	0	0	0
Total	4	.955	18	14	28	2	7	-1
OF								
1970	Chi-N	1.000	1	1	0	0	0	0
1971	Chi-N	.917	6	10	1	1	0	0
1972	Chi-N	1.000	1	1	0	0	0	0
Total	3	.929	8	12	1	1	0	0
1B								
1974	Chi-A	1.000	3	13	0	0	3	0

■ Nelson Santovenia C

YEAR	TM/L	PCT	G	PO	A	E	DP	FR
1987	Mon-N	1.000	1	1	0	0	0	0
1988	Mon-N	.983	86	457	63	9	7	3
1989	Mon-N	.981	89	561	66	12	7	12
1990	Mon-N	.980	51	264	24	6	7	2
Total	4	.982	227	1283	153	7	21	17
1B								
1988	Mon-N	1.000	1	8	0	0	0	0
1989	Mon-N	1.000	1	3	0	0	1	0
Total	2	1.000	2	11	0	0	1	0

■ Bill Sarni C

YEAR	TM/L	PCT	G	PO	A	E	DP	FR
1951	StL-N	.984	35	107	13	2	3	0
1952	StL-N	1.000	3	19	0	0	0	2
1954	StL-N	.996	118	486	41	2	12	-13
1955	StL-N	.987	99	482	39	7	8	-7
1956	StL-N	.992	41	219	25	2	1	3
	NY-N	.993	78	367	36	3	9	-6
	Yr	.992	119	586	61	5	10	-3
Total	5	.991	374	1680	154	6	33	-21

■ Mackey Sasser C

YEAR	TM/L	PCT	G	PO	A	E	DP	FR
1987	SF-N	1.000	1	7	0	0	0	0
	Pit-N	1.000	5	22	0	0	0	-1
	Yr	1.000	6	29	0	0	0	-1
1988	NY-N	.977	42	235	17	6	2	9
1989	NY-N	.992	62	335	19	3	3	0
1990	NY-N	.975	87	498	43	14	4	-10
Total	4	.981	197	1097	79	3	9	-2
3B								
1988	NY-N	—	1	0	0	0	0	0
1989	NY-N	—	1	0	0	0	1	0
Total	2	—	2	0	0	0	1	0
OF								
1988	NY-N	—	1	0	0	0	0	0
1B								
1990	NY-N	1.000	1	3	0	0	0	0

■ Tom Satriano C

YEAR	TM/L	PCT	G	PO	A	E	DP	FR
1963	LA-A	1.000	2	5	1	0	0	0
1964	LA-A	.993	25	132	9	1	0	0
1965	Cal-A	1.000	12	62	5	0	1	1
1966	Cal-A	.991	43	196	16	2	3	-5
1967	Cal-A	.968	23	110	12	4	2	-4
1968	Cal-A	.989	85	404	40	5	6	-7
1969	Cal-A	1.000	36	180	14	0	4	0
	Bos-A	.978	44	248	17	6	1	-2
	Yr	.987	80	428	31	6	5	-2
1970	Bos-A	.985	51	318	19	5	5	0
Total	8	.987	321	1655	133	3	22	-17
3B								
1961	LA-A	.915	23	17	48	6	6	1
1962	LA-A	.833	5	2	8	2	1	0
1963	LA-A	.952	13	8	32	2	2	3
1964	LA-A	.917	38	12	43	5	3	-1
1965	Cal-A	1.000	15	5	11	0	1	0
1966	Cal-A	.926	25	17	33	4	3	-2
1967	Cal-A	.962	38	19	56	3	4	-2
1968	Cal-A	.913	11	8	13	2	2	-1
Total	8	.933	168	88	244	4	22	-2
1B								
1963	LA-A	.800	1	4	0	1	0	0
1964	LA-A	.992	32	237	17	2	29	0
1965	Cal-A	1.000	3	5	0	0	0	0
1966	Cal-A	1.000	36	70	6	0	7	1
1967	Cal-A	1.000	5	8	0	0	1	0
1968	Cal-A	1.000	1	5	1	0	0	0
1969	Cal-A	1.000	5	34	2	0	3	0
Total	7	.992	83	363	26	3	40	1
2B								
1961	LA-A	.920	10	11	12	2	1	-1
1964	LA-A	1.000	1	1	2	0	0	0
1965	Cal-A	.966	12	11	17	1	2	0
1966	Cal-A	1.000	4	0	3	0	0	-2
1967	Cal-A	1.000	15	13	17	0	3	-1
1968	Cal-A	.967	14	16	13	1	3	-1
1969	Cal-A	1.000	2	1	3	0	0	0
Total	7	.968	58	53	67	4	9	-5
SS								
1961	LA-A	1.000	1	1	1	0	0	0
1964	LA-A	1.000	2	1	1	0	0	0
Total	2	1.000	3	2	2	0	0	0

■ Eddie Sauer OF

YEAR	TM/L	PCT	G	PO	A	E	DP	FR
1943	Chi-N	1.000	13	37	1	0	0	1
1944	Chi-N	.960	12	23	1	1	0	0
1945	Chi-N	1.000	26	44	1	0	1	0
1949	StL-N	1.000	10	12	1	0	0	-1
	Bos-N	.972	71	134	3	4	1	1
	Yr	.974	81	146	4	4	1	0
Total	4	.981	132	250	7	5	2	1

■ Hank Sauer OF

YEAR	TM/L	PCT	G	PO	A	E	DP	FR
1941	Cin-N	.957	8	21	1	1	1	1
1945	Cin-N	.972	28	69	0	2	0	0
1948	Cin-N	.973	132	270	14	8	6	4
1949	Cin-N	.956	39	102	6	5	0	3
	Chi-N	.981	96	199	10	4	2	0
	Yr	.972	135	301	16	9	2	3
1950	Chi-N	.965	125	236	12	9	1	-1
1951	Chi-N	.981	132	286	19	6	2	9
1952	Chi-N	.983	151	327	17	6	3	12
1953	Chi-N	.970	105	221	5	7	1	1
1954	Chi-N	.963	141	282	8	11	2	-1
1955	Chi-N	.984	68	122	4	2	1	-6
1956	StL-N	1.000	37	55	2	0	1	-5
1957	NY-N	.992	98	125	4	1	0	-15
1958	SF-N	.950	67	93	3	5	1	-9
1959	SF-N	—	1	0	0	0	0	0
Total	14	.974	1228	2408	105	7	21	-7
1B								
1942	Cin-N	.976	4	37	4	1	8	0
1945	Cin-N	.973	3	31	5	1	4	1
1948	Cin-N	.990	12	89	8	1	4	0
1949	Cin-N	1.000	1	1	0	0	0	0
1950	Chi-N	.976	18	145	17	4	11	2
Total	5	.980	38	303	34	7	27	3

■ Ted Savage OF

YEAR	TM/L	PCT	G	PO	A	E	DP	FR
1962	Phi-N	.974	109	185	4	5	1	-3
1963	Pit-N	.943	47	47	3	3	1	-2
1965	StL-N	.938	20	29	1	2	0	0
1966	StL-N	1.000	7	9	0	0	0	-1
1967	Chi-N	.979	86	133	5	3	1	-4
1968	Chi-N	1.000	2	3	0	0	0	0
	LA-N	.985	39	61	4	1	1	4
	Yr	.986	41	64	4	1	1	4
1969	Cin-N	.983	17	57	0	1	0	3
1970	Mil-A	.953	82	119	3	6	0	-7
1971	Mil-A	1.000	6	4	0	0	0	-1
	KC-A	1.000	9	4	2	0	0	0
	Yr	1.000	15	8	2	0	0	-1
Total	9	.970	424	651	22	1	4	-11
3B								
1967	Chi-N	1.000	1	0	2	0	1	1
2B								
1969	Cin-N	—	1	0	0	0	0	0
1B								
1970	Mil-A	1.000	1	5	0	0	0	0

■ Bob Saverine 2B

YEAR	TM/L	PCT	G	PO	A	E	DP	FR
1962	Bal-A	1.000	7	11	19	0	3	1
1963	Bal-A	.988	19	37	44	1	8	3
1966	Was-A	.972	70	149	169	9	35	-16
1967	Was-A	.957	48	80	98	8	22	-14
Total	4	.971	144	277	330	8	68	-26
OF								
1963	Bal-A	.976	59	39	1	1	0	1
1964	Bal-A	1.000	2	2	0	0	0	0
1966	Was-A	1.000	9	14	0	0	0	0
1967	Was-A	—	2	0	0	0	0	0
Total	4	.982	72	55	1	1	0	1
SS								
1963	Bal-A	1.000	13	23	44	0	11	7
1964	Bal-A	1.000	15	10	16	0	1	5
1966	Was-A	1.000	11	12	17	0	6	0
1967	Was-A	.923	10	7	17	2	1	-3
Total	4	.986	49	52	94	2	19	9
3B								
1966	Was-A	.964	26	11	42	2	3	-2
1967	Was-A	.882	8	3	12	2	1	-1
Total	2	.944	34	14	54	4	4	-3

■ Carl Sawatski C

YEAR	TM/L	PCT	G	PO	A	E	DP	FR
1950	Chi-N	.983	32	100	19	2	6	-1
1953	Chi-N	.943	15	45	5	3	0	-1
1954	Chi-N	.987	33	133	14	2	4	0
1957	Mil-N	.986	28	121	20	2	2	6
1958	Mil-N	1.000	3	8	3	0	0	1
	Phi-N	.986	53	271	17	4	2	-3
	Yr	.987	56	279	20	4	2	-2
1959	Phi-N	.979	69	306	23	7	4	-14
1960	StL-N	.993	67	279	25	2	5	-7
1961	StL-N	.996	60	218	19	1	3	-6
1962	StL-N	.997	70	354	24	1	4	0
1963	StL-N	.986	27	125	11	2	0	-6
Total	10	.988	457	1960	180	6	30	-31
OF								
1961	StL-N	—	1	0	0	0	0	0

■ Steve Sax 2B

YEAR	TM/L	PCT	G	PO	A	E	DP	FR
1981	LA-N	.975	29	64	93	4	22	2
1982	LA-N	.977	149	347	452	19	83	-9
1983	LA-N	.961	152	331	399	30	74	-30
1984	LA-N	.973	141	318	450	21	99	12
1985	LA-N	.969	135	330	357	22	84	-9
1986	LA-N	.980	154	367	432	16	71	-5
1987	LA-N	.982	152	342	420	14	92	2
1988	LA-N	.981	158	276	429	14	69	-19
1989	NY-A	.987	158	312	460	10	117	-10
1990	NY-A	.987	154	292	457	10	102	-13
Total	10	.977	1382	2979	3949	160	813	-79
3B								
1985	LA-N	1.000	1	0	1	0	0	0
1987	LA-N	—	1	0	0	0	0	0
Total	2	1.000	2	0	1	0	0	0
OF								
1987	LA-N	1.000	1	1	0	0	0	0

■ Lou Say SS

YEAR	TM/L	PCT	G	PO	A	E	DP	FR
1880	Cin-N	.832	48	54	164	44	11	1
1882	Phi-A	.867	49	69	192	40	7	6
1883	Bal-a	.794	74	76	241	82	13	7
1884	Bal-U	.795	78	103	234	87	16	2
	KC-U	.860	16	25	67	15	3	8
	Yr	.808	94	128	301	102	19	10
Total	4	.820	265	327	898	268	50	24
2B								
1884	KC-U	1.000	1	3	1	0	0	0

■ Russ Scarritt OF

YEAR	TM/L	PCT	G	PO	A	E	DP	FR
1929	Bos-A	.944	145	302	16	19	6	1
1930	Bos-A	.967	110	256	5	9	0	4
1931	Bos-A	1.000	9	21	1	0	0	1
1932	Phi-N	1.000	1	2	0	0	0	0
Total	4	.956	265	581	22	8	6	6

■ Les Scarsella 1B

YEAR	TM/L	PCT	G	PO	A	E	DP	FR
1935	Cin-N	1.000	2	17	3	0	2	1
1936	Cin-N	.989	115	1109	84	13	90	2
1937	Cin-N	.984	65	589	37	10	55	-3
1940	Bos-N	.986	15	137	7	2	17	-1
Total	4	.988	197	1852	131	5	164	-1
OF								
1937	Cin-N	.950	14	18	1	1	0	0

■ Paul Schaal 3B

YEAR	TM/L	PCT	G	PO	A	E	DP	FR
1964	LA-A	.882	9	2	13	2	0	-1
1965	Cal-A	.970	153	101	321	13	20	-10
1966	Cal-A	.948	131	97	249	19	21	-2
1967	Cal-A	.960	88	73	156	7	9	-2
1968	Cal-A	.958	58	61	142	9	13	9
1969	KC-A	.897	49	27	77	12	3	-14
1970	KC-A	.938	97	69	159	15	12	-14
1971	KC-A	.940	161	107	335	28	31	-12
1972	KC-A	.947	123	77	245	18	16	-16
1973	KC-A	.913	121	77	237	30	14	-12
1974	KC-A	.949	12	11	26	2	4	1
	Cal-A	.903	51	24	78	11	9	-10
	Yr	.914	63	35	104	13	13	-9
Total	11	.943	1053	726	2038	166	152	-83
2B								
1964	LA-A	1.000	9	3	9	0	2	0
1965	Cal-A	—	1	1	0	0	0	0
1967	Cal-A	1.000	1	1	0	0	0	0
1969	KC-A	.857	6	10	8	3	1	-4
1970	KC-A	.971	6	14	19	1	3	0
Total	5	.941	23	28	36	4	6	-4
SS								
1967	Cal-A	1.000	2	1	2	0	0	0
1969	KC-A	1.000	6	4	18	0	1	1
1970	KC-A	.909	10	12	18	3	4	-2
1972	KC-A	—	1	0	0	0	0	0
Total	4	.952	19	21	38	3	7	-3

■ Germany Schaefer 2B

YEAR	TM/L	PCT	G	PO	A	E	DP	FR
1901	Chi-N	1.000	1	3	2	0	1	0
1905	Det-A	.955	151	403	389	37	35	8
1906	Det-A	.948	114	348	328	37	42	8
1907	Det-A	.961	74	188	206	16	23	-6
1908	Det-A	.949	58	122	160	15	22	-9
1909	Det-A	.966	86	180	273	16	26	14
	Was-A	.941	32	52	91	9	16	0
	Yr	.960	118	232	364	25	42	14
1910	Was-A	.953	35	60	104	8	15	2

YEAR	TM/L	PCT	G	PO	A	E	DP	FR
1912	Was-A	.931	15	30	24	4	2	-7
1913	Was-A	.926	16	26	37	5	5	-1
1914	Was-A	1.000	3	3	1	0	0	0
1915	New-F	1.000	2	1	5	0	2	0
1918	Cle-A	1.000	1	3	3	0	0	0
Total	12	.954	588	1419	1623	147	189	9
1B								
1902	Chi-N	.973	3	35	1	1	2	0
1911	Was-A	.980	108	1038	71	23	57	1
1912	Was-A	.984	15	125	2	2	5	-3
1913	Was-A	.967	6	57	1	2	1	-1
1915	New-F	.991	13	109	6	1	6	0
Total	5	.980	145	1364	81	9	71	-3
3B								
1901	Chi-N	1.000	1	3	2	0	0	0
1902	Chi-N	.864	75	103	152	40	11	-8
1907	Det-A	.946	14	21	32	3	0	2
1908	Det-A	.952	29	35	65	5	1	1
1909	Was-A	.800	1	2	2	1	0	-1
1910	Was-A	1.000	2	1	5	0	0	0
1913	Was-A	1.000	2	2	1	0	0	0
1915	New-F	.878	9	19	17	5	4	1
Total	8	.895	133	186	276	4	16	-5
SS								
1902	Chi-N	.600	1	1	2	2	0	-1
1905	Det-A	1.000	3	7	5	0	0	-1
1906	Det-A	.880	7	20	24	6	3	0
1907	Det-A	.955	18	36	48	4	0	-1
1908	Det-A	.918	68	162	254	37	35	10
Total	5	.919	97	226	333	9	38	7
OF								
1902	Chi-N	1.000	2	4	1	0	1	1
1907	Det-A	—	1	0	0	0	0	0
1909	Det-A	1.000	1	1	0	0	0	0
1910	Was-A	.917	26	29	4	3	1	-2
1911	Was-A	1.000	7	10	0	0	0	-1
1912	Was-A	.900	19	14	4	2	0	-2
1913	Was-A	1.000	1	3	0	0	0	0
1914	Was-A	1.000	3	3	1	0	0	0
1915	New-F	.952	17	17	3	1	0	-2
1916	NY-A	—	1	0	0	0	0	0
Total	10	.940	78	81	13	6	2	-6

■ Jimmie Schaffer C

YEAR	TM/L	PCT	G	PO	A	E	DP	FR
1961	StL-N	.996	68	244	23	1	6	4
1962	StL-N	.993	69	134	10	1	1	7
1963	Chi-N	.996	54	231	23	1	3	0
1964	Chi-N	.970	43	143	19	5	1	-7
1965	Chi-N	1.000	14	50	7	0	2	3
	NY-N	.968	21	60	1	2	0	-1
1966	Phi-N	.952	6	17	3	1	1	-1
1967	Phi-N	1.000	1	5	0	0	0	0
1968	Cin-N	1.000	2	4	0	0	0	-1
Total	8	.989	278	888	86	1	14	4

■ Roy Schalk 2B

YEAR	TM/L	PCT	G	PO	A	E	DP	FR
1932	NY-A	.867	3	4	9	2	1	1
1944	Chi-A	.964	142	360	391	28	109	-16
1945	Chi-A	.977	133	380	389	18	90	6
Total	3	.970	278	744	789	8	200	-11
SS								
1944	Chi-A	.966	5	6	22	1	3	1

■ Ray Schalk C

YEAR	TM/L	PCT	G	PO	A	E	DP	FR
1912	Chi-A	.917	23	115	40	14	4	3
1913	Chi-A	.980	125	599	154	15	18	-1
1914	Chi-A	.974	125	613	183	21	20	6
1915	Chi-A	.984	134	655	159	13	8	-4
1916	Chi-A	.988	124	653	166	10	25	8
1917	Chi-A	.981	139	624	148	15	18	4
1918	Chi-A	.978	106	422	114	12	15	-4
1919	Chi-A	.981	129	551	130	13	14	0
1920	Chi-A	.986	151	581	138	10	19	-1
1921	Chi-A	.985	126	453	129	9	19	8
1922	Chi-A	.989	142	591	150	8	16	19
1923	Chi-A	.983	121	481	93	10	20	4
1924	Chi-A	.959	56	176	55	10	8	7
1925	Chi-A	.983	125	368	99	8	15	2
1926	Chi-A	.977	80	251	45	7	6	-7
1927	Chi-A	1.000	15	24	8	0	1	1
1928	Chi-A	1.000	1	4	0	0	0	0
1929	NY-N	1.000	5	7	0	0	0	-1
Total	18	.981	1727	7168	1811	175	226	46

■ Wally Schang C

YEAR	TM/L	PCT	G	PO	A	E	DP	FR
1913	Phi-A	.967	72	317	97	14	9	-5
1914	Phi-A	.956	100	498	154	30	11	2
1915	Phi-A	.945	26	110	46	9	1	-1
1916	Phi-A	.935	36	136	67	14	6	1
1917	Phi-A	.956	80	267	102	17	11	-9
1918	Bos-A	.962	57	202	52	10	4	-9
1919	Bos-A	.972	103	359	131	14	15	-3
1920	Bos-A	.958	73	285	76	16	8	-5
1921	NY-A	.969	132	500	101	19	13	-6
1922	NY-A	.976	119	456	102	14	12	1
1923	NY-A	.970	81	292	60	11	6	-8
1924	NY-A	.972	108	423	89	15	9	-2
1925	NY-A	.974	58	172	55	6	8	3
1926	StL-A	.968	82	224	75	10	7	-1
1927	StL-A	.976	75	213	73	7	10	-8
1928	StL-A	.984	82	263	46	5	5	-13
1929	StL-A	.988	85	268	56	4	6	-6
1930	Phi-A	.973	36	126	18	4	2	3
1931	Det-A	.965	30	91	20	4	6	0
Total	19	.967	1435	5202	1420	223	149	-66
OF								
1915	Phi-A	.857	41	66	12	13	2	1
1916	Phi-A	.966	61	130	10	5	0	5
1917	Phi-A	1.000	6	8	1	0	1	0

YEAR	TM/L	PCT	G	PO	A	E	DP	FR
1918	Bos-A	.914	16	31	1	3	0	-1
1920	Bos-A	.980	40	92	7	2	0	1
1926	StL-A	1.000	3	8	0	0	0	0
Total	6	.941	167	335	31	3	3	6
3B								
1915	Phi-A	.890	43	64	81	18	9	-1
1917	Phi-A	.933	12	18	24	3	1	0
1918	Bos-A	.769	5	2	8	3	1	-2
Total	3	.891	60	84	113	4	11	-3
SS								
1918	Bos-A	.667	1	1	1	1	0	-1

■ Art Scharein 3B

YEAR	TM/L	PCT	G	PO	A	E	DP	FR
1932	StL-A	.965	77	100	172	10	22	18
1933	StL-A	.949	95	113	206	17	31	15
Total	2	.956	172	213	378	7	53	33
SS								
1932	StL-A	.875	3	5	9	2	2	-1
1933	StL-A	.956	24	28	59	4	10	-1
Total	2	.944	27	33	68	6	12	-2
2B								
1932	StL-A	1.000	2	2	8	0	2	1
1933	StL-A	.974	7	17	21	1	2	-1
Total	2	.980	9	19	29	1	4	0

■ George Scharein SS

YEAR	TM/L	PCT	G	PO	A	E	DP	FR
1937	Phi-N	.947	146	335	456	44	98	10
1938	Phi-N	.921	77	151	208	31	39	-3
1939	Phi-N	.958	117	258	331	26	69	-9
1940	Phi-N	.839	7	13	13	5	2	-1
Total	4	.943	347	757	1008	106	208	-3
2B								
1938	Phi-N	.973	39	95	119	6	18	1
3B								
1938	Phi-N	—	1	0	0	0	0	0

■ Al Scheer OF

YEAR	TM/L	PCT	G	PO	A	E	DP	FR
1913	Bro-N	.800	6	3	1	1	0	-2
1914	Ind-F	.926	102	150	13	13	2	-5
1915	New-F	.971	155	287	16	9	5	-2
Total	3	.953	263	440	30	3	7	-9
2B								
1914	Ind-F	1.000	4	2	6	0	0	0
SS								
1914	Ind-F	1.000	1	0	2	0	0	0

■ Bob Scheffing C

YEAR	TM/L	PCT	G	PO	A	E	DP	FR
1941	Chi-N	.966	34	126	17	5	1	-3
1942	Chi-N	.986	32	122	16	2	6	4
1946	Chi-N	1.000	40	97	10	0	3	-6
1947	Chi-N	.984	97	379	52	7	4	-5
1948	Chi-N	.989	78	332	36	4	5	-5
1949	Chi-N	.977	40	152	18	4	3	-3
1950	Chi-N	.917	3	11	0	1	1	0
	Cin-N	1.000	11	43	2	0	0	-3
	Yr	.982	14	54	2	1	1	-3
1951	Chi-N	.976	41	150	13	4	1	-3
	StL-N	1.000	11	32	2	0	0	1
	Yr	.980	52	182	15	4	1	-2
Total	8	.984	387	1444	166	7	24	-23

■ Ted Scheffler OF

YEAR	TM/L	PCT	G	PO	A	E	DP	FR
1888	Det-N	.847	27	49	1	9	1	-5
1890	Roc-a	.911	119	196	29	22	6	9
Total	2	.899	146	245	30	1	7	4
C								
1890	Roc-a	1.000	1	1	0	0	0	0

■ Frank Scheibeck SS

YEAR	TM/L	PCT	G	PO	A	E	DP	FR
1887	Cle-a	.500	1	0	3	3	0	-1
1888	Det-N	.500	1	2	0	2	0	-1
1890	Tol-a	.883	134	282	412	92	35	1
1894	Pit-N	.891	11	23	26	6	4	-6
	Was-N	.876	52	108	204	44	15	5
	Yr	.878	63	131	230	50	19	-1
1895	Was-N	.888	44	95	142	30	16	-1
1899	Was-N	.877	27	46	75	17	3	-10
1901	Cle-A	.897	92	176	268	51	26	-14
Total	7	.884	362	732	1130	245	99	-27
OF								
1894	Pit-N	.786	9	10	1	3	0	-2
2B								
1894	Pit-N	.923	2	8	4	1	1	0
1895	Was-N	.750	2	7	5	4	1	0
1906	Det-A	.889	3	8	8	2	2	-1
Total	3	.851	7	23	17	7	4	-1
3B								
1887	Cle-a	.500	1	1	0	1	0	0
1894	Pit-N	.909	3	3	7	1	1	0
1895	Was-N	.833	2	3	2	1	0	0
Total	3	.842	6	7	9	3	1	0

■ Richie Scheinblum OF

YEAR	TM/L	PCT	G	PO	A	E	DP	FR
1967	Cle-A	.943	18	33	0	2	0	-1
1968	Cle-A	1.000	16	34	0	0	0	1
1969	Cle-A	.974	50	71	4	2	1	0
1971	Was-A	.933	13	23	5	2	1	3
1972	KC-A	.965	119	215	6	8	2	-3
1973	Cin-N	.960	19	22	2	1	1	-1
	Cal-A	.969	54	92	3	3	0	-4
1974	Cal-A	.929	8	13	0	1	0	0
	KC-A	—	2	0	0	0	0	0
	Yr	.929	10	13	0	1	0	0
Total	7	.965	299	503	20	9	5	-5

■ Hank Schenz 2B

YEAR	TM/L	PCT	G	PO	A	E	DP	FR
1948	Chi-N	.974	78	184	190	10	45	-4
1950	Pit-N	.987	21	35	39	1	16	1
1951	Pit-N	.961	19	39	35	3	17	-3
Total	3	.974	118	258	264	4	78	-6

YEAR	TM/L	PCT	G	PO	A	E	DP	FR
3B								
1946	Chi-N	1.000	5	2	4	0	1	0
1947	Chi-N	.917	5	2	9	1	0	0
1948	Chi-N	1.000	5	3	6	0	0	-1
1949	Chi-N	1.000	5	1	9	0	3	1
1950	Pit-N	1.000	12	5	13	0	3	1
1951	Pit-N	1.000	2	1	1	0	0	0
Total	6	.982	34	14	42	1	7	1
SS								
1950	Pit-N	1.000	4	7	7	0	1	0

■ Chuck Schilling 2B

YEAR	TM/L	PCT	G	PO	A	E	DP	FR
1961	Bos-A	.991	158	397	449	8	121	15
1962	Bos-A	.985	118	267	331	9	85	13
1963	Bos-A	.985	143	276	369	10	74	-14
1964	Bos-A	.974	42	89	101	5	20	0
1965	Bos-A	.976	41	90	116	5	22	10
Total	5	.985	502	1119	1366	7	322	24

■ Larry Schlafly 2B

YEAR	TM/L	PCT	G	PO	A	E	DP	FR
1902	Chi-N	.842	4	7	9	3	0	-3
1906	Was-A	.961	123	341	358	28	42	14
1907	Was-A	.928	24	67	49	9	5	-9
1914	Buf-F	.951	23	50	66	6	7	2
Total	4	.954	174	465	482	6	54	4
1B								
1914	Buf-F	1.000	7	63	4	0	2	1
OF								
1902	Chi-N	1.000	5	4	0	0	0	-1
1914	Buf-F	1.000	1	2	0	0	0	0
Total	2	1.000	6	6	0	0	0	0
3B								
1902	Chi-N	1.000	2	3	6	0	1	1
1914	Buf-F	1.000	1	1	2	0	0	0
Total	2	1.000	3	4	8	0	1	1
C								
1914	Buf-F	1.000	1	0	1	0	0	0

■ Admiral Schlei C

YEAR	TM/L	PCT	G	PO	A	E	DP	FR
1904	Cin-N	.977	88	384	123	12	5	11
1905	Cin-N	.962	89	398	153	22	16	16
1906	Cin-N	.961	91	455	139	24	8	7
1907	Cin-N	.980	67	277	111	8	6	7
1908	Cin-N	.962	88	355	96	18	10	-7
1909	NY-N	.963	89	493	127	24	9	5
1910	NY-N	.986	49	165	43	3	4	0
Total	7	.968	561	2527	792	111	58	39
1B								
1905	Cin-N	.984	6	57	3	1	1	0
1906	Cin-N	.983	21	216	17	4	13	1
1907	Cin-N	.889	3	8	0	1	0	0
Total	3	.980	30	281	20	6	14	1
OF								
1907	Cin-N	.667	2	2	0	1	0	-1

■ Norm Schlueter C

YEAR	TM/L	PCT	G	PO	A	E	DP	FR
1938	Chi-A	.952	34	107	13	6	3	-3
1939	Chi-A	.988	32	81	2	1	0	1
1944	Cle-A	.985	43	122	9	2	4	-7
Total	3	.974	109	310	24	9	7	-9

■ Ray Schmandt 1B

YEAR	TM/L	PCT	G	PO	A	E	DP	FR
1915	StL-A	1.000	1	8	0	0	0	0
1919	Bro-N	.991	12	102	7	1	7	1
1920	Bro-N	.995	20	165	17	1	16	3
1921	Bro-N	.989	92	941	52	11	74	0
1922	Bro-N	.989	110	1017	65	12	83	5
Total	5	.990	235	2233	141	5	180	9
2B								
1918	Bro-N	.934	34	79	90	12	8	-4
1919	Bro-N	.911	18	32	50	8	6	1
Total	2	.926	52	111	140	0	14	-3
3B								
1919	Bro-N	.867	6	4	9	2	0	-1

■ Boss Schmidt C

YEAR	TM/L	PCT	G	PO	A	E	DP	FR
1906	Det-A	.958	67	257	104	16	4	7
1907	Det-A	.944	103	446	132	34	14	4
1908	Det-A	.951	121	541	184	37	12	7
1909	Det-A	.955	81	315	107	20	7	-7
1910	Det-A	.973	66	239	80	9	1	-6
1911	Det-A	1.000	9	29	10	0	0	-1
Total	6	.955	447	1827	617	116	38	4
OF								
1909	Det-A	—	1	0	0	0	0	0
1911	Det-A	—	1	0	0	0	0	0
Total	2	—	2	0	0	0	0	0

■ Butch Schmidt 1B

YEAR	TM/L	PCT	G	PO	A	E	DP	FR
1913	Bos-N	.983	22	166	12	3	5	1
1914	Bos-N	.990	147	1485	88	16	109	3
1915	Bos-N	.987	127	1221	60	17	80	-4
Total	3	.988	296	2872	160	6	194	0

■ Mike Schmidt 3B

YEAR	TM/L	PCT	G	PO	A	E	DP	FR
1972	Phi-N	.964	11	6	21	1	3	2
1973	Phi-N	.954	125	101	251	17	30	21
1974	Phi-N	.954	162	134	404	26	40	26
1975	Phi-N	.954	151	132	368	24	30	27
1976	Phi-N	.961	160	139	377	21	29	25
1977	Phi-N	.964	149	106	396	15	33	29
1978	Phi-N	.963	139	98	324	16	34	10
1979	Phi-N	.954	154	117	361	23	36	18
1980	Phi-N	.946	149	98	372	27	31	23
1981	Phi-N	.956	101	74	249	15	20	22
1982	Phi-N	.950	148	110	324	23	28	19
1983	Phi-N	.959	153	107	332	19	29	24
1984	Phi-N	.941	145	85	329	26	19	12
1985	Phi-N	.927	54	31	109	11	8	-1
1986	Phi-N	.980	124	78	220	6	27	-4
1987	Phi-N	.971	138	87	315	12	28	14

YEAR	TM/L	PCT	G	PO	A	E	DP	FR
1988	Phi-N	.939	104	73	222	19	17	3
1989	Phi-N	.918	42	18	71	8	8	-5
Total	18	.955	2212	1591	5045	313	450	265

1B

YEAR	TM/L	PCT	G	PO	A	E	DP	FR
1973	Phi-N	.947	2	14	4	1	2	1
1984	Phi-N	1.000	2	8	1	0	1	0
1985	Phi-N	.993	106	880	83	7	89	6
1986	Phi-N	.993	35	269	18	2	26	-3
1987	Phi-N	.982	9	51	3	1	7	-1
1988	Phi-N	1.000	3	3	1	0	0	0
Total	6	.992	157	1225	110	1	125	3

SS

YEAR	TM/L	PCT	G	PO	A	E	DP	FR
1973	Phi-N	1.000	2	0	1	0	0	0
1975	Phi-N	.935	10	7	22	2	2	-3
1977	Phi-N	1.000	2	2	4	0	1	0
1978	Phi-N	1.000	1	0	1	0	0	0
1979	Phi-N	1.000	2	1	2	0	2	0
1983	Phi-N	1.000	2	1	1	0	0	0
1984	Phi-N	—	1	0	0	0	0	0
1985	Phi-N	1.000	1	0	1	0	0	0
1987	Phi-N	1.000	3	0	1	0	0	0
Total	9	.957	24	11	33	2	5	-3

2B

YEAR	TM/L	PCT	G	PO	A	E	DP	FR
1972	Phi-N	.889	1	4	4	1	0	0
1973	Phi-N	1.000	4	4	0	0	0	0
1977	Phi-N	.667	1	1	1	1	0	0
Total	3	.875	6	9	5	2	0	0

■ Bob Schmidt C

YEAR	TM/L	PCT	G	PO	A	E	DP	FR
1958	SF-N	.982	123	616	54	12	10	-4
1959	SF-N	1.000	70	307	30	0	1	-1
1960	SF-N	.981	108	631	31	13	6	-4
1961	SF-N	1.000	2	17	1	0	0	1
	Cin-N	.993	27	137	6	1	1	1
	Yr	.994	29	154	7	1	1	2
1962	Was-A	.997	88	342	40	1	3	-2
1963	Was-A	1.000	6	18	0	0	0	-1
1965	NY-A	.990	20	93	4	1	0	0
Total	7	.988	444	2161	166	8	21	-8

■ Walter Schmidt C

YEAR	TM/L	PCT	G	PO	A	E	DP	FR
1916	Pit-N	.976	57	232	88	8	6	-1
1917	Pit-N	.978	61	229	84	7	9	9
1918	Pit-N	.981	104	373	153	10	19	15
1919	Pit-N	.982	85	315	110	8	8	0
1920	Pit-N	.971	92	323	109	13	10	-5
1921	Pit-N	.986	111	438	120	8	15	15
1922	Pit-N	.995	40	159	22	1	1	-5
1923	Pit-N	.981	96	279	88	7	10	-10
1924	Pit-N	.986	57	166	51	3	6	1
1925	StL-N	.967	31	84	33	4	2	6
Total	10	.980	734	2598	858	9	86	15

■ Dave Schneck OF

YEAR	TM/L	PCT	G	PO	A	E	DP	FR
1972	NY-N	.985	33	63	1	1	0	0
1973	NY-N	1.000	12	28	0	0	2	0
1974	NY-N	.974	84	179	7	5	2	11
Total	3	.979	129	270	8	6	2	13

■ Red Schoendienst 2B

YEAR	TM/L	PCT	G	PO	A	E	DP	FR
1945	StL-N	1.000	1	0	1	0	0	0
1946	StL-N	.984	128	340	354	11	87	0
1947	StL-N	.976	142	357	404	19	109	-4
1948	StL-N	.980	96	230	269	10	57	1
1949	StL-N	.987	138	399	424	11	105	25
1950	StL-N	.985	143	393	403	12	124	5
1951	StL-N	.990	124	339	386	7	113	12
1952	StL-N	.977	142	399	424	19	108	30
1953	StL-N	.983	140	365	430	14	109	25
1954	StL-N	.980	144	394	477	18	137	33
1955	StL-N	.985	142	296	381	10	96	-15
1956	StL-N	.995	36	99	93	1	27	-1
	NY-N	.993	85	199	215	3	52	-11
	Yr	.993	121	298	308	4	79	-12
1957	NY-N	.984	57	141	166	5	41	-2
	Mil-N	.987	92	238	282	7	72	6
	Yr	.986	149	379	448	12	113	4
1958	Mil-N	.987	105	233	301	7	77	1
1959	Mil-N	.667	4	1	1	1	0	0
1960	Mil-N	.964	62	120	148	10	34	-17
1961	StL-N	.955	32	43	42	4	10	-10
1962	StL-N	.986	21	30	42	1	10	0
Total	18	.983	1834	4616	5243	170	1368	78

OF

YEAR	TM/L	PCT	G	PO	A	E	DP	FR
1945	StL-N	.983	118	286	10	5	1	6
1947	StL-N	1.000	1	1	0	0	0	0
1949	StL-N	.800	2	4	0	1	0	-1
1957	Mil-N	—	2	0	0	0	0	0
Total	4	.980	123	291	10	6	1	5

SS

YEAR	TM/L	PCT	G	PO	A	E	DP	FR
1945	StL-N	.875	10	16	19	5	4	-5
1946	StL-N	1.000	4	5	6	0	3	0
1949	StL-N	.964	14	21	33	2	5	0
1950	StL-N	.969	10	30	33	2	10	3
1951	StL-N	.941	8	15	33	3	7	4
1952	StL-N	.909	3	3	7	1	1	-1
Total	6	.944	49	90	131	3	30	1

3B

YEAR	TM/L	PCT	G	PO	A	E	DP	FR
1946	StL-N	.949	12	18	19	2	6	0
1947	StL-N	1.000	5	6	13	0	2	2
1949	StL-N	.947	6	4	14	1	0	0
1950	StL-N	1.000	1	2	1	0	0	0
1952	StL-N	1.000	11	15	29	0	2	4
1962	StL-N	1.000	4	3	6	0	0	0
Total	6	.977	39	48	82	3	10	6

■ Jumbo Schoeneck 1B

YEAR	TM/L	PCT	G	PO	A	E	DP	FR
1884	CP-U	.956	90	916	24	43	27	0
	Bal-U	.962	16	147	7	6	3	1
	Yr	.957	106	1063	31	49	30	1
1888	Ind-N	.974	48	501	16	14	19	-1
1889	Ind-N	.978	16	164	12	4	7	2
Total	3	.964	170	1728	59	7	56	2

■ Dick Schofield SS

YEAR	TM/L	PCT	G	PO	A	E	DP	FR
1953	StL-N	.917	15	19	36	5	8	10
1954	StL-N	1.000	11	4	3	0	1	14
1955	StL-N	1.000	3	1	1	0	0	3
1956	StL-N	.923	9	11	13	2	4	-1
1957	StL-N	.948	23	21	34	3	8	9
1958	StL-N	.932	27	43	81	9	13	-5
	Pit-N	1.000	5	11	15	0	5	0
	Yr	.943	32	54	96	9	18	-5
1959	Pit-N	.923	8	23	25	4	4	1
1960	Pit-N	.947	23	43	64	6	16	7
1961	Pit-N	.975	9	15	24	1	7	5
1962	Pit-N	1.000	1	2	1	0	1	0
1963	Pit-N	.966	117	232	366	21	95	13
1964	Pit-N	.950	111	184	349	28	78	2
1965	Pit-N	.974	28	49	99	4	26	4
	SF-N	.984	93	145	274	7	52	-6
	Yr	.981	121	194	373	11	78	-2
1966	SF-N	1.000	8	10	13	0	3	2
	NY-N	.909	19	26	64	9	11	5
	LA-N	1.000	3	2	5	0	0	-1
1967	LA-N	.976	69	107	213	8	37	-1
1968	StL-N	.973	43	44	66	3	7	3
1969	Bos-A	.926	11	13	12	2	3	-2
1970	Bos-A	1.000	3	0	4	0	0	0
1971	Mil-A	1.000	4	2	0	0	0	-1
	StL-N	.935	17	12	31	3	6	0
Total	19	.961	660	1019	1793	115	385	61

2B

YEAR	TM/L	PCT	G	PO	A	E	DP	FR
1959	Pit-N	.980	28	65	80	3	21	10
1960	Pit-N	1.000	10	15	13	0	2	2
1961	Pit-N	.947	5	8	10	1	2	2
1962	Pit-N	1.000	2	2	8	0	1	0
1963	Pit-N	.981	20	47	56	2	12	-3
1967	LA-N	1.000	4	2	4	0	0	0
1968	StL-N	.975	23	65	50	3	15	6
1969	Bos-A	.981	37	81	124	4	25	7
1970	Bos-A	.969	15	28	35	2	6	-2
1971	Mil-A	1.000	2	0	1	0	0	0
	StL-N	1.000	13	17	26	0	6	1
Total	10	.980	159	330	407	5	90	23

3B

YEAR	TM/L	PCT	G	PO	A	E	DP	FR
1958	Pit-N	—	2	0	0	0	0	0
1960	Pit-N	1.000	1	0	1	0	0	0
1961	Pit-N	.923	11	4	20	2	1	3
1962	Pit-N	.933	20	14	28	3	2	-6
1963	Pit-N	—	1	0	0	0	0	0
1966	LA-N	.923	19	9	39	4	0	-2
1967	LA-N	1.000	2	0	1	0	0	0
1969	Bos-A	.944	9	3	14	1	2	0
1970	Bos-A	.895	15	9	25	4	2	-2
1971	Mil-A	1.000	12	4	9	0	2	-1
	StL-N	1.000	3	0	4	0	0	0
Total	10	.929	95	43	141	4	9	-8

OF

YEAR	TM/L	PCT	G	PO	A	E	DP	FR
1959	Pit-N	1.000	3	2	0	0	0	0
1961	Pit-N	1.000	3	3	0	0	0	0
1969	Bos-A	—	5	0	0	0	0	0
Total	3	1.000	11	5	0	0	0	0

■ Dick Schofield SS

YEAR	TM/L	PCT	G	PO	A	E	DP	FR
1983	Cal-A	.929	21	24	67	7	10	4
1984	Cal-A	.982	140	218	420	12	95	3
1985	Cal-A	.963	147	261	397	25	108	1
1986	Cal-A	.972	137	246	389	18	103	15
1987	Cal-A	.984	131	204	348	9	76	-18
1988	Cal-A	.983	155	278	492	13	125	21
1989	Cal-A	.983	90	118	276	7	56	-8
1990	Cal-A	.966	99	170	318	17	77	12
Total	8	.975	920	1519	2707	108	650	30

2B

YEAR	TM/L	PCT	G	PO	A	E	DP	FR
1987	Cal-A	1.000	2	1	3	0	0	0

■ Otto Schomberg 1B

YEAR	TM/L	PCT	G	PO	A	E	DP	FR
1886	Pit-a	.966	72	702	6	25	34	-7
1887	Ind-N	.958	112	1216	28	55	76	-10
1888	Ind-N	.965	15	136	0	5	8	-2
Total	3	.961	199	2054	34	5	118	-19

OF

YEAR	TM/L	PCT	G	PO	A	E	DP	FR
1887	Ind-N	1.000	1	1	0	0	0	0
1888	Ind-N	.857	15	15	3	3	0	-1
Total	2	.864	16	16	3	3	0	-1

■ Ossee Schreckengost C

YEAR	TM/L	PCT	G	PO	A	E	DP	FR
1897	Lou-N	1.000	1	2	1	0	0	0
1898	Cle-N	.860	9	33	10	7	1	0
1899	Cle-N	.911	39	104	60	16	6	-5
	StL-N	.950	25	75	40	6	5	4
	Yr	.927	64	179	100	22	11	-1
1901	Bos-A	.926	72	273	102	30	8	3
1902	Phi-A	.960	71	367	108	20	3	23
1903	Phi-A	.975	77	514	106	16	4	19
1904	Phi-A	.979	84	589	76	14	5	6
1905	Phi-A	.984	114	790	115	15	11	11
1906	Phi-A	.971	89	532	110	19	7	7
1907	Phi-A	.985	99	640	145	12	4	16
1908	Phi-A	.978	65	352	91	10	3	9
	Chi-A	.982	6	50	5	1	1	4
	Yr	.978	71	402	96	11	4	13
Total	11	.970	751	4321	969	166	58	97

1B

YEAR	TM/L	PCT	G	PO	A	E	DP	FR
1899	StL-N	1.000	1	9	0	0	0	0
	Cle-N	1.000	1	14	0	0	0	0
	StL-N	.963	41	432	9	17	30	-6
	Yr	.965	43	455	9	17	30	-6
1901	Bos-A	1.000	4	28	0	0	1	0
1902	Cle-A	.967	17	168	7	6	5	-1
	Phi-A	.972	7	68	1	2	2	-1
	Yr	.968	24	236	8	8	7	-2
1903	Phi-A	.978	10	83	4	2	4	0
1904	Phi-A	1.000	9	77	1	0	0	-1
1905	Phi-A	1.000	2	10	0	0	0	0
1906	Phi-A	1.000	4	36	2	0	1	0
1907	Phi-A	1.000	2	3	0	0	0	0
1908	Phi-A	1.000	1	2	0	0	1	0
Total	9	.972	99	930	24	7	44	-9

OF

YEAR	TM/L	PCT	G	PO	A	E	DP	FR
1899	StL-N	—	1	0	0	0	0	0
	Cle-N	1.000	1	1	0	0	0	0
	Yr	1.000	2	1	0	0	0	0
1902	Phi-A	.000	1	0	0	1	0	-1
Total	2	.500	3	1	0	1	0	-1

SS

YEAR	TM/L	PCT	G	PO	A	E	DP	FR
1899	Cle-N	—	1	0	0	0	0	0

2B

YEAR	TM/L	PCT	G	PO	A	E	DP	FR
1899	StL-N	.750	1	2	1	1	0	-1

■ Pop Schriver C

YEAR	TM/L	PCT	G	PO	A	E	DP	FR
1886	Bro-a	1.000	3	8	4	0	0	1
1888	Phi-N	.870	27	148	39	28	1	-2
1889	Phi-N	.920	48	233	76	27	4	5
1890	Phi-N	.916	34	187	43	21	4	2
1891	Chi-N	.964	27	135	27	6	3	3
1892	Chi-N	.929	82	367	102	36	5	-10
1893	Chi-N	.926	56	215	62	22	8	2
1894	Chi-N	.923	88	290	91	32	12	-4
1895	NY-N	.898	18	66	22	10	1	-2
1897	Cin-N	.959	53	147	42	8	3	-5
1898	Pit-N	.957	92	302	95	18	6	-5
1899	Pit-N	.958	78	275	94	16	6	6
1900	Pit-N	.959	24	95	21	5	1	-4
1901	Pit-N	.971	24	91	43	4	2	1
Total	14	.934	654	2559	761	233	56	-12

1B

YEAR	TM/L	PCT	G	PO	A	E	DP	FR
1890	Phi-N	.959	10	67	4	3	7	0
1891	Chi-N	—	2	0	0	0	0	0
1894	Cin-N	.947	2	14	4	1	1	1
1895	NY-N	.913	6	61	2	6	5	-1
1898	Pit-N	1.000	1	5	0	0	0	0
1899	Pit-N	1.000	8	81	1	0	3	-1
1900	Pit-N	—	1	0	0	0	0	0
1901	StL-N	.971	19	182	18	6	11	2
Total	8	.965	49	410	29	6	27	1

OF

YEAR	TM/L	PCT	G	PO	A	E	DP	FR
1886	Bro-a	.667	5	4	2	3	0	0
1888	Phi-N	—	1	0	0	0	0	0
1890	Phi-N	1.000	2	4	0	0	0	0
1892	Chi-N	.929	10	12	1	1	0	-2
1893	Chi-N	.909	5	9	1	1	0	0
Total	5	.868	23	29	4	5	0	-2

3B

YEAR	TM/L	PCT	G	PO	A	E	DP	FR
1888	Phi-N	.786	1	2	9	3	1	-1
1889	Phi-N	.667	1	2	2	2	0	-1
1890	Phi-N	.767	8	10	13	7	1	-3
1894	Chi-N	.867	3	4	9	2	0	0
Total	4	.785	18	18	33	4	2	-5

SS

YEAR	TM/L	PCT	G	PO	A	E	DP	FR
1888	Phi-N	.808	6	6	15	5	1	-2
1894	Chi-N	.800	3	2	2	1	0	0
Total	2	.806	9	8	17	6	1	-2

2B

YEAR	TM/L	PCT	G	PO	A	E	DP	FR
1889	Phi-N	.794	6	6	21	7	2	-1
1890	Phi-N	.778	3	4	3	2	0	-1
Total	2	.791	9	10	24	9	2	-2

■ Bill Schroeder C

YEAR	TM/L	PCT	G	PO	A	E	DP	FR
1983	Mil-A	.980	23	92	5	2	1	-3
1984	Mil-A	.987	58	274	24	4	2	-5
1985	Mil-A	.987	48	211	23	3	4	-8
1986	Mil-A	.995	35	190	14	1	3	-4
1987	Mil-A	.995	67	363	26	2	4	-8
1988	Mil-A	1.000	30	145	10	0	1	2
1989	Cal-A	.991	33	194	27	2	2	7
1990	Cal-A	1.000	15	74	7	0	2	1
Total	8	.992	309	1543	136	4	19	-18

1B

YEAR	TM/L	PCT	G	PO	A	E	DP	FR
1984	Mil-A	1.000	1	3	0	0	0	0
1985	Mil-A	1.000	5	5	0	1	0	0
1986	Mil-A	1.000	19	117	11	0	10	0
1987	Mil-A	1.000	4	10	1	0	4	0
1988	Mil-A	1.000	10	52	11	0	2	3
1989	Cal-A	.984	8	58	5	1	8	0
1990	Cal-A	1.000	3	26	3	0	0	0
Total	7	.997	46	271	31	1	25	3

■ Rich Schu 3B

YEAR	TM/L	PCT	G	PO	A	E	DP	FR
1984	Phi-N	.952	15	7	13	1	3	0
1985	Phi-N	.933	111	86	191	20	19	-10
1986	Phi-N	.913	58	42	94	13	6	1
1987	Phi-N	.905	45	24	62	9	2	1
1988	Bal-A	.937	72	56	108	11	7	-11
1989	Det-A	.934	83	52	119	12	11	-3
1990	Cal-A	.918	38	16	74	8	9	4
Total	7	.927	422	283	661	74	57	-18

1B

YEAR	TM/L	PCT	G	PO	A	E	DP	FR
1987	Phi-N	.994	28	169	9	1	9	-2
1988	Bal-A	1.000	4	38	2	0	1	0
1989	Det-A	1.000	3	3	2	0	0	0
1990	Cal-A	.989	15	85	4	1	7	-1
Total	4	.994	50	294	16	2	17	-3

2B

YEAR	TM/L	PCT	G	PO	A	E	DP	FR
1989	Bal-A	1.000	1	1	0	0	0	0
	Det-A	1.000	5	3	5	0	2	1

YEAR	TM/L	PCT	G	PO	A	E	DP	FR
	Yr	1.000	6	4	5	0	2	1
1990	Cal-A	.750	1	3	3	2	0	-1
Total	2	.882	7	7	8	2	2	0
	OF							
1990	Cal-A	—	4	0	0	0	0	0
	SS							
1989	Det-A	1.000	3	1	1	0	1	0

■ Heinie Schuble SS

YEAR	TM/L	PCT	G	PO	A	E	DP	FR
1927	StL-N	.915	65	120	192	29	36	-7
1929	Det-A	.886	86	141	216	46	43	-10
1932	Det-A	.949	16	42	52	5	14	5
1933	Det-A	.875	2	3	4	1	0	0
1934	Det-A	1.000	3	3	5	0	0	0
Total	5	.906	172	309	469	1	93	-12
	3B							
1929	Det-A	.667	2	1	1	1	0	0
1932	Det-A	.941	76	70	152	14	10	3
1933	Det-A	.951	23	16	42	3	1	2
1934	Det-A	1.000	2	0	2	0	0	0
1935	Det-A	.714	2	1	4	2	2	0
1936	StL-N	—	1	0	0	0	0	0
Total	6	.935	106	88	201	0	13	7
	2B							
1933	Det-A	—	1	0	0	0	0	0
1934	Det-A	1.000	1	1	2	0	1	0
1935	Det-A	—	1	0	0	0	0	0
Total	3	1.000	3	1	2	0	1	0

■ Wes Schulmerich OF

YEAR	TM/L	PCT	G	PO	A	E	DP	FR
1931	Bos-N	.966	87	190	6	7	0	-2
1932	Bos-N	.968	101	232	11	8	5	2
1933	Bos-N	.980	21	46	3	1	0	1
	Phi-N	.977	97	210	6	5	0	-3
	Yr	.978	118	256	9	6	0	-2
1934	Phi-N	.963	13	25	1	1	0	-1
	Cin-N	.976	56	121	1	3	1	-3
	Yr	.974	69	146	2	4	1	-4
Total	4	.971	375	824	28	5	6	-6

■ Frank Schulte OF

YEAR	TM/L	PCT	G	PO	A	E	DP	FR
1904	Chi-N	.949	20	34	3	2	0	0
1905	Chi-N	.981	123	189	14	4	0	-6
1906	Chi-N	.975	146	218	18	6	7	0
1907	Chi-N	.973	92	132	11	4	1	-3
1908	Chi-N	.994	102	145	8	1	2	-6
1909	Chi-N	.968	140	169	14	6	1	-13
1910	Chi-N	.968	150	221	18	8	5	-11
1911	Chi-N	.971	154	246	19	8	8	-9
1912	Chi-N	.952	139	219	19	12	6	-12
1913	Chi-N	.956	130	181	13	9	2	-16
1914	Chi-N	.954	134	217	9	11	2	-14
1915	Chi-N	.962	147	280	24	12	3	-10
1916	Chi-N	.951	67	108	8	6	0	-2
	Pit-N	.968	48	89	2	3	0	-4
	Yr	.958	115	197	10	9	0	-6
1917	Pit-N	.963	28	49	3	2	0	-2
	Phi-N	.923	42	47	1	4	0	-8
	Yr	.943	70	96	4	6	0	-10
1918	Was-A	.969	75	145	10	5	4	1
Total	15	.966	1737	2689	194	103	41	-95

■ Fred Schulte OF

YEAR	TM/L	PCT	G	PO	A	E	DP	FR
1927	StL-A	.916	49	117	3	11	0	-2
1928	StL-A	.973	143	419	21	12	6	17
1929	StL-A	.989	116	361	12	4	2	13
1930	StL-A	.966	98	250	5	9	2	-1
1931	StL-A	.971	134	361	13	11	4	6
1932	StL-A	.986	129	331	9	5	1	-5
1933	Was-A	.980	142	433	10	9	4	14
1934	Was-A	.986	134	351	5	5	0	-3
1935	Was-A	.980	56	97	2	2	0	-3
1936	Pit-N	.977	55	129	1	3	1	0
1937	Pit-N	.800	4	4	0	1	0	0
Total	11	.976	1060	2853	81	2	20	36
	1B							
1930	StL-A	.961	5	47	2	2	4	0
1932	StL-A	.933	5	39	3	3	3	0
Total	2	.948	10	86	5	5	7	0

■ Johnny Schulte C

YEAR	TM/L	PCT	G	PO	A	E	DP	FR
1923	StL-A	1.000	1	4	1	0	1	1
1927	StL-N	.956	59	172	45	10	6	3
1928	Phi-N	.949	34	70	23	5	4	-5
1929	StL-N	.978	30	74	16	2	3	1
1932	StL-A	.864	6	18	1	3	1	1
	Bos-N	1.000	10	17	1	0	0	1
Total	5	.957	140	355	87	0	15	0
	1B							
1923	StL-A	1.000	1	1	0	0	0	0

■ Howie Schultz 1B

YEAR	TM/L	PCT	G	PO	A	E	DP	FR
1943	Bro-N	.986	45	386	33	6	27	2
1944	Bro-N	.988	136	1091	85	14	90	0
1945	Bro-N	.984	38	334	32	6	35	3
1946	Bro-N	.989	87	576	58	7	65	5
1947	Bro-N	1.000	1	0	0	0	0	0
	Phi-N	.993	114	986	67	7	92	-1
	Yr	.993	115	987	67	7	92	-1
1948	Phi-N	1.000	3	21	2	0	3	0
	Cin-N	.982	26	156	5	3	14	-3
	Yr	.984	29	177	7	3	17	-3
Total	5	.989	450	3551	282	3	326	6

■ Joe Schultz OF

YEAR	TM/L	PCT	G	PO	A	E	DP	FR
1913	Bos-N	1.000	5	10	0	0	0	0
1916	Pit-N	.923	6	11	1	1	0	0
1919	StL-N	1.000	49	75	6	0	1	-3
1920	StL-N	.945	80	147	7	9	3	-4
1921	StL-N	.977	67	120	7	3	4	-2
1922	StL-N	.976	89	195	7	5	1	0

YEAR	TM/L	PCT	G	PO	A	E	DP	FR
1923	StL-N	1.000	2	5	0	0	0	0
1924	StL-N	1.000	2	1	0	0	0	-1
	Phi-N	.960	76	137	7	6	0	-4
	Yr	.960	78	138	7	6	0	-5
1925	Phi-N	.923	20	34	2	3	1	0
	Cin-N	.950	15	17	2	1	0	-1
	Yr	.932	35	51	4	4	1	-1
Total	9	.966	411	752	39	8	10	-15
	3B							
1915	Bro-N	.894	27	43	41	10	3	-4
1916	Pit-N	.921	24	39	31	6	1	-5
1919	StL-N	—	1	0	0	0	0	0
1921	StL-N	.769	3	3	7	3	0	0
Total	4	.896	55	85	79	9	4	-9
	2B							
1912	Bos-N	.824	4	6	8	3	1	0
1913	Bos-N	1.000	1	1	1	0	0	0
1915	Chi-N	.857	2	3	3	1	0	0
1916	Pit-N	.840	24	25	54	15	2	-10
1919	StL-N	.840	6	12	9	4	1	-3
1925	Cin-N	—	1	0	0	0	0	0
Total	6	.841	38	47	75	3	4	-13
	SS							
1915	Bro-N	1.000	1	0	2	0	0	0
1916	Pit-N	—	1	0	0	0	0	0
Total	2	1.000	2	0	2	0	0	0
	1B							
1921	StL-N	1.000	2	14	0	0	0	0

■ Al Schweitzer OF

YEAR	TM/L	PCT	G	PO	A	E	DP	FR
1908	StL-A	.952	55	86	14	5	3	5
1909	StL-A	.933	22	26	2	2	0	-3
1910	StL-A	.937	109	149	15	11	3	-4
1911	StL-A	.934	68	100	13	8	4	-1
Total	4	.940	254	361	44	6	10	-3

■ Mike Scioscia C

YEAR	TM/L	PCT	G	PO	A	E	DP	FR
1980	LA-N	.992	54	226	26	2	5	3
1981	LA-N	.987	91	493	48	7	4	-2
1982	LA-N	.986	123	631	57	10	10	-6
1983	LA-N	1.000	11	55	4	0	0	-3
1984	LA-N	.985	112	701	64	12	8	13
1985	LA-N	.986	139	818	66	13	8	1
1986	LA-N	.982	119	756	64	15	4	-1
1987	LA-N	.989	138	925	80	11	11	10
1988	LA-N	.991	123	748	63	7	10	7
1989	LA-N	.988	130	822	82	11	12	18
1990	LA-N	.989	132	842	58	10	9	3
Total	11	.987	1172	7017	612	8	81	43

■ Daryl Sconiers 1B

YEAR	TM/L	PCT	G	PO	A	E	DP	FR
1981	Cal-A	1.000	12	95	8	0	11	1
1982	Cal-A	1.000	3	23	1	0	5	0
1983	Cal-A	.986	57	473	23	7	46	-5
1984	Cal-A	.990	41	355	26	4	27	-1
1985	Cal-A	.973	6	35	1	1	2	-1
Total	5	.989	119	981	59	2	91	-6
	OF							
1983	Cal-A	.000	1	0	0	1	0	0

■ Tony Scott OF

YEAR	TM/L	PCT	G	PO	A	E	DP	FR
1973	Mon-N	.000	3	0	0	1	0	1
1974	Mon-N	1.000	16	7	0	0	0	1
1975	Mon-N	.962	71	94	6	4	0	7
1977	StL-N	.996	99	223	5	1	0	9
1978	StL-N	.946	77	100	6	6	0	-2
1979	StL-N	.984	151	427	14	7	5	10
1980	StL-N	.997	144	324	5	1	2	-8
1981	StL-N	1.000	44	120	2	0	0	-3
	Hou-N	.985	55	127	5	2	0	-1
	Yr	.992	99	247	7	2	0	3
1982	Hou-N	.982	129	262	7	5	0	-9
1983	Hou-N	1.000	61	89	2	0	1	-1
1984	Hou-N	1.000	6	8	0	0	0	-1
	Mon-N	1.000	17	22	1	0	0	-1
	Yr	1.000	23	30	1	0	0	0
Total	11	.986	853	1803	53	7	8	11

■ Donnie Scott C

YEAR	TM/L	PCT	G	PO	A	E	DP	FR
1983	Tex-A	1.000	2	8	2	0	0	1
1984	Tex-A	.974	80	400	41	12	9	7
1985	Sea-A	.981	74	277	31	6	1	-6
Total	3	.977	156	685	74	8	10	2

■ Pete Scott OF

YEAR	TM/L	PCT	G	PO	A	E	DP	FR
1926	Chi-N	.968	59	114	7	4	2	4
1927	Chi-N	.986	36	70	3	1	1	-2
1928	Pit-N	.979	42	90	5	2	5	4
Total	3	.976	137	274	15	7	8	6
	1B							
1928	Pit-N	.980	8	96	3	2	1	-1
	3B							
1926	Chi-N	.800	1	2	2	1	0	0

■ George Scott 1B

YEAR	TM/L	PCT	G	PO	A	E	DP	FR
1966	Bos-A	.991	158	1362	112	14	130	5
1967	Bos-A	.987	152	1321	94	19	115	-4
1968	Bos-A	.987	112	807	55	11	68	1
1969	Bos-A	.994	53	436	23	3	49	-2
1970	Bos-A	.990	59	480	36	5	42	0
1971	Bos-A	.992	143	1256	75	11	122	-7
1972	Mil-A	.992	139	1180	73	10	106	-2
1973	Mil-A	.994	157	1388	118	9	144	7
1974	Mil-A	.992	148	1345	114	12	137	7
1975	Mil-A	.989	144	1202	109	14	118	4
1976	Mil-A	.991	155	1393	107	13	133	-2
1977	Bos-A	.985	157	1446	115	24	150	0
1978	Bos-A	.991	113	1052	55	10	99	-8
1979	Bos-A	.986	41	400	25	6	40	-2
	KC-A	.989	41	335	21	4	27	-4
	NY-A	1.000	1	0	0	0	0	0

YEAR	TM/L	PCT	G	PO	A	E	DP	FR
	Yr	.987	83	737	46	10	67	-6
Total	14	.990	1773	15405	1132	165	1480	-7
	3B							
1966	Bos-A	.818	5	0	9	2	1	0
1967	Bos-A	—	2	0	0	0	0	0
1968	Bos-A	1.000	6	3	10	0	1	1
1969	Bos-A	.954	109	106	203	15	29	-3
1970	Bos-A	.934	68	71	113	13	13	-8
1972	Mil-A	.922	23	13	46	5	2	-3
1975	Mil-A	.909	5	3	7	1	1	-1
1979	KC-A	—	1	0	0	0	0	0
Total	8	.942	219	196	388	6	47	-14

■ Everett Scott SS

YEAR	TM/L	PCT	G	PO	A	E	DP	FR
1914	Bos-A	.949	143	324	408	39	50	-10
1915	Bos-A	.961	100	198	298	20	31	4
1916	Bos-A	.967	121	217	339	19	36	7
1917	Bos-A	.953	157	315	483	39	64	8
1918	Bos-A	.976	126	270	419	17	35	17
1919	Bos-A	.976	138	276	423	17	63	7
1920	Bos-A	.973	154	330	496	23	64	17
1921	Bos-A	.972	154	380	528	26	94	38
1922	NY-A	.966	154	302	538	30	74	19
1923	NY-A	.961	152	245	414	27	65	-11
1924	NY-A	.966	153	322	455	27	80	10
1925	NY-A	.988	18	39	45	1	16	3
	Was-A	.932	30	55	81	10	18	2
	Yr	.952	48	94	126	11	34	5
1926	Chi-N	.955	39	70	120	9	20	5
	Cin-N	.875	4	8	6	2	0	0
Total	13	.965	1643	3351	5053	306	710	116
	3B							
1916	Bos-A	1.000	1	0	1	0	0	0
1925	Was-A	1.000	2	2	4	0	1	1
Total	2	1.000	3	2	5	0	1	1
	2B							
1916	Bos-A	1.000	1	0	2	0	0	0

■ Milt Scott 1B

YEAR	TM/L	PCT	G	PO	A	E	DP	FR
1882	Chi-N	1.000	1	3	0	0	0	0
1884	Det-N	.968	110	1120	26	38	37	-1
1885	Det-N	.967	38	394	18	14	17	2
	Pit-a	.986	55	623	16	9	28	3
1886	Bal-a	.974	137	1347	59	38	38	9
Total	4	.973	341	3487	119	9	120	13

■ Rod Scott 2B

YEAR	TM/L	PCT	G	PO	A	E	DP	FR
1975	KC-A	1.000	9	5	2	0	1	2
1976	Mon-N	1.000	6	2	3	0	1	0
1977	Oak-A	.963	71	139	175	12	31	-16
1978	Chi-N	.963	6	16	10	1	1	-1
1979	Mon-N	.980	113	301	324	13	71	-1
1980	Mon-N	.982	129	287	380	12	73	-13
1981	Mon-N	.983	93	187	278	8	41	-15
1982	Mon-N	.971	12	17	17	1	3	-1
	NY-A	1.000	4	5	8	0	0	1
Total	8	.979	443	959	1197	7	222	-42
	SS							
1975	KC-A	.867	8	3	10	2	1	4
1976	Mon-N	1.000	3	4	5	0	1	0
1977	Oak-A	.945	70	59	95	9	18	-13
1978	Chi-N	.917	6	4	7	1	1	-1
1979	Mon-N	.952	39	61	97	8	11	-16
1980	Mon-N	.945	21	52	52	6	15	-4
1982	NY-A	.963	6	9	17	1	5	0
Total	7	.946	153	192	283	7	52	-30
	3B							
1977	Oak-A	1.000	5	2	3	0	0	0
1978	Chi-N	.929	59	43	101	11	15	-6
Total	2	.931	64	45	104	1	15	-6
	OF							
1977	Oak-A	—	1	0	0	0	0	0
1978	Chi-N	.938	10	14	1	1	0	-1
Total	2	.938	11	14	1	1	0	-1

■ Jimmy Sebring OF

YEAR	TM/L	PCT	G	PO	A	E	DP	FR
1902	Pit-N	.974	19	33	5	1	2	4
1903	Pit-N	.927	124	208	20	18	11	7
1904	Pit-N	.959	80	146	16	7	5	8
	Cin-N	1.000	56	88	11	0	3	4
	Yr	.974	136	234	27	7	8	12
1905	Cin-N	.885	56	63	6	9	2	-6
1909	Bro-N	.951	25	35	4	2	1	-2
	Was-A	—	1	0	0	0	0	0
Total	5	.945	361	573	62	7	24	15

■ Bob Seeds OF

YEAR	TM/L	PCT	G	PO	A	E	DP	FR
1930	Cle-A	.953	70	156	6	8	0	2
1931	Cle-A	.966	33	56	1	2	0	-3
1932	Cle-A	—	1	0	0	0	0	0
	Chi-A	.964	112	234	7	9	1	-4
	Yr	.964	113	234	7	9	1	-4
1933	Bos-A	.959	32	43	4	2	0	2
1934	Bos-A	—	1	0	0	0	0	0
	Cle-A	.977	48	83	2	2	0	-4
	Yr	.977	49	83	2	2	0	-4
1936	NY-A	1.000	9	20	1	0	0	1
1938	NY-N	.987	76	147	6	2	2	-3
1939	NY-N	.975	50	77	2	2	0	0
1940	NY-N	.985	40	64	3	1	0	-3
Total	9	.970	472	880	32	8	3	-17
	1B							
1931	Cle-A	1.000	2	5	3	0	0	1
1933	Bos-A	.985	41	379	18	6	33	-1
Total	2	.985	43	386	21	6	33	0
	3B							
1936	NY-N	.889	3	4	4	1	1	0

■ Pat Seerey OF

YEAR	TM/L	PCT	G	PO	A	E	DP	FR
1943	Cle-A	.974	16	35	3	1	0	1

YEAR	TM/L	PCT	G	PO	A	E	DP	FR
1944	Cle-A	.986	86	196	8	3	1	4
1945	Cle-A	.975	117	227	7	6	3	-7
1946	Cle-A	.981	115	248	4	5	1	-11
1947	Cle-A	.957	68	105	7	5	1	-2
1948	Cle-A	1.000	7	6	0	0	0	-2
	Chi-A	.981	93	198	9	4	5	1
	Yr	.982	100	204	9	4	5	-1
1949	Chi-A	1.000	2	1	0	0	0	0
Total	7	.978	504	1016	38	4	11	-16

■ Emmett Seery OF

YEAR	TM/L	PCT	G	PO	A	E	DP	FR
1884	Bal-U	.828	103	157	26	38	3	6
	KC-U	—	1	0	0	0	0	0
	Yr	.828	104	157	26	38	3	6
1885	StL-N	.874	59	95	16	16	1	5
1886	StL-N	.883	126	176	20	26	2	-3
1887	Ind-N	.891	122	220	25	30	2	7
1888	Ind-N	.939	133	258	19	18	6	9
1889	Ind-N	.909	127	220	20	24	4	0
1890	Bro-P	.894	104	216	21	28	3	7
1891	Cin-a	.898	97	160	17	20	3	3
1892	Lou-N	.961	42	65	9	3	1	3
Total	9	.896	914	1567	173	203	25	37
	C							
1884	Bal-U	.917	3	8	3	1	0	1
	3B							
1884	Bal-U	1.000	2	1	1	0	1	0
1885	StL-N	.750	1	1	2	1	0	0
Total	2	.833	3	2	3	1	1	0
	SS							
1887	Ind-N	—	1	0	0	0	0	0
1888	Ind-N	.800	1	2	2	1	0	0
Total	2	.800	2	2	2	1	0	0

■ Kevin Seitzer 3B

YEAR	TM/L	PCT	G	PO	A	E	DP	FR
1986	KC-A	1.000	3	0	1	0	0	0
1987	KC-A	.947	141	105	292	22	32	6
1988	KC-A	.938	147	93	297	26	33	3
1989	KC-A	.950	133	112	272	20	28	-8
1990	KC-A	.953	152	100	262	18	31	-5
Total	5	.947	602	410	1124	6	124	-4
	1B							
1986	KC-A	.987	22	210	17	3	17	0
1987	KC-A	.990	25	183	23	2	19	2
1989	KC-A	—	2	0	0	0	0	0
Total	3	.989	49	393	40	5	36	2
	OF							
1986	KC-A	1.000	5	14	1	0	0	1
1987	KC-A	1.000	3	2	0	0	0	0
1988	KC-A	—	1	0	0	0	0	0
1989	KC-A	1.000	3	1	0	0	0	0
Total	4	1.000	12	17	1	0	0	1
	2B							
1990	KC-A	.974	10	18	19	1	5	-4
	SS							
1989	KC-A	1.000	6	5	5	0	2	-1

■ Kip Selbach OF

YEAR	TM/L	PCT	G	PO	A	E	DP	FR
1894	Was-N	.915	80	153	8	15	2	-4
1895	Was-N	.912	118	289	21	30	5	13
1896	Was-N	.946	126	303	13	18	3	7
1897	Was-N	.955	124	305	14	15	2	13
1898	Was-N	.948	131	320	24	19	6	19
1899	Cin-N	.953	140	355	27	19	10	17
1900	NY-N	.951	141	327	25	18	8	10
1901	NY-N	.942	125	215	11	14	2	-10
1902	Bal-A	.941	127	286	17	19	3	9
1903	Was-A	.956	140	251	10	12	2	-3
1904	Was-A	.931	48	103	5	8	1	3
	Bos-A	.961	98	190	8	8	2	1
	Yr	.950	146	293	13	16	3	4
1905	Bos-A	.928	112	186	8	15	1	-1
1906	Bos-A	.966	58	109	6	4	2	1
Total	13	.944	1568	3392	197	214	49	75
	SS							
1894	Was-N	.822	19	52	54	23	5	-5
1895	Was-N	.837	6	15	26	8	1	1
1898	Was-N	1.000	1	0	6	0	0	1
Total	3	.832	26	67	86	1	6	-3
	2B							
1895	Was-N	.971	5	16	17	1	1	2
	3B							
1903	Was-A	1.000	1	0	1	0	0	0

■ George Selkirk OF

YEAR	TM/L	PCT	G	PO	A	E	DP	FR
1934	NY-A	.989	46	90	3	1	1	0
1935	NY-A	.975	127	269	9	7	1	2
1936	NY-A	.974	135	290	10	8	3	1
1937	NY-A	.987	69	140	9	2	1	1
1938	NY-A	.973	95	176	7	5	3	-3
1939	NY-A	.989	124	254	4	3	1	-5
1940	NY-A	.962	111	220	9	9	6	-3
1941	NY-A	.967	47	84	4	3	2	0
1942	NY-A	1.000	19	36	0	0	0	-1
Total	9	.977	773	1559	55	8	18	-8

■ Andy Seminick C

YEAR	TM/L	PCT	G	PO	A	E	DP	FR
1943	Phi-N	.930	22	79	14	7	2	0
1944	Phi-N	.963	11	45	7	2	0	0
1945	Phi-N	.979	70	198	30	5	3	1
1946	Phi-N	.974	118	461	61	14	12	-6
1947	Phi-N	.978	107	438	53	11	6	9
1948	Phi-N	.965	124	541	74	22	8	7
1949	Phi-N	.975	98	411	54	12	6	7
1950	Phi-N	.976	124	551	54	15	9	4
1951	Phi-N	.979	91	378	47	9	6	-3
1952	Cin-N	.973	99	416	47	13	7	-4
1953	Cin-N	.982	112	436	44	9	2	-6
1954	Cin-N	.989	82	327	44	4	11	3
1955	Cin-N	1.000	5	26	0	0	0	2

YEAR	TM/L	PCT	G	PO	A	E	DP	FR
	Phi-N	.994	88	435	45	3	6	10
	Yr	.994	93	461	45	3	6	12
1956	Phi-N	.976	54	266	23	7	2	-8
1957	Phi-N	1.000	8	22	1	0	0	1
Total	15	.977	1213	5030	598	133	80	17
	OF							
1943	Phi-N	1.000	1	4	0	0	0	0
1944	Phi-N	1.000	7	13	1	0	1	1
1945	Phi-N	1.000	1	2	0	0	0	0
Total	3	1.000	9	19	1	0	1	1
	3B							
1945	Phi-N	.733	4	2	9	4	0	-1

■ Bill Serena 3B

YEAR	TM/L	PCT	G	PO	A	E	DP	FR
1949	Chi-N	.923	11	9	15	2	0	-4
1950	Chi-N	.945	125	122	274	23	24	-2
1951	Chi-N	.941	12	15	17	2	1	-4
1952	Chi-N	.971	58	70	100	5	5	-4
1953	Chi-N	.958	28	29	40	3	7	-2
1954	Chi-N	.933	12	3	25	2	0	-3
Total	6	.951	246	248	471	7	37	-19
	2B							
1952	Chi-N	.989	49	128	134	3	25	3
1953	Chi-N	.983	49	106	120	4	24	-13
1954	Chi-N	1.000	2	2	1	0	0	0
Total	3	.986	100	236	255	7	49	-10

■ Hank Severeid C

YEAR	TM/L	PCT	G	PO	A	E	DP	FR
1911	Cin-N	.913	22	51	12	6	2	-3
1912	Cin-N	.943	20	85	14	6	2	-7
1913	Cin-N	1.000	2	2	0	0	0	0
1915	StL-A	.966	64	247	66	11	2	-10
1916	StL-A	.976	89	313	99	10	6	-16
1917	StL-A	.966	139	529	156	24	10	-19
1918	StL-A	.946	42	148	44	11	4	-5
1919	StL-A	.983	103	401	106	9	12	-5
1920	StL-A	.983	117	480	111	10	11	2
1921	StL-A	.972	126	481	117	17	11	-4
1922	StL-A	.984	133	552	123	11	10	6
1923	StL-A	.993	116	511	88	4	9	8
1924	StL-A	.989	130	443	104	6	12	-3
1925	StL-A	.993	31	114	24	1	3	-1
	Was-A	.986	35	129	16	2	3	2
	Yr	.990	66	243	40	3	6	1
1926	Was-A	.977	16	36	6	1	1	2
	NY-A	.988	40	135	26	2	3	-3
	Yr	.985	56	171	32	3	4	-1
Total	15	.978	1225	4657	1112	131	101	-56
	1B							
1912	Cin-N	.976	7	39	2	1	1	0
1916	StL-A	1.000	1	6	0	0	0	0
1917	StL-A	1.000	1	3	1	0	0	0
Total	3	.981	9	48	3	1	1	0
	OF							
1912	Cin-N	.889	6	8	0	1	0	-1
1913	Cin-N	—	1	0	0	0	0	0
Total	2	.889	7	8	0	1	0	-1
	3B							
1916	StL-A	1.000	1	1	0	0	0	0

■ Luke Sewell C

YEAR	TM/L	PCT	G	PO	A	E	DP	FR
1921	Cle-A	1.000	3	7	4	0	0	1
1922	Cle-A	.963	39	108	21	5	2	0
1923	Cle-A	.833	7	5	5	2	0	0
1924	Cle-A	.959	57	171	42	9	5	5
1925	Cle-A	.971	66	216	54	8	13	7
1926	Cle-A	.983	125	437	91	9	3	1
1927	Cle-A	.963	126	402	119	20	14	-2
1928	Cle-A	.972	118	430	117	16	13	14
1929	Cle-A	.966	124	433	81	18	11	5
1930	Cle-A	.974	76	283	49	9	5	-2
1931	Cle-A	.980	104	384	61	9	5	-8
1932	Cle-A	.978	84	306	50	8	8	3
1933	Was-A	.990	141	516	61	6	12	-7
1934	Was-A	.994	50	143	23	1	6	-3
1935	Chi-A	.988	112	399	83	6	10	6
1936	Chi-A	.984	126	461	87	9	12	12
1937	Chi-A	.985	118	502	72	9	11	6
1938	Chi-A	.985	65	205	55	4	7	7
1939	Cle-A	.966	15	24	4	1	0	1
1942	StL-A	.944	6	12	5	1	1	1
Total	20	.978	1562	5444	1084	150	138	45
	OF							
1925	Cle-A	1.000	2	6	0	0	0	0
1934	Was-A	.944	7	14	3	1	1	2
Total	2	.958	9	20	3	1	1	2
	1B							
1934	Was-A	1.000	6	57	3	0	4	0
1939	Cle-A	—	1	0	0	0	0	0
Total	2	1.000	7	57	3	0	4	0
	2B							
1934	Was-A	1.000	1	1	1	0	1	0
	3B							
1934	Was-A	—	1	0	0	0	0	0

■ Joe Sewell SS

YEAR	TM/L	PCT	G	PO	A	E	DP	FR
1920	Cle-A	.884	22	44	70	15	11	3
1921	Cle-A	.944	154	319	480	47	75	-3
1922	Cle-A	.939	139	295	462	49	72	12
1923	Cle-A	.951	153	286	497	59	82	5
1924	Cle-A	.960	153	349	514	36	76	21
1925	Cle-A	.967	153	314	529	29	80	18
1926	Cle-A	.955	154	326	463	37	86	3
1927	Cle-A	.962	153	361	480	33	80	6
1928	Cle-A	.963	137	297	438	28	103	19
Total	9	.951	1216	2591	3933	333	665	84
	3B							
1928	Cle-A	.943	19	22	61	5	3	8
1929	Cle-A	.975	152	163	336	13	28	15

YEAR	TM/L	PCT	G	PO	A	E	DP	FR
1930	Cle-A	.950	97	83	184	14	16	0
1931	NY-A	.952	121	131	227	18	14	-2
1932	NY-A	.974	123	122	221	9	15	2
1933	NY-A	.964	131	123	224	13	27	3
Total	6	.963	643	644	1253	2	103	26
	2B							
1922	Cle-A	.954	12	27	35	3	7	3
1925	Cle-A	1.000	3	10	6	0	0	-1
1931	NY-A	1.000	1	1	3	0	1	0
Total	3	.965	16	38	44	3	8	2

■ Jimmy Sexton SS

YEAR	TM/L	PCT	G	PO	A	E	DP	FR
1977	Sea-A	.929	12	12	40	4	10	3
1978	Hou-N	.981	58	59	95	3	18	-3
1979	Hou-N	.943	11	10	23	2	6	6
1982	Oak-A	.957	47	56	101	7	17	-4
1983	StL-N	1.000	4	2	7	0	2	1
Total	5	.962	132	139	266	6	53	3
	3B							
1978	Hou-N	.750	8	0	3	1	0	0
1979	Hou-N	1.000	4	1	0	0	0	0
1981	Oak-A	1.000	1	0	3	0	0	0
1982	Oak-A	.923	8	7	17	2	1	2
1983	StL-N	1.000	2	2	1	0	0	0
Total	5	.919	23	10	24	3	1	3
	2B							
1978	Hou-N	.900	3	3	6	1	1	0
1979	Hou-N	1.000	2	0	1	0	0	0
Total	2	.909	5	3	7	1	1	0

■ Socks Seybold OF

YEAR	TM/L	PCT	G	PO	A	E	DP	FR
1899	Cin-N	.917	22	40	4	4	0	1
1901	Phi-A	.954	100	157	10	8	2	-6
1902	Phi-A	.963	136	246	11	10	3	2
1903	Phi-A	.964	120	177	9	7	4	0
1904	Phi-A	.975	129	180	12	5	5	2
1905	Phi-A	.983	133	215	13	4	5	9
1906	Phi-A	.925	114	150	10	13	3	-5
1907	Phi-A	.973	147	201	19	6	7	1
1908	Phi-A	.921	34	32	3	3	0	-3
Total	9	.961	935	1398	91	0	29	1
	1B							
1901	Phi-A	.987	14	144	7	2	7	0
1903	Phi-A	.966	18	163	8	6	6	-1
1904	Phi-A	.960	13	92	4	4	4	-1
Total	3	.972	45	399	19	2	17	-2

■ Cy Seymour OF

YEAR	TM/L	PCT	G	PO	A	E	DP	FR
1896	NY-N	—	1	0	0	0	0	-1
1897	NY-N	1.000	6	9	0	0	0	-1
1898	NY-N	.875	35	49	7	8	2	-2
1899	NY-N	.846	8	9	2	2	0	-1
1900	NY-N	.667	3	4	0	2	0	-1
1901	Bal-N	.945	133	271	23	17	4	14
1902	Bal-A	.956	72	121	9	6	2	1
	Cin-N	.920	61	139	10	13	3	3
1903	Cin-N	.902	135	318	14	36	2	5
1904	Cin-N	.951	130	308	20	17	4	13
1905	Cin-N	.947	149	347	25	21	12	12
1906	Cin-N	.968	79	202	10	7	3	10
	NY-N	.978	72	129	7	3	3	-2
	Yr	.972	151	331	17	10	6	8
1907	NY-N	.975	126	300	8	8	4	3
1908	NY-N	.949	155	340	29	20	9	11
1909	NY-N	.968	74	138	11	5	3	0
1910	NY-N	.936	76	137	9	10	1	-3
1913	Bos-N	.950	18	34	4	2	0	2
Total	16	.945	1333	2855	188	177	52	63
	1B							
1899	NY-N	.781	3	24	1	7	2	-1
1900	NY-N	1.000	1	1	0	0	0	0
1901	Bal-A	.889	1	7	1	1	1	0
Total	3	.810	5	32	2	8	3	-1
	3B							
1899	NY-N	.667	1	1	1	1	0	0
1902	Cin-N	1.000	1	0	4	0	0	1
Total	2	.857	2	1	5	1	0	1
	2B							
1898	NY-N	1.000	1	1	1	0	0	0

■ Tillie Shafer 3B

YEAR	TM/L	PCT	G	PO	A	E	DP	FR
1909	NY-N	.750	16	11	19	10	1	-2
1910	NY-N	.889	8	5	11	2	2	4
1912	NY-N	.920	16	15	31	4	0	1
1913	NY-N	.923	79	115	136	21	11	-5
Total	4	.903	119	146	197	7	14	-2
	2B							
1909	NY-N	.918	13	19	37	5	1	2
1910	NY-N	1.000	1	0	2	0	0	0
1912	NY-N	.936	15	16	28	3	3	1
1913	NY-N	.930	25	44	63	8	7	-4
Total	4	.929	55	79	130	6	11	-1
	SS							
1910	NY-N	—	2	0	0	0	0	0
1912	NY-N	.879	31	49	60	15	7	-9
1913	NY-N	.875	16	32	52	12	8	-1
Total	3	.877	49	81	112	7	15	-10
	OF							
1909	NY-N	1.000	2	3	0	0	0	0
1913	NY-N	.938	15	27	3	2	0	0
Total	2	.943	17	30	3	2	0	0

■ Orator Shaffer OF

YEAR	TM/L	PCT	G	PO	A	E	DP	FR
1877	Lou-N	.835	60	121	21	28	1	13
1878	Ind-N	.842	63	105	28	25	2	6
1879	Chi-N	.801	72	99	50	37	3	19
1880	Cle-N	.901	83	128	35	18	5	15
1881	Cle-N	.880	85	122	24	20	4	0
1882	Cle-N	.805	84	111	17	31	2	-10
1883	Buf-N	.861	95	182	41	36	3	20

YEAR	TM/L	PCT	G	PO	A	E	DP	FR
1884	StL-U	.870	100	110	24	20	3	-1
1885	StL-N	.918	69	106	28	12	0	10
	Phi-a	1.000	2	1	0	0	0	-1
1886	Phi-a	.815	21	40	4	10	2	0
1890	Phi-a	.958	98	143	17	7	6	1
Total	11	.865	832	1268	289	244	31	72
	2B							
1884	StL-U	.864	7	22	16	6	1	-2
	1B							
1877	Lou-N	1.000	1	12	0	0	0	0
1884	StL-U	—	1	0	0	0	0	0
1890	Phi-a	.966	3	26	2	1	1	0
Total	3	.976	5	38	2	1	1	0
	3B							
1879	Chi-N	.500	1	0	1	1	0	0

■ Art Shamsky   OF

YEAR	TM/L	PCT	G	PO	A	E	DP	FR
1965	Cin-N	.966	18	26	2	1	0	1
1966	Cin-N	.973	74	104	3	3	1	-2
1967	Cin-N	.984	40	59	2	1	1	0
1968	NY-N	.993	82	128	6	1	2	-1
1969	NY-N	.992	78	117	2	1	2	-4
1970	NY-N	1.000	58	104	2	0	1	1
1971	NY-N	.984	38	57	6	1	1	3
Total	7	.987	388	595	23	8	8	-2
	1B							
1965	Cin-N	1.000	1	5	0	0	0	0
1968	NY-N	.983	17	111	6	2	6	-2
1969	NY-N	.987	9	75	0	1	5	-2
1970	NY-N	.995	56	378	35	2	29	0
1971	NY-N	1.000	1	2	0	0	1	0
1972	Chi-N	1.000	4	30	1	0	1	0
Total	6	.992	88	601	42	5	42	-4

■ Wally Shaner   OF

YEAR	TM/L	PCT	G	PO	A	E	DP	FR
1923	Cle-A	1.000	2	2	0	0	0	-1
1926	Bos-A	.965	48	106	3	4	2	0
1927	Bos-A	.955	108	220	13	11	1	-8
1929	Cin-N	1.000	2	6	0	0	0	0
Total	4	.959	160	334	16	5	3	-9
	1B							
1927	Bos-A	.933	1	11	3	1	2	1
1929	Cin-N	1.000	8	74	1	0	9	-1
Total	2	.989	9	85	4	1	11	0
	3B							
1923	Cle-A	—	1	0	0	0	0	0

■ Howie Shanks   OF

YEAR	TM/L	PCT	G	PO	A	E	DP	FR
1912	Was-A	.962	114	189	14	8	2	-2
1913	Was-A	.978	109	207	13	5	3	3
1914	Was-A	.954	139	276	14	14	3	0
1915	Was-A	.982	80	151	13	3	1	5
1916	Was-A	.987	88	203	19	3	4	16
1917	Was-A	.977	26	73	12	2	3	11
1918	Was-A	.957	64	149	7	7	1	2
1919	Was-A	.952	6	19	1	1	1	2
1920	Was-A	1.000	35	74	2	0	0	-1
1922	Was-A	.971	27	65	3	2	2	2
1923	Bos-A	1.000	6	10	1	0	0	0
1924	Bos-A	1.000	4	3	0	0	0	-1
1925	NY-A	1.000	4	4	0	0	0	0
Total	13	.971	702	1423	99	5	20	36
	3B							
1915	Was-A	.915	49	57	94	14	10	4
1916	Was-A	.959	31	45	49	4	3	-3
1918	Was-A	.941	3	5	11	1	1	2
1920	Was-A	.951	63	102	131	12	4	-4
1921	Was-A	.960	154	218	330	23	35	6
1922	Was-A	.920	54	61	112	15	14	5
1923	Bos-A	.939	83	89	173	17	16	-8
1924	Bos-A	.960	22	37	58	4	9	8
1925	NY-A	.938	26	32	29	4	2	-4
Total	9	.946	485	646	987	4	94	6
	SS							
1916	Was-A	.846	8	11	22	6	4	-1
1917	Was-A	.929	90	205	255	35	44	2
1919	Was-A	.922	94	238	260	42	25	-8
1920	Was-A	1.000	1	1	4	0	0	0
1923	Bos-A	.833	1	1	4	1	0	0
1924	Bos-A	.972	41	62	75	4	15	1
Total	6	.928	235	518	620	8	88	-6
	2B							
1915	Was-A	.975	10	18	21	1	4	-1
1918	Was-A	.950	48	130	136	14	20	-4
1919	Was-A	.924	34	72	98	14	8	-5
1920	Was-A	.889	5	5	11	2	2	-1
1921	Was-A	—	1	0	0	0	0	0
1923	Bos-A	.961	38	92	82	7	18	-10
1924	Bos-A	.833	2	4	1	1	0	-1
1925	NY-A	.978	21	32	58	2	11	-1
Total	8	.949	159	353	407	1	63	-23
	1B							
1916	Was-A	.933	7	54	2	4	4	-1
1917	Was-A	.947	2	18	0	1	2	-1
1920	Was-A	.975	14	112	6	3	6	-1
1924	Bos-A	1.000	2	16	1	0	1	0
Total	4	.963	25	200	9	8	13	-3

■ Dan Shannon   2B

YEAR	TM/L	PCT	G	PO	A	E	DP	FR
1889	Lou-a	.910	121	307	391	69	59	7
1890	Phi-P	.926	19	37	51	7	4	-4
	NY-P	.908	77	162	262	43	35	3
	Yr	.911	96	199	313	50	39	-1
1891	Was-a	.960	5	15	9	1	0	-1
Total	3	.911	222	521	713	120	98	5
	SS							
1890	NY-P	.857	6	9	15	4	0	-2
1891	Was-a	.878	14	30	42	10	6	1
Total	2	.873	20	39	57	4	6	-1

YEAR	TM/L	PCT	G	PO	A	E	DP	FR
■ Red Shannon 2B								
1915	Bos-N	1.000	1	1	3	0	0	1
1918	Phi-A	.921	26	50	90	12	14	0
1919	Phi-A	.948	37	66	116	10	10	-5
	Bos-A	.973	79	171	228	11	40	-4
	Yr	.966	116	237	344	21	50	-9
1920	Was-A	.970	16	26	39	2	0	-5
Total	4	.958	159	314	476	5	64	-13
	SS							
1917	Phi-A	.875	10	18	31	7	2	0
1918	Phi-A	.898	45	105	133	27	26	-4
1920	Was-A	.919	31	47	77	11	14	-12
	Phi-A	.945	24	43	77	7	9	-1
	Yr	.931	55	90	154	18	23	-13
1926	Chi-N	.957	13	25	42	3	6	-2
Total	4	.916	123	238	360	5	57	-19
	3B							
1920	Was-A	.906	15	16	32	5	0	-2

■ Mike Shannon   3B

YEAR	TM/L	PCT	G	PO	A	E	DP	FR
1967	StL-N	.919	122	88	239	29	18	-11
1968	StL-N	.952	156	110	310	21	25	-7
1969	StL-N	.945	149	123	258	22	22	-19
1970	StL-N	.919	51	32	59	8	4	-13
Total	4	.938	478	353	866	0	69	-50
	OF							
1962	StL-N	1.000	7	7	1	0	0	1
1963	StL-N	.944	26	15	2	1	0	2
1964	StL-N	.983	88	110	7	2	2	-7
1965	StL-N	.994	101	170	5	1	1	-2
1966	StL-N	.985	129	247	10	4	4	7
1967	StL-N	1.000	6	10	2	0	0	1
Total	6	.987	357	559	27	8	7	2
	C							
1965	StL-N	1.000	4	23	1	0	1	1
1966	StL-N	1.000	1	1	0	0	0	0
Total	2	1.000	5	24	1	0	1	1

■ Spike Shannon   OF

YEAR	TM/L	PCT	G	PO	A	E	DP	FR
1904	StL-N	.978	133	246	18	6	10	9
1905	StL-N	.984	140	299	7	5	3	1
1906	StL-N	.972	80	165	9	5	3	6
	NY-N	.958	76	109	4	5	2	-7
	Yr	.966	156	274	13	10	5	-1
1907	NY-N	.977	155	282	18	7	3	2
1908	NY-N	.976	74	114	8	3	3	-3
	Pit-N	.947	32	88	2	5	0	1
	Yr	.964	106	202	10	8	3	-2
Total	5	.974	690	1303	66	6	24	9

■ Billy Shantz   C

YEAR	TM/L	PCT	G	PO	A	E	DP	FR
1954	Phi-A	.975	51	170	28	5	1	-12
1955	KC-A	.990	78	261	27	3	8	-11
1960	NY-A	1.000	1	1	0	0	0	0
Total	3	.984	130	432	55	8	9	-23

■ Dick Sharon   OF

YEAR	TM/L	PCT	G	PO	A	E	DP	FR
1973	Det-A	.970	91	124	5	4	1	7
1974	Det-A	.989	56	84	3	1	1	-2
1975	SD-N	.948	57	91	1	5	0	0
Total	3	.969	204	299	9	0	2	5

■ Bill Sharp   OF

YEAR	TM/L	PCT	G	PO	A	E	DP	FR
1973	Chi-A	.981	70	146	10	3	2	7
1974	Chi-A	.986	99	210	3	3	0	-2
1975	Chi-A	.941	14	16	0	1	0	-1
	Mil-A	.984	124	294	12	2	4	10
	Yr	.991	138	310	12	3	4	9
1976	Mil-A	.975	56	108	7	3	2	5
Total	4	.985	363	774	32	2	8	19

■ Bud Sharpe   1B

YEAR	TM/L	PCT	G	PO	A	E	DP	FR
1905	Bos-N	1.000	1	9	0	0	0	0
1910	Bos-N	.987	113	1122	81	16	72	7
	Pit-N	1.000	4	37	3	0	0	0
	Yr	.987	117	1159	84	16	72	7
Total	2	.987	118	1168	84	6	72	7
	OF							
1905	Bos-N	.904	42	55	11	7	3	2
	C							
1905	Bos-N	1.000	3	9	9	0	0	1

■ Mike Sharperson   3B

YEAR	TM/L	PCT	G	PO	A	E	DP	FR
1987	LA-N	1.000	7	3	15	0	0	1
1988	LA-N	1.000	6	4	0	0	0	-1
1989	LA-N	—	2	0	0	0	0	0
1990	LA-N	.949	106	70	153	12	10	8
Total	4	.953	121	77	168	2	10	8
	2B							
1987	Tor-A	.971	32	64	69	4	16	-5
	LA-N	.933	6	1	13	1	2	1
1988	LA-N	.949	20	11	26	2	6	1
1989	LA-N	1.000	4	7	4	0	2	0
1990	LA-N	.957	9	10	12	1	1	-1
Total	4	.964	71	93	124	8	27	-4
	SS							
1988	LA-N	1.000	4	4	5	0	0	0
1989	LA-N	1.000	1	3	0	0	0	0
1990	LA-N	.977	15	17	26	1	7	0
Total	3	.982	20	21	34	1	7	0
	1B							
1989	LA-N	1.000	2	4	1	0	0	0
1990	LA-N	.983	6	55	2	1	5	-1
Total	2	.984	8	59	3	1	5	-1

■ Al Shaw   OF

YEAR	TM/L	PCT	G	PO	A	E	DP	FR
1907	StL-N	.947	9	17	1	1	0	-1
1908	StL-N	.931	91	179	23	15	7	9
1909	StL-N	.940	92	189	14	13	1	-1
1914	Bro-F	.955	102	198	14	10	4	1
1915	KC-F	.942	124	184	11	12	0	-14

YEAR	TM/L	PCT	G	PO	A	E	DP	FR
Total	5	.942	418	767	63	1	12	-6
	SS							
1908	StL-N	.750	4	7	5	4	1	-2
	3B							
1908	StL-N	—	1	0	0	0	0	0

■ Al Shaw   C

YEAR	TM/L	PCT	G	PO	A	E	DP	FR
1901	Det-A	.938	42	134	46	12	5	0
1907	Bos-A	.971	73	294	106	12	10	15
1908	Chi-A	.953	29	87	15	5	1	3
1909	Bos-N	.975	14	58	21	2	0	4
Total	4	.961	158	573	188	1	16	22
	1B							
1901	Det-A	.945	9	83	3	5	7	-1
1907	Bos-A	.667	1	2	0	1	1	0
Total	2	.936	10	85	3	6	8	-1
	3B							
1901	Det-A	1.000	2	0	1	0	0	0
	SS							
1901	Det-A	—	1	0	0	0	0	0

■ Marty Shay   SS

YEAR	TM/L	PCT	G	PO	A	E	DP	FR
1916	Chi-N	.917	2	6	5	1	2	0
1924	Bos-N	1.000	1	1	1	0	0	0
1901	Cle-A	.901	19	38	53	10	3	-4
1904	StL-N	.911	97	153	319	46	30	-8
1905	StL-N	.889	39	90	110	25	8	-13
1907	NY-N	.867	9	12	27	6	2	-1
Total	6	.903	167	300	515	8	45	-26
	2B							
1924	Bos-N	.950	19	37	39	4	10	-11
1904	StL-N	1.000	2	0	5	0	0	1
1905	StL-N	.953	39	82	120	10	14	-1
1907	NY-N	.931	13	28	26	4	1	-5
Total	4	.949	73	147	190	8	25	-16
	OF							
1907	NY-N	—	2	0	0	0	0	-1

■ Merv Shea   C

YEAR	TM/L	PCT	G	PO	A	E	DP	FR
1927	Det-A	.949	31	94	17	6	1	0
1928	Det-A	.951	30	93	24	6	2	4
1929	Det-A	.964	46	157	32	7	4	-6
1933	Bos-A	1.000	16	48	11	0	2	-2
	StL-A	.995	85	328	60	2	15	8
	Yr	.996	101	376	71	2	17	6
1934	Chi-A	.972	60	240	35	8	4	2
1935	Chi-A	.990	43	161	30	2	2	8
1936	Chi-A	1.000	14	32	3	0	0	0
1937	Chi-A	.966	25	91	21	4	1	2
1938	Bro-N	.977	47	149	19	4	2	-1
1939	Det-A	.500	4	1	0	1	0	-1
1944	Phi-N	.952	6	18	2	1	0	0
Total	11	.976	407	1412	254	1	33	14

■ Dave Shean   2B

YEAR	TM/L	PCT	G	PO	A	E	DP	FR
1906	Phi-A	.980	22	41	58	2	5	-2
1909	Phi-N	.982	14	24	31	1	3	-1
	Bos-N	.956	72	164	209	17	34	8
	Yr	.960	86	188	240	18	37	7
1910	Bos-N	.953	148	408	493	44	92	42
1911	Chi-N	.947	23	43	64	6	5	0
1917	Cin-N	.961	131	332	412	30	69	19
1918	Bos-A	.967	115	241	341	20	38	-8
1919	Bos-A	.981	29	70	85	3	18	4
Total	7	.961	554	1323	1693	123	264	62
	SS							
1908	Phi-N	.871	14	27	34	9	2	-6
1909	Phi-N	1.000	1	3	3	0	0	0
1911	Chi-N	.929	19	37	42	6	12	1
1912	Bos-N	.917	4	2	9	1	2	-1
Total	4	.908	38	69	88	6	16	-6
	1B							
1909	Phi-N	.990	11	96	1	1	3	-2
	OF							
1909	Phi-N	1.000	3	8	1	0	0	1
	3B							
1911	Chi-N	1.000	1	1	1	0	0	0

■ Jimmy Sheckard   OF

YEAR	TM/L	PCT	G	PO	A	E	DP	FR
1897	Bro-N	.800	2	4	0	1	0	0
1898	Bro-N	.926	105	213	12	18	2	-3
1899	Bal-N	.943	146	298	33	20	14	21
1900	Bro-N	.925	78	171	13	15	3	2
1901	Bro-N	.944	121	287	15	18	5	10
1902	Bal-N	1.000	4	5	0	0	0	-1
	Bro-N	.964	123	284	12	11	5	8
1903	Bro-N	.951	139	314	36	18	7	23
1904	Bro-N	.956	141	291	16	14	5	9
1905	Bro-N	.967	129	266	24	10	6	15
1906	Chi-N	.986	146	264	13	4	1	0
1907	Chi-N	.975	142	222	13	6	2	-11
1908	Chi-N	.955	115	201	18	10	3	-2
1909	Chi-N	.967	148	277	18	10	5	-3
1910	Chi-N	.976	143	308	21	8	3	12
1911	Chi-N	.963	156	332	32	14	12	17
1912	Chi-N	.962	146	332	26	14	4	12
1913	StL-N	.953	46	76	6	4	3	-2
	Cin-N	.969	38	58	4	2	0	-2
	Yr	.960	84	134	10	6	3	-4
Total	17	.958	2071	4203	307	197	80	105
	3B							
1898	Bro-N	.500	1	0	1	1	0	-1
1901	Bro-N	.721	12	9	22	12	1	-3
Total	2	.711	13	9	23	3	1	-4
	SS							
1897	Bro-N	.753	11	17	41	19	5	-3
	2B							
1904	Bro-N	.833	2	5	0	1	0	-2
	1B							
1899	Bal-N	1.000	1	8	0	0	0	0

Tommy Sheehan 3B

YEAR	TM/L	PCT	G	PO	A	E	DP	FR
1906	Pit-N	.947	90	104	166	15	11	-5
1907	Pit-N	.941	57	55	137	12	3	3
1908	Bro-N	.930	145	174	280	34	13	-6
Total	3	.938	292	333	583	1	27	-8
	SS							
1907	Pit-N	.860	10	19	24	7	0	-4

Earl Sheely 1B

YEAR	TM/L	PCT	G	PO	A	E	DP	FR
1921	Chi-A	.988	154	1637	119	22	121	5
1922	Chi-A	.993	149	1512	103	12	101	2
1923	Chi-A	.992	156	1563	96	14	113	-1
1924	Chi-A	.991	146	1423	79	14	97	-10
1925	Chi-A	.988	153	1565	95	20	136	-5
1926	Chi-A	.995	144	1386	84	8	87	0
1927	Chi-A	.982	36	315	15	6	25	-4
1929	Pit-N	.996	139	1292	83	5	102	9
1931	Bos-N	.992	143	1374	70	12	108	-3
Total	9	.991	1220	12067	744	113	890	-16

Larry Sheets OF

YEAR	TM/L	PCT	G	PO	A	E	DP	FR
1984	Bal-A	1.000	7	12	1	0	0	1
1985	Bal-A	.875	9	7	0	1	0	-1
1986	Bal-A	.984	32	60	1	1	1	0
1987	Bal-A	.975	124	229	5	6	2	-7
1988	Bal-A	.974	76	139	9	4	0	-1
1990	Det-A	.981	79	98	7	2	1	-5
Total	6	.976	327	545	23	4	4	-13
	1B							
1985	Bal-A	1.000	1	5	1	0	1	0
1986	Bal-A	.958	4	18	5	1	3	1
1987	Bal-A	.941	3	14	2	1	1	0
1988	Bal-A	1.000	3	20	3	0	3	0
Total	4	.971	11	57	11	2	8	1
	C							
1986	Bal-A	.917	6	10	1	1	0	-1
	3B							
1986	Bal-A	1.000	2	2	1	0	0	0

Gary Sheffield 3B

YEAR	TM/L	PCT	G	PO	A	E	DP	FR
1989	Mil-A	.937	21	15	44	4	4	1
1990	Mil-A	.934	125	98	254	25	16	-4
Total	2	.934	146	113	298	9	20	-3
	SS							
1988	Mil-A	.967	24	39	48	3	9	-10
1989	Mil-A	.959	70	85	194	12	40	-18
Total	2	.961	94	124	242	5	49	-28

John Shelby OF

YEAR	TM/L	PCT	G	PO	A	E	DP	FR
1981	Bal-A	1.000	4	1	0	0	0	0
1982	Bal-A	1.000	24	20	1	0	1	1
1983	Bal-A	.981	115	200	9	4	3	-8
1984	Bal-A	.993	124	261	9	2	1	1
1985	Bal-A	.981	59	148	3	3	0	7
1986	Bal-A	.978	121	222	5	5	2	-6
1987	Bal-A	1.000	19	25	0	0	0	1
	LA-N	.972	117	269	9	8	3	6
1988	LA-N	.982	140	329	7	6	1	0
1989	LA-N	.991	98	220	3	2	1	-5
1990	LA-N	1.000	12	8	0	0	0	0
	Det-A	.973	68	138	5	4	3	3
Total	10	.982	901	1841	51	4	15	0
	2B							
1985	Bal-A	1.000	1	0	1	0	0	0

Jack Shepard C

YEAR	TM/L	PCT	G	PO	A	E	DP	FR
1953	Pit-N	.750	2	6	0	2	0	0
1954	Pit-N	.977	67	257	46	7	5	2
1955	Pit-N	.982	77	288	34	6	6	-9
1956	Pit-N	.990	86	356	36	4	4	1
Total	4	.982	232	907	116	9	15	-6
	1B							
1956	Pit-N	1.000	2	3	0	0	0	0

Pat Sheridan OF

YEAR	TM/L	PCT	G	PO	A	E	DP	FR
1981	KC-A	1.000	3	2	0	0	0	0
1983	KC-A	.988	100	237	6	3	2	3
1984	KC-A	.986	134	273	8	4	1	-3
1985	KC-A	.983	69	116	3	2	0	-6
1986	Det-A	.977	90	172	1	4	0	3
1987	Det-A	.976	137	236	6	6	1	-9
1988	Det-A	.981	111	203	2	4	0	-8
1989	Det-A	.982	35	52	2	1	1	-1
	SF-N	.983	66	111	2	2	0	3
Total	8	.982	745	1402	30	6	5	-18

Norm Sherry C

YEAR	TM/L	PCT	G	PO	A	E	DP	FR
1959	LA-N	1.000	2	4	0	0	0	-1
1960	LA-N	.993	44	282	15	2	3	-4
1961	LA-N	.993	45	253	16	2	3	4
1962	LA-N	.992	34	221	13	2	2	9
1963	NY-N	.980	61	265	26	6	6	3
Total	5	.989	186	1025	70	2	14	11

Billy Shindle 3B

YEAR	TM/L	PCT	G	PO	A	E	DP	FR
1887	Det-N	.818	21	24	30	12	5	-5
1888	Bal-a	.922	135	218	340	47	26	37
1889	Bal-A	.862	138	225	323	88	25	20
1890	Phi-P	.571	2	2	2	3	0	-2
1891	Phi-N	.874	100	153	248	58	24	5
1892	Bal-N	.882	134	200	382	78	27	38
1893	Bal-N	.885	125	176	308	63	24	8
1894	Bro-N	.897	116	192	226	48	12	1
1895	Bro-N	.897	116	142	257	46	16	0
1896	Bro-N	.912	131	144	251	38	20	-12
1897	Bro-N	.904	134	185	241	45	13	-12
1898	Bro-N	.911	120	154	278	42	23	7
Total	12	.892	1272	1815	2886	568	215	85
	SS							
1886	Det-N	.900	7	3	24	3	1	1
1890	Phi-P	.856	130	266	442	119	67	10
1891	Phi-N	1.000	3	4	12	0	1	1
1892	Bal-N	.803	9	25	24	12	1	-2
Total	4	.857	149	298	502	134	70	10
	OF							
1887	Det-N	.500	1	1	0	1	0	-1

Ralph Shinners OF

YEAR	TM/L	PCT	G	PO	A	E	DP	FR
1922	NY-N	.915	37	84	2	8	2	0
1923	NY-N	1.000	6	8	0	0	0	3
1925	StL-N	.982	66	161	2	3	1	1
Total	3	.959	109	253	4	1	3	4

Tim Shinnick 2B

YEAR	TM/L	PCT	G	PO	A	E	DP	FR
1890	Lou-a	.925	130	288	351	52	42	-24
1891	Lou-a	.915	120	226	332	52	45	-19
Total	2	.920	250	514	683	104	87	-43
	3B							
1890	Lou-a	.917	3	9	2	1	3	0
1891	Lou-a	.760	7	8	11	6	2	-2
Total	2	.811	10	17	13	7	5	-2
	SS							
1891	Lou-a	1.000	1	2	2	0	0	0

Bill Shipke 3B

YEAR	TM/L	PCT	G	PO	A	E	DP	FR
1907	Was-A	.944	63	57	127	11	2	7
1908	Was-A	.932	110	111	190	22	11	-6
1909	Was-A	.905	6	5	14	2	1	2
Total	3	.935	179	173	331	5	14	3
	2B							
1906	Cle-A	.933	2	6	8	1	2	2
1908	Chi-A	.000	1	0	0	1	0	-1
Total	2	.875	3	6	8	2	2	1
	SS							
1909	Was-A	1.000	2	1	0	0	0	0

Art Shires 1B

YEAR	TM/L	PCT	G	PO	A	E	DP	FR
1928	Chi-A	.990	32	282	28	3	22	3
1929	Chi-A	.991	90	815	58	8	78	1
1930	Chi-A	.979	33	317	15	7	18	-2
	Was-A	.982	21	151	11	3	19	0
	Yr	.980	54	468	26	10	37	-2
1932	Bos-N	.988	80	715	48	9	61	-2
Total	4	.988	256	2280	160	0	198	0
	2B							
1929	Chi-A	.909	3	6	4	1	1	-1

George Shoch OF

YEAR	TM/L	PCT	G	PO	A	E	DP	FR
1886	Was-N	.882	25	28	2	4	0	-4
1887	Was-N	.897	63	115	15	15	3	6
1888	Was-N	.892	35	59	7	8	1	0
1889	Was-N	.905	29	49	8	6	1	3
1892	Bal-N	.938	12	29	1	2	0	1
1893	Bro-N	.892	46	84	7	11	0	-2
1894	Bro-N	.926	35	82	5	7	1	-1
1895	Bro-N	.952	39	74	5	4	1	0
1896	Bro-N	1.000	10	15	0	0	0	-2
1897	Bro-N	1.000	4	4	0	0	0	-1
Total	10	.912	298	539	50	7	7	0
	SS							
1886	Was-N	.667	1	1	1	1	0	-1
1887	Was-N	.780	6	10	22	9	2	-1
1888	Was-N	.900	52	84	168	28	6	5
1889	Was-N	1.000	1	3	1	0	0	0
1891	Mil-a	.932	25	51	85	10	4	4
1892	Bal-N	.872	57	96	197	43	17	-1
1893	Bro-N	.918	11	25	42	6	2	2
1894	Bro-N	.929	6	18	21	3	3	1
1895	Bro-N	.889	6	8	16	3	1	-1
1896	Bro-N	1.000	1	3	1	0	1	0
1897	Bro-N	.870	13	39	41	12	5	-3
Total	11	.890	179	338	595	115	41	5
	2B							
1887	Was-N	.857	1	0	6	1	0	0
1888	Was-N	.000	1	0	0	2	0	-2
1893	Bro-N	.833	3	2	3	1	2	0
1894	Bro-N	.914	9	13	19	3	1	-3
1895	Bro-N	.893	13	13	37	6	3	-5
1896	Bro-N	.941	62	103	184	18	16	-10
1897	Bro-N	.941	68	188	240	27	25	8
Total	7	.933	157	319	489	8	47	-12
	3B							
1891	Mil-a	.861	9	13	18	5	0	-1
1892	Bal-N	.813	7	8	18	6	0	0
1893	Bro-N	.927	37	48	66	9	5	-3
1894	Bro-N	.925	14	17	32	4	1	1
1895	Bro-N	.889	3	3	5	1	1	0
1896	Bro-N	.909	3	3	7	1	0	0
Total	6	.902	73	92	146	6	7	-4

Tom Shopay OF

YEAR	TM/L	PCT	G	PO	A	E	DP	FR
1967	NY-A	.917	7	9	2	1	0	0
1969	NY-A	1.000	11	26	0	0	0	1
1971	Bal-A	1.000	13	18	1	0	0	0
1972	Bal-A	1.000	3	4	0	0	0	1
1975	Bal-A	1.000	13	12	0	0	0	2
1976	Bal-A	1.000	11	6	0	0	0	0
1977	Bal-A	1.000	52	53	2	0	1	5
Total	7	.993	110	128	5	1	1	9
	C							
1975	Bal-A	1.000	1	5	3	0	0	2
1976	Bal-A	1.000	1	8	1	0	0	1
Total	2	1.000	2	13	4	0	0	2

Chick Shorten OF

YEAR	TM/L	PCT	G	PO	A	E	DP	FR
1915	Bos-A	1.000	5	6	1	0	0	0
1916	Bos-A	1.000	33	46	0	0	0	-8
1917	Bos-A	.977	43	82	2	2	0	-5
1919	Det-A	.973	75	143	2	4	2	-6
1920	Det-A	.989	99	168	14	2	3	-1
1921	Det-A	.981	51	101	3	2	2	-4
1922	StL-A	1.000	31	58	2	0	1	-2
1924	Cin-N	1.000	15	13	1	0	0	-3
Total	8	.985	352	617	25	0	8	-29

Burt Shotton OF

YEAR	TM/L	PCT	G	PO	A	E	DP	FR
1909	StL-A	.915	17	41	2	4	0	1
1911	StL-A	.950	139	356	21	20	2	7
1912	StL-A	.941	154	381	20	25	7	6
1913	StL-A	.951	146	357	29	20	11	13
1914	StL-A	.940	152	359	15	24	4	2
1915	StL-A	.931	154	295	15	23	4	-3
1916	StL-A	.950	157	357	25	20	6	-10
1917	StL-A	.923	107	182	10	16	6	-12
1918	Was-A	.942	122	277	15	18	6	6
1919	StL-N	.927	67	104	10	9	2	-7
1920	StL-N	.959	51	85	9	4	2	1
1921	StL-N	.958	11	21	2	1	1	2
1922	StL-N	1.000	3	1	0	0	0	0
Total	13	.942	1280	2816	173	184	51	26

George Shuba OF

YEAR	TM/L	PCT	G	PO	A	E	DP	FR
1948	Bro-N	.936	56	87	1	6	1	-5
1950	Bro-N	.984	27	56	4	1	2	2
1952	Bro-N	.992	67	116	2	1	0	-6
1953	Bro-N	.984	44	59	1	1	1	-6
1954	Bro-N	.913	13	21	0	2	0	-1
1955	Bro-N	.909	9	10	1	1	0	-1
Total	6	.967	216	349	8	2	4	-17

Frank Shugart SS

YEAR	TM/L	PCT	G	PO	A	E	DP	FR
1890	Chi-P	.881	25	35	69	14	10	-5
1891	Pit-N	.902	75	172	235	44	34	4
1892	Pit-N	.886	134	303	466	99	43	7
1893	Pit-N	.882	51	98	178	37	15	-3
	StL-N	.835	23	35	76	22	8	-5
	Yr	.868	74	133	254	59	23	-8
1894	StL-N	.891	7	25	16	5	2	-1
1895	Lou-N	.874	88	178	258	63	39	-19
1897	Phi-N	.872	40	104	128	34	15	-5
1901	Chi-A	.885	107	223	338	73	32	-8
Total	8	.883	550	1173	1764	391	198	-35
	OF							
1890	Chi-P	1.000	5	3	2	0	1	0
1892	Pit-N	1.000	1	2	1	0	0	1
1893	StL-N	.907	28	59	9	7	1	3
1894	StL-N	.912	122	276	26	29	2	-1
1895	Lou-N	.897	27	65	5	8	3	1
Total	5	.911	183	405	43	4	7	4
	3B							
1893	StL-N	.853	9	13	16	5	2	-1
1894	StL-N	.704	7	8	11	8	2	-2
Total	2	.787	16	21	27	3	4	-3
	C							
1892	Pit-N	.923	2	4	8	1	0	1

Norm Siebern 1B

YEAR	TM/L	PCT	G	PO	A	E	DP	FR
1959	NY-A	1.000	2	15	2	0	1	0
1960	KC-A	.988	69	626	39	8	58	-4
1961	KC-A	.989	109	907	76	11	88	-1
1962	KC-A	.994	162	1405	127	10	122	5
1963	KC-A	.991	131	1193	102	12	95	4
1964	Bal-A	.995	149	1171	101	6	121	4
1965	Bal-A	.991	76	631	48	6	64	2
1966	Cal-A	.992	99	814	65	7	96	3
1967	SF-N	1.000	15	88	5	0	7	0
	Bos-A	.981	13	47	5	1	2	0
1968	Bos-A	1.000	2	8	1	0	1	0
Total	10	.992	827	6905	571	1	655	13
	OF							
1956	NY-A	.971	51	100	1	3	0	-3
1958	NY-A	.982	133	259	8	5	2	2
1959	NY-A	.989	93	175	1	2	0	-3
1960	KC-A	.987	75	151	4	2	0	2
1961	KC-A	.989	47	83	3	1	1	-1
1963	KC-A	1.000	16	30	1	0	0	0
1967	SF-N	1.000	2	3	0	0	0	0
	Bos-A	1.000	1	0	1	0	0	1
1968	Bos-A	—	2	0	0	0	0	0
Total	8	.984	420	801	19	3	3	-2

Dick Siebert 1B

YEAR	TM/L	PCT	G	PO	A	E	DP	FR
1932	Bro-N	1.000	2	13	0	0	0	0
1937	StL-N	.979	7	44	3	1	2	-1
1938	Phi-A	1.000	46	403	41	0	35	5
1939	Phi-A	.991	99	874	74	9	73	5
1940	Phi-A	.985	154	1322	119	22	112	8
1941	Phi-A	.990	123	1102	106	12	95	6
1942	Phi-A	.989	152	1345	104	16	109	-2
1943	Phi-A	.990	145	1332	111	15	117	4
1944	Phi-A	.993	74	661	48	5	60	1
1945	Phi-A	.991	147	1427	135	14	129	10
Total	10	.990	949	8523	741	4	732	36
	OF							
1936	Bro-N	1.000	1	0	1	0	0	1
1944	Phi-A	.954	58	98	5	5	0	-1
Total	2	.954	59	98	6	5	0	0

Ruben Sierra OF

YEAR	TM/L	PCT	G	PO	A	E	DP	FR
1986	Tex-A	.972	107	200	7	6	1	-2
1987	Tex-A	.963	157	272	17	11	6	1
1988	Tex-A	.979	153	310	11	7	3	2
1989	Tex-A	.973	162	313	13	9	2	4
1990	Tex-A	.967	151	283	7	10	1	-5
Total	5	.971	730	1378	55	3	13	0

Roy Sievers 1B

YEAR	TM/L	PCT	G	PO	A	E	DP	FR
1952	StL-A	.968	7	58	3	2	8	-1
1953	StL-A	.992	76	604	31	5	64	-6
1954	Was-A	1.000	8	54	5	0	7	0
1955	Was-A	.997	17	112	5	1	16	-2
1956	Was-A	.990	76	638	51	7	75	1
1957	Was-A	.988	21	159	9	2	21	-2

YEAR	TM/L	PCT	G	PO	A	E	DP	FR
1958	Was-A	.989	33	260	21	3	36	0
1959	Was-A	.989	93	846	72	10	72	5
1960	Chi-A	.993	114	1079	63	8	117	-5
1961	Chi-A	.993	132	1096	94	8	93	1
1962	Phi-N	.991	130	975	93	10	102	4
1963	Phi-N	.989	126	981	77	12	93	0
1964	Phi-N	.992	33	241	15	2	22	-2
	Was-A	1.000	15	87	11	0	15	1
1965	Was-A	1.000	7	51	1	0	6	-1
Total	14	.991	888	7241	551	0	747	-7

OF

YEAR	TM/L	PCT	G	PO	A	E	DP	FR
1949	StL-A	.973	125	314	14	9	1	10
1950	StL-A	.983	78	222	12	4	3	5
1951	StL-A	.985	25	63	1	1	0	2
1954	Was-A	.971	133	296	10	9	1	3
1955	Was-A	.988	129	247	5	3	0	-4
1956	Was-A	.987	78	146	3	2	1	-5
1957	Was-A	.985	130	254	6	4	2	0
1958	Was-A	.991	114	216	5	2	0	-1
1959	Was-A	.960	13	24	0	1	0	-1
1960	Chi-A	1.000	6	6	0	0	0	0
1962	Phi-N	1.000	7	2	0	0	0	0
Total	11	.981	838	1790	56	5	8	9

3B

YEAR	TM/L	PCT	G	PO	A	E	DP	FR
1949	StL-A	.933	7	3	11	1	1	1
1950	StL-A	.939	21	26	36	4	3	-2
1955	Was-A	1.000	2	4	7	0	0	1
Total	3	.946	30	33	54	5	4	0

■ Charlie Silvera C

YEAR	TM/L	PCT	G	PO	A	E	DP	FR
1948	NY-A	1.000	4	17	1	0	0	0
1949	NY-A	.985	51	177	22	3	5	4
1950	NY-A	.959	15	46	1	2	1	3
1951	NY-A	1.000	18	66	6	0	2	0
1952	NY-A	1.000	20	54	8	0	1	-3
1953	NY-A	.992	39	113	15	1	1	6
1954	NY-A	.962	18	72	5	3	1	6
1955	NY-A	1.000	11	47	4	0	1	3
1956	NY-A	.909	7	9	1	1	0	-1
1957	Chi-N	.982	26	97	11	2	2	3
Total	10	.985	209	698	74	2	14	21

3B

YEAR	TM/L	PCT	G	PO	A	E	DP	FR
1953	NY-A	1.000	1	1	0	0	0	0

■ Al Simmons OF

YEAR	TM/L	PCT	G	PO	A	E	DP	FR
1924	Phi-A	.976	152	390	17	10	4	6
1925	Phi-A	.966	153	447	8	16	2	5
1926	Phi-A	.975	147	333	11	9	5	-4
1927	Phi-A	.985	105	247	10	4	2	3
1928	Phi-A	.988	114	231	10	3	2	2
1929	Phi-A	.989	142	349	19	4	2	17
1930	Phi-A	.990	136	275	10	3	1	6
1931	Phi-A	.987	128	287	10	4	0	8
1932	Phi-A	.980	154	290	9	6	4	-7
1933	Chi-A	.990	145	372	15	4	1	14
1934	Chi-A	.987	138	286	14	4	3	6
1935	Chi-A	.981	126	349	5	7	1	-4
1936	Det-A	.986	138	352	8	5	1	-8
1937	Was-A	.984	102	240	7	4	5	5
1938	Was-A	.983	117	232	4	4	1	-6
1939	Bos-N	.982	82	158	7	3	2	-4
	Cin-N	.938	5	14	1	1	0	1
	Yr	.978	87	172	8	4	2	-3
1940	Phi-A	.963	18	51	1	2	0	3
1941	Phi-A	1.000	5	16	0	0	0	1
1943	Bos-A	.986	33	66	3	1	1	-1
1944	Phi-A	1.000	2	3	0	0	0	0
Total	20	.982	2142	4988	169	4	37	43

1B

YEAR	TM/L	PCT	G	PO	A	E	DP	FR
1936	Det-A	1.000	1	12	0	0	1	0

■ Hack Simmons 2B

YEAR	TM/L	PCT	G	PO	A	E	DP	FR
1912	NY-A	.946	88	162	207	21	23	-17
1914	Bal-F	.966	26	32	53	3	4	-4
1915	Bal-F	1.000	13	11	20	0	0	-2
Total	3	.953	127	205	280	4	27	-23

OF

YEAR	TM/L	PCT	G	PO	A	E	DP	FR
1910	Det-A	1.000	2	2	0	0	0	0
1914	Bal-F	.894	73	91	10	12	3	-6
1915	Bal-F	.880	13	21	1	3	0	-1
Total	3	.893	88	114	11	5	3	-7

1B

YEAR	TM/L	PCT	G	PO	A	E	DP	FR
1910	Det-A	.984	22	229	13	4	10	0
1912	NY-A	.985	13	131	4	2	7	-1
1914	Bal-F	.967	4	27	2	1	2	0
Total	3	.983	39	387	19	7	19	-1

3B

YEAR	TM/L	PCT	G	PO	A	E	DP	FR
1910	Det-A	.923	7	9	15	2	0	0
1914	Bal-F	1.000	1	0	8	0	0	2
Total	2	.941	8	9	23	2	0	2

SS

YEAR	TM/L	PCT	G	PO	A	E	DP	FR
1912	NY-A	.933	4	6	8	1	0	-1
1914	Bal-F	.857	2	4	2	1	1	-1
Total	2	.909	6	10	10	2	1	-2

■ Ted Simmons C

YEAR	TM/L	PCT	G	PO	A	E	DP	FR
1968	StL-N	1.000	2	3	1	0	0	-1
1969	StL-N	.957	4	22	0	1	0	-1
1970	StL-N	.990	79	466	37	5	2	-1
1971	StL-N	.989	130	747	52	9	11	-13
1972	StL-N	.991	135	842	78	8	6	5
1973	StL-N	.987	153	888	74	13	13	11
1974	StL-N	.986	141	717	82	11	13	-3
1975	StL-N	.983	154	803	62	15	5	-4
1976	StL-N	.993	113	493	66	4	4	-8
1977	StL-N	.987	144	683	75	10	5	-15
1978	StL-N	.988	134	670	88	9	6	-4
1979	StL-N	.985	122	606	69	10	10	-5
1980	StL-N	.985	129	520	71	9	12	-8
1981	Mil-A	.980	75	300	37	7	3	-9
1982	Mil-A	.995	121	570	62	3	8	-1
1983	Mil-A	.975	86	395	41	11	4	-4
1985	Mil-A	.986	15	65	4	1	1	-2
1986	Atl-N	.978	10	40	5	1	0	-2
1987	Atl-N	.987	15	64	10	1	1	-3
1988	Atl-N	.867	10	12	1	2	0	-2
Total	20	.987	1772	8906	915	130	104	-70

1B

YEAR	TM/L	PCT	G	PO	A	E	DP	FR
1972	StL-N	.966	15	125	15	5	9	2
1973	StL-N	.977	6	38	4	1	1	0
1974	StL-N	.962	12	96	5	4	5	-2
1975	StL-N	1.000	2	10	2	0	0	1
1976	StL-N	.988	30	219	21	3	21	1
1981	Mil-A	.974	4	33	4	1	4	0
1984	Mil-A	.995	37	346	27	2	35	0
1985	Mil-A	.992	28	226	17	2	22	-1
1986	Atl-N	.964	14	124	10	5	13	-1
1987	Atl-N	.984	28	216	23	4	24	2
1988	Atl-N	.993	19	128	13	1	8	1
Total	11	.984	195	1561	141	8	142	3

OF

YEAR	TM/L	PCT	G	PO	A	E	DP	FR
1973	StL-N	1.000	2	6	0	0	0	0
1975	StL-N	1.000	2	5	0	0	0	0
1976	StL-N	1.000	7	11	0	0	0	0
1977	StL-N	—	1	0	0	0	0	0
1978	StL-N	.971	23	33	0	1	0	-2
1980	StL-N	.889	5	8	0	1	0	-1
Total	6	.969	40	63	0	2	0	-3

3B

YEAR	TM/L	PCT	G	PO	A	E	DP	FR
1976	StL-N	.571	2	3	1	3	0	-2
1984	Mil-A	.838	14	6	25	6	2	-1
1985	Mil-A	1.000	2	0	5	0	0	0
1986	Atl-N	1.000	9	3	3	0	0	0
1987	Atl-N	1.000	2	2	2	0	0	0
Total	5	.847	29	14	36	9	2	-3

■ Hank Simon OF

YEAR	TM/L	PCT	G	PO	A	E	DP	FR
1887	Cle-a	1.000	3	3	0	0	0	-1
1890	Bro-a	.951	89	176	17	10	4	6
	Syr-a	.941	38	62	2	4	1	-3
	Yr	.948	127	238	19	14	5	3
Total	2	.949	130	241	19	4	5	2

■ Mike Simon C

YEAR	TM/L	PCT	G	PO	A	E	DP	FR
1909	Pit-N	.917	9	28	5	3	1	0
1910	Pit-N	1.000	14	40	12	0	0	-4
1911	Pit-N	.968	68	320	75	13	6	0
1912	Pit-N	.991	40	172	43	2	5	4
1913	Pit-N	.975	92	393	151	14	6	23
1914	StL-F	.984	78	433	132	9	9	12
1915	Bro-F	.992	45	175	60	2	4	0
Total	7	.979	346	1561	478	3	31	35

■ Harry Simpson OF

YEAR	TM/L	PCT	G	PO	A	E	DP	FR
1951	Cle-A	.971	68	132	3	4	1	0
1952	Cle-A	.088	127	226	11	3	4	-3
1953	Cle-A	.968	69	118	4	4	0	-4
1955	KC-A	.978	100	262	5	6	2	-2
1956	KC-A	.965	111	188	3	7	2	-11
1957	KC-A	.968	21	29	1	1	0	-1
	NY-A	.952	42	55	5	3	1	-3
	Yr	.957	63	84	6	4	1	-4
1958	NY-A	1.000	15	21	0	0	0	-1
	KC-A	.962	11	24	1	1	0	0
	Yr	.979	26	45	1	1	0	-1
1959	Chi-A	.947	12	18	0	1	0	-2
	Pit-N	1.000	3	5	0	0	0	0
Total	8	.974	579	1078	33	0	10	-27

1B

YEAR	TM/L	PCT	G	PO	A	E	DP	FR
1951	Cle-A	.988	50	326	17	4	28	-2
1952	Cle-A	.993	28	276	8	2	21	-5
1953	Cle-A	1.000	2	12	0	0	1	0
1955	KC-A	1.000	3	10	2	0	2	1
1956	KC-A	.986	32	269	15	4	32	-3
1957	KC-A	.996	27	243	23	1	21	2
	NY-A	1.000	21	143	6	0	18	-1
	Yr	.998	48	386	31	1	39	1
1958	KC-A	.990	43	384	18	4	44	-4
1959	KC-A	1.000	4	30	2	0	2	0
	Chi-N	.900	1	9	0	1	0	-1
	Yr	.976	5	39	2	1	2	-1
Total	8	.991	211	1702	93	6	169	-13

■ Joe Simpson OF

YEAR	TM/L	PCT	G	PO	A	E	DP	FR
1975	LA-N	1.000	6	5	0	0	0	1
1976	LA-N	1.000	20	24	0	0	0	1
1977	LA-N	.957	28	21	1	1	1	2
1978	LA-N	1.000	10	8	0	0	0	1
1979	Sea-A	.966	105	162	10	6	4	-7
1980	Sea-A	.977	119	205	10	5	1	-21
1981	Sea-A	.978	88	219	5	5	1	-3
1982	Sea-A	.984	97	177	7	3	0	-3
1983	KC-A	.988	38	75	4	1	2	8
Total	9	.978	511	896	37	0	9	-21

1B

YEAR	TM/L	PCT	G	PO	A	E	DP	FR
1977	LA-N	1.000	1	3	1	0	0	0
1980	Sea-A	.895	3	15	2	2	2	0
1983	KC-A	.995	54	167	14	1	18	2
Total	3	.985	58	185	17	3	20	2

■ Dick Simpson OF

YEAR	TM/L	PCT	G	PO	A	E	DP	FR
1962	LA-A	1.000	4	7	0	0	0	1
1964	LA-A	1.000	16	27	0	0	0	0
1965	Cal-A	.875	8	14	0	2	0	-1
1966	Cin-N	.921	64	35	0	3	0	-1
1967	Cin-N	.973	26	34	2	1	0	4
1968	StL-N	1.000	22	26	1	0	0	0
	Hou-N	.970	49	63	2	2	1	-6
	Yr	.979	71	89	3	2	1	-6
1969	NY-A	1.000	5	4	1	0	0	0
	Sea-A	1.000	17	22	0	0	0	0
	Yr	1.000	22	26	1	0	0	0
Total	7	.967	211	232	6	8	1	-3

■ Duke Sims C

YEAR	TM/L	PCT	G	PO	A	E	DP	FR
1964	Cle-A	1.000	1	13	0	0	0	0
1965	Cle-A	.980	40	228	22	5	2	-2
1966	Cle-A	.975	48	260	15	7	2	-5
1967	Cle-A	.989	85	561	56	7	7	-3
1968	Cle-A	.983	84	523	41	10	7	0
1969	Cle-A	.991	102	634	51	6	8	-4
1970	Cle-A	.993	39	277	13	2	2	-2
1971	LA-N	.992	74	345	33	3	5	0
1972	LA-N	.989	48	244	17	3	4	-1
	Det-A	.994	25	145	10	1	1	-2
1973	Det-A	.979	68	375	39	9	7	3
	NY-A	1.000	1	8	1	0	0	1
	Yr	.979	69	383	40	9	7	4
1974	NY-A	1.000	1	6	0	0	0	0
	Tex-A	.970	30	143	21	5	4	-3
	Yr	.971	31	149	21	5	4	-3
Total	11	.986	646	3762	319	8	49	-18

1B

YEAR	TM/L	PCT	G	PO	A	E	DP	FR
1968	Cle-A	.972	31	191	19	6	16	0
1969	Cle-A	1.000	1	1	0	0	0	0
1970	Cle-A	.985	29	180	18	3	15	1
Total	3	.978	61	372	37	9	31	1

OF

YEAR	TM/L	PCT	G	PO	A	E	DP	FR
1968	Cle-A	1.000	4	8	0	0	0	0
1969	Cle-A	1.000	3	4	1	0	0	1
1970	Cle-A	.944	36	48	3	3	1	-1
1972	Det-A	.750	4	6	0	2	0	-1
1973	Det-A	1.000	6	6	0	0	0	0
1974	Tex-A	—	1	0	0	0	0	0
Total	6	.938	54	72	4	5	1	-1

■ Matt Sinatro C

YEAR	TM/L	PCT	G	PO	A	E	DP	FR
1981	Atl-N	1.000	12	56	10	0	1	4
1982	Atl-N	1.000	35	112	25	0	1	4
1983	Atl-N	.967	7	24	5	1	0	2
1984	Atl-N	1.000	2	4	0	0	0	0
1987	Oak-A	1.000	6	4	0	0	0	0
1988	Oak-A	1.000	9	21	2	0	1	2
1989	Det-A	1.000	13	42	2	0	0	0
1990	Sea-A	.992	28	112	16	1	1	6
Total	8	.995	112	375	60	2	4	18

■ Ken Singleton OF

YEAR	TM/L	PCT	G	PO	A	E	DP	FR
1970	NY-N	.968	51	90	1	3	0	-3
1971	NY-N	.974	96	143	5	4	0	-6
1972	Mon-N	.972	137	236	9	7	3	-2
1973	Mon-N	.983	161	278	20	5	3	2
1974	Mon-N	.955	143	224	7	11	0	-12
1975	Bal-A	.990	155	283	9	3	2	-11
1976	Bal-A	.983	134	278	9	5	2	-4
1977	Bal-A	.986	150	278	8	4	2	-6
1978	Bal-A	.976	140	244	1	6	0	-15
1979	Bal-A	.981	143	247	8	5	2	-9
1980	Bal-A	.984	151	248	3	4	1	-19
1981	Bal-A	1.000	72	125	2	0	2	-7
1982	Bal-A	1.000	5	10	0	0	0	0
Total	13	.980	1538	2684	82	7	17	-92

■ Fred Sington OF

YEAR	TM/L	PCT	G	PO	A	E	DP	FR
1934	Was-A	.933	9	13	1	1	0	-1
1935	Was-A	.889	4	7	1	1	0	1
1936	Was-A	.946	25	52	1	3	0	-2
1937	Was-A	.961	64	120	4	5	0	-4
1938	Bro-N	1.000	17	29	0	0	0	-2
1939	Bro-N	.978	22	44	1	1	1	-1
Total	6	.961	141	265	8	1	1	-9

■ George Sisler 1B

YEAR	TM/L	PCT	G	PO	A	E	DP	FR
1915	StL-A	.989	36	357	18	4	20	-1
1916	StL-A	.985	141	1510	83	24	85	-3
1917	StL-A	.985	133	1384	101	22	97	5
1918	StL-A	.990	114	1244	95	13	64	8
1919	StL-A	.991	131	1249	120	13	62	13
1920	StL-A	.990	154	1477	140	16	87	15
1921	StL-A	.993	138	1267	108	10	86	8
1922	StL-A	.988	141	1293	125	17	116	12
1924	StL-A	.984	151	1326	112	23	115	1
1925	StL-A	.983	150	1343	131	26	120	10
1926	StL-A	.987	149	1467	87	21	141	-4
1927	StL-A	.984	149	1374	131	24	138	11
1928	Was-A	1.000	5	45	0	0	3	-1
	Bos-N	.988	118	1188	86	15	100	7
1929	Bos-N	.982	154	1398	111	28	131	3
1930	Bos-N	.987	107	915	81	13	103	5
Total	15	.987	1971	18837	1529	269	1468	89

OF

YEAR	TM/L	PCT	G	PO	A	E	DP	FR
1915	StL-A	.946	29	51	2	3	0	-2
1916	StL-A	1.000	3	6	1	0	2	1
1928	Was-A	1.000	5	8	0	0	0	-1
Total	3	.958	37	65	3	3	2	-2

3B

YEAR	TM/L	PCT	G	PO	A	E	DP	FR
1916	StL-A	1.000	2	2	4	0	0	0

2B

YEAR	TM/L	PCT	G	PO	A	E	DP	FR
1917	StL-A	.778	2	2	5	2	0	-1

■ Dick Sisler 1B

YEAR	TM/L	PCT	G	PO	A	E	DP	FR
1946	StL-N	.988	37	292	28	4	31	1
1947	StL-N	.976	10	76	6	2	3	0
1948	Phi-N	.983	120	986	73	18	88	-4
1949	Phi-N	.987	96	815	40	11	73	-9
1952	StL-N	.985	114	1022	84	17	116	2
1953	StL-N	1.000	10	42	6	0	5	1
Total	6	.985	387	3233	237	2	316	-9

YEAR	TM/L	PCT	G	PO	A	E	DP	FR
OF								
1946	StL-N	.957	29	42	3	2	0	0
1947	StL-N	1.000	5	8	0	0	0	0
1950	Phi-N	.987	137	293	9	4	0	4
1951	Phi-N	.968	111	233	8	8	3	-1
1952	Cin-N	1.000	7	11	0	0	0	-1
Total	5	.977	289	587	20	4	3	2
■ Sibby Sisti 2B								
1939	Bos-N	.994	34	91	83	1	24	-1
1940	Bos-N	.983	16	25	33	1	7	0
1941	Bos-N	.875	2	4	3	1	1	-1
1942	Bos-N	.970	124	304	351	20	66	-4
1947	Bos-N	1.000	1	0	1	0	0	0
1948	Bos-N	.972	44	104	107	6	19	-4
1949	Bos-N	.986	21	38	35	1	7	-1
1950	Bos-N	.943	19	42	41	5	8	1
1951	Bos-N	.976	52	129	114	6	23	-6
1952	Bos-N	.966	33	73	70	5	14	-3
1953	Mil-N	1.000	13	10	9	0	1	2
Total	11	.973	359	820	847	6	170	-17
3B								
1939	Bos-N	.935	17	21	37	4	3	3
1940	Bos-N	.936	102	117	192	21	21	-3
1941	Bos-N	.916	137	162	287	41	28	-6
1946	Bos-N	—	1	0	0	0	0	0
1949	Bos-N	1.000	1	1	1	0	1	0
1950	Bos-N	.935	13	14	15	2	0	0
1951	Bos-N	1.000	6	3	3	0	0	0
1952	Bos-N	.879	9	10	19	4	2	0
1953	Mil-N	.778	4	2	5	2	0	1
Total	9	.923	290	330	559	4	55	-5
SS								
1939	Bos-N	.949	10	24	32	3	5	-2
1941	Bos-N	.667	2	3	1	2	0	-2
1947	Bos-N	.947	51	93	121	12	24	-9
1948	Bos-N	.927	26	36	66	8	13	-1
1949	Bos-N	.937	18	32	42	5	3	-6
1950	Bos-N	.931	23	14	13	2	3	-1
1951	Bos-N	.944	55	91	113	12	24	-17
1952	Bos-N	.929	18	25	40	5	6	-5
1953	Mil-N	1.000	6	1	4	0	2	1
Total	9	.939	209	319	432	9	80	-42
OF								
1942	Bos-N	1.000	1	2	0	0	0	0
1949	Bos-N	.989	48	85	2	1	0	-2
1950	Bos-N	—	1	0	0	0	0	0
1951	Bos-N	—	1	0	0	0	0	0
1952	Bos-N	.944	23	34	0	2	0	-1
Total	5	.976	74	121	2	3	0	-3
1B								
1950	Bos-N	1.000	1	2	0	0	0	0
1951	Bos-N	1.000	1	8	0	0	0	0
Total	2	1.000	2	10	0	0	0	0
■ Ted Sizemore 2B								
1969	LA-N	.979	118	283	331	13	76	0
1970	LA-N	.984	86	194	232	7	47	-7
1971	StL-N	.976	93	206	237	11	55	-3
1972	StL-N	.976	111	222	342	14	68	0
1973	StL-N	.981	139	312	463	15	83	10
1974	StL-N	.980	128	335	412	15	109	14
1975	StL-N	.972	153	329	405	21	82	-25
1976	LA-N	.986	71	168	191	5	51	4
1977	Phi-N	.986	152	348	427	11	104	9
1978	Phi-N	.978	107	232	302	12	61	4
1979	Chi-N	.973	96	230	312	15	68	15
	Bos-A	.993	26	53	85	1	24	9
1980	Bos-A	.927	8	16	22	3	7	3
Total	12	.979	1288	2928	3761	143	835	33
SS								
1969	LA-N	.948	46	64	138	11	17	-5
1970	LA-N	.917	2	6	5	1	3	0
1971	StL-N	.965	39	52	140	7	24	2
1974	StL-N	.000	1	0	0	1	0	-1
Total	4	.953	88	122	283	0	44	-4
OF								
1969	LA-N	—	1	0	0	0	0	0
1970	LA-N	.917	9	9	2	1	0	1
1971	StL-N	1.000	15	19	1	0	0	1
1974	StL-N	1.000	1	1	0	0	0	0
Total	4	.970	26	29	3	1	0	2
3B								
1971	StL-N	1.000	1	0	1	0	0	0
1973	StL-N	1.000	3	1	0	0	1	0
1976	LA-N	.500	3	2	0	2	0	-1
Total	3	.667	7	3	1	2	1	-1
C								
1976	LA-N	1.000	2	8	0	0	0	0
1979	Bos-A	1.000	2	2	0	0	0	0
Total	2	1.000	4	10	0	0	0	0
■ Dave Skaggs C								
1977	Bal-A	.995	80	344	34	2	4	-1
1978	Bal-A	.988	35	149	17	2	2	4
1979	Bal-A	.984	63	222	24	4	1	3
1980	Bal-A	1.000	2	8	1	0	1	1
	Cal-A	.968	24	86	5	3	2	-10
	Yr	.971	26	94	6	3	3	-9
Total	4	.988	204	809	81	1	10	-3
■ Joel Skinner C								
1983	Chi-A	.960	6	20	4	1	1	2
1984	Chi-A	.989	43	171	11	2	1	9
1985	Chi-A	.971	21	94	8	3	0	3
1986	NY-A	.981	54	280	22	6	5	5
	Chi-A	.988	60	227	15	3	4	-7
	Yr	.984	114	507	37	9	9	-2
1987	NY-A	.984	64	232	18	4	2	-4

YEAR	TM/L	PCT	G	PO	A	E	DP	FR
1988	NY-A	.990	85	395	16	4	5	-7
1989	Cle-A	.990	79	280	22	3	1	-4
1990	Cle-A	.996	49	222	16	1	3	0
Total	8	.987	461	1921	132	7	22	-3
OF								
1988	NY-A	—	2	0	0	0	0	0
1B								
1988	NY-A	1.000	1	1	0	0	0	0
■ Bob Skinner OF								
1954	Pit-N	—	2	0	0	0	0	0
1956	Pit-N	.977	36	40	2	1	0	-3
1957	Pit-N	.963	93	172	9	7	2	0
1958	Pit-N	.977	141	232	19	6	2	-1
1959	Pit-N	.964	142	285	9	11	1	2
1960	Pit-N	.981	141	250	13	5	2	-1
1961	Pit-N	.973	97	175	5	5	1	-2
1962	Pit-N	.960	139	210	6	9	0	-9
1963	Pit-N	.983	32	57	1	1	0	-2
	Cin-N	1.000	51	74	3	0	1	-2
	Yr	.993	83	131	4	1	1	-4
1964	Cin-N	.913	12	20	1	2	0	0
	StL-N	.938	31	42	3	3	0	0
	Yr	.930	43	62	4	5	0	0
1965	StL-N	.935	33	43	0	3	0	-4
Total	11	.969	950	1600	71	3	9	-22
1B								
1954	Pit-N	.986	118	1026	84	16	87	-2
1956	Pit-N	.995	23	176	6	1	21	-4
1957	Pit-N	.985	9	60	6	1	7	0
1959	Pit-N	—	1	0	0	0	0	0
Total	4	.987	151	1262	96	8	115	-6
3B								
1956	Pit-N	1.000	1	1	0	0	0	0
1957	Pit-N	1.000	1	0	2	0	0	0
Total	2	1.000	2	1	2	0	0	0
■ Lou Skizas OF								
1956	KC-A	.975	74	148	9	4	0	2
1957	KC-A	.976	76	119	5	3	2	-6
1958	Det-A	.750	5	3	0	1	0	-1
1959	Chi-A	1.000	6	6	1	0	0	0
Total	4	.973	161	276	15	8	2	-5
3B								
1957	KC-A	.945	32	29	57	5	3	-4
1958	Det-A	.800	4	1	7	2	0	-1
Total	2	.931	36	30	64	7	3	-5
■ Bill Skowron 1B								
1954	NY-A	.986	61	395	28	6	48	-1
1955	NY-A	.989	74	517	37	6	63	-2
1956	NY-A	.993	120	968	80	7	138	3
1957	NY-A	.992	115	1026	86	9	116	6
1958	NY-A	.993	118	1040	71	8	112	0
1959	NY-A	.991	72	626	43	6	68	0
1960	NY-A	.991	142	1202	115	12	130	9
1961	NY-A	.993	149	1228	102	10	146	-5
1962	NY-A	.991	135	1054	77	10	101	-5
1963	LA-N	.991	66	518	34	5	44	-1
1964	Was-A	.994	66	591	40	4	41	-2
	Chi-A	.998	70	621	40	1	53	-1
	Yr	.996	136	1212	80	5	94	-3
1965	Chi-A	.994	145	1297	74	8	116	-3
1966	Chi-A	.991	98	722	60	7	75	0
1967	Cal-A	.988	32	238	16	3	15	-1
Total	14	.992	1463	12043	903	102	1266	1
3B								
1954	NY-A	1.000	5	1	11	0	0	1
1955	NY-A	.857	3	3	3	1	0	-1
1956	NY-A	.875	2	1	6	1	0	0
1958	NY-A	.286	2	1	1	5	0	-2
1963	LA-N	—	1	0	0	0	0	0
Total	5	.794	13	6	21	7	0	-2
2B								
1954	NY-A	.900	2	3	6	1	0	0
■ Gordon Slade SS								
1930	Bro-N	.938	21	22	53	5	13	10
1931	Bro-N	.947	82	173	274	25	54	12
1932	Bro-N	.943	55	101	148	15	30	4
1933	Bro-N	.941	31	34	61	6	11	3
1934	Cin-N	.952	97	200	315	26	60	0
1935	Cin-N	.927	30	53	74	10	14	-7
Total	6	.945	316	583	925	7	182	22
2B								
1933	StL-N	—	1	0	0	0	0	0
1934	Cin-N	.991	39	102	128	2	23	1
1935	Cin-N	.983	19	23	35	1	6	-4
Total	3	.987	59	125	163	3	29	-3
3B								
1931	Bro-N	.750	2	1	2	1	0	0
1932	Bro-N	.973	23	18	53	2	6	7
1935	Cin-N	1.000	7	2	6	0	0	0
Total	3	.965	32	21	61	3	6	7
OF								
1935	Cin-N	1.000	8	13	0	0	0	-1
■ Jimmy Slagle OF								
1899	Was-N	.953	146	407	20	21	8	20
1900	Phi-N	.922	141	320	22	29	5	1
1901	Phi-N	.930	48	108	12	9	3	6
	Bos-N	.935	66	89	11	7	3	-2
	Yr	.932	114	197	23	16	6	4
1902	Chi-N	.965	113	262	15	10	5	7
1903	Chi-N	.936	139	292	16	21	8	2
1904	Chi-N	.921	120	194	15	18	7	-2
1905	Chi-N	.962	155	306	27	13	6	5
1906	Chi-N	.976	127	276	9	7	5	2
1907	Chi-N	.962	136	239	15	10	5	-10
1908	Chi-N	.976	101	199	6	5	2	-6

YEAR	TM/L	PCT	G	PO	A	E	DP	FR
Total	10	.950	1292	2692	168	150	57	23
■ Mike Slattery OF								
1884	Bos-U	.802	96	140	26	41	3	5
1888	NY-N	.919	103	187	16	18	3	-1
1889	NY-N	.852	12	21	2	4	1	0
1890	NY-P	.905	97	175	5	19	1	-14
1891	Cin-N	.941	41	91	4	6	1	0
	Was-a	.862	15	24	1	4	1	-2
Total	5	.883	364	638	54	2	10	-12
1B								
1884	Bos-U	.941	11	91	5	6	4	1
■ Don Slaught C								
1982	KC-A	.994	43	156	7	1	1	2
1983	KC-A	.964	79	299	18	12	7	-5
1984	KC-A	.982	123	547	44	11	8	-13
1985	Tex-A	.990	102	550	33	6	4	-10
1986	Tex-A	.993	91	533	40	4	1	-5
1987	Tex-A	.985	85	429	39	7	5	2
1988	NY-A	.979	94	496	24	11	4	-13
1989	NY-A	.991	105	493	44	5	8	-6
1990	Pit-N	.979	78	345	36	8	4	-4
Total	9	.985	800	3848	285	5	42	-52
■ Enos Slaughter OF								
1938	StL-N	.970	92	189	7	6	0	0
1939	StL-N	.968	149	348	18	12	5	14
1940	StL-N	.989	132	267	8	3	5	0
1941	StL-N	.947	108	173	5	10	1	-14
1942	StL-N	.987	151	287	15	4	2	2
1946	StL-N	.981	156	284	23	6	6	1
1947	StL-N	.982	142	306	15	6	5	4
1948	StL-N	.971	146	330	9	10	1	-11
1949	StL-N	.983	150	330	10	6	1	-2
1950	StL-N	.978	145	260	9	6	1	-6
1951	StL-N	.995	106	198	10	1	3	-3
1952	StL-N	.989	137	250	11	3	3	0
1953	StL-N	.996	137	235	2	1	0	-11
1954	NY-A	.974	30	37	0	1	0	-6
1955	KC-A	.985	77	126	5	2	2	-5
1956	KC-A	.981	56	105	1	2	0	-5
	NY-A	1.000	20	28	1	0	0	-3
	Yr	.985	76	133	2	2	0	-8
1957	NY-A	1.000	64	97	2	0	0	-6
1958	NY-A	.957	35	43	1	2	0	-3
1959	NY-A	.964	26	27	0	1	0	-2
	Mil-N	1.000	5	5	0	0	0	-1
Total	19	.980	2064	3925	152	2	35	-58
■ Tod Sloan OF								
1913	StL-A	.950	7	17	2	1	1	2
1917	StL-A	.963	77	120	10	5	4	-3
1919	StL-A	.933	20	23	5	2	1	-1
Total	3	.957	104	160	17	8	6	-2
■ Roy Smalley SS								
1975	Tex-A	.941	59	80	175	16	30	3
1976	Tex-A	.929	5	3	10	1	1	0
	Min-A	.967	103	189	338	18	70	5
	Yr	.966	108	192	348	19	71	5
1977	Min-A	.958	150	255	504	33	116	19
1978	Min-A	.970	157	287	527	25	121	18
1979	Min-A	.968	161	296	572	29	144	33
1980	Min-A	.975	125	210	446	17	100	21
1981	Min-A	.946	37	52	89	8	14	-12
1982	Min-A	1.000	4	5	16	0	2	1
	NY-A	.977	89	109	238	8	42	-18
	Yr	.979	93	114	254	8	44	-17
1983	NY-A	.959	91	125	230	15	40	-14
1984	NY-A	.963	13	5	21	1	2	0
	Chi-A	1.000	3	2	1	0	0	0
	Yr	.967	16	7	22	1	2	0
1985	Min-A	.987	49	57	91	2	16	-20
1986	Min-A	.963	19	11	15	1	4	-4
1987	Min-A	1.000	4	2	1	0	0	0
Total	13	.966	1069	1688	3274	174	702	32
3B								
1982	NY-A	.953	53	28	113	7	11	0
1983	NY-A	.932	26	11	57	5	7	0
1984	NY-A	.905	35	17	78	10	8	2
	Chi-A	.947	38	15	57	4	6	-5
	Yr	.923	73	32	135	14	14	-3
1985	Min-A	.980	14	9	41	1	2	5
1986	Min-A	1.000	8	3	19	0	1	1
1987	Min-A	.850	14	7	10	3	0	-2
Total	6	.939	188	90	375	0	35	1
2B								
1975	Tex-A	.955	19	28	57	4	14	1
1976	Tex-A	.963	38	82	99	7	19	-5
1982	NY-A	—	1	0	0	0	0	0
Total	3	.960	58	110	156	1	33	-4
1B								
1979	Min-A	1.000	1	9	0	0	2	0
1980	Min-A	1.000	3	16	2	0	3	0
1981	Min-A	1.000	1	10	0	0	0	0
1983	NY-A	.994	22	153	8	1	11	-1
1984	NY-A	.978	5	44	0	1	7	-1
	Chi-A	1.000	1	7	1	0	1	0
	Yr	.981	6	51	1	1	8	-1
1985	Min-A	1.000	1	4	1	0	1	0
Total	6	.992	34	243	12	2	24	-2
C								
1975	Tex-A	—	1	0	0	0	0	0
■ Roy Smalley SS								
1948	Chi-N	.941	124	189	351	34	70	9
1949	Chi-N	.947	132	265	438	39	91	14
1950	Chi-N	.945	154	332	541	51	115	21
1951	Chi-N	.953	74	117	190	15	42	-13

YEAR	TM/L	PCT	G	PO	A	E	DP	FR
1952	Chi-N	.952	82	139	200	17	33	-11
1953	Chi-N	.932	77	153	191	25	39	-6
1954	Mil-N	.950	9	9	10	1	5	2
1955	Phi-N	.974	87	136	205	9	32	-15
1956	Phi-N	.949	60	81	142	12	32	-1
1957	Phi-N	.941	20	11	21	2	5	1
1958	Phi-N	.714	1	3	2	2	1	0
Total	11	.947	820	1435	2291	207	465	1
		2B						
1954	Mil-N	1.000	7	13	15	0	5	2
1955	Phi-N	—	1	0	0	0	0	0
Total	2	1.000	8	13	15	0	5	2
		1B						
1954	Mil-N	1.000	2	14	1	0	1	0
		3B						
1955	Phi-N	1.000	1	2	1	0	0	0

■ Will Smalley   3B
YEAR	TM/L	PCT	G	PO	A	E	DP	FR
1890	Cle-N	.895	136	**221**	**327**	64	**27**	**18**
1891	Was-a	.762	9	12	20	10	1	-2
Total	2	.887	145	233	347	4	28	16
		2B						
1891	Was-a	.833	2	2	3	1	1	0

■ Aleck Smith   C
YEAR	TM/L	PCT	G	PO	A	E	DP	FR
1897	Bro-N	.903	43	111	47	17	7	-5
1898	Bro-N	.906	20	63	24	9	4	-2
1899	Bro-N	.917	17	52	14	6	1	-3
	Bal-N	.951	36	109	26	7	3	-2
	Yr	.939	53	161	40	13	4	-5
1900	Bro-N	.833	1	3	2	1	0	0
1901	NY-N	.962	24	106	22	5	2	0
1902	Bal-A	.947	27	65	25	5	2	-5
1903	Bos-A	.932	10	44	11	4	1	1
1904	Chi-N	1.000	1	1	1	0	1	0
1906	NY-N	1.000	8	26	5	0	1	-1
Total	9	.933	187	580	177	4	22	-17
		OF						
1897	Bro-N	.939	18	27	4	2	1	0
1898	Bro-N	.909	26	40	0	4	1	-6
1899	Bal-N	—	2	0	0	0	0	-1
1902	Bal-A	.909	4	10	0	1	0	0
1904	Chi-N	.778	6	7	0	2	0	-2
1906	NY-N	—	1	0	0	0	0	0
Total	6	.907	57	84	4	9	2	-9
		1B						
1897	Bro-N	.981	6	50	3	1	2	0
1898	Bro-N	—	1	0	0	0	0	0
1899	Bal-A	1.000	1	5	0	0	0	0
1902	Bal-A	1.000	7	60	1	0	3	-1
1906	NY-N	1.000	3	15	2	0	3	0
Total	5	.993	18	130	6	1	8	-1
		3B						
1898	Bro-N	.444	2	0	4	5	0	-2
1900	Bro-N	.875	6	6	8	2	0	-2
1902	Bal-A	1.000	1	0	1	0	0	0
1904	Chi-N	1.000	1	0	2	0	0	0
Total	4	.750	10	6	15	7	0	-4
		2B						
1898	Bro-N	1.000	2	3	5	0	0	0
1902	Bal-A	.875	3	0	7	1	0	0
Total	2	.938	5	3	12	1	0	0

■ Al Smith   OF
YEAR	TM/L	PCT	G	PO	A	E	DP	FR
1953	Cle-A	.920	39	67	2	6	0	-6
1954	Cle-A	.984	109	241	8	4	1	3
1955	Cle-A	.977	120	206	5	5	1	-6
1956	Cle-A	.981	122	248	6	5	1	1
1957	Cle-A	.981	58	100	3	2	1	-1
1958	Chi-A	.970	138	249	9	8	2	-3
1959	Chi-A	.980	128	283	8	6	2	7
1960	Chi-A	.966	141	252	5	9	2	-6
1961	Chi-A	.977	71	123	3	3	0	-3
1962	Chi-A	.964	39	47	6	2	0	1
1963	Bal-A	.971	97	160	6	5	0	-6
1964	Cle-A	1.000	48	64	2	0	0	1
	Bos-A	.909	8	10	0	1	0	0
	Yr	.987	56	74	2	1	0	1
Total	12	.974	1118	2050	63	6	10	-18
		3B						
1953	Cle-A	—	2	0	0	0	0	0
1954	Cle-A	.889	21	23	25	6	3	-7
1955	Cle-A	.929	45	33	59	7	4	-10
1956	Cle-A	.923	28	22	38	5	2	-6
1957	Cle-A	.913	84	95	156	24	16	-9
1958	Chi-A	—	1	0	0	0	0	0
1959	Chi-A	—	1	0	0	0	0	0
1961	Chi-A	.948	80	58	161	12	12	-7
1962	Chi-A	.935	105	76	185	18	8	-21
1964	Cle-A	—	1	0	0	0	0	0
	Bos-A	.917	10	8	14	2	1	-1
	Yr	.917	11	8	14	2	1	-1
Total	10	.928	378	315	638	4	46	-61
		SS						
1954	Cle-A	1.000	4	1	1	0	0	0
1955	Cle-A	1.000	5	2	3	0	1	-1
Total	2	1.000	9	3	4	0	1	-1
		2B						
1955	Cle-A	1.000	1	1	0	0	0	0
1956	Cle-A	—	1	0	0	0	0	0
Total	2	1.000	2	1	0	0	0	0

■ Tony Smith   SS
YEAR	TM/L	PCT	G	PO	A	E	DP	FR
1907	Was-A	.920	51	99	141	21	11	-9
1910	Bro-N	.941	101	254	318	36	57	13
1911	Bro-N	.870	10	14	33	7	5	1
Total	3	.931	162	367	492	4	73	5
		3B						
1910	Bro-N	.950	6	8	11	1	0	0

YEAR	TM/L	PCT	G	PO	A	E	DP	FR
		2B						
1911	Bro-N	.923	3	7	5	1	2	-1

■ Billy Smith   2B
YEAR	TM/L	PCT	G	PO	A	E	DP	FR
1977	Bal-A	.991	104	260	272	5	78	3
1978	Bal-A	.986	83	146	208	5	43	-1
1979	Bal-A	.980	63	107	142	5	33	-7
1981	SF-N	1.000	5	3	8	0	1	0
Total	4	.987	255	516	630	5	155	-5
		SS						
1975	Cal-A	.932	50	80	98	13	19	-8
1976	Cal-A	.625	10	0	5	3	1	-1
1977	Bal-A	.750	5	1	2	1	0	-1
1978	Bal-A	1.000	2	1	2	0	0	0
1979	Bal-A	.833	5	1	9	2	2	-1
1981	SF-N	.971	21	27	39	2	9	-1
Total	6	.927	93	110	155	1	31	-12
		1B						
1975	Cal-A	1.000	6	15	1	0	0	0
1977	Bal-A	.750	2	3	0	1	0	0
Total	2	.950	8	18	1	1	0	0
		3B						
1975	Cal-A	.000	2	0	0	1	0	0
1977	Bal-A	1.000	1	4	4	0	2	2
1981	SF-N	1.000	3	2	3	0	1	0
Total	3	.929	6	6	7	1	3	2

■ Bobby Gene Smith   OF
YEAR	TM/L	PCT	G	PO	A	E	DP	FR
1957	StL-N	.973	79	138	6	4	4	11
1958	StL-N	1.000	27	57	2	0	0	2
1959	StL-N	.971	32	31	3	1	1	3
1960	Phi-N	1.000	70	125	4	0	1	5
1961	Phi-N	.971	47	91	8	3	1	-7
1962	NY-N	1.000	6	12	0	0	0	0
	Chi-N	1.000	7	9	1	0	0	0
	StL-N	1.000	80	65	4	0	1	3
	Yr	1.000	93	86	5	0	1	3
1965	Cal-A	1.000	15	22	1	0	0	0
Total	7	.986	363	550	29	8	8	31
		3B						
1960	Phi-N	1.000	1	1	0	0	0	0

■ Reggie Smith   OF
YEAR	TM/L	PCT	G	PO	A	E	DP	FR
1966	Bos-A	.944	6	17	0	1	0	0
1967	Bos-A	.983	144	335	10	6	3	7
1968	Bos-A	.985	155	**390**	8	6	1	5
1969	Bos-A	.959	139	321	8	**14**	1	-1
1970	Bos-A	.977	145	361	**15**	9	1	13
1971	Bos-A	.966	**159**	386	15	**14**	2	18
1972	Bos-A	.981	129	247	8	5	2	3
1973	Bos-A	.983	104	275	8	5	1	16
1974	StL-N	.976	132	275	9	7	3	3
1975	StL-N	.963	69	126	3	5	0	-3
1976	StL-N	1.000	16	41	5	0	0	4
	LA-N	.985	58	130	3	2	2	2
	Yr	.989	74	171	8	2	2	6
1977	LA N	.980	140	240	7	5	0	-7
1978	LA-N	.950	126	220	8	12	4	-7
1979	LA-N	.988	62	159	5	2	0	6
1980	LA-N	.994	84	153	15	1	5	6
Total	15	.976	1668	3676	127	4	25	63
		1B						
1973	Bos-A	1.000	1	7	0	0	1	0
1974	StL-N	1.000	1	11	0	0	0	0
1975	StL-N	.982	66	524	33	10	51	-4
1976	StL-N	.986	17	128	10	2	16	0
1981	LA-N	1.000	2	15	1	0	1	0
1982	SF-N	.982	99	792	78	16	61	2
Total	6	.983	186	1477	122	8	130	-2
		3B						
1975	StL-N	1.000	1	0	3	0	0	0
1976	StL-N	1.000	13	15	29	0	2	2
	LA-N	1.000	1	0	1	0	0	0
	Yr	1.000	14	15	30	0	2	2
Total	2	1.000	15	15	33	0	2	2
		2B						
1967	Bos-A	.976	6	18	22	1	8	4

■ Pop Smith   2B
YEAR	TM/L	PCT	G	PO	A	E	DP	FR
1880	Cin-N	.855	83	282	243	**89**	32	-10
1881	Wor-N	.941	3	8	8	1	0	0
	Buf-N	.840	3	14	7	4	4	-1
	Yr	.881	6	22	15	5	4	-1
1883	Col-a	.889	73	250	247	62	38	17
1884	Col-a	.905	108	324	**394**	75	55	**29**
1885	Pit-a	.922	106	**372**	384	64	53	**33**
1886	Pit-a	.912	28	88	98	18	8	4
1887	Pit-N	.914	89	225	298	49	32	-8
1888	Pit-N	.905	56	131	184	33	24	-4
1889	Pit-N	.938	9	31	29	4	5	1
1890	Bos-N	.918	**134**	234	401	**57**	41	-20
1891	Was-a	.919	19	53	61	10	11	5
Total	11	.904	711	2012	2354	466	303	46
		SS						
1882	Lou-a	.778	3	4	10	4	0	0
1886	Pit-a	**.895**	98	132	356	57	28	16
1887	Pit-N	.922	33	71	119	16	7	4
1888	Pit-N	.901	75	91	247	37	18	3
1889	Pit-N	.897	58	93	187	32	21	4
	Bos-N	.890	59	121	170	36	23	0
	Yr	.894	117	214	357	68	44	4
1890	Bos-N	.800	1	2	2	1	0	0
1891	Was-a	.833	5	6	19	5	1	2
Total	7	.897	332	520	1110	188	98	29
		3B						
1881	Buf-N	.838	10	16	15	6	0	-2
1883	Col-a	.875	24	35	49	12	2	1
1889	Pit-N	1.000	3	6	6	0	2	1
1891	Was-a	.786	4	4	7	3	0	0

YEAR	TM/L	PCT	G	PO	A	E	DP	FR
Total	4	.868	41	61	77	1	4	0
		OF						
1881	Wor-N	.955	8	17	4	1	1	2
1882	Bal-a	.500	1	1	0	1	0	0
1889	Pit-N	1.000	3	2	0	0	0	0
Total	3	.923	12	20	4	2	1	2
		C						
1886	Pit-a	1.000	1	1	2	0	0	0

■ Charley Smith   3B
YEAR	TM/L	PCT	G	PO	A	E	DP	FR
1960	LA-N	.953	18	14	27	2	2	0
1961	LA-N	1.000	4	4	3	0	1	0
	Phi-N	.924	94	75	194	22	19	2
	Yr	.926	98	79	197	22	20	2
1962	Chi-A	.944	54	26	76	6	12	2
1964	Chi-A	1.000	2	2	10	0	2	3
	NY-N	.917	85	89	166	23	9	-3
1965	NY-N	.957	131	119	281	18	27	10
1966	StL-N	.964	107	84	213	11	26	-1
1967	NY-A	.947	115	92	283	21	22	11
1968	NY-A	.961	13	19	30	2	3	4
Total	8	.945	623	524	1283	105	123	28
		SS						
1961	LA-N	.917	3	3	8	1	0	0
	Phi-N	.914	14	25	28	5	8	-4
	Yr	.914	17	28	36	6	8	-4
1963	Chi-A	1.000	1	3	5	0	4	2
1964	NY-N	.938	36	50	55	7	17	-11
1965	NY-N	1.000	6	3	6	0	1	0
1966	StL-N	1.000	1	5	3	0	1	0
Total	5	.937	61	89	105	3	31	-13
		OF						
1964	NY-N	.947	13	18	0	1	0	3
		2B						
1965	NY-N	1.000	1	1	1	0	1	0

■ Earl Smith   OF
YEAR	TM/L	PCT	G	PO	A	E	DP	FR
1916	Chi-N	.800	7	4	0	1	0	-2
1917	StL-A	.977	51	114	12	3	5	6
1918	StL-A	.952	81	164	14	9	4	1
1919	StL-A	.971	68	155	13	5	4	10
1920	StL-A	.927	15	34	4	3	1	3
1921	StL-A	.889	4	8	0	1	0	-1
	Was-A	.949	43	84	10	5	2	4
	Yr	.944	47	92	10	6	2	3
1922	Was-A	.917	49	88	12	9	3	1
Total	7	.952	318	651	65	6	19	22
		3B						
1920	StL-A	.916	70	73	146	20	2	-8
1921	StL-A	.878	13	20	23	6	0	-3
	Was-A	.667	1	1	1	1	0	-1
	Yr	.865	14	21	24	7	0	-4
1922	Was-A	1.000	2	4	4	0	0	0
Total	3	.910	86	98	174	7	2	-12

■ Earl Smith   C
YEAR	TM/L	PCT	G	PO	A	E	DP	FR
1919	NY-N	.973	14	26	10	1	0	-2
1920	NY-N	.976	82	252	73	8	12	-5
1921	NY-N	.965	78	195	56	9	4	-10
1922	NY-N	.978	75	214	56	6	3	-1
1923	NY-N	.975	12	32	7	1	2	2
	Bos-N	.975	54	141	51	5	7	-3
	Yr	.975	66	173	58	6	9	-1
1924	Bos-N	.946	13	40	13	3	1	-1
	Pit-N	.974	35	127	23	4	3	1
	Yr	.967	48	167	36	7	4	0
1925	Pit-N	.968	96	317	77	13	15	12
1926	Pit-N	.964	98	307	63	14	10	4
1927	Pit-N	.986	61	187	32	3	2	-4
1928	Pit-N	.967	28	78	11	3	2	-4
	StL-N	1.000	18	52	6	0	2	-1
	Yr	.980	46	130	17	3	4	-5
1929	StL-N	.962	50	131	21	6	1	-5
1930	StL-N	.913	6	18	3	2	0	1
Total	12	.971	720	2117	502	8	64	-16
		2B						
1919	NY-N	—	1	0	0	0	0	0

■ Elmer Smith   OF
YEAR	TM/L	PCT	G	PO	A	E	DP	FR
1886	Cin-a	1.000	1	1	0	0	0	0
1887	Cin-a	1.000	2	2	0	1	0	-1
1888	Cin-a	—	2	0	0	0	0	-1
1892	Pit-N	.885	124	223	15	31	0	-4
1893	Pit-N	.921	128	271	20	25	7	3
1894	Pit-N	.933	125	275	18	21	8	4
1895	Pit-N	.896	123	250	16	31	2	-3
1896	Pit-N	.946	122	302	14	18	6	9
1897	Pit-N	.904	123	245	19	28	1	3
1898	Cin-N	.949	123	280	15	16	5	4
1899	Cin-N	.922	87	178	12	16	3	-1
1900	Cin-N	.930	27	63	3	5	1	0
	NY-N	.953	83	91	10	5	2	-8
	Yr	.944	110	154	13	10	3	-8
1901	Pit-N	1.000	1	2	0	0	0	0
	Bos-N	.833	15	19	1	4	0	-3
	Yr	.846	16	21	1	4	0	-3
Total	13	.921	1086	2202	143	200	35	2

■ Elmer Smith   OF
YEAR	TM/L	PCT	G	PO	A	E	DP	FR
1914	Cle-A	1.000	13	29	2	0	0	1
1915	Cle-A	.923	123	202	15	18	4	0
1916	Cle-A	.966	57	77	7	3	3	-2
	Was-A	.988	45	75	5	1	1	1
	Yr	.976	102	152	12	4	4	-1
1917	Was-A	.901	29	60	4	7	0	0
	Cle-A	.986	40	64	5	1	2	-1
	Yr	.943	69	124	9	8	2	-1
1919	Cle-A	.957	111	167	12	8	6	-6
1920	Cle-A	.970	129	217	8	7	1	-8
1921	Cle-A	.971	127	183	16	6	1	-8

YEAR	TM/L	PCT	G	PO	A	E	DP	FR
1922	Bos-A	.947	58	117	7	7	3	2
	NY-A	.933	11	13	1	1	1	-2
	Yr	.945	69	130	8	8	4	0
1923	NY-A	.948	47	86	5	5	2	-2
1925	Cin-N	.967	80	139	8	5	5	-8
Total	10	.957	870	1429	95	9	31	-33

■ Fred Smith 3B

YEAR	TM/L	PCT	G	PO	A	E	DP	FR
1913	Bos-N	.920	59	64	85	13	4	-13
1914	Buf-F	.930	127	170	229	30	14	-1
1915	Buf-F	1.000	1	0	1	0	0	0
	Bro-F	.925	15	21	41	5	5	5
	Yr	.926	16	21	42	5	5	5
1917	StL-N	.950	51	62	110	9	5	6
Total	4	.932	253	317	466	7	28	-3

SS

YEAR	TM/L	PCT	G	PO	A	E	DP	FR
1913	Bos-N	.862	11	21	29	8	4	-1
1914	Buf-F	.942	19	44	53	6	9	1
1915	Buf-F	.920	32	77	96	15	14	3
	Bro-F	.920	94	203	281	42	24	-3
	Yr	.920	126	280	377	57	38	0
1917	StL-N	1.000	1	1	1	0	1	0
Total	4	.919	157	346	460	1	52	0

2B

YEAR	TM/L	PCT	G	PO	A	E	DP	FR
1913	Bos-N	.897	14	16	36	6	3	0
1917	StL-N	1.000	2	0	2	0	0	0
Total	2	.900	16	16	38	6	3	0

OF

YEAR	TM/L	PCT	G	PO	A	E	DP	FR
1913	Bos-N	1.000	4	3	0	0	0	0

1B

YEAR	TM/L	PCT	G	PO	A	E	DP	FR
1914	Buf-F	1.000	1	2	0	0	0	0

OF

YEAR	TM/L	PCT	G	PO	A	E	DP	FR
1890	Tol-a	.875	3	6	1	1	0	0

■ George Smith 2B

YEAR	TM/L	PCT	G	PO	A	E	DP	FR
1963	Det-A	.982	52	120	157	5	28	11
1964	Det-A	1.000	3	2	5	0	2	1
1965	Det-A	.984	22	30	31	1	10	3
1966	Bos-A	.969	109	239	287	17	76	14
Total	4	.974	186	391	480	3	116	29

SS

YEAR	TM/L	PCT	G	PO	A	E	DP	FR
1965	Det-A	1.000	3	1	1	0	0	0
1966	Bos-A	.913	19	29	44	7	9	2
Total	2	.915	22	30	45	7	9	2

3B

YEAR	TM/L	PCT	G	PO	A	E	DP	FR
1965	Det-A	1.000	3	2	1	0	0	0

■ Heinie Smith 2B

YEAR	TM/L	PCT	G	PO	A	E	DP	FR
1897	Lou-N	.928	21	46	57	8	8	-2
1898	Lou-N	.910	33	74	87	16	8	-6
1899	Pit-N	.851	15	34	46	14	3	-3
1901	NY-N	.969	7	13	18	1	0	-1
1902	NY-N	.953	138	347	403	37	58	4
1903	Det-A	.928	93	200	267	36	30	-2
Total	6	.934	307	714	878	112	107	-10

SS

YEAR	TM/L	PCT	G	PO	A	E	DP	FR
1899	Pit-N	—	1	0	0	0	0	0

■ Germany Smith SS

YEAR	TM/L	PCT	G	PO	A	E	DP	FR
1884	Alt-U	.871	25	40	88	19	1	6
	Cle-N	.904	30	44	107	16	3	10
1885	Bro-a	.884	108	161	455	81	23	40
1886	Bro-a	.860	105	142	381	85	30	13
1887	Bro-a	.886	101	157	387	70	23	32
1888	Bro-a	.844	103	155	352	94	29	6
1889	Bro-a	.899	120	182	417	67	37	-3
1890	Bro-N	.904	129	232	468	74	49	4
1891	Cin-N	.909	138	240	507	75	40	11
1892	Cin-N	.920	139	239	561	70	55	25
1893	Cin-N	.934	130	250	500	53	67	20
1894	Cin-N	.911	127	233	501	72	75	20
1895	Cin-N	.923	127	251	457	59	58	2
1896	Cin-N	.926	120	207	407	49	47	-10
1897	Bro-N	.908	112	201	399	61	36	-11
1898	Cin-N	.904	51	79	167	26	14	-7
Total	15	.902	1665	2813	6154	971	587	158

2B

YEAR	TM/L	PCT	G	PO	A	E	DP	FR
1884	Cle-N	.879	42	111	136	34	23	-1
1888	Bro-a	—	1	0	0	0	0	0
Total	2	.879	43	111	136	4	23	-1

OF

YEAR	TM/L	PCT	G	PO	A	E	DP	FR
1886	Bro-a	—	1	0	0	0	0	0
1889	Bro-a	—	1	0	0	0	0	0
Total	2	—	2	0	0	0	0	0

3B

YEAR	TM/L	PCT	G	PO	A	E	DP	FR
1887	Bro-a	.750	2	4	2	2	0	0

C

YEAR	TM/L	PCT	G	PO	A	E	DP	FR
1886	Bro-a	—	1	0	0	0	0	0

■ Hal Smith C

YEAR	TM/L	PCT	G	PO	A	E	DP	FR
1956	StL-N	.982	66	300	34	6	3	-3
1957	StL-N	.990	97	468	42	5	8	1
1958	StL-N	.989	71	346	22	4	4	-1
1959	StL-N	.989	141	758	60	9	13	4
1960	StL-N	.990	124	664	61	7	9	17
1961	StL-N	.993	45	261	28	2	6	17
1965	Pit-N	1.000	4	13	0	0	0	2
Total	7	.989	548	2810	247	3	43	37

■ Hal Smith C

YEAR	TM/L	PCT	G	PO	A	E	DP	FR
1955	Bal-A	.986	125	497	58	8	9	-1
1956	Bal-A	.994	71	313	33	2	11	3
	KC-A	.986	37	183	22	3	3	2
	Yr	.991	108	496	55	5	14	5
1957	KC-A	.983	103	463	55	9	8	0
1958	KC-A	.994	31	149	19	1	4	2
1959	KC-A	.964	22	125	10	5	5	1
1960	Pit-N	.985	71	356	30	6	5	-6
1961	Pit-N	.990	65	290	18	3	1	0
1962	Hou-N	.986	92	570	65	9	9	1
1963	Hou-N	.985	11	65	2	1	1	-3
1964	Cin-N	.983	20	105	8	2	1	-3
Total	10	.986	648	3116	320	9	57	-4

3B

YEAR	TM/L	PCT	G	PO	A	E	DP	FR
1958	KC-A	.949	43	44	87	7	9	-1
1959	KC-A	.953	77	85	119	10	10	6
1962	Hou-N	.875	6	0	7	1	0	0
Total	3	.950	126	129	213	8	19	5

1B

YEAR	TM/L	PCT	G	PO	A	E	DP	FR
1958	KC-A	1.000	14	120	6	0	6	-1
1962	Hou-N	1.000	2	10	0	0	1	0
Total	2	1.000	16	130	6	0	7	-1

■ Harry Smith C

YEAR	TM/L	PCT	G	PO	A	E	DP	FR
1901	Phi-A	.969	9	21	10	1	0	-2
1902	Pit-N	.972	50	265	49	9	3	-3
1903	Pit-N	.974	60	259	75	9	2	-4
1904	Pit-N	.964	44	153	61	8	6	-3
1905	Pit-N	1.000	1	4	1	0	1	0
1906	Pit-N	.800	1	4	0	1	0	0
1907	Pit-N	.939	18	46	16	4	2	-2
1908	Bos-N	.975	38	143	52	5	2	0
1909	Bos-N	.972	31	133	39	5	5	2
1910	Bos-N	.949	38	138	66	11	3	3
Total	10	.967	290	1166	369	3	24	-9

OF

YEAR	TM/L	PCT	G	PO	A	E	DP	FR
1901	Phi-A	.000	1	0	0	2	0	-1
1903	Pit-N	—	1	0	0	0	0	0
1904	Pit-N	1.000	3	2	0	0	1	-1
Total	3	.500	5	2	0	2	1	-2

■ Jack Smith OF

YEAR	TM/L	PCT	G	PO	A	E	DP	FR
1915	StL-N	1.000	4	5	0	0	0	-1
1916	StL-N	.949	120	212	12	12	4	-16
1917	StL-N	.961	128	233	12	10	6	-20
1918	StL-N	.941	42	87	9	6	6	2
1919	StL-N	.960	111	197	19	9	6	1
1920	StL-N	.963	83	144	12	6	1	-3
1921	StL-N	.955	103	179	11	9	3	-8
1922	StL-N	.951	136	282	11	15	3	-17
1923	StL-N	.974	109	247	11	7	3	3
1924	StL-N	.968	114	251	18	9	8	10
1925	StL-N	.958	64	152	7	7	2	4
1926	Bos-N	.973	83	206	8	6	0	-1
1927	Bos-N	.950	48	106	7	6	1	3
1928	Bos-N	.988	65	165	4	2	0	-4
1929	Bos-N	.833	9	10	0	2	0	0
Total	15	.961	1219	2476	141	106	43	-47

■ Red Smith 3B

YEAR	TM/L	PCT	G	PO	A	E	DP	FR
1911	Bro-N	.900	28	30	51	9	7	-2
1912	Bro-N	.938	125	156	251	27	16	5
1913	Bro-N	.933	151	175	295	34	13	-3
1914	Bro-N	.937	90	136	193	22	16	12
	Bos-N	.937	60	84	139	15	12	10
	Yr	.937	150	220	332	37	28	22
1915	Bos-N	.947	157	170	292	26	26	-6
1916	Bos-N	.928	150	166	299	36	15	-4
1917	Bos-N	.925	147	141	264	33	27	-21
1918	Bos-N	.922	119	123	291	35	16	4
1919	Bos-N	.928	23	29	61	7	4	5
Total	9	.932	1050	1210	2136	244	152	0

OF

YEAR	TM/L	PCT	G	PO	A	E	DP	FR
1919	Bos-N	.981	48	99	3	2	0	0

■ Jimmy Smith SS

YEAR	TM/L	PCT	G	PO	A	E	DP	FR
1914	Chi-F	1.000	3	3	5	0	2	1
1915	Chi-F	.904	92	187	246	46	28	-12
	Bal-F	.883	33	86	87	23	9	-4
	Yr	.898	125	273	333	69	37	-16
1916	Pit-N	.929	27	51	66	9	6	1
1917	NY-N	.971	7	15	19	1	0	0
1918	Bos-N	.868	9	28	31	9	5	0
1919	Cin-N	.962	5	9	16	1	3	0
1922	Phi-N	.952	23	43	56	5	13	-2
Total	7	.910	199	422	526	4	66	-16

2B

YEAR	TM/L	PCT	G	PO	A	E	DP	FR
1915	Chi-F	.000	1	0	0	1	0	-1
1917	NY-N	.971	29	38	64	3	5	-2
1918	Bos-N	1.000	10	17	11	0	1	0
1919	Cin-N	.917	4	6	5	1	2	0
1921	Phi-N	.971	66	125	239	11	19	8
1922	Phi-N	.954	13	24	38	3	3	-1
Total	6	.968	123	210	357	9	30	4

3B

YEAR	TM/L	PCT	G	PO	A	E	DP	FR
1916	Pit-N	.864	6	7	12	3	0	-1
1918	Bos-N	.938	5	6	9	1	1	0
1919	Cin-N	1.000	6	2	5	0	0	0
1922	Phi-N	—	1	0	0	0	0	0
Total	4	.911	18	15	26	4	1	-1

OF

YEAR	TM/L	PCT	G	PO	A	E	DP	FR
1918	Bos-N	.875	6	14	0	2	0	-1
1919	Cin-N	.500	4	1	0	1	0	0
Total	2	.833	10	15	0	3	0	-1

■ Dwight Smith OF

YEAR	TM/L	PCT	G	PO	A	E	DP	FR
1989	Chi-N	.975	102	188	7	5	3	-1
1990	Chi-N	.986	81	139	4	2	2	-3
Total	2	.980	183	327	11	7	5	-4

■ Lonnie Smith OF

YEAR	TM/L	PCT	G	PO	A	E	DP	FR
1978	Phi-N	1.000	11	5	1	0	0	2
1979	Phi-N	1.000	11	19	1	0	0	2
1980	Phi-N	.969	82	121	2	4	0	-10
1981	Phi-N	.971	51	89	10	3	2	3
1982	StL-N	.970	149	303	16	10	3	6
1983	StL-N	.941	126	225	14	15	4	-2
1984	StL-N	.948	140	184	18	11	0	-11
1985	StL-N	1.000	20	43	0	0	1	-3
	KC-A	.958	119	195	10	9	3	-9
1986	KC-A	.965	118	245	5	9	1	-2
1987	KC-A	.915	32	52	2	5	0	-3
1988	Atl-N	.968	35	59	2	2	0	-1
1989	Atl-N	.993	132	289	3	2	0	4
1990	Atl-N	.956	122	254	6	12	2	1
Total	13	.956	1156	2083	91	2	16	-23

■ Ozzie Smith SS

YEAR	TM/L	PCT	G	PO	A	E	DP	FR
1978	SD-N	.970	159	264	548	25	98	**26**
1979	SD-N	.976	155	256	**555**	20	86	**20**
1980	SD-N	.974	158	288	**621**	24	113	**41**
1981	SD-N	**.976**	110	220	**422**	16	72	**26**
1982	StL-N	**.984**	139	279	**535**	13	101	**33**
1983	StL-N	.975	158	**304**	519	21	100	18
1984	StL-N	**.982**	124	233	437	12	**94**	**26**
1985	StL-N	**.983**	158	264	549	14	111	15
1986	StL-N	**.978**	144	229	453	15	**96**	-9
1987	StL-N	**.987**	158	245	**516**	10	**111**	19
1988	StL-N	.972	150	234	**519**	22	79	**23**
1989	StL-N	.976	**153**	209	**483**	17	73	6
1990	StL-N	.980	140	212	378	12	66	-13
Total	13	.978	1906	3237	6535	221	1200	231

■ Bob Smith SS

YEAR	TM/L	PCT	G	PO	A	E	DP	FR
1923	Bos-N	.944	101	234	360	35	68	12
1924	Bos-N	.958	80	180	273	20	55	7
1925	Bos-N	.906	21	45	70	12	13	4
1929	Bos-N	.966	5	9	19	1	4	3
1933	Cin-N	—	1	0	0	0	0	0
Total	5	.946	208	468	722	8	140	26

2B

YEAR	TM/L	PCT	G	PO	A	E	DP	FR
1923	Bos-N	1.000	8	22	28	0	10	2
1925	Bos-N	.943	15	32	51	5	6	-1
1932	Chi-N	1.000	2	1	10	0	1	2
Total	3	.966	25	55	89	5	17	3

3B

YEAR	TM/L	PCT	G	PO	A	E	DP	FR
1924	Bos-N	.951	23	18	40	3	5	1

OF

YEAR	TM/L	PCT	G	PO	A	E	DP	FR
1925	Bos-N	1.000	1	0	1	0	0	1

■ Syd Smith C

YEAR	TM/L	PCT	G	PO	A	E	DP	FR
1908	Phi-A	.975	31	158	39	5	6	-1
	StL-A	.977	24	137	32	4	1	9
	Yr	.976	55	295	71	9	7	8
1910	Cle-A	.958	9	33	13	2	3	0
1911	Cle-A	.979	48	270	62	7	10	9
1914	Pit-N	1.000	3	12	3	0	0	0
Total	4	.977	115	610	149	8	20	17

1B

YEAR	TM/L	PCT	G	PO	A	E	DP	FR
1908	Phi-A	.968	6	57	4	2	0	0
1911	Cle-A	—	1	0	0	0	0	0
Total	2	.968	7	57	4	2	0	0

OF

YEAR	TM/L	PCT	G	PO	A	E	DP	FR
1908	Phi-A	—	1	0	0	0	0	0

3B

YEAR	TM/L	PCT	G	PO	A	E	DP	FR
1911	Cle-A	—	1	0	0	0	0	0

■ Willie Smith OF

YEAR	TM/L	PCT	G	PO	A	E	DP	FR
1964	LA-A	.977	87	128	2	3	0	-7
1965	Cal-A	.980	123	187	10	4	1	-3
1966	Cle-A	.974	52	71	4	2	1	-2
1967	Cle-A	.800	4	4	0	1	0	-1
1968	Cle-A	1.000	1	1	0	0	0	0
	Chi-N	1.000	38	42	1	0	0	-6
1969	Chi-N	.929	33	26	0	2	0	-4
1970	Chi-N	—	1	0	0	0	0	0
Total	7	.975	339	459	17	2	2	-23

1B

YEAR	TM/L	PCT	G	PO	A	E	DP	FR
1965	Cal-A	.917	2	9	2	1	1	0
1967	Cle-A	1.000	3	8	0	0	0	0
1968	Cle-A	1.000	7	51	2	0	5	0
	Chi-N	1.000	4	16	1	0	0	0
1969	Chi-N	.994	24	159	9	1	14	-2
1970	Chi-N	.994	43	318	11	2	32	-5
1971	Chi-N	1.000	10	80	9	0	10	1
Total	6	.994	93	641	34	4	62	-6

■ Homer Smoot OF

YEAR	TM/L	PCT	G	PO	A	E	DP	FR
1902	StL-N	.931	129	**284**	14	22	5	-1
1903	StL-N	.942	129	231	14	15	3	-7
1904	StL-N	.966	137	270	17	10	6	2
1905	StL-N	.975	138	295	18	8	6	1
1906	StL-N	.953	86	174	8	9	4	2
	Cin-N	.944	59	109	10	7	0	1
	Yr	.950	145	283	18	16	4	3
Total	5	.953	678	1363	81	1	24	-2

■ John Sneed OF

YEAR	TM/L	PCT	G	PO	A	E	DP	FR
1884	Ind-a	.817	17	45	4	11	0	0
1890	Tol-a	.889	9	11	5	2	1	2
	Col-a	.883	126	161	20	24	5	-7
	Yr	.883	135	172	25	26	6	-5
1891	Col-a	.894	99	142	10	18	4	-4
Total	3	.879	261	359	39	5	10	-9

SS

YEAR	TM/L	PCT	G	PO	A	E	DP	FR
1890	Col-a	.769	2	5	5	3	0	-1

■ Duke Snider OF

YEAR	TM/L	PCT	G	PO	A	E	DP	FR
1947	Bro-N	.980	25	48	0	1	0	1
1948	Bro-N	.989	47	87	5	1	0	2
1949	Bro-N	.984	145	355	12	6	2	-2
1950	Bro-N	.983	151	378	15	7	1	4
1951	Bro-N	.987	150	382	12	5	1	-4
1952	Bro-N	.992	141	341	13	3	3	0
1953	Bro-N	.987	151	370	7	5	3	-6
1954	Bro-N	.981	148	360	8	7	1	-9
1955	Bro-N	.989	146	348	9	4	1	-5
1956	Bro-N	.984	150	358	11	6	1	-4
1957	Bro-N	.990	136	304	6	3	1	-12
1958	LA-N	.987	92	151	4	2	0	-19
1959	LA-N	.975	107	157	2	4	1	-9

YEAR	TM/L	PCT	G	PO	A	E	DP	FR
1960	LA-N	.965	75	108	3	4	1	-4
1961	LA-N	.975	66	113	6	3	3	3
1962	LA-N	.967	39	56	3	2	0	-2
1963	NY-N	.986	106	139	5	2	0	-11
1964	SF-N	.979	43	44	2	1	0	-3
Total	18	.985	1918	4099	123	6	18	-79

■ Fred Snodgrass OF

YEAR	TM/L	PCT	G	PO	A	E	DP	FR
1909	NY-N	.921	20	31	4	3	1	0
1910	NY-N	.970	101	214	12	7	1	-3
1911	NY-N	.973	149	293	31	9	8	3
1912	NY-N	.948	116	229	25	14	4	1
1913	NY-N	.968	133	312	19	11	2	1
1914	NY-N	.977	96	200	11	5	4	3
1915	NY-N	.935	75	160	12	12	2	-1
	Bos-N	.938	18	44	1	3	0	0
	Yr	.935	93	204	13	15	2	-1
1916	Bos-N	.983	110	274	19	5	5	9
Total	8	.965	818	1757	134	9	27	13

1B

YEAR	TM/L	PCT	G	PO	A	E	DP	FR
1909	NY-N	—	1	0	0	0	0	0
1910	NY-N	.978	9	81	8	2	4	1
1911	NY-N	1.000	1	11	1	0	0	0
1912	NY-N	.977	27	243	10	6	12	-2
1913	NY-N	1.000	3	5	0	0	0	0
1914	NY-N	.984	14	112	10	2	6	1
1915	Bos-N	.973	5	35	1	1	2	0
Total	7	.979	60	487	30	1	24	0

C

YEAR	TM/L	PCT	G	PO	A	E	DP	FR
1908	NY-N	1.000	3	4	1	0	0	1
1909	NY-N	1.000	2	7	0	0	0	0
1910	NY-N	.875	1	5	2	1	1	0
Total	3	.950	6	16	3	1	1	1

3B

YEAR	TM/L	PCT	G	PO	A	E	DP	FR
1910	NY-N	—	1	0	0	0	0	0
1911	NY-N	1.000	1	1	5	0	0	1
1914	NY-N	1.000	1	1	0	0	0	0
Total	3	1.000	3	2	5	0	0	1

2B

YEAR	TM/L	PCT	G	PO	A	E	DP	FR
1912	NY-N	.500	1	0	1	1	0	-1
1913	NY-N	—	1	0	0	0	0	0
1914	NY-N	—	1	0	0	0	0	0
Total	3	.500	3	0	1	1	0	-1

■ Pop Snyder C

YEAR	TM/L	PCT	G	PO	A	E	DP	FR
1876	Lou-N	.833	55	249	86	67	2	7
1877	Lou-N	.910	61	292	102	39	8	16
1878	Bos-N	.912	58	344	92	42	2	0
1879	Bos-N	.925	80	398	142	44	10	20
1881	Bos-N	.897	60	261	105	42	0	13
1882	Cin-a	.916	70	358	92	41	3	12
1883	Cin-a	.919	57	283	71	31	4	8
1884	Cin-a	.922	65	341	135	40	5	19
1885	Cin-a	.880	38	185	64	34	3	-1
1886	Cin-a	.874	41	184	73	37	4	-9
1887	Cle-a	.905	63	314	143	48	8	17
1888	Cle-a	.901	58	308	130	48	11	10
1889	Cle-N	.907	22	88	39	13	5	2
1890	Cle-P	.958	13	52	16	3	1	4
1891	Was-a	1.000	3	19	5	0	0	1
Total	15	.904	744	3676	1295	529	66	119

1B

YEAR	TM/L	PCT	G	PO	A	E	DP	FR
1882	Cin-a	.867	2	10	3	2	0	1
1884	Cin-a	1.000	2	18	1	0	1	0
1885	Cin-a	.875	1	7	0	1	0	0
1886	Cin-a	.962	19	144	7	6	7	1
1887	Cle-a	.969	13	90	5	3	4	1
1888	Cle-a	1.000	4	25	1	0	1	0
1891	Was-a	1.000	4	32	1	0	0	0
Total	7	.966	45	326	18	2	13	3

OF

YEAR	TM/L	PCT	G	PO	A	E	DP	FR
1876	Lou-N	.800	4	3	1	1	1	0
1877	Lou-N	—	1	0	0	0	0	0
1878	Bos-N	—	2	0	0	0	0	0
1879	Bos-N	—	2	0	0	0	0	0
1881	Bos-N	—	1	0	0	0	0	0
1882	Cin-a	.000	1	0	0	1	0	-1
1884	Cin-a	.833	1	4	1	1	0	1
1886	Cin-a	1.000	1	1	0	0	0	0
1888	Cle-a	1.000	3	2	0	0	0	-1
1891	Was-a	—	1	0	0	0	0	0
Total	10	.800	17	10	2	3	1	-1

SS

YEAR	TM/L	PCT	G	PO	A	E	DP	FR
1877	Lou-N	.500	1	0	1	1	0	0
1881	Bos-N	.800	1	0	4	1	0	0
1883	Cin-a	.667	2	3	7	5	0	0
Total	3	.682	4	3	12	7	0	0

2B

YEAR	TM/L	PCT	G	PO	A	E	DP	FR
1881	Bos-N	.500	1	0	1	1	0	0

■ Frank Snyder C

YEAR	TM/L	PCT	G	PO	A	E	DP	FR
1912	StL-N	.919	11	25	9	3	0	0
1913	StL-N	.956	7	31	12	2	0	2
1914	StL-N	.979	98	419	130	12	12	4
1915	StL-N	.983	142	592	204	14	9	7
1916	StL-N	.973	72	310	115	12	8	8
1917	StL-N	.975	94	341	133	12	10	0
1918	StL-N	.959	27	104	37	6	3	1
1919	StL-N	.983	48	149	80	4	4	4
	NY-N	.983	31	83	33	2	2	-4
	Yr	.983	79	232	113	6	6	0
1920	NY-N	.978	84	269	92	8	6	1
1921	NY-N	.985	101	299	98	6	7	4
1922	NY-N	.980	97	272	74	7	10	-4
1923	NY-N	.990	112	428	90	5	12	2
1924	NY-N	.987	110	308	79	5	8	-17
1925	NY-N	.985	96	336	71	6	7	2
1926	NY-N	.981	55	168	38	4	3	-1
1927	StL-N	.981	62	174	37	4	5	-1
Total	16	.981	1247	4308	1332	112	106	8

1B

YEAR	TM/L	PCT	G	PO	A	E	DP	FR
1916	StL-N	.984	46	421	23	7	27	1
1918	StL-N	1.000	3	23	3	0	1	1
1919	StL-N	1.000	1	12	0	0	0	0
Total	3	.986	50	456	26	7	28	2

SS

YEAR	TM/L	PCT	G	PO	A	E	DP	FR
1916	StL-N	—	1	0	0	0	0	0

2B

YEAR	TM/L	PCT	G	PO	A	E	DP	FR
1917	StL-N	1.000	1	0	1	0	0	0

■ Jerry Snyder SS

YEAR	TM/L	PCT	G	PO	A	E	DP	FR
1952	Was-A	.818	4	3	6	2	0	0
1953	Was-A	.988	17	28	54	1	10	7
1954	Was-A	.978	48	81	145	5	31	10
1955	Was-A	.944	20	12	5	1	0	-3
1956	Was-A	.968	35	47	106	5	23	-3
1957	Was-A	.966	15	17	39	2	8	0
1958	Was-A	—	1	0	0	0	0	0
Total	7	.971	140	188	355	6	72	11

2B

YEAR	TM/L	PCT	G	PO	A	E	DP	FR
1952	Was-A	.965	19	34	49	3	12	7
1953	Was-A	.818	4	5	4	2	0	0
1954	Was-A	.833	3	7	3	2	1	-1
1955	Was-A	.977	22	66	63	3	24	4
1956	Was-A	.897	7	17	18	4	5	-1
1957	Was-A	1.000	13	26	14	0	7	0
1958	Was-A	1.000	2	8	2	0	1	0
Total	7	.958	70	163	153	4	50	9

3B

YEAR	TM/L	PCT	G	PO	A	E	DP	FR
1957	Was-A	.857	1	0	6	1	1	1

■ Cory Snyder OF

YEAR	TM/L	PCT	G	PO	A	E	DP	FR
1986	Cle-A	.987	74	150	4	2	1	-4
1987	Cle-A	.971	139	283	16	9	3	6
1988	Cle-A	.985	141	314	16	5	0	11
1989	Cle-A	.997	125	291	18	1	5	16
1990	Cle-A	.975	120	224	11	6	2	-1
Total	5	.983	599	1262	65	3	11	28

SS

YEAR	TM/L	PCT	G	PO	A	E	DP	FR
1986	Cle-A	.937	34	53	66	8	20	-6
1987	Cle-A	.918	18	30	37	6	6	-6
1989	Cle-A	1.000	7	6	14	0	2	0
1990	Cle-A	.923	5	5	7	1	2	-2
Total	4	.936	64	94	124	5	30	-14

3B

YEAR	TM/L	PCT	G	PO	A	E	DP	FR
1986	Cle-A	1.000	11	10	14	0	1	-1

■ Russ Snyder OF

YEAR	TM/L	PCT	G	PO	A	E	DP	FR
1959	KC-A	.986	64	127	9	2	2	5
1960	KC-A	.986	91	135	4	2	2	-8
1961	Bal-A	.966	108	168	3	6	0	-12
1962	Bal-A	.974	121	218	8	6	2	0
1963	Bal-A	.988	130	238	5	3	1	-3
1964	Bal-A	.971	40	34	0	1	0	-3
1965	Bal-A	1.000	106	188	4	0	0	0
1966	Bal-A	.986	104	209	6	3	2	6
1967	Bal-A	.985	69	127	3	2	0	-1
1968	Chi-A	1.000	22	22	0	0	0	-4
	Cle-A	.991	54	106	4	1	3	2
	Yr	.992	76	128	4	1	3	-2
1969	Cle-A	.961	84	144	2	6	1	-4
1970	Mil-A	.966	106	140	1	5	0	-25
Total	12	.981	1099	1856	49	7	13	-47

1B

YEAR	TM/L	PCT	G	PO	A	E	DP	FR
1968	Cle-A	1.000	1	5	0	0	0	0

■ Eric Soderholm 3B

YEAR	TM/L	PCT	G	PO	A	E	DP	FR
1971	Min-A	.942	20	17	48	4	2	3
1972	Min-A	.942	79	66	163	14	17	1
1973	Min-A	.921	33	26	67	8	5	0
1974	Min-A	.956	130	100	273	17	19	-6
1975	Min-A	.969	113	94	277	12	14	13
1977	Chi-A	.978	126	99	249	8	18	0
1978	Chi-A	.964	128	128	245	14	17	0
1979	Chi-A	.986	56	55	154	3	12	15
	Tex-A	.944	37	20	48	4	5	2
	Yr	.975	93	75	202	7	17	17
1980	NY-A	.952	37	15	65	4	4	-1
Total	9	.962	759	620	1589	8	113	27

SS

YEAR	TM/L	PCT	G	PO	A	E	DP	FR
1973	Min-A	—	1	0	0	0	0	0
1974	Min-A	1.000	1	1	0	0	0	0
Total	2	1.000	2	1	0	0	0	0

1B

YEAR	TM/L	PCT	G	PO	A	E	DP	FR
1979	Tex-A	.909	2	9	1	1	0	0

2B

YEAR	TM/L	PCT	G	PO	A	E	DP	FR
1978	Chi-A	1.000	1	0	4	0	0	0

■ Rick Sofield OF

YEAR	TM/L	PCT	G	PO	A	E	DP	FR
1979	Min-A	.954	35	61	1	3	1	-1
1980	Min-A	.979	126	267	7	6	0	-2
1981	Min-A	.983	34	54	5	1	0	1
Total	3	.975	195	382	13	0	1	-2

■ Tony Solaita 1B

YEAR	TM/L	PCT	G	PO	A	E	DP	FR
1968	NY-A	1.000	1	5	0	0	1	0
1974	KC-A	.991	65	508	40	5	36	3
1975	KC-A	.994	35	282	28	2	24	3
1976	KC-A	.974	5	34	3	1	1	0
	Cal-A	.998	54	451	54	1	32	8
	Yr	.996	59	485	57	2	33	8
1977	Cal-A	.990	91	641	57	7	50	1
1978	Cal-A	1.000	11	85	7	0	7	0
1979	Mon-N	.989	13	83	6	1	7	0
	Tor-A	1.000	6	39	4	0	8	1
Total	7	.993	281	2128	199	7	166	17

OF

YEAR	TM/L	PCT	G	PO	A	E	DP	FR
1974	KC-A	—	1	0	0	0	0	0

■ Moose Solters OF

YEAR	TM/L	PCT	G	PO	A	E	DP	FR
1934	Bos-A	.933	89	197	11	15	1	5
1935	Bos-A	.966	21	54	2	2	1	3
	StL-A	.989	127	328	18	4	1	19
	Yr	.985	148	382	20	6	2	22
1936	StL-A	.956	147	356	16	17	5	10
1937	Cle-A	.953	149	283	19	15	3	1
1938	Cle-A	.969	46	91	4	3	3	0
1939	Cle-A	.915	25	42	1	4	0	-2
	StL-A	.935	30	70	2	5	0	-1
	Yr	.927	55	112	3	9	0	-3
1940	Chi-A	.971	107	266	6	8	2	5
1941	Chi-A	.966	63	135	7	5	1	-1
1943	Chi-A	.941	21	30	2	2	0	-3
Total	9	.960	825	1852	88	0	17	36

■ Joe Sommer OF

YEAR	TM/L	PCT	G	PO	A	E	DP	FR
1880	Cin-N	.913	22	38	4	4	1	0
1882	Cin-a	.925	80	188	9	16	2	4
1883	Cin-a	.854	94	171	11	31	1	-1
1884	Bal-a	.857	9	16	8	4	1	5
1885	Bal-a	.921	107	230	14	21	2	13
1886	Bal-a	.900	95	186	12	22	4	9
1887	Bal-a	.902	110	187	15	22	4	-2
1888	Bal-a	.871	44	54	7	9	1	-2
1889	Bal-a	.929	105	172	24	15	7	10
1890	Cle-N	.789	9	15	0	4	0	-2
	Bal-a	.892	38	69	5	9	3	1
Total	10	.901	713	1326	109	157	26	35

3B

YEAR	TM/L	PCT	G	PO	A	E	DP	FR
1880	Cin-N	.667	1	2	0	1	0	-1
1883	Cin-a	.833	3	4	6	2	0	0
1884	Bal-a	.841	97	118	168	54	10	1
1885	Bal-a	.571	2	2	2	3	0	-1
1886	Bal-a	.919	11	16	18	3	0	2
1887	Bal-a	.762	10	14	18	10	2	-1
Total	6	.834	124	156	212	3	12	0

2B

YEAR	TM/L	PCT	G	PO	A	E	DP	FR
1884	Bal-a	1.000	1	4	0	0	0	-1
1886	Bal-a	.924	32	84	86	14	9	3
1887	Bal-a	.883	13	35	48	11	4	3
1888	Bal-a	.857	2	2	4	1	0	-1
Total	4	.910	48	125	138	6	13	4

SS

YEAR	TM/L	PCT	G	PO	A	E	DP	FR
1880	Cin-N	—	1	0	0	0	0	0
1885	Bal-a	1.000	2	2	4	0	0	0
1886	Bal-a	.688	3	2	9	5	1	-1
1887	Bal-a	.800	2	1	3	1	0	0
1888	Bal-a	.883	34	53	98	20	12	-1
1889	Bal-a	1.000	1	1	2	0	0	0
Total	6	.871	43	59	116	6	13	-2

1B

YEAR	TM/L	PCT	G	PO	A	E	DP	FR
1885	Bal-a	1.000	1	11	0	0	0	0
1888	Bal-a	1.000	1	6	0	0	0	0
Total	2	1.000	2	17	1	0	0	0

C

YEAR	TM/L	PCT	G	PO	A	E	DP	FR
1880	Cin-N	1.000	1	2	0	0	0	0

■ Sammy Sosa OF

YEAR	TM/L	PCT	G	PO	A	E	DP	FR
1989	Tex-A	.944	19	33	1	2	0	-2
	Chi-A	.969	33	61	1	2	0	1
	Yr	.960	52	94	2	4	0	-1
1990	Chi-A	.962	152	315	14	13	1	4
Total	2	.962	204	409	16	7	1	3

■ Denny Sothern OF

YEAR	TM/L	PCT	G	PO	A	E	DP	FR
1926	Phi-N	.975	13	38	1	1	0	1
1928	Phi-N	.964	136	358	19	14	7	5
1929	Phi-N	.967	71	193	9	7	2	0
1930	Phi-N	.967	84	217	15	8	3	7
	Pit-N	.971	13	34	0	1	0	1
	Yr	.967	97	251	15	9	3	8
1931	Bro-N	.958	10	23	0	1	0	1
Total	5	.966	327	863	44	2	12	15

■ Bud Souchock OF

YEAR	TM/L	PCT	G	PO	A	E	DP	FR
1949	Chi-A	.951	39	96	1	5	0	0
1951	Det-A	.941	59	92	3	6	1	-1
1952	Det-A	.964	56	103	4	4	2	0
1953	Det-A	.962	80	144	7	6	3	-1
1954	Det-A	1.000	9	13	0	0	0	0
Total	5	.957	243	448	15	1	6	-2

1B

YEAR	TM/L	PCT	G	PO	A	E	DP	FR
1946	NY-A	.964	20	180	9	7	19	-2
1948	NY-A	.988	32	231	13	3	25	-2
1949	Chi-A	.996	30	250	20	1	30	2
1951	Det-A	1.000	1	1	0	0	0	0
1952	Det-A	.989	9	81	6	1	4	0
1953	Det-A	1.000	1	3	0	0	0	0
Total	6	.985	93	746	48	2	78	-2

3B

YEAR	TM/L	PCT	G	PO	A	E	DP	FR
1951	Det-A	.833	3	2	3	1	1	0
1952	Det-A	.914	13	11	21	3	1	1
1954	Det-A	1.000	2	2	4	0	0	0
Total	3	.915	18	15	28	4	2	1

2B

YEAR	TM/L	PCT	G	PO	A	E	DP	FR
1951	Det-A	1.000	1	1	1	0	0	0

■ Billy Southworth OF

YEAR	TM/L	PCT	G	PO	A	E	DP	FR
1913	Cle-A	—	1	0	0	0	0	0
1915	Cle-A	.942	44	90	7	6	3	1
1918	Pit-N	.980	64	137	12	3	4	6
1919	Pit-N	.968	121	253	17	9	5	4
1920	Pit-N	.991	142	337	12	3	3	8
1921	Bos-N	.975	141	288	25	8	6	4
1922	Bos-N	.955	41	100	7	5	2	0
1923	Bos-N	.943	151	326	22	21	6	5
1924	NY-N	.935	75	167	5	12	2	-1
1925	NY-N	.919	119	289	7	11	1	-10
1926	NY-N	.970	29	62	2	2	1	-2

YEAR	TM/L	PCT	G	PO	A	E	DP	FR
	StL-N	.971	99	228	5	7	0	-4
	Yr	.971	128	290	7	9	1	-6
1927	StL-N	.970	83	153	6	5	2	-8
1929	StL-N	1.000	5	12	0	0	0	0
Total	13	.965	1115	2442	127	2	33	5

2B

YEAR	TM/L	PCT	G	PO	A	E	DP	FR
1923	Bos-N	.875	2	3	4	1	0	-2

■ Dick Spalding OF

YEAR	TM/L	PCT	G	PO	A	E	DP	FR
1927	Phi-N	.992	113	250	7	2	1	-1
1928	Was-A	1.000	11	9	0	0	0	-3
Total	2	.993	124	259	7	2	1	-4

■ Al Spangler OF

YEAR	TM/L	PCT	G	PO	A	E	DP	FR
1959	Mil-N	1.000	4	6	0	0	0	0
1960	Mil-N	.989	92	88	4	1	1	8
1961	Mil-N	1.000	44	56	2	0	0	1
1962	Hou-N	.960	121	183	7	8	2	-4
1963	Hou-N	.987	113	215	5	3	1	2
1964	Hou-N	.964	127	185	3	7	1	-11
1965	Hou-N	.956	33	40	3	2	0	-2
	Cal-A	.973	24	36	0	1	0	-1
1966	Cal-A	1.000	3	3	0	0	0	0
1967	Chi-N	.986	41	71	0	1	0	-1
1968	Chi-N	.973	48	71	2	2	1	-3
1969	Chi-N	.950	58	75	1	4	0	-8
1970	Chi-N	1.000	6	5	0	0	0	1
Total	12	.973	714	1034	27	9	6	-18

■ Bob Speake OF

YEAR	TM/L	PCT	G	PO	A	E	DP	FR
1955	Chi-N	.959	55	90	4	4	1	-6
1957	Chi-N	.974	60	143	5	4	0	3
1958	SF-N	.938	10	13	2	1	0	1
Total	3	.966	125	246	11	9	1	-2

1B

YEAR	TM/L	PCT	G	PO	A	E	DP	FR
1955	Chi-N	.974	8	69	7	2	7	0
1957	Chi-N	.992	39	337	36	3	21	3
Total	2	.989	47	406	43	5	28	3

■ Tris Speaker OF

YEAR	TM/L	PCT	G	PO	A	E	DP	FR
1907	Bos-A	1.000	4	4	2	0	1	1
1908	Bos-A	1.000	31	57	8	0	3	4
1909	Bos-A	.973	142	319	35	10	12	22
1910	Bos-A	.957	140	337	20	16	7	15
1911	Bos-A	.956	138	297	26	15	5	6
1912	Bos-A	.958	153	372	35	18	9	21
1913	Bos-A	.942	139	374	30	25	7	24
1914	Bos-A	.968	156	423	29	15	12	28
1915	Bos-A	.976	150	378	21	10	8	13
1916	Cle-A	.975	151	359	25	10	10	9
1917	Cle-A	.980	142	365	23	8	5	8
1918	Cle-A	.973	127	352	15	10	6	11
1919	Cle-A	.983	134	375	25	7	6	19
1920	Cle-A	.977	148	363	24	9	8	9
1921	Cle-A	.984	128	345	15	6	2	10
1922	Cle-A	.983	109	281	13	5	6	8
1923	Cle-A	.968	150	369	26	13	7	10
1924	Cle-A	.963	128	323	20	13	3	5
1925	Cle-A	.967	109	311	16	11	9	10
1926	Cle-A	.981	149	394	20	8	7	10
1927	Was-A	.967	120	278	12	10	5	1
1928	Phi-A	.975	50	111	8	3	1	1
Total	22	.970	2698	6787	448	222	139	245
1914	Bos-A	1.000	1	2	0	0	1	0
1927	Was-A	.987	17	145	12	2	18	1
Total	2	.988	18	147	12	2	19	1

■ Chris Speier SS

YEAR	TM/L	PCT	G	PO	A	E	DP	FR
1971	SF-N	.958	156	239	517	33	95	-12
1972	SF-N	.974	150	243	517	20	69	-5
1973	SF-N	.956	150	255	470	33	92	-10
1974	SF-N	.969	135	210	445	21	82	3
1975	SF-N	.982	136	247	420	12	81	1
1976	SF-N	.974	135	225	441	18	81	-2
1977	SF-N	.920	5	3	20	2	2	2
	Mon-N	.970	138	230	435	21	75	-11
	Yr	.968	143	239	455	23	77	-9
1978	Mon-N	.975	148	245	467	18	93	1
1979	Mon-N	.970	112	194	355	17	52	4
1980	Mon-N	.965	127	187	396	21	62	0
1981	Mon-N	.964	96	175	280	17	57	-11
1982	Mon-N	.982	155	291	405	13	76	-21
1983	Mon-N	.962	74	107	196	12	31	-9
1984	Mon-N	.960	13	7	17	1	4	-3
	StL-N	.983	34	49	124	3	25	9
	Min-A	.977	12	14	28	1	6	-3
	Yr	.971	25	21	45	2	10	-6
1985	Chi-N	.964	58	61	125	7	33	2
1986	Chi-N	.975	23	32	46	2	11	5
1987	SF-N	.982	22	16	40	1	8	0
1988	SF-N	.978	12	15	29	1	7	-1
1989	SF-N	.933	9	6	8	1	1	-2
Total	19	.970	1900	3057	5781	275	1043	-63

3B

YEAR	TM/L	PCT	G	PO	A	E	DP	FR
1975	SF-N	1.000	1	0	1	0	0	0
1976	SF-N	.889	5	4	4	1	2	0
1980	Mon-N	1.000	1	0	1	0	0	0
1983	Mon-N	.895	12	10	7	2	1	-1
1984	Mon-N	1.000	4	0	9	0	0	1
	StL-N	1.000	2	0	2	0	0	0
	Yr	1.000	6	0	11	0	0	1
1985	Chi-N	.935	31	5	24	2	1	-1
1986	Chi-N	.984	53	21	42	1	3	2
1987	SF-N	.991	44	22	84	1	10	4
1988	SF-N	1.000	22	9	26	0	1	2
1989	SF-N	1.000	9	2	4	0	0	0
Total	10	.975	184	73	204	7	18	7

2B

YEAR	TM/L	PCT	G	PO	A	E	DP	FR
1973	SF-N	1.000	1	0	1	0	0	0
1974	SF-N	1.000	4	5	8	0	2	0
1976	SF-N	1.000	7	8	18	0	2	1
1983	Mon-N	—	2	0	0	0	0	0
1985	Chi-N	.961	13	21	28	2	9	1
1986	Chi-N	1.000	7	9	18	0	1	2
1987	SF-N	.989	55	80	105	2	23	-3
1988	SF-N	.985	45	46	87	2	18	1
1989	SF-N	1.000	4	7	7	0	4	0
Total	9	.987	138	176	272	6	59	2

1B

YEAR	TM/L	PCT	G	PO	A	E	DP	FR
1976	SF-N	1.000	1	4	1	0	0	0
1989	SF-N	1.000	1	4	1	0	1	0
Total	2	1.000	2	8	2	0	1	0

■ Stan Spence OF

YEAR	TM/L	PCT	G	PO	A	E	DP	FR
1940	Bos-A	1.000	15	15	0	0	0	-1
1941	Bos-A	1.000	52	97	6	0	2	3
1942	Was-A	.973	149	395	7	11	0	-5
1943	Was-A	.983	148	396	12	7	1	1
1944	Was-A	.989	150	434	29	5	9	17
1946	Was-A	.982	150	412	15	8	3	4
1947	Was-A	.984	142	408	12	7	3	3
1948	Bos-A	.977	92	206	4	5	1	-2
1949	Bos-A	1.000	5	14	1	0	0	1
	StL-A	.995	85	205	10	1	2	0
	Yr	.996	90	219	11	1	2	1
Total	9	.984	988	2582	96	4	21	21

1B

YEAR	TM/L	PCT	G	PO	A	E	DP	FR
1941	Bos-A	1.000	1	2	0	0	0	-1
1944	Was-A	.952	3	20	0	1	0	-1
1948	Bos-A	.991	14	110	6	1	6	-1
1949	StL-A	—	1	0	0	0	0	0
Total	4	.986	19	132	6	2	6	-2

■ Daryl Spencer SS

YEAR	TM/L	PCT	G	PO	A	E	DP	FR
1952	NY-N	1.000	3	6	9	0	1	1
1953	NY-N	.927	53	80	137	17	26	-4
1956	NY-N	.979	66	113	169	6	33	-2
1957	NY-N	.950	110	213	342	29	95	8
1958	SF-N	.955	134	238	438	32	95	1
1959	SF-N	1.000	4	0	4	0	2	1
1960	StL-N	.946	138	215	323	31	66	-24
1961	StL-N	.956	37	66	109	8	26	-1
	LA-A	1.000	3	6	7	0	2	0
	Yr	.959	40	72	116	8	28	-1
1962	LA-N	1.000	10	3	13	0	3	2
Total	9	.953	558	940	1551	123	349	-18

2B

YEAR	TM/L	PCT	G	PO	A	E	DP	FR
1953	NY-N	.962	32	66	85	6	23	-1
1956	NY-N	.974	70	161	175	9	36	-5
1957	NY-N	.975	36	80	112	5	23	6
1958	SF-N	.967	17	24	34	2	7	-1
1959	SF-N	.970	151	350	413	24	82	-5
1960	StL-N	.984	16	27	36	1	8	0
Total	6	.971	322	708	855	7	179	-7

3B

YEAR	TM/L	PCT	G	PO	A	E	DP	FR
1952	NY-N	1.000	3	1	5	0	0	0
1953	NY-N	.899	36	33	47	9	3	-5
1956	NY-N	.940	12	14	33	3	5	5
1957	NY-N	.880	6	8	14	3	0	0
1961	LA-N	.964	57	42	92	5	14	4
1962	LA-N	.925	57	35	88	10	4	5
1963	LA-N	1.000	3	2	3	0	0	0
	Cin-N	.979	48	45	92	3	9	3
	Yr	.979	51	47	95	3	9	3
Total	7	.944	222	180	374	3	35	12

■ Tubby Spencer C

YEAR	TM/L	PCT	G	PO	A	E	DP	FR
1905	StL-A	.962	34	134	41	7	1	-6
1906	StL-A	.935	54	226	60	20	3	-5
1907	StL-A	.957	63	250	80	15	6	-2
1908	StL-A	.983	88	398	109	9	9	0
1909	Bos-A	.992	26	94	24	1	0	-5
1911	Phi-A	.925	11	47	15	5	2	-1
1916	Det-A	.988	19	58	21	1	1	-7
1917	Det-A	.970	62	250	57	7	10	2
1918	Det-A	.966	48	153	46	7	3	-12
Total	9	.966	405	1610	453	2	35	-40

1B

YEAR	TM/L	PCT	G	PO	A	E	DP	FR
1918	Det-A	—	1	0	0	0	0	0

■ Jim Spencer 1B

YEAR	TM/L	PCT	G	PO	A	E	DP	FR
1968	Cal-A	.994	19	152	18	1	15	3
1969	Cal-A	.991	107	926	66	9	81	-1
1970	Cal-A	.995	142	1212	85	7	131	-1
1971	Cal-A	.996	145	1296	93	5	117	2
1972	Cal-A	.990	35	267	22	3	25	1
1973	Cal-A	1.000	26	204	7	0	24	-2
	Tex-A	.999	99	790	67	1	86	5
	Yr	.999	125	994	74	1	110	3
1974	Tex-A	.998	60	389	27	1	36	1
1975	Tex-A	.995	99	844	70	5	92	5
1976	Chi-A	.998	143	1206	112	2	116	8
1977	Chi-A	.991	125	977	90	10	76	2
1978	NY-A	1.000	15	90	7	0	4	1
1979	NY-A	.992	26	232	17	2	35	0
1980	NY-A	.990	75	567	41	6	51	2
1981	NY-A	.995	25	172	17	0	17	2
	Oak-A	.997	48	344	36	1	30	2
	Yr	.998	73	516	53	1	47	4
1982	Oak-A	.992	32	230	22	2	20	2
Total	15	.995	1221	9898	797	5	956	32

OF

YEAR	TM/L	PCT	G	PO	A	E	DP	FR
1972	Cal-A	1.000	24	22	1	0	0	-1

■ Roy Spencer C

YEAR	TM/L	PCT	G	PO	A	E	DP	FR
1925	Pit-N	.905	11	18	1	2	2	-2
1926	Pit-N	.972	12	29	3	1	0	-1
1927	Pit-N	.974	34	98	15	3	2	3
1929	Was-A	.967	41	128	20	5	2	-1
1930	Was-A	.989	93	395	44	5	3	4
1931	Was-A	.985	145	642	69	11	9	7
1932	Was-A	.978	98	313	44	8	9	-10
1933	Cle-A	.990	72	258	42	3	4	5
1934	Cle-A	1.000	4	7	2	0	0	1
1936	NY-N	1.000	14	18	3	0	0	1
1937	Bro-N	1.000	45	177	27	0	2	9
1938	Bro-N	.968	16	55	5	2	0	0
Total	8	.984	585	2138	275	0	33	16

■ Bill Spiers SS

YEAR	TM/L	PCT	G	PO	A	E	DP	FR
1989	Mil-A	.962	89	138	264	16	57	12
1990	Mil-A	.976	111	159	326	12	72	-6
Total	2	.969	200	297	590	8	129	6

3B

YEAR	TM/L	PCT	G	PO	A	E	DP	FR
1989	Mil-A	.882	12	10	20	4	1	1

2B

YEAR	TM/L	PCT	G	PO	A	E	DP	FR
1989	Mil-A	1.000	4	6	11	0	1	1

1B

YEAR	TM/L	PCT	G	PO	A	E	DP	FR
1989	Mil-A	.909	2	10	0	1	3	0

■ Ed Spiezio 3B

YEAR	TM/L	PCT	G	PO	A	E	DP	FR
1965	StL-N	1.000	3	1	7	0	0	0
1966	StL-N	.885	19	14	32	6	3	-4
1967	StL-N	.962	19	15	35	2	4	1
1968	StL-N	1.000	2	1	4	0	0	0
1969	SD-N	.939	98	93	198	19	10	1
1970	SD-N	.953	93	66	178	12	10	2
1971	SD-N	.962	91	57	168	9	12	1
1972	SD-N	1.000	5	2	4	0	1	-2
	Chi-A	.952	74	67	172	12	11	7
Total	4	.949	404	316	798	0	51	6

OF

YEAR	TM/L	PCT	G	PO	A	E	DP	FR
1967	StL-N	1.000	7	9	0	0	0	0
1968	StL-N	1.000	11	19	1	0	1	1
1969	SD-N	—	1	0	0	0	0	0
1971	SD-N	—	1	0	0	0	0	0
Total	4	1.000	20	28	1	0	1	1

■ Charlie Spikes OF

YEAR	TM/L	PCT	G	PO	A	E	DP	FR
1972	NY-A	1.000	9	14	1	0	1	0
1973	Cle-A	.964	111	202	13	8	0	1
1974	Cle-A	.968	154	284	16	10	3	-5
1975	Cle-A	.974	103	176	13	5	5	-2
1976	Cle-A	.985	98	185	7	3	0	-2
1977	Cle-A	.972	27	34	1	1	1	-4
1978	Det-A	.909	9	9	1	1	1	-2
1979	Atl-N	.842	15	16	0	3	0	-3
1980	Atl-N	1.000	7	4	0	0	0	0
Total	9	.969	533	924	52	1	11	-17

■ Harry Spilman 1B

YEAR	TM/L	PCT	G	PO	A	E	DP	FR
1979	Cin-N	1.000	12	62	2	0	3	0
1980	Cin-N	.986	18	132	13	2	11	1
1981	Cin-N	.929	2	12	1	1	0	0
	Hou-N	1.000	13	46	2	0	3	0
	Yr	.984	15	58	3	1	3	0
1982	Hou-N	.989	11	86	5	1	5	-1
1983	Hou-N	1.000	19	124	7	0	5	-1
1984	Hou-N	.978	18	130	6	3	14	-2
1985	Hou-N	1.000	19	131	4	0	15	-1
1986	Det-A	1.000	1	4	0	0	0	0
	SF-N	.994	19	138	15	1	8	2
1987	SF-N	.976	9	39	1	1	4	1
1988	SF-N	1.000	6	18	1	0	3	0
	Hou-N	1.000	1	5	0	0	0	0
	Yr	1.000	7	23	1	0	3	0
1989	Hou-N	1.000	9	47	4	0	2	0
Total	11	.991	157	974	61	9	73	-3

3B

YEAR	TM/L	PCT	G	PO	A	E	DP	FR
1979	Cin-N	1.000	4	2	9	0	0	0
1980	Cin-N	1.000	1	0	2	0	0	0
1981	Cin-N	1.000	3	4	2	0	0	0
1986	Det-A	1.000	2	1	1	0	0	0
	SF-N	.667	5	1	1	1	0	-1
1987	SF-N	.875	10	1	6	1	1	-1
Total	5	.938	25	9	21	2	1	-2

C

YEAR	TM/L	PCT	G	PO	A	E	DP	FR
1980	Cin-N	—	1	0	0	0	0	0
1983	Hou-N	1.000	6	14	1	0	0	-1
1984	Hou-N	1.000	8	13	3	0	0	-1
1985	Hou-N	1.000	2	3	0	0	0	0
1986	Det-A	1.000	1	2	0	0	0	0
	SF-N	—	1	0	0	0	0	0
1987	SF-N	—	1	0	0	0	0	0
1988	SF-N	1.000	2	1	1	0	0	0
1989	SF-N	—	1	0	0	0	0	0
Total	8	1.000	23	33	5	0	0	-2

OF

YEAR	TM/L	PCT	G	PO	A	E	DP	FR
1980	Cin-N	—	2	0	0	0	0	0
1986	SF-N	—	1	0	0	0	0	0
1988	SF-N	1.000	1	1	1	1	0	0
Total	3	.500	4	0	1	1	0	0

2B

YEAR	TM/L	PCT	G	PO	A	E	DP	FR
1986	SF-N	1.000	1	1	1	0	0	0

■ Al Spohrer C

YEAR	TM/L	PCT	G	PO	A	E	DP	FR
1928	NY-N	1.000	2	2	0	0	0	0
	Bos-N	.976	48	102	22	3	1	-5
	Yr	.977	50	104	22	3	1	-5
1929	Bos-N	.954	109	314	57	18	5	-9
1930	Bos-N	.957	108	322	36	16	4	-17
1931	Bos-N	.982	111	392	54	8	5	-1
1932	Bos-N	.973	100	374	62	4	2	10
1933	Bos-N	.972	65	150	26	5	4	-6
1934	Bos-N	.977	98	296	45	8	5	4
1935	Bos-N	.958	90	230	45	12	4	-11
Total	8	.972	731	2182	347	4	30	-39

Freddy Spurgeon 2B

YEAR	TM/L	PCT	G	PO	A	E	DP	FR
1924	Cle-A	.882	3	5	10	2	0	1
1925	Cle-A	.970	46	101	127	7	17	-5
1926	Cle-A	.962	149	341	479	32	93	-8
1927	Cle-A	.938	52	124	150	18	28	-8
Total	4	.958	250	571	766	9	138	-20
				3B				
1925	Cle-A	.927	56	54	123	14	13	2
				SS				
1925	Cle-A	.750	3	3	9	4	1	-1

Mike Squires 1B

YEAR	TM/L	PCT	G	PO	A	E	DP	FR
1975	Chi-A	.988	20	155	12	2	14	0
1977	Chi-A	1.000	1	8	1	0	0	0
1978	Chi-A	.997	45	361	20	1	29	-2
1979	Chi-A	.995	110	741	60	4	62	4
1980	Chi-A	.995	114	904	68	5	79	4
1981	Chi-A	.992	88	729	58	6	68	1
1982	Chi-A	.995	109	512	48	3	59	7
1983	Chi-A	.996	124	515	40	2	55	6
1984	Chi-A	1.000	77	226	16	0	29	2
Total	9	.995	688	4151	323	3	395	22
				3B				
1983	Chi-A	—	1	0	0	0	0	0
1984	Chi-A	1.000	13	3	9	0	0	1
Total	2	1.000	14	3	9	0	0	1
				OF				
1979	Chi-A	1.000	1	3	0	0	0	0
1981	Chi-A	—	1	0	0	0	0	0
1984	Chi-A	1.000	3	5	0	0	0	0
Total	3	1.000	5	8	0	0	0	0
				C				
1980	Chi-A	1.000	2	1	0	0	0	0

Marv Staehle 2B

YEAR	TM/L	PCT	G	PO	A	E	DP	FR
1966	Chi-A	1.000	6	9	14	0	5	1
1967	Chi-A	1.000	17	27	32	0	3	1
1969	Mon-N	.944	4	6	11	1	2	-1
1970	Mon-N	.963	91	152	208	14	53	-12
1971	Atl-N	1.000	7	21	25	0	5	3
Total	5	.971	125	215	290	5	68	-8
				SS				
1967	Chi-A	1.000	5	2	3	0	1	0
1970	Mon-N	1.000	1	1	2	0	0	0
Total	2	1.000	6	3	5	0	1	0
				3B				
1971	Atl-N	1.000	1	0	3	0	0	1

General Stafford OF

YEAR	TM/L	PCT	G	PO	A	E	DP	FR
1890	Buf-P	.714	4	5	0	2	0	-1
1893	NY-N	.901	67	129	8	15	4	-7
1894	NY-N	.778	5	7	0	2	0	-1
1895	NY-N	.846	12	20	2	4	0	-1
1896	NY-N	.897	53	78	9	10	2	-4
1897	NY-N	1.000	5	4	0	0	0	-1
	Lou-N	1.000	7	15	0	0	0	0
	Yr	1.000	12	19	0	0	0	-1
1898	Lou-N	.949	22	33	4	2	3	0
	Bos-N	.909	35	59	1	6	0	-4
	Yr	.924	57	92	5	8	3	-4
1899	Bos-N	.956	41	86	0	4	0	-5
Total	8	.911	251	436	24	5	9	-24
				2B				
1894	NY-N	1.000	1	3	1	0	0	0
1895	NY-N	.911	109	242	329	56	44	-8
1898	Lou-N	.901	28	58	78	15	6	-9
1899	Bos-N	.840	5	8	13	4	3	-1
	Was-N	.951	17	27	31	3	2	-5
	Yr	.919	22	35	44	7	5	-6
Total	4	.910	160	338	452	8	55	-23
				SS				
1896	NY-N	.941	6	15	17	2	3	0
1897	NY-N	.615	2	4	4	5	1	-2
	Lou-N	.887	103	197	353	70	33	-12
	Yr	.882	105	201	357	75	34	-14
1899	Bos-N	.826	5	9	10	4	0	-2
	Was-N	.848	13	35	43	14	8	0
	Yr	.843	18	44	53	18	8	-2
Total	3	.879	129	260	427	5	45	-16
				3B				
1894	NY-N	.750	6	8	10	6	1	-2
1895	NY-N	.889	2	3	5	1	0	0
1897	Lou-N	1.000	1	2	3	0	0	0
1898	Lou-N	1.000	1	1	4	0	0	1
1899	Was-N	.800	2	3	1	1	0	-1
Total	5	.833	12	17	23	8	1	-2
				1B				
1894	NY-N	.917	1	11	0	1	2	0
1898	Bos-N	1.000	1	11	1	0	0	0
Total	2	.958	2	22	1	1	2	0

Steve Staggs 2B

YEAR	TM/L	PCT	G	PO	A	E	DP	FR
1977	Tor-A	.965	72	169	194	13	35	-14
1978	Oak-A	.976	40	56	65	3	10	-3
Total	2	.968	112	225	259	6	45	-17
				SS				
1978	Oak-A	1.000	2	2	1	0	0	0
				3B				
1978	Oak-A	1.000	2	1	2	0	0	0

Chick Stahl OF

YEAR	TM/L	PCT	G	PO	A	E	DP	FR
1897	Bos-N	.928	111	164	17	14	4	-3
1898	Bos-N	.968	125	199	14	7	4	-1
1899	Bos-N	.969	148	253	26	9	6	6
1900	Bos-N	.968	135	277	22	10	4	9
1901	Bos-A	.957	131	277	12	13	3	-1
1902	Bos-A	.953	125	244	19	13	2	-4
1903	Bos-A	.961	74	135	11	6	2	-2
1904	Bos-A	.961	157	293	6	12	0	-14
1905	Bos-A	.977	134	249	11	6	4	-5
1906	Bos-A	.961	155	344	24	15	9	10
Total	10	.961	1295	2435	162	105	38	-5

Jake Stahl 1B

YEAR	TM/L	PCT	G	PO	A	E	DP	FR
1904	Was-A	.978	119	1202	85	29	52	3
1905	Was-A	.986	140	1343	94	21	51	2
1906	Was-A	.983	136	1322	78	24	51	2
1908	NY-A	.986	6	67	3	1	0	0
	Bos-A	.984	78	830	43	14	34	-2
	Yr	.984	84	897	46	15	34	-2
1909	Bos-A	.986	126	1353	50	20	57	-11
1910	Bos-A	.985	142	1488	60	23	46	-7
1912	Bos-A	.980	92	853	49	18	37	-2
Total	7	.983	839	8458	462	150	328	-19
				OF				
1903	Bos-A	1.000	1	1	0	0	0	0
1904	Was-A	.938	23	57	4	4	1	3
1908	NY-A	.933	68	111	14	9	3	4
Total	3	.935	92	169	18	3	4	7
				C				
1903	Bos-A	.956	28	104	27	6	0	-1

Larry Stahl OF

YEAR	TM/L	PCT	G	PO	A	E	DP	FR
1964	KC-A	.955	10	20	1	1	1	0
1965	KC-A	1.000	21	47	1	0	0	2
1966	KC-A	.980	94	142	6	3	1	-1
1967	NY-N	.969	43	90	4	3	0	6
1968	NY-N	.983	47	110	5	2	1	6
1969	SD-N	.981	37	48	3	1	0	1
1970	SD-N	1.000	20	16	1	0	0	0
1971	SD-N	.987	75	141	11	2	4	6
1972	SD-N	.986	76	139	4	2	1	-2
1973	Cin-N	1.000	29	27	3	0	2	-1
Total	10	.983	452	780	39	4	10	17
				1B				
1968	NY-N	1.000	9	45	3	0	3	0
1969	SD-N	.990	13	88	13	1	8	3
1971	SD-N	1.000	7	60	1	0	3	-1
1972	SD-N	1.000	1	2	0	0	0	0
1973	Cin-N	1.000	2	17	0	0	1	-1
Total	5	.996	32	212	17	1	15	1

Roy Staiger 3B

YEAR	TM/L	PCT	G	PO	A	E	DP	FR
1975	NY-N	1.000	13	5	11	0	0	1
1976	NY-N	.967	93	55	209	9	18	20
1977	NY-N	.934	36	23	76	7	4	6
1979	NY-A	1.000	4	2	7	0	1	0
Total	4	.960	146	85	303	6	23	27
				SS				
1976	NY-N	—	1	0	0	0	0	0
1977	NY-N	—	1	0	0	0	0	0
Total	2	—	2	0	0	0	0	0

Tuck Stainback OF

YEAR	TM/L	PCT	G	PO	A	E	DP	FR
1934	Chi-N	.955	96	185	4	9	1	-4
1935	Chi-N	.932	28	40	1	3	0	-1
1936	Chi-N	1.000	26	38	1	0	0	1
1937	Chi-N	.901	49	99	4	2	1	5
1938	StL-N	1.000	2	8	0	0	0	1
	Phi-N	.980	25	47	1	1	0	1
	Bro-N	.981	23	52	1	1	0	0
	Yr	.982	50	107	2	2	0	2
1939	Bro-N	.938	55	121	0	8	0	-1
1940	Det-A	.968	9	26	4	1	0	4
1941	Det-A	.948	80	107	3	6	0	1
1942	NY-A	1.000	3	6	0	0	0	1
1943	NY-A	.993	61	141	3	1	2	3
1944	NY-A	.957	24	44	1	2	0	0
1945	NY-A	.968	83	233	10	8	6	6
1946	Phi-A	.963	66	153	5	6	1	1
Total	13	.965	630	1300	38	8	11	18
				3B				
1934	Chi-N	1.000	1	1	1	0	0	0

Virgil Stallcup SS

YEAR	TM/L	PCT	G	PO	A	E	DP	FR
1947	Cin-N	—	1	0	0	0	0	0
1948	Cin-N	.956	148	264	433	32	84	0
1949	Cin-N	.962	141	256	437	27	87	-10
1950	Cin-N	.973	136	253	389	18	79	-5
1951	Cin-N	.969	117	190	333	17	61	-8
1952	Cin-N	—	1	0	0	0	0	0
	StL-N	1.000	12	5	16	0	4	2
	Yr	1.000	13	5	16	0	4	2
Total	6	.965	556	968	1608	4	315	-21

Oscar Stanage C

YEAR	TM/L	PCT	G	PO	A	E	DP	FR
1906	Cin-N	1.000	1	1	0	0	0	0
1909	Det-A	.964	77	324	80	15	12	-9
1910	Det-A	.952	84	344	148	25	6	-3
1911	Det-A	.952	141	599	212	41	13	-15
1912	Det-A	.950	120	440	168	32	14	-27
1913	Det-A	.960	77	277	106	16	6	-9
1914	Det-A	.960	122	532	190	30	11	-6
1915	Det-A	.964	100	395	111	19	0	-9
1916	Det-A	.969	94	392	110	16	11	-9
1917	Det-A	.977	95	385	88	11	13	-4
1918	Det-A	.980	47	188	54	5	9	-7
1919	Det-A	.974	36	149	39	5	8	1
1920	Det-A	.958	77	248	75	14	4	-9
1925	Det-A	1.000	3	2	0	0	0	-1
Total	14	.961	1074	4276	1381	229	107	107
				1B				
1918	Det-A	.923	5	46	2	4	1	-1
1919	Det-A	1.000	1	1	0	0	0	0
Total	2	.925	6	47	2	4	1	-1
				SS				
1918	Det-A	—	1	0	0	0	0	0

Eddie Stanky 2B

YEAR	TM/L	PCT	G	PO	A	E	DP	FR
1943	Chi-N	.966	131	362	416	27	78	15
1944	Chi-N	.875	3	4	3	1	3	0
	Bro-N	.961	58	132	138	11	28	-9
	Yr	.958	61	136	141	12	31	-9
1945	Bro-N	.962	153	429	441	34	101	9
1946	Bro-N	.977	141	356	359	17	88	-5
1947	Bro-N	.985	146	402	406	12	123	6
1948	Bos-N	.981	66	168	202	7	45	5
1949	Bos-N	.979	135	357	354	15	92	-9
1950	NY-N	.976	151	407	418	20	128	2
1951	NY-N	.977	140	356	412	18	117	-1
1952	StL-N	1.000	20	41	44	0	9	-1
1953	StL-N	1.000	8	16	22	0	4	1
Total	11	.975	1152	3030	3215	162	816	13
				SS				
1943	Chi-N	.947	12	16	20	2	7	-2
1944	Chi-N	1.000	3	1	1	0	0	0
	Bro-N	.952	35	67	71	7	5	-9
	Yr	.952	38	68	72	7	5	-9
1945	Bro-N	—	1	0	0	0	0	0
Total	3	.951	51	84	92	9	12	-11
				3B				
1943	Chi-N	.750	2	1	5	2	0	-1
1944	Chi-N	.875	3	3	11	2	1	2
	Bro-N	—	1	0	0	0	0	0
	Yr	.875	4	3	11	2	1	2
Total	2	.833	6	4	16	4	1	1

Fred Stanley SS

YEAR	TM/L	PCT	G	PO	A	E	DP	FR
1969	Sea-A	.962	15	22	28	2	8	-4
1971	Cle-A	.971	55	60	143	6	28	6
1972	Cle-A	.917	5	5	6	1	0	-3
	SD-N	.967	17	16	13	1	3	-1
1973	NY-A	.981	21	39	66	2	11	2
1974	NY-A	.973	19	9	27	1	4	5
1975	NY-A	.977	83	105	189	7	36	-2
1976	NY-A	.983	110	145	251	7	36	-23
1977	NY-A	.958	42	30	38	3	5	1
1978	NY-A	.959	71	81	131	9	22	-6
1979	NY-A	.978	31	23	68	2	18	9
1980	NY-A	.923	19	16	44	5	9	3
1981	Oak-A	.986	62	94	118	3	25	-16
1982	Oak-A	.963	98	112	223	13	42	-21
Total	13	.971	648	757	1345	2	247	-50
				2B				
1969	Sea-A	1.000	1	0	1	0	0	0
1970	Mil-A	1.000	2	1	1	0	0	2
1971	Cle-A	1.000	3	1	2	0	1	0
1972	Cle-A	1.000	1	0	1	0	0	0
	SD-N	.989	21	45	47	1	13	4
1973	NY-A	1.000	3	3	6	0	0	1
1974	NY-A	.982	15	23	32	0	10	7
1975	NY-A	.982	33	54	54	2	17	4
1976	NY-A	.800	3	3	1	1	0	-1
1977	NY-A	1.000	2	4	5	0	2	1
1978	NY-A	1.000	11	7	19	0	4	2
1979	NY-A	.960	8	9	15	1	3	3
1980	NY-A	.980	17	21	27	1	8	3
1981	Oak-A	1.000	6	2	0	0	0	0
1982	Oak-A	1.000	2	4	3	0	1	0
Total	14	.985	128	177	216	6	59	26
				3B				
1972	SD-N	1.000	4	2	8	0	0	0
1975	NY-A	1.000	1	2	6	0	0	2
1977	NY-A	1.000	3	2	5	0	0	1
1978	NY-A	1.000	4	0	2	0	0	0
1979	NY-A	.875	16	5	30	5	2	2
1980	NY-A	.944	12	2	15	1	1	1
Total	6	.929	40	13	66	6	3	6
				1B				
1979	NY-A	1.000	1	5	0	0	0	0
				OF				
1979	NY-A	—	1	0	0	0	0	0

Joe Stanley OF

YEAR	TM/L	PCT	G	PO	A	E	DP	FR
1902	Was-A	.833	3	5	0	1	0	-1
1903	Bos-N	.902	77	117	21	15	2	5
1904	Bos-N	.800	3	2	2	1	0	1
1905	Was-A	.944	27	47	4	3	0	0
1906	Was-A	.934	63	78	7	6	0	-5
1909	Chi-N	.947	16	17	1	1	0	-4
Total	6	.918	189	266	35	7	2	-4
				SS				
1903	Bos-N	.500	1	2	2	4	0	-1

Mickey Stanley OF

YEAR	TM/L	PCT	G	PO	A	E	DP	FR
1964	Det-A	1.000	4	5	0	0	0	0
1965	Det-A	.986	29	69	1	1	0	2
1966	Det-A	1.000	82	163	6	0	1	12
1967	Det-A	.982	128	216	3	4	2	-2
1968	Det-A	1.000	130	297	7	0	2	0
1969	Det-A	.985	101	190	2	3	0	0
1970	Det-A	1.000	132	317	3	0	0	3
1971	Det-A	.988	139	315	10	4	3	4
1972	Det-A	.994	139	309	9	2	1	1
1973	Det-A	.993	157	420	10	3	3	10
1974	Det-A	.992	91	252	4	2	2	3
1975	Det-A	.983	28	58	1	1	0	1
1976	Det-A	.969	38	60	2	2	0	-3
1977	Det-A	.972	57	101	2	3	0	-1
1978	Det-A	.960	34	47	1	2	0	-4
Total	15	.991	1289	2819	61	7	14	26
				1B				
1967	Det-A	1.000	8	48	4	0	3	1
1968	Det-A	.982	15	99	8	2	9	0
1969	Det-A	1.000	4	42	1	0	2	-1
1970	Det-A	.986	9	67	6	1	10	0
1974	Det-A	.980	12	89	10	2	9	1
1975	Det-A	1.000	14	119	7	0	8	0

YEAR	TM/L	PCT	G	PO	A	E	DP	FR
1976	Det-A	.992	17	117	9	1	10	0
1977	Det-A	1.000	3	26	0	0	3	0
1978	Det-A	1.000	12	126	8	0	8	0
Total	9	.992	94	733	53	6	62	1
		SS						
1968	Det-A	.944	9	9	25	2	2	-1
1969	Det-A	.972	59	110	135	7	22	-14
1976	Det-A	1.000	3	0	2	0	0	0
1977	Det-A	.800	3	1	3	1	0	0
Total	4	.966	74	120	165	0	24	-15
		3B						
1975	Det-A	.952	7	6	14	1	1	2
1976	Det-A	.975	11	7	32	1	3	3
Total	2	.967	18	13	46	2	4	5
		2B						
1968	Det-A	—	1	0	0	0	0	0
1974	Det-A	—	1	0	0	0	0	-1
1976	Det-A	.833	2	3	2	1	1	-1
Total	3	.833	4	3	2	1	1	-2

■ **Mike Stanley C**

YEAR	TM/L	PCT	G	PO	A	E	DP	FR
1986	Tex-A	1.000	4	14	2	0	1	0
1987	Tex-A	.980	61	330	17	7	1	-10
1988	Tex-A	.991	64	310	14	3	3	0
1989	Tex-A	.978	25	82	6	2	1	-3
1990	Tex-A	.985	63	244	20	4	0	-2
Total	5	.985	217	980	59	6	6	-15
		1B						
1987	Tex-A	1.000	12	58	9	0	6	2
1988	Tex-A	.970	6	30	2	1	2	0
1989	Tex-A	.973	7	35	1	1	2	-1
1990	Tex-A	1.000	6	14	1	0	2	0
Total	4	.987	31	137	13	2	12	1
		3B						
1986	Tex-A	.857	7	0	6	1	1	0
1988	Tex-A	.667	2	2	0	1	0	-1
1989	Tex-A	1.000	3	0	1	0	0	0
1990	Tex-A	1.000	8	3	4	0	0	0
Total	4	.889	20	5	11	2	1	-1
		OF						
1986	Tex-A	—	1	0	0	0	0	0
1987	Tex-A	1.000	1	1	0	0	0	0
Total	2	1.000	2	1	0	0	0	0

■ **Leroy Stanton OF**

YEAR	TM/L	PCT	G	PO	A	E	DP	FR
1970	NY-N	1.000	1	1	0	0	0	0
1971	NY-N	1.000	5	9	0	0	0	-1
1972	Cal-A	.983	124	225	6	4	2	1
1973	Cal-A	.965	107	160	5	6	2	-9
1974	Cal-A	.975	114	226	11	6	0	4
1975	Cal-A	.961	131	230	16	10	2	0
1976	Cal-A	.985	79	128	1	2	0	-4
1977	Sea-A	.953	91	175	9	9	2	1
1978	Sea-A	1.000	30	59	1	0	0	-1
Total	9	.972	682	1213	49	7	8	-9

■ **Dave Stapleton 1B**

YEAR	TM/L	PCT	G	PO	A	E	DP	FR
1980	Bos-A	.989	8	84	9	1	11	1
1981	Bos-A	.992	12	126	4	1	10	-2
1982	Bos-A	.991	106	964	77	9	98	3
1983	Bos-A	.993	145	1242	95	9	129	-1
1984	Bos-A	1.000	10	86	8	0	5	1
1985	Bos-A	.929	8	12	1	1	3	0
1986	Bos-A	1.000	29	79	7	0	10	1
Total	7	.993	318	2593	201	1	266	3
		2B						
1980	Bos-A	.979	94	178	327	11	90	10
1981	Bos-A	.967	23	61	58	4	19	1
1982	Bos-A	.980	9	28	22	1	3	-1
1983	Bos-A	.944	5	7	10	1	3	-1
1985	Bos-A	1.000	14	29	35	0	8	2
1986	Bos-A	1.000	6	6	7	0	3	2
Total	6	.978	151	309	459	7	126	13
		SS						
1981	Bos-A	.948	33	52	93	8	18	-7
1982	Bos-A	.973	27	35	73	3	14	0
Total	2	.958	60	87	166	1	32	-7
		3B						
1980	Bos-A	1.000	2	1	2	0	0	0
1981	Bos-A	.946	25	21	49	4	3	1
1982	Bos-A	1.000	5	5	7	0	1	0
1986	Bos-A	1.000	2	0	2	0	0	0
Total	4	.956	34	27	60	4	4	1
		OF						
1980	Bos-A	1.000	6	6	0	0	0	0
1982	Bos-A	—	1	0	0	0	0	0
Total	2	1.000	7	6	0	0	0	0

■ **Willie Stargell OF**

YEAR	TM/L	PCT	G	PO	A	E	DP	FR
1962	Pit-N	.929	9	12	1	1	0	-1
1963	Pit-N	.953	65	78	3	4	0	-9
1964	Pit-N	.900	59	79	2	9	0	-6
1965	Pit-N	.965	137	208	12	8	3	-5
1966	Pit-N	.945	127	180	9	11	0	-8
1967	Pit-N	.938	98	140	12	10	1	-4
1968	Pit-N	.945	113	144	12	9	0	-10
1969	Pit-N	.970	116	159	4	5	1	-9
1970	Pit-N	.976	125	184	16	5	1	-1
1971	Pit-N	.984	135	237	8	4	4	-5
1972	Pit-N	.962	32	50	1	2	0	-2
1973	Pit-N	.975	142	261	14	7	1	1
1974	Pit-N	.967	135	253	8	9	1	-5
Total	13	.961	1293	1985	102	4	12	-64
		1B						
1963	Pit-N	.969	16	148	9	5	18	-1
1964	Pit-N	.998	50	486	22	1	50	-4
1965	Pit-N	1.000	7	60	2	0	5	-1
1966	Pit-N	1.000	15	120	4	0	17	-2
1967	Pit-N	.997	37	307	15	1	25	-2

YEAR	TM/L	PCT	G	PO	A	E	DP	FR
1968	Pit-N	1.000	13	110	7	0	12	-1
1969	Pit-N	.989	23	174	10	2	20	-2
1970	Pit-N	1.000	1	0	1	0	0	0
1972	Pit-N	.984	101	881	40	15	96	-10
1974	Pit-N	1.000	1	3	0	0	0	0
1975	Pit-N	.992	122	1121	54	10	112	-10
1976	Pit-N	.988	111	1037	53	13	76	-10
1977	Pit-N	.986	55	449	27	7	26	-1
1978	Pit-N	.994	112	875	57	6	76	-2
1979	Pit-N	.997	113	949	47	3	102	-6
1980	Pit-N	.992	54	460	33	4	54	0
1981	Pit-N	1.000	9	70	0	0	10	-2
1982	Pit-N	1.000	8	43	3	0	2	0
Total	18	.991	848	7293	384	7	701	-54

■ **Joe Start 1B**

YEAR	TM/L	PCT	G	PO	A	E	DP	FR
1876	NY-N	.964	56	547	10	21	11	3
1877	Har-N	.964	60	704	10	27	25	-2
1878	Chi-N	.957	61	719	13	33	28	-2
1879	Pro-N	.973	65	779	11	22	24	0
1880	Pro-N	.971	82	954	10	29	30	-3
1881	Pro-N	.963	79	837	17	33	50	-4
1882	Pro-N	.974	82	905	21	25	54	2
1883	Pro-N	.957	87	923	29	43	48	-1
1884	Pro-N	.980	93	939	21	20	31	1
1885	Pro-N	.972	101	1036	35	31	42	1
1886	Was-N	.973	31	348	7	10	16	-2
Total	11	.968	797	8691	184	294	359	-7
		OF						
1879	Pro-N	—	1	0	0	0	0	0

■ **Jigger Statz OF**

YEAR	TM/L	PCT	G	PO	A	E	DP	FR
1919	NY-N	.977	18	43	0	1	0	1
1920	NY-N	.944	12	16	1	1	1	0
	Bos-N	1.000	2	1	0	0	0	-1
1922	Chi-N	.959	110	309	16	14	4	6
1923	Chi-N	.975	154	438	26	12	7	13
1924	Chi-N	.961	131	373	22	16	5	13
1925	Chi-N	.943	37	112	3	7	0	3
1927	Bro-N	.990	122	371	14	4	5	11
1928	Bro-N	.965	52	107	3	4	2	3
Total	8	.969	638	1770	85	9	24	49
		2B						
1919	NY-N	1.000	5	2	0	0	0	0
1924	Chi-N	.727	1	4	4	3	0	-1
1927	Bro-N	1.000	1	0	1	0	0	0
1928	Bro-N	1.000	1	1	0	0	0	0
Total	4	.800	8	7	5	3	0	-1

■ **Rusty Staub OF**

YEAR	TM/L	PCT	G	PO	A	E	DP	FR
1963	Hou-N	.989	49	82	5	1	0	3
1964	Hou-N	.936	38	70	3	5	0	0
1965	Hou-N	.951	112	202	12	11	1	4
1966	Hou-N	.962	148	289	13	12	2	11
1967	Hou-N	.962	144	269	10	11	2	6
1968	Hou-N	.923	15	23	1	2	0	-1
1969	Mon-N	.966	156	265	16	10	2	5
1970	Mon-N	.985	160	308	14	5	4	8
1971	Mon-N	.945	162	290	20	18	5	2
1972	NY-N	.982	65	108	4	2	2	-4
1973	NY-N	.978	152	297	17	7	5	9
1974	NY-N	.983	147	262	19	5	5	5
1975	NY-N	.986	153	267	15	4	3	2
1976	Det-A	.970	126	218	8	7	3	-10
1979	Mon-N	1.000	1	1	0	0	0	0
1980	Tex-A	1.000	14	19	4	0	1	2
1982	NY-N	.959	27	43	4	2	0	-1
1983	NY-N	.800	5	4	0	1	0	-1
1985	NY-N	1.000	1	1	0	0	0	0
Total	19	.969	1675	3018	165	103	35	40
		1B						
1963	Hou-N	.989	109	881	58	10	52	-3
1964	Hou-N	.992	49	442	27	4	34	-1
1965	Hou-N	1.000	1	1	0	0	0	0
1966	Hou-N	1.000	2	2	0	0	1	1
1968	Hou-N	.992	147	1313	93	11	100	0
1979	Mon-N	.994	22	155	7	1	11	-2
1980	Tex-A	.977	30	243	10	6	27	-4
1981	NY-N	.989	41	339	20	4	26	-2
1982	NY-N	.976	18	129	15	0	12	1
1983	NY-N	.976	5	36	5	1	6	0
1984	NY-N	1.000	3	13	0	0	2	0
Total	11	.990	426	3554	237	7	271	-10

■ **Ecky Stearns 1B**

YEAR	TM/L	PCT	G	PO	A	E	DP	FR
1882	Cin-a	.931	35	305	5	23	16	-3
1883	Bal-a	.947	92	984	38	57	38	3
1884	Bal-a	.949	100	959	48	54	36	4
1885	Bal-a	.973	63	605	19	17	35	2
	Buf-N	.941	12	93	3	6	3	-1
Total	5	.956	437	4344	169	206	203	6
		OF						
1880	Buf-N	.774	20	21	3	7	1	-3
1882	Cin-a	.824	12	23	5	6	0	2
1883	Bal-a	.500	1	1	0	1	0	0
1885	Bal-a	1.000	3	3	0	0	0	-1
Total	4	.800	36	48	8	4	1	-2
		SS						
1880	Buf-N	.750	1	0	3	1	1	0
1881	Det-N	.714	3	1	9	4	1	-1
1882	Cin-a	1.000	1	2	4	0	0	0
1885	Buf-N	.821	19	32	46	17	4	-6
Total	4	.815	24	35	62	2	6	-7
		C						
1880	Buf-N	.800	8	16	12	7	1	-2
1885	Bal-a	.889	2	7	1	1	0	0
	Buf-N	.909	2	6	4	1	0	1
Total	2	.836	12	29	17	9	1	-1

YEAR	TM/L	PCT	G	PO	A	E	DP	FR
		3B						
1880	Buf-N	.615	5	2	6	5	0	-2
1889	KC-a	.667	4	2	4	3	0	-1
Total	2	.636	9	4	10	8	0	-3
		2B						
1882	Cin-a	.900	2	7	2	1	0	-2
1884	Bal-a	—	1	0	0	0	0	0
Total	2	.900	3	7	2	1	0	-2

■ **John Stearns C**

YEAR	TM/L	PCT	G	PO	A	E	DP	FR
1974	Phi-N	1.000	1	1	0	0	0	-1
1975	NY-N	.994	54	297	40	2	9	6
1976	NY-N	.987	30	200	20	3	2	3
1977	NY-N	.982	127	742	76	15	12	4
1978	NY-N	.985	141	711	84	12	7	-3
1979	NY-N	.983	121	628	85	12	11	6
1980	NY-N	.985	74	432	41	7	6	0
1981	NY-N	.983	66	302	38	6	7	-4
1982	NY-N	.987	81	379	61	6	9	-4
1984	NY-N	1.000	4	20	1	0	1	-1
Total	10	.985	699	3712	446	3	64	6
		1B						
1977	NY-N	.943	6	30	3	2	3	0
1979	NY-N	1.000	16	114	8	0	16	0
1980	NY-N	.993	16	120	18	1	10	4
1981	NY-N	1.000	9	58	8	0	4	1
1984	NY-N	1.000	2	8	1	0	3	0
Total	5	.992	49	330	38	3	36	5
		3B						
1978	NY-N	—	1	0	0	0	0	0
1979	NY-N	.905	11	5	14	2	2	-1
1980	NY-N	1.000	1	0	3	0	1	0
1981	NY-N	.857	4	0	6	1	0	0
1982	NY-N	.818	12	5	13	4	0	-3
Total	5	.868	29	10	36	7	3	-4
		OF						
1979	NY-N	.778	6	7	0	2	0	-1

■ **Dave Stegman OF**

YEAR	TM/L	PCT	G	PO	A	E	DP	FR
1978	Det-A	1.000	7	11	0	0	0	0
1979	Det-A	1.000	12	35	0	0	0	3
1980	Det-A	.988	57	82	1	1	0	0
1983	Chi-A	1.000	29	31	1	0	0	-1
1984	Chi-A	.985	46	65	1	1	0	4
Total	5	.991	151	224	3	2	0	6

■ **Bill Stein 3B**

YEAR	TM/L	PCT	G	PO	A	E	DP	FR
1972	StL-N	1.000	4	1	4	0	0	-2
1973	StL-N	1.000	1	0	1	0	0	0
1974	Chi-A	.871	11	7	20	4	0	-2
1975	Chi-A	.917	24	16	39	5	5	1
1976	Chi-A	.943	58	35	98	8	5	-3
1977	Sea-A	.964	147	146	255	15	20	-11
1978	Sea-A	.929	111	72	244	24	21	-6
1979	Sea-A	.959	67	45	120	7	13	6
1980	Sea-A	.972	34	31	75	3	4	4
1981	Tex-A	.941	7	4	12	1	0	1
1982	Tex-A	.986	28	13	55	1	5	6
1983	Tex-A	.943	10	5	28	2	3	2
1984	Tex-A	—	3	0	0	0	0	0
1985	Tex-A	.952	11	5	15	1	1	2
Total	14	.950	516	380	966	1	77	-2
		2B						
1975	Chi-A	.974	28	71	79	4	16	3
1976	Chi-A	.960	58	118	143	11	34	-8
1979	Sea-A	1.000	17	18	42	0	7	5
1980	Sea-A	.986	14	37	36	1	13	4
1981	Tex-A	1.000	3	2	3	0	1	1
1982	Tex-A	.957	34	46	65	5	21	-4
1983	Tex-A	.975	32	56	62	3	20	-2
1984	Tex-A	.967	11	12	17	1	3	-2
1985	Tex-A	1.000	3	2	2	0	1	1
Total	9	.970	200	362	449	5	116	-2
		1B						
1973	StL-N	1.000	1	21	0	0	1	-1
1976	Chi-A	1.000	1	3	0	0	0	0
1980	Sea-A	1.000	8	51	4	0	4	0
1981	Tex-A	1.000	20	146	10	0	9	0
1982	Tex-A	1.000	2	7	0	0	0	0
1983	Tex-A	1.000	23	161	13	0	17	1
1984	Tex-A	1.000	3	4	0	0	1	0
1985	Tex-A	.977	8	40	3	1	2	0
Total	8	.998	67	433	30	1	35	0
		OF						
1972	StL-N	1.000	4	4	0	0	0	-1
1973	StL-N	1.000	10	16	0	0	0	0
1975	Chi-A	—	1	0	0	0	0	0
1976	Chi-A	1.000	1	3	0	0	0	0
1981	Tex-A	.933	8	13	1	1	0	0
1982	Tex-A	1.000	1	5	0	0	0	0
1985	Tex-A	1.000	3	5	0	0	0	0
Total	7	.979	28	46	1	1	0	-2
		SS						
1976	Chi-A	1.000	1	2	2	0	0	0
1977	Sea-A	—	2	0	0	0	0	0
1979	Sea-A	1.000	3	1	0	0	0	0
1981	Tex-A	1.000	1	1	0	0	0	0
1982	Tex-A	1.000	6	1	0	0	0	0
Total	5	1.000	13	5	4	0	1	0

■ **Terry Steinbach C**

YEAR	TM/L	PCT	G	PO	A	E	DP	FR
1986	Oak-A	.962	5	21	4	1	1	0
1987	Oak-A	.986	107	640	40	10	6	-12
1988	Oak-A	.983	84	484	48	9	5	5
1989	Oak-A	.985	103	529	43	9	6	-5
1990	Oak-A	.988	83	396	31	5	1	-9
Total	5	.985	382	2070	166	4	19	-15
		3B						
1987	Oak-A	1.000	10	1	4	0	0	0

YEAR	TM/L	PCT	G	PO	A	E	DP	FR
1988	Oak-A	1.000	9	3	9	0	1	0
1989	Oak-A	1.000	3	2	1	0	1	0
Total	3	1.000	22	6	14	0	2	0
1B								
1987	Oak-A	1.000	1	1	0	0	0	0
1988	Oak-A	1.000	8	48	1	0	4	-1
1989	Oak-A	.983	10	55	3	1	7	-1
1990	Oak-A	1.000	3	5	0	0	0	0
Total	4	.991	22	109	4	1	11	-2
OF								
1988	Oak-A	1.000	1	1	0	0	0	0
1989	Oak-A	.963	14	26	0	1	0	-1
Total	2	.964	15	27	0	1	0	-1

■ Hank Steinbacher OF

YEAR	TM/L	PCT	G	PO	A	E	DP	FR
1937	Chi-A	.960	15	24	0	1	0	-3
1938	Chi-A	.963	101	202	7	8	2	-3
1939	Chi-A	1.000	22	38	1	0	0	-2
Total	3	.968	138	264	8	9	2	-8

■ Harry Steinfeldt 3B

YEAR	TM/L	PCT	G	PO	A	E	DP	FR
1898	Cin-N	.867	22	36	49	13	3	1
1899	Cin-N	.885	59	87	128	28	4	-2
1900	Cin-N	.922	67	107	175	24	11	10
1901	Cin-N	.886	55	60	127	24	5	5
1902	Cin-N	.912	129	190	315	**49**	**29**	**21**
1903	Cin-N	.937	104	159	212	25	11	5
1904	Cin-N	.887	98	153	168	41	13	-7
1905	Chi-N	.919	103	152	221	33	16	**14**
1906	Chi-N	**.954**	**150**	160	253	20	13	-17
1907	Chi-N	**.967**	151	161	307	16	18	-6
1908	Chi-N	.940	150	166	275	28	15	-12
1909	Chi-N	.940	151	183	299	31	16	10
1910	Chi-N	**.946**	128	137	246	22	16	0
1911	Bos-N	.810	19	23	24	11	2	-5
Total	14	.926	1386	1774	2799	365	172	17
2B								
1898	Cin-N	.917	31	68	87	14	11	-1
1899	Cin-N	.939	40	88	111	13	13	-3
1900	Cin-N	.945	64	197	217	24	41	25
1901	Cin-N	.940	50	138	142	18	23	5
1905	Cin-N	1.000	1	0	2	0	0	0
1906	Cin-N	1.000	1	0	1	0	0	0
Total	6	.938	187	491	560	9	88	26
OF								
1898	Cin-N	.896	29	64	5	8	0	0
1899	Cin-N	1.000	2	3	0	0	0	0
1900	Cin-N	1.000	2	1	0	0	0	1
1902	Cin-N	.667	1	1	1	1	1	1
1905	Cin-N	1.000	1	1	0	0	0	0
Total	5	.894	35	70	6	9	1	0
SS								
1898	Cin-N	.815	5	7	15	5	1	0
1899	Cin-N	.895	8	11	23	4	2	-1
1900	Cin-N	1.000	2	4	11	0	0	2
1903	Cin-N	.901	14	42	49	10	1	2
Total	4	.805	29	64	98	9	4	3
1B								
1898	Cin-N	.967	4	27	2	1	2	0
1905	Cin-N	1.000	1	1	0	0	0	0
Total	2	.968	5	28	2	1	2	0

■ Casey Stengel OF

YEAR	TM/L	PCT	G	PO	A	E	DP	FR
1912	Bro-N	.902	17	36	1	4	0	-2
1913	Bro-N	.960	119	270	16	12	1	-2
1914	Bro-N	.964	121	173	15	7	3	-11
1915	Bro-N	.959	129	220	13	10	2	-6
1916	Bro-N	.965	121	206	14	8	4	-5
1917	Bro-N	.969	150	256	**30**	9	**9**	5
1918	Pit-N	.973	37	64	7	2	3	2
1919	Pit-N	.957	87	195	7	9	3	1
1920	Phi-N	.954	118	212	16	11	1	-3
1921	Phi-N	.969	15	26	5	1	2	0
	NY-N	.875	8	7	0	1	0	0
	Yr	.950	23	33	5	2	2	2
1922	NY-N	.969	77	179	7	6	2	-6
1923	NY-N	.983	57	115	4	2	1	-3
1924	Bos-N	.978	126	211	12	5	4	-9
1925	Bos-N	1.000	1	1	0	0	0	0
Total	14	.964	1183	2171	147	7	35	-37

■ Rennie Stennett 2B

YEAR	TM/L	PCT	G	PO	A	E	DP	FR
1971	Pit-N	.954	36	82	106	9	22	2
1972	Pit-N	.977	49	129	162	7	42	12
1973	Pit-N	.981	84	210	248	9	64	13
1974	Pit-N	.980	154	**441**	475	19	115	13
1975	Pit-N	.979	144	379	463	18	98	13
1976	Pit-N	.981	157	**430**	502	18	111	18
1977	Pit-N	.982	113	269	315	11	70	-7
1978	Pit-N	.971	80	164	208	11	40	-11
1979	Pit-N	.974	102	172	282	12	63	6
1980	SF-N	.973	111	244	293	15	53	-13
1981	SF-N	1.000	19	48	46	0	9	-2
Total	11	.978	1049	2568	3100	129	687	44
SS								
1972	Pit-N	.933	6	5	9	1	2	-1
1973	Pit-N	.971	43	67	100	5	20	-12
1976	Pit-N	.857	4	2	4	1	0	-1
Total	3	.964	53	74	113	7	22	-14
OF								
1972	Pit-N	.970	41	63	2	2	1	-1
1973	Pit-N	1.000	5	4	0	0	0	0
1974	Pit-N	1.000	2	3	0	0	0	0
Total	3	.973	48	70	2	2	1	-1
3B								
1978	Pit-N	.833	6	3	7	2	0	-1

■ Jake Stenzel OF

YEAR	TM/L	PCT	G	PO	A	E	DP	FR
1890	Chi-N	.857	6	6	0	1	0	-1
1892	Pit-N	1.000	2	3	1	0	0	0

YEAR	TM/L	PCT	G	PO	A	E	DP	FR
1893	Pit-N	.905	45	82	4	9	2	-4
1894	Pit-N	.925	131	311	23	27	6	-1
1895	Pit-N	.912	129	257	23	27	6	-5
1896	Pit-N	.922	114	247	13	22	5	-3
1897	Bal-N	.932	131	264	12	20	2	-11
1898	Bal-N	.926	35	57	6	5	1	-2
	StL-N	.943	108	257	8	16	2	0
	Yr	.940	143	314	14	21	3	-2
1899	StL-N	.949	33	71	3	4	1	-1
	Cin-N	1.000	7	14	0	0	0	-1
	Yr	.957	40	85	3	4	1	-2
Total	9	.927	741	1569	93	131	25	-29
C								
1890	Chi-N	.969	6	25	6	1	0	-2
1892	Pit-N	1.000	1	0	1	0	0	0
1893	Pit-N	.757	12	23	5	9	1	-4
Total	3	.857	19	48	12	0	1	-6
SS								
1893	Pit-N	.778	1	2	5	2	0	-1
2B								
1893	Pit-N	1.000	1	2	4	0	0	0
1B								
1896	Pit-N	.750	1	3	0	1	0	0

■ Gene Stephens OF

YEAR	TM/L	PCT	G	PO	A	E	DP	FR
1952	Bos-A	.962	13	24	1	1	0	0
1953	Bos-A	.966	72	113	2	4	0	-7
1955	Bos-A	.947	75	82	7	5	1	3
1956	Bos-A	.983	71	57	2	1	0	8
1957	Bos-A	.987	90	70	4	1	2	-1
1958	Bos-A	.975	110	149	5	4	2	2
1959	Bos-A	.981	85	141	11	3	0	4
1960	Bos-A	.951	31	56	2	3	0	-1
	Bal-A	.992	77	124	5	1	0	5
	Yr	.979	108	180	7	4	0	4
1961	Bal-A	1.000	30	34	2	0	1	1
	KC-A	.968	54	114	6	4	4	4
	Yr	.975	84	148	8	4	5	5
1963	Chi-A	.909	5	8	2	1	0	1
1964	Chi-A	.969	59	91	2	3	1	4
Total	11	.973	772	1063	51	1	11	23

■ Jim Stephens C

YEAR	TM/L	PCT	G	PO	A	E	DP	FR
1907	StL-A	.967	56	200	63	9	4	-3
1908	StL-A	.960	45	193	68	11	4	0
1909	StL-A	.980	72	335	103	9	9	3
1910	StL-A	.971	96	418	**156**	17	**18**	3
1911	StL-A	.949	66	223	94	17	7	-3
1912	StL-A	.954	66	262	110	18	10	3
Total	6	.965	401	1631	594	1	52	3

■ Vern Stephens SS

YEAR	TM/L	PCT	G	PO	A	E	DP	FR
1941	StL-A	.500	1	0	1	1	0	0
1942	StL-A	.944	144	290	415	**42**	82	-10
1943	StL-A	.943	123	220	339	34	51	-26
1944	StL-A	.954	143	239	480	35	71	-4
1945	StL-A	**.961**	144	256	439	28	69	-17
1946	StL-A	.950	112	224	343	30	71	0
1947	StL-A	.970	149	283	**494**	24	113	12
1948	Bos-A	.971	**155**	269	**540**	**24**	113	10
1949	Bos-A	.966	**155**	257	**508**	27	**128**	4
1950	Bos-A	.981	146	258	431	13	115	0
1951	Bos-A	1.000	2	0	2	0	0	0
1952	Bos-A	.957	53	89	154	11	40	1
1953	Chi-A	1.000	1	0	1	0	0	0
Total	13	.960	1330	2385	4150	269	853	-30
3B								
1945	StL-A	.867	4	2	11	2	2	0
1951	Bos-A	.978	89	105	207	7	19	**14**
1952	Bos-A	.949	29	21	73	5	8	3
1953	Chi-A	.990	38	30	67	1	7	-3
	StL-A	.954	46	54	91	7	9	-2
	Yr	.968	84	84	158	8	16	-5
1954	Bal-A	.966	96	102	186	10	19	-6
1955	Bal-A	1.000	2	0	2	0	0	-1
	Chi-A	1.000	18	13	37	0	4	4
	Yr	1.000	20	13	39	0	4	3
Total	6	.969	322	327	674	2	68	9
OF								
1943	StL-A	1.000	11	20	3	0	0	2

■ Riggs Stephenson OF

YEAR	TM/L	PCT	G	PO	A	E	DP	FR
1922	Cle-A	1.000	3	1	0	0	0	-1
1923	Cle-A	—	3	0	0	0	0	-1
1924	Cle-A	1.000	7	12	1	0	0	0
1925	Cle-A	.946	16	33	2	2	1	1
1926	Chi-N	.950	74	126	7	7	0	-8
1927	Chi-N	.975	146	297	18	8	5	-1
1928	Chi-N	.982	135	268	10	5	1	-2
1929	Chi-N	.984	130	245	9	4	4	-6
1930	Chi-N	.958	80	132	5	6	1	-9
1931	Chi-N	.985	66	134	1	2	1	-7
1932	Chi-N	.984	147	298	7	5	2	-10
1933	Chi-N	.985	91	187	5	3	2	-3
1934	Chi-N	1.000	15	26	3	0	1	1
Total	13	.978	913	1759	68	2	18	-46
2B								
1921	Cle-A	.942	54	122	153	17	30	-2
1922	Cle-A	.949	25	44	67	6	6	0
1923	Cle-A	.970	66	205	214	13	49	10
1924	Cle-A	.961	58	114	179	12	20	-13
Total	4	.958	203	485	613	8	105	-5
3B								
1921	Cle-A	1.000	2	0	2	0	2	1
1922	Cle-A	.952	34	31	69	5	5	-4
1923	Cle-A	1.000	2	2	2	0	0	0
1927	Chi-N	.905	6	12	7	2	2	-1
Total	4	.947	44	45	80	7	9	-4

YEAR	TM/L	PCT	G	PO	A	E	DP	FR

■ John Stephenson C

YEAR	TM/L	PCT	G	PO	A	E	DP	FR
1965	NY-N	.981	47	146	13	3	1	-8
1966	NY-N	.973	52	187	30	6	4	-1
1967	Chi-N	1.000	13	67	8	0	2	0
1969	SF-N	.941	9	15	1	1	0	-2
1970	SF-N	1.000	9	52	8	0	1	3
1971	Cal-A	.992	88	434	33	4	3	-8
1972	Cal-A	.993	56	273	12	2	2	-7
1973	Cal-A	.980	56	232	11	5	1	-8
Total	8	.986	330	1406	116	1	14	-31
3B								
1964	NY-N	.800	14	6	18	6	1	-2
1969	SF-N	.000	1	0	0	2	0	-1
Total	2	.750	15	6	18	8	1	-3
OF								
1964	NY-N	1.000	8	4	0	0	0	0
1965	NY-N	1.000	2	1	0	0	0	0
1966	NY-N	—	1	0	0	0	0	0
1970	SF-N	—	1	0	0	0	0	0
Total	4	1.000	12	5	0	0	0	0

■ Chuck Stevens 1B

YEAR	TM/L	PCT	G	PO	A	E	DP	FR
1941	StL-A	.966	4	28	0	1	3	-1
1946	StL-A	**.995**	120	1020	86	6	98	3
1948	StL-A	.991	85	737	56	7	89	1
Total	3	.993	209	1785	142	4	190	3

■ Ed Stevens 1B

YEAR	TM/L	PCT	G	PO	A	E	DP	FR
1945	Bro-N	.987	55	478	38	7	40	0
1946	Bro-N	.986	99	716	48	11	59	-4
1947	Bro-N	.971	4	29	4	1	2	1
1948	Pit-N	**.996**	117	1021	83	4	94	5
1949	Pit-N	.995	58	533	58	3	65	10
1950	Pit-N	1.000	12	92	8	0	11	1
Total	6	.992	345	2869	239	6	271	13

■ Bud Stewart OF

YEAR	TM/L	PCT	G	PO	A	E	DP	FR
1941	Pit-N	.962	41	71	5	3	2	-1
1942	Pit-N	1.000	34	69	1	0	0	-1
1948	Was-A	.975	114	265	5	7	1	-1
1949	Was-A	.982	105	207	8	4	3	-5
1950	Was-A	.991	100	202	10	2	3	-1
1951	Chi-A	.983	63	111	4	2	0	-3
1952	Chi-A	.982	60	108	1	2	0	-4
1953	Chi-A	1.000	16	12	0	0	0	-2
1954	Chi-A	1.000	2	3	0	0	0	0
Total	9	.982	535	1048	34	0	9	-18
3B								
1942	Pit-N	.906	10	12	17	3	0	-2
2B								
1942	Pit-N	1.000	6	6	5	0	0	-1

■ Glen Stewart SS

YEAR	TM/L	PCT	G	PO	A	E	DP	FR
1940	NY-N	.913	5	7	14	2	3	1
1943	Phi-N	.947	77	128	232	20	41	-10
1944	Phi-N	.977	32	49	79	3	11	0
Total	3	.953	114	184	325	5	55	-9
3B								
1940	NY-N	.875	6	0	7	1	0	0
1944	Phi-N	.963	83	77	181	10	12	4
Total	2	.960	89	77	188	1	12	4
2B								
1943	Phi-N	.972	18	49	54	3	9	2
1944	Phi-N	1.000	1	0	3	0	0	0
Total	2	.972	19	49	57	3	9	2
1B								
1943	Phi-N	1.000	8	44	0	0	0	-1
C								
1943	Phi-N	1.000	1	1	0	0	0	0

■ Jimmy Stewart OF

YEAR	TM/L	PCT	G	PO	A	E	DP	FR
1964	Chi-N	.750	4	3	0	1	0	-1
1965	Chi-N	.955	55	80	4	4	0	-3
1966	Chi-N	1.000	15	31	1	0	0	1
1967	Chi-N	1.000	6	0	1	0	0	1
1969	Cin-N	.973	66	68	4	2	0	1
1970	Cin-N	1.000	48	15	1	0	0	1
1971	Cin-N	1.000	19	4	0	0	0	0
1972	Hou-N	1.000	11	5	0	0	0	0
1973	Hou-N	1.000	3	2	0	0	0	0
Total	9	.969	227	208	11	7	0	0
2B								
1963	Chi-N	1.000	1	2	4	0	1	0
1964	Chi-N	.981	61	130	180	6	40	0
1966	Chi-N	1.000	4	5	2	0	0	-1
1967	Chi-N	.867	5	7	6	2	3	2
1969	Cin-N	.978	18	17	28	1	6	-1
1970	Cin-N	1.000	18	19	18	0	3	1
1971	Cin-N	1.000	6	9	14	0	3	-1
1972	Hou-N	1.000	8	6	13	0	0	-1
1973	Hou-N	—	1	0	0	0	0	0
Total	9	.981	122	195	265	9	56	-1
SS								
1963	Chi-N	.973	9	11	25	1	7	0
1964	Chi-N	.972	45	84	127	6	24	-6
1965	Chi-N	.958	48	37	54	4	11	-10
1966	Chi-N	—	2	0	0	0	0	0
1967	Chi-A	.750	2	2	1	1	1	0
1969	Cin-N	—	1	0	0	0	0	-1
Total	6	.966	107	134	207	2	43	-17
3B								
1964	Chi-N	1.000	1	0	1	0	0	0
1966	Chi-N	—	1	0	0	0	0	0
1969	Cin-N	.933	6	4	10	1	3	0
1970	Cin-N	.958	9	6	17	1	5	2
1971	Cin-N	.800	9	8	0	2	0	-1
1972	Hou-N	1.000	2	1	0	0	0	0
1973	Hou-N	1.000	8	3	17	0	2	1
Total	7	.944	37	14	53	4	10	2

YEAR	TM/L	PCT	G	PO	A	E	DP	FR
1B								
1970	Cin-N	.667	1	4	0	2	0	-1
1972	Hou-N	1.000	9	71	5	0	5	0
Total	2	.976	10	75	5	2	5	-1
C								
1970	Cin-N	1.000	1	2	0	0	0	0

■ **Kurt Stillwell SS**

YEAR	TM/L	PCT	G	PO	A	E	DP	FR
1986	Cin-N	.951	80	107	205	16	40	-2
1987	Cin-N	.914	51	74	117	18	22	-16
1988	KC-A	.976	124	170	349	13	60	-18
1989	KC-A	.970	130	179	334	16	65	-32
1990	KC-A	.957	141	181	350	24	79	-20
Total	5	.960	526	711	1355	7	266	-88
2B								
1987	Cin-N	.975	37	61	97	4	15	-3
3B								
1987	Cin-N	.977	20	9	33	1	1	-2

■ **Bob Stinson C**

YEAR	TM/L	PCT	G	PO	A	E	DP	FR
1969	LA-N	.952	4	20	0	1	0	1
1970	LA-N	1.000	3	3	0	0	0	0
1971	StL-N	.971	6	34	0	1	0	3
1972	Hou-N	.964	12	25	2	1	0	-4
1973	Mon-N	.979	35	174	9	4	2	-2
1974	Mon-N	1.000	29	122	14	0	4	0
1975	KC-A	.993	59	256	31	2	4	7
1976	KC-A	.979	79	304	30	7	4	-6
1977	Sea-A	.984	99	494	43	9	11	-7
1978	Sea-A	.987	123	472	60	7	7	-18
1979	Sea-A	.978	91	376	29	9	2	-7
1980	Sea-A	.979	45	135	8	3	2	-9
Total	12	.984	585	2415	226	4	36	-42
OF								
1971	StL-N	1.000	3	2	0	0	0	0
1972	Hou-N	1.000	3	1	0	0	0	0
1975	KC-A	1.000	1	1	0	0	0	0
Total	3	1.000	7	4	0	0	0	0
3B								
1973	Mon-N	—	1	0	0	0	0	0
1B								
1975	KC-A	—	1	0	0	0	0	0
2B								
1975	KC-A	1.000	1	0	2	0	0	0

■ **Snuffy Stirnweiss 2B**

YEAR	TM/L	PCT	G	PO	A	E	DP	FR
1943	NY-A	1.000	4	14	8	0	5	0
1944	NY-A	.982	154	433	481	17	113	19
1945	NY-A	.970	152	432	492	29	119	25
1946	NY-A	.979	46	88	141	5	30	-3
1947	NY-A	.983	148	337	402	13	107	-10
1948	NY-A	.993	141	346	364	5	103	-11
1949	NY-A	.974	51	121	106	6	34	4
1950	NY-A	1.000	4	1	2	0	0	1
	StL-A	.975	62	159	154	8	44	-15
	Yr	.975	66	160	156	8	44	-14
1951	Cle-A	.992	25	47	74	1	17	7
Total	9	.980	787	1978	2224	4	572	17
3B								
1946	NY-A	.991	79	66	152	2	18	-1
1949	NY-A	1.000	4	3	3	0	0	0
1950	StL-A	.955	31	32	52	4	7	-8
1951	Cle-A	1.000	2	2	3	0	1	0
1952	Cle-A	—	1	0	0	0	0	0
Total	5	.981	117	103	210	6	26	-9
SS								
1943	NY-A	.938	68	110	192	20	50	-6
1946	NY-A	.917	4	5	6	1	1	-1
1950	StL-A	.875	5	4	3	1	0	-1
Total	3	.936	77	119	201	2	51	-8

■ **Jack Stivetts OF**

YEAR	TM/L	PCT	G	PO	A	E	DP	FR
1889	StL-a	—	1	0	0	0	0	0
1890	StL-a	.864	10	16	3	3	2	1
1891	StL-a	.941	24	29	3	2	2	-1
1092	Bos-N	.914	10	31	1	3	2	-1
1893	Bos-N	.941	8	15	1	1	0	0
1894	Bos-N	.800	16	30	2	8	1	-2
1895	Bos-N	1.000	2	4	0	0	0	0
1896	Bos-N	.833	12	19	1	4	0	-2
1897	Bos-N	.926	29	47	3	4	1	-3
1898	Bos-N	.909	14	19	1	2	0	-3
1899	Cle-N	1.000	7	11	1	0	0	0
Total	11	.898	141	221	16	7	8	-11
1B								
1890	StL-a	.962	3	25	0	1	1	0
1892	Bos-N	.833	1	5	0	1	1	0
1894	Bos-N	.971	4	30	4	1	3	1
1895	Bos-N	.981	5	48	3	1	4	0
1896	Bos-N	.936	5	41	3	3	1	0
1897	Bos-N	.944	2	16	1	1	2	0
1898	Bos-N	.972	10	69	1	2	3	-1
Total	7	.961	30	234	12	0	15	0
3B								
1893	Bos-N	.700	3	3	4	3	1	-2
1896	Bos-N	.250	1	0	1	3	0	-1
1899	Cle-N	1.000	1	0	1	0	0	0
Total	3	.600	5	3	6	6	1	-3
SS								
1898	Bos-N	.786	4	3	8	3	0	-2
1899	Cle-N	.750	1	1	2	1	0	-1
Total	2	.778	5	4	10	4	0	-3
2B								
1897	Bos-N	.875	2	2	5	1	0	-1
1898	Bos-N	.813	2	6	7	3	1	0
Total	2	.833	4	8	12	4	1	-1

■ **Milt Stock 3B**

YEAR	TM/L	PCT	G	PO	A	E	DP	FR
1914	NY-N	.939	113	95	261	23	17	14
1915	Phi-N	.971	55	62	106	5	7	2

YEAR	TM/L	PCT	G	PO	A	E	DP	FR
1916	Phi-N	.955	117	128	213	16	22	-6
1917	Phi-N	.942	133	132	255	24	16	-11
1918	Phi-N	.946	123	132	273	23	16	-5
1919	StL-N	.931	58	51	139	14	15	6
1920	StL-N	.939	155	158	300	30	23	-8
1921	StL-N	.940	149	148	243	25	21	-22
1922	StL-N	.950	149	172	245	22	22	-8
1923	StL-N	.955	150	165	261	20	24	-14
1924	Bro-N	.931	142	139	200	25	14	-23
1925	Bro-N	.957	5	10	12	1	1	2
Total	12	.945	1349	1392	2508	228	198	-73
2B								
1919	StL-N	.966	77	168	254	15	32	11
1923	StL-N	1.000	1	1	0	0	0	0
1925	Bro-N	.978	141	305	477	18	74	-2
1926	Bro-N	.923	3	4	8	1	1	-1
Total	4	.973	222	478	739	4	107	8
SS								
1913	NY-N	.838	7	12	19	6	4	2
1914	NY-N	1.000	1	2	5	0	1	1
1915	Phi-N	1.000	4	2	2	0	0	0
1916	Phi-N	.907	15	22	46	7	7	0
1917	Phi-N	.920	19	44	60	9	4	2
1922	StL-N	1.000	1	3	2	0	0	0
Total	6	.909	47	85	134	2	15	5

■ **George Stone OF**

YEAR	TM/L	PCT	G	PO	A	E	DP	FR
1905	StL-A	.954	154	278	15	14	5	1
1906	StL-A	.968	154	295	10	10	3	-1
1907	StL-A	.970	155	276	12	9	5	-3
1908	StL-A	.947	148	274	11	16	3	0
1909	StL-A	.928	81	147	8	12	4	2
1910	StL-A	.972	145	220	20	7	2	-3
Total	6	.958	837	1490	76	8	22	-4

■ **Ron Stone OF**

YEAR	TM/L	PCT	G	PO	A	E	DP	FR
1966	KC-A	1.000	4	2	0	0	0	0
1969	Phi-N	.978	69	85	6	2	0	-3
1970	Phi-N	.968	99	148	5	5	0	-3
1971	Phi-N	.964	51	76	5	3	0	0
1972	Phi-N	1.000	15	24	3	0	0	3
Total	5	.973	238	335	19	0	0	-3
1B								
1966	KC-A	.875	3	12	2	2	3	0
1970	Phi-N	.941	6	16	0	1	1	-1
1971	Phi-N	.947	3	17	1	1	2	0
Total	3	.923	12	45	3	4	6	-1

■ **Jeff Stone OF**

YEAR	TM/L	PCT	G	PO	A	E	DP	FR
1983	Phi-N	—	1	0	0	0	0	0
1984	Phi-N	.916	46	75	1	7	0	-7
1985	Phi-N	.966	69	82	4	3	0	-10
1986	Phi-N	.982	58	103	8	2	1	0
1987	Phi-N	1.000	25	32	3	0	1	-1
1988	Bal-A	.963	21	23	3	1	1	0
1989	Tex-A	—	3	0	0	0	0	0
	Bos-A	1.000	11	8	0	0	0	1
	Yr	1.000	14	8	0	0	0	1
Total	7	.963	234	323	19	3	3	-17

■ **John Stone OF**

YEAR	TM/L	PCT	G	PO	A	E	DP	FR
1928	Det-A	.962	26	49	2	2	0	-1
1929	Det-A	.986	36	68	4	1	0	-1
1930	Det-A	.966	108	222	5	8	1	0
1931	Det-A	.959	147	319	11	14	6	4
1932	Det-A	.961	142	334	11	14	2	7
1933	Det-A	.970	141	280	11	9	1	-3
1934	Was-A	.966	112	245	13	9	3	6
1935	Was-A	.955	114	224	12	11	4	-1
1936	Was-A	.967	114	249	12	9	5	4
1937	Was-A	.984	137	300	15	5	3	6
1938	Was-A	.974	53	107	5	3	0	-3
Total	11	.967	1130	2397	101	5	25	18

■ **Lin Storti 3B**

YEAR	TM/L	PCT	G	PO	A	E	DP	FR
1931	StL-A	.926	67	78	134	17	20	7
1932	StL-A	.956	51	50	81	6	8	-4
1933	StL-A	.934	32	41	58	7	11	1
Total	3	.936	150	169	273	0	39	4
2B								
1930	StL-A	.975	6	19	20	1	8	1
1931	StL-A	.966	7	13	15	1	4	2
1933	StL-A	.992	24	64	55	1	15	-3
Total	3	.984	37	96	90	3	27	0

■ **George Stovall 1B**

YEAR	TM/L	PCT	G	PO	A	E	DP	FR
1904	Cle-A	.978	38	376	22	9	18	-1
1905	Cle-A	.975	60	661	53	18	28	4
1906	Cle-A	.985	55	617	40	10	46	2
1907	Cle-A	.983	122	1381	68	25	90	-4
1908	Cle-A	.990	132	1508	86	16	79	3
1909	Cle-A	.988	145	1478	109	19	80	10
1910	Cle-A	.988	132	1404	91	18	60	7
1911	Cle-A	.986	118	1073	87	17	56	8
1912	StL-A	.983	94	845	68	16	64	5
1913	StL-A	.988	76	751	65	10	38	7
1914	KC-F	.989	116	1201	70	14	82	5
1915	KC-F	.987	129	1417	87	20	61	5
Total	12	.986	1217	12712	846	192	702	51
2B								
1904	Cle-A	.921	9	13	22	3	2	0
1905	Cle-A	.944	46	97	107	12	7	-9
1906	Cle-A	.953	19	30	52	4	6	-2
1910	Cle-A	—	2	0	0	0	0	0
1911	Cle-A	.800	2	3	5	2	0	-1
Total	5	.940	78	143	186	1	15	-12
3B								
1904	Cle-A	—	1	0	0	0	0	0
1906	Cle-A	.920	30	19	61	7	1	-4
1907	Cle-A	1.000	2	1	3	0	0	0

YEAR	TM/L	PCT	G	PO	A	E	DP	FR
1914	KC-F	—	1	0	0	0	0	0
Total	4	.923	34	20	64	7	1	-4
OF								
1904	Cle-A	1.000	3	2	0	0	0	-1
1905	Cle-A	1.000	4	6	1	0	0	1
1908	Cle-A	1.000	5	12	1	0	0	1
Total	3	1.000	12	20	2	0	0	1
SS								
1908	Cle-A	1.000	1	3	1	0	0	0

■ **Harry Stovey OF**

YEAR	TM/L	PCT	G	PO	A	E	DP	FR
1880	Wor-N	.860	46	68	6	12	1	-5
1881	Wor-N	.886	18	30	1	4	0	-3
1882	Wor-N	.813	41	88	12	23	2	3
1883	Phi-a	.500	3	1	1	2	0	-1
1885	Phi-a	.817	30	50	8	13	2	1
1886	Phi-a	.870	63	142	12	23	4	8
1887	Phi-a	.902	80	195	16	23	1	10
1888	Phi-a	.943	118	204	12	13	4	4
1889	Phi-a	.897	137	284	38	37	9	18
1890	Bos-P	.921	117	186	24	18	3	3
1891	Bos-N	.910	134	232	22	25	4	9
1892	Bos-N	.901	38	79	3	9	1	0
	Bal-N	.913	64	109	6	11	2	-2
	Yr	.908	102	188	9	20	3	-2
1893	Bal-N	.864	7	18	1	3	0	0
	Bro-N	.901	48	115	3	13	0	-3
	Yr	.895	55	133	4	16	0	-3
Total	13	.896	944	1801	165	229	33	42
1B								
1880	Wor-N	.952	37	448	12	23	20	0
1881	Wor-N	.955	57	578	16	28	26	-3
1882	Wor-N	.956	43	469	13	22	25	0
1883	Phi-a	.965	93	984	22	37	31	1
1884	Phi-a	.960	104	1061	32	45	46	-1
1885	Phi-a	.967	82	877	28	31	47	3
1886	Phi-a	.953	62	656	13	33	26	-5
1887	Phi-a	.971	46	418	19	13	21	2
1888	Phi-a	.992	13	125	4	1	6	0
1889	Phi-a	1.000	1	3	0	0	0	0
1890	Bos-P	.750	1	3	0	1	0	0
1891	Bos-N	1.000	1	1	0	0	0	0
1892	Bal-N	.936	10	97	5	7	4	-1
Total	13	.961	550	5720	164	241	252	-4

■ **Joe Strain 2B**

YEAR	TM/L	PCT	G	PO	A	E	DP	FR
1979	SF-N	.982	67	147	188	6	32	-1
1980	SF-N	.989	42	85	102	2	15	-10
1981	Chi-N	.975	20	38	81	3	10	7
Total	3	.983	129	270	371	1	57	-4
3B								
1979	SF-N	1.000	1	0	1	0	0	0
1980	SF-N	.875	6	3	11	2	1	0
Total	2	.882	7	3	12	2	1	0
SS								
1980	SF-N	—	1	0	0	0	0	0

■ **Sammy Strang 3B**

YEAR	TM/L	PCT	G	PO	A	E	DP	FR
1900	Chi-N	.887	16	16	31	6	3	-4
1901	NY-N	.877	91	127	194	45	16	11
1902	Chi-N	.890	137	170	334	62	21	5
	Chi-N	.857	2	3	3	1	0	-1
1903	Bro-N	.914	124	147	245	37	13	-6
1904	Bro-N	.780	12	13	19	9	2	-4
1905	NY-N	—	1	0	0	0	0	0
1906	NY-N	.900	3	1	8	1	0	1
1907	NY-N	.929	7	3	10	1	0	0
Total	8	.891	393	480	844	162	55	2
2B								
1900	Chi-N	.875	2	2	5	1	0	-2
1901	NY-N	.935	37	54	104	11	10	-6
1902	Chi-N	1.000	2	2	1	0	0	-2
1903	Bro-N	.917	3	7	4	1	0	-2
1904	Bro-N	.910	63	100	164	26	13	-26
1905	NY-N	.920	47	77	118	17	9	-8
1906	NY-N	.944	57	116	173	17	13	7
1907	NY-N	.952	13	27	32	3	3	-4
1908	NY-N	.863	14	22	41	10	5	-1
Total	9	.924	238	407	642	6	55	-42
OF								
1901	NY-N	.500	5	2	0	2	0	-2
1903	Bro-N	1.000	8	12	2	0	0	0
1905	NY-N	.911	38	47	4	5	0	-4
1906	NY-N	.937	39	57	2	4	0	-4
1907	NY-N	.947	70	112	13	7	5	2
1908	NY-N	1.000	5	3	2	0	0	-1
Total	6	.934	165	233	23	8	5	-9
SS								
1896	Lou-N	.803	14	19	30	12	5	-8
1900	Chi-N	.809	9	12	26	9	2	-6
1901	NY-N	.857	4	6	6	2	1	-3
1904	Bro-N	.429	1	1	2	4	0	-3
1905	NY-N	.906	9	7	22	3	2	-3
1906	NY-N	.842	4	5	11	3	1	-1
1907	NY-N	1.000	1	1	3	0	0	0
1908	NY-N	.800	3	4	4	2	0	-1
Total	8	.820	45	55	104	5	11	-23
1B								
1905	NY-N	1.000	1	3	0	0	0	0
1906	NY-N	1.000	1	6	0	0	0	0
1907	NY-N	.971	5	31	3	1	0	0
Total	3	.977	7	40	3	1	0	0

■ **Alan Strange SS**

YEAR	TM/L	PCT	G	PO	A	E	DP	FR
1934	StL-A	.955	125	260	392	31	84	4
1935	StL-A	.960	49	105	135	10	28	2
	Was-A	.974	16	26	49	2	11	3
	Yr	.963	65	131	184	12	39	5
1940	StL-A	.962	35	65	112	7	24	2

YEAR	TM/L	PCT	G	PO	A	E	DP	FR
1941	StL-A	.973	32	66	79	4	17	2
1942	StL-A	.933	3	7	7	1	0	0
Total	5	.959	260	529	774	5	164	13
		3B						
1941	StL-A	1.000	1	0	1	0	0	0
1942	StL-A	.935	10	8	21	2	3	4
Total	2	.938	11	8	22	2	3	4
		2B						
1940	StL-A	1.000	4	8	16	0	4	1
1942	StL-A	1.000	1	1	0	0	0	0
Total	2	1.000	5	9	16	0	4	1
		1B						
1941	StL-A	1.000	2	8	0	0	0	0

■ Scott Stratton OF

YEAR	TM/L	PCT	G	PO	A	E	DP	FR
1888	Lou-a	.821	38	40	6	10	0	-4
1889	Lou-a	.915	29	45	9	5	1	2
1890	Lou-a	.917	5	11	0	1	0	0
1891	Lou-a	1.000	6	6	1	0	0	-1
1892	Lou-N	.818	17	13	5	4	0	-1
1893	Lou-N	.884	23	34	4	5	2	0
1894	Lou-N	1.000	5	8	2	0	1	1
	Chi-N	1.000	5	9	0	0	0	0
	Yr	1.000	10	17	2	0	1	1
1895	Chi-N	.714	4	5	0	2	0	-2
Total	8	.880	132	171	27	7	4	-5
		1B						
1889	Lou-a	.940	17	146	10	10	11	1
1891	Lou-a	.930	8	75	5	6	6	0
1892	Lou-N	.944	6	48	3	3	4	0
1893	Lou-N	1.000	1	7	0	0	0	0
1894	Chi-N	.944	2	17	0	1	2	-1
Total	5	.940	34	293	18	20	23	0

■ Darryl Strawberry OF

YEAR	TM/L	PCT	G	PO	A	E	DP	FR
1983	NY-N	.984	117	232	8	4	0	1
1984	NY-N	.980	146	276	11	6	3	5
1985	NY-N	.991	110	211	5	2	2	0
1986	NY-N	.975	131	226	10	6	3	-2
1987	NY-N	.972	151	272	6	8	3	-3
1988	NY-N	.971	150	297	4	9	3	1
1989	NY-N	.972	131	272	4	8	2	3
1990	NY-N	.989	149	268	10	3	4	3
Total	8	.979	1085	2054	58	6	20	8

■ Gabby Street C

YEAR	TM/L	PCT	G	PO	A	E	DP	FR
1904	Cin-N	.973	11	55	17	2	0	5
1905	Cin-N	1.000	1	3	3	0	0	1
	Bos-N	1.000	3	10	4	0	0	-1
	Cin-N	.975	26	110	46	4	1	4
	Yr	.978	30	**123**	53	4	**1**	4
1908	Was-A	.973	128	578	167	21	14	-1
1909	Was-A	.981	**137**	**714**	**210**	18	**18**	**11**
1910	Was-A	**.978**	86	417	151	13	8	10
1911	Was-A	.973	71	362	102	13	10	6
1912	NY-A	.958	29	141	43	8	4	0
1931	StL-N	1.000	1	1	1	0	0	0
Total	8	.975	493	2391	744	9	55	35

■ Cub Stricker 2B

YEAR	TM/L	PCT	G	PO	A	E	DP	FR
1882	Phi-a	.904	72	239	**251**	52	29	**23**
1883	Phi-a	.837	88	253	223	**93**	23	-20
1884	Phi-a	.870	107	280	257	**80**	40	-33
1885	Phi-a	.879	106	284	304	**81**	41	-13
1887	Cle-a	.912	126	**461**	365	80	61	12
1888	Cle-a	.929	**122**	**387**	361	57	58	21
1889	Cle-N	.932	**135**	434	429	63	65	3
1890	Cle-P	.905	109	295	353	68	57	2
1891	Bos-a	.942	139	**405**	**418**	51	**78**	**24**
1892	StL-N	.939	27	66	72	9	8	-4
	Bal-N	.918	75	212	224	39	31	2
	Yr	.923	102	278	296	48	39	-2
1893	Was-N	.903	39	131	130	28	22	7
Total	11	.907	1145	3447	3387	701	513	24
		SS						
1887	Cle-a	.722	6	7	19	10	2	-2
1889	Cle-N	.917	1	3	8	1	0	2
1890	Cle-P	.839	20	30	85	22	4	4
1892	StL-N	1.000	1	1	2	0	0	0
1893	Was-N	.813	4	5	8	3	0	-1
Total	5	.824	32	46	122	6	6	3
		OF						
1882	Phi-a	1.000	1	1	0	0	0	0
1884	Phi-a	1.000	1	1	0	0	0	0
1888	Cle-a	.929	6	10	3	1	0	2
1893	Was-N	.963	12	23	3	1	1	2
Total	4	.953	20	35	6	2	1	4
		3B						
1893	Was-N	.778	4	9	5	4	0	-1
		C						
1883	Phi-a	.833	2	7	3	2	0	0
1884	Phi-a	—	1	0	0	0	0	0
Total	2	.833	3	7	3	2	0	0

■ George Strickland SS

YEAR	TM/L	PCT	G	PO	A	E	DP	FR
1950	Pit-N	.978	19	22	23	1	7	3
1951	Pit-N	.943	125	222	386	37	89	11
1952	Pit-N	.945	28	47	90	8	24	9
	Cle-A	.964	30	64	95	6	18	10
1953	Cle-A	.974	122	238	400	17	**103**	16
1954	Cle-A	.961	112	193	321	21	61	-12
1955	Cle-A	**.976**	128	221	360	14	84	8
1956	Cle-A	.978	28	32	56	2	10	3
1957	Cle-A	.972	23	24	46	2	13	3
1959	Cle-A	.953	50	80	145	11	42	-3
1960	Cle-A	.962	14	6	19	1	5	1
Total	10	.963	679	1149	1941	120	456	49
		2B						
1951	Pit-N	1.000	13	33	40	0	8	1
1952	Pit-N	.953	45	95	127	11	30	6

YEAR	TM/L	PCT	G	PO	A	E	DP	FR
	Cle-A	—	1	0	0	0	0	0
1956	Cle-A	.986	28	73	69	2	21	12
1957	Cle-A	.980	48	108	93	4	22	9
1959	Cle-A	.900	4	4	5	1	1	-1
1960	Cle-A	1.000	2	1	1	0	1	0
Total	6	.973	141	314	335	8	83	27
		3B						
1950	Pit-N	1.000	1	0	1	0	0	0
1952	Pit-N	1.000	1	5	1	0	2	1
1956	Cle-A	.971	26	13	20	1	3	1
1957	Cle-A	1.000	19	14	25	0	3	3
1959	Cle-A	.971	80	69	131	6	11	-5
1960	Cle-A	1.000	12	4	11	0	0	0
Total	6	.977	139	105	189	7	19	0
		1B						
1952	Pit-N	1.000	1	1	0	0	0	0
1953	Cle-A	—	1	0	0	0	0	0
Total	2	1.000	2	1	0	0	0	0

■ George Strief 2B

YEAR	TM/L	PCT	G	PO	A	E	DP	FR
1879	Cle-N	.835	16	35	41	15	4	-10
1882	Pit-a	.917	**78**	241	200	40	28	-1
1883	StL-a	.899	67	205	214	47	28	7
1884	StL-a	.778	3	12	9	6	4	-1
	KC-U	.900	15	56	52	12	9	8
	CP-U	.905	15	34	33	7	1	-2
	Yr	.902	30	90	85	19	10	6
1885	Phi-a	.900	7	20	16	4	5	-2
Total	5	.899	201	603	565	131	79	-1
		OF						
1879	Cle-N	.918	55	104	8	10	0	0
1883	StL-a	1.000	15	15	3	0	0	-1
1884	StL-a	.848	44	51	5	10	0	-2
	Cle-N	1.000	6	6	2	0	0	1
1885	Phi-a	1.000	8	13	4	0	0	2
Total	4	.913	128	189	22	0	0	0
		3B						
1884	Cle-N	.833	2	2	3	1	0	-1
1885	Phi-a	.828	19	18	35	11	0	-2
Total	2	.829	21	20	38	2	0	-3
		SS						
1882	Pit-a	.889	1	0	8	1	1	1
1885	Phi-a	.905	10	11	27	4	5	-1
Total	2	.902	11	11	35	5	6	0
		1B						
1884	StL-a	1.000	1	13	0	0	0	0

■ Lou Stringer 2B

YEAR	TM/L	PCT	G	PO	A	E	DP	FR
1941	Chi-N	.960	137	356	**455**	34	84	**22**
1942	Chi-N	.955	113	268	343	**29**	59	2
1946	Chi-N	.956	62	135	150	13	17	-5
1948	Bos-A	.947	2	5	13	1	5	2
1949	Bos-A	.978	9	25	20	1	12	3
1950	Bos-A	1.000	1	1	2	0	0	1
Total	6	.958	324	790	983	8	177	25
		SS						
1941	Chi-N	.714	7	3	7	4	1	-2
1946	Chi-N	1.000	1	0	2	0	0	0
1950	Bos-A	1.000	1	0	1	0	1	0
Total	3	.765	9	3	10	4	2	-2
		3B						
1942	Chi-N	—	1	0	0	0	0	0
1946	Chi-N	—	1	0	0	0	0	0
1950	Bos-A	.778	3	3	4	2	1	2
Total	3	.778	5	3	4	2	1	2

■ Joe Stripp 3B

YEAR	TM/L	PCT	G	PO	A	E	DP	FR
1928	Cin-N	.906	17	15	33	5	2	-2
1929	Cin-N	.960	55	49	120	7	4	9
1930	Cin-N	.974	48	52	95	4	7	3
1931	Cin-N	.957	96	101	191	13	22	3
1932	Bro-N	.954	93	92	201	14	22	**13**
1933	Bro-N	.967	140	170	264	15	17	5
1934	Bro-N	.941	96	93	147	15	**20**	-6
1935	Bro-N	.962	88	63	162	9	17	8
1936	Bro-N	**.968**	106	132	174	10	13	8
1937	Bro-N	.971	66	75	91	5	4	-2
1938	StL-N	.977	51	53	76	3	9	-8
	Bos-N	.966	58	61	111	6	12	1
	Yr	.971	109	114	187	9	21	-7
Total	11	.961	914	956	1665	106	149	32
		1B						
1930	Cin-N	.996	75	722	38	3	76	-3
1931	Cin-N	.989	9	82	6	1	15	0
1932	Bro-N	.988	43	393	36	5	39	3
1934	Bro-N	1.000	7	63	5	0	5	0
1935	Bro-N	.992	15	117	7	1	7	0
1937	Bro-N	.985	14	127	5	2	6	-2
Total	6	.993	163	1504	97	2	148	-2
		OF						
1928	Cin-N	.931	21	27	0	2	0	-3
1935	Bro-N	—	1	0	0	0	0	0
Total	2	.931	22	27	0	2	0	-3
		SS						
1928	Cin-N	1.000	1	0	1	0	0	0
1934	Bro-N	.500	1	1	0	1	0	-1
1937	Bro-N	.857	3	6	6	2	3	-2
Total	3	.824	5	7	7	3	3	-3
		2B						
1929	Cin-N	—	2	0	0	0	0	0

■ Ed Stroud OF

YEAR	TM/L	PCT	G	PO	A	E	DP	FR
1966	Chi-A	1.000	11	20	0	0	0	0
1967	Chi-A	1.000	12	14	2	0	1	2
	Was-A	.983	79	117	1	2	0	0
	Yr	.985	91	131	3	2	1	2
1968	Was-A	.979	84	139	2	3	1	-4
1969	Was-A	.982	85	109	1	2	0	1
1970	Was-A	.993	118	271	8	2	3	12

YEAR	TM/L	PCT	G	PO	A	E	DP	FR
1971	Chi-A	1.000	44	51	0	0	0	-5
Total	6	.988	433	721	14	9	5	6

■ Amos Strunk OF

YEAR	TM/L	PCT	G	PO	A	E	DP	FR
1908	Phi-A	.903	11	27	1	3	1	1
1909	Phi-A	1.000	9	10	2	0	0	-1
1910	Phi-A	1.000	14	33	1	0	0	1
1911	Phi-A	.958	62	127	11	6	4	2
1912	Phi-A	**.990**	116	278	16	3	3	10
1913	Phi-A	.962	81	168	9	7	3	-2
1914	Phi-A	**.987**	120	280	14	4	3	8
1915	Phi-A	.980	111	225	24	5	4	14
1916	Phi-A	.978	143	291	20	7	5	2
1917	Phi-A	**.986**	146	346	13	5	5	-2
1918	Bos-A	**.988**	113	230	13	3	4	-5
1919	Bos-A	.968	48	118	4	4	0	-1
	Phi-A	.981	52	98	7	2	0	1
	Yr	.974	100	216	11	6	0	0
1920	Phi-A	.990	54	97	2	1	0	-4
	Chi-A	.981	49	98	3	2	0	-1
	Yr	.985	103	195	5	3	0	-5
1921	Chi-A	.970	111	214	10	7	2	-8
1922	Chi-A	.989	74	170	9	2	2	2
1923	Chi-A	1.000	5	13	0	0	0	0
1924	Phi-A	1.000	8	7	0	0	0	-3
Total	17	.980	1327	2830	159	1	36	14
		1B						
1911	Phi-A	.857	2	18	0	3	1	-1
1915	Phi-A	.980	19	188	8	4	17	-2
1916	Phi-A	.988	7	77	4	1	9	0
1922	Chi-A	1.000	7	73	4	0	0	0
1923	Chi-A	.833	2	5	0	1	0	0
Total	5	.977	37	361	16	9	27	-3

■ Dick Stuart 1B

YEAR	TM/L	PCT	G	PO	A	E	DP	FR
1958	Pit-N	.973	64	529	49	**16**	69	0
1959	Pit-N	.976	105	831	81	**22**	87	1
1960	Pit-N	.986	108	920	77	**14**	90	-1
1961	Pit-N	.983	132	1152	99	**21**	**141**	-1
1962	Pit-N	.982	101	868	78	**17**	98	2
1963	Bos-A	.979	**155**	**1207**	134	**29**	100	**9**
1964	Bos-A	.981	**155**	1159	104	**24**	105	2
1965	Phi-N	.989	143	1119	98	17	100	6
1966	NY-N	.974	23	216	13	6	20	-1
	LA-N	.991	25	191	21	2	16	3
	Yr	.982	48	407	34	8	36	2
1969	Cal-A	.991	13	102	4	1	11	-1
Total	10	.982	1024	8294	758	169	837	19
		OF						
1959	Pit-N	—	1	0	0	0	0	0
1961	Pit-N	—	1	0	0	0	0	0
Total	2	—	2	0	0	0	0	0
		3B						
1965	Phi-N	—	1	0	0	0	0	0

■ Franklin Stubbs 1B

YEAR	TM/L	PCT	G	PO	A	E	DP	FR
1984	LA-N	.993	51	395	37	3	31	4
1985	LA-N	1.000	4	11	0	0	1	0
1986	LA-N	1.000	13	38	4	0	1	0
1987	LA-N	**.994**	111	802	78	5	65	7
1988	LA-N	.978	84	521	57	13	41	6
1989	LA-N	1.000	7	18	2	0	2	0
1990	Hou-N	.991	72	497	42	5	42	-2
Total	7	.990	342	2282	220	6	183	15
		OF						
1984	LA-N	.957	20	22	0	1	0	-1
1986	LA-N	.969	124	206	10	7	2	-2
1987	LA-N	1.000	18	28	1	0	0	0
1988	LA-N	1.000	13	9	0	0	0	0
1989	LA-N	.948	28	52	3	3	3	4
1990	Hou-N	.991	71	112	1	1	0	-4
Total	6	.974	274	429	15	2	5	-3

■ Bobby Sturgeon SS

YEAR	TM/L	PCT	G	PO	A	E	DP	FR
1940	Chi-N	.848	7	19	20	7	5	2
1941	Chi-N	.956	126	215	366	27	68	-4
1942	Chi-N	.982	29	43	64	2	15	8
1946	Chi-N	.934	72	109	158	19	31	-12
1947	Chi-N	.975	45	75	120	5	24	6
1948	Bos-N	.875	4	4	3	1	0	-1
Total	6	.951	283	465	731	1	143	-1
		2B						
1941	Chi-N	—	1	0	0	0	0	0
1942	Chi-N	.988	32	69	99	2	18	12
1946	Chi-N	.971	21	51	51	3	13	-1
1947	Chi-N	.992	30	60	72	1	18	5
1948	Bos-N	.938	18	36	40	5	9	-2
Total	5	.978	102	216	262	1	58	14
		3B						
1941	Chi-N	—	1	0	0	0	0	0
1942	Chi-N	1.000	2	1	0	0	0	0
1947	Chi-N	1.000	5	2	10	0	1	2
1948	Bos-N	.857	4	3	3	1	0	-1
Total	4	.950	12	6	13	1	1	1

■ Ken Suarez C

YEAR	TM/L	PCT	G	PO	A	E	DP	FR
1966	KC-A	.954	34	145	20	8	7	5
1967	KC-A	.979	36	170	20	4	2	7
1968	Cle-A	1.000	12	22	1	0	0	2
1969	Cle-A	.991	36	191	20	2	3	6
1971	Cle-A	.993	48	268	14	2	3	8
1972	Tex-A	.965	17	53	2	2	0	1
1973	Tex-A	.989	90	501	44	6	4	2
Total	7	.984	273	1350	121	4	19	31
		2B						
1968	Cle-A	1.000	1	0	1	0	0	0
		3B						
1968	Cle-A	—	1	0	0	0	0	0
		OF						
1968	Cle-A	—	1	0	0	0	0	0

Bill Sudakis 3B

YEAR	TM/L	PCT	G	PO	A	E	DP	FR
1968	LA-N	.953	24	25	57	4	3	4
1969	LA-N	.946	121	98	272	21	26	11
1970	LA-N	.911	37	27	85	11	8	2
1971	LA-N	1.000	3	2	7	0	1	1
1973	Tex-A	.962	29	32	45	3	1	-4
1974	NY-A	.800	3	1	3	1	0	0
Total	6	.942	217	185	469	0	39	14

C

YEAR	TM/L	PCT	G	PO	A	E	DP	FR
1970	LA-N	.983	38	161	14	3	1	-6
1971	LA-N	1.000	19	85	9	0	0	0
1972	NY-N	1.000	5	37	1	0	0	0
1973	Tex-A	1.000	9	25	3	0	1	0
1974	NY-A	1.000	1	2	0	0	0	0
1975	Cal-A	.941	5	15	1	1	0	-1
	Cle-A	1.000	6	15	2	0	0	0
	Yr	.971	11	30	3	1	0	-1
Total	6	.989	83	340	30	4	2	-7

1B

YEAR	TM/L	PCT	G	PO	A	E	DP	FR
1970	LA-N	1.000	1	4	1	0	0	0
1971	LA-N	—	1	0	0	0	0	0
1972	NY-N	.967	7	51	7	2	3	1
1973	Tex-A	.994	24	156	14	1	19	1
1974	NY-A	.990	33	277	23	3	31	2
1975	Cal-A	1.000	2	16	0	0	0	0
	Cle-A	1.000	12	75	4	0	10	-1
	Yr	1.000	14	91	4	0	10	-1
Total	6	.991	80	579	49	6	63	3

OF

YEAR	TM/L	PCT	G	PO	A	E	DP	FR
1970	LA-N	1.000	3	2	0	0	0	0
1971	LA-N	1.000	1	3	0	0	0	0
1973	Tex-A	.750	2	3	0	1	0	0
Total	3	.889	6	8	0	1	0	0

Pete Suder 2B

YEAR	TM/L	PCT	G	PO	A	E	DP	FR
1942	Phi-A	.988	31	63	95	2	20	4
1943	Phi-A	.971	95	231	269	15	58	-5
1946	Phi-A	.983	12	35	23	1	7	-2
1947	Phi-A	.986	140	304	413	10	94	-16
1948	Phi-A	.988	148	342	461	10	114	-1
1949	Phi-A	.975	89	203	259	12	85	5
1950	Phi-A	.979	47	112	126	5	47	-1
1951	Phi-A	.987	103	274	313	8	93	7
1952	Phi-A	.991	43	104	109	2	32	0
1953	Phi-A	.985	38	89	105	3	23	-3
1954	Phi-A	.961	35	71	75	6	23	4
1955	KC-A	.990	24	51	44	1	17	-3
Total	12	.982	805	1879	2292	5	613	-11

3B

YEAR	TM/L	PCT	G	PO	A	E	DP	FR
1941	Phi-A	.957	136	175	271	20	25	-8
1942	Phi-A	.959	34	38	56	4	8	1
1943	Phi-A	.975	32	33	46	2	8	-2
1946	Phi-A	.968	33	34	57	3	9	-1
1947	Phi-A	1.000	2	2	2	0	0	0
1949	Phi-A	.955	36	37	70	5	9	2
1950	Phi-A	.972	11	14	21	1	4	0
1951	Phi-A	1.000	3	3	1	0	1	0
1952	Phi-A	.917	16	13	31	4	2	0
1953	Phi-A	.974	72	89	174	7	19	8
1954	Phi-A	.977	20	26	59	2	2	6
Total	11	.963	395	464	788	8	87	6

SS

YEAR	TM/L	PCT	G	PO	A	E	DP	FR
1941	Phi-A	.929	3	5	8	1	3	1
1942	Phi-A	.954	69	141	193	16	31	-3
1943	Phi-A	1.000	5	8	8	0	2	0
1946	Phi-A	.959	67	151	204	15	39	6
1947	Phi-A	.778	3	4	3	2	2	0
1949	Phi-A	1.000	2	0	2	0	0	0
1950	Phi-A	.935	10	13	30	3	2	0
1951	Phi-A	.966	18	44	41	3	13	2
1952	Phi-A	.967	17	19	39	2	6	4
1953	Phi-A	.957	7	11	11	1	2	-1
1954	Phi-A	.750	2	3	0	1	0	-1
Total	11	.955	203	399	539	4	100	8

1B

YEAR	TM/L	PCT	G	PO	A	E	DP	FR
1946	Phi-A	.962	3	25	0	1	1	-1
1950	Phi-A	1.000	4	28	4	0	2	1
Total	2	.983	7	53	4	1	3	0

OF

YEAR	TM/L	PCT	G	PO	A	E	DP	FR
1946	Phi-A	.500	2	2	0	2	0	-1

Joe Sugden C

YEAR	TM/L	PCT	G	PO	A	E	DP	FR
1893	Pit-N	.956	27	81	27	5	3	0
1894	Pit-N	.910	31	105	27	13	4	-4
1895	Pit-N	.903	49	176	57	25	4	3
1896	Pit-N	.952	70	284	70	18	12	2
1897	Pit-N	.941	81	317	82	25	6	-4
1898	StL-N	.937	60	181	88	18	8	2
1899	Cle-N	.935	66	196	108	21	11	1
1901	Chi-A	.970	42	179	47	7	4	4
1902	StL-A	.956	61	192	67	12	9	-3
1903	StL-A	.983	66	321	81	7	6	5
1904	StL-A	.989	79	370	94	5	11	1
1905	StL-A	.983	76	420	112	9	6	23
Total	12	.957	708	2822	860	165	84	30

1B

YEAR	TM/L	PCT	G	PO	A	E	DP	FR
1896	Pit-N	.961	7	46	3	2	4	0
1897	Pit-N	.929	3	25	1	2	2	0
1898	StL-N	.987	8	74	3	1	4	0
1899	Cle-N	1.000	3	14	3	0	3	1
1901	Chi-A	1.000	5	21	2	0	0	1
1902	StL-A	.950	4	18	1	1	0	0
1903	StL-A	.986	8	70	3	1	4	0
1904	StL-A	.986	28	275	8	4	11	-3
1905	StL-A	.989	9	89	2	1	1	-1
1912	Det-A	.941	1	13	3	1	0	1
Total	10	.981	76	645	29	3	29	-1

OF

YEAR	TM/L	PCT	G	PO	A	E	DP	FR
1894	Pit-N	.833	1	3	2	1	0	1
1896	Pit-N	.875	4	7	0	1	0	-1
1898	StL-N	.895	15	17	0	2	1	-3
1899	Cle-N	1.000	4	3	0	0	0	-1
Total	4	.889	24	30	2	4	1	-4

3B

YEAR	TM/L	PCT	G	PO	A	E	DP	FR
1894	Pit-N	.800	4	6	6	3	1	-1
1899	Cle-N	.000	1	0	0	2	0	-1
Total	2	.706	5	6	6	5	1	-2

SS

YEAR	TM/L	PCT	G	PO	A	E	DP	FR
1894	Pit-N	.778	3	6	8	4	0	-2

Gus Suhr 1B

YEAR	TM/L	PCT	G	PO	A	E	DP	FR
1930	Pit-N	.992	151	1445	79	13	**142**	-7
1931	Pit-N	.993	76	684	39	5	72	0
1932	Pit-N	.988	**154**	1388	84	**18**	111	-10
1933	Pit-N	.991	**154**	1451	90	14	115	-4
1934	Pit-N	.994	151	1326	75	9	108	-5
1935	Pit-N	.989	149	1315	73	15	83	-6
1936	Pit-N	**.993**	**156**	1432	93	10	100	-4
1937	Pit-N	.993	**151**	1452	91	11	108	-4
1938	Pit-N	.993	145	**1512**	81	12	**150**	-2
1939	Pit-N	.993	52	521	23	4	42	-4
	Phi-N	.995	60	520	37	3	50	1
	Yr	.994	112	1041	60	7	92	-3
1940	Phi-N	.967	7	57	1	2	5	-2
Total	11	.992	1406	13103	766	116	1086	-53

OF

YEAR	TM/L	PCT	G	PO	A	E	DP	FR
1935	Pit-N	1.000	2	1	0	0	0	0

Clyde Sukeforth C

YEAR	TM/L	PCT	G	PO	A	E	DP	FR
1927	Cin-N	.970	24	52	12	2	1	1
1928	Cin-N	.966	26	48	8	2	1	1
1929	Cin-N	.981	76	171	40	4	4	-8
1930	Cin-N	.976	82	234	46	7	8	-3
1931	Cin-N	.965	106	300	59	**13**	9	-8
1932	Bro-N	.991	36	95	13	1	2	-3
1933	Bro-N	.983	18	50	7	1	2	3
1934	Bro-N	1.000	18	38	4	0	2	0
1945	Bro-N	.947	13	53	1	3	0	-3
Total	9	.974	399	1041	190	3	29	-20

Dan Sullivan C

YEAR	TM/L	PCT	G	PO	A	E	DP	FR
1882	Lou-a	.878	54	294	95	54	3	11
1883	Lou-a	.897	32	149	34	21	2	-8
1884	Lou-a	.930	63	340	61	30	2	-17
1885	Lou-a	.948	13	58	15	4	0	0
	StL-a	.956	13	64	22	4	1	2
	Yr	.952	26	122	37	8	1	2
1886	Pit-a	.600	1	2	1	2	0	-1
Total	5	.908	176	907	228	115	8	-13

3B

YEAR	TM/L	PCT	G	PO	A	E	DP	FR
1882	Lou-a	.789	10	14	16	8	0	-2
1883	Lou-a	.500	2	4	0	4	0	-2
Total	2	.739	12	18	16	2	0	-4

OF

YEAR	TM/L	PCT	G	PO	A	E	DP	FR
1882	Lou-a	.667	4	2	2	2	0	0
1883	Lou-a	.667	2	4	0	2	0	0
1884	Lou-a	1.000	1	1	0	0	0	0
Total	3	.692	7	7	2	4	0	0

1B

YEAR	TM/L	PCT	G	PO	A	E	DP	FR
1885	StL-a	.923	4	35	1	3	2	0

SS

YEAR	TM/L	PCT	G	PO	A	E	DP	FR
1882	Lou-a	1.000	1	1	2	0	1	1
1883	Lou-a	1.000	1	0	1	0	0	0
Total	2	1.000	2	1	3	0	1	1

Denny Sullivan OF

YEAR	TM/L	PCT	G	PO	A	E	DP	FR
1905	Was-A	1.000	3	3	0	0	0	-1
1907	Bos-A	.975	143	296	16	8	3	1
1908	Bos-A	.981	97	193	18	4	4	8
	Cle-A	1.000	2	2	0	0	0	0
	Yr	.982	99	195	18	4	4	8
1909	Cle-A	—	2	0	0	0	0	-1
Total	4	.978	247	494	34	2	7	7

Haywood Sullivan C

YEAR	TM/L	PCT	G	PO	A	E	DP	FR
1955	Bos-A	1.000	2	11	1	0	0	1
1957	Bos-A	1.000	1	2	0	0	0	0
1959	Bos-A	1.000	2	4	0	0	0	1
1960	Bos-A	.992	50	237	13	2	5	5
1961	KC-A	.984	88	387	32	7	7	-6
1962	KC-A	.980	94	447	31	**10**	2	-9
1963	KC-A	.992	37	226	15	2	3	7
Total	7	.985	274	1314	92	1	17	-1

1B

YEAR	TM/L	PCT	G	PO	A	E	DP	FR
1961	KC-A	.983	16	101	12	2	12	1
1962	KC-A	1.000	1	2	0	0	0	0
Total	2	.983	17	103	12	2	12	1

OF

YEAR	TM/L	PCT	G	PO	A	E	DP	FR
1961	KC-A	.857	5	6	0	1	0	-1

Chub Sullivan 1B

YEAR	TM/L	PCT	G	PO	A	E	DP	FR
1877	Cin-N	.921	8	66	1	4	1	-1
1878	Cin-N	**.975**	**61**	680	**23**	18	33	**5**
1880	Wor-N	.983	43	447	12	8	19	3
Total	3	.976	112	1193	36	0	53	7

John Sullivan OF

YEAR	TM/L	PCT	G	PO	A	E	DP	FR
1920	Bos-N	.977	66	115	10	3	2	-1
1921	Chi-N	.962	66	122	3	5	0	-7
Total	2	.969	132	237	13	8	2	-8

1B

YEAR	TM/L	PCT	G	PO	A	E	DP	FR
1920	Bos-N	.980	6	49	1	1	4	-1

John Sullivan SS

YEAR	TM/L	PCT	G	PO	A	E	DP	FR
1942	Was-A	.936	92	217	235	31	51	-11
1943	Was-A	.946	133	276	445	41	89	11
1944	Was-A	.934	138	276	426	**50**	89	-14
1947	Was-A	.963	40	83	128	8	27	7
1948	Was-A	.951	57	94	138	12	33	1
1949	StL-A	.942	71	117	144	16	35	-11
Total	6	.942	531	1063	1516	158	324	-17

3B

YEAR	TM/L	PCT	G	PO	A	E	DP	FR
1949	StL-A	.931	23	22	32	4	5	1

2B

YEAR	TM/L	PCT	G	PO	A	E	DP	FR
1947	Was-A	1.000	1	2	3	0	2	1
1948	Was-A	.920	4	6	17	2	1	1
1949	StL-A	1.000	6	12	11	0	2	1
Total	3	.962	11	20	31	2	5	3

Joe Sullivan SS

YEAR	TM/L	PCT	G	PO	A	E	DP	FR
1893	Was-N	.860	128	233	396	102	34	-29
1894	Was-N	.844	6	16	11	5	1	-2
	Phi-N	.887	75	169	224	50	32	-16
	Yr	.884	81	185	235	55	33	-18
1895	Phi-N	.879	89	182	270	62	32	-18
1896	Phi-N	.667	2	2	4	3	1	-2
Total	4	.872	300	602	905	222	100	-67

OF

YEAR	TM/L	PCT	G	PO	A	E	DP	FR
1894	Was-N	—	1	0	0	1	0	0
1895	Phi-N	.929	6	13	0	1	0	-1
1896	Phi-N	.962	45	99	3	4	0	-2
	StL-N	.955	45	81	4	4	1	-3
	Yr	.959	90	180	7	8	1	-5
Total	3	.957	97	193	7	9	1	-6

2B

YEAR	TM/L	PCT	G	PO	A	E	DP	FR
1894	Was-N	.900	8	18	27	5	1	-1
1896	StL-N	.964	7	12	15	1	0	-2
Total	2	.923	15	30	42	6	1	-2

3B

YEAR	TM/L	PCT	G	PO	A	E	DP	FR
1894	Was-N	1.000	1	4	2	0	0	0
1896	Phi-N	—	2	0	0	0	0	0
Total	2	.909	3	4	2	0	0	0

Marc Sullivan C

YEAR	TM/L	PCT	G	PO	A	E	DP	FR
1982	Bos-A	1.000	2	9	2	0	1	1
1984	Bos-A	.950	2	19	0	1	0	1
1985	Bos-A	.993	32	129	8	1	1	4
1986	Bos-A	.986	41	203	13	3	1	-5
1987	Bos-A	.994	60	303	29	2	6	1
Total	5	.990	137	663	52	7	9	2

Marty Sullivan OF

YEAR	TM/L	PCT	G	PO	A	E	DP	FR
1887	Chi-N	.847	115	189	10	**36**	0	-8
1888	Chi-N	.927	75	114	13	10	7	3
1889	Ind-N	.910	64	133	9	14	4	-5
1890	Bos-N	.951	120	241	13	13	1	2
1891	Bos-N	.926	17	24	1	2	0	-2
	Cle-N	—	1	0	0	0	0	0
	Yr	.926	18	24	1	2	0	-2
Total	5	.909	392	701	46	5	12	-10

1B

YEAR	TM/L	PCT	G	PO	A	E	DP	FR
1889	Ind-N	.983	5	58	0	1	4	-1

3B

YEAR	TM/L	PCT	G	PO	A	E	DP	FR
1890	Bos-N	1.000	1	1	3	0	0	0

Billy Sullivan C

YEAR	TM/L	PCT	G	PO	A	E	DP	FR
1932	Chi-A	.867	5	12	1	2	0	-2
1933	Chi-A	.857	8	21	3	4	0	-3
1936	Cle-A	.968	72	324	40	12	8	-2
1937	Cle-A	.949	38	146	20	9	1	-5
1938	StL-A	**.990**	99	441	65	5	10	-2
1939	StL-A	.960	19	88	8	4	4	-2
1940	Det-A	.976	57	292	29	8	4	1
1941	Det-A	.976	63	339	33	9	7	5
1942	Bro-N	.962	41	140	13	6	2	-1
1947	Pit-N	1.000	12	42	4	0	1	1
Total	10	.972	414	1845	216	9	37	-10

1B

YEAR	TM/L	PCT	G	PO	A	E	DP	FR
1931	Chi-A	1.000	1	6	0	0	1	0
1932	Chi-A	.990	52	485	35	5	42	2
1933	Chi-A	.982	22	211	12	4	22	0
1935	Cin-N	.992	40	350	31	3	35	3
1936	Cle-A	1.000	3	25	3	0	4	1
1937	Cle-A	1.000	5	62	1	0	3	1
1938	StL-A	1.000	6	43	4	0	7	0
1939	StL-A	.963	4	24	2	1	5	0
Total	8	.990	133	1196	88	3	119	5

3B

YEAR	TM/L	PCT	G	PO	A	E	DP	FR
1931	Chi-A	.912	83	96	152	**24**	9	-8
1932	Chi-A	.880	17	14	30	6	4	-2
1935	Cin-N	.980	15	18	30	1	5	2
1936	Cle-A	1.000	5	6	9	0	1	0
1937	Cle-A	1.000	1	1	2	0	0	0
1940	Det-A	.900	6	4	14	2	1	0
Total	6	.919	127	139	237	3	20	-8

OF

YEAR	TM/L	PCT	G	PO	A	E	DP	FR
1931	Chi-A	1.000	2	2	0	0	0	-1
1932	Chi-A	.600	3	3	0	2	0	-1
1936	Cle-A	—	1	0	0	0	0	0
1939	StL-A	.954	59	139	7	7	3	4
Total	4	.944	65	144	7	9	3	2

2B

YEAR	TM/L	PCT	G	PO	A	E	DP	FR
1935	Cin-N	.889	6	15	17	4	1	-3

Billy Sullivan C

YEAR	TM/L	PCT	G	PO	A	E	DP	FR
1899	Bos-N	.952	22	94	26	6	3	6
1900	Bos-N	.974	66	227	71	8	10	1
1901	Chi-A	**.967**	97	396	104	17	**13**	-1
1902	Chi-A	.967	70	242	81	11	8	-2
1903	Chi-A	.988	31	123	35	2	1	-2
1904	Chi-A	.964	**107**	463	**130**	22	10	2
1905	Chi-A	.974	92	389	104	13	8	4
1906	Chi-A	**.974**	118	475	134	16	7	-5
1907	Chi-A	.983	108	477	117	10	12	4
1908	Chi-A	**.985**	**137**	553	156	11	11	-21
1909	Chi-A	.983	97	452	119	10	6	5
1910	Chi-A	.976	45	290	71	9	5	13

YEAR	TM/L	PCT	G	PO	A	E	DP	FR
1911	Chi-A	**.986**	89	447	114	8	13	1
1912	Chi-A	.975	41	147	52	5	4	1
1914	Chi-A	1.000	1	1	0	0	0	0
1916	Det-A	—	1	0	0	0	0	0
Total	16	.976	1122	4776	1314	148	111	-7

1B

YEAR	TM/L	PCT	G	PO	A	E	DP	FR
1902	Chi-A	1.000	2	11	0	0	2	0
1905	Chi-A	1.000	2	15	0	0	2	0
Total	2	1.000	4	26	0	0	4	0

2B

YEAR	TM/L	PCT	G	PO	A	E	DP	FR
1900	Bos-N	1.000	1	3	3	0	1	0
1907	Chi-A	1.000	1	2	2	0	1	0
Total	2	1.000	2	5	5	0	2	0

3B

YEAR	TM/L	PCT	G	PO	A	E	DP	FR
1901	Chi-A	.000	1	0	0	2	0	-1
1905	Chi-A	—	1	0	0	0	0	0
Total	2	.000	2	0	0	2	0	-1

OF

YEAR	TM/L	PCT	G	PO	A	E	DP	FR
1902	Chi-A	1.000	2	1	0	0	0	0

SS

YEAR	TM/L	PCT	G	PO	A	E	DP	FR
1900	Bos-N	.833	1	2	3	1	0	0

■ Homer Summa OF

YEAR	TM/L	PCT	G	PO	A	E	DP	FR
1920	Pit-N	.950	6	18	1	1	0	1
1922	Cle-A	1.000	12	14	3	0	0	0
1923	Cle-A	.951	136	216	15	12	5	-13
1924	Cle-A	.941	95	167	10	11	2	-6
1925	Cle-A	.966	54	83	2	3	0	-8
1926	Cle-A	.975	154	328	18	9	5	7
1927	Cle-A	.955	145	242	12	12	3	-8
1928	Cle-A	.971	132	223	12	7	5	-4
1929	Phi-A	.980	24	48	1	1	0	-5
1930	Phi-A	.938	15	29	1	2	0	0
Total	10	.961	773	1368	75	8	20	-36

3B

YEAR	TM/L	PCT	G	PO	A	E	DP	FR
1925	Cle-A	.714	2	3	2	2	0	-1

■ Champ Summers OF

YEAR	TM/L	PCT	G	PO	A	E	DP	FR
1974	Oak-A	1.000	12	6	0	0	0	0
1975	Chi-N	.889	18	16	0	2	0	-2
1976	Chi-N	.964	26	26	1	1	0	-1
1977	Cin-N	1.000	16	23	1	0	0	1
1978	Cin-N	.933	12	14	0	1	0	-2
1979	Cin-N	.941	13	15	1	1	0	-1
	Det-A	.989	69	87	3	1	0	-6
1980	Det-A	.953	47	60	1	3	0	-5
1981	Det-A	.964	18	26	1	1	0	-1
1982	SF-N	.913	31	40	2	4	0	-3
1983	SF-N	1.000	1	2	0	0	0	0
Total	10	.959	263	315	10	4	0	-20

1B

YEAR	TM/L	PCT	G	PO	A	E	DP	FR
1976	Chi-N	1.000	10	69	4	0	10	0
1979	Cin-N	.979	6	41	5	1	4	0
	Det-A	1.000	4	23	1	0	1	0
1980	Det-A	—	1	0	0	0	0	0
1982	SF-N	1.000	3	6	1	0	0	0
1984	SD-N	1.000	8	53	1	0	8	-1
Total	5	.995	32	192	12	1	23	-1

C

YEAR	TM/L	PCT	G	PO	A	E	DP	FR
1976	Chi-N	—	1	0	0	0	0	0

3B

YEAR	TM/L	PCT	G	PO	A	E	DP	FR
1977	Cin-N	1.000	1	1	1	0	1	0

■ Billy Sunday OF

YEAR	TM/L	PCT	G	PO	A	E	DP	FR
1883	Chi-N	.647	14	10	1	6	0	-5
1884	Chi-N	.663	43	45	8	27	1	-9
1885	Chi-N	.825	46	46	6	11	2	-8
1886	Chi-N	.914	28	50	3	5	0	0
1887	Chi-N	.766	50	78	4	25	2	-7
1888	Pit-N	.939	120	**297**	27	21	5	**16**
1889	Pit-N	.946	81	157	17	10	2	9
1890	Pit-N	.883	86	181	23	27	9	7
	Phi-N	.950	31	69	7	4	2	5
	Yr	.900	117	250	30	31	11	12
Total	8	.883	499	933	96	136	23	8

■ Jim Sundberg C

YEAR	TM/L	PCT	G	PO	A	E	DP	FR
1974	Tex-A	.990	132	722	69	8	**15**	5
1975	Tex-A	.981	**155**	**791**	101	17	11	5
1976	Tex-A	**.991**	**140**	**719**	**96**	7	**11**	**16**
1977	Tex-A	**.994**	149	**801**	103	5	**12**	**22**
1978	Tex-A	**.997**	148	**769**	91	3	**14**	**16**
1979	Tex-A	**.995**	**150**	**754**	75	4	**14**	9
1980	Tex-A	.993	**151**	**853**	76	7	7	7
1981	Tex-A	.996	98	464	**52**	2	9	-3
1982	Tex-A	.991	132	607	69	6	**15**	-1
1983	Tex-A	.993	131	618	56	5	2	5
1984	Mil-A	**.995**	109	556	55	3	6	6
1985	KC-A	.992	112	572	41	5	10	-6
1986	KC-A	**.995**	134	686	46	4	11	-1
1987	Chi-N	.994	57	273	34	2	2	8
1988	Chi-N	1.000	20	88	7	0	1	-1
	Tex-A	1.000	36	141	9	0	2	-2
1989	Chi-N	.992	73	353	27	3	3	2
Total	16	.993	1927	9767	1007	1	145	87

OF

YEAR	TM/L	PCT	G	PO	A	E	DP	FR
1981	Tex-A	1.000	2	1	0	0	0	0
1982	Tex-A	1.000	1	5	0	0	0	0
Total	2	1.000	3	6	0	0	0	0

■ B.J. Surhoff C

YEAR	TM/L	PCT	G	PO	A	E	DP	FR
1987	Mil-A	.984	98	645	49	11	10	6
1988	Mil-A	.990	106	525	42	6	2	-6
1989	Mil-A	.985	106	526	51	9	6	-6
1990	Mil-A	.985	125	615	53	10	10	-7
Total	4	.986	435	2311	195	6	28	-13

3B

YEAR	TM/L	PCT	G	PO	A	E	DP	FR
1987	Mil-A	1.000	10	2	6	0	2	0
1988	Mil-A	.987	20	23	52	1	1	-1
1989	Mil-A	.917	6	4	7	1	1	0
1990	Mil-A	.867	11	4	9	2	1	-1
Total	4	.964	58	33	74	4	5	-2

1B

YEAR	TM/L	PCT	G	PO	A	E	DP	FR
1987	Mil-A	1.000	1	1	1	0	0	0
1988	Mil-A	.500	2	1	0	1	0	0
Total	2	.750	3	2	1	1	0	0

SS

YEAR	TM/L	PCT	G	PO	A	E	DP	FR
1988	Mil-A	1.000	1	1	0	0	0	0

OF

YEAR	TM/L	PCT	G	PO	A	E	DP	FR
1988	Mil-A	—	1	0	0	0	0	0

■ George Susce C

YEAR	TM/L	PCT	G	PO	A	E	DP	FR
1929	Phi-N	.900	11	9	0	1	0	-1
1932	Det-A	1.000	2	1	0	0	0	0
1939	Pit-N	.984	31	111	14	2	2	3
1940	StL-A	.984	61	168	21	3	3	7
1941	Cle-A	1.000	1	1	0	0	0	0
1942	Cle-A	1.000	2	2	0	0	0	0
1943	Cle-A	1.000	3	0	2	0	0	0
1944	Cle-A	.948	29	78	13	5	3	2
Total	8	.974	140	370	50	1	8	11

■ Sy Sutcliffe C

YEAR	TM/L	PCT	G	PO	A	E	DP	FR
1884	Chi-N	.976	4	34	6	1	1	4
1885	Chi-N	.838	11	46	11	11	0	-3
	StL-N	.881	14	59	15	10	0	0
	Yr	.862	25	105	26	21	0	-3
1888	Det-N	.872	14	75	34	16	5	3
1889	Cle-N	.892	37	179	70	30	3	10
1890	Cle-P	.864	84	264	115	**50**	9	0
1891	Was-a	.905	22	65	30	10	3	1
Total	6	.887	186	722	281	128	21	15

1B

YEAR	TM/L	PCT	G	PO	A	E	DP	FR
1888	Det-N	.917	5	54	1	5	2	-1
1889	Cle-N	.987	8	74	4	1	7	1
1892	Bal-N	.958	66	678	24	31	39	-7
Total	3	.958	79	806	29	7	48	-7

OF

YEAR	TM/L	PCT	G	PO	A	E	DP	FR
1885	Chi-N	.500	1	1	0	1	0	0
	StL-N	.500	2	2	1	3	0	0
	Yr	.500	3	3	1	4	0	0
1888	Det-N	.750	4	3	0	1	0	0
1889	Cle-N	—	1	0	0	0	0	0
1890	Cle-P	.852	15	19	4	4	1	0
1891	Was-a	.918	35	50	6	5	1	0
Total	5	.860	58	75	11	4	2	0

SS

YEAR	TM/L	PCT	G	PO	A	E	DP	FR
1888	Det-N	.901	24	39	88	14	6	6
1890	Cle-P	.714	4	3	7	4	1	-1
1891	Was-a	.571	3	3	5	6	0	-3
Total	3	.858	31	45	100	4	7	2

3B

YEAR	TM/L	PCT	G	PO	A	E	DP	FR
1890	Cle-P	—	2	0	0	0	0	0
1891	Was-a	—	1	0	0	0	0	0
Total	2	—	3	0	0	0	0	0
1888	Det-N	.625	2	1	4	3	0	-1

■ Gary Sutherland 2B

YEAR	TM/L	PCT	G	PO	A	E	DP	FR
1968	Phi-N	.968	17	25	36	2	6	-1
1969	Mon-N	.971	139	318	381	21	**110**	11
1970	Mon-N	.975	97	178	254	11	72	5
1971	Mon-N	.963	56	90	142	9	38	11
1972	Hou-N	—	1	0	0	0	0	0
1973	Hou-N	.971	14	37	31	2	11	-4
1974	Det-A	.976	147	337	360	17	101	-25
1975	Det-A	.968	128	278	365	21	83	-7
1976	Det-A	.984	42	73	117	3	31	1
	Mil-A	.955	45	83	87	8	21	0
	Yr	.970	87	156	204	11	52	1
1977	SD-N	.943	30	26	40	4	10	-4
1978	StL-N	1.000	1	0	3	0	0	2
Total	11	.971	717	1445	1816	8	483	-11

SS

YEAR	TM/L	PCT	G	PO	A	E	DP	FR
1966	Phi-N	1.000	1	1	2	0	1	1
1967	Phi-N	.928	66	77	115	15	33	-14
1968	Phi-N	.974	10	10	27	1	3	-1
1969	Mon-N	1.000	15	8	8	0	2	-1
1970	Mon-N	.933	15	4	10	1	1	-1
1971	Mon-N	.934	46	64	107	12	21	-11
1973	Hou-N	—	1	0	0	0	0	0
1974	Det-A	.900	10	2	7	1	1	-1
Total	8	.936	164	166	276	0	62	-28

3B

YEAR	TM/L	PCT	G	PO	A	E	DP	FR
1968	Phi-N	1.000	10	7	10	0	1	0
1970	Mon-N	—	1	0	0	0	0	0
1971	Mon-N	1.000	2	3	4	0	1	0
1972	Hou-N	1.000	1	1	2	0	0	0
1974	Det-A	1.000	4	1	13	0	1	1
1977	SD-N	1.000	21	6	13	0	0	0
Total	6	1.000	39	18	42	0	3	1

OF

YEAR	TM/L	PCT	G	PO	A	E	DP	FR
1967	Phi-N	1.000	25	33	0	0	0	0
1968	Phi-N	1.000	7	6	0	0	0	0
1969	Mon-N	1.000	1	2	0	0	0	0
1971	Mon-N	—	4	0	0	0	0	0
Total	4	1.000	37	41	0	0	0	0

1B

YEAR	TM/L	PCT	G	PO	A	E	DP	FR
1976	Mil-A	1.000	2	5	0	0	0	0
1977	SD-N	.875	4	7	0	1	2	0
Total	2	.923	6	12	0	1	2	0

■ Ezra Sutton 3B

YEAR	TM/L	PCT	G	PO	A	E	DP	FR
1876	Phi-N	.679	8	11	8	9	0	-2
1877	Bos-N	.821	22	38	31	15	2	-5
1878	Bos-N	.888	59	80	118	25	8	-2
1879	Bos-N	.814	33	36	43	18	3	-11
1880	Bos-N	.897	37	64	66	15	5	0
1881	Bos-N	.877	81	114	157	38	10	-3
1882	Bos-N	.856	77	98	146	41	6	-3
1883	Bos-N	.866	93	120	152	42	14	-1
1884	Bos-N	**.908**	**110**	119	186	31	7	-3
1885	Bos-N	.875	91	132	168	43	**18**	3
1886	Bos-N	.874	28	34	63	14	5	2
1887	Bos-N	.861	11	18	13	5	1	-1
1888	Bos-N	.859	27	32	47	13	4	-4
Total	13	.871	677	896	1198	309	83	-30

SS

YEAR	TM/L	PCT	G	PO	A	E	DP	FR
1877	Bos-N	.882	36	66	91	21	8	-3
1878	Bos-N	1.000	1	2	3	0	1	1
1879	Bos-N	.884	51	53	167	29	15	-1
1880	Bos-N	.896	39	50	122	20	14	4
1881	Bos-N	.800	2	0	4	1	0	0
1882	Bos-N	.917	4	6	5	1	0	-1
1883	Bos-N	1.000	1	2	5	0	0	1
1885	Bos-N	.886	16	12	50	8	6	-3
1886	Bos-N	.883	28	29	84	15	7	-2
1887	Bos-N	.875	37	113	174	41	10	25
1888	Bos-N	.600	1	1	2	2	0	-1
Total	11	.883	216	334	707	138	61	20

OF

YEAR	TM/L	PCT	G	PO	A	E	DP	FR
1876	Phi-N	.818	4	8	1	2	0	0
1883	Bos-N	1.000	1	1	0	0	0	0
1886	Bos-N	.859	43	74	5	13	1	-2
1887	Bos-N	.875	18	21	0	3	0	-2
Total	4	.859	66	104	6	8	1	-4

2B

YEAR	TM/L	PCT	G	PO	A	E	DP	FR
1876	Phi-N	.832	15	47	32	16	7	-2
1885	Bos-N	1.000	2	3	4	0	0	0
1886	Bos-N	.873	18	44	52	14	6	-3
1887	Bos-N	.890	13	26	47	9	1	-4
Total	4	.867	48	120	135	9	14	-9

1B

YEAR	TM/L	PCT	G	PO	A	E	DP	FR
1876	Phi-N	.915	29	324	11	31	6	0
1885	Bos-N	.833	1	10	0	2	0	0
Total	2	.913	30	334	11	3	6	0

■ Dale Sveum SS

YEAR	TM/L	PCT	G	PO	A	E	DP	FR
1986	Mil-A	.945	13	18	34	3	5	-2
1987	Mil-A	.965	142	221	361	21	82	-13
1988	Mil-A	.955	127	208	370	**27**	93	-6
1990	Mil-A	.889	5	3	5	1	1	-1
Total	4	.959	287	450	770	2	181	-22

3B

YEAR	TM/L	PCT	G	PO	A	E	DP	FR
1986	Mil-A	.865	65	45	122	**26**	8	-4
1990	Mil-A	.918	22	17	28	4	2	-2
Total	2	.876	87	62	150	0	10	-6

2B

YEAR	TM/L	PCT	G	PO	A	E	DP	FR
1986	Mil-A	.981	13	29	23	1	6	-2
1987	Mil-A	.966	13	21	35	2	7	-1
1988	Mil-A	1.000	1	1	5	0	1	1
1990	Mil-A	.981	16	22	30	1	6	-1
Total	4	.976	43	73	93	4	20	-3

1B

YEAR	TM/L	PCT	G	PO	A	E	DP	FR
1990	Mil-A	1.000	5	17	0	0	1	-1

■ Harry Swacina 1B

YEAR	TM/L	PCT	G	PO	A	E	DP	FR
1907	Pit-N	.996	26	246	12	1	9	-1
1908	Pit-N	.983	50	501	19	9	19	-5
1914	Bal-F	.985	**158**	**1616**	**104**	26	74	**10**
1915	Bal-F	.986	75	735	57	11	50	**6**
Total	4	.986	309	3098	192	7	152	10

2B

YEAR	TM/L	PCT	G	PO	A	E	DP	FR
1915	Bal-F	1.000	1	0	1	0	0	0

■ Evar Swanson OF

YEAR	TM/L	PCT	G	PO	A	E	DP	FR
1929	Cin-N	.970	142	317	9	10	2	-2
1930	Cin-N	.963	71	178	5	7	1	3
1932	Chi-A	.960	14	24	0	1	0	-3
1933	Chi-A	.973	139	281	7	8	0	-8
1934	Chi-A	.980	105	193	4	4	1	-6
Total	5	.971	471	993	25	0	4	-16

■ Ed Swartwood OF

YEAR	TM/L	PCT	G	PO	A	E	DP	FR
1881	Buf-N	.500	1	1	0	1	0	0
1882	Pit-a	.788	73	99	9	29	2	-8
1883	Pit-a	.816	37	71	9	18	0	3
1884	Pit-a	.804	79	109	22	32	2	-3
1885	Bro-a	.851	95	140	8	26	0	-9
1886	Bro-a	.884	122	189	**32**	29	4	7
1887	Bro-a	.835	91	129	23	30	5	1
1890	Tol-a	.925	126	224	23	20	2	8
1892	Pit-N	.933	13	22	6	2	2	4
Total	9	.856	637	984	132	187	17	3

1B

YEAR	TM/L	PCT	G	PO	A	E	DP	FR
1882	Pit-a	.921	4	34	1	3	1	0
1883	Pit-a	.936	60	632	23	45	28	0
1884	Pit-a	.919	22	238	12	22	18	-1
1885	Bro-a	1.000	4	36	1	0	1	0
Total	4	.933	90	940	37	0	48	-1

C

YEAR	TM/L	PCT	G	PO	A	E	DP	FR
1883	Pit-a	—	3	0	0	0	0	0
1885	Bro-a	1.000	1	3	0	0	0	0
1886	Bro-a	1.000	1	1	1	0	0	0
Total	3	1.000	5	4	1	0	0	0

3B

YEAR	TM/L	PCT	G	PO	A	E	DP	FR
1884	Pit-a	1.000	1	2	2	0	0	0

SS

YEAR	TM/L	PCT	G	PO	A	E	DP	FR
1885	Bro-a	—	1	0	0	0	0	0

■ Charlie Sweasy 2B

YEAR	TM/L	PCT	G	PO	A	E	DP	FR
1876	Cin-N	.864	55	167	158	51	**30**	3
1878	Pro-N	.846	55	141	183	59	20	-8
Total	2	.855	110	308	341	110	50	-5
1876	Cin-N	.400	1	2	0	3	0	-1

■ Jeff Sweeney C

YEAR	TM/L	PCT	G	PO	A	E	DP	FR
1908	NY-A	.955	25	122	26	7	2	1

YEAR	TM/L	PCT	G	PO	A	E	DP	FR
1909	NY-A	.947	62	274	83	**20**	7	3
1910	NY-A	.974	77	388	106	13	2	6
1911	NY-A	.964	83	394	94	18	8	-4
1912	NY-A	.955	108	**548**	167	**34**	9	0
1913	NY-A	.964	112	511	**180**	26	9	10
1914	NY-A	.980	78	369	120	10	7	1
1915	NY-A	.975	53	213	59	7	4	-6
1919	Pit-N	.944	15	34	17	3	2	-3
Total	9	.964	613	2853	852	138	50	8
1B								
1908	NY-A	.923	1	12	0	1	0	0
1909	NY-A	.952	3	19	1	1	1	0
1913	NY-A	1.000	1	1	0	0	0	0
Total	3	.943	5	32	1	2	1	0
OF								
1908	NY-A	.000	1	0	0	1	0	-1
1913	NY-A	—	1	0	0	0	0	-1
Total	2	.000	2	0	0	1	0	-2

■ Bill Sweeney 2B

YEAR	TM/L	PCT	G	PO	A	E	DP	FR
1907	Bos-N	.900	5	14	13	3	1	-1
1908	Bos-N	1.000	1	1	2	0	0	0
1911	Bos-N	.944	136	**372**	410	**46**	61	**11**
1912	Bos-N	.959	**153**	**459**	**475**	**40**	**76**	**27**
1913	Bos-N	.939	137	301	391	**45**	42	1
1914	Chi-N	.954	134	301	426	35	40	15
Total	6	.949	566	1448	1717	169	220	53
3B								
1907	Bos-N	.871	23	36	52	13	5	1
1908	Bos-N	.930	123	174	277	34	14	12
1909	Bos-N	.903	112	156	243	**43**	14	3
1910	Bos-N	.948	21	39	53	5	2	7
Total	4	.916	279	405	625	5	35	23
SS								
1907	Chi-N	.571	3	2	6	6	0	-4
	Bos-N	.934	15	19	38	4	3	1
	Yr	.867	18	21	44	10	3	-3
1908	Bos-N	.750	3	0	3	1	0	0
1909	Bos-N	.943	26	66	83	9	12	3
1910	Bos-N	.903	110	232	300	**57**	52	-11
Total	4	.907	157	319	430	7	67	-11
1B								
1907	Bos-N	1.000	1	4	0	0	0	0
1910	Bos-N	.979	17	168	16	4	19	2
Total	2	.979	18	172	16	4	19	2
OF								
1907	Bos-N	.800	11	13	3	4	0	-1

■ Bill Sweeney 1B

YEAR	TM/L	PCT	G	PO	A	E	DP	FR
1928	Det-A	.993	75	677	55	5	51	**5**
1930	Bos-A	.997	56	541	30	2	49	0
1931	Bos-A	**.993**	124	1283	92	9	89	10
Total	3	.994	255	2501	177	6	189	15
OF								
1928	Det-A	1.000	3	3	0	0	0	-1
3B								
1930	Bos-A	—	1	0	0	0	0	0

■ Rick Sweet C

YEAR	TM/L	PCT	G	PO	A	E	DP	FR
1978	SD-N	.984	76	337	33	6	3	3
1982	Sea-A	.993	83	431	26	3	6	-6
1983	Sea-A	.987	85	413	34	6	6	-3
Total	3	.988	244	1181	93	5	15	-6

■ Bob Swift C

YEAR	TM/L	PCT	G	PO	A	E	DP	FR
1940	StL-A	.980	128	389	55	9	8	-20
1941	StL-A	.985	58	180	22	3	3	-4
1942	StL-A	1.000	28	81	11	0	2	-1
	Phi-A	.970	60	253	39	9	3	2
	Yr	.977	88	334	50	9	5	1
1943	Det-A	.976	77	278	53	8	9	-3
1944	Det-A	.982	76	288	48	6	4	1
1945	Det-A	.988	94	358	60	5	12	1
1946	Det-A	.980	42	187	14	4	2	-4
1947	Det-A	.989	97	401	45	5	6	0
1948	Det-A	.991	111	470	55	5	10	7
1949	Det-A	.989	69	232	26	3	6	1
1950	Det-A	.995	66	201	20	1	3	8
1951	Det-A	.982	43	146	17	3	3	2
1952	Det-A	.977	28	118	12	3	1	6
1953	Det-A	1.000	2	13	0	0	0	1
Total	14	.985	980	3601	477	4	75	-3

■ Steve Swisher C

YEAR	TM/L	PCT	G	PO	A	E	DP	FR
1974	Chi-N	.987	90	493	50	7	8	-1
1975	Chi-N	.979	93	426	36	10	5	-8
1976	Chi-N	.983	107	574	49	11	6	-3
1977	Chi-N	.976	72	327	38	9	3	-3
1978	StL-N	.991	42	202	13	2	0	6
1979	StL-N	.974	33	105	6	3	2	1
1980	StL-N	.957	8	21	1	1	0	0
1981	SD-N	.971	10	33	1	1	0	0
1982	SD-N	.981	26	93	9	2	0	1
Total	9	.982	481	2274	203	6	24	-7

■ Ron Swoboda OF

YEAR	TM/L	PCT	G	PO	A	E	DP	FR
1965	NY-N	.947	112	188	9	11	2	-2
1966	NY-N	.987	97	145	7	2	0	-4
1967	NY-N	.957	108	190	8	9	0	0
1968	NY-N	.975	125	217	14	6	4	4
1969	NY-N	.988	97	163	5	2	0	-2
1970	NY-N	.984	100	117	3	2	1	-14
1971	Mon-N	.977	26	39	3	1	0	2
	NY-A	.965	47	80	2	3	0	-2
1972	NY-A	.983	35	56	2	1	1	0
1973	NY-A	1.000	20	23	0	0	0	2
Total	9	.972	767	1218	53	7	8	-16
1B								
1967	NY-N	.976	20	143	17	4	7	2
1972	NY-A	1.000	2	5	0	0	1	0
Total	2	.976	22	148	17	4	8	2

■ Lou Sylvester OF

YEAR	TM/L	PCT	G	PO	A	E	DP	FR
1884	Cin-U	.792	81	110	23	35	2	2
1886	Lou-a	.913	45	54	9	6	3	0
	Cin-a	.909	17	26	4	3	2	1
	Yr	.912	62	80	13	9	5	1
1887	StL-a	.923	29	53	7	5	3	3
Total	3	.854	172	243	43	9	10	6
SS								
1884	Cin-U	.000	2	0	0	3	0	-1
2B								
1887	StL-a	.750	1	2	1	1	1	0

■ Pat Tabler 1B

YEAR	TM/L	PCT	G	PO	A	E	DP	FR
1984	Cle-A	.998	67	433	39	1	46	0
1985	Cle-A	.983	92	739	72	14	77	3
1986	Cle-A	.990	107	846	84	9	87	3
1987	Cle-A	.984	82	650	75	**12**	49	6
1988	Cle-A	1.000	10	74	5	0	5	0
	KC-A	.917	7	40	4	4	6	-1
	Yr	.969	17	114	9	4	11	-1
1989	KC-A	.993	20	126	13	1	10	1
1990	KC-A	1.000	5	31	1	0	6	0
Total	7	.987	390	2939	293	1	286	12
OF								
1983	Cle-A	.948	88	180	4	10	0	-4
1984	Cle-A	.973	43	72	1	2	1	-1
1988	KC-A	.986	37	68	1	1	0	-3
1989	KC-A	.970	55	89	8	3	1	0
1990	KC-A	.986	42	68	4	1	1	1
	NY-N	1.000	10	20	1	0	1	1
Total	5	.968	275	497	19	7	4	-6
3B								
1982	Chi-N	.949	25	23	33	3	3	-5
1983	Cle-A	.986	25	17	51	1	6	-2
1984	Cle-A	.950	36	27	49	4	7	-9
1985	Cle-A	1.000	4	4	3	0	0	0
1988	KC-A	—	1	0	0	0	0	0
1989	KC-A	—	1	0	0	0	0	0
1990	KC-A	.875	6	2	5	1	0	0
Total	7	.960	98	73	141	9	16	-16
2B								
1981	Chi-N	.982	35	70	93	3	17	1
1983	Cle-A	—	2	0	0	0	0	0
1984	Cle-A	—	1	0	0	0	0	0
1985	Cle-A	1.000	1	1	2	0	1	0
1989	KC-A	1.000	3	2	4	0	0	0
Total	5	.983	42	73	99	3	18	1

■ Jim Tabor 3B

YEAR	TM/L	PCT	G	PO	A	E	DP	FR
1938	Bos-A	.889	11	15	25	5	2	1
1939	Bos-A	.923	148	144	**338**	**40**	32	7
1940	Bos-A	.926	120	143	267	**33**	25	5
1941	Bos-A	.930	125	123	277	**30**	24	2
1942	Bos-A	.924	138	**168**	236	**33**	24	-9
1943	Bos-A	.938	133	135	261	**26**	**32**	-8
1944	Bos-A	.950	114	125	258	20	14	3
1946	Phi-N	.954	124	156	221	18	**17**	-3
1947	Phi-N	.916	67	68	96	15	8	-17
Total	9	.933	980	1077	1979	220	178	-19
SS								
1938	Bos-A	.727	2	3	5	3	3	0
OF								
1943	Bos-A	1.000	2	2	0	0	0	0

■ Doug Taitt OF

YEAR	TM/L	PCT	G	PO	A	E	DP	FR
1928	Bos-A	.975	139	251	19	7	**8**	5
1929	Bos-A	.955	21	39	3	2	1	0
	Chi-A	.966	30	52	4	2	2	0
	Yr	.961	51	91	7	4	3	0
1931	Phi-N	.990	38	95	4	1	0	3
Total	3	.975	228	437	30	2	11	8

■ Bob Talbot OF

YEAR	TM/L	PCT	G	PO	A	E	DP	FR
1953	Chi-N	1.000	7	20	3	0	1	3
1954	Chi-N	.985	111	245	10	4	1	-10
Total	2	.986	118	265	13	4	2	-7

■ Lee Tannehill 3B

YEAR	TM/L	PCT	G	PO	A	E	DP	FR
1904	Chi-A	.947	153	180	**369**	31	**22**	**28**
1905	Chi-A	.931	142	168	**358**	**39**	**17**	**28**
1906	Chi-A	.951	99	131	**278**	21	12	**36**
1907	Chi-A	.912	31	21	82	10	3	4
1908	Chi-A	.935	136	135	**341**	33	15	**17**
1909	Chi-A	.941	91	103	168	17	11	-8
1910	Chi-A	.955	6	9	12	1	0	0
1911	Chi-A	.900	7	4	14	2	3	-1
1912	Chi-A	.667	3	2	2	2	1	0
Total	9	.938	668	753	1624	156	84	104
SS								
1903	Chi-A	.908	138	291	457	76	**58**	-4
1906	Chi-A	.941	17	42	54	6	1	4
1907	Chi-A	.929	2	4	9	1	1	1
1908	Chi-A	.909	5	7	13	2	6	1
1909	Chi-A	.940	64	126	251	24	21	15
1910	Chi-A	.947	38	52	126	10	15	1
1911	Chi-A	.957	102	262	380	29	37	**33**
1912	Chi-A	—	1	0	0	0	0	0
Total	8	.933	367	784	1290	148	139	51
1B								
1910	Chi-A	.991	23	206	18	2	6	3
1911	Chi-A	1.000	5	52	3	0	1	0
Total	2	.993	28	258	21	2	7	3
2B								
1911	Chi-A	.959	27	67	96	7	12	10

■ Chuck Tanner OF

YEAR	TM/L	PCT	G	PO	A	E	DP	FR
1955	Mil-N	.981	62	101	4	2	0	-5
1956	Mil-N	.800	8	4	0	1	0	-2
1957	Mil-N	1.000	18	35	0	0	0	-1
	Chi-N	.988	82	156	5	2	2	-11
	Yr	.990	100	191	5	2	2	-12
1958	Chi-N	.955	15	21	0	1	0	-2
1959	Cle-A	1.000	10	18	0	0	0	-1
1960	Cle-A	1.000	4	5	0	0	0	0
1961	LA-A	—	1	0	0	0	0	0
1962	LA-A	—	2	0	0	0	0	0
Total	8	.983	202	340	9	6	2	-22

■ El Tappe C

YEAR	TM/L	PCT	G	PO	A	E	DP	FR
1954	Chi-N	.986	46	185	22	3	2	5
1955	Chi-N	1.000	2	3	1	0	0	1
1956	Chi-N	1.000	3	4	0	0	0	0
1958	Chi-N	.962	16	46	4	2	0	0
1960	Chi-N	.992	49	215	27	2	4	9
1962	Chi-N	1.000	26	101	13	0	4	4
Total	6	.989	142	554	67	7	10	19

■ Dan Tartabull OF

YEAR	TM/L	PCT	G	PO	A	E	DP	FR
1986	Sea-A	.953	101	157	7	8	0	-12
1987	KC-A	.976	149	228	11	6	1	-12
1988	KC-A	.963	130	227	8	9	1	-7
1989	KC-A	.982	71	108	3	2	0	-7
1990	KC-A	.965	52	81	1	3	0	-7
Total	5	.967	503	801	30	8	2	-45
2B								
1984	Sea-A	1.000	1	1	1	0	1	0
1986	Sea-A	.947	31	76	101	10	28	6
Total	2	.947	32	77	102	10	29	6
SS								
1984	Sea-A	.931	8	7	20	2	4	1
1985	Sea-A	.940	16	26	37	4	11	-3
Total	2	.938	24	33	57	6	15	-2
3B								
1985	Sea-A	1.000	4	2	6	0	0	0
1986	Sea-A	1.000	1	0	3	0	0	0
Total	2	1.000	5	2	9	0	0	0

■ Jose Tartabull OF

YEAR	TM/L	PCT	G	PO	A	E	DP	FR
1962	KC-A	.974	85	185	6	5	0	7
1963	KC-A	.986	71	135	3	2	1	-1
1964	KC-A	.978	59	42	3	1	1	4
1965	KC-A	.986	54	133	5	2	0	7
1966	KC-A	1.000	33	70	1	0	0	0
	Bos-A	.989	46	90	1	1	0	0
	Yr	.994	79	160	2	1	0	0
1967	Bos-A	.989	83	90	3	1	1	-5
1968	Bos-A	.984	43	59	1	1	0	0
1969	Oak-A	.993	63	134	2	1	0	-1
1970	Oak-A	1.000	6	3	0	0	0	1
Total	9	.986	543	941	25	4	3	12

■ Willie Tasby OF

YEAR	TM/L	PCT	G	PO	A	E	DP	FR
1958	Bal-A	1.000	16	30	0	0	0	0
1959	Bal-A	.968	137	320	13	**11**	**4**	-3
1960	Bal-A	.980	36	47	1	1	0	0
	Bos-A	.979	102	232	6	5	1	-2
	Yr	.979	138	279	7	6	1	-2
1961	Was-A	.985	139	332	5	5	0	-5
1962	Was-A	.933	10	14	0	1	0	-1
	Cle-A	1.000	66	105	1	0	0	-1
	Yr	.992	76	119	1	1	0	-2
1963	Cle-A	.981	37	53	0	1	0	-2
Total	6	.980	543	1133	26	4	5	-14
3B								
1962	Cle-A	1.000	1	0	1	0	0	0
2B								
1963	Cle-A	1.000	1	1	0	0	0	0

■ Pop Tate C

YEAR	TM/L	PCT	G	PO	A	E	DP	FR
1885	Bos-N	.865	4	19	13	5	0	3
1886	Bos-N	.885	31	163	44	27	2	-4
1887	Bos-N	.924	53	209	109	26	6	10
1888	Bos-N	.854	41	188	64	43	6	-4
1889	Bal-a	.938	62	306	75	25	3	-3
1890	Bal-a	.923	11	33	15	4	1	-2
Total	6	.905	202	918	320	130	18	0
1B								
1889	Bal-a	.931	10	65	2	5	1	-1
1890	Bal-a	.965	8	79	3	3	2	0
Total	2	.949	18	144	5	8	3	-1
OF								
1887	Bos-N	.909	8	8	2	1	0	1
1888	Bos-N	—	1	0	0	0	0	0
Total	2	.909	9	8	2	1	0	1

■ Bennie Tate C

YEAR	TM/L	PCT	G	PO	A	E	DP	FR
1924	Was-A	.841	14	33	4	7	0	-3
1925	Was-A	.955	14	36	6	2	2	2
1926	Was-A	.960	45	109	35	6	3	-4
1927	Was-A	.977	39	148	24	4	4	4
1928	Was-A	.985	30	111	21	2	1	2
1929	Was-A	.971	74	291	49	10	10	-2
1930	Was-A	.933	9	12	2	1	0	-1
	Chi-A	.981	70	219	40	5	5	-10
	Yr	.978	79	231	42	6	**5**	-11
1931	Chi-A	.987	85	310	69	5	11	7
1932	Chi-A	1.000	4	9	3	0	0	0
	Bos-A	.974	76	244	50	8	7	-6
	Yr	.975	80	253	53	8	7	-6
1934	Chi-N	1.000	8	12	3	0	0	-3
Total	10	.974	468	1534	306	0	43	-15

■ Don Taussig OF

YEAR	TM/L	PCT	G	PO	A	E	DP	FR
1958	SF-N	1.000	36	28	0	0	0	0
1961	StL-N	.992	87	123	6	1	2	8
1962	Hou-N	1.000	4	10	0	0	0	1
Total	3	.994	127	161	6	1	2	9

■ Jackie Tavener SS

YEAR	TM/L	PCT	G	PO	A	E	DP	FR
1921	Det-A	1.000	2	3	4	0	0	1

YEAR	TM/L	PCT	G	PO	A	E	DP	FR
1925	Det-A	.963	134	229	398	24	73	7
1926	Det-A	.952	**156**	300	470	39	**92**	9
1927	Det-A	.948	114	246	356	33	79	4
1928	Det-A	.944	131	302	405	42	81	14
1929	Cle-A	.945	89	158	275	25	59	23
Total	6	.951	626	1238	1908	163	384	58

■ **Frank Taveras SS**

YEAR	TM/L	PCT	G	PO	A	E	DP	FR
1972	Pit-N	1.000	4	2	2	0	1	-1
1974	Pit-N	.941	124	170	321	31	60	-17
1975	Pit-N	.953	132	200	369	28	74	-15
1976	Pit-N	.952	141	210	481	35	74	-5
1977	Pit-N	.962	146	178	449	25	62	-22
1978	Pit-N	.946	157	216	448	38	80	-29
1979	Pit-N	.935	11	17	26	3	4	-4
	NY-N	.966	153	270	438	25	88	-22
	Yr	.964	164	287	464	28	92	-26
1980	NY-N	.959	140	237	347	25	63	-39
1981	NY-N	.931	79	120	202	24	44	-22
1982	Mon-N	.947	26	20	16	2	5	-2
Total	10	.953	1113	1640	3099	236	555	178
			2B					
1982	Mon-N	.958	19	38	54	4	13	1

■ **Tony Taylor 2B**

YEAR	TM/L	PCT	G	PO	A	E	DP	FR
1958	Chi-N	.968	137	311	374	23	103	10
1959	Chi-N	.970	149	352	**456**	25	105	11
1960	Chi-N	.977	19	36	50	2	20	-2
	Phi-N	.968	123	283	356	21	67	-6
	Yr	.969	142	319	406	23	87	-8
1961	Phi-N	.980	91	231	270	10	74	-1
1962	Phi-N	.972	150	372	385	22	101	-15
1963	Phi-N	**.986**	149	319	396	10	86	-9
1964	Phi-N	.977	150	325	358	16	94	-20
1965	Phi-N	.958	86	169	220	17	51	-3
1966	Phi-N	.988	68	137	182	4	36	1
1967	Phi-N	.972	42	64	73	4	23	-5
1968	Phi-N	.923	5	3	9	1	1	0
1969	Phi-N	.970	57	122	139	8	44	-6
1970	Phi-N	.996	59	151	132	1	41	-5
1971	Phi-N	1.000	14	27	34	0	11	2
	Det-A	.995	51	114	107	1	29	1
1972	Det-A	.966	67	121	108	8	25	-8
1973	Det-A	.987	72	134	165	4	37	-13
1974	Phi-N	1.000	4	1	2	0	1	0
1975	Phi-N	.800	3	2	2	1	1	0
1976	Phi-N	—	2	0	0	0	0	0
Total	19	.976	1498	3274	3818	178	950	-68
			3B					
1958	Chi-N	—	1	0	0	0	0	0
1960	Phi-N	1.000	4	2	5	0	0	0
1961	Phi-N	1.000	3	2	9	0	0	1
1963	Phi-N	1.000	13	6	16	0	2	0
1965	Phi-N	1.000	5	0	2	0	1	0
1966	Phi-N	.968	52	50	99	5	9	4
1967	Phi-N	.991	44	35	81	1	5	0
1968	Phi-N	.966	138	112	315	15	25	16
1969	Phi-N	.967	71	57	150	7	8	5
1970	Phi-N	.968	38	41	81	4	7	4
1971	Phi-N	.975	11	10	29	1	1	3
	Det-A	1.000	3	1	2	0	0	0
1972	Det-A	1.000	8	5	14	0	1	1
1973	Det-A	1.000	4	0	1	0	0	0
1974	Phi-N	1.000	5	1	1	0	0	0
1975	Phi-N	.913	16	10	32	4	1	2
1976	Phi-N	1.000	1	0	1	0	1	0
Total	16	.969	417	332	838	7	61	36
			1B					
1967	Phi-N	.991	58	422	25	4	45	-2
1968	Phi-N	—	1	0	0	0	0	0
1969	Phi-N	1.000	10	83	5	0	14	0
1971	Phi-N	1.000	2	21	1	0	2	0
1972	Det-A	1.000	1	4	0	0	0	0
1973	Det-A	1.000	6	17	2	0	0	0
1974	Phi-N	1.000	7	32	1	0	0	-1
1975	Phi-N	1.000	4	22	1	0	0	0
Total	8	.994	89	601	35	4	61	-3
			OF					
1970	Phi-N	1.000	18	28	1	0	0	0
1973	Det-A	—	1	0	0	0	0	0
Total	2	1.000	19	28	1	0	0	0
			SS					
1959	Chi-N	1.000	2	3	0	0	0	-1
1962	Phi-N	—	2	0	0	0	0	0
1967	Phi-N	1.000	3	3	3	0	0	0
1970	Phi-N	1.000	1	0	1	0	0	0
Total	4	1.000	8	6	4	0	0	-1

■ **Carl Taylor C**

YEAR	TM/L	PCT	G	PO	A	E	DP	FR
1968	Pit-N	.979	29	82	10	2	1	-5
1972	KC-A	.982	21	101	6	2	2	-2
1973	KC-A	.980	63	267	20	6	2	1
Total	3	.980	113	450	36	0	5	-6
			OF					
1968	Pit-N	1.000	2	1	0	0	0	0
1969	Pit-N	.914	36	50	3	5	2	1
1970	StL-N	.986	46	66	3	1	1	-1
1971	Pit-N	1.000	6	4	0	0	0	0
	KC-A	.964	12	27	0	1	0	1
1972	KC-A	1.000	7	5	0	0	0	0
Total	5	.958	109	153	6	7	3	1
			1B					
1969	Pit-N	.987	24	217	13	3	24	0
1970	StL-N	.983	15	109	6	2	10	-1
1972	KC-A	.981	6	50	2	1	3	-1
1973	KC-A	1.000	2	3	0	0	0	0
Total	4	.985	47	379	21	6	37	-2
			3B					
1970	StL-N	1.000	1	1	2	0	0	0
1972	KC-A	1.000	5	1	4	0	0	0
Total	2	1.000	6	2	6	0	0	0

■ **Danny Taylor OF**

YEAR	TM/L	PCT	G	PO	A	E	DP	FR
1926	Was-A	1.000	12	17	1	0	0	-1
1929	Chi-N	1.000	1	1	0	0	0	0
1930	Chi-N	.971	52	97	3	3	0	-5
1931	Chi-N	.989	67	170	3	2	0	-5
1932	Chi-N	.900	6	18	0	2	0	0
	Bro-N	.989	96	271	8	3	1	-1
	Yr	.983	102	289	8	5	1	-1
1933	Bro-N	.977	91	247	4	6	1	0
1934	Bro-N	.975	108	188	8	5	1	-9
1935	Bro-N	.970	99	193	4	6	0	-7
1936	Bro-N	.981	31	49	2	1	1	-2
Total	9	.979	563	1251	33	8	4	-30

■ **Harry Taylor 1B**

YEAR	TM/L	PCT	G	PO	A	E	DP	FR
1890	Lou-a	.982	118	1301	51	25	54	3
1891	Lou-a	.979	92	927	45	21	56	3
1892	Lou-a	.979	34	346	19	8	22	0
1893	Bal-N	.976	88	882	43	23	58	-3
Total	4	.979	332	3456	158	7	190	3
			OF					
1892	Lou-N	.923	73	121	10	11	3	1
			2B					
1890	Lou-a	.857	4	8	10	3	1	-2
1891	Lou-a	1.000	1	2	4	0	1	0
1892	Lou-N	.928	14	25	39	5	3	-6
Total	3	.917	19	35	53	8	5	-8
			SS					
1890	Lou-a	.900	12	21	51	8	4	4
1892	Lou-N	1.000	2	1	2	0	0	0
Total	2	.904	14	22	53	8	4	4
			3B					
1891	Lou-a	—	1	0	0	0	0	0
1892	Lou-N	.643	5	5	4	5	1	-3
Total	2	.643	6	5	4	5	1	-3
			C					
1890	Lou-a	—	1	0	0	0	0	0
1891	Lou-a	—	1	0	0	0	0	0
Total	2	—	2	0	0	0	0	0

■ **Zack Taylor C**

YEAR	TM/L	PCT	G	PO	A	E	DP	FR
1920	Bro-N	.882	9	11	4	2	0	-1
1921	Bro-N	.965	30	106	33	5	5	0
1922	Bro-N	.950	6	16	3	1	0	-1
1923	Bro-N	.967	84	354	118	16	6	15
1924	Bro-N	**.988**	93	388	96	6	13	-9
1925	Bro-N	.959	96	294	102	17	12	-9
1926	Bos-N	.985	123	394	**123**	8	17	2
1927	Bos-N	.988	27	137	28	2	3	12
	NY-N	.972	81	267	51	9	8	-4
	Yr	.978	108	404	79	11	11	8
1928	Bos-N	.985	124	367	83	7	8	-11
1929	Bos-N	.965	31	101	35	5	3	6
	Chi-N	.979	64	247	36	6	4	-1
	Yr	.974	95	348	71	11	7	5
1930	Chi-N	1.000	28	92	18	0	1	0
1931	Chi-N	1.000	5	5	2	0	0	0
1932	Chi-N	1.000	14	39	4	0	1	3
1933	Chi-N	1.000	12	8	0	0	0	0
1934	NY-A	1.000	3	3	2	0	0	0
1935	Bro-N	.970	26	51	14	2	2	1
Total	16	.977	856	2880	752	6	83	3

■ **Hawk Taylor C**

YEAR	TM/L	PCT	G	PO	A	E	DP	FR
1957	Mil-N	—	1	0	0	0	0	0
1961	Mil-N	—	1	0	0	0	0	0
1964	NY-N	.981	45	182	28	4	5	1
1965	NY-N	.962	15	46	5	2	0	-2
1966	NY-N	1.000	29	80	13	0	3	-4
1967	NY-N	.955	12	56	8	3	1	6
	Cal-A	1.000	19	84	10	0	2	2
1969	KC-A	1.000	6	19	1	0	0	-1
1970	KC-A	1.000	3	7	0	0	0	0
Total	8	.984	131	474	65	9	11	2
			OF					
1958	Mil-N	1.000	4	5	0	0	0	0
1961	Mil-N	1.000	5	8	1	0	0	1
1962	Mil-N	.960	11	23	1	1	0	1
1963	Mil-N	1.000	8	14	0	0	0	0
1964	NY-N	.966	16	28	0	1	0	-1
1969	KC-A	.909	18	19	1	2	1	0
Total	6	.962	62	97	3	4	1	1
			1B					
1965	NY-N	.857	1	5	1	1	0	0
1966	NY-N	.956	13	60	5	3	7	0
1970	KC-A	.875	1	5	2	1	1	0
Total	3	.940	15	70	8	5	8	0

■ **Sammy Taylor C**

YEAR	TM/L	PCT	G	PO	A	E	DP	FR
1958	Chi-N	.988	87	460	23	6	4	-12
1959	Chi-N	.982	109	497	37	10	1	-15
1960	Chi-N	.978	43	152	24	4	2	-9
1961	Chi-N	.989	75	319	25	4	5	-8
1962	Chi-N	1.000	6	23	1	0	0	-1
	NY-N	.991	50	202	25	2	3	-9
	Yr	.992	56	225	26	2	3	-10
1963	NY-N	1.000	13	55	3	0	1	0
	Cin-N	.833	2	5	0	1	0	-1
	Cle-A	1.000	2	8	2	0	1	-1
	Yr	1.000	15	63	5	0	2	-1
Total	6	.986	387	1721	140	7	17	-56

■ **Birdie Tebbetts C**

YEAR	TM/L	PCT	G	PO	A	E	DP	FR
1936	Det-A	.982	10	51	5	1	0	2
1937	Det-A	.963	48	155	25	7	1	-4
1938	Det-A	.985	53	108	20	2	4	-4
1939	Det-A	.970	100	449	**64**	**16**	10	**15**
1940	Det-A	.975	107	572	**89**	**17**	10	**18**
1941	Det-A	.977	98	461	**83**	13	11	6
1942	Det-A	.977	97	**446**	69	**12**	10	6
1946	Det-A	.982	87	486	53	10	4	-1
1947	Det-A	1.000	20	95	15	0	3	8
	Bos-A	.974	89	332	50	10	7	-2
	Yr	.980	109	427	65	**10**	10	6
1948	Bos-A	.981	126	470	56	10	8	-9
1949	Bos-A	.980	118	481	51	**11**	13	-6
1950	Bos-A	.988	74	285	44	4	5	-6
1951	Cle-A	.977	44	145	27	4	1	-1
1952	Cle-A	.980	37	131	15	2	0	-4
Total	14	.978	1108	4667	666	119	87	18

■ **George Tebeau OF**

YEAR	TM/L	PCT	G	PO	A	E	DP	FR
1887	Cin-a	.887	84	175	14	24	2	4
1888	Cin-a	.911	121	195	20	21	3	4
1889	Cin-a	.887	134	241	18	33	3	-5
1890	Tol-a	.951	94	182	14	10	1	3
1894	Was-N	.857	61	118	8	21	1	-9
	Cle-N	.928	27	63	1	5	2	-3
	Yr	.880	88	181	9	26	3	-12
1895	Cle-N	.873	49	52	3	8	0	-9
Total	6	.900	570	1026	78	122	12	-15
			1B					
1889	Cin-a	.889	1	8	0	1	1	0
1894	Cle-N	.932	12	109	1	8	11	-3
1895	Cle-N	.980	42	428	22	9	12	0
Total	3	.969	55	545	23	8	24	-3
			3B					
1894	Cle-N	.833	1	2	3	1	0	0

■ **Patsy Tebeau 1B**

YEAR	TM/L	PCT	G	PO	A	E	DP	FR
1892	Cle-N	.977	4	40	2	1	2	0
1893	Cle-N	.980	57	561	39	12	27	3
1894	Cle-N	.977	115	1077	46	26	66	-6
1895	Cle-N	.992	49	473	19	4	28	-1
1896	Cle-N	.985	122	**1340**	75	21	**88**	5
1897	Cle-N	**.994**	92	912	44	6	47	0
1898	Cle-N	.984	91	956	43	16	43	1
1899	StL-N	.980	65	648	22	14	33	-3
Total	8	.984	595	6007	290	100	334	-1
			3B					
1887	Chi-N	.855	20	19	34	9	4	-3
1889	Cle-N	.897	**136**	185	287	54	26	-1
1890	Cle-P	**.872**	110	**204**	246	66	25	13
1891	Cle-N	.884	61	102	150	33	13	6
1892	Cle-N	.911	74	99	156	25	17	0
1893	Cle-N	.888	56	91	138	29	8	3
1894	Cle-N	.778	2	4	3	2	0	-1
1895	Cle-N	.897	6	10	16	3	1	2
1896	Cle-N	.867	7	17	9	4	0	-1
1897	Cle-N	.857	2	5	1	1	0	-1
1898	Cle-N	.875	3	3	4	1	0	-1
1899	StL-N	.667	1	1	1	1	0	0
Total	12	.887	478	740	1045	228	94	16
			2B					
1892	Cle-N	.960	5	12	12	1	3	1
1893	Cle-N	.842	3	7	9	3	1	0
1894	Cle-N	.941	10	29	35	4	7	3
1895	Cle-N	.986	9	36	33	1	3	5
1896	Cle-N	.955	5	10	11	1	2	2
1897	Cle-N	.945	18	33	53	5	2	1
1898	Cle-N	.943	34	85	98	11	8	2
1899	StL-N	1.000	1	5	2	0	0	0
Total	8	.948	85	217	253	6	26	14
			SS					
1892	Cle-N	.556	3	3	2	4	0	-2
1894	Cle-N	—	1	0	0	0	0	0
1896	Cle-N	.923	1	5	7	1	1	2
1897	Cle-N	1.000	1	7	1	0	2	0
1898	Cle-N	.938	7	13	17	2	4	0
1899	StL-N	.903	11	22	43	7	1	1
1900	StL-N	.700	1	4	3	3	0	0
Total	7	.882	25	54	73	7	8	1
			OF					
1891	Cle-N	—	1	0	0	0	0	0

■ **Johnny Temple 2B**

YEAR	TM/L	PCT	G	PO	A	E	DP	FR
1952	Cin-N	.984	22	63	57	2	18	-1
1953	Cin-N	.964	44	71	90	6	20	10
1954	Cin-N	.973	144	**428**	374	22	117	-10
1955	Cin-N	.971	149	408	410	24	**119**	-2
1956	Cin-N	.981	**154**	**389**	**432**	16	89	-6
1957	Cin-N	.974	145	391	372	20	81	-21
1958	Cin-N	.979	141	**395**	353	16	90	-19
1959	Cin-N	.974	149	322	390	19	96	-26
1960	Cle-A	.974	77	169	164	9	55	-26
1961	Cle-A	.969	129	239	317	18	79	-30
1962	Bal-A	.971	71	141	169	6	41	-19
	Hou-N	.941	26	37	59	6	6	-8
1963	Hou-N	.970	61	119	142	8	18	-14
Total	12	.974	1312	3172	3329	172	829	172
			3B					
1960	Cle-A	.976	17	13	27	1	3	-4
1962	Hou-N	—	1	0	0	0	0	0
1963	Hou-N	.901	29	27	46	8	1	-6
Total	3	.926	47	40	73	9	4	-10
			SS					
1955	Cin-N	—	1	0	0	0	0	0
			OF					
1956	Cin-N	—	1	0	0	0	0	0
			1B					
1958	Cin-N	1.000	1	1	1	0	1	0

Garry Templeton SS

YEAR	TM/L	PCT	G	PO	A	E	DP	FR
1976	StL-N	.922	53	111	172	24	41	1
1977	StL-N	.958	151	285	453	32	98	-3
1978	StL-N	.953	155	285	523	40	108	23
1979	StL-N	.960	150	292	525	34	102	18
1980	StL-N	.959	115	223	451	29	85	28
1981	StL-N	.960	76	160	272	18	54	5
1982	SD-N	.961	136	220	422	26	70	-24
1983	SD-N	.960	123	219	355	24	66	-14
1984	SD-N	.960	146	225	407	26	79	-23
1985	SD-N	.968	148	245	460	23	96	-7
1986	SD-N	.966	144	207	358	20	60	-28
1987	SD-N	.972	146	253	447	20	77	9
1988	SD-N	.968	105	168	316	16	62	15
1989	SD-N	.970	140	232	409	20	74	13
1990	SD-N	.957	135	214	367	26	74	-9
Total	15	.961	1923	3339	5937	378	1146	4

3B

YEAR	TM/L	PCT	G	PO	A	E	DP	FR
1988	SD-N	1.000	2	2	0	0	0	0

Gene Tenace C

YEAR	TM/L	PCT	G	PO	A	E	DP	FR
1969	Oak-A	1.000	13	61	6	0	0	0
1970	Oak-A	.990	30	180	18	2	7	3
1971	Oak-A	.994	52	300	20	2	3	-6
1972	Oak-A	.979	49	266	18	6	1	-5
1973	Oak-A	.992	33	123	9	1	4	-2
1974	Oak-A	.982	79	293	42	6	3	-4
1975	Oak-A	.984	125	541	63	10	10	-12
1976	Oak-A	.983	65	263	25	5	3	-16
1977	SD-N	.980	99	523	61	12	9	-9
1978	SD-N	.991	71	276	42	3	7	-2
1979	SD-N	.998	94	413	51	1	10	1
1980	SD-N	.979	104	415	46	10	7	-8
1981	StL-N	.980	38	126	18	3	1	-6
1982	StL-N	.994	37	149	21	1	0	1
1983	Pit-N	.944	3	16	1	1	0	-1
Total	15	.986	892	3945	441	63	65	-66

1B

YEAR	TM/L	PCT	G	PO	A	E	DP	FR
1972	Oak-A	1.000	7	49	3	0	4	0
1973	Oak-A	.989	134	1095	61	13	104	-9
1974	Oak-A	.995	106	816	41	4	80	-5
1975	Oak-A	.998	68	401	21	1	27	-3
1976	Oak-A	.995	70	577	31	3	47	-5
1977	SD-N	.997	36	280	27	1	20	4
1978	SD-N	.993	80	668	37	5	61	-2
1979	SD-N	.989	72	582	32	7	55	-3
1980	SD-N	.993	19	125	10	1	9	1
1981	StL-N	1.000	7	39	4	0	3	1
1982	StL-N	1.000	7	39	3	0	4	0
1983	Pit-N	.989	19	83	5	1	6	-1
Total	12	.993	625	4754	275	36	420	-22

3B

YEAR	TM/L	PCT	G	PO	A	E	DP	FR
1972	Oak-A	.750	2	1	2	1	0	0
1977	SD-N	.932	14	17	24	3	4	-1
1978	SD-N	—	1	0	0	0	0	0
Total	3	.917	17	18	26	4	4	-1

OF

YEAR	TM/L	PCT	G	PO	A	E	DP	FR
1971	Oak-A	—	1	0	0	0	0	0
1972	Oak-A	1.000	9	11	0	0	0	0
1983	Pit-N	—	1	0	0	0	0	0
Total	3	1.000	11	11	0	0	0	0

2B

YEAR	TM/L	PCT	G	PO	A	E	DP	FR
1972	Oak-A	1.000	2	2	0	0	0	-1
1973	Oak-A	1.000	1	0	1	0	0	0
1974	Oak-A	1.000	3	1	0	0	0	0
Total	3	1.000	6	3	1	0	0	-1

Fred Tenney 1B

YEAR	TM/L	PCT	G	PO	A	E	DP	FR
1894	Bos-N	—	1	0	0	0	0	0
1897	Bos-N	.988	128	1248	81	16	69	5
1898	Bos-N	.980	117	1090	66	23	71	5
1899	Bos-N	.978	150	1474	99	35	107	10
1900	Bos-N	.981	111	1021	82	21	50	9
1901	Bos-N	.976	113	1059	86	28	58	8
1902	Bos-N	.985	134	1251	105	21	75	13
1903	Bos-N	.974	122	1145	93	33	60	8
1904	Bos-N	.986	144	1445	115	22	66	9
1905	Bos-N	.982	148	1556	152	32	68	21
1906	Bos-N	.983	143	1456	118	28	78	10
1907	Bos-N	.989	149	1587	113	19	86	9
1908	NY-N	.990	156	1624	117	18	68	10
1909	NY-N	.986	98	1046	72	16	53	8
1911	Bos-N	.985	96	901	64	15	47	3
Total	15	.983	1810	17903	1363	327	956	128

OF

YEAR	TM/L	PCT	G	PO	A	E	DP	FR
1894	Bos-N	.846	6	9	2	2	0	0
1895	Bos-N	.885	28	40	6	6	1	-2
1896	Bos-N	.957	60	81	9	4	1	-4
1897	Bos-N	1.000	4	2	1	0	0	-1
1904	Bos-N	.857	4	6	0	1	0	-1
1911	Bos-N	—	2	0	0	0	0	0
Total	6	.923	104	138	18	13	2	-8

C

YEAR	TM/L	PCT	G	PO	A	E	DP	FR
1894	Bos-N	.893	20	55	20	9	3	0
1895	Bos-N	.989	21	69	18	1	1	-1
1896	Bos-N	.930	27	102	31	10	3	4
1898	Bos-N	—	1	0	0	0	0	0
1901	Bos-N	.923	2	10	2	1	0	-1
Total	5	.936	71	236	71	21	7	2

Frank Tepedino 1B

YEAR	TM/L	PCT	G	PO	A	E	DP	FR
1967	NY-A	1.000	1	2	0	0	0	0
1970	NY-A	—	1	10	0	0	0	0
1971	Mil-A	.986	28	189	22	3	18	3
1973	Atl-N	.992	58	331	28	3	30	2
1974	Atl-N	.988	46	307	26	4	35	1
Total	5	.989	134	839	76	10	83	6

OF

YEAR	TM/L	PCT	G	PO	A	E	DP	FR
1969	NY-A	.950	13	19	0	1	0	-1
1970	NY-A	—	1	0	0	0	0	0
1971	NY-A	1.000	1	1	0	0	0	0
Total	3	.952	15	20	0	1	0	-1

Jerry Terrell 3B

YEAR	TM/L	PCT	G	PO	A	E	DP	FR
1973	Min-A	.957	30	21	46	3	7	0
1974	Min-A	.983	21	14	43	1	6	9
1975	Min-A	1.000	12	7	29	0	3	2
1976	Min-A	.923	26	14	34	4	6	3
1977	Min-A	.953	59	30	91	6	10	2
1978	KC-A	.968	25	21	40	2	4	5
1979	KC-A	.963	19	5	21	1	1	2
Total	7	.961	192	112	304	17	37	23

SS

YEAR	TM/L	PCT	G	PO	A	E	DP	FR
1973	Min-A	.962	81	119	211	13	36	-16
1974	Min-A	.960	34	41	80	5	15	12
1975	Min-A	.947	41	56	106	9	29	-9
1976	Min-A	.959	16	28	42	3	9	4
1977	Min-A	.974	7	15	23	1	6	2
1978	KC-A	.949	11	17	20	2	3	-1
1979	KC-A	—	1	0	0	0	0	0
Total	7	.958	191	276	482	33	98	-8

2B

YEAR	TM/L	PCT	G	PO	A	E	DP	FR
1973	Min-A	.972	14	28	41	2	12	4
1974	Min-A	.980	26	44	55	2	14	10
1975	Min-A	.987	39	68	89	2	20	4
1976	Min-A	.988	31	37	46	1	12	4
1977	Min-A	1.000	14	4	14	0	4	1
1978	KC-A	1.000	31	28	39	0	6	1
1979	KC-A	1.000	7	5	7	0	3	0
1980	KC-A	1.000	3	3	4	0	2	2
Total	8	.987	165	217	295	7	73	26

1B

YEAR	TM/L	PCT	G	PO	A	E	DP	FR
1974	Min-A	1.000	2	9	1	0	0	0
1975	Min-A	.985	15	126	6	2	8	-1
1977	Min-A	1.000	1	9	1	0	0	0
1978	KC-A	1.000	5	22	4	0	2	1
1980	KC-A	1.000	3	18	2	0	0	1
Total	5	.990	26	184	14	2	10	1

OF

YEAR	TM/L	PCT	G	PO	A	E	DP	FR
1973	Min-A	1.000	1	2	0	0	0	0
1974	Min-A	.857	3	6	0	1	0	0
1975	Min-A	.923	6	10	2	1	0	0
1976	Min-A	1.000	6	3	0	0	0	0
1977	Min-A	—	1	0	0	0	0	0
1980	KC-A	1.000	7	8	0	0	0	1
Total	6	.939	24	29	2	2	0	1

Bill Terry 1B

YEAR	TM/L	PCT	G	PO	A	E	DP	FR
1923	NY-N	1.000	2	22	1	0	1	0
1924	NY-N	.988	35	325	14	4	30	-2
1925	NY-N	.990	126	1270	77	14	83	4
1926	NY-N	.979	38	391	31	9	36	3
1927	NY-N	.993	150	1621	105	12	135	5
1928	NY-N	.993	149	1584	78	12	148	-2
1929	NY-N	.994	149	1575	111	11	146	7
1930	NY-N	.990	154	1538	128	17	128	13
1931	NY-N	.990	153	1411	105	16	108	9
1932	NY-N	.991	154	1493	137	14	125	14
1933	NY-N	.992	117	1246	76	11	103	1
1934	NY-N	.994	153	1592	105	10	131	6
1935	NY-N	.996	143	1379	99	6	105	6
1936	NY-N	.996	56	525	41	2	55	3
Total	14	.992	1579	15972	1108	138	1334	67

OF

YEAR	TM/L	PCT	G	PO	A	E	DP	FR
1926	NY-N	1.000	14	27	3	0	0	1
1929	NY-N	.000	1	0	0	1	0	0
Total	2	.968	15	27	3	1	0	1

Zeb Terry SS

YEAR	TM/L	PCT	G	PO	A	E	DP	FR
1916	Chi-A	.935	93	148	243	27	36	-10
1917	Chi-A	1.000	1	0	1	0	0	-1
1918	Bos-N	.977	27	57	114	4	14	8
1919	Pit-N	.960	127	207	395	25	41	-31
1920	Chi-N	.962	70	153	249	16	32	9
1922	Chi-N	.952	4	10	10	1	2	0
Total	6	.956	322	575	1012	73	125	-25

2B

YEAR	TM/L	PCT	G	PO	A	E	DP	FR
1920	Chi-N	.976	63	138	222	9	30	5
1921	Chi-N	.972	122	272	413	20	57	6
1922	Chi-N	.964	125	298	442	28	75	8
Total	3	.969	310	708	1077	57	162	19

3B

YEAR	TM/L	PCT	G	PO	A	E	DP	FR
1922	Chi-N	1.000	3	2	9	0	0	1

Wayne Terwilliger 2B

YEAR	TM/L	PCT	G	PO	A	E	DP	FR
1949	Chi-N	.978	34	77	103	4	11	4
1950	Chi-N	.967	126	314	380	24	80	-8
1951	Chi-N	.969	49	136	142	9	37	-4
	Bro-N	.949	24	31	44	4	9	6
	Yr	.964	73	167	186	13	46	2
1953	Was-A	.982	133	333	395	13	108	5
1954	Was-A	.972	90	213	243	13	72	11
1955	NY-N	.985	78	212	240	7	70	27
1956	NY-N	.958	6	14	9	1	3	2
1959	KC-A	.972	63	144	166	9	42	20
1960	KC-A	1.000	2	1	1	0	1	0
Total	8	.974	605	1475	1723	84	433	63

3B

YEAR	TM/L	PCT	G	PO	A	E	DP	FR
1950	Chi-N	—	1	0	0	0	0	0
1951	Bro-N	1.000	1	0	1	0	1	0
1954	Was-A	.972	10	11	24	1	4	3
1955	NY-N	—	1	0	0	0	0	0
1959	KC-A	—	1	0	0	0	0	0
Total	5	.973	14	11	25	1	5	3

SS

YEAR	TM/L	PCT	G	PO	A	E	DP	FR
1954	Was-A	.833	3	3	7	2	1	-1
1955	NY-N	—	1	0	0	0	0	0
1959	KC-A	1.000	2	0	1	0	0	0
Total	3	.846	6	3	8	2	1	-1

1B

YEAR	TM/L	PCT	G	PO	A	E	DP	FR
1950	Chi-N	—	1	0	0	0	0	0

OF

YEAR	TM/L	PCT	G	PO	A	E	DP	FR
1950	Chi-N	—	1	0	0	0	0	0

Mickey Tettleton C

YEAR	TM/L	PCT	G	PO	A	E	DP	FR
1984	Oak-A	.992	32	112	10	1	1	0
1985	Oak-A	.989	76	344	24	4	9	0
1986	Oak-A	.984	89	463	32	8	6	-2
1987	Oak-A	.987	80	433	28	6	1	3
1988	Bal-A	.992	80	361	31	3	1	-9
1989	Bal-A	.994	75	297	42	2	1	-3
1990	Bal-A	.991	90	425	37	4	3	-13
Total	7	.990	522	2435	204	28	22	-24

1B

YEAR	TM/L	PCT	G	PO	A	E	DP	FR
1987	Oak-A	1.000	1	2	1	0	0	0
1990	Bal-A	.971	5	32	2	1	1	-1
Total	2	.974	6	34	3	1	1	-1

OF

YEAR	TM/L	PCT	G	PO	A	E	DP	FR
1990	Bal-A	1.000	1	1	0	0	0	0

Tim Teufel 2B

YEAR	TM/L	PCT	G	PO	A	E	DP	FR
1983	Min-A	.990	18	46	55	1	14	-1
1984	Min-A	.984	157	315	485	13	81	-12
1985	Min-A	.980	137	237	352	12	67	-33
1986	NY-N	.971	84	133	173	9	28	-18
1987	NY-N	.972	92	138	213	10	43	-12
1988	NY-N	.981	84	153	212	7	48	12
1989	NY-N	.960	40	56	87	6	14	-3
1990	NY-N	.970	24	29	35	2	5	-4
Total	8	.978	636	1107	1612	60	300	-71

1B

YEAR	TM/L	PCT	G	PO	A	E	DP	FR
1986	NY-N	1.000	3	10	1	0	0	0
1987	NY-N	.667	1	1	1	1	1	0
1988	NY-N	1.000	3	22	1	0	1	0
1989	NY-N	.983	33	205	25	4	16	3
1990	NY-N	.991	24	106	9	1	11	0
Total	5	.984	64	344	37	6	29	3

3B

YEAR	TM/L	PCT	G	PO	A	E	DP	FR
1986	NY-N	—	1	0	0	0	0	0
1990	NY-N	.952	10	6	14	1	0	0
Total	2	.952	11	6	14	1	0	0

SS

YEAR	TM/L	PCT	G	PO	A	E	DP	FR
1983	Min-A	1.000	1	1	3	0	0	0

Moe Thacker C

YEAR	TM/L	PCT	G	PO	A	E	DP	FR
1958	Chi-N	.952	9	34	6	2	1	0
1960	Chi-N	.980	50	170	23	4	2	5
1961	Chi-N	.973	25	67	5	2	0	0
1962	Chi-N	.996	65	219	34	1	8	14
1963	StL-N	1.000	3	9	1	0	0	1
Total	5	.984	152	499	69	9	11	20

Ron Theobald 2B

YEAR	TM/L	PCT	G	PO	A	E	DP	FR
1971	Mil-A	.973	111	233	311	15	81	1
1972	Mil-A	.988	113	193	299	6	68	-13
Total	2	.980	224	426	610	21	149	-12

SS

YEAR	TM/L	PCT	G	PO	A	E	DP	FR
1971	Mil-A	—	1	0	0	0	0	0

3B

YEAR	TM/L	PCT	G	PO	A	E	DP	FR
1971	Mil-A	1.000	1	0	1	0	0	0

Tommy Thevenow SS

YEAR	TM/L	PCT	G	PO	A	E	DP	FR
1924	StL-N	.951	23	61	95	8	15	8
1925	StL-N	.950	50	98	169	14	18	3
1926	StL-N	.956	156	371	597	45	98	18
1927	StL-N	.945	59	111	199	18	38	7
1928	StL-N	.931	64	100	158	19	29	-5
1929	Phi-N	.953	90	188	296	24	56	3
1930	Phi-N	.941	156	344	554	56	113	-2
1931	Pit-N	.964	120	245	432	25	92	9
1932	Pit-N	.918	29	62	84	13	18	-3
1933	Pit-N	.909	3	5	5	1	2	-1
1934	Pit-N	—	1	0	0	0	0	-2
1935	Pit-N	.986	13	33	36	1	6	0
1936	Cin-N	.945	68	116	160	16	30	-9
1937	Bos-N	.969	12	11	20	1	2	1
1938	Pit-N	.905	4	6	13	2	6	1
Total	15	.950	848	1751	2818	243	523	28

2B

YEAR	TM/L	PCT	G	PO	A	E	DP	FR
1933	Pit-N	.975	61	137	172	8	31	-12
1934	Pit-N	.969	75	178	199	12	33	-14
1935	Pit-N	.919	8	15	19	3	1	-1
1936	Cin-N	.947	33	56	68	7	16	-2
1937	Bos-N	.875	2	2	5	1	0	0
1938	Pit-N	1.000	9	7	16	0	1	1
Total	6	.966	188	395	479	31	82	-28

3B

YEAR	TM/L	PCT	G	PO	A	E	DP	FR
1928	StL-N	1.000	3	4	7	0	0	1
1932	Pit-N	.984	22	20	42	1	6	2
1933	Pit-N	1.000	1	1	3	0	0	0
1934	Pit-N	.944	44	36	81	7	4	-2
1935	Pit-N	.951	82	94	161	13	11	5
1936	Cin-N	1.000	12	6	20	0	3	2
1937	Bos-N	.889	6	1	7	1	1	0
1938	Pit-N	1.000	1	0	2	0	0	0
Total	8	.957	171	162	323	22	25	8

1B

YEAR	TM/L	PCT	G	PO	A	E	DP	FR
1928	StL-N	1.000	1	0	1	0	0	0

Andres Thomas SS

YEAR	TM/L	PCT	G	PO	A	E	DP	FR
1985	Atl-N	.920	10	6	17	2	2	3
1986	Atl-N	.958	97	143	290	19	62	26
1987	Atl-N	.953	81	128	276	20	56	9
1988	Atl-N	.959	150	230	456	29	89	-8
1989	Atl-N	.956	138	231	400	29	81	6
1990	Atl-N	.967	72	103	193	10	41	2

YEAR	TM/L	PCT	G	PO	A	E	DP	FR
Total	6	.958	548	841	1632	109	331	38

3B

YEAR	TM/L	PCT	G	PO	A	E	DP	FR
1990	Atl-N	1.000	5	1	7	0	2	1

■ Pinch Thomas C

YEAR	TM/L	PCT	G	PO	A	E	DP	FR
1912	Bos-A	.966	8	42	14	2	1	2
1913	Bos-A	.983	31	135	41	3	2	2
1914	Bos-A	.966	64	235	47	10	6	-2
1915	Bos-A	.969	82	325	81	13	7	4
1916	Bos-A	.981	90	321	86	8	7	-8
1917	Bos-A	**.986**	77	296	69	5	8	4
1918	Cle-A	.948	24	85	24	6	1	0
1919	Cle-A	.980	21	39	9	1	0	-2
1920	Cle-A	1.000	7	14	3	0	0	1
1921	Cle-A	.882	19	27	3	4	0	-7
Total	10	.973	423	1519	377	2	32	-6

1B

YEAR	TM/L	PCT	G	PO	A	E	DP	FR
1914	Bos-A	1.000	1	1	0	0	0	0

■ Derrel Thomas 2B

YEAR	TM/L	PCT	G	PO	A	E	DP	FR
1971	Hou-N	1.000	1	3	2	0	1	1
1972	SD-N	.967	83	197	239	15	52	-5
1973	SD-N	.975	47	96	97	5	27	-9
1974	SD-N	.976	104	232	294	13	45	6
1975	SF-N	.974	141	348	372	19	100	-7
1976	SF-N	.964	69	160	212	14	52	2
1977	SF-N	.948	27	49	78	7	11	-1
1978	SD-N	.969	40	90	98	6	25	10
1979	LA-N	1.000	5	5	9	0	1	1
1980	LA-N	.974	18	28	48	2	13	5
1981	LA-N	.986	30	73	71	2	16	1
1982	LA-N	.986	18	28	44	1	8	2
1983	LA-N	.926	9	13	12	2	4	-1
1984	Mon-N	.925	15	16	21	3	6	-3
1985	Phi-N	.000	1	0	0	1	0	-1
Total	15	.970	608	1338	1597	0	361	1

OF

YEAR	TM/L	PCT	G	PO	A	E	DP	FR
1972	SD-N	.857	3	6	0	1	0	0
1974	SD-N	.983	20	58	0	1	0	2
1975	SF-N	1.000	1	1	0	0	0	0
1976	SF-N	1.000	2	3	0	0	0	0
1977	SF-N	.991	78	202	10	2	2	7
1978	SD-N	.991	77	103	5	1	1	6
1979	LA-N	.996	119	269	10	1	4	-3
1980	LA-N	.987	52	75	2	1	3	3
1981	LA-N	.889	18	15	1	2	1	0
1982	LA-N	1.000	28	21	0	0	0	0
1983	LA-N	.990	82	97	3	1	0	4
1984	Mon-N	1.000	48	28	0	0	0	0
	Cal-A	.889	7	8	0	1	0	-2
1985	Phi-N	1.000	7	7	1	0	0	1
Total	13	.988	542	893	32	1	9	18

SS

YEAR	TM/L	PCT	G	PO	A	E	DP	FR
1972	SD-N	.953	49	87	118	10	25	-13
1973	SD-N	.914	74	115	227	32	39	-5
1974	SD-N	.667	5	1	1	1	0	-1
1976	SF-N	.667	1	0	2	1	0	0
1977	SF-N	.971	26	42	59	3	10	-1
1979	LA-N	.889	3	4	4	1	0	-1
1980	LA-N	.946	49	74	119	11	25	1
1981	LA-N	.921	26	42	63	9	13	-6
1982	LA-N	.842	6	5	11	3	6	0
1983	LA-N	.979	13	19	28	1	7	3
1984	Mon-N	.963	62	73	111	7	27	-23
	Cal-A	1.000	4	3	1	0	1	-2
1985	Phi-N	.906	21	21	37	6	4	-7
Total	12	.937	339	486	781	5	157	-55

3B

YEAR	TM/L	PCT	G	PO	A	E	DP	FR
1974	SD-N	.952	22	19	41	3	6	-1
1976	SF-N	1.000	1	0	1	0	0	0
1977	SF-N	.833	6	2	8	2	1	-1
1978	SD-N	.964	26	22	59	3	4	5
1979	LA-N	.921	18	20	15	3	3	0
1980	LA-N	1.000	4	1	3	0	0	1
1981	LA-N	.923	10	3	9	1	0	0
1982	LA-N	1.000	14	4	3	0	0	0
1983	LA-N	.929	7	5	8	1	0	1
1984	Mon-N	1.000	4	1	3	0	0	0
	Cal-A	1.000	3	1	0	0	0	0
1985	Phi-N	—	1	0	0	0	0	0
Total	11	.946	116	78	150	3	14	5

1B

YEAR	TM/L	PCT	G	PO	A	E	DP	FR
1977	SF-N	1.000	3	12	3	0	0	1
1978	SD-N	.983	14	113	6	2	9	0
1979	LA-N	—	1	0	0	0	0	0
1984	Mon-N	—	1	0	0	0	0	0
Total	4	.985	19	125	9	2	9	1

C

YEAR	TM/L	PCT	G	PO	A	E	DP	FR
1980	LA-N	1.000	5	25	3	0	0	1
1985	Phi-N	1.000	1	3	0	0	0	0
Total	2	1.000	6	28	3	0	0	1

■ Frank Thomas OF

YEAR	TM/L	PCT	G	PO	A	E	DP	FR
1951	Pit-N	1.000	37	87	5	0	2	3
1952	Pit-N	1.000	5	8	1	0	0	0
1953	Pit-N	.976	118	306	17	8	1	21
1954	Pit-N	.989	**153**	418	**14**	5	2	3
1955	Pit-N	.984	139	307	8	5	3	6
1956	Pit-N	1.000	56	95	3	0	1	1
1957	Pit-N	.975	59	105	14	3	3	7
1958	Pit-N	.947	8	18	0	1	0	0
1959	Cin-N	.909	33	40	0	4	0	-2
1960	Chi-N	.964	49	77	3	3	0	-1
1961	Chi-N	1.000	10	9	2	0	0	0
	Mil-N	.954	109	202	4	10	0	-5
	Yr	.956	119	211	6	10	0	-5
1962	NY-N	.962	126	216	14	9	0	2
1963	NY-N	.988	96	158	8	2	1	-1

YEAR	TM/L	PCT	G	PO	A	E	DP	FR
1964	NY-N	1.000	31	58	2	0	1	-1
1965	Phi-N	1.000	12	10	1	0	0	0
	Hou-N	—	1	0	0	0	0	0
	Mil-N	1.000	3	2	0	0	0	0
	Yr	1.000	16	12	1	0	0	0
Total	15	.978	1045	2116	96	0	14	33

3B

YEAR	TM/L	PCT	G	PO	A	E	DP	FR
1956	Pit-N	.942	111	118	176	18	21	-8
1957	Pit-N	.920	31	27	53	7	4	-4
1958	Pit-N	.926	139	122	240	**29**	21	-32
1959	Cin-N	.927	64	55	111	13	8	-9
1960	Chi-N	.930	33	25	55	6	4	-7
1962	NY-N	.867	10	7	19	4	1	-2
1963	NY-N	.000	1	0	0	1	0	0
1964	NY-N	1.000	2	1	2	0	0	0
1965	Phi-N	.500	1	0	1	1	0	0
	Hou-N	—	2	0	0	0	0	0
	Yr	.500	3	0	1	1	0	0
Total	9	.928	394	355	657	59	59	-62

1B

YEAR	TM/L	PCT	G	PO	A	E	DP	FR
1957	Pit-N	.977	71	597	52	15	53	-2
1958	Pit-N	1.000	2	20	3	0	1	1
1959	Cin-N	.984	14	111	15	2	11	2
1960	Chi-N	.983	50	426	34	8	36	-1
1961	Chi-N	1.000	6	41	2	0	2	-1
	Mil-N	1.000	11	48	4	0	6	0
	Yr	1.000	17	89	6	0	8	-1
1962	NY-N	.989	11	88	3	1	7	-2
1963	NY-N	.994	15	146	9	1	9	0
1964	NY-N	.994	19	142	14	1	11	1
	Phi-N	.976	36	297	28	8	37	1
	Yr	.982	55	439	42	9	48	2
1965	Phi-N	.989	11	88	4	1	10	-1
	Hou-N	.984	16	118	6	2	11	-1
	Mil-N	.979	6	44	3	1	3	0
	Yr	.985	33	250	13	4	24	-2
Total	9	.983	268	2166	177	0	197	-3

2B

YEAR	TM/L	PCT	G	PO	A	E	DP	FR
1956	Pit-N	1.000	4	3	0	0	0	0

■ Fred Thomas 3B

YEAR	TM/L	PCT	G	PO	A	E	DP	FR
1918	Bos-A	.968	41	54	97	5	4	5
1919	Phi-A	.945	124	168	242	24	14	-5
1920	Phi-A	.960	61	78	140	9	9	1
	Was-A	1.000	2	1	8	0	0	2
	Yr	.962	63	79	148	9	9	3
Total	3	.954	228	301	487	8	27	3

SS

YEAR	TM/L	PCT	G	PO	A	E	DP	FR
1918	Bos-A	—	1	0	0	0	0	0
1920	Phi-A	.952	12	27	33	3	4	-1
Total	2	.952	13	27	33	3	4	-1

■ George Thomas OF

YEAR	TM/L	PCT	G	PO	A	E	DP	FR
1958	Det-A	—	1	0	0	0	0	0
1961	Det-A	—	2	0	0	0	0	0
	LA-A	.986	45	71	0	1	0	-3
	Yr	.986	47	71	0	1	0	-3
1962	LA-A	.957	51	107	4	5	1	3
1963	LA-A	.941	39	63	1	4	0	-2
	Det-A	1.000	40	83	0	0	0	4
	Yr	.974	79	146	1	4	0	2
1964	Det-A	.988	90	164	4	2	1	4
1965	Det-A	.948	59	87	4	5	0	3
1966	Bos-A	1.000	48	84	4	0	0	3
1967	Bos-A	.973	43	36	0	1	0	0
1968	Bos-A	1.000	9	9	0	0	0	1
1969	Bos-A	1.000	12	7	0	0	0	0
1970	Bos-A	.972	26	35	0	1	0	-2
1971	Bos-A	1.000	5	2	0	0	0	-1
	Min-A	1.000	11	4	0	0	0	-1
	Yr	1.000	16	6	0	0	0	-2
Total	12	.976	481	752	17	9	2	9

3B

YEAR	TM/L	PCT	G	PO	A	E	DP	FR
1957	Det-A	.000	1	0	0	1	0	0
1961	LA-A	.880	38	25	63	12	5	-7
1963	LA-A	1.000	10	5	18	0	1	1
1964	Det-A	1.000	1	1	1	0	0	0
1966	Bos-A	1.000	6	7	8	0	1	1
1969	Bos-A	1.000	1	0	1	0	0	0
1970	Bos-A	.750	6	5	4	3	1	-3
1971	Min-A	.667	1	1	1	1	0	-1
Total	8	.892	64	44	96	7	8	-9

1B

YEAR	TM/L	PCT	G	PO	A	E	DP	FR
1963	LA-A	.914	4	27	5	3	3	1
1966	Bos-A	1.000	2	4	0	0	0	0
1967	Bos-A	.952	3	17	3	1	0	1
1969	Bos-A	.976	10	75	5	2	9	0
1971	Min-A	—	1	0	0	0	0	0
Total	7	.958	20	123	13	6	12	2

C

YEAR	TM/L	PCT	G	PO	A	E	DP	FR
1966	Bos-A	1.000	2	4	0	0	0	0
1967	Bos-A	1.000	1	4	1	0	0	0
1969	Bos-A	1.000	1	3	0	0	0	0
Total	3	1.000	4	11	1	0	0	0

2B

YEAR	TM/L	PCT	G	PO	A	E	DP	FR
1963	Det-A	—	1	1	0	0	0	0
1965	Det-A	1.000	1	1	0	0	0	1
Total	2	1.000	2	1	0	0	0	1

SS

YEAR	TM/L	PCT	G	PO	A	E	DP	FR
1961	Det-A	1.000	1	3	1	0	1	4

■ Ira Thomas C

YEAR	TM/L	PCT	G	PO	A	E	DP	FR
1906	NY-A	.938	42	145	38	12	1	-5
1907	NY-A	.953	61	257	90	17	7	8
1908	Det-A	.972	29	124	15	4	3	-6
1909	Phi-A	**.985**	84	479	112	9	5	11
1910	Phi-A	.967	60	324	86	14	8	8
1911	Phi-A	.974	103	499	150	17	12	6

YEAR	TM/L	PCT	G	PO	A	E	DP	FR
1912	Phi-A	.971	48	207	58	8	5	-1
1913	Phi-A	.983	21	88	25	2	1	3
1914	Phi-A	1.000	1	6	1	0	0	1
1915	Phi-A	1.000	1	0	1	0	0	0
Total	10	.970	450	2129	576	3	42	25

1B

YEAR	TM/L	PCT	G	PO	A	E	DP	FR
1907	NY-A	1.000	2	7	2	0	1	1

■ Gorman Thomas OF

YEAR	TM/L	PCT	G	PO	A	E	DP	FR
1973	Mil-A	.957	50	87	1	4	1	-1
1974	Mil-A	1.000	13	26	0	0	0	-1
1975	Mil-A	.961	113	215	5	9	1	-8
1976	Mil-A	.986	94	210	4	3	0	-1
1978	Mil-A	.983	137	345	5	6	0	-9
1979	Mil-A	.991	152	435	4	4	0	-3
1980	Mil-A	.985	**160**	455	6	7	1	-2
1981	Mil-A	.979	97	221	8	5	3	-6
1982	Mil-A	.991	157	427	11	4	4	3
1983	Mil-A	.992	46	126	0	1	0	0
	Cle-A	.982	106	313	7	6	2	8
	Yr	.985	152	439	7	7	2	8
1984	Sea-A	1.000	34	45	2	0	0	-6
Total	11	.984	1159	2905	53	9	12	-26

1B

YEAR	TM/L	PCT	G	PO	A	E	DP	FR
1986	Mil-A	.980	6	47	3	1	3	-1

3B

YEAR	TM/L	PCT	G	PO	A	E	DP	FR
1973	Mil-A	1.000	1	1	0	0	0	0
1976	Mil-A	.500	1	1	0	1	0	-1
Total	2	.667	2	2	0	1	0	-1

■ Lee Thomas OF

YEAR	TM/L	PCT	G	PO	A	E	DP	FR
1961	LA-A	.966	86	159	9	6	1	0
1962	LA-A	.972	74	133	5	4	1	-1
1963	LA-A	.986	43	71	1	1	1	-2
1964	LA-A	.949	47	71	4	4	1	-3
	Bos-A	.995	107	176	6	1	1	2
	Yr	.981	154	247	10	5	2	-1
1965	Bos-A	.968	20	29	1	1	0	0
1966	Chi-N	1.000	17	23	1	0	0	-2
1967	Chi-N	.969	43	60	2	2	0	-4
1968	Hou-N	.973	48	67	5	2	0	-1
Total	8	.975	485	789	34	1	5	-11

1B

YEAR	TM/L	PCT	G	PO	A	E	DP	FR
1961	LA-A	.982	34	267	10	5	26	-5
1962	LA-A	.982	90	735	42	14	66	-9
1963	LA-A	.996	104	961	84	4	88	6
1964	LA-A	1.000	1	2	0	0	0	0
	Bos-A	1.000	1	3	0	0	0	0
	Yr	1.000	2	5	0	0	0	0
1965	Bos-A	.984	127	1035	97	18	86	8
1966	Atl-N	.987	36	281	26	4	22	2
	Chi-N	.992	20	121	8	1	13	0
	Yr	.989	56	402	34	5	35	2
1967	Chi-N	1.000	10	71	5	0	9	0
1968	Hou-N	1.000	2	13	3	0	3	1
Total	8	.988	425	3489	275	6	313	3

■ Roy Thomas OF

YEAR	TM/L	PCT	G	PO	A	E	DP	FR
1899	Phi-N	.952	135	313	22	17	8	6
1900	Phi-N	.958	139	303	19	14	6	-2
1901	Phi-N	.967	129	283	9	10	2	-2
1902	Phi-N	.974	138	277	23	8	3	5
1903	Phi-N	.963	130	**318**	19	13	3	14
1904	Phi-N	.974	139	**321**	21	9	4	**15**
1905	Phi-N	.983	147	**373**	**27**	7	6	**19**
1906	Phi-N	**.986**	142	340	12	5	**7**	10
1907	Phi-N	.980	121	274	15	6	4	5
1908	Phi-N	1.000	6	13	0	0	0	-1
	Pit-N	.975	101	269	7	7	4	5
	Yr	.976	107	282	7	7	4	4
1909	Bos-N	.976	76	155	9	4	1	-1
1910	Phi-N	.952	20	38	2	2	0	0
1911	Phi-N	1.000	11	14	3	0	0	1
Total	13	.972	1434	3291	188	102	48	74

1B

YEAR	TM/L	PCT	G	PO	A	E	DP	FR
1899	Phi-N	.979	14	141	1	3	6	-2

■ Valmy Thomas C

YEAR	TM/L	PCT	G	PO	A	E	DP	FR
1957	NY-N	.991	88	396	31	4	8	2
1958	SF-N	.992	61	244	17	2	4	2
1959	Phi-N	.980	65	310	25	7	3	**16**
1960	Bal-N	1.000	8	27	2	0	1	1
1961	Cle-A	.988	27	151	17	2	6	9
Total	5	.988	249	1128	92	5	22	30

3B

YEAR	TM/L	PCT	G	PO	A	E	DP	FR
1959	Phi-N	1.000	1	0	0	0	0	0

■ Gary Thomasson OF

YEAR	TM/L	PCT	G	PO	A	E	DP	FR
1972	SF-N	1.000	2	1	0	0	0	0
1973	SF-N	.952	43	77	2	4	1	1
1974	SF-N	.981	76	149	4	3	1	1
1975	SF-N	.978	74	172	9	4	2	9
1976	SF-N	.959	54	114	2	5	0	-2
1977	SF-N	.959	113	255	9	11	1	2
1978	Oak-A	.969	44	89	4	3	0	-1
	NY-A	.972	50	101	4	3	1	8
	Yr	.971	94	190	8	6	1	7
1979	LA-N	.980	100	194	4	4	1	-1
1980	LA-N	.974	31	36	1	1	0	-1
Total	9	.970	587	1188	32	8	7	16

1B

YEAR	TM/L	PCT	G	PO	A	E	DP	FR
1972	SF-N	1.000	7	59	1	0	7	-1
1973	SF-N	.992	47	235	13	2	14	-1
1974	SF-N	.961	15	86	13	4	8	2
1975	SF-N	.977	17	121	9	3	12	0
1976	SF-N	.980	39	322	18	7	28	-2
1977	SF-N	.981	31	149	9	3	14	-1
1978	Oak-A	.962	5	22	3	1	0	0
1979	LA-N	—	1	0	0	0	0	0
1980	LA-N	1.000	1	2	0	0	0	0

YEAR	TM/L	PCT	G	PO	A	E	DP	FR
Total	9	.982	163	996	66	0	83	-3
■ Tim Thompson C								
1954	Bro-N	.909	2	10	0	1	0	0
1956	KC-A	.981	68	328	38	7	7	3
1957	KC-A	.993	62	272	29	2	7	-3
1958	Det-A	1.000	4	8	1	0	0	-1
Total	4	.986	136	618	68	0	14	-1
OF								
1954	Bro-N	—	1	0	0	0	0	0
■ Danny Thompson SS								
1970	Min-A	.958	6	9	14	1	1	0
1971	Min-A	1.000	1	0	1	0	0	0
1972	Min-A	.957	144	247	468	32	76	-9
1973	Min-A	.950	95	131	326	24	50	7
1974	Min-A	.963	88	127	183	12	39	-24
1975	Min-A	.941	100	138	245	24	40	-22
1976	Min-A	.988	34	58	103	2	23	-2
	Tex-A	.953	10	14	27	2	5	-2
	Yr	.981	44	72	130	4	28	-4
Total	7	.956	478	724	1367	7	234	-52
3B								
1970	Min-A	1.000	37	3	11	0	3	1
1971	Min-A	.897	17	9	17	3	2	0
1973	Min-A	—	1	0	0	0	0	0
1974	Min-A	.929	5	4	9	1	2	0
1975	Min-A	.909	7	4	16	2	1	0
1976	Tex-A	.976	39	28	54	2	3	-5
Total	6	.951	106	48	107	8	11	-4
2B								
1970	Min-A	.986	81	144	204	5	35	-13
1971	Min-A	.909	3	4	6	1	0	0
1975	Min-A	1.000	1	5	0	0	0	0
1976	Tex-A	1.000	14	18	36	0	4	0
Total	4	.986	99	171	246	6	39	-13
■ Don Thompson OF								
1949	Bos-N	.800	2	4	0	1	0	0
1951	Bro-N	.987	61	75	3	1	1	4
1953	Bro-N	.989	81	84	5	1	1	3
1954	Bro-N	1.000	29	14	1	0	0	1
Total	4	.984	173	177	9	3	2	8
■ Hank Thompson 3B								
1949	NY-N	1.000	1	1	5	0	0	1
1950	NY-N	.944	138	136	303	26	43	4
1951	NY-N	.925	71	64	120	15	16	-14
1952	NY-N	.929	46	47	96	11	8	5
1953	NY-N	.956	101	90	194	13	18	-2
1954	NY-N	.945	130	125	267	23	27	-4
1955	NY-N	.943	124	104	262	22	23	2
1956	NY-N	.908	44	25	94	12	7	2
Total	8	.941	655	592	1341	122	142	-6
2B								
1947	StL-A	.957	19	55	55	5	15	1
1949	NY-N	.961	69	197	175	15	44	-9
1952	NY-N	.933	4	7	7	1	2	0
1953	NY-N	1.000	1	1	0	0	0	0
1954	NY-N	1.000	2	1	1	0	0	0
1955	NY-N	1.000	7	9	12	0	2	0
Total	6	.961	102	270	250	1	63	-8
OF								
1950	NY-N	1.000	10	18	2	0	1	1
1952	NY-N	.979	72	182	5	4	1	-1
1953	NY-N	1.000	9	8	1	0	0	0
1954	NY-N	1.000	1	0	1	0	0	1
1956	NY-N	.857	10	11	1	2	0	0
Total	5	.974	102	219	10	6	2	1
SS								
1955	NY-N	.800	1	2	2	1	0	-1
1956	NY-N	—	1	0	0	0	0	0
Total	2	.800	2	2	2	1	0	-1
■ Jason Thompson 1B								
1976	Det-A	.994	117	1157	88	8	104	2
1977	Det-A	.991	150	**1599**	97	18	**135**	-7
1978	Det-A	.993	151	1503	92	11	**153**	-5
1979	Det-A	.994	140	1176	91	8	135	-1
1980	Det-A	1.000	36	328	30	0	33	4
	Cal-A	1.000	47	351	21	0	33	-3
	Yr	1.000	83	679	51	0	66	1
1981	Pit-N	.989	78	590	46	7	65	-1
1982	Pit-N	.993	155	1395	105	10	114	-1
1983	Pit-N	.993	151	1266	89	9	131	-6
1984	Pit-N	.990	152	**1337**	74	**14**	111	-10
1985	Pit-N	.992	114	995	82	9	69	2
1986	Mon-N	.962	15	121	4	5	7	2
Total	11	.992	1314	11818	819	7	1090	-29
■ Fresco Thompson 2B								
1925	Pit-N	.977	12	19	24	1	6	-2
1926	NY-N	1.000	2	2	8	0	0	-1
1927	Phi-N	.963	153	**424**	485	35	97	-5
1928	Phi-N	.966	152	409	509	32	109	9
1929	Phi-N	.965	148	**395**	512	33	103	12
1930	Phi-N	.955	112	287	386	32	95	1
1931	Bro-N	.946	43	89	120	12	36	-3
Total	7	.962	622	1625	2044	145	446	11
SS								
1931	Bro-N	.960	10	9	15	1	4	1
3B								
1931	Bro-N	1.000	5	4	0	0	0	-1
■ Milt Thompson OF								
1984	Atl-N	.956	25	37	6	2	1	0
1985	Atl-N	.964	49	78	2	3	0	-2
1986	Phi-N	.991	89	212	1	2	1	0
1987	Phi-N	.989	146	354	4	4	1	2
1988	Phi-N	.983	112	278	5	5	1	2
1989	StL-N	.978	147	348	5	8	1	-7

YEAR	TM/L	PCT	G	PO	A	E	DP	FR
1990	StL-N	.971	116	232	4	7	0	-4
Total	7	.981	684	1539	27	1	5	-9
■ Robby Thompson 2B								
1986	SF-N	.976	149	255	450	17	97	1
1987	SF-N	.972	126	246	341	17	99	6
1988	SF-N	.978	134	255	365	14	88	-9
1989	SF-N	.989	148	307	425	8	88	5
1990	SF-N	.989	142	287	441	8	**94**	**28**
Total	5	.981	699	1350	2022	4	466	31
SS								
1986	SF-N	1.000	1	0	1	0	0	0
■ Tommy Thompson OF								
1933	Bos-N	1.000	24	64	3	0	0	2
1934	Bos-N	.964	82	205	12	8	3	9
1935	Bos-N	.965	85	184	9	7	3	1
1936	Bos-N	.930	39	94	3	0	0	2
1939	StL-A	.977	23	40	3	1	0	-2
Total	5	.975	253	587	30	6	6	12
1B								
1936	Bos-N	.983	25	265	17	5	19	0
1938	Chi-A	1.000	1	2	0	0	1	0
Total	2	.983	26	267	17	5	20	0
■ Sam Thompson OF								
1885	Det-N	.885	62	84	24	14	0	7
1886	Det-N	.945	122	194	29	13	**11**	9
1887	Det-N	.909	**127**	217	24	24	7	3
1888	Det-N	.882	56	86	4	12	0	-7
1889	Phi-N	.901	128	173	19	21	7	-8
1890	Phi-N	.939	132	170	29	13	5	2
1891	Phi-N	.937	133	234	**32**	18	6	19
1892	Phi-N	.937	**153**	223	28	17	7	4
1893	Phi-N	.931	131	171	17	14	3	-11
1894	Phi-N	**.977**	99	159	12	4	2	-4
1895	Phi-N	.943	118	186	31	13	2	12
1896	Phi-N	**.974**	119	231	**28**	7	**11**	**18**
1897	Phi-N	.833	3	4	1	1	0	0
1898	Phi-N	1.000	14	19	5	0	0	2
1906	Det-A	1.000	8	14	0	0	0	0
Total	15	.935	1405	2165	283	171	61	46
3B								
1885	Det-N	1.000	1	2	0	0	0	0
1B								
1893	Phi-N	.875	1	7	0	1	0	0
■ Scot Thompson OF								
1978	Chi-N	1.000	5	6	0	0	0	-1
1979	Chi-N	.971	100	161	7	5	3	-4
1980	Chi-N	.963	66	100	4	4	2	-2
1981	Chi-N	.980	30	49	1	1	0	-1
1982	Chi-N	1.000	23	36	2	0	1	2
1983	Chi-N	1.000	29	29	0	0	0	-2
1984	SF-N	.875	6	7	0	1	0	0
1985	Mon-N	1.000	3	1	1	0	0	1
Total	8	.973	262	389	15	1	6	-7
1B								
1978	Chi-N	1.000	2	8	1	0	1	0
1980	Chi-N	1.000	12	49	2	0	6	0
1981	Chi-N	.875	3	7	0	1	0	0
1982	Chi-N	1.000	4	3	1	0	0	0
1983	Chi-N	—	1	0	0	0	0	0
1984	SF-N	.998	87	555	36	1	48	0
1985	SF-N	.995	24	168	16	1	13	2
	Mon-N	1.000	3	11	1	0	1	0
	Yr	.995	27	179	17	1	14	2
Total	7	.997	136	801	57	3	69	2
■ Bobby Thomson OF								
1947	NY-N	.980	127	330	12	7	2	6
1948	NY-N	.970	125	313	10	10	2	9
1949	NY-N	.982	**156**	488	10	9	4	14
1950	NY-N	.978	149	394	15	9	5	5
1951	NY-N	.966	77	168	3	6	1	-2
1952	NY-N	.994	63	152	3	1	0	5
1953	NY-N	.983	154	391	16	7	0	-1
1954	Mil-N	.980	26	45	3	1	2	1
1955	Mil-N	.969	91	182	5	6	0	-2
1956	Mil-N	.974	136	257	7	7	0	-4
1957	Mil-N	.988	38	78	2	1	0	0
	NY-N	.992	71	124	2	1	0	0
	Yr	.990	109	202	4	2	0	-2
1958	Chi-N	.989	148	353	13	4	3	-3
1959	Chi-N	.987	116	223	9	3	4	3
1960	Bos-A	.971	27	65	1	2	1	2
	Bal-A	—	2	0	0	0	0	0
	Yr	.971	29	65	1	2	1	2
Total	14	.980	1506	3563	111	74	24	31
3B								
1946	NY-N	.935	16	18	25	3	0	0
1951	NY-N	.942	69	90	136	14	13	-6
1952	NY-N	.940	91	82	184	17	13	-4
1956	Mil-N	.833	3	5	10	3	0	1
1957	NY-N	1.000	1	0	3	0	0	1
1958	Chi-N	.889	4	5	3	1	1	0
Total	6	.937	184	200	361	38	27	-8
2B								
1947	NY-N	.904	9	27	20	5	4	-1
1B								
1960	Bos-A	.833	1	10	0	2	2	-1
■ Dickie Thon SS								
1979	Cal-A	.846	8	3	8	2	1	-1
1980	Cal-A	.928	22	24	66	7	12	-6
1981	Cal-A	.935	13	12	17	2	2	0
1982	Hou-N	.975	119	177	399	15	80	6
1983	Hou-N	.966	154	258	**533**	28	114	**21**
1984	Hou-N	1.000	5	8	13	0	1	0
1985	Hou-N	.967	79	106	218	11	48	7

YEAR	TM/L	PCT	G	PO	A	E	DP	FR
1986	Hou-N	.972	104	142	210	10	39	-2
1987	Hou-N	.925	31	21	53	6	7	-8
1988	SD-N	.954	70	82	168	12	28	-20
1989	Phi-N	.972	129	174	380	16	65	16
1990	Phi-N	.964	148	222	439	25	**86**	3
Total	12	.965	882	1229	2504	134	483	16
2B								
1979	Cal-A	.923	24	34	38	6	12	2
1980	Cal-A	.988	21	39	46	1	15	-4
1981	Hou-N	.950	28	37	39	4	10	-5
1982	Hou-N	—	1	0	0	0	0	0
1988	SD-N	1.000	2	2	2	0	1	0
Total	5	.956	76	112	125	1	38	-7
3B								
1979	Cal-A	1.000	1	1	0	0	0	0
1980	Cal-A	.909	10	4	16	2	1	-2
1981	Hou-N	1.000	5	4	7	0	1	0
1982	Hou-N	.905	8	6	13	2	2	0
1988	SD-N	1.000	1	0	1	0	0	0
Total	5	.929	25	15	37	4	4	-2
1B								
1980	Cal-A	1.000	1	3	0	0	0	0
■ Jack Thoney OF								
1902	Cle-A	1.000	2	6	0	0	0	0
1903	Cle-A	.889	24	50	6	7	1	1
1904	Was-A	.860	17	33	4	6	2	2
	NY-A	.926	10	21	4	2	0	2
	Yr	.886	27	54	8	8	2	4
1908	Bos-A	.948	101	208	12	12	6	8
1909	Bos-A	.960	10	23	1	1	1	1
Total	5	.929	164	341	27	8	6	14
3B								
1902	Bal-A	.778	3	3	4	2	0	-1
1903	Cle-A	.800	2	2	2	1	1	0
1904	NY-A	.826	26	33	38	15	2	-1
Total	3	.820	31	38	44	8	3	-2
2B								
1902	Cle-A	.891	14	21	36	7	1	-5
1903	Cle-A	.857	5	13	5	3	1	0
Total	2	.882	19	34	41	0	2	-5
SS								
1902	Cle-A	.776	11	21	17	11	3	-11
■ Andy Thornton 1B								
1973	Chi-N	.989	9	81	10	1	3	2
1974	Chi-N	.992	90	760	70	7	61	**8**
1975	Chi-N	.988	113	982	77	13	88	3
1976	Chi-N	.987	25	202	19	3	17	1
	Mon-N	.994	43	326	26	2	43	1
	Yr	.991	68	528	45	5	60	2
1977	Cle-A	.995	117	1026	71	6	97	-2
1978	Cle-A	.995	145	1327	106	7	106	4
1979	Cle-A	.994	130	1089	82	7	100	-3
1981	Cle-A	.986	11	67	5	1	7	0
1982	Cle-A	1.000	8	76	5	0	5	0
1983	Cle-A	.991	27	201	21	2	20	2
1984	Cle-A	.979	11	86	9	2	11	0
Total	11	.992	729	6223	501	1	558	16
OF								
1976	Mon-N	.938	11	14	1	1	0	-1
3B								
1974	Chi-N	—	1	0	0	0	0	0
1975	Chi-N	1.000	2	2	0	0	0	0
Total	2	1.000	3	2	0	0	0	0
■ Jim Thorpe OF								
1913	NY-N	.944	9	15	2	1	1	1
1914	NY-N	.750	4	3	0	1	0	0
1915	NY-N	.933	15	28	0	2	0	-1
1917	Cin-N	.962	69	143	7	6	2	0
	NY-N	.939	18	31	0	2	0	-2
	Yr	.958	87	174	7	8	2	-2
1918	NY-N	.983	44	57	2	1	1	1
1919	NY-N	1.000	2	2	0	0	0	0
	Bos-N	.926	38	73	2	6	0	-3
	Yr	.928	40	75	2	6	0	-3
Total	6	.951	199	352	13	9	4	-4
1B								
1919	Bos-N	.867	2	13	0	2	1	-1
■ Marv Throneberry 1B								
1955	NY-A	1.000	1	3	1	0	0	0
1958	NY-A	.991	40	315	21	3	42	0
1959	NY-A	.989	54	337	27	4	40	1
1960	KC-A	.991	71	508	40	5	56	1
1961	KC-A	.996	30	241	25	1	31	3
	Bal-A	.973	11	61	10	2	6	1
	Yr	.991	41	302	35	3	37	4
1962	NY-N	.981	97	785	77	17	87	1
1963	NY-N	1.000	3	9	0	0	1	0
Total	7	.987	307	2259	201	2	263	10
OF								
1958	NY-A	.875	5	7	0	1	0	0
1959	NY-A	.983	13	9	2	0	0	1
1961	KC-A	1.000	10	16	0	0	0	0
	Bal-A	.923	15	12	0	1	0	-2
	Yr	.966	25	28	0	1	0	-2
1962	Bal-A	1.000	2	3	0	0	0	0
Total	6	.961	45	47	2	2	0	-1
■ Faye Throneberry OF								
1952	Bos-A	.955	86	141	9	7	**5**	-4
1955	Bos-A	.960	34	69	3	3	0	-1
1956	Bos-A	.909	13	20	0	2	0	-1
1957	Was-A	.983	58	116	2	2	0	0
1958	Was-A	—	26	35	1	0	0	-1
1959	Was-A	.953	86	136	7	7	2	-4
1960	Was-A	.947	34	52	2	3	0	-3
1961	LA-A	1.000	5	8	1	0	0	1

YEAR	TM/L	PCT	G	PO	A	E	DP	FR
Total	8	.962	342	577	25	4	7	-13

Gary Thurman OF

YEAR	TM/L	PCT	G	PO	A	E	DP	FR
1987	KC-A	.971	27	61	5	2	1	5
1988	KC-A	.949	32	36	1	2	0	0
1989	KC-A	.949	60	54	2	3	0	2
1990	KC-A	1.000	21	32	0	0	0	-1
Total	4	.965	140	183	8	7	1	6

Bob Thurman OF

YEAR	TM/L	PCT	G	PO	A	E	DP	FR
1955	Cin-N	.949	36	54	2	3	0	-3
1956	Cin-N	.953	29	39	2	2	1	-2
1957	Cin-N	.987	44	75	3	1	1	-2
1958	Cin-N	.976	41	80	2	2	1	0
Total	4	.970	150	248	9	8	3	-7

Mike Tiernan OF

YEAR	TM/L	PCT	G	PO	A	E	DP	FR
1887	NY-N	.865	103	150	10	25	3	-8
1888	NY-N	**.960**	113	174	16	8	2	0
1889	NY-N	.896	122	179	19	23	3	-4
1890	NY-N	.896	133	210	13	26	5	-16
1891	NY-N	.901	134	138	16	17	4	-9
1892	NY-N	.899	116	155	15	19	2	-3
1893	NY-N	.927	125	178	12	15	2	-9
1894	NY-N	.922	111	169	9	15	1	-11
1895	NY-N	.946	119	184	8	11	2	-5
1896	NY-N	.970	**133**	213	15	7	4	-2
1897	NY-N	.931	127	178	11	14	2	-11
1898	NY-N	.973	103	130	12	4	2	-12
1899	NY-N	.938	35	42	3	3	1	-4
Total	13	.924	1474	2100	159	187	32	-94

Cotton Tierney 2B

YEAR	TM/L	PCT	G	PO	A	E	DP	FR
1920	Pit-N	.964	10	19	34	2	4	-1
1921	Pit-N	.965	72	152	182	12	33	-24
1922	Pit-N	.964	105	179	302	18	52	-34
1923	Pit-N	.941	29	65	94	10	22	-3
	Phi-N	.975	115	249	416	17	82	17
	Yr	.968	144	314	510	27	104	14
1924	Bos-N	.964	115	235	399	24	88	0
1925	Bro-N	1.000	1	4	3	0	2	0
Total	6	.966	447	903	1430	3	283	-45

3B

1921	Pit-N	.940	32	39	55	6	4	-3
1922	Pit-N	.667	1	1	1	1	0	-1
1923	Phi-N	1.000	2	2	2	0	0	0
1924	Bos-N	.971	22	31	35	2	5	-1
1925	Bro-N	.963	61	54	102	6	6	-1
Total	5	.955	118	127	195	5	15	-6

OF

1921	Pit-N	1.000	4	8	1	0	0	1
1922	Pit-N	.833	2	4	1	1	0	0
1923	Phi-N	1.000	7	7	3	0	1	2
Total	3	.960	13	19	5	1	1	3

SS

1920	Pit-N	1.000	2	1	6	0	0	0
1921	Pit-N	1.000	3	1	5	0	0	0
1922	Pit-N	1.000	1	0	1	0	0	0
Total	3	1.000	6	2	12	0	0	0

1B

1925	Bro-N	1.000	1	2	0	0	0	0

Bob Tillman C

YEAR	TM/L	PCT	G	PO	A	E	DP	FR
1962	Bos-A	.983	66	389	19	7	1	-4
1963	Bos-A	.992	95	621	26	5	5	1
1964	Bos-A	.989	131	897	49	11	5	-10
1965	Bos-A	.988	106	676	45	9	6	-8
1966	Bos-A	.990	72	372	24	4	5	-4
1967	Bos-A	.977	26	120	10	3	3	2
	NY-A	.970	15	83	14	3	3	0
	Yr	.974	41	203	24	6	6	2
1968	Atl-N	.990	75	359	29	4	7	4
1969	Atl-N	.988	69	309	15	4	5	-10
1970	Atl-N	.988	70	404	22	5	0	-1
Total	9	.988	725	4230	253	5	40	-30

Joe Tinker SS

YEAR	TM/L	PCT	G	PO	A	E	DP	FR
1902	Chi-N	.906	124	243	**453**	**72**	46	4
1903	Chi-N	.906	107	229	362	61	37	2
1904	Chi-N	.925	140	327	465	64	54	19
1905	Chi-N	.940	149	345	527	56	**67**	17
1906	Chi-N	**.944**	147	288	472	45	55	5
1907	Chi-N	.939	113	215	390	39	45	14
1908	Chi-N	**.958**	**157**	314	**570**	39	48	30
1909	Chi-N	**.940**	143	320	470	50	49	16
1910	Chi-N	.942	132	277	411	42	54	16
1911	Chi-N	**.937**	143	333	486	55	56	23
1912	Chi-N	.943	142	**354**	470	50	73	25
1913	Cin-N	.968	101	223	320	18	34	17
1914	Chi-F	.947	125	271	408	38	48	19
1915	Chi-F	.914	16	16	37	5	2	-2
1916	Chi-N	.909	4	3	7	1	0	-1
Total	15	.938	1743	3758	5848	635	668	204

3B

1902	Chi-N	.926	8	10	15	2	1	0
1903	Chi-N	.902	19	17	38	6	0	-2
1906	Chi-N	.750	1	1	2	1	0	-1
1913	Cin-N	.969	9	14	17	1	0	0
1915	Chi-F	.909	4	2	8	1	0	0
1916	Chi-N	1.000	2	1	2	0	0	0
Total	6	.920	43	45	82	1	1	-3

2B

1915	Chi-F	.917	5	9	13	2	2	0

OF

1904	Chi-N	1.000	1	1	0	0	0	0

Eric Tipton OF

YEAR	TM/L	PCT	G	PO	A	E	DP	FR
1939	Phi-A	.942	34	65	0	4	0	-1
1940	Phi-A	1.000	2	3	0	0	0	0
1941	Phi-A	1.000	1	2	0	0	0	0
1942	Cin-N	.977	58	126	3	3	0	1
1943	Cin-N	.984	139	298	8	5	2	-4
1944	Cin-N	.983	139	329	8	6	1	-1
1945	Cin-N	.970	83	192	2	6	1	-3
Total	7	.977	456	1015	21	4	4	-8

Joe Tipton C

YEAR	TM/L	PCT	G	PO	A	E	DP	FR
1948	Cle-A	.971	40	84	18	3	4	0
1949	Chi-A	.992	53	203	32	2	4	2
1950	Phi-A	.987	59	201	24	3	3	-4
1951	Phi-A	.969	72	230	52	9	12	1
1952	Phi-A	.990	23	80	16	1	1	-3
	Cle-A	.971	35	118	18	4	1	-8
	Yr	.979	58	198	34	5	2	-11
1953	Cle-A	1.000	46	114	18	0	1	-7
1954	Was-A	.992	52	220	30	2	6	4
Total	7	.984	380	1250	208	4	32	-15

John Titus OF

YEAR	TM/L	PCT	G	PO	A	E	DP	FR
1903	Phi-N	.952	72	126	13	7	2	3
1904	Phi-N	.952	140	258	21	14	7	8
1905	Phi-N	.962	147	255	24	11	4	8
1906	Phi-N	.974	142	236	23	7	5	7
1907	Phi-N	.928	142	198	21	17	3	-5
1908	Phi-N	.963	149	215	22	9	3	-3
1909	Phi-N	.971	149	241	23	8	6	5
1910	Phi-N	.976	142	226	22	6	4	-3
1911	Phi-N	.979	60	85	10	2	3	-2
1912	Phi-N	.917	42	53	2	5	1	-10
	Bos-N	.965	96	152	12	6	1	-10
	Yr	.952	138	205	14	11	2	-20
1913	Bos-N	.919	75	94	8	9	1	-11
Total	11	.959	1356	2139	201	101	40	-13

Jack Tobin OF

YEAR	TM/L	PCT	G	PO	A	E	DP	FR
1914	StL-F	.952	132	185	31	11	3	5
1915	StL-F	.965	**158**	279	21	11	3	3
1916	StL-A	.842	41	46	2	9	0	-9
1918	StL-A	.971	122	244	20	8	**8**	-1
1919	StL-A	.953	123	247	16	13	5	2
1920	StL-A	.960	147	293	18	13	1	4
1921	StL-A	.956	150	277	**28**	14	5	8
1922	StL-A	.940	145	221	15	15	5	-8
1923	StL-A	.969	151	269	14	9	3	-9
1924	StL-A	.957	132	251	19	12	5	2
1925	StL-A	1.000	39	61	1	0	0	-5
1926	Was-A	1.000	7	10	0	0	0	-2
	Bos-A	.966	51	79	7	3	1	-3
	Yr	.970	58	89	7	3	1	-5
1927	Bos-A	.947	93	152	10	9	4	-5
Total	13	.957	1491	2614	202	127	43	-18

1B

1925	StL-A	.947	3	18	0	1	2	-1

Al Todd C

YEAR	TM/L	PCT	G	PO	A	E	DP	FR
1932	Phi-N	.899	25	58	4	7	2	-4
1933	Phi-N	.983	34	92	21	2	3	5
1934	Phi-N	.976	82	291	32	8	7	-2
1935	Phi-N	.968	87	292	37	11	5	-13
1936	Pit-N	.976	70	332	39	9	2	1
1937	Pit-N	.972	**128**	**603**	89	**20**	**15**	-3
1938	Pit-N	.985	**132**	**574**	89	10	7	**9**
1939	Bro-N	.985	73	284	35	5	5	**8**
1940	Chi-N	.984	104	418	59	8	11	-6
1943	Chi-N	.986	17	62	6	1	2	4
Total	10	.977	752	3006	411	1	59	-1

OF

1933	Phi-N	1.000	2	5	0	0	0	0

Phil Todt 1B

YEAR	TM/L	PCT	G	PO	A	E	DP	FR
1924	Bos-A	.983	18	158	11	3	8	-1
1925	Bos-A	.991	140	1408	100	13	126	3
1926	Bos-A	.988	154	**1755**	**126**	**22**	114	10
1927	Bos-A	.991	139	1401	112	13	121	9
1928	Bos-A	**.997**	144	1486	94	5	96	3
1929	Bos-A	.991	153	1467	102	14	128	3
1930	Bos-A	.993	104	1001	65	8	84	**3**
1931	Phi-A	.995	52	403	13	2	36	-4
Total	8	.992	904	9079	623	0	713	26

OF

1924	Bos-A	1.000	4	1	0	0	0	-2

Bobby Tolan OF

YEAR	TM/L	PCT	G	PO	A	E	DP	FR
1965	StL-N	.970	17	32	0	1	0	-1
1966	StL-N	.952	26	39	1	2	0	-1
1967	StL-N	.992	80	118	4	1	1	4
1968	StL-N	.967	67	116	3	4	1	0
1969	Cin-N	.974	150	**362**	6	10	3	1
1970	Cin-N	.978	150	349	7	8	0	3
1972	Cin-N	.990	149	**401**	9	4	3	6
1973	Cin-N	.966	120	279	9	10	1	-1
1974	SD-N	.971	88	161	5	5	0	-2
1975	SD-N	.971	120	230	5	7	1	-4
1976	Phi-N	.955	35	41	1	2	0	-1
1977	Pit-N	1.000	2	3	0	0	0	0
1979	SD-N	—	1	0	0	0	0	0
Total	13	.976	1005	2131	50	4	10	4

1B

1966	StL-N	1.000	1	2	0	0	0	0
1967	StL-N	1.000	13	107	5	0	7	-1
1968	StL-N	1.000	9	83	9	0	7	1
1975	SD-N	1.000	27	106	15	0	7	3
1976	Phi-N	.992	50	354	13	3	36	-6
1977	Phi-N	.944	5	16	1	1	1	0
	Pit-N	1.000	20	106	6	0	9	0
	Yr	.992	25	122	7	1	10	0
1979	SD-N	1.000	5	10	0	0	2	0
Total	7	.995	130	784	51	4	69	-3

Wayne Tolleson SS

YEAR	TM/L	PCT	G	PO	A	E	DP	FR
1981	Tex-A	—	2	0	0	0	0	-1
1982	Tex-A	.958	26	47	68	5	20	5
1983	Tex-A	.988	26	22	57	1	12	-4
1984	Tex-A	1.000	7	2	8	0	1	0
1985	Tex-A	.972	81	96	182	8	37	-5
1986	Chi-A	.974	18	13	25	1	3	-2
	NY-A	.981	56	87	177	5	35	6
	Yr	.981	74	100	202	6	38	4
1987	NY-A	.970	119	162	321	15	64	-4
1988	NY-A	—	1	0	0	0	0	0
1989	NY-A	.975	28	25	54	2	10	6
1990	NY-A	.983	45	43	72	2	22	16
Total	10	.974	409	497	964	9	204	17

2B

1982	Tex-A	—	1	0	0	0	0	0
1983	Tex-A	.972	112	246	315	16	69	-6
1984	Tex-A	.979	109	191	276	10	61	-7
1985	Tex-A	.965	29	44	65	4	11	4
1988	NY-A	.981	12	20	33	1	7	4
1989	NY-A	1.000	13	6	15	0	5	3
1990	NY-A	1.000	13	14	14	0	4	0
Total	8	.976	292	524	720	1	158	-2

3B

1981	Tex-A	1.000	6	5	8	0	0	0
1982	Tex-A	1.000	4	0	2	0	0	0
1984	Tex-A	1.000	5	2	3	0	0	0
1985	Tex-A	.895	12	9	8	2	0	-1
1986	Chi-A	.955	65	37	113	7	9	-8
	NY-A	.938	7	5	10	1	2	1
	Yr	.954	72	42	123	8	11	-7
1987	NY-A	1.000	3	0	5	0	2	1
1988	NY-A	.935	10	8	21	2	2	2
1989	NY-A	.912	28	14	38	5	5	1
1990	NY-A	—	3	0	0	0	0	0
Total	9	.944	143	80	208	7	20	-4

OF

1984	Tex-A	—	1	0	0	0	0	0
1986	Chi-A	1.000	2	2	0	0	0	0
Total	2	1.000	3	2	0	0	0	0

Phil Tomney SS

YEAR	TM/L	PCT	G	PO	A	E	DP	FR
1888	Lou-a	.882	34	40	117	21	7	6
1889	Lou-a	.857	112	229	454	114	57	27
1890	Lou-a	**.902**	108	180	406	64	31	**18**
Total	3	.878	254	449	977	199	95	51

Bert Tooley SS

YEAR	TM/L	PCT	G	PO	A	E	DP	FR
1911	Bro-N	.925	114	226	340	46	42	-8
1912	Bro-N	.885	76	147	214	47	23	-15
Total	2	.909	190	373	554	3	65	-23

Specs Toporcer SS

YEAR	TM/L	PCT	G	PO	A	E	DP	FR
1921	StL-N	1.000	2	1	5	0	0	0
1922	StL-N	.939	91	168	246	27	34	-22
1923	StL-N	.952	33	62	77	7	18	-6
1924	StL-N	.942	25	32	49	5	6	-7
1925	StL-N	.960	66	141	215	15	40	-3
1926	StL-N	1.000	5	2	3	0	0	0
1927	StL-N	.917	27	37	62	9	13	-6
Total	7	.946	249	443	657	3	111	-44

2B

1921	StL-N	.938	12	24	37	4	6	0
1922	StL-N	1.000	1	1	2	0	0	0
1923	StL-N	.945	52	130	162	17	39	-6
1924	StL-N	.800	3	2	2	1	0	-1
1925	StL-N	.960	7	8	16	1	1	0
1926	StL-N	.983	27	22	35	1	3	-9
1927	StL-N	1.000	2	3	2	0	1	0
1928	StL-N	1.000	1	5	0	0	1	-1
Total	8	.949	105	195	256	4	51	-17

3B

1922	StL-N	.818	6	2	7	2	1	-1
1923	StL-N	1.000	1	1	1	0	0	0
1924	StL-N	.974	33	22	54	2	2	-8
1926	StL-N	1.000	1	0	2	0	0	0
1927	StL-N	.980	54	49	95	3	8	-5
Total	5	.971	95	74	159	7	11	-14

1B

1923	StL-N	—	1	0	0	0	0	0
1927	StL-N	.909	1	9	1	1	1	0
1928	StL-N	1.000	1	7	3	0	0	1
Total	3	.952	3	16	4	1	1	1

OF

1922	StL-N	.667	1	2	0	1	0	-1

Jeff Torborg C

YEAR	TM/L	PCT	G	PO	A	E	DP	FR
1964	LA-N	.977	27	80	4	2	1	-2
1965	LA-N	.991	53	300	19	3	1	3
1966	LA-N	.986	45	269	17	4	2	6
1967	LA-N	.989	75	413	30	5	3	11
1968	LA-N	.991	37	206	20	2	1	10
1969	LA-N	.996	50	251	26	1	5	11
1970	LA-N	.983	63	275	16	5	2	9
1971	Cal-A	.987	49	208	17	3	9	5
1972	Cal-A	.998	58	383	28	1	5	**15**
1973	Cal-A	.991	102	613	37	6	2	8
Total	10	.990	559	2998	214	2	31	76

Earl Torgeson 1B

YEAR	TM/L	PCT	G	PO	A	E	DP	FR
1947	Bos-N	.984	117	1033	76	**18**	83	-1
1948	Bos-N	.993	129	1069	81	8	85	1
1949	Bos-N	.988	25	242	8	3	25	2
1950	Bos-N	.986	**156**	1365	110	**21**	126	0
1951	Bos-N	.988	155	1330	107	**17**	137	-1
1952	Bos-N	.989	105	931	73	11	86	0
1953	Phi-N	.987	105	916	65	13	83	-3
1954	Phi-N	.990	133	1146	74	12	103	-10
1955	Phi-N	.995	43	349	26	2	27	-1
	Det-A	.992	83	695	53	6	79	0
1956	Det-A	.992	83	623	32	5	62	-6
1957	Det-A	1.000	17	98	7	0	11	0

YEAR	TM/L	PCT	G	PO	A	E	DP	FR
	Chi-A	.998	70	612	29	1	72	-5
	Yr	.999	87	710	36	1	83	-5
1958	Chi-A	.978	73	470	30	11	54	-2
1959	Chi-A	.983	103	717	37	13	58	-6
1960	Chi-A	.983	10	54	4	1	3	0
1961	Chi-A	1.000	1	1	0	0	0	0
	NY-A	.969	8	29	2	1	7	0
	Yr	.970	9	30	2	1	7	0
Total	15	.989	1416	11680	814	143	1097	-37

OF

YEAR	TM/L	PCT	G	PO	A	E	DP	FR
1952	Bos-N	.833	5	4	1	1	0	0
1957	Chi-A	—	1	0	0	0	0	0
Total	2	.833	6	4	1	1	0	0

■ Frank Torre 1B

YEAR	TM/L	PCT	G	PO	A	E	DP	FR
1956	Mil-N	.993	89	390	42	3	34	5
1957	Mil-N	.996	117	859	71	4	89	1
1958	Mil-N	.994	122	960	80	6	85	6
1959	Mil-N	.994	87	622	46	4	43	0
1960	Mil-N	1.000	17	105	4	0	12	-1
1962	Phi-N	.980	76	347	37	8	40	3
1963	Phi-N	.989	56	253	28	3	26	5
Total	7	.993	564	3536	308	8	329	19

■ Joe Torre C

YEAR	TM/L	PCT	G	PO	A	E	DP	FR
1961	Mil-N	.982	112	494	50	10	4	-9
1962	Mil-N	.986	63	325	39	5	4	5
1963	Mil-N	.994	105	584	46	4	9	-7
1964	Mil-N	.995	96	518	46	3	4	-10
1965	Mil-N	.991	100	589	43	6	4	-5
1966	Atl-N	.984	114	607	67	11	9	-3
1967	Atl-N	.991	114	580	63	6	12	-6
1968	Atl-N	.996	92	492	37	2	7	-15
1969	StL-N	.990	17	90	8	1	0	-1
1970	StL-N	.987	90	571	29	8	4	-2
Total	10	.990	903	4850	428	6	57	-53

1B

YEAR	TM/L	PCT	G	PO	A	E	DP	FR
1963	Mil-N	.995	37	335	30	2	36	2
1964	Mil-N	.993	70	563	48	4	49	2
1965	Mil-N	.996	49	433	30	2	39	1
1966	Atl-N	.997	36	267	20	1	24	0
1967	Atl-N	.991	23	205	18	2	21	2
1968	Atl-N	1.000	29	241	11	0	19	0
1969	StL-N	.996	144	1270	83	6	117	-2
1970	StL-N	1.000	1	12	0	0	0	0
1972	StL-N	.984	27	234	16	4	17	0
1973	StL-N	.993	114	833	60	6	80	1
1974	StL-N	.992	139	1165	102	10	144	7
1975	NY-N	.968	24	111	9	4	12	-1
1976	NY-N	.989	78	590	49	7	40	3
1977	NY-N	.988	16	83	2	1	9	-2
Total	14	.993	787	6342	478	9	607	13

3B

YEAR	TM/L	PCT	G	PO	A	E	DP	FR
1970	StL-N	.948	73	68	133	11	12	-6
1971	StL-N	.951	161	136	271	21	22	-17
1972	StL-N	.963	117	102	182	11	17	-15
1973	StL-N	.951	58	48	68	6	3	-13
1974	StL-N	.871	18	8	19	4	1	-4
1975	NY-N	.950	83	61	148	11	14	0
1976	NY-N	1.000	4	3	3	0	2	0
1977	NY-N	1.000	1	0	1	0	0	0
Total	8	.951	515	426	825	4	71	-55

OF

YEAR	TM/L	PCT	G	PO	A	E	DP	FR
1963	Mil-N	—	2	0	0	0	0	0

■ Gil Torres SS

YEAR	TM/L	PCT	G	PO	A	E	DP	FR
1945	Was-A	.953	145	272	437	35	65	-21
1946	Was-A	.939	31	57	82	9	17	-2
Total	2	.951	176	329	519	4	82	-23

3B

YEAR	TM/L	PCT	G	PO	A	E	DP	FR
1944	Was-A	.952	123	120	297	21	25	9
1945	Was-A	1.000	2	2	3	0	0	0
1946	Was-A	1.000	18	18	42	0	3	3
Total	3	.958	143	140	342	1	28	12

2B

YEAR	TM/L	PCT	G	PO	A	E	DP	FR
1944	Was-A	.979	10	22	24	1	5	1
1946	Was-A	.905	7	6	13	2	0	0
Total	2	.956	17	28	37	3	5	1

1B

YEAR	TM/L	PCT	G	PO	A	E	DP	FR
1944	Was-A	.929	4	25	1	2	5	-1

■ Felix Torres 3B

YEAR	TM/L	PCT	G	PO	A	E	DP	FR
1962	LA-A	.938	123	110	250	24	20	-3
1963	LA-A	.939	122	101	237	22	29	-4
1964	LA-A	.970	72	73	122	6	10	0
Total	3	.945	317	284	609	2	59	-7

1B

YEAR	TM/L	PCT	G	PO	A	E	DP	FR
1963	LA-A	.900	2	9	0	1	1	0
1964	LA-A	.944	3	16	1	1	2	0
Total	2	.929	5	25	1	2	3	0

■ Hector Torres SS

YEAR	TM/L	PCT	G	PO	A	E	DP	FR
1968	Hou-N	.958	127	159	391	24	55	-4
1969	Hou-N	.944	22	30	38	4	7	0
1970	Hou-N	.947	22	26	45	4	7	0
1971	Chi-N	.962	18	11	40	2	6	1
1972	Mon-N	.982	16	24	31	1	5	2
1973	Hou-N	.952	22	18	62	4	7	6
1975	SD-N	.971	75	97	272	11	45	12
1976	SD-N	.949	63	64	160	12	29	-16
1977	Tor-A	.980	68	82	165	5	29	0
Total	9	.962	433	511	1204	7	190	1

2B

YEAR	TM/L	PCT	G	PO	A	E	DP	FR
1968	Hou-N	1.000	1	0	2	0	0	0
1970	Hou-N	1.000	6	8	6	0	2	1
1971	Chi-N	.857	4	1	5	1	1	0
1972	Mon-N	.965	60	86	132	8	28	11
1973	Hou-N	.964	13	14	13	1	3	1
1975	SD-N	.984	16	24	36	1	10	0
1976	SD-N	1.000	3	5	3	0	1	0
1977	Tor-A	.965	23	61	75	5	9	-2
Total	8	.967	126	199	272	6	54	11

3B

YEAR	TM/L	PCT	G	PO	A	E	DP	FR
1972	Mon-N	1.000	1	2	4	0	1	1
1975	SD-N	.974	42	7	30	1	0	0
1976	SD-N	1.000	4	3	5	0	0	0
1977	Tor-A	1.000	2	1	0	0	0	0
Total	4	.981	49	13	39	1	1	1

OF

YEAR	TM/L	PCT	G	PO	A	E	DP	FR
1972	Mon-N	—	2	0	0	0	0	0

■ Rusty Torres OF

YEAR	TM/L	PCT	G	PO	A	E	DP	FR
1971	NY-A	1.000	5	13	0	0	0	0
1972	NY-A	.978	62	86	4	2	0	-4
1973	Cle-A	.976	114	191	9	5	1	-4
1974	Cle-A	.959	94	110	8	5	0	7
1976	Cal-A	.990	105	195	5	2	0	-5
1977	Cal-A	.984	54	60	1	1	0	3
1978	Chi-A	.964	14	27	0	1	0	-1
1979	Chi-A	.976	85	117	4	3	0	-13
1980	KC-A	.973	40	67	4	2	1	6
Total	9	.977	573	866	35	1	2	-11

3B

YEAR	TM/L	PCT	G	PO	A	E	DP	FR
1976	Cal-A	—	1	0	0	0	0	0

■ Cesar Tovar OF

YEAR	TM/L	PCT	G	PO	A	E	DP	FR
1965	Min-A	1.000	2	3	0	0	0	0
1966	Min-A	1.000	24	53	2	0	1	2
1967	Min-A	.994	74	169	5	1	3	7
1968	Min-A	.966	78	138	4	5	1	0
1969	Min-A	.983	113	225	9	4	3	-6
1970	Min-A	.977	151	370	12	9	1	8
1971	Min-A	.986	154	348	14	5	3	15
1972	Min-A	.983	139	287	10	5	2	6
1973	Phi-N	.953	24	40	1	2	1	-2
1974	Tex-A	.980	135	331	13	7	3	16
1975	Tex-A	.919	31	56	1	5	0	-5
1976	Oak-A	.958	20	23	0	1	0	0
Total	12	.980	945	2043	71	4	18	41

3B

YEAR	TM/L	PCT	G	PO	A	E	DP	FR
1965	Min-A	.889	2	0	8	1	0	1
1967	Min-A	.947	70	60	101	9	8	-6
1968	Min-A	.933	75	48	147	14	8	6
1969	Min-A	.950	20	12	26	2	2	1
1970	Min-A	.625	4	2	3	3	0	-2
1971	Min-A	.857	7	3	9	2	1	-1
1973	Phi-N	.928	46	34	56	7	7	-10
1975	Oak-A	1.000	3	1	1	0	1	0
Total	8	.931	227	160	351	8	27	-11

2B

YEAR	TM/L	PCT	G	PO	A	E	DP	FR
1965	Min-A	.800	4	2	6	2	2	0
1966	Min-A	.978	76	154	205	8	33	-5
1967	Min-A	.971	36	69	66	4	11	-3
1968	Min-A	.964	18	29	24	2	6	-1
1969	Min-A	.962	41	78	99	7	25	7
1970	Min-A	.931	8	17	10	2	5	-3
1971	Min-A	1.000	2	1	4	0	1	1
1973	Phi-N	.969	22	39	56	3	24	-4
1975	Tex-A	1.000	1	1	2	0	0	0
	Oak-A	1.000	4	1	1	0	0	0
	Yr	1.000	5	2	3	0	0	0
1976	NY-A	1.000	3	4	8	0	2	1
Total	10	.969	215	395	481	8	109	-7

SS

YEAR	TM/L	PCT	G	PO	A	E	DP	FR
1965	Min-A	—	1	0	0	0	0	0
1966	Min-A	.950	31	47	67	6	10	-6
1967	Min-A	.875	9	9	12	3	1	-2
1968	Min-A	.947	35	31	59	5	9	-6
1975	Oak-A	1.000	1	0	1	0	0	0
Total	5	.942	77	87	139	4	20	-14

1B

YEAR	TM/L	PCT	G	PO	A	E	DP	FR
1968	Min-A	1.000	1	0	1	0	0	0

C

YEAR	TM/L	PCT	G	PO	A	E	DP	FR
1968	Min-A	1.000	1	1	0	0	0	0

■ George Townsend C

YEAR	TM/L	PCT	G	PO	A	E	DP	FR
1887	Phi-a	.865	28	99	42	22	1	-6
1888	Phi-a	.912	42	225	76	29	2	1
1890	Bal-a	.930	18	72	34	8	2	2
1891	Bal-a	.909	58	191	68	26	5	-10
Total	4	.905	146	587	220	5	10	-13

OF

YEAR	TM/L	PCT	G	PO	A	E	DP	FR
1887	Phi-a	1.000	3	3	0	0	0	-1
1891	Bal-a	1.000	3	1	0	0	0	-1
Total	2	1.000	6	4	0	0	0	-2

■ Jim Traber 1B

YEAR	TM/L	PCT	G	PO	A	E	DP	FR
1986	Bal-A	.988	29	224	21	3	28	-1
1988	Bal-A	.990	57	459	58	5	51	7
1989	Bal-A	.998	69	514	54	1	59	6
Total	3	.993	155	1197	133	9	138	12

OF

YEAR	TM/L	PCT	G	PO	A	E	DP	FR
1986	Bal-A	.913	8	19	2	2	0	1
1988	Bal-A	.958	11	22	1	1	0	0
Total	2	.936	19	41	3	3	0	1

■ Dick Tracewski SS

YEAR	TM/L	PCT	G	PO	A	E	DP	FR
1962	LA-N	1.000	4	1	4	0	0	4
1963	LA-N	.957	81	92	196	13	32	17
1964	LA-N	.944	19	25	42	4	9	4
1965	LA-N	.862	7	7	18	4	0	0
1966	Det-A	.917	3	2	9	1	2	1
1967	Det-A	.965	44	31	52	3	12	3
1968	Det-A	.982	51	60	108	3	19	-7
1969	Det-A	.957	41	37	53	4	15	10
Total	8	.958	250	255	482	2	89	32

2B

YEAR	TM/L	PCT	G	PO	A	E	DP	FR
1963	LA-N	.971	23	13	20	1	2	2
1964	LA-N	.970	56	98	130	7	24	-4
1965	LA-N	.962	14	14	11	1	1	-1
1966	Det-A	.947	70	69	91	9	25	10
1967	Det-A	1.000	12	14	25	0	5	5
1968	Det-A	1.000	14	15	30	0	5	2
1969	Det-A	.977	13	19	24	1	4	5
Total	7	.968	202	242	331	9	66	19

3B

YEAR	TM/L	PCT	G	PO	A	E	DP	FR
1964	LA-N	.949	30	29	46	4	2	0
1965	LA-N	.950	53	30	103	7	6	9
1967	Det-A	1.000	10	9	13	0	0	1
1968	Det-A	.929	16	7	19	2	3	-1
1969	Det-A	1.000	6	3	10	0	1	2
Total	5	.954	115	78	191	3	12	11

■ Bill Traffley C

YEAR	TM/L	PCT	G	PO	A	E	DP	FR
1878	Chi-N	1.000	2	7	3	0	0	0
1883	Cin-a	.851	29	121	33	27	2	3
1884	Bal-a	.926	47	321	57	30	6	-4
1885	Bal-a	.943	61	357	105	28	6	12
1886	Bal-a	.952	25	163	35	10	4	0
Total	5	.927	164	969	233	5	18	11

OF

YEAR	TM/L	PCT	G	PO	A	E	DP	FR
1884	Bal-a	1.000	6	6	0	0	0	-1
1885	Bal-a	.750	10	2	1	1	0	-3
Total	2	.900	16	8	1	1	0	-4

2B

YEAR	TM/L	PCT	G	PO	A	E	DP	FR
1885	Bal-a	.800	3	6	6	3	1	-1

SS

YEAR	TM/L	PCT	G	PO	A	E	DP	FR
1883	Cin-a	.500	2	0	1	1	0	0

1B

YEAR	TM/L	PCT	G	PO	A	E	DP	FR
1884	Bal-a	1.000	1	9	0	0	0	0

■ Walt Tragesser C

YEAR	TM/L	PCT	G	PO	A	E	DP	FR
1913	Bos-N	1.000	2	1	0	0	0	0
1915	Bos-N	.944	7	15	2	1	1	1
1916	Bos-N	.971	29	73	27	3	2	4
1917	Bos-N	.971	94	433	105	16	11	-1
1918	Bos-N	.833	7	4	1	1	0	1
1919	Bos-N	.959	14	27	20	2	1	0
	Phi-N	.953	34	155	49	10	6	4
	Yr	.954	48	182	69	12	7	4
1920	Phi-N	.944	52	157	46	12	4	-12
Total	7	.961	239	865	250	5	25	-3

■ Alan Trammell SS

YEAR	TM/L	PCT	G	PO	A	E	DP	FR
1977	Det-A	.961	19	15	34	2	5	-7
1978	Det-A	.979	139	239	421	14	95	6
1979	Det-A	.961	142	245	388	26	99	-13
1980	Det-A	.980	144	225	412	13	89	-27
1981	Det-A	.983	105	181	347	9	65	6
1982	Det-A	.978	157	259	459	16	97	-8
1983	Det-A	.979	140	236	367	13	71	-18
1984	Det-A	.980	114	180	314	10	71	-12
1985	Det-A	.977	149	225	400	15	89	-16
1986	Det-A	.969	149	238	445	22	99	6
1987	Det-A	.971	149	222	421	19	94	-10
1988	Det-A	.980	125	195	355	11	67	-7
1989	Det-A	.985	117	188	396	9	71	12
1990	Det-A	.979	142	232	409	14	102	1
Total	14	.977	1791	2880	5168	193	1114	-87

■ Cecil Travis SS

YEAR	TM/L	PCT	G	PO	A	E	DP	FR
1936	Was-A	.938	71	135	213	23	53	-10
1937	Was-A	.965	129	229	396	23	99	-11
1938	Was-A	.950	143	304	457	40	113	3
1939	Was-A	.958	118	194	359	24	74	-4
1940	Was-A	.918	23	48	75	11	20	5
1941	Was-A	.964	136	279	388	25	99	0
1946	Was-A	.959	75	133	196	14	45	-12
1947	Was-A	.972	15	25	44	2	9	-2
Total	8	.955	710	1347	2128	162	512	-31

3B

YEAR	TM/L	PCT	G	PO	A	E	DP	FR
1933	Was-A	.974	15	8	30	1	1	4
1934	Was-A	.937	99	88	210	20	23	3
1935	Was-A	.963	114	136	254	15	29	20
1936	Was-A	.800	2	2	2	1	0	0
1940	Was-A	.934	113	116	205	27	30	11
1941	Was-A	.964	16	14	39	2	4	2
1945	Was-A	.920	14	18	28	4	4	0
1946	Was-A	.897	56	54	94	17	15	-7
1947	Was-A	.932	39	28	68	7	6	-1
Total	9	.939	468	464	990	4	112	32

OF

YEAR	TM/L	PCT	G	PO	A	E	DP	FR
1935	Was-A	.970	16	28	4	1	1	2
1936	Was-A	.942	53	91	6	6	1	-2
Total	2	.949	69	119	10	7	2	0

2B

YEAR	TM/L	PCT	G	PO	A	E	DP	FR
1936	Was-A	.963	4	16	10	1	4	0

■ Pie Traynor 3B

YEAR	TM/L	PCT	G	PO	A	E	DP	FR
1921	Pit-N	.917	3	3	8	1	0	0
1922	Pit-N	.945	124	147	216	21	21	-3
1923	Pit-N	.950	152	189	306	26	30	8
1924	Pit-N	.968	141	179	268	15	31	9
1925	Pit-N	.957	150	226	303	24	41	23
1926	Pit-N	.952	148	182	279	23	32	4
1927	Pit-N	.962	143	212	265	19	23	12
1928	Pit-N	.946	144	175	296	27	15	4
1929	Pit-N	.951	130	148	238	20	23	-1
1930	Pit-N	.941	130	130	268	25	18	5
1931	Pit-N	.925	155	172	284	37	21	-9
1932	Pit-N	.936	127	173	222	27	16	-1
1933	Pit-N	.946	154	176	300	27	16	-1
1934	Pit-N	.954	110	116	176	14	16	-10
1935	Pit-N	.888	59	59	84	18	2	-3
1937	Pit-N	1.000	3	2	8	0	0	1
Total	16	.947	1863	2289	3521	324	303	36

SS

YEAR	TM/L	PCT	G	PO	A	E	DP	FR
1920	Pit-N	.860	17	35	39	12	4	-6
1921	Pit-N	1.000	1	1	1	0	0	0
1922	Pit-N	.910	18	39	62	10	7	0

YEAR	TM/L	PCT	G	PO	A	E	DP	FR
1923	Pit-N	1.000	1	2	4	0	0	0
1925	Pit-N	1.000	1	2	2	0	1	0
1926	Pit-N	.960	3	9	15	1	1	2
1927	Pit-N	.976	9	13	28	1	2	1
Total	7	.913	50	101	151	4	15	-3
1B								
1935	Pit-N	—	1	0	0	0	0	0

■ George Treadway OF

YEAR	TM/L	PCT	G	PO	A	E	DP	FR
1893	Bal-N	.901	115	192	27	24	4	8
1894	Bro-N	.892	122	274	16	35	2	1
1895	Bro-N	.886	86	117	7	16	4	-9
1896	Lou-N	.500	1	3	0	3	0	0
Total	4	.891	324	586	50	8	10	0
1B								
1894	Bro-N	—	1	0	0	0	0	0
1896	Lou-N	.824	1	13	1	3	0	0
Total	2	.824	2	13	1	3	0	0

■ Jeff Treadway 2B

YEAR	TM/L	PCT	G	PO	A	E	DP	FR
1987	Cin-N	.958	21	44	48	4	14	-7
1988	Cin-N	.984	97	188	252	7	49	3
1989	Atl-N	.981	123	271	336	12	80	3
1990	Atl-N	.976	122	241	360	15	72	10
Total	4	.979	363	744	996	8	215	9
3B								
1988	Cin-N	.667	2	1	1	1	1	0
1989	Atl-N	1.000	6	2	5	0	0	0
Total	2	.900	8	3	6	1	1	0

■ Mike Tresh C

YEAR	TM/L	PCT	G	PO	A	E	DP	FR
1938	Chi-A	.978	10	37	8	1	1	2
1939	Chi-A	.985	119	480	59	8	7	1
1940	Chi-A	.983	135	619	69	12	7	8
1941	Chi-A	.981	115	488	81	11	12	11
1942	Chi-A	.977	72	258	37	7	2	-5
1943	Chi-A	.982	85	321	62	7	4	0
1944	Chi-A	.981	93	370	47	8	5	-3
1945	Chi-A	.984	150	575	102	11	7	-3
1946	Chi-A	.995	79	330	48	2	13	14
1947	Chi-A	.975	89	313	38	9	10	-7
1948	Chi-A	.983	34	99	16	2	1	0
1949	Cle-A	1.000	2	8	0	0	3	6
Total	12	.983	1019	3961	575	8	72	24

■ Tom Tresh OF

YEAR	TM/L	PCT	G	PO	A	E	DP	FR
1962	NY-A	.958	43	89	3	4	0	-1
1963	NY-A	.981	144	305	6	6	1	-7
1964	NY-A	.996	146	259	7	1	0	0
1965	NY-A	.970	154	283	11	9	1	6
1966	NY-A	.985	84	181	12	3	3	12
1967	NY-A	.972	118	198	9	6	1	-1
1968	NY-A	.979	27	45	1	1	0	-1
1969	Det-A	.955	11	20	1	1	0	0
Total	8	.979	727	1380	50	1	6	8
SS								
1961	NY-A	1.000	3	3	7	0	1	3
1962	NY-A	.970	111	201	312	16	51	-14
1968	NY-A	.951	119	199	409	31	70	9
1969	NY-A	.980	41	76	122	4	20	0
	Det-A	.965	77	118	187	11	38	-19
	Yr	.971	118	194	309	15	58	-19
Total	4	.963	351	597	1037	2	180	-21
3B								
1966	NY-A	.961	64	43	179	9	15	15
1969	Det-A	.800	1	1	3	1	0	0
Total	2	.958	65	44	182	0	15	15

■ Alex Trevino C

YEAR	TM/L	PCT	G	PO	A	E	DP	FR
1978	NY-N	1.000	5	12	3	0	0	0
1979	NY-N	.976	36	208	31	6	7	9
1980	NY-N	.977	86	443	63	12	5	-4
1981	NY-N	.963	45	211	22	9	1	3
1982	Cin-N	.979	116	725	61	17	7	4
1983	Cin-N	.987	63	359	28	5	2	10
1984	Cin-N	1.000	4	4	1	0	0	0
	Atl-N	.989	79	399	60	5	5	6
	Yr	.989	83	403	61	5	5	6
1985	SF-N	.978	55	299	19	7	1	0
1986	LA-N	.969	63	304	45	11	4	-5
1987	LA-N	.987	45	205	22	3	3	-2
1988	Hou-N	.977	74	360	24	9	5	-8
1989	Hou-N	.989	32	163	11	2	2	-3
1990	Hou-N	.992	30	124	7	1	0	6
	NY-N	.929	7	25	1	2	0	1
	Cin-N	1.000	2	9	0	0	0	1
	Yr	.982	39	158	8	3	0	8
Total	13	.979	742	3850	398	9	42	18
3B								
1978	NY-N	1.000	1	0	1	0	0	0
1979	NY-N	.945	27	15	37	3	6	2
1980	NY-N	.826	14	6	13	4	2	-2
1981	NY-N	—	1	0	0	0	0	0
1982	Cin-N	—	2	0	0	0	0	0
1983	Cin-N	1.000	4	0	3	0	0	0
1985	SF-N	—	1	0	0	0	0	0
1987	LA-N	—	1	0	0	0	0	0
1989	Hou-N	1.000	2	1	1	0	0	0
Total	9	.917	53	22	55	7	8	0
2B								
1979	NY-N	1.000	8	6	3	0	1	0
1980	NY-N	1.000	1	1	0	0	0	0
1981	NY-N	1.000	1	0	3	0	0	0
1983	Cin-N	1.000	1	0	1	0	1	0
Total	4	1.000	14	8	7	0	1	0
OF								
1981	NY-N	1.000	2	3	0	0	0	0
1987	LA-N	1.000	2	1	0	0	0	0
1988	Hou-N	—	1	0	0	0	0	0
Total	3	1.000	5	4	0	0	0	0

YEAR	TM/L	PCT	G	PO	A	E	DP	FR
1B								
1986	LA-N	1.000	1	0	1	0	0	0
1989	Hou-N	1.000	2	9	1	0	0	0
1990	Hou-N	.938	1	14	1	1	0	0
Total	3	.963	4	23	3	1	0	0

■ Gus Triandos C

YEAR	TM/L	PCT	G	PO	A	E	DP	FR
1953	NY-A	.947	5	17	1	1	0	0
1954	NY-A	—	1	0	0	0	0	0
1955	Bal-A	.979	36	127	13	3	3	-2
1956	Bal-A	.989	89	417	50	5	12	5
1957	Bal-A	.992	120	580	64	5	13	-2
1958	Bal-A	.987	132	698	61	10	11	1
1959	Bal-A	.981	125	597	63	13	5	5
1960	Bal-A	.989	105	516	45	6	5	-6
1961	Bal-A	.989	114	642	55	8	9	7
1962	Bal-A	.985	63	355	28	6	2	0
1963	Det-A	.998	90	535	29	1	4	-4
1964	Phi-N	.985	64	371	24	6	4	3
1965	Phi-N	.975	28	144	10	4	2	-4
	Hou-N	.970	20	124	5	4	0	-2
	Yr	.973	48	268	15	8	2	-6
Total	13	.987	992	5123	448	2	70	1
1B								
1953	NY-A	.991	12	100	6	1	8	0
1955	Bal-A	.989	103	839	69	10	92	2
1956	Bal-A	.983	52	373	39	7	27	5
1964	Phi-N	1.000	1	8	1	0	0	0
Total	4	.988	168	1320	115	8	127	7
3B								
1955	Bal-A	1.000	1	0	2	0	0	0

■ Manny Trillo 2B

YEAR	TM/L	PCT	G	PO	A	E	DP	FR
1973	Oak-A	.941	16	15	17	2	5	5
1974	Oak-A	.949	21	31	43	4	10	6
1975	Chi-N	.967	153	350	509	29	103	16
1976	Chi-N	.981	156	349	527	17	103	19
1977	Chi-N	.970	149	330	467	25	81	30
1978	Chi-N	.978	149	354	505	19	99	29
1979	Phi-N	.985	118	270	368	10	84	5
1980	Phi-N	.987	140	360	467	11	91	19
1981	Phi-N	.987	94	245	286	7	61	11
1982	Phi-N	.994	149	343	441	5	101	5
1983	Cle-A	.989	87	172	269	5	58	3
	Mon-N	.979	31	57	86	3	23	-6
1984	SF-N	.988	96	215	287	6	67	-7
1985	SF-N	.981	120	262	357	12	73	3
1986	Chi-N	.950	6	8	11	1	4	1
1987	Chi-N	1.000	10	7	7	0	1	-1
1988	Chi-N	.980	13	14	34	1	7	0
1989	Cin-N	1.000	10	21	18	0	2	-3
Total	17	.981	1518	3403	4699	157	973	135
3B								
1984	SF-N	1.000	4	3	7	0	0	-1
1985	SF-N	.833	1	1	4	1	0	1
1986	Chi-N	.949	53	26	49	4	3	0
1987	Chi N	.926	35	7	18	2	2	-2
1988	Chi-N	.975	17	4	35	1	4	2
Total	5	.951	110	41	113	8	9	0
1B								
1986	Chi-N	1.000	11	80	3	0	7	-1
1987	Chi-N	.994	47	283	23	2	32	-1
1988	Chi-N	.994	24	154	6	1	7	-2
1989	Cin-N	1.000	3	6	0	0	0	0
Total	4	.995	85	523	32	3	46	-4
SS								
1975	Chi-N	—	1	0	0	0	0	0
1976	Chi-N	1.000	1	1	0	0	0	0
1987	Chi-N	1.000	6	4	5	0	0	-1
1988	Chi-N	1.000	7	5	6	0	1	0
1989	Cin-N	.000	1	0	0	1	0	-1
Total	5	.955	16	10	11	1	1	-2

■ Coaker Triplett OF

YEAR	TM/L	PCT	G	PO	A	E	DP	FR
1938	Chi-N	1.000	9	15	1	0	0	0
1941	StL-N	.965	46	78	4	3	0	-1
1942	StL-N	.966	46	82	2	3	0	1
1943	StL-N	1.000	6	13	0	0	0	0
	Phi-N	.970	90	184	11	6	0	0
	Yr	.972	96	197	11	6	0	0
1944	Phi-N	.989	44	90	3	1	1	0
1945	Phi-N	.945	92	202	3	12	1	-4
Total	6	.965	333	664	24	5	2	-4

■ Hal Trosky 1B

YEAR	TM/L	PCT	G	PO	A	E	DP	FR
1933	Cle-A	.990	11	91	4	1	6	-1
1934	Cle-A	.986	154	1487	86	22	145	0
1935	Cle-A	.993	153	1567	88	11	129	1
1936	Cle-A	.985	151	1367	85	22	126	1
1937	Cle-A	.993	152	1403	76	10	131	-2
1938	Cle-A	.993	148	1232	102	10	121	4
1939	Cle-A	.992	118	1004	97	9	97	11
1940	Cle-A	.991	139	1207	70	11	129	-7
1941	Cle-A	.989	85	727	54	9	77	-3
1944	Chi-A	.993	130	1310	57	9	122	-9
1946	Chi-A	.991	80	729	33	7	63	-8
Total	11	.991	1321	12124	752	121	1146	-13
2B								
1936	Cle-A	1.000	1	1	1	0	0	0

■ Sam Trott C

YEAR	TM/L	PCT	G	PO	A	E	DP	FR
1880	Bos-N	.893	36	170	56	27	0	5
1881	Det-N	.868	6	27	6	5	0	-3
1882	Det-N	.890	23	172	38	26	3	7
1883	Det-N	.864	34	160	43	32	4	-1
1884	Bal-a	.931	60	491	87	43	10	13
1885	Bal-A	.817	8	86	26	15	6	-2
1887	Bal-a	.915	69	373	102	44	6	3
1888	Bal-a	.908	27	156	32	19	4	-4
Total	8	.906	272	1635	390	211	33	18

YEAR	TM/L	PCT	G	PO	A	E	DP	FR
2B								
1882	Det-N	.889	3	4	4	1	0	0
1883	Det-N	.882	42	102	92	26	16	-11
1884	Bal-a	.943	6	16	17	2	3	1
1885	Bal-a	.778	2	3	4	2	0	-1
1887	Bal-a	.886	11	29	33	8	4	2
1888	Bal-a	.750	1	2	4	2	0	0
Total	6	.883	65	156	154	1	23	-9
OF								
1880	Bos-N	.875	4	7	0	1	0	-1
1882	Det-N	1.000	2	4	0	0	0	0
1883	Det-N	1.000	6	4	0	0	0	0
1884	Bal-a	.875	5	6	1	1	2	0
1885	Bal-a	.500	4	2	0	2	0	-2
1887	Bal-a	1.000	3	1	1	0	0	0
1888	Bal-a	.667	3	2	0	1	0	-1
Total	7	.848	27	26	2	5	2	-4
1B								
1882	Det-N	.966	3	27	1	1	1	0
1883	Det-N	1.000	1	7	0	0	0	0
1887	Bal-a	.962	2	25	0	1	1	0
1888	Bal-a	1.000	1	4	0	0	0	0
Total	4	.970	7	63	1	2	2	0
SS								
1882	Det-N	.643	3	0	9	5	2	-1
1885	Bal-a	.500	1	0	2	2	0	-1
1887	Bal-a	—	1	0	0	0	0	0
Total	3	.611	5	0	11	7	2	-2
3B								
1882	Det-N	1.000	1	0	1	0	0	0

■ Dasher Troy 2B

YEAR	TM/L	PCT	G	PO	A	E	DP	FR
1881	Det-N	.895	4	7	10	2	4	-2
1882	Det-N	.847	31	74	76	27	9	-14
1883	NY-N	.879	73	187	226	57	23	-13
1884	NY-a	.879	107	224	314	74	25	-21
1885	NY-a	.866	42	124	103	35	17	-11
Total	5	.873	257	616	729	195	78	-61
SS								
1882	Det-N	.641	11	3	22	14	0	-6
	Pro-N	.750	4	2	13	5	1	-1
	Yr	.678	15	5	35	19	1	-7
1883	NY-N	.797	12	15	36	13	3	-4
1885	NY-a	—	1	0	0	0	0	0
Total	3	.740	28	20	71	2	4	-11
3B								
1881	Det-N	.792	7	6	13	5	0	-2
OF								
1885	NY-a	.571	2	4	0	3	0	-1

■ Frank Truesdale 2B

YEAR	TM/L	PCT	G	PO	A	E	DP	FR
1910	StL-N	.914	122	279	313	56	41	-8
1914	NY-A	.947	67	121	185	17	19	-1
1918	Bos-A	.913	10	14	28	4	2	-1
Total	3	.924	199	414	526	7	62	-10
3B								
1914	NY-A	.857	4	2	4	1	1	0

■ Tommy Tucker 1B

YEAR	TM/L	PCT	G	PO	A	E	DP	FR
1887	Bal-a	.976	136	1346	50	35	49	4
1888	Bal-a	.975	129	1354	59	36	64	4
1889	Bal-a	.964	123	1144	45	44	63	-0
1890	Bos-N	.979	132	1341	39	29	53	-2
1891	Bos-N	.976	140	1313	55	34	66	-3
1892	Bos-N	.972	149	1484	51	45	96	-12
1893	Bos-N	.980	121	1252	39	27	89	-11
1894	Bos-N	.985	123	1108	69	18	82	2
1895	Bos-N	.978	125	1159	82	28	78	5
1896	Bos-N	.985	122	1214	72	20	72	3
1897	Bos-N	.957	4	41	4	2	0	1
	Was-N	.984	93	856	42	15	58	-3
	Yr	.982	97	897	46	17	58	-2
1898	Bro-N	.991	73	797	49	8	44	7
	StL-N	.973	72	755	36	22	40	0
	Yr	.982	145	1552	85	30	84	7
1899	Cle-N	.977	127	1229	58	30	71	-1
Total	13	.978	1669	16393	749	393	925	-7
OF								
1888	Bal-a	.846	7	11	0	2	0	0
1889	Bal-a	.857	12	21	3	4	0	0
1894	Bos-N	—	1	0	0	0	0	-1
Total	3	.854	20	32	3	6	0	-2

■ Thurman Tucker OF

YEAR	TM/L	PCT	G	PO	A	E	DP	FR
1942	Chi-A	.900	5	8	1	1	0	-1
1943	Chi-A	.988	132	399	14	5	1	13
1944	Chi-A	.991	120	414	12	4	2	16
1946	Chi-A	.990	110	276	11	3	1	-1
1947	Chi-A	.978	65	171	5	4	2	4
1948	Cle-A	1.000	66	172	5	0	2	-4
1949	Cle-A	.984	42	119	2	2	0	3
1950	Cle-A	.968	34	58	2	2	1	2
Total	8	.988	574	1617	52	1	9	32

■ Tuck Turner OF

YEAR	TM/L	PCT	G	PO	A	E	DP	FR
1893	Phi-N	.933	36	79	5	6	2	-2
1894	Phi-N	.916	78	134	7	13	1	-9
1895	Phi-N	.847	55	89	5	17	0	-8
1896	Phi-N	.905	8	15	4	2	0	2
	StL-N	.961	51	69	4	3	1	-5
	Yr	.948	59	84	8	5	1	-3
1897	StL-N	.945	102	146	10	9	3	-7
1898	StL-N	.929	34	50	2	4	1	-3
Total	6	.920	364	582	37	4	8	-32

■ Jerry Turner OF

YEAR	TM/L	PCT	G	PO	A	E	DP	FR
1974	SD-N	1.000	13	14	1	0	0	-2
1975	SD-N	.909	4	10	0	1	0	0
1976	SD-N	.960	74	115	6	5	0	-8
1977	SD-N	.947	69	114	10	7	2	0

YEAR	TM/L	PCT	G	PO	A	E	DP	FR
1978	SD-N	.970	58	91	5	3	0	-1
1979	SD-N	.958	115	197	7	9	2	-7
1980	SD-N	1.000	34	44	2	0	1	-3
1981	SD-N	.833	4	5	0	1	0	0
	Chi-A	1.000	1	2	0	0	0	0
1982	Det-A	.909	13	10	0	1	0	0
1983	SD-N	—	1	0	0	0	0	0
Total	10	.959	386	602	31	7	5	-21

■ Terry Turner SS

YEAR	TM/L	PCT	G	PO	A	E	DP	FR
1904	Cle-A	.940	111	191	376	36	28	3
1905	Cle-A	.945	155	288	434	42	49	-25
1906	Cle-A	.960	147	287	570	36	61	24
1907	Cle-A	.950	139	258	477	39	67	-3
1908	Cle-A	.959	17	27	66	4	4	0
1909	Cle-A	.957	26	52	82	6	14	1
1910	Cle-A	.973	94	194	320	14	42	5
1911	Cle-A	.854	10	26	15	7	4	-3
1913	Cle-A	.963	21	29	49	3	8	1
1917	Cle-A	—	1	0	0	0	0	0
1918	Cle-A	—	1	0	0	0	0	0
1919	Phi-A	.946	19	27	61	5	11	1
Total	12	.952	741	1379	2450	192	288	4

3B

YEAR	TM/L	PCT	G	PO	A	E	DP	FR
1901	Pit-N	.833	2	3	7	2	0	1
1910	Cle-A	.939	46	38	101	9	6	-4
1911	Cle-A	.970	94	114	208	10	10	7
1912	Cle-A	.951	103	129	199	17	21	-3
1913	Cle-A	.954	71	91	136	11	27	4
1914	Cle-A	.963	104	138	229	14	23	17
1915	Cle-A	.970	20	10	54	2	3	4
1916	Cle-A	.963	77	87	173	10	10	3
1917	Cle-A	.980	40	41	58	2	3	-4
1918	Cle-A	.969	46	33	93	4	3	-3
1919	Phi-A	1.000	1	3	1	0	0	0
Total	11	.960	604	687	1259	1	106	22

2B

YEAR	TM/L	PCT	G	PO	A	E	DP	FR
1909	Cle-A	.969	26	60	94	5	7	10
1910	Cle-A	.957	9	17	28	2	2	1
1911	Cle-A	.966	14	34	22	2	2	-2
1913	Cle-A	.976	25	68	94	4	0	11
1914	Cle-A	.989	17	30	61	1	0	4
1915	Cle-A	.965	51	82	136	8	11	-12
1916	Cle-A	.981	42	77	135	4	18	2
1917	Cle-A	.981	23	45	61	2	4	2
1918	Cle-A	.992	26	44	77	1	3	0
1919	Phi-A	.965	17	31	52	3	5	1
Total	10	.975	250	488	760	2	52	17

OF

YEAR	TM/L	PCT	G	PO	A	E	DP	FR
1908	Cle-A	.952	36	38	2	2	0	-5

■ Tom Turner C

YEAR	TM/L	PCT	G	PO	A	E	DP	FR
1940	Chi-A	.969	29	110	13	4	0	2
1941	Chi-A	.979	35	166	21	4	3	5
1942	Chi-A	.971	54	199	35	7	5	-1
1943	Chi-A	.978	49	186	34	5	5	6
1944	Chi-A	.968	36	121	15	6	3	-2
	StL-A	.969	11	28	3	1	0	-1
	Yr	.960	47	149	18	7	3	4
Total	5	.972	214	810	121	7	16	9

■ Bill Tuttle OF

YEAR	TM/L	PCT	G	PO	A	E	DP	FR
1952	Det-A	1.000	6	19	0	0	0	1
1954	Det-A	.985	145	364	18	6	3	-1
1955	Det-A	.985	154	442	12	7	2	9
1956	Det-A	.976	137	348	13	9	2	5
1957	Det-A	.982	128	331	5	6	1	-3
1958	KC-A	.988	145	311	12	4	2	-2
1959	KC-A	.984	121	294	17	5	3	6
1960	KC-A	.988	148	381	16	5	3	10
1961	KC-A	.951	25	58	0	3	0	0
	Min-A	.986	64	72	1	1	1	2
	Yr	.970	89	130	1	4	1	2
1962	Min-A	.973	104	71	2	2	0	1
1963	Min-A	1.000	14	7	1	0	1	2
Total	11	.983	1191	2698	97	8	18	30

3B

YEAR	TM/L	PCT	G	PO	A	E	DP	FR
1961	Min-A	.943	85	66	165	14	15	3

2B

YEAR	TM/L	PCT	G	PO	A	E	DP	FR
1961	Min-A	1.000	2	3	1	0	0	0

■ Larry Twitchell OF

YEAR	TM/L	PCT	G	PO	A	E	DP	FR
1886	Det-N	1.000	2	1	0	0	0	0
1887	Det-N	.871	53	84	4	13	1	-5
1888	Det-N	.885	131	195	13	27	4	-9
1889	Cle-N	.916	134	220	10	21	0	-11
1890	Cle-P	.821	56	61	8	15	1	-9
	Buf-P	.918	32	42	3	4	1	-3
	Yr	.857	88	103	11	19	2	-12
1891	Col-a	.887	56	67	4	9	0	-10
1892	Was-N	.897	48	73	5	9	1	-3
1893	Lou-N	.874	45	91	6	14	0	-2
1894	Lou-N	.908	51	103	15	12	4	6
Total	9	.890	608	937	68	124	12	-46

1B

YEAR	TM/L	PCT	G	PO	A	E	DP	FR
1890	Buf-P	1.000	3	15	2	0	0	1

SS

YEAR	TM/L	PCT	G	PO	A	E	DP	FR
1892	Was-N	.813	3	7	6	3	0	-2

3B

YEAR	TM/L	PCT	G	PO	A	E	DP	FR
1892	Was-N	.000	1	0	0	1	0	0

■ George Twombly OF

YEAR	TM/L	PCT	G	PO	A	E	DP	FR
1914	Cin-N	.968	68	111	11	4	2	-1
1915	Cin-N	1.000	24	30	2	0	0	1
1916	Cin-N	1.000	1	2	0	0	0	0
1917	Bos-N	.943	29	49	1	3	1	-4
1919	Was-A	—	1	0	0	0	0	0
Total	5	.967	123	192	14	7	3	-4

1B

YEAR	TM/L	PCT	G	PO	A	E	DP	FR
1917	Bos-N	.923	1	12	0	1	0	0

■ Jim Tyrone OF

YEAR	TM/L	PCT	G	PO	A	E	DP	FR
1972	Chi-N	1.000	4	6	1	0	0	2
1974	Chi-N	.962	32	24	1	1	0	-1
1975	Chi-N	1.000	8	7	1	0	0	0
1977	Oak-A	.950	81	167	5	9	0	0
Total	4	.955	125	204	8	0	0	1

3B

YEAR	TM/L	PCT	G	PO	A	E	DP	FR
1974	Chi-N	1.000	1	2	1	0	0	0

1B

YEAR	TM/L	PCT	G	PO	A	E	DP	FR
1977	Oak-A	1.000	1	1	0	0	0	0

SS

YEAR	TM/L	PCT	G	PO	A	E	DP	FR
1977	Oak-A	—	1	0	0	0	0	0

■ Ty Tyson OF

YEAR	TM/L	PCT	G	PO	A	E	DP	FR
1926	NY-N	.980	92	232	9	5	5	2
1927	NY-N	.929	41	73	5	6	1	-4
1928	Bro-N	.965	55	130	6	5	3	4
Total	3	.966	188	435	20	6	9	2

■ Mike Tyson 2B

YEAR	TM/L	PCT	G	PO	A	E	DP	FR
1972	StL-N	.981	11	20	31	1	3	5
1973	StL-N	1.000	16	37	49	0	12	6
1974	StL-N	.976	12	16	24	1	7	4
1975	StL-N	.966	24	29	57	3	8	1
1976	StL-N	.971	74	158	237	12	54	8
1977	StL-N	.979	135	267	423	15	99	22
1978	StL-N	.977	124	246	306	13	78	0
1979	StL-N	.975	71	125	184	8	42	8
1980	Chi-N	.968	117	222	329	18	69	9
1981	Chi-N	.940	36	50	76	8	14	1
Total	10	.973	620	1170	1716	9	386	64

SS

YEAR	TM/L	PCT	G	PO	A	E	DP	FR
1972	StL-N	.846	2	6	5	2	1	-1
1973	StL-N	.944	128	202	352	33	68	-25
1974	StL-N	.955	143	231	410	30	108	11
1975	StL-N	.971	95	154	246	12	44	-13
1981	Chi-N	—	1	0	0	0	0	0
Total	5	.954	369	593	1013	7	221	-28

3B

YEAR	TM/L	PCT	G	PO	A	E	DP	FR
1975	StL-N	1.000	5	1	5	0	0	0

■ Bob Uecker C

YEAR	TM/L	PCT	G	PO	A	E	DP	FR
1962	Mil-N	.982	24	101	10	2	4	5
1963	Mil-N	.958	6	21	2	1	1	1
1964	StL-N	.987	40	201	20	3	2	4
1965	StL-N	.985	49	240	29	4	1	-1
1966	Phi-N	.985	76	368	33	6	7	1
1967	Phi-N	.973	17	67	5	2	0	0
	Atl-N	.972	59	281	31	9	3	9
	Yr	.972	76	348	36	11	3	9
Total	6	.981	271	1279	130	7	18	19

■ Ted Uhlaender OF

YEAR	TM/L	PCT	G	PO	A	E	DP	FR
1965	Min-A	1.000	4	7	1	0	0	1
1966	Min-A	.985	100	258	4	4	2	9
1967	Min-A	.996	118	255	6	1	3	3
1968	Min-A	.986	129	283	3	4	1	-6
1969	Min-A	.997	150	278	8	1	1	-1
1970	Cle-A	.991	134	225	5	2	1	-15
1971	Cle-A	.992	131	245	6	2	0	-9
1972	Cin-N	.976	27	37	3	1	0	0
Total	8	.991	793	1588	36	5	8	-18

■ Tom Umphlett OF

YEAR	TM/L	PCT	G	PO	A	E	DP	FR
1953	Bos-A	.983	136	382	12	7	1	1
1954	Was-A	.989	101	169	13	2	4	-3
1955	Was-A	.988	103	237	8	3	1	-5
Total	3	.986	340	788	33	2	6	-7

■ Bob Unglaub 1B

YEAR	TM/L	PCT	G	PO	A	E	DP	FR
1905	Bos-A	.976	2	40	1	1	1	0
1907	Bos-A	.986	139	1504	84	22	68	-1
1908	Bos-A	.980	72	744	50	16	22	2
	Was-A	1.000	4	39	4	0	4	1
	Yr	.981	76	783	54	16	26	3
1909	Was-A	.992	57	555	36	5	31	2
1910	Was-A	.985	124	1230	79	20	51	6
Total	5	.986	398	4112	254	4	177	10

2B

YEAR	TM/L	PCT	G	PO	A	E	DP	FR
1904	NY-A	.786	4	4	7	3	1	-1
	Bos-A	1.000	2	3	2	0	0	0
	Yr	.842	6	7	9	3	1	-1
1905	Bos-A	.928	21	25	39	5	2	2
1908	Was-A	.928	39	44	98	11	2	6
1909	Was-A	.857	4	4	8	2	0	-1
Total	4	.918	70	80	154	1	5	6

2B

YEAR	TM/L	PCT	G	PO	A	E	DP	FR
1904	Bos-A	.625	3	4	1	3	0	-2
1905	Bos-A	.902	7	22	15	4	0	-1
1908	Was-A	.974	27	67	80	4	10	4
1909	Was-A	.970	25	54	76	4	7	4
Total	4	.955	62	147	172	5	17	5

OF

YEAR	TM/L	PCT	G	PO	A	E	DP	FR
1909	Was-A	.966	42	56	1	2	1	-4

SS

YEAR	TM/L	PCT	G	PO	A	E	DP	FR
1904	NY-A	1.000	1	1	0	0	0	0
	Bos-A	—	1	0	0	0	0	0
	Yr	1.000	2	1	0	0	0	0

■ Al Unser C

YEAR	TM/L	PCT	G	PO	A	E	DP	FR
1942	Det-A	1.000	4	11	3	0	0	1
1943	Det-A	.982	37	143	20	3	4	-3
1944	Det-A	—	1	0	0	0	0	0
1945	Cin-N	.956	61	207	30	11	5	0
Total	4	.967	103	361	53	4	9	-2

2B

YEAR	TM/L	PCT	G	PO	A	E	DP	FR
1944	Det-A	.864	5	12	7	3	2	-4

■ Del Unser OF

YEAR	TM/L	PCT	G	PO	A	E	DP	FR
1968	Was-A	.988	156	388	22	5	10	13
1969	Was-A	.972	149	339	8	10	3	-2

YEAR	TM/L	PCT	G	PO	A	E	DP	FR
1970	Was-A	.984	103	173	8	3	2	-12
1971	Was-A	.981	151	394	10	8	2	19
1972	Cle-A	.989	119	248	10	3	1	-4
1973	Phi-N	.988	132	329	14	4	4	12
1974	Phi-N	.981	135	300	13	6	0	1
1975	Phi-N	.987	144	362	13	5	2	9
1976	NY-N	.995	77	180	5	1	0	0
	Mon-N	.983	65	108	5	2	2	-3
	Yr	.990	142	288	10	3	2	-3
1977	Mon-N	.976	72	120	2	3	0	-3
1978	Mon-N	.986	33	70	2	1	0	3
1979	Phi-N	.978	30	44	0	1	0	-1
1980	Phi-N	1.000	23	49	0	0	0	3
1981	Phi-N	1.000	16	19	0	0	0	1
1982	Phi-N	—	2	0	0	0	0	0
Total	15	.984	1407	3123	112	2	26	36

1B

YEAR	TM/L	PCT	G	PO	A	E	DP	FR
1968	Was-A	1.000	1	4	0	0	0	0
1977	Mon-N	1.000	27	160	11	0	15	0
1978	Mon-N	.994	64	162	10	1	16	0
1979	Phi-N	.975	22	74	5	2	6	0
1980	Phi-N	1.000	31	67	13	0	7	4
1981	Phi-N	1.000	18	44	5	0	4	1
1982	Phi-N	1.000	5	9	1	0	1	0
Total	7	.995	168	520	45	3	49	5

■ Willie Upshaw 1B

YEAR	TM/L	PCT	G	PO	A	E	DP	FR
1978	Tor-A	.963	10	50	2	2	4	-1
1980	Tor-A	.983	14	51	7	1	11	1
1981	Tor-A	1.000	14	58	5	0	7	0
1982	Tor-A	.989	155	1438	101	17	123	-2
1983	Tor-A	.985	159	1294	117	21	131	3
1984	Tor-A	.990	151	1246	103	14	133	-3
1985	Tor-A	.992	147	1157	104	10	111	1
1986	Tor-A	.992	154	1314	131	12	118	5
1987	Tor-A	.993	146	1169	127	9	114	12
1988	Cle-A	.991	144	1162	102	12	93	0
Total	10	.990	1094	8939	799	8	845	16

OF

YEAR	TM/L	PCT	G	PO	A	E	DP	FR
1978	Tor-A	.943	52	81	2	5	1	5
1980	Tor-A	—	1	0	0	0	0	0
1981	Tor-A	1.000	14	14	1	0	1	1
Total	3	.951	67	95	3	5	2	6

■ Tom Upton SS

YEAR	TM/L	PCT	G	PO	A	E	DP	FR
1950	StL-A	.946	115	198	328	30	65	-11
1951	StL-A	.949	47	80	105	10	33	-4
1952	Was-A	1.000	3	3	8	0	1	2
Total	3	.948	165	281	441	0	99	-13

2B

YEAR	TM/L	PCT	G	PO	A	E	DP	FR
1950	StL-A	1.000	2	0	1	0	0	0

3B

YEAR	TM/L	PCT	G	PO	A	E	DP	FR
1950	StL-A	1.000	1	1	4	0	0	1

■ Billy Urbanski SS

YEAR	TM/L	PCT	G	PO	A	E	DP	FR
1931	Bos-N	.972	19	27	43	2	8	-2
1932	Bos-N	.946	136	316	461	44	91	1
1933	Bos-N	.953	143	299	473	38	91	-4
1934	Bos-N	.961	146	298	457	31	84	-10
1935	Bos-N	.939	129	258	356	40	52	-27
1936	Bos-N	.937	80	188	211	27	56	-19
Total	6	.949	653	1386	2001	182	382	-61

3B

YEAR	TM/L	PCT	G	PO	A	E	DP	FR
1931	Bos-N	.961	68	76	145	9	15	13
1936	Bos-N	.963	38	36	69	4	7	1
Total	2	.962	106	112	214	3	22	14

■ Jose Uribe SS

YEAR	TM/L	PCT	G	PO	A	E	DP	FR
1984	StL-N	.955	5	7	14	1	4	0
1985	SF-N	.961	145	209	438	26	77	-2
1986	SF-N	.977	156	249	444	16	95	12
1987	SF-N	.971	95	145	286	13	62	11
1988	SF-N	.970	140	212	404	19	77	-3
1989	SF-N	.973	150	225	436	18	85	1
1990	SF-N	.965	134	182	373	20	73	15
Total	7	.970	825	1229	2395	113	473	41

2B

YEAR	TM/L	PCT	G	PO	A	E	DP	FR
1984	StL-N	1.000	1	0	1	0	0	0
1985	SF-N	—	1	0	0	0	0	0
Total	2	1.000	2	0	1	0	0	0

■ Bob Usher OF

YEAR	TM/L	PCT	G	PO	A	E	DP	FR
1946	Cin-N	.982	80	102	8	2	3	7
1947	Cin-N	1.000	8	16	1	0	0	1
1950	Cin-N	.985	93	190	7	3	1	3
1951	Cin-N	.974	98	218	9	6	4	10
1957	Cle-A	1.000	4	3	0	0	0	0
	Was-A	.979	95	228	7	5	2	-2
	Yr	.979	99	231	7	5	2	-2
Total	5	.980	378	757	32	6	10	19

3B

YEAR	TM/L	PCT	G	PO	A	E	DP	FR
1946	Cin-N	1.000	1	2	1	0	0	0
1957	Cle-A	—	1	0	0	0	0	0
Total	2	1.000	2	2	1	0	0	0

■ Mike Vail OF

YEAR	TM/L	PCT	G	PO	A	E	DP	FR
1975	NY-N	.971	36	92	9	3	1	8
1976	NY-N	.941	35	63	1	4	0	-2
1977	NY-N	.965	85	159	5	6	2	0
1978	Cle-A	1.000	9	18	0	0	0	0
	Chi-N	.981	45	50	1	1	0	-7
1979	Chi-N	.964	39	51	3	2	0	-5
1980	Chi-N	.963	77	126	5	5	1	-6
1981	Cin-N	1.000	3	3	0	0	0	0
1982	Cin-N	.963	77	72	7	1	0	1
1983	SF-N	1.000	2	1	0	0	0	0
	Mon-N	.958	15	19	4	1	0	2
	Yr	.960	17	20	4	1	0	2
1984	LA-N	—	1	0	0	0	0	0
Total	10	.968	399	654	35	3	4	-9

(continued)

1B

YEAR	TM/L	PCT	G	PO	A	E	DP	FR
1983	SF-N	1.000	4	24	0	0	0	-1
	Mon-N	1.000	1	6	1	0	1	0
	Yr	1.000	5	30	1	0	1	-1

3B

YEAR	TM/L	PCT	G	PO	A	E	DP	FR
1978	Chi-N	—	1	0	0	0	0	0
1979	Chi-N	1.000	2	0	1	0	0	0
1983	Mon-N	—	1	0	0	0	0	0
Total	3	1.000	4	0	1	0	0	0

■ Sandy Valdespino OF

YEAR	TM/L	PCT	G	PO	A	E	DP	FR
1965	Min-A	.990	57	94	4	1	1	0
1966	Min-A	1.000	23	36	0	0	0	-2
1967	Min-A	.977	65	40	3	1	0	3
1968	Atl-N	.976	20	40	0	1	0	-1
1969	Hou-A	.976	29	37	3	1	0	-2
	Sea-A	.889	7	23	1	3	0	2
1970	Mil-A	—	1	0	0	0	0	0
1971	KC-A	.950	15	18	1	1	0	-3
Total	7	.974	217	288	12	8	1	-3

■ Jose Valdivielso SS

YEAR	TM/L	PCT	G	PO	A	E	DP	FR
1955	Was-A	.956	94	160	317	22	69	9
1956	Was-A	.947	90	144	266	23	58	**16**
1959	Was-A	1.000	21	13	18	0	6	5
1960	Was-A	.954	115	178	294	23	68	9
1961	Min-A	.971	43	49	87	4	18	0
Total	5	.955	363	544	982	72	219	39

3B

YEAR	TM/L	PCT	G	PO	A	E	DP	FR
1960	Was-A	1.000	1	1	0	0	0	0
1961	Min-A	.800	14	2	2	1	0	-1
Total	2	.833	15	3	2	1	0	-1

2B

YEAR	TM/L	PCT	G	PO	A	E	DP	FR
1961	Min-A	.971	15	16	18	1	2	-1

■ Ellis Valentine OF

YEAR	TM/L	PCT	G	PO	A	E	DP	FR
1975	Mon-N	.867	11	12	1	2	1	-1
1976	Mon-N	.972	88	162	12	5	4	3
1977	Mon-N	.972	126	232	9	7	1	-3
1978	Mon-N	.970	146	296	**24**	10	3	11
1979	Mon-N	.983	144	281	10	5	2	1
1980	Mon-N	.970	83	154	6	5	1	-2
1981	Mon-N	1.000	21	32	2	0	0	-2
	NY-N	.957	47	83	6	4	0	0
	Yr	.969	68	115	8	4	0	-2
1982	NY-N	.983	98	159	10	3	4	-2
1983	Cal-A	.963	85	152	5	6	1	-5
1985	Tex-A	1.000	7	7	0	0	0	-1
Total	10	.972	856	1570	85	47	17	-1

■ Fred Valentine OF

YEAR	TM/L	PCT	G	PO	A	E	DP	FR
1959	Bal-A	.889	8	7	1	1	0	0
1963	Bal-A	1.000	10	15	0	0	0	-1
1964	Was-A	.978	57	86	2	2	1	-3
1965	Was-A	1.000	11	23	0	0	0	0
1966	Was-A	.980	138	290	6	6	2	7
1967	Was-A	.989	136	258	7	3	0	-10
1968	Was-A	1.000	27	34	2	0	1	-2
	Bal-A	.972	26	33	2	1	1	0
	Yr	.986	53	67	4	1	2	-2
Total	7	.983	413	746	20	13	5	-8

1B

YEAR	TM/L	PCT	G	PO	A	E	DP	FR
1966	Was-A	.938	2	14	1	1	1	0

■ Bobby Valentine SS

YEAR	TM/L	PCT	G	PO	A	E	DP	FR
1971	LA-N	.961	37	43	80	5	17	4
1972	LA-N	.948	10	23	32	3	6	0
1973	Cal-A	.948	25	38	72	6	11	-3
1974	Cal-A	.954	36	42	82	6	6	-6
1977	SD-N	.962	10	11	14	1	1	-1
	NY-N	.974	14	9	29	1	6	0
	Yr	.969	24	20	43	2	7	-1
1979	Sea-A	.971	29	11	23	1	3	-7
Total	6	.957	161	177	332	23	50	-13

OF

YEAR	TM/L	PCT	G	PO	A	E	DP	FR
1971	LA-N	1.000	11	14	1	0	0	1
1972	LA-N	1.000	16	25	0	0	0	0
1973	Cal-A	1.000	8	25	3	0	0	4
1974	Cal-A	.950	62	113	2	6	0	-3
1975	Cal-A	1.000	2	2	0	0	0	0
	SD-N	1.000	4	4	0	0	0	-1
1976	SD-N	1.000	10	18	2	0	1	1
1979	Sea-A	1.000	15	17	3	0	0	0
Total	7	.974	128	218	11	6	1	2

2B

YEAR	TM/L	PCT	G	PO	A	E	DP	FR
1971	LA-N	.959	21	49	45	4	13	-5
1972	LA-N	.976	49	110	132	6	28	3
1974	Cal-A	—	1	0	0	0	0	0
1978	NY-N	.977	45	76	92	4	13	-9
1979	Sea-A	1.000	4	0	2	0	0	0
Total	5	.973	120	235	271	14	54	-11

3B

YEAR	TM/L	PCT	G	PO	A	E	DP	FR
1971	LA-N	.905	23	17	50	7	1	1
1972	LA-N	.878	39	20	81	14	4	-1
1974	Cal-A	.881	15	5	32	5	4	-2
1975	Cal-A	.750	2	2	1	1	0	-1
1977	SD-N	.947	10	3	15	1	2	0
	NY-N	1.000	4	1	2	0	1	0
	Yr	.955	14	4	17	1	3	0
1978	NY-N	.905	9	2	17	2	0	0
1979	Sea-A	.933	4	4	10	1	2	1
Total	7	.894	106	54	208	31	14	-2

1B

YEAR	TM/L	PCT	G	PO	A	E	DP	FR
1975	Cal-A	.958	3	23	0	1	2	-1
1976	SD-N	1.000	4	37	4	0	1	0
1977	SD-N	1.000	1	1	0	0	1	0
	NY-N	1.000	15	94	4	0	5	-1
	Yr	1.000	16	95	4	0	6	-1
Total	3	.994	23	155	8	1	9	-2

C

YEAR	TM/L	PCT	G	PO	A	E	DP	FR
1979	Sea-A	—	2	0	0	0	0	0

■ Dave Valle C

YEAR	TM/L	PCT	G	PO	A	E	DP	FR
1984	Sea-A	1.000	13	56	5	0	0	2
1985	Sea-A	.976	31	117	7	3	0	-2
1986	Sea-A	.982	12	53	1	1	0	-3
1987	Sea-A	.989	75	420	34	5	2	1
1988	Sea-A	.989	84	484	47	6	7	6
1989	Sea-A	.993	93	496	52	4	3	-3
1990	Sea-A	**.997**	104	631	44	2	9	0
Total	7	.991	412	2257	190	21	21	1

1B

YEAR	TM/L	PCT	G	PO	A	E	DP	FR
1986	Sea-A	.975	4	37	2	1	3	-1
1987	Sea-A	1.000	2	2	0	0	0	0
1988	Sea-A	1.000	1	6	0	0	1	0
1990	Sea-A	1.000	1	2	0	0	0	0
Total	4	.980	8	47	2	1	4	-1

OF

YEAR	TM/L	PCT	G	PO	A	E	DP	FR
1987	Sea-A	—	1	0	0	0	0	0

■ Elmer Valo OF

YEAR	TM/L	PCT	G	PO	A	E	DP	FR
1940	Phi-A	1.000	6	18	0	0	0	1
1941	Phi-A	1.000	10	22	0	0	0	-1
1942	Phi-A	.964	122	264	5	10	0	-2
1943	Phi-A	.986	63	134	4	2	0	-4
1946	Phi-A	.974	90	182	7	5	0	-1
1947	Phi-A	.973	104	205	9	6	0	-3
1948	Phi-A	.983	109	231	4	4	1	-5
1949	Phi-A	.981	150	395	8	8	0	8
1950	Phi-A	.982	117	264	9	5	3	2
1951	Phi-A	.981	116	247	5	5	0	-2
1952	Phi-A	.962	121	223	7	9	1	-6
1953	Phi-A	1.000	25	46	1	0	1	0
1954	Phi-A	.965	62	135	3	5	1	-2
1955	KC-A	.987	72	147	5	2	2	-3
1956	KC-A	—	1	0	0	0	0	0
	Phi-A	.966	87	167	4	6	0	-1
1957	Bro-N	1.000	36	57	0	0	0	-4
1958	LA-N	1.000	26	24	0	0	0	-4
1959	Cle-A	1.000	2	1	0	0	0	0
1960	NY-A	—	2	0	0	0	0	0
	Was-A	1.000	6	5	1	0	0	0
	Yr	1.000	8	5	1	0	0	0
1961	Min-A	1.000	1	2	0	0	0	0
	Phi-N	—	1	0	0	0	0	0
Total	20	.977	1329	2769	72	67	9	-27

■ Bill VanDyke OF

YEAR	TM/L	PCT	G	PO	A	E	DP	FR
1890	Tol-a	.924	110	168	15	15	0	-4
1892	StL-N	.875	4	7	0	1	0	-1
1893	Bos-N	1.000	3	4	0	0	0	-1
Total	3	.924	117	179	15	16	0	-6

3B

YEAR	TM/L	PCT	G	PO	A	E	DP	FR
1890	Tol-a	.816	18	29	33	14	3	-3

2B

YEAR	TM/L	PCT	G	PO	A	E	DP	FR
1890	Tol-a	.857	2	4	2	1	0	-1

C

YEAR	TM/L	PCT	G	PO	A	E	DP	FR
1890	Tol-a	1.000	1	10	2	0	0	2

■ Dave VanGorder C

YEAR	TM/L	PCT	G	PO	A	E	DP	FR
1982	Cin-N	.986	51	273	18	4	3	-2
1984	Cin-N	.996	36	194	11	0	1	1
1985	Cin-N	.989	70	255	11	3	2	-4
1986	Cin-N	1.000	7	20	0	0	0	1
1987	Bal-A	.978	12	44	1	1	0	0
Total	5	.990	176	786	41	8	6	-4

1B

YEAR	TM/L	PCT	G	PO	A	E	DP	FR
1984	Cin-N	—	1	0	0	0	0	0

■ George VanHaltren OF

YEAR	TM/L	PCT	G	PO	A	E	DP	FR
1887	Chi-N	.927	27	37	1	3	1	-4
1888	Chi-N	.872	57	73	9	12	0	-3
1889	Chi-N	.898	130	222	25	28	3	0
1890	Bro-P	.896	67	113	16	15	1	2
1891	Bal-a	.882	81	143	21	22	7	6
1892	Bal-N	.850	129	217	27	43	5	0
	Pit-N	.905	13	18	1	2	1	-2
	Yr	.854	142	235	28	45	6	-2
1893	Pit-N	.869	111	227	24	38	3	-6
1894	NY-N	.914	137	299	29	31	5	-2
1895	NY-N	.914	131	252	26	26	3	-3
1896	NY-N	.952	133	272	25	15	4	4
1897	NY-N	.937	129	267	31	20	4	9
1898	NY-N	.917	156	299	22	29	5	-2
1899	NY-N	.932	151	284	31	23	8	2
1900	NY-N	.939	141	325	28	23	7	10
1901	NY-N	.941	135	263	23	18	5	4
1902	NY-N	.925	24	43	6	4	1	2
1903	NY-N	.959	75	136	3	6	1	-6
Total	17	.915	1827	3490	348	358	64	11

SS

YEAR	TM/L	PCT	G	PO	A	E	DP	FR
1889	Chi-N	.765	3	4	9	4	2	-1
1890	Bro-P	.917	3	5	6	1	1	0
1891	Bal-a	.836	59	126	164	57	15	-17
1892	Bal-N	.688	2	5	6	5	1	-1
1893	Pit-N	.841	12	16	37	10	3	-1
Total	5	.831	79	156	222	77	22	-20

2B

YEAR	TM/L	PCT	G	PO	A	E	DP	FR
1889	Chi-N	1.000	1	4	1	0	0	0
1891	Bal-a	.750	2	3	0	1	0	-1
1893	Pit-N	.909	2	2	8	1	0	0
Total	3	.900	5	9	9	2	0	-1

3B

YEAR	TM/L	PCT	G	PO	A	E	DP	FR
1892	Bal-N	.933	3	6	8	1	0	1

1B

YEAR	TM/L	PCT	G	PO	A	E	DP	FR
1892	Bal-N	1.000	2	24	0	0	1	0

■ Maurice VanRobays OF

YEAR	TM/L	PCT	G	PO	A	E	DP	FR
1939	Pit-N	.919	25	33	1	3	0	-5
1940	Pit-N	.963	143	276	10	11	3	-5
1941	Pit-N	.974	121	292	9	8	3	6
1942	Pit-N	.986	84	199	6	3	3	6
1943	Pit-N	.940	60	120	5	8	1	-5
1946	Pit-N	.955	37	62	1	3	0	-5
Total	6	.966	470	982	32	36	10	-8

1B

YEAR	TM/L	PCT	G	PO	A	E	DP	FR
1940	Pit-N	—	1	0	0	0	0	0
1946	Pit-N	1.000	2	8	1	0	0	0
Total	2	1.000	3	8	1	0	0	0

3B

YEAR	TM/L	PCT	G	PO	A	E	DP	FR
1939	Pit-N	1.000	1	3	2	0	1	1

■ Andy VanSlyke OF

YEAR	TM/L	PCT	G	PO	A	E	DP	FR
1983	StL-N	.974	69	108	4	3	1	-1
1984	StL-N	1.000	81	88	5	0	0	0
1985	StL-N	.996	142	234	13	1	**4**	-4
1986	StL-N	.969	110	211	11	7	2	1
1987	Pit-N	.988	150	328	10	4	**6**	1
1988	Pit-N	.991	152	**406**	12	4	2	10
1989	Pit-N	.989	123	338	9	4	**5**	7
1990	Pit-N	.976	133	326	6	8	0	-4
Total	8	.986	960	2039	70	31	20	10

1B

YEAR	TM/L	PCT	G	PO	A	E	DP	FR
1983	StL-N	.974	9	71	5	2	13	-1
1984	StL-N	.996	30	245	9	1	30	-3
1985	StL-N	1.000	2	3	0	0	2	0
1986	StL-N	.996	38	204	23	1	23	2
1987	Pit-N	1.000	1	10	0	0	3	0
1989	Pit-N	1.000	2	6	0	0	1	0
Total	6	.993	82	539	37	4	72	-2

3B

YEAR	TM/L	PCT	G	PO	A	E	DP	FR
1983	StL-N	.987	30	24	50	1	2	0
1984	StL-N	.929	32	24	68	7	10	3
Total	2	.954	62	48	118	8	12	3

■ Arky Vaughan SS

YEAR	TM/L	PCT	G	PO	A	E	DP	FR
1932	Pit-N	.934	128	247	403	**46**	74	-20
1933	Pit-N	.945	**152**	310	487	**46**	95	-9
1934	Pit-N	.952	**149**	329	480	41	77	3
1935	Pit-N	.950	137	249	422	35	55	-11
1936	Pit-N	.945	**156**	**327**	477	47	86	-11
1937	Pit-N	.956	108	231	335	26	58	0
1938	Pit-N	.961	**147**	**306**	**507**	33	**107**	18
1939	Pit-N	.962	**152**	330	**531**	34	103	8
1940	Pit-N	.942	**155**	308	**542**	**52**	94	-13
1941	Pit-N	.958	97	172	289	20	42	-13
1942	Bro-N	1.000	5	11	16	0	4	1
1943	Bro-N	.965	99	175	291	17	55	-14
Total	12	.951	1485	2995	4780	397	850	-40

3B

YEAR	TM/L	PCT	G	PO	A	E	DP	FR
1940	Pit-N	1.000	2	1	4	0	0	0
1941	Pit-N	.917	3	2	9	1	1	0
1942	Bro-N	.959	119	118	208	14	18	-11
1943	Bro-N	.973	55	62	84	4	2	-11
1947	Bro-N	1.000	10	7	20	0	3	1
1948	Bro-N	1.000	8	0	10	0	1	0
Total	6	.965	197	190	335	9	25	-21

OF

YEAR	TM/L	PCT	G	PO	A	E	DP	FR
1937	Pit-N	.963	12	26	0	1	0	-1
1947	Bro-N	1.000	22	49	0	0	0	0
1948	Bro-N	1.000	26	47	4	0	0	1
Total	3	.992	60	122	4	1	0	0

2B

YEAR	TM/L	PCT	G	PO	A	E	DP	FR
1942	Bro-N	1.000	1	1	0	0	0	0

■ Fred Vaughn 2B

YEAR	TM/L	PCT	G	PO	A	E	DP	FR
1944	Was-A	.942	26	61	70	8	16	-1
1945	Was-A	.946	76	177	189	21	35	-4
Total	2	.945	102	238	259	29	51	-5

3B

YEAR	TM/L	PCT	G	PO	A	E	DP	FR
1944	Was-A	.818	3	1	8	2	0	0

SS

YEAR	TM/L	PCT	G	PO	A	E	DP	FR
1945	Was-A	—	1	0	0	0	0	0

■ Greg Vaughn OF

YEAR	TM/L	PCT	G	PO	A	E	DP	FR
1989	Mil-A	.943	24	32	1	2	0	-2
1990	Mil-A	.967	106	195	8	7	1	-5
Total	2	.963	130	227	9	9	1	-7

■ Farmer Vaughn C

YEAR	TM/L	PCT	G	PO	A	E	DP	FR
1886	Cin-a	.917	1	8	3	1	0	1
1888	Lou-a	.889	25	124	45	21	4	0
1889	Lou-a	.900	54	234	107	38	4	4
1890	NY-P	.877	30	102	19	17	3	-10
1891	Cin-a	.923	44	170	58	19	6	9
	Mil-a	.924	20	103	19	10	5	2
	Yr	.923	64	273	77	29	11	11
1892	Cin-N	.929	67	249	63	24	12	-12
1893	Cin-N	**.969**	80	270	77	11	10	0
1894	Cin-N	.918	43	150	41	17	1	-2
1895	Cin-N	.934	77	262	78	24	10	7
1896	Cin-N	.953	57	168	53	11	6	1
1897	Cin-N	.929	15	51	14	5	1	0
1898	Cin-N	.941	33	103	41	9	4	1
1899	Cin-N	.915	7	32	11	4	2	2
Total	13	.926	553	2026	629	211	68	3

1B

YEAR	TM/L	PCT	G	PO	A	E	DP	FR
1889	Lou-a	.977	18	160	8	4	14	1
1891	Cin-a	1.000	2	8	0	0	1	0
	Mil-a	.941	4	30	2	2	0	0
	Yr	.952	6	38	2	2	1	0
1892	Cin-N	.969	14	120	3	4	8	-2
1893	Cin-N	.983	21	217	14	4	15	1
1894	Cin-N	.981	27	198	13	4	17	1
1895	Cin-N	.956	15	115	16	6	3	3
1896	Cin-N	.984	57	572	29	10	35	0
1897	Cin-N	.986	35	342	17	5	19	0
1898	Cin-N	.979	39	359	9	8	24	-3
1899	Cin-N	.982	21	206	13	4	10	1

YEAR	TM/L	PCT	G	PO	A	E	DP	FR
Total	10	.980	253	2327	124	1	146	2

OF

YEAR	TM/L	PCT	G	PO	A	E	DP	FR
1888	Lou-a	.863	28	40	4	7	2	-1
1889	Lou-a	.862	20	47	3	8	0	1
1890	NY-P	.923	12	10	2	1	0	-2
1891	Cin-a	1.000	6	9	0	0	0	-1
	Mil-a	1.000	1	2	0	0	0	0
	Yr	1.000	7	11	0	0	0	-1
1892	Cin-N	.870	11	19	1	3	0	-1
1893	Cin-N	.820	23	46	4	11	2	0
1894	Cin-N	.857	8	9	3	2	0	0
1899	Cin-N	1.000	1	1	0	0	0	0
Total	8	.862	110	183	17	2	4	-4

3B

YEAR	TM/L	PCT	G	PO	A	E	DP	FR
1889	Lou-a	.750	3	0	3	1	0	0
1890	NY-P	.000	1	0	0	1	0	-1
1891	Cin-a	.800	2	2	2	1	0	-1
1892	Cin-N	.905	6	6	13	2	2	1
1895	Cin-N	1.000	1	0	2	0	0	0
Total	5	.848	13	8	20	5	2	-1

SS

YEAR	TM/L	PCT	G	PO	A	E	DP	FR
1894	Cin-N	.800	3	5	7	3	1	0

2B

YEAR	TM/L	PCT	G	PO	A	E	DP	FR
1890	NY-P	1.000	1	1	1	0	0	0
1895	Cin-N	1.000	1	2	0	0	0	0
Total	2	1.000	2	3	1	0	0	0

■ Bobby Vaughn 2B

YEAR	TM/L	PCT	G	PO	A	E	DP	FR
1909	NY-A	.882	4	10	5	2	0	-2
1915	StL-F	.953	127	249	357	30	43	-5
Total	2	.951	131	259	362	2	43	-7

SS

YEAR	TM/L	PCT	G	PO	A	E	DP	FR
1909	NY-A	—	1	0	0	0	0	0
1915	StL-F	.875	12	15	13	4	4	-2
Total	2	.875	13	15	13	4	4	-2

3B

YEAR	TM/L	PCT	G	PO	A	E	DP	FR
1915	StL-F	.917	8	10	12	2	1	-1

■ Bobby Veach OF

YEAR	TM/L	PCT	G	PO	A	E	DP	FR
1912	Det-A	.927	22	46	5	4	0	2
1913	Det-A	.917	135	250	16	24	3	-5
1914	Det-A	.965	145	282	22	11	6	3
1915	Det-A	.975	152	297	19	8	4	2
1916	Det-A	.967	150	342	14	12	4	4
1917	Det-A	.956	154	356	17	17	5	4
1918	Det-A	.977	127	277	14	7	3	3
1919	Det-A	.967	138	338	14	12	3	11
1920	Det-A	.967	154	357	26	13	4	15
1921	Det-A	.974	149	384	21	11	4	15
1922	Det-A	.982	154	375	16	7	3	8
1923	Det-A	.943	85	127	6	8	0	-14
1924	Bos-A	.956	130	270	15	13	2	-1
1925	Bos-A	1.000	1	3	0	0	0	0
	NY-A	.957	33	38	6	2	1	-7
	Was-A	.923	11	12	0	1	0	-3
	Yr	.952	45	53	6	3	1	-10
Total	14	.964	1740	3754	211	150	42	37

■ Coot Veal SS

YEAR	TM/L	PCT	G	PO	A	E	DP	FR
1958	Det-A	.981	58	95	160	5	30	-8
1959	Det-A	.962	72	57	96	6	16	10
1960	Det-A	.988	22	26	53	1	10	-1
1961	Was-A	.974	63	130	172	8	43	0
1963	Det-A	.980	12	14	35	1	1	4
Total	5	.976	227	322	516	1	100	5

3B

YEAR	TM/L	PCT	G	PO	A	E	DP	FR
1960	Det-A	1.000	3	2	1	0	0	0

2B

YEAR	TM/L	PCT	G	PO	A	E	DP	FR
1960	Det-A	1.000	1	2	1	0	0	0

■ Randy Velarde 3B

YEAR	TM/L	PCT	G	PO	A	E	DP	FR
1988	NY-A	.880	11	4	18	3	1	1
1989	NY-A	.954	27	18	44	3	7	0
1990	NY-A	.945	74	43	128	10	11	8
Total	3	.941	112	65	190	6	19	9

SS

YEAR	TM/L	PCT	G	PO	A	E	DP	FR
1987	NY-A	.933	8	8	20	2	3	0
1988	NY-A	.967	14	14	15	1	1	-1
1989	NY-A	.962	9	8	17	1	9	2
1990	NY-A	.979	15	21	26	1	6	3
Total	4	.963	46	51	78	5	19	4

2B

YEAR	TM/L	PCT	G	PO	A	E	DP	FR
1988	NY-A	.967	24	54	65	4	24	8
1990	NY-A	.833	3	0	5	1	1	-1
Total	2	.961	27	54	70	5	25	7

OF

YEAR	TM/L	PCT	G	PO	A	E	DP	FR
1990	NY-A	1.000	5	6	0	0	0	0

■ Otto Velez OF

YEAR	TM/L	PCT	G	PO	A	E	DP	FR
1973	NY-A	.959	23	45	2	2	0	-1
1974	NY-A	.500	3	1	0	1	0	0
1976	NY-A	.979	24	46	1	1	1	1
1977	Tor-A	.973	79	140	5	4	1	-5
1978	Tor-A	.982	74	150	10	3	4	5
1979	Tor-A	.971	73	130	3	4	1	3
Total	6	.973	276	512	21	5	7	3

1B

YEAR	TM/L	PCT	G	PO	A	E	DP	FR
1974	NY-A	.986	21	136	5	2	8	-2
1975	NY-A	1.000	1	11	0	0	1	0
1976	NY-A	.978	8	43	1	1	4	-1
1978	Tor-A	1.000	1	11	2	0	0	1
1979	Tor-A	1.000	6	29	2	0	2	0
1980	Tor-A	.975	3	36	3	1	2	0
1981	Tor-A	1.000	1	9	0	0	0	0
Total	7	.986	41	275	13	4	17	-2

3B

YEAR	TM/L	PCT	G	PO	A	E	DP	FR
1974	NY-A	1.000	2	3	3	0	0	0
1976	NY-A	—	1	0	0	0	0	0
Total	2	1.000	3	3	3	0	0	0

■ Max Venable OF

YEAR	TM/L	PCT	G	PO	A	E	DP	FR
1979	SF-N	.914	25	30	2	3	0	0
1980	SF-N	1.000	40	61	0	0	0	-3
1981	SF-N	1.000	5	12	0	0	0	0
1982	SF-N	.986	53	66	6	1	2	5
1983	SF-N	.993	66	141	5	1	0	6
1984	Mon-N	1.000	27	33	0	0	0	-1
1985	Cin-N	1.000	39	60	3	0	0	3
1986	Cin-N	.969	57	63	0	2	0	-1
1987	Cin-N	1.000	4	3	0	0	0	0
1989	Cal-A	1.000	13	21	0	0	0	-3
1990	Cal-A	.975	77	112	3	3	1	-2
Total	11	.984	406	602	19	0	3	4

■ Robin Ventura 3B

YEAR	TM/L	PCT	G	PO	A	E	DP	FR
1989	Chi-A	.962	16	17	33	2	2	2
1990	Chi-A	.939	147	116	268	25	32	0
Total	2	.941	163	133	301	7	34	2

1B

YEAR	TM/L	PCT	G	PO	A	E	DP	FR
1990	Chi-A	—	1	0	0	0	0	0

■ Emil Verban 2B

YEAR	TM/L	PCT	G	PO	A	E	DP	FR
1944	StL-N	.968	146	319	380	23	105	-6
1945	StL-N	.978	155	398	406	18	95	-19
1946	Phi-N	.963	138	353	381	28	83	-3
1947	Phi-N	.982	155	450	453	17	111	17
1948	Phi-N	.975	54	104	126	6	25	-4
	Chi-N	.964	56	134	164	11	47	6
	Yr	.969	110	238	290	17	72	2
1949	Chi-N	.965	88	218	249	17	60	3
1950	Chi-N	.966	8	11	17	1	6	6
	Bos-N	.833	2	7	3	2	2	1
	Yr	.927	10	18	20	3	8	7
Total	7	.971	802	1994	2179	123	534	1

SS

YEAR	TM/L	PCT	G	PO	A	E	DP	FR
1950	Chi-N	1.000	3	2	1	0	0	0

3B

YEAR	TM/L	PCT	G	PO	A	E	DP	FR
1950	Chi-N	.000	1	0	1	0	0	0

OF

YEAR	TM/L	PCT	G	PO	A	E	DP	FR
1950	Chi-N	—	1	0	0	0	0	0

■ Johnny Vergez 3B

YEAR	TM/L	PCT	G	PO	A	E	DP	FR
1931	NY-N	.932	152	146	268	30	23	-3
1932	NY-N	.935	111	94	208	21	22	6
1933	NY-N	.928	123	101	222	25	17	-14
1934	NY-N	.943	104	86	195	17	11	10
1935	Phi-N	.953	148	188	222	20	25	-6
1936	Phi-N	.964	12	12	15	1	2	0
	StL-N	.929	8	7	6	1	1	0
	Yr	.952	20	19	21	2	3	0
Total	6	.939	658	634	1136	115	101	-7

SS

YEAR	TM/L	PCT	G	PO	A	E	DP	FR
1932	NY-N	.667	1	0	4	2	0	-1
1935	Phi-N	—	2	0	0	0	0	0
Total	2	.667	3	0	4	2	0	-1

■ Mickey Vernon 1B

YEAR	TM/L	PCT	G	PO	A	E	DP	FR
1939	Was-A	.985	75	690	40	11	75	-3
1940	Was-A	1.000	4	41	2	0	5	0
1941	Was-A	.992	132	1186	80	10	122	-6
1942	Was-A	.982	151	1360	95	26	109	-8
1943	Was-A	.990	143	1351	75	14	125	-11
1946	Was-A	.990	147	1320	101	15	133	-1
1947	Was-A	.987	154	1299	106	19	123	-4
1948	Was-A	.989	150	1297	113	15	128	5
1949	Cle-A	.991	153	1438	155	14	168	19
1950	Cle-A	.996	25	216	17	1	28	1
	Was-A	.985	85	743	61	8	93	1
	Yr	.991	110	959	78	9	121	2
1951	Was-A	.994	137	1157	87	8	121	-4
1952	Was-A	.993	152	1291	115	10	139	1
1953	Was-A	.992	152	1376	94	12	158	-3
1954	Was-A	.992	148	1365	76	11	144	-9
1955	Was-A	.994	144	1258	69	8	137	-8
1956	Bos-A	.989	108	930	58	11	96	-3
1957	Bos-A	.992	70	662	51	6	47	4
1958	Cle-A	.987	96	774	50	11	90	-2
1959	Mil-N	.983	10	54	4	1	3	0
Total	19	.990	2237	19808	1448	211	2044	-31

OF

YEAR	TM/L	PCT	G	PO	A	E	DP	FR
1959	Mil-N	.917	4	11	0	1	0	0

■ Zoilo Versalles SS

YEAR	TM/L	PCT	G	PO	A	E	DP	FR
1959	Was-A	.943	29	41	59	6	13	3
1960	Was-A	.935	15	30	42	5	6	-1
1961	Min-A	.952	129	229	371	30	74	-2
1962	Min-A	.970	160	335	501	26	127	32
1963	Min-A	.961	159	301	448	30	87	-2
1964	Min-A	.957	160	271	427	31	89	-17
1965	Min-A	.950	160	248	487	39	105	2
1966	Min-A	.942	135	195	377	35	69	-17
1967	Min-A	.958	159	229	454	30	81	2
1968	LA-N	.949	119	204	380	28	62	8
1969	Cle-A	1.000	3	1	6	0	1	0
	Was-A	.935	13	10	33	3	2	-1
	Yr	.943	16	11	39	3	3	-1
1971	Atl-N	.948	24	32	60	5	11	-11
Total	12	.956	1265	2126	3645	268	727	-4

3B

YEAR	TM/L	PCT	G	PO	A	E	DP	FR
1969	Cle-A	.972	30	28	42	2	8	-3
	Was-A	.846	5	1	10	2	1	0
	Yr	.953	35	29	52	4	9	-3
1971	Atl-N	.902	30	29	45	8	2	-3
Total	2	.928	52	58	97	2	11	-6

2B

YEAR	TM/L	PCT	G	PO	A	E	DP	FR
1969	Cle-A	.955	46	72	83	4	16	-9
	Was-A	1.000	6	9	11	0	1	0
	Yr	.978	52	81	94	4	17	-9
1971	Atl-N	1.000	1	2	2	0	0	0
Total	2	.978	53	83	96	4	17	-9

■ Tom Veryzer SS

YEAR	TM/L	PCT	G	PO	A	E	DP	FR
1973	Det-A	.857	18	6	12	3	1	-5
1974	Det-A	.927	20	18	33	4	4	-10
1975	Det-A	.960	128	215	358	24	62	-4
1976	Det-A	.966	97	164	313	17	53	-1
1977	Det-A	.969	124	185	377	18	62	10
1978	Cle-A	.963	129	177	375	21	58	-5
1979	Cle-A	.974	148	238	446	18	90	4
1980	Cle-A	.971	108	169	331	15	59	-1
1981	Cle-A	.970	75	121	207	10	48	-7
1982	NY-N	.868	16	19	14	5	0	-3
1983	Chi-N	.978	28	23	65	2	16	7
1984	Chi-N	.966	36	37	48	3	10	-3
Total	12	.966	927	1372	2579	140	463	-18

2B

YEAR	TM/L	PCT	G	PO	A	E	DP	FR
1982	NY-N	.962	26	21	30	2	4	2
1984	Chi-N	.957	4	7	15	1	3	1
Total	2	.961	30	28	45	3	7	3

3B

YEAR	TM/L	PCT	G	PO	A	E	DP	FR
1983	Chi-N	1.000	17	4	7	0	1	0
1984	Chi-N	.000	5	0	0	1	0	-1
Total	2	.917	22	4	7	1	1	-1

■ Sammy Vick OF

YEAR	TM/L	PCT	G	PO	A	E	DP	FR
1917	NY-A	.882	10	14	1	2	0	-1
1918	NY-A	—	1	0	0	0	0	0
1919	NY-A	.952	100	166	11	9	2	-4
1920	NY-A	.949	33	56	0	3	0	-4
1921	Bos-A	1.000	14	21	1	0	0	-1
Total	5	.951	158	257	13	4	2	-10

■ Sam Vico 1B

YEAR	TM/L	PCT	G	PO	A	E	DP	FR
1948	Det-A	.988	142	1169	85	15	112	-3
1949	Det-A	.985	53	372	32	6	36	2
Total	2	.987	195	1541	117	1	148	-1

■ Jim Viox 2B

YEAR	TM/L	PCT	G	PO	A	E	DP	FR
1912	Pit-N	—	1	0	0	0	0	0
1913	Pit-N	.959	124	223	314	23	29	-38
1914	Pit-N	.939	138	250	400	42	43	-23
1915	Pit-N	.954	134	239	362	29	35	-20
1916	Pit-N	.937	25	33	56	6	6	-13
Total	5	.949	422	745	1132	100	113	-94

3B

YEAR	TM/L	PCT	G	PO	A	E	DP	FR
1912	Pit-N	.957	10	5	17	1	0	0
1915	Pit-N	.946	13	10	25	2	0	-2
1916	Pit-N	.900	11	8	19	3	0	-3
Total	3	.933	34	23	61	6	0	-5

SS

YEAR	TM/L	PCT	G	PO	A	E	DP	FR
1912	Pit-N	.926	8	12	13	2	2	-3
1913	Pit-N	.844	10	18	20	7	1	-4
1914	Pit-N	.500	2	1	2	3	0	-2
Total	3	.846	20	31	35	2	3	-9

OF

YEAR	TM/L	PCT	G	PO	A	E	DP	FR
1912	Pit-N	.800	3	4	0	1	0	-1
1914	Pit-N	1.000	2	5	0	0	0	0
1915	Pit-N	1.000	2	3	0	0	0	0
Total	3	.923	7	12	0	1	0	-1

■ Bill Virdon OF

YEAR	TM/L	PCT	G	PO	A	E	DP	FR
1955	StL-N	.966	142	339	7	12	1	-8
1956	StL-N	.982	24	53	2	1	0	2
	Pit-N	.989	130	334	10	4	2	0
	Yr	.988	154	387	12	5	2	2
1957	Pit-N	.986	141	403	13	6	2	6
1958	Pit-N	.993	143	401	11	3	0	4
1959	Pit-N	.979	144	404	16	9	5	16
1960	Pit-N	.983	109	272	10	5	0	3
1961	Pit-N	.985	145	384	6	6	4	5
1962	Pit-N	.976	156	360	11	9	0	-1
1963	Pit-N	.988	142	323	6	4	2	1
1964	Pit-N	.976	134	243	5	6	1	-12
1965	Pit-N	.970	128	260	3	8	1	-8
1968	Pit-N	1.000	4	1	0	0	0	0
Total	12	.982	1542	3777	100	3	18	8

■ Ozzie Virgil C

YEAR	TM/L	PCT	G	PO	A	E	DP	FR
1980	Phi-N	1.000	1	4	0	0	0	-1
1981	Phi-N	1.000	1	2	0	0	0	0
1982	Phi-N	.964	35	173	14	7	3	4
1983	Phi-N	.966	51	228	24	9	2	-5
1984	Phi-N	.992	137	722	58	6	6	-4
1985	Phi-N	.994	120	667	52	4	11	-4
1986	Atl-N	.984	111	682	93	13	9	14
1987	Atl-N	.989	122	654	74	8	12	-2
1988	Atl-N	.990	96	448	45	5	3	-11
1989	Tor-A	1.000	1	1	0	0	0	0
1990	Tor-A	1.000	2	1	0	0	0	0
Total	11	.987	677	3582	360	2	46	-9

■ Ozzie Virgil 3B

YEAR	TM/L	PCT	G	PO	A	E	DP	FR
1956	NY-N	.800	3	3	1	1	1	-2
1957	NY-N	.926	62	27	111	11	10	12
1958	Det-A	.981	49	55	101	3	7	3
1960	Det-A	.974	42	28	46	2	7	5
1961	Det-A	.938	9	9	6	1	2	-1
	KC-A	.818	4	2	7	2	1	0
	Yr	.889	13	11	13	3	3	-1
1965	Pit-N	.900	7	1	8	1	0	0
1966	SF-N	.960	13	4	20	1	1	1
Total	7	.951	189	129	300	2	29	18

C

YEAR	TM/L	PCT	G	PO	A	E	DP	FR
1960	Det-A	1.000	1	2	1	0	0	0
1961	Det-A	1.000	3	2	1	0	0	0
	KC-A	1.000	3	8	1	0	0	0
	Yr	1.000	6	10	2	0	0	0
1965	Pit-N	1.000	15	29	2	0	1	0
1966	SF-N	.984	13	57	4	1	0	1
Total	4	.991	35	98	9	1	1	1

(continued — Ozzie Virgil)

OF

YEAR	TM/L	PCT	G	PO	A	E	DP	FR
1957	NY-N	.974	24	37	0	1	0	0
1966	SF-N	1.000	2	2	0	0	0	0
Total	2	.975	26	39	0	1	0	0

2B

YEAR	TM/L	PCT	G	PO	A	E	DP	FR
1960	Det-A	1.000	8	11	24	0	2	2
1961	Det-A	—	1	0	0	0	0	0
1965	Pit-N	1.000	5	6	7	0	3	1
1966	SF-N	1.000	2	1	0	0	0	0
Total	4	1.000	16	18	31	0	5	3

SS

YEAR	TM/L	PCT	G	PO	A	E	DP	FR
1957	NY-N	—	1	0	0	0	0	0
1960	Det-A	.926	5	11	14	2	4	1
1961	Det-A	1.000	1	2	2	0	0	0
Total	3	.935	7	13	16	2	4	1

1B

YEAR	TM/L	PCT	G	PO	A	E	DP	FR
1966	SF-N	.980	5	46	2	1	4	0

■ Jake Virtue 1B

YEAR	TM/L	PCT	G	PO	A	E	DP	FR
1890	Cle-N	.982	62	633	21	12	33	0
1891	Cle-N	.972	139	**1465**	44	44	70	-10
1892	Cle-N	.984	147	1500	61	26	58	-4
1893	Cle-N	.975	73	777	47	21	48	2
1894	Cle-N	1.000	2	16	1	0	0	0
Total	5	.978	423	4391	174	103	209	-12

OF

YEAR	TM/L	PCT	G	PO	A	E	DP	FR
1893	Cle-N	.933	13	26	2	2	0	0
1894	Cle-N	.885	21	43	3	6	0	-2
Total	2	.902	34	69	5	8	0	-2

SS

YEAR	TM/L	PCT	G	PO	A	E	DP	FR
1893	Cle-N	.926	5	11	14	2	0	0

3B

YEAR	TM/L	PCT	G	PO	A	E	DP	FR
1893	Cle-N	.864	5	6	13	3	2	0

OF

YEAR	TM/L	PCT	G	PO	A	E	DP	FR
1894	Cle-N	.909	3	6	4	1	0	0

■ Joe Visner OF

YEAR	TM/L	PCT	G	PO	A	E	DP	FR
1885	Bal-a	.750	4	6	0	2	0	-1
1889	Bro-a	.955	29	40	2	2	1	-3
1890	Pit-P	.893	127	198	18	26	4	-6
1891	Was-a	.806	17	23	2	6	0	-1
	StL-a	1.000	6	7	1	0	0	0
	Yr	.846	23	30	3	6	0	-1
Total	4	.892	183	274	23	6	5	-11

C

YEAR	TM/L	PCT	G	PO	A	E	DP	FR
1889	Bro-a	.871	53	197	72	40	7	-15
1891	Was-a	.500	1	2	0	2	0	-1
Total	2	.866	54	199	72	2	7	-16

3B

YEAR	TM/L	PCT	G	PO	A	E	DP	FR
1891	Was-a	1.000	1	1	1	0	0	0

■ Ossie Vitt 3B

YEAR	TM/L	PCT	G	PO	A	E	DP	FR
1912	Det-A	.966	24	30	55	3	4	1
1913	Det-A	.907	17	19	49	7	1	5
1914	Det-A	.950	16	15	42	3	3	3
1915	Det-A	**.964**	151	191	324	19	19	14
1916	Det-A	**.964**	151	208	385	22	**32**	**28**
1917	Det-A	.940	140	164	260	27	18	-17
1918	Det-A	.953	66	106	137	12	15	6
1919	Bos-A	**.970**	133	169	**308**	15	24	14
1920	Bos-A	.986	64	61	148	3	5	-3
1921	Bos-A	.962	71	63	138	8	14	-2
Total	10	.960	833	1026	1846	119	135	49

2B

YEAR	TM/L	PCT	G	PO	A	E	DP	FR
1912	Det-A	.947	15	29	42	4	3	1
1913	Det-A	.960	78	151	234	16	24	1
1914	Det-A	.964	36	48	112	6	10	-1
1915	Det-A	1.000	2	0	1	0	0	0
1918	Det-A	.955	9	20	22	2	2	-1
1920	Bos-A	.951	21	38	60	5	12	-3
Total	6	.958	161	286	471	33	51	-3

OF

YEAR	TM/L	PCT	G	PO	A	E	DP	FR
1912	Det-A	.929	28	50	2	4	1	-2
1913	Det-A	1.000	2	4	0	0	0	0
1914	Det-A	1.000	2	5	0	0	0	0
1918	Det-A	1.000	3	2	0	0	0	-1
1921	Bos-A	1.000	3	2	0	0	0	-1
Total	5	.942	38	63	2	4	1	-4

SS

YEAR	TM/L	PCT	G	PO	A	E	DP	FR
1914	Det-A	1.000	1	0	1	0	0	0
1916	Det-A	1.000	2	2	4	0	0	0
Total	2	1.000	3	2	5	0	0	0

1B

YEAR	TM/L	PCT	G	PO	A	E	DP	FR
1921	Bos-A	.909	2	10	0	1	2	0

■ Omar Vizquel SS

YEAR	TM/L	PCT	G	PO	A	E	DP	FR
1989	Sea-A	.971	143	208	388	18	102	11
1990	Sea-A	.980	81	103	239	7	48	-2
Total	2	.974	224	311	627	25	150	9

■ Clyde Vollmer OF

YEAR	TM/L	PCT	G	PO	A	E	DP	FR
1942	Cin-N	1.000	11	32	0	0	0	1
1946	Cin-N	1.000	7	9	0	0	0	-1
1947	Cin-N	.984	66	125	2	2	0	7
1948	Cin-N	—	2	0	0	0	0	0
	Was-A	1.000	1	3	0	0	0	0
1949	Was-A	.982	114	324	3	6	1	1
1950	Was-A	1.000	3	5	1	0	0	0
	Bos-A	.954	39	80	3	4	0	-2
	Yr	.957	42	85	4	4	0	-2
1951	Bos-A	.986	106	206	5	3	0	-4
1952	Bos-A	1.000	70	143	3	0	1	0
1953	Was-A	.979	106	227	8	5	1	3
1954	Was-A	1.000	26	33	2	0	1	-3
Total	10	.984	551	1187	27	20	4	2

■ Joe Vosmik OF

YEAR	TM/L	PCT	G	PO	A	E	DP	FR
1930	Cle-A	.933	5	13	1	1	1	1
1931	Cle-A	.970	147	315	12	10	2	6
1932	Cle-A	**.989**	153	432	12	5	4	**22**
1933	Cle-A	.985	113	242	15	4	3	6
1934	Cle-A	.976	104	199	7	5	2	-2
1935	Cle-A	.986	**150**	347	5	5	3	2
1936	Cle-A	.978	136	258	11	6	1	-4
1937	StL-A	.972	143	333	12	10	4	6
1938	Bos-A	.978	146	302	14	7	4	3
1939	Bos-A	.974	144	296	9	8	0	-4
1940	Bro-N	.976	99	193	9	5	1	-1
1941	Bro-N	1.000	18	12	0	0	0	-4
1944	Was-A	1.000	12	16	0	0	0	-1
Total	13	.979	1370	2958	107	66	25	30

■ Bill Voss OF

YEAR	TM/L	PCT	G	PO	A	E	DP	FR
1965	Chi-A	1.000	10	12	0	0	0	-1
1966	Chi-A	1.000	1	1	0	0	0	0
1967	Chi-A	1.000	11	14	0	0	0	1
1968	Chi-A	.963	55	73	5	3	3	-2
1969	Cal-A	.995	111	175	11	1	3	0
1970	Cal-A	.979	55	86	7	2	1	2
1971	Mil-A	.987	79	151	1	2	1	-3
1972	Cal-A	.929	11	13	0	1	0	-1
	Oak-A	1.000	34	59	3	0	0	2
	StL-N	1.000	2	4	0	0	0	0
	Yr	.944	13	17	0	1	0	-1
Total	8	.986	369	588	27	9	8	-2

1B

YEAR	TM/L	PCT	G	PO	A	E	DP	FR
1969	Cal-A	1.000	2	12	0	0	1	0

■ George Vukovich OF

YEAR	TM/L	PCT	G	PO	A	E	DP	FR
1980	Phi-N	.933	28	14	0	1	0	1
1981	Phi-N	1.000	9	10	0	0	0	0
1982	Phi-N	.977	102	168	4	4	3	-1
1983	Cle-A	.986	122	203	3	3	0	-15
1984	Cle-A	.994	130	316	13	2	5	14
1985	Cle-A	.988	137	250	4	3	0	-11
Total	6	.987	528	961	24	13	8	-12

■ John Vukovich 3B

YEAR	TM/L	PCT	G	PO	A	E	DP	FR
1970	Phi-N	1.000	1	1	4	0	0	1
1971	Phi-N	.956	74	58	137	9	8	10
1973	Mil-A	.948	40	28	63	5	3	-4
1974	Mil-A	.966	12	8	20	1	0	2
1975	Cin-N	.925	31	12	37	4	4	7
1976	Cin-N	1.000	4	1	2	0	0	0
1979	Phi-N	1.000	7	0	9	0	1	1
1980	Phi-N	.958	34	14	32	2	0	2
1981	Phi-N	.800	9	0	4	1	0	1
Total	9	.951	212	122	308	22	16	20

2B

YEAR	TM/L	PCT	G	PO	A	E	DP	FR
1974	Mil-A	.960	11	11	13	1	4	0
1979	Phi-N	1.000	3	2	4	0	0	0
1980	Phi-N	1.000	9	3	2	0	0	-1
1981	Phi-N	1.000	1	1	0	0	0	0
Total	4	.973	24	17	19	1	4	-1

SS

YEAR	TM/L	PCT	G	PO	A	E	DP	FR
1970	Phi-N	.778	2	3	4	2	1	0
1973	Mil-A	1.000	1	2	2	0	2	0
1974	Mil-A	.945	12	17	35	3	6	0
1980	Phi-N	1.000	5	1	1	0	0	0
Total	4	.929	20	23	42	5	9	0

1B

YEAR	TM/L	PCT	G	PO	A	E	DP	FR
1973	Mil-A	1.000	13	56	3	0	2	0
1974	Mil-A	1.000	4	10	0	0	0	0
1976	Phi-N	1.000	1	5	0	0	0	0
1980	Phi-N	—	1	0	0	0	0	0
1981	Phi-N	1.000	1	3	0	0	0	0
Total	5	1.000	20	74	3	0	2	0

■ Heinie Wagner SS

YEAR	TM/L	PCT	G	PO	A	E	DP	FR
1902	NY-N	.862	17	31	44	12	5	-3
1907	Bos-A	.931	109	283	387	50	31	4
1908	Bos-A	.939	153	**373**	**569**	61	51	32
1909	Bos-A	.933	123	282	413	50	40	14
1910	Bos-A	.927	140	303	424	57	40	-12
1911	Bos-A	.867	32	75	94	26	14	-5
1912	Bos-A	.922	144	332	391	61	43	-13
1913	Bos-A	.938	105	274	311	39	36	5
1916	Bos-A	1.000	1	1	1	0	0	0
Total	9	.928	824	1954	2634	356	260	22

2B

YEAR	TM/L	PCT	G	PO	A	E	DP	FR
1906	Bos-A	.943	9	16	34	3	2	1
1907	Bos-A	—	1	0	0	0	0	0
1909	Bos-A	1.000	1	1	2	0	0	0
1911	Bos-A	.946	40	106	106	12	11	1
1913	Bos-A	.933	4	7	7	1	1	-1
1915	Bos-A	.927	79	161	195	28	18	-16
1916	Bos-A	1.000	1	1	1	0	0	0
1918	Bos-A	.900	2	2	7	1	2	0
Total	8	.935	137	294	352	45	34	-15

3B

YEAR	TM/L	PCT	G	PO	A	E	DP	FR
1907	Bos-A	.875	1	1	6	1	0	1
1915	Bos-A	1.000	1	3	2	0	0	1
1916	Bos-A	1.000	4	3	10	0	0	2
1918	Bos-A	—	1	0	0	0	0	0
Total	4	.962	7	7	18	1	0	3

OF

YEAR	TM/L	PCT	G	PO	A	E	DP	FR
1915	Bos-A	—	1	0	0	0	0	0

■ Hal Wagner C

YEAR	TM/L	PCT	G	PO	A	E	DP	FR
1937	Phi-A	1.000	1	1	0	0	1	0
1938	Phi-A	.972	30	87	16	3	2	-1
1939	Phi-A	1.000	5	11	3	0	0	1
1940	Phi-A	.964	28	91	16	4	4	2
1941	Phi-A	.976	42	144	19	4	4	2
1942	Phi-A	.986	94	371	47	6	7	-1
1943	Phi-A	.980	99	340	56	8	3	-7
1944	Phi-A	1.000	1	1	0	0	0	0
	Bos-A	.970	64	299	29	10	4	0
	Yr	.971	65	**300**	30	10	4	0
1946	Bos-A	.983	116	553	39	10	3	-9
1947	Bos-A	.978	21	82	9	2	1	-1
	Det-A	.990	71	275	22	3	3	-4
	Yr	.987	92	357	31	5	4	-5
1948	Det-A	.989	52	162	12	2	4	-4
	Phi-N	1.000	1	3	2	0	0	1
1949	Phi-N	.750	1	3	0	1	0	0
Total	12	.981	626	2423	271	53	36	-22

■ Honus Wagner SS

YEAR	TM/L	PCT	G	PO	A	E	DP	FR
1901	Pit-N	.918	61	177	224	36	31	12
1902	Pit-N	.893	44	89	145	28	12	0
1903	Pit-N	.933	111	303	397	50	**51**	**25**
1904	Pit-N	.929	121	274	367	49	46	-5
1905	Pit-N	.935	145	353	517	60	64	19
1906	Pit-N	.941	137	334	473	51	**57**	**24**
1907	Pit-N	.938	138	314	428	49	32	5
1908	Pit-N	.943	151	**354**	469	50	47	-7
1909	Pit-N	.940	136	344	430	49	**58**	6
1910	Pit-N	.935	138	**337**	413	52	62	1
1911	Pit-N	.932	101	221	312	39	55	7
1912	Pit-N	**.962**	143	341	462	32	**74**	23
1913	Pit-N	**.962**	105	289	323	24	47	13
1914	Pit-N	**.950**	132	322	424	39	45	7
1915	Pit-N	**.948**	131	298	395	38	53	-3
1916	Pit-N	.942	92	226	261	30	32	-13
1917	Pit-N	1.000	1	0	1	0	0	0
Total	17	.940	1887	4576	6041	676	766	114

OF

YEAR	TM/L	PCT	G	PO	A	E	DP	FR
1897	Lou-N	.908	52	101	17	12	5	4
1899	Lou-N	.968	61	107	14	4	5	6
1900	Pit-N	.965	118	181	11	7	4	-3
1901	Pit-N	.976	54	79	2	2	0	-6
1902	Pit-N	1.000	61	121	11	0	2	7
1903	Pit-N	.955	12	20	1	1	0	0
1904	Pit-N	.929	8	13	0	1	0	-1
1905	Pit-N	1.000	2	10	0	0	0	1
1906	Pit-N	1.000	2	4	0	0	0	0
1909	Pit-N	—	1	0	0	0	0	-1
1911	Pit-N	.500	1	1	0	1	0	0
Total	11	.961	372	637	56	8	16	7

1B

YEAR	TM/L	PCT	G	PO	A	E	DP	FR
1898	Lou-N	.972	75	729	41	22	44	1
1899	Lou-N	.957	4	42	3	2	2	0
1900	Pit-N	1.000	3	16	0	0	1	0
1902	Pit-N	.988	32	315	15	4	19	0
1903	Pit-N	.985	6	63	3	1	2	0
1904	Pit-N	.969	3	30	1	1	0	-1
1907	Pit-N	1.000	4	44	1	0	1	-1
1910	Pit-N	1.000	11	103	13	0	5	3
1911	Pit-N	.974	28	250	9	7	21	-3
1914	Pit-N	1.000	1	5	3	0	0	1
1915	Pit-N	1.000	10	101	8	0	6	1
1916	Pit-N	.985	24	183	11	3	13	0
1917	Pit-N	.985	47	433	22	7	27	-1
Total	13	.981	248	2314	130	7	141	0

3B

YEAR	TM/L	PCT	G	PO	A	E	DP	FR
1898	Lou-N	.924	65	101	118	18	11	-5
1899	Lou-N	.928	75	90	168	20	10	-2
1900	Pit-N	.848	9	7	21	5	1	-1
1901	Pit-N	.897	24	37	50	10	3	2
1906	Pit-N	.500	1	0	1	1	0	0
1914	Pit-N	.926	17	17	33	4	1	-1
1917	Pit-N	.948	18	32	23	3	0	-3
Total	7	.920	209	284	414	61	26	-10

2B

YEAR	TM/L	PCT	G	PO	A	E	DP	FR
1897	Lou-N	.915	9	23	20	4	2	-1
1898	Lou-N	.943	10	17	33	3	2	0
1899	Lou-N	.949	7	21	16	2	3	-2
1900	Pit-N	.962	7	12	13	1	3	-3
1901	Pit-N	1.000	1	4	4	0	0	0
1902	Pit-N	1.000	1	6	5	0	0	2
1904	Pit-N	1.000	2	2	8	0	0	0
1910	Pit-N	.750	2	3	0	1	0	-1
1915	Pit-N	1.000	12	22	25	0	3	-4
1916	Pit-N	.900	4	8	10	2	1	-2
1917	Pit-N	1.000	2	1	5	0	0	0
Total	11	.952	57	118	140	3	14	-11

■ Leon Wagner OF

YEAR	TM/L	PCT	G	PO	A	E	DP	FR
1958	SF-N	.949	57	89	5	5	0	-5
1959	SF-N	.941	28	48	0	3	0	-2
1960	StL-N	.963	32	48	4	2	0	0
1961	LA-A	.971	116	187	12	6	2	-2
1962	LA-A	.972	156	269	7	8	1	-6
1963	LA-A	.960	141	254	7	**11**	1	-6
1964	Cle-A	.959	**163**	254	5	11	0	-7
1965	Cle-A	.957	134	175	3	8	0	-12
1966	Cle-A	.990	139	185	4	2	0	-13
1967	Cle-A	.980	117	142	4	3	1	-12
1968	Cle-A	.500	10	3	0	3	0	-3
	Chi-A	.941	46	48	0	3	0	-9
	Yr	.895	56	51	0	6	0	-12
1969	SF-N	1.000	1	3	0	0	0	0
Total	12	.964	1140	1705	51	65	5	-77

■ Mark Wagner SS

YEAR	TM/L	PCT	G	PO	A	E	DP	FR
1976	Det-A	.947	39	60	135	11	25	9
1977	Det-A	.923	21	15	57	6	10	-1
1978	Det-A	.964	35	55	79	5	18	-6
1979	Det-A	.974	41	31	83	3	18	3
1980	Det-A	.935	28	39	47	6	7	1
1981	Tex-A	.964	43	39	68	4	13	3
1982	Tex-A	.955	60	77	197	13	32	-1
1983	Tex-A	1.000	2	2	4	0	0	1
1984	Oak-A	.951	57	53	63	6	14	7
Total	9	.953	326	371	733	54	137	16

2B

YEAR	TM/L	PCT	G	PO	A	E	DP	FR
1977	Det-A	1.000	1	0	1	0	0	0

YEAR	TM/L	PCT	G	PO	A	E	DP	FR
1978	Det-A	1.000	4	2	2	0	0	-1
1979	Det-A	.960	29	57	63	5	10	4
1980	Det-A	1.000	6	4	5	0	1	1
1981	Tex-A	.985	4	13	51	1	5	16
1984	Oak-A	1.000	8	3	4	0	0	1
Total 6		.972	52	79	126	6	16	21
3B								
1979	Det-A	—	2	0	0	0	0	0
1980	Det-A	.900	9	0	9	1	0	1
1981	Tex-A	1.000	2	2	4	0	0	1
1984	Oak-A	1.000	15	17	16	0	1	4
Total 4		.980	28	19	29	1	1	6

■ Kermit Wahl 3B

YEAR	TM/L	PCT	G	PO	A	E	DP	FR
1944	Cin-N	—	1	0	0	0	0	0
1945	Cin-N	.875	7	4	10	2	0	0
1947	Cin-N	.964	20	24	30	2	2	4
1950	Phi-A	.946	61	70	141	12	11	6
1951	Phi-A	.967	18	21	37	2	4	2
	StL-A	.950	6	7	12	1	3	0
	Yr	.962	24	28	49	3	7	2
Total 5		.949	113	126	230	9	20	12
SS								
1945	Cin-N	.959	31	59	83	6	9	1
1947	Cin-N	1.000	9	12	18	0	2	2
1950	Phi-A	.957	18	38	52	4	16	5
Total 3		.963	58	109	153	0	27	8
2B								
1945	Cin-N	.948	32	76	87	9	13	3
1947	Cin-N	1.000	2	3	2	0	1	0
1950	Phi-A	.875	2	3	4	1	2	0
Total 3		.946	36	82	93	0	16	3

■ Eddie Waitkus 1B

YEAR	TM/L	PCT	G	PO	A	E	DP	FR
1941	Chi-N	.949	9	71	3	4	8	-1
1946	Chi-N	.996	106	992	81	4	76	4
1947	Chi-N	.994	126	1161	101	8	109	8
1948	Chi-N	.992	116	1064	92	9	77	7
1949	Phi-N	.994	54	452	36	3	51	1
1950	Phi-N	.993	154	1387	99	10	142	-2
1951	Phi-N	.992	144	1214	94	10	121	-2
1952	Phi-N	.991	146	1281	95	12	119	-2
1953	Phi-N	.989	59	480	37	6	65	-1
1954	Bal-A	1.000	78	618	48	0	72	1
1955	Bal-A	.974	26	180	9	5	15	-2
	Phi-N	.996	31	250	21	1	31	0
Total 11		.993	1049	9150	716	2	886	11
OF								
1948	Chi-N	.977	20	43	0	1	0	-2

■ Dick Wakefield OF

YEAR	TM/L	PCT	G	PO	A	E	DP	FR
1941	Det-A	1.000	1	1	0	0	0	0
1943	Det-A	.959	155	314	11	14	1	-7
1944	Det-A	.963	78	155	3	6	1	-4
1946	Det-A	.964	104	210	6	8	1	-1
1947	Det-A	.950	101	197	10	11	2	-1
1948	Det-A	.948	86	198	3	11	1	0
1949	Det-A	1.000	32	71	3	0	1	1
Total 7		.959	557	1146	36	0	7	-12

■ Rube Walker C

YEAR	TM/L	PCT	G	PO	A	E	DP	FR
1948	Chi-N	.980	44	178	22	4	3	-3
1949	Chi-N	.964	43	166	23	7	2	-5
1950	Chi-N	.975	62	240	34	7	6	1
1951	Chi-N	.969	31	111	15	4	2	-4
	Bro-N	.972	22	62	8	2	0	-5
	Yr	.970	53	173	23	6	2	-9
1952	Bro-N	.987	40	217	16	3	2	6
1953	Bro-N	.978	28	120	12	3	2	1
1954	Bro-N	.996	47	259	19	1	4	1
1955	Bro-N	.987	35	147	10	2	3	1
1956	Bro-N	.986	43	184	20	3	4	-2
1957	Bro-N	.992	50	230	20	2	3	-6
1958	LA-N	.985	20	62	5	1	1	-1
Total 11		.982	465	1976	204	9	32	-16

■ Frank Walker OF

YEAR	TM/L	PCT	G	PO	A	E	DP	FR
1918	Det-A	.922	45	102	6	9	1	-2
1920	Phi-A	.983	24	57	1	1	0	-1
1921	Phi-A	.961	19	46	3	2	0	1
1925	NY-N	.960	21	45	3	2	1	2
Total 4		.949	109	250	12	4	2	0

■ Tilly Walker OF

YEAR	TM/L	PCT	G	PO	A	E	DP	FR
1911	Was-A	.917	94	163	14	16	1	-1
1912	Was-A	.837	34	35	6	8	3	-2
1913	StL-A	.911	23	36	5	4	0	0
1914	StL-A	.972	145	311	30	10	5	16
1915	StL-A	.940	139	333	27	23	5	15
1916	Bos-A	.959	128	290	12	13	4	-3
1917	Bos-A	.972	96	225	20	7	7	6
1918	Phi-A	.953	109	242	24	13	4	9
1919	Phi-A	.933	115	253	13	19	4	-4
1920	Phi-A	.940	149	318	26	22	5	6
1921	Phi-A	.955	142	337	24	17	3	9
1922	Phi-A	.956	148	309	19	15	4	-2
1923	Phi-A	1.000	26	52	1	0	1	2
Total 13		.949	1348	2904	221	167	46	43
2B								
1912	Was-A	1.000	1	2	0	0	0	0

■ Duane Walker OF

YEAR	TM/L	PCT	G	PO	A	E	DP	FR
1982	Cin-N	.992	69	110	7	1	1	-1
1983	Cin-N	.956	60	104	4	5	0	2
1984	Cin-N	.950	68	110	3	6	0	0
1985	Cin-N	.882	10	15	0	2	0	0
	Tex-N	1.000	32	51	6	0	1	3
1988	StL-N	—	4	0	0	0	0	0
Total 5		.967	243	390	20	4	2	4
1B								
1988	StL-N	1.000	1	2	0	0	0	0

■ Dixie Walker OF

YEAR	TM/L	PCT	G	PO	A	E	DP	FR
1931	NY-A	1.000	2	3	0	0	0	0
1933	NY-A	.962	77	194	7	8	1	8
1934	NY-A	1.000	1	1	0	0	0	0
1935	NY-A	.750	2	3	0	1	0	0
1936	NY-A	1.000	5	9	0	0	0	0
	Chi-A	1.000	17	46	2	0	0	2
	Yr	1.000	22	55	2	0	0	2
1937	Chi-A	.952	154	270	10	14	1	-13
1938	Det-A	.979	114	224	8	5	1	-3
1939	Det-A	.970	37	93	4	3	1	3
	Bro-N	.968	59	144	5	5	3	0
1940	Bro-N	.973	136	360	6	10	3	2
1941	Bro-N	.976	146	309	19	8	8	7
1942	Bro-N	.986	110	207	8	3	2	-1
1943	Bro-N	.969	136	262	20	9	2	2
1944	Bro-N	.962	140	260	17	11	4	-4
1945	Bro-N	.992	153	346	18	3	4	10
1946	Bro-N	.969	149	237	15	8	3	-12
1947	Bro-N	.964	147	261	9	10	0	-14
1948	Pit-N	.977	112	168	4	4	0	-18
1949	Pit-N	.984	39	58	2	1	0	-5
Total 18		.972	1736	3455	154	103	33	-36
1B								
1949	Pit-N	.900	3	24	3	3	2	0

■ Gee Walker OF

YEAR	TM/L	PCT	G	PO	A	E	DP	FR
1931	Det-A	.953	44	99	2	5	1	-3
1932	Det-A	.949	116	309	9	17	1	-3
1933	Det-A	.942	113	234	10	15	3	-1
1934	Det-A	.947	80	191	5	11	2	4
1935	Det-A	.954	85	204	2	10	1	0
1936	Det-A	.948	125	280	14	16	5	6
1937	Det-A	.956	151	316	9	15	2	-6
1938	Chi-A	.958	107	197	9	9	2	-11
1939	Chi-A	.967	147	365	11	13	3	9
1940	Was-A	.967	140	285	10	10	2	-2
1941	Cle-A	.982	105	257	9	5	0	7
1942	Cin-N	.973	110	277	7	8	2	-1
1943	Cin-N	.980	106	231	8	5	3	-11
1944	Cin-N	.967	117	293	3	10	0	-2
1945	Cin-N	.962	67	123	4	5	1	-9
Total 15		.961	1613	3661	112	154	28	-23
3B								
1945	Cin-N	.778	3	4	3	2	0	-2

■ Greg Walker 1B

YEAR	TM/L	PCT	G	PO	A	E	DP	FR
1983	Chi-A	.985	59	426	19	7	40	-7
1984	Chi-A	.995	101	791	51	4	66	-2
1985	Chi-A	.994	151	1217	97	8	116	-3
1986	Chi-A	.993	77	670	57	5	57	-1
1987	Chi-A	.994	154	1402	80	9	135	-14
1988	Chi-A	.993	98	935	41	7	93	-14
1989	Chi-A	.987	48	373	17	5	38	-6
1990	Chi-A	1.000	1	14	1	0	2	0
Total 8		.993	689	5828	363	5	547	-47

■ Harry Walker OF

YEAR	TM/L	PCT	G	PO	A	E	DP	FR
1940	StL-N	1.000	7	21	2	0	0	3
1941	StL-N	.875	5	7	0	1	0	0
1942	StL-N	.968	56	115	6	4	0	6
1943	StL-N	.965	144	321	14	12	4	-10
1946	StL-N	.974	92	215	11	6	2	7
1947	StL-N	.938	10	15	0	1	0	-1
	Phi-N	.966	127	350	15	13	2	11
	Yr	.964	137	365	15	14	2	10
1948	Phi-N	.981	81	198	6	4	1	0
1949	StL-N	.947	39	69	3	4	0	-5
	Cin-N	.963	77	177	7	7	1	-3
	Yr	.959	116	246	10	11	1	-8
1950	StL-N	.969	46	92	3	3	0	2
1951	StL-N	1.000	6	10	0	0	0	-1
1955	StL-N	1.000	1	2	1	0	1	1
Total 11		.968	691	1592	68	5	11	14
1B								
1946	StL-N	.984	8	58	4	1	3	0
1947	Phi-N	1.000	4	18	0	0	2	0
1948	Phi-N	1.000	4	22	1	0	1	0
1949	Cin-N	—	1	0	0	0	0	0
1950	StL-N	1.000	2	10	0	0	1	0
1951	StL-N	1.000	1	10	1	0	2	0
Total 6		.992	20	118	6	1	9	0
2B								
1942	StL-N	1.000	2	1	0	0	0	0
1943	StL-N	.500	1	1	0	1	0	-1
Total 2		.667	3	2	0	1	0	-1
3B								
1948	Phi-N	1.000	1	0	1	0	0	0

■ Hub Walker OF

YEAR	TM/L	PCT	G	PO	A	E	DP	FR
1931	Det-A	.961	66	170	4	7	1	0
1935	Det-A	1.000	7	19	0	0	0	1
1936	Cin-N	.970	73	158	4	5	2	2
1937	Cin-N	.993	58	135	5	1	3	0
1945	Det-A	1.000	7	5	0	0	0	0
Total 5		.975	211	487	13	3	6	3
2B								
1937	Cin-N	1.000	3	2	0	0	0	0
C								
1936	Cin-N	1.000	1	1	0	0	0	0
1B								
1936	Cin-N	1.000	1	3	0	0	0	0

■ Larry Walker OF

YEAR	TM/L	PCT	G	PO	A	E	DP	FR
1989	Mon-N	1.000	15	19	2	0	1	0
1990	Mon-N	.985	124	249	12	4	5	5
Total 2		.986	139	268	14	4	6	5

■ Oscar Walker OF

YEAR	TM/L	PCT	G	PO	A	E	DP	FR
1880	Buf-N	.846	11	19	3	4	1	1
1882	StL-a	.846	75	158	18	32	4	8
1884	Bro-a	.868	59	87	12	15	0	2
Total 3		.853	145	264	33	1	5	11
1B								
1879	Buf-N	.946	72	828	30	49	52	3
1880	Buf-N	.917	24	248	7	23	16	-2
1882	StL-a	1.000	1	12	0	0	1	0
1884	Bro-a	.961	36	389	8	16	12	-2
Total 4		.945	133	1477	45	8	81	-1
2B								
1882	StL-a	1.000	1	2	0	0	0	0

■ Curt Walker OF

YEAR	TM/L	PCT	G	PO	A	E	DP	FR
1920	NY-N	1.000	4	5	0	0	0	0
1921	NY-N	.978	58	122	11	3	3	6
	Phi-N	.970	21	30	2	1	0	-4
	Yr	.976	79	152	13	4	3	2
1922	Phi-N	.955	147	295	24	15	8	2
1923	Phi-N	.947	137	284	19	17	5	3
1924	Phi-N	.900	20	26	1	3	1	-4
	Cin-N	.978	109	213	14	5	4	2
	Yr	.969	129	239	15	8	5	-2
1925	Cin-N	.983	141	332	12	6	4	0
1926	Cin-N	.961	152	325	21	14	8	2
1927	Cin-N	.957	141	316	15	15	8	2
1928	Cin-N	.955	122	289	9	14	3	4
1929	Cin-N	.969	138	298	11	10	2	-2
1930	Cin-N	.965	120	241	5	9	2	-9
Total 11		.963	1310	2776	144	112	48	2
1B								
1923	Phi-N	—	1	0	0	0	0	0

■ Bobby Wallace SS

YEAR	TM/L	PCT	G	PO	A	E	DP	FR
1899	StL-N	.919	100	238	386	55	40	21
1900	StL-N	.934	126	327	447	55	31	3
1901	StL-N	.929	134	326	542	66	67	30
1902	StL-A	.948	131	299	474	42	64	10
1903	StL-A	.924	135	282	468	62	53	18
1904	StL-A	.947	139	303	482	44	37	8
1905	StL-A	.935	156	385	506	62	40	19
1906	StL-A	.949	138	309	461	41	47	3
1907	StL-A	.941	147	338	517	54	52	8
1908	StL-A	.951	137	286	510	41	45	18
1909	StL-A	.946	87	193	279	27	34	9
1910	StL-A	.948	99	258	344	33	37	17
1911	StL-A	.943	124	280	417	42	47	1
1912	StL-A	.942	87	185	271	28	29	5
1913	StL-A	.931	39	67	96	12	8	-9
1914	StL-A	.889	19	26	46	9	2	-11
1915	StL-A	.848	9	11	17	5	4	1
1916	StL-A	.923	5	5	7	1	0	1
1917	StL-N	.909	2	4	6	1	0	-1
1918	StL-N	.904	12	20	27	5	5	-1
Total 20		.938	1826	4142	6303	685	642	150
3B								
1897	Cle-N	.928	130	190	249	34	10	3
1898	Cle-N	.936	141	201	329	36	19	18
1899	StL-N	.929	52	84	150	18	13	17
1900	StL-N	1.000	1	2	2	0	0	0
1909	StL-A	.955	29	49	57	5	5	1
1910	StL-A	.940	39	58	100	10	6	4
1912	StL-A	.947	10	15	21	2	6	3
1913	StL-A	1.000	7	8	23	0	0	3
1914	StL-A	1.000	2	1	3	0	0	0
1916	StL-A	.958	9	3	20	1	1	4
1917	StL-N	1.000	5	1	0	0	0	0
1918	StL-N	.750	1	1	2	1	0	0
Total 12		.936	426	613	956	107	60	53
2B								
1898	Cle-N	.965	13	47	36	3	4	-1
1911	StL-A	1.000	1	2	0	0	2	0
1912	StL-A	.933	2	10	4	1	0	0
1918	StL-N	.959	17	40	54	4	8	3
Total 4		.960	33	99	94	8	14	2
OF								
1896	Cle-N	.950	23	35	3	2	0	-2
1897	Cle-N	.667	1	1	1	1	0	0
1902	StL-A	1.000	1	2	0	0	0	0
Total 3		.933	25	38	4	3	0	-2
1B								
1896	Cle-N	1.000	1	2	0	0	0	0

■ Tim Wallach 3B

YEAR	TM/L	PCT	G	PO	A	E	DP	FR
1981	Mon-N	.972	15	12	23	1	1	-2
1982	Mon-N	.948	156	132	287	23	23	-5
1983	Mon-N	.956	156	151	265	19	25	-7
1984	Mon-N	.959	160	162	332	22	29	16
1985	Mon-N	.967	154	148	383	18	34	37
1986	Mon-N	.958	132	94	270	16	26	15
1987	Mon-N	.952	150	128	292	21	21	0
1988	Mon-N	.962	153	123	328	18	31	12
1989	Mon-N	.958	153	113	302	18	20	6
1990	Mon-N	.954	161	128	309	21	23	4
Total 10		.958	1390	1191	2791	176	233	76
OF								
1980	Mon-N	1.000	3	2	0	0	0	0
1981	Mon-N	1.000	35	55	3	0	1	1
1982	Mon-N	—	2	0	0	0	0	0
Total 3		1.000	40	57	3	0	1	1
1B								
1980	Mon-N	1.000	1	10	0	0	0	0
1981	Mon-N	1.000	16	140	5	0	7	-2
1982	Mon-N	—	1	0	0	0	0	0
Total 3		1.000	18	150	5	0	7	-2
SS								
1984	Mon-N	—	1	0	0	0	0	-1
2B								
1988	Mon-N	1.000	1	1	1	0	1	0

YEAR	TM/L	PCT	G	PO	A	E	DP	FR
Jack Wallaesa SS								
1940	Phi-A	.903	6	9	19	3	3	1
1942	Phi-A	.920	36	62	76	12	16	-7
1946	Phi-A	.916	59	111	130	22	31	-16
1947	Chi-A	.968	27	55	94	5	22	8
1948	Chi-A	1.000	5	11	17	0	5	0
Total	5	.933	133	248	336	2	77	-14
OF								
1947	Chi-A	1.000	22	74	1	0	0	4
1948	Chi-A	—	1	0	0	0	0	0
Total	2	1.000	23	74	1	0	0	4
3B								
1947	Chi-A	1.000	1	1	1	0	0	0
Dennis Walling 3B								
1983	Hou-N	.906	13	8	21	3	1	0
1984	Hou-N	.956	52	30	100	6	14	2
1985	Hou-N	.938	51	31	104	9	9	1
1986	Hou-N	.960	102	59	156	9	6	1
1987	Hou-N	.948	79	72	109	10	13	-4
1988	Hou-N	.950	51	33	99	7	14	9
	StL-N	.846	5	0	11	2	2	0
	Yr	.941	56	33	110	9	16	9
1989	StL-N	.714	9	0	5	2	0	-1
1990	StL-N	1.000	11	6	19	0	1	1
Total	8	.947	373	239	624	8	60	9
OF								
1975	Oak-A	1.000	3	3	0	0	0	0
1976	Oak-A	.889	3	8	0	1	0	0
1977	Hou-N	1.000	5	14	0	0	0	0
1978	Hou-N	.980	78	140	4	3	2	3
1979	Hou-N	.985	42	65	2	1	0	0
1980	Hou-N	1.000	19	20	0	0	0	-1
1981	Hou-N	1.000	27	38	1	0	1	-1
1982	Hou-N	1.000	32	38	3	0	0	1
1983	Hou-N	.846	13	11	0	2	0	-1
1984	Hou-N	1.000	6	3	0	0	0	0
1985	Hou-N	.923	13	12	0	1	0	0
1986	Hou-N	1.000	11	19	1	0	0	0
1987	Hou-N	1.000	7	8	1	0	0	0
1988	Hou-N	1.000	1	2	0	0	0	0
	StL-N	1.000	11	12	0	0	0	-1
	Yr	1.000	12	14	0	0	0	-1
1989	StL-N	1.000	6	9	0	0	0	0
1990	StL-N	1.000	8	11	1	0	0	1
Total	16	.982	285	413	13	8	3	1
1B								
1980	Hou-N	.989	63	505	31	6	46	-3
1981	Hou-N	.990	27	188	8	2	17	-3
1982	Hou-N	.993	20	129	8	1	8	-1
1983	Hou-N	.992	42	115	8	1	12	0
1984	Hou-N	.988	16	83	2	1	7	-2
1985	Hou-N	.993	46	283	20	2	22	-1
1986	Hou-N	1.000	4	30	4	0	2	1
1987	Hou-N	1.000	16	95	9	0	8	0
1988	Hou-N	1.000	3	21	1	0	1	0
	StL-N	1.000	1	5	1	0	0	0
	Yr	1.000	4	26	2	0	1	0
1989	StL-N	.969	20	58	4	2	4	-1
1990	StL-N	1.000	15	86	6	0	4	0
Total	11	.991	273	1598	102	5	131	-10
Joe Wallis OF								
1975	Chi-N	1.000	15	31	1	0	0	0
1976	Chi-N	.976	90	193	11	5	3	7
1977	Chi-N	.974	35	36	2	1	0	0
1978	Chi-N	1.000	25	36	1	0	0	1
	Oak-A	.980	80	187	7	4	5	4
1979	Oak-A	1.000	23	41	1	0	0	-3
Total	5	.982	268	524	23	0	8	9
Lee Walls OF								
1952	Pit-N	1.000	19	44	2	0	1	2
1956	Pit-N	.967	133	284	10	10	1	6
1957	Pit-N	1.000	7	13	1	0	0	1
	Chi-N	.984	94	174	6	3	0	0
	Yr	.985	101	187	7	3	0	1
1958	Chi-N	.992	132	241	10	2	1	1
1959	Chi-N	.967	119	203	1	7	0	-10
1960	Cin-N	.960	24	46	2	2	1	0
	Phi-N	.952	13	20	0	1	0	-1
	Yr	.958	37	66	2	3	1	-1
1961	Phi-N	1.000	17	23	1	0	1	0
1962	LA-N	.929	17	12	1	1	0	0
1963	LA-N	1.000	18	12	0	0	0	0
1964	LA-N	1.000	6	1	0	0	0	0
Total	10	.977	599	1073	34	6	5	-1
3B								
1956	Pit-N	.500	1	0	1	1	0	0
1957	Chi-N	1.000	1	1	0	0	0	0
1960	Phi-N	.947	34	25	47	4	4	-7
1961	Phi-N	.924	26	22	39	5	3	-3
1962	LA-N	1.000	4	1	7	0	0	0
1963	LA-N	1.000	2	1	9	0	1	2
Total	6	.939	68	50	103	0	8	-8
1B								
1960	Cin-N	1.000	2	9	0	0	1	0
	Phi-N	.970	7	30	2	1	4	-1
	Yr	.976	9	39	2	1	5	-1
1961	Phi-N	.987	28	202	19	3	29	-1
1962	LA-N	.989	11	85	4	1	4	-1
1963	LA-N	.978	5	42	3	1	2	0
Total	4	.985	53	368	28	6	40	-3
C								
1964	LA-N	—	1	0	0	0	0	0
Jimmy Walsh OF								
1912	Phi-A	.947	30	70	1	4	1	0
1913	Phi-A	.961	90	184	11	8	4	1
1914	NY-A	.977	41	81	4	2	0	-1
	Phi-A	.966	56	107	7	4	3	0
	Yr	.971	97	188	11	6	3	-1
1915	Phi-A	.976	109	231	15	6	1	8
1916	Phi-A	.939	113	172	13	12	4	0
	Bos-A	1.000	6	4	0	0	0	-2
	Yr	.940	119	176	13	12	4	-2
1917	Bos-A	.982	47	103	8	2	0	0
Total	6	.964	492	952	59	8	13	6
3B								
1914	Phi-A	.714	3	0	5	2	0	-1
1915	Phi-A	1.000	2	7	1	0	0	-1
1916	Bos-A	1.000	2	3	3	0	0	-1
Total	3	.905	7	10	9	2	0	-2
1B								
1914	Phi-A	.971	3	32	2	1	3	0
1915	Phi-A	1.000	1	2	0	0	0	0
1916	Phi-A	1.000	1	6	0	0	0	0
Total	3	.977	5	40	2	1	3	0
SS								
1914	Phi-A	1.000	1	1	2	0	0	0
Jimmy Walsh 3B								
1910	Phi-N	.636	5	2	5	4	0	-2
1911	Phi-N	.818	7	10	8	4	0	-2
1912	Phi-N	.952	12	6	14	1	2	0
1913	Phi-N	.000	1	0	0	1	0	-1
1914	Bal-F	.932	113	125	217	25	18	3
1915	Bal-F	.936	106	131	190	22	15	-9
	StL-F	.913	9	7	14	2	0	-1
	Yr	.934	115	138	204	24	15	-10
Total	6	.925	253	281	448	9	35	-12
2B								
1910	Phi-N	.947	26	53	72	7	8	5
1911	Phi-N	.971	14	26	41	2	8	2
1912	Phi-N	.944	31	57	94	9	10	0
1913	Phi-N	1.000	6	9	9	0	3	1
1914	Bal-F	—	1	0	0	0	0	0
Total	5	.953	78	145	216	8	29	8
OF								
1910	Phi-N	.938	26	59	1	4	0	-1
1911	Phi-N	.962	48	73	3	3	0	-4
1913	Phi-N	—	1	0	0	0	0	0
1914	Bal-F	—	1	0	0	0	0	0
Total	4	.951	76	132	4	7	0	-5
SS								
1910	Phi-N	.795	9	8	23	8	3	-3
1911	Phi-N	.943	9	15	18	2	3	-1
1913	Phi-N	1.000	3	0	1	0	0	0
1914	Bal-F	.800	1	1	3	1	0	0
Total	4	.863	22	24	45	1	6	-4
C								
1911	Phi-N	.968	4	21	9	1	3	2
1912	Phi-N	1.000	5	6	4	0	0	1
Total	2	.976	9	27	13	1	3	3
1B								
1911	Phi-N	1.000	1	3	0	0	0	0
Roxy Walters C								
1915	NY-A	1.000	2	8	3	0	1	2
1916	NY-A	.974	65	346	102	12	13	**16**
1917	NY-A	.968	57	263	73	11	6	11
1918	NY-A	.953	50	199	47	12	6	-5
1919	Bos-A	.982	47	162	54	4	3	5
1920	Bos-A	.980	85	351	94	9	15	8
1921	Bos-A	.990	54	232	53	3	11	**15**
1922	Bos-A	.967	36	117	30	5	5	6
1923	Bos-A	.974	36	111	36	4	2	6
1924	Cle-A	.979	25	66	26	2	3	6
1925	Cle-A	1.000	5	8	7	0	1	0
Total	11	.975	462	1863	525	2	66	70
OF								
1918	NY-A	.933	9	12	2	1	1	0
2B								
1923	Bos-A	1.000	1	0	2	0	0	0
1924	Cle-A	1.000	7	9	8	0	1	0
Total	2	1.000	8	9	10	0	1	0
1B								
1920	Bos-A	1.000	2	3	0	0	0	0
Ken Walters OF								
1960	Phi-N	.988	119	220	17	3	4	6
1961	Phi-N	.975	56	73	4	2	0	0
1963	Cin-N	.889	21	16	0	2	0	-2
Total	3	.979	196	309	21	7	4	4
1B								
1961	Phi-N	1.000	5	23	3	0	3	0
1963	Cin-N	1.000	1	8	0	0	0	0
Total	2	1.000	6	31	3	0	3	0
3B								
1961	Phi-N	—	1	0	0	0	0	0
Bucky Walters 3B								
1931	Bos-N	.947	6	5	13	1	0	0
1932	Bos-N	.910	22	17	44	6	8	2
1933	Bos-A	.940	43	42	84	8	11	2
1934	Bos-A	.906	23	33	54	9	6	6
	Phi-N	.950	80	74	136	11	12	-6
1935	Phi-N	—	1	0	0	0	0	0
1936	Phi-N	1.000	1	0	1	0	0	0
1937	Phi-N	1.000	8	5	9	0	1	0
Total	7	.937	184	176	341	5	38	4
2B								
1931	Bos-N	1.000	3	2	9	0	2	0
1933	Bos-A	.951	7	16	23	2	3	-1
1934	Phi-N	.941	3	9	7	1	0	-1
1935	Phi-N	.889	2	1	7	1	0	0
1936	Phi-N	1.000	1	0	1	0	0	0
Total	5	.949	16	28	47	4	5	-2
OF								
1935	Phi-N	1.000	5	7	1	0	0	0
1942	Cin-N	—	1	0	0	0	0	0
Total	2	1.000	6	7	1	0	0	0
Danny Walton OF								
1969	Sea-A	.976	23	40	0	1	0	-3
1970	Mil-A	.965	114	162	4	6	0	-11
1971	Mil-A	.923	19	24	0	2	0	-3
	NY-A	1.000	4	4	0	0	0	-1
	Yr	.933	23	28	0	2	0	-4
1973	Min-A	1.000	18	18	0	0	0	2
Total	4	.966	178	248	4	9	0	-16
1B								
1975	Min-A	.962	7	24	1	1	4	0
1977	Hou-N	.956	5	41	2	2	1	0
Total	2	.958	12	65	3	3	5	0
3B								
1971	Mil-A	—	1	0	0	0	0	0
1973	Min-A	1.000	1	0	3	0	0	1
Total	2	1.000	2	0	3	0	0	1
C								
1975	Min-A	1.000	2	3	0	0	0	0
Jerome Walton OF								
1989	Chi-N	.990	115	289	2	3	1	-2
1990	Chi-N	.977	98	247	3	6	0	-2
Total	2	.984	213	536	5	9	1	-4
Bill Wambsganss 2B								
1914	Cle-A	.833	4	7	8	3	0	-1
1915	Cle-A	.938	78	138	237	25	24	5
1916	Cle-A	.958	24	39	76	5	11	0
1917	Cle-A	.951	137	304	441	**38**	**70**	**15**
1918	Cle-A	.952	87	204	251	23	35	-2
1919	Cle-A	.963	139	342	436	**30**	60	11
1920	Cle-A	.960	153	414	489	**38**	75	8
1921	Cle-A	.963	103	268	255	20	51	-20
1922	Cle-A	.961	125	297	376	27	72	-8
1923	Cle-A	.963	86	247	272	20	47	5
1924	Bos-A	.963	**156**	**463**	494	37	**100**	14
1925	Bos-A	.957	103	254	326	26	60	4
1926	Phi-A	1.000	8	4	5	0	0	0
Total	13	.958	1203	2981	3666	292	605	31
SS								
1914	Cle-A	.921	36	65	109	15	16	0
1916	Cle-A	.925	106	208	325	43	38	-8
1922	Cle-A	.825	16	29	4	7	7	-19
1923	Cle-A	1.000	2	5	3	0	0	0
1926	Phi-A	.923	17	10	26	3	5	0
Total	5	.920	177	317	467	8	66	-27
3B								
1915	Cle-A	.909	35	31	69	10	4	2
1916	Cle-A	.778	5	5	9	4	4	-1
1921	Cle-A	1.000	2	3	8	0	0	2
1923	Cle-A	1.000	4	3	3	0	0	0
Total	4	.903	46	42	89	4	8	3
1B								
1917	Cle-A	1.000	3	28	2	0	0	0
1925	Bos-A	.981	6	47	4	1	5	0
Total	2	.988	9	75	6	1	5	0
Lloyd Waner OF								
1927	Pit-N	.976	**150**	396	9	10	0	-11
1928	Pit-N	.980	152	418	15	9	4	3
1929	Pit-N	.987	151	**450**	22	6	6	11
1930	Pit-N	.983	65	165	6	3	1	1
1931	Pit-N	.979	153	**484**	20	11	5	11
1932	Pit-N	.986	131	**426**	9	6	0	5
1933	Pit-N	.982	114	267	9	5	2	3
1934	Pit-N	.979	139	**405**	8	9	1	8
1935	Pit-N	.989	121	350	5	4	1	4
1936	Pit-N	.984	92	245	2	4	2	-3
1937	Pit-N	.988	123	312	8	4	0	2
1938	Pit-N	.986	144	341	15	5	5	-3
1939	Pit-N	.992	92	225	9	2	1	2
1940	Pit-N	1.000	42	90	3	1	1	4
1941	Pit-N	1.000	1	4	0	0	0	0
	Bos-N	.969	15	30	1	1	0	1
	Cin-N	.986	44	68	3	1	1	-3
	Yr	.981	60	102	4	2	1	-2
1942	Phi-N	.967	75	170	6	6	0	-4
1944	Bro-N	1.000	4	3	0	0	0	0
	Pit-N	1.000	7	9	0	0	0	-1
	Yr	1.000	11	12	0	0	0	-1
1945	Pit-N	1.000	3	2	1	0	0	1
Total	18	.983	1818	4860	151	7	30	33
2B								
1927	Pit-N	1.000	1	1	0	0	0	0
1931	Pit-N	1.000	1	1	2	0	0	0
Total	2	1.000	2	2	2	0	0	0
3B								
1939	Pit-N	1.000	1	2	4	0	1	1
Paul Waner OF								
1926	Pit-N	.976	139	307	21	8	3	6
1927	Pit-N	.980	143	326	20	7	4	9
1928	Pit-N	.975	131	299	14	8	0	7
1929	Pit-N	.986	143	328	15	5	5	7
1930	Pit-N	.959	143	344	9	15	4	2
1931	Pit-N	.976	138	342	**28**	9	**8**	**19**
1932	Pit-N	.974	**154**	367	13	10	3	2
1933	Pit-N	.981	**154**	346	16	7	2	3
1934	Pit-N	.985	145	323	15	5	1	6
1935	Pit-N	.983	136	283	13	5	2	0
1936	Pit-N	.960	145	323	15	14	7	7
1937	Pit-N	.970	150	271	16	9	3	-2
1938	Pit-N	.977	147	284	11	7	0	-4
1939	Pit-N	.978	106	206	12	5	4	1
1940	Pit-N	.985	45	62	3	1	0	-6

YEAR	TM/L	PCT	G	PO	A	E	DP	FR
1941	Bro-N	.923	9	12	0	1	0	-2
	Bos-N	.965	77	129	7	5	3	-6
	Yr	.961	86	141	7	6	3	-8
1942	Bos-N	.969	94	150	6	5	3	-9
1943	Bro-N	.960	57	116	4	5	1	-2
1944	Bro-N	.983	32	54	3	1	0	0
Total	19	.975	2288	4872	241	132	53	38

1B

YEAR	TM/L	PCT	G	PO	A	E	DP	FR
1927	Pit-N	.973	14	104	5	3	8	-2
1928	Pit-N	.984	24	234	8	4	17	-2
1929	Pit-N	1.000	7	70	3	0	2	0
1931	Pit-N	1.000	10	99	3	0	10	-1
1937	Pit-N	.938	3	27	3	2	3	0
1940	Pit-N	.989	8	88	6	1	12	0
1941	Bos-N	.909	7	19	1	2	0	-1
Total	7	.982	73	641	29	2	52	-6

■ Pee-Wee Wanninger SS

YEAR	TM/L	PCT	G	PO	A	E	DP	FR
1925	NY-A	.944	111	214	296	30	59	-6
1927	Bos-A	.890	15	27	46	9	11	-1
	Cin-N	.953	28	61	100	8	21	6
Total	2	.941	154	302	442	7	91	-1

3B

YEAR	TM/L	PCT	G	PO	A	E	DP	FR
1925	NY-A	1.000	3	4	7	0	2	1

2B

YEAR	TM/L	PCT	G	PO	A	E	DP	FR
1925	NY-A	.800	1	1	3	1	0	-1

■ Aaron Ward 2B

YEAR	TM/L	PCT	G	PO	A	E	DP	FR
1918	NY-A	1.000	3	3	4	0	1	1
1919	NY-A	1.000	1	1	1	0	0	0
1921	NY-A	.961	124	260	412	27	35	5
1922	NY-A	.974	152	358	489	23	73	2
1923	NY-A	.980	152	387	493	18	86	14
1924	NY-A	.973	120	303	385	19	60	8
1925	NY-A	.966	113	246	317	20	57	-12
1926	NY-A	1.000	4	13	7	0	0	-3
1927	Chi-A	.963	139	275	437	27	66	-20
1928	Cle-A	1.000	1	0	1	0	0	0
Total	10	.970	809	1846	2546	134	378	-5

3B

YEAR	TM/L	PCT	G	PO	A	E	DP	FR
1919	NY-A	1.000	3	0	4	0	0	1
1920	NY-A	.965	114	132	303	16	23	16
1921	NY-A	.977	33	44	84	3	33	14
1922	NY-A	1.000	2	0	1	0	0	0
1925	NY-A	1.000	10	18	19	0	2	1
1926	NY-A	—	1	0	0	0	0	0
1927	Chi-A	1.000	6	8	13	0	0	1
1928	Cle-A	.818	3	1	8	2	2	2
Total	8	.968	172	203	432	1	60	35

SS

YEAR	TM/L	PCT	G	PO	A	E	DP	FR
1917	NY-A	.926	7	12	13	2	3	-2
1918	NY-A	.941	12	12	20	2	4	3
1919	NY-A	.917	2	4	7	1	1	1
1920	NY-A	.975	12	37	41	2	13	6
1924	NY-A	—	1	0	0	0	0	0
1928	Cle-A	.778	2	3	4	2	2	0
Total	6	.944	36	68	85	9	23	8

1B

YEAR	TM/L	PCT	G	PO	A	E	DP	FR
1919	NY-A	1.000	5	38	2	0	4	0

OF

YEAR	TM/L	PCT	G	PO	A	E	DP	FR
1918	NY-A	1.000	4	8	1	0	0	0

■ Chuck Ward SS

YEAR	TM/L	PCT	G	PO	A	E	DP	FR
1917	Pit-N	.912	112	206	312	50	49	-27
1920	Bro-N	.928	19	46	44	7	5	-9
1921	Bro-N	.937	12	25	34	4	7	4
1922	Bro-N	.934	31	54	88	10	13	-4
Total	4	.919	174	331	478	1	74	-36

3B

YEAR	TM/L	PCT	G	PO	A	E	DP	FR
1917	Pit-N	.941	5	4	12	1	0	0
1918	Bro-N	1.000	2	0	3	0	0	-1
1919	Bro-N	.920	45	47	79	11	0	-6
1922	Bro-N	1.000	2	0	1	0	0	0
Total	4	.924	54	51	95	2	0	-7

2B

YEAR	TM/L	PCT	G	PO	A	E	DP	FR
1917	Pit-N	.975	8	16	23	1	4	0

■ Piggy Ward OF

YEAR	TM/L	PCT	G	PO	A	E	DP	FR
1889	Phi-N	.333	1	1	0	2	0	-1
1891	Pit-N	.833	5	5	0	1	0	-1
1892	Bal-N	.892	43	53	13	8	4	4
1893	Bal-N	.846	9	21	1	4	0	0
	Cin-N	.827	40	54	8	13	4	-2
	Yr	.832	49	75	9	17	4	-2
1894	Was-N	.885	12	22	1	3	1	-1
Total	5	.852	110	156	23	1	9	-1

2B

YEAR	TM/L	PCT	G	PO	A	E	DP	FR
1889	Phi-N	.848	6	12	16	5	0	-2
1892	Bal-N	.939	7	16	15	2	2	-1
1894	Was-N	.900	79	167	237	45	21	-20
Total	3	.899	92	195	268	2	23	-23

SS

YEAR	TM/L	PCT	G	PO	A	E	DP	FR
1892	Bal-N	.778	5	5	16	6	1	-2
1894	Was-N	.800	3	5	7	3	0	-1
Total	2	.786	8	10	23	9	1	-3

1B

YEAR	TM/L	PCT	G	PO	A	E	DP	FR
1893	Bal-N	.909	2	20	0	2	0	-1
	Cin-N	1.000	1	2	0	0	0	0
	Yr	.917	3	22	0	2	0	-1

3B

YEAR	TM/L	PCT	G	PO	A	E	DP	FR
1883	Phi-N	1.000	1	0	2	0	0	-1
1894	Was-N	.667	1	1	1	1	0	-1
Total	2	.800	2	1	3	1	0	-1

C

YEAR	TM/L	PCT	G	PO	A	E	DP	FR
1892	Bal-N	1.000	1	10	0	0	0	1

■ Gary Ward OF

YEAR	TM/L	PCT	G	PO	A	E	DP	FR
1979	Min-A	1.000	5	8	0	0	0	0
1980	Min-A	1.000	12	14	0	0	0	-3
1981	Min-A	.975	80	185	8	5	4	6

YEAR	TM/L	PCT	G	PO	A	E	DP	FR
1982	Min-A	.989	150	343	13	4	3	10
1983	Min-A	.978	152	374	24	9	6	21
1984	Tex-A	.987	148	376	11	5	1	-4
1985	Tex-A	.969	153	304	11	10	2	1
1986	Tex-A	.996	104	237	8	1	3	9
1987	NY-A	.985	94	200	2	3	0	-1
1988	NY-A	.992	54	130	0	1	0	4
1989	NY-A	1.000	6	7	0	0	0	-1
	Det-A	.990	51	101	2	1	1	1
	Yr	.991	57	108	2	1	1	0
1990	Det-A	.988	85	157	2	2	1	-5
Total	12	.984	1094	2436	81	41	21	38

1B

YEAR	TM/L	PCT	G	PO	A	E	DP	FR
1987	NY-A	.989	15	118	8	0	11	0
1988	NY-A	.989	11	90	4	1	9	-1
1989	Det-A	.986	26	126	14	2	14	1
1990	Det-A	1.000	2	7	0	0	0	0
Total	4	.992	54	341	26	3	34	0

3B

YEAR	TM/L	PCT	G	PO	A	E	DP	FR
1988	NY-A	1.000	2	0	1	0	0	0

■ Monte Ward SS

YEAR	TM/L	PCT	G	PO	A	E	DP	FR
1881	Pro-N	.819	13	20	39	13	4	-2
1882	Pro-N	.833	4	18	12	6	1	2
1883	NY-N	.900	2	3	6	1	0	0
1885	NY-N	.904	111	167	350	55	36	8
1886	NY-N	.870	122	91	369	69	36	-10
1887	NY-N	.919	129	226	469	61	53	29
1888	NY-N	.857	122	185	331	86	39	-2
1889	NY-N	.890	108	229	319	68	38	6
1890	Bro-P	.878	128	303	450	105	59	21
1891	Bro-N	.878	87	180	296	66	28	-1
Total	10	.885	826	1422	2641	530	294	51

2B

YEAR	TM/L	PCT	G	PO	A	E	DP	FR
1883	NY-N	.857	1	2	4	1	0	0
1884	NY-N	.886	47	95	177	35	17	5
1889	NY-N	.818	7	16	20	8	0	-3
1891	Bro-N	.949	18	55	56	6	8	0
1892	Bro-N	.920	148	377	472	74	48	3
1893	NY-N	.918	134	348	464	73	41	7
1894	NY-N	.924	136	331	446	64	52	5
Total	7	.916	491	1224	1639	261	166	17

OF

YEAR	TM/L	PCT	G	PO	A	E	DP	FR
1879	Pro-N	.727	8	7	1	3	0	-1
1880	Pro-N	.500	2	1	1	2	0	0
1881	Pro-N	.887	40	57	14	9	0	2
1882	Pro-N	.824	50	69	20	19	3	3
1883	NY-N	.859	56	118	28	24	2	13
1884	NY-N	.847	59	103	13	21	2	-1
Total	6	.847	215	355	77	8	7	16

3B

YEAR	TM/L	PCT	G	PO	A	E	DP	FR
1879	Pro-N	.845	16	17	32	9	2	1
1880	Pro-N	.892	25	30	69	12	4	9
1883	NY-N	.739	5	6	11	6	0	-1
Total	3	.859	46	53	112	7	6	9

■ Pete Ward 3B

YEAR	TM/L	PCT	G	PO	A	E	DP	FR
1963	Chi-A	.923	154	156	302	38	27	-5
1964	Chi-A	.958	138	126	309	19	24	13
1965	Chi-A	.952	134	97	319	21	22	9
1966	Chi-A	.978	16	10	34	1	3	2
1967	Chi-A	.909	22	7	33	4	3	-3
1968	Chi-A	.946	77	59	151	12	7	-12
1969	Chi-A	.961	21	15	34	2	1	-2
Total	7	.945	562	470	1182	7	87	2

OF

YEAR	TM/L	PCT	G	PO	A	E	DP	FR
1962	Bal-A	1.000	6	10	0	0	0	-1
1966	Chi-A	.989	59	83	3	1	1	-5
1967	Chi-A	.991	89	107	3	1	0	-11
1968	Chi-A	1.000	22	28	1	0	1	-2
1969	Chi-A	1.000	9	11	2	0	0	0
Total	5	.992	185	239	9	2	2	-18

1B

YEAR	TM/L	PCT	G	PO	A	E	DP	FR
1966	Chi-A	.960	5	19	5	1	2	1
1967	Chi-A	.994	39	295	19	2	23	-3
1968	Chi-A	1.000	31	200	18	0	17	0
1969	Chi-A	.994	25	167	12	1	12	0
1970	NY-A	1.000	13	83	3	0	7	-1
Total	5	.995	113	802	57	4	61	-3

2B

YEAR	TM/L	PCT	G	PO	A	E	DP	FR
1963	Chi-A	1.000	1	1	0	0	0	0
1965	Chi-A	1.000	1	0	1	0	0	0
Total	2	1.000	2	1	1	0	0	0

SS

YEAR	TM/L	PCT	G	PO	A	E	DP	FR
1963	Chi-A	1.000	1	1	0	1	0	0

■ Preston Ward 1B

YEAR	TM/L	PCT	G	PO	A	E	DP	FR
1948	Bro-N	.990	38	268	20	3	21	-2
1950	Chi-N	.995	76	734	73	4	78	9
1953	Chi-N	1.000	7	49	1	0	9	-1
	Pit-N	.991	78	693	64	7	65	4
	Yr	.991	85	742	65	7	74	3
1954	Pit-N	.984	48	338	41	6	31	4
1955	Pit-N	.998	48	384	35	1	41	3
1956	Cle-A	.988	60	226	21	3	20	2
1957	Cle-A	1.000	1	3	0	0	0	0
1958	Cle-A	1.000	21	135	12	0	12	0
	KC-A	.989	39	346	23	4	28	-1
	Yr	.992	60	481	35	4	40	-1
1959	KC-A	.982	22	161	7	3	14	-2
Total	9	.992	438	3337	297	1	319	16

OF

YEAR	TM/L	PCT	G	PO	A	E	DP	FR
1953	Chi-N	.961	27	49	0	2	0	-2
1954	Pit-N	.932	42	74	8	6	3	0
1955	Pit-N	1.000	1	0	0	0	0	0
1956	Pit-N	1.000	5	2	0	0	0	-1
	Cle-A	1.000	17	29	1	0	0	1
1958	KC-A	1.000	2	3	0	0	0	0

YEAR	TM/L	PCT	G	PO	A	E	DP	FR
1959	KC-A	.000	1	0	0	1	0	0
Total	6	.949	95	157	9	9	3	-2

3B

YEAR	TM/L	PCT	G	PO	A	E	DP	FR
1954	Pit-N	.900	11	7	20	3	0	-1
1956	Pit-N	1.000	5	3	3	0	0	-3
1958	Cle-A	.957	24	16	28	2	2	-4
	KC-A	.905	34	23	53	8	4	-6
	Yr	.923	58	39	81	10	6	-10
Total	3	.922	74	49	104	3	6	-14

■ Fred Warner 3B

YEAR	TM/L	PCT	G	PO	A	E	DP	FR
1879	Cle-N	.827	54	78	109	39	5	0
1883	Phi-N	.775	38	46	54	29	4	-10
1884	Bro-a	.824	84	94	149	52	13	-6
Total	3	.815	176	218	312	120	22	-16

SS

YEAR	TM/L	PCT	G	PO	A	E	DP	FR
1878	Ind-N	.907	41	41	124	17	9	-3

OF

YEAR	TM/L	PCT	G	PO	A	E	DP	FR
1876	Phi-N	.600	1	3	0	2	0	0
1878	Ind-N	.750	2	3	0	1	0	0
1879	Cle-N	.816	21	36	4	9	0	-1
1883	Phi-N	1.000	1	3	0	0	0	1
Total	4	.806	25	45	5	2	0	0

1B

YEAR	TM/L	PCT	G	PO	A	E	DP	FR
1879	Cle-N	1.000	1	13	0	0	0	0

■ John Warner C

YEAR	TM/L	PCT	G	PO	A	E	DP	FR
1895	Bos-N	.917	3	7	4	1	0	0
	Lou-N	.931	64	195	47	18	4	-11
	Yr	.930	67	202	51	19	4	-11
1896	Lou-N	.939	32	132	38	11	4	8
	NY-N	.922	19	68	15	7	0	2
	Yr	.934	51	200	53	18	4	10
1897	NY-N	.952	110	513	127	32	17	16
1898	NY-N	.968	109	536	139	22	10	17
1899	NY-N	.952	82	312	123	22	8	13
1900	NY-N	.948	31	98	49	8	5	2
1901	NY-N	.967	84	361	107	16	11	-3
1902	Bos-A	.979	64	252	81	7	8	5
1903	NY-N	.986	85	450	123	8	9	10
1904	NY-N	.982	86	427	115	10	7	1
1905	StL-N	.958	41	165	63	10	4	2
	Det-A	.974	36	185	40	6	2	1
	Yr	.974	81	348	136	13	5	16
1906	Det-A	.978	49	193	79	6	3	7
	Was-A	.968	32	155	57	7	2	9
	Yr	.974	81	348	136	13	5	16
1907	Was-A	.971	64	271	64	10	4	-9
1908	Was-A	.982	41	178	38	4	2	1
Total	14	.966	1032	4498	1309	205	100	71

1B

YEAR	TM/L	PCT	G	PO	A	E	DP	FR
1895	Lou-N	.895	3	16	1	2	1	0
1896	Lou-N	1.000	1	7	1	0	0	0
1899	NY-N	1.000	3	17	2	0	1	1
1908	Was-A	1.000	1	3	0	0	0	0
Total	4	.959	8	43	4	2	2	1

2B

YEAR	TM/L	PCT	G	PO	A	E	DP	FR
1895	Lou-N	1.000	1	1	2	0	0	0

OF

YEAR	TM/L	PCT	G	PO	A	E	DP	FR
1898	NY-N	—	1	0	0	0	0	0

■ Jack Warner 3B

YEAR	TM/L	PCT	G	PO	A	E	DP	FR
1925	Det-A	1.000	10	3	15	0	3	-2
1926	Det-A	.956	95	105	175	13	9	-3
1927	Det-A	.947	138	156	277	24	34	-5
1928	Det-A	.944	52	62	107	10	6	5
1930	Bro-N	1.000	8	5	12	0	0	2
1931	Bro-N	1.000	1	0	1	0	0	0
1933	Phi-N	.939	30	26	66	6	8	4
Total	7	.950	334	357	653	3	60	1

2B

YEAR	TM/L	PCT	G	PO	A	E	DP	FR
1933	Phi-N	.973	71	177	224	11	45	-1

SS

YEAR	TM/L	PCT	G	PO	A	E	DP	FR
1926	Det-A	1.000	3	3	2	0	1	0
1928	Det-A	.917	7	9	13	2	4	0
1929	Bro-N	.945	17	34	52	5	8	-2
1931	Bro-N	1.000	2	2	4	0	0	2
1933	Phi-N	1.000	1	0	1	0	0	0
Total	5	.945	30	48	72	7	13	0

■ Bennie Warren C

YEAR	TM/L	PCT	G	PO	A	E	DP	FR
1939	Phi-N	.958	17	60	8	3	2	-4
1940	Phi-N	.975	97	326	63	10	9	-3
1941	Phi-N	.973	110	412	84	14	16	-4
1942	Phi-N	.978	78	264	50	9	4	-2
1946	NY-N	.965	30	103	8	4	0	1
1947	NY-N	1.000	3	2	0	0	0	-1
Total	6	.972	335	1167	213	0	31	-13

1B

YEAR	TM/L	PCT	G	PO	A	E	DP	FR
1940	Phi-N	.000	1	0	0	1	0	0
1942	Phi-N	.800	1	3	1	1	0	0
Total	2	.667	2	3	1	2	0	0

■ Rabbit Warstler SS

YEAR	TM/L	PCT	G	PO	A	E	DP	FR
1930	Bos-A	.947	54	100	149	14	30	-3
1931	Bos-A	.938	19	28	32	4	6	0
1932	Bos-A	.939	107	254	373	41	84	28
1933	Bos-A	.951	87	150	275	22	40	1
1934	Phi-A	.800	2	4	4	2	1	-1
1936	Bos-N	.948	74	157	278	24	59	13
1937	Bos-N	.942	149	298	493	49	85	-11
1938	Bos-N	.937	135	285	428	48	76	-6
1939	Bos-N	.953	49	96	145	12	35	-3
1940	Bos-N	—	1	0	0	0	0	0
	Chi-N	.939	28	49	90	9	13	-1
	Yr	.939	29	49	90	9	13	-1
Total	10	.942	705	1421	2267	225	429	17

2B

YEAR	TM/L	PCT	G	PO	A	E	DP	FR
1931	Bos-A	.933	42	74	135	15	20	1
1934	Phi-A	.969	107	228	392	20	87	17
1935	Phi-A	.959	136	308	482	34	94	2

YEAR	TM/L	PCT	G	PO	A	E	DP	FR
1936	Phi-A	.973	66	139	265	11	45	11
1938	Bos-N	.964	7	10	17	1	0	-1
1939	Bos-N	.970	43	89	135	7	36	1
1940	Bos-N	.974	24	32	43	2	15	0
	Chi-N	.948	17	41	51	5	7	0
	Yr	.960	41	73	94	7	22	0
Total	7	.963	442	921	1520	5	304	31
3B								
1931	Bos-A	1.000	1	1	1	0	0	0
1935	Phi-A	1.000	2	1	4	0	0	0
1939	Bos-N	.968	21	9	21	1	4	3
1940	Bos-N	—	2	0	0	0	0	0
Total	4	.974	26	11	26	1	4	3

■ Carl Warwick OF

YEAR	TM/L	PCT	G	PO	A	E	DP	FR
1961	LA-N	1.000	12	2	0	0	0	0
	StL-N	.970	48	94	2	3	1	-1
	Yr	.970	60	96	2	3	1	1
1962	StL-N	1.000	10	9	1	0	0	0
	Hou-N	.986	128	262	12	4	1	-3
	Yr	.986	138	271	13	4	1	-3
1963	Hou-N	.988	141	240	7	3	2	-2
1964	StL-N	.933	49	53	3	4	2	-1
1965	StL-N	.960	21	23	1	1	0	0
	Bal-A	1.000	3	3	0	0	0	-1
1966	Chi-N	1.000	10	8	1	0	0	1
Total	6	.980	422	694	27	5	6	-5
1B								
1963	Hou-N	1.000	2	20	1	0	0	0
1965	StL-N	1.000	4	23	0	0	4	0
Total	2	1.000	6	43	1	0	4	0

■ Jimmy Wasdell OF

YEAR	TM/L	PCT	G	PO	A	E	DP	FR
1937	Was-A	1.000	7	14	1	0	1	1
1938	Was-A	1.000	6	14	0	0	0	0
1940	Bro-N	.947	42	70	1	4	0	-5
1941	Bro-N	.956	54	84	2	4	0	-5
1942	Pit-N	.957	97	191	8	9	1	-8
1943	Phi-N	.974	56	108	5	3	0	-1
1944	Phi-N	.980	121	243	6	5	0	-8
1945	Phi-N	.967	65	142	4	5	1	-1
1946	Phi-N	.923	11	12	0	1	0	-3
	Cle-A	.000	3	0	0	1	0	0
Total	9	.966	462	878	27	2	3	-30
1B								
1937	Was-A	.995	21	182	10	1	18	-1
1938	Was-A	.996	26	220	12	1	26	-1
1939	Was-A	.964	28	255	15	10	24	-2
1940	Was-A	1.000	8	76	2	0	8	-1
	Bro-N	.977	17	122	5	3	9	-3
1941	Bro-N	1.000	15	101	5	0	5	-1
1942	Pit-N	.967	7	55	4	2	4	0
1943	Phi-N	.988	82	749	56	10	62	0
1944	Phi-N	1.000	4	43	0	0	6	-1
1945	Phi-N	.989	63	597	43	7	51	0
1946	Phi-N	1.000	2	3	1	0	1	0
	Cle-A	.939	4	28	3	2	0	0
Total	10	.986	277	2431	156	6	222	-10

■ Claudell Washington OF

YEAR	TM/L	PCT	G	PO	A	E	DP	FR
1974	Oak-A	.985	32	63	2	1	0	1
1975	Oak-A	.978	148	305	8	7	1	-2
1976	Oak-A	.963	126	276	10	11	2	0
1977	Tex-A	.978	127	255	11	6	3	3
1978	Tex-A	.917	7	11	0	1	0	-1
	Chi-A	.959	82	159	6	7	0	-2
	Yr	.957	89	170	6	8	0	-3
1979	Chi-A	.974	122	256	7	7	3	1
1980	Chi-A	.933	23	41	1	3	1	-2
	NY-N	.978	70	123	12	3	1	0
1981	Atl-N	.993	79	145	5	1	0	-4
1982	Atl-N	.950	139	221	9	12	3	-10
1983	Atl-N	.974	128	218	8	6	3	-4
1984	Atl-N	.967	107	170	4	6	0	-9
1985	Atl-N	.962	99	122	3	5	1	-20
1986	Atl-N	.957	38	44	1	2	0	-7
	NY-A	.985	39	66	0	1	0	-2
1987	NY-A	.988	72	166	3	2	1	3
1988	NY-A	.984	117	309	5	5	1	-2
1989	Cal-A	.975	100	187	6	5	2	-4
1990	Cal-A	1.000	9	19	1	0	0	0
	NY-A	1.000	21	42	2	0	0	1
	Yr	1.000	30	61	3	0	0	1
Total	17	.973	1685	3198	104	1	22	-60

■ Ron Washington SS

YEAR	TM/L	PCT	G	PO	A	E	DP	FR
1977	LA-N	.857	10	4	14	3	2	-2
1981	Min-A	.951	26	58	79	7	19	2
1982	Min-A	.972	91	127	186	9	38	-34
1983	Min-A	.962	81	121	204	13	49	-18
1984	Min-A	.978	71	60	114	4	19	-16
1985	Min-A	.951	31	20	38	3	5	-3
1986	Min-A	1.000	7	1	2	0	1	0
1987	Bal-A	—	1	0	0	0	0	0
1988	Cle-A	.933	54	83	141	16	26	-14
Total	9	.958	372	474	778	5	159	-85
2B								
1982	Min-A	.975	37	74	82	4	20	-10
1983	Min-A	.967	14	19	39	2	5	1
1984	Min-A	1.000	9	17	17	0	5	0
1985	Min-A	.953	24	31	50	4	8	-3
1986	Min-A	.917	16	10	12	2	3	-1
1987	Bal-A	1.000	3	3	2	0	0	0
1988	Cle-A	1.000	7	5	11	0	1	1
1989	Hou-N	—	1	0	0	0	0	0
Total	8	.969	111	159	213	2	42	-12
3B								
1982	Min-A	1.000	1	1	1	0	0	0
1983	Min-A	.750	1	0	3	1	0	0

YEAR	TM/L	PCT	G	PO	A	E	DP	FR
1984	Min-A	1.000	2	0	3	0	0	0
1985	Min-A	1.000	7	3	12	0	1	2
1986	Min-A	1.000	3	1	6	0	2	1
1987	Bal-A	1.000	20	15	40	0	3	4
1988	Cle-A	.944	8	7	10	1	2	0
1989	Hou-N	1.000	1	0	1	0	0	0
Total	8	.981	43	26	76	2	8	7
OF								
1981	Min-A	.875	2	6	1	1	0	1
1987	Bal-A	1.000	2	1	0	0	0	0
Total	2	.889	4	7	1	1	0	1
1B								
1985	Min-A	1.000	1	1	0	0	0	0

■ U L Washington SS

YEAR	TM/L	PCT	G	PO	A	E	DP	FR
1977	KC-A	.872	9	13	21	5	4	0
1978	KC-A	.927	49	47	55	8	8	-8
1979	KC-A	.970	50	62	131	6	31	-3
1980	KC-A	.957	152	237	467	32	86	-26
1981	KC-A	.973	98	135	297	12	58	-21
1982	KC-A	.961	117	173	371	22	63	-11
1983	KC-A	.947	140	201	448	36	91	-10
1984	KC-A	.961	61	81	166	10	40	0
1985	Mon-N	.968	9	5	25	1	7	-1
1986	Pit-N	.947	51	50	92	8	25	-8
1987	Pit-N	.833	1	1	4	1	0	0
Total	11	.956	737	1005	2077	141	413	-88
2B								
1978	KC-A	.986	19	32	37	1	10	-2
1979	KC-A	.949	46	112	111	12	37	4
1985	Mon-N	.978	43	70	104	4	22	-7
1986	Pit-N	1.000	3	0	5	0	0	0
Total	4	.965	111	214	257	7	69	-5
3B								
1979	KC-A	1.000	1	0	1	0	0	0
1985	Mon-N	.500	3	1	1	2	0	-1
1987	Pit-N	—	1	0	0	0	0	0
Total	3	.600	5	1	2	2	0	-1

■ John Wathan C

YEAR	TM/L	PCT	G	PO	A	E	DP	FR
1976	KC-A	.984	23	57	4	1	1	-1
1977	KC-A	.993	35	130	9	1	0	-1
1978	KC-A	.977	21	78	6	2	0	0
1979	KC-A	.987	23	70	5	1	0	-2
1980	KC-A	.982	77	306	25	6	5	-7
1981	KC-A	.979	73	300	26	7	1	-8
1982	KC-A	.980	120	463	38	10	3	-18
1983	KC-A	.985	92	360	32	6	5	-9
1984	KC-A	.975	59	213	21	6	2	4
1985	KC-A	.986	49	247	28	4	6	20
Total	10	.982	572	2224	194	4	23	-22
1B								
1976	KC-A	1.000	3	6	0	0	0	0
1977	KC-A	.963	5	26	0	1	2	-1
1978	KC-A	1.000	47	307	22	0	20	1
1979	KC-A	.993	49	264	19	2	30	0
1980	KC-A	.992	12	112	7	1	14	-1
1981	KC-A	1.000	1	1	0	0	0	0
1982	KC-A	1.000	3	19	2	0	2	0
1983	KC-A	.989	37	244	26	3	24	0
1984	KC-A	1.000	33	91	10	0	8	2
1985	KC-A	1.000	6	12	1	0	0	0
Total	10	.994	196	1082	87	7	100	1
OF								
1979	KC-A	1.000	3	2	0	0	0	0
1980	KC-A	.982	35	54	1	1	0	-3
1981	KC-A	1.000	16	15	2	0	0	1
1983	KC-A	1.000	9	11	0	0	0	0
1984	KC-A	—	1	0	0	0	0	0
Total	5	.988	64	82	3	1	0	-2

■ George Watkins OF

YEAR	TM/L	PCT	G	PO	A	E	DP	FR
1930	StL-N	.956	89	163	10	8	4	-3
1931	StL-N	.958	129	263	12	12	4	-1
1932	StL-N	.949	120	267	11	15	1	2
1933	StL-N	.953	135	295	9	15	3	-1
1934	NY-N	.944	81	165	3	10	1	-12
1935	Phi-N	.958	148	325	18	15	4	5
1936	Phi-N	.889	17	23	1	3	1	-3
	Bro-N	.969	98	183	5	6	1	-5
	Yr	.959	115	206	6	9	2	-8
Total	7	.954	817	1684	69	4	19	-18
1B								
1930	StL-N	.976	13	116	8	3	12	0
2B								
1930	StL-N	—	1	0	0	0	0	0

■ Bob Watson 1B

YEAR	TM/L	PCT	G	PO	A	E	DP	FR
1967	Hou-N	.958	3	21	2	1	0	0
1969	Hou-N	1.000	5	34	3	0	4	0
1970	Hou-N	.992	83	695	39	6	54	-7
1971	Hou-N	.986	45	339	16	5	28	-6
1972	Hou-N	1.000	2	13	1	0	3	0
1973	Hou-N	.987	26	150	2	2	7	-4
1974	Hou-N	1.000	35	96	5	0	7	-1
1975	Hou-N	.993	118	1077	69	8	106	-1
1976	Hou-N	.990	155	1395	96	15	126	-2
1977	Hou-N	.994	146	1331	118	9	100	12
1978	Hou-N	.993	128	974	95	9	63	10
1979	Hou-N	.993	44	371	33	3	23	3
	Cle-A	.988	58	525	47	7	58	2
1980	NY-A	.990	104	851	63	9	87	-2
1981	NY-A	.997	50	367	25	1	42	-1
1982	NY-A	1.000	6	40	0	0	5	0
	Atl-N	1.000	27	206	8	0	18	-3
1983	Atl-N	.984	34	280	19	5	23	-3
1984	Atl-N	.983	19	165	12	3	17	1
Total	17	.991	1088	8930	653	3	771	-3

YEAR	TM/L	PCT	G	PO	A	E	DP	FR
OF								
1968	Hou-N	.885	40	46	0	6	0	-8
1969	Hou-N	1.000	6	7	0	0	0	0
1970	Hou-N	1.000	1	1	0	0	0	0
1971	Hou-N	.985	87	131	2	2	0	-8
1972	Hou-N	.978	143	218	6	5	0	-10
1973	Hou-N	.969	142	271	8	9	0	-2
1974	Hou-N	.981	140	202	7	4	2	-16
1975	Hou-N	1.000	9	12	1	0	0	0
1982	Atl-N	1.000	2	2	0	0	0	0
Total	9	.972	570	890	24	6	2	-44
C								
1969	Hou-N	1.000	1	5	0	0	0	0
1970	Hou-N	1.000	6	11	1	0	0	0
1973	Hou-N	.929	3	12	1	1	0	-1
Total	3	.968	10	28	2	1	0	-1

■ Johnny Watwood OF

YEAR	TM/L	PCT	G	PO	A	E	DP	FR
1929	Chi-A	.942	77	188	7	12	2	-2
1930	Chi-A	.968	52	117	5	4	0	1
1931	Chi-A	.944	102	259	13	16	2	3
1932	Chi-A	.960	13	23	1	1	0	-1
	Bos-A	.945	46	101	3	6	0	-2
	Yr	.948	59	124	4	7	0	-3
1933	Bos-A	.950	9	19	0	1	0	0
Total	5	.948	299	707	29	0	4	-1
1B								
1930	Chi-A	.989	62	590	41	7	59	2
1931	Chi-A	1.000	4	18	1	0	1	0
1932	Bos-A	.959	18	149	16	7	17	1
1939	Phi-N	.933	2	14	0	1	0	-1
Total	4	.982	86	771	58	5	77	2

■ Roy Weatherly OF

YEAR	TM/L	PCT	G	PO	A	E	DP	FR
1936	Cle-A	.973	84	164	15	5	2	5
1937	Cle-A	.964	38	48	6	2	1	-1
1938	Cle-A	.975	55	110	7	3	3	5
1939	Cle-A	.961	76	146	3	6	1	-6
1940	Cle-A	.969	135	370	10	12	3	5
1941	Cle-A	.968	88	208	1	7	1	-10
1942	Cle-A	.991	117	324	7	3	4	0
1943	NY-A	.983	68	174	2	3	0	-3
1950	NY-N	1.000	15	21	2	0	0	0
Total	9	.975	676	1565	53	1	15	-5
3B								
1937	Cle-A	—	1	0	0	0	0	0

■ Buck Weaver SS

YEAR	TM/L	PCT	G	PO	A	E	DP	FR
1912	Chi-A	.915	147	342	425	71	53	-6
1913	Chi-A	.929	151	392	520	70	73	34
1914	Chi-A	.928	134	367	389	59	50	5
1915	Chi-A	.939	148	281	470	49	54	1
1916	Chi-A	.954	66	142	192	16	27	-2
1917	Chi-A	.983	10	20	39	1	9	5
1918	Chi-A	.941	98	191	319	32	50	0
1919	Chi-A	.966	43	87	141	8	14	3
1920	Chi-A	.963	25	56	75	5	18	1
Total	9	.935	822	1878	2570	311	348	41
3B								
1916	Chi-A	.941	85	124	193	20	22	9
1917	Chi-A	.949	107	154	218	20	18	4
1918	Chi-A	.966	11	10	18	1	0	-1
1919	Chi-A	.963	97	113	200	12	14	-3
1920	Chi-A	.933	127	153	276	31	15	-11
Total	5	.946	427	554	905	4	69	-2
2B								
1918	Chi-A	1.000	1	0	2	0	1	0

■ Farmer Weaver OF

YEAR	TM/L	PCT	G	PO	A	E	DP	FR
1888	Lou-a	.878	26	37	6	6	0	-2
1889	Lou-a	.918	123	249	30	25	4	0
1890	Lou-a	.933	127	227	23	18	4	1
1891	Lou-a	.956	132	294	33	15	7	17
1892	Lou-N	.902	122	185	18	22	3	-5
1893	Lou-N	.913	85	151	17	16	2	4
1894	Lou-N	.958	35	60	8	3	0	2
	Pit-N	.750	1	3	0	1	0	0
	Yr	.947	36	63	8	4	0	2
Total	7	.927	651	1206	135	106	20	17
C								
1889	Lou-a	1.000	2	4	1	0	0	0
1891	Lou-a	.947	4	16	2	1	0	0
1892	Lou-N	.853	15	48	16	11	1	-6
1893	Lou-N	.962	21	57	20	3	3	-5
1894	Lou-N	.912	17	47	15	6	4	-1
	Pit-N	.943	14	38	12	3	5	-1
	Yr	.926	31	85	27	9	9	-2
Total	5	.920	73	210	66	4	13	-13
SS								
1890	Lou-a	.714	2	4	1	2	1	-1
1894	Pit-N	.851	12	26	31	10	1	-7
Total	2	.838	14	30	32	2	2	-8
1B								
1892	Lou-N	.824	1	12	2	3	1	0
1894	Lou-N	.978	10	84	4	2	5	-1
Total	2	.953	11	96	6	5	6	-1
3B								
1889	Lou-a	1.000	1	3	0	0	0	0
1890	Lou-a	.600	1	2	1	2	0	-1
1894	Pit-N	.909	5	6	4	1	0	-1
Total	3	.850	7	9	8	3	0	-2
2B								
1889	Lou-a	.625	1	3	2	3	0	-1
1894	Lou-N	1.000	1	0	1	0	0	0
Total	2	.667	2	3	3	3	0	-1

■ Skeeter Webb SS

YEAR	TM/L	PCT	G	PO	A	E	DP	FR
1932	StL-N	—	1	0	0	0	0	0
1938	Cle-A	.964	13	25	28	2	7	-1
1939	Cle-A	.932	81	165	203	27	40	-8

YEAR	TM/L	PCT	G	PO	A	E	DP	FR
1940	Chi-A	.964	7	9	18	1	2	-1
1941	Chi-A	.842	5	5	11	3	1	1
1944	Chi-A	.944	135	202	461	39	81	-8
1945	Det-A	.957	104	215	343	25	71	**20**
1946	Det-A	1.000	8	8	12	0	2	2
1947	Det-A	.800	6	0	4	1	1	0
1948	Phi-A	.952	8	12	28	2	5	2
Total	10	.946	368	641	1108	100	210	7

2B

YEAR	TM/L	PCT	G	PO	A	E	DP	FR
1938	Cle-A	.600	2	2	1	2	0	-1
1940	Chi-A	.969	74	143	229	12	44	-9
1941	Chi-A	.940	18	45	49	6	12	5
1942	Chi-A	.961	29	62	87	6	14	1
1943	Chi-A	.953	54	118	169	14	35	-3
1944	Chi-A	1.000	5	19	19	0	7	4
1945	Det-A	1.000	11	30	25	0	8	3
1946	Det-A	.972	50	97	143	7	28	13
1947	Det-A	.992	30	52	74	1	9	12
1948	Phi-A	1.000	9	12	14	0	7	1
Total	10	.967	282	580	810	8	164	26

3B

YEAR	TM/L	PCT	G	PO	A	E	DP	FR
1938	Cle-A	1.000	3	2	3	0	0	0
1940	Chi-A	—	1	0	0	0	0	0
1941	Chi-A	.900	3	5	4	1	0	0
Total	3	.933	7	7	7	1	0	0

■ Earl Webb OF

YEAR	TM/L	PCT	G	PO	A	E	DP	FR
1927	Chi-N	.959	86	171	14	8	5	1
1928	Chi-N	.986	31	65	4	1	0	1
1930	Bos-A	.959	116	200	8	9	4	-5
1931	Bos-A	.948	151	270	21	**16**	5	-2
1932	Bos-A	.964	50	74	7	3	2	-6
	Det-A	.955	85	163	8	8	0	-2
	Yr	.958	135	237	15	11	2	-8
1933	Det-A	1.000	2	1	0	0	0	-1
	Chi-A	1.000	16	20	2	0	0	0
	Yr	1.000	18	21	2	0	0	-1
Total	6	.958	537	964	64	5	16	-14

1B

YEAR	TM/L	PCT	G	PO	A	E	DP	FR
1932	Bos-A	.938	2	14	1	1	2	0
1933	Chi-A	.941	10	108	3	7	8	-2
Total	2	.940	12	122	4	8	10	-2

■ Mitch Webster OF

YEAR	TM/L	PCT	G	PO	A	E	DP	FR
1983	Tor-A	1.000	7	5	0	0	0	0
1984	Tor-A	.875	10	14	0	2	0	1
1985	Tor-A	—	2	0	0	0	0	0
	Mon-N	.993	64	133	3	1	0	3
1986	Mon-N	.977	146	325	12	8	3	6
1987	Mon-N	.982	153	266	8	5	0	-4
1988	Chi-N	.971	65	169	1	5	0	0
	Mon-N	.994	71	153	2	1	0	-1
	Yr	.982	136	322	3	6	0	-1
1989	Chi-N	.965	74	161	3	6	0	1
1990	Cle-A	.991	118	330	1	3	0	3
Total	8	.981	710	1556	30	1	3	9

1B

YEAR	TM/L	PCT	G	PO	A	E	DP	FR
1984	Tor-A	1.000	1	2	0	0	1	0
1990	Cle-A	.895	3	15	2	2	2	0
Total	2	.905	4	17	2	2	3	0

■ Ray Webster 1B

YEAR	TM/L	PCT	G	PO	A	E	DP	FR
1967	KC-A	.989	83	615	41	7	42	-3
1968	Oak-A	.988	55	454	27	6	33	-1
1969	Oak-A	1.000	13	89	8	0	6	1
1970	SD-N	.981	15	99	7	2	14	-1
1971	Oak-A	1.000	1	1	0	0	0	0
	Chi-N	1.000	1	2	1	0	1	0
Total	5	.989	168	1260	84	5	96	-4

OF

YEAR	TM/L	PCT	G	PO	A	E	DP	FR
1967	KC-A	.963	15	24	2	1	1	1
1970	SD-N	—	1	0	0	0	0	0
Total	2	.963	16	24	2	1	1	1

■ Phil Weintraub 1B

YEAR	TM/L	PCT	G	PO	A	E	DP	FR
1935	NY-N	.975	19	148	11	4	9	0
1938	Phi-N	.988	98	913	75	12	70	2
1944	NY-N	.992	99	928	72	8	72	3
1945	NY-N	.993	77	774	60	6	49	3
Total	4	.990	293	2763	218	0	200	8

OF

YEAR	TM/L	PCT	G	PO	A	E	DP	FR
1933	NY-N	.667	6	4	0	2	0	-2
1934	NY-N	.944	20	34	0	2	0	-3
1935	NY-N	1.000	7	4	0	0	0	0
1937	Cin-N	.976	47	78	3	2	1	-4
	NY-N	1.000	1	1	0	0	0	0
	Yr	.976	48	79	3	2	1	-4
Total	4	.954	81	121	3	6	1	-9

■ Al Weis 2B

YEAR	TM/L	PCT	G	PO	A	E	DP	FR
1962	Chi-A	.500	1	0	1	1	0	0
1963	Chi-A	.990	48	88	103	2	28	12
1964	Chi-A	.966	116	199	255	16	64	14
1965	Chi-A	.975	74	109	122	6	27	**24**
1966	Chi-A	.987	96	130	173	4	44	**32**
1967	Chi-A	.986	32	25	46	1	2	8
1968	NY-N	.981	29	42	62	2	15	3
1969	NY-N	.970	43	73	90	5	23	9
1970	NY-N	.952	44	60	59	6	10	1
1971	NY-N	1.000	5	4	3	0	1	0
Total	10	.975	488	730	914	3	214	103

SS

YEAR	TM/L	PCT	G	PO	A	E	DP	FR
1962	Chi-A	.882	4	3	12	2	0	0
1963	Chi-A	.926	27	35	65	8	13	3
1964	Chi-A	.762	9	4	12	5	1	-2
1965	Chi-A	1.000	7	6	7	0	4	2
1966	Chi-A	.917	18	21	45	6	8	5
1967	Chi-A	1.000	13	5	16	0	3	3
1968	NY-N	.958	59	96	180	12	28	3
1969	NY-N	.960	52	65	128	8	27	4
1970	NY-N	.949	15	15	22	2	3	2
Total	9	.945	204	250	487	3	87	20

3B

YEAR	TM/L	PCT	G	PO	A	E	DP	FR
1962	Chi-A	—	1	0	0	0	0	0
1963	Chi-A	—	1	0	0	0	0	0
1965	Chi-A	1.000	2	1	1	0	0	0
1968	NY-N	1.000	2	0	2	0	0	0
1969	NY-N	—	1	0	0	0	0	0
1971	NY-N	1.000	2	1	3	0	1	1
Total	6	1.000	9	2	6	0	1	1

OF

YEAR	TM/L	PCT	G	PO	A	E	DP	FR
1964	Chi-A	1.000	2	2	0	0	0	0
1965	Chi-A	1.000	2	1	0	0	0	0
Total	2	1.000	4	3	0	0	0	0

■ Walt Weiss SS

YEAR	TM/L	PCT	G	PO	A	E	DP	FR
1987	Oak-A	.974	11	8	30	1	4	5
1988	Oak-A	.979	147	254	431	15	83	10
1989	Oak-A	.953	84	106	195	15	44	-14
1990	Oak-A	.979	137	194	373	12	77	-26
Total	4	.974	379	562	1029	3	208	-25

■ Johnny Welaj OF

YEAR	TM/L	PCT	G	PO	A	E	DP	FR
1939	Was-A	.975	55	113	2	3	1	-1
1940	Was-A	.978	53	132	1	3	0	3
1941	Was-A	.979	19	47	0	1	0	1
1943	Phi-A	.960	72	187	3	8	0	2
Total	4	.970	199	479	6	5	1	5

■ Curt Welch OF

YEAR	TM/L	PCT	G	PO	A	E	DP	FR
1884	Tol-a	.888	107	**207**	24	29	3	16
1885	StL-a	**.946**	112	**236**	25	15	5	14
1886	StL-a	**.952**	138	**297**	19	16	4	**15**
1887	StL-a	.941	123	**336**	29	23	7	**21**
1888	Phi-a	.952	135	272	23	15	6	6
1889	Phi-a	.923	125	282	30	26	10	8
1890	Phi-a	.919	103	225	24	22	8	14
	Bal-a	.974	17	35	3	1	1	2
	Yr	.926	120	260	27	23	9	16
1891	Bal-a	.946	113	258	25	16	4	11
1892	Bal-N	.905	63	129	4	14	1	-4
	Cin-N	.925	25	60	2	5	1	0
	Yr	.911	88	189	6	19	2	-4
1893	Lou-N	.912	14	29	2	3	0	0
Total	10	.933	1075	2366	210	185	50	103

2B

YEAR	TM/L	PCT	G	PO	A	E	DP	FR
1884	Tol-a	1.000	2	0	3	0	1	1
1886	StL-a	.600	2	3	0	2	1	-1
1887	StL-a	.765	8	21	18	12	3	-2
1888	Phi-a	.636	3	5	2	4	0	-1
1891	Bal-a	.941	21	48	79	8	14	8
Total	5	.873	36	77	102	6	19	5

1B

YEAR	TM/L	PCT	G	PO	A	E	DP	FR
1884	Tol-a	.833	1	5	0	1	0	0
1887	StL-a	1.000	1	13	0	0	0	0
1890	Bal-a	1.000	2	9	0	0	0	0
Total	3	.964	4	27	0	1	0	0

C

YEAR	TM/L	PCT	G	PO	A	E	DP	FR
1884	Tol-a	.667	2	0	2	1	0	0

SS

YEAR	TM/L	PCT	G	PO	A	E	DP	FR
1891	Bal-a	1.000	2	0	2	0	0	0

■ Frank Welch OF

YEAR	TM/L	PCT	G	PO	A	E	DP	FR
1919	Phi-A	.909	15	38	2	4	0	0
1920	Phi-A	.937	97	194	14	14	4	-5
1921	Phi-A	.943	104	251	16	16	1	3
1922	Phi-A	.949	104	191	12	11	2	0
1923	Phi-A	.967	117	253	13	9	4	3
1924	Phi-A	.985	74	120	15	2	2	1
1925	Phi-A	.968	57	85	6	3	3	-3
1926	Phi-A	.975	49	75	4	2	1	-5
1927	Bos-A	1.000	6	9	3	0	1	2
Total	9	.955	623	1216	85	1	18	-4

■ Brad Wellman 2B

YEAR	TM/L	PCT	G	PO	A	E	DP	FR
1982	SF-N	1.000	2	0	1	0	0	0
1983	SF-N	.965	74	91	160	9	20	1
1984	SF-N	.977	54	103	151	6	23	8
1985	SF-N	.983	36	55	60	2	11	-1
1986	SF-N	—	1	0	0	0	0	0
1987	LA-N	1.000	1	0	1	0	0	0
1988	KC-A	.972	46	54	85	4	21	13
1989	KC-A	.995	64	74	128	1	27	15
Total	8	.978	278	377	586	2	108	36

SS

YEAR	TM/L	PCT	G	PO	A	E	DP	FR
1983	SF-N	1.000	2	3	7	0	1	1
1984	SF-N	.967	34	43	102	5	14	8
1985	SF-N	.750	3	1	2	1	2	0
1986	SF-N	1.000	8	3	7	0	0	0
1987	LA-N	1.000	1	1	1	0	0	0
1988	KC-A	.929	15	13	13	2	4	0
1989	KC-A	.989	34	30	56	1	15	5
Total	7	.969	97	94	188	9	36	14

3B

YEAR	TM/L	PCT	G	PO	A	E	DP	FR
1984	SF-N	1.000	9	5	5	0	0	0
1985	SF-N	.902	25	10	45	6	2	-1
1986	SF-N	1.000	1	0	3	0	1	1
1987	LA-N	1.000	1	2	1	0	1	1
1988	KC-A	1.000	4	0	3	0	2	1
1989	KC-A	—	3	0	0	0	0	0
Total	6	.925	43	17	57	6	6	2

■ Jimmy Welsh OF

YEAR	TM/L	PCT	G	PO	A	E	DP	FR
1925	Bos-N	.960	116	237	**27**	11	7	5
1926	Bos-N	.965	129	283	**23**	11	**8**	8
1927	Bos-N	.969	129	377	24	13	6	10
1928	NY-N	.981	117	310	8	6	3	-3
1929	NY-N	.940	35	43	4	3	1	-6
	Bos-N	.979	51	177	6	4	1	13
	Yr	.970	86	220	10	7	2	7
1930	Bos-N	.980	110	329	8	7	2	9
Total	6	.971	687	1756	100	5	28	36

2B

YEAR	TM/L	PCT	G	PO	A	E	DP	FR
1925	Bos-N	1.000	3	4	9	0	0	-1

1B

YEAR	TM/L	PCT	G	PO	A	E	DP	FR
1927	Bos-N	1.000	1	4	0	0	0	0

■ Billy Werber 3B

YEAR	TM/L	PCT	G	PO	A	E	DP	FR
1930	NY-A	—	1	0	0	0	0	0
1933	NY-A	—	1	0	0	0	0	0
	Bos-A	.936	38	39	63	7	7	-1
	Yr	.936	39	39	**63**	7	7	**-1**
1934	Bos-A	.941	130	136	323	29	25	23
1935	Bos-A	.942	123	**174**	264	27	20	17
1936	Bos-A	.935	101	112	161	19	16	-14
1937	Phi-A	.958	125	132	260	17	25	0
1938	Phi-A	.935	134	168	266	30	21	0
1939	Cin-N	.933	147	165	**308**	**34**	**32**	**13**
1940	Cin-N	**.962**	143	139	287	17	24	3
1941	Cin-N	.959	107	120	256	16	30	12
1942	Cin-N	.927	93	79	227	24	14	10
Total	11	.944	1143	1264	2415	220	214	63

SS

YEAR	TM/L	PCT	G	PO	A	E	DP	FR
1930	NY-A	.955	3	12	9	1	3	1
1933	Bos-A	.910	71	128	194	32	36	-15
1934	Bos-A	.889	22	43	69	14	14	-3
Total	3	.906	96	183	272	7	53	-17

OF

YEAR	TM/L	PCT	G	PO	A	E	DP	FR
1936	Bos-A	.980	45	90	6	2	0	1
1937	Phi-A	1.000	3	9	0	0	0	0
Total	2	.981	48	99	6	2	0	1

2B

YEAR	TM/L	PCT	G	PO	A	E	DP	FR
1933	Bos-A	1.000	2	2	2	0	0	0
1936	Bos-A	—	1	0	0	0	0	0
Total	2	1.000	3	2	2	0	0	0

■ Perry Werden 1B

YEAR	TM/L	PCT	G	PO	A	E	DP	FR
1890	Tol-a	.972	124	1178	59	**35**	57	4
1891	Bal-a	.980	139	1422	58	30	79	1
1892	StL-N	.982	149	1467	102	28	81	12
1893	StL-N	.968	124	1194	81	**42**	75	2
1897	Lou-N	.984	**131**	**1318**	116	23	70	**18**
Total	5	.978	667	6579	416	158	362	37

OF

YEAR	TM/L	PCT	G	PO	A	E	DP	FR
1884	StL-U	1.000	6	3	0	0	0	-2
1888	Was-N	.857	3	6	0	1	0	0
1890	Tol-a	1.000	5	12	2	0	0	2
1893	StL-N	.500	1	0	1	1	0	0
Total	4	.923	15	21	3	2	0	0

■ Don Werner C

YEAR	TM/L	PCT	G	PO	A	E	DP	FR
1975	Cin-N	.923	7	10	2	1	0	1
1976	Cin-N	1.000	3	7	2	0	0	1
1977	Cin-N	1.000	10	40	4	0	2	1
1978	Cin-N	.987	49	214	21	3	4	5
1980	Cin-N	.962	24	119	6	5	1	1
1982	Tex-A	.980	22	91	5	2	2	1
Total	6	.979	115	481	40	1	9	10

■ Joe Werrick 3B

YEAR	TM/L	PCT	G	PO	A	E	DP	FR
1886	Lou-a	.853	136	162	257	72	9	-1
1887	Lou-a	.831	136	153	286	**89**	12	0
1888	Lou-a	.811	89	96	170	62	9	-14
Total	3	.834	361	411	713	223	30	-15

SS

YEAR	TM/L	PCT	G	PO	A	E	DP	FR
1884	StP-U	.756	9	8	26	11	0	0
1888	Lou-a	.776	11	12	33	13	0	-2
Total	2	.767	20	20	59	4	0	-2

2B

YEAR	TM/L	PCT	G	PO	A	E	DP	FR
1888	Lou-a	.949	8	24	32	3	2	4

OF

YEAR	TM/L	PCT	G	PO	A	E	DP	FR
1888	Lou-a	.750	3	3	0	1	0	-1

■ Don Wert 3B

YEAR	TM/L	PCT	G	PO	A	E	DP	FR
1963	Det-A	.957	47	33	99	6	6	4
1964	Det-A	.965	142	126	283	15	30	1
1965	Det-A	**.976**	**161**	163	331	12	33	5
1966	Det-A	.972	150	128	253	11	20	-18
1967	Det-A	.978	140	112	280	9	21	-5
1968	Det-A	.966	150	142	284	15	22	-6
1969	Det-A	.966	129	114	259	13	20	0
1970	Det-A	.953	117	94	191	14	20	-2
1971	Was-A	.818	12	7	2	1	1	-1
Total	9	.968	1043	914	1987	7	173	-22

2B

YEAR	TM/L	PCT	G	PO	A	E	DP	FR
1963	Det-A	.968	21	36	54	3	10	0
1965	Det-A	1.000	1	1	0	0	0	0
1970	Det-A	1.000	2	1	2	0	0	0
1971	Was-A	1.000	1	2	1	0	0	-1
Total	4	.970	25	40	57	3	10	-1

SS

YEAR	TM/L	PCT	G	PO	A	E	DP	FR
1963	Det-A	.973	8	16	20	1	4	-1
1964	Det-A	.947	4	8	10	1	3	-1
1965	Det-A	1.000	3	0	6	0	1	0
1967	Det-A	1.000	1	1	2	0	0	1
1968	Det-A	1.000	1	2	0	0	0	0
1971	Was-A	1.000	7	5	15	0	1	-2
Total	6	.977	25	32	53	2	10	-4

■ Vic Wertz OF

YEAR	TM/L	PCT	G	PO	A	E	DP	FR
1947	Det-A	.965	82	160	6	6	0	-7
1948	Det-A	.954	98	196	11	10	3	-4
1949	Det-A	.981	**155**	302	14	6	4	-5
1950	Det-A	.967	145	286	5	10	3	-12
1951	Det-A	.989	131	254	7	3	1	-4
1952	Det-A	.986	79	134	8	2	3	-1
	StL-A	.955	36	64	0	3	0	-6
	Yr	.976	115	198	8	5	3	-6
1953	StL-A	.974	121	243	15	7	4	6
1954	Bal-A	.963	27	47	5	2	1	1

YEAR	TM/L	PCT	G	PO	A	E	DP	FR
	Cle-A	1.000	5	10	0	0	0	0
	Yr	.969	32	57	5	2	1	1
1955	Cle-A	1.000	9	13	1	0	1	0
Total	9	.973	888	1709	72	9	20	-32
1B								
1954	Cle-A	.989	83	557	52	7	57	2
1955	Cle-A	.984	63	449	33	8	49	-3
1956	Cle-A	.991	133	971	77	9	99	1
1957	Cle-A	.988	139	1025	83	14	122	-2
1958	Cle-A	.980	8	44	5	1	5	0
1959	Bos-A	.992	64	440	38	4	44	2
1960	Bos-A	.987	117	841	78	12	89	3
1961	Bos-A	.991	86	664	67	7	65	4
1962	Det-A	.988	16	75	9	1	5	0
1963	Min-A	1.000	6	32	5	0	2	1
Total	10	.989	715	5098	447	3	537	8

■ Max West OF

YEAR	TM/L	PCT	G	PO	A	E	DP	FR
1938	Bos-N	.986	109	205	6	3	2	-7
1939	Bos-N	.974	124	287	8	8	2	3
1940	Bos-N	.975	102	220	16	6	1	8
1941	Bos-N	.981	132	302	13	6	5	6
1942	Bos-N	.965	50	106	4	4	0	0
1946	Cin-N	.952	58	112	6	6	3	-3
1948	Pit-N	1.000	16	11	0	0	0	-1
Total	7	.975	591	1243	53	3	13	6
1B								
1938	Bos-N	.985	7	63	2	1	2	-1
1940	Bos-N	.986	36	338	24	5	33	0
1942	Bos-N	.991	85	807	47	8	67	0
1946	Bos-N	1.000	1	3	0	0	0	0
1948	Pit-N	.991	32	198	20	2	14	1
Total	5	.989	161	1409	93	6	116	-1

■ Sam West OF

YEAR	TM/L	PCT	G	PO	A	E	DP	FR
1927	Was-A	.939	18	28	3	2	0	-1
1928	Was-A	.996	116	210	13	1	0	-10
1929	Was-A	.978	139	376	25	9	8	15
1930	Was-A	.972	118	310	8	9	1	3
1931	Was-A	.990	127	402	13	4	3	21
1932	Was-A	.979	143	450	15	10	7	14
1933	StL-A	.988	127	329	14	4	3	7
1934	StL-A	.972	120	303	14	9	3	5
1935	StL-A	.989	135	449	7	5	2	13
1936	StL-A	.983	148	442	10	8	2	4
1937	StL-A	.987	105	298	17	4	6	8
1938	StL-A	.971	41	101	0	3	0	0
	Was-A	.983	85	221	4	4	3	-5
	Yr	.979	126	322	4	7	3	-5
1939	Was-A	.992	89	232	7	2	3	-3
1940	Was-A	1.000	9	18	0	0	0	0
1941	Was-A	1.000	8	19	0	0	0	0
1942	Chi-A	.983	45	112	1	2	1	0
Total	16	.983	1573	4300	151	6	42	71
1B								
1939	Was-A	.972	17	133	6	4	9	-2
1940	Was-A	.990	12	95	7	1	13	0
Total	2	.980	29	228	13	5	22	-2

■ Wally Westlake OF

YEAR	TM/L	PCT	G	PO	A	E	DP	FR
1947	Pit-N	.988	109	239	8	3	0	-6
1948	Pit-N	.976	125	274	8	7	2	1
1949	Pit-N	.982	143	319	12	6	4	3
1950	Pit-N	.991	123	329	4	3	3	-1
1951	Pit-N	1.000	11	17	2	0	1	1
	StL-N	.982	68	154	7	3	1	0
	Yr	.984	79	171	9	3	2	1
1952	StL-N	1.000	15	60	3	0	0	7
	Cin-N	.992	56	127	5	1	0	4
	Cle-A	1.000	28	44	4	0	2	3
	Yr	1.000	43	104	7	0	2	10
1953	Cle-A	.963	72	128	3	5	2	-5
1954	Cle-A	.964	70	131	1	5	0	-5
1955	Cle-A	1.000	7	10	1	0	0	1
	Bal-A	1.000	7	8	0	0	0	-2
	Yr	1.000	14	18	1	0	0	-1
Total	9	.983	834	1840	58	3	15	1
3B								
1951	Pit-N	.908	34	32	87	12	12	5

■ Wes Westrum C

YEAR	TM/L	PCT	G	PO	A	E	DP	FR
1947	NY-N	1.000	2	8	2	0	0	0
1948	NY-N	.981	63	179	25	4	4	8
1949	NY-N	.980	62	224	18	5	4	0
1950	NY-N	.999	139	608	71	1	21	10
1951	NY-N	.987	122	554	62	8	9	8
1952	NY-N	.978	112	481	64	12	11	-3
1953	NY-N	.982	106	441	53	9	9	4
1954	NY-N	.985	98	419	45	7	8	12
1955	NY-N	.987	68	280	27	4	5	10
1956	NY-N	.982	67	297	27	6	7	15
1957	NY-N	.966	63	148	21	6	4	2
Total	11	.985	902	3639	415	2	82	66
3B								
1953	NY-N	1.000	1	0	3	0	0	0

■ Bert Whaling C

YEAR	TM/L	PCT	G	PO	A	E	DP	FR
1913	Bos-N	.990	77	328	84	4	4	2
1914	Bos-N	.981	59	272	91	7	7	11
1915	Bos-N	.986	69	292	68	5	2	1
Total	3	.986	205	892	243	6	13	14

■ Mack Wheat C

YEAR	TM/L	PCT	G	PO	A	E	DP	FR
1915	Bro-N	.957	8	19	3	1	1	0
1916	Bro-N	1.000	2	5	0	0	0	0
1917	Bro-N	.968	18	68	22	3	0	3
1918	Bro-N	.966	38	151	50	7	1	-1
1919	Bro-N	.944	38	131	39	10	3	-4
1920	Phi-N	.961	74	262	105	15	8	9
1921	Phi-N	.980	9	39	11	1	1	4

YEAR	TM/L	PCT	G	PO	A	E	DP	FR
Total	7	.961	187	675	230	7	14	11
OF								
1917	Bro-N	1.000	9	9	1	0	0	1
1918	Bro-N	.917	7	11	0	1	0	-1
Total	2	.955	16	20	1	1	0	0

■ Zach Wheat OF

YEAR	TM/L	PCT	G	PO	A	E	DP	FR
1909	Bro-N	.952	26	54	5	3	1	2
1910	Bro-N	.962	156	354	21	15	6	11
1911	Bro-N	.955	136	287	12	14	0	-1
1912	Bro-N	.968	120	285	13	10	2	6
1913	Bro-N	.978	135	338	13	8	7	13
1914	Bro-N	.962	144	331	21	14	5	13
1915	Bro-N	.953	144	345	18	18	4	15
1916	Bro-N	.975	149	333	14	9	0	8
1917	Bro-N	.979	98	216	12	5	5	7
1918	Bro-N	.979	105	219	11	5	2	2
1919	Bro-N	.971	137	297	9	9	2	-1
1920	Bro-N	.971	148	287	10	9	5	-6
1921	Bro-N	.965	148	283	18	11	3	-5
1922	Bro-N	.991	152	317	14	3	1	-1
1923	Bro-N	.908	87	135	4	14	1	-15
1924	Bro-N	.965	139	288	13	11	4	4
1925	Bro-N	.962	149	320	7	13	2	-9
1926	Bro-N	.955	102	202	9	10	3	-4
1927	Phi-A	.983	62	105	8	2	1	-3
Total	19	.966	2337	4996	232	183	54	36

■ Harry Wheeler OF

YEAR	TM/L	PCT	G	PO	A	E	DP	FR
1879	Cin-N	1.000	1	2	0	0	0	0
1880	Cle-N	1.000	1	2	0	0	0	0
	Cin-N	.750	17	37	5	14	1	1
	Yr	.759	18	39	5	14	1	1
1882	Cin-a	.808	64	94	11	25	1	-4
1883	Col-a	.803	82	130	13	35	1	-2
1884	StL-a	.600	5	6	0	4	0	-1
	KC-U	.769	13	29	1	9	0	-1
	CP-U	.774	37	45	3	14	0	-5
	Bal-U	.815	17	18	4	5	0	-1
	Yr	.781	67	92	8	28	0	-6
Total	5	.791	237	363	37	106	3	-12
1B								
1882	Cin-a	.892	12	80	3	10	10	-1
2B								
1883	Col-a	1.000	1	1	2	0	1	0

■ Bobby Wheelock SS

YEAR	TM/L	PCT	G	PO	A	E	DP	FR
1887	Bos-N	.878	20	33	68	14	5	1
1890	Col-a	.885	52	92	162	33	12	-1
1891	Col-a	.899	136	248	474	81	65	19
Total	3	.894	208	373	704	128	82	19
OF								
1887	Bos-N	.878	28	35	1	5	0	-4
2B								
1887	Bos-N	.727	4	5	3	3	0	-2

■ Pete Whisenant OF

YEAR	TM/L	PCT	G	PO	A	E	DP	FR
1952	Bos-N	.973	14	34	4	1	2	3
1955	StL-N	.964	40	76	4	3	1	6
1956	Chi-N	.992	93	242	6	2	0	0
1957	Cin-N	.982	43	54	0	1	0	2
1958	Cin-N	1.000	66	122	3	0	1	3
1959	Cin-N	.966	21	27	1	1	1	-1
1960	Cle-A	1.000	2	1	0	0	0	0
	Was-A	1.000	47	68	2	0	0	2
	Yr	1.000	49	69	2	0	0	2
1961	Min-A	1.000	5	2	0	0	0	0
	Cin-N	1.000	12	4	0	0	0	0
Total	8	.988	343	630	18	8	5	15
2B								
1958	Cin-N	—	1	0	0	0	0	0
C								
1961	Cin-N	.500	1	0	1	1	0	0
3B								
1961	Cin-N	1.000	1	0	1	0	0	0

■ Lew Whistler 1B

YEAR	TM/L	PCT	G	PO	A	E	DP	FR
1890	NY-N	.982	45	490	10	9	28	-2
1891	NY-N	.982	7	54	1	1	3	-1
1892	Bal-N	.973	51	540	26	16	21	-1
	Lou-N	.978	72	773	32	18	52	-2
	Yr	.976	123	1313	58	34	73	-3
1893	Lou-N	.946	13	132	8	8	8	0
	StL-N	1.000	1	10	0	0	1	0
	Yr	.949	14	142	8	8	9	0
Total	4	.976	189	1999	77	2	113	-6
SS								
1891	NY-N	.852	33	52	104	27	7	-5
OF								
1891	NY-N	.742	22	22	1	8	0	-6
1892	Bal-N	—	1	0	0	0	0	0
1893	StL-N	.923	9	11	1	1	0	-1
Total	3	.795	32	33	2	9	0	-7
2B								
1891	NY-N	.806	6	12	17	7	1	-1
1892	Lou-N	.958	10	16	30	2	2	1
Total	2	.893	16	28	47	9	3	0
3B								
1891	NY-N	.571	5	3	5	6	0	-4

■ Lou Whitaker 2B

YEAR	TM/L	PCT	G	PO	A	E	DP	FR
1977	Det-A	1.000	9	17	18	0	2	-4
1978	Det-A	.978	136	301	458	17	95	-11
1979	Det-A	.986	126	280	369	9	103	2
1980	Det-A	.985	143	340	428	12	93	-3
1981	Det-A	.985	108	227	354	9	77	5
1982	Det-A	.988	149	331	470	10	120	12
1983	Det-A	.983	160	299	447	13	92	-13
1984	Det-A	.979	142	290	405	15	83	-11
1985	Det-A	.985	150	314	414	11	101	-16

YEAR	TM/L	PCT	G	PO	A	E	DP	FR
1986	Det-A	.984	141	276	421	11	98	-1
1987	Det-A	.976	148	275	416	17	99	-14
1988	Det-A	.984	110	218	284	8	53	-23
1989	Det-A	.985	146	327	393	11	99	-1
1990	Det-A	.991	130	286	372	6	98	12
Total	14	.984	1798	3781	5249	149	1213	-66

■ Steve Whitaker OF

YEAR	TM/L	PCT	G	PO	A	E	DP	FR
1966	NY-A	.955	31	61	3	3	0	1
1967	NY-A	.982	114	202	12	4	6	5
1968	NY-A	.917	14	20	2	2	0	-1
1969	Sea-A	.962	39	45	5	2	0	2
1970	SF-N	.857	9	6	0	1	0	-1
Total	5	.967	207	334	22	2	6	6

■ Devon White OF

YEAR	TM/L	PCT	G	PO	A	E	DP	FR
1985	Cal-A	1.000	16	10	1	0	0	2
1986	Cal-A	.961	28	49	0	2	0	3
1987	Cal-A	.980	159	424	16	9	3	25
1988	Cal-A	.976	116	364	7	9	2	10
1989	Cal-A	.989	154	430	10	5	3	10
1990	Cal-A	.972	122	302	11	9	4	3
Total	6	.979	595	1579	45	4	12	53

■ Don White OF

YEAR	TM/L	PCT	G	PO	A	E	DP	FR
1948	Phi-A	.957	54	108	3	5	1	-1
1949	Phi-A	.989	47	89	4	1	0	0
Total	2	.971	101	197	7	6	1	-1
3B								
1948	Phi-A	.923	17	14	34	4	5	1
1949	Phi-A	.875	4	2	5	1	2	0
Total	2	.917	21	16	39	5	7	1

■ Frank White 2B

YEAR	TM/L	PCT	G	PO	A	E	DP	FR
1973	KC-A	.952	11	19	40	3	12	2
1974	KC-A	.962	50	67	84	6	23	11
1975	KC-A	.987	67	124	179	4	35	10
1976	KC-A	.973	130	256	391	18	76	16
1977	KC-A	.989	152	310	434	8	86	-3
1978	KC-A	.978	140	325	385	16	96	-17
1979	KC-A	.982	125	317	332	12	78	-22
1980	KC-A	.988	153	395	448	10	103	-7
1981	KC-A	.988	93	226	263	6	70	-17
1982	KC-A	.978	144	361	389	17	99	-15
1983	KC-A	.990	145	390	442	8	123	7
1984	KC-A	.985	129	299	425	11	97	13
1985	KC-A	.980	149	342	490	17	101	11
1986	KC-A	.987	151	316	439	10	91	0
1987	KC-A	.987	152	320	458	10	89	8
1988	KC-A	.994	148	293	426	4	88	7
1989	KC-A	.985	132	238	407	10	64	7
1990	KC-A	.978	79	142	218	8	51	3
Total	18	.984	2150	4740	6250	178	1382	14
SS								
1973	KC-A	.937	37	52	81	9	24	5
1974	KC-A	.967	29	37	81	4	16	13
1975	KC-A	.953	42	55	86	7	20	4
1976	KC-A	.964	37	41	92	5	14	5
1977	KC-A	1.000	4	0	3	0	0	0
1986	KC-A	1.000	1	1	2	0	1	0
Total	6	.955	150	186	345	5	75	27
3B								
1974	KC-A	.951	16	15	24	2	1	1
1975	KC-A	1.000	4	1	7	0	1	1
1986	KC-A	—	1	0	0	0	0	0
Total	3	.959	21	16	31	2	2	2
OF								
1989	KC-A	—	1	0	0	0	0	0
1990	KC-A	—	1	0	0	0	0	0
Total	2	—	2	0	0	0	0	0
C								
1975	KC-A	.833	1	2	3	1	0	0

■ Deacon White 3B

YEAR	TM/L	PCT	G	PO	A	E	DP	FR
1876	Chi-N	—	1	0	0	0	0	0
1878	Cin-N	1.000	1	0	1	0	0	0
1881	Buf-N	.875	7	16	12	4	1	-1
1882	Buf-N	.837	63	59	111	33	6	-12
1883	Buf-N	.797	77	84	128	54	8	-12
1884	Buf-N	.825	108	113	198	66	11	-8
1885	Buf-N	.888	98	118	198	40	12	1
1886	Det-N	.847	124	131	245	68	18	-9
1887	Det-N	.848	106	133	225	64	18	-2
1888	Det-N	.857	125	146	244	65	19	-3
1889	Pit-N	.872	52	68	95	24	7	-8
1890	Buf-P	.905	64	86	161	26	18	16
Total	12	.853	826	954	1618	444	118	-38
C								
1876	Chi-N	.844	63	295	50	64	3	3
1877	Bos-N	.830	7	39	5	9	0	-2
1878	Cin-N	.909	48	262	66	33	4	-4
1879	Cin-N	.901	59	307	92	44	3	5
1881	Buf-N	.870	4	17	3	3	0	-1
1882	Buf-N	.874	20	114	39	22	2	5
1883	Buf-N	.913	22	99	37	13	3	7
1884	Buf-N	1.000	3	17	5	0	2	2
Total	8	.885	226	1150	297	188	17	15
1B								
1876	Chi-N	.833	3	15	0	3	0	-1
1877	Bos-N	.963	35	324	13	13	16	2
1879	Cin-N	.955	2	18	3	1	0	0
1880	Cin-N	.958	3	23	0	1	2	0
1881	Buf-N	.943	26	256	8	16	10	-1
1887	Det-N	.950	2	18	1	1	0	0
1889	Pit-N	.941	3	30	2	2	3	0
1890	Buf-P	.970	57	582	40	19	33	4
Total	8	.960	131	1266	67	6	65	5
OF								
1876	Chi-N	.800	3	8	0	2	0	0
1877	Bos-N	.926	19	21	4	2	0	0

YEAR	TM/L	PCT	G	PO	A	E	DP	FR
1878	Cin-N	.760	16	15	4	6	0	-3
1879	Cin-N	.714	21	24	1	10	0	-6
1880	Cin-N	.738	33	36	9	16	1	-3
1881	Buf-N	.711	17	19	8	11	0	-1
1887	Det-N	1.000	3	1	1	0	0	1
Total	7	.763	112	124	27	7	1	-12
2B								
1880	Cin-N	—	1	0	0	0	0	0
1881	Buf-N	.807	25	63	88	36	18	-4
Total	2	.807	26	63	88	6	18	-4
SS								
1890	Buf-P	.600	1	2	1	2	1	-1

■ **Jerry White** OF

YEAR	TM/L	PCT	G	PO	A	E	DP	FR
1974	Mon-N	1.000	7	6	0	0	0	0
1975	Mon-N	.976	30	81	1	2	1	5
1976	Mon-N	.982	92	157	4	3	0	-6
1977	Mon-N	1.000	8	5	0	0	0	-1
1978	Mon-N	—	3	0	0	0	0	0
	Chi-N	.981	54	102	4	2	1	5
	Yr	.981	57	102	4	2	1	5
1979	Mon-N	.983	43	55	2	1	1	-1
1980	Mon-N	.946	84	101	5	6	1	-2
1981	Mon-N	.952	39	58	2	3	1	-1
1982	Mon-N	1.000	30	40	1	0	0	-1
1983	Mon-N	1.000	13	13	0	0	0	0
1986	StL-N	1.000	6	5	0	0	0	0
Total	11	.974	409	623	19	7	5	-2

■ **Jo-Jo White** OF

YEAR	TM/L	PCT	G	PO	A	E	DP	FR
1932	Det-A	.962	48	96	6	4	2	0
1933	Det-A	.977	54	122	4	3	1	0
1934	Det-A	.959	100	225	9	10	2	-3
1935	Det-A	.962	98	247	7	10	1	-4
1936	Det-A	.938	18	14	1	1	0	1
1937	Det-A	.973	82	216	4	6	0	-7
1938	Det-A	.967	55	141	4	5	0	5
1943	Phi-A	.966	133	335	8	12	2	-6
1944	Phi-A	.949	74	162	5	9	2	0
	Cin-N	1.000	23	55	4	0	0	2
Total	9	.965	685	1613	52	0	10	-12
SS								
1944	Phi-A	—	1	0	0	0	0	0

■ **Roy White** OF

YEAR	TM/L	PCT	G	PO	A	E	DP	FR
1965	NY-A	1.000	10	13	0	0	0	-1
1966	NY-A	.957	82	153	3	7	0	-1
1967	NY-A	.968	36	59	1	2	0	-4
1968	NY-A	.997	154	283	14	1	4	8
1969	NY-A	.989	126	267	9	3	1	8
1970	NY-A	.994	161	315	6	2	0	-1
1971	NY-A	1.000	145	306	8	0	1	2
1972	NY-A	.994	155	323	8	2	1	3
1973	NY-A	.977	162	339	4	8	0	-2
1974	NY-A	.993	67	141	2	1	1	-4
1975	NY-A	.984	135	303	11	5	0	7
1976	NY-A	.987	156	380	9	5	1	5
1977	NY-A	.981	135	301	7	6	4	5
1978	NY-A	.992	74	128	1	1	0	-8
1979	NY-A	1.000	27	45	3	0	0	-1
Total	15	.988	1625	3356	86	3	13	16
3B								
1967	NY-A	.857	17	20	28	8	1	-5
1B								
1975	NY-A	.983	7	58	1	1	3	-2
2B								
1965	NY-A	1.000	1	3	4	0	0	0
1966	NY-A	1.000	2	6	3	0	2	0
Total	2	1.000	3	9	7	0	2	0

■ **Sammy White** C

YEAR	TM/L	PCT	G	PO	A	E	DP	FR
1951	Bos-A	1.000	4	15	1	0	2	0
1952	Bos-A	.983	110	464	59	9	7	-2
1953	Bos-A	.986	131	588	68	9	9	8
1954	Bos-A	.979	133	677	80	16	11	14
1955	Bos-A	.984	143	671	71	12	8	-1
1956	Bos-A	.984	114	547	60	10	13	7
1957	Bos-A	.985	111	489	49	8	13	-5
1958	Bos-A	.988	102	450	38	6	8	-3
1959	Bos-A	.990	119	557	56	6	6	-1
1961	Mil-N	.974	20	107	5	3	0	3
1962	Phi-N	.975	40	173	19	5	4	5
Total		.984	1027	4738	506	4	83	25

■ **Bill White** 1B

YEAR	TM/L	PCT	G	PO	A	E	DP	FR
1956	NY-N	.989	138	1256	111	15	106	3
1958	SF-N	1.000	3	17	1	0	2	0
1959	StL-N	.995	71	404	25	2	32	-1
1960	StL-N	.990	123	994	65	11	109	-5
1961	StL-N	.989	151	1373	104	17	125	-2
1962	StL-N	.993	146	1221	94	9	114	1
1963	StL-N	.991	162	1389	105	13	126	-1
1964	StL-N	.996	160	1513	101	6	125	0
1965	StL-N	.992	144	1308	109	11	114	9
1966	Phi-N	.994	158	1422	109	9	118	7
1967	Phi-N	.993	95	775	52	6	85	1
1968	Phi-N	.994	111	982	77	6	94	4
1969	StL-N	1.000	15	81	7	0	7	1
Total	13	.992	1477	12735	960	105	1157	17
OF								
1956	NY-N	—	2	0	0	0	0	0
1958	SF-N	1.000	2	2	0	0	0	0
1959	StL-N	.962	92	175	2	7	1	-2
1960	StL-N	.970	29	64	1	2	0	0
1962	StL-N	.977	27	39	3	1	2	0
Total	5	.966	152	280	6	0	3	-2

■ **Bill White** SS

YEAR	TM/L	PCT	G	PO	A	E	DP	FR
1884	Pit-a	.807	60	58	185	58	12	-10
1886	Lou-a	.871	135	212	430	95	48	17
1887	Lou-a	.869	132	204	431	96	45	22
1888	Lou-a	.816	38	52	130	41	5	-3
	StL-a	.892	74	132	205	41	10	-3
	Yr	.864	112	184	335	82	15	-6
Total	4	.860	439	658	1381	331	120	23
3B								
1884	Pit-a	.800	10	11	21	8	2	0
1888	Lou-a	.905	11	11	27	4	1	1
Total	2	.854	21	22	48	2	3	1
OF								
1884	Pit-a	.667	4	6	0	3	0	-1
2B								
1888	StL-a	1.000	2	4	6	0	0	0

■ **Burgess Whitehead** 2B

YEAR	TM/L	PCT	G	PO	A	E	DP	FR
1933	StL-N	1.000	3	1	4	0	0	1
1934	StL-N	.962	48	88	140	9	27	4
1935	StL-N	.980	80	172	218	8	43	4
1936	NY-N	.969	153	442	552	32	107	29
1937	NY-N	.974	152	394	514	24	106	26
1939	NY-N	.970	91	232	320	17	60	18
1940	NY-N	.986	57	164	200	5	45	19
1941	NY-N	.970	104	288	285	18	60	0
1946	Pit-N	.963	30	66	64	5	14	-6
Total	9	.972	718	1847	2297	118	462	95
3B								
1934	StL-N	.962	28	30	47	3	6	2
1935	StL-N	.950	8	7	12	1	2	1
1939	NY-N	1.000	1	1	1	0	1	0
1940	NY-N	.947	74	68	130	11	5	-6
1941	NY-N	—	1	0	0	0	0	0
1946	Pit-N	1.000	4	0	1	0	0	0
Total	6	.952	116	106	191	5	14	-3
SS								
1933	StL-N	1.000	9	3	3	0	1	0
1934	StL-N	.948	29	40	33	4	5	-6
1935	StL-N	.950	6	9	10	1	2	0
1939	NY-N	1.000	4	7	15	0	2	2
1940	NY-N	1.000	4	6	6	0	0	0
1946	Pit-N	1.000	1	0	1	0	0	0
Total	6	.964	53	65	68	5	10	-4

■ **Fred Whitfield** 1B

YEAR	TM/L	PCT	G	PO	A	E	DP	FR
1962	StL-N	.987	38	282	25	4	32	1
1963	Cle-A	.987	92	690	51	10	64	-3
1964	Cle-A	.992	79	596	36	5	63	-2
1965	Cle-A	.993	122	932	80	7	79	6
1966	Cle-A	.991	132	1104	76	11	96	-2
1967	Cle-A	.993	66	494	49	4	51	4
1968	Cin-N	.981	41	285	21	6	28	-1
1969	Cin-N	.985	14	57	8	1	5	1
1970	Mon-N	.976	4	34	7	1	3	2
Total	9	.990	588	4474	353	9	421	6

■ **Terry Whitfield** OF

YEAR	TM/L	PCT	G	PO	A	E	DP	FR
1974	NY-A	—	1	0	0	0	0	0
1975	NY-A	.978	25	42	3	1	0	1
1976	NY-A	—	1	0	0	0	0	0
1977	SF-N	.972	84	167	4	5	0	0
1978	SF-N	.988	140	249	7	3	2	-6
1979	SF-N	.957	106	167	10	8	3	-6
1980	SF-N	.987	95	140	11	2	1	0
1984	LA-N	.988	58	76	4	1	0	-1
1985	LA-N	.926	28	23	2	2	0	-1
1986	LA-N	1.000	1	1	0	0	0	0
Total	10	.976	539	865	41	2	6	-13

■ **Ed Whiting** C

YEAR	TM/L	PCT	G	PO	A	E	DP	FR
1882	Bal-a	.834	72	299	108	81	6	-4
1883	Lou-a	.884	50	244	62	40	5	-4
1884	Lou-a	.891	40	199	54	31	6	-2
1886	Was-N	.919	6	22	12	3	0	-1
Total	4	.866	168	764	236	155	17	-11
OF								
1882	Bal-a	.500	2	1	0	1	0	-1
1883	Lou-a	.857	6	11	1	2	0	0
1884	Lou-a	.875	2	6	1	1	0	1
Total	3	.833	10	18	2	4	0	0
1B								
1882	Bal-a	.875	3	20	1	3	3	0
1883	Lou-a	.833	1	10	0	2	0	0
1884	Lou-a	.913	2	20	1	2	4	0
Total	3	.881	6	50	2	7	7	0
2B								
1883	Lou-a	.800	2	4	4	2	1	0
3B								
1883	Lou-a	1.000	1	1	1	0	0	0

■ **Dick Whitman** OF

YEAR	TM/L	PCT	G	PO	A	E	DP	FR
1946	Bro-N	1.000	85	178	5	0	0	7
1947	Bro-N	1.000	3	7	0	0	0	0
1948	Bro-N	.990	48	93	3	1	0	1
1949	Bro-N	.952	11	20	0	1	0	-1
1950	Phi-N	.983	32	56	2	1	0	1
1951	Phi-N	—	6	0	0	0	0	0
Total	6	.992	185	354	10	3	0	8

■ **Pinky Whitney** 3B

YEAR	TM/L	PCT	G	PO	A	E	DP	FR
1928	Phi-N	.955	149	171	293	22	27	3
1929	Phi-N	.967	154	168	333	17	29	21
1930	Phi-N	.965	148	186	313	18	29	20
1931	Phi-N	.948	128	131	217	19	21	-6
1932	Phi-N	.960	151	177	276	19	31	4
1933	Phi-N	.963	30	30	48	3	6	-4
	Bos-N	.971	85	77	187	8	15	4
	Yr	.969	115	107	235	11	21	0
1934	Bos-N	.968	111	105	227	11	11	4
1935	Bos-N	.958	74	83	144	10	8	4
1936	Bos-N	.971	10	15	18	1	2	1
	Phi-N	.955	111	106	212	15	15	11
	Yr	.956	121	121	230	16	17	12
1937	Phi-N	.982	130	136	238	7	17	4
1938	Phi-N	.934	75	68	131	14	8	-1
1939	Phi-N	1.000	2	2	3	0	0	0
Total	12	.961	1358	1455	2640	164	219	65
2B								
1932	Phi-N	.944	5	17	17	2	5	1
1933	Bos-N	1.000	18	39	53	0	8	-4
1934	Bos-N	.968	36	65	116	6	19	-1
1935	Bos-N	.975	49	113	161	7	17	1
1936	Phi-N	—	1	0	0	0	0	0
1938	Phi-N	1.000	2	4	1	0	0	0
1939	Phi-N	1.000	8	8	17	0	2	0
Total	7	.976	119	246	365	5	51	-3
1B								
1938	Phi-N	1.000	4	29	2	0	6	0
1939	Phi-N	.991	12	96	10	1	11	1
Total	2	.993	16	125	12	1	17	1
SS								
1934	Bos-N	1.000	2	2	2	0	1	0

■ **Art Whitney** 3B

YEAR	TM/L	PCT	G	PO	A	E	DP	FR
1880	Wor-N	.860	76	83	162	40	6	-1
1881	Det-N	.849	58	73	141	38	10	7
1882	Det-N	.854	22	40	42	14	3	0
1884	Pit-a	.916	21	29	47	7	1	4
1885	Pit-a	.933	8	7	21	2	1	2
1886	Pit-a	.906	95	120	209	34	17	12
1887	Pit-N	.924	119	166	237	33	13	-3
1888	NY-N	.887	90	90	184	35	11	8
1889	NY-N	.882	129	160	265	57	27	-2
1890	NY-P	.865	88	129	172	47	11	-3
1891	Cin-a	.903	93	129	198	35	12	-5
	StL-a	.867	3	0	13	2	0	2
	Yr	.902	96	129	211	37	12	-3
Total	11	.888	802	1026	1691	344	112	21
SS								
1882	Pro-N	.784	11	7	33	11	2	-2
	Det-N	.857	8	18	24	7	4	1
	Yr	.820	19	25	57	18	6	-1
1884	Pit-a	.833	1	3	2	1	0	-1
1885	Pit-a	.918	75	95	219	28	21	-13
1886	Pit-a	.872	42	48	136	27	13	0
1890	NY-P	.830	31	47	85	27	12	-9
Total	5	.877	168	218	499	101	52	-24
OF								
1884	Pit-a	1.000	1	1	0	0	0	0
1885	Pit-a	1.000	3	2	0	0	0	-1
Total	2	1.000	4	3	0	0	0	-1
2B								
1885	Pit-a	.842	4	12	4	3	1	-2

■ **Jim Whitney** OF

YEAR	TM/L	PCT	G	PO	A	E	DP	FR
1881	Bos-N	.700	15	6	1	3	0	-1
1882	Bos-N	.625	9	5	0	3	0	-2
1883	Bos-N	.795	40	55	7	16	0	-5
1884	Bos-N	.947	15	18	0	1	0	-2
1885	Bos-N	.892	17	31	2	4	0	0
1886	KC-N	.844	22	18	9	5	1	0
1887	Was-N	.667	7	3	1	2	0	0
1888	Was-N	.500	3	1	0	1	0	0
1889	Ind-N	1.000	1	1	0	0	0	0
1890	Phi-a	—	1	0	0	0	0	0
Total	10	.819	130	138	20	5	1	-10
1B								
1881	Bos-N	.938	2	15	0	1	0	0
1882	Bos-N	.929	6	39	0	3	0	-1
1883	Bos-N	.917	3	22	0	2	2	-1
1884	Bos-N	.924	15	108	1	9	1	-2
1885	Bos-N	.870	5	37	3	6	3	0
1888	Was-N	1.000	1	8	0	0	0	0
Total	6	.917	31	229	4	1	6	-4
3B								
1884	Bos-N	1.000	1	1	1	0	0	0
1886	KC-N	.571	1	1	3	3	0	0
Total	2	.667	2	2	4	3	0	0

■ **Ernie Whitt** C

YEAR	TM/L	PCT	G	PO	A	E	DP	FR
1976	Bos-A	1.000	8	24	0	0	0	-1
1977	Tor-A	1.000	14	62	4	0	0	2
1978	Tor-A	1.000	1	7	1	0	0	0
1980	Tor-A	.986	105	436	56	7	11	5
1981	Tor-A	.991	72	297	46	3	5	9
1982	Tor-A	.982	98	406	30	8	0	1
1983	Tor-A	.992	119	554	50	5	4	6
1984	Tor-A	.994	118	583	40	4	8	12
1985	Tor-A	.988	134	649	38	8	6	4
1986	Tor-A	.991	129	709	41	7	7	-5
1987	Tor-A	.994	131	803	55	5	10	5
1988	Tor-A	.994	123	643	43	4	10	-5
1989	Tor-A	.992	115	550	43	5	5	-1
1990	Atl-N	.991	59	492	46	3	1	2
Total	14	.991	1226	6019	489	9	67	34

■ **Possum Whitted** OF

YEAR	TM/L	PCT	G	PO	A	E	DP	FR
1913	StL-N	.989	41	84	5	1	0	1
1914	StL-N	.000	3	0	0	0	1	0
	Bos-N	.967	38	84	4	3	1	1
	Yr	.957	41	84	4	4	1	1
1915	Phi-N	.978	119	266	7	6	2	-7
1916	Phi-N	.964	136	285	13	11	3	5
1917	Phi-N	.977	141	275	19	7	0	5
1918	Phi-N	.982	22	52	3	1	1	2
1919	Phi-N	.955	47	97	9	5	0	1
	Pit-N	1.000	1	1	0	0	0	0
	Yr	.955	48	98	9	5	0	1
1920	Pit-N	—	1	0	0	0	0	0
1921	Pit-N	.988	102	247	9	3	6	5
Total	9	.975	651	1391	69	8	13	13

YEAR	TM/L	PCT	G	PO	A	E	DP	FR
3B								
1912	StL-N	.857	12	19	17	6	1	-3
1913	StL-N	.931	22	28	53	6	99	22
1914	StL-N	.889	5	6	10	2	1	-1
	Bos-N	1.000	4	3	5	0	1	0
	Yr	.923	9	9	15	2	2	-1
1917	Phi-N	.920	7	10	13	2	1	0
1919	Pit-N	1.000	2	1	1	0	0	0
1920	Pit-N	.961	125	166	229	16	16	-3
Total	6	.946	177	233	328	2	119	15
1B								
1913	StL-N	1.000	2	26	1	0	2	0
1914	Bos-N	.972	4	30	5	1	3	1
1915	Phi-N	.956	7	73	14	4	3	3
1916	Phi-N	.971	16	98	3	3	5	-1
1917	Phi-N	1.000	10	21	1	0	1	0
1918	Phi-N	—	1	0	0	0	0	0
1919	Phi-N	1.000	2	9	0	0	0	0
	Pit-N	.988	33	311	27	4	21	3
	Yr	.989	35	320	27	4	21	3
1920	Pit-N	1.000	10	97	5	0	8	0
1921	Pit-N	1.000	7	29	4	0	4	1
Total	9	.984	92	694	60	2	47	7
2B								
1913	StL-N	.892	7	9	24	4	0	0
1914	StL-N	—	1	0	0	0	0	0
	Bos-N	.933	15	39	45	6	4	2
	Yr	.933	16	39	45	6	4	2
1917	Phi-N	1.000	1	0	2	0	0	0
1919	Phi-N	.972	26	72	65	4	8	-2
Total	4	.948	50	120	136	4	12	0
SS								
1913	StL-N	.927	38	78	124	16	16	-1
1914	Bos-N	.778	3	5	2	2	0	-1
Total	2	.921	41	83	126	8	16	-2
■ Al Wickland OF								
1913	Cin-N	.983	24	57	2	1	1	3
1914	Chi-F	.962	157	252	23	11	3	1
1915	Chi-F	.946	24	32	3	2	2	-2
	Pit-F	.968	109	234	11	8	0	4
	Yr	.966	133	266	14	10	2	2
1918	Bos-N	.975	95	183	11	5	2	-1
1919	NY-A	1.000	15	14	0	0	0	-4
Total	5	.968	424	772	50	7	8	-1
■ Whitey Wietelmann SS								
1939	Bos-N	.953	22	36	66	5	10	1
1940	Bos-N	1.000	3	4	6	0	2	1
1941	Bos-N	.941	5	11	11	0	3	1
1942	Bos-N	.941	11	19	29	3	6	0
1943	Bos-N	.957	153	307	**581**	40	91	20
1944	Bos-N	.954	103	215	287	24	60	-5
1945	Bos-N	.958	39	79	104	8	18	4
1946	Bos-N	.915	16	28	26	5	5	-4
1947	Pit-N	.885	22	31	38	9	6	-7
Total	9	.952	374	730	1148	4	201	11
2B								
1939	Bos-N	1.000	1	2	3	0	2	1
1940	Bos-N	.962	15	14	11	1	5	1
1941	Bos-N	1.000	10	14	16	0	0	1
1942	Bos-N	—	1	0	0	0	0	0
1944	Bos-N	.951	23	54	62	6	14	-1
1945	Bos-N	.972	87	222	232	13	58	-1
1946	Bos-N	1.000	4	5	3	0	0	-1
1947	Pit-N	.947	14	30	24	3	8	-6
Total	8	.968	155	341	351	4	87	-6
3B								
1940	Bos-N	.923	9	2	10	1	2	1
1941	Bos-N	1.000	2	1	2	0	0	0
1944	Bos-N	1.000	1	0	2	0	1	0
1945	Bos-N	1.000	2	2	2	0	0	0
1946	Bos-N	.938	8	5	10	1	1	-1
1947	Pit-N	.857	6	1	5	1	0	0
Total	6	.933	28	11	31	3	4	0
1B								
1947	Pit-N	1.000	1	7	1	0	0	0
■ Al Wiggins 2B								
1982	SD-N	—	1	0	0	0	0	0
1984	SD-N	.962	157	**391**	410	32	95	-29
1985	SD-N	1.000	9	22	21	0	4	-3
	Bal-A	.960	76	148	186	14	58	-24
1986	Bal-A	.978	66	121	151	6	40	-19
1987	Bal-A	.983	33	78	98	3	21	1
Total	5	.967	342	760	866	5	218	-74
OF								
1981	SD-N	.750	4	6	0	2	0	0
1982	SD-N	.967	68	140	8	5	2	2
1983	SD-N	.992	105	242	6	2	1	8
1987	Bal-A	.889	5	8	0	1	0	-1
Total	4	.976	182	396	14	0	3	9
1B								
1983	SD-N	.984	45	330	29	6	30	0
■ Del Wilber C								
1946	StL-N	1.000	4	13	0	0	0	1
1947	StL-N	.983	34	108	10	2	2	1
1948	StL-N	.949	26	67	7	4	1	-3
1949	StL-N	1.000	2	5	1	0	0	0
1951	Phi-N	.978	73	326	26	8	5	5
1952	Bos-A	.995	39	160	22	1	5	1
1953	Bos-A	.980	28	90	7	2	0	-2
1954	Bos-A	.950	18	49	8	3	2	-5
Total	8	.978	224	818	81	0	15	-2
1B								
1953	Bos-A	1.000	2	18	0	0	2	0
■ Rob Wilfong 2B								
1977	Min-A	.959	66	114	164	12	40	4
1978	Min-A	.986	80	152	196	5	37	6
1979	Min-A	.979	133	287	379	14	92	**22**
1980	Min-A	**.995**	120	238	337	3	85	-3
1981	Min-A	.980	93	183	268	9	52	0
1982	Min-A	.980	22	31	67	2	19	0
	Cal-A	.982	28	35	72	2	13	15
	Yr	.981	50	66	139	4	32	15
1983	Cal-A	.995	39	92	110	1	26	8
1984	Cal-A	.975	97	161	266	11	48	4
1985	Cal-A	.986	69	124	216	5	45	**21**
1986	Cal-A	.982	90	135	257	7	48	9
1987	SF-N	.833	2	2	3	1	2	-2
Total	11	.982	839	1554	2335	2	507	84
3B								
1982	Cal-A	.933	5	1	13	1	0	3
1983	Cal-A	.978	13	11	33	1	6	3
Total	2	.967	18	12	46	2	6	6
OF								
1979	Min-A	—	3	0	0	0	0	0
1980	Min-A	.889	6	7	1	1	0	0
1982	Cal-A	1.000	3	1	1	0	0	1
Total	3	.909	12	8	2	1	0	1
SS								
1982	Cal-A	1.000	2	1	2	0	0	1
1983	Cal-A	1.000	6	4	1	0	1	0
1984	Cal-A	.750	4	1	2	1	0	-1
Total	3	.917	12	6	5	1	1	0
■ Joe Wilhoit OF								
1916	Bos-N	.979	108	177	12	4	3	-3
1917	Bos-N	.928	52	70	7	6	1	-6
	Pit-N	1.000	3	1	0	0	0	0
	NY-N	1.000	11	15	1	0	0	-1
	Yr	.941	66	86	9	6	1	-7
1918	NY-N	.975	55	71	7	2	2	2
1919	Bos-A	1.000	5	8	0	0	0	-1
Total	4	.969	234	342	28	2	6	-9
1B								
1917	Pit-N	1.000	1	2	0	0	0	0
■ Curt Wilkerson SS								
1983	Tex-A	1.000	9	11	25	0	3	1
1984	Tex-A	.944	116	151	285	26	50	-21
1985	Tex-A	.954	56	59	85	7	26	8
1987	Tex-A	.946	33	41	47	5	8	6
1988	Tex-A	.974	24	29	46	2	6	4
1989	Chi-N	1.000	7	2	3	0	1	0
1990	Chi-N	1.000	1	0	2	0	0	0
Total	8	.953	356	418	767	8	144	-7
2B								
1983	Tex-A	1.000	2	7	6	0	2	1
1984	Tex-A	.978	47	76	106	4	23	-7
1985	Tex-A	.969	19	40	54	3	15	5
1986	Tex-A	.968	60	66	114	6	30	7
1987	Tex-A	1.000	28	31	46	0	9	5
1988	Tex-A	.970	87	153	240	12	52	5
1989	Chi-N	.987	15	26	50	1	7	6
1990	Chi-N	.946	14	24	29	3	3	2
Total	8	.974	272	423	645	9	141	24
3B								
1983	Tex-A	.000	2	0	0	1	0	0
1987	Tex-A	.923	18	7	5	1	1	-1
1988	Tex-A	.944	11	4	13	1	0	1
1989	Chi-N	.881	26	14	38	7	2	-2
1990	Chi-N	.888	52	25	62	11	4	-6
Total	5	.889	109	50	118	1	7	-8
OF								
1989	Chi-N	—	1	0	0	0	0	0
1990	Chi-N	—	1	0	0	0	0	0
Total	2	—	2	0	0	0	0	0
■ Bob Will OF								
1957	Chi-N	.963	30	51	1	2	0	1
1958	Chi-N	—	1	0	0	0	0	0
1960	Chi-N	.992	121	224	10	2	2	1
1961	Chi-N	1.000	30	33	0	0	0	-1
1962	Chi-N	1.000	9	14	0	0	0	0
Total	5	.988	191	322	11	4	2	1
1B								
1961	Chi-N	.750	1	3	0	1	1	0
1963	Chi-N	1.000	1	10	0	0	1	0
Total	2	.929	2	13	0	1	2	0
■ Jerry Willard C								
1984	Cle-A	.981	76	335	35	7	7	0
1985	Cle-A	.990	96	427	52	5	11	1
1986	Oak-A	.994	71	300	12	2	1	-12
1990	Chi-N	—	1	0	0	0	0	0
Total	4	.988	244	1062	99	4	19	-11
1B								
1987	Oak-A	1.000	1	1	0	0	0	0
3B								
1987	Oak-A	—	1	0	0	0	0	0
■ Rip Williams C								
1911	Bos-A	.978	38	182	42	5	0	4
1912	Was-A	.978	48	234	74	7	6	3
1913	Was-A	.985	18	51	14	1	1	-4
1914	Was-A	.975	44	181	54	6	0	-4
1915	Was-A	.967	40	213	51	9	4	5
1916	Was-A	.993	23	119	19	1	3	-5
1918	Cle-A	—	1	0	0	0	0	0
Total	7	.977	212	980	254	9	14	-1
1B								
1911	Bos-A	.975	57	545	31	15	28	-2
1913	Was-A	.986	9	64	6	1	5	1
1914	Was-A	1.000	8	71	4	0	0	0
1915	Was-A	.994	15	149	16	1	6	3
1916	Was-A	.982	34	269	11	5	18	-3
1918	Cle-A	.980	21	190	10	4	11	-1
Total	6	.981	144	1288	78	6	68	-2
1913	Was-A	1.000	5	2	1	0	0	-1
1914	Was-A	—	1	0	0	0	0	0
Total	2	1.000	6	2	1	0	0	-1
3B								
1915	Was-A	1.000	1	1	0	0	0	0
1916	Was-A	1.000	1	2	0	0	0	0
Total	2	1.000	2	3	0	0	0	0
■ Gus Williams OF								
1911	StL-A	.867	7	13	0	2	0	-1
1912	StL-A	.930	62	94	12	8	3	2
1913	StL-A	.951	143	225	26	13	7	4
1914	StL-A	.933	142	200	24	16	2	2
1915	StL-A	.949	35	35	2	2	1	-5
Total	5	.939	389	567	64	1	13	2
■ Billy Williams OF								
1959	Chi-N	1.000	10	18	0	0	0	1
1960	Chi-N	.962	12	25	0	1	0	-1
1961	Chi-N	.954	135	220	19	**11**	3	-6
1962	Chi-N	.967	159	273	18	10	4	4
1963	Chi-N	.987	160	298	13	4	2	5
1964	Chi-N	.950	**162**	233	14	13	0	-10
1965	Chi-N	.968	**164**	296	10	10	2	0
1966	Chi-N	.976	**162**	319	9	8	3	8
1967	Chi-N	.989	**162**	271	3	3	1	-8
1968	Chi-N	.967	**163**	261	4	9	0	-12
1969	Chi-N	.957	159	250	15	12	2	-1
1970	Chi-N	.989	**160**	259	13	3	1	-1
1971	Chi-N	.977	154	284	8	7	3	-3
1972	Chi-N	.984	144	233	9	4	0	-7
1973	Chi-N	.985	138	253	14	4	1	3
1974	Chi-N	.973	43	69	4	2	2	-1
1976	Oak-A	—	1	0	0	0	0	0
Total	17	.973	2088	3562	143	101	24	-29
1B								
1972	Chi-N	1.000	5	42	4	0	5	1
1973	Chi-N	.989	19	167	20	2	14	3
1974	Chi-N	.986	65	566	49	9	48	2
1975	Oak-A	.971	7	30	3	1	5	0
Total	4	.987	96	805	76	2	72	6
■ Davey Williams 2B								
1949	NY-N	.953	13	19	22	2	5	-10
1951	NY-N	1.000	22	38	43	0	7	2
1952	NY-N	.973	138	279	375	18	102	-15
1953	NY-N	.982	95	191	254	8	54	0
1954	NY-N	**.982**	142	353	396	14	112	-7
1955	NY-N	.968	71	139	162	10	39	-8
Total	6	.978	481	1019	1252	2	319	-38
■ Dewey Williams C								
1944	Chi-N	.981	77	317	50	7	7	3
1945	Chi-N	.978	54	114	20	3	1	2
1946	Chi-N	1.000	2	3	1	0	0	0
1947	Chi-N	—	1	0	0	0	0	0
1948	Cin-N	.961	47	137	11	6	1	-3
Total	5	.976	181	571	82	6	9	2
■ Earl Williams C								
1971	Atl-N	.981	72	375	35	8	4	-5
1972	Atl-N	.980	116	584	49	13	7	-12
1973	Bal-A	.987	95	407	33	6	5	-8
1974	Bal-A	.983	75	308	33	6	5	-10
1975	Atl-N	.967	11	52	6	2	3	1
1976	Atl-N	.995	38	178	10	1	0	-8
	Mon-N	1.000	13	40	5	0	4	1
	Yr	.996	51	218	15	1	4	-7
1977	Oak-A	.989	36	165	21	2	2	-2
Total	7	.984	456	2109	192	8	30	-43
1B								
1970	Atl-N	1.000	4	20	1	0	1	0
1971	Atl-N	.995	31	194	8	1	25	-3
1972	Atl-N	1.000	20	140	8	0	10	0
1973	Bal-A	.994	42	326	19	2	36	-2
1974	Bal-A	.995	47	399	17	2	39	-4
1975	Atl-N	.989	90	844	50	10	77	-4
1976	Atl-N	1.000	17	120	8	0	9	0
	Mon-N	.981	47	377	41	8	37	5
	Yr	.986	64	497	49	8	46	5
1977	Oak-A	.993	29	140	5	1	12	-2
Total	8	.991	327	2560	157	4	246	-10
3B								
1970	Atl-N	1.000	3	3	7	0	3	1
1971	Atl-N	.918	42	27	74	9	9	0
1972	Atl-N	.821	21	16	30	10	1	-4
Total	3	.892	66	46	111	9	13	-3
■ Eddie Williams 3B								
1987	Cle-A	.982	22	17	37	1	6	2
1988	Cle-A	1.000	10	3	18	0	0	2
1989	Chi-A	.909	65	37	123	16	21	1
1990	SD-N	.897	13	5	21	3	2	-1
Total	4	.929	110	62	199	0	29	4
OF								
1986	Cle-A	—	4	0	0	0	0	0
■ Dib Williams 2B								
1930	Phi-A	.951	39	71	102	9	14	4
1931	Phi-A	1.000	10	15	23	0	4	1
1932	Phi-A	.952	53	122	175	15	30	8
1933	Phi-A	.941	29	52	76	8	16	2
1934	Phi-A	.956	53	110	171	13	31	0
1935	Phi-A	1.000	2	0	5	0	0	2
	Bos-A	.972	29	53	52	3	8	-4
	Yr	.973	31	53	57	3	8	-6
Total	6	.955	215	423	604	8	103	5

YEAR	TM/L	PCT	G	PO	A	E	DP	FR
SS								
1930	Phi-A	.966	19	37	47	3	9	-1
1931	Phi-A	.931	72	152	214	27	59	6
1932	Phi-A	.800	3	2	6	2	2	-1
1933	Phi-A	.921	84	199	243	38	34	-11
1934	Phi-A	1.000	2	1	3	0	0	0
1935	Bos-A	.947	15	35	37	4	8	-5
Total	6	.930	195	426	550	4	112	-12
3B								
1930	Phi-A	1.000	1	1	2	0	0	0
1935	Bos-A	.952	30	34	65	5	5	3
Total	2	.953	31	35	67	5	5	3
1B								
1933	Phi-A	.938	2	14	1	1	1	0
1935	Bos-A	1.000	1	5	0	0	0	0
Total	2	.952	3	19	1	1	1	0
OF								
1931	Phi-A	1.000	1	1	0	0	0	0
■ Cy Williams OF								
1912	Chi-N	1.000	22	36	3	0	0	2
1913	Chi-N	.976	44	77	4	2	0	-1
1914	Chi-N	.941	27	46	2	3	0	1
1915	Chi-N	.968	149	347	14	12	2	-3
1916	Chi-N	.989	116	260	7	3	0	-8
1917	Chi-N	.960	136	340	23	15	4	9
1918	Phi-N	.968	91	229	10	8	4	-4
1919	Phi-N	.970	108	278	13	9	2	0
1920	Phi-N	.972	147	388	22	12	4	6
1921	Phi-N	.979	146	382	29	9	5	10
1922	Phi-N	.973	150	376	19	11	2	-2
1923	Phi-N	.981	135	350	9	7	3	-7
1924	Phi-N	.962	145	368	13	15	0	-6
1925	Phi-N	.989	96	173	12	2	3	-1
1926	Phi-N	.963	93	143	14	6	3	-7
1927	Phi-N	.970	130	241	22	8	8	1
1928	Phi-N	1.000	69	118	9	0	0	-2
1929	Phi-N	.966	11	27	1	1	0	2
1930	Phi-N	1.000	3	1	0	0	0	0
Total	19	.973	1818	4180	226	123	40	-10
■ Jimmy Williams 2B								
1901	Bal-A	.935	130	339	412	52	47	-2
1902	Bal-A	.945	104	248	332	34	46	8
1903	NY-A	.957	132	266	438	32	59	16
1904	NY-A	.951	146	315	465	40	52	17
1905	NY-A	.964	129	335	332	25	51	5
1906	NY-A	.958	139	326	412	32	34	11
1907	NY-A	.966	139	357	393	26	45	-1
1908	StL-A	.963	148	352	445	31	50	5
1909	StL-A	.962	109	221	280	20	42	-6
Total	9	.955	1176	2759	3509	292	426	53
3B								
1899	Pit-N	.902	152	251	354	66	14	7
1900	Pit-N	.889	103	153	254	51	21	7
1902	Bal-A	.821	19	27	37	14	1	-4
Total	3	.891	274	431	645	131	36	10
SS								
1900	Pit-N	.824	4	3	11	3	1	-1
1B								
1902	Bal-A	—	1	0	0	0	0	0
■ Ken Williams OF								
1915	Cin-N	.948	62	117	11	7	4	4
1916	Cin-N	.955	10	19	2	1	1	2
1919	StL-A	.937	63	168	10	12	3	4
1920	StL-A	.961	138	331	17	14	6	8
1921	StL-A	.932	145	331	24	26	3	7
1922	StL-A	.970	153	372	16	12	4	7
1923	StL-A	.967	145	333	23	12	5	10
1924	StL-A	.968	109	257	13	9	2	6
1925	StL-A	.955	102	242	11	12	4	5
1926	StL-A	.948	92	189	12	11	2	1
1927	StL-A	.965	113	260	15	10	4	6
1928	Bos-A	.971	127	254	10	8	0	-3
1929	Bos-A	.963	39	75	3	3	2	-5
Total	13	.958	1298	2918	167	107	40	52
1B								
1929	Bos-A	1.000	2	8	0	0	1	0
2B								
1926	StL-A	—	1	0	0	0	0	0
■ Ken Williams OF								
1986	Chi-A	1.000	10	18	1	0	1	1
1987	Chi-A	.981	115	303	5	6	2	2
1988	Chi-A	.959	38	68	2	3	1	0
1989	Det-A	.979	87	180	11	4	3	5
1990	Det-A	1.000	47	67	5	0	2	8
	Tor-A	1.000	30	36	0	0	0	1
	Yr	1.000	77	103	5	0	2	9
Total	5	.982	327	672	24	3	9	17
3B								
1988	Chi-A	.860	32	19	67	14	3	1
1B								
1989	Det-A	—	1	0	0	0	0	0
■ Matt Williams 3B								
1987	SF-N	.968	17	6	24	1	3	3
1988	SF-N	.967	43	35	83	4	5	9
1989	SF-N	.961	73	71	126	8	10	8
1990	SF-N	.959	159	140	306	19	33	4
Total	4	.961	292	252	539	2	51	24
SS								
1987	SF-N	.975	70	104	210	8	49	18
1988	SF-N	.927	14	13	25	3	4	0
1989	SF-N	.968	30	19	42	2	5	-1
Total	3	.969	114	136	277	3	58	17
■ Reggie Williams OF								
1985	LA-N	.900	15	8	1	1	0	2

YEAR	TM/L	PCT	G	PO	A	E	DP	FR
1986	LA-N	.984	124	179	5	3	2	-17
1987	LA-N	.913	30	21	0	2	0	0
1988	Cle-A	1.000	11	13	1	0	0	-1
Total	4	.974	180	221	7	6	2	-16
■ Dick Williams OF								
1951	Bro-N	1.000	15	21	1	0	0	-2
1952	Bro-N	1.000	25	41	1	0	0	-2
1953	Bro-N	.923	24	24	0	2	0	-2
1954	Bro-N	1.000	14	12	0	0	0	-2
1956	Bal-A	.990	81	205	2	2	0	-2
1957	Bal-A	1.000	26	46	3	0	2	3
	Cle-A	.973	37	72	1	2	0	0
	Yr	.984	63	118	4	2	2	3
1958	Bal-A	1.000	70	147	6	0	1	4
1959	KC-A	1.000	23	31	0	0	0	1
1960	KC-A	1.000	25	67	3	0	0	4
1961	Bal-A	.968	75	86	4	3	1	-9
1962	Bal-A	1.000	29	46	0	0	0	-4
1963	Bos-A	1.000	7	2	0	0	0	0
1964	Bos-A	1.000	5	12	0	0	0	1
Total	13	.989	456	812	21	9	4	-7
3B								
1952	Bro-N	1.000	1	0	1	0	0	0
1956	Bal-A	.875	4	4	3	1	0	-1
1957	Bal-A	.961	15	21	28	2	1	0
	Cle-A	.930	19	23	30	4	5	-1
	Yr	.944	34	44	58	6	6	-1
1958	Bal-A	.919	45	32	47	7	5	-2
1959	KC-A	.957	80	83	164	11	10	-4
1960	KC-A	.951	57	62	111	9	13	-1
1961	Bal-A	—	2	0	0	0	0	0
1962	Bal-A	—	4	0	0	0	0	0
1963	Bos-A	.976	17	16	25	1	1	-4
1964	Bos-A	.960	13	7	17	1	4	3
Total	10	.949	257	248	426	6	39	-10
1B								
1952	Bro-N	1.000	1	10	1	0	2	0
1956	Bal-A	1.000	10	36	7	0	4	2
1957	Bal-A	1.000	12	82	10	0	12	2
1958	Bal-A	.995	26	175	6	1	21	-2
1959	KC-A	.992	32	233	16	2	32	-1
1960	KC-A	.992	34	247	17	2	15	0
1961	Bal-A	1.000	20	123	12	0	10	0
1962	Bal-A	1.000	21	134	13	0	13	0
1963	Bos-A	1.000	11	46	3	0	3	-1
1964	Bos-A	1.000	21	31	4	0	2	1
Total	10	.996	188	1117	89	5	114	1
2B								
1956	Bal-A	.900	10	4	5	1	0	-1
1958	Bal-A	1.000	7	5	2	0	0	-1
1959	KC-A	1.000	3	2	1	0	0	-1
Total	3	.950	20	11	8	1	0	-3
■ Ted Williams OF								
1939	Bos-A	.945	149	318	11	19	3	-2
1940	Bos-A	.960	143	302	13	13	2	0
1941	Bos-A	.961	133	262	11	11	2	-5
1942	Bos-A	.988	150	312	15	4	4	4
1946	Bos-A	.971	150	325	7	10	2	-1
1947	Bos-A	.975	156	347	10	9	2	3
1948	Bos-A	.983	134	289	9	5	2	-1
1949	Bos-A	.983	155	337	12	6	3	0
1950	Bos-A	.956	86	165	7	8	0	-4
1951	Bos-A	.988	147	315	12	4	6	1
1952	Bos-A	1.000	2	4	0	0	0	0
1953	Bos-A	.970	26	31	1	1	1	-5
1954	Bos-A	.982	115	213	5	4	1	-7
1955	Bos-A	.989	91	170	5	2	0	-4
1956	Bos-A	.973	110	174	7	5	2	-10
1957	Bos-A	.995	125	215	2	1	0	-9
1958	Bos-A	.973	114	154	3	7	0	-17
1959	Bos-A	.970	76	94	4	3	0	-11
1960	Bos-A	.993	87	131	6	1	1	-4
Total	19	.974	2151	4158	140	113	30	-67
■ Walt Williams OF								
1964	Hou-N	1.000	5	4	0	0	0	0
1967	Chi-A	.983	73	112	6	2	2	-2
1968	Chi-A	1.000	34	47	2	0	1	-2
1969	Chi-A	.985	111	183	13	3	4	1
1970	Chi-A	.949	79	119	12	7	1	-1
1971	Chi-A	1.000	90	157	4	0	2	-3
1972	Chi-A	.990	57	93	6	1	2	0
1973	Cle-A	.990	61	123	7	4	0	0
1974	NY-A	.955	24	20	1	1	0	1
1975	NY-A	.982	31	55	1	1	0	-1
Total	10	.981	565	913	52	9	12	-7
2B								
1975	NY-A	1.000	6	2	3	0	0	0
3B								
1971	Chi-A	1.000	1	0	1	0	0	0
1972	Chi-A	—	1	0	0	0	0	0
Total	2	1.000	2	0	1	0	0	0
■ Woody Williams 2B								
1943	Cin-N	.986	12	32	38	1	5	3
1944	Cin-N	.971	155	377	542	27	97	15
1945	Cin-N	.969	133	295	393	22	61	-10
Total	3	.971	300	704	973	0	163	8
SS								
1938	Bro-N	.931	18	26	28	4	4	-6
1943	Cin-N	.700	5	4	3	3	1	-1
Total	2	.897	23	30	31	7	5	-7
3B								
1938	Bro-N	1.000	1	2	0	0	0	0
1943	Cin-N	.778	7	1	6	2	1	0
Total	2	.818	8	3	6	2	1	0

YEAR	TM/L	PCT	G	PO	A	E	DP	FR
■ Ned Williamson 3B								
1878	Ind-N	.867	63	88	128	33	6	-4
1879	Chi-N	.871	70	84	193	41	13	18
1880	Chi-N	.893	63	83	143	27	5	12
1881	Chi-N	.909	76	117	194	31	10	20
1882	Chi-N	.881	83	108	210	43	16	15
1883	Chi-N	.807	97	111	252	87	20	17
1884	Chi-N	.861	99	121	250	60	25	23
1885	Chi-N	.892	113	113	258	45	18	11
1890	Chi-P	.809	52	53	91	34	6	-11
Total	9	.866	716	878	1719	401	119	101
SS								
1881	Chi-N	.929	2	6	7	1	1	1
1886	Chi-N	.869	121	161	355	78	36	-1
1887	Chi-N	.890	127	133	361	61	31	-31
1888	Chi-N	.884	132	120	375	65	48	-11
1889	Chi-N	.844	47	48	130	33	7	-24
1890	Chi-P	.825	21	22	58	17	6	-9
Total	6	.874	450	490	1286	255	129	-75
C								
1879	Chi-N	.844	4	22	5	5	0	0
1880	Chi-N	.929	11	57	22	6	2	1
1881	Chi-N	—	1	0	0	0	0	0
1883	Chi-N	.900	3	4	5	1	0	0
1884	Chi-N	.885	10	34	20	7	1	1
1885	Chi-N	1.000	1	6	1	0	0	0
1886	Chi-N	.667	4	1	1	1	0	1
Total	7	.899	34	124	54	0	3	3
2B								
1880	Chi-N	.947	3	7	11	1	2	0
1881	Chi-N	.875	4	11	17	4	2	1
Total	2	.902	7	18	28	5	4	1
1B								
1879	Chi-N	.963	6	77	1	3	2	0
■ Bump Wills 2B								
1977	Tex-A	.982	150	321	492	15	89	4
1978	Tex-A	.981	156	350	526	17	84	21
1979	Tex-A	.976	146	337	468	20	95	7
1980	Tex-A	.984	144	340	473	13	112	19
1981	Tex-A	.983	101	268	326	10	70	8
1982	Chi-N	.963	103	199	297	19	45	-18
Total	6	.979	800	1815	2582	4	495	41
SS								
1977	Tex-A	—	2	0	0	0	0	0
1B								
1977	Tex-A	—	1	0	0	0	0	0
■ Maury Wills SS								
1959	LA-N	.966	82	121	220	12	39	2
1960	LA-N	.945	145	260	431	40	78	21
1961	LA-N	.959	148	253	428	29	104	12
1962	LA-N	.956	165	295	493	36	86	-5
1963	LA-N	.959	109	171	322	21	47	-6
1964	LA-N	.963	149	273	422	27	77	-5
1965	LA-N	.970	155	267	535	25	89	21
1966	LA-N	.967	139	227	453	23	79	9
1967	Pit-N	1.000	2	4	3	0	1	0
1968	Pit-N	.977	10	10	32	1	5	0
1969	Mon-N	.950	46	72	139	11	31	-3
	LA-N	.969	104	168	357	17	61	7
	Yr	.963	150	240	496	28	92	4
1970	LA-N	.959	126	171	396	24	58	-19
1971	LA-N	.978	144	220	484	16	86	1
1972	LA-N	.984	31	38	89	2	18	-5
Total	14	.963	1555	2550	4804	284	859	28
3B								
1963	LA-N	.944	33	26	59	5	7	1
1964	LA-N	1.000	6	2	6	0	0	0
1966	LA-N	1.000	4	4	7	0	1	0
1967	Pit-N	.948	144	98	343	24	31	10
1968	Pit-N	.957	141	105	276	17	27	-9
1970	LA-N	1.000	1	0	1	0	0	0
1971	LA-N	.667	4	0	2	1	1	0
1972	LA-N	1.000	26	1	14	0	2	1
Total	8	.953	362	236	708	7	69	3
2B								
1969	Mon-N	—	1	0	0	0	0	0
■ Walt Wilmot OF								
1888	Was-N	.872	119	260	19	41	4	11
1889	Was-N	.927	108	232	22	20	4	14
1890	Chi-N	.938	139	320	26	23	4	10
1891	Chi-N	.922	121	223	15	20	0	-5
1892	Chi-N	.903	92	197	8	22	0	2
1893	Chi-N	.873	93	198	16	31	1	0
1894	Chi-N	.872	133	264	16	41	5	4
1895	Chi-N	.914	108	226	19	23	5	4
1897	NY-N	.938	9	13	2	1	0	0
1898	NY-N	.886	34	35	4	5	0	-5
Total	10	.903	956	1968	147	227	23	24
■ Art Wilson C								
1909	NY-N	.985	19	55	12	1	1	-4
1910	NY-N	.975	25	95	22	3	4	-1
1911	NY-N	.963	64	200	34	9	2	-6
1912	NY-N	.960	61	213	30	10	5	1
1913	NY-N	.965	49	127	38	6	4	7
1914	Chi-F	.932	132	674	212	24	19	13
1915	Chi-F	.980	87	391	96	10	6	-8
1916	Pit-N	.981	39	167	37	4	4	-8
	Chi-N	.953	34	140	43	9	2	-4
	Yr	.967	73	307	80	13	6	-12
1917	Chi-N	.968	75	361	92	15	5	8
1918	Bos-N	.977	85	292	96	9	4	-11
1919	Bos-N	.977	64	213	82	7	4	-2
1920	Bos-N	.667	2	1	1	1	0	-1
1921	Cle-A	1.000	2	1	1	0	0	0
Total	13	.972	738	2930	796	108	60	-16

YEAR	TM/L	PCT	G	PO	A	E	DP	FR
		3B						
1920	Bos-N	1.000	6	3	4	0	0	-1
		1B						
1910	NY-N	—	1	0	0	0	0	0
1919	Bos-N	1.000	1	1	0	0	0	0
Total	2	1.000	2	1	0	0	0	0

■ Frank Wilson OF

YEAR	TM/L	PCT	G	PO	A	E	DP	FR
1924	Bos-N	.973	55	140	5	4	1	2
1925	Bos-N	1.000	10	23	1	0	0	1
1926	Bos-N	.934	56	121	6	9	1	-1
1928	StL-A	—	1	0	0	0	0	0
Total	4	.958	122	284	12	3	2	2

■ Glenn Wilson OF

YEAR	TM/L	PCT	G	PO	A	E	DP	FR
1982	Det-A	.987	80	215	8	3	1	3
1983	Det-A	.988	143	225	12	3	2	-12
1984	Phi-N	.968	109	147	4	5	0	-5
1985	Phi-N	.968	158	343	18	12	4	15
1986	Phi-N	.989	154	331	20	4	5	16
1987	Phi-N	.968	154	315	18	11	2	10
1988	Sea-A	.980	75	140	4	3	1	-1
	Pit-N	.985	35	66	1	1	1	-1
1989	Pit-N	.977	85	163	4	4	0	-4
	Hou-N	.966	25	50	6	2	1	3
	Yr	.974	110	213	10	6	1	-1
1990	Hou-N	.975	108	225	12	6	6	6
Total	9	.977	1126	2220	107	4	23	30
		1B						
1989	Pit-N	1.000	10	36	3	0	1	0
1990	Hou-N	1.000	1	2	0	0	0	0
Total	2	1.000	11	38	3	0	1	0
		3B						
1984	Phi-N	.818	4	6	3	2	0	-2

■ Jimmy Wilson C

YEAR	TM/L	PCT	G	PO	A	E	DP	FR
1923	Phi-N	.960	69	235	50	12	10	-1
1924	Phi-N	.968	82	240	93	11	14	6
1925	Phi-N	.982	89	275	50	6	9	-9
1926	Phi-N	.950	79	228	78	16	5	1
1927	Phi-N	.975	124	377	82	12	12	-18
1928	Phi-N	.990	20	75	21	1	4	1
	StL-N	.983	120	394	82	8	13	0
	Yr	.985	140	469	103	9	17	1
1929	StL-N	.972	119	410	80	14	16	4
1930	StL-N	.987	99	456	67	7	11	10
1931	StL-N	.985	110	498	75	9	15	10
1932	StL-N	.982	75	326	55	7	9	2
1933	StL-N	.982	107	498	58	10	13	2
1934	Phi-N	.987	77	265	42	4	7	2
1935	Phi-N	.982	78	329	44	7	9	8
1936	Phi-N	.960	63	187	31	9	5	-6
1937	Phi-N	.978	22	76	12	2	1	-1
1938	Phi-N	1.000	1	1	1	0	0	0
1939	Cin-N	—	1	0	0	0	0	0
1940	Cin-N	.982	16	46	10	1	0	3
Total	18	.977	1351	4916	931	136	153	14
		1B						
1924	Phi-N	.900	2	9	0	1	2	0
1932	StL-N	.950	3	17	2	1	2	0
1934	Phi-N	—	1	0	0	0	0	0
1936	Phi-N	1.000	1	9	0	0	0	0
1937	Phi-N	.947	2	17	1	1	1	0
Total	5	.948	9	52	3	3	5	0
		OF						
1923	Phi-N	.500	2	3	0	3	0	-1
1924	Phi-N	—	1	0	0	0	0	0
1925	Phi-N	—	1	0	0	0	0	0
Total	3	.500	4	3	0	3	0	-1
		2B						
1932	StL-N	1.000	1	1	1	0	0	0
1934	Phi-N	—	1	0	0	0	0	0
1935	Phi-N	—	1	0	0	0	0	0
Total	3	1.000	3	1	1	0	0	0

■ Chief Wilson OF

YEAR	TM/L	PCT	G	PO	A	E	DP	FR
1908	Pit-N	.955	144	258	20	13	3	1
1909	Pit-N	.957	154	292	19	14	7	6
1910	Pit-N	.972	146	255	23	8	3	-1
1911	Pit-N	.977	146	273	20	7	10	3
1912	Pit-N	.961	152	324	20	14	5	-5
1913	Pit-N	.969	155	301	14	10	3	-4
1914	StL-N	.983	154	312	34	6	11	14
1915	StL-N	.984	105	234	20	4	3	4
1916	StL-N	.955	113	181	11	9	3	-7
Total	9	.968	1269	2430	181	5	48	11

■ Hack Wilson OF

YEAR	TM/L	PCT	G	PO	A	E	DP	FR
1923	NY-N	.857	3	6	0	1	0	0
1924	NY-N	.967	103	230	8	8	2	-10
1925	NY-N	.975	50	75	3	2	2	-8
1926	Chi-N	.973	140	348	11	10	5	0
1927	Chi-N	.967	146	400	13	14	3	-6
1928	Chi-N	.960	143	321	11	14	2	-13
1929	Chi-N	.970	150	380	14	12	4	-7
1930	Chi-N	.951	155	357	9	19	2	-10
1931	Chi-N	.978	103	210	9	5	1	-2
1932	Bro-N	.955	125	220	14	11	4	-10
1933	Bro-N	.963	90	181	3	7	0	-6
1934	Bro-N	.974	43	71	3	2	3	-4
	Phi-N	1.000	6	11	0	0	0	0
	Yr	.977	49	82	3	2	3	-4
Total	12	.965	1257	2810	98	105	28	-76
		2B						
1933	Bro-N	.906	5	11	18	3	3	0

■ Parke Wilson C

YEAR	TM/L	PCT	G	PO	A	E	DP	FR
1893	NY-N	.969	31	106	20	4	1	-7
1894	NY-N	.841	34	108	19	24	2	-8
1895	NY-N	.938	53	214	56	18	8	5
1896	NY-N	.936	71	256	64	22	4	-2
1897	NY-N	.929	30	123	20	11	3	0
1899	NY-N	.925	31	96	27	10	3	-4
Total	6	.926	250	903	206	9	21	-16
		1B						
1894	NY-N	.955	15	138	9	7	7	0
1895	NY-N	.943	11	95	5	6	12	-1
1896	NY-N	.957	2	22	0	1	0	-1
1897	NY-N	.989	10	88	4	1	6	0
1899	NY-N	.972	29	254	19	8	24	2
Total	5	.965	67	597	37	3	49	0
		SS						
1899	NY-N	.843	19	42	60	19	6	-3
		3B						
1895	NY-N	.688	3	4	7	5	0	0
1899	NY-N	.823	15	17	34	11	1	-1
Total	2	.795	18	21	41	6	1	-1
		OF						
1897	NY-N	1.000	4	11	0	0	0	0
1898	NY-N	1.000	1	2	0	0	0	0
1899	NY-N	.875	6	7	0	1	0	-2
Total	3	.952	11	20	0	1	0	-2
		2B						
1897	NY-N	.667	1	0	2	1	0	0

■ Red Wilson C

YEAR	TM/L	PCT	G	PO	A	E	DP	FR
1951	Chi-A	1.000	4	9	2	0	0	-1
1952	Chi-A	1.000	2	8	1	0	0	1
1953	Chi-A	.981	63	282	24	6	1	9
1954	Chi-A	1.000	8	44	3	0	1	4
	Det-A	.996	53	245	25	1	7	2
	Yr	.997	61	289	28	1	8	6
1955	Det-A	.984	72	292	25	5	5	-6
1956	Det-A	.991	78	393	34	4	7	4
1957	Det-A	1.000	60	280	29	0	5	1
1958	Det-A	.992	101	565	34	5	6	7
1959	Det-A	.988	64	374	25	5	8	2
1960	Det-A	.980	45	229	17	5	0	0
	Cle-A	.989	30	163	17	2	1	7
	Yr	.984	75	392	34	7	1	7
Total	10	.990	580	2884	236	3	41	30

■ Bill Wilson OF

YEAR	TM/L	PCT	G	PO	A	E	DP	FR
1950	Chi-A	1.000	2	3	0	0	0	0
1953	Chi-A	1.000	3	9	0	0	0	0
1954	Chi-A	.943	19	33	0	2	0	1
	Phi-A	.989	91	270	7	3	4	5
	Yr	.984	110	303	7	5	4	6
1955	KC-A	.969	82	186	4	6	0	2
Total	4	.979	197	501	11	1	4	8

■ Bill Wilson C

YEAR	TM/L	PCT	G	PO	A	E	DP	FR
1890	Pit-N	.874	38	174	69	35	5	-1
1897	Lou-N	.940	103	338	113	29	7	2
1898	Lou-N	.895	28	86	33	14	1	-3
Total	3	.912	169	598	215	8	13	-2
		OF						
1890	Pit-N	.805	25	54	8	15	3	3
		1B						
1890	Pit-N	.956	18	167	8	8	15	0
1898	Lou-N	.857	1	11	1	2	1	0
Total	2	.949	19	178	9	0	16	0
		SS						
1890	Pit-N	.778	1	0	5	2	1	0
		3B						
1897	Lou-N	.667	1	1	1	1	0	0

■ Mookie Wilson OF

YEAR	TM/L	PCT	G	PO	A	E	DP	FR
1980	NY-N	.973	26	72	1	2	0	2
1981	NY-N	.983	80	226	3	4	2	3
1982	NY-N	.988	156	415	12	5	4	9
1983	NY-N	.984	148	422	5	7	1	5
1984	NY-N	.990	146	396	8	4	6	11
1985	NY-N	.964	83	216	0	8	0	0
1986	NY-N	.979	114	228	7	5	2	3
1987	NY-N	.963	109	205	3	8	2	1
1988	NY-N	.976	104	200	4	5	1	2
1989	NY-N	.975	71	152	2	4	0	4
	Tor-A	.991	54	111	2	1	1	-5
1990	Tor-A	.992	141	370	5	3	2	1
Total	11	.982	1232	3013	52	6	21	36

■ Willie Wilson OF

YEAR	TM/L	PCT	G	PO	A	E	DP	FR
1976	KC-A	.875	6	6	1	1	0	2
1977	KC-A	.960	9	24	0	1	0	1
1978	KC-A	.978	112	171	6	4	2	-14
1979	KC-A	.985	152	384	12	6	0	14
1980	KC-A	.988	159	482	9	6	1	24
1981	KC-A	.987	101	299	14	4	3	22
1982	KC-A	.987	135	376	4	5	0	13
1983	KC-A	.976	136	354	3	9	0	-9
1984	KC-A	.990	128	383	6	4	2	2
1985	KC-A	.995	140	378	4	2	1	-5
1986	KC-A	.993	155	408	4	3	2	-3
1987	KC-A	.997	143	342	3	1	1	-1
1988	KC-A	.989	142	365	1	4	0	-6
1989	KC-A	.977	108	252	2	6	0	-6
1990	KC-A	.994	106	187	2	0	1	-6
Total	15	.988	1732	4411	71	6	13	28

■ Bobby Wine SS

YEAR	TM/L	PCT	G	PO	A	E	DP	FR
1960	Phi-N	1.000	4	9	10	0	4	0
1962	Phi-N	.979	89	140	237	8	51	4
1963	Phi-N	.971	132	220	359	17	73	14
1964	Phi-N	.965	108	153	257	15	55	9
1965	Phi-N	.967	135	221	387	21	84	22
1966	Phi-N	.974	40	56	94	4	19	12
1967	Phi-N	.980	134	201	390	12	90	28
1968	Phi-N	.972	25	37	67	3	11	3
1969	Mon-N	.949	118	208	367	31	96	17
1970	Mon-N	.976	159	284	481	19	137	20
1971	Mon-N	.982	119	221	321	10	76	2
1972	Mon-N	.917	4	4	7	1	2	2
Total	12	.971	1067	1754	2974	141	698	133
		3B						
1962	Phi-N	1.000	20	9	26	0	3	2
1963	Phi-N	1.000	8	4	10	0	0	1
1964	Phi-N	1.000	16	6	9	0	2	2
1968	Phi-N	1.000	1	0	1	0	1	0
1969	Mon-N	—	1	0	0	0	0	0
1972	Mon-N	1.000	21	8	7	0	0	3
Total	6	1.000	67	27	53	0	6	8
		1B						
1965	Phi-N	1.000	4	2	0	0	1	0
1967	Phi-N	1.000	2	5	2	0	1	1
1969	Mon-N	1.000	1	6	0	0	2	0
Total	3	1.000	7	13	2	0	4	1
		OF						
1966	Phi-N	1.000	2	1	0	0	0	0
1972	Mon-N	1.000	1	0	1	0	0	0

■ Dave Winfield OF

YEAR	TM/L	PCT	G	PO	A	E	DP	FR
1973	SD-N	.956	36	64	1	3	0	-2
1974	SD-N	.960	131	276	11	12	2	-7
1975	SD-N	.972	138	302	9	9	1	-5
1976	SD-N	.982	134	304	15	6	4	12
1977	SD-N	.972	156	368	15	11	3	16
1978	SD-N	.979	154	321	7	7	1	0
1979	SD-N	.986	157	344	14	5	3	11
1980	SD-N	.987	159	273	20	4	4	-2
1981	NY-A	.985	102	196	1	3	0	-6
1982	NY-A	.974	135	279	17	8	2	8
1983	NY-A	.978	151	313	5	7	2	-4
1984	NY-A	.994	140	306	3	2	1	1
1985	NY-A	.991	152	316	13	3	3	6
1986	NY-A	.982	145	292	9	5	5	0
1987	NY-A	.989	145	253	6	3	1	-10
1988	NY-A	.989	141	276	3	3	1	-7
1990	NY-A	1.000	12	12	0	0	0	-2
	Cal-A	.989	108	165	7	2	1	-10
	Yr	.989	120	177	7	2	1	-12
Total	17	.981	2296	4660	156	3	34	23
		1B						
1973	SD-N	1.000	1	1	0	0	0	0
1978	SD-N	1.000	2	7	1	0	0	0
Total	2	1.000	3	8	1	0	0	0
		3B						
1986	NY-A	—	2	0	0	0	0	0

■ Al Wingo OF

YEAR	TM/L	PCT	G	PO	A	E	DP	FR
1919	Phi-A	.815	15	21	1	5	0	-3
1924	Det-A	.925	43	59	3	5	2	-8
1925	Det-A	.971	122	282	16	9	6	8
1926	Det-A	.923	74	155	13	14	2	4
1927	Det-A	.891	34	43	6	6	2	-3
1928	Det-A	.968	71	144	5	5	1	-3
Total	6	.944	359	704	44	4	13	-5
		3B						
1926	Det-A	—	2	0	0	0	0	0

■ Ivey Wingo C

YEAR	TM/L	PCT	G	PO	A	E	DP	FR
1911	StL-N	.916	18	65	22	8	3	0
1912	StL-N	.957	92	360	148	23	11	3
1913	StL-N	.945	98	346	132	28	12	0
1914	StL-N	.958	70	272	93	16	7	-2
1915	Cin-N	.966	98	413	124	19	15	3
1916	Cin-N	.958	107	463	170	28	15	7
1917	Cin-N	.967	120	459	151	21	12	-4
1918	Cin-N	.973	93	315	111	12	13	-5
1919	Cin-N	.969	75	266	106	12	6	4
1920	Cin-N	.958	107	368	115	21	14	-11
1921	Cin-N	.959	92	318	101	18	11	6
1922	Cin-N	.964	78	211	81	11	6	3
1923	Cin-N	.969	57	172	44	7	2	3
1924	Cin-N	.989	65	215	50	3	7	4
1925	Cin-N	.965	55	154	38	7	7	3
1926	Cin-N	1.000	7	12	1	0	0	0
1929	Cin-N	—	1	0	0	0	0	0
Total	17	.962	1233	4409	1487	234	141	14
		OF						
1913	StL-N	—	1	0	0	0	0	0
1914	StL-N	1.000	4	4	0	0	0	0
1915	Cin-N	.667	1	2	0	1	0	0
1918	Cin-N	.857	5	6	0	1	0	0
1921	Cin-N	.000	1	0	0	1	0	0
Total	5	.800	12	12	0	3	0	0
		1B						
1913	StL-N	.947	5	47	7	3	2	1
1924	Cin-N	1.000	1	5	0	0	0	0
Total	2	.952	6	52	7	3	2	1
		2B						
1920	Cin-N	1.000	2	2	2	0	0	0

■ Herm Winningham OF

YEAR	TM/L	PCT	G	PO	A	E	DP	FR
1984	NY-N	1.000	10	7	0	0	0	-1
1985	Mon-N	.983	116	229	6	4	2	-10
1986	Mon-N	.980	66	97	2	2	1	2
1987	Mon-N	.975	131	225	5	6	1	-14
1988	Mon-N	.982	30	56	0	1	0	1
	Cin-N	1.000	42	72	1	0	0	3
	Yr	.992	72	128	1	1	0	4
1989	Cin-N	.980	85	146	3	3	0	3
1990	Cin-N	.964	64	89	3	0	0	0
Total	7	.983	544	921	20	6	4	-14
		SS						
1986	Mon-N	—	1	0	0	0	0	0

■ Tom Winsett OF

YEAR	TM/L	PCT	G	PO	A	E	DP	FR
1931	Bos-A	1.000	8	13	1	0	0	0

YEAR	TM/L	PCT	G	PO	A	E	DP	FR
1933	Bos-A	1.000	4	1	0	0	0	-1
1935	StL-N	—	2	0	0	0	0	0
1936	Bro-N	1.000	21	42	3	0	0	0
1937	Bro-N	.960	101	209	6	9	1	-1
1938	Bro-N	.882	9	15	0	2	0	-1
Total	6	.963	145	280	10	1	1	-3

■ Sam Wise SS

1882	Bos-N	.852	72	84	197	49	13	-8
1883	Bos-N	.823	96	134	274	**88**	21	-2
1884	Bos-N	.884	107	156	307	61	16	6
1885	Bos-N	.858	79	135	270	67	29	13
1886	Bos-N	.808	18	24	39	15	2	-9
1887	Bos-N	.869	72	152	233	58	22	2
1888	Bos-N	.888	89	179	271	57	34	10
1889	Was-N	.818	26	40	72	25	9	-7
1891	Bal-a	.867	4	4	9	2	2	0
Total	9	.859	563	908	1672	422	148	5

2B

1884	Bos-N	.824	7	19	23	9	5	1
1885	Bos-N	.918	22	56	67	11	6	0
1886	Bos-N	.850	20	41	44	15	4	-11
1887	Bos-N	.873	16	40	49	13	5	-7
1888	Bos-N	.875	2	4	3	1	0	0
1889	Was-N	.916	72	170	225	36	26	-14
1890	Buf-P	.906	119	328	375	73	58	5
1891	Bal-a	.888	99	225	299	66	30	-13
1893	Was-N	.924	91	315	302	51	45	17
Total	9	.904	448	1198	1387	275	179	-22

1B

1886	Bos-N	.956	57	527	17	25	21	-3
1888	Bos-N	.957	5	43	2	2	3	0
Total	2	.956	62	570	19	7	24	-3

3B

1881	Det-N	.571	1	1	3	3	0	0
1882	Bos-N	.615	6	6	2	5	0	-4
1888	Bos-N	.917	6	6	5	1	0	0
1889	Was-N	.810	13	26	25	12	1	-1
1893	Was-N	.794	31	30	78	28	8	-3
Total	5	.788	57	69	113	9	9	-8

OF

1885	Bos-N	.857	6	5	1	1	0	0
1887	Bos-N	.821	27	39	7	10	2	-2
1888	Bos-N	.909	4	10	0	1	0	0
1889	Was-N	.769	10	9	1	3	0	-1
Total	4	.828	47	63	9	5	2	-3

■ Tex Wisterzil 3B

1914	Bro-F	**.956**	149	**207**	294	23	24	15
1915	Bro-F	.949	31	45	67	6	7	3
	Chi-F	.955	6	8	13	1	0	1
	StL-F	.939	8	13	18	2	0	2
	Chi-F	.968	42	57	96	5	6	9
	Yr	.958	87	123	194	14	13	15
Total	2	.957	236	330	488	7	37	30

■ Mickey Witek 2B

1940	NY-N	.960	32	65	105	7	16	5
1941	NY-N	.933	23	70	70	10	17	2
1942	NY-N	**.978**	147	371	**441**	18	72	-1
1943	NY-N	.967	**153**	**401**	**505**	**31**	90	**16**
1946	NY-N	.962	42	102	100	8	19	-6
1947	NY-N	.983	40	102	125	4	27	12
Total	6	.969	437	.1111	1346	8	241	28

SS

1940	NY-N	.958	89	192	307	22	46	14

3B

1946	NY-N	.878	35	36	50	12	4	-6
1947	NY-N	.750	3	3	3	2	1	-1
Total	2	.868	38	39	53	4	5	-7

■ Whitey Witt OF

1917	Phi-A	.944	7	15	2	1	0	1
1919	Phi-A	.972	59	134	3	4	0	-1
1920	Phi-A	.960	50	70	2	3	0	-2
1921	Phi-A	.959	**154**	288	15	13	3	-2
1922	NY-A	.976	139	312	9	8	1	-5
1923	NY-A	**.979**	144	357	14	8	4	2
1924	NY-A	.976	144	362	11	9	1	-1
1925	NY-A	1.000	10	19	1	0	0	-1
1926	Bro-N	.920	22	44	2	4	1	3
Total	9	.971	729	1601	59	0	10	-11

SS

1916	Phi-A	.902	142	**299**	423	**78**	**59**	-1
1917	Phi-A	.935	111	190	354	38	41	3
1920	Phi-A	1.000	2	0	1	0	0	0
Total	3	.916	255	489	778	116	100	2

2B

1919	Phi-A	.951	56	132	162	15	25	-2
1920	Phi-A	.966	10	29	27	2	5	-1
Total	2	.954	66	161	189	7	30	-3

3B

1917	Phi-A	.947	6	4	14	1	0	1
1919	Phi-A	1.000	2	1	1	0	0	0
Total	2	.952	8	5	15	1	0	1

■ John Wockenfuss C

1974	Det-A	.932	13	45	10	4	1	-1
1975	Det-A	.982	34	195	23	4	4	5
1976	Det-A	.941	59	221	19	15	5	-9
1977	Det-A	.985	37	175	20	3	2	5
1979	Det-A	.983	20	109	8	2	0	5
1980	Det-A	.978	25	123	10	3	2	1
1981	Det-A	1.000	5	15	1	0	0	0
1982	Det-A	.981	24	91	10	2	0	3
1983	Det-A	1.000	29	141	11	0	2	3
1984	Phi-N	.943	21	92	7	6	1	-5
1985	Phi-N	1.000	2	5	0	0	0	0
Total	11	.972	269	1212	119	9	17	7

1B

YEAR	TM/L	PCT	G	PO	A	E	DP	FR
1979	Det-A	.996	31	205	18	1	22	2
1980	Det-A	.983	52	415	35	8	41	1
1981	Det-A	.984	25	179	5	3	27	-3
1982	Det-A	1.000	17	122	3	0	9	-2
1983	Det-A	.979	13	84	10	2	8	1
1984	Phi-N	.996	39	231	13	1	20	-1
1985	Phi-N	1.000	7	39	1	0	5	-1
Total	7	.989	184	1275	85	5	132	-3

OF

1977	Det-A	1.000	9	6	0	0	0	0
1978	Det-A	.978	60	89	2	2	0	4
1979	Det-A	1.000	6	4	0	0	0	0
1980	Det-A	1.000	23	37	2	0	1	1
1981	Det-A	1.000	1	3	0	0	0	0
1982	Det-A	1.000	10	15	1	0	0	1
1983	Det-A	—	1	0	0	0	0	0
Total	7	.988	110	154	5	2	1	6

3B

1982	Det-A	—	1	0	0	0	0	0
1983	Det-A	—	1	0	0	0	0	0
1984	Phi-N	—	2	0	0	0	0	0
Total	3	—	4	0	0	0	0	0

■ Jim Wohlford OF

1973	KC-A	1.000	13	31	2	0	1	2
1974	KC-A	.982	138	273	7	5	4	-6
1975	KC-A	.953	102	175	9	9	1	-4
1976	KC-A	.975	93	189	6	5	0	-3
1977	Mil-A	.981	125	246	6	5	1	-3
1978	Mil-A	.982	35	52	2	1	0	-2
1979	Mil-A	.969	55	126	0	4	0	2
1980	SF-N	.989	49	89	2	1	0	0
1981	SF-N	1.000	10	3	1	0	0	-2
1982	SF-N	.992	72	122	4	1	0	-2
1983	Mon-N	.988	61	80	2	1	0	3
1984	Mon-N	.989	59	85	3	1	1	-5
1985	Mon-N	1.000	43	58	1	0	0	-1
1986	Mon-N	1.000	22	21	1	0	0	-1
Total	14	.980	877	1550	46	3	8	-22

2B

1972	KC-A	.950	8	7	12	1	1	-2
1976	KC-A	1.000	1	1	2	0	1	0
1977	Mil-A	1.000	1	0	1	0	0	0
Total	3	.958	10	8	15	1	2	-2

3B

1980	SF-N	.500	1	0	1	1	0	0
1984	Mon-N	1.000	2	0	1	0	1	0
1986	Mon-N	1.000	6	1	5	0	0	0
Total	3	.889	9	1	7	1	1	0

■ Jimmy Wolf OF

1882	Lou-a	.902	70	71	**21**	10	2	2
1883	Lou-a	.890	78	157	29	23	**6**	**18**
1884	Lou-a	.884	101	173	26	26	4	4
1885	Lou-a	.917	111	180	19	18	4	0
1886	Lou-a	.934	122	197	28	16	5	11
1887	Lou-a	.940	128	207	27	15	5	9
1888	Lou-a	.886	85	113	19	17	4	3
1889	Lou-a	.946	88	159	16	10	2	6
1890	Lou-a	.939	123	199	16	14	5	-1
1891	Lou-a	.938	133	185	28	19	5	5
1892	StL-N	1.000	3	1	0	0	0	-1
Total	11	.918	1042	1642	229	168	42	56

SS

1882	Lou-a	.809	9	14	24	9	1	-3
1883	Lou-a	.652	5	3	12	8	2	-2
1884	Lou-a	.833	1	1	4	1	0	0
1888	Lou-a	.825	39	62	131	41	9	2
1889	Lou-a	.862	10	27	23	8	4	-3
Total	5	.818	64	107	194	7	16	-6

1B

1882	Lou-a	.867	1	13	0	2	0	0
1884	Lou-a	1.000	1	16	0	0	0	0
1886	Lou-a	.931	8	64	3	5	7	0
1887	Lou-a	.917	11	95	4	9	6	-1
1888	Lou-a	1.000	1	3	0	0	0	0
1889	Lou-a	.979	16	135	5	3	14	0
1891	Lou-a	.973	5	35	1	1	4	0
Total	7	.949	43	361	13	0	31	-1

C

1883	Lou-a	.908	20	84	25	11	1	1
1884	Lou-a	.893	11	37	13	6	0	-1
1885	Lou-a	.750	2	2	1	1	0	0
1886	Lou-a	.692	3	6	3	4	1	0
1888	Lou-a	.700	3	4	3	3	0	-1
Total	5	.877	39	133	45	5	3	-1

3B

1884	Lou-a	.000	1	0	0	2	0	0
1885	Lou-a	.800	1	1	3	1	0	0
1888	Lou-a	.917	4	7	15	2	0	3
1889	Lou-a	.760	7	7	12	6	0	-3
1890	Lou-a	.892	12	11	22	4	1	-1
1891	Lou-a	1.000	1	2	2	0	1	0
Total	6	.845	26	28	54	5	2	-2

2B

1883	Lou-a	—	1	0	0	0	0	0
1886	Lou-a	.800	1	0	4	1	0	0
1889	Lou-a	.902	13	34	40	8	3	-2
Total	3	.897	15	34	44	9	3	-2

■ Larry Wolfe 3B

1977	Min-A	1.000	8	9	13	0	1	0
1978	Min-A	.953	81	60	143	10	9	5
1979	Bos-A	.933	9	10	18	2	3	1
1980	Bos-A	1.000	14	3	8	0	2	1
Total	4	.957	112	82	182	2	15	7

2B

YEAR	TM/L	PCT	G	PO	A	E	DP	FR
1979	Bos-A	.963	27	28	50	3	11	4

SS

1978	Min-A	.929	7	6	20	2	2	1
1979	Bos-A	1.000	2	2	1	0	1	0
Total	2	.935	9	8	21	2	3	1

C

1979	Bos-A	1.000	1	2	0	0	0	0

1B

1979	Bos-A	1.000	1	6	1	0	0	0

■ Harry Wolter OF

1907	Cin-N	1.000	4	6	0	0	0	0
	StL-N	.962	12	20	5	1	1	4
	Yr	.969	16	26	5	1	1	4
1909	Bos-A	.783	9	17	1	5	0	0
1910	NY-A	.940	129	192	11	13	3	-3
1911	NY-A	.951	113	178	18	10	8	4
1912	NY-A	.923	9	11	1	1	0	-1
1913	NY-A	.946	121	228	15	14	1	-7
1917	Chi-N	.942	97	131	14	9	5	-7
Total	7	.941	494	783	65	3	18	-10

1B

1909	Bos-A	.978	17	169	12	4	5	0
1910	NY-A	—	2	0	0	0	0	0
1911	NY-A	.889	2	14	2	2	1	0
1917	Chi-N	1.000	1	3	0	0	0	0
Total	4	.971	22	186	14	6	6	0

■ Harry Wolverton 3B

1898	Chi-N	.848	13	21	35	10	1	3
1899	Chi-N	.860	98	123	227	57	12	-5
1900	Chi-N	.875	3	2	5	1	0	-2
	Phi-N	.881	101	122	234	48	16	-9
	Yr	**.881**	104	124	239	49	16	-11
1901	Phi-N	.921	93	114	190	26	9	3
1902	Was-N	.904	59	86	139	24	8	3
	Phi-N	.931	34	44	91	10	11	9
1903	Phi-N	**.941**	123	182	247	27	8	1
1904	Phi-N	.925	102	143	191	27	15	1
1905	Bos-N	.934	122	139	256	28	12	4
1912	NY-A	.821	8	13	10	5	1	-1
Total	9	.909	756	989	1625	263	93	7

SS

1899	Chi-N	.667	1	1	1	1	0	-1

■ George Wood OF

1880	Wor-N	.887	80	123	10	17	0	-7
1881	Det-N	.862	80	132	18	24	4	-3
1882	Det-N	.884	**84**	161	14	23	**8**	1
1883	Det-N	.876	99	**226**	15	34	3	7
1884	Det-N	.896	**114**	190	17	24	1	3
1885	Det-N	.885	70	112	11	16	1	2
1886	Phi-N	.904	97	148	13	17	2	-4
1887	Phi-N	.873	104	155	10	24	2	-8
1888	Phi-N	.905	104	175	15	20	3	2
1889	Phi-N	.915	92	164	9	16	1	-4
	Bal-a	1.000	3	4	0	0	0	0
1890	Phi-P	.895	132	254	**35**	34	9	14
1891	Phi-a	.939	122	221	25	16	**10**	11
1892	Bal-N	.911	21	35	6	4	1	2
	Cin-N	.863	30	39	5	7	1	-2
	Yr	.885	51	74	11	11	2	0
Total	13	.895	1232	2139	203	276	46	14

3B

1880	Wor-N	1.000	2	2	1	0	0	0
1884	Det-N	1.000	1	0	1	0	0	0
1885	Det-N	.907	12	13	26	4	2	0
1886	Phi-N	.833	3	2	3	1	0	-1
1887	Phi-N	.667	3	3	2	2	0	-1
1888	Phi-N	.667	2	1	3	2	0	-1
1890	Phi-P	1.000	1	1	0	0	0	0
1891	Phi-a	.765	6	7	6	4	0	-2
Total	8	.843	30	28	42	3	3	-6

SS

1885	Det-N	.750	1	0	3	1	0	-1
1886	Phi-N	.852	6	6	17	4	1	-1
1887	Phi-N	.929	3	3	10	1	0	-1
1889	Phi-N	.893	6	7	18	3	0	-1
1891	Phi-a	.769	5	8	12	6	3	-2
Total	5	.848	21	24	60	5	4	-6

2B

1887	Phi-N	.941	3	4	12	1	2	1

1B

1880	Wor-N	1.000	1	3	0	0	1	0

■ Jake Wood 2B

1961	Det-A	.969	**162**	380	396	**25**	83	-27
1962	Det-A	.950	90	185	197	**20**	33	-31
1963	Det-A	.958	81	188	202	17	47	-11
1964	Det-A	1.000	10	17	13	0	4	-1
1965	Det-A	.977	20	47	38	2	11	-1
1966	Det-A	.968	52	109	100	7	25	-11
1967	Det-A	.889	2	3	5	1	1	0
Total	7	.963	417	929	951	2	204	-82

1B

1964	Det-A	.989	11	81	7	1	6	0
1965	Det-A	1.000	1	10	0	0	1	0
1966	Det-A	1.000	2	14	0	0	1	0
1967	Det-A	1.000	2	9	0	0	2	0
Total	4	.992	16	114	7	1	10	0

3B

1963	Det-A	1.000	1	2	0	0	0	0
1964	Det-A	.833	6	5	10	3	3	-1
1965	Det-A	—	1	0	0	0	0	0
1966	Det-A	.333	4	1	0	2	0	-1
Total	4	.783	12	8	10	5	3	-2

OF

1964	Det-A	.667	1	2	0	1	0	0

YEAR	TM/L	PCT	G	PO	A	E	DP	FR
1967	Cin-N	1.000	2	3	0	0	0	0
Total	2	.833	3	5	0	1	0	0
SS								
1965	Det-A	—	1	0	0	0	0	0
■ Joe Wood OF								
1918	Cle-A	.962	95	193	10	8	4	-1
1919	Cle-A	.932	64	90	6	7	1	-8
1920	Cle-A	.987	55	71	5	1	0	-7
1921	Cle-A	.973	64	105	3	3	1	-13
1922	Cle-A	.960	141	249	18	11	5	2
Total	5	.962	419	708	42	0	11	-27
2B								
1918	Cle-A	.934	19	47	67	8	3	2
1B								
1918	Cle-A	.971	4	33	0	1	0	-1
■ Ken Wood OF								
1948	StL-A	1.000	5	10	1	0	0	0
1949	StL-A	—	3	0	0	0	0	0
1950	StL-A	.952	94	162	16	9	2	-4
1951	StL-A	.959	100	179	7	8	0	-6
1952	Bos-A	.889	13	8	0	1	0	-1
	Was-A	.954	56	161	6	8	1	7
	Yr	.951	69	169	6	9	1	6
1953	Was-A	1.000	7	13	1	0	1	0
Total	6	.956	278	533	31	6	4	-4
■ Bob Wood C								
1898	Cin-N	.943	29	104	28	8	1	1
1899	Cin-N	.937	53	160	49	14	3	-11
1900	Cin-N	.967	18	59	29	3	2	-1
1901	Cin-N	.952	84	307	106	21	11	-2
1902	Cle-A	.940	52	169	52	14	4	-8
1904	Det-A	.974	47	232	69	8	5	9
1905	Det-A	.886	7	26	13	5	0	0
Total	7	.951	290	1057	346	3	26	-12
3B								
1899	Cin-N	1.000	2	2	2	0	0	0
1900	Cin-N	.800	15	9	27	9	3	-6
1901	Cle-A	.900	4	6	12	2	1	2
1902	Cle-A	1.000	1	1	4	0	0	1
Total	4	.851	22	18	45	1	4	-3
1B								
1898	Cin-N	1.000	1	4	0	0	0	0
1899	Cin-N	1.000	1	8	0	0	2	0
1901	Cle-A	1.000	1	9	0	0	0	0
1902	Cle-A	.973	16	173	10	5	7	0
Total	4	.976	19	194	10	5	9	0
OF								
1898	Cin-N	1.000	1	1	1	0	0	1
1899	Cin-N	1.000	2	4	1	0	0	1
1900	Cin-N	1.000	1	1	0	0	0	0
1901	Cle-A	.857	3	5	1	1	0	0
1902	Cle-A	1.000	2	1	0	0	0	-1
Total	5	.938	9	12	3	1	0	1
2B								
1901	Cle-A	1.000	1	0	1	0	0	0
1902	Cle-A	1.000	1	3	3	0	0	0
Total	2	1.000	2	3	4	0	0	0
SS								
1901	Cle-A	.667	1	1	1	1	0	-1
■ Larry Woodall C								
1920	Det-A	.988	15	59	20	1	0	2
1921	Det-A	.966	25	48	8	2	1	-7
1922	Det-A	.977	40	117	11	3	1	-10
1923	Det-A	.983	60	140	32	3	2	-5
1924	Det-A	.986	62	174	41	3	5	0
1925	Det-A	.967	75	165	38	7	4	-7
1926	Det-A	.979	59	149	37	4	3	-4
1927	Det-A	.997	86	265	72	1	6	4
1928	Det-A	.992	62	218	44	2	3	5
Total	9	.984	484	1335	303	6	25	-22
■ Gene Woodling OF								
1943	Cle-A	1.000	6	8	1	0	0	-1
1946	Cle-A	1.000	37	81	0	0	0	1
1947	Pit-N	.968	21	59	1	2	0	2
1949	NY-A	.982	98	163	5	3	1	-11
1950	NY-A	.993	118	263	16	2	3	10
1951	NY-A	.993	116	265	5	2	0	5
1952	NY-A	.996	118	241	12	1	4	6
1953	NY-A	.996	119	240	6	1	2	-1
1954	NY-A	.983	89	164	5	3	1	-4
1955	Bal-A	1.000	44	76	1	0	1	-4
	Cle-A	.993	70	129	4	1	0	-3
	Yr	.995	114	205	5	1	1	-7
1956	Cle-A	.981	85	154	3	3	0	-9
1957	Cle-A	.992	113	225	10	2	0	6
1958	Bal-A	.974	116	181	7	5	1	-8
1959	Bal-A	.981	124	210	2	4	0	-10
1960	Bal-A	.995	124	202	7	1	0	-4
1961	Was-A	.988	90	154	8	2	0	-8
1962	NY-N	.953	30	41	0	2	0	-6
	NY-N	.986	48	68	0	1	0	-6
Total	17	.989	1566	2924	93	5	13	-45
■ Al Woods OF								
1977	Tor-A	.969	115	215	6	7	1	-4
1978	Tor-A	.978	60	131	2	3	0	-8
1979	Tor-A	.967	127	251	10	9	2	-1
1980	Tor-A	.991	88	205	5	2	1	-2
1981	Tor-A	.973	77	179	4	5	0	1
1982	Tor-A	.970	64	96	2	3	1	-4
Total	6	.974	531	1077	29	9	5	-14
■ Gary Woods OF								
1976	Oak-A	1.000	4	7	0	0	0	1
1977	Tor-A	.994	60	154	4	1	0	0
1978	Tor-A	1.000	6	12	0	0	0	0

YEAR	TM/L	PCT	G	PO	A	E	DP	FR
1980	Hou-N	1.000	14	19	1	0	0	-1
1981	Hou-N	.984	40	61	1	1	0	0
1982	Chi-N	1.000	103	161	6	0	1	-7
1983	Chi-N	.971	73	97	4	3	2	1
1984	Chi-N	1.000	62	53	2	0	1	2
1985	Chi-N	1.000	56	42	1	0	0	1
Total	9	.992	418	606	19	5	4	-3
2B								
1983	Chi-N	—	1	0	0	0	0	0
1984	Chi-N	1.000	3	1	1	0	0	0
Total	2	1.000	4	1	1	0	0	0
■ Ron Woods OF								
1969	Det-A	1.000	7	6	0	0	0	1
	NY-A	1.000	67	129	2	0	0	-6
	Yr	1.000	74	135	2	0	0	-5
1970	NY-A	.974	78	108	6	3	1	-7
1971	NY-A	.929	9	13	0	1	0	0
	Mon-N	.989	45	87	5	1	1	2
1972	Mon-N	.991	73	110	2	1	0	-2
1973	Mon-N	.977	114	208	7	5	1	-11
1974	Mon-N	.987	61	75	0	1	0	1
Total	6	.984	454	736	22	2	3	-22
■ Woody Woodward SS								
1963	Mil-N	1.000	5	1	6	0	0	4
1964	Mil-N	1.000	18	16	39	0	8	7
1965	Mil-N	.977	107	146	243	9	61	10
1966	Atl-N	.958	73	108	191	13	32	-3
1967	Atl-N	1.000	16	30	46	0	5	1
1968	Atl-N	.973	6	13	23	1	3	3
	Cin-N	.968	41	57	95	5	16	-4
	Yr	.969	47	70	118	6	19	-1
1969	Cin-N	.966	93	147	248	14	36	-2
1970	Cin-N	.973	77	101	226	9	48	0
1971	Cin-N	.987	85	101	193	4	42	-10
Total	9	.974	521	720	1310	5	251	6
2B								
1964	Mil-N	.958	40	55	60	5	19	5
1965	Mil-N	1.000	8	4	9	0	1	1
1966	Atl-N	.973	79	154	208	10	46	-2
1967	Atl-N	.982	120	270	339	11	81	8
1968	Atl-N	—	1	0	0	0	0	0
	Cin-N	1.000	9	1	4	0	1	1
	Yr	1.000	10	1	4	0	1	1
1969	Cin-N	1.000	2	1	1	0	0	0
1970	Cin-N	1.000	10	17	13	0	3	1
1971	Cin-N	1.000	9	15	17	0	5	1
Total	8	.978	278	517	651	6	156	15
3B								
1964	Mil-N	1.000	7	3	3	0	0	1
1968	Atl-N	1.000	2	0	1	0	0	0
1970	Cin-N	1.000	20	7	11	0	3	1
1971	Cin-N	.949	63	13	43	3	2	4
Total	4	.964	92	23	58	3	5	6
1B								
1964	Mil-N	1.000	1	1	0	0	0	0
1968	Cin-N	—	1	0	0	0	0	0
1970	Cin-N	1.000	2	6	0	0	1	0
Total	3	1.000	4	7	0	0	1	0
■ Chuck Workman OF								
1938	Cle-A	.500	1	1	0	1	0	0
1943	Bos-N	.988	149	310	22	4	7	3
1944	Bos-N	.983	103	161	16	3	3	-7
1945	Bos-N	.981	24	53	0	1	0	-2
1946	Bos-N	.920	12	22	1	2	0	0
	Pit-N	1.000	40	110	4	0	1	7
	Yr	.986	52	132	5	2	1	7
Total	5	.985	329	657	43	1	11	1
3B								
1943	Bos-N	1.000	1	2	2	0	0	0
1944	Bos-N	.958	19	25	44	3	4	2
1945	Bos-N	.910	107	97	205	30	18	-15
1946	Pit-N	.000	1	0	0	1	0	0
Total	4	.917	128	124	251	4	22	-13
1B								
1943	Bos-N	.946	3	31	4	2	2	0
■ Craig Worthington 3B								
1988	Bal-A	.961	26	20	53	3	4	1
1989	Bal-A	.951	145	113	277	20	22	-10
1990	Bal-A	.945	131	90	218	18	28	-12
Total	3	.950	302	223	548	1	54	-21
■ Red Worthington OF								
1931	Bos-N	.988	124	242	8	3	1	-7
1932	Bos-N	.987	104	216	8	3	2	-5
1933	Bos-N	.900	10	17	1	2	0	-1
1934	Bos-N	.920	11	23	0	2	0	-1
Total	4	.981	249	498	17	0	3	-14
■ Chuck Wortman SS								
1916	Chi-N	.908	69	124	191	32	24	-21
1917	Chi-N	.918	65	85	162	22	26	-8
1918	Chi-N	1.000	4	5	2	0	0	1
Total	3	.913	138	214	355	4	50	-28
2B								
1917	Chi-N	1.000	1	0	2	0	0	0
1918	Chi-N	.864	9	8	11	3	1	1
Total	2	.875	9	8	13	3	1	1
3B								
1917	Chi-N	—	1	0	0	0	0	0
■ Glenn Wright SS								
1924	Pit-N	.946	153	310	601	52	102	11
1925	Pit-N	.939	153	338	530	56	109	1
1926	Pit-N	.927	116	242	382	49	82	-13
1927	Pit-N	.942	143	296	430	45	82	-17
1928	Pit-N	.927	101	194	301	39	59	-24
1929	Bro-N	.667	3	2	2	2	0	-3

YEAR	TM/L	PCT	G	PO	A	E	DP	FR
1930	Bro-N	.964	134	297	462	28	97	-2
1931	Bro-N	.942	75	151	255	25	52	6
1932	Bro-N	.939	122	231	386	40	83	8
1933	Bro-N	.936	51	95	124	15	29	-4
Total	10	.941	1051	2156	3473	351	695	-37
1B								
1928	Pit-N	1.000	1	1	0	0	0	0
1932	Bro-N	1.000	2	4	1	0	1	0
1933	Bro-N	.972	9	65	5	2	6	0
Total	3	.974	12	70	6	2	7	0
2B								
1935	Chi-A	.943	7	13	20	2	3	0
3B								
1925	Pit-N	—	1	0	0	0	0	0
1933	Bro-N	.750	2	1	5	2	0	0
Total	2	.750	3	1	5	2	0	0
OF								
1928	Pit-N	—	1	0	0	0	0	0
■ George Wright SS								
1876	Bos-N	.888	68	89	251	43	16	14
1877	Bos-N	.857	3	4	8	2	1	-1
1878	Bos-N	.947	59	72	197	15	24	11
1879	Pro-N	.924	85	96	319	34	17	20
1880	Bos-N	1.000	1	0	3	0	0	0
1881	Bos-N	.963	7	7	19	1	3	-3
1882	Pro-N	.873	46	46	133	26	16	-6
Total	7	.911	269	314	930	121	77	35
2B								
1876	Bos-N	.900	2	7	2	1	0	-1
1877	Bos-N	.878	58	171	209	53	28	9
Total	2	.878	60	178	211	4	28	8
■ George Wright OF								
1982	Tex-A	.981	149	398	14	8	3	5
1983	Tex-A	.985	161	460	6	7	1	5
1984	Tex-A	.983	80	175	3	3	0	1
1985	Tex-A	.991	102	213	8	2	2	4
1986	Tex-A	.969	42	61	2	2	0	1
	Mon-N	1.000	32	48	2	0	0	0
Total	5	.984	566	1355	35	2	6	16
■ Taffy Wright OF								
1938	Was-A	.982	60	107	3	2	3	-3
1939	Was-A	.950	123	236	10	13	4	-6
1940	Chi-A	.963	144	278	11	11	2	-7
1941	Chi-A	.973	134	279	8	8	3	-6
1942	Chi-A	.968	81	176	6	6	1	1
1946	Chi-A	.991	107	217	5	2	0	-5
1947	Chi-A	.971	100	198	6	6	1	-5
1948	Chi-A	.987	114	227	9	3	3	-4
1949	Phi-A	.970	35	60	5	2	0	-2
Total	9	.972	898	1778	63	3	17	-37
■ Tom Wright OF								
1950	Bos-A	.953	24	40	1	2	1	-1
1951	Bos-A	.950	18	19	0	1	0	-4
1952	StL-A	.976	18	38	2	1	0	1
	Chi-A	.969	34	60	2	2	0	-1
	Yr	.971	52	98	4	3	0	0
1953	Chi-A	.978	33	44	1	1	0	-3
1954	Was-A	1.000	43	84	0	0	0	-3
Total	5	.977	170	285	6	7	1	-11
■ Russ Wrightstone 3B								
1920	Phi-N	.934	56	75	109	13	7	6
1921	Phi-N	.922	54	58	108	14	6	3
1922	Phi-N	.973	40	28	79	3	4	2
1923	Phi-N	.942	72	73	121	12	11	-6
1924	Phi-N	.944	97	114	154	16	19	-5
1925	Phi-N	.964	11	7	20	1	1	-1
1926	Phi-N	.953	37	33	68	5	9	3
1927	Phi-N	—	1	0	0	0	0	0
Total	8	.942	368	388	659	4	57	1
1B								
1922	Phi-N	1.000	2	9	0	0	2	0
1925	Phi-N	.974	6	35	3	1	5	0
1926	Phi-N	.977	53	482	30	12	48	-1
1927	Phi-N	.989	136	1268	90	15	114	2
1928	Phi-N	.800	4	6	2	2	0	0
	NY-N	1.000	2	4	0	0	0	0
	Yr	.857	6	10	2	2	0	0
Total	5	.985	203	1804	125	0	169	1
OF								
1921	Phi-N	.937	37	67	7	5	0	-1
1924	Phi-N	—	1	0	0	0	0	0
1925	Phi-N	.937	45	72	2	5	3	-5
1926	Phi-N	1.000	5	5	1	0	0	1
1928	Phi-N	.936	26	43	1	3	1	-3
Total	5	.938	114	187	11	3	4	-8
SS								
1920	Phi-N	1.000	2	1	0	0	0	0
1922	Phi-N	.966	35	81	148	8	21	11
1923	Phi-N	.991	21	45	66	1	11	1
1924	Phi-N	.895	5	5	12	2	1	0
1925	Phi-N	.900	12	17	19	4	2	-4
Total	5	.963	75	149	245	5	35	8
2B								
1920	Phi-N	—	1	0	0	0	0	0
1921	Phi-N	1.000	4	10	19	0	0	2
1923	Phi-N	.956	9	14	29	2	8	1
1924	Phi-N	.917	9	20	13	3	3	-2
1925	Phi-N	.886	10	21	18	5	3	-6
1926	Phi-N	.965	13	29	26	2	7	-2
1927	Phi-N	—	1	0	0	0	0	0
Total	7	.943	47	94	105	2	21	8
■ Zeke Wrigley SS								
1896	Was-N	1.000	1	2	7	0	0	2
1897	Was-N	.888	33	75	115	24	8	0

YEAR	TM/L	PCT	G	PO	A	E	DP	FR
1898	Was-N	.895	97	252	326	68	42	11
1899	Bro-N	.870	14	33	34	10	4	-5
Total 4		.892	145	362	482	102	54	8
OF								
1897	Was-N	.885	36	44	10	7	4	0
1898	Was-N	1.000	3	1	0	0	0	-1
Total 2		.887	39	45	10	7	4	-1
3B								
1897	Was-N	.852	30	34	64	17	4	0
1898	Was-N	—	1	0	0	0	0	0
1899	NY-N	.818	5	1	8	2	0	-1
	Bro-N	1.000	1	1	0	0	0	0
	Yr	.833	6	2	8	2	0	-1
Total 3		.850	37	36	72	9	4	-1
2B								
1896	Was-N	.909	3	2	8	1	0	1
1897	Was-N	.955	9	22	20	2	2	-1
1898	Was-N	.940	11	31	32	4	3	1
Total 3		.943	23	55	60	7	5	1
■ Butch Wynegar C								
1976	Min-A	.978	137	650	78	**16**	6	-9
1977	Min-A	.993	142	676	84	5	8	-11
1978	Min-A	.988	131	582	70	8	12	-3
1979	Min-A	.992	146	653	65	6	10	-6
1980	Min-A	.988	142	670	72	9	**13**	2
1981	Min-A	.995	37	162	24	1	4	2
1982	Min-A	.986	24	128	9	2	4	-2
	NY-A	.993	62	395	17	3	6	-1
	Yr	.991	86	523	26	5	10	-3
1983	NY-A	.985	93	480	29	8	4	-13
1984	NY-A	.993	126	757	59	6	9	-4
1985	NY-A	.990	96	547	34	6	7	-6
1986	NY-A	.994	57	325	22	2	1	-2
1987	Cal-A	.994	28	162	12	1	3	2
1988	Cal-A	.981	26	94	8	2	1	-1
Total 13		.989	1247	6281	583	5	88	-52
3B								
1977	Min-A	—	1	0	0	0	0	0
1978	Min-A	—	1	0	0	0	0	0
Total 2		—	2	0	0	0	0	0
■ Jim Wynn OF								
1963	Hou-N	.963	53	99	5	4	1	0
1964	Hou-N	.958	64	129	8	6	3	1
1965	Hou-N	.978	155	**382**	13	9	1	14
1966	Hou-N	.978	104	259	6	6	4	6
1967	Hou-N	.968	157	**364**	4	12	1	5
1968	Hou-N	.988	153	298	**20**	4	**8**	17
1969	Hou-N	.985	149	318	9	5	3	6
1970	Hou-N	.987	151	293	14	4	4	8
1971	Hou-N	.988	116	232	9	3	**5**	4
1972	Hou-N	.983	144	284	8	5	2	5
1973	Hou-N	.986	133	270	9	4	1	4
1974	LA-N	.992	148	365	10	3	3	7
1975	LA-N	.983	120	282	6	5	2	-3
1976	Atl-N	.971	138	287	17	9	2	10
1977	NY-N	1.000	8	21	1	0	0	1
	Mil-A	.967	17	29	0	1	0	-3
	Yr	.981	25	50	1	1	0	-2
Total 15		.981	1810	3912	139	0	40	82
SS								
1963	Hou-N	.926	21	22	28	4	2	-7
3B								
1963	Hou-N	1.000	2	3	0	0	0	-1
■ Marvell Wynne OF								
1983	Pit-N	.983	102	223	3	4	2	-5
1984	Pit-N	.990	154	373	8	4	1	-1
1985	Pit-N	.987	99	229	7	3	1	2
1986	SD-N	.986	125	203	3	3	2	-9
1987	SD-N	.981	71	100	2	2	0	1
1988	SD-N	.987	113	216	5	3	2	-12
1989	SD-N	.971	96	160	7	5	2	-4
	Chi-N	.944	13	17	0	1	0	-2
	Yr	.968	109	177	7	6	2	-6
1990	Chi-N	.991	66	108	3	1	2	3
Total 8		.985	839	1629	38	6	12	-27
■ Johnny Wyrostek OF								
1942	Pit-N	1.000	8	18	1	0	1	0
1943	Pit-N	.919	20	34	0	3	0	0
1946	Phi-N	.981	142	**388**	18	8	4	**12**
1947	Phi-N	.971	126	261	11	8	2	-2
1948	Cin-N	.977	130	331	8	8	1	-2
1949	Cin-N	.971	129	293	10	9	1	-1
1950	Cin-N	.980	129	238	8	5	0	-3
1951	Cin-N	.970	139	255	8	8	2	-10
1952	Cin-N	1.000	29	70	6	0	0	4
	Phi-N	.972	88	202	10	6	1	8
	Yr	.980	117	272	16	6	1	12
1953	Phi-N	.962	110	192	11	8	2	-2
1954	Phi-N	.990	55	90	5	1	1	0
Total 11		.975	1105	2372	96	4	15	-3
1B								
1943	Pit-N	—	1	0	0	0	0	0
1950	Cin-N	1.000	4	20	2	0	4	0
1952	Cin-N	1.000	1	8	0	0	1	0
1954	Phi-N	.985	22	187	9	3	20	-3
Total 4		.987	28	215	11	3	25	-3
3B								
1943	Pit-N	.500	2	0	1	1	0	0
2B								
1943	Pit-N	.000	1	0	0	1	0	-1
■ Carl Yastrzemski OF								
1961	Bos-A	.963	147	248	12	10	1	-6
1962	Bos-A	.969	160	329	**15**	**11**	3	12
1963	Bos-A	.980	151	283	**18**	6	3	8
1964	Bos-A	.973	148	372	**19**	11	3	**18**

YEAR	TM/L	PCT	G	PO	A	E	DP	FR
1965	Bos-A	.987	130	222	11	3	2	5
1966	Bos-A	.985	158	310	**15**	5	2	11
1967	Bos-A	.978	161	297	13	7	1	7
1968	Bos-A	.991	155	301	12	3	3	12
1969	Bos-A	.985	143	246	**17**	4	2	4
1970	Bos-A	.953	69	120	3	6	0	-4
1971	Bos-A	.993	146	281	**16**	2	**4**	6
1972	Bos-A	.974	83	141	10	4	1	2
1973	Bos-A	1.000	14	30	0	0	0	-1
1974	Bos-A	.962	63	99	2	4	1	-6
1975	Bos-A	1.000	8	15	1	0	0	0
1976	Bos-A	.980	51	93	3	2	0	-3
1977	Bos-A	**1.000**	140	287	**16**	0	1	8
1978	Bos-A	.986	71	136	8	2	2	-4
1979	Bos-A	.970	36	63	1	2	0	-3
1980	Bos-A	1.000	39	65	3	0	1	-2
1982	Bos-A	1.000	2	3	0	0	0	-1
1983	Bos-A	—	1	0	0	0	0	0
Total 22		.981	2076	3941	195	2	30	64
1B								
1968	Bos-A	1.000	3	14	1	0	1	0
1969	Bos-A	.990	22	181	21	2	29	3
1970	Bos-A	.990	94	696	61	8	62	1
1972	Bos-A	.990	42	357	33	4	34	3
1973	Bos-A	.994	107	912	56	6	85	-5
1974	Bos-A	.997	84	707	44	2	67	-2
1975	Bos-A	.996	140	1202	87	5	103	-2
1976	Bos-A	.998	94	829	52	2	78	-5
1977	Bos-A	1.000	7	57	6	0	4	1
1978	Bos-A	.993	50	387	41	3	47	3
1979	Bos-A	.996	51	466	55	2	42	8
1980	Bos-A	.977	16	160	10	4	19	-1
1981	Bos-A	.992	39	353	34	3	26	2
1982	Bos-A	1.000	14	116	10	0	12	1
1983	Bos-A	1.000	2	22	1	0	1	0
Total 15		.994	765	6459	512	1	610	7
3B								
1964	Bos-A	1.000	2	0	5	0	1	1
1973	Bos-A	.893	31	37	63	12	2	-5
Total 2		.897	33	37	68	2	3	-4
■ George Yeager C								
1897	Bos-N	.970	13	54	10	2	0	3
1898	Bos-N	.951	37	160	33	10	2	0
1899	Bos-N	.833	1	9	1	2	0	1
1901	Cle-A	.964	25	90	45	5	1	5
	Pit-N	.971	20	81	20	3	2	-2
1902	NY-N	.946	27	123	36	9	5	0
	Bal-A	.930	11	38	15	4	0	1
Total 5		.953	134	555	160	5	10	8
1B								
1896	Bos-N	1.000	2	13	0	0	3	0
1898	Bos-N	.985	17	129	5	2	4	0
1901	Cle-A	.963	5	50	2	2	2	0
	Pit-N	.923	1	12	0	1	0	0
1902	NY-N	.968	3	29	1	1	1	0
Total 4		.976	28	233	8	6	10	0
OF								
1897	Bos-N	.944	10	15	2	1	0	0
1898	Bos-N	.737	9	13	1	5	0	-2
1899	Bos-N	1.000	2	2	0	0	0	-1
1901	Cle-A	.667	3	5	1	3	0	0
1902	NY-N	—	1	0	0	0	0	0
Total 5		.813	25	35	4	9	0	-3
2B								
1897	Bos-N	.885	4	7	16	3	1	-1
1901	Cle-A	.667	2	1	3	2	0	-1
Total 2		.844	6	8	19	5	1	-2
3B								
1897	Bos-N	.444	1	1	3	5	0	-1
1901	Pit-N	.875	4	4	10	2	4	1
Total 2		.720	5	5	13	7	4	0
SS								
1898	Bos-N	.500	2	1	1	2	0	-1
■ Joe Yeager 3B								
1899	Bro-N	1.000	1	1	0	0	0	0
1900	Bro-N	—	1	0	0	0	0	0
1902	Det-A	.750	1	2	1	1	0	0
1903	Det-A	.921	107	126	176	26	9	-10
1905	NY-A	.923	91	103	173	23	6	-2
1906	NY-A	1.000	3	3	5	0	0	0
1907	StL-A	.938	91	108	194	20	12	3
Total 7		.927	295	343	549	70	27	-9
SS								
1898	Bro-N	1.000	2	4	7	0	0	0
1899	Bro-N	.914	11	16	37	5	8	3
1901	Det-A	.902	12	18	37	6	8	2
1902	Det-A	.875	3	4	10	2	1	0
1903	Det-A	.889	1	1	7	1	1	1
1905	NY-A	.934	21	45	69	8	8	1
1906	NY-A	.905	22	31	45	8	6	-2
1907	StL-A	.935	10	18	40	4	4	3
1908	StL-A	1.000	1	1	2	0	0	0
Total 9		.920	83	137	254	4	36	8
2B								
1898	Bro-N	—	1	0	0	0	0	0
1901	Det-A	1.000	1	2	1	0	0	0
1902	Det-A	.958	12	16	30	2	1	-3
1906	NY-A	.973	13	35	36	2	3	1
1907	StL-A	.934	17	46	53	7	0	1
1908	StL-A	1.000	4	4	10	0	0	0
Total 6		.955	48	103	130	1	4	-1
OF								
1898	Bro-N	1.000	4	7	1	0	0	0
1899	Bro-N	1.000	1	1	0	0	0	0
1902	Det-A	.960	13	23	1	1	0	0
Total 3		.971	18	31	2	1	0	0

YEAR	TM/L	PCT	G	PO	A	E	DP	FR
■ Steve Yeager C								
1972	LA-N	.984	35	220	19	4	2	8
1973	LA-N	.981	50	230	24	5	2	5
1974	LA-N	.992	93	552	58	5	4	**14**
1975	LA-N	.992	135	**806**	62	7	4	**11**
1976	LA-N	.985	115	522	**77**	9	9	8
1977	LA-N	.977	123	690	89	**18**	12	11
1978	LA-N	.988	91	373	55	5	3	**11**
1979	LA-N	.984	103	513	56	9	7	**11**
1980	LA-N	.984	95	382	36	7	5	4
1981	LA-N	.994	40	142	13	1	1	1
1982	LA-N	.990	76	338	42	4	8	6
1983	LA-N	.985	112	579	63	10	10	-6
1984	LA-N	.994	65	317	30	2	1	-6
1985	LA-N	.992	48	212	28	2	2	8
1986	Sea-A	.989	49	234	22	0	5	0
Total 15		.987	1230	6110	674	8	75	86
■ Eric Yelding OF								
1989	Hou-N	.889	8	7	1	1	0	1
1990	Hou-N	.971	94	230	5	7	2	-3
Total 2		.968	102	237	6	8	2	-2
SS								
1989	Hou-N	1.000	15	10	26	0	4	3
1990	Hou-N	.958	40	64	97	7	16	-6
Total 2		.966	55	74	123	7	20	-3
2B								
1989	Hou-N	.962	13	20	30	2	5	4
1990	Hou-N	.953	10	21	20	2	3	-1
Total 2		.958	23	41	50	4	8	3
3B								
1990	Hou-N	.667	3	0	2	1	0	0
■ Steve Yerkes 2B								
1911	Bos-A	.959	14	40	30	3	2	-3
1912	Bos-A	.943	131	244	323	34	39	-15
1913	Bos-A	.957	129	220	341	25	31	-19
1914	Bos-A	.972	91	177	241	12	38	4
1915	Pit-F	**.967**	114	242	322	19	38	0
1916	Chi-N	.919	41	79	114	17	14	1
Total 6		.956	520	1002	1371	110	162	-32
SS								
1909	Bos-A	1.000	2	1	2	0	0	-1
1911	Bos-A	.927	116	232	337	45	37	-16
1914	Pit-F	.974	39	89	139	6	13	7
1915	Pit-F	.844	8	13	14	5	4	-3
Total 4		.937	165	335	492	6	54	-13
3B								
1911	Bos-A	.902	11	16	21	4	0	-1
■ Rudy York 1B								
1937	Det-A	1.000	2	11	2	0	0	1
1938	Det-A	1.000	1	4	0	0	1	0
1939	Det-A	1.000	19	151	1	0	17	-3
1940	Det-A	.990	**155**	1390	107	15	101	5
1941	Det-A	.986	**155**	1393	110	**21**	111	-1
1942	Det-A	.988	152	1413	**146**	19	117	**15**
1943	Det-A	.990	**155**	1349	**149**	15	105	**18**
1944	Det-A	.989	151	1453	107	**17**	**163**	5
1945	Det-A	.988	**155**	**1464**	113	**19**	142	-2
1946	Bos-A	.994	154	**1327**	116	8	**154**	6
1947	Bos-A	.995	48	395	36	2	45	1
	Chi-A	.995	102	932	71	5	106	-1
	Yr	.995	150	1327	107	7	151	0
1948	Phi-A	.988	14	77	5	1	10	0
Total 12		.990	1263	11359	963	122	1072	44
C								
1934	Det-A	1.000	2	4	2	0	0	0
1937	Det-A	.960	54	190	27	9	6	-8
1938	Det-A	.990	116	406	70	5	10	2
1939	Det-A	.985	67	283	38	5	5	-4
Total 4		.982	239	883	137	9	21	-10
3B								
1937	Det-A	.925	41	45	66	9	5	-10
OF								
1938	Det-A	.815	14	21	1	5	0	-2
■ Tom York OF								
1876	Har-N	.899	67	153	8	18	1	2
1877	Har-N	.865	56	130	5	21	1	0
1878	Pro-N	.873	62	89	14	15	3	3
1879	Pro-N	.898	81	114	9	14	2	-5
1880	Pro-N	.934	53	94	5	7	1	-3
1881	Pro-N	.859	**85**	159	17	29	1	-3
1882	Pro-N	.873	81	154	11	24	3	-3
1883	Cle-N	.864	**100**	176	15	30	3	-1
1884	Bal-a	.843	83	100	7	20	1	-5
1885	Bal-a	.938	22	41	4	3	1	1
Total 10		.878	690	1210	95	181	17	-14
■ Ed Yost C								
1980	Mil-A	1.000	15	41	5	0	0	2
1981	Mil-A	.956	16	37	6	2	2	2
1982	Mil-A	.977	39	121	6	3	2	-1
1983	Mil-A	.971	61	252	16	8	2	-5
1984	Tex-A	.995	78	368	20	2	1	-4
1985	Mon-N	.962	5	24	1	1	0	1
Total 6		.982	214	843	54	6	7	-5
■ Eddie Yost 3B								
1944	Was-A	.917	3	6	5	1	0	0
1946	Was-A	1.000	7	7	10	0	1	0
1947	Was-A	.958	114	125	198	14	11	-9
1948	Was-A	.966	124	**189**	240	15	21	-13
1949	Was-A	.954	122	158	232	19	23	-2
1950	Was-A	.945	155	**205**	307	**30**	**45**	-2
1951	Was-A	.954	152	**203**	234	21	22	-26
1952	Was-A	.962	**157**	212	249	18	26	-35
1953	Was-A	.965	152	**190**	300	18	31	-13
1954	Was-A	.968	**155**	**170**	**347**	17	29	3

YEAR	TM/L	PCT	G	PO	A	E	DP	FR
1955	Was-A	.943	107	100	217	19	22	-6
1956	Was-A	.963	**135**	**164**	303	18	**31**	**11**
1957	Was-A	.952	107	109	207	16	18	-11
1958	Was-A	**.964**	114	109	186	11	20	-15
1959	Det-A	**.962**	146	**168**	259	17	21	-11
1960	Det-A	.933	142	155	208	**26**	18	-27
1961	LA-A	.964	67	57	103	6	4	-10
1962	LA-A	.950	28	29	47	4	2	-2
Total	18	.957	2008	2356	3659	270	345	167

OF

YEAR	TM/L	PCT	G	PO	A	E	DP	FR
1951	Was-A	1.000	3	6	0	0	0	0
1956	Was-A	1.000	8	18	0	0	0	0
1958	Was-A	1.000	4	1	0	0	0	0
Total	3	1.000	15	25	0	0	0	0

1B

YEAR	TM/L	PCT	G	PO	A	E	DP	FR
1958	Was-A	1.000	2	12	1	0	1	0
1962	LA-A	1.000	7	40	1	0	3	-1
Total	2	1.000	9	52	2	0	4	-1

SS

YEAR	TM/L	PCT	G	PO	A	E	DP	FR
1944	Was-A	.800	2	3	1	1	0	-1

2B

YEAR	TM/L	PCT	G	PO	A	E	DP	FR
1959	Det-A	1.000	1	0	1	0	0	0

■ **Del Young**   SS

YEAR	TM/L	PCT	G	PO	A	E	DP	FR
1938	Phi-N	.933	87	156	263	30	44	-1
1939	Phi-N	.946	55	70	104	10	16	-15
1940	Phi-N	.962	6	13	12	1	3	0
Total	3	.938	148	239	379	1	63	-16

2B

YEAR	TM/L	PCT	G	PO	A	E	DP	FR
1937	Phi-N	.950	108	200	333	28	63	11
1938	Phi-N	.966	17	40	44	3	8	-1
1939	Phi-N	.937	17	39	50	6	12	-3
1940	Phi-N	.955	5	10	11	1	1	0
Total	4	.950	147	289	438	8	84	7

■ **Don Young**   OF

YEAR	TM/L	PCT	G	PO	A	E	DP	FR
1965	Chi-N	.933	11	14	0	1	0	-1
1969	Chi-N	.975	100	191	4	5	0	-7
Total	2	.972	111	205	4	6	0	-8

■ **Gerald Young**   OF

YEAR	TM/L	PCT	G	PO	A	E	DP	FR
1987	Hou-N	.980	67	143	5	3	1	2
1988	Hou-N	.992	145	357	10	3	1	6
1989	Hou-N	**.998**	143	**412**	**15**	1	**5**	**19**
1990	Hou-N	.990	50	99	4	1	1	2
Total	4	.992	405	1011	34	8	8	29

■ **Pep Young**   2B

YEAR	TM/L	PCT	G	PO	A	E	DP	FR
1933	Pit-N	1.000	1	2	1	0	0	2
1934	Pit-N	1.000	2	3	6	0	1	3
1935	Pit-N	.952	107	282	315	30	47	-11
1936	Pit-N	.966	123	318	361	24	39	-24
1937	Pit-N	.988	30	73	92	2	14	3
1938	Pit-N	.973	149	370	**554**	26	**120**	**32**
1939	Pit-N	.967	84	202	270	16	61	3
1940	Pit-N	.909	33	51	79	13	9	-6
1945	StL-N	1.000	3	5	4	0	1	0
Total	9	.964	532	1306	1682	111	292	2

SS

YEAR	TM/L	PCT	G	PO	A	E	DP	FR
1933	Pit-N	—	1	0	0	0	0	0
1934	Pit-N	1.000	2	1	3	0	0	0
1935	Pit-N	.933	4	7	7	1	0	-1
1937	Pit-N	.942	45	84	160	15	34	13
1940	Pit-N	.900	7	6	12	2	6	1
1945	StL-N	.978	11	23	21	1	3	0
Total	6	.945	70	121	203	9	43	13

3B

YEAR	TM/L	PCT	G	PO	A	E	DP	FR
1935	Pit-N	.923	6	8	4	1	0	-1
1937	Pit-N	.942	39	38	76	7	4	2
1940	Pit-N	1.000	5	4	7	0	1	0
1941	Cin-N	.923	3	5	7	1	1	1
1945	StL-N	.889	9	3	5	1	0	0
Total	5	.940	62	58	99	0	6	2

OF

YEAR	TM/L	PCT	G	PO	A	E	DP	FR
1935	Pit-N	1.000	6	18	0	0	0	0

■ **Mike Young**   OF

YEAR	TM/L	PCT	G	PO	A	E	DP	FR
1982	Bal-A	1.000	1	1	0	0	0	0
1983	Bal-A	.929	22	25	1	2	0	2
1984	Bal-A	.982	115	216	4	4	0	-8
1985	Bal-A	.975	90	190	6	5	0	1
1986	Bal-A	.962	69	149	1	6	0	-2
1987	Bal-A	.975	60	117	0	3	0	-6
1988	Phi-N	.938	42	76	0	5	0	-1
	Mil-A	—	2	0	0	0	0	0
1989	Cle-A	1.000	1	1	0	0	0	0
Total	8	.969	402	775	12	5	0	-14

■ **Babe Young**   1B

YEAR	TM/L	PCT	G	PO	A	E	DP	FR
1939	NY-N	.982	22	214	9	4	18	-2
1940	NY-N	.992	147	1505	86	13	112	-2
1941	NY-N	.986	150	1395	87	21	124	-3
1942	NY-N	.983	18	159	12	3	11	0
1946	NY-N	.988	49	452	24	6	25	-4
1947	Cin-N	.990	93	730	56	8	66	-1
1948	Cin-N	.993	31	261	21	2	31	0
	StL-N	.996	35	266	8	1	23	-4
	Yr	.995	66	527	29	3	54	-4
Total	7	.989	545	4982	303	8	410	-16

OF

YEAR	TM/L	PCT	G	PO	A	E	DP	FR
1942	NY-N	.972	54	101	4	3	2	-4
1946	NY-N	.976	24	40	0	1	0	-2
1948	Cin-N	1.000	1	2	0	0	0	0
Total	3	.974	79	143	4	4	2	-6

■ **Ralph Young**   2B

YEAR	TM/L	PCT	G	PO	A	E	DP	FR
1915	Det-A	.950	119	233	371	**32**	44	8
1916	Det-A	.966	146	345	419	27	55	-3
1917	Det-A	.958	141	300	**449**	33	46	8
1918	Det-A	.939	91	190	271	**30**	28	-12

YEAR	TM/L	PCT	G	PO	A	E	DP	FR
1919	Det-A	.970	120	296	388	21	38	16
1920	Det-A	.969	150	405	436	27	46	-11
1921	Det-A	.947	106	285	270	31	44	-23
1922	Phi-A	.960	120	302	350	27	53	-15
Total	8	.959	993	2356	2954	228	354	-32

SS

YEAR	TM/L	PCT	G	PO	A	E	DP	FR
1913	NY-A	.857	7	11	19	5	3	1
1916	Det-A	.957	6	26	18	2	1	2
1919	Det-A	.943	5	16	17	2	1	1
Total	3	.922	18	53	54	9	5	4

3B

YEAR	TM/L	PCT	G	PO	A	E	DP	FR
1916	Det-A	1.000	1	2	1	0	0	0

■ **Bobby Young**   2B

YEAR	TM/L	PCT	G	PO	A	E	DP	FR
1951	StL-A	.980	147	361	462	17	**118**	1
1952	StL-A	.984	149	380	407	13	**127**	-9
1953	StL-A	.977	148	397	363	18	120	-17
1954	Bal-A	.976	127	299	310	15	76	-14
1955	Bal-A	.985	58	121	146	4	42	3
	Cle-A	.983	11	24	33	1	14	6
	Yr	.985	69	145	179	5	56	9
1958	Phi-N	.968	21	28	33	2	6	-2
Total	6	.980	661	1610	1754	0	503	-32

3B

YEAR	TM/L	PCT	G	PO	A	E	DP	FR
1948	StL-N	1.000	1	2	0	0	0	1
1955	Cle-A	1.000	1	0	1	0	0	0
Total	2	1.000	2	2	1	0	0	1

■ **Joel Youngblood**   OF

YEAR	TM/L	PCT	G	PO	A	E	DP	FR
1976	Cin-N	.938	9	14	1	1	1	1
1977	StL-N	1.000	11	7	0	0	0	0
	NY-N	1.000	22	36	3	0	0	3
	Yr	1.000	33	43	3	0	0	3
1978	NY-N	.989	50	86	8	1	1	7
1979	NY-N	.985	147	308	18	5	3	11
1980	NY-N	.984	121	292	18	5	**6**	**20**
1981	NY-N	.962	41	70	6	3	0	-1
1982	NY-N	.969	63	88	5	3	1	0
	Mon-N	1.000	35	49	1	0	0	0
	Yr	.979	98	137	6	3	1	0
1983	SF-N	.968	22	28	2	1	0	0
1984	SF-N	1.000	11	9	0	0	0	0
1985	SF-N	.955	56	103	4	5	0	0
1986	SF-N	1.000	45	49	2	0	1	-3
1987	SF-N	1.000	22	24	2	0	0	1
1988	SF-N	.980	45	48	0	1	0	-2
1989	Cin-N	.970	45	31	1	1	1	-5
Total	14	.981	745	1242	71	6	14	32

3B

YEAR	TM/L	PCT	G	PO	A	E	DP	FR
1976	Cin-N	.750	6	1	2	1	1	0
1977	StL-N	.875	6	1	6	1	0	0
	NY-N	.960	10	9	15	1	2	1
	Yr	.939	16	10	21	2	2	1
1978	NY-N	.913	9	5	16	2	1	1
1979	NY-N	.926	12	8	17	2	1	-1
1980	NY-N	.889	21	15	33	6	3	-1
1982	NY-N	—	1	0	0	0	0	0
1983	SF-N	.923	28	22	38	5	2	-4
1984	SF-N	.887	117	87	195	**36**	11	-23
1985	SF-N	.667	1	0	2	1	0	0
1986	SF-N	1.000	5	0	1	0	0	0
1987	SF-N	1.000	2	0	1	0	0	0
Total	11	.896	218	148	326	5	21	-27

2B

YEAR	TM/L	PCT	G	PO	A	E	DP	FR
1976	Cin-N	—	1	0	0	0	0	0
1977	NY-N	.954	33	54	70	6	19	1
1978	NY-N	.979	39	67	72	3	19	1
1979	NY-N	.956	13	21	22	2	6	-3
1980	NY-N	.926	6	11	14	2	2	-1
1982	NY-N	.900	8	11	16	3	2	-2
1983	SF-N	.948	64	97	142	13	26	-25
1984	SF-N	.944	5	6	11	1	1	-1
1986	SF-N	1.000	4	0	3	0	0	0
Total	9	.954	173	267	350	0	75	-30

1B

YEAR	TM/L	PCT	G	PO	A	E	DP	FR
1986	SF-N	.913	7	18	3	2	3	0

SS

YEAR	TM/L	PCT	G	PO	A	E	DP	FR
1978	NY-N	1.000	1	2	0	0	0	-1
1982	NY-N	.667	1	1	1	1	0	-1
1986	SF-N	.857	1	1	5	1	0	-1
Total	3	.833	3	4	6	2	0	-2

C

YEAR	TM/L	PCT	G	PO	A	E	DP	FR
1976	Cin-N	—	1	0	0	0	0	0

■ **Ross Youngs**   OF

YEAR	TM/L	PCT	G	PO	A	E	DP	FR
1917	NY-N	1.000	7	16	2	0	1	1
1918	NY-N	.950	120	192	16	11	3	-9
1919	NY-N	.942	130	235	**23**	16	**7**	-1
1920	NY-N	.935	153	288	**26**	**22**	**7**	0
1921	NY-N	.978	137	247	16	6	5	-9
1922	NY-N	.942	147	280	**28**	**19**	6	1
1923	NY-N	.959	152	282	22	13	7	-1
1924	NY-N	.955	132	236	17	12	3	-4
1925	NY-N	.952	127	214	24	12	2	-7
1926	NY-N	.974	94	170	18	5	5	-2
Total	10	.953	1199	2160	192	116	46	-31

2B

YEAR	TM/L	PCT	G	PO	A	E	DP	FR
1918	NY-N	.917	7	5	6	1	0	-2
1924	NY-N	1.000	2	1	2	0	0	0
1925	NY-N	.813	3	5	8	3	1	-2
Total	3	.871	12	11	16	4	1	-4

■ **Robin Yount**   SS

YEAR	TM/L	PCT	G	PO	A	E	DP	FR
1974	Mil-A	.962	107	148	327	19	55	-11
1975	Mil-A	.939	145	273	402	**44**	80	-23
1976	Mil-A	.963	**161**	**290**	510	31	104	-4
1977	Mil-A	.964	153	256	449	26	94	-9
1978	Mil-A	.959	125	246	453	30	78	22
1979	Mil-A	.969	149	267	517	25	97	5

YEAR	TM/L	PCT	G	PO	A	E	DP	FR
1980	Mil-A	.961	133	239	455	28	89	0
1981	Mil-A	**.985**	93	161	370	8	83	**28**
1982	Mil-A	.969	154	253	**489**	24	95	-4
1983	Mil-A	.973	139	256	420	19	86	-5
1984	Mil-A	.971	120	199	402	18	80	15
Total	11	.964	1479	2588	4794	272	941	14

OF

YEAR	TM/L	PCT	G	PO	A	E	DP	FR
1976	Mil-A	—	1	0	0	0	0	0
1985	Mil-A	.970	108	258	4	8	2	-11
1986	Mil-A	**.997**	131	352	9	1	4	6
1987	Mil-A	.987	150	380	5	5	2	4
1988	Mil-A	.996	**158**	444	12	2	2	8
1989	Mil-A	.981	143	361	8	7	2	0
1990	Mil-A	.991	157	**422**	3	4	0	-1
Total	7	.988	848	2217	41	7	12	6

1B

YEAR	TM/L	PCT	G	PO	A	E	DP	FR
1985	Mil-A	1.000	2	9	1	0	0	0
1986	Mil-A	.929	3	13	0	1	1	-1
Total	2	.958	5	22	1	1	1	-1

■ **Sal Yvars**   C

YEAR	TM/L	PCT	G	PO	A	E	DP	FR
1947	NY-N	1.000	1	3	1	0	0	0
1948	NY-N	1.000	15	50	8	0	2	2
1949	NY-N	1.000	2	11	1	0	0	1
1950	NY-N	.963	9	22	4	1	0	2
1951	NY-N	.942	23	46	3	3	1	-3
1952	NY-N	.988	59	202	40	3	3	**8**
1953	NY-N	1.000	20	70	8	0	1	1
	StL-N	.989	26	76	12	1	3	2
	Yr	.994	46	146	20	1	4	3
1954	StL-N	1.000	21	46	9	0	1	-2
Total	8	.987	176	526	86	8	11	11

■ **Al Zarilla**   OF

YEAR	TM/L	PCT	G	PO	A	E	DP	FR
1943	StL-A	.962	60	123	5	5	2	-2
1944	StL-A	.977	79	167	4	4	1	-2
1946	StL-A	.973	107	236	13	7	**6**	7
1947	StL-A	.986	110	209	6	3	0	-6
1948	StL-A	.962	136	322	5	13	0	0
1949	StL-A	1.000	15	19	0	0	0	-4
	Bos-A	.984	122	241	6	4	4	-7
	Yr	.985	137	260	6	4	4	-11
1950	Bos-A	.976	128	230	12	6	1	-7
1951	Chi-A	.983	117	164	7	3	2	-17
1952	Chi-A	.974	32	35	2	1	0	-4
	StL-A	.976	35	77	5	2	0	2
	Yr	.968	86	141	10	5	0	-2
1953	Bos-A	.947	18	17	1	1	0	-1
Total	10	.974	978	1869	69	1	16	-41

■ **Norm Zauchin**   1B

YEAR	TM/L	PCT	G	PO	A	E	DP	FR
1951	Bos-A	.957	4	20	2	1	8	0
1955	Bos-A	**.995**	126	1137	84	6	106	1
1956	Bos-A	.990	31	189	10	2	18	-1
1957	Bos-A	.972	36	194	15	6	28	0
1958	Was-A	.995	91	749	56	4	74	2
1959	Was-A	.995	19	203	6	1	17	-2
Total	6	.993	307	2492	173	0	251	0

■ **Joe Zdeb**   OF

YEAR	TM/L	PCT	G	PO	A	E	DP	FR
1977	KC-A	.970	93	93	4	3	0	-1
1978	KC-A	.957	52	65	2	3	0	-3
1979	KC-A	1.000	9	13	0	0	0	0
Total	3	.967	154	171	6	6	0	-4

3B

YEAR	TM/L	PCT	G	PO	A	E	DP	FR
1977	KC-A	—	1	0	0	0	0	0
1978	KC-A	—	1	0	0	0	0	0
Total	2	—	2	0	0	0	0	0

2B

YEAR	TM/L	PCT	G	PO	A	E	DP	FR
1978	KC-A	1.000	1	1	0	0	0	0

■ **Rollie Zeider**   2B

YEAR	TM/L	PCT	G	PO	A	E	DP	FR
1910	Chi-A	.931	87	205	242	33	31	5
1911	Chi-A	.865	9	20	12	5	0	-4
1913	Chi-A	1.000	1	0	1	0	0	0
	NY-A	.950	19	51	44	5	2	-4
	Yr	.950	20	51	45	5	2	-4
1915	Chi-F	.941	83	208	240	28	39	4
1916	Chi-N	.959	33	59	81	6	7	-6
1917	Chi-N	.977	24	51	76	3	13	4
1918	Chi-N	.956	79	142	207	16	22	-11
Total	7	.945	335	736	903	6	114	-12

3B

YEAR	TM/L	PCT	G	PO	A	E	DP	FR
1910	Chi-A	.870	4	7	13	3	1	2
1911	Chi-A	.957	10	10	12	1	1	-2
1912	Chi-A	.938	56	57	108	11	11	1
1913	Chi-A	1.000	6	8	9	0	0	1
	NY-A	1.000	2	2	3	0	0	0
	Yr	1.000	8	10	12	0	0	1
1914	Chi-F	.936	117	151	217	25	27	0
1915	Chi-F	.960	30	40	57	4	0	-1
1916	Chi-N	.928	55	59	108	13	10	1
1917	Chi-N	.926	26	20	55	6	6	0
1918	Chi-N	1.000	1	1	1	0	0	0
Total	9	.937	307	355	583	3	56	2

SS

YEAR	TM/L	PCT	G	PO	A	E	DP	FR
1910	Chi-A	.900	45	100	117	24	15	-8
1911	Chi-A	.886	17	34	44	10	5	-2
1912	Chi-A	1.000	1	3	1	0	0	0
1913	NY-A	.901	24	48	52	11	9	-9
1914	Chi-F	.667	1	0	2	1	0	0
1915	Chi-F	.945	21	33	53	5	8	-2
1916	Chi-N	.900	5	9	9	2	2	-2
1917	Chi-N	.901	48	77	95	19	16	-24
Total	8	.904	162	304	373	2	55	-47

1B

YEAR	TM/L	PCT	G	PO	A	E	DP	FR
1911	Chi-A	.997	29	295	22	1	10	3
1912	Chi-A	.979	66	682	54	16	28	**5**
1913	Chi-A	1.000	3	7	2	0	0	1

YEAR	TM/L	PCT	G	PO	A	E	DP	FR
	NY-A	.976	4	37	3	1	2	0
	Yr	.980	7	44	5	1	2	1
1916	Chi-N	1.000	2	6	0	0	0	0
1917	Chi-N	1.000	1	2	0	0	0	0
1918	Chi-N	1.000	1	4	1	0	0	0
Total	6	.984	106	1033	82	8	40	9
	OF							
1916	Chi-N	1.000	7	7	1	0	0	0
1917	Chi-N	1.000	1	1	0	0	0	0
Total	2	1.000	8	8	1	0	0	0

■ Todd Zeile C

YEAR	TM/L	PCT	G	PO	A	E	DP	FR
1989	StL-N	.971	23	125	10	4	1	-1
1990	StL-N	.988	105	533	56	7	3	-7
Total	2	.985	128	658	66	1	4	-8
	3B							
1990	StL-N	.883	24	11	42	7	2	-2
	1B							
1990	StL-N	.991	11	104	8	1	7	0
	OF							
1990	StL-N	—	1	0	0	0	0	0

■ Gus Zernial OF

YEAR	TM/L	PCT	G	PO	A	E	DP	FR
1949	Chi-A	1.000	46	73	4	0	0	-4
1950	Chi-A	.969	137	306	9	10	2	1
1951	Chi-A	.933	4	13	1	1	0	1
	Phi-A	.974	138	321	17	9	3	12
	Yr	.972	142	334	18	10	3	13
1952	Phi-A	.972	141	302	6	9	0	0
1953	Phi-A	.972	141	300	17	9	2	7
1954	Phi-A	.953	90	180	4	9	1	-7
1955	KC-A	.964	103	231	9	9	4	6
1956	KC-A	.984	69	111	9	2	1	-3
1957	KC-A	.952	113	213	4	**11**	1	-5
1958	Det-A	.939	24	30	1	2	0	-4
1959	Det-A	1.000	1	1	0	0	0	0
Total	11	.968	1007	2081	81	1	14	4
	1B							
1954	Phi-A	1.000	2	5	0	0	0	0
1957	KC-A	.833	1	4	1	1	0	0
1959	Det-A	.972	32	197	10	6	20	-3
Total	3	.969	35	206	11	7	20	-3

■ Benny Zientara 2B

YEAR	TM/L	PCT	G	PO	A	E	DP	FR
1941	Cin-N	.914	6	14	18	3	3	1
1946	Cin-N	.970	39	92	131	7	27	20
1947	Cin-N	.976	100	243	247	12	53	-17
1948	Cin-N	.990	60	143	140	3	32	**12**
Total	4	.976	205	492	536	5	115	16
	3B							
1946	Cin-N	.965	36	22	88	4	11	4
1947	Cin-N	1.000	13	5	11	0	0	0
1948	Cin-N	1.000	3	1	1	0	0	0
Total	3	.970	52	28	100	4	11	4
	SS							
1948	Cin-N	1.000	2	2	3	0	0	0

■ Chief Zimmer C

YEAR	TM/L	PCT	G	PO	A	E	DP	FR
1884	Det-N	.830	6	28	11	8	3	0
1886	NY-a	.893	6	33	17	6	0	3
1887	Cle-a	.923	12	47	13	5	1	-4
1888	Cle-a	.917	59	311	111	38	6	7
1889	Cle-N	.931	81	315	131	33	**10**	10
1890	Cle-N	.937	**125**	480	**188**	**45**	**14**	12
1891	Cle-N	.936	**116**	**476**	**181**	45	7	15
1892	Cle-N	.938	111	514	122	42	11	6
1893	Cle-N	.968	56	169	73	8	10	9
1894	Cle-N	**.963**	89	289	100	15	**16**	7
1895	Cle-N	.975	84	318	77	10	2	8
1896	Cle-N	**.972**	91	338	81	12	9	10
1897	Cle-N	.976	80	278	81	9	10	6
1898	Cle-N	.970	19	78	20	3	2	4
1899	Cle-N	.957	20	58	30	4	4	-1
	Lou-N	.985	62	184	77	4	6	0
	Yr	.978	82	**242**	107	8	10	-1
1900	Pit-N	.961	78	318	100	17	8	6
1901	Pit-N	.975	68	285	69	9	4	-8
1902	Pit-N	.969	41	202	48	8	8	-1
1903	Phi-N	.968	35	162	50	7	4	4
Total	19	.952	1239	4883	1580	328	135	93
	1B							
1887	Cle-a	.895	2	17	0	2	1	-1
1888	Cle-a	1.000	3	31	2	0	0	1
1889	Cle-N	.913	3	21	0	2	1	-1
1895	Cle-N	.958	3	21	2	1	3	0
1899	Lou-N	.960	11	116	4	5	3	-1
1900	Pit-N	1.000	2	25	0	0	1	0
1902	Pit-N	—	1	0	0	0	0	0
Total	7	.960	25	231	9	0	9	-2
	OF							
1884	Det-N	1.000	2	3	0	0	0	0
1888	Cle-a	.667	3	3	1	2	1	0
Total	2	.778	5	6	1	2	1	0
	3B							
1891	Cle-N	1.000	1	1	3	0	0	0
1893	Cle-N	—	1	0	0	0	0	0
1896	Cle-N	—	1	0	0	0	0	0

YEAR	TM/L	PCT	G	PO	A	E	DP	FR
Total	3	1.000	3	1	3	0	0	0
	SS							
1888	Cle-a	1.000	1	0	1	0	0	0

■ Don Zimmer 3B

YEAR	TM/L	PCT	G	PO	A	E	DP	FR
1955	Bro-N	1.000	8	2	8	0	0	1
1956	Bro-N	1.000	3	2	1	0	1	0
1957	Bro-N	.957	39	44	68	5	3	4
1958	LA-N	.914	12	12	20	3	1	1
1959	LA-N	1.000	5	5	13	0	0	2
1960	Chi-N	.918	45	38	51	8	5	-5
1961	Chi-N	.786	5	2	9	3	1	-1
1962	NY-N	.961	14	12	37	2	3	5
	Cin-N	.949	43	45	66	6	6	0
	Yr	.952	57	57	103	8	9	5
1963	LA-N	.933	10	3	11	1	0	2
	Was-A	.935	78	88	173	18	17	2
1964	Was-A	.955	87	68	143	10	6	-12
1965	Was-A	.919	26	19	49	6	3	-1
Total	11	.941	375	340	649	2	46	-2
	2B							
1955	Bro-N	.976	62	154	166	8	54	8
1956	Bro-N	1.000	1	0	1	0	0	0
1957	Bro-N	.939	5	15	16	2	4	2
1958	LA-N	1.000	1	4	3	0	1	0
1959	LA-N	1.000	1	0	1	0	0	0
1960	Chi-N	.980	75	170	215	8	25	11
1961	Chi-N	.973	116	282	323	17	99	2
1962	Cin-N	.939	17	20	26	3	5	0
1963	LA-N	1.000	1	0	2	0	0	0
	Was-A	1.000	2	2	4	0	1	0
1964	Was-A	1.000	1	1	1	0	0	0
1965	Was-A	1.000	12	12	14	0	3	0
Total	11	.974	294	660	772	8	192	23
	SS							
1954	Bro-N	.939	13	14	32	3	6	3
1955	Bro-N	.938	21	28	33	4	9	0
1956	Bro-N	.944	8	8	9	1	3	1
1957	Bro-N	.952	37	55	102	8	17	3
1958	LA-N	.965	114	265	372	23	100	**31**
1959	LA-N	.972	88	115	226	10	43	0
1960	Chi-N	1.000	5	3	8	0	1	1
1962	Cin-N	—	1	0	0	0	0	0
1963	LA-N	.500	1	0	1	1	0	0
Total	9	.962	288	488	783	0	179	39
	C							
1964	Was-A	—	2	0	0	0	0	0
1965	Was-A	.966	33	150	18	6	1	-7
Total	2	.966	35	150	18	6	1	-7
	OF							
1958	LA-N	—	1	0	0	0	0	0
1960	Chi-N	—	2	0	0	0	0	0
1961	Chi-N	—	1	0	0	0	0	0
1964	Was-A	1.000	4	3	0	0	0	0
Total	4	1.000	8	3	0	0	0	0

■ Eddie Zimmerman 3B

YEAR	TM/L	PCT	G	PO	A	E	DP	FR
1906	StL-N	.929	5	7	6	1	0	0
1911	Bro-N	**.961**	122	167	229	16	24	3
Total	2	.960	127	174	235	7	24	3

■ Jerry Zimmerman C

YEAR	TM/L	PCT	G	PO	A	E	DP	FR
1961	Cin-N	.975	76	374	22	10	8	3
1962	Min-A	.992	34	111	9	1	0	2
1963	Min-A	1.000	39	116	8	0	0	6
1964	Min-A	.993	63	264	22	2	1	6
1965	Min-A	**.997**	82	321	22	1	5	**12**
1966	Min-A	.996	59	264	16	1	5	**9**
1967	Min-A	.992	104	572	44	5	7	**14**
1968	Min-A	.991	24	109	7	1	0	5
Total	8	.991	481	2131	150	1	26	57

■ Heinie Zimmerman 3B

YEAR	TM/L	PCT	G	PO	A	E	DP	FR
1908	Chi-N	.800	1	1	3	1	0	0
1909	Chi-N	.911	16	34	38	7	1	6
1910	Chi-N	.987	23	37	38	1	4	0
1911	Chi-N	.868	20	25	34	9	2	-2
1912	Chi-N	.916	121	142	242	**35**	16	3
1913	Chi-N	.912	125	139	232	**36**	18	4
1914	Chi-N	.897	118	141	197	**39**	13	-14
1915	Chi-N	.909	36	39	71	11	3	-2
1916	Chi-N	.932	85	88	198	21	11	9
	NY-N	.943	40	38	77	7	5	-3
	Yr	.935	125	126	**275**	28	16	**6**
1917	NY-N	.947	149	148	349	28	22	14
1918	NY-N	.955	100	128	209	16	8	-4
1919	NY-N	.940	123	122	**268**	**25**	15	-1
Total	12	.928	957	1082	1956	236	118	10
	2B							
1907	Chi-N	.789	4	7	8	4	2	1
1908	Chi-N	.923	20	41	43	7	2	0
1909	Chi-N	.945	27	66	55	7	7	-3
1910	Chi-N	.948	32	73	73	8	15	-1
1911	Chi-N	.946	108	256	304	32	42	0
1914	Chi-N	.924	12	25	36	5	3	-2
1915	Chi-N	.943	100	211	267	29	30	-8
1916	Chi-N	.932	14	22	46	5	6	-1

YEAR	TM/L	PCT	G	PO	A	E	DP	FR
	NY-N	1.000	1	1	0	0	0	0
	Yr	.932	15	23	46	5	6	-1
1917	NY-N	.900	5	6	3	1	2	-1
Total	9	.940	323	708	835	8	109	-22
	SS							
1907	Chi-N	1.000	1	1	0	0	0	0
1908	Chi-N	.750	1	1	2	1	0	-1
1909	Chi-N	.857	12	28	32	10	4	1
1910	Chi-N	.827	26	46	69	24	9	-9
1914	Chi-N	.870	15	30	37	10	3	-5
1915	Chi-N	1.000	4	2	6	0	2	1
1916	Chi-N	.933	4	6	8	1	1	-1
Total	7	.854	63	114	154	6	19	-14
	1B							
1910	Chi-N	1.000	1	3	0	0	0	0
1911	Chi-N	.992	11	107	10	1	8	2
1912	Chi-N	.982	22	212	11	4	15	-1
1918	NY-N	.995	19	184	10	1	7	0
Total	4	.989	53	506	31	6	30	1
	OF							
1907	Chi-N	1.000	1	2	0	0	0	0
1908	Chi-N	1.000	8	5	0	0	0	-3
1910	Chi-N	1.000	4	5	1	0	0	0
Total	3	1.000	13	12	1	0	0	-3

■ Guy Zinn OF

YEAR	TM/L	PCT	G	PO	A	E	DP	FR
1911	NY-A	.923	8	10	2	1	0	0
1912	NY-A	.893	106	158	9	20	1	-9
1913	Bos-N	.948	35	83	8	5	1	5
1914	Bal-F	.935	57	82	5	6	1	-5
1915	Bal-F	.949	88	139	11	8	4	-5
Total	5	.927	294	472	35	0	7	-14

■ Richie Zisk OF

YEAR	TM/L	PCT	G	PO	A	E	DP	FR
1971	Pit-N	1.000	6	7	0	0	0	-1
1972	Pit-N	.938	12	14	1	1	0	-1
1973	Pit-N	.987	84	139	12	2	4	1
1974	Pit-N	.985	141	312	9	5	3	6
1975	Pit-N	.975	140	264	7	7	1	0
1976	Pit-N	.987	152	300	11	4	2	0
1977	Chi-A	.982	109	210	9	4	3	2
1978	Tex-A	.988	90	155	6	2	0	-10
1979	Tex-A	.972	134	234	10	7	**6**	-5
1980	Tex-A	.980	37	45	3	1	1	-2
Total	10	.981	905	1680	68	3	20	-13

■ Billy Zitzmann OF

YEAR	TM/L	PCT	G	PO	A	E	DP	FR
1919	Pit-N	.917	8	11	0	1	0	-1
	Cin-N	—	1	0	0	0	0	0
	Yr	.917	9	11	0	1	0	-1
1925	Cin-N	.959	89	135	5	6	0	-12
1926	Cin-N	.965	31	55	0	2	0	0
1927	Cin-N	.958	60	135	2	6	0	-1
1928	Cin-N	.958	78	155	4	7	2	-5
1929	Cin-N	.940	22	47	0	3	0	0
Total	6	.956	289	538	11	5	2	-19
	SS							
1925	Cin-N	1.000	1	1	1	0	0	0
1927	Cin-N	.906	8	12	17	3	0	-2
Total	2	.912	9	13	18	3	0	-2
	1B							
1929	Cin-N	.938	5	30	0	2	1	-1
	3B							
1927	Cin-N	.778	3	2	5	2	0	0
1928	Cin-N	1.000	1	0	1	0	0	0
Total	2	.800	4	2	6	2	0	0

■ Paul Zuvella SS

YEAR	TM/L	PCT	G	PO	A	E	DP	FR
1982	Atl-N	.800	1	0	4	1	0	1
1983	Atl-N	.750	2	1	2	1	0	-2
1984	Atl-N	1.000	6	6	9	0	3	0
1985	Atl-N	.958	33	57	81	6	23	3
1986	NY-A	.966	21	30	54	3	12	4
1987	NY-A	1.000	6	3	7	0	0	-1
1988	Cle-A	.959	49	77	112	8	21	-3
1989	Cle-A	.963	15	10	16	1	1	0
Total	8	.959	133	184	285	0	60	0
	2B							
1984	Atl-N	1.000	6	7	12	0	3	1
1985	Atl-N	.986	42	55	88	2	15	5
1987	NY-A	1.000	7	17	18	0	5	0
Total	3	.990	55	79	118	2	23	6
	3B							
1985	Atl-N	1.000	5	0	4	0	1	0
1987	NY-A	—	1	0	0	0	0	0
1989	Cle-A	.923	5	4	8	1	0	0
Total	3	.941	11	4	12	1	1	-1

■ Dutch Zwilling OF

YEAR	TM/L	PCT	G	PO	A	E	DP	FR
1910	Chi-N	.940	27	45	2	3	1	-2
1914	Chi-F	.962	154	**340**	15	14	3	2
1915	Chi-F	.979	148	**356**	20	8	6	8
1916	Chi-N	1.000	11	11	0	0	0	-2
Total	4	.969	339	752	37	5	10	6
	1B							
1915	Chi-F	1.000	3	3	0	0	0	0

The Annual Record

The Annual Record

This section contains the season-by-season standings and records for all teams since 1871, plus 28 statistical categories for each team's batting and baserunning, and 26 categories for its pitching and fielding. In those years in which major league play consisted of more than one league, the statistics are presented in the order of the leagues' founding: that is, the National Association comes first; the National League record precedes those of all its rivals; the American Association precedes the Union Association and Players League; and the American League follows the National League but precedes the Federal League.

The figure for the leading team in a given category is displayed in boldface. Where data are unavailable, the statistical column is blank. In the case of the National Association, much of the data that had been missing from the records for the five years of its existence, 1871–1875, are at last available. A research project of the Society for American Baseball Research to reconstruct all data from this period, based on original box scores and play-by-plays collected over decades by Michael Stagno of New York, is still in progress, though. It is hoped that additional, authoritative records can be developed for the next edition of *Total Baseball*.

Also presented here are the top three to five players/pitchers in up to 48 categories per season. When fewer than 48 categories are shown, it means that official records are lacking; that data is not reconstructible at present, which is the case for records of stolen bases before 1886 (with the single exception, to date, being 1871); or that available data is not meaningful, such as for Relief Runs or Relief Ranking in the early years of this century. When fewer than five individuals appear in a given category, credible standouts are lacking, as in the case of Stolen Base Wins in most years. The criterion used for identifying pitching leaders is a minimum of one inning pitched per scheduled game; for batters the criterion employed is the one officially in place at the time or, in the absence of any known practice, 3.1 plate appearances per scheduled game.

Ties in counting stats are common, and occasionally they are so numerous that space does not permit listing all the players by name; ties for fifth place are not shown. Highly uncommon are ties in stats based on a large array of data, as with batting averages, on base percentages, earned run averages, and sabermetric stats such as Runs Created, Total Average, or the various Linear Weights measures. Where rounding off has created the appearance of a tie, the true leader—as extra decimal places for a complete calculation would have revealed—is listed first. An example is the AL batting race of 1949, in which

George Kell and Ted Williams are both shown as hitting .343; Kell in fact hit .3429 and Williams .3428. Both men are credited with batting averages of .343, but Kell, the actual leader, is listed first. (This procedure does not hold for calculated stats based on pitchers' won-lost percentages, where the narrow array of data frequently produces actual ties.)

For additional useful information about a team in a given year, we refer the reader to the Home/Road section, the preceding registers, and the various rosters. Team abbreviations used in the Annual Record are to be found on the last page of this book.

The abbreviations employed in the team statistical reviews of the Annual Record, plus brief descriptions of what the less common statistics measure, follow. For fuller explanations, see the general introduction to Part Two, and for more technical information about formulas and computation, see the Glossary. Also included below are descriptions of statistics computed for league-leading players shown in the Annual Record.

Batting and Baserunning

G	Games played
W	Wins
L	Losses
PCT	Percentage of games won
GB	Games Behind the league or division leader
R	Runs scored
OR	Opponents' Runs scored
AB	At-Bats
H	Hits
2B	Doubles
3B	Triples
HR	Home Runs
BB	Bases on Balls
SO	Strikeouts
AVG	Batting Average
OBP	On Base Percentage
SLG	Slugging Average
PRO	Production (On Base Percentage plus Slugging Average)

PRO⁺ Normalized and park-adjusted Production. A figure of 100 is a league-average performance.

BR Batting Runs (Linear Weights measure of runs contributed *beyond* what a league-average batter or team might have contributed, defined as zero.)

/A Adjusted (Signifies that the stat to the immediate left, in this instance Batting Runs, is here normalized to league average and adjusted for home-park factor. A mark of 100 is a league-average performance. Pitcher batting is removed from all league batting statistics before normalization for a variety of reasons expanded upon in the Glossary.)

PF Park Factor (Calculated separately for batters and pitchers: above 100 signifies a park favorable to hitters, below 100 signifies a park favorable to pitchers; see Home/Road section and Glossary for further data and technical information.)

CHI Clutch Hitting Index (Calculated for individuals, actual RBIs over expected RBIs, adjusted for league average and position in batting order; calculated for teams, actual runs scored divided by Batting Runs. Marks above the median of 100 are superior. See Glossary for precise formula.)

RC Runs Created (Bill James's formulation for run contribution from a variety of batting and baserunning events; many different formulas are applied, depending on data available; see Glossary.)

SB Stolen Bases (1886 to the present.)

CS Caught Stealing (Available 1915, 1916 for players with more than 20 steals, 1920–1925, 1951–1990 NL; 1914–1915, 1916 for players with more than 20 steals, 1920–1990 AL.)

SBA Stolen Base Average (Stolen bases divided by attempts; availability dependent upon CS, as shown above.)

SBR Stolen Base Runs (Linear Weights measure of runs contributed *beyond* what a league-average base stealer or team might have gained, defined as zero; individual SBRs are calculated on the basis of a 66.7 percent success rate, the rate necessary to produce benefit, while team SBRs are normalized to the success rate for the league in that season; availability dependent upon CS.)

Pitching and Fielding

CG Complete Games

SH Shutouts (Individual and combined when calculated for teams; individual only for top five leaders.)

SV Saves (Employing definition in force at the time, and 1969 definition for years prior to 1969.)

IP Innings Pitched (Fractional innings given for teams; rounded-off whole innings for individuals.)

H Hits allowed

H/G Hits allowed per Game (Game defined as nine innings.)

HR Home Runs allowed

BB Bases on Balls allowed

SO Strikeouts

RAT Hits allowed plus walks allowed per nine innings.

ERA Earned Run Average

ERA⁺ Normalized and park-adjusted ERA. A mark of 100 is a league-average performance, while marks over 100 are superior to league average and those below 100 indicate poor pitching performance.

OAV Opponents' Batting Average

OOB Opponents' On Base Percentage

PR Pitching Runs (Linear Weights measure of runs saved *beyond* what a league-average pitcher or team might have saved, defined as zero.)

/A Adjusted (Signifies that the stat to the immediate left, in this instance Pitching Runs, is here normalized to league average and adjusted for home-park factor.)

PF Park Factor (Calculated separately for batters and pitchers; above 100 signifies a park favorable to hitters, below 100 signifies a park favorable to pitchers; see Home/Road section and Glossary for further data and technical information.)

CPI Clutch Pitching Index (Expected runs over actual runs, with 100 being a league-average performance and marks above 100 indicating better than expected results. See Glossary.)

FA Fielding Average

E Errors

DP Double Plays

FW Fielding Wins (Fielding Runs divided by the number of runs required to create an additional win beyond average; average is defined as a team record of .500 because a league won-lost average must be .500. For more technical data about Runs Per Win and Fielding Run formulas, see Glossary.)

PW Pitching Wins (Adjusted Pitching Runs divided by the number of runs required to create an additional win beyond average; average is defined as a team record of .500 because a league won-lost average must be .500. For more technical data about Runs Per Win and Pitching Run formulas, see Glossary.)

BW Batting Wins (Adjusted Batting Runs divided by the number of runs required to create an additional win beyond average; average is defined as a team record of .500 because a league won-lost average must be .500. For more technical data about Runs Per Win and Batting Run formulas, see Glossary.)

SBW Stolen Base Wins (Stolen Base Runs divided by the number of runs required to create an additional win beyond average; average is defined as a team record of .500 because a league won-lost average must be .500. For more technical data about Runs Per Win and Stolen Base Run formulas, see Glossary.)

DIF Differential (Difference between the team's actual won-lost record and that predicted by the total of its Pitching Wins, Batting Wins, Fielding Wins, and Stolen Base Wins; indicates the extent to which a team outperformed or underperformed its talent.)

Other stats carried only on an individual basis in the Annual Record portion of *Total Baseball* are as follows:

Total Average Tom Boswell's formulation for offensive contribution from a variety of batting and baserunning events; calculated to make use of the maximum available data.

Fielding Runs The Linear Weights measure of runs saved *beyond* what a league-average player at that position might have saved, defined as zero; calculated to take into account the particular demands of the different positions. See Glossary for formulas.

Total Player Rating The sum of a player's Adjusted Batting Runs, Fielding Runs, and Base Stealing Runs, minus his positional adjustment, all divided by the Runs Per Win factor for that year (generally around 10, historically in the 9–11 range).

Bases on Balls Per Game Game defined as nine innings; league leaders calculated on the basis of fewest walks per nine innings.

Strikeouts Per Game Game defined as nine innings; league leaders calculated on the basis of most strikeouts per nine innings.

Starter Runs Identical to Pitching Runs but confined to starting pitchers, defined as pitchers who average more than three innings per appearance.

Relief Runs Identical to Pitching Runs but confined to relief pitchers.

Relief Ranking Adjusted Relief Runs, weighted for the greater value of a bullpen "closer" who limits his opponents' scoring in the late innings; see Glossary for formula. Relief Runs will tend to benefit long and middle relievers, who are effective over many innings, while Relief Ranking will tend to benefit relievers with perhaps fewer innings but more saves and decisions.

Total Pitcher Index The sum of a pitcher's Pitching Runs, Batting Runs (in the AL since 1973, zero), and Fielding Runs, all divided by the Runs Per Win factor for that year (generally around 10, historically in the 9–11 range).

Total Baseball Ranking The "MVP" of statistics, this ranks pitchers and position players by the total runs contributed in all their endeavors, revealing the most valuable performers in a given year. For rare individuals like Babe Ruth in his Red Sox years, or Bob Caruthers, both of whom played a position in the field when they were not pitching, the TPR will sum up their records in both endeavors.

How to Read a Team Line

TEAM	G	W	L	PCT	GB	R	OR	AB	H	2B	3B	HR	BB	SO	AVG	OBP	SLG	PRO	PRO+	BR	/A	PF	CHI	RC	SB	CS	SBA	SBR
EAST																												
NY	160	100	60	.625		**703**	**532**	5408	1387	251	24	**152**	544	842	.256	**.328**	**.396**	**.724**	119	95	125	95	97	**717**	140	51	45	-11
PIT	160	85	75	.531	15	651	616	5379	1327	240	45	110	**553**	947	.247	.321	.369	.690	105	33	41	99	99	648	119	60	57	-15
MON	163	81	81	.500	20	628	592	5573	1400	260	**48**	107	454	1053	.251	.311	.373	.684	97	12	-17	105	97	636	189	89	**61**	**-9**
CHI	163	77	85	.475	24	660	694	5675	**1481**	**262**	46	113	403	910	**.261**	.312	.383	.695	100	31	2	105	99	673	120	46	43	-11
STL	162	76	86	.469	25	578	633	5518	1373	207	33	71	484	**827**	.249	.312	.337	.649	92	-46	-52	101	98	601	**234**	64	60	-16
PHI	162	65	96	.404	35.5	597	734	5403	1294	246	31	106	489	981	.239	.308	.355	.663	94	-21	-34	102	99	599	112	49	45	-11
WEST																												
LA	162	94	67	.584		628	544	5431	1346	217	25	99	437	947	.248	.308	.352	.660	99	-31	-11	97	**106**	590	131	46	51	-16
CIN	161	87	74	.540	7	641	596	5426	1334	246	25	122	479	922	.246	.311	.368	.679	97	6	-18	104	102	639	207	56	52	-13
SD	161	83	78	.516	11	594	583	5366	1325	205	35	94	494	892	.247	.313	.351	.664	98	-18	-6	98	99	594	123	50	49	-13
SF	162	83	79	.512	11.5	670	626	5450	1353	227	44	113	550	1023	.248	.321	.368	.689	108	32	59	96	101	650	121	78	**61**	-12
HOU	162	82	80	.506	12.5	617	631	5494	1338	239	31	96	474	840	.244	.308	.351	.659	98	-31	-6	96	103	604	198	71	54	-10
ATL	160	54	106	.338	39.5	555	741	5440	1319	228	28	96	432	848	.242	.301	.348	.649	87	-55	-85	105	99	549	95	69	56	-12
TOT	969					7522		65563	16277	2828	415	1279	5793	11032	.248	.313	.363	.675							1789	729	71	99

TEAM	CG	SH	SV	IP	H	H/G	HR	BB	SO	RAT	ERA	ERA+	OAV	OOB	PR	/A	PF	CPI	FA	E	DP	FW	PW	BW	SBW	DIF
EAST																										
NY	31	22	46	1439	**1253**	7.8	78	404	**1100**	10.6	2.91	111	**.234**	**.292**	86	49	93	97	**.981**	115	127	.9	5.3	**13.5**	-2.1	2.4
PIT	12	11	46	1440²	1349	8.4	108	469	790	11.6	3.47	98	.250	.313	-3	-10	99	101	.980	125	128	.3	-1.1	4.4	-2.5	3.8
MON	18	12	43	1482²	1310	8.0	122	476	923	11.1	3.08	**117**	.237	.302	59	**84**	104	**105**	.978	142	145	-.5	**9.1**	-1.8	**-1.9**	-4.9
CHI	30	10	29	1464¹	1494	9.2	115	490	897	12.4	3.84	94	.264	.326	-64	-38	105	102	.980	125	128	.5	-4.1	.2	-2.1	1.5
STL	17	14	42	1470²	1387	8.5	91	486	881	11.6	3.47	100	.251	.314	-3	0	101	99	**.981**	121	131	.6	.0	-5.6	-2.6	2.6
PHI	16	6	36	1433	1447	9.1	118	628	859	13.3	4.14	86	.264	.344	-110	-92	103	102	.976	145	139	-.7	-9.9	-3.7	-2.1	.9
WEST																										
LA	**32**	**24**	49	1463¹	1291	7.9	84	473	1029	11.0	2.96	112	.237	.300	78	59	97	102	.977	142	126	-.5	6.4	-1.2	-2.6	11.5
CIN	24	13	43	1455	1271	7.9	121	564	934	11.1	3.35	107	.236	.305	16	37	104	98	.980	125	131	.4	4.0	-1.9	-2.3	6.4
SD	30	9	39	1449²	1332	8.3	112	439	885	11.1	3.28	104	.246	.306	27	18	99	102	**.981**	120	**147**	.6	1.9	-.6	-2.3	2.9
SF	25	13	42	1462¹	1323	8.1	99	422	875	10.9	3.39	96	.242	.300	10	-20	95	93	.980	129	145	.2	-2.2	6.4	-2.2	-.2
HOU	21	15	40	1474²	1339	8.2	123	478	1049	11.3	3.41	97	.242	.307	6	-14	96	99	.978	138	124	-.3	-1.5	-.6	-2.0	5.4
ATL	14	4	25	1446	1481	9.2	108	524	810	12.7	4.09	90	.267	.336	-103	-66	107	100	.976	151	138	-1.1	-7.1	-9.2	-2.2	-6.4
TOT	270	153	480	17481¹		8.4				11.6	3.45		.248	.313					.979	1578	1609					

The Los Angeles Dodgers had a miracle season in 1988, winning the National League pennant and the World Series against seemingly far superior opponents, the New York Mets and the Oakland Athletics, respectively. But their first miracle was to win the National League's Western Division title after finishing 73–89 in each of the previous two seasons. How did they win the West? With mirrors, mostly, for they had below-average fielding and hitting that should have negated their outstanding pitching.

Let's just track the Dodgers' performance in some of the key categories to show how illuminating a close examination of team data in the Annual Record can be. The Dodgers' on base percentage (OBP) and slugging average (SLG) reveal them to have been a weak hitting club, and their Adjusted Production (PRO+) is worse still, for they scored fewer runs in their park than might have been expected from the total run-scoring picture at Chavez Ravine (Park Factor 106). However, their Clutch Hitting Index (CHI) was the best in their division, testifying to their character, their good fortune, or both. Their Stolen Base Average was above average, but still only accounted for 12 extra runs over the course of the season, so this wasn't the secret of their success.

The pitching numbers are superlative—fewest runs allowed in the West and lowest ERA—despite the fact that Cincinnati held opponents to a lower batting average (OAV) and San Francisco to a lower on base percentage (OOB). Their West-leading Clutch Pitching Index (CPI) suggests that Dodger hurlers pulled their belts a notch tighter when men were on base, and their Home Runs allowed (HR) gives another tip that they knew how to stay away from the big inning. And maybe all those Shutouts (SH) are indicative of the many games they won while scoring few runs themselves.

Look at their batting (which cost them 7.4 wins in the BW, or Batting Wins, column) and baserunning and fielding (which are a virtual wash at +0.4 and −0.6, respectively, in the SBW and FW columns), and notice that their pitching, good as it was, only supplied 11.4 wins beyond average (.500). On balance, then, their offense and defense combined to produce only four wins beyond average. They should have finished with a record of 85–77, or four games beyond the 81–81 league average. Instead they finished 94–67, nine wins beyond their expectations, as indicated in the Differential (DIF) column. Maybe it was manager Tommy Lasorda's doing after all.

TEAM	G	W	L	PCT	GB	R	OR	AB	H	2B	3B	HR	BB	SO	AVG	OBP	SLG	PRO	PRO+	BR	/A	PF	CHI	RC	SB	CS	SBA	SBR
ATH	28	21	7	.750		376	266	1281	410	66	27	9	46	23	.320	.344	.435	.779	125	38	41	99	107	216	56			
BOS	31	20	10	.667	2	401	303	1372	426	70	37	3	60	19	.310	.339	.422	.761	115	33	22	103	108	227	73			
CHI	28	19	9	.679	2	302	241	1196	323	52	21	10	60	22	.270	.305	.374	.679	85	-6	-37	111	103	161	69			
MUT	33	16	17	.485	7.5	302	313	1404	403	43	21	1	33	15	.287	.303	.350	.653	96	-19	11	91	94	167	46			
OLY	32	15	15	.500	7	310	303	1353	375	54	26	6	48	13	.277	.302	.369	.671	97	-11	5	95	97	169	48			
TRO	29	13	15	.464	8	351	362	1248	384	51	34	6	49	19	.308	.334	.417	.751	114	25	20	101	106	199	62			
CLE	29	10	19	.345	11.5	249	341	1186	328	35	40	7	26	25	.277	.292	.391	.683	101	-6	9	95	88	144	18			
KEK	19	7	12	.368	9.5	137	243	746	178	19	8	2	33	9	.239	.271	.294	.565	62	-33	-36	102	90	65	16			
ROK	25	4	21	.160	15.5	231	287	1036	274	44	25	3	38	30	.264	.291	.364	.655	92	-15	-3	96	96	128	53			
TOT	127					2659		10822	3101	434	239	47	393	175	.287	.312	.384	.695							441			

TEAM	CG	SH	SV	IP	H	H/G	HR	BB	SO	RAT	ERA	ERA+	OAV	OOB	PR	/A	PF	CPI	FA	E	DP	FW	PW	BW	SBW	DIF
ATH	27	0	0	249	329	11.9	3	53	16	13.8	4.95	81	.284	.315	-20	-25	95	85	.845	194	13	1.1	-1.6	2.7		4.8
BOS	22	1	3	276	367	12.0	2	42	23	13.3	3.55	117	.273	.295	20	18	99	101	.834	243	24	-.3	1.2	1.4		2.7
CHI	25	0	1	251	308	11.0	6	28	22	12.0	2.76	166	.264	.281	40	50	109	121	.828	231	16	-.9	3.3	-2.4		5.0
MUT	32	1	0	293	373	11.5	7	42	22	12.7	3.72	102	.270	.292	16	2	90	98	.840	235	14	1.0	.1	.7		-2.3
OLY	32	0	0	282	371	11.8	4	45	13	13.3	4.37	95	.280	.304	-4	-6	99	90	.850	218	20	1.5	-.4	.3		-1.4
TRO	28	0	0	250	431	15.5	4	75	12	18.2	5.51	76	.341	.378	-35	-36	100	118	.845	198	22	1.3	-2.3	1.3		-1.3
CLE	23	0	0	254	346	12.3	13	53	33	14.1	4.11	100	.282	.312	3	0	98	107	.819	234	15	-.6	.0	.6		-4.5
KEK	19	1	0	169	261	13.9	5	21	17	15.0	5.17	88	.305	.321	-17	-11	108	93	.803	163	8	-.9	-.7	-2.3		1.5
ROK	23	1	0	226	315	12.5	3	34	16	13.9	4.30	95	.282	.303	-2	-5	97	91	.821	220	14	-1.5	-.3	-.2		-6.5
TOT	231	4	4	2250		12.4				14.0	4.22		.287	.312					.833	1936	146					

Runs
Barnes-Bos 66
Birdsall-Bos 51
Radcliff-Ath 47
Cuthbert-Ath 47
Waterman-Oly 46

Hits
McVey-Bos 66
Meyerle-Ath 64
Barnes-Bos 63
Start-Mut 58
King-Tro 57

Doubles
Anson-Rok 11

Triples
Bass-Cle 10
Wolters-Mut 9
Barnes-Bos 9
Pratt-Cle 8

Home Runs
Treacey-Chi 4
Pike-Tro 4
Meyerle-Ath 4

Total Bases
Meyerle-Ath 91
Barnes-Bos 91
Pike-Tro 85
McVey-Bos 85
King-Tro 79

Runs Batted In
Wolters-Mut 44
McVey-Bos 43
Meyerle-Ath 40
Pike-Tro 39

Runs Produced
Barnes-Bos 100
McVey-Bos 86
Meyerle-Ath 81
King-Tro 79
Pike-Tro 78

Bases On Balls
Pinkham-Chi 18
Wright-Bos 13
Barnes-Bos 13
Wood-Chi 11

Batting Average
Meyerle-Ath 492
McVey-Bos 431
Wright-Bos 412
Barnes-Bos 401
King-Tro 396

On Base Percentage
Meyerle-Ath 500
Wright-Bos 453
Barnes-Bos 447
McVey-Bos 435
Wood-Chi 425

Slugging Average
Meyerle-Ath 700
Pike-Tro 654
Bass-Cle 640
Wright-Bos 625
Barnes-Bos 580

Production
Meyerle-Ath 1.200
Wright-Bos 1.078
Pike-Tro 1.054
Barnes-Bos 1.027
McVey-Bos 991

Adjusted Production
Meyerle-Ath 243
Wright-Bos 199
Pike-Tro 194
Wolters-Mut 188
Barnes-Bos 186

Batter Runs
Meyerle-Ath 22.6
Barnes-Bos 18.9
Pike-Tro 15.5
McVey-Bos 15.5
Wood-Chi 14.2

Adjusted Batter Runs
Meyerle-Ath 22.9
Barnes-Bos 17.6
Pike-Tro 15.1
Wolters-Mut 14.8
McVey-Bos 14.3

Clutch Hitting Index
McMullin-Tro 173
Barrows-Bos 162
Brainard-Oly 155
Wolters-Mut 147
Ferguson-Mut 141

Runs Created
Meyerle-Ath 49
Barnes-Bos 47
Wood-Chi 41
McVey-Bos 41
Pike-Tro 36

Total Average
Meyerle-Ath 1.470
Wright-Bos 1.383
Wood-Chi 1.250
Barnes-Bos 1.223
Pike-Tro 1.148

Stolen Bases
McGeary-Tro 20
Wood-Chi 18
Cuthbert-Ath 16
Leonard-Oly 14
Eggler-Mut 14

Stolen Base Average

Stolen Base Runs

Fielding Runs

Total Player Rating
Meyerle-Ath 1.3
Barnes-Bos 1.1
Pike-Tro 1.0
McVey-Bos 9
King-Tro 8

Wins
Spalding-Bos 19
Zettlein-Chi 18
McBride-Ath 18
Wolters-Mut 16

Win Percentage
McBride-Ath 783
Zettlein-Chi 667
Spalding-Bos 655
Wolters-Mut 500

Games
Wolters-Mut 32
Spalding-Bos 31
Brainard-Oly 30
McMullin-Tro 29

Complete Games
Wolters-Mut 31
Brainard-Oly 30
McMullin-Tro 28
Zettlein-Chi 25
McBride-Ath 25

Shutouts
Wolters-Mut 1
Spalding-Bos 1
Mathews-Kek 1
Fisher-Rok 1

Saves
Wright-Bos 3
Pinkham-Chi 1

Innings Pitched
Wolters-Mut 283.0
Brainard-Oly 264.0
Spalding-Bos 257.1
McMullin-Tro 249.0
Zettlein-Chi 240.2

Fewest Hits/Game
McBride-Ath 10.97
Zettlein-Chi 11.14
McBride-Ath 11.55
Spalding-Bos 11.65
Pratt-Cle 11.86

Fewest BB/Game
Zettlein-Chi 93
Mathews-Kek 1.12
Wolters-Mut 1.24
Brainard-Oly 1.26
Fisher-Rok 1.31

Strikeouts
Pratt-Cle 33
Spalding-Bos 23
Zettlein-Chi 22
Wolters-Mut 22
Mathews-Kek 17

Strikeouts/Game
Pratt-Cle 1.32
Mathews-Kek 91
Zettlein-Chi 82
Spalding-Bos 80
Wolters-Mut 70

Ratio
Zettlein-Chi 12.08
Wolters-Mut 12.21
Spalding-Bos 12.98
McBride-Ath 13.18
Brainard-Oly 13.57

Earned Run Average
Zettlein-Chi 2.73
Spalding-Bos 3.36
Wolters-Mut 3.43
Pratt-Cle 3.77
Fisher-Rok 4.35

Adjusted ERA
Zettlein-Chi 168
Spalding-Bos 124
Wolters-Mut 110
Pratt-Cle 110
Fisher-Rok 94

Opponents' Batting Avg.
Wolters-Mut 263
Zettlein-Chi 267
Spalding-Bos 268
Pratt-Cle 277
McBride-Ath 280

Opponents' On Base Pct.
Zettlein-Chi 283
Wolters-Mut 285
Spalding-Bos 290
Fisher-Rok 302
McBride-Ath 307

Starter Runs
Zettlein-Chi 39.8
Wolters-Mut 24.7
Spalding-Bos 24.7
Pratt-Cle 11.3
Stearns-Oly 3.4

Adjusted Starter Runs
Zettlein-Chi 49.7
Spalding-Bos 22.9
Wolters-Mut 11.2
Pratt-Cle 9.0
Stearns-Oly 3.3

Clutch Pitching Index
Zettlein-Chi 124
McMullin-Tro 118
Pratt-Cle 110
Spalding-Bos 101
Wolters-Mut 99

Relief Runs
Pinkham-Chi 8

Adjusted Relief Runs
Pinkham-Chi 1.3

Relief Ranking
Pinkham-Chi 1.4

Total Pitcher Index
Zettlein-Chi 3.0
Wolters-Mut 1.7
Spalding-Bos 1.6
Pratt-Cle 7
Stearns-Oly 1

Total Baseball Ranking
Zettlein-Chi 3.0
Wolters-Mut 1.7
Spalding-Bos 1.6
Meyerle-Ath 1.3
Barnes-Bos 1.1

TEAM	G	W	L	PCT	GB	R	OR	AB	H	2B	3B	HR	BB	SO	AVG	OBP	SLG	PRO	PRO+	BR	/A	PF	CHI	RC	SB	CS	SBA	SBR
BOS	48	39	8	.830		521	**236**	2137	677	**114**	31	7	25		**.317**	.325	**.409**	**.734**	120	64	39	105	100	**291**				
BAL	58	35	19	.648	7.5	**617**	434	2576	**747**	94	**35**	**14**	28		.290	.298	.370	.668	102	19	-5	105	**108**	**291**				
MUT	56	34	20	.630	8.5	523	362	2423	668	86	13	4	57		.276	.292	.327	.619	99	-17	16	94	103	237				
ATH	47	30	14	.682	7.5	539	349	2140	678	77	23	4	**66**		**.317**	**.337**	.380	.717	**122**	58	**56**	100	102	281				
TRO	25	15	10	.600	13	273	191	1124	329	56	11	5	6		.293	.296	.375	.671	106	9	5	101	110	128				
ATL	37	9	28	.243	25	237	473	1466	370	46	10	0	17		.252	.261	.297	.558	63	-42	-95	117	87	117				
CLE	22	6	16	.273	20.5	174	254	935	272	37	6	0	15		.291	.302	.343	.645	106	1	12	95	86	99				
MAN	24	5	19	.208	22.5	220	348	1015	305	31	8	1	7		.300	.305	.350	.655	110	4	16	94	99	111				
ECK	29	3	26	.103	27	152	413	1075	235	26	6	0	15		.219	.229	.254	.483	58	-58	-23	85	88	64				
OLY	9	2	7	.222	18	54	140	363	93	12	3	0	5		.256	.266	.306	.572	82	-8	-4	95	77	30				
NAT	11	0	11	.0	21	80	190	460	105	3	2	0	1		.228	.230	.243	.473	41	-26	-42	117	111	26				
TOT	183					3390		15714	4479	582	148	35	242	0	.285	.296	.348	.644										

TEAM	CG	SH	SV	IP	H	H/G	HR	BB	SO	RAT	ERA	ERA+	OAV	OOB	PR	/A	PF	CPI	FA	E	DP	FW	PW	BW	SBW	DIF
BOS	41	3	1	430¹	**438**	9.2	0	28		9.7	1.99	188	.240	.252	82	83	100	119					5.8	2.7		7.0
BAL	48	1	1	515²	566	9.9	3	66		11.0	3.02	124	.243	.263	39	41	101	85					2.9	-.3		5.5
MUT	**54**	3	0	512	618	10.9	2	31		11.4	2.55	135	.269	.279	66	50	93	**124**					3.5	1.1		2.4
ATH	47	1	0	419	513	11.0	3	26		11.6	3.01	121	.267	.277	33	28	98	104					1.9	**3.9**		2.2
TRO	17	2	0	225	282	11.3	2	10		11.7	3.08	120	.272	.279	15	15	100	105					1.0	.3		1.1
ATL	37	0	0	336	561	15.0	6	**17**		15.5	5.06	91	.322	.329	-50	-17	124	99					-1.2	-6.6		-1.7
CLE	15	0	0	199	289	13.1	6	19		13.9	4.57	80	.289	.302	-18	-20	98	89					-1.4	.8		-4.4
MAN	22	0	0	211	368	15.7	5	12		16.2	5.97	61	.320	.327	-52	-53	99	84					-3.7	1.1		-4.4
ECK	28	0	0	259¹	503	17.5	6	23		18.3	5.73	61	.354	.364	-57	-65	93	112					-4.5	-1.6		-5.4
OLY	9	0	0	79	147	16.7	0	5		17.3	6.38	58	.331	.339	-23	-23	99	84					-1.6	-.3		-.6
NAT	11	0	0	99	194	17.6	2	5		18.1	6.91	68	.340	.346	-35	-24	127	84					-1.7	-2.9		-.9
TOT	329	10	2	3285¹		12.3				12.9	3.72		.285	.296												

Runs
Eggler-Mut........ 95
Wright-Bos........ 87
Cuthbert-Ath...... 82
Barnes-Bos....... 81
Hatfield-Mut...... 75

Hits
Eggler-Mut........ 97
Barnes-Bos....... 97
Force-Tro-Bal..... 93
Hatfield-Mut...... 91
Cuthbert-Ath...... 90

Doubles
Barnes-Bos....... 28
Eggler-Mut........ 20
Wright-Bos........ 16
Hall-Bal........... 14
Fisler-Ath......... 14

Triples
Hall-Bal........... 8
Gould-Bos......... 8
Anson-Ath......... 7
Meyerle-Ath....... 6

Home Runs
Pike-Bal.......... 6
Gedney-Tro-Eck.... 3

Total Bases
Barnes-Bos...... 132
Pike-Bal......... 120
Wright-Bos....... 119
Eggler-Mut....... 117
Hall-Bal.......... 115

Runs Batted In

Runs Produced
Eggler-Mut........ 95
Wright-Bos........ 85
Cuthbert-Ath...... 81
Barnes-Bos....... 80
Hatfield-Mut...... 74

Bases On Balls
Mack-Ath......... 23
Anson-Ath........ 16
McMullin-Mut..... 11

Batting Average
Barnes-Bos.......422
Anson-Ath........414
Force-Tro-Bal.....406
Hastings-Cle-Bal..360
McGeary-Ath.....358

On Base Percentage
Anson-Ath........455
Barnes-Bos.......444
Force-Tro-Bal.....411
Hastings-Cle-Bal..370
White-Cle.........366

Slugging Average
Barnes-Bos.......574
Anson-Ath........521
Meyerle-Ath......479
Force-Tro-Bal....476
Wright-Bos.......467

Production
Barnes-Bos.....1.017
Anson-Ath.......975
Force-Tro-Bal....887
Spalding-Bos.....815
Wright-Bos.......813

Adjusted Production
Barnes-Bos...... 200
Anson-Ath....... 199
Force-Tro-Bal.... 168
White-Cle........ 146
Hastings-Cle-Bal.. 146

Batter Runs
Barnes-Bos...... 29.2
Anson-Ath....... 25.5
Force-Tro-Bal.... 18.6
Spalding-Bos..... 13.5
Wright-Bos....... 13.5

Adjusted Batter Runs
Barnes-Bos...... 26.5
Anson-Ath....... 25.3
Spalding-Bos.... 19.3
Force-Tro-Bal.... 17.3
Eggler-Mut....... 15.8

Clutch Hitting Index

Runs Created
Barnes-Bos....... 60
Anson-Ath........ 52
Force-Tro-Bal.... 46
Eggler-Mut........ 43
Wright-Bos....... 42

Total Average
Barnes-Bos.....1.060
Anson-Ath......1.016
Force-Tro-Bal....816
Wood-Tro-Eck.....725
Wright-Bos.......720

Stolen Bases

Stolen Base Average

Stolen Base Runs

Fielding Runs

Total Player Rating
Anson-Ath........1.5
Barnes-Bos.......1.4
Eggler-Mut.......1.3
Force-Tro-Bal....1.0
Cuthbert-Ath.......8

Wins
Spalding-Bos...... 38
Cummings-Mut.... 33
McBride-Ath...... 30
Mathews-Bal...... 25
Zettlein-Tro-Eck.... 15

Win Percentage
Spalding-Bos......826
McBride-Ath......682
Cummings-Mut.....623
Mathews-Bal......581
Zettlein-Tro-Eck....484

Games
Cummings-Mut.... 55
Mathews-Bal...... 49
Spalding-Bos..... 48
McBride-Ath...... 47
Britt-Atl........... 37

Complete Games
Cummings-Mut.... 53
McBride-Ath...... 47
Spalding-Bos..... 41
Mathews-Bal...... 39
Britt-Atl........... 37

Shutouts
Spalding-Bos....... 3
Cummings-Mut.... 3
Zettlein-Tro-Eck.... 2
McBride-Ath...... 1
Fisher-Bal......... 1

Saves
Wright-Bos......... 1
Fisher-Bal......... 1

Innings Pitched
Cummings-Mut.. 497.0
McBride-Ath....419.0
Mathews-Bal... 405.1
Spalding-Bos... 404.2
Britt-Atl......... 336.0

Fewest Hits/Game
Fisher-Bal....... 7.26
Spalding-Bos..... 9.16
Mathews-Bal... 10.59
Zettlein-Tro-Eck.. 10.75
Cummings-Mut.. 10.87

Fewest BB/Game
Buttery-Man.......18
Martin-Tro-Eck.....44
Stearns-Nat........45
Britt-Atl...........46
Zettlein-Tro-Eck.....48

Strikeouts

Strikeouts/Game

Ratio
Fisher-Bal....... 8.16
Spalding-Bos.....9.79
Zettlein-Tro-Eck.. 11.22
Cummings-Mut.. 11.39
McBride-Ath....11.58

Earned Run Average
Spalding-Bos.....1.98
Cummings-Mut...2.52
Fisher-Bal.......2.53
Zettlein-Tro-Eck...2.67
McBride-Ath.....3.01

Adjusted ERA
Spalding-Bos.... 188
Fisher-Bal...... 148
Cummings-Mut... 137
Zettlein-Tro-Eck... 136
McBride-Ath..... 121

Opponents' Batting Avg.
Fisher-Bal.......189
Spalding-Bos.....241
Mathews-Bal.....257
Zettlein-Tro-Eck...265
McBride-Ath.....268

Opponents' On Base Pct.
Fisher-Bal........207
Spalding-Bos.....253
Zettlein-Tro-Eck....273
McBride-Ath.....278
Mathews-Bal.....278

Starter Runs
Spalding-Bos.....78.1
Cummings-Mut... 66.3
McBride-Ath..... 33.1
Zettlein-Tro-Eck... 30.6
Mathews-Bal..... 25.4

Adjusted Starter Runs
Spalding-Bos.... 78.6
Cummings-Mut... 51.1
McBride-Ath..... 28.7
Zettlein-Tro-Eck... 28.4
Mathews-Bal..... 26.8

Clutch Pitching Index
Cummings-Mut... 127
Spalding-Bos..... 120
Zettlein-Tro-Eck... 114
Martin-Tro-Eck... 109
McBride-Ath..... 104

Relief Runs
Wright-Bos........ 4.6

Adjusted Relief Runs
Wright-Bos........ 4.6

Relief Ranking
Wright-Bos........ 2.0

Total Pitcher Index
Spalding-Bos...... 7.2
Cummings-Mut.... 3.1
McBride-Ath..... 2.1
Zettlein-Tro-Eck.... 1.7
Mathews-Bal...... 1.4

Total Baseball Ranking
Spalding-Bos......7.2
Cummings-Mut.... 3.1
McBride-Ath..... 2.1
Zettlein-Tro-Eck.... 1.7
Anson-Ath........ 1.5

TEAM	G	W	L	PCT	GB	R	OR	AB	H	2B	3B	HR	BB	SO	AVG	OBP	SLG	PRO	PRO+	BR	/A	PF	CHI	RC	SB	CS	SBA	SBR
BOS	60	43	16	.729		739	460	2747	934	137	46	13	64		.340	.355	.438	.793	127	122	73	108	105	437				
PHI	53	36	17	.679	4	526	396	2324	645	76	26	6	62		.278	.296	.340	.636	88	-20	-38	104	111	240				
BAL	57	34	22	.607	7.5	644	451	2571	814	123	37	12	40		.317	.327	.407	.734	120	61	63	100	107	351				
MUT	53	29	24	.547	11	424	385	2210	619	68	39	6	40		.280	.293	.354	.647	95	-13	-9	99	94	235				
ATH	52	28	23	.549	11	474	403	2263	674	76	22	4	34		.298	.308	.356	.664	93	0	-35	108	100	255				
ATL	55	17	37	.315	23.5	366	549	2208	582	60	27	6	52		.264	.281	.323	.604	91	-45	4	89	86	205				
WAS	39	8	31	.205	25	283	485	1557	412	41	27	3	18		.265	.273	.331	.604	84	-33	-22	97	96	144				
RES	23	2	21	.87	23	98	299	865	203	22	7	0	6		.235	.240	.276	.516	60	-44	-30	92	72	59				
MAR	6	0	6	.0	16.5	26	152	215	34	5	0	0	0		.158	.158	.181	.339	2	-23	-12	77	121	6				
TOT	199					3580		16960	4917	608	231	50	316	0	.290	.303	.362	.665										

TEAM	CG	SH	SV	IP	H	H/G	HR	BB	SO	RAT	ERA	ERA+	OAV	OOB	PR	/A	PF	CPI	FA	E	DP	FW	PW	BW	SBW	DIF
BOS	48	1	6	536	710	11.9	5	34		12.5	3.09	119	.288	.298	30	34	102	112					2.4	5.2		5.9
PHI	50	0	0	481	628	11.8	3	44		12.6	2.98	123	.285	.300	33	35	101	115					2.5	-2.7		9.7
BAL	55	1	0	509¹	676	11.9	4	43		12.7	3.20	112	.284	.296	22	22	100	105					1.6	4.5		-.0
MUT	48	2	0	477	535	10.1	5	69		11.4	2.91	120	.253	.277	36	31	97	91					2.2	-.6		.9
ATH	44	3	2	475	559	10.6	3	57		11.7	3.07	123	.259	.278	27	37	105	87					2.6	-2.5		2.4
ATL	52	1	0	500²	733	13.2	7	42		13.9	3.94	85	.301	.313	-18	-32	93	101					-2.3	.3		-8.0
WAS	39	0	0	346	591	15.4	11	18		15.8	5.05	73	.333	.339	-55	-51	103	102					-3.6	-1.6		-6.3
RES	22	0	0	207	340	14.8	8	9		15.2	5.17	72	.308	.314	-36	-33	103	83					-2.3	-2.1		-5.0
MAR	6	0	0	54	144	24.0	4	0		24.0	10.17	35	.396	.396	-39	-39	100	85					-2.8	-.8		.6
TOT	364	8	8	3586		12.3				13.1	3.60		.290	.303												

Runs
Barnes-Bos 125
Wright-Bos 99
Spalding-Bos 84
Leonard-Bos 81
Eggler-Mut 81

Hits
Barnes-Bos 137
Wright-Bos 124
White-Bos 122
Spalding-Bos 107
O'Rourke-Bos 100

Doubles
Barnes-Bos 28
O'Rourke-Bos 22
White-Bos 20
Pike-Bal 18
Carey-Bal 18

Triples
Barnes-Bos 10
White-Bos 8
Pike-Bal 8
Holdsworth-Mut 8
Beals-Was 8

Home Runs
Pike-Bal 4
Wright-Bos 3
McVey-Bal 3
Barnes-Bos 3

Total Bases
Barnes-Bos 194
Wright-Bos 160
White-Bos 158
Pike-Bal 135
O'Rourke-Bos 131

Runs Batted In

Runs Produced
Barnes-Bos 122
Wright-Bos 96
Spalding-Bos 83
Leonard-Bos 81
Eggler-Mut 81

Bases On Balls
Barnes-Bos 18
Mack-Phi 16
O'Rourke-Bos 15
Malone-Phi 14

Batting Average
Barnes-Bos ...... .428
White-Bos .... .394
Anson-Ath .... .393
McVey-Bal .... .380
Wright-Bos ...... .379

On Base Percentage
Barnes-Bos ...... .459
Anson-Ath .... .405
O'Rourke-Bos ... .397
Wright-Bos ...... .394
White-Bos .... .394

Slugging Average
Barnes-Bos ...... .606
McVey-Bal .... .521
White-Bos .... .510
Wright-Bos ...... .489
Meyerle-Phi ..... .485

Production
Barnes-Bos 1.065
McVey-Bal .... .911
White-Bos .... .903
Wright-Bos ...... .883
O'Rourke-Bos ... .873

Adjusted Production
Barnes-Bos 194
McVey-Bal 166
White-Bos 151
Pabor-Atl 148
Wright-Bos 146

Batter Runs
Barnes-Bos 43.6
White-Bos 23.3
Wright-Bos 23.1
O'Rourke-Bos ... 19.2
Anson-Ath 15.3

Adjusted Batter Runs
Barnes-Bos 37.8
Spalding-Bos ... 21.3
White-Bos 17.9
Wright-Bos 17.3
McVey-Bal 15.2

Clutch Hitting Index

Runs Created
Barnes-Bos 91
Wright-Bos 65
White-Bos 64
O'Rourke-Bos 53
Anson-Ath 46

Total Average
Barnes-Bos 1.158
McVey-Bal .... .866
White-Bos .... .840
O'Rourke-Bos ... .834
Wright-Bos ...... .828

Stolen Bases

Stolen Base Average

Stolen Base Runs

Fielding Runs

Total Player Rating
Barnes-Bos 2.3
White-Bos 1.3
Wright-Bos 1.2
Pabor-Atl 1.1
O'Rourke-Bos 1.1

Wins
Spalding-Bos 41
Zettlein-Phi 36
Mathews-Mut 29
Cummings-Bal 28
McBride-Ath 24

Win Percentage
Spalding-Bos .... .745
Zettlein-Phi ..... .706
Cummings-Bal ... .667
McBride-Ath ..... .558
Mathews-Mut .... .558

Games
Spalding-Bos 60
Britt-Atl 54
Mathews-Mut 52
Zettlein-Phi 51
McBride-Ath 46

Complete Games
Britt-Atl 51
Zettlein-Phi 49
Spalding-Bos 48
Mathews-Mut 47
Cummings-Bal 42

Shutouts
McBride-Ath 3
Mathews-Mut 2
Spalding-Bos 1
Cummings-Bal 1
Britt-Atl 1

Saves
Wright-Bos 5
Fisher-Ath 2
Spalding-Bos 1

Innings Pitched
Spalding-Bos 500.2
Britt-Atl 481.0
Zettlein-Phi 460.0
Mathews-Mut ... 442.2

Fewest Hits/Game
Fisher-Ath 9.53
Mathews-Mut 9.88
McBride-Ath 10.81
Cummings-Bal .. 11.03
Zettlein-Phi 11.62

Fewest BB/Game
Stearns-Was ...... .35
Campbell-Res ..... .38
Spalding-Bos ..... .50
Britt-Atl .... .71
Cummings-Bal .... .78

Strikeouts

Strikeouts/Game

Ratio
Fisher-Ath 10.59
Mathews-Mut ... 11.14
Cummings-Bal .. 11.80
McBride-Ath ... 11.90
Spalding-Bos ... 12.15

Earned Run Average
Cummings-Bal ... 2.76
Mathews-Mut ... 2.85
Zettlein-Phi 2.88
Spalding-Bos ... 2.97
McBride-Ath 3.06

Adjusted ERA
Cummings-Bal ... 130
Zettlein-Phi 127
Spalding-Bos 124
McBride-Ath 123
Mathews-Mut ... 123

Opponents' Batting Avg.
Fisher-Ath ...... .228
Mathews-Mut ... .250
McBride-Ath .... .266
Cummings-Bal .. .270
Zettlein-Phi .... .285

Opponents' On Base Pct.
Fisher-Ath ...... .247
Mathews-Mut ... .273
Cummings-Bal .. .284
McBride-Ath .... .285
Spalding-Bos ... .294

Starter Runs
Mathews-Mut ... 36.9
Zettlein-Phi 36.8
Cummings-Bal .. 35.7
Spalding-Bos ... 35.1
McBride-Ath 22.7

Adjusted Starter Runs
Zettlein-Phi 39.4
Spalding-Bos 39.1
Cummings-Bal ... 35.7
Mathews-Mut ... 32.1
McBride-Ath 30.3

Clutch Pitching Index
Greyson-Was 127
Zettlein-Phi 118
Spalding-Bos 112
Cummings-Bal ... 107
Brainard-Bal 103

Relief Runs

Adjusted Relief Runs

Relief Ranking

Total Pitcher Index
Spalding-Bos 4.4
Cummings-Bal 2.7
McBride-Ath 2.5
Zettlein-Phi 2.3
Mathews-Mut 2.0

Total Baseball Ranking
Spalding-Bos 4.4
Cummings-Bal 2.7
McBride-Ath 2.5
Barnes-Bos 2.3
Zettlein-Phi 2.3

TEAM	G	W	L	PCT	GB	R	OR	AB	H	2B	3B	HR	BB	SO	AVG	OBP	SLG	PRO	PRO+	BR	/A	PF	CHI	RC	SB	CS	SBA	SBR
BOS	71	52	18	.743		735	415	3122	981	130	57	18	32		.314	.321	.410	.731	127	114	82	106	108	421				
MUT	65	42	23	.646	7.5	500	377	2719	709	100	31	8	38		.261	.271	.329	.600	89	-18	-35	104	105	249				
ATH	55	33	22	.600	11.5	441	344	2260	646	87	17	6	24		.286	.293	.347	.640	97	15	-20	109	104	236				
PHI	58	29	29	.500	17	476	428	2432	690	74	51	3	28		.284	.292	.360	.652	106	25	9	104	102	262				
CHI	59	28	31	.475	18.5	418	480	2457	690	89	3	3	34		.281	.291	.323	.614	98	-3	-7	101	94	237				
ATL	56	22	33	.400	22.5	301	449	2165	497	50	11	1	32		.230	.241	.264	.505	71	-82	-36	88	96	141				
HAR	53	16	37	.302	27.5	371	471	2140	587	92	19	2	26		.274	.283	.338	.621	95	0	-19	105	95	210				
BAL	47	9	38	.191	31.5	227	505	1781	435	53	8	1	24		.244	.254	.285	.539	74	-47	-44	99	82	132				
TOT	232					3469		19076	5235	675	197	42	238	0	.274	.283	.337	.620										

TEAM	CG	SH	SV	IP	H	H/G	HR	BB	SO	RAT	ERA	ERA+	OAV	OOB	PR	/A	PF	CPI	FA	E	DP	FW	PW	BW	SBW	DIF
BOS	65	4	3	633	777	11.0	1	27		11.4	2.36	126	.274	.281	44	42	99	123					3.3	6.4		7.4
MUT	62	4	0	586	658	10.1	3	40		10.7	2.30	134	.259	.270	45	51	103	111					4.0	-2.7		8.3
ATH	55	0	0	487	514	9.5	5	29		10.0	2.55	124	.240	.251	24	33	106	80					2.6	-1.6		4.5
PHI	56	3	0	524	666	11.4	4	21		11.8	2.95	103	.275	.281	2	4	101	100					.3	.7		-1.0
CHI	58	3	0	533²	696	11.7	7	48		12.5	3.25	94	.285	.299	-15	-11	102	106					-.9	-.5		-.1
ATL	56	1	0	506	621	11.0	16	13		11.3	3.20	88	.267	.271	-11	-21	94	90					-1.6	-2.8		-1.1
HAR	45	0	1	481	660	12.3	2	23		12.8	3.54	89	.287	.294	-28	-20	105	94					-1.6	-1.5		-7.5
BAL	43	0	0	420	643	13.8	4	37		14.6	4.31	71	.306	.318	-61	-58	102	96					-4.5	-3.4		-6.6
TOT	440	15	4	4170²		11.3				11.8	3.00		.274	.283												

Runs
McVey-Bos 91
O'Rourke-Bos 82
Spalding-Bos 80
Wright-Bos 76
White-Bos 75

Hits
McVey-Bos 124
Spalding-Bos 119
Leonard-Bos 109
Wright-Bos 106
White-Bos 106

Doubles
Pike-Har 24
McVey-Bos 22
Meyerle-Chi 20
Leonard-Bos 18
Burdock-Mut 16

Triples
Wright-Bos 15
Craver-Phi 11
Holdsworth-Phi 9
York-Phi 8

Home Runs
O'Rourke-Bos 5
McVey-Bos 4
White-Bos 3
Clapp-Ath 3

Total Bases
McVey-Bos 166
Wright-Bos 153
O'Rourke-Bos ... 144
Spalding-Bos 136
Leonard-Bos 135

Runs Batted In

Runs Produced
McVey-Bos 87
Spalding-Bos 80
O'Rourke-Bos 77
Wright-Bos 74

Bases On Balls
Nelson-Mut 9
Stearns-Har 8
Hatfield-Mut 8
Barnes-Bos 8

Batting Average
Meyerle-Chi ...... .403
McVey-Bos ...... .364
Craver-Phi .... .352
Barnes-Bos ...... .344
Pike-Har .... .340

On Base Percentage
Meyerle-Chi ...... .410
McVey-Bos ...... .364
Barnes-Bos ...... .363
Craver-Phi .... .362
McMullin-Ath ..... .357

Slugging Average
Pike-Har .... .496
Meyerle-Chi ...... .494
Wright-Bos .... .489
McVey-Bos ...... .487
Craver-Phi .... .483

Production
Meyerle-Chi ...... .904
McVey-Bos ...... .850
Craver-Phi .... .845
Wright-Bos .... .842
Pike-Har .... .836

Adjusted Production
Meyerle-Chi 185
Craver-Phi 161
McVey-Bos 159
Wright-Bos 156
Pike-Har 155

Batter Runs
McVey-Bos 24.7
Meyerle-Chi 23.6
Wright-Bos 22.1
Craver-Phi 19.1
Pike-Har 15.8

Adjusted Batter Runs
Meyerle-Chi 23.1
McVey-Bos 21.2
Spalding-Bos 20.8
Wright-Bos 18.9
Craver-Phi 17.4

Clutch Hitting Index

Runs Created
McVey-Bos 62
Wright-Bos 55
Meyerle-Chi 53
Craver-Phi 48
O'Rourke-Bos 47

Total Average
Meyerle-Chi ...... .848
Wright-Bos .... .773
Craver-Phi .... .769
McVey-Bos ...... .765
Pike-Har .... .752

Stolen Bases

Stolen Base Average

Stolen Base Runs

Fielding Runs

Total Player Rating
McVey-Bos 1.8
Meyerle-Chi 1.7
Craver-Phi 1.3
Wright-Bos 1.1
Pike-Har 1.0

Wins
Spalding-Bos 52
Mathews-Mut 42
McBride-Ath 33
Cummings-Phi 28
Zettlein-Chi 27

Win Percentage
Spalding-Bos ..... .765
Mathews-Mut ..... .656
McBride-Ath ..... .600
Cummings-Phi .... .519
Zettlein-Chi ...... .474

Games
Spalding-Bos 71
Mathews-Mut 65
Zettlein-Chi 57
McBride-Ath 55
Bond-Atl 55

Complete Games
Spalding-Bos 65
Mathews-Mut 62
Zettlein-Chi 57
McBride-Ath 55
Bond-Atl 55

Shutouts
Spalding-Bos 4
Mathews-Mut 4
Zettlein-Chi 3
Cummings-Phi 3
Bond-Atl 1

Saves
Wright-Bos 3
Stearns-Har 1

Innings Pitched
Spalding-Bos 616.1
Mathews-Mut ... 578.0
Zettlein-Chi 515.2
Bond-Atl 497.0
McBride-Ath 487.0

Fewest Hits/Game
McBride-Ath 9.50
Mathews-Mut ... 10.07
Spalding-Bos ... 11.00
Bond-Atl 11.03
Cummings-Phi ... 11.24

Fewest BB/Game
Bond-Atl .... .18
Fisher-Har .... .28
Spalding-Bos ...... .34
Cummings-Phi ..... .39
McBride-Ath .... .54

Strikeouts

Strikeouts/Game

Ratio
McBride-Ath 10.03
Mathews-Mut ... 10.68
Bond-Atl 11.21
Spalding-Bos ... 11.33
Cummings-Phi ... 11.63

Earned Run Average
Mathews-Mut 2.30
Spalding-Bos 2.35
McBride-Ath 2.55
Cummings-Phi ... 2.88
Fisher-Har 3.04

Adjusted ERA
Mathews-Mut 134
Spalding-Bos 126
McBride-Ath 124
Cummings-Phi ... 106
Fisher-Har 104

Opponents' Batting Avg.
McBride-Ath ..... .241
Mathews-Mut ... .258
Bond-Atl .... .268
Cummings-Phi ... .271
Spalding-Bos .... .273

Opponents' On Base Pct.
McBride-Ath ..... .251
Mathews-Mut ... .270
Bond-Atl .... .271
Cummings-Phi ... .278
Spalding-Bos .... .279

Starter Runs
Mathews-Mut ... 44.5
Spalding-Bos ... 44.3
McBride-Ath 24.2
Cummings-Phi ... 6.5

Adjusted Starter Runs
Mathews-Mut ... 50.3
Spalding-Bos ... 42.0
McBride-Ath 33.3
Cummings-Phi ... 8.6
Fisher-Har 4.2

Clutch Pitching Index
Spalding-Bos 120
Mathews-Mut 110
Zettlein-Chi 105
Cummings-Phi 99
Brainard-Bal 99

Relief Runs

Adjusted Relief Runs

Relief Ranking

Total Pitcher Index
Spalding-Bos 5.0
Mathews-Mut 3.8
McBride-Ath 2.2
Cummings-Phi 6
Hatfield-Mut 0

Total Baseball Ranking
Spalding-Bos 5.0
Mathews-Mut 3.8
McBride-Ath 2.2
McVey-Bos 1.8
Meyerle-Chi 1.7

TEAM	G	W	L	PCT	GB	R	OR	AB	H	2B	3B	HR	BB	SO	AVG	OBP	SLG	PRO	PRO+	BR	/A	PF	CHI	RC	SB	CS	SBA	SBR
BOS	82	71	8	.899	—	831	343	3516	1124	157	54	14	31		.320	.326	.407	.733	150	184	163	104	112	478				
HAR	86	54	28	.659	18.5	557	343	3342	873	98	34	2	40		.261	.270	.313	.583	99	12	-14	105	103	289				
ATH	77	53	20	.726	15	699	402	3245	940	126	61	10	40		.290	.298	.375	.673	121	107	49	111	112	372				
STL	70	39	29	.574	26.5	386	369	2679	641	84	27	0	33		.239	.249	.291	.540	97	-28	10	91	97	198				
PHI	70	37	31	.544	28.5	470	376	2717	681	65	28	5	22		.251	.257	.301	.558	91	-12	-28	104	113	215				
MUT	71	30	38	.441	35.5	328	425	2683	626	84	24	7	21		.233	.239	.290	.529	80	-37	-62	106	85	191				
CHI	69	30	37	.448	35	379	416	2658	697	85	13	0	24		.262	.269	.304	.573	100	1	-2	101	90	223				
NH	47	7	40	.149	48	170	397	1708	374	42	12	2	13		.219	.225	.261	.486	81	-47	-7	86	76	103				
WAS	28	5	23	.179	40.5	107	338	997	194	12	11	0	5		.195	.199	.229	.428	51	-47	-41	96	97	46				
RS	19	4	15	.211	37	60	161	688	138	20	1	0	14		.201	.217	.233	.450	64	-26	-15	90	71	36				
CEN	14	2	12	.143	36.5	70	138	529	126	19	3	0	8		.238	.250	.285	.535	94	-5	1	92	88	39				
ATL	44	2	42	.45	51.5	132	438	1547	304	32	9	2	10		.197	.202	.233	.435	59	-69	-37	87	75	74				
WES	13	1	12	.77	37	45	88	449	81	9	6	0	1		.180	.182	.227	.409	40	-23	-26	105	95	19				
TOT	345					4234		26758	6799	833	283	42	262	0	.254	.261	.311	.572										

TEAM	CG	SH	SV	IP	H	H/G	HR	BB	SO	RAT	ERA	ERA+	OAV	OOB	PR	/A	PF	CPI	FA	E	DP	FW	PW	BW	SBW	DIF
BOS	60	10	17	732	752	9.2	2	29		9.6	1.70	140	.249	.256	62	54	96	136					4.6	13.9		12.9
HAR	83	13	0	771	706	8.2	4	16		8.4	1.61	161	.227	.231	72	84	105	106					7.2	-1.2		7.0
ATH	75	6	0	687	776	10.2	4	40		10.7	2.11	125	.268	.278	26	40	107	137					3.4	4.2		8.9
STL	67	5	1	630	634	9.1	3	20		9.3	2.11	105	.239	.245	24	7	90	96					.6	.9		3.5
PHI	64	5	0	627	650	9.3	6	30		9.8	2.15	117	.243	.252	21	25	102	103					2.1	-2.4		3.3
MUT	70	2	0	637²	716	10.1	3	24		10.4	2.40	108	.258	.264	4	13	105	106					1.1	-5.3		.2
CHI	65	7	0	625	652	9.4	0	28		9.8	2.40	104	.244	.252	3	7	102	89					.6	-.2		-3.9
NH	40	0	0	426	500	10.6	5	22		11.0	3.34	68	.254	.263	-41	-51	92	76					-4.4	-.6		-11.5
WAS	23	0	0	250²	399	14.3	6	11		14.7	4.85	54	.313	.319	-66	-62	107	94					-5.3	-3.5		-.2
RS	16	2	0	171	207	10.9	0	3		11.1	3.37	72	.264	.266	-17	-18	98	78					-1.5	-1.3		-2.7
CEN	14	0	0	126	170	12.1	0	3		12.4	3.93	61	.277	.280	-20	-21	98	78					-1.8	.0		-3.3
ATL	31	0	0	396	531	12.1	9	22		12.6	3.95	58	.284	.293	-65	-72	94	90					-6.2	-3.2		-10.7
WES	13	0	0	112	110	8.8	0	14		10.0	2.81	96	.225	.247	-4	-1	110	65					-.0	-2.2		-3.2
TOT	621	50	18	6191¹		9.9				10.3	2.46		.254	.261												

Runs
Barnes-Bos 114
Wright-Bos 105
O'Rourke-Bos 98
McVey-Bos 88
Leonard-Bos 87

Hits
Barnes-Bos 142
McVey-Bos 137
White-Bos 136
Wright-Bos 135
Leonard-Bos 127

Doubles
McVey-Bos 33
Barnes-Bos 22
Pike-StL 21
Force-Ath 21
White-Bos 20

Triples
Craver-Cen-Ath 13
Hall-Ath 13
Pike-StL 10
Meyerle-Phi 9
McVey-Bos 9

Home Runs
O'Rourke-Bos 6
Hall-Ath 5
Start-Mut 4
Hallinan-Wes-Mut .. 3
McVey-Bos 3

Total Bases
McVey-Bos 197
Barnes-Bos 179
Wright-Bos 170
White-Bos 167
Hall-Ath 160

Runs Batted In
Barnes-Bos 113
Wright-Bos 104
O'Rourke-Bos 92
Leonard-Bos 86
McVey-Bos 85

Runs Produced
Barnes-Bos 113
Wright-Bos 104
O'Rourke-Bos 92
Leonard-Bos 86
McVey-Bos 85

Bases On Balls
Harbidge-Har 12
Dehlman-StL 11
O'Rourke-Bos 10
Nelson-Mut 10
Hastings-Chi 9

Batting Average
White-Bos .... .366
Barnes-Bos .... .361
McVey-Bos .... .352
Pike-StL .... .343
Wright-Bos .... .333

On Base Percentage
Barnes-Bos .... .373
White-Bos .... .369
McVey-Bos .... .354
Pike-StL .... .349
Anson-Ath .... .336

Slugging Average
McVey-Bos ...... .506
Pike-StL .... .474
Craver-Cen-Ath ... .458
Barnes-Bos ...... .455
White-Bos .... .449

Production
McVey-Bos .... .860
Barnes-Bos ...... .828
Pike-StL .... .824
White-Bos .... .818
Craver-Cen-Ath ... .778

Adjusted Production
Pike-StL 200
McVey-Bos 187
Barnes-Bos 178
White-Bos 175
Luff-NH 161

Batter Runs
McVey-Bos 35.0
Barnes-Bos 32.3
White-Bos 28.9
Pike-StL 24.7
Wright-Bos 23.0

Adjusted Batter Runs
McVey-Bos 32.8
Barnes-Bos 30.0
Pike-StL 29.1
White-Bos 26.8
Wright-Bos 20.7

Clutch Hitting Index

Runs Created
McVey-Bos 71
Barnes-Bos 68
White-Bos 63
Wright-Bos 59
Pike-StL 53

Total Average
McVey-Bos .... .786
Barnes-Bos ...... .741
Pike-StL .... .737
White-Bos .... .716
Craver-Cen-Ath ... .683

Stolen Bases

Stolen Base Average

Stolen Base Runs

Fielding Runs

Total Player Rating
McVey-Bos 2.6
Pike-StL 2.5
White-Bos 2.4
Barnes-Bos 2.3
Wright-Bos 1.6

Wins
Spalding-Bos 55
McBride-Ath 44
Cummings-Har 35
Bradley-StL 33

Win Percentage
Spalding-Bos ...... .917
Manning-Bos ...... .882
McBride-Ath ...... .759
Cummings-Har .... .745
Zettlein-Chi-Phi ... .569

Games
Spalding-Bos 72
Mathews-Mut 70
McBride-Ath 60
Bradley-StL 60
Zettlein-Chi-Phi ... 52

Complete Games
Mathews-Mut 69
McBride-Ath 59
Bradley-StL 57
Spalding-Bos 52
Zettlein-Chi-Phi ... 49

Shutouts
Zettlein-Chi-Phi ... 7
Spalding-Bos 7
Cummings-Har 7
McBride-Ath 6
Bond-Har 6

Saves
Spalding-Bos 8
Manning-Bos 7
McVey-Bos 1
Heifer-Bos 1
Galvin-StL 1

Innings Pitched
Mathews-Mut ... 626.2
Spalding-Bos ... 575.0
McBride-Ath ... 538.0
Bradley-StL 535.2
Zettlein-Chi-Phi .. 462.1

Fewest Hits/Game
Borden-Phi 6.41
Galvin-StL 7.69
Bond-Har 7.70
Cummings-Har ... 8.55
Fisher-Phi 8.71

Fewest BB/Game
Cummings-Har ..... .13
Blong-RS .... .14
Galvin-StL .... .15
Spalding-Bos ...... .22
Fisher-Phi .... .23

Strikeouts

Strikeouts/Game

Ratio
Borden-Phi 7.36
Galvin-StL 7.84
Bond-Har 7.95
Cummings-Har .. 8.68
Fisher-Phi 8.93

Earned Run Average
Spalding-Bos 1.52
Bond-Har 1.56
Cummings-Har ... 1.60
Borden-Phi 1.64
Fisher-Phi 1.92

Adjusted ERA
Bond-Har 166
Cummings-Har ... 162
Spalding-Bos 156
Borden-Phi 154
McBride-Ath 134

Opponents' Batting Avg.
Borden-Phi ...... .181
Galvin-StL .... .209
Bond-Har .... .215
Fisher-Phi .... .232
Cummings-Har ... .235

Opponents' On Base Pct.
Borden-Phi ...... .203
Galvin-StL .... .213
Bond-Har .... .220
Fisher-Phi .... .237
Cummings-Har ... .237

Starter Runs
Spalding-Bos 60.2
Cummings-Har ... 40.0
Bond-Har 35.3
McBride-Ath 29.1
Bradley-StL 24.5

Adjusted Starter Runs
Spalding-Bos 54.4
Cummings-Har ... 46.1
Bond-Har 40.4
McBride-Ath 40.0
Zettlein-Chi-Phi .. 24.0

Clutch Pitching Index
McBride-Ath 143
Spalding-Bos 140
Manning-Bos 124
Cummings-Har ... 114
Knight-Ath 113

Relief Runs

Adjusted Relief Runs

Relief Ranking

Total Pitcher Index
Spalding-Bos 6.6
Bond-Har 4.4
McBride-Ath 4.2
Cummings-Har 3.8
Fisher-Phi 2.0

Total Baseball Ranking
Spalding-Bos 6.6
Bond-Har 4.4
McBride-Ath 4.2
Cummings-Har 3.8
McVey-Bos 2.6

TEAM	G	W	L	PCT	GB	R	OR	AB	H	2B	3B	HR	BB	SO	AVG	OBP	SLG	PRO	PRO+	BR	/A	PF	CHI	RC	SB	CS	SBA	SBR
CHI	66	52	14	.788		624	257	2748	926	131	32	8	70	45	.337	.353	.417	.770	140	160	110	112	107	415				
STL	64	45	19	.703	6	386	229	2478	642	73	27	2	59	63	.259	.276	.313	.589	102	-5	15	95	103	219				
HAR	69	47	21	.691	6	429	261	2664	711	96	22	2	39	78	.267	.277	.322	.599	92	1	-32	108	106	244				
BOS	70	39	31	.557	15	471	450	2722	723	96	24	9	58	98	.266	.281	.328	.609	102	11	4	102	110	257				
LOU	69	30	36	.455	22	280	344	2570	641	68	14	6	24	98	.249	.256	.294	.550	71	-41	-110	118	81	198				
NY	57	21	35	.375	26	260	412	2180	494	39	15	2	18	35	.227	.233	.261	.494	74	-75	-32	87	102	136				
PHI	60	14	45	.237	34.5	378	534	2387	646	79	35	7	27	36	.271	.279	.342	.621	107	16	19	99	100	233				
CIN	65	9	56	.138	42.5	238	579	2372	555	51	12	4	41	136	.234	.247	.271	.518	86	-62	-9	86	79	163				
TOT	260					3066		20121	5338	633	181	40	336	589	.265	.277	.321	.598										

TEAM	CG	SH	SV	IP	H	H/G	HR	BB	SO	RAT	ERA	ERA+	OAV	OOB	PR	/A	PF	CPI	FA	E	DP	FW	PW	BW	SBW	DIF
CHI	59	9	4	592¹	608	9.2	6	29	51	9.7	1.76	139	.247	.256	35	44	106	101	.899	282	33	6.0	3.9	9.7		-.5
STL	63	16	0	577	472	7.4	3	39	103	8.0	1.22	175	.207	.221	69	58	93	66	.902	268	33	6.1	5.1	1.3		.5
HAR	69	11	0	624	570	8.2	2	27	114	8.6	1.67	142	.226	.234	43	48	103	70	.887	337	27	4.0	4.2	-2.8		7.6
BOS	49	3	7	632	732	10.4	7	104	77	11.9	2.51	90	.270	.297	-13	-17	98	109	.860	442	42	-1.1	-1.5	.4		6.3
LOU	67	5	0	643	605	8.5	3	38	125	9.0	1.69	160	.231	.242	43	73	118	80	.875	397	44	.9	6.4	-9.7		-.7
NY	56	2	0	530	718	12.2	8	24	37	12.6	2.94	73	.302	.309	-37	-47	93	115	.825	473	18	-6.8	-4.1	-2.8		6.7
PHI	53	1	2	550	783	12.8	2	41	22	13.5	3.22	75	.313	.324	-55	-48	105	115	.839	456	32	-5.0	-4.2	1.7		-8.0
CIN	57	0	0	591	850	12.9	9	34	60	13.5	3.62	61	.315	.324	-86	-93	95	105	.841	469	45	-4.1	-8.2	-.8		-10.4
TOT	473	47	13	4739¹		10.1				10.8	2.31		.265	.277					.866	3124	274					

Runs		Hits		Doubles		Triples		Home Runs		Total Bases	
Barnes-Chi	126	Barnes-Chi	138	Hines-Chi	21	Barnes-Chi	14	Hall-Phi	5	Barnes-Chi	190
G.Wright-Bos	72	Peters-Chi	111	Higham-Har	21	Hall-Phi	13	Jones-Cin	4	Hall-Phi	146
Peters-Chi	70	Anson-Chi	110	Barnes-Chi	21	Pike-StL	10			Anson-Chi	139
White-Chi	66	McVey-Chi	107	Pike-StL	19	Meyerle-Phi	8			Hines-Chi	134
Burdock-Har	66	White-Chi	104								

Runs Batted In		Runs Produced		Bases On Balls		Batting Average		On Base Percentage		Slugging Average	
White-Chi	60	Barnes-Chi	184	Barnes-Chi	20	Barnes-Chi	.429	Barnes-Chi	.462	Barnes-Chi	.590
Hines-Chi	59	White-Chi	125	O'Rourke-Bos	15	Hall-Phi	.366	Hall-Phi	.384	Hall-Phi	.545
Barnes-Chi	59	Anson-Chi	120	Burdock-Har	13	Anson-Chi	.356	Anson-Chi	.380	Pike-StL	.472
Anson-Chi	59	Hines-Chi	119	Glenn-Chi	12	Peters-Chi	.351	White-Chi	.358	Anson-Chi	.450
McVey-Chi	53	Peters-Chi	116	Anson-Chi	12	McVey-Chi	.347	O'Rourke-Bos	.358	Meyerle-Phi	.449

Production		Adjusted Production		Batter Runs		Adjusted Batter Runs		Clutch Hitting Index		Runs Created	
Barnes-Chi	1.052	Barnes-Chi	222	Barnes-Chi	50.0	Barnes-Chi	44.0	White-Chi	165	Barnes-Chi	90
Hall-Phi	.929	Hall-Phi	208	Hall-Phi	29.1	Hall-Phi	29.4	Hines-Chi	151	Hall-Phi	57
Anson-Chi	.830	Pike-StL	178	Anson-Chi	24.2	Pike-StL	22.0	Schafer-Bos	145	Anson-Chi	54
Pike-StL	.813	Meyerle-Phi	165	Pike-StL	19.7	Anson-Chi	18.5	Battin-StL	144	Peters-Chi	48
Meyerle-Phi	.797	Jones-Cin	162	O'Rourke-Bos	19.1	O'Rourke-Bos	18.4	Spalding-Chi	139	O'Rourke-Bos	48

Total Average		Stolen Bases		Stolen Base Average		Stolen Base Runs		Fielding Runs		Total Player Rating	
Barnes-Chi	1.141							Somerville-Lou	29.6	Barnes-Chi	4.2
Hall-Phi	.906							Force-Phi-NY	21.2	Anson-Chi	2.6
Anson-Chi	.759							Battin-StL	13.7	Hall-Phi	2.3
Pike-StL	.738							G.Wright-Bos	13.2	G.Wright-Bos	2.0
Meyerle-Phi	.698							Anson-Chi	12.9	Battin-StL	1.9

Wins		Win Percentage		Games		Complete Games		Shutouts		Saves	
Spalding-Chi	47	Spalding-Chi	.797	Devlin-Lou	68	Devlin-Lou	66	Bradley-StL	16	Manning-Bos	5
Bradley-StL	45	Manning-Bos	.783	Bradley-StL	64	Bradley-StL	63	Spalding-Chi	9	Zettlein-Phi	2
Bond-Har	31	Bond-Har	.705	Spalding-Chi	61	Mathews-NY	55	Bond-Har	6	McVey-Chi	2
Devlin-Lou	30	Bradley-StL	.703	Mathews-NY	56	Spalding-Chi	54	Devlin-Lou	5		
Mathews-NY	21	Cummings-Har	.667	Bond-Har	45	Bond-Har	45	Cummings-Har	5		

Innings Pitched		Fewest Hits/Game		Fewest BB/Game		Strikeouts		Strikeouts/Game		Ratio	
Devlin-Lou	622.0	Bradley-StL	7.38	Zettlein-Phi	.23	Devlin-Lou	122	Bond-Har	1.94	Bradley-StL	7.98
Bradley-StL	573.0	Bond-Har	7.83	Fisher-Cin	.24	Bradley-StL	103	Devlin-Lou	1.77	Bond-Har	8.12
Spalding-Chi	528.2	Devlin-Lou	8.19	Bond-Har	.29	Bond-Har	88	Bradley-StL	1.62	Devlin-Lou	8.73
Mathews-NY	516.0	Cummings-Har	8.96	Mathews-NY	.42	Spalding-Chi	39	Borden-Bos	1.40	Cummings-Har	9.54
Bond-Har	408.0	Spalding-Chi	9.23	Williams-Cin	.43	Mathews-NY	37	Fisher-Cin	1.14	Spalding-Chi	9.67

Earned Run Average		Adjusted ERA		Opponents' Batting Avg.		Opponents' On Base Pct.		Starter Runs		Adjusted Starter Runs	
Bradley-StL	1.23	Bradley-StL	174	Bradley-StL	.208	Bradley-StL	.221	Bradley-StL	68.9	Devlin-Lou	79.8
Devlin-Lou	1.56	Devlin-Lou	174	Bond-Har	.218	Bond-Har	.224	Devlin-Lou	51.5	Bradley-StL	57.9
Cummings-Har	1.67	Cummings-Har	142	Devlin-Lou	.226	Devlin-Lou	.237	Spalding-Chi	32.5	Spalding-Chi	40.5
Bond-Har	1.68	Bond-Har	141	Cummings-Har	.242	Cummings-Har	.254	Bond-Har	28.6	Bond-Har	31.5
Spalding-Chi	1.75	Spalding-Chi	139	Spalding-Chi	.247	Spalding-Chi	.256	Cummings-Har	15.4	Cummings-Har	16.9

Clutch Pitching Index		Relief Runs		Adjusted Relief Runs		Relief Ranking		Total Pitcher Index		Total Baseball Ranking	
Knight-Phi	133							Devlin-Lou	8.7	Devlin-Lou	8.7
Mathews-NY	116							Bradley-StL	5.5	Bradley-StL	5.5
Dean-Cin	111							Spalding-Chi	5.3	Spalding-Chi	5.3
Manning-Bos	108							Bond-Har	3.5	Barnes-Chi	4.0
Borden-Bos	107							Cummings-Har	.7	Bond-Har	3.5

1877 National League

TEAM	G	W	L	PCT	GB	R	OR	AB	H	2B	3B	HR	BB	SO	AVG	OBP	SLG	PRO	PRO+	BR	/A	PF	CHI	RC	SB	CS	SBA	SBR
BOS	61	42	18	.700		419	263	2368	700	91	37	4	65	121	.296	.314	.370	.684	113	47	34	104	104	283				
LOU	61	35	25	.583	7	339	288	2355	659	75	36	9	58	140	.280	.297	.354	.651	91	19	-43	118	92	254				
HAR	60	31	27	.534	10	341	311	2358	637	63	31	4	30	97	.270	.279	.328	.607	105	-16	21	89	103	222				
STL	60	28	32	.467	14	284	318	2178	531	51	36	1	57	147	.244	.263	.302	.565	84	-45	-27	95	101	177				
CHI	60	26	33	.441	15.5	366	375	2273	633	79	30	0	57	111	.278	.296	.340	.636	92	8	-32	112	105	234				
CIN	58	15	42	.263	25.5	291	485	2135	545	72	34	6	78	110	.255	.282	.329	.611	106	-10	26	89	93	203				
TOT	180					2040		13667	3705	431	204	24	345	726	.271	.289	.338	.627										

TEAM	CG	SH	SV	IP	H	H/G	HR	BB	SO	RAT	ERA	ERA+	OAV	OOB	PR	/A	PF	CPI	FA	E	DP	FW	PW	BW	SBW	DIF
BOS	61	7	0	548	557	9.1	5	38	177	9.8	2.15	130	.248	.261	39	39	100	98	.889	290	36	1.2	3.5	3.0		4.3
LOU	61	4	0	559	617	9.9	4	41	141	10.6	2.25	147	.264	.276	34	65	118	112	.904	267	37	2.4	5.8	-3.8		.7
HAR	59	4	0	544	572	9.5	2	56	99	10.4	2.32	105	.254	.273	29	6	87	100	.885	313	32	-.2	.5	1.9		-.2
STL	52	1	0	541	582	9.7	2	92	132	11.2	2.66	98	.259	.288	8	-3	93	99	.892	281	29	1.4	-.3	-2.4		-.7
CHI	45	3	3	534	630	10.6	7	58	92	11.6	3.37	88	.277	.295	-33	-23	106	90	.883	313	43	-.2	-2.0	-2.9		1.6
CIN	48	1	1	515	747	13.1	4	61	85	14.1	4.19	63	.320	.337	-79	-88	94	103	.851	394	33	-4.7	-7.8	2.3		-3.3
TOT	326	20	4	3241		10.3				11.2	2.81		.271	.289					.884	1858	210					

Runs		Hits		Doubles		Triples		Home Runs		Total Bases	
O'Rourke-Bos	68	J.White-Bos	103	Anson-Chi	19	J.White-Bos	11	Pike-Cin	4	J.White-Bos	145
G.Wright-Bos	58	McVey-Chi	98	York-Har	16	Jones-Cin-Chi-Cin	8	Shaffer-Lou	2	McVey-Chi	121
McVey-Chi	58	O'Rourke-Bos	96	Manning-Cin	16	Hall-Lou	8	Jones-Cin-Chi-Cin	2	O'Rourke-Bos	118
Start-Har	55	Cassidy-Har	95	G.Wright-Bos	15	Brown-Bos	8	J.White-Bos	2	Hall-Lou	118
		Start-Har	90	Hall-Lou	15			Snyder-Lou	2	Cassidy-Har	115

Runs Batted In		Runs Produced		Bases On Balls		Batting Average		On Base Percentage		Slugging Average	
J.White-Bos	49	J.White-Bos	98	O'Rourke-Bos	20	J.White-Bos	.387	O'Rourke-Bos	.407	J.White-Bos	.545
Peters-Chi	41	McVey-Chi	94	Jones-Cin-Chi-Cin	15	Cassidy-Har	.378	J.White-Bos	.405	Jones-Cin-Chi-Cin	.471
Sutton-Bos	39	G.Wright-Bos	93	Hall-Lou	12	McVey-Chi	.368	McVey-Chi	.387	Cassidy-Har	.458
Jones-Cin-Chi-Cin	38	O'Rourke-Bos	91	Booth-Cin	12	O'Rourke-Bos	.362	Cassidy-Har	.386	McVey-Chi	.455
York-Har	37	Jones-Cin-Chi-Cin	89	Force-StL	11	Anson-Chi	.337	Anson-Chi	.360	O'Rourke-Bos	.445

Production		Adjusted Production		Batter Runs		Adjusted Batter Runs		Clutch Hitting Index		Runs Created	
J.White-Bos	.950	J.White-Bos	190	J.White-Bos	28.2	J.White-Bos	26.8	Ferguson-Har	165	J.White-Bos	60
O'Rourke-Bos	.852	Cassidy-Har	184	O'Rourke-Bos	21.2	Cassidy-Har	21.6	Croft-StL	162	O'Rourke-Bos	49
Cassidy-Har	.844	Jones-Cin-Chi-Cin	175	McVey-Chi	18.9	O'Rourke-Bos	19.7	Bond-Bos	150	McVey-Chi	48
McVey-Chi	.842	O'Rourke-Bos	162	Cassidy-Har	17.6	Jones-Cin-Chi-Cin	19.4	Spalding-Chi	150	Cassidy-Har	45
Jones-Cin-Chi-Cin	.824	Manning-Cin	157	Jones-Cin-Chi-Cin	15.6	Manning-Cin	15.0	Sutton-Bos	146	Hall-Lou	43

Total Average		Stolen Bases	Stolen Base Average	Stolen Base Runs	Fielding Runs		Total Player Rating	
J.White-Bos	.939				Gerhardt-Lou	19.8	Jones-Cin-Chi-Cin	2.5
O'Rourke-Bos	.817				Peters-Chi	19.1	J.White-Bos	2.2
Jones-Cin-Chi-Cin	.776				Ferguson-Har	17.3	Peters-Chi	1.8
McVey-Chi	.768				Snyder-Lou	15.1	Anson-Chi	1.8
Cassidy-Har	.756				Shaffer-Lou	13.2	Gerhardt-Lou	1.8

Wins		Win Percentage		Games		Complete Games		Shutouts		Saves	
Bond-Bos	40	Bond-Bos	.702	Devlin-Lou	61	Devlin-Lou	61	Bond-Bos	6	McVey-Chi	2
Devlin-Lou	35	Devlin-Lou	.583	Bond-Bos	58	Bond-Bos	58	Larkin-Har	4	Spalding-Chi	1
Larkin-Har	29	Larkin-Har	.537	Larkin-Har	56	Larkin-Har	55	Devlin-Lou	4	Manning-Cin	1
Nichols-StL	18	Nichols-StL	.439	Bradley-Chi	50	Nichols-StL	35	Bradley-Chi	2		
Bradley-Chi	18	Bradley-Chi	.439	Nichols-StL	42	Bradley-Chi	35				

Innings Pitched		Fewest Hits/Game		Fewest BB/Game		Strikeouts		Strikeouts/Game		Ratio	
Devlin-Lou	559.0	Bond-Bos	9.16	Bond-Bos	.62	Bond-Bos	170	Mitchell-Cin	3.69	Bond-Bos	9.78
Bond-Bos	521.0	Larkin-Har	9.16	Devlin-Lou	.66	Devlin-Lou	141	Bond-Bos	2.94	Larkin-Har	10.11
Larkin-Har	501.0	Nichols-StL	9.67	Cummings-Cin	.75	Larkin-Har	96	Blong-StL	2.45	Devlin-Lou	10.59
Bradley-Chi	394.0	Blong-StL	9.75	Bradley-Chi	.89	Nichols-StL	80	Devlin-Lou	2.27	Nichols-StL	11.03
Nichols-StL	350.0	Devlin-Lou	9.93	Larkin-Har	.95	Bradley-Chi	59	Nichols-StL	2.06	Bradley-Chi	11.22

Earned Run Average		Adjusted ERA		Opponents' Batting Avg.		Opponents' On Base Pct.		Starter Runs		Adjusted Starter Runs	
Bond-Bos	2.11	Devlin-Lou	147	Bond-Bos	.249	Bond-Bos	.261	Bond-Bos	40.5	Devlin-Lou	65.4
Larkin-Har	2.14	Bond-Bos	133	Larkin-Har	.249	Larkin-Har	.268	Larkin-Har	37.3	Bond-Bos	40.5
Devlin-Lou	2.25	Larkin-Har	114	Nichols-StL	.259	Devlin-Lou	.277	Devlin-Lou	34.4	Larkin-Har	16.3
Nichols-StL	2.60	Nichols-StL	100	Blong-StL	.261	Nichols-StL	.285	Reis-Chi	8.2	Reis-Chi	8.9
Blong-StL	2.74	Blong-StL	95	Devlin-Lou	.264	Bradley-Chi	.288	Nichols-StL	8.2		

Clutch Pitching Index		Relief Runs	Adjusted Relief Runs	Relief Ranking	Total Pitcher Index		Total Baseball Ranking	
Mathews-Cin	126				Devlin-Lou	7.0	Devlin-Lou	7.0
Devlin-Lou	112				Bond-Bos	3.7	Bond-Bos	3.7
Booth-Cin	108				Larkin-Har	1.5	Jones-Cin-Chi-Cin	2.5
Larkin-Har	102				Reis-Chi	.7	J.White-Bos	2.2
Bond-Bos	100						Peters-Chi	1.8

TEAM	G	W	L	PCT	GB	R	OR	AB	H	2B	3B	HR	BB	SO	AVG	OBP	SLG	PRO	PRO+	BR	/A	PF	CHI	RC	SB	CS	SBA	SBR
BOS	60	41	19	.683		298	241	2220	535	75	25	2	35	154	.241	.253	.300	.553	78	-34	-57	108	109	173				
CIN	61	37	23	.617	4	333	281	2281	629	67	22	5	58	141	.276	.294	.331	.625	120	21	51	91	98	227				
PRO	62	33	27	.550	8	353	337	2298	604	107	30	8	50	218	.263	.279	.346	.625	109	19	20	100	104	227				
CHI	61	30	30	.500	11	371	331	2333	677	91	20	3	88	157	.290	.316	.350	.666	115	56	34	107	96	265				
IND	63	24	36	.400	17	293	328	2300	542	76	15	3	64	197	.236	.256	.286	.542	94	-42	1	87	105	173				
MIL	61	15	45	.250	26	256	386	2212	552	65	20	2	69	214	.250	.272	.300	.572	86	-17	-37	107	87	185				
TOT	184					1904		13644	3539	481	132	23	364	1081	.259	.279	.319	.598										

TEAM	CG	SH	SV	IP	H	H/G	HR	BB	SO	RAT	ERA	ERA+	OAV	OOB	PR	/A	PF	CPI	FA	E	DP	FW	PW	BW	SBW	DIF
BOS	58	9	0	544	595	9.8	6	38	184	10.5	2.32	102	.264	.276	0	2	102	102	.914	228	48	3.5	.2	-5.3		12.6
CIN	61	6	0	548	546	9.0	2	63	220	10.0	1.84	116	.246	.267	28	17	92	107	.900	269	37	1.5	1.6	4.8		-.9
PRO	59	6	0	556	609	9.9	5	86	173	11.3	2.38	93	.264	.291	-4	-10	96	109	.892	311	42	-.5	-.9	1.9		2.6
CHI	61	1	0	551	577	9.4	4	35	175	10.0	2.37	102	.256	.267	-3	3	105	88	.891	304	37	-.4	.3	3.2		-3.0
IND	59	2	1	578	621	9.7	3	87	182	11.0	2.32	87	.261	.287	-1	-18	88	106	.898	290	37	.9	-1.7	.0		-5.3
MIL	54	1	0	547	589	9.7	3	55	147	10.6	2.60	101	.261	.279	-17	1	114	89	.866	376	32	-4.4	.0	-3.5		-7.2
TOT	352	25	1	3324		9.6				10.6	2.30		.259	.279					.893	1778	233					

Runs		Hits		Doubles		Triples		Home Runs		Total Bases	
Higham-Pro	60	Start-Chi	100	Higham-Pro	22	York-Pro	10	Hines-Pro	4	York-Pro	125
Start-Chi	58	Dalrymple-Mil	96	Brown-Pro	21	O'Rourke-Bos	7	Jones-Cin	3	Start-Chi	125
York-Pro	56	Hines-Pro	92	York-Pro	19	Jones-Cin	7	McVey-Cin	2	Hines-Pro	125
Anson-Chi	55	Ferguson-Chi	91	Shaffer-Ind	19			McKelvy-Ind	2	Shaffer-Ind	121
Dalrymple-Mil	52			O'Rourke-Bos	17					Higham-Pro	117

Runs Batted In		Runs Produced		Bases On Balls		Batting Average		On Base Percentage		Slugging Average	
Hines-Pro	50	Anson-Chi	95	Remsen-Chi	17	Hines-Pro	.358	Ferguson-Chi	.375	Hines-Pro	.486
Brown-Pro	43	Hines-Pro	88	Larkin-Chi	17	Dalrymple-Mil	.354	Anson-Chi	.372	York-Pro	.465
Anson-Chi	40	Higham-Pro	88	Shaffer-Ind	13	Ferguson-Chi	.351	Shaffer-Ind	.369	Shaffer-Ind	.455
Jones-Cin	39	Jones-Cin	86	Clapp-Ind	13	Start-Chi	.351	Dalrymple-Mil	.368	Brown-Pro	.453
Ferguson-Chi	39	Brown-Pro	86	Anson-Chi	13	Anson-Chi	.341	Hines-Pro	.363	Jones-Cin	.441

Production		Adjusted Production		Batter Runs		Adjusted Batter Runs		Clutch Hitting Index		Runs Created	
Hines-Pro	.849	Shaffer-Ind	196	Hines-Pro	20.0	Shaffer-Ind	24.7	McClellan-Chi	193	Hines-Pro	47
Shaffer-Ind	.824	Hines-Pro	177	Shaffer-Ind	19.6	Hines-Pro	20.2	Hague-Pro	166	Shaffer-Ind	46
Start-Chi	.794	Jones-Cin	163	Start-Chi	17.2	York-Pro	16.2	McKelvy-Ind	164	Start-Chi	46
York-Pro	.793	York-Pro	159	Dalrymple-Mil	16.4	Larkin-Chi	16.2	Redmond-Mil	148	Dalrymple-Mil	43
Dalrymple-Mil	.789	Brown-Pro	153	York-Pro	16.1	Jones-Cin	16.1	Harbidge-Chi	145	York-Pro	42

Total Average		Stolen Bases		Stolen Base Average		Stolen Base Runs		Fielding Runs		Total Player Rating	
Hines-Pro	.770							Burdock-Bos	21.4	Ferguson-Chi	3.1
Shaffer-Ind	.761							Hague-Pro	18.7	Shaffer-Ind	2.3
York-Pro	.715							Ferguson-Chi	17.6	Burdock-Bos	2.2
Brown-Pro	.692							Wright-Bos	10.5	Brown-Pro	1.7
Start-Chi	.686							Kelly-Cin	8.8	Gerhardt-Cin	1.6

Wins		Win Percentage		Games		Complete Games		Shutouts		Saves	
Bond-Bos	40	Bond-Bos	.678	Bond-Bos	59	Bond-Bos	57	Bond-Bos	9	Healey-Pro-Ind	1
W.White-Cin	30	Ward-Pro	.629	Larkin-Chi	56	Larkin-Chi	56	Ward-Pro	6		
Larkin-Chi	29	W.White-Cin	.588	W.White-Cin	52	W.White-Cin	52	W.White-Cin	5		
Ward-Pro	22	Larkin-Chi	.527	Weaver-Mil	45	Weaver-Mil	39				
Nolan-Ind	13			Nolan-Ind	38						

Innings Pitched		Fewest Hits/Game		Fewest BB/Game		Strikeouts		Strikeouts/Game		Ratio	
Bond-Bos	532.2	Mitchell-Cin	7.76	Weaver-Mil	.49	Bond-Bos	182	Mitchell-Cin	5.74	Weaver-Mil	9.21
Larkin-Chi	506.0	Ward-Pro	8.30	Larkin-Chi	.55	W.White-Cin	169	Wheeler-Pro	3.63	Ward-Pro	9.22
W.White-Cin	468.0	Weaver-Mil	8.72	Bond-Bos	.56	Larkin-Chi	163	W.White-Cin	3.25	Larkin-Chi	9.64
Weaver-Mil	383.0	Larkin-Chi	9.09	Nichols-Pro	.73	Nolan-Ind	125	Nolan-Ind	3.24	Mitchell-Cin	9.79
Nolan-Ind	347.0	W.White-Cin	9.17	W.White-Cin	.87	Ward-Pro	116	Ward-Pro	3.13	W.White-Cin	10.04

Earned Run Average		Adjusted ERA		Opponents' Batting Avg.		Opponents' On Base Pct.		Starter Runs		Adjusted Starter Runs	
Ward-Pro	1.51	Ward-Pro	146	Mitchell-Cin	.221	Weaver-Mil	.252	Ward-Pro	29.5	Weaver-Mil	28.6
McCormick-Ind	1.69	Weaver-Mil	134	Ward-Pro	.233	Ward-Pro	.252	W.White-Cin	26.8	Ward-Pro	25.7
W.White-Cin	1.79	McCormick-Ind	120	Weaver-Mil	.242	Larkin-Chi	.261	Weaver-Mil	15.1	Bond-Bos	17.6
Weaver-Mil	1.95	W.White-Cin	119	Larkin-Chi	.249	Mitchell-Cin	.263	Bond-Bos	14.4	W.White-Cin	17.6
Bond-Bos	2.06	Bond-Bos	114	W.White-Cin	.251	W.White-Cin	.268	McCormick-Ind	8.0	Larkin-Chi	10.2

Clutch Pitching Index		Relief Runs		Adjusted Relief Runs		Relief Ranking		Total Pitcher Index		Total Baseball Ranking	
McCormick-Ind	144							Weaver-Mil	2.8	Ferguson-Chi	3.1
Healey-Pro-Ind	116							Ward-Pro	2.7	Weaver-Mil	2.8
Nichols-Pro	113							Larkin-Chi	2.1	Ward-Pro	2.7
W.White-Cin	112							Bond-Bos	1.6	Shaffer-Ind	2.3
Bond-Bos	108							W.White-Cin	.6	Burdock-Bos	2.2

TEAM	G	W	L	PCT	GB	R	OR	AB	H	2B	3B	HR	BB	SO	AVG	OBP	SLG	PRO	PRO+	BR	/A	PF	CHI	RC	SB	CS	SBA	SBR
PRO	85	59	25	.702		612	355	3392	1003	142	55	12	91	172	.296	.314	.381	.695	134	110	117	98	103	416				
BOS	84	54	30	.643	5	562	348	3217	883	138	51	20	90	222	.274	.294	.368	.662	118	68	57	102	107	357				
BUF	79	46	32	.590	10	394	365	2906	733	105	54	2	78	314	.252	.272	.328	.600	97	1	-8	102	95	265				
CHI	83	46	33	.582	10.5	437	411	3116	808	167	32	3	73	294	.259	.276	.336	.612	98	14	-12	106	96	297				
CIN	81	43	37	.538	14	485	464	3085	813	127	53	8	66	207	.264	.279	.347	.626	114	27	48	95	105	306				
CLE	82	27	55	.329	31	322	461	2987	666	116	29	4	37	214	.223	.232	.285	.517	72	-82	-77	99	96	203				
SYR	71	22	48	.314	30	276	462	2611	592	61	19	5	28	238	.227	.235	.270	.505	77	-81	-40	89	97	170				
TRO	77	19	56	.253	35.5	321	543	2841	673	102	24	4	45	182	.237	.249	.294	.543	86	-53	-26	93	93	213				
TOT	321					3409		24155	6171	958	317	58	508	1843	.255	.271	.329	.599										

TEAM	CG	SH	SV	IP	H	H/G	HR	BB	SO	RAT	ERA	ERA+	OAV	OOB	PR	/A	PF	CPI	FA	E	DP	FW	PW	BW	SBW	DIF
PRO	73	3	2	776	765	8.9	9	62	329	9.6	2.18	108	.241	.255	27	15	94	96	.902	382	41	1.8	1.4	10.8		3.0
BOS	80	13	0	753	757	9.0	9	46	230	9.6	2.19	114	.244	.255	25	24	100	98	.913	319	58	4.9	2.2	5.3		-.3
BUF	78	8	0	713	698	8.8	3	47	198	9.4	2.34	112	.239	.251	12	22	105	84	.906	331	62	2.9	2.0	-.7		2.8
CHI	82	6	0	744	762	9.2	5	57	211	9.9	2.46	105	.248	.261	3	9	103	91	.900	381	52	1.3	.8	-1.1		5.4
CIN	79	4	0	726	756	9.4	11	81	246	10.4	2.29	102	.251	.270	16	3	93	108	.877	454	48	-3.1	.3	4.4		1.4
CLE	79	3	0	741	818	9.9	4	116	287	11.3	2.65	95	.262	.288	-12	-11	100	108	.889	406	42	-.3	-1.0	-7.1		-5.6
SYR	64	5	0	649	775	10.7	4	52	132	11.5	3.19	74	.277	.291	-49	-59	95	97	.873	398	37	-2.7	-5.4	-3.7		-1.2
TRO	75	3	0	695	840	10.9	13	47	210	11.5	2.80	89	.280	.291	-23	-23	100	115	.875	460	44	-4.4	-2.1	-2.4		-9.6
TOT	610	45	2	5797		9.6				10.4	2.50		.255	.271					.892	3131	384					

Runs		Hits		Doubles		Triples		Home Runs		Total Bases	
Jones-Bos	85	Hines-Pro	146	Eden-Cle	31	Dickerson-Cin	14	Jones-Bos	9	Hines-Pro	197
Hines-Pro	81	O'Rourke-Pro	126	York-Pro	25	Williamson-Chi	13	O'Rourke-Bos	6	Jones-Bos	181
Wright-Pro	79	Kelly-Cin	120	Hines-Pro	25	Kelly-Cin	12	Brouthers-Tro	4	Kelly-Cin	170
Kelly-Cin	78	Jones-Bos	112	Dalrymple-Chi	25	O'Rourke-Bos	11	Eden-Cle	3	O'Rourke-Pro	166
Dickerson-Cin	73	J.White-Cin	110	Houck-Bos	24					O'Rourke-Bos	165

Runs Batted In		Runs Produced		Bases On Balls		Batting Average		On Base Percentage		Slugging Average	
O'Rourke-Bos	62	Jones-Bos	138	Jones-Bos	29	Hines-Pro	.357	O'Rourke-Pro	.371	O'Rourke-Bos	.521
Jones-Bos	62	Hines-Pro	131	Williamson-Chi	24	O'Rourke-Pro	.348	Hines-Pro	.369	Jones-Bos	.510
Dickerson-Cin	57	Dickerson-Cin	128	York-Pro	19	Kelly-Cin	.348	Jones-Bos	.367	Kelly-Cin	.493
McVey-Cin	55	O'Rourke-Bos	125	Richardson-Buf	16	O'Rourke-Bos	.341	Kelly-Cin	.363	Hines-Pro	.482
		Kelly-Cin	123	Barnes-Cin	16	J.White-Cin	.330	O'Rourke-Bos	.357	O'Rourke-Pro	.459

Production		Adjusted Production		Batter Runs		Adjusted Batter Runs		Clutch Hitting Index		Runs Created	
O'Rourke-Bos	.877	Kelly-Cin	188	Jones-Bos	33.1	Hines-Pro	33.8	Gerhardt-Cin	162	Hines-Pro	75
Jones-Bos	.877	Jones-Bos	182	Hines-Pro	32.9	Jones-Bos	31.9	Brown-Pro-Chi	148	Jones-Bos	68
Kelly-Cin	.855	O'Rourke-Bos	181	Kelly-Cin	28.1	Kelly-Cin	30.6	Morrill-Bos	145	Kelly-Cin	63
Hines-Pro	.851	Hines-Pro	181	O'Rourke-Bos	28.0	O'Rourke-Pro	28.0	McVey-Cin	137	O'Rourke-Pro	63
O'Rourke-Pro	.829	O'Rourke-Pro	174	O'Rourke-Pro	27.2	O'Rourke-Bos	27.0	J.White-Cin	134	O'Rourke-Bos	60

Total Average		Stolen Bases	Stolen Base Average	Stolen Base Runs	Fielding Runs		Total Player Rating	
Jones-Bos	.864				Wright-Pro	20.4	Kelly-Cin	4.0
O'Rourke-Bos	.828				Snyder-Bos	19.9	Jones-Bos	3.7
Kelly-Cin	.791				Shaffer-Chi	18.5	Williamson-Chi	3.3
Hines-Pro	.779				Williamson-Chi	18.0	Hines-Pro	3.3
O'Rourke-Pro	.758				Fulmer-Buf	17.5	Wright-Pro	3.2

Wins		Win Percentage		Games		Complete Games		Shutouts		Saves	
Ward-Pro	47	Ward-Pro	.712	W.White-Cin	76	W.White-Cin	75	Bond-Bos	12	Ward-Pro	1
W.White-Cin	43	Bond-Bos	.694	Ward-Pro	70	Galvin-Buf	65	Galvin-Buf	6	Mathews-Pro	1
Bond-Bos	43	Hankinson-Chi	.600	Galvin-Buf	66	Bond-Bos	60	McCormick-Syr	5		
Galvin-Buf	37	W.White-Cin	.581	Bond-Bos	64	McCormick-Cle	59	W.White-Cin	4		
Larkin-Chi	31	Galvin-Buf	.578	McCormick-Cle	62	Ward-Pro	58	Larkin-Chi	4		

Innings Pitched		Fewest Hits/Game		Fewest BB/Game		Strikeouts		Strikeouts/Game		Ratio	
W.White-Cin	680.0	McGunnigle-Buf	8.48	Bond-Bos	.39	Ward-Pro	239	McGunnigle-Buf	4.65	Bond-Bos	9.19
Galvin-Buf	593.0	Ward-Pro	8.75	Galvin-Buf	.47	W.White-Cin	232	Mathews-Pro	4.29	Ward-Pro	9.31
Ward-Pro	587.0	Bond-Bos	8.80	Bradley-Tro	.48	McCormick-Cle	197	Mitchell-Cle	4.16	Galvin-Buf	9.35
Bond-Bos	555.1	Galvin-Buf	8.88	Larkin-Chi	.53	Bond-Bos	155	Ward-Pro	3.66	Larkin-Chi	9.54
McCormick-Cle	546.1	W.White-Cin	8.95	Ward-Pro	.55	Larkin-Chi	142	McCormick-Cle	3.25	McGunnigle-Buf	9.68

Earned Run Average		Adjusted ERA		Opponents' Batting Avg.		Opponents' On Base Pct.		Starter Runs		Adjusted Starter Runs	
Bond-Bos	1.96	Bond-Bos	127	McGunnigle-Buf	.233	Bond-Bos	.248	W.White-Cin	38.6	Bond-Bos	32.3
W.White-Cin	1.99	W.White-Cin	117	Ward-Pro	.239	Ward-Pro	.250	Bond-Bos	33.0	W.White-Cin	26.2
Ward-Pro	2.15	Galvin-Buf	115	Bond-Bos	.240	Galvin-Buf	.251	Ward-Pro	22.8	Galvin-Buf	22.2
Salisbury-Tro	2.22	Salisbury-Tro	112	Galvin-Buf	.241	Larkin-Chi	.255	Galvin-Buf	14.5	Ward-Pro	13.7
Galvin-Buf	2.28	Ward-Pro	110	W.White-Cin	.243	McGunnigle-Buf	.257	Goldsmith-Tro	6.5	Larkin-Chi	7.4

Clutch Pitching Index		Relief Runs	Adjusted Relief Runs	Relief Ranking	Total Pitcher Index		Total Baseball Ranking	
Salisbury-Tro	134				Bond-Bos	3.9	Kelly-Cin	4.0
Bradley-Tro	114				Ward-Pro	3.2	Bond-Bos	3.9
W.White-Cin	112				Galvin-Buf	3.0	Jones-Bos	3.7
Mathews-Pro	111				McCormick-Cle	.7	Williamson-Chi	3.3
McCormick-Cle	108				Goldsmith-Tro	.6	Hines-Pro	3.3

TEAM	G	W	L	PCT	GB	R	OR	AB	H	2B	3B	HR	BB	SO	AVG	OBP	SLG	PRO	PRO+	BR	/A	PF	CHI	RC	SB	CS	SBA	SBR
CHI	86	67	17	.798		538	317	3135	876	164	39	4	104	217	.279	.305	.360	.663	118	81	56	106	109	350				
PRO	87	52	32	.619	15	419	299	3196	793	114	34	8	89	186	.248	.268	.313	.581	101	-5	8	97	101	275				
CLE	85	47	37	.560	20	387	337	3002	726	130	52	7	75	241	.242	.260	.327	.587	102	0	8	98	99	262				
TRO	83	41	42	.494	25.5	392	438	3007	755	114	37	5	119	261	.251	.280	.319	.599	99	14	-6	105	95	275				
WOR	85	40	43	.482	26.5	412	370	3024	699	129	52	8	82	276	.231	.251	.316	.567	85	-20	-54	109	110	246				
BOS	86	40	44	.476	27	416	456	3080	779	134	41	20	106	218	.253	.278	.343	.621	114	35	47	97	94	300				
BUF	85	24	58	.293	42	331	502	2962	669	104	37	3	90	328	.226	.249	.289	.538	82	-47	-54	102	97	218				
CIN	83	21	59	.263	44	296	472	2895	649	91	36	7	75	266	.224	.244	.288	.532	81	-53	-48	99	91	208				
TOT	340					3191		24301	5946	980	328	62	740	1993	.245	.267	.320	.587										

TEAM	CG	SH	SV	IP	H	H/G	HR	BB	SO	RAT	ERA	ERA+	OAV	OOB	PR	/A	PF	CPI	FA	E	DP	FW	PW	BW	SBW	DIF
CHI	80	8	3	775	622	7.2	8	129	367	8.7	1.93	126	.208	.241	38	42	102	82	.913	329	41	2.3	4.1	5.4		13.2
PRO	75	13	2	799	663	7.5	7	51	286	8.0	1.64	134	.214	.226	64	49	93	86	.910	357	53	1.1	4.8	.8		3.4
CLE	83	7	1	759²	685	8.1	4	98	289	9.3	1.90	124	.228	.252	40	38	99	102	.910	330	52	2.0	3.7	.8		-1.5
TRO	81	4	0	738	763	9.3	8	113	173	10.7	2.74	92	.253	.280	-30	-18	106	99	.899	366	58	-.3	-1.7	-.6		2.2
WOR	68	7	5	762²	709	8.4	13	97	297	9.5	2.27	115	.233	.257	9	28	109	95	.906	355	49	.7	2.7	-5.2		.3
BOS	70	4	0	744²	840	10.2	2	86	187	11.2	3.08	74	.270	.290	-58	-67	96	98	.901	367	54	.3	-6.5	4.6		-.4
BUF	72	6	1	739	879	10.7	10	78	186	11.7	3.09	79	.281	.298	-59	-52	104	109	.891	408	55	-2.1	-5.1	-5.2		-4.6
CIN	79	3	0	713¹	785	9.9	10	88	208	11.0	2.44	102	.265	.286	-4	3	105	122	.876	437	49	-4.1	.3	-4.7		-10.6
TOT	608	52	12	6031¹		8.9				10.0	2.37		.245	.267					.901	2949	411					

Runs		Hits		Doubles		Triples		Home Runs		Total Bases	
Dalrymple-Chi	91	Dalrymple-Chi	126	Dunlap-Cle	27	Stovey-Wor	14	Stovey-Wor	6	Dalrymple-Chi	175
Stovey-Wor	76	Anson-Chi	120	Dalrymple-Chi	25	Dalrymple-Chi	12	J.O'Rourke-Bos	6	Stovey-Wor	161
Kelly-Chi	72	Gore-Chi	116	Anson-Chi	24	J.O'Rourke-Bos	11	Jones-Bos	5	J.O'Rourke-Bos	160
J.O'Rourke-Bos	71	Hines-Pro	115	Gore-Chi	23	Hornung-Buf	11	Dunlap-Cle	4	Dunlap-Cle	160
Gore-Chi	70	Connor-Tro	113	J.O'Rourke-Bos	22	Phillips-Cle	10			Connor-Tro	156

Runs Batted In		Runs Produced		Bases On Balls		Batting Average		On Base Percentage		Slugging Average	
Anson-Chi	74	Kelly-Chi	131	Ferguson-Tro	24	Gore-Chi	.360	Gore-Chi	.399	Gore-Chi	.463
Kelly-Chi	60	Dalrymple-Chi	127	J.O'Rourke-Bos	21	Anson-Chi	.337	Anson-Chi	.362	Connor-Tro	.459
Gore-Chi	47	Anson-Chi	127	Gore-Chi	21	Connor-Tro	.332	Connor-Tro	.357	Dalrymple-Chi	.458
Connor-Tro	47	Gore-Chi	115	Clapp-Cin	21	Dalrymple-Chi	.330	Dalrymple-Chi	.335	Stovey-Wor	.454
J.O'Rourke-Bos	45	J.O'Rourke-Bos	110	Crowley-Buf	19	Burns-Chi	.309	Burns-Chi	.333	J.O'Rourke-Bos	.441

Production		Adjusted Production		Batter Runs		Adjusted Batter Runs		Clutch Hitting Index		Runs Created	
Gore-Chi	.862	Gore-Chi	180	Gore-Chi	30.4	Gore-Chi	27.8	Anson-Chi	171	Gore-Chi	61
Connor-Tro	.816	Connor-Tro	166	Connor-Tro	25.4	Connor-Tro	23.1	Kelly-Chi	165	Dalrymple-Chi	60
Dalrymple-Chi	.793	Jones-Bos	159	Dalrymple-Chi	24.5	Dalrymple-Chi	21.6	Richmond-Wor	153	Connor-Tro	57
Anson-Chi	.781	J.O'Rourke-Bos	158	Anson-Chi	22.9	J.O'Rourke-Bos	21.5	Hanlon-Cle	146	Anson-Chi	55
J.O'Rourke-Bos	.756	Dalrymple-Chi	156	J.O'Rourke-Bos	19.9	Anson-Chi	20.1	Whitney-Wor	145	J.O'Rourke-Bos	52

Total Average		Stolen Bases	Stolen Base Average	Stolen Base Runs	Fielding Runs		Total Player Rating	
Gore-Chi	.825				Irwin-Wor	31.0	Irwin-Wor	3.3
Connor-Tro	.744				Force-Buf	30.8	Clapp-Cin	2.9
Dalrymple-Chi	.695				Bradley-Pro	18.8	Gore-Chi	2.7
Anson-Chi	.691				Shaffer-Cle	15.0	Dunlap-Cle	2.5
J.O'Rourke-Bos	.688				Ward-Pro	13.8	Dalrymple-Chi	2.1

Wins		Win Percentage		Games		Complete Games		Shutouts		Saves	
McCormick-Cle	45	Goldsmith-Chi	.875	Richmond-Wor	74	McCormick-Cle	72	Ward-Pro	8	Richmond-Wor	3
Corcoran-Chi	43	Corcoran-Chi	.754	McCormick-Cle	74	Welch-Tro	64	McCormick-Cle	7	Corey-Wor	2
Ward-Pro	39	Ward-Pro	.619	Ward-Pro	70	Ward-Pro	59	Richmond-Wor	5	Corcoran-Chi	2
Welch-Tro	34	McCormick-Cle	.616	Welch-Tro	65	W.White-Cin	58	Galvin-Buf	5		
Richmond-Wor	32	Welch-Tro	.531								

Innings Pitched		Fewest Hits/Game		Fewest BB/Game		Strikeouts		Strikeouts/Game		Ratio	
McCormick-Cle	657.2	Keefe-Tro	6.09	Bradley-Pro	.28	Corcoran-Chi	268	Corcoran-Chi	4.50	Bradley-Pro	7.53
Ward-Pro	595.0	Corcoran-Chi	6.78	Galvin-Buf	.63	McCormick-Cle	260	Goldsmith-Chi	3.85	Keefe-Tro	7.54
Richmond-Wor	590.2	Bradley-Pro	7.26	Ward-Pro	.68	Richmond-Wor	243	Richmond-Wor	3.70	Ward-Pro	8.26
Welch-Tro	574.0	Ward-Pro	7.58	Weidman-Buf	.71	Ward-Pro	230	Keefe-Tro	3.69	Corcoran-Chi	8.44
Corcoran-Chi	536.1	Corey-Wor	7.95	Goldsmith-Chi	.77	W.White-Cin	161	McCormick-Cle	3.56	Goldsmith-Chi	8.86

Earned Run Average		Adjusted ERA		Opponents' Batting Avg.		Opponents' On Base Pct.		Starter Runs		Adjusted Starter Runs	
Keefe-Tro	.86	Keefe-Tro	294	Keefe-Tro	.182	Bradley-Pro	.216	Ward-Pro	42.0	McCormick-Cle	36.8
Bradley-Pro	1.38	Bradley-Pro	160	Corcoran-Chi	.198	Keefe-Tro	.216	McCormick-Cle	38.5	Ward-Pro	30.8
Ward-Pro	1.74	Goldsmith-Chi	138	Bradley-Pro	.209	Ward-Pro	.232	Corcoran-Chi	25.5	Richmond-Wor	29.5
Goldsmith-Chi	1.75	McCormick-Cle	127	Ward-Pro	.217	Corcoran-Chi	.236	Bradley-Pro	21.7	Corcoran-Chi	28.3
McCormick-Cle	1.85	Ward-Pro	127	Corey-Wor	.225	Goldsmith-Chi	.244	Keefe-Tro	17.7	W.White-Cin	19.6

Clutch Pitching Index		Relief Runs	Adjusted Relief Runs	Relief Ranking	Total Pitcher Index		Total Baseball Ranking	
W.White-Cin	130				McCormick-Cle	3.9	McCormick-Cle	3.9
Poorman-Buf-Chi	115				Corcoran-Chi	3.4	Corcoran-Chi	3.4
Galvin-Buf	113				Ward-Pro	3.3	Irwin-Wor	3.3
Bond-Bos	111				Richmond-Wor	2.3	Ward-Pro	3.3
Purcell-Cin	109				Keefe-Tro	2.2	Bradley-Pro	3.2

1881 National League

TEAM	G	W	L	PCT	GB	R	OR	AB	H	2B	3B	HR	BB	SO	AVG	OBP	SLG	PRO	PRO+	BR	/A	PF	CHI	RC	SB	CS	SBA	SBR
CHI	84	56	28	.667		550	379	3114	918	157	36	12	140	224	.295	.325	.380	.705	119	85	63	105	105	394				
PRO	85	47	37	.560	9	447	426	3077	780	144	37	11	146	214	.253	.287	.335	.622	99	-3	4	98	104	304				
BUF	83	45	38	.542	10.5	440	447	3019	797	157	50	12	108	270	.264	.289	.361	.650	108	22	27	99	99	323				
DET	84	41	43	.488	15	439	429	2995	780	131	53	17	136	250	.260	.293	.357	.650	102	22	4	104	99	320				
TRO	85	39	45	.464	17	399	429	3046	754	124	31	5	140	240	.248	.281	.314	.595	85	-31	-53	105	100	275				
BOS	83	38	45	.458	17.5	349	410	2916	733	121	27	5	110	193	.251	.279	.317	.596	94	-30	-11	95	92	264				
CLE	85	36	48	.429	20	392	414	3117	796	120	39	7	132	224	.255	.286	.326	.612	100	-15	8	95	93	297				
WOR	83	32	50	.390	23	410	492	3093	781	114	31	7	121	169	.253	.281	.316	.597	86	-30	-54	106	102	281				
TOT	336					3426		24377	6339	1068	304	76	1033	1784	.260	.289	.338	.627										

TEAM	CG	SH	SV	IP	H	H/G	HR	BB	SO	RAT	ERA	ERA+	OAV	OOB	PR	/A	PF	CPI	FA	E	DP	FW	PW	BW	SBW	DIF
CHI	81	9	0	744²	722	8.7	14	122	228	10.2	2.43	113	.243	.273	28	25	99	97	.916	309	54	2.1	2.3	5.9		3.7
PRO	76	7	0	757²	756	9.0	5	138	264	10.6	2.40	111	.248	.281	31	21	96	102	.896	390	66	-2.0	2.0	.4		4.7
BUF	72	5	0	742¹	881	10.7	9	89	185	11.8	2.84	98	.282	.302	-5	-4	100	115	.892	408	48	-3.4	-.4	2.5		4.8
DET	83	10	0	744²	785	9.5	8	137	265	11.1	2.65	110	.259	.291	10	22	105	105	.906	338	80	.5	2.1	.4		-3.9
TRO	85	8	0	770	813	9.5	11	159	207	11.4	2.97	99	.259	.295	-16	-1	106	97	.917	311	70	2.2	-.0	-5.0		-.1
BOS	72	6	3	730²	763	9.4	9	143	199	11.2	2.72	98	.257	.291	4	-5	96	102	.909	325	54	1.0	-.5	-1.0		-3.0
CLE	82	2	0	760	737	8.7	9	126	240	10.2	2.68	98	.243	.273	8	-4	94	86	.904	348	68	.2	-.4	.7		-6.6
WOR	80	5	0	737¹	882	10.8	11	120	196	12.2	3.54	85	.284	.310	-62	-42	109	97	.903	353	50	-.5	-3.9	-5.0		.5
TOT	631	52	3	5987¹		9.5				11.1	2.78		.260	.289					.905	2782	490					

Runs		Hits		Doubles		Triples		Home Runs		Total Bases	
Gore-Chi	86	Anson-Chi	137	Kelly-Chi	27	Rowe-Buf	11	Brouthers-Buf	8	Anson-Chi	175
Kelly-Chi	84	Dalrymple-Chi	117	Hines-Pro	27	Phillips-Cle	10	Bennett-Det	7	Dunlap-Cle	156
Dalrymple-Chi	72	Dickerson-Wor	116	Stovey-Wor	25			Farrell-Pro	5	Kelly-Chi	153
O'Rourke-Buf	71			Dunlap-Cle	25			Burns-Chi	4	Dalrymple-Chi	150
Farrell-Pro	69			White-Buf	24					Dickerson-Wor	149

Runs Batted In		Runs Produced		Bases On Balls		Batting Average		On Base Percentage		Slugging Average	
Anson-Chi	82	Anson-Chi	148	Clapp-Cle	35	Anson-Chi	.399	Anson-Chi	.442	Brouthers-Buf	.541
Bennett-Det	64	Kelly-Chi	137	York-Pro	29	Start-Pro	.328	York-Pro	.362	Anson-Chi	.510
Kelly-Chi	55	Gore-Chi	129	Ferguson-Tro	29	Dunlap-Cle	.325	Brouthers-Buf	.361	Bennett-Det	.478
		Knight-Det	118	Farrell-Pro	29	Dalrymple-Chi	.323	Dunlap-Cle	.358	Dunlap-Cle	.444
		Richardson-Buf	113			Kelly-Chi	.323	Gore-Chi	.354	Kelly-Chi	.433

Production		Adjusted Production		Batter Runs		Adjusted Batter Runs		Clutch Hitting Index		Runs Created	
Anson-Chi	.952	Anson-Chi	189	Anson-Chi	38.9	Anson-Chi	36.5	Anson-Chi	169	Anson-Chi	79
Brouthers-Buf	.902	Brouthers-Buf	182	Brouthers-Buf	24.1	Brouthers-Buf	24.6	Ward-Pro	167	Dunlap-Cle	57
Bennett-Det	.819	Dunlap-Cle	159	Dunlap-Cle	20.0	Dunlap-Cle	22.6	White-Buf	149	Kelly-Chi	55
Dunlap-Cle	.802	York-Pro	150	Bennett-Det	18.3	York-Pro	18.6	Richmond-Wor	147	Brouthers-Buf	54
York-Pro	.790	Bennett-Det	149	Kelly-Chi	18.0	Bennett-Det	16.5	Radbourn-Pro	146	Dalrymple-Chi	54

Total Average		Stolen Bases	Stolen Base Average	Stolen Base Runs	Fielding Runs		Total Player Rating	
Anson-Chi	.976				Richardson-Buf	24.6	Richardson-Buf	3.2
Brouthers-Buf	.891				Force-Pro	24.2	Anson-Chi	3.0
Bennett-Det	.770				Ewing-Tro	23.5	Dunlap-Cle	2.9
York-Pro	.745				Williamson-Chi	22.2	Bennett-Det	2.7
Dunlap-Cle	.734				Bennett-Det	13.1	Williamson-Chi	2.7

Wins		Win Percentage		Games		Complete Games		Shutouts		Saves	
Whitney-Bos	31	Radbourn-Pro	.694	Whitney-Bos	66	Whitney-Bos	57	Derby-Det	9	Mathews-Pro-Bos	2
Corcoran-Chi	31	Corcoran-Chi	.689	McCormick-Cle	59	McCormick-Cle	57	Whitney-Bos	6	Morrill-Bos	1
Derby-Det	29	Goldsmith-Chi	.649	Galvin-Buf	56	Derby-Det	55	Goldsmith-Chi	5		
Galvin-Buf	28	Welch-Tro	.538	Derby-Det	56	Richmond-Wor	50	Galvin-Buf	5		
McCormick-Cle	26	Galvin-Buf	.538	Richmond-Wor	53	Galvin-Buf	48				

Innings Pitched		Fewest Hits/Game		Fewest BB/Game		Strikeouts		Strikeouts/Game		Ratio	
Whitney-Bos	552.1	McCormick-Cle	8.28	Galvin-Buf	.87	Derby-Det	212	Derby-Det	3.86	Weidman-Det	9.39
McCormick-Cle	526.0	Weidman-Det	8.45	Weidman-Det	.94	McCormick-Cle	178	Corcoran-Chi	3.40	McCormick-Cle	9.72
Derby-Det	494.2	Radbourn-Pro	8.55	Goldsmith-Chi	1.20	Whitney-Bos	162	Ward-Pro	3.25	Goldsmith-Chi	10.15
Galvin-Buf	474.0	Corcoran-Chi	8.62	Richmond-Wor	1.32	Richmond-Wor	156	Radbourn-Pro	3.24	Radbourn-Pro	10.32
Richmond-Wor	462.1	Ward-Pro	8.89	McCormick-Cle	1.44	Corcoran-Chi	150	McCormick-Cle	3.05	Ward-Pro	10.34

Earned Run Average		Adjusted ERA		Opponents' Batting Avg.		Opponents' On Base Pct.		Starter Runs		Adjusted Starter Runs	
Weidman-Det	1.80	Weidman-Det	162	McCormick-Cle	.234	Weidman-Det	.257	Derby-Det	31.6	Derby-Det	39.4
Ward-Pro	2.13	Derby-Det	133	Weidman-Det	.238	McCormick-Cle	.264	Ward-Pro	23.8	Galvin-Buf	21.4
Derby-Det	2.20	Ward-Pro	125	Radbourn-Pro	.240	Goldsmith-Chi	.272	Galvin-Buf	21.2	Ward-Pro	19.4
Corcoran-Chi	2.31	Corcoran-Chi	118	Corcoran-Chi	.241	Radbourn-Pro	.276	Corcoran-Chi	20.4	Corcoran-Chi	18.8
Galvin-Buf	2.37	Galvin-Buf	117	Ward-Pro	.247	Ward-Pro	.276	McCormick-Cle	19.3	Weidman-Det	14.3

Clutch Pitching Index		Relief Runs	Adjusted Relief Runs	Relief Ranking	Total Pitcher Index		Total Baseball Ranking	
Galvin-Buf	126				Derby-Det	3.0	Richardson-Buf	3.2
Derby-Det	115				Galvin-Buf	2.6	Derby-Det	3.0
Mathews-Pro-Bos	114				Ward-Pro	1.9	Anson-Chi	3.0
Ward-Pro	110				Whitney-Bos	1.7	Dunlap-Cle	2.9
Weidman-Det	109				Corcoran-Chi	1.4	Williamson-Chi	2.8

TEAM	G	W	L	PCT	GB	R	OR	AB	H	2B	3B	HR	BB	SO	AVG	OBP	SLG	PRO	PRO+	BR	/A	PF	CHI	RC	SB	CS	SBA	SBR
CHI	84	55	29	.655		604	353	3225	892	209	54	15	142	262	.277	.307	.389	.696	118	82	59	105	108	395				
PRO	84	52	32	.619	3	463	356	3104	776	121	53	11	102	255	.250	.274	.334	.608	96	-15	-14	100	105	291				
BUF	84	45	39	.536	10	500	461	3128	858	146	47	18	116	228	.274	.300	.368	.668	112	50	41	102	98	355				
BOS	85	45	39	.536	10	472	414	3118	823	114	50	15	134	244	.264	.294	.347	.641	106	23	22	100	97	326				
CLE	84	42	40	.512	12	402	411	3009	716	139	40	20	122	261	.238	.268	.331	.599	96	-23	-8	97	95	273				
DET	86	42	41	.506	12.5	407	488	3144	724	117	44	19	122	308	.230	.259	.314	.573	84	-52	-51	100	99	262				
TRO	85	35	48	.422	19.5	430	522	3057	747	116	59	12	109	298	.244	.270	.333	.603	98	-19	2	95	100	282				
WOR	84	18	66	.214	37	379	652	2984	689	109	57	16	113	303	.231	.259	.322	.581	84	-42	-52	102	95	255				
TOT	338					3657		24769	6225	1071	404	126	960	2159	.251	.279	.342	.622										

TEAM	CG	SH	SV	IP	H	H/G	HR	BB	SO	RAT	ERA	ERA+	OAV	OOB	PR	/A	PF	CPI	FA	E	DP	FW	PW	BW	SBW	DIF
CHI	83	7	0	763²	667	7.9	13	102	279	9.1	2.22	129	.221	.247	56	54	99	90	.899	376	54	.1	4.9	5.4		2.6
PRO	80	10	1	752	690	8.3	12	87	273	9.3	2.27	123	.230	.251	51	44	97	95	.900	371	67	.4	4.0	-1.3		6.9
BUF	79	3	0	737	778	9.5	16	114	287	10.9	3.25	90	.255	.282	-29	-26	101	93	.911	315	42	3.3	-2.4	3.7		-1.7
BOS	81	4	0	749	738	8.9	10	77	352	9.8	2.80	102	.243	.261	7	4	99	87	.910	314	37	3.6	.4	2.0		-2.9
CLE	81	4	0	751²	743	8.9	22	132	232	10.5	2.75	101	.243	.274	10	2	97	101	.905	358	71	1.1	.2	-.7		.5
DET	82	7	0	793	808	9.2	19	129	354	10.6	2.98	98	.249	.277	-8	-5	101	96	.894	396	44	-.4	-.5	-4.6		6.0
TRO	81	6	0	757	837	10.0	13	168	189	11.9	3.08	91	.264	.301	-16	-22	98	111	.887	432	70	-2.5	-2.0	.2		-2.2
WOR	75	0	0	738¹	964	11.8	21	151	195	13.6	3.75	83	.298	.329	-71	-53	107	119	.878	468	66	-4.6	-4.8	-4.7		-9.9
TOT	642	41	1	6041²		9.3				10.7	2.89		.251	.279					.898	3030	451					

Runs
Gore-Chi 99
Dalrymple-Chi 96
Stovey-Wor 90
Kelly-Chi 81
Purcell-Buf 79

Hits
Brouthers-Buf 129
Anson-Chi 126

Doubles
Kelly-Chi 37
Anson-Chi 29
Hines-Pro 28
Williamson-Chi 27
Glasscock-Cle 27

Triples
Connor-Tro 18
Wood-Det 12
Corey-Wor 12

Home Runs
Wood-Det 7
Muldoon-Cle 6
Brouthers-Buf 6

Total Bases
Brouthers-Buf 192
Connor-Tro 185
Hines-Pro 177
Anson-Chi 174
Dalrymple-Chi 167

Runs Batted In
Anson-Chi 83
Brouthers-Buf 63
Williamson-Chi 60
Richardson-Buf 57
Kelly-Chi 55

Runs Produced
Anson-Chi 151
Gore-Chi 147
Kelly-Chi 135
Dalrymple-Chi ... 131
Brouthers-Buf 128

Bases On Balls
Gore-Chi 29
Williamson-Chi 27
Shaffer-Cle 27
Hanlon-Det 26

Batting Average
Brouthers-Buf .... .368
Anson-Chi .... .362
Connor-Tro ...... .330
Start-Pro .... .329
Whitney-Bos ..... .323

On Base Percentage
Brouthers-Buf .... .403
Anson-Chi .... .397
Whitney-Bos ..... .382
Gore-Chi .... .369
Connor-Tro ...... .354

Slugging Average
Brouthers-Buf .... .547
Connor-Tro ...... .530
Whitney-Bos ..... .510
Anson-Chi .... .500
Hines-Pro .... .467

Production
Brouthers-Buf ..... .950
Anson-Chi .... .897
Whitney-Bos ...... .892
Connor-Tro ...... .884
Hines-Pro .... .793

Adjusted Production
Brouthers-Buf 198
Connor-Tro 188
Whitney-Bos 183
Anson-Chi 177
Hines-Pro 151

Batter Runs
Brouthers-Buf 39.1
Anson-Chi 32.7
Connor-Tro 29.7
Whitney-Bos 23.7
Gore-Chi 22.2

Adjusted Batter Runs
Brouthers-Buf 38.2
Connor-Tro 32.1
Anson-Chi 30.3
Whitney-Bos 27.8
Hines-Pro 20.7

Clutch Hitting Index
Anson-Chi 167
Pfeffer-Tro 159
Holbert-Tro 152
Rowen-Bos 150
Williamson-Chi ... 142

Runs Created
Brouthers-Buf 79
Anson-Chi 71
Connor-Tro 67
Hines-Pro 59
Gore-Chi 59

Total Average
Brouthers-Buf ..... .959
Whitney-Bos ...... .894
Anson-Chi .... .874
Connor-Tro ...... .846
Gore-Chi .... .736

Stolen Bases

Stolen Base Average

Stolen Base Runs

Fielding Runs
Glasscock-Cle 23.9
A.Irwin-Wor 20.7
Evans-Wor 18.6
Dunlap-Cle 17.5
Williamson-Chi ... 15.4

Total Player Rating
Glasscock-Cle 4.4
Williamson-Chi ... 2.5
Dunlap-Cle 2.5
Connor-Tro 2.5
Bennett-Det 2.3

Wins
McCormick-Cle 36
Radbourn-Pro 33
Goldsmith-Chi 28
Galvin-Buf 28
Corcoran-Chi 27

Win Percentage
Corcoran-Chi ..... .692
Radbourn-Pro ..... .623
Goldsmith-Chi .... .622
Ward-Pro .... .613
Mathews-Bos ..... .559

Games
McCormick-Cle 68
Radbourn-Pro 55
Galvin-Buf 52
Whitney-Bos 49
Richmond-Wor 48

Complete Games
McCormick-Cle 65
Radbourn-Pro 51
Galvin-Buf 48
Whitney-Bos 46
Goldsmith-Chi 45

Shutouts
Radbourn-Pro 6
Welch-Tro 5

Saves
Ward-Pro 1

Innings Pitched
McCormick-Cle .. 595.2
Radbourn-Pro ... 474.0
Galvin-Buf 445.1
Whitney-Bos 420.0

Fewest Hits/Game
Corcoran-Chi 7.11
Radbourn-Pro 8.15
McCormick-Cle ... 8.31
Goldsmith-Chi ... 8.38
Ward-Pro 8.45

Fewest BB/Game
Mathews-Bos ...... .69
Galvin-Buf .... .81
Goldsmith-Chi .... .84
Weidman-Det ...... .85
Whitney-Bos ...... .88

Strikeouts
Radbourn-Pro 201
McCormick-Cle ... 200
Derby-Det 182
Whitney-Bos 180
Corcoran-Chi 170

Strikeouts/Game
Mathews-Bos 4.83
Derby-Det 4.52
Corcoran-Chi 4.30
Daily-Buf 4.08
Whitney-Bos 3.86

Ratio
Corcoran-Chi 8.70
Radbourn-Pro 9.11
Goldsmith-Chi 9.22
Weidman-Det 9.42
Mathews-Bos 9.47

Earned Run Average
Corcoran-Chi 1.95
Radbourn-Pro ... 2.09
McCormick-Cle ... 2.37
Goldsmith-Chi ... 2.42
Keefe-Tro 2.50

Adjusted ERA
Corcoran-Chi 147
Radbourn-Pro ... 134
Goldsmith-Chi ... 118
McCormick-Cle ... 118
Keefe-Tro 113

Opponents' Batting Avg.
Corcoran-Chi ..... .205
Radbourn-Pro ... .228
McCormick-Cle ... .231
Goldsmith-Chi .... .233
Ward-Pro .... .234

Opponents' On Base Pct.
Corcoran-Chi ..... .240
Radbourn-Pro ... .248
Goldsmith-Chi .... .250
Weidman-Det .... .254
Mathews-Bos .... .255

Starter Runs
Radbourn-Pro 42.0
Corcoran-Chi 37.0
McCormick-Cle ... 34.0
Goldsmith-Chi ... 20.8
Keefe-Tro 16.2

Adjusted Starter Runs
Radbourn-Pro 37.6
Corcoran-Chi 35.9
McCormick-Cle ... 27.5
Goldsmith-Chi ... 19.5
Weidman-Det ... 13.5

Clutch Pitching Index
F.Mountain-Wor ... 121
Corey-Wor 120
Richmond-Wor ... 116
Welch-Tro 113
Egan-Tro 112

Relief Runs

Adjusted Relief Runs

Relief Ranking

Total Pitcher Index
Whitney-Bos 3.7
Radbourn-Pro 3.3
Corcoran-Chi 3.2
Keefe-Tro 2.1
McCormick-Cle 1.8

Total Baseball Ranking
Glasscock-Cle 4.4
Whitney-Bos 3.7
Radbourn-Pro 3.3
Corcoran-Chi 3.2
Dunlap-Cle 2.5

TEAM	G	W	L	PCT	GB	R	OR	AB	H	2B	3B	HR	BB	SO	AVG	OBP	SLG	PRO	PRO+	BR	/A	PF	CHI	RC	SB	CS	SBA	SBR
CIN	80	55	25	.688		489	268	3007	795	95	47	5	102	204	.264	.289	.332	.621	106	38	11	106	104	295				
PHI	75	41	34	.547	11.5	406	389	2707	660	89	21	5	125	164	.244	.277	.298	.575	87	-3	-49	112	104	229				
LOU	80	42	38	.525	13	443	352	2806	728	110	28	9	128	193	.259	.292	.328	.620	120	37	61	94	99	275				
PIT	79	39	39	.500	15	428	418	2904	730	110	59	18	90	183	.251	.274	.348	.622	118	35	54	95	95	284				
STL	80	37	43	.463	18	399	496	2865	663	87	41	11	112	226	.231	.260	.302	.562	89	-18	-34	104	101	231				
BAL	74	19	54	.260	32.5	273	515	2583	535	60	24	4	72	215	.207	.229	.254	.483	71	-86	-57	92	96	153				
TOT	234					2438		16872	4111	551	220	52	629	1185	.244	.271	.312	.582										

TEAM	CG	SH	SV	IP	H	H/G	HR	BB	SO	RAT	ERA	ERA+	OAV	OOB	PR	/A	PF	CPI	FA	E	DP	FW	PW	BW	SBW	DIF
CIN	77	11	0	721¹	609	7.6	7	125	165	9.2	1.65	161	.213	.247	83	80	99	119	.907	332	41	3.7	7.3	1.0		2.9
PHI	72	2	0	663	682	9.3	13	99	190	10.6	2.97	100	.249	.275	-21	0	111	97	.895	361	36	1.2	.0	-4.5		6.8
LOU	73	6	0	693¹	637	8.3	6	112	240	9.7	2.03	122	.228	.258	50	33	92	113	.893	385	57	1.3	3.0	5.6		-7.9
PIT	77	2	0	696²	694	9.0	4	82	252	10.0	2.79	93	.243	.264	-8	-14	97	90	.889	397	40	.5	-1.3	5.0		-4.1
STL	75	3	1	688¹	729	9.5	7	103	225	10.9	2.92	96	.254	.280	-17	-8	105	101	.875	446	41	-1.6	-.7	-3.1		2.4
BAL	64	1	0	646¹	760	10.6	15	108	113	12.1	3.88	71	.274	.301	-86	-81	102	94	.859	490	41	-5.0	-7.4	-5.2		.2
TOT	438	25	1	4109		9.0				10.4	2.68		.244	.271					.886	2411	256					

Runs
Swartwood-Pit 86
Sommer-Cin 82
Carpenter-Cin 78
Browning-Lou 67
Birchall-Phi 65

Hits
Carpenter-Cin 120
Browning-Lou 109
Swartwood-Pit 107
Sommer-Cin 102
W.Gleason-StL 100

Doubles
Swartwood-Pit 18
Mansell-Pit 18
Browning-Lou 17
Taylor-Pit 16
Cuthbert-StL 16

Triples
Mansell-Pit 16
Taylor-Pit 13
Wheeler-Cin 11
Swartwood-Pit 11
Wolf-Lou........... 8

Home Runs
Walker-StL 7
Browning-Lou 5
Swartwood-Pit 4

Total Bases
Swartwood-Pit ... 159
Mansell-Pit 152
Carpenter-Cin ... 148
Browning-Lou 147
Taylor-Pit 135

Runs Batted In

Runs Produced
Swartwood-Pit 82
Sommer-Cin 81
Carpenter-Cin 77
Birchall-Phi 65

Bases On Balls
J.Gleason-StL 27
Browning-Lou 26
Sommer-Cin 24
J.Reccius-Lou 23
Swartwood-Pit 21

Batting Average
Browning-Lou 378
Carpenter-Cin 342
Swartwood-Pit 329
O'Brien-Phi 303
Wolf-Lou..........299

On Base Percentage
Browning-Lou 430
Swartwood-Pit 370
Carpenter-Cin 360
O'Brien-Phi 339
Sommer-Cin 333

Slugging Average
Browning-Lou 510
Swartwood-Pit 489
Taylor-Pit 452
Mansell-Pit 438
Carpenter-Cin 422

Production
Browning-Lou 940
Swartwood-Pit 859
Carpenter-Cin 782
O'Brien-Phi 758
Taylor-Pit 749

Adjusted Production
Browning-Lou 230
Swartwood-Pit ... 197
Taylor-Pit 157
Carpenter-Cin ... 153
Mansell-Pit 150

Batter Runs
Browning-Lou 35.3
Swartwood-Pit ...29.3
Carpenter-Cin ... 22.0
Taylor-Pit 14.5
Mansell-Pit 14.5

Adjusted Batter Runs
Browning-Lou 37.9
Swartwood-Pit ...31.5
Carpenter-Cin ...18.9
Mansell-Pit 16.7
Taylor-Pit 16.4

Clutch Hitting Index

Runs Created
Browning-Lou 65
Swartwood-Pit 60
Carpenter-Cin 55
Mansell-Pit 45
Sommer-Cin 44

Total Average
Browning-Lou 966
Swartwood-Pit 826
Carpenter-Cin 684
O'Brien-Phi 679
Taylor-Pit 660

Stolen Bases

Stolen Base Average

Stolen Base Runs

Fielding Runs
Stricker-Phi 22.5
Snyder-Cin 12.6
White-Cin 11.8
Browning-Lou 11.8
Mullane-Lou...... 10.1

Total Player Rating
Browning-Lou 4.7
Swartwood-Pit ... 2.0
Mansell-Pit 1.7
Snyder-Cin........ 1.6
W.Gleason-StL 1.5

Wins
White-Cin 40
Mullane-Lou....... 30
Weaver-Phi 26
McGinnis-StL...... 25
Salisbury-Pit 20

Win Percentage
White-Cin 769
Weaver-Phi 634
McGinnis-StL......595
Mullane-Lou.......556
Salisbury-Pit 526

Games
Mullane-Lou....... 55
White-Cin 54
Landis-Phi-Bal.... 44
McGinnis-StL...... 44
Weaver-Phi 42

Complete Games
White-Cin 52
Mullane-Lou....... 51
McGinnis-StL...... 42
Weaver-Phi 41
Salisbury-Pit 38

Shutouts
White-Cin 8
Mullane-Lou....... 5
McGinnis-StL...... 3
McCormick-Cin 3
Weaver-Phi 2

Saves
Fusselback-StL 1

Innings Pitched
White-Cin 480.0
Mullane-Lou...... 460.1
McGinnis-StL... 379.1
Weaver-Phi 371.0
Landis-Phi-Bal...358.0

Fewest Hits/Game
Hecker-Lou 6.49
McCormick-Cin ... 7.25
Driscoll-Pit 7.25
White-Cin 7.71
Geis-Bal 7.90

Fewest BB/Game
Hecker-Lou 43
Driscoll-Pit 54
Weaver-Phi .... .85
Salisbury-Pit 99
Landis-Phi-Bal....1.18

Strikeouts
Mullane-Lou...... 170
Salisbury-Pit 135
McGinnis-StL..... 134
White-Cin 122
Weaver-Phi 104

Strikeouts/Game
Salisbury-Pit 3.63
Arundel-Pit....... 3.53
Mullane-Lou...... 3.32
McGinnis-StL..... 3.18
J.Reccius-Lou ... 2.94

Ratio
Hecker-Lou 6.92
Driscoll-Pit 7.79
McCormick-Cin ... 8.97
White-Cin 9.04
Salisbury-Pit 9.46

Earned Run Average
Driscoll-Pit 1.21
Hecker-Lou 1.30
McCormick-Cin ... 1.52
White-Cin 1.54
Mullane-Lou......1.88

Adjusted ERA
Driscoll-Pit 216
Hecker-Lou 190
McCormick-Cin ... 175
White-Cin 173
Mullane-Lou...... 131

Opponents' Batting Avg.
Hecker-Lou 188
McCormick-Cin ...206
Driscoll-Pit 206
White-Cin 216
Geis-Bal 220

Opponents' On Base Pct.
Hecker-Lou 199
Driscoll-Pit 218
McCormick-Cin ...243
White-Cin 244
Salisbury-Pit 253

Starter Runs
White-Cin 61.1
Mullane-Lou...... 41.2
Driscoll-Pit 32.9
McCormick-Cin ... 28.5
Hecker-Lou 16.0

Adjusted Starter Runs
White-Cin 59.5
Driscoll-Pit 31.2
Mullane-Lou...... 30.0
McCormick-Cin ... 27.8
McGinnis-StL..... 14.2

Clutch Pitching Index
White-Cin 124
McCormick-Cin ... 121
Mullane-Lou...... 120
J.Reccius-Lou 119
Driscoll-Pit 113

Relief Runs

Adjusted Relief Runs

Relief Ranking

Total Pitcher Index
White-Cin 7.7
Mullane-Lou....... 5.0
Driscoll-Pit 2.4
McCormick-Cin ... 2.2
Weaver-Phi 1.4

Total Baseball Ranking
White-Cin 7.7
Mullane-Lou....... 5.0
Browning-Lou 4.7
Hecker-Lou 2.7
Driscoll-Pit 2.4

TEAM	G	W	L	PCT	GB	R	OR	AB	H	2B	3B	HR	BB	SO	AVG	OBP	SLG	PRO	PRO+	BR	/A	PF	CHI	RC	SB	CS	SBA	SBR
BOS	98	63	35	.643		669	456	3657	1010	209	86	34	123	423	.276	.300	.408	.708	114	68	54	102	104	459				
CHI	98	59	39	.602	4	679	540	3658	1000	277	61	13	129	399	.273	.298	.393	.691	105	49	14	106	109	439				
PRO	98	58	40	.592	5	636	436	3685	1001	189	59	21	149	309	.272	.300	.372	.672	104	29	13	103	104	422				
CLE	100	55	42	.567	7.5	476	443	3457	852	184	38	8	139	374	.246	.276	.329	.605	88	-52	-45	99	97	321				
BUF	98	52	45	.536	10.5	614	576	3729	1058	184	59	8	147	342	.284	.311	.371	.682	107	-17	-10	99	97	441				
NY	98	46	50	.479	16	530	577	3524	900	139	69	24	127	297	.255	.281	.354	.635	96	-17	-10	99	99	360				
DET	101	40	58	.408	23	524	650	3726	931	164	48	13	166	378	.250	.282	.330	.612	93	-45	-18	96	96	355				
PHI	99	17	81	.173	46	437	887	3576	859	181	48	3	141	355	.240	.269	.320	.589	89	-73	-23	91	89	316				
TOT	395					4565		29012	7611	1527	468	124	1121	2877	.262	.290	.360	.650										

TEAM	CG	SH	SV	IP	H	H/G	HR	BB	SO	RAT	ERA	ERA+	OAV	OOB	PR	/A	PF	CPI	FA	E	DP	FW	PW	BW	SBW	DIF
BOS	89	6	3	860	853	8.9	11	90	538	9.9	2.55	122	.243	.262	55	52	99	95	.901	409	58	3.1	4.5	4.7		1.6
CHI	91	5	1	862	942	9.8	21	123	299	11.1	2.78	115	.262	.286	34	40	102	113	.879	543	76	-3.5	3.5	1.2		8.8
PRO	88	4	1	871	827	8.5	12	111	376	9.7	2.37	130	.235	.259	74	69	98	96	.903	419	75	2.7	6.0	1.1		-.8
CLE	92	5	2	879	818	8.4	7	217	402	10.6	2.22	142	.232	.276	89	90	100	111	.909	389	69	4.6	7.9	-3.9		-2.0
BUF	90	5	2	859¹	971	10.2	12	101	362	11.2	3.32	96	.268	.288	-17	-13	101	96	.895	445	52	1.4	-1.1	2.7		.6
NY	87	5	0	866	907	9.4	19	170	323	11.2	2.94	105	.253	.287	18	14	99	103	.890	468	52	.2	1.2	-.9		-2.6
DET	89	5	2	894¹	1026	10.3	22	184	324	12.2	3.58	87	.271	.305	-44	-47	99	100	.893	470	77	.9	-4.1	-1.6		-4.2
PHI	91	3	0	864²	1267	13.2	20	125	253	14.5	5.34	58	.322	.343	-211	-216	98	94	.858	639	62	-8.0	-18.9	-2.0		-3.2
TOT	717	38	11	6956¹		9.8				11.3	3.14		.262	.290					.891	3782	521					

Runs
Hornung-Bos	107
Gore-Chi	105
O'Rourke-Buf	102
Sutton-Bos	101
Hines-Pro	94

Hits
Brouthers-Buf	159
O'Rourke-Buf	146
O'Rourke-Buf	143
Sutton-Bos	134
Wood-Det	133

Doubles
Williamson-Chi	49
Brouthers-Buf	41
Burns-Chi	37
Anson-Chi	36

Triples
Brouthers-Buf	17
Morrill-Bos	16
Sutton-Bos	15
Connor-NY	15

Home Runs
Ewing-NY	10
Hornung-Bos	8
Denny-Pro	8
Ward-NY	7
Morrill-Bos	6

Total Bases
Brouthers-Buf	243
Morrill-Bos	212
Connor-NY	207
Sutton-Bos	201
Hornung-Bos	199

Runs Batted In
Brouthers-Buf	97
Burdock-Bos	88
Sutton-Bos	73
Morrill-Bos	68
Anson-Chi	68

Runs Produced
Brouthers-Buf	179
Sutton-Bos	171
Hornung-Bos	165
Burdock-Bos	163

Bases On Balls
York-Cle	37
Hanlon-Det	34
Powell-Det	28
Shaffer-Buf	27
Gore-Chi	27

Batting Average
Brouthers-Buf	.374
Connor-NY	.357
Gore-Chi	.334
Burdock-Bos	.330
O'Rourke-Buf	.328

On Base Percentage
Brouthers-Buf	.397
Connor-NY	.394
Gore-Chi	.377
Dunlap-Cle	.361
Burdock-Bos	.353

Slugging Average
Brouthers-Buf	.572
Morrill-Bos	.525
Connor-NY	.506
Sutton-Bos	.486
Ewing-NY	.481

Production
Brouthers-Buf	.969
Connor-NY	.900
Morrill-Bos	.868
Gore-Chi	.849
Sutton-Bos	.836

Adjusted Production
Brouthers-Buf	186
Connor-NY	173
Morrill-Bos	155
Bennett-Det	155
Sutton-Bos	147

Batter Runs
Brouthers-Buf	44.4
Connor-NY	34.6
Morrill-Bos	27.6
Gore-Chi	26.5
Sutton-Bos	24.4

Adjusted Batter Runs
Brouthers-Buf	42.9
Connor-NY	35.3
Whitney-Bos	29.6
Morrill-Bos	26.0
Bennett-Det	23.9

Clutch Hitting Index
Burdock-Bos	159
Anson-Chi	146
Brouthers-Buf	143
Burns-Chi	137
Start-Pro	136

Runs Created
Brouthers-Buf	99
Connor-NY	84
Morrill-Bos	75
Sutton-Bos	72
Gore-Chi	72

Total Average
Brouthers-Buf	.974
Connor-NY	.882
Morrill-Bos	.825
Gore-Chi	.812
Bennett-Det	.783

Stolen Bases

Stolen Base Average

Stolen Base Runs

Fielding Runs
Farrell-Pro	24.1
Richardson-Buf	22.2
Shaffer-Buf	19.9
Glasscock-Cle	17.8
Williamson-Chi	17.1

Total Player Rating
Richardson-Buf	2.9
Brouthers-Buf	2.8
Farrell-Pro	2.8
Gore-Chi	2.8
Wood-Det	2.8

Wins
Radbourn-Pro	48
Galvin-Buf	46
Whitney-Bos	37
Corcoran-Chi	34
McCormick-Cle	28

Win Percentage
McCormick-Cle	.700
Radbourn-Pro	.658
Buffinton-Bos	.641
Whitney-Bos	.638
Corcoran-Chi	.630

Games
Radbourn-Pro	76
Galvin-Buf	76
Coleman-Phi	65
Whitney-Bos	62
Corcoran-Chi	56

Complete Games
Galvin-Buf	72
Radbourn-Pro	66
Coleman-Phi	59
Whitney-Bos	54
Corcoran-Chi	51

Shutouts
Galvin-Buf	5
Welch-NY	4
Radbourn-Pro	4
Daily-Cle	4
Buffinton-Bos	4

Saves
Whitney-Bos	2
Weidman-Det	2

Innings Pitched
Galvin-Buf	656.1
Radbourn-Pro	632.1
Coleman-Phi	538.1
Whitney-Bos	514.0
Corcoran-Chi	473.2

Fewest Hits/Game
Sawyer-Cle	7.60
Radbourn-Pro	8.01
McCormick-Cle	8.32
Daily-Cle	8.56
Whitney-Bos	8.61

Fewest BB/Game
Whitney-Bos	.61
Galvin-Buf	.69
Radbourn-Pro	.80
Coleman-Phi	.80
Goldsmith-Chi	.92

Strikeouts
Whitney-Bos	345
Radbourn-Pro	315
Galvin-Buf	279
Corcoran-Chi	216
Buffinton-Bos	188

Strikeouts/Game
Whitney-Bos	6.04
Buffinton-Bos	5.08
Sawyer-Cle	4.85
Radbourn-Pro	4.48
Corcoran-Chi	4.10

Ratio
Radbourn-Pro	8.81
Whitney-Bos	9.23
Galvin-Buf	9.96
McCormick-Cle	10.03
Ward-NY	10.04

Earned Run Average
McCormick-Cle	1.84
Radbourn-Pro	2.05
Whitney-Bos	2.24
Sawyer-Cle	2.36
Daily-Cle	2.42

Adjusted ERA
McCormick-Cle	171
Radbourn-Pro	150
Whitney-Bos	138
Sawyer-Cle	133
Daily-Cle	130

Opponents' Batting Avg.
Sawyer-Cle	.215
Radbourn-Pro	.224
McCormick-Cle	.231
Daily-Cle	.236
Whitney-Bos	.237

Opponents' On Base Pct.
Radbourn-Pro	.241
Whitney-Bos	.250
Galvin-Buf	.264
McCormick-Cle	.266
Ward-NY	.266

Starter Runs
Radbourn-Pro	76.4
Whitney-Bos	51.2
McCormick-Cle	49.2
Corcoran-Chi	34.1
Galvin-Buf	30.8

Adjusted Starter Runs
Radbourn-Pro	72.7
McCormick-Cle	49.7
Whitney-Bos	49.2
Corcoran-Chi	37.3
Galvin-Buf	33.5

Clutch Pitching Index
McCormick-Cle	121
Shaw-Det	118
O'Neill-NY	116
Goldsmith-Chi	115
Burns-Det	112

Relief Runs

Adjusted Relief Runs

Relief Ranking

Total Pitcher Index
Radbourn-Pro	8.5
Whitney-Bos	7.3
McCormick-Cle	5.2
Corcoran-Chi	3.3
Galvin-Buf	2.6

Total Baseball Ranking
Radbourn-Pro	8.5
Whitney-Bos	7.3
McCormick-Cle	5.2
Corcoran-Chi	3.3
Ward-NY	3.1

1883 American Association

TEAM	G	W	L	PCT	GB	R	OR	AB	H	2B	3B	HR	BB	SO	AVG	OBP	SLG	PRO	PRO+	BR	/A	PF	CHI	RC	SB	CS	SBA	SBR
PHI	98	66	32	.673		720	547	3714	972	149	50	20	194	268	.262	.298	.345	.643	101	42	-7	109	115	392				
STL	98	65	33	.663	1	549	409	3495	892	118	46	7	125	240	.255	.281	.321	.602	91	-11	-42	106	104	323				
CIN	98	61	37	.622	5	662	413	3669	961	122	74	34	139	261	.262	.289	.363	.652	105	47	12	106	107	395				
NY	97	54	42	.563	11	498	405	3534	883	111	58	6	142	259	.250	.279	.319	.598	92	-16	-37	104	93	322				
LOU	98	52	45	.536	13.5	564	562	3553	891	114	64	14	140	305	.251	.279	.331	.610	107	-3	39	92	103	336				
COL	97	32	65	.330	33.5	476	659	3553	854	101	79	15	134	410	.240	.268	.326	.594	102	-23	21	92	90	318				
PIT	98	31	67	.316	35	525	728	3609	892	120	58	13	162	345	.247	.280	.323	.603	101	-10	15	95	95	334				
BAL	96	28	68	.292	37	471	742	3534	870	125	49	5	162	331	.246	.279	.314	.593	91	-20	-36	103	88	317				
TOT	390					4465		28661	7215	960	478	114	1198	2419	.252	.282	.331	.612										

TEAM	CG	SH	SV	IP	H	H/G	HR	BB	SO	RAT	ERA	ERA+	OAV	OOB	PR	/A	PF	CPI	FA	E	DP	FW	PW	BW	SBW	DIF
PHI	92	1	0	873	921	9.5	22	95	347	10.5	2.88	121	.254	.273	40	58	106	113	.865	584	40	-4.1	5.1	-.6		16.6
STL	93	9	1	879¹	729	7.5	7	150	325	9.0	2.23	156	.211	.244	104	122	106	97	.909	388	62	4.5	10.7	-3.7		4.5
CIN	96	8	0	866²	766	8.0	17	168	215	9.7	2.26	144	.222	.258	99	95	99	115	.905	383	57	4.7	8.4	1.1		-2.1
NY	97	6	0	874	749	7.7	12	123	480	9.0	2.90	114	.216	.243	38	39	101	78	.905	391	45	4.1	3.4	-3.3		1.7
LOU	96	7	0	873²	987	10.2	7	110	269	11.3	3.50	85	.267	.288	-19	-51	90	101	.886	478	67	.6	-4.5	3.4		4.0
COL	90	4	0	840¹	980	10.5	16	211	222	12.8	3.96	78	.273	.313	-62	-83	93	105	.874	535	69	-2.1	-7.3	1.8		-8.9
PIT	82	1	1	867²	1140	11.8	21	151	271	13.4	4.62	69	.298	.324	-127	-136	97	102	.884	504	55	-.6	-12.0	1.3		-6.8
BAL	86	1	0	844²	943	10.0	12	190	290	12.1	4.08	85	.265	.302	-73	-57	105	93	.855	624	44	-6.3	-5.0	-3.2		-5.6
TOT	732	37	2	6919¹		9.4				10.9	3.30		.252	.282					.885	3887	439					

Runs
Stovey-Phi 110
Reilly-Cin 103
Carpenter-Cin 99
Knight-Phi 98

Hits
Swartwood-Pit . . . 147
Reilly-Cin 136
Carpenter-Cin . . . 129
Stovey-Phi 127
Nelson-NY 127

Doubles
Stovey-Phi 31
Swartwood-Pit 24
Knight-Phi 23
Hayes-Pit 23

Triples
Smith-Col 17
Reilly-Cin 14
Kuehne-Col 14
Mansell-Pit 13
Mann-Col 13

Home Runs
Stovey-Phi 14
Jones-Cin 10
Reilly-Cin 9
Fulmer-Cin 5
Brown-Col 5

Total Bases
Stovey-Phi 212
Reilly-Cin 212
Swartwood-Pit . . . 196
Jones-Cin 184
W.Gleason-StL . . . 167

Runs Batted In

Runs Produced
Knight-Phi 97
Stovey-Phi 96
Carpenter-Cin 96
Reilly-Cin 94
Birchall-Phi 94

Bases On Balls
Stearns-Bal 34
Nelson-NY 31
Moynahan-Phi 30
J.Gleason-StL-Lou . . 29
Clinton-Bal 27

Batting Average
Swartwood-Pit 356
Browning-Lou 338
Clinton-Bal 313
Reilly-Cin 311
Moynahan-Phi 308

On Base Percentage
Swartwood-Pit 391
Browning-Lou 378
Clinton-Bal 357
Moynahan-Phi 356
Nelson-NY 353

Slugging Average
Stovey-Phi 504
Reilly-Cin 485
Swartwood-Pit 475
Jones-Cin 471
Browning-Lou 464

Production
Swartwood-Pit 866
Stovey-Phi 846
Browning-Lou 842
Reilly-Cin 810
Jones-Cin 799

Adjusted Production
Swartwood-Pit . . . 186
Browning-Lou . . . 184
Stovey-Phi 156
Reilly-Cin 148
Jones-Cin 145

Batter Runs
Swartwood-Pit . . . 35.0
Stovey-Phi 31.5
Browning-Lou . . . 27.4
Reilly-Cin 26.1
Jones-Cin 22.8

Adjusted Batter Runs
Swartwood-Pit . . . 38.0
Browning-Lou . . . 31.8
Stovey-Phi 25.8
Reilly-Cin 22.1
Jones-Cin 19.1

Clutch Hitting Index

Runs Created
Swartwood-Pit 79
Stovey-Phi 74
Reilly-Cin 71
Browning-Lou 64
Jones-Cin 62

Total Average
Swartwood-Pit 827
Stovey-Phi 810
Browning-Lou 797
Jones-Cin 739
Reilly-Cin 734

Stolen Bases

Stolen Base Average

Stolen Base Runs

Fielding Runs
Battin-Pit 29.0
Holbert-NY 26.9
Richmond-Col 25.5
Latham-StL 22.0
Gerhardt-Lou 20.4

Total Player Rating
Smith-Col 3.2
Swartwood-Pit 3.1
Richmond-Col 3.0
Gerhardt-Lou 2.4
Browning-Lou 2.1

Wins
White-Cin 43
Keefe-NY 41
Mullane-StL 35
Mathews-Phi 30
McGinnis-StL 28

Win Percentage
Mullane-StL 700
Mathews-Phi 698
Bradley-Phi 696
White-Cin 662
McGinnis-StL 636

Games
Keefe-NY 68
White-Cin 65
Mountain-Col 59
Mullane-StL 53
Hecker-Lou 51

Complete Games
Keefe-NY 68
White-Cin 64
Mountain-Col 57
Mullane-StL 49
Hecker-Lou 49

Shutouts
White-Cin 6
McGinnis-StL 6
Keefe-NY 5
Weaver-Lou 4
Mountain-Col 4

Saves
Mullane-StL 1
Barr-Pit 1

Innings Pitched
Keefe-NY 619.0
White-Cin 577.0
Mountain-Col . . . 503.0
Mullane-StL 460.2
Hecker-Lou 451.0

Fewest Hits/Game
Keefe-NY 7.07
Mullane-StL 7.27
White-Cin 7.38
McGinnis-StL 7.64
Deagle-Cin 8.27

Fewest BB/Game
Mathews-Phi 73
Weaver-Lou 82
Lynch-NY 88
Bradley-Phi 92
Driscoll-Pit 1.04

Strikeouts
Keefe-NY 361
Mathews-Phi 203
Mullane-StL 191
Mountain-Col . . . 159
Hecker-Lou 153

Strikeouts/Game
Keefe-NY 5.25
Mathews-Phi 4.80
Lynch-NY 4.20
Mullane-StL 3.73
Henderson-Bal . . . 3.64

Ratio
Keefe-NY 8.49
Mullane-StL 8.71
White-Cin 9.00
McGinnis-StL 9.27
Bradley-Phi 9.95

Earned Run Average
White-Cin 2.09
Mullane-StL 2.19
Deagle-Cin 2.31
McGinnis-StL 2.33
Keefe-NY 2.41

Adjusted ERA
Mullane-StL 159
White-Cin 156
McGinnis-StL 150
Mathews-Phi 142
Deagle-Cin 141

Opponents' Batting Avg.
Keefe-NY 202
Mullane-StL 207
White-Cin 209
McGinnis-StL 215
Deagle-Cin 229

Opponents' On Base Pct.
Keefe-NY 233
Mullane-StL 238
White-Cin 244
McGinnis-StL 249
Bradley-Phi 263

Starter Runs
White-Cin 77.4
Keefe-NY 60.8
Mullane-StL 56.8
McGinnis-StL 41.2
Mathews-Phi 35.6

Adjusted Starter Runs
White-Cin 75.1
Mullane-StL 66.6
Keefe-NY 62.4
McGinnis-StL 49.3
Mathews-Phi 43.7

Clutch Pitching Index
Mathews-Phi 127
Corey-Phi 124
McCormick-Cin . . . 123
Valentine-Col 122
Deagle-Cin 117

Relief Runs

Adjusted Relief Runs

Relief Ranking

Total Pitcher Index
White-Cin 6.9
Keefe-NY 6.7
Mullane-StL 6.7
McGinnis-StL 4.2
Mathews-Phi 3.3

Total Baseball Ranking
White-Cin 6.9
Keefe-NY 6.7
Mullane-StL 6.7
McGinnis-StL 4.2
Mathews-Phi 3.3

TEAM	G	W	L	PCT	GB	R	OR	AB	H	2B	3B	HR	BB	SO	AVG	OBP	SLG	PRO	PRO+	BR	/A	PF	CHI	RC	SB	CS	SBA	SBR
PRO	114	84	28	.750		665	388	4093	987	153	43	21	300	469	.241	.293	.315	.608	97	-17	-2	98	107	387				
BOS	116	73	38	.658	10.5	684	468	4189	1063	179	60	36	207	660	.254	.289	.351	.640	104	17	22	99	104	435				
BUF	114	64	47	.577	19.5	700	626	4197	1099	163	69	39	215	458	.262	.298	.361	.659	106	46	27	103	102	463				
NY	116	62	50	.554	22	693	623	4124	1053	149	67	23	249	492	.255	.298	.341	.639	101	20	4	102	105	429				
CHI	112	62	50	.554	22	834	647	4182	1176	162	50	142	264	469	.281	.324	.446	.770	132	201	145	109	98	619				
PHI	113	39	73	.348	45	549	824	3998	934	149	39	14	209	512	.234	.272	.301	.573	88	-71	-42	95	101	335				
CLE	113	35	77	.313	49	458	716	3934	934	147	49	16	170	576	.237	.269	.312	.581	83	-62	-82	103	85	338				
DET	114	28	84	.250	56	445	736	3966	824	114	47	31	207	699	.208	.247	.284	.531	74	-130	-93	94	93	285				
TOT	456					5028		32683	8070	1216	424	322	1821	4335	.247	.287	.340	.626										

TEAM	CG	SH	SV	IP	H	H/G	HR	BB	SO	RAT	ERA	ERA+	OAV	OOB	PR	/A	PF	CPI	FA	E	DP	FW	PW	BW	SBW	DIF
PRO	107	16	2	1036¹	825	7.2	26	172	639	8.7	1.61	176	.206	.239	157	140	95	104	.918	398	50	5.1	12.5	-.2		10.5
BOS	109	14	2	1037	932	8.1	30	135	742	9.3	2.47	116	.227	.251	58	46	97	85	.921	384	46	6.3	4.1	2.0		5.1
BUF	108	14	1	1001	1041	9.4	46	189	534	11.1	2.95	106	.253	.286	3	20	105	105	.905	462	71	1.7	1.8	2.4		2.6
NY	111	4	0	1014	1011	9.0	28	161	567	11.9	3.12	95	.245	.301	-15	-16	100	100	.896	514	69	-.6	-1.4	.4		7.7
CHI	106	9	0	997¹	1028	9.3	83	231	472	11.4	3.03	104	.252	.292	-6	12	106	114	.886	595	107	-5.9	1.1	13.0		-2.2
PHI	106	3	1	981	1090	10.0	38	254	411	12.3	3.93	76	.266	.309	-103	-103	100	92	.889	536	67	-2.5	-9.2	-3.8		-1.5
CLE	107	7	0	994²	1046	9.5	35	269	482	11.9	3.43	92	.255	.301	-49	-31	106	96	.897	512	75	-1.2	-2.8	-7.3		-9.7
DET	109	3	0	984²	1097	10.0	36	245	488	12.3	3.38	86	.266	.308	-44	-53	97	105	.887	549	60	-3.0	-4.7	-8.3		-12.0
TOT	863	70	6	8046		9.0				11.1	2.98		.247	.287					.900	3950	545					

Runs	Hits	Doubles	Triples	Home Runs	Total Bases
Kelly-Chi 120	Sutton-Bos 162	Hines-Pro 36	Ewing-NY 20	Williamson-Chi 27	Dalrymple-Chi 263
O'Rourke-Buf 119	O'Rourke-Buf 162	O'Rourke-Buf 33	Brouthers-Buf 15	Pfeffer-Chi 25	Anson-Chi 258
Hornung-Bos 119	Dalrymple-Chi 161	Anson-Chi 30	Rowe-Buf 14	Dalrymple-Chi 22	Pfeffer-Chi 240
Dalrymple-Chi 111	Kelly-Chi 160	Manning-Phi 29	Phillips-Cle 12	Anson-Chi 21	Kelly-Chi 237
Anson-Chi 108	Anson-Chi 159		McKinnon-NY 12	Brouthers-Buf 14	Williamson-Chi ... 231

Runs Batted In	Runs Produced	Bases On Balls	Batting Average	On Base Percentage	Slugging Average
Anson-Chi 102	Kelly-Chi 202	Gore-Chi 61	Kelly-Chi .... .354	Kelly-Chi .... .414	Brouthers-Buf .... .563
Pfeffer-Chi 101	Anson-Chi 189	Kelly-Chi 46	O'Rourke-Buf ..... .347	Gore-Chi .... .404	Williamson-Chi ... .554
Kelly-Chi 95	Pfeffer-Chi 181	Hines-Pro 44	Sutton-Bos ...... .346	O'Rourke-Buf ..... .392	Anson-Chi .... .543
Williamson-Chi 84	O'Rourke-Buf 177	Williamson-Chi 42	Anson-Chi .... .335	Sutton-Bos ...... .384	Kelly-Chi .... .524
Connor-NY 82	Connor-NY 176		Brouthers-Buf .... .327	Brouthers-Buf .... .378	Pfeffer-Chi .... .514

Production	Adjusted Production	Batter Runs	Adjusted Batter Runs	Clutch Hitting Index	Runs Created
Brouthers-Buf .... .941	Brouthers-Buf 186	Kelly-Chi 48.8	Kelly-Chi 42.6	Dorgan-NY 142	Kelly-Chi 100
Kelly-Chi .... .938	Kelly-Chi 178	Anson-Chi 44.6	Brouthers-Buf 39.4	Caskin-NY 140	Anson-Chi 99
Anson-Chi .... .916	Anson-Chi 170	Brouthers-Buf 41.2	Anson-Chi 38.3	McKinnon-NY 135	O'Rourke-Buf 90
Williamson-Chi .... .898	O'Rourke-Buf 168	O'Rourke-Buf 38.8	O'Rourke-Buf 36.7	Morrill-Bos 135	Dalrymple-Chi 88
O'Rourke-Buf .... .872	Sutton-Bos 164	Williamson-Chi ... 36.7	Sutton-Bos 33.9	Lillie-Buf 128	Brouthers-Buf 87

Total Average	Stolen Bases	Stolen Base Average	Stolen Base Runs	Fielding Runs	Total Player Rating
Kelly-Chi .... .969				Pfeffer-Chi 45.8	Pfeffer-Chi 6.3
Brouthers-Buf .... .959				Williamson-Chi 24.0	Williamson-Chi ... 4.5
Anson-Chi .... .908				Lillie-Buf 14.8	Kelly-Chi 3.5
Williamson-Chi .... .907				Mulvey-Phi 10.7	Glasscock-Cle 2.7
O'Rourke-Buf .... .849				Hanlon-Det 10.4	Brouthers-Buf 2.6

Wins	Win Percentage	Games	Complete Games	Shutouts	Saves
Radbourn-Pro 59	Radbourn-Pro ..... .831	Radbourn-Pro 75	Radbourn-Pro 73	Galvin-Buf 12	Morrill-Bos 2
Buffinton-Bos 48	Buffinton-Bos ..... .750	Galvin-Buf 72	Galvin-Buf 71	Radbourn-Pro 11	Sweeney-Pro 1
Galvin-Buf 46	Sweeney-Pro ..... .680	Buffinton-Bos 67	Buffinton-Bos 63	Buffinton-Bos 8	Radbourn-Pro 1
Welch-NY 39	Galvin-Buf .... .676	Welch-NY 65	Welch-NY 62	L.Corcoran-Chi ... 7	O'Rourke-Buf 1
L.Corcoran-Chi 35	Welch-NY .... .650	L.Corcoran-Chi 60	L.Corcoran-Chi ... 57	Whitney-Bos 6	Ferguson-Phi 1

Innings Pitched	Fewest Hits/Game	Fewest BB/Game	Strikeouts	Strikeouts/Game	Ratio
Radbourn-Pro ... 678.2	Sweeney-Pro 6.23	Whitney-Bos .... .72	Radbourn-Pro 441	Clarkson-Chi 7.78	Sweeney-Pro 7.41
Galvin-Buf 636.1	Radbourn-Pro 7.00	Galvin-Buf .... .89	Buffinton-Bos 417	Whitney-Bos 7.23	Whitney-Bos 8.01
Buffinton-Bos ... 587.0	Clarkson-Chi 7.17	Buffinton-Bos 1.17	Galvin-Buf 369	Getzien-Det 6.54	Radbourn-Pro 8.30
Welch-NY 557.1	Getzien-Det 7.21	Sweeney-Pro 1.18	Welch-NY 345	Buffinton-Bos 6.39	Getzien-Det 8.74
L.Corcoran-Chi .. 516.2	Whitney-Bos 7.29	Coleman-Phi 1.28	L.Corcoran-Chi ... 272	Sweeney-Pro 5.90	Galvin-Buf 8.90

Earned Run Average	Adjusted ERA	Opponents' Batting Avg.	Opponents' On Base Pct.	Starter Runs	Adjusted Starter Runs
Radbourn-Pro 1.38	Radbourn-Pro 205	Sweeney-Pro ..... .185	Sweeney-Pro ..... .212	Radbourn-Pro ... 120.5	Radbourn-Pro 109.3
Sweeney-Pro 1.55	Sweeney-Pro 183	Radbourn-Pro .... .203	Whitney-Bos ..... .225	Galvin-Buf 69.5	Galvin-Buf 80.5
Getzien-Det 1.95	Galvin-Buf 157	Clarkson-Chi ..... .207	Radbourn-Pro .... .232	Buffinton-Bos 54.2	Buffinton-Bos 47.8
Galvin-Buf 1.99	Getzien-Det 148	Getzien-Det ...... .207	Getzien-Det ...... .241	Sweeney-Pro 35.1	L.Corcoran-Chi ... 42.3
Whitney-Bos 2.09	Clarkson-Chi 147	Whitney-Bos ..... .209	Galvin-Buf .... .244	Whitney-Bos 33.2	Sweeney-Pro 31.5

Clutch Pitching Index	Relief Runs	Adjusted Relief Runs	Relief Ranking	Total Pitcher Index	Total Baseball Ranking
Meinke-Det 119				Radbourn-Pro 10.4	Radbourn-Pro 10.4
L.Corcoran-Chi ... 114				Galvin-Buf 7.0	Galvin-Buf 7.0
Weidman-Det 111				Buffinton-Bos 6.1	Pfeffer-Chi 6.2
Radbourn-Pro 111				L.Corcoran-Chi ... 4.9	Buffinton-Bos 6.1
Serad-Buf 108				Whitney-Bos 4.5	L.Corcoran-Chi ... 4.9

TEAM	G	W	L	PCT	GB	R	OR	AB	H	2B	3B	HR	BB	SO	AVG	OBP	SLG	PRO	PRO+	BR	/A	PF	CHI	RC	SB	CS	SBA	SBR
NY	112	75	32	.701		734	423	4012	1052	155	64	22	203	315	.262	.304	.349	.653	122	82	98	97	107	436				
COL	110	69	39	.639	6.5	585	459	3759	901	107	96	40	196	404	.240	.288	.351	.639	123	59	104	92	93	390				
LOU	110	68	40	.630	7.5	573	425	3957	1004	152	69	17	146	408	.254	.286	.340	.626	115	41	69	95	91	395				
STL	110	67	40	.626	8	658	539	3952	986	151	60	11	174	339	.249	.288	.326	.614	102	28	5	104	107	381				
CIN	112	68	41	.624	8	754	512	4090	1037	109	96	36	154	404	.254	.289	.354	.643	109	65	35	104	102	429				
BAL	108	63	43	.594	11.5	636	515	3845	896	133	84	32	211	545	.233	.284	.336	.620	103	38	15	104	102	377				
PHI	108	61	46	.570	14	700	546	3959	1057	167	100	26	153	425	.267	.301	.379	.680	119	112	72	107	100	463				
TOL	110	46	58	.442	27.5	463	571	3712	859	153	48	8	157	541	.231	.268	.305	.573	89	-26	-45	104	88	310				
BRO	109	40	64	.385	33.5	476	644	3763	845	112	47	16	179	417	.225	.263	.292	.555	86	-48	-51	101	93	296				
RIC	46	12	30	.286	30.5	194	294	1469	325	40	33	7	53	284	.221	.260	.308	.568	92	-13	-10	99	94	120				
PIT	110	30	78	.278	45.5	406	725	3689	777	105	50	2	143	411	.211	.248	.268	.516	72	-96	-104	102	90	251				
IND	110	29	78	.271	46	462	755	3813	890	129	62	20	125	560	.233	.262	.315	.577	96	-25	-5	97	86	323				
WAS	63	12	51	.190	41	248	481	2166	434	61	24	6	102	377	.200	.242	.259	.501	78	-67	-29	88	97	139				
TOT	659					6889		46186	11063	1574	833	243	1996	5430	.240	.271	.325	.597										

TEAM	CG	SH	SV	IP	H	H/G	HR	BB	SO	RAT	ERA	ERA+	OAV	OOB	PR	/A	PF	CPI	FA	E	DP	FW	PW	BW	SBW	DIF
NY	111	9	0	984²	800	7.3	15	119	611	8.4	2.46	126	.210	.234	85	70	96	89	.907	441	42	2.3	6.4	9.0		3.8
COL	102	8	1	962¹	815	7.6	22	172	526	9.2	2.68	113	.217	.251	59	35	93	96	.908	433	74	2.3	3.2	9.5		.0
LOU	101	6	0	989²	836	7.6	9	97	470	8.5	2.17	141	.216	.236	117	98	95	103	.912	426	84	2.6	9.0	6.3		-3.9
STL	99	8	0	987	881	8.0	16	172	477	9.6	2.67	122	.226	.259	62	64	101	103	.900	490	65	-.2	5.8	.5		7.4
CIN	111	11	0	983²	956	8.7	27	181	308	10.4	3.33	100	.241	.275	-9	0	103	98	.909	430	82	2.8	.0	3.2		7.5
BAL	105	8	1	955²	869	8.2	16	219	635	10.2	2.71	128	.229	.271	56	79	107	110	.899	461	61	.7	7.2	1.4		.7
PHI	105	5	0	948²	920	8.7	16	127	530	9.9	3.42	99	.241	.265	-18	-2	105	89	.901	457	63	.9	-.2	6.6		.2
TOL	103	9	1	946	885	8.4	12	169	501	10.0	3.06	111	.235	.267	18	35	105	96	.900	469	67	.7	3.2	-4.1		-5.8
BRO	105	6	0	948²	996	9.4	20	163	378	11.0	3.79	87	.256	.286	-58	-51	102	94	.889	520	68	-1.6	-4.7	-4.7		-1.0
RIC	45	1	0	370¹	402	9.8	14	52	167	11.0	4.52	73	.262	.286	-52	-49	102	84	.874	239	27	-1.5	-4.5	-.9		-2.1
PIT	108	4	0	943¹	1059	10.1	25	216	338	12.2	4.35	77	.269	.307	-116	-103	104	95	.889	523	71	-1.6	-9.4	-9.5		-3.5
IND	107	2	0	937²	1001	9.6	30	199	479	11.5	4.20	78	.259	.295	-100	-99	101	92	.889	515	45	-1.2	-9.0	-.5		-13.8
WAS	62	3	0	543²	643	10.6	21	110	235	12.5	4.01	76	.279	.312	-46	-59	93	111	.858	400	40	-5.3	-5.4	-2.6		-6.2
TOT	1264	80	3	11501¹		8.7				10.2	3.24		.240	.271					.897	5804	789					

Runs		Hits		Doubles		Triples		Home Runs		Total Bases	
Stovey-Phi	124	Orr-NY	162	Barkley-Tol	39	Stovey-Phi	23	Reilly-Cin	11	Reilly-Cin	247
Jones-Cin	117	Reilly-Cin	152	Browning-Lou	33	Reilly-Cin	19	Stovey-Phi	10	Orr-NY	247
Latham-StL	115	Esterbrook-NY	150	Orr-NY	32	Mann-Col	18	Orr-NY	9	Stovey-Phi	244
Reilly-Cin	114	Browning-Lou	150	Esterbrook-NY	29	Peltz-Ind	17	Mann-Col	7	Jones-Cin	222
Nelson-NY	114	Jones-Cin	148	Lewis-StL	25	Jones-Cin	17	Jones-Cin	7	Browning-Lou	211

Runs Batted In		Runs Produced		Bases On Balls		Batting Average		On Base Percentage		Slugging Average	
		Stovey-Phi	114	Nelson-NY	74	Orr-NY	.354	Jones-Cin	.376	Reilly-Cin	.551
		Latham-StL	114	Geer-Bro	38	Reilly-Cin	.339	Nelson-NY	.375	Stovey-Phi	.545
		Nelson-NY	113	Jones-Cin	37	Browning-Lou	.336	Stovey-Phi	.368	Orr-NY	.539
		Jones-Cin	110	Macullar-Bal	36	Stovey-Phi	.326	Fennelly-Was-Cin	.367	Fennelly-Was-Cin	.480
		Esterbrook-NY	109	Richmond-Col	35	Lewis-StL	.323	Reilly-Cin	.366	Browning-Lou	.472

Production		Adjusted Production		Batter Runs		Adjusted Batter Runs		Clutch Hitting Index		Runs Created	
Reilly-Cin	.918	Orr-NY	199	Stovey-Phi	46.2	Orr-NY	45.3			Reilly-Cin	93
Stovey-Phi	.913	Fennelly-Was-Cin	190	Reilly-Cin	45.9	Reilly-Cin	42.7			Stovey-Phi	92
Orr-NY	.901	Reilly-Cin	190	Orr-NY	43.4	Stovey-Phi	41.6			Orr-NY	92
Fennelly-Was-Cin	.847	Stovey-Phi	185	Jones-Cin	40.4	Jones-Cin	36.9			Jones-Cin	85
Jones-Cin	.846	Browning-Lou	180	Browning-Lou	32.9	Browning-Lou	36.1			Browning-Lou	77

Total Average		Stolen Bases		Stolen Base Average		Stolen Base Runs		Fielding Runs		Total Player Rating	
Stovey-Phi	.907							Latham-StL	40.1	Barkley-Tol	4.6
Reilly-Cin	.899							Smith-Col	29.1	Latham-StL	4.5
Orr-NY	.855							Gerhardt-Lou	27.3	Smith-Col	4.0
Jones-Cin	.830							Barkley-Tol	25.0	Fennelly-Was-Cin	3.7
Fennelly-Was-Cin	.824							Nicol-StL	23.4	Esterbrook-NY	3.5

Wins		Win Percentage		Games		Complete Games		Shutouts		Saves	
Hecker-Lou	52	Morris-Col	.723	Hecker-Lou	75	Hecker-Lou	72	White-Cin	7	O'Day-Tol	1
Lynch-NY	37	Hecker-Lou	.722	Mullane-Tol	67	Mullane-Tol	64	Mullane-Tol	7	Mountain-Col	1
Keefe-NY	37	Foutz-StL	.714	McKeon-Ind	61	McKeon-Ind	59	Hecker-Lou	6	T.Burns-Bal	1
Mullane-Tol	36	Lynch-NY	.712	Keefe-NY	58	Keefe-NY	57				
		Keefe-NY	.685	Terry-Bro	56	Terry-Bro	54				

Innings Pitched		Fewest Hits/Game		Fewest BB/Game		Strikeouts		Strikeouts/Game		Ratio	
Hecker-Lou	670.2	Morris-Col	7.02	Driscoll-Lou	.62	Hecker-Lou	385	Henderson-Bal	7.09	Hecker-Lou	7.81
Mullane-Tol	567.0	Hecker-Lou	7.06	Hecker-Lou	.75	Henderson-Bal	346	Davis-StL	6.49	Morris-Col	8.09
McKeon-Ind	512.0	Keefe-NY	7.10	Lynch-NY	.78	Mullane-Tol	325	Morris-Col	6.33	Lynch-NY	8.35
Keefe-NY	491.2	Mountain-Col	7.21	E.Dugan-Ric	.81	Keefe-NY	323	Mathews-Phi	5.98	Keefe-NY	8.48
Lynch-NY	487.0	Foutz-StL	7.27	McGinnis-StL	.89	McKeon-Ind	308	Keefe-NY	5.91	Foutz-StL	8.84

Earned Run Average		Adjusted ERA		Opponents' Batting Avg.		Opponents' On Base Pct.		Starter Runs		Adjusted Starter Runs	
Hecker-Lou	1.80	Hecker-Lou	171	Morris-Col	.203	Hecker-Lou	.221	Hecker-Lou	107.6	Hecker-Lou	94.6
Foutz-StL	2.18	Foutz-StL	150	Hecker-Lou	.204	Morris-Col	.227	Keefe-NY	52.2	Mullane-Tol	55.7
Morris-Col	2.18	Morris-Col	139	Keefe-NY	.205	Lynch-NY	.233	Morris-Col	50.8	Keefe-NY	44.7
Keefe-NY	2.29	Keefe-NY	136	Mountain-Col	.208	Keefe-NY	.236	Mullane-Tol	45.3	Henderson-Bal	40.9
Mountain-Col	2.45	Mullane-Tol	135	Foutz-StL	.209	Foutz-StL	.243	Lynch-NY	32.5	Morris-Col	40.3

Clutch Pitching Index		Relief Runs		Adjusted Relief Runs		Relief Ranking		Total Pitcher Index		Total Baseball Ranking	
O'Neill-StL	122							Hecker-Lou	12.5	Hecker-Lou	12.5
Hamill-Was	115							Mullane-Tol	8.9	Mullane-Tol	8.9
Foutz-StL	112							Keefe-NY	5.3	Keefe-NY	5.3
Henderson-Bal	111							Henderson-Bal	4.4	Barkley-Tol	4.6
White-Cin	110							Morris-Col	3.9	Latham-StL	4.5

TEAM	G	W	L	PCT	GB	R	OR	AB	H	2B	3B	HR	BB	SO	AVG	OBP	SLG	PRO	PRO+	BR	/A	PF	CHI	RC	SB	CS	SBA	SBR
STL	114	94	19	.832		887	429	4285	1251	259	41	32	181	542	.292	.321	.394	.715	138	182	158	104	103	555				
MIL	12	8	4	.667	35.5	53	34	395	88	25	0	0	20	70	.223	.260	.286	.546	158	-4	25	54	89	30				
CIN	105	69	36	.657	21	703	466	3786	1027	118	63	26	147	482	.271	.298	.356	.654	113	85	37	108	102	413				
BAL	106	58	47	.552	32	662	627	3883	952	150	26	17	144	652	.245	.272	.310	.582	88	-6	-70	110	109	336				
BOS	111	58	51	.532	34	636	558	3940	928	168	32	19	128	787	.236	.260	.309	.569	94	-27	-17	98	107	324				
CP	93	41	50	.451	42	438	482	3212	742	127	26	10	119	505	.231	.258	.296	.554	88	-35	-31	99	92	252				
WAS	114	47	65	.420	46.5	572	679	3926	931	120	26	4	118	558	.237	.259	.284	.543	87	-58	-37	97	102	296				
PHI	67	21	46	.313	50	414	545	2518	618	108	35	7	103	405	.245	.275	.324	.599	112	10	39	93	101	230				
STP	9	2	6	.250	39.5	24	57	272	49	13	1	0	7	47	.180	.201	.235	.436	88	-13	6	54	81	13				
ALT	25	6	19	.240	44	90	216	899	223	30	6	2	22	130	.248	.266	.301	.567	91	-6	-7	101	67	74				
KC	82	16	63	.203	61	311	618	2802	557	104	15	6	123	529	.199	.232	.253	.485	74	-94	-35	87	88	169				
WIL	18	2	16	.111	44.5	35	114	521	91	8	8	2	22	123	.175	.208	.232	.440	48	-25	-27	103	60	26				
TOT	428					4825		30439	7457	1230	279	125	1134	4830	.245	.272	.316	.588										

TEAM	CG	SH	SV	IP	H	H/G	HR	BB	SO	RAT	ERA	ERA+	OAV	OOB	PR	/A	PF	CPI	FA	E	DP	FW	PW	BW	SBW	DIF
STL	104	8	6	993	838	7.6	9	110	550	8.6	1.96	151	.213	.235	116	109	98	104	.888	554	79	3.8	9.5	13.8		10.3
MIL	12	3	0	104	49	4.2	1	13	139	5.4	2.25	73	.131	.160	8	-7	54	11	.892	53	4	.6	-.6	2.2		-.2
CIN	95	11	1	914[1]	831	8.2	17	90	503	9.1	2.38	133	.226	.244	64	78	105	100	.882	532	45	2.6	6.8	3.2		3.9
BAL	92	4	0	946[2]	1002	9.5	24	177	628	11.2	3.20	103	.254	.286	-20	10	110	107	.872	616	53	-.8	.9	-6.1		11.6
BOS	100	5	1	953[1]	885	8.4	17	110	753	9.4	2.70	109	.230	.252	33	24	98	94	.868	633	39	-.3	2.1	-1.5		3.2
CP	86	6	0	803[2]	743	8.3	12	137	679	9.9	2.18	138	.229	.260	73	73	100	121	.882	459	38	2.8	6.4	-2.7		-11.0
WAS	94	4	0	953[2]	992	9.4	16	168	684	10.9	4.63	86	.251	.281	-44	-50	98	94	.869	625	55	.7	-4.4	-3.2		-2.1
PHI	64	1	0	593[1]	726	11.0	7	105	310	12.6	4.63	62	.282	.310	-106	-116	95	89	.841	501	36	-5.3	-10.2	3.4		-.5
STP	7	1	0	71	72	9.1	1	27	44	12.5	3.17	52	.247	.311	-1	-12	54	116	.872	47	6	.2	-1.1	.5		-1.6
ALT	20	0	0	219[2]	292	12.0	3	52	93	14.1	4.67	70	.299	.335	-40	-34	109	103	.862	156	4	-.6	-3.0	-.6		-2.3
KC	70	0	0	702[2]	862	11.0	14	127	334	12.7	4.07	68	.283	.311	-82	-102	92	103	.861	520	51	-2.5	-8.9	-3.1		-9.0
WIL	15	0	0	142	165	10.5	4	18	113	11.6	3.04	108	.273	.294	0	3	109	125	.860	104	10	-.1	.3	-2.4		-4.8
TOT	759	43	8	7397[1]		9.1				10.5	3.01		.245	.272					.872	4800	420					

Runs
Dunlap-StL....... 160
Shaffer-StL 130
Seery-Bal-KC 115
Robinson-Bal..... 101
Rowe-StL 95

Hits
Dunlap-StL....... 185
Shaffer-StL....... 168
Moore-Was 155
Seery-Bal-KC 146
Rowe-StL 142

Doubles
Shaffer-StL 40
Dunlap-StL 39
Rowe-StL.......... 32
O'Brien-Bos 31
Gleason-StL....... 30

Triples
Burns-Cin......... 12
Rowe-StL 11
Shaffer-StL 10

Home Runs
Dunlap-StL........ 13
Crane-Bos 12
Levis-Bal-Was 6

Total Bases
Dunlap-StL........ 279
Shaffer-StL........ 234
Rowe-StL......... 208
Crane-Bos 193
Seery-Bal-KC 192

Runs Batted In

Runs Produced
Dunlap-StL....... 147
Shaffer-StL....... 128
Seery-Bal-KC ... 113
Robinson-Bal...... 99
Rowe-StL 91

Bases On Balls
Robinson-Bal...... 37
Shaffer-StL 30
Dunlap-StL........ 29
Harbidge-Cin 25
Gleason-StL....... 23

Batting Average
Dunlap-StL........412
Hoover-Phi.......364
Shaffer-StL.......360
Moore-Was 336
Gleason-StL......324

On Base Percentage
Dunlap-StL........448
Shaffer-StL.......398
Hoover-Phi.......390
Moore-Was 363
Gleason-StL......361

Slugging Average
Dunlap-StL........621
Shaffer-StL.......501
Hoover-Phi.......495
Burns-Cin........457
Crane-Bos 451

Production
Dunlap-StL...... 1.069
Shaffer-StL 899
Hoover-Phi.......885
Gleason-StL......802
Moore-Was 777

Adjusted Production
Dunlap-StL....... 249
Hoover-Phi....... 213
Shaffer-StL 195
Moore-Was 168
Gleason-StL...... 164

Batter Runs
Dunlap-StL....... 72.5
Shaffer-StL 49.1
Moore-Was 28.9
Gleason-StL...... 28.3
Hoover-Phi....... 27.0

Adjusted Batter Runs
Dunlap-StL....... 69.9
Shaffer-StL 46.5
Moore-Was 31.3
Hoover-Phi....... 30.3
Gleason-StL...... 26.1

Clutch Hitting Index

Runs Created
Dunlap-StL....... 128
Shaffer-StL 96
Moore-Was 71
Seery-Bal-KC 67
Rowe-StL......... 65

Total Average
Dunlap-StL...... 1.167
Shaffer-StL 883
Hoover-Phi.......846
Gleason-StL......738
Moore-Was 686

Stolen Bases

Stolen Base Average

Stolen Base Runs

Fielding Runs
Dunlap-StL....... 30.5
Fusselback-Bal ... 15.9
Robinson-Bal.... 15.4
Krieg-CP 15.3
Wise-Was 12.2

Total Player Rating
Dunlap-StL........ 8.1
Shaffer-StL 3.6
Hoover-Phi....... 2.5
Robinson-Bal.... 2.2
Glasscock-Cin 2.0

Wins
W.Sweeney-Bal 40
Daily-CP-Was 28
Taylor-StL........ 25
Bradley-Cin 25
Sweeney-StL 24

Win Percentage
McCormick-Cin ...875
Taylor-StL.........862
Boyle-StL.........833
Sweeney-StL 774
W.Sweeney-Bal ...656

Games
W.Sweeney-Bal 62
Daily-CP-Was 58
Wise-Was 50
Bakely-Phi-Wil-KC . 46
Bradley-Cin 41

Complete Games
W.Sweeney-Bal 58
Daily-CP-Was 56
Bakely-Phi-Wil-KC . 43
Bradley-Cin 36
Shaw-Bos 35

Shutouts
McCormick-Cin 7
Daily-CP-Was 5
Shaw-Bos 5
W.Sweeney-Bal 4

Saves
Taylor-StL.......... 4
Sylvester-Cin 1
Dunlap-StL......... 1
Brown-Bos 1
Boyle-StL.......... 1

Innings Pitched
W.Sweeney-Bal .. 538.0
Daily-CP-Was ... 500.2
Bakely-Phi-Wil-KC 394.2
Wise-Was 364.1
Bradley-Cin 342.0

Fewest Hits/Game
McCormick-Cin ... 6.47
Shaw-Bos 6.47
Sweeney-StL 6.87
Boyle-StL 7.08
Werden-StL 7.20

Fewest BB/Game
Sweeney-StL 43
McCormick-Cin ...60
Boyle-StL 60
Bradley-Cin 61
Murphy-Wil-Alt 62

Strikeouts
Daily-CP-Was 483
W.Sweeney-Bal .. 374
Shaw-Bos 309
Wise-Was 268
Burke-Bos 255

Strikeouts/Game
Shaw-Bos 8.81
Daily-CP-Was ... 8.68
Gagus-Was 7.92
Robinson-Bal..... 7.32
Burke-Bos 7.13

Ratio
McCormick-Cin ...7.07
Sweeney-StL 7.31
Shaw-Bos 7.53
Boyle-StL 7.68
Werden-StL 8.60

Earned Run Average
McCormick-Cin ... 1.54
Taylor-StL........ 1.68
Boyle-StL......... 1.74
Shaw-Bos 1.77
Sweeney-StL 1.83

Adjusted ERA
McCormick-Cin ... 205
Taylor-StL........ 176
Boyle-StL......... 170
Shaw-Bos 166
Sweeney-StL 162

Opponents' Batting Avg.
McCormick-Cin 188
Shaw-Bos 188
Sweeney-StL 197
Boyle-StL.........202
Werden-StL 205

Opponents' On Base Pct.
McCormick-Cin 202
Sweeney-StL 207
Shaw-Bos 212
Boyle-StL.........215
Werden-StL 235

Starter Runs
Shaw-Bos 43.7
Taylor-StL........ 39.0
Sweeney-StL 35.7
McCormick-Cin ... 34.3
Daily-CP-Was ... 32.6

Adjusted Starter Runs
W.Sweeney-Bal ... 42.7
Shaw-Bos 41.0
McCormick-Cin ... 37.7
Taylor-StL........ 37.4
Sweeney-StL 34.0

Clutch Pitching Index
Hodnett-StL 139
Robinson-Bal..... 131
Taylor-StL........ 127
W.Sweeney-Bal ... 109
Murphy-Wil-Alt ... 109

Relief Runs

Adjusted Relief Runs

Relief Ranking

Total Pitcher Index
Taylor-StL......... 5.7
Sweeney-StL 5.0
Burns-Cin......... 4.8
W.Sweeney-Bal ... 3.8
Shaw-Bos 3.7

Total Baseball Ranking
Dunlap-StL........ 8.1
Taylor-StL........ 5.7
Sweeney-StL 5.0
Burns-Cin......... 4.8
W.Sweeney-Bal ... 3.8

1885 National League

TEAM	G	W	L	PCT	GB	R	OR	AB	H	2B	3B	HR	BB	SO	AVG	OBP	SLG	PRO	PRO+	BR	/A	PF	CHI	RC	SB	CS	SBA	SBR
CHI	113	87	25	.777		834	470	4093	1079	184	75	54	340	429	.264	.320	.385	.705	114	143	54	115	113	517				
NY	112	85	27	.759	2	691	370	4029	1085	150	82	16	221	312	.269	.307	.359	.666	121	82	89	99	106	456				
PHI	111	56	54	.509	30	513	511	3893	891	156	35	20	220	401	.229	.270	.302	.572	90	-44	-33	98	101	326				
PRO	110	53	57	.482	33	442	531	3727	820	114	30	6	265	430	.220	.272	.272	.544	82	-73	-53	96	96	282				
BOS	113	46	66	.411	41	528	589	3950	915	144	53	22	190	522	.232	.267	.312	.579	94	-40	-18	96	103	337				
DET	108	41	67	.380	44	514	442	3773	917	149	66	25	216	451	.243	.284	.337	.621	104	17	15	100	93	371				
BUF	112	38	74	.339	49	495	761	3900	980	149	50	23	179	380	.251	.284	.333	.617	100	11	-4	103	89	378				
STL	111	36	72	.333	49	390	593	3758	829	121	21	8	214	412	.221	.263	.270	.533	81	-91	-57	94	89	273				
TOT	445					4407		31123	7516	1167	412	174	1845	3337	.241	.284	.322	.606										

TEAM	CG	SH	SV	IP	H	H/G	HR	BB	SO	RAT	ERA	ERA+	OAV	OOB	PR	/A	PF	CPI	FA	E	DP	FW	PW	BW	SBW	DIF
CHI	108	14	4	1015^2	868	7.7	37	202	458	9.5	2.23	136	.220	.258	65	90	108	102	.904	496	80	-2.4	8.5	5.1		19.9
NY	109	16	1	992	755	6.8	11	266	519	9.3	1.72	155	.200	.253	120	103	95	105	.929	331	85	6.0	9.7	8.4		4.9
PHI	108	10	0	976	860	7.9	18	218	378	9.9	2.39	117	.225	.267	46	43	99	98	.906	447	66	-.3	4.0	-3.1		.3
PRO	108	8	0	960^2	912	8.5	18	235	371	10.7	2.71	98	.238	.282	11	-4	95	101	.903	459	70	-1.1	-.4	-5.0		4.5
BOS	111	10	0	981	1045	9.6	26	188	480	11.3	3.03	88	.260	.293	-22	-37	95	107	.901	478	79	-1.5	-3.5	-1.7		-3.4
DET	105	6	1	954^1	966	9.1	18	224	475	11.2	2.88	99	.250	.291	-6	-4	101	105	.901	463	61	-1.7	-.4	1.4		-12.3
BUF	107	4	1	956	1175	11.1	31	234	320	13.3	4.29	69	.288	.327	-156	-141	105	99	.901	464	65	-.9	-13.3	-.4		-3.4
STL	107	4	0	965^1	935	8.7	15	278	337	11.3	3.37	82	.242	.293	-58	-66	97	87	.916	398	67	2.3	-6.2	-5.4		-8.7
TOT	863	72	7	7801		8.7				10.8	2.82		.241	.284					.908	3536	573					

Runs
Kelly-Chi 124
O'Rourke-NY 119
Gore-Chi 115
Dalrymple-Chi 109
Connor-NY 102

Hits
Connor-NY 169
Brouthers-Buf 146
Anson-Chi 144
Sutton-Bos 143
O'Rourke-NY 143

Doubles
Anson-Chi 35
Brouthers-Buf 32
Rowe-Buf 28
Dalrymple-Chi 27
Mulvey-Phi 25

Triples
O'Rourke-NY 16
Connor-NY 15
Gore-Chi 13
Bennett-Det 13

Home Runs
Dalrymple-Chi 11
Kelly-Chi 9

Total Bases
Connor-NY 225
Brouthers-Buf 221
Dalrymple-Chi 219
Anson-Chi 214
O'Rourke-NY 211

Runs Batted In
Anson-Chi 108
Kelly-Chi 75
Pfeffer-Chi 73
Burns-Chi 71

Runs Produced
Anson-Chi 201
Kelly-Chi 190
Gore-Chi 167
Connor-NY 166
Dalrymple-Chi 159

Bases On Balls
Williamson-Chi . . . 75
Gore-Chi 68
Morrill-Bos 64
Connor-NY 51

Batting Average
Connor-NY 371
Brouthers-Buf 359
Dorgan-NY 326
Richardson-Buf 319
Gore-Chi 313

On Base Percentage
Connor-NY 435
Brouthers-Buf 408
Gore-Chi 405
Hanlon-Det 372
Anson-Chi 357

Slugging Average
Brouthers-Buf 543
Connor-NY 495
Ewing-NY 471
Anson-Chi 461
Richardson-Buf 458

Production
Brouthers-Buf 951
Connor-NY 929
Gore-Chi 858
Anson-Chi 819
Bennett-Det 812

Adjusted Production
Connor-NY 203
Brouthers-Buf 200
Bennett-Det 161
Ewing-NY 159
O'Rourke-NY 158

Batter Runs
Connor-NY 51.7
Brouthers-Buf 46.8
Gore-Chi 40.6
Anson-Chi 31.7
O'Rourke-NY 29.5

Adjusted Batter Runs
Connor-NY 52.6
Brouthers-Buf 45.1
O'Rourke-NY 30.5
Gore-Chi 30.5
Richardson-Buf . . . 24.9

Clutch Hitting Index
Williamson-Chi . . . 170
Anson-Chi 169
Pfeffer-Chi 159
Gerhardt-NY 150
White-Buf 140

Runs Created
Connor-NY 100
Brouthers-Buf 92
Gore-Chi 83
Anson-Chi 78
O'Rourke-NY 77

Total Average
Brouthers-Buf 977
Connor-NY 965
Gore-Chi 884
Bennett-Det 808
Anson-Chi 775

Stolen Bases

Stolen Base Average

Stolen Base Runs

Fielding Runs
Dunlap-StL 25.2
Pfeffer-Chi 24.5
Fogarty-Phi 22.0
Glasscock-StL 18.9
Wise-Bos 13.5

Total Player Rating
Dunlap-StL 4.5
Richardson-Buf 3.8
Wise-Bos 3.5
Connor-NY 3.4
Glasscock-StL 3.4

Wins
Clarkson-Chi 53
Welch-NY 44
Keefe-NY 32
Radbourn-Pro 28

Win Percentage
Welch-NY 800
Clarkson-Chi 768
McCormick-Pro-Chi . . .750
Keefe-NY 711
Radbourn-Pro 571

Games
Clarkson-Chi 70
Welch-NY 56
Whitney-Bos 51
Buffinton-Bos 51
Daily-Phi 50

Complete Games
Clarkson-Chi 68
Welch-NY 55
Whitney-Bos 50

Shutouts
Clarkson-Chi 10
Welch-NY 7
Keefe-NY 7
Shaw-Pro 6
Buffinton-Bos 6

Saves
Williamson-Chi 2
Pfeffer-Chi 2
Welch-NY 1
Galvin-Buf 1
Baldwin-Det 1

Innings Pitched
Clarkson-Chi . . . 623.0
Welch-NY 492.0
Radbourn-Pro . . . 445.2
Whitney-Bos 441.1
Daily-Phi 440.0

Fewest Hits/Game
Keefe-NY 6.72
Welch-NY 6.80
Baldwin-Det 6.88
Clarkson-Chi 7.18
Daily-Phi 7.57

Fewest BB/Game
Whitney-Bos 75
Galvin-Buf 1.17
Clarkson-Chi 1.40
Baldwin-Det 1.41
C.Sweeney-StL . . 1.64

Strikeouts
Clarkson-Chi 308
Welch-NY 258
Buffinton-Bos 242
Keefe-NY 230
Whitney-Bos 200

Strikeouts/Game
Baldwin-Det 6.78
Keefe-NY 5.20
Buffinton-Bos 5.01
Welch-NY 4.72
Clarkson-Chi 4.45

Ratio
Baldwin-Det 8.28
Clarkson-Chi 8.58
Keefe-NY 9.05
Welch-NY 9.20
Daily-Phi 9.41

Earned Run Average
Keefe-NY 1.58
Welch-NY 1.66
Clarkson-Chi 1.85
Baldwin-Det 1.86
Radbourn-Pro 2.20

Adjusted ERA
Keefe-NY 168
Clarkson-Chi 164
Welch-NY 160
Baldwin-Det 153
Daily-Phi 126

Opponents' Batting Avg.
Keefe-NY 198
Welch-NY 200
Baldwin-Det 202
Clarkson-Chi 209
Daily-Phi 217

Opponents' On Base Pct.
Baldwin-Det 233
Clarkson-Chi 240
Keefe-NY 249
Welch-NY 253
Daily-Phi 257

Starter Runs
Clarkson-Chi 67.0
Welch-NY 63.0
Keefe-NY 54.6
Radbourn-Pro 30.5
Daily-Phi 29.7

Adjusted Starter Runs
Clarkson-Chi 82.0
Welch-NY 54.7
Keefe-NY 47.9
Daily-Phi 28.2
Ferguson-Phi 25.4

Clutch Pitching Index
Getzien-Det 118
Radbourn-Pro 114
Whitney-Bos 112
Keefe-NY 110
Serad-Buf 108

Relief Runs

Adjusted Relief Runs

Relief Ranking

Total Pitcher Index
Clarkson-Chi 9.5
Welch-NY 4.9
Ferguson-Phi 4.6
Keefe-NY 4.6
Radbourn-Pro 3.8

Total Baseball Ranking
Clarkson-Chi 9.5
Welch-NY 4.9
Ferguson-Phi 4.6
Keefe-NY 4.6
Dunlap-StL 4.5

TEAM	G	W	L	PCT	GB	R	OR	AB	H	2B	3B	HR	BB	SO	AVG	OBP	SLG	PRO	PRO+	BR	/A	PF	CHI	RC	SB	CS	SBA	SBR
STL	112	79	33	.705		677	461	3972	979	132	57	17	234	282	.246	.297	.321	.618	97	14	-16	105	107	388				
CIN	112	63	49	.563	16	642	575	4050	1046	108	77	26	153	420	.258	.294	.342	.636	105	31	19	102	99	417				
PIT	111	56	55	.505	22.5	547	539	3975	955	123	79	5	189	537	.240	.282	.315	.597	96	-18	-9	99	92	362				
PHI	113	55	57	.491	24	564	691	4142	1099	169	76	30	223	410	.265	.310	.365	.675	113	90	51	106	105	480				
LOU	112	53	59	.473	26	564	598	3969	986	126	83	19	152	448	.248	.281	.336	.617	101	2	3	100	93	384				
BRO	112	53	59	.473	26	624	650	3943	966	121	65	14	238	324	.245	.295	.319	.614	100	9	5	101	100	381				
NY	108	44	64	.407	33	526	688	3731	921	123	57	21	217	428	.247	.295	.327	.622	111	16	61	92	88	369				
BAL	110	41	68	.376	36.5	541	683	3820	837	124	59	17	279	529	.219	.280	.296	.576	90	-39	-29	99	96	324				
TOT	445					4885		31602	7789	1026	553	149	1685	3378	.246	.285	.328	.613										

TEAM	CG	SH	SV	IP	H	H/G	HR	BB	SO	RAT	ERA	ERA+	OAV	OOB	PR	/A	PF	CPI	FA	E	DP	FW	PW	BW	SBW	DIF
STL	111	11	0	1002	879	7.9	12	168	378	9.4	2.44	134	.226	.258	89	92	101	99	.920	381	64	3.0	8.3	-1.4		13.2
CIN	102	7	1	999[1]	998	9.0	24	250	330	11.2	3.26	100	.249	.293	-1	0	100	103	.911	423	86	.8	.0	1.7		4.5
PIT	104	8	0	1011	918	8.2	14	201	454	10.0	2.92	110	.232	.269	36	32	99	92	.912	422	77	.6	2.9	-.8		-2.2
PHI	105	5	0	1003[1]	1038	9.3	11	212	506	11.2	3.23	106	.256	.293	1	22	106	103	.901	483	79	-2.2	2.0	4.6		-5.4
LOU	109	3	1	1002	927	8.3	13	217	462	10.3	2.68	120	.235	.275	63	60	99	105	.905	460	75	-1.2	5.4	.3		-7.5
BRO	110	3	1	991[2]	955	8.7	27	211	436	10.6	3.46	95	.242	.281	-23	-18	102	89	.910	434	56	.2	-1.6	.5		-2.0
NY	103	2	0	937	1015	9.7	36	204	408	11.7	4.15	71	.265	.302	-94	-124	91	91	.901	452	62	-1.6	-11.2	5.5		-2.8
BAL	104	2	4	971	1059	9.8	12	222	395	11.9	3.90	83	.266	.305	-70	-70	100	94	.910	418	71	.6	-6.3	-2.6		-5.2
TOT	848	41	7	7917[1]		8.9				10.8	3.24		.246	.285					.909	3473	570					

Runs
Stovey-Phi 130
Larkin-Phi 114
Jones-Cin 108
Nelson-NY 98
Browning-Lou 98

Hits
Browning-Lou 174
Jones-Cin 157
Stovey-Phi 153
Orr-NY 152
Larkin-Phi 149

Doubles
Larkin-Phi 37
Browning-Lou 34
Orr-NY 29
Stovey-Phi 27

Triples
Orr-NY 21
Kuehne-Pit 19
Wolf-Lou 17
Jones-Cin 17
Fennelly-Cin 17

Home Runs
Stovey-Phi 13
Fennelly-Cin 10
Browning-Lou 9
Larkin-Phi 8
Orr-NY 6

Total Bases
Browning-Lou 255
Orr-NY 241
Larkin-Phi 238
Stovey-Phi 237
Jones-Cin 225

Runs Batted In
Stovey-Phi 117
Larkin-Phi 106
Jones-Cin 103
Nelson-NY 97
Browning-Lou 89

Runs Produced
Stovey-Phi 117
Larkin-Phi 106
Jones-Cin 103
Nelson-NY 97
Browning-Lou 89

Bases On Balls
Nelson-NY 61
Macullar-Bal 49
Hotaling-Bro 49
Stovey-Phi 39

Batting Average
Browning-Lou 362
Orr-NY 342
Larkin-Phi 329
Jones-Cin 322
Stovey-Phi 315

On Base Percentage
Browning-Lou 393
Larkin-Phi 372
Stovey-Phi 371
Brown-Pit 366
Phillips-Bro 364

Slugging Average
Orr-NY 543
Browning-Lou 530
Larkin-Phi 525
Stovey-Phi 488
Jones-Cin 462

Production
Browning-Lou 923
Orr-NY 901
Larkin-Phi 897
Stovey-Phi 858
Jones-Cin 824

Adjusted Production
Orr-NY 201
Browning-Lou 193
Larkin-Phi 174
Stovey-Phi 163
Jones-Cin 159

Batter Runs
Browning-Lou 48.4
Larkin-Phi 41.7
Orr-NY 39.5
Stovey-Phi 39.5
Jones-Cin 33.0

Adjusted Batter Runs
Browning-Lou 48.6
Orr-NY 44.7
Larkin-Phi 37.5
Stovey-Phi 34.9
Jones-Cin 31.6

Clutch Hitting Index

Runs Created
Browning-Lou 103
Larkin-Phi 91
Stovey-Phi 90
Orr-NY 88
Jones-Cin 83

Total Average
Browning-Lou 912
Larkin-Phi 885
Orr-NY 863
Stovey-Phi 841
Jones-Cin 773

Stolen Bases

Stolen Base Average

Stolen Base Runs

Fielding Runs
G.Smith-Bro......39.9
Smith-Pit 33.2
Houck-Phi 21.8
Hankinson-NY ... 18.0
Corkhill-Cin 17.1

Total Player Rating
Browning-Lou 4.2
Larkin-Phi 3.8
G.Smith-Bro...... 3.8
Smith-Pit 3.4
Jones-Cin 3.3

Wins
Caruthers-StL 40
Morris-Pit 39
Porter-Bro 33
Foutz-StL 33

Win Percentage
Caruthers-StL 755
Foutz-StL 702
Mathews-Phi 638
Morris-Pit 619
Porter-Bro 611

Games
Morris-Pit 63
Henderson-Bal 61
Porter-Bro 54
Hecker-Lou 53
Caruthers-StL 53

Complete Games
Morris-Pit 63
Henderson-Bal 59
Porter-Bro 53
Caruthers-StL 53
Hecker-Lou 51

Shutouts
Morris-Pit 7
Caruthers-StL 6
McGinnis-StL 3

Saves
Burns-Bal 3
Terry-Bro 1
Sommer-Bal 1
Reccius-Lou 1
Corkhill-Cin 1

Innings Pitched
Morris-Pit 581.0
Henderson-Bal .. 539.1
Caruthers-StL 482.1
Porter-Bro 481.2
Hecker-Lou 480.0

Fewest Hits/Game
Morris-Pit 7.11
Mays-Lou 7.74
Foutz-StL 7.75
McGinnis-StL ... 7.87
Porter-Bro 7.98

Fewest BB/Game
Lynch-NY 1.00
Hecker-Lou 1.01
Caruthers-StL 1.06
Mathews-Phi 1.21
McGinnis-StL..... 1.53

Strikeouts
Morris-Pit 298
Mathews-Phi 286
Henderson-Bal ... 263
Hecker-Lou 209
Porter-Bro 197

Strikeouts/Game
Mathews-Phi 6.09
Cushman-Phi-NY . 5.50
Morris-Pit 4.62
Henderson-Bal ... 4.39
Harkins-Bro 4.33

Ratio
Morris-Pit 8.67
Caruthers-StL 9.09
McGinnis-StL..... 9.40
Hecker-Lou 9.52
Mathews-Phi 9.61

Earned Run Average
Caruthers-StL 2.07
Hecker-Lou 2.17
Morris-Pit 2.35
Mathews-Phi 2.43
Foutz-StL 2.63

Adjusted ERA
Caruthers-StL 158
Hecker-Lou 148
Mathews-Phi 141
Morris-Pit 137
Foutz-StL 125

Opponents' Batting Avg.
Morris-Pit 208
Mays-Lou 222
Foutz-StL 223
McGinnis-StL.....225
Porter-Bro 228

Opponents' On Base Pct.
Morris-Pit 243
Caruthers-StL 251
McGinnis-StL.....258
Hecker-Lou 260
Mathews-Phi 262

Starter Runs
Caruthers-StL 62.9
Morris-Pit 57.4
Hecker-Lou 57.0
Mathews-Phi 38.2
Foutz-StL 28.0

Adjusted Starter Runs
Caruthers-StL 64.6
Hecker-Lou 55.8
Morris-Pit 55.6
Mathews-Phi 47.2
Foutz-StL 29.4

Clutch Pitching Index
Hecker-Lou 120
Caruthers-StL 111
Mathews-Phi 106
Mountjoy-Cin-Bal . 105
Henderson-Bal ... 100

Relief Runs

Adjusted Relief Runs

Relief Ranking

Total Pitcher Index
Hecker-Lou 7.0
Caruthers-StL 7.0
Morris-Pit 4.6
Foutz-StL 4.1
Mathews-Phi 3.8

Total Baseball Ranking
Hecker-Lou 7.0
Caruthers-StL 7.0
Morris-Pit 4.6
Browning-Lou 4.2
Foutz-StL 4.1

TEAM	G	W	L	PCT	GB	R	OR	AB	H	2B	3B	HR	BB	SO	AVG	OBP	SLG	PRO	PRO+	BR	/A	PF	CHI	RC	SB	CS	SBA	SBR
CHI	126	90	34	.726		900	555	4378	1223	198	87	53	460	513	.279	.348	.401	.749	115	176	71	115	104	701	213			
DET	126	87	36	.707	2.5	829	538	4501	1260	176	81	53	374	426	.280	.335	.390	.725	122	137	116	103	100	670	194			
NY	124	75	44	.630	12.5	692	558	4298	1156	175	68	21	237	410	.269	.307	.356	.663	105	29	22	101	102	531	155			
PHI	119	71	43	.623	14	621	498	4072	976	145	66	26	282	516	.240	.289	.327	.616	91	-36	-41	101	106	461	226			
BOS	118	56	61	.479	30.5	657	661	4180	1085	151	59	24	250	537	.260	.301	.341	.642	104	0	25	96	104	489	156			
STL	126	43	79	.352	46	547	712	4250	1001	183	46	30	235	656	.236	.276	.321	.597	91	-70	-29	94	96	430	156			
KC	126	30	91	.248	58.5	494	872	4236	967	177	48	19	269	608	.228	.274	.306	.580	76	-91	-132	106	90	392	96			
WAS	125	28	92	.233	60	445	791	4082	856	135	51	23	265	582	.210	.258	.285	.543	73	-142	-106	94	93	345	143			
TOT	495					5185		33997	8524	1340	506	249	2372	4248	.251	.300	.342	.641							1339			

TEAM	CG	SH	SV	IP	H	H/G	HR	BB	SO	RAT	ERA	ERA+	OAV	OOB	PR	/A	PF	CPI	FA	E	DP	FW	PW	BW	SBW	DIF
CHI	116	8	3	1097²	988	8.1	49	262	647	10.2	2.54	143	.230	.274	93	133	110	109	.912	475	82	-1.8	12.0	6.4		11.4
DET	122	8	0	1103²	995	8.1	20	270	592	10.3	2.85	116	.230	.276	55	55	100	91	.928	373	82	3.7	5.0	10.5		6.3
NY	119	3	1	1067	1028	8.7	23	278	582	11.0	2.85	112	.242	.289	53	42	97	105	.929	359	70	4.1	3.8	2.0		5.6
PHI	110	10	2	1045²	923	7.9	29	264	540	10.2	2.45	134	.227	.274	99	97	100	106	.921	393	46	1.3	8.8	-3.7		7.6
BOS	116	3	0	1029	1049	9.2	33	298	511	11.8	3.24	98	.253	.303	6	-7	96	106	.906	457	63	-2.4	-.6	2.3		-1.8
STL	118	6	0	1032¹	1050	9.2	34	392	501	12.6	3.41	94	.253	.317	-11	-21	97	108	.912	452	92	-.6	-1.9	-2.6		-12.9
KC	117	4	0	1066²	1345	11.3	27	246	442	13.4	4.84	78	.295	.331	-182	-127	114	91	.910	482	79	-2.2	-11.5	-11.9		-4.9
WAS	116	4	0	1041	1147	9.9	34	379	500	13.2	4.30	76	.268	.328	-114	-117	99	94	.910	458	69	-1.1	-10.6	-9.6		-10.8
TOT	934	46	6	8483		9.0				11.6	3.31		.251	.300					.916	3449	583					

Runs
Kelly-Chi 155
Gore-Chi 150
Brouthers-Det 139
Richardson-Det . . . 125
Anson-Chi 117

Hits
Richardson-Det . . . 189
Anson-Chi 187
Brouthers-Det 181
Kelly-Chi 175
Connor-NY 172

Doubles
Brouthers-Det 40
Anson-Chi 35
Kelly-Chi 32
Hines-Was 30

Triples
Connor-NY 20
Wood-Phi 15
Brouthers-Det 15
Thompson-Det 13

Home Runs
Richardson-Det 11
Brouthers-Det 11
Anson-Chi 10
Hines-Was 9
Denny-StL 9

Total Bases
Brouthers-Det 284
Anson-Chi 274
Richardson-Det . . . 271
Connor-NY 262
Kelly-Chi 241

Runs Batted In
Anson-Chi 147
Pfeffer-Chi 95
Thompson-Det 89
Rowe-Det 87
Ward-NY 81

Runs Produced
Anson-Chi 254
Kelly-Chi 230
Gore-Chi 207
Brouthers-Det 200
Thompson-Det 182

Bases On Balls
Gore-Chi 102
Kelly-Chi 83
Williamson-Chi 80
Brouthers-Det 66
Radford-KC 58

Batting Average
Kelly-Chi 388
Anson-Chi 371
Brouthers-Det 370
Connor-NY 355
Richardson-Det 351

On Base Percentage
Kelly-Chi 483
Brouthers-Det 445
Gore-Chi 434
Anson-Chi 433
Connor-NY 405

Slugging Average
Brouthers-Det 581
Anson-Chi 544
Connor-NY 540
Kelly-Chi 534
Richardson-Det 504

Production
Brouthers-Det . . . 1.026
Kelly-Chi 1.018
Anson-Chi 977
Connor-NY 945
Richardson-Det 906

Adjusted Production
Brouthers-Det 204
Connor-NY 183
Kelly-Chi 181
Anson-Chi 170
Richardson-Det . . . 169

Batter Runs
Brouthers-Det 65.9
Kelly-Chi 64.3
Anson-Chi 58.2
Connor-NY 48.7
Richardson-Det . . . 47.4

Adjusted Batter Runs
Brouthers-Det 63.6
Kelly-Chi 52.7
Connor-NY 48.0
Anson-Chi 46.1
Richardson-Det . . . 45.0

Clutch Hitting Index
Pfeffer-Chi 164
Dorgan-NY 162
Anson-Chi 151
White-Det 148
Ward-NY 147

Runs Created
Kelly-Chi 146
Brouthers-Det 139
Anson-Chi 134
Richardson-Det . . . 129
Connor-NY 116

Total Average
Kelly-Chi 1.366
Brouthers-Det . . . 1.205
Anson-Chi 1.129
Gore-Chi 1.042
Richardson-Det . . 1.029

Stolen Bases
Andrews-Phi 56
Kelly-Chi 53
Hanlon-Det 50
Richardson-Det 42
Radford-KC 39

Stolen Base Average

Stolen Base Runs

Fielding Runs
Denny-StL 28.4
Knowles-Was 26.2
Dunlap-StL-Det . . . 25.3
Glasscock-StL 22.0
Johnston-Bos 15.2

Total Player Rating
Richardson-Det 5.2
Kelly-Chi 5.1
Glasscock-StL 4.5
Dunlap-StL-Det 3.9
Denny-StL 3.3

Wins
Keefe-NY 42
Baldwin-Det 42
Clarkson-Chi 36
Welch-NY 33
McCormick-Chi 31

Win Percentage
Flynn-Chi 793
Ferguson-Phi 769
Baldwin-Det 764
McCormick-Chi 738
Getzien-Det 732

Games
Keefe-NY 64
Welch-NY 59
Radbourn-Bos 58
Baldwin-Det 56
Clarkson-Chi 55

Complete Games
Keefe-NY 62
Radbourn-Bos 57
Welch-NY 56
Baldwin-Det 55
Clarkson-Chi 50

Shutouts
Baldwin-Det 7
Ferguson-Phi 4
Casey-Phi 4

Saves
Ferguson-Phi 2
Williamson-Chi 1
Ryan-Chi 1
Flynn-Chi 1
Devlin-NY 1

Innings Pitched
Keefe-NY 540.0
Radbourn-Bos . . . 509.1
Welch-NY 500.0
Baldwin-Det 487.0
Clarkson-Chi 466.2

Fewest Hits/Game
Baldwin-Det 6.86
Ferguson-Phi 7.21
Flynn-Chi 7.25
Stemmeyer-Bos . . 7.74
Casey-Phi 7.95

Fewest BB/Game
Whitney-KC 1.26
Ferguson-Phi 1.57
Clarkson-Chi 1.66
Keefe-NY 1.67
Baldwin-Det 1.85

Strikeouts
Baldwin-Det 323
Clarkson-Chi 313
Keefe-NY 291
Welch-NY 272
Stemmeyer-Bos . . 239

Strikeouts/Game
Stemmeyer-Det . . 6.17
Clarkson-Chi 6.04
Baldwin-Det 5.97
Boyle-StL 5.51
Healy-StL 5.42

Ratio
Baldwin-Det 8.70
Ferguson-Phi 8.78
Flynn-Chi 9.46
Keefe-NY 9.63
Clarkson-Chi 9.74

Earned Run Average
Ferguson-Phi 1.98
Baldwin-Det 2.24
Flynn-Chi 2.24
Boyle-StL 2.40
Clarkson-Chi 2.41

Adjusted ERA
Ferguson-Phi 167
Flynn-Chi 162
Clarkson-Chi 151
Baldwin-Det 148
Casey-Phi 137

Opponents' Batting Avg.
Baldwin-Det 202
Ferguson-Phi 211
Flynn-Chi 211
Stemmeyer-Bos . . .223
Casey-Phi 227

Opponents' On Base Pct.
Baldwin-Det 244
Ferguson-Phi 245
Flynn-Chi 259
Keefe-NY 263
Clarkson-Chi 265

Starter Runs
Ferguson-Phi 58.3
Baldwin-Det 57.9
Clarkson-Chi 46.4
Keefe-NY 46.4
Casey-Phi 36.5

Adjusted Starter Runs
Clarkson-Chi 63.7
Baldwin-Det 58.1
Ferguson-Phi 57.9
Keefe-NY 40.4
Flynn-Chi 39.9

Clutch Pitching Index
Boyle-StL 160
McCormick-Chi . . . 120
Welch-NY 118
Kirby-StL 112
Casey-Phi 110

Relief Runs

Adjusted Relief Runs

Relief Ranking

Total Pitcher Index
Ferguson-Phi 7.8
Clarkson-Chi 6.9
Baldwin-Det 6.1
Flynn-Chi 4.7
Keefe-NY 3.8

Total Baseball Ranking
Ferguson-Phi 7.8
Clarkson-Chi 6.9
Baldwin-Det 6.1
Kelly-Chi 5.1
Richardson-Det . . . 5.0

TEAM	G	W	L	PCT	GB	R	OR	AB	H	2B	3B	HR	BB	SO	AVG	OBP	SLG	PRO	PRO+	BR	/A	PF	CHI	RC	SB	CS	SBA	SBR
STL	139	93	46	.669		944	592	5009	1365	206	85	20	400	425	.273	.333	.360	.693	116	126	87	105	100	729	336			
PIT	140	80	57	.584	12	810	647	4854	1171	186	96	16	478	713	.241	.314	.329	.643	107	43	47	100	96	598	260			
BRO	141	76	61	.555	16	832	832	5053	1261	196	80	16	433	523	.250	.311	.330	.641	105	35	27	101	97	610	248			
LOU	138	66	70	.485	25.5	833	805	4921	1294	182	88	20	410	558	.263	.323	.348	.671	108	86	39	106	94	634	202			
CIN	141	65	73	.471	27.5	883	865	4915	1225	145	95	45	374	633	.249	.311	.345	.656	107	57	35	103	103	599	185			
PHI	139	63	72	.467	28	772	942	4856	1142	192	82	21	378	697	.235	.296	.321	.617	97	-9	-16	101	99	560	284			
NY	137	53	82	.393	38	628	766	4683	1047	108	72	18	330	578	.224	.279	.289	.568	85	-89	-55	96	95	422	120			
BAL	139	48	83	.366	41	625	878	4639	945	124	51	8	379	603	.204	.269	.258	.527	71	-150	-131	98	104	404	269			
TOT	557					6327		38930	9450	1339	649	164	3182	4730	.243	.300	.323	.623						1904				

TEAM	CG	SH	SV	IP	H	H/G	HR	BB	SO	RAT	ERA	ERA+	OAV	OOB	PR	/A	PF	CPI	FA	E	DP	FW	PW	BW	SBW	DIF
STL	134	14	2	1229[1]	1087	8.0	13	329	583	10.4	2.52	136	.226	.276	126	124	100	108	.915	494	96	3.3	10.9	7.6		1.7
PIT	137	15	1	1226	1130	8.3	10	299	515	10.5	2.83	120	.234	.278	84	74	98	100	.917	487	90	3.9	6.5	4.1		-3.0
BRO	138	6	0	1234[2]	1202	8.8	17	464	540	12.1	3.42	102	.243	.308	3	9	101	102	.900	610	87	-2.2	.8	2.4		6.5
LOU	131	5	2	1209[2]	1109	8.3	16	432	720	11.5	3.07	119	.233	.296	51	76	106	103	.901	593	89	-1.9	6.7	3.4		-10.2
CIN	129	3	0	1247[2]	1267	9.1	25	481	495	12.6	4.18	84	.252	.317	-102	-95	102	91	.905	582	122	-.8	-8.3	3.1		2.0
PHI	134	4	0	1218[2]	1308	9.7	35	388	513	12.5	3.97	88	.262	.315	-71	-65	102	100	.894	637	99	-4.0	-5.7	-1.4		6.6
NY	134	5	0	1186[1]	1148	8.7	23	386	559	11.6	3.50	97	.243	.300	-7	-13	99	96	.907	544	81	.3	-1.1	-4.8		-8.9
BAL	134	5	0	1206[2]	1197	8.9	25	403	805	11.9	4.08	84	.247	.305	-84	-89	99	87	.910	523	59	1.8	-7.8	-11.5		.0
TOT	1071	57	5	9759		8.7				11.6	3.45		.243	.300					.906	4470	723					

Runs		Hits		Doubles		Triples		Home Runs		Total Bases	
Latham-StL	152	Orr-NY	193	Larkin-Phi	36	Orr-NY	31	McPhee-Cin	8	Orr-NY	301
McPhee-Cin	139	O'Neill-StL	190	McClellan-Bro	33	Coleman-Phi-Pit	17	Stovey-Phi	7	O'Neill-StL	255
Larkin-Phi	133	Larkin-Phi	180	Welch-StL	31	Kuehne-Pit	17	Orr-NY	7	Larkin-Phi	254
McClellan-Bro	131	Latham-StL	174	Barkley-Pit	31	Fennelly-Cin	17			Welch-StL	221
Pinkney-Bro	119	Phillips-Bro	160	Browning-Lou	29	Larkin-Phi	16			McPhee-Cin	221

Runs Batted In	Runs Produced		Bases On Balls		Batting Average		On Base Percentage		Slugging Average	
	Latham-StL	151	Swartwood-Bro	70	Browning-Lou	.340	Larkin-Phi	.390	Orr-NY	.527
	McPhee-Cin	131	Pinkney-Bro	70	Orr-NY	.338	Browning-Lou	.389	Larkin-Phi	.450
	Larkin-Phi	131	Mack-Lou	68	O'Neill-StL	.328	O'Neill-StL	.385	Browning-Lou	.441
	McClellan-Bro	130	Kerins-Lou	66	Larkin-Phi	.319	Stovey-Phi	.377	O'Neill-StL	.440
	Pinkney-Bro	119			Latham-StL	.301	Swartwood-Bro	.377	Stovey-Phi	.440

Production		Adjusted Production		Batter Runs		Adjusted Batter Runs		Clutch Hitting Index	Runs Created	
Orr-NY	.890	Orr-NY	188	Orr-NY	47.2	Caruthers-StL	51.3		Orr-NY	118
Larkin-Phi	.839	Larkin-Phi	163	Larkin-Phi	42.6	Orr-NY	51.1		Larkin-Phi	114
Browning-Lou	.830	Stovey-Phi	156	Caruthers-StL	42.1	Larkin-Phi	41.7		Stovey-Phi	109
O'Neill-StL	.826	O'Neill-StL	153	O'Neill-StL	39.9	Hecker-Lou	36.7		O'Neill-StL	104
Stovey-Phi	.817	Browning-Lou	153	Stovey-Phi	33.3	O'Neill-StL	35.5		Latham-StL	104

Total Average		Stolen Bases		Stolen Base Average	Stolen Base Runs	Fielding Runs		Total Player Rating	
Stovey-Phi	1.009	Stovey-Phi	68			Kerins-Lou	40.8	Kerins-Lou	4.9
Larkin-Phi	.914	Latham-StL	60			McPhee-Cin	30.5	McPhee-Cin	4.2
Robinson-StL	.903	Welch-StL	59			Hankinson-NY	25.4	Orr-NY	3.8
Orr-NY	.897	Robinson-StL	51			Smith-Pit	20.8	Carroll-Pit	3.6
Browning-Lou	.873	McClellan-Bro	43			White-Lou	17.3	Larkin-Phi	3.6

Wins		Win Percentage		Games		Complete Games		Shutouts		Saves	
Morris-Pit	41	Foutz-StL	.719	Kilroy-Bal	68	Ramsey-Lou	66	Morris-Pit	12	Morris-Pit	1
Foutz-StL	41	Caruthers-StL	.682	Ramsey-Lou	67	Kilroy-Bal	66	Foutz-StL	11	Hudson-StL	1
Ramsey-Lou	38	Morris-Pit	.672	Morris-Pit	64	Morris-Pit	63	Terry-Bro	5	Foutz-StL	1
Mullane-Cin	33	Hudson-StL	.615	Mullane-Cin	63	Mullane-Cin	55	Kilroy-Bal	5	Ely-Lou	1
Caruthers-StL	30	Atkinson-Phi	.595	Foutz-StL	59	Foutz-StL	55	Ramsey-Lou	3		

Innings Pitched		Fewest Hits/Game		Fewest BB/Game		Strikeouts		Strikeouts/Game		Ratio	
Ramsey-Lou	588.2	Ramsey-Lou	6.83	Galvin-Pit	1.55	Kilroy-Bal	513	Kilroy-Bal	7.92	Morris-Pit	9.29
Kilroy-Bal	583.0	Kilroy-Bal	7.35	Morris-Pit	1.91	Ramsey-Lou	499	Ramsey-Lou	7.63	Caruthers-StL	9.50
Morris-Pit	555.1	Morris-Pit	7.37	Caruthers-StL	2.00	Morris-Pit	326	Morris-Pit	5.28	Ramsey-Lou	10.00
Mullane-Cin	529.2	Foutz-StL	7.46	McGinnis-StL-Bal	2.27	Foutz-StL	283	Miller-Phi	5.25	Foutz-StL	10.04
Foutz-StL	504.0	Caruthers-StL	7.51	Atkinson-Phi	2.29	Mullane-Cin	250	Terry-Bro	5.06	Kilroy-Bal	10.16

Earned Run Average		Adjusted ERA		Opponents' Batting Avg.		Opponents' On Base Pct.		Starter Runs		Adjusted Starter Runs	
Foutz-StL	2.11	Foutz-StL	163	Ramsey-Lou	.201	Morris-Pit	.255	Foutz-StL	75.0	Ramsey-Lou	78.0
Caruthers-StL	2.32	Ramsey-Lou	149	Kilroy-Bal	.213	Caruthers-StL	.259	Ramsey-Lou	65.4	Foutz-StL	74.4
Ramsey-Lou	2.45	Caruthers-StL	148	Morris-Pit	.213	Ramsey-Lou	.269	Morris-Pit	61.7	Morris-Pit	57.8
Morris-Pit	2.45	Morris-Pit	138	Foutz-StL	.215	Foutz-StL	.270	Caruthers-StL	48.3	Caruthers-StL	47.9
Galvin-Pit	2.67	Hecker-Lou	127	Caruthers-StL	.216	Kilroy-Bal	.272	Galvin-Pit	37.4	Hecker-Lou	36.1

Clutch Pitching Index		Relief Runs	Adjusted Relief Runs	Relief Ranking	Total Pitcher Index		Total Baseball Ranking	
Galvin-Pit	122				Caruthers-StL	9.5	Caruthers-StL	9.5
Foutz-StL	118				Foutz-StL	8.9	Foutz-StL	8.9
McGinnis-StL-Bal	116				Hecker-Lou	7.1	Hecker-Lou	7.1
Hart-Phi	115				Ramsey-Lou	6.6	Ramsey-Lou	6.6
Miller-Phi	114				Morris-Pit	4.4	Kerins-Lou	4.9

TEAM	G	W	L	PCT	GB	R	OR	AB	H	2B	3B	HR	BB	SO	AVG	OBP	SLG	PRO	PRO+	BR	/A	PF	CHI	RC	SB	CS	SBA	SBR
DET	127	79	45	.637		969	714	4689	1404	213	126	55	352	258	.299	.353	.434	.787	120	146	120	103	102	833	267			
PHI	128	75	48	.610	3.5	901	702	4630	1269	213	89	47	385	346	.274	.337	.389	.726	101	48	2	106	106	744	355			
CHI	127	71	50	.587	6.5	813	716	4350	1177	178	98	80	407	400	.271	.336	.412	.748	100	74	-24	113	98	748	382			
NY	129	68	55	.553	10.5	816	723	4516	1259	167	93	48	361	326	.279	.339	.389	.728	113	49	85	95	98	753	415			
BOS	127	61	60	.504	16.5	831	792	4531	1255	185	94	53	340	392	.277	.333	.394	.727	106	44	43	100	101	736	373			
PIT	125	55	69	.444	24	621	750	4414	1141	183	78	20	319	381	.258	.314	.349	.663	95	-55	-8	94	88	567	221			
WAS	126	46	76	.377	32	601	818	4314	1039	149	63	49	269	339	.241	.292	.337	.629	84	-113	-74	95	97	535	334			
IND	127	37	89	.294	43	628	965	4368	1080	162	70	33	300	379	.247	.302	.339	.641	86	-91	-64	96	95	562	334			
TOT	508					6180		35812	9624	1450	711	383	2733	2821	.269	.321	.381	.702							2681			

TEAM	CG	SH	SV	IP	H	H/G	HR	BB	SO	RAT	ERA	ERA+	OAV	OOB	PR	/A	PF	CPI	FA	E	DP	FW	PW	BW	SBW	DIF
DET	122	3	1	1116¹	1172	9.4	52	344	337	12.2	3.95	102	.262	.315	12	9	99	96	.926	394	92	3.3	.8	10.2		2.8
PHI	119	7	1	1132²	1173	9.3	48	305	435	11.7	3.47	121	.259	.306	72	92	104	103	.913	471	76	-.4	7.8	.2		5.9
CHI	117	4	3	1126	1156	9.2	55	338	510	11.9	3.46	129	.258	.310	73	125	110	106	.915	472	99	-.6	10.6	-2.0		2.6
NY	123	5	1	1113³	1115	9.0	27	373	412	12.0	3.59	104	.253	.311	56	19	93	96	.921	431	83	1.8	1.6	7.2		-4.1
BOS	123	4	1	1100²	1226	10.0	55	396	254	13.3	4.41	91	.274	.333	-43	-45	100	97	.905	522	94	-3.1	-3.8	3.6		3.8
PIT	123	3	0	1108²	1287	10.4	39	246	248	12.4	4.12	94	.282	.319	-8	-31	95	98	.921	425	70	1.4	-2.6	-.7		-5.1
WAS	124	4	0	1090¹	1216	10.0	47	299	396	12.5	4.19	96	.274	.320	-17	-19	100	96	.910	483	77	-1.4	-1.6	-6.3		-5.8
IND	118	4	1	1088	1289	10.7	60	431	245	14.2	5.24	79	.286	.348	-144	-135	102	91	.912	479	105	-1.0	-11.4	-5.4		-8.2
TOT	969	34	8	8876¹		9.8				12.5	4.05		.269	.321					.915	3677	696					

Runs
Brouthers-Det ... 153
Rowe-Det ... 135
Richardson-Det ... 131
Kelly-Bos ... 120

Hits
Thompson-Det ... 203
Ward-NY ... 184
Richardson-Det ... 178
Rowe-Det ... 171
Brouthers-Det ... 169

Doubles
Brouthers-Det ... 36
Kelly-Bos ... 34
Denny-Ind ... 34
Anson-Chi ... 33

Triples
Thompson-Det ... 23
Connor-NY ... 22
Johnston-Bos ... 20
Brouthers-Det ... 20
Wood-Phi ... 19

Home Runs
W.O'Brien-Was ... 19
Connor-NY ... 17
Pfeffer-Chi ... 16
Wood-Phi ... 14

Total Bases
Thompson-Det ... 311
Brouthers-Det ... 281
Richardson-Det ... 263
Denny-Ind ... 256
Connor-NY ... 255

Runs Batted In
Thompson-Det ... 166
Connor-NY ... 104
Anson-Chi ... 102
Brouthers-Det ... 101
Denny-Ind ... 97

Runs Produced
Thompson-Det ... 273
Brouthers-Det ... 242
Rowe-Det ... 225
Richardson-Det ... 217
Anson-Chi ... 202

Bases On Balls
Fogarty-Phi ... 82
Connor-NY ... 75
Williamson-Chi ... 73
Seery-Ind ... 71
Brouthers-Det ... 71

Batting Average
Thompson-Det ... .372
Anson-Chi ... .347
Brouthers-Det ... .338
Ward-NY ... .338
Wise-Bos ... .334

On Base Percentage
Brouthers-Det ... .426
Anson-Chi ... .422
Thompson-Det ... .416
Schomberg-Ind ... .397
Kelly-Bos ... .393

Slugging Average
Thompson-Det ... .571
Brouthers-Det ... .562
Connor-NY ... .541
Wise-Bos ... .522
Anson-Chi ... .517

Production
Brouthers-Det ... .988
Thompson-Det ... .987
Anson-Chi ... .939
Connor-NY ... .933
Wise-Bos ... .913

Adjusted Production
Brouthers-Det ... 169
Thompson-Det ... 168
Connor-NY ... 166
Carroll-Pit ... 155
Wise-Bos ... 153

Batter Runs
Thompson-Det ... 52.5
Brouthers-Det ... 51.8
Anson-Chi ... 40.6
Connor-NY ... 38.4
Wise-Bos ... 32.9

Adjusted Batter Runs
Thompson-Det ... 49.5
Brouthers-Det ... 48.9
Connor-NY ... 42.6
Wise-Bos ... 32.8
Ferguson-Phi ... 30.6

Clutch Hitting Index
O'Rourke-NY ... 167
Thompson-Det ... 143
Mulvey-Phi ... 140
McGeachey-Ind ... 132
Donnelly-Was ... 129

Runs Created
Thompson-Det ... 142
Brouthers-Det ... 138
Kelly-Bos ... 129
Ward-NY ... 125
Connor-NY ... 120

Total Average
Brouthers-Det ... 1.184
Kelly-Bos ... 1.146
Connor-NY ... 1.131
Thompson-Det ... 1.094
Fogarty-Phi ... 1.085

Stolen Bases
Ward-NY ... 111
Fogarty-Phi ... 102
Kelly-Bos ... 84
Hanlon-Det ... 69
Glasscock-Ind ... 62

Stolen Base Average

Stolen Base Runs

Fielding Runs
Glasscock-Ind ... 35.1
Ward-NY ... 29.4
Fogarty-Phi ... 28.9
Pfeffer-Chi ... 25.1
Denny-Ind ... 22.6

Total Player Rating
Thompson-Det ... 4.4
Denny-Ind ... 4.0
Fogarty-Phi ... 3.5
Ward-NY ... 3.4
Richardson-Det ... 3.3

Wins
Clarkson-Chi ... 38
Keefe-NY ... 35
Getzien-Det ... 29
Galvin-Pit ... 28
Casey-Phi ... 28

Win Percentage
Getzien-Det ... .690
Ferguson-Phi ... .688
Casey-Phi ... .683
Keefe-NY ... .648
Clarkson-Chi ... .644

Games
Clarkson-Chi ... 60
Keefe-NY ... 56
Radbourn-Bos ... 50
Galvin-Pit ... 49
Whitney-Was ... 47

Complete Games
Clarkson-Chi ... 56
Keefe-NY ... 54
Radbourn-Bos ... 48
Galvin-Pit ... 47
Whitney-Was ... 46

Shutouts
Casey-Phi ... 4
Whitney-Was ... 3
Madden-Bos ... 3
Healy-Ind ... 3

Saves
VanHaltren-Chi ... 1
Twitchell-Det ... 1
Tiernan-NY ... 1
Stemmeyer-Bos ... 1
Pettit-Chi ... 1
Ferguson-Phi ... 1
Fast-Ind ... 1
Baldwin-Chi ... 1

Innings Pitched
Clarkson-Chi ... 523.0
Keefe-NY ... 478.2
Galvin-Pit ... 440.2
Radbourn-Bos ... 425.0
Whitney-Was ... 404.2

Fewest Hits/Game
Conway-Det ... 8.14
Keefe-NY ... 8.40
Casey-Phi ... 8.69
Welch-NY ... 8.82
Clarkson-Chi ... 8.83

Fewest BB/Game
Whitney-Was ... .93
Galvin-Pit ... 1.37
Ferguson-Phi ... 1.42
Clarkson-Chi ... 1.58
Boyle-Ind ... 1.89

Strikeouts
Clarkson-Chi ... 237
Keefe-NY ... 186
Baldwin-Chi ... 164
Buffinton-Phi ... 160
Whitney-Was ... 146

Strikeouts/Game
Baldwin-Chi ... 4.42
Gilmore-Was ... 4.37
Buffinton-Phi ... 4.33
VanHaltren-Chi ... 4.25
Clarkson-Chi ... 4.08

Ratio
Clarkson-Chi ... 10.41
Ferguson-Phi ... 10.41
Keefe-NY ... 10.44
Whitney-Was ... 10.50
Conway-Det ... 11.03

Earned Run Average
Casey-Phi ... 2.86
Conway-Det ... 2.90
Ferguson-Phi ... 3.00
Clarkson-Chi ... 3.08
Keefe-NY ... 3.10

Adjusted ERA
Casey-Phi ... 147
Clarkson-Chi ... 145
Ferguson-Phi ... 140
Conway-Det ... 139
Baldwin-Chi ... 131

Opponents' Batting Avg.
Conway-Det ... .235
Keefe-NY ... .240
Casey-Phi ... .247
Welch-NY ... .249
Clarkson-Chi ... .250

Opponents' On Base Pct.
Clarkson-Chi ... .282
Ferguson-Phi ... .282
Keefe-NY ... .282
Whitney-Was ... .283
Conway-Det ... .294

Starter Runs
Clarkson-Chi ... 56.2
Casey-Phi ... 51.5
Keefe-NY ... 50.3
Galvin-Pit ... 37.2
Whitney-Was ... 37.0

Adjusted Starter Runs
Clarkson-Chi ... 80.2
Casey-Phi ... 58.4
Ferguson-Phi ... 39.9
Baldwin-Chi ... 39.5
Whitney-Was ... 36.4

Clutch Pitching Index
Casey-Phi ... 114
VanHaltren-Chi ... 112
Baldwin-Chi ... 112
Galvin-Pit ... 108
Ferguson-Phi ... 103

Relief Runs

Adjusted Relief Runs

Relief Ranking

Total Pitcher Index
Clarkson-Chi ... 8.7
Ferguson-Phi ... 6.6
Whitney-Was ... 4.6
Casey-Phi ... 4.2
Keefe-NY ... 3.7

Total Baseball Ranking
Clarkson-Chi ... 8.7
Ferguson-Phi ... 6.6
Whitney-Was ... 4.6
Thompson-Det ... 4.4
Casey-Phi ... 4.2

TEAM	G	W	L	PCT	GB	R	OR	AB	H	2B	3B	HR	BB	SO	AVG	OBP	SLG	PRO	PRO+	BR	/A	PF	CHI	RC	SB	CS	SBA	SBR
STL	138	95	40	.704		1131	761	5048	1550	261	78	39	442	340	.307	.371	.413	.784	113	168	68	111	102	1012	581			
CIN	136	81	54	.600	14	892	745	4797	1285	179	102	37	382	366	.268	.329	.371	.700	99	5	-10	102	100	778	527			
BAL	141	77	58	.570	18	975	861	4825	1337	202	100	31	469	334	.277	.349	.380	.729	115	67	119	94	100	852	545			
LOU	139	76	60	.559	19.5	956	854	4916	1420	194	98	27	436	356	.289	.352	.385	.737	109	77	59	102	96	850	466			
PHI	137	64	69	.481	30	893	890	4954	1370	231	84	29	321	388	.277	.327	.375	.702	100	4	3	100	98	782	476			
BRO	138	60	74	.448	34.5	904	918	4913	1281	200	82	25	456	365	.261	.330	.350	.680	93	-22	-33	101	101	720	409			
NY	138	44	89	.331	50	754	1093	4820	1197	193	66	21	463	463	.248	.318	.329	.647	89	-80	-40	96	92	615	305			
CLE	133	39	92	.298	54	729	1112	4649	1170	178	77	14	375	463	.252	.314	.332	.646	88	-82	-60	98	94	611	355			
TOT	550					7234		38922	10610	1638	687	223	3320	3075	.273	.330	.367	.697							3664			

TEAM	CG	SH	SV	IP	H	H/G	HR	BB	SO	RAT	ERA	ERA+	OAV	OOB	PR	/A	PF	CPI	FA	E	DP	FW	PW	BW	SBW	DIF
STL	132	7	2	1199^1	1254	9.4	19	323	334	11.8	3.77	120	.259	.306	68	99	106	93	.916	481	86	3.6	8.0	5.5		10.4
CIN	129	11	1	1182^2	1202	9.1	28	396	330	12.2	3.58	120	.254	.311	92	94	100	101	.916	484	106	3.0	7.6	-.8		3.7
BAL	132	8	0	1220	1288	9.5	16	418	470	12.6	3.87	106	.261	.319	57	29	95	97	.907	549	66	.8	2.3	9.6		-3.3
LOU	133	3	1	1205^2	1274	9.5	31	357	544	12.2	3.82	115	.261	.312	62	74	102	98	.903	574	83	-.9	6.0	4.8		-1.9
PHI	131	5	1	1186^1	1227	9.3	29	433	417	12.6	4.59	93	.257	.319	-39	-41	100	83	.907	528	95	1.0	-3.3	.2		-.4
BRO	132	3	3	1185^1	1348	10.2	27	454	332	13.7	4.47	96	.276	.338	-23	-24	100	97	.905	562	88	-.5	-1.9	-2.7		-1.9
NY	132	1	0	1180^1	1545	11.8	39	406	316	14.9	5.28	80	.305	.357	-130	-137	99	98	.894	632	102	-4.0	-11.1	-3.2		-4.2
CLE	127	2	1	1136	1472	11.7	34	533	332	15.9	4.99	87	.303	.372	-88	-81	102	109	.898	576	97	-2.2	-6.6	-4.9		-12.9
TOT	1048	40	9	9495^2		10.1				13.2	4.29		.273	.330					.906	4386	723					

Runs		Hits		Doubles		Triples		Home Runs		Total Bases	
O'Neill-StL	167	O'Neill-StL	225	O'Neill-StL	52	Poorman-Phi	19	O'Neill-StL	14	O'Neill-StL	357
Latham-StL	163	Browning-Lou	220	Lyons-Phi	43	O'Neill-StL	19	Reilly-Cin	10	Browning-Lou	299
Griffin-Bal	142	Lyons-Phi	209	Reilly-Cin	35	McPhee-Cin	19	Burns-Bal	9	Lyons-Phi	298
Poorman-Phi	140	Latham-StL	198	Latham-StL	35	Kerins-Lou	19			Burns-Bal	286
Comiskey-StL	139	Burns-Bal	188	Browning-Lou	35	Davis-Bal	19			Reilly-Cin	263
						Burns-Bal	19				

Runs Batted In		Runs Produced		Bases On Balls		Batting Average		On Base Percentage		Slugging Average	
		Latham-StL	161	Radford-NY	106	O'Neill-StL	.435	O'Neill-StL	.490	O'Neill-StL	.691
		O'Neill-StL	153	Robinson-StL	92	Browning-Lou	.402	Browning-Lou	.464	Caruthers-StL	.547
		Griffin-Bal	139	Nicol-Cin	86	Lyons-Phi	.367	Caruthers-StL	.463	Browning-Lou	.547
		Poorman-Phi	136	Mack-Lou	83	Caruthers-StL	.357	Robinson-StL	.445	Lyons-Phi	.523
				Fennelly-Cin	82	Foutz-StL	.357	Lyons-Phi	.421	Burns-Bal	.519

Production		Adjusted Production		Batter Runs		Adjusted Batter Runs		Clutch Hitting Index		Runs Created	
O'Neill-StL	1.180	O'Neill-StL	208	O'Neill-StL	87.9	O'Neill-StL	77.6			O'Neill-StL	194
Browning-Lou	1.011	Browning-Lou	181	Browning-Lou	62.5	Browning-Lou	60.5			Browning-Lou	191
Caruthers-StL	1.010	Burns-Bal	172	Lyons-Phi	48.5	Burns-Bal	51.6			Lyons-Phi	160
Lyons-Phi	.943	Caruthers-StL	166	Burns-Bal	45.5	Lyons-Phi	48.4			Burns-Bal	146
Burns-Bal	.933	Lyons-Phi	165	Caruthers-StL	44.0	Caruthers-StL	36.2			Latham-StL	146

Total Average		Stolen Bases		Stolen Base Average		Stolen Base Runs		Fielding Runs		Total Player Rating	
O'Neill-StL	1.514	Nicol-Cin	138					Smith-Bro	32.0	O'Neill-StL	5.3
Browning-Lou	1.422	Latham-StL	129					McPhee-Cin	26.2	Browning-Lou	4.3
Caruthers-StL	1.368	Comiskey-StL	117					Kerins-Lou	24.6	Caruthers-StL	4.0
Robinson-StL	1.197	Browning-Lou	103					White-Lou	21.5	Kerins-Lou	3.2
Lyons-Phi	1.175	McPhee-Cin	95					Welch-StL	19.4	Lyons-Phi	3.1

Wins		Win Percentage		Games		Complete Games		Shutouts		Saves	
Kilroy-Bal	46	Caruthers-StL	.763	Kilroy-Bal	69	Kilroy-Bal	66	Mullane-Cin	6	Terry-Bro	3
Ramsey-Lou	37	King-StL	.727	Ramsey-Lou	65	Ramsey-Lou	61	Kilroy-Bal	6		
Smith-Cin	34	Kilroy-Bal	.708	Smith-Bal	58	Smith-Bal	54	Smith-Cin	3		
King-StL	32	Foutz-StL	.676	Weyhing-Phi	55	Weyhing-Phi	53	Seward-Phi	3		
Mullane-Cin	31	Smith-Cin	.667	Seward-Phi	55	Seward-Phi	52				

Innings Pitched		Fewest Hits/Game		Fewest BB/Game		Strikeouts		Strikeouts/Game		Ratio	
Kilroy-Bal	589.1	Smith-Cin	8.05	Hecker-Lou	1.58	Ramsey-Lou	355	Ramsey-Lou	5.70	Caruthers-StL	10.50
Ramsey-Lou	561.0	Seward-Phi	8.51	Caruthers-StL	1.61	Kilroy-Bal	217	Morrison-Cle	4.49	Smith-Cin	10.58
Smith-Bal	491.1	Toole-Bro	8.63	Lynch-NY	1.73	Smith-Bal	206	Terry-Bro	3.91	Seward-Phi	11.19
Seward-Phi	470.2	Ramsey-Lou	8.73	Foutz-StL	2.39	Weyhing-Phi	193	Smith-Bal	3.77	Kilroy-Bal	11.33
Weyhing-Phi	466.1	Caruthers-StL	8.89	Kilroy-Bal	2.40	Smith-Cin	176	Weyhing-Phi	3.72	Ramsey-Lou	11.41

Earned Run Average		Adjusted ERA		Opponents' Batting Avg.		Opponents' On Base Pct.		Starter Runs		Adjusted Starter Runs	
Smith-Cin	2.94	Smith-Cin	147	Smith-Cin	.231	Caruthers-StL	.281	Kilroy-Bal	80.0	Smith-Cin	68.1
Kilroy-Bal	3.07	Caruthers-StL	137	Seward-Phi	.241	Smith-Cin	.283	Smith-Cin	67.3	Kilroy-Bal	67.0
Mullane-Cin	3.24	Kilroy-Bal	133	Toole-Bro	.243	Seward-Phi	.294	Ramsey-Lou	53.5	Ramsey-Lou	59.3
Caruthers-StL	3.30	Mullane-Cin	133	Ramsey-Lou	.245	Kilroy-Bal	.297	Mullane-Cin	48.5	Mullane-Cin	49.3
Ramsey-Lou	3.43	Ramsey-Lou	128	Caruthers-StL	.249	Ramsey-Lou	.298	Caruthers-StL	37.6	Caruthers-StL	46.7

Clutch Pitching Index		Relief Runs		Adjusted Relief Runs		Relief Ranking		Total Pitcher Index		Total Baseball Ranking	
Daily-Cle	132							Kilroy-Bal	7.2	Caruthers-StL	7.9
Morrison-Cle	114							Smith-Cin	5.7	Kilroy-Bal	7.2
Crowell-Cle	114							Mullane-Cin	4.4	Smith-Cin	5.7
Chamberlain-Lou	110							Caruthers-StL	4.0	O'Neill-StL	5.3
Porter-Bro	107							Ramsey-Lou	3.4	Mullane-Cin	4.4

TEAM	G	W	L	PCT	GB	R	OR	AB	H	2B	3B	HR	BB	SO	AVG	OBP	SLG	PRO	PRO+	BR	/A	PF	CHI	RC	SB	CS	SBA	SBR
NY	138	84	47	.641		659	479	4747	1149	130	76	55	270	456	.242	.287	.336	.623	107	33	40	99	100	562	314			
CHI	136	77	58	.570	9	734	659	4616	1201	147	95	77	290	563	.260	.308	.383	.691	119	139	95	107	98	649	287			
PHI	132	69	61	.531	14.5	535	509	4528	1021	151	46	16	268	485	.225	.276	.290	.566	83	-49	-80	105	97	441	246			
BOS	137	70	64	.522	15.5	669	619	4834	1183	167	89	56	282	524	.245	.291	.351	.642	110	63	52	102	96	593	293			
DET	134	68	63	.519	16	721	629	4849	1275	177	72	51	307	396	.263	.313	.361	.674	123	122	122	100	94	623	193			
PIT	139	66	68	.493	19.5	534	580	4713	1070	150	49	14	194	583	.227	.264	.289	.553	91	-79	-31	92	100	446	287			
IND	136	50	85	.370	36	603	603	4623	1100	180	33	34	236	492	.238	.281	.313	.594	95	-10	-21	102	101	518	350			
WAS	136	48	86	.358	37.5	482	731	4546	944	98	49	30	246	499	.208	.255	.271	.526	79	-116	-82	94	100	408	331			
TOT	544					4937		37456	8943	1200	509	333	2093	3998	.239	.279	.325	.604							2301			

TEAM	CG	SH	SV	IP	H	H/G	HR	BB	SO	RAT	ERA	ERA+	OAV	OOB	PR	/A	PF	CPI	FA	E	DP	FW	PW	BW	SBW	DIF
NY	133	20	1	1208	906	6.7	27	308	724	9.0	1.96	139	.200	.251	116	102	96	93	.924	432	76	1.2	10.0	3.9		3.3
CHI	123	13	1	1186¹	1139	8.6	63	308	588	11.0	2.96	102	.243	.290	-16	6	106	105	.927	417	112	1.7	.6	9.3		-2.1
PHI	125	16	3	1167	1072	8.3	26	196	519	9.8	2.38	124	.235	.266	58	73	104	101	.924	424	70	.6	7.2	-7.9		4.1
BOS	134	7	0	1225¹	1104	8.1	36	269	484	10.1	2.61	109	.231	.273	30	30	100	97	.917	494	91	-2.2	3.0	5.1		-2.8
DET	130	10	1	1199	1115	8.4	44	183	522	9.7	2.74	100	.237	.266	12	0	97	93	.919	463	83	-1.1	.0	12.0		-8.4
PIT	135	13	0	1203¹	1190	8.9	23	223	367	10.6	2.67	99	.248	.282	21	-2	94	104	.927	416	88	2.3	-.2	-3.0		.0
IND	132	6	0	1187²	1260	9.5	64	308	388	11.9	3.81	77	.262	.306	-129	-114	104	95	.922	449	84	-.0	-11.2	-2.1		-4.2
WAS	133	6	0	1179¹	1157	8.8	50	298	406	11.1	3.54	79	.247	.292	-93	-98	98	88	.913	494	69	-2.4	-9.6	-8.1		1.1
TOT	1045	91	6	9556		8.4				10.4	2.83		.239	.279					.922	3589	673					

Runs
Brouthers-Det 118
Ryan-Chi 115
Johnston-Bos 102
Anson-Chi 101
Connor-NY 98

Hits
Ryan-Chi 182
Anson-Chi 177
Johnston-Bos 173
Brouthers-Det ... 160
White-Det 157

Doubles
Ryan-Chi 33
Brouthers-Det ... 33
Johnston-Bos 31
Denny-Ind 27
Hines-Ind 26

Triples
Johnston-Bos 18
Connor-NY 17
Nash-Bos 15
Ewing-NY 15

Home Runs
Ryan-Chi 16
Connor-NY 14
Johnston-Bos 12
Denny-Ind 12
Anson-Chi 12

Total Bases
Ryan-Chi 283
Johnston-Bos 276
Anson-Chi 257
Brouthers-Det ... 242
Connor-NY 231

Runs Batted In
Anson-Chi 84
Nash-Bos 75
Rowe-Det 74
Williamson-Chi ... 73

Runs Produced
Brouthers-Det ... 175
Anson-Chi 173
Ryan-Chi 163
Johnston-Bos 158
Connor-NY 155

Bases On Balls
Connor-NY 73
Hoy-Was 69
Brouthers-Det ... 68
Williamson-Chi ... 65
Seery-Ind 64

Batting Average
Anson-Chi .... .344
Ryan-Chi .... .332
Kelly-Bos .... .318
Brouthers-Det ..... .307
Ewing-NY .... .306

On Base Percentage
Anson-Chi .... .400
Brouthers-Det ..... .399
Connor-NY .... .389
Ryan-Chi .... .377
Hoy-Was .... .374

Slugging Average
Ryan-Chi .... .515
Anson-Chi .... .499
Connor-NY .... .480
Kelly-Bos .... .480
Johnston-Bos ...... .472

Production
Anson-Chi .... .899
Ryan-Chi .... .892
Connor-NY .... .869
Brouthers-Det .... .862
Kelly-Bos .... .848

Adjusted Production
Connor-NY 181
Brouthers-Det ... 177
Anson-Chi 175
Ryan-Chi 172
Kelly-Bos 168

Batter Runs
Ryan-Chi 50.7
Anson-Chi 50.5
Brouthers-Det ... 48.0
Connor-NY 44.9
Kelly-Bos 34.5

Adjusted Batter Runs
Brouthers-Det ... 48.0
Connor-NY 45.7
Anson-Chi 45.5
Ryan-Chi 45.5
Kelly-Bos 33.5

Clutch Hitting Index
Burns-Chi 163
Rowe-Det 148
Bassett-Ind 148
Williamson-Chi .. 140
Smith-Pit 139

Runs Created
Ryan-Chi 133
Anson-Chi 117
Brouthers-Det ... 113
Connor-NY 103
Kelly-Bos 101

Total Average
Ryan-Chi 1.044
Kelly-Bos 1.007
Anson-Chi .... .985
Brouthers-Det ... .983
Connor-NY .... .982

Stolen Bases
Hoy-Was 82
Seery-Ind 80
Sunday-Pit 71
Pfeffer-Chi 64
Ryan-Chi 60

Stolen Base Average

Stolen Base Runs

Fielding Runs
Pfeffer-Chi 39.4
Nash-Bos 25.1
Denny-Ind 25.0
Burns-Chi 17.8
Sunday-Pit 15.8

Total Player Rating
Nash-Bos 5.2
Ryan-Chi 4.7
Pfeffer-Chi 4.6
Anson-Chi 4.1
Ewing-NY 3.9

Wins
Keefe-NY 35
Clarkson-Bos 33
Conway-Det 30
Morris-Pit 29
Buffinton-Phi 28

Win Percentage
Keefe-NY .... .745
Conway-Det .... .682
Sanders-Phi .... .655
Krock-Chi .... .641
Clarkson-Bos ...... .623

Games
Morris-Pit 55
Clarkson-Bos 54
Keefe-NY 51
Galvin-Pit 50
Welch-NY 47

Complete Games
Morris-Pit 54
Clarkson-Bos 53
Galvin-Pit 49
Keefe-NY 48
Welch-NY 47

Shutouts
Sanders-Phi 8
Keefe-NY 8
Galvin-Pit 6
Buffinton-Phi 6

Saves
Wood-Phi 2
VanHaltren-Chi 1
Tyng-Phi 1
Twitchell-Det 1
Crane-NY 1

Innings Pitched
Clarkson-Bos ... 483.1
Morris-Pit 480.0
Galvin-Pit 437.1
Keefe-NY 434.1
Welch-NY 425.1

Fewest Hits/Game
Keefe-NY 6.55
Titcomb-NY 6.81
Welch-NY 6.94
Conway-Det 7.25
Buffinton-Phi 7.28

Fewest BB/Game
Sanders-Phi 1.08
Galvin-Pit 1.09
Krock-Chi 1.19
Getzien-Det 1.20
Madden-Bos 1.31

Strikeouts
Keefe-NY 333
Clarkson-Bos 223
Getzien-Det 202
Buffinton-Phi ... 199
O'Day-Was 186

Strikeouts/Game
Keefe-NY 6.90
Titcomb-NY 5.89
Baldwin-Chi 5.63
VanHaltren-Chi ... 5.09
Getzien-Det 4.50

Ratio
Keefe-NY 8.43
Conway-Det 8.56
Buffinton-Phi 8.61
Gruber-Det 8.89
Titcomb-NY 8.91

Earned Run Average
Keefe-NY 1.74
Sanders-Phi 1.90
Buffinton-Phi 1.91
Welch-NY 1.93
Sowders-Bos 2.07

Adjusted ERA
Keefe-NY 156
Sanders-Phi 156
Buffinton-Phi ... 154
Welch-NY 141
Sowders-Bos 137

Opponents' Batting Avg.
Keefe-NY .... .196
Titcomb-NY .... .202
Welch-NY .... .205
Conway-Det .... .213
Buffinton-Phi ..... .213

Opponents' On Base Pct.
Keefe-NY .... .239
Conway-Det .... .242
Buffinton-Phi ..... .243
Gruber-Det .... .249
Titcomb-NY .... .249

Starter Runs
Keefe-NY 52.6
Welch-NY 42.8
Buffinton-Phi 40.9
Sanders-Phi 28.6
Morris-Pit 28.0

Adjusted Starter Runs
Keefe-NY 47.3
Buffinton-Phi 46.2
Welch-NY 37.6
Sanders-Phi 32.2
Sowders-Bos 26.7

Clutch Pitching Index
Baldwin-Chi 126
Gleason-Phi 117
Morris-Pit 113
Burdick-Ind 112
Sowders-Bos 110

Relief Runs

Adjusted Relief Runs

Relief Ranking

Total Pitcher Index
Buffinton-Phi 5.8
Sanders-Phi 5.2
Keefe-NY 4.2
Conway-Det 3.9
Welch-NY 3.7

Total Baseball Ranking
Buffinton-Phi 5.8
Nash-Bos 5.2
Sanders-Phi 5.2
Ryan-Chi 4.7
Pfeffer-Chi 4.6

TEAM	G	W	L	PCT	GB	R	OR	AB	H	2B	3B	HR	BB	SO	AVG	OBP	SLG	PRO	PRO+	BR	/A	PF	CHI	RC	SB	CS	SBA	SBR
STL	137	92	43	.681		789	501	4755	1189	149	47	36	410	521	.250	.316	.324	.640	101	74	-4	111	99	651	468			
BRO	143	88	52	.629	6.5	758	584	4871	1177	172	70	25	353	439	.242	.300	.321	.621	106	37	39	100	99	584	334			
PHI	136	81	52	.609	10	827	594	4828	1209	183	89	31	303	473	.250	.305	.344	.649	115	79	84	99	103	656	434			
CIN	137	80	54	.597	11.5	745	628	4801	1161	132	82	32	345	555	.242	.301	.323	.624	102	41	7	105	98	623	469			
BAL	137	57	80	.416	36	653	779	4656	1068	162	70	19	298	479	.229	.284	.306	.590	98	-16	2	97	96	511	326			
CLE	135	50	82	.379	40.5	651	839	4603	1076	128	59	12	315	559	.234	.294	.295	.589	98	-12	5	98	96	516	353			
LOU	139	48	87	.356	44	689	870	4881	1177	183	67	14	322	604	.241	.297	.315	.612	105	21	37	98	92	565	318			
KC	132	43	89	.326	47.5	579	896	4588	1000	142	61	19	288	604	.218	.273	.288	.561	80	-64	-107	106	94	441	257			
TOT	548					5691		37983	9057	1251	545	188	2634	4234	.238	.288	.315	.603						2959				

TEAM	CG	SH	SV	IP	H	H/G	HR	BB	SO	RAT	ERA	ERA+	OAV	OOB	PR	/A	PF	CPI	FA	E	DP	FW	PW	BW	SBW	DIF
STL	132	12	0	1212²	939	7.0	19	225	517	8.6	2.09	156	.206	.243	130	156	107	89	.924	430	73	3.4	14.4	-.4		7.0
BRO	138	9	0	1286¹	1059	7.4	15	285	577	9.4	2.33	128	.216	.260	104	91	97	93	.918	502	88	.6	8.4	3.6		5.4
PHI	133	13	0	1208²	988	7.4	14	324	596	9.8	2.41	124	.215	.267	86	76	98	94	.919	475	73	.7	7.0	7.8		-1.0
CIN	132	10	2	1237²	1103	8.0	19	310	539	10.3	2.73	116	.230	.277	45	57	103	96	.923	456	100	2.0	5.3	.6		5.1
BAL	130	3	0	1200¹	1162	8.7	23	419	525	11.9	3.78	79	.245	.306	-96	-107	97	87	.920	461	88	1.7	-9.9	.2		-3.5
CLE	131	6	1	1171	1235	9.5	38	389	500	12.5	3.72	83	.261	.317	-86	-80	102	102	.915	488	87	-.2	-7.4	.5		-8.8
LOU	133	6	0	1231¹	1264	9.2	28	281	599	11.3	3.25	95	.256	.296	-25	-24	100	101	.900	609	75	-6.2	-2.2	3.4		-14.5
KC	128	4	0	1157²	1306	10.2	32	401	381	13.3	4.29	80	.274	.331	-158	-112	112	97	.914	507	95	-1.9	-10.3	-9.9		-.9
TOT	1057	63	3	9705²		8.4				10.8	3.06		.238	.288					.917	3928	679					

Runs
Pinkney-Bro...... 134
Collins-Lou-Bro... 133
Stovey-Phi...... 127
Welch-Phi...... 125
Latham-StL...... 119

Hits
O'Neill-StL...... 177
Reilly-Cin...... 169
McKean-Cle...... 164
Collins-Lou-Bro... 162
Corkhill-Cin-Bro.. 160

Doubles
Collins-Lou-Bro... 31
Wolf-Lou........ 28
Reilly-Cin........ 28
Larkin-Phi........ 28

Triples
Stovey-Phi...... 20
Burns-Bal-Bro.... 15
McKean-Cle...... 15
Reilly-Cin........ 14
Foutz-Bro........ 13

Home Runs
Larkin-Phi........ 13
Stovey-Phi....... 9
Reilly-Cin......... 7

Total Bases
Reilly-Cin........ 264
Stovey-Phi....... 244
O'Neill-StL...... 236
McKean-Cle...... 233
Burns-Bal-Bro.... 230

Runs Batted In
Reilly-Cin........ 103
Larkin-Phi....... 101
Foutz-Bro........ 99
O'Neill-StL....... 98
Corkhill-Cin-Bro... 93

Runs Produced
Reilly-Cin........ 202
O'Neill-StL...... 189
Foutz-Bro........ 187
Larkin-Phi....... 186
Welch-Phi........ 185

Bases On Balls
Robinson-StL...... 116
Fennelly-Cin-Phi.. 72
Nicol-Cin......... 67
McTamany-KC..... 67
Pinkney-Bro....... 66

Batting Average
O'Neill-StL........335
Reilly-Cin.........321
Browning-Lou.....313
Collins-Lou-Bro....307
McKean-Cle.......299

On Base Percentage
Robinson-StL.....400
O'Neill-StL.......390
Browning-Lou.....380
Collins-Lou-Bro....373
Stovey-Phi.......365

Slugging Average
Reilly-Cin.........501
Stovey-Phi.......460
O'Neill-StL.......446
Browning-Lou.....436
Burns-Bal-Bro....435

Production
Reilly-Cin.........864
O'Neill-StL.......836
Stovey-Phi.......825
Browning-Lou.....816
Collins-Lou-Bro....796

Adjusted Production
Reilly-Cin........ 171
Browning-Lou.... 169
Stovey-Phi....... 169
Collins-Lou-Bro... 162
Burns-Bal-Bro.... 155

Batter Runs
Reilly-Cin....... 43.8
O'Neill-StL...... 41.7
Stovey-Phi...... 39.9
Collins-Lou-Bro... 34.7
Burns-Bal-Bro.... 29.8

Adjusted Batter Runs
Stovey-Phi...... 40.5
Reilly-Cin....... 40.1
Collins-Lou-Bro.. 36.3
O'Neill-StL...... 33.0
Burns-Bal-Bro.... 31.1

Clutch Hitting Index
Gleason-Phi...... 154
Smith-Bro........ 151
Fennelly-Cin-Phi.. 149
Gilks-Cle........ 144
Lyons-StL....... 142

Runs Created
Reilly-Cin........ 129
Stovey-Phi....... 124
Collins-Lou-Bro... 112
Welch-Phi........ 106
O'Neill-StL....... 105

Total Average
Reilly-Cin....... 1.064
Stovey-Phi...... 1.048
Collins-Lou-Bro....956
Robinson-StL.....934
Browning-Lou.....928

Stolen Bases
Latham-StL...... 109
Nicol-Cin........ 103
Welch-Phi......... 95
McCarthy-StL..... 93
Stovey-Phi........ 87

Stolen Base Average

Stolen Base Runs

Fielding Runs
Shindle-Bal......36.8
McPhee-Cin......31.3
McCarthy-StL.... 29.8
Davis-KC........ 29.8
Easterday-KC....26.4

Total Player Rating
Collins-Lou-Bro.... 4.1
Stovey-Phi....... 3.5
McPhee-Cin...... 3.4
McKean-Cle...... 3.1
Davis-KC......... 3.1

Wins
King-StL......... 45
Seward-Phi...... 35
Caruthers-Bro..... 29
Weyhing-Phi....... 28
Viau-Cin.......... 27

Win Percentage
Hudson-StL........714
Chamberlain-Lou-StL .694
King-StL..........682
Caruthers-Bro.....659
Viau-Cin..........659

Games
King-StL........ 66
Bakely-Cle........ 61
Seward-Phi...... 57
Porter-KC........ 55
Cunningham-Bal... 51

Complete Games
King-StL........ 64
Bakely-Cle........ 60
Seward-Phi...... 57
Porter-KC........ 53
Cunningham-Bal... 50

Shutouts
Seward-Phi....... 6
King-StL.......... 6
Smith-Cin......... 5
Hudson-StL........ 5

Saves
Mullane-Cin........ 1
Gilks-Cle.......... 1

Innings Pitched
King-StL........585.2
Bakely-Cle......532.2
Seward-Phi....518.2
Porter-KC.......474.0
Cunningham-Bal . 453.1

Fewest Hits/Game
Terry-Bro........ 6.69
King-StL......... 6.72
Seward-Phi...... 6.73
Chamberlain-Lou-StL 6.95
Hughes-Bro...... 6.97

Fewest BB/Game
King-StL......... 1.17
Caruthers-Bro..... 1.22
Hudson-StL...... 1.59
Ewing-Lou....... 1.60
Hecker-Lou...... 1.73

Strikeouts
Seward-Phi...... 272
King-StL........ 258
Ramsey-Lou..... 228
Bakely-Cle....... 212
Weyhing-Phi...... 204

Strikeouts/Game
Terry-Bro........ 6.37
Ramsey-Lou..... 5.99
Chamberlain-Lou-StL 5.14
Smith-Bal-Phi.... 4.90
Seward-Phi...... 4.72

Ratio
King-StL........ 7.88
Seward-Phi...... 8.94
Caruthers-Bro.... 8.96
Hudson-StL...... 9.24
Foutz-Bro....... 9.26

Earned Run Average
King-StL......... 1.64
Seward-Phi...... 2.01
Terry-Bro........ 2.03
Hughes-Bro...... 2.13
Chamberlain-Lou-StL 2.19

Adjusted ERA
King-StL........ 198
Seward-Phi...... 148
Terry-Bro........ 147
Chamberlain-Lou-StL 143
Hughes-Bro...... 140

Opponents' Batting Avg.
Terry-Bro.........200
King-StL..........200
Seward-Phi......201
Chamberlain-Lou-StL .206
Hughes-Bro......206

Opponents' On Base Pct.
King-StL..........227
Seward-Phi......250
Caruthers-Bro.....250
Hudson-StL......256
Foutz-Bro.........257

Starter Runs
King-StL......... 92.0
Seward-Phi...... 60.2
Hughes-Bro...... 37.3
Weyhing-Phi...... 36.3
Chamberlain-Lou-StL 29.7

Adjusted Starter Runs
King-StL........104.9
Seward-Phi...... 56.0
Hughes-Bro...... 34.1
Weyhing-Phi...... 33.0
Chamberlain-Lou-StL 32.4

Clutch Pitching Index
Hecker-Lou..... 108
Sullivan-KC...... 105
Ramsey-Lou..... 104
Terry-Bro........ 104
Bakely-Cle....... 103

Relief Runs

Adjusted Relief Runs

Relief Ranking

Total Pitcher Index
King-StL......... 11.8
Seward-Phi....... 5.2
Weyhing-Phi....... 3.6
Hudson-StL....... 3.5
Chamberlain-Lou-StL . 2.9

Total Baseball Ranking
King-StL......... 11.8
Seward-Phi....... 5.2
Collins-Lou-Bro.... 4.1
Caruthers-Bro..... 3.7
Weyhing-Phi....... 3.6

TEAM	G	W	L	PCT	GB	R	OR	AB	H	2B	3B	HR	BB	SO	AVG	OBP	SLG	PRO	PRO+	BR	/A	PF	CHI	RC	SB	CS	SBA	SBR
NY	131	83	43	.659	—	935	708	4671	1319	208	77	52	538	386	.282	.360	.393	.753	118	120	118	100	103	785	292			
BOS	133	83	45	.648	1	826	626	4628	1251	196	54	42	471	450	.270	.343	.363	.706	99	38	-8	106	102	707	331			
CHI	136	67	65	.508	19	867	814	4849	1274	184	66	79	518	516	.263	.338	.377	.715	102	48	7	105	101	716	243			
PHI	130	63	64	.496	20.5	742	748	4695	1248	215	52	44	393	353	.266	.327	.362	.689	91	0	-66	109	97	660	269			
PIT	134	61	71	.462	25	726	801	4748	1202	209	65	42	420	467	.253	.320	.351	.671	105	-31	43	90	97	622	231			
CLE	136	61	72	.459	25.5	656	720	4673	1167	131	59	25	429	417	.250	.318	.319	.637	86	-80	-65	98	95	563	237			
IND	135	59	75	.440	28	819	894	4879	1356	228	35	62	377	447	.278	.335	.377	.712	105	39	23	102	98	719	252			
WAS	127	41	83	.331	41	632	892	4395	1105	151	57	25	466	456	.251	.329	.329	.658	97	-37	7	94	91	566	232			
TOT	531					6203		37538	9922	1522	465	371	3612	3492	.264	.329	.359	.688						2087				

TEAM	CG	SH	SV	IP	H	H/G	HR	BB	SO	RAT	ERA	ERA+	OAV	OOB	PR	/A	PF	CPI	FA	E	DP	FW	PW	BW	SBW	DIF
NY	118	6	3	1151	1064	8.3	38	523	542	12.4	3.47	114	.237	.317	70	60	98	97	.920	437	90	-.3	5.2	10.2		4.9
BOS	121	10	4	1166	1152	8.9	41	413	497	12.1	3.36	124	.249	.311	86	105	104	102	.926	413	105	1.2	9.1	-.7		9.4
CHI	123	6	2	1237	1313	9.6	71	408	434	12.5	3.73	112	.263	.319	41	60	104	104	.923	463	91	-.8	5.2	.6		-4.0
PHI	106	4	2	1153¹	1288	10.1	33	428	443	13.4	4.00	109	.273	.333	2	45	108	101	.915	466	92	-2.0	3.9	-5.7		3.3
PIT	125	5	1	1130²	1296	10.3	42	374	345	13.3	4.51	83	.278	.332	-60	-94	93	92	.929	385	94	2.8	-8.1	3.7		-3.4
CLE	132	6	1	1191²	1182	8.9	36	519	435	12.8	3.66	110	.250	.324	47	49	100	99	.936	365	108	4.2	4.2	-5.6		-8.3
IND	109	3	2	1174¹	1365	10.5	73	420	408	13.7	4.85	86	.281	.338	-107	-87	104	93	.926	420	102	1.2	-7.5	2.0		-3.6
WAS	113	1	0	1103	1261	10.3	37	527	388	14.6	4.68	85	.278	.353	-79	-88	98	97	.905	519	91	-5.2	-7.6	.6		-8.8
TOT	947	41	15	9307		9.6				13.1	4.02		.264	.329					.923	3468	773					

Runs
Tiernan-NY 147
Duffy-Chi 144
Ryan-Chi 140
Gore-NY 132
Glasscock-Ind 128

Hits
Glasscock-Ind 205
Brouthers-Bos 181
Ryan-Chi 177
Duffy-Chi 172
VanHaltren-Chi ... 168

Doubles
Kelly-Bos 41
Glasscock-Ind 40
Thompson-Phi 36
O'Rourke-NY 36
Richardson-Bos ... 33

Triples
Wilmot-Was 19
Fogarty-Phi 17
Connor-NY 17
Tiernan-NY 14
Ryan-Chi 14

Home Runs
Thompson-Phi 20
Denny-Ind 18
Ryan-Chi 17
Connor-NY 13
Duffy-Chi 12

Total Bases
Ryan-Chi 287
Glasscock-Ind 272
Thompson-Phi 262
Connor-NY 262
Tiernan-NY 248

Runs Batted In
Connor-NY 130
Brouthers-Bos 118
Anson-Chi 117
Denny-Ind 112
Thompson-Phi 111

Runs Produced
Connor-NY 234
Duffy-Chi 221
Brouthers-Bos 216
Tiernan-NY 210
Anson-Chi 210

Bases On Balls
Tiernan-NY 96
Connor-NY 93
Radford-Cle 91
Anson-Chi 86
Carroll-Pit 85

Batting Average
Brouthers-Bos ... .373
Glasscock-Ind ... .352
Tiernan-NY ...... .335
Carroll-Pit ..... .330
Ewing-NY .... .327

On Base Percentage
Carroll-Pit ..... .486
Brouthers-Bos ... .462
Tiernan-NY ...... .447
Connor-NY .... .426
Gore-NY .... .416

Slugging Average
Connor-NY .... .528
Brouthers-Bos ... .507
Ryan-Chi .... .498
Tiernan-NY ...... .497
Thompson-Phi .... .492

Production
Carroll-Pit ...... .970
Brouthers-Bos .... .969
Connor-NY .... .955
Tiernan-NY .... .944
Ryan-Chi .... .886

Adjusted Production
Carroll-Pit 192
Connor-NY 168
Tiernan-NY 165
Brouthers-Bos 163
Wilmot-Was 147

Batter Runs
Brouthers-Bos ... 50.7
Tiernan-NY 48.3
Connor-NY 47.3
Carroll-Pit 38.7
Ryan-Chi 36.7

Adjusted Batter Runs
Tiernan-NY 48.1
Connor-NY 47.1
Brouthers-Bos ... 45.6
Carroll-Pit 44.6
Ryan-Chi 31.8

Clutch Hitting Index
Quinn-NY 144
Dunlap-Pit 144
Richardson-NY 144
Whitney-NY 144
Nash-Bos 138

Runs Created
Ryan-Chi 132
Glasscock-Ind 132
Tiernan-NY 129
Brouthers-Bos 127
Connor-NY 124

Total Average
Carroll-Pit 1.263
Tiernan-NY 1.151
Brouthers-Bos ... 1.145
Connor-NY 1.115
Ryan-Chi 1.023

Stolen Bases
Fogarty-Phi 99
Kelly-Bos 68
Brown-Bos 63
Ward-NY 62
Glasscock-Ind 57

Stolen Base Average

Stolen Base Runs

Fielding Runs
Glasscock-Ind ... 34.9
Pfeffer-Chi 20.6
Fogarty-Phi 17.5
Ewing-NY 14.7
Wilmot-Was 13.5

Total Player Rating
Glasscock-Ind 5.8
Tiernan-NY 3.4
Ewing-NY 3.2
Brouthers-Bos 3.2
Carroll-Pit 3.0

Wins
Clarkson-Bos 49
Keefe-NY 28
Buffinton-Phi 28
Welch-NY 27
Galvin-Pit 23

Win Percentage
Clarkson-Bos .... .721
Welch-NY .... .692
Keefe-NY .... .683
Radbourn-Bos .... .645
Buffinton-Phi ... .636

Games
Clarkson-Bos 73
Staley-Pit 49
Keefe-NY 47
Buffinton-Phi 47
Boyle-Ind 46

Complete Games
Clarkson-Bos 68
Staley-Pit 46
Welch-NY 39
O'Brien-Cle 39

Shutouts
Clarkson-Bos 8
Galvin-Pit 4

Saves
Sowders-Bos-Pit .. 2
Welch-NY 2
Bishop-Chi 2

Innings Pitched
Clarkson-Bos ... 620.0
Staley-Pit 420.0
Buffinton-Phi .. 380.0
Boyle-Ind 378.2
Welch-NY 375.0

Fewest Hits/Game
Keefe-NY 7.66
Welch-NY 8.16
Clarkson-Bos 8.55
Crane-NY 8.65
Hutchinson-Chi .. 8.66

Fewest BB/Game
Galvin-Pit 2.06
Boyle-Ind 2.26
Radbourn-Bos 2.34
Dwyer-Chi 2.35
Sanders-Phi 2.47

Strikeouts
Clarkson-Bos 284
Keefe-NY 209
Staley-Pit 159
Buffinton-Phi 153
Getzien-Ind 139

Strikeouts/Game
Keefe-NY 5.17
Crane-NY 5.09
Rusie-Ind 4.36
Healy-Was-Chi ... 4.35
Clarkson-Bos 4.12

Ratio
Keefe-NY 11.40
Clarkson-Bos ... 11.50
Radbourn-Bos ... 11.50
Welch-NY 11.74
Staley-Pit 11.76

Earned Run Average
Clarkson-Bos 2.73
Bakely-Cle 2.96
Welch-NY 3.02
Buffinton-Phi ... 3.24
Keefe-NY 3.31

Adjusted ERA
Clarkson-Bos 153
Bakely-Cle 136
Buffinton-Phi 134
Welch-NY 131
Sanders-Phi 123

Opponents' Batting Avg.
Keefe-NY .... .223
Welch-NY .... .234
Clarkson-Bos .... .243
Crane-NY .... .245
Hutchinson-Chi .. .245

Opponents' On Base Pct.
Keefe-NY .... .299
Clarkson-Bos .... .301
Radbourn-Bos .... .301
Welch-NY .... .305
Staley-Pit ...... .306

Starter Runs
Clarkson-Bos 89.2
Welch-NY 41.7
Bakely-Cle 36.1
Buffinton-Phi ... 32.9
Keefe-NY 28.7

Adjusted Starter Runs
Clarkson-Bos 99.4
Buffinton-Phi ... 47.0
Welch-NY 38.5
Bakely-Cle 36.5
Sanders-Phi 31.3

Clutch Pitching Index
Casey-Phi 114
Clarkson-Bos 113
Sanders-Phi 112
Bakely-Cle 111
Crane-NY 109

Relief Runs

Adjusted Relief Runs

Relief Ranking

Total Pitcher Index
Clarkson-Bos 10.4
Buffinton-Phi ... 4.3
Sanders-Phi 3.4
Bakely-Cle 3.4
Welch-NY 3.0

Total Baseball Ranking
Clarkson-Bos 10.4
Glasscock-Ind ... 5.8
Buffinton-Phi ... 4.3
Sanders-Phi 3.4
Tiernan-NY 3.4

TEAM	G	W	L	PCT	GB	R	OR	AB	H	2B	3B	HR	BB	SO	AVG	OBP	SLG	PRO	PRO+	BR	/A	PF	CHI	RC	SB	CS	SBA	SBR
BRO	140	93	44	.679		995	706	4815	1265	188	79	47	550	401	.263	.344	.364	.708	107	60	57	100	109	756	389			
STL	141	90	45	.667	2	957	680	4939	1312	211	64	58	493	477	.266	.339	.370	.709	95	56	-56	113	104	751	336			
PHI	138	75	58	.564	16	880	787	4868	1339	239	65	43	534	496	.275	.354	.377	.731	116	103	115	99	91	758	252			
CIN	141	76	63	.547	18	897	769	4844	1307	197	96	52	452	511	.270	.340	.382	.722	108	74	49	103	98	806	462			
BAL	139	70	65	.519	22	791	795	4756	1209	155	68	20	418	536	.254	.325	.328	.653	90	-37	-51	102	100	624	311			
COL	140	60	78	.435	33.5	779	924	4816	1247	171	95	36	507	609	.259	.335	.356	.691	108	26	68	95	90	693	304			
KC	139	55	82	.401	38	852	1031	4947	1256	162	76	18	430	626	.254	.322	.328	.650	86	-47	-96	106	105	692	472			
LOU	140	27	111	.196	66.5	632	1091	4955	1249	170	75	22	320	521	.252	.303	.330	.633	87	-90	-72	98	85	571	203			
TOT	559					6783		38940	10184	1493	618	296	3704	4177	.262	.326	.354	.680							2729			

TEAM	CG	SH	SV	IP	H	H/G	HR	BB	SO	RAT	ERA	ERA+	OAV	OOB	PR	/A	PF	CPI	FA	E	DP	FW	PW	BW	SBW	DIF
BRO	120	10	1	1212²	1205	8.9	33	400	471	11.9	3.61	103	.251	.309	30	14	97	91	.928	421	92	4.6	1.2	4.8		13.9
STL	121	7	3	1237²	1166	8.5	39	413	617	11.5	3.00	141	.241	.301	115	166	110	102	.925	438	100	3.8	14.0	-4.7		9.4
PHI	130	9	1	1199¹	1200	9.0	35	509	479	12.8	3.53	107	.252	.325	42	32	98	102	.920	465	120	1.7	2.7	9.7		-5.6
CIN	114	3	8	1243	1270	9.2	35	475	562	12.6	3.50	111	.256	.321	46	53	101	102	.926	440	121	3.7	4.5	4.1		-5.8
BAL	128	10	1	1192	1168	8.8	27	424	540	12.0	3.56	111	.249	.311	38	49	103	91	.907	536	104	-2.1	4.1	-4.3		4.7
COL	114	9	4	1199	1274	9.6	33	551	610	13.7	4.39	82	.264	.339	-72	-103	94	91	.915	497	92	.3	-8.7	5.8		-6.4
KC	128	0	2	1204¹	1373	10.3	51	457	447	13.7	4.36	96	.278	.339	-68	-24	109	98	.899	611	109	-6.3	-2.0	-8.1		2.9
LOU	127	2	1	1226¹	1529	11.2	43	475	451	14.7	4.81	80	.296	.356	-132	-133	100	99	.906	584	117	-4.5	-11.3	-6.1		-20.1
TOT	982	50	21	9714¹		9.4				12.9	3.84		.262	.326					.916	3992	855					

Runs
Stovey-Phi 152
Griffin-Bal 152
O'Brien-Bro 146
Hamilton-KC 144
Collins-Bro 139

Hits
Tucker-Bal 196
Orr-Col 183
Holliday-Cin 181
O'Neill-StL 179
Shindle-Bal 178

Doubles
Welch-Phi 39
Stovey-Phi 38
Lyons-Phi 36
O'Neill-StL 33
Long-KC 32

Triples
Marr-Col 15
Griffin-Bal 14
Beard-Cin 14

Home Runs
Stovey-Phi 19
Holliday-Cin 19
Duffee-StL 15
Milligan-StL 12

Total Bases
Stovey-Phi 292
Holliday-Cin 280
Tucker-Bal 255
O'Neill-StL 255
Orr-Col 250

Runs Batted In
Stovey-Phi 119
Foutz-Bro 113
O'Neill-StL 110
Bierbauer-Phi 105
Holliday-Cin 104

Runs Produced
Stovey-Phi 252
Foutz-Bro 225
O'Neill-StL 224
O'Brien-Bro 221
Hamilton-KC 218

Bases On Balls
Robinson-StL 118
McTamany-Col . . . 116
Griffin-Bal 91
Marr-Col 87
Hamilton-KC 87

Batting Average
Tucker-Bal 372
O'Neill-StL 335
Lyons-Phi 329
Orr-Col 327
Holliday-Cin 321

On Base Percentage
Tucker-Bal 450
Larkin-Phi 428
Lyons-Phi 426
O'Neill-StL 419
Hamilton-KC 413

Slugging Average
Stovey-Phi 525
Holliday-Cin 497
Tucker-Bal 484
O'Neill-StL 478
Lyons-Phi 469

Production
Tucker-Bal 934
Stovey-Phi 918
O'Neill-StL 897
Lyons-Phi 895
Holliday-Cin 869

Adjusted Production
Tucker-Bal 166
Stovey-Phi 165
Lyons-Phi 160
Larkin-Phi 148
Holliday-Cin 145

Batter Runs
Tucker-Bal 49.8
Stovey-Phi 44.6
O'Neill-StL 41.7
Lyons-Phi 41.0
Larkin-Phi 36.0

Adjusted Batter Runs
Tucker-Bal 48.2
Stovey-Phi 46.1
Lyons-Phi 42.4
Larkin-Phi 37.4
Marr-Col 34.7

Clutch Hitting Index
Hornung-Bal 149
Robinson-StL 144
Mack-Bal 141
Foutz-Bro 139
Manning-KC 136

Runs Created
Tucker-Bal 147
Stovey-Phi 143
Hamilton-KC 136
O'Brien-Bro 129
Holliday-Cin 124

Total Average
Tucker-Bal 1.187
Hamilton-KC 1.134
Stovey-Phi 1.125
O'Brien-Bro 1.020
O'Neill-StL 1.014

Stolen Bases
Hamilton-KC 111
O'Brien-Bro 91
Long-KC 89
Nicol-Cin 80
Latham-StL 69

Stolen Base Average

Stolen Base Runs

Fielding Runs
McPhee-Cin 41.1
Bierbauer-Phi 36.5
Long-KC 32.2
Tomney-Lou 26.7
Shindle-Bal 20.3

Total Player Rating
Stovey-Phi 4.9
Lyons-Phi 4.3
Bierbauer-Phi 4.3
Marr-Col 3.9
Milligan-StL 3.9

Wins
Caruthers-Bro 40
King-StL 35
Duryea-Cin 32
Chamberlain-StL . . . 32
Weyhing-Phi 30

Win Percentage
Caruthers-Bro 784
King-StL 686
Chamberlain-StL . . .681
Lovett-Bro 630
Duryea-Cin 627

Games
Baldwin-Col 63
Kilroy-Bal 59
King-StL 56
Caruthers-Bro 56
Weyhing-Phi 54

Complete Games
Kilroy-Bal 55
Baldwin-Col 54
Weyhing-Phi 50
King-StL 47
Caruthers-Bro 46

Shutouts
Caruthers-Bro 7
Baldwin-Col 6
Kilroy-Bal 5
Foreman-Bal 5
Weyhing-Phi 4

Saves
Mullane-Cin 5

Innings Pitched
Baldwin-Col 513.2
Kilroy-Bal 480.2
King-StL 458.0
Weyhing-Phi 449.0
Caruthers-Bro . . . 445.0

Fewest Hits/Game
Stivetts-StL 7.18
Weyhing-Phi 7.66
Terry-Bro 7.87
Foreman-Bal 7.91
Baldwin-Col 8.02

Fewest BB/Game
Caruthers-Bro 2.10
Conway-KC 2.42
King-StL 2.46
Lovett-Bro 2.55
Swartzel-KC 2.57

Strikeouts
Baldwin-Col 368
Kilroy-Bal 217
Weyhing-Phi 213
Chamberlain-StL . . 202
King-StL 188

Strikeouts/Game
Stivetts-StL 6.71
Baldwin-Col 6.45
Terry-Bro 5.13
Sowders-KC 5.06
Gastright-Col 4.65

Ratio
Stivetts-StL 10.38
Foreman-Bal 10.89
Caruthers-Bro . . . 11.08
Duryea-Cin 11.20
Terry-Bro 11.35

Earned Run Average
Stivetts-StL 2.25
Duryea-Cin 2.56
Kilroy-Bal 2.85
Weyhing-Phi 2.95
Chamberlain-StL . . 2.97

Adjusted ERA
Stivetts-StL 187
Duryea-Cin 152
Chamberlain-StL . . 142
Kilroy-Bal 138
King-StL 134

Opponents' Batting Avg.
Stivetts-StL 212
Weyhing-Phi 223
Terry-Bro 228
Foreman-Bal 229
Baldwin-Col 231

Opponents' On Base Pct.
Stivetts-StL 280
Foreman-Bal 290
Caruthers-Bro 294
Duryea-Cin 296
Terry-Bro 299

Starter Runs
Duryea-Cin 57.3
Kilroy-Bal 53.3
Weyhing-Phi 44.8
Chamberlain-StL . . 41.1
King-StL 35.6

Adjusted Starter Runs
Duryea-Cin 59.5
Chamberlain-StL . . 58.7
Kilroy-Bal 58.4
King-StL 54.8
Stivetts-StL 41.9

Clutch Pitching Index
Mullane-Cin 114
Duryea-Cin 112
Kilroy-Bal 108
Hughes-Bro 107
Smith-Cin 107

Relief Runs

Adjusted Relief Runs

Relief Ranking

Total Pitcher Index
Kilroy-Bal 7.1
Duryea-Cin 6.0
Chamberlain-StL . . 5.1
King-StL 5.0
Caruthers-Bro 4.3

Total Baseball Ranking
Kilroy-Bal 7.1
Duryea-Cin 6.0
Chamberlain-StL . . 5.1
King-StL 5.0
Stovey-Phi 4.9

TEAM	G	W	L	PCT	GB	R	OR	AB	H	2B	3B	HR	BB	SO	AVG	OBP	SLG	PRO	PRO+	BR	/A	PF	CHI	RC	SB	CS	SBA	SBR
BRO	129	86	43	.667		884	620	4419	1166	184	75	43	517	361	.264	.346	.369	.715	114	90	87	100	110	702	349			
CHI	139	84	53	.613	6	847	692	4891	1271	147	59	67	516	514	.260	.336	.355	.691	103	54	22	104	101	712	329			
PHI	133	78	54	.591	9.5	823	707	4707	1267	220	78	23	522	403	.269	.350	.364	.714	112	96	76	103	96	735	335			
CIN	134	77	55	.583	10.5	753	633	4644	1204	150	120	27	433	377	.259	.329	.361	.690	108	42	45	100	97	670	312			
BOS	134	76	57	.571	12	763	593	4722	1220	175	62	31	530	515	.258	.342	.341	.683	98	46	-15	108	94	665	285			
NY	135	63	68	.481	24	713	698	4832	1250	208	89	25	350	478	.259	.315	.354	.669	100	1	0	100	95	647	289			
CLE	136	44	88	.333	43.5	630	832	4633	1073	132	59	21	497	474	.232	.312	.299	.611	85	-79	-64	98	95	491	152			
PIT	138	23	113	.169	66.5	597	1235	4739	1088	160	43	20	408	458	.230	.300	.294	.594	89	-116	-29	88	94	492	208			
TOT	539					6010		37587	9539	1376	585	257	3773	3580	.254	.322	.342	.664							2259			

TEAM	CG	SH	SV	IP	H	H/G	HR	BB	SO	RAT	ERA	ERA+	OAV	OOB	PR	/A	PF	CPI	FA	E	DP	FW	PW	BW	SBW	DIF
BRO	115	6	2	1145	1102	8.7	27	401	403	11.8	3.06	112	.245	.307	64	47	96	100	.940	320	92	4.5	4.2	7.7		5.1
CHI	126	6	3	1237¹	1103	8.0	41	481	504	11.5	3.24	113	.231	.302	43	55	103	89	.940	344	89	4.9	4.9	2.0		3.8
PHI	122	9	2	1194²	1210	9.1	22	486	507	12.8	3.32	110	.255	.324	31	43	102	103	.929	398	122	.4	3.8	6.8		1.0
CIN	124	9	1	1190²	1097	8.3	42	407	488	11.4	2.79	127	.237	.299	102	100	100	105	.933	382	106	1.6	8.9	4.0		-3.5
BOS	132	13	1	1187	1132	8.6	27	354	506	11.3	2.93	128	.243	.297	82	107	105	98	.935	359	77	3.0	9.5	-1.3		-1.7
NY	115	6	1	1177	1029	7.9	14	607	612	12.5	3.06	114	.228	.319	65	56	98	98	.921	449	104	-2.3	5.0	.0		-5.1
CLE	129	2	0	1184¹	1322	10.0	32	464	303	13.6	4.13	86	.274	.337	-75	-73	100	96	.930	405	108	.6	-6.5	-5.7		-10.4
PIT	119	3	0	1176¹	1520	11.6	52	573	381	16.0	5.97	55	.304	.375	-314	-350	92	88	.897	607	94	-11.5-31.1		-2.6		.1
TOT	982	54	10	9492¹		9.0				12.6	3.56		.254	.322					.928	3264	792					

Runs		Hits		Doubles		Triples		Home Runs		Total Bases	
Collins-Bro	148	Thompson-Phi	172	Thompson-Phi	41	Reilly-Cin	26	Wilmot-Chi	13	Tiernan-NY	274
Carroll-Chi	134	Glasscock-NY	172	Glasscock-NY	32	McPhee-Cin	22	Tiernan-NY	13	Reilly-Cin	261
Hamilton-Phi	133	Tiernan-NY	168	Collins-Bro	32	Tiernan-NY	21	Burns-Bro	13	Thompson-Phi	243
Tiernan-NY	132	Reilly-Cin	166	Myers-Phi	29	Beard-Cin	15	Long-Bos	8	Wilmot-Chi	237
McPhee-Cin	125	Carroll-Chi	166	O'Brien-Bro	28					Glasscock-NY	225

Runs Batted In		Runs Produced		Bases On Balls		Batting Average		On Base Percentage		Slugging Average	
Burns-Bro	128	Burns-Bro	217	Anson-Chi	113	Glasscock-NY	.336	Anson-Chi	.443	Tiernan-NY	.495
Anson-Chi	107	Thompson-Phi	214	McKean-Cle	87	Hamilton-Phi	.325	Hamilton-Phi	.430	Clements-Phi	.472
Thompson-Phi	102	Collins-Bro	214	Allen-Phi	87	Clements-Phi	.315	Pinkney-Bro	.411	Reilly-Cin	.472
Wilmot-Chi	99	Wilmot-Chi	200	Collins-Bro	85	Thompson-Phi	.313	McKean-Cle	.401	Burns-Bro	.464
Foutz-Bro	98	Foutz-Bro	199	Hamilton-Phi	83	Knight-Cin	.312	Glasscock-NY	.395	Burkett-NY	.461

Production		Adjusted Production		Batter Runs		Adjusted Batter Runs		Clutch Hitting Index		Runs Created	
Tiernan-NY	.880	Tiernan-NY	158	Tiernan-NY	39.8	Tiernan-NY	39.6	Burns-Bro	144	Hamilton-Phi	132
Clements-Phi	.864	Clements-Phi	150	Anson-Chi	39.3	Anson-Chi	35.7	Mayer-Phi	142	Tiernan-NY	130
Anson-Chi	.844	Pinkney-Bro	148	Hamilton-Phi	33.3	McKean-Cle	32.5	Anson-Chi	139	Wilmot-Chi	113
Pinkney-Bro	.842	Glasscock-NY	145	Pinkney-Bro	32.5	Pinkney-Bro	32.1	Hornung-NY	139	Glasscock-NY	113
Glasscock-NY	.834	McKean-Cle	144	McKean-Cle	30.8	Hamilton-Phi	31.2	Clarke-NY	134	Collins-Bro	111

Total Average		Stolen Bases		Stolen Base Average	Stolen Base Runs	Fielding Runs		Total Player Rating	
Hamilton-Phi	1.170	Hamilton-Phi	102			Allen-Phi	39.3	McPhee-Cin	4.4
Tiernan-NY	1.047	Collins-Bro	85			McPhee-Cin	30.3	Glasscock-NY	4.1
Pinkney-Bro	1.015	Sunday-Pit-Phi	84			Glasscock-NY	20.2	Allen-Phi	3.4
Anson-Chi	1.009	Wilmot-Chi	76			Smalley-Cle	18.2	Hamilton-Phi	2.7
Collins-Bro	1.005	Tiernan-NY	56			Myers-Phi	14.4	Clements-Phi	2.7

Wins		Win Percentage		Games		Complete Games		Shutouts		Saves	
W.Hutchinson-Chi	42	Lovett-Bro	.732	W.Hutchinson-Chi	71	W.Hutchinson-Chi	65	Nichols-Bos	7	W.Hutchinson-Chi	2
Gleason-Phi	38	Gleason-Phi	.691	Rusie-NY	67	Rusie-NY	56	Rhines-Cin	6	Gleason-Phi	2
Lovett-Bro	30	Luby-Chi	.690	Gleason-Phi	60	Gleason-Phi	54	Gleason-Phi	6	Foutz-Bro	2
Rusie-NY	29	Caruthers-Bro	.676	Beatin-Cle	54	Beatin-Cle	53	W.Hutchinson-Chi	5		
Rhines-Cin	28	W.Hutchinson-Chi	.627	Nichols-Bos	48	Nichols-Bos	47				

Innings Pitched		Fewest Hits/Game		Fewest BB/Game		Strikeouts		Strikeouts/Game		Ratio	
W.Hutchinson-Chi	603.0	Rusie-NY	7.15	Young-Cle	1.95	Rusie-NY	341	Rusie-NY	5.59	Rhines-Cin	10.09
Rusie-NY	548.2	Mullane-Cin	7.54	Duryea-Cin	1.97	W.Hutchinson-Chi	289	Nichols-Bos	4.71	Nichols-Bos	10.32
Gleason-Phi	506.0	W.Hutchinson-Chi	7.54	Getzien-Bos	2.11	Nichols-Bos	222	Terry-Bro	4.50	W.Hutchinson-Chi	10.51
Beatin-Cle	474.1	Rhines-Cin	7.56	Nichols-Bos	2.38	Gleason-Phi	222	W.Hutchinson-Chi	4.31	Young-Cle	10.79
Nichols-Bos	424.0	Luby-Chi	7.60	Rhines-Cin	2.53	Terry-Bro	185	Sharrott-NY	4.11	Luby-Chi	10.79

Earned Run Average		Adjusted ERA		Opponents' Batting Avg.		Opponents' On Base Pct.		Starter Runs		Adjusted Starter Runs	
Rhines-Cin	1.95	Rhines-Cin	182	Rusie-NY	.212	Rhines-Cin	.275	Rhines-Cin	71.8	Nichols-Bos	71.3
Nichols-Bos	2.23	Nichols-Bos	168	Mullane-Cin	.221	Nichols-Bos	.279	Nichols-Bos	62.8	Rhines-Cin	71.3
Mullane-Cin	2.24	Mullane-Cin	159	W.Hutchinson-Chi	.221	W.Hutchinson-Chi	.283	Rusie-NY	61.1	W.Hutchinson-Chi	63.6
Rusie-NY	2.56	Gleason-Phi	139	Rhines-Cin	.221	Young-Cle	.289	W.Hutchinson-Chi	57.6	Gleason-Phi	57.0
Gleason-Phi	2.63	Rusie-NY	137	Luby-Chi	.222	Luby-Chi	.289	Gleason-Phi	52.2	Rusie-NY	57.0

Clutch Pitching Index		Relief Runs	Adjusted Relief Runs	Relief Ranking	Total Pitcher Index		Total Baseball Ranking	
Mullane-Cin	126				Nichols-Bos	7.0	Nichols-Bos	7.0
Vickery-Phi	113				Rusie-NY	6.8	Rusie-NY	6.8
Rhines-Cin	112				Rhines-Cin	6.4	Rhines-Cin	6.4
Gleason-Phi	109				W.Hutchinson-Chi	6.0	W.Hutchinson-Chi	6.0
Nichols-Bos	107				Gleason-Phi	4.8	Gleason-Phi	4.8

TEAM	G	W	L	PCT	GB	R	OR	AB	H	2B	3B	HR	BB	SO	AVG	OBP	SLG	PRO	PRO+	BR	/A	PF	CHI	RC	SB	CS	SBA	SBR
LOU	136	88	44	.667		819	**588**	4687	**1310**	156	65	15	410	**460**	**.279**	.344	.350	.694	115	71	88	98	99	698	341			
COL	140	79	55	.590	10	831	617	4741	1225	159	77	16	**545**	557	.258	.340	.335	.675	114	49	**102**	93	**100**	677	353			
STL	139	78	58	.574	12	**870**	736	4800	1308	178	73	48	474	490	.273	**.349**	**.370**	**.719**	105	119	8	114	96	**746**	307			
TOL	134	68	64	.515	20	739	689	4575	1152	152	**108**	24	486	558	.252	.331	.348	.679	105	45	24	103	93	683	**421**			
ROC	133	63	63	.500	22	709	711	4553	1088	131	64	31	446	538	.239	.314	.316	.630	100	-33	22	93	**100**	564	310			
BAL	38	15	19	.441	24	182	192	1213	278	34	16	2	125	152	.229	.315	.289	.604	81	-18	-26	105	**100**	145	101			
SYR	128	55	72	.433	30.5	698	831	4469	1158	151	59	14	457	482	.259	.332	.329	.661	112	18	87	90	94	600	292			
PHI	132	54	78	.409	34	702	945	4490	1057	**181**	51	24	475	540	.235	.320	.314	.634	96	-22	-2	97	98	563	305			
BRO	100	26	73	.263	45.5	492	733	3475	769	116	47	13	328	456	.221	.294	.293	.587	82	-82	-62	97	103	362	182			
TOT	540					6042		37003	9345	1258	560	187	3746	4233	.253	.321	.332	.653							2612			

TEAM	CG	SH	SV	IP	H	H/G	HR	BB	SO	RAT	ERA	ERA+	OAV	OOB	PR	/A	PF	CPI	FA	E	DP	FW	PW	BW	SBW	DIF
LOU	114	13	7	1206	1120	8.4	18	293	587	10.5	2.57	149	.239	.284	172	169	100	113	.934	380	79	2.8	14.9	7.7		-3.4
COL	120	14	3	1214^{2}	976	7.2	20	471	624	10.7	2.99	120	.213	.287	118	79	93	90	.932	396	101	2.6	7.0	9.0		-6.5
STL	118	4	1	1195^{1}	1127	8.5	38	447	733	11.9	3.67	117	.242	.308	25	82	112	94	.916	478	93	-1.8	7.2	.7		3.9
TOL	122	4	2	1159^{1}	1122	8.7	23	429	533	12.0	3.56	111	.246	.311	38	48	102	98	.925	419	75	.4	4.2	2.1		-4.8
ROC	122	5	2	1161^{2}	1115	8.6	19	530	477	12.7	3.56	100	.245	.324	38	-2	92	103	.926	416	95	.4	-.2	1.9		-2.2
BAL	36	1	0	315^{1}	307	8.8	3	123	134	12.3	4.00	101	.247	.315	-4	1	105	87	.928	109	21	.6	.0	-2.3		-.4
SYR	115	5	0	1089^{2}	1158	9.6	28	518	454	13.8	4.98	71	.264	.342	-135	-173	92	86	.925	391	90	.9	-15.2	7.7		-1.8
PHI	119	3	2	1132	1405	11.2	17	514	461	15.3	5.22	73	.295	.364	-171	-177	99	96	.918	452	93	-1.6	-15.6	-.2		5.3
BRO	96	0	0	879	1011	10.4	21	421	230	14.7	4.71	83	.280	.355	-82	-81	101	100	.909	404	92	-4.4	-7.1	-5.5		-6.5
TOT	962	49	17	9353		9.0				12.6	3.86		.253	.321					.923	3445	739					

Runs	Hits	Doubles	Triples	Home Runs	Total Bases
McTamany-Col ... 140	Wolf-Lou........ 197	Childs-Syr 33	Werden-Tol........ 20	Campau-StL 9	Wolf-Lou........ 260
McCarthy-StL 137	McCarthy-StL 192	Wolf-Lou.......... 29	Johnson-Col 18	Cartwright-StL 8	McCarthy-StL 256
Fuller-StL 118	Johnson-Col 186	Lyons-Phi.......... 29	Alvord-Tol......... 16	Stivetts-StL 7	Johnson-Col 248
Sneed-Tol-Col 117	Childs-Syr 170		Sneed-Tol-Col 15	Lyons-Phi.......... 7	Childs-Syr 237
Welch-Phi-Bal 116	Taylor-Lou 169				Werden-Tol....... 227

Runs Batted In	Runs Produced	Bases On Balls	Batting Average	On Base Percentage	Slugging Average
McTamany-Col ... 139		McTamany-Col ... 112	Wolf-Lou.........363	Lyons-Phi.........458	Lyons-Phi........531
McCarthy-StL 131		Crooks-Col 96	Lyons-Phi.........354	Swartwood-Tol 442	Childs-Syr 481
Fuller-StL 117		Swartwood-Tol 80	McCarthy-StL 350	Childs-Syr 434	Wolf-Lou........479
Sneed-Tol-Col 115		Werden-Tol........ 78	Johnson-Col 346	McCarthy-StL 430	McCarthy-StL 467
Taylor-Lou 115		Scheffler-Roc 78	Childs-Syr 345	Wright-Syr 427	Johnson-Col 461

Production	Adjusted Production	Batter Runs	Adjusted Batter Runs	Clutch Hitting Index	Runs Created
Lyons-Phi........989	Lyons-Phi........ 200	McCarthy-StL 47.6	Childs-Syr 54.6		McCarthy-StL 150
Childs-Syr 915	Childs-Syr 191	Childs-Syr 46.5	Wolf-Lou......... 46.6		Wolf-Lou........ 132
Wolf-Lou........898	Wolf-Lou........ 172	Wolf-Lou......... 44.6	Johnson-Col 45.3		Childs-Syr 130
McCarthy-StL 898	Johnson-Col 171	Lyons-Phi........ 42.0	Lyons-Phi........ 43.6		Johnson-Col 122
Swartwood-Tol 885	Swartwood-Tol ... 160	Swartwood-Tol ... 41.7	Swartwood-Tol ... 39.5		Werden-Tol....... 118

Total Average	Stolen Bases	Stolen Base Average	Stolen Base Runs	Fielding Runs	Total Player Rating
Lyons-Phi.......1.215	McCarthy-StL 83			Gerhardt-Bro-StL . 41.5	Childs-Syr 6.1
McCarthy-StL 1.169	Scheffler-Roc 77			Reilly-Col 28.2	Lyons-Phi........ 4.4
Childs-Syr 1.149	VanDyke-Tol 73			Ely-Syr 19.4	O'Connor-Col 4.1
Swartwood-Tol ...1.135	Welch-Phi-Bal 72			Tomney-Lou...... 17.6	Swartwood-Tol ... 3.5
Werden-Tol......1.071				Welch-Phi-Bal 15.7	Wolf-Lou......... 3.3

Wins	Win Percentage	Games	Complete Games	Shutouts	Saves
McMahon-Phi-Bal .. 36	Stratton-Lou 708	McMahon-Phi-Bal .. 60	McMahon-Phi-Bal .. 55	Chamberlain-StL-Col 6	Goodall-Lou........ 4
Stratton-Lou 34	Chamberlain-StL-Col .682	Barr-Roc 57	Barr-Roc 52	Stratton-Lou 4	Knauss-Col 2
Gastright-Col 30	Gastright-Col 682	Stivetts-StL 54	Stratton-Lou 44	Gastright-Col 4	Ehret-Lou 2
Barr-Roc 28	Ehret-Lou........641	Stratton-Lou 50	Healy-Tol 44	Ehret-Lou 4	
Stivetts-StL 27	McMahon-Phi-Bal .632	Gastright-Col 48			

Innings Pitched	Fewest Hits/Game	Fewest BB/Game	Strikeouts	Strikeouts/Game	Ratio
McMahon-Phi-Bal 509.0	Knauss-Col 6.73	Stratton-Lou 1.27	McMahon-Phi-Bal . 291	Ramsey-StL...... 6.63	Stratton-Lou 9.58
Barr-Roc 493.1	Gastright-Col 7.00	Ehret-Lou 1.98	Stivetts-StL 289	Stivetts-StL 6.20	Gastright-Col 10.02
Stratton-Lou 431.0	Easton-Col 7.50	Ramsey-StL 2.63	Ramsey-StL 257	Meakim-Lou 5.77	Knauss-Col 10.19
Stivetts-StL 419.1	Chamberlain-StL-Col 7.50	Smith-Tol 2.83	Healy-Tol 225	Chamberlain-StL-Col 5.49	Healy-Tol 10.48
Gastright-Col 401.1	Healy-Tol 7.54	McMahon-Phi-Bal 2.94	Barr-Roc 209	Healy-Tol 5.21	Ehret-Lou....... 10.78

Earned Run Average	Adjusted ERA	Opponents' Batting Avg.	Opponents' On Base Pct.	Starter Runs	Adjusted Starter Runs
Stratton-Lou 2.36	Stratton-Lou 163	Knauss-Col 202	Stratton-Lou 265	Stratton-Lou 72.0	Stratton-Lou 71.1
Ehret-Lou 2.53	Ehret-Lou........ 152	Gastright-Col 208	Gastright-Col 274	Ehret-Lou 53.1	Ehret-Lou 52.3
Knauss-Col 2.81	Healy-Tol 136	Easton-Col 220	Knauss-Col 277	Healy-Tol 42.0	Healy-Tol 45.5
Chamberlain-StL-Col 2.83	Meakim-Lou 132	Chamberlain-StL-Col .220	Healy-Tol 283	Gastright-Col..... 41.3	Stivetts-StL 36.7
Healy-Tol 2.89	Chamberlain-StL-Col 131	Healy-Tol 221	Ehret-Lou 288	Barr-Roc 33.8	McMahon-Phi-Bal 33.4

Clutch Pitching Index	Relief Runs	Adjusted Relief Runs	Relief Ranking	Total Pitcher Index	Total Baseball Ranking
Ehret-Lou........ 121				Stratton-Lou 9.1	Stratton-Lou 9.1
Titcomb-Roc 116				Stivetts-StL 5.9	Childs-Syr 6.1
Daily-Bro-Lou 108				Healy-Tol......... 4.7	Stivetts-StL 5.9
Stratton-Lou 107				Ehret-Lou......... 4.4	Healy-Tol 4.7
Chamberlain-StL-Col 107				McMahon-Phi-Bal .. 3.9	Lyons-Phi......... 4.4

TEAM	G	W	L	PCT	GB	R	OR	AB	H	2B	3B	HR	BB	SO	AVG	OBP	SLG	PRO	PRO+	BR	/A	PF	CHI	RC	SB	CS	SBA	SBR
BOS	130	81	48	.628		992	767	4626	1306	223	76	54	652	435	.282	.376	.398	.774	106	105	44	107	99	869	412			
BRO	133	76	56	.576	6.5	964	893	4887	1354	186	93	34	502	369	.277	.349	.374	.723	94	4	-52	106	104	752	272			
NY	132	74	57	.565	8	1018	875	4913	1393	204	97	66	486	364	.284	.352	.405	.757	100	56	-24	109	104	800	231			
CHI	138	75	62	.547	10	886	770	4968	1311	200	95	31	492	410	.264	.335	.361	.696	89	-48	-86	104	100	712	276			
PHI	132	68	63	.519	14	941	855	4855	1348	187	113	49	431	321	.278	.343	.393	.736	100	16	-4	102	102	742	203			
PIT	128	60	68	.469	20.5	835	892	4577	1192	168	113	35	569	375	.260	.349	.369	.718	107	0	72	92	95	694	249			
CLE	131	55	75	.423	26.5	849	1027	4804	1373	213	94	27	509	345	.286	.360	.386	.746	115	47	121	92	89	751	180			
BUF	134	36	96	.273	46.5	793	1199	4795	1249	180	64	20	541	367	.260	.347	.337	.684	98	-52	24	92	91	632	160			
TOT	529					7278		38425	10526	1561	745	316	4182	2986	.274	.345	.378	.723							1983			

TEAM	CG	SH	SV	IP	H	H/G	HR	BB	SO	RAT	ERA	ERA+	OAV	OOB	PR	/A	PF	CPI	FA	E	DP	FW	PW	BW	SBW	DIF
BOS	105	6	2	1137¹	1291	10.2	49	467	345	13.9	3.79	116	.273	.339	55	75	104	107	.918	460	109	1.7	6.0	3.5		5.3
BRO	111	4	7	1184	1334	10.1	26	570	377	14.5	3.95	113	.272	.348	37	65	105	103	.909	531	114	-1.8	5.2	-4.1		10.7
NY	111	3	6	1172¹	1219	9.4	37	569	449	13.7	4.17	109	.257	.336	7	47	107	89	.921	450	94	2.8	3.8	-1.9		3.9
CHI	124	5	2	1219¹	1238	9.1	27	503	460	12.9	3.39	128	.252	.321	113	128	103	97	.918	492	107	1.6	10.2	-6.9		1.5
PHI	118	4	2	1154¹	1292	10.1	33	495	361	13.9	4.05	105	.271	.339	22	27	101	97	.910	510	118	-.7	2.2	-.3		1.4
PIT	121	7	0	1116²	1267	10.2	32	334	318	12.9	4.22	93	.273	.322	1	-39	92	86	.907	512	80	-1.7	-3.1	5.7		-4.9
CLE	115	1	0	1143²	1386	10.9	45	571	325	15.4	4.23	94	.287	.362	0	-32	94	110	.907	533	103	-2.3	-2.6	9.7		-14.8
BUF	125	2	0	1141	1499	11.8	67	673	351	17.1	6.11	67	.304	.387	-238	-256	97	91	.914	491	116	.8	-20.4	1.9		-12.3
TOT	930	32	19	9268²		10.2				14.3	4.23		.274	.345					.913	3979	841					

Runs		Hits		Doubles		Triples		Home Runs		Total Bases	
Duffy-Chi	161	Duffy-Chi	191	Browning-Cle	40	Visner-Pit	22	Connor-NY	14	Shindle-Phi	281
Brown-Bos	146	Ward-Bro	189	Beckley-Pit	38	Beckley-Pit	22	Richardson-Bos	13	Duffy-Chi	280
Stovey-Bos	142	Shindle-Phi	188	O'Rourke-NY	37	Shindle-Phi	21	Stovey-Bos	12	Beckley-Pit	276
Ward-Bro	134	Browning-Cle	184	Duffy-Chi	36	Fields-Pit	20	Shindle-Phi	10	Richardson-Bos	274
Connor-NY	133	Richardson-Bos	181	Brouthers-Bos	36	Joyce-Bro	18	Gore-NY	10	Connor-NY	265

Runs Batted In		Runs Produced		Bases On Balls		Batting Average		On Base Percentage		Slugging Average	
Richardson-Bos	146	Richardson-Bos	259	Joyce-Bro	123	Browning-Cle	.373	Brouthers-Bos	.466	Connor-NY	.548
Orr-Bro	124	Duffy-Chi	236	Robinson-Pit	101	Orr-Bro	.373	Browning-Cle	.459	Orr-Bro	.537
Beckley-Pit	120	Connor-NY	222	Brouthers-Bos	99	O'Rourke-NY	.360	Connor-NY	.450	Beckley-Pit	.535
O'Rourke-NY	115	Bierbauer-Bro	220	Hoy-Buf	94	Connor-NY	.349	Robinson-Pit	.434	Browning-Cle	.517
Larkin-Cle	112	Beckley-Pit	220			Ryan-Chi	.340	Gore-NY	.432	O'Rourke-NY	.515

Production		Adjusted Production		Batter Runs		Adjusted Batter Runs		Clutch Hitting Index		Runs Created	
Connor-NY	.998	Browning-Cle	177	Connor-NY	49.1	Browning-Cle	54.6	Nash-Bos	130	Duffy-Chi	141
Browning-Cle	.976	Beckley-Pit	158	Browning-Cle	46.7	Larkin-Cle	40.7	McGeachey-Bro	129	Browning-Cle	136
Orr-Bro	.952	Larkin-Cle	156	Brouthers-Bos	39.6	Connor-NY	40.6	Rowe-Buf	127	Stovey-Bos	134
Gore-NY	.931	Connor-NY	154	Orr-Bro	34.4	Beckley-Pit	37.8	Farrell-Chi	125	Connor-NY	132
O'Rourke-NY	.925	Orr-Bro	147	Larkin-Cle	32.6	Brouthers-Bos	33.1	Fogarty-Phi	124	Shindle-Phi	126

Total Average		Stolen Bases		Stolen Base Average		Stolen Base Runs		Fielding Runs		Total Player Rating	
Stovey-Bos	1.210	Stovey-Bos	97					Richardson-Bos	25.3	Browning-Cle	4.2
Connor-NY	1.194	Brown-Bos	79					Bierbauer-Bro	24.8	Ward-Bro	3.2
Browning-Cle	1.191	Duffy-Chi	78					Pfeffer-Chi	24.1	W.Ewing-NY	3.1
Brouthers-Bos	1.149	Hanlon-Pit	65					Farrell-Chi	23.8	Connor-NY	3.1
Gore-NY	1.129	Ward-Bro	63					Ward-Bro	21.3	Shindle-Phi	2.7

Wins		Win Percentage		Games		Complete Games		Shutouts		Saves	
Baldwin-Chi	34	Daley-Bos	.720	Baldwin-Chi	59	Baldwin-Chi	54	King-Chi	4	Hemming-Cle-Bro	3
Weyhing-Bro	30	Radbourn-Bos	.692	King-Chi	56	King-Chi	48	Weyhing-Bro	3	O'Day-NY	3
King-Chi	30	Knell-Phi	.667	Weyhing-Bro	49	Staley-Pit	44	Staley-Pit	3		
Radbourn-Bos	27	Gumbert-Bos	.657	Gruber-Cle	48	Gruber-Cle	39				
Gumbert-Bos	23	Weyhing-Bro	.652	Staley-Pit	46	Weyhing-Bro	38				

Innings Pitched		Fewest Hits/Game		Fewest BB/Game		Strikeouts		Strikeouts/Game		Ratio	
Baldwin-Chi	501.0	King-Chi	8.20	Staley-Pit	1.72	Baldwin-Chi	211	J.Ewing-NY	4.88	Staley-Pit	10.82
King-Chi	461.0	Crane-NY	8.80	Sanders-Phi	1.79	King-Chi	185	Daley-Bos	4.21	King-Chi	11.38
Weyhing-Bro	390.0	Hemming-Cle-Bro	8.88	Galvin-Pit	2.03	Weyhing-Bro	177	Weyhing-Bro	4.08	Radbourn-Bos	11.86
Staley-Pit	387.2	Baldwin-Chi	8.95	Morris-Pit	2.18	Staley-Pit	145	McGill-Cle	4.02	Keefe-NY	12.30
Gruber-Cle	383.1	Keefe-NY	8.96	Radbourn-Bos	2.62	J.Ewing-NY	145	Haddock-Buf	3.81	Sanders-Phi	12.49

Earned Run Average		Adjusted ERA		Opponents' Batting Avg.		Opponents' On Base Pct.		Starter Runs		Adjusted Starter Runs	
King-Chi	2.69	King-Chi	161	King-Chi	.232	Staley-Pit	.285	King-Chi	78.6	King-Chi	84.2
Staley-Pit	3.23	Keefe-NY	134	Crane-NY	.245	King-Chi	.296	Baldwin-Chi	51.4	Baldwin-Chi	57.5
Baldwin-Chi	3.31	Radbourn-Bos	133	Hemming-Cle-Bro	.247	Radbourn-Bos	.304	Staley-Pit	43.2	Radbourn-Bos	41.4
Radbourn-Bos	3.31	Baldwin-Chi	131	Baldwin-Chi	.248	Keefe-NY	.312	Radbourn-Bos	35.2	Weyhing-Bro	37.0
Keefe-NY	3.38	Weyhing-Bro	124	Keefe-NY	.249	Sanders-Phi	.316	Weyhing-Bro	27.2	Keefe-NY	29.5

Clutch Pitching Index		Relief Runs		Adjusted Relief Runs		Relief Ranking		Total Pitcher Index		Total Baseball Ranking	
Daley-Bos	121							King-Chi	7.1	King-Chi	7.1
O'Brien-Cle	119							Baldwin-Chi	5.1	Baldwin-Chi	5.1
McGill-Cle	112							Radbourn-Bos	3.8	Browning-Cle	4.2
Gruber-Cle	111							Sanders-Phi	2.7	Radbourn-Bos	3.8
Sowders-Bro	111							Keefe-NY	2.2	Ward-Bro	3.2

TEAM	G	W	L	PCT	GB	R	OR	AB	H	2B	3B	HR	BB	SO	AVG	OBP	SLG	PRO	PRO+	BR	/A	PF	CHI	RC	SB	CS	SBA	SBR
BOS	140	87	51	.630		847	658	4956	1264	181	80	54	532	538	.255	.337	.357	.694	98	68	-25	112	99	711	289			
CHI	137	82	53	.607	3.5	832	730	4873	1233	159	88	60	526	457	.253	.332	.359	.691	109	58	62	99	100	676	238			
NY	136	71	61	.538	13	754	711	4833	1271	189	72	46	438	394	.263	.329	.360	.689	112	49	79	96	94	663	224			
PHI	138	68	69	.496	18.5	756	773	4929	1244	180	51	21	482	412	.252	.326	.322	.648	93	-11	-30	103	99	609	232			
CLE	141	65	74	.468	22.5	835	888	5074	1294	183	88	22	519	464	.255	.330	.339	.669	98	22	-10	104	102	663	242			
BRO	137	61	76	.445	25.5	765	820	4748	1233	200	69	23	464	435	.260	.330	.345	.675	104	30	35	99	99	669	337			
CIN	138	56	81	.409	30.5	646	790	4791	1158	148	90	40	414	439	.242	.308	.335	.643	94	-32	-37	101	91	584	244			
PIT	137	55	80	.407	30.5	679	744	4794	1148	148	71	29	427	503	.239	.308	.318	.626	92	-56	-37	98	98	547	205			
TOT	552					6114		38998	9845	1388	609	295	3802	3642	.252	.319	.342	.661							2011			

TEAM	CG	SH	SV	IP	H	H/G	HR	BB	SO	RAT	ERA	ERA+	OAV	OOB	PR	/A	PF	CPI	FA	E	DP	FW	PW	BW	SBW	DIF
BOS	126	9	6	1241²	1223	8.9	51	364	525	11.5	2.76	132	.248	.299	80	122	109	106	.938	358	96	4.7	10.9	-2.2		4.7
CHI	114	6	3	1220²	1207	8.9	53	475	477	12.4	3.47	95	.249	.316	-17	-23	99	93	.932	397	119	1.5	-2.1	5.5		9.5
NY	117	11	3	1204	1098	8.2	27	593	651	12.6	2.99	107	.233	.319	47	27	96	100	.933	384	104	2.2	2.4	7.1		-6.6
PHI	105	3	5	1229¹	1280	9.4	29	505	343	13.1	3.73	91	.258	.327	-53	-46	102	91	.925	443	108	-1.3	-4.1	-2.7		7.6
CLE	118	1	3	1244	1371	9.9	24	466	400	13.3	3.50	99	.269	.331	-21	-6	103	102	.920	485	86	-3.5	-.5	-.9		.4
BRO	121	8	3	1204²	1272	9.5	40	459	407	12.9	3.86	86	.261	.325	-68	-74	99	90	.924	432	73	-.8	-6.6	3.1		-3.2
CIN	125	6	1	1218²	1234	9.1	40	465	393	12.5	3.55	95	.253	.318	-28	-24	101	91	.931	409	101	.9	-2.1	-3.3		-8.0
PIT	122	7	2	1197²	1160	8.7	31	465	446	12.2	2.89	114	.245	.312	61	51	98	104	.917	475	76	-3.6	4.6	-3.3		-10.1
TOT	948	51	26	9760²		9.1				12.6	3.34		.252	.319					.928	3383	763					

Runs
Hamilton-Phi 141
Long-Bos 129
Childs-Cle 120
Latham-Cin 119
Stovey-Bos 118

Hits
Hamilton-Phi 179
McKean-Cle 170
Tiernan-NY 166
Davis-Cle 165
O'Rourke-NY 164

Doubles
Griffin-Bro 36
Davis-Cle 35
Stovey-Bos 31
Tiernan-NY 30

Triples
Stovey-Bos 20
Beckley-Pit 19
McPhee-Cin....... 16
Ryan-Chi 15
Virtue-Cle 14

Home Runs
Tiernan-NY 16
Stovey-Bos 16
Wilmot-Chi 11
Long-Bos 10

Total Bases
Stovey-Bos 271
Tiernan-NY 268
Long-Bos 239
Davis-Cle 233
Beckley-Pit....... 232

Runs Batted In
Anson-Chi 120
Stovey-Bos 95
O'Rourke-NY 95
Nash-Bos 95
Connor-NY 94

Runs Produced
Davis-Cle 201
Childs-Cle 201
Hamilton-Phi 199
Connor-NY 199
Stovey-Bos 197

Bases On Balls
Hamilton-Phi 102
Childs-Cle 97
Connor-NY 83
Long-Bos 80
Pfeffer-Chi 79

Batting Average
Hamilton-Phi 340
Holliday-Cin 319
Browning-Pit-Cin..317
Clements-Phi.....310
Tiernan-NY 306

On Base Percentage
Hamilton-Phi 453
Connor-NY 399
Childs-Cle 395
Browning-Pit-Cin..395
Tiernan-NY 388

Slugging Average
Stovey-Bos 498
Tiernan-NY 494
Holliday-Cin 473
Connor-NY.......449
Ryan-Chi 434

Production
Tiernan-NY 882
Hamilton-Phi 874
Stovey-Bos 870
Holliday-Cin 848
Connor-NY.......848

Adjusted Production
Tiernan-NY 165
Connor-NY....... 155
Hamilton-Phi 154
Holliday-Cin 148
Browning-Pit-Cin.. 142

Batter Runs
Hamilton-Phi 45.6
Tiernan-NY 39.5
Stovey-Bos 36.7
Connor-NY....... 32.2
Holliday-Cin 25.7

Adjusted Batter Runs
Hamilton-Phi 43.4
Tiernan-NY 43.0
Connor-NY....... 35.5
Stovey-Bos 26.3
Holliday-Cin 25.2

Clutch Hitting Index
Anson-Chi 151
Brodie-Bos 139
Nash-Bos........ 133
Myers-Phi 132
Zimmer-Cle 129

Runs Created
Hamilton-Phi 155
Tiernan-NY 128
Stovey-Bos 125
Long-Bos 116
Latham-Cin 112

Total Average
Hamilton-Phi 1.270
Tiernan-NY 1.045
Stovey-Bos 1.041
Latham-Cin 974
Connor-NY.......968

Stolen Bases
Hamilton-Phi 111
Latham-Cin 87
Griffin-Bro 65
Long-Bos 60

Stolen Base Average

Stolen Base Runs

Fielding Runs
Richardson-NY ... 49.1
Griffin-Bro 25.7
Pfeffer-Chi 25.0
McPhee-Cin...... 23.3
Latham-Cin 20.8

Total Player Rating
Richardson-NY 4.5
Latham-Cin 3.8
Hamilton-Phi 3.7
Pfeffer-Chi 3.2
Long-Bos 3.2

Wins
Hutchinson-Chi 44
Rusie-NY 33
Clarkson-Bos 33
Nichols-Bos 30
Young-Cle 27

Win Percentage
J.Ewing-NY 724
Hutchinson-Chi ...698
Staley-Pit-Bos 649
Nichols-Bos 638
Clarkson-Bos 635

Games
Hutchinson-Chi 66
Rusie-NY 61
Young-Cle 55
Clarkson-Bos 55

Complete Games
Hutchinson-Chi 56
Rusie-NY 52
Baldwin-Pit 48
Clarkson-Bos 47
Nichols-Bos 45

Shutouts
Rusie-NY 6
Nichols-Bos 5
J.Ewing-NY 5
Hutchinson-Chi 4

Saves
Nichols-Bos 3
Clarkson-Bos 3
Young-Cle 2
Thornton-Phi 2

Innings Pitched
Hutchinson-Chi .. 561.0
Rusie-NY 500.1
Clarkson-Bos 460.2
Baldwin-Pit 437.2
Mullane-Cin 426.1

Fewest Hits/Game
Rusie-NY 7.03
Baldwin-Pit 7.92
J.Ewing-NY 7.92
Hutchinson-Chi ... 8.15
Mullane-Cin 8.23

Fewest BB/Game
Nichols-Bos 2.18
Staley-Pit-Bos 2.22
Galvin-Pit 2.26
Radbourn-Cin 2.56
Hutchinson-Chi ... 2.86

Strikeouts
Rusie-NY 337
Hutchinson-Chi ... 261
Nichols-Bos 240
Baldwin-Pit 197
King-Pit 160

Strikeouts/Game
Rusie-NY 6.06
Nichols-Bos 5.07
J.Ewing-NY 4.61
Hutchinson-Chi ... 4.19
Baldwin-Pit 4.05

Ratio
Nichols-Bos 10.91
Staley-Pit-Bos ... 10.92
Hutchinson-Chi ... 11.01
J.Ewing-NY 11.43
Clarkson-Bos ... 11.51

Earned Run Average
J.Ewing-NY 2.27
Nichols-Bos 2.39
Rusie-NY 2.55
Staley-Pit-Bos ... 2.58
Baldwin-Pit 2.76

Adjusted ERA
Nichols-Bos 153
J.Ewing-NY 141
Staley-Pit-Bos .. 138
Clarkson-Bos 131
Rusie-NY 125

Opponents' Batting Avg.
Rusie-NY 207
Baldwin-Pit 228
J.Ewing-NY 228
Hutchinson-Chi ...233
Mullane-Cin 234

Opponents' On Base Pct.
Nichols-Bos 289
Staley-Pit-Bos 289
Hutchinson-Chi ...290
J.Ewing-NY 298
Clarkson-Bos 300

Starter Runs
Nichols-Bos 45.2
Rusie-NY 43.9
Hutchinson-Chi .. 33.5
J.Ewing-NY 32.1
Baldwin-Pit 28.6

Adjusted Starter Runs
Nichols-Bos 59.7
Clarkson-Bos 43.9
Rusie-NY 35.7
Staley-Pit-Bos ... 35.5
Hutchinson-Chi ... 31.4

Clutch Pitching Index
Viau-Cle 113
Caruthers-Bro 112
Nichols-Bos 112
Galvin-Pit 106
J.Ewing-NY 106

Relief Runs

Adjusted Relief Runs

Relief Ranking

Total Pitcher Index
Nichols-Bos 6.0
Clarkson-Bos 5.2
Rusie-NY 3.6
Staley-Pit-Bos ... 3.2
Hutchinson-Chi ... 2.5

Total Baseball Ranking
Nichols-Bos 6.0
Clarkson-Bos 5.2
Richardson-NY ... 4.5
Latham-Cin 3.8
Hamilton-Phi 3.7

TEAM	G	W	L	PCT	GB	R	OR	AB	H	2B	3B	HR	BB	SO	AVG	OBP	SLG	PRO	PRO+	BR	/A	PF	CHI	RC	SB	CS	SBA	SBR
BOS	139	93	42	.689		1028	675	4889	1341	163	100	52	651	499	.274	.367	.380	.747	123	149	161	99	104	868	447			
STL	138	85	51	.625	8.5	976	753	5005	1330	169	51	58	625	440	.266	.357	.355	.712	97	88	-40	115	103	753	283			
MIL	36	21	15	.583	22.5	227	156	1271	332	58	15	13	107	114	.261	.333	.361	.694	88	9	-33	120	103	173	47			
BAL	139	71	64	.526	22	850	798	4771	1217	142	99	30	551	553	.255	.346	.345	.691	104	45	36	101	99	705	342			
PHI	143	73	66	.525	22	817	794	5039	1301	182	123	55	447	548	.258	.328	.376	.704	105	46	20	103	93	686	149			
COL	138	61	76	.445	33	702	777	4697	1113	154	61	20	529	530	.237	.319	.308	.627	92	-69	-23	94	97	565	280			
CIN	101	43	57	.430	32.5	549	643	3574	838	105	58	28	428	385	.234	.322	.320	.642	83	-33	-85	109	96	432	164			
LOU	139	54	83	.394	40	713	890	4833	1247	130	69	17	443	473	.258	.329	.324	.653	95	-29	-19	99	92	606	230			
WAS	139	44	91	.326	49	691	1067	4715	1183	147	84	19	468	485	.251	.328	.330	.658	100	-20	16	95	90	597	219			
TOT	556					6553		38794	9902	1250	660	292	4249	4027	.255	.329	.344	.673							2161			

TEAM	CG	SH	SV	IP	H	H/G	HR	BB	SO	RAT	ERA	ERA+	OAV	OOB	PR	/A	PF	CPI	FA	E	DP	FW	PW	BW	SBW	DIF
BOS	108	9	7	1219²	1158	8.5	42	497	524	12.2	3.03	115	.242	.313	94	62	94	105	.934	392	115	4.2	5.3	13.9		2.1
STL	103	8	5	1222²	1106	8.1	50	576	621	12.4	3.27	129	.233	.316	61	126	113	97	.920	468	91	-.5	10.9	-3.4		10.1
MIL	35	3	0	309²	291	8.5	6	120	137	11.9	2.50	176	.240	.309	41	64	118	118	.922	116	20	.2	5.5	-2.8		.1
BAL	118	6	2	1217	1238	9.2	33	472	408	12.6	3.43	109	.255	.321	38	40	100	99	.915	503	103	-2.4	3.4	3.1		-.6
PHI	135	3	0	1233²	1274	9.3	35	520	533	13.1	4.01	95	.258	.328	-40	-27	103	89	.933	389	109	5.1	-2.3	1.7		-1.0
COL	118	6	0	1213¹	1141	8.5	29	588	502	12.8	3.75	92	.240	.324	-3	-39	93	87	.935	379	126	4.7	-3.4	-2.0		-6.9
CIN	86	2	1	902	921	9.2	20	446	331	13.6	3.43	120	.255	.337	28	67	111	107	.913	389	68	-3.1	5.8	-7.3		-2.3
LOU	128	9	1	1226	1353	9.9	33	464	485	13.3	4.27	85	.271	.333	-75	-85	98	89	.922	458	113	.3	-7.3	-1.6		-5.8
WAS	123	2	2	1181	1420	10.8	44	566	486	15.1	4.83	77	.288	.361	-145	-144	101	96	.900	589	95	-7.5	-12.4	1.4		-5.0
TOT	954	48	18	9725		9.2				13.1	3.72		.255	.329					.922	3683	840					

Runs
Brown-Bos 177
VanHaltren-Bal ... 136
Hoy-StL 136
Duffy-Bos 134
McCarthy-StL 127

Hits
Brown-Bos 189
VanHaltren-Bal ... 180
Duffy-Bos 180
McCarthy-StL 179
Brouthers-Bos.... 170

Doubles
Milligan-Phi 35
Brown-Bos 30
O'Neill-StL 28
Duffee-Col 28
Larkin-Phi 27

Triples
Brown-Bos 21
Brouthers-Bos 19
Canavan-Cin-Mil ... 18
Werden-Bal 18

Home Runs
Farrell-Bos 12
Milligan-Phi 11
Lyons-StL 11

Total Bases
Brown-Bos 276
VanHaltren-Bal ... 251
Brouthers-Bos.... 249
Duffy-Bos 243
McCarthy-StL 236

Runs Batted In
Farrell-Bos 110
Duffy-Bos 110
Brouthers-Bos 109
Milligan-Phi 106
Werden-Bal 104

Runs Produced
Brown-Bos 243
Duffy-Bos 235
Brouthers-Bos 221
McCarthy-StL 214
VanHaltren-Bal ... 210

Bases On Balls
Hoy-StL 119
Crooks-Col 103
McTamany-Col-Phi 101
Radford-Bos 96
Johnson-Bal 89

Batting Average
Brouthers-Bos.....350
Duffy-Bos 336
Brown-Bos 321
O'Neill-StL 321
VanHaltren-Bal 318

On Base Percentage
Brouthers-Bos.....471
Lyons-StL 445
Hoy-StL 424
Seery-Cin.........423
Duffy-Bos 408

Slugging Average
Brouthers-Bos.....512
Milligan-Phi 505
Farrell-Bos 474
Brown-Bos 469
Cross-Phi.........458

Production
Brouthers-Bos....983
Milligan-Phi 903
Lyons-StL 900
Brown-Bos 865
Duffy-Bos 861

Adjusted Production
Brouthers-Bos 188
Milligan-Phi 157
Brown-Bos 153
Duffy-Bos 152
Farrell-Bos 151

Batter Runs
Brouthers-Bos ...59.1
Lyons-StL 41.2
Brown-Bos 37.9
Milligan-Phi 35.5
Duffy-Bos 34.5

Adjusted Batter Runs
Brouthers-Bos 60.5
Brown-Bos 39.4
Duffy-Bos 35.9
Milligan-Phi 33.1
VanHaltren-Bal ...31.5

Clutch Hitting Index
Sneed-Col 154
Comiskey-StL 144
Wolf-Lou 143
Radford-Bos 138
Johnson-Bal 132

Runs Created
Brown-Bos 155
Duffy-Bos 137
Brouthers-Bos ... 135
VanHaltren-Bal ... 133
Hoy-StL 114

Total Average
Brouthers-Bos...1.237
Brown-Bos 1.140
Duffy-Bos 1.104
VanHaltren-Bal ..1.039
Lyons-StL 1.036

Stolen Bases
Brown-Bos 106
Duffy-Bos 85
VanHaltren-Bal ... 75
Hoy-StL 59
Radford-Bos 55

Stolen Base Average

Stolen Base Runs

Fielding Runs
Stricker-Bos 24.2
Farrell-Bos 21.0
Radford-Bos 19.9
Crooks-Col 19.6
Eagan-StL 19.5

Total Player Rating
Farrell-Bos 4.5
Brouthers-Bos..... 4.0
Crooks-Col 3.7
Welch-Bal 3.0
Radford-Bos 3.0

Wins
McMahon-Bal 35
Haddock-Bos 34
Stivetts-StL 33
Weyhing-Phi....... 31
Buffinton-Bos 29

Win Percentage
Buffinton-Bos 763
Haddock-Bos 756
Weyhing-Phi 608
Stivetts-StL 600
McMahon-Bal 593

Games
Stivetts-StL 64
McMahon-Bal 61
Knell-Col 58
Carsey-Was 54
Weyhing-Phi....... 52

Complete Games
McMahon-Bal 53
Weyhing-Phi....... 51
Knell-Col 47
Carsey-Was 46
Chamberlain-Phi ... 44

Shutouts
McMahon-Bal 5
Knell-Col 5
Haddock-Bos 5

Saves
Buffinton-Bos 3
O'Brien-Bos........ 2
Daley-Bos 2

Innings Pitched
McMahon-Bal ... 503.0
Knell-Col 462.0
Weyhing-Phi 450.0
Stivetts-StL 440.0
Carsey-Was 415.0

Fewest Hits/Game
Knell-Col 7.07
Stivetts-StL 7.30
Buffinton-Bos 7.50
Crane-Cin........ 7.78
Haddock-Bos ... 7.82

Fewest BB/Game
Stratton-Lou 1.78
Sanders-Phi...... 2.30
McMahon-Bal ... 2.67
Ehret-Lou 2.85
Griffith-StL-Bos ... 2.90

Strikeouts
Stivetts-StL 259
Knell-Col 228
Weyhing-Phi...... 219
McMahon-Bal ... 219
Chamberlain-Phi .. 204

Strikeouts/Game
Meekin-Lou 5.68
Stivetts-StL 5.30
McGill-Cin-StL 4.96
Daley-Bos 4.83
Chamberlain-Phi .. 4.53

Ratio
Buffinton-Bos ... 10.47
Haddock-Bos 11.07
Knell-Col 11.47
McMahon-Bal ... 11.49
Weyhing-Phi 11.78

Earned Run Average
Crane-Cin........2.45
Haddock-Bos 2.49
Buffinton-Bos 2.55
McMahon-Bal ...2.81
Stivetts-StL 2.86

Adjusted ERA
Crane-Cin........ 168
Stivetts-StL 147
Haddock-Bos 140
Buffinton-Bos 137
Mains-Cin-Mil 134

Opponents' Batting Avg.
Knell-Col 209
Stivetts-StL 215
Buffinton-Bos 219
Crane-Cin.........225
Haddock-Bos 226

Opponents' On Base Pct.
Buffinton-Bos 281
Haddock-Bos 293
Knell-Col 300
McMahon-Bal ...301
Weyhing-Phi......306

Starter Runs
Haddock-Bos 51.9
McMahon-Bal ...50.9
Buffinton-Bos 47.3
Stivetts-StL 41.8
Knell-Col 40.9

Adjusted Starter Runs
Stivetts-StL 65.5
McMahon-Bal ...51.7
Crane-Cin........46.2
Haddock-Bos 42.2
Buffinton-Bos 38.0

Clutch Pitching Index
Daley-Bos 129
Crane-Cin........ 122
O'Brien-Bos...... 117
Mains-Cin-Mil 117
McMahon-Bal ... 105

Relief Runs

Adjusted Relief Runs

Relief Ranking

Total Pitcher Index
Stivetts-StL 8.1
Haddock-Bos 5.1
McMahon-Bal 4.7
Buffinton-Bos 3.8
Crane-Cin.........3.5

Total Baseball Ranking
Stivetts-StL 8.1
Haddock-Bos 5.1
McMahon-Bal 4.7
Farrell-Bos 4.5
Brouthers-Bos.....4.0

TEAM	G	W	L	PCT	GB	R	OR	AB	H	2B	3B	HR	BB	SO	AVG	OBP	SLG	PRO	PRO+	BR	/A	PF	CHI	RC	SB	CS	SBA	SBR
BOS	152	102	48	.680		862	649	5301	1324	203	51	34	526	488	.250	.325	.327	.652	95	32	-39	109	106	689	338			
CLE	153	93	56	.624	8.5	855	613	5412	1375	196	96	26	552	536	.254	.328	.340	.668	104	62	30	104	99	694	225			
BRO	158	95	59	.617	9	935	733	5485	1439	183	105	30	629	506	.262	.344	.350	.694	121	124	154	96	99	822	409			
PHI	155	87	66	.569	16.5	860	690	5413	1420	225	95	50	528	515	.262	.334	.367	.701	119	121	123	100	94	753	216			
CIN	155	82	68	.547	20	766	731	5349	1288	155	75	44	503	474	.241	.311	.322	.633	99	-8	2	99	99	635	270			
PIT	155	80	73	.523	23.5	802	796	5469	1288	143	108	38	435	453	.236	.297	.322	.619	93	-43	-46	100	107	604	222			
CHI	147	70	76	.479	30	635	735	5063	1188	149	92	26	427	482	.235	.299	.316	.615	92	-45	-50	101	92	561	233			
NY	153	71	80	.470	31.5	811	826	5291	1326	173	85	39	510	469	.251	.320	.338	.658	107	39	51	98	100	686	301			
LOU	154	63	89	.414	40	649	804	5334	1208	133	61	18	433	508	.226	.290	.284	.574	86	-119	-57	92	99	533	275			
WAS	153	58	93	.384	44.5	731	869	5204	1245	149	78	37	529	553	.239	.314	.319	.633	100	-3	19	97	96	624	276			
STL	155	56	94	.373	46	703	922	5259	1187	138	53	45	607	491	.226	.312	.298	.610	95	-39	0	95	94	568	209			
BAL	152	46	101	.313	54.5	779	1020	5296	1342	160	111	30	499	480	.253	.325	.343	.668	105	58	32	103	93	680	227			
TOT	921					9388		63876	15630	2007	1010	417	6178	5955	.245	.311	.327	.639						3201				

TEAM	CG	SH	SV	IP	H	H/G	HR	BB	SO	RAT	ERA	ERA+	OAV	OOB	PR	/A	PF	CPI	FA	E	DP	FW	PW	BW	SBW	DIF
BOS	142	15	1	1336	1156	7.8	41	460	509	10.9	2.86	123	.224	.288	63	95	107	91	.929	454	127	.5	8.8	-3.6		21.3
CLE	140	11	2	1336	1178	7.9	28	413	472	10.7	2.41	140	.227	.285	129	143	103	104	.935	407	95	3.4	13.2	2.8		-.9
BRO	132	12	5	1405²	1285	8.2	26	600	597	12.1	3.25	97	.233	.309	5	-13	96	92	.940	398	98	4.8	-1.2	14.3		.2
PHI	131	10	5	1379	1297	8.5	24	492	502	11.7	2.93	111	.239	.302	54	47	99	99	.939	393	128	4.5	4.4	11.4		-9.8
CIN	131	8	2	1377¹	1327	8.7	39	535	437	12.2	3.17	103	.243	.311	17	14	99	101	.939	402	140	4.0	1.3	.2		1.5
PIT	130	3	1	1347¹	1300	8.7	28	537	455	12.3	3.10	106	.244	.313	27	27	100	102	.927	483	113	-.7	2.5	-4.3		6.0
CHI	133	6	1	1298	1269	8.8	35	424	518	11.7	3.16	105	.246	.303	17	20	101	97	.932	424	85	1.3	1.9	-4.6		-1.5
NY	139	5	1	1322²	1165	7.9	32	635	641	12.2	3.29	98	.227	.312	-1	-11	98	91	.912	565	97	-5.8	-1.0	4.7		-2.4
LOU	147	9	0	1346	1358	9.1	26	447	430	12.1	3.34	92	.251	.309	-7	-40	93	95	.928	471	133	-.2	-3.7	-5.3		-3.8
WAS	129	5	3	1315¹	1293	8.8	40	556	479	12.7	3.46	94	.247	.319	-25	-32	99	98	.916	547	122	-4.8	-3.0	1.8		-11.5
STL	139	4	1	1344²	1466	9.8	47	543	478	13.4	4.20	76	.267	.333	-137	-151	97	93	.929	452	100	1.1	-14.0	.0		-6.1
BAL	131	2	2	1298²	1537	10.7	51	536	437	14.4	4.28	81	.283	.348	-144	-121	105	104	.910	584	100	-7.1	-11.2	3.0		-12.1
TOT	1624	90	24	16106²		8.7				12.2	3.28		.245	.311					.928	5580	1338					

Split Season: First-half Winner BOS (52-22); Second-half Winner CLE (53-23)

Runs
Childs-Cle 136
Hamilton-Phi 132
Duffy-Bos 125
Connor-Phi 123
Brouthers-Bro 121

Hits
Brouthers-Bro 197
Thompson-Phi.... 186
Duffy-Bos 184
Hamilton-Phi 183
Long-Bos 181

Doubles
Connor-Phi 37
Long-Bos 33
Delahanty-Phi 30
Brouthers-Bro 30
Zimmer-Cle 29

Triples
Delahanty-Phi 21
Virtue-Cle 20
Brouthers-Bro 20
Dahlen-Chi 19
Beckley-Pit 19

Home Runs
Holliday-Cin 13
Connor-Phi 12
Ryan-Chi 10
Beckley-Pit........ 10
Thompson-Phi.... 9

Total Bases
Brouthers-Bro 282
Holliday-Cin 270
Thompson-Phi ... 263
Connor-Phi 261
Duffy-Bos 251

Runs Batted In
Brouthers-Bro 124
Thompson-Phi.... 104
Larkin-Was 96
Burns-Bro 96
Beckley-Pit........ 96

Runs Produced
Brouthers-Bro 240
Thompson-Phi ... 204
Duffy-Bos 201
Holliday-Cin 192

Bases On Balls
Crooks-StL 136
Childs-Cle 117
Connor-Phi 116
McCarthy-Bos 93

Batting Average
Brouthers-Bro 335
Hamilton-Phi 330
Childs-Cle 317
Burns-Bro 315
Delahanty-Phi 306

On Base Percentage
Childs-Cle 443
Brouthers-Bro 432
Hamilton-Phi 423
Connor-Phi 420
Crooks-StL 400

Slugging Average
Delahanty-Phi 495
Brouthers-Bro 480
Connor-Phi 463
Burns-Bro 454
Holliday-Cin 449

Production
Brouthers-Bro 911
Connor-Phi 883
Delahanty-Phi 855
Burns-Bro 849
Childs-Cle 841

Adjusted Production
Brouthers-Bro 185
Connor-Phi 170
Burns-Bro 165
Delahanty-Phi 160
Hamilton-Phi 155

Batter Runs
Brouthers-Bro .. 58.4
Connor-Phi 52.1
Childs-Cle 47.0
Hamilton-Phi ... 40.4
Burns-Bro 38.8

Adjusted Batter Runs
Brouthers-Bro .. 61.8
Connor-Phi 52.4
Childs-Cle 43.4
Burns-Bro 41.8
Hamilton-Phi ... 40.6

Clutch Hitting Index
McKean-Cle 159
Nash-Bos 158
Larkin-Was 152
Corcoran-Bro 138
Comiskey-Cin 137

Runs Created
Brouthers-Bro ... 138
Hamilton-Phi 123
Connor-Phi 122
VanHaltren-Bal-Pit 117
Holliday-Cin 114

Total Average
Brouthers-Bro ... 1.056
Connor-Phi 1.018
Hamilton-Phi ... 1.005
Childs-Cle .... .982
Burns-Bro .... .943

Stolen Bases
Ward-Bro 88
Brown-Lou 78
Latham-Cin 66
Hoy-Was 60
Dahlen-Chi 60

Stolen Base Average

Stolen Base Runs

Fielding Runs
D.Richardson-Was 57.6
Shindle-Bal 35.5
Bierbauer-Pit 31.7
McPhee-Cin 25.3
Dahlen-Chi 25.2

Total Player Rating
Brouthers-Bro 5.7
Dahlen-Chi 5.0
Hamilton-Phi 4.6
McPhee-Cin 4.5
D.Richardson-Was . 4.2

Wins
Hutchinson-Chi 37
Young-Cle 36
Stivetts-Bos 35
Nichols-Bos 35
Weyhing-Phi....... 32

Win Percentage
Young-Cle 750
Terry-Bal-Pit.......692
Haddock-Bro 690
Staley-Bos 688

Games
Hutchinson-Chi 75
Rusie-NY 64
Killen-Was 60
Weyhing-Phi....... 59
Baldwin-Pit 56

Complete Games
Hutchinson-Chi 67
Rusie-NY 58
Nichols-Bos 49
Young-Cle 48

Shutouts
Young-Cle 9
Weyhing-Phi........ 6
Stein-Bro 6

Saves
Weyhing-Phi........ 3
Duryea-Cin-Was 2

Innings Pitched
Hutchinson-Chi .. 627.0
Rusie-NY 532.0
Weyhing-Phi.... 469.2
Killen-Was 459.2

Fewest Hits/Game
Mullane-Cin 6.77
Rusie-NY 6.85
Terry-Bal-Pit...... 6.94
Young-Cle 7.21
Duryea-Cin-Was .. 7.25

Fewest BB/Game
Stratton-Lou 1.79
Dwyer-StL-Cin 2.03
Sanders-Lou 2.08
Young-Cle 2.34
Ehret-Pit 2.36

Strikeouts
Hutchinson-Chi ... 316
Rusie-NY 288
Weyhing-Phi..... 202
Stein-Bro 190
Nichols-Bos 187

Strikeouts/Game
Kennedy-Bro 5.09
Rusie-NY 4.87
Hutchinson-Chi ... 4.54
Stein-Bro 4.53
Crane-NY 4.30

Ratio
Young-Cle 9.56
Nichols-Bos 10.43
Keefe-Phi 10.46
Duryea-Cin-Was .. 10.52
Stratton-Lou 10.54

Earned Run Average
Young-Cle 1.93
Keefe-Phi 2.36
J.Clarkson-Bos-Cle ..2.48
Cuppy-Cle 2.51
Terry-Bal-Pit...... 2.57

Adjusted ERA
Young-Cle 176
J.Clarkson-Bos-Cle . 139
Keefe-Phi 138
Cuppy-Cle 135
Davies-Cle 131

Opponents' Batting Avg.
Mullane-Cin ...... .201
Rusie-NY .... .203
Terry-Bal-Pit...... .205
Young-Cle .... .211
Duryea-Cin-Was ...212

Opponents' On Base Pct.
Young-Cle .... .262
Nichols-Bos ...... .279
Keefe-Phi .... .279
Duryea-Cin-Was ...281
Stratton-Lou ..... .281

Starter Runs
Young-Cle 68.3
Hutchinson-Chi ... 37.8
J.Clarkson-Bos-Cle . 35.0
Weyhing-Phi...... 32.4
Keefe-Phi 32.3

Adjusted Starter Runs
Young-Cle 73.4
J.Clarkson-Bos-Cle .. 41.3
Hutchinson-Chi ... 39.6
Cuppy-Cle 36.5
Nichols-Bos 33.6

Clutch Pitching Index
Sullivan-Cin 131
Galvin-Pit-StL 120
Luby-Chi 114
McMahon-Bal ... 113
Vickery-Bal 112

Relief Runs

Adjusted Relief Runs

Relief Ranking

Total Pitcher Index
Young-Cle 7.1
Hutchinson-Chi ... 4.5
Stivetts-Bos 4.5
Cuppy-Cle 4.0
J.Clarkson-Bos-Cle . 3.6

Total Baseball Ranking
Young-Cle 7.1
Brouthers-Bro 5.7
Dahlen-Chi 5.0
Hamilton-Phi 4.6
McPhee-Cin 4.5

1893 National League

TEAM	G	W	L	PCT	GB	R	OR	AB	H	2B	3B	HR	BB	SO	AVG	OBP	SLG	PRO	PRO+	BR	/A	PF	CHI	RC	SB	CS	SBA	SBR
BOS	131	86	43	.667		1008	795	4678	1358	178	50	65	561	292	.290	.372	.391	.763	101	70	2	108	109	790	243			
PIT	131	81	48	.628	5	970	766	4834	1447	176	127	37	537	273	.299	.377	.411	.788	118	113	129	98	98	848	210			
CLE	129	73	55	.570	12.5	976	839	4747	1425	222	98	32	532	229	.300	.374	.408	.782	107	100	48	106	102	841	252			
PHI	133	72	57	.558	14	1011	841	5151	1553	246	90	80	468	335	.301	.368	.431	.799	119	125	127	100	97	912	202			
NY	136	68	64	.515	19.5	941	845	4858	1424	182	101	61	504	279	.293	.366	.410	.776	112	85	81	100	98	860	299			
CIN	131	65	63	.508	20.5	759	814	4617	1195	161	65	29	532	256	.259	.342	.341	.683	85	-71	-91	102	98	634	238			
BRO	130	65	63	.508	20.5	775	845	4511	1200	173	83	45	473	296	.266	.341	.371	.712	99	-29	8	95	99	659	213			
BAL	130	60	70	.462	26.5	820	893	4651	1281	164	86	27	537	323	.275	.359	.365	.724	97	3	-14	102	96	711	233			
CHI	128	56	71	.441	29	829	874	4664	1299	186	93	32	465	262	.279	.348	.379	.727	101	-3	13	98	99	722	255			
STL	135	57	75	.432	30.5	745	829	4879	1288	152	98	10	524	251	.264	.343	.341	.684	87	-71	-72	100	91	674	250			
LOU	126	50	75	.400	34	759	942	4566	1185	177	73	19	485	306	.260	.338	.343	.681	94	-76	-11	92	101	612	203			
WAS	130	40	89	.310	46	722	1032	4742	1260	180	83	23	524	237	.266	.347	.353	.700	94	-43	-19	97	88	650	154			
TOT	785					10315		56898	15915	2197	1047	460	6142	3339	.280	.350	.379	.729							2752			

TEAM	CG	SH	SV	IP	H	H/G	HR	BB	SO	RAT	ERA	ERA+	OAV	OOB	PR	/A	PF	CPI	FA	E	DP	FW	PW	BW	SBW	DIF
BOS	115	2	2	1163²	1314	10.2	66	402	253	13.3	4.43	111	.276	.333	30	64	106	98	.936	353	118	1.8	5.2	.2		14.3
PIT	104	8	1	1167	1232	9.5	29	504	280	13.4	4.08	112	.263	.335	75	60	98	98	.938	347	112	2.1	4.9	10.6		-1.1
CLE	110	2	2	1140¹	1361	10.7	35	356	242	13.6	4.20	116	.287	.337	59	86	105	104	.929	395	92	-.9	7.1	3.9		-1.1
PHI	107	4	2	1189	1359	10.3	30	521	283	14.2	4.68	98	.279	.348	-1	-13	98	95	.944	318	121	4.1	-1.1	10.4		-5.9
NY	111	6	4	1211¹	1271	9.4	36	581	395	13.8	4.29	108	.262	.341	49	48	100	96	.927	432	95	-1.8	3.9	6.6		-6.7
CIN	97	4	5	1172	1305	10.0	38	542	258	14.2	4.59	104	.283	.348	9	24	103	96	.943	321	138	3.6	2.0	-7.5		2.9
BRO	109	3	3	1154	1262	9.8	41	547	297	14.1	4.55	97	.270	.346	15	-15	95	96	.930	385	88	-.2	-1.2	.7		1.8
BAL	104	1	2	1123²	1325	10.6	29	534	275	14.9	4.97	96	.285	.358	-38	-26	102	95	.929	384	95	-.1	-2.1	-1.1		-1.6
CHI	101	4	5	1117¹	1278	10.3	26	553	273	14.7	4.81	96	.279	.357	-17	-26	99	95	.922	421	92	-2.5	-2.1	1.1		-3.9
STL	114	3	4	1207	1292	9.6	38	542	301	13.7	4.06	116	.266	.339	80	88	101	102	.930	398	110	-.0	7.2	-5.9		-10.2
LOU	114	4	1	1080	1431	11.9	38	479	190	15.9	5.90	75	.309	.374	-148	-180	94	92	.937	330	111	2.2	-14.8	-.9		.9
WAS	110	2	0	1139	1485	11.7	54	574	292	16.3	5.56	83	.306	.379	-113	-119	99	101	.912	497	96	-6.5	-9.8	-1.6		-6.7
TOT	1296	43	31	13864¹		10.3				14.3	4.66		.280	.350					.931	4581	1268					

Runs		Hits		Doubles		Triples		Home Runs		Total Bases	
Long-Bos	149	Thompson-Phi	222	Thompson-Phi	37	Werden-StL	29	Delahanty-Phi	19	Delahanty-Phi	347
Duffy-Bos	147	Delahanty-Phi	219	Delahanty-Phi	35	Davis-NY	27	Clements-Phi	17	Thompson-Phi	318
Delahanty-Phi	145	Duffy-Bos	203	Tebeau-Cle	32	McKean-Cle	24	Tiernan-NY	14	Davis-NY	304
Childs-Cle	145	Davis-NY	195	Beckley-Pit	32	Smith-Pit	23	Lowe-Bos	14	Smith-Pit	272
Burkett-Cle	145	Ward-NY	193			Beckley-Pit	19				

Runs Batted In		Runs Produced		Bases On Balls		Batting Average		On Base Percentage		Slugging Average	
Delahanty-Phi	146	Delahanty-Phi	272	Crooks-StL	121	Hamilton-Phi	.380	Hamilton-Phi	.490	Delahanty-Phi	.583
McKean-Cle	133	Duffy-Bos	259	Childs-Cle	120	Thompson-Phi	.370	Childs-Cle	.463	Davis-NY	.554
Thompson-Phi	126	Thompson-Phi	245	Radford-Was	105	Delahanty-Phi	.368	Burkett-Cle	.459	Thompson-Phi	.530
Nash-Bos	123	Ewing-Cle	233	McGraw-Bal	101	Duffy-Bos	.363	McGraw-Bal	.454	Smith-Pit	.525
Ewing-Cle	122	McKean-Cle	232	Burkett-Cle	98	Davis-NY	.355	Smith-Pit	.435	Hamilton-Phi	.524

Production		Adjusted Production		Batter Runs		Adjusted Batter Runs		Clutch Hitting Index		Runs Created	
Hamilton-Phi	1.014	Hamilton-Phi	172	Delahanty-Phi	54.6	Delahanty-Phi	54.9	Anson-Chi	172	Delahanty-Phi	167
Delahanty-Phi	1.007	Delahanty-Phi	169	Burkett-Cle	45.3	Thompson-Phi	45.6	Vaughn-Cin	172	Thompson-Phi	146
Davis-NY	.964	Smith-Pit	160	Thompson-Phi	45.3	Smith-Pit	45.0	Nash-Bos	149	Davis-NY	143
Smith-Pit	.960	Davis-NY	157	Smith-Pit	43.1	Davis-NY	41.4	McCarthy-Bos	140	Burkett-Cle	137
Thompson-Phi	.954	Thompson-Phi	155	Davis-NY	41.8	Hamilton-Phi	41.2	Lyons-Pit	139	Smith-Pit	133

Total Average		Stolen Bases		Stolen Base Average	Stolen Base Runs	Fielding Runs		Total Player Rating	
Hamilton-Phi	1.386	T.Brown-Lou	66			McPhee-Cin	34.0	Delahanty-Phi	6.5
Burkett-Cle	1.186	Dowd-StL	59			Delahanty-Phi	30.8	Davis-NY	3.5
Delahanty-Phi	1.173	Latham-Cin	57			T.Brown-Lou	27.1	Smith-Pit	3.4
Smith-Pit	1.121	Burke-NY	54			G.Smith-Cin	19.5	Hamilton-Phi	3.4
Davis-NY	1.107	Brodie-StL-Bal	49			Allen-Phi	18.4	McPhee-Cin	3.4

Wins		Win Percentage		Games		Complete Games		Shutouts		Saves	
Killen-Pit	36	Gastright-Pit-Bos	.750	Rusie-NY	56	Rusie-NY	50	Rusie-NY	4	Mullane-Cin-Bal	2
Young-Cle	34	Killen-Pit	.720	Killen-Pit	55	Nichols-Bos	43	Ehret-Pit	4	Baldwin-Pit-NY	2
Nichols-Bos	34	Nichols-Bos	.708	Young-Cle	53	Young-Cle	42			Dwyer-Cin	2
Rusie-NY	33	Young-Cle	.680	Nichols-Bos	52	Kennedy-Bro	40			Donnelly-Chi	2
Kennedy-Bro	25	Staley-Bos	.643	Mullane-Cin-Bal	49					Colcolough-Pit	2

Innings Pitched		Fewest Hits/Game		Fewest BB/Game		Strikeouts		Strikeouts/Game		Ratio	
Rusie-NY	482.0	Young-Cle	8.42	Young-Cle	2.19	Rusie-NY	208	Rusie-NY	3.88	Nichols-Bos	11.52
Nichols-Bos	425.0	Breitenstein-StL	8.44	Nichols-Bos	2.50	Kennedy-Bro	107	Meekin-Was	3.34	Young-Cle	11.60
Young-Cle	422.2	Killen-Pit	8.70	Cuppy-Cle	2.77	Young-Cle	102	Hawley-StL	2.89	Killen-Pit	11.73
Killen-Pit	415.0	Kennedy-Bro	8.84	Staley-Bos	2.77	Breitenstein-StL	102	Terry-Pit	2.75	Breitenstein-StL	12.11
		Stein-Bro	8.87	Stratton-Lou	2.89	Weyhing-Phi	101	Hawke-StL-Bal	2.74	Stein-Bro	12.46

Earned Run Average		Adjusted ERA		Opponents' Batting Avg.		Opponents' On Base Pct.		Starter Runs		Adjusted Starter Runs	
Breitenstein-StL	3.18	Breitenstein-StL	149	Rusie-NY	.240	Nichols-Bos	.302	Rusie-NY	76.8	Rusie-NY	76.3
Rusie-NY	3.23	Young-Cle	145	Breitenstein-StL	.241	Young-Cle	.304	Breitenstein-StL	63.3	Young-Cle	71.4
Young-Cle	3.36	Rusie-NY	144	Killen-Pit	.246	Killen-Pit	.306	Young-Cle	61.1	Nichols-Bos	67.1
Ehret-Pit	3.44	Nichols-Bos	140	Kennedy-Bro	.249	Breitenstein-StL	.313	Nichols-Bos	54.3	Breitenstein-StL	66.1
Clarkson-StL	3.48	Clarkson-StL	136	Stein-Bro	.250	Stein-Bro	.319	Killen-Pit	47.1	Killen-Pit	41.9

Clutch Pitching Index		Relief Runs	Adjusted Relief Runs	Relief Ranking	Total Pitcher Index		Total Baseball Ranking	
Esper-Was	118				Rusie-NY	7.1	Rusie-NY	7.1
Clarkson-StL	111				Young-Cle	6.2	Delahanty-Phi	6.5
McNabb-Bal	109				Nichols-Bos	5.6	Young-Cle	6.2
Cuppy-Cle	108				Breitenstein-StL	5.5	Nichols-Bos	5.6
Rusie-NY	108				Killen-Pit	4.8	Breitenstein-StL	5.5

TEAM	G	W	L	PCT	GB	R	OR	AB	H	2B	3B	HR	BB	SO	AVG	OBP	SLG	PRO	PRO+	BR	/A	PF	CHI	RC	SB	CS	SBA	SBR
BAL	129	89	39	.695		1171	819	4799	1647	271	150	33	516	200	.343	.418	.483	.901	117	188	144	104	99	1131	324			
NY	137	88	44	.667	3	940	789	4806	1446	197	96	43	476	217	.301	.368	.409	.777	93	-51	-43	99	102	860	319			
BOS	133	83	49	.629	8	1221	1002	5011	1658	272	94	103	535	261	.331	.401	.484	.885	110	151	68	108	104	1095	241			
PHI	129	71	57	.555	18	1143	966	4967	1732	252	131	40	496	245	.349	.414	.476	.890	123	172	198	97	96	1120	273			
BRO	134	70	61	.534	20.5	1021	1007	4816	1507	228	130	42	466	294	.313	.378	.440	.818	110	20	89	93	102	930	282			
CLE	130	68	61	.527	21.5	932	896	4764	1442	241	90	37	471	301	.303	.368	.414	.782	90	-40	-76	104	101	828	220			
PIT	132	65	65	.500	25	955	972	4676	1458	222	124	48	434	208	.312	.379	.443	.822	105	26	35	99	98	903	256			
CHI	135	57	75	.432	34	1041	1066	4960	1555	265	86	65	496	298	.314	.380	.441	.821	97	28	-26	105	100	979	327			
STL	133	56	76	.424	35	771	954	4610	1320	171	113	54	442	289	.286	.354	.408	.762	89	-84	-84	100	91	750	190			
CIN	132	55	75	.423	35	910	1085	4671	1374	224	67	61	508	252	.294	.368	.410	.778	89	-45	-81	104	100	804	215			
WAS	132	45	87	.341	46	882	1122	4581	1317	218	118	59	617	375	.287	.381	.425	.806	103	9	39	97	90	857	249			
LOU	130	36	94	.277	54	692	1001	4482	1206	173	88	42	350	364	.269	.330	.375	.705	80	-183	-121	93	97	641	217			
TOT	793					11679		57143	17662	2734	1287	627	5807	3304	.309	.373	.435	.808							3113			

TEAM	CG	SH	SV	IP	H	H/G	HR	BB	SO	RAT	ERA	ERA+	OAV	OOB	PR	/A	PF	CPI	FA	E	DP	FW	PW	BW	SBW	DIF
BAL	97	1	11	1116¹	1371	11.1	31	472	275	14.9	5.00	109	.299	.364	39	55	103	95	.944	293	105	5.6	4.2	11.0		4.1
NY	111	5	5	1212	1292	9.6	37	539	395	13.6	3.83	137	.270	.345	199	187	99	105	.924	443	101	-1.6	14.3	-3.3		12.5
BOS	108	3	1	1166	1529	11.8	89	411	262	15.0	5.41	105	.313	.366	-12	32	107	99	.925	415	120	-.7	2.5	10.0		
PHI	102	3	4	1125²	1482	11.8	62	469	262	15.6	5.63	90	.314	.376	-39	-67	96	96	.935	338	111	3.0	-5.1	15.2		-6.1
BRO	105	3	5	1162¹	1447	11.2	41	555	285	15.5	5.51	90	.302	.374	-25	-74	93	92	.928	390	85	.9	-5.7	6.8		2.4
CLE	107	6	1	1124¹	1390	11.1	54	435	254	14.6	4.97	110	.301	.361	43	59	103	98	.935	344	107	2.9	4.5	-5.8		1.9
PIT	106	2	0	1164²	1552	12.0	39	457	304	15.5	5.60	93	.317	.375	-37	-49	98	94	.936	354	106	2.6	-3.8	2.7		-1.6
CHI	117	0	0	1148	1561	12.2	43	557	281	16.6	5.68	99	.321	.391	-46	-11	106	100	.918	452	113	-2.4	-.8	-2.0		-3.7
STL	114	2	0	1161	1418	11.0	48	500	319	14.9	5.29	102	.298	.365	3	14	102	92	.923	426	109	-1.3	1.1	-6.4		-3.3
CIN	110	4	3	1147¹	1585	12.4	85	491	219	16.3	5.99	93	.324	.386	-85	-56	104	99	.925	423	119	-1.3	-4.3	-6.2		1.8
WAS	102	0	4	1107	1573	12.8	59	446	190	16.4	5.51	95	.331	.388	-24	-32	99	107	.908	499	81	-5.6	-2.5	3.0		-15.9
LOU	113	2	1	1096²	1462	12.0	39	475	258	15.9	5.45	93	.316	.380	-16	-44	96	99	.920	428	130	-1.9	-3.4	-9.3		-14.4
TOT	1292	31	35	13731¹		11.6				15.4	5.32		.309	.373					.927	4805	1287					

Runs
Hamilton-Phi 192
Kelley-Bal 165
Keeler-Bal 165
Duffy-Bos 160
Lowe-Bos 158

Hits
Duffy-Bos 237
Hamilton-Phi 220
Keeler-Bal 219
Lowe-Bos 212
Brodie-Bal 210

Doubles
Duffy-Bos 51
Kelley-Bal 48
Wilmot-Chi 45

Triples
Reitz-Bal 31
Thompson-Phi 27
Treadway-Bro 26
Connor-NY-StL 25
Brouthers-Bal 23

Home Runs
Duffy-Bos 18
Lowe-Bos 17
Joyce-Was 17
Dahlen-Chi 15

Total Bases
Duffy-Bos 374
Lowe-Bos 319
Kelley-Bal 305
Keeler-Bal 305
Stenzel-Pit 303

Runs Batted In
Duffy-Bos 145
Thompson-Phi.... 141
E.Delahanty-Phi . 131
Wilmot-Chi 130

Runs Produced
Duffy-Bos 287
Hamilton-Phi 275
E.Delahanty-Phi .. 274
Kelley-Bal 270
Wilmot-Chi 259

Bases On Balls
Hamilton-Phi 126
Kelley-Bal 107
Childs-Cle 107
Nash-Bos 91
McGraw-Bal....... 91

Batting Average
Duffy-Bos........440
Thompson-Phi.....407
E.Delahanty-Phi ..407
Hamilton-Phi 404
Kelley-Bal........393

On Base Percentage
Hamilton-Phi 523
Kelley-Bal 502
Duffy-Bos........502
Joyce-Was 496
E.Delahanty-Phi ...478

Slugging Average
Duffy-Bos........694
Thompson-Phi.....686
Joyce-Was 648
Kelley-Bal 602
E.Delahanty-Phi ..585

Production
Duffy-Bos 1.196
Thompson-Phi... 1.145
Joyce-Was 1.143
Kelley-Bal 1.104
E.Delahanty-Phi . 1.063

Adjusted Production
Joyce-Was 182
Thompson-Phi... 179
Duffy-Bos 174
E.Delahanty-Phi . 161
Kelley-Bal 160

Batter Runs
Duffy-Bos....... 77.2
Kelley-Bal........ 61.7
Hamilton-Phi 61.5
Thompson-Phi... 50.6
Joyce-Was 48.3

Adjusted Batter Runs
Duffy-Bos....... 68.3
Hamilton-Phi 64.7
Kelley-Bal....... 56.7
Thompson-Phi... 52.9
Joyce-Was 50.9

Clutch Hitting Index
Robinson-Bal.... 152
Shindle-Bro 137
Decker-Chi....... 136
Ward-NY......... 136
Bierbauer-Pit 136

Runs Created
Duffy-Bos 217
Hamilton-Phi 206
Kelley-Bal 181
Stenzel-Pit 165
Thompson-Phi.... 152

Total Average
Duffy-Bos 1.619
Hamilton-Phi 1.605
Joyce-Was 1.528
Kelley-Bal 1.503
Thompson-Phi... 1.409

Stolen Bases
Hamilton-Phi 98
McGraw-Bal....... 78
Wilmot-Chi 74
T.Brown-Lou 66
Lange-Chi 65

Stolen Base Average

Stolen Base Runs

Fielding Runs
Jennings-Bal 33.1
Dahlen-Chi......31.6
McPhee-Cin......31.2
Farrell-NY........30.9
Reitz-Bal 26.4

Total Player Rating
Dahlen-Chi 4.9
Duffy-Bos........ 4.9
E.Delahanty-Phi .. 4.6
Hamilton-Phi 4.6
Kelley-Bal........ 3.8

Wins
Rusie-NY 36
Meekin-NY 33
Nichols-Bos 32
Stein-Bro 27
Breitenstein-StL ... 27

Win Percentage
Meekin-NY........786
McMahon-Bal 758
Rusie-NY 735
Nichols-Bos.......711
Stein-Bro 659

Games
Breitenstein-StL ... 56
Rusie-NY 54
Hawley-StL 53
Young-Cle 52
Meekin-NY 52

Complete Games
Breitenstein-StL ... 46
Rusie-NY 45
Young-Cle 44
Nichols-Bos 40
Meekin-NY 40

Shutouts
Rusie-NY 3
Nichols-Bos 3
Cuppy-Cle 3

Saves
Mullane-Bal-Cle..... 4
Mercer-Was 3
Hawke-Bal 3

Innings Pitched
Breitenstein-StL . 447.1
Rusie-NY 444.0
Meekin-NY 409.0
Young-Cle 408.2
Nichols-Bos 407.0

Fewest Hits/Game
Rusie-NY 8.64
Meekin-NY 8.89
Stein-Bro 9.93
Breitenstein-StL . 10.00
Clarkson-Cle 10.33

Fewest BB/Game
Young-Cle 2.33
Menefee-Lou-Pit .. 2.48
Gleason-StL-Bal .. 2.54
Staley-Bos 2.63
Nichols-Bos 2.68

Strikeouts
Rusie-NY 195
Breitenstein-StL .. 140
Meekin-NY 133
Hawley-StL 120
Nichols-Bos 113

Strikeouts/Game
Rusie-NY 3.95
Hawke-Bal 2.99
Wadsworth-Lou... 2.97
Meekin-NY 2.93
Chamberlain-Cin .. 2.89

Ratio
Meekin-NY ... 12.65
Rusie-NY 12.69
Young-Cle 13.08
Clarkson-Cle ... 13.08
Taylor-Phi 13.38

Earned Run Average
Rusie-NY 2.78
Meekin-NY 3.70
Mercer-Was 3.76
Young-Cle 3.94
Taylor-Phi....... 4.08

Adjusted ERA
Rusie-NY 189
Meekin-NY 142
Mercer-Was 140
Young-Cle 138
McMahon-Bal 129

Opponents' Batting Avg.
Rusie-NY 250
Meekin-NY 256
Stein-Bro 277
Breitenstein-StL ...279
Clarkson-Cle 285

Opponents' On Base Pct.
Meekin-NY 328
Rusie-NY 329
Young-Cle 336
Clarkson-Cle 336
Taylor-Phi........341

Starter Runs
Rusie-NY 125.3
Meekin-NY 73.6
Young-Cle 62.4
Mercer-Was 57.7
Taylor-Phi........ 41.0

Adjusted Starter Runs
Rusie-NY 121.3
Meekin-NY 70.0
Young-Cle 68.7
Mercer-Was 55.5
Nichols-Bos 41.5

Clutch Pitching Index
Mercer-Was 132
Rusie-NY 124
Terry-Pit-Chi 117
Hemming-Lou-Bal . 109
Killen-Pit 109

Relief Runs

Adjusted Relief Runs

Relief Ranking

Total Pitcher Index
Rusie-NY 10.9
Meekin-NY 5.9
Young-Cle 5.4
Mercer-Was 4.7
Nichols-Bos 3.7

Total Baseball Ranking
Rusie-NY 10.9
Meekin-NY 5.9
Young-Cle 5.4
Dahlen-Chi 4.9
Duffy-Bos........ 4.9

TEAM	G	W	L	PCT	GB	R	OR	AB	H	2B	3B	HR	BB	SO	AVG	OBP	SLG	PRO	PRO+	BR	/A	PF	CHI	RC	SB	CS	SBA	SBR
BAL	132	87	43	.669		1009	646	4725	1530	235	89	25	355	243	.324	.384	.427	.811	111	109	84	103	103	916	310			
CLE	131	84	46	.646	3	917	720	4658	1423	194	67	29	472	361	.305	.375	.395	.770	99	43	-7	106	100	779	187			
PHI	133	78	53	.595	9.5	1068	957	5037	1664	272	73	61	463	262	.330	.394	.450	.844	123	178	174	100	96	1027	276			
CHI	133	72	58	.554	15	866	854	4708	1401	171	85	55	422	344	.298	.346	.405	.766	96	23	-31	106	97	801	260			
BRO	133	71	60	.542	16.5	867	834	4717	1330	189	77	39	397	318	.282	.346	.379	.725	100	-48	22	92	105	699	183			
BOS	132	71	60	.542	16.5	907	826	4715	1369	197	57	54	500	236	.290	.365	.391	.756	93	13	-56	108	101	763	199			
PIT	134	71	61	.538	17	811	787	4645	1349	190	89	26	376	299	.290	.352	.386	.738	101	-23	23	95	97	740	257			
CIN	132	66	64	.508	21	903	854	4684	1395	235	105	36	414	249	.298	.359	.416	.775	100	35	0	104	101	838	326			
NY	132	66	65	.504	21.5	852	834	4605	1324	191	90	32	454	292	.288	.355	.389	.744	99	-11	9	98	101	759	292			
WAS	132	43	85	.336	43	837	1048	4577	1314	207	101	55	518	396	.287	.366	.412	.778	107	48	59	99	92	797	237			
STL	135	39	92	.298	48.5	747	1032	4781	1344	155	88	38	384	279	.281	.338	.374	.712	90	-75	-62	99	94	691	205			
LOU	133	35	96	.267	52.5	698	1090	4724	1320	171	73	34	346	323	.279	.339	.368	.707	93	-81	-26	94	89	658	156			
TOT	796					10482		56576	16763	2407	994	484	5101	3602	.296	.354	.400	.754							2888			

TEAM	CG	SH	SV	IP	H	H/G	HR	BB	SO	RAT	ERA	ERA+	OAV	OOB	PR	/A	PF	CPI	FA	E	DP	FW	PW	BW	SBW	DIF
BAL	104	10	4	1134.1	1216	9.6	31	430	244	13.1	3.80	125	.270	.334	122	117	100	102	.946	288	108	5.4	9.5	6.8		.4
CLE	108	6	3	1143.2	1272	10.0	33	346	326	12.7	3.90	128	.277	.328	110	136	104	99	.936	348	77	1.8	11.0	-.6		6.7
PHI	106	2	7	1161	1467	11.4	36	485	330	15.1	5.47	88	.304	.367	-88	-88	100	91	.933	369	93	1.0	-7.1	14.1		4.5
CHI	119	3	1	1150.0	1422	11.1	38	432	297	14.5	4.67	109	.299	.357	13	51	106	101	.928	401	113	-.8	4.1	-2.5		6.2
BRO	103	5	6	1150.2	1360	10.6	41	395	216	13.7	4.94	89	.289	.345	-21	-71	92	89	.941	325	96	3.5	-5.8	1.8		6.0
BOS	116	4	4	1175.1	1364	10.4	56	363	370	13.2	4.27	119	.286	.337	65	106	107	100	.934	364	104	1.1	8.6	-4.5		.3
PIT	106	4	6	1171.2	1263	9.7	17	500	382	13.5	4.05	111	.271	.342	94	59	95	97	.930	392	95	-.1	4.8	1.9		-1.5
CIN	97	2	6	1147.1	1451	11.4	39	362	245	14.2	4.81	103	.304	.353	-4	19	104	98	.931	377	112	.4	1.5	.0		-.9
NY	115	6	1	1147.1	1359	10.7	34	415	409	13.9	4.51	103	.290	.348	33	15	97	98	.922	438	106	-3.0	1.2	.7		1.6
WAS	99	0	5	1101.2	1507	12.3	55	465	258	16.1	5.28	91	.321	.382	-61	-60	100	107	.917	447	96	-3.5	-4.9	4.8		-17.4
STL	105	1	1	1152.1	1562	12.2	64	439	280	15.6	5.76	84	.319	.375	-126	-120	101	96	.930	380	94	.7	-9.7	-5.0		-12.5
LOU	104	3	1	1117.1	1520	12.2	40	470	245	16.0	5.90	78	.319	.381	-139	-158	97	93	.913	477	104	-5.1	-12.8	-2.1		-10.5
TOT	1282	46	45	13753.1		11.0				14.3	4.78		.296	.354					.930	4606	1198					

Runs
Hamilton-Phi 166
Keeler-Bal 162
Jennings-Bal 159
Burkett-Cle 153
Delahanty-Phi 149

Hits
Burkett-Cle 225
Keeler-Bal 213
Thompson-Phi 211
Jennings-Bal 204
Hamilton-Phi 201

Doubles
Delahanty-Phi 49
Thompson-Phi 45
Jennings-Bal 41
Stenzel-Pit 38
Griffin-Bro 38

Triples
Selbach-Was 22
Tiernan-NY 21
Thompson-Phi 21
Cooley-StL 20

Home Runs
Thompson-Phi 18
Joyce-Was 17
Clements-Phi 13
Delahanty-Phi 11

Total Bases
Thompson-Phi 352
Delahanty-Phi ... 296
Burkett-Cle 288
McKean-Cle 283
Kelley-Bal 283

Runs Batted In
Thompson-Phi 165
Kelley-Bal 134
Brodie-Bal 134
Jennings-Bal 125
McKean-Cle 119

Runs Produced
Jennings-Bal 280
Thompson-Phi 278
Kelley-Bal 272
Delahanty-Phi ... 244
McKean-Cle 242

Bases On Balls
Joyce-Was 96
Hamilton-Phi 96
Griffin-Bro 93
Delahanty-Phi 86
Kelley-Bal 77

Batting Average
Burkett-Cle ..... .409
Delahanty-Phi ... .404
Thompson-Phi .... .392
Lange-Chi .... .389
Hamilton-Phi .... .389

On Base Percentage
Delahanty-Phi ... .500
Hamilton-Phi .... .490
Burkett-Cle ..... .486
McGraw-Bal ...... .459
Lange-Chi .... .456

Slugging Average
Thompson-Phi .... .654
Delahanty-Phi ... .617
Lange-Chi .... .575
Kelley-Bal ...... .546
Stenzel-Pit ..... .539

Production
Delahanty-Phi ... 1.117
Thompson-Phi 1.085
Lange-Chi 1.032
Burkett-Cle 1.009
Kelley-Bal 1.003

Adjusted Production
Delahanty-Phi 189
Thompson-Phi 179
Stenzel-Pit 165
Lange-Chi 157
Hamilton-Phi 157

Batter Runs
Delahanty-Phi ... 67.9
Thompson-Phi 58.7
Burkett-Cle 56.0
Hamilton-Phi 51.3
Kelley-Bal 49.0

Adjusted Batter Runs
Delahanty-Phi ... 67.6
Thompson-Phi 58.3
Hamilton-Phi 50.9
Burkett-Cle 49.8
Stenzel-Pit 49.1

Clutch Hitting Index
Brodie-Bal 163
Cross-Phi 149
Hassamaer-Was-Lou .. 139
Childs-Cle 136
McCarthy-Bos 135

Runs Created
Hamilton-Phi 177
Delahanty-Phi 175
Thompson-Phi 167
Burkett-Cle 164
Lange-Chi 160

Total Average
Delahanty-Phi ... 1.517
Hamilton-Phi 1.443
Lange-Chi 1.373
Kelley-Bal 1.289
Thompson-Phi 1.269

Stolen Bases
Hamilton-Phi 97
Lange-Chi 67
McGraw-Bal 61
Kelley-Bal 54

Fielding Runs
Jennings-Bal 35.7
Dahlen-Chi 35.2
Fuller-NY 34.2
Cross-Phi 33.4
Collins-Bos-Lou .. 19.0

Total Player Rating
Jennings-Bal 6.5
Delahanty-Phi 4.9
Thompson-Phi 4.8
Kelley-Bal 3.8
Griffin-Bro 3.5

Wins
Young-Cle 35
Hoffer-Bal 31
Hawley-Pit 31

Win Percentage
Hoffer-Bal ...... .838
Young-Cle .... .778
Rhines-Cin ...... .655

Games
Hawley-Pit 56
Breitenstein-StL .. 54
Rusie-NY 49

Complete Games
Breitenstein-StL .. 46
Hawley-Pit 44
Rusie-NY 42
Nichols-Bos 42
Griffith-Chi 39

Shutouts
Young-Cle 4
Rusie-NY 4
McMahon-Bal 4
Hoffer-Bal 4
Hawley-Pit 4

Saves
Parrott-Cin 3
Nichols-Bos 3
Beam-Phi 3

Innings Pitched
Hawley-Pit 444.1
Breitenstein-StL . 429.2
Rusie-NY 393.1
Nichols-Bos 379.2
Young-Cle 369.2

Fewest Hits/Game
Foreman-Pit 8.44
Hoffer-Bal 8.48
Rusie-NY 8.79
Young-Cle 8.84
Maul-Was 9.02

Fewest BB/Game
Young-Cle 1.83
Clarke-NY 1.92
Nichols-Bos 2.04
Staley-StL 2.21
Taylor-Phi 2.23

Strikeouts
Rusie-NY 201
Hawley-Pit 142
Nichols-Bos 140
Breitenstein-StL . 127
Young-Cle 121

Strikeouts/Game
Rusie-NY 4.60
McGill-Phi 4.32
Foreman-Pit 3.48
Stivetts-Bos 3.43
Nichols-Bos 3.32

Ratio
Young-Cle 10.66
Maul-Was 11.48
Hawley-Pit 11.57
Nichols-Bos 11.92
Hoffer-Bal 12.04

Earned Run Average
Maul-Was 2.45
Hawley-Pit 3.18
Hoffer-Bal 3.21
Foreman-Pit 3.22
Young-Cle 3.26

Adjusted ERA
Maul-Was 195
Young-Cle 153
Nichols-Bos 149
Hoffer-Bal 148
Hawley-Pit 142

Opponents' Batting Avg.
Foreman-Pit ..... .245
Hoffer-Bal ...... .246
Rusie-NY .... .252
Young-Cle .... .253
Maul-Was .... .257

Opponents' On Base Pct.
Young-Cle .... .290
Maul-Was .... .306
Hawley-Pit ...... .307
Nichols-Bos ..... .314
Hoffer-Bal ...... .316

Starter Runs
Hawley-Pit 78.8
Young-Cle 62.2
Nichols-Bos 57.5
Hoffer-Bal 54.6
Cuppy-Cle 48.3

Adjusted Starter Runs
Nichols-Bos 71.0
Young-Cle 70.6
Hawley-Pit 65.8
Cuppy-Cle 56.4
Hoffer-Bal 53.8

Clutch Pitching Index
Maul-Was 134
Mercer-Was 122
Clarke-NY 116
Foreman-Cin 111
Griffith-Chi 111

Total Pitcher Index
Hawley-Pit 6.8
Young-Cle 6.5
Cuppy-Cle 5.9
Nichols-Bos 5.8
Griffith-Chi 4.6

Total Baseball Ranking
Hawley-Pit 6.8
Jennings-Bal 6.5
Young-Cle 6.5
Cuppy-Cle 5.9
Nichols-Bos 5.8

TEAM	G	W	L	PCT	GB	R	OR	AB	H	2B	3B	HR	BB	SO	AVG	OBP	SLG	PRO	PRO+	BR	/A	PF	CHI	RC	SB	CS	SBA	SBR
BAL	132	90	39	.698		995	662	4719	1548	207	100	23	386	201	.328	.393	.429	.822	122	167	155	101	101	993	441			
CLE	135	80	48	.625	9.5	840	650	4856	1463	207	72	28	436	316	.301	.363	.391	.754	99	43	-4	106	96	772	175			
CIN	128	77	50	.606	12	783	620	4360	1283	204	73	20	382	226	.294	.357	.388	.745	96	22	-27	107	102	747	350			
BOS	132	74	57	.565	17	860	761	4717	1416	175	74	36	414	274	.300	.363	.392	.755	100	43	-4	106	101	777	241			
CHI	132	71	57	.555	18.5	815	799	4582	1311	182	97	34	409	290	.286	.349	.390	.739	97	10	-20	104	102	759	332			
PIT	131	66	63	.512	24	787	741	4701	1371	169	94	27	387	286	.292	.353	.385	.738	105	9	41	96	97	733	217			
NY	133	64	67	.489	27	829	821	4661	1383	159	87	40	439	271	.297	.364	.394	.758	110	49	71	97	97	787	274			
PHI	130	62	68	.477	28.5	890	891	4680	1382	234	84	49	488	297	.295	.363	.413	.776	112	74	83	99	101	790	191			
WAS	133	58	73	.443	33	818	920	4639	1328	179	79	45	516	365	.286	.365	.388	.753	105	46	46	100	95	770	258			
BRO	133	58	73	.443	33	692	764	4548	1292	174	87	28	344	269	.284	.340	.379	.719	101	-27	16	94	93	669	198			
STL	131	40	90	.308	50.5	593	929	4520	1162	134	78	37	332	300	.257	.313	.346	.659	82	-131	-100	96	94	561	185			
LOU	134	38	93	.290	53	653	997	4588	1197	142	80	37	371	427	.261	.322	.351	.673	86	-105	-74	96	96	596	195			
TOT	792					9555		55571	16136	2166	1005	404	4854	3522	.290	.347	.387	.735							3057			

TEAM	CG	SH	SV	IP	H	H/G	HR	BB	SO	RAT	ERA	ERA+	OAV	OOB	PR	/A	PF	CPI	FA	E	DP	FW	PW	BW	SBW	DIF
BAL	115	9	1	1168[1]	1281	9.9	22	339	302	12.5	3.67	116	.277	.326	88	76	98	98	.945	296	114	2.6	6.4	13.2		3.2
CLE	113	9	5	1195[2]	1363	10.3	27	280	336	12.4	3.46	131	.284	.324	118	140	104	107	.949	288	117	3.6	11.9	-.3		.9
CIN	105	12	4	1108	1240	10.1	27	310	219	12.6	3.67	125	.281	.328	84	114	106	101	.951	252	107	4.7	9.7	-2.3		1.4
BOS	110	6	3	1155[2]	1254	9.8	57	397	277	12.9	3.78	120	.274	.332	74	96	104	104	.934	368	94	-1.7	8.1	-.3		2.4
CHI	118	2	1	1161	1302	10.1	30	467	353	13.7	4.41	103	.281	.347	-7	14	104	93	.934	366	115	-1.6	1.2	-1.7		9.1
PIT	108	8	1	1159[1]	1286	10.0	18	439	362	13.4	4.30	98	.279	.342	7	-14	96	90	.941	317	103	1.2	-1.2	3.5		-2.0
NY	104	1	2	1136[2]	1303	10.3	33	403	312	13.5	4.54	92	.286	.344	-23	-44	96	90	.933	365	90	-1.3	-3.7	6.0		-2.4
PHI	107	3	2	1117	1473	11.9	39	387	243	15.0	5.20	83	.315	.368	-104	-112	99	96	.941	313	112	1.3	-9.5	7.0		-1.9
WAS	106	2	3	1136[2]	1435	11.4	24	435	292	14.8	4.61	95	.306	.365	-31	-27	101	102	.927	398	99	-3.3	-2.3	3.9		-5.8
BRO	97	3	1	1144	1353	10.6	39	400	259	13.8	4.25	97	.292	.348	13	-17	95	101	.945	297	104	2.7	-1.4	1.4		-10.2
STL	115	1	1	1130[2]	1448	11.5	40	456	279	15.2	5.33	82	.309	.370	-121	-124	100	93	.936	345	73	-.5	-10.5	-8.5		-5.5
LOU	108	1	4	1148[2]	1398	11.0	48	541	288	15.2	5.12	84	.298	.370	-98	-103	99	95	.916	475	110	-7.8	-8.7	-6.3		-4.7
TOT	1306	57	28	13761[2]		10.6				13.7	4.36		.290	.347					.938	4080	1238					

Runs		Hits		Doubles		Triples		Home Runs		Total Bases	
Burkett-Cle	160	Burkett-Cle	240	Delahanty-Phi	44	VanHaltren-NY	21	Joyce-Was-NY	13	Burkett-Cle	317
Keeler-Bal	153	Keeler-Bal	210	Miller-Cin	38	McCreery-Lou	21	Delahanty-Phi	13	Delahanty-Phi	315
Hamilton-Bos	152	Jennings-Bal	209	Kelley-Bal	31	Kelley-Bal	19	Thompson-Phi	12	Kelley-Bal	282
Kelley-Bal	148	Delahanty-Phi	198	Dahlen-Chi	30	Dahlen-Chi	19	Connor-StL	11	VanHaltren-NY	272
Dahlen-Chi	137	VanHaltren-NY	197			Clarke-Lou	18			Keeler-Bal	270

Runs Batted In		Runs Produced		Bases On Balls		Batting Average		On Base Percentage		Slugging Average	
Delahanty-Phi	126	Jennings-Bal	246	Hamilton-Bos	110	Burkett-Cle	.410	Hamilton-Bos	.477	Delahanty-Phi	.631
Jennings-Bal	121	Delahanty-Phi	244	Joyce-Was-NY	101	Jennings-Bal	.401	Jennings-Bal	.472	Dahlen-Chi	.553
Duffy-Bos	113	Kelley-Bal	240	Childs-Cle	100	Delahanty-Phi	.397	Delahanty-Phi	.472	McCreery-Lou	.546
McKean-Cle	112	Keeler-Bal	231	Kelley-Bal	91	Keeler-Bal	.386	Joyce-Was-NY	.470	Kelley-Bal	.543
		Burkett-Cle	226	Tiernan-NY	77	Tiernan-NY	.369	Kelley-Bal	.469	Burkett-Cle	.541

Production		Adjusted Production		Batter Runs		Adjusted Batter Runs		Clutch Hitting Index		Runs Created	
Delahanty-Phi	1.103	Delahanty-Phi	194	Delahanty-Phi	66.3	Delahanty-Phi	67.4	Reitz-Bal	176	Kelley-Bal	178
Kelley-Bal	1.013	Kelley-Bal	167	Kelley-Bal	56.4	Kelley-Bal	55.0	Anson-Chi	165	Delahanty-Phi	170
Burkett-Cle	1.002	Joyce-Was-NY	165	Burkett-Cle	56.3	Joyce-Was-NY	51.2	Duffy-Bos	157	Burkett-Cle	166
Dahlen-Chi	.990	Tiernan-NY	162	Joyce-Was-NY	50.1	Burkett-Cle	50.6	McPhee-Cin	156	Hamilton-Bos	159
Joyce-Was-NY	.988	E.Smith-Pit	161	Hamilton-Bos	46.5	Tiernan-NY	48.3	Cross-NY	150	Jennings-Bal	157

Total Average		Stolen Bases		Stolen Base Average		Stolen Base Runs		Fielding Runs		Total Player Rating	
Kelley-Bal	1.430	Kelley-Bal	87					Childs-Cle	42.2	Childs-Cle	6.6
Delahanty-Phi	1.405	Lange-Chi	84					Jennings-Bal	34.4	Jennings-Bal	6.6
Hamilton-Bos	1.316	Hamilton-Bos	83					Dahlen-Chi	24.6	Delahanty-Phi	6.3
Joyce-Was-NY	1.306	Miller-Cin	76					Corcoran-Bro	23.6	Dahlen-Chi	5.4
Jennings-Bal	1.263	Doyle-Bal	73					Clingman-Lou	23.6	Joyce-Was-NY	4.2

Wins		Win Percentage		Games		Complete Games		Shutouts		Saves	
Nichols-Bos	30	Hoffer-Bal	.781	Killen-Pit	52	Killen-Pit	44	Young-Cle	5	Young-Cle	3
Killen-Pit	30	Hemming-Bal	.714	Young-Cle	51	Young-Cle	42	Killen-Pit	5	Hill-Lou	2
Young-Cle	28	F.Foreman-Cin	.714	Nichols-Bos	49	Mercer-Was	38			Fisher-Cin	2
Meekin-NY	26	Dwyer-Cin	.686	Hawley-Pit	49						
		Nichols-Bos	.682	Clarke-NY	48						

Innings Pitched		Fewest Hits/Game		Fewest BB/Game		Strikeouts		Strikeouts/Game		Ratio	
Killen-Pit	432.1	Rhines-Cin	8.06	Young-Cle	1.35	Young-Cle	140	Briggs-Chi	3.90	Rhines-Cin	11.08
Young-Cle	414.1	Hawley-Pit	9.10	Clarke-NY	1.54	Hawley-Pit	137	Pond-Bal	3.36	Cuppy-Cle	11.64
Hawley-Pit	378.0	Sullivan-NY	9.13	Dwyer-Cin	1.87	Killen-Pit	134	McJames-Was	3.31	Young-Cle	11.71
Nichols-Bos	372.1	Friend-Chi	9.23	Cuppy-Cle	1.89	Breitenstein-StL	114	Hawley-Pit	3.26	Nichols-Bos	11.80
Mercer-Was	366.1	Hoffer-Bal	9.23	Griffith-Chi	1.98	Meekin-NY	110	Young-Cle	3.04	Dwyer-Cin	11.88

Earned Run Average		Adjusted ERA		Opponents' Batting Avg.		Opponents' On Base Pct.		Starter Runs		Adjusted Starter Runs	
Rhines-Cin	2.45	Rhines-Cin	188	Rhines-Cin	.238	Rhines-Cin	.300	Nichols-Bos	63.2	Nichols-Bos	70.6
Nichols-Bos	2.83	Nichols-Bos	160	Hawley-Pit	.261	Cuppy-Cle	.311	Young-Cle	51.5	Young-Cle	59.6
Cuppy-Cle	3.12	Dwyer-Cin	146	Sullivan-NY	.261	Young-Cle	.312	Cuppy-Cle	49.3	Cuppy-Cle	56.2
Dwyer-Cin	3.15	Cuppy-Cle	145	Friend-Chi	.264	Nichols-Bos	.314	Killen-Pit	45.3	Dwyer-Cin	46.7
Young-Cle	3.24	Young-Cle	140	Hoffer-Bal	.264	Dwyer-Cin	.315	Dwyer-Cin	38.7	Killen-Pit	37.5

Clutch Pitching Index		Relief Runs		Adjusted Relief Runs		Relief Ranking		Total Pitcher Index		Total Baseball Ranking	
Nichols-Bos	120							Young-Cle	6.9	Young-Cle	6.9
Wallace-Cle	118							Nichols-Bos	6.3	Childs-Cle	6.6
Payne-Bro	113							Cuppy-Cle	6.2	Jennings-Bal	6.6
Dwyer-Cin	111							Dwyer-Cin	4.5	Delahanty-Phi	6.3
Mercer-Was	108							Killen-Pit	4.1	Nichols-Bos	6.3

TEAM	G	W	L	PCT	GB	R	OR	AB	H	2B	3B	HR	BB	SO	AVG	OBP	SLG	PRO	PRO+	BR	/A	PF	CHI	RC	SB	CS	SBA	SBR
BOS	135	93	39	.705		1025	665	4937	1574	230	83	45	423	262	.319	.378	.426	.804	112	137	85	106	106	906	233			
BAL	136	90	40	.692	2	964	674	4872	1584	243	66	19	437	256	.325	.394	.414	.808	121	157	157	100	97	976	401			
NY	137	83	48	.634	9.5	895	695	4844	1449	188	84	31	404	327	.299	.361	.392	.753	109	44	66	97	104	824	328			
CIN	134	76	56	.576	17	763	705	4524	1311	219	69	22	380	218	.290	.352	.383	.735	94	10	-40	107	99	696	194			
CLE	132	69	62	.527	23.5	773	680	4604	1374	192	88	16	435	344	.298	.364	.389	.753	100	44	2	105	94	735	181			
WAS	135	61	71	.462	32	781	793	4636	1376	194	77	36	374	348	.297	.357	.395	.752	105	37	40	100	96	746	208			
BRO	136	61	71	.462	32	802	845	4810	1343	202	72	24	351	255	.279	.335	.366	.701	96	-54	-9	95	107	670	187			
PIT	135	60	71	.458	32.5	676	835	4590	1266	140	108	25	359	334	.276	.337	.370	.707	96	-42	-13	96	93	645	170			
CHI	138	59	73	.447	34	832	894	4803	1356	189	97	38	430	317	.282	.347	.386	.733	96	4	-26	104	102	754	264			
PHI	134	55	77	.417	38	752	792	4756	1392	213	83	40	399	299	.293	.353	.398	.751	107	32	52	97	91	743	163			
LOU	134	52	78	.400	40	669	859	4520	1197	160	70	40	370	453	.265	.329	.358	.687	91	-74	-48	97	97	612	195			
STL	132	29	102	.221	63.5	588	1083	4642	1277	149	67	31	354	314	.275	.336	.356	.692	90	-64	-48	98	82	629	172			
TOT	809					9520		56538	16499	2319	964	367	4716	3727	.292	.346	.386	.733							2696			

TEAM	CG	SH	SV	IP	H	H/G	HR	BB	SO	RAT	ERA	ERA+	OAV	OOB	PR	/A	PF	CPI	FA	E	DP	FW	PW	BW	SBW	DIF
BOS	115	8	7	1194¹	1273	9.6	39	393	329	12.6	3.65	122	.271	.327	86	107	104	99	.951	272	80	3.9	9.2	7.3		6.6
BAL	118	3	0	1197²	1296	9.7	18	382	361	12.6	3.55	117	.274	.328	100	80	97	99	.951	277	110	3.8	6.9	13.4		.9
NY	118	8	3	1187¹	1214	9.2	26	486	456	12.9	3.47	120	.263	.333	110	88	96	102	.930	397	109	-3.3	7.5	5.7		7.6
CIN	100	4	2	1156²	1375	10.7	18	329	270	13.3	4.09	111	.293	.340	28	58	106	97	.948	273	100	3.7	5.0	-3.4		4.7
CLE	111	6	0	1119¹	1297	10.4	32	289	277	12.8	3.95	114	.288	.331	44	66	104	97	.950	261	74	4.2	5.7	.2		-6.5
WAS	103	7	5	1148	1383	10.8	27	400	348	14.0	4.01	108	.296	.351	37	40	101	107	.933	369	103	-1.9	3.4	3.4		-9.9
BRO	114	4	2	1194²	1417	10.7	34	410	256	13.8	4.60	89	.292	.348	-39	-67	95	92	.936	364	99	-1.5	-5.7	-.8		3.0
PIT	112	2	2	1153¹	1397	10.9	22	318	342	13.4	4.67	89	.297	.342	-47	-65	97	87	.936	346	70	-.5	-5.6	-1.1		1.7
CHI	131	2	1	1197	1485	11.2	30	433	361	14.4	4.53	98	.302	.359	-30	-11	104	100	.932	391	111	-2.9	-.9	-2.2		-.9
PHI	115	4	2	1155¹	1415	11.0	28	364	253	13.9	4.60	91	.299	.349	-38	-52	97	93	.944	296	72	2.3	-4.5	4.5		-13.3
LOU	114	2	0	1138	1363	10.8	39	459	267	14.4	4.42	96	.294	.358	-14	-21	99	102	.929	395	84	-3.6	-1.8	-4.1		-3.5
STL	109	1	1	1127¹	1584	12.6	54	453	207	16.3	6.21	71	.329	.387	-238	-227	102	91	.933	375	84	-2.7	-19.4	-4.1		-10.2
TOT	1360	51	25	13969		10.6				13.7	4.31		.292	.346					.939	4018	1096					

Runs
Hamilton-Bos 152
Keeler-Bal 145
Griffin-Bro 136
Jones-Bro 134
Jennings-Bal 133

Hits
Keeler-Bal 239
F.Clarke-Lou 202
Delahanty-Phi 200
Burkett-Cle 198
Lajoie-Phi 197

Doubles
Stenzel-Bal 43
Lajoie-Phi 40
Delahanty-Phi 40
Wallace-Cle 33
Ryan-Chi 33

Triples
Davis-Pit 28
Lajoie-Phi 23
Wallace-Cle 21
Keeler-Bal 19

Home Runs
Duffy-Bos 11
Davis-NY 10
Lajoie-Phi 9
Beckley-NY-Cin 8

Total Bases
Lajoie-Phi 310
Keeler-Bal 304
Delahanty-Phi 285
F.Clarke-Lou 276
Duffy-Bos 265

Runs Batted In
Davis-NY 136
Collins-Bos 132
Duffy-Bos 129
Lajoie-Phi 127
Kelley-Bal 118

Runs Produced
Duffy-Bos 248
Davis-NY 238
Collins-Bos 229
Kelley-Bal 226

Bases On Balls
Hamilton-Bos 105
McGraw-Bal 99
Griffin-Bro 81
Selbach-Was 80
Joyce-NY 78

Batting Average
Keeler-Bal .... .424
F.Clarke-Lou .... .390
Burkett-Cle .... .383
Delahanty-Phi .... .377
Kelley-Bal .... .362

On Base Percentage
McGraw-Bal .... .471
Burkett-Cle .... .468
Keeler-Bal .... .464
Jennings-Bal .... .463
Hamilton-Bos .... .461

Slugging Average
Lajoie-Phi .... .569
Keeler-Bal .... .539
Delahanty-Phi .... .538
F.Clarke-Lou .... .533
Davis-NY .... .509

Production
Keeler-Bal 1.003
F.Clarke-Lou .... .994
Delahanty-Phi .... .981
Lajoie-Phi .... .960
Burkett-Cle .... .944

Adjusted Production
F.Clarke-Lou 170
Keeler-Bal 167
Delahanty-Phi 165
Lajoie-Phi 158
Kelley-Bal 150

Batter Runs
Keeler-Bal 54.1
F.Clarke-Lou 50.1
Delahanty-Phi 47.1
Burkett-Cle 44.0
Kelley-Bal 39.2

Adjusted Batter Runs
Keeler-Bal 54.1
F.Clarke-Lou 53.2
Delahanty-Phi 49.5
Lajoie-Phi 40.5
Kelley-Bal 39.2

Clutch Hitting Index
Gleason-NY 163
Lowe-Bos 147
Shindle-Bro 147
Collins-Bos 144
Anson-Chi 143

Runs Created
Keeler-Bal 175
F.Clarke-Lou 157
Delahanty-Phi 141
Davis-NY 137
Stenzel-Bal 135

Total Average
F.Clarke-Lou 1.269
Keeler-Bal 1.262
Jennings-Bal 1.251
Hamilton-Bos ... 1.162
Kelley-Bal 1.143

Stolen Bases
Lange-Chi 73
Stenzel-Bal 69
Hamilton-Bos 66
Davis-NY 65
Keeler-Bal 64

Stolen Base Average

Stolen Base Runs

Fielding Runs
Clingman-Lou 29.2
Cross-StL 28.1
Jennings-Bal 27.2
Davis-NY 22.0
Reitz-Bal 21.4

Total Player Rating
Jennings-Bal 5.6
Davis-NY 4.9
F.Clarke-Lou 4.2
Delahanty-Phi 4.1
Childs-Cle 3.8

Wins
Nichols-Bos 31
Rusie-NY 28
Klobedanz-Bos 26
Corbett-Bal 24
Breitenstein-Cin 23

Win Percentage
Klobedanz-Bos .... .788
Nops-Bal .... .769
Corbett-Bal .... .750
Nichols-Bos .... .738
Rusie-NY .... .737

Games
Young-Cle 46
Nichols-Bos 46
Donahue-StL 46
Mercer-Was 45

Complete Games
Killen-Pit 38
Griffith-Chi 38
Donahue-StL 38
Nichols-Bos 37
Kennedy-Bro 36

Shutouts
Mercer-Was 3
McJames-Was 3

Saves
Nichols-Bos 3

Innings Pitched
Nichols-Bos 368.0
Donahue-StL 348.0
Griffith-Chi 343.2
Kennedy-Bro 343.1
Killen-Pit 337.1

Fewest Hits/Game
Seymour-NY 8.23
Rusie-NY 8.77
Nichols-Bos 8.85
Hill-Lou 9.45
Corbett-Bal 9.49

Fewest BB/Game
Young-Cle 1.32
Tannehill-Pit 1.52
Nichols-Bos 1.66
Cuppy-Cle 1.68
Killen-Pit 2.03

Strikeouts
McJames-Was 156
Seymour-NY 149
Corbett-Bal 149
Rusie-NY 135
Nichols-Bos 127

Strikeouts/Game
Seymour-NY 4.83
McJames-Was 4.34
Corbett-Bal 4.28
Rusie-NY 3.77
Nichols-Bos 3.11

Ratio
Nichols-Bos 10.52
Rusie-NY 11.20
Cuppy-Cle 11.37
Nops-Bal 11.71
Young-Cle 11.87

Earned Run Average
Rusie-NY 2.54
Nichols-Bos 2.64
Nops-Bal 2.81
Corbett-Bal 3.11
Powell-Cle 3.16

Adjusted ERA
Nichols-Bos 169
Rusie-NY 163
Nops-Bal 148
Powell-Cle 142
Cuppy-Cle 142

Opponents' Batting Avg.
Seymour-NY .... .242
Rusie-NY .... .254
Nichols-Bos .... .256
Hill-Lou .... .268
Corbett-Bal .... .269

Opponents' On Base Pct.
Nichols-Bos .... .290
Rusie-NY .... .303
Cuppy-Cle .... .306
Nops-Bal .... .312
Young-Cle .... .315

Starter Runs
Nichols-Bos 68.1
Rusie-NY 63.3
Corbett-Bal 41.8
Mercer-Was 38.9
Nops-Bal 36.6

Adjusted Starter Runs
Nichols-Bos 74.6
Rusie-NY 57.7
Mercer-Was 40.0
Corbett-Bal 36.8
Nops-Bal 33.1

Clutch Pitching Index
Mercer-Was 124
Nops-Bal 116
Rusie-NY 114
Dwyer-Cin 113
McJames-Was 112

Relief Runs

Adjusted Relief Runs

Relief Ranking

Total Pitcher Index
Nichols-Bos 7.1
Rusie-NY 5.7
Mercer-Was 4.3
Corbett-Bal 3.3
Breitenstein-Cin ... 3.3

Total Baseball Ranking
Nichols-Bos 7.1
Rusie-NY 5.7
Jennings-Bal 5.6
Davis-NY 4.9
Mercer-Was 4.3

TEAM	G	W	L	PCT	GB	R	OR	AB	H	2B	3B	HR	BB	SO	AVG	OBP	SLG	PRO	PRO+	BR	/A	PF	CHI	RC	SB	CS	SBA	SBR
BOS	152	102	47	.685		872	614	5276	1531	190	55	53	405	303	.290	.344	.377	.721	108	94	53	105	102	763	172			
BAL	154	96	53	.644	6	933	623	5242	1584	154	77	12	519	316	.302	.382	.368	.750	120	178	163	102	97	853	250			
CIN	157	92	60	.605	11.5	831	740	5334	1448	207	101	19	455	300	.271	.333	.359	.692	99	41	-12	107	102	711	165			
CHI	152	85	65	.567	17.5	828	679	5219	1431	175	84	18	476	394	.274	.343	.350	.692	106	51	52	100	101	720	220			
CLE	156	81	68	.544	21	730	683	5246	1379	162	56	18	545	306	.263	.337	.325	.662	98	0	11	99	94	622	93			
PHI	150	78	71	.523	24	823	784	5118	1431	238	81	33	472	382	.280	.348	.377	.725	121	105	137	96	96	754	182			
NY	157	77	73	.513	25.5	837	800	5349	1422	190	86	34	428	372	.266	.328	.353	.681	106	18	42	97	105	706	214			
PIT	152	72	76	.486	29.5	634	694	5087	1313	140	88	14	336	343	.258	.312	.328	.640	91	-57	-43	98	94	569	107			
LOU	154	70	81	.464	33	728	833	5193	1389	150	71	32	375	429	.267	.324	.342	.666	99	-9	3	98	98	668	235			
BRO	149	54	91	.372	46	638	811	5126	1314	156	66	17	328	314	.256	.309	.322	.631	88	-74	-71	100	97	565	130			
WAS	155	51	101	.336	52.5	704	939	5257	1423	177	80	36	370	386	.271	.327	.355	.682	103	18	20	100	91	692	197			
STL	154	39	111	.260	63.5	571	929	5214	1290	149	55	13	383	402	.247	.309	.305	.614	81	-103	-120	102	87	536	104			
TOT	921					9129		62661	16955	2088	900	299	5092	4247	.271	.325	.347	.672						2069				

TEAM	CG	SH	SV	IP	H	H/G	HR	BB	SO	RAT	ERA	ERA+	OAV	OOB	PR	/A	PF	CPI	FA	E	DP	FW	PW	BW	SBW	DIF
BOS	127	9	7	1340	1186	8.0	37	470	432	11.1	2.98	124	.236	.301	93	105	102	93	.950	310	102	3.1	9.8	5.0		9.6
BAL	138	12	0	1323	1236	8.4	17	400	422	11.1	2.90	123	.246	.301	103	98	99	95	.947	326	105	2.5	9.2	15.2		-5.4
CIN	131	10	2	1385¹	1484	9.6	16	449	294	12.6	3.50	110	.272	.327	16	50	106	99	.950	325	128	2.9	4.7	-1.1		9.5
CHI	137	13	0	1342²	1357	9.1	17	364	323	11.5	2.83	126	.261	.309	115	110	99	107	.936	412	149	-2.9	10.3	4.9		-2.3
CLE	142	9	0	1334	1429	9.6	26	309	339	11.7	3.20	113	.272	.312	59	59	100	102	.952	301	95	4.2	5.5	1.0		-4.2
PHI	129	10	0	1288¹	1440	10.1	23	399	325	12.8	3.72	92	.280	.332	-17	-42	95	99	.937	379	102	-1.2	-3.9	12.8		-4.2
NY	141	9	1	1353²	1359	9.0	21	587	558	12.9	3.44	101	.259	.334	24	4	96	101	.932	447	113	-4.2	.4	3.9		1.9
PIT	131	10	3	1323²	1400	9.5	14	346	330	11.9	3.41	104	.269	.315	28	21	99	94	.946	340	105	1.4	2.0	-4.0		-1.3
LOU	137	4	0	1334	1457	9.8	33	470	271	13.0	4.24	84	.276	.335	-94	-100	99	88	.939	382	114	-.8	-9.3	.3		4.4
BRO	134	1	0	1298²	1446	10.0	34	476	294	13.3	4.01	89	.280	.340	-59	-63	99	97	.947	334	125	1.3	-5.9	-6.6		-7.3
WAS	129	0	1	1307	1577	10.9	29	450	371	14.0	4.52	81	.296	.351	-133	-127	101	94	.929	443	119	-4.2	-11.9	1.9		-10.8
STL	133	0	2	1324¹	1584	10.8	32	372	288	13.3	4.53	83	.294	.340	-136	-111	105	89	.939	388	97	-1.2	-10.4	-11.2		-13.2
TOT	1609	87	16	15954²		9.6				12.4	3.60		.271	.325					.942	4387	1354					

Runs
McGraw-Bal 143
Jennings-Bal 135
VanHaltren-NY 129
Keeler-Bal 126
Cooley-Phi 123

Hits
Keeler-Bal 216
Burkett-Cle 213
VanHaltren-NY 204
Lajoie-Phi 197

Doubles
Lajoie-Phi 43
Delahanty-Phi 36
Dahlen-Chi 35
Collins-Bos 35
Anderson-Bro-Was . 33

Triples
Anderson-Bro-Was .. 22
VanHaltren-NY 16
Hoy-Lou 16

Home Runs
Collins-Bos 15
Wagner-Lou 10
Joyce-NY 10
Anderson-Bro-Was .. 9
McKean-Cle 9

Total Bases
Collins-Bos 286
Lajoie-Phi 280
VanHaltren-NY 270
Anderson-Bro-Was 257
Cooley-Phi 256

Runs Batted In
Lajoie-Phi 127
Collins-Bos 111
Kelley-Bal 110
Duffy-Bos 108
McGann-Bal 106

Runs Produced
Lajoie-Phi 234
Jennings-Bal 221
Delahanty-Phi 203
Collins-Bos 203
McGann-Bal 200

Bases On Balls
McGraw-Bal 112
Joyce-NY 88
Hamilton-Bos 87
Flick-Phi 86
Jennings-Bal 78

Batting Average
Keeler-Bal .... .385
Hamilton-Bos ..... .369
McGraw-Bal ...... .342
Smith-Cin .... .342
Burkett-Cle .... .341

On Base Percentage
Hamilton-Bos ..... .480
McGraw-Bal ...... .475
Jennings-Bal ..... .454
Flick-Phi .... .430
Delahanty-Phi .... .426

Slugging Average
Anderson-Bro-Was .494
Collins-Bos ...... .479
Lajoie-Phi .... .461
Delahanty-Phi .... .454
Hamilton-Bos ..... .453

Production
Hamilton-Bos .... .933
Delahanty-Phi .... .880
Flick-Phi .... .878
Jennings-Bal ..... .875
McGraw-Bal ..... .871

Adjusted Production
Hamilton-Bos 163
Delahanty-Phi 163
Flick-Phi 162
Jennings-Bal 152
McGraw-Bal 151

Batter Runs
McGraw-Bal 47.3
Jennings-Bal 46.1
Hamilton-Bos 45.1
Delahanty-Phi 42.5
Flick-Phi 37.2

Adjusted Batter Runs
Delahanty-Phi 46.1
McGraw-Bal 45.6
Jennings-Bal 44.5
Hamilton-Bos 41.5
Flick-Phi 40.3

Clutch Hitting Index
Kelley-Bal 169
Hartman-NY 158
McGann-Bal 151
Duffy-Bos 147
Connor-Chi 147

Runs Created
Delahanty-Phi 134
McGraw-Bal 120
Hamilton-Bos 120
Ryan-Chi 118
Jennings-Bal 118

Total Average
Hamilton-Bos ... 1.262
McGraw-Bal 1.115
Delahanty-Phi ... 1.082
Jennings-Bal 1.047
Flick-Phi 1.035

Stolen Bases
Delahanty-Phi 58
Hamilton-Bos 54
DeMontreville-Bal .. 49
Dexter-Lou 44
McGraw-Bal 43

Stolen Base Average

Stolen Base Runs

Fielding Runs
Davis-NY 35.8
Dahlen-Chi 25.3
Selbach-Was 20.2
Gleason-NY 19.4
Cross-StL 18.4

Total Player Rating
Dahlen-Chi 4.8
Jennings-Bal 4.7
Davis-NY 4.7
Collins-Bos 4.4
Delahanty-Phi 3.9

Wins
Nichols-Bos 31
Cunningham-Lou .. 28
McJames-Bal 27
Hawley-Cin 27
Lewis-Bos 26

Win Percentage
Lewis-Bos .... .765
Maul-Bal .... .741
Nichols-Bos ..... .721
Hawley-Cin ...... .711
Griffith-Chi ..... .706

Games
Taylor-StL 50
Nichols-Bos 50
Young-Cle 46

Complete Games
Taylor-StL 42
Cunningham-Lou .. 41
Young-Cle 40
Nichols-Bos 40
McJames-Bal 40

Shutouts
Powell-Cle 6
Piatt-Phi 6
Tannehill-Pit 5
Nichols-Bos 5
Hughes-Bal 5

Saves
Nichols-Bos 4
Tannehill-Pit 2
Lewis-Bos 2
Hickman-Bos 2
Dammann-Cin 2

Innings Pitched
Taylor-StL 397.1
Nichols-Bos 388.0
Young-Cle 377.2
McJames-Bal ... 374.0
Cunningham-Lou 362.0

Fewest Hits/Game
Nichols-Bos 7.33
Willis-Bos 7.64
Lewis-Bos 7.67
Maul-Bal 7.77
McJames-Bal 7.87

Fewest BB/Game
Young-Cle .... .98
Dwyer-Cin 1.58
Cunningham-Lou . 1.62
Tannehill-Pit 1.74
Griffith-Chi 1.77

Strikeouts
Seymour-NY 239
McJames-Bal 178
Willis-Bos 160
Nichols-Bos 138
Piatt-Phi 121

Strikeouts/Game
Seymour-NY 6.03
Willis-Bos 4.63
McJames-Bal ... 4.28
Doheny-NY 4.06
Piatt-Phi 3.56

Ratio
Nichols-Bos 9.30
Maul-Bal 9.61
Griffith-Chi 10.20
Young-Cle 10.20
McJames-Bal ... 10.59

Earned Run Average
Griffith-Chi 1.88
Maul-Bal 2.10
Nichols-Bos 2.13
McJames-Bal 2.36
Callahan-Chi 2.46

Adjusted ERA
Griffith-Chi 190
Nichols-Bos 173
Maul-Bal 170
McJames-Bal ... 152
Callahan-Chi 145

Opponents' Batting Avg.
Nichols-Bos ...... .221
Willis-Bos .... .229
Lewis-Bos .... .229
Maul-Bal .... .232
McJames-Bal ... .234

Opponents' On Base Pct.
Nichols-Bos ...... .265
Maul-Bal .... .272
Griffith-Chi ..... .283
Young-Cle .... .283
McJames-Bal ... .291

Starter Runs
Nichols-Bos 63.3
Griffith-Chi 62.4
McJames-Bal ... 51.7
Young-Cle 45.2
Maul-Bal 39.9

Adjusted Starter Runs
Nichols-Bos 67.1
Griffith-Chi 61.5
McJames-Bal ... 50.7
Young-Cle 45.5
Maul-Bal 39.3

Clutch Pitching Index
Griffith-Chi 127
Orth-Phi 117
Dammann-Cin ... 116
Callahan-Chi 112
Doheny-NY 110

Relief Runs

Adjusted Relief Runs

Relief Ranking

Total Pitcher Index
Nichols-Bos 6.9
Griffith-Chi 6.2
Young-Cle 5.7
McJames-Bal 4.2
Callahan-Chi 4.1

Total Baseball Ranking
Nichols-Bos 6.9
Griffith-Chi 6.2
Young-Cle 5.7
Dahlen-Chi 4.8
Jennings-Bal 4.7

TEAM	G	W	L	PCT	GB	R	OR	AB	H	2B	3B	HR	BB	SO	AVG	OBP	SLG	PRO	PRO+	BR	/A	PF	CHI	RC	SB	CS	SBA	SBR
BRO	150	101	47	.682		892	658	4937	1436	178	97	27	477	263	.291	.368	.383	.751	111	108	90	102	100	815	271			
BOS	153	95	57	.625	8	858	645	5290	1517	178	90	39	431	269	.287	.345	.377	.722	96	44	-33	110	100	771	185			
PHI	154	94	58	.618	9	916	743	5353	1613	241	83	31	441	341	.301	.363	.395	.758	120	118	146	97	97	864	212			
BAL	152	86	62	.581	15	827	691	5073	1509	204	71	17	418	383	.297	.365	.376	.741	106	90	48	105	94	849	364			
STL	155	84	67	.556	18.5	819	739	5304	1514	172	88	47	468	262	.285	.347	.378	.725	104	51	32	102	94	787	210			
CIN	156	83	67	.553	19	856	770	5225	1439	194	105	13	485	295	.275	.344	.360	.704	99	16	1	102	103	744	228			
PIT	154	76	73	.510	25.5	834	765	5450	1574	196	121	27	384	345	.289	.342	.384	.726	107	48	50	100	95	797	179			
CHI	152	75	73	.507	26	812	765	5148	1428	173	82	27	406	342	.277	.337	.359	.696	101	-4	17	97	103	723	247			
LOU	155	75	77	.493	28	827	775	5307	1484	192	68	40	436	375	.280	.343	.364	.707	102	18	18	100	99	760	233			
NY	152	60	90	.400	42	734	863	5092	1431	161	65	23	387	360	.281	.337	.352	.689	100	-17	10	97	97	699	234			
WAS	155	54	98	.355	49	743	983	5256	1429	162	87	47	350	341	.272	.327	.363	.690	98	-23	-13	99	96	698	176			
CLE	154	20	134	.130	84	529	1252	5279	1333	142	50	12	289	280	.253	.299	.305	.604	78	-185	-125	93	87	533	127			
TOT	921					9647		62714	17707	2193	1007	350	4972	3856	.282	.335	.366	.701						2666				

TEAM	CG	SH	SV	IP	H	H/G	HR	BB	SO	RAT	ERA	ERA+	OAV	OOB	PR	/A	PF	CPI	FA	E	DP	FW	PW	BW	SBW	DIF
BRO	121	9	9	1269¹	1320	9.4	32	463	331	12.6	3.25	120	.268	.331	84	92	102	108	.948	314	125	2.9	8.3	8.2		7.6
BOS	138	13	4	1348	1273	8.5	44	432	385	11.4	3.26	127	.249	.308	87	132	108	91	.952	303	124	4.0	12.0	-3.0		6.1
PHI	129	15	2	1333¹	1398	9.4	17	370	281	11.9	3.47	106	.270	.318	56	30	96	92	.940	379	110	-.4	2.7	13.2		2.4
BAL	133	9	4	1304¹	1403	9.7	13	349	294	12.1	3.31	120	.274	.321	77	93	103	99	.949	308	96	3.5	8.4	4.4		-4.3
STL	134	7	1	1340²	1476	9.9	41	321	331	12.1	3.36	118	.279	.320	73	90	103	104	.939	397	117	-1.3	8.2	2.9		-1.3
CIN	130	8	5	1361	1484	9.8	26	370	360	12.3	3.70	106	.277	.324	23	32	102	93	.947	339	111	2.3	2.9	.0		2.7
PIT	117	9	4	1364	1464	9.7	27	437	334	12.5	3.60	106	.274	.329	38	32	99	97	.945	361	98	.7	2.9	4.5		-6.6
CHI	147	8	1	1331¹	1433	9.7	20	330	313	11.9	3.37	111	.275	.318	71	54	97	97	.935	428	145	-3.5	4.9	1.5		-1.9
LOU	134	5	2	1351²	1509	10.0	33	323	287	12.2	3.45	112	.282	.323	60	60	100	102	.939	394	101	-1.1	5.4	1.6		-7.0
NY	138	4	0	1278¹	1454	10.2	19	628	397	14.7	4.29	87	.286	.364	-63	-78	97	99	.932	433	140	-3.8	-7.1	.9		-5.0
WAS	131	3	0	1300¹	1649	11.4	35	422	328	14.3	4.93	79	.309	.359	-156	-149	101	91	.935	403	99	-1.6	-13.5	-1.2		-5.7
CLE	138	0	0	1264	1844	13.1	43	527	215	16.9	6.37	58	.339	.398	-353	-379	95	91	.937	388	121	-.9	-34.3	-11.3		-10.4
TOT	1590	90	32	15846¹		10.1				12.9	3.85		.282	.335					.942	4447	1387					

Runs
McGraw-Bal	140
Keeler-Bro	140
Thomas-Phi	137
Delahanty-Phi	135
Williams-Pit	126

Hits
Delahanty-Phi	238
Burkett-StL	221
Williams-Pit	219
Keeler-Bro	216
Tenney-Bos	209

Doubles
Delahanty-Phi	55
Wagner-Lou	43
Holmes-Bal	31
Long-Bos	30
Duffy-Bos	29

Triples
Williams-Pit	27
Freeman-Was	25
Stahl-Bos	19
Tenney-Bos	17
McCarthy-Pit	17

Home Runs
Freeman-Was	25
Wallace-StL	12
Williams-Pit	9
Mertes-Chi	9
Delahanty-Phi	9

Total Bases
Delahanty-Phi	338
Freeman-Was	331
Williams-Pit	328
Stahl-Bos	284
Wagner-Lou	282

Runs Batted In
Delahanty-Phi	137
Freeman-Was	122
Williams-Pit	116
Wagner-Lou	113
Wallace-StL	108

Runs Produced
Delahanty-Phi	263
Williams-Pit	233
Wagner-Lou	204
Freeman-Was	204

Bases On Balls
McGraw-Bal	124
Thomas-Phi	115
VanHaltren-NY	74
Childs-StL	74

Batting Average
Delahanty-Phi	.410
Burkett-StL	.396
McGraw-Bal	.391
Keeler-Bro	.379
Williams-Pit	.355

On Base Percentage
McGraw-Bal	.547
Delahanty-Phi	.464
Burkett-StL	.463
Thomas-Phi	.457
Stahl-Bos	.426

Slugging Average
Delahanty-Phi	.582
Freeman-Was	.563
Williams-Pit	.532
Burkett-StL	.500
Wagner-Lou	.494

Production
Delahanty-Phi	1.046
McGraw-Bal	.994
Burkett-StL	.963
Williams-Pit	.947
Freeman-Was	.924

Adjusted Production
Delahanty-Phi	196
McGraw-Bal	169
Burkett-StL	163
Williams-Pit	162
Freeman-Was	156

Batter Runs
Delahanty-Phi	70.1
McGraw-Bal	58.4
Burkett-StL	53.7
Williams-Pit	50.9
Stahl-Bos	44.6

Adjusted Batter Runs
Delahanty-Phi	73.2
McGraw-Bal	54.4
Burkett-StL	51.7
Williams-Pit	51.1
Freeman-Was	39.5

Clutch Hitting Index
Corcoran-Cin	150
Flick-Phi	143
Duffy-Bos	140
Lauder-Phi	139
Lowe-Bos	138

Runs Created
Delahanty-Phi	175
Williams-Pit	151
Burkett-StL	144
McGraw-Bal	141
Stahl-Bos	139

Total Average
McGraw-Bal	1.601
Delahanty-Phi	1.245
Burkett-StL	1.107
Stahl-Bos	1.051
Williams-Pit	1.050

Stolen Bases
Sheckard-Bal	77
McGraw-Bal	73
Heidrick-StL	55
Holmes-Bal	50
Clarke-Lou	49

Stolen Base Average

Stolen Base Runs

Fielding Runs
G.Davis-NY	46.3
Wallace-StL	38.3
Cross-Cle-StL	32.9
Gleason-NY	25.7
Collins-Bos	21.0

Total Player Rating
G.Davis-NY	6.2
Delahanty-Phi	5.7
Wallace-StL	5.3
Williams-Pit	5.1
McGraw-Bal	5.0

Wins
McGinnity-Bal	28
Hughes-Bro	28
Willis-Bos	27
Young-StL	26
Tannehill-Pit	24

Win Percentage
Hughes-Bro	.824
Willis-Bos	.771
Hahn-Cin	.742
Donahue-Phi	.724
Kennedy-Bro	.710

Games
Leever-Pit	51
Powell-StL	48
McGinnity-Bal	48
Young-StL	44
Carrick-NY	44

Complete Games
Young-StL	40
Powell-StL	40
Carrick-NY	40
Taylor-Chi	39
McGinnity-Bal	38

Shutouts
Willis-Bos	5

Saves
Leever-Pit	3

Innings Pitched
Leever-Pit	379.0
Powell-StL	373.0
Young-StL	369.1
McGinnity-Bal	366.1
Carrick-NY	361.2

Fewest Hits/Game
Willis-Bos	7.28
Hughes-Bro	7.71
Hahn-Cin	8.16
Seymour-NY	8.28
Leever-Pit	8.38

Fewest BB/Game
Young-StL	1.07
Cuppy-StL	1.36
Tannehill-Pit	1.47
Woods-Lou	1.79
Phillippe-Lou	1.79

Strikeouts
Hahn-Cin	145
Seymour-NY	142
Leever-Pit	121
Willis-Bos	120
Doheny-NY	115

Strikeouts/Game
Seymour-NY	4.76
Hahn-Cin	4.22
Doheny-NY	3.90
McJames-Bro	3.43
Willis-Bos	3.15

Ratio
Young-StL	10.04
Hahn-Cin	10.14
Willis-Bos	10.35
Nichols-Bos	10.70
Kitson-Bal	10.78

Earned Run Average
Willis-Bos	2.50
Young-StL	2.58
McGinnity-Bal	2.68
Hahn-Cin	2.68
Hughes-Bro	2.68

Adjusted ERA
Willis-Bos	166
Young-StL	154
McGinnity-Bal	148
Hahn-Cin	146
Hughes-Bro	146

Opponents' Batting Avg.
Willis-Bos	.222
Hughes-Bro	.232
Hahn-Cin	.242
Seymour-NY	.245
Leever-Pit	.247

Opponents' On Base Pct.
Young-StL	.282
Hahn-Cin	.284
Willis-Bos	.288
Nichols-Bos	.295
Kitson-Bal	.297

Starter Runs
Young-StL	52.0
Willis-Bos	51.6
McGinnity-Bal	47.7
Hahn-Cin	40.2
Kitson-Bal	40.0

Adjusted Starter Runs
Willis-Bos	63.1
Young-StL	57.0
McGinnity-Bal	52.2
Nichols-Bos	44.5
Kitson-Bal	44.1

Clutch Pitching Index
Kennedy-Bro	129
Tannehill-Pit	120
Dowling-Lou	116
Woods-Lou	115
Callahan-Chi	114

Relief Runs

Adjusted Relief Runs

Relief Ranking

Total Pitcher Index
Young-StL	6.0
Willis-Bos	5.9
McGinnity-Bal	4.6
Tannehill-Pit	4.5
Hughes-Bro	4.5

Total Baseball Ranking
G.Davis-NY	6.2
Young-StL	6.0
Willis-Bos	5.9
Delahanty-Phi	5.7
Wallace-StL	5.3

TEAM	G	W	L	PCT	GB	R	OR	AB	H	2B	3B	HR	BB	SO	AVG	OBP	SLG	PRO	PRO+	BR	/A	PF	CHI	RC	SB	CS	SBA	SBR
BRO	142	82	54	.603		816	722	4860	1423	199	81	26	421	272	.293	.354	.383	.737	104	78	33	106	100	774	274			
PIT	140	79	60	.568	4.5	733	613	4817	1312	185	100	26	327	321	.272	.326	.368	.694	98	-7	-12	101	102	651	174			
PHI	141	75	63	.543	8	810	791	4969	1439	187	82	29	440	374	.290	.355	.378	.733	110	76	82	99	97	757	205			
BOS	142	66	72	.478	17	778	739	4952	1403	163	68	48	395	278	.283	.342	.373	.715	93	35	-57	112	99	710	182			
STL	142	65	75	.464	19	744	748	4877	1420	141	81	36	406	318	.291	.354	.375	.729	109	69	74	99	91	753	243			
CHI	146	65	75	.464	19	635	751	4907	1276	202	51	33	343	383	.260	.315	.342	.657	92	-70	-42	96	95	603	189			
CIN	144	62	77	.446	21.5	703	745	5026	1335	178	83	33	333	408	.266	.315	.354	.669	94	-56	-37	98	101	632	183			
NY	141	60	78	.435	23	713	823	4724	1317	177	61	23	369	343	.279	.335	.357	.692	103	-4	28	95	100	660	236			
TOT	569					5932		39132	10925	1432	607	254	3034	2697	.279	.331	.366	.697						1686				

TEAM	CG	SH	SV	IP	H	H/G	HR	BB	SO	RAT	ERA	ERA+	OAV	OOB	PR	/A	PF	CPI	FA	E	DP	FW	PW	BW	SBW	DIF
BRO	104	8	4	1225²	1370	10.1	30	405	300	13.0	3.89	99	.282	.337	-26	-8	104	96	.948	303	102	2.6	-.7	3.0		9.1
PIT	114	11	1	1229	1232	9.0	24	295	415	11.2	3.06	119	.260	.304	86	77	98	94	.945	322	106	1.1	7.0	-1.1		2.5
PHI	116	7	3	1248²	1506	10.9	29	402	284	13.8	4.12	88	.297	.349	-59	-71	98	100	.945	330	125	.8	-6.5	7.5		4.2
BOS	116	8	2	1240¹	1263	9.2	59	463	340	12.5	3.72	111	.263	.328	-3	55	112	95	.953	273	86	4.4	5.0	-5.2		-7.2
STL	117	12	0	1217¹	1373	10.2	37	299	325	12.4	3.75	97	.284	.325	-7	-16	98	96	.943	331	73	.8	-1.5	6.8		-11.1
CHI	137	9	1	1271	1375	9.7	21	324	357	12.0	3.23	112	.275	.319	65	52	98	102	.933	418	98	-3.9	4.8	-3.8		-2.0
CIN	118	9	1	1274²	1383	9.8	28	404	399	12.6	3.83	96	.276	.330	-19	-23	99	92	.945	341	120	.5	-2.1	-3.4		-2.5
NY	114	4	0	1207¹	1423	10.6	26	442	277	13.9	3.96	91	.293	.352	-35	-47	98	104	.928	439	124	-6.0	-4.3	2.6		-1.3
TOT	936	68	12	9914		9.9				12.7	3.69		.279	.331					.942	2757	834					

Runs
Thomas-Phi 132
Slagle-Phi 115
VanHaltren-NY 114
Barrett-Cin 114
Wagner-Pit 107

Hits
Keeler-Bro 204
Burkett-StL 203
Wagner-Pit 201
Flick-Phi 200
Beckley-Cin 190

Doubles
Wagner-Pit 45
Lajoie-Phi 33
Flick-Phi 32
Delahanty-Phi 32
VanHaltren-NY..... 30

Triples
Wagner-Pit 22
Kelley-Bro 17
Hickman-NY 17
Stahl-Bos 16
Flick-Phi 16

Home Runs
Long-Bos 12
Flick-Phi 11
Donlin-StL 10
Hickman-NY 9
Sullivan-Bos 8

Total Bases
Wagner-Pit 302
Flick-Phi 297
Burkett-StL 265
Keeler-Bro 253
Beckley-Cin 242

Runs Batted In
Flick-Phi 110
Delahanty-Phi 109
Wagner-Pit 100
Collins-Bos 95
Beckley-Cin 94

Runs Produced
Flick-Phi 205
Wagner-Pit 203
Collins-Bos 193
Beckley-Cin 190
Delahanty-Phi 189

Bases On Balls
Thomas-Phi 115
Hamilton-Bos 107
McGraw-StL 85
Dahlen-Bro 73

Batting Average
Wagner-Pit .... .381
Flick-Phi .... .367
Burkett-StL .... .363
Keeler-Bro .... .362
McGraw-StL ...... .344

On Base Percentage
McGraw-StL ...... .502
Hamilton-Bos .... .449
Thomas-Phi ...... .447
Flick-Phi .... .439
Wagner-Pit .... .431

Slugging Average
Wagner-Pit .... .573
Flick-Phi .... .545
Lajoie-Phi .... .510
Kelley-Bro .... .485
Hickman-NY ...... .482

Production
Wagner-Pit 1.004
Flick-Phi .... .984
McGraw-StL ..... .918
Burkett-StL ...... .904
Selbach-NY ...... .881

Adjusted Production
Wagner-Pit 178
Flick-Phi 175
McGraw-StL 159
Burkett-StL 153
Selbach-NY 153

Batter Runs
Flick-Phi 55.0
Wagner-Pit 54.3
Burkett-StL 41.1
McGraw-StL 36.7
Selbach-NY 34.8

Adjusted Batter Runs
Flick-Phi 55.7
Wagner-Pit 53.7
Burkett-StL 41.8
Selbach-NY 38.7
McGraw-StL 37.2

Clutch Hitting Index
Cross-Phi 153
Jennings-Bro 146
Delahanty-Phi 138
Dahlen-Bro 135
Lowe-Bos 132

Runs Created
Wagner-Pit 150
Flick-Phi 149
Burkett-StL 131
Keeler-Bro 120
Selbach-NY 119

Total Average
McGraw-StL 1.251
Wagner-Pit 1.184
Flick-Phi 1.165
Burkett-StL 1.017
Selbach-NY 1.014

Stolen Bases
VanHaltren-NY 45
Donovan-StL 45
Barrett-Cin 44
Keeler-Bro 41

Stolen Base Average

Stolen Base Runs

Fielding Runs
Steinfeldt-Cin 35.9
Lajoie-Phi 29.5
Davis-NY 29.1
Dahlen-Bro 19.3
Bradley-Chi 16.8

Total Player Rating
Lajoie-Phi 5.2
Davis-NY 4.9
Flick-Phi 4.2
Wagner-Pit 3.3
Selbach-NY 3.3

Wins
McGinnity-Bro 28
Tannehill-Pit 20
Phillippe-Pit 20
Kennedy-Bro 20
Dinneen-Bos 20

Win Percentage
McGinnity-Bro .... .778
Tannehill-Pit ...... .769
Fraser-Phi .... .625
Phillippe-Pit ...... .606
Kennedy-Bro ..... .606

Games
Carrick-NY 45
McGinnity-Bro 44
Scott-Cin 43
Kennedy-Bro 42

Complete Games
Hawley-NY 34
Dinneen-Bos 33

Shutouts
Young-StL 4
Nichols-Bos 4
Hahn-Cin 4
Griffith-Chi 4

Saves
Kitson-Bro 4
Bernhard-Phi 2

Innings Pitched
McGinnity-Bro ... 343.0
Carrick-NY 341.2
Hawley-NY 329.1
Scott-Cin 323.0
Young-StL 321.1

Fewest Hits/Game
Waddell-Pit 7.59
Garvin-Chi 8.22
Nichols-Bos 8.36
Dinneen-Bos 8.53
Hahn-Cin 8.78

Fewest BB/Game
Young-StL 1.01
Phillippe-Pit 1.35
Tannehill-Pit 1.65
Scott-Cin 1.84
Griffith-Chi 1.85

Strikeouts
Waddell-Pit 130
Hahn-Cin 127
Young-StL 115
Garvin-Chi 107
Dinneen-Bos 107

Strikeouts/Game
Waddell-Pit 5.61
Garvin-Chi 3.91
Hahn-Cin 3.77
Newton-Cin 3.38
Leever-Pit 3.25

Ratio
Waddell-Pit 9.96
Phillippe-Pit 10.19
Young-StL 10.45
Garvin-Chi 10.52
Griffith-Chi 10.74

Earned Run Average
Waddell-Pit 2.37
Garvin-Chi 2.41
Taylor-Chi 2.55
Leever-Pit 2.71
Phillippe-Pit 2.84

Adjusted ERA
Waddell-Pit 153
Garvin-Chi 149
Taylor-Chi 141
Nichols-Bos 134
Leever-Pit 134

Opponents' Batting Avg.
Waddell-Pit .... .229
Garvin-Chi .... .243
Nichols-Bos ...... .246
Dinneen-Bos ..... .250
Hahn-Cin .... .255

Opponents' On Base Pct.
Waddell-Pit .... .280
Phillippe-Pit ...... .285
Young-StL .... .290
Garvin-Chi .... .291
Griffith-Chi .... .296

Starter Runs
Garvin-Chi 35.1
Waddell-Pit 30.7
McGinnity-Bro ... 28.8
Taylor-Chi 28.3
Phillippe-Pit 26.5

Adjusted Starter Runs
Dinneen-Bos 35.9
McGinnity-Bro ... 34.2
Garvin-Chi 32.6
Waddell-Pit 29.1
Nichols-Bos 27.0

Clutch Pitching Index
Fraser-Phi 128
Taylor-Chi 117
Carrick-NY 113
Donahue-Phi 112
McGinnity-Bro ... 108

Relief Runs

Adjusted Relief Runs

Relief Ranking

Total Pitcher Index
Dinneen-Bos 4.0
Garvin-Chi 3.0
Tannehill-Pit 2.8
McGinnity-Bro 2.6
Waddell-Pit 2.6

Total Baseball Ranking
Lajoie-Phi 5.2
Davis-NY 4.9
Flick-Phi 4.2
Dinneen-Bos 4.0
Wagner-Pit 3.4

1901 National League

TEAM	G	W	L	PCT	GB	R	OR	AB	H	2B	3B	HR	BB	SO	AVG	OBP	SLG	PRO	PRO+	BR	/A	PF	CHI	RC	SB	CS	SBA	SBR
PIT	140	90	49	.647		776	534	4913	1407	182	92	29	386	493	.286	.343	.379	.722	114	110	90	103	100	739	203			
PHI	140	83	57	.593	7.5	668	543	4793	1275	194	58	24	430	549	.266	.333	.346	.679	102	41	27	102	96	649	199			
BRO	137	79	57	.581	9.5	744	600	4879	1399	206	93	32	312	449	.287	.332	.387	.719	113	96	78	103	101	713	178			
STL	142	76	64	.543	14.5	792	689	5039	1430	187	94	39	314	540	.284	.330	.381	.711	120	84	117	95	105	727	190			
BOS	140	69	69	.500	20.5	531	556	4746	1180	135	36	28	303	519	.249	.298	.310	.608	76	-88	-145	109	97	514	158			
CHI	140	53	86	.381	37	578	699	4844	1250	153	61	18	314	532	.258	.307	.326	.633	94	-47	-22	96	98	569	204			
NY	141	52	85	.380	37	544	755	4839	1225	167	46	19	303	575	.253	.301	.318	.619	90	-72	-47	96	96	524	133			
CIN	142	52	87	.374	38	561	818	4914	1232	173	70	38	323	584	.251	.300	.338	.638	99	-45	-1	93	92	565	137			
TOT	561					5194		38967	10398	1397	550	227	2685	4241	.267	.314	.348	.662						1402				

TEAM	CG	SH	SV	IP	H	H/G	HR	BB	SO	RAT	ERA	ERA+	OAV	OOB	PR	/A	PF	CPI	FA	E	DP	FW	PW	BW	SBW	DIF
PIT	119	15	4	1244²	1198	8.7	20	244	505	10.8	2.58	126	.251	.296	102	93	98	106	.950	287	97	1.2	9.1	8.8		1.4
PHI	125	15	2	1246²	1221	8.8	19	259	480	11.0	2.87	119	.255	.299	62	72	102	98	.954	262	65	2.7	7.1	2.6		.6
BRO	111	7	5	1213²	1244	9.2	18	435	583	12.8	3.14	107	.263	.332	23	27	101	111	.950	281	99	1.2	2.6	7.6		-.5
STL	118	5	5	1269²	1333	9.4	39	332	445	12.1	3.68	86	.268	.320	-50	-71	96	93	.949	305	108	.4	-7.0	11.5		1.1
BOS	128	11	0	1263	1196	8.5	29	349	558	11.3	2.90	125	.248	.304	58	99	109	99	.952	282	89	1.5	9.7	-14.2		3.0
CHI	131	2	0	1241²	1348	9.8	27	324	586	12.5	3.33	97	.274	.326	-1	-13	97	106	.943	336	87	-1.8	-1.3	-2.2		-11.3
NY	118	11	1	1232	1389	10.1	24	377	542	13.3	3.87	85	.282	.340	-75	-78	100	100	.941	348	81	-2.3	-7.6	-4.6		-1.9
CIN	126	4	0	1265²	1469	10.4	51	365	542	13.5	4.17	77	.288	.343	-120	-138	96	100	.940	355	102	-2.6	-13.5	-.0		-1.2
TOT	976	70	17	9977		9.4				12.2	3.32		.267	.314					.947	2456	728					

Runs
Burkett-StL	142
Keeler-Bro	123
Beaumont-Pit	120
Clarke-Pit	118
Sheckard-Bro	116

Hits
Burkett-StL	226
Keeler-Bro	202
Sheckard-Bro	196
Wagner-Pit	194
Delahanty-Phi	192

Doubles
Delahanty-Phi	38
Daly-Bro	38
Wagner-Pit	37
Beckley-Cin	36
Wallace-StL	34

Triples
Sheckard-Bro	19
Flick-Phi	17

Home Runs
Crawford-Cin	16
Sheckard-Bro	11
Burkett-StL	10

Total Bases
Burkett-StL	306
Sheckard-Bro	296
Delahanty-Phi	286
Wagner-Pit	271

Runs Batted In
Wagner-Pit	126
Delahanty-Phi	108
Sheckard-Bro	104
Crawford-Cin	104

Runs Produced
Wagner-Pit	221
Sheckard-Bro	209
Burkett-StL	207
Delahanty-Phi	206
Flick-Phi	192

Bases On Balls
Thomas-Phi	100
Hartsel-Chi	74
Davis-Bro-Pit	66
Delahanty-Phi	65
Hamilton-Bos	64

Batting Average
Burkett-StL	.376
Delahanty-Phi	.354
Sheckard-Bro	.354
Wagner-Pit	.353
Keeler-Bro	.339

On Base Percentage
Thomas-Phi	.436
Burkett-StL	.434
Delahanty-Phi	.426
Wagner-Pit	.415
Hartsel-Chi	.414

Slugging Average
Sheckard-Bro	.534
Delahanty-Phi	.528
Crawford-Cin	.524
Burkett-StL	.509
Flick-Phi	.500

Production
Delahanty-Phi	.954
Burkett-StL	.944
Sheckard-Bro	.942
Wagner-Pit	.909
Crawford-Cin	.902

Adjusted Production
Burkett-StL	185
Delahanty-Phi	175
Crawford-Cin	174
Sheckard-Bro	170
Hartsel-Chi	166

Batter Runs
Burkett-StL	58.3
Delahanty-Phi	54.7
Sheckard-Bro	50.9
Wagner-Pit	46.0
Hartsel-Chi	44.4

Adjusted Batter Runs
Burkett-StL	62.4
Delahanty-Phi	53.1
Sheckard-Bro	48.9
Hartsel-Chi	47.3
Wagner-Pit	43.8

Clutch Hitting Index
Ganzel-NY	163
Dexter-Chi	158
Wagner-Pit	155
Long-Bos	155
Dahlen-Bro	149

Runs Created
Burkett-StL	149
Delahanty-Phi	139
Sheckard-Bro	138
Wagner-Pit	137
Hartsel-Chi	130

Total Average
Delahanty-Phi	1.094
Wagner-Pit	1.065
Sheckard-Bro	1.064
Burkett-StL	1.053
Hartsel-Chi	1.027

Stolen Bases
Wagner-Pit	49
Hartsel-Chi	41
Strang-NY	40
Harley-Cin	37
Beaumont-Pit	36

Stolen Base Average

Stolen Base Runs

Fielding Runs
Wallace-StL	29.6
Davis-NY	23.1
Flick-Phi	14.9
Dahlen-Bro	13.5
Daly-Bro	11.1

Total Player Rating
Wallace-StL	5.8
Wagner-Pit	5.0
Davis-NY	4.8
Burkett-StL	4.5
Sheckard-Bro	4.2

Wins
Donovan-Bro	25
Harper-StL	23
Phillippe-Pit	22
Hahn-Cin	22

Win Percentage
Chesbro-Pit	.677
Phillippe-Pit	.647
Tannehill-Pit	.643
Harper-StL	.639
Kitson-Bro	.633

Games
Taylor-NY	45
Powell-StL	45
Donovan-Bro	45
Hahn-Cin	42
Mathewson-NY	40

Complete Games
Hahn-Cin	41
Taylor-NY	37
Mathewson-NY	36
Donovan-Bro	36
Donahue-Phi	34

Shutouts
Willis-Bos	6
Orth-Phi	6
Chesbro-Pit	6

Saves
Powell-StL	3
Donovan-Bro	3
Sudhoff-StL	2
Phillippe-Pit	2
Kitson-Bro	2

Innings Pitched
Hahn-Cin	375.1
Taylor-NY	353.1
Donovan-Bro	351.0
Powell-StL	338.1
Mathewson-NY	336.0

Fewest Hits/Game
Townsend-Phi	7.39
Mathewson-NY	7.71
Willis-Bos	7.72
Orth-Phi	7.99
Chesbro-Pit	8.17

Fewest BB/Game
Orth-Phi	1.02
Phillippe-Pit	1.16
Tannehill-Pit	1.28
Duggleby-Phi	1.31
Powell-StL	1.33

Strikeouts
Hahn-Cin	239
Donovan-Bro	226
Hughes-Chi	225
Mathewson-NY	221
Waddell-Pit-Chi	172

Strikeouts/Game
Hughes-Chi	6.57
Waddell-Pit-Chi	6.16
Mathewson-NY	5.92
Donovan-Bro	5.79
Hahn-Cin	5.73

Ratio
Orth-Phi	9.27
Phillippe-Pit	9.79
Tannehill-Pit	10.17
Chesbro-Pit	10.17
Willis-Bos	10.35

Earned Run Average
Tannehill-Pit	2.18
Phillippe-Pit	2.22
Orth-Phi	2.27
Willis-Bos	2.36
Chesbro-Pit	2.38

Adjusted ERA
Willis-Bos	153
Tannehill-Pit	150
Orth-Phi	150
Phillippe-Pit	147
Chesbro-Pit	137

Opponents' Batting Avg.
Townsend-Phi	.223
Mathewson-NY	.230
Willis-Bos	.231
Orth-Phi	.237
Chesbro-Pit	.241

Opponents' On Base Pct.
Orth-Phi	.264
Phillippe-Pit	.275
Tannehill-Pit	.283
Chesbro-Pit	.283
Willis-Bos	.286

Starter Runs
Phillippe-Pit	36.2
Mathewson-NY	34.0
Orth-Phi	32.9
Willis-Bos	32.7
Tannehill-Pit	32.1

Adjusted Starter Runs
Willis-Bos	42.6
Orth-Phi	35.3
Phillippe-Pit	34.4
Mathewson-NY	33.3
Tannehill-Pit	30.5

Clutch Pitching Index
Kitson-Bro	123
Taylor-Chi	118
Hughes-Bro	115
Taylor-NY	114
Tannehill-Pit	111

Relief Runs

Adjusted Relief Runs

Relief Ranking

Total Pitcher Index
Orth-Phi	4.8
Phillippe-Pit	4.4
Willis-Bos	4.3
Mathewson-NY	4.0
Tannehill-Pit	3.4

Total Baseball Ranking
Wallace-StL	5.8
Wagner-Pit	5.0
Orth-Phi	4.8
Davis-NY	4.8
Burkett-StL	4.5

TEAM	G	W	L	PCT	GB	R	OR	AB	H	2B	3B	HR	BB	SO	AVG	OBP	SLG	PRO	PRO+	BR	/A	PF	CHI	RC	SB	CS	SBA	SBR
CHI	137	83	53	.610		819	631	4725	1303	173	89	32	475	337	.276	.349	.370	.719	109	55	75	97	102	742	280			
BOS	138	79	57	.581	4	759	608	4866	1353	183	104	37	331	282	.278	.330	.381	.711	105	25	38	98	99	693	157			
DET	136	74	61	.548	8.5	741	694	4676	1303	180	80	29	380	346	.279	.340	.370	.710	99	30	-2	105	97	690	204			
PHI	137	74	62	.544	9	805	761	4882	1409	239	87	35	301	344	.289	.336	.395	.731	105	56	23	104	101	732	173			
BAL	135	68	65	.511	13.5	760	750	4589	1348	179	111	24	369	377	.294	.353	.397	.750	110	94	62	104	94	745	207			
WAS	138	61	73	.455	21	682	771	4772	1282	191	83	33	356	340	.269	.325	.364	.689	99	-9	2	98	94	631	127			
CLE	138	55	82	.401	28.5	667	831	4833	1311	197	68	12	243	326	.271	.313	.348	.661	93	-65	-35	96	101	588	125			
MIL	139	48	89	.350	35.5	641	828	4795	1250	192	66	26	325	384	.261	.313	.345	.658	93	-65	-28	95	95	602	176			
TOT	549					5874		38138	10559	1534	688	228	2780	2736	.277	.326	.371	.697							1449			

TEAM	CG	SH	SV	IP	H	H/G	HR	BB	SO	RAT	ERA	ERA+	OAV	OOB	PR	/A	PF	CPI	FA	E	DP	FW	PW	BW	SBW	DIF
CHI	110	11	2	1218¹	1250	9.2	27	312	394	11.5	2.98	117	.262	.307	92	67	95	103	.941	345	100	.9	6.0	6.8		1.3
BOS	123	7	1	1217	1178	8.7	33	294	396	10.9	3.04	116	.251	.295	84	65	96	91	.943	337	104	1.6	5.9	3.4		.2
DET	118	8	2	1188²	1326	10.0	22	313	307	12.4	3.30	116	.279	.323	47	70	105	106	.930	410	127	-3.3	6.3	-.2		3.7
PHI	124	6	1	1200²	1346	10.1	20	374	350	12.9	4.00	94	.280	.332	-45	-31	103	91	.942	337	93	1.4	-2.8	2.1		5.3
BAL	115	4	3	1158	1313	10.2	21	344	271	12.9	3.73	104	.282	.331	-8	16	106	99	.926	401	76	-2.9	1.4	5.6		-2.6
WAS	118	8	2	1183	1396	10.6	51	284	308	12.8	4.09	89	.290	.330	-56	-57	100	96	.943	323	97	2.4	-5.1	.2		-3.5
CLE	122	7	4	1182¹	1365	10.4	22	464	334	13.9	4.12	86	.286	.349	-59	-75	97	98	.942	329	99	2.1	-6.8	-3.2		-5.6
MIL	107	3	4	1218	1383	10.2	32	395	376	13.1	4.06	89	.282	.336	-53	-63	98	94	.934	393	106	-1.8	-5.7	-2.5		-10.5
TOT	937	54	19	9566		9.9				12.5	3.66		.277	.326					.938	2875	802					

Runs
Lajoie-Phi 145
Jones-Chi 120
Williams-Bal 113
Hoy-Chi 112
Barrett-Det 110

Hits
Lajoie-Phi 232
Anderson-Mil 190
Collins-Bos 187
Waldron-Mil-Was . . 186
Dungan-Was 179

Doubles
Lajoie-Phi 48
Anderson-Mil 46
Collins-Bos 42
Farrell-Was 32

Triples
Williams-Bal 21
Keister-Bal 21
Mertes-Chi 17
Stahl-Bos 16
Collins-Bos 16

Home Runs
Lajoie-Phi 14
Freeman-Bos 12
Grady-Was 9

Total Bases
Lajoie-Phi 350
Collins-Bos 279
Anderson-Mil 274
Freeman-Bos 255
Williams-Bal 248

Runs Batted In
Lajoie-Phi 125
Freeman-Bos 114
Anderson-Mil 99
Mertes-Chi 98
Williams-Bal 96

Runs Produced
Lajoie-Phi 256
Williams-Bal 202
Collins-Bos 196
Freeman-Bos 190
Mertes-Chi 187

Bases On Balls
Hoy-Chi 86
Jones-Chi 84
Barrett-Det 76
McFarland-Chi 75
McGraw-Bal 61

Batting Average
Lajoie-Phi 426
Donlin-Bal 340
Freeman-Bos 339
Seybold-Phi 334
Collins-Bos 332

On Base Percentage
Lajoie-Phi 462
Jones-Chi 411
Donlin-Bal 409
Hoy-Chi 405
Freeman-Bos 401

Slugging Average
Lajoie-Phi 643
Freeman-Bos 520
Seybold-Phi 503
Williams-Bal 495
Collins-Bos 495

Production
Lajoie-Phi 1.105
Freeman-Bos 922
Seybold-Phi 899
Donlin-Bal 883
Williams-Bal 883

Adjusted Production
Lajoie-Phi 198
Freeman-Bos 159
Collins-Bos 144
Seybold-Phi 144
Donlin-Bal 141

Batter Runs
Lajoie-Phi 75.3
Freeman-Bos 36.8
McGraw-Bal 31.8
Donlin-Bal 31.0
Williams-Bal 31.0

Adjusted Batter Runs
Lajoie-Phi 71.7
Freeman-Bos 38.2
Collins-Bos 31.6
McGraw-Bal 29.9
Donlin-Bal 27.7

Clutch Hitting Index
Burke-Mil-Chi 151
Keister-Bal 142
Hartman-Chi 140
Freeman-Bos 131
Elberfeld-Det 131

Runs Created
Lajoie-Phi 179
Collins-Bos 116
Anderson-Mil 114
Freeman-Bos 113
Donlin-Bal 109

Total Average
Lajoie-Phi 1.324
Donlin-Bal 1.000
Freeman-Bos 997
Seybold-Phi 960
Williams-Bal 956

Stolen Bases
Isbell-Chi 52
Mertes-Chi 46
Seymour-Bal 38
Jones-Chi 38

Stolen Base Average

Stolen Base Runs

Fielding Runs
Lajoie-Phi 28.7
Elberfeld-Det 22.6
Conroy-Mil 19.8
Clingman-Was 17.8
Farrell-Was 16.6

Total Player Rating
Lajoie-Phi 8.4
Elberfeld-Det 4.1
Collins-Bos 3.8
Donlin-Bal 3.0
Pickering-Cle 2.6

Wins
Young-Bos 33
McGinnity-Bal 26
Griffith-Chi 24
Miller-Det 23
Fraser-Phi 22

Win Percentage
Griffith-Chi 774
Young-Bos 767
Callahan-Chi 652
Patten-Was 643
Miller-Det 639

Games
McGinnity-Bal 48
Dowling-Mil-Cle . . . 43
Young-Bos 43
Carrick-Was 42
Patterson-Chi 41

Complete Games
McGinnity-Bal 39
Young-Bos 38
Miller-Det 35
Fraser-Phi 35
Carrick-Was 34

Shutouts
Young-Bos 5
Griffith-Chi 5
Patterson-Chi 4
Patten-Was 4
Moore-Cle 4

Saves
Hoffer-Cle 3
Garvin-Mil 2

Innings Pitched
McGinnity-Bal . . . 382.0
Young-Bos 371.1
Miller-Det 332.0
Fraser-Phi 331.0
Carrick-Was 324.0

Fewest Hits/Game
Young-Bos 7.85
Callahan-Chi 8.15
Moore-Cle 8.38
Lewis-Bos 8.51
Winter-Bos 8.74

Fewest BB/Game
Young-Bos 90
Gear-Was 1.21
Lee-Was 1.55
Griffith-Chi 1.69
Cronin-Det 1.72

Strikeouts
Young-Bos 158
Patterson-Chi 127
Dowling-Mil-Cle . . . 124
Garvin-Mil 122
Fraser-Phi 110

Strikeouts/Game
Garvin-Mil 4.27
Patten-Was 3.86
Young-Bos 3.83
Patterson-Chi 3.66
Dowling-Mil-Cle . . . 3.65

Ratio
Young-Bos 8.75
Callahan-Chi 10.24
Griffith-Chi 10.97
Lewis-Bos 11.10
Plank-Phi 11.12

Earned Run Average
Young-Bos 1.62
Callahan-Chi 2.42
Yeager-Det 2.61
Griffith-Chi 2.67
Winter-Bos 2.80

Adjusted ERA
Young-Bos 217
Yeager-Det 147
Callahan-Chi 143
Griffith-Chi 130
Miller-Det 130

Opponents' Batting Avg.
Young-Bos 232
Callahan-Chi 239
Moore-Cle 244
Lewis-Bos 247
Winter-Bos 252

Opponents' On Base Pct.
Young-Bos 252
Callahan-Chi 283
Griffith-Chi 297
Lewis-Bos 300
Plank-Phi 300

Starter Runs
Young-Bos 84.1
Callahan-Chi 29.6
Griffith-Chi 29.5
Miller-Det 26.1
Yeager-Det 23.2

Adjusted Starter Runs
Young-Bos 78.5
Miller-Det 32.8
Yeager-Det 27.3
Callahan-Chi 25.2
Griffith-Chi 24.1

Clutch Pitching Index
Katoll-Chi 121
Yeager-Det 117
Siever-Det 114
Young-Bos 111
Sparks-Mil 111

Relief Runs

Adjusted Relief Runs

Relief Ranking

Total Pitcher Index
Young-Bos 7.8
Callahan-Chi 4.3
Yeager-Det 3.8
Miller-Det 3.7
Griffith-Chi 3.5

Total Baseball Ranking
Lajoie-Phi 8.4
Young-Bos 7.8
Callahan-Chi 4.3
Elberfeld-Det 4.1
Yeager-Det 3.8

1902 National League

TEAM	G	W	L	PCT	GB	R	OR	AB	H	2B	3B	HR	BB	SO	AVG	OBP	SLG	PRO	PRO+	BR	/A	PF	CHI	RC	SB	CS	SBA	SBR
PIT	142	103	36	.741		775	440	4926	1410	189	95	18	372	446	.286	.345	.374	.719	125	167	146	104	103	744	222			
BRO	141	75	63	.543	27.5	564	519	4845	1242	147	49	19	319	489	.256	.310	.319	.629	100	9	5	101	98	552	145			
BOS	142	73	64	.533	29	572	516	4728	1178	142	39	14	398	481	.249	.313	.305	.618	97	0	-5	101	101	541	189			
CIN	141	70	70	.500	33.5	633	566	4908	1383	188	77	18	297	465	.282	.328	.362	.690	110	110	56	110	93	654	131			
CHI	141	68	69	.496	34	530	501	4802	1200	131	40	6	353	565	.250	.307	.298	.605	96	-26	-9	97	98	539	222			
STL	140	56	78	.418	44.5	517	695	4751	1226	116	37	10	273	438	.258	.306	.304	.610	98	-21	1	96	97	516	158			
PHI	138	56	81	.409	46	484	649	4615	1139	110	43	5	356	481	.247	.306	.293	.599	91	-34	-34	100	95	473	108			
NY	139	48	88	.353	53.5	401	590	4571	1088	147	34	8	252	530	.238	.283	.290	.573	83	-84	-79	99	90	451	187			
TOT	562					4476		38146	9866	1170	414	98	2620	3895	.259	.306	.319	.625							1362			

TEAM	CG	SH	SV	IP	H	H/G	HR	BB	SO	RAT	ERA	ERA+	OAV	OOB	PR	/A	PF	CPI	FA	E	DP	FW	PW	BW	SBW	DIF
PIT	131	21	3	1264²	1142	8.1	4	250	564	10.3	2.30	119	.241	.287	67	60	98	93	.958	247	87	3.4	6.3	15.4		8.4
BRO	132	14	3	1256	1113	8.0	10	363	536	10.8	2.69	102	.237	.298	11	9	99	86	.952	275	79	1.5	.9	.5		3.0
BOS	124	14	4	1259²	1233	8.8	16	372	523	11.8	2.61	108	.256	.315	23	29	102	109	.959	240	90	3.8	3.1	-.5		-1.9
CIN	130	9	1	1239	1228	8.9	15	352	430	11.9	2.67	112	.258	.317	14	43	108	108	.945	322	118	-1.4	4.5	5.9		-9.1
CHI	132	17	2	1275¹	1235	8.7	9	279	437	11.0	2.21	122	.254	.300	80	68	97	113	.945	327	111	-1.7	7.2	-.9		-5.0
STL	112	7	4	1227²	1399	10.3	16	338	400	13.0	3.47	79	.286	.337	-95	-101	99	102	.944	336	107	-2.4	-10.7	.1		1.9
PHI	118	8	3	1211	1323	9.8	12	334	504	12.7	3.50	80	.278	.332	-97	-93	101	95	.946	305	81	-.7	-9.8	-3.6		1.6
NY	118	11	1	1226¹	1193	8.8	16	332	501	11.6	2.82	99	.255	.311	-5	-2	101	98	.943	330	104	-2.1	-.2	-8.3		-9.3
TOT	997	101	21	9959²		8.9				11.6	2.78		.259	.306					.949	2382	777					

Runs		Hits		Doubles		Triples		Home Runs		Total Bases	
Wagner-Pit	105	Beaumont-Pit	193	Wagner-Pit	30	Leach-Pit	22	Leach-Pit	6	Crawford-Cin	256
Clarke-Pit	103	Keeler-Bro	186	Clarke-Pit	27	Crawford-Cin	22	Beckley-Cin	5	Wagner-Pit	247
Beaumont-Pit	100	Crawford-Cin	185	Cooley-Bos	26	Wagner-Pit	16	Sheckard-Bro	4	Beckley-Cin	227
Leach-Pit	97	Wagner-Pit	176	Dahlen-Bro	25	Clarke-Pit	14	McCreery-Bro	4	Beaumont-Pit	226
Crawford-Cin	92	Beckley-Cin	175	Beckley-Cin	23	Gremminger-Bos	12			Leach-Pit	219

Runs Batted In		Runs Produced		Bases On Balls		Batting Average		On Base Percentage		Slugging Average	
Wagner-Pit	91	Wagner-Pit	193	R.Thomas-Phi	107	Beaumont-Pit	.357	R.Thomas-Phi	.415	Wagner-Pit	.463
Leach-Pit	85	Leach-Pit	176	Lush-Bos	76	Crawford-Cin	.333	Tenney-Bos	.410	Crawford-Cin	.461
Crawford-Cin	78	Crawford-Cin	167	Tenney-Bos	73	Keeler-Bro	.333	Clarke-Pit	.408	Clarke-Pit	.449
Dahlen-Bro	74	Beaumont-Pit	167	Sheckard-Bro	57	Wagner-Pit	.330	Beaumont-Pit	.403	Beckley-Cin	.427
		Clarke-Pit	154			Beckley-Cin	.330	Wagner-Pit	.391	Leach-Pit	.426

Production		Adjusted Production		Batter Runs		Adjusted Batter Runs		Clutch Hitting Index		Runs Created	
Clarke-Pit	.856	Clarke-Pit	161	Wagner-Pit	40.5	Wagner-Pit	38.3	Hartman-StL	173	Wagner-Pit	117
Wagner-Pit	.854	Wagner-Pit	160	Crawford-Cin	40.2	Clarke-Pit	36.1	Bransfield-Pit	155	Beaumont-Pit	109
Crawford-Cin	.848	Beaumont-Pit	151	Clarke-Pit	38.1	Crawford-Cin	34.0	Ritchey-Pit	145	Crawford-Cin	108
Beaumont-Pit	.821	Crawford-Cin	150	Beaumont-Pit	35.3	Beaumont-Pit	33.0	McCreery-Bro	144	Clarke-Pit	99
Beckley-Cin	.803	Tenney-Bos	144	Tenney-Bos	30.4	Tenney-Bos	29.8	Dahlen-Bro	141	Beckley-Cin	94

Total Average		Stolen Bases		Stolen Base Average	Stolen Base Runs	Fielding Runs		Total Player Rating	
Clarke-Pit	.975	Wagner-Pit	42			Farrell-StL	33.3	Wagner-Pit	4.4
Wagner-Pit	.958	Slagle-Chi	40			Lowe-Chi	26.0	Leach-Pit	4.0
Beaumont-Pit	.865	Donovan-StL	34			H.Long-Bos	22.5	Farrell-StL	3.9
Crawford-Cin	.865	Beaumont-Pit	33			Steinfeldt-Cin	21.2	Tenney-Bos	3.8
Tenney-Bos	.848	Smith-NY	32			Leach-Pit	12.7	Crawford-Cin	2.9

Wins		Win Percentage		Games		Complete Games		Shutouts		Saves	
Chesbro-Pit	28	Chesbro-Pit	.824	Willis-Bos	51	Willis-Bos	45	Mathewson-NY	8	Willis-Bos	3
Willis-Bos	27	Doheny-Pit	.800	Pittinger-Bos	46	Pittinger-Bos	36	Chesbro-Pit	8	M.O'Neill-StL	2
Pittinger-Bos	27	Tannehill-Pit	.769	Yerkes-StL	39	Hahn-Cin	35	Taylor-Chi	7	Newton-Bro	2
Taylor-Chi	23	Phillippe-Pit	.690			White-Phi	34	Pittinger-Bos	7	Leever-Pit	2
Hahn-Cin	23	Leever-Pit	.682			Taylor-Chi	33	Hahn-Cin	6		

Innings Pitched		Fewest Hits/Game		Fewest BB/Game		Strikeouts		Strikeouts/Game		Ratio	
Willis-Bos	410.0	Newton-Bro	7.08	Phillippe-Pit	.86	Willis-Bos	225	White-Phi	5.44	Taylor-Chi	8.95
Pittinger-Bos	389.1	McGinnity-NY	7.18	Tannehill-Pit	.97	White-Phi	185	Mathewson-NY	5.17	Tannehill-Pit	9.27
Taylor-Chi	324.2	Taylor-Chi	7.51	Menefee-Chi	1.19	Pittinger-Bos	174	Donovan-Bro	5.14	McGinnity-NY	9.53
Hahn-Cin	321.0	Donovan-Bro	7.56	Taylor-Chi	1.19	Donovan-Bro	170	Willis-Bos	4.94	Hahn-Cin	9.70
White-Phi	306.0	Chesbro-Pit	7.61	Leever-Pit	1.26	Mathewson-NY	159	Wicker-StL	4.61	Phillippe-Pit	9.73

Earned Run Average		Adjusted ERA		Opponents' Batting Avg.		Opponents' On Base Pct.		Starter Runs		Adjusted Starter Runs	
Taylor-Chi	1.33	Taylor-Chi	203	Newton-Bro	.217	Taylor-Chi	.259	Taylor-Chi	52.2	Taylor-Chi	49.3
Hahn-Cin	1.77	Hahn-Cin	169	McGinnity-NY	.219	Tannehill-Pit	.266	Hahn-Cin	36.1	Hahn-Cin	43.7
Tannehill-Pit	1.95	Poole-Pit-Cin	142	Taylor-Chi	.227	McGinnity-NY	.272	Willis-Bos	26.5	Willis-Bos	28.4
Lundgren-Chi	1.97	Tannehill-Pit	140	Donovan-Bro	.228	Hahn-Cin	.275	Phillippe-Pit	22.0	Mathewson-NY	21.2
Phillippe-Pit	2.05	Lundgren-Chi	137	Chesbro-Pit	.229	Phillippe-Pit	.276	Tannehill-Pit	21.3	Phillippe-Pit	20.6

Clutch Pitching Index		Relief Runs	Adjusted Relief Runs	Relief Ranking	Total Pitcher Index		Total Baseball Ranking	
Lundgren-Chi	144				Taylor-Chi	6.9	Taylor-Chi	6.9
Eason-Chi-Bos	140				Hahn-Cin	4.9	Hahn-Cin	4.9
Poole-Pit-Cin	140				Tannehill-Pit	3.7	Wagner-Pit	4.6
Taylor-NY	124				Phillips-Cin	3.3	Leach-Pit	4.0
Taylor-Chi	121				Mathewson-NY	2.9	Farrell-StL	3.9

TEAM	G	W	L	PCT	GB	R	OR	AB	H	2B	3B	HR	BB	SO	AVG	OBP	SLG	PRO	PRO+	BR	/A	PF	CHI	RC	SB	CS	SBA	SBR
PHI	137	83	53	.610		775	636	4762	1369	235	67	38	343	293	.287	.340	.389	.729	105	63	34	104	105	729	201			
STL	140	78	58	.574	5	619	607	4736	1254	208	61	29	373	327	.265	.324	.353	.677	96	-24	-14	99	95	613	137			
BOS	138	77	60	.562	6.5	664	600	4875	1356	195	95	42	275	375	.278	.322	.383	.705	100	14	-5	103	96	672	132			
CHI	138	74	60	.552	8	675	602	4654	1248	170	50	14	411	381	.268	.333	.335	.668	97	-27	2	96	104	642	265			
CLE	137	69	67	.507	14	686	667	4840	1401	248	68	33	308	356	.289	.336	.389	.725	113	54	81	96	93	712	140			
WAS	138	61	75	.449	22	707	790	4734	1338	262	66	47	329	296	.283	.336	.396	.732	110	64	59	101	97	697	121			
DET	137	52	83	.385	30.5	566	657	4644	1167	141	55	22	359	287	.251	.312	.320	.632	81	-95	-107	102	100	527	130			
BAL	141	50	88	.362	34	715	848	4760	1318	202	107	33	417	429	.277	.342	.385	.727	105	64	33	104	95	723	189			
TOT	553					5407		38005	10451	1661	569	258	2815	2744	.275	.325	.369	.694							1315			

TEAM	CG	SH	SV	IP	H	H/G	HR	BB	SO	RAT	ERA	ERA+	OAV	OOB	PR	/A	PF	CPI	FA	E	DP	FW	PW	BW	SBW	DIF
PHI	114	5	2	1216¹	1292	9.6	33	368	455	12.3	3.29	111	.273	.325	38	50	103	105	.953	270	75	1.4	4.7	3.2		5.6
STL	120	7	2	1244	1273	9.2	36	343	348	11.7	3.34	106	.265	.314	32	25	99	96	.953	274	122	1.5	2.4	-1.3		7.4
BOS	123	6	1	1238	1217	8.8	27	326	431	11.2	3.02	118	.257	.305	75	74	100	96	.955	263	101	2.0	7.0	-.5		.0
CHI	116	11	0	1221²	1269	9.3	30	331	346	11.8	3.41	99	.268	.316	21	-4	95	95	.955	257	125	2.3	-.4	.2		4.9
CLE	116	16	3	1204¹	1199	9.0	26	411	361	12.0	3.28	105	.260	.320	38	20	96	97	.950	287	96	.3	1.9	7.7		-8.9
WAS	130	2	1	1207²	1403	10.5	56	312	300	12.8	4.36	85	.291	.334	-105	-88	104	91	.945	316	70	-1.3	-8.3	5.6		-2.9
DET	116	9	3	1190²	1267	9.6	20	370	245	12.4	3.56	102	.273	.327	1	9	102	96	.943	332	111	-2.5	.9	-10.2		-3.7
BAL	119	3	1	1210¹	1531	11.4	30	354	258	14.0	4.33	87	.309	.355	-101	-76	106	102	.938	357	109	-3.5	-7.2	3.1		-11.4
TOT	954	59	13	9733		9.7				12.3	3.57		.275	.325					.949	2356	809					

Runs
Hartsel-Phi....... 109
Fultz-Phi......... 109
Strang-Chi....... 108
Bradley-Cle 104
Delahanty-Was ... 103

Hits
Hickman-Bos-Cle . 193
L.Cross-Phi 187
Bradley-Cle 187
Delahanty-Was ... 178
Freeman-Bos..... 174

Doubles
Delahanty-Was 43
Davis-Phi 43
L.Cross-Phi 39
Bradley-Cle 39
Freeman-Bos...... 38

Triples
Williams-Bal....... 21
Freeman-Bos...... 19
Ferris-Bos 14
Delahanty-Was 14
Hickman-Bos-Cle .. 13

Home Runs
Seybold-Phi 16
Hickman-Bos-Cle .. 11
Freeman-Bos...... 11
Bradley-Cle 11
Delahanty-Was 10

Total Bases
Hickman-Bos-Cle . 288
Freeman-Bos..... 283
Bradley-Cle 283
Delahanty-Was ... 279
Seybold-Phi 264

Runs Batted In
Freeman-Bos..... 121
Hickman-Bos-Cle . 110
L.Cross-Phi 108
Seybold-Phi 97

Runs Produced
L.Cross-Phi 198
Delahanty-Was ... 186
Freeman-Bos..... 185
Davis-Phi 175
Hickman-Bos-Cle . 173

Bases On Balls
Hartsel-Phi........ 87
Strang-Chi 76
Barrett-Det 74
Burkett-StL 71
Davis-Chi 65

Batting Average
Delahanty-Was ... .376
Hickman-Bos-Cle .361
Dougherty-Bos ... .342
L.Cross-Phi ...... .342
Bradley-Cle ...... .340

On Base Percentage
Delahanty-Was ... .454
Dougherty-Bos ... .411
Barrett-Det ...... .397
Jones-Chi......... .394
Selbach-Bal ...... .394

Slugging Average
Delahanty-Was ... .590
Hickman-Bos-Cle . .539
Bradley-Cle ...... .515
Seybold-Phi ...... .506
Freeman-Bos..... .502

Production
Delahanty-Was .. 1.044
Hickman-Bos-Cle .926
Bradley-Cle ...... .890
Seybold-Phi ...... .881
Williams-Bal...... .864

Adjusted Production
Delahanty-Was ... 189
Hickman-Bos-Cle . 161
Bradley-Cle 153
Seybold-Phi 138
Williams-Bal 134

Batter Runs
Delahanty-Was ... 58.5
Hickman-Bos-Cle . 37.6
Lajoie-Phi-Cle 33.3
Bradley-Cle 32.2
Seybold-Phi 29.9

Adjusted Batter Runs
Delahanty-Was ... 58.0
Hickman-Bos-Cle . 39.5
Lajoie-Phi-Cle 35.3
Bradley-Cle 35.2
Seybold-Phi 26.8

Clutch Hitting Index
Davis-Chi 159
L.Cross-Phi 153
Mertes-Chi 151
Daly-Chi 126
Anderson-StL 126

Runs Created
Delahanty-Was ... 137
Hickman-Bos-Cle . 118
Bradley-Cle 114
Freeman-Bos..... 109
L.Cross-Phi 105

Total Average
Delahanty-Was .. 1.227
Hickman-Bos-Cle .935
Bradley-Cle ...... .895
Hartsel-Phi....... .895
Seybold-Phi ...... .894

Stolen Bases
Hartsel-Phi........ 47
Mertes-Chi 46
Fultz-Phi 44

Stolen Base Average

Stolen Base Runs

Fielding Runs
Ferris-Bos 26.6
Schreck-Cle-Phi .. 20.3
Padden-StL 17.9
Jones-Chi........ 12.5
Coughlin-Was 11.8

Total Player Rating
Lajoie-Phi-Cle 6.2
Delahanty-Was 5.0
Bradley-Cle 4.0
Hickman-Bos-Cle .. 3.1
Davis-Chi 2.7

Wins
Young-Bos 32
Waddell-Phi 24
Powell-StL 22
F.Donahue-StL..... 22
Dinneen-Bos 21

Win Percentage
Bernhard-Phi-Cle ..783
Waddell-Phi 774
Young-Bos 744
F.Donahue-StL.....667
Griffith-Chi 625

Games
Young-Bos 45
Powell-StL 42
Dinneen-Bos 42
Wiltse-Phi-Bal 38
Orth-Was 38

Complete Games
Young-Bos 41
Dinneen-Bos 39
Powell-StL 36
Orth-Was 36

Shutouts
Joss-Cle 5
Siever-Det 4
Moore-Cle 4
Mercer-Det 4

Saves
Powell-StL 2

Innings Pitched
Young-Bos 384.2
Dinneen-Bos 371.1
Powell-StL 328.1
Orth-Was 324.0
F.Donahue-StL... 316.1

Fewest Hits/Game
Bernhard-Phi-Cle . 7.01
Waddell-Phi 7.30
Joss-Cle 7.52
Siever-Det 7.93
Winter-Bos....... 7.97

Fewest BB/Game
Orth-Was 1.11
Young-Bos 1.24
Bernhard-Phi-Cle . 1.47
Siever-Det 1.53
Plank-Phi 1.83

Strikeouts
Waddell-Phi 210
Young-Bos 160
Powell-StL 137
Dinneen-Bos 136
Plank-Phi 107

Strikeouts/Game
Waddell-Phi 6.84
Powell-StL 3.76
Young-Bos 3.74
Joss-Cle 3.54
Piatt-Chi 3.51

Ratio
Bernhard-Phi-Cle . 8.48
Waddell-Phi 9.38
Young-Bos 9.43
Siever-Det 9.46
Joss-Cle 10.02

Earned Run Average
Siever-Det 1.91
Waddell-Phi 2.05
Bernhard-Phi-Cle . 2.15
Young-Bos 2.15
Garvin-Chi 2.21

Adjusted ERA
Siever-Det 191
Waddell-Phi 179
Young-Bos 166
Bernhard-Phi-Cle . 160
Garvin-Chi 153

Opponents' Batting Avg.
Bernhard-Phi-Cle . .216
Waddell-Phi ...... .223
Joss-Cle .... .228
Siever-Det .... .237
Winter-Bos........ .238

Opponents' On Base Pct.
Bernhard-Phi-Cle . .250
Waddell-Phi ...... .269
Young-Bos .... .270
Siever-Det .... .271
Joss-Cle .... .282

Starter Runs
Young-Bos 60.6
Waddell-Phi 46.6
Bernhard-Phi-Cle . 35.7
Siever-Det 34.7
F.Donahue-StL.... 28.5

Adjusted Starter Runs
Young-Bos 60.6
Waddell-Phi 49.5
Siever-Det 36.2
Bernhard-Phi-Cle . 32.6
F.Donahue-StL.... 26.9

Clutch Pitching Index
Garvin-Chi 123
Shields-Bal-StL ... 122
Moore-Cle 117
Husting-Bos-Phi .. 117
F.Donahue-StL.... 106

Relief Runs

Adjusted Relief Runs

Relief Ranking

Total Pitcher Index
Young-Bos 5.8
Waddell-Phi 5.7
Bernhard-Phi-Cle . 3.2
Siever-Det 2.9
F.Donahue-StL.... 2.5

Total Baseball Ranking
Lajoie-Phi-Cle 6.2
Young-Bos 5.8
Waddell-Phi 5.7
Delahanty-Was ... 5.0
Bradley-Cle 4.0

TEAM	G	W	L	PCT	GB	R	OR	AB	H	2B	3B	HR	BB	SO	AVG	OBP	SLG	PRO	PRO+	BR	/A	PF	CHI	RC	SB	CS	SBA	SBR
PIT	141	91	49	.650		793	613	4988	1429	208	110	34	364		.286	.335	.393	.728	112	90	68	103	101	744	172			
NY	142	84	55	.604	6.5	729	567	4741	1290	181	49	20	379		.272	.326	.344	.670	95	-3	-28	104	109	654	264			
CHI	139	82	56	.594	8	695	599	4733	1300	191	62	9	422		.275	.334	.347	.681	105	19	37	97	101	665	259			
CIN	141	74	65	.532	16.5	765	656	4857	1399	228	92	28	403		.288	.343	.390	.733	106	102	26	111	98	727	144			
BRO	139	70	66	.515	19	667	682	4534	1201	177	56	15	379		.265	.341	.339	.680	105	26	45	97	97	647	159			
BOS	140	58	80	.420	32	578	699	4682	1145	176	47	25	398		.245	.304	.318	.622	88	-84	-57	96	101	526	159			
PHI	139	49	86	.363	39.5	617	738	4781	1283	186	62	12	338		.268	.317	.341	.658	99	-28	-5	97	96	587	120			
STL	139	43	94	.314	46.5	505	795	4689	1176	138	65	8	277		.251	.293	.313	.606	82	-118	-97	97	96	503	171			
TOT	560					5349		38005	10223	1485	543	151	3103	3767	.269	.324	.349	.673							1562			

TEAM	CG	SH	SV	IP	H	H/G	HR	BB	SO	RAT	ERA	ERA+	OAV	OOB	PR	/A	PF	CPI	FA	E	DP	FW	PW	BW	SBW	DIF
PIT	117	16	5	1251¹	1215	8.7	9	384	454	11.8	2.91	111	.254	.315	48	43	99	99	.951	295	100	1.6	4.1	6.5		8.8
NY	115	8	8	1262²	1257	9.0	20	371	628	11.9	2.95	113	.258	.315	43	56	102	102	.951	287	87	2.3	5.4	-2.7		9.5
CHI	117	6	6	1240¹	1182	8.6	14	354	451	11.4	2.77	113	.249	.307	67	45	96	97	.942	338	78	-1.6	4.3	3.6		6.7
CIN	126	11	1	1230	1277	9.3	14	378	480	12.6	3.07	116	.268	.330	25	64	109	109	.946	312	84	.4	6.1	2.5		-4.6
BRO	118	11	4	1221¹	1276	9.4	18	377	438	12.7	3.44	92	.275	.338	-24	-38	98	103	.951	284	98	2.0	-3.6	4.3		-.7
BOS	125	8	1	1228²	1310	9.6	30	460	516	13.4	3.34	96	.277	.348	-10	-20	98	115	.939	361	89	-3.0	-1.9	-5.5		-.6
PHI	126	5	3	1212¹	1347	10.0	21	425	381	13.6	3.96	82	.285	.352	-94	-96	100	100	.947	300	76	1.0	-9.2	-.5		-9.8
STL	111	4	2	1212¹	1353	10.0	25	430	419	13.6	3.67	89	.284	.350	-54	-56	100	107	.940	354	111	-2.7	-5.4	-9.3		-8.1
TOT	955	69	30	9859		9.3				12.6	3.26		.269	.324					.946	2531	723					

Runs	Hits	Doubles	Triples	Home Runs	Total Bases
Beaumont-Pit 137	Beaumont-Pit 209	Steinfeldt-Cin 32	Wagner-Pit 19	Sheckard-Bro 9	Beaumont-Pit 272
Donlin-Cin 110	Seymour-Cin 191	Mertes-NY 32	Donlin-Cin 18		Seymour-Cin 267
Browne-NY 105	Browne-NY 185	Clarke-Pit 32	Leach-Pit 17		Wagner-Pit 265
Slagle-Chi 104	Wagner-Pit 182				Donlin-Cin 256
Strang-Bro 101	Donlin-Cin 174				Sheckard-Bro 245

Runs Batted In	Runs Produced	Bases On Balls	Batting Average	On Base Percentage	Slugging Average
Mertes-NY 104	Beaumont-Pit 198	Thomas-Phi 107	Wagner-Pit .... .355	Thomas-Phi .... .450	Clarke-Pit .... .532
Wagner-Pit 101	Mertes-NY 197	Dahlen-Bro 82	Clarke-Pit .... .351	Bresnahan-NY .... .435	Wagner-Pit .... .518
Doyle-Bro 91	Wagner-Pit 193	Slagle-Chi 81	Donlin-Cin .... .351	Chance-Chi .... .428	Donlin-Cin .... .516
Leach-Pit 87	Leach-Pit 177	Chance-Chi 78	Bresnahan-NY .... .350	Sheckard-Bro .... .417	Bresnahan-NY .... .493
Steinfeldt-Cin 83	Doyle-Bro 175		Seymour-Cin .... .342	Donlin-Cin .... .417	Steinfeldt-Cin .... .481

Production	Adjusted Production	Batter Runs	Adjusted Batter Runs	Clutch Hitting Index	Runs Created
Clarke-Pit .... .940	Clarke-Pit 164	Donlin-Cin 43.2	Sheckard-Bro 41.8	Doyle-Bro 153	Sheckard-Bro 135
Donlin-Cin .... .933	Sheckard-Bro 161	Wagner-Pit 41.5	Wagner-Pit 39.3	Corcoran-Cin 153	Wagner-Pit 130
Bresnahan-NY .... .927	Bresnahan-NY 160	Sheckard-Bro 39.6	Donlin-Cin 35.3	Chance-Chi 138	Donlin-Cin 121
Wagner-Pit .... .924	Wagner-Pit 160	Clarke-Pit 37.1	Clarke-Pit 35.2	Dobbs-Chi-Bro 138	Beaumont-Pit 118
Sheckard-Bro .... .893	Chance-Chi 154	Bresnahan-NY 36.9	Bresnahan-NY 34.6	Dahlen-Bro 132	Chance-Chi 115

Total Average	Stolen Bases	Stolen Base Average	Stolen Base Runs	Fielding Runs	Total Player Rating
Chance-Chi 1.141	Sheckard-Bro 67			Farrell-StL 28.1	Wagner-Pit 6.5
Sheckard-Bro 1.125	Chance-Chi 67			Wagner-Pit 24.6	Sheckard-Bro 5.4
Bresnahan-NY 1.117	Wagner-Pit 46			Sheckard-Bro 23.4	Thomas-Phi 3.8
Wagner-Pit 1.076	Strang-Bro 46			Moran-Bos 21.2	Farrell-StL 3.4
Donlin-Cin 1.050	Mertes-NY 45			Ritchey-Pit 19.0	Dahlen-Bro 3.2

Wins	Win Percentage	Games	Complete Games	Shutouts	Saves
McGinnity-NY 31	Leever-Pit .... .781	McGinnity-NY 55	McGinnity-NY 44	Leever-Pit 7	Miller-NY 3
Mathewson-NY 30	Phillippe-Pit .... .735	Mathewson-NY 45	Mathewson-NY 37	Schmidt-Bro 5	Lundgren-Chi 3
Phillippe-Pit 25	Weimer-Chi .... .714	Pittinger-Bos 44	Pittinger-Bos 35	Hahn-Cin 5	
Leever-Pit 25	Mathewson-NY .... .698	Schmidt-Bro 40	Hahn-Cin 34	Phillippe-Pit 4	
	Wicker-StL-Chi .... .690		Taylor-Chi 33	Jones-Bro 4	

Innings Pitched	Fewest Hits/Game	Fewest BB/Game	Strikeouts	Strikeouts/Game	Ratio
McGinnity-NY 434.0	Weimer-Chi 7.69	Phillippe-Pit .... .90	Mathewson-NY 267	Mathewson-NY 6.56	Phillippe-Pit 9.39
Mathewson-NY 366.1	Mathewson-NY 7.89	Hahn-Cin 1.43	McGinnity-NY 171	Piatt-Bos 4.97	Taylor-Chi 9.77
Pittinger-Bos 351.2	Taylor-Chi 7.98	Taylor-Chi 1.64	Garvin-Bro 154	Garvin-Bro 4.65	Leever-Pit 10.13
Jones-Bro 324.1	Leever-Pit 8.07	McFarland-StL 1.89	Pittinger-Bos 140	Weimer-Chi 4.09	Mathewson-NY 10.59
Taylor-Chi 312.1	McGinnity-NY 8.11	Leever-Pit 1.90	Weimer-Chi 128	Willis-Bos 4.05	Hahn-Cin 10.70

Earned Run Average	Adjusted ERA	Opponents' Batting Avg.	Opponents' On Base Pct.	Starter Runs	Adjusted Starter Runs
Leever-Pit 2.06	Leever-Pit 157	Weimer-Chi .... .225	Phillippe-Pit .... .263	Mathewson-NY 40.7	McGinnity-NY 44.0
Mathewson-NY 2.26	Mathewson-NY 148	Mathewson-NY .... .231	Taylor-Chi .... .273	McGinnity-NY 40.2	Mathewson-NY 43.9
Weimer-Chi 2.30	Hahn-Cin 141	Taylor-Chi .... .235	Leever-Pit .... .282	Leever-Pit 38.0	Leever-Pit 37.0
Phillippe-Pit 2.43	McGinnity-NY 138	McGinnity-NY .... .236	Mathewson-NY .... .287	Weimer-Chi 30.2	Hahn-Cin 33.8
McGinnity-NY 2.43	Weimer-Chi 136	Leever-Pit .... .238	McGinnity-NY .... .291	Taylor-Chi 28.2	Weimer-Chi 26.0

Clutch Pitching Index	Relief Runs	Adjusted Relief Runs	Relief Ranking	Total Pitcher Index	Total Baseball Ranking
Brown-StL 157				Mathewson-NY 4.8	Wagner-Pit 6.5
Pittinger-Bos 129				McGinnity-NY 3.9	Sheckard-Bro 5.4
Malarkey-Bos 119				Leever-Pit 3.4	Mathewson-NY 4.8
Piatt-Bos 118				Hahn-Cin 3.3	McGinnity-NY 3.9
Poole-Cin 117				Ewing-Cin 3.1	Thomas-Phi 3.8

TEAM	G	W	L	PCT	GB	R	OR	AB	H	2B	3B	HR	BB	SO	AVG	OBP	SLG	PRO	PRO+	BR	/A	PF	CHI	RC	SB	CS	SBA	SBR
BOS	141	91	47	.659		**708**	504	4919	**1336**	222	113	**48**	262	561	**.272**	.308	**.392**	**.700**	111	**92**	60	105	103	**669**	141			
PHI	137	75	60	.556	14.5	597	519	4673	1236	227	68	32	268	513	.264	.304	.363	.667	103	39	13	105	99	589	157			
CLE	140	77	63	.550	15	639	579	4773	1265	**231**	95	31	259	595	.265	.303	.373	.676	112	51	**61**	98	102	622	175			
NY	136	72	62	.537	17	579	573	4565	1136	193	62	18	**332**	465	.249	.300	.330	.630	91	-13	-48	106	**106**	527	160			
DET	137	65	71	.478	25	567	573	4582	1229	162	91	12	292	526	.268	**.312**	.351	.663	110	37	53	97	94	578	128			
STL	139	65	74	.468	26.5	500	525	4639	1133	166	68	12	271	539	.244	.286	.317	.603	90	-61	-45	97	100	473	101			
CHI	138	60	77	.438	30.5	516	613	4670	1152	176	49	14	325	537	.247	.296	.314	.610	95	-45	-19	96	98	516	**180**			
WAS	140	43	94	.314	47.5	437	691	4613	1066	172	72	17	257	**463**	.231	.272	.311	.583	80	-97	-108	102	96	445	131			
TOT	554					4543		37434	9553	1549	618	184	2266	4199	.255	.298	.344	.642							1173			

TEAM	CG	SH	SV	IP	H	H/G	HR	BB	SO	RAT	ERA	ERA+	OAV	OOB	PR	/A	PF	CPI	FA	E	DP	FW	PW	BW	SBW	DIF
BOS	123	**20**	4	1255	1142	8.2	22	269	579	10.1	2.57	118	.242	.283	55	64	102	100	.959	239	86	2.3	**6.6**	6.2		6.9
PHI	112	10	1	1207	**1124**	8.4	20	315	**728**	10.7	2.98	103	.246	.295	-1	9	103	94	**.960**	217	66	**3.2**	.9	1.3		2.0
CLE	**125**	20	1	1243²	1161	8.4	**16**	271	521	10.4	2.73	105	.246	.287	32	17	96	98	.946	322	**99**	-3.2	1.8	6.3		2.1
NY	111	7	2	1201¹	1171	8.8	19	245	463	10.6	3.08	101	.254	.292	-15	5	105	93	.953	264	87	.0	.5	-5.0		9.4
DET	123	15	2	1196	1169	8.8	19	336	554	11.3	2.75	106	.255	.306	27	20	98	**112**	.950	281	82	-.9	2.1	5.5		-9.7
STL	124	12	3	1222¹	1220	9.0	26	**237**	511	10.7	2.77	105	.259	.295	26	18	98	108	.953	268	94	.2	1.9	-4.7		-1.9
CHI	114	9	**4**	1235	1233	9.0	24	287	391	11.1	3.02	93	.259	.301	-7	-28	95	102	.949	297	85	-1.8	-2.9	-2.0		-1.8
WAS	122	6	3	1223²	1333	9.8	38	306	452	12.1	3.82	82	.276	.319	-116	-93	106	96	.954	260	86	.8	-9.7	-11.2		-5.4
TOT	954	99	20	9784		8.8				10.9	2.96		.255	.298					.953	2148	685					

Runs	Hits	Doubles	Triples	Home Runs	Total Bases
Dougherty-Bos ... 106	Dougherty-Bos ... 195	Seybold-Phi 45	Crawford-Det 25	Freeman-Bos 13	Freeman-Bos 281
Bradley-Cle ... 101	Crawford-Det 184	Lajoie-Cle 41	Bradley-Cle 22	Hickman-Cle 12	Crawford-Det 269
Keeler-NY ... 95	Parent-Bos 170	Freeman-Bos 39	Freeman-Bos 20	Ferris-Bos 9	Bradley-Cle 266
Barrett-Det 95	Bay-Cle 169	Bradley-Cle 36	Parent-Bos 17	Seybold-Phi 8	Lajoie-Cle 251
Bay-Cle 94	Bradley-Cle 168	Anderson-StL 34	Collins-Bos 17		Dougherty-Bos ... 250

Runs Batted In	Runs Produced	Bases On Balls	Batting Average	On Base Percentage	Slugging Average
Freeman-Bos 104	Lajoie-Cle 176	Barrett-Det 74	Lajoie-Cle .... .344	Barrett-Det .... .401	Lajoie-Cle .... .518
Hickman-Cle 97	Crawford-Det 173	Lush-Det 70	Crawford-Det ..... .335	Hartsel-Phi .... .391	Bradley-Cle ...... .496
Lajoie-Cle 93	Freeman-Bos 165	Pickering-Phi 53	Dougherty-Bos .... .331	Lush-Det .... .377	Freeman-Bos ..... .496
L.Cross-Phi 90	Bradley-Cle 163	Burkett-StL 52	Barrett-Det .... .315	Lajoie-Cle .... .375	Crawford-Det ..... .489
Crawford-Det 89	Dougherty-Bos ... 161	Flick-Cle 51	Bradley-Cle .... .313	Green-Chi .... .368	Hartsel-Phi .... .477

Production	Adjusted Production	Batter Runs	Adjusted Batter Runs	Clutch Hitting Index	Runs Created
Lajoie-Cle .... .893	Lajoie-Cle 171	Lajoie-Cle 37.8	Lajoie-Cle 38.9	Gochnauer-Cle ... 168	Crawford-Det 109
Hartsel-Phi .... .868	Crawford-Det 161	Crawford-Det ... 35.3	Crawford-Det 37.2	L.Cross-Phi 152	Dougherty-Bos ... 109
Crawford-Det ..... .853	Hartsel-Phi 155	Bradley-Cle 31.3	Bradley-Cle 32.5	Williams-NY 152	Lajoie-Cle 106
Bradley-Cle ...... .840	Bradley-Cle 155	Barrett-Det 29.1	Barrett-Det 31.1	Ganzel-NY 143	Bradley-Cle 103
Freeman-Bos ..... .819	Green-Chi 146	Hartsel-Phi 29.0	Green-Chi 27.3	Elberfeld-Det-NY .. 133	Barrett-Det 97

Total Average	Stolen Bases	Stolen Base Average	Stolen Base Runs	Fielding Runs	Total Player Rating
Hartsel-Phi .... .934	Bay-Cle 45			Lajoie-Cle 40.1	Lajoie-Cle 8.1
Lajoie-Cle .... .931	Pickering-Phi 40			Criger-Bos 22.2	Bradley-Cle 4.3
Barrett-Det .... .856	Holmes-Was-Chi ... 35			Schreckengost-Phi 18.3	Crawford-Det 3.3
Crawford-Det ..... .852	Dougherty-Bos ... 35			Wallace-StL 18.1	Barrett-Det 3.0
Bradley-Cle ...... .848	Conroy-NY 33			Williams-NY 15.6	Elberfeld-Det-NY ... 3.0

Wins	Win Percentage	Games	Complete Games	Shutouts	Saves
Young-Bos 28	Young-Bos .... .757	Plank-Phi 43	Young-Bos 34	Young-Bos 7	Young-Bos 2
Plank-Phi 23	Hughes-Bos ...... .741	Mullin-Det 41	Waddell-Phi 34	Mullin-Det 6	Powell-StL 2
	Moore-Cle .... .679	Young-Bos 40	Donovan-Det 34	Dinneen-Bos 6	Orth-Was 2
	Dinneen-Bos ..... .618	Flaherty-Chi 40		Sudhoff-StL 5	Mullin-Det 2
	Plank-Phi .... .590	Chesbro-NY 40		Hughes-Bos 5	Dinneen-Bos 2

Innings Pitched	Fewest Hits/Game	Fewest BB/Game	Strikeouts	Strikeouts/Game	Ratio
Young-Bos 341.2	Moore-Cle 7.12	Young-Bos .... .97	Waddell-Phi 302	Waddell-Phi 8.39	Joss-Cle 8.53
Plank-Phi 336.0	Donovan-Det 7.24	Bernhard-Cle 1.14	Donovan-Det 187	Donovan-Det 5.48	Young-Bos 8.72
Chesbro-NY 324.2	Joss-Cle 7.36	Donahue-StL-Cle.. 1.14	Young-Bos 176	Moore-Cle 5.38	Bernhard-Cle 9.34
Waddell-Phi 324.0	Waddell-Phi 7.61	Joss-Cle 1.17	Plank-Phi 176	Powell-StL 4.97	Moore-Cle 9.38
Mullin-Det 320.2	Dinneen-Bos 7.68	Tannehill-NY 1.28	Mullin-Det 170	Mullin-Det 4.77	Dinneen-Bos 9.66

Earned Run Average	Adjusted ERA	Opponents' Batting Avg.	Opponents' On Base Pct.	Starter Runs	Adjusted Starter Runs
Moore-Cle 1.74	Moore-Cle 164	Moore-Cle .... .217	Joss-Cle .... .250	Moore-Cle 33.5	Young-Bos 36.1
Young-Bos 2.08	Young-Bos 146	Donovan-Det ..... .220	Young-Bos .... .254	Young-Bos 33.4	Moore-Cle 30.5
Bernhard-Cle 2.12	Bernhard-Cle 135	Joss-Cle .... .223	Bernhard-Cle ..... .267	White-Chi 27.7	Dinneen-Bos 25.8
White-Chi 2.13	Dinneen-Bos 134	Waddell-Phi ...... .229	Moore-Cle .... .268	Mullin-Det 25.5	Plank-Phi 24.9
Joss-Cle 2.19	White-Chi 132	Dinneen-Bos ..... .230	Dinneen-Bos ..... .274	Joss-Cle 24.4	Mullin-Det 23.6

Clutch Pitching Index	Relief Runs	Adjusted Relief Runs	Relief Ranking	Total Pitcher Index	Total Baseball Ranking
Kitson-Det 128				Young-Bos 5.1	Lajoie-Cle 8.1
Mullin-Det 122				Mullin-Det 4.0	Young-Bos 5.1
Donahue-StL-Cle.. 120				White-Chi 3.2	Bradley-Cle 4.3
Plank-Phi 112				Joss-Cle 2.7	Mullin-Det 4.0
Moore-Cle 111				Dinneen-Bos 2.6	Crawford-Det...... 3.3

TEAM	G	W	L	PCT	GB	R	OR	AB	H	2B	3B	HR	BB	SO	AVG	OBP	SLG	PRO	PRO+	BR	/A	PF	CHI	RC	SB	CS	SBA	SBR
NY	158	106	47	.693		744	476	5150	1347	202	65	31	434		.262	.319	.344	.663	108	78	51	104	106	691	283			
CHI	156	93	60	.608	13	599	517	5210	1294	157	62	22	298		.248	.289	.315	.604	93	-37	-37	100	104	569	227			
CIN	157	88	65	.575	18	695	547	5231	1332	189	92	21	399		.255	.307	.338	.645	98	43	-12	109	104	630	179			
PIT	156	87	66	.569	19	675	592	5160	1333	164	102	15	391		.258	.311	.338	.649	106	49	32	103	102	627	178			
STL	155	75	79	.487	31.5	602	595	5104	1292	175	66	24	343		.253	.300	.327	.627	106	8	35	96	98	590	199			
BRO	154	56	97	.366	50	497	614	4917	1142	159	53	15	411		.232	.291	.295	.586	91	-54	-39	98	93	511	205			
BOS	155	55	98	.359	51	491	749	5135	1217	153	50	24	316		.237	.281	.300	.581	90	-75	-53	97	93	498	143			
PHI	155	52	100	.342	53.5	571	784	5103	1268	170	54	23	377		.248	.300	.316	.616	101	-7	14	96	95	560	159			
TOT	623					4874		41010	10225	1369	544	175	2969	4277	.249	.300	.322	.622							1573			

TEAM	CG	SH	SV	IP	H	H/G	HR	BB	SO	RAT	ERA	ERA+	OAV	OOB	PR	/A	PF	CPI	FA	E	DP	FW	PW	BW	SBW	DIF
NY	127	21	15	1396²	1151	7.4	36	349	707	9.9	2.17	125	.222	.276	86	83	100	98	.956	294	93	2.3	8.8	5.4		13.0
CHI	139	18	6	1383²	1150	7.5	15	402	618	10.3	2.30	115	.224	.285	65	53	97	95	.954	298	89	1.8	5.6	-3.9		13.0
CIN	142	12	2	1392²	1256	8.1	14	343	502	10.7	2.34	125	.241	.294	59	87	107	107	.954	301	81	1.7	9.2	-1.3		1.8
PIT	133	15	1	1348¹	1273	8.5	13	379	455	11.4	2.89	95	.247	.306	-24	-23	100	95	.955	291	93	2.2	-2.4	3.4		7.3
STL	146	7	2	1368	1286	8.5	23	319	529	10.8	2.64	102	.238	.286	13	4	99	89	.952	307	83	1.1	.4	3.7		-7.2
BRO	135	12	2	1337¹	1281	8.6	27	414	453	11.8	2.70	101	.255	.319	4	3	100	116	.945	343	87	-1.4	.3	-4.1		-15.3
BOS	136	13	0	1348¹	1405	9.4	25	500	544	13.1	3.43	80	.272	.342	-105	-105	101	108	.945	353	91	-1.9	-11.1	-5.6		-2.9
PHI	131	10	2	1339¹	1418	9.5	22	425	469	12.9	3.39	79	.269	.332	-99	-109	98	103	.936	403	93	-5.1	-11.5	1.5		-8.9
TOT	1089	108	30	10914¹		8.4				11.3	2.73		.249	.300					.950	2590	710					

Runs		Hits		Doubles		Triples		Home Runs		Total Bases	
Browne-NY	99	Beaumont-Pit	185	Wagner-Pit	44	Lumley-Bro	18	Lumley-Bro	9	Wagner-Pit	255
Wagner-Pit	97	Beckley-StL	179	Mertes-NY	28	Wagner-Pit	14	Brain-StL	7	Lumley-Bro	247
Beaumont-Pit	97	Wagner-Pit	171	Delahanty-Bos	27	Tinker-Chi	13			Seymour-Cin	233
Huggins-Cin	96	Browne-NY	169	Seymour-Cin	26	Seymour-Cin	13			Beaumont-Pit	230
		Seymour-Cin	166	Dahlen-NY	26	Kelley-Cin	13			Beckley-StL	222

Runs Batted In		Runs Produced		Bases On Balls		Batting Average		On Base Percentage		Slugging Average	
Dahlen-NY	80	Wagner-Pit	168	Thomas-Phi	102	Wagner-Pit	.349	Wagner-Pit	.419	Wagner-Pit	.520
Mertes-NY	78	Mertes-NY	157	Huggins-Cin	88	Beckley-StL	.325	Thomas-Phi	.411	Seymour-Cin	.439
Lumley-Bro	78	Lumley-Bro	148	Devlin-NY	62	Seymour-Cin	.313	Huggins-Cin	.375	Chance-Chi	.430
Wagner-Pit	75	Dahlen-NY	148	Wagner-Pit	59	Chance-Chi	.310	Beckley-StL	.365	Lumley-Bro	.428
Corcoran-Cin	74	Beaumont-Pit	148	Ritchey-Pit	59	Beaumont-Pit	.301	Devlin-NY	.364	Brain-StL	.408

Production		Adjusted Production		Batter Runs		Adjusted Batter Runs		Clutch Hitting Index		Runs Created	
Wagner-Pit	.939	Wagner-Pit	187	Wagner-Pit	52.8	Wagner-Pit	51.1	Dahlen-NY	170	Wagner-Pit	133
Chance-Chi	.792	Chance-Chi	146	Thomas-Phi	28.3	Thomas-Phi	30.6	Corcoran-Cin	159	Lumley-Bro	94
Seymour-Cin	.787	Beckley-StL	146	Seymour-Cin	25.5	Beckley-StL	27.3	Bransfield-Pit	154	Mertes-NY	92
Beckley-StL	.768	Thomas-Phi	142	Donlin-Cin-NY	24.4	Grady-StL	24.9	Cooley-Bos	144	Beaumont-Pit	92
Thomas-Phi	.756	Lumley-Bro	138	Beckley-StL	24.4	Chance-Chi	23.5	Kelley-Cin	141	Beckley-StL	91

Total Average		Stolen Bases		Stolen Base Average		Stolen Base Runs		Fielding Runs		Total Player Rating	
Wagner-Pit	1.150	Wagner-Pit	53					Leach-Pit	35.8	Wagner-Pit	4.7
Chance-Chi	.875	Mertes-NY	47					Evers-Chi	31.3	Leach-Pit	4.3
Thomas-Phi	.855	Dahlen-NY	47					Dahlen-NY	27.6	Thomas-Phi	4.2
Mertes-NY	.805	McGann-NY	42					Tinker-Chi	19.3	Evers-Chi	3.2
Devlin-NY	.771	Chance-Chi	42					Farrell-StL	16.3	Chance-Chi	3.1

Wins		Win Percentage		Games		Complete Games		Shutouts		Saves	
McGinnity-NY	35	McGinnity-NY	.814	McGinnity-NY	51	Willis-Bos	39	McGinnity-NY	9	McGinnity-NY	5
Mathewson-NY	33	Mathewson-NY	.733	Mathewson-NY	48	Taylor-NY	39	Harper-Cin	6	Wiltse-NY	3
Harper-Cin	23	Harper-Cin	.719	Jones-Bro	46	McGinnity-NY	38			Briggs-Chi	3
Taylor-NY	21	Flaherty-Pit	.679	Willis-Bos	43	Jones-Bro	38			Ames-NY	3
Nichols-StL	21			Fraser-Phi	42						

Innings Pitched		Fewest Hits/Game		Fewest BB/Game		Strikeouts		Strikeouts/Game		Ratio	
McGinnity-NY	408.0	Brown-Chi	6.57	Hahn-Cin	1.06	Mathewson-NY	212	Wiltse-NY	5.74	Brown-Chi	8.94
Jones-Bro	377.0	Weimer-Chi	6.71	Phillippe-Pit	1.40	Willis-Bos	196	Mathewson-NY	5.19	McGinnity-NY	8.96
Mathewson-NY	367.2	McGinnity-NY	6.77	Nichols-StL	1.42	Weimer-Chi	177	Weimer-Chi	5.19	Hahn-Cin	9.07
Taylor-StL	352.0	Garvin-Bro	6.99	Kellum-Cin	1.84	Pittinger-Bos	146	Willis-Bos	5.04	Nichols-StL	9.17
Willis-Bos	350.0	Taylor-NY	7.02	McFarland-StL	1.87	McGinnity-NY	144	Phillippe-Pit	4.43	Mathewson-NY	9.50

Earned Run Average		Adjusted ERA		Opponents' Batting Avg.		Opponents' On Base Pct.		Starter Runs		Adjusted Starter Runs	
McGinnity-NY	1.61	McGinnity-NY	169	Brown-Chi	.199	Brown-Chi	.253	McGinnity-NY	50.6	McGinnity-NY	50.1
Garvin-Bro	1.68	Garvin-Bro	162	Weimer-Chi	.204	Nichols-StL	.256	Mathewson-NY	28.4	Hahn-Cin	28.5
Brown-Chi	1.86	Brown-Chi	142	McGinnity-NY	.206	McGinnity-NY	.256	Weimer-Chi	28.0	Mathewson-NY	28.0
Weimer-Chi	1.91	Hahn-Cin	142	Taylor-NY	.214	Hahn-Cin	.262	Nichols-StL	25.0	Weimer-Chi	25.6
Nichols-StL	2.02	Weimer-Chi	139	Garvin-Bro	.218	Mathewson-NY	.270	Hahn-Cin	22.2	Nichols-StL	23.6

Clutch Pitching Index		Relief Runs		Adjusted Relief Runs		Relief Ranking		Total Pitcher Index		Total Baseball Ranking	
Garvin-Bro	158							McGinnity-NY	6.0	McGinnity-NY	6.0
O'Neill-StL	136							Mathewson-NY	4.4	Wagner-Pit	4.7
Briggs-Chi	131							Flaherty-Pit	3.5	Mathewson-NY	4.4
Jones-Bro	121							Hahn-Cin	3.4	Leach-Pit	4.3
Mitchell-Phi-Bro	119							Weimer-Chi	2.8	Thomas-Phi	4.2

TEAM	G	W	L	PCT	GB	R	OR	AB	H	2B	3B	HR	BB	SO	AVG	OBP	SLG	PRO	PRO+	BR	/A	PF	CHI	RC	SB	CS	SBA	SBR
BOS	157	95	59	.617		608	466	5231	1294	194	105	26	347	570	.247	.294	.340	.634	102	41	9	106	101	584	101			
NY	155	92	59	.609	1.5	598	526	5220	1354	195	91	27	312	548	.259	.301	.347	.648	106	66	39	105	96	625	163			
CHI	156	89	65	.578	6	600	482	5027	1217	193	68	14	373	586	.242	.294	.316	.610	104	6	27	96	108	567	216			
CLE	154	86	65	.570	7.5	647	482	5152	1340	225	90	27	307	714	.260	.302	.354	.656	115	78	82	99	103	638	178			
PHI	155	81	70	.536	12.5	557	503	5088	1266	197	77	31	313	605	.249	.292	.336	.628	101	30	3	105	97	569	137			
STL	156	65	87	.428	29	481	604	5291	1266	153	53	10	332	609	.239	.284	.294	.578	95	-54	-19	94	95	512	150			
DET	162	62	90	.408	32	505	627	5321	1231	154	69	11	344	635	.231	.278	.292	.570	89	-69	-51	97	101	494	112			
WAS	157	38	113	.252	55.5	437	743	5149	1170	171	57	10	283	759	.227	.267	.288	.555	83	-96	-87	98	98	463	150			
TOT	626					4433		41479	10138	1482	610	156	2611	5026	.244	.289	.321	.610						1207				

TEAM	CG	SH	SV	IP	H	H/G	HR	BB	SO	RAT	ERA	ERA+	OAV	OOB	PR	/A	PF	CPI	FA	E	DP	FW	PW	BW	SBW	DIF
BOS	148	21	1	1406	1208	7.7	31	233	612	9.2	2.12	126	.233	.266	74	86	103	103	.962	242	83	1.6	9.6	1.0		5.8
NY	123	15	1	1380²	1180	7.7	29	311	684	9.7	2.57	106	.232	.276	4	21	104	90	.958	275	90	-.8	2.3	4.4		10.6
CHI	134	26	3	1380	1161	7.6	13	303	550	9.5	2.30	107	.229	.273	45	22	95	94	.964	238	95	1.7	2.5	3.0		4.8
CLE	141	20	0	1356²	1273	8.4	10	285	627	10.3	2.22	114	.249	.289	56	47	98	117	.959	255	86	.4	5.3	9.2		-4.3
PHI	136	26	0	1361¹	1149	7.6	13	366	887	10.0	2.35	114	.230	.282	37	49	103	98	.959	250	67	.8	5.5	.3		-1.1
STL	135	13	1	1410	1335	8.5	25	333	577	10.6	2.83	88	.251	.295	-36	-54	96	99	.960	267	78	-.2	-6.0	-2.1		-2.7
DET	143	15	2	1430	1345	8.5	16	433	556	11.2	2.77	92	.249	.305	-27	-35	98	104	.959	273	92	.0	-3.9	-5.7		-4.5
WAS	137	7	4	1359²	1487	9.8	19	347	533	12.1	3.62	73	.279	.323	-154	-145	102	98	.951	314	97	-3.1	-16.2	-9.7		-8.4
TOT	1097	143	12	11084¹		8.2				10.4	2.60		.244	.289					.959	2114	688					

Runs		Hits		Doubles		Triples		Home Runs		Total Bases	
Dougherty-Bos-NY	113	Lajoie-Cle	208	Lajoie-Cle	49	Stahl-Bos	19	Davis-Phi	10	Lajoie-Cle	305
Flick-Cle	97	Keeler-NY	186	Collins-Bos	33	Freeman-Bos	19	Murphy-Phi	7	Flick-Cle	260
Bradley-Cle	94	Bradley-Cle	183	Bradley-Cle	32	Cassidy-Was	19	Freeman-Bos	7	Freeman-Bos	246
Lajoie-Cle	92	Dougherty-Bos-NY	181			Murphy-Phi	17			Bradley-Cle	246
		Flick-Cle	177			Flick-Cle	17				

Runs Batted In		Runs Produced		Bases On Balls		Batting Average		On Base Percentage		Slugging Average	
Lajoie-Cle	102	Lajoie-Cle	188	Barrett-Det	79	Lajoie-Cle	.376	Lajoie-Cle	.405	Lajoie-Cle	.552
Freeman-Bos	84	Bradley-Cle	172	Burkett-StL	78	Keeler-NY	.343	Keeler-NY	.382	Flick-Cle	.449
Bradley-Cle	83	Parent-Bos	156	Hartsel-Phi	75	Flick-Cle	.306	Flick-Cle	.362	Murphy-Phi	.440
Anderson-NY	82	Collins-Bos	149	Selbach-Was-Bos	72	Bradley-Cle	.300	Stahl-Bos	.359	Hickman-Cle-Det	.437
		Murphy-Phi	148	Lush-Cle	72	Seybold-Phi	.292	Burkett-StL	.358	Stahl-Bos	.416

Production		Adjusted Production		Batter Runs		Adjusted Batter Runs		Clutch Hitting Index		Runs Created	
Lajoie-Cle	.957	Lajoie-Cle	205	Lajoie-Cle	61.3	Lajoie-Cle	61.8	Anderson-NY	145	Lajoie-Cle	139
Flick-Cle	.811	Flick-Cle	159	Flick-Cle	37.5	Flick-Cle	38.0	Williams-NY	143	Flick-Cle	112
Keeler-NY	.791	Keeler-NY	146	Stahl-Bos	32.2	Keeler-NY	29.2	Tannehill-Chi	140	Keeler-NY	98
Stahl-Bos	.775	Stahl-Bos	139	Keeler-NY	31.9	Stahl-Bos	28.5	Jones-StL	135	Stahl-Bos	97
Murphy-Phi	.754	Hickman-Cle-Det	139	Davis-Phi	28.0	Davis-Phi	25.9	Davis-Chi	133	Bradley-Cle	93

Total Average		Stolen Bases		Stolen Base Average	Stolen Base Runs	Fielding Runs		Total Player Rating	
Lajoie-Cle	1.046	Flick-Cle	38			Tannehill-Chi	27.8	Lajoie-Cle	6.8
Flick-Cle	.868	Bay-Cle	38			Davis-Chi	16.8	Flick-Cle	4.3
Keeler-NY	.779	Heidrick-StL	35			Williams-NY	16.8	Bradley-Cle	4.0
Stahl-Bos	.765	Davis-Chi	32			Carr-Det-Cle	15.9	Murphy-Phi	3.6
Murphy-Phi	.728	Conroy-NY	30			Elberfeld-NY	15.3	Davis-Chi	3.0

Wins		Win Percentage		Games		Complete Games		Shutouts		Saves	
Chesbro-NY	41	Chesbro-NY	.774	Chesbro-NY	55	Chesbro-NY	48	Young-Bos	10	Patten-Was	3
Young-Bos	26	Tannehill-Bos	.656	Powell-NY	47	Mullin-Det	42	Waddell-Phi	8		
Plank-Phi	26	Smith-Chi	.640	Waddell-Phi	46	Young-Bos	40	White-Chi	7		
Waddell-Phi	25	Bernhard-Cle	.639	Patten-Was	45	Waddell-Phi	39	Plank-Phi	7		
		Dinneen-Bos	.622	Mullin-Det	45	Powell-NY	38	Mullin-Det	7		

Innings Pitched		Fewest Hits/Game		Fewest BB/Game		Strikeouts		Strikeouts/Game		Ratio	
Chesbro-NY	454.2	Chesbro-NY	6.69	Young-Bos	.69	Waddell-Phi	349	Waddell-Phi	8.20	Young-Bos	8.43
Powell-NY	390.1	Owen-Chi	6.94	Tannehill-Bos	1.05	Chesbro-NY	239	Bender-Phi	6.58	Chesbro-NY	8.43
Waddell-Phi	383.0	Smith-Chi	6.98	Patterson-Chi	1.31	Powell-NY	202	Moore-Cle	5.49	Owen-Chi	8.69
Mullin-Det	382.1	Gibson-Bos	7.12	Joss-Cle	1.40	Plank-Phi	201	Plank-Phi	5.06	Joss-Cle	8.89
Young-Bos	380.0	Waddell-Phi	7.21	Altrock-Chi	1.41	Young-Bos	200	Glade-StL	4.86	Tannehill-Bos	9.23

Earned Run Average		Adjusted ERA		Opponents' Batting Avg.		Opponents' On Base Pct.		Starter Runs		Adjusted Starter Runs	
Joss-Cle	1.59	Waddell-Phi	165	Chesbro-NY	.208	Young-Bos	.249	Waddell-Phi	41.5	Chesbro-NY	45.0
Waddell-Phi	1.62	Joss-Cle	159	Owen-Chi	.214	Chesbro-NY	.249	Chesbro-NY	39.2	Waddell-Phi	44.8
White-Chi	1.78	Chesbro-NY	149	Smith-Chi	.215	Owen-Chi	.254	Young-Bos	26.6	Young-Bos	29.8
Chesbro-NY	1.82	White-Chi	138	Gibson-Bos	.219	Joss-Cle	.259	Owen-Chi	22.9	Joss-Cle	20.2
Owen-Chi	1.94	Young-Bos	136	Waddell-Phi	.221	Tannehill-Bos	.266	Joss-Cle	21.5	Plank-Phi	20.2

Clutch Pitching Index		Relief Runs	Adjusted Relief Runs	Relief Ranking	Total Pitcher Index		Total Baseball Ranking	
White-Chi	152				Chesbro-NY	6.8	Chesbro-NY	6.8
Siever-StL	136				Waddell-Phi	4.4	Lajoie-Cle	6.8
Bernhard-Cle	133				Owen-Chi	3.4	Waddell-Phi	4.4
Waddell-Phi	125				Tannehill-Bos	3.2	Flick-Cle	4.3
Donahue-Cle	120				Mullin-Det	3.1	Bradley-Cle	4.0

TEAM	G	W	L	PCT	GB	R	OR	AB	H	2B	3B	HR	BB	SO	AVG	OBP	SLG	PRO	PRO+	BR	/A	PF	CHI	RC	SB	CS	SBA	SBR
NY	155	105	48	.686		778	505	5094	1392	191	88	39	517		.273	.340	.368	.708	118	131	117	102	101	772	291			
PIT	155	96	57	.627	9	692	570	5213	1385	190	91	22	382		.266	.316	.350	.666	105	43	26	103	101	674	202			
CHI	155	92	61	.601	13	667	442	5108	1249	157	82	12	448		.245	.305	.314	.619	89	-31	-56	104	109	609	267			
PHI	155	83	69	.546	21.5	708	602	5243	1362	187	82	16	406		.260	.325	.336	.649	106	16	40	96	106	644	180			
CIN	155	79	74	.516	26	735	698	5205	1401	160	101	27	434		.269	.325	.354	.679	101	74	3	111	102	696	181			
STL	154	58	96	.377	47.5	535	734	5066	1254	140	85	20	391		.248	.301	.321	.622	97	-32	-12	97	91	565	162			
BOS	156	51	103	.331	54.5	468	731	5190	1217	148	52	17	302		.234	.277	.293	.570	79	-134	-120	98	96	479	132			
BRO	155	48	104	.316	56.5	506	807	5100	1255	154	60	29	327		.246	.292	.317	.609	97	-62	-15	93	91	554	186			
TOT	620					5089		41219	10515	1327	641	182	3207	4462	.255	.309	.332	.641						1601				

TEAM	CG	SH	SV	IP	H	H/G	HR	BB	SO	RAT	ERA	ERA+	OAV	OOB	PR	/A	PF	CPI	FA	C	DP	FW	PW	BW	SBW	DIF
NY	117	18	15	1370	1160	7.6	25	364	760	10.2	2.39	122	.228	.284	91	79	98	97	.960	258	93	2.3	8.2	12.2		5.8
PIT	113	12	6	1382²	1270	8.3	11	389	512	11.2	2.86	104	.247	.308	19	16	100	98	.961	255	112	2.5	1.7	2.7		12.7
CHI	133	23	2	1407	1135	7.3	15	385	627	10.0	2.04	146	.224	.285	148	143	99	110	.962	248	99	2.9	14.9	-5.8		3.5
PHI	119	12	5	1399	1303	8.4	21	411	516	11.5	2.81	104	.253	.316	28	12	97	109	.957	275	99	1.2	1.2	4.2		.4
CIN	119	10	2	1366	1409	9.3	22	439	547	12.5	3.01	109	.271	.334	-2	41	110	119	.953	310	122	-1.0	4.3	.3		-1.1
STL	135	10	2	1347²	1431	9.6	28	367	411	12.3	3.59	83	.275	.329	-89	-92	99	100	.957	274	83	1.2	-9.6	-1.2		-9.3
BOS	139	14	0	1382²	1390	9.0	36	433	533	12.1	3.52	88	.264	.325	-81	-68	103	98	.951	325	89	-1.8	-7.1	-12.5		-4.6
BRO	125	7	3	1347	1416	9.5	24	476	556	13.1	3.76	77	.274	.342	-114	-132	96	101	.937	408	101	-7.2	-13.7	-1.6		-5.5
TOT	1000	106	35	11002		8.6				11.6	2.99		.255	.309					.954	2353	798					

Runs
Donlin-NY	124
Thomas-Phi	118
Huggins-Cin	117
Wagner-Pit	114

Hits
Seymour-Cin	219
Donlin-NY	216
Wagner-Pit	199
Barry-Chi-Cin	182
Magee-Phi	180

Doubles
Seymour-Cin	40
Titus-Phi	36
Wagner-Pit	32
Donlin-NY	31
Ritchey-Pit	29

Triples
Seymour-Cin	21
Mertes-NY	17
Magee-Phi	17
Smoot-StL	16
Donlin-NY	16

Home Runs
Odwell-Cin	9
Seymour-Cin	8
Lumley-Bro	7
Donlin-NY	7
Dahlen-NY	7

Total Bases
Seymour-Cin	325
Donlin-NY	300
Wagner-Pit	277
Magee-Phi	253
Titus-Phi	239

Runs Batted In
Seymour-Cin	121
Mertes-NY	108
Wagner-Pit	101
Magee-Phi	98
Titus-Phi	89

Runs Produced
Wagner-Pit	209
Seymour-Cin	208
Donlin-NY	197
Magee-Phi	193
Titus-Phi	186

Bases On Balls
Huggins-Cin	103
Slagle-Chi	97
Thomas-Phi	93
Chance-Chi	78
Titus-Phi	69

Batting Average
Seymour-Cin	.377
Wagner-Pit	.363
Donlin-NY	.356
Thomas-Phi	.317
Chance-Chi	.316

On Base Percentage
Chance-Chi	.430
Seymour-Cin	.427
Wagner-Pit	.420
Thomas-Phi	.414
Donlin-NY	.411

Slugging Average
Seymour-Cin	.559
Wagner-Pit	.505
Donlin-NY	.495
Titus-Phi	.436
McGann-NY	.434

Production
Seymour-Cin	.987
Wagner-Pit	.926
Donlin-NY	.906
Chance-Chi	.863
Titus-Phi	.822

Adjusted Production
Seymour-Cin	177
Wagner-Pit	174
Donlin-NY	169
Chance-Chi	154
Titus-Phi	153

Batter Runs
Seymour-Cin	65.8
Donlin-NY	52.5
Wagner-Pit	51.7
Chance-Chi	33.2
Titus-Phi	32.7

Adjusted Batter Runs
Seymour-Cin	58.1
Donlin-NY	50.9
Wagner-Pit	50.0
Titus-Phi	35.3
Thomas-Phi	31.4

Clutch Hitting Index
Mertes-NY	162
Dahlen-NY	147
Chance-Chi	146
Wolverton-Bos	140
Corcoran-Cin	139

Runs Created
Seymour-Cin	152
Wagner-Pit	144
Donlin-NY	141
Magee-Phi	108
Mertes-NY	101

Total Average
Wagner-Pit	1.112
Seymour-Cin	1.097
Chance-Chi	1.067
Donlin-NY	.997
Mertes-NY	.851

Stolen Bases
Maloney-Chi	59
Devlin-NY	59
Wagner-Pit	57
Mertes-NY	52
Magee-Phi	48

Stolen Base Average

Stolen Base Runs

Fielding Runs
Huggins-Cin	35.9
Gilbert-NY	26.2
Tenney-Bos	21.3
Wagner-Pit	20.3
Dahlen-NY	19.8

Total Player Rating
Wagner-Pit	7.4
Huggins-Cin	6.1
Thomas-Phi	4.1
Titus-Phi	3.4

Wins
Mathewson-NY	31
Pittinger-Phi	23
Ames-NY	22
McGinnity-NY	21

Win Percentage
Leever-Pit	.800
Mathewson-NY	.775
Ames-NY	.733
Wiltse-NY	.714
Lynch-Pit	.680

Games
Pittinger-Phi	46
McGinnity-NY	46
Young-Bos	43
Mathewson-NY	43
Overall-Cin	42

Complete Games
Young-Bos	41
Willis-Bos	36
Fraser-Bos	35
Taylor-StL	34

Shutouts
Mathewson-NY	8
Young-Bos	7
Reulbach-Chi	5
Phillippe-Pit	5
Briggs-Chi	5

Saves
Elliott-NY	6
Wiltse-NY	4
McGinnity-NY	3

Innings Pitched
Young-Bos	378.0
Willis-Bos	342.0
Mathewson-NY	339.0
Pittinger-Phi	337.0
Fraser-Bos	334.0

Fewest Hits/Game
Reulbach-Chi	6.41
Mathewson-NY	6.69
Wicker-Chi	7.03
Lundgren-Chi	7.03
Wiltse-NY	7.22

Fewest BB/Game
Phillippe-Pit	1.55
Brown-Chi	1.59
Young-Bos	1.69
Mathewson-NY	1.70
McGinnity-NY	2.00

Strikeouts
Mathewson-NY	206
Ames-NY	198
Overall-Cin	173
Ewing-Cin	164
Young-Bos	156

Strikeouts/Game
Ames-NY	6.78
Wiltse-NY	5.48
Mathewson-NY	5.47
Overall-Cin	4.90
Scanlan-Bro	4.86

Ratio
Mathewson-NY	8.42
Reulbach-Chi	9.22
Phillippe-Pit	9.45
Wicker-Chi	9.46
Brown-Chi	9.54

Earned Run Average
Mathewson-NY	1.27
Reulbach-Chi	1.42
Wicker-Chi	2.02
Briggs-Chi	2.14
Brown-Chi	2.17

Adjusted ERA
Mathewson-NY	229
Reulbach-Chi	210
Wicker-Chi	147
Briggs-Chi	139
Brown-Chi	137

Opponents' Batting Avg.
Reulbach-Chi	.201
Mathewson-NY	.205
Wiltse-NY	.219
Lundgren-Chi	.220
Wicker-Chi	.221

Opponents' On Base Pct.
Mathewson-NY	.245
Reulbach-Chi	.266
Brown-Chi	.271
Phillippe-Pit	.274
Wicker-Chi	.276

Starter Runs
Mathewson-NY	64.7
Reulbach-Chi	51.1
Phillippe-Pit	24.7
Sparks-Phi	23.4
Brown-Chi	22.8

Adjusted Starter Runs
Mathewson-NY	62.0
Reulbach-Chi	50.4
Ewing-Cin	27.2
Phillippe-Pit	24.7
Brown-Chi	22.2

Clutch Pitching Index
Chech-Cin	136
Duggleby-Phi	131
Briggs-Chi	124
Overall-Cin	123
Case-Pit	119

Relief Runs

Adjusted Relief Runs

Relief Ranking

Total Pitcher Index
Mathewson-NY	8.9
Reulbach-Chi	4.9
Ewing-Cin	3.2
Wiltse-NY	2.4
Brown-Chi	2.3

Total Baseball Ranking
Mathewson-NY	8.9
Wagner-Pit	7.4
Seymour-Cin	6.1
Huggins-Cin	5.4
Reulbach-Chi	4.9

TEAM	G	W	L	PCT	GB	R	OR	AB	H	2B	3B	HR	BB	SO	AVG	OBP	SLG	PRO	PRO+	BR	/A	PF	CHI	RC	SB	CS	SBA	SBR
PHI	152	92	56	.622		**623**	492	5146	1310	**256**	51	24	376		**.255**	**.305**	**.338**	**.643**	**110**	65	55	102	97	**623**	190			
CHI	158	92	60	.605	2	612	**451**	5114	1213	200	55	11	439		.237	.297	.304	.601	102	-1	23	96	105	563	194			
DET	154	79	74	.516	15.5	512	602	4971	1209	190	54	13	375		.243	.296	.311	.607	99	3	0	101	91	531	129			
BOS	153	78	74	.513	16	579	564	5049	1179	165	69	29	486		.234	.301	.311	.612	100	18	11	101	98	542	131			
CLE	155	76	78	.494	19	567	587	5166	**1318**	211	**72**	18	286		**.255**	.294	.334	.628	105	31	23	101	95	594	188			
NY	152	71	78	.477	21.5	586	622	4957	1228	163	61	23	360		.248	.299	.319	.618	93	20	-43	111	102	563	**200**			
WAS	154	64	87	.424	29.5	559	623	5015	1121	193	68	22	298		.224	.267	.302	.569	90	-70	-47	96	115	479	169			
STL	156	54	99	.353	40.5	511	608	5204	1205	153	49	16	362		.232	.282	.289	.571	92	-63	-32	95	99	490	130			
TOT	617					4549		40622	9783	1531	479	156	2982	5107	.241	.293	.314	.606							1331			

TEAM	CG	SH	SV	IP	H	H/G	HR	BB	SO	RAT	ERA	ERA+	OAV	OOB	PR	/A	PF	CPI	FA	E	DP	FW	PW	BW	SBW	DIF
PHI	117	**19**	0	1383¹	**1137**	7.4	21	409	895	10.1	2.19	121	.227	.285	69	67	100	**109**	.957	265	64	.2	7.4	**6.0**		4.4
CHI	131	16	0	1427	1163	7.3	**11**	329	613	9.4	**1.99**	**124**	**.226**	**.272**	**104**	71	93	107	**.968**	217	95	4.1	7.8	2.5		1.5
DET	124	17	1	1348	1226	8.2	11	474	578	11.4	2.83	96	.246	.311	-27	-19	103	104	.957	265	80	.5	-2.1	.0		4.1
BOS	124	15	1	1356¹	1198	7.9	33	**292**	652	9.9	2.84	95	.240	.282	-28	-26	102	90	.953	294	75	-1.6	-2.9	1.2		5.2
CLE	**140**	16	0	1363¹	1251	8.3	23	334	555	10.5	2.85	92	.246	.292	-29	-33	99	96	.963	229	84	3.0	-3.6	2.5		-2.9
NY	88	**19**	**4**	1353²	1235	8.2	26	396	642	10.8	2.93	100	.245	.301	-41	-1	111	98	.952	293	88	-1.6	-.1	-4.7		3.0
WAS	118	12	1	1362¹	1250	8.3	12	385	539	10.8	2.87	92	.246	.299	-33	-35	100	97	.951	318	76	-3.1	-3.8	-5.2		.6
STL	134	11	2	1384²	1245	8.1	19	389	633	10.6	2.74	93	.243	.296	-13	-32	96	99	.955	295	78	-1.3	-3.5	-3.5		-14.2
TOT	976	125	9	10978²		8.0				10.4	2.65		.241	.293					.957	2176	640					

Runs
Davis-Phi 93
Jones-Chi 91
Bay-Cle 90
Hartsel-Phi 88
Keeler-NY 81

Hits
Stone-StL 187
Davis-Phi 173
Crawford-Det 171
Keeler-NY 169
Bay-Cle 166

Doubles
Davis-Phi 47
Crawford-Det 38
Hickman-Det-Was . . 37
Seybold-Phi 37

Triples
Flick-Cle 18
Ferris-Bos 16
Turner-Cle 14
Stone-StL 13
Burkett-Bos 13

Home Runs
Davis-Phi 8
Stone-StL 7

Total Bases
Stone-StL 259
Davis-Phi 256
Crawford-Det 247
Hickman-Det-Was . 232
Flick-Cle 231

Runs Batted In
Davis-Phi 83
L.Cross-Phi 77
Donahue-Chi 76
Crawford-Det 75
Turner-Cle 72

Runs Produced
Davis-Phi 168
Donahue-Chi 146
L.Cross-Phi 146
Crawford-Det 142
Murphy-Phi 136

Bases On Balls
Hartsel-Phi 121
Jones-Chi 73
Selbach-Bos 67
Burkett-Bos 67
Davis-Chi 60

Batting Average
Flick-Cle 308
Keeler-NY 302
Bay-Cle 301
Crawford-Det 297
Stone-StL 296

On Base Percentage
Hartsel-Phi 408
Flick-Cle 374
Crawford-Det 354
Keeler-NY 352
Selbach-Bos 351

Slugging Average
Flick-Cle 462
Crawford-Det 430
Davis-Phi 422
Stone-StL 410
Hickman-Det-Was . .405

Production
Flick-Cle 836
Crawford-Det 783
Davis-Phi 754
Hartsel-Phi 754
Stone-StL 752

Adjusted Production
Flick-Cle 165
Crawford-Det 149
Stone-StL 148
Hartsel-Phi 140
Davis-Phi 139

Batter Runs
Flick-Cle 37.5
Hartsel-Phi 34.2
Crawford-Det 31.7
Stone-StL 27.2
Davis-Phi 26.1

Adjusted Batter Runs
Flick-Cle 36.7
Hartsel-Phi 33.1
Crawford-Det 31.3
Stone-StL 30.9
Davis-Phi 25.1

Clutch Hitting Index
Donahue-Chi 152
Gleason-StL 145
L.Cross-Phi 136
Jones-StL 128
Stahl-Was 124

Runs Created
Flick-Cle 103
Stone-StL 101
Davis-Phi 100
Crawford-Det 98
Hartsel-Phi 96

Total Average
Flick-Cle 922
Hartsel-Phi 882
Crawford-Det 790
Davis-Phi 772
Stone-StL 739

Stolen Bases
Hoffman-Phi 46
Fultz-NY 44
Stahl-Was 41
Hartsel-Phi 37

Stolen Base Average

Stolen Base Runs

Fielding Runs
Cassidy-Was 33.1
Tannehill-StL 27.8
Wallace-StL 19.0
McIntyre-Det 16.4
Jones-Was 16.1

Total Player Rating
Davis-Chi 4.2
Wallace-StL 4.1
Crawford-Det 3.9
Flick-Cle 3.3
Stone-StL 2.7

Wins
Waddell-Phi 27
Plank-Phi 24
Killian-Det 23
Altrock-Chi 23
Tannehill-Bos 22

Win Percentage
Waddell-Phi 730
Tannehill-Bos 710
Coakley-Phi 692
Plank-Phi 667
Altrock-Chi 657

Games
Waddell-Phi 46
Mullin-Det 44
Patten-Was 42
Owen-Chi 42

Complete Games
Plank-Phi 35
Mullin-Det 35
Howell-StL 35
Killian-Det 33
Owen-Chi 32

Shutouts
Killian-Det 8
Waddell-Phi 7
Tannehill-Bos 6
Orth-NY 6
Hughes-Was 6

Saves
Buchanan-StL 2

Innings Pitched
Mullin-Det 347.2
Plank-Phi 346.2
Owen-Chi 334.0
Waddell-Phi 328.2
Howell-StL 323.0

Fewest Hits/Game
Waddell-Phi 6.33
Smith-Chi 6.63
Young-Bos 6.96
Howell-StL 7.02
White-Chi 7.05

Fewest BB/Game
Young-Bos 84
Joss-Cle 1.45
Owen-Chi 1.51
Bernhard-Cle 1.76
Altrock-Chi 1.80

Strikeouts
Waddell-Phi 287
Young-Bos 210
Plank-Phi 210
Howell-StL 198
Smith-Chi 171

Strikeouts/Game
Waddell-Phi 7.86
Young-Bos 5.89
Bender-Phi 5.58
Howell-StL 5.52
Hogg-NY 5.49

Ratio
Young-Bos 7.80
Waddell-Phi 8.79
Owen-Chi 8.95
White-Chi 9.06
Joss-Cle 9.19

Earned Run Average
Waddell-Phi 1.48
White-Chi 1.76
Young-Bos 1.82
Coakley-Phi 1.84
Altrock-Chi 1.88

Adjusted ERA
Waddell-Phi 179
Young-Bos 147
Coakley-Phi 144
White-Chi 140
Chesbro-NY 133

Opponents' Batting Avg.
Waddell-Phi 200
Smith-Chi 208
Young-Bos 216
Howell-StL 217
White-Chi 218

Opponents' On Base Pct.
Young-Bos 236
Waddell-Phi 258
Owen-Chi 261
White-Chi 264
Joss-Cle 267

Starter Runs
Waddell-Phi 42.7
Young-Bos 29.3
Altrock-Chi 26.9
White-Chi 25.6
Howell-StL 24.0

Adjusted Starter Runs
Waddell-Phi 42.7
Young-Bos 30.9
Chesbro-NY 24.6
Coakley-Phi 23.0
Altrock-Chi 20.3

Clutch Pitching Index
Coakley-Phi 144
Altrock-Chi 122
Waddell-Phi 117
Mullin-Det 115
Townsend-Was . . . 113

Relief Runs

Adjusted Relief Runs

Relief Ranking

Total Pitcher Index
Waddell-Phi 4.6
Howell-StL 4.6
Chesbro-NY 3.1
Young-Bos 3.1
Altrock-Chi 2.9

Total Baseball Ranking
Waddell-Phi 4.6
Howell-StL 4.6
Davis-Chi 4.2
Wallace-StL 4.1
Crawford-Det 3.9

TEAM	G	W	L	PCT	GB	R	OR	AB	H	2B	3B	HR	BB	SO	AVG	OBP	SLG	PRO	PRO+	BR	/A	PF	CHI	RC	SB	CS	SBA	SBR
CHI	155	116	36	.763		705	381	5018	1316	181	71	20	448		.262	.323	.339	.662	109	84	51	106	109	683	283			
NY	153	96	56	.632	20	625	510	4768	1217	162	53	15	563		.255	.334	.321	.655	110	84	72	102	100	642	288			
PIT	154	93	60	.608	23.5	623	470	5030	1313	164	67	12	424		.261	.318	.327	.645	105	57	32	104	101	615	162			
PHI	154	71	82	.464	45.5	528	564	4911	1183	197	47	12	432		.241	.302	.307	.609	98	-5	-5	100	98	542	180			
BRO	153	66	86	.434	50	496	625	4897	1156	141	68	25	388		.236	.292	.308	.600	103	-27	15	92	97	523	175			
CIN	155	64	87	.424	51.5	533	582	5025	1198	140	71	16	395		.238	.294	.304	.598	90	-30	-54	104	102	532	170			
STL	154	52	98	.347	63	470	607	5075	1195	137	69	10	361		.235	.286	.296	.582	93	-61	-38	96	96	490	110			
BOS	152	49	102	.325	66.5	408	649	4925	1115	136	43	16	356		.226	.279	.281	.560	84	-96	-82	97	93	437	93			
TOT	615					4388		39649	9693	1258	489	126	3367	4537	.244	.304	.310	.614							1461			

TEAM	CG	SH	SV	IP	H	H/G	HR	BB	SO	RAT	ERA	ERA+	OAV	OOB	PR	/A	PF	CPI	FA	E	DP	FW	PW	BW	SBW	DIF
CHI	125	30	10	1388¹	1018	6.6	12	446	702	9.8	1.75	150	.206	.279	134	135	100	106	.969	194	100	4.5	15.0	5.7		14.8
NY	105	19	18	1334¹	1207	8.1	13	394	639	11.0	2.49	104	.241	.299	20	14	99	100	.963	233	84	1.8	1.6	8.0		8.7
PIT	116	27	2	1358	1234	8.2	13	309	532	10.5	2.21	120	.245	.294	62	69	102	112	.964	228	109	2.2	7.7	3.6		3.1
PHI	108	21	5	1354¹	1201	8.0	18	436	500	11.3	2.58	101	.235	.303	6	0	99	97	.956	271	83	-.6	.0	-.6		-4.3
BRO	119	22	11	1348²	1255	8.4	15	453	476	11.7	3.13	80	.249	.315	-75	-93	96	91	.955	283	73	-1.5	-10.3	1.7		.2
CIN	126	12	5	1369²	1248	8.2	14	470	567	11.6	2.69	102	.249	.320	-9	5	105	108	.959	262	97	.0	.6	-6.0		-6.1
STL	118	4	2	1354	1246	8.3	17	479	559	11.9	3.04	86	.245	.318	-63	-64	100	95	.957	272	92	-.7	-7.1	-4.2		-11.0
BOS	137	10	0	1334¹	1291	8.7	24	436	562	12.0	3.14	85	.260	.327	-75	-70	102	103	.947	337	102	-5.2	-7.8	-9.1		-4.4
TOT	954	145	53	10841²		8.1				11.2	2.62		.244	.304					.959	2080	740					

Runs
Wagner-Pit 103
Chance-Chi 103
Sheckard-Chi 90
Nealon-Pit 82

Hits
Wagner-Pit 176
Wagner-Pit 175
Seymour-Cin-NY . . 165
Magee-Phi 159
Huggins-Cin 159

Doubles
Wagner-Pit 38
Magee-Phi 36
Bransfield-Phi 28
Steinfeldt-Chi 27
Sheckard-Chi 27

Triples
Schulte-Chi 13
Clarke-Pit 13
Nealon-Pit 12
Lumley-Bro 12

Home Runs
Jordan-Bro 12
Lumley-Bro 9
Seymour-Cin-NY 8
Schulte-Chi 7

Total Bases
Wagner-Pit 237
Steinfeldt-Chi 232
Lumley-Bro 231
Magee-Phi 229
Schulte-Chi 223

Runs Batted In
Steinfeldt-Chi 83
Nealon-Pit 83
Seymour-Cin-NY . . . 80
Jordan-Bro 78

Runs Produced
Wagner-Pit 172
Chance-Chi 171
Nealon-Pit 162
Steinfeldt-Chi 161
Seymour-Cin-NY . . 142

Bases On Balls
Thomas-Phi 107
Bresnahan-NY 81
Titus-Phi 78
Dahlen-NY 76
Devlin-NY 74

Batting Average
Wagner-Pit 339
Steinfeldt-Chi 327
Lumley-Bro 324
Chance-Chi 319
Clarke-Pit 309

On Base Percentage
Chance-Chi 406
Wagner-Pit 406
Bresnahan-NY 401
Devlin-NY 390
Thomas-Phi 387

Slugging Average
Lumley-Bro 477
Wagner-Pit 459
Steinfeldt-Chi 430
Chance-Chi 430
Jordan-Bro 422

Production
Wagner-Pit 865
Lumley-Bro 863
Chance-Chi 837
Steinfeldt-Chi 811
Clarke-Pit 782

Adjusted Production
Lumley-Bro 186
Wagner-Pit 165
Chance-Chi 154
Jordan-Bro 154
Steinfeldt-Chi 147

Batter Runs
Wagner-Pit 43.0
Lumley-Bro 38.3
Chance-Chi 36.7
Steinfeldt-Chi 33.3
Devlin-NY 28.7

Adjusted Batter Runs
Lumley-Bro 42.6
Wagner-Pit 40.5
Chance-Chi 33.5
Steinfeldt-Chi 29.8
Devlin-NY 27.5

Clutch Hitting Index
Tinker-Chi 161
Nealon-Pit 156
Ritchey-Pit 138
Mertes-NY-StL . . . 135
Jordan-Bro 133

Runs Created
Wagner-Pit 121
Chance-Chi 111
Lumley-Bro 107
Steinfeldt-Chi 104
Magee-Phi 101

Total Average
Chance-Chi 1.025
Wagner-Pit 1.021
Lumley-Bro 960
Devlin-NY 923
Bresnahan-NY 859

Stolen Bases
Chance-Chi 57
Magee-Phi 55
Devlin-NY 54
Wagner-Pit 53
Evers-Chi 49

Stolen Base Average

Stolen Base Runs

Fielding Runs
Devlin-NY 28.0
Brain-Bos 25.7
Wagner-Pit 23.8
Gilbert-NY 22.6
Huggins-Cin 21.5

Total Player Rating
Wagner-Pit 7.6
Devlin-NY 5.5
Lumley-Bro 4.5
Huggins-Cin 4.0
Bresnahan-NY 3.6

Wins
McGinnity-NY 27
Brown-Chi 26
Willis-Pit 23
C.Mathewson-NY . . 22
Leever-Pit 22

Win Percentage
Reulbach-Chi 826
Brown-Chi 813
Leever-Pit 759
Lundgren-Chi 739
Pfiester-Chi 714

Games
McGinnity-NY 45
Young-Bos 43
Sparks-Phi 42
Duggleby-Phi 42

Complete Games
Young-Bos 37
Pfeffer-Bos 33

Shutouts
Brown-Chi 9
Leifield-Pit 8

Saves
Ferguson-NY 7
Wiltse-NY 6
Stricklett-Bro 5

Innings Pitched
Young-Bos 358.1
McGinnity-NY . . . 339.2
Willis-Pit 322.0
Sparks-Phi 316.2
Lindaman-Bos . . . 307.1

Fewest Hits/Game
Reulbach-Chi 5.33
Pfiester-Chi 6.21
Brown-Chi 6.43
Beebe-Chi-StL 6.67
Lundgren-Chi 6.93

Fewest BB/Game
Phillippe-Pit 1.07
Leever-Pit 1.66
Sparks-Phi 1.76
Ewing-Cin 1.88
McGinnity-NY 1.88

Strikeouts
Beebe-Chi-StL 171
Pfeffer-Bos 158
Ames-NY 156
Pfiester-Chi 153

Strikeouts/Game
Ames-NY 6.90
Beebe-Chi-StL 6.67
Pfiester-Chi 5.49
Overall-Cin-Chi . . . 5.05
Lush-Phi 4.84

Ratio
Brown-Chi 8.53
Pfiester-Chi 8.94
Sparks-Phi 8.98
Reulbach-Chi 9.66
Ewing-Cin 9.70

Earned Run Average
Brown-Chi 1.04
Pfiester-Chi 1.51
Reulbach-Chi 1.65
Willis-Pit 1.73
Leifield-Pit 1.87

Adjusted ERA
Brown-Chi 254
Pfiester-Chi 175
Reulbach-Chi 159
Willis-Pit 154
Leifield-Pit 143

Opponents' Batting Avg.
Reulbach-Chi 175
Pfiester-Chi 194
Brown-Chi 202
Beebe-Chi-StL 209
Sparks-Phi 211

Opponents' On Base Pct.
Brown-Chi 252
Sparks-Phi 257
Pfiester-Chi 258
Phillippe-Pit 276
Reulbach-Chi 278

Starter Runs
Brown-Chi 48.9
Willis-Pit 31.9
Pfiester-Chi 31.1
Reulbach-Chi 23.6
Leifield-Pit 21.6

Adjusted Starter Runs
Brown-Chi 49.1
Willis-Pit 33.3
Pfiester-Chi 31.3
Reulbach-Chi 23.8
Leifield-Pit 22.7

Clutch Pitching Index
Willis-Pit 144
Brown-Chi 132
Lindaman-Bos 130
Leifield-Pit 125
Lush-Phi 118

Relief Runs
Ferguson-NY 3

Adjusted Relief Runs
Ferguson-NY 1

Relief Ranking
Ferguson-NY 0

Total Pitcher Index
Brown-Chi 6.5
Willis-Pit 4.5
Taylor-StL-Chi 3.3
Reulbach-Chi 2.9
Weimer-Cin 2.9

Total Baseball Ranking
Wagner-Pit 7.6
Brown-Chi 6.5
Devlin-NY 5.5
Willis-Pit 4.5
Lumley-Bro 4.5

TEAM	G	W	L	PCT	GB	R	OR	AB	H	2B	3B	HR	BB	SO	AVG	OBP	SLG	PRO	PRO+	BR	/A	PF	CHI	RC	SB	CS	SBA	SBR
CHI	154	93	58	.616		570	460	4925	1133	152	52	7	453		.230	.295	.286	.581	91	-47	-32	97	110	519	214			
NY	155	90	61	.596	3	644	543	5095	1354	166	77	17	331		.266	.311	.339	.650	100	58	0	110	103	632	192			
CLE	157	89	64	.582	5	663	482	5426	1516	240	73	12	330		.279	.321	.357	.678	121	113	120	99	93	726	203			
PHI	149	78	67	.538	12	561	542	4883	1206	213	49	32	366		.247	.302	.330	.632	101	30	13	103	97	570	166			
STL	154	76	73	.510	16	558	498	5030	1244	145	60	20	366		.247	.298	.312	.610	102	-6	18	96	101	568	221			
DET	151	71	78	.477	21	518	599	4930	1195	154	64	10	333		.242	.290	.306	.596	91	-33	-47	103	101	530	205			
WAS	151	55	95	.367	37.5	518	664	4956	1180	144	65	26	306		.238	.282	.309	.591	96	-44	-17	95	103	527	233			
BOS	155	49	105	.318	45.5	462	706	5168	1223	160	75	13	298		.237	.278	.304	.582	89	-64	-62	100	92	493	99			
TOT	613					4494		40413	10051	1374	515	137	2802	4561	.249	.297	.318	.616							1533			

TEAM	CG	SH	SV	IP	H	H/G	HR	BB	SO	RAT	ERA	ERA+	OAV	OOB	PR	/A	PF	CPI	FA	E	DP	FW	PW	BW	SBW	DIF
CHI	117	32	3	1375¹	1212	7.9	11	255	543	9.6	2.13	119	.239	.275	85	62	94	105	.963	243	80	1.8	6.8	-3.5		12.4
NY	99	18	5	1357²	1236	8.2	21	351	605	10.5	2.78	107	.245	.295	-13	27	110	95	.957	272	69	.1	3.0	.0		11.4
CLE	133	27	4	1412²	1197	7.6	16	365	530	10.0	2.09	125	.232	.283	94	83	97	110	.967	216	111	3.9	9.1	13.2		-13.7
PHI	107	19	4	1322	1135	7.7	9	425	749	10.6	2.60	105	.235	.297	13	15	101	96	.957	267	86	-.2	1.6	1.4		2.7
STL	133	17	5	1357²	1132	7.5	14	314	558	9.6	2.23	116	.229	.275	69	53	96	96	.954	290	80	-1.1	5.8	2.0		-5.2
DET	128	7	4	1334¹	1398	9.4	14	389	469	12.1	3.06	90	.272	.323	-55	-42	103	110	.959	260	86	.4	-4.6	-5.2		5.9
WAS	115	13	1	1322²	1331	9.1	15	451	558	12.1	3.25	81	.264	.324	-82	-89	98	102	.955	279	78	-.8	-9.8	-1.9		-7.6
BOS	124	6	6	1382	1360	8.9	37	285	549	10.7	3.41	81	.262	.300	-110	-105	102	87	.949	335	84	-3.9	-11.5	-6.8		-5.8
TOT	956	139	32	10864¹		8.3				10.6	2.69		.249	.297					.958	2162	674					

Runs
Flick-Cle	98
Keeler-NY	96
Hartsel-Phi	96
Davis-Phi	94
Stone-StL	91

Hits
Lajoie-Cle	214
Stone-StL	208
Flick-Cle	194
Chase-NY	193
Keeler-NY	180

Doubles
Lajoie-Cle	48
Davis-Phi	40
Flick-Cle	33
Turner-Cle	27
Davis-Chi	26

Triples
Flick-Cle	22
Stone-StL	20
Crawford-Det	16
Ferris-Bos	13

Home Runs
Davis-Phi	12
Hickman-Was	9
Stone-StL	6
Seybold-Phi	5

Total Bases
Stone-StL	291
Lajoie-Cle	280
Flick-Cle	274
Davis-Phi	253
Chase-NY	236

Runs Batted In
Davis-Phi	96
Lajoie-Cle	91
Davis-Chi	80
Williams-NY	77
Chase-NY	76

Runs Produced
Lajoie-Cle	179
Davis-Phi	178
Chase-NY	160
Flick-Cle	159
Stone-StL	156

Bases On Balls
Hartsel-Phi	88
Jones-Chi	83
W.Hahn-NY-Chi	72
Wallace-StL	58
McIntyre-Det	56

Batting Average
Stone-StL	.358
Lajoie-Cle	.355
Chase-NY	.323
Flick-Cle	.311
Keeler-NY	.304

On Base Percentage
Stone-StL	.411
Lajoie-Cle	.386
Flick-Cle	.366
Hartsel-Phi	.361
Davis-Phi	.350

Slugging Average
Stone-StL	.501
Lajoie-Cle	.465
Davis-Phi	.459
Flick-Cle	.439
Crawford-Det	.407

Production
Stone-StL	.912
Lajoie-Cle	.851
Davis-Phi	.809
Flick-Cle	.805
Crawford-Det	.746

Adjusted Production
Stone-StL	196
Lajoie-Cle	171
Flick-Cle	156
Davis-Phi	150
Hemphill-StL	133

Batter Runs
Stone-StL	57.1
Lajoie-Cle	44.5
Flick-Cle	37.6
Davis-Phi	33.1
Crawford-Det	21.5

Adjusted Batter Runs
Stone-StL	59.9
Lajoie-Cle	45.3
Flick-Cle	38.5
Davis-Phi	31.2
Hemphill-StL	20.6

Clutch Hitting Index
Davis-Phi	180
Wallace-StL	152
Williams-NY	152
Coughlin-Det	145
Stahl-Was	144

Runs Created
Stone-StL	139
Lajoie-Cle	120
Flick-Cle	119
Davis-Phi	100
Chase-NY	94

Total Average
Stone-StL	1.013
Flick-Cle	.853
Lajoie-Cle	.851
Davis-Phi	.833
Hartsel-Phi	.748

Stolen Bases
Flick-Cle	39
Anderson-Was	39
Isbell-Chi	37
Altizer-Was	37
Donahue-Chi	36

Stolen Base Average

Stolen Base Runs

Fielding Runs
Tannehill-Chi	39.6
Lajoie-Cle	31.9
Turner-Cle	23.6
Schlafly-Was	14.0
McIntyre-Det	11.9

Total Player Rating
Lajoie-Cle	8.0
Stone-StL	5.6
Turner-Cle	4.3
Davis-Phi	2.9
Tannehill-Chi	2.8

Wins
Orth-NY	27
Chesbro-NY	24
Rhoads-Cle	22
Owen-Chi	22

Win Percentage
Plank-Phi	.760
White-Chi	.750
Joss-Cle	.700
Rhoads-Cle	.688
Owen-Chi	.629

Games
Chesbro-NY	49
Orth-NY	45
Waddell-Phi	43
Hess-Cle	43
Owen-Chi	42

Complete Games
Orth-NY	36
Mullin-Det	35
Hess-Cle	33
Rhoads-Cle	31

Shutouts
Walsh-Chi	10
Joss-Cle	9
Waddell-Phi	8

Saves
Hess-Cle	3
Bender-Phi	3

Innings Pitched
Orth-NY	338.2
Hess-Cle	333.2
Mullin-Det	330.0
Chesbro-NY	325.0
Rhoads-Cle	315.0

Fewest Hits/Game
Pelty-StL	6.53
White-Chi	6.57
Walsh-Chi	6.95
Joss-Cle	7.02
Powell-StL	7.23

Fewest BB/Game
Young-Cle	.78
Altrock-Chi	1.31
Joss-Cle	1.37
White-Chi	1.56
Jacobson-StL	1.57

Strikeouts
Waddell-Phi	196
Falkenberg-Was	178
Walsh-Chi	171
Hess-Cle	167
Bender-Phi	159

Strikeouts/Game
Waddell-Phi	6.47
Bender-Phi	6.00
Walsh-Chi	5.53
Falkenberg-Was	5.36
Powell-StL	4.87

Ratio
White-Chi	8.12
Joss-Cle	8.39
Pelty-StL	8.56
Walsh-Chi	8.83
Glade-StL	9.25

Earned Run Average
White-Chi	1.52
Pelty-StL	1.59
Joss-Cle	1.72
Powell-StL	1.77
Rhoads-Cle	1.80

Adjusted ERA
White-Chi	167
Pelty-StL	163
Joss-Cle	152
Powell-StL	146
Rhoads-Cle	146

Opponents' Batting Avg.
Pelty-StL	.206
White-Chi	.207
Walsh-Chi	.217
Joss-Cle	.218
Powell-StL	.223

Opponents' On Base Pct.
White-Chi	.244
Joss-Cle	.250
Pelty-StL	.254
Walsh-Chi	.260
Glade-StL	.269

Starter Runs
Pelty-StL	31.9
Hess-Cle	31.7
Rhoads-Cle	31.1
Joss-Cle	30.3
White-Chi	28.6

Adjusted Starter Runs
Hess-Cle	29.1
Pelty-StL	28.8
Rhoads-Cle	28.7
Joss-Cle	28.1
White-Chi	24.9

Clutch Pitching Index
Rhoads-Cle	128
Siever-Det	124
Donahue-Det	120
Smith-Was	120
Owen-Chi	120

Relief Runs

Adjusted Relief Runs

Relief Ranking

Total Pitcher Index
Joss-Cle	3.8
Pelty-StL	3.7
Orth-NY	3.6
White-Chi	3.6
Hess-Cle	3.1

Total Baseball Ranking
Lajoie-Cle	8.0
Stone-StL	5.6
Turner-Cle	4.3
Joss-Cle	3.8
Pelty-StL	3.7

TEAM	G	W	L	PCT	GB	R	OR	AB	H	2B	3B	HR	BB	SO	AVG	OBP	SLG	PRO	PRO+	BR	/A	PF	CHI	RC	SB	CS	SBA	SBR
CHI	155	107	45	.704		572	390	4892	1224	162	48	13	435		.250	.311	.311	.622	97	25	-8	106	104	585	235			
PIT	157	91	63	.591	17	634	510	4957	1261	133	78	19	469		.254	.319	.324	.643	109	62	54	101	106	633	264			
PHI	149	83	64	.565	21.5	512	476	4725	1113	162	65	12	424		.236	.299	.305	.604	99	-9	-1	99	104	504	154			
NY	155	82	71	.536	25.5	574	510	4874	1222	160	48	23	516		.251	.322	.317	.639	106	61	44	103	97	601	205			
BRO	153	65	83	.439	40	446	522	4895	1135	142	63	18	336		.232	.281	.298	.579	97	-59	-17	92	97	478	121			
CIN	156	66	87	.431	41.5	526	519	4966	1226	126	90	15	372		.247	.299	.318	.617	97	7	-15	104	99	556	158			
BOS	152	58	90	.392	47	502	652	5020	1222	142	61	22	413		.243	.301	.309	.610	100	0	1	100	95	532	118			
STL	155	52	101	.340	55.5	419	606	5008	1163	121	51	19	312		.232	.277	.288	.565	87	-84	-66	97	96	464	125			
TOT	616					4185		39337	9566	1148	504	141	3277	4217	.243	.301	.309	.610						1380				

TEAM	CG	SH	SV	IP	H	H/G	HR	BB	SO	RAT	ERA	ERA+	OAV	OOB	PR	/A	PF	CPI	FA	E	DP	FW	PW	BW	SBW	DIF
CHI	113	32	8	1370¹	1054	6.9	11	402	586	9.8	1.73	144	.216	.281	111	115	101	107	.967	211	110	3.1	13.1	-.9		15.8
PIT	111	24	5	1363	1207	8.0	12	368	497	10.7	2.30	106	.241	.299	25	18	98	103	.959	256	75	.2	2.0	6.1		5.6
PHI	110	21	4	1299¹	1095	7.6	13	422	499	10.9	2.43	99	.233	.303	4	-3	98	98	.957	256	104	-.7	-.3	-.1		10.6
NY	109	22	13	1371	1219	8.0	25	369	655	10.7	2.45	101	.237	.293	2	1	100	94	.963	232	75	1.6	.1	5.0		-1.2
BRO	125	20	1	1356¹	1218	8.1	16	463	479	11.4	2.38	98	.248	.318	12	-8	95	117	.959	262	94	-.7	-.9	-1.9		-5.5
CIN	118	10	2	1351¹	1223	8.1	16	444	481	11.5	2.41	107	.250	.321	8	25	105	118	.963	227	118	2.1	2.8	-1.7		-13.7
BOS	121	9	2	1338²	1324	8.9	28	458	426	12.4	3.33	76	.268	.338	-129	-119	103	101	.961	249	128	.1	-13.5	.1		-2.7
STL	126	19	2	1361²	1212	8.0	20	500	594	11.6	2.70	93	.242	.317	-35	-30	101	101	.948	340	105	-5.8	-3.4	-7.5		-7.8
TOT	933	157	37	10811²		8.0				11.1	2.46		.243	.301					.960	2033	809					

Runs
Shannon-NY 104
Leach-Pit 102
Wagner-Pit 98
Clarke-Pit 97
Tenney-Bos 83

Hits
Beaumont-Bos ... 187
Wagner-Pit 180
Leach-Pit 166
Magee-Phi 165
Mitchell-Cin 163

Doubles
Wagner-Pit 38
Magee-Phi 28
Steinfeldt-Chi 25
Seymour-NY 25
Brain-Bos 24

Triples
Ganzel-Cin 16
Alperman-Bro 16
Wagner-Pit 14
Beaumont-Bos 14
Clarke-Pit 13

Home Runs
Brain-Bos 10
Lumley-Bro 9
Murray-StL 7
Wagner-Pit 6
Browne-NY 5

Total Bases
Wagner-Pit 264
Beaumont-Bos ... 246
Magee-Phi 229
Leach-Pit 221
Brain-Bos 214

Runs Batted In
Magee-Phi 85
Wagner-Pit 82
Abbaticchio-Pit ... 82
Seymour-NY 75
Steinfeldt-Chi 70

Runs Produced
Wagner-Pit 174
Magee-Phi 156
Clarke-Pit 154
Abbaticchio-Pit .. 143
Leach-Pit 141

Bases On Balls
Thomas-Phi 83
Huggins-Cin 83
Tenney-Bos 82
Shannon-NY 82
Anderson-Pit 80

Batting Average
Wagner-Pit ...... .350
Magee-Phi .... .328
Beaumont-Bos ... .322
Leach-Pit .... .303
Seymour-NY ..... .294

On Base Percentage
Wagner-Pit ...... .403
Magee-Phi .... .392
Clarke-Pit ...... .374
Jordan-Bro ...... .370
Thomas-Phi ...... .369

Slugging Average
Wagner-Pit ...... .513
Magee-Phi .... .455
Lumley-Bro ...... .425
Beaumont-Bos ... .424
Brain-Bos .... .420

Production
Wagner-Pit ...... .915
Magee-Phi .... .847
Beaumont-Bos ... .787
Clarke-Pit ...... .764
Leach-Pit .... .755

Adjusted Production
Wagner-Pit 187
Magee-Phi 171
Beaumont-Bos ... 149
Lumley-Bro 145
Jordan-Bro 144

Batter Runs
Wagner-Pit 50.4
Magee-Phi 38.6
Beaumont-Bos ... 30.2
Clarke-Pit 25.5
Leach-Pit 22.7

Adjusted Batter Runs
Wagner-Pit 49.6
Magee-Phi 39.4
Beaumont-Bos ... 30.4
Jordan-Bro 24.8
Clarke-Pit 24.7

Clutch Hitting Index
Abbaticchio-Pit ... 194
Seymour-NY 152
Steinfeldt-Chi 152
Magee-Phi 142
Ganzel-Cin 129

Runs Created
Wagner-Pit 135
Magee-Phi 111
Beaumont-Bos ... 102
Leach-Pit 98
Clarke-Pit 91

Total Average
Wagner-Pit 1.107
Magee-Phi .... .970
Clarke-Pit ...... .843
Leach-Pit .... .798
Beaumont-Bos ... .784

Stolen Bases
Wagner-Pit 61
Magee-Phi 46
Evers-Chi 46
Leach-Pit 43
Devlin-NY 38

Stolen Base Average

Stolen Base Runs

Fielding Runs
Evers-Chi 27.6
Brain-Bos 24.8
Mitchell-Cin 22.3
Byrne-StL 21.4
Tinker-Chi 14.5

Total Player Rating
Wagner-Pit 6.6
Magee-Phi 4.6
Brain-Bos 4.6
Mitchell-Cin 3.3
Beaumont-Bos ... 3.3

Wins
C.Mathewson-NY .. 24
Overall-Chi 23
Sparks-Phi 22
Willis-Pit 21

Win Percentage
Reulbach-Chi ... .810
Brown-Chi .... .769
Overall-Chi ..... .767
Sparks-Phi ...... .733
Lundgren-Chi .... .720

Games
McGinnity-NY 47
McGlynn-StL 45
C.Mathewson-NY .. 41
Ewing-Cin 41

Complete Games
McGlynn-StL 33
Ewing-Cin 32
C.Mathewson-NY .. 31
Karger-StL 28
Willis-Pit 27

Shutouts
Overall-Chi 8
C.Mathewson-NY ... 8
Lundgren-Chi 7

Saves
McGinnity-NY 4
Overall-Chi 3
Brown-Chi 3

Innings Pitched
McGlynn-StL 352.1
Ewing-Cin 332.2
C.Mathewson-NY 315.0
McGinnity-NY ... 310.1
Karger-StL 310.0

Fewest Hits/Game
Lundgren-Chi 5.65
Pfiester-Chi 6.60
Overall-Chi 6.75
Camnitz-Pit 6.75
Reulbach-Chi 6.89

Fewest BB/Game
Phillippe-Pit ... 1.51
C.Mathewson-NY . 1.51
Brown-Chi 1.55
McGinnity-NY 1.68
Sparks-Phi 1.73

Strikeouts
C.Mathewson-NY . 178
Ewing-Cin 147
Ames-NY 146
Beebe-StL 141
Overall-Chi 139

Strikeouts/Game
Ames-NY 5.63
Beebe-StL 5.32
C.Mathewson-NY . 5.09
Overall-Chi 4.71
Reulbach-Chi 4.50

Ratio
C.Mathewson-NY . 8.71
Brown-Chi 8.73
Pfiester-Chi 9.05
Karger-StL 9.44
Overall-Chi 9.46

Earned Run Average
Pfiester-Chi 1.15
Lundgren-Chi 1.17
Brown-Chi 1.39
Leever-Pit 1.66
Reulbach-Chi 1.69

Adjusted ERA
Pfiester-Chi 216
Lundgren-Chi 212
Brown-Chi 179
Ewing-Cin 149
Reulbach-Chi 148

Opponents' Batting Avg.
Lundgren-Chi .... .185
Overall-Chi ..... .206
Pfiester-Chi .... .207
Camnitz-Pit ..... .211
C.Mathewson-NY . .212

Opponents' On Base Pct.
C.Mathewson-NY . .247
Brown-Chi .... .262
Pfiester-Chi .... .263
Karger-StL ...... .265
Overall-Chi ..... .266

Starter Runs
Lundgren-Chi 29.7
Pfiester-Chi 28.4
Brown-Chi 27.8
Ewing-Cin 27.1
Overall-Chi 22.7

Adjusted Starter Runs
Ewing-Cin 31.7
Lundgren-Chi 30.3
Pfiester-Chi 28.9
Brown-Chi 28.5
Overall-Chi 23.4

Clutch Pitching Index
Coakley-Cin 137
Pastorius-Bro 133
Lundgren-Chi 130
McIntire-Bro 129
Brown-StL-Phi 129

Relief Runs

Adjusted Relief Runs

Relief Ranking

Total Pitcher Index
Brown-Chi 3.9
Overall-Chi 3.4
Lundgren-Chi 3.3
Ewing-Cin 3.0
Pfiester-Chi 2.9

Total Baseball Ranking
Wagner-Pit 6.6
Magee-Phi 4.6
Brain-Bos 4.6
Brown-Chi 3.9
Overall-Chi 3.4

TEAM	G	W	L	PCT	GB	R	OR	AB	H	2B	3B	HR	BB	SO	AVG	OBP	SLG	PRO	PRO+	BR	/A	PF	CHI	RC	SB	CS	SBA	SBR
DET	153	92	58	.613		694	532	5204	1383	179	75	11	315		.266	.308	.335	.643	108	63	42	104	110	630	192			
PHI	150	88	57	.607	1.5	582	511	5008	1274	223	43	22	384		.254	.307	.329	.636	107	56	42	102	95	584	137			
CHI	157	87	64	.576	5.5	588	474	5070	1205	149	33	5	421		.238	.296	.283	.579	94	-36	-16	97	111	512	175			
CLE	158	85	67	.559	8	530	525	5068	1221	182	68	11	335		.241	.288	.310	.598	97	-14	-18	101	97	541	193			
NY	152	70	78	.473	21	605	665	5044	1258	150	67	15	304		.249	.292	.315	.607	92	-1	-45	108	111	552	206			
STL	155	69	83	.454	24	542	555	5224	1324	154	64	9	370		.253	.303	.313	.616	104	20	21	100	91	570	144			
BOS	155	59	90	.396	32.5	464	558	5235	1224	154	48	18	305		.234	.276	.292	.568	88	-71	-65	99	93	485	125			
WAS	154	49	102	.325	43.5	506	691	5112	1243	134	58	12	390		.243	.297	.299	.596	105	-12	32	92	92	550	223			
TOT	617					4511		40965	10132	1325	456	103	2824	4479	.247	.296	.309	.605							1395			

TEAM	CG	SH	SV	IP	H	H/G	HR	BB	SO	RAT	ERA	ERA+	OAV	OOB	PR	/A	PF	CPI	FA	E	DP	FW	PW	BW	SBW	DIF
DET	120	15	7	1370²	1281	8.4	7	380	512	10.9	2.33	112	.250	.302	31	39	102	113	.959	260	79	1.0	4.3	4.6		7.1
PHI	106	27	6	1354²	1106	7.3	13	378	789	9.9	2.35	111	.225	.281	29	37	102	90	.958	263	67	.4	4.1	4.6		6.4
CHI	112	17	9	1406¹	1279	8.2	13	305	604	10.1	2.22	108	.245	.287	49	26	94	107	.966	233	101	3.4	2.9	-1.8		7.0
CLE	127	20	5	1392²	1253	8.1	8	362	513	10.4	2.26	111	.243	.293	43	35	99	107	.960	264	137	1.3	3.9	-2.0		5.8
NY	94	10	5	1333²	1327	9.0	13	428	511	11.8	3.03	92	.264	.321	-72	-39	110	103	.947	334	79	-4.4	-4.3	-5.0		9.6
STL	129	15	9	1381¹	1254	8.2	17	352	463	10.5	2.61	96	.245	.293	-10	-15	99	96	.959	266	97	.8	-1.7	2.3		-8.5
BOS	100	17	7	1414	1222	7.8	22	337	517	9.9	2.45	105	.237	.284	14	14	101	94	.959	274	100	.2	1.5	-7.2		-10.1
WAS	106	12	5	1351¹	1383	9.2	10	344	570	11.5	3.11	78	.268	.313	-85	-105	95	97	.951	311	69	-2.5	-11.6	3.5		-15.9
TOT	894	133	53	11004²		8.3				10.6	2.54		.247	.296					.957	2205	729					

Runs
Crawford-Det 102
D.Jones-Det 101
Cobb-Det 97
Hartsel-Phi 93
Hahn-Chi 87

Hits
Cobb-Det 212
Stone-StL 191
Crawford-Det 188
Ganley-Was 167
Flick-Cle 166

Doubles
Davis-Phi 37
Crawford-Det 34
J.Collins-Bos-Phi . . 30
Lajoie-Cle 30
Seybold-Phi 29

Triples
Flick-Cle 18
Crawford-Det 17
Cobb-Det 14
Unglaub-Bos 13

Home Runs
Davis-Phi 8
Seybold-Phi 5
Hoffman-NY 5
Cobb-Det 5

Total Bases
Cobb-Det 283
Crawford-Det 268
Stone-StL 238
Davis-Phi 232
Flick-Cle 226

Runs Batted In
Cobb-Det 119
Seybold-Phi 92
Davis-Phi 87
Crawford-Det 81
Wallace-StL 70

Runs Produced
Cobb-Det 211
Crawford-Det 179
Davis-Phi 163
Seybold-Phi 145
Donahue-Chi 143

Bases On Balls
Hartsel-Phi 106
Hahn-Chi 84
Jones-Chi 67
Flick-Cle 64
D.Jones-Det 60

Batting Average
Cobb-Det 350
Crawford-Det 323
Stone-StL 320
Flick-Cle 302
Nicholls-Phi 302

On Base Percentage
Hartsel-Phi 405
Stone-StL 382
Flick-Cle 375
Cobb-Det 375
Crawford-Det 363

Slugging Average
Cobb-Det 468
Crawford-Det 460
Flick-Cle 412
Stone-StL 399
Davis-Phi 399

Production
Cobb-Det 843
Crawford-Det 824
Flick-Cle 787
Stone-StL 781
Hartsel-Phi 771

Adjusted Production
Cobb-Det 165
Crawford-Det 159
Flick-Cle 152
Stone-StL 152
Hartsel-Phi 145

Batter Runs
Cobb-Det 44.2
Crawford-Det 39.5
Stone-StL 35.1
Hartsel-Phi 34.4
Flick-Cle 33.7

Adjusted Batter Runs
Cobb-Det 41.9
Crawford-Det 37.2
Stone-StL 35.3
Flick-Cle 33.2
Hartsel-Phi 32.9

Clutch Hitting Index
Wallace-StL 155
Davis-Chi 144
Seybold-Phi 144
Rohe-Chi 141
Cobb-Det 138

Runs Created
Cobb-Det 129
Crawford-Det 108
Flick-Cle 104
Stone-StL 104
Hartsel-Phi 87

Total Average
Cobb-Det 906
Flick-Cle 864
Hartsel-Phi 855
Crawford-Det 820
Stone-StL 790

Stolen Bases
Cobb-Det 49
Flick-Cle 41
Conroy-NY 41
Ganley-Was 40
Altizer-Was 38

Stolen Base Average

Stolen Base Runs

Fielding Runs
Lajoie-Cle 45.0
Donahue-Chi 20.7
Ferris-Bos 14.6
D.Jones-Det 13.0
Murphy-Phi 12.7

Total Player Rating
Lajoie-Cle 6.7
Cobb-Det 4.9
Crawford-Det 4.0
Flick-Cle 2.8
Schreckengost-Phi . 2.8

Wins
White-Chi 27
Joss-Cle 27
Killian-Det 25
Donovan-Det 25

Win Percentage
Donovan-Det 862
Dygert-Phi 724
Joss-Cle 711
Smith-Chi 697
White-Chi 675

Games
Walsh-Chi 56
White-Chi 46
Mullin-Det 46
Waddell-Phi 44

Complete Games
Walsh-Chi 37
Mullin-Det 35
Joss-Cle 34
Young-Bos 33
Plank-Phi 33

Shutouts
Plank-Phi 8
Waddell-Phi 7
Young-Bos 6
White-Chi 6
Joss-Cle 6

Saves
Dinneen-Bos-StL . . . 4
Walsh-Chi 4
Hughes-Was 4

Innings Pitched
Walsh-Chi 422.1
Mullin-Det 357.1
Plank-Phi 343.2
Young-Bos 343.1
Joss-Cle 338.2

Fewest Hits/Game
Dygert-Phi 6.88
Winter-Bos 6.94
Walsh-Chi 7.27
Howell-StL 7.34
Donovan-Det 7.37

Fewest BB/Game
White-Chi 1.18
Altrock-Chi 1.31
Young-Bos 1.34
Bender-Phi 1.40
Joss-Cle 1.44

Strikeouts
Waddell-Phi 232
Walsh-Chi 206
Plank-Phi 183
Dygert-Phi 151
Young-Bos 147

Strikeouts/Game
Waddell-Phi 7.33
Dygert-Phi 5.19
Plank-Phi 4.79
Bender-Phi 4.60
Walsh-Chi 4.39

Ratio
Young-Bos 8.83
Joss-Cle 8.85
Bender-Phi 8.99
Winter-Bos 9.08
Walsh-Chi 9.12

Earned Run Average
Walsh-Chi 1.60
Killian-Det 1.78
Joss-Cle 1.83
Howell-StL 1.93
Young-Bos 1.99

Adjusted ERA
Walsh-Chi 150
Killian-Det 146
Joss-Cle 136
Howell-StL 130
Young-Bos 129

Opponents' Batting Avg.
Dygert-Phi 214
Winter-Bos 216
Walsh-Chi 224
Howell-StL 225
Donovan-Det 226

Opponents' On Base Pct.
Young-Bos 259
Joss-Cle 260
Bender-Phi 263
Winter-Bos 265
Walsh-Chi 266

Starter Runs
Walsh-Chi 44.2
Killian-Det 26.6
Joss-Cle 26.6
Howell-StL 21.3
Young-Bos 20.9

Adjusted Starter Runs
Walsh-Chi 37.3
Killian-Det 28.8
Joss-Cle 25.2
Young-Bos 22.2
Howell-StL 20.2

Clutch Pitching Index
Killian-Det 143
Hogg-NY 125
Liebhardt-Cle 124
Rhoads-Cle 117
Walsh-Chi 115

Relief Runs

Adjusted Relief Runs

Relief Ranking

Total Pitcher Index
Walsh-Chi 6.7
Killian-Det 4.6
Howell-StL 3.9
Joss-Cle 3.3
Orth-NY 2.1

Total Baseball Ranking
Lajoie-Cle 6.7
Walsh-Chi 6.7
Cobb-Det 4.9
Killian-Det 4.6
Crawford-Det 4.0

1908 National League

TEAM	G	W	L	PCT	GB	R	OR	AB	H	2B	3B	HR	BB	SO	AVG	OBP	SLG	PRO	PRO+	BR	/A	PF	CHI	RC	SB	CS	SBA	SBR
CHI	158	99	55	.643		624	461	5085	1267	196	56	19	418		.249	.306	.321	.627	104	51	28	104	107	574	212			
PIT	155	98	56	.636	1	585	469	5109	1263	162	98	25	420		.247	.304	.332	.636	112	65	65	100	99	572	186			
NY	157	98	56	.636	1	652	456	5006	1339	182	43	20	494		.267	.333	.333	.666	116	128	102	105	99	627	181			
PHI	155	83	71	.539	16	504	445	5012	1223	194	68	11	334		.244	.291	.316	.607	99	10	-6	103	96	522	200			
CIN	155	73	81	.474	26	489	544	4879	1108	129	77	14	372		.227	.282	.294	.576	94	-39	-24	97	105	463	196			
BOS	156	63	91	.409	36	537	622	5131	1228	137	43	17	414		.239	.296	.293	.589	98	-13	-4	98	104	489	134			
BRO	154	53	101	.344	46	377	516	4897	1044	110	60	28	323		.213	.262	.277	.539	83	-105	-85	96	96	385	113			
STL	154	49	105	.318	50	371	626	4959	1105	134	57	17	282		.223	.265	.283	.548	87	-94	-70	95	91	409	150			
TOT	622					4139		40078	9577	1244	502	151	3057	4180	.239	.293	.306	.599							1372			

TEAM	CG	SH	SV	IP	H	H/G	HR	BB	SO	RAT	ERA	ERA+	OAV	OOB	PR	/A	PF	CPI	FA	E	DP	FW	PW	BW	SBW	DIF
CHI	108	29	12	1433²	1137	7.1	20	437	668	10.1	2.14	109	.221	.287	32	30	100	97	.969	205	76	3.7	3.5	3.3		11.5
PIT	100	24	9	1402¹	1142	7.3	16	406	468	10.3	2.12	107	.222	.286	34	24	97	97	.964	226	74	1.9	2.8	7.5		8.8
NY	95	25	18	1411	1214	7.7	26	288	656	9.8	2.14	112	.232	.277	31	38	102	96	.962	250	79	.4	4.4	11.8		4.3
PHI	116	22	6	1393	1167	7.5	8	379	476	10.3	2.10	115	.234	.294	38	45	103	107	.963	238	75	1.0	5.2	-.7		.4
CIN	110	17	8	1384	1218	7.9	19	415	433	10.9	2.37	96	.243	.306	-4	-18	98	108	.959	255	72	-.2	-2.1	-2.8		1.0
BOS	92	14	1	1404²	1262	8.1	29	423	416	11.2	2.79	86	.245	.309	-69	-67	102	97	.962	253	90	.0	-7.8	-.5		-5.9
BRO	118	20	4	1369	1165	7.7	17	444	535	11.0	2.47	94	.235	.306	-18	-23	99	101	.961	247	66	.3	-2.7	-9.9		-11.7
STL	97	13	4	1368	1217	8.0	16	430	528	11.1	2.64	89	.232	.295	-44	-50	100	86	.946	348	68	-6.8	-5.8	-8.1		-7.2
TOT	836	164	62	11165²		7.7				10.6	2.35		.239	.293					.961	2022	600					

Runs
Tenney-NY 101
Wagner-Pit 100
Leach-Pit 93
Evers-Chi 83
Clarke-Pit 83

Hits
Wagner-Pit 201
Donlin-NY 198
Murray-StL 167
Lobert-Cin 167
Bransfield-Phi 160

Doubles
Wagner-Pit 39
Magee-Phi 30
Chance-Chi 27
Knabe-Phi 26
Donlin-NY 26

Triples
Wagner-Pit 19
Lobert-Cin 18
Magee-Phi 16
Leach-Pit 16

Home Runs
Jordan-Bro 12
Wagner-Pit 10
Murray-StL 7
Tinker-Chi 6
Donlin-NY 6

Total Bases
Wagner-Pit 308
Donlin-NY 268
Murray-StL 237
Lobert-Cin 232
Leach-Pit 222

Runs Batted In
Wagner-Pit 109
Donlin-NY 106
Seymour-NY 92
Bransfield-Phi 71
Tinker-Chi 68

Runs Produced
Wagner-Pit 199
Donlin-NY 171
Tenney-NY 148
Seymour-NY 147

Bases On Balls
Bresnahan-NY 83
Tenney-NY 72
Evers-Chi 66
Clarke-Pit 65

Batting Average
Wagner-Pit 354
Donlin-NY 334
Bransfield-Phi 304
Evers-Chi 300
Lobert-Cin 293

On Base Percentage
Wagner-Pit 410
Evers-Chi 396
Bresnahan-NY 395
Donlin-NY 359
Bridwell-NY 356

Slugging Average
Wagner-Pit 542
Donlin-NY 452
Magee-Phi 417
Lobert-Cin 407
Murray-StL 400

Production
Wagner-Pit 952
Donlin-NY 811
Evers-Chi 771
Magee-Phi 764
Bresnahan-NY 753

Adjusted Production
Wagner-Pit 206
Donlin-NY 154
Lobert-Cin 147
Evers-Chi 143
Magee-Phi 141

Batter Runs
Wagner-Pit 65.2
Donlin-NY 36.6
Bresnahan-NY 26.5
Evers-Chi 26.0
Lobert-Cin 25.9

Adjusted Batter Runs
Wagner-Pit 65.2
Donlin-NY 33.8
Lobert-Cin 27.6
Evers-Chi 24.0
Bresnahan-NY 24.0

Clutch Hitting Index
Seymour-NY 175
Abbaticchio-Pit 154
Steinfeldt-Chi 150
McGann-Bos 150
Donlin-NY 137

Runs Created
Wagner-Pit 146
Donlin-NY 106
Lobert-Cin 96
Murray-StL 89
Magee-Phi 87

Total Average
Wagner-Pit 1.131
Evers-Chi 887
Magee-Phi 827
Donlin-NY 813
Lobert-Cin 806

Stolen Bases
Wagner-Pit 53
Murray-StL 48
Lobert-Cin 47
Magee-Phi 40
Evers-Chi 36

Stolen Base Average

Stolen Base Runs

Fielding Runs
Dahlen-Bos 37.5
Tinker-Chi 30.4
Ritchey-Bos 15.6
Devlin-NY 12.8
Burch-Bro 12.6

Total Player Rating
Wagner-Pit 6.3
Tinker-Chi 4.4
Donlin-NY 3.7
Dahlen-Bos 3.5
Clarke-Pit 3.0

Wins
Mathewson-NY 37
Brown-Chi 29
Reulbach-Chi 24

Win Percentage
Reulbach-Chi 774
Mathewson-NY 771
Brown-Chi 763
Maddox-Pit 742
Leever-Pit 682

Games
Mathewson-NY 56
Raymond-StL 48
McQuillan-Phi 48
Reulbach-Chi 46

Complete Games
Mathewson-NY 34
Wilhelm-Bro 33
McQuillan-Phi 32
Wiltse-NY 30
Rucker-Bro 30

Shutouts
Mathewson-NY 11
Brown-Chi 9

Saves
McGinnity-NY 5
Mathewson-NY 5
Brown-Chi 5
Overall-Chi 4
Ewing-Cin 3

Innings Pitched
Mathewson-NY . . 390.2
McQuillan-Phi . . 359.2
Rucker-Bro 333.1
Wilhelm-Bro 332.0
Wiltse-NY 330.0

Fewest Hits/Game
Brown-Chi 6.17
Raymond-StL 6.55
Mathewson-NY . . . 6.57
McQuillan-Phi 6.58
Overall-Chi 6.60

Fewest BB/Game
Mathewson-NY 97
Brown-Chi 1.41
Sparks-Phi 1.74
Ewing-Cin 1.75
Campbell-Cin 1.79

Strikeouts
Mathewson-NY . . . 259
Rucker-Bro 199
Overall-Chi 167
Raymond-StL 145
Reulbach-Chi 133

Strikeouts/Game
Overall-Chi 6.68
Mathewson-NY . . . 5.97
Rucker-Bro 5.37
Camnitz-Pit 4.49
Ferguson-Bos 4.24

Ratio
Mathewson-NY . . . 7.60
Brown-Chi 7.72
McQuillan-Phi 9.01
Willis-Pit 9.28
Ewing-Cin 9.47

Earned Run Average
Mathewson-NY . . . 1.43
Brown-Chi 1.47
McQuillan-Phi 1.53
Camnitz-Pit 1.56
Coakley-Cin-Chi . . 1.78

Adjusted ERA
Mathewson-NY . . . 168
Brown-Chi 159
McQuillan-Phi 158
Camnitz-Pit 146
Richie-Phi 132

Opponents' Batting Avg.
Beebe-StL 193
Brown-Chi 195
Mathewson-NY 200
McQuillan-Phi 207
Raymond-StL 207

Opponents' On Base Pct.
Mathewson-NY 225
Brown-Chi 232
Willis-Pit 262
McQuillan-Phi 263
Beebe-StL 267

Starter Runs
Mathewson-NY . . . 39.8
McQuillan-Phi 32.7
Brown-Chi 30.4
Camnitz-Pit 20.7
Wilhelm-Bro 17.5

Adjusted Starter Runs
Mathewson-NY . . . 42.1
McQuillan-Phi 35.2
Brown-Chi 30.2
Camnitz-Pit 19.0
Wilhelm-Bro 16.8

Clutch Pitching Index
Coakley-Cin-Chi . . 139
McGinnity-NY 138
Richie-Phi 131
Fraser-Chi 130
Rucker-Bro 123

Relief Runs

Adjusted Relief Runs

Relief Ranking

Total Pitcher Index
Mathewson-NY 6.4
McQuillan-Phi 3.9
Brown-Chi 3.8
Reulbach-Chi 1.9
Wilhelm-Bro 1.9

Total Baseball Ranking
Mathewson-NY 6.4
Wagner-Pit 6.3
Tinker-Chi 4.4
McQuillan-Phi 3.9
Brown-Chi 3.8

TEAM	G	W	L	PCT	GB	R	OR	AB	H	2B	3B	HR	BB	SO	AVG	OBP	SLG	PRO	PRO+	BR	/A	PF	CHI	RC	SB	CS	SBA	SBR
DET	154	90	63	.588		647	547	5115	1347	199	86	19	320		.263	.307	.347	.654	116	104	81	104	101	593	165			
CLE	157	90	64	.584	0.5	568	457	5108	1221	188	58	18	364		.239	.290	.309	.599	101	12	9	100	102	514	177			
CHI	156	88	64	.579	1.5	537	470	5027	1127	145	41	3	463		.224	.290	.271	.561	91	-41	-32	98	106	465	209			
STL	155	83	69	.546	6.5	544	483	5151	1261	173	52	20	343		.245	.292	.310	.602	102	18	14	101	97	505	126			
BOS	155	75	79	.487	15.5	564	513	5048	1239	117	88	14	289		.245	.286	.312	.598	99	6	-8	103	106	496	167			
PHI	157	68	85	.444	22	486	562	5065	1131	183	50	21	368		.223	.276	.292	.568	86	-41	-77	107	98	441	116			
WAS	155	67	85	.441	22.5	479	539	5041	1186	132	74	8	368		.235	.287	.296	.583	105	-12	32	92	92	479	170			
NY	155	51	103	.331	39.5	459	713	5046	1190	142	50	13	288		.236	.277	.292	.569	90	-42	-47	101	96	467	231			
TOT	622					4284		40601	9702	1279	499	116	2803	4928	.239	.288	.304	.592						1361				

TEAM	CG	SH	SV	IP	H	H/G	HR	BB	SO	RAT	ERA	ERA+	OAV	OOB	PR	/A	PF	CPI	FA	E	DP	FW	PW	BW	SBW	DIF
DET	119	15	5	1374¹	1313	8.6	12	318	553	11.1	2.40	100	.254	.305	-2	2	101	118	.953	305	95	-2.1	.2	9.2		6.1
CLE	108	18	5	1424¹	1172	7.4	16	328	548	9.7	2.02	118	.228	.279	58	56	100	107	.962	257	95	1.6	6.4	1.0		4.0
CHI	107	23	10	1414	1170	7.4	11	284	623	9.4	2.22	104	.225	.269	25	13	97	88	.966	232	82	3.2	1.5	-3.7		11.0
STL	107	15	5	1397	1151	7.4	7	387	607	10.3	2.15	111	.230	.293	37	36	100	109	.964	237	97	2.7	4.1	1.6		-1.4
BOS	102	12	7	1380¹	1200	7.8	18	364	624	10.5	2.28	108	.237	.294	16	26	103	110	.955	297	71	-1.4	3.0	-.9		-2.6
PHI	102	23	4	1400¹	1186	7.6	10	409	740	10.6	2.56	100	.232	.296	-26	-4	107	94	.957	272	68	.6	-.5	-8.8		.2
WAS	105	15	7	1392²	1238	8.0	16	347	649	10.5	2.34	97	.241	.294	7	-13	96	106	.958	275	89	.1	-1.5	3.7		-11.3
NY	91	11	3	1366	1286	8.5	26	457	584	12.0	3.16	78	.250	.321	-116	-105	104	98	.947	337	78	-4.1	-12.0	-5.4		-4.5
TOT	841	132	46	11149		7.8				10.5	2.39		.239	.288					.958	2212	675					

Runs
McIntyre-Det 105
Crawford-Det 102
Schaefer-Det 96
Jones-Chi 92
Stone-StL 89

Hits
Cobb-Det 188
Crawford-Det 184
McIntyre-Det 168
Lajoie-Cle 168
Stone-StL 165

Doubles
Cobb-Det 36
Rossman-Det 33
Crawford-Det 33
Lajoie-Cle 32
Stovall-Cle 29

Triples
Cobb-Det 20
Stahl-NY-Bos 16
Crawford-Det 16
Gessler-Bos 14

Home Runs
Crawford-Det 7
Hinchman-Cle 6
Niles-NY-Bos 5
Stone-StL 5
Davis-Phi 5

Total Bases
Cobb-Det 276
Crawford-Det 270
Rossman-Det 219
McIntyre-Det 218
Lajoie-Cle 218

Runs Batted In
Cobb-Det 108
Crawford-Det 80
Lajoie-Cle 74
Ferris-StL 74
Rossman-Det 71

Runs Produced
Cobb-Det 192
Crawford-Det 175
Lajoie-Cle 149
Schaefer-Det 145
Jones-Chi 141

Bases On Balls
Hartsel-Phi 93
Jones-Chi 86
McIntyre-Det 83
J.Clarke-Cle 76
Davis-Phi 61

Batting Average
Cobb-Det .... .324
Crawford-Det ..... .311
Gessler-Bos ...... .308
Hemphill-NY ...... .297
McIntyre-Det ...... .295

On Base Percentage
McIntyre-Det ...... .385
Gessler-Bos ...... .381
Hartsel-Phi .... .371
Hemphill-NY ...... .371
Cobb-Det .... .361

Slugging Average
Cobb-Det .... .475
Crawford-Det ..... .457
Gessler-Bos ...... .423
Rossman-Det ..... .418
McIntyre-Det ..... .383

Production
Cobb-Det .... .836
Crawford-Det ..... .809
Gessler-Bos ...... .804
McIntyre-Det ..... .768
Rossman-Det .... .746

Adjusted Production
Cobb-Det 167
Gessler-Bos 159
Crawford-Det 158
McIntyre-Det 146
Rossman-Det 139

Batter Runs
Cobb-Det 43.6
Crawford-Det 39.1
McIntyre-Det 35.9
Gessler-Bos 31.1
Hemphill-NY 23.5

Adjusted Batter Runs
Cobb-Det 41.1
Crawford-Det 36.5
McIntyre-Det 33.3
Gessler-Bos 29.7
Hemphill-NY 22.9

Clutch Hitting Index
Wallace-StL 148
Ferris-StL 146
Cobb-Det 135
Gessler-Bos 130
Murphy-Phi 128

Runs Created
Cobb-Det 112
Crawford-Det 99
McIntyre-Det 91
Hemphill-NY 82
Lajoie-Cle 81

Total Average
Cobb-Det .... .888
Gessler-Bos ...... .844
McIntyre-Det ..... .800
Hemphill-NY ..... .792
Crawford-Det .... .791

Stolen Bases
Dougherty-Chi 47
Hemphill-NY 42
Schaefer-Det 40
Cobb-Det 39
J.Clarke-Cle 37

Stolen Base Average

Stolen Base Runs

Fielding Runs
Lajoie-Cle 49.3
McBride-Was 32.9
Wagner-Bos 31.7
Tannehill-Chi 18.0
Wallace-StL 18.0

Total Player Rating
Lajoie-Cle 7.5
McIntyre-Det 4.6
Cobb-Det 4.2
McBride-Was 3.8
Wallace-StL 3.3

Wins
Walsh-Chi 40
Summers-Det 24
Joss-Cle 24
Young-Bos 21
Waddell-StL 19

Win Percentage
Walsh-Chi .... .727
Donovan-Det ..... .720
Joss-Cle .... .686
Summers-Det .... .667
Young-Bos .... .656

Games
Walsh-Chi 66
Vickers-Phi 53
Chesbro-NY 45
Waddell-StL 43
Hughes-Was 43

Complete Games
Walsh-Chi 42
Young-Bos 30
Joss-Cle 29
Howell-StL 27
Mullin-Det 26

Shutouts
Walsh-Chi 11
Joss-Cle 9
Vickers-Phi 6
Johnson-Was 6
Donovan-Det 6

Saves
Walsh-Chi 6
Hughes-Was 4
Waddell-StL 3

Innings Pitched
Walsh-Chi 464.0
Joss-Cle 325.0
Howell-StL 324.1
Vickers-Phi 317.0
Summers-Det ... 301.0

Fewest Hits/Game
Joss-Cle 6.42
Smith-Chi 6.44
Walsh-Chi 6.65
Johnson-Was 6.78
Berger-Cle 6.86

Fewest BB/Game
Joss-Cle .... .83
Burns-Was .... .98
Walsh-Chi 1.09
Young-Bos 1.11
Summers-Det 1.64

Strikeouts
Walsh-Chi 269
Waddell-StL 232
Hughes-Was 165
Dygert-Phi 164
Johnson-Was 160

Strikeouts/Game
Waddell-StL 7.31
Dygert-Phi 6.18
Johnson-Was 5.60
Hughes-Was 5.37
Donovan-Det 5.23

Ratio
Joss-Cle 7.31
Walsh-Chi 7.91
Young-Bos 8.07
Burns-Was 8.56
Smith-Chi 8.71

Earned Run Average
Joss-Cle 1.16
Young-Bos 1.26
Walsh-Chi 1.42
Johnson-Was 1.64
Summers-Det 1.64

Adjusted ERA
Joss-Cle 205
Young-Bos 194
Walsh-Chi 163
Summers-Det 147
Johnson-Was 139

Opponents' Batting Avg.
Joss-Cle .... .197
Smith-Chi .... .203
Walsh-Chi .... .203
Johnson-Was .... .211
Young-Bos .... .213

Opponents' On Base Pct.
Joss-Cle .... .218
Walsh-Chi .... .232
Young-Bos .... .240
Smith-Chi .... .256
Burns-Was .... .257

Starter Runs
Walsh-Chi 50.0
Joss-Cle 44.2
Young-Bos 37.3
Summers-Det 24.8
Johnson-Was 21.2

Adjusted Starter Runs
Walsh-Chi 46.0
Joss-Cle 44.0
Young-Bos 39.5
Summers-Det 25.6
Rhoads-Cle 18.4

Clutch Pitching Index
Summers-Det 148
Willett-Det 144
Rhoads-Cle 142
Howell-StL 127
Chech-Cle 125

Relief Runs

Adjusted Relief Runs

Relief Ranking

Total Pitcher Index
Walsh-Chi 7.2
Joss-Cle 6.1
Young-Bos 4.2
Rhoads-Cle 3.0
Howell-StL 2.4

Total Baseball Ranking
Lajoie-Cle 7.5
Walsh-Chi 7.2
Joss-Cle 6.1
McIntyre-Det 4.6
Young-Bos 4.2

TEAM	G	W	L	PCT	GB	R	OR	AB	H	2B	3B	HR	BB	SO	AVG	OBP	SLG	PRO	PRO+	BR	/A	PF	CHI	RC	SB	CS	SBA	SBR
PIT	153	110	42	.724		699	447	5129	1332	218	92	25	479		.260	.327	.353	.680	108	100	52	108	103	656	185			
CHI	155	104	49	.680	6.5	635	390	4999	1227	203	60	20	420		.245	.308	.322	.630	99	7	-6	102	112	562	187			
NY	158	92	61	.601	18.5	623	546	5218	1327	173	68	26	530		.254	.329	.328	.657	109	70	61	102	95	640	234			
CIN	156	77	76	.503	33.5	606	599	5088	1273	159	72	22	478		.250	.319	.323	.642	106	35	39	99	100	618	280			
PHI	154	74	79	.484	36.5	516	518	5034	1228	185	53	12	369		.244	.303	.309	.612	95	-25	-28	101	96	534	185			
BRO	155	55	98	.359	55.5	444	627	5056	1157	176	59	16	330		.229	.279	.296	.575	87	-97	-77	96	98	456	141			
STL	154	54	98	.355	56	583	731	5108	1242	148	56	15	568		.243	.326	.303	.629	108	25	60	94	97	556	161			
BOS	155	45	108	.294	65.5	435	683	5017	1121	124	43	15	400		.223	.285	.274	.559	75	-115	-140	105	99	435	135			
TOT	620					4541		40649	9907	1386	503	151	3574	4397	.244	.310	.314	.624							1508			

TEAM	CG	SH	SV	IP	H	H/G	HR	BB	SO	RAT	ERA	ERA+	OAV	OOB	PR	/A	PF	CPI	FA	E	DP	FW	PW	BW	SBW	DIF
PIT	93	21	11	1401²	1174	7.5	12	320	490	9.9	2.07	131	.231	.283	81	99	105	97	.964	228	100	3.4	11.0	5.8		13.8
CHI	111	32	11	1399¹	1094	7.0	6	364	680	9.6	1.75	145	.214	.272	130	124	98	94	.962	244	95	2.6	13.8	-.7		11.8
NY	105	17	15	1440²	1248	7.8	29	397	695	10.5	2.27	112	.237	.295	50	42	98	103	.954	307	99	-1.1	4.7	6.8		5.2
CIN	91	10	8	1407	1233	7.9	5	510	477	11.4	2.52	103	.239	.314	10	9	100	100	.952	309	120	-1.5	1.0	4.3		-3.4
PHI	89	17	6	1391	1190	7.7	23	472	612	11.0	2.44	106	.234	.304	23	20	100	99	.962	241	97	2.7	2.2	-3.1		-4.3
BRO	126	18	3	1384¹	1277	8.3	31	528	594	12.1	3.10	83	.256	.333	-78	-83	100	101	.955	282	86	.2	-9.2	-8.5		-3.9
STL	84	5	4	1379²	1368	8.9	22	483	435	12.4	3.41	74	.263	.330	-125	-138	97	92	.950	322	90	-2.5	-15.3	6.7		-10.8
BOS	98	12	6	1370²	1329	8.7	23	543	414	12.6	3.20	88	.262	.338	-92	-60	109	103	.948	342	101	-3.7	-6.7	-15.5		-5.6
TOT	797	132	64	11174¹		8.0				11.2	2.59		.244	.310					.956	2275	788					

Runs
Leach-Pit	126
Clarke-Pit	97
Byrne-StL-Pit	92
Wagner-Pit	92

Hits
Doyle-NY	172
Grant-Phi	170
Wagner-Pit	168
Konetchy-StL	165
Burch-Bro	163

Doubles
Wagner-Pit	39
Magee-Phi	33
J.Miller-Pit	31
Sheckard-Chi	29
Leach-Pit	29

Triples
Mitchell-Cin	17
Magee-Phi	14
Konetchy-StL	14
J.Miller-Pit	13

Home Runs
Murray-NY	7
Leach-Pit	6
Doyle-NY	6
Becker-Bos	6
Wagner-Pit	5

Total Bases
Wagner-Pit	242
Doyle-NY	239
Konetchy-StL	228
Mitchell-Cin	225
J.Miller-Pit	222

Runs Batted In
Wagner-Pit	100
Murray-NY	91
J.Miller-Pit	87
Mitchell-Cin	86
Konetchy-StL	80

Runs Produced
Wagner-Pit	187
Mitchell-Cin	165
Konetchy-StL	164
Leach-Pit	163
Clarke-Pit	162

Bases On Balls
Clarke-Pit	80
Byrne-StL-Pit	78
Evers-Chi	73
Sheckard-Chi	72
Bridwell-NY	67

Batting Average
Wagner-Pit	.339
Mitchell-Cin	.310
Hoblitzel-Cin	.308
Doyle-NY	.302
Bridwell-NY	.294

On Base Percentage
Wagner-Pit	.420
Bridwell-NY	.386
Clarke-Pit	.384
Mitchell-Cin	.378
Evers-Chi	.369

Slugging Average
Wagner-Pit	.489
Mitchell-Cin	.430
Doyle-NY	.419
Hoblitzel-Cin	.418
Magee-Phi	.398

Production
Wagner-Pit	.909
Mitchell-Cin	.808
Hoblitzel-Cin	.782
Doyle-NY	.779
Konetchy-StL	.762

Adjusted Production
Wagner-Pit	168
Mitchell-Cin	152
Konetchy-StL	145
Hoblitzel-Cin	144
Doyle-NY	140

Batter Runs
Wagner-Pit	48.1
Mitchell-Cin	30.3
Doyle-NY	26.2
Clarke-Pit	25.4
Konetchy-StL	24.9

Adjusted Batter Runs
Wagner-Pit	43.3
Mitchell-Cin	30.8
Konetchy-StL	28.9
Doyle-NY	25.3
Hoblitzel-Cin	24.8

Clutch Hitting Index
Murray-NY	152
Abstein-Pit	151
Wagner-Pit	150
Lobert-Cin	146
J.Miller-Pit	145

Runs Created
Wagner-Pit	117
Mitchell-Cin	98
Doyle-NY	96
Clarke-Pit	92
Konetchy-StL	92

Total Average
Wagner-Pit	1.058
Mitchell-Cin	.884
Clarke-Pit	.821
Doyle-NY	.809
Konetchy-StL	.791

Stolen Bases
Bescher-Cin	54
Murray-NY	48
Egan-Cin	39
Magee-Phi	38
Burch-Bro	38

Stolen Base Average

Stolen Base Runs

Fielding Runs
Doolan-Phi	24.8
Egan-Cin	24.3
Byrne-StL-Pit	20.8
Bergen-Bro	20.6
Tinker-Chi	16.0

Total Player Rating
Wagner-Pit	5.5
Mitchell-Cin	3.5
Konetchy-StL	3.4
Devlin-NY	3.2
Egan-Cin	2.9

Wins
M.Brown-Chi	27
Mathewson-NY	25
S.Camnitz-Pit	25
Willis-Pit	22

Win Percentage
Mathewson-NY	.806
S.Camnitz-Pit	.806
M.Brown-Chi	.750
Pfiester-Chi	.739
Leifield-Pit	.704

Games
M.Brown-Chi	50
Mattern-Bos	47
Gaspar-Cin	44
Beebe-StL	44

Complete Games
M.Brown-Chi	32
Bell-Bro	29
Rucker-Bro	28
Mathewson-NY	26

Shutouts
Overall-Chi	9
Mathewson-NY	8
M.Brown-Chi	8

Saves
M.Brown-Chi	7
Crandall-NY	6

Innings Pitched
M.Brown-Chi	342.2
Mattern-Bos	316.1
Rucker-Bro	309.1
Moore-Phi	299.2
Willis-Pit	289.2

Fewest Hits/Game
Mathewson-NY	6.28
Fromme-Cin	6.28
Overall-Chi	6.44
M.Brown-Chi	6.46
S.Camnitz-Pit	6.58

Fewest BB/Game
Mathewson-NY	1.18
M.Brown-Chi	1.39
Wiltse-NY	1.70
Maddox-Pit	1.73
McQuillan-Phi	1.96

Strikeouts
Overall-Chi	205
Rucker-Bro	201
Moore-Phi	173
M.Brown-Chi	172
Ames-NY	156

Strikeouts/Game
Overall-Chi	6.47
Rucker-Bro	5.85
Ames-NY	5.75
Marquard-NY	5.67
Moore-Phi	5.20

Ratio
Mathewson-NY	7.45
M.Brown-Chi	8.04
S.Camnitz-Pit	8.97
Overall-Chi	9.22
McQuillan-Phi	9.34

Earned Run Average
Mathewson-NY	1.14
M.Brown-Chi	1.31
Overall-Chi	1.42
S.Camnitz-Pit	1.62
Reulbach-Chi	1.78

Adjusted ERA
Mathewson-NY	223
M.Brown-Chi	193
Overall-Chi	178
S.Camnitz-Pit	167
Reulbach-Chi	142

Opponents' Batting Avg.
Overall-Chi	.198
Mathewson-NY	.200
Fromme-Cin	.201
M.Brown-Chi	.202
Moore-Phi	.210

Opponents' On Base Pct.
Mathewson-NY	.228
M.Brown-Chi	.239
Overall-Chi	.262
S.Camnitz-Pit	.267
McQuillan-Phi	.271

Starter Runs
M.Brown-Chi	48.6
Mathewson-NY	44.2
Overall-Chi	37.0
S.Camnitz-Pit	30.4
Reulbach-Chi	23.6

Adjusted Starter Runs
M.Brown-Chi	46.5
Mathewson-NY	43.0
Overall-Chi	35.2
S.Camnitz-Pit	34.3
Adams-Pit	23.2

Clutch Pitching Index
Richie-Phi-Bos	126
Corridon-Phi	123
Sallee-StL	119
Wilhelm-Bro	117
Marquard-NY	117

Relief Runs

Adjusted Relief Runs

Relief Ranking

Total Pitcher Index
Mathewson-NY	6.9
M.Brown-Chi	5.5
Overall-Chi	5.0
S.Camnitz-Pit	3.6
Reulbach-Chi	3.0

Total Baseball Ranking
Mathewson-NY	6.9
Wagner-Pit	5.5
M.Brown-Chi	5.5
Overall-Chi	5.0
S.Camnitz-Pit	3.6

TEAM	G	W	L	PCT	GB	R	OR	AB	H	2B	3B	HR	BB	SO	AVG	OBP	SLG	PRO	PRO+	BR	/A	PF	CHI	RC	SB	CS	SBA	SBR
DET	158	98	54	.645		666	493	5095	1360	209	58	19	397		.267	.325	.342	.667	113	98	73	104	103	660	280			
PHI	153	95	58	.621	3.5	605	408	4905	1257	186	88	21	403		.256	.321	.343	.664	114	91	80	102	97	613	205			
BOS	152	88	63	.583	9.5	597	550	4979	1307	151	69	20	348		.263	.321	.333	.654	111	73	61	102	99	599	215			
CHI	159	78	74	.513	20	492	463	5017	1110	145	56	4	441		.221	.292	.275	.567	89	-71	-48	96	103	474	191			
NY	153	74	77	.490	23.5	590	587	4981	1234	143	61	16	407		.248	.313	.311	.624	103	25	21	101	105	547	187			
CLE	155	71	82	.464	27.5	493	532	5044	1214	173	81	10	283		.241	.287	.313	.600	92	-28	-49	104	99	500	174			
STL	154	61	89	.407	36	441	575	4964	1151	116	45	10	331		.232	.287	.279	.566	91	-78	-41	93	100	436	136			
WAS	156	42	110	.276	56	380	656	4983	1112	149	41	9	321		.223	.276	.275	.551	83	-107	-82	95	91	419	136			
TOT	620					4264		39968	9745	1272	499	109	2931	4921	.244	.303	.309	.611							1544			

TEAM	CG	SH	SV	IP	H	H/G	HR	BB	SO	RAT	ERA	ERA+	OAV	OOB	PR	/A	PF	CPI	FA	E	DP	FW	PW	BW	SBW	DIF
DET	117	17	12	1420¹	1254	7.9	16	359	528	10.6	2.26	111	.237	.293	32	40	102	100	.959	276	87	.4	4.5	8.3		8.8
PHI	110	27	3	1378	1069	7.0	9	386	728	9.9	1.93	124	.216	.282	82	72	97	96	.961	245	92	1.8	8.2	9.1		-.6
BOS	75	11	15	1360¹	1214	8.0	18	384	555	10.9	2.59	96	.242	.303	-18	-15	101	96	.955	292	95	-1.3	-1.7	6.9		8.6
CHI	115	26	4	1430¹	1190	7.5	8	341	671	10.6	2.05	114	.230	.284	66	44	95	98	.964	246	101	2.4	5.0	-5.5		.0
NY	94	18	7	1350¹	1223	8.2	21	422	597	11.4	2.65	95	.247	.316	-26	-21	102	104	.948	329	94	-3.6	-2.4	2.4		2.1
CLE	110	15	3	1361	1211	8.0	9	349	569	10.6	2.40	106	.250	.306	10	20	103	106	.957	278	110	-.0	2.3	-5.6		-2.1
STL	105	21	4	1354²	1287	8.6	16	383	620	11.4	2.88	84	.260	.319	-61	-72	98	101	.958	267	107	.5	-8.2	-4.7		-1.6
WAS	99	11	2	1375¹	1288	8.4	12	424	653	11.6	3.04	80	.247	.311	-86	-95	98	87	.957	280	100	-.1	-10.8	-9.3		-13.8
TOT	825	146	50	11030¹		7.9				10.8	2.47		.244	.303					.957	2213	786					

Runs
Cobb-Det 116
Bush-Det 114
Collins-Phi 104
Lord-Bos 86
Crawford-Det 83

Hits
Cobb-Det 216
Collins-Phi 198
Crawford-Det 185
Speaker-Bos 168
Lord-Bos 166

Doubles
Crawford-Det 35
Lajoie-Cle 33
Cobb-Det 33
Collins-Phi 30
Murphy-Phi 28

Triples
Baker-Phi 19
Murphy-Phi 14
Crawford-Det 14

Home Runs
Cobb-Det 9
Speaker-Bos 7
Stahl-Bos 6
Crawford-Det 6
Murphy-Phi 5

Total Bases
Cobb-Det 296
Crawford-Det 266
Collins-Phi 257
Baker-Phi 242
Speaker-Bos 241

Runs Batted In
Cobb-Det 107
Crawford-Det 97
Baker-Phi 85
Speaker-Bos 77
Davis-Phi 75

Runs Produced
Cobb-Det 214
Crawford-Det 174
Collins-Phi 157
Baker-Phi 154
Bush-Det 147

Bases On Balls
Bush-Det 88
Collins-Phi 62
Demmitt-NY 55
McIntyre-Det 54

Batting Average
Cobb-Det 377
Collins-Phi 346
Lajoie-Cle 324
Crawford-Det 314
Lord-Bos 311

On Base Percentage
Cobb-Det 431
Collins-Phi 416
Bush-Det 380
Lajoie-Cle 378
Stahl-Bos 377

Slugging Average
Cobb-Det 517
Crawford-Det 452
Collins-Phi 449
Baker-Phi 447
Speaker-Bos 443

Production
Cobb-Det 947
Collins-Phi 865
Crawford-Det 817
Stahl-Bos 812
Lajoie-Cle 809

Adjusted Production
Cobb-Det 191
Collins-Phi 170
Stahl-Bos 153
Crawford-Det 151
Speaker-Bos 151

Batter Runs
Cobb-Det 63.3
Collins-Phi 48.9
Crawford-Det 36.7
Speaker-Bos 31.6
Lajoie-Cle 28.8

Adjusted Batter Runs
Cobb-Det 60.6
Collins-Phi 47.6
Crawford-Det 33.9
Speaker-Bos 30.3
Stahl-Bos 27.4

Clutch Hitting Index
Engle-NY 153
Davis-Phi 143
Gessler-Bos-Was . . . 137
Ferris-StL 135
Baker-Phi 134

Runs Created
Cobb-Det 159
Collins-Phi 134
Crawford-Det 108
Speaker-Bos 99
Baker-Phi 90

Total Average
Cobb-Det 1.193
Collins-Phi 1.048
Stahl-Bos 857
Speaker-Bos 854
Crawford-Det 851

Stolen Bases
Cobb-Det 76
Collins-Phi 67
Bush-Det 53
Lord-Bos 36
Dougherty-Chi 36

Stolen Base Average

Stolen Base Runs

Fielding Runs
Speaker-Bos 22.4
Lajoie-Cle 18.9
Parent-Chi 16.5
McConnell-Bos 14.4
Engle-NY 14.3

Total Player Rating
Cobb-Det 6.4
Collins-Phi 5.7
Speaker-Bos 5.2
Lajoie-Cle 4.7
Baker-Phi 2.7

Wins
Mullin-Det 29
Smith-Chi 25
Willett-Det 21

Win Percentage
Mullin-Det 784
Krause-Phi 692
Bender-Phi 692
Summers-Det 679
Willett-Det 677

Games
Smith-Chi 51
Arellanes-Bos 45
Groom-Was 44
Willett-Det 41

Complete Games
Smith-Chi 37
Young-Cle 30
Mullin-Det 29
Johnson-Was 27
Morgan-Bos-Phi . . . 26

Shutouts
Walsh-Chi 8
Smith-Chi 7
Krause-Phi 7
Coombs-Phi 6

Saves
Arellanes-Bos 8
Powell-StL 3

Innings Pitched
Smith-Chi 365.0
Mullin-Det 303.2
Johnson-Was 297.0
Young-Cle 295.0
Morgan-Bos-Phi . 293.8

Fewest Hits/Game
Morgan-Bos-Phi . . 6.26
Krause-Phi 6.38
Walsh-Chi 6.49
Cicotte-Bos 6.59
Wood-Bos 6.78

Fewest BB/Game
Joss-Cle 1.15
White-Chi 1.57
Powell-StL 1.58
Bender-Phi 1.62
Summers-Det 1.66

Strikeouts
Smith-Chi 177
Johnson-Was 164
Berger-Cle 162
Bender-Phi 161
Waddell-StL 141

Strikeouts/Game
Berger-Cle 5.90
Krause-Phi 5.87
Bender-Phi 5.80
Waddell-StL 5.76
Bailey-StL 5.16

Ratio
Walsh-Chi 8.60
Joss-Cle 8.64
Smith-Chi 8.73
Bender-Phi 8.86
Krause-Phi 9.00

Earned Run Average
Krause-Phi 1.39
Walsh-Chi 1.41
Bender-Phi 1.66
Joss-Cle 1.71
Killian-Det 1.71

Adjusted ERA
Krause-Phi 172
Walsh-Chi 166
Joss-Cle 149
Killian-Det 146
Bender-Phi 145

Opponents' Batting Avg.
Morgan-Bos-Phi . . .202
Walsh-Chi 203
Krause-Phi 204
Wood-Bos 209
Cicotte-Bos 210

Opponents' On Base Pct.
Walsh-Chi 253
Bender-Phi 254
Joss-Cle 255
Smith-Chi 257
Krause-Phi 266

Starter Runs
Walsh-Chi 27.2
Smith-Chi 27.2
Krause-Phi 25.5
Bender-Phi 22.6
Morgan-Bos-Phi . . 21.5

Adjusted Starter Runs
Krause-Phi 23.8
Walsh-Chi 23.8
Joss-Cle 22.7
Smith-Chi 21.7
Bender-Phi 20.6

Clutch Pitching Index
Burns-Was-Chi . . . 142
Killian-Det 132
Brockett-NY 132
Waddell-StL 125
Bailey-StL 117

Relief Runs

Adjusted Relief Runs

Relief Ranking

Total Pitcher Index
Smith-Chi 4.3
Walsh-Chi 4.2
Bender-Phi 3.0
Plank-Phi 2.8
Lake-NY 2.5

Total Baseball Ranking
Cobb-Det 6.4
Collins-Phi 5.7
Speaker-Bos 5.2
Lajoie-Cle 4.7
Smith-Chi 4.3

TEAM	G	W	L	PCT	GB	R	OR	AB	H	2B	3B	HR	BB	SO	AVG	OBP	SLG	PRO	PRO+	BR	/A	PF	CHI	RC	SB	CS	SBA	SBR
CHI	154	104	50	.675		712	499	4977	1333	219	84	34	542	501	.268	.344	.366	.710	113	81	85	99	101	696	173			
NY	155	91	63	.591	13	715	567	5061	1391	204	83	31	562	489	.275	.354	.366	.720	115	106	105	100	97	759	282			
PIT	154	86	67	.562	17.5	655	576	5125	1364	214	83	33	437	524	.266	.328	.360	.688	100	30	-6	106	100	655	148			
PHI	157	78	75	.510	25.5	674	639	5171	1319	223	71	22	506	559	.255	.328	.338	.665	96	-3	-24	103	106	641	199			
CIN	156	75	79	.487	29	620	684	5121	1326	150	79	23	529	515	.259	.332	.333	.665	104	0	27	96	98	669	310			
BRO	156	64	90	.416	40	497	623	5125	1174	166	73	25	434	706	.229	.294	.305	.599	82	-131	-112	97	101	506	151			
STL	153	63	90	.412	40.5	639	718	4912	1217	167	70	15	655	581	.248	.345	.319	.664	102	19	42	96	99	609	179			
BOS	157	53	100	.346	50.5	495	701	5123	1260	173	49	31	359	540	.246	.301	.317	.618	81	-98	-125	105	96	536	152			
TOT	621					5007		40615	10384	1516	592	214	4024	4415	.256	.328	.338	.666							1594			

TEAM	CG	SH	SV	IP	H	H/G	HR	BB	SO	RAT	ERA	ERA+	OAV	OOB	PR	/A	PF	CPI	FA	E	DP	FW	PW	BW	SBW	DIF
CHI	100	25	13	1378²	1171	7.6	18	474	609	11.0	2.51	115	.235	.307	79	53	95	95	.963	230	110	2.1	5.6	8.9		10.4
NY	96	9	10	1391²	1290	8.3	30	397	717	11.2	2.68	110	.250	.308	53	43	98	99	.955	291	117	-1.7	4.5	11.1		.1
PIT	73	13	12	1376	1254	8.2	20	392	479	11.1	2.83	109	.249	.311	29	38	102	93	.961	245	102	1.1	4.0	-.6		5.0
PHI	84	17	9	1411¹	1297	8.3	36	547	657	12.1	3.05	102	.252	.330	-4	9	103	101	.960	258	132	.6	.9	-2.5		2.4
CIN	86	16	11	1386²	1334	8.7	27	528	497	12.5	3.08	94	.260	.337	-9	-29	96	105	.955	291	103	-1.6	-3.1	2.8		-.2
BRO	103	15	5	1420¹	1331	8.4	17	545	555	12.1	3.07	99	.259	.334	-6	-9	100	101	.964	235	125	2.0	-.9	-11.8		-2.3
STL	81	4	14	1337¹	1396	9.4	30	541	466	13.3	3.78	79	.275	.349	-111	-119	98	96	.959	261	109	.0	-12.5	4.4		-5.4
BOS	72	12	9	1390¹	1328	8.6	36	599	531	12.8	3.22	103	.265	.349	-29	14	110	110	.954	305	137	-2.4	1.5	-13.2		-9.5
TOT	695	111	83	11092¹		8.4				12.0	3.02		.256	.328					.959	2116	935					

Runs		Hits		Doubles		Triples		Home Runs		Total Bases	
Magee-Phi	110	Wagner-Pit	178	Byrne-Pit	43	Mitchell-Cin	18	Schulte-Chi	10	Magee-Phi	263
Huggins-StL	101	Byrne-Pit	178	Magee-Phi	39	Magee-Phi	17	Beck-Bos	10	Schulte-Chi	257
Byrne-Pit	101	Wheat-Bro	172	Wheat-Bro	36	Konetchy-StL	16	Doyle-NY	8	Byrne-Pit	251
Doyle-NY	97	Magee-Phi	172	Merkle-NY	35	Hofman-Chi	16	Daubert-Bro	8	Wheat-Bro	244
Bescher-Cin	95	Hoblitzel-Cin	170	Wagner-Pit	34					Wagner-Pit	240

Runs Batted In		Runs Produced		Bases On Balls		Batting Average		On Base Percentage		Slugging Average	
Magee-Phi	123	Magee-Phi	227	Huggins-StL	116	Magee-Phi	.331	Magee-Phi	.445	Magee-Phi	.507
Mitchell-Cin	88	Wagner-Pit	167	Evers-Chi	108	Hofman-Chi	.325	Snodgrass-NY	.440	Hofman-Chi	.461
Murray-NY	87	Hofman-Chi	166	Magee-Phi	94	Snodgrass-NY	.321	Evers-Chi	.413	Schulte-Chi	.460
Hofman-Chi	86	Mitchell-Cin	162	Titus-Phi	93	Wagner-Pit	.320	Hofman-Chi	.406	Merkle-NY	.441
Wagner-Pit	81	Konetchy-StL	162	Sheckard-Chi	83	Bates-Phi	.305	Huggins-StL	.399	Snodgrass-NY	.432

Production		Adjusted Production		Batter Runs		Adjusted Batter Runs		Clutch Hitting Index		Runs Created	
Magee-Phi	.952	Magee-Phi	172	Magee-Phi	54.9	Magee-Phi	52.6	Magee-Phi	162	Magee-Phi	139
Snodgrass-NY	.871	Snodgrass-NY	154	Hofman-Chi	32.4	Hofman-Chi	32.9	Evans-StL	158	Byrne-Pit	104
Hofman-Chi	.867	Hofman-Chi	154	Snodgrass-NY	31.9	Snodgrass-NY	31.9	Murray-NY	146	Wagner-Pit	103
Konetchy-StL	.822	Konetchy-StL	145	Konetchy-StL	28.0	Konetchy-StL	30.5	Steinfeldt-Chi	145	Hofman-Chi	102
Wagner-Pit	.822	Schulte-Chi	137	Wagner-Pit	27.9	Wagner-Pit	23.9	Devlin-NY	143	Doyle-NY	101

Total Average		Stolen Bases		Stolen Base Average	Stolen Base Runs	Fielding Runs		Total Player Rating	
Magee-Phi	1.205	Bescher-Cin	70			Shean-Bos	42.5	Magee-Phi	4.1
Snodgrass-NY	1.071	Murray-NY	57			Doolan-Phi	20.7	Konetchy-StL	3.9
Hofman-Chi	.975	Paskert-Cin	51			Collins-Bos	17.5	Wagner-Pit	3.4
Konetchy-StL	.884	Magee-Phi	49			Tinker-Chi	15.5	Hofman-Chi	3.2
Paskert-Cin	.884	Devore-NY	43			Knabe-Phi	13.9	Mowrey-StL	2.8

Wins		Win Percentage		Games		Complete Games		Shutouts		Saves	
Mathewson-NY	27	Cole-Chi	.833	Mattern-Bos	51	Rucker-Bro	27	Rucker-Bro	6	Gaspar-Cin	7
Brown-Chi	25	Crandall-NY	.810	Gaspar-Cin	48	Mathewson-NY	27	Moore-Phi	6	Brown-Chi	7
Moore-Phi	22	Mathewson-NY	.750			Brown-Chi	27	Mattern-Bos	6	Crandall-NY	5
Suggs-Cin	20	Adams-Pit	.667			Bell-Bro	25	Brown-Chi	6	Richie-Bos-Chi	4
Cole-Chi	20	Brown-Chi	.641			Barger-Bro	25			Phillippe-Pit	4

Innings Pitched		Fewest Hits/Game		Fewest BB/Game		Strikeouts		Strikeouts/Game		Ratio	
Rucker-Bro	320.1	Cole-Chi	6.53	Suggs-Cin	1.62	Moore-Phi	185	Drucke-NY	6.31	Brown-Chi	9.87
Mathewson-NY	318.1	Scanlan-Bro	7.25	Mathewson-NY	1.70	Mathewson-NY	184	Frock-Pit-Bos	5.98	Mathewson-NY	10.04
Bell-Bro	310.0	Moore-Phi	7.25	Crandall-NY	1.86	Frock-Pit-Bos	171	Moore-Phi	5.88	Bell-Bro	10.25
Mattern-Bos	305.0	Drucke-NY	7.27	Brown-Chi	1.95	Drucke-NY	151	Mathewson-NY	5.20	Adams-Pit	10.40
Brown-Chi	295.1	Ames-NY	7.61	Wiltse-NY	1.99	Rucker-Bro	147	Ames-NY	4.44	Crandall-NY	10.44

Earned Run Average		Adjusted ERA		Opponents' Batting Avg.		Opponents' On Base Pct.		Starter Runs		Adjusted Starter Runs	
Cole-Chi	1.80	Cole-Chi	159	Cole-Chi	.211	Brown-Chi	.277	Mathewson-NY	40.0	Mathewson-NY	37.6
Brown-Chi	1.86	Mathewson-NY	156	Drucke-NY	.228	Mathewson-NY	.286	Brown-Chi	38.2	Brown-Chi	33.3
Mathewson-NY	1.89	Brown-Chi	155	Moore-Phi	.228	Crandall-NY	.289	Cole-Chi	32.5	Cole-Chi	28.5
Ames-NY	2.22	Adams-Pit	138	Brown-Chi	.232	Adams-Pit	.291	McQuillan-Phi	24.2	McQuillan-Phi	25.8
Adams-Pit	2.24	Ames-NY	133	Scanlan-Bro	.234	Bell-Bro	.296	Adams-Pit	21.3	Adams-Pit	23.1

Clutch Pitching Index		Relief Runs	Adjusted Relief Runs	Relief Ranking	Total Pitcher Index		Total Baseball Ranking	
Cole-Chi	136				Mathewson-NY	5.8	Mathewson-NY	5.8
Brown-Bos	122				Brown-Chi	3.9	Magee-Phi	4.1
Barger-Bro	122				Cole-Chi	3.3	Brown-Chi	3.9
Mathewson-NY	117				McQuillan-Phi	2.8	Konetchy-StL	3.8
Curtis-Bos	116				Brown-Bos	2.3	Wagner-Pit	3.4

TEAM	G	W	L	PCT	GB	R	OR	AB	H	2B	3B	HR	BB	SO	AVG	OBP	SLG	PRO	PRO+	BR	/A	PF	CHI	RC	SB	CS	SBA	SBR
PHI	155	102	48	.680		673	441	5156	1373	191	105	19	409		.266	.326	.355	.681	120	104	109	99	99	665	207			
NY	156	88	63	.583	14.5	626	557	5051	1254	164	75	20	464		.248	.320	.322	.642	101	44	10	106	102	614	288			
DET	155	86	68	.558	18	679	582	5039	1317	190	72	28	459		.261	.329	.344	.673	109	96	57	107	102	655	249			
BOS	158	81	72	.529	22.5	638	564	5204	1350	175	87	43	430		.259	.323	.351	.674	114	93	78	102	94	656	194			
CLE	161	71	81	.467	32	548	657	5385	1316	188	64	9	366		.244	.297	.308	.605	93	-36	-43	101	99	549	189			
CHI	156	68	85	.444	35.5	457	479	5024	1058	115	58	7	403		.211	.275	.261	.536	76	-149	-125	96	111	415	183			
WAS	157	66	85	.437	36.5	501	550	4989	1175	145	46	9	449		.236	.309	.288	.597	96	-31	-4	95	94	508	192			
STL	158	47	107	.305	57	451	743	5077	1105	131	60	12	415		.218	.281	.274	.555	84	-116	-80	94	101	438	169			
TOT	628					4573		40925	9948	1299	567	147	3395	5276	.243	.308	.313	.621						1671				

TEAM	CG	SH	SV	IP	H	H/G	HR	BB	SO	RAT	ERA	ERA+	OAV	OOB	PR	/A	PF	CPI	FA	E	DP	FW	PW	BW	SBW	DIF
PHI	123	24	5	1421²	1103	7.0	8	450	789	10.2	1.79	133	.220	.292	115	91	94	111	.965	230	117	3.8	10.1	12.1		.9
NY	110	14	8	1399	1238	8.0	16	364	654	10.7	2.61	102	.242	.300	-14	3	106	90	.956	285	95	.2	.3	1.1		10.8
DET	108	17	5	1380¹	1257	8.2	34	460	532	11.6	2.82	93	.248	.319	-47	-27	104	101	.956	288	79	-.0	-3.0	6.3		5.8
BOS	100	12	6	1430	1236	7.8	30	414	670	10.7	2.45	104	.235	.296	9	14	101	94	.954	309	80	-1.1	1.6	8.7		-4.6
CLE	92	13	5	1467	1386	8.5	10	487	614	11.9	2.88	90	.259	.328	-59	-50	103	103	.964	247	112	3.4	-5.6	-4.8		1.9
CHI	103	23	7	1421	1130	7.2	15	381	785	9.8	2.03	118	.221	.280	77	55	95	91	.954	314	100	-1.7	6.1	-13.9		1.0
WAS	119	19	3	1377¹	1223	8.0	19	374	675	10.8	2.46	101	.245	.305	8	4	99	102	.959	264	99	1.8	.4	-.4		-11.3
STL	100	9	3	1391	1356	8.8	15	532	557	12.6	3.09	80	.265	.340	-89	-95	98	106	.943	385	113	-6.3	-10.6	-8.9		-4.3
TOT	855	131	42	11287¹		7.9				11.0	2.52		.243	.308					.956	2322	795					

Runs
Cobb-Det	106
Lajoie-Cle	94
Speaker-Bos	92
Bush-Det	90
Milan-Was	89

Hits
Lajoie-Cle	227
Cobb-Det	194
Collins-Phi	188
Speaker-Bos	183
Crawford-Det	170

Doubles
Lajoie-Cle	51
Cobb-Det	35
Lewis-Bos	29
Murphy-Phi	28
Oldring-Phi	27

Triples
Crawford-Det	19
Lord-Cle-Phi	18
Murphy-Phi	18
Stahl-Bos	16
Cree-NY	16

Home Runs
Stahl-Bos	10
Lewis-Bos	8
Cobb-Det	8
Speaker-Bos	7
Crawford-Det	5

Total Bases
Lajoie-Cle	304
Cobb-Det	279
Speaker-Bos	252
Crawford-Det	249
Murphy-Phi	244

Runs Batted In
Crawford-Det	120
Cobb-Det	91
Collins-Phi	81
Stahl-Bos	77
Lajoie-Cle	76

Runs Produced
Crawford-Det	198
Cobb-Det	189
Lajoie-Cle	166
Collins-Phi	159
Baker-Phi	155

Bases On Balls
Bush-Det	78
Milan-Was	71
Wolter-NY	66
Cobb-Det	64

Batting Average
Lajoie-Cle	.384
Cobb-Det	.383
Speaker-Bos	.340
Collins-Phi	.322
Oldring-Phi	.308

On Base Percentage
Cobb-Det	.456
Lajoie-Cle	.445
Speaker-Bos	.404
Collins-Phi	.381
Milan-Was	.379

Slugging Average
Cobb-Det	.551
Lajoie-Cle	.514
Speaker-Bos	.468
Murphy-Phi	.436
Oldring-Phi	.430

Production
Cobb-Det	1.008
Lajoie-Cle	.960
Speaker-Bos	.873
Collins-Phi	.798
Cree-NY	.775

Adjusted Production
Cobb-Det	202
Lajoie-Cle	198
Speaker-Bos	169
Collins-Phi	151
Murphy-Phi	143

Batter Runs
Lajoie-Cle	68.2
Cobb-Det	67.9
Speaker-Bos	44.9
Collins-Phi	32.9
Murphy-Phi	23.6

Adjusted Batter Runs
Lajoie-Cle	67.4
Cobb-Det	64.0
Speaker-Bos	43.5
Collins-Phi	33.6
Murphy-Phi	24.2

Clutch Hitting Index
Crawford-Det	178
LaPorte-NY	166
McBride-Was	143
Purtell-Chi-Bos	138
Moriarty-Det	137

Runs Created
Cobb-Det	156
Lajoie-Cle	147
Collins-Phi	122
Speaker-Bos	115
Crawford-Det	89

Total Average
Cobb-Det	1.321
Lajoie-Cle	1.085
Speaker-Bos	.972
Collins-Phi	.959
Cree-NY	.820

Stolen Bases
Collins-Phi	81
Cobb-Det	65
Zeider-Chi	49
Bush-Det	49
Milan-Was	44

Stolen Base Average

Stolen Base Runs

Fielding Runs
Collins-Phi	35.4
McBride-Was	26.7
Wallace-StL	21.1
Lajoie-Cle	16.7
Speaker-Bos	15.2

Total Player Rating
Lajoie-Cle	8.0
Cobb-Det	7.2
Collins-Phi	6.4
Speaker-Bos	5.6
Wallace-StL	3.2

Wins
Coombs-Phi	31
Ford-NY	26
Johnson-Was	25
Bender-Phi	23
Mullin-Det	21

Win Percentage
Bender-Phi	.821
Ford-NY	.813
Coombs-Phi	.775
Donovan-Det	.708
Mullin-Det	.636

Games
Walsh-Chi	45
Johnson-Was	45
Coombs-Phi	45
Scott-Chi	41

Complete Games
Johnson-Was	38
Coombs-Phi	35
Walsh-Chi	33
Ford-NY	29
Mullin-Det	27

Shutouts
Coombs-Phi	13
Johnson-Was	8
Ford-NY	8
Walsh-Chi	7

Saves
Walsh-Chi	5
Browning-Det	3

Innings Pitched
Johnson-Was	374.0
Walsh-Chi	369.2
Coombs-Phi	353.0
Ford-NY	299.2
Morgan-Phi	290.2

Fewest Hits/Game
Ford-NY	5.83
Walsh-Chi	5.89
Coombs-Phi	6.32
Johnson-Was	6.47
Bender-Phi	6.55

Fewest BB/Game
Walsh-Chi	1.49
Young-Cle	1.49
Collins-Bos	1.51
Bender-Phi	1.69
Johnson-Was	1.83

Strikeouts
Johnson-Was	313
Walsh-Chi	258
Coombs-Phi	224
Ford-NY	209
Bender-Phi	155

Strikeouts/Game
Johnson-Was	7.53
Wood-Bos	6.57
Walsh-Chi	6.28
Ford-NY	6.28
Coombs-Phi	5.71

Ratio
Walsh-Chi	7.47
Ford-NY	8.17
Bender-Phi	8.60
Johnson-Was	8.61
Collins-Bos	9.09

Earned Run Average
Walsh-Chi	1.27
Coombs-Phi	1.30
Johnson-Was	1.35
Morgan-Phi	1.55
Bender-Phi	1.58

Adjusted ERA
Walsh-Chi	189
Johnson-Was	185
Coombs-Phi	182
Ford-NY	161
Collins-Bos	157

Opponents' Batting Avg.
Walsh-Chi	.187
Ford-NY	.188
Coombs-Phi	.201
Hall-Bos	.207
Bender-Phi	.207

Opponents' On Base Pct.
Walsh-Chi	.226
Ford-NY	.245
Bender-Phi	.255
Johnson-Was	.262
Collins-Bos	.264

Starter Runs
Walsh-Chi	51.3
Johnson-Was	48.5
Coombs-Phi	47.7
Morgan-Phi	31.2
Ford-NY	28.8

Adjusted Starter Runs
Johnson-Was	47.4
Walsh-Chi	46.3
Coombs-Phi	41.9
Ford-NY	33.4
Morgan-Phi	26.5

Clutch Pitching Index
Morgan-Phi	142
Olmstead-Chi	142
Vaughn-NY	121
Wood-Bos	117
Coombs-Phi	114

Relief Runs

Adjusted Relief Runs

Relief Ranking

Total Pitcher Index
Walsh-Chi	7.0
Johnson-Was	5.2
Coombs-Phi	4.5
Ford-NY	4.0
Bender-Phi	3.6

Total Baseball Ranking
Lajoie-Cle	8.0
Cobb-Det	7.2
Walsh-Chi	7.0
Collins-Phi	6.4
Speaker-Bos	5.6

TEAM	G	W	L	PCT	GB	R	OR	AB	H	2B	3B	HR	BB	SO	AVG	OBP	SLG	PRO	PRO+	BR	/A	PF	CHI	RC	SB	CS	SBA	SBR
NY	154	99	54	.647		756	542	5006	1399	225	103	41	530	506	.279	.358	.390	.748	112	109	88	103	96	820	347			
CHI	157	92	62	.597	7.5	757	607	5130	1335	218	101	54	585	617	.260	.341	.374	.715	106	44	42	100	102	729	214			
PIT	155	85	69	.552	14.5	744	557	5137	1345	206	106	49	525	583	.262	.336	.372	.708	101	28	2	104	104	698	160			
PHI	153	79	73	.520	19.5	658	669	5044	1307	214	56	60	490	588	.259	.328	.359	.687	97	-10	-18	101	100	647	153			
STL	158	75	74	.503	22	671	745	5132	1295	199	85	26	592	650	.252	.337	.339	.676	98	-17	1	97	99	651	175			
CIN	159	70	83	.458	29	682	706	5291	1379	180	105	21	578	594	.261	.337	.346	.683	101	-9	16	96	97	716	289			
BRO	154	64	86	.427	33.5	539	659	5059	1198	151	71	28	425	683	.237	.301	.311	.612	80	-151	-123	96	105	528	184			
BOS	156	44	107	.291	54	699	1021	5308	1417	249	54	37	554	577	.267	.340	.355	.695	93	10	-47	108	98	696	169			
TOT	623					5506		41107	10675	1642	681	316	4279	4798	.260	.335	.356	.691							1691			

TEAM	CG	SH	SV	IP	H	H/G	HR	BB	SO	RAT	ERA	ERA+	OAV	OOB	PR	/A	PF	CPI	FA	E	DP	FW	PW	BW	SBW	DIF
NY	95	19	13	1368	1267	8.3	33	369	771	11.0	2.69	125	.246	.300	106	99	99	97	.959	256	86	.5	9.9	8.8		3.2
CHI	85	12	16	1411	1270	8.1	26	525	582	11.7	2.90	114	.245	.320	77	61	97	100	.960	260	114	.6	6.1	4.2		4.1
PIT	91	13	11	1380[1]	1249	8.1	36	375	605	10.8	2.84	121	.248	.305	85	87	101	97	.963	232	131	2.1	8.7	.2		-3.0
PHI	90	20	10	1373[1]	1285	8.4	43	598	697	12.7	3.30	104	.254	.340	14	19	101	104	.963	231	113	1.9	1.9	-1.8		1.0
STL	88	6	10	1402[1]	1296	8.3	39	701	561	13.2	3.68	91	.253	.349	-45	-51	99	97	.960	261	106	.6	-5.1	.1		4.9
CIN	77	4	12	1425	1410	8.9	36	476	557	12.3	3.26	101	.264	.332	20	4	97	103	.955	295	108	-1.4	.4	1.6		-7.1
BRO	81	13	10	1371[2]	1310	8.6	27	566	533	12.6	3.39	98	.263	.343	0	-12	98	103	.962	241	112	1.4	-1.2	-12.4		1.1
BOS	73	5	7	1374	1570	10.3	76	672	486	15.1	5.08	75	.296	.381	-258	-195	113	96	.947	347	110	-5.0	-19.6	-4.7		-2.2
TOT	680	92	89	11105[2]		8.6				12.4	3.39		.260	.335					.958	2123	880					

Runs		Hits		Doubles		Triples		Home Runs		Total Bases	
Sheckard-Chi	121	Miller-Bos	192	Konetchy-StL	38	Doyle-NY	25	Schulte-Chi	21	Schulte-Chi	308
Huggins-StL	106	Hoblitzel-Cin	180	Miller-Bos	36	Mitchell-Cin	22	Luderus-Phi	16	Doyle-NY	277
Bescher-Cin	106	Daubert-Bro	176	Wilson-Pit	34	Schulte-Chi	21	Magee-Phi	15	Luderus-Phi	260
Schulte-Chi	105	Schulte-Chi	173	Herzog-Bos-NY	33	Zimmerman-Chi	17	Doyle-NY	13	Hoblitzel-Cin	258
Doyle-NY	102	Luderus-Phi	166	Sweeney-Bos	33	Byrne-Pit	17			Wilson-Pit	257

Runs Batted In		Runs Produced		Bases On Balls		Batting Average		On Base Percentage		Slugging Average	
Wilson-Pit	107	Schulte-Chi	191	Sheckard-Chi	147	Wagner-Pit	.334	Sheckard-Chi	.434	Schulte-Chi	.534
Schulte-Chi	107	Konetchy-StL	172	Bates-Cin	103	Miller-Bos	.333	Wagner-Pit	.423	Doyle-NY	.527
Luderus-Phi	99	Wilson-Pit	167	Bescher-Cin	102	Sweeney-Bos	.314	Bates-Cin	.415	Wagner-Pit	.507
Magee-Phi	94	Wagner-Pit	167	Huggins-StL	96	Doyle-NY	.310	Sweeney-Bos	.404	Magee-Phi	.483
		Sheckard-Chi	167	Knabe-Phi	94	Daubert-Bro	.307	Doyle-NY	.397	Wilson-Pit	.472

Production		Adjusted Production		Batter Runs		Adjusted Batter Runs		Clutch Hitting Index		Runs Created	
Wagner-Pit	.930	Schulte-Chi	155	Schulte-Chi	40.6	Schulte-Chi	40.4	Hofman-Chi	155	Schulte-Chi	127
Doyle-NY	.924	Wagner-Pit	154	Doyle-NY	39.3	Doyle-NY	37.0	Miller-Pit	138	Doyle-NY	124
Schulte-Chi	.918	Doyle-NY	153	Wagner-Pit	38.8	Wagner-Pit	36.4	Grant-Cin	136	Bescher-Cin	114
Magee-Phi	.849	Magee-Phi	135	Sheckard-Chi	31.7	Sheckard-Chi	31.6	Mitchell-Cin	130	Wagner-Pit	109
Wilson-Pit	.826	Konetchy-StL	132	Clarke-Pit	27.0	Bates-Cin	26.6	Magee-Phi	130	Miller-Bos	107

Total Average		Stolen Bases		Stolen Base Average		Stolen Base Runs		Fielding Runs		Total Player Rating	
Doyle-NY	1.077	Bescher-Cin	80					Tinker-Chi	23.4	Sheckard-Chi	4.3
Wagner-Pit	1.057	Devore-NY	61					Doolan-Phi	20.3	Wagner-Pit	4.2
Schulte-Chi	1.015	Snodgrass-NY	51					Herzog-Bos-NY	17.8	Herzog-Bos-NY	3.2
Sheckard-Chi	1.003	Merkle-NY	49					Ingerton-Bos	17.8	Tinker-Chi	2.6
Bates-Cin	.943							Sheckard-Chi	17.1	Schulte-Chi	2.6

Wins		Win Percentage		Games		Complete Games		Shutouts		Saves	
Alexander-Phi	28	Marquard-NY	.774	Brown-Chi	53	Alexander-Phi	31	Alexander-Phi	7	Brown-Chi	13
Mathewson-NY	26	Crandall-NY	.750	Harmon-StL	51	Mathewson-NY	29	Adams-Pit	6	Crandall-NY	5
Marquard-NY	24	Cole-Chi	.720	Rucker-Bro	48	Harmon-StL	28				
Harmon-StL	23	Alexander-Phi	.683	Alexander-Phi	48	Leifield-Pit	26				
		Mathewson-NY	.667			Adams-Pit	24				

Innings Pitched		Fewest Hits/Game		Fewest BB/Game		Strikeouts		Strikeouts/Game		Ratio	
Alexander-Phi	367.0	Alexander-Phi	6.99	Mathewson-NY	1.11	Marquard-NY	237	Marquard-NY	7.68	Adams-Pit	9.30
Harmon-StL	348.0	Marquard-NY	7.16	Adams-Pit	1.29	Alexander-Phi	227	Alexander-Phi	5.57	Ames-NY	10.01
Leifield-Pit	318.0	Rucker-Bro	7.27	Steele-Pit-Bro	1.71	Rucker-Bro	190	Rucker-Bro	5.42	Mathewson-NY	10.03
Rucker-Bro	315.2	Ames-NY	7.46	Brown-Chi	1.83	Moore-Phi	174	Ames-NY	5.18	Steele-Pit-Bro	10.33
Moore-Phi	308.1	Harmon-StL	7.50	Wiltse-NY	1.87	Harmon-StL	144	Moore-Phi	5.08	Alexander-Phi	10.35

Earned Run Average		Adjusted ERA		Opponents' Batting Avg.		Opponents' On Base Pct.		Starter Runs		Adjusted Starter Runs	
Mathewson-NY	1.99	Mathewson-NY	168	Alexander-Phi	.219	Adams-Pit	.271	Mathewson-NY	47.7	Mathewson-NY	46.4
Richie-Chi	2.31	Adams-Pit	147	Marquard-NY	.219	Ames-NY	.277	Adams-Pit	34.5	Adams-Pit	35.5
Adams-Pit	2.33	Richie-Chi	143	Ames-NY	.223	Mathewson-NY	.283	Alexander-Phi	33.3	Alexander-Phi	34.9
Marquard-NY	2.50	Marquard-NY	134	Rucker-Bro	.226	Wiltse-NY	.292	Richie-Chi	30.3	Leifield-Pit	27.9
Alexander-Phi	2.57	Alexander-Phi	133	Keefe-Cin	.229	Alexander-Phi	.293	Marquard-NY	27.6	Richie-Chi	27.8

Clutch Pitching Index		Relief Runs		Adjusted Relief Runs		Relief Ranking		Total Pitcher Index		Total Baseball Ranking	
Moore-Phi	130	Richter-Chi	1.6	Richter-Chi	1.1	Richter-Chi	.8	Mathewson-NY	5.9	Mathewson-NY	5.9
Mathewson-NY	122							Leifield-Pit	3.6	Sheckard-Chi	4.3
Richie-Chi	119							Alexander-Phi	3.4	Wagner-Pit	4.2
Leifield-Pit	117							Adams-Pit	3.4	Leifield-Pit	3.6
Gaspar-Cin	115							Crandall-NY	2.7	Alexander-Phi	3.4

TEAM	G	W	L	PCT	GB	R	OR	AB	H	2B	3B	HR	BB	SO	AVG	OBP	SLG	PRO	PRO+	BR	/A	PF	CHI	RC	SB	CS	SBA	SBR
PHI	152	101	50	.669		861	601	5199	1540	237	93	35	424		.296	.357	.398	.755	119	108	121	98	104	821	226			
DET	154	89	65	.578	13.5	831	776	5294	1544	230	96	30	471		.292	.355	.388	.743	107	91	54	105	102	825	276			
CLE	156	80	73	.523	22	691	712	5321	1501	238	81	20	354		.282	.333	.369	.702	100	1	-7	101	97	716	209			
CHI	154	77	74	.510	24	719	624	5213	1401	179	92	20	385		.269	.325	.350	.675	97	-45	-22	97	108	659	201			
BOS	153	78	75	.510	24	680	643	5014	1379	203	66	35	506		.275	.350	.363	.713	105	39	45	99	91	710	190			
NY	153	76	76	.500	25.5	684	724	5052	1374	190	96	25	493		.272	.344	.362	.706	96	24	-21	107	94	724	269			
WAS	154	64	90	.416	38.5	625	766	5065	1308	159	54	16	466		.258	.330	.320	.650	88	-74	-60	98	100	607	215			
STL	152	45	107	.296	56.5	567	812	4996	1192	187	63	17	460		.239	.307	.311	.618	81	-141	-114	96	105	515	125			
TOT	614					5658		41154	11239	1623	641	198	3559	5093	.273	.338	.358	.696							1711			

TEAM	CG	SH	SV	IP	H	H/G	HR	BB	SO	RAT	ERA	ERA+	OAV	OOB	PR	/A	PF	CPI	FA	E	DP	FW	PW	BW	SBW	DIF
PHI	97	13	13	1375²	1343	8.8	17	487	739	12.5	3.01	105	.263	.337	50	20	94	106	.964	225	100	4.9	2.0	11.9		6.8
DET	108	8	3	1387²	1514	9.8	28	460	538	13.3	3.73	93	.283	.347	-60	-44	104	97	.951	318	78	-1.0	-4.3	5.3		12.0
CLE	93	6	6	1390²	1376	8.9	16	550	673	12.9	3.36	101	.265	.344	-3	7	102	99	.954	302	108	.3	.7	-.7		3.2
CHI	87	17	11	1386¹	1349	8.8	22	384	752	11.5	2.97	108	.255	.309	57	37	96	88	.961	252	98	3.4	3.6	-2.2		-3.3
BOS	87	10	8	1351²	1314	8.7	21	475	713	12.2	2.74	119	.263	.333	89	78	98	114	.949	323	93	-1.4	7.7	4.4		-9.2
NY	91	5	3	1360²	1404	9.3	26	406	667	12.3	3.54	101	.269	.328	-30	9	108	89	.949	328	99	-1.7	.9	-2.1		2.9
WAS	106	13	3	1354¹	1471	9.8	39	410	628	12.8	3.52	93	.276	.334	-26	-37	98	96	.953	305	90	-.1	-3.6	-5.9		-3.4
STL	92	8	1	1332²	1465	9.9	29	463	383	13.4	3.86	87	.277	.342	-76	-73	101	90	.945	358	104	-3.8	-7.2	-11.2		-8.8
TOT	761	80	48	10939¹		9.2				12.6	3.34		.273	.338					.953	2411	770					

Runs
Cobb-Det 147
Jackson-Cle 126
Bush-Det 126
Milan-Was 109
Crawford-Det 109

Hits
Cobb-Det 248
Jackson-Cle 233
Crawford-Det 217
Baker-Phi 198
Milan-Was 194

Doubles
Cobb-Det 47
Jackson-Cle 45
Baker-Phi 42
Lord-Phi 37
LaPorte-StL 37

Triples
Cobb-Det 24
Cree-NY 22
Jackson-Cle 19
Lord-Chi 18
Wolter-NY 15

Home Runs
Baker-Phi 11
Speaker-Bos 8
Cobb-Det 8

Total Bases
Cobb-Det 367
Jackson-Cle 337
Crawford-Det 302
Baker-Phi 301
Cree-NY 267

Runs Batted In
Cobb-Det 127
Crawford-Det 115
Baker-Phi 115
Bodie-Chi 97
Delahanty-Det 94

Runs Produced
Cobb-Det 266
Crawford-Det 217
Jackson-Cle 202
Baker-Phi 200

Bases On Balls
Bush-Det 98
Milan-Was 74
Gessler-Was 74
Hooper-Bos 73
Austin-StL 69

Batting Average
Cobb-Det .... .420
Jackson-Cle ...... .408
Crawford-Det ..... .378
Collins-Phi .... .365
Cree-NY .... .348

On Base Percentage
Jackson-Cle ...... .468
Cobb-Det .... .467
Collins-Phi .... .451
Crawford-Det ..... .438
Speaker-Bos ...... .418

Slugging Average
Cobb-Det .... .621
Jackson-Cle ...... .590
Crawford-Det ..... .526
Cree-NY .... .513
Baker-Phi .... .508

Production
Cobb-Det 1.088
Jackson-Cle 1.058
Crawford-Det ..... .964
Collins-Phi .... .932
Cree-NY .... .928

Adjusted Production
Cobb-Det 193
Jackson-Cle 192
Collins-Phi 163
Crawford-Det 160
Speaker-Bos 158

Batter Runs
Cobb-Det 78.4
Jackson-Cle 71.8
Crawford-Det 52.4
Collins-Phi 43.0
Cree-NY 39.9

Adjusted Batter Runs
Cobb-Det 74.4
Jackson-Cle 70.8
Crawford-Det 48.4
Collins-Phi 44.3
Speaker-Bos 39.0

Clutch Hitting Index
Stovall-Cle 176
Hartzell-NY 153
Bodie-Chi 147
McBride-Was 141
Gessler-Was 141

Runs Created
Cobb-Det 207
Jackson-Cle 175
Crawford-Det 147
Cree-NY 129
Baker-Phi 127

Total Average
Cobb-Det 1.464
Jackson-Cle 1.308
Collins-Phi 1.125
Crawford-Det ... 1.120
Cree-NY 1.103

Stolen Bases
Cobb-Det 83
Milan-Was 58
Cree-NY 48
Callahan-Chi 45
Lord-Chi 43

Stolen Base Average

Stolen Base Runs

Fielding Runs
Tannehill-Chi 42.5
Gardner-Bos 23.7
McBride-Was 23.5
Bush-Det 16.7
Austin-StL 16.3

Total Player Rating
Cobb-Det 7.0
Jackson-Cle 6.5
Collins-Phi 4.5
Baker-Phi 3.4
Speaker-Bos 3.3

Wins
Coombs-Phi 28
Walsh-Chi 27
Johnson-Was 25

Win Percentage
Bender-Phi ...... .773
Gregg-Cle .... .767
Plank-Phi .... .742
Coombs-Phi ..... .700
Morgan-Phi ..... .682

Games
Walsh-Chi 56
Coombs-Phi 47
Wood-Bos 44
Caldwell-NY 41

Complete Games
Johnson-Was 36
Walsh-Chi 33
Ford-NY 26
Coombs-Phi 26

Shutouts
Plank-Phi 6
Johnson-Was 6
Wood-Bos 5
Walsh-Chi 5
Gregg-Cle 5

Saves
Walsh-Chi 4
Plank-Phi 4
Hall-Bos 4
Wood-Bos 3
Bender-Phi 3

Innings Pitched
Walsh-Chi 368.2
Coombs-Phi 336.2
Johnson-Was ... 323.1
Ford-NY 281.1
Wood-Bos 275.2

Fewest Hits/Game
Gregg-Cle 6.33
Wood-Bos 7.38
Krapp-Cle 7.62
Morgan-Phi 7.82
Scott-Chi 7.91

Fewest BB/Game
White-Chi 1.47
Lake-StL 1.67
Walsh-Chi 1.76
Warhop-NY 1.89
Powell-StL 1.91

Strikeouts
Walsh-Chi 255
Wood-Bos 231
Johnson-Was 207
Coombs-Phi 185
Ford-NY 158

Strikeouts/Game
Wood-Bos 7.54
Walsh-Chi 6.23
Lange-Chi 5.79
Johnson-Was ... 5.76
Kahler-Cle 5.66

Ratio
Gregg-Cle 9.86
Walsh-Chi 9.91
Wood-Bos 10.22
Johnson-Was .. 10.30
Ford-NY 10.59

Earned Run Average
Gregg-Cle 1.80
Johnson-Was ... 1.89
Wood-Bos 2.02
Plank-Phi 2.10
Bender-Phi 2.16

Adjusted ERA
Gregg-Cle 189
Johnson-Was 173
Wood-Bos 162
Ford-NY 158
Plank-Phi 149

Opponents' Batting Avg.
Gregg-Cle ...... .205
Wood-Bos ...... .223
Krapp-Cle ...... .232
Ford-NY .... .237
Johnson-Was ... .238

Opponents' On Base Pct.
Walsh-Chi ...... .280
Johnson-Was ... .283
Wood-Bos ...... .284
Gregg-Cle ...... .286
Ford-NY .... .291

Starter Runs
Johnson-Was ... 51.9
Walsh-Chi 45.8
Gregg-Cle 41.8
Wood-Bos 40.3
Plank-Phi 35.2

Adjusted Starter Runs
Johnson-Was ... 49.8
Gregg-Cle 43.7
Ford-NY 41.2
Walsh-Chi 40.8
Wood-Bos 38.2

Clutch Pitching Index
Plank-Phi 133
Pape-Bos 130
Cicotte-Bos 122
Bender-Phi 117
Willett-Det 111

Relief Runs

Adjusted Relief Runs

Relief Ranking

Total Pitcher Index
Johnson-Was 5.9
Walsh-Chi 5.4
Wood-Bos 4.9
Gregg-Cle 4.2
Ford-NY 4.0

Total Baseball Ranking
Cobb-Det 7.0
Jackson-Cle 6.5
Johnson-Was 5.9
Walsh-Chi 5.4
Wood-Bos 4.9

TEAM	G	W	L	PCT	GB	R	OR	AB	H	2B	3B	HR	BB	SO	AVG	OBP	SLG	PRO	PRO+	BR	/A	PF	CHI	RC	SB	CS	SBA	SBR
NY	154	103	48	.682		823	571	5067	1451	231	89	47	514	497	.286	.360	.395	.755	109	89	67	103	104	830	319			
PIT	152	93	58	.616	10	751	565	5252	1493	222	129	39	420	514	.284	.340	.398	.738	109	44	55	98	99	767	177			
CHI	152	91	59	.607	11.5	756	668	5048	1398	245	90	43	560	615	.277	.354	.387	.741	109	62	64	100	98	750	164			
CIN	155	75	78	.490	29	656	722	5115	1310	183	89	21	479	492	.256	.323	.339	.662	89	-89	-67	97	107	639	248			
PHI	152	73	79	.480	30.5	670	688	5077	1354	244	68	43	464	615	.267	.332	.367	.699	90	-22	-67	107	99	671	159			
STL	153	63	90	.412	41	659	830	5092	1366	190	77	27	508	620	.268	.340	.352	.692	97	-26	-9	98	97	675	193			
BRO	153	58	95	.379	46	651	754	5141	1377	220	73	32	490	584	.268	.336	.358	.694	99	-27	0	96	96	677	179			
BOS	155	52	101	.340	52	693	861	5361	1465	227	68	35	454	690	.273	.335	.361	.696	94	-27	-39	102	99	693	137			
TOT	613					5659		41153	11214	1762	683	287	3889	4627	.272	.340	.369	.710							1576			

TEAM	CG	SH	SV	IP	H	H/G	HR	BB	SO	RAT	ERA	ERA+	OAV	OOB	PR	/A	PF	CPI	FA	E	DP	FW	PW	BW	SBW	DIF
NY	93	8	15	1369²	1352	8.9	36	338	652	11.3	2.58	130	.252	.300	124	118	99	94	.956	280	123	-2.1	11.6	6.6		11.4
PIT	94	18	7	1385	1268	8.2	28	497	664	11.8	2.85	114	.243	.315	84	59	96	90	.972	169	125	6.0	5.8	5.4		.3
CHI	80	15	9	1358²	1307	8.7	33	493	554	12.2	3.42	97	.250	.320	-3	-18	98	80	.960	249	125	-.0	-1.8	6.3		11.5
CIN	86	13	10	1377²	1455	9.5	28	452	561	12.9	3.42	98	.269	.333	-3	-13	99	93	.960	249	102	.4	-1.3	-6.6		6.0
PHI	82	10	9	1355	1381	9.2	43	515	616	12.9	3.25	111	.264	.335	22	53	106	100	.963	231	98	1.3	5.2	-6.6		-3.0
STL	62	6	12	1353	1466	9.8	31	560	487	13.7	3.85	89	.275	.348	-68	-63	101	93	.957	274	113	-1.8	-6.2	-.9		-4.7
BRO	71	10	8	1357	1399	9.3	45	510	553	12.9	3.64	92	.264	.332	-36	-48	98	88	.959	255	96	-.3	-4.7	.0		-13.4
BOS	92	5	5	1390²	1544	10.0	43	521	542	13.6	4.17	86	.280	.347	-118	-98	105	87	.954	297	129	-3.2	-9.6	-3.8		-7.8
TOT	660	85	75	10946²		9.2				12.7	3.40		.272	.340					.960	2004	911					

Runs
Bescher-Cin 120
Carey-Pit 114
Paskert-Phi 102
Campbell-Bos 102

Hits
Zimmerman-Chi . . 207
Sweeney-Bos 204
Campbell-Bos 185
Doyle-NY 184
Wagner-Pit 181

Doubles
Zimmerman-Chi . . . 41
Paskert-Phi 37
Wagner-Pit 35
Miller-Pit 33
Doyle-NY 33

Triples
Wilson-Pit 36
Wagner-Pit 20
Murray-NY 20
Daubert-Bro 16

Home Runs
Zimmerman-Chi . . . 14
Schulte-Chi 12
Wilson-Pit 11
Merkle-NY 11
Cravath-Phi 11

Total Bases
Zimmerman-Chi . . 318
Wilson-Pit 299
Wagner-Pit 277
Sweeney-Bos 264
Doyle-NY 263

Runs Batted In
Wagner-Pit 102
Sweeney-Bos 100
Zimmerman-Chi . . . 99
Wilson-Pit 95
Murray-NY 92

Runs Produced
Wagner-Pit 186
Sweeney-Bos 183
Zimmerman-Chi . . 180
Doyle-NY 178
Carey-Pit 175

Bases On Balls
Sheckard-Chi 122
Paskert-Phi 91
Huggins-StL 87
Bescher-Cin 83
Titus-Phi-Bos 82

Batting Average
Zimmerman-Chi . .372
Sweeney-Bos 344
Evers-Chi 341
Doyle-NY 330
Wagner-Pit 324

On Base Percentage
Evers-Chi 431
Huggins-StL 422
Paskert-Phi 420
Zimmerman-Chi . .418
Sweeney-Bos 416

Slugging Average
Zimmerman-Chi . .571
Wilson-Pit 513
Wagner-Pit 496
Doyle-NY 471
Cravath-Phi 470

Production
Zimmerman-Chi . .989
Wagner-Pit 891
Evers-Chi 873
Doyle-NY 864
Titus-Phi-Bos 862

Adjusted Production
Zimmerman-Chi . . 169
Wagner-Pit 145
Evers-Chi 139
Wilson-Pit 134
Konetchy-StL 134

Batter Runs
Zimmerman-Chi . . 49.8
Wagner-Pit 32.1
Sweeney-Bos 30.9
Evers-Chi 29.1
Meyers-NY 28.2

Adjusted Batter Runs
Zimmerman-Chi . . 50.0
Wagner-Pit 33.3
Sweeney-Bos 29.5
Evers-Chi 29.3
Meyers-NY 26.7

Clutch Hitting Index
Murray-NY 139
Miller-Pit 131
Mitchell-Cin 127
Tinker-Chi 126
Mowrey-StL 123

Runs Created
Zimmerman-Chi . . 141
Sweeney-Bos 123
Wagner-Pit 118
Doyle-NY 116
Paskert-Phi 108

Total Average
Zimmerman-Chi . 1.100
Wagner-Pit 976
Paskert-Phi 965
Evers-Chi 962
Doyle-NY 955

Stolen Bases
Bescher-Cin 67
Carey-Pit 45
Snodgrass-NY 43
Murray-NY 38

Stolen Base Average

Stolen Base Runs

Fielding Runs
Sweeney-Bos 26.9
Tinker-Chi 24.7
Wagner-Pit 22.9
Herzog-NY 19.2
Fletcher-NY 15.8

Total Player Rating
Wagner-Pit 6.7
Zimmerman-Chi . . . 5.0
Sweeney-Bos 4.9
Evers-Chi 3.0
Tinker-Chi 2.7

Wins
Marquard-NY 26
Cheney-Chi 26
Hendrix-Pit 24
Mathewson-NY . . . 23
Camnitz-Pit 22

Win Percentage
Hendrix-Pit 727
Cheney-Chi 722
Tesreau-NY 708
Marquard-NY 703
Richie-Chi 667

Games
Benton-Cin 50
Sallee-StL 48
Alexander-Phi 46
Rucker-Bro 45
Seaton-Phi 44

Complete Games
Cheney-Chi 28
Mathewson-NY . . . 27
Alexander-Phi 26
Suggs-Cin 25
Hendrix-Pit 25

Shutouts
Rucker-Bro 6
Suggs-Cin 5
O'Toole-Pit 5

Saves
Sallee-StL 6
Rucker-Bro 4
Reulbach-Chi 4
Mathewson-NY 4

Innings Pitched
Alexander-Phi . . . 310.1
Mathewson-NY . . 310.0
Cheney-Chi 303.1
Suggs-Cin 303.0
Benton-Cin 302.0

Fewest Hits/Game
Tesreau-NY 6.56
Robinson-Pit 7.51
O'Toole-Pit 7.75
Cheney-Chi 7.77
Brown-Bos 7.81

Fewest BB/Game
Mathewson-NY 99
Robinson-Pit 1.54
Suggs-Cin 1.66
Ames-NY 1.76
Adams-Pit 1.85

Strikeouts
Alexander-Phi 195
Hendrix-Pit 176
Marquard-NY 175
Benton-Cin 162
Rucker-Bro 151

Strikeouts/Game
Alexander-Phi 5.66
Hendrix-Pit 5.49
Marquard-NY 5.35
Tyler-Bos 5.06
O'Toole-Pit 4.90

Ratio
Robinson-Pit 9.57
Mathewson-NY . . 10.07
Rucker-Bro 10.49
Tesreau-NY 10.85
Adams-Pit 10.94

Earned Run Average
Tesreau-NY 1.96
Mathewson-NY . . . 2.12
Rucker-Bro 2.21
Robinson-Pit 2.26
Ames-NY 2.46

Adjusted ERA
Tesreau-NY 172
Mathewson-NY . . . 159
Rucker-Bro 151
Rixey-Phi 145
Robinson-Pit 144

Opponents' Batting Avg.
Tesreau-NY 199
Cheney-Chi 228
Brown-Bos 228
Robinson-Pit 230
O'Toole-Pit 235

Opponents' On Base Pct.
Mathewson-NY . . .275
Robinson-Pit 276
Rucker-Bro 289
Tesreau-NY 292
Adams-Pit 294

Starter Runs
Mathewson-NY . . 44.1
Rucker-Bro 39.4
Tesreau-NY 38.8
Marquard-NY 27.3
Sallee-StL 26.0

Adjusted Starter Runs
Mathewson-NY . . 43.0
Tesreau-NY 37.9
Rucker-Bro 37.4
Alexander-Phi . . . 27.7
Sallee-StL 26.6

Clutch Pitching Index
Ames-NY 117
Geyer-StL 112
Benton-Cin 108
Yingling-Bro 107
O'Toole-Pit 106

Relief Runs

Adjusted Relief Runs

Relief Ranking

Total Pitcher Index
Mathewson-NY 5.1
Rucker-Bro 4.3
Hendrix-Pit 4.1
Tesreau-NY 3.8
Alexander-Phi 2.9

Total Baseball Ranking
Wagner-Pit 6.7
Mathewson-NY 5.1
Zimmerman-Chi . . . 4.9
Sweeney-Bos 4.9
Rucker-Bro 4.3

TEAM	G	W	L	PCT	GB	R	OR	AB	H	2B	3B	HR	BB	SO	AVG	OBP	SLG	PRO	PRO+	BR	/A	PF	CHI	RC	SB	CS	SBA	SBR
BOS	154	105	47	.691		799	544	5071	1404	269	84	29	565		.277	.355	.380	.735	110	104	69	105	100	752	185			
WAS	154	91	61	.599	14	698	581	5075	1298	202	86	20	472		.256	.324	.341	.665	94	-31	-35	101	108	645	274			
PHI	153	90	62	.592	15	779	658	5111	1442	204	108	22	485		.282	.349	.377	.726	117	83	108	96	101	763	258			
CHI	158	78	76	.506	28	638	646	5182	1321	174	80	17	423		.255	.317	.329	.646	92	-67	-45	97	102	610	205			
CLE	155	75	78	.490	30.5	676	680	5133	1403	219	77	12	407		.273	.353	.353	.686	97	5	-16	103	98	671	194			
DET	154	69	84	.451	36.5	720	777	5143	1376	189	86	19	530		.268	.343	.349	.692	106	26	48	97	100	705	270			
STL	157	53	101	.344	53	552	764	5080	1262	166	71	19	449		.248	.315	.320	.635	90	-85	-60	96	94	565	176			
NY	153	50	102	.329	55	630	842	5092	1320	168	79	18	463		.259	.329	.334	.663	89	-31	-71	106	97	638	247			
TOT	619					5492		40887	10826	1591	671	156	3794	5150	.265	.333	.348	.681						1809				

TEAM	CG	SH	SV	IP	H	H/G	HR	BB	SO	RAT	ERA	ERA+	OAV	OOB	PR	/A	PF	CPI	FA	E	DP	FW	PW	BW	SBW	DIF
BOS	108	18	6	1362	1243	8.2	18	385	712	11.0	2.76	124	.247	.305	88	103	102	98	.957	267	88	2.4	10.3	6.9		9.4
WAS	98	11	7	1375²	1219	8.0	24	525	828	11.8	2.70	124	.241	.319	98	104	100	108	.954	297	92	.7	10.4	-3.5		7.5
PHI	95	11	9	1357	1273	8.4	12	518	601	12.3	3.32	93	.258	.336	2	-31	93	99	.959	263	115	2.5	-3.1	10.8		3.8
CHI	85	14	16	1413	1397	8.9	26	426	697	11.8	3.06	105	.263	.322	44	26	96	104	.956	291	102	1.5	2.6	-4.5		1.4
CLE	94	7	7	1352²	1367	9.1	15	523	622	12.9	3.30	104	.271	.345	5	21	103	110	.954	287	124	1.4	2.1	-1.6		-3.4
DET	107	7	5	1367¹	1424	9.4	16	517	506	13.2	3.77	87	.274	.346	-65	-70	98	98	.950	338	91	-1.7	-7.0	4.8		-3.6
STL	85	8	5	1369²	1433	9.4	17	442	547	12.7	3.71	90	.276	.340	-55	-54	100	97	.947	341	127	-1.6	-5.4	-6.0		-11.1
NY	105	5	3	1335	1448	9.8	28	436	637	13.0	4.13	88	.282	.343	-116	-70	108	92	.940	382	77	-4.4	-7.0	-7.1		-7.5
TOT	777	81	58	10932¹		8.9				12.3	3.34		.265	.333					.952	2466	816					

Runs
Collins-Phi 137
Speaker-Bos 136
Jackson-Cle 121
Cobb-Det 119
Baker-Phi 116

Hits
Cobb-Det 227
Jackson-Cle 226
Speaker-Bos 222
Baker-Phi 200

Doubles
Speaker-Bos 53
Jackson-Cle 44
Baker-Phi 40
Lewis-Bos 36

Triples
Jackson-Cle 26
Cobb-Det 23
Crawford-Det 21
Baker-Phi 21
Gardner-Bos 18

Home Runs
Speaker-Bos 10
Baker-Phi 10
Cobb-Det 7

Total Bases
Jackson-Cle 331
Speaker-Bos 329
Cobb-Det 324
Baker-Phi 312
Crawford-Det 273

Runs Batted In
Baker-Phi 130
Lewis-Bos 109
Crawford-Det 109
McInnis-Phi 101

Runs Produced
Baker-Phi 236
Speaker-Bos 216
Jackson-Cle 208
Collins-Phi 201
Cobb-Det 195

Bases On Balls
Bush-Det 117
Collins-Phi 101
Rath-Chi 95
Shotton-StL 86
Speaker-Bos 82

Batting Average
Cobb-Det 410
Jackson-Cle 395
Speaker-Bos 383
Lajoie-Cle 368
Collins-Phi 348

On Base Percentage
Speaker-Bos 464
Jackson-Cle 458
Cobb-Det 458
Collins-Phi 450
Lajoie-Cle 414

Slugging Average
Cobb-Det 586
Jackson-Cle 579
Speaker-Bos 567
Baker-Phi 541
Crawford-Det 470

Production
Cobb-Det 1.043
Jackson-Cle 1.036
Speaker-Bos 1.031
Baker-Phi 945
Collins-Phi 885

Adjusted Production
Cobb-Det 204
Jackson-Cle 190
Speaker-Bos 185
Baker-Phi 176
Collins-Phi 159

Batter Runs
Speaker-Bos 72.8
Jackson-Cle 70.3
Cobb-Det 67.9
Baker-Phi 49.2
Collins-Phi 43.7

Adjusted Batter Runs
Cobb-Det 70.2
Speaker-Bos 68.8
Jackson-Cle 67.8
Baker-Phi 52.0
Collins-Phi 46.7

Clutch Hitting Index
Lewis-Bos 151
Gandil-Was 145
McInnis-Phi 140
Lajoie-Cle 140
Crawford-Det 135

Runs Created
Speaker-Bos 175
Cobb-Det 174
Jackson-Cle 166
Baker-Phi 140
Collins-Phi 136

Total Average
Cobb-Det 1.328
Speaker-Bos 1.310
Jackson-Cle 1.249
Collins-Phi 1.130
Baker-Phi 1.082

Stolen Bases
Milan-Was 88
Collins-Phi 63
Cobb-Det 61
Speaker-Bos 52
Zeider-Chi 47

Stolen Base Average

Stolen Base Runs

Fielding Runs
McBride-Was 31.2
Bush-Det 29.0
Louden-Det 22.5
Speaker-Bos 21.0
Rath-Chi 18.3

Total Player Rating
Speaker-Bos 7.8
Jackson-Cle 6.9
Cobb-Det 6.0
Collins-Phi 5.8
Baker-Phi 5.8

Wins
Wood-Bos 34
Johnson-Was 33
Walsh-Chi 27
Plank-Phi 26
Groom-Was 24

Win Percentage
Wood-Bos 872
Plank-Phi 813
Johnson-Was 733
Bedient-Bos 690
Coombs-Phi 677

Games
Walsh-Chi 62
Johnson-Was 50
Wood-Bos 43
Groom-Was 43
Benz-Chi 42

Complete Games
Wood-Bos 35
Johnson-Was 34
Walsh-Chi 32
Ford-NY 30

Shutouts
Wood-Bos 10
Johnson-Was 7
Walsh-Chi 6
Plank-Phi 5
Collins-Bos 4

Saves
Walsh-Chi 10
Warhop-NY 3
Mogridge-Chi 3
Lange-Chi 3
Dubuc-Det 3

Innings Pitched
Walsh-Chi 393.0
Johnson-Was 368.0
Wood-Bos 344.0
Groom-Was 316.0
Ford-NY 291.2

Fewest Hits/Game
Johnson-Was 6.33
Wood-Bos 6.99
Houck-Phi 7.37
Walsh-Chi 7.60
O'Brien-Bos 7.74

Fewest BB/Game
Bender-Phi 1.74
Johnson-Was 1.86
Collins-Bos 1.90
Powell-StL 1.99
Warhop-NY 2.06

Strikeouts
Johnson-Was 303
Wood-Bos 258
Walsh-Chi 254
Gregg-Cle 184
Groom-Was 179

Strikeouts/Game
Johnson-Was 7.41
Wood-Bos 6.75
Gregg-Cle 6.10
Walsh-Chi 5.82
Lange-Chi 5.23

Ratio
Johnson-Was 8.58
Wood-Bos 9.44
Walsh-Chi 9.78
Bedient-Bos 10.29
Collins-Bos 10.66

Earned Run Average
Johnson-Was 1.39
Wood-Bos 1.91
Walsh-Chi 2.15
Plank-Phi 2.22
Collins-Bos 2.53

Adjusted ERA
Johnson-Was 240
Wood-Bos 179
Walsh-Chi 149
Plank-Phi 140
Collins-Bos 135

Opponents' Batting Avg.
Johnson-Was 196
Wood-Bos 216
Walsh-Chi 231
Houck-Phi 234
Dubuc-Det 235

Opponents' On Base Pct.
Johnson-Was 248
Wood-Bos 272
Walsh-Chi 279
Bedient-Bos 288
Collins-Bos 297

Starter Runs
Johnson-Was 79.5
Wood-Bos 54.6
Walsh-Chi 51.8
Plank-Phi 32.3
Groom-Was 25.2

Adjusted Starter Runs
Johnson-Was 80.0
Wood-Bos 57.7
Walsh-Chi 46.5
O'Brien-Bos 25.7
Groom-Was 25.7

Clutch Pitching Index
Hughes-Was 129
McConnell-NY 121
Cashion-Was 120
Kahler-Cle 120
Plank-Phi 119

Relief Runs

Adjusted Relief Runs

Relief Ranking

Total Pitcher Index
Johnson-Was 9.8
Wood-Bos 8.3
Walsh-Chi 6.0
McConnell-NY 3.1
Plank-Phi 2.8

Total Baseball Ranking
Johnson-Was 9.8
Wood-Bos 8.3
Speaker-Bos 7.8
Jackson-Cle 6.9
Cobb-Det 6.0

TEAM	G	W	L	PCT	GB	R	OR	AB	H	2B	3B	HR	BB	SO	AVG	OBP	SLG	PRO	PRO+	BR	/A	PF	CHI	RC	SB	CS	SBA	SBR
NY	156	101	51	.664		684	515	5218	1427	226	71	30	444	501	.273	.338	.361	.699	105	43	38	101	99	708	296			
PHI	159	88	63	.583	12.5	693	636	5400	1433	257	78	73	383	578	.265	.318	.382	.700	101	29	1	104	100	695	156			
CHI	155	88	65	.575	13.5	720	630	5022	1289	195	96	59	554	634	.257	.335	.369	.704	106	52	50	100	104	683	181			
PIT	155	78	71	.523	21.5	673	585	5252	1383	210	86	35	391	545	.263	.319	.356	.675	103	-12	16	96	106	641	181			
BOS	154	69	82	.457	31.5	641	690	5145	1318	191	60	32	448	640	.256	.326	.335	.661	93	-25	-37	102	103	619	177			
BRO	152	65	84	.436	34.5	595	613	5165	1394	193	86	39	361	555	.270	.321	.363	.684	98	4	-13	103	94	646	188			
CIN	156	64	89	.418	37.5	607	717	5132	1339	170	96	27	458	579	.261	.325	.347	.672	98	-9	-5	100	96	639	226			
STL	153	51	99	.340	49	528	755	4967	1229	152	72	15	451	573	.247	.316	.316	.632	88	-77	-68	99	97	550	171			
TOT	620					5141		41301	10812	1594	645	310	3530	4605	.262	.325	.354	.679							1576			

TEAM	CG	SH	SV	IP	H	H/G	HR	BB	SO	RAT	ERA	ERA+	OAV	OOB	PR	/A	PF	CPI	FA	E	DP	FW	PW	BW	SBW	DIF
NY	82	12	11	1422	1276	8.1	38	315	651	10.2	2.42	128	.243	.288	122	107	97	99	.961	254	107	-.6	11.1	4.0		10.5
PHI	77	20	11	1455¹	1407	8.7	40	512	667	12.1	3.15	106	.260	.329	6	27	104	103	.968	214	112	2.2	2.8	.1		7.4
CHI	89	12	15	1372¹	1330	8.7	39	478	556	12.1	3.13	101	.259	.327	9	5	99	103	.959	260	106	-1.1	.5	5.2		6.9
PIT	74	9	7	1400	1344	8.6	26	434	590	11.6	2.90	104	.259	.320	46	16	94	104	.964	226	94	1.1	1.7	1.7		-.9
BOS	105	13	3	1373¹	1343	8.8	37	419	597	11.8	3.19	103	.263	.324	0	11	103	100	.957	273	82	-2.0	1.1	-3.8		-1.8
BRO	70	9	7	1373	1287	8.4	33	439	548	11.6	3.13	105	.255	.321	10	22	103	97	.961	243	125	-.3	2.3	-1.4		-10.1
CIN	71	10	10	1380	1398	9.1	40	456	522	12.4	3.46	94	.273	.338	-39	-35	101	102	.961	251	104	-.4	-3.6	-.5		-7.9
STL	74	6	11	1351²	1423	9.5	57	476	464	13.0	4.23	76	.279	.346	-155	-151	101	92	.965	219	113	1.3	-15.7	-7.1		-2.5
TOT	642	91	75	11127²		8.7				11.9	3.20		.262	.325					.962	1940	843					

Runs		Hits		Doubles		Triples		Home Runs		Total Bases	
Leach-Chi	99	Cravath-Phi	179	Smith-Bro	40	Saier-Chi	21	Cravath-Phi	19	Cravath-Phi	298
Carey-Pit	99	Daubert-Bro	178	Burns-NY	37	Miller-Pit	20	Luderus-Phi	18	Luderus-Phi	254
Lobert-Phi	98	Burns-NY	173	Magee-Phi	36	Konetchy-StL	17	Saier-Chi	14	Saier-Chi	249
Saier-Chi	94	Lobert-Phi	172	Cravath-Phi	34	Wilson-Pit	14	Magee-Phi	11	Miller-Pit	243
Magee-Phi	92	Carey-Pit	172			Cravath-Phi	14	Wilson-Pit	10	Lobert-Phi	243

Runs Batted In		Runs Produced		Bases On Balls		Batting Average		On Base Percentage		Slugging Average	
Cravath-Phi	128	Cravath-Phi	187	Bescher-Cin	94	Daubert-Bro	.350	Huggins-StL	.432	Cravath-Phi	.568
Zimmerman-Chi	95	Saier-Chi	172	Huggins-StL	92	Cravath-Phi	.341	Cravath-Phi	.407	Zimmerman-Chi	.490
Saier-Chi	92	Miller-Pit	158	Leach-Chi	77	Viox-Pit	.317	Daubert-Bro	.405	Saier-Chi	.480
Miller-Pit	90	Zimmerman-Chi	155	Bridwell-Chi	74	Zimmerman-Chi	.313	Viox-Pit	.399	Magee-Phi	.479
Luderus-Phi	86	Magee-Phi	151			Magee-Phi	.306	Leach-Chi	.391	Smith-Bro	.441

Production		Adjusted Production		Batter Runs		Adjusted Batter Runs		Clutch Hitting Index		Runs Created	
Cravath-Phi	.974	Cravath-Phi	169	Cravath-Phi	50.5	Cravath-Phi	47.8	Zimmerman-Chi	143	Cravath-Phi	124
Zimmerman-Chi	.868	Zimmerman-Chi	147	Saier-Chi	27.5	Viox-Pit	27.7	Doyle-NY	139	Saier-Chi	100
Saier-Chi	.850	Viox-Pit	142	Zimmerman-Chi	26.3	Saier-Chi	27.4	Cravath-Phi	134	Lobert-Phi	94
Magee-Phi	.848	Saier-Chi	141	Daubert-Bro	25.2	Zimmerman-Chi	26.2	Miller-Pit	131	Daubert-Bro	94
Daubert-Bro	.829	Magee-Phi	136	Viox-Pit	24.8	Daubert-Bro	23.5	Murray-NY	123	Smith-Bro	91

Total Average		Stolen Bases		Stolen Base Average		Stolen Base Runs		Fielding Runs		Total Player Rating	
Cravath-Phi	1.058	Carey-Pit	61					Evers-Chi	29.9	Tinker-Cin	3.6
Saier-Chi	.927	Myers-Bos	57					Whitted-StL	22.7	Cravath-Phi	3.5
Zimmerman-Chi	.925	Lobert-Phi	41					Carey-Pit	19.5	Evers-Chi	3.4
Magee-Phi	.905	Burns-NY	40					Magee-StL	18.4	Zimmerman-Chi	2.9
Leach-Chi	.895	Cutshaw-Bro	39					Cutshaw-Bro	17.6	Wagner-Pit	2.8

Wins		Win Percentage		Games		Complete Games		Shutouts		Saves	
Seaton-Phi	27	Humphries-Chi	.800	Cheney-Chi	54	Tyler-Bos	28	Alexander-Phi	9	Cheney-Chi	11
Mathewson-NY	25	Alexander-Phi	.733	Seaton-Phi	52	Mathewson-NY	25	Seaton-Phi	5	Brown-Cin	6
Marquard-NY	23	Marquard-NY	.697	Sallee-StL	50	Cheney-Chi	25			Sallee-StL	5
Tesreau-NY	22	Mathewson-NY	.694	Alexander-Phi	47	Adams-Pit	24				
Alexander-Phi	22	Seaton-Phi	.692	Camnitz-Pit-Phi	45	Alexander-Phi	23				

Innings Pitched		Fewest Hits/Game		Fewest BB/Game		Strikeouts		Strikeouts/Game		Ratio	
Seaton-Phi	322.1	Tesreau-NY	7.09	Mathewson-NY	.62	Seaton-Phi	168	Tesreau-NY	5.33	Mathewson-NY	9.18
Adams-Pit	313.2	Seaton-Phi	7.32	Humphries-Chi	1.19	Tesreau-NY	167	Hendrix-Pit	5.15	Adams-Pit	9.18
Alexander-Phi	306.1	Allen-Bro	7.42	Adams-Pit	1.41	Alexander-Phi	159	Marquard-NY	4.72	Marquard-NY	9.38
Mathewson-NY	306.0	Pearce-Chi	7.55	Marquard-NY	1.53	Marquard-NY	151	Seaton-Phi	4.69	Humphries-Chi	9.70
Cheney-Chi	305.0	Tyler-Bos	7.59	Suggs-Cin	1.58	Adams-Pit	144	Alexander-Phi	4.67	Demaree-NY	9.87

Earned Run Average		Adjusted ERA		Opponents' Batting Avg.		Opponents' On Base Pct.		Starter Runs		Adjusted Starter Runs	
Mathewson-NY	2.06	Mathewson-NY	151	Tesreau-NY	.220	Mathewson-NY	.266	Mathewson-NY	38.7	Mathewson-NY	35.9
Adams-Pit	2.15	Tesreau-NY	143	Seaton-Phi	.226	Adams-Pit	.267	Adams-Pit	36.4	Adams-Pit	29.8
Tesreau-NY	2.17	Demaree-NY	141	Allen-Bro	.231	Marquard-NY	.273	Tesreau-NY	32.2	Tesreau-NY	29.5
Demaree-NY	2.21	Adams-Pit	140	Pearce-Chi	.234	Humphries-Chi	.277	Marquard-NY	22.3	Seaton-Phi	26.2
Pearce-Chi	2.31	Brennan-Phi	139	Tyler-Bos	.235	Demaree-NY	.286	Demaree-NY	21.9	Brennan-Phi	21.5

Clutch Pitching Index		Relief Runs		Adjusted Relief Runs		Relief Ranking		Total Pitcher Index		Total Baseball Ranking	
Brennan-Phi	128	Crandall-NY-StL-NY	3.7	Crandall-NY-StL-NY	2.8	Crandall-NY-StL-NY	2.1	Mathewson-NY	4.4	Mathewson-NY	4.4
Packard-Cin	127							Adams-Pit	4.0	Adams-Pit	4.0
Brown-Cin	119							Tesreau-NY	3.4	Tinker-Cin	3.6
Ames-NY-Cin	119							Tyler-Bos	2.8	Cravath-Phi	3.5
Pearce-Chi	112							Seaton-Phi	2.4	Evers-Chi	3.4

TEAM	G	W	L	PCT	GB	R	OR	AB	H	2B	3B	HR	BB	SO	AVG	OBP	SLG	PRO	PRO+	BR	/A	PF	CHI	RC	SB	CS	SBA	SBR
PHI	153	96	57	.627		794	592	5043	1412	223	80	33	534	547	.280	.356	.376	.732	123	135	149	98	105	747	221			
WAS	155	90	64	.584	6.5	596	561	5074	1281	156	81	19	440	595	.252	.317	.326	.643	93	-33	-45	102	105	593	287			
CLE	155	86	66	.566	9.5	633	536	5030	1348	205	74	16	420	557	.268	.331	.348	.679	101	29	10	103	99	635	191			
BOS	151	79	71	.527	15.5	631	610	4965	1334	220	101	17	466	534	.269	.336	.364	.700	109	67	51	103	95	664	189			
CHI	153	78	74	.513	17.5	488	498	4822	1139	157	66	24	398	550	.236	.299	.311	.610	85	-93	-87	99	100	496	156			
DET	153	66	87	.431	30	624	716	5064	1344	180	101	24	496	501	.265	.336	.355	.691	110	56	65	99	93	669	218			
NY	153	57	94	.377	38	529	668	4880	1157	155	45	8	534	617	.237	.320	.292	.612	84	-74	-75	100	101	525	203			
STL	155	57	96	.373	39	528	642	5031	1193	179	73	18	449	769	.237	.305	.312	.617	89	-81	-64	97	101	536	209			
TOT	614					4823		39909	10208	1475	621	159	3737	4670	.256	.325	.336	.661							1674			

TEAM	CG	SH	SV	IP	H	H/G	HR	BB	SO	RAT	ERA	ERA+	OAV	OOB	PR	/A	PF	CPI	FA	E	DP	FW	PW	BW	SBW	DIF
PHI	69	17	22	1351¹	1200	8.0	24	532	630	11.8	3.19	86	.228	.304	-39	-65	94	70	.966	212	108	3.2	-6.9	15.9		7.3
WAS	78	23	20	1396	1175	7.6	35	465	757	11.0	2.73	108	.224	.296	30	33	101	80	.960	261	122	.3	3.5	-4.8		14.0
CLE	93	18	5	1386²	1278	8.3	19	502	689	11.8	2.54	119	.248	.320	59	73	104	108	.962	242	124	1.5	7.8	1.1		-.4
BOS	83	12	10	1358¹	1318	8.7	6	441	709	11.9	2.94	100	.258	.321	-1	-3	100	95	.961	237	84	1.4	-.3	5.4		-2.5
CHI	84	17	8	1360¹	1189	7.9	10	438	602	11.0	2.33	125	.236	.302	90	88	100	97	.960	255	104	.5	9.4	-9.3		1.4
DET	90	4	7	1360	1359	9.0	13	504	468	12.6	3.38	86	.264	.336	-68	-70	100	94	.954	300	105	-2.4	-7.5	6.9		-7.6
NY	75	8	7	1344	1318	8.8	31	455	530	12.2	3.27	91	.259	.327	-51	-41	102	94	.954	293	94	-1.9	-4.4	-8.0		-4.2
STL	104	14	5	1382¹	1369	8.9	21	454	476	12.2	3.06	96	.266	.331	-20	-21	100	103	.954	301	125	-2.2	-2.2	-6.8		-8.2
TOT	676	113	84	10939		8.4				11.8	2.93		.256	.325					.959	2101	866					

Runs
Collins-Phi 125
Baker-Phi 116
Jackson-Cle 109
Shotton-StL 105
J.Murphy-Phi 105

Hits
Jackson-Cle 197
Crawford-Det 193
Baker-Phi 190
Speaker-Bos 189
Collins-Phi 184

Doubles
Jackson-Cle 39
Speaker-Bos 35
Baker-Phi 34
Crawford-Det 32

Triples
Crawford-Det 23
Speaker-Bos 22
Jackson-Cle 17
Williams-StL 16
Cobb-Det 16

Home Runs
Baker-Phi 12
Crawford-Det 9
Bodie-Chi 8
Jackson-Cle 7

Total Bases
Crawford-Det 298
Jackson-Cle 291
Baker-Phi 278
Speaker-Bos 277
Collins-Phi 242

Runs Batted In
Baker-Phi 117
McInnis-Phi 90
Lewis-Bos 90
Pratt-StL 87
Barry-Phi 85

Runs Produced
Baker-Phi 221
Collins-Phi 195
Jackson-Cle 173
Oldring-Phi 167
McInnis-Phi 165

Bases On Balls
Shotton-StL 99
Collins-Phi 85
Wolter-NY 80
Jackson-Cle 80
Bush-Det 80

Batting Average
Cobb-Det .... .390
Jackson-Cle ..... .373
Speaker-Bos ..... .363
Collins-Phi .... .345
Baker-Phi .... .337

On Base Percentage
Cobb-Det .... .467
Jackson-Cle ..... .460
Collins-Phi .... .441
Speaker-Bos ..... .441
Baker-Phi .... .413

Slugging Average
Jackson-Cle ...... .551
Cobb-Det .... .535
Speaker-Bos ..... .533
Baker-Phi .... .493
Crawford-Det .... .489

Production
Jackson-Cle 1.011
Cobb-Det 1.002
Speaker-Bos ..... .974
Baker-Phi .... .906
Collins-Phi .... .894

Adjusted Production
Cobb-Det 196
Jackson-Cle 190
Speaker-Bos 180
Baker-Phi 169
Collins-Phi 165

Batter Runs
Jackson-Cle 65.5
Speaker-Bos 55.9
Cobb-Det 51.9
Baker-Phi 46.0
Collins-Phi 45.7

Adjusted Batter Runs
Jackson-Cle 63.6
Speaker-Bos 54.3
Cobb-Det 52.7
Baker-Phi 47.5
Collins-Phi 47.3

Clutch Hitting Index
Barry-Phi 176
Lewis-Bos 155
McInnis-Phi 142
Turner-Cle 142
Baker-Phi 140

Runs Created
Jackson-Cle 144
Speaker-Bos 135
Collins-Phi 125
Baker-Phi 125
Cobb-Det 121

Total Average
Cobb-Det 1.310
Jackson-Cle 1.215
Speaker-Bos 1.193
Collins-Phi 1.111
Baker-Phi 1.029

Stolen Bases
Milan-Was 75
Moeller-Was 62
Collins-Phi 55
Cobb-Det 51
Speaker-Bos 46

Stolen Base Average

Stolen Base Runs

Fielding Runs
Weaver-Chi 33.6
Speaker-Bos 23.7
Turner-Cle 16.2
Collins-Phi 15.7
Shotton-StL 12.8

Total Player Rating
Speaker-Bos 7.3
Collins-Phi 6.1
Baker-Phi 6.1
Jackson-Cle 6.0
Cobb-Det 5.2

Wins
Johnson-Was 36
Falkenberg-Cle ... 23
Russell-Chi 22
Bender-Phi 21

Win Percentage
Johnson-Was ... .837
Bush-Phi .... .714
Boehling-Was ... .708
Collins-Bos ...... .704
Falkenberg-Cle ... .697

Games
Russell-Chi 52
Scott-Chi 48
Johnson-Was 48
Bender-Phi 48
S.Gregg-Cle 44

Complete Games
Johnson-Was 29
Russell-Chi 26
Scott-Chi 25

Shutouts
Johnson-Was 11
Russell-Chi 8
Plank-Phi 7
Falkenberg-Cle 6

Saves
Bender-Phi 13
Hughes-Was 6
Bedient-Bos 5

Innings Pitched
Johnson-Was ... 346.0
Russell-Chi 316.2
Scott-Chi 312.1
S.Gregg-Cle 285.2
Falkenberg-Cle .. 276.0

Fewest Hits/Game
Johnson-Was 6.03
Mitchell-Cle 6.35
Engel-Was 6.78
Leverenz-StL 7.06
Russell-Chi 7.11

Fewest BB/Game
Johnson-Was ..... .99
Collins-Bos 1.35
Mitchell-StL 1.72
Plank-Phi 2.11
Weilman-StL 2.15

Strikeouts
Johnson-Was 243
S.Gregg-Cle 166
Falkenberg-Cle ... 166
Scott-Chi 158
Groom-Was 156

Strikeouts/Game
Johnson-Was 6.32
Mitchell-Cle 5.85
Plank-Phi 5.60
Falkenberg-Cle ... 5.41
Groom-Was 5.31

Ratio
Johnson-Was 7.26
Russell-Chi 9.55
Scott-Chi 10.00
Cicotte-Chi 10.07
Plank-Phi 10.13

Earned Run Average
Johnson-Was 1.14
Cicotte-Chi 1.58
Scott-Chi 1.90
Russell-Chi 1.90
Mitchell-Cle 1.91

Adjusted ERA
Johnson-Was 258
Cicotte-Chi 185
Mitchell-Cle 159
Scott-Chi 154
Russell-Chi 153

Opponents' Batting Avg.
Johnson-Was ..... .187
Mitchell-Cle ..... .199
Engel-Was .... .207
Houck-Phi .... .214
Russell-Chi ...... .219

Opponents' On Base Pct.
Johnson-Was ..... .217
Russell-Chi ...... .273
Bender-Phi .... .277
Cicotte-Chi ...... .281
Scott-Chi .... .281

Starter Runs
Johnson-Was 68.6
Cicotte-Chi 40.2
Russell-Chi 36.1
Scott-Chi 35.7
Mitchell-Cle 24.6

Adjusted Starter Runs
Johnson-Was 69.3
Cicotte-Chi 40.0
Russell-Chi 35.8
Scott-Chi 35.4
Mitchell-Cle 27.2

Clutch Pitching Index
Blanding-Cle 141
S.Gregg-Cle 130
Ford-NY 123
Baumgardner-StL .. 118
Cicotte-Chi 114

Relief Runs

Adjusted Relief Runs

Relief Ranking

Total Pitcher Index
Johnson-Was 9.5
Cicotte-Chi 5.1
Russell-Chi 3.7
Scott-Chi 3.1
Boehling-Was 2.7

Total Baseball Ranking
Johnson-Was 9.5
Speaker-Bos 7.3
Collins-Phi 6.1
Baker-Phi 6.1
Jackson-Cle 6.0

TEAM	G	W	L	PCT	GB	R	OR	AB	H	2B	3B	HR	BB	SO	AVG	OBP	SLG	PRO	PRO+	BR	/A	PF	CHI	RC	SB	CS	SBA	SBR
BOS	158	94	59	.614		657	548	5206	1307	213	60	35	502	617	.251	.323	.335	.658	102	17	20	99	103	618	139			
NY	156	84	70	.545	10.5	672	576	5146	1363	222	59	30	447	479	.265	.330	.348	.678	111	53	73	97	103	655	239			
STL	157	81	72	.529	13	558	540	5046	1249	203	65	33	445	618	.248	.314	.333	.647	100	-8	·0	99	95	585	204			
CHI	156	78	76	.506	16.5	605	638	5050	1229	199	74	42	501	577	.243	.317	.337	.654	101	7	8	100	100	595	164			
BRO	154	75	79	.487	19.5	622	618	5152	1386	172	90	31	376	559	.269	.323	.355	.678	105	43	29	102	97	636	173			
PHI	154	74	80	.481	20.5	651	687	5110	1345	211	52	62	472	570	.263	.329	.361	.690	105	69	30	107	97	654	145			
PIT	158	69	85	.448	25.5	503	540	5145	1197	148	79	18	416	608	.233	.295	.303	.598	87	-100	-74	96	101	503	147			
CIN	157	60	94	.390	34.5	530	651	4991	1178	142	64	16	441	627	.236	.305	.300	.605	83	-78	-95	103	104	517	224			
TOT	625					4798		40846	10254	1510	543	267	3600	4655	.251	.317	.334	.651							1435			

TEAM	CG	SH	SV	IP	H	H/G	HR	BB	SO	RAT	ERA	ERA+	OAV	OOB	PR	/A	PF	CPI	FA	E	DP	FW	PW	BW	SBW	DIF
BOS	104	19	6	1421	1272	8.1	38	477	606	11.4	2.74	100	.248	.318	6	1	99	102	.963	246	143	1.8	.1	2.2		13.4
NY	88	20	9	1390²	1298	8.4	47	367	563	11.0	2.94	90	.252	.306	-24	-46	95	92	.961	254	119	1.1	-5.0	7.9		3.0
STL	84	16	12	1424²	1279	8.1	26	422	531	11.1	2.38	117	.249	.313	63	64	100	112	.964	239	109	2.2	6.9	.0		-4.6
CHI	70	14	11	1389¹	1169	7.6	37	528	651	11.2	2.71	103	.232	.310	11	8	100	92	.951	310	87	-2.7	.9	.9		2.0
BRO	80	11	11	1368¹	1282	8.4	36	466	605	11.8	2.82	101	.255	.323	-4	6	103	105	.961	248	112	1.2	.6	3.1		-7.0
PHI	85	14	7	1379¹	1403	9.2	26	452	650	12.4	3.06	96	.270	.335	-42	-21	105	106	.950	324	81	-3.9	-2.3	3.2		-.0
PIT	86	10	11	1405	1272	8.1	27	392	488	10.9	2.70	98	.249	.307	12	-9	95	95	.966	223	96	3.4	-1.0	-8.0		-2.4
CIN	74	15	15	1387¹	1259	8.2	30	489	607	11.7	2.94	100	.248	.320	-23	-2	105	95	.952	314	113	-2.9	-.2	-10.2		-3.7
TOT	671	119	82	11165²		8.2				11.4	2.78		.251	.317					.958	2158	860					

Runs
Burns-NY 100
Magee-Phi 96
Daubert-Bro....... 89
Saier-Chi 87
Doyle-NY 87

Hits
Magee-Phi 171
Wheat-Bro 170
Burns-NY 170
Zimmerman-Chi ... 167
Becker-Phi 167

Doubles
Magee-Phi 39
Zimmerman-Chi ... 36
Burns-NY 35
Connolly-Bos...... 28

Triples
Carey-Pit 17
Zimmerman-Chi ... 12
Wilson-StL 12
Cutshaw-Bro 12

Home Runs
Cravath-Phi 19
Saier-Chi 18
Magee-Phi 15
Luderus-Phi 12

Total Bases
Magee-Phi 277
Cravath-Phi 249
Wheat-Bro 241
Zimmerman-Chi .. 239
Burns-NY 234

Runs Batted In
Magee-Phi 103
Cravath-Phi 100
Wheat-Bro 89
J.Miller-StL 88
Zimmerman-Chi ... 87

Runs Produced
Magee-Phi 184
Zimmerman-Chi ... 158
Cravath-Phi 157
Burns-NY 157
J.Miller-StL 151

Bases On Balls
Huggins-StL 105
Saier-Chi 94
Burns-NY 89
Evers-Bos 87
Cravath-Phi 83

Batting Average
Daubert-Bro....... .329
Becker-Phi........ .325
Dalton-Bro .... .319
Wheat-Bro .... .319
Stengel-Bro ...... .316

On Base Percentage
Stengel-Bro ...... .404
Burns-NY .... .403
Cravath-Phi ...... .402
Huggins-StL ...... .396
Dalton-Bro .... .396

Slugging Average
Magee-Phi .... .509
Cravath-Phi ...... .499
Wheat-Bro .... .452
Becker-Phi .... .446
Daubert-Bro ...... .432

Production
Cravath-Phi ...... .901
Magee-Phi .... .890
Wheat-Bro .... .830
Stengel-Bro ...... .829
Burns-NY .... .820

Adjusted Production
Cravath-Phi 157
Magee-Phi 154
Burns-NY 149
Stengel-Bro 143
Wheat-Bro 143

Batter Runs
Cravath-Phi 42.7
Magee-Phi 40.7
Burns-NY 34.0
Connolly-Bos..... 31.0
Wheat-Bro 29.3

Adjusted Batter Runs
Cravath-Phi 38.7
Magee-Phi 36.5
Burns-NY 36.3
Connolly-Bos..... 31.3
Wheat-Bro 27.9

Clutch Hitting Index
Fletcher-NY 151
Maranville-Bos ... 148
Cutshaw-Bro 144
J.Miller-StL 143
Schmidt-Bos 141

Runs Created
Burns-NY 113
Magee-Phi 111
Cravath-Phi 108
Wheat-Bro 96
Saier-Chi 89

Total Average
Burns-NY .... .997
Cravath-Phi ...... .997
Magee-Phi .... .965
Stengel-Bro ...... .904
Wheat-Bro .... .857

Stolen Bases
Burns-NY 62
Herzog-Cin 46
Dolan-StL 42
Carey-Pit 38

Stolen Base Average

Stolen Base Runs

Fielding Runs
Maranville-Bos ... 51.8
Herzog-Cin 30.6
Cutshaw-Bro 27.5
Smith-Bro-Bos ... 22.6
Stock-NY 15.1

Total Player Rating
Maranville-Bos 5.1
Magee-Phi 4.5
Smith-Bro-Bos 4.3
Herzog-Cin 4.1
Wheat-Bro 3.9

Wins
Rudolph-Bos 27
Alexander-Phi 27
Tesreau-NY 26
James-Bos 26
Mathewson-NY ... 24

Win Percentage
James-Bos .... .788
Doak-StL .... .760
Rudolph-Bos ..... .730
Tesreau-NY .... .722
Pfeffer-Bro .... .657

Games
Cheney-Chi 50
Mayer-Phi 48
Ames-Cin 47

Complete Games
Alexander-Phi 32
Rudolph-Bos 31
James-Bos 30
Mathewson-NY ... 29
Pfeffer-Bro 27

Shutouts
Tesreau-NY 8
Doak-StL 7
Rudolph-Bos 6
Cheney-Chi 6
Alexander-Phi 6

Saves
Sallee-StL 6
Ames-Cin 6
Cheney-Chi 5
Pfeffer-Bro 4
McQuillan-Pit....... 4

Innings Pitched
Alexander-Phi ... 355.0
Rudolph-Bos 336.1
James-Bos 332.1
Tesreau-NY 322.1
Mayer-Phi 321.0

Fewest Hits/Game
Tesreau-NY 6.65
Doak-StL 6.79
Cheney-Chi 6.91
Douglas-Cin...... 6.99
James-Bos 7.07

Fewest BB/Game
Mathewson-NY ... .66
Adams-Pit 1.24
Marquard-NY 1.58
Rudolph-Bos 1.63
Alexander-Phi 1.93

Strikeouts
Alexander-Phi 214
Tesreau-NY 189
Vaughn-Chi 165
Cheney-Chi 157
James-Bos 156

Strikeouts/Game
Alexander-Phi 5.43
Tesreau-NY 5.28
Vaughn-Chi 5.06
G.Tyler-Bos 4.64
Ragan-Bro 4.58

Ratio
Rudolph-Bos 9.45
Adams-Pit 9.51
Mathewson-NY ... 9.78
Doak-StL 10.09
Pfeffer-Bro 10.34

Earned Run Average
Doak-StL 1.72
James-Bos 1.90
Pfeffer-Bro 1.97
Vaughn-Chi 2.05
Sallee-StL 2.10

Adjusted ERA
Doak-StL 162
James-Bos 145
Pfeffer-Bro 145
Vaughn-Chi 135
Sallee-StL 133

Opponents' Batting Avg.
Tesreau-NY ...... .209
Cheney-Chi ...... .215
Doak-StL .... .216
Vaughn-Chi ...... .222
Douglas-Cin....... .223

Opponents' On Base Pct.
Adams-Pit .... .276
Rudolph-Bos ..... .276
Mathewson-NY ... .278
Alexander-Phi ..... .290
Doak-StL .... .290

Starter Runs
James-Bos 32.8
Doak-StL 30.2
Pfeffer-Bro 28.5
Vaughn-Chi 23.9
Sallee-StL 21.4

Adjusted Starter Runs
James-Bos 31.6
Pfeffer-Bro 30.9
Doak-StL 30.4
Vaughn-Chi 23.6
Alexander-Phi 21.8

Clutch Pitching Index
Cooper-Pit 126
James-Bos 121
Crutcher-Bos..... 120
Perritt-StL 116
Sallee-StL 116

Relief Runs

Adjusted Relief Runs

Relief Ranking

Total Pitcher Index
James-Bos 3.9
Doak-StL 3.6
Alexander-Phi 3.2
Pfeffer-Bro 3.0
Vaughn-Chi 2.5

Total Baseball Ranking
Maranville-Bos 5.1
Magee-Phi 4.5
Smith-Bro-Bos 4.3
Herzog-Cin 4.1
Wheat-Bro 3.9

TEAM	G	W	L	PCT	GB	R	OR	AB	H	2B	3B	HR	BB	SO	AVG	OBP	SLG	PRO	PRO+	BR	/A	PF	CHI	RC	SB	CS	SBA	SBR
PHI	158	99	53	.651		749	529	5126	1392	165	80	29	545	517	.272	.348	.352	.700	122	112	132	97	107	662	231	188	100	-3
BOS	159	91	62	.595	8.5	589	511	5117	1278	226	85	18	490	549	.250	.320	.338	.658	105	26	26	100	98	567	177	176	64	14
WAS	158	81	73	.526	19	572	519	5108	1245	176	81	18	470	640	.244	.313	.320	.633	94	-16	-30	103	102	544	220	163	72	6
DET	157	80	73	.523	19.5	615	618	5102	1318	195	84	25	557	537	.258	.336	.344	.680	108	76	57	103	93	630	211	154	68	5
STL	159	71	82	.464	28.5	523	615	5101	1241	185	75	17	423	863	.243	.306	.319	.625	98	-37	-15	96	99	516	233	189	74	12
NY	157	70	84	.455	30	538	550	4992	1144	149	52	12	577	711	.229	.315	.287	.602	88	-59	-56	100	105	484	251	191	72	14
CHI	157	70	84	.455	30	487	560	5040	1205	161	71	19	408	609	.239	.302	.311	.613	92	-58	-50	99	96	497	167	152	68	5
CLE	157	51	102	.333	48.5	538	709	5157	1262	178	70	10	450	685	.245	.310	.312	.622	90	-38	-60	104	100	517	167	157	70	5
TOT	631					4611		40743	10085	1435	598	148	3920	5111	.248	.319	.323	.642							1657	1370	55	-324

TEAM	CG	SH	SV	IP	H	H/G	HR	BB	SO	RAT	ERA	ERA+	OAV	OOB	PR	/A	PF	CPI	FA	E	DP	FW	PW	BW	SBW	DIF
PHI	89	24	17	1404	1264	8.1	18	521	720	11.6	2.78	95	.248	.321	-6	-24	96	100	.966	213	116	3.5	-2.7	14.6	4.2	3.4
BOS	88	24	8	1427¹	1212	7.6	18	397	605	10.3	2.36	114	.237	.296	58	49	98	95	.963	242	99	1.8	5.4	2.9	6.0	-1.7
WAS	75	25	20	1420²	1170	7.4	20	520	784	11.0	2.54	109	.232	.311	30	35	101	97	.961	254	116	1.0	3.9	-3.3	5.2	-2.7
DET	81	14	12	1412	1285	8.2	17	498	567	11.8	2.86	98	.248	.322	-18	-9	103	97	.958	286	101	-1.1	-1.0	6.3	5.0	-5.8
STL	81	15	11	1410²	1309	8.4	20	540	553	12.1	2.85	95	.250	.326	-17	-21	99	103	.952	317	114	-2.7	-2.3	-1.7	5.8	-4.6
NY	98	9	5	1397¹	1277	8.2	30	390	563	10.9	2.81	98	.250	.307	-12	-10	101	94	.963	238	93	1.9	-1.1	-6.2	6.0	-7.6
CHI	74	17	11	1398²	1207	7.8	15	401	660	10.5	2.48	108	.238	.298	39	29	98	92	.955	299	90	-1.9	3.2	-5.5	5.0	-7.9
CLE	69	9	3	1391²	1365	8.8	10	666	688	13.4	3.21	90	.267	.356	-74	-55	105	110	.953	300	119	-1.9	-6.1	-6.6	5.0	-15.9
TOT	655	137	87	11262¹		8.1				11.5	2.73		.248	.319					.959	2149	848					

Runs
Collins-Phi 122
Speaker-Bos 101
Murphy-Phi 101
Bush-Det 97

Hits
Speaker-Bos 193
Crawford-Det 183
Baker-Phi 182
McInnis-Phi 181
Collins-Phi 181

Doubles
Speaker-Bos 46
Lewis-Bos 37
Pratt-StL 34
Collins-Chi 34
Leary-StL 28

Triples
Crawford-Det 26
Gardner-Bos 19
Speaker-Bos 18
C.Walker-StL 16
Hooper-Bos 15

Home Runs
Baker-Phi 9
Crawford-Det 8
C.Walker-StL 6
Fournier-Chi 6

Total Bases
Speaker-Bos 287
Crawford-Det 281
Baker-Phi 252
Pratt-StL 240
Collins-Phi 238

Runs Batted In
Crawford-Det 104
McInnis-Phi 95
Speaker-Bos 90
Baker-Phi 89
Collins-Phi 85

Runs Produced
Collins-Phi 205
Speaker-Bos 187
Crawford-Det 170
McInnis-Phi 168
Baker-Phi 164

Bases On Balls
Bush-Det 112
Collins-Phi 97
Murphy-Phi 87
Speaker-Bos 77
Maisel-NY 76

Batting Average
Collins-Phi .... .344
Speaker-Bos ...... .338
Jackson-Cle .... .338
Baker-Phi .... .319
Crawford-Det ..... .314

On Base Percentage
Collins-Phi .... .452
Speaker-Bos ...... .423
Jackson-Cle .... .399
Crawford-Det ..... .388
Baker-Phi .... .380

Slugging Average
Speaker-Bos ...... .503
Crawford-Det ..... .483
Jackson-Cle .... .464
Collins-Phi .... .452
Baker-Phi .... .442

Production
Speaker-Bos ..... .926
Collins-Phi .... .904
Crawford-Det .... .871
Jackson-Cle ...... .862
Baker-Phi .... .822

Adjusted Production
Speaker-Bos 178
Collins-Phi 178
Crawford-Det 157
Jackson-Cle 153
Baker-Phi 152

Batter Runs
Speaker-Bos 54.9
Collins-Phi 51.6
Cobb-Det 42.3
Crawford-Det 42.1
Jackson-Cle 31.6

Adjusted Batter Runs
Speaker-Bos 54.9
Collins-Phi 53.9
Cobb-Det 41.0
Crawford-Det 40.0
Baker-Phi 33.4

Clutch Hitting Index
McInnis-Phi 171
Lewis-Bos 146
Veach-Det 135
Shanks-Was 134
Gandil-Was 133

Runs Created
Speaker-Bos 124
Collins-Phi 120
Crawford-Det 113
Baker-Phi 95
C.Walker-StL 87

Total Average
Collins-Phi .... .984
Speaker-Bos ...... .943
Crawford-Det .... .867
Jackson-Cle ...... .835
C.Walker-StL ..... .776

Stolen Bases
Maisel-NY 74
Collins-Phi 58
Speaker-Bos 42
Shotton-StL 40

Stolen Base Average
Maisel-NY 81.3
Sweeney-NY 76.0
Chapman-Cle 72.7
Moriarty-Det 69.4
Peckinpaugh-NY .. 69.1

Stolen Base Runs
Maisel-NY 12.0
Sweeney-NY 2.1
Kopf-Phi 1.8
Chapman-Cle 1.8

Fielding Runs
Bush-Det 33.6
Speaker-Bos 27.7
Gandil-Was 23.7
Boone-NY 22.7
Turner-Cle 21.3

Total Player Rating
Speaker-Bos 7.4
Collins-Phi 5.7
Bush-Det 5.1
Baker-Phi 4.3
C.Walker-StL 3.6

Wins
Johnson-Was 28
Coveleski-Det ... 22
Collins-Bos 20
Leonard-Bos 19

Win Percentage
Bender-Phi .... .850
Leonard-Bos ..... .792
Plank-Phi .... .682
Shawkey-Phi ..... .667
Caldwell-NY ..... .654

Games
Johnson-Was 51
Ayers-Was 49
Shaw-Was 48
Benz-Chi 48

Complete Games
Johnson-Was 33
Coveleski-Det ... 23
Dauss-Det 22
Caldwell-NY 22

Shutouts
Johnson-Was 9
Leonard-Bos 7
Bender-Phi 7
Collins-Bos 6

Saves
Shaw-Was 4
Mitchell-StL 4
Faber-Chi 4
Dauss-Det 4
Bentley-Was 4

Innings Pitched
Johnson-Was ... 371.2
Coveleski-Det ... 303.1
Hamilton-StL ... 302.1
Dauss-Det 302.0
Weilman-StL ... 299.0

Fewest Hits/Game
Leonard-Bos 5.57
Caldwell-NY 6.46
Shaw-Was 6.93
Johnson-Was 6.95
Foster-Bos 6.97

Fewest BB/Game
McHale-NY 1.55
Russell-Chi 1.77
Johnson-Was 1.79
Warhop-NY 1.83
Ayers-Was 1.83

Strikeouts
Johnson-Was 225
Mitchell-Cle 179
Leonard-Bos 176
Shaw-Was 164
Dauss-Det 150

Strikeouts/Game
Leonard-Bos 7.05
Mitchell-Cle 6.27
Shaw-Was 5.74
Johnson-Was 5.45
Bender-Phi 5.38

Ratio
Leonard-Bos 8.29
Caldwell-NY 8.79
Johnson-Was 9.01
Foster-Bos 9.48
Ayers-Was 9.60

Earned Run Average
Leonard-Bos ...... .96
Foster-Bos 1.70
Johnson-Was 1.72
Caldwell-NY 1.94
Cicotte-Chi 2.04

Adjusted ERA
Leonard-Bos 279
Johnson-Was 161
Foster-Bos 158
Caldwell-NY 142
Cicotte-Chi 131

Opponents' Batting Avg.
Leonard-Bos ..... .180
Caldwell-NY ..... .205
Shaw-Was .... .216
Johnson-Was ..... .217
Foster-Bos .... .218

Opponents' On Base Pct.
Leonard-Bos ..... .246
Caldwell-NY ..... .260
Johnson-Was ..... .265
Foster-Bos .... .274
Benz-Chi .... .282

Starter Runs
Leonard-Bos 44.3
Johnson-Was 41.9
Foster-Bos 24.3
Weilman-StL 21.8
Cicotte-Chi 20.8

Adjusted Starter Runs
Johnson-Was 43.4
Leonard-Bos 43.0
Foster-Bos 23.2
Weilman-StL 20.7
Caldwell-NY 19.2

Clutch Pitching Index
Hagerman-Cle 126
Steen-Cle 123
Shawkey-Phi 109
James-StL 106
Bender-Phi 106

Relief Runs

Adjusted Relief Runs

Relief Ranking

Total Pitcher Index
Johnson-Was 6.4
Leonard-Bos 4.4
Cicotte-Chi 2.9
Foster-Bos 2.7
Coveleski-Det 2.4

Total Baseball Ranking
Speaker-Bos 7.3
Johnson-Was 6.4
Collins-Phi 5.7
Bush-Det 5.1
Leonard-Bos 4.4

1914 Federal League

TEAM	G	W	L	PCT	GB	R	OR	AB	H	2B	3B	HR	BB	SO	AVG	OBP	SLG	PRO	PRO+	BR	/A	PF	CHI	RC	SB	CS	SBA	SBR
IND	157	88	65	.575		762	622	5176	1474	230	90	33	470	668	.285	.349	.383	.732	104	106	35	111	100	763	273			
CHI	157	87	67	.565	1.5	621	517	5098	1314	227	50	52	520	645	.258	.331	.352	.683	108	19	57	94	94	653	171			
BAL	160	84	70	.545	4.5	645	628	5120	1374	222	67	32	487	589	.268	.337	.357	.694	101	38	17	103	94	670	152			
BUF	155	80	71	.530	7	620	602	5064	1264	177	74	38	430	589	.250	.311	.336	.647	89	-54	-67	102	108	585	228			
BRO	157	77	77	.500	11.5	662	677	5221	1402	225	85	42	404	665	.269	.326	.368	.694	105	29	34	99	99	680	220			
KC	154	67	84	.444	20	644	683	5127	1369	226	77	39	399	621	.267	.324	.364	.688	107	17	42	96	99	650	171			
PIT	154	64	86	.427	22.5	605	698	5114	1339	180	90	34	410	575	.262	.321	.352	.673	99	-7	-1	99	96	624	153			
STL	154	62	89	.411	25	565	697	5078	1254	193	65	26	503	662	.247	.319	.326	.645	86	-51	-84	105	96	577	113			
TOT	624					5124		40998	10790	1680	598	296	3623	5186	.263	.323	.355	.678						1481				

TEAM	CG	SH	SV	IP	H	H/G	HR	BB	SO	RAT	ERA	ERA+	OAV	OOB	PR	/A	PF	CPI	FA	E	DP	FW	PW	BW	SBW	DIF
IND	104	15	9	1397²	1352	8.7	29	476	664	12.1	3.06	113	.280	.351	22	62	108	122	.956	289	113	-1.2	6.4	3.6		2.6
CHI	93	17	8	1420¹	1204	7.6	43	393	650	10.3	2.44	121	.237	.296	120	79	92	100	.962	249	114	1.1	8.2	5.9		-5.2
BAL	88	15	13	1392	1389	9.0	34	392	732	11.7	3.13	108	.281	.338	11	36	105	114	.960	263	105	.6	3.7	1.8		.9
BUF	89	15	16	1387	1249	8.1	45	505	662	11.7	3.16	104	.269	.346	6	19	103	115	.962	242	109	1.3	2.0	-7.0		8.2
BRO	91	11	9	1385¹	1375	8.9	31	559	636	12.9	3.33	96	.285	.365	-19	-21	100	121	.956	283	120	-.9	-2.2	3.5		-.5
KC	82	10	12	1361	1387	9.2	37	445	600	12.5	3.41	91	.266	.330	-30	-48	96	96	.957	279	135	-.9	-5.0	4.4		-7.0
PIT	97	9	6	1370	1416	9.3	39	444	510	12.4	3.56	89	.283	.345	-54	-58	99	105	.960	253	92	.6	-6.0	-.1		-5.4
STL	97	9	6	1367²	1418	9.3	38	409	661	12.3	3.59	94	.268	.325	-57	-32	105	90	.957	273	94	-.6	-3.3	-8.7		-.9
TOT	741	101	79	11081		8.8				12.0	3.20		.263	.323					.959	2131	882					

Runs
Kauff-Ind 120
McKechnie-Ind ... 107
Duncan-Bal 99
Kenworthy-KC 93
Evans-Bro 93

Hits
Kauff-Ind 211
Zwilling-Chi 185
Evans-Bro 179
Oakes-Pit 178
Hanford-Buf 174

Doubles
Kauff-Ind 44
Evans-Bro 41
Kenworthy-KC..... 40
Zwilling-Chi 38

Triples
Evans-Bro 15
Esmond-Ind 15
Kenworthy-KC..... 14

Home Runs
Zwilling-Chi 16
Kenworthy-KC 15
Hanford-Buf....... 13
Evans-Bro 12

Total Bases
Kauff-Ind 305
Zwilling-Chi 287
Kenworthy-KC.... 286
Evans-Bro 286
Hanford-Buf 267

Runs Batted In
LaPorte-Ind 107
Evans-Bro 96
Zwilling-Chi 95
Kauff-Ind 95
Kenworthy-KC..... 91

Runs Produced
Kauff-Ind 207
LaPorte-Ind 189
Evans-Bro 177
Zwilling-Chi 170
Kenworthy-KC.... 169

Bases On Balls
Wickland-Chi 81
Agler-Buf 77
Kauff-Ind 72

Batting Average
Kauff-Ind 370
Evans-Bro 348
Campbell-Ind 318
Kenworthy-KC....317
Louden-Buf 313

On Base Percentage
Kauff-Ind 447
Evans-Bro 416
Lennox-Pit 414
Meyer-Bal 395
Wilson-Chi 394

Slugging Average
Evans-Bro 556
Kauff-Ind 534
Kenworthy-KC....525
Lennox-Pit 493
Zwilling-Chi 485

Production
Kauff-Ind 981
Evans-Bro 973
Lennox-Pit 907
Kenworthy-KC....896
Wilson-Chi 860

Adjusted Production
Evans-Bro 178
Kauff-Ind 163
Kenworthy-KC....162
Lennox-Pit 160
Wilson-Chi 155

Batter Runs
Kauff-Ind 61.6
Evans-Bro 50.7
Kenworthy-KC....36.3
Lennox-Pit 35.1
Zwilling-Chi 29.6

Adjusted Batter Runs
Kauff-Ind 53.6
Evans-Bro 51.2
Kenworthy-KC....39.1
Lennox-Pit 35.7
Zwilling-Chi 33.9

Clutch Hitting Index
LaPorte-Ind 176
Swacina-Bal 160
Carr-Ind 148
Wisterzil-Bro 139
Stovall-KC 138

Runs Created
Kauff-Ind 156
Evans-Bro 124
Kenworthy-KC.... 113
Zwilling-Chi 108
Lennox-Pit 96

Total Average
Kauff-Ind 1.278
Evans-Bro 1.087
Lennox-Pit 1.034
Kenworthy-KC....995
Wilson-Chi 939

Stolen Bases
Kauff-Ind 75
McKechnie-Ind ... 47
Myers-Bro 43
Chadbourne-KC ... 42

Stolen Base Average

Stolen Base Runs

Fielding Runs
Doolan-Bal 29.3
McKechnie-Ind ... 23.0
Kenworthy-KC....20.8
Rariden-Ind 19.2
Tinker-Chi 19.1

Total Player Rating
Kenworthy-KC..... 6.2
Kauff-Ind 6.2
Wilson-Chi 5.1
Evans-Bro 4.2
McKechnie-Ind 3.0

Wins
Hendrix-Chi 29
Quinn-Bal 26
Seaton-Bro 25
Falkenberg-Ind ... 25
Suggs-Bal 24

Win Percentage
Ford-Buf 778
Hendrix-Chi 744
Quinn-Bal 650
Seaton-Bro 641
Suggs-Bal 632

Games
Hendrix-Chi 49
Falkenberg-Ind ... 49
Wilhelm-Bal 47
Suggs-Bal 46
Quinn-Bal 46

Complete Games
Hendrix-Chi 34
Falkenberg-Ind ... 33
Moseley-Ind 29
Quinn-Bal 27

Shutouts
Falkenberg-Ind 9
Seaton-Bro 7
Suggs-Bal 6
Hendrix-Chi 6

Saves
Ford-Buf 6
Wilhelm-Bal 5
Packard-KC 5
Hendrix-Chi 5

Innings Pitched
Falkenberg-Ind .. 377.1
Hendrix-Chi 362.0
Quinn-Bal 342.2
Suggs-Bal 319.1
Moseley-Ind 316.2

Fewest Hits/Game
Hendrix-Chi 6.51
Ford-Buf 6.91
Krapp-Buf 7.05
Fiske-Chi 7.32
Watson-Chi-StL .. 7.34

Fewest BB/Game
Ford-Buf 1.49
Suggs-Bal 1.61
Quinn-Bal 1.71
Hendrix-Chi 1.91
Keupper-StL 2.07

Strikeouts
Falkenberg-Ind ... 236
Moseley-Ind 205
Hendrix-Chi 189
Seaton-Bro 172
Groom-StL 167

Strikeouts/Game
Davenport-StL.... 5.93
Moseley-Ind 5.83
Falkenberg-Ind ... 5.63
Groom-StL 5.36
Seaton-Bro 5.11

Ratio
Hendrix-Chi 8.55
Ford-Buf 8.66
Falkenberg-Ind .. 10.16
Fiske-Chi 10.32
Lange-Chi 10.42

Earned Run Average
Hendrix-Chi 1.69
Ford-Buf 1.82
Watson-Chi-StL .. 2.01
Falkenberg-Ind ... 2.22
Lange-Chi 2.23

Adjusted ERA
Ford-Buf 181
Hendrix-Chi 174
Falkenberg-Ind ... 156
Watson-Chi-StL .. 152
Lange-Chi 132

Opponents' Batting Avg.
Hendrix-Chi 203
Krapp-Buf 210
Ford-Buf 214
Cullop-KC 215
Lange-Chi 224

Opponents' On Base Pct.
Hendrix-Chi 251
Ford-Buf 254
Cullop-KC 275
Lange-Chi 282
Falkenberg-Ind ...284

Starter Runs
Hendrix-Chi 60.9
Falkenberg-Ind .. 41.4
Ford-Buf 38.1
Watson-Chi-StL .. 30.2
Cullop-KC 28.3

Adjusted Starter Runs
Falkenberg-Ind .. 52.3
Hendrix-Chi 50.6
Ford-Buf 40.4
Quinn-Bal 29.2
Watson-Chi-StL .. 26.4

Clutch Pitching Index
Dickson-Pit 130
Mullin-Ind 128
Lafitte-Bro 122
Watson-Chi-StL .. 114
Kaiserling-Ind ... 109

Relief Runs

Adjusted Relief Runs

Relief Ranking

Total Pitcher Index
Hendrix-Chi 6.9
Falkenberg-Ind ... 5.8
Quinn-Bal 4.4
Ford-Buf 4.2
Krapp-Buf 3.0

Total Baseball Ranking
Hendrix-Chi 6.9
Kenworthy-KC..... 6.2
Kauff-Ind 6.2
Falkenberg-Ind ... 5.8
Wilson-Chi 5.1

TEAM	G	W	L	PCT	GB	R	OR	AB	H	2B	3B	HR	BB	SO	AVG	OBP	SLG	PRO	PRO+	BR	/A	PF	CHI	RC	SB	CS	SBA	SBR
PHI	153	90	62	.592	—	589	463	4916	1216	202	39	58	460	600	.247	.316	.340	.656	103	31	24	101	101	550	121	113	100	-25
BOS	157	83	69	.546	7	582	545	5070	1219	231	57	17	549	620	.240	.321	.319	.640	104	15	41	96	98	554	121	98	49	0
BRO	154	80	72	.526	10	536	560	5120	1268	165	75	14	313	496	.248	.295	.317	.612	89	-55	-64	102	107	496	131	126	72	-4
CHI	156	73	80	.477	17.5	570	620	5114	1246	212	66	53	393	639	.244	.303	.342	.645	101	4	3	100	100	555	166	124	63	0
PIT	156	73	81	.474	18	557	520	5113	1259	197	91	24	419	656	.246	.309	.334	.643	102	8	15	99	97	563	182	111	64	-4
STL	157	72	81	.471	18.5	590	601	5106	1297	159	92	20	457	658	.254	.320	.333	.653	103	30	28	100	98	568	162	144	69	2
CIN	160	71	83	.461	20	516	585	5231	1323	194	84	15	360	512	.253	.308	.331	.639	98	-4	-14	102	90	553	156	142	67	2
NY	155	69	83	.454	21	582	628	5218	1312	195	68	24	315	547	.251	.300	.329	.629	102	-26	6	94	109	526	155	137	67	1
TOT	624					4522		40888	10140	1555	572	225	3266	4728	.248	.309	.331	.640							1194	995	55	-238

TEAM	CG	SH	SV	IP	H	H/G	HR	BB	SO	RAT	ERA	ERA+	OAV	OOB	PR	/A	PF	CPI	FA	E	DP	FW	PW	BW	SBW	DIF
PHI	98	20	8	1374¹	1161	7.6	26	342	652	10.0	2.17	126	.234	.287	87	84	100	103	.966	216	99	.8	9.3	2.7	.5	.6
BOS	95	17	13	1405²	1257	8.0	23	366	630	10.7	2.57	100	.245	.302	26	0	94	100	.966	213	115	1.4	.0	4.6	3.3	-2.3
BRO	87	16	8	1389²	1252	8.1	29	473	499	11.6	2.66	104	.245	.317	13	17	101	108	.963	238	96	-.5	1.9	-7.1	2.9	6.9
CHI	71	18	8	1399	1272	8.2	28	480	657	11.6	3.11	89	.246	.316	-57	-54	101	91	.958	268	94	-2.3	-6.0	.3	3.3	1.2
PIT	91	18	11	1380	1229	8.0	21	384	544	10.8	2.60	105	.245	.304	22	19	99	100	.966	214	100	1.2	2.1	1.7	2.9	-11.9
STL	79	13	9	1400²	1320	8.5	30	402	538	11.3	2.89	96	.256	.314	-21	-17	101	101	.964	235	109	-.0	-1.9	3.1	3.5	-9.2
CIN	80	19	12	1432¹	1304	8.2	28	497	572	11.6	2.84	101	.249	.320	-15	1	104	104	.966	222	148	1.1	.1	-1.6	3.5	-9.2
NY	78	15	9	1385	1350	8.8	40	325	637	11.2	3.11	82	.259	.308	-56	-86	93	94	.960	256	119	-1.6	-9.6	.7	3.4	.1
TOT	679	136	78	11166²		8.2				11.1	2.75		.248	.309					.964	1862	880					

Runs
Cravath-Phi 89
Doyle-NY 86
Bancroft-Phi 85
Burns-NY 83
O'Mara-Bro 77

Hits
Doyle-NY 189
Griffith-Cin 179
Hinchman-Pit 177
Groh-Cin 170
Burns-NY 169

Doubles
Doyle-NY 40
Luderus-Phi 36
Saier-Chi 35
Smith-Bos 34
Magee-Bos 34

Triples
Long-StL 25
J.Wagner-Pit 17
Griffith-Cin 16
Hinchman-Pit 14
Burns-NY 14

Home Runs
Cravath-Phi 24
Williams-Chi 13
Schulte-Chi 12
Saier-Chi 11
Becker-Phi 11

Total Bases
Cravath-Phi 266
Doyle-NY 261
Griffith-Cin 254
Hinchman-Pit 253
J.Wagner-Pit 239

Runs Batted In
Cravath-Phi 115
Magee-Bos 87
Griffith-Cin 85
J.Wagner-Pit 78
Hinchman-Pit 77

Runs Produced
Cravath-Phi 180
Magee-Bos 157
Doyle-NY 152
Hinchman-Pit 144
Miller-StL 143

Bases On Balls
Cravath-Phi 86
Bancroft-Phi 77
Viox-Pit 75
Huggins-StL 74
Smith-Bos 67

Batting Average
Doyle-NY .... .320
Luderus-Phi ...... .315
Griffith-Cin ...... .307
Hinchman-Pit .... .307
Daubert-Bro ...... .301

On Base Percentage
Cravath-Phi ...... .393
Luderus-Phi ...... .376
Daubert-Bro ...... .369
Hinchman-Pit .... .368
Doyle-NY .... .358

Slugging Average
Cravath-Phi ...... .510
Luderus-Phi ...... .457
Long-StL .... .446
Saier-Chi .... .445
Doyle-NY .... .442

Production
Cravath-Phi ...... .902
Luderus-Phi ...... .833
Hinchman-Pit .... .807
Doyle-NY .... .799
Saier-Chi .... .795

Adjusted Production
Cravath-Phi 170
Doyle-NY 150
Luderus-Phi 150
Hinchman-Pit 146
Saier-Chi 140

Batter Runs
Cravath-Phi 46.8
Luderus-Phi 30.3
Hinchman-Pit 29.7
Doyle-NY 27.1
Griffith-Cin 25.4

Adjusted Batter Runs
Cravath-Phi 46.1
Doyle-NY 30.8
Hinchman-Pit 30.6
Luderus-Phi 29.7
Griffith-Cin 24.2

Clutch Hitting Index
Fletcher-NY 156
Magee-Bos 153
Miller-StL 149
Schmidt-Bos 145
Cutshaw-Bro 143

Runs Created
Cravath-Phi 105
Doyle-NY 94
Hinchman-Pit 94
Luderus-Phi 87
Griffith-Cin 85

Total Average
Cravath-Phi ...... .942
Saier-Chi .... .819
Luderus-Phi ...... .799
Hinchman-Pit .... .741
Doyle-NY .... .714

Stolen Bases
Carey-Pit 36
Herzog-Cin 35
Saier-Chi 29
Baird-Pit 29
Cutshaw-Bro 28

Stolen Base Average
Bresnahan-Chi ... 86.4
Saier-Chi 76.3
Baird-Pit 70.7
Robertson-NY ... 68.8
Herzog-Cin 68.6

Stolen Base Runs
Bresnahan-Chi 3.9
Saier-Chi 3.3
Costello-Pit 1.5
Baird-Pit 1.5
Gerber-Pit 1.2

Fielding Runs
Fletcher-NY 34.1
Herzog-Cin 30.9
Maranville-Bos ... 20.9
Carey-Pit 17.6
Cutshaw-Bro 16.8

Total Player Rating
Cravath-Phi 4.5
Luderus-Phi 3.4
Herzog-Cin 3.3
Groh-Cin 3.0
Snyder-StL 2.8

Wins
Alexander-Phi 31
Rudolph-Bos 22
Mayer-Phi 21
Mamaux-Pit 21
Vaughn-Chi 20

Win Percentage
Alexander-Phi .... .756
Toney-Cin .... .739
Mamaux-Pit ...... .724
Vaughn-Chi ...... .625
Coombs-Bro ..... .600

Games
Hughes-Bos 50
Dale-Cin 49
Alexander-Phi 49
Schneider-Cin 48
Sallee-StL 46

Complete Games
Alexander-Phi 36
Rudolph-Bos 30
Pfeffer-Bro 26
Harmon-Pit 25
Tesreau-NY 24

Shutouts
Alexander-Phi 12
Tesreau-NY 8
Mamaux-Pit 8
Toney-Cin 6
Pfeffer-Bro 6

Saves
Hughes-Bos 9
Benton-Cin-NY 5
Lavender-Chi 4
Cooper-Pit 4

Innings Pitched
Alexander-Phi ... 376.1
Rudolph-Bos 341.1
Tesreau-NY 306.0
Dale-Cin 296.2
Pfeffer-Bro 291.2

Fewest Hits/Game
Alexander-Phi ... 6.05
Toney-Cin 6.47
Mamaux-Pit 6.51
Hughes-Bos 6.68
Zabel-Chi 6.85

Fewest BB/Game
Mathewson-NY ... .97
Humphries-Chi ... 1.21
Adams-Pit 1.25
Alexander-Phi ... 1.53
Rudolph-Bos 1.69

Strikeouts
Alexander-Phi 241
Tesreau-NY 176
Hughes-Bos 171
Mamaux-Pit 152
Vaughn-Chi 148

Strikeouts/Game
Alexander-Phi 5.76
Hughes-Bos 5.49
Mamaux-Pit 5.44
Douglas-Cin-Bro-Chi ... 5.26
Tesreau-NY 5.18

Ratio
Alexander-Phi 7.82
Hughes-Bos 8.89
Tesreau-NY 9.26
Toney-Cin 9.54
Adams-Pit 9.73

Earned Run Average
Alexander-Phi ... 1.22
Toney-Cin 1.58
Mamaux-Pit 2.04
Pfeffer-Bro 2.10
Hughes-Bos 2.12

Adjusted ERA
Alexander-Phi 224
Toney-Cin 181
Mamaux-Pit 134
Pfeffer-Bro 132
Hughes-Bos 122

Opponents' Batting Avg.
Alexander-Phi .... .191
Toney-Cin .... .207
Mamaux-Pit ..... .208
Hughes-Bos ..... .213
Tesreau-NY ..... .215

Opponents' On Base Pct.
Alexander-Phi .... .234
Hughes-Bos ...... .265
Tesreau-NY ...... .269
Toney-Cin .... .278
Adams-Pit .... .280

Starter Runs
Alexander-Phi 63.8
Toney-Cin 28.9
Pfeffer-Bro 21.0
Mamaux-Pit 19.8
Hughes-Bos 19.5

Adjusted Starter Runs
Alexander-Phi 63.4
Toney-Cin 31.6
Pfeffer-Bro 21.9
Mamaux-Pit 19.2
Hughes-Bos 14.5

Clutch Pitching Index
Humphries-Chi ... 139
Perritt-NY 122
Schneider-Cin 121
Rixey-Phi 120
Stroud-NY 118

Relief Runs

Adjusted Relief Runs

Relief Ranking

Total Pitcher Index
Alexander-Phi 8.5
Toney-Cin 3.2
Pfeffer-Bro 2.6
Mayer-Phi 2.0
Schneider-Cin 1.9

Total Baseball Ranking
Alexander-Phi 8.5
Cravath-Phi 4.5
Luderus-Phi 3.4
Herzog-Cin 3.3
Toney-Cin 3.2

1915 American League

TEAM	G	W	L	PCT	GB	R	OR	AB	H	2B	3B	HR	BB	SO	AVG	OBP	SLG	PRO	PRO+	BR	/A	PF	CHI	RC	SB	CS	SBA	SBR
BOS	155	101	50	.669		668	499	5024	1308	202	76	14	527	476	.260	.336	.339	.675	110	46	65	97	100	611	118	117	63	-2
DET	156	100	54	.649	2.5	778	597	5128	1372	207	94	23	681	527	.268	.357	.358	.715	114	131	98	105	101	711	241	146	70	2
CHI	155	93	61	.604	9.5	717	509	4914	1269	163	102	25	583	575	.258	.345	.348	.693	109	83	64	103	102	637	233	183	72	12
WAS	155	85	68	.556	17	569	491	5029	1225	152	79	12	458	541	.244	.312	.312	.624	91	-51	-54	101	103	535	186	106	60	-3
NY	154	69	83	.454	32.5	584	588	4982	1162	167	50	31	570	669	.233	.317	.305	.622	91	-45	-43	100	103	523	198	133	69	-1
STL	159	63	91	.409	39.5	521	679	5112	1255	166	65	19	472	765	.246	.315	.315	.630	97	-43	-19	96	91	535	202	160	70	6
CLE	154	57	95	.375	44.5	539	670	5034	1210	169	79	20	490	681	.240	.312	.317	.629	91	-42	-53	102	95	526	138	117	63	-2
PHI	154	43	109	.283	58.5	545	888	5081	1204	183	72	16	436	634	.237	.304	.311	.615	91	-73	-55	97	103	507	127	89	59	-8
TOT	621					4921		40304	10005	1409	617	160	4217	4868	.248	.325	.326	.651							1443	1051	58	-197

TEAM	CG	SH	SV	IP	H	H/G	HR	BB	SO	RAT	ERA	ERA+	OAV	OOB	PR	/A	PF	CPI	FA	E	DP	FW	PW	BW	SBW	DIF
BOS	81	19	15	1397	1164	7.5	18	446	634	10.7	2.39	116	.231	.299	84	58	95	97	.964	226	95	2.5	6.2	6.9	2.4	7.6
DET	86	10	19	1413¹	1259	8.0	14	489	550	11.5	2.86	106	.243	.315	11	24	103	93	.961	258	107	.5	2.6	10.4	2.8	6.7
CHI	91	16	9	1401	1242	8.0	14	350	635	10.4	2.43	122	.241	.294	78	84	101	95	.965	222	95	2.7	8.9	6.8	3.9	-6.3
WAS	87	21	13	1393²	1161	7.5	12	455	715	10.7	2.31	127	.232	.302	96	95	100	102	.964	230	101	2.2	10.1	-5.7	2.3	-.4
NY	101	12	2	1382²	1272	8.3	41	517	559	12.0	3.06	96	.253	.329	-19	-20	100	104	.966	217	118	2.9	-2.1	-4.6	2.5	-5.8
STL	76	6	7	1403	1256	8.1	21	612	566	12.4	3.04	94	.249	.337	-17	-30	98	103	.949	336	144	-4.3	-3.2	-2.0	3.3	-7.7
CLE	62	11	10	1372	1287	8.4	18	518	610	12.0	3.13	99	.255	.328	-30	-13	104	98	.957	280	82	-1.2	-1.4	-5.6	2.4	-13.2
PHI	78	6	2	1348¹	1358	9.1	22	827	588	15.0	4.29	69	.277	.388	-203	-202	100	102	.947	338	118	-5.0	-21.5	-5.8	1.8	-2.5
TOT	662	101	77	11111		8.1				11.8	2.93		.248	.325					.959	2107	860					

Runs
Cobb-Det 144
E.Collins-Chi 118
Vitt-Det 116
Speaker-Bos 108
Chapman-Cle 101

Hits
Cobb-Det 208
Crawford-Det 183
Veach-Det 178
Speaker-Bos 176
Pratt-StL 175

Doubles
Veach-Det 40
Pratt-StL 31
Lewis-Bos 31
Crawford-Det 31
Cobb-Det 31

Triples
Crawford-Det...... 19
Fournier-Chi...... 18
Roth-Chi-Cle 17
J.Collins-Chi 17
Chapman-Cle 17

Home Runs
Roth-Chi-Cle 7
Oldring-Phi......... 6

Total Bases
Cobb-Det 274
Crawford-Det..... 267
Veach-Det 247
Pratt-StL 237
E.Collins-Chi 227

Runs Batted In
Veach-Det 112
Crawford-Det..... 112
Cobb-Det 99
J.Collins-Chi 85
J.Jackson-Cle-Chi . 81

Runs Produced
Cobb-Det 240
E.Collins-Chi 191
Veach-Det 190
Crawford-Det.... 188
Speaker-Bos 177

Bases On Balls
E.Collins-Chi 119
Shotton-StL 118
Cobb-Det 118
Bush-Det 118
Hooper-Bos 89

Batting Average
Cobb-Det .... .369
E.Collins-Chi ..... .332
Fournier-Chi ...... .322
Speaker-Bos ..... .322
McInnis-Phi ...... .314

On Base Percentage
Cobb-Det .... .486
E.Collins-Chi ..... .460
Fournier-Chi ...... .429
Speaker-Bos ..... .416
Shotton-StL ...... .409

Slugging Average
Fournier-Chi ...... .491
Cobb-Det .... .487
J.Jackson-Cle-Chi .445
Crawford-Det..... .436
E.Collins-Chi ..... .436

Production
Cobb-Det .... .973
Fournier-Chi...... .920
E.Collins-Chi ..... .896
J.Jackson-Cle-Chi .830
Speaker-Bos ..... .827

Adjusted Production
Cobb-Det 182
Fournier-Chi...... 170
E.Collins-Chi 163
Speaker-Bos 152
J.Jackson-Cle-Chi 145

Batter Runs
Cobb-Det 71.6
E.Collins-Chi 51.9
Fournier-Chi 40.9
Speaker-Bos 35.0
Veach-Det 32.3

Adjusted Batter Runs
Cobb-Det 67.9
E.Collins-Chi 49.7
Fournier-Chi 39.3
Speaker-Bos 37.2
Shotton-StL 30.1

Clutch Hitting Index
Veach-Det 158
J.Collins-Chi 140
Gardner-Bos 133
Schalk-Chi 133
Crawford-Det..... 130

Runs Created
Cobb-Det 155
E.Collins-Chi 116
Crawford-Det..... 102
Speaker-Bos 97
Veach-Det 97

Total Average
Cobb-Det 1.170
E.Collins-Chi ..... .971
Fournier-Chi...... .964
Speaker-Bos ..... .801
Crawford-Det..... .774

Stolen Bases
Cobb-Det 96
Maisel-NY 51
E.Collins-Chi 46
Shotton-StL 43
J.Milan-Was 40

Stolen Base Average
Schang-Phi 85.7
Maisel-NY 81.0
Foster-Was 76.9
Moeller-Was 76.2
Roth-Chi-Cle 72.2

Stolen Base Runs
Maisel-NY 8.1
Cobb-Det 6.0
Schang-Phi 3.6
Moeller-Was 3.6
Williams-StL....... 2.7

Fielding Runs
Boone-NY 20.8
C.Walker-StL..... 14.8
Vitt-Det 14.4
Lajoie-Phi 14.1
Speaker-Bos 13.4

Total Player Rating
Cobb-Det 6.5
E.Collins-Chi 5.9
Speaker-Bos 3.8
Chapman-Cle 3.6
Fournier-Chi...... 3.5

Wins
Johnson-Was 27
Scott-Chi 24
Faber-Chi 24
Dauss-Det 24
Coveleski-Det 22

Win Percentage
Wood-Bos .... .750
Shore-Bos .... .704
Foster-Bos .... .704
Ruth-Bos .... .692
Scott-Chi .... .686

Games
Faber-Chi 50
Coveleski-Det 50
Scott-Chi 48
Jones-Cle 48

Complete Games
Johnson-Was 35
Caldwell-NY 31
Dauss-Det 27
Scott-Chi 23
Dubuc-Det 22

Shutouts
Scott-Chi 7
Johnson-Was 7
Morton-Cle 6
Foster-Bos 5
Dubuc-Det 5

Saves
Mays-Bos 7

Innings Pitched
Johnson-Was ... 336.2
Coveleski-Det ... 312.2
Dauss-Det 309.2
Caldwell-NY 305.0
Faber-Chi 299.2

Fewest Hits/Game
Leonard-Bos 6.38
Ruth-Bos 6.86
Wood-Bos 6.86
Johnson-Was 6.90
Morton-Cle 7.09

Fewest BB/Game
Johnson-Was 1.50
Ayers-Was 1.62
Benz-Chi 1.62
Russell-Chi 1.84
Cicotte-Chi 1.93

Strikeouts
Johnson-Was 203
Faber-Chi 182
Wyckoff-Phi...... 157
Coveleski-Det 150
Mitchell-Cle 149

Strikeouts/Game
Leonard-Bos 5.69
Mitchell-Cle 5.68
Faber-Chi........ 5.47
Johnson-Was 5.43
Lowdermilk-StL-Det . 5.32

Ratio
Johnson-Was 8.90
Morton-Cle 9.41
Wood-Bos 9.44
Ayers-Was 9.50
Benz-Chi 9.63

Earned Run Average
Wood-Bos 1.49
Johnson-Was 1.55
Shore-Bos 1.64
Scott-Chi 2.03
Fisher-NY........ 2.11

Adjusted ERA
Johnson-Was 188
Wood-Bos 186
Shore-Bos 169
Scott-Chi 146
Morton-Cle 142

Opponents' Batting Avg.
Leonard-Bos ..... .208
Ruth-Bos .... .212
Johnson-Was ..... .214
Morton-Cle ...... .216
Wood-Bos .... .216

Opponents' On Base Pct.
Johnson-Was ..... .260
Morton-Cle ...... .268
Wood-Bos .... .275
Benz-Chi .... .276
Ayers-Was .... .276

Starter Runs
Johnson-Was 51.7
Shore-Bos 35.5
Scott-Chi 29.5
Wood-Bos 25.2
Foster-Bos 23.2

Adjusted Starter Runs
Johnson-Was 51.3
Shore-Bos 31.1
Scott-Chi 30.9
Morton-Cle 24.1
Benz-Chi 22.7

Clutch Pitching Index
Hamilton-StL 125
Shore-Bos 122
Foster-Bos 121
Fisher-NY........ 119
Wood-Bos 118

Relief Runs

Adjusted Relief Runs

Relief Ranking

Total Pitcher Index
Johnson-Was 6.8
Shore-Bos 3.6
Scott-Chi 3.2
Wood-Bos 3.1
Dauss-Det 3.1

Total Baseball Ranking
Johnson-Was 6.8
Cobb-Det 6.5
E.Collins-Chi 5.9
Speaker-Bos 3.8
Chapman-Cle 3.6

TEAM	G	W	L	PCT	GB	R	OR	AB	H	2B	3B	HR	BB	SO	AVG	OBP	SLG	PRO	PRO+	BR	/A	PF	CHI	RC	SB	CS	SBA	SBR
CHI	155	86	66	.566		640	538	5133	1320	185	77	50	444	590	.257	.320	.352	.672	111	28	63	94	102	650	161			
STL	159	87	67	.565		634	527	5145	1344	199	81	23	576	502	.261	.340	.345	.685	103	67	34	105	92	698	195			
PIT	156	86	67	.562	0.5	592	524	5040	1318	180	80	20	448	561	.262	.326	.341	.667	103	25	30	99	95	655	224			
KC	153	81	72	.529	5.5	547	551	4937	1206	200	66	28	368	503	.244	.303	.329	.632	96	-46	-22	96	103	559	144			
NEW	155	80	72	.526	6	585	562	5097	1283	210	80	17	438	550	.252	.315	.334	.649	104	-9	-25	99	99	618	184			
BUF	153	74	78	.487	12	574	634	5065	1261	193	68	40	420	587	.249	.309	.338	.647	95	-20	-32	102	102	594	184			
BRO	153	70	82	.461	16	647	673	5035	1348	205	75	36	473	654	.268	.336	.360	.696	112	77	81	99	97	704	249			
BAL	154	47	107	.305	40	550	760	5060	1235	196	53	36	470	641	.244	.313	.325	.638	92	-28	-46	103	97	578	128			
TOT	619					4769		40512	10315	1568	580	250	3637	4588	.255	.316	.340	.656							1469			

TEAM	CG	SH	SV	IP	H	H/G	HR	BB	SO	RAT	ERA	ERA+	OAV	OOB	PR	/A	PF	CPI	FA	E	DP	FW	PW	BW	SBW	DIF
CHI	97	21	10	1397²	1232	7.9	33	402	576	10.7	2.64	106	.235	.294	60	22	92	90	.964	233	102	.4	2.4	6.8		.4
STL	94	24	9	1426	1267	8.0	22	396	698	10.7	2.73	117	.244	.301	47	72	105	94	.967	212	111	2.0	7.7	3.7		-3.4
PIT	88	16	12	1382¹	1273	8.3	37	441	517	11.4	2.79	108	.261	.326	36	32	99	116	.971	182	98	3.5	3.4	3.2		-.7
KC	95	16	11	1359	1210	8.0	29	390	526	10.8	2.82	103	.254	.315	31	14	96	105	.962	246	96	-.5	1.5	-2.4		5.9
NEW	100	16	7	1406²	1308	8.4	15	453	581	11.6	2.60	109	.278	.348	66	37	94	139	.963	239	124	.0	4.0	2.7		-2.7
BUF	79	14	11	1360	1271	8.4	34	553	594	12.3	3.38	92	.257	.335	-52	-41	103	99	.964	232	112	.3	-4.4	-3.4		5.6
BRO	78	10	16	1355²	1299	8.6	27	536	467	12.3	3.37	90	.258	.333	-50	-52	100	97	.955	290	103	-3.1	-5.6	8.7		-6.0
BAL	85	5	7	1360¹	1455	9.6	53	466	570	13.0	3.96	81	.295	.361	-139	-116	105	108	.957	273	140	-2.0	-12.5	-5.0		-10.5
TOT	716	122	83	11047²		8.4				11.6	3.03		.255	.316					.963	1907	886					

Runs		Hits		Doubles		Triples		Home Runs		Total Bases	
Borton-StL	97	Tobin-StL	184	Evans-Bro-Bal	34	Mann-Chi	19	Chase-Buf	17	Konetchy-Pit	278
Berghammer-Pit	96	Konetchy-Pit	181	Zwilling-Chi	32	Konetchy-Pit	18	Zwilling-Chi	13	Chase-Buf	267
Evans-Bro-Bal	94	Evans-Bro-Bal	171	Konetchy-Pit	31	Kelly-Pit	17	Kauff-Bro	12	Tobin-StL	254
Tobin-StL	92	Kauff-Bro	165	Chase-Buf	31	Gilmore-KC	15	Konetchy-Pit	10	Kauff-Bro	246
Kauff-Bro	92	Chase-Buf	165					Walsh-Bal-StL	9	Zwilling-Chi	242

Runs Batted In		Runs Produced		Bases On Balls		Batting Average		On Base Percentage		Slugging Average	
Zwilling-Chi	94	Borton-StL	177	Borton-StL	92	Kauff-Bro	.342	Kauff-Bro	.446	Kauff-Bro	.509
Konetchy-Pit	93	Kauff-Bro	163	Kauff-Bro	85	Magee-Bro	.323	W.Miller-StL	.400	Konetchy-Pit	.483
Chase-Buf	89	Konetchy-Pit	162	Berghammer-Pit	83	Konetchy-Pit	.314	Borton-StL	.395	Chase-Buf	.471
Kauff-Bro	83	Evans-Bro-Bal	157	W.Miller-StL	79	Flack-Chi	.314	Evans-Bro-Bal	.392	Zwilling-Chi	.442
Borton-StL	83	Chase-Buf	157			Campbell-New	.310	Cooper-Bro	.388	Mann-Chi	.438

Production		Adjusted Production		Batter Runs		Adjusted Batter Runs		Clutch Hitting Index		Runs Created	
Kauff-Bro	.955	Kauff-Bro	184	Kauff-Bro	53.5	Kauff-Bro	53.9	Oakes-Pit	146	Kauff-Bro	132
Konetchy-Pit	.846	Konetchy-Pit	150	Konetchy-Pit	32.6	Konetchy-Pit	33.2	Borton-StL	142	Konetchy-Pit	111
Evans-Bro-Bal	.818	Zwilling-Chi	147	Evans-Bro-Bal	31.0	Zwilling-Chi	30.2	Engle-Buf	140	Tobin-StL	106
Zwilling-Chi	.808	Mann-Chi	143	Borton-StL	26.7	Evans-Bro-Bal	30.0	F.Smith-Buf-Bro	134	Zwilling-Chi	99
Mann-Chi	.795	Flack-Chi	141	Zwilling-Chi	26.3	Wilson-Chi	26.8	Zwilling-Chi	128	Evans-Bro-Bal	99

Total Average		Stolen Bases		Stolen Base Average	Stolen Base Runs	Fielding Runs		Total Player Rating	
Kauff-Bro	1.233	Kauff-Bro	55			Doolan-Bal-Chi	32.1	Kauff-Bro	6.5
Konetchy-Pit	.884	Mowrey-Pit	40			Rariden-New	21.0	Rariden-New	4.0
Cooper-Bro	.868	Kelly-Pit	38			Cooper-Bro	18.3	Cooper-Bro	4.0
W.Miller-StL	.863	Flack-Chi	37			Johnson-StL	17.7	Konetchy-Pit	3.7
Zwilling-Chi	.857	Magee-Bro	34			Perring-KC	14.8	Zwilling-Chi	3.3

Wins		Win Percentage		Games		Complete Games		Shutouts		Saves	
McConnell-Chi	25	McConnell-Chi	.714	Davenport-StL	55	Davenport-StL	30	Davenport-StL	10	Bedient-Buf	10
Allen-Pit	23	Brown-Chi	.680	Bedient-Buf	53	Hendrix-Chi	26	Plank-StL	6	Barger-Pit	6
Davenport-StL	22	Reulbach-New	.677	Crandall-StL	51	Schulz-Buf	25	Allen-Pit	6	Wiltse-Bro	5
Cullop-KC	22	Cullop-KC	.667	Johnson-KC	46	Allen-Pit	24			Upham-Bro	5
		Plank-StL	.656								

Innings Pitched		Fewest Hits/Game		Fewest BB/Game		Strikeouts		Strikeouts/Game		Ratio	
Davenport-StL	392.2	Davenport-StL	6.88	Plank-StL	1.81	Davenport-StL	229	Anderson-Buf	5.33	Plank-StL	9.02
Crandall-StL	312.2	Main-KC	7.08	Bender-Bal	1.87	Schulz-Buf	160	Davenport-StL	5.25	Davenport-StL	9.19
Schulz-Buf	309.2	Plank-StL	7.11	Hearn-Pit	1.90	McConnell-Chi	151	Plank-StL	4.93	Brown-Chi	9.90
McConnell-Chi	303.0	Brown-Chi	7.20	Cullop-KC	1.99	Plank-StL	147	Bailey-Bal-Chi	4.91	Anderson-Buf	10.01
Cullop-KC	302.1	Anderson-Buf	7.20	Quinn-Bal	2.07			Groom-StL	4.78	Reulbach-New	10.17

Earned Run Average		Adjusted ERA		Opponents' Batting Avg.		Opponents' On Base Pct.		Starter Runs		Adjusted Starter Runs	
Moseley-New	1.91	Plank-StL	154	Davenport-StL	.215	Plank-StL	.262	Davenport-StL	36.3	Davenport-StL	43.4
Plank-StL	2.08	Moseley-New	149	Plank-StL	.218	Davenport-StL	.268	Moseley-New	33.3	Plank-StL	33.3
Brown-Chi	2.09	Davenport-StL	145	Brown-Chi	.220	Brown-Chi	.279	Plank-StL	28.4	Moseley-New	27.7
McConnell-Chi	2.20	Brown-Chi	133	Main-KC	.222	Anderson-Buf	.285	McConnell-Chi	28.1	Crandall-StL	21.0
Davenport-StL	2.20	Reulbach-New	127	Anderson-Buf	.222	Reulbach-New	.287	Brown-Chi	24.6	McConnell-Chi	19.9

Clutch Pitching Index		Relief Runs	Adjusted Relief Runs	Relief Ranking	Total Pitcher Index		Total Baseball Ranking	
Moran-New	129				Crandall-StL	4.4	Kauff-Bro	6.5
Kaiserling-New	127				Plank-StL	4.0	Crandall-StL	4.4
Rogge-Pit	127				McConnell-Chi	3.1	Rariden-New	4.0
Moseley-New	122				Brown-Chi	3.0	Cooper-Bro	4.0
Suggs-Bal	118				Davenport-StL	2.9	Plank-StL	4.0

TEAM	G	W	L	PCT	GB	R	OR	AB	H	2B	3B	HR	BB	SO	AVG	OBP	SLG	PRO	PRO+	BR	/A	PF	CHI	RC	SB	CS	SBA	SBR
BRO	156	94	60	.610		585	471	5234	**1366**	195	80	28	355	**550**	**.261**	**.313**	**.345**	**.658**	105	**46**	31	103	99	**645**	187			
PHI	154	91	62	.595	2.5	581	489	4985	1244	**223**	53	42	399	571	.250	.310	.341	.651	102	34	15	104	104	593	149			
BOS	158	89	63	.586	4	542	**453**	5075	1181	166	73	22	**437**	646	.233	.299	.307	.606	96	-37	-13	96	**108**	535	141			
NY	155	86	66	.566	7	**597**	504	5152	1305	188	74	42	356	558	.253	.307	.343	.650	**111**	31	**59**	95	106	617	**206**			
CHI	156	67	86	.438	26.5	520	541	5179	1237	194	56	**46**	399	662	.239	.298	.325	.623	87	-17	-75	111	99	559	133			
PIT	157	65	89	.422	29	484	586	5181	1246	147	**91**	20	372	618	.240	.298	.316	.614	94	-31	-35	101	95	556	173			
STL	153	60	93	.392	33.5	476	629	5030	1223	155	74	25	335	651	.243	.295	.318	.613	94	-34	-30	99	98	535	182			
CIN	155	60	93	.392	33.5	505	617	5254	1336	187	88	14	362	573	.254	.307	.331	.638	104	13	26	98	91	596	157			
TOT	622					4290		41090	10138	1455	589	239	3015	4829	.247	.303	.328	.632						1328				

TEAM	CG	SH	SV	IP	H	H/G	HR	BB	SO	RAT	ERA	ERA+	OAV	OOB	PR	/A	PF	CPI	FA	E	DP	FW	PW	BW	SBW	DIF
BRO	96	22	9	1427.1	**1201**	7.6	24	372	634	10.2	**2.12**	**126**	**.232**	.288	**78**	**86**	102	103	.965	224	90	1.2	**9.8**	3.5		2.4
PHI	**97**	**25**	9	1382.1	1238	8.1	28	**295**	601	10.3	2.36	112	.244	.291	39	43	101	101	.963	234	119	.4	4.9	1.7		7.5
BOS	**97**	23	11	1415.2	1206	7.7	24	325	**644**	9.9	2.19	113	.235	.284	65	44	95	99	**.967**	212	124	2.1	5.0	-1.5		7.3
NY	88	22	12	1397.1	1267	8.2	41	310	638	10.4	2.60	93	.244	.292	1	-27	93	95	.966	217	108	1.5	-3.1	**6.7**		4.8
CHI	72	17	13	1416.2	1265	8.0	32	365	616	10.6	2.65	110	.243	.298	-5	38	111	94	.957	286	104	-2.6	4.3	-8.6		-2.7
PIT	88	11	7	1419.2	1277	8.1	24	443	596	11.1	2.76	97	.246	.310	-23	-14	103	97	.959	260	97	-.9	-1.6	-4.0		-5.5
STL	58	13	**15**	1355	1331	8.8	31	445	529	12.1	3.14	84	.265	.330	-79	-77	101	**104**	.957	278	124	-2.4	-8.8	-3.4		-1.9
CIN	86	7	6	1408	1356	8.7	35	458	569	11.9	3.10	84	.260	.325	-76	-81	99	101	.965	228	**126**	.9	-9.3	3.0		-11.1
TOT	682	140	82	11222		8.1				10.8	2.61		.247	.303					.963	1939	892					

Runs
Burns-NY 105
Carey-Pit 90
Robertson-NY 88
Groh-Cin 85
Paskert-Phi 82

Hits
Chase-Cin 184
Robertson-NY 180
Z.Wheat-Bro 177
Hinchman-Pit 175
Burns-NY 174

Doubles
Niehoff-Phi 42
Z.Wheat-Bro 32
Paskert-Phi 30

Triples
Hinchman-Pit 16
Roush-NY-Cin 15
Kauff-NY 15
Hornsby-StL 15

Home Runs
Williams-Chi 12
Robertson-NY 12
Cravath-Phi 11
Z.Wheat-Bro 9
Kauff-NY 9

Total Bases
Z.Wheat-Bro 262
Robertson-NY 250
Chase-Cin 249
Hinchman-Pit 237
Burns-NY 229

Runs Batted In
Zimmerman-Chi-NY 83
Chase-Cin 82
Hinchman-Pit 76
Kauff-NY 74
Z.Wheat-Bro 73

Runs Produced
Zimmerman-Chi-NY 153
Robertson-NY 145
Chase-Cin 143
Konetchy-Bos 143
Burns-NY 141

Bases On Balls
Groh-Cin 84
Saier-Phi 79
Bancroft-Phi 74
Kauff-NY 68
Cravath-Phi 64

Batting Average
Chase-Cin 339
Daubert-Bro 316
Hinchman-Pit 315
Hornsby-StL 313
Z.Wheat-Bro 312

On Base Percentage
Cravath-Phi 379
Hinchman-Pit 378
Williams-Chi 372
Daubert-Bro 371
Groh-Cin 370

Slugging Average
Z.Wheat-Bro 461
Chase-Cin 459
Williams-Chi 459
Hornsby-StL 444
Cravath-Phi 440

Production
Williams-Chi 831
Z.Wheat-Bro 828
Chase-Cin 822
Cravath-Phi 819
Hornsby-StL 814

Adjusted Production
Chase-Cin 155
Hornsby-StL 150
Z.Wheat-Bro 149
Cravath-Phi 146
Hinchman-Pit 146

Batter Runs
Z.Wheat-Bro 34.5
Hinchman-Pit 31.1
Chase-Cin 30.2
Cravath-Phi 28.7
Hornsby-StL 28.2

Adjusted Batter Runs
Z.Wheat-Bro 32.9
Chase-Cin 31.5
Hinchman-Pit 30.6
Hornsby-StL 28.5
Cravath-Phi 26.9

Clutch Hitting Index
Mowrey-Bro 157
Magee-Bos 156
Zimmerman-Chi-NY 145
Fletcher-NY 139
Cutshaw-Bro 138

Runs Created
Z.Wheat-Bro 103
Hinchman-Pit 96
Chase-Cin 93
Hornsby-StL 88
Carey-Pit 87

Total Average
Williams-Chi 863
Cravath-Phi 857
Z.Wheat-Bro 844
Hornsby-StL 826
Hinchman-Pit 797

Stolen Bases
Carey-Pit 63
Kauff-NY 40
Bescher-StL 39
Burns-NY 37
Herzog-Cin-NY 34

Stolen Base Average
Carey-Pit 76.8
Bescher-StL 76.5
Daubert-Bro 75.0
Maranville-Bos . . . 68.1
Chase-Cin 66.7

Stolen Base Runs
Carey-Pit 7.5
Bescher-StL 4.5
Daubert-Bro 2.1
Maranville-Bos 6

Fielding Runs
Betzel-StL 29.3
Bancroft-Phi 24.5
Carey-Pit 22.9
Maranville-Bos . . . 21.5
Doyle-NY-Chi 20.0

Total Player Rating
Groh-Cin 5.0
Carey-Pit 4.3
Fletcher-NY 4.2
Z.Wheat-Bro 4.1
Doyle-NY-Chi 4.1

Wins
Alexander-Phi 33
Pfeffer-Bro 25
Rixey-Phi 22
Mamaux-Pit 21

Win Percentage
Hughes-Bos 842
Alexander-Phi 733
Pfeffer-Bro 694
Rixey-Phi 688
Benton-NY 667

Games
Meadows-StL 51
Alexander-Phi 48
Mamaux-Pit 45
Ames-StL 45

Complete Games
Alexander-Phi 38
Pfeffer-Bro 30
Rudolph-Bos 27
Mamaux-Pit 26
Demaree-Phi 25

Shutouts
Alexander-Phi 16
Tyler-Bos 6
Pfeffer-Bro 6

Saves
Ames-StL 8
Packard-Chi 5
Marquard-Bro 5
Hughes-Bos 5

Innings Pitched
Alexander-Phi . . . 388.2
Pfeffer-Bro 328.2
Rudolph-Bos 312.0
Mamaux-Pit 310.0
Toney-Cin 300.0

Fewest Hits/Game
Cheney-Bro 6.33
Hughes-Bos 6.76
Cooper-Pit 6.91
Miller-Pit 7.02
Ragan-Bos 7.07

Fewest BB/Game
Rudolph-Bos 1.10
Alexander-Phi 1.16
Demaree-Phi 1.52
Sallee-StL-NY 1.63
Marquard-Bro 1.67

Strikeouts
Alexander-Phi 167
Cheney-Bro 166
Mamaux-Pit 163
Toney-Cin 146
Vaughn-Chi 144

Strikeouts/Game
Cheney-Bro 5.91
Hughes-Bos 5.42
Hendrix-Chi 4.83
Mamaux-Pit 4.73
Marquard-Bro 4.70

Ratio
Rudolph-Bos 8.86
Alexander-Phi 8.87
Marquard-Bro 9.09
McConnell-Chi 9.30
Ragan-Bos 9.40

Earned Run Average
Alexander-Phi 1.55
Marquard-Bro 1.58
Rixey-Phi 1.85
Cooper-Pit 1.87
Pfeffer-Bro 1.92

Adjusted ERA
Alexander-Phi 171
Marquard-Bro 169
Cooper-Pit 144
Rixey-Phi 143
Pfeffer-Bro 140

Opponents' Batting Avg.
Cheney-Bro 198
Cooper-Pit 215
Hughes-Bos 215
Ragan-Bos 218
McConnell-Chi 223

Opponents' On Base Pct.
Rudolph-Bos 261
Alexander-Phi 262
Marquard-Bro 267
Ragan-Bos 270
McConnell-Chi 271

Starter Runs
Alexander-Phi 45.8
Schupp-NY 26.7
Pfeffer-Bro 25.4
Rixey-Phi 24.3
Marquard-Bro 23.5

Adjusted Starter Runs
Alexander-Phi 47.3
Pfeffer-Bro 27.7
Rixey-Phi 25.4
Marquard-Bro 24.9
Schupp-NY 23.8

Clutch Pitching Index
Dell-Bro 124
Sallee-StL-NY 117
Meadows-StL 116
Schulz-Cin 114
Alexander-Phi 114

Relief Runs

Adjusted Relief Runs

Relief Ranking

Total Pitcher Index
Alexander-Phi . . . 7.1
Pfeffer-Bro 3.8
Rixey-Phi 3.2
Cooper-Pit 2.6
Tyler-Bos 2.5

Total Baseball Ranking
Alexander-Phi 7.1
Groh-Cin 5.0
Carey-Pit 4.3
Fletcher-NY 4.2
Z.Wheat-Bro 4.1

TEAM	G	W	L	PCT	GB	R	OR	AB	H	2B	3B	HR	BB	SO	AVG	OBP	SLG	PRO	PRO+	BR	/A	PF	CHI	RC	SB	CS	SBA	SBR
BOS	156	91	63	.591		550	**480**	5018	1246	197	56	14	464	**482**	.248	.317	.318	.635	96	-19	-21	100	100	580	129			
CHI	155	89	65	.578	2	601	497	5081	1277	194	**100**	17	447	591	.251	.319	.339	.658	102	18	11	101	102	638	197			
DET	155	87	67	.565	4	**670**	595	5193	**1371**	202	96	17	545	529	**.264**	**.337**	**.350**	**.687**	109	78	57	104	101	**700**	190			
NY	156	80	74	.519	11	577	561	5198	1277	194	59	**35**	490	632	.246	.318	.326	.644	97	-3	-15	102	100	613	179			
STL	158	79	75	.513	12	588	545	5159	1262	181	50	14	**627**	640	.245	.331	.307	.638	102	2	30	95	99	620	**234**			
CLE	157	77	77	.500	14	630	602	5064	1264	**233**	66	16	522	605	.250	.324	.331	.655	97	17	-16	106	**106**	625	160			
WAS	159	76	77	.497	14.5	536	543	5114	1238	170	60	12	535	597	.242	.320	.306	.626	96	-29	-15	98	98	579	185			
PHI	154	36	117	.235	54.5	447	776	5010	1212	169	65	19	406	631	.242	.303	.313	.616	94	-60	-37	96	91	538	151			
TOT	625					4599		40837	10147	1540	552	144	4062	4707	.248	.321	.324	.645							1425			

TEAM	CG	SH	SV	IP	H	H/G	HR	BB	SO	RAT	ERA	ERA+	OAV	OOB	PR	/A	PF	CPI	FA	E	DP	FW	PW	BW	SBW	DIF
BOS	76	**24**	16	1410²	1221	7.8	**10**	463	584	11.0	2.48	112	.239	.307	54	44	98	99	**.972**	183	108	**3.0**	4.9	-2.3		8.4
CHI	73	20	15	1412¹	**1189**	7.6	14	**405**	644	10.3	**2.36**	117	**.236**	.296	72	61	98	96	.968	205	**134**	1.5	**6.8**	1.2		2.5
DET	81	8	13	1410	1254	8.0	11	578	531	12.1	2.97	96	.248	.332	-22	-18	101	100	.968	211	110	1.1	-2.0	**6.3**		4.5
NY	84	12	**17**	1428	1249	7.9	37	476	616	11.2	2.77	104	.244	.314	7	17	102	100	.967	219	119	.7	1.9	-1.7		2.0
STL	74	9	13	1443²	1292	8.1	15	478	505	11.3	2.58	106	.247	.315	38	26	97	105	.963	248	120	-.9	2.9	3.3		-3.3
CLE	65	9	16	1410	1383	8.8	17	467	537	12.0	2.90	103	.263	.328	-12	15	106	**107**	.965	232	130	.0	1.7	-1.8		.1
WAS	85	11	7	1432	1271	8.0	14	540	**706**	11.6	2.66	103	.246	.322	25	11	97	105	.964	232	119	.2	1.2	-1.7		-.2
PHI	**94**	11	3	1343²	1311	8.8	26	715	575	13.8	3.92	73	.267	.363	-163	-157	102	97	.951	314	126	-5.5	-17.4	-4.1		-13.5
TOT	632	104	100	11290¹		8.1				11.6	2.82		.248	.321					.965	1844	966					

Runs
Cobb-Det	113
Graney-Cle	106
Speaker-Cle	102
Shotton-StL	97
Veach-Det	92

Hits
Speaker-Cle	211
Jackson-Chi	202
Cobb-Det	201
Sisler-StL	177
Shotton-StL	174

Doubles
Speaker-Cle	41
Graney-Cle	41
Jackson-Chi	40
Pratt-StL	35
Veach-Det	33

Triples
Jackson-Chi	21
E.Collins-Chi	17
Witt-Phi	15
Veach-Det	15

Home Runs
Pipp-NY	12
Baker-NY	10
Schang-Phi	7
Felsch-Chi	7

Total Bases
Jackson-Chi	293
Speaker-Cle	274
Cobb-Det	267
Veach-Det	245

Runs Batted In
Pratt-StL	103
Pipp-NY	93
Veach-Det	91
Speaker-Cle	79
Jackson-Chi	78

Runs Produced
Veach-Det	180
Speaker-Cle	179
Cobb-Det	176
Jackson-Chi	166
Pratt-StL	162

Bases On Balls
Shotton-StL	111
Graney-Cle	102
E.Collins-Chi	86
Speaker-Cle	82
Hooper-Bos	80

Batting Average
Speaker-Cle	.386
Cobb-Det	.371
Jackson-Chi	.341
Strunk-Phi	.316
Gardner-Bos	.308

On Base Percentage
Speaker-Cle	.470
Cobb-Det	.452
E.Collins-Chi	.405
Jackson-Chi	.393
Strunk-Phi	.393

Slugging Average
Speaker-Cle	.502
Jackson-Chi	.495
Cobb-Det	.493
Veach-Det	.433
Felsch-Chi	.427

Production
Speaker-Cle	.972
Cobb-Det	.944
Jackson-Chi	.888
Strunk-Phi	.814
E.Collins-Chi	.802

Adjusted Production
Speaker-Cle	181
Cobb-Det	177
Jackson-Chi	165
Strunk-Phi	151
E.Collins-Chi	139

Batter Runs
Speaker-Cle	64.6
Cobb-Det	57.5
Jackson-Chi	44.9
E.Collins-Chi	30.5
Strunk-Phi	30.2

Adjusted Batter Runs
Speaker-Cle	60.8
Cobb-Det	55.3
Jackson-Chi	44.2
Strunk-Phi	32.8
E.Collins-Chi	29.8

Clutch Hitting Index
Pratt-StL	158
Gandil-Cle	151
Marsans-StL	143
Heilmann-Det	138
Burns-Det	137

Runs Created
Cobb-Det	136
Speaker-Cle	132
Jackson-Chi	119
E.Collins-Chi	99
Veach-Det	94

Total Average
Cobb-Det	1.071
Speaker-Cle	1.017
Jackson-Chi	.876
E.Collins-Chi	.814
Graney-Cle	.761

Stolen Bases
Cobb-Det	68
Marsans-StL	46
Shotton-StL	41
E.Collins-Chi	40
Speaker-Cle	35

Stolen Base Average
Cobb-Det	73.9
Hooper-Bos	71.1
Schalk-Chi	69.8
Roth-Cle	67.4
Shanks-Was	65.7

Stolen Base Runs
Cobb-Det	6.0
Hooper-Bos	1.5
Schalk-Chi	1.2
Roth-Cle	.3

Fielding Runs
Lavan-StL	34.2
Lajoie-Phi	30.4
Vitt-Det	27.6
Pratt-StL	22.4
Milan-Was	16.5

Total Player Rating
Speaker-Cle	6.0
Cobb-Det	5.6
Pratt-StL	4.1
Lavan-StL	3.7
Jackson-Chi	3.6

Wins
Johnson-Was	25
Shawkey-NY	24
Ruth-Bos	23
Coveleski-Det	21
Dauss-Det	19

Win Percentage
Cicotte-Chi	.682
Ruth-Bos	.657
Coveleski-Det	.656
Faber-Chi	.654
Shawkey-NY	.632

Games
Davenport-StL	59
Russell-Chi	56
Shawkey-NY	53
Gallia-Was	49

Complete Games
Johnson-Was	36
Myers-Phi	31
Bush-Phi	25
Ruth-Bos	23
Coveleski-Det	22

Shutouts
Ruth-Bos	9
Bush-Phi	8
Leonard-Bos	6
Russell-Chi	5

Saves
Shawkey-NY	8
Russell-NY	6
Leonard-Bos	6
Cicotte-Chi	5
Bagby-Cle	5

Innings Pitched
Johnson-Was	371.0
Coveleski-Det	324.1
Ruth-Bos	323.2
Myers-Phi	315.0
Davenport-StL	290.2

Fewest Hits/Game
Ruth-Bos	6.40
Shawkey-NY	6.64
Cicotte-Chi	6.64
Bush-Phi	6.97
Johnson-Was	7.04

Fewest BB/Game
Russell-Chi	1.43
Cullop-NY	1.72
Coveleski-Det	1.75
Shore-Bos	1.95
Johnson-Was	1.99

Strikeouts
Johnson-Was	228
Myers-Phi	182
Ruth-Bos	170
Bush-Phi	157
Harper-Was	149

Strikeouts/Game
Williams-Chi	5.54
Johnson-Was	5.53
Russell-NY	5.46
Harper-Was	5.37
Myers-Phi	5.20

Ratio
Russell-Chi	8.51
Johnson-Was	9.24
Shawkey-NY	9.47
Coveleski-Det	9.77
Ruth-Bos	9.90

Earned Run Average
Ruth-Bos	1.75
Cicotte-Chi	1.78
Johnson-Was	1.89
Coveleski-Det	1.97
Faber-Chi	2.02

Adjusted ERA
Ruth-Bos	158
Cicotte-Chi	155
Johnson-Was	145
Coveleski-Det	145
Cullop-NY	141

Opponents' Batting Avg.
Ruth-Bos	.201
Shawkey-NY	.209
Cicotte-Chi	.218
Bush-Phi	.219
Johnson-Was	.220

Opponents' On Base Pct.
Russell-Chi	.254
Johnson-Was	.270
Shawkey-NY	.273
Ruth-Bos	.280
Coveleski-Det	.282

Starter Runs
Ruth-Bos	38.5
Johnson-Was	38.4
Coveleski-Det	30.7
Cicotte-Chi	21.7
Weilman-StL	20.6

Adjusted Starter Runs
Ruth-Bos	36.4
Johnson-Was	35.4
Coveleski-Det	32.1
Shawkey-NY	20.7
Cicotte-Chi	20.3

Clutch Pitching Index
Cicotte-Chi	117
Gallia-Was	117
Mogridge-NY	113
Fisher-NY	113
Weilman-StL	113

Relief Runs

Adjusted Relief Runs

Relief Ranking

Total Pitcher Index
Ruth-Bos	5.9
Coveleski-Det	4.4
Johnson-Was	4.3
Mays-Bos	3.1
Cicotte-Chi	2.6

Total Baseball Ranking
Speaker-Cle	6.0
Ruth-Bos	5.9
Cobb-Det	5.6
Coveleski-Det	4.4
Johnson-Was	4.3

TEAM	G	W	L	PCT	GB	R	OR	AB	H	2B	3B	HR	BB	SO	AVG	OBP	SLG	PRO	PRO+	BR	/A	PF	CHI	RC	SB	CS	SBA	SBR
NY	158	98	56	.636		635	457	5211	1360	170	71	39	373	533	.261	.317	.343	.660	112	50	67	97	105	610	162			
PHI	154	87	65	.572	10	578	500	5084	1262	225	60	38	435	533	.248	.310	.339	.649	100	29	5	104	100	573	109			
STL	154	82	70	.539	15	531	567	5083	1271	159	93	26	359	652	.250	.303	.333	.636	103	2	17	97	98	552	159			
CIN	157	78	76	.506	20	601	611	5251	1385	196	100	26	312	477	.264	.309	.354	.663	113	48	71	96	101	607	153			
CHI	157	74	80	.481	24	552	567	5135	1229	194	67	17	415	599	.239	.299	.313	.612	86	-34	-77	108	106	524	127			
BOS	157	72	81	.471	25.5	536	552	5201	1280	169	75	22	427	587	.246	.309	.320	.629	105	-1	31	94	96	563	155			
BRO	156	70	81	.464	26.5	511	559	5251	1299	159	78	25	334	527	.247	.296	.322	.618	92	-31	-45	103	98	534	130			
PIT	157	51	103	.331	47	464	595	5169	1230	160	61	9	399	580	.238	.298	.298	.596	86	-60	-78	103	94	506	150			
TOT	625					4408		41385	10316	1432	605	202	3054	4488	.249	.305	.328	.633						1145				

TEAM	CG	SH	SV	IP	H	H/G	HR	BB	SO	RAT	ERA	ERA+	OAV	OOB	PR	/A	PF	CPI	FA	E	DP	FW	PW	BW	SBW	DIF
NY	92	18	14	1426²	1221	7.7	29	327	551	9.9	2.27	112	.233	.282	68	42	94	97	.968	208	122	1.8	4.7	7.6		6.9
PHI	102	22	5	1389	1258	8.2	25	327	617	10.5	2.46	114	.245	.295	38	52	104	102	.967	212	112	1.2	5.9	.6		3.4
STL	66	16	10	1392²	1257	8.1	29	421	502	11.1	3.03	89	.248	.310	-50	-54	99	92	.967	221	153	.6	-6.1	1.9		9.5
CIN	94	12	6	1397¹	1363	8.8	20	404	492	11.6	2.70	97	.261	.318	0	-14	97	112	.962	247	120	-.7	-1.6	8.0		-4.8
CHI	79	15	9	1404	1303	8.4	34	374	654	10.9	2.62	110	.253	.307	13	40	107	108	.959	267	121	-1.9	4.5	-8.7		3.1
BOS	105	22	3	1424²	1309	8.3	19	371	593	10.8	2.77	92	.246	.304	-10	-37	94	96	.966	224	122	.7	-4.2	3.5		-4.6
BRO	99	8	9	1421¹	1288	8.2	32	405	582	11.0	2.78	100	.246	.306	-12	0	103	98	.962	245	102	-.7	.0	-5.1		.2
PIT	84	17	6	1417²	1318	8.4	14	432	509	11.3	3.01	94	.252	.314	-48	-29	105	94	.961	251	119	-.9	-3.3	-8.8		-13.0
TOT	721	130	62	11273¹		8.2				10.9	2.70		.249	.305					.964	1875	971					

Runs
Burns-NY 103
Groh-Cin 91
Kauff-NY 89
Hornsby-StL 86

Hits
Groh-Cin 182
Burns-NY 180
Roush-Cin 178
Zimmerman-NY ... 174
Carey-Pit 174

Doubles
Groh-Cin 39
Merkle-Bro-Chi 31
Smith-Bos 31
Cravath-Phi 29
Chase-Cin 28

Triples
Hornsby-StL 17
Cravath-Phi 16
Chase-Cin 15
Roush-Cin 14
Long-StL 14

Home Runs
Robertson-NY 12
Cravath-Phi 12
Hornsby-StL 8

Total Bases
Hornsby-StL 253
Groh-Cin 246
Burns-NY 246
Cravath-Phi 238

Runs Batted In
Zimmerman-NY ... 102
Chase-Cin 86
Cravath-Phi 83
Stengel-Bro 73
Luderus-Phi 72

Runs Produced
Zimmerman-NY 158
Chase-Cin 153
Kauff-NY 152
Roush-Cin 145
Hornsby-StL 144

Bases On Balls
Burns-NY 75
Groh-Cin 71
Cravath-Phi 70
Luderus-Phi 65
Paskert-Phi 62

Batting Average
Roush-Cin 341
Hornsby-StL 327
Kauff-NY 308
Groh-Cin 304
Burns-NY 302

On Base Percentage
Groh-Cin 385
Hornsby-StL 385
Burns-NY 380
Roush-Cin 379
Kauff-NY 379

Slugging Average
Hornsby-StL 484
Cravath-Phi 473
Roush-Cin 454
Burns-NY 412
Groh-Cin 411

Production
Hornsby-StL 868
Cravath-Phi 842
Roush-Cin 833
Groh-Cin 796
Burns-NY 792

Adjusted Production
Hornsby-StL 170
Roush-Cin 162
Cravath-Phi 151
Groh-Cin 150
Burns-NY 148

Batter Runs
Hornsby-StL 39.6
Cravath-Phi 34.7
Groh-Cin 33.5
Roush-Cin 32.3
Burns-NY 32.2

Adjusted Batter Runs
Hornsby-StL 41.2
Groh-Cin 36.2
Roush-Cin 34.6
Burns-NY 34.3
Cravath-Phi 32.3

Clutch Hitting Index
Zimmerman-NY ... 171
Ward-Pit 143
Luderus-Phi 143
Deal-Chi 141
Chase-Cin 141

Runs Created
Burns-NY 105
Groh-Cin 102
Hornsby-StL 102
Carey-Pit 94
Roush-Cin 93

Total Average
Hornsby-StL 906
Cravath-Phi 870
Burns-NY 868
Roush-Cin 843
Groh-Cin 815

Stolen Bases
Carey-Pit 46
Burns-NY 40
Kauff-NY 30
Maranville-Bos 27
Baird-Pit-StL 26

Stolen Base Average

Stolen Base Runs

Fielding Runs
Bancroft-Phi 27.8
Fletcher-NY 27.4
Hornsby-StL 21.2
Carey-Pit 20.2
Shean-Cin 18.7

Total Player Rating
Hornsby-StL 7.0
Groh-Cin 4.6
Burns-NY 3.9
Carey-Pit 3.9
Fletcher-NY 3.5

Wins
Alexander-Phi 30
Toney-Cin 24
Vaughn-Chi 23
Schupp-NY 21
Schneider-Cin 20

Win Percentage
Schupp-NY 750
Sallee-NY 720
Perritt-NY 708
Alexander-Phi 698
Nehf-Bos 680

Games
Douglas-Chi....... 51
Barnes-Bos 50
Schneider-Cin 46
Alexander-Phi 45
Doak-StL 44

Complete Games
Alexander-Phi 34
Toney-Cin 31
Vaughn-Chi 27
Barnes-Bos 27
Schupp-NY 25

Shutouts
Alexander-Phi 8
Toney-Cin 7
Cooper-Pit 7
Schupp-NY 6

Saves
Sallee-NY 4

Innings Pitched
Alexander-Phi ... 387.2
Toney-Cin 339.2
Schneider-Cin ... 333.2
Cooper-Pit 297.2
Vaughn-Chi 295.2

Fewest Hits/Game
Schupp-NY 6.68
Anderson-NY 6.78
Nehf-Bos 7.60
Pfeffer-Bro 7.61
Tyler-Bos 7.64

Fewest BB/Game
Alexander-Phi ... 1.30
Sallee-NY 1.42
Nehf-Bos 1.50
Barnes-Bos 1.53
Douglas-Chi..... 1.53

Strikeouts
Alexander-Phi 200
Vaughn-Chi 195
Douglas-Chi 151
Schupp-NY 147
Schneider-Cin ... 138

Strikeouts/Game
Vaughn-Chi 5.94
Schupp-NY 4.86
Alexander-Phi ... 4.64
Douglas-Chi 4.63
Marquard-Bro ... 4.53

Ratio
Anderson-NY..... 8.78
Schupp-NY 9.13
Alexander-Phi 9.24
Nehf-Bos 9.26
Barnes-Bos 9.58

Earned Run Average
Anderson-NY..... 1.44
Alexander-Phi ... 1.83
Perritt-NY 1.88
Schupp-NY 1.95
Vaughn-Chi 2.01

Adjusted ERA
Anderson-NY 176
Alexander-Phi ... 153
Vaughn-Chi 144
Perritt-NY 135
Schupp-NY 130

Opponents' Batting Avg.
Schupp-NY 209
Anderson-NY 209
Nehf-Bos 231
Marquard-Bro 232
Pfeffer-Bro 234

Opponents' On Base Pct.
Anderson-NY 255
Schupp-NY 265
Alexander-Phi 266
Nehf-Bos 268
Barnes-Bos 277

Starter Runs
Alexander-Phi 37.4
Vaughn-Chi 22.8
Schupp-NY 22.7
Anderson-NY 22.7
Schneider-Cin ... 22.2

Adjusted Starter Runs
Alexander-Phi 41.6
Vaughn-Chi 28.8
Anderson-NY..... 19.8
Schneider-Cin 18.7
Schupp-NY 17.9

Clutch Pitching Index
Schneider-Cin 145
Vaughn-Chi 120
Perritt-NY 118
Hendrix-Chi 117
Mayer-Phi 114

Relief Runs

Adjusted Relief Runs

Relief Ranking

Total Pitcher Index
Alexander-Phi 5.9
Vaughn-Chi 3.7
Rixey-Phi 2.3
Anderson-NY...... 1.9
Cooper-Pit 1.8

Total Baseball Ranking
Hornsby-StL 7.0
Alexander-Phi 5.9
Groh-Cin 4.6
Burns-NY 3.9
Carey-Pit 3.9

TEAM	G	W	L	PCT	GB	R	OR	AB	H	2B	3B	HR	BB	SO	AVG	OBP	SLG	PRO	PRO+	BR	/A	PF	CHI	RC	SB	CS	SBA	SBR
CHI	156	100	54	.649		656	464	5057	1281	152	81	18	522	479	.253	.329	.326	.655	102	36	24	102	108	615	219			
BOS	157	90	62	.592	9	555	454	5048	1243	198	64	14	466	473	.246	.314	.319	.633	100	-9	-3	99	99	558	105			
CLE	156	88	66	.571	12	584	543	4994	1224	218	64	13	549	596	.245	.324	.322	.646	95	21	-21	107	99	595	210			
DET	154	78	75	.510	21.5	639	577	5093	1317	204	77	25	483	476	.259	.328	.344	.672	111	61	63	100	102	630	163			
WAS	157	74	79	.484	25.5	543	566	5142	1238	173	70	4	500	574	.241	.313	.304	.617	95	-33	-26	99	101	548	166			
NY	155	71	82	.464	28.5	524	558	5136	1226	172	52	27	496	535	.239	.310	.308	.618	93	-33	-38	101	97	544	136			
STL	155	57	97	.370	43	510	687	5091	1250	183	63	15	405	540	.246	.305	.315	.620	97	-38	-17	96	99	535	157			
PHI	154	55	98	.359	44.5	529	691	5109	1296	177	62	17	435	519	.254	.316	.323	.639	101	0	7	99	94	566	112			
TOT	622					4540		40670	10075	1477	533	133	3856	4192	.248	.318	.320	.638							1268			

TEAM	CG	SH	SV	IP	H	H/G	HR	BB	SO	RAT	ERA	ERA+	OAV	OOB	PR	/A	PF	CPI	FA	E	DP	FW	PW	BW	SBW	DIF
CHI	78	22	21	1424¹	1236	7.8	10	413	517	10.6	2.16	123	.237	.298	79	76	100	102	.967	204	117	2.3	8.5	2.7		9.6
BOS	115	15	7	1421¹	1197	7.6	12	413	509	10.5	2.20	117	.231	.294	73	60	97	95	.972	183	116	3.9	6.7	-.3		3.8
CLE	73	20	22	1412²	1270	8.1	17	438	451	11.1	2.52	112	.247	.310	22	48	106	101	.964	242	136	-.5	5.3	-2.3		8.5
DET	78	20	15	1396¹	1209	7.8	12	504	516	11.4	2.56	103	.239	.315	16	13	99	99	.964	234	95	-.1	1.4	7.0		-6.8
WAS	84	21	10	1415	1228	7.8	12	536	637	11.5	2.77	95	.240	.317	-17	-23	99	92	.961	251	127	-1.0	-2.6	-2.9		4.0
NY	87	10	6	1411¹	1280	8.2	29	427	571	11.1	2.66	101	.251	.313	0	3	101	102	.965	225	129	.6	.3	-4.2		-2.2
STL	66	12	12	1385¹	1320	8.6	19	537	429	12.3	3.20	81	.257	.332	-83	-95	98	94	.957	281	139	-3.4	-10.6	-1.9		-4.1
PHI	80	8	8	1365²	1310	8.6	22	516	516	12.5	3.27	84	.261	.338	-91	-78	103	97	.961	251	106	-1.3	-8.7	.8		-12.3
TOT	661	128	101	11232		8.1				11.4	2.66		.248	.318					.964	1871	965					

Runs	Hits	Doubles	Triples	Home Runs	Total Bases
Bush-Det 112	Cobb-Det 225	Cobb-Det 44	Cobb-Det 24	Pipp-NY 9	Cobb-Det 335
Cobb-Det 107	Sisler-StL 190	Speaker-Cle 42	Jackson-Chi 17	Veach-Det 8	Veach-Det 261
Chapman-Cle 98	Speaker-Cle 184	Veach-Det 31	Judge-Was 15	Bodie-Phi 7	Speaker-Cle 254
Jackson-Chi...... 91	Veach-Det 182	Sisler-StL 30	Chapman-Cle 13		Sisler-StL 244
E.Collins-Chi 91		Roth-Cle 30			Bodie-Phi 233

Runs Batted In	Runs Produced	Bases On Balls	Batting Average	On Base Percentage	Slugging Average
Veach-Det 103	Cobb-Det 203	Graney-Cle 94	Cobb-Det .... .383	Cobb-Det .... .444	Cobb-Det .... .570
Felsch-Chi 102	Veach-Det 174	E.Collins-Chi 89	Sisler-StL .... .353	Speaker-Cle ...... .432	Speaker-Cle ...... .486
Cobb-Det 102	Felsch-Chi 171	Hooper-Bos 80	Speaker-Cle ...... .352	Veach-Det .... .393	Veach-Det .... .457
Heilmann-Det..... 86	Jackson-Chi...... 161	Bush-Det 80	Veach-Det .... .319	Sisler-StL .... .390	Sisler-StL .... .453
Jackson-Chi...... 75	E.Collins-Chi 158	Leibold-Chi 74	Felsch-Chi .... .308	E.Collins-Chi ..... .389	Jackson-Chi...... .429

Production	Adjusted Production	Batter Runs	Adjusted Batter Runs	Clutch Hitting Index	Runs Created
Cobb-Det 1.014	Cobb-Det 210	Cobb-Det 74.4	Cobb-Det 74.7	Bates-Phi 156	Cobb-Det 162
Speaker-Cle 918	Speaker-Cle 168	Speaker-Cle 51.2	Felsch-Chi 46.8	Felsch-Chi 155	Speaker-Cle 120
Veach-Det 850	Sisler-StL 163	Veach-Det 40.1	Veach-Det 40.3	Heilmann-Det..... 142	Veach-Det 110
Sisler-StL 843	Veach-Det 160	Sisler-StL 34.0	Sisler-StL 36.1	Schalk-Chi 141	Sisler-StL 102
Jackson-Chi......805	Jackson-Chi...... 142	Jackson-Chi...... 28.8	Jackson-Chi...... 27.5	Roth-Cle 135	Chapman-Cle 98

Total Average	Stolen Bases	Stolen Base Average	Stolen Base Runs	Fielding Runs	Total Player Rating
Cobb-Det 1.253	Cobb-Det 55			Chapman-Cle 24.4	Cobb-Det 8.4
Speaker-Cle 1.056	E.Collins-Chi 53			Felsch-Chi 19.1	Chapman-Cle 5.4
Veach-Det 905	Chapman-Cle 52			Wambsganss-Cle . 15.3	Speaker-Cle 5.0
Sisler-StL 900	Roth-Cle 51			Ainsmith-Was 15.0	Veach-Det 3.9
E.Collins-Chi 873	Sisler-StL 37			Pratt-StL 14.8	Sisler-StL 3.8

Wins	Win Percentage	Games	Complete Games	Shutouts	Saves
Cicotte-Chi 28	Russell-Chi 750	Danforth-Chi 50	Ruth-Bos 35	Coveleski-Cle 9	Danforth-Chi 9
Ruth-Bos 24	Mays-Bos 710	Cicotte-Chi 49	Johnson-Was 30	Johnson-Was 8	Bagby-Cle 7
Johnson-Was 23	Cicotte-Chi 700	Bagby-Cle 49	Cicotte-Chi 29	Bagby-Cle 8	Boland-Det 6
Bagby-Cle 23	Williams-Chi 680	Sothoron-StL 48	Mays-Bos 27	Cicotte-Chi 7	Coumbe-Cle 5
Mays-Bos 22	Ruth-Bos 649				

Innings Pitched	Fewest Hits/Game	Fewest BB/Game	Strikeouts	Strikeouts/Game	Ratio
Cicotte-Chi 346.2	Coveleski-Cle ... 6.09	Russell-Chi 1.52	Johnson-Was 188	Johnson-Was 5.16	Cicotte-Chi 8.28
Johnson-Was ... 328.0	Cicotte-Chi 6.39	Mogridge-NY 1.79	Cicotte-Chi 150	Harper-Was 4.97	Coveleski-Cle ... 8.96
Ruth-Bos 326.1	Ruth-Bos 6.73	Cicotte-Chi 1.82	Leonard-Bos 144	Bush-Phi 4.67	Johnson-Was 9.33
Bagby-Cle 320.2	Johnson-Was ... 7.11	Johnson-Was 1.84	Coveleski-Cle 133	Leonard-Bos 4.40	Russell-Chi 9.65
Coveleski-Cle ... 298.1	Mays-Bos 7.16	Bagby-Cle 2.05	Ruth-Bos 128	Danforth-Chi 4.11	Mays-Bos 9.90

Earned Run Average	Adjusted ERA	Opponents' Batting Avg.	Opponents' On Base Pct.	Starter Runs	Adjusted Starter Runs
Cicotte-Chi 1.53	Cicotte-Chi 174	Coveleski-Cle 194	Cicotte-Chi 248	Cicotte-Chi 43.6	Cicotte-Chi 43.4
Mays-Bos 1.74	Coveleski-Cle ... 157	Cicotte-Chi .... .203	Coveleski-Cle 261	Mays-Bos 29.5	Coveleski-Cle ... 33.9
Coveleski-Cle ... 1.81	Mays-Bos 148	Ruth-Bos .... .211	Johnson-Was .... .270	Coveleski-Cle ... 28.3	Bagby-Cle 31.0
Faber-Chi 1.92	Bagby-Cle 144	Johnson-Was .... .220	Russell-Chi 279	Bagby-Cle 24.9	Mays-Bos 26.9
Russell-Chi 1.95	Faber-Chi 138	Mays-Bos 221	Mays-Bos 282	Ruth-Bos 23.6	Ruth-Bos 20.6

Clutch Pitching Index	Relief Runs	Adjusted Relief Runs	Relief Ranking	Total Pitcher Index	Total Baseball Ranking
Faber-Chi 136				Cicotte-Chi 5.0	Cobb-Det 8.4
Ayers-Was 128				Mays-Bos 5.0	Chapman-Cle 5.4
James-Det 127				Ruth-Bos 4.6	Cicotte-Chi 5.0
Morton-Cle 117				Bagby-Cle 3.7	Speaker-Cle 5.0
Mitchell-Det 116				Coveleski-Cle 3.0	Mays-Bos 5.0

TEAM	G	W	L	PCT	GB	R	OR	AB	H	2B	3B	HR	BB	SO	AVG	OBP	SLG	PRO	PRO+	BR	/A	PF	CHI	RC	SB	CS	SBA	SBR
CHI	131	84	45	.651		538	393	4325	1147	164	53	21	358	343	.265	.325	.342	.667	106	48	36	102	102	528	159			
NY	124	71	53	.573	10.5	480	415	4164	1081	150	53	13	271	365	.260	.310	.330	.640	102	1	9	98	107	459	130			
CIN	129	68	60	.531	15.5	530	496	4265	1185	165	84	15	304	303	.278	.330	.366	.696	120	86	94	98	96	551	128			
PIT	126	65	60	.520	17	466	412	4091	1016	107	72	15	371	285	.248	.315	.321	.636	95	1	-14	104	102	467	200			
BRO	126	57	69	.452	25.5	360	463	4212	1052	121	62	10	212	326	.250	.291	.315	.606	90	-52	-50	100	91	411	113			
PHI	125	55	68	.447	26	430	507	4192	1022	158	28	25	346	400	.244	.305	.313	.618	88	-28	-59	107	100	432	97			
BOS	124	53	71	.427	28.5	424	469	4162	1014	107	59	13	350	438	.244	.307	.307	.614	97	-31	-11	96	99	426	83			
STL	131	51	78	.395	33	454	527	4369	1066	147	64	27	329	461	.244	.301	.325	.626	99	-20	-3	97	100	461	119			
TOT	508					3682		33780	8583	1119	475	139	2541	2921	.254	.311	.328	.638						1029				

TEAM	CG	SH	SV	IP	H	H/G	HR	BB	SO	RAT	ERA	ERA+	OAV	OOB	PR	/A	PF	CPI	FA	E	DP	FW	PW	BW	SBW	DIF
CHI	92	23	8	1197	1050	7.9	13	296	472	10.3	2.18	128	.239	.290	77	80	101	104	.966	188	91	.5	8.9	4.0		6.1
NY	74	18	11	1111²	1002	8.1	20	228	330	10.1	2.64	100	.243	.286	15	-1	95	87	.971	152	78	2.1	-.1	1.0		6.0
CIN	84	14	6	1142¹	1136	9.0	19	381	321	12.1	3.00	89	.267	.331	-30	-42	97	109	.964	192	127	.0	-4.7	10.5		-1.9
PIT	85	10	7	1140¹	1005	7.9	13	299	367	10.5	2.48	116	.243	.299	36	51	104	99	.966	179	108	.6	5.7	-1.6		-2.2
BRO	85	17	2	1131¹	1024	8.1	22	320	395	10.9	2.81	99	.248	.306	-5	-4	101	95	.963	193	74	-.3	-.4	-5.6		.3
PHI	78	10	6	1139²	1086	8.6	22	369	312	11.7	3.15	95	.258	.322	-49	-20	109	96	.961	211	91	-1.5	-2.2	-6.6		3.9
BOS	96	13	0	1117¹	1111	8.9	14	277	340	11.4	2.90	93	.266	.315	-16	-26	97	102	.965	184	89	.0	-2.9	-1.2		-5.0
STL	72	3	5	1193	1148	8.7	16	352	361	11.6	2.96	91	.260	.321	-26	-33	98	101	.962	220	116	-1.5	-3.7	-.3		-7.9
TOT	666	108	45	9172²		8.4				11.1	2.76		.254	.311					.965	1519	774					

Runs		Hits		Doubles		Triples		Home Runs		Total Bases	
Groh-Cin	86	Hollocher-Chi	161	Groh-Cin	28	Daubert-Bro	15	Cravath-Phi	8	Hollocher-Chi	202
Burns-NY	80	Groh-Cin	158	Mann-Chi	27	Wickland-Bos	13	Williams-Phi	6	Roush-Cin	198
Flack-Chi	74	Roush-Cin	145	Cravath-Phi	27	S.Magee-Cin	13	Cruise-StL	6	Groh-Cin	195
Hollocher-Chi	72	Youngs-NY	143	Meusel-Phi	25	L.Magee-Cin	13			Mann-Chi	188
		Merkle-Chi	143	Merkle-Chi	25					Merkle-Chi	187

Runs Batted In		Runs Produced		Bases On Balls		Batting Average		On Base Percentage		Slugging Average	
S.Magee-Cin	76	Burns-NY	127	Carey-Pit	62	Z.Wheat-Bro	.335	Groh-Cin	.395	Roush-Cin	.455
Cutshaw-Pit	68	Paskert-Chi	126	Flack-Chi	56	Roush-Cin	.333	Hollocher-Chi	.379	Daubert-Bro	.429
Luderus-Phi	67	Mann-Chi	122	Groh-Cin	54	Groh-Cin	.320	J.Smith-Bos	.373	Hornsby-StL	.416
J.Smith-Bos	65	Groh-Cin	122	Cravath-Phi	54	Hollocher-Chi	.316	S.Magee-Cin	.370	S.Magee-Cin	.415
Merkle-Chi	65	S.Magee-Cin	120	Bancroft-Phi	54	Daubert-Bro	.308	Z.Wheat-Bro	.369	Wickland-Bos	.398

Production		Adjusted Production		Batter Runs		Adjusted Batter Runs		Clutch Hitting Index		Runs Created	
Roush-Cin	.823	Roush-Cin	153	Groh-Cin	26.4	Groh-Cin	27.4	S.Magee-Cin	170	Hollocher-Chi	84
Groh-Cin	.791	Groh-Cin	144	Roush-Cin	24.3	Roush-Cin	25.2	Konetchy-Bos	160	Groh-Cin	83
Daubert-Bro	.789	S.Magee-Cin	142	Hollocher-Chi	23.0	Hollocher-Chi	21.6	J.Smith-Bos	157	Roush-Cin	77
S.Magee-Cin	.785	Daubert-Bro	141	S.Magee-Cin	19.2	S.Magee-Cin	20.0	Paulette-StL	142	Carey-Pit	74
Hollocher-Chi	.775	Wickland-Bos	139	Daubert-Bro	18.2	Daubert-Bro	18.4	Luderus-Phi	140	Burns-NY	73

Total Average		Stolen Bases		Stolen Base Average		Stolen Base Runs		Fielding Runs		Total Player Rating	
Roush-Cin	.848	Carey-Pit	58					Fletcher-NY	22.3	Groh-Cin	3.5
Carey-Pit	.844	Burns-NY	40					Bancroft-Phi	17.9	Fisher-StL	3.5
Wickland-Bos	.812	Hollocher-Chi	26					Schmidt-Pit	15.4	Hornsby-StL	3.3
Burns-NY	.809	Cutshaw-Pit	25					Carey-Pit	13.2	L.Magee-Cin	2.9
S.Magee-Cin	.804	Baird-StL	25					Hornsby-StL	10.6	J.Smith-Bos	2.6

Wins		Win Percentage		Games		Complete Games		Shutouts		Saves	
Vaughn-Chi	22	Hendrix-Chi	.741	Grimes-Bro	40	Nehf-Bos	28	Vaughn-Chi	8	Toney-Cin-NY	3
Hendrix-Chi	20	Tyler-Chi	.704	Cooper-Pit	38	Vaughn-Chi	27	Grimes-Bro	7	Oeschger-Phi	3
Tyler-Chi	19	Mayer-Phi-Pit	.696	Eller-Cin	37	Cooper-Pit	26	Tyler-Chi	6	Cooper-Pit	3
Grimes-Bro	19	Vaughn-Chi	.688			Tyler-Chi	22	Perritt-NY	6	Anderson-NY	3
Cooper-Pit	19	Grimes-Bro	.679			Hendrix-Chi	21				

Innings Pitched		Fewest Hits/Game		Fewest BB/Game		Strikeouts		Strikeouts/Game		Ratio	
Vaughn-Chi	290.1	Vaughn-Chi	6.70	Sallee-NY	.82	Vaughn-Chi	148	Vaughn-Chi	4.59	Sallee-NY	9.14
Nehf-Bos	284.1	Grimes-Bro	7.01	Perritt-NY	1.47	Cooper-Pit	117	Cooper-Pit	3.85	Vaughn-Chi	9.27
Cooper-Pit	273.1	Cooper-Pit	7.21	G.Smith-Cin-NY-Bro	1.50	Grimes-Bro	113	Grimes-Bro	3.77	Grimes-Bro	9.68
Grimes-Bro	269.2	Tyler-Chi	7.28	Toney-Cin-NY	1.54	Tyler-Chi	102	Cheney-Bro	3.72	Cooper-Pit	9.68
Tyler-Chi	269.1	Oeschger-Phi	7.78	Demaree-NY	1.58	Nehf-Bos	96	May-StL	3.60	Tyler-Chi	9.69

Earned Run Average		Adjusted ERA		Opponents' Batting Avg.		Opponents' On Base Pct.		Starter Runs		Adjusted Starter Runs	
Vaughn-Chi	1.74	Vaughn-Chi	160	Vaughn-Chi	.208	Sallee-NY	.259	Vaughn-Chi	33.1	Vaughn-Chi	33.8
Tyler-Chi	2.00	Tyler-Chi	139	Grimes-Bro	.216	Vaughn-Chi	.266	Tyler-Chi	22.7	Cooper-Pit	23.3
Cooper-Pit	2.11	Cooper-Pit	136	Cooper-Pit	.223	Grimes-Bro	.276	Cooper-Pit	19.9	Tyler-Chi	23.3
Douglas-Chi	2.13	Douglas-Chi	131	Tyler-Chi	.226	Perritt-NY	.278	Grimes-Bro	18.8	Grimes-Bro	19.4
Grimes-Bro	2.14	Grimes-Bro	130	Oeschger-Phi	.238	Cooper-Pit	.279	Hamilton-Pit	11.6	Hamilton-Pit	12.2

Clutch Pitching Index		Relief Runs		Adjusted Relief Runs		Relief Ranking		Total Pitcher Index		Total Baseball Ranking	
Bressler-Cin	123							Vaughn-Chi	4.4	Vaughn-Chi	4.4
Mayer-Phi-Pit	117							Tyler-Chi	3.3	Groh-Cin	3.5
Schneider-Cin	113							Cooper-Pit	2.7	Fisher-StL	3.5
Eller-Cin	112							Grimes-Bro	2.7	Hornsby-StL	3.3
Demaree-NY	112							Hogg-Phi	2.0	Tyler-Chi	3.3

TEAM	G	W	L	PCT	GB	R	OR	AB	H	2B	3B	HR	BB	SO	AVG	OBP	SLG	PRO	PRO+	BR	/A	PF	CHI	RC	SB	CS	SBA	SBR
BOS	126	75	51	.595		474	380	3982	990	159	54	15	406	324	.249	.322	.327	.649	102	5	12	98	105	465	110			
CLE	129	73	54	.575	2.5	504	447	4166	1084	176	67	9	491	386	.260	.344	.341	.685	102	68	22	110	93	552	165			
WAS	130	72	56	.563	4	461	412	4472	1144	156	49	4	376	361	.256	.318	.315	.633	97	-20	-11	98	99	492	137			
NY	126	60	63	.488	13.5	493	475	4224	1085	160	45	20	367	370	.257	.320	.330	.650	98	2	-8	102	106	482	88			
STL	123	58	64	.475	15	426	448	4019	1040	152	40	5	397	340	.259	.331	.320	.651	98	11	24	97	93	476	138			
CHI	124	57	67	.460	17	457	446	4132	1057	136	55	8	375	358	.256	.322	.321	.643	98	-4	-8	101	101	469	116			
DET	128	55	71	.437	20	476	557	4262	1063	141	56	13	452	380	.249	.325	.318	.643	103	-1	18	96	101	488	123			
PHI	130	52	76	.406	24	412	538	4278	1039	124	44	22	343	485	.243	.303	.308	.611	88	-58	-63	101	102	431	83			
TOT	508					3703		33535	8502	1204	410	96	3207	3004	.254	.323	.322	.646						960				

TEAM	CG	SH	SV	IP	H	H/G	HR	BB	SO	RAT	ERA	ERA+	OAV	OOB	PR	/A	PF	CPI	FA	E	DP	FW	PW	BW	SBW	DIF
BOS	105	26	2	1120	931	7.5	9	380	392	10.8	2.31	116	.231	.302	58	47	97	95	.971	152	89	2.5	5.2	1.3		2.9
CLE	78	5	13	1161	1126	8.7	9	343	364	11.5	2.64	114	.261	.318	17	45	108	105	.962	207	82	-.7	5.0	2.5		2.7
WAS	75	19	8	1227	1021	7.5	10	395	505	10.6	2.14	127	.230	.298	86	79	98	99	.960	226	85	-1.8	8.8	-1.2		2.2
NY	59	8	13	1157¹	1103	8.6	25	463	370	12.5	3.00	94	.261	.339	-29	-23	102	107	.970	161	137	1.9	-2.6	-.9		.0
STL	67	8	8	1111¹	993	8.0	11	402	346	11.5	2.75	99	.245	.319	2	-2	99	95	.963	190	86	-.2	-.2	2.7		-5.3
CHI	76	9	8	1126	1092	8.7	9	300	349	11.3	2.73	100	.261	.313	4	-2	99	97	.967	169	98	1.2	-.2	-.9		-5.1
DET	74	8	7	1160²	1130	8.8	10	437	371	12.4	3.40	78	.262	.335	-81	-99	96	89	.960	212	77	-1.1	-11.0	2.0		2.1
PHI	80	13	9	1155	1105	8.6	13	479	279	12.6	3.23	91	.265	.346	-58	-39	106	102	.959	228	136	-1.9	-4.4	-7.0		1.3
TOT	614	96	68	9218¹		8.3				11.6	2.77		.254	.323					.964	1545	800					

Runs
Chapman-Cle 84
T.Cobb-Det 83
Hooper-Bos 81
Bush-Det 74
Speaker-Cle 73

Hits
Burns-Phi 178
T.Cobb-Det 161
Sisler-StL 154
Baker-NY 154
Speaker-Cle 150

Doubles
Speaker-Cle 33
Ruth-Bos 26
Hooper-Bos 26
Baker-NY 24

Triples
Veach-Det 14
Hooper-Bos 13
Roth-Cle 12

Home Runs
Walker-Phi 11
Veach-Det 11
Burns-Phi 6
Baker-NY 6

Total Bases
Burns-Phi 236
T.Cobb-Det 217
Baker-NY 206
Speaker-Cle 205
Sisler-StL 199

Runs Batted In
Veach-Det 78
Burns-Phi 70
Wood-Cle 66
Ruth-Bos 66
T.Cobb-Det 64

Runs Produced
T.Cobb-Det 144
Veach-Det 134
Speaker-Cle 134
Burns-Phi 125
Hooper-Bos 124

Bases On Balls
Chapman-Cle 84
Bush-Det 79
Hooper-Bos 75
E.Collins-Chi 73
Shotton-Was 67

Batting Average
T.Cobb-Det ..... .382
Burns-Phi ..... .352
Sisler-StL ..... .341
Speaker-Cle ..... .318
Baker-NY ..... .306

On Base Percentage
T.Cobb-Det ..... .440
E.Collins-Chi ..... .407
Speaker-Cle ..... .403
Sisler-StL ..... .400
Hooper-Bos ..... .391

Slugging Average
T.Cobb-Det ..... .515
Burns-Phi ..... .467
Sisler-StL ..... .440
Speaker-Cle ..... .435
Walker-Phi ..... .423

Production
T.Cobb-Det 1.131
Sisler-StL ..... .970
Speaker-Cle ..... .931
Roth-Cle ..... .929
Hooper-Bos ..... .875

T.Cobb-Det ..... .955
Burns-Phi ..... .857
Sisler-StL ..... .841
Speaker-Cle ..... .839
Hooper-Bos ..... .796

Adjusted Production
T.Cobb-Det 196
Sisler-StL 159
Burns-Phi 157
Hooper-Bos 142
Speaker-Cle 140

Batter Runs
T.Cobb-Det 44.0
Ruth-Bos 34.8
Burns-Phi 32.8
Speaker-Cle 31.3
Sisler-StL 28.8

Adjusted Batter Runs
T.Cobb-Det 45.9
Ruth-Bos 35.4
Burns-Phi 32.3
Sisler-StL 30.3
Speaker-Cle 26.2

Clutch Hitting Index
McInnis-Bos 159
Demmitt-StL 148
Gandil-Chi 147
Roth-Cle 145
Shanks-Was 144

Runs Created
T.Cobb-Det 104
Burns-Phi 93
Speaker-Cle 92
Sisler-StL 90
Hooper-Bos 85

Total Average
T.Cobb-Det 1.131
Sisler-StL ..... .970
Speaker-Cle ..... .931
Roth-Cle ..... .929
Hooper-Bos ..... .875

Stolen Bases
Sisler-StL 45
Roth-Cle 35
T.Cobb-Det 34
Chapman-Cle 30
Speaker-Cle 27

Stolen Base Average

Stolen Base Runs

Fielding Runs
Peckinpaugh-NY 25.0
Scott-Bos 17.5
Dugan-Phi 17.1
Gedeon-StL 15.8
J.Collins-Chi 14.1

Total Player Rating
T.Cobb-Det 4.7
Ruth-Bos 4.1
Sisler-StL 3.5
Speaker-Cle 3.4
Burns-Phi 3.3

Wins
Johnson-Was 23
Coveleski-Cle 22
Mays-Bos 21
Perry-Phi 20
Bagby-Cle 17

Win Percentage
Jones-Bos ..... .762
Johnson-Was ..... .639
Coveleski-Cle ..... .629
Mays-Bos ..... .618
Shaw-Was ..... .571

Games
Mogridge-NY 45
Bagby-Cle 45
Perry-Phi 44
Shaw-Was 41
Ayers-Was 40

Complete Games
Perry-Phi 30
Mays-Bos 30
Johnson-Was 29
Bush-Bos 26
Coveleski-Cle 25

Shutouts
Mays-Bos 8
Johnson-Was 8
Bush-Bos 7
Jones-Bos 5

Saves
Mogridge-NY 7
Bagby-Cle 6
Russell-NY 4
Geary-Phi 4

Innings Pitched
Perry-Phi 332.1
Johnson-Was 325.0
Coveleski-Cle 311.0
Mays-Bos 293.1
Bush-Bos 272.2

Fewest Hits/Game
Sothoron-StL 6.55
Johnson-Was 6.67
Harper-Was 6.71
Ruth-Bos 6.76
Mays-Bos 7.06

Fewest BB/Game
Cicotte-Chi 1.35
Mogridge-NY 1.62
Benz-Chi 1.64
Enzmann-Cle 1.91
Johnson-Was 1.94

Strikeouts
Johnson-Was 162
Shaw-Was 129
Bush-Bos 125
Morton-Cle 123
Mays-Bos 114

Strikeouts/Game
Morton-Cle 5.16
Shaw-Was 4.81
Johnson-Was 4.49
Bush-Bos 4.13
Love-NY 3.74

Ratio
Johnson-Was 8.83
Ruth-Bos 9.52
Sothoron-StL 9.56
Coveleski-Cle 9.87
Mays-Bos 9.88

Earned Run Average
Johnson-Was 1.27
Coveleski-Cle 1.82
Sothoron-StL 1.94
Perry-Phi 1.98
Bush-Bos 2.11

Adjusted ERA
Johnson-Was 214
Coveleski-Cle 164
Perry-Phi 148
Sothoron-StL 141
Mogridge-NY 129

Opponents' Batting Avg.
Sothoron-StL ..... .205
Johnson-Was ..... .210
Harper-Was ..... .212
Ruth-Bos ..... .214
Mays-Bos ..... .221

Opponents' On Base Pct.
Johnson-Was ..... .260
Sothoron-StL ..... .274
Ruth-Bos ..... .277
Coveleski-Cle ..... .279
Mays-Bos ..... .284

Starter Runs
Johnson-Was 54.1
Coveleski-Cle 32.8
Perry-Phi 29.4
Bush-Bos 20.0
Sothoron-StL 19.4

Adjusted Starter Runs
Johnson-Was 52.3
Coveleski-Cle 40.6
Perry-Phi 35.1
Sothoron-StL 18.5
Bush-Bos 17.1

Clutch Pitching Index
Perry-Phi 125
Mogridge-NY 123
Coumbe-Cle 119
Russell-NY 119
Shellenback-Chi 116

Relief Runs
Houck-StL 3.1

Adjusted Relief Runs
Houck-StL 2.8

Relief Ranking
Houck-StL 2.3

Total Pitcher Index
Johnson-Was 7.4
Coveleski-Cle 4.7
Mays-Bos 4.0
Perry-Phi 3.6
Bush-Bos 3.0

Total Baseball Ranking
Johnson-Was 7.4
Ruth-Bos 5.1
Coveleski-Cle 4.7
T.Cobb-Det 4.6
Mays-Bos 4.0

TEAM	G	W	L	PCT	GB	R	OR	AB	H	2B	3B	HR	BB	SO	AVG	OBP	SLG	PRO	PRO+	BR	/A	PF	CHI	RC	SB	CS	SBA	SBR
CIN	140	96	44	.686		577	401	4577	1204	135	83	20	405	368	.263	.327	.342	.669	109	43	56	97	104	560	143			
NY	140	87	53	.621	9	605	470	4664	1254	204	64	40	328	407	.269	.322	.366	.688	113	64	69	99	106	587	157			
CHI	140	75	65	.536	21	454	407	4581	1174	166	58	21	298	359	.256	.308	.332	.640	97	-13	-15	101	93	505	150			
PIT	139	71	68	.511	24.5	472	466	4538	1132	130	82	17	344	405	.249	.304	.325	.631	91	-24	-43	104	99	498	196			
BRO	141	69	71	.493	27	525	513	4844	1272	167	66	25	258	405	.263	.304	.340	.644	96	-12	-22	102	103	525	112			
BOS	140	57	82	.410	38.5	465	563	4746	1201	142	62	24	355	481	.253	.311	.324	.635	100	-16	5	96	92	520	145			
STL	138	54	83	.394	40.5	463	552	4588	1175	163	52	18	304	418	.256	.305	.326	.631	101	-27	3	94	98	491	148			
PHI	138	47	90	.343	47.5	510	699	4746	1191	208	50	42	323	469	.251	.303	.342	.645	92	-8	-44	107	101	521	114			
TOT	558					4071		37284	9603	1315	517	207	2615	3288	.258	.311	.337	.648						1165				

TEAM	CG	SH	SV	IP	H	H/G	HR	BB	SO	RAT	ERA	ERA+	OAV	OOB	PR	/A	PF	CPI	FA	E	DP	FW	PW	BW	SBW	DIF
CIN	89	23	9	1274	1104	7.8	21	298	407	10.0	2.23	124	.238	.287	95	75	95	104	.974	151	98	2.7	8.3	6.2		8.7
NY	72	11	13	1256	1153	8.3	34	305	340	10.6	2.70	104	.246	.296	28	13	96	96	.964	216	96	-1.0	1.4	7.7		8.9
CHI	80	21	5	1265	1127	8.0	14	294	495	10.3	2.21	130	.242	.291	97	92	99	106	.969	185	87	.7	10.2	-1.7		-4.3
PIT	91	17	4	1249	1113	8.0	23	263	391	10.2	2.88	105	.243	.290	3	18	104	84	.970	165	89	1.8	2.0	-4.8		2.5
BRO	98	12	1	1281	1256	8.8	21	292	476	11.1	2.73	109	.261	.308	25	32	102	106	.963	219	84	-1.1	3.6	-2.4		-1.0
BOS	79	5	9	1270[1]	1313	9.3	29	337	374	11.8	3.17	90	.276	.326	-36	-44	98	107	.966	204	111	-.4	-4.9	.6		-7.8
STL	55	6	8	1217[1]	1146	8.5	25	415	414	11.9	3.23	86	.256	.326	-43	-60	96	97	.963	214	112	-1.1	-6.7	.3		-7.1
PHI	93	6	2	1252	1391	10.0	40	408	397	13.3	4.14	78	.293	.355	-171	-128	111	100	.963	218	112	-1.3	-14.2	-4.9		-1.1
TOT	657	101	51	10064[2]		8.6				11.2	2.91		.258	.311					.967	1572	789					

Runs
Burns-NY 86
Groh-Cin 79
Daubert-Cin 79
Rath-Cin 77

Hits
Olson-Bro 164
Hornsby-StL 163
Roush-Cin 162
Burns-NY 162

Doubles
Youngs-NY 31
Luderus-Phi 30
Burns-NY 30
Kauff-NY 27
Meusel-Phi 26

Triples
Southworth-Pit 14
Myers-Bro 14
Roush-Cin 13

Home Runs
Cravath-Phi 12
Kauff-NY 10
Williams-Phi 9
Hornsby-StL 8
Doyle-NY 7

Total Bases
Myers-Bro 223
Hornsby-StL 220
Z.Wheat-Bro 219
Roush-Cin 216
Burns-NY 216

Runs Batted In
Myers-Bro 73
Roush-Cin 71
Hornsby-StL 71
Kauff-NY 67
Groh-Cin 63

Runs Produced
Roush-Cin 141
Groh-Cin 137
Hornsby-StL 131

Bases On Balls
Burns-NY 82
Rath-Cin 64
Groh-Cin 56
Luderus-Phi 54
Boeckel-Pit-Bos . . . 53

Batting Average
Roush-Cin 321
Hornsby-StL 318
Youngs-NY 311
Groh-Cin 310
Stock-StL 307

On Base Percentage
Burns-NY 396
Groh-Cin 392
Hornsby-StL 384
Youngs-NY 384
Roush-Cin 380

Slugging Average
Myers-Bro 436
Groh-Cin 431
Hornsby-StL 430
Roush-Cin 429
Kauff-NY 422

Production
Groh-Cin 823
Hornsby-StL 814
Roush-Cin 809
Burns-NY 801
Youngs-NY 799

Adjusted Production
Hornsby-StL 154
Groh-Cin 151
Roush-Cin 147
Burns-NY 142
Youngs-NY 142

Batter Runs
Cravath-Phi 32.2
Burns-NY 30.0
Hornsby-StL 28.5
Groh-Cin 27.4
Roush-Cin 26.6

Adjusted Batter Runs
Hornsby-StL 32.0
Burns-NY 30.7
Cravath-Phi 30.4
Groh-Cin 28.7
Roush-Cin 28.1

Clutch Hitting Index
Kopf-Cin 146
Zimmerman-NY . . . 141
Merkle-Chi 140
Neale-Cin 138
Deal-Chi 127

Runs Created
Burns-NY 98
Hornsby-StL 90
Roush-Cin 88
Youngs-NY 85
Groh-Cin 83

Total Average
Burns-NY 909
Groh-Cin 887
Youngs-NY 846
Hornsby-StL 837
Roush-Cin 830

Stolen Bases
Burns-NY 40
Cutshaw-Pit 36
Bigbee-Pit 31
Smith-StL 30

Stolen Base Average

Stolen Base Runs

Fielding Runs
Maranville-Bos . . . 28.7
Fletcher-NY 24.0
Stock-StL 16.8
Killefer-Chi 16.3
Rath-Cin 13.1

Total Player Rating
Maranville-Bos 4.4
Hornsby-StL 3.9
Stock-StL 3.9
Roush-Cin 3.1
Groh-Cin 3.0

Wins
J.Barnes-NY 25
Vaughn-Chi 21
Sallee-Cin 21

Win Percentage
Ruether-Cin 760
Sallee-Cin 750
J.Barnes-NY 735
Eller-Cin 679
Adams-Pit 630

Games
Tuero-StL 45
Meadows-StL-Phi . . 40
Vaughn-Chi 38
Eller-Cin 38
J.Barnes-NY 38

Complete Games
Cooper-Pit 27
Pfeffer-Bro 26
Vaughn-Chi 25
Rudolph-Bos 24

Shutouts
Alexander-Chi 9
Eller-Cin 7
Adams-Pit 6
Fisher-Cin 5

Saves
Tuero-StL 4

Innings Pitched
Vaughn-Chi 306.2
J.Barnes-NY 295.2
Cooper-Pit 286.2
Rudolph-Bos 273.2
Nehf-Bos-NY 270.2

Fewest Hits/Game
Alexander-Chi 6.89
Cooper-Pit 7.19
Ruether-Cin 7.23
Carlson-Pit 7.28
Fisher-Cin 7.28

Fewest BB/Game
Adams-Pit 79
Sallee-Cin 79
J.Barnes-NY 1.07
Cadore-Bro 1.40
Alexander-Chi 1.46

Strikeouts
Vaughn-Chi 141
Eller-Cin 137
Alexander-Chi 121
Meadows-StL-Phi . . 116
Cooper-Pit 106

Strikeouts/Game
Eller-Cin 4.97
Alexander-Chi 4.63
Meadows-StL-Phi 4.17
Vaughn-Chi 4.14
Grimes-Bro 4.07

Ratio
Adams-Pit 8.17
Alexander-Chi 8.35
J.Barnes-NY 9.13
Fisher-Cin 9.29
Miller-Pit 9.33

Earned Run Average
Alexander-Chi 1.72
Vaughn-Chi 1.79
Ruether-Cin 1.82
Toney-NY 1.84
Adams-Pit 1.98

Adjusted ERA
Alexander-Chi 167
Vaughn-Chi 161
Ruether-Cin 152
Toney-NY 152
Adams-Pit 152

Opponents' Batting Avg.
Alexander-Chi 211
Adams-Pit 220
Ruether-Cin 223
Cooper-Pit 225
Nehf-Bos-NY 225

Opponents' On Base Pct.
Adams-Pit 241
Alexander-Chi 245
J.Barnes-NY 260
Fisher-Cin 271
Miller-Pit 272

Starter Runs
Vaughn-Chi 38.1
Alexander-Chi 31.0
Ruether-Cin 29.4
Adams-Pit 27.1
Rudolph-Bos 22.5

Adjusted Starter Runs
Vaughn-Chi 37.0
Adams-Pit 30.3
Alexander-Chi 30.1
Ruether-Cin 25.7
Rudolph-Bos 20.8

Clutch Pitching Index
Rudolph-Bos 141
Smith-Bro 141
Martin-Chi 122
Jacobs-Phi-StL . . . 122
Toney-NY 120

Relief Runs

Adjusted Relief Runs

Relief Ranking

Total Pitcher Index
Alexander-Chi 4.2
Vaughn-Chi 4.0
Ruether-Cin 3.3
Adams-Pit 3.0
Rudolph-Bos 2.8

Total Baseball Ranking
Maranville-Bos 4.4
Alexander-Chi 4.2
Vaughn-Chi 4.0
Hornsby-StL 3.9
Stock-StL 3.9

TEAM	G	W	L	PCT	GB	R	OR	AB	H	2B	3B	HR	BB	SO	AVG	OBP	SLG	PRO	PRO+	BR	/A	PF	CHI	RC	SB	CS	SBA	SBR
CHI	140	88	52	.629		667	534	4675	1343	218	70	25	427	358	.287	.351	.380	.731	110	69	66	100	103	674	150			
CLE	139	84	55	.604	3.5	636	537	4565	1268	254	71	25	498	367	.278	.354	.381	.735	105	78	42	106	98	667	113			
NY	141	80	59	.576	7.5	578	506	4775	1275	193	49	45	386	479	.267	.326	.356	.682	96	-19	-23	101	103	590	101			
DET	140	80	60	.571	8	618	578	4665	1319	222	84	23	429	427	.283	.346	.381	.727	112	60	73	98	97	659	121			
STL	140	67	72	.482	20.5	533	567	4672	1234	187	73	31	391	443	.264	.326	.355	.681	94	-21	-35	103	97	575	74			
BOS	138	66	71	.482	20.5	564	552	4548	1188	181	49	33	471	411	.261	.336	.344	.680	102	-10	22	94	101	577	108			
WAS	142	56	84	.400	32	533	570	4757	1238	177	63	24	416	511	.260	.325	.339	.664	92	-46	-40	99	100	571	142			
PHI	140	36	104	.257	52	457	742	4730	1156	175	71	35	349	565	.244	.300	.334	.634	82	-107	-113	101	100	505	103			
TOT	560					4586		37387	10021	1607	530	241	3367	3561	.268	.333	.359	.692						912				

TEAM	CG	SH	SV	IP	H	H/G	HR	BB	SO	RAT	ERA	ERA+	OAV	OOB	PR	/A	PF	CPI	FA	E	DP	FW	PW	BW	SBW	DIF
CHI	88	14	3	1265²	1245	8.9	25	342	468	11.5	3.04	105	.261	.315	26	19	99	93	.969	176	116	1.6	2.0	6.9		7.5
CLE	80	10	10	1245	1242	9.0	19	362	432	11.8	2.94	114	.264	.321	38	53	104	98	.965	201	102	-.0	5.5	4.4		4.6
NY	85	14	7	1287	1143	8.0	47	433	500	11.3	2.82	113	.240	.308	57	53	99	92	.968	193	108	.7	5.5	-2.4		6.7
DET	85	10	4	1256	1254	9.0	35	431	428	12.3	3.30	97	.265	.331	-11	-13	99	99	.964	205	81	-.2	-1.4	7.6		3.9
STL	78	14	4	1256	1255	9.0	35	421	415	12.3	3.13	106	.262	.328	12	24	103	99	.963	215	98	-.8	2.5	-3.7		-.5
BOS	89	15	8	1224¹	1251	9.2	16	420	380	12.5	3.31	91	.275	.340	-11	-40	94	101	.975	140	118	3.8	-4.2	2.3		-4.4
WAS	68	13	10	1274¹	1237	8.7	20	451	536	12.2	3.01	106	.259	.327	30	27	99	99	.960	227	86	-1.4	2.8	-4.2		-11.2
PHI	72	1	3	1239¹	1371	10.0	44	503	417	13.8	4.26	80	.291	.363	-143	-117	106	96	.956	257	96	-3.5	-12.2	-11.8		-6.4
TOT	645	91	49	100047²		9.0				12.2	3.22		.268	.333					.965	1614	805					

Runs
Ruth-Bos 103
Sisler-StL 96
Cobb-Det 92
Weaver-Chi 89
Peckinpaugh-NY ... 89

Hits
Veach-Det 191
Cobb-Det 191
Jackson-Chi 181
Sisler-StL 180
Rice-Was 179

Doubles
Veach-Det 45
Speaker-Cle 38
Cobb-Det 36
O'Neill-Cle 35

Triples
Veach-Det 17
Sisler-StL 15
Heilmann-Det 15
Jackson-Chi 14
Cobb-Det 13

Home Runs
Ruth-Bos 29
C.Walker-Phi 10
Sisler-StL 10
Baker-NY 10
Smith-Cle 9

Total Bases
Ruth-Bos 284
Veach-Det 279
Sisler-StL 271
Jackson-Chi 261

Runs Batted In
Ruth-Bos 114
Veach-Det 101
Jackson-Chi 96
Heilmann-Det 93
Lewis-NY 89

Runs Produced
Ruth-Bos 188
Veach-Det 185
Sisler-StL 169
Jackson-Chi 168
E.Collins-Chi 163

Bases On Balls
Graney-Cle 105
Ruth-Bos 101
Judge-Was 81
Hooper-Bos 79
Bush-Det 75

Batting Average
Cobb-Det .... .384
Veach-Det .... .355
Sisler-StL .... .352
Jackson-Chi ..... .351
Tobin-StL .... .327

On Base Percentage
Ruth-Bos .... .456
Cobb-Det .... .429
Jackson-Chi ..... .422
Leibold-Chi ..... .404
E.Collins-Chi .... .400

Slugging Average
Ruth-Bos .... .657
Sisler-StL .... .530
Veach-Det .... .519
Cobb-Det .... .515
Jackson-Chi ..... .506

Production
Ruth-Bos 1.114
Cobb-Det .... .944
Jackson-Chi ..... .928
Sisler-StL .... .921
Veach-Det .... .916

Adjusted Production
Ruth-Bos 224
Cobb-Det 168
Veach-Det 160
Jackson-Chi 159
Sisler-StL 153

Batter Runs
Ruth-Bos 66.5
Jackson-Chi 41.7
Cobb-Det 41.6
Veach-Det 37.7
Sisler-StL 35.8

Adjusted Batter Runs
Ruth-Bos 69.9
Cobb-Det 43.0
Jackson-Chi 41.5
Veach-Det 39.2
Sisler-StL 34.3

Clutch Hitting Index
Lewis-NY 152
Gardner-Cle 143
Jones-Det 141
Felsch-Chi 140
Veach-Det 135

Runs Created
Ruth-Bos 138
Cobb-Det 115
Jackson-Chi 115
Veach-Det 114
Sisler-StL 110

Total Average
Ruth-Bos 1.358
Cobb-Det 1.056
Sisler-StL 1.000
Jackson-Chi ..... .997
Veach-Det .... .968

Stolen Bases
E.Collins-Chi 33
Sisler-StL 28
Cobb-Det 28
Rice-Was 26

Stolen Base Average

Stolen Base Runs

Fielding Runs
Pratt-NY 28.0
Peckinpaugh-NY .. 27.8
Felsch-Chi 21.4
Speaker-Cle 19.1
Young-Det 17.3

Total Player Rating
Ruth-Bos 7.0
Peckinpaugh-NY ... 5.4
Pratt-NY 4.4
Veach-Det 4.2
Sisler-StL 3.8

Wins
Cicotte-Chi 29
Coveleski-Cle 24
Williams-Chi 23
Dauss-Det 21

Win Percentage
Cicotte-Chi 806
Dauss-Det 700
Williams-Chi 676
Pennock-Bos 667
Coveleski-Cle 667

Games
Shaw-Was 45
Russell-NY-Bos.... 44
Kinney-Phi 43
Coveleski-Cle 43

Complete Games
Cicotte-Chi 30
Williams-Chi 27
Johnson-Was 27
Mays-Bos-NY 26
Coveleski-Cle 24

Shutouts
Johnson-Was 7

Saves
Russell-NY-Bos..... 5
Shawkey-NY 5
Shaw-Was 5
Coveleski-Cle 4

Innings Pitched
Shaw-Was 306.2
Cicotte-Chi 306.2
Williams-Chi.... 297.0
Johnson-Was .. 290.1
Coveleski-Cle .. 286.0

Fewest Hits/Game
Johnson-Was ... 7.28
Thormahlen-NY ... 7.39
Shawkey-NY 7.51
Cicotte-Chi 7.51
Mays-Bos-NY ... 7.68

Fewest BB/Game
Cicotte-Chi 1.44
Johnson-Was 1.58
Bagby-Cle 1.64
Williams-Chi 1.76
Coveleski-Cle 1.89

Strikeouts
Johnson-Was 147
Shaw-Was 128
Williams-Chi 125
Shawkey-NY 122
Coveleski-Cle 118

Strikeouts/Game
Erickson-Det-Was . 5.52
Russell-NY-Bos .. 4.80
Johnson-Was ... 4.56
Kinney-Phi 4.31
Leonard-Det 4.22

Ratio
Cicotte-Chi 9.01
Johnson-Was 9.08
Williams-Chi 10.12
Thormahlen-NY .. 10.49
Quinn-NY 10.59

Earned Run Average
Johnson-Was 1.49
Cicotte-Chi 1.82
Weilman-StL 2.07
Mays-Bos-NY 2.10
Sothoron-StL 2.20

Adjusted ERA
Johnson-Was ... 215
Cicotte-Chi 175
Weilman-StL 160
Sothoron-StL..... 151
Mays-Bos-NY 147

Opponents' Batting Avg.
Johnson-Was .... .219
Cicotte-Chi ...... .228
Thormahlen-NY ...228
Shawkey-NY 231
Mays-Bos-NY 233

Opponents' On Base Pct.
Johnson-Was ..... .259
Cicotte-Chi ...... .261
Williams-Chi .... .289
Morton-Cle ...... .293
Quinn-NY .... .295

Starter Runs
Johnson-Was 56.0
Cicotte-Chi 47.8
Mays-Bos-NY ... 33.3
Sothoron-StL..... 30.7
Coveleski-Cle 19.4

Adjusted Starter Runs
Johnson-Was 55.3
Cicotte-Chi 46.3
Sothoron-StL..... 33.4
Mays-Bos-NY 29.4
Coveleski-Cle ... 23.2

Clutch Pitching Index
Weilman-StL 119
Sothoron-StL..... 114
Ehmke-Det....... 113
Harper-Was 107
Pennock-Bos 107

Relief Runs
Phillips-Cle....... 1.7

Adjusted Relief Runs
Phillips-Cle........ 2.4

Relief Ranking
Phillips-Cle........ 2.0

Total Pitcher Index
Johnson-Was 6.6
Cicotte-Chi....... 4.8
Mays-Bos-NY 3.8
Coveleski-Cle 3.3
Sothoron-StL...... 2.6

Total Baseball Ranking
Ruth-Bos 7.1
Johnson-Was 6.6
Peckinpaugh-NY ... 5.4
Cicotte-Chi........ 4.8
Pratt-NY 4.4

TEAM	G	W	L	PCT	GB	R	OR	AB	H	2B	3B	HR	BB	SO	AVG	OBP	SLG	PRO	PRO+	BR	/A	PF	CHI	RC	SB	CS	SBA	SBR
BRO	155	93	61	.604		660	528	5399	1493	205	99	28	359	391	.277	.324	.367	.691	99	19	0	103	103	637	70	80	54	-7
NY	155	86	68	.558	7	682	543	5309	1427	210	76	46	432	545	.269	.327	.363	.690	104	23	29	99	107	628	131	113	68	-6
CIN	154	82	71	.536	10.5	639	569	5176	1432	169	76	18	382	367	.277	.332	.349	.681	102	11	19	99	104	602	158	128	65	0
PIT	155	79	75	.513	14	530	552	5219	1342	162	90	16	374	405	.257	.310	.332	.642	86	-66	-84	103	98	544	181	117	64	-2
STL	155	75	79	.487	18	675	682	5495	1589	238	96	32	373	484	.289	.337	.385	.722	117	83	106	96	94	704	126	114	64	-3
CHI	154	75	79	.487	18	619	635	5117	1350	223	67	34	428	421	.264	.326	.354	.680	98	7	-5	102	101	589	115	129	67	-1
BOS	153	62	90	.408	30	523	670	5218	1358	168	86	23	385	488	.260	.315	.339	.654	97	-44	-17	96	93	557	88	98	59	-5
PHI	153	62	91	.405	30.5	565	714	5264	1385	229	54	64	283	531	.263	.305	.364	.669	92	-29	-57	105	99	577	100	83	58	-9
TOT	617					4893		42197	11376	1604	644	261	3016	3632	.270	.322	.357	.679							969	862	53	-226

TEAM	CG	SH	SV	IP	H	H/G	HR	BB	SO	RAT	ERA	ERA+	OAV	OOB	PR	/A	PF	CPI	FA	E	DP	FW	PW	BW	SBW	DIF
BRO	89	17	10	1427.1	1381	8.7	25	327	553	10.9	2.62	122	.258	.304	80	91	102	102	.966	226	118	-.2	9.7	.0	2.3	4.1
NY	86	18	9	1408.2	1379	8.8	44	297	380	10.8	2.80	107	.261	.302	51	30	96	96	.969	210	137	.8	3.2	3.1	2.4	-.5
CIN	90	12	9	1391.2	1327	8.6	26	393	435	11.3	2.90	105	.256	.312	36	22	97	97	.968	200	125	1.3	2.4	2.0	3.0	-3.2
PIT	92	17	10	1415.1	1389	8.8	25	280	444	10.8	2.89	111	.260	.301	38	50	103	91	.971	186	119	2.2	5.4	-9.0	2.8	.6
STL	72	9	12	1426.2	1488	9.4	30	479	529	12.8	3.43	87	.276	.342	-47	-71	95	103	.961	256	136	-2.0	-7.6	11.4	2.7	-6.5
CHI	95	13	9	1388.2	1459	9.5	37	382	508	12.1	3.27	98	.276	.327	-20	-9	102	102	.965	225	112	-.2	-1.0	-.5	2.9	-3.2
BOS	93	14	6	1386.1	1464	9.5	39	415	368	12.4	3.54	86	.280	.337	-62	-75	97	100	.964	239	125	-1.1	-8.0	-1.8	2.5	-5.5
PHI	77	8	11	1380.2	1480	9.6	35	444	419	12.8	3.63	94	.284	.345	-76	-34	109	102	.964	232	135	-.7	-3.6	-6.1	2.1	-6.1
TOT	694	108	76	11225.1		9.1				11.7	3.13		.270	.322					.966	1774	1007					

Runs
Burns-NY 115
Bancroft-Phi-NY .. 102
Daubert-Cin 97
Hornsby-StL 96
Youngs-NY 92

Hits
Hornsby-StL 218
Youngs-NY 204
Stock-StL 204
Roush-Cin 196
Williams-Phi 192

Doubles
Hornsby-StL 44
Bancroft-Phi-NY ... 36
Williams-Phi 36
Myers-Bro 36
Burns-NY 35

Triples
Myers-Bro 22
Hornsby-StL 20
Roush-Cin 16
Maranville-Bos ... 15
Bigbee-Pit 15

Home Runs
Williams-Phi 15
Meusel-Phi 14
Kelly-NY 11
Robertson-Chi..... 10
McHenry-StL 10

Total Bases
Hornsby-StL 329
Williams-Phi 293
Youngs-NY 277
Wheat-Bro 270
Myers-Bro 269

Runs Batted In
Kelly-NY 94
Hornsby-StL 94
Roush-Cin 90
Duncan-Cin 83
Myers-Bro 80

Runs Produced
Hornsby-StL 181
Roush-Cin 167
Youngs-NY 164
Stock-StL 161
Myers-Bro 159

Bases On Balls
Burns-NY 76
Youngs-NY 75
Paskert-Chi 64
Hornsby-StL 60
Groh-Cin 60

Batting Average
Hornsby-StL ...... .370
Youngs-NY .... .351
Roush-Cin .... .339
Wheat-Bro .... .328
Williams-Phi ...... .325

On Base Percentage
Hornsby-StL ...... .431
Youngs-NY .... .427
Roush-Cin .... .386
Wheat-Bro .... .385
Groh-Cin .... .375

Slugging Average
Hornsby-StL ..... .559
Williams-Phi ..... .497
Youngs-NY .... .477
Meusel-Phi ...... .473
Wheat-Bro .... .463

Production
Hornsby-StL ..... .990
Youngs-NY ...... .904
Williams-Phi ...... .861
Wheat-Bro .... .848
Roush-Cin .... .839

Adjusted Production
Hornsby-StL 190
Youngs-NY 161
Roush-Cin 142
Williams-Phi 139
Wheat-Bro 138

Batter Runs
Hornsby-StL 62.6
Youngs-NY 47.1
Williams-Phi 32.1
Wheat-Bro 31.9
Roush-Cin 29.7

Adjusted Batter Runs
Hornsby-StL 65.2
Youngs-NY 47.9
Roush-Cin 30.7
Wheat-Bro 29.8
Williams-Phi 29.0

Clutch Hitting Index
Whitted-Pit 176
Kopf-Cin 172
Duncan-Cin 153
Kelly-NY 142
Paskert-Chi 138

Runs Created
Hornsby-StL 138
Youngs-NY 118
Williams-Phi 103
Wheat-Bro 102
Roush-Cin 98

Total Average
Hornsby-StL 1.008
Youngs-NY ...... .896
Williams-Phi ...... .817
Wheat-Bro .... .801
Roush-Cin .... .784

Stolen Bases
Carey-Pit 52
Carey-Cin 36
Frisch-NY 34
Bigbee-Pit 31
Neale-Cin 29

Stolen Base Average
Carey-Pit 83.9
Frisch-NY 75.6
Neale-Cin 70.7
Bigbee-Pit 67.4
Meusel-Phi....... 60.7

Stolen Base Runs
Carey-Pit 9.6
Frisch-NY 3.6
Neale-Cin 1.5
Tragesser-Phi 1.2
Gowdy-Bos 1.2

Fielding Runs
Bancroft-Phi-NY .. 39.0
Lavan-StL 16.2
Maranville-Bos ... 14.3
Terry-Chi 14.0
Neale-Cin 12.9

Total Player Rating
Hornsby-StL 7.7
Bancroft-Phi-NY .. 5.2
Youngs-NY 3.6
Roush-Cin 3.2
Williams-Phi 2.6

Wins
Alexander-Chi 27
Cooper-Pit 24
Grimes-Bro 23
Toney-NY 21
Nehf-NY 21

Win Percentage
Grimes-Bro .... .676
Alexander-Chi .... .659
Toney-NY .... .656
Pfeffer-Bro .... .640
Nehf-NY .... .636

Games
Haines-StL 47
Douglas-NY 46
Alexander-Chi 46
Scott-Bos 44
Cooper-Pit 44

Complete Games
Alexander-Chi 33
Cooper-Pit 28
Rixey-Phi 25
Grimes-Bro 25
Vaughn-Chi 24

Shutouts
Adams-Pit 8
Alexander-Chi 7

Saves
Sherdel-StL 6
McQuillan-Bos..... 5
Alexander-Chi 5
Hubbell-NY-Phi 4
Mamaux-Bro 4

Innings Pitched
Alexander-Chi ... 363.1
Cooper-Pit 327.0
Grimes-Bro 303.2
Haines-StL 301.2
Vaughn-Chi 301.0

Fewest Hits/Game
Luque-Cin 7.28
Ruether-Cin 7.96
Grimes-Bro 8.03
Mamaux-Bro 8.12
Adams-Pit 8.21

Fewest BB/Game
Adams-Pit .... .62
Cooper-Pit 1.43
Nehf-NY 1.44
Benton-NY 1.44
Marquard-Bro 1.66

Strikeouts
Alexander-Chi 173
Vaughn-Chi 131
Grimes-Bro 131
Haines-StL 120
Schupp-StL 119

Strikeouts/Game
Mamaux-Bro 4.77
Alexander-Chi 4.29
Schupp-StL 4.27
Marquard-Bro 4.22
Sherdel-StL 3.92

Ratio
Adams-Pit 8.86
Alexander-Chi ... 10.03
Luque-Cin 10.05
J.Barnes-NY 10.12
Grimes-Bro 10.14

Earned Run Average
Alexander-Chi 1.91
Adams-Pit 2.16
Grimes-Bro 2.22
Cooper-Pit 2.39
Ruether-Cin 2.47

Adjusted ERA
Alexander-Chi 168
Adams-Pit 149
Grimes-Bro 144
Cooper-Pit 134
Vaughn-Chi 126

Opponents' Batting Avg.
Luque-Cin .... .225
Grimes-Bro ...... .238
Adams-Pit .... .244
Ponder-Pit ...... .246
Ruether-Cin ..... .247

Opponents' On Base Pct.
Adams-Pit .... .259
Grimes-Bro ...... .282
Alexander-Chi .... .285
Luque-Cin .... .286
Ponder-Pit ...... .286

Starter Runs
Alexander-Chi 49.5
Grimes-Bro 30.7
Adams-Pit 28.5
Cooper-Pit 26.8
Vaughn-Chi 19.8

Adjusted Starter Runs
Alexander-Chi 52.4
Grimes-Bro 33.0
Adams-Pit 30.9
Cooper-Pit 29.8
Vaughn-Chi 22.2

Clutch Pitching Index
Meadows-Phi 121
Alexander-Chi 120
Vaughn-Chi 119
Fillingim-Bos 118
Benton-NY 115

Relief Runs

Adjusted Relief Runs

Relief Ranking

Total Pitcher Index
Alexander-Chi 6.8
Grimes-Bro 5.3
Smith-Bro 3.2
Cooper-Pit 2.9
Adams-Pit 2.7

Total Baseball Ranking
Hornsby-StL 7.7
Alexander-Chi 6.8
Grimes-Bro 5.3
Bancroft-Phi-NY .. 5.2
Youngs-NY........ 3.6

TEAM	G	W	L	PCT	GB	R	OR	AB	H	2B	3B	HR	BB	SO	AVG	OBP	SLG	PRO	PRO+	BR	/A	PF	CHI	RC	SB	CS	SBA	SBR
CLE	154	98	56	.636		857	642	5196	1574	300	95	35	576	379	.303	.376	.417	.793	112	125	101	103	98	827	73	92	61	-8
CHI	154	96	58	.623	2	794	665	5328	1574	263	98	37	471	353	.295	.357	.402	.759	107	49	49	100	100	769	112	96	61	-7
NY	154	95	59	.617	3	838	629	5176	1448	268	71	115	539	626	.280	.350	.426	.776	107	71	45	104	105	773	64	82	57	-9
STL	154	76	77	.497	21.5	797	766	5358	1651	279	83	50	427	339	.308	.363	.419	.782	109	93	70	103	95	822	118	79	58	-10
BOS	154	72	81	.471	25.5	650	698	5199	1397	216	71	22	533	429	.269	.342	.350	.692	92	-69	-37	96	97	637	98	111	66	-5
WAS	153	68	84	.447	29	723	802	5251	1526	233	81	36	433	543	.291	.351	.386	.737	103	7	26	97	98	718	161	114	63	-3
DET	155	61	93	.396	37	652	833	5215	1408	228	72	30	479	391	.270	.334	.359	.693	91	-79	-60	98	100	640	76	66	51	-10
PHI	156	48	106	.312	50	558	834	5256	1324	220	49	44	353	593	.252	.305	.338	.643	74	-187	-194	101	105	543	50	67	57	-13
TOT	617					5869		41979	11902	2007	620	369	3811	3653	.284	.347	.387	.734							752	707	52	-198

TEAM	CG	SH	SV	IP	H	H/G	HR	BB	SO	RAT	ERA	ERA+	OAV	OOB	PR	/A	PF	CPI	FA	E	DP	FW	PW	BW	SBW	DIF
CLE	94	11	7	1377	1448	9.5	31	401	466	12.3	3.41	111	.276	.331	57	58	100	98	.971	184	124	2.1	5.6	9.8	1.6	1.8
CHI	109	9	10	1386²	1467	9.5	45	405	438	12.3	3.59	105	.279	.334	30	23	99	98	.968	198	142	1.2	2.2	4.8	1.7	9.1
NY	88	15	11	1368	1414	9.3	48	420	480	12.3	3.32	115	.269	.327	71	75	101	99	.969	194	129	1.4	7.3	4.4	1.5	3.4
STL	84	9	14	1378²	1481	9.7	53	578	444	13.7	4.03	97	.283	.358	-37	-22	103	99	.963	233	119	-1.2	-2.1	6.8	1.4	-5.4
BOS	92	11	6	1395¹	1481	9.6	39	461	481	12.7	3.82	95	.278	.339	-4	-29	96	93	.972	183	131	2.2	-2.8	-3.6	1.9	-2.2
WAS	81	10	10	1367	1521	10.0	51	520	418	13.7	4.17	89	.288	.356	-57	-69	98	97	.963	232	95	-1.3	-6.7	2.5	2.1	-4.7
DET	74	9	7	1385	1487	9.7	46	561	483	13.7	4.04	92	.283	.359	-38	-51	98	99	.964	230	95	-.9	-4.9	-5.8	1.4	-5.7
PHI	79	6	2	1380¹	1612	10.5	56	461	423	13.8	3.93	102	.301	.361	-21	11	106	110	.959	266	125	-3.3	1.1	-18.8	1.1	-9.1
TOT	701	80	67	11038		9.7				13.1	3.79		.284	.347					.966	1720	960					

Runs
Ruth-NY 158
Speaker-Cle 137
Sisler-StL 137
E.Collins-Chi 115

Hits
Sisler-StL 257
E.Collins-Chi 222
Jackson-Chi 218
Jacobson-StL 216
Speaker-Cle 214

Doubles
Speaker-Cle 50
Sisler-StL 49
Jackson-Chi 42

Triples
Jackson-Chi 20
Sisler-StL 18
Hooper-Bos 17

Home Runs
Ruth-NY 54
Sisler-StL 19
C.Walker-Phi 17
Felsch-Chi 14

Total Bases
Sisler-StL 399
Ruth-NY 388
Jackson-Chi 336
Speaker-Cle 310
Jacobson-StL 305

Runs Batted In
Ruth-NY 137
Sisler-StL 122
Jacobson-StL 122
Jackson-Chi 121
Gardner-Cle 118

Runs Produced
Ruth-NY 241
Sisler-StL 240
Speaker-Cle 236
Jackson-Chi 214
Jacobson-StL 210

Bases On Balls
Ruth-NY 148
Speaker-Cle 97
Hooper-Bos 88
Young-Det 85
Roth-Was 75

Batting Average
Sisler-StL .... .407
Speaker-Cle ...... .388
Jackson-Chi ..... .382
Ruth-NY .... .376
E.Collins-Chi ..... .369

On Base Percentage
Ruth-NY .... .530
Speaker-Cle ...... .483
Sisler-StL .... .449
Jackson-Chi ..... .444
E.Collins-Chi ..... .436

Slugging Average
Ruth-NY .... .847
Sisler-StL .... .632
Jackson-Chi ..... .589
Speaker-Cle ...... .562
Felsch-Chi .... .540

Production
Ruth-NY 1.378
Sisler-StL 1.082
Speaker-Cle 1.045
Jackson-Chi ... 1.033
E.Collins-Chi ..... .925

Adjusted Production
Ruth-NY 252
Sisler-StL 179
Jackson-Chi 172
Speaker-Cle 171
E.Collins-Chi 145

Batter Runs
Ruth-NY 113.2
Sisler-StL 73.2
Speaker-Cle 65.7
Jackson-Chi 58.4
E.Collins-Chi 40.8

Adjusted Batter Runs
Ruth-NY 110.5
Sisler-StL 70.7
Speaker-Cle 63.2
Jackson-Chi 58.4
E.Collins-Chi 40.8

Clutch Hitting Index
Gardner-Cle 168
Roth-Was 141
Pratt-NY 138
Jacobson-StL 134
Smith-Cle 133

Runs Created
Ruth-NY 211
Sisler-StL 176
Speaker-Cle 152
Jackson-Chi 145
E.Collins-Chi 132

Total Average
Ruth-NY 1.797
Sisler-StL 1.207
Speaker-Cle 1.165
Jackson-Chi ... 1.088
E.Collins-Chi ..... .972

Stolen Bases
Rice-Was 63
Sisler-StL 42
Roth-Was 24
Menosky-Bos 23
Tobin-StL 21

Stolen Base Average
Sisler-StL 71.2
E.Collins-Chi 70.4
Williams-StL 69.2
Rice-Was 67.7
Roth-Was 66.7

Stolen Base Runs
Sisler-StL 2.4
Burns-Phi-Cle ... 1.5
Smith-StL 9
Rice-Was 9
E.Collins-Chi 9

Fielding Runs
Perkins-Phi 23.5
Ward-NY 21.8
Rice-Was 21.4
Pinelli-Det 19.9
Felsch-Chi 17.7

Total Player Rating
Ruth-NY 8.8
Sisler-StL 8.3
E.Collins-Chi 5.3
Speaker-Cle 5.2
Jackson-Chi 3.9

Wins
Bagby-Cle 31
Mays-NY 26
Coveleski-Cle 24
Faber-Chi 23
Williams-Chi 22

Win Percentage
Bagby-Cle .... .721
Mays-NY .... .703
Kerr-Chi .... .700
Cicotte-Chi .... .677

Games
Bagby-Cle 48
Ayers-Det 46
Mays-NY 45
Kerr-Chi 45
Zachary-Was 44

Complete Games
Bagby-Cle 30
Faber-Chi 28
Cicotte-Chi 28
Mays-NY 26
Coveleski-Cle 26

Shutouts
Mays-NY 6
Shocker-StL 5
Shawkey-NY 5

Saves
Shocker-StL 5
Kerr-Chi 5
Burwell-StL 4

Innings Pitched
Bagby-Cle 339.2
Faber-Chi 319.0
Coveleski-Cle .. 315.0
Mays-NY 312.0
Cicotte-Chi 303.1

Fewest Hits/Game
Coveleski-Cle 8.11
Shocker-StL 8.21
Collins-NY 8.22
Shawkey-NY 8.27
Davis-StL 8.35

Fewest BB/Game
Quinn-NY 1.71
Coveleski-Cle 1.86
Bagby-Cle 2.09
Cicotte-Chi 2.20
Perry-Phi 2.22

Strikeouts
Coveleski-Cle 133
Williams-Chi 128
Shawkey-NY 126
Faber-Chi 108
Shocker-StL 107

Strikeouts/Game
Ayers-Det 4.44
Shawkey-NY 4.24
Harper-Bos 3.93
Shocker-StL 3.92
Williams-Chi 3.85

Ratio
Coveleski-Cle ... 10.09
Shocker-StL ... 10.92
Rommel-Phi 10.99
Shawkey-NY 11.16
Bagby-Cle 11.18

Earned Run Average
Shawkey-NY 2.45
Coveleski-Cle ... 2.49
Shocker-StL 2.71
Rommel-Phi 2.85
Bagby-Cle 2.89

Adjusted ERA
Shawkey-NY 155
Coveleski-Cle 153
Shocker-StL 144
Rommel-Phi 141
Bagby-Cle 131

Opponents' Batting Avg.
Coveleski-Cle .... .243
Collins-NY ...... .247
Shawkey-NY .... .248
Shocker-StL ..... .248
Ehmke-Det ...... .253

Opponents' On Base Pct.
Coveleski-Cle .... .285
Shocker-StL .... .305
Shawkey-NY .... .308
Quinn-NY .... .308
Rommel-Phi ..... .309

Starter Runs
Coveleski-Cle 45.6
Shawkey-NY 39.6
Bagby-Cle 33.9
Shocker-StL 29.4
Faber-Chi 28.2

Adjusted Starter Runs
Coveleski-Cle 45.7
Shawkey-NY 40.3
Bagby-Cle 34.1
Shocker-StL 32.7
Faber-Chi 27.2

Clutch Pitching Index
Naylor-Phi 130
Harper-Bos 128
Davis-StL 117
Oldham-Det 116
Perry-Phi 113

Relief Runs

Adjusted Relief Runs

Relief Ranking

Total Pitcher Index
Coveleski-Cle 5.4
Shawkey-NY 3.7
Mays-NY 3.5
Shocker-StL 3.5
Bagby-Cle 3.4

Total Baseball Ranking
Ruth-NY 8.8
Sisler-StL 8.4
Coveleski-Cle 5.4
E.Collins-Chi 5.3
Speaker-Cle 5.2

TEAM	G	W	L	PCT	GB	R	OR	AB	H	2B	3B	HR	BB	SO	AVG	OBP	SLG	PRO	PRO+	BR	/A	PF	CHI	RC	SB	CS	SBA	SBR
NY	153	94	59	.614		840	637	5278	1575	237	93	75	469	390	.298	.359	.421	.780	111	94	92	100	104	795	137	114	66	-4
PIT	154	90	63	.588	4	692	595	5379	1533	231	104	37	341	371	.285	.330	.387	.717	92	-36	-54	103	102	684	134	93	58	-6
STL	154	87	66	.569	7	809	681	5309	1635	260	88	83	382	452	.308	.358	.437	.795	118	114	128	98	98	816	94	94	62	-8
BOS	153	79	74	.516	15	721	697	5385	1561	209	100	61	377	470	.290	.339	.400	.739	106	6	45	95	100	718	94	100	62	-6
BRO	152	77	75	.507	16.5	667	681	5263	1476	209	85	59	325	400	.280	.325	.386	.711	89	-51	-75	104	104	655	91	73	54	-10
CIN	153	70	83	.458	24	618	649	5112	1421	221	94	20	375	308	.278	.333	.370	.703	96	-55	-23	95	98	623	117	120	69	-4
CHI	153	64	89	.418	30	668	773	5321	1553	234	56	37	343	374	.292	.339	.378	.717	94	-30	-30	100	98	671	70	97	58	-5
PHI	154	51	103	.331	43.5	617	919	5329	1512	238	50	88	294	615	.284	.324	.397	.721	88	-36	-90	108	94	668	66	80	58	-10
TOT	613					5632		42376	12266	1839	670	460	2906	3380	.289	.338	.397	.736							803	771	51	-221

TEAM	CG	SH	SV	IP	H	H/G	HR	BB	SO	RAT	ERA	ERA+	OAV	OOB	PR	/A	PF	CPI	FA	E	DP	FW	PW	BW	SBW	DIF
NY	71	9	18	1372¹	1497	9.8	79	295	357	11.9	3.55	103	.285	.325	34	16	97	102	.971	187	155	1.3	1.6	9.1	2.3	3.2
PIT	88	10	10	1415²	1448	9.2	37	322	500	11.5	3.17	121	.270	.316	96	103	101	96	.973	172	129	2.3	10.2	-5.3	2.1	4.3
STL	70	10	16	1371²	1486	9.8	61	399	464	12.6	3.62	101	.282	.337	24	5	97	102	.965	219	130	-.6	.5	12.6	1.9	-4.0
BOS	74	11	12	1385	1488	9.7	54	420	382	12.6	3.90	94	.280	.337	-18	-38	97	93	.969	199	122	.5	-3.8	4.4	2.1	-.9
BRO	82	8	12	1363¹	1556	10.3	46	361	471	12.9	3.70	105	.293	.342	12	28	103	103	.964	232	142	-1.5	2.8	-7.4	1.7	5.4
CIN	83	7	9	1363	1500	9.9	37	305	408	12.0	3.46	103	.286	.328	48	16	95	100	.969	193	139	.9	1.6	-2.3	2.3	-9.1
CHI	73	7	7	1363	1605	10.6	67	409	441	13.6	4.39	87	.302	.357	-92	-88	101	99	.974	166	129	2.5	-8.7	-3.0	2.2	-5.6
PHI	82	5	8	1348²	1665	11.1	79	371	333	13.8	4.48	94	.308	.356	-104	-38	112	99	.955	295	127	-5.2	-3.8	-8.9	1.7	-9.9
TOT	623	67	92	10982²		10.0				12.6	3.78		.289	.338					.967	1663	1073					

Runs
Hornsby-StL 131
Frisch-NY 121
Bancroft-NY 121
Powell-Bos 114
Burns-NY 111

Hits
Hornsby-StL 235
Frisch-NY 211
C.Bigbee-Pit 204
Johnston-Bro 203

Doubles
Hornsby-StL 44
Kelly-NY 42
Johnston-Bro 41
Grimes-Chi 38
McHenry-StL 37

Triples
Powell-Bos 18
Hornsby-StL 18
Grimm-Pit 17
Frisch-NY 17
C.Bigbee-Pit 17

Home Runs
Kelly-NY 23
Hornsby-StL 21
Williams-Phi 18
McHenry-StL 17
Fournier-StL 16

Total Bases
Hornsby-StL 378
Kelly-NY 310
McHenry-StL 305
Meusel-Phi-NY 302
Frisch-NY 300

Runs Batted In
Hornsby-StL 126
Kelly-NY 122
Youngs-NY 102
McHenry-StL 102
Frisch-NY 100

Runs Produced
Hornsby-StL 236
Frisch-NY 213
Kelly-NY 194
Youngs-NY 189
Bancroft-NY 182

Bases On Balls
Burns-NY 80
Youngs-NY 71
Grimes-Chi 70
Carey-Pit 70
Bancroft-NY 66

Batting Average
Hornsby-StL ...... .397
McHenry-StL ...... .350
Fournier-StL ..... .343
Meusel-Phi-NY .... .343
Frisch-NY .... .341

On Base Percentage
Hornsby-StL ...... .458
Youngs-NY .... .411
Fournier-StL ..... .409
Grimes-Chi .... .406
Carey-Pit .... .395

Slugging Average
Hornsby-StL ...... .639
McHenry-StL ...... .531
Kelly-NY .... .528
Meusel-Phi-NY .... .515
Fournier-StL ..... .505

Production
Hornsby-StL 1.097
McHenry-StL ...... .924
Fournier-StL ..... .914
Meusel-Phi-NY .... .895
Kelly-NY .... .884

Adjusted Production
Hornsby-StL 191
McHenry-StL 145
Fournier-StL 144
Kelly-NY 131
Youngs-NY 129

Batter Runs
Hornsby-StL 74.4
Fournier-StL 34.5
McHenry-StL 33.5
Meusel-Phi-NY 27.6
Frisch-NY 24.8

Adjusted Batter Runs
Hornsby-StL 76.1
Fournier-StL 36.1
McHenry-StL 35.0
Cruise-Bos 27.1
Roush-Cin 25.6

Clutch Hitting Index
Youngs-NY 166
Lavan-StL 152
Barnhart-Pit 133
Myers-Bro 130
Kelly-NY 125

Runs Created
Hornsby-StL 169
Frisch-NY 118
Fournier-StL 114
McHenry-StL 111
Meusel-Phi-NY 110

Total Average
Hornsby-StL 1.203
Frisch-NY .... .902
Fournier-StL ..... .882
Carey-Pit .... .868
Youngs-NY .... .860

Stolen Bases
Frisch-NY 49
Carey-Pit 37
Johnston-Bro 28
Bohne-Cin 26
Maranville-Pit ... 25

Stolen Base Average
Frisch-NY 79.0
Carey-Pit 75.5
Maisel-Chi 70.8
Maranville-Pit ... 67.6
Johnston-Bro 63.6

Stolen Base Runs
Frisch-NY 6.9
Carey-Pit 3.9
Stock-StL 1.5
Cutshaw-Pit 1.2

Fielding Runs
Lavan-StL 18.5
Bancroft-NY 17.4
C.Bigbee-Pit 16.6
Ford-Bos 16.0
Deal-Chi 14.1

Total Player Rating
Hornsby-StL 6.7
Bancroft-NY 4.8
Frisch-NY 3.6
McHenry-StL 2.5
Kelly-NY 2.5

Wins
Grimes-Bro 22
Cooper-Pit 22
Oeschger-Bos 20
Nehf-NY 20
Rixey-Cin 19

Win Percentage
Doak-StL .... .714
Nehf-NY .... .667
Grimes-Bro .... .629
Barnes-NY .... .625
Toney-NY .... .621

Games
Scott-StL 47
Oeschger-Bos 46
McQuillan-Bos 45
Watson-Bos 44
Fillingim-Bos 44

Complete Games
Grimes-Bro 30
Cooper-Pit 29
Luque-Cin 25

Shutouts
Oeschger-Bos 3
J.Morrison-Pit ... 3
Mitchell-Bro 3
Luque-Cin 3
Haines-StL 3
Fillingim-Bos 3
Douglas-NY 3
Alexander-Chi 3

Saves
North-StL 7
Barnes-NY 6
McQuillan-Bos 5

Innings Pitched
Cooper-Pit 327.0
Luque-Cin 304.0
Grimes-Bro 302.1
Rixey-Cin 301.0
Oeschger-Bos 299.0

Fewest Hits/Game
Glazner-Pit 8.23
Adams-Pit 8.72
Oeschger-Bos 9.12
Pertica-StL 9.16
Nehf-NY 9.18

Fewest BB/Game
Adams-Pit 1.01
Alexander-Chi 1.18
Barnes-NY 1.53
Hubbell-Phi 1.55
Doak-StL 1.60

Strikeouts
Grimes-Bro 136
Cooper-Pit 134
Luque-Cin 102
McQuillan-Bos 94

Strikeouts/Game
Grimes-Bro 4.05
Cooper-Pit 3.69
Doak-StL 3.58
Martin-Chi 3.56
Glazner-Pit 3.38

Ratio
Adams-Pit 9.73
Glazner-Pit 10.92
Nehf-NY 11.15
Luque-Cin 11.34
Alexander-Chi 11.43

Earned Run Average
Doak-StL 2.59
Adams-Pit 2.64
Glazner-Pit 2.77
Rixey-Cin 2.78
Grimes-Bro 2.83

Adjusted ERA
Adams-Pit 145
Doak-StL 142
Glazner-Pit 138
Grimes-Bro 137
Mitchell-Bro 134

Opponents' Batting Avg.
Glazner-Pit ...... .250
Adams-Pit .... .251
Pertica-StL ...... .267
Watson-Bos .... .270
Nehf-NY .... .271

Opponents' On Base Pct.
Adams-Pit .... .272
Glazner-Pit ...... .306
Nehf-NY .... .311
Luque-Cin .... .312
Doak-StL .... .313

Starter Runs
Rixey-Cin 33.4
Grimes-Bro 32.0
Doak-StL 27.6
Glazner-Pit 26.3
Adams-Pit 20.2

Adjusted Starter Runs
Grimes-Bro 35.5
Glazner-Pit 27.6
Rixey-Cin 26.6
Doak-StL 24.9
Cooper-Pit 21.2

Clutch Pitching Index
Barnes-NY 124
Mitchell-Bro 118
Doak-StL 116
Rixey-Cin 113
Grimes-Bro 112

Relief Runs
North-StL 2.3
Sallee-NY 1.5

Adjusted Relief Runs
North-StL 1.1
Sallee-NY 2

Relief Ranking
North-StL 1.1
Sallee-NY 2

Total Pitcher Index
Grimes-Bro 4.4
Mitchell-Bro 3.0
Rixey-Cin 2.5
Adams-Pit 2.4
Doak-StL 2.4

Total Baseball Ranking
Hornsby-StL 6.7
Bancroft-NY 4.8
Grimes-Bro 4.4
Frisch-NY 3.6
Mitchell-Bro 3.0

TEAM	G	W	L	PCT	GB	R	OR	AB	H	2B	3B	HR	BB	SO	AVG	OBP	SLG	PRO	PRO+	BR	/A	PF	CHI	RC	SB	CS	SBA	SBR
NY	153	98	55	.641		**948**	708	5249	1576	285	87	**134**	588	569	.300	.375	**.464**	**.839**	116	**142**	124	102	102	**929**	89	64	53	-12
CLE	154	94	60	.610	4.5	925	712	5383	1656	**355**	90	42	**623**	376	.308	.383	.430	.813	111	112	99	102	100	916	50	42	44	-13
STL	154	81	73	.526	17.5	835	845	5442	1655	246	**106**	67	413	407	.304	.357	.425	.782	98	28	-18	106	102	827	92	71	**62**	-15
WAS	154	80	73	.523	18	704	738	5294	1468	240	96	42	462	472	.277	.342	.383	.725	94	-79	-41	95	101	712	**111**	66	52	-10
BOS	154	75	79	.487	23.5	668	**696**	5206	1440	248	69	17	428	**344**	.277	.335	.361	.696	84	-132	-111	97	**107**	642	83	65	56	-13
DET	154	71	82	.464	27	883	852	5461	**1724**	268	100	58	582	376	**.316**	**.385**	.433	.818	115	120	**128**	99	94	921	95	89	61	-9
CHI	154	62	92	.403	36.5	683	858	5329	1509	242	82	35	445	474	.283	.343	.379	.722	90	-85	-74	99	99	696	97	93	60	**-7**
PHI	155	53	100	.346	45	657	894	5465	1497	256	64	82	424	565	.274	.331	.389	.720	87	-101	-104	101	96	710	68	55	48	-11
TOT	616					6303		42829	12525	2140	694	477	3965	3583	.292	.356	.408	.765							685	545	56	-121

TEAM	CG	SH	SV	IP	H	H/G	HR	BB	SO	RAT	ERA	ERA+	OAV	OOB	PR	/A	PF	CPI	FA	E	DP	FW	PW	BW	SBW	DIF
NY	**92**	8	15	1364	**1461**	9.6	51	470	481	13.1	**3.82**	111	**.276**	.341	69	62	99	99	.965	222	138	-.3	**5.8**	11.6	.3	4.1
CLE	81	11	14	1377	1534	10.0	**43**	431	475	13.0	3.90	109	.287	.344	58	55	100	100	.967	204	124	.8	5.1	9.3	.2	1.6
STL	77	9	9	1379	1543	10.1	71	557	478	14.0	4.61	97	.288	.360	-50	-21	105	94	.964	224	127	-.3	-2.0	-1.7	.0	7.9
WAS	80	10	10	1383²	1568	10.2	51	442	452	13.3	3.97	104	.291	.348	47	21	96	102	.963	235	153	-.9	2.0	-3.8	.5	5.8
BOS	88	9	5	1364¹	1521	10.0	53	452	446	13.3	3.98	106	.290	.351	45	37	99	104	**.975**	**157**	151	**3.5**	3.5	-10.4	.2	1.2
DET	73	4	**16**	1386¹	1634	10.6	71	495	452	14.2	4.40	97	.297	.361	-18	-20	100	102	.963	232	107	-.8	-1.9	**12.0**	.6	-15.4
CHI	84	7	9	1365¹	1603	10.6	52	549	392	14.4	4.94	86	.302	.371	-99	-107	99	94	.969	200	**155**	1.0	-10.0	-6.9	.4	.1
PHI	75	2	7	1400¹	1645	10.6	85	548	431	14.3	4.61	97	.300	.367	-51	-24	104	102	.958	274	144	-3.1	-2.2	-9.7	.4	-8.9
TOT	650	60	85	11020		10.2				13.7	4.28		.292	.356					.965	1748	1099					

Runs
Ruth-NY 177
Tobin-StL 132
Peckinpaugh-NY 128
Sisler-StL 125
Cobb-Det 124

Hits
Heilmann-Det 237
Tobin-StL 236
Sisler-StL 216
Jacobson-StL 211
Veach-Det 207

Doubles
Speaker-Cle 52
Ruth-NY 44
Veach-Det 43
Heilmann-Det 43
Meusel-NY 40

Triples
Tobin-StL 18
Sisler-StL 18
Shanks-Was 18

Home Runs
Ruth-NY 59
Williams-StL 24
Meusel-NY 24
C.Walker-Phi 23
Heilmann-Det 19

Total Bases
Ruth-NY 457
Heilmann-Det 365
Meusel-NY 334
Tobin-StL 327
Sisler-StL 326

Runs Batted In
Ruth-NY 171
Heilmann-Det 139
Meusel-NY 135
Veach-Det 128
Gardner-Cle 120

Runs Produced
Ruth-NY 289
Heilmann-Det 234
Veach-Det 222
Gardner-Cle 218
Sisler-StL 217

Bases On Balls
Ruth-NY 144
Blue-Det 103
Peckinpaugh-NY 84
J.Sewell-Cle 80
Schang-NY 78

Batting Average
Heilmann-Det .394
Cobb-Det .389
Ruth-NY .378
Sisler-StL .371
Speaker-Cle .362

On Base Percentage
Ruth-NY .512
Cobb-Det .452
Heilmann-Det .444
Speaker-Cle .439
Williams-StL .429

Slugging Average
Ruth-NY .846
Heilmann-Det .606
Cobb-Det .596
Williams-StL .561
Sisler-StL .560

Production
Ruth-NY 1.358
Heilmann-Det 1.051
Cobb-Det 1.048
Williams-StL .990
Speaker-Cle .977

Adjusted Production
Ruth-NY 236
Heilmann-Det 167
Cobb-Det 167
Speaker-Cle 146
Williams-StL 142

Batter Runs
Ruth-NY 119.2
Heilmann-Det 58.4
Cobb-Det 50.3
Williams-StL 42.5
Speaker-Cle 38.2

Adjusted Batter Runs
Ruth-NY 117.3
Heilmann-Det 59.3
Cobb-Det 51.0
Williams-StL 37.5
Speaker-Cle 37.1

Clutch Hitting Index
Gardner-Cle 164
Pratt-Bos 145
Severeid-StL 132
Pipp-NY 128
J.Sewell-Cle 127

Runs Created
Ruth-NY 238
Heilmann-Det 159
Cobb-Det 134
Sisler-StL 133
Williams-StL 130

Total Average
Ruth-NY 1.745
Cobb-Det 1.132
Heilmann-Det 1.121
Speaker-Cle 1.040
Williams-StL 1.037

Stolen Bases
Sisler-StL 35
Harris-Was 29
Rice-Was 25
Johnson-Chi 22
Cobb-Det 22

Stolen Base Average
Judge-Was 77.8
Harris-Was 76.3
Sisler-StL 76.1
Meusel-NY 73.9
Rice-Was 67.6

Stolen Base Runs
Sisler-StL 3.9
Harris-Was 3.3
Judge-Was 2.7
Welch-Phi 1.8

Fielding Runs
Scott-Bos 38.1
Collins-Chi 27.1
Dykes-Phi 25.0
Ward-NY 18.8
Johnson-Chi 18.0

Total Player Rating
Ruth-NY 9.6
Cobb-Det 4.8
Collins-Chi 4.0
Sisler-StL 4.0
Speaker-Cle 3.2

Wins
Shocker-StL 27
Mays-NY 27
Faber-Chi 25
Jones-Bos 23
Coveleski-Cle 23

Win Percentage
Mays-NY .750
Shocker-StL .692
Bush-Bos .640
Coveleski-Cle .639
Faber-Chi .625

Games
Mays-NY 49
Shocker-StL 47
Bayne-StL 47
Rommel-Phi 46

Complete Games
Faber-Chi 32
Shocker-StL 30
Mays-NY 30
Coveleski-Cle 28

Shutouts
Jones-Bos 5
Shocker-StL 4
Mogridge-Was 4
Faber-Chi 4

Saves
Middleton-Det 7
Mays-NY 7

Innings Pitched
Mays-NY 336.2
Faber-Chi 330.2
Shocker-StL 326.2
Coveleski-Cle 315.0
Kerr-Chi 308.2

Fewest Hits/Game
Faber-Chi 7.97
Bush-Bos 8.63
Mays-NY 8.88
Shawkey-NY 9.00
Johnson-Was 9.03

Fewest BB/Game
Hasty-Phi 2.01
Mays-NY 2.03
Mogridge-Was 2.06
Bagby-Cle 2.07
Zachary-Was 2.12

Strikeouts
Johnson-Was 143
Shocker-StL 132
Shawkey-NY 126
Faber-Chi 124
Leonard-Det 120

Strikeouts/Game
Johnson-Was 4.88
Shawkey-NY 4.63
Bayne-StL 4.50
Leonard-Det 4.41
Mails-Cle 4.03

Ratio
Faber-Chi 10.53
Mays-NY 11.15
Mogridge-Was 11.69
Shocker-StL 12.04
Jones-Bos 12.11

Earned Run Average
Faber-Chi 2.48
Mogridge-Was 3.00
Mays-NY 3.05
Hoyt-NY 3.09
Jones-Bos 3.22

Adjusted ERA
Faber-Chi 171
Mays-NY 139
Mogridge-Was 137
Hoyt-NY 137
Jones-Bos 131

Opponents' Batting Avg.
Faber-Chi .242
Mays-NY .257
Bush-Bos .260
Shawkey-NY .263
Johnson-Was .263

Opponents' On Base Pct.
Faber-Chi .297
Mays-NY .303
Mogridge-Was .313
Shocker-StL .319
Johnson-Was .326

Starter Runs
Faber-Chi 66.3
Mays-NY 46.2
Mogridge-Was 41.0
Hoyt-NY 37.3
Jones-Bos 35.1

Adjusted Starter Runs
Faber-Chi 64.6
Mays-NY 44.4
Hoyt-NY 35.8
Mogridge-Was 35.7
Shocker-StL 33.6

Clutch Pitching Index
Russell-Bos 122
Zachary-Was 118
Keefe-Phi 114
Uhle-Cle 108
Sothoron-StL-Bos-Cle 108

Relief Runs

Adjusted Relief Runs

Relief Ranking

Total Pitcher Index
Faber-Chi 6.2
Mays-NY 5.9
Shocker-StL 4.0
Jones-Bos 3.3
Hoyt-NY 3.2

Total Baseball Ranking
Ruth-NY 9.2
Faber-Chi 6.2
Mays-NY 5.9
Cobb-Det 4.8
Collins-Chi 4.0

TEAM	G	W	L	PCT	GB	R	OR	AB	H	2B	3B	HR	BB	SO	AVG	OBP	SLG	PRO	PRO+	BR	/A	PF	CHI	RC	SB	CS	SBA	SBR
NY	156	93	61	.604		852	658	5454	1661	253	90	80	448	421	.305	.363	.428	.791	109	77	70	101	99	848	116	83	59	-10
CIN	156	86	68	.558	7	766	677	5282	1561	226	99	45	436	381	.296	.353	.401	.754	101	8	22	98	99	737	130	136	70	0
STL	154	85	69	.552	8	863	819	5425	1634	280	88	107	447	425	.301	.357	.444	.801	117	91	127	95	99	860	73	63	47	-8
PIT	155	85	69	.552	8	865	736	5521	1698	239	110	52	423	326	.308	.360	.419	.779	105	56	46	101	102	848	145	59	56	-15
CHI	156	80	74	.519	13	771	808	5335	1564	248	71	42	525	447	.293	.359	.390	.749	97	7	-7	102	98	752	97	108	66	-6
BRO	155	76	78	.494	17	743	754	5413	1569	235	76	56	339	318	.290	.335	.392	.727	93	-57	-50	99	105	709	79	60	48	-10
PHI	154	57	96	.373	35.5	738	920	5459	1537	268	55	116	450	611	.282	.341	.415	.756	92	-2	-76	110	94	771	48	60	56	-15
BOS	154	53	100	.346	39.5	596	822	5161	1355	162	73	32	387	451	.263	.317	.341	.658	78	-178	-145	96	106	566	67	65	54	-12
TOT	620					6194		43050	12579	1911	662	530	3455	3380	.292	.348	.404	.753							755	634	54	-153

TEAM	CG	SH	SV	IP	H	H/G	HR	BB	SO	RAT	ERA	ERA+	OAV	OOB	PR	/A	PF	CPI	FA	E	DP	FW	PW	BW	SBW	DIF
NY	76	7	15	1396[1]	1454	9.4	71	393	388	12.0	3.45	116	.271	.323	99	83	98	99	.970	194	145	1.1	7.8	6.6	.9	-.4
CIN	88	8	3	1385[2]	1481	9.6	49	326	357	11.9	3.53	113	.277	.322	86	69	97	95	.968	205	147	.4	6.5	2.1	1.8	-1.8
STL	60	8	12	1362[2]	1609	10.6	61	447	465	13.9	4.44	87	.299	.358	-51	-87	94	98	.961	239	122	-2.0	-8.2	12.0	1.1	5.2
PIT	88	15	7	1387[1]	1613	10.5	52	358	490	13.0	3.98	102	.296	.342	17	13	99	99	.970	187	126	1.5	1.2	4.3	.4	.5
CHI	74	8	12	1397[2]	1579	10.2	77	475	402	13.6	4.34	97	.292	.355	-37	-23	102	99	.968	204	154	.5	-2.2	-.7	1.2	4.1
BRO	82	12	8	1385[2]	1568	10.2	74	490	499	13.6	4.05	100	.291	.354	7	1	99	105	.967	208	139	.1	.0	-4.7	.9	2.6
PHI	73	6	5	1372	1692	11.1	89	460	394	14.4	4.64	101	.307	.364	-82	6	114	102	.965	225	152	-1.1	.6	-7.2	.4	-12.2
BOS	63	7	6	1348	1565	10.4	57	489	360	13.9	4.37	91	.298	.361	-41	-57	98	100	.965	215	121	-.4	-5.4	-13.7	.7	-4.7
TOT	604	71	68	11035[1]		10.2				13.3	4.10		.292	.348					.967	1677	1106					

Runs
Hornsby-StL	141
Carey-Pit	140
Smith-StL	117
Bancroft-NY	117
Maranville-Pit	115

Hits
Hornsby-StL	250
Bigbee-Pit	215
Bancroft-NY	209
Carey-Pit	207
Daubert-Cin	205

Doubles
Hornsby-StL	46
Grimes-Chi	45
Duncan-Cin	44
Bancroft-NY	41
Hollocher-Chi	37

Triples
Daubert-Cin	22
Meusel-NY	17
Maranville-Pit	15
Bigbee-Pit	15

Home Runs
Hornsby-StL	42
Williams-Phi	26
Lee-Phi	17
Kelly-NY	17

Total Bases
Hornsby-StL	450
Meusel-NY	314
Wheat-Bro	302
Williams-Phi	300
Daubert-Cin	300

Runs Batted In
Hornsby-StL	152
Meusel-NY	132
Wheat-Bro	112
Kelly-NY	107

Runs Produced
Hornsby-StL	251
Meusel-NY	216
Bigbee-Pit	207
Carey-Pit	200
Wheat-Bro	188

Bases On Balls
Hornsby-StL	80
O'Farrell-Chi	79
Bancroft-NY	79
Burns-Cin	78
Grimes-Chi	75

Batting Average
Hornsby-StL	.401
Grimes-Chi	.354
Miller-Chi	.352
Bigbee-Pit	.350
Tierney-Pit	.345

On Base Percentage
Hornsby-StL	.459
Grimes-Chi	.442
O'Farrell-Chi	.439
Carey-Pit	.408
Bigbee-Pit	.405

Slugging Average
Hornsby-StL	.722
Grimes-Chi	.572
Tierney-Pit	.515
Williams-Phi	.514
Miller-Chi	.511

Production
Hornsby-StL	1.181
Grimes-Chi	1.014
Williams-Phi	.905
Miller-Chi	.899
Walker-Phi	.899

Adjusted Production
Hornsby-StL	210
Grimes-Chi	157
Daubert-Cin	130
Wheat-Bro	129
Miller-Chi	128

Batter Runs
Hornsby-StL	90.0
Grimes-Chi	47.1
Williams-Phi	27.5
Walker-Phi	26.3
Daubert-Cin	24.7

Adjusted Batter Runs
Hornsby-StL	94.2
Grimes-Chi	45.6
Daubert-Cin	26.4
Wheat-Bro	25.0
Russell-Pit	23.7

Clutch Hitting Index
Terry-Chi	146
Meusel-NY	135
Traynor-Pit	133
Pinelli-Cin	125
Tierney-Pit	124

Runs Created
Hornsby-StL	200
Carey-Pit	131
Grimes-Chi	130
Walker-Phi	118
Bigbee-Pit	116

Total Average
Hornsby-StL	1.353
Grimes-Chi	1.107
Carey-Pit	.995
O'Farrell-Chi	.951
Walker-Phi	.918

Stolen Bases
Carey-Pit	51
Frisch-NY	31
Burns-Cin	30
Maranville-Pit	24
Bigbee-Pit	24

Stolen Base Average
Carey-Pit	96.2
Traynor-Pit	85.0
Smith-StL	72.0
Johnston-Bro	66.7
Youngs-NY	65.4

Stolen Base Runs
Carey-Pit	14.1
Traynor-Pit	3.3
Kelly-NY	1.8
T.Griffith-Bro	1.5
Smith-StL	1.2

Fielding Runs
Parkinson-Phi	31.0
Bancroft-NY	21.9
Pinelli-Cin	21.1
Carey-Pit	14.7
Bigbee-Pit	14.7

Total Player Rating
Hornsby-StL	7.6
Carey-Pit	4.3
Bancroft-NY	3.9
Grimes-Chi	3.7
O'Farrell-Chi	3.2

Wins
Rixey-Cin	25
Cooper-Pit	23
Ruether-Bro	21
Pfeffer-StL	19
Nehf-NY	19

Win Percentage
Donohue-Cin	.667
Rixey-Cin	.658
Couch-Cin	.640
Ruether-Bro	.636
Cooper-Pit	.622

Games
North-Pit	53
Sherdel-StL	47
Ryan-NY	46
Oeschger-Bos	46
Morrison-Pit	45

Complete Games
Cooper-Pit	27
Ruether-Bro	26
Rixey-Cin	26

Shutouts
Vance-Bro	5
Morrison-Pit	5
Cooper-Pit	4
Adams-Pit	4
Sherdel-StL	3

Saves
Jonnard-NY	5
North-StL	4

Innings Pitched
Rixey-Cin	313.1
Cooper-Pit	294.2
Morrison-Pit	286.1
Nehf-NY	268.1
Ruether-Bro	267.1

Fewest Hits/Game
Douglas-NY	8.79
Osborne-Chi	8.95
Ryan-NY	9.11
Luque-Cin	9.17
Vance-Bro	9.49

Fewest BB/Game
Adams-Pit	.79
Alexander-Chi	1.25
Rixey-Cin	1.29
Donohue-Cin	1.60
J.Barnes-NY	1.61

Strikeouts
Vance-Bro	134
Cooper-Pit	129
Ring-Phi	116
Morrison-Pit	104
Grimes-Bro	99

Strikeouts/Game
Vance-Bro	4.91
Ring-Phi	4.19
Osborne-Chi	3.96
Cooper-Pit	3.94
Doak-StL	3.64

Ratio
Douglas-NY	11.02
Adams-Pit	11.03
Rixey-Cin	11.09
Donohue-Cin	11.34
Luque-Cin	11.69

Earned Run Average
Douglas-NY	2.63
Ryan-NY	3.01
Donohue-Cin	3.12
Cooper-Pit	3.18
Nehf-NY	3.29

Adjusted ERA
Douglas-NY	152
Weinert-Phi	137
Ryan-NY	133
Cooper-Pit	128
Donohue-Cin	128

Opponents' Batting Avg.
Douglas-NY	.257
Luque-Cin	.268
Ryan-NY	.269
Osborne-Chi	.271
Rixey-Cin	.275

Opponents' On Base Pct.
Douglas-NY	.302
Rixey-Cin	.303
Adams-Pit	.307
J.Barnes-NY	.311
Donohue-Cin	.312

Starter Runs
Cooper-Pit	30.2
Donohue-Cin	26.2
Douglas-NY	25.8
Nehf-NY	24.2
Ryan-NY	23.3

Adjusted Starter Runs
Cooper-Pit	29.4
Douglas-NY	24.1
Weinert-Phi	23.4
Donohue-Cin	23.2
Nehf-NY	21.3

Clutch Pitching Index
Weinert-Phi	129
Ryan-NY	116
Cooper-Pit	113
Morrison-Pit	111
McQuillan-Bos-NY	110

Relief Runs
McNamara-Bos	13.2
Causey-NY	7.2
Braxton-Bos	5.4
Mamaux-Bro	3.9
V.Barnes-NY	3.5

Adjusted Relief Runs
McNamara-Bos	12.4
Causey-NY	6.4
Braxton-Bos	4.6
Mamaux-Bro	3.6
V.Barnes-NY	3.0

Relief Ranking
McNamara-Bos	11.0
Causey-NY	5.9
Mamaux-Bro	2.1
Braxton-Bos	1.9
Jonnard-NY	1.3

Total Pitcher Index
Cooper-Pit	3.6
Meadows-Phi	2.5
Douglas-NY	2.5
Nehf-NY	2.4
Aldridge-Chi	2.3

Total Baseball Ranking
Hornsby-StL	7.6
Carey-Pit	4.3
Bancroft-NY	3.9
Grimes-Chi	3.7
Cooper-Pit	3.6

TEAM	G	W	L	PCT	GB	R	OR	AB	H	2B	3B	HR	BB	SO	AVG	OBP	SLG	PRO	PRO+	BR	/A	PF	CHI	RC	SB	CS	SBA	SBR
NY	154	94	60	.610		758	**618**	5245	1504	220	75	95	497	532	.287	.353	.412	.765	102	36	19	102	99	774	62	59	55	-14
STL	154	93	61	.604	1	**867**	643	5416	**1693**	291	**94**	98	473	381	.313	**.372**	**.455**	**.827**	116	**157**	**130**	104	96	**924**	**132**	73	57	-11
DET	155	79	75	.513	15	828	791	5360	1641	250	87	54	530	378	.306	**.372**	.415	.787	114	94	118	97	98	848	78	61	52	-12
CLE	155	78	76	.506	16	768	817	5293	1544	**320**	73	32	**554**	331	.292	.364	.398	.762	104	43	37	101	97	792	89	58	53	-13
CHI	155	77	77	.500	17	691	691	5267	1463	243	62	45	482	463	.278	.343	.373	.716	92	-51	-47	100	101	690	106	84	**61**	-10
WAS	154	69	85	.448	25	650	706	5201	1395	229	76	45	458	442	.268	.334	.367	.701	92	-83	-47	95	103	659	94	54	47	-11
PHI	155	65	89	.422	29	705	830	5211	1409	229	63	**111**	437	591	.270	.331	.402	.733	93	-35	-53	103	104	697	60	63	57	-14
BOS	154	61	93	.396	33	598	769	5288	1392	250	55	45	366	455	.263	.316	.357	.673	81	-148	-142	99	**105**	600	60	63	53	-12
TOT	618					5865		42281	12041	2032	585	525	3797	3573	.285	.348	.398	.746							681	515	57	-104

TEAM	CG	SH	SV	IP	H	H/G	HR	BB	SO	RAT	ERA	ERA+	OAV	OOB	PR	/A	PF	CPI	FA	E	DP	FW	PW	BW	SBW	DIF
NY	**100**	7	14	1393²	1402	9.1	73	423	458	11.9	3.39	118	.267	.324	99	90	99	101	**.975**	157	124	2.0	8.7	1.8	-.0	4.5
STL	79	8	**22**	1392	1412	9.1	71	**419**	**534**	12.1	3.38	122	.267	.327	100	114	103	103	.968	201	158	-.5	11.1	12.6	.2	-7.4
DET	67	7	15	1391	1554	10.1	62	473	461	13.7	4.27	91	.287	.354	-36	-64	96	97	.970	191	133	.2	-6.2	11.5	.1	-3.5
CLE	76	**14**	7	1383²	1605	10.4	58	464	489	13.7	4.59	87	.296	.356	-85	-92	99	93	.968	202	147	-.5	-8.9	3.6	.0	6.8
CHI	86	13	8	1403²	1472	9.4	57	529	484	13.0	3.94	103	.278	.346	14	15	101	98	**.975**	155	143	**2.2**	1.5	-4.6	**.3**	.6
WAS	84	13	10	1362¹	1485	9.8	49	500	422	13.4	3.81	101	.286	.354	33	5	96	**107**	.969	196	**168**	-.2	.5	-4.6	.2	-3.9
PHI	73	4	6	1362¹	1573	10.4	107	469	373	13.7	4.59	92	.296	.357	-84	-54	105	99	.966	215	118	-1.2	-5.2	-5.1	-.0	-.3
BOS	71	10	6	1373¹	1508	9.9	**48**	503	359	13.5	4.30	95	.286	.353	-40	-31	102	94	.965	224	145	-1.8	-3.0	-13.8	.1	2.5
TOT	636	76	88	11062		9.8				13.1	4.03		.285	.348					.969	1541	1136					

Runs
Sisler-StL 134
Blue-Det 131
Williams-StL 128
Tobin-StL 122

Hits
Sisler-StL 246
Cobb-Det 211
Tobin-StL 207
Veach-Det 202

Doubles
Speaker-Cle 48
Pratt-Bos 44
Sisler-StL 42
Cobb-Det 42

Triples
Sisler-StL 18
Jacobson-StL 16
Cobb-Det 16
Judge-Was 15
Mostil-Chi 14

Home Runs
Williams-StL 39
Walker-Phi 37
Ruth-NY 35
Miller-Phi 21
Heilmann-Det 21

Total Bases
Williams-StL 367
Sisler-StL 348
Walker-Phi 310
Cobb-Det 297
Tobin-StL 296

Runs Batted In
Williams-StL 155
Veach-Det 126
McManus-StL 109
Sisler-StL 105
Jacobson-StL 102

Runs Produced
Williams-StL 244
Sisler-StL 231
Veach-Det 213
Cobb-Det 194
McManus-StL 186

Bases On Balls
Witt-NY 89
Ruth-NY 84
Blue-Det 82
Speaker-Cle 77
Williams-StL 74

Batting Average
Sisler-StL 420
Cobb-Det 401
Speaker-Cle 378
Heilmann-Det 356
Miller-Phi 335

On Base Percentage
Speaker-Cle 474
Sisler-StL 467
Cobb-Det 462
Ruth-NY 434
Heilmann-Det 432

Slugging Average
Ruth-NY 672
Williams-StL 627
Speaker-Cle 606
Heilmann-Det 598
Sisler-StL 594

Production
Ruth-NY 1.106
Speaker-Cle 1.080
Sisler-StL 1.061
Williams-StL 1.040
Heilmann-Det 1.030

Adjusted Production
Ruth-NY 181
Speaker-Cle 178
Cobb-Det 172
Heilmann-Det 172
Sisler-StL 169

Batter Runs
Sisler-StL 64.4
Williams-StL 56.1
Speaker-Cle 52.8
Cobb-Det 52.4
Ruth-NY 50.5

Adjusted Batter Runs
Sisler-StL 61.6
Cobb-Det 54.8
Williams-StL 53.2
Speaker-Cle 52.3
Ruth-NY 49.2

Clutch Hitting Index
J.Sewell-Cle 142
O'Neill-Cle 138
Veach-Det 137
Jacobson-StL 136
Wood-Cle 136

Runs Created
Sisler-StL 162
Williams-StL 150
Cobb-Det 133
Speaker-Cle 127
Ruth-NY 120

Total Average
Speaker-Cle 1.272
Ruth-NY 1.246
Sisler-StL 1.203
Williams-StL 1.137
Heilmann-Det 1.135

Stolen Bases
Sisler-StL 51
Williams-StL 37
Harris-Was 25
Johnson-Chi 21

Stolen Base Average
Jacobson-StL 76.0
Sisler-StL 72.9
Harris-Was 69.4
Rice-Was 69.0
Rigney-Det 68.0

Stolen Base Runs
Sisler-StL 3.9
Veach-Det 2.1
Jacobson-StL 2.1
Evans-Cle 2.1
Shanks-Was 1.8

Fielding Runs
Harris-Was 26.4
Peckinpaugh-Was . . 22.2
Scott-NY 19.1
Schalk-Chi 18.8
J.Sewell-Cle 14.7

Total Player Rating
Sisler-StL 6.3
Speaker-Cle 5.0
Williams-StL 4.6
Cobb-Det 4.1
Ruth-NY 3.7

Wins
Rommel-Phi 27
Bush-NY 26
Shocker-StL 24
Uhle-Cle 22
Faber-Chi 21

Win Percentage
Bush-NY 788
Rommel-Phi 675
Shawkey-NY 625
Pillette-Det 613
Hoyt-NY 613

Games
Rommel-Phi 51
Uhle-Cle 50
Shocker-StL 48
Harriss-Phi 47

Complete Games
Faber-Chi 31
Shocker-StL 29
Uhle-Cle 23
Johnson-Was 23

Shutouts
Uhle-Cle 5

Saves
Jones-NY 8
Pruett-StL 7
Wright-StL 5

Innings Pitched
Faber-Chi 352.0
Shocker-StL 348.0
Shawkey-NY 299.2
Rommel-Phi 294.0
Uhle-Cle 287.1

Fewest Hits/Game
Davis-StL 8.36
Bush-NY 8.46
Faber-Chi 8.54
Shawkey-NY 8.59
Wright-StL 8.65

Fewest BB/Game
Shocker-StL 1.47
Vangilder-StL 1.76
Mays-NY 1.88
Kolp-StL 1.91
Hasty-Phi 1.92

Strikeouts
Shocker-StL 149
Faber-Chi 148
Shawkey-NY 130
Ehmke-Det 108
Johnson-Was 105

Strikeouts/Game
Morton-Cle 4.53
Harriss-Phi 4.00
Shawkey-NY 3.90
Shocker-StL 3.85
Faber-Chi 3.78

Ratio
Faber-Chi 10.82
Shocker-StL 11.02
Rommel-Phi 11.08
Vangilder-StL 11.09
Quinn-Bos 11.43

Earned Run Average
Faber-Chi 2.81
Pillette-Det 2.85
Shawkey-NY 2.91
Wright-StL 2.92
Shocker-StL 2.97

Adjusted ERA
Faber-Chi 144
Wright-StL 141
Shocker-StL 139
Shawkey-NY 137
Pillette-Det 136

Opponents' Batting Avg.
Davis-StL 250
Bush-NY 252
Faber-Chi 252
Shawkey-NY 256
Pillette-Det 258

Opponents' On Base Pct.
Faber-Chi 299
Shocker-StL 304
Rommel-Phi 309
Vangilder-StL 310
Quinn-Bos 311

Starter Runs
Faber-Chi 47.7
Shocker-StL 40.9
Shawkey-NY 37.2
Pillette-Det 36.0
Johnson-Was 32.4

Adjusted Starter Runs
Faber-Chi 48.8
Shocker-StL 44.8
Shawkey-NY 36.0
Rommel-Phi 31.5
Pillette-Det 31.1

Clutch Pitching Index
Mogridge-Was 124
Wright-StL 118
Johnson-Was 114
Pillette-Det 110
Shawkey-NY 109

Relief Runs
Murray-NY 4

Adjusted Relief Runs
Murray-NY 2

Relief Ranking
Murray-NY 1

Total Pitcher Index
Faber-Chi 4.8
Shocker-StL 4.5
Rommel-Phi 3.3
Shawkey-NY 3.3
Vangilder-StL 3.2

Total Baseball Ranking
Sisler-StL 6.3
Speaker-Cle 5.0
Faber-Chi 4.8
Williams-StL 4.6
Shocker-StL 4.5

1923 National League

TEAM	G	W	L	PCT	GB	R	OR	AB	H	2B	3B	HR	BB	SO	AVG	OBP	SLG	PRO	PRO+	BR	/A	PF	CHI	RC	SB	CS	SBA	SBR
NY	153	95	58	.621		854	679	5452	1610	248	76	85	487	406	.295	.356	.415	.771	110	72	81	99	103	816	106	70	56	-12
CIN	154	91	63	.591	4.5	708	629	5278	1506	237	95	45	439	367	.285	.344	.392	.736	102	0	14	98	96	707	96	105	65	-7
PIT	154	87	67	.565	8.5	786	696	5405	1592	224	111	49	407	362	.295	.347	.404	.751	101	26	9	102	103	766	154	75	54	-9
CHI	154	83	71	.539	12.5	756	704	5259	1516	243	52	90	455	485	.288	.343	.406	.754	103	33	32	100	99	735	89	61	46	0
STL	154	79	74	.516	16	746	732	5526	1582	274	76	63	438	446	.286	.343	.398	.741	103	5	21	98	97	761	181	143	73	-8
BRO	155	76	78	.494	19.5	753	741	5476	1559	214	81	62	425	382	.285	.340	.387	.727	99	-19	2	97	102	730	71	50	52	-15
BOS	155	54	100	.351	41.5	636	798	5329	1455	213	58	32	429	404	.273	.331	.353	.684	89	-98	-67	96	99	625	57	80	61	-12
PHI	155	50	104	.325	45.5	748	1008	5491	1528	259	39	112	414	556	.278	.333	.401	.734	88	-14	-100	112	101	729	70	73	54	-10
TOT	617					5987		43216	12348	1912	588	538	3494	3408	.286	.343	.395	.737							824	657	56	-146

TEAM	CG	SH	SV	IP	H	H/G	HR	BB	SO	RAT	ERA	ERA+	OAV	OOB	PR	/A	PF	CPI	FA	E	DP	FW	PW	BW	SBW	DIF
NY	62	10	18	1378	1440	9.4	82	424	453	12.3	3.90	98	.271	.327	14	-13	96	93	.972	176	141	2.4	-1.3	7.8	.6	9.0
CIN	88	11	9	1391¹	1465	9.5	29	359	450	12.0	3.21	120	.272	.322	120	98	97	101	.969	202	144	.9	9.4	1.3	1.1	1.2
PIT	92	5	9	1376¹	1313	8.6	53	402	414	11.4	3.87	103	.246	.302	18	19	100	70	.971	179	157	2.3	1.8	.9	.9	4.1
CHI	80	8	11	1366²	1419	9.3	86	435	408	12.4	3.82	105	.269	.328	26	25	100	96	.967	208	144	.5	2.4	3.1	1.8	-1.8
STL	77	9	7	1398¹	1539	9.9	70	456	398	13.1	3.87	101	.283	.344	19	4	98	104	.963	232	141	-.9	.4	2.0	1.0	-.0
BRO	94	8	5	1396²	1522	9.8	54	477	549	13.1	3.74	103	.280	.343	38	19	97	103	.955	293	137	-4.4	1.8	.2	.3	1.1
BOS	54	13	7	1392²	1662	10.7	64	394	351	13.5	4.21	94	.301	.352	-33	-40	100	102	.964	230	157	-.7	-3.8	-6.4	.6	-12.6
PHI	68	3	8	1376¹	1801	11.8	100	549	384	15.6	5.34	86	.321	.386	-205	-114	115	102	.966	217	172	.0	-11.0	-9.6	.8	-7.3
TOT	615	67	74	11076¹		9.9				12.9	3.99		.286	.343					.966	1737	1193					

Runs		Hits		Doubles		Triples		Home Runs		Total Bases	
Youngs-NY	121	Frisch-NY	223	Roush-Cin	41	Traynor-Pit	19	Williams-Phi	41	Frisch-NY	311
Carey-Pit	120	Statz-Chi	209	Tierney-Pit-Phi	36	Carey-Pit	19	Fournier-Bro	22	Williams-Phi	308
Frisch-NY	116	Traynor-Pit	208	Grantham-Chi	36	Roush-Cin	18	Miller-Chi	20	Fournier-Bro	303
Johnston-Bro	111	Johnston-Bro	203	Bottomley-StL	34	Southworth-Bos	16	Meusel-NY	19	Traynor-Pit	301
Statz-Chi	110	Youngs-NY	200					Hornsby-StL	17	Statz-Chi	288

Runs Batted In		Runs Produced		Bases On Balls		Batting Average		On Base Percentage		Slugging Average	
Meusel-NY	125	Frisch-NY	215	Burns-Cin	101	Hornsby-StL	.384	Hornsby-StL	.459	Hornsby-StL	.627
Williams-Phi	114	Meusel-NY	208	Sand-Phi	82	Bottomley-StL	.371	Bottomley-StL	.425	Fournier-Bro	.588
Frisch-NY	111	Youngs-NY	205	Youngs-NY	73	Fournier-Bro	.351	Youngs-NY	.412	Williams-Phi	.576
Kelly-NY	103	Traynor-Pit	197	Carey-Pit	73	Roush-Cin	.351	Fournier-Bro	.411	Bottomley-StL	.535
Fournier-Bro	102	Carey-Pit	177	Grantham-Chi	71	Frisch-NY	.348	O'Farrell-Chi	.408	Roush-Cin	.531

Production		Adjusted Production		Batter Runs		Adjusted Batter Runs		Clutch Hitting Index		Runs Created	
Hornsby-StL	1.086	Hornsby-StL	188	Hornsby-StL	52.1	Hornsby-StL	53.3	Stock-StL	159	Fournier-Bro	125
Fournier-Bro	.999	Fournier-Bro	165	Fournier-Bro	43.7	Fournier-Bro	45.7	McInnis-Bos	145	Frisch-NY	123
Bottomley-StL	.960	Bottomley-StL	155	Bottomley-StL	39.2	Bottomley-StL	40.7	Meusel-NY	137	Hornsby-StL	120
Williams-Phi	.947	Roush-Cin	149	Roush-Cin	34.0	Roush-Cin	35.5	Kelly-NY	123	Bottomley-StL	117
Roush-Cin	.938	Frisch-NY	133	Williams-Phi	33.2	Frisch-NY	29.5	Grimm-Pit	122	Carey-Pit	117

Total Average		Stolen Bases		Stolen Base Average		Stolen Base Runs		Fielding Runs		Total Player Rating	
Hornsby-StL	1.194	Carey-Pit	51	Carey-Pit	86.4	Carey-Pit	10.5	Bancroft-NY	21.3	Fournier-Bro	3.9
Fournier-Bro	1.071	Grantham-Chi	43	Smith-StL	74.4	Smith-StL	3.0	Johnston-Bro	19.5	Carey-Pit	3.6
Bottomley-StL	.976	Smith-StL	32	Frisch-NY	70.7	Rawlings-Pit	2.7	Tierney-Pit-Phi	15.5	Bancroft-NY	3.5
Williams-Phi	.966	Heathcote-Chi	32	Traynor-Pit	68.3			Carey-Pit	14.9	Johnston-Bro	3.4
Carey-Pit	.928			Heathcote-Chi	65.3			R.Smith-Bos	14.0	Hargrave-Cin	3.2

Wins		Win Percentage		Games		Complete Games		Shutouts		Saves	
Luque-Cin	27	Luque-Cin	.771	Ryan-NY	45	Grimes-Bro	33	Luque-Cin	6	Jonnard-NY	5
Morrison-Pit	25	Ryan-NY	.762	Jonnard-NY	45	Luque-Cin	28	J.Barnes-NY-Bos	5	Ryan-NY	4
Alexander-Chi	22	Scott-NY	.696	Oeschger-Bos	44	Morrison-Pit	27	McQuillan-NY	5		
Grimes-Bro	21	Morrison-Pit	.658	J.Barnes-NY-Bos	43	Cooper-Pit	26				
Donohue-Cin	21	Alexander-Chi	.647	Genewich-Bos	43	Alexander-Chi	26				

Innings Pitched		Fewest Hits/Game		Fewest BB/Game		Strikeouts		Strikeouts/Game		Ratio	
Grimes-Bro	327.0	Luque-Cin	7.80	Alexander-Chi	.89	Vance-Bro	197	Vance-Bro	6.32	Alexander-Chi	9.97
Luque-Cin	322.0	Vance-Bro	8.44	C.Adams-Phi	1.42	Luque-Cin	151	Luque-Cin	4.22	Luque-Cin	10.40
Rixey-Cin	309.0	Morrison-Pit	8.56	Genewich-Bos	1.82	Grimes-Bro	119	Bentley-NY	3.93	Ryan-NY	11.31
Alexander-Chi	305.0	Keen-Chi	8.59	Rixey-Cin	1.89	Morrison-Pit	114	Osborne-Chi	3.46	Aldridge-Chi	11.49
Ring-Phi	304.1	Aldridge-Chi	8.67	Meadows-Phi-Pit	2.15	Ring-Phi	112	Morrison-Pit	3.40	McQuillan-NY	11.56

Earned Run Average		Adjusted ERA		Opponents' Batting Avg.		Opponents' On Base Pct.		Starter Runs		Adjusted Starter Runs	
Luque-Cin	1.93	Luque-Cin	200	Luque-Cin	.235	Alexander-Chi	.277	Luque-Cin	73.9	Luque-Cin	69.1
Rixey-Cin	2.80	Rixey-Cin	138	Vance-Bro	.250	Luque-Cin	.291	Rixey-Cin	41.1	Rixey-Cin	36.5
Keen-Chi	3.00	Keen-Chi	133	Aldridge-Chi	.251	Aldridge-Chi	.307	Alexander-Chi	27.4	Alexander-Chi	27.4
Kaufmann-Chi	3.10	Kaufmann-Chi	129	Morrison-Pit	.253	Ryan-NY	.308	Haines-StL	26.1	Ring-Phi	24.3
Haines-StL	3.11	Alexander-Chi	125	Osborne-Chi	.255	McQuillan-NY	.315	Kaufmann-Chi	20.6	Haines-StL	23.2

Clutch Pitching Index		Relief Runs		Adjusted Relief Runs		Relief Ranking		Total Pitcher Index		Total Baseball Ranking	
Kaufmann-Chi	118	Decatur-Bro	15.3	Decatur-Bro	14.0	Decatur-Bro	8.7	Luque-Cin	7.3	Luque-Cin	7.3
Rixey-Cin	116	Jonnard-NY	7.6	Jonnard-NY	5.7	Jonnard-NY	4.4	Rixey-Cin	3.3	Fournier-Bro	3.9
Genewich-Bos	116	Keck-Cin	2.6	Keck-Cin	1.3	Keck-Cin	1.3	Alexander-Chi	3.2	Carey-Pit	3.6
Doak-StL	116	V.Barnes-NY	.5					Kaufmann-Chi	2.2	Bancroft-NY	3.5
Luque-Cin	115							Haines-StL	2.1	Johnston-Bro	3.4

TEAM	G	W	L	PCT	GB	R	OR	AB	H	2B	3B	HR	BB	SO	AVG	OBP	SLG	PRO	PRO+	BR	/A	PF	CHI	RC	SB	CS	SBA	SBR
NY	152	98	54	.645		823	622	5347	1554	231	79	105	521	516	.291	.357	.422	.779	108	73	60	102	101	811	69	74	58	-12
DET	155	83	71	.539	16	831	741	5266	1579	270	69	41	596	385	.300	.377	.401	.778	113	91	106	98	98	827	87	62	52	-12
CLE	153	82	71	.536	16.5	888	746	5290	1594	301	75	59	633	384	.301	.381	.420	.801	117	135	136	100	100	869	79	77	60	-12
WAS	155	75	78	.490	23.5	720	747	5244	1436	224	93	26	532	448	.274	.346	.367	.713	97	-45	-7	95	103	693	102	67	53	-11
STL	154	74	78	.487	24	688	720	5298	1489	248	62	82	442	423	.281	.339	.398	.737	93	-14	-54	106	96	724	64	54	50	-13
PHI	153	69	83	.454	29	661	761	5196	1407	229	64	53	445	517	.271	.333	.370	.703	88	-73	-82	101	103	653	72	62	55	-13
CHI	156	69	85	.448	30	692	741	5246	1463	254	57	42	532	458	.279	.350	.373	.723	97	-25	-15	99	96	706	191	119	68	-4
BOS	154	61	91	.401	37	584	809	5181	1354	253	54	34	391	480	.261	.318	.351	.669	80	-142	-145	101	103	578	77	91	57	-6
TOT	616					5887		42068	11876	2010	553	442	4092	3611	.282	.351	.388	.739							741	606	55	-140

TEAM	CG	SH	SV	IP	H	H/G	HR	BB	SO	RAT	ERA	ERA+	OAV	OOB	PR	/A	PF	CPI	FA	E	DP	FW	PW	BW	SBW	DIF
NY	101	9	10	1380²	1365	8.9	68	491	506	12.3	3.62	109	.263	.330	54	48	99	96	.977	144	131	3.3	4.6	5.8	.5	7.7
DET	61	9	12	1373²	1502	9.8	58	449	447	13.1	4.09	94	.282	.345	-16	-33	97	96	.968	200	103	.0	-3.2	10.3	.5	-1.7
CLE	77	10	11	1376	1517	9.9	36	466	407	13.2	3.91	101	.284	.346	10	4	100	97	.964	226	143	-1.7	.4	13.2	.5	-6.9
WAS	71	8	16	1374²	1531	10.0	56	559	474	14.0	3.98	95	.291	.363	0	-30	95	110	.966	216	182	-.9	-2.9	-.7	.6	2.3
STL	83	10	10	1373¹	1430	9.4	59	528	488	13.2	3.93	106	.275	.347	8	37	105	98	.971	177	145	1.4	3.6	-5.2	.5	-2.2
PHI	65	7	12	1364²	1465	9.7	68	550	400	13.5	4.08	101	.280	.351	-15	1	103	99	.965	221	127	-1.4	.0	-7.9	.5	1.8
CHI	74	5	11	1397	1512	9.7	49	534	467	13.4	4.05	98	.283	.352	-9	-12	99	99	.971	184	138	1.1	-1.2	-1.5	1.3	-7.9
BOS	77	3	11	1372	1534	10.1	48	520	412	13.9	4.20	98	.294	.365	-32	-15	103	104	.963	232	126	-2.0	-1.5	-14.0	1.1	1.3
TOT	609	61	93	11012		9.7				13.3	3.98		.282	.351					.968	1600	1095					

Runs
Ruth-NY	151
Speaker-Cle	133
Jamieson-Cle	130
Heilmann-Det	121
Rice-Was	117

Hits
Jamieson-Cle	222
Speaker-Cle	218
Heilmann-Det	211
Ruth-NY	205
Tobin-StL	202

Doubles
Speaker-Cle	59
Burns-Bos	47
Ruth-NY	45
Heilmann-Det	44
J.Sewell-Cle	41

Triples
Rice-Was	18
Goslin-Was	18
Tobin-StL	15
Mostil-Chi	15

Home Runs
Ruth-NY	41
Williams-StL	29
Heilmann-Det	18
Speaker-Cle	17
Hauser-Phi	17

Total Bases
Ruth-NY	399
Speaker-Cle	350
Williams-StL	346
Heilmann-Det	331
Tobin-StL	303

Runs Batted In
Speaker-Cle	130
Ruth-NY	130
Heilmann-Det	115
J.Sewell-Cle	109
Pipp-NY	108

Runs Produced
Speaker-Cle	246
Ruth-NY	240
Heilmann-Det	218
J.Sewell-Cle	204
Rice-Was	189

Bases On Balls
Ruth-NY	170
J.Sewell-Cle	98
Blue-Det	96
Speaker-Cle	93
Collins-Chi	84

Batting Average
Heilmann-Det	.403
Ruth-NY	.393
Speaker-Cle	.380
Collins-Chi	.360
Williams-StL	.357

On Base Percentage
Ruth-NY	.545
Heilmann-Det	.481
Speaker-Cle	.469
J.Sewell-Cle	.456
Collins-Chi	.455

Slugging Average
Ruth-NY	.764
Heilmann-Det	.632
Williams-StL	.623
Speaker-Cle	.610
Harris-Bos	.520

Production
Ruth-NY	1.309
Heilmann-Det	1.113
Speaker-Cle	1.079
Williams-StL	1.062
J.Sewell-Cle	.935

Adjusted Production
Ruth-NY	238
Heilmann-Det	195
Speaker-Cle	183
Williams-StL	168
J.Sewell-Cle	147

Batter Runs
Ruth-NY	119.1
Speaker-Cle	70.9
Heilmann-Det	70.7
Williams-StL	61.2
J.Sewell-Cle	42.8

Adjusted Batter Runs
Ruth-NY	117.7
Heilmann-Det	72.2
Speaker-Cle	71.1
Williams-StL	56.8
J.Sewell-Cle	42.9

Clutch Hitting Index
Pipp-NY	160
J.Sewell-Cle	144
Sheely-Chi	142
Rigney-Det	134
Judge-Was	130

Runs Created
Ruth-NY	223
Speaker-Cle	166
Heilmann-Det	159
Williams-StL	148
J.Sewell-Cle	128

Total Average
Ruth-NY	1.683
Heilmann-Det	1.284
Speaker-Cle	1.227
Williams-StL	1.144
J.Sewell-Cle	1.025

Stolen Bases
Collins-Chi	49
Mostil-Chi	41
Harris-Was	23
Rice-Was	20
Jamieson-Cle	19

Stolen Base Average
Rice-Was	71.4
Mostil-Chi	70.7
Collins-Chi	62.8
Jamieson-Cle	61.3
Harris-Was	59.0

Stolen Base Runs
Mostil-Chi	2.1
Barrett-Chi	1.8
Veach-Det	1.2
Rice-Was	1.2

Fielding Runs
Peckinpaugh-Was	22.9
Mostil-Chi	22.0
Lutzke-Cle	20.4
Flagstead-Det-Bos	20.1
Harris-Was	19.7

Total Player Rating
Ruth-NY	10.5
Speaker-Cle	6.1
J.Sewell-Cle	5.9
Heilmann-Det	5.7
Williams-StL	4.7

Wins
Uhle-Cle	26
Jones-NY	21
Dauss-Det	21
Shocker-StL	20
Ehmke-Bos	20

Win Percentage
Pennock-NY	.760
Jones-NY	.724
Hoyt-NY	.654
Shocker-StL	.625
Uhle-Cle	.619

Games
Rommel-Phi	56
Uhle-Cle	54
Russell-Was	52
Cole-Det	52
Dauss-Det	50

Complete Games
Uhle-Cle	29
Ehmke-Bos	28
Shocker-StL	24
Dauss-Det	22
Bush-NY	22

Shutouts
Coveleski-Cle	5
Vangilder-StL	4
Dauss-Det	4

Saves
Russell-Was	9
Quinn-Bos	7
Harriss-Phi	6

Innings Pitched
Uhle-Cle	357.2
Ehmke-Bos	316.2
Dauss-Det	316.0
Rommel-Phi	297.2
Vangilder-StL	282.1

Fewest Hits/Game
Shawkey-NY	8.07
Hoyt-NY	8.56
Bush-NY	8.59
Russell-Was	8.78
Danforth-StL	8.79

Fewest BB/Game
Shocker-StL	1.59
Coveleski-Cle	1.66
Thurston-StL-Chi	1.75
Quinn-Bos	1.96
Dauss-Det	2.22

Strikeouts
Johnson-Was	130
Shawkey-NY	125
Bush-NY	125
Ehmke-Bos	121

Strikeouts/Game
Johnson-Det	4.75
Johnson-Was	4.48
Shawkey-NY	4.35
Bush-NY	4.08
Harriss-Phi	3.83

Ratio
Shocker-StL	11.16
Hoyt-NY	11.20
Pennock-NY	11.52
Jones-NY	11.63
Coveleski-Cle	11.64

Earned Run Average
Coveleski-Cle	2.76
Hoyt-NY	3.02
Russell-Was	3.03
Vangilder-StL	3.06
Mogridge-Was	3.11

Adjusted ERA
Coveleski-Cle	143
Vangilder-StL	136
Hoyt-NY	131
Thurston-StL-Chi	127
Rommel-Phi	126

Opponents' Batting Avg.
Shawkey-NY	.246
Hoyt-NY	.253
Jones-NY	.257
Faber-Chi	.259
Bush-NY	.260

Opponents' On Base Pct.
Shocker-StL	.306
Hoyt-NY	.307
Faber-Chi	.311
Jones-NY	.312
Pennock-NY	.314

Starter Runs
Coveleski-Cle	30.9
Vangilder-StL	28.9
Hoyt-NY	25.6
Rommel-Phi	23.7
Pennock-NY	22.4

Adjusted Starter Runs
Vangilder-StL	34.8
Coveleski-Cle	30.4
Rommel-Phi	27.8
Hoyt-NY	24.4
Shocker-StL	23.5

Clutch Pitching Index
Thurston-StL-Chi	139
Russell-Was	128
Mogridge-Was	122
Vangilder-StL	121
Coveleski-Cle	121

Relief Runs

Adjusted Relief Runs

Relief Ranking

Total Pitcher Index
Rommel-Phi	3.6
Vangilder-StL	3.3
Coveleski-Cle	2.6
Bush-NY	2.4
Uhle-Cle	2.4

Total Baseball Ranking
Ruth-NY	10.5
Speaker-Cle	6.1
J.Sewell-Cle	5.9
Heilmann-Det	5.7
Williams-StL	4.7

TEAM	G	W	L	PCT	GB	R	OR	AB	H	2B	3B	HR	BB	SO	AVG	OBP	SLG	PRO	PRO+	BR	/A	PF	CHI	RC	SB	CS	SBA	SBR
NY	154	93	60	.608		857	641	5445	1634	269	81	95	467	479	.300	.358	.432	.790	120	124	144	97	102	849	82	53	50	-13
BRO	154	92	62	.597	1.5	717	675	5339	1534	227	54	72	447	357	.287	.345	.391	.736	105	19	41	97	99	725	34	46	48	-14
PIT	153	90	63	.588	3	724	588	5288	1517	222	122	43	366	396	.287	.336	.399	.735	100	11	0	102	103	714	181	92	66	-11
CIN	153	83	70	.542	10	649	579	5301	1539	236	111	36	349	334	.290	.337	.397	.734	102	8	18	99	93	698	103	98	60	-6
CHI	154	81	72	.529	12	698	699	5134	1419	207	59	66	469	521	.276	.340	.378	.718	96	-9	-15	101	103	652	137	149	71	2
STL	154	65	89	.422	28.5	740	750	5349	1552	270	87	67	382	418	.290	.341	.411	.752	107	42	54	98	100	740	86	86	55	-6
PHI	152	55	96	.364	37	676	849	5306	1459	256	56	94	382	452	.275	.328	.397	.725	88	-12	-96	112	99	687	57	67	55	-12
BOS	154	53	100	.346	40	520	800	5283	1355	194	52	25	354	451	.256	.306	.327	.633	77	-180	-150	96	103	532	74	68	55	-12
TOT	614					5581		42445	12009	1881	622	498	3216	3408	.283	.337	.392	.729		754	659						53	-168

TEAM	CG	SH	SV	IP	H	H/G	HR	BB	SO	RAT	ERA	ERA+	OAV	OOB	PR	/A	PF	CPI	FA	E	DP	FW	PW	BW	SBW	DIF
NY	71	4	21	1378²	1464	9.6	77	392	406	12.2	3.62	101	.273	.325	38	6	95	100	.971	186	160	.4	.6	14.3	.8	.4
BRO	97	10	5	1376¹	1432	9.4	58	403	638	12.2	3.64	103	.269	.325	35	16	97	96	.968	196	121	-.2	1.6	4.1	.7	8.8
PIT	85	15	5	1382	1387	9.0	42	323	364	11.3	3.27	117	.267	.312	91	87	99	97	.971	183	161	.5	8.6	.0	1.0	3.4
CIN	77	14	9	1378	1408	9.2	30	293	451	11.3	3.12	121	.266	.308	114	99	97	97	.966	217	142	-1.4	9.8	1.8	1.5	-5.2
CHI	85	4	6	1380²	1459	9.5	89	438	416	12.5	3.83	102	.275	.333	6	11	101	101	.966	218	153	-1.4	1.1	-1.5	2.3	4.0
STL	79	7	6	1364²	1528	10.1	69	486	393	13.5	4.15	91	.289	.354	-42	-56	98	104	.969	188	162	.3	-5.6	5.4	1.5	-13.6
PHI	59	7	10	1354¹	1689	11.2	84	469	349	14.5	4.87	92	.313	.371	-151	-59	115	103	.972	175	168	.8	-5.9	-9.5	.9	-6.9
BOS	66	10	4	1379¹	1607	10.5	49	402	364	13.3	4.46	86	.301	.353	-91	-99	99	96	.973	168	154	1.4	-9.8	-14.9	.9	-1.1
TOT	619	71	66	10994		9.8				12.6	3.87		.283	.337					.970	1531	1221					

Runs
Hornsby-StL 121
Frisch-NY 121
Carey-Pit 113
Youngs-NY 112
Williams-Phi 101

Hits
Hornsby-StL 227
Wheat-Bro 212
Frisch-NY 198
High-Bro 191
Fournier-Bro 188

Doubles
Hornsby-StL 43
Wheat-Bro 41
Kelly-NY 37

Triples
Roush-Cin 21
Maranville-Pit ... 20
Wright-Pit 18
Cuyler-Pit 16
Frisch-NY 15

Home Runs
Fournier-Bro 27
Hornsby-StL 25
Williams-Phi 24
Kelly-NY 21

Total Bases
Hornsby-StL 373
Wheat-Bro 311
Williams-Phi 308
Kelly-NY 303
Fournier-Bro 302

Runs Batted In
Kelly-NY 136
Fournier-Bro 116
Wright-Pit 111
Bottomley-StL 111
Meusel-NY 102

Runs Produced
Kelly-NY 206
Hornsby-StL 190
Wright-Pit 184
Bottomley-StL 184
Frisch-NY 183

Bases On Balls
Hornsby-StL 89
Fournier-Bro 83
Youngs-NY 77
Williams-Phi 67
Friberg-Chi 66

Batting Average
Hornsby-StL .... .424
Wheat-Bro ..... .375
Youngs-NY ..... .356
Cuyler-Pit ...... .354
Roush-Cin ...... .348

On Base Percentage
Hornsby-StL .... .507
Youngs-NY ..... .441
Fournier-Bro .... .428
Wheat-Bro ..... .428
Williams-Phi .... .403

Slugging Average
Hornsby-StL .... .696
Williams-Phi .... .552
Wheat-Bro ..... .549
Cuyler-Pit ...... .539
Fournier-Bro .... .536

Production
Hornsby-StL 1.203
Wheat-Bro ...... .978
Fournier-Bro ..... .965
Youngs-NY ...... .962
Williams-Phi ...... .955

Adjusted Production
Hornsby-StL 223
Wheat-Bro 165
Fournier-Bro 162
Youngs-NY 161
Cuyler-Pit 147

Batter Runs
Hornsby-StL 94.1
Wheat-Bro 48.2
Fournier-Bro 48.1
Youngs-NY 45.3
Williams-Phi 42.0

Adjusted Batter Runs
Hornsby-StL 95.5
Fournier-Bro 50.7
Wheat-Bro 50.6
Youngs-NY 47.3
Williams-Phi 32.8

Clutch Hitting Index
Friberg-Chi 164
Meusel-NY 158
Wright-Pit 152
Griffith-Bro 145
Brown-Bro 145

Runs Created
Hornsby-StL 186
Fournier-Bro 133
Wheat-Bro 132
Youngs-NY 123
Williams-Phi 121

Total Average
Hornsby-StL 1.424
Fournier-Bro 1.045
Youngs-NY 1.023
Wheat-Bro 1.014
Cuyler-Pit ...... .990

Stolen Bases
Carey-Pit 49
Cuyler-Pit 32
Heathcote-Chi 26
Traynor-Pit 24
Smith-StL 24

Stolen Base Average
Carey-Pit 79.0
Cuyler-Pit 74.4
Frisch-NY 71.0
Critz-Cin 63.3
Smith-StL 60.0

Stolen Base Runs
Carey-Pit 6.9
Cuyler-Pit 3.0
Hartnett-Chi 1.8

Fielding Runs
Pinelli-Cin 26.7
Frisch-NY 24.9
Ford-Phi 11.9
Statz-Chi 11.7
Wright-Pit 10.7

Total Player Rating
Hornsby-StL 7.5
Wheat-Bro 4.9
Fournier-Bro 4.9
Frisch-NY 4.4
Youngs-NY 3.8

Wins
Vance-Bro 28
Grimes-Bro 22
Mays-Cin 20
Cooper-Pit 20
Kremer-Pit 18

Win Percentage
Yde-Pit .... .842
Vance-Bro .... .824
Bentley-NY ...... .762
Mays-Cin .... .690
Kremer-Pit ...... .643

Games
Morrison-Pit 41
Kremer-Pit 41
Keen-Chi 40
Sheehan-Cin 39

Complete Games
Vance-Bro 30
Grimes-Bro 30
Cooper-Pit 25
Barnes-Bos 21
Aldridge-Chi 20

Shutouts
Yde-Pit 4
Sothoron-StL 4
Rixey-Cin 4
Kremer-Pit 4
Cooper-Pit 4
Barnes-Bos 4

Saves
May-Cin 6
Ryan-NY 5
Jonnard-NY 5

Innings Pitched
Grimes-Bro 310.2
Vance-Bro 308.2
Cooper-Pit 268.2
Barnes-Bos 267.2
Kremer-Pit 259.1

Fewest Hits/Game
Vance-Bro 6.94
Yde-Pit 7.93
Morrison-Pit 8.07
Doak-StL-Bro 8.14
Rixey-Cin 8.27

Fewest BB/Game
Benton-Cin 1.33
Alexander-Chi 1.33
Cooper-Pit 1.34
Mays-Cin 1.43
Donohue-Cin 1.46

Strikeouts
Vance-Bro 262
Grimes-Bro 135
Luque-Cin 86
Morrison-Pit 85
Kaufmann-Chi 79

Strikeouts/Game
Vance-Bro 7.64
Grimes-Bro 3.91
Nehf-NY 3.77
Luque-Cin 3.53
Kaufmann-Chi 3.41

Ratio
Vance-Bro 9.45
Rixey-Cin 10.12
Benton-Cin 10.73
Doak-StL-Bro 10.87
McQuillan-NY 10.96

Earned Run Average
Vance-Bro 2.16
McQuillan-NY 2.69
Rixey-Cin 2.76
Benton-Cin 2.77
Yde-Pit 2.83

Adjusted ERA
Vance-Bro 174
Rixey-Cin 137
McQuillan-NY 136
Benton-Cin 136
Yde-Pit 136

Opponents' Batting Avg.
Vance-Bro .... .213
Yde-Pit .... .244
Morrison-Pit ..... .245
Rixey-Cin .... .246
Doak-StL-Bro .... .249

Opponents' On Base Pct.
Vance-Bro .... .269
Rixey-Cin .... .285
Benton-Cin ...... .297
Alexander-Chi .... .299
Nehf-NY .... .301

Starter Runs
Vance-Bro 58.6
Rixey-Cin 29.4
McQuillan-NY 24.0
Yde-Pit 22.3
Barnes-NY 20.5

Adjusted Starter Runs
Vance-Bro 54.5
Rixey-Cin 26.7
Yde-Pit 21.7
McQuillan-NY 19.9
Kremer-Pit 18.6

Clutch Pitching Index
Sherdel-StL 117
Sothoron-StL 115
Ring-Phi 113
McQuillan-NY 113
Aldridge-Chi 110

Relief Runs
Jonnard-NY 14.5
May-Cin 9.5
Stone-Pit 6.5

Adjusted Relief Runs
Jonnard-NY 12.5
May-Cin 8.4
Stone-Pit 6.3

Relief Ranking
Jonnard-NY 12.9
May-Cin 5.7
Stone-Pit 5.3

Total Pitcher Index
Vance-Bro 5.4
Mays-Cin 3.2
Rixey-Cin 2.8
Yde-Pit 2.6
Cooper-Pit 2.3

Total Baseball Ranking
Hornsby-StL 7.5
Vance-Bro 5.4
Wheat-Bro 4.9
Fournier-Bro 4.9
Frisch-NY 4.4

TEAM	G	W	L	PCT	GB	R	OR	AB	H	2B	3B	HR	BB	SO	AVG	OBP	SLG	PRO	PRO+	BR	/A	PF	CHI	RC	SB	CS	SBA	SBR
WAS	156	92	62	.597		755	**613**	5304	1558	255	**88**	22	513	392	.294	.361	.387	.748	101	-7	17	97	98	761	115	87	60	**-9**
NY	153	89	63	.586	2	798	667	5240	1516	248	86	**98**	478	420	.289	.352	**.426**	**.778**	106	29	30	100	102	790	69	64	52	-11
DET	156	86	68	.558	6	**849**	796	5389	**1604**	315	76	35	**607**	400	**.298**	**.373**	.404	.777	**107**	53	65	98	100	837	100	76	59	-12
STL	153	74	78	.487	17	769	809	5236	1543	266	62	67	465	**349**	.295	.356	.408	.764	96	9	-37	106	101	762	85	85	59	**-9**
PHI	152	71	81	.467	20	685	778	5184	1459	251	59	63	374	482	.281	.334	.389	.723	90	-76	-82	101	**105**	675	79	66	53	-11
CLE	153	67	86	.438	24.5	755	814	5332	1580	306	59	41	492	371	.296	.361	.399	.760	99	8	-1	101	97	786	84	51	49	-13
BOS	157	67	87	.435	25	737	806	5340	1481	302	63	30	603	417	.277	.356	.374	.730	93	-41	-41	100	99	741	79	61	55	-14
CHI	154	66	87	.431	25.5	793	858	5255	1512	254	58	41	604	418	.288	.365	.382	.747	101	-5	19	97	103	763	**138**	86	**61**	-10
TOT	617					6141		42280	12253	2197	551	397	4136	3249	.290	.358	.397	.755							749	576	57	-120

TEAM	CG	SH	SV	IP	H	H/G	HR	BB	SO	RAT	ERA	ERA+	OAV	OOB	PR	/A	PF	CPI	FA	E	DP	FW	PW	BW	SBW	DIF
WAS	74	**13**	25	1383	**1329**	8.6	34	505	469	12.2	**3.34**	121	.258	.330	135	106	95	99	.972	171	149	1.3	**10.0**	1.6	.6	1.5
NY	76	**13**	13	1359¹	1483	9.8	59	522	**487**	13.4	3.86	108	.284	.352	55	44	98	**107**	**.974**	156	131	2.0	4.2	2.8	.4	3.6
DET	60	5	20	1394²	1582	10.2	55	**465**	439	13.5	4.19	98	.291	.352	5	-12	97	100	.971	187	142	.4	-1.1	**6.1**	.3	3.3
STL	65	11	7	1353¹	1511	10.0	68	517	386	13.8	4.57	90	.288	.357	-51	-9	107	95	.969	184	142	.3	-.8	-3.5	**.6**	1.5
PHI	68	8	10	1345	1527	10.2	43	597	371	14.4	4.39	98	.292	.367	-23	-15	101	101	.971	180	**157**	.5	-1.4	-7.7	.4	3.3
CLE	**87**	7	7	1349	1603	10.7	43	503	312	14.3	4.40	97	.300	.364	-25	-20	101	101	.967	205	130	-1.0	-1.9	-.0	.2	-6.7
BOS	73	8	16	1391¹	1563	10.1	43	523	414	13.9	4.35	100	.289	.359	-19	1	103	97	.967	210	126	-1.0	.0	-3.9	.1	-5.3
CHI	76	1	11	1370²	1635	10.7	52	512	360	14.3	4.74	87	.304	.368	-77	-95	97	98	.963	229	136	-2.4	-9.0	1.8	.5	-1.4
TOT	579	66	109	10946¹		10.1				13.7	4.23		.290	.358					.969	1522	1113					

Runs
Ruth-NY 143
Cobb-Det 115
Collins-Chi 108
Hooper-Chi 107
Heilmann-Det. 107

Hits
Rice-Was 216
Jamieson-Cle 213
Cobb-Det 211
Ruth-NY 200
Goslin-Was 199

Doubles
J.Sewell-Cle 45
Heilmann-Det. 45
Wambsganss-Bos . . 41
Jacobson-StL 41
Meusel-NY 40

Triples
Pipp-NY 19
Goslin-Was 17
Heilmann-Det 16
Rice-Was 14
Jacobson-SLL 12

Home Runs
Ruth-NY 46
Hauser-Phi 27
Jacobson-StL 19
Williams-StL 18
Boone-Bos 13

Total Bases
Ruth-NY 391
Jacobson-StL 306
Heilmann-Det 304
Goslin-Was 299
Hauser-Phi 290

Runs Batted In
Goslin-Was 129
Ruth-NY 121
Meusel-NY 120
Hauser-Phi 115
Heilmann-Det. . . . 114

Runs Produced
Ruth-NY 218
Goslin-Was 217
Heilmann-Det. . . . 211
J.Sewell-Cle 201
Meusel-NY 201

Bases On Balls
Ruth-NY 142
Rigney-Det 102
Sheely-Chi 95
Collins-Chi 89
Cobb-Det 85

Batting Average
Ruth-NY 378
Jamieson-Cle 359
Falk-Chi 352
Collins-Chi 349
Heilmann-Det. 346

On Base Percentage
Ruth-NY 513
Collins-Chi 441
Speaker-Cle 432
Heilmann-Det. 428
Sheely-Chi 426

Slugging Average
Ruth-NY 739
Heilmann-Det. 533
Williams-StL 533
Jacobson-StL 528
Goslin-Was 516

Production
Ruth-NY 1.252
Heilmann-Det. 961
Williams-StL 958
Speaker-Cle 943
Goslin-Was 937

Adjusted Production
Ruth-NY 221
Heilmann-Det. . . . 149
Goslin-Was 145
Speaker-Cle 141
Williams-StL 137

Batter Runs
Ruth-NY 100.8
Heilmann-Det. . . . 40.4
Goslin-Was 35.6
Speaker-Cle 32.4
Collins-Chi 30.5

Adjusted Batter Runs
Ruth-NY 100.9
Heilmann-Det. . . . 41.8
Goslin-Was 38.2
Collins-Chi 33.1
Speaker-Cle 31.5

Clutch Hitting Index
Kamm-Chi 150
Pratt-Det 149
Rigney-Det 148
Sheely-Chi 143
Veach-Bos 142

Runs Created
Ruth-NY 205
Heilmann-Det. . . . 134
Goslin-Was 126
Cobb-Det 121
Collins-Chi 119

Total Average
Ruth-NY 1.558
Heilmann-Det. . . . 1.042
Williams-StL 1.039
Speaker-Cle 988
Collins-Chi 976

Stolen Bases
Collins-Chi 42
Meusel-NY 26
Rice-Was 24
Cobb-Det 23
Jamieson-Cle 21

Stolen Base Average
Collins-Chi 71.2
Jamieson-Cle . . . 65.6
Harris-Was 65.5
Meusel-NY 65.0
Rice-Was 64.9

Stolen Base Runs
Collins-Chi 2.4

Fielding Runs
J.Sewell-Cle 21.2
Lutzke-Cle 19.3
Dykes-Phi 15.9
Jacobson-StL 15.8
Wambsganss-Bos . 14.5

Total Player Rating
Ruth-NY 8.4
J.Sewell-Cle 4.2
Heilmann-Det 3.7
Rigney-Det 3.3
Collins-Chi 3.0

Wins
Johnson-Was 23
Pennock-NY 21
Thurston-Chi 20
Shaute-Cle 20
Ehmke-Bos 19

Win Percentage
Johnson-Was 767
Pennock-NY 700
Whitehill-Det 654
Zachary-Was 625

Games
Marberry-Was 50
Holloway-Det 49
Shaute-Cle 46
Hoyt-NY 46
Ehmke-Bos 45

Complete Games
Thurston-Chi 28
Ehmke-Bos 26
Pennock-NY 25
Shaute-Cle 21
Rommel-Phi 21

Shutouts
Johnson-Was 6
Davis-StL 5
Shocker-StL 4
Pennock-NY 4
Ehmke-Bos 4

Saves
Marberry-Was 15
Russell-Was 8
Quinn-Bos 7
Dauss-Det 6
Connally-Chi 6

Innings Pitched
Ehmke-Bos 315.0
Thurston-Chi 291.0
Pennock-NY 286.1
Shaute-Cle 283.0
Rommel-Phi 278.0

Fewest Hits/Game
Johnson-Was 7.55
Collins-Det 8.29
Marberry-Was 8.75
Zachary-Was 8.79
Wingard-StL 8.88

Fewest BB/Game
Smith-Cle 1.53
Thurston-Chi 1.86
Shocker-StL 1.90
Pennock-NY 2.01
Quinn-Bos 2.05

Strikeouts
Johnson-Was 158
Ehmke-Bos 119
Shawkey-NY 114
Pennock-NY 101
Shocker-StL 88

Strikeouts/Game
Johnson-Was 5.12
Shawkey-NY 4.94
Ehmke-Bos 3.40
Shocker-StL 3.22
Pennock-NY 3.17

Ratio
Johnson-Was . . . 10.37
Collins-Det 11.08
Zachary-Was 11.28
Smith-Cle 11.48
Pennock-NY 11.54

Earned Run Average
Johnson-Was 2.72
Zachary-Was 2.75
Pennock-NY 2.83
Baumgartner-Phi. . 2.88
Smith-Cle 3.02

Adjusted ERA
Baumgartner-Phi. . 149
Johnson-Was 148
Pennock-NY 147
Zachary-Was 147
Smith-Cle 142

Opponents' Batting Avg.
Johnson-Was 224
Collins-Det 249
Marberry-Was 262
Wingard-StL 262
Davis-StL 263

Opponents' On Base Pct.
Johnson-Was 284
Collins-Det 307
Smith-Cle 312
Pennock-NY 314
Zachary-Was 315

Starter Runs
Johnson-Was 46.5
Pennock-NY 44.6
Smith-Cle 33.4
Zachary-Was 33.2
Baumgartner-Phi. . 27.1

Adjusted Starter Runs
Pennock-NY 42.3
Johnson-Was 40.5
Smith-Cle 34.5
Ehmke-Bos 31.9
Zachary-Was 28.9

Clutch Pitching Index
Baumgartner-Phi. . 132
Pennock-NY 117
Zachary-Was 113
Ferguson-Bos 113
Hoyt-NY 112

Relief Runs
Speece-Was 9.5

Adjusted Relief Runs
Speece-Was 8.4

Relief Ranking
Speece-Was 4.2

Total Pitcher Index
Johnson-Was 4.4
Pennock-NY 3.9
Smith-Cle 3.6
Zachary-Was 3.4
Bush-NY 3.1

Total Baseball Ranking
Ruth-NY 8.4
Johnson-Was 4.4
J.Sewell-Cle 4.2
Pennock-NY 3.9
Heilmann-Det 3.7

TEAM	G	W	L	PCT	GB	R	OR	AB	H	2B	3B	HR	BB	SO	AVG	OBP	SLG	PRO	PRO+	BR	/A	PF	CHI	RC	SB	CS	SBA	SBR
PIT	153	95	58	.621		912	715	5372	1651	316	105	78	499	363	.307	.369	.449	.818	107	116	62	107	101	909	159	63	53	-12
NY	152	86	66	.566	8.5	736	702	5327	1507	239	61	61	411	494	.283	.337	.415	.752	101	-25	5	96	100	742	79	65	55	-13
CIN	153	80	73	.523	15	690	643	5233	1490	221	90	44	409	327	.285	.339	.387	.726	93	-65	-46	98	99	680	108	107	66	-7
STL	153	77	76	.503	18	828	764	5329	1592	292	80	109	446	414	.299	.356	.445	.801	107	72	54	102	98	846	70	51	44	-10
BOS	153	70	83	.458	25	708	802	5365	1567	260	70	41	405	380	.292	.345	.390	.735	101	-47	21	91	97	722	77	72	62	-15
PHI	153	68	85	.444	27	812	930	5412	1598	288	58	100	456	542	.295	.354	.425	.779	95	35	-34	109	99	814	48	59	49	-11
BRO	153	68	85	.444	27	786	866	5468	1617	250	80	64	437	383	.296	.351	.406	.757	101	-5	16	97	101	787	37	30	38	-13
CHI	154	68	86	.442	27.5	723	773	5353	1473	254	70	86	397	470	.275	.329	.397	.726	88	-76	-87	102	104	700	94	70	65	-17
TOT	612					6195		42859	12495	2120	614	636	3460	3373	.292	.348	.414	.762							672	517	57	-108

TEAM	CG	SH	SV	IP	H	H/G	HR	BB	SO	RAT	ERA	ERA+	OAV	OOB	PR	/A	PF	CPI	FA	E	DP	FW	PW	BW	SBW	DIF
PIT	77	2	13	1354²	1526	10.1	81	387	386	12.9	3.87	115	.286	.339	59	88	105	105	.964	224	171	-.9	8.2	5.8	.1	5.2
NY	80	6	8	1354	1532	10.2	73	408	446	13.0	3.94	102	.288	.341	48	16	95	104	.968	199	129	.5	1.5	.5	.0	7.5
CIN	92	11	12	1375¹	1447	9.5	35	324	437	11.8	3.38	121	.271	.317	135	110	96	95	.968	203	161	.3	10.3	-4.3	.6	-3.4
STL	82	8	7	1335²	1480	10.0	86	470	428	13.4	4.36	99	.283	.347	-13	-7	101	96	.966	204	156	.3	-.7	5.1	.3	-4.5
BOS	77	5	4	1366²	1567	10.3	67	458	351	13.4	4.39	91	.290	.348	-19	-58	94	96	.964	221	145	-.7	-5.4	2.0	-.1	-2.2
PHI	69	8	9	1350²	1753	11.7	117	444	371	14.8	5.02	95	.315	.367	-113	-38	112	103	.966	211	147	-.1	-3.6	-3.2	.2	-1.9
BRO	82	4	4	1350²	1608	10.7	75	477	518	14.1	4.77	88	.301	.362	-75	-90	98	97	.966	210	130	-.0	-8.4	1.5	.0	-1.6
CHI	75	5	10	1370	1575	10.3	102	485	435	13.7	4.41	98	.291	.353	-21	-13	101	102	.969	198	161	.7	-1.2	-8.1	-.3	-.0
TOT	634	49	67	10857²		10.4				13.4	4.27		.292	.348					.966	1670	1200					

Runs
Cuyler-Pit 144
Hornsby-StL 133
Wheat-Bro 125
Traynor-Pit 114
Blades-StL 112

Hits
Bottomley-StL 227
Wheat-Bro 221
Cuyler-Pit 220
Hornsby-StL 203
Stock-Bro 202

Doubles
Bottomley-StL 44
Cuyler-Pit 43
Wheat-Bro 42
Hornsby-StL 41
Burrus-Bos 41

Triples
Cuyler-Pit 26
Walker-Cin 16
Roush-Cin 16
Fournier-Bro 16

Home Runs
Hornsby-StL 39
Hartnett-Chi 24
Fournier-Bro 22
Meusel-NY 21
Bottomley-StL 21

Total Bases
Hornsby-StL 381
Cuyler-Pit 369
Bottomley-StL ... 358
Wheat-Bro 333
Fournier-Bro 310

Runs Batted In
Hornsby-StL 143
Fournier-Bro 130
Bottomley-StL ... 128
Wright-Pit 121
Barnhart-Pit 114

Runs Produced
Hornsby-StL 237
Cuyler-Pit 228
Wheat-Bro 214
Traynor-Pit 214
Fournier-Bro 207

Bases On Balls
Fournier-Bro 86
Hornsby-StL 83
Moore-NY 73
Youngs-NY 66
Carey-Pit 66

Batting Average
Hornsby-StL 403
Bottomley-StL 367
Wheat-Bro 359
Cuyler-Pit 357
Fournier-Bro 350

On Base Percentage
Hornsby-StL 489
Fournier-Bro 446
Blades-StL 423
Cuyler-Pit 423
Carey-Pit 418

Slugging Average
Hornsby-StL 756
Cuyler-Pit 598
Bottomley-StL 578
Fournier-Bro 569
Harper-Phi 558

Production
Hornsby-StL 1.245
Cuyler-Pit 1.021
Fournier-Bro ... 1.015
Bottomley-StL 992
Blades-StL 958

Adjusted Production
Hornsby-StL 208
Fournier-Bro 162
Cuyler-Pit 148
Bottomley-StL ... 147
Wheat-Bro 143

Batter Runs
Hornsby-StL 87.1
Cuyler-Pit 53.1
Fournier-Bro 50.1
Bottomley-StL ... 45.5
Wheat-Bro 35.0

Adjusted Batter Runs
Hornsby-StL 85.3
Fournier-Bro 52.4
Cuyler-Pit 46.9
Bottomley-StL ... 43.5
Wheat-Bro 37.3

Clutch Hitting Index
Barnhart-Pit 170
Traynor-Pit 137
E.Brown-Phi 133
Wright-Pit 131
Fournier-Bro 130

Runs Created
Hornsby-StL 187
Cuyler-Pit 158
Bottomley-StL ... 145
Fournier-Bro 141
Wheat-Bro 134

Total Average
Hornsby-StL 1.539
Cuyler-Pit 1.141
Fournier-Bro ... 1.117
Bottomley-StL ... 1.025
Carey-Pit 1.011

Stolen Bases
Carey-Pit 46
Cuyler-Pit 41
Adams-Chi 26
Roush-Cin 22
Frisch-NY 21

Stolen Base Average
Smith-StL 90.9
Carey-Pit 80.7
Cuyler-Pit 75.9
Moore-Pit 73.1
Adams-Chi 68.4

Stolen Base Runs
Carey-Pit 7.2
Smith-StL 4.8
Cuyler-Pit 4.5
Stock-Bro 1.8
Grantham-Pit 1.8

Fielding Runs
Adams-Chi 28.1
Traynor-Pit 22.9
Critz-Cin 21.6
Pinelli-Cin 20.8
Kelly-NY 17.5

Total Player Rating
Hornsby-StL 5.8
Cuyler-Pit 4.9
Traynor-Pit 3.5
Fournier-Bro 3.5
Bancroft-Bos 3.4

Wins
Vance-Bro 22
Rixey-Cin 21
Donohue-Cin 21
Meadows-Pit 19

Win Percentage
Sherdel-StL 714
Vance-Bro 710
Aldridge-Pit 682
Kremer-Pit 680
Rixey-Cin 656

Games
Morrison-Pit....... 44
Donohue-Cin 42
Bush-Chi 42
Osborne-Bro 41
Kremer-Pit 40

Complete Games
Donohue-Cin 27
Vance-Bro 26
Rixey-Cin 22
Luque-Cin 22
Ring-Phi 21

Shutouts
Vance-Bro 4
Luque-Cin 4
Carlson-Phi 4
Donohue-Cin 3

Saves
Morrison-Pit........ 4
Bush-Chi 4

Innings Pitched
Donohue-Cin 301.0
Luque-Cin 291.0
Rixey-Cin 287.1
Ring-Phi 270.0
Vance-Bro 265.1

Fewest Hits/Game
Luque-Cin 8.13
Benton-Bos 8.35
Vance-Bro 8.38
Aldridge-Pit 9.20
Donohue-Cin 9.27

Fewest BB/Game
Alexander-Chi 1.11
Donohue-Cin 1.47
Rixey-Cin 1.47
Cooney-Bos 1.83
Sherdel-StL 1.89

Strikeouts
Vance-Bro 221
Luque-Cin 140
Ring-Phi 93
Blake-Chi 93
Aldridge-Pit 88

Strikeouts/Game
Vance-Bro 7.50
Luque-Cin 4.33
Sothoron-StL 3.87
Bush-Chi 3.76
Aldridge-Pit 3.71

Ratio
Luque-Cin 10.61
Donohue-Cin ... 10.79
Vance-Bro 10.96
Rixey-Cin 11.15
Alexander-Chi .. 11.52

Earned Run Average
Luque-Cin 2.63
Rixey-Cin 2.88
Donohue-Cin 3.08
Benton-Bos 3.09
Sherdel-StL 3.11

Adjusted ERA
Luque-Cin 156
Rixey-Cin 143
Sherdel-StL 139
Donohue-Cin 133
Benton-Bos 130

Opponents' Batting Avg.
Luque-Cin 239
Benton-Bos 249
Vance-Bro 250
Donohue-Cin 268
Scott-NY 269

Opponents' On Base Pct.
Luque-Cin 291
Donohue-Cin 299
Vance-Bro 304
Rixey-Cin 307
Cooney-Bos 312

Starter Runs
Luque-Cin 53.0
Rixey-Cin 44.2
Donohue-Cin 39.7
Scott-NY 29.6
Sherdel-StL 25.8

Adjusted Starter Runs
Luque-Cin 47.9
Rixey-Cin 39.2
Donohue-Cin 34.4
Sherdel-StL 27.0
Alexander-Chi ... 24.4

Clutch Pitching Index
Nehf-NY 122
Yde-Pit 117
Sherdel-StL 109
Rixey-Cin 108
Morrison-Pit...... 107

Relief Runs
Huntzinger-NY..... 5.5

Adjusted Relief Runs
Huntzinger-NY.....3.9

Relief Ranking
Huntzinger-NY.....3.2

Total Pitcher Index
Luque-Cin 5.6
Donohue-Cin 3.8
Rixey-Cin 3.6
Scott-NY 2.9
Sherdel-StL 2.8

Total Baseball Ranking
Hornsby-StL 5.8
Luque-Cin 5.6
Cuyler-Pit 4.9
Donohue-Cin 3.8
Rixey-Cin 3.6

TEAM	G	W	L	PCT	GB	R	OR	AB	H	2B	3B	HR	BB	SO	AVG	OBP	SLG	PRO	PRO+	BR	/A	PF	CHI	RC	SB	CS	SBA	SBR
WAS	152	96	55	.636		829	**670**	5206	1577	251	71	56	533	427	.303	.373	.411	.784	106	39	54	98	100	816	**134**	88	59	-8
PHI	153	88	64	.579	8.5	831	713	5399	**1659**	298	79	76	453	432	**.307**	.364	.434	.798	101	54	1	107	97	857	67	59	50	-11
STL	154	82	71	.536	15	900	906	5440	1620	**304**	68	**110**	498	375	.298	.360	**.439**	.799	102	52	10	105	**105**	859	85	78	61	-12
DET	156	81	73	.526	16.5	**903**	829	5371	1621	277	**84**	50	640	386	.302	**.379**	.413	.792	**108**	63	75	99	102	**872**	97	63	51	-11
CHI	154	79	75	.513	18.5	811	770	5224	1482	299	59	38	**662**	405	.284	.370	.385	.755	102	-6	37	95	101	781	129	88	**63**	-10
CLE	155	70	84	.455	27.5	782	817	5436	1613	285	58	52	520	379	.297	.361	.399	.760	97	-11	-17	101	98	795	90	76	55	-9
NY	156	69	85	.448	28.5	706	774	5353	1471	247	74	**110**	470	482	.275	.336	.410	.746	95	-60	-45	98	96	738	67	73	57	-11
BOS	152	47	105	.309	49.5	639	922	5166	1375	257	64	41	513	422	.266	.336	.364	.700	83	-130	-129	100	100	647	42	56	50	-12
TOT	616					6401		42595	12418	2218	557	533	4289	3308	.292	.360	.408	.768							711	581	55	-134

TEAM	CG	SH	SV	IP	H	H/G	HR	BB	SO	RAT	ERA	ERA+	OAV	OOB	PR	/A	PF	CPI	FA	E	DP	FW	PW	BW	SBW	DIF
WAS	69	10	21	1358¹	**1426**	9.4	49	543	464	13.3	3.70	114	.276	.349	105	79	96	**106**	.972	170	166	1.8	7.3	5.0	**.8**	5.6
PHI	61	8	18	1381²	1468	9.6	60	544	**495**	13.3	3.87	120	.275	**.347**	80	119	106	101	.966	211	148	-.6	**11.0**	.0	.5	.9
STL	67	7	10	1379²	1598	10.4	99	675	419	15.0	4.92	95	.299	.382	-80	-39	106	103	.964	226	164	-1.4	-3.6	.9	.5	9.1
DET	66	2	18	1383²	1582	10.3	70	556	419	14.2	4.61	94	.295	.366	-32	-46	98	99	.972	173	143	1.9	-4.3	**6.9**	.5	-1.2
CHI	71	**12**	13	1385²	1583	10.3	69	**493**	375	13.6	4.29	97	.295	.357	16	-21	95	103	.968	200	162	.2	-1.9	3.4	.6	-.3
CLE	**93**	6	9	1372¹	1604	10.5	**41**	**493**	345	14.0	4.49	98	.295	.358	-14	-9	101	95	.967	210	146	-.4	-.8	-1.6	.7	-5.0
NY	80	8	13	1387²	1560	10.1	78	505	492	13.6	4.33	98	.288	.353	9	-10	97	99	**.974**	160	150	2.7	-.9	-4.2	.5	-6.1
BOS	68	6	6	1326²	1615	11.0	67	510	310	14.7	4.97	92	.307	.373	-84	-62	103	98	.957	271	150	-4.2	-5.7	-11.9	.5	-7.5
TOT	575	59	108	10975²		10.2				14.0	4.39		.292	.360					.968	1621	1229					

Runs		Hits		Doubles		Triples		Home Runs		Total Bases	
Mostil-Chi	135	Simmons-Phi	253	McManus-StL	44	Goslin-Was	20	Meusel-NY	33	Simmons-Phi	392
Simmons-Phi	122	Rice-Was	227	Simmons-Phi	43	Mostil-Chi	16	Williams-StL	25	Meusel-NY	338
Combs-NY	117	Heilmann-Det	225	Sheely-Chi	43	Sisler-StL	15	Ruth-NY	25	Goslin-Was	329
Goslin-Was	116	Sisler-StL	224	Burns-Cle	41			Simmons-Phi	24	Heilmann-Det	326
Rice-Was	111	J.Sewell-Cle	204					Gehrig-NY	20	Sisler-StL	311

Runs Batted In		Runs Produced		Bases On Balls		Batting Average		On Base Percentage		Slugging Average	
Meusel-NY	138	Simmons-Phi	227	Mostil-Chi	90	Heilmann-Det	.393	Speaker-Cle	.479	Simmons-Phi	.599
Heilmann-Det	134	Heilmann-Det	218	Kamm-Chi	90	Speaker-Cle	.389	Cobb-Det	.468	Cobb-Det	.598
Simmons-Phi	129	Goslin-Was	211	Collins-Chi	87	Simmons-Phi	.387	Collins-Chi	.461	Speaker-Cle	.578
Goslin-Was	113	Meusel-NY	206	Bishop-Phi	87	Cobb-Det	.378	Heilmann-Det	.457	Heilmann-Det	.569
Sheely-Chi	111	Rice-Was	197	Blue-Det	83	Wingo-Det	.370	Wingo-Det	.456	Goslin-Was	.547

Production		Adjusted Production		Batter Runs		Adjusted Batter Runs		Clutch Hitting Index		Runs Created	
Cobb-Det	1.066	Cobb-Det	171	Heilmann-Det	52.5	Heilmann-Det	53.8	Galloway-Phi	155	Simmons-Phi	155
Speaker-Cle	1.057	Speaker-Cle	166	Simmons-Phi	51.4	Speaker-Cle	46.4	Blue-Det	148	Heilmann-Det	149
Heilmann-Det	1.026	Heilmann-Det	161	Speaker-Cle	47.0	Cobb-Det	46.3	Collins-Chi	144	Goslin-Was	131
Simmons-Phi	1.018	Wingo-Det	151	Cobb-Det	45.3	Simmons-Phi	45.3	Falk-Chi	136	Speaker-Cle	123
Wingo-Det	.983	Simmons-Phi	146	Wingo-Det	35.3	Wingo-Det	36.3	J.Sewell-Cle	133	Cobb-Det	118

Total Average		Stolen Bases		Stolen Base Average		Stolen Base Runs		Fielding Runs		Total Player Rating	
Speaker-Cle	1.231	Mostil-Chi	43	Blue-Det	79.2	Goslin-Was	3.0	Flagstead-Bos	20.0	J.Sewell-Cle	4.4
Cobb-Det	1.206	Rice-Was	26	Goslin-Was	76.5	Haney-Det	2.7	J.Sewell-Cle	16.3	Speaker-Cle	4.3
Heilmann-Det	1.113	Goslin-Was	26	Collins-Chi	76.0	Blue-Det	2.7	O'Rourke-Det	14.6	Heilmann-Det	3.3
Wingo-Det	1.041			Rice-Was	70.3	Collins-Chi	2.1	Goslin-Was	13.6	Goslin-Was	3.3
Collins-Chi	1.028			Mostil-Chi	67.2	Peckinpaugh-Was	1.5	Sisler-StL	10.8	Cobb-Det	3.1

Wins		Win Percentage		Games		Complete Games		Shutouts		Saves	
Rommel-Phi	21	Coveleski-Was	.800	Marberry-Was	55	Smith-Cle	22	Lyons-Chi	5	Marberry-Was	15
Lyons-Chi	21	Johnson-Was	.741	Walberg-Phi	53	Ehmke-Bos	22	Gray-Phi	4	Doyle-Det	8
Johnson-Was	20	Ruether-Was	.720	Vangilder-StL	52	Pennock-NY	21	Giard-StL	4	Connally-Chi	8
Coveleski-Was	20	Blankenship-Chi	.680	Rommel-Phi	52	Lyons-Chi	19			Walberg-Phi	7
Harriss-Phi	19	Rommel-Phi	.677	Pennock-NY	47	Wingfield-Bos	18				

Innings Pitched		Fewest Hits/Game		Fewest BB/Game		Strikeouts		Strikeouts/Game		Ratio	
Pennock-NY	277.0	Johnson-Was	8.29	Smith-Cle	1.82	Grove-Phi	116	Grove-Phi	5.30	Pennock-NY	11.05
Lyons-Chi	262.2	Blankenship-Chi	8.46	Quinn-Bos-Phi	1.85	Johnson-Was	108	Johnson-Was	4.24	Blankenship-Chi	11.13
Rommel-Phi	261.0	Coveleski-Was	8.59	Shocker-NY	2.14	Harriss-Phi	95	Shawkey-NY	3.92	Coveleski-Was	11.39
Ehmke-Bos	260.2	Pennock-NY	8.68	Faber-Chi	2.23	Ehmke-Bos	95	Walberg-Phi	3.85	Johnson-Was	11.63
Wingfield-Bos	254.1	Gray-Phi	8.79	Pennock-NY	2.31	Jones-NY	92	Gray-Phi	3.54	Gray-Phi	11.71

Earned Run Average		Adjusted ERA		Opponents' Batting Avg.		Opponents' On Base Pct.		Starter Runs		Adjusted Starter Runs	
Coveleski-Was	2.84	Coveleski-Was	149	Johnson-Was	.243	Pennock-NY	.303	Pennock-NY	44.2	Pennock-NY	40.2
Pennock-NY	2.96	Pennock-NY	144	Blankenship-Chi	.253	Blankenship-Chi	.308	Coveleski-Was	41.7	Coveleski-Was	37.2
Blankenship-Chi	3.03	Gray-Phi	142	Pennock-NY	.254	Johnson-Was	.311	Blankenship-Chi	35.3	Harriss-Phi	32.5
Johnson-Was	3.07	Johnson-Was	138	Coveleski-Was	.255	Coveleski-Was	.312	Johnson-Was	33.8	Gray-Phi	31.2
Dauss-Det	3.16	Blankenship-Chi	137	Gray-Phi	.260	Gray-Phi	.319	Lyons-Chi	33.3	Johnson-Was	29.6

Clutch Pitching Index		Relief Runs		Adjusted Relief Runs		Relief Ranking		Total Pitcher Index		Total Baseball Ranking	
Dauss-Det	119	Marberry-Was	9.6	Marberry-Was	7.8	Marberry-Was	13.4	Johnson-Was	4.0	J.Sewell-Cle	4.4
Shocker-NY	114	Gregg-Was	2.3	Gregg-Was	.9	Gregg-Was	.5	Harriss-Phi	3.3	Speaker-Cle	4.3
Zachary-Was	113							Pennock-NY	3.3	Johnson-Was	4.0
Lyons-Chi	111							Rommel-Phi	3.2	Heilmann-Det	3.3
Shawkey-NY	110							Coveleski-Was	2.9	Goslin-Was	3.3

TEAM	G	W	L	PCT	GB	R	OR	AB	H	2B	3B	HR	BB	SO	AVG	OBP	SLG	PRO	PRO+	BR	/A	PF	CHI	RC	SB	CS	SBA	SBR
STL	156	89	65	.578		817	678	5381	1541	259	82	90	478	518	.286	.348	.415	.763	106	76	48	104	102	770	83			
CIN	157	87	67	.565	2	747	651	5320	1541	242	120	35	454	333	.290	.349	.400	.749	109	52	70	97	97	738	51			
PIT	157	84	69	.549	4.5	769	689	5312	1514	243	106	44	434	350	.285	.343	.396	.739	98	28	-9	105	104	713	91			
CHI	155	82	72	.532	7	682	602	5229	1453	291	49	66	445	447	.278	.338	.390	.728	99	7	-1	101	96	685	85			
NY	151	74	77	.490	13.5	663	668	5167	1435	214	58	73	339	420	.278	.325	.384	.709	97	-35	-26	99	104	631	94			
BRO	155	71	82	.464	17.5	623	705	5130	1348	246	62	40	475	464	.263	.329	.358	.687	91	-64	-53	99	100	607	76			
BOS	153	66	86	.434	22	624	719	5216	1444	209	62	16	426	348	.277	.335	.350	.685	98	-65	-2	91	99	612	81			
PHI	152	58	93	.384	29.5	687	900	5254	1479	244	50	75	422	479	.281	.337	.390	.727	96	5	-30	105	98	683	47			
TOT	618					5612		42009	11755	1948	589	439	3473	3359	.280	.338	.386	.724						608				

TEAM	CG	SH	SV	IP	H	H/G	HR	BB	SO	RAT	ERA	ERA+	OAV	OOB	PR	/A	PF	CPI	FA	E	DP	FW	PW	BW	SBW	DIF
STL	90	10	6	1398²	1423	9.2	76	397	365	11.8	3.67	106	.268	.322	24	36	102	96	.969	198	141	.3	3.6	4.7		3.4
CIN	88	14	8	1408²	1449	9.3	40	324	424	11.5	3.42	108	.270	.315	63	42	97	95	.972	183	160	1.3	4.2	6.9		-2.4
PIT	83	12	18	1379¹	1422	9.3	50	455	387	12.5	3.67	107	.271	.334	24	41	103	99	.965	220	161	-.9	4.1	-.9		5.2
CHI	77	13	14	1378¹	1407	9.2	39	486	508	12.6	3.26	118	.273	.340	86	89	101	113	.974	162	174	2.4	8.8	-.0		-6.1
NY	61	4	15	1341²	1370	9.2	70	427	419	12.2	3.77	100	.268	.327	8	-2	98	96	.970	186	150	.7	-.2	-2.6		.6
BRO	83	5	9	1361²	1440	9.5	50	472	517	12.8	3.82	100	.275	.338	0	0	100	98	.963	229	95	-1.5	.0	-5.2		1.3
BOS	60	9	9	1365¹	1536	10.1	46	455	408	13.4	4.01	88	.293	.354	-27	-70	93	105	.967	208	150	-.5	-6.9	-.2		-2.4
PHI	68	5	5	1334¹	1699	11.5	68	454	331	14.7	5.03	82	.315	.370	-179	-133	108	98	.964	224	153	-1.5	-13.1	-3.0		.0
TOT	610	72	84	10968		9.6				12.7	3.82		.280	.338					.968	1610	1184					

Runs		Hits		Doubles		Triples		Home Runs		Total Bases	
Cuyler-Pit	113	Brown-Bos	201	Bottomley-StL	40	Waner-Pit	22	Wilson-Chi	21	Bottomley-StL	305
Waner-Pit	101	Cuyler-Pit	197	Roush-Cin	37	Walker-Cin	20	Bottomley-StL	19	L.Bell-StL	301
Southworth-NY-StL	99	Adams-Chi	193	Wilson-Chi	36	Traynor-Pit	17	Williams-Phi	18	Wilson-Chi	285
Sand-Phi	99	L.Bell-StL	189					L.Bell-StL	17	Waner-Pit	283
								Southworth-NY-StL	16	Cuyler-Pit	282

Runs Batted In		Runs Produced		Bases On Balls		Batting Average		On Base Percentage		Slugging Average	
Bottomley-StL	120	Bottomley-StL	199	Wilson-Chi	69	Waner-Pit	.336	Waner-Pit	.413	Wilson-Chi	.539
Wilson-Chi	109	Cuyler-Pit	197	Waner-Pit	66	Leach-Phi	.329	Blades-StL	.409	Waner-Pit	.528
L.Bell-StL	100	Wilson-Chi	185	Sand-Phi	66	Brown-Bos	.328	Wilson-Chi	.406	L.Bell-StL	.518
Southworth-NY-StL	99	Southworth-NY-StL	182	Bancroft-Bos	64	L.Bell-StL	.325	Grantham-Pit	.400	Bottomley-StL	.506
Pipp-Cin	99	Hornsby-StL	178	Blades-StL	62	Roush-Cin	.323	Bancroft-Bos	.399	Herman-Bro	.500

Production		Adjusted Production		Batter Runs		Adjusted Batter Runs		Clutch Hitting Index		Runs Created	
Wilson-Chi	.944	Wilson-Chi	150	Waner-Pit	39.5	Wilson-Chi	38.3	Pipp-Cin	142	Waner-Pit	115
Waner-Pit	.941	Waner-Pit	144	Wilson-Chi	39.2	Waner-Pit	35.6	Butler-Bro	135	Wilson-Chi	115
L.Bell-StL	.901	Herman-Bro	136	L.Bell-StL	31.6	L.Bell-StL	28.5	Traynor-Pit	130	L.Bell-StL	112
Grantham-Pit	.890	L.Bell-StL	135	Williams-Phi	29.8	Williams-Phi	27.4	Burrus-Bos	125	Bottomley-StL	109
Herman-Bro	.875	Grantham-Pit	131	Bottomley-StL	25.2	Herman-Bro	23.3	Critz-Cin	124	Cuyler-Pit	105

Total Average		Stolen Bases		Stolen Base Average		Stolen Base Runs		Fielding Runs		Total Player Rating	
Wilson-Chi	1.031	Cuyler-Pit	35					Critz-Cin	24.0	Waner-Pit	3.5
Waner-Pit	1.022	Adams-Chi	27					Friberg-Phi	22.4	Wilson-Chi	3.2
Grantham-Pit	.938	Frisch-NY	23					Cooney-Chi	19.4	Cuyler-Pit	2.4
Blades-StL	.938	Douthit-StL	23					Thevenow-StL	18.4	Adams-Chi	2.3
L.Bell-StL	.929	Youngs-NY	21					Dressen-Cin	17.0	Jackson-NY	2.2

Wins		Win Percentage		Games		Complete Games		Shutouts		Saves	
Rhem-StL	20	Kremer-Pit	.769	Scott-NY	50	Mays-Cin	24	Donohue-Cin	5	Davies-NY	6
Meadows-Pit	20	Rhem-StL	.741	Willoughby-Phi	47	Petty-Bro	23	R.Smith-Bos	4	Scott-NY	5
Kremer-Pit	20	Meadows-Pit	.690	Donohue-Cin	47	Root-Chi	21	Blake-Chi	4	Kremer-Pit	5
Donohue-Cin	20	Mays-Cin	.613	Ulrich-Phi	45	Rhem-StL	20			Ehrhardt-Bro	4
Mays-Cin	19	Donohue-Cin	.588	May-Cin	45	Carlson-Phi	20				

Innings Pitched		Fewest Hits/Game		Fewest BB/Game		Strikeouts		Strikeouts/Game		Ratio	
Donohue-Cin	285.2	Petty-Bro	8.03	Donohue-Cin	1.23	Vance-Bro	140	Vance-Bro	7.46	Alexander-Chi-StL	10.06
Mays-Cin	281.0	Greenfield-NY	8.33	Alexander-Chi-StL	1.39	Root-Chi	127	May-Cin	5.53	Petty-Bro	10.71
Petty-Bro	275.2	Rhem-StL	8.41	Carlson-Phi	1.58	May-Cin	103	Jones-Chi	4.49	Kremer-Pit	10.74
Root-Chi	271.1	Jones-Chi	8.48	Mays-Cin	1.70	Benton-Bos	103	Blake-Chi	4.33	Donohue-Cin	10.90
Carlson-Phi	267.1	Bush-Chi	8.52	Lucas-Cin	1.75	Petty-Bro	101	Root-Chi	4.21	Mays-Cin	10.99

Earned Run Average		Adjusted ERA		Opponents' Batting Avg.		Opponents' On Base Pct.		Starter Runs		Adjusted Starter Runs	
Kremer-Pit	2.61	Kremer-Pit	151	Petty-Bro	.240	Alexander-Chi-StL	.281	Kremer-Pit	31.3	Kremer-Pit	34.1
Root-Chi	2.82	Root-Chi	136	Alexander-Chi-StL	.250	Petty-Bro	.296	Root-Chi	30.3	Root-Chi	30.9
Petty-Bro	2.84	Petty-Bro	134	Rhem-StL	.250	Kremer-Pit	.296	Petty-Bro	30.1	Petty-Bro	30.0
Bush-Chi	2.86	Bush-Chi	134	Greenfield-NY	.251	Donohue-Cin	.298	Fitzsimmons-NY	23.0	Carlson-Phi	27.0
Barnes-NY	2.87	Barnes-NY	131	Kremer-Pit	.252	Rhem-StL	.305	Mays-Cin	21.4	Fitzsimmons-NY	21.3

Clutch Pitching Index		Relief Runs		Adjusted Relief Runs		Relief Ranking		Total Pitcher Index		Total Baseball Ranking	
Jones-Chi	122	Hallahan-StL	1.1	Hallahan-StL	1.6	Hallahan-StL	1.3	Kremer-Pit	3.6	Kremer-Pit	3.6
Blake-Chi	119							Mays-Cin	3.1	Waner-Pit	3.5
Fitzsimmons-NY	118							Carlson-Phi	2.8	Wilson-Chi	3.2
Wertz-Bos	117							Root-Chi	2.6	Mays-Cin	3.1
Root-Chi	111							Petty-Bro	2.4	Carlson-Phi	2.8

TEAM	G	W	L	PCT	GB	R	OR	AB	H	2B	3B	HR	BB	SO	AVG	OBP	SLG	PRO	PRO+	BR	/A	PF	CHI	RC	SB	CS	SBA	SBR
NY	155	91	63	.591		**847**	713	5221	1508	262	75	**121**	642	580	.289	**.369**	**.437**	**.806**	118	123	134	98	98	866	79	60	55	-14
CLE	154	88	66	.571	3	738	612	5293	1529	333	49	27	455	331	.289	.349	.386	.735	97	-16	-22	101	**103**	735	88	44	44	-12
PHI	150	83	67	.553	6	677	**570**	5046	1359	259	65	61	523	449	.269	.341	.383	.724	89	-38	-78	106	101	680	56	49	53	-16
WAS	152	81	69	.540	8	802	761	5223	1525	244	**97**	43	555	369	**.292**	.364	.401	.765	108	48	66	98	**103**	780	**122**	89	**63**	-10
CHI	155	81	72	.529	9.5	730	665	5220	1508	314	60	32	556	381	.289	.361	.390	.751	105	24	50	96	96	761	121	77	55	**-9**
DET	157	79	75	.513	12	793	830	5315	**1547**	281	90	36	599	423	.291	.367	.394	.765	104	52	42	101	99	800	88	72	57	-12
STL	155	62	92	.403	29	682	845	5259	1449	253	78	72	437	465	.276	.335	.394	.729	91	-37	-70	105	100	698	62	71	55	-11
BOS	154	46	107	.301	44.5	562	835	5185	1325	249	54	32	465	450	.256	.321	.343	.664	81	-155	-132	97	101	586	48	51	48	-13
TOT	616					5831		41762	11750	2195	568	424	4232	3448	.281	.351	.392	.743							664	513	56	-108

TEAM	CG	SH	SV	IP	H	H/G	HR	BB	SO	RAT	ERA	ERA+	OAV	OOB	PR	/A	PF	CPI	FA	E	DP	FW	PW	BW	SBW	DIF
NY	63	4	20	1372¹	1442	9.5	56	478	486	12.8	3.86	100	.273	.337	24	-1	96	96	.966	210	117	-1.1	-.0	**13.0**	-.0	2.3
CLE	**96**	11	4	1374	1412	9.2	49	**450**	381	12.5	3.40	119	.271	.334	94	101	101	105	.972	173	153	1.1	9.8	-2.1	.2	2.1
PHI	62	10	16	1346	**1362**	9.1	38	451	**571**	12.3	**3.00**	139	**.268**	.330	152	174	104	114	.972	171	131	.9	**16.9**	-7.6	-.2	-1.9
WAS	65	5	**26**	1349¹	1489	9.9	45	566	418	14.0	4.34	89	.287	.361	-47	-71	96	98	.969	184	129	.2	-6.9	6.4	.3	5.9
CHI	85	**11**	12	1380	1426	9.3	47	506	458	12.7	3.74	103	.271	.336	42	16	96	96	**.973**	165	122	**1.6**	1.6	4.8	**.4**	-3.9
DET	57	10	18	1394²	1570	10.1	58	555	469	14.0	4.41	92	.291	.362	-60	-54	101	99	.969	193	151	.0	-5.2	4.1	.2	2.9
STL	64	5	9	1368	1549	10.2	86	654	337	14.7	4.66	92	.296	.378	-98	-59	107	105	.963	235	**167**	-2.6	-5.7	-6.8	.2	-.1
BOS	53	6	5	1362	1520	10.0	45	546	336	13.9	4.72	86	.293	.364	-107	-100	101	92	.970	193	143	-.2	-9.7	-12.8	.0	-7.9
TOT	545	62	110	10946¹		9.7				13.3	4.02		.281	.351					.969	1524	1113					

Runs		Hits		Doubles		Triples		Home Runs		Total Bases	
Ruth-NY	139	Rice-Was	216	Burns-Cle	64	Gehrig-NY	20	Ruth-NY	47	Ruth-NY	365
Gehrig-NY	135	Burns-Cle	216	Simmons-Phi	53	Gehringer-Det	17	Simmons-Phi	19	Simmons-Phi	329
Mostil-Chi	120	Goslin-Was	201	Speaker-Cle	52	Mostil-Chi	15	Lazzeri-NY	18	Gehrig-NY	314
Combs-NY	113	Simmons-Phi	199	Jacobson-StL-Bos	51	Goslin-Was	15	Williams-StL	17	Goslin-Was	308
Goslin-Was	105	Mostil-Chi	197	Gehrig-NY	47			Goslin-Was	17	Burns-Cle	298

Runs Batted In		Runs Produced		Bases On Balls		Batting Average		On Base Percentage		Slugging Average	
Ruth-NY	146	Ruth-NY	238	Ruth-NY	144	Manush-Det	.378	Ruth-NY	.516	Ruth-NY	.737
Lazzeri-NY	114	Gehrig-NY	226	Bishop-Phi	116	Ruth-NY	.372	Heilmann-Det	.445	Simmons-Phi	.564
Burns-Cle	114	Burns-Cle	207	Rigney-Bos	108	Heilmann-Det	.367	Bishop-Phi	.431	Manush-Det	.564
Simmons-Phi	109	Goslin-Was	196	Gehrig-NY	105	Burns-Cle	.358	Goslin-Was	.425	Gehrig-NY	.549
		Falk-Chi	186	Speaker-Cle	94	Goslin-Was	.354	Manush-Det	.421	Goslin-Was	.542

Production		Adjusted Production		Batter Runs		Adjusted Batter Runs		Clutch Hitting Index		Runs Created	
Ruth-NY	1.253	Ruth-NY	228	Ruth-NY	97.4	Ruth-NY	98.7	Judge-Was	144	Ruth-NY	196
Manush-Det	.985	Goslin-Was	155	Gehrig-NY	44.2	Gehrig-NY	45.5	Haney-Bos	138	Gehrig-NY	137
Heilmann-Det	.979	Gehrig-NY	154	Goslin-Was	42.3	Goslin-Was	44.3	Dugan-NY	136	Goslin-Was	131
Gehrig-NY	.969	Manush-Det	153	Heilmann-Det	41.7	Heilmann-Det	40.8	Sheely-Chi	135	Simmons-Phi	127
Goslin-Was	.967	Heilmann-Det	152	Manush-Det	38.2	Manush-Det	37.3	Burns-Cle	132	Mostil-Chi	122

Total Average		Stolen Bases		Stolen Base Average		Stolen Base Runs		Fielding Runs		Total Player Rating	
Ruth-NY	1.606	Mostil-Chi	35	McNeely-Was	75.0	Mostil-Chi	2.1	Dykes-Phi	26.4	Ruth-NY	8.1
Gehrig-NY	1.058	Rice-Was	25	Hunnefield-Chi	72.7	McNeely-Was	1.8	Rigney-Bos	19.6	Goslin-Was	4.7
Heilmann-Det	1.040	Hunnefield-Chi	24	Mostil-Chi	71.4	Kamm-Chi	1.8	Goslin-Was	18.5	Mostil-Chi	3.8
Manush-Det	1.029	McNeely-Was	18	J.Sewell-Cle	70.8	Hunnefield-Chi	1.8	Regan-Bos	17.4	Kamm-Chi	3.5
Goslin-Was	1.008	J.Sewell-Cle	17	Lazzeri-NY	69.6	Speaker-Cle	1.2	Mostil-Chi	17.1	Rigney-Bos	3.5

Wins		Win Percentage		Games		Complete Games		Shutouts		Saves	
Uhle-Cle	27	Uhle-Cle	.711	Marberry-Was	64	Uhle-Cle	32	Wells-Det	4	Marberry-Was	22
Pennock-NY	23	Pennock-NY	.676	Pate-Phi	47	Lyons-Chi	24			Dauss-Det	9
Shocker-NY	19	Shocker-NY	.633	Grove-Phi	45	Johnson-Was	22			Pate-Phi	6
Lyons-Chi	18	Faber-Chi	.625	Thomas-Chi	44	Grove-Phi	20			Grove-Phi	6
		Hoyt-NY	.571			Pennock-NY	19			Jones-NY	5

Innings Pitched		Fewest Hits/Game		Fewest BB/Game		Strikeouts		Strikeouts/Game		Ratio	
Uhle-Cle	318.1	Grove-Phi	7.92	Pennock-NY	1.45	Grove-Phi	194	Grove-Phi	6.77	Pennock-NY	11.52
Lyons-Chi	283.2	Thomas-Chi	8.13	Smith-Cle	1.48	Uhle-Cle	159	Thomas-Chi	4.59	Rommel-Phi	11.55
Pennock-NY	266.1	Uhle-Cle	8.48	Quinn-Phi	1.98	Thomas-Chi	127	Uhle-Cle	4.50	Johnson-Was	11.59
Johnson-Was	261.2	Lyons-Chi	8.50	Rommel-Phi	2.22	Johnson-Was	125	Johnson-Was	4.30	Grove-Phi	11.65
Shocker-NY	258.1	Buckeye-Cle	8.69	Wingfield-Bos	2.36	Whitehill-Det	109	Whitehill-Det	3.89	Lyons-Chi	11.90

Earned Run Average		Adjusted ERA		Opponents' Batting Avg.		Opponents' On Base Pct.		Starter Runs		Adjusted Starter Runs	
Grove-Phi	2.51	Grove-Phi	166	Thomas-Chi	.244	Pennock-NY	.313	Grove-Phi	43.1	Grove-Phi	47.4
Uhle-Cle	2.83	Uhle-Cle	143	Grove-Phi	.244	Rommel-Phi	.314	Uhle-Cle	42.1	Uhle-Cle	43.3
Lyons-Chi	3.01	Rommel-Phi	135	Lyons-Chi	.252	Hoyt-NY	.316	Lyons-Chi	31.6	Lyons-Chi	26.7
Rommel-Phi	3.08	Buckeye-Cle	131	Uhle-Cle	.253	Johnson-Was	.317	Coveleski-Was	24.5	Rommel-Phi	26.3
Buckeye-Cle	3.10	Lyons-Chi	128	Levsen-Cle	.261	Shocker-NY	.318	Rommel-Phi	22.7	Walberg-Phi	22.9

Clutch Pitching Index		Relief Runs		Adjusted Relief Runs		Relief Ranking		Total Pitcher Index		Total Baseball Ranking	
Wingard-StL	128	Pate-Phi	16.4	Pate-Phi	18.3	Marberry-Was	21.2	Uhle-Cle	4.7	Ruth-NY	8.1
Zachary-StL	122	Marberry-Was	15.6	Marberry-Was	13.2	Pate-Phi	15.3	Grove-Phi	4.1	Goslin-Was	4.7
Grove-Phi	119	Braxton-NY	10.0	Braxton-NY	8.8	Braxton-NY	7.7	Lyons-Chi	3.0	Uhle-Cle	4.7
Coveleski-Was	117	Russell-Bos	4.7	Russell-Bos	5.3	Russell-Bos	2.4	Zachary-StL	2.7	Grove-Phi	4.1
Buckeye-Cle	114							Rommel-Phi	2.6	Mostil-Chi	3.8

1927 National League

TEAM	G	W	L	PCT	GB	R	OR	AB	H	2B	3B	HR	BB	SO	AVG	OBP	SLG	PRO	PRO+	BR	/A	PF	CHI	RC	SB	CS	SBA	SBR
PIT	156	94	60	.610		817	659	5397	1648	257	78	54	437	355	.305	.361	.412	.773	105	98	47	107	100	790	65			
STL	153	92	61	.601	1.5	754	665	5207	1450	264	79	84	484	511	.278	.343	.408	.751	103	47	25	103	101	723	110			
NY	155	92	62	.597	2	817	720	5372	1594	251	62	109	461	462	.297	.356	.427	.783	116	113	114	100	98	805	73			
CHI	153	85	68	.556	8.5	750	661	5303	1505	266	63	74	481	492	.284	.346	.400	.746	105	43	41	100	99	730	65			
CIN	153	75	78	.490	18.5	643	653	5185	1439	222	77	29	402	332	.278	.332	.367	.699	95	-46	-24	97	99	628	62			
BRO	154	65	88	.425	28.5	541	619	5193	1314	195	74	39	368	494	.253	.306	.342	.648	78	-151	-153	100	101	539	106			
BOS	155	60	94	.390	34	651	771	5370	1498	216	61	37	346	363	.279	.326	.363	.689	97	-72	-16	92	103	626	100			
PHI	155	51	103	.331	43	678	903	5317	1487	216	46	57	434	482	.280	.337	.370	.707	93	-29	-38	101	100	660	68			
TOT	617					5651		42344	11935	1887	540	483	3413	3491	.282	.339	.386	.725						649				

TEAM	CG	SH	SV	IP	H	H/G	HR	BB	SO	RAT	ERA	ERA+	OAV	OOB	PR	/A	PF	CPI	FA	E	DP	FW	PW	BW	SBW	DIF
PIT	90	10	10	1385	1400	9.1	58	418	435	12.0	3.66	112	.266	.323	39	68	105	95	.969	187	130	.6	6.7	4.6		5.0
STL	89	14	11	1367[1]	1416	9.3	72	363	394	11.8	3.57	110	.270	.320	51	56	101	99	.966	213	170	-1.0	5.5	2.5		8.5
NY	65	7	16	1381[2]	1520	9.9	77	453	442	13.0	3.97	97	.282	.341	-8	-17	98	102	.969	195	160	.1	-1.7	11.3		5.3
CHI	75	11	5	1385	1439	9.4	50	514	465	12.9	3.65	106	.273	.341	40	31	99	104	.971	181	152	.8	3.1	4.0		.6
CIN	87	12	12	1368	1472	9.7	36	316	407	11.9	3.54	107	.281	.324	56	36	97	100	.973	165	160	1.6	3.6	-2.4		-4.3
BRO	74	7	10	1375[1]	1382	9.0	63	418	574	11.9	3.36	118	.265	.322	85	90	101	103	.963	229	117	-1.8	8.9	-15.1		-3.5
BOS	52	3	11	1390	1602	10.4	43	468	402	13.6	4.22	88	.296	.355	-47	-78	95	102	.963	231	130	-1.8	-7.7	-1.6		-5.9
PHI	81	5	6	1355[1]	1710	11.4	84	462	377	14.7	5.36	77	.316	.374	-217	-186	106	96	.972	169	152	1.5	-18.4	-3.8		-5.4
TOT	613	69	81	11007[2]		9.8				12.7	3.91		.282	.339					.969	1570	1171					

Runs		Hits		Doubles		Triples		Home Runs		Total Bases	
L.Waner-Pit	133	P.Waner-Pit	237	Stephenson-Chi	46	P.Waner-Pit	18	Wilson-Chi	30	P.Waner-Pit	342
Hornsby-NY	133	L.Waner-Pit	223	P.Waner-Pit	42	Bottomley-StL	15	Williams-Phi	30	Hornsby-NY	333
Wilson-Chi	119	Frisch-StL	208	Lindstrom-NY	36	Thompson-Phi	14	Hornsby-NY	26	Wilson-Chi	319
P.Waner-Pit	114	Hornsby-NY	205	Dressen-Cin	36	Terry-NY	13	Terry-NY	20	Terry-NY	307
Frisch-StL	112	Stephenson-Chi	199	Brown-Bos	35	Wilson-Chi	12	Bottomley-StL	19	Bottomley-StL	292

Runs Batted In		Runs Produced		Bases On Balls		Batting Average		On Base Percentage		Slugging Average	
P.Waner-Pit	131	P.Waner-Pit	236	Hornsby-NY	86	P.Waner-Pit	.380	Hornsby-NY	.448	Hornsby-NY	.586
Wilson-Chi	129	Hornsby-NY	232	Harper-NY	84	Hornsby-NY	.361	P.Waner-Pit	.437	Wilson-Chi	.579
Hornsby-NY	125	Wilson-Chi	218	Grantham-Pit	74	L.Waner-Pit	.355	Harper-NY	.435	P.Waner-Pit	.549
Bottomley-StL	124	Terry-NY	202	Bottomley-StL	74	Stephenson-Chi	.344	Stephenson-Chi	.415	Terry-NY	.529
Terry-NY	121	Bottomley-StL	200			Traynor-Pit	.342	Harris-Pit	.402	Bottomley-StL	.509

Production		Adjusted Production		Batter Runs		Adjusted Batter Runs		Clutch Hitting Index		Runs Created	
Hornsby-NY	1.035	Hornsby-NY	175	Hornsby-NY	62.5	Hornsby-NY	62.7	Wright-Pit	157	Hornsby-NY	148
P.Waner-Pit	.986	Wilson-Chi	159	P.Waner-Pit	55.6	P.Waner-Pit	49.7	Bressler-Cin	155	P.Waner-Pit	145
Wilson-Chi	.980	P.Waner-Pit	152	Wilson-Chi	45.7	Wilson-Chi	45.6	Traynor-Pit	142	Wilson-Chi	126
Harper-NY	.930	Harper-NY	149	Harper-NY	37.1	Harper-NY	37.2	Farrell-NY-Bos	141	Stephenson-Chi	117
Terry-NY	.907	Stephenson-Chi	141	Stephenson-Chi	35.7	Stephenson-Chi	35.6	Felix-Bro	131	Bottomley-StL	112

Total Average		Stolen Bases		Stolen Base Average		Stolen Base Runs		Fielding Runs		Total Player Rating	
Hornsby-NY	1.190	Frisch-StL	48					Frisch-StL	48.6	Frisch-StL	6.6
Wilson-Chi	1.088	Carey-Bro	32					Jackson-NY	27.9	Hornsby-NY	6.1
P.Waner-Pit	1.062	Hendrick-Bro	29					Friberg-Phi	25.3	Jackson-NY	5.3
Harper-NY	1.037	Adams-Chi	26					Beck-Chi	22.0	P.Waner-Pit	4.9
Stephenson-Chi	.955	Richbourg-Bos	24					Cooney-Chi-Phi	14.8	Wilson-Chi	3.3

Wins		Win Percentage		Games		Complete Games		Shutouts		Saves	
Root-Chi	26	Benton-Bos-NY	.708	Scott-Phi	48	Vance-Bro	25	Haines-StL	6	Sherdel-StL	6
Haines-StL	24	Haines-StL	.706	Root-Chi	48	Meadows-Pit	25	Root-Chi	4	Nehf-Cin-Chi	5
Hill-Pit	22	Kremer-Pit	.704	Ehrhardt-Bro	46	Haines-StL	25	Lucas-Cin	4	Mogridge-Bos	5
Alexander-StL	21	Grimes-NY	.704	Henry-NY	45	Hill-Pit	22	Kremer-Pit	3	Henry-NY	4
		Alexander-StL	.677	May-Cin	44	Alexander-StL	22				

Innings Pitched		Fewest Hits/Game		Fewest BB/Game		Strikeouts		Strikeouts/Game		Ratio	
Root-Chi	309.0	Vance-Bro	7.97	Alexander-StL	1.28	Vance-Bro	184	Vance-Bro	6.06	Alexander-StL	10.07
Haines-StL	300.2	Kremer-Pit	8.16	Lucas-Cin	1.46	Root-Chi	145	Elliott-Bro	4.73	Lucas-Cin	10.14
Meadows-Pit	299.1	Haines-StL	8.17	Donohue-Cin	1.51	May-Cin	121	May-Cin	4.62	Kremer-Pit	10.27
Hill-Pit	277.2	Bush-Chi	8.24	Carlson-Phi-Chi	1.63	Grimes-NY	102	Pruett-Phi	4.35	Vance-Bro	10.44
Vance-Bro	273.1	Hill-Pit	8.43	Henry-NY	1.70	Petty-Bro	101	Root-Chi	4.22	Petty-Bro	10.60

Earned Run Average		Adjusted ERA		Opponents' Batting Avg.		Opponents' On Base Pct.		Starter Runs		Adjusted Starter Runs	
Kremer-Pit	2.47	Kremer-Pit	166	Vance-Bro	.239	Alexander-StL	.286	Alexander-StL	41.5	Alexander-StL	42.5
Alexander-StL	2.52	Alexander-StL	157	Kremer-Pit	.244	Lucas-Cin	.287	Haines-StL	39.8	Kremer-Pit	41.1
Vance-Bro	2.70	Vance-Bro	147	Haines-StL	.245	Kremer-Pit	.289	Vance-Bro	36.9	Haines-StL	40.8
Haines-StL	2.72	Haines-StL	145	Hill-Pit	.249	Vance-Bro	.291	Kremer-Pit	36.3	Vance-Bro	38.2
Petty-Bro	2.98	Petty-Bro	133	Bush-Chi	.250	Petty-Bro	.293	Petty-Bro	28.1	Petty-Bro	29.4

Clutch Pitching Index		Relief Runs		Adjusted Relief Runs		Relief Ranking		Total Pitcher Index		Total Baseball Ranking	
Blake-Chi	117	Clark-Bro	13.0	Clark-Bro	13.4	Clark-Bro	15.5	Alexander-StL	5.0	Frisch-StL	6.6
McWeeny-Bro	116	Ehrhardt-Bro	3.6	Cvengros-Pit	4.5	Ehrhardt-Bro	4.0	Haines-StL	4.2	Hornsby-NY	6.1
R.Smith-Bos	114	Cvengros-Pit	3.3	Ehrhardt-Bro	4.1	Cvengros-Pit	2.4	Kremer-Pit	3.9	Jackson-NY	5.3
Donohue-Cin	111	Songer-Pit-NY	1.9	Songer-Pit-NY	1.7	Songer-Pit-NY	2.3	Vance-Bro	3.5	Alexander-StL	5.0
Alexander-StL	109	H.Bell-StL	.1			H.Bell-StL	.0	Hill-Pit	3.0	P.Waner-Pit	4.9

TEAM	G	W	L	PCT	GB	R	OR	AB	H	2B	3B	HR	BB	SO	AVG	OBP	SLG	PRO	PRO+	BR	/A	PF	CHI	RC	SB	CS	SBA	SBR
NY	155	110	44	.714		975	599	5347	1644	291	103	158	635	605	.307	.383	.489	.872	135	235	258	97	95	1016	90	64	57	-14
PHI	155	91	63	.591	19	841	726	5296	1606	281	70	56	551	326	.303	.372	.414	.786	103	79	35	106	99	839	98	63	53	-12
WAS	157	85	69	.552	25	782	730	5389	1549	268	87	29	498	359	.287	.351	.386	.737	97	-24	-14	99	104	758	133	52	50	-13
DET	156	82	71	.536	27.5	845	805	5299	1533	282	100	51	587	420	.289	.363	.409	.772	104	47	36	101	103	814	141	73	59	-13
CHI	153	70	83	.458	39.5	662	708	5157	1433	285	61	36	493	389	.278	.344	.378	.722	94	-53	-34	98	95	685	90	75	56	-10
CLE	153	66	87	.431	43.5	668	766	5202	1471	321	52	26	381	366	.283	.337	.379	.716	90	-69	-74	101	99	668	63	72	56	-11
STL	155	59	94	.386	50.5	724	904	5220	1440	262	59	55	443	420	.276	.338	.380	.718	88	-67	-91	103	106	683	91	66	54	-12
BOS	154	51	103	.331	59	597	856	5207	1348	271	78	28	430	456	.259	.320	.357	.677	81	-148	-132	98	100	614	82	46	46	-13
TOT	619					6094		42117	12024	2261	610	439	4018	3341	.285	.352	.399	.751							788	511	61	-69

TEAM	CG	SH	SV	IP	H	H/G	HR	BB	SO	RAT	ERA	ERA+	OAV	OOB	PR	/A	PF	CPI	FA	E	DP	FW	PW	BW	SBW	DIF
NY	82	11	20	1389²	1403	9.1	42	409	431	11.9	3.20	120	.267	.322	144	99	93	104	.969	195	123	.7	9.4	24.5	-.5	-1.1
PHI	66	8	25	1384	1467	9.5	65	442	553	12.6	3.97	107	.277	.337	25	45	103	97	.970	190	124	1.0	4.3	3.3	-.3	5.7
WAS	62	10	23	1402	1444	9.3	53	491	497	12.7	3.97	102	.270	.336	26	13	98	93	.969	195	125	.8	1.2	-1.3	-.4	7.6
DET	75	5	17	1387²	1542	10.0	52	577	421	14.0	4.14	102	.289	.364	0	9	102	106	.968	206	173	.1	.9	3.4	-.4	1.5
CHI	85	10	8	1367	1467	9.7	55	440	365	12.7	3.91	103	.282	.342	34	19	98	101	.971	178	131	1.6	1.8	-3.2	-.1	-6.5
CLE	72	5	8	1353¹	1542	10.3	37	508	366	13.9	4.27	98	.294	.361	-20	-11	102	102	.968	201	146	.2	-1.0	-7.0	-.2	-2.4
STL	80	4	8	1353¹	1592	10.6	79	604	385	14.7	4.95	88	.303	.377	-122	-91	105	101	.960	248	166	-2.5	-8.6	-8.6	-.3	2.6
BOS	63	6	7	1366¹	1603	10.6	56	558	381	14.5	4.72	89	.304	.376	-88	-77	102	102	.964	228	167	-1.4	-7.3	-12.5	-.4	-4.4
TOT	585	59	116	11003¹		9.9				13.4	4.14		.285	.352					.967	1641	1155					

Runs		Hits		Doubles		Triples		Home Runs		Total Bases	
Ruth-NY	158	Combs-NY	231	Gehrig-NY	52	Combs-NY	23	Ruth-NY	60	Gehrig-NY	447
Gehrig-NY	149	Gehrig-NY	218	Burns-Cle	51	Manush-Det	18	Gehrig-NY	47	Ruth-NY	417
Combs-NY	137	Sisler-StL	201	Heilmann-Det	50	Gehrig-NY	18	Lazzeri-NY	18	Combs-NY	331
Gehringer-Det	110	Heilmann-Det	201	J.Sewell-Cle	48	Goslin-Was	15	Williams-StL	17	Heilmann-Det	311
Heilmann-Det	106	Goslin-Was	194	Meusel-NY	47	Rice-Was	14	Simmons-Phi	15	Goslin-Was	300

Runs Batted In		Runs Produced		Bases On Balls		Batting Average		On Base Percentage		Slugging Average	
Gehrig-NY	175	Gehrig-NY	277	Ruth-NY	138	Heilmann-Det	.398	Ruth-NY	.487	Ruth-NY	.772
Ruth-NY	164	Ruth-NY	262	Gehrig-NY	109	Gehrig-NY	.373	Heilmann-Det	.475	Gehrig-NY	.765
Heilmann-Det	120	Heilmann-Det	212	Bishop-Phi	105	Fothergill-Det	.359	Gehrig-NY	.474	Heilmann-Det	.616
Goslin-Was	120	Goslin-Was	203	Heilmann-Det	72	Cobb-Phi	.357	Bishop-Phi	.442	Williams-StL	.525
Fothergill-Det	114	Fothergill-Det	198	Blue-Det	71	Combs-NY	.356	Cobb-Phi	.440	Goslin-Was	.516

Production		Adjusted Production		Batter Runs		Adjusted Batter Runs		Clutch Hitting Index		Runs Created	
Ruth-NY	1.259	Ruth-NY	229	Gehrig-NY	100.8	Gehrig-NY	103.5	J.Sewell-Cle	133	Gehrig-NY	212
Gehrig-NY	1.240	Gehrig-NY	224	Ruth-NY	100.7	Ruth-NY	103.3	Cobb-Phi	130	Ruth-NY	208
Heilmann-Det	1.091	Heilmann-Det	179	Heilmann-Det	62.3	Heilmann-Det	61.3	Fothergill-Det	129	Heilmann-Det	150
Fothergill-Det	.929	Combs-NY	143	Simmons-Phi	44.1	Simmons-Phi	40.9	Hale-Phi	126	Combs-NY	138
Williams-StL	.928	Fothergill-Det	138	Combs-NY	37.1	Combs-NY	39.8	Barrett-Chi	124	Goslin-Was	119

Total Average		Stolen Bases		Stolen Base Average		Stolen Base Runs		Fielding Runs		Total Player Rating	
Ruth-NY	1.571	Sisler-StL	27	Harris-Was	85.7	Sisler-StL	3.9	Gehringer-Det	19.8	Ruth-NY	8.9
Gehrig-NY	1.500	Meusel-NY	24	Sisler-StL	79.4	Harris-Was	3.6	Falk-Chi	18.2	Gehrig-NY	8.2
Heilmann-Det	1.265	Neun-Det	22	Goslin-Was	77.8	Goslin-Was	2.7	Metzler-Chi	15.7	Heilmann-Det	4.2
Williams-StL	.959	Lazzeri-NY	22	Rice-Was	76.0			Bluege-Was	15.0	Simmons-Phi	3.6
Combs-NY	.955	Cobb-Phi	22	Neun-Det	75.9			Koenig-NY	13.8	Gehringer-Det	3.2

Wins		Win Percentage		Games		Complete Games		Shutouts		Saves	
Lyons-Chi	22	Hoyt-NY	.759	Braxton-Was	58	Lyons-Chi	30	Lisenbee-Was	4	Moore-NY	13
Hoyt-NY	22	Shocker-NY	.750	Marberry-Was	56	Thomas-Chi	24			Braxton-Was	13
Grove-Phi	20	Moore-NY	.731	Grove-Phi	51	Hoyt-NY	23			Marberry-Was	9
		Pennock-NY	.704	Moore-NY	50	Gaston-StL	21			Grove-Phi	9
		Lisenbee-Was	.667	Walberg-Phi	46						

Innings Pitched		Fewest Hits/Game		Fewest BB/Game		Strikeouts		Strikeouts/Game		Ratio	
Thomas-Chi	307.2	Moore-NY	7.82	Quinn-Phi	1.65	Grove-Phi	174	Grove-Phi	5.97	Moore-NY	10.35
Lyons-Chi	307.2	Thomas-Chi	7.93	Shocker-NY	1.85	Walberg-Phi	136	Braxton-Was	5.56	Braxton-Was	10.37
Hudlin-Cle	264.2	Pipgras-NY	8.01	Hoyt-NY	1.90	Thomas-Chi	107	Walberg-Phi	4.91	Lyons-Chi	10.47
Grove-Phi	262.1	Hadley-Was	8.02	Braxton-Was	1.91	Lisenbee-Was	105	Pipgras-NY	4.38	Hoyt-NY	10.53
Hoyt-NY	256.1	Lisenbee-Was	8.22	Lyons-Chi	1.96	Braxton-Was	96	Ruffing-Bos	4.38	Thomas-Chi	10.71

Earned Run Average		Adjusted ERA		Opponents' Batting Avg.		Opponents' On Base Pct.		Starter Runs		Adjusted Starter Runs	
Moore-NY	2.28	Moore-NY	169	Moore-NY	.234	Moore-NY	.289	Lyons-Chi	44.4	Lyons-Chi	41.3
Hoyt-NY	2.63	Hoyt-NY	146	Thomas-Chi	.244	Braxton-Was	.289	Moore-NY	43.9	Moore-NY	37.1
Shocker-NY	2.84	Lyons-Chi	143	Hadley-Was	.244	Lyons-Chi	.292	Hoyt-NY	42.8	Thomas-Chi	36.3
Lyons-Chi	2.84	Hadley-Was	142	Lisenbee-Was	.245	Hoyt-NY	.294	Thomas-Chi	39.4	Hoyt-NY	34.7
Hadley-Was	2.85	Braxton-Was	137	Braxton-Was	.246	Thomas-Chi	.303	Shocker-NY	28.9	Grove-Phi	31.2

Clutch Pitching Index		Relief Runs		Adjusted Relief Runs		Relief Ranking		Total Pitcher Index		Total Baseball Ranking	
Ruether-NY	121	Braxton-Was	20.4	Braxton-Was	19.1	Braxton-Was	24.6	Lyons-Chi	4.7	Ruth-NY	8.9
Gibson-Det	119	Burke-Was	1.9	G.Smith-Det	2.3	G.Smith-Det	1.5	Moore-NY	3.8	Gehrig-NY	8.2
Pennock-NY	118	G.Smith-Det	1.8	Burke-Was	1.1	Burke-Was	.5	Hoyt-NY	3.3	Lyons-Chi	4.7
Zachary-StL-Was	115							Hadley-Was	2.9	Heilmann-Det	4.2
Stoner-Det	114							Thomas-Chi	2.7	Moore-NY	3.8

TEAM	G	W	L	PCT	GB	R	OR	AB	H	2B	3B	HR	BB	SO	AVG	OBP	SLG	PRO	PRO+	BR	/A	PF	CHI	RC	SB	CS	SBA	SBR
STL	154	95	59	.617		807	636	5357	1505	292	70	113	568	438	.281	.353	.425	.778	108	73	59	102	99	802	82			
NY	155	93	61	.604	2	807	653	5459	1600	276	59	118	444	376	.293	.349	.430	.779	109	68	65	100	100	805	62			
CHI	154	91	63	.591	4	714	615	5260	1460	251	64	92	508	517	.278	.345	.402	.747	103	11	21	99	97	728	83			
PIT	152	85	67	.559	9	837	704	5371	1659	246	100	52	435	352	.309	.364	.421	.785	107	89	59	104	103	809	64			
CIN	153	78	74	.513	16	648	686	5184	1449	229	67	32	386	330	.280	.333	.368	.701	91	-75	-63	98	104	630	83			
BRO	155	77	76	.503	17.5	665	640	5243	1393	229	70	66	557	510	.266	.340	.374	.714	94	-45	-34	99	98	673	81			
BOS	153	50	103	.327	44.5	631	878	5228	1439	241	41	52	447	377	.275	.335	.367	.702	94	-69	-32	95	98	643	60			
PHI	152	43	109	.283	51	660	957	5234	1396	257	47	85	503	510	.267	.333	.382	.715	89	-48	-72	103	99	667	53			
TOT	614					5769		42336	11901	2021	518	610	3848	3410	.281	.344	.397	.741							568			

TEAM	CG	SH	SV	IP	H	H/G	HR	BB	SO	RAT	ERA	ERA+	OAV	OOB	PR	/A	PF	CPI	FA	E	DP	FW	PW	BW	SBW	DIF
STL	83	4	21	1415¹	1470	9.3	86	399	422	12.1	3.38	118	.270	.323	95	96	100	104	.974	160	134	1.3	9.4	5.8		1.5
NY	79	7	16	1394	1454	9.4	77	405	399	12.1	3.67	106	.273	.327	48	36	98	98	.972	178	175	.3	3.5	6.4		5.8
CHI	75	12	14	1380²	1383	9.0	56	508	531	12.5	3.40	113	.267	.336	89	67	96	105	.975	156	176	1.6	6.5	2.1		3.8
PIT	82	8	11	1354	1422	9.5	66	446	385	12.6	3.95	103	.274	.334	5	14	102	93	.967	201	123	-1.3	1.4	5.8		3.1
CIN	68	11	11	1371²1516		9.9	58	410	355	12.7	3.94	100	.289	.342	6	1	99	100	.974	162	194	1.1	.0	-6.2		6.9
BRO	75	16	15	1396	1378	8.9	59	468	551	12.1	3.25	122	.260	.324	113	110	100	101	.965	217	113	-2.0	10.8	-3.3		-4.9
BOS	54	1	6	1360	1596	10.6	100	524	343	14.2	4.83	81	.297	.363	-128	-140	98	97	.969	193	141	-.7	-13.7	-3.1		-9.0
PHI	42	4	11	1352²	1654	11.0	108	671	403	15.7	5.52	77	.314	.396	-231	-193	107	100	.971	181	171	-.0	-18.9	-7.0		-7.0
TOT	558	63	105	11024¹		9.7				13.0	3.98		.281	.344					.971	1448	1227					

Runs
P.Waner-Pit 142
Bottomley-StL 123
L.Waner-Pit 121
Douthit-StL 111
Frisch-StL 107

Hits
Lindstrom-NY 231
P.Waner-Pit 223
L.Waner-Pit 221
Richbourg-Bos ... 206
Traynor-Pit 192

Doubles
P.Waner-Pit 50
Hafey-StL 46
Hornsby-Bos 42
Bottomley-StL 42
Lindstrom-NY 39

Triples
Bottomley-StL 20
P.Waner-Pit 19
L.Waner-Pit 14
Bressler-Bro 13
Bissonette-Bro 13

Home Runs
Wilson-Chi 31
Bottomley-StL 31
Hafey-StL 27
Bissonette-Bro ... 25
Hornsby-Bos 21

Total Bases
Bottomley-StL 362
Lindstrom-NY 330
P.Waner-Pit 329
Bissonette-Bro ... 319
Hafey-StL 314

Runs Batted In
Bottomley-StL 136
Traynor-Pit 124
Wilson-Chi 120
Hafey-StL 111
Lindstrom-NY 107

Runs Produced
Bottomley-StL 228
P.Waner-Pit 222
Traynor-Pit 212
Lindstrom-NY 192
Hafey-StL 185

Bases On Balls
Hornsby-Bos 107
Douthit-StL 84
Bressler-Bro 80
Wilson-Chi 77
P.Waner-Pit 77

Batting Average
Hornsby-Bos 387
P.Waner-Pit 370
Lindstrom-NY 358
Sisler-Bos 340
Herman-Bro 340

On Base Percentage
Hornsby-Bos 498
P.Waner-Pit 446
Grantham-Pit 408
Stephenson-Chi ..407
Wilson-Chi 404

Slugging Average
Hornsby-Bos 632
Bottomley-StL 628
Hafey-StL 604
Wilson-Chi 588
P.Waner-Pit 547

Production
Hornsby-Bos ... 1.130
Bottomley-StL ... 1.030
Wilson-Chi 992
P.Waner-Pit 992
Hafey-StL 990

Adjusted Production
Hornsby-Bos 204
Bottomley-StL 163
Wilson-Chi 159
Hafey-StL 152
P.Waner-Pit 152

Batter Runs
Hornsby-Bos 72.5
P.Waner-Pit 53.4
Bottomley-StL 52.5
Wilson-Chi 42.1
Hafey-StL 38.5

Adjusted Batter Runs
Hornsby-Bos 76.3
Bottomley-StL 51.0
P.Waner-Pit 50.0
Wilson-Chi 43.1
Bissonette-Bro ... 37.5

Clutch Hitting Index
Traynor-Pit 172
Walker-Cin 137
Whitney-Phi 134
Ford-Cin 133
Wilson-Phi-StL ... 131

Runs Created
Hornsby-Bos 154
P.Waner-Pit 145
Bottomley-StL 142
Bissonette-Bro ... 125
Wilson-Chi 122

Total Average
Hornsby-Bos ... 1.409
Bottomley-StL ... 1.147
P.Waner-Pit ... 1.100
Wilson-Chi 1.090
Hafey-StL 1.055

Stolen Bases
Cuyler-Chi 37
Frisch-StL 29
Walker-Cin 19
Thompson-Phi..... 19

Stolen Base Average

Stolen Base Runs

Fielding Runs
Maguire-Chi 50.5
Jackson-NY 28.3
Douthit-StL 21.2
Lindstrom-NY 15.1
Leach-Phi 12.6

Total Player Rating
Hornsby-Bos ... 5.2
Jackson-NY 4.6
P.Waner-Pit 4.5
Lindstrom-NY ... 4.3
Hartnett-Chi 3.9

Wins
Grimes-Pit 25
Benton-NY 25
Vance-Bro 22
Sherdel-StL 21

Win Percentage
Benton-NY 735
Haines-StL 714
Bush-Chi 714
Fitzsimmons-NY ..690
Vance-Bro 688

Games
Grimes-Pit 48
Kolp-Cin 44
Rixey-Cin 43

Complete Games
Grimes-Pit 28
Benton-NY 28
Vance-Bro 24
Sherdel-StL 20
Haines-StL 20

Shutouts
Vance-Bro 4
McWeeny-Bro 4
Lucas-Cin 4
Grimes-Pit 4
Blake-Chi 4

Saves
Sherdel-StL 5
Haid-StL 5
Carlson-Chi 4
Benton-NY 4

Innings Pitched
Grimes-Pit 330.2
Benton-NY 310.1
Rixey-Cin 291.1
Vance-Bro 280.1
Fitzsimmons-NY . 261.1

Fewest Hits/Game
Vance-Bro 7.26
Blake-Chi 7.82
Malone-Chi 7.83
McWeeny-Bro ... 8.04
Root-Chi........ 8.13

Fewest BB/Game
Alexander-StL 1.37
Sherdel-StL 2.03
Benton-NY 2.06
Rixey-Cin 2.07
Grimes-Pit 2.10

Strikeouts
Vance-Bro 200
Malone-Chi 155
Root-Chi......... 122
Grimes-Pit 97
Benton-NY 90

Strikeouts/Game
Vance-Bro 6.42
Malone-Chi 5.57
Root-Chi........ 4.63
Clark-Bro 3.93
Ring-Phi 3.75

Ratio
Vance-Bro 9.79
Benton-NY 10.73
Grimes-Pit 10.81
Lucas-Cin....... 11.08
Alexander-StL .. 11.12

Earned Run Average
Vance-Bro 2.09
Blake-Chi 2.47
Nehf-Chi........ 2.65
Clark-Bro 2.68
Benton-NY 2.73

Adjusted ERA
Vance-Bro 190
Blake-Chi 156
Clark-Bro 148
Nehf-Chi........ 145
Benton-NY 143

Opponents' Batting Avg.
Vance-Bro 221
McWeeny-Bro 235
Malone-Chi 236
Blake-Chi 240
Root-Chi.........242

Opponents' On Base Pct.
Vance-Bro 277
Grimes-Pit 297
Benton-NY 300
Sherdel-StL 303
Lucas-Cin.........304

Starter Runs
Vance-Bro 59.0
Benton-NY 43.3
Blake-Chi 40.5
Grimes-Pit 36.3
Malone-Chi 31.9

Adjusted Starter Runs
Vance-Bro 58.5
Benton-NY 40.6
Grimes-Pit 38.8
Blake-Chi 36.7
Sherdel-StL 31.2

Clutch Pitching Index
Nehf-Chi......... 133
Bush-Chi 117
Blake-Chi 115
Kolp-Cin 114
Rhem-StL 114

Relief Runs

Adjusted Relief Runs

Relief Ranking

Total Pitcher Index
Vance-Bro 6.4
Grimes-Pit 5.8
Benton-NY 3.8
Blake-Chi 3.6
Sherdel-StL 3.1

Total Baseball Ranking
Vance-Bro 6.4
Grimes-Pit 5.8
Hornsby-Bos 5.2
Jackson-NY 4.6
P.Waner-Pit 4.5

TEAM	G	W	L	PCT	GB	R	OR	AB	H	2B	3B	HR	BB	SO	AVG	OBP	SLG	PRO	PRO+	BR	/A	PF	CHI	RC	SB	CS	SBA	SBR
NY	154	101	53	.656		894	685	5337	1578	269	79	133	562	544	.296	.365	.450	.815	123	146	169	97	100	888	51	51	53	-16
PHI	153	98	55	.641	2.5	829	615	5226	1540	323	75	89	533	442	.295	.363	.436	.799	111	115	95	103	97	843	59	48	48	-13
STL	154	82	72	.532	19	772	742	5217	1431	276	76	63	548	479	.274	.346	.393	.739	96	2	-20	103	104	736	76	43	47	-14
WAS	155	75	79	.487	26	718	705	5320	1510	277	93	40	481	390	.284	.346	.393	.739	100	1	6	99	97	743	110	59	56	-15
CHI	155	72	82	.468	29	656	725	5207	1405	231	77	24	469	488	.270	.334	.358	.692	88	-87	-76	99	102	641	139	82	59	-10
DET	154	68	86	.442	33	744	804	5292	1476	265	97	62	469	438	.279	.340	.401	.741	98	-1	-12	102	102	730	113	77	57	-10
CLE	155	62	92	.403	39	674	830	5386	1535	299	61	34	377	426	.285	.335	.382	.717	93	-48	-55	101	98	696	50	45	44	-12
BOS	154	57	96	.373	43.5	589	770	5132	1356	260	62	38	389	512	.264	.319	.361	.680	85	-118	-104	98	100	602	99	64	59	-15
TOT	617					5876		42117	11831	2200	620	483	3828	3719	.281	.344	.397	.741							697	469	60	-71

TEAM	CG	SH	SV	IP	H	H/G	HR	BB	SO	RAT	ERA	ERA+	OAV	OOB	PR	/A	PF	CPI	FA	E	DP	FW	PW	BW	SBW	DIF
NY	82	13	21	1375¹	1466	9.6	59	452	487	12.7	3.74	101	.276	.335	46	3	93	102	.968	194	136	-.0	.3	16.3	-.7	8.1
PHI	81	15	16	1367²	1349	8.9	66	424	607	11.8	3.36	119	.259	.317	102	97	99	99	.970	181	124	.6	9.4	9.2	-.4	2.7
STL	80	6	15	1374¹	1487	9.7	93	454	456	12.8	4.17	101	.281	.340	-20	3	104	100	.969	189	146	.2	.3	-1.9	-.5	6.9
WAS	77	15	10	1384	1420	9.2	40	466	462	12.5	3.88	103	.271	.334	24	18	99	94	.972	178	146	1.0	1.7	.6	-.6	-4.7
CHI	88	6	11	1378	1516	9.9	66	501	418	13.4	3.98	102	.286	.352	8	7	100	107	.970	186	149	.5	.7	-7.3	-.0	1.3
DET	65	5	16	1372	1481	9.7	58	567	451	13.7	4.32	95	.280	.354	-42	-33	102	97	.965	218	140	-1.5	-3.2	-1.2	-.0	-3.1
CLE	71	4	15	1378	1615	10.5	52	511	416	14.2	4.47	93	.303	.368	-65	-51	103	105	.965	221	187	-1.6	-4.9	-5.3	-.3	-2.9
BOS	70	5	9	1352	1492	9.9	49	452	407	13.2	4.39	93	.287	.349	-53	-44	102	94	.971	178	139	.9	-4.3	-10.1	-.6	-5.5
TOT	614	69	113	10981¹		9.7				13.0	4.04		.281	.344					.969	1545	1167					

Runs
Ruth-NY 163
Gehrig-NY 139
Combs-NY 118
Blue-StL 116
Gehringer-Det 108

Hits
Manush-StL 241
Gehrig-NY 210
Rice-Was 202
Combs-NY 194
Gehringer-Det 193

Doubles
Manush-StL 47
Gehrig-NY 47
Meusel-NY 45
Schulte-StL 44
Lind-Cle 42

Triples
Combs-NY 21
Manush-StL 20
Gehringer-Det 16

Home Runs
Ruth-NY 54
Gehrig-NY 27
Goslin-Was 17
Hauser-Phi 16
Simmons-Phi 15

Total Bases
Ruth-NY 380
Manush-StL 367
Gehrig-NY 364
Combs-NY 290
Heilmann-Det..... 283

Runs Batted In
Ruth-NY 142
Gehrig-NY 142
Meusel-NY 113
Manush-StL 108

Runs Produced
Gehrig-NY 254
Ruth-NY 251
Manush-StL 199
Blue-StL 182
Meusel-NY 179

Bases On Balls
Ruth-NY 135
Blue-StL 105
Bishop-Phi 97
Gehrig-NY 95
Judge-Was 80

Batting Average
Goslin-Was 379
Manush-StL 378
Gehringer-NY 374
Simmons-Phi 351
Miller-Phi 329

On Base Percentage
Gehrig-NY 467
Ruth-NY 461
Goslin-Was 442
Bishop-Phi 435
Manush-StL 414

Slugging Average
Ruth-NY 709
Gehrig-NY 648
Goslin-Was 614
Manush-StL 575
Simmons-Phi 558

Production
Ruth-NY 1.170
Gehrig-NY 1.115
Goslin-Was 1.056
Manush-StL 989
Simmons-Phi 954

Adjusted Production
Ruth-NY 210
Gehrig-NY 196
Goslin-Was 176
Manush-StL 153
Simmons-Phi 144

Batter Runs
Ruth-NY 83.9
Gehrig-NY 76.0
Manush-StL 50.3
Goslin-Was 49.0
Foxx-Phi......... 30.5

Adjusted Batter Runs
Ruth-NY 86.6
Gehrig-NY 78.6
Goslin-Was 49.4
Manush-StL 47.7
Foxx-Phi......... 28.9

Clutch Hitting Index
Meusel-NY 149
Judge-Was 144
Cissell-Chi 141
Kress-StL 136
Kamm-Chi 133

Runs Created
Ruth-NY 182
Gehrig-NY 169
Manush-StL 150
Goslin-Was 125
Combs-NY 114

Total Average
Ruth-NY 1.405
Gehrig-NY 1.256
Goslin-Was 1.203
Manush-StL ... 1.040
Simmons-Phi 951

Stolen Bases
Myer-Bos 30
Mostil-Chi 23
Rice-Det 20
Cissell-Chi 18
Bluege-Was 18

Stolen Base Average
Rice-Was 84.2
Goslin-Was 84.2
Judge-Was 80.0
Manush-StL 77.3

Stolen Base Runs
Rice-Was 3.0
Goslin-Was 3.0
Reynolds-Chi 2.7
Judge-Was........ 2.4
Manush-StL 2.1

Fielding Runs
Gerber-StL-Bos ... 32.0
J.Sewell-Cle 27.0
Jamieson-Cle 19.9
Mostil-Chi 17.8
Schulte-StL 17.3

Total Player Rating
Ruth-NY 6.9
Gehrig-NY 5.3
J.Sewell-Cle 5.1
Goslin-Was 4.5
Manush-StL 4.1

Wins
Pipgras-NY 24
Grove-Phi 24
Hoyt-NY 23
Crowder-StL 21
Gray-StL 20

Win Percentage
Crowder-StL 808
Hoyt-NY 767
Grove-Phi 750
Pennock-NY 739
Quinn-Phi 720

Games
Marberry-Was 48
Morris-Bos........ 47
Pipgras-NY 46
Rommel-Phi 43

Complete Games
Ruffing-Bos 25
Thomas-Chi 24
Grove-Phi......... 24
Pipgras-NY 22

Shutouts
Pennock-NY 5
Quinn-Phi 4
Pipgras-NY 4
Jones-Was 4
Grove-Phi 4

Saves
Hoyt-NY 8
Hudlin-Cle 7
Lyons-Chi 6
Braxton-Was 6

Innings Pitched
Pipgras-NY 300.2
Ruffing-Bos 289.1
Thomas-Chi 283.0
Hoyt-NY 273.0
Gray-StL 262.2

Fewest Hits/Game
Braxton-Was 7.30
Grove-Phi 7.84
Earnshaw-Phi 8.13
Jones-Was 8.37
Johnson-NY 8.50

Fewest BB/Game
Rommel-Phi...... 1.35
Quinn-Phi 1.45
Pennock-NY 1.71
Braxton-Was 1.81
Russell-Bos 1.83

Strikeouts
Grove-Phi........ 183
Pipgras-NY 139
Thomas-Chi 129
Ruffing-Bos 118
Earnshaw-Phi ... 117

Strikeouts/Game
Earnshaw-Phi 6.65
Grove-Phi 6.29
Johnson-NY 4.97
Walberg-Phi 4.28
Whitehill-Det 4.26

Ratio
Braxton-Was 9.32
Grove-Phi 10.08
Rommel-Phi 10.62
Pennock-NY 10.88
Hoyt-NY 11.21

Earned Run Average
Braxton-Was 2.51
Pennock-NY 2.56
Grove-Phi 2.58
Jones-Was 2.84
Quinn-Phi 2.90

Adjusted ERA
Braxton-Was 159
Grove-Phi 155
Pennock-NY 147
Jones-Was 141
Quinn-Phi 138

Opponents' Batting Avg.
Braxton-Was 222
Grove-Phi 229
Earnshaw-Phi 240
Johnson-NY 250
Jones-Was 252

Opponents' On Base Pct.
Braxton-Was 267
Grove-Phi 277
Rommel-Phi 295
Pennock-NY 302
Thomas-Chi 310

Starter Runs
Grove-Phi........ 42.4
Braxton-Was 37.0
Pennock-NY 34.7
Thomas-Chi 30.0
Jones-Was 29.8

Adjusted Starter Runs
Grove-Phi........ 41.5
Braxton-Was 36.2
Thomas-Chi 30.2
Gray-StL......... 29.4
Jones-Was 29.0

Clutch Pitching Index
Miller-Cle 119
Quinn-Phi 119
Blankenship-Chi .. 114
Pennock-NY 113
Adkins-Chi 113

Relief Runs

Adjusted Relief Runs
Simmons-Bos 5

Relief Ranking
Simmons-Bos 1

Total Pitcher Index
Grove-Phi......... 3.9
Jones-Was 3.7
Braxton-Was 3.2
Gray-StL.......... 3.1
Thomas-Chi 2.9

Total Baseball Ranking
Ruth-NY 6.9
Gehrig-NY 5.3
J.Sewell-Cle 5.1
Goslin-Was 4.5
Manush-StL 4.1

TEAM	G	W	L	PCT	GB	R	OR	AB	H	2B	3B	HR	BB	SO	AVG	OBP	SLG	PRO	PRO+	BR	/A	PF	CHI	RC	SB	CS	SBA	SBR
CHI	156	98	54	.645		982	758	5471	1655	310	46	139	589	567	.303	.373	.452	.825	110	92	90	100	104	916	103			
PIT	154	88	65	.575	10.5	904	780	5490	1663	285	116	60	503	335	.303	.364	.430	.794	100	28	7	102	104	850	94			
NY	152	84	67	.556	13.5	897	709	5388	1594	251	47	136	482	405	.296	.358	.436	.794	103	18	20	100	106	827	85			
STL	154	78	74	.513	20	831	806	5364	1569	310	84	100	490	455	.293	.354	.438	.792	100	12	3	101	100	819	72			
PHI	154	71	82	.464	27.5	897	1032	5484	1693	305	51	153	573	470	.309	.377	.467	.844	107	125	69	107	92	951	59			
BRO	153	70	83	.458	28.5	755	888	5273	1535	282	69	99	504	454	.291	.355	.427	.782	102	0	17	98	93	792	80			
CIN	155	66	88	.429	33	686	760	5269	1478	258	79	34	412	347	.281	.336	.379	.715	87	-132	-94	95	102	664	134			
BOS	154	56	98	.364	43	657	876	5291	1481	252	77	33	408	432	.280	.335	.375	.710	85	-141	-108	96	99	659	65			
TOT	616					6609		43030	12668	2253	569	754	3961	3465	.294	.357	.426	.783						692				

TEAM	CG	SH	SV	IP	H	H/G	HR	BB	SO	RAT	ERA	ERA+	OAV	OOB	PR	/A	PF	CPI	FA	E	DP	FW	PW	BW	SBW	DIF
CHI	79	14	21	1398²	1542	9.9	77	564	548	13.7	4.16	111	.285	.354	86	69	98	107	.975	154	169	1.4	6.3	8.2		6.1
PIT	79	5	13	1379	1530	10.0	96	439	409	13.0	4.36	109	.284	.340	53	62	101	98	.970	181	136	-.2	5.6	.6		5.5
NY	68	9	13	1372	1536	10.1	102	387	431	12.7	3.97	115	.287	.337	113	93	97	109	.975	158	163	.9	8.5	1.8		-2.7
STL	83	6	8	1359²	1604	10.6	101	474	453	13.9	4.66	100	.296	.356	7	-1	99	102	.971	174	149	.2	-.0	.3		1.6
PHI	45	5	24	1348	1743	11.6	122	616	369	16.0	6.13	85	.324	.397	-212	-141	110	99	.969	191	153	-.8	-12.8	6.3		1.8
BRO	59	8	16	1358	1553	10.3	92	549	549	14.2	4.92	94	.289	.359	-32	-48	98	95	.968	192	113	-.9	-4.4	1.5		-2.8
CIN	75	5	8	1369¹	1558	10.2	61	413	347	13.1	4.41	103	.291	.345	45	21	97	97	.974	162	148	.9	1.9	-8.6		-5.3
BOS	78	4	12	1352²	1604	10.7	103	530	366	14.4	5.12	91	.301	.367	-61	-68	99	99	.967	204	146	-1.5	-6.2	-9.8		-3.5
TOT	566	56	115	10937¹		10.4				13.9	4.71		.294	.357					.971	1416	1177					

Runs		Hits		Doubles		Triples		Home Runs		Total Bases	
Hornsby-Chi	156	O'Doul-Phi	254	Frederick-Bro	52	L.Waner-Pit	20	Klein-Phi	43	Hornsby-Chi	409
O'Doul-Phi	152	L.Waner-Pit	234	Hornsby-Chi	47	P.Waner-Pit	15	Ott-NY	42	Klein-Phi	405
Ott-NY	138	Hornsby-Chi	229	Hafey-StL	47	Walker-Cin	15	Wilson-Chi	39	O'Doul-Phi	397
Wilson-Chi	135	Terry-NY	226	Klein-Phi	45	Whitney-Phi	14	Hornsby-Chi	39	Wilson-Chi	355
L.Waner-Pit	134	Klein-Phi	219	Kelly-Cin	45			O'Doul-Phi	32	Herman-Bro	348

Runs Batted In		Runs Produced		Bases On Balls		Batting Average		On Base Percentage		Slugging Average	
Wilson-Chi	159	Hornsby-Chi	266	Ott-NY	113	O'Doul-Phi	.398	O'Doul-Phi	.465	Hornsby-Chi	.679
Ott-NY	151	Wilson-Chi	255	Grantham-Pit	93	Herman-Bro	.381	Hornsby-Chi	.459	Klein-Phi	.657
Hornsby-Chi	149	Ott-NY	247	P.Waner-Pit	89	Hornsby-Chi	.380	Ott-NY	.449	Ott-NY	.635
Klein-Phi	145	O'Doul-Phi	242	Hornsby-Chi	87	Terry-NY	.372	Stephenson-Chi	.445	Hafey-StL	.632
Bottomley-StL	137	Klein-Phi	228	Walker-Cin	85	Stephenson-Chi	.362	Cuyler-Chi	.438	O'Doul-Phi	.622

Production		Adjusted Production		Batter Runs		Adjusted Batter Runs		Clutch Hitting Index		Runs Created	
Hornsby-Chi	1.139	Hornsby-Chi	178	Hornsby-Chi	74.1	Hornsby-Chi	73.9	Sheely-Pit	148	Hornsby-Chi	183
O'Doul-Phi	1.087	Ott-NY	166	O'Doul-Phi	68.5	O'Doul-Phi	62.0	Comorosky-Pit	144	O'Doul-Phi	180
Ott-NY	1.084	Herman-Bro	160	Ott-NY	58.4	Ott-NY	58.7	Kelly-Cin	143	Klein-Phi	158
Klein-Phi	1.065	O'Doul-Phi	157	Klein-Phi	53.2	Herman-Bro	51.4	Grimm-Chi	137	Ott-NY	157
Herman-Bro	1.047	Wilson-Chi	155	Herman-Bro	49.6	Wilson-Chi	48.8	Traynor-Pit	133	Wilson-Chi	148

Total Average		Stolen Bases		Stolen Base Average	Stolen Base Runs	Fielding Runs		Total Player Rating	
Hornsby-Chi	1.338	Cuyler-Chi	43			Whitney-Phi	21.3	Hornsby-Chi	7.0
Ott-NY	1.287	Swanson-Cin	33			Maranville-Bos	19.5	Ott-NY	5.2
O'Doul-Phi	1.247	Frisch-StL	24			Jackson-NY	19.2	Jackson-NY	4.3
Herman-Bro	1.205	Herman-Bro	21			English-Chi	15.4	O'Doul-Phi	4.2
Cuyler-Chi	1.181	Allen-Cin	21			Ott-NY	13.2	Whitney-Phi	3.7

Wins		Win Percentage		Games		Complete Games		Shutouts		Saves	
Malone-Chi	22	Root-Chi	.760	Bush-Chi	50	Lucas-Cin	28	Malone-Chi	5	Morrison-Bro	8
Root-Chi	19	Bush-Chi	.720	Willoughby-Phi	49			Root-Chi	4	Bush-Chi	8
Lucas-Cin	19	Grimes-Pit	.708	Sweetland-Phi	43			Fitzsimmons-NY	4	Koupal-Bro-Phi	6
		Malone-Chi	.688	Root-Chi	43						
		Kremer-Pit	.643	Collins-Phi	43						

Innings Pitched		Fewest Hits/Game		Fewest BB/Game		Strikeouts		Strikeouts/Game		Ratio	
Clark-Bro	279.0	Lucas-Cin	8.90	Vance-Bro	1.83	Malone-Chi	166	Malone-Chi	5.60	Lucas-Cin	10.87
Root-Chi	272.0	Hubbell-NY	9.17	Lucas-Cin	1.93	Clark-Bro	140	Vance-Bro	4.90	Hubbell-NY	11.62
Bush-Chi	270.2	Kremer-Pit	9.18	Petty-Pit	2.05	Vance-Bro	126	Clark-Bro	4.52	Kremer-Pit	11.65
Lucas-Cin	270.0	Johnson-StL	9.18	Hubbell-NY	2.25	Root-Chi	124	May-Cin	4.16	Petty-Pit	11.67
Hubbell-NY	268.0	Bush-Chi	9.21	Clark-Bro	2.29	Hubbell-NY	106	Root-Chi	4.10	Vance-Bro	11.67

Earned Run Average		Adjusted ERA		Opponents' Batting Avg.		Opponents' On Base Pct.		Starter Runs		Adjusted Starter Runs	
Walker-NY	3.09	Grimes-Pit	152	Lucas-Cin	.257	Lucas-Cin	.297	Grimes-Pit	40.8	Grimes-Pit	42.2
Grimes-Pit	3.13	Walker-NY	148	Johnson-StL	.265	Hubbell-NY	.313	Root-Chi	37.4	Root-Chi	34.4
Root-Chi	3.47	Root-Chi	133	Hubbell-NY	.265	Clark-Bro	.316	Malone-Chi	33.8	Malone-Chi	30.8
Malone-Chi	3.57	Johnson-StL	129	Bush-Chi	.265	Vance-Bro	.316	Lucas-Cin	33.3	Walker-NY	29.5
Lucas-Cin	3.60	Malone-Chi	129	Grimes-Pit	.269	Petty-Pit	.317	Walker-NY	32.0	Lucas-Cin	28.8

Clutch Pitching Index		Relief Runs		Adjusted Relief Runs	Relief Ranking	Total Pitcher Index		Total Baseball Ranking	
Mitchell-StL	129	Hill-Pit-StL	2.9	Hill-Pit-StL	3.3	Hill-Pit-StL	2.0	Grimes-Pit	5.0	Hornsby-Chi	7.0
Walker-NY	129	Cvengros-Chi	.5			Root-Chi	2.8	Ott-NY	5.2
Sweetland-Phi	116					Lucas-Cin	2.7	Grimes-Pit	5.0
Grimes-Pit	116					Malone-Chi	2.6	Jackson-NY	4.3
Malone-Chi	115					Bush-Chi	2.4	O'Doul-Phi	4.2

TEAM	G	W	L	PCT	GB	R	OR	AB	H	2B	3B	HR	BB	SO	AVG	OBP	SLG	PRO	PRO+	BR	/A	PF	CHI	RC	SB	CS	SBA	SBR
PHI	151	104	46	.693		901	**615**	5204	1539	288	76	122	543	440	.296	**.365**	.451	**.816**	111	**113**	85	104	**102**	875	61	38	39	-11
NY	154	88	66	.571	18	899	775	5379	1587	262	74	**142**	554	518	.295	.364	.450	.814	**123**	111	**162**	93	100	892	51	44	53	-18
CLE	152	81	71	.533	24	717	736	5187	1525	294	79	62	453	**363**	.294	.353	.417	.770	99	23	-4	104	92	759	75	85	**62**	-11
STL	154	79	73	.520	26	733	713	5174	1426	277	64	46	589	431	.276	.352	.381	.733	90	-32	-61	104	100	723	72	46	43	-11
WAS	153	71	81	.467	34	730	776	5237	1445	244	66	48	556	400	.276	.347	.375	.722	90	-55	-60	101	**102**	706	86	61	59	-16
DET	155	70	84	.455	36	**926**	928	5592	**1671**	339	97	110	521	496	**.299**	.360	**.453**	.813	113	110	106	100	101	**914**	95	72	55	**-10**
CHI	152	59	93	.388	46	627	792	5248	1406	240	74	37	425	436	.268	.325	.363	.688	82	-133	-123	99	101	631	**106**	67	55	-12
BOS	155	58	96	.377	48	605	803	5160	1377	285	69	28	413	494	.267	.325	.365	.690	85	-129	-111	98	99	616	85	80	59	**-10**
TOT	613					6138		42181	11976	2229	599	595	4054	3578	.284	.349	.407	.756							631	493	56	-106

TEAM	CG	SH	SV	IP	H	H/G	HR	BB	SO	RAT	ERA	ERA+	OAV	OOB	PR	/A	PF	CPI	FA	E	DP	FW	PW	BW	SBW	DIF
PHI	70	9	**24**	1357	**1371**	9.1	73	487	**573**	12.4	3.44	123	.263	.328	121	118	100	105	**.975**	**146**	117	**2.6**	**11.1**	8.0	.2	7.1
NY	64	12	18	1366²	1475	9.7	83	485	484	13.1	4.19	92	.277	.340	6	-51	91	96	.971	178	152	.8	-4.8	**15.3**	-.4	.1
CLE	80	8	10	1352	1570	10.5	56	488	389	13.9	4.05	109	.295	.357	27	56	105	**109**	.968	198	**162**	-.6	5.3	-.4	.2	.4
STL	83	**15**	10	1371	1469	9.6	100	**462**	415	12.8	4.08	108	.279	.339	24	51	104	102	**.975**	156	148	2.2	4.8	-5.8	.2	1.5
WAS	62	3	17	1354²	1429	9.5	**48**	496	494	12.9	4.34	98	.275	.342	-14	-15	100	89	.968	195	156	-.3	-1.4	-5.7	-.3	2.6
DET	82	5	9	1390¹	1641	10.6	73	646	467	15.0	4.96	86	.300	.377	-111	-104	101	100	.961	242	149	-3.0	-9.8	10.0	**.3**	-4.5
CHI	78	5	7	1357²	1481	9.8	84	505	328	13.4	4.41	97	.284	.351	-26	-21	101	98	.970	188	153	.0	-2.0	-11.6	.1	-3.6
BOS	**84**	9	5	1366²	1537	10.1	78	496	416	13.6	4.43	96	.291	.355	-28	-24	101	101	.965	218	159	-1.6	-2.3	-10.5	.3	-5.0
TOT	603		66	100	10916		9.9				13.4	4.24		.284	.349					.969	1521	1196					

Runs		Hits		Doubles		Triples		Home Runs		Total Bases	
Gehringer-Det	131	Gehringer-Det	215	Manush-StL	45	Gehringer-Det	19	Ruth-NY	46	Simmons-Phi	373
Johnson-Det	128	Alexander-Det	215	Johnson-Det	45	Scarritt-Bos	17	Gehrig-NY	35	Alexander-Det	363
Gehrig-NY	127	Simmons-Phi	212	Gehringer-Det	45	E.Miller-Phi	16	Simmons-Phi	34	Ruth-NY	348
Foxx-Phi	123	Fonseca-Cle	209	Fonseca-Cle	44			Foxx-Phi	33	Gehringer-Det	337
Ruth-NY	121	Manush-StL	204					Alexander-Det	25		

Runs Batted In		Runs Produced		Bases On Balls		Batting Average		On Base Percentage		Slugging Average	
Simmons-Phi	157	Simmons-Phi	237	Bishop-Phi	128	Fonseca-Cle	.369	Foxx-Phi	.463	Ruth-NY	.697
Ruth-NY	154	Ruth-NY	229	Blue-StL	126	Simmons-Phi	.365	Gehrig-NY	.431	Simmons-Phi	.642
Alexander-Det	137	Gehringer-Det	224	Gehrig-NY	122	Manush-StL	.355	Ruth-NY	.430	Foxx-Phi	.625
Gehrig-NY	126	Alexander-Det	222	Foxx-Phi	103	Lazzeri-NY	.354	Lazzeri-NY	.429	Gehrig-NY	.584
Heilmann-Det	120	Gehrig-NY	218	Cronin-Was	85	Foxx-Phi	.354	Fonseca-Cle	.426	Alexander-Det	.580

Production		Adjusted Production		Batter Runs		Adjusted Batter Runs		Clutch Hitting Index		Runs Created	
Ruth-NY	1.128	Ruth-NY	199	Foxx-Phi	63.1	Ruth-NY	66.9	Kress-StL	144	Foxx-Phi	154
Foxx-Phi	1.088	Foxx-Phi	171	Ruth-NY	61.9	Foxx-Phi	60.2	West-Was	141	Ruth-NY	150
Simmons-Phi	1.040	Gehrig-NY	170	Gehrig-NY	51.6	Gehrig-NY	57.4	Heilmann-Det	139	Gehrig-NY	146
Gehrig-NY	1.015	Lazzeri-NY	164	Simmons-Phi	50.3	Lazzeri-NY	49.3	Schulte-StL	136	Simmons-Phi	145
Lazzeri-NY	.991	Simmons-Phi	158	Lazzeri-NY	43.9	Simmons-Phi	47.4	Cochrane-Phi	130	Alexander-Det	140

Total Average		Stolen Bases		Stolen Base Average		Stolen Base Runs		Fielding Runs		Total Player Rating	
Ruth-NY	1.288	Gehringer-Det	27	Gehringer-Det	75.0	Gehringer-Det	2.7	Durocher-NY	26.2	Simmons-Phi	5.4
Foxx-Phi	1.261	Cissell-Chi	26	E.Miller-Phi	72.7	E.Miller-Phi	1.8	Kerr-Chi	24.0	Ruth-NY	4.8
Gehrig-NY	1.151	E.Miller-Phi	24	Myer-Was	72.0	Kamm-Chi	1.5	Melillo-StL	22.5	Lazzeri-NY	4.2
Simmons-Phi	1.097	Rothrock-Bos	23	Reynolds-Chi	67.9	Myer-Was	1.2	Simmons-Phi	17.3	Cochrane-Phi	3.6
Lazzeri-NY	1.041	Johnson-Det	20	Rice-Was	66.7	Goslin-Was	1.2	West-Was	15.0	Gehringer-Det	3.6

Wins		Win Percentage		Games		Complete Games		Shutouts		Saves	
Earnshaw-Phi	24	Grove-Phi	.769	Marberry-Was	49	Thomas-Chi	24	MacFayden-Bos	4	Marberry-Was	11
Ferrell-Cle	21	Earnshaw-Phi	.750	Earnshaw-Phi	44	Uhle-Det	23	Gray-StL	4	Moore-NY	8
Grove-Phi	20	Ferrell-Cle	.677	Gray-StL	43	Gray-StL	23	Crowder-StL	4	Shores-Phi	7
Marberry-Was	19	Walberg-Phi	.621	Ferrell-Cle	43	Hudlin-Cle	22	Blaeholder-StL	4	Ferrell-Cle	5
		Marberry-Was	.613			Lyons-Chi	21				

Innings Pitched		Fewest Hits/Game		Fewest BB/Game		Strikeouts		Strikeouts/Game		Ratio	
Gray-StL	305.0	Earnshaw-Phi	8.23	Russell-Bos	1.58	Grove-Phi	170	Grove-Phi	5.56	Marberry-Was	11.07
Hudlin-Cle	280.1	Wells-NY	8.33	Pennock-NY	1.60	Earnshaw-Phi	149	Earnshaw-Phi	5.27	Thomas-Chi	11.44
Grove-Phi	275.1	Marberry-Was	8.38	Thomas-Chi	2.08	Pipgras-NY	125	Pipgras-NY	4.99	Grove-Phi	11.83
Walberg-Phi	267.2	Walberg-Phi	8.61	Uhle-Det	2.10	Marberry-Was	121	Hadley-Was	4.52	Walberg-Phi	11.94
Crowder-StL	266.2	McKain-Chi	9.00	Quinn-Phi	2.18			Marberry-Was	4.35	Faber-Chi	11.96

Earned Run Average		Adjusted ERA		Opponents' Batting Avg.		Opponents' On Base Pct.		Starter Runs		Adjusted Starter Runs	
Grove-Phi	2.81	Grove-Phi	150	Earnshaw-Phi	.241	Marberry-Was	.308	Grove-Phi	43.7	Grove-Phi	43.3
Marberry-Was	3.06	Marberry-Was	139	Wells-NY	.248	Thomas-Chi	.310	Marberry-Was	32.9	Hudlin-Cle	34.3
Thomas-Chi	3.19	Thomas-Chi	134	Marberry-Was	.252	Grove-Phi	.316	Thomas-Chi	30.3	Marberry-Was	32.8
Earnshaw-Phi	3.29	Hudlin-Cle	133	Walberg-Phi	.254	Hudlin-Cle	.318	Hudlin-Cle	28.1	Thomas-Chi	31.4
Hudlin-Cle	3.34	Earnshaw-Phi	129	Grove-Phi	.262	Walberg-Phi	.320	Earnshaw-Phi	27.0	Earnshaw-Phi	26.6

Clutch Pitching Index		Relief Runs		Adjusted Relief Runs		Relief Ranking		Total Pitcher Index		Total Baseball Ranking	
McKain-Chi	130	Moore-NY	7					Grove-Phi	3.9	Simmons-Phi	5.4
N.Gaston-Bos	117							Hudlin-Cle	3.9	Ruth-NY	4.8
Shaute-Cle	116							Marberry-Was	3.0	Lazzeri-NY	4.2
Ferrell-Cle	116							Thomas-Chi	3.0	Grove-Phi	3.9
Collins-StL	113							Ferrell-Cle	2.9	Hudlin-Cle	3.9

TEAM	G	W	L	PCT	GB	R	OR	AB	H	2B	3B	HR	BB	SO	AVG	OBP	SLG	PRO	PRO+	BR	/A	PF	CHI	RC	SB	CS	SBA	SBR
STL	154	92	62	.597		1004	784	5512	1732	373	89	104	479	496	.314	.372	.471	.843	104	72	42	103	104	944	72			
CHI	156	90	64	.584	2	998	870	5581	1722	305	72	171	588	635	.309	.378	.481	.859	111	110	103	101	98	1001	70			
NY	154	87	67	.565	5	959	814	5553	1769	264	83	143	422	382	.319	.369	.473	.842	110	67	85	98	101	941	59			
BRO	154	86	68	.558	6	871	738	5433	1654	303	73	122	446	541	.304	.364	.454	.818	103	21	32	99	97	881	53			
PIT	154	80	74	.519	12	891	928	5346	1622	285	119	86	494	449	.303	.365	.449	.814	100	15	12	100	101	862	76			
BOS	154	70	84	.455	22	693	835	5356	1503	246	78	66	332	397	.281	.326	.393	.719	80	-185	-156	97	105	669	69			
CIN	154	59	95	.383	33	665	857	5245	1475	265	67	74	445	489	.281	.339	.400	.739	87	-134	-91	95	94	703	48			
PHI	156	52	102	.338	40	944	1199	5667	1783	345	44	126	450	459	.315	.367	.458	.825	97	37	-28	107	100	929	34			
TOT	618					7025		43693	13260	2386	625	892	3691	3848	.303	.360	.448	.808							481			

TEAM	CG	SH	SV	IP	H	H/G	HR	BB	SO	RAT	ERA	ERA+	OAV	OOB	PR	/A	PF	CPI	FA	E	DP	FW	PW	BW	SBW	DIF
STL	63	5	21	1380²	1595	10.4	87	477	641	13.7	4.39	114	.293	.353	88	94	101	104	.970	183	176	.2	8.3	3.7		2.8
CHI	67	6	12	1403²	1642	10.5	111	528	601	14.1	4.80	102	.293	.357	26	13	98	99	.973	170	167	1.0	1.1	9.1		1.7
NY	64	6	19	1363¹	1546	10.2	117	439	522	13.3	4.61	103	.289	.347	54	18	95	99	.974	164	144	1.3	1.6	7.5		-.3
BRO	74	13	15	1372	1480	9.7	115	394	526	12.4	4.03	122	.277	.329	143	133	99	102	.972	174	167	.7	11.7	2.8		-6.2
PIT	80	7	13	1361¹	1730	11.4	128	438	393	14.5	5.24	95	.313	.366	-40	-39	100	101	.965	216	164	-1.8	-3.4	1.1		7.1
BOS	71	6	11	1361	1624	10.7	117	475	424	14.0	4.91	100	.302	.360	8	3	99	102	.971	178	167	.4	.3	-13.8		6.1
CIN	61	6	11	1335	1650	11.1	75	394	361	13.9	5.08	95	.304	.354	-15	-36	97	92	.973	161	164	1.4	-3.2	-8.0		-8.2
PHI	54	3	7	1372²	1993	13.1	142	543	384	16.8	6.71	81	.345	.405	-265	-189	110	99	.962	239	169	-3.0	-16.7	-2.5		-2.9
TOT	534	52	109	10949²		10.9				14.1	4.97		.303	.360					.970	1485	1318					

Runs
Klein-Phi 158
Cuyler-Chi 155
English-Chi 152
Wilson-Chi 146
Herman-Bro 143

Hits
Terry-NY 254
Klein-Phi 250
Herman-Bro 241
Lindstrom-NY 231
Cuyler-Chi 228

Doubles
Klein-Phi 59
Cuyler-Chi 50
Herman-Bro 48
Comorosky-Pit 47
Frisch-StL 46

Tripels
Comorosky-Pit 23
P.Waner-Pit 18
English-Chi 17
Cuyler-Chi 17
Terry-NY 15

Home Runs
Wilson-Chi 56
Klein-Phi 40
Berger-Bos 38
Hartnett-Chi 37
Herman-Bro 35

Total Bases
Klein-Phi 445
Wilson-Chi 423
Herman-Bro 416
Terry-NY 392
Cuyler-Chi 351

Runs Batted In
Wilson-Chi 190
Klein-Phi 170
Cuyler-Chi 134
Herman-Bro 130
Terry-NY 129

Runs Produced
Klein-Phi 288
Wilson-Chi 280
Cuyler-Chi 276
Terry-NY 245
Herman-Bro 238

Bases On Balls
Wilson-Chi 105
Ott-NY 103
English-Chi 100
Grantham-Pit 81
Suhr-Pit 80

Batting Average
Terry-NY 401
Herman-Bro 393
Klein-Phi 386
O'Doul-Phi 383
Lindstrom-NY 379

On Base Percentage
Ott-NY 458
Herman-Bro 455
Wilson-Chi 454
O'Doul-Phi 453
Terry-NY 452

Slugging Average
Wilson-Chi 723
Klein-Phi 687
Herman-Bro 678
Hafey-StL 652
Hartnett-Chi 630

Production
Wilson-Chi 1.177
Herman-Bro 1.132
Klein-Phi 1.123
Terry-NY 1.071
Hafey-StL 1.059

Adjusted Production
Wilson-Chi 177
Herman-Bro 171
Terry-NY 159
Klein-Phi 155
Ott-NY 152

Batter Runs
Wilson-Chi 75.4
Herman-Bro 68.7
Klein-Phi 67.3
Terry-NY 57.6
O'Doul-Phi 46.9

Adjusted Batter Runs
Wilson-Chi 74.7
Herman-Bro 70.0
Klein-Phi 59.8
Terry-NY 59.8
Ott-NY 47.3

Clutch Hitting Index
Traynor-Pit 155
Thevenow-Phi ... 144
Whitney-Phi 140
Wright-Bro 130
Grimm-Chi 121

Runs Created
Wilson-Chi 189
Klein-Phi 186
Herman-Bro 183
Terry-NY 170
Cuyler-Chi 148

Total Average
Wilson-Chi 1.411
Herman-Bro 1.351
Klein-Phi 1.274
Ott-NY 1.224
Terry-NY 1.208

Stolen Bases
Cuyler-Chi 37
P.Waner-Pit 18
Herman-Bro 18

Stolen Base Average

Stolen Base Runs

Fielding Runs
Klein-Phi 27.9
Frisch-StL 27.7
Whitney-Phi 20.3
Cuyler-Chi 16.4
Heilmann-Cin 14.9

Total Player Rating
Klein-Phi 6.6
Terry-NY 5.7
Frisch-StL 5.1
Wilson-Chi 4.7
Lindstrom-NY 4.2

Wins
Malone-Chi 20
Kremer-Pit 20
Fitzsimmons-NY ... 19

Win Percentage
Fitzsimmons-NY ...731
Malone-Chi 690
Brame-Pit 680
Kremer-Pit 625
Hallahan-StL 625

Games
Elliott-Phi 48
Collins-Phi 47
Bush-Chi 46
Pruett-NY 45
Malone-Chi 45

Complete Games
Malone-Chi 22
Brame-Pit 22
French-Pit 21
Vance-Bro 20
Seibold-Bos 20

Shutouts
Vance-Bro 4
Root-Chi 4
Hubbell-NY 3
French-Pit 3

Saves
Bell-StL 8
Heving-NY 6
Clark-Bro 6

Innings Pitched
Kremer-Pit 276.0
French-Pit 274.2
Malone-Chi 271.2
Vance-Bro 258.2
Seibold-Bos 251.0

Fewest Hits/Game
Vance-Bro 8.39
Hallahan-StL 8.84
Fitzsimmons-NY . 9.23
Elliott-Bro 9.26
Clark-Bro 9.41

Fewest BB/Game
Clark-Phi 1.71
Kolp-Cin 1.82
Johnson-StL 1.82
Lucas-Cin 1.88
Vance-Bro 1.91

Strikeouts
Hallahan-StL 177
Vance-Bro 173
Malone-Chi 142
Root-Chi.......... 124
Hubbell-NY 117

Strikeouts/Game
Hallahan-StL 6.71
Vance-Bro 6.02
Root-Chi 5.07
Malone-Chi 4.70
Johnson-StL 4.41

Ratio
Vance-Bro 10.47
Clark-Bro 11.11
Kolp-Cin 11.44
Fitzsimmons-NY .11.63
Johnson-StL ... 12.33

Earned Run Average
Vance-Bro 2.61
Hubbell-NY 3.87
Walker-NY 3.93
Malone-Chi 3.94
Elliott-Bro 3.95

Adjusted ERA
Vance-Bro 188
Elliott-Bro 124
Malone-Chi 124
Grimes-Bos-StL ... 123
Hubbell-NY 122

Opponents' Batting Avg.
Vance-Bro .... .246
Hallahan-StL .... .260
Fitzsimmons-NY .266
Walker-NY ...... .268
Malone-Chi ..... .271

Opponents' On Base Pct.
Vance-Bro .... .289
Clark-Bro .... .306
Fitzsimmons-NY .314
Kolp-Cin .... .314
Hubbell-NY ..... .327

Starter Runs
Vance-Bro 67.9
Malone-Chi 31.1
Hubbell-NY 29.5
Walker-NY 28.5
Seibold-Bos 23.7

Adjusted Starter Runs
Vance-Bro 66.0
Malone-Chi 28.5
Hubbell-NY 23.2
Seibold-Bos 22.7
Walker-NY 22.2

Clutch Pitching Index
Grimes-Bos-StL .. 119
Smith-Bos 117
Haines-StL 109
Vance-Bro 108
Seibold-Bos 107

Relief Runs
Bell-StL 13.7
Lindsey-StL 6.4
Johnson-Cin 3

Adjusted Relief Runs
Bell-StL 14.3
Lindsey-StL 6.9

Relief Ranking
Bell-StL 10.0
Lindsey-StL 7.8

Total Pitcher Index
Vance-Bro 5.6
Malone-Chi 2.8
Grimes-Bos-StL .. 2.3
Fitzsimmons-NY .. 2.1
Collins-Phi 1.8

Total Baseball Ranking
Klein-Phi 6.6
Terry-NY 5.7
Vance-Bro 5.6
Frisch-StL 5.1
Wilson-Chi 4.7

TEAM	G	W	L	PCT	GB	R	OR	AB	H	2B	3B	HR	BB	SO	AVG	OBP	SLG	PRO	PRO+	BR	/A	PF	CHI	RC	SB	CS	SBA	SBR
PHI	154	102	52	.662		951	751	5345	1573	319	74	125	599	531	.294	.369	.452	.821	108	102	64	104	100	913	48	33	36	-11
WAS	154	94	60	.610	8	892	689	5370	1620	300	98	57	537	438	.302	.369	.426	.795	105	59	55	100	99	860	101	67	65	-18
NY	154	86	68	.558	16	1062	898	5448	1683	298	110	152	644	569	.309	.384	.488	.872	130	207	245	96	99	1035	91	60	48	-10
CLE	154	81	73	.526	21	890	915	5439	1654	358	59	72	490	461	.304	.364	.431	.795	102	54	21	104	99	863	51	47	49	-14
DET	154	75	79	.487	27	783	833	5297	1504	298	90	82	461	508	.284	.344	.421	.765	96	-17	-32	102	98	771	98	70	59	-13
STL	154	64	90	.416	38	751	886	5278	1415	289	67	75	497	550	.268	.333	.391	.724	85	-95	-122	103	104	696	93	71	55	-11
CHI	154	62	92	.403	40	729	884	5419	1496	256	90	63	389	479	.276	.328	.391	.719	89	-110	-81	97	102	705	74	40	42	-12
BOS	154	52	102	.338	50	612	814	5286	1393	257	68	47	358	552	.264	.313	.365	.678	79	-191	-159	96	100	608	42	35	45	-16
TOT	616					6670		42882	12338	2375	656	673	3975	4088	.288	.351	.421	.772							598	423	59	-73

TEAM	CG	SH	SV	IP	H	H/G	HR	BB	SO	RAT	ERA	ERA+	OAV	OOB	PR	/A	PF	CPI	FA	E	DP	FW	PW	BW	SBW	DIF
PHI	72	8	21	1371	1457	9.6	84	488	672	12.9	4.28	109	.273	.337	55	58	101	98	.975	145	121	3.0	5.2	5.8	-.2	11.1
WAS	78	6	14	1369	1367	9.0	52	504	524	12.5	3.96	116	.263	.332	103	96	99	97	.974	157	150	2.3	8.7	5.0	-.8	1.9
NY	65	7	15	1367²	1586	10.4	93	524	572	14.1	4.88	88	.290	.355	-35	-90	93	98	.965	207	132	-.7	-8.1	22.2	-.0	-4.2
CLE	68	5	14	1360	1663	11.0	85	528	41	14.6	4.88	99	.304	.368	-35	-9	104	107	.962	237	156	-2.5	-.8	1.9	-.4	5.9
DET	68	4	17	1351²	1507	10.0	86	570	574	14.0	4.70	102	.285	.359	-8	13	103	102	.967	192	156	.2	1.2	-2.9	-.3	-.1
STL	68	5	10	1371²	1639	10.8	124	449	470	13.9	5.07	96	.300	.356	-64	-30	105	101	.970	188	152	.4	-2.7	-11.0	-.2	.5
CHI	63	2	10	1361	1629	10.8	74	407	471	13.6	4.71	98	.300	.352	-10	-14	99	101	.962	235	136	-2.4	-1.3	-7.3	-.2	-3.7
BOS	78	4	5	1360¹	1505	10.0	75	488	356	13.3	4.68	98	.283	.346	-5	-11	99	95	.968	196	161	-.0	-1.0	-14.4	-.6	-8.9
TOT	560	41	106	10912¹		10.2				13.6	4.65		.288	.351					.968	1557	1164					

Runs
Simmons-Phi 152
Ruth-NY 150
Gehringer-Det 144
Gehrig-NY 143
Combs-NY 129

Hits
Hodapp-Cle 225
Gehrig-NY 220
Simmons-Phi 211
Rice-Was 207
Morgan-Cle 204

Doubles
Hodapp-Cle 51
Manush-StL-Was . . . 49
Morgan-Cle 47
Gehringer-Det 47

Triples
Combs-NY 22
Reynolds-Chi 18
Gehrig-NY 17
Simmons-Phi 16

Home Runs
Ruth-NY 49
Gehrig-NY 41
Goslin-Was-StL 37
Foxx-Phi 37
Simmons-Phi 36

Total Bases
Gehrig-NY 419
Simmons-Phi 392
Ruth-NY 379
Foxx-Phi 358

Runs Batted In
Gehrig-NY 174
Simmons-Phi 165
Foxx-Phi 156
Ruth-NY 153
Goslin-Was-StL . . . 138

Runs Produced
Simmons-Phi 281
Gehrig-NY 276
Ruth-NY 254
Foxx-Phi 246
Cronin-Was 240

Bases On Balls
Ruth-NY 136
Bishop-Phi 128
Gehrig-NY 101
Foxx-Phi 93
Blue-StL 81

Batting Average
Simmons-Phi 381
Gehrig-NY 379
Ruth-NY 359
Reynolds-Chi 359
Cochrane-Phi 357

On Base Percentage
Ruth-NY 493
Gehrig-NY 473
Foxx-Phi 429
Bishop-Phi 426
Combs-NY 424

Slugging Average
Ruth-NY 732
Gehrig-NY 721
Simmons-Phi 708
Foxx-Phi 637

Production
Ruth-NY 1.225
Gehrig-NY 1.194
Simmons-Phi 1.130
Foxx-Phi 1.066
Morgan-Cle 1.014

Adjusted Production
Ruth-NY 216
Gehrig-NY 207
Simmons-Phi 173
Foxx-Phi 159
Morgan-Cle 148

Batter Runs
Ruth-NY 89.5
Gehrig-NY 88.4
Simmons-Phi 64.2
Foxx-Phi 57.0
Morgan-Cle 46.3

Adjusted Batter Runs
Ruth-NY 93.7
Gehrig-NY 92.7
Simmons-Phi 60.5
Foxx-Phi 52.9
Morgan-Cle 42.8

Clutch Hitting Index
Lazzeri-NY 146
Rice-Det-NY 142
Cronin-Was 130
Alexander-Det 130
Hodapp-Cle 123

Runs Created
Gehrig-NY 195
Ruth-NY 191
Simmons-Phi 163
Foxx-Phi 154
Morgan-Cle 144

Total Average
Ruth-NY 1.509
Gehrig-NY 1.389
Simmons-Phi 1.272
Foxx-Phi 1.184
Morgan-Cle 1.089

Stolen Bases
McManus-Det 23
Gehringer-Det 19
Goslin-Was-StL 17
Johnson-Det 17
Cronin-Was 17

Stolen Base Average
Reynolds-Chi 80.0
McManus-Det 74.2
Cissell-Chi 64.0
Johnson-Det 63.0
Cronin-Was 63.0

Stolen Base Runs
Lary-NY 3.0
Reynolds-Chi 2.4
McManus-Det 2.1

Fielding Runs
Melillo-StL 26.8
Cronin-Was 26.2
Goldman-Cle 20.7
Oliver-Bos 15.2
Kamm-Chi 14.9

Total Player Rating
Ruth-NY 7.5
Cronin-Was 6.6
Gehrig-NY 6.3
Simmons-Phi 5.5
Cochrane-Phi 4.1

Wins
Grove-Phi 28
Ferrell-Cle 25
Lyons-Chi 22
Earnshaw-Phi 22
Stewart-StL 20

Win Percentage
Grove-Phi 848
Marberry-Was 750
Jones-Was 682
Ferrell-Cle 658
Ruffing-Bos-NY . . .652

Games
Grove-Phi 50
Earnshaw-Phi 49
Pipgras-NY 44
Johnson-NY 44
Ferrell-Cle 43

Complete Games
Lyons-Chi 29
Crowder-StL-Was . . 25
Ferrell-Cle 25
Stewart-StL 23
Grove-Phi 22

Shutouts
Pipgras-NY 3
Earnshaw-Phi 3
Brown-Cle 3

Saves
Grove-Phi 9
Braxton-Was-Chi . . . 6
Quinn-Phi 6
Sullivan-Det 5
McKain-Chi 5

Innings Pitched
Lyons-Chi 297.2
Ferrell-Cle 296.2
Earnshaw-Phi . . . 296.0
Grove-Phi 291.0
Crowder-StL-Was 279.2

Fewest Hits/Game
Hadley-Was 8.37
Grove-Phi 8.44
Collins-StL 8.81
Crowder-StL-Was 8.88
Gaston-Bos 8.97

Fewest BB/Game
Pennock-NY 1.15
Lyons-Chi 1.72
Grove-Phi 1.86
Russell-Bos 2.08
Brown-Cle 2.15

Strikeouts
Grove-Phi 209
Earnshaw-Phi 193
Hadley-Was 162
Ferrell-Cle 143
Ruffing-Bos-NY . . . 131

Strikeouts/Game
Grove-Phi 6.46
Johnson-NY 5.90
Earnshaw-Phi 5.87
Hadley-Was 5.60
Ruffing-Bos-NY . . . 5.32

Ratio
Grove-Phi 10.45
Stewart-StL 11.69
Lyons-Chi 11.79
Marberry-Was . . . 11.82
Caraway-Chi 11.82

Earned Run Average
Grove-Phi 2.54
Ferrell-Cle 3.31
Stewart-StL 3.45
Uhle-Det 3.65
Hadley-Was 3.73

Adjusted ERA
Grove-Phi 184
Ferrell-Cle 146
Stewart-StL 141
Uhle-Det 131
Sorrell-Det 124

Opponents' Batting Avg.
Grove-Phi 247
Hadley-Was 247
Crowder-StL-Was . .259
Collins-StL 259
Gaston-Bos 259

Opponents' On Base Pct.
Grove-Phi 288
Stewart-StL 315
Lyons-Chi 319
Marberry-Was 321
Crowder-StL-Was . .321

Starter Runs
Grove-Phi 68.3
Ferrell-Cle 44.2
Stewart-StL 35.9
Lyons-Chi 28.7
Hadley-Was 26.4

Adjusted Starter Runs
Grove-Phi 69.0
Ferrell-Cle 50.0
Stewart-StL 42.7
Uhle-Det 30.4
Lyons-Chi 27.8

Clutch Pitching Index
Henry-Chi 122
Harder-Cle 115
Sorrell-Det 115
Hoyt-NY-Det 113
Ferrell-Cle 113

Relief Runs
Quinn-Phi 2.3

Adjusted Relief Runs
Quinn-Phi 2.5

Relief Ranking
Quinn-Phi 4.5

Total Pitcher Index
Grove-Phi 6.6
Ferrell-Cle 5.3
Stewart-StL 4.5
Lyons-Chi 3.7
Uhle-Det 3.4

Total Baseball Ranking
Ruth-NY 7.6
Grove-Phi 6.6
Cronin-Was 6.6
Gehrig-NY 6.3
Simmons-Phi 5.5

TEAM	G	W	L	PCT	GB	R	OR	AB	H	2B	3B	HR	BB	SO	AVG	OBP	SLG	PRO	PRO+	BR	/A	PF	CHI	RC	SB	CS	SBA	SBR
STL	154	101	53	.656		815	614	5435	1554	353	74	60	432	475	.286	.342	.411	.753	104	61	33	104	107	787	114			
NY	153	87	65	.572	13	768	599	5372	1554	251	64	101	383	395	.289	.340	.416	.756	111	61	77	98	103	776	83			
CHI	156	84	70	.545	17	828	710	5451	1578	340	66	84	577	641	.289	.360	.422	.782	115	131	118	102	97	865	49			
BRO	153	79	73	.520	21	681	673	5309	1464	240	77	71	409	512	.276	.330	.390	.721	100	-2	-5	99	101	705	45			
PIT	155	75	79	.487	26	636	691	5360	1425	243	70	41	493	454	.266	.330	.360	.690	92	-53	-45	99	98	667	59			
PHI	155	66	88	.429	35	684	828	5375	1502	299	52	81	437	492	.279	.336	.400	.736	96	27	-27	108	95	745	42			
BOS	156	64	90	.416	37	533	680	5296	1367	221	59	34	368	430	.258	.309	.341	.650	84	-136	-111	96	98	580	46			
CIN	154	58	96	.377	43	592	742	5343	1439	241	70	21	403	463	.269	.323	.352	.675	93	-84	-42	94	99	631	24			
TOT	618					5537		42941	11883	2188	532	493	3502	3862	.277	.334	.387	.721							462			

TEAM	CG	SH	SV	IP	H	H/G	HR	BB	SO	RAT	ERA	ERA+	OAV	OOB	PR	/A	PF	CPI	FA	E	DP	FW	PW	BW	SBW	DIF
STL	80	17	20	1384²	1470	9.6	65	449	626	12.6	3.45	114	.273	.331	63	73	102	110	.974	160	169	1.0	7.3	3.3		12.5
NY	90	17	12	1360²	1341	8.9	71	422	570	11.8	3.30	112	.255	.313	85	58	96	100	.974	159	126	1.0	5.8	7.7		-3.4
CHI	80	8	8	1385²	1448	9.4	54	524	541	13.0	3.97	97	.267	.336	-17	-18	100	94	.973	169	141	.6	-1.8	11.7		-3.5
BRO	64	9	18	1356	1520	10.1	56	351	546	12.5	3.84	99	.283	.329	3	-5	99	100	.969	187	154	-.7	-.5	.3		3.9
PIT	89	9	5	1390	1489	9.6	55	442	345	12.6	3.66	105	.273	.330	31	27	100	102	.968	194	167	-.9	2.7	-4.5		.7
PHI	60	6	16	1360¹	1603	10.6	75	511	499	14.2	4.58	93	.293	.357	-108	-50	110	100	.966	210	149	-1.9	-5.0	-2.7		-1.5
BOS	78	12	9	1380¹	1465	9.6	66	406	419	12.3	3.90	97	.272	.325	-5	-17	98	94	.973	170	141	.5	-1.7	-11.0		-.8
CIN	70	7	6	1345	1545	10.3	51	399	317	13.1	4.22	89	.293	.346	-52	-72	97	101	.973	165	194	.7	-7.2	-4.2		-8.3
TOT	611	85	94	10962²		9.8				12.8	3.86		.277	.334					.971	1414	1241					

Runs
Terry-NY	121
Klein-Phi	121
English-Chi	117
Ott-NY	104
Cuyler-Chi	100

Hits
L.Waner-Pit	214
Terry-NY	213
English-Chi	202
Cuyler-Chi	202
Klein-Phi	200

Doubles
Adams-StL	46
Berger-Bos	44
Terry-NY	43
Herman-Bro	43
Bartell-Phi	43

Triples
Terry-NY	20
Herman-Bro	16
Traynor-Pit	15
Bissonette-Bro	14

Home Runs
Klein-Phi	31
Ott-NY	29
Berger-Bos	19
Herman-Bro	18
Arlett-Phi	18

Total Bases
Klein-Phi	347
Terry-NY	323
Herman-Bro	320
Berger-Bos	316
Cuyler-Chi	290

Runs Batted In
Klein-Phi	121
Ott-NY	115
Terry-NY	112
Traynor-Pit	103
Herman-Bro	97

Runs Produced
Terry-NY	224
Klein-Phi	211
Ott-NY	190
Traynor-Pit	182
Cuyler-Chi	179

Bases On Balls
Ott-NY	80
P.Waner-Pit	73
Cuyler-Chi	72
Grantham-Pit	71
English-Chi	68

Batting Average
Hafey-StL	.349
Terry-NY	.349
Klein-Phi	.337
O'Doul-Bro	.336
Grimm-Chi	.331

On Base Percentage
Hafey-StL	.404
Cuyler-Chi	.404
P.Waner-Pit	.404
Grantham-Pit	.400
Klein-Phi	.398

Slugging Average
Klein-Phi	.584
Hafey-StL	.569
Ott-NY	.545
Terry-NY	.529
Herman-Bro	.525

Production
Klein-Phi	.982
Hafey-StL	.973
Ott-NY	.937
Terry-NY	.926
Berger-Bos	.892

Adjusted Production
Ott-NY	153
Hafey-StL	153
Terry-NY	150
Klein-Phi	149
Berger-Bos	143

Batter Runs
Klein-Phi	48.9
Terry-NY	39.0
Hafey-StL	36.2
Ott-NY	35.0
Hornsby-Chi	33.5

Adjusted Batter Runs
Klein-Phi	42.8
Terry-NY	40.9
Ott-NY	36.6
Berger-Bos	34.4
Hafey-StL	34.0

Clutch Hitting Index
Sheely-Bos	163
Traynor-Pit	148
Frisch-StL	143
Cuccinello-Cin	138
Gelbert-StL	127

Runs Created
Klein-Phi	140
Terry-NY	130
Cuyler-Chi	122
Berger-Bos	122
Herman-Bro	118

Total Average
Hafey-StL	1.055
Klein-Phi	1.051
Ott-NY	1.031
Terry-NY	.955
Cuyler-Chi	.925

Stolen Bases
Frisch-StL	28
Herman-Bro	17
Martin-StL	16
Adams-StL	16
Watkins-StL	15

Stolen Base Average

Stolen Base Runs

Fielding Runs
P.Waner-Pit	18.5
Frisch-StL	16.3
Gelbert-StL	12.9
Crabtree-Cin	12.7
Hurst-Phi	11.4

Total Player Rating
Terry-NY	3.7
P.Waner-Pit	3.7
Klein-Phi	3.0
Berger-Bos	3.0
Cuccinello-Cin	2.9

Wins
Meine-Pit	19
Hallahan-StL	19
J.Elliott-Phi	19

Win Percentage
Derringer-StL	.692
Hallahan-StL	.679
Bush-Chi	.667
Grimes-StL	.654

Games
J.Elliott-Phi	52
Johnson-Cin	42
Collins-Phi	42

Complete Games
Lucas-Cin	24
Brandt-Bos	23
Meine-Pit	22
Hubbell-NY	21
French-Pit	20

Shutouts
Walker-NY	6
Hubbell-NY	4
Fitzsimmons-NY	4
Derringer-StL	4

Saves
Quinn-Bro	15
Lindsey-StL	7
J.Elliott-Phi	5
Hallahan-StL	4
Collins-Phi	4

Innings Pitched
Meine-Pit	284.0
French-Pit	275.2
Johnson-Cin	262.1
Fitzsimmons-NY	253.2
Root-Chi	251.0

Fewest Hits/Game
Hubbell-NY	7.66
Walker-NY	7.97
Brandt-Bos	8.21
Fitzsimmons-NY	8.59
Root-Chi	8.61

Fewest BB/Game
Johnson-StL	1.40
Lucas-Cin	1.47
Cantwell-Bos	1.96
Clark-Bro	2.01
Zachary-Bos	2.08

Strikeouts
Hallahan-StL	159
Hubbell-NY	155
Vance-Bro	150
Derringer-StL	134
Root-Chi	131

Strikeouts/Game
Vance-Bro	6.17
Hallahan-StL	5.75
Derringer-StL	5.70
Hubbell-NY	5.63
Root-Chi	4.70

Ratio
Hubbell-NY	10.23
Walker-NY	10.49
Johnson-StL	10.50
Fitzsimmons-NY	10.79
Brandt-Bos	11.12

Earned Run Average
Walker-NY	2.26
Hubbell-NY	2.65
Brandt-Bos	2.92
Meine-Pit	2.98
Johnson-StL	3.00

Adjusted ERA
Walker-NY	164
Hubbell-NY	139
Benge-Phi	134
Johnson-StL	131
Brandt-Bos	130

Opponents' Batting Avg.
Hubbell-NY	.227
Walker-NY	.231
Brandt-Bos	.244
Fitzsimmons-NY	.251
Root-Chi	.252

Opponents' On Base Pct.
Hubbell-NY	.282
Walker-NY	.283
Johnson-StL	.286
Fitzsimmons-NY	.296
Cantwell-Bos	.301

Starter Runs
Walker-NY	42.7
Hubbell-NY	33.5
Meine-Pit	27.9
Brandt-Bos	26.3
Fitzsimmons-NY	22.9

Adjusted Starter Runs
Walker-NY	38.2
Benge-Phi	29.4
Hubbell-NY	28.8
Meine-Pit	27.3
Brandt-Bos	24.2

Clutch Pitching Index
Benton-Cin	125
Dudley-Phi	120
Grimes-StL	114
Hallahan-StL	113
Derringer-StL	112

Relief Runs
Lindsey-StL	9.1
Quinn-Bro	8.6
Moore-Bro	.5

Adjusted Relief Runs
Lindsey-StL	9.6
Quinn-Bro	8.2
Moore-Bro	.0

Relief Ranking
Quinn-Bro	14.6
Lindsey-StL	13.6
Moore-Bro	.0

Total Pitcher Index
Fitzsimmons-NY	3.6
Brandt-Bos	3.3
Hubbell-NY	3.1
Walker-NY	2.9
Benge-Phi	2.7

Total Baseball Ranking
Terry-NY	3.7
P.Waner-Pit	3.7
Fitzsimmons-NY	3.6
Brandt-Bos	3.3
Hubbell-NY	3.1

TEAM	G	W	L	PCT	GB	R	OR	AB	H	2B	3B	HR	BB	SO	AVG	OBP	SLG	PRO	PRO+	BR	/A	PF	CHI	RC	SB	CS	SBA	SBR
PHI	153	107	45	.704		858	626	5377	1544	311	64	118	528	543	.287	.355	.435	.790	106	93	45	106	98	843	25	23	34	-13
NY	155	94	59	.614	13.5	1067	760	5608	1667	277	78	155	748	554	.297	.383	.457	.840	134	220	267	94	100	1016	138	68	67	-19
WAS	156	92	62	.597	16	843	691	5576	1588	308	93	49	481	459	.285	.345	.400	.745	100	8	3	101	103	774	72	64	49	-9
CLE	155	78	76	.506	30	885	833	5445	1612	321	69	71	555	433	.296	.363	.419	.782	105	91	46	106	100	840	63	60	55	-14
STL	154	63	91	.409	45	722	870	5374	1455	287	62	76	488	580	.271	.333	.390	.723	91	-39	-66	104	98	696	73	80	59	-10
BOS	153	62	90	.408	45	625	800	5379	1409	289	34	37	405	565	.262	.315	.349	.664	84	-153	-110	95	102	596	42	43	42	-11
DET	154	61	93	.396	47	651	836	5430	1456	292	69	43	480	468	.268	.330	.371	.701	87	-78	-104	103	92	675	117	75	64	-15
CHI	156	56	97	.366	51.5	704	939	5481	1423	238	69	27	483	445	.260	.323	.343	.666	86	-145	-98	94	108	632	94	39	38	-10
TOT	618					6355		43670	12154	2323	538	576	4168	4047	.278	.344	.396	.740							624	452	58	-83

TEAM	CG	SH	SV	IP	H	H/G	HR	BB	SO	RAT	ERA	ERA+	OAV	OOB	PR	/A	PF	CPI	FA	E	DP	FW	PW	BW	SBW	DIF
PHI	97	12	16	1365¹	1342	8.8	73	457	574	11.9	3.47	130	.258	.319	138	155	103	107	.976	141	151	3.2	14.4	4.2	-.2	9.4
NY	78	4	17	1410¹	1461	9.3	67	543	686	12.9	4.20	94	.263	.331	28	-37	91	94	.972	169	131	1.7	-3.4	24.9	-.8	-4.8
WAS	60	7	24	1394¹	1434	9.3	73	498	582	12.6	3.76	114	.264	.327	95	81	98	104	.976	142	148	3.3	7.5	.3	.1	3.7
CLE	76	6	9	1354²	1577	10.5	64	561	470	14.4	4.63	100	.286	.354	-37	-1	106	100	.963	232	143	-2.0	-.0	4.3	-.3	-.8
STL	65	4	10	1362	1623	10.7	84	444	436	13.8	4.76	97	.292	.347	-57	-18	106	99	.963	232	160	-2.1	-1.7	-6.1	.0	-4.1
BOS	61	5	10	1366²	1559	10.3	54	473	365	13.5	4.60	94	.284	.344	-33	-44	98	95	.970	188	127	.4	-4.1	-10.2	-.0	-.0
DET	86	5	6	1384¹	1549	10.1	79	597	511	14.1	4.54	100	.282	.355	-32	0	105	102	.964	220	139	-1.4	.0	-9.7	-.4	-4.5
CHI	54	6	10	1390¹	1611	10.4	82	588	420	14.4	5.04	85	.287	.358	-101	-121	97	96	.961	245	131	-2.7	-11.3	-9.1	.0	2.6
TOT	577		49	102	11028		9.9				13.5	4.38		.278	.344					.968	1569	1130					

Runs
Gehrig-NY 163
Ruth-NY 149
Averill-Cle 140
Combs-NY 120
Chapman-NY 120

Hits
Gehrig-NY 211
Averill-Cle 209
Simmons-Phi 200
Ruth-NY 199
Webb-Bos 196

Doubles
Webb-Bos 67
Alexander-Det 47
Kress-StL 46
Cronin-Was 44

Triples
Johnson-Det 19
Gehrig-NY 15
Blue-Chi 15
Vosmik-Cle 14
Reynolds-Chi 14

Home Runs
Ruth-NY 46
Gehrig-NY 46
Averill-Cle 32
Foxx-Phi 30
Goslin-StL 24

Total Bases
Gehrig-NY 410
Ruth-NY 374
Averill-Cle 361
Simmons-Phi 329
Goslin-StL 328

Runs Batted In
Gehrig-NY 184
Ruth-NY 163
Averill-Cle 143
Simmons-Phi 128
Cronin-Was 126

Runs Produced
Gehrig-NY 301
Ruth-NY 266
Averill-Cle 251
Chapman-NY 225
Cronin-Was 217

Bases On Balls
Ruth-NY 128
Blue-Chi 127
Gehrig-NY 117
Bishop-Phi 112
Lary-NY 88

Batting Average
Simmons-Phi ..... .390
Ruth-NY .... .373
Morgan-Cle ...... .351
Cochrane-Phi ..... .349
Gehrig-NY .... .341

On Base Percentage
Ruth-NY .... .495
Morgan-Cle ...... .451
Gehrig-NY .... .446
Simmons-Phi ..... .444
Blue-Chi .... .430

Slugging Average
Ruth-NY .... .700
Gehrig-NY .... .662
Simmons-Phi ..... .641
Averill-Cle .... .576
Foxx-Phi .... .567

Production
Ruth-NY 1.195
Gehrig-NY 1.108
Simmons-Phi 1.085
Averill-Cle .... .979
Cochrane-Phi .... .976

Adjusted Production
Ruth-NY 223
Gehrig-NY 199
Simmons-Phi 172
Webb-Bos 151
Goslin-StL 147

Batter Runs
Ruth-NY 91.5
Gehrig-NY 79.9
Simmons-Phi 59.6
Averill-Cle 48.2
Goslin-StL 44.7

Adjusted Batter Runs
Ruth-NY 96.4
Gehrig-NY 85.3
Simmons-Phi 55.1
Averill-Cle 43.1
Goslin-StL 41.6

Clutch Hitting Index
Kamm-Chi-Cle 145
Vosmik-Cle 139
Bluege-Was 136
Cronin-Was 134
Lary-NY 132

Runs Created
Ruth-NY 192
Gehrig-NY 185
Simmons-Phi 145
Averill-Cle 144
Goslin-StL 137

Total Average
Ruth-NY 1.487
Gehrig-NY 1.267
Simmons-Phi 1.199
Morgan-Cle 1.046
Cochrane-Phi 1.033

Stolen Bases
Chapman-NY 61
Johnson-Det 33
Burns-StL 19
Lazzeri-NY 18
Cissell-Chi 18

Stolen Base Average
Cissell-Chi 75.0
Reynolds-Chi 73.9
Chapman-NY 72.6
Lazzeri-NY 66.7
Bluege-Was 61.5

Stolen Base Runs
Chapman-NY 4.5
H.Walker-Det 2.4
Blue-Chi 2.1
Cissell-Chi 1.8

Fielding Runs
Melillo-StL 33.1
McManus-Det-Bos 21.1
West-Was 21.0
Burns-StL 18.4
Rhyne-Bos 16.9

Total Player Rating
Ruth-NY 6.8
Gehrig-NY 5.4
Simmons-Phi 5.0
Cronin-Was 4.6
Cochrane-Phi 4.5

Wins
Grove-Phi 31
Ferrell-Cle 22
Gomez-NY 21
Earnshaw-Phi 21
Walberg-Phi 20

Win Percentage
Grove-Phi .... .886
Marberry-Was .... .800
Mahaffey-Phi ..... .789
Earnshaw-Phi .... .750
Gomez-NY .... .700

Games
Hadley-Was 55
Moore-Bos 53
Caraway-Chi 51
Frasier-Chi 46
Fischer-Was 46

Complete Games
Grove-Phi 27
Ferrell-Cle 27
Earnshaw-Phi 23
Whitehill-Det 22
Stewart-StL 20

Shutouts
Grove-Phi 4
Earnshaw-Phi 3

Saves
Moore-Bos 10
Hadley-Was 8
Marberry-Was 7
Kimsey-StL 7
Earnshaw-Phi 6

Innings Pitched
Walberg-Phi 291.0
Grove-Phi 288.2
Earnshaw-Phi 281.2
Ferrell-Cle 276.1
Whitehill-Det 271.1

Fewest Hits/Game
Hadley-Was 7.26
Gomez-NY 7.63
Grove-Phi 7.76
Johnson-NY 8.07
Earnshaw-Phi 8.15

Fewest BB/Game
Pennock-NY 1.43
Gray-StL 1.88
Grove-Phi 1.93
Brown-Cle 2.12
Blaeholder-StL ... 2.23

Strikeouts
Grove-Phi 175
Earnshaw-Phi 152
Gomez-NY 150
Ruffing-NY 132
Hadley-Was 124

Strikeouts/Game
Hadley-Was 6.21
Gomez-NY 5.56
Bridges-Det 5.46
Grove-Phi 5.46
Ruffing-NY 5.01

Ratio
Grove-Phi 9.73
Earnshaw-Phi ... 10.64
Gomez-NY 10.93
Coffman-StL 11.27
Uhle-Det 11.33

Earned Run Average
Grove-Phi 2.06
Gomez-NY 2.67
Hadley-Was 3.06
Brown-Was 3.20
Marberry-Was 3.45

Adjusted ERA
Grove-Phi 218
Gomez-NY 149
Hadley-Was 140
Brown-Was 134
Uhle-Det 131

Opponents' Batting Avg.
Hadley-Was ...... .218
Gomez-NY .... .226
Grove-Phi .... .229
Johnson-NY ...... .234
Earnshaw-Phi .... .236

Opponents' On Base Pct.
Grove-Phi .... .271
Earnshaw-Phi .... .288
Gomez-NY .... .295
Coffman-StL ..... .298
Uhle-Det .... .304

Starter Runs
Grove-Phi 74.5
Gomez-NY 46.2
Brown-Was 33.9
Hadley-Was 26.4
Marberry-Was 22.6

Adjusted Starter Runs
Grove-Phi 78.1
Gomez-NY 35.1
Brown-Was 31.3
Ferrell-Cle 26.9
Earnshaw-Phi 25.6

Clutch Pitching Index
Grove-Phi 118
Faber-Chi 116
Whitehill-Det 115
Pennock-NY 110
Brown-Was 110

Relief Runs

Adjusted Relief Runs
Kimsey-StL 2.6

Relief Ranking
Kimsey-StL 2.9

Total Pitcher Index
Grove-Phi 7.5
Ferrell-Cle 5.0
Brown-Was 3.5
Earnshaw-Phi 3.1
Gomez-NY 2.9

Total Baseball Ranking
Grove-Phi 7.5
Ruth-NY 6.8
Gehrig-NY 5.4
Ferrell-Cle 5.0
Simmons-Phi 5.0

TEAM	G	W	L	PCT	GB	R	OR	AB	H	2B	3B	HR	BB	SO	AVG	OBP	SLG	PRO	PRO+	BR	/A	PF	CHI	RC	SB	CS	SBA	SBR
CHI	154	90	64	.584		720	633	5462	1519	296	60	69	398	514	.278	.330	.392	.722	101	0	7	99	101	728	48			
PIT	154	86	68	.558	4	701	711	5421	1543	274	90	48	358	385	.285	.333	.395	.728	102	9	21	98	99	729	71			
BRO	154	81	73	.526	9	752	747	5433	1538	296	59	110	388	574	.283	.334	.420	.754	110	55	69	98	99	778	61			
PHI	154	78	76	.506	12	844	796	5510	1608	330	67	122	446	547	.292	.348	.442	.790	105	45	112	98		870	71			
BOS	155	77	77	.500	13	649	655	5506	1460	262	53	63	347	496	.265	.311	.366	.677	90	-93	-66	96	105	643	36			
STL	156	72	82	.468	18	684	717	5458	1467	307	51	76	420	514	.269	.324	.385	.709	93	-26	-46	103	100	702	92			
NY	154	72	82	.468	18	755	706	5530	1527	263	54	116	348	391	.276	.322	.406	.728	103	1	15	98	107	735	31			
CIN	155	60	94	.390	30	575	715	5443	1429	265	68	47	436	436	.263	.320	.362	.682	92	-76	-52	97	90	654	35			
TOT	618					5680		43763	12091	2293	502	651	3141	3857	.276	.328	.396	.724							445			

TEAM	CG	SH	SV	IP	H	H/G	HR	BB	SO	RAT	ERA	ERA+	OAV	OOB	PR	/A	PF	CPI	FA	E	DP	FW	PW	BW	SBW	DIF
CHI	79	9	7	1401	1444	9.3	68	409	527	12.1	3.44	109	.264	.318	67	49	97	102	.973	173	146	.4	4.8	.7		7.1
PIT	71	12	12	1377	1472	9.6	86	338	377	11.9	3.75	102	.269	.314	20	10	98	96	.969	185	124	-.4	1.0	2.1		6.3
BRO	61	7	16	1379²	1538	10.0	72	403	497	12.8	4.27	89	.282	.334	-60	-68	98	94	.971	183	169	-.3	-6.7	6.8		4.2
PHI	59	4	17	1384	1589	10.3	107	450	459	13.5	4.47	99	.287	.344	-90	-9	114	100	.968	194	133	-.9	-.9	4.5		-1.6
BOS	72	8	8	1414	1483	9.4	61	420	440	12.3	3.53	107	.272	.327	55	35	97	105	.976	152	145	1.7	3.5	-6.5		1.3
STL	70	13	9	1396	1533	9.9	76	455	681	13.0	3.97	99	.281	.339	-14	-5	101	104	.971	175	155	.4	-.5	-4.6		-.3
NY	57	3	16	1375¹	1533	10.0	112	387	506	12.7	3.83	97	.280	.330	7	-17	96	108	.969	191	143	-.7	-1.7	1.5		-4.1
CIN	83	6	6	1394²	1505	9.7	69	276	359	11.6	3.79	102	.273	.310	14	9	99	92	.971	178	129	.1	.9	-5.1		-12.9
TOT	552	62	91	11121²		9.8				12.5	3.88		.276	.328					.971	1431	1144					

Runs
Klein-Phi 152
Terry-NY 124
O'Doul-Bro 120
Ott-NY 119
Bartell-Phi 118

Hits
Klein-Phi 226
Terry-NY 225
O'Doul-Bro 219
P.Waner-Pit 215
Herman-Chi 206

Doubles
P.Waner-Pit 62
Klein-Phi 50
Stephenson-Chi . . . 49
Bartell-Phi 48

Triples
Herman-Cin 19
Suhr-Pit 16
Klein-Phi 15

Home Runs
Ott-NY 38
Klein-Phi 38
Terry-NY 28
Hurst-Phi 24
Wilson-Bro 23

Total Bases
Klein-Phi 420
Terry-NY 373
Ott-NY 340
O'Doul-Bro 330
P.Waner-Pit 321

Runs Batted In
Hurst-Phi 143
Klein-Phi 137
Whitney-Phi 124
Wilson-Bro 123
Ott-NY 123

Runs Produced
Klein-Phi 251
Hurst-Phi 228
Terry-NY 213
Whitney-Phi 204
Ott-NY 204

Bases On Balls
Ott-NY 100
Hurst-Phi 65
Bartell-Phi 64
Suhr-Pit 63

Batting Average
O'Doul-Bro 368
Terry-NY 350
Klein-Phi 348
P.Waner-Pit 341
Hurst-Phi 339

On Base Percentage
Ott-NY 424
O'Doul-Bro 423
Hurst-Phi 412
Klein-Phi 404
P.Waner-Pit 397

Slugging Average
Klein-Phi 646
Ott-NY 601
Terry-NY 580
O'Doul-Bro 555
Hurst-Phi 547

Production
Klein-Phi 1.050
Ott-NY 1.025
O'Doul-Bro 978
Terry-NY 962
Hurst-Phi 959

Adjusted Production
Ott-NY 175
O'Doul-Bro 164
Klein-Phi 158
Terry-NY 158
Herman-Cin 152

Batter Runs
Klein-Phi 68.2
Ott-NY 59.8
O'Doul-Bro 51.2
Terry-NY 46.4
Hurst-Phi 46.2

Adjusted Batter Runs
Ott-NY 61.5
Klein-Phi 58.1
O'Doul-Bro 52.8
Terry-NY 48.1
Herman-Cin 40.5

Clutch Hitting Index
Whitney-Phi 153
Hurst-Phi 145
Wilson-Bro 142
Hogan-NY 134
Piet-Pit 132

Runs Created
Klein-Phi 171
Ott-NY 151
O'Doul-Bro 142
Terry-NY 142
Hurst-Phi 134

Total Average
Klein-Phi 1.182
Ott-NY 1.166
O'Doul-Bro 1.059
Hurst-Phi 1.042
Terry-NY 981

Stolen Bases
Klein-Phi 20
Piet-Pit 19
Watkins-StL 18
Frisch-StL 18
G.Davis-Phi 16

Stolen Base Average

Stolen Base Runs

Fielding Runs
Jurges-Chi 31.7
Cuccinello-Bro . . . 19.0
Herman-Chi 16.8
Frisch-StL 16.4
Stripp-Bro 15.9

Total Player Rating
Klein-Phi 5.4
Terry-NY 5.2
Ott-NY 5.0
Herman-Cin 4.4
Herman-Chi 3.3

Wins
Warneke-Chi 22
Clark-Bro 20
Bush-Chi 19

Win Percentage
Warneke-Chi 786
Bush-Chi 633
Rhem-StL-Phi 625
Clark-Bro 625
Hubbell-NY 621

Games
French-Pit 47
Dean-StL 46
Carleton-StL 44
Collins-Phi 43

Complete Games
Lucas-Cin 28
Warneke-Chi 25
Hubbell-NY 22

Shutouts
Warneke-Chi 4
Swetonic-Pit 4
Dean-StL 4

Saves
Quinn-Bro 8
Benge-Phi 6
Luque-NY 5
Cantwell-Bos 5

Innings Pitched
Dean-StL 286.0
Hubbell-NY 284.0
Warneke-Chi 277.0
French-Pit 274.1
Clark-Bro 273.0

Fewest Hits/Game
Swetonic-Pit . . . 7.41
Brown-Bos 7.90
Warneke-Chi 8.03
Hubbell-NY 8.24
Malone-Chi 8.43

Fewest BB/Game
Swift-Pit 1.09
Lucas-Cin 1.17
Hubbell-NY 1.27
Benton-Cin 1.35
Betts-Bos 1.42

Strikeouts
Dean-StL 191
Hubbell-NY 137
Malone-Chi 120
Carleton-StL 113
Brown-Bos 110

Strikeouts/Game
Dean-StL 6.01
Hallahan-StL 5.51
Vance-Bro 5.28
Carleton-StL 5.18
Brown-Bos 4.65

Ratio
Hubbell-NY 9.63
Swift-Pit 9.78
Lucas-Cin 9.92
Warneke-Chi 10.17
Swetonic-Pit 10.46

Earned Run Average
Warneke-Chi 2.37
Hubbell-NY 2.50
Betts-Bos 2.80
Swetonic-Pit 2.82
Lucas-Cin 2.94

Adjusted ERA
Warneke-Chi 159
Hubbell-NY 148
Swetonic-Pit 135
Betts-Bos 134
Lucas-Cin 131

Opponents' Batting Avg.
Swetonic-Pit 221
Warneke-Chi 237
Hubbell-NY 238
Brown-Bos 238
Malone-Chi 244

Opponents' On Base Pct.
Hubbell-NY 268
Swift-Pit 272
Lucas-Cin 274
Warneke-Chi 283
Swetonic-Pit 286

Starter Runs
Warneke-Chi 46.4
Hubbell-NY 43.4
Lucas-Cin 28.1
Betts-Bos 26.5
French-Pit 26.2

Adjusted Starter Runs
Warneke-Chi 42.9
Hubbell-NY 38.1
Lucas-Cin 27.4
French-Pit 24.2
Betts-Bos 23.6

Clutch Pitching Index
Bush-Chi 123
French-Pit 123
Zachary-Bos 117
Hallahan-StL 113
Derringer-StL 113

Relief Runs
Quinn-Bro 5.6
Frankhouse-Bos . . . 3.8

Adjusted Relief Runs
Quinn-Bro 5.0
Frankhouse-Bos . . . 2.4

Relief Ranking
Quinn-Bro 6.2
Frankhouse-Bos . . . 2.0

Total Pitcher Index
Hubbell-NY 5.0
Warneke-Chi 4.5
Lucas-Cin 2.8
Betts-Bos 2.4
Dean-StL 2.3

Total Baseball Ranking
Klein-Phi 5.4
Terry-NY 5.2
Hubbell-NY 5.0
Ott-NY 5.0
Warneke-Chi 4.5

TEAM	G	W	L	PCT	GB	R	OR	AB	H	2B	3B	HR	BB	SO	AVG	OBP	SLG	PRO	PRO+	BR	/A	PF	CHI	RC	SB	CS	SBA	SBR
NY	156	107	47	.695		1002	724	5477	1564	279	82	160	766	527	.286	.376	.454	.830	127	172	215	95	99	961	77	66	63	-17
PHI	154	94	60	.610	13	981	752	5537	1606	303	52	172	647	630	.290	.366	.457	.823	114	148	118	104	100	951	38	23	27	-8
WAS	154	93	61	.604	14	840	716	5515	1565	303	100	61	505	442	.284	.347	.408	.755	102	8	18	99	103	793	70	47	64	-23
CLE	153	87	65	.572	19	845	747	5412	1544	310	74	78	566	454	.285	.357	.413	.770	98	44	-8	107	99	811	52	54	46	-10
DET	153	76	75	.503	29.5	799	787	5409	1479	291	80	80	486	523	.273	.335	.401	.736	92	-34	-65	104	105	741	103	49	52	-16
STL	154	63	91	.409	44	736	898	5449	1502	274	69	67	507	528	.276	.339	.388	.727	88	-44	-89	106	97	726	69	62	54	-13
CHI	152	49	102	.325	56.5	667	897	5336	1426	274	56	36	459	386	.267	.327	.360	.687	89	-121	-70	94	101	642	89	58	52	-13
BOS	154	43	111	.279	64	566	915	5295	1331	253	57	53	469	539	.251	.314	.351	.665	80	-170	-148	97	94	593	46	46	47	-13
TOT	615					6436		43430	12017	2287	570	707	4405	4029	.277	.346	.404	.750							544	405	57	-79

TEAM	CG	SH	SV	IP	H	H/G	HR	BB	SO	RAT	ERA	ERA+	OAV	OOB	PR	/A	PF	CPI	FA	E	DP	FW	PW	BW	SBW	DIF
NY	96	11	15	1408	1425	9.1	93	561	780	12.8	3.98	102	.260	.331	77	15	91	101	.969	188	124	.2	1.4	19.9	-.6	9.2
PHI	95	10	10	1386	1477	9.6	112	511	591	13.0	4.45	102	.271	.335	3	11	101	98	.979	124	142	3.8	1.0	10.9	.2	1.1
WAS	66	11	22	1383¹	1463	9.5	73	526	437	13.0	4.16	104	.271	.337	49	24	96	100	.979	125	157	3.8	2.2	1.7	-1.2	9.6
CLE	94	6	8	1377¹	1506	9.8	70	446	439	12.8	4.12	115	.273	.329	55	95	106	98	.969	191	129	-.2	8.8	-.7	.0	3.2
DET	67	9	17	1362²	1421	9.4	89	592	521	13.5	4.30	109	.268	.345	27	61	105	102	.969	187	154	.0	5.6	-6.0	-.6	1.4
STL	63	7	11	1376²	1592	10.4	103	574	496	14.3	5.01	97	.289	.359	-80	-23	108	100	.969	188	156	.0	-2.1	-8.2	-.3	-3.4
CHI	50	2	12	1348²	1551	10.4	88	580	379	14.4	4.82	90	.287	.359	-51	-74	97	101	.958	264	170	-4.6	-6.8	-6.5	-.3	-8.3
BOS	42	3	7	1362	1574	10.4	79	612	365	14.6	5.02	90	.289	.364	-81	-79	100	99	.963	233	165	-2.6	-7.3	-13.7	-.3	-10.1
TOT	573	59	102	11004²		9.8				13.6	4.48		.277	.346					.969	1500	1197					

Runs
Foxx-Phi 151
Simmons-Phi 144
Combs-NY 143
Gehrig-NY 138
Manush-Was 121

Hits
Simmons-Phi 216
Manush-Was 214
Foxx-Phi 213
Gehrig-NY 208
Averill-Cle 198

Doubles
McNair-Phi 47
Gehringer-Det 44
Cronin-Was 43

Triples
Cronin-Was 18
Myer-Was 16
Lazzeri-NY 16
Chapman-NY 15

Home Runs
Foxx-Phi 58
Ruth-NY 41
Simmons-Phi 35
Gehrig-NY 34
Averill-Cle 32

Total Bases
Foxx-Phi 438
Gehrig-NY 370
Simmons-Phi 367
Averill-Cle 359
Manush-Was 325

Runs Batted In
Foxx-Phi 169
Simmons-Phi 151
Gehrig-NY 151
Ruth-NY 137
Averill-Cle 124

Runs Produced
Foxx-Phi 262
Simmons-Phi 260
Gehrig-NY 255
Manush-Was 223
Ruth-NY 216

Bases On Balls
Ruth-NY 130
Foxx-Phi 116
Bishop-Phi 110
Gehrig-NY 108
Cochrane-Phi 100

Batting Average
Foxx-Phi 364
Gehrig-NY .... .349
Manush-Was .... .342
Ruth-NY .... .341
Walker-Det .... .323

On Base Percentage
Ruth-NY .... .489
Foxx-Phi .... .469
Gehrig-NY .... .451
Bishop-Phi .... .412
Cochrane-Phi 412

Slugging Average
Foxx-Phi 749
Ruth-NY .... .661
Gehrig-NY .... .621
Averill-Cle .... .569
Simmons-Phi 548

Production
Foxx-Phi 1.218
Ruth-NY 1.150
Gehrig-NY 1.072
Averill-Cle .... .961
Cochrane-Phi .... .921

Adjusted Production
Ruth-NY 206
Foxx-Phi 203
Gehrig-NY 184
Lazzeri-NY 140
Averill-Cle 137

Batter Runs
Foxx-Phi 96.7
Ruth-NY 71.2
Gehrig-NY 68.6
Averill-Cle 41.1
Alexander-Det-Bos 31.8

Adjusted Batter Runs
Foxx-Phi 93.4
Ruth-NY 75.3
Gehrig-NY 73.5
Averill-Cle 35.0
Alexander-Det-Bos 32.8

Clutch Hitting Index
Cronin-Was 141
Dykes-Phi 134
Kamm-Cle 129
Lazzeri-NY 127
Cissell-Chi-Cle 126

Runs Created
Foxx-Phi 207
Gehrig-NY 168
Ruth-NY 157
Averill-Cle 140
Simmons-Phi 134

Total Average
Foxx-Phi 1.451
Ruth-NY 1.432
Gehrig-NY 1.188
Cochrane-Phi ... 1.000
Averill-Cle .... .991

Stolen Bases
Chapman-NY 38
Walker-Det 30
Johnson-Det-Bos .. 20
Cissell-Chi-Cle 18

Stolen Base Average
Walker-Det 83.3
Johnson-Det-Bos . 76.9
Blue-Chi 73.9
Chapman-NY 67.9
Burns-StL 60.7

Stolen Base Runs
Walker-Det 5.4
Johnson-Det-Bos .. 2.4
Blue-Chi 1.5

Fielding Runs
Warstler-Bos 28.0
Vosmik-Cle 21.6
Appling-Chi 18.1
West-Was 14.0
Cochrane-Phi 12.0

Total Player Rating
Foxx-Phi 6.4
Ruth-NY 5.5
Cochrane-Phi 4.2
Gehrig-NY 4.2
Cronin-Was 3.7

Wins
Crowder-Was 26
Grove-Phi 25
Gomez-NY 24
Ferrell-Cle 23
Weaver-Was 22

Win Percentage
Allen-NY .... .810
Gomez-NY .... .774
Ruffing-NY .... .720
Grove-Phi .... .714
Weaver-Was ...... .688

Games
Marberry-Was 54
Gray-StL 52
Crowder-Was 50

Complete Games
Grove-Phi 27
Ferrell-Cle 26
Ruffing-NY 22

Shutouts
Grove-Phi 4
Bridges-Det 4

Saves
Marberry-Was 13
Moore-Bos-NY 8
Hogsett-Det 7
Grove-Phi 7
Faber-Chi 6

Innings Pitched
Crowder-Was .. 327.0
Grove-Phi 291.2
Ferrell-Cle 287.2
Walberg-Phi 272.0
Gomez-NY 265.1

Fewest Hits/Game
Allen-NY 7.59
Ruffing-NY 7.61
Bridges-Det 7.79
Grove-Phi 8.30
Crowder-Was 8.78

Fewest BB/Game
Brown-Cle 1.71
Crowder-Was ... 2.12
Gray-StL 2.31
Harder-Cle 2.40
Grove-Phi 2.44

Strikeouts
Ruffing-NY 190
Grove-Phi 188
Gomez-NY 176
Hadley-Chi-StL ... 145
Pipgras-NY 111

Strikeouts/Game
Ruffing-NY 6.60
Gomez-NY 5.97
Grove-Phi 5.80
Hadley-Chi-StL ... 5.26
Allen-NY 5.11

Ratio
Grove-Phi 10.77
Crowder-Was ... 10.90
Allen-NY 11.39
Ruffing-NY 11.71
Sorrell-Det 12.06

Earned Run Average
Grove-Phi 2.84
Ruffing-NY 3.09
Lyons-Chi 3.28
Crowder-Was ... 3.33
Bridges-Det 3.36

Adjusted ERA
Grove-Phi 159
Bridges-Det 140
Hogsett-Det 133
Lyons-Chi 132
Ruffing-NY 132

Opponents' Batting Avg.
Ruffing-NY .... .226
Allen-NY .... .228
Bridges-Det ...... .233
Grove-Phi .... .241
Crowder-Was 252

Opponents' On Base Pct.
Grove-Phi .... .292
Crowder-Was ... .295
Allen-NY .... .306
Ruffing-NY ...... .311
Brown-Cle ...... .314

Starter Runs
Grove-Phi 53.2
Crowder-Was ... 41.7
Ruffing-NY 39.9
Lyons-Chi 30.8
Ferrell-Cle 26.2

Adjusted Starter Runs
Grove-Phi 54.6
Crowder-Was ... 35.7
Ferrell-Cle 34.6
Bridges-Det 30.0
Ruffing-NY 28.3

Clutch Pitching Index
Hogsett-Det 129
Lyons-Chi 120
Weiland-Bos 117
Bridges-Det 116
Gaston-Chi 115

Relief Runs
Faber-Chi 8.8
Kimsey-StL-Chi ... 6.5

Adjusted Relief Runs
Kimsey-StL-Chi ... 9.5
Faber-Chi 7.0

Relief Ranking
Kimsey-StL-Chi ... 8.9
Faber-Chi 8.6

Total Pitcher Index
Grove-Phi 5.0
Ferrell-Cle 4.0
Ruffing-NY 3.6
Crowder-Was 3.2
Harder-Cle 3.0

Total Baseball Ranking
Foxx-Phi 6.4
Ruth-NY 5.5
Grove-Phi 5.0
Cochrane-Phi 4.2
Gehrig-NY 4.2

1933 National League

TEAM	G	W	L	PCT	GB	R	OR	AB	H	2B	3B	HR	BB	SO	AVG	OBP	SLG	PRO	PRO+	BR	/A	PF	CHI	RC	SB	CS	SBA	SBR
NY	156	91	61	.599		636	515	5461	1437	204	41	82	377	477	.263	.312	.361	.673	99	-13	-3	98	104	667	31			
PIT	154	87	67	.565	5	667	619	5429	1548	249	84	39	366	334	.285	.333	.383	.716	111	71	72	100	96	750	34			
CHI	154	86	68	.558	6	646	536	5255	1422	256	51	72	392	475	.271	.325	.380	.705	107	47	48	100	99	705	52			
BOS	156	83	71	.539	9	552	531	5243	1320	217	56	54	326	428	.252	.299	.345	.644	98	-69	-19	92	103	588	25			
STL	154	82	71	.536	9.5	687	609	5387	1486	256	61	57	391	528	.276	.329	.378	.707	102	53	20	105	102	726	99			
BRO	157	65	88	.425	26.5	617	695	5367	1413	224	51	62	397	453	.263	.316	.359	.675	103	-7	19	96	101	662	82			
PHI	152	60	92	.395	31	607	760	5261	1439	240	41	60	381	479	.274	.326	.369	.695	93	32	-45	113	95	689	55			
CIN	153	58	94	.382	33	496	643	5156	1267	208	37	34	349	354	.246	.298	.320	.618	83	-109	-100	99	102	540	30			
TOT	618					4908		42559	11332	1854	422	460	2979	3528	.266	.317	.362	.679						408				

TEAM	CG	SH	SV	IP	H	H/G	HR	BB	SO	RAT	ERA	ERA+	OAV	OOB	PR	/A	PF	CPI	FA	E	DP	FW	PW	BW	SBW	DIF
NY	75	23	15	1408²	1280	8.2	61	400	555	10.9	2.71	118	.249	.307	98	78	96	112	.973	178	156	-.5	8.3	-.3		7.5
PIT	70	16	12	1373¹	1417	9.3	54	313	401	11.5	3.27	101	.264	.307	10	6	99	95	.972	166	133	.2	.6	7.6		1.6
CHI	95	16	9	1362	1308	8.6	51	415	491	11.6	2.93	112	.252	.311	61	52	98	104	.973	168	163	.0	5.5	5.1		-1.6
BOS	85	15	16	1403	1391	8.9	54	355	383	11.3	2.96	103	.261	.308	58	13	92	105	.978	138	148	2.1	1.4	-2.0		4.5
STL	73	11	16	1382²	1391	9.1	55	452	635	12.1	3.37	103	.260	.320	-5	15	104	98	.973	162	119	.4	1.6	2.1		1.4
BRO	71	9	10	1386¹	1502	9.8	51	374	415	12.4	3.73	86	.275	.326	-60	-78	96	95	.971	177	120	-.3	-8.3	2.0		-4.9
PHI	52	10	13	1336²	1563	10.5	87	410	341	13.6	4.34	88	.292	.348	-149	-78	114	101	.970	183	156	-1.1	-8.3	-4.8		-1.9
CIN	74	13	8	1352	1470	9.8	47	257	310	11.6	3.42	99	.279	.314	-12	-5	102	99	.971	177	139	-.6	-.5	-10.6		-6.3
TOT	595	113	99	11004²		9.3				11.9	3.34		.266	.317					.973	1349	1134					

Runs
Martin-StL 122
P.Waner-Pit 101
Klein-Phi........ 101
Ott-NY 98
Medwick-StL 92

Hits
Klein-Phi......... 223
Fullis-Phi........ 200
P.Waner-Pit 191
Traynor-Pit 190
Martin-StL 189

Doubles
Klein-Phi.......... 44
Medwick-StL 40
Lindstrom-Pit 39
P.Waner-Pit 38
Berger-Bos 37

Triples
Vaughan-Pit 19
P.Waner-Pit 16
Martin-StL 12
F.Herman-Chi 12

Home Runs
Klein-Phi.......... 28
Berger-Bos 27
Ott-NY 23
Medwick-StL 18

Total Bases
Klein-Phi......... 365
Berger-Bos 299
Medwick-StL 296
P.Waner-Pit 282
Vaughan-Pit 274

Runs Batted In
Klein-Phi......... 120
Berger-Bos 106
Ott-NY 103
Medwick-StL 98
Vaughan-Pit 97

Runs Produced
Klein-Phi......... 193
Ott-NY 178
Vaughan-Pit 173
Medwick-StL 172
Martin-StL 171

Bases On Balls
Ott-NY 75
Suhr-Pit 72
Martin-StL 67
Vaughan-Pit 64
P.Waner-Pit 60

Batting Average
Klein-Phi..........368
Davis-Phi.........349
Terry-NY 322
Schulmerich-Bos-Phi.318
Martin-StL 316

On Base Percentage
Klein-Phi..........422
Davis-Phi.........395
Vaughan-Pit 388
Martin-StL 387
Terry-NY 375

Slugging Average
Klein-Phi..........602
Berger-Bos 566
F.Herman-Chi 502
Medwick-StL 497
Vaughan-Pit 478

Production
Klein-Phi........1.025
Berger-Bos 932
Davis-Phi........867
Vaughan-Pit 866
F.Herman-Chi......855

Adjusted Production
Berger-Bos 177
Klein-Phi........ 168
Vaughan-Pit 146
F.Herman-Chi..... 142
Ott-NY 139

Batter Runs
Klein-Phi......... 69.1
Berger-Bos 40.5
Vaughan-Pit 35.2
Martin-StL 32.3
Davis-Phi......... 29.8

Adjusted Batter Runs
Klein-Phi......... 60.2
Berger-Bos 45.4
Vaughan-Pit 35.4
Ott-NY 29.5
P.Waner-Pit 28.8

Clutch Hitting Index
Traynor-Pit 139
Hartnett-Chi 130
Bottomley-Cin ... 129
Vaughan-Pit 128
Hurst-Phi 127

Runs Created
Klein-Phi......... 162
Berger-Bos 113
Vaughan-Pit 112
Martin-StL 111
P.Waner-Pit 109

Total Average
Klein-Phi........1.132
Berger-Bos 935
Martin-StL 881
Vaughan-Pit 861
F.Herman-Chi......827

Stolen Bases
Martin-StL 26
Fullis-Phi 18
Frisch-StL 18
Klein-Phi......... 15
Orsatti-StL 14

Stolen Base Average

Stolen Base Runs

Fielding Runs
Critz-NY 46.5
W.Herman-Chi ... 29.4
Jurges-Chi 20.3
Lopez-Bro 17.6
Ryan-NY.......... 17.3

Total Player Rating
Klein-Phi.......... 6.1
Berger-Bos 3.9
Vaughan-Pit 3.7
W.Herman-Chi 3.7
Critz-NY 3.4

Wins
Hubbell-NY 23
Dean-StL 20
Cantwell-Bos 20
Bush-Chi 20
Schumacher-NY ... 19

Win Percentage
Cantwell-Bos 667
Hubbell-NY 657
Meine-Pit 652
Bush-Chi 625
Schumacher-NY ..613

Games
Dean-StL 48
French-Pit 47
Liska-Phi 45
Hubbell-NY 45
Carleton-StL 44

Complete Games
Warneke-Chi 26
Dean-StL 26
Brandt-Bos 23
Hubbell-NY 22

Shutouts
Hubbell-NY 10
Schumacher-NY 7
French-Pit 5

Saves
Collins-Phi 6
Hubbell-NY 5
Harris-Pit 5
Bell-NY 5

Innings Pitched
Hubbell-NY 308.2
Dean-StL 293.0
French-Pit 291.1
Brandt-Bos 287.2
Warneke-Chi 287.1

Fewest Hits/Game
Schumacher-NY .. 6.92
Hubbell-NY 7.46
Parmelee-NY 7.87
Brandt-Bos 8.01
Mungo-Bro 8.09

Fewest BB/Game
Lucas-Cin..........74
Hubbell-NY 1.37
Swift-Pit 1.48
Hansen-Phi 1.60
French-Pit 1.70

Strikeouts
Dean-StL 199
Hubbell-NY 156
Carleton-StL 147
Warneke-Chi 133
Parmelee-NY 132

Strikeouts/Game
Dean-StL 6.11
Parmelee-NY 5.44
Carleton-StL 4.78
Hubbell-NY 4.55
Warneke-Chi 4.17

Ratio
Hubbell-NY 8.92
Schumacher-NY .. 9.88
Betts-Bos 10.41
Swift-Pit 10.47
Brandt-Bos 10.51

Earned Run Average
Hubbell-NY 1.66
Warneke-Chi .. 2.00
Schumacher-NY . 2.16
Brandt-Bos 2.60
Root-Chi......... 2.60

Adjusted ERA
Hubbell-NY 193
Warneke-Chi 163
Schumacher-NY .. 149
Root-Chi......... 126
French-Pit 122

Opponents' Batting Avg.
Schumacher-NY ...214
Hubbell-NY 227
Parmelee-NY 232
Mungo-Bro 236
Warneke-Chi 244

Opponents' On Base Pct.
Hubbell-NY 260
Schumacher-NY ..280
Swift-Pit 285
Betts-Bos.........290
Cantwell-Bos 291

Starter Runs
Hubbell-NY 57.4
Warneke-Chi 42.5
Schumacher-NY . 33.9
Brandt-Bos 23.6
Cantwell-Bos 20.4

Adjusted Starter Runs
Hubbell-NY 53.1
Warneke-Chi 40.4
Schumacher-NY ... 30.2
French-Pit 19.3
Root-Chi......... 18.0

Clutch Pitching Index
Warneke-Chi 131
Root-Chi......... 120
Walker-StL 116
Holley-Phi 115
Hubbell-NY 112

Relief Runs
Bell-NY 15.0
Luque-NY......... 5.8
Harris-Pit 7

Adjusted Relief Runs
Bell-NY 13.6
Luque-NY......... 4.6
Harris-Pit 6

Relief Ranking
Bell-NY 14.2
Luque-NY......... 5.7
Harris-Pit 9

Total Pitcher Index
Hubbell-NY 7.0
Warneke-Chi 6.2
Schumacher-NY .. 3.9
Brandt-Bos 2.4
Bush-Chi 1.9

Total Baseball Ranking
Hubbell-NY 7.0
Warneke-Chi 6.2
Klein-Phi.......... 6.1
Berger-Bos 3.9
Schumacher-NY ... 3.9

TEAM	G	W	L	PCT	GB	R	OR	AB	H	2B	3B	HR	BB	SO	AVG	OBP	SLG	PRO	PRO+	BR	/A	PF	CHI	RC	SB	CS	SBA	SBR
WAS	153	99	53	.651		850	665	5524	1586	281	86	60	539	395	.287	.353	.402	.755	107	46	54	99	102	798	65	50	52	-15
NY	152	91	59	.607	7	927	768	5274	1495	241	75	144	700	506	.283	.369	.440	.809	128	155	201	94	100	880	74	59	53	-13
PHI	152	79	72	.523	19.5	875	853	5330	1519	298	56	139	625	618	.285	.362	.440	.802	117	135	127	101	97	867	33	34	39	-12
CLE	151	75	76	.497	23.5	654	669	5240	1366	218	77	50	448	426	.261	.321	.360	.681	82	-102	-135	105	103	616	36	40	51	-18
DET	155	75	79	.487	25	722	733	5502	1479	283	78	57	475	523	.269	.342	.380	.709	92	-53	-67	102	100	698	68	50	50	-14
CHI	151	67	83	.447	31	683	814	5318	1448	231	53	43	539	416	.272	.342	.360	.702	96	-49	-17	96	96	674	43	46	48	-14
BOS	149	63	86	.423	34.5	700	758	5201	1407	294	56	50	525	464	.271	.339	.377	.716	96	-28	-20	99	98	686	58	37	44	-14
STL	153	55	96	.364	43.5	669	820	5285	1337	244	64	64	520	556	.253	.322	.360	.682	80	-101	-148	106	103	625	70	60	58	-16
TOT	608					6080		42674	11637	2090	545	607	4371	3904	.273	.342	.390	.732							447	376	54	-91

TEAM	CG	SH	SV	IP	H	H/G	HR	BB	SO	RAT	ERA	ERA+	OAV	OOB	PR	/A	PF	CPI	FA	E	DP	FW	PW	BW	SBW	DIF
WAS	68	5	26	1389²	1415	9.2	64	452	447	12.2	3.82	109	.263	.322	71	56	98	98	.979	131	149	2.6	5.3	5.1	-.3	10.3
NY	70	8	22	1354²	1426	9.5	66	612	711	13.6	4.36	89	.267	.344	-12	-72	91	96	.972	165	122	.4	-6.8	19.0	-.1	3.5
PHI	69	6	14	1343²	1523	10.2	77	644	423	14.6	4.81	89	.282	.361	-78	-78	100	99	.966	203	121	-1.9	-7.4	12.0	-.0	.9
CLE	74	12	7	1350	1382	9.2	60	465	437	12.4	3.71	120	.263	.325	86	110	104	102	.974	156	127	.9	10.4	-12.8	-.6	1.6
DET	69	6	17	1398	1415	9.1	84	561	575	12.9	3.95	109	.263	.335	52	56	101	103	.971	178	167	-.2	5.3	-6.3	-.2	-.5
CHI	53	8	13	1371¹	1505	9.9	85	519	423	13.5	4.45	95	.277	.343	-25	-32	99	99	.970	186	143	-1.0	-3.0	-1.6	-.2	-2.2
BOS	60	4	14	1327²	1396	9.5	75	591	467	13.6	4.35	101	.270	.348	-10	4	102	101	.966	204	133	-2.2	.4	-1.9	-.2	-7.5
STL	55	7	10	1360²	1574	10.4	96	531	426	14.0	4.82	97	.289	.353	-81	-25	109	100	.976	149	162	1.5	-2.4	-14.0	-.4	-5.2
TOT	518	56	123	10895²		9.6				13.3	4.28		.273	.342					.972	1372	1124					

Runs		Hits		Doubles		Triples		Home Runs		Total Bases	
Gehrig-NY	138	Manush-Was	221	Cronin-Was	45	Manush-Was	17	Foxx-Phi	48	Foxx-Phi	403
Foxx-Phi	125	Gehringer-Det	204	Johnson-Phi	44	Combs-NY	16	Ruth-NY	34	Gehrig-NY	359
Manush-Was	115	Foxx-Phi	204	Burns-StL	43	Averill-Cle	16	Gehrig-NY	32	Manush-Was	302
Chapman-NY	112	Simmons-Chi	200	Rogell-Det	42	Myer-Was	15	Johnson-Phi	21	Gehringer-Det	294
Cramer-Phi	109	Gehrig-NY	198	Gehringer-Det	42	Reynolds-StL	14	Lazzeri-NY	18	Simmons-Chi	291

Runs Batted In		Runs Produced		Bases On Balls		Batting Average		On Base Percentage		Slugging Average	
Foxx-Phi	163	Gehrig-NY	245	Ruth-NY	114	Foxx-Phi	.356	Cochrane-Phi	.459	Foxx-Phi	.703
Gehrig-NY	139	Foxx-Phi	240	Cochrane-Phi	106	Manush-Was	.336	Foxx-Phi	.449	Gehrig-NY	.605
Simmons-Chi	119	Manush-Was	205	Bishop-Phi	106	Gehrig-NY	.334	Bishop-Phi	.446	Ruth-NY	.582
Cronin-Was	118	Cronin-Was	202	Foxx-Phi	96	Simmons-Chi	.331	Ruth-NY	.442	Cochrane-Phi	.515
Kuhel-Was	107	Chapman-NY	201	Swanson-Chi	93	Gehringer-Det	.325	Gehrig-NY	.424	Johnson-Phi	.505

Production		Adjusted Production		Batter Runs		Adjusted Batter Runs		Clutch Hitting Index		Runs Created	
Foxx-Phi	1.153	Foxx-Phi	199	Foxx-Phi	82.7	Foxx-Phi	81.9	Cronin-Was	147	Foxx-Phi	184
Gehrig-NY	1.030	Gehrig-NY	181	Gehrig-NY	59.5	Gehrig-NY	64.7	Melillo-StL	136	Gehrig-NY	151
Ruth-NY	1.023	Ruth-NY	180	Ruth-NY	49.5	Ruth-NY	53.9	Ferrell-StL-Bos	134	Ruth-NY	124
Cochrane-Phi	.974	Cochrane-Phi	156	Cochrane-Phi	41.6	Cochrane-Phi	40.9	Bluege-Was	133	Gehringer-Det	117
Johnson-Phi	.892	Dickey-NY	138	Johnson-Phi	26.8	Lazzeri-NY	26.3	R.Johnson-Bos	127	Manush-Was	111

Total Average		Stolen Bases		Stolen Base Average		Stolen Base Runs		Fielding Runs		Total Player Rating	
Foxx-Phi	1.348	Chapman-NY	27	Walker-Det	74.3	Walker-Det	2.4	Melillo-StL	23.3	Foxx-Phi	7.0
Ruth-NY	1.172	Walker-Det	26	Kuhel-Was	68.0	Werber-NY-Bos	1.5	Rogell-Det	19.5	Gehrig-NY	4.2
Cochrane-Phi	1.118	Swanson-Chi	19	Swanson-Chi	63.3	Stumpf-Bos	1.2	Simmons-Chi	14.3	Cronin-Was	4.1
Gehrig-NY	1.098	Kuhel-Was	17	Chapman-NY	60.0			Scharein-StL	14.0	Cochrane-Phi	3.6
Johnson-Phi	.940							Schulte-Was	13.6	Ruth-NY	3.5

Wins		Win Percentage		Games		Complete Games		Shutouts		Saves	
Grove-Phi	24	Grove-Phi	.750	Crowder-Was	52	Grove-Phi	21	Hildebrand-Cle	6	Russell-Was	13
Crowder-Was	24	Whitehill-Was	.733	Russell-Was	50	Whitehill-Was	19	Gomez-NY	4	Hogsett-Det	9
Whitehill-Was	22	Stewart-Was	.714	Welch-Bos	47	Hadley-StL	19	Blaeholder-StL	3	Moore-NY	8
		Allen-NY	.682	Kline-Bos	46	Ruffing-NY	18			Heving-Chi	6
										Grove-Phi	6

Innings Pitched		Fewest Hits/Game		Fewest BB/Game		Strikeouts		Strikeouts/Game		Ratio	
Hadley-StL	316.2	Bridges-Det	7.42	Brown-Cle	1.65	Gomez-NY	163	Gomez-NY	6.25	Marberry-Det	11.10
Crowder-Was	299.1	Weiland-Bos	8.20	Marberry-Det	2.30	Hadley-StL	149	Allen-NY	5.80	Stewart-Was	11.24
Grove-Phi	275.1	Allen-NY	8.33	Stewart-Was	2.34	Ruffing-NY	122	Ruffing-NY	4.67	Harder-Cle	11.53
Whitehill-Was	270.0	Gomez-NY	8.36	Harder-Cle	2.38	Bridges-Det	120	Bridges-Det	4.64	Brown-Cle	11.58
Blaeholder-StL	255.2	Hildebrand-Cle	8.37	Blaeholder-StL	2.43	Allen-NY	119	Fischer-Det	4.58	Weaver-Was	11.88

Earned Run Average		Adjusted ERA		Opponents' Batting Avg.		Opponents' On Base Pct.		Starter Runs		Adjusted Starter Runs	
Harder-Cle	2.95	Harder-Cle	151	Bridges-Det	.226	Marberry-Det	.302	Harder-Cle	37.4	Harder-Cle	41.9
Bridges-Det	3.09	Bridges-Det	140	Gomez-NY	.240	Stewart-Was	.304	Grove-Phi	33.0	Grove-Phi	33.1
Gomez-NY	3.18	Grove-Phi	134	Allen-NY	.242	Harder-Cle	.309	Bridges-Det	30.8	Pearson-Cle	31.8
Grove-Phi	3.20	Marberry-Det	131	Weiland-Bos	.244	Brown-Cle	.310	Pearson-Cle	29.4	Bridges-Det	31.6
Weaver-Was	3.25	Brown-Cle	130	Hildebrand-Cle	.245	Grove-Phi	.316	Gomez-NY	28.6	Marberry-Det	27.2

Clutch Pitching Index		Relief Runs		Adjusted Relief Runs		Relief Ranking		Total Pitcher Index		Total Baseball Ranking	
Cain-Phi	125	Russell-Was	22.0	Russell-Was	20.6	Russell-Was	31.8	Harder-Cle	5.0	Foxx-Phi	7.0
Jones-Chi	124	Heving-Chi	21.1	Heving-Chi	20.6	Heving-Chi	21.2	Bridges-Det	3.4	Harder-Cle	5.0
Harder-Cle	115	Faber-Chi	8.1	Faber-Chi	7.7	Gray-StL	6.7	Pearson-Cle	3.3	Gehrig-NY	4.2
Whitehill-Was	112	Burke-Was	7.4	Gray-StL	6.9	Burke-Was	6.6	Grove-Phi	2.6	Cronin-Was	4.1
Grove-Phi	111	Herring-Det	3.0	Burke-Was	6.7	Faber-Chi	6.6	Whitehill-Was	2.4	Cochrane-Phi	3.6

TEAM	G	W	L	PCT	GB	R	OR	AB	H	2B	3B	HR	BB	SO	AVG	OBP	SLG	PRO	PRO+	BR	/A	PF	CHI	RC	SB	CS	SBA	SBR
STL	154	95	58	.621		799	656	5502	1582	294	75	104	392	535	.288	.337	.425	.762	102	63	15	107	101	796	69			
NY	153	93	60	.608	2	760	583	5396	1485	240	41	126	406	526	.275	.329	.405	.734	104	8	25	98	105	736	19			
CHI	152	86	65	.570	8	705	639	5347	1494	263	44	101	375	630	.279	.330	.402	.732	103	5	19	98	99	719	59			
BOS	152	78	73	.517	16	683	714	5370	1460	233	44	83	375	440	.272	.323	.378	.701	100	-51	2	93	104	660	30			
PIT	151	74	76	.493	19.5	735	713	5361	1541	281	77	52	440	398	.287	.344	.398	.742	101	34	17	102	99	742	44			
BRO	153	71	81	.467	23.5	748	795	5427	1526	284	52	79	548	555	.281	.350	.396	.746	111	51	87	95	95	782	55			
PHI	149	56	93	.376	37	675	794	5218	1480	286	35	56	398	534	.284	.338	.384	.722	87	-2	-94	113	98	685	52			
CIN	152	52	99	.344	42	590	801	5361	1428	227	65	55	313	532	.266	.311	.364	.675	88	-104	-87	98	99	603	34			
TOT	608					5695		42982	11996	2108	433	656	3247	4150	.279	.333	.394	.727							362			

TEAM	CG	SH	SV	IP	H	H/G	HR	BB	SO	RAT	ERA	ERA+	OAV	OOB	PR	/A	PF	CPI	FA	E	DP	FW	PW	BW	SBW	DIF
STL	78	15	16	1386²	1463	9.5	77	411	689	12.4	3.69	115	.268	.323	57	82	104	101	.972	166	141	.3	8.0	1.5		8.7
NY	68	13	30	1370	1384	9.1	75	351	499	11.5	3.19	121	.260	.308	132	102	95	105	.972	179	141	-.5	9.9	2.4		4.6
CHI	73	11	9	1361¹	1432	9.5	80	417	633	12.3	3.76	103	.269	.324	46	18	95	101	.977	137	135	1.9	1.8	1.9		5.0
BOS	62	12	20	1359²	1512	10.0	78	405	462	12.8	4.11	93	.279	.331	-7	-44	94	97	.972	169	120	.0	-4.3	.2		6.6
PIT	63	8	8	1329²	1523	10.3	78	354	487	12.9	4.20	98	.284	.332	-19	-13	101	98	.975	145	118	1.4	-1.3	1.7		-2.8
BRO	66	6	12	1354¹	1540	10.2	81	475	520	13.6	4.48	87	.284	.345	-62	-87	96	97	.970	180	141	-.6	-8.5	8.5		-4.4
PHI	52	8	15	1297	1501	10.4	126	437	416	13.6	4.76	99	.288	.346	-100	-3	116	99	.966	197	140	-1.8	-.3	-9.2		-7.2
CIN	51	3	19	1347²	1645	11.0	61	389	438	13.8	4.37	93	.298	.348	-45	-42	101	102	.970	181	136	-.7	-4.1	-8.5		-10.2
TOT	513	76	129	10806¹		10.0				12.9	4.06		.279	.333					.972	1354	1072					

Runs		Hits		Doubles		Triples		Home Runs		Total Bases	
P.Waner-Pit	122	P.Waner-Pit	217	Cuyler-Chi	42	Medwick-StL	18	Ott-NY	35	Collins-StL	369
Ott-NY	119	Terry-NY	213	Allen-Phi	42	P.Waner-Pit	16	Collins-StL	35	Ott-NY	344
Collins-StL	116	Collins-StL	200	Vaughan-Pit	41	Suhr-Pit	13	Berger-Bos	34	Berger-Bos	336
Vaughan-Pit	115	Medwick-StL	198	Medwick-StL	40	Collins-StL	12	Hartnett-Chi	22	Medwick-StL	328
Medwick-StL	110			Collins-StL	40			Klein-Chi	20	P.Waner-Pit	323

Runs Batted In		Runs Produced		Bases On Balls		Batting Average		On Base Percentage		Slugging Average	
Ott-NY	135	Ott-NY	219	Vaughan-Pit	94	P.Waner-Pit	.362	Vaughan-Pit	.431	Collins-StL	.615
Collins-StL	128	Collins-StL	209	Ott-NY	85	Terry-NY	.354	P.Waner-Pit	.429	Ott-NY	.591
Berger-Bos	121	P.Waner-Pit	198	Koenecke-Bro	70	Cuyler-Chi	.338	Ott-NY	.415	Berger-Bos	.546
Medwick-StL	106	Medwick-StL	198	Leslie-Bro	69	Vaughan-Pit	.333	Terry-NY	.414	P.Waner-Pit	.539
Suhr-Pit	103	Vaughan-Pit	197	P.Waner-Pit	68	Collins-StL	.333	Koenecke-Bro	.411	Medwick-StL	.529

Production		Adjusted Production		Batter Runs		Adjusted Batter Runs		Clutch Hitting Index		Runs Created	
Collins-StL	1.008	Ott-NY	170	Ott-NY	55.2	Ott-NY	57.1	Thevenow-Pit	138	Ott-NY	150
Ott-NY	1.006	Collins-StL	155	Collins-StL	53.3	P.Waner-Pit	48.3	Durocher-StL	137	Collins-StL	148
P.Waner-Pit	.968	P.Waner-Pit	154	P.Waner-Pit	50.2	Collins-StL	48.1	Leslie-Bro	136	P.Waner-Pit	142
Vaughan-Pit	.942	Koenecke-Bro	152	Vaughan-Pit	44.3	Vaughan-Pit	42.5	Jackson-NY	135	Vaughan-Pit	135
Koenecke-Bro	.919	Berger-Bos	148	Terry-NY	31.5	Berger-Bos	35.3	Cuccinello-Bro	134	Terry-NY	122

Total Average		Stolen Bases		Stolen Base Average	Stolen Base Runs	Fielding Runs		Total Player Rating	
Ott-NY	1.075	Martin-StL	23			Critz-NY	25.0	Vaughan-Pit	4.6
Collins-StL	1.046	Cuyler-Chi	15			G.Davis-StL	16.8	P.Waner-Pit	4.5
Vaughan-Pit	1.043	Bartell-Phi	13			W.Herman-Chi	15.6	Collins-StL	4.1
P.Waner-Pit	1.010	Taylor-Bro	12			Hartnett-Chi	13.7	Ott-NY	3.8
Koenecke-Bro	.981					Bartell-Phi	13.5	Hartnett-Chi	3.4

Wins		Win Percentage		Games		Complete Games		Shutouts		Saves	
J.Dean-StL	30	J.Dean-StL	.811	C.Davis-Phi	51	Hubbell-NY	25	J.Dean-StL	7	Hubbell-NY	8
Schumacher-NY	23	Hoyt-Pit	.714	Hansen-Phi	50	J.Dean-StL	24	Hubbell-NY	5	Luque-NY	7
Warneke-Chi	22	Schumacher-NY	.697	J.Dean-StL	50	Warneke-Chi	23	P.Dean-StL	5	J.Dean-StL	7
Hubbell-NY	21	Warneke-Chi	.688	Hubbell-NY	49	Mungo-Bro	22	Lee-Chi	4	Bell-NY	6
		Frankhouse-Bos	.654	French-Pit	49	Brandt-Bos	20				

Innings Pitched		Fewest Hits/Game		Fewest BB/Game		Strikeouts		Strikeouts/Game		Ratio	
Mungo-Bro	315.1	Parmelee-NY	7.90	Hubbell-NY	1.06	J.Dean-StL	195	P.Dean-StL	5.79	Hubbell-NY	9.35
Hubbell-NY	313.0	Hubbell-NY	8.22	Freitas-Cin	1.47	Mungo-Bro	184	J.Dean-StL	5.63	Warneke-Chi	10.53
J.Dean-StL	311.2	J.Dean-StL	8.32	Frey-Cin	1.54	P.Dean-StL	150	Weaver-Chi	5.55	J.Dean-StL	10.66
Schumacher-NY	297.0	Warneke-Chi	8.43	Leonard-Bro	1.62	Warneke-Chi	143	Mungo-Bro	5.25	Hoyt-Pit	10.81
Warneke-Chi	291.1	Mungo-Bro	8.56	Fitzsimmons-NY	1.74	Derringer-Cin	122	Malone-Chi	5.23	Fitzsimmons-NY	10.87

Earned Run Average		Adjusted ERA		Opponents' Batting Avg.		Opponents' On Base Pct.		Starter Runs		Adjusted Starter Runs	
Hubbell-NY	2.30	Hubbell-NY	168	Parmelee-NY	.238	Hubbell-NY	.263	Hubbell-NY	61.3	Hubbell-NY	54.5
J.Dean-StL	2.66	C.Davis-Phi	160	Hubbell-NY	.239	Warneke-Chi	.287	J.Dean-StL	48.7	J.Dean-StL	54.3
Hoyt-Pit	2.93	J.Dean-StL	159	J.Dean-StL	.241	J.Dean-StL	.289	C.Davis-Phi	33.8	C.Davis-Phi	54.0
C.Davis-Phi	2.95	Hoyt-Pit	141	Warneke-Chi	.244	P.Dean-StL	.292	Fitzsimmons-NY	29.8	Hoyt-Pit	25.2
Fitzsimmons-NY	3.04	Walker-StL	135	P.Dean-StL	.248	Hoyt-Pit	.296	Schumacher-NY	29.0	Fitzsimmons-NY	24.1

Clutch Pitching Index		Relief Runs		Adjusted Relief Runs		Relief Ranking		Total Pitcher Index		Total Baseball Ranking	
Walker-StL	137	Haines-StL	5.6	Haines-StL	7.2	Haines-StL	6.0	C.Davis-Phi	6.6	C.Davis-Phi	6.6
Leonard-Bro	121	Bell-NY	2.4	Brennan-Cin	2.4	Brennan-Cin	2.1	Hubbell-NY	5.9	Hubbell-NY	5.9
C.Davis-Phi	120	Brennan-Cin	2.2	Bell-NY	1.2	Bell-NY	1.7	J.Dean-StL	5.8	J.Dean-StL	5.8
Freitas-Cin	111							Schumacher-NY	3.5	Vaughan-Pit	4.6
Frankhouse-Bos	110							Fitzsimmons-NY	3.4	P.Waner-Pit	4.5

TEAM	G	W	L	PCT	GB	R	OR	AB	H	2B	3B	HR	BB	SO	AVG	OBP	SLG	PRO	PRO+	BR	/A	PF	CHI	RC	SB	CS	SBA	SBR
DET	154	101	53	.656		958	708	5475	**1644**	349	53	74	639	528	**.300**	**.376**	.424	**.800**	112	**112**	110	100	104	**905**	124	55	49	-12
NY	154	94	60	.610	7	842	**669**	5368	1494	226	61	135	639	597	.278	.364	.419	.783	116	70	**124**	93	96	848	71	46	48	-14
CLE	154	85	69	.552	16	814	763	5396	1550	340	46	100	526	**433**	.287	.353	.423	.776	105	44	32	102	98	820	52	32	40	-13
BOS	153	76	76	.500	24	820	775	5339	1465	287	**70**	51	610	535	.274	.350	.383	.733	89	-27	-82	107	**108**	748	116	47	**54**	-17
PHI	153	68	82	.453	31	764	838	5317	1491	236	50	**144**	491	584	.280	.343	**.425**	.768	107	20	48	96	97	785	57	35	39	-12
STL	154	67	85	.441	33	674	800	5288	1417	252	59	62	514	631	.268	.335	.373	.708	82	-83	-147	108	98	680	42	31	44	-16
WAS	155	66	86	.434	34	729	806	5448	1512	278	**70**	51	567	447	.278	.348	.382	.730	98	-35	-4	96	95	746	49	42	49	-16
CHI	153	53	99	.349	47	704	946	5301	1395	237	40	71	565	524	.263	.336	.363	.699	84	-96	-119	103	103	672	36	27	36	-13
TOT	615					6305		42932	11968	2205	449	688	4612	4279	.279	.351	.399	.750							547	315	63	-24

TEAM	CG	SH	SV	IP	H	H/G	HR	BB	SO	RAT	ERA	ERA+	OAV	OOB	PR	/A	PF	CPI	FA	E	DP	FW	PW	BW	SBW	DIF
DET	74	**13**	14	1370²	1467	9.6	86	**488**	640	12.9	4.06	108	.273	.335	66	50	98	102	**.974**	159	150	1.2	4.6	10.2	-.8	8.8
NY	**83**	**13**	10	1382²	1349	8.8	71	542	**656**	12.4	3.76	108	**.254**	.324	113	47	90	97	.973	**157**	151	**1.3**	4.4	**11.5**	-1.0	.8
CLE	72	8	19	1367	1476	9.7	**70**	582	554	13.7	4.28	106	.275	.349	33	40	101	101	.972	172	164	.4	3.7	3.0	-.9	1.8
BOS	68	9	9	1361	1527	10.1	**70**	543	538	13.8	4.32	111	.282	.351	27	72	107	103	.969	188	141	-.5	6.7	-7.6	-1.3	2.8
PHI	68	8	8	1337	1429	9.6	84	693	480	14.4	5.01	87	.275	.363	-76	-94	97	94	.967	196	166	-1.0	-8.7	4.5	-.8	-.9
STL	50	6	**20**	1350	1499	10.0	94	632	499	14.3	4.49	111	.283	.360	0	**75**	111	107	.969	187	160	-.4	**7.0**	-13.7	-1.2	-.7
WAS	61	4	12	1381¹	1622	10.6	74	503	412	13.9	4.68	92	.294	.355	-27	-55	96	101	**.974**	162	167	1.0	-5.1	-.4	-1.2	-4.4
CHI	72	5	8	1355	1599	10.6	139	628	506	14.9	5.41	88	.291	.366	-136	-101	105	97	.966	207	126	-1.6	-9.4	-11.1	-.9	-.0
TOT	548	66	100	10904²		9.9				13.8	4.50		.279	.351					.970	1428	1225					

Runs		Hits		Doubles		Triples		Home Runs		Total Bases	
Gehringer-Det	134	Gehringer-Det	214	Greenberg-Det	63	Chapman-NY	13	Gehrig-NY	49	Gehrig-NY	409
Werber-Bos	129	Gehrig-NY	210	Gehringer-Det	50	Manush-Was	11	Foxx-Phi	44	Trosky-Cle	374
Gehrig-NY	128	Trosky-Cle	206	Averill-Cle	48			Trosky-Cle	35	Greenberg-Det	356
Averill-Cle	128	Cramer-Phi	202	Trosky-Cle	45			Johnson-Phi	34	Foxx-Phi	352
Foxx-Phi	120	Greenberg-Det	201	Hale-Cle	44			Averill-Cle	31	Averill-Cle	340

Runs Batted In		Runs Produced		Bases On Balls		Batting Average		On Base Percentage		Slugging Average	
Gehrig-NY	165	Gehringer-Det	250	Foxx-Phi	111	Gehrig-NY	.363	Gehrig-NY	.465	Gehrig-NY	.706
Trosky-Cle	142	Gehrig-NY	244	Gehrig-NY	109	Gehringer-Det	.356	Gehringer-Det	.450	Foxx-Phi	.653
Greenberg-Det	139	Greenberg-Det	231	Ruth-NY	103	Manush-Was	.349	Foxx-Phi	.449	Greenberg-Det	.600
Foxx-Phi	130	Trosky-Cle	224	Myer-Was	102	Simmons-Chi	.344	Cochrane-Det	.428	Trosky-Cle	.598
Gehringer-Det	127	Rogell-Det	211			Greenberg-Det	.339	Myer-Was	.419	Averill-Cle	.569

Production		Adjusted Production		Batter Runs		Adjusted Batter Runs		Clutch Hitting Index		Runs Created	
Gehrig-NY	1.172	Gehrig-NY	213	Gehrig-NY	85.6	Gehrig-NY	91.7	Cronin-Was	153	Gehrig-NY	195
Foxx-Phi	1.102	Foxx-Phi	188	Foxx-Phi	66.4	Foxx-Phi	69.5	Dykes-Chi	148	Foxx-Phi	165
Greenberg-Det	1.005	Greenberg-Det	156	Gehringer-Det	47.8	Gehringer-Det	47.6	Rogell-Det	147	Averill-Cle	145
Trosky-Cle	.987	Trosky-Cle	149	Greenberg-Det	46.7	Greenberg-Det	46.5	R.Johnson-Bos	147	Trosky-Cle	145
Averill-Cle	.982	Averill-Cle	149	Averill-Cle	45.6	Averill-Cle	44.3	Morgan-Bos	143	Gehringer-Det	144

Total Average		Stolen Bases		Stolen Base Average		Stolen Base Runs		Fielding Runs		Total Player Rating	
Gehrig-NY	1.401	Werber-Bos	40	White-Det	82.4	White-Det	4.8	Hale-Cle	25.7	Gehrig-NY	6.0
Foxx-Phi	1.310	White-Det	28	Werber-Bos	72.7	Werber-Bos	3.0	Hemsley-StL	24.0	Gehringer-Det	5.5
Averill-Cle	1.075	Chapman-NY	26	Fox-Det	71.4	Lazzeri-NY	2.7	Werber-Bos	20.3	Foxx-Phi	4.7
Greenberg-Det	1.071	Fox-Det	25	Walker-Det	69.0	Cronin-Was	2.4	Cronin-Was	18.4	Averill-Cle	4.3
Gehringer-Det	1.053	Walker-Det	20	Chapman-NY	61.9			Melillo-StL	18.1	Werber-Bos	3.7

Wins		Win Percentage		Games		Complete Games		Shutouts		Saves	
Gomez-NY	26	Gomez-NY	.839	Russell-Was	54	Gomez-NY	25	Harder-Cle	6	Russell-Was	7
Rowe-Det	24	Rowe-Det	.750	Newsom-StL	47	Bridges-Det	23	Gomez-NY	6	L.Brown-Cle	6
Bridges-Det	22	Marberry-Det	.750	Rowe-Det	45	Lyons-Chi	21	Ruffing-NY	5	Newsom-StL	5
Harder-Cle	20	Auker-Det	.682	Knott-StL	45	Rowe-Det	20	Dietrich-Phi	4		
Ruffing-NY	19	Bridges-Det	.667								

Innings Pitched		Fewest Hits/Game		Fewest BB/Game		Strikeouts		Strikeouts/Game		Ratio	
Gomez-NY	281.2	Gomez-NY	7.13	W.Ferrell-Bos	2.44	Gomez-NY	158	Ruffing-NY	5.23	Gomez-NY	10.19
Bridges-Det	275.0	Ruffing-NY	8.15	Auker-Det	2.46	Bridges-Det	151	Gomez-NY	5.05	Rowe-Det	11.54
Rowe-Det	266.0	Bridges-Det	8.15	Blaeholder-StL	2.61	Ruffing-NY	149	Rowe-Det	5.04	Bridges-Det	11.65
Newsom-StL	262.1	Burke-Was	8.30	Rowe-Det	2.74	Rowe-Det	149	Pearson-Cle	4.95	Murphy-NY	11.66
Ruffing-NY	256.1	Murphy-NY	8.36	Weaver-Was	2.77	Pearson-Cle	140	Bridges-Det	4.94	Harder-Cle	11.77

Earned Run Average		Adjusted ERA		Opponents' Batting Avg.		Opponents' On Base Pct.		Starter Runs		Adjusted Starter Runs	
Gomez-NY	2.33	Harder-Cle	174	Gomez-NY	.215	Gomez-NY	.282	Gomez-NY	67.7	Harder-Cle	55.0
Harder-Cle	2.61	Gomez-NY	174	Ruffing-NY	.236	Ruffing-NY	.310	Harder-Cle	53.6	Gomez-NY	54.2
Murphy-NY	3.12	Ostermueller-Bos	138	Bridges-Det	.241	Rowe-Det	.312	Murphy-NY	31.8	Ostermueller-Bos	29.0
Burke-Was	3.21	Burke-Was	134	Burke-Was	.245	Bridges-Det	.312	Rowe-Det	30.9	Newsom-StL	28.6
Auker-Det	3.42	W.Ferrell-Bos	132	Benton-Phi	.249	Harder-Cle	.316	Bridges-Det	25.4	Rowe-Det	27.7

Clutch Pitching Index		Relief Runs		Adjusted Relief Runs		Relief Ranking		Total Pitcher Index		Total Baseball Ranking	
Harder-Cle	127	Pennock-Bos	10.0	Pennock-Bos	12.1	Bean-Cle	4.1	Harder-Cle	5.5	Gehrig-NY	6.0
Auker-Det	123	McColl-Was	8.0	McColl-Was	5.7	Pennock-Bos	3.9	Gomez-NY	4.7	Harder-Cle	5.5
Ostermueller-Bos	116	Russell-Was	5.8	Bean-Cle	3.9	McColl-Was	3.3	Rowe-Det	3.7	Gehringer-Det	5.5
Murphy-NY	113	Bean-Cle	3.7	Russell-Was	2.6	Russell-Was	2.5	W.Ferrell-Bos	3.1	Gomez-NY	4.7
Coffman-StL	109			Wells-StL	2.1	Wells-StL	1.7	Ostermueller-Bos	3.0	Foxx-Phi	4.7

TEAM	G	W	L	PCT	GB	R	OR	AB	H	2B	3B	HR	BB	SO	AVG	OBP	SLG	PRO	PRO+	BR	/A	PF	CHI	RC	SB	CS	SBA	SBR
CHI	154	100	54	.649		847	597	5486	1581	303	62	88	464	471	.288	.347	.414	.761	110	81	76	101	102	812	66			
STL	154	96	58	.623	4	829	625	5457	1548	286	59	86	404	521	.284	.335	.405	.740	100	33	3	104	109	759	71			
NY	156	91	62	.595	8.5	770	675	5623	1608	248	56	123	392	479	.286	.336	.416	.752	109	54	67	98	96	797	32			
PIT	153	86	67	.562	13.5	743	647	5415	1543	255	90	66	457	437	.285	.343	.402	.745	102	49	25	103	96	758	30			
BRO	154	70	83	.458	29.5	711	767	5410	1496	235	62	59	430	520	.277	.333	.376	.709	99	-20	-4	98	101	691	60			
CIN	154	68	85	.444	31.5	646	772	5296	1403	244	68	73	392	547	.265	.319	.378	.697	95	-50	-28	97	98	658	72			
PHI	156	64	89	.418	35.5	685	871	5442	1466	249	32	92	392	661	.269	.322	.378	.700	85	-46	-119	110	101	681	52			
BOS	153	38	115	.248	61.5	575	852	5309	1396	233	33	75	353	436	.263	.311	.362	.673	93	-97	-40	92	95	596	20			
TOT	617					5806		43438	12041	2053	462	662	3284	4072	.277	.331	.391	.722							403			

TEAM	CG	SH	SV	IP	H	H/G	HR	BB	SO	RAT	ERA	ERA+	OAV	OOB	PR	/A	PF	CPI	FA	E	DP	FW	PW	BW	SBW	DIF
CHI	81	12	14	1394¹	1417	9.1	85	400	589	11.9	3.26	121	.263	.316	117	103	98	111	.970	186	163	.3	10.0	7.4		5.3
STL	73	10	18	1383²	1447	9.4	68	382	594	12.1	3.54	116	.267	.318	74	87	102	102	.972	164	133	1.6	8.5	.3		8.7
NY	76	10	11	1403²	1433	9.2	106	411	524	12.0	3.78	102	.262	.317	37	11	96	99	.972	174	129	1.1	1.1	6.5		5.8
PIT	76	15	11	1365²	1428	9.4	63	312	549	11.6	3.42	120	.264	.307	91	103	102	98	.968	190	94	.0	10.0	2.4		-2.9
BRO	62	11	20	1358	1519	10.1	88	436	480	13.1	4.22	94	.281	.336	-30	-36	99	100	.969	188	146	.2	-3.5	-.4		-2.8
CIN	59	9	13	1356	1490	9.9	65	438	500	13.0	4.30	93	.278	.336	-42	-48	99	94	.966	204	139	-.7	-4.7	-2.7		-.4
PHI	53	8	15	1374²	1652	10.8	106	505	475	14.4	4.76	95	.294	.358	-112	-34	113	102	.963	228	145	-2.0	-3.3	-11.6		4.3
BOS	54	6	5	1330	1645	11.1	81	404	355	14.0	4.93	77	.303	.353	-134	-169	94	97	.967	197	101	-.4	-16.4	-3.9		-17.8
TOT	534	81	107	10966		9.9				12.7	4.02		.277	.331					.968	1531	1050					

Runs
Galan-Chi 133
Medwick-StL 132
Martin-StL 121
Ott-NY 113
Herman-Chi 113

Hits
Herman-Chi 227
Medwick-StL 224

Doubles
Herman-Chi 57
Medwick-StL 46
Allen-Phi.......... 46
Martin-StL 41
Galan-Chi 41

Triples
Goodman-Cin 18
L.Waner-Pit 14
Medwick-StL 13

Home Runs
Berger-Bos 34
Ott-NY 31
Camilli-Phi 25
Medwick-StL 23
J.Collins-StL 23

Total Bases
Medwick-StL 365
Ott-NY 329
Berger-Bos 323
Herman-Chi 317
Leiber-NY 314

Runs Batted In
Berger-Bos 130
Medwick-StL 126
J.Collins-StL 122
Ott-NY 114
Leiber-NY 107

Runs Produced
Medwick-StL 235
J.Collins-StL 208
Galan-Chi 200
Ott-NY 196
Leiber-NY 195

Bases On Balls
Vaughan-Pit 97
Galan-Chi 87
Ott-NY 82
Suhr-Pit 70
Frey-Bro 66

Batting Average
Vaughan-Pit 385
Medwick-StL 353
Herman-Chi 341
Terry-NY 341
Leiber-NY 331

On Base Percentage
Vaughan-Pit 491
Ott-NY 407
Hack-Chi 406
Galan-Chi 399
P.Waner-Pit 392

Slugging Average
Vaughan-Pit 607
Medwick-StL 576
Ott-NY 555
Berger-Bos 548
J.Collins-StL 529

Production
Vaughan-Pit 1.098
Medwick-StL 962
Ott-NY 962
J.Collins-StL 915
Berger-Bos 903

Adjusted Production
Vaughan-Pit 187
Ott-NY 159
Berger-Bos 151
Medwick-StL 149
Leiber-NY 143

Batter Runs
Vaughan-Pit 71.9
Ott-NY 47.6
Medwick-StL 46.0
J.Collins-StL 35.0
Leiber-NY 34.3

Adjusted Batter Runs
Vaughan-Pit 69.5
Ott-NY 49.1
Medwick-StL 42.7
Berger-Bos 36.1
Leiber-NY 35.8

Clutch Hitting Index
Leslie-Bro 146
Young-Pit 138
Jurges-Chi 131
Durocher-StL..... 130
J.Collins-StL 124

Runs Created
Vaughan-Pit 163
Ott-NY 144
Medwick-StL 139
Galan-Chi 133
J.Collins-StL 125

Total Average
Vaughan-Pit 1.317
Ott-NY 1.037
Medwick-StL 948
Galan-Chi 937
J.Collins-StL 930

Stolen Bases
Galan-Chi 22
Martin-StL 20
Bordagaray-Bro ... 18
Hack-Chi 14
Goodman-Cin 14

Stolen Base Average

Stolen Base Runs

Fielding Runs
Jurges-Chi 30.3
Herman-Chi 19.0
Hartnett-Chi 14.0
Allen-Phi......... 11.9
T.Moore-StL 11.6

Total Player Rating
Vaughan-Pit 6.1
Herman-Chi 5.5
Ott-NY 4.5
Hartnett-Chi 4.2
Berger-Bos 3.5

Wins
J.Dean-StL 28
Hubbell-NY 23
Derringer-Cin 22
Warneke-Chi 20
Lee-Chi........... 20

Win Percentage
Lee-Chi............769
Castleman-NY 714
J.Dean-StL........700
Schumacher-NY ..679
Hubbell-NY 657

Games
Jorgens-Phi 53
J.Dean-StL 50
Bivin-Phi 47
Smith-Bos 46
P.Dean-StL........ 46

Complete Games
J.Dean-StL 29
Hubbell-NY 24
Blanton-Pit 23
Warneke-Chi 20
Derringer-Cin...... 20

Shutouts
Weaver-Pit 4
Mungo-Bro 4
French-Chi 4
Fitzsimmons-NY 4
Blanton-Pit......... 4

Saves
Leonard-Bro 8
Johnson-Phi 6
Hoyt-Pit 6

Innings Pitched
J.Dean-StL 324.1
Hubbell-NY 302.2
Derringer-Cin ... 276.2
P.Dean-StL 269.2

Fewest Hits/Game
Blanton-Pit 7.79
Schumacher-NY .. 8.08
Parmelee-NY 8.52
Swift-Pit 8.53
Hollingsworth-Cin . 8.57

Fewest BB/Game
Clark-Bro 1.22
Hubbell-NY 1.46
Hoyt-Pit 1.48
Derringer-Cin..... 1.59
Johnson-Phi 1.60

Strikeouts
J.Dean-StL 182
Hubbell-NY 150
Mungo-Bro 143
P.Dean-StL 143
Blanton-Pit 142

Strikeouts/Game
Mungo-Bro 6.00
J.Dean-StL 5.05
Blanton-Pit 5.02
P.Dean-StL 4.77
Hollingsworth-Cin . 4.62

Ratio
Blanton-Pit....... 9.80
Swift-Pit 10.21
Clark-Bro 10.61
Warneke-Chi 10.66
Schumacher-NY . 10.66

Earned Run Average
Blanton-Pit 2.58
Swift-Pit 2.70
Schumacher-NY .. 2.89
French-Chi 2.96
Lee-Chi........... 2.96

Adjusted ERA
Blanton-Pit 159
Swift-Pit 152
Schumacher-NY .. 133
French-Chi 133
Lee-Chi........... 133

Opponents' Batting Avg.
Blanton-Pit........229
Schumacher-NY ..238
Hollingsworth-Cin ..243
Swift-Pit 247
P.Dean-StL 249

Opponents' On Base Pct.
Blanton-Pit........272
Swift-Pit 282
Clark-Bro 289
Schumacher-NY ..292
P.Dean-StL 292

Starter Runs
Blanton-Pit....... 40.6
Schumacher-NY . 32.9
J.Dean-StL....... 32.9
Swift-Pit 30.0
Lee-Chi.......... 29.6

Adjusted Starter Runs
Blanton-Pit....... 43.0
J.Dean-StL 35.8
Swift-Pit 31.9
Schumacher-NY . 28.1
Lee-Chi.......... 27.1

Clutch Pitching Index
French-Chi 126
Zachary-Bro 121
Walker-StL 116
Lee-Chi.......... 111
Hallahan-StL 111

Relief Runs

Adjusted Relief Runs

Relief Ranking

Total Pitcher Index
Blanton-Pit........ 4.2
Schumacher-NY .. 3.8
J.Dean-StL....... 3.5
Swift-Pit 3.1
Lee-Chi........... 2.9

Total Baseball Ranking
Vaughan-Pit 6.1
Herman-Chi 5.5
Ott-NY 4.5
Hartnett-Chi 4.2
Blanton-Pit........ 4.2

TEAM	G	W	L	PCT	GB	R	OR	AB	H	2B	3B	HR	BB	SO	AVG	OBP	SLG	PRO	PRO+	BR	/A	PF	CHI	RC	SB	CS	SBA	SBR
DET	152	93	58	.616		919	665	5423	1573	301	83	106	627	456	.290	.366	.435	.801	116	95	122	97	104	885	70	45	56	-19
NY	149	89	60	.597	3	818	632	5214	1462	255	70	104	604	469	.280	.358	.416	.774	111	42	84	94	102	799	68	46	45	-12
CLE	156	82	71	.536	12	776	739	5534	1573	324	77	93	460	567	.284	.341	.421	.762	100	3	-11	102	99	796	63	54	55	-16
BOS	154	78	75	.510	16	718	732	5288	1458	281	63	69	609	470	.276	.353	.392	.745	91	-10	-62	107	94	757	89	59	52	-13
CHI	153	74	78	.487	19.5	738	750	5314	1460	262	42	74	580	405	.275	.348	.382	.730	91	-40	-59	103	101	733	46	28	35	-12
WAS	154	67	86	.438	27	823	903	5592	1591	255	95	32	595	406	.285	.357	.381	.738	99	-18	8	97	104	787	54	37	51	-19
STL	155	65	87	.428	28.5	718	930	5365	1446	291	51	73	593	561	.270	.344	.384	.728	89	-48	-83	105	98	735	45	25	33	-11
PHI	149	58	91	.389	34	710	869	5269	1470	243	44	112	475	602	.279	.341	.406	.747	98	-22	-16	99	98	738	42	35	51	-19
TOT	611					6220		42999	12033	2212	525	663	4543	3936	.280	.351	.402	.753							477	329	59	-53

TEAM	CG	SH	SV	IP	H	H/G	HR	BB	SO	RAT	ERA	ERA+	OAV	OOB	PR	/A	PF	CPI	FA	E	DP	FW	PW	BW	SBW	DIF
DET	87	16	11	1364	1440	9.5	78	522	584	13.1	3.82	109	.270	.339	96	52	94	107	.978	128	154	2.3	4.9	11.4	-1.1	.0
NY	76	12	13	1331	1276	8.6	91	516	594	12.2	3.60	112	.250	.321	125	65	91	101	.974	151	114	.8	6.1	7.9	-.5	.3
CLE	67	12	21	1396	1527	9.8	68	457	498	12.9	4.15	108	.277	.334	47	54	101	97	.972	177	147	-.3	5.1	-1.0	-.9	2.6
BOS	82	6	11	1376	1520	9.9	67	520	470	13.5	4.05	117	.280	.345	62	106	107	106	.969	194	136	-1.4	9.9	-5.8	-.6	-.7
CHI	80	8	8	1360²	1443	9.5	105	574	436	13.5	4.38	106	.272	.345	11	36	104	100	.976	146	133	1.3	3.4	-5.5	-.5	-.7
WAS	67	5	12	1378²	1672	10.9	89	613	456	15.1	5.25	82	.301	.374	-121	-142	97	99	.972	171	186	-.0	-13.3	.7	-1.1	4.2
STL	42	4	15	1380¹	1667	10.9	92	640	435	15.2	5.26	91	.297	.370	-123	-71	108	97	.970	187	138	-.9	-6.6	-7.8	-.4	4.7
PHI	58	7	10	1326¹	1486	10.1	73	704	469	15.0	5.12	89	.284	.372	-97	-84	102	96	.968	190	150	-1.4	-7.9	-1.5	-1.1	-4.5
TOT	559	70	101	10913		9.9				13.8	4.46		.280	.351					.972	1344	1158					

Runs		Hits		Doubles		Triples		Home Runs		Total Bases	
Gehrig-NY	125	Vosmik-Cle	216	Vosmik-Cle	47	Vosmik-Cle	20	Greenberg-Det	36	Greenberg-Det	389
Gehringer-Det	123	Myer-Was	215	Greenberg-Det	46	Stone-Was	18	Foxx-Phi	36	Foxx-Phi	340
Greenberg-Det	121	Cramer-Phi	214	Solters-Bos-StL	45	Greenberg-Det	16	Gehrig-NY	30	Vosmik-Cle	333
Foxx-Phi	118	Greenberg-Det	203	Fox-Det	38	Cronin-Bos	14	Johnson-Phi	28	Solters-Bos-StL	314
Chapman-NY	118			Chapman-NY	38	Averill-Cle	13	Trosky-Cle	26	Gehrig-NY	312

Runs Batted In		Runs Produced		Bases On Balls		Batting Average		On Base Percentage		Slugging Average	
Greenberg-Det	170	Greenberg-Det	255	Gehrig-NY	132	Myer-Was	.349	Gehrig-NY	.466	Foxx-Phi	.636
Gehrig-NY	119	Gehrig-NY	214	Appling-Chi	122	Vosmik-Cle	.348	Foxx-Phi	.461	Greenberg-Det	.628
Foxx-Phi	115	Gehringer-Det	212	Foxx-Phi	114	Foxx-Phi	.346	Cochrane-Det	.452	Gehrig-NY	.583
Trosky-Cle	113	Myer-Was	210	Myer-Was	96	Cramer-Phi	.332	Myer-Was	.440	Vosmik-Cle	.537
Solters-Bos-StL	112	Foxx-Phi	197	Cochrane-Det	96	Gehringer-Det	.330	Appling-Chi	.437	Fox-Det	.513

Production		Adjusted Production		Batter Runs		Adjusted Batter Runs		Clutch Hitting Index		Runs Created	
Foxx-Phi	1.096	Foxx-Phi	182	Foxx-Phi	67.2	Foxx-Phi	67.9	Goslin-Det	144	Foxx-Phi	163
Gehrig-NY	1.049	Gehrig-NY	180	Gehrig-NY	61.6	Gehrig-NY	66.4	Owen-Det	139	Greenberg-Det	161
Greenberg-Det	1.039	Greenberg-Det	171	Greenberg-Det	57.5	Greenberg-Det	60.7	Powell-Was	134	Gehrig-NY	154
Vosmik-Cle	.946	Vosmik-Cle	140	Vosmik-Cle	38.3	Myer-Was	39.6	Dykes-Chi	126	Vosmik-Cle	137
Gehringer-Det	.911	Myer-Was	139	Myer-Was	36.5	Vosmik-Cle	36.7	Stone-Was	125	Myer-Was	132

Total Average		Stolen Bases		Stolen Base Average		Stolen Base Runs		Fielding Runs		Total Player Rating	
Foxx-Phi	1.288	Werber-Bos	29	Lary-Was-StL	87.5	Lary-Was-StL	6.0	Travis-Was	21.9	Foxx-Phi	5.6
Gehrig-NY	1.230	Lary-Was-StL	28	Werber-Bos	80.6	Werber-Bos	4.5	Solters-Bos-StL	21.8	Myer-Was	4.8
Greenberg-Det	1.138	Almada-Bos	20	Almada-Bos	69.0	Solters-Bos-StL	2.1	Appling-Chi	21.3	Greenberg-Det	4.6
Cochrane-Det	1.000	White-Det	19	White-Det	65.5	Hughes-Cle	2.1	Melillo-StL-Bos	18.6	Gehrig-NY	4.5
Vosmik-Cle	.980	Chapman-NY	17	Chapman-NY	63.0			Werber-Bos	17.2	Appling-Chi	4.3

Wins		Win Percentage		Games		Complete Games		Shutouts		Saves	
W.Ferrell-Bos	25	Auker-Det	.720	VanAtta-NY-StL	58	W.Ferrell-Bos	31	Rowe-Det	6	Knott-StL	7
Harder-Cle	22	Broaca-NY	.682	Walkup-StL	55	Grove-Bos	23	Harder-Cle	4		
Bridges-Det	21	Bridges-Det	.677	Andrews-StL	50	Bridges-Det	23	Bridges-Det	4		
Grove-Bos	20	Harder-Cle	.667	Thomas-StL	49	Rowe-Det	21				
Rowe-Det	19	Lyons-Chi	.652	Knott-StL	48						

Innings Pitched		Fewest Hits/Game		Fewest BB/Game		Strikeouts		Strikeouts/Game		Ratio	
W.Ferrell-Bos	322.1	Allen-NY	8.03	Harder-Cle	1.66	Bridges-Det	163	Allen-NY	6.09	Grove-Bos	11.11
Harder-Cle	287.1	Ruffing-NY	8.15	Grove-Bos	2.14	Rowe-Det	140	Bridges-Det	5.35	Rowe-Det	11.17
Whitehill-Was	279.1	Gomez-NY	8.16	Rowe-Det	2.22	Gomez-NY	138	Gomez-NY	5.05	Ruffing-NY	11.27
Rowe-Det	275.2	Whitehead-Chi	8.46	Andrews-StL	2.24	Grove-Bos	121	VanAtta-NY-StL	4.63	Allen-NY	11.37
Bridges-Det	274.1	Grove-Bos	8.87	Hudlin-Cle	2.37	Allen-NY	113	Rowe-Det	4.57	Gomez-NY	11.38

Earned Run Average		Adjusted ERA		Opponents' Batting Avg.		Opponents' On Base Pct.		Starter Runs		Adjusted Starter Runs	
Grove-Bos	2.70	Grove-Bos	176	Allen-NY	.238	Rowe-Det	.301	Grove-Bos	53.1	Grove-Bos	61.9
Lyons-Chi	3.02	Lyons-Chi	153	Ruffing-NY	.239	Grove-Bos	.302	Harder-Cle	37.2	W.Ferrell-Bos	43.9
Ruffing-NY	3.12	Harder-Cle	137	Gomez-NY	.242	Ruffing-NY	.303	Gomez-NY	34.8	Harder-Cle	38.8
Gomez-NY	3.18	Andrews-StL	135	Whitehead-Chi	.250	Allen-NY	.307	W.Ferrell-Bos	33.6	Lyons-Chi	33.9
Harder-Cle	3.29	W.Ferrell-Bos	135	Broaca-NY	.254	Harder-Cle	.307	Ruffing-NY	32.9	Andrews-StL	29.6

Clutch Pitching Index		Relief Runs		Adjusted Relief Runs		Relief Ranking		Total Pitcher Index		Total Baseball Ranking	
Lyons-Chi	124	L.Brown-Cle	11.4	L.Brown-Cle	12.1	L.Brown-Cle	14.2	W.Ferrell-Bos	7.1	W.Ferrell-Bos	7.1
Bridges-Det	113	Hogsett-Det	9.9	Hogsett-Det	6.8	Hogsett-Det	8.4	Grove-Bos	6.0	Grove-Bos	6.0
Auker-Det	112	DeShong-NY	9.2	DeShong-NY	6.0	DeShong-NY	4.5	Harder-Cle	4.2	Foxx-Phi	5.6
Grove-Bos	112	Murphy-NY	4.9	Wilson-Bos	3.7	Wilson-Bos	3.8	Lyons-Chi	3.3	Myer-Was	4.8
Tietje-Chi	110	Wilson-Bos	1.7					Ruffing-NY	3.2	Greenberg-Det	4.6

1936 National League

TEAM	G	W	L	PCT	GB	R	OR	AB	H	2B	3B	HR	BB	SO	AVG	OBP	SLG	PRO	PRO+	BR	/A	PF	CHI	RC	SB	CS	SBA	SBR
NY	154	92	62	.597		742	621	5449	1529	237	48	97	431	**452**	.281	.337	.395	.732	104	19	27	99	99	744	31			
STL	155	87	67	.565	5	795	794	5537	1554	**332**	60	88	442	577	.281	.336	**.410**	**.746**	106	40	**42**	100	**103**	772	**69**			
CHI	154	87	67	.565	5	755	**603**	5409	1545	275	36	76	491	462	**.286**	**.349**	.392	.741	103	44	27	102	97	757	68			
PIT	156	84	70	.545	8	**804**	718	5586	**1596**	283	**80**	60	**517**	502	**.286**	**.349**	.397	**.746**	104	**56**	38	102	100	**798**	37			
CIN	154	74	80	.481	18	722	760	5393	1476	224	73	82	410	584	.274	.329	.388	.717	105	-13	31	94	103	699	68			
BOS	157	71	83	.461	21	631	715	5478	1450	207	45	67	433	582	.265	.322	.356	.678	94	-85	-38	94	98	635	23			
BRO	156	67	87	.435	25	662	752	5574	1518	263	43	33	390	458	.272	.323	.353	.676	87	-91	-98	101	103	649	55			
PHI	154	54	100	.351	38	726	874	5465	1538	250	46	**103**	451	586	.281	.339	.401	.740	95	32	-40	110	96	757	50			
TOT	620					5837		43891	12206	2071	431	606	3565	4203	.278	.335	.386	.722							401			

TEAM	CG	SH	SV	IP	H	H/G	HR	BB	SO	RAT	ERA	ERA+	OAV	OOB	PR	/A	PF	CPI	FA	E	DP	FW	PW	BW	SBW	DIF
NY	60	12	22	1385²	1458	9.5	75	401	500	12.2	**3.46**	113	.273	.326	86	66	97	110	.974	168	164	1.1	6.4	2.6		4.8
STL	65	5	**24**	1398	1610	10.4	89	434	559	13.4	4.47	88	.288	.343	-71	-83	98	98	.974	156	134	1.9	-8.1	**4.1**		12.1
CHI	**77**	**18**	10	1382¹	**1413**	**9.2**	77	434	597	12.2	3.54	113	**.264**	.323	73	**68**	99	104	**.976**	**146**	156	**2.4**	6.6	2.6		-1.6
PIT	67	5	12	1395¹	1475	9.5	74	**379**	559	12.1	3.89	104	.268	**.318**	19	25	101	92	.967	199	113	-.5	2.4	3.7		1.4
CIN	50	6	23	1367¹	1576	10.4	51	418	459	13.3	4.22	91	.287	.340	-30	-61	95	90	.969	191	150	-.2	-6.0	3.0		.1
BOS	61	7	13	1413¹	1566	10.0	69	451	421	13.0	3.94	97	.280	.337	11	-17	95	103	.971	189	**175**	.1	-1.7	-3.7		-.8
BRO	59	7	18	1403	1466	9.4	84	528	**651**	13.0	3.98	104	.266	.333	5	21	103	97	.966	208	107	-1.0	2.0	-9.6		-1.5
PHI	51	7	14	1365¹	1630	10.7	87	515	454	14.4	4.64	98	.292	.355	-94	-17	113	100	.959	252	144	-3.7	-1.7	-3.9		-13.8
TOT	490	67	136	11110¹		9.9				12.9	4.02		.278	.335					.969	1509	1143					

Runs
Vaughan-Pit	122
J.Martin-StL	121
Ott-NY	120
Medwick-StL	115
Suhr-Pit	111

Hits
Medwick-StL	223
P.Waner-Pit	218
Demaree-Chi	212
Herman-Chi	211
Moore-NY	205

Doubles
Medwick-StL	64
Herman-Chi	57
P.Waner-Pit	53
Moore-StL	39
Moore-Bos	38

Triples
Goodman-Cin	14
Medwick-StL	13
Camilli-Phi	13

Home Runs
Ott-NY	33
Camilli-Phi	28
Klein-Chi-Phi	25
Berger-Bos	25
Mize-StL	19

Total Bases
Medwick-StL	367
Ott-NY	314
Klein-Chi-Phi	308
Camilli-Phi	306
P.Waner-Pit	304

Runs Batted In
Medwick-StL	138
Ott-NY	135
Suhr-Pit	118
Klein-Chi-Phi	104

Runs Produced
Medwick-StL	235
Ott-NY	222
Suhr-Pit	218
P.Waner-Pit	196
Vaughan-Pit	191

Bases On Balls
Vaughan-Pit	118
Camilli-Phi	116
Ott-NY	111
Suhr-Pit	95
Hack-Chi	89

Batting Average
P.Waner-Pit	.373
Medwick-StL	.351
Demaree-Chi	.350
Vaughan-Pit	.335
Herman-Chi	.334

On Base Percentage
Vaughan-Pit	.453
Ott-NY	.448
P.Waner-Pit	.446
Camilli-Phi	.441
Suhr-Pit	.410

Slugging Average
Ott-NY	.588
Camilli-Phi	.577
Medwick-StL	.577
P.Waner-Pit	.520
Klein-Chi-Phi	.512

Production
Ott-NY	1.036
Camilli-Phi	1.018
P.Waner-Pit	.965
Medwick-StL	.964
Vaughan-Pit	.927

Adjusted Production
Ott-NY	179
Medwick-StL	157
Camilli-Phi	156
P.Waner-Pit	156
Vaughan-Pit	146

Batter Runs
Ott-NY	61.9
Camilli-Phi	58.0
P.Waner-Pit	51.4
Vaughan-Pit	47.3
Medwick-StL	46.9

Adjusted Batter Runs
Ott-NY	62.8
Camilli-Phi	50.1
P.Waner-Pit	49.5
Medwick-StL	47.2
Vaughan-Pit	45.3

Clutch Hitting Index
Brubaker-Pit	160
Suhr-Pit	145
Young-Pit	141
Cuccinello-Bos	130
Galan-Chi	130

Runs Created
Ott-NY	153
Camilli-Phi	148
Medwick-StL	141
P.Waner-Pit	140
Vaughan-Pit	137

Total Average
Ott-NY	1.188
Camilli-Phi	1.162
Vaughan-Pit	1.034
P.Waner-Pit	1.016
Medwick-StL	.956

Stolen Bases
J.Martin-StL	23
S.Martin-StL	17
Hack-Chi	17
Chiozza-Phi	17

Stolen Base Average

Stolen Base Runs

Fielding Runs
Bartell-NY	44.8
Whitehead-NY	29.2
Kampouris-Cin	28.2
Berres-Bro	23.6
Cuccinello-Bos	21.9

Total Player Rating
Bartell-NY	5.6
Medwick-StL	5.0
Ott-NY	4.9
Herman-Chi	4.9
P.Waner-Pit	4.8

Wins
Hubbell-NY	26
J.Dean-StL	24
Derringer-Cin	19

Win Percentage
Hubbell-NY	.813
Lucas-Pit	.789
French-Chi	.667
J.Dean-StL	.649
Lee-Chi	.621

Games
Derringer-Cin	51
J.Dean-StL	51
Passeau-Phi	49
M.Brown-Pit	47

Complete Games
J.Dean-StL	28
Hubbell-NY	25
Mungo-Bro	22
MacFayden-Bos	21
Lee-Chi	20

Shutouts
Warneke-Chi	4
Walters-Phi	4
Smith-NY	4
Lee-Chi	4
French-Chi	4
Carleton-Chi	4
Blanton-Pit	4

Saves
J.Dean-StL	11
Brennan-Cin	9
Smith-Bos	8
Johnson-Phi	7
Coffman-NY	7

Innings Pitched
J.Dean-StL	315.0
Mungo-Bro	311.2
Hubbell-NY	304.0
Derringer-Cin	282.1
MacFayden-Bos	266.2

Fewest Hits/Game
Hubbell-NY	7.85
Mungo-Bro	7.94
Lee-Chi	8.28
J.Dean-StL	8.86
Blanton-Pit	8.97

Fewest BB/Game
Lucas-Pit	1.33
Derringer-Cin	1.34
J.Dean-StL	1.51
Hubbell-NY	1.69
Gabler-NY	1.89

Strikeouts
Mungo-Bro	238
J.Dean-StL	195
Blanton-Pit	127
Hubbell-NY	123
Derringer-Cin	121

Strikeouts/Game
Mungo-Bro	6.87
J.Dean-StL	5.57
Blanton-Pit	4.85
Weaver-Pit	4.31
Warneke-Chi	4.23

Ratio
Hubbell-NY	9.68
J.Dean-StL	10.46
Lucas-Pit	10.61
Blanton-Pit	11.19
Davis-Phi-Chi	11.35

Earned Run Average
Hubbell-NY	2.31
MacFayden-Bos	2.87
Gabler-NY	3.12
J.Dean-StL	3.17
Lucas-Pit	3.18

Adjusted ERA
Hubbell-NY	169
MacFayden-Bos	134
Passeau-Phi	130
Lucas-Pit	128
Gabler-NY	125

Opponents' Batting Avg.
Mungo-Bro	.234
Hubbell-NY	.236
Lee-Chi	.246
J.Dean-StL	.253
Blanton-Pit	.257

Opponents' On Base Pct.
Hubbell-NY	.276
J.Dean-StL	.285
Lucas-Pit	.287
Blanton-Pit	.301
Mungo-Bro	.305

Starter Runs
Hubbell-NY	57.7
MacFayden-Bos	34.0
J.Dean-StL	29.6
Mungo-Bro	23.1
Lee-Chi	20.4

Adjusted Starter Runs
Hubbell-NY	53.5
MacFayden-Bos	28.5
Mungo-Bro	27.0
J.Dean-StL	26.9
Passeau-Phi	25.4

Clutch Pitching Index
Schumacher-NY	120
Gabler-NY	119
Chaplin-Bos	111
Smith-NY	110
Carleton-Chi	109

Relief Runs
Bryant-Chi	4.6
Coffman-NY	1.4

Adjusted Relief Runs
Bryant-Chi	4.4
Johnson-Phi	2.9

Relief Ranking
Johnson-Phi	3.2
Bryant-Chi	2.1

Total Pitcher Index
Hubbell-NY	5.7
Passeau-Phi	3.2
MacFayden-Bos	2.7
Walters-Phi	2.3
Mungo-Bro	2.3

Total Baseball Ranking
Hubbell-NY	5.7
Bartell-NY	5.6
Medwick-StL	5.0
Ott-NY	4.9
Herman-Chi	4.9

TEAM	G	W	L	PCT	GB	R	OR	AB	H	2B	3B	HR	BB	SO	AVG	OBP	SLG	PRO	PRO+	BR	/A	PF	CHI	RC	SB	CS	SBA	SBR
NY	155	102	51	.667		1065	731	5591	1676	315	83	182	700	594	.300	.381	.483	.864	124	162	193	97	100	1056	76	40	44	-13
DET	154	83	71	.539	19.5	921	871	5464	1638	326	55	94	640	462	.300	.377	.431	.808	105	57	54	100	98	912	72	49	53	-16
CHI	153	81	70	.536	20	920	873	5466	1597	282	56	60	684	417	.292	.374	.397	.771	93	-8	-40	104	104	851	66	29	35	-11
WAS	153	82	71	.536	20	889	799	5433	1601	293	84	62	576	398	.295	.365	.414	.779	104	-6	42	94	104	847	103	42	55	-19
CLE	157	80	74	.519	22.5	921	862	5646	1715	357	82	123	514	470	.304	.364	.461	.825	109	70	62	101	96	948	66	53	49	-13
BOS	155	74	80	.481	28.5	775	764	5383	1485	288	62	86	584	465	.276	.349	.400	.749	86	-71	-120	106	98	773	54	44	47	-14
STL	155	57	95	.375	44.5	804	1064	5391	1502	299	66	79	625	627	.279	.356	.403	.759	91	-50	-74	103	99	804	62	20	30	-11
PHI	154	53	100	.346	49	714	1045	5373	1443	240	60	72	524	590	.269	.336	.376	.712	83	-150	-133	98	102	694	59	43	59	-22
TOT	618					7009		43747	12657	2400	548	758	4847	4023	.289	.363	.421	.784							558	320	64	-24

TEAM	CG	SH	SV	IP	H	H/G	HR	BB	SO	RAT	ERA	ERA+	OAV	OOB	PR	/A	PF	CPI	FA	E	DP	FW	PW	BW	SBW	DIF
NY	77	6	21	1400¹	1474	9.5	84	663	624	13.8	4.17	112	.270	.351	134	75	92	108	.973	163	148	.8	6.6	17.0	-.9	1.9
DET	76	13	13	1360	1568	10.4	100	562	526	14.2	5.00	99	.289	.358	6	-6	98	100	.975	153	159	1.3	-.5	4.8	-1.1	1.6
CHI	80	5	8	1365	1603	10.6	104	578	414	14.5	5.06	103	.293	.363	-3	20	103	102	.973	168	174	.4	1.8	-3.5	-.7	7.6
WAS	78	8	14	1345²	1484	9.9	73	588	462	14.0	4.58	104	.279	.353	68	29	95	101	.970	182	163	-.4	2.6	3.7	-1.4	1.0
CLE	74	6	12	1389¹	1604	10.4	73	607	619	14.5	4.83	104	.289	.362	31	31	100	102	.971	178	154	.0	2.7	5.5	-.9	-4.4
BOS	78	11	9	1372¹	1501	9.8	78	552	584	13.6	4.39	121	.276	.345	99	141	106	102	.972	165	139	.7	12.5	-10.6	-1.0	-4.6
STL	54	3	13	1348¹	1776	11.9	115	609	399	16.2	6.24	86	.314	.385	-180	-129	107	95	.969	188	143	-.6	-11.4	-6.5	-.7	.2
PHI	68	3	12	1352¹	1645	10.9	131	696	405	15.7	6.08	84	.299	.380	-156	-146	101	94	.965	209	152	-1.9	-12.9	-11.7	-1.7	4.7
TOT	585	55	102	10933¹		10.4				14.6	5.04		.289	.363					.971	1406	1232					

Runs		Hits		Doubles		Triples		Home Runs		Total Bases	
Gehrig-NY	167	Averill-Cle	232	Gehringer-Det	60	Rolfe-NY	15	Gehrig-NY	49	Trosky-Cle	405
Clift-StL	145	Gehringer-Det	227	Walker-Det	55	DiMaggio-NY	15	Trosky-Cle	42	Gehrig-NY	403
Gehringer-Det	144	Trosky-Cle	216	Chapman-NY-Was	50	Averill-Cle	15	Foxx-Bos	41	Averill-Cle	385
Crosetti-NY	137	Bell-StL	212	Hale-Cle	50	R.Johnson-Phi	14	DiMaggio-NY	29	Foxx-Bos	369
Averill-Cle	136	Radcliff-Chi	207					Averill-Cle	28	DiMaggio-NY	367

Runs Batted In		Runs Produced		Bases On Balls		Batting Average		On Base Percentage		Slugging Average	
Trosky-Cle	162	Gehrig-NY	270	Gehrig-NY	130	Appling-Chi	.388	Gehrig-NY	.478	Gehrig-NY	.696
Gehrig-NY	152	Bonura-Chi	246	Lary-StL	117	Averill-Cle	.378	Appling-Chi	.474	Trosky-Cle	.644
Foxx-Bos	143	Gehringer-Det	245	Clift-StL	115	Gehringer-Det	.354	Foxx-Bos	.440	Foxx-Bos	.631
Bonura-Chi	138	Trosky-Cle	244	Foxx-Bos	105	Gehrig-NY	.354	Averill-Cle	.438	Averill-Cle	.627
Solters-StL	134	Averill-Cle	234	Lazzeri-NY	97	Walker-Det	.353	Gehringer-Det	.431	DiMaggio-NY	.576

Production		Adjusted Production		Batter Runs		Adjusted Batter Runs		Clutch Hitting Index		Runs Created	
Gehrig-NY	1.174	Gehrig-NY	193	Gehrig-NY	82.2	Gehrig-NY	85.8	Appling-Chi	154	Gehrig-NY	199
Foxx-Bos	1.071	Averill-Cle	159	Foxx-Bos	56.8	Averill-Cle	55.6	Bonura-Chi	148	Averill-Cle	168
Averill-Cle	1.065	Foxx-Bos	153	Averill-Cle	56.4	Foxx-Bos	51.2	Sewell-Chi	137	Foxx-Bos	168
Trosky-Cle	1.026	Trosky-Cle	148	Gehringer-Det	43.0	Gehringer-Det	42.7	Owen-Det	137	Gehringer-Det	157
Gehringer-Det	.987	Stone-Was	145	Trosky-Cle	41.9	Trosky-Cle	41.1	Vosmik-Cle	135	Trosky-Cle	150

Total Average		Stolen Bases		Stolen Base Average		Stolen Base Runs		Fielding Runs		Total Player Rating	
Gehrig-NY	1.426	Lary-StL	37	Lary-StL	80.4	Lary-StL	5.7	Hayes-Chi	17.1	Gehringer-Det	6.0
Foxx-Bos	1.238	Powell-Was-NY	26	Crosetti-NY	72.0	Hill-Was	3.3	Hale-Cle	16.5	Gehrig-NY	5.6
Averill-Cle	1.171	Werber-Bos	23	Powell-Was-NY	70.3	Stone-Was	2.4	Gehringer-Det	15.7	Appling-Chi	5.3
Appling-Chi	1.088	Chapman-NY-Was	20	Chapman-NY-Was	69.0	Sewell-Chi	2.1	Appling-Chi	15.2	Dickey-NY	3.9
Gehringer-Det	1.075	Hughes-Cle	20	Hughes-Cle	69.0			Bonura-Chi	11.9	Averill-Cle	3.7

Wins		Win Percentage		Games		Complete Games		Shutouts		Saves	
Bridges-Det	23	Pearson-NY	.731	VanAtta-StL	52	W.Ferrell-Bos	28	Grove-Bos	6	Malone-NY	9
Kennedy-Chi	21	Kennedy-Chi	.700	Knott-StL	47	Bridges-Det	26	Bridges-Det	5	Knott-StL	6
Ruffing-NY	20	Bridges-Det	.676			Ruffing-NY	25	Rowe-Det	4	Murphy-NY	5
W.Ferrell-Bos	20	Allen-Cle	.667			Newsom-Was	24	Newsom-Was	4	Brown-Chi	5
Allen-Cle	20	Rowe-Det	.655			Grove-Bos	22	Allen-Cle	4	Hildebrand-Cle	4

Innings Pitched		Fewest Hits/Game		Fewest BB/Game		Strikeouts		Strikeouts/Game		Ratio	
W.Ferrell-Bos	301.0	Pearson-NY	7.71	Lyons-Chi	2.23	Bridges-Det	175	Allen-Cle	6.11	Grove-Bos	10.87
Bridges-Det	294.2	Grove-Bos	8.42	Grove-Bos	2.31	Allen-Cle	165	Bridges-Det	5.35	Rowe-Det	12.18
Newsom-Was	285.2	Allen-Cle	8.67	Rowe-Det	2.35	Newsom-Was	156	Gomez-NY	5.01	Ruffing-NY	12.19
Kennedy-Chi	274.1	Gomez-NY	8.78	Andrews-StL	2.35	Grove-Bos	130	Newsom-Was	4.91	Allen-Cle	12.30
Ruffing-NY	271.0	Bridges-Det	8.83	Marcum-Bos	2.69	Pearson-NY	118	Pearson-NY	4.76	Appleton-Was	12.45

Earned Run Average		Adjusted ERA		Opponents' Batting Avg.		Opponents' On Base Pct.		Starter Runs		Adjusted Starter Runs	
Grove-Bos	2.81	Grove-Bos	189	Pearson-NY	.233	Grove-Bos	.297	Grove-Bos	62.8	Grove-Bos	70.6
Allen-Cle	3.44	Allen-Cle	146	Grove-Bos	.246	Rowe-Det	.321	Bridges-Det	46.9	Bridges-Det	44.1
Appleton-Was	3.53	Bridges-Det	137	Gomez-NY	.254	Ruffing-NY	.323	Allen-Cle	43.0	Allen-Cle	43.0
Bridges-Det	3.60	Appleton-Was	135	Appleton-Was	.254	Appleton-Was	.324	Ruffing-NY	35.7	W.Ferrell-Bos	37.8
Pearson-NY	3.71	Kelley-Phi	132	Bridges-Det	.255	Bridges-Det	.326	Appleton-Was	33.9	Kelley-Phi	32.4

Clutch Pitching Index		Relief Runs		Adjusted Relief Runs		Relief Ranking		Total Pitcher Index		Total Baseball Ranking	
Hadley-NY	116	Lee-Cle	2.1	Gumpert-Phi	2.3	Brown-Chi	2.0	Grove-Bos	6.6	Grove-Bos	6.6
Kelley-Phi	115	Gumpert-Phi	1.9	Lee-Cle	2.1	Lee-Cle	1.3	W.Ferrell-Bos	4.5	Gehringer-Det	6.0
Grove-Bos	115	Kimsey-Det	1.1	Brown-Chi	1.9	Gumpert-Phi	1.2	Bridges-Det	4.2	Gehrig-NY	5.6
Bridges-Det	109	Brown-Chi	.5	Kimsey-Det	.6	Kimsey-Det	.6	Allen-Cle	3.9	Appling-Chi	5.3
Thomas-StL	107							Ruffing-NY	3.7	W.Ferrell-Bos	4.5

1937 National League

TEAM	G	W	L	PCT	GB	R	OR	AB	H	2B	3B	HR	BB	SO	AVG	OBP	SLG	PRO	PRO+	BR	/A	PF	CHI	RC	SB	CS	SBA	SBR
NY	152	95	57	.625		732	602	5329	1484	251	41	111	412	492	.278	.334	.403	.737	104	40	31	101	100	734	45			
CHI	154	93	61	.604	3	811	682	5349	1537	253	74	96	538	496	.287	.355	.416	.771	111	117	87	104	98	816	71			
PIT	154	86	68	.558	10	704	646	5433	1550	223	86	47	463	480	.285	.343	.384	.727	104	30	30	100	96	734	32			
STL	157	81	73	.526	15	789	733	5476	1543	264	67	94	385	569	.282	.331	.406	.737	103	36	21	102	107	744	78			
BOS	152	79	73	.520	16	579	556	5124	1265	200	41	63	485	707	.247	.314	.339	.653	91	-108	-47	91	102	565	45			
BRO	155	62	91	.405	33.5	616	772	5295	1401	258	53	37	469	583	.265	.327	.354	.681	89	-56	-67	102	96	629	69			
PHI	155	61	92	.399	34.5	724	869	5424	1482	258	37	103	478	640	.273	.334	.391	.725	95	21	-36	108	100	730	66			
CIN	155	56	98	.364	40	612	707	5230	1329	215	59	73	437	586	.254	.315	.360	.675	93	-77	-43	95	102	599	53			
TOT	617					5567		42660	11591	1922	458	624	3667	4553	.272	.332	.382	.714						459				

TEAM	CG	SH	SV	IP	H	H/G	HR	BB	SO	RAT	ERA	ERA+	OAV	OOB	PR	/A	PF	CPI	FA	E	DP	FW	PW	BW	SBW	DIF
NY	67	11	17	1361	1341	8.9	85	404	653	11.7	3.43	113	.258	.314	73	69	99	102	.974	159	143	.9	6.8	3.1		8.2
CHI	73	11	13	1381¹	1434	9.3	91	502	596	12.8	3.97	100	.266	.331	-9	0	102	99	.975	151	141	1.5	.0	8.6		5.9
PIT	67	12	17	1366¹	1398	9.2	71	428	643	12.2	3.56	108	.263	.321	52	44	99	101	.970	181	135	-.2	4.4	3.0		1.8
STL	81	10	4	1392	1546	10.0	95	448	571	13.0	3.98	100	.280	.336	-10	0	102	105	.973	164	127	1.0	.0	2.1		1.0
BOS	85	16	10	1359¹	1344	8.9	60	372	387	11.4	3.22	111	.259	.310	104	55	92	103	.975	157	128	1.0	5.5	-4.7		1.2
BRO	63	5	8	1362²	1470	9.7	68	476	592	13.0	4.13	98	.274	.336	-32	-14	103	96	.964	217	127	-2.2	-1.4	-6.6		-4.3
PHI	59	6	15	1373²	1629	10.7	116	501	529	14.2	5.05	86	.297	.359	-174	-113	111	97	.970	184	157	-.3	-11.2	-3.6		-.4
CIN	64	10	18	1358¹	1428	9.5	38	533	581	13.1	3.94	95	.270	.339	-3	-31	95	97	.966	208	139	-1.6	-3.1	-4.3		-12.0
TOT	559	81	102	10954²		9.5				12.7	3.91		.272	.332					.971	1421	1097					

Runs
Medwick-StL 111
Herman-Chi 106
Hack-Chi 106
Galan-Chi 104
Demaree-Chi 104

Hits
Medwick-StL 237
P.Waner-Pit 219
Mize-StL 204
Demaree-Chi 199
Herman-Chi 189

Doubles
Medwick-StL 56
Mize-StL 40
Bartell-NY 38
Phelps-Bro 37
Moore-NY 37

Triples
Vaughan-Pit 17
Suhr-Pit 14
Handley-Pit 12
Goodman-Cin 12
Herman-Chi 11

Home Runs
Ott-NY 31
Medwick-StL 31
Camilli-Phi 27
Mize-StL 25
Galan-Chi 18

Total Bases
Medwick-StL 406
Mize-StL 333
Demaree-Chi 298
Ott-NY 285
Camilli-Phi 279

Runs Batted In
Medwick-StL 154
Demaree-Chi 115
Mize-StL 113
Suhr-Pit 97
Ott-NY 95

Runs Produced
Medwick-StL 234
Demaree-Chi 202
Mize-StL 191
Hack-Chi 167
P.Waner-Pit 166

Bases On Balls
Ott-NY 102
Camilli-Phi 90
Suhr-Pit 83
Hack-Chi 83
Galan-Chi 79

Batting Average
Medwick-StL 374
Mize-StL 364
P.Waner-Pit 354
Whitney-Phi 341
Camilli-Phi 339

On Base Percentage
Camilli-Phi 446
Mize-StL 427
Medwick-StL 414
P.Waner-Pit 413
Ott-NY 408

Slugging Average
Medwick-StL 641
Mize-StL 595
Camilli-Phi 587
Ott-NY 523
Demaree-Chi 485

Production
Medwick-StL 1.056
Camilli-Phi 1.034
Mize-StL 1.021
Ott-NY 931
Herman-Chi 875

Adjusted Production
Medwick-StL 179
Mize-StL 171
Camilli-Phi 165
Ott-NY 149
P.Waner-Pit 132

Batter Runs
Medwick-StL 68.8
Mize-StL 57.4
Camilli-Phi 54.9
Ott-NY 41.2
Hartnett-Chi 31.1

Adjusted Batter Runs
Medwick-StL 67.2
Mize-StL 56.0
Camilli-Phi 49.5
Ott-NY 40.3
P.Waner-Pit 29.8

Clutch Hitting Index
Suhr-Pit 151
Durocher-StL 144
Scharein-Phi 142
Jurges-Chi 134
Todd-Pit 130

Runs Created
Medwick-StL 170
Mize-StL 150
Camilli-Phi 137
Ott-NY 128
P.Waner-Pit 118

Total Average
Camilli-Phi 1.189
Medwick-StL 1.113
Mize-StL 1.097
Ott-NY 1.021
Vaughan-Pit 864

Stolen Bases
Galan-Chi 23
Hack-Chi 16

Stolen Base Average

Stolen Base Runs

Fielding Runs
Bartell-NY 37.5
Whitehead-NY 26.1
Riggs-Cin 19.5
Herman-Chi 18.6
Young-Pit 18.1

Total Player Rating
Bartell-NY 6.2
Medwick-StL 5.8
Herman-Chi 4.9
Camilli-Phi 4.5
Ott-NY 3.6

Wins
Hubbell-NY 22
Turner-Bos 20
Melton-NY 20
Fette-Bos 20
Warneke-StL 18

Win Percentage
Hubbell-NY 733
Melton-NY 690
Fette-Bos 667
Carleton-Chi 667
Turner-Bos 645

Games
Mulcahy-Phi 56
Jorgens-Phi 52

Complete Games
Turner-Bos 24
Fette-Bos 23
Weiland-StL 21

Shutouts
Turner-Bos 5
Grissom-Cin 5
Fette-Bos 5

Saves
Melton-NY 7
Brown-Pit 7
Grissom-Cin 6
Root-Chi 5
Hollingsworth-Cin ... 5

Innings Pitched
Passeau-Phi ... 292.1
Lee-Chi 272.1
Weiland-StL ... 264.1
Hubbell-NY 261.2
Fette-Bos 259.0

Fewest Hits/Game
Mungo-Bro 7.60
Grissom-Cin ... 7.77
Melton-NY 7.84
Carleton-Chi .. 7.91
Turner-Bos 7.99

Fewest BB/Game
J.Dean-StL 1.51
Root-Chi 1.61
Hoyt-Pit-Bro ... 1.66
Turner-Bos 1.82
Castleman-NY .. 1.85

Strikeouts
Hubbell-NY 159
Grissom-Cin 149
Blanton-Pit 143
Melton-NY 142

Strikeouts/Game
Mungo-Bro 6.82
Grissom-Cin ... 6.00
Bauers-Pit 5.66
Henshaw-Bro ... 5.64
LaMaster-Phi... 5.51

Ratio
Turner-Bos 9.82
Melton-NY 10.05
Castleman-NY .. 10.16
Root-Chi 10.53
J.Dean-StL 10.72

Earned Run Average
Turner-Bos 2.38
Melton-NY 2.61
J.Dean-StL 2.69
Bauers-Pit 2.88
Fette-Bos 2.88

Adjusted ERA
Turner-Bos 150
Melton-NY 149
J.Dean-StL 148
Mungo-Bro 139
Bauers-Pit 134

Opponents' Batting Avg.
Mungo-Bro 229
Grissom-Cin 232
Melton-NY 233
Turner-Bos 235
Carleton-Chi 236

Opponents' On Base Pct.
Turner-Bos 274
Melton-NY 280
Castleman-NY 287
Root-Chi.........290
J.Dean-StL.......291

Starter Runs
Turner-Bos 43.5
Melton-NY 35.8
Fette-Bos 29.5
MacFayden-Bos .. 26.9
J.Dean-StL 26.7

Adjusted Starter Runs
Melton-NY 35.0
Turner-Bos 34.2
J.Dean-StL 28.2
Bauers-Pit 20.5
Mungo-Bro 20.1

Clutch Pitching Index
Johnson-StL 128
Brandt-Pit 124
Weiland-StL 115
Frankhouse-Bro .. 113
MacFayden-Bos .. 112

Relief Runs
Coffman-NY 7.8
Hutchinson-Bos ... 1.8

Adjusted Relief Runs
Coffman-NY 7.5

Relief Ranking
Coffman-NY 9.9

Total Pitcher Index
Turner-Bos 3.9
Melton-NY 3.4
J.Dean-StL 2.8
Mungo-Bro 2.6
Bauers-Pit 2.4

Total Baseball Ranking
Bartell-NY 6.2
Medwick-StL 5.8
Herman-Chi 4.9
Camilli-Phi 4.5
Turner-Bos 3.9

TEAM	G	W	L	PCT	GB	R	OR	AB	H	2B	3B	HR	BB	SO	AVG	OBP	SLG	PRO	PRO+	BR	/A	PF	CHI	RC	SB	CS	SBA	SBR
NY	157	102	52	.662		979	671	5487	1554	282	73	174	709	607	.283	.369	.456	.825	113	112	106	101	103	952	60	36	38	-11
DET	155	89	65	.578	13	935	841	5516	1611	309	62	150	656	711	.292	.370	.452	.822	110	106	87	102	100	947	89	45	54	-18
CHI	154	86	68	.558	16	780	730	5277	1478	280	76	67	549	447	.280	.350	.400	.750	95	-37	-36	100	103	763	70	34	39	-12
CLE	156	83	71	.539	19	817	768	5353	1499	304	76	103	570	551	.280	.352	.423	.775	100	4	0	101	101	813	78	51	57	-18
BOS	154	80	72	.526	21	821	775	5354	1506	269	64	100	601	557	.281	.357	.411	.768	96	0	-30	104	101	804	79	61	52	-12
WAS	158	73	80	.477	28.5	757	841	5578	1559	245	84	47	591	503	.279	.351	.379	.730	94	-73	-35	96	100	767	61	35	40	-13
PHI	154	54	97	.358	46.5	699	854	5228	1398	278	60	94	583	557	.267	.341	.397	.738	93	-62	-49	98	97	732	95	48	55	-18
STL	156	46	108	.299	56	715	1023	5510	1573	327	44	71	514	510	.285	.348	.399	.747	93	-46	-50	101	93	780	30	27	33	-11
TOT	622					6503		43303	12178	2294	539	806	4773	4443	.281	.355	.415	.770							562	337	63	-33

TEAM	CG	SH	SV	IP	H	H/G	HR	BB	SO	RAT	ERA	ERA+	OAV	OOB	PR	/A	PF	CPI	FA	E	DP	FW	PW	BW	SBW	DIF
NY	82	15	21	1396	1417	9.1	92	506	652	12.5	3.65	122	.261	.325	150	123	96	103	.972	170	134	.2	11.3	9.7	-.6	4.4
DET	70	6	11	1378	1521	9.9	102	635	485	14.2	4.87	96	.279	.356	-38	-29	101	95	.976	147	149	1.4	-2.7	8.0	-1.3	6.5
CHI	70	15	21	1351¹	1435	9.6	115	532	533	13.2	4.17	110	.272	.341	67	65	100	104	.971	174	173	-.2	6.0	-3.3	-.7	7.3
CLE	64	4	15	1364²	1529	10.1	61	566	630	14.0	4.39	105	.285	.356	34	32	100	102	.974	159	153	.8	2.9	.0	-1.3	3.6
BOS	74	6	14	1366	1520	10.0	92	597	682	14.0	4.48	106	.279	.352	21	40	103	100	.970	177	139	-.4	3.7	-2.8	-.7	4.2
WAS	75	5	14	1398²	1498	9.6	90	671	524	14.1	4.58	97	.274	.356	7	-22	96	99	.972	170	181	.3	-2.0	-3.2	-.8	2.3
PHI	65	6	9	1335	1490	10.0	105	613	469	14.3	4.85	97	.280	.357	-34	-20	102	97	.967	198	150	-1.7	-1.8	-4.5	-1.3	-12.2
STL	55	2	8	1363	1768	11.7	143	653	468	16.2	6.00	80	.315	.389	-209	-177	105	100	.972	173	166	-.0	-16.2	-4.6	-.6	-9.5
TOT	555	59	113	10952²		10.0				14.1	4.62		.281	.355					.972	1368	1245					

Runs		Hits		Doubles		Triples		Home Runs		Total Bases	
DiMaggio-NY	151	Bell-StL	218	Bell-StL	51	Walker-Chi	16	DiMaggio-NY	46	DiMaggio-NY	418
Rolfe-NY	143	DiMaggio-NY	215	Greenberg-Det	49	Kreevich-Chi	16	Greenberg-Det	40	Greenberg-Det	397
Gehrig-NY	138	Walker-Det	213	Moses-Phi	48	Stone-Was	15	Gehrig-NY	37	Gehrig-NY	366
Greenberg-Det	137	Lewis-Was	210	Vosmik-StL	47	DiMaggio-NY	15	Foxx-Bos	36	Moses-Phi	357
Gehringer-Det	133	Gehringer-Det	209	Lary-Cle	46	Greenberg-Det	14	York-Det	35	Trosky-Cle	329

Runs Batted In		Runs Produced		Bases On Balls		Batting Average		On Base Percentage		Slugging Average	
Greenberg-Det	183	Greenberg-Det	280	Gehrig-NY	127	Gehringer-Det	.371	Gehrig-NY	.473	DiMaggio-NY	.673
DiMaggio-NY	167	DiMaggio-NY	272	Greenberg-Det	102	Gehrig-NY	.351	Greenberg-Det	.458	Greenberg-Det	.668
Gehrig-NY	159	Gehrig-NY	260	Foxx-Bos	99	DiMaggio-NY	.346	Greenberg-Det	.436	Gehrig-NY	.643
Dickey-NY	133	Gehringer-Det	215	Johnson-Phi	98	Bonura-Chi	.345	Johnson-Phi	.425	Bonura-Chi	.573
Trosky-Cle	128	Foxx-Bos	202	Clift-StL	98	Travis-Was	.344	Dickey-NY	.417	Dickey-NY	.570

Production		Adjusted Production		Batter Runs		Adjusted Batter Runs		Clutch Hitting Index		Runs Created	
Gehrig-NY	1.116	Gehrig-NY	177	Gehrig-NY	73.3	Gehrig-NY	72.7	Hayes-Chi	146	Gehrig-NY	181
Greenberg-Det	1.105	Greenberg-Det	171	Greenberg-Det	67.2	Greenberg-Det	65.2	Higgins-Bos	138	Greenberg-Det	178
DiMaggio-NY	1.085	DiMaggio-NY	168	DiMaggio-NY	61.3	DiMaggio-NY	60.7	Myer-Was	135	DiMaggio-NY	173
Dickey-NY	.987	Johnson-Phi	147	Gehringer-Det	44.0	Gehringer-Det	42.1	Greenberg-Det	128	Gehringer-Det	140
Bonura-Chi	.984	Bonura-Chi	146	Dickey-NY	37.5	Dickey-NY	37.0	Hale-Cle	127	Clift-StL	134

Total Average		Stolen Bases		Stolen Base Average		Stolen Base Runs		Fielding Runs		Total Player Rating	
Gehrig-NY	1.339	Chapman-Was-Bos	35	Hill-Was-Phi	81.8	Chapman-Was-Bos	3.3	Clift-StL	41.0	Clift-StL	7.0
Greenberg-Det	1.277	Werber-Phi	35	Walker-Det	76.7	Hill-Was-Phi	3.0	Lake-Cle	25.9	Gehringer-Det	5.6
DiMaggio-NY	1.207	Walker-Det	23	Pytlak-Cle	76.2	Werber-Phi	2.7	Hayes-Chi	20.5	DiMaggio-NY	5.6
Gehringer-Det	1.089			Chapman-Was-Bos	74.5	Walker-Det	2.7	Appling-Chi	13.8	Dickey-NY	5.2
Johnson-Phi	1.083			Werber-Phi	72.9	Kreevich-Chi	2.4	Hughes-Cle	11.8	Greenberg-Det	4.7

Wins		Win Percentage		Games		Complete Games		Shutouts		Saves	
Gomez-NY	21	Allen-Cle	.938	Brown-Chi	53	W.Ferrell-Bos-Was	26	Gomez-NY	6	Brown-Chi	18
Ruffing-NY	20	Stratton-Chi	.750	Wilson-Bos	51	Gomez-NY	25	Stratton-Chi	5	Murphy-NY	10
Lawson-Det	18	Ruffing-NY	.741	Newsom-Was-Bos	41	Ruffing-NY	22	Whitehead-Chi	4	Wilson-Bos	7
Grove-Bos	17	Lawson-Det	.720	Kelley-Phi	41	Grove-Bos	21	Ruffing-NY	4	Malone-NY	6
Auker-Det	17	Gomez-NY	.656	Heving-Cle	40	DeShong-Was	20	Appleton-Was	4		

Innings Pitched		Fewest Hits/Game		Fewest BB/Game		Strikeouts		Strikeouts/Game		Ratio	
W.Ferrell-Bos-Was	281.0	Gomez-NY	7.53	Stratton-Chi	2.02	Gomez-NY	194	Gomez-NY	6.27	Stratton-Chi	9.89
Gomez-NY	278.1	Stratton-Chi	7.76	Hudlin-Cle	2.20	Newsom-Was-Bos	166	Wilson-Bos	5.57	Gomez-NY	10.57
Newsom-Was-Bos	275.8	Smith-Phi	8.15	Marcum-Bos	2.30	Grove-Bos	153	Newsom-Was-Bos	5.43	Ruffing-NY	10.92
DeShong-Was	264.1	Allen-Cle	8.17	Ruffing-NY	2.39	Feller-Cle	150	Grove-Bos	5.26	Allen-Cle	11.55
Grove-Bos	262.0	Ruffing-NY	8.50	Lyons-Chi	2.39	Bridges-Det	138	Bridges-Det	5.06	Lee-Chi	11.87

Earned Run Average		Adjusted ERA		Opponents' Batting Avg.		Opponents' On Base Pct.		Starter Runs		Adjusted Starter Runs	
Gomez-NY	2.33	Stratton-Chi	191	Gomez-NY	.223	Stratton-Chi	.280	Gomez-NY	70.9	Gomez-NY	65.5
Stratton-Chi	2.40	Gomez-NY	191	Stratton-Chi	.234	Gomez-NY	.287	Ruffing-NY	46.6	Grove-Bos	50.2
Allen-Cle	2.55	Allen-Cle	181	Smith-Phi	.242	Ruffing-NY	.296	Grove-Bos	46.5	Ruffing-NY	41.6
Ruffing-NY	2.98	Grove-Bos	157	Allen-Cle	.244	Lee-Chi	.312	Stratton-Chi	40.6	Stratton-Chi	40.2
Grove-Bos	3.02	Ruffing-NY	149	Ruffing-NY	.247	Allen-Cle	.313	Allen-Cle	39.8	Allen-Cle	39.6

Clutch Pitching Index		Relief Runs		Adjusted Relief Runs		Relief Ranking		Total Pitcher Index		Total Baseball Ranking	
Allen-Cle	120	Brown-Chi	13.3	Brown-Chi	13.1	Brown-Chi	21.9	Gomez-NY	6.1	Clift-StL	7.0
Whitehead-Chi	119	Cohen-Was	9.2	Cohen-Was	8.1	Cohen-Was	9.2	Grove-Bos	4.6	Gomez-NY	6.1
Knott-StL	112	Murphy-NY	5.5	Fink-Phi	5.9	Murphy-NY	5.3	Stratton-Chi	4.1	Gehringer-Det	5.6
Grove-Bos	111	Fink-Phi	5.1	Murphy-NY	3.3	Fink-Phi	2.2	Ruffing-NY	3.9	DiMaggio-NY	5.6
Galehouse-Cle	110	Wyatt-Cle	1.5	Wyatt-Cle	1.4	Wyatt-Cle	.8	Allen-Cle	3.4	Dickey-NY	5.2

TEAM	G	W	L	PCT	GB	R	OR	AB	H	2B	3B	HR	BB	SO	AVG	OBP	SLG	PRO	PRO+	BR	/A	PF	CHI	RC	SB	CS	SBA	SBR
CHI	154	89	63	.586		713	598	5333	1435	242	70	65	522	476	.269	.338	.377	.715	100	25	6	103	101	689	49			
PIT	152	86	64	.573	2	707	630	5422	1511	265	66	65	485	409	.279	.340	.388	.728	106	48	43	101	96	727	47			
NY	152	83	67	.553	5	705	637	5255	1424	210	36	125	465	528	.271	.334	.396	.730	106	45	39	101	99	715	31			
CIN	151	82	68	.547	6	723	634	5391	1495	251	57	110	366	518	.277	.327	.406	.733	109	43	61	101	99	720	19			
BOS	153	77	75	.507	12	561	618	5250	1311	199	39	54	424	548	.250	.309	.333	.642	91	-118	-51	90	103	549	49			
STL	156	71	80	.470	17.5	725	721	5528	1542	288	74	91	412	492	.279	.331	.407	.738	103	56	17	106	97	752	55			
BRO	151	69	80	.463	18.5	704	710	5142	1322	225	79	61	611	615	.257	.338	.367	.705	97	13	-2	102	103	671	66			
PHI	151	45	105	.300	43	550	840	5192	1318	233	29	40	423	507	.254	.312	.333	.645	85	-110	-91	97	101	549	38			
TOT	610					5388		42513	11358	1913	450	611	3708	4093	.267	.329	.376	.705							354			

TEAM	CG	SH	SV	IP	H	H/G	HR	BB	SO	RAT	ERA	ERA+	OAV	OOB	PR	/A	PF	CPI	FA	E	DP	FW	PW	BW	SBW	DIF
CHI	67	16	18	1396²	1414	9.1	71	454	583	12.1	3.37	113	.262	.321	64	66	101	105	.978	135	151	2.3	6.6	.6		3.5
PIT	57	8	15	1379²	1406	9.2	71	432	557	12.2	3.46	109	.265	.324	49	50	100	106	.974	163	168	.5	5.0	4.3		1.2
NY	59	8	18	1349	1370	9.1	87	389	497	11.9	3.62	104	.260	.314	24	20	99	97	.973	168	147	.2	2.0	3.9		1.9
CIN	72	11	16	1362	1329	8.8	75	463	542	11.9	3.62	101	.253	.316	24	3	96	94	.971	172	133	-.1	.3	6.1		.7
BOS	83	15	12	1380	1375	9.0	66	465	413	12.2	3.40	101	.258	.321	58	2	91	103	.972	173	136	-.0	.2	-5.1		6.0
STL	58	10	16	1384²	1482	9.6	77	474	534	12.8	3.84	103	.272	.332	-8	16	104	102	.967	199	145	-1.4	1.6	1.7		-6.4
BRO	56	12	14	1332	1464	9.9	88	446	469	13.1	4.07	96	.278	.338	-42	-25	103	102	.973	157	148	.8	-2.5	-.2		-3.5
PHI	68	3	6	1329¹	1516	10.3	76	582	492	14.4	4.93	79	.284	.357	-169	-155	103	92	.966	201	135	-1.8	-15.6	-9.2		-3.4
TOT	520	83	115	10913¹		9.4				12.6	3.78		.267	.329					.972	1368	1163					

Runs
Ott-NY 116
Hack-Chi 109
Camilli-Bro 106
Goodman-Cin 103
Medwick-StL 100

Hits
McCormick-Cin 209
Hack-Chi 195
L.Waner-Pit 194
Medwick-StL 190
Mize-StL 179

Doubles
Medwick-StL 47
McCormick-Cin 40
Young-Pit 36
Martin-Phi 36

Triples
Mize-StL 16
Gutteridge-StL 15
Suhr-Pit 14
Riggs-Cin 13
Koy-Bro 13

Home Runs
Ott-NY 36
Goodman-Cin 30
Mize-StL 27
Camilli-Bro 24
Rizzo-Pit 23

Total Bases
Mize-StL 326
Medwick-StL 316
Ott-NY 307
Goodman-Cin 303
Rizzo-Pit 285

Runs Batted In
Medwick-StL 122
Ott-NY 116
Rizzo-Pit 111
McCormick-Cin 106
Mize-StL 102

Runs Produced
Medwick-StL 201
Ott-NY 196
McCormick-Cin 190
Rizzo-Pit 185
Camilli-Bro 182

Bases On Balls
Camilli-Bro 119
Ott-NY 118
Vaughan-Pit 104
Hack-Chi 94
Suhr-Pit 87

Batting Average
Lombardi-Cin .342
Mize-StL .337
McCormick-Cin .327
Medwick-StL .322
Vaughan-Pit .322

On Base Percentage
Ott-NY .442
Vaughan-Pit .433
Mize-StL .422
Hack-Chi .411
Suhr-Pit .394

Slugging Average
Mize-StL .614
Ott-NY .583
Medwick-StL .536
Goodman-Cin .533
Lombardi-Cin .524

Production
Mize-StL 1.036
Ott-NY 1.024
Lombardi-Cin .915
Medwick-StL .905
Goodman-Cin .901

Adjusted Production
Ott-NY 178
Mize-StL 172
Lombardi-Cin 154
Goodman-Cin 149
Vaughan-Pit 140

Batter Runs
Ott-NY 61.9
Mize-StL 59.2
Vaughan-Pit 36.4
Medwick-StL 34.4
Goodman-Cin 33.5

Adjusted Batter Runs
Ott-NY 61.3
Mize-StL 55.3
Vaughan-Pit 35.9
Goodman-Cin 35.5
Lombardi-Cin 33.5

Clutch Hitting Index
Durocher-Bro 146
Arnovich-Phi 139
Lavagetto-Bro 135
Todd-Pit 132
Young-Pit 129

Runs Created
Ott-NY 149
Mize-StL 141
Hack-Chi 119
Goodman-Cin 116
Vaughan-Pit 115

Total Average
Ott-NY 1.164
Mize-StL 1.104
Camilli-Bro .964
Vaughan-Pit .960
Goodman-Cin .908

Stolen Bases
Hack-Chi 16
Lavagetto-Bro 15
Koy-Bro 15
Vaughan-Pit 14
Gutteridge-StL 14

Stolen Base Average

Stolen Base Runs

Fielding Runs
Young-Pit 31.8
Herman-Chi 24.8
Bartell-NY 22.4
Vaughan-Pit 18.3
Arnovich-Phi 18.1

Total Player Rating
Vaughan-Pit 6.3
Ott-NY 5.7
Mize-StL 4.1
Young-Pit 3.7
Medwick-StL 3.6

Wins
Lee-Chi 22
Derringer-Cin 21
Bryant-Chi 19
Weiland-StL 16

Win Percentage
Lee-Chi .710
Bryant-Chi .633
Brown-Pit .625
VanderMeer-Cin .600
Derringer-Cin .600

Games
Coffman-NY 51
Brown-Pit 51
McGee-StL 47
Mulcahy-Phi 46

Complete Games
Derringer-Cin 26
Turner-Bos 22
Walters-Phi-Cin 20
MacFayden-Bos 19
Lee-Chi 19

Shutouts
Lee-Chi 9
MacFayden-Bos 5
Warneke-StL 4
Derringer-Cin 4

Saves
Coffman-NY 12
Root-Chi 8
Hamlin-Bro 6
Errickson-Bos 6

Innings Pitched
Derringer-Cin 307.0
Lee-Chi 291.0
Bryant-Chi 270.1
Turner-Bos 268.0
Mulcahy-Phi 267.1

Fewest Hits/Game
VanderMeer-Cin 7.07
Bauers-Pit 7.67
Bryant-Chi 7.82
MacFayden-Bos 8.52
Klinger-Pit 8.59

Fewest BB/Game
Davis-StL 1.40
Derringer-Cin 1.44
Hubbell-NY 1.66
Root-Chi 1.68
Turner-Bos 1.81

Strikeouts
Bryant-Chi 135
Derringer-Cin 132
VanderMeer-Cin 125
Lee-Chi 121

Strikeouts/Game
Hubbell-NY 5.23
VanderMeer-Cin 4.99
Weiland-StL 4.61
Bryant-Chi 4.49

Ratio
Hubbell-NY 10.36
Derringer-Cin 10.67
Root-Chi 10.92
Turner-Bos 10.95
Lee-Chi 11.04

Earned Run Average
Lee-Chi 2.66
Root-Chi 2.86
Derringer-Cin 2.93
MacFayden-Bos 2.95
Klinger-Pit 2.99

Adjusted ERA
Lee-Chi 144
Root-Chi 134
Fitzsimmons-Bro 129
Klinger-Pit 127
Derringer-Cin 124

Opponents' Batting Avg.
VanderMeer-Cin .213
Bauers-Pit .233
Bryant-Chi .235
MacFayden-Bos .247
Schumacher-NY .248

Opponents' On Base Pct.
Hubbell-NY .285
Derringer-Cin .291
Root-Chi .294
Lohrman-NY .294
Schumacher-NY .299

Starter Runs
Lee-Chi 36.3
Derringer-Cin 29.1
Bryant-Chi 20.6
MacFayden-Bos 20.3
Bauers-Pit 19.2

Adjusted Starter Runs
Lee-Chi 37.6
Derringer-Cin 24.3
Bryant-Chi 21.8
Fitzsimmons-Bro 19.8
Bauers-Pit 19.4

Clutch Pitching Index
Lee-Chi 119
Pressnell-Bro 111
Blanton-Pit 111
Tamulis-Bro 110
Fette-Bos 110

Relief Runs
Brown-NY 19.8
Russell-Chi 5.0
Coffman-NY 3.8

Adjusted Relief Runs
Brown-NY 19.6
Russell-Chi 5.5
Coffman-NY 3.5

Relief Ranking
Brown-NY 18.1
Coffman-NY 4.3
Russell-Chi 3.7

Total Pitcher Index
Lee-Chi 4.2
Fitzsimmons-Bro 2.7
Bryant-Chi 2.4
Derringer-Cin 2.2
Bauers-Pit 2.0

Total Baseball Ranking
Vaughan-Pit 6.3
Ott-NY 5.7
Lee-Chi 4.2
Mize-StL 4.1
Young-Pit 3.7

TEAM	G	W	L	PCT	GB	R	OR	AB	H	2B	3B	HR	BB	SO	AVG	OBP	SLG	PRO	PRO+	BR	/A	PF	CHI	RC	SB	CS	SBA	SBR
NY	157	99	53	.651		**966**	710	5410	1480	283	63	**174**	749	616	.274	.366	**.446**	**.812**	110	77	81	100	**104**	926	91	28	46	-18
BOS	150	88	61	.591	9.5	902	751	5230	1566	298	56	98	650	463	**.299**	**.378**	.434	**.812**	105	87	49	105	100	881	55	51	53	-16
CLE	153	86	66	.566	13	847	782	5356	1506	**300**	**89**	113	550	605	.281	.350	.434	.784	104	9	25	98	102	832	83	36	40	**-12**
DET	155	84	70	.545	16	862	795	5270	1434	219	52	137	695	581	.272	.359	.411	.770	93	0	-47	106	104	813	76	41	51	-17
WAS	152	75	76	.497	23.5	814	873	5474	**1602**	278	72	85	573	379	.293	.362	.416	.778	108	12	69	93	96	845	65	37	42	-13
CHI	149	65	83	.439	32	709	752	5199	1439	239	55	67	514	489	.277	.343	.383	.726	86	-90	-108	102	101	700	56	39	48	-16
STL	156	55	97	.362	44	755	962	5333	1498	273	36	92	590	528	.281	.355	.397	.752	95	-37	-34	100	96	774	51	40	45	-14
PHI	154	53	99	.349	46	726	956	5229	1410	243	62	98	605	590	.270	.348	.396	.744	95	-56	-34	97	96	741	65	53	**54**	-16
TOT	613					6581		42501	11935	2133	485	864	4926	4251	.281	.358	.415	.773							542	325	63	-31

TEAM	CG	SH	SV	IP	H	H/G	HR	BB	SO	RAT	ERA	ERA+	OAV	OOB	PR	/A	PF	CPI	FA	E	DP	FW	PW	BW	SBW	DIF
NY	**91**	11	13	1382	1436	9.4	85	566	567	**13.1**	3.91	116	.267	.338	134	95	95	106	.973	169	177	.5	8.6	7.3	-1.3	7.9
BOS	67	10	15	1316¹	1472	10.1	102	**528**	484	13.8	4.46	111	.281	.349	48	69	103	103	.968	190	172	-1.1	6.2	4.4	-1.1	5.1
CLE	68	5	**17**	1353	**1416**	9.4	100	681	717	14.1	4.60	101	.268	.355	29	6	97	99	.974	151	145	1.2	.5	2.3	-.7	6.7
DET	75	3	11	1348¹	1532	10.2	110	608	435	14.4	4.79	104	.286	.361	0	32	104	103	**.976**	147	172	1.6	2.9	-4.2	-1.2	7.9
WAS	59	6	11	1360¹	1472	9.7	92	655	515	14.3	4.94	91	.275	.358	-22	-64	94	94	.970	180	**179**	-.5	-5.8	6.2	-.8	.3
CHI	83	5	9	1316¹	1449	9.9	101	550	432	13.8	4.36	112	.279	.350	62	77	102	**106**	.967	196	155	-1.6	7.0	-9.8	-1.1	-3.6
STL	71	3	7	1344²	1584	10.6	132	737	632	15.7	5.80	86	.294	.382	-151	-124	104	96	.975	**145**	163	**1.8**	-11.2	-3.1	-.9	-7.6
PHI	56	4	12	1324	1573	10.7	142	599	473	14.9	5.48	88	.291	.364	-101	-95	101	96	.965	206	119	-1.8	-8.6	-3.1	-1.1	-8.5
TOT	570	47	95	10745		10.0				14.3	4.79		.281	.358					.971	1384	1282					

Runs
Greenberg-Det ... 144
Foxx-Bos ... 139
Gehringer-Det ... 133
Rolfe-NY ... 132
DiMaggio-NY ... 129

Hits
Vosmik-Bos ... 201
Cramer-Bos ... 198
Almada-Was-StL ... 197
Foxx-Bos ... 197
Rolfe-NY ... 196

Doubles
Cronin-Bos ... 51
McQuinn-StL ... 42
Trosky-Cle ... 40
Chapman-Bos ... 40
Vosmik-Bos ... 37

Triples
Heath-Cle ... 18
Averill-Cle ... 15
DiMaggio-NY ... 13

Home Runs
Greenberg-Det ... 58
Foxx-Bos ... 50
Clift-StL ... 34
York-Det ... 33
DiMaggio-NY ... 32

Total Bases
Foxx-Bos ... 398
Greenberg-Det ... 380
DiMaggio-NY ... 348
Johnson-Phi ... 311
Heath-Cle ... 302

Runs Batted In
Foxx-Bos ... 175
Greenberg-Det ... 146
DiMaggio-NY ... 140
York-Det ... 127
Clift-StL ... 118

Runs Produced
Foxx-Bos ... 264
DiMaggio-NY ... 237
Greenberg-Det ... 232
Gehringer-Det ... 220
Clift-StL ... 203

Bases On Balls
Greenberg-Det ... 119
Foxx-Bos ... 119
Clift-StL ... 118
Gehringer-Det ... 113
Gehrig-NY ... 107

Batting Average
Foxx-Bos ... .349
Heath-Cle ... .343
Chapman-Bos ... .340
Myer-Was ... .336
Travis-Was ... .335

On Base Percentage
Foxx-Bos ... .462
Myer-Was ... .454
Greenberg-Det ... .438
Averill-Cle ... .429
Cronin-Bos ... .428

Slugging Average
Foxx-Bos ... .704
Greenberg-Det ... .683
Heath-Cle ... .602
DiMaggio-NY ... .581
York-Det ... .579

Production
Foxx-Bos ... 1.166
Greenberg-Det ... 1.122
York-Det ... .995
Heath-Cle ... .985
Dickey-NY ... .981

Adjusted Production
Foxx-Bos ... 180
Greenberg-Det ... 167
Heath-Cle ... 146
Dickey-NY ... 144
Clift-StL ... 143

Batter Runs
Foxx-Bos ... 78.2
Greenberg-Det ... 66.0
Clift-StL ... 37.7
Cronin-Bos ... 34.8
York-Det ... 33.9

Adjusted Batter Runs
Foxx-Bos ... 73.9
Greenberg-Det ... 60.7
Clift-StL ... 37.9
Johnson-Phi ... 35.0
Averill-Cle ... 33.3

Clutch Hitting Index
Higgins-Bos ... 166
Heffner-StL ... 152
Doerr-Bos ... 127
Radcliff-Chi ... 126
R.Ferrell-Was ... 123

Runs Created
Foxx-Bos ... 189
Greenberg-Det ... 172
DiMaggio-NY ... 136
Clift-StL ... 133
Gehrig-NY ... 131

Total Average
Foxx-Bos ... 1.392
Greenberg-Det ... 1.306
Clift-StL ... 1.104
York-Det ... 1.104
Dickey-NY ... 1.083

Stolen Bases
Crosetti-NY ... 27
Lary-Cle ... 23
Werber-Phi ... 19
Lewis-Was ... 17
Fox-Det ... 16

Stolen Base Average
Lary-Cle ... 79.3
Fox-Det ... 69.6
Crosetti-NY ... 69.2
Lewis-Was ... 65.4
Werber-Phi ... 55.9

Stolen Base Runs
Gehringer-Det ... 3.6
Rolfe-NY ... 3.3
Lary-Cle ... 3.3
Hale-Cle ... 1.8

Fielding Runs
Gordon-NY ... 23.7
Crosetti-NY ... 17.6
Clift-StL ... 14.0
Rogell-Det ... 7.5
Cronin-Bos ... 7.2

Total Player Rating
Foxx-Bos ... 5.2
Clift-StL ... 5.0
Cronin-Bos ... 4.0
Greenberg-Det ... 4.0
Dickey-NY ... 3.3

Wins
Ruffing-NY ... 21
Newsom-StL ... 20
Gomez-NY ... 18
Harder-Cle ... 17
Feller-Cle ... 17

Win Percentage
Ruffing-NY ... .750
Pearson-NY ... .696
Harder-Cle ... .630
Stratton-Chi ... .625
Feller-Cle ... .607

Games
Humphries-Cle ... 45
Newsom-StL ... 44
E.Smith-Phi ... 43
Bagby-Bos ... 43
Appleton-Was ... 43

Complete Games
Newsom-StL ... 31
Ruffing-NY ... 22
Gomez-NY ... 20
Feller-Cle ... 20
Caster-Phi ... 20

Shutouts
Gomez-NY ... 4
Wilson-Bos ... 3
Ruffing-NY ... 3
Leonard-Was ... 3

Saves
Murphy-NY ... 11
McKain-Bos ... 6
Humphries-Cle ... 6
Potter-Phi ... 5
Appleton-Was ... 5

Innings Pitched
Newsom-StL ... 329.2
Caster-Phi ... 281.1
Feller-Cle ... 277.2
Ruffing-NY ... 247.1
Lee-Chi ... 245.1

Fewest Hits/Game
Feller-Cle ... 7.29
Allen-Cle ... 8.51
Pearson-NY ... 8.82
Rigney-Chi ... 8.84
Hadley-NY ... 8.87

Fewest BB/Game
Leonard-Was ... 2.14
Harder-Cle ... 2.33
Lyons-Chi ... 2.40
Chandler-NY ... 2.46
Thomas-Phi ... 2.63

Strikeouts
Feller-Cle ... 240
Newsom-StL ... 226
H.Mills-StL ... 134
Gomez-NY ... 129
Ruffing-NY ... 127

Strikeouts/Game
Feller-Cle ... 7.78
Newsom-StL ... 6.17
H.Mills-StL ... 5.73
Grove-Bos ... 5.44
Allen-Cle ... 5.04

Ratio
Leonard-Was ... 11.32
Ruffing-NY ... 11.94
Stratton-Chi ... 12.03
Chandler-NY ... 12.14
Harder-Cle ... 12.15

Earned Run Average
Grove-Bos ... 3.08
Ruffing-NY ... 3.31
Gomez-NY ... 3.35
Leonard-Was ... 3.43
Lee-Chi ... 3.49

Adjusted ERA
Grove-Bos ... 160
Lee-Chi ... 140
Rigney-Chi ... 138
Ruffing-NY ... 137
Gomez-NY ... 135

Opponents' Batting Avg.
Feller-Cle ... .220
Allen-Cle ... .246
Hadley-NY ... .254
Stratton-Chi ... .255
Rigney-Chi ... .256

Opponents' On Base Pct.
Leonard-Was ... .305
Stratton-Chi ... .315
Ruffing-NY ... .317
Harder-Cle ... .319
Grove-Bos ... .319

Starter Runs
Ruffing-NY ... 40.6
Gomez-NY ... 38.2
Lee-Chi ... 35.6
Leonard-Was ... 33.8
Grove-Bos ... 31.1

Adjusted Starter Runs
Lee-Chi ... 38.4
Grove-Bos ... 33.7
Ruffing-NY ... 33.6
Gomez-NY ... 31.4
Leonard-Was ... 27.0

Clutch Pitching Index
Lyons-Chi ... 125
Gill-Det ... 119
Grove-Bos ... 118
Rigney-Chi ... 117
Ruffing-NY ... 110

Relief Runs
Murphy-NY ... 5.6
McKain-Bos ... 3.0

Adjusted Relief Runs
McKain-Bos ... 4.6
Murphy-NY ... 3.0

Relief Ranking
McKain-Bos ... 4.4
Murphy-NY ... 3.8

Total Pitcher Index
Lee-Chi ... 4.2
Ruffing-NY ... 3.9
Grove-Bos ... 3.1
Gomez-NY ... 2.9
Leonard-Was ... 2.8

Total Baseball Ranking
Foxx-Bos ... 5.2
Clift-StL ... 5.0
Lee-Chi ... 4.2
Cronin-Bos ... 4.0
Greenberg-Det ... 4.0

TEAM	G	W	L	PCT	GB	R	OR	AB	H	2B	3B	HR	BB	SO	AVG	OBP	SLG	PRO	PRO+	BR	/A	PF	CHI	RC	SB	CS	SBA	SBR
CIN	156	97	57	.630		767	595	5378	1493	269	60	98	500	538	.278	.343	.405	.748	106	51	47	101	102	759	46			
STL	155	92	61	.601	4.5	779	633	5447	1601	332	62	98	475	566	.294	.354	.432	.786	110	122	78	106	94	834	44			
BRO	157	84	69	.549	12.5	708	645	5350	1420	265	57	78	564	631	.265	.338	.380	.718	95	0	-25	104	102	697	59			
CHI	156	84	70	.545	13	724	678	5293	1407	263	62	91	523	553	.266	.336	.391	.727	99	10	-1	102	103	702	61			
NY	151	77	74	.510	18.5	703	685	5129	1395	211	38	116	498	499	.272	.340	.396	.736	103	28	22	101	101	683	26			
PIT	153	68	85	.444	28.5	666	721	5269	1453	261	60	63	477	420	.276	.338	.384	.722	101	4	14	98	97	687	44			
BOS	152	63	88	.417	32.5	572	659	5286	1395	199	39	56	366	494	.264	.314	.348	.662	90	-116	-67	93	104	575	41			
PHI	152	45	106	.298	50.5	553	856	5133	1341	232	40	49	421	486	.261	.318	.351	.669	88	-97	-77	97	99	570	47			
TOT	616					5472		42285	11505	2032	418	649	3824	4187	.272	.335	.386	.721							368			

TEAM	CG	SH	SV	IP	H	H/G	HR	BB	SO	RAT	ERA	ERA+	OAV	OOB	PR	/A	PF	CPI	FA	E	DP	FW	PW	BW	SBW	DIF
CIN	86	13	9	1403²	1340	8.6	81	499	637	12.0	3.27	117	.254	.322	100	87	98	107	.974	162	170	.6	8.7	4.7		6.0
STL	45	18	32	1384²	1377	9.0	76	498	603	12.3	3.59	115	.260	.326	50	79	105	100	.971	177	140	-.2	7.9	7.8		.0
BRO	69	9	13	1410¹	1431	9.1	93	399	528	11.9	3.64	110	.263	.317	42	59	103	97	.972	176	157	-.0	5.9	-2.5		4.1
CHI	72	8	13	1392¹	1504	9.7	74	430	584	12.6	3.80	104	.275	.330	17	20	101	101	.970	186	126	-.6	2.0	-.1		5.7
NY	55	6	20	1319	1412	9.6	86	477	505	13.1	4.07	96	.274	.339	-22	-19	100	100	.975	153	151	.8	-1.9	2.2		.4
PIT	53	10	15	1354	1537	10.2	70	423	464	13.2	4.15	92	.287	.341	-35	-49	98	100	.972	168	153	.1	-4.9	1.4		-5.1
BOS	68	11	15	1358¹	1400	9.3	63	513	430	12.8	3.71	100	.270	.338	31	-2	94	104	.971	181	178	-.6	-.2	-6.7		-5.0
PHI	67	3	12	1326²	1502	10.2	106	579	447	14.4	5.17	77	.288	.364	-184	-170	102	93	.970	171	136	-.0	-17.0	-7.7		-5.7
TOT	515	78	129	10949		9.5				12.8	3.92		.272	.335					.972	1374	1211					

Runs		Hits		Doubles		Triples		Home Runs		Total Bases	
Werber-Cin	115	McCormick-Cin	209	Slaughter-StL	52	Herman-Chi	18	Mize-StL	28	Mize-StL	353
Hack-Chi	112	Medwick-StL	201	Medwick-StL	48	Goodman-Cin	16	Ott-NY	27	McCormick-Cin	312
Herman-Chi	111	Mize-StL	197	Mize-StL	44	Mize-StL	14	Camilli-Bro	26	Medwick-StL	307
Camilli-Bro	105	Slaughter-StL	193	McCormick-Cin	41	Camilli-Bro	12	Leiber-Chi	24	Camilli-Bro	296
		Brown-StL	192					Lombardi-Cin	20	Slaughter-StL	291

Runs Batted In		Runs Produced		Bases On Balls		Batting Average		On Base Percentage		Slugging Average	
McCormick-Cin	128	McCormick-Cin	209	Camilli-Bro	110	Mize-StL	.349	Ott-NY	.449	Mize-StL	.626
Medwick-StL	117	Medwick-StL	201	Ott-NY	100	McCormick-Cin	.332	Mize-StL	.444	Ott-NY	.581
Mize-StL	108	Mize-StL	184	Mize-StL	92	Medwick-StL	.332	Camilli-Bro	.409	Camilli-Bro	.524
Camilli-Bro	104	Camilli-Bro	183	Werber-Cin	91	P.Waner-Pit	.328	Goodman-Cin	.401	Goodman-Cin	.515
Leiber-Chi	88	Herman-Chi	174	Lavagetto-Bro	78	Arnovich-Phi	.324	Arnovich-Phi	.397	Medwick-StL	.507

Production		Adjusted Production		Batter Runs		Adjusted Batter Runs		Clutch Hitting Index		Runs Created	
Mize-StL	1.070	Mize-StL	174	Mize-StL	68.7	Mize-StL	64.0	McCormick-Cin	136	Mize-StL	162
Ott-NY	1.030	Ott-NY	173	Ott-NY	45.9	Ott-NY	45.5	Bonura-NY	132	Camilli-Bro	128
Camilli-Bro	.933	Camilli-Bro	144	Camilli-Bro	41.8	Camilli-Bro	39.0	May-Phi	130	Medwick-StL	114
Goodman-Cin	.916	Goodman-Cin	144	Leiber-Chi	30.5	Leiber-Chi	29.6	Medwick-StL	130	Ott-NY	112
Medwick-StL	.886	West-Bos	139	Goodman-Cin	29.8	Goodman-Cin	29.5	G.Russell-Chi	125	McCormick-Cin	110

Total Average		Stolen Bases		Stolen Base Average	Stolen Base Runs	Fielding Runs		Total Player Rating	
Mize-StL	1.194	Handley-Pit	17			Frey-Cin	15.1	Mize-StL	4.2
Ott-NY	1.194	Hack-Chi	17			Jurges-NY	14.9	Frey-Cin	3.8
Camilli-Bro	.995	Werber-Cin	15			Slaughter-StL	14.3	Ott-NY	3.8
Goodman-Cin	.941	Lavagetto-Bro	14			Werber-Cin	12.6	Vaughan-Pit	3.5
Frey-Cin	.860	Hassett-Bos	13			Arnovich-Phi	12.3	Goodman-Cin	3.2

Wins		Win Percentage		Games		Complete Games		Shutouts		Saves	
Walters-Cin	27	Derringer-Cin	.781	Shoun-StL	53	Walters-Cin	31	Fette-Bos	6	Shoun-StL	9
Derringer-Cin	25	Walters-Cin	.711	Sewell-Pit	52	Derringer-Cin	28	Posedel-Bos	5	Bowman-StL	9
Davis-StL	22	French-Chi	.652	Bowman-StL	51	Lee-Chi	20	Derringer-Cin	5	Davis-StL	7
Hamlin-Bro	20	Gumbert-NY	.621	Davis-StL	49	Hamlin-Bro	19	McGee-StL	4	Brown-NY	7
Lee-Chi	19	Hamlin-Bro	.606	Brown-Pit	47	Posedel-Bos	18			Brown-Pit	7

Innings Pitched		Fewest Hits/Game		Fewest BB/Game		Strikeouts		Strikeouts/Game		Ratio	
Walters-Cin	319.0	Walters-Cin	7.05	Derringer-Cin	1.05	Passeau-Phi-Chi	137	Cooper-StL	5.55	Hubbell-NY	10.29
Derringer-Cin	301.0	Bowman-StL	7.49	Hubbell-NY	1.40	Walters-Cin	137	Tamulis-Bro	4.71	Walters-Cin	10.30
Lee-Chi	282.1	Moore-Cin	8.49	Davis-StL	1.74	Cooper-StL	130	French-Chi	4.55	Hamlin-Bro	10.31
Passeau-Phi-Chi	274.1	Hamlin-Bro	8.51	Hamlin-Bro	1.80	Derringer-Cin	128	Passeau-Phi-Chi	4.49	Derringer-Cin	10.73
Hamlin-Bro	269.2	Hubbell-NY	8.77	Root-Chi	1.83	Lee-Chi	105	Bowman-StL	4.15	Bowman-StL	10.74

Earned Run Average		Adjusted ERA		Opponents' Batting Avg.		Opponents' On Base Pct.		Starter Runs		Adjusted Starter Runs	
Walters-Cin	2.29	Walters-Cin	168	Walters-Cin	.220	Hubbell-NY	.280	Walters-Cin	57.8	Walters-Cin	54.7
Bowman-StL	2.60	Bowman-StL	158	Bowman-StL	.232	Hamlin-Bro	.285	Derringer-Cin	33.0	Derringer-Cin	30.1
Hubbell-NY	2.75	Hubbell-NY	143	Hamlin-Bro	.248	Walters-Cin	.291	Casey-Bro	24.9	Bowman-StL	28.4
Casey-Bro	2.93	Casey-Bro	137	Hubbell-NY	.249	Derringer-Cin	.295	Bowman-StL	24.7	Casey-Bro	27.7
Derringer-Cin	2.93	Derringer-Cin	131	Moore-Cin	.254	Bowman-StL	.302	Thompson-Cin	23.3	Thompson-Cin	21.8

Clutch Pitching Index		Relief Runs		Adjusted Relief Runs		Relief Ranking		Total Pitcher Index		Total Baseball Ranking	
Brown-Pit	120	J.Russell-Chi	1.9	Shoun-StL	4.1	Shoun-StL	2.2	Walters-Cin	8.0	Walters-Cin	8.0
Shoffner-Bos-Cin	115	Shoun-StL	1.8	J.Russell-Chi	2.0	J.Russell-Chi	2.1	Casey-Bro	3.2	Mize-StL	4.2
Casey-Bro	113							Davis-StL	2.9	Frey-Cin	3.8
Cooper-StL	113							Derringer-Cin	2.8	Ott-NY	3.8
Moore-Cin	113							Bowman-StL	2.5	Vaughan-Pit	3.5

TEAM	G	W	L	PCT	GB	R	OR	AB	H	2B	3B	HR	BB	SO	AVG	OBP	SLG	PRO	PRO+	BR	/A	PF	CHI	RC	SB	CS	SBA	SBR
NY	152	106	45	.702		967	556	5300	1521	259	55	166	701	543	.287	.374	.451	.825	118	134	146	98	102	923	72	37	41	-13
BOS	152	89	62	.589	17	890	795	5308	1543	287	57	124	591	505	.291	.363	.436	.799	105	78	47	104	101	831	42	44	52	-17
CLE	154	87	67	.565	20.5	797	700	5316	1490	291	79	85	557	574	.280	.350	.413	.763	104	4	31	97	100	775	72	46	47	-13
CHI	155	85	69	.552	22.5	755	737	5279	1451	220	56	64	579	502	.275	.349	.374	.723	88	-61	-81	103	103	708	113	61	56	-14
DET	155	81	73	.526	26.5	849	762	5326	1487	277	67	124	620	592	.279	.356	.426	.782	98	43	-17	108	100	821	88	38	40	-12
WAS	153	65	87	.428	41.5	702	797	5334	1483	249	79	44	547	460	.278	.346	.379	.725	98	-61	-2	93	95	718	94	47	54	-17
PHI	153	55	97	.362	51.5	711	1022	5309	1438	282	55	98	503	532	.271	.336	.400	.736	96	-54	-37	98	97	713	60	34	39	-12
STL	156	43	111	.279	64.5	733	1035	5422	1453	242	50	91	559	606	.268	.339	.381	.720	88	-78	-95	102	100	706	48	38	49	-17
TOT	615					6404		42594	11866	2107	498	796	4657	4314	.279	.352	.407	.759							589	345	63	-29

TEAM	CG	SH	SV	IP	H	H/G	HR	BB	SO	RAT	ERA	ERA+	OAV	OOB	PR	/A	PF	CPI	FA	E	DP	FW	PW	BW	SBW	DIF
NY	87	15	26	1348²	1208	8.1	85	567	565	11.9	3.31	132	.240	.319	196	156	94	107	.978	126	159	2.9	14.4	13.5	-.8	.6
BOS	52	4	20	1350²	1533	10.2	77	543	539	14.0	4.56	104	.286	.354	9	25	102	102	.970	180	147	.0	2.3	4.3	-1.2	8.0
CLE	69	10	13	1364²	1394	9.2	75	602	614	13.3	4.08	108	.266	.344	81	48	95	103	.970	180	148	.2	4.4	2.9	-.8	3.3
CHI	62	5	21	1377	1470	9.6	99	454	535	12.7	4.31	110	.274	.333	47	64	102	98	.972	167	140	1.0	5.9	-7.5	-.9	9.6
DET	64	8	16	1367¹	1430	9.4	104	574	633	13.3	4.29	114	.267	.341	49	90	106	100	.967	198	147	-.6	8.3	-1.6	-.8	-1.3
WAS	72	4	10	1354²	1420	9.4	75	602	521	13.6	4.60	94	.270	.347	2	-38	94	94	.966	205	167	-1.1	-3.5	-.2	-1.2	-5.0
PHI	50	6	12	1342²	1687	11.3	148	579	397	15.3	5.79	81	.306	.374	-174	-161	102	99	.964	210	131	-1.4	-14.8	-3.4	-.6	-.6
STL	56	3	3	1371¹	1724	11.3	133	739	516	16.4	6.01	81	.309	.393	-212	-174	105	100	.968	199	144	-.6	-16.0	-8.8	-1.2	-7.4
TOT	512	55	121	10877		9.8				13.8	4.62		.279	.352					.969	1465	1183					

Runs
Rolfe-NY 139
Williams-Bos 131
Foxx-Bos 130
McCosky-Det 120
Johnson-Phi 115

Hits
Rolfe-NY 213
McQuinn-StL 195
Keltner-Cle 191
McCosky-Det 190
Williams-Bos 185

Doubles
Rolfe-NY 46
Williams-Bos 44
Greenberg-Det ... 42
McQuinn-StL 37
Keltner-Cle 35

Triples
Lewis-Bos 16
McCosky-Det 14
McQuinn-StL 13
Campbell-Cle 13

Home Runs
Foxx-Bos 35
Greenberg-Det ... 33
Williams-Bos 31
DiMaggio-NY 30
Gordon-NY 28

Total Bases
Williams-Bos 344
Foxx-Bos 324
Rolfe-NY 321
McQuinn-StL 318
Greenberg-Det ... 311

Runs Batted In
Williams-Bos 145
DiMaggio-NY 126
Johnson-Phi 114
Greenberg-Det ... 112

Runs Produced
Williams-Bos 245
Johnson-Phi 206
Rolfe-NY 205
DiMaggio-NY 204
Foxx-Bos 200

Bases On Balls
Clift-StL 111
Williams-Bos 107
Appling-Chi 105
Selkirk-NY 103
Johnson-Phi 99

Batting Average
DiMaggio-NY ..... .381
Foxx-Bos .... .360
Johnson-Phi ...... .338
Trosky-Cle ...... .335
Keller-NY .... .334

On Base Percentage
Foxx-Bos .... .464
Selkirk-NY ...... .452
DiMaggio-NY ..... .448
Keller-NY .... .447
Johnson-Phi ..... .440

Slugging Average
DiMaggio-NY ..... .694
Foxx-Bos .... .671
Greenberg-Det ... .622
Williams-Bos ..... .609
Trosky-Cle .... .589

Production
Foxx-Bos 1.158
DiMaggio-NY 1.119
Williams-Bos 1.045
Greenberg-Det .. 1.042
Trosky-Cle .... .994

Adjusted Production
DiMaggio-NY 185
Foxx-Bos 185
Williams-Bos 158
Trosky-Cle 157
Johnson-Phi 156

Batter Runs
Foxx-Bos 66.1
Williams-Bos 56.3
DiMaggio-NY 56.0
Greenberg-Det .. 47.3
Johnson-Phi 45.7

Adjusted Batter Runs
Foxx-Bos 63.2
DiMaggio-NY 57.1
Williams-Bos 52.9
Johnson-Phi 47.5
Greenberg-Det .. 41.3

Clutch Hitting Index
Wright-Was 140
Walker-Chi 131
Keller-NY 128
Vosmik-Bos 127
McNair-Chi....... 126

Runs Created
Williams-Bos 157
Foxx-Bos 150
DiMaggio-NY 139
Johnson-Phi 138
Greenberg-Det ... 136

Total Average
Foxx-Bos 1.304
DiMaggio-NY 1.242
Williams-Bos 1.161
Greenberg-Det .. 1.152
Selkirk-NY 1.121

Stolen Bases
Case-Was 51
Kreevich-Chi 23
Fox-Det 23
McCosky-Det..... 20

Stolen Base Average
McCosky-Det ... 83.3
Kuhel-Chi 78.3
Chapman-Cle ... 75.0
Case-Was 75.0
Walker-Chi 73.9

Stolen Base Runs
Case-Was 5.1
McCosky-Det...... 3.6
Welaj-Was 2.7
Kuhel-Chi 2.4
Henrich-NY 2.1

Fielding Runs
Doerr-Bos 27.3
Tebbetts-Det 14.7
Lewis-Was 13.6
Clift-StL 12.0
Trosky-Cle 11.3

Total Player Rating
Foxx-Bos 5.3
DiMaggio-NY 5.3
Johnson-Phi 4.9
Williams-Bos 4.2
Dickey-NY 3.8

Wins
Feller-Cle 24
Ruffing-NY 21
Newsom-StL-Det... 20
Leonard-Was 20
Bridges-Det 17

Win Percentage
Grove-Bos .... .789
Ruffing-NY .... .750
Feller-Cle .... .727
Leonard-Was ..... .714
Bridges-Det ...... .708

Games
Brown-Chi 61
Dean-Phi 54
Dickman-Bos 48
Heving-Bos 46

Complete Games
Newsom-StL-Det... 24
Feller-Cle 24
Ruffing-NY 22
Leonard-Was 21
Grove-Bos 17

Shutouts
Ruffing-NY 5
Feller-Cle 4
Newsom-StL-Det.... 3

Saves
Murphy-NY 19
Brown-Chi 18
Heving-Bos 7
Dean-Phi 7
Appleton-Was 6

Innings Pitched
Feller-Cle 296.2
Newsom-StL-Det . 291.2
Leonard-Was 269.1
Lee-Chi.......... 235.0
Ruffing-NY 233.1

Fewest Hits/Game
Feller-Cle 6.89
Hadley-NY 7.71
Gomez-NY 7.86
Ruffing-NY 8.14
Chase-Was 8.34

Fewest BB/Game
Lyons-Chi 1.36
Leonard-Was 1.97
Beckmann-Phi ... 2.38
Lee-Chi.......... 2.68
Grove-Bos 2.73

Strikeouts
Feller-Cle 246
Newsom-StL-Det.. 192
Bridges-Det 129
Rigney-Chi 119
Chase-Was 118

Strikeouts/Game
Feller-Cle 7.46
Newsom-StL-Det . 5.92
Bridges-Det 5.86
Rigney-Chi 4.90
Gomez-NY 4.64

Ratio
Lyons-Chi 9.85
Ruffing-NY 11.11
Leonard-Was ... 11.26
Grove-Bos 11.26
Feller-Cle 11.29

Earned Run Average
Grove-Bos 2.54
Lyons-Chi 2.76
Feller-Cle 2.85
Ruffing-NY 2.93
Hadley-NY 2.98

Adjusted ERA
Grove-Bos 186
Lyons-Chi 171
Feller-Cle 154
Ruffing-NY 149
Hadley-NY 146

Opponents' Batting Avg.
Feller-Cle .... .210
Gomez-NY ...... .235
Hadley-NY ...... .237
Ruffing-NY ...... .240
Bridges-Det ...... .243

Opponents' On Base Pct.
Lyons-Chi .... .276
Ruffing-NY ...... .301
Feller-Cle .... .303
Bridges-Det ..... .304
Leonard-Was ..... .305

Starter Runs
Feller-Cle 58.3
Grove-Bos 44.0
Ruffing-NY 43.8
Lyons-Chi 35.6
Newsom-StL-Det.. 33.7

Adjusted Starter Runs
Feller-Cle 51.1
Grove-Bos 46.3
Newsom-StL-Det . 42.3
Lyons-Chi 37.8
Ruffing-NY 36.9

Clutch Pitching Index
Hadley-NY 132
Grove-Bos 126
Trout-Det 116
Harder-Cle 116
Milnar-Cle 110

Relief Runs
Heving-Bos 10.9
Brown-Chi 9.7
Dickman-Bos 2.3
Murphy-NY 1.5
Appleton-Was 7

Adjusted Relief Runs
Heving-Bos 12.2
Brown-Chi 11.2
Dickman-Bos 3.7

Relief Ranking
Brown-Chi 21.7
Heving-Bos 16.1
Dickman-Bos..... 3.6

Total Pitcher Index
Feller-Cle 5.3
Ruffing-NY 4.3
Grove-Bos 4.3
Lyons-Chi 4.1
Newsom-StL-Det . 3.6

Total Baseball Ranking
Feller-Cle 5.3
Foxx-Bos 5.3
DiMaggio-NY 5.3
Johnson-Phi 4.9
Ruffing-NY 4.3

TEAM	G	W	L	PCT	GB	R	OR	AB	H	2B	3B	HR	BB	SO	AVG	OBP	SLG	PRO	PRO+	BR	/A	PF	CHI	RC	SB	CS	SBA	SBR
CIN	155	100	53	.654		707	528	5372	1427	264	38	89	453	503	.266	.327	.379	.706	100	6	0	101	103	672	72			
BRO	156	88	65	.575	12	697	621	5470	1421	256	70	93	522	570	.260	.327	.383	.710	96	15	-27	106	98	692	56			
STL	156	84	69	.549	16	747	699	5499	1514	266	61	119	479	610	.275	.336	.411	.747	105	83	43	106	96	764	97			
PIT	156	78	76	.506	22.5	809	783	5466	1511	276	68	76	553	494	.276	.346	.394	.740	111	84	89	99	104	757	69			
CHI	154	75	79	.487	25.5	681	636	5389	1441	272	48	86	482	566	.267	.331	.384	.715	106	25	38	98	97	691	63			
NY	152	72	80	.474	27.5	663	659	5324	1423	201	46	91	453	478	.267	.329	.374	.703	99	3	-2	101	98	653	45			
BOS	152	65	87	.428	34.5	623	745	5329	1366	219	50	59	402	581	.256	.311	.349	.660	93	-82	-45	95	108	581	48			
PHI	153	50	103	.327	50	494	750	5137	1225	180	35	75	435	527	.238	.300	.331	.631	83	-132	-106	96	96	512	25			
TOT	617					5421		42986	11328	1934	416	688	3779	4329	.264	.326	.376	.702							475			

TEAM	CG	SH	SV	IP	H	H/G	HR	BB	SO	RAT	ERA	ERA+	OAV	OOB	PR	/A	PF	CPI	FA	E	DP	FW	PW	BW	SBW	DIF
CIN	91	10	11	1407²	1263	8.1	73	445	557	11.0	3.05	124	.240	.302	124	115	98	102	.981	117	158	2.9	11.6	.0		9.0
BRO	65	17	14	1433	1366	8.6	101	393	639	11.2	3.50	114	.248	.301	55	78	104	95	.970	183	110	-.3	7.9	-2.7		6.7
STL	71	10	14	1396	1457	9.4	83	488	550	12.7	3.83	104	.266	.329	2	23	104	102	.971	174	134	.1	2.3	4.3		.7
PIT	49	8	24	1388²	1569	10.2	72	492	491	13.6	4.36	87	.282	.344	-79	-85	99	99	.966	217	161	-2.0	-8.6	9.0		2.6
CHI	69	12	14	1392	1418	9.2	74	430	564	12.1	3.54	106	.262	.318	47	31	97	103	.968	199	143	-1.2	3.1	3.8		-7.8
NY	57	11	18	1360¹	1383	9.1	110	473	606	12.4	3.79	102	.261	.324	8	13	101	104	.977	139	132	1.6	1.3	-.2		-6.7
BOS	76	9	12	1359	1444	9.6	83	573	435	13.6	4.36	85	.273	.348	-76	-97	97	100	.970	184	169	-.6	-9.8	-4.6		4.0
PHI	66	5	8	1357	1429	9.5	92	475	485	12.8	4.40	89	.269	.332	-82	-74	101	93	.970	181	136	-.4	-7.5	-10.7		-7.9
TOT	544	82	115	11093²		9.2				12.4	3.85		.264	.326					.972	1394	1143					

Runs
Vaughan-Pit	113
Mize-StL	111
Werber-Cin	105
Frey-Cin	102
Hack-Chi	101

Hits
F.McCormick-Cin	191
Hack-Chi	191
Mize-StL	182
Vaughan-Pit	178
Medwick-StL-Bro	175

Doubles
F.McCormick-Cin	44
Vaughan-Pit	40
Gleeson-Chi	39
Hack-Chi	38
Walker-Bro	37

Triples
Vaughan-Pit	15
Ross-Bos	14
Slaughter-StL	13
Mize-StL	13
Camilli-Bro	13

Home Runs
Mize-StL	43
Nicholson-Chi	25
Rizzo-Pit-Cin-Phi	24
Camilli-Bro	23

Total Bases
Mize-StL	368
F.McCormick-Cin	298
Medwick-StL-Bro	280
Camilli-Bro	271
Vaughan-Pit	269

Runs Batted In
Mize-StL	137
F.McCormick-Cin	127
VanRobays-Pit	116
Fletcher-Pit	104
Young-NY	101

Runs Produced
Mize-StL	205
Vaughan-Pit	201
F.McCormick-Cin	201
VanRobays-Pit	187
Fletcher-Pit	182

Bases On Balls
Fletcher-Pit	119
Ott-NY	100
Camilli-Bro	89
Vaughan-Pit	88
Mize-StL	82

Batting Average
Hack-Chi	.317
Mize-StL	.314
Gleeson-Chi	.313
F.McCormick-Cin	.309
Walker-Bro	.308

On Base Percentage
Fletcher-Pit	.418
Ott-NY	.407
Mize-StL	.404
Camilli-Bro	.397
Hack-Chi	.395

Slugging Average
Mize-StL	.636
Nicholson-Chi	.534
Camilli-Bro	.529
Slaughter-StL	.504
F.McCormick-Cin	.482

Production
Mize-StL	1.039
Camilli-Bro	.926
Nicholson-Chi	.899
Slaughter-StL	.874
Ott-NY	.864

Adjusted Production
Mize-StL	173
Nicholson-Chi	148
Camilli-Bro	144
Gleeson-Chi	139
Fletcher-Pit	137

Batter Runs
Mize-StL	63.9
Camilli-Bro	38.7
Fletcher-Pit	31.8
Ott-NY	31.7
Vaughan-Pit	28.8

Adjusted Batter Runs
Mize-StL	59.6
Camilli-Bro	34.5
Fletcher-Pit	32.4
Ott-NY	31.1
Nicholson-Chi	29.9

Clutch Hitting Index
VanRobays-Pit	167
Fletcher-Pit	151
F.McCormick-Cin	141
Young-NY	134
West-Bos	131

Runs Created
Mize-StL	152
Camilli-Bro	114
Vaughan-Pit	113
Hack-Chi	112
Ott-NY	107

Total Average
Mize-StL	1.135
Camilli-Bro	1.005
Fletcher-Pit	.930
Ott-NY	.915
Nicholson-Chi	.901

Stolen Bases
Frey-Cin	22
Hack-Chi	21
Moore-StL	18
Werber-Cin	16
Reese-Bro	15

Stolen Base Average

Stolen Base Runs

Fielding Runs
Witek-NY	19.0
Herman-Chi	18.9
Frey-Cin	18.2
Miller-Bos	14.7
Moore-StL	14.1

Total Player Rating
Vaughan-Pit	5.2
Hack-Chi	4.0
Mize-StL	3.9
Miller-Bos	3.6
Frey-Cin	3.1

Wins
Walters-Cin	22
Passeau-Chi	20
Derringer-Cin	20

Win Percentage
Fitzsimmons-Bro	.889
Sewell-Pit	.762
Walters-Cin	.688
Thompson-Cin	.640
Derringer-Cin	.625

Games
Shoun-StL	54
Brown-Pit	48
Passeau-Chi	46
Casey-Bro	44
Raffensberger-Chi	43

Complete Games
Walters-Cin	29
Derringer-Cin	26
Mulcahy-Phi	21
Passeau-Chi	20
Higbe-Phi	20

Shutouts
Wyatt-Bro	5
Salvo-Bos	5

Saves
Brown-NY	7
Brown-Pit	7
Beggs-Cin	7
Shoun-StL	5
Passeau-Chi	5

Innings Pitched
Walters-Cin	305.0
Derringer-Cin	296.2
Higbe-Phi	283.0
Passeau-Chi	280.2
Mulcahy-Phi	280.0

Fewest Hits/Game
Walters-Cin	7.11
Higbe-Phi	7.70
Thompson-Cin	7.87
Casey-Bro	7.95
Sullivan-Bos	7.97

Fewest BB/Game
Derringer-Cin	1.46
Turner-Cin	1.54
Hamlin-Bro	1.68
Davis-StL-Bro	1.79
Warneke-StL	1.82

Strikeouts
Higbe-Phi	137
Wyatt-Bro	124
Passeau-Chi	124
Schumacher-NY	123

Strikeouts/Game
Melton-NY	4.91
Schumacher-NY	4.88
Wyatt-Bro	4.66
Hamlin-Bro	4.49
Higbe-Phi	4.36

Ratio
Derringer-Cin	9.95
Walters-Cin	9.97
Passeau-Chi	10.33
Turner-Cin	10.54
Tamulis-Bro	10.73

Earned Run Average
Walters-Cin	2.48
Passeau-Chi	2.50
Sewell-Pit	2.80
Turner-Cin	2.89
Olsen-Chi	2.97

Adjusted ERA
Walters-Cin	153
Passeau-Chi	150
Sewell-Pit	136
Turner-Cin	131
Hamlin-Bro	131

Opponents' Batting Avg.
Walters-Cin	.220
Higbe-Phi	.232
Thompson-Cin	.233
Passeau-Chi	.237
Casey-Bro	.237

Opponents' On Base Pct.
Derringer-Cin	.276
Passeau-Chi	.278
Walters-Cin	.283
Tamulis-Bro	.288
Hamlin-Bro	.292

Starter Runs
Walters-Cin	46.4
Passeau-Chi	42.0
Derringer-Cin	25.8
Sewell-Pit	22.1
Turner-Cin	20.0

Adjusted Starter Runs
Walters-Cin	44.3
Passeau-Chi	38.9
Derringer-Cin	23.8
Warneke-StL	21.8
Sewell-Pit	21.3

Clutch Pitching Index
Errickson-Bos	124
Olsen-Chi	119
Schumacher-NY	113
Turner-Cin	113
Hamlin-Bro	111

Relief Runs
Beggs-Cin	15.8
Russell-StL	8.1
Raffensberger-Chi	6.0
MacFayden-Pit	3.0
Joiner-NY	2.7

Adjusted Relief Runs
Beggs-Cin	15.3
Russell-StL	8.9
Raffensberger-Chi	4.8
Brown-NY	2.9
Joiner-NY	2.9

Relief Ranking
Beggs-Cin	30.0
Russell-StL	10.8
Raffensberger-Chi	6.2
Brown-NY	3.6
Pressnell-Bro	3.6

Total Pitcher Index
Walters-Cin	5.0
Passeau-Chi	4.8
Warneke-StL	2.7
Sewell-Pit	2.7
Schumacher-NY	2.3

Total Baseball Ranking
Vaughan-Pit	5.2
Walters-Cin	5.0
Passeau-Chi	4.8
Hack-Chi	4.0
Mize-StL	3.9

TEAM	G	W	L	PCT	GB	R	OR	AB	H	2B	3B	HR	BB	SO	AVG	OBP	SLG	PRO	PRO+	BR	/A	PF	CHI	RC	SB	CS	SBA	SBR
DET	155	90	64	.584		888	717	5418	1549	312	65	134	664	556	.286	.366	.442	.808	105	124	49	110	97	913	66	39	44	-14
CLE	155	89	65	.578	1	710	637	5361	1422	287	61	101	519	597	.265	.332	.398	.730	97	-42	-20	97	99	724	53	36	45	-15
NY	155	88	66	.571	2	817	671	5286	1371	243	66	155	648	606	.259	.344	.418	.762	107	25	55	96	103	789	59	35	44	-15
CHI	155	82	72	.532	8	735	672	5386	1499	238	63	73	496	569	.278	.340	.387	.727	92	-40	-49	101	101	713	52	60	58	-14
BOS	154	82	72	.532	8	872	825	5481	1566	301	80	145	590	597	.286	.356	.449	.805	109	109	77	104	97	889	55	49	46	-12
STL	156	67	87	.435	23	757	882	5416	1423	278	58	118	556	642	.263	.333	.401	.734	94	-34	-50	102	103	744	51	40	47	-15
WAS	154	64	90	.416	26	665	811	5365	1453	266	67	52	468	504	.271	.331	.374	.705	95	-84	-35	94	99	690	94	40	46	-15
PHI	154	54	100	.351	36	703	932	5304	1391	242	53	105	556	656	.262	.334	.387	.721	94	-52	-36	98	100	704	48	33	42	-14
TOT	619					6147		43017	11674	2167	513	883	4497	4727	.271	.342	.407	.750							478	332	59	-55

TEAM	CG	SH	SV	IP	H	H/G	HR	BB	SO	RAT	ERA	ERA+	OAV	OOB	PR	/A	PF	CPI	FA	E	DP	FW	PW	BW	SBW	DIF
DET	59	10	23	1375¹	1425	9.3	102	570	752	13.2	4.01	119	.265	.338	56	113	109	105	.968	194	116	-.7	10.7	4.6	-.7	-1.0
CLE	72	13	22	1375	1328	8.7	86	512	686	12.2	3.63	116	.254	.323	114	89	96	102	.975	149	164	1.7	8.4	-1.9	-.8	4.5
NY	76	10	14	1373	1389	9.1	119	511	559	12.6	3.89	104	.261	.328	75	22	92	104	.975	152	158	1.6	2.1	5.2	-.8	2.9
CHI	83	10	18	1386²	1335	8.7	111	480	574	11.9	3.74	118	.249	.312	99	105	101	96	.969	185	125	-.2	9.9	-4.6	-.9	.7
BOS	51	4	16	1379²	1568	10.2	124	625	613	14.5	4.89	92	.283	.359	-77	-59	103	101	.972	173	156	.4	-5.6	7.3	-.5	3.4
STL	64	4	9	1373¹	1592	10.4	113	646	439	14.8	5.12	89	.290	.367	-113	-82	105	100	.974	158	179	1.3	-7.7	-4.7	-.8	1.9
WAS	74	6	7	1350	1494	10.0	93	618	618	14.2	4.59	91	.281	.358	-31	-63	95	103	.968	194	166	-.7	-5.9	-3.3	-.8	-2.3
PHI	72	4	12	1345	1543	10.3	135	534	488	14.0	5.22	85	.282	.348	-124	-115	101	91	.960	238	131	-3.1	-10.9	-3.4	-.7	-5.0
TOT	551	61	121	10958		9.6				13.4	4.38		.271	.342					.970	1443	1195					

Runs
Williams-Bos 134
Greenberg-Det ... 129
McCosky-Det 123
Gordon-NY 112
Kuhel-Chi 111

Hits
Radcliff-StL 200
McCosky-Det..... 200
Cramer-Bos 200
Appling-Chi 197
Wright-Chi 196

Doubles
Greenberg-Det ... 50
York-Det 46
Boudreau-Cle 46
Williams-Bos 43
Moses-Phi 41

Triples
McCosky-Det..... 19
Keller-NY 15
Finney-Bos 15
Williams-Bos 14
Appling-Chi 13

Home Runs
Greenberg-Det ... 41
Foxx-Bos 36
York-Det 33
Johnson-Phi 31
DiMaggio-NY 31

Total Bases
Greenberg-Det ... 384
York-Det 343
Williams-Bos 333
DiMaggio-NY 318
Gordon-NY 315

Runs Batted In
Greenberg-Det ... 150
York-Det 134
DiMaggio-NY 133
Foxx-Bos 119
Williams-Bos 113

Runs Produced
Greenberg-Det ... 238
Williams-Bos 224
York-Det 206
DiMaggio-NY 195
Cronin-Bos 191

Bases On Balls
Keller-NY 106
Clift-StL 104
Gehringer-Det 101
Foxx-Bos 101
Williams-Bos 96

Batting Average
DiMaggio-NY 352
Appling-Chi 348
Williams-Bos 344
Radcliff-StL 342
Greenberg-Det 340

On Base Percentage
Williams-Bos 442
Greenberg-Det 433
Gehringer-Det 428
DiMaggio-NY 425
Appling-Chi 420

Slugging Average
Greenberg-Det 670
DiMaggio-NY 626
Williams-Bos 594
York-Det 583
Foxx-Bos 581

Production
Greenberg-Det ...1.103
DiMaggio-NY 1.051
Williams-Bos 1.036
York-Det 993
Foxx-Bos 993

Adjusted Production
DiMaggio-NY 176
Greenberg-Det ... 166
Williams-Bos 159
Foxx-Bos 148
Keller-NY 142

Batter Runs
Greenberg-Det ... 68.8
Williams-Bos 57.2
DiMaggio-NY 50.8
York-Det 47.3
Foxx-Bos 42.6

Adjusted Batter Runs
Greenberg-Det ... 60.7
Williams-Bos 53.8
DiMaggio-NY 53.7
Foxx-Bos 39.5
York-Det 39.1

Clutch Hitting Index
Tresh-Chi 142
Heffner-StL 127
Bloodworth-Was .. 125
DiMaggio-NY 124
Bell-Cle 123

Runs Created
Greenberg-Det ... 171
Williams-Bos 154
York-Det 147
DiMaggio-NY 135
Foxx-Bos 124

Total Average
Greenberg-Det ...1.215
Williams-Bos 1.122
DiMaggio-NY 1.098
York-Det 1.050
Foxx-Bos 1.026

Stolen Bases
Case-Was 35
Walker-Was 21
Gordon-NY 18
Lewis-Was 15
Kreevich-Chi 15

Stolen Base Average
Walker-Was 84.0
Case-Was 77.8
Gordon-NY 69.2

Stolen Base Runs
Case-Was 4.5
Walker-Was 3.9
Gehringer-Det 3.0
Bartell-Det 2.4
Rosar-NY 1.5

Fielding Runs
Heffner-StL 19.1
Doerr-Bos 18.3
Tebbetts-Det 17.8
Travis-Was 15.7
DiMaggio-Bos 15.1

Total Player Rating
Greenberg-Det 4.7
DiMaggio-NY 4.1
Williams-Bos 4.0
Travis-Was 3.7
Gordon-NY 3.6

Wins
Feller-Cle 27
Newsom-Det 21
Milnar-Cle 18
Hudson-Was 17

Win Percentage
Rowe-Det 842
Newsom-Det 808
Feller-Cle 711
Smith-Cle 682
Milnar-Cle 643

Games
Feller-Cle 43
Benton-Det 42
Wilson-Bos 41
Heusser-Phi....... 41
Dobson-Cle 40

Complete Games
Feller-Cle 31
Lee-Chi 24
Leonard-Was 23

Shutouts
Milnar-Cle 4
Lyons-Chi 4
Feller-Cle 4

Saves
Benton-Det 17
Brown-Chi 10
Murphy-NY 9

Innings Pitched
Feller-Cle 320.1
Leonard-Was ... 289.0
Rigney-Chi 280.2
Newsom-Det ... 264.0
Auker-StL....... 263.2

Fewest Hits/Game
Feller-Cle 6.88
Rigney-Chi 7.70
Smith-Chi 7.77
Bridges-Det 7.79
Newsom-Det 8.01

Fewest BB/Game
Lyons-Chi 1.79
Lee-Chi 2.21
Rowe-Det........ 2.29
Leonard-Was ... 2.43
Russo-NY 2.61

Strikeouts
Feller-Cle 261
Newsom-Det 164
Rigney-Chi 141
Bridges-Det 133
Chase-Was 129

Strikeouts/Game
Feller-Cle 7.33
Bridges-Det 6.06
Wilson-Bos 5.82
Newsom-Det 5.59
Smith-Chi 5.17

Ratio
Feller-Cle 10.34
Rigney-Chi 10.65
Lyons-Chi 10.87
Lee-Chi 11.09
Russo-NY 11.27

Earned Run Average
Feller-Cle 2.61
Newsom-Det 2.83
Rigney-Chi 3.11
Smith-Chi 3.21
Chase-Was 3.23

Adjusted ERA
Newsom-Det 168
Feller-Cle 161
Rigney-Chi 142
Bridges-Det 141
Smith-Chi 138

Opponents' Batting Avg.
Feller-Cle 210
Smith-Chi 228
Bridges-Det 229
Rigney-Chi 230
Newsom-Det 238

Opponents' On Base Pct.
Feller-Cle 285
Lyons-Chi 287
Rigney-Chi 292
Lee-Chi 300
Russo-NY 303

Starter Runs
Feller-Cle 63.0
Newsom-Det 45.6
Rigney-Chi 39.7
Chase-Was 33.4
Milnar-Cle 30.0

Adjusted Starter Runs
Feller-Cle 57.1
Newsom-Det 56.5
Rigney-Chi 40.9
Bridges-Det 30.5
Smith-Chi 27.9

Clutch Pitching Index
Chase-Was 134
Leonard-Was 122
Newsom-Det 119
Smith-Cle 117
Milnar-Cle 115

Relief Runs
Eisenstat-Cle 9.9
Trotter-StL 6.7
Brown-Chi 5.1
Murphy-NY 4.8

Adjusted Relief Runs
Trotter-StL 8.9
Eisenstat-Cle 8.6
Brown-Chi 5.4
Benton-Det 2.9
Murphy-NY 2.4

Relief Ranking
Trotter-StL 11.1
Brown-Chi 9.3
Benton-Det 6.7
Eisenstat-Cle 6.5
Murphy-NY 4.8

Total Pitcher Index
Newsom-Det 5.4
Feller-Cle 5.3
Rigney-Chi 4.0
Rowe-Det......... 3.0
Smith-Chi 2.8

Total Baseball Ranking
Newsom-Det 5.4
Feller-Cle 5.3
Greenberg-Det ... 4.7
DiMaggio-NY 4.1
Rigney-Chi 4.0

TEAM	G	W	L	PCT	GB	R	OR	AB	H	2B	3B	HR	BB	SO	AVG	OBP	SLG	PRO	PRO+	BR	/A	PF	CHI	RC	SB	CS	SBA	SBR
BRO	157	100	54	.649		800	581	5485	1494	286	69	101	600	535	.272	.347	.405	.752	113	128	98	104	98	792	36			
STL	155	97	56	.634	2.5	734	589	5457	1482	254	56	70	540	543	.272	.340	.377	.717	102	62	16	107	99	719	47			
CIN	154	88	66	.571	12	616	564	5218	1288	213	33	64	477	428	.247	.313	.337	.650	88	-71	-72	100	108	556	68			
PIT	156	81	73	.526	19	690	643	5297	1417	233	65	56	547	516	.268	.338	.368	.706	105	39	41	100	99	670	59			
NY	156	74	79	.484	25.5	667	706	5395	1401	248	35	95	504	518	.260	.326	.371	.697	100	15	1	102	98	659	36			
CHI	155	70	84	.455	30	666	670	5230	1323	239	25	99	559	670	.253	.327	.365	.692	104	9	32	96	101	642	39			
BOS	156	62	92	.403	38	592	720	5414	1357	231	38	48	471	608	.251	.312	.334	.646	91	-81	-53	96	103	568	61			
PHI	155	43	111	.279	57	501	793	5233	1277	188	38	64	451	596	.244	.307	.331	.638	89	-96	-71	96	92	528	65			
TOT	622					5266		42729	11039	1892	359	597	4149	4414	.258	.326	.361	.688						411				

TEAM	CG	SH	SV	IP	H	H/G	HR	BB	SO	RAT	ERA	ERA+	OAV	OOB	PR	/A	PF	CPI	FA	E	DP	FW	PW	BW	SBW	DIF
BRO	66	17	22	1421	1236	7.8	81	495	603	11.1	3.14	117	.232	.299	77	82	101	93	.974	162	125	.9	8.4	10.1		3.6
STL	64	15	20	1416¹	1289	8.2	85	502	659	11.5	3.19	118	.241	.309	69	90	104	101	.973	172	146	.2	9.2	1.4		9.4
CIN	89	19	10	1386²	1300	8.4	61	510	627	11.9	3.17	114	.250	.319	71	66	99	106	.975	152	147	1.3	6.8	-7.4		10.4
PIT	71	8	12	1374¹	1392	9.1	66	492	410	12.4	3.48	104	.259	.323	22	18	99	102	.968	196	130	-1.1	1.8	4.2		-.9
NY	55	12	18	1391²	1455	9.4	90	539	566	13.0	3.94	94	.269	.337	-48	-38	102	102	.974	160	144	.9	-3.9	.1		.4
CHI	74	8	9	1364²	1431	9.4	60	449	548	12.5	3.72	94	.267	.326	-13	-32	97	98	.970	180	139	-.3	-3.3	3.3		-6.7
BOS	62	10	9	1385²	1440	9.4	75	554	446	13.2	3.95	90	.268	.340	-48	-58	98	102	.969	191	174	-.9	-6.0	-5.4		-2.7
PHI	35	4	9	1372¹	1499	9.8	79	606	552	14.0	4.50	82	.278	.354	-132	-121	102	98	.969	187	147	-.7	-12.4	-7.3		-13.6
TOT	516	93	109	11112²		8.9				12.4	3.63		.258	.326					.972	1400	1152					

Runs
Reiser-Bro 117
Hack-Chi 111
Medwick-Bro 100
Rucker-NY 95
Fletcher-Pit 95

Hits
Hack-Chi 186
Reiser-Bro 184
Litwhiler-Phi...... 180
Rucker-NY 179
Medwick-Bro 171

Doubles
Reiser-Bro 39
Mize-StL 39
Rucker-NY 38
Dallessandro-Chi .. 36

Triples
Reiser-Bro 17
Fletcher-Pit 13
Hopp-StL 11
Medwick-Bro 10
Elliott-Pit.......... 10

Home Runs
Camilli-Bro 34
Ott-NY 27
Nicholson-Chi 26
Young-NY 25
Dahlgren-Bos-Chi .. 23

Total Bases
Reiser-Bro 299
Camilli-Bro 294
Medwick-Bro 278
Litwhiler-Phi 275
Young-NY 265

Runs Batted In
Camilli-Bro 120
Young-NY 104
Mize-StL 100
DiMaggio-Pit 100
Nicholson-Chi 98

Runs Produced
Reiser-Bro 179
Camilli-Bro 178
Medwick-Bro 170
Young-NY 169
Fletcher-Pit 158

Bases On Balls
Fletcher-Pit 118
Camilli-Bro 104
Ott-NY 100
Hack-Chi 99

Batting Average
Reiser-Bro 343
Medwick-Bro 318
Hack-Chi 317
Mize-StL 317
Etten-Phi 311

On Base Percentage
Fletcher-Pit 421
Hack-Chi 417
Camilli-Bro 407
Reiser-Bro 406
Mize-StL 406

Slugging Average
Reiser-Bro 558
Camilli-Bro 556
Mize-StL 535
Medwick-Bro 517
Slaughter-StL 496

Production
Reiser-Bro 964
Camilli-Bro 962
Mize-StL 941
Ott-NY 898
Slaughter-StL 886

Adjusted Production
Reiser-Bro 163
Camilli-Bro 162
Mize-StL 153
Ott-NY 149
Fletcher-Pit 148

Batter Runs
Camilli-Bro 50.2
Reiser-Bro 48.0
Mize-StL 40.2
Ott-NY 38.7
Fletcher-Pit 38.2

Adjusted Batter Runs
Camilli-Bro 47.1
Reiser-Bro 45.1
Fletcher-Pit 38.5
Ott-NY 37.3
Hack-Chi 36.7

Clutch Hitting Index
Lavagetto-Bro 173
VanRobays-Pit.... 154
Dallessandro-Chi . 150
Elliott-Pit......... 141
Bragan-Phi....... 134

Runs Created
Camilli-Bro 128
Reiser-Bro 124
Ott-NY 115
Hack-Chi 114
Fletcher-Pit 111

Total Average
Camilli-Bro 1.057
Reiser-Bro 1.006
Mize-StL 991
Ott-NY 976
Fletcher-Pit 965

Stolen Bases
Murtaugh-Phi 18
Benjamin-Phi 17
Handley-Pit 16
Frey-Cin 16
Hopp-StL 15

Stolen Base Average

Stolen Base Runs

Fielding Runs
May-Phi 25.2
Stringer-Chi 20.1
Litwhiler-Phi 15.2
Werber-Cin 12.5
Miller-Bos 12.2

Total Player Rating
Reiser-Bro 4.9
Litwhiler-Phi 3.2
Camilli-Bro 2.9
Ott-NY 2.8
Fletcher-Pit 2.7

Wins
Wyatt-Bro........ 22
Higbe-Bro 22
Walters-Cin 19
E.Riddle-Cin...... 19

Win Percentage
E.Riddle-Cin......826
Higbe-Bro 710
White-StL 708
Wyatt-Bro........688
Warneke-StL 654

Games
Higbe-Bro 48
Pearson-Phi 46
Casey-Bro 45
Hutchings-Cin-Bos .. 44
Johnson-Bos 43

Complete Games
Walters-Cin 27
Wyatt-Bro 23
Tobin-Bos......... 20
Passeau-Chi 20

Shutouts
Wyatt-Bro........ 7
VanderMeer-Cin .. 6
Walters-Cin 5
Davis-Bro.......... 5

Saves
Brown-NY 8
Crouch-Phi-StL 7
Casey-Bro 7
Pearson-Phi 6

Innings Pitched
Walters-Cin 302.0
Higbe-Bro 298.0
Wyatt-Bro...... 288.1
Sewell-Pit....... 249.0
Warneke-StL 246.0

Fewest Hits/Game
VanderMeer-Cin .. 6.84
Wyatt-Bro........ 6.96
White-StL 7.24
Higbe-Bro 7.37
E.Riddle-Cin......7.48

Fewest BB/Game
Passeau-Chi 2.03
Derringer-Cin..... 2.13
Lohrman-NY 2.26
Tobin-Bos......... 2.27
Lee-Chi........... 2.31

Strikeouts
VanderMeer-Cin .. 202
Wyatt-Bro....... 176
Walters-Cin 129
Higbe-Bro 121
M.Cooper-StL 118

Strikeouts/Game
VanderMeer-Cin .. 8.03
M.Cooper-StL .. 5.69
Wyatt-Bro....... 5.49
White-StL 5.01
Melton-NY 4.63

Ratio
Wyatt-Bro........ 9.58
E.Riddle-Cin..... 10.14
White-StL 10.50
Tobin-Bos....... 10.93
Sewell-Pit....... 11.28

Earned Run Average
E.Riddle-Cin...... 2.24
Wyatt-Bro...... 2.34
White-StL 2.40
VanderMeer-Cin .. 2.82
Walters-Cin 2.83

Adjusted ERA
E.Riddle-Cin...... 160
White-StL 157
Wyatt-Bro....... 157
VanderMeer-Cin .. 127
Walters-Cin 127

Opponents' Batting Avg.
Wyatt-Bro.........212
VanderMeer-Cin ..214
White-StL 217
Higbe-Bro 220
E.Riddle-Cin.......224

Opponents' On Base Pct.
Wyatt-Bro.........270
E.Riddle-Cin......282
White-StL 287
Sewell-Pit........299
Tobin-Bos.........300

Starter Runs
Wyatt-Bro....... 41.4
E.Riddle-Cin..... 33.5
White-StL 28.8
Walters-Cin 26.9
VanderMeer-Cin .. 20.4

Adjusted Starter Runs
Wyatt-Bro........ 42.4
E.Riddle-Cin..... 32.6
White-StL 31.8
Walters-Cin 25.7
VanderMeer-Cin .. 19.5

Clutch Pitching Index
V.Olsen-Chi 120
Heintzelman-Pit.. 117
Butcher-Pit... 112
Johnson-Bos 111
Walters-Cin 111

Relief Runs
Pressnell-Chi...... 4.3
Brown-NY 2.0
Pearson-Phi........9
Sullivan-Bos-Pit......0

Adjusted Relief Runs
Pressnell-Chi..... 3.3
Brown-NY 2.4
Pearson-Phi...... 1.9

Relief Ranking
Pressnell-Chi..... 3.5
Brown-NY 3.0
Pearson-Phi...... 2.5

Total Pitcher Index
Wyatt-Bro.......... 5.3
E.Riddle-Cin....... 3.8
Walters-Cin 3.2
White-StL 3.1
Gumbert-NY-StL ... 2.6

Total Baseball Ranking
Wyatt-Bro.......... 5.3
Reiser-Bro......... 4.9
E.Riddle-Cin....... 3.8
Walters-Cin 3.2
Litwhiler-Phi....... 3.2

TEAM	G	W	L	PCT	GB	R	OR	AB	H	2B	3B	HR	BB	SO	AVG	OBP	SLG	PRO	PRO+	BR	/A	PF	CHI	RC	SB	CS	SBA	SBR
NY	156	101	53	.656		830	631	5444	1464	243	60	151	616	565	.269	.346	.419	.765	110	64	74	99	103	822	51	33	44	-16
BOS	155	84	70	.545	17	865	750	5359	1517	304	55	124	683	567	.283	.366	.430	.796	115	136	118	102	98	872	67	51	54	-16
CHI	156	77	77	.500	24	638	649	5404	1376	245	47	47	510	476	.255	.322	.343	.665	84	-127	-117	99	106	612	91	53	50	-13
DET	155	75	79	.487	26	686	743	5370	1412	247	55	81	602	584	.263	.340	.375	.715	87	-26	-99	110	96	713	43	28	36	-12
CLE	155	75	79	.487	26	677	668	5283	1350	249	84	103	512	605	.256	.323	.393	.716	100	-39	-3	95	100	691	63	47	57	-19
WAS	156	70	84	.455	31	728	798	5521	1502	257	80	52	470	488	.272	.331	.376	.707	98	-52	-17	95	106	702	79	36	39	-12
STL	157	70	84	.455	31	765	823	5408	1440	281	58	91	775	552	.266	.360	.390	.750	102	56	30	103	93	804	50	39	50	-17
PHI	154	64	90	.416	37	713	840	5336	1431	240	69	85	574	588	.268	.340	.387	.727	101	-6	12	98	99	711	27	36	42	-13
TOT	622					5902		43125	11492	2066	508	734	4742	4425	.266	.341	.389	.730							471	323	59	-52

TEAM	CG	SH	SV	IP	H	H/G	HR	BB	SO	RAT	ERA	ERA+	OAV	OOB	PR	/A	PF	CPI	FA	E	DP	FW	PW	BW	SBW	DIF
NY	75	13	26	1396¹	1309	8.4	81	598	589	12.4	3.53	112	.247	.325	96	63	95	102	.973	165	196	.5	6.1	7.2	-.9	11.1
BOS	70	8	11	1372	1453	9.5	88	611	574	13.7	4.19	100	.269	.346	-5	-2	101	102	.972	172	139	.0	-.2	11.4	-.9	-3.4
CHI	106	14	4	1416	1362	8.7	89	521	564	12.1	3.52	116	.251	.320	98	90	99	102	.971	180	145	-.3	8.7	-11.3	-.6	3.6
DET	52	8	16	1381²	1399	9.1	80	645	697	13.4	4.18	109	.259	.340	-4	56	110	96	.969	186	129	-.7	5.4	-9.6	-.5	3.4
CLE	68	10	19	1377	1366	8.9	71	660	617	13.4	3.90	101	.259	.344	38	6	95	103	.976	142	158	1.7	.6	-.3	-1.2	-2.8
WAS	69	8	7	1389¹	1524	9.9	69	603	544	13.9	4.35	93	.279	.352	-31	-47	98	101	.969	187	169	-.7	-4.6	-1.6	-.5	.5
STL	65	7	10	1389	1563	10.1	120	549	454	13.8	4.72	91	.283	.350	-87	-64	104	99	.975	151	156	1.3	-6.2	2.9	-1.0	-4.0
PHI	64	3	18	1365¹	1516	10.0	136	557	386	13.8	4.83	87	.279	.348	-103	-97	101	97	.967	200	150	-1.6	-9.4	1.2	-.6	-2.6
TOT	569	71	111	11086²		9.3				13.3	4.15		.266	.341					.972	1383	1242					

Runs	Hits	Doubles	Triples	Home Runs	Total Bases
Williams-Bos 135	Travis-Was 218	Boudreau-Cle 45	Heath-Cle 20	Williams-Bos 37	DiMaggio-NY 348
DiMaggio-NY 122	Heath-Cle 199	DiMaggio-NY 43	Travis-Was 19	Keller-NY 33	Heath-Cle 343
DiMaggio-Bos 117	DiMaggio-NY 193	Judnich-StL 40	Keltner-Cle 13	Henrich-NY 31	Williams-Bos 335
Clift-StL 108	Appling-Chi 186	Travis-Was 39		DiMaggio-NY 30	Travis-Was 316
	Williams-Bos 185	Kuhel-Chi 39		York-Det 27	S.Chapman-Phi ... 300

Runs Batted In	Runs Produced	Bases On Balls	Batting Average	On Base Percentage	Slugging Average
DiMaggio-NY 125	Williams-Bos 218	Williams-Bos 145	Williams-Bos ..... .406	Williams-Bos ..... .551	Williams-Bos ..... .735
Heath-Cle 123	DiMaggio-NY 217	Cullenbine-StL ... 121	Travis-Was ...... .359	Cullenbine-StL ... .452	DiMaggio-NY ..... .643
Keller-NY 122	Travis-Was 200	Clift-StL 113	DiMaggio-NY ..... .357	DiMaggio-NY ..... .440	Heath-Cle .... .586
Williams-Bos 120	Keller-NY 191	Keller-NY 102	Heath-Cle .... .340	Keller-NY .... .416	Keller-NY .... .580
York-Det 111	Heath-Cle 188		Siebert-Phi ...... .334	Foxx-Bos .... .412	S.Chapman-Phi ... .543

Production	Adjusted Production	Batter Runs	Adjusted Batter Runs	Clutch Hitting Index	Runs Created
Williams-Bos 1.286	Williams-Bos 232	Williams-Bos 102.0	Williams-Bos 100.3	Berardino-StL 165	Williams-Bos 202
DiMaggio-NY 1.083	DiMaggio-NY 186	DiMaggio-NY 64.3	DiMaggio-NY 65.4	Cullenbine-StL ... 136	DiMaggio-NY 162
Keller-NY .... .996	Heath-Cle 165	Keller-NY 45.7	Heath-Cle 48.6	Tabor-Bos 135	Heath-Cle 138
Heath-Cle .... .982	Keller-NY 163	Heath-Cle 44.8	Keller-NY 46.7	Wright-Chi 135	Keller-NY 134
Travis-Was .... .930	Travis-Was 152	Cullenbine-StL ... 38.3	Travis-Was 41.8	Vernon-Was 133	Travis-Was 131

Total Average	Stolen Bases	Stolen Base Average	Stolen Base Runs	Fielding Runs	Total Player Rating
Williams-Bos 1.688	Case-Was 33	Kuhel-Chi 80.0	Case-Was 4.5	Bloodworth-Was .. 34.7	Williams-Bos 8.0
DiMaggio-NY 1.208	Kuhel-Chi 20	Case-Was 78.6	Kuhel-Chi 3.0	Rizzuto-NY 22.5	DiMaggio-NY 6.0
Keller-NY 1.099	Heath-Cle 18	Kreevich-Chi 77.3	Kreevich-Chi 2.1	Rizzuto-NY 15.6	Travis-Was 4.5
Cullenbine-StL ... 1.023	Tabor-Bos 17	Tabor-Bos 65.4	Fox-Bos 1.5	Case-Was 13.5	Keltner-Cle 3.9
Heath-Cle 1.000	Kreevich-Chi 17	Heath-Cle 60.0		Boudreau-Cle 13.1	Keller-NY 3.9

Wins	Win Percentage	Games	Complete Games	Shutouts	Saves
Feller-Cle 25	Gomez-NY .... .750	Feller-Cle 44	Lee-Chi 30	Feller-Cle 6	Murphy-NY 15
Lee-Chi 22	Ruffing-NY ...... .714	Newsom-Det 43	Feller-Cle 28	Leonard-Was 4	Ferrick-Phi 7
H.Newsome-Bos ... 19	Benton-Det ...... .714	Brown-Cle 41	Smith-Chi 21	Humphries-Chi 4	Benton-Det 7
Leonard-Was 18	Lee-Chi .... .667	Ryba-Bos 40	Lyons-Chi 19	Chandler-NY 4	Ryba-Bos 6
	Feller-Cle .... .658	Benton-Det 38	Leonard-Was 19		

Innings Pitched	Fewest Hits/Game	Fewest BB/Game	Strikeouts	Strikeouts/Game	Ratio
Feller-Cle 343.0	Benton-Det 7.42	Lyons-Chi 1.78	Feller-Cle 260	Feller-Cle 6.82	Lee-Chi 10.61
Lee-Chi 300.1	Feller-Cle 7.45	Leonard-Was 1.90	Newsom-Det 175	Newsom-Det 6.29	Ruffing-NY 11.25
Smith-Chi 263.1	Lee-Chi 7.73	Muncrief-StL 2.23	Lee-Chi 130	Newhouser-Det ... 5.51	Benton-Det 11.30
Leonard-Was 256.0	Donald-NY 7.98	Ruffing-NY 2.62	Rigney-Chi 119	Harris-Bos 5.15	Chandler-NY 11.33
Newsom-Det 250.1	Chandler-NY 8.03	Lee-Chi 2.76		Rigney-Chi 4.52	Lyons-Chi 11.53

Earned Run Average	Adjusted ERA	Opponents' Batting Avg.	Opponents' On Base Pct.	Starter Runs	Adjusted Starter Runs
Lee-Chi 2.37	Lee-Chi 173	Benton-Det ...... .221	Lee-Chi .... .293	Lee-Chi 59.4	Lee-Chi 57.7
Benton-Det 2.97	Benton-Det 153	Feller-Cle .... .226	Benton-Det ...... .302	Feller-Cle 38.1	Feller-Cle 30.2
Wagner-Bos 3.07	Wagner-Bos 136	Lee-Chi .... .232	Ruffing-NY ...... .306	Smith-Chi 28.4	Benton-Det 27.6
Russo-NY 3.09	Smith-Chi 129	Donald-NY ...... .237	Chandler-NY ..... .307	Russo-NY 24.6	Smith-Chi 26.9
Feller-Cle 3.15	Harris-Bos 128	Chandler-NY ..... .239	Lyons-Chi .... .308	Wagner-Bos 22.3	Wagner-Bos 22.8

Clutch Pitching Index	Relief Runs	Adjusted Relief Runs	Relief Ranking	Total Pitcher Index	Total Baseball Ranking
Lee-Chi 122	Murphy-NY 18.6	Murphy-NY 16.8	Murphy-NY 28.8	Lee-Chi 6.5	Williams-Bos 8.0
Wagner-Bos 120	Heving-Cle 14.6	Heving-Cle 12.9	Heving-Cle 13.6	Smith-Chi 3.1	Lee-Chi 6.5
Gomez-NY 115	Carrasquel-Was ... 7.5	Carrasquel-Was ... 6.4	Carrasquel-Was ... 5.1	Feller-Cle 2.9	DiMaggio-NY 6.0
Marchildon-Phi ... 115	Brown-Cle 7.3	Brown-Cle 5.5	Brown-Cle 4.9	Russo-NY 2.3	Travis-Was 4.5
Smith-Chi 112		Thomas-Det 2.7	Thomas-Det 1.5	Benton-Det 2.3	Keltner-Cle 3.9

TEAM	G	W	L	PCT	GB	R	OR	AB	H	2B	3B	HR	BB	SO	AVG	OBP	SLG	PRO	PRO+	BR	/A	PF	CHI	RC	SB	CS	SBA	SBR
STL	156	106	48	.688		755	482	5421	1454	282	69	60	551	507	.268	.338	.379	.717	108	109	62	108	103	718	71			
BRO	155	104	50	.675	2	742	510	5285	1398	263	34	62	572	484	.265	.338	.362	.700	110	80	70	102	107	671	79			
NY	154	85	67	.559	20	675	600	5210	1323	162	35	109	558	511	.254	.330	.361	.691	108	59	55	101	102	627	39			
CIN	154	76	76	.500	29	527	545	5260	1216	198	39	66	483	549	.231	.299	.321	.620	88	-80	-78	100	102	519	42			
PIT	151	66	81	.449	36.5	585	631	5104	1250	173	49	54	537	536	.245	.320	.330	.650	94	-14	-28	103	102	556	41			
CHI	155	68	86	.442	38	591	665	5352	1360	224	41	75	509	607	.254	.321	.353	.674	108	23	46	96	93	619	61			
BOS	150	59	89	.399	44	515	645	5077	1216	210	19	68	474	507	.240	.307	.329	.636	93	-47	-35	98	97	520	49			
PHI	151	42	109	.278	62.5	394	706	5060	1174	168	37	44	392	488	.232	.289	.306	.595	84	-124	-95	95	89	451	37			
TOT	613					4784		41769	10391	1680	323	538	4076	4189	.249	.318	.343	.661						419				

TEAM	CG	SH	SV	IP	H	H/G	HR	BB	SO	RAT	ERA	ERA+	OAV	OOB	PR	/A	PF	CPI	FA	E	DP	FW	PW	BW	SBW	DIF
STL	70	18	15	1410^1	1192	7.6	49	473	651	10.7	2.55	134	.227	.294	120	137	103	102	.972	169	137	-.1	14.7	6.7		7.8
BRO	67	16	24	1398^2	1205	7.8	73	493	612	11.1	2.84	115	.231	.301	72	64	98	101	.977	138	150	1.7	6.9	7.5		10.9
NY	70	12	13	1370	1299	8.5	94	493	497	11.9	3.31	101	.249	.316	0	7	101	104	.977	138	128	1.6	.8	5.9		.7
CIN	80	12	8	1411^2	1213	7.7	47	526	616	11.2	2.82	117	.230	.302	77	73	99	97	.971	177	158	-.7	7.8	-8.4		1.2
PIT	64	13	11	1351^1	1376	9.2	62	435	426	12.1	3.58	94	.262	.320	-40	-30	102	97	.969	184	128	-1.3	-3.2	-3.0		.0
CHI	71	10	14	1400^2	1447	9.3	70	525	507	12.8	3.60	89	.266	.333	-44	-62	97	105	.973	170	136	-.2	-6.7	4.9		-7.1
BOS	68	9	8	1334	1326	8.9	82	518	414	12.6	3.76	89	.259	.331	-65	-62	101	100	.976	142	138	1.1	-6.7	-3.8		-5.7
PHI	51	2	6	1341	1328	8.9	61	605	472	13.1	4.12	80	.260	.341	-120	-121	100	93	.968	194	147	-1.9	-13.0	-10.2		-8.4
TOT	541	92	99	11017^2		8.5				11.9	3.31		.249	.318					.973	1312	1122					

Runs
Ott-NY	118
Slaughter-StL	100
Mize-NY	97
Hack-Chi	91

Hits
Slaughter-StL	188
Nicholson-Chi	173
Medwick-Bro	166
Hack-Chi	166
Elliott-Pit	166

Doubles
Marion-StL	38
Medwick-Bro	37
Hack-Chi	36
Herman-Bro	34
Reiser-Bro	33

Triples
Slaughter-StL	17
Nicholson-Chi	11
Musial-StL	10
Litwhiler-Phi	9

Home Runs
Ott-NY	30
Mize-NY	26
Camilli-Bro	26
Nicholson-Chi	21
West-Bos	16

Total Bases
Slaughter-StL	292
Mize-NY	282
Nicholson-Chi	280
Ott-NY	273
Camilli-Bro	247

Runs Batted In
Mize-NY	110
Camilli-Bro	109
Slaughter-StL	98
Medwick-Bro	96
Ott-NY	93

Runs Produced
Slaughter-StL	185
Ott-NY	181
Mize-NY	181
Camilli-Bro	172
Medwick-Bro	161

Bases On Balls
Ott-NY	109
Fletcher-Pit	105
Camilli-Bro	97
Hack-Chi	94
Slaughter-StL	88

Batting Average
Slaughter-StL	.318
Musial-StL	.315
Reiser-Bro	.310
Mize-NY	.305
Novikoff-Chi	.300

On Base Percentage
Fletcher-Pit	.417
Ott-NY	.415
Slaughter-StL	.412
Hack-Chi	.402
Musial-StL	.397

Slugging Average
Mize-NY	.521
Ott-NY	.497
Slaughter-StL	.494
Musial-StL	.490
Nicholson-Chi	.476

Production
Ott-NY	.912
Slaughter-StL	.906
Mize-NY	.901
Musial-StL	.888
Nicholson-Chi	.859

Adjusted Production
Ott-NY	165
Mize-NY	161
Nicholson-Chi	156
Slaughter-StL	153
Musial-StL	148

Batter Runs
Slaughter-StL	49.8
Ott-NY	49.3
Mize-NY	40.8
Nicholson-Chi	37.6
Musial-StL	35.0

Adjusted Batter Runs
Ott-NY	49.0
Slaughter-StL	44.6
Mize-NY	40.4
Nicholson-Chi	40.2
Hack-Chi	32.4

Clutch Hitting Index
Medwick-Bro	154
F.McCormick-Cin	135
Elliott-Pit	134
Camilli-Bro	127
Herman-Bro	125

Runs Created
Slaughter-StL	128
Ott-NY	122
Nicholson-Chi	112
Mize-NY	110
Hack-Chi	100

Total Average
Ott-NY	.990
Slaughter-StL	.966
Musial-StL	.926
Mize-NY	.911
Camilli-Bro	.888

Stolen Bases
Reiser-Bro	20
Reese-Bro	15
Fernandez-Bos	15
Merullo-Chi	14
Hopp-StL	14

Stolen Base Average

Stolen Base Runs

Fielding Runs
Reese-Bro	17.4
May-Phi	17.2
DiMaggio-Pit	14.0
Fletcher-Pit	11.5
Nicholson-Chi	10.0

Total Player Rating
Nicholson-Chi	4.9
Slaughter-StL	4.6
Ott-NY	4.5
Musial-StL	3.3
Reese-Bro	3.1

Wins
M.Cooper-StL	22
Beazley-StL	21
Wyatt-Bro	19
Passeau-Chi	19
VanderMeer-Cin	18

Win Percentage
French-Bro	.789
Casey-Bro	.778
M.Cooper-StL	.759
Wyatt-Bro	.731
Davis-Bro	.714

Games
Adams-NY	61
Casey-Bro	50
Podgajny-Phi	43
Beazley-StL	43

Complete Games
Tobin-Bos	28
Passeau-Chi	24
M.Cooper-StL	22
Walters-Cin	21
VanderMeer-Cin	21

Shutouts
M.Cooper-StL	10
Sewell-Pit	5
Javery-Bos	5
Davis-Bro	5

Saves
Casey-Bro	13
Adams-NY	11
Beggs-Cin	8
Sain-Bos	6
Gumbert-StL	5

Innings Pitched
Tobin-Bos	287.2
M.Cooper-StL	278.2
Passeau-Chi	278.1
Starr-Cin	276.2
Javery-Bos	261.0

Fewest Hits/Game
M.Cooper-StL	6.69
VanderMeer-Cin	6.93
Higbe-Bro	7.31
Starr-Cin	7.42
Beazley-StL	7.57

Fewest BB/Game
Warneke-StL-Chi	1.79
Lohrman-StL-NY	1.85
Hubbell-NY	1.94
Derringer-Cin	2.11
M.Cooper-StL	2.20

Strikeouts
VanderMeer-Cin	186
M.Cooper-StL	152
Higbe-Bro	115
Walters-Cin	109
Melton-Phi	107

Strikeouts/Game
VanderMeer-Cin	6.86
Lanier-StL	5.20
M.Cooper-StL	4.91
Higbe-Bro	4.67
Melton-Phi	4.60

Ratio
M.Cooper-StL	9.04
Lohrman-StL-NY	10.07
Davis-Bro	10.35
Warneke-StL-Chi	10.39
Wyatt-Bro	10.56

Earned Run Average
M.Cooper-StL	1.78
Beazley-StL	2.13
Davis-Bro	2.36
VanderMeer-Cin	2.43
Lohrman-StL-NY	2.48

Adjusted ERA
M.Cooper-StL	193
Beazley-StL	161
Davis-Bro	138
Lohrman-StL-NY	136
VanderMeer-Cin	135

Opponents' Batting Avg.
M.Cooper-StL	.204
VanderMeer-Cin	.208
Higbe-Bro	.223
Wyatt-Bro	.225
Starr-Cin	.226

Opponents' On Base Pct.
M.Cooper-StL	.258
Lohrman-StL-NY	.281
Wyatt-Bro	.286
Warneke-StL-Chi	.286
Davis-Bro	.287

Starter Runs
M.Cooper-StL	47.6
Beazley-StL	28.3
French-Bro	24.4
VanderMeer-Cin	23.8
Davis-Bro	21.8

Adjusted Starter Runs
M.Cooper-StL	51.0
Beazley-StL	30.9
French-Bro	23.5
VanderMeer-Cin	23.0
Davis-Bro	20.6

Clutch Pitching Index
Bithorn-Chi	130
Passeau-Chi	121
Beazley-StL	114
Schumacher-NY	113
Carpenter-NY	112

Relief Runs
Adams-NY	14.4
Casey-Bro	13.2
Beggs-Cin	11.6
Shoun-StL-Cin	9.4
Webber-Bro	2.0

Adjusted Relief Runs
Adams-NY	14.8
Casey-Bro	12.6
Beggs-Cin	11.3
Shoun-StL-Cin	9.1
Webber-Bro	1.7

Relief Ranking
Adams-NY	20.9
Beggs-Cin	15.0
Casey-Bro	12.4
Shoun-StL-Cin	4.4
Webber-Bro	1.6

Total Pitcher Index
M.Cooper-StL	5.5
Beazley-StL	3.5
French-Bro	3.0
Walters-Cin	2.9
Davis-Bro	2.7

Total Baseball Ranking
M.Cooper-StL	5.5
Nicholson-Chi	4.9
Slaughter-StL	4.6
Ott-NY	4.5
Beazley-StL	3.5

TEAM	G	W	L	PCT	GB	R	OR	AB	H	2B	3B	HR	BB	SO	AVG	OBP	SLG	PRO	PRO+	BR	/A	PF	CHI	RC	SB	CS	SBA	SBR
NY	154	103	51	.669		801	507	5305	1429	223	57	108	591	556	.269	.346	.394	.740	118	104	117	98	104	759	69	33	44	-16
BOS	152	93	59	.612	9	761	594	5248	1451	244	55	103	591	508	.276	.352	.403	.755	116	132	109	103	96	774	68	61	58	-16
STL	151	82	69	.543	19.5	730	637	5229	1354	239	62	98	609	607	.259	.338	.385	.723	109	68	58	102	101	703	37	38	40	-12
CLE	156	75	79	.487	28	590	659	5317	1344	223	58	50	500	544	.253	.320	.345	.665	99	-42	-3	94	96	596	69	74	65	-16
DET	156	73	81	.474	30	589	587	5327	1313	217	37	76	509	476	.246	.314	.344	.658	85	-56	-109	108	98	582	39	40	38	-10
CHI	148	66	82	.446	34	538	609	4949	1215	214	36	25	497	427	.246	.316	.318	.634	87	-86	-71	98	102	520	114	70	65	-17
WAS	151	62	89	.411	39.5	653	817	5295	1364	224	49	40	581	536	.258	.333	.341	.674	97	-13	-6	99	101	641	98	29	31	-9
PHI	154	55	99	.357	48	549	801	5285	1315	213	46	33	440	490	.249	.309	.325	.634	85	-100	-96	99	101	536	44	45	59	-21
TOT	611					5211		41955	10785	1797	400	533	4318	4144	.257	.329	.357	.686							538	390	58	-72

TEAM	CG	SH	SV	IP	H	H/G	HR	BB	SO	RAT	ERA	ERA+	OAV	OOB	PR	/A	PF	CPI	FA	E	DP	FW	PW	BW	SBW	DIF
NY	88	18	17	1375	1259	8.2	71	431	558	11.2	2.91	118	.244	.304	114	81	94	108	.976	142	190	2.0	8.3	12.0	-.7	4.4
BOS	84	11	17	1358²	1260	8.3	65	553	500	12.1	3.44	108	.246	.322	32	43	102	99	.974	157	156	1.0	4.4	11.2	-.7	1.1
STL	68	12	13	1363	1387	9.2	63	505	488	12.7	3.59	103	.262	.329	9	17	101	103	.972	167	143	.4	1.7	5.9	-.3	-1.3
CLE	61	12	11	1402²	1353	8.7	61	560	448	12.4	3.59	96	.253	.326	9	-22	94	99	.974	163	175	1.0	-2.3	-.3	-.7	.3
DET	65	12	14	1399¹	1321	8.5	60	598	671	12.5	3.13	126	.247	.326	81	127	108	111	.969	194	142	-.8	13.0	-11.2	-.0	-5.0
CHI	86	8	8	1314¹	1304	8.9	74	473	432	12.3	3.58	100	.257	.324	11	2	98	102	.970	173	144	-.1	.2	-7.3	-.8	-.0
WAS	68	12	11	1346²	1496	10.0	50	558	496	13.8	4.58	80	.279	.348	-138	-139	100	91	.962	222	133	-2.7	-14.2	-.6	.0	4.0
PHI	67	5	9	1374²	1404	9.2	89	639	546	13.5	4.45	85	.263	.344	-120	-101	103	93	.969	188	124	-.6	-10.3	-9.8	-1.2	-.0
TOT	587	90	100	10934¹		8.9				12.6	3.66		.257	.329					.971	1406	1207					

Runs		Hits		Doubles		Triples		Home Runs		Total Bases	
Williams-Bos	141	Pesky-Bos	205	Kolloway-Chi	40	Spence-Was	15	Williams-Bos	36	Williams-Bos	338
DiMaggio-NY	123	Spence-Was	203	Clift-StL	39	Heath-Cle	13	Laabs-StL	27	DiMaggio-NY	304
DiMaggio-Bos	110	Williams-Bos	186	Heath-Cle	37	DiMaggio-NY	13	Keller-NY	26	Keller-NY	279
Clift-StL	108	DiMaggio-NY	186	DiMaggio-Bos	36	McQuillen-StL	12	York-Det	21	Spence-Was	272
Keller-NY	106	Keltner-Cle	179					DiMaggio-NY	21	DiMaggio-Bos	272

Runs Batted In		Runs Produced		Bases On Balls		Batting Average		On Base Percentage		Slugging Average	
Williams-Bos	137	Williams-Bos	242	Williams-Bos	145	Williams-Bos	.356	Williams-Bos	.499	Williams-Bos	.648
DiMaggio-NY	114	DiMaggio-NY	216	Keller-NY	114	Pesky-Bos	.331	Keller-NY	.417	Keller-NY	.513
Keller-NY	108	Keller-NY	188	Fleming-Cle	106	Spence-Was	.323	Judnich-StL	.413	Judnich-StL	.499
Gordon-NY	103	Gordon-NY	173	Clift-StL	106	Gordon-NY	.322	Fleming-Cle	.412	DiMaggio-NY	.498
Doerr-Bos	102	Spence-Was	169	Cullenbine-StL-Was	92	Case-Was	.320	Gordon-NY	.409	Laabs-StL	.498

Production		Adjusted Production		Batter Runs		Adjusted Batter Runs		Clutch Hitting Index		Runs Created	
Williams-Bos	1.147	Williams-Bos	214	Williams-Bos	92.6	Williams-Bos	90.1	Lupien-Bos	135	Williams-Bos	185
Keller-NY	.930	Keller-NY	164	Keller-NY	46.9	Keller-NY	48.4	Siebert-Phi	132	Keller-NY	131
Judnich-StL	.912	Gordon-NY	156	Gordon-NY	38.6	Gordon-NY	40.0	Kuhel-Chi	130	DiMaggio-NY	120
Gordon-NY	.900	Judnich-StL	153	Judnich-StL	35.4	Fleming-Cle	36.3	Doerr-Bos	130	Spence-Was	111
Laabs-StL	.878	DiMaggio-NY	148	DiMaggio-NY	34.5	DiMaggio-NY	36.0	Cullenbine-StL-Was	126	Gordon-NY	108

Total Average		Stolen Bases		Stolen Base Average		Stolen Base Runs		Fielding Runs		Total Player Rating	
Williams-Bos	1.394	Case-Was	44	Case-Was	88.0	Case-Was	9.6	Rizzuto-NY	25.0	Williams-Bos	8.3
Keller-NY	1.038	Vernon-Was	25	Vernon-Was	80.6	Vernon-Was	3.9	Pesky-Bos	17.7	Gordon-NY	4.9
Judnich-StL	.950	Rizzuto-NY	22	Rizzuto-NY	78.6	Rizzuto-NY	3.0	Keltner-Cle	15.6	Keller-NY	4.2
Gordon-NY	.891	Kuhel-Chi	22	Appling-Chi	77.3	Keller-NY	3.0	York-Det	15.4	Pesky-Bos	4.0
Laabs-StL	.878			Kuhel-Chi	71.0	Appling-Chi	2.1	DiMaggio-Bos	14.4	Rizzuto-NY	3.8

Wins		Win Percentage		Games		Complete Games		Shutouts		Saves	
Hughson-Bos	22	Bonham-NY	.808	Haynes-Chi	40	Hughson-Bos	22	Bonham-NY	6	Murphy-NY	11
Bonham-NY	21	Borowy-NY	.789	Caster-StL	39	Bonham-NY	22			Haynes-Chi	6
Marchildon-Phi	17	Hughson-Bos	.786			Lyons-Chi	20			Brown-Bos	6
Bagby-Cle	17	Chandler-NY	.762			Hudson-Was	19			Newhouser-Det	5
Chandler-NY	16	Bagby-Cle	.654							Caster-StL	5

Innings Pitched		Fewest Hits/Game		Fewest BB/Game		Strikeouts		Strikeouts/Game		Ratio	
Hughson-Bos	281.0	Newhouser-Det	6.71	Bonham-NY	.96	Newsom-Was	113	Newhouser-Det	5.05	Bonham-NY	8.92
Bagby-Cle	270.2	Niggeling-StL	7.55	Lyons-Chi	1.30	Hughson-Bos	113	Bridges-Det	5.02	Lyons-Chi	9.73
Auker-StL	249.0	Dobson-Bos	7.64	Ruffing-NY	1.91	Marchildon-Phi	110	Trucks-Det	4.88	Ruffing-NY	10.55
Marchildon-Phi	244.0	Trucks-Det	7.89	Breuer-NY	2.03	Benton-Det	110	Newsom-Was	4.76	Breuer-NY	10.68
Hudson-Was	239.1	Chandler-NY	7.89	Bagby-Cle	2.13	Niggeling-StL	107	Niggeling-StL	4.67	Hughson-Bos	10.70

Earned Run Average		Adjusted ERA		Opponents' Batting Avg.		Opponents' On Base Pct.		Starter Runs		Adjusted Starter Runs	
Lyons-Chi	2.10	Lyons-Chi	172	Newhouser-Det	.207	Bonham-NY	.259	Bonham-NY	34.8	Hughson-Bos	35.5
Bonham-NY	2.27	Newhouser-Det	161	Niggeling-StL	.226	Lyons-Chi	.275	Hughson-Bos	33.2	Newhouser-Det	30.6
Chandler-NY	2.38	Bonham-NY	152	Dobson-Bos	.231	Ruffing-NY	.292	Lyons-Chi	31.3	Lyons-Chi	30.1
Newhouser-Det	2.45	Chandler-NY	145	Trucks-Det	.231	Breuer-NY	.295	Chandler-NY	28.5	Bonham-NY	29.4
Borowy-NY	2.52	Trucks-Det	144	Borowy-NY	.233	Hughson-Bos	.296	Humphries-Chi	24.8	Benton-Det	26.5

Clutch Pitching Index		Relief Runs		Adjusted Relief Runs		Relief Ranking		Total Pitcher Index		Total Baseball Ranking	
Chandler-NY	136	Ferrick-Cle	15.0	Ferrick-Cle	13.2	Haynes-Chi	14.2	Hughson-Bos	4.1	Williams-Bos	8.3
Lyons-Chi	131	Haynes-Chi	11.9	Haynes-Chi	11.2	Caster-StL	10.0	Lyons-Chi	4.0	Gordon-NY	4.9
Hollingsworth-StL	123	Caster-StL	7.5	Caster-StL	7.9	Ferrick-Cle	8.4	Newhouser-Det	3.5	Keller-NY	4.2
Humphries-Chi	121	Murphy-NY	1.6	Brown-Bos	2.0	Brown-Bos	4.0	Chandler-NY	3.3	Hughson-Bos	4.1
Niggeling-StL	119	Brown-Bos	1.5	Murphy-NY	.2	Murphy-NY	.5	Humphries-Chi	2.8	Pesky-Bos	4.0

TEAM	G	W	L	PCT	GB	R	OR	AB	H	2B	3B	HR	BB	SO	AVG	OBP	SLG	PRO	PRO+	BR	/A	PF	CHI	RC	SB	CS	SBA	SBR
STL	157	105	49	.682		679	475	5438	1515	259	72	70	428	438	.279	.333	.391	.724	110	92	64	104	95	720	40			
CIN	155	87	67	.565	18	608	543	5329	1362	229	47	43	445	476	.256	.315	.340	.655	96	-34	-25	99	106	581	49			
BRO	153	81	72	.529	23.5	716	674	5309	1444	263	35	39	580	422	.272	.346	.357	.703	109	70	68	100	104	675	58			
PIT	157	80	74	.519	25	669	605	5353	1401	240	73	42	573	566	.262	.335	.357	.692	102	45	23	103	100	657	64			
CHI	154	74	79	.484	30.5	632	600	5279	1380	207	56	52	574	522	.261	.336	.351	.687	106	38	47	99	97	641	53			
BOS	153	68	85	.444	36.5	465	612	5196	1213	202	36	39	469	609	.233	.299	.309	.608	82	-120	-111	99	98	491	56			
PHI	157	64	90	.416	41	571	676	5297	1321	186	36	66	499	556	.249	.316	.335	.651	97	-37	-12	96	100	565	29			
NY	156	55	98	.359	49.5	558	713	5290	1309	153	33	81	480	470	.247	.313	.335	.648	92	-47	-51	101	100	552	35			
TOT	621					4898		42491	10945	1739	388	432	4048	4059	.258	.324	.347	.672							384			

TEAM	CG	SH	SV	IP	H	H/G	HR	BB	SO	RAT	ERA	ERA+	OAV	OOB	PR	/A	PF	CPI	FA	E	DP	FW	PW	BW	SBW	DIF
STL	94	21	15	1427	1241	7.8	33	477	639	10.9	2.57	131	.236	.301	129	125	99	104	.976	151	183	.9	13.4	6.8		6.9
CIN	78	18	17	1404	1298	8.3	38	579	498	12.1	3.13	106	.250	.327	38	27	98	105	.980	125	193	2.2	2.9	-2.7		7.6
BRO	50	13	22	1369²	1230	8.1	59	637	588	12.5	3.88	86	.235	.322	-76	-79	99	81	.972	168	137	-.3	-8.4	7.3		6.0
PIT	74	11	12	1404	1424	9.1	44	422	396	11.9	3.08	113	.263	.318	46	59	103	107	.973	170	159	-.2	6.3	2.5		-5.5
CHI	67	13	14	1386	1378	8.9	53	394	513	11.6	3.31	101	.257	.310	11	3	99	95	.973	168	138	-.3	.3	5.0		-7.6
BOS	87	13	4	1397²	1361	8.8	66	441	409	11.8	3.25	105	.254	.314	20	24	101	100	.972	176	139	-.8	2.6	-11.9		1.6
PHI	66	10	14	1392²	1430	9.2	59	451	431	12.3	3.79	89	.265	.324	-62	-63	100	93	.969	189	143	-1.3	-6.7	-1.3		-3.7
NY	35	6	19	1394²	1473	9.5	80	626	588	13.7	4.08	84	.271	.349	-107	-98	102	101	.973	166	140	-.0	-10.5	-5.4		-5.5
TOT	551	105	117	11175²		8.7				12.1	3.38		.258	.324					.974	1313	1232					

Runs
Vaughan-Bro 112
Musial-StL 108
Nicholson-Chi 95
Cavarretta-Chi 93
Stanky-Chi 92

Hits
Musial-StL 220
Witek-NY 195
Herman-Bro 193
Nicholson-Chi 188
Vaughan-Bro 186

Doubles
Musial-StL 48
Herman-Bro 41
DiMaggio-Pit 41
Vaughan-Bro 39
Holmes-Bos 33

Triples
Musial-StL 20
Klein-StL 14
Lowrey-Chi 12
Elliott-Pit.......... 12

Home Runs
Nicholson-Chi 29
Ott-NY 18
Northey-Phi 16
Triplett-StL-Phi..... 15
DiMaggio-Pit 15

Total Bases
Musial-StL 347
Nicholson-Chi 323
Elliott-Pit........ 258
Klein-StL 257

Runs Batted In
Nicholson-Chi 128
Elliott-Pit......... 101
Herman-Bro 100
DiMaggio-Pit 88

Runs Produced
Nicholson-Chi 194
Musial-StL 176
Elliott-Pit....... 176
Herman-Bro 174
Vaughan-Bro 173

Bases On Balls
Galan-Bro 103
Ott-NY 95
Fletcher-Pit....... 95
Stanky-Chi 92
Tipton-Cin 85

Batting Average
Musial-StL .... .357
Herman-Bro ...... .330
Elliott-Pit....... .315
Witek-NY .... .314
Nicholson-Chi ...... .309

On Base Percentage
Musial-StL .... .425
Galan-Bro .... .412
Herman-Bro ...... .398
Fletcher-Pit....... .395
Tipton-Cin .... .395

Slugging Average
Musial-StL .... .562
Nicholson-Chi ..... .531
Elliott-Pit........ .444
Kurowski-StL..... .439
Northey-Phi ...... .430

Production
Musial-StL .... .988
Nicholson-Chi 917
Elliott-Pit........ .820
Tipton-Cin .... .819
Galan-Bro .... .818

Adjusted Production
Musial-StL 176
Nicholson-Chi 166
Tipton-Cin 138
Galan-Bro 136
Herman-Bro 135

Batter Runs
Musial-StL 65.5
Nicholson-Chi 47.7
Galan-Bro 28.5
Herman-Bro 28.0
Elliott-Pit....... 26.5

Adjusted Batter Runs
Musial-StL 62.3
Nicholson-Chi 48.8
Galan-Bro 28.3
Herman-Bro 27.9
Tipton-Cin 26.7

Clutch Hitting Index
Herman-Bro 153
Miller-Cin 149
Elliott-Pit......... 133
Wasdell-Pit-Phi ... 130
Stanky-Chi 127

Runs Created
Musial-StL 147
Nicholson-Chi 129
Herman-Bro 97
Vaughan-Bro 96
Elliott-Pit....... 96

Total Average
Musial-StL 1.039
Nicholson-Chi .... .944
Ott-NY .... .895
Galan-Bro .... .876
Tipton-Cin .... .825

Stolen Bases
Vaughan-Bro 20
Lowrey-Chi 13
Workman-Bos 12
Russell-Pit 12
Gustine-Pit 12

Stolen Base Average

Stolen Base Runs

Fielding Runs
Miller-Cin 26.6
Marion-StL 25.3
Wietelmann-Bos .. 20.0
Mueller-Cin 19.6
Witek-NY 15.5

Total Player Rating
Musial-StL 7.1
Nicholson-Chi 4.9
Galan-Bro 3.5
Marion-StL....... 3.4
Mueller-Cin 3.4

Wins
Sewell-Pit......... 21
Riddle-Cin 21
M.Cooper-StL 21
Bithorn-Chi 18
Javery-Bos 17

Win Percentage
M.Cooper-StL 724
Sewell-Pit........ .700
Lanier-StL .... .682
Riddle-Cin .... .656
Bithorn-Chi ...... .600

Games
Adams-NY 70
Webber-Bro 54
Head-Bro 47
Shoun-Cin 45
Mungo-NY 45

Complete Games
Sewell-Pit......... 25
Tobin-Bos 24
M.Cooper-StL 24
Andrews-Bos...... 23

Shutouts
Bithorn-Chi 7
M.Cooper-StL 6

Saves
Webber-Bro 10
Adams-NY 9
Shoun-Cin 7
Head-Bro 6
Beggs-Cin 6

Innings Pitched
Javery-Bos 303.0
VanderMeer-Cin . 289.0
Andrews-Bos... 283.2
M.Cooper-StL... 274.0
Sewell-Pit....... 265.1

Fewest Hits/Game
Wyatt-Bro........ 6.92
VanderMeer-Cin . 7.10
M.Cooper-StL.... 7.49
Krist-StL......... 7.72
Barrett-Chi-Phi ... 7.94

Fewest BB/Game
Rowe-Phi 1.31
Wyse-Chi 1.96
Derringer-Chi 2.02
Davis-Bro 2.14
Wyatt-Bro........ 2.14

Strikeouts
VanderMeer-Cin .. 174
M.Cooper-StL 141
Javery-Bos 134
Lanier-StL 123
Higbe-Bro 108

Strikeouts/Game
VanderMeer-Cin ..5.42
Higbe-Bro 5.25
Lanier-StL 5.19
M.Cooper-StL 4.63
Head-Bro 4.40

Ratio
Wyatt-Bro........ 9.07
Rowe-Phi 10.22
M.Cooper-StL 10.25
Bithorn-Chi 10.56
Andrews-Bos..... 10.60

Earned Run Average
Lanier-StL 1.90
M.Cooper-StL ... 2.30
Wyatt-Bro........ 2.49
Sewell-Pit........ 2.54
Andrews-Bos..... 2.57

Adjusted ERA
Lanier-StL 177
M.Cooper-StL 146
Sewell-Pit........ 137
Wyatt-Bro........ 135
Butcher-Pit....... 134

Opponents' Batting Avg.
Wyatt-Bro........ .207
VanderMeer-Cin . .224
M.Cooper-StL .... .226
Krist-StL......... .233
Barrett-Chi-Phi ...237

Opponents' On Base Pct.
Wyatt-Bro........ .255
Rowe-Phi .... .276
M.Cooper-StL .... .286
Andrews-Bos..... .291
Bithorn-Chi ...... .293

Starter Runs
Lanier-StL 35.2
M.Cooper-StL 33.0
Andrews-Bos..... 25.6
Sewell-Pit........ 24.7
Riddle-Cin 21.9

Adjusted Starter Runs
Lanier-StL 34.7
M.Cooper-StL 32.4
Sewell-Pit........ 27.5
Andrews-Bos..... 26.6
Pollet-StL 21.2

Clutch Pitching Index
Lanier-StL 151
Butcher-Pit....... 122
Sewell-Pit........ 121
Riddle-Cin 118
Tobin-Bos 113

Relief Runs
Beggs-Cin 13.4
Adams-NY 8.8
Prim-Chi 5.6
Brandt-Pit......... 1.6

Adjusted Relief Runs
Beggs-Cin 12.5
Adams-NY 9.7
Prim-Chi 5.2
Brandt-Pit........ 2.2

Relief Ranking
Beggs-Cin 14.1
Adams-NY 12.6
Prim-Chi 5.7
Brandt-Pit......... 1.7

Total Pitcher Index
Sewell-Pit......... 4.0
Lanier-StL 3.7
Tobin-Bos 3.6
M.Cooper-StL 3.3
Andrews-Bos..... 3.2

Total Baseball Ranking
Musial-StL 7.1
Nicholson-Chi 4.9
Sewell-Pit........ 4.0
Lanier-StL 3.7
Tobin-Bos 3.6

TEAM	G	W	L	PCT	GB	R	OR	AB	H	2B	3B	HR	BB	SO	AVG	OBP	SLG	PRO	PRO+	BR	/A	PF	CHI	RC	SB	CS	SBA	SBR
NY	155	98	56	.636		669	542	5282	1350	218	59	100	624	562	.256	.337	.376	.713	114	97	92	101	95	683	46	60	50	-11
WAS	153	84	69	.549	13.5	666	595	5233	1328	245	50	47	605	579	.254	.336	.347	.683	110	45	67	96	103	656	142	55	52	-14
CLE	153	82	71	.536	15.5	600	577	5265	1344	246	45	55	567	521	.255	.329	.350	.679	111	33	69	94	94	626	47	58	53	-13
CHI	155	82	72	.532	16	573	594	5252	1297	193	46	33	561	581	.247	.322	.320	.642	94	-31	-30	100	101	570	173	87	62	-10
DET	155	78	76	.506	20	632	560	5364	1401	200	47	77	483	553	.261	.324	.359	.683	98	32	-14	108	99	620	40	43	41	-11
STL	153	72	80	.474	25	596	604	5175	1269	229	36	78	569	646	.245	.322	.349	.671	99	14	1	102	98	603	37	43	51	-17
BOS	155	68	84	.447	29	563	607	5392	1314	223	42	57	486	591	.244	.308	.332	.640	91	-47	-56	102	101	570	86	61	54	-13
PHI	155	49	105	.318	49	497	717	5244	1219	174	44	26	430	465	.232	.294	.297	.591	78	-136	-133	100	111	466	55	42	44	-13
TOT	617					4796		42207	10522	1728	369	473	4325	4498	.249	.322	.341	.663							626	449	58	-81

TEAM	CG	SH	SV	IP	H	H/G	HR	BB	SO	RAT	ERA	ERA+	OAV	OOB	PR	/A	PF	CPI	FA	E	DP	FW	PW	BW	SBW	DIF
NY	83	14	13	1415[1]	1229	7.8	60	489	653	11.0	2.93	110	.233	.300	58	45	98	95	.974	160	166	.2	4.9	10.0	-.0	6.0
WAS	61	16	21	1388	1293	8.4	48	540	495	12.0	3.18	101	.246	.318	17	3	97	99	.971	179	145	-1.0	.3	7.2	-.4	1.3
CLE	64	14	20	1406[1]	1234	7.9	52	606	585	11.9	3.15	99	.239	.321	22	-6	94	100	.975	157	183	.3	-.6	7.5	-.3	-1.3
CHI	70	12	19	1400[1]	1352	8.7	54	501	476	12.1	3.20	104	.254	.323	14	21	101	105	.973	166	167	-.0	2.3	-3.2	.0	6.0
DET	67	18	20	1411[2]	1226	7.8	51	549	706	11.4	3.00	117	.233	.308	45	81	107	95	.971	177	130	-.7	8.8	-1.5	-.0	-5.4
STL	64	10	14	1385	1397	9.1	74	488	572	12.4	3.41	97	.262	.327	-17	-13	101	106	.975	152	127	.6	-1.4	.1	-.7	-2.5
BOS	62	13	16	1426[1]	1369	8.6	61	615	513	12.6	3.45	96	.256	.335	-24	-22	101	105	.976	153	179	.6	-2.4	-6.1	-.3	.0
PHI	73	5	13	1394	1421	9.2	73	536	503	12.9	4.05	84	.265	.336	-116	-101	103	94	.973	162	148	.1	-10.9	-14.4	-.3	-2.5
TOT	544	102	136	11227		8.4				12.0	3.30		.249	.322					.973	1306	1245					

Runs
Case-Was 102
Keller-NY 97
Wakefield-Det 91
York-Det 90
Vernon-Was 89

Hits
Wakefield-Det 200
Appling-Chi 192
Cramer-Det 182
Case-Was 180

Doubles
Wakefield-Det 38
Case-Was 36
Gutteridge-StL 35
Etten-NY 35

Triples
Moses-Chi 12
Lindell-NY 12
York-Det 11
Keller-NY 11
Spence-Was 10

Home Runs
York-Det 34
Keller-NY 31
Stephens-StL 22
Heath-Cle 18

Total Bases
York-Det 301
Wakefield-Det 275
Keller-NY 269
Doerr-Bos 249
Stephens-StL 247

Runs Batted In
York-Det 118
Etten-NY 107
Johnson-NY 94
Stephens-StL 91
Spence-Was 88

Runs Produced
York-Det 174
Etten-NY 171
Wakefield-Det 163
Johnson-NY 159
Case-Was 153

Bases On Balls
Keller-NY 106
Gordon-NY 98
Cullenbine-Cle 96
Boudreau-Cle 90
Appling-Chi 90

Batting Average
Appling-Chi 328
Wakefield-Det 316
Cramer-Det 300
Case-Was 294
Curtright-Chi 291

On Base Percentage
Appling-Chi 419
Cullenbine-Cle 407
Keller-NY 396
Boudreau-Cle 388
Curtright-Chi 382

Slugging Average
York-Det 527
Keller-NY 525
Stephens-StL 482
Heath-Cle 481
Wakefield-Det 434

Production
Keller-NY 922
York-Det 893
Heath-Cle 850
Stephens-StL 839
Appling-Chi 825

Adjusted Production
Keller-NY 167
Heath-Cle 157
York-Det 148
Cullenbine-Cle 146
Appling-Chi 142

Batter Runs
Keller-NY 45.8
York-Det 41.0
Appling-Chi 35.0
Wakefield-Det 28.8
Cullenbine-Cle 27.4

Adjusted Batter Runs
Keller-NY 45.3
York-Det 35.9
Appling-Chi 35.1
Cullenbine-Cle 31.1
Heath-Cle 28.1

Clutch Hitting Index
Sullivan-Was 175
Johnson-NY 157
Siebert-Phi 150
Etten-NY 144
Higgins-Det 143

Runs Created
Keller-NY 116
Appling-Chi 109
York-Det 108
Wakefield-Det 101
Spence-Was 93

Total Average
Keller-NY 979
York-Det 871
Appling-Chi 841
Heath-Cle 828
Cullenbine-Cle 816

Stolen Bases
Case-Was 61
Moses-Chi 56
Tucker-Chi 29
Appling-Chi 27
Vernon-Was 24

Stolen Base Average
Case-Was 81.3
Moses-Chi 80.0
Appling-Chi 77.1
Vernon-Was 75.0
Fox-Bos 73.3

Stolen Base Runs
Case-Was 9.9
Moses-Chi 8.4
Culberson-Bos 4.2
Appling-Chi 3.3
Vernon-Was 2.4

Fielding Runs
Boudreau-Cle 28.3
Gordon-NY 25.7
Clift-StL-Was 18.3
York-Det 17.6
Bloodworth-Det . . . 17.2

Total Player Rating
Boudreau-Cle 5.5
Gordon-NY 5.2
York-Det 5.1
Appling-Chi 5.0
Keller-NY 4.7

Wins
Trout-Det 20
Chandler-NY 20
Wynn-Was 18
Smith-Cle 17
Bagby-Cle 17

Win Percentage
Chandler-NY 833
Smith-Cle 708
Bonham-NY 652
Trout-Det 625
Grove-Chi 625

Games
Brown-Bos 49
Trout-Det 44
Wolff-Phi 41
Ryba-Bos 40
Carrasquel-Was . . . 39

Complete Games
Hughson-Bos 20
Chandler-NY 20
Wensloff-NY 18
Trout-Det 18
Grove-Chi 18

Shutouts
Trout-Det 5
Chandler-NY 5
Hughson-Bos 4
Bonham-NY 4

Saves
Maltzberger-Chi . . . 14
Heving-Cle 9
Brown-Bos 9
Murphy-NY 8
Caster-StL 8

Innings Pitched
Bagby-Cle 273.0
Hughson-Bos 266.0
Wynn-Was 256.2
Chandler-NY 253.0
Trout-Det 246.2

Fewest Hits/Game
Reynolds-Cle 6.34
Niggeling-StL-Was 6.66
Haefner-Was 6.86
Chandler-NY 7.01
Wensloff-NY 7.21

Fewest BB/Game
Leonard-Was 1.88
Chandler-NY 1.92
Bonham-NY 2.07
Muncrief-StL 2.11
Trucks-Det 2.31

Strikeouts
Reynolds-Cle 151
Newhouser-Det . . . 144
Chandler-NY 134
Bridges-Det 124
Trucks-Det 118

Strikeouts/Game
Reynolds-Cle 6.84
Newhouser-Det . . . 6.62
Bridges-Det 5.82
Trucks-Det 5.24
Chandler-NY 4.77

Ratio
Chandler-NY 9.07
Trucks-Det 9.90
Bonham-NY 9.97
Wensloff-NY 10.07
Niggeling-StL-Was 10.24

Earned Run Average
Chandler-NY 1.64
Bonham-NY 2.27
Haefner-Was 2.29
Bridges-Det 2.39
Trout-Det 2.48

Adjusted ERA
Chandler-NY 197
Bridges-Det 147
Trout-Det 142
Bonham-NY 141
Haefner-Was 140

Opponents' Batting Avg.
Reynolds-Cle 202
Niggeling-StL-Was .204
Haefner-Was 208
Chandler-NY 215
Wensloff-NY 219

Opponents' On Base Pct.
Chandler-NY 261
Trucks-Det 276
Wensloff-NY 282
Bonham-NY 282
Niggeling-StL-Was .282

Starter Runs
Chandler-NY 46.6
Bonham-NY 25.6
Trout-Det 22.3
Hughson-Bos 19.4
Bridges-Det 19.2

Adjusted Starter Runs
Chandler-NY 44.4
Trout-Det 28.5
Bridges-Det 24.0
Bonham-NY 23.6
Hughson-Bos 19.9

Clutch Pitching Index
Hughson-Bos 124
Muncrief-StL 120
Bonham-NY 116
Galehouse-StL . . . 115
Candini-Was 115

Relief Runs
Brown-Bos 12.2
Caster-StL 10.0
Maltzberger-Chi . . . 9.1
Naymick-Cle 6.9
Murphy-NY 5.9

Adjusted Relief Runs
Brown-Bos 12.3
Caster-StL 10.2
Maltzberger-Chi . . . 9.6
Naymick-Cle 5.6
Murphy-NY 5.3

Relief Ranking
Caster-StL 19.2
Brown-Bos 17.0
Maltzberger-Chi . . . 12.7
Murphy-NY 12.6
Naymick-Cle 6.9

Total Pitcher Index
Chandler-NY 6.5
Trout-Det 4.1
Bridges-Det 2.9
Bonham-NY 2.2
Grove-Chi 1.9

Total Baseball Ranking
Chandler-NY 6.5
Boudreau-Cle 5.5
Gordon-NY 5.2
York-Det 5.1
Appling-Chi 5.0

1944 National League

TEAM	G	W	L	PCT	GB	R	OR	AB	H	2B	3B	HR	BB	SO	AVG	OBP	SLG	PRO	PRO+	BR	/A	PF	CHI	RC	SB	CS	SBA	SBR
STL	157	105	49	.682		772	490	5475	1507	274	59	100	544	473	.275	.344	.402	.746	113	110	97	102	98	775	37			
PIT	158	90	63	.588	14.5	744	662	5428	1441	248	80	70	573	616	.265	.338	.379	.717	103	58	29	104	102	707	87			
CIN	155	89	65	.578	16	573	537	5271	1340	229	31	51	423	391	.254	.313	.338	.651	92	-73	-49	96	101	558	51			
CHI	157	75	79	.487	30	702	669	5462	1425	236	46	93	520	521	.261	.328	.360	.688	100	-1	3	99	104	658	53			
NY	155	67	87	.435	38	682	773	5306	1398	191	47	93	512	480	.263	.331	.370	.701	103	22	23	100	100	656	38			
BOS	155	65	89	.422	40	593	674	5282	1299	250	39	79	456	509	.246	.308	.353	.661	88	-60	-86	104	101	586	37			
BRO	155	63	91	.409	42	690	832	5393	1450	255	51	56	486	451	.269	.331	.366	.697	103	16	27	98	101	664	43			
PHI	154	61	92	.399	43.5	539	658	5301	1331	199	42	55	470	500	.251	.316	.336	.652	92	-69	-47	97	92	571	32			
TOT	623					5295		42918	11191	1882	395	575	3984	3941	.261	.326	.363	.689							378			

TEAM	CG	SH	SV	IP	H	H/G	HR	BB	SO	RAT	ERA	ERA+	OAV	OOB	PR	/A	PF	CPI	FA	E	DP	FW	PW	BW	SBW	DIF
STL	89	26	12	1427	1228	7.7	55	468	637	10.8	2.67	132	.233	.298	148	134	98	103	.982	112	162	3.7	13.8	10.0		.6
PIT	77	10	19	1414¹	1466	9.3	65	435	452	12.2	3.44	108	.265	.320	27	44	103	103	.970	191	122	-1.1	4.5	3.0		7.1
CIN	93	17	12	1398¹	1292	8.3	60	390	369	10.9	2.97	117	.245	.300	98	79	97	99	.978	137	153	2.0	8.1	-5.0		6.9
CHI	70	11	13	1400²	1484	9.5	75	458	545	12.5	3.59	98	.273	.331	3	-8	98	108	.970	186	151	-.8	-.8	.3		-.6
NY	47	4	21	1363²	1413	9.3	116	587	499	13.4	4.29	85	.265	.341	-102	-94	102	98	.971	179	128	-.5	-9.6	2.4		-2.2
BOS	70	13	12	1388¹	1430	9.3	80	527	454	12.8	3.67	104	.267	.335	-9	22	106	106	.971	182	160	-.7	2.3	-8.8		-4.7
BRO	50	4	13	1367²	1471	9.7	75	660	487	14.3	4.68	76	.273	.356	-162	-171	98	93	.966	197	112	-1.7	-17.6	2.8		2.4
PHI	66	11	6	1395¹	1407	9.1	49	459	496	12.2	3.64	99	.260	.321	-4	-4	100	93	.972	177	138	-.5	-.4	-4.8		-9.8
TOT	562	96	108	11155¹		9.0				12.4	3.61		.261	.326					.972	1361	1126					

Runs
Nicholson-Chi ... 116
Musial-StL ... 112
Russell-Pit ... 109
Hopp-StL ... 106
Cavarretta-Chi ... 106

Hits
Musial-StL ... 197
Cavarretta-Chi ... 197
Holmes-Bos ... 195
Walker-Bro ... 191
Russell-Pit ... 181

Doubles
Musial-StL ... 51
Galan-Bro ... 43
Holmes-Bos ... 42

Triples
Barrett-Pit ... 19
Elliott-Pit ... 16
Cavarretta-Chi ... 15
Russell-Pit ... 14
Musial-StL ... 14

Home Runs
Nicholson-Chi ... 33
Ott-NY ... 26
Northey-Phi ... 22
McCormick-Cin ... 20
Kurowski-StL ... 20

Total Bases
Nicholson-Chi ... 317
Musial-StL ... 312
Holmes-Bos ... 288
Walker-Bro ... 283
Northey-Phi ... 283

Runs Batted In
Nicholson-Chi ... 122
Elliott-Pit ... 108
Northey-Phi ... 104
Sanders-StL ... 102
McCormick-Cin ... 102

Runs Produced
Nicholson-Chi ... 205
Musial-StL ... 194
Elliott-Pit ... 183
Cavarretta-Chi ... 183

Bases On Balls
Galan-Bro ... 101
Nicholson-Chi ... 93
Ott-NY ... 90
Musial-StL ... 90
Barrett-Pit ... 86

Batting Average
Walker-Bro ... .357
Musial-StL ... .347
Medwick-NY ... .337
Hopp-StL ... .336
Cavarretta-Chi ... .321

On Base Percentage
Musial-StL ... .440
Walker-Bro ... .434
Galan-Bro ... .426
Ott-NY ... .423
Hopp-StL ... .404

Slugging Average
Musial-StL ... .549
Nicholson-Chi ... .545
Ott-NY ... .544
Walker-Bro ... .529
Hopp-StL ... .499

Production
Musial-StL ... .990
Ott-NY ... .967
Walker-Bro ... .963
Nicholson-Chi ... .935
Galan-Bro ... .922

Adjusted Production
Musial-StL ... 174
Walker-Bro ... 173
Ott-NY ... 171
Nicholson-Chi ... 162
Galan-Bro ... 162

Batter Runs
Musial-StL ... 60.9
Walker-Bro ... 51.2
Nicholson-Chi ... 47.4
Galan-Bro ... 46.5
Ott-NY ... 40.4

Adjusted Batter Runs
Musial-StL ... 59.6
Walker-Bro ... 52.4
Nicholson-Chi ... 47.9
Galan-Bro ... 47.8
Ott-NY ... 40.6

Clutch Hitting Index
Elliott-Pit ... 146
Olmo-Bro ... 143
Medwick-NY ... 136
Dahlgren-Pit ... 129
Sanders-StL ... 129

Runs Created
Musial-StL ... 145
Nicholson-Chi ... 132
Walker-Bro ... 128
Galan-Bro ... 123
Russell-Pit ... 112

Total Average
Musial-StL ... 1.095
Ott-NY ... 1.087
Walker-Bro ... 1.034
Nicholson-Chi ... 1.002
Galan-Bro ... .992

Stolen Bases
Barrett-Pit ... 28
Lupien-Phi ... 18
Hughes-Chi ... 16
Hopp-StL ... 15
Kerr-NY ... 14

Stolen Base Average

Stolen Base Runs

Fielding Runs
Kerr-NY ... 16.8
Luby-NY ... 16.4
Williams-Cin ... 15.0
Pafko-Chi ... 12.7
Miller-Cin ... 12.4

Total Player Rating
Musial-StL ... 6.0
Walker-Bro ... 3.8
Galan-Bro ... 3.7
Nicholson-Chi ... 3.5
Kerr-NY ... 3.3

Wins
Walters-Cin ... 23
M.Cooper-StL ... 22
Voiselle-NY ... 21
Sewell-Pit ... 21
Tobin-Bos ... 18

Win Percentage
Wilks-StL ... .810
Brecheen-StL ... .762
M.Cooper-StL ... .759
Walters-Cin ... .742
Sewell-Pit ... .636

Games
Adams-NY ... 65
Webber-NY ... 48
Rescigno-Pit ... 48
Voiselle-NY ... 43
Tobin-Bos ... 43

Complete Games
Tobin-Bos ... 28
Walters-Cin ... 27
Voiselle-NY ... 25
Sewell-Pit ... 24
M.Cooper-StL ... 22

Shutouts
M.Cooper-StL ... 7
Walters-Cin ... 6
Tobin-Bos ... 5
Lanier-StL ... 5
Butcher-Pit ... 5

Saves
Adams-NY ... 13
Schmidt-StL ... 5
Rescigno-Pit ... 5
Davis-Bro ... 4
Cuccurullo-Pit ... 4

Innings Pitched
Voiselle-NY ... 312.2
Tobin-Bos ... 299.1
Sewell-Pit ... 286.0
Walters-Cin ... 285.0
Raffensberger-Phi 258.2

Fewest Hits/Game
Walters-Cin ... 7.36
Wilks-StL ... 7.50
Lanier-StL ... 7.70
Heusser-Cin ... 7.71
Voiselle-NY ... 7.94

Fewest BB/Game
Raffensberger-Phi . 1.57
Strincevich-Pit ... 1.75
Davis-Bro ... 1.81
Shoun-Cin ... 1.87
Derringer-Chi ... 1.95

Strikeouts
Voiselle-NY ... 161
Lanier-StL ... 141
Javery-Bos ... 137
Raffensberger-Phi ... 136

Strikeouts/Game
Lanier-StL ... 5.66
Javery-Bos ... 4.85
Raffensberger-Phi 4.73
Voiselle-NY ... 4.63
Melton-Bro ... 4.37

Ratio
Wilks-StL ... 9.66
Heusser-Cin ... 9.72
De LaCruz-Cin ... 10.16
Walters-Cin ... 10.23
M.Cooper-StL ... 10.41

Earned Run Average
Heusser-Cin ... 2.38
Walters-Cin ... 2.40
M.Cooper-StL ... 2.46
Wilks-StL ... 2.64
Lanier-StL ... 2.65

Adjusted ERA
Heusser-Cin ... 146
Walters-Cin ... 145
M.Cooper-StL ... 143
Wilks-StL ... 133
Lanier-StL ... 133

Opponents' Batting Avg.
Walters-Cin ... .219
Wilks-StL ... .227
Heusser-Cin ... .231
Voiselle-NY ... .232
Lanier-StL ... .234

Opponents' On Base Pct.
Wilks-StL ... .275
Heusser-Cin ... .275
Walters-Cin ... .281
De LaCruz-Cin ... .284
Raffensberger-Phi ..285

Starter Runs
Walters-Cin ... 38.3
M.Cooper-StL ... 32.2
Munger-StL ... 30.5
Heusser-Cin ... 26.3
Lanier-StL ... 24.0

Adjusted Starter Runs
Walters-Cin ... 34.4
M.Cooper-StL ... 29.8
Munger-StL ... 29.4
Tobin-Bos ... 27.0
Ostermueller-Bro-Pit 23.9

Clutch Pitching Index
Fleming-Chi ... 121
Ostermueller-Bro-Pit . 120
Chipman-Bro-Chi . 119
Wyse-Chi ... 113
Javery-Bos ... 111

Relief Runs
Karl-Phi ... 12.7
Donnelly-StL ... 12.6

Adjusted Relief Runs
Karl-Phi ... 12.7
Donnelly-StL ... 11.9

Relief Ranking
Karl-Phi ... 7.1
Donnelly-StL ... 4.9

Total Pitcher Index
Walters-Cin ... 4.7
Tobin-Bos ... 4.4
Munger-StL ... 3.3
M.Cooper-StL ... 2.9
Ostermueller-Bro-Pit .. 2.6

Total Baseball Ranking
Musial-StL ... 6.0
Walters-Cin ... 4.7
Tobin-Bos ... 4.4
Walker-Bro ... 3.8
Galan-Bro ... 3.7

TEAM	G	W	L	PCT	GB	R	OR	AB	H	2B	3B	HR	BB	SO	AVG	OBP	SLG	PRO	PRO+	BR	/A	PF	CHI	RC	SB	CS	SBA	SBR
STL	154	89	65	.578		684	587	5269	1328	223	45	72	531	604	.252	.323	.352	.675	93	-3	-39	106	109	629	44	33	43	-15
DET	156	88	66	.571	1	658	581	5344	1405	220	44	60	532	500	.263	.332	.354	.686	96	21	-14	106	100	641	61	55	56	-16
NY	154	83	71	.539	6	674	617	5331	1410	216	74	96	523	627	.264	.333	.387	.720	108	75	54	103	95	707	91	31	36	-11
BOS	156	77	77	.500	12	739	676	5400	1456	277	56	69	522	505	.270	.336	.380	.716	112	73	81	99	103	710	60	40	53	-19
PHI	155	72	82	.468	17	525	594	5312	1364	169	47	36	422	490	.257	.314	.327	.641	90	-72	-62	99	95	547	42	32	38	-12
CLE	155	72	82	.468	17	643	677	5481	1458	270	50	70	512	593	.266	.331	.372	.703	111	46	70	96	93	684	48	42	53	-18
CHI	154	71	83	.461	18	543	662	5292	1307	210	55	23	439	448	.247	.307	.320	.627	86	-96	-87	99	104	533	66	47	47	-13
WAS	154	64	90	.416	25	592	664	5319	1386	186	42	33	470	477	.261	.324	.330	.654	97	-40	-11	96	101	594	127	59	56	-15
TOT	619					5058		42748	11114	1771	413	459	3951	4244	.260	.325	.353	.678							539	339	61	-41

TEAM	CG	SH	SV	IP	H	H/G	HR	BB	SO	RAT	ERA	ERA+	OAV	OOB	PR	/A	PF	CPI	FA	E	DP	FW	PW	BW	SBW	DIF
STL	71	16	17	1397¹	1392	9.0	58	469	581	12.1	3.17	114	.258	.319	40	66	105	105	.972	171	142	.5	6.9	-4.1	-1.0	9.7
DET	87	20	8	1400	1373	8.8	39	452	568	11.9	3.09	116	.257	.317	53	75	104	103	.970	190	184	-.5	7.9	-1.5	-1.1	6.2
NY	78	9	13	1390¹	1351	8.7	82	532	529	12.3	3.39	103	.256	.326	6	15	102	105	.974	156	170	1.3	1.6	5.7	-.6	-2.0
BOS	58	7	17	1394¹	1404	9.1	66	592	524	13.0	3.82	89	.262	.338	-60	-65	99	98	.972	171	154	.6	-6.8	8.5	-1.4	-.8
PHI	72	10	14	1397¹	1345	8.7	58	390	534	11.4	3.26	107	.251	.306	26	35	102	93	.971	176	127	.2	3.7	-6.5	-.7	-1.7
CLE	48	7	18	1419¹	1428	9.1	40	621	524	13.2	3.65	90	.264	.343	-34	-55	96	102	.974	165	192	.9	-5.8	7.4	-1.3	-6.1
CHI	64	5	17	1390²	1411	9.1	68	420	481	12.0	3.58	96	.264	.320	-22	-23	100	97	.970	183	154	-.2	-2.4	-9.1	-.8	6.6
WAS	83	13	11	1381	1410	9.2	48	475	503	12.4	3.49	93	.264	.327	-9	-36	95	99	.964	218	156	-2.3	-3.8	-1.2	-1.0	-4.7
TOT	561	87	115	11170¹		9.0				12.3	3.43		.260	.325					.971	1430	1279					

Runs
Stirnweiss-NY 125
R.Johnson-Bos 106
Cullenbine-Cle 98
Doerr-Bos 95
Metkovich-Bos 94

Hits
Stirnweiss-NY 205
Boudreau-Cle 191
Spence-Was 187
Lindell-NY 178
Rocco-Cle 174

Doubles
Boudreau-Cle 45
Keltner-Cle 41
R.Johnson-Bos ... 40
Fox-Bos 37
Stirnweiss-NY 35

Triples
Stirnweiss-NY 16
Lindell-NY 16
Gutteridge-StL..... 11
Doerr-Bos 10

Home Runs
Etten-NY 22
Stephens-StL 20
York-Det 18
Spence-Was 18
Lindell-NY 18

Total Bases
Lindell-NY 297
Stirnweiss-NY 296
Spence-Was 288
R.Johnson-Bos ... 277

Runs Batted In
Stephens-StL 109
R.Johnson-Bos ... 106
Lindell-NY 103
Spence-Was 100
York-Det 98

Runs Produced
R.Johnson-Bos ... 195
Stephens-StL 180
Lindell-NY 176
Spence-Was 165
Cullenbine-Cle 162

Bases On Balls
Etten-NY 97
R.Johnson-Bos ... 95
Cullenbine-Cle 87
McQuinn-StL 85
Higgins-Det 81

Batting Average
Boudreau-Cle 327
Doerr-Bos 325
R.Johnson-Bos ...324
Stirnweiss-NY 319
Spence-Was 316

On Base Percentage
R.Johnson-Bos ...431
Boudreau-Cle 406
Doerr-Bos 399
Etten-NY 399
Byrnes-StL........396

Slugging Average
Doerr-Bos 528
R.Johnson-Bos ...528
Lindell-NY 500
Spence-Was 486

Production
R.Johnson-Bos 959
Doerr-Bos 927
Spence-Was 877
Etten-NY 865
Lindell-NY 851

Adjusted Production
R.Johnson-Bos ... 175
Doerr-Bos 166
Spence-Was 157
Boudreau-Cle 146
Etten-NY 142

Batter Runs
R.Johnson-Bos ... 52.9
Spence-Was 38.1
Doerr-Bos 38.0
Etten-NY 37.3
Wakefield-Det ... 36.7

Adjusted Batter Runs
R.Johnson-Bos ... 53.7
Spence-Was 41.3
Doerr-Bos 38.7
Boudreau-Cle 35.9
Etten-NY 34.9

Clutch Hitting Index
Christman-StL 145
Carnett-Cle 133
Stephens-StL 131
Torres-Was 124
Trosky-Chi 124

Runs Created
Stirnweiss-NY 128
R.Johnson-Bos ... 124
Spence-Was 118
Etten-NY 114
Boudreau-Cle 112

Total Average
R.Johnson-Bos 987
Doerr-Bos 945
Stirnweiss-NY 910
Etten-NY 879
Spence-Was 856

Stolen Bases
Stirnweiss-NY 55
Case-Was 49
Myatt-Was 26
Moses-Chi 21
Gutteridge-StL..... 20

Stolen Base Average
Stirnweiss-NY 83.3
Moses-Chi 75.0
Case-Was 73.1
Myatt-Was 72.2
Gutteridge-StL.... 71.4

Stolen Base Runs
Stirnweiss-NY 9.9
Case-Was 3.9
Moses-Chi 2.1
Myatt-Was 1.8
Grimes-NY 1.8

Fielding Runs
Mayo-Det 29.4
Boudreau-Cle 25.8
Stirnweiss-NY ... 18.9
Rocco-Cle 17.1
Spence-Was 16.5

Total Player Rating
Boudreau-Cle 7.3
Stirnweiss-NY ... 6.8
R.Johnson-Bos ... 5.2
Spence-Was 5.1
Doerr-Bos 4.8

Wins
Newhouser-Det 29
Trout-Det 27
Potter-StL 19
Hughson-Bos 18

Win Percentage
Hughson-Bos 783
Newhouser-Det 763
Potter-StL 731
Trout-Det 659
Borowy-NY 586

Games
Heving-Cle 63
Berry-Phi 53
Trout-Det 49
Newhouser-Det 47
Klieman-Cle 47

Complete Games
Trout-Det 33
Newhouser-Det ... 25

Shutouts
Trout-Det 7
Newhouser-Det ... 6
Jakucki-StL 4

Saves
Maltzberger-Chi ... 12
Caster-StL 12
Berry-Phi 12
Heving-Cle 10
Barrett-Bos 8

Innings Pitched
Trout-Det 352.1
Newhouser-Det .. 312.1
Newsom-Phi 265.0
Kramer-StL 257.0
Borowy-NY 252.2

Fewest Hits/Game
Gromek-Cle 7.07
Niggeling-Was 7.17
Newhouser-Det .. 7.61
Hughson-Bos 7.61
Borowy-NY 7.98

Fewest BB/Game
Harris-Phi........ 1.34
Leonard-Was 1.45
Bonham-NY 1.73
Gorsica-Det 1.78
Hamlin-Phi 1.80

Strikeouts
Newhouser-Det ... 187
Trout-Det 144
Newsom-Phi 142
Kramer-StL 124
Niggeling-Was 121

Strikeouts/Game
Newhouser-Det ... 5.39
Niggeling-Was 5.29
Gromek-Cle 5.08
Hughson-Bos 4.96
Newsom-Phi 4.82

Ratio
Hughson-Bos 9.52
Trout-Det 10.24
Leonard-Was 10.28
Gromek-Cle 10.30
Newhouser-Det .. 10.58

Earned Run Average
Trout-Det 2.12
Newhouser-Det .. 2.22
Hughson-Bos 2.26
Niggeling-Was 2.32
Kramer-StL 2.49

Adjusted ERA
Trout-Det 168
Newhouser-Det ... 161
Hughson-Bos 151
Kramer-StL 145
Niggeling-Was 141

Opponents' Batting Avg.
Gromek-Cle 219
Niggeling-Was 221
Hughson-Bos 225
Newhouser-Det ...230
Borowy-NY 236

Opponents' On Base Pct.
Hughson-Bos 267
Leonard-Was 284
Trout-Det 284
Gromek-Cle 290
Newhouser-Det ...293

Starter Runs
Trout-Det 51.3
Newhouser-Det ... 42.1
Kramer-StL 27.0
Hughson-Bos 26.5
Niggeling-Was ... 25.5

Adjusted Starter Runs
Trout-Det 56.7
Newhouser-Det .. 46.8
Kramer-StL 31.8
Hughson-Bos 25.8
Borowy-NY 23.9

Clutch Pitching Index
Donald-NY 129
Woods-Bos 122
Smith-Cle 116
Haynes-Chi 116
Bonham-NY 115

Relief Runs
Heving-Cle 19.6
Berry-Phi 18.4
Caster-StL 8.9
Maltzberger-Chi ... 4.8

Adjusted Relief Runs
Berry-Phi 19.1
Heving-Cle 17.9
Caster-StL 10.4
Maltzberger-Chi ... 4.8

Relief Ranking
Berry-Phi 32.4
Heving-Cle 18.2
Caster-StL 17.3
Maltzberger-Chi ... 8.5

Total Pitcher Index
Trout-Det 8.9
Newhouser-Det ... 5.8
Kramer-StL 4.1
Hughson-Bos 2.7
Borowy-NY 2.3

Total Baseball Ranking
Trout-Det 8.9
Boudreau-Cle 7.3
Stirnweiss-NY ... 6.8
Newhouser-Det 5.8
R.Johnson-Bos 5.2

1945 National League

TEAM	G	W	L	PCT	GB	R	OR	AB	H	2B	3B	HR	BB	SO	AVG	OBP	SLG	PRO	PRO+	BR	/A	PF	CHI	RC	SB	CS	SBA	SBR
CHI	155	98	56	.636		735	532	5298	1465	229	52	57	554	462	.277	.349	.372	.721	109	53	67	98	99	714	69			
STL	155	95	59	.617	3	756	583	5487	1498	256	44	64	515	488	.273	.338	.371	.709	101	25	8	102	103	716	55			
BRO	155	87	67	.565	11	795	724	5418	1468	257	71	57	629	434	.271	.349	.376	.725	108	66	71	99	102	746	75			
PIT	155	82	72	.532	16	753	686	5343	1425	259	56	72	590	480	.267	.342	.377	.719	102	45	17	104	102	701	81			
NY	154	78	74	.513	19	668	700	5350	1439	175	35	114	501	457	.269	.336	.379	.715	103	33	22	102	93	692	38			
BOS	154	67	85	.441	30	721	728	5441	1453	229	25	101	520	510	.267	.334	.374	.708	102	20	16	101	100	692	82			
CIN	154	61	93	.396	37	536	694	5283	1317	221	26	56	392	532	.249	.304	.333	.637	84	-121	-106	98	98	537	71			
PHI	154	46	108	.299	52	548	865	5203	1278	197	27	56	449	501	.246	.307	.326	.633	84	-121	-102	97	102	527	54			
TOT	618					5512		42823	11343	1823	336	577	4150	3864	.265	.333	.364	.696						525				

TEAM	CG	SH	SV	IP	H	H/G	HR	BB	SO	RAT	ERA	ERA+	OAV	OOB	PR	/A	PF	CPI	FA	E	DP	FW	PW	BW	SBW	DIF
CHI	86	15	14	1366²	1301	8.6	57	385	541	11.3	2.98	123	.249	.303	124	102	96	102	.980	121	124	3.4	10.2	6.7		.7
STL	77	18	9	1408²	1351	8.6	70	497	510	12.0	3.24	116	.253	.320	87	78	99	106	.977	137	150	2.4	7.8	.8		7.0
BRO	61	7	18	1392¹	1357	8.8	74	586	557	12.0	3.70	101	.253	.330	14	7	99	98	.962	230	144	-3.2	.7	7.1		5.4
PIT	73	8	16	1387¹	1477	9.6	61	455	518	12.7	3.76	105	.272	.330	5	27	104	100	.971	178	141	-.0	2.7	1.7		.7
NY	53	13	21	1374²	1401	9.2	85	528	530	12.8	4.06	96	.262	.332	-39	-22	103	95	.973	166	112	.6	-2.2	2.2		1.4
BOS	57	7	13	1391²	1474	9.5	99	557	404	13.3	4.04	95	.271	.341	-36	-32	101	104	.969	193	160	-1.1	-3.2	1.6		-6.3
CIN	77	11	6	1365²	1438	9.5	70	534	372	13.2	4.00	94	.270	.340	-30	-36	99	100	.976	146	138	1.8	-3.6	-10.6		-3.6
PHI	31	4	26	1352²	1544	10.3	61	608	432	14.5	4.64	83	.285	.360	-126	-122	101	97	.962	234	150	-3.5	-12.2	-10.2		-5.0
TOT	515	83	123	11039¹		9.2				12.8	3.80		.265	.333					.971	1405	1119					

Runs
Stanky-Bro 128
Rosen-Bro 126
Holmes-Bos 125
Galan-Bro 114
Hack-Chi 110

Hits
Holmes-Bos 224
Rosen-Bro 197
Hack-Chi 193
Clay-Cin 184

Doubles
Holmes-Bos 47
Walker-Bro 42
Galan-Bro 36
Elliott-Pit 36
Cavarretta-Chi 34

Triples
Olmo-Bro 13
Pafko-Chi 12
Rucker-NY 11
Rosen-Bro 11
Cavarretta-Chi 10

Home Runs
Holmes-Bos 28
Workman-Bos 25
Adams-Phi-StL . . . 22
Ott-NY 21
Kurowski-StL 21

Total Bases
Holmes-Bos 367
Adams-Phi-StL . . . 279
Rosen-Bro 279
Walker-Bro 266
Kurowski-StL 261

Runs Batted In
Walker-Bro 124
Holmes-Bos 117
Pafko-Chi 110
Olmo-Bro 110
Adams-Phi-StL . . . 109

Runs Produced
Walker-Bro 218
Holmes-Bos 214
Galan-Bro 197
Adams-Phi-StL . . . 191
Rosen-Bro 189

Bases On Balls
Stanky-Bro 148
Galan-Bro 114
Hack-Chi 99
Nicholson-Chi 92
Sanders-StL 83

Batting Average
Cavarretta-Chi 355
Holmes-Bos 352
Rosen-Bro 325
Hack-Chi 323
Kurowski-StL 323

On Base Percentage
Cavarretta-Chi 449
Galan-Bro 423
Hack-Chi 420
Holmes-Bos 420
Stanky-Bro 417

Slugging Average
Holmes-Bos 577
Kurowski-StL 511
Cavarretta-Chi 500
Ott-NY 499
Olmo-Bro 462

Production
Holmes-Bos 997
Cavarretta-Chi . . .949
Ott-NY 910
Kurowski-StL 894
Galan-Bro 864

Adjusted Production
Holmes-Bos 175
Cavarretta-Chi . . . 167
Ott-NY 150
Kurowski-StL 144
Galan-Bro 142

Batter Runs
Holmes-Bos 62.9
Cavarretta-Chi . . . 46.4
Galan-Bro 36.8
Ott-NY 33.4
Kurowski-StL 30.7

Adjusted Batter Runs
Holmes-Bos 62.5
Cavarretta-Chi . . . 47.8
Galan-Bro 37.4
Ott-NY 32.5
Hack-Chi 31.0

Clutch Hitting Index
Walker-Bro 157
Elliott-Pit 157
Pafko-Chi 145
Lowrey-Chi 139
Olmo-Bro 136

Runs Created
Holmes-Bos 156
Cavarretta-Chi . . . 119
Galan-Bro 116
Hack-Chi 111
Rosen-Bro 110

Total Average
Holmes-Bos 1.078
Cavarretta-Chi . . . 1.037
Ott-NY 959
Galan-Bro 936
Kurowski-StL 876

Stolen Bases
Schoendienst-StL . . 26
Barrett-Pit 25
Clay-Cin 19

Stolen Base Average

Stolen Base Runs

Fielding Runs
Kerr-NY 28.3
Coscarart-Pit 21.1
Gillenwater-Bos . . 19.1
Hack-Chi 18.0
Mesner-Cin 11.6

Total Player Rating
Holmes-Bos 5.3
Hack-Chi 4.6
Cavarretta-Chi 4.0
Stanky-Bro 3.9
Kurowski-StL 2.9

Wins
Barrett-Bos-StL . . . 23
Wyse-Chi 22
Gregg-Bro 18
Burkhart-StL 18
Passeau-Chi 17

Win Percentage
Brecheen-StL 789
Burkhart-StL 692
Wyse-Chi 688
Barrett-Bos-StL . . .657
Passeau-Chi 654

Games
Karl-Phi 67
Adams-NY 65
Hutchings-Bos . . . 57
Barrett-Bos-StL . . . 45
Fox-Cin 45

Complete Games
Barrett-Bos-StL . . . 24
Wyse-Chi 23
Passeau-Chi 19
Strincevich-Pit 18
Heusser-Cin 18

Shutouts
Passeau-Chi 5
Voiselle-NY 4
Heusser-Cin 4
Donnelly-StL 4
Burkhart-StL 4

Saves
Karl-Phi 15
Adams-NY 15
Rescigno-Pit 9

Innings Pitched
Barrett-Bos-StL . . 284.2
Wyse-Chi 278.1
Gregg-Bro 254.1
Roe-Pit 235.0
Voiselle-NY 232.1

Fewest Hits/Game
Prim-Chi 7.73
Brecheen-StL 7.78
Gregg-Bro 7.82
Mungo-NY 7.92
Passeau-Chi 8.13

Fewest BB/Game
Prim-Chi 1.25
Barrett-Bos-StL . . . 1.71
Roe-Pit 1.76
Wyse-Chi 1.78
Strincevich-Pit 1.93

Strikeouts
Roe-Pit 148
Gregg-Bro 139
Voiselle-NY 115
Mungo-NY 101
Hutchings-Bos . . . 99

Strikeouts/Game
Roe-Pit 5.67
Mungo-NY 4.97
Gregg-Bro 4.92
Hutchings-Bos . . . 4.82
Prim-Chi 4.79

Ratio
Prim-Chi 9.04
Roe-Pit 10.53
Passeau-Chi 10.55
Brecheen-StL 10.58
Wyse-Chi 10.74

Earned Run Average
Prim-Chi 2.40
Passeau-Chi 2.46
Brecheen-StL 2.52
Walters-Cin 2.68
Wyse-Chi 2.68

Adjusted ERA
Prim-Chi 152
Brecheen-StL 149
Passeau-Chi 149
Walters-Cin 140
Roe-Pit 137

Opponents' Batting Avg.
Prim-Chi 228
Gregg-Bro 232
Brecheen-StL 238
Mungo-NY 238
Passeau-Chi 238

Opponents' On Base Pct.
Prim-Chi 256
Passeau-Chi 289
Barrett-Bos-StL . . .295
Wyse-Chi 296
Roe-Pit 296

Starter Runs
Wyse-Chi 34.5
Passeau-Chi 33.8
Prim-Chi 25.8
Barrett-Bos-StL . . 25.2
Roe-Pit 24.2

Adjusted Starter Runs
Passeau-Chi 30.1
Wyse-Chi 29.9
Roe-Pit 28.0
Barrett-Bos-StL . . . 23.7
Prim-Chi 23.1

Clutch Pitching Index
Butcher-Pit 124
Logan-Bos 124
Walters-Cin 124
Lee-Phi-Bos 123
Wyse-Chi 117

Relief Runs
Karl-Phi 16.3
Buker-Bro 4.9
Adams-NY 4.7
Chipman-Chi 2.4

Adjusted Relief Runs
Karl-Phi 16.9
Adams-NY 6.1
Buker-Bro 4.4
Chipman-Chi 1.2

Relief Ranking
Karl-Phi 16.6
Adams-NY 11.5
Buker-Bro 4.7
Chipman-Chi 1.4

Total Pitcher Index
Passeau-Chi 3.6
Wyse-Chi 3.1
Walters-Cin 2.7
Roe-Pit 2.6
Prim-Chi 2.5

Total Baseball Ranking
Holmes-Bos 5.3
Hack-Chi 4.6
Cavarretta-Chi 4.0
Stanky-Bro 3.9
Passeau-Chi 3.6

TEAM	G	W	L	PCT	GB	R	OR	AB	H	2B	3B	HR	BB	SO	AVG	OBP	SLG	PRO	PRO+	BR	/A	PF	CHI	RC	SB	CS	SBA	SBR
DET	155	88	65	.575		633	565	5257	1345	**227**	47	77	517	533	.256	.324	.361	.685	97	21	-17	106	102	627	60	54	49	-12
WAS	156	87	67	.565	1.5	622	562	5326	1375	197	**63**	27	545	489	.258	.330	.334	.664	107	-7	45	92	103	612	**110**	65	57	-14
STL	154	81	70	.536	6	597	**548**	5227	1302	215	37	63	500	555	.249	.316	.341	.657	91	-28	-57	105	**105**	584	25	31	35	**-11**
NY	152	81	71	.533	6.5	**676**	606	5176	1343	189	61	**93**	618	567	.259	**.343**	**.373**	**.716**	108	90	62	105	97	**698**	64	43	55	-19
CLE	147	73	72	.503	11	557	548	4898	1249	216	48	65	505	578	.255	.326	.359	.685	108	23	47	96	95	588	19	31	36	**-11**
CHI	150	71	78	.477	15	596	633	5077	1330	204	55	22	470	467	**.262**	.326	.337	.663	100	-12	3	97	**105**	571	78	54	**60**	-19
BOS	157	71	83	.461	17.5	599	674	5367	**1393**	225	44	50	541	534	.260	.330	.346	.676	99	12	-2	102	96	634	72	50	45	**-11**
PHI	153	52	98	.347	34.5	494	638	5296	1297	201	37	33	449	**463**	.245	.306	.316	.622	86	-95	-92	100	98	523	25	45	50	-16
TOT	612					4774		41624	10634	1674	392	430	4145	4186	.255	.325	.346	.671							453	373	55	-87

TEAM	CG	SH	SV	IP	H	H/G	HR	BB	SO	RAT	ERA	ERA+	OAV	OOB	PR	/A	PF	CPI	FA	E	DP	FW	PW	BW	SBW	DIF
DET	78	**19**	16	1393²	1305	8.4	48	538	**588**	12.1	2.99	**118**	.249	.322	58	**81**	105	108	.975	158	173	.4	**8.7**	-1.8	-.1	4.4
WAS	82	**19**	11	1412¹	1307	**8.3**	42	**440**	550	**11.2**	**2.92**	106	**.241**	**.300**	68	27	92	93	.970	183	124	-1.0	2.9	4.8	-.3	3.6
STL	91	10	8	1382²	1307	8.5	59	506	570	11.8	3.14	112	.249	.315	33	57	105	101	.976	143	123	1.2	6.1	-6.1	.0	4.3
NY	78	9	14	1355	1277	8.5	66	485	474	11.8	3.45	100	.249	.315	-13	1	103	93	.971	175	170	-.7	.1	**6.6**	-.9	-.1
CLE	76	14	12	1302¹	**1269**	8.8	**39**	501	497	12.4	3.31	98	.257	.328	7	-9	97	102	**.977**	**126**	149	**1.7**	-1.0	5.0	.0	-5.3
CHI	84	13	13	1330²	1400	9.5	63	448	486	12.7	3.69	90	.270	.331	-48	-55	99	100	.970	180	139	-1.1	-5.9	.3	-.9	4.1
BOS	71	15	13	1390²	1389	9.0	58	656	490	13.4	3.80	90	.263	.348	-67	-60	101	102	.973	169	**198**	-.1	-6.4	-.2	.0	.8
PHI	65	11	8	1381	1380	9.0	55	571	531	12.9	3.62	95	.262	.337	-39	-29	102	101	.973	168	160	-.3	-3.1	-9.9	-.5	-9.2
TOT	625	110	95	10948¹		8.7				12.3	3.36		.255	.325					.973	1302	1236					

Runs
Stirnweiss-NY 107
Stephens-StL 90
Cullenbine-Cle-Det 83

Hits
Stirnweiss-NY 195
Moses-Chi 168
Stephens-StL 165
Hall-Phi.......... 161
Etten-NY 161

Doubles
Moses-Chi 35
Stirnweiss-NY 32
Binks-Was 32
McQuinn-StL 31

Triples
Stirnweiss-NY 22
Moses-Chi 15
Kuhel-Was 13
Dickshot-Chi 10
Peck-Phi.......... 9

Home Runs
Stephens-StL 24
Cullenbine-Cle-Det 18
York-Det 18
Etten-NY 18
Heath-Cle 15

Total Bases
Stirnweiss-NY 301
Stephens-StL 270
Etten-NY 247
York-Det 246
Moses-Chi 239

Runs Batted In
Etten-NY 111
Cullenbine-Cle-Det 93
Stephens-StL 89
York-Det 87
Binks-Was 81

Runs Produced
Etten-NY 170
Stirnweiss-NY 161
Cullenbine-Cle-Det 158
Stephens-StL 155
Kuhel-Was 146

Bases On Balls
Cullenbine-Cle-Det 113
Lake-Bos 106
Grimes-NY 97
Etten-NY 90
Kuhel-Was 79

Batting Average
Stirnweiss-NY 309
Dickshot-Chi 302
Estalella-Phi......299
Myatt-Was 296
Moses-Chi 295

On Base Percentage
Lake-Bos 412
Cullenbine-Cle-Det .402
Estalella-Phi.......399
Grimes-NY 395
Etten-NY 387

Slugging Average
Stirnweiss-NY 476
Stephens-StL 473
Cullenbine-Cle-Det .444
Etten-NY 437
Estalella-Phi.......435

Production
Stirnweiss-NY 862
Cullenbine-Cle-Det .846
Estalella-Phi......834
Stephens-StL 825
Etten-NY 824

Adjusted Production
Stirnweiss-NY 143
Estalella-Phi...... 142
Kuhel-Was 137
Cullenbine-Cle-Det 137
Lake-Bos 136

Batter Runs
Stirnweiss-NY 39.1
Cullenbine-Cle-Det 35.1
Etten-NY 29.9
Heath-Cle 29.4
Lake-Bos 28.7

Adjusted Batter Runs
Stirnweiss-NY 35.8
Heath-Cle 31.3
Cullenbine-Cle-Det 31.1
Lake-Bos 27.3
Etten-NY 26.8

Clutch Hitting Index
Schalk-Chi 158
Michaels-Chi 143
Etten-NY 141
Tresh-Chi 135
Kuhel-Was 131

Runs Created
Stirnweiss-NY 121
Cullenbine-Cle-Det 106
Etten-NY 98
Stephens-StL 98
Moses-Chi 97

Total Average
Cullenbine-Cle-Det .888
Stirnweiss-NY 855
Lake-Bos 849
Etten-NY 794
Estalella-Phi......789

Stolen Bases
Stirnweiss-NY 33
Myatt-Was 30
Case-Was 30
Metkovich-Bos 19
Dickshot-Chi 18

Stolen Base Average
Dickshot-Chi 85.7
Metkovich-Bos ... 76.0
Myatt-Was 73.2
Stirnweiss-NY ... 66.0
Case-Was 65.2

Stolen Base Runs
Dickshot-Chi 3.6
Myatt-Was 2.4
Metkovich-Bos ... 2.1
Crosetti-NY 1.5
Richards-Det 1.2

Fielding Runs
Hall-Phi.......... 26.1
Stirnweiss-NY 25.5
Webb-Det 23.0
Newsome-Bos.... 22.2
Kell-Phi.......... 21.7

Total Player Rating
Stirnweiss-NY 6.6
Lake-Bos 5.3
Cullenbine-Cle-Det 3.6
Mayo-Det 2.5
Moses-Chi 2.5

Wins
Newhouser-Det 25
Ferriss-Bos 21
Wolff-Was........ 20
Gromek-Cle 19

Win Percentage
Newhouser-Det 735
Leonard-Was 708
Gromek-Cle 679
Ferriss-Bos 677
Wolff-Was.........667

Games
Berry-Phi 52
Reynolds-Cle 44
Pieretti-Was 44
Trout-Det 41
Newhouser-Det 40

Complete Games
Newhouser-Det 29
Ferriss-Bos 26
Wolff-Was........ 21
Potter-StL 21
Gromek-Cle 21

Shutouts
Newhouser-Det 8
Ferriss-Bos 5
Benton-Det 5

Saves
Turner-NY 10
Berry-Phi 5

Innings Pitched
Newhouser-Det .. 313.1
Ferriss-Bos 264.2
Newsom-Phi 257.1
Potter-StL 255.1
Gromek-Cle 251.0

Fewest Hits/Game
Newhouser-Det ... 6.86
Wolff-Was........ 7.20
Potter-StL 7.47
Lee-Chi.......... 8.20
Niggeling-Was ... 8.20

Fewest BB/Game
Bonham-NY 1.10
Leonard-Was 1.46
Wolff-Was........ 1.91
Overmire-Det 2.33
Gromek-Cle 2.37

Strikeouts
Newhouser-Det ... 212
Potter-StL 129
Newsom-Phi 127
Reynolds-Cle 112

Strikeouts/Game
Newhouser-Det ... 6.09
Kramer-StL 4.62
Niggeling-Was ... 4.58
Potter-StL 4.55
Newsom-Phi 4.44

Ratio
Wolff-Was........ 9.14
Potter-StL 9.90
Newhouser-Det ... 10.02
Leonard-Was 10.21
Bonham-NY 10.41

Earned Run Average
Newhouser-Det ... 1.81
Benton-Det 2.02
Wolff-Was........ 2.12
Leonard-Was 2.13
Lee-Chi.......... 2.44

Adjusted ERA
Newhouser-Det ... 194
Benton-Det 174
Wolff-Was........ 146
Leonard-Was 146
Potter-StL 143

Opponents' Batting Avg.
Newhouser-Det 211
Wolff-Was........215
Potter-StL 226
Niggeling-Was 240
Benton-Det 241

Opponents' On Base Pct.
Wolff-Was........258
Potter-StL 279
Leonard-Was 279
Newhouser-Det ...281
Bonham-NY 288

Starter Runs
Newhouser-Det ... 54.1
Wolff-Was........ 34.5
Leonard-Was 29.8
Benton-Det 28.7
Potter-StL 25.5

Adjusted Starter Runs
Newhouser-Det ... 59.4
Benton-Det 31.9
Potter-StL 29.8
Wolff-Was........ 27.2
Leonard-Was 23.5

Clutch Pitching Index
Benton-Det 139
Lee-Chi.......... 121
Shirley-StL 116
Hollingsworth-StL . 116
Ferriss-Bos 114

Relief Runs
Berry-Phi 14.7
Holcombe-NY 9.7
Barrett-Bos 7.2
Zoldak-StL 0

Adjusted Relief Runs
Berry-Phi 15.7
Holcombe-NY 10.3
Barrett-Bos 7.5
Zoldak-StL 1.2

Relief Ranking
Berry-Phi 17.6
Holcombe-NY 10.0
Barrett-Bos 6.1
Zoldak-StL 8

Total Pitcher Index
Newhouser-Det 7.9
Potter-StL 3.8
Ferriss-Bos 3.3
Benton-Det 3.1
Leonard-Was 2.6

Total Baseball Ranking
Newhouser-Det 7.9
Stirnweiss-NY 6.6
Lake-Bos 5.3
Potter-StL 3.8
Cullenbine-Cle-Det 3.6

1946 National League

TEAM	G	W	L	PCT	GB	R	OR	AB	H	2B	3B	HR	BB	SO	AVG	OBP	SLG	PRO	PRO+	BR	/A	PF	CHI	RC	SB	CS	SBA	SBR
STL	156	98	58	.628		712	545	5372	1426	265	56	81	530	537	.265	.334	.381	.715	104	54	27	104	105	702	58			
BRO	157	96	60	.615	2	701	570	5285	1376	233	66	55	691	575	.260	.348	.361	.709	105	60	53	101	101	699	100			
CHI	155	82	71	.536	14.5	626	581	5298	1344	223	50	56	586	599	.254	.331	.346	.677	100	-8	4	98	102	622	43			
BOS	154	81	72	.529	15.5	630	592	5225	1377	238	48	44	558	468	.264	.337	.353	.690	100	44	8	101	100	641	60			
PHI	155	69	85	.448	28	560	705	5233	1351	209	40	80	417	590	.258	.315	.359	.674	99	-29	-11	97	99	598	41			
CIN	156	67	87	.435	30	523	570	5291	1262	206	33	65	493	604	.239	.307	.327	.634	88	-100	-77	96	102	546	82			
PIT	155	63	91	.409	34	552	668	5199	1300	202	52	60	592	555	.250	.328	.344	.672	94	-17	-32	103	93	602	48			
NY	154	61	93	.396	36	612	685	5191	1326	176	37	121	532	546	.255	.328	.374	.702	104	27	23	101	97	644	46			
TOT	621					4916		42094	10762	1752	382	562	4399	4474	.256	.329	.355	.684							478			

TEAM	CG	SH	SV	IP	H	H/G	HR	BB	SO	RAT	ERA	ERA+	OAV	OOB	PR	/A	PF	CPI	FA	E	DP	FW	PW	BW	SBW	DIF
STL	75	18	15	1397	1326	8.5	63	493	607	11.9	3.01	115	.253	.321	62	69	101	108	.980	124	167	2.1	7.3	2.9		7.7
BRO	52	14	28	1418	1280	8.1	58	671	647	12.5	3.05	111	.243	.331	57	52	99	107	.972	174	154	-.9	5.5	5.6		7.7
CHI	59	15	11	1393	1370	8.9	58	527	619	12.4	3.24	102	.256	.325	26	15	97	102	.976	146	119	.7	1.6	.4		2.8
BOS	73	10	12	1371	1291	8.5	76	478	566	11.7	3.35	102	.248	.313	9	13	101	93	.972	169	129	-.8	1.4	.8		3.0
PHI	55	11	23	1369	1442	9.5	73	542	490	13.3	3.99	86	.272	.344	-87	-85	101	98	.975	148	144	.6	-9.0	-1.2		1.6
CIN	69	17	11	1413[1]	1334	8.5	70	467	506	11.6	3.08	109	.251	.314	53	41	98	101	.975	155	192	.2	4.4	-8.2		-6.4
PIT	61	10	6	1370	1406	9.2	50	561	458	13.1	3.72	95	.268	.341	-46	-29	103	99	.970	184	127	-1.6	-3.1	-3.4		-5.9
NY	47	8	13	1353[1]	1313	8.7	114	660	581	13.2	3.92	88	.256	.342	-75	-71	101	100	.973	159	121	-.2	-7.5	2.4		-10.7
TOT	491	103	119	11084[2]		8.7				12.5	3.41		.256	.329					.974	1259	1153					

Runs		Hits		Doubles		Triples		Home Runs		Total Bases	
Musial-StL	124	Musial-StL	228	Musial-StL	50	Musial-StL	20	Kiner-Pit	23	Musial-StL	366
Slaughter-StL	100	Walker-Bro	184	Holmes-Bos	35	Reese-Bro	10	Mize-NY	22	Slaughter-StL	283
Stanky-Bro	98	Slaughter-StL	183	Kurowski-StL	32	Cavarretta-Chi	10	Slaughter-StL	18	Ennis-Phi	262
Schoendienst-StL	94	Holmes-Bos	176	Herman-Bro-Bos	31	Walker-Bro	9	Ennis-Phi	17	Walker-Bro	258
Cavarretta-Chi	89	Schoendienst-StL	170							Holmes-Bos	241

Runs Batted In		Runs Produced		Bases On Balls		Batting Average		On Base Percentage		Slugging Average	
Slaughter-StL	130	Slaughter-StL	212	Stanky-Bro	137	Musial-StL	.365	Stanky-Bro	.436	Musial-StL	.587
Walker-Bro	116	Musial-StL	211	Fletcher-Pit	111	Hopp-Bos	.333	Musial-StL	.434	Ennis-Phi	.485
Musial-StL	103	Walker-Bro	187	Cavarretta-Chi	88	Walker-Bro	.319	Cavarretta-Chi	.401	Slaughter-StL	.465
Kurowski-StL	89	Cavarretta-Chi	159	Reese-Bro	87	Ennis-Phi	.313	Herman-Bro-Bos	.395	Kurowski-StL	.462
Kiner-Pit	81	Holmes-Bos	153	Hack-Chi	83	Holmes-Bos	.310	Walker-Bro	.391	Walker-Bro	.448

Production		Adjusted Production		Batter Runs		Adjusted Batter Runs		Clutch Hitting Index		Runs Created	
Musial-StL	1.021	Musial-StL	180	Musial-StL	70.9	Musial-StL	67.7	Walker-Bro	161	Musial-StL	164
Kurowski-StL	.853	Ennis-Phi	144	Mize-NY	43.6	Mize-NY	43.3	Slaughter-StL	152	Slaughter-StL	110
Ennis-Phi	.849	Cavarretta-Chi	140	Kurowski-StL	29.1	Cavarretta-Chi	29.0	Elliott-Pit	137	Walker-Bro	104
Walker-Bro	.839	Walker-Bro	136	Walker-Bro	28.9	Walker-Bro	28.2	Reiser-Bro	130	Kurowski-StL	97
Slaughter-StL	.838	Kurowski-StL	136	Slaughter-StL	28.6	Ennis-Phi	27.2	Cavarretta-Chi	125	Ennis-Phi	96

Total Average		Stolen Bases		Stolen Base Average	Stolen Base Runs	Fielding Runs		Total Player Rating	
Musial-StL	1.114	Reiser-Bro	34			Marion-StL	18.8	Musial-StL	5.5
Stanky-Bro	.890	Haas-Cin	22			Handley-Pit	13.2	Mize-NY	4.1
Reiser-Bro	.877	Hopp-Bos	21			Wyrostek-Phi	12.0	Ennis-Phi	3.8
Kurowski-StL	.855	Adams-Cin	16			Ennis-Phi	11.9	Kurowski-StL	2.9
Walker-Bro	.848	Walker-Bro	14			Mueller-Cin	8.7	Cavarretta-Chi	2.9

Wins		Win Percentage		Games		Complete Games		Shutouts		Saves	
Pollet-StL	21	Dickson-StL	.714	Trinkle-NY	48	Sain-Bos	24	Brecheen-StL	5	Raffensberger-Phi	6
Sain-Bos	20	Higbe-Bro	.680	Dickson-StL	47	Pollet-StL	22	Blackwell-Cin	5	Pollet-StL	5
Higbe-Bro	17	Pollet-StL	.677	Behrman-Bro	47	Koslo-NY	17	VanderMeer-Cin	4	Karl-Phi	5
Dickson-StL	15	Sain-Bos	.588	Casey-Bro	46	Ostermueller-Pit	16	Pollet-StL	4	Herring-Bro	5
Brecheen-StL	15	Brecheen-StL	.500			Cooper-Bos	15	Cooper-Bos	4	Casey-Bro	5

Innings Pitched		Fewest Hits/Game		Fewest BB/Game		Strikeouts		Strikeouts/Game		Ratio	
Pollet-StL	266.0	Kennedy-NY	7.38	Cooper-Bos	1.76	Schmitz-Chi	135	Higbe-Bro	5.72	Cooper-Bos	9.95
Koslo-NY	265.1	Schmitz-Chi	7.38	Raffensberger-Phi	1.79	Higbe-Bro	134	Schmitz-Chi	5.42	Beggs-Cin	10.18
Sain-Bos	265.0	Blackwell-Cin	7.41	Beggs-Cin	1.85	Sain-Bos	129	Blackwell-Cin	4.63	Sain-Bos	10.66
Brecheen-StL	231.1	Higbe-Bro	7.60	Heusser-Cin	2.09	Koslo-NY	121	Brecheen-StL	4.55	Dickson-StL	10.74
Schmitz-Chi	224.1	Sain-Bos	7.64	Strincevich-Pit	2.25	Brecheen-StL	117	Voiselle-NY	4.50	Pollet-StL	10.79

Earned Run Average		Adjusted ERA		Opponents' Batting Avg.		Opponents' On Base Pct.		Starter Runs		Adjusted Starter Runs	
Pollet-StL	2.10	Pollet-StL	165	Schmitz-Chi	.221	Cooper-Bos	.276	Pollet-StL	38.9	Pollet-StL	40.1
Sain-Bos	2.21	Sain-Bos	155	Kennedy-NY	.224	Beggs-Cin	.287	Sain-Bos	35.5	Sain-Bos	36.0
Beggs-Cin	2.32	Beggs-Cin	144	Blackwell-Cin	.226	Sain-Bos	.294	Brecheen-StL	23.7	Brecheen-StL	24.8
Blackwell-Cin	2.45	Brecheen-StL	139	Higbe-Bro	.229	Dickson-StL	.295	Beggs-Cin	23.1	Beggs-Cin	21.6
Brecheen-StL	2.49	Blackwell-Cin	136	Sain-Bos	.230	Pollet-StL	.300	Blackwell-Cin	20.7	Rowe-Phi	19.9

Clutch Pitching Index		Relief Runs		Adjusted Relief Runs		Relief Ranking		Total Pitcher Index		Total Baseball Ranking	
Hatten-Bro	129	Casey-Bro	15.8	Casey-Bro	15.5	Casey-Bro	24.1	Sain-Bos	5.1	Musial-StL	5.5
Pollet-StL	127	Thompson-NY	14.8	Thompson-NY	15.0	Thompson-NY	23.7	Pollet-StL	4.7	Sain-Bos	5.1
Beggs-Cin	124	Malloy-Cin	5.3	Malloy-Cin	4.8	Malloy-Cin	4.5	Beggs-Cin	2.8	Pollet-StL	4.7
Wyse-Chi	117	Budnick-NY	2.5	Budnick-NY	2.8	Budnick-NY	1.6	Brecheen-StL	2.5	Mize-NY	4.1
Ostermueller-Pit	110	Herring-Bro	.6	Wilks-StL	.5	Wilks-StL	.4	Rowe-Phi	2.3	Ennis-Phi	3.8

TEAM	G	W	L	PCT	GB	R	OR	AB	H	2B	3B	HR	BB	SO	AVG	OBP	SLG	PRO	PRO+	BR	/A	PF	CHI	RC	SB	CS	SBA	SBR
BOS	156	104	50	.675		792	594	5318	1441	268	50	109	687	661	.271	.356	.402	.758	112	136	99	106	101	790	45	36	42	-13
DET	155	92	62	.597	12	704	567	5318	1373	212	41	108	622	616	.258	.337	.374	.711	99	42	2	106	103	698	65	41	49	-16
NY	154	87	67	.565	17	684	547	5139	1275	208	50	136	627	706	.248	.334	.387	.721	106	55	46	101	101	695	48	35	42	-14
WAS	155	76	78	.494	28	608	706	5337	1388	260	63	60	511	641	.260	.327	.366	.693	106	1	38	94	96	653	51	50	54	-16
CHI	155	74	80	.481	30	562	595	5312	1364	206	44	37	501	600	.257	.323	.333	.656	93	-63	-39	96	100	579	78	64	54	-12
CLE	156	68	86	.442	36	537	638	5242	1285	233	56	79	506	697	.245	.313	.356	.669	99	-48	-7	94	94	596	57	49	48	-13
STL	156	66	88	.429	38	621	710	5373	1350	220	46	84	465	713	.251	.313	.356	.669	88	-52	-83	105	108	601	23	35	42	-14
PHI	155	49	105	.318	55	529	680	5200	1317	220	51	40	482	594	.253	.318	.338	.656	90	-67	-63	99	97	574	39	30	42	-15
TOT	621					5037		42239	10793	1827	401	653	4401	5228	.256	.328	.364	.692							406	340	54	-81

TEAM	CG	SH	SV	IP	H	H/G	HR	BB	SO	RAT	ERA	ERA+	OAV	OOB	PR	/A	PF	CPI	FA	E	DP	FW	PW	BW	SBW	DIF
BOS	79	15	20	1396[2]	1359	8.8	89	501	667	12.1	3.38	108	.253	.319	18	43	105	100	.977	139	163	1.5	4.5	10.4	-.3	10.9
DET	94	18	15	1402	1277	8.2	97	497	896	11.5	3.22	114	.240	.307	44	68	104	95	.974	155	138	.5	7.1	.2	-.6	7.8
NY	68	17	17	1361	1232	8.1	66	552	653	11.9	3.13	110	.242	.318	55	47	99	100	.975	150	174	.7	4.9	4.8	-.4	-.0
WAS	71	8	10	1396[1]	1459	9.4	81	547	537	13.1	3.74	89	.268	.338	-36	-60	96	103	.966	211	162	-2.8	-6.3	4.0	-.6	4.7
CHI	62	9	16	1392[1]	1348	8.7	80	508	550	12.1	3.10	110	.254	.322	62	49	97	110	.972	175	170	-.7	5.1	-4.1	-.2	-3.2
CLE	63	16	13	1388[2]	1282	8.3	84	649	789	12.6	3.62	91	.245	.330	-17	-47	94	96	.975	147	147	1.0	-4.9	-.7	-.3	-4.1
STL	63	13	12	1382[1]	1465	9.5	73	573	574	13.3	3.95	94	.272	.343	-68	-33	107	99	.974	159	157	.3	-3.5	-8.7	-.4	1.3
PHI	61	10	5	1342[2]	1371	9.2	83	577	562	13.2	3.90	91	.263	.340	-59	-53	101	98	.971	167	141	-.2	-5.6	-6.6	-.5	-15.1
TOT	561	106	108	11062		8.8				12.5	3.50		.256	.328					.973	1303	1252					

Runs
Williams-Bos 142
Pesky-Bos 115
Lake-Det 105
Keller-NY 98
Doerr-Bos 95

Hits
Pesky-Bos 208
Vernon-Was 207
Appling-Chi 180
Williams-Bos 176
Lewis-Was 170

Doubles
Vernon-Was 51
Spence-Was 50
Pesky-Bos 43
Williams-Bos 37
Doerr-Bos 34

Triples
Edwards-Cle 16
Lewis-Was 13
Kell-Phi-Det 10
Spence-Was 10
Keller-NY 10

Home Runs
Greenberg-Det 44
Williams-Bos 38
Keller-NY 30
Seerey-Cle 26
DiMaggio-NY 25

Total Bases
Williams-Bos 343
Greenberg-Det 316
Vernon-Was 298
Spence-Was 287
Keller-NY 287

Runs Batted In
Greenberg-Det 127
Williams-Bos 123
York-Bos 119
Doerr-Bos 116
Keller-NY 101

Runs Produced
Williams-Bos 227
Doerr-Bos 193
York-Bos 180
Greenberg-Det 174
Keller-NY 169

Bases On Balls
Williams-Bos 156
Keller-NY 113
Lake-Det 103
Cullenbine-Det 88
Henrich-NY 87

Batting Average
Vernon-Was .353
Williams-Bos .342
Pesky-Bos .335
Kell-Phi-Det .322
DiMaggio-Bos .316

On Base Percentage
Williams-Bos .497
Keller-NY .405
Vernon-Was .403
Pesky-Bos .401
DiMaggio-Bos .393

Slugging Average
Williams-Bos .667
Greenberg-Det .604
Keller-NY .533
DiMaggio-NY .511
Edwards-Cle .509

Production
Williams-Bos 1.164
Greenberg-Det .977
Keller-NY .938
Vernon-Was .910
DiMaggio-NY .878

Adjusted Production
Williams-Bos 211
Vernon-Was 163
Greenberg-Det 160
Keller-NY 158
Edwards-Cle 151

Batter Runs
Williams-Bos 94.2
Greenberg-Det 46.1
Keller-NY 45.9
Cullenbine-Det 42.2
Vernon-Was 40.3

Adjusted Batter Runs
Williams-Bos 90.2
Keller-NY 45.0
Vernon-Was 44.4
Greenberg-Det 42.2
Cullenbine-Det 39.5

Clutch Hitting Index
York-Bos 158
Doerr-Bos 147
Travis-Was 141
Berardino-StL 123
DiMaggio-Bos 118

Runs Created
Williams-Bos 188
Keller-NY 127
Vernon-Was 120
Greenberg-Det 119
Pesky-Bos 111

Total Average
Williams-Bos 1.431
Greenberg-Det 1.010
Keller-NY 1.005
Vernon-Was .873
DiMaggio-NY .862

Stolen Bases
Case-Cle 28
Stirnweiss-NY 18
Lake-Det 15

Stolen Base Average
Stirnweiss-NY 75.0
Case-Cle 71.8

Stolen Base Runs
Stirnweiss-NY 1.8
Dillinger-StL 1.8
Case-Cle 1.8
Philley-Chi 1.5
Evers-Det 1.5

Fielding Runs
Doerr-Bos 26.8
Gordon-NY 21.5
Boudreau-Cle 16.2
Chapman-Phi 15.3
Rizzuto-NY 13.1

Total Player Rating
Williams-Bos 8.2
Doerr-Bos 5.0
Greenberg-Det 3.8
Pesky-Bos 3.6
Cullenbine-Det 3.6

Wins
Newhouser-Det 26
Feller-Cle 26
Ferriss-Bos 25
Hughson-Bos 20
Chandler-NY 20

Win Percentage
Ferriss-Bos .806
Newhouser-Det .747
Chandler-NY .714
Harris-Bos .654
Hughson-Bos .645

Games
Feller-Cle 48
Savage-Phi 40
Ferriss-Bos 40
Hughson-Bos 39
Caldwell-Chi 39

Complete Games
Feller-Cle 36
Newhouser-Det 29
Ferriss-Bos 26
Trout-Det 23
Hughson-Bos 21

Shutouts
Feller-Cle 10
Newhouser-Det 6
Hughson-Bos 6
Ferriss-Bos 6
Chandler-NY 6

Saves
Klinger-Bos 9
Caldwell-Chi 8
Murphy-NY 7
Ferrick-Cle-StL 6

Innings Pitched
Feller-Cle 371.1
Newhouser-Det 292.2
Hughson-Bos 278.0
Trout-Det 276.1
Ferriss-Bos 274.0

Fewest Hits/Game
Newhouser-Det 6.61
Feller-Cle 6.71
Chandler-NY 6.99
Embree-Cle 7.65
Bevens-NY 7.68

Fewest BB/Game
Hughson-Bos 1.65
Lopat-Chi 1.87
Leonard-Was 2.00
Flores-Phi 2.21
Ferriss-Bos 2.33

Strikeouts
Feller-Cle 348
Newhouser-Det 275
Hughson-Bos 172
Trucks-Det 161
Trout-Det 151

Strikeouts/Game
Newhouser-Det 8.46
Feller-Cle 8.43
Trucks-Det 6.12
Hutchinson-Det 6.00
Hughson-Bos 5.57

Ratio
Newhouser-Det 9.66
Hughson-Bos 9.87
Chandler-NY 10.18
Lopat-Chi 10.32
Feller-Cle 10.49

Earned Run Average
Newhouser-Det 1.94
Chandler-NY 2.10
Feller-Cle 2.18
Bevens-NY 2.23
Flores-Phi 2.32

Adjusted ERA
Newhouser-Det 189
Chandler-NY 164
Trout-Det 156
Bevens-NY 154
Flores-Phi 153

Opponents' Batting Avg.
Newhouser-Det .201
Feller-Cle .208
Chandler-NY .218
Embree-Cle .227
Bevens-NY .232

Opponents' On Base Pct.
Newhouser-Det .269
Hughson-Bos .274
Chandler-NY .288
Lopat-Chi .288
Feller-Cle .291

Starter Runs
Feller-Cle 54.5
Newhouser-Det 50.9
Chandler-NY 40.2
Trout-Det 35.6
Bevens-NY 35.2

Adjusted Starter Runs
Newhouser-Det 55.8
Feller-Cle 46.5
Trout-Det 40.2
Chandler-NY 38.7
Bevens-NY 33.7

Clutch Pitching Index
Grove-Chi 126
Flores-Phi 121
Trout-Det 119
Haynes-Chi 118
Bevens-NY 115

Relief Runs
Caldwell-Chi 14.3
Lemon-Cle 10.6
Klinger-Bos 7.2
Kinder-StL 1.7

Adjusted Relief Runs
Caldwell-Chi 13.4
Lemon-Cle 8.5
Klinger-Bos 8.2
Kinder-StL 3.9

Relief Ranking
Caldwell-Chi 25.2
Klinger-Bos 9.4
Lemon-Cle 7.6
Kinder-StL 2.5

Total Pitcher Index
Newhouser-Det 6.4
Trout-Det 5.5
Chandler-NY 4.8
Feller-Cle 4.5
Bevens-NY 2.8

Total Baseball Ranking
Williams-Bos 8.2
Newhouser-Det 6.4
Trout-Det 5.5
Doerr-Bos 5.0
Chandler-NY 4.8

TEAM	G	W	L	PCT	GB	R	OR	AB	H	2B	3B	HR	BB	SO	AVG	OBP	SLG	PRO	PRO+	BR	/A	PF	CHI	RC	SB	CS	SBA	SBR
BRO	155	94	60	.610		774	668	5249	1428	241	50	83	732	561	.272	.364	.384	.748	102	62	34	104	98	781	88			
STL	156	89	65	.578	5	780	634	5422	1462	235	65	115	612	511	.270	.347	.401	.748	100	41	9	104	102	762	28			
BOS	154	86	68	.558	8	701	622	5253	1444	265	42	85	558	500	.275	.346	.390	.736	104	19	35	98	97	717	58			
NY	155	81	73	.526	13	830	761	5343	1446	220	48	221	494	568	.271	.335	.454	.789	114	95	90	101	104	809	29			
CIN	154	73	81	.474	21	681	755	5299	1372	242	43	95	539	530	.259	.330	.375	.705	94	-47	-42	99	103	672	46			
CHI	155	69	85	.448	25	567	722	5305	1373	231	48	71	471	578	.259	.321	.361	.682	90	-92	-64	96	94	620	22			
PIT	156	62	92	.403	32	744	817	5307	1385	216	44	156	607	687	.261	.340	.406	.746	102	31	11	103	100	738	30			
PHI	155	62	92	.403	32	589	687	5256	1354	210	52	60	464	594	.258	.321	.352	.673	88	-107	-81	96	101	597	60			
TOT	620					5666		42434	11264	1860	392	886	4477	4529	.265	.338	.390	.729							361			

TEAM	CG	SH	SV	IP	H	H/G	HR	BB	SO	RAT	ERA	ERA+	OAV	OOB	PR	/A	PF	CPI	FA	E	DP	FW	PW	BW	SBW	DIF
BRO	47	14	34	1375	1299	8.5	104	626	592	12.8	3.82	108	.251	.335	37	48	102	100	.978	129	169	.9	4.7	3.3		8.0
STL	65	12	20	1397²	1417	9.1	106	495	642	12.4	3.53	117	.265	.330	82	93	102	110	.979	128	169	1.1	9.1	.9		.9
BOS	74	14	13	1362²	1342	8.9	93	453	494	11.9	3.62	108	.255	.316	66	41	96	95	.974	153	124	-.6	-5.4	8.9		1.2
NY	58	6	14	1363²	1428	9.4	122	590	553	13.4	4.44	92	.266	.341	-57	-55	100	94	.977	138	136	.3	-4.5	-4.1		4.3
CIN	54	13	13	1365¹	1442	9.5	102	589	633	13.5	4.41	93	.273	.348	-53	-46	101	98	.977	138	134	.3	-4.5	-4.1		4.3
CHI	46	8	15	1367	1449	9.5	106	618	571	13.7	4.04	98	.274	.352	3	-12	97	109	.975	150	159	-.4	-1.2	-6.3		-.2
PIT	44	9	13	1374	1488	9.7	155	592	530	13.9	4.68	90	.277	.353	-95	-70	104	101	.975	149	131	-.2	-6.9	1.1		-9.0
PHI	70	8	14	1362	1399	9.2	98	513	514	12.8	3.96	101	.276	.345	15	7	99	108	.974	152	140	-.5	.7	-8.0		-7.2
TOT	458	84	136	10967¹		9.2				13.1	4.06		.265	.338					.976	1154	1162					

Runs		Hits		Doubles		Triples		Home Runs		Total Bases	
Mize-NY	137	Holmes-Bos	191	Miller-Cin	38	Walker-StL-Phi	16	Mize-NY	51	Kiner-Pit	361
Robinson-Bro	125	Walker-StL-Phi	186	R.Elliott-Bos	35	Slaughter-StL	13	Kiner-Pit	51	Mize-NY	360
Kiner-Pit	118	Musial-StL	183	Ryan-Bos	33	Musial-StL	13	Marshall-NY	36	Marshall-NY	310
Musial-StL	113	Gustine-Pit	183	Holmes-Bos	33	Schoendienst-StL	9	W.Cooper-NY	35	W.Cooper-NY	302
Kurowski-StL	108	Baumholtz-Cin	182	Baumholtz-Cin	32	Baumholtz-Cin	9	Thomson-NY	29	Musial-StL	296

Runs Batted In		Runs Produced		Bases On Balls		Batting Average		On Base Percentage		Slugging Average	
Mize-NY	138	Mize-NY	224	Reese-Bro	104	Walker-StL-Phi	.363	Galan-Cin	.449	Kiner-Pit	.639
Kiner-Pit	127	Kiner-Pit	194	Greenberg-Pit	104	R.Elliott-Bos	.317	Walker-StL-Phi	.436	Mize-NY	.614
W.Cooper-NY	122	Musial-StL	189	Stanky-Bro	103	Galan-Cin	.314	Kurowski-StL	.420	W.Cooper-NY	.586
R.Elliott-Bos	113	Kurowski-StL	185	Kiner-Pit	98	Cavarretta-Chi	.314	Kiner-Pit	.417	Kurowski-StL	.544
Marshall-NY	107	R.Elliott-Bos	184	Walker-Bro	97	Kiner-Pit	.313	Walker-Bro	.415	Marshall-NY	.528

Production		Adjusted Production		Batter Runs		Adjusted Batter Runs		Clutch Hitting Index		Runs Created	
Kiner-Pit	1.055	Kiner-Pit	172	Kiner-Pit	61.4	Kiner-Pit	59.1	Walker-Bro	146	Kiner-Pit	154
Mize-NY	.998	Mize-NY	160	Mize-NY	48.3	Mize-NY	47.8	Marion-StL	138	Mize-NY	143
Kurowski-StL	.964	Walker-StL-Phi	150	Kurowski-StL	41.8	R.Elliott-Bos	38.6	Haas-Cin	135	R.Elliott-Bos	120
R.Elliott-Bos	.927	R.Elliott-Bos	148	R.Elliott-Bos	36.8	Kurowski-StL	38.5	Edwards-Bro	135	Kurowski-StL	118
W.Cooper-NY	.926	Kurowski-StL	148	Walker-StL-Phi	35.4	Walker-StL-Phi	37.6	Cavarretta-Chi	131	Musial-StL	118

Total Average		Stolen Bases		Stolen Base Average		Stolen Base Runs		Fielding Runs		Total Player Rating	
Kiner-Pit	1.155	Robinson-Bro	29					Marion-StL	20.1	Kiner-Pit	6.0
Mize-NY	1.060	Reiser-Bro	14					Verban-Phi	16.9	Mize-NY	4.5
Kurowski-StL	1.019	Walker-StL-Phi	13					Gustine-Pit	14.8	Walker-StL-Phi	4.1
Walker-StL-Phi	.979	Hopp-Bos	13					Russell-Pit	14.1	R.Elliott-Bos	3.1
Torgeson-Bos	.973	Torgeson-Bos	11					Kerr-NY	12.1	Reese-Bro	2.6

Wins		Win Percentage		Games		Complete Games		Shutouts		Saves	
Blackwell-Cin	22	Jansen-NY	.808	Trinkle-NY	62	Blackwell-Cin	23	Spahn-Bos	7	Casey-Bro	18
Spahn-Bos	21	Munger-StL	.762	Higbe-Bro-Pit	50	Spahn-Bos	22	Munger-StL	6	Trinkle-NY	10
Sain-Bos	21	Blackwell-Cin	.733	Behrman-Bro-Pit	50	Sain-Bos	22	Blackwell-Cin	6	Gumbert-Cin	10
Jansen-NY	21	Hatten-Bro	.680	Kush-Chi	47	Jansen-NY	20	Dickson-StL	4	Behrman-Bro-Pit	8
Branca-Bro	21	Spahn-Bos	.677	Dickson-StL	47	Leonard-Phi	19	Branca-Bro	4		

Innings Pitched		Fewest Hits/Game		Fewest BB/Game		Strikeouts		Strikeouts/Game		Ratio	
Spahn-Bos	289.2	Taylor-Bro	7.22	Jansen-NY	2.07	Blackwell-Cin	193	Blackwell-Cin	6.36	Spahn-Bos	10.25
Branca-Bro	280.0	Blackwell-Cin	7.48	Rowe-Phi	2.07	Branca-Bro	148	Munger-StL	4.93	Blackwell-Cin	10.75
Blackwell-Cin	273.0	Spahn-Bos	7.61	Leonard-Phi	2.18	Sain-Bos	132	Branca-Bro	4.76	Leonard-Phi	10.84
Sain-Bos	266.0	Lombardi-Bro	8.04	Barrett-Bos	2.26	Spahn-Bos	123	Brazle-StL	4.55	Jansen-NY	10.85
Jansen-NY	248.0	Branca-Bro	8.07	Brazle-StL	2.57	Munger-StL	123	Sain-Bos	4.47	Barrett-Bos	10.89

Earned Run Average		Adjusted ERA		Opponents' Batting Avg.		Opponents' On Base Pct.		Starter Runs		Adjusted Starter Runs	
Spahn-Bos	2.33	Spahn-Bos	167	Taylor-Bro	.225	Spahn-Bos	.283	Spahn-Bos	55.7	Spahn-Bos	50.3
Blackwell-Cin	2.47	Blackwell-Cin	166	Spahn-Bos	.226	Barrett-Bos	.292	Blackwell-Cin	48.2	Blackwell-Cin	49.5
Branca-Bro	2.67	Branca-Bro	155	Blackwell-Cin	.234	Blackwell-Cin	.304	Branca-Bro	43.3	Branca-Bro	45.6
Leonard-Phi	2.68	Leonard-Phi	149	Branca-Bro	.240	Leonard-Phi	.306	Leonard-Phi	36.0	Leonard-Phi	34.6
Brazle-StL	2.84	Brazle-StL	146	Lombardi-Bro	.241	Jansen-NY	.306	Dickson-StL	25.5	Dickson-StL	27.4

Clutch Pitching Index		Relief Runs		Adjusted Relief Runs		Relief Ranking		Total Pitcher Index		Total Baseball Ranking	
Brazle-StL	139	Lanfranconi-Bos	7.9	Lanfranconi-Bos	6.7	Lanfranconi-Bos	7.8	Blackwell-Cin	5.2	Kiner-Pit	6.0
Leonard-Phi	123	Kush-Chi	7.1	Kush-Chi	5.9	Kush-Chi	7.2	Spahn-Bos	5.1	Blackwell-Cin	5.2
Branca-Bro	122	Trinkle-NY	3.3	Trinkle-NY	3.4	Gumbert-Cin	4.9	Branca-Bro	4.0	Spahn-Bos	5.1
Blackwell-Cin	115	Gumbert-Cin	1.8	Gumbert-Cin	2.2	Trinkle-NY	4.7	Leonard-Phi	3.8	Mize-NY	4.5
Jansen-NY	114	Casey-Bro	.6	Casey-Bro	1.2	Casey-Bro	2.6	Dickson-StL	3.0	Walker-StL-Phi	4.1

TEAM	G	W	L	PCT	GB	R	OR	AB	H	2B	3B	HR	BB	SO	AVG	OBP	SLG	PRO	PRO+	BR	/A	PF	CHI	RC	SB	CS	SBA	SBR
NY	155	97	57	.630		794	568	5308	1439	230	72	115	610	581	.271	.349	.407	.756	117	110	116	99	104	780	27	23	35	-13
DET	158	85	69	.552	12	714	642	5276	1363	234	42	103	762	565	.258	.353	.377	.730	105	77	57	103	96	735	52	60	63	-19
BOS	157	83	71	.539	14	720	669	5322	1412	206	54	103	666	590	.265	.349	.382	.731	102	71	22	107	98	734	41	35	36	-10
CLE	157	80	74	.519	17	687	588	5367	1392	234	51	112	502	609	.259	.324	.385	.709	105	9	26	97	105	687	29	25	41	-16
PHI	156	78	76	.506	19	633	614	5198	1311	218	52	61	605	563	.252	.333	.349	.682	94	-23	-35	102	101	635	37	33	45	-16
CHI	155	70	84	.455	27	553	661	5274	1350	211	41	53	492	527	.256	.321	.342	.663	93	-68	-44	96	98	584	91	57	56	-16
WAS	154	64	90	.416	33	496	675	5112	1234	186	48	42	525	534	.241	.313	.321	.634	84	-116	-99	97	98	523	53	51	48	-13
STL	154	59	95	.383	38	564	744	5145	1238	189	52	90	583	664	.241	.320	.350	.670	90	-54	-65	102	98	596	69	49	51	-15
TOT	623					5161		42002	10739	1708	412	679	4745	4633	.256	.333	.364	.698							399	333	55	-79

TEAM	CG	SH	SV	IP	H	H/G	HR	BB	SO	RAT	ERA	ERA+	OAV	OOB	PR	/A	PF	CPI	FA	E	DP	FW	PW	BW	SBW	DIF
NY	73	14	21	1374¹	1221	8.0	95	628	691	12.2	3.39	104	.237	.323	47	21	95	100	.981	109	151	1.5	2.2	12.0	-.3	4.6
DET	77	15	18	1398²	1382	8.9	79	531	648	12.4	3.57	106	.257	.326	20	30	102	100	.975	155	142	-1.0	3.1	5.9	-.9	.9
BOS	64	13	19	1391¹	1383	8.9	84	575	632	12.8	3.81	102	.261	.335	-16	11	105	100	.977	137	172	-.0	1.1	2.3	.0	2.6
CLE	55	13	29	1402¹	1244	8.0	94	628	590	12.2	3.44	101	.240	.325	41	6	94	100	.983	104	178	1.9	.6	2.7	-.6	-1.6
PHI	70	12	15	1391¹	1291	8.4	85	597	493	12.3	3.51	109	.247	.326	29	46	103	99	.976	143	161	-.4	4.8	-3.6	-.6	.9
CHI	47	11	27	1391	1384	9.0	76	603	522	13.0	3.64	100	.261	.339	10	2	99	105	.975	155	180	-1.2	.2	-4.6	-.6	-.9
WAS	67	15	12	1362	1408	9.3	63	579	551	13.2	3.97	94	.267	.341	-40	-37	101	98	.976	143	151	-.5	-3.8	-10.3	-.3	1.9
STL	50	7	13	1365	1426	9.4	103	604	552	13.4	4.33	90	.271	.347	-94	-67	105	98	.977	134	169	.0	-6.9	-6.7	-.5	-3.8
TOT	503	100	154	11076		8.7				12.7	3.71		.256	.333					.977	1080	1304					

Runs
Williams-Bos 125
Henrich-NY 109
Pesky-Bos 106
Stirnweiss-NY 102
DiMaggio-NY 97

Hits
Pesky-Bos 207
Kell-Det 188
Williams-Bos 181
McCosky-Phi 179

Doubles
Boudreau-Cle 45
Williams-Bos 40
Henrich-NY 35
DiMaggio-NY 31

Triples
Henrich-NY 13
Vernon-Was 12
Philley-Chi 11

Home Runs
Williams-Bos 32
Gordon-Cle 29
Heath-StL 27
Cullenbine-Det.... 24
York-Bos-Chi 21

Total Bases
Williams-Bos 335
Gordon-Cle 279
DiMaggio-NY 279
Henrich-NY 267
Pesky-Bos 250

Runs Batted In
Williams-Bos 114
Henrich-NY 98
DiMaggio-NY 97
Jones-Chi-Bos 96

Runs Produced
Williams-Bos 207
Henrich-NY 191
DiMaggio-NY 174
Kell-Det 163
Doerr-Bos 157

Bases On Balls
Williams-Bos 162
Cullenbine-Det.... 137
Lake-Det 120
Joost-Phi 114
Fain-Phi 95

Batting Average
Williams-Bos 343
McCosky-Phi 328
Pesky-Bos 324
Kell-Det 320
Mitchell-Cle 316

On Base Percentage
Williams-Bos 499
Fain-Phi 414
Cullenbine-Det.....401
McCosky-Phi 395
McQuinn-NY 395

Slugging Average
Williams-Bos 634
DiMaggio-NY 522
Gordon-Cle 496
Henrich-NY 485
Heath-StL 485

Production
Williams-Bos 1.133
DiMaggio-NY 913
Henrich-NY 857
Heath-StL.........850
Gordon-Cle 842

Adjusted Production
Williams-Bos 199
DiMaggio-NY 154
Henrich-NY 139
Gordon-Cle 136
Heath-StL........ 133

Batter Runs
Williams-Bos 91.1
DiMaggio-NY 36.5
Henrich-NY 26.4
Fain-Phi 24.7
Cullenbine-Det... 23.9

Adjusted Batter Runs
Williams-Bos 85.5
DiMaggio-NY 37.2
Henrich-NY 27.1
McQuinn-NY 24.0
Fain-Phi 23.5

Clutch Hitting Index
W.Johnson-NY ... 151
Kell-Det 141
Vernon-Was 130
Jones-Chi-Bos ... 129
Chapman-Phi..... 129

Runs Created
Williams-Bos 186
DiMaggio-NY 112
Henrich-NY 104
Pesky-Bos 103
McQuinn-NY 97

Total Average
Williams-Bos 1.391
DiMaggio-NY 918
Cullenbine-Det.....898
Heath-StL.........856
Henrich-NY 849

Stolen Bases
Dillinger-StL 34
Philley-Chi 21
Vernon-Was 12
Pesky-Bos 12

Stolen Base Average
Dillinger-StL 72.3
Philley-Chi 56.8

Stolen Base Runs
Dillinger-StL 2.4
Valo-Phi 1.5
Binks-Phi 1.2

Fielding Runs
Doerr-Bos 23.8
Baker-Chi 18.3
Kell-Det 17.9
Boudreau-Cle 16.7
Rizzuto-NY 16.4

Total Player Rating
Williams-Bos 8.2
Boudreau-Cle 3.9
Cullenbine-Det.... 3.5
DiMaggio-NY 3.5
Kell-Det 3.4

Wins
Feller-Cle 20
Reynolds-NY 19
Marchildon-Phi 19
Hutchinson-Det 18
Dobson-Bos 18

Win Percentage
Reynolds-NY 704
Dobson-Bos 692
Marchildon-Phi ...679
Feller-Cle 645
Hutchinson-Det....643

Games
Klieman-Cle 58
Page-NY 56
Johnson-Bos 45
Savage-Phi 44
Christopher-Phi.... 44

Complete Games
Newhouser-Det ... 24
Wynn-Was 22
Lopat-Chi 22
Marchildon-Phi ... 21
Feller-Cle 20

Shutouts
Feller-Cle 5
Reynolds-NY 4
Masterson-Was 4
Haefner-Was 4

Saves
Page-NY.......... 17
Klieman-Cle 17
Christopher-Phi ... 12
Ferrick-Was 9

Innings Pitched
Feller-Cle 299.0
Newhouser-Det ... 285.0
Marchildon-Phi .. 276.2
Masterson-Was ... 253.0
Lopat-Chi 252.2

Fewest Hits/Game
Shea-NY 6.40
Feller-Cle 6.92
Marchildon-Phi .. 7.42
Embree-Cle 7.58
Masterson-Was ... 7.65

Fewest BB/Game
Galehouse-StL-Bos 2.48
Hutchinson-Det ... 2.50
Lopat-Chi 2.60
Muncrief-StL 2.60
Dobson-Bos 2.87

Strikeouts
Feller-Cle 196
Newhouser-Det ... 176
Masterson-Was ... 135
Reynolds-NY 129
Marchildon-Phi ... 128

Strikeouts/Game
Feller-Cle 5.90
Hughson-Bos 5.66
Newhouser-Det ... 5.56
Trucks-Det 5.38
Kinder-StL 5.09

Ratio
Feller-Cle 10.87
Dobson-Bos 10.90
Shea-NY 11.08
Masterson-Was .. 11.17
Hutchinson-Det .. 11.23

Earned Run Average
Haynes-Chi 2.42
Feller-Cle 2.68
Fowler-Phi 2.81
Lopat-Chi 2.81
Newhouser-Det ... 2.87

Adjusted ERA
Haynes-Chi 151
Fowler-Phi 136
Dobson-Bos 132
Newhouser-Det ... 131
Feller-Cle 130

Opponents' Batting Avg.
Shea-NY..........200
Feller-Cle 215
Marchildon-Phi 224
Reynolds-NY 227
Embree-Cle 233

Opponents' On Base Pct.
Dobson-Bos 299
Feller-Cle 300
Shea-NY..........303
Hutchinson-Det ...304
Lopat-Chi 307

Starter Runs
Feller-Cle 34.1
Newhouser-Det ... 26.3
Haynes-Chi 25.9
Lopat-Chi 25.0
Fowler-Phi 22.6

Adjusted Starter Runs
Newhouser-Det ... 28.3
Feller-Cle 26.7
Fowler-Phi 25.3
Haynes-Chi 24.9
Dobson-Bos 23.8

Clutch Pitching Index
Haynes-Chi 124
Fowler-Phi 119
Lopat-Chi 116
Ferriss-Bos 114
Newsom-Was-NY . 112

Relief Runs
Page-NY 19.2
Christopher-Phi ... 7.2
Klieman-Cle 6.9
Murphy-Bos 5.5
Ferrick-Was 3.7

Adjusted Relief Runs
Page-NY 16.5
Christopher-Phi ... 8.2
Murphy-Bos 6.6
Klieman-Cle 4.6
Ferrick-Was 3.8

Relief Ranking
Page-NY 27.6
Christopher-Phi .. 18.2
Klieman-Cle 6.0
Ferrick-Was 5.9
Maltzberger-Chi ... 1.6

Total Pitcher Index
Newhouser-Det ... 3.6
Hutchinson-Det ... 3.4
Feller-Cle 3.1
Haynes-Chi 3.0
Dobson-Bos 2.5

Total Baseball Ranking
Williams-Bos 8.2
Boudreau-Cle 3.9
Newhouser-Det ... 3.6
Cullenbine-Det.... 3.5
DiMaggio-NY 3.5

TEAM	G	W	L	PCT	GB	R	OR	AB	H	2B	3B	HR	BB	SO	AVG	OBP	SLG	PRO	PRO+	BR	/A	PF	CHI	RC	SB	CS	SBA	SBR
BOS	154	91	62	.595		739	**584**	5297	**1458**	**272**	49	95	671	536	**.275**	**.359**	.399	**.758**	113	95	107	98	92	**784**	43			
STL	155	85	69	.552	6.5	742	646	5302	1396	238	**58**	105	594	521	.263	.340	.389	.729	98	31	-8	106	103	713	24			
BRO	155	84	70	.545	7.5	744	667	5328	1393	256	54	91	601	684	.261	.338	.381	.719	97	13	-10	103	105	709	**114**			
PIT	156	83	71	.539	8.5	706	699	5286	1388	191	54	108	580	578	.263	.338	.380	.718	99	10	-3	102	101	698	68			
NY	155	78	76	.506	13.5	**780**	704	5277	1352	210	49	**164**	599	648	.256	.334	**.408**	.742	106	46	41	101	**106**	731	51			
PHI	155	66	88	.429	25.5	591	729	5287	1367	227	39	91	440	598	.259	.318	.368	.686	93	-62	-49	98	97	625	68			
CIN	153	64	89	.418	27	588	752	5127	1266	221	37	104	478	586	.247	.313	.365	.678	92	-75	-52	97	101	587	42			
CHI	155	64	90	.416	27.5	597	706	5352	1402	225	44	87	443	578	.262	.322	.369	.691	96	-51	-23	96	95	641	39			
TOT	619					5487		42256	11022	1840	384	845	4406	4729	.261	.333	.383	.715							449			

TEAM	CG	SH	SV	IP	H	H/G	HR	BB	SO	RAT	ERA	ERA+	OAV	OOB	PR	/A	PF	CPI	FA	E	DP	FW	PW	BW	SBW	DIF
BOS	**70**	10	17	1389[1]	1354	8.8	93	**430**	579	11.6	**3.37**	114	**.249**	.305	89	70	97	96	.976	143	132	.7	7.0	10.7		-3.9
STL	60	13	18	1368	1392	9.2	103	476	625	12.4	3.91	105	.261	.323	7	27	103	97	**.980**	119	138	2.1	2.7	-.8		4.0
BRO	52	9	**22**	1392[2]	**1328**	8.6	119	633	670	12.9	3.75	106	.253	.337	30	36	101	107	.973	161	151	-.2	3.6	-1.0		4.6
PIT	65	5	19	1371[2]	1373	9.0	120	564	543	12.9	4.15	98	.260	.334	-29	-12	103	98	.977	137	150	1.2	-1.2	-.3		6.3
NY	54	**15**	21	1373	1425	9.3	122	556	527	13.2	3.93	100	.269	.341	4	0	100	**109**	.974	156	134	.1	.0	4.1		-3.2
PHI	61	6	15	1362[1]	1385	9.1	95	556	550	13.0	4.08	97	.262	.334	-18	-20	100	97	.964	210	126	-2.8	-2.0	-4.9		-1.3
CIN	40	8	20	1343[1]	1410	9.4	104	572	599	13.4	4.47	87	.269	.343	-76	-85	99	95	.973	158	135	-.1	-8.5	-5.2		1.3
CHI	51	7	10	1355[1]	1355	9.0	**89**	619	636	13.2	4.00	97	.261	.342	-7	-15	99	101	.972	172	**152**	-.7	-1.5	-2.3		-8.5
TOT	453	73	142	10955[2]		9.1				12.8	3.95		.261	.333					.974	1256	1118					

Runs	Hits	Doubles	Triples	Home Runs	Total Bases
Musial-StL 135	Musial-StL 230	Musial-StL 46	Musial-StL 18	Mize-NY 40	Musial-StL 429
Lockman-NY 117	Holmes-Bos 190	Ennis-Phi 40	Hopp-Pit 12	Kiner-Pit 40	Mize-NY 316
Mize-NY 110	Rojek-Pit 186	Dark-Bos 39	Slaughter-StL 11	Musial-StL 39	Ennis-Phi 309
Robinson-Bro ... 108	Slaughter-StL 176	Robinson-Bro 38	Waitkus-Chi 10	Sauer-Cin 35	Kiner-Pit 296
Kiner-Pit 104	Dark-Bos 175	Holmes-Bos 35	Lockman-NY 10		Pafko-Chi 283

Runs Batted In	Runs Produced	Bases On Balls	Batting Average	On Base Percentage	Slugging Average
Musial-StL 131	Musial-StL 227	R.Elliott-Bos ... 131	Musial-StL 376	Musial-StL 450	Musial-StL 702
Mize-NY 125	Mize-NY 195	Kiner-Pit 112	Ashburn-Phi 333	R.Elliott-Bos 423	Mize-NY 564
Kiner-Pit 123	Kiner-Pit 187	Mize-NY 94	Holmes-Bos 325	Ashburn-Phi......410	Gordon-NY 537
Gordon-NY 107	Robinson-Bro 181		Dark-Bos 322	Slaughter-StL 409	Kiner-Pit 533
Pafko-Chi 101	Gordon-NY 177		Slaughter-StL 321	Mize-NY 395	Ennis-Phi 525

Production	Adjusted Production	Batter Runs	Adjusted Batter Runs	Clutch Hitting Index	Runs Created
Musial-StL 1.152	Musial-StL 196	Musial-StL 90.2	Musial-StL 85.7	Murtaugh-Pit 146	Musial-StL 191
Mize-NY 959	Mize-NY 156	Mize-NY 44.6	Mize-NY 44.1	Jones-StL 140	Mize-NY 131
Gordon-NY 927	Gordon-NY 148	Kiner-Pit 38.5	R.Elliott-Bos 39.1	Stallcup-Cin 139	Kiner-Pit 120
Kiner-Pit 924	Kiner-Pit 145	R.Elliott-Bos 37.8	Kiner-Pit 37.0	Lowrey-Chi 128	R.Elliott-Bos 117
R.Elliott-Bos 897	R.Elliott-Bos 145	Gordon-NY 35.1	Gordon-NY 34.6	Marshall-NY 128	Slaughter-StL 110

Total Average	Stolen Bases	Stolen Base Average	Stolen Base Runs	Fielding Runs	Total Player Rating
Musial-StL 1.298	Ashburn-Phi....... 32			Pafko-Chi........ 12.8	Musial-StL 7.7
Mize-NY 1.032	Reese-Bro 25			Ashburn-Phi...... 12.6	Mize-NY 4.6
R.Elliott-Bos 980	Rojek-Pit 24			Reese-Bro 10.3	Pafko-Chi 4.0
Kiner-Pit 974	Robinson-Bro 22			Marion-StL........ 9.4	Reese-Bro 2.8
Gordon-NY 953	Torgeson-Bos 19			Thomson-NY 9.2	Stanky-Bos 2.7

Wins	Win Percentage	Games	Complete Games	Shutouts	Saves
Sain-Bos 24	Brecheen-StL 741	Gumbert-Cin 61	Sain-Bos 28	Brecheen-StL 7	Gumbert-Cin 17
Brecheen-StL ... 20	Jones-StL 667	Wilks-StL 57	Brecheen-StL 21	Sain-Bos 4	Wilks-StL 13
Schmitz-Chi ... 18	Sain-Bos 615	Higbe-Pit 56	Schmitz-Chi 18	Raffensberger-Cin .. 4	Higbe-Pit 10
Jansen-NY 18	Jansen-NY 600	Jones-NY 55	Spahn-Bos 16	Jansen-NY 4	Trinkle-NY 7
VanderMeer-Cin ... 17	Schmitz-Chi 581	Dobernic-Chi 54	Leonard-Phi 16	Barney-Bro 4	Behrman-Bro....... 7

Innings Pitched	Fewest Hits/Game	Fewest BB/Game	Strikeouts	Strikeouts/Game	Ratio
Sain-Bos 314.2	Schmitz-Chi 6.92	Roe-Bro 1.67	Brecheen-StL 149	Brecheen-StL 5.75	Brecheen-StL 9.41
Jansen-NY 277.0	Barney-Bro 7.04	Jansen-NY 1.75	Barney-Bro 138	Branca-Bro 5.09	Roe-Bro 9.68
Spahn-Bos...... 257.0	Brecheen-StL 7.44	Raffensberger-Cin 1.85	Sain-Bos 137	Barney-Bro 5.04	Schmitz-Chi 10.60
Dickson-StL 252.1	Branca-Bro 7.89	Brecheen-StL 1.89	Jansen-NY 126	Higbe-Pit 4.90	Sain-Bos 11.01
Barney-Bro 246.2	Roe-Bro 7.90	Leonard-Phi...... 2.15	Branca-Bro 122	Meyer-Chi 4.86	Spahn-Bos...... 11.03

Earned Run Average	Adjusted ERA	Opponents' Batting Avg.	Opponents' On Base Pct.	Starter Runs	Adjusted Starter Runs
Brecheen-StL 2.24	Brecheen-StL 183	Schmitz-Chi 215	Brecheen-StL 265	Sain-Bos 47.3	Brecheen-StL 48.0
Leonard-Phi 2.51	Leonard-Phi 157	Barney-Bro 217	Roe-Bro 271	Brecheen-StL 44.5	Sain-Bos 43.0
Sain-Bos 2.60	Roe-Bro 152	Brecheen-StL 222	Schmitz-Chi 295	Leonard-Phi 36.2	Leonard-Phi...... 35.9
Roe-Bro 2.63	Schmitz-Chi 148	Branca-Bro 232	Sain-Bos 296	Schmitz-Chi 35.3	Schmitz-Chi 34.0
Schmitz-Chi 2.64	Sain-Bos 147	Roe-Bro 233	Raffensberger-Cin .296	Roe-Bro 26.1	Roe-Bro 26.8

Clutch Pitching Index	Relief Runs	Adjusted Relief Runs	Relief Ranking	Total Pitcher Index	Total Baseball Ranking
Leonard-Phi 134	Wilks-StL 19.4	Wilks-StL 21.4	Wilks-StL 22.4	Brecheen-StL 5.2	Musial-StL 7.7
Jones-NY 126	Hansen-NY 10.9	Higbe-Pit 12.4	Higbe-Pit 12.4	Sain-Bos 4.6	Brecheen-StL 5.2
Hatten-Bro 124	Minner-Bro 10.5	Minner-Bro 10.8	Minner-Bro 11.3	Schmitz-Chi 3.9	Sain-Bos 4.6
Voiselle-Bos 120	Higbe-Pit 10.4	Hansen-NY 10.7	Gumbert-Cin 9.7	Leonard-Phi...... 3.9	Mize-NY 4.6
Sain-Bos 115	Dobernic-Chi 7.6	Dobernic-Chi 7.2	Trinkle-NY 8.1	Roe-Bro 2.5	Pafko-Chi 4.0

TEAM	G	W	L	PCT	GB	R	OR	AB	H	2B	3B	HR	BB	SO	AVG	OBP	SLG	PRO	PRO+	BR	/A	PF	CHI	RC	SB	CS	SBA	SBR
CLE	156	97	58	.626		840	568	5446	1534	242	54	155	646	575	.282	.360	.431	.791	119	112	131	97	97	868	54	44	46	-13
BOS	155	96	59	.619	1	907	720	5363	1471	277	40	121	823	552	.274	.374	.409	.783	108	116	78	105	104	869	38	17	27	-10
NY	154	94	60	.610	2.5	857	633	5324	1480	251	75	139	623	478	.278	.356	.432	.788	116	99	106	99	103	838	24	24	47	-20
PHI	154	84	70	.545	12.5	729	735	5181	1345	231	47	68	726	523	.260	.353	.362	.715	95	-19	-20	100	102	699	40	32	41	-14
DET	154	78	76	.506	18.5	700	726	5235	1396	219	58	78	671	504	.267	.353	.375	.728	96	0	-19	103	95	723	22	32	44	-16
STL	155	59	94	.386	37	671	849	5303	1438	251	62	63	578	572	.271	.345	.378	.723	95	-20	-38	103	95	711	63	44	50	-16
WAS	154	56	97	.366	40	578	796	5111	1245	203	75	31	568	572	.244	.322	.331	.653	81	-150	-129	97	105	566	76	48	49	-14
CHI	154	51	101	.336	44.5	559	814	5192	1303	172	39	55	595	528	.251	.329	.331	.660	83	-133	-108	97	97	588	46	47	49	-14
TOT	618					5841		42155	11212	1846	450	710	5230	4304	.266	.349	.382	.731							363	288	56	-63

TEAM	CG	SH	SV	IP	H	H/G	HR	BB	SO	RAT	ERA	ERA+	OAV	OOB	PR	/A	PF	CPI	FA	E	DP	FW	PW	BW	SBW	DIF
CLE	66	26	30	1409¹	1246	8.0	82	628	595	12.1	3.22	126	.239	.323	166	130	95	108	.982	114	183	1.4	12.6	12.7	-.5	-6.7
BOS	70	11	13	1379¹	1445	9.4	83	592	513	13.4	4.26	103	.269	.344	4	20	102	99	.981	116	174	1.2	1.9	7.6	-.2	8.0
NY	62	16	24	1365²	1289	8.5	94	641	654	12.9	3.75	109	.250	.336	81	50	95	104	.979	120	161	.9	4.8	10.3	-1.2	2.1
PHI	74	7	18	1368²	1456	9.6	86	638	486	13.9	4.43	97	.275	.354	-20	-20	100	101	.981	113	180	1.3	-1.9	-1.9	-.6	10.1
DET	60	5	22	1377	1367	8.9	92	589	678	12.9	4.15	105	.258	.334	21	33	102	95	.974	155	143	-.9	3.2	-1.8	-.8	1.4
STL	35	4	20	1373¹	1513	9.9	103	737	531	14.9	5.01	91	.281	.370	-109	-68	106	99	.972	168	190	-1.6	-6.6	-3.7	-.8	-4.9
WAS	42	4	22	1357¹	1439	9.5	81	734	446	14.6	4.65	93	.272	.364	-55	-46	101	99	.974	154	144	-.9	-4.5	-12.5	-.6	-2.1
CHI	35	2	23	1345²	1454	9.7	89	673	403	14.4	4.89	87	.279	.365	-89	-93	99	97	.974	160	176	-1.2	-9.0	-10.5	-.6	-3.7
TOT	444	75	172	10976¹		9.2				13.6	4.29		.266	.349					.977	1100	1351					

Runs
Henrich-NY 138
DiMaggio-Bos 127
Williams-Bos ... 124
Pesky-Bos 124
Boudreau-Cle ... 116

Hits
Dillinger-StL 207
Mitchell-Cle 204
Boudreau-Cle 199
DiMaggio-NY 190
Williams-Bos 188

Doubles
Williams-Bos 44
Henrich-NY 42
Majeski-Phi 41
Priddy-StL 40
DiMaggio-Bos 40

Triples
Henrich-NY 14
Stewart-NY-Was ... 13
Yost-Was 11
Mullin-Det 11
DiMaggio-NY 11

Home Runs
DiMaggio-NY 39
Gordon-Cle 32
Keltner-Cle 31
Stephens-Bos 29
Doerr-Bos 27

Total Bases
DiMaggio-NY 355
Henrich-NY 326
Williams-Bos 313
Stephens-Bos 299
Boudreau-Cle 299

Runs Batted In
DiMaggio-NY 155
Stephens-Bos 137
Williams-Bos 127
Gordon-Cle 124
Majeski-Phi 120

Runs Produced
Williams-Bos 226
DiMaggio-NY 226
Stephens-Bos 222
Henrich-NY 213
DiMaggio-Bos 205

Bases On Balls
Williams-Bos 126
Joost-Phi 119
Fain-Phi 113
DiMaggio-Bos 101
Pesky-Bos 99

Batting Average
Williams-Bos 369
Boudreau-Cle 355
Mitchell-Cle 336
Zarilla-StL 329
McCosky-Phi.....326

On Base Percentage
Williams-Bos 497
Boudreau-Cle 453
Appling-Chi 423
Goodman-Bos 414
Fain-Phi 412

Slugging Average
Williams-Bos 615
DiMaggio-NY 598
Henrich-NY 554
Boudreau-Cle 534
Keltner-Cle........522

Production
Williams-Bos 1.112
DiMaggio-NY 994
Boudreau-Cle 987
Henrich-NY 945
Keltner-Cle........917

Adjusted Production
Williams-Bos 185
Boudreau-Cle 166
DiMaggio-NY 164
Henrich-NY 151
Keltner-Cle....... 146

Batter Runs
Williams-Bos 75.7
Boudreau-Cle 52.7
DiMaggio-NY 48.6
Henrich-NY 38.9
Keltner-Cle....... 33.0

Adjusted Batter Runs
Williams-Bos 71.8
Boudreau-Cle 54.8
DiMaggio-NY 49.4
Henrich-NY 39.7
Keltner-Cle....... 35.1

Clutch Hitting Index
Majeski-Phi 141
Fain-Phi 139
Platt-StL 136
Evers-Det 134
Goodman-Bos.... 130

Runs Created
Williams-Bos 172
Boudreau-Cle 143
DiMaggio-NY 140
Henrich-NY 130
Keltner-Cle....... 116

Total Average
Williams-Bos 1.347
Boudreau-Cle ... 1.058
DiMaggio-NY ... 1.012
Henrich-NY 955
Keltner-Cle........918

Stolen Bases
Dillinger-StL 28
Coan-Was 23
Vernon-Was 15
Mitchell-Cle 13

Stolen Base Average
Coan-Was 71.9
Dillinger-StL 71.8

Stolen Base Runs
Robertson-Was 2.4
Tucker-Cle 2.1
DiMaggio-Bos 1.8
Dillinger-StL 1.8

Fielding Runs
Pellagrini-StL 24.0
Priddy-StL 23.5
Hegan-Cle 20.7
Michaels-Chi 13.4
Baker-Chi........ 12.5

Total Player Rating
Williams-Bos 6.3
Boudreau-Cle 6.1
DiMaggio-NY 4.0
Priddy-StL 4.0
Henrich-NY 3.3

Wins
Newhouser-Det 21
Lemon-Cle 20
Bearden-Cle 20
Raschi-NY 19
Feller-Cle 19

Win Percentage
Kramer-Bos 783
Bearden-Cle 741
Raschi-NY 704
Reynolds-NY 696

Games
Page-NY 55
Widmar-StL 49
Biscan-StL 47
Thompson-Was 46

Complete Games
Lemon-Cle 20
Newhouser-Det ... 19
Raschi-NY 18
Feller-Cle 18

Shutouts
Lemon-Cle 10
Raschi-NY 6
Bearden-Cle 6
Dobson-Bos 5

Saves
Christopher-Cle.... 17
Page-NY........... 16
Houtteman-Det ... 10
Ferrick-Was 10
Judson-Chi 8

Innings Pitched
Lemon-Cle 293.2
Feller-Cle 280.1
Newhouser-Det .. 272.1
Dobson-Bos 245.1
Reynolds-NY 236.1

Fewest Hits/Game
Shea-NY 6.76
Lemon-Cle 7.08
Bearden-Cle 7.33
Scarborough-Was 8.06
Trucks-Det 8.08

Fewest BB/Game
Hutchinson-Det ... 1.95
Zoldak-StL-Cle ... 2.42
Lopat-NY 2.62
Kramer-Bos 2.81
Houtteman-Det ... 2.85

Strikeouts
Feller-Cle 164
Lemon-Cle 147
Newhouser-Det ... 143
Brissie-Phi 127
Raschi-NY 124

Strikeouts/Game
Brissie-Phi 5.89
Feller-Cle 5.27
Trucks-Det 5.23
Raschi-NY 5.01
Newhouser-Det ... 4.73

Ratio
Hutchinson-Det ... 11.08
Lemon-Cle 11.12
Raschi-NY 11.52
Newhouser-Det ... 11.53
Bearden-Cle 11.60

Earned Run Average
Bearden-Cle 2.43
Scarborough-Was . 2.82
Lemon-Cle 2.82
Newhouser-Det ... 3.01
Parnell-Bos 3.14

Adjusted ERA
Bearden-Cle 167
Scarborough-Was . 154
Newhouser-Det ... 145
Lemon-Cle 144
Parnell-Bos 140

Opponents' Batting Avg.
Shea-NY 208
Lemon-Cle 216
Bearden-Cle 229
Scarborough-Was .233
Trucks-Det 240

Opponents' On Base Pct.
Hutchinson-Det ...297
Lemon-Cle 302
Scarborough-Was .307
Newhouser-Det ...309
Raschi-NY 310

Starter Runs
Lemon-Cle 48.0
Bearden-Cle 47.5
Newhouser-Det ... 38.8
Scarborough-Was 30.3
Parnell-Bos 27.1

Adjusted Starter Runs
Bearden-Cle 41.6
Newhouser-Det ... 41.1
Lemon-Cle 40.4
Scarborough-Was . 31.5
Parnell-Bos 29.5

Clutch Pitching Index
Bearden-Cle 132
Garver-StL 129
Fowler-Phi 119
Lopat-NY 118
Reynolds-NY 117

Relief Runs
Klieman-Cle 15.0
Christopher-Cle.... 9.1
Thompson-Was.... 6.6
Hiller-NY 1.7
Harris-Phi......... 1.6

Adjusted Relief Runs
Klieman-Cle 12.9
Christopher-Cle.... 7.6
Thompson-Was.... 7.4
Harris-Phi 1.6
Ferrick-Was 1.6

Relief Ranking
Christopher-Cle... 10.7
Klieman-Cle 8.8
Thompson-Was ... 8.6
Ferrick-Was 1.8
Harris-Phi 1.3

Total Pitcher Index
Lemon-Cle 6.4
Bearden-Cle 5.2
Newhouser-Det ... 4.5
Scarborough-Was . 3.3
Garver-StL 3.1

Total Baseball Ranking
Lemon-Cle 6.4
Williams-Bos 6.3
Boudreau-Cle 6.1
Bearden-Cle 5.2
Newhouser-Det ... 4.5

TEAM	G	W	L	PCT	GB	R	OR	AB	H	2B	3B	HR	BB	SO	AVG	OBP	SLG	PRO	PRO+	BR	/A	PF	CHI	RC	SB	CS	SBA	SBR
BRO	156	97	57	.630		879	651	5400	1477	236	47	152	638	570	.274	.354	.419	.773	109	103	73	104	106	815	117			
STL	157	96	58	.623	1	766	616	5463	1513	281	54	102	569	482	.277	.348	.404	.752	103	61	27	105	98	777	17			
PHI	154	81	73	.526	16	662	668	5307	1349	232	55	122	528	670	.254	.325	.388	.713	99	-26	-7	97	98	674	27			
BOS	157	75	79	.487	22	706	719	5336	1376	246	33	103	684	656	.258	.345	.374	.719	104	6	44	95	97	710	28			
NY	156	73	81	.474	24	736	693	5308	1383	203	52	147	613	523	.261	.340	.401	.741	105	36	37	100	99	735	43			
PIT	154	71	83	.461	26	681	760	5214	1350	191	41	126	548	554	.259	.332	.384	.716	95	-13	-30	103	100	682	48			
CIN	156	62	92	.403	35	627	770	5469	1423	264	35	86	429	559	.260	.316	.368	.684	88	-83	-90	101	101	636	31			
CHI	154	61	93	.396	36	593	773	5214	1336	212	53	97	396	573	.256	.312	.373	.685	91	-82	-63	97	100	601	53			
TOT	622					5650		42711	11207	1865	370	935	4405	4587	.262	.334	.389	.723							364			

TEAM	CG	SH	SV	IP	H	H/G	HR	BB	SO	RAT	ERA	ERA+	OAV	OOB	PR	/A	PF	CPI	FA	E	DP	FW	PW	BW	SBW	DIF
BRO	62	15	17	1408²	1306	8.3	132	582	743	12.2	3.80	108	.246	.323	37	46	102	99	.980	122	162	1.5	4.6	7.2		6.7
STL	64	13	19	1407²	1356	8.7	87	507	606	12.1	3.44	121	.252	.319	93	112	103	101	.976	146	149	.3	11.1	2.7		5.0
PHI	58	12	15	1391²	1389	9.0	104	502	495	12.4	3.89	101	.267	.335	22	8	98	105	.974	156	141	-.5	.8	-.7		4.4
BOS	68	12	11	1400	1466	9.4	110	520	589	12.9	3.99	95	.267	.333	8	-32	94	102	.976	148	144	.1	-3.2	4.4		-3.3
NY	68	10	9	1374¹	1328	8.7	132	544	516	12.4	3.82	104	.248	.320	32	24	99	97	.973	161	134	-.6	2.4	3.7		-9.4
PIT	53	9	15	1356	1452	9.6	142	535	556	13.4	4.57	92	.273	.343	-79	-54	104	99	.978	132	173	.9	-5.4	-3.0		1.5
CIN	55	10	6	1401²	1423	9.1	124	640	538	13.4	4.34	96	.263	.345	-46	-24	104	99	.977	138	150	.6	-2.4	-8.9		-4.3
CHI	44	8	17	1357²	1487	9.9	104	575	544	13.8	4.50	90	.278	.351	-69	-70	100	100	.970	186	160	-2.1	-6.9	-6.2		-.7
TOT	472	89	109	11097²		9.1				12.8	4.04		.262	.334					.975	1189	1213					

Runs
Reese-Bro 132
Musial-StL 128
Robinson-Bro 122
Kiner-Pit 116
Schoendienst-StL . 102

Hits
Musial-StL 207
Robinson-Bro 203
Thomson-NY 198
Slaughter-StL 191
Schoendienst-StL . 190

Doubles
Musial-StL 41
Ennis-Phi 39
Robinson-Bro 38
Hatton-Cin 38

Triples
Slaughter-StL 13
Musial-StL 13
Robinson-Bro 12
Ennis-Phi 11
Ashburn-Phi 11

Home Runs
Kiner-Pit 54
Musial-StL 36
Sauer-Cin-Chi 31
Thomson-NY 27
Gordon-NY 26

Total Bases
Musial-StL 382
Kiner-Pit 361
Thomson-NY 332
Ennis-Phi 320
Robinson-Bro 313

Runs Batted In
Kiner-Pit 127
Robinson-Bro 124
Musial-StL 123
Hodges-Bro 115
Ennis-Phi 110

Runs Produced
Robinson-Bro 230
Musial-StL 215
Reese-Bro 189
Kiner-Pit 189
Hodges-Bro 186

Bases On Balls
Kiner-Pit 117
Reese-Bro 116
Stanky-Bos 113
Musial-StL 107
Gordon-NY 95

Batting Average
Robinson-Bro .... .342
Musial-StL .... .338
Slaughter-StL .... .336
Furillo-Bro .... .322
Kiner-Pit .... .310

On Base Percentage
Musial-StL .... .438
Robinson-Bro .... .432
Kiner-Pit .... .432
Slaughter-StL .... .418
Stanky-Bos ...... .417

Slugging Average
Kiner-Pit .... .658
Musial-StL .... .624
Robinson-Bro .... .528
Ennis-Phi .... .525
Thomson-NY .... .518

Production
Kiner-Pit 1.089
Musial-StL 1.062
Robinson-Bro ... .960
Slaughter-StL ... .929
Gordon-NY ...... .909

Adjusted Production
Kiner-Pit 183
Musial-StL 174
Robinson-Bro 150
Gordon-NY 142
Slaughter-StL 141

Batter Runs
Musial-StL 72.4
Kiner-Pit 70.0
Robinson-Bro ... 49.9
Slaughter-StL ... 40.1
Gordon-NY 31.6

Adjusted Batter Runs
Musial-StL 68.5
Kiner-Pit 68.0
Robinson-Bro ... 46.5
Slaughter-StL ... 36.6
Gordon-NY 31.7

Clutch Hitting Index
Marion-StL 136
Hodges-Bro 135
Robinson-Bro 124
Cooper-NY-Cin ... 124
Furillo-Bro 123

Runs Created
Musial-StL 173
Kiner-Pit 163
Robinson-Bro 135
Slaughter-StL 127
Ennis-Phi 118

Total Average
Kiner-Pit 1.247
Musial-StL 1.185
Robinson-Bro .. 1.078
Slaughter-StL ... .971
Gordon-NY ...... .925

Stolen Bases
Robinson-Bro 37
Reese-Bro 26

Stolen Base Average

Stolen Base Runs

Fielding Runs
Schoendienst-StL . 23.9
Ashburn-Phi 18.8
Marion-StL 16.6
Smalley-Chi 13.9
Reich-Chi 13.8

Total Player Rating
Musial-StL 5.4
Kiner-Pit 5.4
Robinson-Bro 5.0
R.Elliott-Bos 3.8
Reese-Bro 3.3

Wins
Spahn-Bos 21
Pollet-StL 20
Raffensberger-Cin . 18

Win Percentage
Roe-Bro .... .714
Pollet-StL .... .690
Newcombe-Bro ... .680
Meyer-Phi .... .680
Munger-StL ...... .652

Games
Wilks-StL 59
Konstanty-Phi 53
Palica-Bro 49
Banta-Bro 48
Muncrief-Pit-Chi ... 47

Complete Games
Spahn-Bos 25
Raffensberger-Cin . 20
Newcombe-Bro 19
Pollet-StL 17
Jansen-NY 17

Shutouts
Raffensberger-Cin .. 5
Pollet-StL 5
Newcombe-Bro 5
Heintzelman-Phi ... 5

Saves
Wilks-StL 9
Potter-Bos 7
Konstanty-Phi 7
Staley-StL 6
Palica-Bro 6

Innings Pitched
Spahn-Bos 302.1
Raffensberger-Cin 284.0
Jansen-NY 259.2
Heintzelman-Phi . 250.0
Newcombe-Bro .. 244.1

Fewest Hits/Game
Staley-StL 8.09
Koslo-NY 8.19
Newcombe-Bro ... 8.21
Kennedy-NY 8.38
Meyer-Phi 8.41

Fewest BB/Game
Koslo-NY 1.83
Roe-Bro 1.86
Werle-Pit 2.08
Jansen-NY 2.15
Leonard-Chi 2.15

Strikeouts
Spahn-Bos 151
Newcombe-Bro ... 149
Jansen-NY 113
Roe-Bro 109
Branca-Bro 109

Strikeouts/Game
Newcombe-Bro ... 5.49
Branca-Bro 5.26
Chambers-Pit 4.72
Roe-Bro 4.61
Spahn-Bos 4.50

Ratio
Koslo-NY 10.02
Staley-StL 10.40
Roe-Bro 10.45
Newcombe-Bro .. 11.01
Spahn-Bos 11.07

Earned Run Average
Koslo-NY 2.50
Staley-StL 2.73
Pollet-StL 2.77
Roe-Bro 2.79
Heintzelman-Phi .. 3.02

Adjusted ERA
Koslo-NY 159
Staley-StL 152
Pollet-StL 150
Roe-Bro 147
Brazle-StL 131

Opponents' Batting Avg.
Staley-StL .... .238
Koslo-NY .... .239
Kennedy-NY ..... .242
Newcombe-Bro ... .243
Spahn-Bos ...... .245

Opponents' On Base Pct.
Koslo-NY .... .278
Staley-StL .... .286
Roe-Bro .... .293
Spahn-Bos ...... .299
Newcombe-Bro ... .301

Starter Runs
Koslo-NY 36.2
Spahn-Bos 32.7
Pollet-StL 32.6
Roe-Bro 29.5
Heintzelman-Phi .. 28.2

Adjusted Starter Runs
Pollet-StL 35.7
Koslo-NY 34.8
Roe-Bro 30.9
Staley-StL 27.2
Heintzelman-Phi .. 25.5

Clutch Pitching Index
Roe-Bro 126
Heintzelman-Phi .. 123
Brazle-StL 121
Jones-NY 116
Dickson-Pit 113

Relief Runs
Erautt-Cin 8.6
Konstanty-Phi 8.5
Hogue-Bos 7.3
Palica-Bro 4.5
Wilks-StL 4.1

Adjusted Relief Runs
Erautt-Cin 10.3
Konstanty-Phi 7.5
Wilks-StL 5.7
Hogue-Bos 5.2
Palica-Bro 5.2

Relief Ranking
Erautt-Cin 12.6
Konstanty-Phi ... 11.0
Palica-Bro 8.9
Wilks-StL 6.6
Hogue-Bos 3.1

Total Pitcher Index
Koslo-NY 3.8
Pollet-StL 3.7
Staley-StL 3.1
Newcombe-Bro ... 3.0
Dickson-Pit 2.9

Total Baseball Ranking
Musial-StL 5.4
Kiner-Pit 5.4
Robinson-Bro 5.0
R.Elliott-Bos 3.8
Koslo-NY 3.8

TEAM	G	W	L	PCT	GB	R	OR	AB	H	2B	3B	HR	BB	SO	AVG	OBP	SLG	PRO	PRO+	BR	/A	PF	CHI	RC	SB	CS	SBA	SBR
NY	155	97	57	.630		829	637	5196	1396	215	60	115	731	539	.269	.362	.400	.762	108	58	58	100	106	790	58	30	38	-13
BOS	155	96	58	.623	1	896	667	5320	1500	272	36	131	835	510	.282	.381	.420	.801	111	147	93	107	100	890	43	25	40	-16
CLE	154	89	65	.578	8	675	574	5221	1358	194	58	112	601	534	.260	.339	.384	.723	98	-29	-14	98	99	696	44	40	50	-17
DET	155	87	67	.565	10	751	655	5259	1405	215	51	88	751	502	.267	.361	.378	.739	101	20	18	100	99	739	39	52	51	-14
PHI	154	81	73	.526	16	726	725	5123	1331	214	49	82	783	493	.260	.361	.369	.730	103	6	30	97	99	719	36	25	33	-11
CHI	154	63	91	.409	34	648	737	5204	1340	207	66	43	702	596	.257	.347	.347	.694	92	-65	-41	97	99	657	62	55	63	-20
STL	155	53	101	.344	44	667	913	5112	1301	213	30	117	631	700	.254	.339	.377	.716	92	-40	-69	104	101	670	38	39	38	-10
WAS	154	50	104	.325	47	584	868	5234	1330	207	41	81	593	495	.254	.333	.356	.689	89	-92	-76	98	95	640	46	33	46	-17
TOT	618					5776		41669	10961	1737	391	769	5627	4369	.263	.353	.379	.732							366	299	55	-69

TEAM	CG	SH	SV	IP	H	H/G	HR	BB	SO	RAT	ERA	ERA+	OAV	OOB	PR	/A	PF	CPI	FA	E	DP	FW	PW	BW	SBW	DIF
NY	59	12	36	1371¹	1231	8.1	98	812	671	13.6	3.69	110	.242	.350	76	53	96	107	.977	138	195	.0	5.2	5.6	-.4	9.6
BOS	84	16	16	1377	1375	9.0	82	661	598	13.5	3.97	110	.262	.347	34	59	104	101	.980	120	207	1.1	5.7	9.1	-.7	3.8
CLE	65	10	19	1383²	1275	8.3	82	611	594	12.4	3.36	119	.247	.328	129	97	95	104	.983	103	192	2.1	9.4	-1.4	-.8	2.7
DET	70	19	12	1393²	1338	8.6	102	628	631	12.8	3.77	110	.253	.335	66	60	99	100	.978	131	174	.4	5.8	1.8	-.5	2.5
PHI	85	9	11	1365	1359	9.0	105	758	490	14.1	4.23	97	.263	.359	-5	-18	98	103	.976	140	217	-.1	-1.8	2.9	-.2	3.2
CHI	57	10	17	1363¹	1362	9.0	108	693	502	13.7	4.30	97	.264	.352	-15	-18	99	99	.977	141	180	-.2	-1.8	-4.0	-1.1	-7.0
STL	43	3	16	1341¹	1583	10.6	113	685	432	15.4	5.21	87	.294	.376	-151	-101	108	98	.971	166	154	-1.6	-9.8	-6.7	-.1	-5.7
WAS	44	9	9	1345²	1438	9.6	79	779	451	15.0	5.10	84	.276	.372	-134	-125	101	91	.973	161	168	-1.4	-12.2	-7.4	-.8	-5.2
TOT	507	88	136	10941		9.0				13.8	4.20		.263	.353					.977	1100	1487					

Runs
Williams-Bos 150
Joost-Phi 128
DiMaggio-Bos 126
Stephens-Bos 113
Pesky-Bos 111

Hits
Mitchell-Cle 203
Williams-Bos 194
DiMaggio-Bos 186
Wertz-Det 185
Pesky-Bos 185

Doubles
Williams-Bos 39
Kell-Det 38
DiMaggio-Bos 34
Zarilla-StL-Bos 33
Stephens-Bos 31

Triples
Mitchell-Cle 23
Dillinger-StL 13
Valo-Phi 12

Home Runs
Williams-Bos 43
Stephens-Bos 39

Total Bases
Williams-Bos 368
Stephens-Bos 329
Wertz-Det 283
Mitchell-Cle 274
Doerr-Bos 269

Runs Batted In
Williams-Bos 159
Stephens-Bos 159
Wertz-Det 133
Doerr-Bos 109
Chapman-Phi..... 108

Runs Produced
Williams-Bos 266
Stephens-Bos 233
Wertz-Det 209
Joost-Phi 186
Doerr-Bos 182

Bases On Balls
Williams-Bos 162
Joost-Phi 149
Fain-Phi 136
Appling-Chi 121
Valo-Phi 119

Batting Average
Kell-Det 343
Williams-Bos 343
Dillinger-StL 324
Mitchell-Cle 317
Doerr-Bos 309

On Base Percentage
Williams-Bos 490
Appling-Chi 439
Joost-Phi 429
Kell-Det 424
Michaels-Chi 417

Slugging Average
Williams-Bos 650
Stephens-Bos 539
Henrich-NY 526
Doerr-Bos 497
Sievers-StL 471

Production
Williams-Bos 1.141
Henrich-NY 942
Stephens-Bos 930
Kell-Det 892
Doerr-Bos 890

Adjusted Production
Williams-Bos 187
Henrich-NY 148
Joost-Phi 138
Kell-Det 136
Stephens-Bos 135

Batter Runs
Williams-Bos 88.9
Stephens-Bos 36.9
Joost-Phi 31.9
DiMaggio-NY 31.7
Henrich-NY 29.7

Adjusted Batter Runs
Williams-Bos 82.6
Joost-Phi 34.6
DiMaggio-NY 31.7
Stephens-Bos 30.8
Henrich-NY 29.7

Clutch Hitting Index
Wertz-Det........ 141
Fain-Phi 137
Lipon-Det 134
Stephens-Bos 129
Doerr-Bos 123

Runs Created
Williams-Bos 193
Stephens-Bos ... 132
Joost-Phi 119
DiMaggio-Bos ... 110
Wertz-Det........ 110

Total Average
Williams-Bos 1.347
Henrich-NY 1.017
Joost-Phi 995
Stephens-Bos 947
Kell-Det 877

Stolen Bases
Dillinger-StL 20
Rizzuto-NY 18
Valo-Phi 14
Philley-Chi 13

Stolen Base Average
Rizzuto-NY 75.0
Dillinger-StL 58.8

Stolen Base Runs
Tebbetts-Bos 1.8
Rizzuto-NY 1.8
Mapes-NY 1.8
Fain-Phi 1.8
Philley-Chi 1.5

Fielding Runs
Doerr-Bos 27.8
Pesky-Bos 21.4
Vernon-Cle 18.8
Evers-Det 12.6
Baker-Chi........ 11.8

Total Player Rating
Williams-Bos 7.5
Doerr-Bos 4.7
Joost-Phi 4.2
Stephens-Bos 3.4
Michaels-Chi 3.3

Wins
Parnell-Bos 25
Kinder-Bos........ 23
Lemon-Cle 22
Raschi-NY 21
Kellner-Phi 20

Win Percentage
Kinder-Bos........793
Parnell-Bos 781
Reynolds-NY 739
Lemon-Cle 688

Games
Page-NY 60
Welteroth-Was ... 52
Ferrick-StL 50
Kennedy-StL 48
Surkont-Chi 44

Complete Games
Parnell-Bos 27
Newhouser-Det ... 22
Lemon-Cle 22
Raschi-NY 21

Shutouts
Trucks-Det 6
Kinder-Bos......... 6
Garcia-Cle 5

Saves
Page-NY 27
Benton-Cle........ 10
Ferrick-StL 6
Paige-Cle 5

Innings Pitched
Parnell-Bos 295.1
Newhouser-Det .. 292.0
Lemon-Cle 279.2
Trucks-Det 275.0
Raschi-NY 274.2

Fewest Hits/Game
Byrne-NY 5.74
Lemon-Cle 6.79
Trucks-Det 6.84
Gray-Det 7.52
Pierce-Chi 7.60

Fewest BB/Game
Hutchinson-Det ... 2.48
Houtteman-Det ... 2.61
Lopat-NY 2.88
Garcia-Cle 3.07
Wynn-Cle 3.12

Strikeouts
Trucks-Det 153
Newhouser-Det ... 144
Lemon-Cle 138
Kinder-Bos 138
Byrne-NY 129

Strikeouts/Game
Byrne-NY 5.92
Trucks-Det 5.01
Pierce-Chi 4.98
Kinder-Bos 4.93
Garcia-Cle 4.82

Ratio
Hutchinson-Det .. 10.49
Trucks-Det 11.03
Garcia-Cle 11.07
Lemon-Cle 11.39
Gumpert-Chi 11.81

Earned Run Average
Garcia-Cle 2.36
Parnell-Bos 2.77
Trucks-Det 2.81
Hutchinson-Det ... 2.96
Lemon-Cle 2.99

Adjusted ERA
Garcia-Cle 169
Parnell-Bos 157
Trucks-Det 148
Hutchinson-Det ... 141
Lemon-Cle 133

Opponents' Batting Avg.
Byrne-NY 183
Lemon-Cle 211
Trucks-Det 211
Gray-Det 227
Pierce-Chi 228

Opponents' On Base Pct.
Hutchinson-Det 290
Trucks-Det 301
Garcia-Cle 308
Lemon-Cle 309
Gumpert-Chi 318

Starter Runs
Parnell-Bos 46.7
Trucks-Det 42.3
Lemon-Cle 37.4
Garcia-Cle 35.9
Benton-Cle....... 31.3

Adjusted Starter Runs
Parnell-Bos 52.1
Trucks-Det 41.1
Garcia-Cle 31.9
Lemon-Cle 31.0
Benton-Cle....... 28.2

Clutch Pitching Index
Garcia-Cle 123
Lopat-NY 122
Wight-Chi 118
Houtteman-Det ... 115
Kinder-Bos....... 114

Relief Runs
Page-NY 24.1
Paige-Cle 10.7
Papish-Cle 6.9
Ferrick-StL 3.7

Adjusted Relief Runs
Page-NY 21.8
Paige-Cle 8.8
Ferrick-StL 7.5
Papish-Cle 5.5
Starr-StL 1.9

Relief Ranking
Page-NY 40.3
Paige-Cle 11.7
Ferrick-StL 7.4
Starr-StL 1.7
Papish-Cle 1.0

Total Pitcher Index
Parnell-Bos 5.7
Lemon-Cle 5.4
Garcia-Cle 3.6
Hutchinson-Det ... 3.3
Trucks-Det 3.2

Total Baseball Ranking
Williams-Bos 7.5
Parnell-Bos 5.7
Lemon-Cle 5.4
Doerr-Bos 4.7
Joost-Phi 4.2

TEAM	G	W	L	PCT	GB	R	OR	AB	H	2B	3B	HR	BB	SO	AVG	OBP	SLG	PRO	PRO+	BR	/A	PF	CHI	RC	SB	CS	SBA	SBR
PHI	157	91	63	.591		722	624	5426	1440	225	55	125	535	569	.265	.334	.396	.730	99	-13	0	98	101	714	33			
BRO	155	89	65	.578	2	847	724	5364	1461	247	46	194	607	632	.272	.349	.444	.793	112	107	92	102	101	833	77			
NY	154	86	68	.558	5	735	643	5238	1352	204	50	133	627	629	.258	.342	.392	.734	99	4	0	101	101	726	42			
BOS	156	83	71	.539	8	785	736	5363	1411	246	36	148	615	616	.263	.342	.405	.747	110	24	70	94	104	750	71			
STL	153	78	75	.510	12.5	693	670	5215	1353	255	50	102	606	604	.259	.339	.386	.725	92	-14	-48	105	99	696	23			
CIN	153	66	87	.431	24.5	654	734	5253	1366	257	27	99	504	497	.260	.327	.376	.703	90	-64	-66	100	102	643	37			
CHI	154	64	89	.418	26.5	643	772	5230	1298	224	47	161	479	767	.248	.315	.401	.716	95	-52	-43	99	99	658	46			
PIT	154	57	96	.373	33.5	681	857	5327	1404	227	59	138	564	693	.264	.338	.406	.744	98	13	-10	103	93	729	43			
TOT	618					5760		42416	11085	1885	370	1100	4537	5007	.261	.336	.401	.737							372			

TEAM	CG	SH	SV	IP	H	H/G	HR	BB	SO	RAT	ERA	ERA+	OAV	OOB	PR	/A	PF	CPI	FA	E	DP	FW	PW	BW	SBW	DIF
PHI	57	13	27	1406	1324	8.5	122	530	620	12.0	3.50	116	.250	.320	100	85	98	105	.975	151	155	.1	8.3	.0		5.6
BRO	62	10	21	1389²	1397	9.0	163	591	772	13.0	4.28	96	.262	.338	-21	-28	99	102	.979	127	183	1.4	-2.7	9.0		4.4
NY	70	19	15	1375	1268	8.3	140	536	596	12.0	3.71	110	.245	.320	65	58	99	100	.977	137	181	.8	5.7	.0		2.6
BOS	88	7	10	1385¹	1411	9.2	129	554	615	13.0	4.14	93	.263	.335	0	-44	93	99	.970	182	146	-1.7	-4.3	6.8		5.1
STL	57	10	14	1356	1398	9.3	119	535	603	13.0	3.97	108	.267	.338	25	48	104	105	.978	130	172	1.1	4.7	-4.7		.4
CIN	67	7	13	1357²	1363	9.0	145	582	686	13.2	4.32	98	.259	.337	-26	-13	102	97	.976	140	132	.5	-1.3	-6.5		-3.3
CHI	55	9	19	1371¹	1452	9.5	130	593	559	13.6	4.28	98	.271	.346	-20	-11	101	103	.968	201	169	-2.8	-1.1	-4.2		-4.4
PIT	42	6	16	1368²	1472	9.7	152	616	556	13.9	4.96	88	.274	.352	-124	-88	106	95	.977	136	165	.8	-8.6	-1.0		-10.7
TOT	498	81	135	11009²		9.1				13.0	4.14		.261	.336					.975	1204	1303					

Runs
Torgeson-Bos 120
Stanky-NY ... 115
Kiner-Pit ... 112
Snider-Bro ... 109
Musial-StL ... 105

Hits
Snider-Bro ... 199
Musial-StL ... 192
Furillo-Bro ... 189
Ennis-Phi ... 185
Waitkus-Phi ... 182

Doubles
Schoendienst-StL .. 43
Musial-StL ... 41
Robinson-Bro ... 39
Kluszewski-Cin ... 37
Dark-NY ... 36

Triples
Ashburn-Phi ... 14
Bell-Pit ... 11
Snider-Bro ... 10
Smalley-Chi ... 9
Schoendienst-StL ... 9

Home Runs
Kiner-Pit ... 47
Pafko-Chi ... 36
Sauer-Chi ... 32
Hodges-Bro ... 32

Total Bases
Snider-Bro ... 343
Musial-StL ... 331
Ennis-Phi ... 328
Kiner-Pit ... 323
Pafko-Chi ... 304

Runs Batted In
Ennis-Phi ... 126
Kiner-Pit ... 118
Hodges-Bro ... 113
Kluszewski-Cin ... 111
Musial-StL ... 109

Runs Produced
Furillo-Bro ... 187
Ennis-Phi ... 187
Musial-StL ... 186
Snider-Bro ... 185
Torgeson-Bos ... 184

Bases On Balls
Stanky-NY ... 144
Kiner-Pit ... 122
Torgeson-Bos ... 119
Westrum-NY ... 92
Reese-Bro ... 91

Batting Average
Musial-StL ... .346
Robinson-Bro ... .328
Snider-Bro ... .321
Ennis-Phi ... .311
Kluszewski-Cin ... .307

On Base Percentage
Stanky-NY ... .460
Musial-StL ... .437
Robinson-Bro ... .423
Glaviano-StL ... .421
Torgeson-Bos ... .412

Slugging Average
Musial-StL ... .596
Pafko-Chi ... .591
Kiner-Pit ... .590
Gordon-Bos ... .557
Snider-Bro ... .553

Production
Musial-StL ... 1.034
Kiner-Pit ... .998
Pafko-Chi ... .989
Gordon-Bos ... .960
Snider-Bro ... .932

Adjusted Production
Musial-StL ... 161
Gordon-Bos ... 160
Pafko-Chi ... 158
Kiner-Pit ... 154
Elliott-Bos ... 143

Batter Runs
Musial-StL ... 57.3
Kiner-Pit ... 48.7
Pafko-Chi ... 41.5
Snider-Bro ... 35.6
Gordon-Bos ... 35.3

Adjusted Batter Runs
Musial-StL ... 53.5
Kiner-Pit ... 46.1
Pafko-Chi ... 42.3
Gordon-Bos ... 39.6
Torgeson-Bos ... 36.5

Clutch Hitting Index
Slaughter-StL ... 158
D.Mueller-NY ... 149
Wyrostek-Cin ... 131
Kluszewski-Cin ... 129
Furillo-Bro ... 128

Runs Created
Musial-StL ... 149
Kiner-Pit ... 133
Snider-Bro ... 131
Pafko-Chi ... 124
Torgeson-Bos ... 121

Total Average
Musial-StL ... 1.139
Kiner-Pit ... 1.071
Pafko-Chi ... 1.057
Stanky-NY ... 1.013
Gordon-Bos ... 1.003

Stolen Bases
Jethroe-Bos ... 35
Reese-Bro ... 17
Snider-Bro ... 16
Torgeson-Bos ... 15
Ashburn-Phi ... 14

Stolen Base Average

Stolen Base Runs

Fielding Runs
Smalley-Chi ... 21.3
Cox-Bro ... 12.0
Lockman-NY ... 11.9
Ryan-Bos-Cin ... 11.6
Robinson-Bro ... 10.6

Total Player Rating
Robinson-Bro ... 4.5
Gordon-Bos ... 4.1
Stanky-NY ... 3.9
Kiner-Pit ... 3.8
Musial-StL ... 3.4

Wins
Spahn-Bos ... 21
Sain-Bos ... 20
Roberts-Phi ... 20

Win Percentage
Maglie-NY ... .818
Konstanty-Phi ... .696
Simmons-Phi ... .680
Roberts-Phi ... .645

Games
Konstanty-Phi ... 74
Dickson-Pit ... 51
Werle-Pit ... 48
Maglie-NY ... 47
Brazle-StL ... 46

Complete Games
Bickford-Bos ... 27
Spahn-Bos ... 25
Sain-Bos ... 25
Roberts-Phi ... 21
Jansen-NY ... 21

Shutouts
Hearn-StL-NY ... 5
Roberts-Phi ... 5
Maglie-NY ... 5
Jansen-NY ... 5

Saves
Konstanty-Phi ... 22
Werle-Pit ... 8
Hogue-Bos ... 7
Branca-Bro ... 7

Innings Pitched
Bickford-Bos ... 311.2
Roberts-Phi ... 304.1
Spahn-Bos ... 293.0
Sain-Bos ... 278.1
Jansen-NY ... 275.0

Fewest Hits/Game
Blackwell-Cin ... 7.00
Maglie-NY ... 7.38
Simmons-Phi ... 7.46
Spahn-Bos ... 7.62
Jansen-NY ... 7.79

Fewest BB/Game
Raffensberger-Cin 1.51
Jansen-NY ... 1.80
Sain-Bos ... 2.26
Roberts-Phi ... 2.28
Roe-Bro ... 2.37

Strikeouts
Spahn-Bos ... 191
Blackwell-Cin ... 188
Jansen-NY ... 161
Simmons-Phi ... 146
Roberts-Phi ... 146

Strikeouts/Game
Blackwell-Cin ... 6.48
Simmons-Phi ... 6.12
Spahn-Bos ... 5.87
Palica-Bro ... 5.86
Jansen-NY ... 5.27

Ratio
Jansen-NY ... 9.62
Roberts-Phi ... 10.68
Brecheen-StL ... 10.97
Spahn-Bos ... 11.06
Simmons-Phi ... 11.24

Earned Run Average
Maglie-NY ... 2.71
Blackwell-Cin ... 2.97
Jansen-NY ... 3.01
Roberts-Phi ... 3.02
Lanier-StL ... 3.13

Adjusted ERA
Maglie-NY ... 151
Blackwell-Cin ... 143
Lanier-StL ... 137
Jansen-NY ... 136
Roberts-Phi ... 134

Opponents' Batting Avg.
Blackwell-Cin ... .210
Simmons-Phi ... .223
Maglie-NY ... .226
Spahn-Bos ... .227
Jansen-NY ... .232

Opponents' On Base Pct.
Jansen-NY ... .271
Roberts-Phi ... .297
Brecheen-StL ... .298
Spahn-Bos ... .299
Blackwell-Cin ... .301

Starter Runs
Roberts-Phi ... 38.0
Jansen-NY ... 34.5
Blackwell-Cin ... 34.1
Maglie-NY ... 32.8
Spahn-Bos ... 31.8

Adjusted Starter Runs
Blackwell-Cin ... 36.7
Roberts-Phi ... 34.8
Jansen-NY ... 33.1
Maglie-NY ... 31.7
Pollet-StL ... 25.9

Clutch Pitching Index
Brazle-StL ... 125
Roe-Bro ... 118
Maglie-NY ... 116
Ramsdell-Bro-Cin ... 115
Minner-Chi ... 113

Relief Runs
Konstanty-Phi ... 24.9
Kramer-NY ... 5.9
Leonard-Chi ... 3.1
VanderMeer-Chi ... 2.9
Smith-Cin ... 2.7

Adjusted Relief Runs
Konstanty-Phi ... 23.3
Kramer-NY ... 5.4
Smith-Cin ... 3.6
Leonard-Chi ... 3.5
VanderMeer-Chi ... 3.4

Relief Ranking
Konstanty-Phi ... 39.4
Kramer-NY ... 5.2
Smith-Cin ... 3.5
Leonard-Chi ... 3.2
VanderMeer-Chi ... 3.0

Total Pitcher Index
Blackwell-Cin ... 3.6
Jansen-NY ... 3.4
Maglie-NY ... 3.4
Roberts-Phi ... 3.2
Hearn-StL-NY ... 2.5

Total Baseball Ranking
Robinson-Bro ... 4.5
Gordon-Bos ... 4.1
Stanky-NY ... 3.9
Kiner-Pit ... 3.8
Blackwell-Cin ... 3.6

TEAM	G	W	L	PCT	GB	R	OR	AB	H	2B	3B	HR	BB	SO	AVG	OBP	SLG	PRO	PRO+	BR	/A	PF	CHI	RC	SB	CS	SBA	SBR
NY	155	98	56	.636		914	691	5361	1511	234	70	159	687	463	.282	.367	.441	.808	116	92	114	97	104	902	41	28	38	-13
DET	157	95	59	.617	3	837	713	5381	1518	285	50	114	722	480	.282	.369	.417	.786	103	60	34	103	97	846	23	40	51	-18
BOS	154	94	60	.610	4	1027	804	5516	1665	287	61	161	719	582	.302	.385	.464	.849	112	185	106	110	103	1014	32	17	25	-9
CLE	155	92	62	.597	6	806	654	5263	1417	222	46	164	693	624	.269	.358	.422	.780	108	39	64	97	98	820	40	34	58	-24
WAS	155	67	87	.435	31	690	813	5251	1365	190	53	76	671	606	.260	.347	.360	.707	91	-92	-54	95	101	690	42	25	30	-10
CHI	156	60	94	.390	38	625	749	5260	1368	172	47	93	551	566	.260	.333	.364	.697	86	-124	-102	97	98	648	19	22	42	-18
STL	154	58	96	.377	40	684	916	5163	1269	235	43	106	690	744	.246	.337	.370	.707	83	-101	-130	104	103	667	39	40	49	-16
PHI	154	52	102	.338	46	670	913	5212	1361	204	53	100	685	493	.261	.349	.378	.727	93	-55	-40	98	94	708	42	25	34	-12
TOT	620					6253		42407	11474	1829	423	973	5418	4558	.271	.356	.402	.759							278	231	55	-54

TEAM	CG	SH	SV	IP	H	H/G	HR	BB	SO	RAT	ERA	ERA+	OAV	OOB	PR	/A	PF	CPI	FA	E	DP	FW	PW	BW	SBW	DIF
NY	66	12	31	1372²	1322	8.7	118	708	712	13.5	4.15	103	.254	.348	65	21	94	102	.980	119	188	1.3	2.0	10.7	-.6	7.6
DET	72	9	20	1407¹	1444	9.2	141	553	576	13.0	4.12	114	.267	.338	70	88	102	105	.981	120	194	1.3	8.2	3.2	-1.0	6.3
BOS	66	6	28	1362¹	1413	9.3	121	748	630	14.4	4.88	100	.270	.364	-45	2	107	97	.981	111	181	1.7	.2	9.9	-.2	5.4
CLE	69	11	16	1378²	1289	8.4	120	647	674	12.8	3.75	115	.247	.333	126	88	95	103	.978	129	160	.7	8.2	6.0	-1.6	1.6
WAS	59	7	18	1364²	1479	9.8	99	648	486	14.2	4.66	96	.277	.358	-11	-24	98	99	.972	167	181	-1.4	-2.2	-5.1	-.3	-1.0
CHI	62	7	9	1365²	1370	9.0	107	734	566	14.0	4.41	102	.262	.355	25	11	98	100	.977	140	181	.2	1.0	-9.6	-1.0	-7.6
STL	56	7	14	1365¹	1629	10.7	129	651	448	15.2	5.20	95	.294	.372	-94	-38	108	100	.967	196	155	-3.1	-3.6	-12.2	-.9	.6
PHI	50	3	18	1346¹	1528	10.2	138	729	466	15.3	5.49	83	.287	.376	-136	-140	99	96	.974	155	208	-.8	-13.1	-3.7	-.5	-6.9
TOT	500	62	154	10963		9.4				14.0	4.58		.271	.356					.976	1137	1448					

Runs
DiMaggio-Bos 131
Stephens-Bos 125
Rizzuto-NY 125
Berra-NY 116

Hits
Kell-Det 218
Rizzuto-NY 200
DiMaggio-Bos ... 193
Berra-NY 192
Stephens-Bos 185

Doubles
Kell-Det 56
Wertz-Det 37
Rizzuto-NY 36
Evers-Det 35
Stephens-Bos 34

Triples
Evers-Det 11
Doerr-Bos 11
DiMaggio-Bos 11

Home Runs
Rosen-Cle 37
Dropo-Bos 34
DiMaggio-NY 32
Stephens-Bos 30
Zernial-Chi 29

Total Bases
Dropo-Bos 326
Stephens-NY 321
Berra-NY 318
Kell-Det 310
DiMaggio-NY 307

Runs Batted In
Stephens-Bos 144
Dropo-Bos 144
Berra-NY 124
Wertz-Det 123
DiMaggio-NY 122

Runs Produced
Stephens-Bos 239
Berra-NY 212
Dropo-Bos 211
Kell-Det 207
DiMaggio-NY 204

Bases On Balls
Yost-Was 141
Fain-Phi 133
Pesky-Bos 104
Joost-Phi 103
Rosen-Cle 100

Batting Average
Goodman-Bos 354
Kell-Det 340
DiMaggio-Bos 328
Doby-Cle 326
Zarilla-Bos 325

On Base Percentage
Doby-Cle 442
Yost-Was 440
Pesky-Bos 437
Fain-Phi 430
Goodman-Bos 427

Slugging Average
DiMaggio-NY 585
Dropo-Bos 583
Evers-Det 551
Doby-Cle 545
Rosen-Cle 543

Production
Doby-Cle .... .986
DiMaggio-NY 979
Dropo-Bos 961
Evers-Det 959
Rosen-Cle 948

Adjusted Production
Doby-Cle 156
DiMaggio-NY 152
Rosen-Cle 146
Evers-Det 139
Berra-NY 136

Batter Runs
Doby-Cle 41.7
Williams-Bos 40.9
DiMaggio-NY 35.4
Rosen-Cle 34.3
Evers-Det 33.5

Adjusted Batter Runs
Doby-Cle 44.3
DiMaggio-NY 37.7
Rosen-Cle 37.2
Williams-Bos 35.7
Evers-Det 31.0

Clutch Hitting Index
Vernon-Cle-Was .. 136
Mele-Was 135
Stephens-Bos 128
Fain-Phi 126
Dropo-Bos 123

Runs Created
Doby-Cle 130
Wertz-Det 128
DiMaggio-NY 125
Berra-NY 125
Rizzuto-NY 124

Total Average
Doby-Cle 1.073
DiMaggio-NY 1.018
Wertz-Det 978
Zarilla-Bos 954
Rosen-Cle 953

Stolen Bases
DiMaggio-Bos 15
Valo-Phi 12
Rizzuto-NY 12
Coan-Was 10
Lipon-Det 9

Stolen Base Average

Stolen Base Runs
DiMaggio-Bos 2.1
Vernon-Cle-Was ... 1.8
Collins-NY 1.5
Avila-Cle 1.5
Jensen-NY 1.2

Fielding Runs
Priddy-Det 31.3
Hegan-Cle 23.5
Pesky-Bos 21.5
Noren-Was 13.4
Carrasquel-Chi ... 11.2

Total Player Rating
Rizzuto-NY 3.6
Priddy-Det 3.3
Berra-NY 3.2
DiMaggio-NY 3.1
Evers-Det 3.1

Wins
R.Lemon-Cle 23
Raschi-NY 21
Houtteman-Det ... 19

Win Percentage
Raschi-NY .... .724
Wynn-Cle 692
Lopat-NY 692
Hutchinson-Det ...680
R.Lemon-Cle 676

Games
Harris-Was 53
Kinder-Bos 48
Ferrick-StL-NY 46
Judson-Chi 46
Brissie-Phi 46

Complete Games
R.Lemon-Cle 22
Garver-StL 22
Parnell-Bos 21
Houtteman-Det ... 21

Shutouts
Houtteman-Det 4

Saves
Harris-Was 15
Page-NY 13
Ferrick-StL-NY 11
Kinder-Bos 9
Brissie-Phi 8

Innings Pitched
R.Lemon-Cle 288.0
Houtteman-Det .. 274.2
Garver-StL 260.0
Raschi-NY 256.2
Parnell-Bos 249.0

Fewest Hits/Game
Wynn-Cle 6.99
Pierce-Chi 7.76
Cain-Chi 8.02
Reynolds-NY 8.04
Raschi-NY 8.14

Fewest BB/Game
Hutchinson-Det ... 1.86
Lopat-NY 2.48
Overmire-StL 2.52
Trout-Det 3.12
Houtteman-Det ... 3.24

Strikeouts
R.Lemon-Cle 170
Reynolds-NY 160
Raschi-NY 155
Wynn-Cle 143
Feller-Cle 119

Strikeouts/Game
Wynn-Cle 6.02
Reynolds-NY 5.98
Raschi-NY 5.44
R.Lemon-Cle 5.31
Byrne-NY 5.22

Ratio
Wynn-Cle 11.41
Lopat-NY 11.92
Houtteman-Det .. 11.93
Raschi-NY 12.31
Feller-Cle 12.32

Earned Run Average
Wynn-Cle 3.20
Garver-StL 3.39
Feller-Cle 3.43
Lopat-NY 3.47
Houtteman-Det ... 3.54

Adjusted ERA
Garver-StL 146
Parnell-Bos 136
Wynn-Cle 135
Houtteman-Det ... 132
Feller-Cle 126

Opponents' Batting Avg.
Wynn-Cle 212
Pierce-Chi 228
Reynolds-NY 242
Raschi-NY 243
Cain-Chi 244

Opponents' On Base Pct.
Wynn-Cle 305
Lopat-NY 317
Houtteman-Det ...322
Feller-Cle 325
Raschi-NY 327

Starter Runs
Garver-StL 34.3
Wynn-Cle 32.7
Houtteman-Det .. 31.7
Feller-Cle 31.7
Lopat-NY 29.2

Adjusted Starter Runs
Garver-StL 45.0
Parnell-Bos 35.5
Houtteman-Det .. 35.1
Wynn-Cle 26.8
Feller-Cle 24.9

Clutch Pitching Index
Garver-StL 119
Hudson-Was 113
R.Lemon-Cle 111
Houtteman-Det .. 110
Parnell-Bos 110

Relief Runs
Judson-Chi 8.0
Aloma-Chi 7.6
Benton-Cle 7.0
Ferrick-StL-NY ... 7.0
Flores-Cle 5.0

Adjusted Relief Runs
Judson-Chi 6.8
Aloma-Chi 6.7
Ferrick-StL-NY ... 6.2
Benton-Cle 5.3
Flores-Cle 3.5

Relief Ranking
Ferrick-StL-NY ... 13.0
Aloma-Chi 6.9
Benton-Cle 5.3
Flores-Cle 4.2
Judson-Chi 2.7

Total Pitcher Index
Garver-StL 5.4
Parnell-Bos 4.0
Houtteman-Det ... 3.5
R.Lemon-Cle 3.4
Wynn-Cle 3.2

Total Baseball Ranking
Garver-StL 5.4
Parnell-Bos 4.0
Rizzuto-NY 3.6
Houtteman-Det ... 3.5
R.Lemon-Cle 3.4

TEAM	G	W	L	PCT	GB	R	OR	AB	H	2B	3B	HR	BB	SO	AVG	OBP	SLG	PRO	PRO+	BR	/A	PF	CHI	RC	SB	CS	SBA	SBR
NY	157	98	59	.624		781	641	5360	1396	201	53	179	671	624	.260	.347	.418	.765	111	91	85	101	97	812	55	34	34	-9
BRO	158	97	60	.618	1	855	672	5492	1511	249	37	184	603	649	.275	.352	.434	.786	115	130	115	102	101	843	89	70	67	-18
STL	155	81	73	.526	15.5	683	671	5317	1404	230	57	95	569	492	.264	.339	.382	.721	99	7	2	101	97	705	30	30	31	-9
BOS	155	76	78	.494	20.5	723	662	5293	1385	234	37	130	565	617	.262	.336	.394	.730	110	20	68	93	102	719	80	34	52	-20
PHI	154	73	81	.474	23.5	648	644	5332	1384	199	47	108	505	525	.260	.326	.375	.701	96	-37	-26	99	99	676	63	28	35	-12
CIN	155	68	86	.442	28.5	559	667	5285	1309	215	33	88	415	577	.248	.304	.351	.655	80	-133	-143	102	104	562	44	40	53	-19
PIT	155	64	90	.416	32.5	689	845	5318	1372	218	56	137	557	615	.258	.331	.397	.728	99	11	-9	103	98	712	29	27	34	-11
CHI	155	62	92	.403	34.5	614	750	5307	1327	200	47	103	477	647	.250	.315	.364	.679	86	-85	-97	102	103	613	63	30	47	-18
TOT	622					5552		42704	11088	1746	367	1024	4362	4746	.260	.331	.390	.721							453	293	61	-39

TEAM	CG	SH	SV	IP	H	H/G	HR	BB	SO	RAT	ERA	ERA+	OAV	OOB	PR	/A	PF	CPI	FA	E	DP	FW	PW	BW	SBW	DIF
NY	64	9	18	1412²	1334	8.5	148	482	625	11.7	3.48	113	.248	.312	75	68	99	104	.972	171	175	-1.0	6.8	8.5	-.4	5.6
BRO	64	10	13	1423¹	1360	8.6	150	549	693	12.2	3.88	101	.253	.325	13	7	99	101	.979	129	192	1.3	.7	11.5	-1.3	6.3
STL	58	9	23	1387²	1391	9.0	119	568	546	12.8	3.95	100	.263	.337	1	1	100	103	.980	125	187	1.3	.1	.2	-.4	2.8
BOS	73	16	12	1389	1378	8.9	96	595	604	13.0	3.75	104	.259	.337	33	-10	93	104	.976	145	157	.3	-1.0	-2.6	-1.5	-5.6
PHI	57	19	15	1384²	1373	8.9	110	497	570	12.3	3.81	101	.258	.324	23	5	97	98	.977	138	146	.6	.5	-2.6	-.7	-1.8
CIN	55	14	23	1390²	1357	8.8	119	490	584	12.2	3.70	110	.254	.322	39	58	103	100	.977	140	141	.5	5.8	-14.3	-1.4	.4
PIT	40	9	22	1380¹	1479	9.6	157	609	580	13.8	4.79	88	.273	.350	-127	-87	107	97	.972	170	178	-1.1	-8.7	-.9	-.6	-1.7
CHI	48	10	10	1385²	1416	9.2	125	572	544	13.1	4.34	94	.265	.339	-58	-37	103	96	.971	181	161	-1.7	-3.7	-9.7	-1.3	1.4
TOT	459	96	136	11154		8.9				12.6	3.96		.260	.331					.975	1199	1337					

Runs		Hits		Doubles		Triples		Home Runs		Total Bases	
Musial-StL	124	Ashburn-Phi	221	Dark-NY	41	Musial-StL	12	Kiner-Pit	42	Musial-StL	355
Kiner-Pit	124	Musial-StL	205	Kluszewski-Cin	35	Bell-Pit	12	Hodges-Bro	40	Kiner-Pit	333
Hodges-Bro	118	Furillo-Bro	197	Robinson-Bro	33	Irvin-NY	11	Campanella-Bro	33	Hodges-Bro	307
Dark-NY	114	Dark-NY	196	Campanella-Bro	33	Jethroe-Bos	10	Thomson-NY	32	Campanella-Bro	298
Robinson-Bro	106	Robinson-Bro	185			Baumholtz-Chi	10	Musial-StL	32		

Runs Batted In		Runs Produced		Bases On Balls		Batting Average		On Base Percentage		Slugging Average	
Irvin-NY	121	Musial-StL	200	Kiner-Pit	137	Musial-StL	.355	Kiner-Pit	.452	Kiner-Pit	.627
Kiner-Pit	109	Kiner-Pit	191	Stanky-NY	127	Ashburn-Phi	.344	Musial-StL	.449	Musial-StL	.614
Gordon-Bos	109	Irvin-NY	191	Westrum-NY	104	Robinson-Bro	.338	Robinson-Bro	.429	Campanella-Bro	.590
Musial-StL	108	Hodges-Bro	181	Torgeson-Bos	102	Campanella-Bro	.325	Irvin-NY	.415	Thomson-NY	.562
Campanella-Bro	108	Gordon-Bos	176	Musial-StL	98	Irvin-NY	.312	Stanky-NY	.401	Hodges-Bro	.527

Production		Adjusted Production		Batter Runs		Adjusted Batter Runs		Clutch Hitting Index		Runs Created	
Kiner-Pit	1.079	Musial-StL	182	Kiner-Pit	70.8	Musial-StL	69.6	Slaughter-StL	147	Musial-StL	169
Musial-StL	1.063	Kiner-Pit	182	Musial-StL	70.1	Kiner-Pit	68.5	Irvin-NY	138	Kiner-Pit	165
Campanella-Bro	.983	Campanella-Bro	158	Robinson-Bro	45.8	Robinson-Bro	44.3	Gordon-Bos	123	Robinson-Bro	133
Robinson-Bro	.957	Robinson-Bro	153	Campanella-Bro	41.7	Campanella-Bro	40.4	Westlake-Pit-StL	121	Irvin-NY	127
Thomson-NY	.947	Thomson-NY	150	Irvin-NY	40.7	Irvin-NY	40.1	Hamner-Phi	118	Hodges-Bro	119

Total Average		Stolen Bases		Stolen Base Average		Stolen Base Runs		Fielding Runs		Total Player Rating	
Kiner-Pit	1.251	Jethroe-Bos	35	Jethroe-Bos	87.5	Jethroe-Bos	7.5	Ashburn-Phi	25.0	Musial-StL	6.8
Musial-StL	1.180	Ashburn-Phi	29	Ashburn-Phi	82.9	Ashburn-Phi	5.1	Robinson-Bro	6.3	Robinson-Bro	6.7
Robinson-Bro	1.034	Robinson-Bro	25	Robinson-Bro	75.8	Robinson-Bro	2.7	Schoendienst-StL	15.5	Kiner-Pit	5.7
Irvin-NY	.985	Torgeson-Bos	20	Torgeson-Bos	64.5	Jackson-Chi	2.4	Hemus-StL	13.4	Irvin-NY	4.8
Campanella-Bro	.978	Reese-Bro	20	Reese-Bro	58.8	Irvin-NY	2.4	Furillo-Bro	12.7	Campanella-Bro	4.7

Wins		Win Percentage		Games		Complete Games		Shutouts		Saves	
Maglie-NY	23	Roe-Bro	.880	Wilks-StL-Pit	65	Spahn-Bos	26	Spahn-Bos	7	Wilks-StL-Pit	13
Jansen-NY	23	Maglie-NY	.793	Werle-Pit	59	Roberts-Phi	22	Roberts-Phi	6	Smith-Cin	11
Spahn-Bos	22	Newcombe-Bro	.690	Konstanty-Phi	58	Maglie-NY	22	Raffensberger-Cin	5	Konstanty-Phi	9
Roe-Bro	22	Jansen-NY	.676	Spencer-NY	57	Roe-Bro	19			Brazle-StL	7
Roberts-Phi	21	Hearn-NY	.654	Brazle-StL	56	Dickson-Pit	19				

Innings Pitched		Fewest Hits/Game		Fewest BB/Game		Strikeouts		Strikeouts/Game		Ratio	
Roberts-Phi	315.0	Maglie-NY	7.67	Raffensberger-Cin	1.38	Spahn-Bos	164	Queen-Pit	6.58	Raffensberger-Cin	9.99
Spahn-Bos	310.2	Newcombe-Bro	7.78	Jansen-NY	1.81	Newcombe-Bro	164	Rush-Chi	5.49	Roberts-Phi	10.03
Maglie-NY	298.0	Blackwell-Cin	7.89	Roberts-Phi	1.83	Maglie-NY	146	Newcombe-Bro	5.43	Jansen-NY	10.11
Dickson-Pit	288.2	Branca-Bro	7.94	Roe-Bro	2.24	Jansen-NY	145	Branca-Bro	5.21	Maglie-NY	10.45
Jansen-NY	278.2	Queen-Pit	7.97	Sain-Bos	2.53	Rush-Chi	129	Spahn-Bos	4.75	Roe-Bro	10.86

Earned Run Average		Adjusted ERA		Opponents' Batting Avg.		Opponents' On Base Pct.		Starter Runs		Adjusted Starter Runs	
Nichols-Bos	2.88	Maglie-NY	134	Maglie-NY	.230	Roberts-Phi	.278	Maglie-NY	34.1	Maglie-NY	32.7
Maglie-NY	2.93	Roe-Bro	129	Newcombe-Bro	.230	Jansen-NY	.279	Spahn-Bos	33.7	Roberts-Phi	28.7
Spahn-Bos	2.98	Jansen-NY	129	Blackwell-Cin	.233	Raffensberger-Cin	.279	Roberts-Phi	32.6	Jansen-NY	27.2
Roberts-Phi	3.03	Nichols-Bos	127	Queen-Pit	.233	Maglie-NY	.289	Jansen-NY	28.6	Roe-Bro	25.3
Jansen-NY	3.04	Roberts-Phi	127	Branca-Bro	.237	Newcombe-Bro	.297	Roe-Bro	26.4	Spahn-Bos	23.8

Clutch Pitching Index		Relief Runs		Adjusted Relief Runs		Relief Ranking		Total Pitcher Index		Total Baseball Ranking	
Roe-Bro	122	Brazle-StL	14.9	Brazle-StL	15.0	Leonard-Chi	24.3	Maglie-NY	3.3	Musial-StL	6.8
Sain-Bos	113	Kennedy-NY	12.9	Wilks-StL-Pit	14.7	Wilks-StL-Pit	14.8	Roberts-Phi	3.2	Robinson-Bro	6.7
Nichols-Bos	112	Perkowski-Cin	12.9	Perkowski-Cin	14.2	Perkowski-Cin	11.6	Spahn-Bos	2.6	Kiner-Pit	5.7
Minner-Chi	111	Wilks-StL-Pit	12.3	Leonard-Chi	13.1	Smith-Cin	11.2	Jansen-NY	2.6	Irvin-NY	4.8
Bickford-Bos	108	Leonard-Chi	11.9	Kennedy-NY	12.6	Brazle-StL	11.1	Newcombe-Bro	2.6	Campanella-Bro	4.7

TEAM	G	W	L	PCT	GB	R	OR	AB	H .	2B	3B	HR	BB	SO	AVG	OBP	SLG	PRO	PRO+	BR	/A	PF	CHI	RC	SB	CS	SBA	SBR
NY	154	98	56	.636		798	621	5194	1395	208	48	**140**	605	547	.269	.349	**.408**	.757	**113**	62	**88**	96	**104**	762	78	39	53	-19
CLE	155	93	61	.604	5	696	**594**	5250	1346	208	35	**140**	606	632	.256	.336	.389	.725	105	0	39	94	98	710	52	35	40	-13
BOS	154	87	67	.565	11	**804**	725	5378	1428	233	32	127	**756**	594	.266	**.358**	.392	.750	98	**64**	-7	110	100	**778**	20	21	34	-13
CHI	155	81	73	.526	17	714	644	5378	**1453**	229	**64**	86	596	524	**.270**	.349	.385	.734	105	23	38	98	95	745	**99**	70	**67**	-18
DET	154	73	81	.474	25	685	741	5336	1413	231	35	104	568	525	.265	.338	.380	.718	98	-13	-15	100	98	697	37	34	34	**-9**
PHI	154	70	84	.455	28	736	745	5277	1381	**262**	43	102	677	565	.262	.349	.386	.735	100	29	13	102	98	745	47	36	51	-19
WAS	154	62	92	.403	36	672	764	5329	1399	242	45	54	560	**515**	.263	.336	.355	.691	92	-59	-46	98	103	648	45	38	43	-13
STL	154	52	102	.338	46	611	882	5219	1288	223	47	86	521	693	.247	.317	.357	.674	83	-101	-121	103	103	592	35	38	47	-16
TOT	617					5716		42361	11103	1836	349	839	4889	4595	.262	.342	.381	.723							413	311	57	-62

TEAM	CG	SH	SV	IP	H	H/G	HR	BB	SO	RAT	ERA	ERA+	OAV	OOB	PR	/A	PF	CPI	FA	E	DP	FW	PW	BW	SBW	DIF
NY	66	**24**	22	1367	1290	8.5	92	562	**664**	12.4	3.56	107	.250	.327	84	40	93	103	.975	144	190	.3	3.9	**8.7**	-1.1	9.2
CLE	**76**	10	19	1391¹	1287	8.3	86	577	642	**12.2**	**3.38**	112	**.245**	.322	114	62	92	103	**.978**	**134**	151	**.9**	6.1	3.8	-.5	5.7
BOS	46	7	**24**	1399	1413	9.1	100	599	658	13.2	4.14	108	.264	.341	-2	50	108	100	.977	141	184	.5	4.9	-.7	-.5	5.8
CHI	74	11	14	1418¹	1353	8.6	109	**549**	572	12.2	3.50	115	.251	.322	97	**83**	98	**105**	.975	151	176	.0	**8.2**	3.7	-1.0	-6.9
DET	51	8	17	1384	1385	9.0	102	602	597	13.2	4.29	97	.261	.341	-26	-17	101	96	.973	163	166	-.7	-1.7	-1.5	-.1	-.0
PHI	52	7	22	1358	1421	9.4	109	569	437	13.4	4.47	96	.272	.347	-52	-28	104	98	.978	136	**204**	.8	-2.8	1.3	-1.1	-5.2
WAS	58	6	13	1366¹	1429	9.4	110	630	475	13.7	4.49	91	.268	.348	-55	-59	99	97	.973	160	148	-.5	-5.8	-4.5	-.5	-3.6
STL	56	5	9	1370¹	1525	10.0	131	801	550	15.5	5.18	85	.282	.378	-160	-119	107	101	.971	172	179	-1.2	-11.7	-11.9	-.8	.6
TOT	479	78	140	11054¹		9.0				13.2	4.12		.262	.342					.975	1201	1398					

<table>
<tr><td colspan="2">Runs</td><td colspan="2">Hits</td><td colspan="2">Doubles</td><td colspan="2">Triples</td><td colspan="2">Home Runs</td><td colspan="2">Total Bases</td></tr>
</table>

Runs
DiMaggio-Bos 113
Minoso-Cle-Chi ... 112
Yost-Was 109
Williams-Bos 109
Joost-Phi 107

Hits
Kell-Det 191
Fox-Chi 189
DiMaggio-Bos 189
Minoso-Cle-Chi ... 173
Williams-Bos 169

Doubles
Yost-Was 36
Mele-Was 36
Kell-Det 36

Triples
Minoso-Cle-Chi 14
Coleman-StL-Chi ... 12
Fox-Chi........... 12
Young-StL 9

Home Runs
Zernial-Chi-Phi ... 33
Williams-Bos 30
Robinson-Chi 29

Total Bases
Williams-Bos 295
Zernial-Chi-Phi ... 292
Robinson-Chi 279
Berra-NY 269
DiMaggio-Bos 267

Runs Batted In
Zernial-Chi-Phi ... 129
Williams-Bos 126
Robinson-Chi 117
Easter-Cle 103
Rosen-Cle 102

Runs Produced
Williams-Bos 205
Zernial-Chi-Phi ... 188
Minoso-Cle-Chi ... 178
Robinson-Chi 173
DiMaggio-Bos 173

Bases On Balls
Williams-Bos 144
Yost-Was 126
Joost-Phi 106
Doby-Cle 101
Rosen-Cle 85

Batting Average
Fain-Phi 344
Minoso-Cle-Chi ...326
Kell-Det 319
Williams-Bos 318
Fox-Chi...........313

On Base Percentage
Williams-Bos 464
Fain-Phi 451
Doby-Cle 428
Yost-Was 423
Minoso-Cle-Chi ...422

Slugging Average
Williams-Bos 556
Doby-Cle 512
Zernial-Chi-Phi ...511
Wertz-Det........511
Minoso-Cle-Chi ...500

Production
Williams-Bos 1.019
Doby-Cle 941
Minoso-Cle-Chi ...922
Fain-Phi 921
Wertz-Det........894

Adjusted Production
Doby-Cle 163
Williams-Bos 159
Minoso-Cle-Chi ... 152
Fain-Phi 146
Wertz-Det 140

Batter Runs
Williams-Bos 62.8
Minoso-Cle-Chi ... 38.2
Doby-Cle 37.0
Fain-Phi 33.8
Joost-Phi 30.5

Adjusted Batter Runs
Williams-Bos 55.0
Doby-Cle 40.7
Minoso-Cle-Chi ... 39.9
Fain-Phi 32.5
Yost-Was 31.7

Clutch Hitting Index
Mele-Was........ 147
Noren-NY 140
Busby-Chi 132
Vernon-Was 128
Williams-Bos 124

Runs Created
Williams-Bos 152
Minoso-Cle-Chi ... 120
Yost-Was 117
Joost-Phi 115
Doby-Cle 108

Total Average
Williams-Bos 1.177
Doby-Cle 1.031
Minoso-Cle-Chi ...987
Fain-Phi 959
Yost-Was 909

Stolen Bases
Minoso-Cle-Chi ... 31
Busby-Chi 26
Rizzuto-NY 18

Stolen Base Average
Rizzuto-NY 85.7
Minoso-Cle-Chi ... 75.6
Busby-Chi 70.3

Stolen Base Runs
Rizzuto-NY 3.6
Minoso-Cle-Chi ... 3.3
Carrasquel-Chi ... 1.8

Fielding Runs
Coan-Was 24.3
Noren-Was....... 16.1
Stephens-Bos 14.1
Fain-Phi 13.6
Zernial-Chi-Phi ... 13.0

Total Player Rating
Williams-Bos 5.3
Fain-Phi 4.1
Joost-Phi 3.8
Berra-NY 3.5
Doby-Cle 2.9

Wins
Feller-Cle 22
Raschi-NY 21
Lopat-NY 21

Win Percentage
Feller-Cle 733
Lopat-NY 700
Reynolds-NY 680
Raschi-NY 677
Shantz-Phi 643

Games
Kinder-Bos........ 63
Brissie-Phi-Cle ... 56
Garcia-Cle 47
Scheib-Phi 46

Complete Games
Garver-StL 24
Wynn-Cle 21
Lopat-NY 20
Pierce-Chi 18

Shutouts
Reynolds-NY 7
Raschi-NY 4
Lopat-NY 4
Feller-Cle 4

Saves
Kinder-Bos........ 14
Scheib-Phi 10
Brissie-Phi-Cle ... 9
Reynolds-NY 7
Garcia-Cle 6

Innings Pitched
Wynn-Cle 274.1
Lemon-Cle 263.1
Raschi-NY 258.1
Garcia-Cle 254.0
Feller-Cle 249.2

Fewest Hits/Game
Reynolds-NY 6.96
McDermott-Bos... 7.38
Wynn-Cle 7.45
Rogovin-Det-Chi .. 7.85
Lopat-NY 8.02

Fewest BB/Game
Hutchinson-Det .. 1.29
Lopat-NY 2.72
Pierce-Chi 2.73
Hooper-Phi 2.90
Garcia-Cle 2.91

Strikeouts
Raschi-NY 164
Wynn-Cle 133
Lemon-Cle 132
Gray-Det 131
McDermott-Bos... 127

Strikeouts/Game
McDermott-Bos... 6.65
Gray-Det 5.97
Raschi-NY 5.71
Reynolds-NY 5.13
Lemon-Cle 4.51

Ratio
Lopat-NY 10.85
Rogovin-Det-Chi . 10.97
Wynn-Cle 11.06
Hutchinson-Det .. 11.13
Reynolds-NY 11.24

Earned Run Average
Rogovin-Det-Chi .. 2.78
Lopat-NY 2.91
Wynn-Cle 3.02
Pierce-Chi 3.03
Reynolds-NY 3.05

Adjusted ERA
Rogovin-Det-Chi .. 146
Parnell-Bos 137
McDermott-Bos... 133
Pierce-Chi 133
Lopat-NY 131

Opponents' Batting Avg.
Reynolds-NY 213
Wynn-Cle 225
McDermott-Bos....226
Rogovin-Det-Chi ..235
Lopat-NY 239

Opponents' On Base Pct.
Lopat-NY 298
Rogovin-Det-Chi .. .301
Wynn-Cle 301
Hutchinson-Det 302
Reynolds-NY 304

Starter Runs
Wynn-Cle 33.6
Rogovin-Det-Chi .. 32.2
Lopat-NY 31.5
Pierce-Chi 29.1
Garcia-Cle 27.3

Adjusted Starter Runs
Rogovin-Det-Chi .. 30.5
Parnell-Bos 29.5
Pierce-Chi 26.7
Lopat-NY 23.8
Wynn-Cle 23.4

Clutch Pitching Index
Parnell-Bos 119
Pierce-Chi 113
Rogovin-Det-Chi .. 111
Feller-Cle 109
Raschi-NY 108

Relief Runs
Kinder-Bos....... 22.2
Brissie-Phi-Cle ... 7.5
Ostrowski-NY 6.7
Masterson-Bos ... 5.2

Adjusted Relief Runs
Kinder-Bos....... 26.9
Aloma-Chi 17.1
Masterson-Bos ... 7.4
Brissie-Phi-Cle ... 3.6
Ostrowski-NY 3.6

Relief Ranking
Kinder-Bos....... 31.5
Aloma-Chi 15.0
Harris-Was....... 4.3
Masterson-Bos ... 3.9
Ostrowski-NY 3.8

Total Pitcher Index
Parnell-Bos 3.6
Rogovin-Det-Chi .. 3.2
Garver-StL 2.9
Lopat-NY 2.6
Pierce-Chi 2.5

Total Baseball Ranking
Williams-Bos 5.3
Fain-Phi 4.1
Joost-Phi 3.8
Parnell-Bos 3.6
Berra-NY 3.5

1952 National League

TEAM	G	W	L	PCT	GB	R	OR	AB	H	2B	3B	HR	BB	SO	AVG	OBP	SLG	PRO	PRO+	BR	/A	PF	CHI	RC	SB	CS	SBA	SBR
BRO	155	96	57	.627		775	603	5266	1380	199	32	153	663	699	.262	.348	.399	.747	112	107	99	101	100	754	90	49	51	-15
NY	154	92	62	.597	4.5	722	639	5229	1337	186	56	151	536	672	.256	.329	.399	.728	107	56	51	101	103	712	30	31	38	-13
STL	154	88	66	.571	8.5	677	630	5200	1386	247	54	97	537	479	.267	.340	.391	.731	109	68	67	100	95	708	33	32	46	-17
PHI	154	87	67	.565	9.5	657	552	5205	1353	237	45	93	540	534	.260	.332	.376	.708	104	26	33	99	98	671	60	41	47	-15
CHI	155	77	77	.500	19.5	628	631	5330	1408	223	45	107	422	712	.264	.321	.383	.704	100	5	-2	101	97	652	50	40	46	-15
CIN	154	69	85	.448	27.5	615	659	5234	1303	212	45	104	480	709	.249	.314	.366	.680	95	-35	-33	100	102	610	32	42	48	-15
BOS	155	64	89	.418	32	569	651	5221	1214	187	31	110	483	711	.233	.301	.343	.644	88	-101	-78	97	105	555	58	34	41	-13
PIT	155	42	112	.273	54.5	515	793	5193	1201	181	30	92	486	724	.231	.300	.331	.631	78	-124	-141	103	101	530	43	41	50	-17
TOT	618					5158		41878	10582	1672	338	907	4147	5240	.253	.323	.374	.697							396	310	56	-66

TEAM	CG	SH	SV	IP	H	H/G	HR	BB	SO	RAT	ERA	ERA+	OAV	OOB	PR	/A	PF	CPI	FA	E	DP	FW	PW	BW	SBW	DIF
BRO	45	11	24	1399[1]	1295	8.3	121	544	773	12.0	3.53	103	.246	.320	31	16	98	103	.982	106	169	2.0	1.7	10.2	-.7	6.3
NY	49	12	31	1371	1282	8.4	121	538	655	12.2	3.59	103	.247	.322	21	16	99	103	.974	158	175	-.8	1.7	5.3	-.5	9.3
STL	49	12	27	1361[1]	1274	8.4	119	501	712	11.9	3.66	101	.246	.316	10	7	100	98	.977	141	159	.1	.7	6.9	-.9	4.1
PHI	80	17	16	1386[2]	1306	8.5	95	373	609	11.0	3.07	119	.248	.300	102	89	98	104	.975	150	145	-.4	9.2	3.4	-.7	-1.6
CHI	59	15	15	1386[1]	1265	8.2	101	534	661	11.9	3.58	107	.240	.314	22	41	103	94	.976	146	123	-.1	4.2	-.2	-.7	-3.2
CIN	56	11	12	1363[1]	1377	9.1	111	517	579	12.8	4.01	94	.266	.337	-42	-36	101	103	.982	107	145	1.9	-3.7	-3.4	-.7	-2.1
BOS	63	11	13	1396	1388	8.9	106	525	687	12.5	3.78	96	.259	.328	-7	-26	97	102	.975	154	143	-.5	-2.7	-8.1	-.5	-.7
PIT	43	5	8	1363[2]	1395	9.2	133	615	564	13.4	4.65	86	.265	.345	-138	-98	107	94	.970	182	167	-2.0	-10.1	-14.6	-.9	-7.4
TOT	444	94	146	11027[2]		8.6				12.2	3.73		.253	.323					.976	1144	1226					

Runs
Musial-StL	105
Hemus-StL	105
Robinson-Bro	104
Lockman-NY	99
Reese-Bro	94

Hits
Musial-StL	194
Schoendienst-StL	188
Adams-Cin	180
Dark-NY	177
Lockman-NY	176

Doubles
Musial-StL	42
Schoendienst-StL	40
McMillan-Cin	32
Sauer-Chi	31
Ashburn-Phi	31

Triples
Thomson-NY	14
Slaughter-StL	12
Kluszewski-Cin	11
Ennis-Phi	10

Home Runs
Sauer-Chi	37
Kiner-Pit	37
Hodges-Bro	32
Mathews-Bos	25
Gordon-Bos	25

Total Bases
Musial-StL	311
Sauer-Chi	301
Thomson-NY	293
Ennis-Phi	281
Snider-Bro	264

Runs Batted In
Sauer-Chi	121
Thomson-NY	108
Ennis-Phi	107
Hodges-Bro	102
Slaughter-StL	101

Runs Produced
Ennis-Phi	177
Musial-StL	175
Thomson-NY	173
Sauer-Chi	173
Slaughter-StL	163

Bases On Balls
Kiner-Pit	110
Hodges-Bro	107
Robinson-Bro	106
Musial-StL	96
Hemus-StL	96

Batting Average
Musial-StL	.336
Kluszewski-Cin	.320
Robinson-Bro	.308
Snider-Bro	.303
Schoendienst-StL	.303

On Base Percentage
Robinson-Bro	.440
Musial-StL	.432
Hemus-StL	.392
Hodges-Bro	.386
Slaughter-StL	.386

Slugging Average
Musial-StL	.538
Sauer-Chi	.531
Kluszewski-Cin	.509
Kiner-Pit	.500
Hodges-Bro	.500

Production
Musial-StL	.970
Robinson-Bro	.904
Kluszewski-Cin	.892
Sauer-Chi	.892
Hodges-Bro	.886

Adjusted Production
Musial-StL	167
Robinson-Bro	149
Kluszewski-Cin	146
Gordon-Bos	144
Sauer-Chi	143

Batter Runs
Musial-StL	55.7
Robinson-Bro	41.9
Sauer-Chi	32.8
Kiner-Pit	32.7
Hodges-Bro	32.4

Adjusted Batter Runs
Musial-StL	55.6
Robinson-Bro	41.1
Sauer-Chi	31.9
Hodges-Bro	31.6
Kiner-Pit	30.8

Clutch Hitting Index
Slaughter-StL	161
Hatton-Cin	140
Campanella-Bro	139
Ennis-Phi	130
Thomson-NY	122

Runs Created
Musial-StL	141
Robinson-Bro	116
Sauer-Chi	111
Kiner-Pit	111
Hodges-Bro	106

Total Average
Musial-StL	1.017
Robinson-Bro	.995
Kiner-Pit	.955
Hodges-Bro	.921
Sauer-Chi	.886

Stolen Bases
Reese-Bro	30
Jethroe-Bos	28
Robinson-Bro	24
Ashburn-Phi	16

Stolen Base Average
Reese-Bro	85.7
Robinson-Bro	77.4
Jethroe-Bos	75.7
Ashburn-Phi	59.3

Stolen Base Runs
Reese-Bro	6.0
Robinson-Bro	3.0
Jethroe-Bos	3.0
Davis-Pit	1.5
Slaughter-StL	1.2

Fielding Runs
Schoendienst-StL	32.9
Logan-Bos	17.6
Ashburn-Phi	13.1
Baumholtz-Chi	12.1
Wyrostek-Cin-Phi	11.6

Total Player Rating
Robinson-Bro	5.5
Schoendienst-StL	4.9
Musial-StL	4.2
Sauer-Chi	4.0
Hemus-StL	3.1

Wins
Roberts-Phi	28
Maglie-NY	18
Staley-StL	17
Rush-Chi	17
Raffensberger-Cin	17

Win Percentage
Wilhelm-NY	.833
Roberts-Phi	.800
Black-Bro	.789
Maglie-NY	.692
Hacker-Chi	.625

Games
Wilhelm-NY	71
Black-Bro	56
Yuhas-StL	54
Smith-Cin	53
Main-Pit	48

Complete Games
Roberts-Phi	30
Dickson-Pit	21
Spahn-Bos	19
Raffensberger-Cin	18
Rush-Chi	17

Shutouts
Simmons-Phi	6
Raffensberger-Cin	6

Saves
Brazle-StL	16
Black-Bro	15
Wilhelm-NY	11
Leonard-Chi	11

Innings Pitched
Roberts-Phi	330.0
Spahn-Bos	290.0
Dickson-Pit	277.2
Rush-Chi	250.1
Raffensberger-Cin	247.0

Fewest Hits/Game
Hacker-Chi	7.01
Wilhelm-NY	7.17
Erskine-Bro	7.27
Rush-Chi	7.37
Loes-Bro	7.40

Fewest BB/Game
Roberts-Phi	1.23
Hacker-Chi	1.51
Raffensberger-Cin	1.64
Staley-StL	1.95
Drews-Phi	2.05

Strikeouts
Spahn-Bos	183
Rush-Chi	157
Roberts-Phi	148
Mizell-StL	146
Simmons-Phi	141

Strikeouts/Game
Mizell-StL	6.92
Simmons-Phi	6.30
Wilhelm-NY	6.10
Wade-Bro	5.90
Erskine-Bro	5.70

Ratio
Hacker-Chi	8.56
Roberts-Phi	9.33
Erskine-Bro	10.45
Rush-Chi	10.50
Drews-Phi	10.59

Earned Run Average
Wilhelm-NY	2.43
Hacker-Chi	2.58
Roberts-Phi	2.59
Loes-Bro	2.69
Rush-Chi	2.70

Adjusted ERA
Wilhelm-NY	152
Hacker-Chi	149
Rush-Chi	143
Roberts-Phi	141
Loes-Bro	135

Opponents' Batting Avg.
Hacker-Chi	.212
Rush-Chi	.216
Wilhelm-NY	.220
Erskine-Bro	.220
Loes-Bro	.224

Opponents' On Base Pct.
Hacker-Chi	.247
Roberts-Phi	.263
Rush-Chi	.282
Erskine-Bro	.289
Spahn-Bos	.291

Starter Runs
Roberts-Phi	41.8
Rush-Chi	28.8
Drews-Phi	25.8
Raffensberger-Cin	25.4
Spahn-Bos	24.3

Adjusted Starter Runs
Roberts-Phi	39.0
Rush-Chi	32.1
Raffensberger-Cin	26.6
Hacker-Chi	26.2
Drews-Phi	23.8

Clutch Pitching Index
Roe-Bro	127
Church-Phi-Cin	119
Wilhelm-NY	119
Raffensberger-Cin	117
Maglie-NY	116

Relief Runs
Black-Bro	25.0
Wilhelm-NY	23.1
Brazle-StL	12.3
Leonard-Chi	11.6
Yuhas-StL	11.2

Adjusted Relief Runs
Black-Bro	23.5
Wilhelm-NY	22.5
Leonard-Chi	12.5
Brazle-StL	12.1
Yuhas-StL	11.0

Relief Ranking
Black-Bro	33.9
Wilhelm-NY	26.4
Brazle-StL	20.9
Yuhas-StL	15.4
Leonard-Chi	11.4

Total Pitcher Index
Rush-Chi	4.6
Roberts-Phi	4.1
Erskine-Bro	2.5
Spahn-Bos	2.5
Raffensberger-Cin	2.4

Total Baseball Ranking
Robinson-Bro	5.5
Schoendienst-StL	4.9
Rush-Chi	4.6
Musial-StL	4.2
Roberts-Phi	4.1

TEAM	G	W	L	PCT	GB	R	OR	AB	H	2B	3B	HR	BB	SO	AVG	OBP	SLG	PRO	PRO+	BR	/A	PF	CHI	RC	SB	CS	SBA	SBR
NY	154	95	59	.617		727	557	5294	1411	221	56	129	566	652	.267	.341	.403	.744	121	89	127	94	99	758	52	42	47	-15
CLE	155	93	61	.604	2	763	606	5330	1399	211	49	148	626	749	.262	.342	.404	.746	121	95	137	94	102	759	46	39	45	-14
CHI	156	81	73	.526	14	610	568	5316	1337	199	38	80	541	521	.252	.327	.348	.675	93	-34	-39	101	98	633	61	38	46	-15
PHI	155	79	75	.513	16	664	723	5163	1305	212	35	89	683	561	.253	.343	.359	.702	95	26	-14	106	99	659	52	43	48	-15
WAS	157	78	76	.506	17	598	608	5357	1282	225	44	50	580	607	.239	.317	.326	.643	87	-97	-74	97	107	572	48	37	44	-14
BOS	154	76	78	.494	19	668	658	5246	1338	233	34	113	542	739	.255	.328	.377	.705	95	14	-35	108	103	659	59	47	52	-16
STL	155	64	90	.416	31	604	733	5353	1340	225	46	82	540	720	.250	.322	.356	.678	92	-38	-56	103	99	631	30	34	40	-13
DET	156	50	104	.325	45	557	738	5258	1278	190	37	103	553	605	.243	.318	.352	.670	92	-51	-56	101	94	594	27	38	49	-17
TOT	621					5191		42317	10690	1716	339	794	4631	5154	.253	.330	.365	.695							375	318	54	-77

TEAM	CG	SH	SV	IP	H	H/G	HR	BB	SO	RAT	ERA	ERA+	OAV	OOB	PR	/A	PF	CPI	FA	E	DP	FW	PW	BW	SBW	DIF
NY	72	21	27	1381	1240	8.1	94	581	666	12.1	3.14	106	.242	.324	81	27	90	110	.979	127	199	.8	2.8	13.2	-.5	1.8
CLE	80	19	18	1407	1278	8.2	94	556	671	11.9	3.32	101	.241	.316	55	3	91	99	.975	155	141	-.8	.3	14.2	-.4	2.7
CHI	53	15	28	1416²	1251	7.9	86	578	774	11.7	3.25	112	.237	.315	66	62	99	98	.980	123	158	1.1	6.4	-4.0	-.5	1.1
PHI	73	11	16	1384¹	1402	9.1	113	526	562	12.8	4.15	95	.262	.332	-73	-30	108	94	.977	140	148	.0	-3.1	-1.5	-.5	7.0
WAS	75	10	15	1429²	1405	8.8	78	577	574	12.7	3.37	105	.257	.331	47	29	97	108	.978	132	152	.6	3.0	-7.7	-.4	5.5
BOS	53	7	24	1372¹	1332	8.7	107	623	624	13.1	3.80	104	.256	.340	-19	20	107	104	.976	145	181	-.3	2.1	-3.6	-.6	1.5
STL	48	6	18	1399	1388	8.9	111	598	581	13.0	4.12	95	.259	.338	-68	-31	107	97	.974	155	176	-.8	-3.2	-5.8	-.3	-2.8
DET	51	10	14	1388¹	1394	9.0	111	591	702	13.0	4.25	90	.261	.338	-89	-68	104	94	.975	152	145	-.6	-7.1	-5.8	-.7	-12.8
TOT	505	99	160	11178¹		8.6				12.5	3.67		.253	.330					.977	1129	1300					

Runs
Doby-Cle 104
Avila-Cle 102
Rosen-Cle 101
Berra-NY 97
Minoso-Chi 96

Hits
Fox-Chi 192
Avila-Cle 179
Robinson-Chi 176
Fain-Phi 176

Doubles
Fain-Phi 43
Mantle-NY 37
Vernon-Was 33
Robinson-Chi 33

Triples
Avila-Cle 11
Simpson-Cle 10
Rizzuto-NY 10
Fox-Chi........... 10

Home Runs
Doby-Cle 32
Easter-Cle 31
Berra-NY 30
Dropo-Bos-Det 29
Zernial-Phi 29

Total Bases
Rosen-Cle 297
Mantle-NY 291
Dropo-Bos-Det .. 282
Doby-Cle 281
Robinson-Chi 277

Runs Batted In
Rosen-Cle 105
Robinson-Chi ... 104
Doby-Cle 104
Zernial-Phi 100
Berra-NY 98

Runs Produced
Rosen-Cle 178
Doby-Cle 176
Berra-NY 165
Robinson-Chi 161
Mantle-NY 158

Bases On Balls
Yost-Was 129
Joost-Phi 122
Fain-Phi 105
Valo-Phi 101
Doby-Cle 90

Batting Average
Fain-Phi .... .327
Mitchell-Cle ..... .323
Mantle-NY .... .311
Kell-Det-Bos ..... .311
Goodman-Bos .... .306

On Base Percentage
Fain-Phi .... .438
Valo-Phi .... .432
Mantle-NY .... .394
Joost-Phi .... .388
Rosen-Cle .... .387

Slugging Average
Doby-Cle .... .541
Mantle-NY ...... .530
Rosen-Cle .... .524
Easter-Cle .... .513
Wertz-Det-StL ... .506

Production
Mantle-NY ...... .924
Doby-Cle .... .924
Rosen-Cle ...... .911
Wertz-Det-StL ... .887
Fain-Phi .... .867

Adjusted Production
Doby-Cle 166
Mantle-NY 166
Rosen-Cle 162
Easter-Cle 144
Wertz-Det-StL ... 143

Batter Runs
Mantle-NY 40.3
Rosen-Cle 38.6
Doby-Cle 37.9
Fain-Phi 36.3
Robinson-Chi 28.3

Adjusted Batter Runs
Mantle-NY 44.4
Rosen-Cle 43.2
Doby-Cle 42.2
Fain-Phi 31.9
Robinson-Chi 27.7

Clutch Hitting Index
Runnels-Was 130
McDougald-NY ... 125
Vernon-Was 125
Jensen-NY-Was... 121
Robinson-Chi 120

Runs Created
Mantle-NY 123
Doby-Cle 116
Rosen-Cle 115
Robinson-Chi 113
Fain-Phi 107

Total Average
Doby-Cle .... .974
Mantle-NY ...... .961
Wertz-Det-StL ... .912
Rosen-Cle .... .900
Valo-Phi .... .873

Stolen Bases
Minoso-Chi 22
Rivera-StL-Chi 21
Jensen-NY-Was.... 18
Rizzuto-NY 17
Throneberry-Bos .. 16

Stolen Base Average
Jensen-NY-Was ... 75.0
Rizzuto-NY 73.9
Rivera-StL-Chi 70.0
Throneberry-Bos . 69.6
Minoso-Chi 57.9

Stolen Base Runs
Jensen-NY-Was.... 1.8
Rizzuto-NY 1.5
Michaels-Was-StL-Phi 1.2
.... 1.2
Porter-StL 1.2
Goodman-Bos 1.2

Fielding Runs
Goodman-Bos 21.0
Rizzuto-NY 18.9
Martin-NY 18.3
Hatfield-Bos-Det .. 17.8
Fain-Phi 16.0

Total Player Rating
Doby-Cle 4.3
Fain-Phi 3.8
Mantle-NY 3.5
Berra-NY 3.3
Goodman-Bos 3.0

Wins
Shantz-Phi 24
Wynn-Cle 23
Lemon-Cle 22
Garcia-Cle 22
Reynolds-NY 20

Win Percentage
Shantz-Phi .... .774
Raschi-NY .... .727
Reynolds-NY ..... .714
Lemon-Cle .... .667
Garcia-Cle .... .667

Games
Kennedy-Chi 47
Paige-StL 46
Garcia-Cle 46
Hooper-Phi 43

Complete Games
Lemon-Cle 28
Shantz-Phi 27
Reynolds-NY 24
Wynn-Cle 19
Garcia-Cle 19

Shutouts
Reynolds-NY 6
Garcia-Cle 6
Shantz-Phi 5
Lemon-Cle 5

Saves
Dorish-Chi 11
Paige-StL 10
Sain-NY 7

Innings Pitched
Lemon-Cle 309.2
Garcia-Cle 292.1
Wynn-Cle 285.2
Shantz-Phi 279.2
Pierce-Chi 255.1

Fewest Hits/Game
Lemon-Cle 6.86
Raschi-NY 7.02
Reynolds-NY 7.15
Dobson-Chi 7.36
Shantz-Phi 7.40

Fewest BB/Game
Shantz-Phi 2.03
Pillette-StL 2.41
Marrero-Was 2.59
Houtteman-Det ... 2.65
Garcia-Cle 2.68

Strikeouts
Reynolds-NY 160
Wynn-Cle 153
Shantz-Phi 152
Pierce-Chi 144
Garcia-Cle 143

Strikeouts/Game
McDermott-Bos ... 6.50
Reynolds-NY 5.89
Trucks-Det 5.89
Gray-Det 5.54
Grissom-Chi 5.26

Ratio
Shantz-Phi 9.56
Dobson-Chi 10.05
Lemon-Cle 10.09
Pierce-Chi 10.43
Raschi-NY 10.94

Earned Run Average
Reynolds-NY 2.06
Garcia-Cle 2.37
Shantz-Phi 2.48
Lemon-Cle 2.50
Dobson-Chi 2.51

Adjusted ERA
Reynolds-NY 161
Shantz-Phi 160
Dobson-Chi 145
Pierce-Chi 142
Garcia-Cle 141

Opponents' Batting Avg.
Lemon-Cle ...... .208
Raschi-NY ...... .216
Reynolds-NY .... .218
Dobson-Chi ..... .222
Shantz-Phi ...... .225

Opponents' On Base Pct.
Shantz-Phi ...... .272
Lemon-Cle ...... .279
Dobson-Chi ..... .280
Pierce-Chi ...... .289
Reynolds-NY .... .300

Starter Runs
Reynolds-NY 43.8
Garcia-Cle 42.4
Lemon-Cle 40.4
Shantz-Phi 37.2
Pierce-Chi 31.3

Adjusted Starter Runs
Shantz-Phi 46.0
Reynolds-NY 34.2
Garcia-Cle 31.6
Pierce-Chi 30.5
Lemon-Cle 29.1

Clutch Pitching Index
Garcia-Cle 127
Byrd-Phi 126
Reynolds-NY 125
Porterfield-Was ... 120
Hudson-Was-Bos . 117

Relief Runs
Dorish-Chi 12.2
Kennedy-Chi 6.9
Consuegra-Was ... 5.1
Brissie-Cle 1.8
Littlefield-Det-StL .. 1.4

Adjusted Relief Runs
Dorish-Chi 11.9
Kennedy-Chi 6.7
Consuegra-Was ... 4.1
Littlefield-Det-StL .. 3.3
White-Det 8

Relief Ranking
Dorish-Chi 17.4
Kennedy-Chi 4.4
Consuegra-Was ... 3.6
Littlefield-Det-StL .. 2.6
White-Det 1.1

Total Pitcher Index
Shantz-Phi 5.6
Lemon-Cle 4.5
Reynolds-NY 3.4
Garcia-Cle 3.3
Pierce-Chi 3.3

Total Baseball Ranking
Shantz-Phi 5.6
Lemon-Cle 4.5
Doby-Cle 4.3
Fain-Phi 3.8
Mantle-NY 3.5

TEAM	G	W	L	PCT	GB	R	OR	AB	H	2B	3B	HR	BB	SO	AVG	OBP	SLG	PRO	PRO+	BR	/A	PF	CHI	RC	SB	CS	SBA	SBR
BRO	155	105	49	.682		955	689	5373	1529	274	59	208	655	686	.285	.366	.474	.840	121	188	171	102	101	963	90	47	48	-14
MIL	157	92	62	.597	13	738	589	5349	1422	227	52	156	439	637	.266	.325	.415	.740	104	-21	24	94	104	727	46	27	36	-13
STL	157	83	71	.539	22	768	713	5397	1474	281	56	140	574	617	.273	.347	.424	.771	107	53	53	100	95	806	18	22	38	-15
PHI	156	83	71	.539	22	716	666	5290	1400	228	62	115	530	597	.265	.336	.396	.731	96	-24	-19	99	101	727	42	21	36	-14
NY	155	70	84	.455	35	768	747	5362	1452	195	45	176	499	608	.271	.336	.422	.758	101	20	6	102	101	771	31	21	37	-15
CIN	155	68	86	.442	37	714	788	5343	1396	190	34	166	485	701	.261	.325	.403	.728	94	-41	-46	101	103	711	25	20	35	-14
CHI	155	65	89	.422	40	633	835	5272	1372	204	57	137	514	746	.260	.328	.399	.727	92	-40	-56	102	92	697	49	21	38	-16
PIT	154	50	104	.325	55	622	887	5253	1297	178	49	99	524	715	.247	.319	.356	.675	82	-129	-124	99	103	614	41	39	51	-18
TOT	622					5914		42639	11342	1777	414	1197	4220	5307	.266	.335	.411	.747							342	218	61	-27

TEAM	CG	SH	SV	IP	H	H/G	HR	BB	SO	RAT	ERA	ERA+	OAV	OOB	PR	/A	PF	CPI	FA	E	DP	FW	PW	BW	SBW	DIF
BRO	51	11	29	1380²	1337	8.7	169	509	817	12.1	4.10	104	.252	.320	28	24	99	97	.980	118	161	1.7	2.3	16.5	-1.0	8.6
MIL	72	14	15	1387	1282	8.3	107	539	738	12.0	3.30	119	.244	.317	152	96	92	106	.976	143	169	.4	9.2	2.3	-.9	4.0
STL	51	11	36	1386²	1406	9.1	139	533	732	12.9	4.23	101	.261	.333	9	4	99	98	.977	138	161	.7	.4	5.1	-1.1	1.0
PHI	76	13	15	1369²	1410	9.3	138	410	637	12.1	3.80	111	.264	.320	74	62	98	104	.975	147	161	.0	6.0	-1.8	-1.0	2.8
NY	46	10	20	1365²	1403	9.2	146	610	647	13.4	4.25	101	.264	.342	5	6	100	103	.975	151	151	-.2	.6	.6	-1.1	-6.9
CIN	47	7	15	1365	1484	9.8	179	488	506	13.2	4.64	94	.278	.342	-52	-42	102	102	.978	129	176	1.1	-4.0	-4.4	-1.0	-.6
CHI	38	3	22	1359	1491	9.9	151	554	623	13.8	4.79	93	.275	.347	-75	-50	104	97	.967	193	141	-2.5	-4.8	-5.4	-1.2	2.0
PIT	49	4	10	1358	1529	10.1	168	577	607	14.1	5.22	86	.284	.356	-141	-112	104	96	.973	163	139	-.9	-10.8	-11.9	-1.4	-2.0
TOT	430	73	162	10971²		9.3				12.9	4.29		.266	.335					.975	1182	1259					

Runs		Hits		Doubles		Triples		Home Runs		Total Bases	
Snider-Bro	132	Ashburn-Phi	205	Musial-StL	53	Gilliam-Bro	17	Mathews-Mil	47	Snider-Bro	370
Musial-StL	127	Musial-StL	200	Dark-NY	41	Bruton-Mil	14	Snider-Bro	42	Mathews-Mil	363
Dark-NY	126	Snider-Bro	198	Snider-Bro	38	Hemus-StL	11	Campanella-Bro	41	Musial-StL	361
Gilliam-Bro	125	Dark-NY	194	Furillo-Bro	38	Fondy-Chi	11	Kluszewski-Cin	40	Kluszewski-Cin	325
		Schoendienst-StL	193	Bell-Cin	37			Kiner-Pit-Chi	35	Bell-Cin	320

Runs Batted In		Runs Produced		Bases On Balls		Batting Average		On Base Percentage		Slugging Average	
Campanella-Bro	142	Snider-Bro	216	Musial-StL	105	Furillo-Bro	.344	Musial-StL	.437	Snider-Bro	.627
Mathews-Mil	135	Musial-StL	210	Kiner-Pit-Chi	100	Schoendienst-StL	.342	Robinson-Bro	.425	Mathews-Mil	.627
Snider-Bro	126	Campanella-Bro	204	Gilliam-Bro	100	Musial-StL	.337	Snider-Bro	.419	Campanella-Bro	.611
Ennis-Phi	125	Mathews-Mil	198	Mathews-Mil	99	Snider-Bro	.336	Irvin-NY	.406	Musial-StL	.609
Hodges-Bro	122			Hemus-StL	86	Mueller-NY	.333	Mathews-Mil	.406	Furillo-Bro	.580

Production		Adjusted Production		Batter Runs		Adjusted Batter Runs		Clutch Hitting Index		Runs Created	
Snider-Bro	1.046	Mathews-Mil	175	Musial-StL	62.7	Musial-StL	62.8	Slaughter-StL	153	Musial-StL	166
Musial-StL	1.046	Musial-StL	169	Snider-Bro	59.3	Mathews-Mil	60.2	Ennis-Phi	141	Snider-Bro	161
Mathews-Mil	1.033	Snider-Bro	165	Mathews-Mil	54.9	Snider-Bro	57.4	Jablonski-StL	139	Mathews-Mil	157
Campanella-Bro	1.006	Campanella-Bro	154	Campanella-Bro	42.9	Campanella-Bro	41.3	Robinson-Bro	135	Campanella-Bro	128
Furillo-Bro	.973	Furillo-Bro	146	Kluszewski-Cin	35.0	Kluszewski-Cin	34.4	Campanella-Bro	128	Kluszewski-Cin	126

Total Average		Stolen Bases		Stolen Base Average		Stolen Base Runs		Fielding Runs		Total Player Rating	
Musial-StL	1.143	Bruton-Mil	26	Robinson-Bro	81.0	Reese-Bro	3.0	Schoendienst-StL	25.3	Schoendienst-StL	5.7
Snider-Bro	1.134	Reese-Bro	22	Reese-Bro	78.6	Robinson-Bro	2.7	Ashburn-Phi	21.9	Mathews-Mil	5.3
Mathews-Mil	1.119	Gilliam-Bro	21	Bruton-Mil	70.3	Torgeson-Phi	1.5	Thomas-Pit	20.8	Musial-StL	4.9
Campanella-Bro	1.048	Robinson-Bro	17	Snider-Bro	69.6	Miksis-Chi	1.5	Logan-Mil	20.6	Campanella-Bro	4.8
Robinson-Bro	.988	Snider-Bro	16	Gilliam-Bro	60.0	Jeffcoat-Chi	1.5	Jeffcoat-Chi	15.1	Snider-Bro	4.3

Wins		Win Percentage		Games		Complete Games		Shutouts		Saves	
Spahn-Mil	23	Erskine-Bro	.769	Wilhelm-NY	68	Roberts-Phi	33	Haddix-StL	6	Brazle-StL	18
Roberts-Phi	23	Spahn-Mil	.767	Brazle-StL	60	Spahn-Mil	24	Spahn-Mil	5	Wilhelm-NY	15
Haddix-StL	20	Meyer-Bro	.750	Hetki-Pit	54	Simmons-Phi	19	Roberts-Phi	5	Hughes-Bro	9
Erskine-Bro	20	Burdette-Mil	.750	Smith-Cin	50	Haddix-StL	19	Simmons-Phi	4	Leonard-Chi	8
Staley-StL	18	Haddix-StL	.690			Erskine-Bro	16	Erskine-Bro	4	Burdette-Mil	8

Innings Pitched		Fewest Hits/Game		Fewest BB/Game		Strikeouts		Strikeouts/Game		Ratio	
Roberts-Phi	346.2	Spahn-Mil	7.15	Roberts-Phi	1.58	Roberts-Phi	198	Mizell-StL	6.94	Spahn-Mil	9.55
Spahn-Mil	265.2	Gomez-NY	7.32	Raffensberger-Cin	1.71	Erskine-Bro	187	Erskine-Bro	6.82	Roberts-Phi	10.05
Haddix-StL	253.0	Mizell-StL	7.74	Minner-Chi	1.79	Mizell-StL	173	Antonelli-Mil	6.72	Haddix-StL	10.42
Erskine-Bro	246.2	Erskine-Bro	7.77	Staley-StL	2.11	Haddix-StL	163	Klippstein-Chi	6.07	Simmons-Phi	11.19
Simmons-Phi	238.0	Haddix-StL	7.83	Hacker-Chi	2.19	Spahn-Mil	148	Haddix-StL	5.80	Erskine-Bro	11.35

Earned Run Average		Adjusted ERA		Opponents' Batting Avg.		Opponents' On Base Pct.		Starter Runs		Adjusted Starter Runs	
Spahn-Mil	2.10	Spahn-Mil	187	Spahn-Mil	.217	Spahn-Mil	.270	Spahn-Mil	64.5	Roberts-Phi	56.1
Roberts-Phi	2.75	Roberts-Phi	153	Gomez-NY	.218	Roberts-Phi	.276	Roberts-Phi	59.1	Spahn-Mil	53.8
Haddix-StL	3.06	Haddix-StL	139	Mizell-StL	.227	Haddix-StL	.287	Haddix-StL	34.5	Haddix-StL	33.6
Antonelli-Mil	3.18	Simmons-Phi	131	Erskine-Bro	.230	Hacker-Chi	.299	Simmons-Phi	28.3	Simmons-Phi	26.3
Simmons-Phi	3.21	Gomez-NY	126	Haddix-StL	.232	Simmons-Phi	.302	Buhl-Mil	22.5	Gomez-NY	20.2

Clutch Pitching Index		Relief Runs		Adjusted Relief Runs		Relief Ranking		Total Pitcher Index		Total Baseball Ranking	
Raffensberger-Cin	115	Wilhelm-NY	20.1	Wilhelm-NY	20.1	Labine-Bro	27.9	Spahn-Mil	6.2	Spahn-Mil	6.2
Dickson-Pit	112	Labine-Bro	18.5	Labine-Bro	18.2	Wilhelm-NY	23.4	Roberts-Phi	5.9	Roberts-Phi	5.9
Drews-Phi	112	Johnson-Mil	14.6	White-StL	12.0	White-StL	16.3	Haddix-StL	4.5	Schoendienst-StL	5.7
Burdette-Mil	110	White-StL	12.3	Johnson-Mil	11.3	Johnson-Mil	8.8	Simmons-Phi	2.0	Mathews-Mil	5.3
Roe-Bro	108	Hughes-Bro	7.8	Hughes-Bro	7.6	Hughes-Bro	7.3	Gomez-NY	2.0	Musial-StL	4.9

TEAM	G	W	L	PCT	GB	R	OR	AB	H	2B	3B	HR	BB	SO	AVG	OBP	SLG	PRO	PRO+	BR	/A	PF	CHI	RC	SB	CS	SBA	SBR
NY	151	99	52	.656		801	547	5194	1420	226	52	139	656	644	.273	.359	.417	.776	120	113	137	97	100	809	34	44	47	-14
CLE	155	92	62	.597	8.5	770	627	5285	1426	201	29	160	609	683	.270	.349	.410	.759	114	77	95	97	100	780	33	29	38	-13
CHI	156	89	65	.578	11.5	716	592	5212	1345	226	53	74	601	530	.258	.341	.364	.705	93	-16	-36	103	106	666	73	55	59	-18
BOS	153	84	69	.549	16	656	632	5246	1385	255	37	101	496	601	.264	.343	.384	.716	94	-9	-44	105	98	683	33	45	43	-11
WAS	152	76	76	.500	23.5	687	614	5149	1354	230	53	69	596	604	.263	.343	.368	.711	100	-5	11	98	102	675	65	36	46	-16
DET	158	60	94	.390	40.5	695	923	5553	1479	259	44	108	506	603	.266	.331	.387	.718	100	-9	0	99	99	716	30	35	43	-14
PHI	157	59	95	.383	41.5	632	799	5455	1398	205	38	116	498	602	.256	.331	.372	.693	88	-60	-86	104	99	658	41	24	36	-13
STL	154	54	100	.351	46.5	555	778	5264	1310	214	25	112	507	644	.249	.317	.363	.680	87	-82	-94	102	93	606	17	34	49	-18
TOT	618					5512		42358	11117	1816	331	879	4469	4911	.262	.336	.383	.720							326	302	52	-82

TEAM	CG	SH	SV	IP	H	H/G	HR	BB	SO	RAT	ERA	ERA+	OAV	OOB	PR	/A	PF	CPI	FA	E	DP	FW	PW	BW	SBW	DIF
NY	50	18	39	1358¹	1286	8.5	94	500	604	12.1	3.20	115	.250	.321	119	74	92	110	.979	126	182	.3	7.4	13.7	-.4	2.4
CLE	81	11	15	1373	1311	8.6	92	519	586	12.2	3.64	103	.253	.325	53	16	94	99	.979	127	197	.4	1.6	9.5	-.3	3.7
CHI	57	17	33	1403²	1299	8.3	113	583	714	12.2	3.41	118	.245	.323	91	95	101	105	.980	125	144	.6	9.5	-3.6	-.8	6.3
BOS	41	15	37	1373	1333	8.7	92	584	642	12.7	3.58	118	.254	.331	63	95	105	104	.975	148	173	-.9	9.5	-4.4	-.0	3.3
WAS	76	16	10	1344²	1313	8.8	112	478	515	12.2	3.66	106	.257	.324	49	34	98	103	.979	120	173	.7	3.4	1.1	-.6	-4.6
DET	50	2	16	1415	1633	10.4	154	585	645	14.4	5.25	77	.291	.362	-197	-186	102	96	.978	135	149	.1	-18.6	.0	-.4	1.9
PHI	51	7	11	1409	1475	9.4	121	594	566	13.6	4.67	92	.270	.348	-105	-60	107	93	.977	137	161	-.0	-6.0	-8.6	-.3	-3.1
STL	28	10	24	1383²	1467	9.5	101	626	639	13.8	4.48	94	.272	.351	-73	-42	105	97	.974	152	165	-1.0	-4.2	-9.4	-.8	-7.6
TOT	434	96	185	11060¹		9.0				12.9	3.99		.262	.336					.978	1070	1344					

Runs	Hits	Doubles	Triples	Home Runs	Total Bases
Rosen-Cle 115	Kuenn-Det 209	Vernon-Was 43	Rivera-Chi 16	Rosen-Cle 43	Rosen-Cle 367
Yost-Was 107	Vernon-Was 205	Kell-Bos 41	Vernon-Was 11	Zernial-Phi 42	Vernon-Was 315
Mantle-NY 105	Rosen-Cle 201	White-Bos 34	Piersall-Bos 9	Doby-Cle 29	Zernial-Phi 311
Minoso-Chi 104	Philley-Phi 188	Kuenn-Det 33	Philley-Phi 9	Berra-NY 27	Philley-Phi 263
Vernon-Was 101	Busby-Was 183	Goodman-Bos 33		Boone-Cle-Det 26	Berra-NY 263

Runs Batted In	Runs Produced	Bases On Balls	Batting Average	On Base Percentage	Slugging Average
Rosen-Cle 145	Rosen-Cle 217	Yost-Was 123	Vernon-Was 337	Woodling-NY 429	Rosen-Cle 613
Vernon-Was 115	Vernon-Was 201	Fain-Chi 108	Rosen-Cle 336	Rosen-Cle 422	Zernial-Phi 559
Boone-Cle-Det ... 114	Minoso-Chi 193	Doby-Cle 96	Goodman-Bos 313	Minoso-Chi 410	Berra-NY 523
Zernial-Phi 108	Boone-Cle-Det 182	Gernert-Bos....... 88	Minoso-Chi 313	Fain-Chi 405	Boone-Cle-Det 519
Berra-NY 108	Mantle-NY 176	Rosen-Cle 85	Busby-Was 312	Yost-Was 403	Vernon-Was 518

Production	Adjusted Production	Batter Runs	Adjusted Batter Runs	Clutch Hitting Index	Runs Created
Rosen-Cle 1.034	Rosen-Cle 181	Rosen-Cle 63.3	Rosen-Cle 65.5	Dropo-Det 143	Rosen-Cle 155
Vernon-Was 921	Vernon-Was 151	Vernon-Was 39.7	Vernon-Was 41.5	Minoso-Chi 134	Vernon-Was 127
Zernial-Phi 914	Woodling-NY 147	Minoso-Chi 30.6	Boone-Cle-Det ... 31.5	Boone-Cle-Det ... 133	Zernial-Phi 113
Boone-Cle-Det 909	Boone-Cle-Det 146	Boone-Cle-Det ... 30.5	Mantle-NY 29.4	Rizzuto-NY 132	Boone-Cle-Det ... 106
Woodling-NY 898	Mantle-NY 145	Zernial-Phi 30.4	Woodling-NY 29.2	Jensen-Was 129	Minoso-Chi 106

Total Average	Stolen Bases	Stolen Base Average	Stolen Base Runs	Fielding Runs	Total Player Rating
Rosen-Cle 1.078	Minoso-Chi 25	Jensen-Was 69.2	Michaels-Phi 2.1	Strickland-Cle ... 15.6	Rosen-Cle 5.6
Mantle-NY 943	Rivera-Chi 22	Minoso-Chi 61.0	Coan-Was 2.1	Piersall-Bos 15.2	Vernon-Was 3.3
Boone-Cle-Det 925	Jensen-Was....... 18	Rivera-Chi 59.5	Zernial-Phi 1.2	Hunter-StL 14.6	Zernial-Phi 3.2
Zernial-Phi 917	Philley-Phi 13		Souchock-Det 9	Busby-Was 13.7	Berra-NY 3.1
Doby-Cle 912	Busby-Was 13		Philley-Phi 9	Avila-Cle 13.4	Boone-Cle-Det ... 2.9

Wins	Win Percentage	Games	Complete Games	Shutouts	Saves
Porterfield-Was 22	Lopat-NY 800	Kinder-Bos........ 69	Porterfield-Was 24	Porterfield-Was 9	Kinder-Bos........ 27
Parnell-Bos 21	Ford-NY 750	Stuart-StL 60	R.Lemon-Cle 23	Pierce-Chi 7	Dorish-Chi 18
R.Lemon-Cle 21	Parnell-Bos 724	Martin-Phi 58	Garcia-Cle 21	Trucks-StL-Chi..... 5	Reynolds-NY 13
Trucks-StL-Chi..... 20	Porterfield-Was ...688	Paige-StL 57	Pierce-Chi 19	Parnell-Bos 5	Paige-StL 11
		Dorish-Chi 55	Trucks-StL-Chi 17	R.Lemon-Cle 5	Sain-NY 9

Innings Pitched	Fewest Hits/Game	Fewest BB/Game	Strikeouts	Strikeouts/Game	Ratio
R.Lemon-Cle 286.2	Pierce-Chi 7.16	Lopat-NY 1.61	Pierce-Chi 186	Pierce-Chi 6.17	Raschi-NY 10.24
Garcia-Cle 271.2	McDermott-Bos ... 7.37	Sain-NY 2.14	Trucks-StL-Chi ... 149	Gray-Det 5.88	Lopat-NY 10.35
Pierce-Chi 271.1	Raschi-NY 7.46	A.Kellner-Phi 2.28	Wynn-Cle 138	Masterson-Was ... 5.14	Pierce-Chi 10.65
Trucks-StL-Chi .. 264.1	Masterson-Was ... 7.85	Porterfield-Was ... 2.58	Parnell-Bos 136	Parnell-Bos 5.08	Porterfield-Was .. 11.19
Porterfield-Was .. 255.0	Trucks-StL-Chi.... 7.97	Hoeft-Det 2.64	Garcia-Cle 134	Trucks-StL-Chi ... 5.07	Sain-NY 11.29

Earned Run Average	Adjusted ERA	Opponents' Batting Avg.	Opponents' On Base Pct.	Starter Runs	Adjusted Starter Runs
Lopat-NY 2.42	Lopat-NY 152	Pierce-Chi 218	Raschi-NY 283	Pierce-Chi 38.4	Pierce-Chi 39.3
Pierce-Chi 2.72	Pierce-Chi 148	McDermott-Bos....224	Lopat-NY 288	Trucks-StL-Chi.... 31.3	Trucks-StL-Chi.... 33.9
Trucks-StL-Chi.... 2.93	McDermott-Bos... 140	Raschi-NY 224	Pierce-Chi 292	Lopat-NY 31.2	Parnell-Bos 30.6
Sain-NY 3.00	Trucks-StL-Chi ... 139	Masterson-Was ...232	Masterson-Was 304	Parnell-Bos 25.0	McDermott-Bos... 27.4
Ford-NY 3.00	Parnell-Bos 137	Trucks-StL-Chi 238	Garcia-Cle 307	Ford-NY 22.9	Lopat-NY 25.1

Clutch Pitching Index	Relief Runs	Adjusted Relief Runs	Relief Ranking	Total Pitcher Index	Total Baseball Ranking
Ford-NY 127	Kinder-Bos 25.5	Kinder-Bos 28.0	Kinder-Bos....... 53.6	McDermott-Bos.... 3.8	Rosen-Cle 5.6
Lopat-NY 123	Dorish-Chi 9.7	Dorish-Chi 10.1	Dorish-Chi 12.8	Trucks-StL-Chi.... 3.7	McDermott-Bos.... 3.8
Sain-NY 118	Kuzava-NY 7.0	Paige-StL 8.7	Paige-StL 9.9	Pierce-Chi 3.4	Trucks-StL-Chi.... 3.7
R.Lemon-Cle 113	Bearden-Chi 6.9	Bearden-Chi 7.1	Bearden-Chi 6.5	Kinder-Bos........ 3.2	Pierce-Chi 3.4
Parnell-Bos 112	Paige-StL 6.1	Kuzava-NY........ 3.9	Kuzava-NY........ 4.5	Parnell-Bos 3.2	Vernon-Was 3.3

TEAM	G	W	L	PCT	GB	R	OR	AB	H	2B	3B	HR	BB	SO	AVG	OBP	SLG	PRO	PRO+	BR	/A	PF	CHI	RC	SB	CS	SBA	SBR
NY	154	97	57	.630		732	**550**	5245	1386	194	42	**186**	522	561	.264	.335	.424	.759	102	17	13	101	102	747	30	23	31	**-11**
BRO	154	92	62	.597	5	778	740	5251	1418	246	56	**186**	**634**	625	.270	.353	**.444**	**.797**	**109**	**100**	**77**	103	96	**821**	46	39	**56**	-21
MIL	154	89	65	.578	8	670	556	5261	1395	217	41	139	471	619	.265	.330	.401	.731	102	-32	13	94	101	697	54	31	36	1
PHI	154	75	79	.487	22	659	614	5184	1384	243	**58**	102	604	620	.267	.345	.395	.740	99	-1	0	100	94	707	30	27	43	-17
CIN	154	74	80	.481	23	729	763	5234	1369	221	46	147	557	645	.262	.336	.406	.742	96	-7	-26	103	**105**	726	47	30	41	-15
STL	154	72	82	.468	25	**799**	790	5405	**1518**	**285**	58	119	582	586	**.281**	**.354**	.421	.775	107	65	59	101	102	807	**63**	46	53	-17
CHI	154	64	90	.416	33	700	766	5359	1412	229	45	159	478	693	.263	.327	.412	.739	96	-20	-27	101	103	717	46	31	37	-12
PIT	154	53	101	.344	44	557	845	5088	1260	181	57	76	566	737	.248	.326	.350	.676	83	-118	-107	99	98	596	21	13	26	**-11**
TOT	616					5624		42027	11142	1816	403	1114	4414	5086	.265	.338	.407	.745							337	240	58	-42

TEAM	CG	SH	SV	IP	H	H/G	HR	BB	SO	RAT	ERA	ERA+	OAV	OOB	PR	/A	PF	CPI	FA	E	DP	FW	PW	BW	SBW	DIF
NY	45	**19**	33	1390	**1258**	8.1	113	613	692	12.3	3.09	130	**.243**	.327	150	**145**	99	113	.975	154	172	-.5	**14.4**	1.3	-.6	5.5
BRO	39	8	**36**	1393²	1399	9.0	164	533	762	12.6	4.31	95	.261	.330	-36	-34	100	93	.978	129	138	.8	-3.4	7.6	-1.5	11.5
MIL	63	13	21	1394²	1296	8.4	**106**	553	698	12.1	3.19	117	.250	.325	137	83	92	110	**.981**	**116**	171	**1.5**	8.2	1.3	-.6	1.5
PHI	**78**	14	12	1365¹	1329	8.8	133	**450**	570	**11.8**	3.59	112	.256	**.317**	72	67	99	106	.975	145	133	-.0	6.6	.0	-1.2	-7.4
CIN	34	8	27	1367¹	1491	9.8	169	547	537	13.6	4.50	93	.282	.353	-65	-46	103	105	.977	137	**194**	.4	-4.6	-2.6	-1.0	4.7
STL	40	11	18	1390¹	1484	9.6	170	535	680	13.4	4.50	91	.275	.345	-65	-59	101	100	.976	146	178	-.0	-5.8	5.8	-1.2	-3.8
CHI	41	6	19	1374¹	1375	9.0	131	619	622	13.2	4.51	93	.263	.344	-66	-46	103	92	.974	154	164	-.5	-4.6	-2.7	-.7	-4.6
PIT	37	4	15	1346	1510	10.1	128	564	525	14.0	4.92	85	.287	.358	-126	-109	103	95	.971	173	136	-1.6	-10.8	-10.6	-.6	-.5
TOT	377	83	181	11021²		9.1				12.9	4.07		.265	.338					.976	1154	1286					

Runs
Snider-Bro	120
Musial-StL	120
Mays-NY	119
Ashburn-Phi	111
Gilliam-Bro	107

Hits
Mueller-NY	212
Snider-Bro	199
Musial-StL	195
Mays-NY	195
Moon-StL	193

Doubles
Musial-StL	41
Snider-Bro	39
Repulski-StL	39
Hamner-Phi	39

Triples
Mays-NY	13
Hamner-Phi	11
Snider-Bro	10

Home Runs
Kluszewski-Cin	49
Hodges-Bro	42
Sauer-Chi	41
Mays-NY	41

Total Bases
Snider-Bro	378
Mays-NY	377
Kluszewski-Cin	368
Musial-StL	359
Hodges-Bro	335

Runs Batted In
Kluszewski-Cin	141
Snider-Bro	130
Hodges-Bro	130
Musial-StL	126
Ennis-Phi	119

Runs Produced
Musial-StL	211
Snider-Bro	210
Kluszewski-Cin	196
Hodges-Bro	194

Bases On Balls
Ashburn-Phi	125
Mathews-Mil	113
Musial-StL	103
Thompson-NY	90
Reese-Bro	90

Batting Average
Mays-NY	.345
Mueller-NY	.342
Snider-Bro	.341
Musial-StL	.330
Kluszewski-Cin	.326

On Base Percentage
Ashburn-Phi	.442
Musial-StL	.433
Mathews-Mil	.428
Snider-Bro	.427
Mays-NY	.415

Slugging Average
Mays-NY	.667
Snider-Bro	.647
Kluszewski-Cin	.642
Musial-StL	.607
Mathews-Mil	.603

Production
Mays-NY	1.083
Snider-Bro	1.074
Kluszewski-Cin	1.052
Musial-StL	1.040
Mathews-Mil	1.031

Adjusted Production
Mathews-Mil	177
Mays-NY	176
Snider-Bro	170
Musial-StL	166
Kluszewski-Cin	165

Batter Runs
Snider-Bro	64.6
Mays-NY	61.8
Musial-StL	60.7
Kluszewski-Cin	57.1
Mathews-Mil	48.6

Adjusted Batter Runs
Snider-Bro	62.1
Mays-NY	61.4
Musial-StL	60.1
Kluszewski-Cin	54.9
Mathews-Mil	53.2

Clutch Hitting Index
Ennis-Phi	154
Jablonski-StL	148
Post-Cin	131
Furillo-Bro	128
Hodges-Bro	118

Runs Created
Snider-Bro	161
Mays-NY	155
Musial-StL	153
Kluszewski-Cin	151
Mathews-Mil	131

Total Average
Mathews-Mil	1.169
Mays-NY	1.158
Snider-Bro	1.156
Kluszewski-Cin	1.117
Musial-StL	1.087

Stolen Bases
Bruton-Mil	34
Temple-Cin	21
Fondy-Chi	20
Moon-StL	18
Ashburn-Phi	11

Stolen Base Average
Fondy-Chi	80.0
Temple-Cin	75.0
Bruton-Mil	72.3
Moon-StL	64.3

Stolen Base Runs
Fondy-Chi	3.0
Bruton-Mil	2.4
Temple-Cin	2.1
Torgeson-Phi	1.5

Fielding Runs
Schoendienst-StL	32.9
Grammas-StL	29.8
Logan-Mil	14.4
Crandall-Mil	13.2
Ashburn-Phi	12.9

Total Player Rating
Mays-NY	6.5
Mathews-Mil	5.1
Schoendienst-StL	4.7
Musial-StL	4.6
Snider-Bro	4.5

Wins
Roberts-Phi	23
Spahn-Mil	21
Antonelli-NY	21
Haddix-StL	18
Erskine-Bro	18

Win Percentage
Antonelli-NY	.750
Lawrence-StL	.714
Gomez-NY	.654
Spahn-Mil	.636
Roberts-Phi	.605

Games
Hughes-Bro	60
Hetki-Pit	58
Brazle-StL	58
Wilhelm-NY	57
Grissom-NY	56

Complete Games
Roberts-Phi	29
Spahn-Mil	23
Simmons-Phi	21
Antonelli-NY	18

Shutouts
Antonelli-NY	6

Saves
Hughes-Bro	24
Smith-Cin	20
Grissom-NY	19
Jolly-Mil	10
Hetki-Pit	9

Innings Pitched
Roberts-Phi	336.2
Spahn-Mil	283.1
Erskine-Bro	260.1
Haddix-StL	259.2
Antonelli-NY	258.2

Fewest Hits/Game
Antonelli-NY	7.27
Roberts-Phi	7.73
Conley-Mil	7.92
Lawrence-StL	8.00
Wehmeier-Cin-Phi	8.02

Fewest BB/Game
Roberts-Phi	1.50
Minner-Chi	2.06
Hacker-Chi	2.10
Burdette-Mil	2.34
Meyer-Bro	2.45

Strikeouts
Roberts-Phi	185
Haddix-StL	184
Erskine-Bro	166
Antonelli-NY	152
Spahn-Mil	136

Strikeouts/Game
Haddix-StL	6.38
Erskine-Bro	5.74
Littlefield-Pit	5.34
Antonelli-NY	5.29
Conley-Mil	5.23

Ratio
Roberts-Phi	9.36
Antonelli-NY	10.72
Burdette-Mil	10.97
Spahn-Mil	11.09
Hacker-Chi	11.23

Earned Run Average
Antonelli-NY	2.30
Burdette-Mil	2.76
Simmons-Phi	2.81
Gomez-NY	2.88
Conley-Mil	2.96

Adjusted ERA
Antonelli-NY	176
Simmons-Phi	144
Gomez-NY	140
Roberts-Phi	136
Burdette-Mil	135

Opponents' Batting Avg.
Antonelli-NY	.219
Roberts-Phi	.231
Simmons-Phi	.239
Littlefield-Pit	.239
Wehmeier-Cin-Phi	.239

Opponents' On Base Pct.
Roberts-Phi	.267
Antonelli-NY	.293
Spahn-Mil	.302
Burdette-Mil	.302
Hacker-Chi	.304

Starter Runs
Antonelli-NY	51.0
Roberts-Phi	41.3
Simmons-Phi	35.5
Burdette-Mil	34.7
Gomez-NY	29.3

Adjusted Starter Runs
Antonelli-NY	50.0
Roberts-Phi	40.1
Simmons-Phi	34.6
Gomez-NY	28.4
Burdette-Mil	25.5

Clutch Pitching Index
Gomez-NY	130
Dickson-Phi	123
Fowler-Cin	116
Conley-Mil	116
Antonelli-NY	115

Relief Runs
Wilhelm-NY	24.4
Grissom-NY	23.4
Jolly-Mil	20.4
Johnson-Mil	13.9
Smith-Cin	12.7

Adjusted Relief Runs
Wilhelm-NY	23.9
Grissom-NY	22.9
Jolly-Mil	16.1
Smith-Cin	13.7
Johnson-Mil	10.1

Relief Ranking
Grissom-NY	36.6
Wilhelm-NY	34.3
Smith-Cin	27.5
Jolly-Mil	25.4
Hughes-Bro	15.6

Total Pitcher Index
Antonelli-NY	5.5
Roberts-Phi	3.4
Simmons-Phi	3.1
Gomez-NY	3.0
Spahn-Mil	2.5

Total Baseball Ranking
Mays-NY	6.5
Antonelli-NY	5.5
Mathews-Mil	5.1
Schoendienst-StL	4.7
Musial-StL	4.6

TEAM	G	W	L	PCT	GB	R	OR	AB	H	2B	3B	HR	BB	SO	AVG	OBP	SLG	PRO	PRO+	BR	/A	PF	CHI	RC	SB	CS	SBA	SBR
CLE	156	111	43	.721		746	504	5222	1368	188	39	156	637	668	.262	.345	.403	.748	109	76	64	102	102	739	30	33	40	-13
NY	155	103	51	.669	8	805	563	5226	1400	215	59	133	650	632	.268	.351	.408	.759	118	101	123	97	106	768	34	41	51	-17
CHI	155	94	60	.610	17	711	521	5168	1382	203	47	94	604	536	.267	.350	.379	.729	102	51	28	103	101	700	98	58	53	-13
BOS	156	69	85	.448	42	700	728	5399	1436	244	41	123	654	660	.266	.348	.395	.743	99	73	-1	111	93	749	51	30	36	-12
DET	155	68	86	.442	43	584	664	5233	1351	215	41	90	492	603	.258	.324	.367	.691	96	-36	-23	98	97	609	48	44	55	-19
WAS	155	66	88	.429	45	632	680	5249	1292	188	69	81	610	719	.246	.328	.355	.683	98	-43	-7	95	103	631	37	21	28	-10
BAL	154	54	100	.351	57	483	668	5206	1309	195	49	52	468	634	.251	.316	.338	.654	91	-103	-55	93	91	553	30	31	53	-22
PHI	156	51	103	.331	60	542	875	5206	1228	191	41	94	504	677	.236	.307	.342	.649	83	-116	-117	100	105	553	30	29	35	-11
TOT	621					5203		41909	10766	1639	386	823	4619	5129	.257	.334	.373	.707							358	287	56	-64

TEAM	CG	SH	SV	IP	H	H/G	HR	BB	SO	RAT	ERA	ERA+	OAV	OOB	PR	/A	PF	CPI	FA	E	DP	FW	PW	BW	SBW	DIF
CLE	77	12	36	1419¹	1220	7.7	89	486	678	10.9	2.78	132	.232	.299	148	140	99	100	.979	128	148	.7	14.5	6.6	-.5	12.7
NY	51	16	37	1379¹	1284	8.4	86	552	655	12.2	3.26	105	.251	.327	70	26	92	107	.979	126	198	.8	2.7	12.7	-.9	10.7
CHI	60	23	33	1383	1255	8.2	94	517	701	11.6	3.05	122	.243	.314	103	104	100	105	.982	108	149	1.8	10.7	2.9	-.5	2.1
BOS	41	10	22	1412¹	1434	9.1	118	612	707	13.3	4.01	102	.265	.343	-45	15	110	101	.972	176	163	-2.0	1.5	-.1	-.4	-7.1
DET	58	13	13	1383	1375	8.9	138	506	603	12.5	3.81	97	.261	.330	-12	-17	99	103	.978	129	131	.6	-1.8	-2.4	-1.1	-4.4
WAS	69	10	7	1383¹	1396	9.1	79	573	562	13.0	3.84	93	.265	.340	-17	-43	96	99	.977	137	172	.2	-4.4	-.7	-.2	-5.8
BAL	58	6	8	1373¹	1279	8.4	78	688	668	13.0	3.88	92	.249	.340	-23	-45	96	94	.975	147	152	-.4	-4.6	-5.7	-1.4	-10.8
PHI	49	3	13	1371¹	1523	10.0	141	685	555	14.7	5.18	75	.284	.370	-221	-193	105	95	.972	169	163	-1.6	-19.9	-12.1	-.3	7.9
TOT	463	93	169	11105		8.7				12.6	3.72		.257	.334					.977	1120	1276					

Runs
Mantle-NY	129
Minoso-Chi	119
Avila-Cle	112
Fox-Chi	111
Carrasquel-Chi	106

Hits
Kuenn-Det	201
Fox-Chi	201
Avila-Cle	189
Busby-Was	187
Minoso-Chi	182

Doubles
Vernon-Was	33
Smith-Cle	29
Minoso-Chi	29

Triples
Minoso-Chi	18
Runnels-Was	15
Vernon-Was	14
Mantle-NY	12
Tuttle-Det	11

Home Runs
Doby-Cle	32
Williams-Bos	29
Mantle-NY	27
Jensen-Bos	25

Total Bases
Minoso-Chi	304
Vernon-Was	294
Mantle-NY	285
Berra-NY	285
Doby-Cle	279

Runs Batted In
Doby-Cle	126
Berra-NY	125
Jensen-Bos	117
Minoso-Chi	116

Runs Produced
Minoso-Chi	216
Mantle-NY	204
Berra-NY	191
Doby-Cle	188
Jensen-Bos	184

Bases On Balls
Williams-Bos	136
Yost-Was	131
Mantle-NY	102
Smith-Cle	88

Batting Average
Williams-Bos	.345
Avila-Cle	.341
Minoso-Chi	.320
Noren-NY	.319
Fox-Chi	.319

On Base Percentage
Williams-Bos	.516
Minoso-Chi	.416
Rosen-Cle	.412
Mantle-NY	.411
Yost-Was	.406

Slugging Average
Williams-Bos	.635
Minoso-Chi	.535
Mantle-NY	.525
Rosen-Cle	.506
Vernon-Was	.492

Production
Williams-Bos	1.151
Minoso-Chi	.951
Mantle-NY	.936
Rosen-Cle	.918
Avila-Cle	.882

Adjusted Production
Williams-Bos	193
Mantle-NY	160
Minoso-Chi	154
Rosen-Cle	148
Noren-NY	140

Batter Runs
Williams-Bos	70.9
Minoso-Chi	47.3
Mantle-NY	42.8
Rosen-Cle	34.2
Avila-Cle	31.5

Adjusted Batter Runs
Williams-Bos	64.6
Mantle-NY	45.2
Minoso-Chi	44.8
Rosen-Cle	33.2
Avila-Cle	30.3

Clutch Hitting Index
Berra-NY	143
Sievers-Was	136
Doby-Cle	135
Jensen-Bos	135
Rosen-Cle	128

Runs Created
Williams-Bos	139
Mantle-NY	127
Minoso-Chi	125
Avila-Cle	109
Doby-Cle	108

Total Average
Williams-Bos	1.452
Mantle-NY	1.013
Minoso-Chi	.969
Rosen-Cle	.959
Doby-Cle	.862

Stolen Bases
Jensen-Bos	22
Rivera-Chi	18
Minoso-Chi	18
Jacobs-Phi	17
Busby-Was	17

Stolen Base Average
Busby-Was	89.5
Jacobs-Phi	85.0
Jensen-Bos	75.9
Rivera-Chi	64.3
Fox-Chi	64.0

Stolen Base Runs
Busby-Was	3.9
Jacobs-Phi	3.3
Jensen-Bos	2.4
Cavarretta-Chi	1.2

Fielding Runs
Coleman-NY	17.9
Carey-NY	16.7
Lepcio-Bos	16.1
Bolling-Bos	15.3
Power-Phi	14.7

Total Player Rating
Williams-Bos	5.5
Minoso-Chi	5.2
Avila-Cle	4.4
Mantle-NY	3.8
Berra-NY	3.4

Wins
Wynn-Cle	23
Lemon-Cle	23
Grim-NY	20
Trucks-Chi	19
Garcia-Cle	19

Win Percentage
Consuegra-Chi	.842
Grim-NY	.769
Lemon-Cle	.767
Garcia-Cle	.704
Houtteman-Cle	.682

Games
Dixon-Was-Phi	54
Martin-Phi-Chi	48
Pascual-Was	48
Kinder-Bos	48

Complete Games
Porterfield-Was	21
Lemon-Cle	21
Wynn-Cle	20
Gromek-Det	17

Shutouts
Trucks-Chi	5
Garcia-Cle	5

Saves
Sain-NY	22
Kinder-Bos	15
Narleski-Cle	13

Innings Pitched
Wynn-Cle	270.2
Trucks-Chi	264.2
Garcia-Cle	258.2
Lemon-Cle	258.1
Gromek-Det	252.2

Fewest Hits/Game
Turley-Bal	6.48
Ford-NY	7.26
Wynn-Cle	7.48
Coleman-Bal	7.48
Reynolds-NY	7.61

Fewest BB/Game
Lopat-NY	1.75
Gromek-Det	2.03
Garver-Det	2.27
Garcia-Cle	2.47
Zuverink-Det	2.75

Strikeouts
Turley-Bal	185
Wynn-Cle	155
Trucks-Chi	152
Pierce-Chi	148
Harshman-Chi	134

Strikeouts/Game
Pierce-Cle	7.06
Harshman-Chi	6.81
Turley-Bal	6.73
Hoeft-Det	5.86
Reynolds-NY	5.72

Ratio
Garcia-Cle	10.19
Wynn-Cle	10.24
Garver-Det	10.30
Gromek-Det	10.86
Trucks-Chi	10.88

Earned Run Average
Garcia-Cle	2.64
Lemon-Cle	2.72
Wynn-Cle	2.73
Gromek-Det	2.74
Trucks-Chi	2.79

Adjusted ERA
Garcia-Cle	139
Lemon-Cle	135
Wynn-Cle	135
Gromek-Det	135
Trucks-Chi	134

Opponents' Batting Avg.
Turley-Bal	.203
Wynn-Cle	.225
Ford-NY	.227
Trucks-Chi	.228
Garcia-Cle	.229

Opponents' On Base Pct.
Garcia-Cle	.284
Wynn-Cle	.284
Garver-Det	.287
Gromek-Det	.297
Trucks-Chi	.297

Starter Runs
Garcia-Cle	31.0
Wynn-Cle	30.0
Lemon-Cle	28.9
Gromek-Det	27.5
Trucks-Chi	27.5

Adjusted Starter Runs
Garcia-Cle	29.6
Wynn-Cle	28.5
Trucks-Chi	27.8
Lemon-Cle	27.5
Gromek-Det	26.7

Clutch Pitching Index
Keegan-Chi	126
Gromek-Det	116
Houtteman-Cle	114
Lopat-NY	114
Harshman-Chi	114

Relief Runs
Mossi-Cle	18.5
Narleski-Cle	14.8
Dorish-Chi	12.1
Miller-Det	9.8
Sain-NY	4.9

Adjusted Relief Runs
Mossi-Cle	18.0
Narleski-Cle	14.3
Dorish-Chi	12.2
Miller-Det	9.6
Kinder-Bos	5.9

Relief Ranking
Mossi-Cle	15.2
Narleski-Cle	13.4
Dorish-Chi	11.6
Kinder-Bos	9.7
Sain-NY	4.9

Total Pitcher Index
Lemon-Cle	4.0
Garcia-Cle	2.9
Trucks-Chi	2.9
Wynn-Cle	2.8
Garver-Det	2.7

Total Baseball Ranking
Williams-Bos	5.5
Minoso-Chi	5.2
Avila-Cle	4.4
Lemon-Cle	4.0
Mantle-NY	3.8

TEAM	G	W	L	PCT	GB	R	OR	AB	H	2B	3B	HR	BB	SO	AVG	OBP	SLG	PRO	PRO+	BR	/A	PF	CHI	RC	SB	CS	SBA	SBR
BRO	154	98	55	.641		857	650	5193	1406	230	44	201	674	718	.271	.359	.448	.807	115	142	122	103	100	834	79	56	68	-23
MIL	154	85	69	.552	13.5	743	668	5277	1377	219	55	182	504	735	.261	.329	.427	.756	109	27	62	95	102	733	42	27	28	-8
NY	154	80	74	.519	18.5	702	673	5288	1377	173	34	169	497	581	.260	.328	.402	.730	97	-14	-15	100	102	699	38	22	44	-19
PHI	154	77	77	.500	21.5	675	666	5092	1300	214	50	132	652	673	.255	.344	.395	.738	102	14	26	98	95	692	44	32	42	-15
CIN	154	75	79	.487	23.5	761	684	5270	1424	216	28	181	556	657	.270	.344	.425	.769	103	63	21	106	99	773	51	36	46	-16
CHI	154	72	81	.471	26	626	713	5214	1287	187	55	164	428	806	.247	.307	.398	.705	91	-74	-71	100	103	623	37	35	43	-14
STL	154	68	86	.442	30.5	654	757	5266	1375	228	36	143	458	597	.261	.344	.400	.724	96	-29	-28	100	99	662	64	59	58	-16
PIT	154	60	94	.390	38.5	560	767	5173	1262	210	60	91	471	652	.244	.310	.361	.671	84	-126	-116	99	100	567	22	22	28	-9
TOT	616					5578		41773	10808	1677	362	1263	4240	5419	.259	.330	.407	.737							377	289	57	-59

TEAM	CG	SH	SV	IP	H	H/G	HR	BB	SO	RAT	ERA	ERA+	OAV	OOB	PR	/A	PF	CPI	FA	E	DP	FW	PW	BW	SBW	DIF
BRO	46	11	37	1378	1296	8.5	168	483	773	11.7	3.68	110	.248	.314	54	57	101	100	.978	133	156	.5	5.7	12.1	-1.5	4.8
MIL	61	5	12	1383	1339	8.7	138	591	654	12.7	3.85	98	.255	.333	29	-13	93	102	.975	152	155	-.6	-1.3	6.2	-.0	3.8
NY	52	6	14	1386²	1347	8.7	155	560	721	12.7	3.77	107	.256	.333	41	39	100	107	.976	142	165	.0	3.9	-1.5	-1.1	1.8
PHI	58	11	21	1356²	1291	8.6	161	477	657	11.9	3.93	101	.251	.317	16	6	98	96	.981	110	117	1.8	.6	2.6	-.7	-4.2
CIN	38	12	22	1363	1373	9.1	161	443	576	12.1	3.95	107	.263	.324	13	43	105	102	.977	139	169	.2	4.3	2.1	-.8	-7.7
CHI	47	10	23	1378¹	1306	8.5	153	601	686	12.6	4.17	98	.251	.332	-20	-13	101	95	.975	147	147	-.3	-1.3	-7.0	-.6	4.8
STL	42	10	15	1376²	1376	9.0	185	549	730	12.9	4.56	89	.261	.336	-80	-76	101	95	.975	146	152	-.2	-7.5	-2.8	-.8	2.4
PIT	41	5	16	1362	1480	9.8	142	536	622	13.5	4.39	94	.280	.350	-53	-42	102	104	.972	166	175	-1.4	-4.2	-11.5	-.1	.2
TOT	385	70	160	10984¹		8.9				12.5	4.04		.259	.330					.976	1135	1236					

Runs
Snider-Bro 126
Mays-NY 123
Post-Cin 116
Kluszewski-Cin . . . 116
Gilliam-Bro 110

Hits
Kluszewski-Cin . . . 192
Aaron-Mil 189
Bell-Cin 188
Post-Cin 186

Doubles
Logan-Mil 37
Aaron-Mil 37
Snider-Bro 34
Post-Cin 33
Ashburn-Phi 32

Triples
Mays-NY 13
Long-Pit 13
Bruton-Mil 12
Clemente-Pit 11

Home Runs
Mays-NY 51
Kluszewski-Cin . . . 47
Banks-Chi 44
Snider-Bro 42
Mathews-Mil 41

Total Bases
Mays-NY 382
Kluszewski-Cin . . . 358
Banks-Chi 355
Post-Cin 345
Snider-Bro 338

Runs Batted In
Snider-Bro 136
Mays-NY 127
Ennis-Phi 120
Banks-Chi 117
Kluszewski-Cin . . . 113

Runs Produced
Snider-Bro 220
Mays-NY 199
Post-Cin 185
Aaron-Mil 184
Kluszewski-Cin . . . 182

Bases On Balls
Mathews-Mil 109
Ashburn-Phi 105
Snider-Bro 104
Thompson-NY 84

Batting Average
Ashburn-Phi 338
Mays-NY 319
Musial-StL 319
Campanella-Bro . . .318
Aaron-Mil 314

On Base Percentage
Ashburn-Phi 449
Snider-Bro 421
Mathews-Mil 417
Musial-StL 411
Mays-NY 404

Slugging Average
Mays-NY 659
Snider-Bro 628
Mathews-Mil 601
Banks-Chi 596
Kluszewski-Cin 585

Production
Mays-NY 1.063
Snider-Bro 1.050
Mathews-Mil 1.018
Campanella-Bro . . .985
Musial-StL 977

Adjusted Production
Mays-NY 176
Mathews-Mil 175
Snider-Bro 169
Musial-StL 156
Campanella-Bro . . 153

Batter Runs
Mays-NY 62.3
Snider-Bro 58.9
Mathews-Mil 50.0
Musial-StL 46.5
Kluszewski-Cin . . . 44.9

Adjusted Batter Runs
Mays-NY 62.2
Snider-Bro 56.8
Mathews-Mil 53.6
Musial-StL 46.5
Kluszewski-Cin . . . 40.2

Clutch Hitting Index
Jones-Phi 136
Mueller-NY 136
Ennis-Phi 136
Snider-Bro 126
Campanella-Bro . . 124

Runs Created
Mays-NY 157
Snider-Bro 145
Kluszewski-Cin . . . 136
Musial-StL 131
Mathews-Mil 131

Total Average
Mays-NY 1.180
Snider-Bro 1.147
Mathews-Mil 1.124
Musial-StL 1.020
Campanella-Bro . 1.000

Stolen Bases
Bruton-Mil 25
Mays-NY 24
Boyer-StL 22
Temple-Cin 19
Gilliam-Bro 15

Stolen Base Average
Mays-NY 85.7
Temple-Cin 82.6
Bruton-Mil 69.4
Boyer-StL 56.4

Stolen Base Runs
Mays-NY 4.8
Temple-Cin 3.3
Robinson-Bro 1.8
Blaylock-Phi 1.2

Fielding Runs
McMillan-Cin 16.6
O'Connell-Mil 15.8
Groat-Pit 15.4
Mays-NY 14.2
Clemente-Pit 12.3

Total Player Rating
Mays-NY 7.6
Snider-Bro 4.7
Mathews-Mil 4.6
Banks-Chi 4.4
Musial-StL 4.1

Wins
Roberts-Phi 23
Newcombe-Bro 20
Spahn-Mil 17
Nuxhall-Cin 17

Win Percentage
Newcombe-Bro 800
Roberts-Phi 622
Nuxhall-Cin 586
Spahn-Mil 548

Games
Labine-Bro 60
Wilhelm-NY 59
LaPalme-StL 56
Grissom-NY 55
Freeman-Cin 52

Complete Games
Roberts-Phi 26
Newcombe-Bro . . 17
Spahn-Mil 16

Shutouts
Nuxhall-Cin 5
Jones-Chi 4
Dickson-Phi 4

Saves
Meyer-Phi 16
Roebuck-Bro 12
Labine-Bro 11
Freeman-Cin 11
Grissom-NY 8

Innings Pitched
Roberts-Phi 305.0
Nuxhall-Cin 257.0
Spahn-Mil 245.2
Jones-Chi 241.2
Antonelli-NY 235.1

Fewest Hits/Game
Jones-Chi 6.52
Buhl-Mil 7.50
Rush-Chi 7.85
Antonelli-NY 7.88
Dickson-Phi 7.92

Fewest BB/Game
Newcombe-Bro . . . 1.46
Roberts-Phi 1.56
Hacker-Chi 1.82
Friend-Pit 2.34
Spahn-Mil 2.38

Strikeouts
Jones-Chi 198
Roberts-Phi 160
Haddix-StL 150
Newcombe-Bro . . . 143
Antonelli-NY 143

Strikeouts/Game
Jones-Chi 7.37
Haddix-StL 6.49
Podres-Bro 6.44
Conley-Mil 6.09
Newcombe-Bro . . . 5.51

Ratio
Newcombe-Bro . . 10.05
Roberts-Phi 10.24
Friend-Pit 10.42
Hacker-Chi 10.44
Rush-Chi 10.73

Earned Run Average
Friend-Pit 2.83
Newcombe-Bro . . . 3.20
Buhl-Mil 3.21
Spahn-Mil 3.26
Roberts-Phi 3.28

Adjusted ERA
Friend-Pit 145
Newcombe-Bro . . . 127
Nuxhall-Cin 122
Roberts-Phi 121
Antonelli-NY 121

Opponents' Batting Avg.
Jones-Chi 206
Buhl-Mil 227
Rush-Chi 234
Antonelli-NY 234
Dickson-Phi 238

Opponents' On Base Pct.
Roberts-Phi 280
Newcombe-Bro 280
Hacker-Chi 285
Friend-Pit 294
Rush-Chi 295

Starter Runs
Friend-Pit 26.9
Roberts-Phi 25.8
Newcombe-Bro . . . 21.8
Spahn-Mil 21.2
Antonelli-NY 18.6

Adjusted Starter Runs
Friend-Pit 28.6
Roberts-Phi 23.5
Newcombe-Bro . . . 22.5
Nuxhall-Cin 21.9
Schmidt-StL 18.5

Clutch Pitching Index
Minner-Chi 122
Spahn-Mil 114
Jackson-StL 113
Law-Pit 109
Friend-Pit 109

Relief Runs
Freeman-Cin 19.1
Miller-Phi 16.2
LaPalme-StL 13.1
Labine-Bro 12.8
Jeffcoat-Chi 12.2

Adjusted Relief Runs
Freeman-Cin 21.1
Miller-Phi 15.5
LaPalme-StL 13.4
Labine-Bro 13.1
Jeffcoat-Chi 12.7

Relief Ranking
Freeman-Cin 28.5
Miller-Phi 19.1
Jeffcoat-Chi 17.6
Labine-Bro 17.0
Bessent-Bro 13.3

Total Pitcher Index
Newcombe-Bro . . . 4.3
Roberts-Phi 3.3
Friend-Pit 3.1
Nuxhall-Cin 2.5
Freeman-Cin 2.3

Total Baseball Ranking
Mays-NY 7.6
Snider-Bro 4.7
Mathews-Mil 4.6
Banks-Chi 4.4
Newcombe-Bro . . . 4.3

TEAM	G	W	L	PCT	GB	R	OR	AB	H	2B	3B	HR	BB	SO	AVG	OBP	SLG	PRO	PRO+	BR	/A	PF	CHI	RC	SB	CS	SBA	SBR
NY	154	96	58	.623		762	569	5161	1342	179	55	175	609	658	.260	.343	.418	.761	112	71	81	98	101	759	55	25	42	-17
CLE	154	93	61	.604	3	698	601	5146	1325	195	31	148	723	715	.257	.353	.394	.747	104	60	34	104	93	741	28	24	36	-13
CHI	155	91	63	.591	5	725	557	5220	1401	204	36	116	567	595	.268	.347	.388	.735	101	31	11	103	101	712	69	45	56	-19
BOS	154	84	70	.545	12	755	652	5273	1392	241	39	137	567	733	.264	.348	.394	.742	100	77	53	109	97	773	43	17	23	-8
DET	154	79	75	.513	17	775	658	5283	1407	211	38	130	641	583	.266	.348	.394	.742	99	46	62	98	104	736	41	22	49	-22
KC	155	63	91	.409	33	638	911	5335	1395	189	46	121	463	725	.261	.323	.382	.705	94	-39	-46	101	100	637	22	36	42	-13
BAL	156	57	97	.370	39	540	754	5257	1263	177	39	54	560	742	.240	.316	.320	.636	82	-158	-110	93	103	532	34	46	52	-16
WAS	154	53	101	.344	43	598	789	5142	1277	178	54	80	538	654	.248	.324	.351	.675	93	-85	-48	95	102	586	25	32	38	-12
TOT	618					5491		41817	10802	1574	338	961	4808	5405	.258	.339	.381	.720							317	247	56	-52

TEAM	CG	SH	SV	IP	H	H/G	HR	BB	SO	RAT	ERA	ERA+	OAV	OOB	PR	/A	PF	CPI	FA	E	DP	FW	PW	BW	SBW	DIF
NY	52	19	33	1372¹	1163	7.6	108	689	731	12.4	3.23	116	.231	.328	110	77	95	107	.978	128	180	.5	7.7	8.1	-1.0	3.7
CLE	45	15	36	1386¹	1285	8.3	111	557	877	12.1	3.39	118	.245	.320	88	92	101	101	.981	108	152	1.7	9.2	3.4	-.6	2.4
CHI	55	20	23	1378	1301	8.5	111	497	720	11.9	3.37	117	.250	.318	90	88	100	103	.981	111	147	1.5	8.8	1.1	-1.2	3.8
BOS	44	9	34	1384¹	1333	8.7	128	582	674	12.7	3.72	115	.253	.331	37	87	108	102	.977	136	140	.0	8.7	1.3	-.1	-2.9
DET	66	16	12	1380¹	1381	9.0	126	517	629	12.6	3.79	101	.260	.330	25	7	97	102	.976	139	159	-.2	.7	6.2	-1.5	-3.2
KC	29	9	22	1382	1486	9.7	175	707	572	14.6	5.35	78	.278	.367	-213	-180	105	94	.976	146	174	-.5	-18.0	-4.6	-.6	9.8
BAL	35	10	20	1388²	1403	9.1	103	625	595	13.4	4.21	91	.266	.347	-38	-61	96	98	.972	167	159	-1.7	-6.1	-11.0	-.9	-.2
WAS	37	10	16	1354²	1450	9.6	99	634	607	14.2	4.62	83	.278	.362	-99	-119	97	98	.974	154	170	-1.0	-11.9	-4.8	-.5	-5.7
TOT	363	108	196	11026²		8.8				13.0	3.96		.258	.339					.977	1089	1281					

Runs
Smith-Cle	123
Mantle-NY	121
Kaline-Det	121
Tuttle-Det	102
Kuenn-Det	101

Hits
Kaline-Det	200
Fox-Chi	198
Power-KC	190
Kuenn-Det	190
Smith-Cle	186

Doubles
Kuenn-Det	38
Power-KC	34
Goodman-Bos	31
White-Bos	30
Finigan-KC	30

Triples
Mantle-NY	11
Carey-NY	11
Power-KC	10

Home Runs
Mantle-NY	37
Zernial-KC	30
Williams-Bos	28

Total Bases
Kaline-Det	321
Mantle-NY	316
Power-KC	301
Smith-Cle	287
Jensen-Bos	275

Runs Batted In
Jensen-Bos	116
Boone-Det	116
Berra-NY	108
Sievers-Was	106
Kaline-Det	102

Runs Produced
Kaline-Det	196
Jensen-Bos	185
Mantle-NY	183
Smith-Cle	178
Tuttle-Det	166

Bases On Balls
Mantle-NY	113
Goodman-Bos	99
Yost-Was	95
Fain-Det-Cle	94
Smith-Cle	93

Batting Average
Kaline-Det	.340
Power-KC	.319
Kell-Chi	.312
Fox-Chi	.311
Kuenn-Det	.306

On Base Percentage
Mantle-NY	.433
Kaline-Det	.425
Smith-Cle	.411
Yost-Was	.410
Goodman-Bos	.397

Slugging Average
Mantle-NY	.611
Kaline-Det	.546
Doby-Cle	.505
Power-KC	.505
Sievers-Was	.489

Production
Mantle-NY	1.044
Kaline-Det	.971
Smith-Cle	.884
Doby-Cle	.877
Power-KC	.862

Adjusted Production
Mantle-NY	181
Kaline-Det	163
Sievers-Was	136
Vernon-Was	133
Smith-Cle	132

Batter Runs
Williams-Bos	59.3
Mantle-NY	59.0
Kaline-Det	50.2
Smith-Cle	34.7
Valo-KC	24.8

Adjusted Batter Runs
Mantle-NY	60.2
Williams-Bos	55.0
Kaline-Det	52.0
Smith-Cle	31.7
Valo-KC	24.4

Clutch Hitting Index
Kell-Chi	148
Boone-Det	148
Jensen-Bos	130
Sievers-Was	129
Berra-NY	127

Runs Created
Mantle-NY	148
Kaline-Det	135
Smith-Cle	128
Power-KC	103
Jensen-Bos	102

Total Average
Mantle-NY	1.206
Kaline-Det	.993
Smith-Cle	.928
Doby-Cle	.884
Jensen-Bos	.849

Stolen Bases
Rivera-Chi	25
Minoso-Chi	19
Jensen-Bos	16
Busby-Was-Chi	12
Smith-Cle	11

Stolen Base Average
Minoso-Chi	70.4
Jensen-Bos	69.6
Rivera-Chi	61.0

Stolen Base Runs
Torgeson-Det	2.7
Busby-Was-Chi	1.8
Mantle-NY	1.8
Klaus-Bos	1.8

Fielding Runs
Fox-Chi	26.9
McDougald-NY	19.4
Miranda-Bal	19.0
Lopez-KC	15.1
Power-KC	13.9

Total Player Rating
Mantle-NY	5.7
Williams-Bos	4.6
Kaline-Det	4.4
Fox-Chi	3.6
McDougald-NY	3.3

Wins
F.Sullivan-Bos	18
Lemon-Cle	18
Ford-NY	18
Wynn-Cle	17
Turley-NY	17

Win Percentage
Byrne-NY	.762
Ford-NY	.720
Hoeft-Det	.696
Lemon-Cle	.643
Donovan-Chi	.625

Games
Narleski-Cle	60
Mossi-Cle	57
Gorman-KC	57
Dorish-Chi-Bal	48
Moore-Bal	46

Complete Games
Ford-NY	18
Hoeft-Det	17

Shutouts
Hoeft-Det	7
Wynn-Cle	6
Turley-NY	6
Pierce-Chi	6

Saves
Narleski-Cle	19
Kinder-Bos	18
Gorman-KC	18
Konstanty-NY	11
Morgan-NY	10

Innings Pitched
F.Sullivan-Bos	260.0
Ford-NY	253.2
Turley-NY	246.2
Wilson-Bal	235.1
Lary-Det	235.0

Fewest Hits/Game
Turley-NY	6.13
Score-Cle	6.26
Ford-NY	6.67
Pierce-Chi	7.09
Harshman-Chi	7.23

Fewest BB/Game
Gromek-Det	1.84
Donovan-Chi	2.31
Garcia-Cle	2.39
Garver-Det	2.61
Porterfield-Was	2.73

Strikeouts
Score-Cle	245
Turley-NY	210
Pierce-Chi	157
Ford-NY	137
Hoeft-Det	133

Strikeouts/Game
Score-Cle	9.70
Turley-NY	7.66
Pierce-Chi	6.87
Harshman-Chi	5.82
Hoeft-Det	5.44

Ratio
Pierce-Chi	10.02
Ford-NY	10.71
Hoeft-Det	10.96
Wilson-Bal	11.13
Wynn-Cle	11.35

Earned Run Average
Pierce-Chi	1.97
Ford-NY	2.63
Wynn-Cle	2.82
Score-Cle	2.85
F.Sullivan-Bos	2.91

Adjusted ERA
Pierce-Chi	201
F.Sullivan-Bos	148
Ford-NY	143
Wynn-Cle	142
Score-Cle	140

Opponents' Batting Avg.
Turley-NY	.193
Score-Cle	.194
Ford-NY	.208
Pierce-Chi	.213
Harshman-Chi	.224

Opponents' On Base Pct.
Pierce-Chi	.277
Ford-NY	.297
Hoeft-Det	.298
Wilson-Bal	.300
Wynn-Cle	.307

Starter Runs
Pierce-Chi	45.5
Ford-NY	37.6
F.Sullivan-Bos	30.4
Wynn-Cle	29.2
Score-Cle	28.1

Adjusted Starter Runs
Pierce-Chi	45.2
F.Sullivan-Bos	39.9
Ford-NY	31.5
Wynn-Cle	29.9
Score-Cle	28.8

Clutch Pitching Index
Pierce-Chi	119
Byrne-NY	119
F.Sullivan-Bos	116
Lary-Det	115
Schmitz-Was	115

Relief Runs
Consuegra-Chi	18.6
Mossi-Cle	13.9
Konstanty-NY	13.4
Kiely-Bos	11.6
Dorish-Chi-Bal	10.4

Adjusted Relief Runs
Consuegra-Chi	18.4
Kiely-Bos	14.9
Mossi-Cle	14.2
Konstanty-NY	11.6
Hurd-Bos	11.4

Relief Ranking
Kinder-Bos	21.1
Hurd-Bos	19.5
Consuegra-Chi	16.7
Konstanty-NY	16.7
Mossi-Cle	14.5

Total Pitcher Index
Pierce-Chi	4.7
F.Sullivan-Bos	3.9
Ford-NY	3.4
Wynn-Cle	3.1
Wight-Cle-Bal	2.4

Total Baseball Ranking
Mantle-NY	5.7
Pierce-Chi	4.7
Williams-Bos	4.6
Kaline-Det	4.4
F.Sullivan-Bos	3.9

TEAM	G	W	L	PCT	GB	R	OR	AB	H	2B	3B	HR	BB	SO	AVG	OBP	SLG	PRO	PRO+	BR	/A	PF	CHI	RC	SB	CS	SBA	SBR
BRO	154	93	61	.604	.	720	601	5098	1315	212	36	179	649	738	.258	.344	.419	.763	102	81	29	108	97	728	65	37	57	-22
MIL	155	92	62	.597	1	709	569	5207	1350	212	54	177	486	714	.259	.325	.423	.748	112	38	77	94	101	714	29	20	26	-9
CIN	155	91	63	.591	2	775	658	5291	1406	201	32	221	528	760	.266	.338	.441	.779	107	103	59	106	100	789	45	22	46	-20
STL	156	76	78	.494	17	678	698	5378	1443	234	49	124	503	622	.268	.335	.399	.734	103	25	25	100	97	707	41	35	43	-14
PHI	154	71	83	.461	22	668	738	5204	1313	207	49	121	585	673	.252	.331	.381	.712	98	-11	1	98	102	658	45	23	35	-13
NY	154	67	87	.435	26	540	650	5190	1268	192	45	145	402	659	.244	.301	.382	.683	88	-84	-79	99	97	586	67	34	49	-18
PIT	157	66	88	.429	27	588	653	5221	1340	199	57	110	383	752	.257	.310	.380	.690	93	-69	-54	98	102	594	24	33	40	-13
CHI	157	60	94	.390	33	597	708	5260	1281	202	50	142	446	776	.244	.304	.382	.686	90	-78	-66	98	103	606	55	38	49	-17
TOT	621					5275		41849	10716	1659	372	1219	3982	5694	.256	.324	.401	.725							371	242	61	-33

TEAM	CG	SH	SV	IP	H	H/G	HR	BB	SO	RAT	ERA	ERA+	OAV	OOB	PR	/A	PF	CPI	FA	E	DP	FW	PW	BW	SBW	DIF
BRO	46	12	30	1368²	1251	8.2	171	441	772	11.3	3.57	111	.244	.306	30	60	105	97	.981	111	149	1.4	6.1	3.0	-1.8	7.3
MIL	64	12	27	1393¹	1295	8.4	133	467	639	11.5	3.11	111	.246	.311	101	53	92	107	.979	130	159	.3	5.4	7.9	-.5	1.9
CIN	47	4	29	1389	1406	9.1	141	458	653	12.3	3.85	103	.265	.327	-11	20	106	101	.981	113	147	1.3	2.0	6.0	-1.6	6.2
STL	41	12	30	1388²	1339	8.7	155	546	709	12.3	3.97	95	.256	.329	-30	-28	100	98	.978	134	172	.1	-2.9	2.6	-1.0	.2
PHI	57	4	15	1377¹	1407	9.2	172	437	750	12.2	4.20	89	.265	.324	-65	-73	99	95	.975	144	140	-.6	-7.5	.1	-.9	2.9
NY	31	9	28	1378	1287	8.4	144	551	765	12.2	3.78	100	.249	.325	0	1	100	98	.976	144	143	-.6	.1	-8.1	-1.4	-.0
PIT	37	8	24	1376¹	1406	9.2	142	469	662	12.4	3.74	101	.266	.328	4	4	100	100	.973	162	140	-1.5	.4	-5.5	-.9	-3.5
CHI	37	6	17	1392	1325	8.6	161	613	744	12.7	3.96	95	.252	.334	-28	-28	100	100	.976	144	141	-.4	-2.9	-6.8	-1.3	-5.6
TOT	360	67	200	11063¹		8.7				12.1	3.77		.256	.324					.977	1082	1191					

Runs
Robinson-Cin 122
Snider-Bro 112
Aaron-Mil 106
Mathews-Mil 103
Gilliam-Bro 102

Hits
Aaron-Mil 200
Ashburn-Phi...... 190
Virdon-StL-Pit ... 185
Musial-StL 184
Boyer-StL 182

Doubles
Aaron-Mil 34
Snider-Bro 33
Musial-StL 33
Lopata-Phi 33
Bell-Cin 31

Triples
Bruton-Mil 15
Aaron-Mil 14
Walls-Pit 11
Moon-StL 11
Virdon-StL-Pit 10

Home Runs
Snider-Bro 43
Robinson-Cin 38
Adcock-Mil........ 38
Mathews-Mil 37

Total Bases
Aaron-Mil 340
Snider-Bro 324
Mays-NY 322
Robinson-Cin 319
Musial-StL 310

Runs Batted In
Musial-StL 109
Adcock-Mil....... 103
Kluszewski-Cin ... 102
Snider-Bro 101
Boyer-StL 98

Runs Produced
Aaron-Mil 172
Snider-Bro 170
Musial-StL 169
Robinson-Cin 167
Boyer-StL 163

Bases On Balls
Snider-Bro 99
Gilliam-Bro 95
Jones-Phi......... 92
Mathews-Mil 91
Moon-StL.......... 80

Batting Average
Aaron-Mil 328
Virdon-StL-Pit 319
Clemente-Pit 311
Musial-StL 310
Boyer-StL 306

On Base Percentage
Snider-Bro 402
Gilliam-Bro 400
Musial-StL 390
Moon-StL 390
Jones-Phi........387

Slugging Average
Snider-Bro 598
Adcock-Mil.......597
Aaron-Mil 558
Robinson-Cin 558
Mays-NY 557

Production
Snider-Bro 1.000
Robinson-Cin 939
Adcock-Mil.......936
Mays-NY 928
Aaron-Mil........927

Adjusted Production
Adcock-Mil....... 154
Aaron-Mil 154
Snider-Bro 152
Mays-NY 146
Mathews-Mil 146

Batter Runs
Snider-Bro 50.5
Robinson-Cin 39.1
Aaron-Mil 36.3
Musial-StL 36.3
Mays-NY 35.9

Adjusted Batter Runs
Snider-Bro 44.7
Aaron-Mil 40.7
Mays-NY 36.4
Musial-StL 36.3
Robinson-Cin 34.3

Clutch Hitting Index
McMillan-Cin 151
Thomson-Mil 128
Jones-Phi 127
Musial-StL 125
Long-Pit 118

Runs Created
Snider-Bro 128
Robinson-Cin 121
Musial-StL 119
Mays-NY 118
Aaron-Mil 115

Total Average
Snider-Bro 1.052
Mays-NY 972
Robinson-Cin 960
Mathews-Mil 946
Adcock-Mil.......916

Stolen Bases
Mays-NY 40
Gilliam-Bro 21
White-NY 15
Temple-Cin 14
Reese-Bro 13

Stolen Base Average
Mays-NY 80.0
Gilliam-Bro 70.0

Stolen Base Runs
Mays-NY 6.0
Ashburn-Phi..... 2.4
Temple-Cin 1.8
Post-Cin 1.8
Mathews-Mil 1.8

Fielding Runs
McMillan-Cin 29.9
Blasingame-StL... 21.9
Ashburn-Phi..... 20.9
Baker-Chi..... 17.2
Robinson-Bro 14.9

Total Player Rating
Mays-NY 4.5
Aaron-Mil 4.2
McMillan-Cin 3.5
Snider-Bro 3.4
Musial-StL 3.2

Wins
Newcombe-Bro 27
Spahn-Mil 20
Antonelli-NY....... 20

Win Percentage
Newcombe-Bro 794
Buhl-Mil 692
Lawrence-Cin 655
Burdette-Mil.......655
Spahn-Mil 645

Games
Face-Pit 68
Wilhelm-NY 64
Freeman-Cin 64
Labine-Bro 62
Lown-Chi 61

Complete Games
Roberts-Phi 22
Spahn-Mil 20
Friend-Pit 19
Newcombe-Bro 18
Burdette-Mil....... 16

Shutouts
Burdette-Mil....... 6
Newcombe-Bro 5
Antonelli-NY 5
Friend-Pit 4

Saves
Labine-Bro........ 19
Freeman-Cin 18
Lown-Chi 13
Jackson-StL 9
Bessent-Bro 9

Innings Pitched
Friend-Pit 314.1
Roberts-Phi 297.1
Spahn-Mil 281.1
Newcombe-Bro .. 268.0
Kline-Pit 264.0

Fewest Hits/Game
Maglie-Bro 7.26
Newcombe-Bro ... 7.35
Jones-Chi 7.39
Mizell-StL....... 7.42
Craig-Bro 7.64

Fewest BB/Game
Roberts-Phi 1.21
Newcombe-Bro ... 1.54
Spahn-Mil 1.66
Fowler-Cin 1.77
Burdette-Mil...... 1.83

Strikeouts
Jones-Chi........ 176
Haddix-StL-Phi ... 170
Friend-Pit 166
Roberts-Phi 157
Mizell-StL....... 153

Strikeouts/Game
Jones-Chi........ 8.40
Haddix-StL-Phi ... 6.64
Mizell-StL 6.60
Nuxhall-Cin 5.38
Worthington-NY .. 5.16

Ratio
Newcombe-Bro ... 9.00
Spahn-Mil 9.73
Maglie-Bro 9.94
Burdette-Mil..... 10.15
Rush-Chi 10.18

Earned Run Average
Burdette-Mil..... 2.70
Spahn-Mil 2.78
Antonelli-NY...... 2.86
Maglie-Bro....... 2.87
Newcombe-Bro ... 3.06

Adjusted ERA
Maglie-Bro 138
Antonelli-NY..... 132
Newcombe-Bro ... 130
Burdette-Mil..... 128
Spahn-Mil 124

Opponents' Batting Avg.
Newcombe-Bro 221
Jones-Chi........221
Mizell-StL........222
Maglie-Bro 222
Craig-Bro 231

Opponents' On Base Pct.
Newcombe-Bro ...257
Spahn-Mil 276
Maglie-Bro 281
Burdette-Mil......282
Rush-Chi 282

Starter Runs
Spahn-Mil 30.9
Burdette-Mil...... 30.4
Antonelli-NY...... 26.3
Newcombe-Bro ... 21.3
Maglie-Bro 19.0

Adjusted Starter Runs
Newcombe-Bro ... 27.1
Antonelli-NY...... 26.6
Maglie-Bro 23.2
Burdette-Mil...... 21.6
Spahn-Mil 21.2

Clutch Pitching Index
Conley-Mil 127
Klippstein-Cin 111
Kline-Pit 110
Poholsky-StL 108
Jeffcoat-Cin 105

Relief Runs
Grissom-NY 19.8
Acker-Cin 13.1
Bessent-Bro 11.2
R.Miller-Phi 7.3
Labine-Bro 5.5

Adjusted Relief Runs
Grissom-NY 19.9
Acker-Cin 15.0
Bessent-Bro 13.0
Labine-Bro 8.0
Freeman-Cin 7.0

Relief Ranking
Freeman-Cin 13.7
Bessent-Bro 13.6
Labine-Bro 12.9
Acker-Cin 11.7
Grissom-NY 8.3

Total Pitcher Index
Newcombe-Bro 4.0
Antonelli-NY...... 3.1
Spahn-Mil 2.7
Burdette-Mil....... 2.4
Dickson-Phi-StL ... 2.2

Total Baseball Ranking
Mays-NY 4.5
Aaron-Mil 4.2
Newcombe-Bro ... 4.0
McMillan-Cin 3.5
Snider-Bro 3.4

TEAM	G	W	L	PCT	GB	R	OR	AB	H	2B	3B	HR	BB	SO	AVG	OBP	SLG	PRO	PRO+	BR	/A	PF	CHI	RC	SB	CS	SBA	SBR
NY	154	97	57	.630		857	631	5312	1433	193	55	190	615	755	.270	.349	.434	.783	115	80	103	97	106	814	51	37	49	-17
CLE	155	88	66	.571	9	712	581	5148	1256	199	23	153	681	764	.244	.337	.381	.718	92	-34	-49	102	105	681	40	32	40	-13
CHI	154	85	69	.552	12	776	634	5286	1412	218	43	128	619	660	.267	.352	.397	.749	101	30	19	101	102	756	70	33	45	-16
BOS	155	84	70	.545	13	780	751	5349	1473	261	45	139	727	687	.275	.365	.419	.784	100	100	9	112	93	826	28	19	30	-11
DET	155	82	72	.532	15	789	699	5364	1494	209	50	150	644	618	.279	.359	.420	.779	110	84	82	100	97	816	43	26	46	-19
BAL	154	69	85	.448	28	571	705	5090	1242	198	34	91	563	725	.244	.322	.350	.672	89	-122	-68	92	100	572	39	42	48	-15
WAS	155	59	95	.383	38	652	924	5202	1302	198	62	112	690	877	.250	.343	.377	.720	96	-26	-25	100	94	681	37	34	41	-13
KC	154	52	102	.338	45	619	831	5256	1325	204	41	112	480	727	.252	.317	.370	.687	85	-107	-109	100	105	610	40	30	42	-15
TOT	618					5756		42007	10937	1680	353	1075	5019	5813	.260	.343	.394	.737							348	253	58	-46

TEAM	CG	SH	SV	IP	H	H/G	HR	BB	SO	RAT	ERA	ERA+	OAV	OOB	PR	/A	PF	CPI	FA	E	DP	FW	PW	BW	SBW	DIF
NY	50	10	35	1382	1285	8.4	114	652	732	12.9	3.63	107	.248	.337	81	36	93	105	.977	136	214	.6	3.5	10.1	-1.1	6.9
CLE	67	17	24	1384	1233	8.0	116	564	845	11.9	3.32	127	.238	.316	128	135	101	100	.978	129	130	1.0	13.2	-4.8	-.7	2.3
CHI	65	11	13	1389	1351	8.8	118	524	722	12.3	3.73	110	.255	.325	66	57	99	99	.979	122	160	1.3	5.6	1.9	-1.0	.2
BOS	50	8	20	1398	1354	8.7	130	668	712	13.3	4.17	111	.253	.341	0	70	111	96	.972	169	168	-1.2	6.9	.9	-.5	1.0
DET	62	10	15	1379	1389	9.1	140	655	788	13.6	4.06	101	.264	.350	15	8	99	108	.976	140	151	.4	.8	8.0	-1.3	-2.9
BAL	38	10	24	1360²	1362	9.0	99	547	715	12.8	4.20	93	.263	.336	-6	-42	94	93	.977	137	142	.5	-4.1	-6.7	-.9	3.1
WAS	36	1	18	1368²	1539	10.1	171	730	663	15.1	5.33	81	.287	.375	-178	-152	104	99	.972	171	173	-1.3	-14.9	-2.4	-.7	1.3
KC	30	3	18	1370¹	1424	9.4	187	679	636	14.1	4.86	89	.271	.359	-106	-80	104	101	.973	166	187	-1.1	-7.8	-10.7	-.9	-4.5
TOT	398	70	167	11031²		8.9				13.2	4.16		.260	.343					.975	1170	1325					

Runs		Hits		Doubles		Triples		Home Runs		Total Bases	
Mantle-NY	132	Kuenn-Det	196	Piersall-Bos	40	Simpson-KC	11	Mantle-NY	52	Mantle-NY	376
Fox-Chi	109	Kaline-Det	194	Kuenn-Det	32	Minoso-Cle	11	Wertz-Cle	32	Kaline-Det	327
Minoso-Chi	106	Fox-Chi	192	Kaline-Det	32	Lemon-Was	11	Berra-NY	30	Jensen-Bos	287
		Mantle-NY	188			Jensen-Bos	11	Sievers-Was	29	Minoso-Chi	286
		Jensen-Bos	182					Maxwell-Det	28		

Runs Batted In		Runs Produced		Bases On Balls		Batting Average		On Base Percentage		Slugging Average	
Mantle-NY	130	Mantle-NY	210	Yost-Was	151	Mantle-NY	.353	Williams-Bos	.479	Mantle-NY	.705
Kaline-Det	128	Kaline-Det	197	Mantle-NY	112	Williams-Bos	.345	Mantle-NY	.467	Williams-Bos	.605
Wertz-Cle	106	Minoso-Chi	173	Williams-Bos	102	Kuenn-Det	.332	Nieman-Chi-Bal	.438	Maxwell-Det	.534
Simpson-KC	105	Kuenn-Det	172	Doby-Chi	102	Maxwell-Det	.326	Minoso-Chi	.430	Berra-NY	.534
Berra-NY	105	Berra-NY	168	Sievers-Was	100	Nieman-Chi-Bal	.320	Maxwell-Det	.420	Kaline-Det	.530

Production		Adjusted Production		Batter Runs		Adjusted Batter Runs		Clutch Hitting Index		Runs Created	
Mantle-NY	1.172	Mantle-NY	213	Mantle-NY	83.3	Mantle-NY	85.8	Doby-Chi	131	Mantle-NY	188
Williams-Bos	1.084	Williams-Bos	164	Williams-Bos	54.1	Williams-Bos	46.7	Simpson-KC	126	Minoso-Chi	130
Minoso-Chi	.954	Nieman-Chi-Bal	156	Minoso-Chi	43.2	Minoso-Chi	42.1	Triandos-Bal	123	Kaline-Det	129
Maxwell-Det	.954	Maxwell-Det	150	Maxwell-Det	37.5	Maxwell-Det	37.4	Lollar-Chi	122	Williams-Bos	121
Nieman-Chi-Bal	.934	Minoso-Chi	149	Kaline-Det	33.4	Nieman-Chi-Bal	36.5	Wertz-Cle	118	Maxwell-Det	118

Total Average		Stolen Bases		Stolen Base Average		Stolen Base Runs		Fielding Runs		Total Player Rating	
Mantle-NY	1.426	Aparicio-Chi	21	Aparicio-Chi	84.0	Aparicio-Chi	3.9	Kaline-Det	16.1	Mantle-NY	7.9
Williams-Bos	1.255	Rivera-Chi	20	Avila-Cle	81.0	Avila-Cle	2.7	Hegan-Cle	14.7	Kaline-Det	4.2
Minoso-Chi	1.031	Avila-Cle	17	Rivera-Chi	69.0	Mantle-NY	2.4	Buddin-Bos	13.9	Berra-NY	3.7
Maxwell-Det	1.015	Minoso-Chi	12					Piersall-Bos	11.4	Maxwell-Det	3.5
Nieman-Chi-Bal	.955							Yost-Was	10.7	Williams-Bos	3.0

Wins		Win Percentage		Games		Complete Games		Shutouts		Saves	
Lary-Det	21	Ford-NY	.760	Zuverink-Bal	62	Pierce-Chi	21	Score-Cle	5	Zuverink-Bal	16
		Wynn-Cle	.690	Crimian-KC	54	Lemon-Cle	21			Mossi-Cle	11
		Score-Cle	.690	Gorman-KC	52	Lary-Det	20			Morgan-NY	11
		Pierce-Chi	.690	Mossi-Cle	48					Shantz-KC	9
		Brewer-Bos	.679	Delock-Bos	48					Delock-Bos	9

Innings Pitched		Fewest Hits/Game		Fewest BB/Game		Strikeouts		Strikeouts/Game		Ratio	
Lary-Det	294.0	Score-Cle	5.85	Stobbs-Was	2.03	Score-Cle	263	Score-Cle	9.49	Score-Cle	10.58
Wynn-Cle	277.2	Larsen-NY	6.66	Donovan-Chi	2.26	Pierce-Chi	192	Pascual-Was	7.73	Donovan-Chi	10.62
Pierce-Chi	276.1	Harshman-Chi	7.27	Kucks-NY	2.89	Foytack-Det	184	Foytack-Det	6.47	Wynn-Cle	10.66
Foytack-Det	256.0	Brewer-Bos	7.37	Wynn-Cle	2.95	Hoeft-Det	172	Pierce-Chi	6.25	Sturdivant-NY	10.80
Lemon-Cle	255.1	Foytack-Det	7.42	Sturdivant-NY	2.96	Lary-Det	165	Sturdivant-NY	6.25	Ford-NY	10.97

Earned Run Average		Adjusted ERA		Opponents' Batting Avg.		Opponents' On Base Pct.		Starter Runs		Adjusted Starter Runs	
Ford-NY	2.47	Score-Cle	166	Score-Cle	.186	Sturdivant-NY	.291	Score-Cle	45.2	Score-Cle	46.5
Score-Cle	2.53	Ford-NY	156	Larsen-NY	.204	Donovan-Chi	.292	Wynn-Cle	44.3	Wynn-Cle	45.7
Wynn-Cle	2.72	Wynn-Cle	154	Brewer-Bos	.220	Score-Cle	.292	Ford-NY	42.3	Ford-NY	35.0
Lemon-Cle	3.03	Lemon-Cle	139	Harshman-Chi	.221	Wynn-Cle	.294	Lary-Det	32.9	Lemon-Cle	33.3
Harshman-Chi	3.10	Sullivan-Bos	135	Sturdivant-NY	.224	Ford-NY	.303	Lemon-Cle	32.0	Sullivan-Bos	32.2

Clutch Pitching Index		Relief Runs		Adjusted Relief Runs		Relief Ranking		Total Pitcher Index		Total Baseball Ranking	
Lary-Det	117	Narleski-Cle	17.4	Narleski-Cle	17.7	Narleski-Cle	16.1	Wynn-Cle	5.3	Mantle-NY	7.9
Sullivan-Bos	116	Grim-NY	11.5	Grim-NY	9.1	Byerly-Was	9.6	Lemon-Cle	4.5	Wynn-Cle	5.3
Hoeft-Det	116	Byrne-NY	9.7	Byerly-Was	7.9	Delock-Bos	9.2	Score-Cle	4.4	Lemon-Cle	4.5
Ford-NY	114	Byerly-Was	6.9	Byrne-NY	6.1	Grim-NY	9.0	Ford-NY	4.4	Score-Cle	4.4
Stobbs-Was	114	Mossi-Cle	5.5	Mossi-Cle	6.0	Mossi-Cle	8.4	Brewer-Bos	4.3	Ford-NY	4.4

TEAM	G	W	L	PCT	GB	R	OR	AB	H	2B	3B	HR	BB	SO	AVG	OBP	SLG	PRO	PRO+	BR	/A	PF	CHI	RC	SB	CS	SBA	SBR
MIL	155	95	59	.617		772	613	5458	1469	221	62	199	461	729	.269	.329	.442	.771	120	82	131	93	101	787	35	16	25	-9
STL	154	87	67	.565	8	737	666	5472	1497	235	43	132	493	672	.274	.336	.405	.741	102	36	22	102	102	731	58	44	64	-24
BRO	154	84	70	.545	11	690	591	5242	1325	188	38	147	550	848	.253	.328	.387	.715	89	-10	-74	110	104	664	60	34	35	-10
CIN	154	80	74	.519	15	747	781	5389	1452	251	33	187	546	752	.269	.341	.432	.773	105	97	48	107	95	794	51	36	51	-19
PHI	156	77	77	.500	18	623	656	5241	1311	213	44	117	534	758	.250	.325	.375	.700	97	-38	-17	97	98	635	57	26	34	-12
NY	154	69	85	.448	26	643	701	5346	1349	171	54	157	447	669	.252	.313	.393	.706	95	-41	-38	100	103	646	64	38	53	-19
PIT	155	62	92	.403	33	586	696	5402	1447	231	60	92	374	733	.268	.318	.384	.702	96	-45	-24	97	93	649	46	35	40	-13
CHI	156	62	92	.403	33	628	722	5369	1312	223	31	147	461	989	.244	.307	.380	.687	91	-77	-66	98	105	623	28	25	38	-14
TOT	619					5426		42919	11162	1733	365	1178	3866	6150	.260	.325	.400	.724							399	254	61	-32

TEAM	CG	SH	SV	IP	H	H/G	HR	BB	SO	RAT	ERA	ERA+	OAV	OOB	PR	/A	PF	CPI	FA	E	DP	FW	PW	BW	SBW	DIF
MIL	60	9	24	1411	1347	8.6	124	570	693	12.3	3.47	101	.253	.327	64	4	90	107	.981	120	173	1.0	.4	13.3	-.5	3.8
STL	46	11	29	1413¹	1385	8.8	140	506	778	12.2	3.78	105	.256	.323	16	29	102	100	.979	131	168	.4	2.9	2.2	-2.0	6.5
BRO	44	18	29	1399	1285	8.3	144	456	891	11.4	3.35	124	.243	.307	81	126	107	101	.979	127	136	.6	12.8	-7.5	-.6	1.7
CIN	40	5	29	1395²	1486	9.6	179	429	707	12.7	4.62	89	.274	.333	-115	-79	106	95	.982	107	139	1.7	-8.0	4.9	-1.5	6.0
PHI	54	9	23	1401²	1363	8.8	139	412	858	11.5	3.79	100	.254	.309	13	1	98	92	.976	136	117	.2	.1	-1.7	-.8	2.2
NY	35	9	20	1398²	1436	9.2	150	471	701	12.5	4.01	98	.266	.330	-20	-11	101	101	.974	161	180	-1.3	-1.1	-3.9	-1.5	-.2
PIT	47	9	15	1395	1463	9.4	158	421	663	12.3	3.88	98	.269	.325	0	-13	98	105	.972	170	143	-1.7	-1.3	-2.4	-.9	-8.6
CHI	30	5	26	1403¹	1397	9.0	144	601	859	13.0	4.13	94	.260	.339	-39	-40	100	100	.975	149	140	-.5	-4.1	-6.7	-1.0	-2.7
TOT	356	75	195	11217²		9.0				12.23.88			.260	.325					.977	1101	1196					

Runs
Aaron-Mil	118
Banks-Chi	113
Mays-NY	112
Mathews-Mil	109
Blasingame-StL	108

Hits
Schoendienst-NY-Mil	200
Aaron-Mil	198
Robinson-Cin	197
Mays-NY	195
Ashburn-Phi	186

Doubles
Hoak-Cin	39
Musial-StL	38
Bouchee-Phi	35
Banks-Chi	34
Moryn-Chi	33

Triples
Mays-NY	20
Virdon-Pit	11
Mathews-Mil	9
Bruton-Mil	9

Home Runs
Aaron-Mil	44
Banks-Chi	43
Snider-Bro	40
Mays-NY	35
Mathews-Mil	32

Total Bases
Aaron-Mil	369
Mays-NY	366
Banks-Chi	344
Robinson-Cin	323
Mathews-Mil	309

Runs Batted In
Aaron-Mil	132
Ennis-StL	105
Musial-StL	102
Banks-Chi	102
Hodges-Bro	98

Runs Produced
Aaron-Mil	206
Mays-NY	174
Banks-Chi	172
Mathews-Mil	171
Hodges-Bro	165

Bases On Balls
Temple-Cin	94
Ashburn-Phi	94
Mathews-Mil	90
Bouchee-Phi	84
Snider-Bro	77

Batting Average
Musial-StL	.351
Mays-NY	.333
Robinson-Cin	.322
Aaron-Mil	.322
Groat-Pit	.315

On Base Percentage
Musial-StL	.428
Mays-NY	.411
Bouchee-Phi	.396
Ashburn-Phi	.392
Temple-Cin	.391

Slugging Average
Mays-NY	.626
Musial-StL	.612
Aaron-Mil	.600
Snider-Bro	.587
Banks-Chi	.579

Production
Musial-StL	1.040
Mays-NY	1.037
Aaron-Mil	.979
Snider-Bro	.957
Banks-Chi	.942

Adjusted Production
Mays-NY	174
Musial-StL	172
Aaron-Mil	170
Mathews-Mil	157
Banks-Chi	150

Batter Runs
Mays-NY	60.5
Musial-StL	54.1
Aaron-Mil	48.3
Banks-Chi	38.6
Mathews-Mil	38.3

Adjusted Batter Runs
Mays-NY	60.8
Aaron-Mil	53.8
Musial-StL	52.8
Mathews-Mil	43.7
Banks-Chi	39.9

Clutch Hitting Index
Ennis-StL	141
McMillan-Cin	140
Hamner-Phi	134
Moryn-Chi	124
Hoak-Chi	121

Runs Created
Mays-NY	145
Aaron-Mil	136
Musial-StL	129
Mathews-Mil	126
Banks-Chi	123

Total Average
Musial-StL	1.103
Mays-NY	1.092
Aaron-Mil	.988
Mathews-Mil	.973
Snider-Bro	.962

Stolen Bases
Mays-NY	38
Gilliam-Bro	26
Blasingame-StL	21
Temple-Cin	19
Fernandez-Phi	18

Stolen Base Average
Temple-Cin	79.2
Fernandez-Phi	78.3
Gilliam-Bro	72.2
Blasingame-StL	70.0
Mays-NY	66.7

Stolen Base Runs
Temple-Cin	2.7
Fernandez-Phi	2.4
Robinson-Cin	1.8
Gilliam-Bro	1.8

Fielding Runs
Ashburn-Phi	26.5
Blasingame-StL	25.9
Logan-Mil	23.9
Robinson-Cin	20.5
Campanella-Bro	15.9

Total Player Rating
Mays-NY	6.1
Aaron-Mil	5.8
Robinson-Cin	4.5
Mathews-Mil	4.5
Musial-StL	4.3

Wins
Spahn-Mil	21
Sanford-Phi	19
Buhl-Mil	18
Drysdale-Bro	17
Burdette-Mil	17

Win Percentage
Buhl-Mil	.720
Sanford-Phi	.704
Spahn-Mil	.656
Drysdale-Bro	.654
Burdette-Mil	.654

Games
Lown-Chi	67
Face-Pit	59
Labine-Bro	58
Worthington-NY	55
Grissom-NY	55

Complete Games
Spahn-Mil	18
Friend-Pit	17
Gomez-NY	16
Sanford-Phi	15

Shutouts
Podres-Bro	6
Spahn-Mil	4
Newcombe-Bro	4
Drysdale-Bro	4

Saves
Labine-Bro	17
Grissom-NY	14
Lown-Chi	12
Wilhelm-StL	11

Innings Pitched
Friend-Pit	277.0
Spahn-Mil	271.0
Burdette-Mil	256.2
Lawrence-Cin	250.1
Roberts-Phi	249.2

Fewest Hits/Game
Sanford-Phi	7.38
Podres-Bro	7.71
Drott-Chi	7.86
Buhl-Mil	7.93
Worthington-NY	7.99

Fewest BB/Game
Newcombe-Bro	1.49
Roberts-Phi	1.55
Law-Pit	1.67
Purkey-Pit	1.90
Jeffcoat-Cin	2.00

Strikeouts
Jones-StL	188
Drott-Chi	170
Drabowsky-Chi	170
Jones-StL	154
Drysdale-Bro	148

Strikeouts/Game
Jones-StL	7.59
Haddix-Phi	7.17
Sanford-Phi	7.15
Drott-Chi	6.68
Drabowsky-Chi	6.38

Ratio
Podres-Bro	9.78
Roberts-Phi	10.45
Newcombe-Bro	10.56
Spahn-Mil	10.66
Law-Pit	10.74

Earned Run Average
Podres-Bro	2.66
Drysdale-Bro	2.69
Spahn-Mil	2.69
Buhl-Mil	2.74
Law-Pit	2.87

Adjusted ERA
Podres-Bro	156
Drysdale-Bro	155
Law-Pit	132
Spahn-Mil	130
Buhl-Mil	128

Opponents' Batting Avg.
Sanford-Phi	.221
Podres-Bro	.230
Drott-Chi	.234
Drysdale-Bro	.236
Spahn-Mil	.237

Opponents' On Base Pct.
Podres-Bro	.274
Roberts-Phi	.284
Newcombe-Bro	.290
Law-Pit	.291
Spahn-Mil	.293

Starter Runs
Spahn-Mil	35.8
Drysdale-Bro	29.2
Buhl-Mil	27.4
Podres-Bro	26.5
Sanford-Phi	21.0

Adjusted Starter Runs
Drysdale-Bro	36.3
Podres-Bro	32.7
Spahn-Mil	24.3
Sanford-Phi	19.0
Buhl-Mil	18.2

Clutch Pitching Index
Buhl-Mil	135
Barclay-NY	117
Law-Pit	113
Spahn-Mil	109
Antonelli-NY	108

Relief Runs
Farrell-Phi	13.9
Roebuck-Bro	12.5
Grissom-NY	11.6
Face-Pit	8.4
Miller-Phi	8.0

Adjusted Relief Runs
Roebuck-Bro	15.6
Farrell-Phi	13.2
Grissom-NY	12.1
Labine-Bro	8.4
Miller-Phi	7.5

Relief Ranking
Farrell-Phi	20.7
Roebuck-Bro	17.5
Grissom-NY	15.2
Labine-Bro	11.8
Miller-Phi	9.5

Total Pitcher Index
Drysdale-Bro	4.6
Podres-Bro	3.7
Spahn-Mil	2.7
Newcombe-Bro	2.3
Roebuck-Bro	2.2

Total Baseball Ranking
Mays-NY	6.1
Aaron-Mil	5.8
Drysdale-Bro	4.6
Robinson-Cin	4.5
Mathews-Mil	4.5

TEAM	G	W	L	PCT	GB	R	OR	AB	H	2B	3B	HR	BB	SO	AVG	OBP	SLG	PRO	PRO+	BR	/A	PF	CHI	RC	SB	CS	SBA	SBR
NY	154	98	56	.636		**723**	**534**	5271	**1412**	200	**54**	145	562	709	**.268**	.341	**.409**	**.750**	112	76	86	98	99	**729**	49	38	48	-16
CHI	155	90	64	.584	8	707	566	5265	1369	208	41	106	**633**	745	.260	**.347**	.375	.722	103	40	36	101	100	708	**109**	51	52	-15
BOS	154	82	72	.532	16	721	668	5267	1380	**231**	32	153	624	739	.262	.343	.405	.748	103	76	37	106	98	725	29	21	29	**-10**
DET	154	78	76	.506	20	614	614	5348	1376	224	37	116	504	**643**	.257	.324	.378	.702	95	-17	-34	103	96	644	36	47	**62**	-22
BAL	154	76	76	.500	21	597	588	5264	1326	191	39	87	504	699	.252	.321	.353	.674	95	-65	-24	94	101	600	57	35	36	**-10**
CLE	153	76	77	.497	21.5	682	722	5171	1304	199	26	140	591	786	.252	.332	.382	.714	102	10	16	99	**103**	661	40	47	57	-19
KC	154	59	94	.386	38.5	563	710	5170	1262	195	40	**166**	364	760	.244	.297	.394	.691	92	-59	-69	102	100	578	35	27	32	**-10**
WAS	154	55	99	.357	43	603	808	5231	1274	215	38	111	527	733	.244	.318	.363	.681	93	-55	-47	99	102	592	13	38	54	-20
TOT	616					5210		41987	10703	1663	307	1024	4309	5814	.255	.328	.382	.710							368	304	55	-71

TEAM	CG	SH	SV	IP	H	H/G	HR	BB	SO	RAT	ERA	ERA+	OAV	OOB	PR	/A	PF	CPI	FA	E	DP	FW	PW	BW	SBW	DIF
NY	41	13	**42**	1395¹	**1198**	7.7	110	580	**810**	11.7	3.00	120	**.234**	.316	122	91	95	109	.980	123	**183**	.2	9.4	8.9	-.7	3.2
CHI	**59**	16	27	1401²	1305	8.4	124	**470**	665	11.6	3.35	112	.248	.312	68	60	99	102	**.982**	**107**	169	1.1	6.2	3.7	-.6	2.6
BOS	55	9	23	1376²	1391	9.1	116	498	692	12.6	3.88	103	.263	.331	-13	16	105	100	.976	149	179	-1.2	1.7	3.8	-.1	.8
DET	52	9	21	1417²	1330	8.4	147	505	756	11.9	3.56	108	.250	.320	36	47	102	104	.980	121	151	.3	4.9	-3.5	-1.3	.7
BAL	44	13	25	1408	1272	8.1	**95**	493	767	**11.5**	3.46	104	.243	**.311**	50	19	95	92	.981	112	159	.8	2.0	-2.5	-.1	-.2
CLE	46	7	23	1380²	1381	9.0	130	618	807	13.3	4.06	92	.260	.342	-41	-52	98	101	.974	153	154	-1.4	-5.4	1.7	-1.0	5.7
KC	26	6	19	1369²	1344	8.8	153	565	626	12.7	4.19	94	.260	.336	-60	-35	104	99	.979	125	162	.1	-3.6	-7.1	-.1	-6.8
WAS	31	5	16	1377	1482	9.7	149	580	691	13.7	4.85	80	.277	.352	-162	-146	103	95	.979	128	159	-.0	-15.1	-4.9	-1.1	-.9
TOT	354	78	196	11126²		8.7				12.4	3.79		.255	.328					.979	1018	1316					

Runs		Hits		Doubles		Triples		Home Runs		Total Bases	
Mantle-NY	121	Fox-Chi	196	Minoso-Chi	36	Simpson-KC-NY	9	Sievers-Was	42	Sievers-Was	331
Fox-Chi	110	Malzone-Bos	185	Gardner-Bal	36	McDougald-NY	9	Williams-Bos	38	Mantle-NY	315
Piersall-Bos	103	Minoso-Chi	176	Malzone-Bos	31	Bauer-NY	9	Mantle-NY	34	Williams-Bos	307
Sievers-Was	99	Mantle-NY	173	Kuenn-Det	30	Fox-Chi	8	Wertz-Cle	28	Kaline-Det	276
		Kuenn-Det	173			Boyd-Bal	8	Zernial-KC	27	Malzone-Bos	271

Runs Batted In		Runs Produced		Bases On Balls		Batting Average		On Base Percentage		Slugging Average	
Sievers-Was	114	Minoso-Chi	187	Mantle-NY	146	Williams-Bos	.388	Williams-Bos	.528	Williams-Bos	.731
Wertz-Cle	105	Mantle-NY	181	Williams-Bos	119	Mantle-NY	.365	Mantle-NY	.515	Mantle-NY	.665
Minoso-Chi	103	Sievers-Was	171	Smith-Cle	79	Woodling-Cle	.321	Minoso-Chi	.413	Sievers-Was	.579
Malzone-Bos	103	Malzone-Bos	170	Minoso-Chi	79	Boyd-Bal	.318	Woodling-Cle	.412	Woodling-Cle	.521
Jensen-Bos	103	Fox-Chi	165	Wertz-Cle	78	Fox-Chi	.317	Fox-Chi	.404	Wertz-Cle	.485

Production		Adjusted Production		Batter Runs		Adjusted Batter Runs		Clutch Hitting Index		Runs Created	
Williams-Bos	1.259	Williams-Bos	227	Williams-Bos	89.9	Mantle-NY	90.0	Minoso-Chi	147	Mantle-NY	178
Mantle-NY	1.179	Mantle-NY	223	Mantle-NY	88.9	Williams-Bos	86.4	Malzone-Bos	136	Williams-Bos	167
Sievers-Was	.968	Sievers-Was	163	Sievers-Was	47.3	Sievers-Was	48.1	Doby-Cle	135	Sievers-Was	131
Woodling-Cle	.933	Woodling-Cle	155	Woodling-Cle	33.0	Woodling-Cle	33.6	Skowron-NY	133	Fox-Chi	109
Minoso-Chi	.867	Minoso-Chi	136	Minoso-Chi	32.7	Minoso-Chi	32.3	Jensen-Bos	133	Minoso-Chi	106

Total Average		Stolen Bases		Stolen Base Average		Stolen Base Runs		Fielding Runs		Total Player Rating	
Williams-Bos	1.599	Aparicio-Chi	28	Rivera-Chi	90.0	Rivera-Chi	4.2	Bridges-Was	29.3	Mantle-NY	7.8
Mantle-NY	1.534	Rivera-Chi	18	Mantle-NY	84.2	Aparicio-Chi	3.6	Fox-Chi	20.9	Williams-Bos	7.0
Sievers-Was	1.010	Minoso-Chi	18	Aparicio-Chi	77.8	Mantle-NY	3.0	Berra-NY	16.8	Fox-Chi	5.2
Woodling-Cle	.944	Mantle-NY	16	Minoso-Chi	54.5	Landis-Chi	1.8	Phillips-Chi	15.8	McDougald-NY	4.0
Maxwell-Det	.876					Martin-NY-KC	1.5	McDougald-NY	15.1	Sievers-Was	3.9

Wins		Win Percentage		Games		Complete Games		Shutouts		Saves	
Pierce-Chi	20	Sturdivant-NY	.727	Zuverink-Bal	56	Pierce-Chi	16	Wilson-Chi	5	Grim-NY	19
Bunning-Det	20	Donovan-Chi	.727	Hyde-Was	52	Donovan-Chi	16	Turley-NY	4	Narleski-Cle	16
Sturdivant-NY	16	Bunning-Det	.714	Clevenger-Was	52	Brewer-Bos	15	Pierce-Chi	4	Delock-Bos	11
Donovan-Chi	16	Wilson-Chi	.652	Delock-Bos	49					Zuverink-Bal	9
Brewer-Bos	16	Pierce-Chi	.625	Trucks-KC	48					Clevenger-Was	8

Innings Pitched		Fewest Hits/Game		Fewest BB/Game		Strikeouts		Strikeouts/Game		Ratio	
Bunning-Det	267.1	Turley-NY	6.12	F.Sullivan-Bos	1.80	Wynn-Cle	184	Turley-NY	7.76	F.Sullivan-Bos	9.76
Wynn-Cle	263.0	Bunning-Det	7.20	Donovan-Chi	1.84	Bunning-Det	182	Johnson-Bal	6.58	Bunning-Det	10.00
Pierce-Chi	257.0	Foytack-Det	7.43	Shantz-NY	2.08	Johnson-Bal	177	Wynn-Cle	6.30	Donovan-Chi	10.44
Johnson-Bal	242.0	Sturdivant-NY	7.59	Loes-Bal	2.14	Pierce-Chi	171	Bunning-Det	6.13	Johnson-Bal	10.45
F.Sullivan-Bos	240.2	F.Sullivan-Bos	7.70	Bunning-Det	2.42	Turley-NY	152	Pierce-Chi	5.99	Pierce-Chi	10.51

Earned Run Average		Adjusted ERA		Opponents' Batting Avg.		Opponents' On Base Pct.		Starter Runs		Adjusted Starter Runs	
Shantz-NY	2.45	Shantz-NY	147	Turley-NY	.194	F.Sullivan-Bos	.275	Bunning-Det	32.5	Bunning-Det	34.5
Sturdivant-NY	2.54	F.Sullivan-Bos	146	Bunning-Det	.218	Bunning-Det	.279	F.Sullivan-Bos	28.3	F.Sullivan-Bos	33.6
Bunning-Det	2.69	Bunning-Det	143	Foytack-Det	.226	Pierce-Chi	.287	Sturdivant-NY	27.9	Donovan-Chi	23.6
Turley-NY	2.71	Sturdivant-NY	141	F.Sullivan-Bos	.230	Johnson-Bal	.289	Shantz-NY	25.8	Sturdivant-NY	23.4
F.Sullivan-Bos	2.73	Donovan-Chi	135	Sturdivant-NY	.232	Donovan-Chi	.293	Donovan-Chi	24.9	Shantz-NY	22.0

Clutch Pitching Index		Relief Runs		Adjusted Relief Runs		Relief Ranking		Total Pitcher Index		Total Baseball Ranking	
Shantz-NY	131	Staley-Chi	20.2	Staley-Chi	19.6	Grim-NY	23.8	F.Sullivan-Bos	3.8	Mantle-NY	7.8
Sturdivant-NY	121	Zuverink-Bal	16.4	Zuverink-Bal	14.0	Zuverink-Bal	20.3	Bunning-Det	3.5	Williams-Bos	7.0
Narleski-Cle	112	Trucks-KC	9.8	Trucks-KC	12.0	Trucks-KC	16.5	Shantz-NY	3.4	Fox-Chi	5.2
Kemmerer-Bos-Was	110	Grim-NY	9.3	Byerly-Was	8.1	Staley-Chi	13.0	Donovan-Chi	2.8	McDougald-NY	4.0
Donovan-Chi	108	Lehman-Bal	7.6	Grim-NY	7.7	Byerly-Was	10.4	Sturdivant-NY	2.4	Sievers-Was	3.9

TEAM	G	W	L	PCT	GB	R	OR	AB	H	2B	3B	HR	BB	SO	AVG	OBP	SLG	PRO	PRO+	BR	/A	PF	CHI	RC	SB	CS	SBA	SBR
MIL	154	92	62	.597		675	541	5225	1388	221	21	167	478	646	.266	.331	.412	.743	111	14	71	92	98	705	26	8	17	-7
PIT	154	84	70	.545	8	662	607	5247	1386	229	68	134	396	753	.264	.319	.410	.729	100	-20	-2	97	103	669	30	15	47	-23
SF	154	80	74	.519	12	727	698	5318	1399	250	42	170	531	817	.263	.334	.422	.756	107	37	52	98	100	747	64	29	38	-13
CIN	154	76	78	.494	16	695	621	5273	1359	242	40	123	572	765	.258	.333	.389	.722	92	-18	-54	105	104	690	61	38	50	-18
STL	154	72	82	.468	20	619	704	5255	1371	216	39	111	533	637	.261	.331	.380	.711	90	-37	-63	104	97	638	44	43	46	-14
CHI	154	72	82	.468	20	709	725	5289	1402	207	49	182	487	853	.265	.332	.426	.758	107	39	49	98	99	737	39	23	33	-12
LA	154	71	83	.461	21	668	761	5173	1297	166	50	172	495	850	.251	.319	.402	.721	93	-31	-52	103	105	650	73	47	59	-20
PHI	154	69	85	.448	23	664	762	5363	1424	238	56	124	573	871	.266	.341	.400	.741	103	20	29	99	93	729	51	33	36	-11
TOT	616					5419		42143	11026	1769	365	1183	4065	6192	.262	.330	.405	.735							388	236	62	-24

TEAM	CG	SH	SV	IP	H	H/G	HR	BB	SO	RAT	ERA	ERA+	OAV	OOB	PR	/A	PF	CPI	FA	E	DP	FW	PW	BW	SBW	DIF
MIL	72	16	17	1376	1261	8.2	125	426	773	11.2	3.21	110	.243	.304	113	47	89	99	.980	120	152	.8	4.7	7.2	-.4	2.7
PIT	43	10	41	1367	1344	8.8	123	470	679	12.1	3.56	109	.260	.325	59	45	98	105	.978	133	173	.1	4.5	-.2	-2.0	4.5
SF	38	7	25	1389¹	1400	9.1	166	512	775	12.6	3.98	96	.262	.331	-3	-25	97	103	.975	152	156	-.9	-2.5	5.2	-1.0	2.2
CIN	50	7	20	1385¹	1422	9.2	148	419	705	12.1	3.73	111	.267	.323	34	64	105	105	.983	100	148	1.9	6.5	-5.4	-2.4	
STL	45	6	25	1381²	1398	9.1	158	567	822	13.1	4.12	100	.263	.339	-25	1	105	102	.974	153	163	-.9	.1	-6.4	-1.1	3.3
CHI	27	5	24	1361	1322	8.7	142	619	805	13.1	4.22	93	.254	.338	-40	-45	99	94	.975	150	161	-.8	-4.5	4.9	-.9	-3.7
LA	30	7	31	1368¹	1399	9.2	173	606	855	13.4	4.47	92	.266	.346	-79	-56	104	100	.975	146	198	-.6	-5.6	-5.2	-1.7	7.2
PHI	51	6	15	1397	1480	9.5	148	446	778	12.5	4.32	92	.271	.329	-57	-56	100	93	.978	129	136	.3	-5.6	2.9	-.8	-4.8
TOT	356	64	198	11025²		9.0				12.5	3.95		.262	.330					.977	1083	1287					

Runs
Mays-SF 121
Banks-Chi 119
Aaron-Mil 109
Boyer-StL 101
Ashburn-Phi 98

Hits
Ashburn-Phi 215
Mays-SF 208
Aaron-Mil 196
Banks-Chi 193
Cepeda-SF 188

Doubles
Cepeda-SF 38
Groat-StL 36
Musial-StL 35
H.Anderson-Phi . . . 34
Aaron-Mil 34

Triples
Ashburn-Phi 13
Virdon-Pit 11
Mays-SF 11
Banks-Chi 11

Home Runs
Banks-Chi 47
Thomas-Pit 35
Robinson-Cin 31
Mathews-Mil 31
Aaron-Mil 30

Total Bases
Banks-Chi 379
Mays-SF 350
Aaron-Mil 328
Cepeda-SF 309
Thomas-Pit 297

Runs Batted In
Banks-Chi 129
Thomas-Pit 109
H.Anderson-Phi . . . 97
Mays-SF 96
Cepeda-SF 96

Runs Produced
Banks-Chi 201
Mays-SF 188
Aaron-Mil 174
Boyer-StL 168
Thomas-Pit 163

Bases On Balls
Ashburn-Phi 97
Temple-Cin 91
Mathews-Mil 85
Cunningham-StL . . . 82

Batting Average
Ashburn-Phi 350
Mays-SF 347
Musial-StL 337
Aaron-Mil 326
Skinner-Pit 321

On Base Percentage
Ashburn-Phi 441
Musial-StL 426
Mays-SF 423
Temple-Cin 406
Skinner-Pit 390

Slugging Average
Banks-Chi 614
Mays-SF 583
Aaron-Mil 546
Thomas-Pit 528
Musial-StL 528

Production
Mays-SF 1.006
Banks-Chi 984
Musial-StL 953
Aaron-Mil 933
H.Anderson-Phi 900

Adjusted Production
Mays-SF 167
Banks-Chi 157
Aaron-Mil 157
Musial-StL 145
H.Anderson-Phi . . . 137

Batter Runs
Mays-SF 55.3
Banks-Chi 45.7
Aaron-Mil 37.0
Musial-StL 36.7
Ashburn-Phi 36.5

Adjusted Batter Runs
Mays-SF 57.1
Banks-Chi 47.0
Aaron-Mil 43.5
Ashburn-Phi 37.7
Musial-StL 34.2

Clutch Hitting Index
H.Anderson-Phi . . . 121
Spencer-SF 120
Thomas-Pit 119
Groat-Pit 117
Fernandez-Phi 115

Runs Created
Mays-SF 152
Banks-Chi 135
Ashburn-Phi 129
Aaron-Mil 121
Skinner-Pit 102

Total Average
Mays-SF 1.110
Banks-Chi 984
Musial-StL 970
Ashburn-Phi 929
Aaron-Mil 916

Stolen Bases
Mays-SF 31
Ashburn-Phi 30
A.Taylor-Chi 21
Blasingame-StL . . . 20
Gilliam-LA 18

Stolen Base Average
Mays-SF 83.8
Blasingame-StL . . . 80.0
A.Taylor-Chi 77.8
Ashburn-Phi 71.4
Gilliam-LA 62.1

Stolen Base Runs
Mays-SF 5.7
Zimmer-LA 3.0
Blasingame-StL . . . 3.0
A.Taylor-Chi 2.7
Robinson-Cin 2.4

Fielding Runs
Zimmer-LA 32.6
Boyer-StL 24.3
Clemente-Pit 20.6
Mazeroski-Pit 18.8
Ashburn-Phi 14.8

Total Player Rating
Mays-SF 6.7
Banks-Chi 5.3
Ashburn-Phi 4.9
Aaron-Mil 4.3
Boyer-StL 4.1

Wins
Spahn-Mil 22
Friend-Pit 22
Burdette-Mil 20
Roberts-Phi 17
Purkey-Cin 17

Win Percentage
Spahn-Mil 667
Burdette-Mil 667
Friend-Pit 611
Purkey-Cin 607
Antonelli-SF 552

Games
Elston-Chi 69
Klippstein-Cin-LA . . 57
Face-Pit 57
Hobbie-Chi 55

Complete Games
Spahn-Mil 23
Roberts-Phi 21
Burdette-Mil 19
Purkey-Cin 17
Friend-Pit 16

Shutouts
Willey-Mil 4
Witt-Pit 3
Purkey-Cin 3
Jay-Mil 3
Burdette-Mil 3

Saves
Face-Pit 20
Labine-LA 14
Farrell-Phi 11

Innings Pitched
Spahn-Mil 290.0
Burdette-Mil 275.1
Friend-Pit 274.0
Roberts-Phi 269.2

Fewest Hits/Game
Jones-StL 7.34
Koufax-LA 7.49
Miller-SF 7.91
Spahn-Mil 7.98
Brosnan-Chi-StL . . 7.99

Fewest BB/Game
Burdette-Mil 1.63
Roberts-Phi 1.70
Law-Pit 1.73
Purkey-Cin 1.76
Newcombe-LA-Cin 1.93

Strikeouts
Jones-StL 225
Spahn-Mil 150
Podres-LA 143
Antonelli-SF 143
Friend-Pit 135

Strikeouts/Game
Jones-StL 8.10
Koufax-LA 7.43
Drott-Chi 6.83
Podres-LA 6.12
Miller-SF 5.88

Ratio
Spahn-Mil 10.40
Miller-SF 10.43
Roberts-Phi 10.78
Burdette-Mil 10.92
Purkey-Cin 11.23

Earned Run Average
Miller-SF 2.47
Jones-StL 2.88
Burdette-Mil 2.91
Spahn-Mil 3.07
Roberts-Phi 3.24

Adjusted ERA
Miller-SF 154
Jones-StL 143
Roberts-Phi 122
Brosnan-Chi-StL . . 121
Burdette-Mil 121

Opponents' Batting Avg.
Koufax-LA 220
Jones-StL 223
Miller-SF 233
Spahn-Mil 237
Antonelli-SF 239

Opponents' On Base Pct.
Miller-SF 286
Spahn-Mil 288
Roberts-Phi 294
Burdette-Mil 301
Purkey-Cin 306

Starter Runs
Burdette-Mil 31.9
Miller-SF 29.9
Jones-StL 29.8
Spahn-Mil 28.3
Witt-Pit 27.5

Adjusted Starter Runs
Jones-StL 34.7
Miller-SF 27.1
Witt-Pit 26.5
Roberts-Phi 21.6
Burdette-Mil 18.7

Clutch Pitching Index
Haddix-Cin 116
Newcombe-LA-Cin 115
Mizell-StL 114
Miller-SF 110
Podres-LA 109

Relief Runs
Elston-Chi 11.6
Face-Pit 9.9
Henry-Chi 9.7
Schmidt-Cin 8.4
Porterfield-Pit 6.5

Adjusted Relief Runs
Elston-Chi 11.2
Schmidt-Cin 9.9
Henry-Chi 9.4
Face-Pit 9.1
Farrell-Phi 6.4

Relief Ranking
Elston-Chi 20.3
Farrell-Phi 12.0
Face-Pit 11.7
Henry-Chi 10.9
Schmidt-Cin 10.3

Total Pitcher Index
Spahn-Mil 3.5
Burdette-Mil 3.0
Miller-SF 2.9
Jones-StL 2.9
Witt-Pit 2.7

Total Baseball Ranking
Mays-SF 6.7
Banks-Chi 5.3
Ashburn-Phi 4.9
Aaron-Mil 4.3
Boyer-StL 4.1

TEAM	G	W	L	PCT	GB	R	OR	AB	H	2B	3B	HR	BB	SO	AVG	OBP	SLG	PRO	PRO+	BR	/A	PF	CHI	RC	SB	CS	SBA	SBR
NY	155	92	62	.597		759	577	5294	1418	212	39	164	537	822	.268	.338	.416	.754	117	88	111	96	102	746	48	32	37	-12
CHI	155	82	72	.532	10	634	615	5249	1348	191	42	101	518	669	.257	.329	.367	.696	98	-12	1	98	99	647	101	33	47	-17
BOS	155	79	75	.513	13	697	691	5218	1335	229	30	155	638	820	.256	.340	.400	.740	102	70	25	107	96	708	29	22	32	-12
CLE	153	77	76	.503	14.5	694	635	5201	1340	210	31	161	494	819	.258	.327	.403	.730	108	38	54	98	102	677	50	49	60	-20
DET	154	77	77	.500	15	659	606	5194	1384	229	41	109	463	678	.266	.329	.389	.718	95	20	-26	107	100	657	48	32	35	-10
BAL	154	74	79	.484	17.5	521	575	5111	1233	195	19	108	483	731	.241	.310	.350	.660	91	-84	-50	95	95	546	33	35	50	-19
KC	156	73	81	.474	19	642	713	5261	1297	196	50	138	452	747	.247	.309	.381	.690	93	-39	-50	102	106	601	22	36	42	-13
WAS	156	61	93	.396	31	553	747	5156	1240	161	38	121	477	751	.240	.309	.357	.666	90	-77	-64	98	99	555	22	41	49	-16
TOT	619					5159		41684	10595	1623	290	1057	4062	6037	.254	.324	.383	.707							353	280	56	-61

TEAM	CG	SH	SV	IP	H	H/G	HR	BB	SO	RAT	ERA	ERA+	OAV	OOB	PR	/A	PF	CPI	FA	E	DP	FW	PW	BW	SBW	DIF
NY	53	21	33	1379	1201	7.8	116	557	796	11.8	3.22	110	.234	.315	84	48	94	103	.978	128	182	-.1	5.0	11.5	-.4	-.9
CHI	55	15	25	1389²	1296	8.4	152	515	751	11.8	3.61	101	.249	.319	25	4	97	104	.981	114	160	.7	.4	.1	-1.0	4.8
BOS	44	5	28	1380	1396	9.1	121	521	695	12.7	3.92	102	.264	.333	-23	13	106	102	.976	145	172	-1.1	1.3	2.6	-.4	-.4
CLE	51	2	20	1373¹	1283	8.4	123	604	766	12.5	3.73	98	.248	.330	6	-12	97	101	.974	152	171	-1.5	-1.2	5.6	-1.3	-1.0
DET	59	8	19	1357¹	1294	8.6	133	437	797	11.8	3.59	112	.252	.316	26	66	107	101	.982	106	140	1.1	6.8	-2.7	-.2	-5.0
BAL	55	15	28	1369²	1277	8.4	106	403	749	11.3	3.40	106	.249	.308	56	30	95	97	.980	114	159	.6	3.1	-5.2	-1.2	.0
KC	42	9	25	1398¹	1405	9.0	150	467	721	12.2	4.15	94	.261	.324	-59	-37	104	95	.979	125	166	.1	-3.8	-5.2	-.5	5.4
WAS	28	6	28	1376²	1443	9.4	156	558	762	13.3	4.53	84	.271	.343	-116	-109	101	98	.980	118	163	.5	-11.3	-6.6	-.9	2.2
TOT	387	81	206	11024		8.6				12.2	3.77		.254	.324					.979	1002	1313					

Runs
Mantle-NY 127
Runnels-Bos 103
Power-KC-Cle 98
Minoso-Cle 94
Cerv-KC 93

Hits
Fox-Chi.......... 187
Malzone-Bos 185
Power-KC-Cle 184
Runnels-Bos 183
Kuenn-Det 179

Doubles
Kuenn-Det 39
Power-KC-Cle 37
Kaline-Det 34
Runnels-Bos 32
Jensen-Bos 31

Triples
Power-KC-Cle 10
Tuttle-KC 9
Lemon-Was 9
Aparicio-Chi....... 9
Harris-Det 8

Home Runs
Mantle-NY 42
Colavito-Cle 41
Sievers-Was 39
Cerv-KC 38
Jensen-Bos 35

Total Bases
Mantle-NY 307
Cerv-KC 305
Colavito-Cle 303
Sievers-Was 299
Jensen-Bos 293

Runs Batted In
Jensen-Bos 122
Colavito-Cle 113
Sievers-Was 108
Cerv-KC 104
Mantle-NY 97

Runs Produced
Mantle-NY 182
Jensen-Bos 170
Power-KC-Cle 162
Cerv-KC 159

Bases On Balls
Mantle-NY 129
Jensen-Bos 99
Williams-Bos 98
Runnels-Bos 87
Colavito-Cle 84

Batting Average
Williams-Bos 328
Runnels-Bos 322
Kuenn-Det 319
Kaline-Det 313
Power-KC-Cle 312

On Base Percentage
Williams-Bos 462
Mantle-NY 445
Runnels-Bos 418
Colavito-Cle 407
Jensen-Bos 398

Slugging Average
Colavito-Cle 620
Cerv-KC 592
Mantle-NY 592
Williams-Bos 584
Sievers-Was 544

Production
Williams-Bos 1.046
Mantle-NY 1.036
Colavito-Cle 1.027
Cerv-KC 964
Jensen-Bos 933

Adjusted Production
Mantle-NY 189
Colavito-Cle 183
Williams-Bos 174
Cerv-KC 158
Sievers-Was 148

Batter Runs
Mantle-NY 64.2
Williams-Bos 53.6
Colavito-Cle 52.8
Jensen-Bos 42.7
Cerv-KC 40.7

Adjusted Batter Runs
Mantle-NY 66.8
Colavito-Cle 54.4
Williams-Bos 49.7
Cerv-KC 39.5
Jensen-Bos 37.8

Clutch Hitting Index
Courtney-Was 142
Lollar-Chi 137
Jensen-Bos 130
Skowron-NY 125
Harris-Det 120

Runs Created
Mantle-NY 147
Colavito-Cle 122
Jensen-Bos 120
Williams-Bos 112
Runnels-Bos 107

Total Average
Mantle-NY 1.208
Williams-Bos ...1.163
Colavito-Cle ...1.078
Jensen-Bos 980
Cerv-KC 947

Stolen Bases
Aparicio-Chi....... 29
Rivera-Chi 21
Landis-Chi 19
Mantle-NY 18
Minoso-Cle 14

Stolen Base Average
Rivera-Chi 87.5
Mantle-NY 85.7
Aparicio-Chi 82.9
Landis-Chi 73.1

Stolen Base Runs
Aparicio-Chi....... 5.1
Rivera-Chi 4.5
Mantle-NY 3.6
Wilson-Det 3.0

Fielding Runs
Kaline-Det 22.1
Kubek-NY 20.2
Malzone-Bos 16.6
Buddin-Bos 14.6
Cerv-KC 13.4

Total Player Rating
Mantle-NY 5.7
Colavito-Cle 4.7
Cerv-KC 4.4
Runnels-Bos 4.0
Kaline-Det 3.5

Wins
Turley-NY 21
Pierce-Chi 17
McLish-Cle 16
Lary-Det 16

Win Percentage
Turley-NY 750
McLish-Cle 667
Pierce-Chi 607
Portocarrero-Bal ..577
Foytack-Det 536

Games
Clevenger-Was 55
Tomanek-Cle-KC .. 54
Hyde-Was 53
Wall-Bos 52

Complete Games
Turley-NY 19
Pierce-Chi 19
Lary-Det 19
Harshman-Bal 17

Shutouts
Ford-NY 7
Turley-NY 6
Wynn-Chi 4
Ramos-Was 4
Donovan-Chi 4

Saves
Duren-NY 20
Hyde-Was 18
Kiely-Bos 12
Wall-Bos 10

Innings Pitched
Lary-Det 260.1
Ramos-Was 259.1
Donovan-Chi 248.0
Turley-NY 245.1
Pierce-Chi 245.0

Fewest Hits/Game
Turley-NY 6.53
Bell-Cle.......... 6.97
Ford-NY 7.14
Pierce-Chi 7.49
Portocarrero-Bal .. 7.61

Fewest BB/Game
Donovan-Chi 1.92
O'Dell-Bal........ 2.07
Sullivan-Bos 2.21
Lary-Det 2.35
Pierce-Chi 2.42

Strikeouts
Wynn-Chi 179
Bunning-Det 177
Turley-NY 168
Harshman-Bal ... 161
Pascual-Was 146

Strikeouts/Game
Pascual-Was 7.41
Bunning-Det 7.25
Wynn-Chi 6.72
Turley-NY 6.16
Harshman-Bal 6.13

Ratio
Ford-NY 9.81
Pierce-Chi 9.96
Portocarrero-Bal . 10.25
O'Dell-Bal....... 10.41
Harshman-Bal ... 10.74

Earned Run Average
Ford-NY 2.01
Pierce-Chi 2.68
Harshman-Bal ... 2.89
Lary-Det 2.90
O'Dell-Bal....... 2.97

Adjusted ERA
Ford-NY 176
Lary-Det 139
Pierce-Chi 136
Harshman-Bal ... 124
McLish-Cle 122

Opponents' Batting Avg.
Turley-NY 206
Bell-Cle..........213
Ford-NY 217
Pierce-Chi 227
Grant-Cle 228

Opponents' On Base Pct.
Ford-NY 276
Pierce-Chi 280
Portocarrero-Bal ..286
O'Dell-Bal........288
Harshman-Bal 294

Starter Runs
Ford-NY 42.9
Pierce-Chi 29.6
Lary-Det 25.0
Harshman-Bal ... 23.0
Turley-NY 21.7

Adjusted Starter Runs
Ford-NY 37.1
Lary-Det 32.8
Pierce-Chi 26.0
Wilhelm-Cle-Bal .. 18.9
Harshman-Bal ... 18.4

Clutch Pitching Index
McLish-Cle 120
Ford-NY 117
Pierce-Chi 114
Lary-Det 113
Wilson-Chi 110

Relief Runs
Hyde-Was 23.1
Duren-NY 14.7
Kiely-Bos 6.9
Staley-Chi 5.7
Morgan-Det 4.2

Adjusted Relief Runs
Hyde-Was 23.7
Duren-NY 12.7
Kiely-Bos 9.1
Morgan-Det 6.1
Wall-Bos 4.9

Relief Ranking
Hyde-Was 36.2
Duren-NY 22.6
Kiely-Bos 10.1
Wall-Bos 7.5
Morgan-Det 6.4

Total Pitcher Index
Ford-NY 4.4
Lary-Det 3.4
Harshman-Bal 3.1
Pierce-Chi 2.7
Hyde-Was 2.5

Total Baseball Ranking
Mantle-NY 5.7
Colavito-Cle 4.9
Ford-NY 4.4
Cerv-KC 4.4
Runnels-Bos 4.0

TEAM	G	W	L	PCT	GB	R	OR	AB	H	2B	3B	HR	BB	SO	AVG	OBP	SLG	PRO	PRO+	BR	/A	PF	CHI	RC	SB	CS	SBA	SBR
LA	156	88	68	.564		705	670	5282	1360	196	46	148	591	891	.257	.335	.396	.731	94	17	-33	107	99	706	84	51	59	-19
MIL	157	86	70	.551	2	724	623	5388	1426	216	36	177	488	765	.265	.329	.417	.746	114	32	90	92	100	729	41	14	19	-6
SF	154	83	71	.539	4	705	613	5281	1377	239	35	167	473	875	.261	.324	.414	.738	105	16	31	98	101	711	81	34	64	-27
PIT	155	78	76	.506	9	651	680	5369	1414	230	42	112	442	715	.263	.322	.384	.706	94	-38	-31	99	100	653	32	26	29	-9
CIN	154	74	80	.481	13	764	738	5288	1448	258	34	161	499	763	.274	.340	.427	.767	107	76	56	103	101	764	65	28	49	-20
CHI	155	74	80	.481	13	673	688	5296	1321	209	44	163	498	911	.249	.319	.398	.717	98	-22	-14	99	102	673	32	19	28	-10
STL	154	71	83	.461	16	641	725	5317	1432	244	49	118	485	747	.269	.333	.400	.733	95	14	-29	106	92	699	65	53	65	-22
PHI	155	64	90	.416	23	599	725	5109	1237	196	38	113	498	858	.242	.314	.362	.676	85	-91	-101	102	105	574	39	46	41	-10
TOT	620					5462		42330	11015	1788	324	1159	3974	6525	.260	.327	.400	.727							439	271	62	-30

TEAM	CG	SH	SV	IP	H	H/G	HR	BB	SO	RAT	ERA	ERA+	OAV	OOB	PR	/A	PF	CPI	FA	E	DP	FW	PW	BW	SBW	DIF
LA	43	14	26	1411²	1317	8.4	157	614	1077	12.6	3.79	111	.247	.330	24	68	107	103	.981	114	154	1.5	6.8	-3.3	-1.5	6.6
MIL	69	18	18	1400²	1406	9.0	128	429	775	11.9	3.51	101	.260	.316	68	5	90	104	.979	127	138	.8	.5	9.1	-.2	-2.1
SF	52	12	23	1376¹	1279	8.4	139	500	873	11.8	3.47	110	.245	.315	73	52	97	103	.974	152	118	-.8	5.2	3.1	-2.3	.7
PIT	48	7	17	1393¹	1432	9.2	134	418	730	12.1	3.90	99	.267	.322	7	-5	98	100	.975	154	165	-.8	-.5	-3.1	-.5	6.0
CIN	44	7	26	1357¹	1460	9.7	162	456	690	12.9	4.31	94	.275	.336	-54	-39	103	102	.978	126	157	.7	-3.9	5.6	-1.6	-3.8
CHI	30	11	25	1391	1337	8.7	152	519	765	12.2	4.01	98	.253	.323	-9	-9	100	96	.977	140	142	-.0	-.9	-1.4	-.6	-.0
STL	36	8	21	1363	1427	9.4	137	564	846	13.3	4.34	98	.270	.343	-59	-14	107	100	.975	146	158	-.4	-1.4	-2.9	-1.8	.6
PHI	54	8	15	1354	1357	9.0	150	474	769	12.4	4.27	96	.261	.326	-49	-25	104	93	.973	154	132	-.8	-2.5	-10.2	-.6	1.1
TOT	376	85	171	11047¹		9.0				12.4	3.95		.260	.327					.977	1113	1164					

Runs
Pinson-Cin 131
Mays-SF 125
Mathews-Mil 118
Aaron-Mil 116
Robinson-Cin 106

Hits
Aaron-Mil 223
Pinson-Cin 205
Cepeda-SF 192
Temple-Cin 186
Mathews-Mil 182

Doubles
Pinson-Cin 47
Aaron-Mil 46
Mays-SF 43
Cimoli-StL 40

Triples
Neal-LA 11
Moon-LA 11
White-StL 9
Pinson-Cin 9
Dark-Chi 9

Home Runs
Mathews-Mil 46
Banks-Chi 45
Aaron-Mil 39
Robinson-Cin 36
Mays-SF 34

Total Bases
Aaron-Mil 400
Mathews-Mil 352
Banks-Chi 351
Mays-SF 335
Pinson-Cin 330

Runs Batted In
Banks-Chi 143
Robinson-Cin ... 125
Aaron-Mil 123
Bell-Cin 115
Mathews-Mil 114

Runs Produced
Aaron-Mil 200
Robinson-Cin ... 195
Pinson-Cin 195
Mays-SF 195
Banks-Chi 195

Bases On Balls
Gilliam-LA 96
Cunningham-StL .. 88
Moon-LA 81
Mathews-Mil 80
Ashburn-Phi 79

Batting Average
Aaron-Mil .... .355
Cunningham-StL ... .345
Cepeda-SF .... .317
Pinson-Cin .... .316
Mays-SF .... .313

On Base Percentage
Cunningham-StL ... .456
Aaron-Mil .... .406
Robinson-Cin .... .397
Moon-LA .... .396
Mathews-Mil ..... .391

Slugging Average
Aaron-Mil .... .636
Banks-Chi .... .596
Mathews-Mil ..... .593
Robinson-Cin .... .583
Mays-SF .... .583

Production
Aaron-Mil 1.042
Mathews-Mil ..... .984
Robinson-Cin .... .980
Banks-Chi .... .975
Mays-SF .... .967

Adjusted Production
Aaron-Mil 188
Mathews-Mil 172
Mays-SF 157
Banks-Chi 156
Robinson-Cin 152

Batter Runs
Aaron-Mil 62.8
Mathews-Mil 48.4
Banks-Chi 44.4
Robinson-Cin 44.0
Mays-SF 42.6

Adjusted Batter Runs
Aaron-Mil 69.5
Mathews-Mil 55.0
Banks-Chi 45.3
Mays-SF 44.3
Robinson-Cin 41.9

Clutch Hitting Index
Bell-Cin 156
Post-Phi 138
Mazeroski-Pit 129
Robinson-Cin 127
Banks-Chi 126

Runs Created
Aaron-Mil 156
Mathews-Mil 143
Mays-SF 131
Banks-Chi 126
Pinson-Cin 124

Total Average
Aaron-Mil 1.089
Mathews-Mil 1.041
Mays-SF 1.037
Robinson-Cin ... 1.015
Cunningham-StL ... .978

Stolen Bases
Mays-SF 27
A.Taylor-Chi 23
Gilliam-LA 23
Cepeda-SF 23
Pinson-Cin 21

Stolen Base Average
Mays-SF 87.1
Pinson-Cin 77.8
Neal-LA 73.9
A.Taylor-Chi 71.9
Cepeda-SF 71.9

Stolen Base Runs
Mays-SF 5.7
Pinson-Cin 2.7
Temple-Cin 2.4
Aaron-Mil 2.4
Cimoli-StL 2.1

Fielding Runs
Blasingame-StL ... 20.5
Neal-LA 20.0
Virdon-Pit 16.2
H.Anderson-Phi ... 14.3
Boyer-StL 13.5

Total Player Rating
Aaron-Mil 6.6
Banks-Chi 5.4
Mathews-Mil 5.3
Mays-SF 4.8
Pinson-Cin 3.8

Wins
Spahn-Mil 21
S.Jones-SF 21
Burdette-Mil 21
Antonelli-SF 19

Win Percentage
Face-Pit .... .947
Law-Pit .... .667
Antonelli-SF ...... .655
Buhl-Mil .... .625

Games
Henry-Chi 65
Elston-Chi 65
McDaniel-StL 62
McMahon-Mil 60
Miller-SF 59

Complete Games
Spahn-Mil 21
Law-Pit 20
Burdette-Mil 20
Roberts-Phi 19

Shutouts
Spahn-Mil 4
S.Jones-SF 4
Drysdale-LA 4
Craig-LA 4
Burdette-Mil 4
Buhl-Mil 4
Antonelli-SF 4

Saves
McMahon-Mil 15
McDaniel-StL 15
Elston-Chi 13
Henry-Chi 12

Innings Pitched
Spahn-Mil 292.0
Burdette-Mil 289.2
Antonelli-SF 282.0
S.Jones-SF 270.2
Drysdale-LA 270.2

Fewest Hits/Game
Haddix-Pit 7.58
S.Jones-SF 7.71
Hobbie-Chi 7.85
Drysdale-LA 7.88
Antonelli-SF 7.88

Fewest BB/Game
Newcombe-Cin ... 1.09
Burdette-Mil 1.18
Roberts-Phi 1.22
Purkey-Cin 1.78
Law-Pit 1.79

Strikeouts
Drysdale-LA 242
S.Jones-SF 209
Koufax-LA 173
Antonelli-SF 165
McCormick-SF ... 151

Strikeouts/Game
Drysdale-LA 8.05
S.Jones-SF 6.95
Podres-LA 6.69
Broglio-StL 6.60
McCormick-SF ... 6.02

Ratio
Haddix-Pit 9.63
Newcombe-Cin .. 10.05
Conley-Phi 10.15
Law-Pit 10.15
Antonelli-SF 10.40

Earned Run Average
S.Jones-SF 2.83
Miller-SF 2.84
Buhl-Mil 2.86
Spahn-Mil 2.96
Law-Pit 2.98

Adjusted ERA
Conley-Phi 137
S.Jones-SF 135
Miller-SF 134
Law-Pit 130
Jackson-StL 128

Opponents' Batting Avg.
S.Jones-SF ...... .228
Haddix-Pit .... .228
Antonelli-SF ..... .233
Drysdale-LA ..... .233
Conley-Phi ...... .235

Opponents' On Base Pct.
Haddix-Pit .... .273
Newcombe-Cin ... .280
Conley-Phi ...... .281
Law-Pit .... .282
Antonelli-SF ..... .286

Starter Runs
S.Jones-SF 33.7
Spahn-Mil 32.1
Craig-LA 32.0
Law-Pit 28.7
Antonelli-SF 26.7

Adjusted Starter Runs
Craig-LA 36.7
S.Jones-SF 29.6
Jackson-StL 26.6
Law-Pit 26.3
Drysdale-LA 23.1

Clutch Pitching Index
Miller-SF 134
Buhl-Mil 120
Spahn-Mil 105
Jackson-StL 104
S.Jones-SF 104

Relief Runs
Miller-SF 20.5
Henry-Chi 18.9
Face-Pit 12.9
McMahon-Mil ... 12.4
Elston-Chi 6.8

Adjusted Relief Runs
Henry-Chi 18.9
Miller-SF 18.0
Face-Pit 12.1
McMahon-Mil 8.7
Meyer-Phi 7.7

Relief Ranking
Henry-Chi 25.3
Face-Pit 25.1
Miller-SF 16.4
Elston-Chi 13.4
McDaniel-StL ... 12.5

Total Pitcher Index
Craig-LA 3.6
Law-Pit 3.0
Drysdale-LA 3.0
S.Jones-SF 2.6
Conley-Phi 2.6

Total Baseball Ranking
Aaron-Mil 6.6
Banks-Chi 5.4
Mathews-Mil 5.3
Mays-SF 4.8
Pinson-Cin 3.8

TEAM	G	W	L	PCT	GB	R	OR	AB	H	2B	3B	HR	BB	SO	AVG	OBP	SLG	PRO	PRO+	BR	/A	PF	CHI	RC	SB	CS	SBA	SBR
CHI	156	94	60	.610		669	**588**	5297	1325	220	**46**	97	580	**634**	.250	.330	.364	.694	97	-19	-10	99	100	653	**113**	53	**52**	-14
CLE	154	89	65	.578	5	745	646	5288	1390	216	25	**167**	433	721	.263	.323	**.408**	.731	**110**	32	**57**	96	**107**	682	33	36	41	**-13**
NY	155	79	75	.513	15	687	647	5379	**1397**	224	40	153	457	828	.260	.321	.402	.723	106	17	40	97	98	695	45	22	35	**-13**
DET	154	76	78	.494	18	713	732	5211	1346	196	30	160	580	737	.258	**.338**	.400	**.738**	102	57	20	105	97	720	34	17	33	-14
BOS	154	75	79	.487	19	726	696	5225	1335	**248**	28	125	**626**	810	.256	**.338**	.385	.723	99	36	4	105	101	697	68	25	43	-17
BAL	155	74	80	.481	20	551	621	5208	1240	182	23	109	536	690	.238	.312	.345	.657	88	-95	-79	98	96	563	36	24	36	**-13**
KC	154	66	88	.429	28	681	760	5264	1383	231	43	117	481	780	.263	.328	.390	.718	100	16	3	102	99	620	34	24	40	-16
WAS	154	63	91	.409	31	619	701	5092	1205	173	32	163	517	881	.237	.310	.379	.689	94	-42	-38	100	101	594	51	34	46	-16
TOT	618					5391		41964	10621	1690	267	1091	4210	6081	.253	.325	.384	.709							414	235	64	-16

TEAM	CG	SH	SV	IP	H	H/G	HR	BB	SO	RAT	ERA	ERA+	OAV	OOB	PR	/A	PF	CPI	FA	E	DP	FW	PW	BW	SBW	DIF
CHI	44	13	36	1425.1	1297	8.2	129	525	761	11.7	**3.29**	114	.242	.313	90	73	97	106	.979	130	141	.6	7.4	-1.0	-1.2	11.2
CLE	58	7	23	1383.2	**1230**	8.0	148	635	799	12.3	3.75	98	.239	.325	17	-9	95	101	.978	127	138	.7	-.9	5.8	-1.1	7.5
NY	38	**15**	28	1399	1281	8.2	120	594	**836**	12.2	3.60	101	.244	.324	40	6	94	102	.978	131	160	.5	.6	4.0	-1.1	-2.1
DET	53	9	24	1360	1327	8.8	177	432	829	11.9	4.20	97	.253	.316	-51	-21	105	94	.978	124	131	.9	-2.1	2.0	-1.2	-.6
BOS	38	9	25	1364	1386	9.1	135	589	724	13.2	4.17	97	.265	.343	-46	-16	105	104	.978	131	167	.5	-1.6	.4	-1.5	3.0
BAL	45	**15**	30	1400.1	1290	8.3	111	476	735	**11.5**	3.56	106	.246	**.312**	46	34	98	96	.976	146	163	-.4	3.4	-8.0	-1.1	3.0
KC	44	8	21	1360.2	1452	9.6	148	492	703	13.2	4.35	92	.273	.340	-74	-52	104	102	.973	160	156	-1.2	-5.3	.3	-1.4	-3.4
WAS	46	10	21	1360	1358	9.0	123	467	694	12.3	4.01	98	.259	.324	-22	-14	101	96	.973	162	140	-1.4	-1.4	-3.8	-1.4	-6.0
TOT	366	86	208	11053		8.6				12.3	3.86		.253	.325					.977	1111	1196					

Runs
Yost-Det 115
Mantle-NY 104
Power-Cle 102
Jensen-Bos 101
Kuenn-Det 99

Hits
Kuenn-Det 198
Fox-Chi 191
Runnels-Bos 176
Power-Cle 172
Minoso-Cle 172

Doubles
Kuenn-Det 42
Malzone-Bos 34
Fox-Chi 34
Williams-KC 33
Runnels-Bos 33

Triples
Allison-Was 9
McDougald-NY 8

Home Runs
Killebrew-Was 42
Colavito-Cle 42
Lemon-Was 33
Maxwell-Det 31
Mantle-NY 31

Total Bases
Colavito-Cle 301
Killebrew-Was 282
Kuenn-Det 281
Mantle-NY 278
Allison-Was 275

Runs Batted In
Jensen-Bos 112
Colavito-Cle 111
Killebrew-Was 105
Lemon-Was 100
Maxwell-Det 95

Runs Produced
Jensen-Bos 185
Minoso-Cle 163
Malzone-Bos 163
Kuenn-Det 161
Killebrew-Was 161

Bases On Balls
Yost-Det 135
Runnels-Bos 95
Mantle-NY 93
Buddin-Bos 92
Killebrew-Was 90

Batting Average
Kuenn-Det .353
Kaline-Det .327
Runnels-Bos .314
Fox-Chi .306
Minoso-Cle .302

On Base Percentage
Yost-Det .437
Runnels-Bos .415
Kaline-Det .414
Woodling-Bal .405
Kuenn-Det .405

Slugging Average
Kaline-Det .530
Killebrew-Was .516
Mantle-NY .514
Colavito-Cle .512
Lemon-Was .510

Production
Kaline-Det .944
Kuenn-Det .906
Mantle-NY .905
Yost-Det .873
Killebrew-Was .873

Adjusted Production
Mantle-NY 152
Kaline-Det 149
Kuenn-Det 140
Woodling-Bal 139
Killebrew-Was 137

Batter Runs
Kaline-Det 41.6
Yost-Det 37.9
Francona-Cle 36.6
Kuenn-Det 36.2
Mantle-NY 36.0

Adjusted Batter Runs
Francona-Cle 38.5
Mantle-NY 38.5
Kaline-Det 38.0
Yost-Det 33.7
Kuenn-Det 32.4

Clutch Hitting Index
Strickland-Cle 136
Jensen-Bos 135
Woodling-Bal 125
Cerv-KC 124
Williams-KC 120

Runs Created
Mantle-NY 117
Kuenn-Det 117
Yost-Det 115
Kaline-Det 114
Killebrew-Was 103

Total Average
Yost-Det .992
Mantle-NY .985
Kaline-Det .983
Kuenn-Det .903
Jensen-Bos .888

Stolen Bases
Aparicio-Chi 56
Mantle-NY 21
Landis-Chi 20
Jensen-Bos 20
Allison-Was 13

Stolen Base Average
Mantle-NY 87.5
Aparicio-Chi 81.2
Jensen-Bos 80.0
Landis-Chi 69.0

Stolen Base Runs
Aparicio-Chi 9.0
Mantle-NY 4.5
Jensen-Bos 3.0
Malzone-Bos 1.8
Yost-Det 1.5

Fielding Runs
Gardner-Bal 30.5
Minoso-Cle 11.9
Jensen-Bos 10.6
Power-Cle 10.0
Landis-Chi 9.0

Total Player Rating
Mantle-NY 3.8
Kaline-Det 3.6
Francona-Cle 3.4
Runnels-Bos 3.4
Jensen-Bos 3.1

Wins
Wynn-Chi 22
McLish-Cle 19
Shaw-Chi 18

Win Percentage
Shaw-Chi .750
McLish-Cle .704
Wynn-Chi .688
Mossi-Det .654

Games
Staley-Chi 67
Lown-Chi 60
Clevenger-Was 50
Shaw-Chi 47

Complete Games
Pascual-Was 17
Pappas-Bal 15
Mossi-Det 15
Wynn-Chi 14
Bunning-Det 14

Shutouts
Pascual-Was 6
Wynn-Chi 5
Pappas-Bal 4

Saves
Lown-Chi 15
Staley-Chi 14
Loes-Bal 14
Duren-NY 14
Fornieles-Bos 11

Innings Pitched
Wynn-Chi 255.2
Bunning-Det 249.2
Foytack-Det 240.1
Pascual-Was 238.2
McLish-Cle 235.1

Fewest Hits/Game
Score-Cle 6.89
Ditmar-NY 6.95
Wilhelm-Bal 7.09
Wynn-Chi 7.11
O'Dell-Bal 7.36

Fewest BB/Game
Brown-Bal 1.76
Lary-Det 1.86
Garver-KC 1.88
Mossi-Det 1.93
Ramos-Was 2.00

Strikeouts
Bunning-Det 201
Pascual-Was 185
Wynn-Chi 179
Score-Cle 147
Wilhelm-Bal 139

Strikeouts/Game
Score-Cle 8.23
Bunning-Det 7.25
Pascual-Was 6.98
Turley-NY 6.47
Wynn-Chi 6.30

Ratio
Ditmar-NY 9.62
Pascual-Was 10.33
Mossi-Det 10.34
O'Dell-Bal 10.43
Brown-Bal 10.48

Earned Run Average
Wilhelm-Bal 2.19
Pascual-Was 2.64
Shaw-Chi 2.69
Ditmar-NY 2.90
Walker-Bal 2.92

Adjusted ERA
Wilhelm-Bal 173
Pascual-Was 148
Shaw-Chi 140
Walker-Bal 130
O'Dell-Bal 129

Opponents' Batting Avg.
Score-Cle .210
Ditmar-NY .211
Wynn-Chi .216
O'Dell-Bal .220
Wilhelm-Bal .224

Opponents' On Base Pct.
Ditmar-NY .270
Pascual-Was .284
O'Dell-Bal .286
Mossi-Det .286
Brown-Bal .290

Starter Runs
Wilhelm-Bal 42.0
Pascual-Was 32.4
Shaw-Chi 30.0
Ditmar-NY 21.7
Perry-Cle 20.6

Adjusted Starter Runs
Wilhelm-Bal 40.0
Pascual-Was 33.8
Shaw-Chi 27.3
Daley-KC 20.2
O'Dell-Bal 18.8

Clutch Pitching Index
Wilhelm-Bal 132
Daley-KC 122
Ford-NY 119
Shaw-Chi 114
McLish-Cle 114

Relief Runs
Staley-Chi 20.9
Duren-NY 16.9
Shantz-NY 15.6
Coates-NY 11.0
Lown-Chi 10.0

Adjusted Relief Runs
Staley-Chi 19.6
Duren-NY 15.0
Shantz-NY 13.3
Stobbs-Was 9.4
Fornieles-Bos 9.0

Relief Ranking
Staley-Chi 25.0
Duren-NY 22.1
Shantz-NY 14.7
Lown-Chi 12.7
Fornieles-Bos 10.6

Total Pitcher Index
Pascual-Was 4.8
Wilhelm-Bal 3.5
Shaw-Chi 2.8
Daley-KC 2.6
Ford-NY 2.5

Total Baseball Ranking
Pascual-Was 4.8
Mantle-NY 3.8
Kaline-Det 3.6
Wilhelm-Bal 3.5
Francona-Cle 3.4

TEAM	G	W	L	PCT	GB	R	OR	AB	H	2B	3B	HR	BB	SO	AVG	OBP	SLG	PRO	PRO+	BR	/A	PF	CHI	RC	SB	CS	SBA	SBR
PIT	155	95	59	.617		**734**	593	5406	**1493**	**236**	56	120	486	**747**	**.276**	**.338**	**.407**	**.745**	109	**72**	67	101	99	**737**	34	24	37	-14
MIL	154	88	66	.571	7	724	658	5263	1393	198	48	**170**	463	793	.265	.327	**.417**	.744	**117**	60	**108**	93	102	714	69	37	50	-18
STL	155	86	68	.558	9	639	616	5187	1317	213	48	138	501	792	.254	.323	.393	.716	93	13	-42	109	97	652	48	35	41	**-13**
LA	154	82	72	.532	13	662	**593**	5227	1333	216	38	126	529	837	.255	.327	.383	.710	93	6	-36	106	99	659	**95**	53	**56**	-17
SF	156	79	75	.513	16	671	631	5324	1357	220	**62**	130	467	846	.255	.319	.393	.712	106	0	-11	102	97	663	86	45	45	**-13**
CIN	154	67	87	.435	28	640	692	5289	1324	230	40	140	512	858	.250	.320	.388	.708	98	-47	-39	99	**103**	617	73	37	45	-15
CHI	156	60	94	.390	35	634	776	5311	1293	213	48	119	**531**	897	.243	.314	.369	.683	94	-47	-39	99	103	617	51	34	43	-15
PHI	154	59	95	.383	36	546	691	5169	1235	196	44	99	448	1054	.239	.304	.351	.655	84	-101	-101	100	101	546	45	48	53	-16
TOT	619					5250		42176	10745	1722	384	1042	3937	6824	.255	.322	.388	.710							501	313	62	-37

TEAM	CG	SH	SV	IP	H	H/G	HR	BB	SO	RAT	ERA	ERA+	OAV	OOB	PR	/A	PF	CPI	FA	E	DP	FW	PW	BW	SBW	DIF
PIT	47	11	33	1399²	1363	8.8	**105**	386	811	11.3	3.49	107	.257	**.309**	42	40	100	99	**.979**	128	163	.7	4.1	6.9	-1.0	7.2
MIL	**55**	13	28	1387¹	1327	8.6	130	518	807	12.2	3.76	91	.251	.322	0	-51	91	99	.976	141	137	-.0	-5.2	**11.1**	-1.4	6.5
STL	37	11	30	1371	1316	8.6	127	511	906	12.1	3.64	112	.253	.321	18	69	109	**103**	.976	141	152	.0	7.1	-4.3	**-.9**	7.1
LA	46	13	20	1398	**1218**	**7.8**	154	564	**1122**	11.7	**3.40**	**117**	**.233**	.312	56	88	106	103	.979	125	142	.9	**9.1**	-3.7	-1.3	.0
SF	**55**	**16**	26	1396	1288	8.3	107	512	897	11.8	3.44	101	.245	.314	49	5	93	99	.972	**166**	117	-1.3	.5	4.1	-.9	-.5
CIN	33	8	**35**	1390¹	1417	9.2	134	442	740	12.3	4.00	96	.267	.328	-36	-27	102	101	**.979**	125	155	.9	-2.8	-1.1	-1.1	-5.9
CHI	36	6	25	1402²	1393	8.9	152	565	805	12.8	4.35	87	.260	.335	-91	-89	100	96	.977	143	133	-.0	-9.2	-4.0	-1.1	-2.7
PHI	45	6	16	1375¹	1423	9.3	133	439	736	12.3	4.01	97	.269	.328	-38	-19	103	101	.974	155	129	-.8	-2.0	-10.4	-1.2	-3.7
TOT	354	84	213	11120¹		8.7				12.1	3.76		.255	.322					.977	1124	1128					

Runs		Hits		Doubles		Triples		Home Runs		Total Bases	
Bruton-Mil	112	Mays-SF	190	Pinson-Cin	37	Bruton-Mil	13	Banks-Chi	41	Aaron-Mil	334
Mathews-Mil	108	Pinson-Cin	187	Cepeda-SF	36	Pinson-Cin	12	Aaron-Mil	40	Banks-Chi	331
Pinson-Cin	107	Groat-Pit	186	Skinner-Pit	33	Mays-SF	12	Mathews-Mil	39	Mays-SF	330
Mays-SF	107	Bruton-Mil	180	Robinson-Cin	33	Aaron-Mil	11	Boyer-StL	32	Boyer-StL	310
Aaron-Mil	102	Clemente-Pit	179	Banks-Chi	32			Robinson-Cin	31	Pinson-Cin	308

Runs Batted In		Runs Produced		Bases On Balls		Batting Average		On Base Percentage		Slugging Average	
Aaron-Mil	126	Mathews-Mil	193	Ashburn-Chi	116	Groat-Pit	.325	Ashburn-Chi	.416	Robinson-Cin	.595
Mathews-Mil	124	Aaron-Mil	188	Mathews-Mil	111	Larker-LA	.323	Robinson-Cin	.413	Aaron-Mil	.566
Banks-Chi	117	Mays-SF	181	Gilliam-LA	96	Mays-SF	.319	Mathews-Mil	.401	Boyer-StL	.562
Mays-SF	103	Banks-Chi	170	Robinson-Cin	82	Clemente-Pit	.314	Moon-LA	.387	Mays-SF	.555
Boyer-StL	97	Clemente-Pit	167	Spencer-StL	81	Boyer-StL	.304	Mays-SF	.386	Banks-Chi	.554

Production		Adjusted Production		Batter Runs		Adjusted Batter Runs		Clutch Hitting Index		Runs Created	
Robinson-Cin	1.007	Mathews-Mil	170	Robinson-Cin	47.8	Mathews-Mil	51.6	Larker-LA	155	Mathews-Mil	128
Mathews-Mil	.952	Robinson-Cin	169	Mathews-Mil	46.0	Mays-SF	48.0	Clemente-Pit	131	Mays-SF	124
Mays-SF	.941	Mays-SF	164	Mays-SF	43.5	Robinson-Cin	46.8	Skinner-Pit	127	Aaron-Mil	119
Boyer-StL	.934	Aaron-Mil	161	Boyer-StL	37.9	Aaron-Mil	42.9	Bailey-Cin	125	Banks-Chi	113
Aaron-Mil	.925	Banks-Chi	145	Aaron-Mil	37.4	Banks-Chi	35.2	Stuart-Pit	123	Robinson-Cin	113

Total Average		Stolen Bases		Stolen Base Average		Stolen Base Runs		Fielding Runs		Total Player Rating	
Robinson-Cin	1.069	Wills-LA	50	Javier-StL	82.6	Wills-LA	7.8	Mazeroski-Pit	25.4	Mays-SF	5.3
Mathews-Mil	1.029	Pinson-Cin	32	Wills-LA	80.6	Javier-StL	3.3	Wills-LA	20.5	Banks-Chi	5.1
Mays-SF	.953	A.Taylor-Chi-Phi	26	Ashburn-Chi	80.0	Blasingame-SF	3.0	Grammas-StL	19.8	Aaron-Mil	4.8
Aaron-Mil	.935	Mays-SF	25	Pinson-Cin	72.7	Pinson-Cin	2.4	Smith-StL	17.0	Robinson-Cin	4.3
Boyer-StL	.918	Bruton-Mil	22	Mays-SF	71.4	Ashburn-Chi	2.4	Boyer-StL	13.1	Boyer-StL	4.2

Wins		Win Percentage		Games		Complete Games		Shutouts		Saves	
Spahn-Mil	21	Broglio-StL	.700	Face-Pit	68	Spahn-Mil	18	Sanford-SF	6	McDaniel-StL	26
Broglio-StL	21	Law-Pit	.690	McDaniel-StL	65	Law-Pit	18	Drysdale-LA	5	Face-Pit	24
Law-Pit	20	Spahn-Mil	.677	Elston-Chi	60	Burdette-Mil	18			Henry-Cin	17
Burdette-Mil	19	Buhl-Mil	.640	Farrell-Phi	59	Hobbie-Chi	16			Brosnan-Cin	12
		Purkey-Cin	.607	Roebuck-LA	58	Friend-Pit	16				

Innings Pitched		Fewest Hits/Game		Fewest BB/Game		Strikeouts		Strikeouts/Game		Ratio	
Jackson-StL	282.0	Broglio-StL	6.84	Burdette-Mil	1.14	Drysdale-LA	246	Koufax-LA	10.13	Drysdale-LA	9.90
Friend-Pit	275.2	Koufax-LA	6.84	Roberts-Phi	1.29	Koufax-LA	197	Drysdale-LA	8.23	Friend-Pit	10.15
Burdette-Mil	275.2	Williams-LA	7.03	Law-Pit	1.33	S.Jones-SF	190	Williams-LA	7.60	Law-Pit	10.27
Law-Pit	271.2	Drysdale-LA	7.16	Friend-Pit	1.47	Broglio-StL	188	Broglio-StL	7.48	Burdette-Mil	10.35
Drysdale-LA	269.0	Buhl-Mil	7.62	Haddix-Pit	1.98	Friend-Pit	183	S.Jones-SF	7.31	Williams-LA	10.37

Earned Run Average		Adjusted ERA		Opponents' Batting Avg.		Opponents' On Base Pct.		Starter Runs		Adjusted Starter Runs	
McCormick-SF	2.70	Broglio-StL	149	Koufax-LA	.207	Drysdale-LA	.275	McCormick-SF	29.8	Broglio-StL	34.0
Broglio-StL	2.74	Drysdale-LA	140	Williams-LA	.210	Friend-Pit	.281	Drysdale-LA	27.5	Drysdale-LA	33.6
Drysdale-LA	2.84	Simmons-Phi-StL	134	Broglio-StL	.213	Williams-LA	.282	Broglio-StL	25.6	Friend-Pit	22.9
Williams-LA	3.00	Williams-LA	133	Drysdale-LA	.215	Law-Pit	.287	Friend-Pit	23.2	Williams-LA	22.4
Friend-Pit	3.00	Podres-LA	129	Buhl-Mil	.229	Burdette-Mil	.287	Law-Pit	20.6	Podres-LA	22.4

Clutch Pitching Index		Relief Runs		Adjusted Relief Runs		Relief Ranking		Total Pitcher Index		Total Baseball Ranking	
Simmons-Phi-StL	121	McDaniel-StL	21.6	McDaniel-StL	26.0	McDaniel-StL	45.2	Drysdale-LA	4.4	Mays-SF	5.3
Podres-LA	117	Brosnan-Cin	15.4	Brosnan-Cin	16.1	Farrell-Phi	22.2	Broglio-StL	4.1	Banks-Chi	5.1
O'Dell-SF	110	Roebuck-LA	12.8	Roebuck-LA	15.5	Face-Pit	20.3	McDaniel-StL	2.9	Aaron-Mil	4.8
Sadecki-StL	109	Farrell-Phi	12.2	Farrell-Phi	13.6	Brosnan-Cin	17.5	Law-Pit	2.7	Drysdale-LA	4.4
Buhl-Mil	108	Face-Pit	10.9	Face-Pit	10.8	Roebuck-LA	15.5	McCormick-SF	2.7	Robinson-Cin	4.3

TEAM	G	W	L	PCT	GB	R	OR	AB	H	2B	3B	HR	BB	SO	AVG	OBP	SLG	PRO	PRO+	BR	/A	PF	CHI	RC	SB	CS	SBA	SBR
NY	155	97	57	.630		746	627	5290	1377	215	40	193	537	818	.260	.332	.426	.758	116	63	101	94	100	747	37	23	33	-12
BAL	154	89	65	.578	8	682	606	5170	1307	206	33	123	596	801	.253	.334	.377	.711	99	-7	1	99	102	659	37	24	42	-17
CHI	154	87	67	.565	10	741	617	5191	1402	242	38	112	567	648	.270	.348	.396	.744	108	57	63	99	101	726	122	48	53	-16
CLE	154	76	78	.494	21	667	693	5296	1415	218	20	127	444	573	.267	.328	.388	.716	102	-10	10	97	100	673	58	25	32	-11
WAS	154	73	81	.474	24	672	696	5248	1283	205	43	147	584	883	.244	.326	.375	.701	98	-17	-10	99	101	656	52	43	57	-20
DET	154	71	83	.461	26	633	644	5202	1243	188	34	150	636	728	.239	.326	.375	.701	92	-31	-49	103	97	651	66	32	36	-11
BOS	154	65	89	.422	32	658	775	5215	1359	234	32	124	570	798	.261	.336	.389	.725	98	16	-7	104	95	674	34	28	44	-17
KC	155	58	96	.377	39	615	756	5226	1303	212	34	110	513	744	.249	.318	.366	.684	90	-67	-71	101	103	598	16	11	20	-8
TOT	617					5414		41838	10689	1720	274	1086	4447	5993	.255	.331	.388	.718							422	234	64	-13

TEAM	CG	SH	SV	IP	H	H/G	HR	BB	SO	RAT	ERA	ERA+	OAV	OOB	PR	/A	PF	CPI	FA	E	DP	FW	PW	BW	SBW	DIF
NY	38	16	42	1398	1225	7.9	123	609	712	12.0	3.52	102	.237	.321	55	10	93	98	.979	129	162	.2	1.0	10.2	-1.0	9.7
BAL	48	11	22	1375²	1222	8.0	117	552	785	11.8	3.52	108	.241	.319	53	43	98	98	.982	108	172	1.4	4.4	.1	-1.5	7.7
CHI	42	11	26	1381	1338	8.7	127	533	695	12.3	3.60	105	.257	.328	41	26	98	106	.982	109	175	1.4	2.6	6.4	-1.4	1.1
CLE	32	10	30	1382¹	1308	8.5	161	636	771	12.8	3.95	95	.251	.336	-12	-33	97	103	.978	128	165	.2	-3.3	1.0	-.9	2.1
WAS	34	10	35	1405¹	1392	8.9	130	538	775	12.6	3.77	103	.259	.331	15	18	100	103	.973	165	159	-2.1	1.8	-1.0	-1.8	-.8
DET	40	7	25	1405²	1336	8.6	141	474	824	11.9	3.64	109	.250	.317	36	50	102	99	.977	138	138	-.5	5.1	-5.0	-.9	-4.7
BOS	34	6	23	1361	1440	9.5	127	580	767	13.6	4.62	87	.272	.348	-113	-87	104	94	.976	141	156	-.6	-8.8	-.7	-1.5	-.3
KC	44	4	14	1374	1428	9.4	160	525	664	13.1	4.38	91	.271	.342	-76	-60	103	100	.979	127	149	.3	-6.1	-7.2	-.6	-5.4
TOT	312	75	217	11083		8.7				12.5	3.87		.255	.331					.978	1045	1276					

Runs		Hits		Doubles		Triples		Home Runs		Total Bases	
Mantle-NY	119	Minoso-Chi	184	Francona-Cle	36	Fox-Chi	10	Mantle-NY	40	Mantle-NY	294
Maris-NY	98	Robinson-Bal	175	Skowron-NY	34	Robinson-Bal	9	Maris-NY	39	Maris-NY	290
Minoso-Chi	89	Fox-Chi	175	Minoso-Chi	32			Lemon-Was	38	Skowron-NY	284
Landis-Chi	89	Smith-Chi	169	Freese-Chi	32			Colavito-Det	35	Minoso-Chi	284
Sievers-Chi	87	Runnels-Bos	169					Killebrew-Was	31	Lemon-Was	268

Runs Batted In		Runs Produced		Bases On Balls		Batting Average		On Base Percentage		Slugging Average	
Maris-NY	112	Minoso-Chi	174	Yost-Det	125	Runnels-Bos	.320	Yost-Det	.416	Maris-NY	.581
Minoso-Chi	105	Mantle-NY	173	Mantle-NY	111	Smith-Chi	.315	Woodling-Bal	.403	Mantle-NY	.558
Wertz-Bos	103	Maris-NY	171	Allison-Was	92	Minoso-Chi	.311	Runnels-Bos	.403	Killebrew-Was	.534
Lemon-Was	100	Sievers-Chi	152	Woodling-Bal	84	Skowron-NY	.309	Mantle-NY	.402	Sievers-Chi	.534
Gentile-Bal	98	Robinson-Bal	148	Landis-Chi	80	Kuenn-Cle	.308	Sievers-Chi	.399	Skowron-NY	.528

Production		Adjusted Production		Batter Runs		Adjusted Batter Runs		Clutch Hitting Index		Runs Created	
Mantle-NY	.960	Mantle-NY	166	Mantle-NY	43.9	Mantle-NY	48.0	Wertz-Bos	155	Mantle-NY	125
Maris-NY	.955	Maris-NY	164	Williams-Bos	43.5	Williams-Bos	41.9	Power-Cle	135	Maris-NY	111
Sievers-Chi	.933	Sievers-Chi	152	Maris-NY	36.5	Maris-NY	40.2	Minoso-Chi	127	Minoso-Chi	104
Killebrew-Was	.911	Killebrew-Was	145	Sievers-Chi	32.1	Sievers-Chi	32.7	Robinson-Bal	120	Lemon-Was	99
Skowron-NY	.884	Skowron-NY	144	Killebrew-Was	26.9	Skowron-NY	28.3	Aparicio-Chi	119	Francona-Cle	96

Total Average		Stolen Bases		Stolen Base Average		Stolen Base Runs		Fielding Runs		Total Player Rating	
Mantle-NY	1.053	Aparicio-Chi	51	Aparicio-Chi	86.4	Aparicio-Chi	10.5	Aparicio-Chi	30.4	Aparicio-Chi	3.8
Maris-NY	.992	Landis-Chi	23	Kaline-Det	82.6	Landis-Chi	3.3	Boyer-NY	27.6	Mantle-NY	3.7
Sievers-Chi	.960	Green-Was	21	Landis-Chi	79.3	Kaline-Det	3.3	Power-Cle	21.0	Maris-NY	3.6
Killebrew-Was	.936	Kaline-Det	19	Piersall-Cle	78.3	Piersall-Cle	2.4	Fox-Chi	12.3	Williams-Bos	3.4
Lemon-Was	.871	Piersall-Cle	18	Green-Was	72.4	Mantle-NY	2.4	Robinson-Bal	12.2	Runnels-Bos	2.7

Wins		Win Percentage		Games		Complete Games		Shutouts		Saves	
Perry-Cle	18	Perry-Cle	.643	Fornieles-Bos	70	Lary-Det	15	Wynn-Chi	4	Klippstein-Cle	14
Estrada-Bal	18	Ditmar-NY	.625	Staley-Chi	64	Ramos-Was	14	Perry-Cle	4	Fornieles-Bos	14
L.Daley-KC	16	Estrada-Bal	.621	Clevenger-Was	53	Herbert-KC	14	Ford-NY	4	Moore-Chi-Was	13
		Pappas-Bal	.577	Moore-Chi-Was	51	Wynn-Chi	13			R.Shantz-NY	11
				Kutyna-KC	51	L.Daley-KC	13				

Innings Pitched		Fewest Hits/Game		Fewest BB/Game		Strikeouts		Strikeouts/Game		Ratio	
Lary-Det	274.1	Estrada-Bal	6.99	Brown-Bal	1.25	Bunning-Det	201	Bunning-Det	7.18	Brown-Bal	10.08
Ramos-Was	274.0	Turley-NY	7.17	Mossi-Det	1.82	Ramos-Was	160	Bell-Cle	6.34	Bunning-Det	10.43
Perry-Cle	261.1	Barber-Bal	7.33	Hall-KC	1.88	Wynn-Chi	158	Estrada-Bal	6.21	Baumann-Chi	10.83
Herbert-KC	252.2	Bunning-Det	7.75	Lary-Det	2.03	Lary-Det	149	Wynn-Chi	5.99	Mossi-Det	10.86
Bunning-Det	252.0	Ford-NY	7.85	Pierce-Chi	2.11	Estrada-Bal	144	Monbouquette-Bos	5.61	Ford-NY	10.93

Earned Run Average		Adjusted ERA		Opponents' Batting Avg.		Opponents' On Base Pct.		Starter Runs		Adjusted Starter Runs	
Baumann-Chi	2.67	Bunning-Det	142	Estrada-Bal	.218	Brown-Bal	.286	Bunning-Det	30.4	Bunning-Det	32.8
Bunning-Det	2.79	Baumann-Chi	141	Turley-NY	.222	Bunning-Det	.293	Baumann-Chi	24.7	Baumann-Chi	22.8
Brown-Bal	3.06	Brown-Bal	125	Barber-Bal	.226	Mossi-Det	.296	Ditmar-NY	18.0	Herbert-KC	19.7
Ditmar-NY	3.06	Herbert-KC	121	Ford-NY	.235	Ford-NY	.299	Ford-NY	16.9	Pascual-Was	14.5
Ford-NY	3.08	Barber-Bal	118	Bunning-Det	.236	Terry-NY	.300	Herbert-KC	16.7	Kralick-Was	14.2

Clutch Pitching Index		Relief Runs		Adjusted Relief Runs		Relief Ranking		Total Pitcher Index		Total Baseball Ranking	
Ditmar-NY	121	Staley-Chi	18.6	Staley-Chi	17.4	Staley-Chi	32.0	Bunning-Det	3.0	Aparicio-Chi	3.8
Perry-Cle	113	Fornieles-Bos	14.9	Fornieles-Bos	17.0	Fornieles-Bos	25.9	Herbert-KC	2.5	Mantle-NY	3.7
Lee-Was	113	Sisler-Det	12.4	Sisler-Det	13.2	Sisler-Det	20.0	Baumann-Chi	2.3	Maris-NY	3.6
Baumann-Chi	113	Aguirre-Det	10.7	Aguirre-Det	11.6	Aguirre-Det	11.6	Staley-Chi	2.2	Williams-Bos	3.4
Herbert-KC	111	R.Shantz-NY	8.1	Stobbs-Was	7.5	Klippstein-Cle	11.2	Fornieles-Bos	2.0	Bunning-Det	3.0

1961 National League

TEAM	G	W	L	PCT	GB	R	OR	AB	H	2B	3B	HR	BB	SO	AVG	OBP	SLG	PRO	PRO+	BR	/A	PF	CHI	RC	SB	CS	SBA	SBR
CIN	154	93	61	.604	–	710	653	5243	1414	247	35	158	423	761	.270	.328	.421	.749	101	19	10	101	101	713	70	33	38	-12
LA	154	89	65	.578	4	735	697	5189	1358	193	40	157	596	796	.262	.340	.405	.745	94	29	-32	109	100	722	86	45	54	-18
SF	155	85	69	.552	8	773	655	5233	1379	219	32	183	506	764	.264	.332	.423	.755	109	35	60	96	106	719	79	54	50	-13
MIL	155	83	71	.539	10	712	656	5288	1365	199	34	188	534	880	.258	.330	.415	.745	109	19	62	110	98	714	70	43	46	-14
STL	155	80	74	.519	13	703	668	5307	1436	236	51	103	494	745	.271	.336	.393	.729	90	-2	-71	110	100	702	46	28	38	-13
PIT	154	75	79	.487	18	694	675	5311	1448	232	57	128	428	721	.273	.330	.410	.740	100	8	5	100	99	694	26	30	44	-16
CHI	156	64	90	.416	29	689	800	5344	1364	238	51	176	539	1027	.255	.327	.418	.745	100	16	7	101	95	726	35	25	36	-13
PHI	155	47	107	.305	46	584	796	5213	1265	185	50	103	475	928	.243	.311	.357	.668	84	-122	-112	99	102	577	56	30	45	-17
TOT	619					5600		42128	11029	1749	350	1196	3995	6622	.262	.329	.405	.735							468	288	62	-31

TEAM	CG	SH	SV	IP	H	H/G	HR	BB	SO	RAT	ERA	ERA+	OAV	OOB	PR	/A	PF	CPI	FA	E	DP	FW	PW	BW	SBW	DIF
CIN	46	12	40	1370	1300	8.5	147	500	829	12.0	3.78	107	.250	.319	37	42	101	98	.977	134	124	.7	4.2	1.0	-.8	11.0
LA	40	10	35	1378¹	1346	8.8	167	544	1105	12.7	4.04	107	.255	.331	-1	45	108	101	.975	144	162	.1	4.5	-3.2	-1.4	12.0
SF	39	9	30	1388	1306	8.5	152	502	924	11.9	3.77	101	.248	.317	39	5	95	98	.977	133	126	.8	.5	6.0	-.9	1.7
MIL	57	8	16	1391¹	1357	8.8	153	493	652	12.1	3.89	96	.257	.324	21	-23	93	101	.982	111	152	2.0	-2.3	6.2	-1.0	1.1
STL	49	10	24	1368²	1334	8.8	136	570	823	12.7	3.74	118	.256	.332	44	99	109	106	.972	166	165	-1.1	9.8	-7.0	-.9	2.2
PIT	34	9	29	1362	1442	9.5	121	400	759	12.3	3.92	102	.274	.328	17	10	99	102	.975	150	187	-.2	1.0	.5	-1.2	-2.1
CHI	34	6	25	1385	1492	9.7	165	465	755	12.9	4.48	93	.276	.328	-69	-46	104	99	.970	183	175	-2.0	-4.6	.7	-.9	-6.3
PHI	29	9	13	1383¹	1452	9.4	155	521	775	13.1	4.61	88	.273	.342	-88	-81	101	96	.976	146	179	.0	-8.0	-11.1	-1.3	-9.6
TOT	328	73	212	11026²		9.0				12.5	4.03		.262	.329					.976	1167	1270					

Runs
Mays-SF 129
Robinson-Cin 117
Aaron-Mil 115
Boyer-StL 109

Hits
Pinson-Cin 208
Clemente-Pit 201
Aaron-Mil 197
Boyer-StL 194
Cepeda-SF 182

Doubles
Aaron-Mil 39
Pinson-Cin 34
Santo-Chi 32
Robinson-Cin 32
Mays-SF 32

Triples
Altman-Chi 12
White-StL 11
Callison-Phi 11
Boyer-StL 11

Home Runs
Cepeda-SF 46
Mays-SF 40
Robinson-Cin 37
Stuart-Pit 35
Adcock-Mil 35

Total Bases
Aaron-Mil 358
Cepeda-SF 356
Mays-SF 334
Robinson-Cin 333
Clemente-Pit 320

Runs Batted In
Cepeda-SF 142
Robinson-Cin 124
Mays-SF 123
Aaron-Mil 120
Stuart-Pit 117

Runs Produced
Mays-SF 212
Robinson-Cin 204
Cepeda-SF 201
Aaron-Mil 201
Boyer-StL 180

Bases On Balls
Mathews-Mil 93
Moon-LA 89
Mays-SF 81
Gilliam-LA 79

Batting Average
Clemente-Pit ..... .351
Pinson-Cin .... .343
Boyer-StL .... .329
Moon-LA .... .328
Aaron-Mil .... .327

On Base Percentage
Moon-LA .... .438
Robinson-Cin .... .411
Mathews-Mil ...... .405
Boyer-StL .... .400
Mays-SF .... .395

Slugging Average
Robinson-Cin .... .611
Cepeda-SF .... .609
Aaron-Mil .... .594
Mays-SF .... .584
Stuart-Pit .... .581

Production
Robinson-Cin ... 1.022
Aaron-Mil .... .979
Mays-SF .... .979
Cepeda-SF .... .972
Clemente-Pit ..... .951

Adjusted Production
Aaron-Mil 165
Robinson-Cin 164
Mays-SF 162
Cepeda-SF 158
Mathews-Mil 156

Batter Runs
Robinson-Cin 52.4
Aaron-Mil 46.0
Mays-SF 45.8
Cepeda-SF 40.7
Mathews-Mil 40.4

Adjusted Batter Runs
Robinson-Cin 51.5
Aaron-Mil 50.8
Mays-SF 48.7
Mathews-Mil 45.2
Cepeda-SF 43.5

Clutch Hitting Index
Moon-LA 132
Cepeda-SF 123
Stuart-Pit 121
Robinson-Cin 119
Mays-SF 116

Runs Created
Robinson-Cin 137
Aaron-Mil 132
Mays-SF 130
Mathews-Mil 128
Boyer-StL 126

Total Average
Robinson-Cin ... 1.119
Mays-SF 1.017
Moon-LA 1.003
Aaron-Mil .... .993
Mathews-Mil ..... .981

Stolen Bases
Wills-LA 35
Pinson-Cin 23
Robinson-Cin 22
Aaron-Mil 21
Mays-SF 18

Stolen Base Average
Robinson-Cin 88.0
Wills-LA 70.0
Aaron-Mil 70.0
Pinson-Cin 69.7
Mays-SF 66.7

Stolen Base Runs
Robinson-Cin 4.8
Maye-Mil 2.4
Williams-Chi 1.8
Wills-LA 1.5
Gonzalez-Phi 1.5

Fielding Runs
Mazeroski-Pit 30.5
Malkmus-Phi 16.3
Amaro-Phi 14.1
Boyer-StL 13.3
Clemente-Pit 13.0

Total Player Rating
Robinson-Cin 5.4
Clemente-Pit 4.3
Mays-SF 4.3
Aaron-Mil 4.2
Boyer-StL 3.6

Wins
Spahn-Mil 21
Jay-Cin 21
O'Toole-Cin 19

Win Percentage
Podres-LA .... .783
O'Toole-Cin ...... .679
Jay-Cin .... .677
Burdette-Mil ...... .621
Spahn-Mil .... .618

Games
Baldschun-Phi 65
Face-Pit 63
Face-Pit 62
Elston-Chi 58
Anderson-Chi 57

Complete Games
Spahn-Mil 21
Koufax-LA 15
Jay-Cin 14
Burdette-Mil 14

Shutouts
Spahn-Mil 4
Jay-Cin 4

Saves
Miller-SF 17
Face-Pit 17
Henry-Cin 16
Brosnan-Cin 16
L.Sherry-LA 15

Innings Pitched
Burdette-Mil 272.1
Spahn-Mil 262.2
Cardwell-Chi 259.1
Koufax-LA 255.2
O'Toole-Cin 252.2

Fewest Hits/Game
Koufax-LA 7.46
Jay-Cin 7.90
Gibson-StL 7.92
Sadecki-StL 7.92
Spahn-Mil 8.09

Fewest BB/Game
Burdette-Mil 1.09
Friend-Pit 1.72
Purkey-Cin 1.86
Spahn-Mil 2.19
Ellsworth-Chi 2.31

Strikeouts
Koufax-LA 269
Williams-LA 205
Drysdale-LA 182
O'Toole-Cin 178
Gibson-StL 166

Strikeouts/Game
Koufax-LA 9.47
Williams-LA 7.84
Gibson-StL 7.07
Drysdale-LA 6.71
Gibbon-Pit 6.68

Ratio
Spahn-Mil 10.42
Burdette-Mil 10.94
Koufax-LA 10.95
Purkey-Cin 11.03
Jackson-StL 11.22

Earned Run Average
Spahn-Mil 3.02
O'Toole-Cin 3.10
Simmons-StL 3.13
McCormick-SF ... 3.20
Gibson-StL 3.24

Adjusted ERA
Simmons-StL 141
Gibson-StL 136
O'Toole-Cin 131
Spahn-Mil 124
Koufax-LA 123

Opponents' Batting Avg.
Koufax-LA ...... .222
Jay-Cin .... .236
Sadecki-StL .... .238
Gibson-StL ..... .239
O'Toole-Cin .... .240

Opponents' On Base Pct.
Spahn-Mil ...... .293
Koufax-LA ...... .295
Burdette-Mil .... .296
Purkey-Cin ..... .297
Jackson-StL .... .303

Starter Runs
Spahn-Mil 29.7
O'Toole-Cin 26.2
McCormick-SF ... 23.0
Simmons-StL 19.6
Gibson-StL 18.7

Adjusted Starter Runs
Simmons-StL 27.6
Gibson-StL 27.3
O'Toole-Cin 27.1
Koufax-LA 23.3
Spahn-Mil 21.2

Clutch Pitching Index
Simmons-StL 122
Ellsworth-Chi 121
Podres-LA 116
McCormick-SF ... 115
Gibson-StL 114

Relief Runs
Miller-SF 18.6
Perranoski-LA ... 14.1
McMahon-Mil 12.2
Henry-Cin 10.9
Schultz-Chi 9.9

Adjusted Relief Runs
Perranoski-LA ... 17.2
Miller-SF 15.6
Henry-Cin 11.1
Schultz-Chi 11.0
McMahon-Mil 9.2

Relief Ranking
Miller-SF 26.8
Perranoski-LA ... 22.8
Schultz-Chi 21.8
Brosnan-Cin 18.5
Henry-Cin 13.1

Total Pitcher Index
Simmons-StL 3.6
Spahn-Mil 3.4
Gibson-StL 3.1
O'Toole-Cin 2.6
Drysdale-LA 2.3

Total Baseball Ranking
Robinson-Cin 5.4
Clemente-Pit 4.3
Mays-SF 4.3
Aaron-Mil 4.2
Simmons-StL 3.6

TEAM	G	W	L	PCT	GB	R	OR	AB	H	2B	3B	HR	BB	SO	AVG	OBP	SLG	PRO	PRO+	BR	/A	PF	CHI	RC	SB	CS	SBA	SBR
NY	163	109	53	.673		827	612	5559	1461	194	40	240	543	785	.263	.332	.442	.774	118	82	120	95	101	811	28	18	47	-22
DET	163	101	61	.623	8	841	671	5561	1481	215	53	180	673	867	.266	.349	.421	.770	108	96	74	103	99	835	98	36	43	-14
BAL	163	95	67	.586	14	691	588	5481	1393	227	36	149	581	902	.254	.328	.390	.718	100	-15	0	98	96	699	39	30	41	-15
CHI	163	86	76	.531	23	765	726	5556	1475	216	46	138	550	612	.265	.338	.395	.733	103	17	28	98	101	754	100	40	49	-16
CLE	161	78	83	.484	30.5	737	752	5609	1493	257	39	150	492	720	.266	.328	.406	.734	104	9	28	97	99	743	34	11	18	-7
BOS	163	76	86	.469	33	729	792	5508	1401	251	37	112	647	847	.254	.336	.374	.710	93	-21	-38	102	101	704	56	36	67	-28
MIN	161	70	90	.438	38	707	778	5417	1353	215	40	167	597	840	.250	.328	.397	.725	94	-4	-43	106	98	698	47	43	39	-10
LA	162	70	91	.435	38.5	744	784	5424	1331	218	22	189	681	1068	.245	.333	.398	.731	90	12	-71	111	99	734	37	28	42	-16
WAS	161	61	100	.379	47.5	618	776	5366	1307	217	44	119	558	917	.244	.317	.367	.684	90	-82	-71	99	98	625	81	47	53	-17
KC	162	61	100	.379	47.5	683	863	5423	1342	216	47	90	580	772	.247	.323	.354	.677	86	-89	-90	100	107	642	58	22	29	-10
TOT	811					7342		54904	14037	2226	404	1534	5902	8330	.256	.331	.395	.726							578	311	65	-12

TEAM	CG	SH	SV	IP	H	H/G	HR	BB	SO	RAT	ERA	ERA+	OAV	OOB	PR	/A	PF	CPI	FA	E	DP	FW	PW	BW	SBW	DIF
NY	47	14	39	1451	1288	8.0	137	542	866	11.5	3.46	107	.239	.312	90	41	92	99	.980	124	180	1.6	4.1	11.9	-2.0	12.5
DET	62	12	30	1459¹	1404	8.7	170	469	836	11.7	3.55	116	.252	.313	77	89	102	106	.976	146	147	.3	8.8	7.3	-1.3	4.8
BAL	54	21	33	1471¹	1226	7.5	109	617	926	11.5	3.22	121	.227	.310	131	112	97	97	.980	128	173	1.4	11.1	.0	-1.4	2.9
CHI	39	3	33	1448²	1491	9.3	158	498	814	12.4	4.06	97	.267	.328	-5	-22	97	102	.980	128	138	1.4	-2.2	2.8	-1.5	4.5
CLE	35	12	23	1443¹	1426	8.9	178	599	801	12.8	4.15	95	.257	.333	-19	-33	98	102	.977	139	142	.6	-3.3	2.8	-.6	-2.1
BOS	35	6	30	1442²	1472	9.2	167	679	831	13.5	4.29	97	.265	.347	-42	-19	104	105	.977	144	170	.4	-1.9	-3.8	-2.6	2.9
MIN	49	14	23	1432¹	1415	8.9	163	570	914	12.8	4.28	99	.256	.331	-40	-5	105	95	.972	174	150	-1.4	-.5	-4.3	-.9	-3.0
LA	25	5	34	1438	1391	8.7	180	713	973	13.4	4.31	105	.253	.343	-45	31	112	101	.969	192	154	-2.4	3.1	-7.0	-1.5	-2.7
WAS	39	8	21	1425	1405	8.9	131	586	666	12.8	4.23	95	.260	.331	-32	-34	100	96	.975	156	171	-.4	-3.4	-7.0	-1.6	-7.2
KC	32	5	23	1415	1519	9.7	141	629	703	14.0	4.74	87	.275	.354	-113	-98	102	97	.972	175	160	-1.4	-9.7	-8.9	-.9	1.4
TOT	417	100	289	14426²		8.8				12.6	4.02		.256	.331					.976	1506	1585					

Runs
Maris-NY 132
Mantle-NY 132
Colavito-Det 129
Cash-Det 119
Kaline-Det 116

Hits
Cash-Det 193
B.Robinson-Bal ... 192
Kaline-Det 190
Francona-Cle 178
Richardson-NY ... 173

Doubles
Kaline-Det 41
B.Robinson-Bal ... 38
Kubek-NY 38
Siebern-KC 36
Power-Cle 34

Triples
Wood-Det 14
Lumpe-KC 9
Keough-Was 9

Home Runs
Maris-NY 61
Mantle-NY 54
Killebrew-Min 46
Gentile-Bal 46
Colavito-Det....... 45

Total Bases
Maris-NY 366
Cash-Det 354
Mantle-NY 353
Colavito-Det 338
Killebrew-Min 328

Runs Batted In
Maris-NY 142
Gentile-Bal 141
Colavito-Det...... 140
Cash-Det 132
Mantle-NY 128

Runs Produced
Colavito-Det 224
Maris-NY 213
Cash-Det 210
Mantle-NY 206
Gentile-Bal 191

Bases On Balls
Mantle-NY 126
Cash-Det 124
Colavito-Det...... 113
Killebrew-Min 107
Allison-Min 103

Batting Average
Cash-Det .... .361
Kaline-Det .... .324
Piersall-Cle ..... .322
Mantle-NY .... .317
Gentile-Bal ...... .302

On Base Percentage
Cash-Det .... .488
Mantle-NY .... .452
Gentile-Bal ...... .428
Pearson-LA ...... .422
Killebrew-Min .... .409

Slugging Average
Mantle-NY .... .687
Cash-Det .... .662
Gentile-Bal ...... .646
Maris-NY .... .620
Killebrew-Min .... .606

Production
Cash-Det 1.150
Mantle-NY 1.138
Gentile-Bal 1.074
Killebrew-Min ... 1.015
Maris-NY .... .997

Adjusted Production
Mantle-NY 210
Cash-Det 198
Gentile-Bal 187
Maris-NY 170
Killebrew-Min 159

Batter Runs
Cash-Det 86.1
Mantle-NY 76.3
Gentile-Bal 59.1
Killebrew-Min 52.9
Colavito-Det 51.5

Adjusted Batter Runs
Cash-Det 83.9
Mantle-NY 80.2
Gentile-Bal 60.6
Maris-NY 53.8
Colavito-Det...... 49.2

Clutch Hitting Index
Malzone-Bos 134
Allison-Min 129
Siebern-KC 127
Minoso-Chi 126
Yastrzemski-Bos .. 126

Runs Created
Cash-Det 178
Mantle-NY 174
Colavito-Det...... 141
Gentile-Bal 138
Maris-NY 138

Total Average
Mantle-NY 1.384
Cash-Det 1.358
Gentile-Bal 1.196
Killebrew-Min ... 1.098
Colavito-Det..... 1.051

Stolen Bases
Aparicio-Chi 53
Howser-KC 37
Wood-Det......... 30
Hinton-Was 22
Bruton-Det 22

Stolen Base Average
Hinton-Was 81.5
Howser-KC 80.4
Aparicio-Chi 80.3
Geiger-Bos 80.0
Landis-Chi 79.2

Stolen Base Runs
Aparicio-Chi 8.1
Howser-KC 5.7
Wood-Det......... 3.6
Kaline-Det 3.6
Hinton-Was 3.6

Fielding Runs
Boyer-NY 30.6
Power-Cle 18.8
Kaline-Det 18.1
Cottier-Det-Was .. 16.9
Lumpe-KC 16.0

Total Player Rating
Cash-Det 7.3
Mantle-NY 7.2
Colavito-Det 4.8
Kaline-Det 4.8
Gentile-Bal 4.8

Wins
Ford-NY 25
Lary-Det 23
Barber-Bal 18
Bunning-Det 17
Terry-NY 16

Win Percentage
Ford-NY .... .862
Terry-NY .... .842
Arroyo-NY .... .750
Lary-Det .... .719

Games
Arroyo-NY 65
Morgan-LA 59
Lown-Chi 59
Kunkel-KC 58
Fornieles-Bos 57

Complete Games
Lary-Det 22
Pascual-Min 15
Barber-Bal 14

Shutouts
Pascual-Min 8
Barber-Bal 8
Pappas-Bal 4
Lary-Det 4
Bunning-Det 4

Saves
Arroyo-NY 29
Wilhelm-Bal 18
Fornieles-Bos 15
Moore-Min 14
Fox-Det 12

Innings Pitched
Ford-NY 283.0
Lary-Det 275.1
Bunning-Det 268.0
Ramos-Min 264.1
Pascual-Min 252.1

Fewest Hits/Game
Estrada-Bal 6.75
Pappas-Bal 6.79
Barber-Bal 7.03
Pascual-Min 7.31
Donovan-Was 7.36

Fewest BB/Game
Mossi-Det 1.76
Brown-Bal 1.78
Donovan-Was 1.87
Terry-NY 2.01
McClain-Was 2.04

Strikeouts
Pascual-Min 221
Ford-NY 209
Bunning-Det 194
Pizarro-Chi 188
McBride-LA 180

Strikeouts/Game
Pizarro-Chi....... 8.69
Pascual-Min 7.88
Estrada-Bal 6.79
McBride-LA 6.70
Ford-NY 6.65

Ratio
Donovan-Was 9.39
Terry-NY 9.80
Brown-Bal 10.10
Bunning-Det ... 10.48
Lary-Det 10.59

Earned Run Average
Donovan-Was 2.40
Stafford-NY 2.68
Mossi-Det 2.96
Pappas-Bal 3.04
Pizarro-Chi....... 3.05

Adjusted ERA
Donovan-Was 167
Stafford-NY 139
Mossi-Det 139
Schwall-Bos 129
Archer-KC 129

Opponents' Batting Avg.
Estrada-Bal ...... .207
Pappas-Bal ...... .208
Pascual-Min ..... .217
Barber-Bal ...... .218
Donovan-Was .... .224

Opponents' On Base Pct.
Donovan-Was .... .269
Terry-NY .... .277
Bunning-Det ..... .285
Brown-Bal .... .286
Ford-NY .... .292

Starter Runs
Hoeft-Bal 30.7
Donovan-Was 30.4
Stafford-NY 29.2
Mossi-Det 28.5
Ford-NY 25.5

Adjusted Starter Runs
Mossi-Det 30.5
Donovan-Was 30.3
Hoeft-Bal 28.9
Bunning-Det 27.1
Lary-Det 26.5

Clutch Pitching Index
Schwall-Bos 131
Mossi-Det 119
Shaw-Chi-KC 115
Monbouquette-Bos 115
McBride-LA 112

Relief Runs
Arroyo-NY 24.2
Wilhelm-Bal 21.0
Morgan-LA 17.0
Fox-Det 16.6
Lown-Chi 14.2

Adjusted Relief Runs
Morgan-LA 21.9
Arroyo-NY 20.2
Wilhelm-Bal 19.6
Fox-Det 17.1
Lown-Chi 12.9

Relief Ranking
Arroyo-NY 41.6
Wilhelm-Bal 33.0
Morgan-LA 26.9
Fox-Det 26.9
Lown-Chi 17.0

Total Pitcher Index
Lary-Det 3.6
Donovan-Was 3.4
Mossi-Det 3.3
Hoeft-Bal 3.2
Stafford-NY 2.4

Total Baseball Ranking
Cash-Det 7.3
Mantle-NY 7.2
Colavito-Det 4.8
Kaline-Det 4.8
Gentile-Bal 4.8

TEAM	G	W	L	PCT	GB	R	OR	AB	H	2B	3B	HR	BB	SO	AVG	OBP	SLG	PRO	PRO+	BR	/A	PF	CHI	RC	SB	CS	SBA	SBR
SF	165	103	62	.624		**878**	690	5588	**1552**	235	32	**204**	523	822	**.278**	**.344**	**.441**	**.785**	119	**123**	**135**	98	102	**838**	73	50	53	-16
LA	165	102	63	.618	1	842	697	5628	1510	192	**65**	140	572	886	.268	.339	.400	.739	111	41	86	94	**107**	783	**198**	43	45	**-13**
CIN	162	98	64	.605	3.5	802	685	5645	1523	**252**	40	167	498	903	.270	.333	.417	.750	103	54	30	103	102	779	66	39	46	-15
PIT	161	93	68	.578	8	706	**626**	5483	1468	240	**65**	108	432	836	.268	.323	.394	.717	98	-14	-14	100	102	682	50	39	46	-15
MIL	162	86	76	.531	15.5	730	665	5458	1376	204	38	181	581	975	.252	.328	.403	.731	104	16	35	97	99	720	57	27	37	**-13**
STL	163	84	78	.519	17.5	774	664	5643	1528	221	31	137	515	846	.271	.337	.394	.731	93	22	-48	110	102	747	86	41	53	-19
PHI	161	81	80	.503	20	705	759	5420	1410	199	39	142	531	923	.260	.332	.390	.722	103	4	25	97	98	705	79	42	44	**-13**
HOU	162	64	96	.400	36.5	592	717	5558	1370	170	47	105	493	806	.246	.312	.351	.663	90	-116	-61	93	97	605	42	30	41	-15
CHI	162	59	103	.364	42.5	632	827	5534	1398	196	56	126	504	1044	.253	.319	.377	.696	89	-52	-78	104	94	657	78	50	**55**	-17
NY	161	40	120	.250	60.5	617	948	5492	1318	166	40	139	**616**	991	.240	.320	.361	.681	87	-74	-85	102	94	640	59	48	47	**-13**
TOT	812					7278		55449	14453	2075	453	1449	5265	9032	.261	.329	.393	.722							788	409	66	-8

TEAM	CG	SH	SV	IP	H	H/G	HR	BB	SO	RAT	ERA	ERA+	OAV	OOB	PR	/A	PF	CPI	FA	E	DP	FW	PW	BW	SBW	DIF
SF	62	10	39	1461²	1399	8.6	148	503	886	11.9	3.79	100	.250	**.315**	24	0	96	95	.977	142	153	1.0	.0	**13.5**	-1.5	7.6
LA	44	8	46	1488²	**1386**	**8.4**	115	588	**1104**	12.1	3.62	100	**.244**	.319	53	2	92	94	.970	193	144	-2.1	.2	8.6	**-1.2**	14.0
CIN	51	13	35	1460²	1397	8.6	149	567	964	12.4	3.75	107	.254	.329	30	44	102	104	.977	145	144	.6	4.4	3.0	-1.4	10.4
PIT	40	13	41	1432¹	1433	9.0	118	466	897	12.1	**3.37**	117	.261	.322	**90**	88	100	110	.976	152	**177**	.2	8.8	-1.4	-1.4	6.4
MIL	59	10	24	1434²	1443	9.1	151	**407**	802	11.8	3.68	103	.262	.316	42	18	96	103	**.980**	**124**	154	**1.9**	1.8	3.5	**-1.2**	-1.0
STL	53	**17**	25	1463¹	1394	8.6	149	517	914	11.9	3.55	120	.251	.319	63	**116**	98	104	.979	132	170	1.5	**11.6**	-4.8	-1.8	-3.4
PHI	43	7	24	1426²	1469	9.3	155	574	863	13.2	4.28	90	.268	.343	-53	-64	98	102	.977	138	167	1.0	-6.4	2.5	**-1.2**	4.6
HOU	34	9	19	1453²	1446	9.0	**113**	471	1047	12.1	3.83	98	.259	.321	18	-14	95	95	.973	173	149	-1.0	-1.4	-6.1	-1.4	-6.1
CHI	29	4	26	1438¹	1509	9.4	159	601	783	13.5	4.54	91	.272	.348	-95	-62	105	99	.977	146	171	.6	-6.2	-7.8	-1.6	-7.0
NY	43	4	10	1430	1577	9.9	192	571	772	13.8	5.04	83	.280	.352	-174	-136	106	96	.967	210	167	-3.3	-13.6	-8.5	-1.2	-13.4
TOT	458	95	289	14490		9.0				12.5	3.94		.261	.329					.975	1555	1596					

Runs		Hits		Doubles		Triples		Home Runs		Total Bases	
Robinson-Cin	134	H.Davis-LA	230	Robinson-Cin	51	Wills-LA	10	Mays-SF	49	Mays-SF	382
Wills-LA	130	Wills-LA	208	Mays-SF	36	Virdon-Pit	10	H.Aaron-Mil	45	Robinson-Cin	380
Mays-SF	130	Robinson-Cin	208	Groat-Pit	34	W.Davis-LA	10	Robinson-Cin	39	H.Aaron-Mil	366
H.Aaron-Mil	127	White-StL	199			Callison-Phi	10	Banks-Chi	37	H.Davis-LA	356
H.Davis-LA	120	Groat-Pit	199					Cepeda-SF	35	Cepeda-SF	324

Runs Batted In		Runs Produced		Bases On Balls		Batting Average		On Base Percentage		Slugging Average	
H.Davis-LA	153	H.Davis-LA	246	Mathews-Mil	101	H.Davis-LA	.346	Robinson-Cin	.424	Robinson-Cin	.624
Mays-SF	141	Robinson-Cin	231	Gilliam-LA	93	Robinson-Cin	.342	Musial-StL	.420	H.Aaron-Mil	.618
Robinson-Cin	136	Mays-SF	222	Ashburn-NY	81	Musial-StL	.330	Skinner-Pit	.397	Mays-SF	.615
H.Aaron-Mil	128	H.Aaron-Mil	210	Mays-SF	78	White-StL	.324	Altman-Chi	.394	Howard-LA	.560
Howard-LA	119					H.Aaron-Mil	.323	H.Aaron-Mil	.393	H.Davis-LA	.535

Production		Adjusted Production		Batter Runs		Adjusted Batter Runs		Clutch Hitting Index		Runs Created	
Robinson-Cin	1.048	Robinson-Cin	172	Robinson-Cin	66.6	Robinson-Cin	64.0	H.Davis-LA	146	Robinson-Cin	160
H.Aaron-Mil	1.012	H.Aaron-Mil	171	Mays-SF	54.1	H.Aaron-Mil	56.1	Santo-Chi	130	Mays-SF	146
Mays-SF	1.001	Mays-SF	167	H.Aaron-Mil	54.0	Mays-SF	55.5	Howard-LA	127	H.Aaron-Mil	140
Musial-StL	.928	H.Davis-LA	151	H.Davis-LA	37.2	H.Davis-LA	42.2	White-StL	120	H.Davis-LA	129
H.Davis-LA	.914	Howard-LA	149	Altman-Chi	31.5	Skinner-Pit	30.1	Kuenn-SF	118	White-StL	114

Total Average		Stolen Bases		Stolen Base Average		Stolen Base Runs		Fielding Runs		Total Player Rating	
Robinson-Cin	1.125	Wills-LA	104	Mays-SF	90.0	Wills-LA	23.4	Mazeroski-Pit	41.1	Robinson-Cin	6.2
Mays-SF	1.060	W.Davis-LA	32	Wills-LA	88.9	W.Davis-LA	5.4	Callison-Phi	25.4	Mays-SF	5.6
H.Aaron-Mil	1.050	Pinson-Cin	26	W.Davis-LA	82.1	Mays-SF	4.2	Kanehl-NY	18.2	Mazeroski-Pit	4.8
Musial-StL	.957	Javier-StL	26	Clendenon-Pit	80.0	Pinson-Cin	3.0	Burright-LA	14.2	H.Aaron-Mil	4.2
Skinner-Pit	.930	Taylor-Phi	20	Pinson-Cin	76.5			Groat-Pit	13.9	Callison-Phi	4.2

Wins		Win Percentage		Games		Complete Games		Shutouts		Saves	
Drysdale-LA	25	Purkey-Cin	.821	Perranoski-LA	70	Spahn-Mil	22	Gibson-StL	5	Face-Pit	28
Sanford-SF	24	Sanford-SF	.774	Baldschun-Phi	67	O'Dell-SF	20	Friend-Pit	5	Perranoski-LA	20
Purkey-Cin	23	Drysdale-LA	.735	Roebuck-LA	64	Mahaffey-Phi	20			Miller-SF	19
Jay-Cin	21	Pierce-SF	.727	Face-Pit	63	Drysdale-LA	19			McDaniel-StL	14
		Shaw-Mil	.625	Olivo-Pit	62						

Innings Pitched		Fewest Hits/Game		Fewest BB/Game		Strikeouts		Strikeouts/Game		Ratio	
Drysdale-LA	314.1	Koufax-LA	6.54	Shaw-Mil	1.76	Drysdale-LA	232	Koufax-LA	10.55	Koufax-LA	9.42
Purkey-Cin	288.1	Gibson-StL	6.70	Friend-Pit	1.82	Koufax-LA	216	Johnson-Hou	8.13	Farrell-Hou	10.06
O'Dell-SF	280.2	Bennett-Phi	7.42	Spahn-Mil	1.84	Gibson-StL	208	Gibson-StL	8.01	Spahn-Mil	10.23
Mahaffey-Phi	274.0	Drysdale-LA	7.79	Pierce-SF	1.94	Farrell-Hou	203	Bennett-Phi	7.68	Pierce-SF	10.26
Jay-Cin	273.0	Broglio-StL	7.81	Purkey-Cin	2.00	O'Dell-SF	195	Farrell-Hou	7.56	Drysdale-LA	10.34

Earned Run Average		Adjusted ERA		Opponents' Batting Avg.		Opponents' On Base Pct.		Starter Runs		Adjusted Starter Runs	
Koufax-LA	2.54	Gibson-StL	150	Koufax-LA	.197	Koufax-LA	.261	Drysdale-LA	38.6	Purkey-Cin	38.9
Shaw-Mil	2.80	Purkey-Cin	143	Gibson-StL	.204	Farrell-Hou	.280	Purkey-Cin	36.3	Gibson-StL	36.8
Purkey-Cin	2.81	Koufax-LA	143	Bennett-Phi	.224	Drysdale-LA	.283	Koufax-LA	28.7	Broglio-StL	31.4
Drysdale-LA	2.83	Broglio-StL	142	Drysdale-LA	.230	Pierce-SF	.284	Shaw-Mil	28.5	Drysdale-LA	27.8
Gibson-StL	2.85	Shaw-Mil	136	Farrell-Hou	.233	Spahn-Mil	.287	Gibson-StL	28.3	Friend-Pit	25.4

Clutch Pitching Index		Relief Runs		Adjusted Relief Runs		Relief Ranking		Total Pitcher Index		Total Baseball Ranking	
Shaw-Mil	123	Face-Pit	20.8	Face-Pit	20.8	Face-Pit	45.2	Gibson-StL	4.7	Robinson-Cin	6.2
Friend-Pit	119	McMahon-Mil-Hou	19.9	Shantz-Hou-StL	18.9	McMahon-Mil-Hou	26.6	Purkey-Cin	4.2	Mays-SF	5.6
Broglio-StL	116	Shantz-Hou-StL	17.3	McMahon-Mil-Hou	18.1	Shantz-Hou-StL	23.9	Drysdale-LA	3.3	Mazeroski-Pit	4.8
McBean-Pit	114	Umbricht-Hou	14.3	Umbricht-Hou	12.8	Elston-Chi	23.9	Broglio-StL	3.2	Gibson-StL	4.7
Koonce-Chi	111	Perranoski-LA	13.0	Elston-Chi	12.6	Baldschun-Phi	20.3	Spahn-Mil	2.9	Purkey-Cin	4.2

TEAM	G	W	L	PCT	GB	R	OR	AB	H	2B	3B	HR	BB	SO	AVG	OBP	SLG	PRO	PRO+	BR	/A	PF	CHI	RC	SB	CS	SBA	SBR
NY	162	96	66	.593		817	680	5644	1509	240	29	199	584	842	.267	.339	.426	.765	115	87	110	97	99	816	42	29	50	-20
MIN	163	91	71	.562	5	798	713	5561	1445	215	39	185	649	823	.260	.340	.412	.752	104	67	39	104	100	789	33	20	29	-10
LA	162	86	76	.531	10	718	706	5499	1377	232	35	137	602	917	.250	.328	.380	.708	100	-22	1	97	103	698	46	27	48	-20
DET	161	85	76	.528	10.5	758	692	5456	1352	191	36	209	651	894	.248	.332	.411	.743	102	41	15	104	100	757	69	21	30	-11
CHI	162	85	77	.525	11	707	658	5514	1415	250	56	92	620	674	.257	.336	.372	.708	97	-12	-8	100	99	701	76	40	57	-21
CLE	162	80	82	.494	16	682	745	5484	1341	202	22	180	502	939	.245	.314	.388	.702	97	-45	-23	97	103	671	35	16	22	-7
BAL	162	77	85	.475	19	652	680	5491	1363	225	34	156	516	931	.248	.316	.387	.703	99	-41	-6	95	98	665	45	32	59	-25
BOS	160	76	84	.475	19	707	756	5530	1429	257	53	146	525	923	.258	.326	.403	.729	98	9	-13	103	98	716	39	33	36	-11
KC	162	72	90	.444	24	745	837	5576	1467	220	58	116	556	803	.263	.334	.386	.720	96	3	-19	103	102	738	76	21	37	-15
WAS	162	60	101	.373	35.5	599	716	5484	1370	206	38	132	466	789	.250	.310	.373	.683	89	-81	-75	99	97	623	99	53	59	-19
TOT	809					7183		55239	14068	2238	400	1552	5671	8535	.255	.328	.394	.722							560	292	66	-6

TEAM	CG	SH	SV	IP	H	H/G	HR	BB	SO	RAT	ERA	ERA+	OAV	OOB	PR	/A	PF	CPI	FA	E	DP	FW	PW	BW	SBW	DIF
NY	33	10	42	1470¹	1375	8.4	146	499	838	11.6	3.70	101	.247	.312	43	7	94	96	.979	131	151	.4	.7	11.1	-1.9	4.8
MIN	53	11	27	1463¹	1400	8.6	166	493	948	11.9	3.89	105	.253	.319	12	30	103	99	.980	129	173	.5	3.0	3.9	-.9	3.5
LA	23	15	47	1466	1412	8.7	118	616	858	12.8	3.70	104	.252	.332	44	26	97	104	.973	175	153	-2.2	2.6	.1	-1.9	6.4
DET	46	8	35	1443²	1452	9.1	169	503	873	12.4	3.81	107	.258	.323	25	41	103	105	.974	156	114	-1.1	4.1	1.5	-1.0	1.0
CHI	50	13	28	1451²	1380	8.6	123	537	821	12.0	3.73	105	.250	.319	38	28	98	97	.982	110	153	1.6	2.8	-.8	-2.0	2.5
CLE	45	12	31	1441	1410	8.8	174	594	780	12.7	4.14	94	.257	.334	-27	-42	98	102	.978	139	168	-.1	-4.2	-2.3	-.6	6.3
BAL	32	8	33	1462¹	1373	8.5	147	549	898	12.0	3.69	102	.248	.319	45	10	95	101	.980	122	152	.9	1.0	-.6	-2.4	-2.8
BOS	34	12	40	1437²	1416	8.9	159	632	923	13.1	4.22	98	.258	.339	-39	-14	104	101	.979	131	152	.3	-1.4	-1.3	-1.0	-.5
KC	32	4	33	1434	1450	9.1	199	655	825	13.5	4.79	87	.263	.346	-131	-101	105	97	.979	132	131	.3	-10.2	-1.9	-1.4	4.2
WAS	38	11	13	1445	1400	8.7	151	593	771	12.5	4.04	100	.255	.330	-11	0	102	100	.978	139	160	-.1	.0	-7.5	-1.8	-11.0
TOT	386	104	329	14515		8.7				12.4	3.97		.255	.328					.978	1364	1507					

Runs
Pearson-LA 115
Siebern-KC 114
Allison-Min 102
Yastrzemski-Bos . . . 99
Richardson-NY 99

Hits
Richardson-NY . . . 209
Lumpe-KC 193
B.Robinson-Bal . . . 192
Yastrzemski-Bos . . 191
Robinson-Chi 187

Doubles
Robinson-Chi 45
Yastrzemski-Bos . . 43
Bressoud-Bos 40
Richardson-NY 38

Triples
Cimoli-KC 15
Robinson-Chi 10
Lumpe-KC 10
Clinton-Bos 10

Home Runs
Killebrew-Min 48
Cash-Det 39
Wagner-LA 37
Colavito-Det 37

Total Bases
Colavito-Det 309
B.Robinson-Bal . . . 308
Wagner-LA 306
Yastrzemski-Bos . . 303
Killebrew-Min 301

Runs Batted In
Killebrew-Min 126
Siebern-KC 117
Colavito-Det 112
Robinson-Chi 109
Wagner-LA 107

Runs Produced
Siebern-KC 206
Robinson-Chi 187
Rollins-Min 176
Allison-Min 175
Yastrzemski-Bos . . 174

Bases On Balls
Mantle-NY 122
Siebern-KC 110
Killebrew-Min 106
Cash-Det 104
Cunningham-Chi . . 101

Batting Average
Runnels-Bos 326
Mantle-NY 321
Robinson-Chi 312
Hinton-Was 310
Siebern-KC 308

On Base Percentage
Mantle-NY 488
Siebern-KC 416
Cunningham-Chi . . .415
Runnels-Bos 411
Robinson-Chi 387

Slugging Average
Mantle-NY 605
Killebrew-Min 545
Colavito-Det 514
Cash-Det 513
Allison-Min 511

Production
Mantle-NY 1.093
Killebrew-Min 914
Siebern-KC 911
Cash-Det 897
Colavito-Det 889

Adjusted Production
Mantle-NY 198
Siebern-KC 140
Killebrew-Min 137
Cash-Det 134
Colavito-Det 132

Batter Runs
Mantle-NY 57.3
Siebern-KC 41.1
Killebrew-Min 33.1
Colavito-Det 31.4
Kaline-Det 30.7

Adjusted Batter Runs
Mantle-NY 59.1
Siebern-KC 38.6
Killebrew-Min 30.2
Kaline-Det 28.9
Colavito-Det 28.5

Clutch Hitting Index
Robinson-Chi 144
Howard-NY 124
Malzone-Bos 122
J.Thomas-LA 120
Siebern-KC 120

Runs Created
Siebern-KC 129
Mantle-NY 126
Colavito-Det 117
Killebrew-Min 113
Robinson-Chi 113

Total Average
Mantle-NY 1.385
Siebern-KC 956
Cash-Det 950
Killebrew-Min 945
Allison-Min 901

Stolen Bases
Aparicio-Chi 31
Hinton-Was 28
Wood-Det 24
Charles-KC 20

Stolen Base Average
Howser-KC 90.5
Wood-Det 88.9
Charles-KC 83.3
Tartabull-KC 79.2
Hinton-Was 73.7

Stolen Base Runs
Wood-Det 5.4
Howser-KC 4.5
Charles-KC 3.6
Tartabull-KC 2.7
Mantle-NY 2.7

Fielding Runs
Boyer-NY 36.2
Versalles-Min 31.6
Bressoud-Bos 24.5
Kindall-Cle 20.7
Cottier-Was 20.5

Total Player Rating
Mantle-NY 4.4
Boyer-NY 4.0
Colavito-Det 3.7
Kaline-Det 3.6
Bressoud-Bos 3.4

Wins
Terry-NY 23
Pascual-Min 20
Herbert-Chi 20
Donovan-Cle 20
Bunning-Det 19

Win Percentage
Herbert-Chi 690
Ford-NY 680
Donovan-Cle 667
Aguirre-Det 667
Terry-NY 657

Games
Radatz-Bos 62
Wyatt-KC 59

Complete Games
Pascual-Min 18
Kaat-Min 16
Donovan-Cle 16
Terry-NY 14

Shutouts
Pascual-Min 5
Kaat-Min 5
Donovan-Cle 5
Monbouquette-Bos . . 4
McBride-LA 4

Saves
Radatz-Bos 24
Bridges-NY 18
Fox-Det 16
Wilhelm-Bal 15
Bell-Cle 12

Innings Pitched
Terry-NY 298.2
Kaat-Min 269.0
Bunning-Det . . . 258.0
Pascual-Min . . . 257.2
Ford-NY 257.2

Fewest Hits/Game
Aguirre-Det 6.75
Cheney-Was 6.96
Belinsky-LA 7.16
Wilson-Bos 7.67
Stenhouse-Was . . 7.72

Fewest BB/Game
Donovan-Cle 1.69
Terry-NY 1.72
Mossi-Det 1.80
Roberts-Bal 1.93
Pascual-Min 2.06

Strikeouts
Pizarro-Chi 206
Bunning-Det 184
Terry-NY 176
Pizarro-Chi 173
Kaat-Min 173

Strikeouts/Game
Pizarro-Chi 7.66
Cheney-Was 7.63
Pascual-Min 7.20
Belinsky-LA 6.97
Estrada-Bal 6.65

Ratio
Terry-NY 9.55
Aguirre-Det 9.67
Pascual-Min . . . 10.37
Roberts-Bal . . . 10.40
Fisher-Chi 10.59

Earned Run Average
Aguirre-Det 2.21
Roberts-Bal 2.78
Ford-NY 2.90
Chance-LA 2.96
Fisher-Chi 3.10

Adjusted ERA
Aguirre-Det 184
Roberts-Bal 135
Chance-LA 130
Kaat-Min 130
Ford-NY 129

Opponents' Batting Avg.
Aguirre-Det 205
Cheney-Was 213
Belinsky-LA 216
Terry-NY 231
Wilson-Bos 231

Opponents' On Base Pct.
Aguirre-Det 269
Terry-NY 270
Pascual-Min 286
Roberts-Bal 289
Fisher-Chi 293

Starter Runs
Aguirre-Det 42.3
Ford-NY 30.7
Terry-NY 25.8
Roberts-Bal 25.4
Kaat-Min 24.7

Adjusted Starter Runs
Aguirre-Det 44.7
Kaat-Min 28.1
Ford-NY 24.3
Pascual-Min 22.0
Monbouquette-Bos 21.0

Clutch Pitching Index
Chance-LA 114
Roberts-Bal 111
Ramos-Cle 110
Ford-NY 110
Perry-Cle 109

Relief Runs
Radatz-Bos 24.0
Hall-Bal 22.2
Wilhelm-Bal 21.0
Fox-Det 14.6
Fowler-LA 10.0

Adjusted Relief Runs
Radatz-Bos 26.2
Hall-Bal 19.4
Wilhelm-Bal 18.9
Fox-Det 15.2
Fowler-LA 9.0

Relief Ranking
Radatz-Bos 39.7
Wilhelm-Bal 37.9
Hall-Bal 20.0
Fox-Det 18.9
Bridges-NY 10.0

Total Pitcher Index
Kaat-Min 4.0
Aguirre-Det 3.5
Pascual-Min 3.2
Ford-NY 2.9
Herbert-Chi 2.6

Total Baseball Ranking
Mantle-NY 4.4
Kaat-Min 4.0
Boyer-NY 4.0
Colavito-Det 3.7
Kaline-Det 3.6

1963 National League

TEAM	G	W	L	PCT	GB	R	OR	AB	H	2B	3B	HR	BB	SO	AVG	OBP	SLG	PRO	PRO+	BR	/A	PF	CHI	RC	SB	CS	SBA	SBR
LA	163	99	63	.611		640	550	5428	1361	178	34	110	453	867	.251	.311	.357	.668	106	-2	39	93	105	596	124	70	60	-14
STL	162	93	69	.574	6	747	628	5678	1540	231	66	128	458	915	.271	.328	.403	.731	107	119	59	109	99	751	77	42	41	-11
SF	162	88	74	.543	11	725	641	5579	1442	206	35	197	441	889	.258	.318	.414	.732	118	111	117	99	98	712	55	49	54	-17
PHI	162	87	75	.537	12	642	578	5524	1390	228	54	126	403	955	.252	.312	.381	.689	106	28	35	99	96	640	56	39	42	-13
CIN	162	86	76	.531	13	648	594	5416	1333	225	44	122	474	960	.246	.312	.371	.683	100	25	6	103	101	630	92	58	58	-16
MIL	163	84	78	.519	15	677	603	5518	1345	204	39	139	525	954	.244	.314	.370	.684	105	30	36	99	102	643	75	52	47	-12
CHI	162	82	80	.506	17	570	578	5404	1286	205	44	127	439	1049	.238	.300	.363	.663	92	-20	-52	105	97	573	68	60	56	-15
PIT	162	74	88	.457	25	567	595	5536	1385	181	49	108	444	940	.250	.310	.359	.669	98	-1	-4	101	92	603	57	41	42	-12
HOU	162	66	96	.407	33	464	640	5384	1184	170	39	62	456	938	.220	.284	.301	.585	79	-158	-120	94	103	461	39	30	42	-15
NY	162	51	111	.315	48	501	774	5336	1168	156	35	96	457	1078	.219	.286	.315	.601	78	-128	-137	102	106	477	41	52	55	-16
TOT	811					6181		54803	13434	1984	439	1215	4560	9545	.245	.307	.364	.671							684	493	58	-90

TEAM	CG	SH	SV	IP	H	H/G	HR	BB	SO	RAT	ERA	ERA+	OAV	OOB	PR	/A	PF	CPI	FA	E	DP	FW	PW	BW	SBW	DIF
LA	51	24	29	1469²	1329	8.1	111	402	1095	10.8	2.85	106	.239	.294	70	27	92	103	.975	159	129	-.0	2.9	4.2	-.5	11.4
STL	49	17	32	1463	1329	8.2	124	463	978	11.3	3.32	107	.241	.305	-5	36	108	97	.976	147	136	.6	3.9	6.4	-.2	1.3
SF	46	9	30	1469	1380	8.5	126	464	954	11.5	3.35	96	.245	.307	-9	-23	97	99	.975	156	113	.1	-2.5	12.7	-.9	-2.4
PHI	45	12	31	1457¹	1262	7.8	113	553	1052	11.4	3.09	105	.235	.310	32		98	104	.978	142	147	.9	2.5	3.8	-.4	-.8
CIN	55	22	36	1439²	1307	8.2	117	425	1048	11.1	3.29	102	.242	.302	-1	7	102	96	.978	135	127	1.3	.8	.7	-.8	3.0
MIL	56	18	25	1471²	1327	8.1	149	489	924	11.3	3.27	99	.241	.306	3	-7	98	103	.980	129	161	1.8	-.8	3.9	-.3	-1.6
CHI	45	15	28	1457	1357	8.4	119	400	851	11.0	3.08	114	.248	.302	34	69	107	105	.976	155	172	.2	7.5	-5.6	-.6	-.4
PIT	34	16	33	1448	1350	8.4	99	457	900	11.5	3.10	107	.249	.313	31	32	100	107	.972	182	195	-1.4	3.5	-.4	-.3	-8.3
HOU	36	16	20	1450¹	1341	8.3	95	378	937	10.9	3.44	92	.244	.297	-24	-45	96	87	.974	162	100	-.3	-4.9	-13.0	-.6	3.8
NY	42	5	12	1427²	1452	9.2	162	529	806	12.8	4.12	85	.262	.332	-132	-100	106	100	.967	210	151	-3.1	-10.9	-14.9	-.8	-.4
TOT	459	154	276	14553¹		8.3				11.4	3.29		.245	.307					.975	1577	1431					

Runs
H.Aaron-Mil	121
Mays-SF	115
Flood-StL	112
White-StL	106
McCovey-SF	103

Hits
Pinson-Cin	204
Groat-StL	201
H.Aaron-Mil	201
White-StL	200
Flood-StL	200

Doubles
Groat-StL	43
Pinson-Cin	37
Williams-Chi	36
Gonzalez-Phi	36
Callison-Phi	36

Triples
Pinson-Cin	14
Gonzalez-Phi	12
Groat-StL	11
Callison-Phi	11
Brock-Chi	11

Home Runs
McCovey-SF	44
H.Aaron-Mil	44
Mays-SF	38
Cepeda-SF	34
Howard-LA	28

Total Bases
H.Aaron-Mil	370
Mays-SF	347
Pinson-Cin	335
Cepeda-SF	326
White-StL	323

Runs Batted In
H.Aaron-Mil	130
Boyer-StL	111
White-StL	109
Pinson-Cin	106
Mays-SF	103

Runs Produced
H.Aaron-Mil	207
White-StL	188
Pinson-Cin	180
Mays-SF	180
Boyer-StL	173

Bases On Balls
Mathews-Mil	124
Robinson-Cin	81
H.Aaron-Mil	78
Boyer-StL	70
Schofield-Pit	69

Batting Average
H.Davis-LA	.326
Clemente-Pit	.320
Groat-StL	.319
H.Aaron-Mil	.319
Cepeda-SF	.316

On Base Percentage
Mathews-Mil	.400
H.Aaron-Mil	.394
Mays-SF	.384
Robinson-Cin	.381
Groat-StL	.380

Slugging Average
H.Aaron-Mil	.586
Mays-SF	.582
McCovey-SF	.566
Cepeda-SF	.563
Pinson-Cin	.514

Production
H.Aaron-Mil	.980
Mays-SF	.966
Cepeda-SF	.930
McCovey-SF	.916
Pinson-Cin	.864

Adjusted Production
H.Aaron-Mil	180
Mays-SF	176
Cepeda-SF	166
McCovey-SF	161
Mathews-Mil	147

Batter Runs
H.Aaron-Mil	63.0
Mays-SF	55.8
Cepeda-SF	45.4
McCovey-SF	41.1
Mathews-Mil	37.4

Adjusted Batter Runs
H.Aaron-Mil	63.8
Mays-SF	56.5
Cepeda-SF	46.1
McCovey-SF	41.8
Mathews-Mil	38.2

Clutch Hitting Index
Robinson-Cin	147
Fairly-LA	146
Sievers-Phi	141
Boyer-StL	140
Edwards-Cin	130

Runs Created
H.Aaron-Mil	149
Mays-SF	131
White-StL	117
Cepeda-SF	113
Pinson-Cin	113

Total Average
H.Aaron-Mil	1.063
Mays-SF	.984
McCovey-SF	.911
Cepeda-SF	.906
Mathews-Mil	.894

Stolen Bases
Wills-LA	40
H.Aaron-Mil	31
Pinson-Cin	27
Robinson-Cin	26
W.Davis-LA	25

Stolen Base Average
H.Aaron-Mil	86.1
Gilliam-LA	79.2
Pinson-Cin	77.1
Robinson-Cin	72.2
Taylor-Phi	71.9

Stolen Base Runs
H.Aaron-Mil	6.3
Pinson-Cin	3.3
Maye-Mil	3.0
Harper-Cin	3.0
Gilliam-LA	2.7

Fielding Runs
Mazeroski-Pit	56.7
Callison-Phi	20.9
Hubbs-Chi	20.1
Harkness-NY	16.6
Wine-Phi	14.6

Total Player Rating
H.Aaron-Mil	6.1
Mays-SF	6.0
Mazeroski-Pit	5.5
Mathews-Mil	5.1
Callison-Phi	4.6

Wins
Marichal-SF	25
Koufax-LA	25
Spahn-Mil	23
Maloney-Cin	23
Ellsworth-Chi	22

Win Percentage
Perranoski-LA	.842
Koufax-LA	.833
Spahn-Mil	.767
Maloney-Cin	.767
Marichal-SF	.758

Games
Perranoski-LA	69
Baldschun-Phi	65
Bearnarth-NY	58
Sisk-Pit	57
McDaniel-Chi	57

Complete Games
Spahn-Mil	22
Koufax-LA	20
Ellsworth-Chi	19
Marichal-SF	18
Drysdale-LA	17

Shutouts
Koufax-LA	11
Spahn-Mil	7
Simmons-StL	6
Maloney-Cin	6

Saves
McDaniel-Chi	22
Perranoski-LA	21
Face-Pit	16
Baldschun-Phi	16
Henry-Cin	14

Innings Pitched
Marichal-SF	321.1
Drysdale-LA	315.1
Koufax-LA	311.0
Ellsworth-Chi	290.2
Sanford-SF	284.1

Fewest Hits/Game
Koufax-LA	6.19
Culp-Phi	6.55
Maloney-Cin	6.58
Ellsworth-Chi	6.90
Farrell-Hou	7.16

Fewest BB/Game
Friend-Pit	1.47
Farrell-Hou	1.56
Nuxhall-Cin	1.62
Drysdale-LA	1.63
Koufax-LA	1.68

Strikeouts
Koufax-LA	306
Maloney-Cin	265
Drysdale-LA	251
Marichal-SF	248
Gibson-StL	204

Strikeouts/Game
Maloney-Cin	9.53
Koufax-LA	8.86
Culp-Phi	7.79
Short-Phi	7.27
Lemaster-Mil	7.22

Ratio
Koufax-LA	7.96
Farrell-Hou	8.81
Marichal-SF	9.02
Ellsworth-Chi	9.29
Friend-Pit	9.55

Earned Run Average
Koufax-LA	1.88
Ellsworth-Chi	2.11
Friend-Pit	2.34
Marichal-SF	2.41
Simmons-StL	2.48

Adjusted ERA
Ellsworth-Chi	167
Koufax-LA	161
Simmons-StL	143
Friend-Pit	141
Jackson-Chi	137

Opponents' Batting Avg.
Koufax-LA	.189
Maloney-Cin	.202
Culp-Phi	.206
Ellsworth-Chi	.210
Broglio-StL	.216

Opponents' On Base Pct.
Koufax-LA	.230
Marichal-SF	.256
Farrell-Hou	.256
Ellsworth-Chi	.263
Friend-Pit	.269

Starter Runs
Koufax-LA	48.6
Ellsworth-Chi	38.2
Marichal-SF	31.4
Friend-Pit	28.2
Drysdale-LA	23.2

Adjusted Starter Runs
Ellsworth-Chi	45.3
Koufax-LA	39.4
Jackson-Chi	29.2
Friend-Pit	28.5
Marichal-SF	28.2

Clutch Pitching Index
Schwall-Pit	118
Spahn-Mil	115
Short-Phi	111
Cardwell-Pit	110
Buhl-Chi	109

Relief Runs
Perranoski-LA	23.1
Veale-Pit	19.4
Klippstein-Phi	16.9
Woodeshick-Hou	16.6
Baldschun-Phi	12.5

Adjusted Relief Runs
Veale-Pit	19.5
Perranoski-LA	19.3
Klippstein-Phi	16.2
Woodeshick-Hou	14.9
Baldschun-Phi	11.8

Relief Ranking
Perranoski-LA	32.7
Woodeshick-Hou	26.5
Baldschun-Phi	20.6
Veale-Pit	17.5
Klippstein-Phi	16.9

Total Pitcher Index
Ellsworth-Chi	5.3
Jackson-Chi	4.0
Koufax-LA	3.5
Spahn-Mil	3.2
Marichal-SF	3.0

Total Baseball Ranking
H.Aaron-Mil	6.1
Mays-SF	6.0
Mazeroski-Pit	5.5
Ellsworth-Chi	5.3
Mathews-Mil	5.1

TEAM	G	W	L	PCT	GB	R	OR	AB	H	2B	3B	HR	BB	SO	AVG	OBP	SLG	PRO	PRO+	BR	/A	PF	CHI	RC	SB	CS	SBA	SBR
NY	161	104	57	.646		714	547	5506	1387	197	35	188	434	**808**	.252	.310	.403	.713	105	27	32	99	**105**	686	42	26	31	-10
CHI	162	94	68	.580	10.5	683	**544**	5508	1379	208	**40**	114	571	896	.250	.325	.365	.690	100	4	15	98	101	675	64	28	47	-19
MIN	161	91	70	.565	13	**767**	602	5531	**1408**	223	35	**225**	547	912	**.255**	.326	**.430**	**.756**	114	**116**	**103**	102	98	**777**	32	14	23	**-9**
BAL	162	86	76	.531	18.5	644	621	5448	1359	207	32	146	469	940	.249	.312	.380	.692	101	-6	8	98	100	645	**97**	34	**60**	-25
DET	162	79	83	.488	25.5	700	703	5500	1388	195	36	148	**592**	908	.252	**.329**	.382	.711	101	43	20	103	98	699	73	32	35	-10
CLE	162	79	83	.488	25.5	635	702	5496	1314	214	29	169	469	1102	.239	.304	.381	.685	97	-25	-19	99	100	634	59	36	51	-19
BOS	161	76	85	.472	28	666	704	5575	1403	**247**	34	171	475	954	.252	.313	.400	.713	101	31	9	103	96	684	27	16	24	**-9**
KC	162	73	89	.451	31.5	615	704	5495	1356	225	38	95	529	829	.247	.316	.353	.669	89	-40	-66	104	99	616	47	26	52	-22
LA	161	70	91	.435	34	597	660	5506	1378	208	38	95	448	916	.250	.312	.354	.666	97	-52	-13	94	99	608	43	30	37	-12
WAS	162	56	106	.346	48.5	578	812	5446	1237	190	35	138	497	963	.227	.295	.351	.646	86	-94	-92	100	104	569	68	28	43	-16
TOT	808					6599		55011	13609	2114	352	1489	5031	9228	.247	.314	.380	.694							552	270	67	4

TEAM	CG	SH	SV	IP	H	H/G	HR	BB	SO	RAT	ERA	ERA+	OAV	OOB	PR	/A	PF	CPI	FA	E	DP	FW	PW	BW	SBW	DIF
NY	**59**	19	31	1449	**1239**	7.7	115	476	965	10.8	3.07	114	**.231**	.297	89	70	97	98	.982	110	162	1.4	7.4	3.4	-1.1	12.5
CHI	49	**21**	39	1469	1311	8.0	**100**	**440**	932	10.9	**2.97**	118	.238	.299	107	87	97	102	.979	131	163	.3	**9.1**	1.6	-2.0	4.1
MIN	58	13	30	1446¹	1322	8.2	162	459	941	11.2	3.28	111	.241	.303	56	58	100	**105**	.976	144	140	-.5	6.1	**10.8**	-1.0	-4.9
BAL	35	8	**43**	1452	1353	8.4	137	507	913	11.7	3.45	102	.248	.315	28	12	97	104	**.984**	**99**	157	**2.1**	1.3	.8	-2.7	3.5
DET	42	7	28	1456¹	1407	8.7	195	477	930	11.9	3.90	96	.252	.317	-43	-25	103	102	.982	113	124	1.3	-2.6	2.1	-1.1	-1.7
CLE	40	14	25	1469	1390	8.5	176	478	**1018**	11.6	3.79	95	.248	.311	-26	-28	100	98	.977	143	129	-.4	-2.9	-2.0	-2.0	5.4
BOS	29	7	32	1449²	1367	8.5	152	539	1009	12.0	3.97	95	.247	.317	-55	-30	104	93	.978	135	119	-.0	-3.2	.9	-1.0	-1.3
KC	35	11	29	1458	1417	8.7	156	540	887	12.4	3.92	98	.255	.326	-46	-12	106	101	.980	127	131	.5	-1.3	-6.9	-2.3	2.1
LA	30	13	31	1455¹	1317	8.1	120	578	889	12.0	3.52	97	.241	.320	16	-15	94	100	.974	163	155	-1.6	-1.6	-1.4	-1.3	-4.7
WAS	29	8	25	1447	1486	9.2	176	537	744	12.8	4.42	84	.265	.334	-126	-113	102	98	.971	182	**165**	-2.6	-11.9	-9.7	-1.7	.9
TOT	406	121	313	14551²		8.4				11.7	3.63		.247	.314					.978	1347	1445					

Runs
Allison-Min 99
Pearson-LA 92
Yastrzemski-Bos . . . 91
Tresh-NY 91
Colavito-Det 91

Hits
Yastrzemski-Bos . . 183
Ward-Chi 177
Pearson-LA 176
Kaline-Det 172
Fregosi-LA 170

Doubles
Yastrzemski-Bos . . . 40
Ward-Chi 34
Torres-LA 32
Causey-KC 32
Alvis-Cle 32

Triples
Versalles-Min 13
Hinton-Was 12
Fregosi-LA 12
Cimoli-KC 11

Home Runs
Killebrew-Min 45
Stuart-Bos 42
Allison-Min 35
Hall-Min 33
Howard-NY 28

Total Bases
Stuart-Bos 319
Ward-Chi 289
Killebrew-Min 286
Kaline-Det 283
Allison-Min 281

Runs Batted In
Stuart-Bos 118
Kaline-Det 101
Killebrew-Min 96
Colavito-Det 91
Allison-Min 91

Runs Produced
Kaline-Det 163
Colavito-Det 160
Stuart-Bos 157
Allison-Min 155
Siebern-KC 147

Bases On Balls
Yastrzemski-Bos . . . 95
Pearson-LA 92
Allison-Min 90
Cash-Det 89
Colavito-Det 84

Batting Average
Yastrzemski-Bos . . .321
Kaline-Det 312
Rollins-Min 307
Pearson-LA 304
Ward-Chi 295

On Base Percentage
Yastrzemski-Bos . . .419
Pearson-LA 403
Cash-Det 388
Allison-Min 381
Kaline-Det 378

Slugging Average
Killebrew-Min 555
Allison-Min 533
Howard-NY 528
Stuart-Bos 521
Hall-Min 521

Production
Allison-Min 914
Killebrew-Min 908
Yastrzemski-Bos . . .894
Kaline-Det 891
Howard-NY 871

Adjusted Production
Allison-Min 150
Killebrew-Min 147
Yastrzemski-Bos . . 145
Kaline-Det 142
Howard-NY 141

Batter Runs
Yastrzemski-Bos . . 42.0
Allison-Min 38.6
Kaline-Det 34.3
Killebrew-Min 33.5
Cash-Det 28.7

Adjusted Batter Runs
Yastrzemski-Bos . . 39.7
Allison-Min 37.3
Killebrew-Min 32.3
Kaline-Det 32.0
Tresh-NY 29.2

Clutch Hitting Index
Hansen-Chi 137
Siebern-KC 133
Charles-KC 124
Colavito-Det 123
Kaline-Det 123

Runs Created
Yastrzemski-Bos . . 118
Allison-Min 113
Kaline-Det 105
Ward-Chi 104
Pearson-LA 100

Total Average
Allison-Min 967
Yastrzemski-Bos . . .916
Killebrew-Min 907
Tresh-NY 879
Cash-Det 876

Stolen Bases
Aparicio-Bal 40
Hinton-Was 25
Wood-Det 18
Snyder-Bal 18
Pearson-LA 17

Stolen Base Average
Tartabull-KC 94.1
Aparicio-Bal 87.0
Wood-Det 78.3
Snyder-Bal 78.3
Hinton-Was 73.5

Stolen Base Runs
Aparicio-Bal 8.4
Tartabull-KC 4.2
Weis-Chi 3.9
Richardson-NY . . . 3.9
Smith-Bal 2.7

Fielding Runs
Hansen-Chi 27.0
Boyer-NY 22.3
Moran-LA 15.2
Allison-Min 11.4
Cottier-Was 10.9

Total Player Rating
Allison-Min 4.6
Yastrzemski-Bos . . 4.4
Hansen-Chi 3.3
Battey-Min 2.8
Cash-Det 2.4

Wins
Ford-NY 24
Pascual-Min 21
Bouton-NY 21
Monbouquette-Bos . 20
Barber-Bal 20

Win Percentage
Ford-NY 774
Bouton-NY 750
Radatz-Bos 714
Peters-Chi 704
Pascual-Min 700

Games
S.Miller-Bal 71
Radatz-Bos 66
Dailey-Min 66
Lamabe-Bos 65
Wyatt-KC 63

Complete Games
Terry-NY 18
Pascual-Min 18
Stigman-Min 15
Herbert-Chi 14
Aguirre-Det 14

Shutouts
Herbert-Chi 7
Bouton-NY 6

Saves
S.Miller-Bal 27
Radatz-Bos 25
Wyatt-KC 21
Wilhelm-Chi 21
Dailey-Min 21

Innings Pitched
Ford-NY 269.1
Terry-NY 268.0
Monbouquette-Bos . . . .
. . . . 266.2
Barber-Bal 258.2
Roberts-Bal 251.1

Fewest Hits/Game
Downing-NY 5.84
Bouton-NY 6.89
Drabowsky-KC . . . 6.97
Morehead-Bos . . . 7.06
McBride-LA 7.10

Fewest BB/Game
Donovan-Cle 1.22
Terry-NY 1.31
Herbert-Chi 1.40
Monbouquette-Bos 1.42
Roberts-Bal 1.43

Strikeouts
Pascual-Min 202
Bunning-Det 196
Stigman-Min 193
Peters-Chi 189
Ford-NY 189

Strikeouts/Game
Downing-NY 8.76
Ramos-Cle 8.24
Pascual-Min 7.32
Stigman-Min 7.21
Bunning-Det 7.10

Ratio
Terry-NY 9.71
Roberts-Bal 9.78
Ramos-Cle 9.80
Peters-Chi 9.93
Downing-NY 9.94

Earned Run Average
Peters-Chi 2.33
Pizarro-Chi 2.39
Pascual-Min 2.46
Bouton-NY 2.53
Downing-NY 2.56

Adjusted ERA
Peters-Chi 150
Pascual-Min 148
Pizarro-Chi 147
Bouton-NY 139
Stange-Min 139

Opponents' Batting Avg.
Downing-NY 184
Morehead-Bos 211
Bouton-NY 212
Drabowsky-KC 214
Peters-Chi 216

Opponents' On Base Pct.
Roberts-Bal 272
Terry-NY 273
Ramos-Cle 273
Downing-NY 277
Peters-Chi 278

Starter Runs
Peters-Chi 35.0
Pascual-Min 32.2
Bouton-NY 30.6
Pizarro-Chi 29.6
Ford-NY 26.6

Adjusted Starter Runs
Pascual-Min 32.6
Peters-Chi 31.7
Bouton-NY 27.3
Pizarro-Chi 26.6
Ford-NY 23.2

Clutch Pitching Index
Barber-Bal 126
Osteen-Was 120
Stange-Min 120
Segui-KC 115
Pascual-Min 115

Relief Runs
Radatz-Bos 24.4
Dailey-Min 19.8
S.Miller-Bal 17.3
Wilhelm-Chi 15.0
Fowler-LA 12.0

Adjusted Relief Runs
Radatz-Bos 26.7
Dailey-Min 20.0
S.Miller-Bal 16.0
Wilhelm-Chi 13.1
Lamabe-Bos 10.7

Relief Ranking
Radatz-Bos 49.4
S.Miller-Bal 25.4
Dailey-Min 23.6
Wilhelm-Chi 15.8
Kline-Was 14.1

Total Pitcher Index
Peters-Chi 4.3
Pascual-Min 4.2
Pizarro-Chi 2.9
Dailey-Min 2.6
Barber-Bal 2.5

Total Baseball Ranking
Allison-Min 4.6
Yastrzemski-Bos . . 4.4
Peters-Chi 4.3
Pascual-Min 4.2
Hansen-Chi 3.3

1964 National League

TEAM	G	W	L	PCT	GB	R	OR	AB	H	2B	3B	HR	BB	SO	AVG	OBP	SLG	PRO	PRO+	BR	/A	PF	CHI	RC	SB	CS	SBA	SBR
STL	162	93	69	.574		715	652	5625	1531	240	53	109	427	925	.272	.326	.392	.718	100	62	4	109	99	711	73	51	48	-13
PHI	162	92	70	.568	1	693	632	5493	1415	241	51	130	440	924	.258	.317	.391	.708	107	41	49	99	100	672	30	35	42	-14
CIN	163	92	70	.568	1	660	566	5561	1383	220	38	130	457	974	.249	.310	.372	.682	95	-9	-32	104	102	642	90	36	46	-16
SF	162	90	72	.556	3	656	587	5535	1360	185	38	165	505	486	.246	.313	.382	.695	99	16	2	102	97	657	64	35	43	-14
MIL	162	88	74	.543	5	803	744	5591	1522	274	32	159	486	825	.272	.335	.418	.753	118	132	128	101	101	764	53	41	49	-16
PIT	162	80	82	.494	13	663	636	5566	1469	225	54	121	408	970	.264	.317	.389	.706	105	35	36	100	97	668	39	33	40	-13
LA	164	80	82	.494	13	614	572	5499	1375	180	39	79	438	893	.250	.308	.340	.648	95	-69	-22	93	105	581	141	60	60	-17
CHI	162	76	86	.469	17	649	724	5545	1391	239	50	145	499	1041	.251	.316	.390	.706	100	37	10	104	94	679	70	49	45	-11
HOU	162	66	96	.407	27	495	628	5303	1214	162	41	70	381	872	.229	.287	.315	.602	80	-157	-121	94	106	469	40	48	52	-16
NY	163	53	109	.327	40	569	776	5566	1372	195	31	103	353	932	.246	.297	.348	.645	90	-83	-67	98	101	552	36	31	37	-12
TOT	812					6517		55284	14032	2161	427	1211	4394	9256	.254	.313	.374	.687							636	419	60	-60

TEAM	CG	SH	SV	IP	H	H/G	HR	BB	SO	RAT	ERA	ERA+	OAV	OOB	PR	/A	PF	CPI	FA	E	DP	FW	PW	BW	SBW	DIF
STL	47	10	38	1445¹	1405	8.7	133	410	877	11.5	3.43	111	.254	.309	16	59	108	104	.973	172	147	-.7	6.2	.4	-.7	6.8
PHI	37	17	41	1461	1402	8.6	129	440	1009	11.7	3.36	103	.252	.313	27	16	98	106	.975	157	150	.0	1.7	5.2	-.8	4.9
CIN	54	14	35	1467	1306	8.0	112	436	1122	10.9	3.07	118	.238	.298	75	87	102	100	.979	130	137	1.6	9.2	-3.4	-1.0	4.6
SF	48	17	30	1476¹	1348	8.2	118	480	1023	11.4	3.19	112	.241	.305	56	61	101	102	.975	159	136	-.0	6.4	.2	-.8	3.2
MIL	45	14	39	1434²	1411	8.9	160	452	906	11.8	4.12	86	.257	.316	-92	-94	100	94	.977	143	139	.8	-9.9	13.5	-1.0	3.6
PIT	42	14	29	1443²	1429	8.9	92	476	951	12.1	3.52	100	.259	.322	2	-1	99	103	.972	177	179	-1.0	-.1	3.8	-.7	-3.0
LA	47	19	27	1483²	1289	7.8	88	458	1062	10.8	2.95	110	.231	.293	95	46	92	95	.973	170	126	-.5	4.9	-2.3	-1.2	-1.9
CHI	58	11	19	1445	1510	9.4	144	423	737	12.1	4.08	91	.269	.322	-87	-58	105	98	.975	162	147	-.2	-6.1	1.1	-.5	.8
HOU	30	9	31	1428	1421	9.0	105	353	852	11.4	3.41	100	.260	.308	19	0	97	102	.976	149	124	.5	.0	-12.8	-1.0	-1.7
NY	40	10	15	1438²	1511	9.5	130	466	717	12.7	4.25	84	.272	.334	-114	-108	101	98	.974	167	154	-.4	-11.4	-7.1	-.6	-8.5
TOT	448	135	304	14523¹		8.7				11.6	3.54		.254	.313					.975	1586	1439					

Runs		Hits		Doubles		Triples		Home Runs		Total Bases	
Allen-Phi	125	Flood-StL	211	Maye-Mil	44	Santo-Chi	13	Mays-SF	47	Allen-Phi	352
Mays-SF	121	Clemente-Pit	211	Clemente-Pit	40	Allen-Phi	13	Williams-Chi	33	Mays-SF	351
Brock-Chi-StL	111	Williams-Chi	201	Williams-Chi	39	Brock-Chi-StL	11	Hart-SF	31	Williams-Chi	343
Robinson-Cin	103	Allen-Phi	201	Robinson-Cin	38	Pinson-Cin	11	Cepeda-SF	31	Santo-Chi	334
Aaron-Mil	103	Brock-Chi-StL	200	Allen-Phi	38			Callison-Phi	31	Callison-Phi	322

Runs Batted In		Runs Produced		Bases On Balls		Batting Average		On Base Percentage		Slugging Average	
Boyer-StL	119	Boyer-StL	195	Santo-Chi	86	Clemente-Pit	.339	Santo-Chi	.401	Mays-SF	.607
Santo-Chi	114	Allen-Phi	187	Mathews-Mil	85	Carty-Mil	.330	Robinson-Cin	.399	Santo-Chi	.564
Mays-SF	111	Mays-SF	185	Mays-SF	82	Aaron-Mil	.328	Aaron-Mil	.394	Allen-Phi	.557
Torre-Mil	109	Santo-Chi	178	Robinson-Cin	79	Torre-Mil	.321	Carty-Mil	.391	Carty-Mil	.554
Callison-Phi	104	Torre-Mil	176	Boyer-StL	70	Allen-Phi	.318	Clemente-Pit	.391	Robinson-Cin	.548

Production		Adjusted Production		Batter Runs		Adjusted Batter Runs		Clutch Hitting Index		Runs Created	
Mays-SF	.992	Mays-SF	171	Mays-SF	56.5	Mays-SF	55.0	Fairly-LA	148	Mays-SF	136
Santo-Chi	.966	Allen-Phi	163	Santo-Chi	55.1	Santo-Chi	52.1	Boyer-StL	136	Santo-Chi	135
Robinson-Cin	.947	Santo-Chi	162	Allen-Phi	50.5	Allen-Phi	51.5	H.Davis-LA	135	Allen-Phi	135
Carty-Mil	.945	Carty-Mil	162	Robinson-Cin	49.5	Robinson-Cin	47.0	Torre-Mil	132	Robinson-Cin	127
Allen-Phi	.940	Robinson-Cin	158	Williams-Chi	42.5	Aaron-Mil	40.4	Bond-Hou	128	Williams-Chi	125

Total Average		Stolen Bases		Stolen Base Average		Stolen Base Runs		Fielding Runs		Total Player Rating	
Mays-SF	1.059	Wills-LA	53	Harper-Cin	88.9	Wills-LA	5.7	Mazeroski-Pit	33.9	Mays-SF	6.3
Robinson-Cin	1.012	Brock-Chi-StL	43	Aaron-Mil	84.6	Harper-Cin	5.4	Edwards-Cin	22.3	Santo-Chi	6.0
Santo-Chi	.998	W.Davis-LA	42	Robinson-Cin	82.1	W.Davis-LA	4.8	Rodgers-Chi	19.4	Robinson-Cin	5.3
Allen-Phi	.944	Harper-Cin	24	Mays-SF	79.2	Aaron-Mil	4.2	W.Davis-LA	19.2	Aaron-Mil	5.2
Carty-Mil	.920	Robinson-Cin	23	W.Davis-LA	76.4	Robinson-Cin	3.9	Callison-Phi	17.6	Allen-Phi	5.0

Wins		Win Percentage		Games		Complete Games		Shutouts		Saves	
Jackson-Chi	24	Koufax-LA	.792	R.Miller-LA	74	Marichal-SF	22	Koufax-LA	7	Woodeshick-Hou	23
Marichal-SF	21	Marichal-SF	.724	Perranoski-LA	72	Drysdale-LA	21	Law-Pit	5	McBean-Pit	22
Sadecki-StL	20	O'Toole-Cin	.708	Baldschun-Phi	71	Jackson-Chi	19	Fischer-Mil	5	Baldschun-Phi	21
		Bunning-Phi	.704	Taylor-StL	63	Gibson-StL	17	Drysdale-LA	5	McDaniel-Chi	15
		Jackson-Chi	.686	McDaniel-Chi	63	Ellsworth-Chi	16	Bunning-Phi	5		

Innings Pitched		Fewest Hits/Game		Fewest BB/Game		Strikeouts		Strikeouts/Game		Ratio	
Drysdale-LA	321.1	Koufax-LA	6.22	Bunning-Phi	1.46	Veale-Pit	250	Koufax-LA	9.00	Koufax-LA	8.35
Jackson-Chi	297.2	Drysdale-LA	6.78	Bruce-Hou	1.47	Gibson-StL	245	Maloney-Cin	8.92	Drysdale-LA	8.96
Gibson-StL	287.1	Short-Phi	7.10	Law-Pit	1.50	Drysdale-LA	237	Veale-Pit	8.05	Short-Phi	9.34
Bunning-Phi	284.1	Veale-Pit	7.14	Marichal-SF	1.74	Koufax-LA	223	Gibson-StL	7.67	Bunning-Phi	9.75
Veale-Pit	279.2	Maloney-Cin	7.29	Jackson-Chi	1.75	Bunning-Phi	219	Lemaster-Mil	7.53	Jackson-Chi	9.80

Earned Run Average		Adjusted ERA		Opponents' Batting Avg.		Opponents' On Base Pct.		Starter Runs		Adjusted Starter Runs	
Koufax-LA	1.74	Koufax-LA	187	Koufax-LA	.191	Koufax-LA	.241	Drysdale-LA	48.2	Drysdale-LA	37.6
Drysdale-LA	2.18	Short-Phi	157	Drysdale-LA	.207	Drysdale-LA	.256	Koufax-LA	44.6	Koufax-LA	37.2
Short-Phi	2.20	Drysdale-LA	148	Veale-Pit	.217	Short-Phi	.268	Short-Phi	32.7	Marichal-SF	32.5
Marichal-SF	2.48	Marichal-SF	144	Short-Phi	.217	Jackson-Chi	.273	Marichal-SF	31.7	Short-Phi	31.0
Bunning-Phi	2.63	O'Toole-Cin	136	Bolin-SF	.220	Marichal-SF	.273	Bunning-Phi	28.7	Bunning-Phi	26.6

Clutch Pitching Index		Relief Runs		Adjusted Relief Runs		Relief Ranking		Total Pitcher Index		Total Baseball Ranking	
Craig-StL	122	McBean-Pit	16.2	McBean-Pit	16.0	McBean-Pit	26.5	Drysdale-LA	4.8	Mays-SF	6.3
D.Bennett-Phi	119	R.Miller-LA	14.1	Ellis-Cin	14.1	Ellis-Cin	17.1	Marichal-SF	3.5	Santo-Chi	6.0
Farrell-Hou	115	Ellis-Cin	13.1	McCool-Cin	11.9	McCool-Cin	15.2	Koufax-LA	3.4	Robinson-Cin	5.3
Tsitouris-Cin	115	Roebuck-Phi	11.4	Roebuck-Phi	10.8	Roebuck-Phi	13.8	Short-Phi	3.1	Aaron-Mil	5.2
Hendley-SF	110	McCool-Cin	11.1	R.Miller-LA	9.5	Woodeshick-Hou	11.0	Jackson-Chi	2.9	Allen-Phi	5.0

TEAM	G	W	L	PCT	GB	R	OR	AB	H	2B	3B	HR	BB	SO	AVG	OBP	SLG	PRO	PRO+	BR	/A	PF	CHI	RC	SB	CS	SBA	SBR
NY	164	99	63	.611		730	577	5705	1442	208	35	162	520	976	.253	.319	.387	.706	100	13	2	102	105	705	54	18	30	-12
CHI	162	98	64	.605	1	642	501	5491	1356	184	40	106	562	902	.247	.323	.353	.676	97	-31	-12	97	101	643	75	39	57	-22
BAL	163	97	65	.599	2	679	567	5463	1357	229	20	162	537	1019	.248	.319	.387	.706	102	14	16	100	101	671	78	38	40	-12
DET	163	85	77	.525	14	699	678	5513	1394	199	57	157	517	912	.253	.321	.395	.716	103	35	25	102	100	707	60	27	40	-15
LA	162	82	80	.506	17	544	551	5362	1297	186	27	102	472	920	.242	.306	.344	.650	96	-88	-24	90	99	552	49	39	49	-17
MIN	163	79	83	.488	20	737	678	5610	1413	227	46	221	553	1019	.252	.324	.427	.751	113	98	93	101	95	775	46	22	31	-11
CLE	164	79	83	.488	20	689	693	5603	1386	208	22	164	500	1063	.247	.315	.380	.695	99	-7	-1	99	104	666	79	51	62	-21
BOS	162	72	90	.444	27	688	793	5513	1425	253	29	186	504	917	.258	.324	.416	.740	105	76	44	105	94	725	18	16	21	-7
WAS	162	62	100	.383	37	578	733	5396	1246	199	28	125	514	1124	.231	.301	.348	.649	86	-94	-90	100	105	566	47	30	59	-25
KC	163	57	105	.352	42	621	836	5524	1321	216	29	166	548	1104	.239	.313	.379	.692	95	-13	-32	103	96	645	34	20	25	-8
TOT	814					6607		55180	13637	2109	333	1551	5227	9956	.247	.316	.322	.698							540	300	64	-17

TEAM	CG	SH	SV	IP	H	H/G	HR	BB	SO	RAT	ERA	ERA+	OAV	OOB	PR	/A	PF	CPI	FA	E	DP	FW	PW	BW	SBW	DIF
NY	46	18	45	1506^2	1312	7.8	129	504	989	11.0	3.15	115	.234	.300	78	78	100	97	.983	109	158	1.1	8.2	.2	-1.1	9.5
CHI	44	20	45	1467^2	1216	7.5	124	401	955	10.1	2.72	127	.225	.283	147	119	95	100	.981	122	164	.2	12.5	-1.3	-2.1	7.6
BAL	44	17	41	1458^2	1292	8.0	129	456	939	11.0	3.16	113	.238	.302	75	66	99	100	.985	95	159	1.9	6.9	1.7	-1.1	6.5
DET	35	11	35	1453	1343	8.3	164	536	993	12.0	3.84	95	.243	.316	-34	-28	101	95	.982	111	137	1.0	-2.9	2.6	-1.4	4.8
LA	30	28	41	1450^2	1273	7.9	100	530	965	11.5	2.91	113	.235	.309	115	60	91	107	.978	138	168	-.7	6.3	-2.5	-1.6	-.5
MIN	47	4	29	1477^2	1361	8.3	181	545	1099	11.8	3.58	100	.243	.313	8	0	99	102	.977	145	131	-1.1	.0	9.8	-1.0	-9.7
CLE	37	16	37	1487^2	1443	8.7	154	565	1162	12.3	3.75	96	.254	.325	-20	-24	99	103	.981	118	149	.6	-2.5	-.1	-2.0	2.1
BOS	21	9	38	1422	1464	9.3	178	571	1094	13.1	4.50	86	.266	.338	-138	-101	106	97	.977	138	123	-.7	-10.6	4.6	-.5	-1.7
WAS	27	5	26	1435^1	1417	8.9	172	505	794	12.2	3.98	93	.258	.324	-56	-44	102	100	.979	127	145	-.0	-4.6	-9.5	-2.4	-2.4
KC	18	6	27	1455^2	1516	9.4	220	614	966	13.5	4.71	81	.268	.346	-174	-143	105	101	.975	158	152	-1.9	-15.0	-3.4	-.7	-3.1
TOT	349	134	364	14615		8.4				11.8	3.63		.247	.316					.980	1261	1486					

Runs
Oliva-Min	109
Howser-Cle	101
Killebrew-Min	95
Wagner-Cle	94
Versalles-Min	94

Hits
Oliva-Min	217
B.Robinson-Bal	194
Richardson-NY	181
Howard-NY	172
Versalles-Min	171

Doubles
Oliva-Min	43
Bressoud-Bos	41
B.Robinson-Bal	35
Versalles-Min	33

Triples
Versalles-Min	10
Rollins-Min	10
Yastrzemski-Bos	9
Oliva-Min	9
Fregosi-LA	9

Home Runs
Killebrew-Min	49
Powell-Bal	39
Mantle-NY	35
Colavito-KC	34
Stuart-Bos	33

Total Bases
Oliva-Min	374
B.Robinson-Bal	319
Killebrew-Min	316
Colavito-KC	298
Stuart-Bos	296

Runs Batted In
B.Robinson-Bal	118
Stuart-Bos	114
Mantle-NY	111
Killebrew-Min	111
Colavito-KC	102

Runs Produced
B.Robinson-Bal	172
Oliva-Min	171
Mantle-NY	168
Wagner-Cle	163

Bases On Balls
Siebern-Bal	106
Mantle-NY	99
Killebrew-Min	93
Allison-Min	92
Causey-KC	88

Batting Average
Oliva-Min	.323
B.Robinson-Bal	.317
Howard-NY	.313
Mantle-NY	.303
Robinson-Chi	.301

On Base Percentage
Mantle-NY	.426
Allison-Min	.406
Powell-Bal	.400
Robinson-Chi	.388
Kaline-Det	.385

Slugging Average
Powell-Bal	.606
Mantle-NY	.591
Oliva-Min	.557
Allison-Min	.553
Killebrew-Min	.548

Production
Mantle-NY	1.017
Powell-Bal	1.007
Allison-Min	.959
Killebrew-Min	.927
Oliva-Min	.918

Adjusted Production
Mantle-NY	177
Powell-Bal	176
Allison-Min	163
Killebrew-Min	153
Oliva-Min	150

Batter Runs
Mantle-NY	53.0
Allison-Min	45.0
Powell-Bal	44.1
Killebrew-Min	43.1
Oliva-Min	43.0

Adjusted Batter Runs
Mantle-NY	52.0
Allison-Min	44.5
Powell-Bal	44.3
Killebrew-Min	42.6
Oliva-Min	42.5

Clutch Hitting Index
Rodgers-LA	135
B.Robinson-Bal	131
Ward-Chi	130
Stuart-Bos	130
Pepitone-NY	127

Runs Created
Oliva-Min	132
Killebrew-Min	122
Mantle-NY	121
Allison-Min	119
B.Robinson-Bal	115

Total Average
Mantle-NY	1.122
Powell-Bal	1.081
Allison-Min	1.058
Killebrew-Min	.956
Oliva-Min	.894

Stolen Bases
Aparicio-Bal	57
Weis-Chi	22
Davalillo-Cle	21
Howser-Cle	20
Hinton-Was	17

Stolen Base Average
Aparicio-Bal	77.0
Weis-Chi	75.9
Howser-Cle	74.1
Hinton-Was	73.9
Davalillo-Cle	65.6

Stolen Base Runs
Aparicio-Bal	6.9
Tresh-NY	3.9
Wagner-Cle	3.0
Weis-Chi	2.4
Allison-Min	2.4

Fielding Runs
Knoop-LA	37.2
Boyer-NY	19.3
Yastrzemski-Bos	18.4
Green-KC	16.5
Hansen-Chi	15.9

Total Player Rating
Allison-Min	4.4
Oliva-Min	4.4
B.Robinson-Bal	3.9
Powell-Bal	3.9
Ward-Chi	3.7

Wins
Peters-Chi	20
Chance-LA	20
Wickersham-Det	19
Pizarro-Chi	19
Bunker-Bal	19

Win Percentage
Bunker-Bal	.792
Ford-NY	.739
Peters-Chi	.714
Pappas-Bal	.696
Chance-LA	.690

Games
Wyatt-KC	81
Radatz-Bos	79
Wilhelm-Chi	73
McMahon-Cle	70
Miller-Bal	66

Complete Games
Chance-LA	15
Pascual-Min	14
Pappas-Bal	13
Osteen-Was	13
Kaat-Min	13

Shutouts
Chance-LA	11
Ford-NY	8
Pappas-Bal	7
Lolich-Det	6
Monbouquette-Bos	5

Saves
Radatz-Bos	29
Wilhelm-Chi	27
Miller-Bal	23
Wyatt-KC	20
R.Lee-LA	19

Innings Pitched
Chance-LA	278.1
Peters-Chi	273.2
Bouton-NY	271.1
Pascual-Min	267.1
Osteen-Was	257.0

Fewest Hits/Game
Horlen-Chi	6.07
Chance-LA	6.27
Bunker-Bal	6.77
Peters-Chi	7.14
Pizarro-Chi	7.27

Fewest BB/Game
Monbouquette-Bos	1.54
Pappas-Bal	1.72
Newman-LA	1.85
Bouton-NY	1.99
Pizarro-Chi	2.07

Strikeouts
Downing-NY	217
Pascual-Min	213
Chance-LA	207
Peters-Chi	205
Lolich-Det	192

Strikeouts/Game
McDowell-Cle	9.19
Downing-NY	8.00
Pena-KC	7.55
Stigman-Min	7.53
Morehead-Bos	7.51

Ratio
Horlen-Chi	8.59
Chance-LA	9.12
Pizarro-Chi	9.45
Bunker-Bal	9.50
Bouton-NY	9.72

Earned Run Average
Chance-LA	1.65
Horlen-Chi	1.88
Ford-NY	2.13
Peters-Chi	2.50
Pizarro-Chi	2.56

Adjusted ERA
Chance-LA	199
Horlen-Chi	184
Ford-NY	170
Peters-Chi	138
Pizarro-Chi	135

Opponents' Batting Avg.
Horlen-Chi	.190
Chance-LA	.195
Bunker-Bal	.207
Peters-Chi	.219
Pizarro-Chi	.219

Opponents' On Base Pct.
Horlen-Chi	.250
Chance-LA	.261
Pizarro-Chi	.267
Bunker-Bal	.269
Bouton-NY	.273

Starter Runs
Chance-LA	61.1
Horlen-Chi	40.9
Ford-NY	40.6
Peters-Chi	34.2
Pizarro-Chi	28.3

Adjusted Starter Runs
Chance-LA	50.6
Ford-NY	40.5
Horlen-Chi	36.9
Peters-Chi	29.1
Pizarro-Chi	23.7

Clutch Pitching Index
McDowell-Cle	123
Roberts-Bal	121
Kralick-Cle	118
Grant-Cle-Min	112
Peters-Chi	111

Relief Runs
R.Lee-LA	32.2
Wilhelm-Chi	23.9
Radatz-Bos	23.2
Worthington-Min	18.1
Hall-Bal	17.3

Adjusted Relief Runs
Radatz-Bos	27.3
R.Lee-LA	27.0
Wilhelm-Chi	21.4
Stock-Bal-KC	18.6
Worthington-Min	17.8

Relief Ranking
Radatz-Bos	50.4
Wilhelm-Chi	40.7
Worthington-Min	32.0
Kline-Was	28.2
R.Lee-LA	27.9

Total Pitcher Index
Ford-NY	4.9
Chance-LA	4.8
Horlen-Chi	4.4
Peters-Chi	4.1
Pizarro-Chi	2.9

Total Baseball Ranking
Ford-NY	4.9
Chance-LA	4.8
Allison-Min	4.4
Horlen-Chi	4.4
Oliva-Min	4.4

1965 National League

TEAM	G	W	L	PCT	GB	R	OR	AB	H	2B	3B	HR	BB	SO	AVG	OBP	SLG	PRO	PRO+	BR	/A	PF	CHI	RC	SB	CS	SBA	SBR
LA	162	97	65	.599		608	521	5425	1329	193	32	78	492	891	.245	.314	.335	.649	96	-60	-17	93	103	593	172	77	68	-17
SF	163	95	67	.586	2	682	593	5495	1384	169	43	159	476	844	.252	.315	.385	.700	101	24	6	103	101	649	47	27	28	-8
PIT	163	90	72	.556	7	675	580	5686	1506	217	57	111	419	1008	.265	.319	.382	.701	103	27	23	101	97	671	51	38	58	-22
CIN	162	89	73	.549	8	825	704	5658	1544	268	61	183	538	1003	.273	.341	.439	.780	117	188	141	107	95	842	64	37	47	-12
MIL	162	86	76	.531	11	708	633	5542	1419	243	28	196	408	976	.256	.311	.416	.727	110	67	63	101	99	699	64	37	47	-16
PHI	162	85	76	.528	11.5	654	667	5528	1380	205	53	144	494	1091	.250	.315	.384	.699	104	24	35	98	96	665	46	32	41	-14
STL	162	80	81	.497	16.5	707	674	5579	1415	234	46	109	477	882	.254	.316	.371	.687	91	3	-59	109	107	659	100	52	56	-17
CHI	164	72	90	.444	25	635	723	5540	1316	202	33	134	532	948	.238	.309	.358	.667	91	-33	-48	102	101	613	65	47	46	-13
HOU	162	65	97	.401	32	569	711	5483	1299	188	42	97	502	877	.237	.306	.340	.646	95	-72	-27	93	98	574	90	37	45	-15
NY	164	50	112	.309	47	495	752	5441	1202	203	27	107	392	1129	.221	.278	.327	.605	78	-163	-140	96	105	480	28	42	48	-15
TOT	813					6558		55377	13794	2122	422	1318	4730	9649	.249	.313	.374	.687							745	429	63	-33

TEAM	CG	SH	SV	IP	H	H/G	HR	BB	SO	RAT	ERA	ERA+	OAV	OOB	PR	/A	PF	CPI	FA	E	DP	FW	PW	BW	SBW	DIF
LA	58	23	34	1476	1223	7.5	127	425	1079	10.3	2.81	116	.224	.284	119	74	92	99	.979	134	135	.8	7.8	-1.8	-1.4	10.6
SF	42	17	42	1465[1]	1325	8.1	137	408	1060	10.9	3.20	112	.238	.294	55	65	102	98	.976	148	124	.0	6.9	.6	-.5	6.9
PIT	49	17	27	1479	1324	8.1	89	469	882	11.2	3.01	117	.240	.305	86	81	99	103	.977	152	189	-.1	8.6	2.4	-2.0	.1
CIN	43	9	34	1457[1]	1355	8.4	136	587	1113	12.3	3.88	96	.246	.324	-55	-22	106	96	.981	178	142	1.8	-2.3	14.9	-.9	-5.5
MIL	43	4	38	1447[2]	1336	8.3	123	541	966	11.8	3.52	100	.246	.317	3	0	100	101	.974	140	145	.5	.0	6.7	-1.3	-.8
PHI	50	18	21	1468[2]	1426	8.7	116	466	1071	12.0	3.53	98	.256	.320	1	-11	98	104	.975	157	153	-.5	-1.2	3.7	-1.1	3.6
STL	40	11	35	1461[1]	1414	8.7	166	467	916	11.8	3.77	102	.254	.316	-37	12	109	102	.979	130	152	1.1	1.3	-6.2	-1.4	4.8
CHI	33	9	35	1472	1470	9.0	154	481	855	12.1	3.78	98	.260	.321	-39	-15	104	104	.974	171	166	-1.2	-1.6	-5.1	-1.0	-.2
HOU	29	7	26	1461	1459	9.0	123	388	931	11.6	3.84	87	.259	.312	-49	-79	95	94	.974	166	130	-1.0	-8.3	-2.9	-1.2	-2.6
NY	29	11	14	1454[2]	1462	9.0	147	498	776	12.4	4.06	87	.262	.327	-83	-85	100	99	.974	171	153	-1.2	-9.0	-14.8	-1.2	-4.8
TOT	416	126	306	14643		8.5				11.6	3.54		.249	.313					.977	1486	1489					

Runs
Harper-Cin 126
Mays-SF 118
Rose-Cin 117
Williams-Chi 115

Hits
Rose-Cin 209
Pinson-Cin 204
Williams-Chi 203
Clemente-Pit 194
Flood-StL 191

Doubles
H.Aaron-Mil 40
Williams-Chi 39
Rose-Cin 35
Brock-StL 35
Pinson-Cin 34

Triples
Callison-Phi 16
Clendenon-Pit 14
Clemente-Pit 14
Allen-Phi 14
Morgan-Hou 12

Home Runs
Mays-SF 52
McCovey-SF 39
Williams-Chi 34
Santo-Chi 33
Robinson-Cin 33

Total Bases
Mays-SF 360
Williams-Chi 356
Pinson-Cin 324
H.Aaron-Mil 319
Johnson-Cin 317

Runs Batted In
Johnson-Cin 130
Robinson-Cin 113
Mays-SF 112
Williams-Chi 108
Stargell-Pit 107

Runs Produced
Johnson-Cin 190
Williams-Chi 189
Robinson-Cin 189
Rose-Cin 187
Mays-SF 178

Bases On Balls
Morgan-Hou 97
Santo-Chi 88
McCovey-SF 88
Wynn-Hou 84
Harper-Cin 78

Batting Average
Clemente-Pit 329
H.Aaron-Mil 318
Mays-SF 317
Williams-Chi 315
Rose-Cin 312

On Base Percentage
Mays-SF 399
Robinson-Cin 388
H.Aaron-Mil 384
McCovey-SF 383
Rose-Cin 383

Slugging Average
Mays-SF 645
H.Aaron-Mil 560
Williams-Chi 552
Robinson-Cin 540
McCovey-SF 539

Production
Mays-SF 1.044
H.Aaron-Mil 943
Williams-Chi 932
Robinson-Cin 928
McCovey-SF 922

Adjusted Production
Mays-SF 184
H.Aaron-Mil 161
Williams-Chi 155
McCovey-SF 152
Robinson-Cin 148

Batter Runs
Mays-SF 64.7
Williams-Chi 49.3
H.Aaron-Mil 45.9
Robinson-Cin 45.9
McCovey-SF 41.8

Adjusted Batter Runs
Mays-SF 62.9
Williams-Chi 47.5
H.Aaron-Mil 45.6
Robinson-Cin 40.9
McCovey-SF 40.0

Clutch Hitting Index
Johnson-Cin 138
Boyer-StL 138
Fairly-LA 130
Stargell-Pit 130
Banks-Chi 129

Runs Created
Mays-SF 143
Williams-Chi 132
H.Aaron-Mil 122
Santo-Chi 121
Robinson-Cin 120

Total Average
Mays-SF 1.114
H.Aaron-Mil 980
McCovey-SF 945
Robinson-Cin 938
Williams-Chi 935

Stolen Bases
Wills-LA 94
Brock-StL 63
Wynn-Hou 43
Harper-Cin 35
W.Davis-LA 25

Stolen Base Average
Wynn-Hou 91.5
H.Aaron-Mil 85.7
Harper-Cin 85.4
Wills-LA 75.2
W.Davis-LA 73.5

Stolen Base Runs
Wynn-Hou 10.5
Wills-LA 9.6
Harper-Cin 6.9
H.Aaron-Mil 4.8
Allen-Phi 3.3

Fielding Runs
Alley-Pit 29.5
Mazeroski-Pit 25.6
Wine-Phi 21.7
Wills-LA 21.2
Santo-Chi 18.5

Total Player Rating
Mays-SF 7.1
H.Aaron-Mil 5.7
Wynn-Hou 5.4
Santo-Chi 5.2
Williams-Chi 4.6

Wins
Koufax-LA 26
Cloninger-Mil 24
Drysdale-LA 23
Marichal-SF 22
Ellis-Cin 22

Win Percentage
Koufax-LA 765
Maloney-Cin 690
Ellis-Cin 688
Cloninger-Mil 686
Bunning-Phi 679

Games
Abernathy-Chi 84
Woodeshick-Hou-StL . 78
McDaniel-Chi 71
Baldschun-Phi 65

Complete Games
Koufax-LA 27
Marichal-SF 24
Gibson-StL 20
Drysdale-LA 20
Cloninger-Mil 16

Shutouts
Marichal-SF 10
Koufax-LA 8
Veale-Pit 7
Drysdale-LA 7
Bunning-Phi 7

Saves
Abernathy-Chi 31
McCool-Cin 21
Linzy-SF 21

Innings Pitched
Koufax-LA 335.2
Drysdale-LA 308.1
Gibson-StL 299.0
Short-Phi 297.1
Marichal-SF 295.1

Fewest Hits/Game
Koufax-LA 5.79
Maloney-Cin 6.66
Marichal-SF 6.83
Bolin-SF 6.90
Gibson-StL 7.31

Fewest BB/Game
Marichal-SF 1.40
Law-Pit 1.45
Bruce-Hou 1.49
Farrell-Hou 1.51
Johnson-Hou-Mil . 1.87

Strikeouts
Koufax-LA 382
Veale-Pit 276
Gibson-StL 270
Bunning-Phi 268
Maloney-Cin 244

Strikeouts/Game
Koufax-LA 10.24
Veale-Pit 9.34
Maloney-Cin 8.60
Bunning-Phi 8.29
Gibson-StL 8.13

Ratio
Koufax-LA 7.83
Marichal-SF 8.35
Law-Pit 9.11
Bunning-Phi 10.11
Drysdale-LA 10.16

Earned Run Average
Koufax-LA 2.04
Marichal-SF 2.13
Law-Pit 2.15
Maloney-Cin 2.54
Bunning-Phi 2.60

Adjusted ERA
Marichal-SF 169
Law-Pit 163
Koufax-LA 160
Maloney-Cin 148
Shaw-SF 136

Opponents' Batting Avg.
Koufax-LA 179
Marichal-SF 205
Maloney-Cin 206
Bolin-SF 214
Gibson-StL 222

Opponents' On Base Pct.
Koufax-LA 228
Marichal-SF 240
Law-Pit 264
Drysdale-LA 280
Shaw-SF 280

Starter Runs
Marichal-SF 56.0
Koufax-LA 46.1
Law-Pit 33.5
Bunning-Phi 30.4
Maloney-Cin 28.4

Adjusted Starter Runs
Marichal-SF 48.1
Koufax-LA 45.7
Maloney-Cin 34.3
Law-Pit 32.8
Bunning-Phi 27.8

Clutch Pitching Index
Law-Pit 115
Koonce-Chi 112
Culp-Phi 108
Spahn-NY-SF . . . 107
Buhl-Chi 107

Relief Runs
Linzy-SF 19.1
O'Dell-Mil 16.8
McBean-Pit 15.8
Perranoski-LA 15.2
Abernathy-Chi 14.6

Adjusted Relief Runs
Linzy-SF 19.7
Abernathy-Chi 16.8
O'Dell-Mil 16.6
McDaniel-Chi 15.7
McBean-Pit 15.5

Relief Ranking
Linzy-SF 37.4
O'Dell-Mil 27.4
Woodeshick-Hou-StL 23.5
McBean-Pit 20.2
Abernathy-Chi 19.7

Total Pitcher Index
Marichal-SF 5.6
Koufax-LA 5.0
Maloney-Cin 4.6
Law-Pit 4.4
Drysdale-LA 4.1

Total Baseball Ranking
Mays-SF 7.1
H.Aaron-Mil 5.7
Marichal-SF 5.6
Wynn-Hou 5.4
Santo-Chi 5.2

TEAM	G	W	L	PCT	GB	R	OR	AB	H	2B	3B	HR	BB	SO	AVG	OBP	SLG	PRO	PRO+	BR	/A	PF	CHI	RC	SB	CS	SBA	SBR
MIN	162	102	60	.630		774	600	5488	**1396**	257	42	150	554	969	**.254**	.327	.399	.726	107	84	55	104	**106**	730	92	33	57	-23
CHI	162	95	67	.586	7	647	**555**	5509	1354	200	38	125	533	916	.246	.317	.364	.681	106	1	40	94	99	636	50	33	37	-11
BAL	162	94	68	.580	8	641	578	5450	1299	227	38	125	529	907	.238	.309	.363	.672	95	-20	-32	102	103	607	67	31	46	-17
DET	162	89	73	.549	13	680	602	5368	1278	190	27	162	554	952	.238	.314	.374	.688	100	10	3	101	**106**	628	57	41	47	-15
CLE	162	87	75	.537	15	663	613	5469	1367	198	21	156	506	**857**	.250	.317	.379	.696	103	26	20	101	99	667	109	46	49	-15
NY	162	77	85	.475	25	611	604	5470	1286	196	31	149	489	951	.235	.300	.364	.664	94	-41	-36	99	103	593	35	20	29	-10
CAL	162	75	87	.463	27	527	569	5354	1279	200	36	92	443	973	.239	.300	.341	.641	90	-80	-65	98	97	549	107	59	**67**	-22
WAS	162	70	92	.432	32	591	721	5374	1227	179	33	136	570	1125	.228	.306	.350	.656	94	-46	-36	99	100	586	30	19	22	**-7**
BOS	162	62	100	.383	40	669	791	5487	1378	244	40	**165**	607	964	.251	**.329**	**.400**	**.729**	106	95	56	106	90	715	47	24	52	-23
KC	162	59	103	.364	43	585	755	5393	1294	186	**59**	110	521	1020	.240	.311	.358	.669	97	-24	-14	99	96	604	**110**	51	50	-14
TOT	810					6388		54362	13158	2077	365	1370	5306	9634	.242	.313	.369	.682							704	357	66	-2

TEAM	CG	SH	SV	IP	H	H/G	HR	BB	SO	RAT	ERA	ERA+	OAV	OOB	PR	/A	PF	CPI	FA	E	DP	FW	PW	BW	SBW	DIF
MIN	32	12	45	1457[1]	1278	7.9	166	503	934	11.2	3.14	113	.234	.302	52	67	103	**107**	.973	172	158	-2.3	7.1	5.9	-2.4	12.7
CHI	21	14	**53**	1481[2]	1261	**7.7**	122	**460**	946	**10.6**	2.99	107	**.230**	**.294**	76	32	92	98	.980	127	156	.6	3.4	4.3	-1.1	6.9
BAL	32	**15**	41	1477[2]	1268	**7.7**	120	510	939	11.0	**2.98**	116	.233	.302	**77**	**79**	100	104	.980	126	152	.6	**8.4**	-3.4	-1.8	9.1
DET	**45**	14	31	1455	1283	7.9	137	509	1069	11.4	3.35	104	.236	.307	17	19	101	99	**.981**	116	126	1.3	2.0	.3	-1.6	6.0
CLE	41	13	41	1458[1]	**1254**	**7.7**	129	500	**1156**	11.0	3.30	106	.231	.300	26	29	101	94	**.981**	114	127	**1.4**	3.1	2.1	-1.6	1.0
NY	41	11	31	1459[2]	1337	8.2	126	511	1001	11.6	3.28	104	.244	.312	28	19	98	104	.978	137	**166**	-.0	2.0	-3.8	-1.0	-1.1
CAL	39	14	33	1441[2]	1259	7.9	**91**	563	847	11.5	3.17	107	.237	.313	45	36	98	100	**.981**	123	149	.8	3.8	-6.9	-2.3	-1.4
WAS	21	8	40	1435[2]	1376	8.6	160	633	867	12.8	3.93	88	.254	.336	-75	-72	101	105	.977	143	148	-.4	-7.7	-3.8	**-.7**	1.7
BOS	33	9	25	1439[1]	1443	9.0	158	543	993	12.6	4.24	88	.259	.329	-124	-82	108	95	.974	162	129	-1.6	-8.7	**6.0**	-2.4	-12.2
KC	18	7	32	1433	1399	8.8	161	574	882	12.6	4.24	82	.256	.331	-124	-119	101	96	.977	139	142	-.2	-12.7	-1.5	-1.5	-6.2
TOT	323	117	372	14539[1]		8.1				11.6	3.46		.242	.313					.978	1359	1453					

Runs
Versalles-Min 126
Oliva-Min 107
Tresh-NY 94
Buford-Chi 93
Colavito-Cle 92

Hits
Oliva-Min 185
Versalles-Min 182
Colavito-Cle 170
Tresh-NY 168
Fregosi-Cal 167

Doubles
Yastrzemski-Bos 45
Versalles-Min 45
Oliva-Min 40
Tresh-NY 29
Richardson-NY 28

Triples
Versalles-Min 12
Campaneris-KC 12
Aparicio-Bal 10
W.Smith-Cal 9

Home Runs
Conigliaro-Bos 32
Cash-Det 30
Horton-Det 29
Wagner-Cle 28

Total Bases
Versalles-Min 308
Tresh-NY 287
Oliva-Min 283
Colavito-Cle 277
Conigliaro-Bos . . . 267

Runs Batted In
Colavito-Cle 108
Horton-Det 104
Oliva-Min 98
Mantilla-Bos 92
Whitfield-Cle 90

Runs Produced
Oliva-Min 189
Versalles-Min 184
Colavito-Cle 174
Hall-Min 147
Horton-Det 144

Bases On Balls
Colavito-Cle 93
Blefary-Bal 88
Mantilla-Bos 79
Cash-Det 77
Robinson-Chi 76

Batting Average
Oliva-Min 321
Yastrzemski-Bos . . .312
Davalillo-Cle 301
Robinson-Bal 297
Wagner-Cle 294

On Base Percentage
Yastrzemski-Bos . . .398
Colavito-Cle 387
Oliva-Min 384
Blefary-Bal 382
Mantilla-Bos 377

Slugging Average
Yastrzemski-Bos . . .536
Conigliaro-Bos 512
Cash-Det 512
Wagner-Cle 495
Oliva-Min 491

Production
Yastrzemski-Bos . . .935
Cash-Det 886
Oliva-Min 876
Wagner-Cle 866
Colavito-Cle 855

Adjusted Production
Yastrzemski-Bos . . 154
Cash-Det 147
Wagner-Cle 143
Oliva-Min 141
Colavito-Cle 140

Batter Runs
Yastrzemski-Bos . . 41.6
Oliva-Min 35.3
Colavito-Cle 34.6
Cash-Det 31.0
Wagner-Cle 29.6

Adjusted Batter Runs
Yastrzemski-Bos . . 38.0
Colavito-Cle 34.0
Oliva-Min 32.3
Cash-Det 30.4
Wagner-Cle 29.1

Clutch Hitting Index
Mantilla-Bos 146
Colavito-Cle 134
Horton-Det 130
Oliva-Min 130
Powell-Bal 125

Runs Created
Colavito-Cle 110
Oliva-Min 109
Yastrzemski-Bos . . 102
Versalles-Min 102
Tresh-NY 101

Total Average
Yastrzemski-Bos . . .931
Cash-Det 894
Wagner-Cle 882
Blefary-Bal 876
Oliva-Min 863

Stolen Bases
Campaneris-KC 51
Cardenal-Cal 37
Versalles-Min 27
Davalillo-Cle 26
Aparicio-Bal 26

Stolen Base Average
Hinton-Cle 85.0
Versalles-Min 84.4
Howser-Cal 81.0
Davalillo-Cle 78.8
Aparicio-Bal 78.8

Stolen Base Runs
Versalles-Min 5.1
Campaneris-KC . . . 3.9
Davalillo-Cle 3.6
Aparicio-Bal 3.6
Hinton-Cle 3.3

Fielding Runs
Boyer-NY 24.8
Hansen-Chi 16.7
Knoop-Cal 12.8
Conigliaro-Bos . . . 12.3
Adair-Bal 12.1

Total Player Rating
Yastrzemski-Bos . . . 3.8
Weis-Chi 3.6
Oliva-Min 3.6
Colavito-Cle 3.1
Boyer-NY 3.1

Wins
Grant-Min 21
Stottlemyre-NY 20
Kaat-Min 18
McDowell-Cle 17

Win Percentage
Grant-Min 750
McLain-Det 727
Stottlemyre-NY 690
Fisher-Chi 682
Siebert-Cle 667

Games
Fisher-Chi 82
Kline-Was 74
R.Lee-Cal 69
Dickson-KC 68
S.Miller-Bal 67

Complete Games
Stottlemyre-NY 18
McDowell-Cle 14
Grant-Min 14
McLain-Det 13

Shutouts
Grant-Min 6
Stottlemyre-NY 4
McLain-Det 4
Horlen-Chi 4
Chance-Cal 4

Saves
Kline-Was 29
S.Miller-Bal 24
Fisher-Chi 24
R.Lee-Cal 23
Radatz-Bos 22

Innings Pitched
Stottlemyre-NY . . 291.0
McDowell-Cle . . . 273.0
Grant-Min 270.1
Kaat-Min 264.1
Newman-Cal 260.2

Fewest Hits/Game
McDowell-Cle 5.87
Fisher-Chi 6.42
Siebert-Cle 6.63
Richert-Was 6.77
Brunet-Cal 6.81

Fewest BB/Game
Terry-Cle 1.25
Monbouquette-Bos 1.57
Horlen-Chi 1.60
Ford-NY 1.84
Grant-Min 2.03

Strikeouts
McDowell-Cle 325
Lolich-Det 226
McLain-Det 192
Siebert-Cle 191
Downing-NY 179

Strikeouts/Game
McDowell-Cle . . . 10.71
Siebert-Cle 9.11
Lolich-Det 8.35
McLain-Det 7.84
Morehead-Bos . . . 7.61

Ratio
Fisher-Chi 8.87
Siebert-Cle 9.06
Terry-Cle 9.67
McLain-Det 9.72
Newman-Cal 10.01

Earned Run Average
McDowell-Cle 2.18
Fisher-Chi 2.40
Siebert-Cle 2.43
Brunet-Cal 2.56
Richert-Was 2.60

Adjusted ERA
McDowell-Cle 160
Siebert-Cle 143
Perry-Min 135
Richert-Was 134
Pappas-Bal 133

Opponents' Batting Avg.
McDowell-Cle 185
Fisher-Chi 205
Siebert-Cle 206
Brunet-Cal 209
Richert-Was 210

Opponents' On Base Pct.
Siebert-Cle 262
Fisher-Chi 262
Terry-Cle 269
McLain-Det 273
Pappas-Bal 281

Starter Runs
McDowell-Cle 38.9
Stottlemyre-NY . . . 26.8
Siebert-Cle 21.5
Pappas-Bal 21.1
McLain-Det 20.7

Adjusted Starter Runs
McDowell-Cle 39.5
Stottlemyre-NY . . . 25.0
Siebert-Cle 21.9
Kaat-Min 21.4
Pappas-Bal 21.3

Clutch Pitching Index
Kaat-Min 123
Perry-Min 117
Peters-Chi 113
Richert-Was 110
Pappas-Bal 110

Relief Runs
Wilhelm-Chi 26.3
R.Lee-Cal 22.5
S.Miller-Bal 20.9
Fisher-Chi 19.5
Hamilton-NY 13.4

Adjusted Relief Runs
Wilhelm-Chi 22.1
R.Lee-Cal 21.6
S.Miller-Bal 21.0
Fisher-Chi 14.6
Hamilton-NY 13.1

Relief Ranking
S.Miller-Bal 42.7
R.Lee-Cal 32.2
Worthington-Min . . 31.7
Wilhelm-Chi 26.2
Fisher-Chi 22.3

Total Pitcher Index
McDowell-Cle 4.1
Stottlemyre-NY 3.6
Kaat-Min 3.6
Newman-Cal 2.4
R.Lee-Cal 2.3

Total Baseball Ranking
McDowell-Cle 4.1
Yastrzemski-Bos . . 3.8
Stottlemyre-NY 3.6
Weis-Chi 3.6
Kaat-Min 3.6

TEAM	G	W	L	PCT	GB	R	OR	AB	H	2B	3B	HR	BB	SO	AVG	OBP	SLG	PRO	PRO+	BR	/A	PF	CHI	RC	SB	CS	SBA	SBR
LA	162	95	67	.586		606	490	5471	1399	201	27	108	430	830	.256	.316	.362	.678	103	-36	15	92	98	615	94	64	57	-14
SF	161	93	68	.578	1.5	675	626	5539	1373	195	31	181	414	860	.248	.304	.392	.696	96	-13	-32	103	105	633	29	30	34	-10
PIT	162	92	70	.568	3	759	641	5676	1586	238	66	158	405	1011	.279	.331	.428	.759	115	117	116	100	96	779	64	60	64	-19
PHI	162	87	75	.537	8	696	640	5607	1448	224	49	117	510	969	.258	.323	.378	.701	100	12	11	100	101	683	56	42	40	-10
ATL	163	85	77	.525	10	782	683	5617	1476	220	32	207	512	913	.263	.329	.424	.753	113	106	95	102	100	775	59	47	54	-17
STL	162	83	79	.512	12	571	577	5480	1377	196	61	108	345	977	.251	.300	.368	.668	90	-65	-68	101	98	592	144	61	53	-13
CIN	160	76	84	.475	18	692	702	5521	1434	232	33	149	394	877	.260	.311	.395	.706	93	7	-50	109	105	658	70	50	49	-13
HOU	163	72	90	.444	23	612	695	5511	1405	203	35	124	491	885	.255	.320	.365	.685	104	-18	27	93	94	640	90	47	49	-14
NY	161	66	95	.410	28.5	587	761	5371	1286	187	35	98	446	992	.239	.303	.342	.645	87	-98	-83	98	108	546	55	46	48	-14
CHI	162	59	103	.364	36	644	809	5592	1418	203	43	140	457	998	.254	.315	.380	.695	97	-5	-13	101	97	665	76	47	49	-14
TOT	809					6624		55385	14202	2099	412	1378	4404	9312	.256	.315	.384	.699							737	494	60	-74

TEAM	CG	SH	SV	IP	H	H/G	HR	BB	SO	RAT	ERA	ERA+	OAV	OOB	PR	/A	PF	CPI	FA	E	DP	FW	PW	BW	SBW	DIF
LA	52	20	35	1458	1287	7.9	84	356	1084	10.3	2.62	126	.237	.287	159	109	91	102	.979	133	128	.9	11.4	1.6	-.7	.8
SF	52	14	27	1476²	1370	8.3	140	359	973	10.7	3.24	113	.244	.293	60	70	102	96	.974	168	131	-1.2	7.3	-3.4	-.3	9.9
PIT	35	12	43	1463¹	1445	8.9	125	463	898	12.0	3.52	101	.260	.322	13	8	99	105	.978	141	215	.4	.8	12.2	-1.2	-1.2
PHI	52	15	23	1459²	1439	8.9	137	412	928	11.8	3.57	101	.258	.316	5	4	100	102	.982	113	147	2.0	.4	1.2	-.3	2.7
ATL	37	10	36	1469¹	1430	8.8	129	485	884	11.9	3.68	99	.256	.319	-12	-6	101	98	.976	154	139	-.3	-.6	10.0	-1.0	-4.1
STL	47	19	32	1459²	1345	8.3	130	448	892	11.3	3.11	115	.246	.307	79	76	100	107	.977	145	166	.2	8.0	-7.1	-.6	1.5
CIN	28	10	35	1436	1408	8.8	153	490	1043	12.2	4.08	96	.257	.323	-75	-28	108	94	.980	122	133	1.4	-2.9	-5.2	-.6	3.4
HOU	34	13	26	1443²	1468	9.2	130	391	929	11.8	3.76	91	.262	.314	-24	-53	95	96	.972	174	126	-1.4	-5.6	2.8	-.7	-4.2
NY	37	9	22	1427	1497	9.4	166	521	773	12.9	4.17	87	.271	.338	-89	-84	101	104	.975	159	171	-.6	-8.8	-8.7	-.7	4.3
CHI	28	6	24	1458	1513	9.3	184	479	908	12.5	4.33	85	.267	.327	-117	-106	102	97	.974	166	132	-1.0	-11.1	-1.4	-.7	-7.9
TOT	402	128	303	14551¹		8.8				11.7	3.61		.256	.315					.977	1475	1488					

Runs		Hits		Doubles		Triples		Home Runs		Total Bases	
Alou-Atl	122	Alou-Atl	218	Callison-Phi	40	McCarver-StL	13	Aaron-Atl	44	Alou-Atl	355
Aaron-Atl	117	Rose-Cin	205	Rose-Cin	38	Brock-StL	12	Allen-Phi	40	Clemente-Pit	342
Allen-Phi	112	Clemente-Pit	202	Pinson-Cin	35	Clemente-Pit	11	Mays-SF	37	Allen-Phi	331
Clemente-Pit	105	Beckert-Chi	188	Alou-Atl	32			Torre-Atl	36	Aaron-Atl	325
Williams-Chi	100							McCovey-SF	36	Mays-SF	307

Runs Batted In		Runs Produced		Bases On Balls		Batting Average		On Base Percentage		Slugging Average	
Aaron-Atl	127	Aaron-Atl	200	Santo-Chi	95	Alou-Pit	.342	Santo-Chi	.417	Allen-Phi	.632
Clemente-Pit	119	Clemente-Pit	195	Morgan-Hou	89	Alou-Atl	.327	Morgan-Hou	.412	McCovey-SF	.586
Allen-Phi	110	Allen-Phi	182	McCovey-SF	76	Carty-Atl	.326	Allen-Phi	.398	Stargell-Pit	.581
White-Phi	103	White-Phi	166	Aaron-Atl	76	Allen-Phi	.317	Carty-Atl	.396	Torre-Atl	.560
Mays-SF	103			Menke-Atl	71	Clemente-Pit	.317	McCovey-SF	.394	Mays-SF	.556

Production		Adjusted Production		Batter Runs		Adjusted Batter Runs		Clutch Hitting Index		Runs Created	
Allen-Phi	1.030	Allen-Phi	181	Allen-Phi	56.8	Allen-Phi	56.8	White-Phi	135	Allen-Phi	131
McCovey-SF	.979	Stargell-Pit	164	Santo-Chi	51.2	Santo-Chi	50.3	Staub-Hou	135	Santo-Chi	127
Stargell-Pit	.965	McCovey-SF	163	McCovey-SF	46.9	McCovey-SF	45.1	Flood-StL	135	Alou-Atl	123
Santo-Chi	.955	Santo-Chi	161	Torre-Atl	43.0	Torre-Atl	42.0	Aaron-Atl	124	McCovey-SF	119
Torre-Atl	.945	Torre-Atl	157	Stargell-Pit	41.1	Stargell-Pit	41.1	Woodward-Atl	121	Clemente-Pit	119

Total Average		Stolen Bases		Stolen Base Average		Stolen Base Runs		Fielding Runs		Total Player Rating	
Allen-Phi	1.088	Brock-StL	74	Aaron-Atl	87.5	Brock-StL	11.4	Mazeroski-Pit	40.8	Santo-Chi	7.7
McCovey-SF	1.039	Jackson-Hou	49	Brock-StL	80.4	Jackson-Hou	6.3	Santo-Chi	28.4	Clemente-Pit	4.9
Santo-Chi	.988	Wills-LA	38	Jackson-Hou	77.8	Aaron-Atl	4.5	Lanier-SF	28.2	Aaron-Atl	4.8
Stargell-Pit	.980	Phillips-Phi-Chi	32	Harper-Cin	74.4	Harper-Cin	2.7	Maxvill-StL	24.0	Allen-Phi	4.4
Mays-SF	.941	Harper-Cin	29	White-Phi	72.7			Clemente-Pit	15.6	Mazeroski-Pit	4.4

Wins		Win Percentage		Games		Complete Games		Shutouts		Saves	
Koufax-LA	27	Marichal-SF	.806	Carroll-Atl	73	Koufax-LA	27	L.Jackson-Chi-Phi	5	Regan-LA	21
Marichal-SF	25	Koufax-LA	.750	Mikkelsen-Pit	71	Marichal-SF	25	Maloney-Cin	5	McCool-Cin	18
Perry-SF	21	Perry-SF	.724	Knowles-Phi	69	Gibson-StL	20	Koufax-LA	5	Face-Pit	18
Gibson-StL	21	Short-Phi	.667	Regan-LA	65	Short-Phi	19	Jaster-StL	5	Raymond-Hou	16
Short-Phi	20	Maloney-Cin	.667	McDaniel-SF	64	Bunning-Phi	16	Gibson-StL	5	Linzy-SF	16
								Bunning-Phi	5		

Innings Pitched		Fewest Hits/Game		Fewest BB/Game		Strikeouts		Strikeouts/Game		Ratio	
Koufax-LA	323.0	Marichal-SF	6.68	Marichal-SF	1.05	Koufax-LA	317	Koufax-LA	8.83	Marichal-SF	7.88
Bunning-Phi	314.0	Koufax-LA	6.72	Law-Pit	1.22	Bunning-Phi	252	Maloney-Cin	8.65	Koufax-LA	8.86
Marichal-SF	307.1	Gibson-StL	6.74	Perry-SF	1.41	Veale-Pit	229	Sutton-LA	8.34	Gibson-StL	9.41
Gibson-StL	280.1	Maloney-Cin	6.97	Drysdale-LA	1.48	Gibson-StL	225	Veale-Pit	7.68	Bunning-Phi	9.57
Drysdale-LA	273.2	Bolin-SF	6.98	Bunning-Phi	1.58	Marichal-SF	222	Jenkins-Phi-Chi	7.32	Cuellar-Hou	9.70

Earned Run Average		Adjusted ERA		Opponents' Batting Avg.		Opponents' On Base Pct.		Starter Runs		Adjusted Starter Runs	
Koufax-LA	1.73	Koufax-LA	191	Marichal-SF	.202	Marichal-SF	.230	Koufax-LA	67.4	Koufax-LA	56.3
Cuellar-Hou	2.22	Marichal-SF	165	Koufax-LA	.205	Koufax-LA	.253	Marichal-SF	47.2	Marichal-SF	49.2
Marichal-SF	2.23	Cuellar-Hou	154	Gibson-StL	.207	Gibson-StL	.267	Bunning-Phi	41.8	Bunning-Phi	41.4
Bunning-Phi	2.41	Bunning-Phi	149	Bolin-SF	.211	Bunning-Phi	.270	Gibson-StL	36.3	Gibson-StL	35.8
Gibson-StL	2.44	Gibson-StL	147	Maloney-Cin	.214	Cuellar-Hou	.274	Cuellar-Hou	35.1	Cuellar-Hou	30.5

Clutch Pitching Index		Relief Runs		Adjusted Relief Runs		Relief Ranking		Total Pitcher Index		Total Baseball Ranking	
Jackson-StL	117	Regan-LA	25.8	Regan-LA	21.7	Regan-LA	33.9	Marichal-SF	6.4	Santo-Chi	7.7
L.Jackson-Chi-Phi	110	Carroll-Atl	19.8	Carroll-Atl	20.4	McCool-Cin	29.2	Koufax-LA	5.1	Marichal-SF	6.4
Ellsworth-Chi	108	Hoerner-StL	17.5	Hoerner-StL	17.3	Carroll-Atl	22.5	Bunning-Phi	4.2	Koufax-LA	5.1
Johnson-Atl	108	McCool-Cin	13.2	McCool-Cin	16.7	Hoerner-StL	19.0	Gibson-StL	4.1	Clemente-Pit	4.9
Osteen-LA	107	Woodeshick-StL	13.2	McDaniel-SF	13.6	McDaniel-SF	16.6	Jackson-StL	4.0	Aaron-Atl	4.8

TEAM	G	W	L	PCT	GB	R	OR	AB	H	2B	3B	HR	BB	SO	AVG	OBP	SLG	PRO	PRO+	BR	/A	PF	CHI	RC	SB	CS	SBA	SBR
BAL	160	97	63	.606		755	601	5529	1426	243	35	175	514	926	.258	.325	.409	.734	118	114	124	98	100	727	55	43	46	-14
MIN	162	89	73	.549	9	663	581	5390	1341	219	33	144	513	844	.249	.319	.382	.701	100	49	8	106	98	643	67	42	48	-15
DET	162	88	74	.543	10	719	698	5507	1383	224	45	179	551	987	.251	.323	.406	.729	112	102	87	102	96	714	41	34	41	-13
CHI	163	83	79	.512	15	574	517	5348	1235	193	40	87	476	872	.231	.299	.331	.630	93	-82	-40	93	106	539	153	78	66	-15
CLE	162	81	81	.500	17	574	586	5474	1300	156	25	155	450	914	.237	.299	.360	.659	95	-37	-37	100	97	579	53	41	38	-10
CAL	162	80	82	.494	18	604	643	5360	1244	179	54	122	525	1062	.232	.305	.354	.659	97	-28	-11	97	101	582	80	54	59	-18
KC	160	74	86	.463	23	564	648	5328	1259	212	56	70	421	982	.236	.295	.337	.632	89	-83	-63	97	107	535	132	50	46	-12
WAS	159	71	88	.447	25.5	557	659	5318	1245	185	40	126	450	1069	.234	.296	.355	.651	93	-49	-42	99	99	548	53	37	45	-15
BOS	162	72	90	.444	26	655	731	5498	1318	228	44	145	542	1020	.240	.312	.376	.688	93	24	-42	110	98	640	35	24	35	-13
NY	160	70	89	.440	26.5	611	612	5330	1254	182	36	162	485	817	.235	.302	.374	.676	103	-4	18	96	100	598	49	29	45	-17
TOT	806					6276		54082	13005	2021	408	1365	4927	9493	.240	.308	.369	.676							718	432	62	-43

TEAM	CG	SH	SV	IP	H	H/G	HR	BB	SO	RAT	ERA	ERA+	OAV	OOB	PR	/A	PF	CPI	FA	E	DP	FW	PW	BW	SBW	DIF
BAL	23	13	51	1466¹	1267	7.8	127	514	1070	11.1	3.32	100	.233	.302	18	1	97	97	.981	115	142	1.3	.1	13.3	-1.0	3.3
MIN	52	11	28	1438²	1246	7.8	139	392	1015	10.4	3.13	115	.231	.287	48	73	105	97	.977	139	118	.0	7.8	.9	-1.1	.4
DET	36	11	38	1454¹	1356	8.4	185	520	1026	11.9	3.85	90	.247	.317	-66	-59	101	102	.980	120	142	1.1	-6.3	9.3	-.9	3.8
CHI	38	22	34	1475¹	1229	7.5	101	403	896	10.2	2.68	118	.225	.283	123	79	92	100	.976	159	149	-1.1	8.5	-4.3	-1.1	.0
CLE	49	15	28	1467¹	1260	7.7	129	489	1111	10.9	3.23	107	.232	.299	34	34	100	98	.978	138	132	.0	3.7	-4.0	-.6	.8
CAL	31	12	40	1457¹	1364	8.4	136	511	836	11.8	3.56	94	.251	.319	-20	-32	98	105	.979	136	186	.2	-3.4	-1.2	-1.5	4.9
KC	19	11	47	1435	1281	8.0	106	630	854	12.2	3.56	96	.240	.325	-19	-25	99	101	.977	139	154	-.0	-2.7	-6.8	-.8	4.4
WAS	25	6	35	1419	1282	8.1	154	448	866	11.1	3.70	93	.241	.303	-42	-38	101	95	.977	142	139	-.3	-4.1	-4.5	-1.1	1.5
BOS	32	10	31	1463²	1402	8.6	164	577	977	12.4	3.92	97	.252	.327	-78	-17	111	103	.975	155	153	-.9	-1.8	-4.5	-.9	-.8
NY	29	7	32	1415²	1318	8.4	124	443	842	11.3	3.41	97	.247	.308	3	-14	97	102	.977	142	142	-.3	-1.5	1.9	-1.4	-8.3
TOT	334	118	364	14492²		8.1				11.3	3.44		.240	.308					.978	1385	1457					

Runs		Hits		Doubles		Triples		Home Runs		Total Bases	
F.Robinson-Bal	122	Oliva-Min	191	Yastrzemski-Bos	39	Knoop-Cal	11	F.Robinson-Bal	49	F.Robinson-Bal	367
Oliva-Min	99	F.Robinson-Bal	182	B.Robinson-Bal	35	Campaneris-KC	10	Killebrew-Min	39	Oliva-Min	312
Cash-Det	98	Aparicio-Bal	182	F.Robinson-Bal	34	Brinkman-Was	9	Powell-Bal	34	Killebrew-Min	306
Agee-Chi	98	Agee-Chi	172	Oliva-Min	32			Cash-Det	32	Cash-Det	288
		Cash-Det	168	Fregosi-Cal	32			Pepitone-NY	31	Agee-Chi	281

Runs Batted In		Runs Produced		Bases On Balls		Batting Average		On Base Percentage		Slugging Average	
F.Robinson-Bal	122	F.Robinson-Bal	195	Killebrew-Min	103	F.Robinson-Bal	.316	F.Robinson-Bal	.415	F.Robinson-Bal	.637
Killebrew-Min	110	B.Robinson-Bal	168	Foy-Bos	91	Oliva-Min	.307	Kaline-Det	.396	Killebrew-Min	.538
Powell-Bal	109	Agee-Chi	162	F.Robinson-Bal	87	Kaline-Det	.288	Killebrew-Min	.393	Kaline-Det	.534
B.Robinson-Bal	100	Oliva-Min	161	Tresh-NY	86	Powell-Bal	.287	McAuliffe-Det	.375	Powell-Bal	.532
Horton-Det	100	Killebrew-Min	160	Yastrzemski-Bos	84	Killebrew-Min	.281	Powell-Bal	.374	McAuliffe-Det	.509

Production		Adjusted Production		Batter Runs		Adjusted Batter Runs		Clutch Hitting Index		Runs Created	
F.Robinson-Bal	1.052	F.Robinson-Bal	200	F.Robinson-Bal	73.6	F.Robinson-Bal	74.7	Hershberger-KC	134	F.Robinson-Bal	146
Killebrew-Min	.931	Kaline-Det	161	Killebrew-Min	49.9	Killebrew-Min	45.4	Wert-Det	130	Killebrew-Min	122
Kaline-Det	.931	Powell-Bal	159	Kaline-Det	42.1	Kaline-Det	40.7	B.Robinson-Bal	129	Oliva-Min	106
Powell-Bal	.905	Killebrew-Min	155	Powell-Bal	36.3	Powell-Bal	37.2	Powell-Bal	129	Kaline-Det	105
McAuliffe-Det	.884	McAuliffe-Det	148	Oliva-Min	33.2	Mantle-NY	30.3	Horton-Det	128	Cash-Det	101

Total Average		Stolen Bases		Stolen Base Average		Stolen Base Runs		Fielding Runs		Total Player Rating	
F.Robinson-Bal	1.104	Campaneris-KC	52	Campaneris-KC	83.9	Campaneris-KC	9.6	Weis-Chi	36.9	F.Robinson-Bal	6.5
Kaline-Det	.969	Buford-Chi	51	Tartabull-KC-Bos	82.6	Tartabull-KC-Bos	3.3	Tresh-NY	27.0	Tresh-NY	4.0
Killebrew-Min	.967	Agee-Chi	44	Tovar-Min	72.7	Salmon-Cle	2.4	Boyer-NY	19.9	Oliva-Min	3.6
Powell-Bal	.898	Aparicio-Bal	25	Agee-Chi	71.0	Agee-Chi	2.4	Knoop-Cal	16.5	Kaline-Det	3.5
McAuliffe-Det	.877	Cardenal-Cal	24	Buford-Chi	69.9			G.Smith-Bos	15.8	Fregosi-Cal	3.2

Wins		Win Percentage		Games		Complete Games		Shutouts		Saves	
Kaat-Min	25	Siebert-Cle	.667	Fisher-Chi-Bal	67	Kaat-Min	19	Tiant-Cle	5	Aker-KC	32
McLain-Det	20	Kaat-Min	.658	Cox-Was	66	McLain-Det	14	McDowell-Cle	5	Kline-Was	23
Wilson-Bos-Det	18	Wilson-Bos-Det	.621	Aker-KC	66	Wilson-Bos-Det	13	John-Chi	5	Sherry-Det	20
Siebert-Cle	16	Palmer-Bal	.600	Worthington-Min	65	Bell-Cle	12			Fisher-Chi-Bal	19
Palmer-Bal	15	McLain-Det	.588	Kline-Was	63					S.Miller-Bal	18

Innings Pitched		Fewest Hits/Game		Fewest BB/Game		Strikeouts		Strikeouts/Game		Ratio	
Kaat-Min	304.2	McDowell-Cle	6.02	Kaat-Min	1.62	McDowell-Cle	225	McDowell-Cle	10.42	Peters-Chi	8.97
McLain-Det	264.1	Boswell-Min	6.38	Peterson-NY	1.67	Kaat-Min	205	Boswell-Min	9.19	Kaat-Min	9.72
Wilson-Bos-Det	264.0	Peters-Chi	6.86	Grant-Min	1.77	Wilson-Bos-Det	200	Lolich-Det	7.64	Richert-Was	9.74
Chance-Cal	259.2	McLain-Det	6.98	Peters-Chi	1.98	Richert-Was	195	Richert-Was	7.14	Siebert-Cle	9.75
Bell-Cle	254.1	Chance-Cal	7.14	Hargan-Cle	2.11	Bell-Cle	194	Bell-Cle	6.87	Ortega-Was	9.85

Earned Run Average		Adjusted ERA		Opponents' Batting Avg.		Opponents' On Base Pct.		Starter Runs		Adjusted Starter Runs	
Peters-Chi	1.98	Peters-Chi	160	McDowell-Cle	.188	Peters-Chi	.261	Peters-Chi	33.1	Kaat-Min	28.8
Horlen-Chi	2.43	Perry-Min	142	Boswell-Min	.197	Richert-Was	.271	Horlen-Chi	23.5	Peters-Chi	27.1
Hargan-Cle	2.48	Hargan-Cle	138	Peters-Chi	.212	Kaat-Min	.271	Kaat-Min	23.3	Perry-Min	21.7
Perry-Min	2.54	Kaat-Min	131	McLain-Det	.214	Ortega-Was	.276	Hargan-Cle	20.3	Hargan-Cle	20.4
John-Chi	2.62	Horlen-Chi	130	Richert-Was	.215	Siebert-Cle	.278	John-Chi	20.1	Nash-KC	18.9

Clutch Pitching Index		Relief Runs		Adjusted Relief Runs		Relief Ranking		Total Pitcher Index		Total Baseball Ranking	
McNally-Bal	118	Aker-KC	18.1	Aker-KC	17.7	Aker-KC	28.1	Peters-Chi	3.9	F.Robinson-Bal	6.5
Horlen-Chi	114	Wilhelm-Chi	16.0	Wilhelm-Chi	13.7	McMahon-Cle-Bos	20.8	Kaat-Min	3.8	Tresh-NY	4.0
Brunet-Cal	114	S.Miller-Bal	12.1	Worthington-Min	11.5	S.Miller-Bal	18.9	Wilson-Bos-Det	3.4	Peters-Chi	3.9
Perry-Min	113	Fisher-Chi-Bal	10.8	S.Miller-Bal	11.1	Kline-Was	16.8	Perry-Min	2.8	Kaat-Min	3.8
Hargan-Cle	110	Lines-Was	10.7	Lines-Was	10.9	Worthington-Min	14.7	Horlen-Chi	2.2	Oliva-Min	3.6

TEAM	G	W	L	PCT	GB	R	OR	AB	H	2B	3B	HR	BB	SO	AVG	OBP	SLG	PRO	PRO+	BR	/A	PF	CHI	RC	SB	CS	SBA	SBR
STL	161	101	60	.627		695	557	5566	1462	225	40	115	443	919	.263	.322	.379	.701	109	52	60	99	103	676	102	54	52	-14
SF	162	91	71	.562	10.5	652	551	5524	1354	201	39	140	520	978	.245	.315	.372	.687	104	24	32	99	100	641	22	30	37	-12
CHI	162	87	74	.540	14	702	624	5463	1373	211	49	128	509	912	.251	.319	.378	.697	101	44	-15	105	105	654	63	50	57	-18
CIN	162	87	75	.537	14.5	604	563	5519	1366	251	54	109	372	969	.248	.299	.372	.671	87	-19	-88	111	102	592	92	63	53	-12
PHI	162	82	80	.506	19.5	612	581	5401	1306	221	47	103	545	1033	.242	.314	.357	.671	98	0	-6	101	99	604	79	62	54	-13
PIT	163	81	81	.500	20.5	679	693	5724	1585	193	62	91	387	914	.277	.327	.380	.707	108	63	59	101	97	693	79	37	41	-13
ATL	162	77	85	.475	24.5	631	640	5456	1307	191	29	158	512	947	.240	.309	.372	.681	102	10	18	99	100	615	55	45	52	-17
LA	162	73	89	.451	28.5	519	595	5456	1285	203	38	82	485	881	.236	.303	.332	.635	96	-73	-22	92	95	541	56	47	47	-13
HOU	162	69	93	.426	32.5	626	742	5506	1372	259	46	93	537	934	.249	.319	.364	.683	106	20	41	97	97	640	88	38	45	-15
NY	162	61	101	.377	40.5	498	672	5417	1288	178	23	83	362	981	.238	.290	.325	.615	83	-117	-107	98	103	500	58	44	49	-15
TOT	810					6218		55026	13698	2133	427	1102	4672	9468	.249	.312	.363	.675							694	470	60	-73

TEAM	CG	SH	SV	IP	H	H/G	HR	BB	SO	RAT	ERA	ERA+	OAV	OOB	PR	/A	PF	CPI	FA	E	DP	FW	PW	BW	SBW	DIF
STL	44	17	45	1465	1313	8.1	97	431	956	10.9	3.05	108	.239	.298	53	39	97	98	.978	140	127	.0	4.2	6.5	-.7	10.5
SF	64	17	25	1474¹	1283	7.8	113	453	990	10.8	2.92	113	.233	.295	75	60	97	101	.979	134	149	.4	6.5	3.5	-.5	.1
CHI	47	7	28	1457	1352	8.4	142	463	888	11.4	3.48	102	.245	.307	-17	9	105	99	.981	121	143	1.1	1.0	1.6	-1.2	3.9
CIN	34	18	39	1468	1328	8.1	101	498	1065	11.5	3.05	123	.240	.308	53	114	111	104	.980	121	124	1.1	12.3	-9.5	-.5	2.5
PHI	46	17	23	1453²	1372	8.5	86	403	967	11.2	3.10	110	.249	.306	44	49	101	102	.978	137	174	.2	5.3	-.6	-.6	-3.3
PIT	35	5	35	1458¹	1439	8.9	108	561	820	12.5	3.74	90	.260	.332	-58	-60	100	103	.978	141	186	.0	-6.5	6.4	-.6	.7
ATL	35	5	32	1454	1377	8.5	118	449	862	11.6	3.47	96	.251	.312	-15	-24	98	100	.978	138	148	.2	-2.6	1.9	-1.0	-2.5
LA	41	17	24	1473	1421	8.7	93	393	967	11.3	3.21	96	.254	.307	26	-18	92	102	.975	160	144	-1.1	-1.9	-2.4	-.6	-2.0
HOU	35	8	21	1445²	1444	9.0	120	485	1060	12.3	4.03	82	.259	.324	-104	-115	98	93	.974	159	120	-1.0	-12.5	4.4	-.8	-2.1
NY	36	10	19	1433²	1369	8.6	124	536	893	12.1	3.73	91	.252	.323	-56	-54	100	99	.975	157	147	-.9	-5.8	-11.6	-.8	-.8
TOT	417	121	291	14582²		8.5				11.6	3.38		.249	.312					.978	1408	1462					

Runs
Brock-StL 113
Aaron-Atl 113
Santo-Chi 107
Clemente-Pit ... 103
Wynn-Hou 102

Hits
Clemente-Pit 209
Brock-StL 206
Pinson-Cin 187
Wills-Pit 186
Alou-Pit 186

Doubles
Staub-Hou 44
Cepeda-StL 37
Aaron-Atl 37

Triples
Pinson-Cin 13
Williams-Chi 12
Brock-StL 12
Morgan-Hou 11

Home Runs
Aaron-Atl 39
Wynn-Hou 37
Santo-Chi 31
McCovey-SF 31
Hart-SF 29

Total Bases
Aaron-Atl 344
Brock-StL 325
Clemente-Pit 324
Williams-Chi 305
Santo-Chi 300

Runs Batted In
Cepeda-StL 111
Clemente-Pit 110
Aaron-Atl 109
Wynn-Hou 107
Perez-Cin 102

Runs Produced
Clemente-Pit 190
Aaron-Atl 183
Cepeda-StL 177
Santo-Chi 174
Wynn-Hou 172

Bases On Balls
Santo-Chi 96
Morgan-Hou 81
Phillips-Chi 80
Hart-SF 77
Allen-Phi 75

Batting Average
Clemente-Pit ..... .357
Gonzalez-Phi ..... .339
Alou-Pit ..... .338
Flood-StL ..... .335
Staub-Hou ..... .333

On Base Percentage
Allen-Phi ..... .404
Cepeda-StL ..... .403
Staub-Hou ..... .402
Clemente-Pit ..... .402
Santo-Chi ..... .401

Slugging Average
Aaron-Atl ..... .573
Allen-Phi ..... .566
Clemente-Pit ..... .554
McCovey-SF ..... .535
Cepeda-StL ..... .524

Production
Allen-Phi ..... .970
Clemente-Pit ..... .956
Aaron-Atl ..... .946
Cepeda-StL ..... .927
McCovey-SF ..... .916

Adjusted Production
Allen-Phi 173
Clemente-Pit 170
Aaron-Atl 169
Cepeda-StL 166
McCovey-SF 162

Batter Runs
Clemente-Pit 52.1
Aaron-Atl 50.1
Santo-Chi 47.9
Cepeda-StL 47.3
Allen-Phi 46.1

Adjusted Batter Runs
Clemente-Pit 51.8
Aaron-Atl 51.0
Cepeda-StL 48.1
Allen-Phi 45.5
Santo-Chi 44.6

Clutch Hitting Index
Shannon-StL 152
Mazeroski-Pit 134
Cepeda-StL 132
Lanier-SF 130
Boyer-Atl 127

Runs Created
Clemente-Pit 126
Aaron-Atl 126
Santo-Chi 120
Cepeda-StL 118
Hart-SF 111

Total Average
Allen-Phi 1.054
Aaron-Atl ..... .965
Clemente-Pit ..... .959
Cepeda-StL ..... .950
McCovey-SF ..... .941

Stolen Bases
Brock-StL 52
Wills-Pit 29
Morgan-Hou 29
Pinson-Cin 26
Phillips-Chi 24

Stolen Base Average
Morgan-Hou 85.3
Wynn-Hou 80.0
Allen-Phi 80.0
Davis-LA 76.9
Pinson-Cin 76.5

Stolen Base Runs
Morgan-Hou 5.7
Brock-StL 4.8
Pinson-Cin 3.0
Allen-Phi 3.0
Wills-Pit 2.7

Fielding Runs
Santo-Chi 30.6
Lanier-SF 28.9
Wine-Phi 28.9
Fuentes-SF 24.5
Mazeroski-Pit 16.7

Total Player Rating
Santo-Chi 6.7
Aaron-Atl 6.1
Clemente-Pit 5.9
Cepeda-StL 4.6
Allen-Phi 3.9

Wins
McCormick-SF 22
Jenkins-Chi 20
Osteen-LA 17
Bunning-Phi 17

Win Percentage
Hughes-StL ..... .727
McCormick-SF ..... .688
Veale-Pit ..... .667
Jenkins-Chi ..... .606
Jarvis-Atl ..... .600

Games
Perranoski-LA 70
Abernathy-Cin 70
Willis-StL 65
Face-Pit 61

Complete Games
Jenkins-Chi 20
Seaver-NY 18
Perry-SF 18
Marichal-SF 18

Shutouts
Bunning-Phi 6
Osteen-LA 5
Nolan-Cin 5
McCormick-SF 5
L.Jackson-Phi 4

Saves
Abernathy-Cin 28
Linzy-SF 17
Face-Pit 17
Perranoski-LA 16
Hoerner-StL 15

Innings Pitched
Bunning-Phi 302.1
Perry-SF 293.0
Jenkins-Chi 289.1
Osteen-LA 288.1
Drysdale-LA 282.0

Fewest Hits/Game
Hughes-StL 6.64
Wilson-Hou 6.90
Perry-SF 7.10
Queen-Cin 7.13
Niekro-Atl 7.13

Fewest BB/Game
Pappas-Cin 1.57
Osteen-LA 1.62
Johnson-Atl 1.63
Niekro-Chi 1.70
L.Jackson-Phi 1.86

Strikeouts
Bunning-Phi 253
Jenkins-Chi 236
Perry-SF 230
Nolan-Cin 206
Cuellar-Hou 203

Strikeouts/Game
Nolan-Cin 8.18
Veale-Pit 7.94
Carlton-StL 7.83
Wilson-Hou 7.78
Gibson-StL 7.55

Ratio
Hughes-StL 8.78
Bunning-Phi 9.73
Queen-Cin 9.80
Perry-SF 9.80
Niekro-Atl 9.83

Earned Run Average
Niekro-Atl 1.87
Bunning-Phi 2.29
Short-Phi 2.39
Nolan-Cin 2.58
Perry-SF 2.61

Adjusted ERA
Niekro-Atl 178
Bunning-Phi 149
Nolan-Cin 145
Short-Phi 142
Queen-Cin 136

Opponents' Batting Avg.
Hughes-StL ..... .203
Wilson-Hou ..... .209
Perry-SF ..... .214
Queen-Cin ..... .215
Bunning-Phi ..... .217

Opponents' On Base Pct.
Hughes-StL ..... .252
Bunning-Phi ..... .273
Queen-Cin ..... .273
Perry-SF ..... .274
Jenkins-Chi ..... .277

Starter Runs
Bunning-Phi 36.4
Niekro-Atl 34.6
Perry-SF 24.9
Short-Phi 21.8
Nolan-Cin 20.0

Adjusted Starter Runs
Bunning-Phi 37.5
Niekro-Atl 33.4
Nolan-Cin 29.5
Jenkins-Chi 24.0
Short-Phi 22.5

Clutch Pitching Index
Ellis-Cin 123
Niekro-Atl 121
Seaver-NY 114
Marichal-SF 114
Short-Phi 114

Relief Runs
Abernathy-Cin 24.9
Linzy-SF 19.9
Nottebart-Cin 12.8
McBean-Pit 12.1
Farrell-Hou-Phi 11.9

Adjusted Relief Runs
Abernathy-Cin 29.3
Linzy-SF 19.0
Nottebart-Cin 16.1
Farrell-Hou-Phi 12.1
McBean-Pit 12.0

Relief Ranking
Abernathy-Cin 39.7
Linzy-SF 32.5
Hall-Phi 24.2
Farrell-Hou-Phi 20.0
Face-Pit 15.3

Total Pitcher Index
Bunning-Phi 4.2
Niekro-Atl 3.9
Abernathy-Cin 3.3
Nolan-Cin 3.1
Jenkins-Chi 3.0

Total Baseball Ranking
Santo-Chi 6.7
Aaron-Atl 6.1
Clemente-Pit 5.9
Cepeda-StL 4.6
Bunning-Phi 4.2

TEAM	G	W	L	PCT	GB	R	OR	AB	H	2B	3B	HR	BB	SO	AVG	OBP	SLG	PRO	PRO+	BR	/A	PF	CHI	RC	SB	CS	SBA	SBR
BOS	162	92	70	.568		722	614	5471	1394	216	39	158	522	1020	.255	.323	.395	.718	109	118	68	108	100	694	68	59	57	-16
MIN	164	91	71	.562	1	671	590	5458	1309	216	48	131	512	976	.240	.310	.369	.679	98	44	-4	108	104	625	55	37	39	-11
DET	163	91	71	.562	1	683	587	5410	1315	192	36	152	626	994	.243	.327	.376	.703	111	100	83	103	96	681	37	21	35	-14
CHI	162	89	73	.549	3	531	491	5383	1209	181	34	89	480	849	.225	.293	.320	.613	90	-79	-57	96	103	504	124	82	70	-16
CAL	161	84	77	.522	7.5	567	587	5307	1265	170	37	114	453	1021	.238	.302	.349	.651	101	-11	-11	96	99	553	40	36	34	-9
WAS	161	76	85	.472	15.5	550	637	5441	1211	168	25	115	472	1037	.223	.289	.326	.615	91	-80	-56	96	106	512	53	37	52	-19
BAL	161	76	85	.472	15.5	654	592	5456	1312	215	44	138	531	1002	.240	.313	.372	.685	109	54	58	99	99	639	54	37	42	-13
CLE	162	75	87	.463	17	559	613	5461	1282	213	35	131	413	984	.235	.295	.359	.654	98	-14	-19	101	96	563	53	65	61	-16
NY	163	72	90	.444	20	522	621	5443	1225	166	17	100	532	1043	.225	.298	.317	.615	91	-73	-50	96	98	522	63	37	38	-11
KC	161	62	99	.385	29.5	533	660	5349	1244	212	50	69	452	1019	.233	.297	.330	.627	94	-53	-34	97	100	539	132	59	61	-18
TOT	810					5992		54179	12766	1949	365	1197	4993	9945	.236	.305	.351	.656		679	470				59	-77		

TEAM	CG	SH	SV	IP	H	H/G	HR	BB	SO	RAT	ERA	ERA+	OAV	OOB	PR	/A	PF	CPI	FA	E	DP	FW	PW	BW	SBW	DIF
BOS	41	9	44	1459¹	1307	8.1	142	477	1010	11.3	3.36	104	.238	.305	-21	20	108	101	.977	142	142	-.6	2.2	7.5	-.9	2.8
MIN	58	18	24	1461	1336	8.2	115	396	1089	10.9	3.14	110	.242	.298	15	52	107	101	.978	132	123	.1	5.7	-.4	-.3	4.9
DET	46	17	40	1443²	1230	7.7	151	472	1038	10.8	3.32	98	.230	.297	-13	-8	101	97	.978	132	126	.0	-.9	9.2	-.7	2.3
CHI	36	24	39	1490¹	1197	7.2	87	465	927	10.4	2.45	127	.219	.287	128	108	96	106	.979	138	149	-.3	11.9	-6.3	-.9	3.6
CAL	19	14	46	1430¹	1246	7.8	118	525	892	11.4	3.19	98	.236	.310	6	-7	97	105	.982	111	135	1.3	-.8	1.2	-.1	1.9
WAS	24	14	39	1473¹	1334	8.1	113	495	878	11.4	3.38	93	.242	.308	-25	-36	98	98	.978	144	167	-.8	-4.0	-6.2	-1.2	7.7
BAL	29	17	36	1457¹	1218	7.5	116	566	1034	11.2	3.32	95	.227	.305	-14	-27	98	95	.980	124	144	.5	-3.0	6.4	-.6	-7.8
CLE	49	14	27	1477²	1258	7.7	120	559	1189	11.3	3.25	101	.231	.306	-2	3	101	98	.981	116	138	1.0	.3	-2.1	-.9	-4.4
NY	37	16	27	1480²	1375	8.4	110	480	898	11.5	3.24	97	.248	.312	-1	-18	97	106	.976	154	144	-1.3	-2.0	-5.5	-.3	.1
KC	26	10	34	1428	1265	8.0	125	558	990	11.7	3.68	87	.237	.314	-71	-78	99	94	.978	132	120	-.0	-8.6	-3.8	-1.1	-5.0
TOT	365	153	356	14601²		7.9				11.2	3.23		.236	.305					.979	1325	1388					

Runs
Yastrzemski-Bos .. 112
Killebrew-Min 105
Tovar-Min 98
Kaline-Det 94
McAuliffe-Det 92

Hits
Yastrzemski-Bos .. 189
Tovar-Min 173
Scott-Bos 171
Fregosi-Cal 171
B.Robinson-Bal ... 164

Doubles
Oliva-Min 34
Tovar-Min 32
Yastrzemski-Bos .. 31
D.Johnson-Bal 30
Campaneris-KC.... 29

Triples
Blair-Bal 12
Buford-Chi 9

Home Runs
Yastrzemski-Bos ... 44
Killebrew-Min 44
Howard-Was 36
F.Robinson-Bal 30

Total Bases
Yastrzemski-Bos ... 360
Killebrew-Min 305
F.Robinson-Bal ... 276
B.Robinson-Bal ... 265
Howard-Was 265

Runs Batted In
Yastrzemski-Bos .. 121
Killebrew-Min 113
F.Robinson-Bal ... 94
Howard-Was 89
Oliva-Min 83

Runs Produced
Yastrzemski-Bos .. 189
Killebrew-Min ... 174
F.Robinson-Bal ... 147
Kaline-Det 147
B.Robinson-Bal ... 143

Bases On Balls
Killebrew-Min 131
Mantle-NY 107
McAuliffe-Det..... 105
Yastrzemski-Bos .. 91
Kaline-Det 83

Batting Average
Yastrzemski-Bos .. .326
F.Robinson-Bal ... .311
Kaline-Det .... .308
Scott-Bos .... .303
Blair-Bal .... .293

On Base Percentage
Yastrzemski-Bos .. .421
Kaline-Det .... .415
Killebrew-Min .... .413
F.Robinson-Bal ... .408
Mantle-NY .... .394

Slugging Average
Yastrzemski-Bos .. .622
F.Robinson-Bal ... .576
Killebrew-Min .... .558
Kaline-Det .... .541
Howard-Was ..... .511

Production
Yastrzemski-Bos . 1.043
F.Robinson-Bal 984
Killebrew-Min 970
Kaline-Det 957
Mincher-Cal 855

Adjusted Production
Yastrzemski-Bos .. 189
F.Robinson-Bal ... 189
Kaline-Det 176
Killebrew-Min ... 170
Mincher-Cal 156

Batter Runs
Yastrzemski-Bos .. 76.4
Killebrew-Min ... 62.3
F.Robinson-Bal .. 53.3
Kaline-Det 48.4
Scott-Bos 33.8

Adjusted Batter Runs
Yastrzemski-Bos .. 71.0
Killebrew-Min ... 56.8
F.Robinson-Bal ... 53.8
Kaline-Det 46.9
Mincher-Cal 33.4

Clutch Hitting Index
Hershberger-KC .. 134
Pepitone-NY 124
D.Johnson-Bal ... 123
Blefary-Bal....... 121
Oliva-Min 119

Runs Created
Yastrzemski-Bos .. 155
Killebrew-Min 131
F.Robinson-Bal ... 113
Kaline-Det 104
Scott-Bos......... 97

Total Average
Yastrzemski-Bos . 1.134
Killebrew-Min ... 1.058
F.Robinson-Bal ... 1.029
Kaline-Det 1.009
Mantle-NY 874

Stolen Bases
Campaneris-KC.... 55
Buford-Chi 34
Agee-Chi 28
McCraw-Chi 24
Clarke-NY 21

Stolen Base Average
Valentine-Was 85.0
Clarke-NY 84.0
Aparicio-Bal 78.3
Campaneris-KC... 77.5
Agee-Chi 73.7

Stolen Base Runs
Campaneris-KC ... 6.9
Clarke-NY 3.9
Valentine-Was 3.3

Fielding Runs
B.Robinson-Bal ... 30.8
Blair-Bal 15.8
Cullen-Was....... 15.4
Clarke-NY 15.2
Oyler-Det 14.5

Total Player Rating
Yastrzemski-Bos .. 7.7
B.Robinson-Bal ... 5.5
Kaline-Det 5.4
F.Robinson-Bal ... 4.8
Killebrew-Min 4.1

Wins
Wilson-Det 22
Lonborg-Bos 22
Chance-Min 20
Horlen-Chi 19
McLain-Det 17

Win Percentage
Horlen-Chi 731
Lonborg-Bos 710
Wilson-Det 667
Sparma-Det 640
Peters-Chi 593

Games
Locker-Chi 77
Rojas-Cal 72
Kelso-Cal 69
Womack-NY 65
McMahon-Bos-Chi 63

Complete Games
Chance-Min 18
Lonborg-Bos 15
Hargan-Cle 15

Shutouts
McGlothlin-Cal...... 6
Lolich-Det 6
John-Chi 6
Horlen-Chi 6
Hargan-Cle 6

Saves
Rojas-Cal 27
Wyatt-Bos 20
Locker-Chi 20
Womack-NY 18
Worthington-Min ... 16

Innings Pitched
Chance-Min 283.2
Lonborg-Bos 273.1
Wilson-Det 264.0
Kaat-Min 263.1
Peters-Chi 260.0

Fewest Hits/Game
Peters-Chi 6.47
Boswell-Min 6.55
Horlen-Chi 6.56
Siebert-Cle 6.60
Downing-NY 7.05

Fewest BB/Game
Merritt-Min 1.19
Kaat-Min 1.44
Stange-Bos 1.59
Horlen-Chi 2.02
Peterson-NY 2.13

Strikeouts
Lonborg-Bos 246
McDowell-Cle 236
Chance-Min 220
Tiant-Cle 219
Peters-Chi 215

Strikeouts/Game
Tiant-Cle 9.22
McDowell-Cle 8.99
Boswell-Min 8.25
Lonborg-Bos 8.10
Phoebus-Bal 7.75

Ratio
Horlen-Chi 8.72
Merritt-Min 9.21
Siebert-Cle 9.52
John-Chi 9.84
Peters-Chi 10.00

Earned Run Average
Horlen-Chi 2.06
Peters-Chi 2.28
Siebert-Cle...... 2.38
John-Chi 2.47
Merritt-Min 2.53

Adjusted ERA
Horlen-Chi 151
Siebert-Cle 137
Merritt-Min 137
Peters-Chi 136
Chance-Min 127

Opponents' Batting Avg.
Peters-Chi 199
Boswell-Min 202
Siebert-Cle 202
Horlen-Chi 203
Downing-NY 217

Opponents' On Base Pct.
Horlen-Chi 253
Merritt-Min 262
Siebert-Cle 268
John-Chi 277
Peters-Chi 277

Starter Runs
Horlen-Chi 33.6
Peters-Chi 27.3
Merritt-Min 17.7
Siebert-Cle 17.5
Chance-Min 15.8

Adjusted Starter Runs
Horlen-Chi 30.0
Peters-Chi 23.7
Merritt-Min 23.5
Chance-Min 23.0
Siebert-Cle 18.3

Clutch Pitching Index
Clark-Cal 121
Stottlemyre-NY ... 117
Kaat-Min 108
Tiant-Cle 107
Stange-Bos 105

Relief Runs
Wilhelm-Chi 18.9
Drabowsky-Bal ... 17.2
Locker-Chi 15.7
McMahon-Bos-Chi 15.2
Baldwin-Was 11.6

Adjusted Relief Runs
Wilhelm-Chi 17.7
Drabowsky-Bal ... 16.4
McMahon-Bos-Chi 14.5
Locker-Chi 14.0
Baldwin-Was 11.1

Relief Ranking
Wilhelm-Chi 25.1
Drabowsky-Bal ... 23.2
Wyatt-Bos 19.4
Rojas-Cal 17.3
Locker-Chi 17.2

Total Pitcher Index
Horlen-Chi 3.9
Peters-Chi 3.7
Merritt-Min 2.6
Hargan-Cle 2.2
Chance-Min 2.2

Total Baseball Ranking
Yastrzemski-Bos .. 7.7
B.Robinson-Bal ... 5.5
Kaline-Det 5.4
F.Robinson-Bal 4.8
Killebrew-Min 4.1

TEAM	G	W	L	PCT	GB	R	OR	AB	H	2B	3B	HR	BB	SO	AVG	OBP	SLG	PRO	PRO+	BR	/A	PF	CHI	RC	SB	CS	SBA	SBR
STL	162	97	65	.599		583	472	5561	1383	227	48	73	378	897	.249	.300	.346	.646	102	2	9	99	104	581	110	45	48	-14
SF	163	88	74	.543	9	599	529	5441	1301	162	33	108	508	904	.239	.310	.341	.651	103	20	20	100	103	577	50	37	44	-14
CHI	163	84	78	.519	13	612	611	5458	1319	203	43	130	415	854	.242	.300	.366	.666	100	36	-1	107	104	593	41	30	41	-15
CIN	163	83	79	.512	14	690	673	5767	1573	281	36	106	379	938	.273	.322	.389	.711	113	130	93	106	98	688	59	55	57	-17
ATL	163	81	81	.500	16	514	549	5552	1399	179	31	80	414	782	.252	.308	.339	.647	100	9	7	100	90	564	83	44	44	-12
PIT	163	80	82	.494	17	583	532	5569	1404	180	44	80	422	953	.252	.309	.343	.652	104	19	27	99	100	580	130	59	57	-16
PHI	162	76	86	.469	21	543	615	5372	1253	178	30	100	462	1003	.233	.297	.333	.630	96	-23	-23	100	103	527	58	51	47	-12
LA	162	76	86	.469	21	470	509	5354	1234	202	36	67	439	980	.230	.291	.319	.610	97	-60	-18	92	97	501	57	43	48	-15
NY	163	73	89	.451	24	473	499	5503	1252	178	30	81	379	1203	.228	.283	.315	.598	85	-90	-92	101	102	486	72	45	48	-14
HOU	162	72	90	.444	25	510	588	5336	1233	205	28	66	479	988	.231	.300	.317	.617	93	-40	-28	98	100	505	44	51	52	-15
TOT	813					5577		54913	13351	1995	359	891	4275	9502	.243	.302	.341	.643							704	460	60	-64

TEAM	CG	SH	SV	IP	H	H/G	HR	BB	SO	RAT	ERA	ERA+	OAV	OOB	PR	/A	PF	CPI	FA	E	DP	FW	PW	BW	SBW	DIF
STL	63	30	32	1479¹	1282	7.8	82	375	971	10.3	2.49	116	.233	.286	81	66	97	105	.978	140	135	-.0	7.6	1.0	-.9	8.3
SF	77	20	16	1469	1302	8.0	86	344	942	10.2	2.71	109	.235	.283	45	38	99	96	.975	162	125	-1.3	4.4	2.3	-.9	2.5
CHI	46	12	32	1453²	1399	8.7	138	392	894	11.3	3.41	93	.253	.306	-68	-40	106	100	.981	119	149	1.2	-4.6	-.1	-1.0	7.5
CIN	24	16	38	1490¹	1399	8.4	114	573	963	12.2	3.56	89	.249	.324	-95	-66	106	100	.978	144	144	-.2	-7.6	10.7	-1.2	.4
ATL	44	16	29	1474²	1326	8.1	87	362	871	10.5	2.92	103	.241	.292	11	12	100	96	.980	125	139	.9	1.4	.8	-.6	-2.4
PIT	42	19	30	1487	1322	8.0	73	485	897	11.2	2.74	107	.239	.305	40	30	98	107	.979	139	162	.0	3.4	3.1	-1.1	-6.5
PHI	42	12	27	1448¹	1416	8.8	91	421	935	11.7	3.36	89	.257	.314	-60	-57	101	100	.980	127	163	.7	-6.5	-2.6	-.6	4.1
LA	38	23	31	1448²	1293	8.0	65	414	994	10.8	2.69	103	.240	.299	47	12	93	104	.977	144	144	-.3	1.4	-2.1	-1.0	-3.0
NY	45	25	32	1483¹	1250	7.6	87	430	1014	10.5	2.72	111	.229	.291	43	48	101	98	.979	133	142	.4	5.5	-10.6	-.9	-2.5
HOU	50	12	23	1446²	1362	8.5	68	479	1021	11.7	3.26	91	.248	.313	-44	-48	99	96	.975	156	129	-1.0	-5.5	-3.2	-1.0	1.7
TOT	471	185	290	14681		8.2				11.0	2.99		.243	.302					.978	1389	1432					

Runs
Beckert-Chi 98 · Rose-Cin 94 · Perez-Cin 93 · Brock-StL 92 · Williams-Chi 91

Hits
Rose-Cin 210 · Alou-Atl 210 · Beckert-Chi 189 · A.Johnson-Cin 188 · Flood-StL 186

Doubles
Brock-StL 46 · Rose-Cin 42 · Bench-Cin 40 · Staub-Hou 37 · Alou-Atl 37

Triples
Brock-StL 14 · Clemente-Pit 12 · Davis-LA 10 · Allen-Phi 9 · Williams-Chi 8

Home Runs
McCovey-SF 36 · Allen-Phi 33 · Banks-Chi 32 · Williams-Chi 30 · H.Aaron-Atl 29

Total Bases
Williams-Chi 321 · H.Aaron-Atl 302 · Rose-Cin 294 · Alou-Atl 290 · McCovey-SF 285

Runs Batted In
McCovey-SF 105 · Williams-Chi 98 · Santo-Chi 98 · Perez-Cin 92 · Allen-Phi 90

Runs Produced
Perez-Cin 167 · Williams-Chi 159 · Santo-Chi 158 · McCovey-SF 150 · Allen-Phi 144

Bases On Balls
Santo-Chi 96 · Wynn-Hou 90 · Hunt-SF 78 · Allen-Phi 74 · Staub-Hou 73

Batting Average
Rose-Cin .335 · Alou-Pit .332 · Alou-Atl .317 · A.Johnson-Cin .312 · Flood-StL .301

On Base Percentage
Rose-Cin .394 · McCovey-SF .383 · Wynn-Hou .378 · Mays-SF .376 · Staub-Hou .376

Slugging Average
McCovey-SF .545 · Allen-Phi .520 · Williams-Chi .500 · H.Aaron-Atl .498 · Mays-SF .488

Production
McCovey-SF .928 · Allen-Phi .876 · Mays-SF .864 · Rose-Cin .863 · H.Aaron-Atl .855

Adjusted Production
McCovey-SF 176 · Allen-Phi 160 · Mays-SF 158 · Wynn-Hou 158 · H.Aaron-Atl 154

Batter Runs
McCovey-SF 48.8 · Rose-Cin 44.5 · H.Aaron-Atl 39.0 · Wynn-Hou 38.4 · Allen-Phi 38.0

Adjusted Batter Runs
McCovey-SF 48.9 · Rose-Cin 40.5 · Wynn-Hou 39.6 · H.Aaron-Atl 38.8 · Allen-Phi 38.0

Clutch Hitting Index
Hundley-Chi 145 · Santo-Chi 136 · Clendenon-Pit 132 · Perez-Cin 127 · Swoboda-NY 126

Runs Created
Rose-Cin 113 · McCovey-SF 110 · Williams-Chi 107 · H.Aaron-Atl 104 · Alou-Atl 103

Total Average
McCovey-SF .953 · Allen-Phi .869 · Mays-SF .853 · H.Aaron-Atl .852 · Wynn-Hou .826

Stolen Bases
Brock-StL 62 · Wills-Pit 52 · Davis-LA 36 · H.Aaron-Atl 28 · Jones-NY 23

Stolen Base Average
H.Aaron-Atl 84.8 · Brock-StL 83.8 · Taylor-Phi 81.5 · Davis-LA 78.3

Stolen Base Runs
Brock-StL 11.4 · H.Aaron-Atl 5.4 · Davis-LA 4.8 · Taylor-Phi 3.6 · Wills-Pit 3.0

Fielding Runs
Mazeroski-Pit 25.7 · Alley-Pit 25.6 · Kessinger-Chi 17.9 · Santo-Chi 17.3 · Wynn-Hou 16.7

Total Player Rating
H.Aaron-Atl 5.5 · McCovey-SF 5.1 · Wynn-Hou 4.7 · Rose-Cin 4.3 · Santo-Chi 4.1

Wins
Marichal-SF 26 · Gibson-StL 22 · Jenkins-Chi 20

Win Percentage
Blass-Pit .750 · Marichal-SF .743 · Gibson-StL .710 · Briles-StL .633

Games
Abernathy-Cin 78 · Regan-LA-Chi 73 · Carroll-Atl-Cin 68 · Taylor-NY 58 · Linzy-SF 57

Complete Games
Marichal-SF 30 · Gibson-StL 28 · Jenkins-Chi 20 · Perry-SF 19 · Koosman-NY 17

Shutouts
Gibson-StL 13 · Drysdale-LA 8 · Koosman-NY 7 · Blass-Pit 7

Saves
Regan-LA-Chi 25 · Carroll-Atl-Cin 17 · Hoerner-StL 17 · Brewer-LA 14

Innings Pitched
Marichal-SF 326.0 · Jenkins-Chi 308.0 · Gibson-StL 304.2 · Perry-SF 291.0 · Seaver-NY 277.2

Fewest Hits/Game
Gibson-StL 5.85 · Bolin-SF 6.52 · Veale-Pit 6.86 · Jarvis-Atl 7.10 · Moose-Pit 7.14

Fewest BB/Game
Hands-Chi 1.25 · Marichal-SF 1.27 · Seaver-NY 1.56 · Pappas-Cin-Atl 1.57 · Niekro-Atl 1.58

Strikeouts
Gibson-StL 268 · Jenkins-Chi 260 · Singer-LA 227 · Marichal-SF 218 · Sadecki-SF 206

Strikeouts/Game
Singer-LA 7.97 · Gibson-StL 7.92 · Maloney-Cin 7.87 · Jenkins-Chi 7.60 · Wilson-Hou 7.55

Ratio
Gibson-StL 7.89 · Jarvis-Atl 8.93 · Bolin-SF 9.07 · Seaver-NY 9.08 · Hands-Chi 9.15

Earned Run Average
Gibson-StL 1.12 · Bolin-SF 1.99 · Veale-Pit 2.05 · Koosman-NY 2.08 · Blass-Pit 2.12

Adjusted ERA
Gibson-StL 258 · Bolin-SF 148 · Koosman-NY 145 · Veale-Pit 142 · Blass-Pit 138

Opponents' Batting Avg.
Gibson-StL .184 · Bolin-SF .200 · Veale-Pit .211 · Jarvis-Atl .214 · Moose-Pit .218

Opponents' On Base Pct.
Gibson-StL .233 · Jarvis-Atl .255 · Bolin-SF .258 · Seaver-NY .262 · Hands-Chi .264

Starter Runs
Gibson-StL 63.1 · Koosman-NY 26.5 · Veale-Pit 25.4 · Seaver-NY 24.1 · Drysdale-LA 22.3

Adjusted Starter Runs
Gibson-StL 60.0 · Koosman-NY 27.5 · Seaver-NY 25.2 · Veale-Pit 23.8 · Blass-Pit 19.6

Clutch Pitching Index
Blass-Pit 125 · Briles-StL 124 · Koosman-NY 123 · Lemaster-Hou 122 · Drysdale-LA 117

Relief Runs
Kline-Pit 16.4 · Regan-LA-Chi 10.7 · Linzy-SF 9.4 · Grant-LA 9.4 · Abernathy-Cin 7.7

Adjusted Relief Runs
Kline-Pit 15.6 · Regan-LA-Chi 13.0 · Abernathy-Cin 10.3 · Linzy-SF 9.0 · Carroll-Atl-Cin 7.2

Relief Ranking
Kline-Pit 23.4 · Regan-LA-Chi 20.1 · Linzy-SF 17.0 · Abernathy-Cin 13.9 · Upshaw-Atl 9.6

Total Pitcher Index
Gibson-StL 7.9 · Seaver-NY 3.3 · Koosman-NY 2.8 · Marichal-SF 2.8 · Drysdale-LA 2.3

Total Baseball Ranking
Gibson-StL 7.9 · H.Aaron-Atl 5.5 · McCovey-SF 5.1 · Wynn-Hou 4.7 · Rose-Cin 4.3

TEAM	G	W	L	PCT	GB	R	OR	AB	H	2B	3B	HR	BB	SO	AVG	OBP	SLG	PRO	PRO+	BR	/A	PF	CHI	RC	SB	CS	SBA	SBR
DET	164	103	59	.636		671	492	5490	1292	190	39	185	521	964	.235	.309	.385	.694	113	102	84	103	100	646	26	32	34	-10
BAL	162	91	71	.562	12	579	497	5275	1187	215	28	133	570	1019	.225	.306	.352	.658	105	41	40	100	97	585	78	32	48	-18
CLE	162	86	75	.534	16.5	516	504	5416	1266	210	36	75	427	858	.234	.294	.327	.621	96	-33	-24	99	100	525	115	61	56	-14
BOS	162	86	76	.531	17	614	611	5303	1253	207	17	125	523	974	.236	.294	.352	.668	102	62	25	107	99	590	76	62	53	-12
NY	164	83	79	.512	20	536	531	5310	1137	154	34	109	566	958	.214	.293	.318	.611	94	-45	-27	97	106	507	90	50	49	-13
OAK	163	82	80	.506	21	569	544	5406	1300	192	40	94	472	1022	.240	.306	.343	.649	108	19	45	95	99	580	147	61	55	-14
MIN	162	79	83	.488	24	562	546	5373	1274	207	41	105	445	966	.237	.301	.350	.651	99	20	-7	105	99	564	98	54	50	-13
CAL	162	67	95	.414	36	498	615	5331	1209	170	33	83	447	1080	.227	.293	.318	.611	95	-50	-29	96	100	498	62	50	50	-14
CHI	162	67	95	.414	36	463	527	5405	1233	169	33	71	397	840	.228	.286	.311	.597	86	-81	-86	101	99	480	90	50	50	-14
WAS	161	65	96	.404	37.5	524	665	5400	1208	160	37	124	454	960	.224	.289	.336	.625	99	-30	-12	97	101	518	29	19	28	-10
TOT	812					5532		53709	12359	1874	338	1104	4881	9641	.230	.299	.339	.639							811	471	63	-38

TEAM	CG	SH	SV	IP	H	H/G	HR	BB	SO	RAT	ERA	ERA+	OAV	OOB	PR	/A	PF	CPI	FA	E	DP	FW	PW	BW	SBW	DIF
DET	59	19	29	1489²	1180	7.1	129	486	1115	10.3	2.71	111	.217	.285	44	48	101	100	.983	105	133	2.0	5.5	9.6	-.7	5.5
BAL	53	16	31	1451¹	1111	6.9	101	502	1044	10.3	2.66	110	.212	.286	51	42	98	96	.981	120	131	1.0	4.8	4.6	-1.6	1.2
CLE	48	23	32	1464¹	1087	6.7	98	540	1157	10.3	2.66	111	.206	.286	52	49	99	93	.979	127	130	.6	5.6	-2.8	-1.2	3.2
BOS	55	17	31	1447	1303	8.1	115	523	972	11.7	3.33	95	.240	.313	-57	-28	106	100	.979	128	147	.6	-3.2	2.9	-.9	5.7
NY	45	14	27	1467¹	1308	8.0	99	424	831	10.8	2.79	104	.240	.298	30	18	97	108	.979	139	142	.0	2.1	-3.1	-1.0	4.1
OAK	45	18	29	1455²	1220	7.5	124	505	997	10.9	2.94	96	.226	.297	5	-20	95	101	.977	145	136	-.4	-2.3	5.2	-1.2	-.3
MIN	46	14	29	1433¹	1224	7.7	92	414	996	10.5	2.89	107	.229	.289	13	30	104	94	.973	170	117	-2.0	3.4	-.8	-1.0	-1.6
CAL	29	11	31	1437	1234	7.7	131	519	869	11.2	3.43	85	.233	.305	-72	-83	98	94	.977	140	156	-.2	-9.5	-3.3	-1.2	.2
CHI	20	11	40	1468	1290	7.9	97	451	834	11.1	2.75	110	.236	.302	37	45	102	110	.977	151	152	-.8	5.2	-9.9	-1.2	-7.3
WAS	26	11	28	1439²	1402	8.8	118	517	826	12.3	3.64	80	.258	.327	-106	-116	98	104	.976	148	144	-.7	-13.3	-1.4	-.7	.6
TOT	426	154	307	14553¹		7.6				10.9	2.98		.230	.299					.978	1373	1388					

Runs
McAuliffe-Det 95
Yastrzemski-Bos 90
White-NY 89
Tovar-Min 89
Stanley-Det 88

Hits
Campaneris-Oak 177
Tovar-Min 167
F.Howard-Was 164
Aparicio-Chi 164
Yastrzemski-Bos 162

Doubles
Smith-Bos 37
B.Robinson-Bal 36
Yastrzemski-Bos 32
Tovar-Min 31

Triples
Fregosi-Cal 13
McCraw-Chi 12
Stroud-Was 10
McAuliffe-Det 10
Campaneris-Oak 9

Home Runs
F.Howard-Was 44
Horton-Det 36
Harrelson-Bos 35
Jackson-Oak 29

Total Bases
F.Howard-Was 330
Horton-Det 278
Harrelson-Bos 277
Yastrzemski-Bos 267
Northrup-Det 259

Runs Batted In
Harrelson-Bos 109
F.Howard-Was 106
Northrup-Det 90
Powell-Bal 85
Horton-Det 85

Runs Produced
Harrelson-Bos 153
Northrup-Det 145
Yastrzemski-Bos 141
F.Howard-Was 141
Stanley-Det 137

Bases On Balls
Yastrzemski-Bos 119
Mantle-NY 106
Foy-Bos 84
McAuliffe-Det 82
Andrews-Bos 81

Batting Average
Yastrzemski-Bos .301
Cater-Oak .290
Oliva-Min .289
Horton-Det .285
Uhlaender-Min .283

On Base Percentage
Yastrzemski-Bos .429
F.Robinson-Bal .391
Mantle-NY .387
Monday-Oak .373
Andrews-Bos .369

Slugging Average
F.Howard-Was .552
Horton-Det .543
Harrelson-Bos .518
Yastrzemski-Bos .495
Oliva-Min .477

Production
Yastrzemski-Bos .924
Horton-Det .900
F.Howard-Was .892
Harrelson-Bos .877
Oliva-Min .837

Adjusted Production
F.Howard-Was 172
Yastrzemski-Bos 168
Horton-Det 165
Harrelson-Bos 153
F.Robinson-Bal 153

Batter Runs
Yastrzemski-Bos 57.5
F.Howard-Was 45.1
Horton-Det 41.1
Harrelson-Bos 40.2
Freehan-Det 32.7

Adjusted Batter Runs
Yastrzemski-Bos 53.5
F.Howard-Was 47.0
Horton-Det 39.5
Harrelson-Bos 36.4
Freehan-Det 30.9

Clutch Hitting Index
Foy-Bos 137
Powell-Bal 132
Harrelson-Bos 129
Northrup-Det 127
Bando-Oak 126

Runs Created
Yastrzemski-Bos 121
F.Howard-Was 110
Horton-Det 95
Harrelson-Bos 94
Freehan-Det 94

Total Average
Yastrzemski-Bos 1.000
F.Howard-Was .872
Horton-Det .867
F.Robinson-Bal .865
Harrelson-Bos .835

Stolen Bases
Campaneris-Oak 62
Cardenal-Cle 40
Tovar-Min 35
Buford-Bal 27
Foy-Bos 26

Stolen Base Average
McCraw-Chi 80.0
Nelson-Cle 76.7
Foy-Bos 76.5
Clarke-NY 74.1
Campaneris-Oak 73.8

Stolen Base Runs
Campaneris-Oak 5.4
McCraw-Chi 3.0
Foy-Bos 3.0
Tovar-Min 2.7
Nelson-Cle 2.7

Fielding Runs
Clarke-NY 29.5
Aparicio-Chi 24.7
B.Robinson-Bal 16.6
Knoop-Cal 16.0
Unser-Was 13.3

Total Player Rating
Yastrzemski-Bos 6.6
Freehan-Det 4.5
F.Howard-Was 4.4
B.Robinson-Bal 3.6
Harrelson-Bos 3.6

Wins
McLain-Det 31
McNally-Bal 22
Tiant-Cle 21
Stottlemyre-NY 21
Hardin-Bal 18

Win Percentage
McLain-Det .838
Culp-Bos .727
Tiant-Cle .700
Ellsworth-Bos .696
McNally-Bal .688

Games
Wood-Chi 88
Wilhelm-Chi 72
Locker-Chi 70
Perranoski-Min 66

Complete Games
McLain-Det 28
Tiant-Cle 19
Stottlemyre-NY 19
McNally-Bal 18
Hardin-Bal 16

Shutouts
Tiant-Cle 9

Saves
Worthington-Min 18
Wood-Chi 16
Higgins-Was 13

Innings Pitched
McLain-Det 336.0
Chance-Min 292.0
Stottlemyre-NY 278.2
McNally-Bal 273.0
McDowell-Cle 269.0

Fewest Hits/Game
Tiant-Cle 5.30
McNally-Bal 5.77
McDowell-Cle 6.06
Siebert-Cle 6.33
McLain-Det 6.46

Fewest BB/Game
Peterson-NY 1.23
McLain-Det 1.69
Ellsworth-Bos 1.70
Kaat-Min 1.73
McNally-Bal 1.81

Strikeouts
McDowell-Cle 283
McLain-Det 280
Tiant-Cle 264
Chance-Min 234
McNally-Bal 202

Strikeouts/Game
McDowell-Cle 9.47
Tiant-Cle 9.20
Lolich-Det 8.06
Culp-Bos 7.90
McLain-Det 7.50

Ratio
McNally-Bal 7.91
Tiant-Cle 7.98
McLain-Det 8.30
Chance-Min 9.15
Peterson-NY 9.32

Earned Run Average
Tiant-Cle 1.60
McDowell-Cle 1.81
McNally-Bal 1.95
McLain-Det 1.96
John-Chi 1.98

Adjusted ERA
Tiant-Cle 185
McDowell-Cle 164
McLain-Det 154
John-Chi 153
McNally-Bal 150

Opponents' Batting Avg.
Tiant-Cle .168
McNally-Bal .182
McDowell-Cle .189
Siebert-Cle .198
McLain-Det .200

Opponents' On Base Pct.
Tiant-Cle .233
McNally-Bal .234
McLain-Det .243
Chance-Min .261
Nash-Oak .270

Starter Runs
McLain-Det 39.5
Tiant-Cle 38.2
McDowell-Cle 35.0
McNally-Bal 31.4
Bahnsen-NY 27.5

Adjusted Starter Runs
McLain-Det 39.3
Tiant-Cle 38.9
McDowell-Cle 34.4
McNally-Bal 29.7
Bahnsen-NY 25.2

Clutch Pitching Index
Horlen-Chi 133
John-Chi 119
Fisher-Chi 116
McDowell-Cle 113
Bahnsen-NY 111

Relief Runs
Wood-Chi 19.6
Wilhelm-Chi 13.0
Romo-Cle 12.6
McMahon-Chi-Det 9.0
Drabowsky-Bal 7.3

Adjusted Relief Runs
Wood-Chi 20.5
Wilhelm-Chi 13.5
Romo-Cle 12.4
McMahon-Chi-Det 9.4
Locker-Chi 7.4

Relief Ranking
Wood-Chi 33.6
Romo-Cle 14.7
Wilhelm-Chi 14.3
Drabowsky-Bal 9.9
Locker-Chi 8.5

Total Pitcher Index
McLain-Det 4.9
McDowell-Cle 4.0
Tiant-Cle 3.8
McNally-Bal 3.7
John-Chi 3.5

Total Baseball Ranking
Yastrzemski-Bos 6.6
McLain-Det 4.9
Freehan-Det 4.5
F.Howard-Was 4.4
McDowell-Cle 4.0

TEAM	G	W	L	PCT	GB	R	OR	AB	H	2B	3B	HR	BB	SO	AVG	OBP	SLG	PRO	PRO+	BR	/A	PF	CHI	RC	SB	CS	SBA	SBR
EAST																												
NY	162	100	62	.617		632	541	5427	1311	184	41	109	527	1089	.242	.313	.351	.664	91	-51	-64	102	**105**	601	66	43	45	-13
CHI	163	92	70	.568	8	720	611	5530	1400	215	40	142	559	928	.253	.326	.384	.710	93	37	-48	113	102	693	30	32	42	-15
PIT	162	88	74	.543	12	725	652	5626	1557	220	52	119	454	944	**.277**	.336	.398	.734	**115**	84	97	98	97	742	74	34	45	-16
STL	162	87	75	.537	13	595	**540**	5536	1403	**228**	44	90	503	876	.253	.318	.359	.677	95	-24	-25	100	94	632	87	49	52	-16
PHI	162	63	99	.389	37	645	745	5408	1304	227	35	137	549	1130	.241	.314	.372	.686	101	-11	6	97	101	629	73	49	49	-14
MON	162	52	110	.321	48	582	791	5419	1300	202	33	125	529	962	.240	.312	.359	.671	93	-39	-40	100	96	596	52	52	51	-14
WEST																												
ATL	162	93	69	.574		691	631	5460	1411	195	22	141	485	**665**	.258	.323	.380	.703	103	20	18	100	103	655	59	48	48	-13
SF	162	90	72	.556	3	713	636	5474	1325	187	28	136	**711**	1054	.242	.336	.361	.697	103	32	44	98	100	690	71	32	40	-13
CIN	163	89	73	.549	4	798	768	5634	**1558**	224	42	171	474	1042	**.277**	.338	**.422**	**.760**	114	**133**	**98**	105	99	**791**	79	56	**58**	-17
LA	162	85	77	.525	8	645	561	5532	1405	185	**52**	97	484	823	.254	.316	.359	.675	103	-30	16	93	103	626	80	51	47	**-12**
HOU	162	81	81	.500	12	676	668	5348	1284	208	40	104	699	972	.240	.332	.352	.684	101	7	20	98	101	649	**101**	58	55	-15
SD	162	52	110	.321	41	468	746	5357	1203	180	42	99	423	1143	.225	.286	.329	.615	81	-152	-126	96	98	491	45	44	44	**-12**
TOT	973					7890		65751	16461	2455	471	1470	6397	11628	.250	.321	.369	.690							817	548	60	-83

TEAM	CG	SH	SV	IP	H	H/G	HR	BB	SO	RAT	ERA	ERA+	OAV	OOB	PR	/A	PF	CPI	FA	E	DP	FW	PW	BW	SBW	DIF
EAST																										
NY	51	**28**	35	1468¹	**1217**	7.5	119	517	1012	**10.8**	2.99	122	**.226**	.298	99	109	102	99	.980	122	146	1.4	11.4	-6.7	-.6	13.5
CHI	58	22	27	1454¹	1366	8.5	118	475	1017	11.6	3.34	120	.248	.311	40	110	112	101	.979	136	149	.6	**11.5**	-5.0	-.8	4.7
PIT	39	9	33	1445²	1348	8.4	**96**	553	1124	12.1	3.61	97	.248	.321	-2	-20	97	95	.975	155	169	-.5	-2.1	10.2	-.9	.3
STL	63	12	26	1460¹	1289	7.9	99	511	1004	11.3	**2.94**	121	.237	.306	**105**	102	99	**105**	.978	138	144	.5	10.7	-2.6	-.9	-1.6
PHI	47	14	21	1434	1494	9.4	134	570	921	13.2	4.14	86	.269	.342	-87	-95	99	102	.978	137	157	.5	-10.0	.6	-.7	-8.5
MON	26	8	21	1426	1429	9.0	145	702	973	13.8	4.33	85	.263	.352	-116	-103	102	102	.971	184	**179**	-2.1	-10.8	-4.2	-.7	-11.1
WEST																										
ATL	38	7	42	1445	1334	8.3	144	438	893	11.2	3.53	102	.244	.303	10	12	100	95	**.981**	**115**	114	**1.8**	1.3	1.9	-.6	7.7
SF	71	15	17	1473²	1381	8.4	120	461	906	11.5	3.26	108	.249	.309	55	39	97	102	.974	169	155	-1.3	4.1	4.6	-.6	2.2
CIN	23	11	**44**	1465	1478	9.1	149	611	818	13.2	4.11	92	.261	.339	-84	-56	105	102	.974	167	158	-1.1	-5.9	**10.3**	-1.1	5.8
LA	47	20	31	1457	1324	8.2	122	**420**	975	11.0	3.08	108	.242	.300	82	39	93	102	.980	126	130	1.2	4.1	1.7	**-.5**	-2.4
HOU	52	11	34	1435²	1347	8.4	111	547	**1221**	12.1	3.60	98	.246	.319	0	-9	99	96	.975	153	136	-.4	-.9	2.1	-.8	.0
SD	16	9	25	1422¹	1454	9.2	113	592	764	13.2	4.24	83	.266	.342	-102	-111	98	97	.975	156	140	-.5	-11.7	-13.2	-.5	-3.1
TOT	531	166	356	17387¹		8.5				12.1	3.59		.250	.321					.977	1758	1777					

Runs		Hits		Doubles		Triples		Home Runs		Total Bases	
Rose-Cin	120	Alou-Pit	231	Alou-Pit	41	Clemente-Pit	12	McCovey-SF	45	H.Aaron-Atl	332
Bonds-SF	120	Rose-Cin	218	Kessinger-Chi	38	Rose-Cin	11	H.Aaron-Atl	44	Perez-Cin	331
Wynn-Hou	113	Brock-StL	195	Williams-Chi	33	Williams-Chi	10	May-Cin	38	McCovey-SF	322
Kessinger-Chi	109	Tolan-Cin	194	Rose-Cin	33	Tolan-Cin	10	Perez-Cin	37	Rose-Cin	321
Alou-Pit	105	Williams-Chi	188	Brock-StL	33	Brock-StL	10	Wynn-Hou	33	May-Cin	321

Runs Batted In		Runs Produced		Bases On Balls		Batting Average		On Base Percentage		Slugging Average	
McCovey-SF	126	Santo-Chi	191	Wynn-Hou	148	Rose-Cin	.348	McCovey-SF	.458	McCovey-SF	.656
Santo-Chi	123	Perez-Cin	188	McCovey-SF	121	Clemente-Pit	.345	Wynn-Hou	.440	H.Aaron-Atl	.607
Perez-Cin	122	Rose-Cin	186	Staub-Mon	110	Jones-NY	.340	Rose-Cin	.432	Allen-Phi	.573
May-Cin	110	McCovey-SF	182	Morgan-Hou	110	Alou-Pit	.331	Staub-Mon	.427	Stargell-Pit	.556
Banks-Chi	106	Bonds-SF	178	Santo-Chi	96	McCovey-SF	.320	Jones-NY	.424	Clemente-Pit	.544

Production		Adjusted Production		Batter Runs		Adjusted Batter Runs		Clutch Hitting Index		Runs Created	
McCovey-SF	1.114	McCovey-SF	212	McCovey-SF	76.1	McCovey-SF	77.3	Menke-Hou	157	McCovey-SF	151
H.Aaron-Atl	1.005	H.Aaron-Atl	177	H.Aaron-Atl	56.3	H.Aaron-Atl	56.1	Rader-Hou	143	Rose-Cin	138
Clemente-Pit	.958	Clemente-Pit	170	Rose-Cin	56.0	Staub-Mon	52.4	Santo-Chi	143	Staub-Mon	128
Staub-Mon	.953	Wynn-Hou	168	Staub-Mon	52.6	Wynn-Hou	52.4	Banks-Chi	143	H.Aaron-Atl	128
Allen-Phi	.952	Allen-Phi	168	Wynn-Hou	51.0	Rose-Cin	52.0	Pinson-StL	135	Wynn-Hou	126

Total Average		Stolen Bases		Stolen Base Average		Stolen Base Runs		Fielding Runs		Total Player Rating	
McCovey-SF	1.296	Brock-StL	53	Bonds-SF	91.8	Bonds-SF	11.1	Lanier-SF	28.6	McCovey-SF	6.1
Wynn-Hou	1.118	Morgan-Hou	49	Brock-StL	79.1	Brock-StL	7.5	Kessinger-Chi	24.6	Wynn-Hou	5.4
H.Aaron-Atl	1.032	Bonds-SF	45	Morgan-Hou	77.8	Morgan-Hou	6.3	Maxvill-StL	21.1	H.Aaron-Atl	5.1
Staub-Mon	1.018	Wills-Mon-LA	40	Wynn-Hou	76.7	Wynn-Hou	2.7	Grote-NY	17.8	Staub-Mon	4.9
Allen-Phi	.988	Tolan-Cin	26	Alou-Pit	73.3	Millan-Atl	2.4	Money-Phi	17.3	Rose-Cin	4.8

Wins		Win Percentage		Games		Complete Games		Shutouts		Saves	
Seaver-NY	25	Seaver-NY	.781	Granger-Cin	90	Gibson-StL	28	Marichal-SF	8	Gladding-Hou	29
Niekro-Atl	23	Marichal-SF	.656	McGinn-Mon	74	Marichal-SF	27	Osteen-LA	7	Upshaw-Atl	27
Marichal-SF	21	Merritt-Cin	.654	Regan-Chi	71	Perry-SF	26	Jenkins-Chi	7	Granger-Cin	27
Jenkins-Chi	21	Koosman-NY	.654	Carroll-Cin	71	Jenkins-Chi	23	Koosman-NY	6	Brewer-LA	20
		Reed-Atl	.643	Reberger-SD	67	Niekro-Atl	21	Holtzman-Chi	6	Regan-Chi	17

Innings Pitched		Fewest Hits/Game		Fewest BB/Game		Strikeouts		Strikeouts/Game		Ratio	
Perry-SF	325.1	Seaver-NY	6.65	Marichal-SF	1.62	Jenkins-Chi	273	Griffin-Hou	9.56	Marichal-SF	9.13
Osteen-LA	321.0	Maloney-Cin	6.80	Niekro-Atl	1.80	Gibson-StL	269	Wilson-Hou	9.40	Dierker-Hou	9.23
Singer-LA	315.2	Singer-LA	6.96	Jenkins-Chi	2.05	Singer-LA	247	Moose-Pit	8.74	Singer-LA	9.35
Gibson-StL	314.0	Koosman-NY	6.98	Niekro-Chi-SD	2.07	Wilson-Hou	235	Selma-SD-Chi	8.54	Niekro-Atl	9.40
Jenkins-Chi	311.1	Carlton-StL	7.05	Osteen-LA	2.07	Perry-SF	233	Veale-Pit	8.49	Seaver-NY	9.58

Earned Run Average		Adjusted ERA		Opponents' Batting Avg.		Opponents' On Base Pct.		Starter Runs		Adjusted Starter Runs	
Marichal-SF	2.10	Marichal-SF	166	Seaver-NY	.207	Dierker-Hou	.262	Marichal-SF	49.6	Hands-Chi	51.1
Carlton-StL	2.17	Seaver-NY	166	Maloney-Cin	.208	Marichal-SF	.263	Gibson-StL	49.3	Gibson-StL	48.6
Gibson-StL	2.18	Carlton-StL	165	Singer-LA	.210	Singer-LA	.263	Singer-LA	44.0	Marichal-SF	46.5
Seaver-NY	2.21	Gibson-StL	164	Dierker-Hou	.214	Niekro-Atl	.264	Dierker-Hou	42.9	Seaver-NY	44.0
Koosman-NY	2.28	Hands-Chi	162	Carlton-StL	.216	Seaver-NY	.273	Seaver-NY	42.1	Dierker-Hou	41.1

Clutch Pitching Index		Relief Runs		Adjusted Relief Runs		Relief Ranking		Total Pitcher Index		Total Baseball Ranking	
Carlton-StL	122	McGraw-NY	15.1	McGraw-NY	15.7	McGraw-NY	21.2	Gibson-StL	6.2	Gibson-StL	6.2
Perry-SF	117	Granger-Cin	12.8	Granger-Cin	15.5	Granger-Cin	20.9	Marichal-SF	5.6	McCovey-SF	6.1
Veale-Pit	114	Brewer-LA	10.3	DiLauro-NY	8.8	Taylor-NY	15.1	Hands-Chi	5.5	Marichal-SF	5.6
Robertson-Mon	113	Gibbon-SF-Pit	9.5	Gibbon-SF-Pit	8.7	Brewer-LA	14.0	Seaver-NY	5.3	Hands-Chi	5.5
Hands-Chi	111	DiLauro-NY	8.4	Upshaw-Atl	8.2	Gibbon-SF-Pit	13.9	Carlton-StL	4.5	Wynn-Hou	5.4

TEAM	G	W	L	PCT	GB	R	OR	AB	H	2B	3B	HR	BB	SO	AVG	OBP	SLG	PRO	PRO+	BR	/A	PF	CHI	RC	SB	CS	SBA	SBR
EAST																												
BAL	162	109	53	.673		779	**517**	5518	1465	234	29	175	634	**806**	.265	**.346**	.414	**.760**	117	135	**128**	101	96	791	82	45	62	-23
DET	162	90	72	.556	19	701	601	5441	1316	188	29	182	578	922	.242	.318	.387	.705	98	17	-11	104	104	674	35	28	31	**-9**
BOS	162	87	75	.537	22	743	736	5494	1381	234	37	**197**	**658**	923	.251	.335	**.415**	.750	110	110	74	105	95	761	41	47	60	-21
WAS	162	86	76	.531	23	694	644	5447	1365	171	40	148	630	900	.251	.332	.378	.710	110	38	72	95	99	675	52	40	40	-11
NY	162	80	81	.497	28.5	562	587	5308	1247	210	**44**	94	565	840	.235	.310	.344	.654	92	-73	-49	96	99	572	119	74	65	-16
CLE	161	62	99	.385	46.5	573	717	5365	1272	173	24	119	535	906	.237	.309	.345	.654	86	-76	-97	103	101	568	85	37	36	-10
WEST																												
MIN	162	97	65	.599		**790**	618	5677	**1520**	**246**	32	163	599	906	**.268**	.342	.408	.750	113	118	103	102	98	**794**	115	70	66	-18
OAK	162	88	74	.543	9	740	678	5614	1400	210	28	148	617	953	.249	.330	.376	.706	108	32	61	96	103	712	100	39	37	-10
CAL	163	71	91	.438	26	528	652	5316	1221	151	29	88	516	929	.230	.302	.319	.621	84	-136	-103	95	**105**	518	54	38	51	-18
KC	163	69	93	.426	28	586	688	5462	1311	179	32	98	522	901	.240	.311	.338	.649	87	-83	-86	101	102	577	129	70	58	-13
CHI	162	68	94	.420	29	625	723	5450	1346	210	27	112	552	844	.247	.322	.357	.679	91	-24	-56	105	98	638	54	22	28	**-9**
SEA	163	64	98	.395	33	639	799	5444	1276	179	27	125	626	1015	.234	.317	.346	.663	93	-52	-40	98	104	622	**167**	59	**68**	-22
TOT	973					7960		65536	16120	2385	378	1649	7032	10845	.246	.323	.369	.693							1033	570	64	-31

TEAM	CG	SH	SV	IP	H	H/G	HR	BB	SO	RAT	ERA	ERA+	OAV	OOB	PR	/A	PF	CPI	FA	E	DP	FW	PW	BW	SBW	DIF
EAST																										
BAL	50	20	36	1473²	**1194**	7.3	117	498	897	10.5	**2.83**	126	**.222**	**.291**	130	120	98	97	**.984**	101	145	2.2	12.6	13.4	-2.1	1.9
DET	**55**	20	28	1455¹	1250	7.7	128	586	**1032**	11.6	3.31	113	.232	.311	49	67	103	98	.979	130	130	.5	7.0	-1.2	-.7	3.3
BOS	30	7	41	1466²	1423	8.7	155	685	935	13.2	3.92	97	.256	.342	-48	-19	105	106	.975	157	**178**	-1.0	-2.0	7.8	-1.9	3.2
WAS	28	10	41	1447¹	1310	8.1	135	656	835	12.4	3.49	99	.243	.330	21	-3	96	**107**	.978	140	159	-.0	-.3	7.5	-.9	-1.3
NY	53	13	20	1440²	1258	7.9	118	522	801	11.2	3.23	108	.235	.306	62	39	96	97	.979	131	158	.5	4.1	-5.1	-1.4	1.5
CLE	35	8	22	1437	1330	8.3	134	681	1000	12.9	3.94	96	.248	.338	-50	-27	104	99	.976	145	153	-.4	-2.8	-10.2	-.8	-4.4
WEST																										
MIN	41	8	**43**	1497²	1388	8.3	119	524	906	11.7	3.24	113	.246	.314	63	68	101	104	.977	150	177	-.6	7.1	10.8	-1.6	.3
OAK	42	14	36	1480²	1356	8.2	163	586	887	12.0	3.71	93	.245	.321	-15	-45	95	100	.979	136	162	.2	-4.7	6.4	-.8	5.9
CAL	25	9	39	1438¹	1294	8.1	126	517	885	11.7	3.54	98	.241	.314	12	-9	96	96	.978	136	164	.2	-.9	-10.8	-1.6	3.1
KC	42	10	25	1464²	1357	8.3	136	560	894	11.9	3.72	99	.246	.318	-15	-4	102	95	.975	157	114	-1.0	-.4	-9.0	-1.1	-.5
CHI	29	9	25	1437²	1470	9.2	146	564	810	12.9	4.21	92	.267	.339	-93	-55	107	99	.981	122	163	1.0	-5.8	-5.9	-.7	-1.7
SEA	21	6	33	1463²	1490	9.2	172	653	963	13.5	4.35	84	.263	.345	-117	-116	100	101	.974	167	149	-1.5	-12.2	-4.2	-2.0	2.9
TOT	451	134	389	17503¹		8.3				12.1	3.62		.246	.323					.978	1672	1852					

Runs		Hits		Doubles		Triples		Home Runs		Total Bases	
Jackson-Oak	123	Oliva-Min	197	Oliva-Min	39	Unser-Was	8	Killebrew-Min	49	Howard-Was	340
F.Robinson-Bal	111	Clarke-NY	183	Jackson-Oak	36	Smith-Bos	7	Howard-Was	48	Jackson-Oak	334
Howard-Was	111	Blair-Bal	178	Johnson-Bal	34	Clarke-NY	7	Jackson-Oak	47	Killebrew-Min	324
Killebrew-Min	106	Howard-Was	175	Petrocelli-Bos	32			Yastrzemski-Bos	40	Oliva-Min	316
Bando-Oak	106	Horton-Cle	174	Blair-Bal	32			Petrocelli-Bos	40	Petrocelli-Bos	315

Runs Batted In		Runs Produced		Bases On Balls		Batting Average		On Base Percentage		Slugging Average	
Killebrew-Min	140	Killebrew-Min	197	Killebrew-Min	145	Carew-Min	.332	Killebrew-Min	.430	Jackson-Oak	.608
Powell-Bal	121	Jackson-Oak	194	Jackson-Oak	114	Smith-Bos	.309	F.Robinson-Bal	.417	Petrocelli-Bos	.589
Jackson-Oak	118	Bando-Oak	188	Bando-Oak	111	Oliva-Min	.309	Jackson-Oak	.410	Killebrew-Min	.584
Bando-Oak	113	F.Robinson-Bal	179	Howard-Was	102	F.Robinson-Bal	.308	Petrocelli-Bos	.407	Howard-Was	.574
				Yastrzemski-Bos	101	Powell-Bal	.304	Howard-Was	.403	Powell-Bal	.559

Production		Adjusted Production		Batter Runs		Adjusted Batter Runs		Clutch Hitting Index		Runs Created	
Jackson-Oak	1.019	Jackson-Oak	190	Killebrew-Min	65.6	Jackson-Oak	65.1	White-NY	148	Killebrew-Min	146
Killebrew-Min	1.014	Howard-Was	180	Jackson-Oak	62.0	Killebrew-Min	64.0	Foy-KC	134	Jackson-Oak	144
Petrocelli-Bos	.996	Killebrew-Min	177	Howard-Was	56.8	Howard-Was	60.7	Reichardt-Cal	130	Howard-Was	132
Howard-Was	.978	Petrocelli-Bos	167	Petrocelli-Bos	54.8	Petrocelli-Bos	51.1	Cater-Oak	129	Petrocelli-Bos	129
F.Robinson-Bal	.957	F.Robinson-Bal	164	F.Robinson-Bal	49.9	F.Robinson-Bal	49.3	Killebrew-Min	126	F.Robinson-Bal	126

Total Average		Stolen Bases		Stolen Base Average		Stolen Base Runs		Fielding Runs		Total Player Rating	
Killebrew-Min	1.143	Harper-Sea	73	Campaneris-Oak	88.6	Campaneris-Oak	13.8	Cardenas-Min	33.5	Jackson-Oak	6.6
Jackson-Oak	1.139	Campaneris-Oak	62	Alomar-Chi-Cal	87.0	Harper-Sea	11.1	Aparicio-Chi	29.3	Petrocelli-Bos	6.2
Petrocelli-Bos	1.048	Tovar-Min	45	Cardenal-Cle	85.7	Cardenal-Cle	7.2	Knoop-Cal-Chi	24.5	Cardenas-Min	4.6
F.Robinson-Bal	1.026	Kelly-KC	40	Aparicio-Chi	85.7	Tovar-Min	6.3	Quilici-Min	24.2	F.Robinson-Bal	4.2
Howard-Was	1.004	Foy-KC	37	Davis-Sea	82.6	Aparicio-Chi	4.8	B.Robinson-Bal	19.2	Killebrew-Min	4.1

Wins		Win Percentage		Games		Complete Games		Shutouts		Saves	
McLain-Det	24	Palmer-Bal	.800	Wood-Chi	76	Stottlemyre-NY	24	McLain-Det	9	Perranoski-Min	31
Cuellar-Bal	23	Perry-Min	.769	Perranoski-Min	75	McLain-Det	23	Palmer-Bal	6	K.Tatum-Cal	22
		McNally-Bal	.741	Lyle-Bos	71	McDowell-Cle	18	Cuellar-Bal	5	Lyle-Bos	17
		McLain-Det	.727	Locker-Chi-Sea	68	Cuellar-Bal	18			Watt-Bal	16
		Odom-Oak	.714	Segui-Sea	66	Peterson-NY	16			Higgins-Was	16

Innings Pitched		Fewest Hits/Game		Fewest BB/Game		Strikeouts		Strikeouts/Game		Ratio	
McLain-Det	325.0	Messersmith-Cal	6.08	Peterson-NY	1.42	McDowell-Cle	279	McDowell-Cle	8.81	Peterson-NY	9.07
Stottlemyre-NY	303.0	Palmer-Bal	6.51	Bosman-Was	1.82	Lolich-Det	271	Lolich-Det	8.69	Cuellar-Bal	9.07
Cuellar-Bal	290.2	Cuellar-Bal	6.60	McLain-Det	1.86	Messersmith-Cal	211	Messersmith-Cal	7.60	Bosman-Was	9.19
McDowell-Cle	285.0	Lolich-Det	6.86	Perry-Min	2.27	Boswell-Min	190	Butler-KC	7.25	Palmer-Bal	9.75
Lolich-Det	280.2	Odom-Oak	6.96	Cuellar-Bal	2.45			Williams-Cle	7.01	Messersmith-Cal	9.86

Earned Run Average		Adjusted ERA		Opponents' Batting Avg.		Opponents' On Base Pct.		Starter Runs		Adjusted Starter Runs	
Bosman-Was	2.19	Bosman-Was	158	Messersmith-Cal	.190	Cuellar-Bal	.261	Cuellar-Bal	40.0	Cuellar-Bal	38.1
Palmer-Bal	2.34	Palmer-Bal	153	Palmer-Bal	.200	Bosman-Was	.262	Peterson-NY	32.5	McLain-Det	33.7
Cuellar-Bal	2.38	Cuellar-Bal	150	Cuellar-Bal	.204	Peterson-NY	.263	Bosman-Was	30.7	Peterson-NY	28.1
Messersmith-Cal	2.52	Messersmith-Cal	138	Lolich-Det	.210	Palmer-Bal	.272	Messersmith-Cal	30.6	Bosman-Was	27.3
Peterson-NY	2.55	Peterson-NY	136	McDowell-Cle	.213	Messersmith-Cal	.276	McLain-Det	29.8	Messersmith-Cal	26.8

Clutch Pitching Index		Relief Runs		Adjusted Relief Runs		Relief Ranking		Total Pitcher Index		Total Baseball Ranking	
Cox-Was	128	K.Tatum-Cal	21.7	Perranoski-Min	20.6	Perranoski-Min	41.3	Cuellar-Bal	3.9	Jackson-Oak	6.6
Nagy-Bos	119	Perranoski-Min	20.2	K.Tatum-Cal	20.4	K.Tatum-Cal	30.9	Stottlemyre-NY	3.8	Petrocelli-Bos	6.2
Tiant-Cle	118	Watt-Bal	15.6	Watt-Bal	15.1	Watt-Bal	21.1	Peterson-NY	3.3	Cardenas-Min	4.6
John-Chi	114	Roland-Oak	13.7	Lyle-Bos	14.4	Wood-Chi	21.0	McLain-Det	3.2	F.Robinson-Bal	4.2
Wilson-Det	112	Knowles-Was	12.9	Hall-Bal	12.0	Lyle-Bos	19.2	Bosman-Was	3.0	Killebrew-Min	4.1

1970 National League

TEAM	G	W	L	PCT	GB	R	OR	AB	H	2B	3B	HR	BB	SO	AVG	OBP	SLG	PRO	PRO+	BR	/A	PF	CHI	RC	SB	CS	SBA	SBR
EAST																												
PIT	162	89	73	.549		729	664	5637	**1522**	235	**70**	130	444	871	**.270**	.328	.406	.734	105	12	27	98	99	740	66	34	44	-15
CHI	162	84	78	.519	5	806	679	5491	1424	228	44	179	607	844	.259	.335	.415	.750	95	49	-39	112	**104**	773	39	16	27	**-10**
NY	162	83	79	.512	6	695	**630**	5443	1358	211	42	120	684	1062	.249	.336	.370	.706	95	-22	-23	100	98	689	118	54	**67**	-23
STL	162	76	86	.469	13	744	747	5689	1497	218	51	113	569	961	.263	.333	.379	.712	95	-19	-34	102	103	719	117	47	41	**-10**
PHI	161	73	88	.453	15.5	594	730	5456	1299	224	58	101	519	1066	.238	.307	.356	.663	85	-124	-104	97	101	582	72	64	61	-16
MON	162	73	89	.451	16	687	807	5411	1284	211	35	136	659	972	.237	.324	.365	.689	91	-61	-59	100	103	658	65	45	42	-11
WEST																												
CIN	162	102	60	.630		775	681	5540	1498	253	45	**191**	547	984	**.270**	.339	**.436**	**.775**	**112**	94	91	100	94	814	115	52	55	-16
LA	161	87	74	.540	14.5	749	684	5606	1515	233	67	87	541	841	**.270**	.335	.382	.719	103	-3	29	96	102	730	**138**	57	51	-13
SF	162	86	76	.531	16	**831**	826	5578	1460	**257**	35	165	**729**	1005	.262	**.353**	.409	.762	**112**	92	**101**	99	98	**821**	83	27	35	-12
HOU	162	79	83	.488	23	744	763	5574	1446	250	47	129	598	911	.259	.334	.391	.725	104	5	35	96	100	728	114	41	54	-19
ATL	162	76	86	.469	26	736	772	5546	1495	215	24	160	522	**736**	**.270**	.337	.404	.741	99	32	-10	106	97	742	58	34	39	-12
SD	162	63	99	.389	39	681	788	5494	1353	208	36	172	500	1164	.246	.314	.391	.705	97	-48	-19	96	102	669	60	45	54	-18
TOT	971					8771		66465	17151	2743	554	1683	6919	11417	.258	.332	.392	.724							1045	516	67	4

TEAM	CG	SH	SV	IP	H	H/G	HR	BB	SO	RAT	ERA	ERA+	OAV	OOB	PR	/A	PF	CPI	FA	E	DP	FW	PW	BW	SBW	DIF
EAST																										
PIT	36	13	43	1453²	1386	8.6	106	625	990	12.7	3.70	106	.254	.335	56	32	96	**106**	.979	137	**195**	.3	3.2	2.7	-1.5	3.4
CHI	59	9	25	1435	1402	8.8	143	**475**	1000	11.9	3.76	**120**	.255	.318	46	118	111	101	.978	137	146	.3	**11.8**	-3.9	**-1.0**	-4.1
NY	47	10	32	1459²	**1260**	7.8	135	575	1064	11.5	3.45	117	**.232**	**.309**	97	93	99	98	.979	124	136	1.0	9.3	-2.3	-2.3	-3.7
STL	51	11	20	1475²	1483	9.0	**102**	632	960	13.0	4.06	101	.263	.339	-1	9	102	100	.977	150	159	-.4	.9	-3.4	**-1.0**	-1.1
PHI	24	8	36	1461	1483	9.1	132	538	1047	12.7	4.17	96	.265	.333	-20	-29	99	98	**.981**	**114**	134	1.5	-2.9	-10.4	-1.6	5.9
MON	29	10	32	1438²	1434	9.0	162	716	914	13.8	4.50	91	.260	.351	-73	-62	102	101	.977	141	193	.0	-6.2	-5.9	-1.1	5.1
WEST																										
CIN	32	15	**60**	1444²	1370	8.5	118	592	843	12.4	3.69	109	.250	.327	57	55	100	102	.976	151	173	-.5	5.5	9.1	-1.6	8.6
LA	37	**17**	42	1458²	1394	8.6	164	496	880	11.9	3.82	100	.250	.315	36	1	95	99	.978	135	135	.4	.0	2.9	-1.3	4.5
SF	50	7	30	1457²	1514	9.3	156	604	931	13.3	4.50	88	.267	.341	-73	-85	98	98	.973	170	153	-1.5	-8.5	10.1	-1.2	6.2
HOU	36	6	35	1456	1491	9.2	131	577	942	13.0	4.23	92	.265	.338	-30	-57	96	99	.978	140	144	.1	-5.7	3.5	-1.9	2.0
ATL	45	9	24	1430²	1451	9.1	185	478	960	12.3	4.33	99	.260	.322	-44	-6	106	96	.977	141	118	.0	-.6	-1.0	-1.2	-2.3
SD	24	9	32	1440¹	1483	9.3	149	611	886	13.3	4.36	91	.267	.344	-49	-61	98	102	.975	158	159	-.9	-6.1	-1.9	-1.8	-7.3
TOT	470	124	411	17411²		8.9				12.6	4.05		.258	.332					.977	1698	1845					

Runs		Hits		Doubles		Triples		Home Runs		Total Bases	
Williams-Chi	137	Williams-Chi	205	Parker-LA	47	Davis-LA	16	Bench-Cin	45	Williams-Chi	373
Bonds-SF	134	Rose-Cin	205	McCovey-SF	39	Kessinger-Chi	14	Williams-Chi	42	Bench-Cin	355
Rose-Cin	120	Torre-StL	203	Rose-Cin	37	Clemente-Pit	10	Perez-Cin	40	Perez-Cin	346
Brock-StL	114	Brock-StL	202	Dietz-SF	36	Bonds-SF	10	McCovey-SF	39	Bonds-SF	334
Tolan-Cin	112	Alou-Pit	201	Bonds-SF	36					Gaston-SD	317

Runs Batted In		Runs Produced		Bases On Balls		Batting Average		On Base Percentage		Slugging Average	
Bench-Cin	148	Williams-Chi	224	McCovey-SF	137	Carty-Atl	.366	Carty-Atl	.456	McCovey-SF	.612
Williams-Chi	129	Bench-Cin	200	Staub-Mon	112	Torre-StL	.325	McCovey-SF	.446	Perez-Cin	.589
Perez-Cin	129	Perez-Cin	196	Dietz-SF	109	Sanguillen-Pit	.325	Dietz-SF	.430	Bench-Cin	.587
McCovey-SF	126	Bonds-SF	186	Wynn-Hou	106	Williams-Chi	.322	Hickman-Chi	.421	Williams-Chi	.586
H.Aaron-Atl	118			Morgan-Hou	102	Parker-LA	.319	Perez-Cin	.405	Carty-Atl	.584

Production		Adjusted Production		Batter Runs		Adjusted Batter Runs		Clutch Hitting Index		Runs Created	
McCovey-SF	1.058	McCovey-SF	183	McCovey-SF	62.0	McCovey-SF	62.9	Parker-LA	147	Williams-Chi	147
Carty-Atl	1.040	Carty-Atl	167	Carty-Atl	54.4	Perez-Cin	51.8	Santo-Chi	137	McCovey-SF	140
Hickman-Chi	1.003	Perez-Cin	162	Perez-Cin	52.1	Carty-Atl	50.6	Davis-LA	135	Perez-Cin	140
Perez-Cin	.994	Dietz-SF	154	Williams-Chi	51.1	Dietz-SF	41.7	Dietz-SF	132	Bonds-SF	134
Williams-Chi	.979	Hickman-Chi	148	Hickman-Chi	49.5	Williams-Chi	41.0	Menke-Hou	132	Hickman-Chi	129

Total Average		Stolen Bases		Stolen Base Average		Stolen Base Runs		Fielding Runs		Total Player Rating	
McCovey-SF	1.214	Tolan-Cin	57	Henderson-SF	87.0	Bonds-SF	8.4	Maxvill-StL	37.5	McCovey-SF	6.1
Carty-Atl	1.102	Brock-StL	51	Harrelson-NY	85.2	Brock-StL	6.3	Alley-Pit	33.7	Morgan-Hou	4.5
Hickman-Chi	1.080	Bonds-SF	48	Wynn-Hou	82.8	Tolan-Cin	5.1	Mazeroski-Pit	23.9	Bench-Cin	4.5
Perez-Cin	1.045	Morgan-Hou	42	Bonds-SF	82.8	Morgan-Hou	4.8	Rader-Hou	23.8	Bonds-SF	4.3
Williams-Chi	1.018	Davis-LA	38	Cedeno-Hou	81.0	Harrelson-NY	4.5	Wine-Mon	19.7	Perez-Cin	4.0

Wins		Win Percentage		Games		Complete Games		Shutouts		Saves	
Perry-SF	23	Gibson-StL	.767	Herbel-SD-NY	76	Jenkins-Chi	24	Perry-SF	5	Granger-Cin	35
Gibson-StL	23	Nolan-Cin	.720	Selma-Phi	73	Perry-SF	23	Sutton-LA	4	Giusti-Pit	26
Jenkins-Chi	22	Walker-Pit	.714	Linzy-SF-StL	67	Gibson-StL	23	Osteen-LA	4	Brewer-LA	24
Merritt-Cin	20	Perry-SF	.639	Granger-Cin	67	Seaver-NY	19	Morton-Mon	4	Raymond-Mon	23
		Merritt-Cin	.625	Giusti-Pit	66	Dierker-Hou	17	Ellis-Pit	4	Selma-Phi	22

Innings Pitched		Fewest Hits/Game		Fewest BB/Game		Strikeouts		Strikeouts/Game		Ratio	
Perry-SF	328.2	Simpson-Cin	6.39	Jenkins-Chi	1.73	Seaver-NY	283	Seaver-NY	8.76	Jenkins-Chi	9.55
Jenkins-Chi	313.0	Seaver-NY	7.12	Marichal-SF	1.78	Jenkins-Chi	274	Gibson-StL	8.39	Seaver-NY	9.82
Gibson-StL	294.0	Walker-Pit	7.12	Osteen-LA	1.81	Gibson-StL	274	Veale-Pit	7.93	McAndrew-NY	10.06
Seaver-NY	290.2	Gentry-NY	7.41	McAndrew-NY	1.86	Perry-SF	214	Jenkins-Chi	7.88	Perry-SF	10.52
Holtzman-Chi	287.2	Jenkins-Chi	7.62	Merritt-Cin	2.04	Holtzman-Chi	202	Stoneman-Mon	7.63	Gibson-StL	10.84

Earned Run Average		Adjusted ERA		Opponents' Batting Avg.		Opponents' On Base Pct.		Starter Runs		Adjusted Starter Runs	
Seaver-NY	2.82	Seaver-NY	143	Simpson-Cin	.198	Jenkins-Chi	.265	Seaver-NY	39.7	Seaver-NY	38.9
Simpson-Cin	3.02	Simpson-Cin	134	Seaver-NY	.214	Seaver-NY	.273	Perry-SF	30.7	Jenkins-Chi	38.5
Walker-Pit	3.04	Pappas-Atl-Chi	133	Walker-Pit	.219	McAndrew-NY	.281	Gibson-StL	30.2	Holtzman-Chi	35.8
Gibson-StL	3.12	Holtzman-Chi	133	Jenkins-Chi	.224	Perry-SF	.290	Jenkins-Chi	22.7	Gibson-StL	32.4
Koosman-NY	3.14	Jenkins-Chi	133	Gentry-NY	.224	Gibson-StL	.296	Nolan-Cin	21.7	Perry-SF	28.1

Clutch Pitching Index		Relief Runs		Adjusted Relief Runs		Relief Ranking		Total Pitcher Index		Total Baseball Ranking	
Ellis-Pit	119	Selma-Phi	19.4	Selma-Phi	18.5	Selma-Phi	27.9	Seaver-NY	4.7	McCovey-SF	6.1
Morton-Mon	118	Carroll-Cin	16.9	Carroll-Cin	16.8	Granger-Cin	27.2	Gibson-StL	4.5	Seaver-NY	4.7
Coombs-SD	113	Gullett-Cin	13.9	C.Taylor-StL	13.8	Carroll-Cin	24.6	Holtzman-Chi	4.1	Morgan-Hou	4.5
Pappas-Atl-Chi	109	Granger-Cin	13.1	Gullett-Cin	13.8	Hoerner-Phi	21.7	Jenkins-Chi	3.7	Bench-Cin	4.5
Dobson-SD	108	C.Taylor-StL	12.9	Granger-Cin	12.9	McMahon-SF	19.0	Perry-SF	3.0	Gibson-StL	4.5

TEAM	G	W	L	PCT	GB	R	OR	AB	H	2B	3B	HR	BB	SO	AVG	OBP	SLG	PRO	PRO+	BR	/A	PF	CHI	RC	SB	CS	SBA	SBR
EAST																												
BAL	162	108	54	.667		**792**	**574**	5545	1424	213	25	179	717	952	.257	**.346**	.401	.747	111	101	**93**	101	99	**795**	84	39	36	**-9**
NY	163	93	69	.574	15	680	612	5492	1381	208	**41**	111	588	**808**	.251	.327	.365	.692	102	-17	17	95	103	662	105	61	63	-19
BOS	162	87	75	.537	21	786	722	5535	**1450**	**252**	28	**203**	594	855	**.262**	.338	**.428**	**.766**	109	**119**	71	107	98	786	50	48	43	-10
DET	162	79	83	.488	29	666	731	5377	1282	207	38	148	656	825	.238	.325	.374	.699	98	-3	-7	101	99	658	29	30	41	-15
CLE	162	76	86	.469	32	649	675	5463	1358	197	23	183	503	909	.249	.316	.394	.710	96	3	-29	105	97	670	25	36	47	-16
WAS	162	70	92	.432	38	626	689	5460	1302	184	28	138	635	989	.238	.323	.358	.681	98	-35	-2	95	97	638	72	42	47	-15
WEST																												
MIN	162	98	64	.605		744	605	5483	1438	230	**41**	153	501	905	**.262**	.329	.403	.732	106	50	40	101	103	709	57	52	53	-15
OAK	162	89	73	.549	9	678	593	5376	1338	208	24	171	584	977	.249	.327	.392	.719	107	28	52	96	98	689	**131**	68	56	-12
CAL	162	86	76	.531	12	631	630	5532	1391	197	40	114	447	922	.251	.311	.363	.674	95	-63	-39	97	104	622	69	27	33	-11
MIL	163	65	97	.401	33	613	751	5395	1305	202	24	126	592	985	.242	.321	.358	.679	92	-41	-45	101	97	618	91	73	**69**	-19
KC	162	65	97	.401	33	611	705	5503	1341	202	**41**	97	514	958	.244	.311	.348	.659	88	-87	-86	100	**105**	593	97	53	43	**-9**
CHI	162	56	106	.346	42	633	822	5514	1394	192	20	123	477	872	.253	.317	.362	.679	89	-49	-74	104	102	627	53	33	43	-15
TOT	973					8109		65675	16404	2492	373	1746	6808	10957	.250	.324	.379	.703							863	562	61	-77

TEAM	CG	SH	SV	IP	H	H/G	HR	BB	SO	RAT	ERA	ERA+	OAV	OOB	PR	/A	PF	CPI	FA	E	DP	FW	PW	BW	SBW	DIF
EAST																										
BAL	**60**	12	31	1478²	1317	8.0	139	469	941	**11.0**	3.15	116	.239	**.302**	93	82	98	102	.981	117	148	1.1	8.5	9.6	-.3	8.0
NY	36	6	49	1471²	1386	8.5	130	451	777	11.4	3.24	108	.249	.308	77	44	95	103	.980	130	146	.4	4.6	1.8	-1.3	6.6
BOS	38	8	44	1446¹	1391	8.7	156	594	1003	12.6	3.87	102	.251	.328	-25	14	107	100	.974	156	131	-1.2	1.5	7.4	-.4	-1.3
DET	33	9	39	1447¹	1443	9.0	153	623	1045	13.1	4.09	91	.259	.338	-60	-58	100	100	.978	133	142	.2	-6.0	-.7	-.9	5.5
CLE	34	8	35	1451¹	1333	8.3	163	689	**1076**	12.8	3.91	101	.247	.337	-31	8	107	103	.979	133	168	.2	.8	-3.0	-1.0	-2.0
WAS	20	11	40	1457²	1375	8.5	139	611	823	12.4	3.80	94	.251	.330	-13	-39	96	100	**.982**	116	173	1.1	-4.0	-.2	-.9	-7.0
WEST																										
MIN	26	12	**58**	1448¹	1329	8.3	**130**	486	940	11.5	3.23	115	.243	.310	77	78	100	103	.980	123	130	.7	8.1	4.1	-.9	4.9
OAK	33	**15**	40	1442²	**1253**	**7.8**	134	542	858	11.4	3.30	107	**.233**	.308	66	38	95	98	.977	141	152	-.3	3.9	5.4	-.6	-.5
CAL	21	10	49	1462¹	1280	7.9	154	559	922	11.6	3.48	104	.236	.313	37	21	97	99	.980	127	169	.5	2.2	-4.0	-.5	6.8
MIL	31	2	27	1446²	1397	8.7	146	587	895	12.6	4.21	90	.255	.332	-78	-67	102	93	.978	136	142	.0	-6.9	-4.7	-1.3	-3.1
KC	30	11	25	1463²	1346	8.3	138	641	915	12.4	3.78	99	.247	.330	-10	-7	101	99	.976	152	162	-.9	-.7	-8.9	-.3	-5.2
CHI	20	6	30	1430¹	1554	9.8	164	556	762	13.6	4.54	86	.279	.349	-131	-102	105	101	.975	165	**187**	-1.7	-10.6	-7.7	-.9	-4.2
TOT	382	110	467	17447		8.5				12.2	3.71		.250	.324					.978	1629	1850					

Runs
Yastrzemski-Bos .. 125
Tovar-Min 120
White-NY 109
Smith-Bos 109
Harper-Mil 104

Hits
Oliva-Min 204
Johnson-Cal 202
Tovar-Min 195
Yastrzemski-Bos .. 186
White-NY 180

Doubles
Tovar-Min 36
Otis-KC 36
Oliva-Min 36
Harper-Mil 35
Cardenas-Min 34

Triples
Tovar-Min 13
Stanley-Det 11
Otis-KC 9

Home Runs
Howard-Was 44
Killebrew-Min ... 41
Yastrzemski-Bos .. 40
A.Conigliaro-Bos .. 36
Powell-Bal 35

Total Bases
Yastrzemski-Bos .. 335
Oliva-Min 323
Harper-Mil 315
Howard-Was 309
Powell-Bal 289

Runs Batted In
Howard-Was 126
A.Conigliaro-Bos .. 116
Powell-Bal 114
Killebrew-Min ... 113
Oliva-Min 107

Runs Produced
Yastrzemski-Bos .. 187
White-NY 181
Oliva-Min 180
Howard-Was 172
A.Conigliaro-Bos.. 169

Bases On Balls
Howard-Was 132
Yastrzemski-Bos .. 128
Killebrew-Min ... 128
Bando-Oak 118
Buford-Bal 109

Batting Average
Johnson-Cal 329
Yastrzemski-Bos ..329
Oliva-Min 325
Aparicio-Chi.......313
F.Robinson-Bal ...306

On Base Percentage
Yastrzemski-Bos ..453
Howard-Was 420
Powell-Bal 417
Killebrew-Min ...416
Buford-Bal 409

Slugging Average
Yastrzemski-Bos ..592
Powell-Bal 549
Killebrew-Min ...546
Howard-Was 546
Harper-Mil 522

Production
Yastrzemski-Bos . 1.045
Powell-Bal 967
Howard-Was 966
Killebrew-Min ...962
F.Robinson-Bal ...922

Adjusted Production
Yastrzemski-Bos .. 174
Howard-Was 173
Powell-Bal 163
Killebrew-Min ... 161
F.Robinson-Bal ... 151

Batter Runs
Yastrzemski-Bos ..71.7
Howard-Was 54.1
Killebrew-Min ...49.5
Powell-Bal 49.2
Harper-Mil 37.5

Adjusted Batter Runs
Yastrzemski-Bos ..66.4
Howard-Was 57.8
Killebrew-Min ...48.5
Powell-Bal 48.4
Harper-Mil 36.9

Clutch Hitting Index
Piniella-KC 138
A.Conigliaro-Bos . 128
Cater-NY 127
McMullen-Was-Cal 125
B.Robinson-Bal... 123

Runs Created
Yastrzemski-Bos .. 157
Howard-Was 130
Powell-Bal 123
Harper-Mil 122
Killebrew-Min 116

Total Average
Yastrzemski-Bos . 1.170
Powell-Bal 1.034
Howard-Was 1.026
Killebrew-Min ... 1.000
F.Robinson-Bal ...944

Stolen Bases
Campaneris-Oak ... 42
Harper-Mil 38
Alomar-Cal 35
Kelly-KC 34
Otis-KC 33

Stolen Base Average
Otis-KC 94.3
Johnson-Cal 89.5
Campaneris-Oak .. 80.8
Stroud-Was 78.4
Kenney-NY 76.9

Stolen Base Runs
Otis-KC 8.7
Campaneris-Oak .. 6.6
Stroud-Was 3.9
Johnson-Cal 3.9
Alomar-Cal 3.3

Fielding Runs
Knoop-Chi 35.1
Brinkman-Was.... 31.1
Nettles-Cle 28.6
Cullen-Was 26.5
Mitterwald-Min ... 23.9

Total Player Rating
Yastrzemski-Bos .. 5.6
Aparicio-Chi....... 4.1
Powell-Bal 4.0
Oliva-Min 3.9
Harper-Mil 3.9

Wins
Perry-Min 24
McNally-Bal 24
Cuellar-Bal 24
Wright-Cal 22

Win Percentage
Cuellar-Bal 750
McNally-Bal 727
Perry-Min 667
Palmer-Bal 667
Siebert-Bos 652

Games
Wood-Chi 77
Grant-Oak 72
Knowles-Was...... 71
Williams-Min 68

Complete Games
Cuellar-Bal 21
McDowell-Cle 19
Palmer-Bal 17
McNally-Bal 16
Culp-Bos 15

Shutouts
Palmer-Bal 5
Dobson-Oak 5
Peters-Bos 4
Perry-Min 4
Cuellar-Bal 4

Saves
Perranoski-Min 34
McDaniel-NY 29
Timmermann-Det ... 27
Knowles-Was 27
Grant-Oak 24

Innings Pitched
Palmer-Bal 305.0
McDowell-Cle 305.0
Cuellar-Bal 297.2
McNally-Bal 296.0
Perry-Min 278.2

Fewest Hits/Game
Messersmith-Cal .. 6.66
McDowell-Cle 6.96
Segui-Oak 7.22
Johnson-KC 7.49
Culp-Bos 7.56

Fewest BB/Game
Peterson-NY 1.38
Perry-Min 1.84
Cox-Was 2.06
Cuellar-Bal 2.09
Horlen-Chi 2.14

Strikeouts
McDowell-Cle 304
Lolich-Det 230
Johnson-KC 206
Palmer-Bal 199
Culp-Bos 197

Strikeouts/Game
McDowell-Cle 8.97
Johnson-KC 8.66
Cain-Det 7.77
Lolich-Det 7.59
Messersmith-Cal.. 7.49

Ratio
Peterson-NY 10.03
Cuellar-Bal 10.37
Perry-Min 10.46
Blyleven-Min 10.54
Messersmith-Cal. 10.54

Earned Run Average
Segui-Oak 2.56
Palmer-Bal 2.71
Wright-Cal 2.83
Peterson-NY 2.90
McDowell-Cle 2.92

Adjusted ERA
Segui-Oak 139
McDowell-Cle 136
Palmer-Bal 134
Culp-Bos 130
Wright-Cal 128

Opponents' Batting Avg.
Messersmith-Cal ...205
McDowell-Cle 213
Segui-Oak 222
Culp-Bos 224
Johnson-KC 228

Opponents' On Base Pct.
Peterson-NY 280
Cuellar-Bal 286
Perry-Min 287
Blyleven-Min 289
Messersmith-Cal...290

Starter Runs
Palmer-Bal 33.9
McDowell-Cle 26.9
Wright-Cal 25.6
Peterson-NY 23.4
Perry-Min 21.0

Adjusted Starter Runs
McDowell-Cle 35.2
Palmer-Bal 31.6
Culp-Bos 25.6
Wright-Cal 22.7
Perry-Min 21.2

Clutch Pitching Index
Stottlemyre-NY ... 113
Kaat-Min 112
Bahnsen-NY 109
Segui-Oak 108
Wright-Cal 107

Relief Runs
Grant-Oak 25.9
Knowles-Was..... 22.2
Williams-Min 21.8
McDaniel-NY 21.1
Sanders-Mil 20.1

Adjusted Relief Runs
Grant-Oak 23.5
Williams-Min 21.9
Sanders-Mil 20.9
Hall-Min 20.2
Knowles-Was..... 20.1

Relief Ranking
Knowles-Was..... 34.5
McDaniel-NY 31.8
Perranoski-Min ... 30.3
Wood-Chi 29.6
Williams-Min 25.6

Total Pitcher Index
Palmer-Bal 3.3
McDowell-Cle 3.2
Perry-Min 3.0
Grant-Oak 2.8
Peterson-NY 2.6

Total Baseball Ranking
Yastrzemski-Bos .. 5.6
Aparicio-Chi....... 4.1
Powell-Bal 4.0
Oliva-Min 3.9
Harper-Mil 3.9

TEAM	G	W	L	PCT	GB	R	OR	AB	H	2B	3B	HR	BB	SO	AVG	OBP	SLG	PRO	PRO+	BR	/A	PF	CHI	RC	SB	CS	SBA	SBR
EAST																												
PIT	162	97	65	.599		**788**	599	5674	**1555**	223	**61**	154	469	919	.274	.333	**.416**	**.749**	118	121	**124**	100	103	**776**	65	31	36	-11
STL	163	90	72	.556	7	739	699	5610	1542	225	54	95	543	757	**.275**	**.342**	.385	.727	107	91	65	104	100	736	**124**	53	**60**	-19
NY	162	83	79	.512	14	588	**550**	5477	1365	202	29	98	547	958	.249	.321	.351	.672	98	-19	-9	99	95	614	44	32	43	-11
CHI	162	83	79	.512	14	637	648	5438	1401	202	34	128	527	772	.258	.327	.378	.705	92	41	-50	115	95	663	44	32	43	-15
MON	162	71	90	.441	25.5	622	729	5335	1312	197	29	88	543	800	.246	.325	.343	.668	95	-19	-21	100	102	598	51	43	50	-16
PHI	162	67	95	.414	30	558	688	5538	1289	209	35	123	499	1031	.233	.300	.350	.650	90	-73	-72	100	99	586	63	39	44	-14
WEST																												
SF	162	90	72	.556		706	644	5461	1348	224	36	140	**654**	1042	.247	.331	.378	.709	108	57	67	98	101	699	101	36	45	-15
LA	162	89	73	.549	1	663	587	5523	1469	213	38	95	489	755	.266	.328	.370	.698	110	28	66	94	100	661	76	40	47	-15
ATL	162	82	80	.506	8	643	699	5575	1434	192	30	153	434	**747**	.257	.314	.385	.699	97	18	-22	106	98	658	57	46	49	-15
HOU	162	79	83	.488	11	585	567	5492	1319	**230**	52	71	478	888	.240	.304	.340	.644	90	-80	-63	97	**107**	573	101	51	51	-14
CIN	162	79	83	.488	11	586	581	5414	1306	203	28	138	438	907	.241	.301	.366	.667	96	-44	-31	98	103	580	59	33	39	-13
SD	161	61	100	.379	28.5	486	610	5366	1250	184	31	96	438	966	.233	.294	.332	.626	89	-116	-74	93	98	513	70	45	54	-18
TOT	972					7601		65903	16590	2505	457	1379	6059	10542	.252	.318	.366	.685							900	492	65	-24

TEAM	CG	SH	SV	IP	H	H/G	HR	BB	SO	RAT	ERA	ERA+	OAV	OOB	PR	/A	PF	CPI	FA	E	DP	FW	PW	BW	SBW	DIF
EAST																										
PIT	43	15	**48**	1461	1426	8.8	108	470	813	11.9	3.31	102	.256	.318	25	12	98	105	.979	133	164	.0	1.3	**13.3**	-1.0	2.3
STL	56	14	22	1467	1482	9.1	104	576	911	12.9	3.85	93	.263	.335	-63	-41	104	99	.978	142	155	-.4	-4.4	7.0	-1.8	8.6
NY	42	13	22	1466¹	1227	7.5	100	529	1157	11.0	2.99	114	.226	.300	77	68	98	94	.981	114	135	1.2	7.3	-1.0	-1.0	-4.6
CHI	**75**	17	13	1444	1458	9.1	132	411	900	11.8	3.61	109	.262	.316	-22	52	114	101	.980	126	150	.5	5.6	-5.4	-1.4	2.7
MON	49	8	25	1434¹	1418	8.9	133	658	829	13.2	4.12	86	.260	.343	-103	-93	102	100	.976	150	164	-.9	-10.0	-2.3	-1.5	5.1
PHI	31	10	25	1470²	1396	8.5	132	525	838	12.0	3.71	95	.253	.322	-40	-31	102	98	.981	122	158	.7	-3.3	-7.7	-1.3	-2.4
WEST																										
SF	45	14	30	1454²	1324	8.2	128	471	831	11.3	3.32	102	.242	.305	24	12	98	97	.972	179	153	-2.6	1.3	7.2	-1.4	4.5
LA	48	**18**	33	1449²	1363	8.5	110	**399**	853	11.1	3.23	100	.250	.303	37	0	93	98	.979	131	159	.2	.0	7.1	-1.4	2.1
ATL	40	11	31	1474²	1529	9.3	152	485	823	12.5	3.75	99	.269	.330	-46	-5	107	108	.977	146	**180**	-.7	-.5	-2.4	-1.4	5.9
HOU	43	10	25	1471¹	1318	8.1	**75**	475	914	11.3	3.13	107	.240	.308	54	38	97	95	.983	106	152	1.6	4.1	-6.8	-1.3	.3
CIN	27	11	38	1444	1298	8.1	112	501	750	11.4	3.35	100	.243	.311	18	0	97	97	**.984**	**103**	174	**1.8**	.0	-3.3	-1.2	.7
SD	47	10	17	1438	1351	8.5	93	559	923	12.1	3.22	102	.249	.322	38	11	95	106	.974	161	144	-1.6	1.2	-7.9	-1.7	-9.5
TOT	546	151	329	17475²		8.5				11.9	3.47		.252	.318					.979	1613	1888					

Runs
Brock-StL 126
Bonds-SF 110
Stargell-Pit 104
Garr-Atl 101
Torre-StL 97

Hits
Torre-StL 230
Garr-Atl 219
Brock-StL 200
Davis-LA 198

Doubles
Cedeno-Hou 40
Brock-StL 37
Torre-StL 34
Staub-Mon 34
Davis-LA 33

Triples
Morgan-Hou 11
Metzger-Hou 11
Davis-LA 10
Gaston-SD 9

Home Runs
Stargell-Pit 48
H.Aaron-Atl 47
May-Cin 39
Johnson-Phi 34

Total Bases
Torre-StL 352
H.Aaron-Atl 331
Stargell-Pit 321
Bonds-SF 317
Williams-Chi 300

Runs Batted In
Torre-StL 137
Stargell-Pit 125
H.Aaron-Atl 118
Bonds-SF 102
Montanez-Phi 99

Runs Produced
Torre-StL 210
Stargell-Pit 181
Brock-StL 180
Bonds-SF 179
Staub-Mon 172

Bases On Balls
Mays-SF 112
Dietz-SF 97
Bailey-Mon 97
Allen-LA 93
Morgan-Hou 88

Batting Average
Torre-StL 363
Garr-Atl 343
Beckert-Chi 342
Clemente-Pit 341
H.Aaron-Atl 327

On Base Percentage
Mays-SF 429
Torre-StL 424
H.Aaron-Atl 414
Hunt-Mon 403
Stargell-Pit 401

Slugging Average
H.Aaron-Atl 669
Stargell-Pit 628
Torre-StL 555
May-Cin 532
Bonds-SF 512

Production
H.Aaron-Atl 1.082
Stargell-Pit 1.029
Torre-StL 979
Mays-SF 911
Williams-Chi 889

Adjusted Production
H.Aaron-Atl 190
Stargell-Pit 188
Torre-StL 169
Mays-SF 160
Allen-LA 154

Batter Runs
H.Aaron-Atl 65.2
Torre-StL 62.5
Stargell-Pit 58.7
Williams-Chi 39.4
Staub-Mon 38.5

Adjusted Batter Runs
H.Aaron-Atl 61.5
Torre-StL 59.6
Stargell-Pit 59.0
Allen-LA 38.9
Mays-SF 38.5

Clutch Hitting Index
Bailey-Mon 143
Simmons-StL 140
Torre-StL 139
Sanguillen-Pit 136
Fairly-Mon 134

Runs Created
Torre-StL 145
H.Aaron-Atl 137
Stargell-Pit 131
Bonds-SF 115
Brock-StL 114

Total Average
H.Aaron-Atl 1.178
Stargell-Pit 1.117
Mays-SF 1.067
Torre-StL 998
Bonds-SF 876

Stolen Bases
Brock-StL 64
Morgan-Hou 40
Garr-Atl 30

Stolen Base Average
Mays-SF 88.5
Henderson-SF 85.7
Morgan-Hou 83.3
Agee-NY 82.4
Hernandez-SD 80.8

Stolen Base Runs
Brock-StL 7.8
Morgan-Hou 7.2
Mays-SF 5.1
Agee-NY 4.8
Harrelson-NY 4.2

Fielding Runs
Maxvill-StL 29.2
Robertson-Pit 15.2
Helms-Cin 14.4
Barton-SD 12.3
Harrelson-NY 10.7

Total Player Rating
Stargell-Pit 5.1
H.Aaron-Atl 4.7
Torre-StL 4.5
Bonds-SF 4.1
Staub-Mon 3.6

Wins
Jenkins-Chi 24
Seaver-NY 20
Downing-LA 20
Carlton-StL 20
Ellis-Pit 19

Win Percentage
Gullett-Cin 727
Downing-LA 690
Carlton-StL 690
Ellis-Pit 679
Seaver-NY 667

Games
Granger-Cin 70
J.Johnson-SF 67
Marshall-Mon 66
McMahon-SF 61
Carroll-Cin 61

Complete Games
Jenkins-Chi 30
Seaver-NY 21
Stoneman-Mon 20
Gibson-StL 20

Shutouts
Pappas-Chi 5
Gibson-StL 5
Downing-LA 5
Blass-Pit 5

Saves
Giusti-Pit 30
Marshall-Mon 23
Brewer-LA 22
J.Johnson-SF 18
Upshaw-Atl 17

Innings Pitched
Jenkins-Chi 325.0
Stoneman-Mon . . 294.2
Seaver-NY 286.1
Perry-SF 280.0
Marichal-SF 279.0

Fewest Hits/Game
Wilson-Hou 6.55
Seaver-NY 6.60
Kirby-SD 7.17
Gentry-NY 7.39
Stoneman-Mon 7.42

Fewest BB/Game
Jenkins-Chi 1.02
Marichal-SF 1.81
Stone-Atl 1.82
Hands-Chi 1.86
Sutton-LA 1.87

Strikeouts
Seaver-NY 289
Jenkins-Chi 263
Stoneman-Mon 251
Kirby-SD 231
Sutton-LA 194

Strikeouts/Game
Seaver-NY 9.08
Kirby-SD 7.78
Stoneman-Mon 7.67
Jenkins-Chi 7.28
Gentry-NY 6.86

Ratio
Seaver-NY 8.64
Wilson-Hou 9.44
Jenkins-Chi 9.58
Marichal-SF 9.77
Sutton-LA 9.87

Earned Run Average
Seaver-NY 1.76
Roberts-SD 2.10
Wilson-Hou 2.45
Forsch-Hou 2.53
Sutton-LA 2.54

Adjusted ERA
Seaver-NY 194
Roberts-SD 157
Jenkins-Chi 142
Wilson-Hou 137
Forsch-Hou 133

Opponents' Batting Avg.
Wilson-Hou 202
Seaver-NY 206
Kirby-SD 216
Cumberland-SF 223
Gentry-NY 224

Opponents' On Base Pct.
Seaver-NY 253
Wilson-Hou 268
Jenkins-Chi 271
Marichal-SF 274
Nolan-Cin 275

Starter Runs
Seaver-NY 54.3
Roberts-SD 40.9
Wilson-Hou 30.2
Sutton-LA 27.2
Jenkins-Chi 25.2

Adjusted Starter Runs
Seaver-NY 52.4
Jenkins-Chi 42.1
Roberts-SD 35.8
Wilson-Hou 27.2
Niekro-Atl 21.8

Clutch Pitching Index
Roberts-SD 120
Downing-LA 115
Short-Phi 115
Johnson-Pit 112
Wise-Phi 112

Relief Runs
McGraw-NY 21.7
Miller-Chi-SD-Pit . . 20.0
Frisella-NY 14.9
Ray-Hou 14.6
Brewer-LA 14.3

Adjusted Relief Runs
McGraw-NY 21.0
Miller-Chi-SD-Pit . . 18.9
Frisella-NY 14.3
Ray-Hou 13.5
Hoerner-Phi 12.6

Relief Ranking
McGraw-NY 29.0
Miller-Chi-SD-Pit . . 26.7
Frisella-NY 22.7
Brewer-LA 22.3
Ray-Hou 18.4

Total Pitcher Index
Seaver-NY 6.7
Jenkins-Chi 6.7
Roberts-SD 4.4
Wise-Phi 3.4
Wilson-Hou 2.5

Total Baseball Ranking
Seaver-NY 6.7
Jenkins-Chi 6.7
Stargell-Pit 5.1
H.Aaron-Atl 4.7
Torre-StL 4.5

TEAM	G	W	L	PCT	GB	R	OR	AB	H	2B	3B	HR	BB	SO	AVG	OBP	SLG	PRO	PRO+	BR	/A	PF	CHI	RC	SB	CS	SBA	SBR
EAST																												
BAL	158	101	57	.639		**742**	**530**	5303	1382	207	25	158	**672**	844	**.261**	**.349**	.398	**.747**	120	**133**	**138**	99	97	**750**	66	38	47	-16
DET	162	91	71	.562	12	701	645	5502	1399	214	38	**179**	540	854	.254	.327	**.405**	.732	109	88	63	104	97	715	35	43	48	-15
BOS	162	85	77	.525	18	691	667	5401	1360	**246**	28	161	552	871	.252	.325	.397	.722	103	68	23	107	100	686	51	34	41	-13
NY	162	82	80	.506	21	648	641	5413	1377	195	**43**	97	581	**717**	.254	.331	.360	.691	108	22	60	94	99	643	75	55	57	-17
WAS	159	63	96	.396	38.5	537	660	5290	1219	189	30	86	575	956	.230	.309	.326	.635	91	-85	-50	94	102	538	68	45	44	-12
CLE	162	60	102	.370	43	543	747	5467	1303	200	20	109	467	868	.238	.302	.342	.644	80	-82	-138	109	101	558	57	37	46	-16
WEST																												
OAK	161	101	60	.627		691	564	5494	1383	195	25	160	542	1018	.252	.323	.384	.707	109	42	54	98	102	681	80	53	54	-16
KC	161	85	76	.528	16	603	566	5295	1323	225	40	80	490	819	.250	.316	.353	.669	96	-27	-21	99	**104**	594	**130**	46	46	-13
CHI	162	79	83	.488	22.5	617	597	5382	1346	185	30	138	546	870	.250	.327	.373	.700	101	33	13	103	94	661	83	65	**59**	-15
CAL	162	76	86	.469	25.5	511	576	5495	1271	213	18	96	441	827	.231	.292	.329	.621	88	-130	-85	93	**104**	518	72	34	37	**-11**
MIN	160	74	86	.463	26.5	654	670	5414	**1406**	197	31	116	512	846	.260	.326	.372	.698	100	28	8	103	101	641	66	44	54	-18
MIL	161	69	92	.429	32	534	609	5185	1188	160	23	104	543	924	.229	.306	.329	.635	87	-87	-79	99	103	534	82	53	50	-13
TOT	966					7472		64641	15957	2426	351	1484	6477	10414	.247	.320	.364	.684							865	547	61	-68

TEAM	CG	SH	SV	IP	H	H/G	HR	BB	SO	RAT	ERA	ERA+	OAV	OOB	PR	/A	PF	CPI	FA	E	DP	FW	PW	BW	SBW	DIF
EAST																										
BAL	**71**	15	22	1415¹	1257	8.0	125	**416**	793	**10.8**	**2.99**	112	.238	**.296**	74	56	97	101	.981	112	148	.7	6.0	**14.8**	-1.1	1.6
DET	53	11	32	1468¹	1355	8.3	126	609	**1000**	12.3	3.63	99	.246	.327	-28	-7	104	99	**.983**	**106**	156	**1.2**	-.8	6.8	-1.0	3.8
BOS	44	11	35	1443	1424	8.9	136	535	871	12.5	3.80	97	.258	.329	-55	-17	107	100	.981	116	149	.6	-1.8	2.5	-.8	3.5
NY	67	15	12	1452	1382	8.6	126	423	707	11.3	3.43	94	.251	.308	4	-32	93	97	.981	125	159	.1	-3.4	6.5	-1.2	-.9
WAS	30	10	26	1418²	1376	8.7	132	554	762	12.5	3.70	89	.258	.333	-37	-61	96	105	.977	141	170	-1.0	-6.6	-5.4	-.7	-2.9
CLE	21	7	32	1440	1352	8.4	154	770	937	13.6	4.28	89	.251	.350	-130	-72	111	99	.981	116	159	.6	-7.7	-14.8	-1.1	2.1
WEST																										
OAK	57	18	36	1469¹	**1229**	**7.5**	131	501	999	**10.8**	3.05	109	**.228**	.298	67	46	96	97	.981	117	157	.5	4.9	5.8	-1.1	10.3
KC	34	15	**44**	1420¹	1301	8.2	**84**	496	775	11.6	3.25	106	.246	.315	33	28	99	98	.979	132	**178**	-.4	3.0	-2.3	-.8	4.9
CHI	46	19	32	1450¹	1348	8.4	100	468	976	11.4	3.12	**115**	.246	.309	54	**75**	104	101	.975	160	128	-1.9	**8.1**	1.4	-1.0	-8.5
CAL	39	11	32	1481	1246	7.6	101	607	904	11.5	3.10	104	.230	.311	59	22	94	98	.980	131	159	-.2	2.4	-9.1	**-.6**	2.6
MIN	43	9	25	1416²	1384	8.8	139	529	895	12.4	3.81	93	.257	.328	-55	-41	103	100	.980	118	134	.4	-4.4	.9	-1.3	-1.6
MIL	32	**23**	32	1416¹	1303	8.3	130	569	795	12.1	3.38	103	.247	.323	12	13	100	**106**	.977	138	152	-.7	1.4	-8.5	-.8	-2.9
TOT	537	164	360	17291¹		8.3				11.9	3.46		.247	.320					.980	1512	1849					

Runs
Buford-Bal 99
Tovar-Min 94
Murcer-NY 94
Carew-Min 88
Jackson-Oak 87

Hits
Tovar-Min 204
Alomar-Cal 179
Carew-Min 177
Smith-Bos 175
Murcer-NY 175

Doubles
Smith-Bos 33
Schaal-KC 31
Rodriguez-Det 30
Oliva-Min 30

Triples
Patek-KC 11
Carew-Min 10
Blair-Bal 8

Home Runs
Melton-Chi 33
Jackson-Oak 32
Cash-Det 32
Smith-Bos 30

Total Bases
Smith-Bos 302
Jackson-Oak 288
Murcer-NY 287
Melton-Chi 267
Oliva-Min 266

Runs Batted In
Killebrew-Min 119
F.Robinson-Bal 99
Smith-Bos 96
Murcer-NY 94
Bando-Oak 94

Runs Produced
Murcer-NY 163
F.Robinson-Bal . . . 153
Killebrew-Min 152
White-NY 151
Smith-Bos 151

Bases On Balls
Killebrew-Min 114
Yastrzemski-Bos . . 106
Schaal-KC 103
Petrocelli-Bos 91
Murcer-NY 91

Batting Average
Oliva-Min 337
Murcer-NY 331
Rettenmund-Bal . . .318
Tovar-Min 311
Carew-Min 307

On Base Percentage
Murcer-NY 429
Rettenmund-Bal . . .424
Kaline-Det 421
Buford-Bal 415
White-NY 399

Slugging Average
Oliva-Min 546
Murcer-NY 543
Cash-Det 531
F.Robinson-Bal 510
Jackson-Oak 508

Production
Murcer-NY 972
Oliva-Min 918
Cash-Det 905
F.Robinson-Bal 900
Buford-Bal 891

Adjusted Production
Murcer-NY 185
White-NY 155
F.Robinson-Bal . . . 154
Buford-Bal 153
Oliva-Min 152

Batter Runs
Murcer-NY 53.7
Rettenmund-Bal . . 34.8
Buford-Bal 34.5
White-NY 33.7
Oliva-Min 33.6

Adjusted Batter Runs
Murcer-NY 57.6
White-NY 37.7
Rettenmund-Bal . . 35.3
Buford-Bal 35.0
F.Robinson-Bal . . . 33.5

Clutch Hitting Index
Killebrew-Min 163
Powell-Bal 148
Alou-Oak-NY 133
B.Robinson-Bal . . . 131
F.Robinson-Bal . . . 130

Runs Created
Murcer-NY 126
Smith-Bos 106
Jackson-Oak 103
White-NY 103
Rettenmund-Bal . . . 99

Total Average
Murcer-NY 1.035
Buford-Bal 970
Cash-Det 933
F.Robinson-Bal 905
Rettenmund-Bal . . .904

Stolen Bases
Otis-KC 52
Patek-KC 49
Alomar-Cal 39
Campaneris-Oak . . . 34

Stolen Base Average
Harper-Mil 89.3
Otis-KC 86.7
Campaneris-Oak . . 82.9
Pinson-Cle 80.6
Alomar-Cal 79.6

Stolen Base Runs
Otis-KC 10.8
Patek-KC 6.3
Campaneris-Oak . . . 6.0
Harper-Mil 5.7
Alomar-Cal 5.7

Fielding Runs
Nettles-Cle 42.3
Melton-Chi 27.0
Alomar-Cal 21.4
Cullen-Was 20.5
Unser-Was 18.5

Total Player Rating
Murcer-NY 5.2
Nettles-Cle 5.0
Melton-Chi 4.7
Otis-KC 4.2
Smith-Bos 4.0

Wins
Lolich-Det 25
Blue-Oak 24
Wood-Chi 22
McNally-Bal 21
Hunter-Oak 21

Win Percentage
McNally-Bal 808
Dobson-Oak 750
Blue-Oak 750
Dobson-Bal 714

Games
Sanders-Mil 83
Scherman-Det 69
Burgmeier-KC 67
Abernathy-KC 63

Complete Games
Lolich-Det 29
Blue-Oak 24
Wood-Chi 22
Cuellar-Bal 21
Palmer-Bal 20

Shutouts
Blue-Oak 8
Wood-Chi 7
Stottlemyre-NY 7
Bradley-Chi 6

Saves
Sanders-Mil 31
Abernathy-KC 23
Scherman-Det 20
Fingers-Oak 17
Burgmeier-KC 17

Innings Pitched
Lolich-Det 376.0
Wood-Chi 334.0
Blue-Oak 312.0
Cuellar-Bal 292.1
Coleman-Det 286.0

Fewest Hits/Game
Blue-Oak 6.03
McDowell-Cle 6.71
May-Cal 6.91
Messersmith-Cal . . 7.29
Wright-Cal 7.32

Fewest BB/Game
Peterson-NY 1.38
Kline-NY 1.50
Kaat-Min 1.62
Wood-Chi 1.67
Drago-KC 1.72

Strikeouts
Lolich-Det 308
Blue-Oak 301
Coleman-Det 236
Blyleven-Min 224
Wood-Chi 210

Strikeouts/Game
Blue-Oak 8.68
McDowell-Cle 8.05
Johnson-Chi 7.74
Coleman-Det 7.43
Lolich-Det 7.37

Ratio
Blue-Oak 8.68
Wood-Chi 9.19
Kline-NY 9.84
Dobson-Bal 9.98
McNally-Bal 10.07

Earned Run Average
Blue-Oak 1.82
Wood-Chi 1.91
Palmer-Bal 2.68
Hedlund-KC 2.71
Blyleven-Min 2.81

Adjusted ERA
Wood-Chi 188
Blue-Oak 183
Siebert-Bos 127
Hedlund-KC 126
Blyleven-Min 126

Opponents' Batting Avg.
Blue-Oak 189
McDowell-Cle 207
May-Cal 213
Messersmith-Cal . . .218
Palmer-Bal 221

Opponents' On Base Pct.
Blue-Oak 252
Wood-Chi 264
Kline-NY 276
Dobson-Bal 279
Hunter-Oak 282

Starter Runs
Wood-Chi 57.5
Blue-Oak 57.0
Palmer-Bal 24.5
Lolich-Det 22.6
Blyleven-Min 20.0

Adjusted Starter Runs
Wood-Chi 62.2
Blue-Oak 52.6
Lolich-Det 28.0
Blyleven-Min 22.8
Palmer-Bal 21.0

Clutch Pitching Index
Drago-KC 119
Krausse-Mil 118
Johnson-Chi 117
Bosman-Was 112
Wood-Chi 112

Relief Runs
Sanders-Mil 23.4
Burgmeier-KC 17.0
Mingori-Cle 12.8
Queen-Cal 12.3
Grzenda-Was 12.0

Adjusted Relief Runs
Sanders-Mil 23.5
Burgmeier-KC 16.7
Mingori-Cle 15.1
Scherman-Det 11.1
Lee-Bos 10.9

Relief Ranking
Sanders-Mil 41.6
Burgmeier-KC 34.4
Scherman-Det 19.4
Abernathy-KC 13.8
Grzenda-Was 11.4

Total Pitcher Index
Wood-Chi 7.1
Blue-Oak 5.2
Siebert-Bos 3.7
Lolich-Det 2.8
Sanders-Mil 2.7

Total Baseball Ranking
Wood-Chi 7.1
Murcer-NY 5.2
Blue-Oak 5.2
Nettles-Cle 5.0
Melton-Chi 4.7

TEAM	G	W	L	PCT	GB	R	OR	AB	H	2B	3B	HR	BB	SO	AVG	OBP	SLG	PRO	PRO+	BR	/A	PF	CHI	RC	SB	CS	SBA	SBR
EAST																												
PIT	155	96	59	.619		691	512	5490	**1505**	251	47	110	404	871	**.274**	.327	**.397**	**.724**	114	74	86	98	100	**701**	49	30	36	**-12**
CHI	156	85	70	.548	11	685	567	5247	1346	206	40	133	565	815	.257	.332	.387	.719	100	74	9	111	100	670	69	47	**57**	-19
NY	156	83	73	.532	13.5	528	578	5135	1154	175	31	105	589	990	.225	.309	.332	.641	91	-67	-51	97	98	530	41	41	42	**-12**
STL	156	75	81	.481	21.5	568	600	5326	1383	214	42	70	437	793	.260	.319	.355	.674	99	-13	-5	99	96	591	104	48	53	-16
MON	156	70	86	.449	26.5	513	609	5156	1205	156	22	91	474	828	.234	.304	.325	.629	83	-91	-101	102	101	513	68	66	55	**-12**
PHI	156	59	97	.378	37.5	503	635	5248	1240	200	36	98	487	930	.236	.304	.344	.648	87	-64	-79	103	94	545	42	50	48	-13
WEST																												
CIN	154	95	59	.617		707	557	5241	1317	214	44	124	**606**	914	.251	**.333**	.380	.713	**115**	67	**102**	94	104	676	**140**	63	**57**	-14
HOU	153	84	69	.549	10.5	**708**	636	5267	1359	233	38	134	524	907	.258	.329	.393	.722	114	**75**	87	98	103	686	111	56	50	**-12**
LA	155	85	70	.548	10.5	584	527	5270	1349	178	39	98	480	786	.256	.321	.360	.681	102	1	15	98	96	610	82	39	44	-14
ATL	155	70	84	.455	25	628	730	5278	1363	186	17	144	532	**770**	.258	.330	.382	.712	99	60	3	109	94	661	47	35	44	-15
SF	155	69	86	.445	26.5	662	649	5245	1281	211	36	**150**	480	964	.244	.311	.384	.695	101	17	8	101	**107**	630	123	45	51	-16
SD	153	58	95	.379	36.5	488	665	5213	1181	168	38	102	407	976	.227	.284	.332	.616	87	-129	-87	93	106	489	78	46	47	-13
TOT	930					7265		63116	15683	2392	430	1359	5985	10544	.248	.317	.365	.682							954	566	63	-52

TEAM	CG	SH	SV	IP	H	H/G	HR	BB	SO	RAT	ERA	ERA+	OAV	OOB	PR	/A	PF	CPI	FA	E	DP	FW	PW	BW	SBW	DIF
EAST																										
PIT	39	15	48	1414.1	1282	8.2	90	433	838	11.1	2.81	118	.242	.303	101	81	96	**108**	.978	136	**171**	-.0	8.7	9.2	-.8	1.4
CHI	54	19	32	1398.2	1329	8.6	112	**421**	824	11.5	3.22	118	.251	.310	36	**91**	110	105	.979	132	148	.2	**9.8**	1.0	-1.6	-1.9
NY	32	12	41	1414.2	1263	8.0	118	486	**1059**	11.3	3.26	103	.240	.307	29	15	97	99	.980	116	122	1.1	1.6	-5.5	-.8	8.6
STL	**64**	13	13	1399.2	1290	8.3	87	531	912	11.8	3.42	99	.246	.318	5	-2	99	97	.977	141	146	-.3	-.2	-.5	-1.2	-.7
MON	39	11	23	1401.1	1281	8.2	103	579	888	12.1	3.59	99	.245	.323	-21	-6	103	97	.978	134	141	.0	-.6	-10.9	-.8	4.2
PHI	43	13	15	1400	1318	8.5	117	536	927	12.1	3.66	98	.251	.324	-32	-11	104	99	.981	116	142	1.1	-1.2	-8.5	-.9	-9.5
WEST																										
CIN	25	15	**60**	1412.2	1313	8.4	129	435	806	11.3	3.21	100	.247	.306	38	0	93	104	**.982**	110	143	**1.3**	.0	**11.0**	-1.0	6.8
HOU	38	14	31	1385.1	1340	8.7	114	498	971	12.2	3.77	89	.255	.324	-48	-62	97	98	.980	116	151	.9	-6.7	9.4	-.8	4.7
LA	50	**23**	29	1403	**1196**	**7.7**	83	429	856	**10.6**	**2.78**	**120**	**.229**	**.292**	**104**	85	97	96	.974	162	145	-1.5	9.1	1.6	-1.0	-.8
ATL	40	4	27	1377	1412	9.2	155	512	732	12.7	4.27	89	.265	.333	-125	-73	110	97	.974	156	130	-1.1	-7.8	.3	-1.1	2.8
SF	44	8	23	1386.1	1309	8.5	130	507	771	12.0	3.69	94	.250	.320	-37	-32	101	98	.974	156	121	-1.1	-3.4	.9	-1.2	-3.5
SD	39	17	19	1403.2	1350	8.7	121	618	960	12.9	3.78	91	.254	.337	-50	-76	95	103	.976	144	146	-.6	-8.2	-9.4	-.9	.5
TOT	507	164	361	16796.2		8.4				11.8	3.45		.248	.317					.978	1619	1706					

Runs
Morgan-Cin 122
Bonds-SF 118
Wynn-Hou 117
Rose-Cin 107
Cedeno-Hou 103

Hits
Rose-Cin 198
Brock-StL 193
Williams-Chi 191
Simmons-StL 180
Garr-Atl 180

Doubles
Montanez-Phi 39
Cedeno-Hou 39
Simmons-StL 36
Williams-Chi 34

Triples
Bowa-Phi 13
Rose-Cin 11
Sanguillen-Pit 8
Cedeno-Hou 8
Brock-StL 8

Home Runs
Bench-Cin 40
Colbert-SD 38
Williams-Chi 37
Aaron-Atl 34
Stargell-Pit 33

Total Bases
Williams-Chi 348
Cedeno-Hou 300
Bench-Cin 291
May-Hou 290
Colbert-SD 286

Runs Batted In
Bench-Cin 125
Williams-Chi 122
Stargell-Pit 112
Colbert-SD 111
May-Hou 98

Runs Produced
Wynn-Hou 183
Williams-Chi 180
Morgan-Cin 179
Bonds-SF 172
Bench-Cin 172

Bases On Balls
Morgan-Cin 115
Wynn-Hou 103
Bench-Cin 100
Aaron-Atl 92
Evans-Atl 90

Batting Average
Williams-Chi 333
Garr-Atl 325
Baker-Atl 321
Cedeno-Hou 320
Watson-Hou 312

On Base Percentage
Morgan-Cin 419
Williams-Chi 403
Santo-Chi 397
Aaron-Atl 391
Wynn-Hou 391

Slugging Average
Williams-Chi 606
Stargell-Pit 558
Bench-Cin 541
Cedeno-Hou 537
Aaron-Atl 514

Production
Williams-Chi 1.010
Stargell-Pit 935
Bench-Cin 927
Cedeno-Hou 924
Aaron-Atl 906

Adjusted Production
Bench-Cin 171
Stargell-Pit 166
Williams-Chi 166
Cedeno-Hou 163
Hebner-Pit 155

Batter Runs
Williams-Chi 61.1
Bench-Cin 44.0
Cedeno-Hou 42.9
Stargell-Pit 39.6
Morgan-Cin 37.2

Adjusted Batter Runs
Williams-Chi 54.0
Bench-Cin 47.9
Cedeno-Hou 44.3
Morgan-Cin 41.3
Stargell-Pit 40.8

Clutch Hitting Index
Parker-LA 152
Oliver-Pit 137
Torre-StL 135
Evans-Atl 133
Bench-Cin 132

Runs Created
Williams-Chi 137
Morgan-Cin 117
Cedeno-Hou 115
Bench-Cin 110
Rose-Cin 109

Total Average
Williams-Chi 1.050
Morgan-Cin 973
Cedeno-Hou 959
Stargell-Pit 958
Aaron-Atl 945

Stolen Bases
Brock-StL 63
Morgan-Cin 58
Cedeno-Hou 55
Bonds-SF 44
Tolan-Cin 42

Stolen Base Average
Hernandez-SD . . . 88.9
Bond-SF 88.0
Davis-LA 87.0
Brock-StL 77.8
Morgan-Cin 77.3

Stolen Base Runs
Bonds-SF 9.6
Brock-StL 8.1
Morgan-Cin 7.2
Hernandez-SD 5.4
Davis-LA 4.2

Fielding Runs
Helms-Hou 26.5
Money-Phi 20.3
Rader-Hou 18.0
Russell-LA 16.5
Rose-Cin 12.1

Total Player Rating
Morgan-Cin 5.4
Cedeno-Hou 4.9
Bench-Cin 4.9
Williams-Chi 4.3
Rose-Cin 3.7

Wins
Carlton-Phi 27
Seaver-NY 21
Osteen-LA 20
Jenkins-Chi 20

Win Percentage
Nolan-Cin 750
Carlton-Phi 730
Pappas-Chi 708
Blass-Pit 704
Ellis-Pit 682

Games
Marshall-Mon 65
Carroll-Cin 65
Borbon-Cin 62
Ross-SD 60

Complete Games
Carlton-Phi 30
Jenkins-Chi 23
Gibson-StL 23
Wise-StL 20
Sutton-LA 18

Shutouts
Sutton-LA 9
Carlton-Phi 8
Norman-SD 6
Jenkins-Chi 5
Dierker-Hou 5

Saves
Carroll-Cin 37
McGraw-NY 27
Giusti-Pit 22
Marshall-Mon 18

Innings Pitched
Carlton-Phi 346.1
Jenkins-Chi 289.1
Niekro-Atl 282.1
Gibson-StL 278.0
Sutton-LA 272.2

Fewest Hits/Game
Sutton-LA 6.14
Carlton-Phi 6.68
Gibson-StL 7.32
Seaver-NY 7.39
Bryant-SF 7.40

Fewest BB/Game
Pappas-Chi 1.34
Nolan-Cin 1.53
Niekro-Atl 1.69
Ellis-Pit 1.82
Moose-Pit 1.87

Strikeouts
Carlton-Phi 310
Seaver-NY 249
Gibson-StL 208
Sutton-LA 207
Jenkins-Chi 184

Strikeouts/Game
Seaver-NY 8.55
Reuss-Hou 8.16
Koosman-NY 8.12
Carlton-Phi 8.06
Norman-SD 7.10

Ratio
Sutton-LA 8.35
Carlton-Phi 8.97
Nolan-Cin 9.10
McAndrew-NY 9.86
Niekro-Atl 9.95

Earned Run Average
Carlton-Phi 1.97
Nolan-Cin 1.99
Sutton-LA 2.08
Matlack-NY 2.32
Gibson-StL 2.46

Adjusted ERA
Carlton-Phi 182
Nolan-Cin 161
Sutton-LA 160
Matlack-NY 145
Gibson-StL 138

Opponents' Batting Avg.
Sutton-LA 189
Carlton-Phi 206
Gibson-StL 224
Seaver-NY 224
Bryant-SF 224

Opponents' On Base Pct.
Sutton-LA 240
Carlton-Phi 259
Nolan-Cin 262
Niekro-Atl 275
McAndrew-NY 278

Starter Runs
Carlton-Phi 56.9
Sutton-LA 41.6
Gibson-StL 30.7
Matlack-NY 30.6
Nolan-Cin 28.5

Adjusted Starter Runs
Carlton-Phi 62.2
Sutton-LA 38.0
Gibson-StL 29.1
Matlack-NY 28.1
Hooton-Chi 24.4

Clutch Pitching Index
Blass-Pit 131
Nolan-Cin 115
Hooton-Chi 115
Matlack-NY 115
Downing-LA 115

Relief Runs
Marshall-Mon 21.5
McGraw-NY 20.7
Brewer-LA 19.1
R.Hernandez-Pit . . 13.9
Carroll-Cin 12.8

Adjusted Relief Runs
Marshall-Mon 22.8
McGraw-NY 19.6
Brewer-LA 18.0
R.Hernandez-Pit . . 12.8
Giusti-Pit 11.6

Relief Ranking
Marshall-Mon 46.8
Brewer-LA 39.8
McGraw-NY 34.5
Giusti-Pit 23.0
Carroll-Cin 18.5

Total Pitcher Index
Carlton-Phi 7.6
Gibson-StL 4.3
Sutton-LA 4.1
Osteen-LA 3.3
Matlack-NY 3.2

Total Baseball Ranking
Carlton-Phi 7.6
Morgan-Cin 5.4
Cedeno-Hou 4.9
Bench-Cin 4.9
Williams-Chi 4.3

TEAM	G	W	L	PCT	GB	R	OR	AB	H	2B	3B	HR	BB	SO	AVG	OBP	SLG	PRO	PRO+	BR	/A	PF	CHI	RC	SB	CS	SBA	SBR
EAST																												
DET	156	86	70	.551		558	514	5099	1206	179	32	122	483	793	.237	.306	.356	.662	99	18	0	103	101	549	17	21	30	**-11**
BOS	155	85	70	.548	0.5	640	620	5208	1289	**229**	**34**	124	522	858	.248	.320	**.376**	**.696**	108	**83**	52	106	102	**634**	66	30	50	-20
BAL	154	80	74	.519	5	519	**430**	5028	1153	193	29	100	507	935	.229	.304	.339	.643	95	-11	-24	103	100	523	78	41	45	-14
NY	155	79	76	.510	6.5	557	527	5168	1288	201	24	103	491	**689**	.249	.318	.357	.675	110	45	63	97	95	588	71	42	48	-15
CLE	156	72	84	.462	14	472	519	5207	1220	187	18	91	420	762	.234	.295	.330	.625	89	-53	-70	103	97	495	49	53	52	-14
MIL	156	65	91	.417	21	493	595	5124	1204	167	22	88	472	868	.235	.303	.328	.631	95	-34	-23	98	99	495	64	57	52	-13
WEST																												
OAK	155	93	62	.600		604	457	5200	1248	195	29	**134**	463	886	.240	.308	.366	.674	**112**	37	65	95	104	584	87	48	48	-13
CHI	154	87	67	.565	5.5	566	538	5083	1208	170	28	108	511	991	.238	.311	.346	.657	100	14	3	102	103	550	100	52	52	-15
MIN	154	77	77	.500	15.5	537	535	5234	1277	182	31	93	478	905	.244	.311	.344	.655	96	9	-17	105	97	554	53	41	44	-13
KC	154	76	78	.494	16.5	580	545	5167	1317	220	26	78	534	711	**.255**	**.329**	.353	.682	110	65	67	100	95	601	85	44	50	-16
CAL	155	75	80	.484	18	454	533	5165	1249	171	26	78	358	850	.242	.294	.330	.624	97	-54	-24	94	96	487	57	37	43	-14
TEX	154	54	100	.351	38.5	461	628	5029	1092	166	17	56	503	926	.217	.292	.290	.582	82	-114	-91	96	**111**	438	**126**	73	**63**	-15
TOT	929					6441		61712	14751	2260	316	1175	5742	10174	.239	.308	.343	.651							853	539	61	-67

TEAM	CG	SH	SV	IP	H	H/G	HR	BB	SO	RAT	ERA	ERA+	OAV	OOB	PR	/A	PF	CPI	FA	E	DP	FW	PW	BW	SBW	DIF
EAST																										
DET	46	11	33	1388[1]	1212	7.9	101	465	952	11.2	2.96	106	.236	.305	15	28	103	102	**.984**	**96**	137	**1.9**	3.2	.0	**-.6**	3.5
BOS	48	20	25	1382[1]	1309	8.5	101	512	918	12.1	3.47	93	.251	.322	-62	-39	105	100	.978	130	141	-.0	-4.4	5.9	-1.6	7.7
BAL	62	20	21	1371[2]	1116	7.3	85	**395**	788	10.0	**2.53**	121	.223	**.282**	80	82	100	97	.983	100	150	1.6	**9.3**	-2.7	-1.0	-4.2
NY	35	19	39	1373[1]	1306	8.6	87	419	625	11.5	3.05	97	.252	.312	2	-15	96	105	.978	134	**179**	-.3	-1.7	7.2	-1.1	-2.6
CLE	47	13	24	1410	1232	7.9	123	534	846	11.5	2.92	110	.237	.312	22	47	105	**112**	.981	116	157	.8	5.3	-8.0	-1.0	-3.2
MIL	37	14	32	1391[2]	1289	8.3	116	486	740	11.7	3.45	88	.246	.314	-60	-65	99	97	.977	139	145	-.5	-7.4	-2.6	-.8	-1.6
WEST																										
OAK	42	**23**	**43**	1417[2]	1170	7.4	96	418	862	10.2	2.58	110	.225	.285	76	41	93	99	.979	130	146	-.0	4.7	7.4	-.8	4.4
CHI	36	14	42	1385[1]	1269	8.2	94	431	936	11.2	3.12	100	.245	.306	-8	1	102	99	.977	135	136	-.4	.1	.3	-1.1	11.0
MIN	37	17	34	1399[1]	1188	7.6	105	444	838	10.7	2.84	113	.230	.295	34	57	105	99	.974	159	133	-1.8	6.5	-1.9	-.8	-1.9
KC	44	16	29	1381[1]	1293	8.4	**85**	405	801	11.3	3.24	94	.250	.309	-27	-31	99	97	.981	116	164	.7	-3.5	**7.6**	-1.2	-4.6
CAL	57	18	16	1377[2]	**1109**	**7.2**	90	620	**1000**	11.5	3.06	95	**.222**	.311	0	-23	95	96	.981	114	135	.8	-2.6	-2.7	-1.0	2.9
TEX	11	8	34	1374[2]	1258	8.2	92	613	868	12.6	3.53	85	.245	.331	-71	-79	98	99	.972	166	147	-2.2	-9.0	-10.3	-1.1	-.4
TOT	502	193	372	16653[1]		8.0				11.3	3.06		.239	.308					.979	1535	1770					

Runs
Murcer-NY 102
Rudi-Oak 94
Harper-Bos 92
R.Allen-Chi 90
Tovar-Min 86

Hits
Rudi-Oak 181
Piniella-KC 179
Murcer-NY 171
Carew-Min 170
May-Chi 161

Doubles
Piniella-KC 33
Rudi-Oak 32
Murcer-NY 30
White-NY 29
Harper-Bos 29

Triples
Rudi-Oak 9
Fisk-Bos 9
Blair-Bal 8
Murcer-NY 7
Kelly-Chi 7

Home Runs
R.Allen-Chi 37
Murcer-NY 33
Killebrew-Min 26
Epstein-Oak 26

Total Bases
Murcer-NY 314
R.Allen-Chi 305
Rudi-Oak 288
Mayberry-KC 255
Piniella-KC 253

Runs Batted In
R.Allen-Chi 113
Mayberry-KC 100
Murcer-NY 96
Scott-Mil 88
Powell-Bal 81

Runs Produced
R.Allen-Chi 166
Murcer-NY 165
Rudi-Oak 150
Mayberry-KC 140

Bases On Balls
White-NY 99
R.Allen-Chi 99
Killebrew-Min 94
May-Chi 79

Batting Average
Carew-Min 318
Piniella-KC 312
R.Allen-Chi 308
May-Chi 308
Rudi-Oak 305

On Base Percentage
R.Allen-Chi 422
May-Chi 408
Mayberry-KC 396
White-NY 385
Scheinblum-KC . . .385

Slugging Average
R.Allen-Chi 603
Fisk-Bos 538
Murcer-NY 537
Mayberry-KC 507
Epstein-Oak 490

Production
R.Allen-Chi 1.025
Fisk-Bos 909
Mayberry-KC 903
Murcer-NY 900
Epstein-Oak 868

Adjusted Production
R.Allen-Chi 199
Murcer-NY 171
Mayberry-KC 168
Epstein-Oak 166
Fisk-Bos 159

Batter Runs
R.Allen-Chi 66.1
Murcer-NY 44.9
Mayberry-KC 43.0
Fisk-Bos 37.1
May-Chi 36.7

Adjusted Batter Runs
R.Allen-Chi 64.9
Murcer-NY 47.0
Mayberry-KC 43.3
Epstein-Oak 35.8
May-Chi 35.5

Clutch Hitting Index
Billings-Tex 149
Petrocelli-Bos 142
Bando-Oak 141
Yastrzemski-Bos . . 141
Rojas-KC 133

Runs Created
R.Allen-Chi 131
Murcer-NY 114
Mayberry-KC 101
May-Chi 96
Rudi-Oak 95

Total Average
R.Allen-Chi 1.121
Mayberry-KC 910
Fisk-Bos 908
Murcer-NY 888
Epstein-Oak 885

Stolen Bases
Campaneris-Oak . . . 52
Nelson-Tex 51
Patek-KC 33
Kelly-Chi 32
Otis-KC 28

Stolen Base Average
Baylor-Bal 92.3
Patek-KC 82.5
Scott-Mil 80.0
Campaneris-Oak . . 78.8
Harper-Bos 78.1

Stolen Base Runs
Campaneris-Oak . . . 7.2
Baylor-Bal 6.0
Patek-KC 5.7
Nelson-Tex 5.1
Kelly-Chi 4.2

Fielding Runs
Patek-KC 29.5
Rodriguez-Det 24.0
Michael-NY 23.7
Belanger-Bal 20.8
Bell-Cle 12.2

Total Player Rating
R.Allen-Chi 5.3
Murcer-NY 5.0
Fisk-Bos 4.1
Jackson-Oak 3.3
Patek-KC 3.2

Wins
Wood-Chi 24
Perry-Cle 24
Lolich-Det 22

Win Percentage
Hunter-Oak 750
Tiant-Bos 714
Odom-Oak 714
Palmer-Bal 677
Kline-NY 640

Games
Lindblad-Tex 66
Fingers-Oak 65
Granger-Min 63

Complete Games
Perry-Cle 29
Lolich-Det 23
Wood-Chi 20
Ryan-Cal 20
Palmer-Bal 18

Shutouts
Ryan-Cal 9
Wood-Chi 8
Stottlemyre-NY 7

Saves
Lyle-NY 35
Forster-Chi 29
Fingers-Oak 21
Granger-Min 19
Sanders-Mil 17

Innings Pitched
Wood-Chi 376.2
Perry-Cle 342.2
Lolich-Det 327.1
Hunter-Oak 295.1
Blyleven-Min 287.1

Fewest Hits/Game
Ryan-Cal 5.26
Hunter-Oak 6.09
Nelson-KC 6.23
Tiant-Bos 6.44
Messersmith-Cal . . 6.63

Fewest BB/Game
Peterson-NY 1.58
Nelson-KC 1.61
Kline-NY 1.68
Holtzman-Oak . . . 1.76
Wood-Chi 1.77

Strikeouts
Ryan-Cal 329
Lolich-Det 250
Perry-Cle 234
Blyleven-Min 228
Coleman-Det 222

Strikeouts/Game
Ryan-Cal 10.43
Messersmith-Cal . . 7.53
May-Cal 7.41
Bradley-Chi 7.23
Blyleven-Min 7.14

Ratio
Nelson-KC 7.89
Hunter-Oak 8.32
Perry-Cle 9.11
Palmer-Bal 9.51
Wood-Chi 9.70

Earned Run Average
Tiant-Bos 1.91
Perry-Cle 1.92
Hunter-Oak 2.04
Palmer-Bal 2.07
Nelson-KC 2.08

Adjusted ERA
Tiant-Bos 168
Perry-Cle 168
Palmer-Bal 149
Nelson-KC 146
Hunter-Oak 139

Opponents' Batting Avg.
Ryan-Cal 171
Hunter-Oak 189
Nelson-KC 196
Tiant-Bos 202
Perry-Cle 205

Opponents' On Base Pct.
Nelson-KC 236
Hunter-Oak 242
Perry-Cle 261
Palmer-Bal 269
Tiant-Bos 277

Starter Runs
Perry-Cle 43.5
Hunter-Oak 33.4
Palmer-Bal 30.3
Ryan-Cal 24.6
Wood-Chi 23.1

Adjusted Starter Runs
Perry-Cle 49.5
Palmer-Bal 30.7
Hunter-Oak 26.3
Tiant-Bos 25.9
Wood-Chi 25.8

Clutch Pitching Index
Paul-Tex 128
Odom-Oak 124
Wilcox-Cle 119
Lonborg-Mil 112
Lolich-Det 111

Relief Runs
Lyle-NY 13.6
Knowles-Oak 12.3
Bell-Mil 11.0
Forster-Chi 9.0
Abernathy-KC . . . 8.8

Adjusted Relief Runs
Lyle-NY 12.3
Bell-Mil 10.8
Knowles-Oak 10.7
Forster-Chi 9.7
Abernathy-KC . . . 8.6

Relief Ranking
Lyle-NY 23.3
Forster-Chi 16.0
Knowles-Oak 12.9
Abernathy-KC . . . 11.0
Fingers-Oak 8.5

Total Pitcher Index
Perry-Cle 6.6
Palmer-Bal 4.1
Wood-Chi 3.3
Hunter-Oak 3.0
Tiant-Bos 2.8

Total Baseball Ranking
Perry-Cle 6.6
R.Allen-Chi 5.3
Murcer-NY 5.0
Palmer-Bal 4.1
Fisk-Bos 4.1

TEAM	G	W	L	PCT	GB	R	OR	AB	H	2B	3B	HR	BB	SO	AVG	OBP	SLG	PRO	PRO+	BR	/A	PF	CHI	RC	SB	CS	SBA	SBR
EAST																												
NY	161	82	79	.509		608	588	5457	1345	198	24	85	540	805	.246	.317	.338	.655	89	-80	-69	98	103	583	27	22	32	-12
STL	162	81	81	.500	1.5	643	603	5478	1418	240	35	75	531	796	.259	.328	.357	.685	96	-23	-20	100	99	635	100	46	59	-21
PIT	162	80	82	.494	2.5	704	693	5608	1465	257	44	154	432	842	.261	.317	.405	.722	108	30	47	97	101	697	23	30	34	-10
MON	162	79	83	.488	3.5	668	702	5369	1345	190	23	125	**695**	777	.251	.341	.364	.705	98	30	5	104	94	672	77	68	**67**	-19
CHI	161	77	84	.478	5	614	655	5363	1322	201	21	117	575	855	.247	.322	.357	.679	87	-34	-82	107	98	605	65	58	46	**-9**
PHI	162	71	91	.438	11.5	642	717	5546	1381	218	29	134	476	979	.249	.312	.371	.683	92	-39	-56	103	102	641	51	47	51	-16
WEST																												
CIN	162	99	63	.611		741	621	5505	1398	232	34	137	639	947	.254	.335	.383	.718	**110**	43	78	95	102	724	**148**	55	52	-14
LA	162	95	66	.590	3.5	675	**565**	5604	1473	219	29	110	497	795	.263	.326	.371	.697	103	-4	25	96	100	676	109	50	49	-13
SF	162	88	74	.543	11	739	702	5537	1452	212	**52**	161	590	913	.262	.337	.407	.744	107	87	59	104	96	765	112	52	51	-14
HOU	162	82	80	.506	17	681	672	5532	1391	216	35	134	469	962	.251	.314	.376	.690	97	-27	-24	100	106	639	92	48	48	-13
ATL	162	76	85	.472	22.5	**799**	774	5631	1497	219	34	**206**	608	870	**.266**	**.341**	**.427**	**.768**	110	134	82	108	97	826	84	40	45	-14
SD	162	60	102	.370	39	548	770	5457	1330	198	26	112	401	966	.244	.298	.351	.649	92	-109	-56	92	101	566	88	36	44	-15
TOT	971					8062		66087	16817	2600	386	1550	6453	10507	.254	.324	.376	.700							976	552	64	-37

TEAM	CG	SH	SV	IP	H	H/G	HR	BB	SO	RAT	ERA	ERA+	OAV	OOB	PR	/A	PF	CPI	FA	E	DP	FW	PW	BW	SBW	DIF
EAST																										
NY	47	15	40	1465	1345	8.3	127	490	**1027**	11.4	3.26	111	.244	.309	64	57	99	101	.980	126	140	1.1	5.9	-7.2	-.9	2.6
STL	42	14	36	1460²	1366	8.4	**105**	486	867	11.6	3.25	112	.247	.312	66	63	100	100	.975	159	149	-.7	6.6	-2.1	-1.9	-1.9
PIT	26	11	44	1450²	1426	8.8	110	564	839	12.6	3.53	94	.258	.331	-11	-34	96	100	.976	151	156	-.3	-3.5	4.9	-.7	-1.4
MON	26	6	38	1451²	1356	8.4	128	681	866	12.8	3.71	103	.249	.336	-8	16	104	103	.974	163	156	-.9	1.7	.5	-1.6	-1.6
CHI	27	13	40	1437²	1471	9.2	128	**438**	885	12.1	3.66	108	.267	.324	0	45	108	104	.975	157	155	-.7	4.7	-8.5	**-.6**	1.6
PHI	**49**	11	22	1447¹	1435	8.9	131	632	919	13.1	3.99	95	.263	.343	-53	-31	104	103	.979	134	**179**	.7	-3.2	-5.8	-1.3	-.3
WEST																										
CIN	39	**17**	43	1473	1389	8.5	135	518	801	11.8	3.40	100	.251	.319	42	0	93	**105**	**.982**	115	162	**1.8**	.0	8.1	-1.1	9.2
LA	45	15	38	1491	**1270**	**7.7**	129	461	961	**10.6**	**3.00**	115	**.230**	**.293**	**109**	72	94	97	.981	125	166	1.2	**7.5**	2.6	-1.0	4.2
SF	33	8	**44**	1452¹	1442	8.9	145	485	787	12.1	3.79	101	.257	.319	-21	4	104	97	.974	163	138	-.9	.4	6.1	-1.1	2.5
HOU	45	14	26	1460²	1389	8.6	111	575	907	12.3	3.75	97	.251	.325	-13	-18	99	95	.981	116	140	1.7	-1.9	-2.5	-1.0	4.7
ATL	34	9	35	1462	1467	9.0	144	575	803	12.7	4.25	93	.263	.335	-95	-51	107	95	.974	166	142	-1.1	-5.3	**8.5**	-1.1	-5.5
SD	34	10	23	1430	1461	9.2	157	548	845	12.8	4.16	83	.266	.336	-79	-109	95	100	.973	170	152	-1.3	-11.3	-5.8	-1.2	-1.2
TOT	447	143	429	17482		8.7				12.2	3.66		.254	.324					.977	1745	1835					

Runs	Hits	Doubles	Triples	Home Runs	Total Bases
Bonds-SF 131	Rose-Cin 230	Stargell-Pit 43	Metzger-Hou 14	Stargell-Pit 44	Bonds-SF 341
Morgan-Cin 116	Garr-Atl 200	Oliver-Pit 38	Matthews-SF 10	Johnson-Atl 43	Stargell-Pit 337
Rose-Cin 115	Brock-StL 193	Staub-NY 36	Maddox-SF 10	Evans-Atl 41	Evans-Atl 331
Evans-Atl 114	Simmons-StL 192	Simmons-StL 36	Davis-LA 9	Aaron-Atl 40	Johnson-Atl 305
Brock-StL 110	Oliver-Pit 191	Rose-Cin 36		Bonds-SF 39	Oliver-Pit 303

Runs Batted In	Runs Produced	Bases On Balls	Batting Average	On Base Percentage	Slugging Average
Stargell-Pit 119	Bonds-SF 188	Evans-Atl 124	Rose-Cin ..... .338	Singleton-Mon ..... .429	Stargell-Pit ..... .646
May-Hou 105	Stargell-Pit 181	Singleton-Mon 123	Cedeno-Hou ..... .320	Fairly-Mon ..... .422	Evans-Atl ..... .556
Evans-Atl 104	Singleton-Mon 180	Morgan-Cin 111	Maddox-SF ..... .319	Morgan-Cin ..... .408	Johnson-Atl ..... .546
Bench-Cin 104	Baker-Atl 179	McCovey-SF 105	Perez-Cin ..... .314	Evans-Atl ..... .407	Cedeno-Hou ..... .537
Singleton-Mon 103	Evans-Atl 177	Monday-Chi 92	Watson-Hou ..... .312	Watson-Hou ..... .405	Bonds-SF ..... .530

Production	Adjusted Production	Batter Runs	Adjusted Batter Runs	Clutch Hitting Index	Runs Created
Stargell-Pit 1.041	Stargell-Pit 189	Stargell-Pit 57.8	Stargell-Pit 59.5	Bench-Cin 141	Evans-Atl 143
Evans-Atl ..... .964	Perez-Cin 162	Evans-Atl 54.8	Evans-Atl 48.8	Cey-LA 137	Stargell-Pit 136
Perez-Cin ..... .923	Morgan-Cin 157	Aaron-Atl 45.5	Morgan-Cin 45.5	Watson-Hou 131	Bonds-SF 130
Johnson-Atl ..... .917	Evans-Atl 153	Singleton-Mon 44.8	Perez-Cin 44.9	Singleton-Mon 130	Morgan-Cin 128
Cedeno-Hou ..... .914	Cedeno-Hou 151	Morgan-Cin 41.6	Singleton-Mon 42.1	Speier-SF 129	Rose-Cin 119

Total Average	Stolen Bases	Stolen Base Average	Stolen Base Runs	Fielding Runs	Total Player Rating
Stargell-Pit 1.129	Brock-StL 70	Baker-Atl 88.9	Morgan-Cin 11.1	Schmidt-Phi 21.2	Morgan-Cin 5.6
Evans-Atl 1.048	Morgan-Cin 67	Morgan-Cin 81.7	Brock-StL 9.0	Kessinger-Chi 17.0	Stargell-Pit 5.5
Morgan-Cin 1.034	Cedeno-Hou 56	Concepcion-Cin 81.5	Cedeno-Hou 7.8	Cey-LA 16.2	Evans-Atl 5.3
Cedeno-Hou ..... .949	Bonds-SF 43	Cedeno-Hou 78.9	Baker-Atl 5.4	Menke-Cin 16.2	Cedeno-Hou 4.7
Johnson-Atl ..... .947	Lopes-LA 36	Brock-StL 77.8	Garr-Atl 3.9	Unser-Phi 11.9	Bonds-SF 4.2

Wins	Win Percentage	Games	Complete Games	Shutouts	Saves
Bryant-SF 24	John-LA ..... .696	Marshall-Mon 92	Seaver-NY 18	Billingham-Cin 7	Marshall-Mon 31
Seaver-NY 19	Gullett-Cin ..... .692	Borbon-Cin 80	Carlton-Phi 18	Roberts-Hou 6	McGraw-NY 25
Billingham-Cin 19	Bryant-SF ..... .667	Sosa-SF 71	Billingham-Cin 16	Wise-StL 5	Giusti-Pit 20
Sutton-LA 18	Seaver-NY ..... .655	Giusti-Pit 67		Twitchell-Phi 5	Brewer-LA 20
Gullett-Cin 18	Billingham-Cin ..... .655	Segui-StL 65			

Innings Pitched	Fewest Hits/Game	Fewest BB/Game	Strikeouts	Strikeouts/Game	Ratio
Carlton-Phi 293.1	Seaver-NY 6.80	Marichal-SF 1.61	Seaver-NY 251	Seaver-NY 7.79	Seaver-NY 8.91
Billingham-Cin 293.1	Sutton-LA 6.88	Jenkins-Chi 1.89	Carlton-Phi 223	Moore-Mon 7.71	Sutton-LA 9.02
Seaver-NY 290.0	Twitchell-Phi 6.93	Barr-SF 1.91	Matlack-NY 205	Matlack-NY 7.62	Messersmith-LA 10.06
Reuss-Hou 279.1	Wilson-Hou 7.03	Sutton-LA 1.97	Sutton-LA 200	Sutton-LA 7.02	Gibson-StL 10.11
Jenkins-Chi 271.0	Messersmith-LA 7.07	Seaver-NY 1.99		Carlton-Phi 6.84	Rooker-Pit 10.41

Earned Run Average	Adjusted ERA	Opponents' Batting Avg.	Opponents' On Base Pct.	Starter Runs	Adjusted Starter Runs
Seaver-NY 2.08	Seaver-NY 174	Seaver-NY ..... .206	Seaver-NY ..... .254	Seaver-NY 51.0	Seaver-NY 49.5
Sutton-LA 2.42	Twitchell-Phi 152	Sutton-LA ..... .209	Sutton-LA ..... .258	Sutton-LA 35.3	Rogers-Mon 33.8
Twitchell-Phi 2.50	Marshall-Mon 143	Wilson-Hou ..... .213	Messersmith-LA ..... .279	Rogers-Mon 31.5	Twitchell-Phi 32.2
Marshall-Mon 2.66	Sutton-LA 142	Messersmith-LA ..... .214	Gibson-StL ..... .284	Twitchell-Phi 28.8	Sutton-LA 28.9
Messersmith-LA 2.70	Renko-Mon 136	Renko-Mon ..... .218	Briles-Pit ..... .288	Messersmith-LA 26.6	Renko-Mon 27.8

Clutch Pitching Index	Relief Runs	Adjusted Relief Runs	Relief Ranking	Total Pitcher Index	Total Baseball Ranking
Marshall-Mon 134	Borbon-Cin 20.2	Marshall-Mon 22.9	Marshall-Mon 37.7	Seaver-NY 5.9	Seaver-NY 5.9
Roberts-Hou 122	Marshall-Mon 19.8	Borbon-Cin 16.8	Locker-Chi 28.8	Rogers-Mon 4.1	Morgan-Cin 5.6
Twitchell-Phi 121	Giusti-Pit 14.1	Locker-Chi 16.6	Borbon-Cin 23.1	Renko-Mon 3.8	Stargell-Pit 5.5
Grimsley-Cin 116	Moffitt-SF 13.8	Moffitt-SF 15.6	Giusti-Pit 18.3	Marshall-Mon 2.8	Evans-Atl 5.3
Moose-Pit 113	Locker-Chi 13.3	Giusti-Pit 12.6	Scarce-Phi 16.5	Sutton-LA 2.8	Cedeno-Hou 4.7

TEAM	G	W	L	PCT	GB	R	OR	AB	H	2B	3B	HR	BB	SO	AVG	OBP	SLG	PRO	PRO+	BR	/A	PF	CHI	RC	SB	CS	SBA	SBR
EAST																												
BAL	162	97	65	.599		754	561	5537	1474	229	**48**	119	**648**	752	.266	**.348**	.389	.737	107	**61**	**66**	99	98	**765**	**146**	64	50	**-10**
BOS	162	89	73	.549	8	738	647	5513	1472	235	30	147	581	799	.267	.340	**.401**	**.741**	101	58	16	106	98	751	114	45	47	-14
DET	162	85	77	.525	12	642	674	5508	1400	213	32	157	509	722	.254	.322	.390	.712	93	-8	-53	107	95	674	28	30	39	-13
NY	162	80	82	.494	17	641	610	5492	1435	212	17	131	489	**680**	.261	.324	.378	.702	100	-24	0	97	98	655	47	43	52	-17
MIL	162	74	88	.457	23	708	731	5526	1399	229	40	145	563	977	.253	.327	.388	.715	103	2	17	98	101	702	110	66	56	-13
CLE	162	71	91	.438	26	680	826	5592	1429	205	29	**158**	471	793	.256	.317	.387	.704	95	-26	-37	102	102	666	60	68	55	-12
WEST																												
OAK	162	94	68	.580		**758**	615	5507	1431	216	28	147	595	919	.260	.336	.389	.725	**109**	28	64	95	**104**	730	128	57	51	-13
KC	162	88	74	.543	6	755	752	5508	1440	239	40	114	644	696	.261	.342	.381	.723	95	31	-22	108	103	720	105	69	**58**	-13
MIN	162	81	81	.500	13	738	692	5625	**1521**	**240**	44	120	598	954	**.270**	.344	.393	.737	102	56	28	104	97	756	87	46	44	-12
CAL	162	79	83	.488	15	629	657	5505	1395	183	29	93	509	816	.253	.320	.348	.668	95	-83	-30	92	**104**	609	59	47	52	-16
CHI	162	77	85	.475	17	652	705	5475	1400	228	38	111	537	952	.256	.326	.372	.698	92	-27	-50	103	99	647	83	73	**58**	-12
TEX	162	57	105	.352	37	619	844	5488	1397	195	29	110	503	791	.255	.320	.361	.681	94	-62	-33	96	100	629	91	53	48	-12
TOT	972					8314		66276	17193	2624	404	1552	6647	9851	.259	.331	.381	.712							1058	661	62	-78

TEAM	CG	SH	SV	IP	H	H/G	HR	BB	SO	RAT	ERA	ERA+	OAV	OOB	PR	/A	PF	CPI	FA	E	DP	FW	PW	BW	SBW	DIF
EAST																										
BAL	67	14	26	1461²	**1297**	8.0	124	475	715	11.0	3.07	122	.239	.303	121	**108**	98	102	.981	119	184	1.3	**11.0**	6.8	-.3	-2.7
BOS	67	10	33	1440¹	1417	8.9	158	499	808	12.2	3.65	110	.259	.324	26	59	105	**106**	.979	127	162	.8	6.0	1.6	-.8	.2
DET	39	11	**46**	1447²	1468	9.1	154	493	911	12.4	3.90	105	.264	.327	-13	30	107	101	**.982**	**112**	144	**1.7**	3.1	-5.4	-.7	5.3
NY	47	16	39	1427²	1379	8.7	109	**457**	708	11.7	3.34	110	.254	.315	75	51	96	102	.976	156	172	-.8	5.2	.0	-1.1	-4.4
MIL	50	11	28	1454	1476	9.1	119	623	671	13.2	3.98	94	.264	.341	-26	-35	99	101	.977	145	167	-.2	-3.6	1.7	-.7	-4.3
CLE	55	9	21	1464²	1532	9.4	172	602	883	13.4	4.58	85	.270	.344	-124	-108	103	96	.978	139	174	.2	-11.0	-3.8	-.6	5.2
WEST																										
OAK	46	16	41	1457¹	1311	8.1	143	494	797	11.3	3.29	108	.240	.307	85	42	93	100	.978	137	170	.3	4.3	6.5	-.7	2.5
KC	40	7	41	1448²	1521	9.4	114	617	790	13.5	4.19	98	.272	.348	-60	-13	108	100	.974	167	**192**	-1.4	-1.3	-2.3	-.7	12.7
MIN	48	**18**	34	1451²	1443	8.9	115	519	879	12.4	3.77	105	.259	.326	7	30	104	97	.978	139	147	.2	3.1	2.9	-.6	-5.5
CAL	**72**	13	19	1456¹	1351	8.3	**104**	614	**1010**	14.1	3.53	100	.245	.326	46	2	93	98	.975	156	153	-.8	2.3	-3.1	-1.0	2.6
CHI	48	15	35	1456	1484	9.2	110	574	848	13.0	3.86	102	.265	.338	-7	15	104	101	.977	144	165	-.1	1.5	-5.1	-.6	-4.2
TEX	35	10	27	1430	1514	9.5	130	680	831	14.1	4.64	80	.273	.357	-130	-145	98	96	.974	161	164	-1.1	-14.8	-3.4	-.6	-4.2
TOT	614	150	390	17396		8.9				12.5	3.82		.259	.331					.977	1702	1994					

Runs
Jackson-Oak 99
Scott-Mil 98
North-Oak 98
Carew-Min 98
Bando-Oak 97

Hits
Carew-Min 203
May-Mil 189
Murcer-NY 187
Scott-Mil 185
Johnson-Tex 179

Doubles
Garcia-Mil 32
Bando-Oak 32
Scott-Mil 30
Chambliss-Cle 30
Carew-Min 30

Triples
Carew-Min 11
Bumbry-Bal 11
Orta-Chi 10
Coggins-Bal 9
Coluccio-Mil 8

Home Runs
Jackson-Oak 32
Robinson-Cal 30
Burroughs-Tex 30
Bando-Oak 29

Total Bases
Scott-Mil 295
May-Mil 295
Bando-Oak 295
Murcer-NY 286
Jackson-Oak 286

Runs Batted In
Jackson-Oak 117
Scott-Mil 107
Mayberry-KC 100
Bando-Oak 98
Robinson-Cal 97

Runs Produced
Jackson-Oak 184
Scott-Mil 181
Bando-Oak 166
May-Mil 164
Mayberry-KC 161

Bases On Balls
Mayberry-KC 122
Grich-Bal 107
Yastrzemski-Bos . . 105
Tenace-Oak 101
Briggs-Mil 87

Batting Average
Carew-Min 350
Scott-Mil 306
Davis-Bal 306
Murcer-NY 304
May-Mil 303

On Base Percentage
Mayberry-KC 420
Carew-Min 415
Yastrzemski-Bos . . .411
Tenace-Oak 391
Jackson-Oak 387

Slugging Average
Jackson-Oak 531
Bando-Oak 498
Robinson-Cal 489
Scott-Mil 488
Munson-NY 487

Production
Jackson-Oak 918
Mayberry-KC 898
Carew-Min 885
Bando-Oak 876
Yastrzemski-Bos . . .874

Adjusted Production
Jackson-Oak 165
Robinson-Cal 153
Bando-Oak 153
Scott-Mil 144
Carew-Min 143

Batter Runs
Mayberry-KC 41.0
Jackson-Oak 40.5
Carew-Min 38.9
Yastrzemski-Bos . . 36.8
Bando-Oak 35.5

Adjusted Batter Runs
Jackson-Oak 44.2
Bando-Oak 39.5
Carew-Min 36.0
Robinson-Cal 35.6
Mayberry-KC 35.6

Clutch Hitting Index
Davis-Bal 156
May-Chi 139
Darwin-Min 137
Oliva-Min 136
Robinson-Bal 134

Runs Created
Bando-Oak 113
Carew-Min 113
Mayberry-KC 113
Jackson-Oak 112
Scott-Mil 106

Total Average
Mayberry-KC 995
Jackson-Oak 953
Carew-Min 885
Yastrzemski-Bos . . .879
Bando-Oak 876

Stolen Bases
Harper-Bos 54
North-Oak 53
Nelson-Tex 43
Carew-Min 41
Patek-KC 36

Stolen Base Average
Rojas-KC 81.8
Money-Mil 81.5
Harper-Bos 79.4
Baylor-Bal 78.0
Campaneris-Oak . . 77.3

Stolen Base Runs
Harper-Bos 7.8
Campaneris-Oak . . . 4.2
Baylor-Bal 4.2
North-Oak 3.9
Money-Mil 3.6

Fielding Runs
Patek-KC 35.3
Nettles-NY 26.0
Bell-Cle 24.7
North-Oak 21.4
Grich-Bal 21.0

Total Player Rating
Carew-Min 5.1
Grich-Bal 4.3
Smith-Bos 4.2
Jackson-Oak 4.0
Patek-KC 3.7

Wins
Wood-Chi 24
Coleman-Det 23
Palmer-Bal 22

Win Percentage
Hunter-Oak 808
Palmer-Bal 710
Blue-Oak 690
Splittorff-KC 645
Colborn-Mil 625

Games
Hiller-Det 65
Fingers-Oak 62
Bird-KC 54
Knowles-Oak 52

Complete Games
Perry-Cle 29
Ryan-Cal 26
Blyleven-Min 25
Tiant-Bos 23
Colborn-Mil 22

Shutouts
Blyleven-Min 9
Perry-Cle 7
Palmer-Bal 6

Saves
Hiller-Det 38
Lyle-NY 27
Fingers-Oak 22
Bird-KC 20
Acosta-Chi 18

Innings Pitched
Wood-Chi 359.1
Perry-Cle 344.0
Ryan-Cal 326.0
Blyleven-Min 325.0
Singer-Cal 315.2

Fewest Hits/Game
Bibby-Tex 6.04
Ryan-Cal 6.57
Palmer-Bal 6.83
Tiant-Bos 7.18
Blue-Oak 7.30

Fewest BB/Game
Kaat-Min 1.73
Blyleven-Min 1.86
Holtzman-Oak 2.00
Wood-Chi 2.28
Lolich-Det 2.30

Strikeouts
Ryan-Cal 383
Blyleven-Min 258
Singer-Cal 241
Perry-Cle 238
Lolich-Det 214

Strikeouts/Game
Ryan-Cal 10.57
Bibby-Tex 7.74
Blyleven-Min 7.14
Stone-Chi 7.04
Singer-Cal 6.87

Ratio
Tiant-Bos 9.99
Hunter-Oak 10.25
Blyleven-Min 10.30
Palmer-Bal 10.36
Holtzman-Oak . . . 10.44

Earned Run Average
Palmer-Bal 2.40
Blyleven-Min 2.52
Lee-Bos 2.75
Ryan-Cal 2.87
Medich-NY 2.95

Adjusted ERA
Blyleven-Min 157
Palmer-Bal 156
Lee-Bos 146
Medich-NY 124
Ryan-Cal 123

Opponents' Batting Avg.
Bibby-Tex 192
Ryan-Cal 203
Palmer-Bal 211
Tiant-Bos 219
Blue-Oak 224

Opponents' On Base Pct.
Tiant-Bos 281
Hunter-Oak 284
Blyleven-Min 287
Holtzman-Oak 287
Palmer-Bal 289

Starter Runs
Blyleven-Min 46.8
Palmer-Bal 46.6
Ryan-Cal 34.2
Lee-Bos 33.7
Holtzman-Oak 28.1

Adjusted Starter Runs
Blyleven-Min 51.9
Palmer-Bal 43.9
Lee-Bos 40.1
Ryan-Cal 24.4
Perry-Cle 20.8

Clutch Pitching Index
Lee-Bos 119
Forster-Chi 116
Curtis-Bos 113
Drago-KC 112
Bahnsen-Chi 112

Relief Runs
Hiller-Det 33.1
Fingers-Oak 26.7
Reynolds-Bal 23.1
Acosta-Chi 17.1
Jackson-Bal 17.1

Adjusted Relief Runs
Hiller-Det 36.9
Fingers-Oak 22.9
Reynolds-Bal 22.0
Acosta-Chi 18.7
Jackson-Bal 16.3

Relief Ranking
Hiller-Det 64.9
Acosta-Chi 35.5
Fingers-Oak 33.3
Reynolds-Bal 25.5
Lyle-NY 23.8

Total Pitcher Index
Blyleven-Min 5.4
Palmer-Bal 4.7
Lee-Bos 4.6
Hiller-Det 3.9
Colborn-Mil 2.3

Total Baseball Ranking
Blyleven-Min 5.4
Carew-Min 5.1
Palmer-Bal 4.7
Lee-Bos 4.6
Grich-Bal 4.3

TEAM	G	W	L	PCT	GB	R	OR	AB	H	2B	3B	HR	BB	SO	AVG	OBP	SLG	PRO	PRO+	BR	/A	PF	CHI	RC	SB	CS	SBA	SBR
EAST																												
PIT	162	88	74	.543		751	657	5702	**1560**	238	46	114	514	828	.274	.338	.391	.729	114	66	91	96	100	745	55	31	41	-14
STL	161	86	75	.534	1.5	677	643	5620	1492	216	46	83	531	752	.265	.334	.365	.699	101	9	15	99	98	687	172	62	60	-16
PHI	162	80	82	.494	8	676	701	5494	1434	233	50	95	469	822	.261	.322	.373	.695	96	-6	-33	104	104	658	115	58	49	-11
MON	161	79	82	.491	8.5	662	657	5343	1355	201	29	86	652	812	.254	.338	.350	.688	92	2	-34	106	99	657	124	49	50	-14
NY	162	71	91	.438	17	572	646	5468	1286	183	22	96	597	735	.235	.314	.329	.643	86	-98	-86	98	100	571	43	23	32	-11
CHI	162	66	96	.407	22	669	826	5574	1397	221	42	110	621	857	.251	.329	.365	.694	96	0	-28	104	98	668	78	73	70	-19
WEST																												
LA	162	102	60	.630		798	561	5557	1511	231	34	139	597	820	.272	.346	.401	.747	119	103	130	96	102	774	149	75	52	-8
CIN	163	98	64	.605	4	776	631	5535	1437	271	35	135	693	940	.260	.345	.394	.739	114	95	105	99	99	776	146	49	49	-14
ATL	163	88	74	.543	14	661	563	5533	1375	202	37	120	571	772	.249	.321	.363	.684	93	-22	-51	104	101	649	72	44	47	-14
HOU	162	81	81	.500	21	653	632	5489	1441	222	41	110	471	864	.263	.324	.378	.702	106	6	34	96	98	663	108	65	58	-14
SF	162	72	90	.444	30	634	637	5482	1380	228	38	93	548	869	.252	.323	.358	.681	91	-27	-58	105	100	642	107	51	47	-12
SD	162	60	102	.370	42	541	830	5415	1239	196	27	99	564	900	.229	.304	.330	.634	86	-121	-92	96	101	555	85	45	49	-15
TOT	972					8070		66212	16907	2642	447	1280	6828	9971	.255	.328	.367	.695							1254	625	67	1

TEAM	CG	SH	SV	IP	H	H/G	HR	BB	SO	RAT	ERA	ERA+	OAV	OOB	PR	/A	PF	CPI	FA	E	DP	FW	PW	BW	SBW	DIF
EAST																										
PIT	**51**	9	17	1466	1428	8.8	93	543	721	12.3	3.49	99	.256	.325	21	-7	95	100	.975	162	154		-.7	9.5	-1.5	.2
STL	37	13	20	1473¹	1399	8.5	97	616	794	12.5	3.48	103	.253	.331	22	15	99	**104**	.977	147	**192**	.4	1.6	1.6	-1.7	3.7
PHI	46	4	19	1447¹	1394	8.7	111	682	892	13.1	3.91	97	.257	.343	-47	-21	104	101	.976	148	168	.4	-2.2	-3.4	-1.2	5.4
MON	35	8	**27**	1429	1340	8.4	99	544	822	12.0	3.60	107	.248	.321	3	38	106	94	.976	153	157	.0	4.0	-3.5	-1.5	-.5
NY	46	15	14	1470¹	1433	8.8	99	504	908	12.0	3.42	104	.257	.322	32	24	99	102	.975	158	150	-.2	2.5	-9.0	-1.2	-2.2
CHI	23	6	26	1466¹	1593	9.8	122	576	895	13.6	4.28	89	.277	.347	-107	-75	105	100	.969	199	141	-2.6	-7.8	-2.9	-2.0	.3
WEST																										
LA	33	19	23	1465¹	**1272**	7.8	112	464	943	10.8	2.97	114	**.232**	.295	104	69	94	96	.975	157	122	-.2	7.2	**13.5**	-.8	1.3
CIN	34	11	**27**	1466¹	1364	8.4	126	536	875	11.8	3.41	102	.247	.315	33	12	96	100	.979	134	151	1.2	1.2	10.9	-1.5	5.1
ATL	46	**21**	22	1474¹	1343	8.2	97	488	772	11.3	3.05	**124**	.244	.308	92	**118**	104	102	.979	132	161	1.3	**12.3**	-5.3	-1.5	.1
HOU	36	18	18	1450²	1396	8.7	**84**	601	738	12.6	3.46	100	.255	.333	25	0	96	**104**	**.982**	**113**	161	**2.4**	.0	3.5	-1.5	-4.5
SF	27	11	25	1439	1409	8.8	116	559	756	12.5	3.78	101	.256	.327	-25	3	105	97	.972	175	153	-1.2	.3	-6.0	-1.3	-.8
SD	25	7	19	1445²	1536	9.6	124	715	855	14.3	4.58	78	.274	.361	-154	-164	98	99	.973	170	126	-.9	-17.1	-9.6	-1.6	8.2
TOT	439	142	257	17493²		8.7				12.4	3.62		.255	.328					.976	1848	1836					

Runs
Rose-Cin 110
Schmidt-Phi 108
Bench-Cin 108
Morgan-Cin 107
Brock-StL 105

Hits
Garr-Atl 214
Cash-Phi 206
Garvey-LA 200
Oliver-Pit 198
Stennett-Pit 196

Doubles
Rose-Cin 45
Oliver-Pit 38
Bench-Cin 38
Stargell-Pit 37

Triples
Garr-Atl 17
Oliver-Pit 12
Cash-Phi 11
Metzger-Hou 10
Bowa-Phi 10

Home Runs
Schmidt-Phi 36
Bench-Cin 33
Wynn-LA 32
Perez-Cin 28
Cedeno-Hou 26

Total Bases
Bench-Cin 315
Schmidt-Phi 310
Garr-Atl 305
Garvey-LA 301
Oliver-Pit 293

Runs Batted In
Bench-Cin 129
Schmidt-Phi 116
Garvey-LA 111
Wynn-LA 108
Simmons-StL 103

Runs Produced
Bench-Cin 204
Schmidt-Phi 188
Garvey-LA 185
Wynn-LA 180
Cedeno-Hou 171

Bases On Balls
Evans-Atl 126
Morgan-Cin 120
Wynn-LA 108
Schmidt-Phi 106
Rose-Cin 106

Batting Average
Garr-Atl 353
Oliver-Pit 321
Gross-Hou 314
Buckner-LA 314
Madlock-Chi 313

On Base Percentage
Morgan-Cin 430
Stargell-Pit 409
Bailey-Mon 400
Schmidt-Phi 398
Smith-StL 394

Slugging Average
Schmidt-Phi 546
Stargell-Pit 537
Smith-StL 528
Bench-Cin 507
Garr-Atl 503

Production
Stargell-Pit 947
Schmidt-Phi 944
Morgan-Cin 924
Smith-StL 922
Wynn-LA 891

Adjusted Production
Stargell-Pit 169
Morgan-Cin 160
Smith-StL 158
Schmidt-Phi 156
Wynn-LA 154

Batter Runs
Schmidt-Phi 48.3
Morgan-Cin 45.2
Stargell-Pit 44.4
Smith-StL 38.5
Wynn-LA 36.4

Adjusted Batter Runs
Stargell-Pit 46.8
Morgan-Cin 46.2
Schmidt-Phi 45.3
Wynn-LA 39.3
Smith-StL 39.1

Clutch Hitting Index
Cey-LA 140
Singleton-Mon 133
Montanez-Phi 131
Zisk-Pit 129
Simmons-StL 128

Runs Created
Schmidt-Phi 130
Morgan-Cin 125
Stargell-Pit 115
Bench-Cin 114
Garr-Atl 113

Total Average
Morgan-Cin 1.108
Schmidt-Phi 1.017
Stargell-Pit 997
Smith-StL 920
Wynn-LA 915

Stolen Bases
Brock-StL 118
Lopes-LA 59
Morgan-Cin 58
Cedeno-Hou 57
Lintz-Mon 50

Stolen Base Average
Lintz-Mon 87.7
Concepcion-Cin . . . 87.2
Morgan-Cin 82.9
Bonds-SF 78.8
Hernandez-SD 78.7

Stolen Base Runs
Brock-StL 15.6
Lintz-Mon 10.8
Morgan-Cin 10.2
Concepcion-Cin . . . 8.7

Fielding Runs
Cash-Phi 29.1
Schmidt-Phi 26.3
Foli-Mon 19.4
Geronimo-Cin 19.1
Milbourne-Hou 17.9

Total Player Rating
Schmidt-Phi 6.9
Morgan-Cin 5.1
Cash-Phi 4.0
Concepcion-Cin . . . 4.0
Cedeno-Hou 3.8

Wins
P.Niekro-Atl 20
Messersmith-LA 20
Sutton-LA 19
Billingham-Cin 19

Win Percentage
Messersmith-LA 769
Sutton-LA 679
Capra-Atl 667
Torrez-Mon 652
Billingham-Cin 633

Games
Marshall-LA 106
Hardy-SD 76
Borbon-Cin 73
Forsch-Hou 70
Sosa-SF 68

Complete Games
P.Niekro-Atl 18
Carlton-Phi 17
Lonborg-Phi 16
Rooker-Pit 15

Shutouts
Matlack-NY 7
P.Niekro-Atl 6

Saves
Marshall-LA 21
Moffitt-SF 15
Borbon-Cin 14
Giusti-Pit 12

Innings Pitched
P.Niekro-Atl 302.1
Messersmith-LA . . . 292.1
Carlton-Phi 291.0
Lonborg-Phi 283.0
Sutton-LA 276.0

Fewest Hits/Game
Capra-Atl 6.76
Messersmith-LA . . . 6.99
P.Niekro-Atl 7.41
Gullett-Cin 7.44
Wilson-Hou 7.48

Fewest BB/Game
Barr-SF 1.76
Reed-Atl 1.98
Ellis-Pit 2.09
Lonborg-Phi 2.23
Marshall-LA 2.42

Strikeouts
Carlton-Phi 240
Messersmith-LA . . . 221
Seaver-NY 201
P.Niekro-Atl 195
Matlack-NY 195

Strikeouts/Game
Seaver-NY 7.67
Carlton-Phi 7.42
Bonham-Chi 7.08
D'Acquisto-SF 6.99
Norman-Cin 6.81

Ratio
Messersmith-LA . . 9.97
P.Niekro-Atl 10.21
Barr-SF 10.21
Matlack-NY 10.24
Reed-Atl 10.35

Earned Run Average
Capra-Atl 2.28
P.Niekro-Atl 2.38
Matlack-NY 2.41
Marshall-LA 2.42
Messersmith-LA . . 2.59

Adjusted ERA
Capra-Atl 166
P.Niekro-Atl 159
Matlack-NY 148
Marshall-LA 141
Barr-SF 139

Opponents' Batting Avg.
Capra-Atl 208
Messersmith-LA 212
Gullett-Cin 222
P.Niekro-Atl 225
Matlack-NY 226

Opponents' On Base Pct.
Messersmith-LA 278
Matlack-NY 285
P.Niekro-Atl 286
Reed-Atl 286
Capra-Atl 287

Starter Runs
P.Niekro-Atl 41.5
Matlack-NY 35.6
Messersmith-LA . . . 33.5
Capra-Atl 32.2
Rooker-Pit 24.6

Adjusted Starter Runs
P.Niekro-Atl 46.9
Capra-Atl 36.1
Matlack-NY 34.0
Barr-SF 28.1
Messersmith-LA . . 26.4

Clutch Pitching Index
Caldwell-SF 117
Morton-Atl 117
Marshall-LA 116
Schueler-Phi 113
McGlothen-StL 112

Relief Runs
Marshall-LA 27.7
Murray-Mon 21.7
House-Atl 19.3
Taylor-Mon 17.3
C.Carroll-Cin 16.5

Adjusted Relief Runs
Marshall-LA 22.7
Murray-Mon 21.7
House-Atl 21.1
Taylor-Mon 19.9
C.Carroll-Cin 15.0

Relief Ranking
Marshall-LA 31.6
C.Carroll-Cin 24.8
House-Atl 19.9
Taylor-Mon 17.9
Leon-Atl 13.4

Total Pitcher Index
P.Niekro-Atl 5.3
Messersmith-LA . . . 3.8
Barr-SF 3.8
Capra-Atl 3.7
Rooker-Pit 3.3

Total Baseball Ranking
Schmidt-Phi 6.9
P.Niekro-Atl 5.3
Morgan-Cin 5.1
Cash-Phi 4.0
Concepcion-Cin 4.0

TEAM	G	W	L	PCT	GB	R	OR	AB	H	2B	3B	HR	BB	SO	AVG	OBP	SLG	PRO	PRO+	BR	/A	PF	CHI	RC	SB	CS	SBA	SBR
EAST																												
BAL	162	91	71	.562		659	612	5535	1418	226	27	116	509	770	.256	.325	.370	.695	103	-1	19	97	98	671	145	58	55	-15
NY	162	89	73	.549	2	671	623	5524	1451	220	30	101	515	**690**	.263	.328	.368	.696	102	1	19	97	100	666	53	35	39	-12
BOS	162	84	78	.519	7	**696**	661	5499	1449	**236**	31	109	**569**	811	.264	.336	.377	.713	98	39	-7	107	98	699	104	58	60	-18
CLE	162	77	85	.475	14	662	694	5474	1395	201	19	131	432	756	.255	.312	.370	.682	96	-35	-29	99	**108**	610	79	68	53	-10
MIL	162	76	86	.469	15	647	660	5472	1335	228	**49**	120	500	909	.244	.310	.369	.679	95	-40	-36	99	105	622	106	75	59	-12
DET	162	72	90	.444	19	620	768	5568	1375	200	35	131	436	784	.247	.304	.366	.670	88	-63	-86	104	104	607	67	38	39	-14
WEST																												
OAK	162	90	72	.556		689	551	5331	1315	205	37	132	568	876	.247	.324	.373	.697	106	1	43	94	105	648	**164**	93	70	-13
TEX	161	84	76	.525	5	690	698	5449	1482	198	39	99	508	710	**.272**	**.338**	.377	.715	**107**	42	**58**	98	98	677	113	80	53	**-7**
MIN	163	82	80	.506	8	673	669	5632	**1530**	190	37	111	520	791	**.272**	**.338**	.378	.716	102	44	17	104	93	**707**	74	45	46	-13
CHI	163	80	80	.500	9	684	721	5577	1492	225	23	**135**	519	858	.268	.333	**.389**	**.722**	104	49	32	102	95	701	64	53	54	-16
KC	162	77	85	.475	13	667	662	5582	1448	232	42	89	550	768	.259	.329	.364	.693	93	-1	-39	106	99	668	146	76	58	-11
CAL	163	68	94	.420	22	618	657	5401	1372	203	31	95	509	801	.254	.323	.356	.679	100	-29	8	94	98	615	119	79	58	-10
TOT	973					7976		66044	17062	2564	400	1369	6135	9524	.258	.325	.371	.697							1234	758	62	-84

TEAM	CG	SH	SV	IP	H	H/G	HR	BB	SO	RAT	ERA	ERA+	OAV	OOB	PR	/A	PF	CPI	FA	E	DP	FW	PW	BW	SBW	DIF
EAST																										
BAL	57	**16**	25	1474	1393	8.5	101	480	701	11.6	3.27	105	.253	.315	56	29	95	102	**.980**	128	174	1.0	3.0	2.0	-.8	4.8
NY	53	13	24	1455¹	1402	8.7	104	528	829	12.1	3.31	105	.255	.324	49	28	96	**106**	.977	142	158	.2	2.9	2.0	-.5	3.4
BOS	**71**	12	18	1455¹	1462	9.0	126	463	751	12.1	3.72	103	.262	.322	-16	20	106	99	.977	145	156	.0	2.1	-.7	-1.1	2.8
CLE	45	9	27	1445²	1419	8.8	138	479	650	12.0	3.80	95	.259	.323	-29	-30	100	98	.977	146	157	-.0	-3.1	-3.0	-.3	2.5
MIL	43	11	24	1457²	1476	9.1	126	493	621	12.3	3.76	96	.265	.328	-23	-23	100	102	**.980**	**127**	168	1.1	-2.4	-3.8	-.5	.6
DET	54	7	15	1455²	1443	8.9	148	621	869	13.0	4.16	91	.262	.340	-87	-58	105	99	.975	158	155	-.7	-6.1	-9.0	-.4	7.2
WEST																										
OAK	49	12	28	1439²	**1322**	**8.3**	**90**	430	755	**11.1**	**2.95**	112	.246	.305	106	58	92	103	.977	141	154	.3	**6.1**	4.5	-.6	-1.2
TEX	62	**16**	12	1433²	1423	8.9	126	449	871	12.0	3.82	93	.259	.320	-32	-41	99	95	.974	163	164	-1.1	-4.3	**6.1**	.0	3.3
MIN	43	11	**29**	1455¹	1436	8.9	115	513	934	12.3	3.64	103	.259	.326	-4	17	104	100	.976	151	164	-.3	1.8	1.8	-.6	-1.7
CHI	55	11	**29**	1465²	1470	9.0	103	548	826	12.7	3.94	95	.263	.334	-51	-34	103	96	.977	147	**188**	-.0	-3.6	3.3	-.9	1.2
KC	54	13	17	1471²	1477	9.0	91	482	731	12.2	3.51	100	.262	.324	17	50	106	100	.976	152	166	-.4	5.2	-4.1	-.4	-4.4
CAL	64	13	12	1439	1339	8.4	101	649	**986**	12.7	3.52	98	.248	.334	15	-13	95	102	.976	147	150	-.0	-1.4	.8	-.3	-12.1
TOT	650	144	260	17448²		8.8				12.2	3.62		.258	.325					.977	1747	1954					

Runs
Yastrzemski-Bos	93
Grich-Bal	92
Jackson-Oak	90
Otis-KC	87
Carew-Min	86

Hits
Carew-Min	218
Davis-Bal	181
Money-Mil	178
K.Henderson-Chi	176
Rudi-Oak	174

Doubles
Rudi-Oak	39
Scott-Mil	36
McRae-KC	36
K.Henderson-Chi	35
Burroughs-Tex	33

Triples
Rivers-Cal	11
Otis-KC	9

Home Runs
R.Allen-Chi	32
Jackson-Oak	29
Tenace-Oak	26
Darwin-Min	25
Burroughs-Tex	25

Total Bases
Rudi-Oak	287
K.Henderson-Chi	281
Burroughs-Tex	279
Carew-Min	267

Runs Batted In
Burroughs-Tex	118
Bando-Oak	103
Rudi-Oak	99
K.Henderson-Chi	95
Darwin-Min	94

Runs Produced
Burroughs-Tex	177
Bando-Oak	165
Yastrzemski-Bos	157
Grich-Bal	155
Jackson-Oak	154

Bases On Balls
Tenace-Oak	110
Yastrzemski-Bos	104
Burroughs-Tex	91
Grich-Bal	90

Batting Average
Carew-Min	.364
Orta-Chi	.316
McRae-KC	.310
Piniella-NY	.305
Maddox-NY	.303

On Base Percentage
Carew-Min	.435
Yastrzemski-Bos	.421
Burroughs-Tex	.405
Maddox-NY	.397
Jackson-Oak	.396

Slugging Average
R.Allen-Chi	.563
Jackson-Oak	.514
Burroughs-Tex	.504
Rudi-Oak	.484
Freehan-Det	.479

Production
R.Allen-Chi	.942
Jackson-Oak	.910
Burroughs-Tex	.908
Carew-Min	.880
Yastrzemski-Bos	.866

Adjusted Production
Jackson-Oak	171
Burroughs-Tex	164
R.Allen-Chi	164
Carew-Min	148
Robinson-Cal-Cle	143

Batter Runs
Burroughs-Tex	45.3
Carew-Min	44.7
Jackson-Oak	41.0
R.Allen-Chi	39.3
Yastrzemski-Bos	38.1

Adjusted Batter Runs
Burroughs-Tex	47.1
Jackson-Oak	45.2
Carew-Min	41.8
R.Allen-Chi	37.9
Yastrzemski-Bos	33.3

Clutch Hitting Index
Bando-Oak	154
Davis-Bal	130
Petrocelli-Bos	129
Murcer-NY	128
Burroughs-Tex	126

Runs Created
Carew-Min	118
Burroughs-Tex	113
Jackson-Oak	109
Yastrzemski-Bos	102
K.Henderson-Chi	100

Total Average
Jackson-Oak	.992
R.Allen-Chi	.953
Burroughs-Tex	.919
Yastrzemski-Bos	.900
Carew-Min	.879

Stolen Bases
North-Oak	54
Carew-Min	38
Lowenstein-Cle	36
Campaneris-Oak	34
Patek-KC	33

Stolen Base Average
Jackson-Oak	83.3
Coggins-Bal	81.3
Pinson-KC	80.8
Otis-KC	78.3
Money-Mil	76.0

Stolen Base Runs
Jackson-Oak	4.5
Coggins-Bal	4.2
Pinson-KC	3.3
Miller-Bos	2.7
Blair-Bal	2.7

Fielding Runs
Terrell-Min	31.4
Rodriguez-Det	21.6
Robinson-Bal	19.2
Doyle-Cal	16.4
North-Oak	16.2

Total Player Rating
Carew-Min	6.0
Jackson-Oak	5.3
Grich-Bal	4.6
Robinson-Bal	3.3
Burroughs-Tex	2.9

Wins
Jenkins-Tex	25
Hunter-Oak	25

Win Percentage
Cuellar-Bal	.688
Jenkins-Tex	.676
Hunter-Oak	.676
Tiant-Bos	.629

Games
Fingers-Oak	76
Murphy-Mil	70
Foucault-Tex	69
Lyle-NY	66
Campbell-Min	63

Complete Games
Jenkins-Tex	29
G.Perry-Cle	28
Lolich-Det	27
Ryan-Cal	26
Tiant-Bos	25

Shutouts
Tiant-Bos	7
Jenkins-Tex	6
Hunter-Oak	6
Cuellar-Bal	5
Bibby-Tex	5

Saves
Forster-Chi	24
Murphy-Mil	20
Campbell-Min	19
Buskey-NY-Cle	18
Fingers-Oak	18

Innings Pitched
Ryan-Cal	332.2
Jenkins-Tex	328.1
G.Perry-Cle	322.1
Wood-Chi	320.1
Hunter-Oak	318.1

Fewest Hits/Game
Ryan-Cal	5.98
G.Perry-Cle	6.42
DalCanton-KC	6.93
Hassler-Cal	7.33
Hunter-Oak	7.58

Fewest BB/Game
Jenkins-Tex	1.23
Hunter-Oak	1.30
Holtzman-Oak	1.80
Kaat-Chi	2.04
Wright-Mil	2.09

Strikeouts
Ryan-Cal	367
Blyleven-Min	249
Jenkins-Tex	225
G.Perry-Cle	216
Lolich-Det	202

Strikeouts/Game
Ryan-Cal	9.93
Blyleven-Min	7.98
Jenkins-Tex	6.17
Busby-KC	6.10
G.Perry-Cle	6.03

Ratio
Hunter-Oak	8.99
Jenkins-Tex	9.29
G.Perry-Cle	9.35
Grimsley-Bal	10.53
Blyleven-Min	10.57

Earned Run Average
Hunter-Oak	2.49
G.Perry-Cle	2.51
Hassler-Cal	2.61
Blyleven-Min	2.66
Fitzmorris-KC	2.79

Adjusted ERA
G.Perry-Cle	144
Blyleven-Min	141
Fitzmorris-KC	137
Hunter-Oak	133
Hassler-Cal	132

Opponents' Batting Avg.
Ryan-Cal	.190
G.Perry-Cle	.204
DalCanton-KC	.211
Hassler-Cal	.225
Hunter-Oak	.229

Opponents' On Base Pct.
Hunter-Oak	.260
Jenkins-Tex	.264
G.Perry-Cle	.272
Blyleven-Min	.292
Tiant-Bos	.293

Starter Runs
Hunter-Oak	39.9
G.Perry-Cle	39.6
Blyleven-Min	29.9
Jenkins-Tex	29.0
Ryan-Cal	26.7

Adjusted Starter Runs
G.Perry-Cle	39.4
Blyleven-Min	34.1
Tiant-Bos	31.9
Hunter-Oak	29.3
Jenkins-Tex	27.0

Clutch Pitching Index
Goltz-Min	124
Hassler-Cal	121
Lee-Bos	119
Fitzmorris-KC	116
Tanana-Cal	113

Relief Runs
Lyle-NY	24.8
Murphy-Mil	23.4
Foucault-Tex	22.0
Lindblad-Oak	17.5
Hiller-Det	16.3

Adjusted Relief Runs
Murphy-Mil	23.4
Lyle-NY	23.2
Foucault-Tex	21.1
Hiller-Det	19.4
Campbell-Min	15.2

Relief Ranking
Murphy-Mil	42.9
Hiller-Det	39.8
Lyle-NY	28.8
Foucault-Tex	26.4
Campbell-Min	22.4

Total Pitcher Index
G.Perry-Cle	4.4
Blyleven-Min	3.7
Tiant-Bos	3.2
Jenkins-Tex	2.9
Hunter-Oak	2.8

Total Baseball Ranking
Carew-Min	6.0
Jackson-Oak	5.3
Grich-Bal	4.6
G.Perry-Cle	4.4
Blyleven-Min	3.7

TEAM	G	W	L	PCT	GB	R	OR	AB	H	2B	3B	HR	BB	SO	AVG	OBP	SLG	PRO	PRO+	BR	/A	PF	CHI	RC	SB	CS	SBA	SBR
EAST																												
PIT	161	92	69	.571		712	565	5489	1444	255	47	**138**	468	832	.263	.325	**.402**	.727	108	44	49	99	102	709	49	28	36	-12
PHI	162	86	76	.531	6.5	735	694	5592	1506	**283**	42	125	610	960	.269	.344	**.402**	.746	108	98	70	104	94	785	126	57	61	-19
NY	162	82	80	.506	10.5	646	625	5587	1430	217	34	101	501	805	.256	.321	.361	.682	99	-35	-4	95	102	639	32	26	30	**-9**
STL	163	82	80	.506	10.5	662	689	5597	**1527**	239	46	81	444	649	.273	.329	.375	.704	98	7	-16	104	99	683	116	49	62	-22
MON	162	75	87	.463	17.5	601	690	5518	1346	216	31	98	579	954	.244	.319	.348	.667	87	-62	-90	104	99	623	108	58	48	-10
CHI	162	75	87	.463	17.5	712	827	5470	1419	229	41	95	650	802	.259	.341	.368	.709	98	33	3	104	100	702	67	55	53	-14
WEST																												
CIN	162	108	54	.667		**840**	586	5581	1515	278	37	124	**691**	916	.271	**.355**	.401	**.756**	**113**	128	115	102	103	**829**	168	36	40	-12
LA	162	88	74	.543	20	648	**534**	5453	1355	217	31	118	611	825	.248	.328	.365	.693	103	-9	19	96	98	667	138	52	57	-18
SF	161	80	81	.497	27.5	659	671	5447	1412	235	45	84	604	775	.259	.336	.365	.701	96	11	-16	104	98	673	99	47	45	-12
SD	162	71	91	.438	37	552	683	5429	1324	215	22	78	506	754	.244	.313	.335	.648	91	-99	-58	94	99	571	85	50	53	-16
ATL	161	67	94	.416	40.5	583	739	5424	1323	179	28	107	543	759	.244	.315	.346	.661	85	-74	-98	104	101	587	55	38	42	-13
HOU	162	64	97	.398	43.5	664	711	5515	1401	218	**54**	84	523	762	.254	.322	.359	.681	102	-35	12	93	**105**	643	133	62	60	-16
TOT	971					8014		66102	17002	2781	458	1233	6730	9793	.257	.329	.369	.698							1176	558	68	18

TEAM	CG	SH	SV	IP	H	H/G	HR	BB	SO	RAT	ERA	ERA+	OAV	OOB	PR	/A	PF	CPI	FA	E	DP	FW	PW	BW	SBW	DIF
EAST																										
PIT	43	14	31	1437¹	1302	8.2	**79**	551	768	11.7	3.01	**118**	.242	.315	98	**85**	98	103	.976	151	147	.2	**8.9**	5.1	-1.4	-1.3
PHI	33	11	30	1455	1353	8.4	111	546	897	11.9	3.82	98	.248	.319	-32	-15	103	89	.976	152	156	.2	-1.6	7.3	-2.1	1.2
NY	40	14	31	1466	1344	8.3	99*	580	**989**	12.0	3.39	102	.245	.320	37	10	95	98	.976	151	144	.3	1.0	-.4	**-1.1**	1.2
STL	33	13	36	1454²	1452	9.0	98	571	824	12.7	3.57	105	.259	.331	8	29	104	102	.973	171	140	-.8	3.0	-1.7	-2.5	2.9
MON	30	12	25	1480	1448	8.8	102	665	831	13.1	3.72	103	.258	.341	-16	16	106	103	.973	180	**179**	-1.3	1.7	-9.4	-1.2	4.3
CHI	27	8	33	1444¹	1587	9.9	130	551	850	13.6	4.49	86	.281	.349	-139	-104	106	98	.972	179	152	-1.3	-10.9	.3	-1.6	7.4
WEST																										
CIN	22	8	**50**	1459	1422	8.8	112	487	663	12.0	3.37	107	.257	.320	40	36	99	105	**.984**	102	173	**3.0**	3.8	**12.0**	-1.4	9.6
LA	51	18	21	1469²	1215	7.4	104	**448**	894	10.4	**2.92**	116	**.224**	.287	114	78	94	88	.979	127	106	1.6	8.1	2.0	-2.0	-2.7
SF	37	9	24	1432²	1406	8.8	92	612	856	12.9	3.74	102	.259	.338	-18	9	105	101	.976	146	164	.5	.9	-1.7	-1.4	1.1
SD	40	12	20	1463¹	1494	9.2	99	521	713	12.5	3.48	100	.266	.331	22	-1	96	**107**	.971	188	163	-1.8	-.1	-6.1	-1.8	-.2
ATL	32	4	24	1430	1543	9.7	101	519	669	13.3	3.91	96	.277	.344	-46	-22	104	105	.972	175	147	-1.1	-2.3	-10.2	-1.5	1.7
HOU	39	6	25	1458¹	1436	8.9	106	679	839	13.3	4.04	83	.261	.346	-67	-108	93	99	.979	137	166	1.1	-11.3	1.3	-1.8	-5.7
TOT	427	129	350	17450¹		8.8				12.4	3.62		.257	.329					.976	1859	1837					

Runs		Hits		Doubles		Triples		Home Runs		Total Bases	
Rose-Cin	112	Cash-Phi	213	Rose-Cin	47	Garr-Atl	11	Schmidt-Phi	38	Luzinski-Phi	322
Cash-Phi	111	Rose-Cin	210	Cash-Phi	40	Parker-Pit	10	Kingman-NY	36	Garvey-LA	314
Lopes-LA	108	Garvey-LA	210	Oliver-Pit	39	Kessinger-Chi	10	Luzinski-Phi	34	Parker-Pit	302
Morgan-Cin	107	Simmons-StL	193	Bench-Cin	39	Joshua-SF	10	Bench-Cin	28	Schmidt-Phi	294
Thomas-SF	99	Millan-NY	191	Garvey-LA	38	Gross-Hou	10			Rose-Cin	286

Runs Batted In		Runs Produced		Bases On Balls		Batting Average		On Base Percentage		Slugging Average	
Luzinski-Phi	120	Morgan-Cin	184	Morgan-Cin	132	Madlock-Chi	.354	Morgan-Cin	.471	Parker-Pit	.541
Bench-Cin	110	Staub-NY	179	Wynn-LA	110	Simmons-StL	.332	Wynn-LA	.407	Luzinski-Phi	.540
Perez-Cin	109	Rose-Cin	179	Evans-Atl	105	Sanguillen-Pit	.328	Rose-Cin	.407	Schmidt-Phi	.523
Staub-NY	105	Luzinski-Phi	171	Schmidt-Phi	101	Morgan-Cin	.327	Madlock-Chi	.406	Bench-Cin	.519
		Bench-Cin	165			Watson-Hou	.324	Murcer-SF	.404	Foster-Cin	.518

Production		Adjusted Production		Batter Runs		Adjusted Batter Runs		Clutch Hitting Index		Runs Created	
Morgan-Cin	.979	Morgan-Cin	168	Morgan-Cin	57.1	Morgan-Cin	55.9	Montanez-Phi-SF	148	Morgan-Cin	145
Luzinski-Phi	.939	Luzinski-Phi	152	Luzinski-Phi	47.5	Luzinski-Phi	44.5	Perez-Cin	144	Luzinski-Phi	128
Parker-Pit	.899	Watson-Hou	152	Simmons-StL	35.7	Simmons-StL	33.3	Morales-Chi	144	Rose-Cin	120
Stargell-Pit	.894	Parker-Pit	148	Thornton-Chi	35.4	Thornton-Chi	33.2	Murcer-SF	143	Schmidt-Phi	113
Schmidt-Phi	.890	Stargell-Pit	147	Schmidt-Phi	33.7	Parker-Pit	32.2	Trillo-Chi	143	Simmons-StL	108

Total Average		Stolen Bases		Stolen Base Average		Stolen Base Runs		Fielding Runs		Total Player Rating	
Morgan-Cin	1.279	Lopes-LA	77	Morgan-Cin	87.0	Lopes-LA	15.9	Schmidt-Phi	24.0	Morgan-Cin	7.0
Luzinski-Phi	.956	Morgan-Cin	67	Lopes-LA	86.5	Morgan-Cin	14.1	Evans-Atl	23.4	Schmidt-Phi	5.8
Schmidt-Phi	.943	Brock-StL	56	Maddox-SF-Phi	86.2	Brock-StL	7.2	Maddox-SF-Phi	18.8	Bench-Cin	3.6
Bench-Cin	.901	Cedeno-Hou	50	Winfield-SD	85.2	Concepcion-Cin	6.3	Mackanin-Mon	18.2	Evans-Atl	3.5
Stargell-Pit	.895	Cardenal-Chi	34	Concepcion-Cin	84.6	Maddox-SF-Phi	5.1	Trillo-Chi	16.0	Simmons-StL	3.4

Wins		Win Percentage		Games		Complete Games		Shutouts		Saves	
Seaver-NY	22	Gullett-Cin	.789	Garber-Atl	71	Messersmith-LA	19	Messersmith-LA	7	Hrabosky-StL	22
Jones-SD	20	Seaver-NY	.710	McEnaney-Cin	70	Jones-SD	18	Reuss-Pit	6	Eastwick-Cin	22
Messersmith-LA	19	Hooton-Chi-LA	.667	Tomlin-SD	67	Seaver-NY	15	Jones-SD	6	Giusti-Pit	17
Hooton-Chi-LA	18	Murray-Mon	.652	Borbon-Cin	67	Reuss-Pit	15	Seaver-NY	5	McEnaney-Cin	15
Reuss-Pit	18			Garman-StL	66					Knowles-Chi	15

Innings Pitched		Fewest Hits/Game		Fewest BB/Game		Strikeouts		Strikeouts/Game		Ratio	
Messersmith-LA	321.2	Messersmith-LA	6.83	Nolan-Cin	1.24	Seaver-NY	243	Montefusco-SF	7.94	Jones-SD	9.41
Jones-SD	285.0	Seaver-NY	6.97	Jones-SD	1.77	Montefusco-SF	215	Richard-Hou	7.80	Sutton-LA	9.45
Seaver-NY	280.1	Warthen-Mon	6.98	Reed-Atl-StL	1.91	Messersmith-LA	213	Seaver-NY	7.80	Messersmith-LA	9.65
Morton-Atl	277.2	Sutton-LA	7.15	Rau-LA	2.13	Carlton-Phi	192	Warthen-Mon	6.87	Hooton-Chi-LA	9.89
Niekro-Atl	275.2	Hooton-Chi-LA	7.29	Barr-SF	2.14	Richard-Hou	176	Carlton-Phi	6.77	Nolan-Cin	9.91

Earned Run Average		Adjusted ERA		Opponents' Batting Avg.		Opponents' On Base Pct.		Starter Runs		Adjusted Starter Runs	
Jones-SD	2.24	Jones-SD	155	Messersmith-LA	.213	Sutton-LA	.264	Messersmith-LA	47.4	Messersmith-LA	39.5
Messersmith-LA	2.29	Messersmith-LA	148	Sutton-LA	.213	Jones-SD	.271	Jones-SD	43.7	Jones-SD	39.0
Seaver-NY	2.38	Seaver-NY	145	Seaver-NY	.214	Hooton-Chi-LA	.276	Seaver-NY	38.8	Seaver-NY	33.5
Reuss-Pit	2.54	Reuss-Pit	139	Warthen-Mon	.217	Messersmith-LA	.276	Reuss-Pit	28.5	Reuss-Pit	26.4
Forsch-StL	2.86	Montefusco-SF	132	Hooton-Chi-LA	.219	Nolan-Cin	.278	Sutton-LA	21.3	Montefusco-SF	24.8

Clutch Pitching Index		Relief Runs		Adjusted Relief Runs		Relief Ranking		Total Pitcher Index		Total Baseball Ranking	
Reuss-Pit	122	Hrabosky-StL	21.2	Hrabosky-StL	22.6	Hrabosky-StL	44.9	Jones-SD	4.8	Morgan-Cin	7.0
Niekro-Atl	122	Apodaca-NY	20.1	Apodaca-NY	18.5	Apodaca-NY	20.1	Messersmith-LA	4.3	Schmidt-Phi	5.8
Blair-Mon	114	Hilgendorf-Phi	15.9	Hilgendorf-Phi	17.1	Garman-StL	18.4	Seaver-NY	4.1	Jones-SD	4.8
Koosman-NY	113	McEnaney-Cin	11.6	Garman-StL	12.0	Hilgendorf-Phi	15.9	Forsch-StL	3.9	Messersmith-LA	4.3
Barr-SF	110	Garman-StL	10.8	McEnaney-Cin	11.3	McGraw-Phi	13.9	Reuss-Pit	3.4	Seaver-NY	4.1

TEAM	G	W	L	PCT	GB	R	OR	AB	H	2B	3B	HR	BB	SO	AVG	OBP	SLG	PRO	PRO+	BR	/A	PF	CHI	RC	SB	CS	SBA	SBR
EAST																												
BOS	160	95	65	.594		**796**	709	5448	**1500**	284	44	134	565	741	**.275**	**.347**	**.417**	**.764**	105	**108**	**49**	109	99	**776**	66	58	50	-12
BAL	159	90	69	.566	4.5	682	553	5474	1382	224	33	124	580	834	.252	.328	.373	.701	104	-13	31	94	100	680	104	55	52	-14
NY	160	83	77	.519	12	681	588	5415	1430	230	39	110	486	710	.264	.328	.382	.710	102	-2	16	97	101	665	102	59	53	-13
CLE	159	79	80	.497	15.5	688	703	5404	1409	201	25	**153**	525	**667**	.261	.329	.392	.721	103	17	17	100	99	672	106	89	63	-10
MIL	162	68	94	.420	28	675	792	5378	1343	242	34	146	553	922	.250	.323	.389	.712	99	-1	-4	101	99	663	65	64	50	-10
DET	159	57	102	.358	37.5	570	786	5366	1338	171	39	125	383	872	.249	.303	.366	.669	84	-93	-121	104	101	573	63	57	53	-14
WEST																												
OAK	162	98	64	.605		758	606	5415	1376	220	33	151	609	846	.254	.335	.391	.726	**107**	34	**49**	98	104	725	183	82	61	-11
KC	162	91	71	.562	7	710	649	5491	1431	263	**58**	118	591	675	.261	.336	.394	.730	103	40	21	103	96	736	155	75	55	-10
TEX	162	79	83	.488	19	714	733	5599	1431	208	17	134	**613**	863	.256	.332	.371	.703	98	-9	-3	99	102	693	102	62	53	-12
MIN	159	76	83	.478	20.5	724	736	5514	1497	215	28	121	563	746	.271	.343	.386	.729	103	46	31	102	97	732	81	48	48	-13
CHI	161	75	86	.466	22.5	655	703	5490	1400	209	38	94	611	800	.255	.334	.358	.692	94	-23	-32	101	97	659	101	54	53	-15
CAL	161	72	89	.447	25.5	628	723	5377	1324	195	41	55	593	811	.246	.324	.328	.652	91	-98	-49	93	**106**	596	**220**	108	**67**	-7
TOT	963					8281		65371	16861	2662	429	1465	6672	9487	.258	.330	.379	.709							1348	811	62	-81

TEAM	CG	SH	SV	IP	H	H/G	HR	BB	SO	RAT	ERA	ERA+	OAV	OOB	PR	/A	PF	CPI	FA	E	DP	FW	PW	BW	SBW	DIF
EAST																										
BOS	62	11	31	1436²	1463	9.2	145	**490**	720	12.4	3.98	102	.265	.327	-32	14	108	99	.977	139	142	.9	1.4	**5.0**	-.5	8.2
BAL	**70**	**19**	21	1451	1285	8.0	110	500	717	11.1	**3.17**	111	.241	**.308**	98	54	93	100	**.983**	**107**	**175**	**2.6**	5.5	3.2	-.7	-.0
NY	**70**	11	20	1424	1325	8.4	104	502	809	11.7	3.29	111	.249	.316	77	56	96	103	.978	135	148	1.1	5.7	1.6	-.6	-4.8
CLE	37	6	33	1435¹	1395	8.7	136	599	800	12.7	3.84	98	.257	.335	-10	-9	100	103	.978	134	156	1.1	-.9	1.7	-.3	-2.1
MIL	36	10	34	1431²	1496	9.4	133	624	643	13.7	4.34	88	.270	.350	-89	-80	101	100	.971	180	162	-1.4	-8.2	-.4	-.3	-2.7
DET	52	10	17	1396	1496	9.6	137	533	787	13.3	4.27	94	.274	.342	-76	-40	106	100	.972	173	141	-1.1	-4.1	-12.4	-.7	-4.2
WEST																										
OAK	36	10	**44**	1448	**1267**	**7.9**	102	523	784	11.4	3.27	111	**.236**	**.308**	81	57	96	94	.977	143	140	.7	5.8	**5.0**	-.4	5.8
KC	52	11	25	1456²	1422	8.8	108	498	815	12.0	3.47	111	.257	.322	50	**62**	102	102	.976	155	151	.0	**6.3**	2.1	-.3	1.8
TEX	60	16	17	1465²	1456	8.9	123	518	792	12.4	3.86	97	.261	.328	-13	-17	99	98	.971	191	173	-2.0	-1.7	-.3	-.5	2.5
MIN	57	7	22	1423	1381	8.7	137	617	846	12.9	4.05	95	.256	.337	-42	-30	102	98	.973	170	147	-.9	-3.1	3.2	-.6	-2.0
CHI	34	7	39	1452¹	1489	9.2	107	655	799	13.5	3.93	99	.268	.349	-24	-9	103	105	.978	140	155	.9	-.9	-3.3	-.8	-1.3
CAL	59	**19**	16	1453¹	1386	8.6	123	613	**975**	12.6	3.89	91	.253	.332	-17	-55	94	97	.971	184	164	-1.6	-5.6	-5.0	-.0	3.8
TOT	625	137	319	17273²		8.8				12.5	3.78		.258	.330					.975	1851	1854					

Runs		Hits		Doubles		Triples		Home Runs		Total Bases	
Lynn-Bos	103	Brett-KC	195	Lynn-Bos	47	Rivers-Cal	13	Scott-Mil	36	Scott-Mil	318
Mayberry-KC	95	Carew-Min	192	Jackson-Oak	39	Brett-KC	13	Jackson-Oak	36	Mayberry-KC	303
Bonds-NY	93	Munson-NY	190	McRae-KC	38	Orta-Chi	10	Mayberry-KC	34	Jackson-Oak	303
Rice-Bos	92	C.Washington-Oak	182	Mayberry-KC	38	Cowens-KC	8	Bonds-NY	32	Lynn-Bos	299
				Chambliss-NY	38					Brett-KC	289

Runs Batted In		Runs Produced		Bases On Balls		Batting Average		On Base Percentage		Slugging Average	
Scott-Mil	109	Lynn-Bos	187	Mayberry-KC	119	Carew-Min	.359	Carew-Min	.428	Lynn-Bos	.566
Mayberry-KC	106	Munson-NY	173	Singleton-Bal	118	Lynn-Bos	.331	Mayberry-KC	.419	Mayberry-KC	.547
Lynn-Bos	105	Rice-Bos	172	Grich-Bal	107	Munson-NY	.318	Singleton-Bal	.418	Powell-Cle	.524
Jackson-Oak	104	Mayberry-KC	167	Tenace-Oak	106	Rice-Bos	.309	Harrah-Tex	.406	Scott-Mil	.515
		Brett-KC	162	Harrah-Tex	98	C.Washington-Oak	.308	Lynn-Bos	.405	Bonds-NY	.512

Production		Adjusted Production		Batter Runs		Adjusted Batter Runs		Clutch Hitting Index		Runs Created	
Lynn-Bos	.971	Mayberry-KC	167	Mayberry-KC	56.0	Mayberry-KC	54.0	Munson-NY	142	Mayberry-KC	135
Mayberry-KC	.966	Lynn-Bos	158	Lynn-Bos	49.4	Singleton-Bal	46.4	Stanton-Cal	140	Lynn-Bos	120
Carew-Min	.926	Carew-Min	158	Carew-Min	44.4	Lynn-Bos	43.6	Robinson-Bal	136	Singleton-Bal	118
Powell-Cle	.906	Singleton-Bal	156	Singleton-Bal	41.3	Carew-Min	43.0	May-Bal	132	Carew-Min	118
Bonds-NY	.891	Bonds-NY	154	Bonds-NY	35.4	Bonds-NY	37.3	McRae-KC	127	Harrah-Tex	105

Total Average		Stolen Bases		Stolen Base Average		Stolen Base Runs		Fielding Runs		Total Player Rating	
Mayberry-KC	1.059	Rivers-Cal	70	Hisle-Min	85.0	Rivers-Cal	12.6	Belanger-Bal	28.0	Harrah-Tex	6.2
Lynn-Bos	1.000	C.Washington-Oak	40	Bumbry-Bal	84.2	Patek-KC	5.4	Dent-Chi	27.2	Grich-Bal	5.3
Carew-Min	.986	Otis-KC	39	Rivers-Cal	83.3	Otis-KC	5.1	Grich-Bal	24.0	Carew-Min	5.3
Tenace-Oak	.919	Carew-Min	35	Alomar-NY	82.4	Carew-Min	5.1	Henderson-Chi	20.2	Mayberry-KC	4.9
Harrah-Tex	.914	Remy-Cal	34	Patek-KC	82.1	Alomar-NY	4.8	Rodriguez-Det	18.2	Lynn-Bos	4.9

Wins		Win Percentage		Games		Complete Games		Shutouts		Saves	
Palmer-Bal	23	Torrez-Bal	.690	Fingers-Oak	75	Hunter-NY	30	Palmer-Bal	10	Gossage-Chi	26
Hunter-NY	23	Leonard-KC	.682	Lindblad-Oak	68	G.Perry-Cle-Tex	25	Hunter-NY	7	Fingers-Oak	24
Blue-Oak	22	Palmer-Bal	.676	Gossage-Chi	62	Palmer-Bal	25			Murphy-Mil	20
Torrez-Bal	20	Blue-Oak	.667	LaRoche-Cle	61	Jenkins-Tex	22			LaRoche-Cle	17
Kaat-Chi	20	Lee-Bos	.654	Foucault-Tex	59	Blyleven-Min	20			Drago-Bos	15

Innings Pitched		Fewest Hits/Game		Fewest BB/Game		Strikeouts		Strikeouts/Game		Ratio	
Hunter-NY	328.0	Hunter-NY	6.80	Jenkins-Tex	1.87	Tanana-Cal	269	Tanana-Cal	9.41	Hunter-NY	9.22
Palmer-Bal	323.0	Ryan-Cal	6.91	G.Perry-Cle-Tex	2.06	G.Perry-Cle-Tex	233	Ryan-Cal	8.45	Palmer-Bal	9.33
G.Perry-Cle-Tex	305.2	Palmer-Bal	7.05	Grimsley-Bal	2.15	Blyleven-Min	233	Blyleven-Min	7.61	Blyleven-Min	10.02
Kaat-Chi	303.2	Eckersley-Cle	7.09	Palmer-Bal	2.23	Palmer-Bal	193	Eckersley-Cle	7.33	Tanana-Cal	10.18
Wood-Chi	291.1	Blyleven-Min	7.15	Hunter-NY	2.28	Blue-Oak	189	G.Perry-Cle-Tex	6.86	G.Perry-Cle-Tex	10.33

Earned Run Average		Adjusted ERA		Opponents' Batting Avg.		Opponents' On Base Pct.		Starter Runs		Adjusted Starter Runs	
Palmer-Bal	2.09	Palmer-Bal	168	Hunter-NY	.208	Hunter-NY	.263	Palmer-Bal	60.6	Palmer-Bal	51.0
Hunter-NY	2.58	Eckersley-Cle	145	Ryan-Cal	.213	Palmer-Bal	.267	Hunter-NY	43.7	Hunter-NY	38.7
Eckersley-Cle	2.60	Hunter-NY	141	Eckersley-Cle	.215	Blyleven-Min	.283	Tanana-Cal	33.0	Tanana-Cal	26.4
Tanana-Cal	2.62	Tanana-Cal	135	Palmer-Bal	.216	G.Perry-Cle-Tex	.284	Eckersley-Cle	24.4	Blyleven-Min	26.0
Figueroa-Cal	2.91	Blyleven-Min	128	Blyleven-Min	.219	Tanana-Cal	.288	Blyleven-Min	23.7	Kaat-Chi	25.7

Clutch Pitching Index		Relief Runs		Adjusted Relief Runs		Relief Ranking		Total Pitcher Index		Total Baseball Ranking	
Kaat-Chi	119	Gossage-Chi	30.5	Gossage-Chi	18.2	Gossage-Chi	47.7	Palmer-Bal	5.8	Harrah-Tex	6.2
Eckersley-Cle	116	Todd-Oak	20.2	Todd-Oak	18.2	LaRoche-Cle	19.5	Hunter-NY	3.7	Palmer-Bal	5.8
Torrez-Bal	111	LaRoche-Cle	14.6	LaRoche-Cle	14.6	Todd-Oak	18.8	Gossage-Chi	3.4	Grich-Bal	5.3
Osteen-Chi	110	Lindblad-Oak	14.4	Hiller-Det	14.5	Hiller-Det	15.7	Tanana-Cal	3.0	Carew-Min	5.3
Hargan-Tex	108	Hiller-Det	12.7	Lindblad-Oak	12.3	Fingers-Oak	14.1	Blyleven-Min	3.0	Mayberry-KC	4.9

1976 National League

TEAM	G	W	L	PCT	GB	R	OR	AB	H	2B	3B	HR	BB	SO	AVG	OBP	SLG	PRO	PRO+	BR	/A	PF	CHI	RC	SB	CS	SBA	SBR
EAST																												
PHI	162	101	61	.623		770	557	5528	1505	259	45	110	542	793	.272	.342	.395	.737	111	106	86	103	101	746	127	70	54	**-10**
PIT	162	92	70	.568	9	708	630	5604	1499	249	56	110	433	807	.267	.323	.391	.714	107	50	44	101	102	700	130	45	45	-13
NY	162	86	76	.531	15	615	**538**	5415	1334	198	34	102	561	797	.246	.320	.352	.672	102	-18	19	94	99	608	66	58	56	-15
CHI	162	75	87	.463	26	611	728	5519	1386	216	24	105	490	834	.251	.316	.356	.672	88	-26	-83	109	99	605	74	74	57	-11
STL	162	72	90	.444	29	629	671	5516	1432	243	57	63	512	860	.260	.325	.359	.684	99	1	-4	101	97	644	123	55	49	-12
MON	162	55	107	.340	46	531	734	5428	1275	224	32	94	433	841	.235	.293	.340	.633	81	-108	-134	104	102	539	86	44	47	-14
WEST																												
CIN	162	102	60	.630		**857**	633	5702	**1599**	271	63	141	**681**	902	**.280**	**.360**	**.424**	**.784**	**125**	214	197	102	95	**907**	210	57	55	-15
LA	162	92	70	.568	10	608	543	5472	1371	200	34	91	486	744	.251	.315	.349	.664	95	-38	-25	98	101	604	144	55	50	-13
HOU	162	80	82	.494	22	625	657	5464	1401	195	50	66	530	719	.256	.325	.347	.672	106	-19	38	91	101	622	150	57	53	-14
SF	162	74	88	.457	28	595	686	5452	1340	211	37	85	518	778	.246	.314	.345	.659	90	-47	-66	103	100	591	88	55	51	-13
SD	162	73	89	.451	29	570	662	5369	1327	216	37	64	488	**716**	.247	.313	.337	.650	97	-64	-12	92	100	570	92	46	47	-13
ATL	162	70	92	.432	32	620	700	5345	1309	170	30	82	589	811	.245	.322	.334	.656	86	-43	-83	106	**104**	579	74	61	56	-14
TOT	972					7739		65814	16778	2652	499	1113	6263	9602	.255	.323	.361	.684							1364	677	67	3

TEAM	CG	SH	SV	IP	H	H/G	HR	BB	SO	RAT	ERA	ERA+	OAV	OOB	PR	/A	PF	CPI	FA	E	DP	FW	PW	BW	SBW	DIF
EAST																										
PHI	34	9	44	1459	1377	8.5	98	397	918	11.1	3.08	**115**	.249	.302	68	**76**	101	102	.981	115	148	1.7	**8.1**	9.1	**-1.1**	2.1
PIT	45	12	35	1466¹	1402	8.6	95	460	762	11.5	3.36	104	.253	.312	22	19	100	99	.975	163	142	-1.0	2.0	4.7	-1.4	6.7
NY	53	18	25	1449	1248	7.8	97	419	1025	10.5	2.94	112	**.233**	.291	90	57	94	95	.979	131	116	.8	6.1	2.0	-1.6	-2.3
CHI	27	12	33	1471¹	1511	9.2	123	490	850	12.4	3.93	98	.268	.329	-70	-12	110	100	.978	140	145	.3	-1.3	-8.8	-1.2	5.0
STL	35	15	26	1453²	1416	8.8	91	581	731	12.4	3.60	98	.258	.332	-16	-10	101	103	.973	174	163	-1.7	-1.1	-.4	-1.3	-4.5
MON	26	10	21	1440	1442	9.0	89	659	783	13.4	3.99	93	.265	.350	-78	-44	106	102	.976	155	**179**	-.6	-4.7	-14.2	-1.5	-5.0
WEST																										
CIN	33	12	**45**	1471	1436	8.8	100	491	790	11.9	3.51	100	.258	.320	0	0	100	101	**.984**	102	157	2.5	.0	20.9	-1.6	-.8
LA	47	17	28	1470²	1330	8.1	97	479	747	11.2	3.02	112	.243	.307	79	59	97	**104**	.980	128	154	1.0	6.3	-2.7	-1.4	7.8
HOU	42	17	29	1444¹	1349	8.4	82	662	780	12.7	3.56	90	.249	.334	-9	-58	91	101	.978	140	155	.3	-6.2	-4.0	-1.5	2.3
SF	27	**18**	31	1461²	1464	9.0	**68**	518	746	12.3	3.53	103	.262	.327	-4	16	104	100	.971	186	153	-2.4	1.7	-7.0	-1.4	2.1
SD	47	11	18	1432¹	1368	8.6	87	543	652	12.1	3.65	90	.253	.323	-23	-60	93	95	.978	141	148	.2	-6.4	-1.3	-1.4	.8
ATL	33	13	27	1438	1435	9.0	86	564	818	12.8	3.86	98	.261	.334	-57	-11	108	97	.973	167	151	-1.3	-1.2	-8.8	-1.5	1.8
TOT	449	164	362	17457¹		8.6				12.0	3.50		.255	.323					.977	1742	1811					

Runs
Rose-Cin 130
Morgan-Cin 113
Schmidt-Phi 112
Griffey-Cin 111
Monday-Chi 107

Hits
Rose-Cin 215
Montanez-SF-Atl .. 206
Garvey-LA 200
Buckner-LA 193

Doubles
Rose-Cin 42
Johnstone-Phi 38
Maddox-Phi 37
Garvey-LA 37

Triples
Cash-Phi 12
Geronimo-Cin 11
Parker-Pit 10
W.Davis-SD 10

Home Runs
Schmidt-Phi 38
Kingman-NY 37
Monday-Chi 32
Foster-Cin 29
Morgan-Cin 27

Total Bases
Schmidt-Phi 306
Rose-Cin 299
Foster-Cin 298
Garvey-LA 284

Runs Batted In
Foster-Cin 121
Morgan-Cin 111
Schmidt-Phi 107
Watson-Hou 102
Luzinski-Phi 95

Runs Produced
Morgan-Cin 197
Rose-Cin 183
Schmidt-Phi 181
Griffey-Cin 179
Foster-Cin 178

Bases On Balls
Wynn-Atl 127
Morgan-Cin 114
Schmidt-Phi 100
Cey-LA 89
Rose-Cin 86

Batting Average
Madlock-Chi 339
Griffey-Cin 336
Maddox-Phi 330
Rose-Cin 323
Morgan-Cin 320

On Base Percentage
Morgan-Cin 453
Madlock-Chi 415
Rose-Cin 406
Griffey-Cin 403
Cey-LA 389

Slugging Average
Morgan-Cin 576
Foster-Cin 530
Schmidt-Phi 524
Monday-Chi 507
Kingman-NY 506

Production
Morgan-Cin 1.029
Madlock-Chi 915
Schmidt-Phi 904
Foster-Cin 899
Rose-Cin 855

Adjusted Production
Morgan-Cin 186
Watson-Hou 151
Schmidt-Phi 150
Foster-Cin 149
Madlock-Chi 146

Batter Runs
Morgan-Cin 61.4
Schmidt-Phi 42.7
Madlock-Chi 40.6
Rose-Cin 39.6
Foster-Cin 36.7

Adjusted Batter Runs
Morgan-Cin 59.9
Schmidt-Phi 40.4
Rose-Cin 37.7
Watson-Hou 35.4
Foster-Cin 35.2

Clutch Hitting Index
Simmons-StL...... 133
Watson-Hou 132
Cruz-StL......... 128
Brock-StL 127
Milner-NY 126

Runs Created
Morgan-Cin 144
Rose-Cin 123
Schmidt-Phi 121
Foster-Cin 111
Griffey-Cin 109

Total Average
Morgan-Cin 1.319
Schmidt-Phi 944
Foster-Cin 911
Madlock-Chi 882
Griffey-Cin 876

Stolen Bases
Lopes-LA 63
Morgan-Cin 60
Taveras-Pit 58
Cedeno-StL 58
Brock-StL 56

Stolen Base Average
Morgan-Cin 87.0
Lopes-LA 86.3
Foster-Cin 85.0
Taveras-Pit 84.1
Geronimo-Cin 81.5

Stolen Base Runs
Lopes-LA 12.9
Morgan-Cin 12.6
Taveras-Pit 10.8
Cedeno-Hou 8.4
Cabell-Hou 5.7

Fielding Runs
Schmidt-Phi 24.7
Trillo-Chi 18.3
Maddox-Phi 17.8
Stennett-Pit 17.4
Royster-Atl 16.6

Total Player Rating
Schmidt-Phi 6.4
Morgan-Cin 5.8
Foster-Cin 4.4
Maddox-Phi 3.9
Cey-LA 3.9

Wins
Jones-SD 22
Sutton-LA 21
Koosman-NY 21
Richard-Hou 20
Carlton-Phi 20

Win Percentage
Carlton-Phi 741
Candelaria-Pit 696
Sutton-LA 677
Koosman-NY 677
Rooker-Pit 652

Games
Murray-Mon 81
Metzger-SD 77
Hough-LA 77
Eastwick-Cin 71
Borbon-Cin 69

Complete Games
Jones-SD 25
Koosman-NY 17
Matlack-NY 16
Sutton-LA 15
Richard-Hou 14

Shutouts
Montefusco-SF 6
Matlack-NY 6
Seaver-NY 5
Jones-SD 5

Saves
Eastwick-Cin 26
Lockwood-NY 19
Forsch-Hou 19
Hough-LA 18
Metzger-SD 16

Innings Pitched
Jones-SD 315.1
Richard-Hou .. 291.0
Seaver-NY 271.0
Niekro-Atl 270.2
Sutton-LA 267.2

Fewest Hits/Game
Richard-Hou 6.84
Seaver-NY 7.01
Candelaria-Pit 7.08
Messersmith-Atl .. 7.21
Falcone-StL 7.34

Fewest BB/Game
Nolan-Cin 1.02
Kaat-Phi 1.27
Jones-SD 1.43
Matlack-NY 1.96
Lonborg-Phi 2.03

Strikeouts
Seaver-NY 235
Richard-Hou 214
Koosman-NY 200
Carlton-Phi 195
Niekro-Atl 173

Strikeouts/Game
Seaver-NY 7.80
Koosman-NY 7.28
Carlton-Phi 6.95
Richard-Hou 6.62
Zachry-Cin 6.31

Ratio
Jones-SD 9.36
Candelaria-Pit ... 9.61
Seaver-NY 9.70
Nolan-Cin 9.78
Koosman-NY 9.90

Earned Run Average
Denny-StL 2.52
Rau-LA 2.57
Seaver-NY 2.59
Koosman-NY 2.69
Zachry-Cin 2.74

Adjusted ERA
Denny-StL 140
Rau-LA 132
Zachry-Cin 128
Montefusco-SF ... 128
Seaver-NY 127

Opponents' Batting Avg.
Richard-Hou 212
Seaver-NY 213
Candelaria-Pit 216
Messersmith-Atl ...219
Falcone-StL 222

Opponents' On Base Pct.
Jones-SD 267
Candelaria-Pit 273
Seaver-NY 273
Nolan-Cin 276
Koosman-NY 279

Starter Runs
Seaver-NY 27.4
Jones-SD 26.7
Richard-Hou 24.2
Rau-LA 23.9
Denny-StL 22.5

Adjusted Starter Runs
Denny-StL 23.3
Montefusco-SF ... 22.1
Seaver-NY 21.2
Rau-LA 20.8
Burris-Chi 20.8

Clutch Pitching Index
Rau-LA 139
Denny-StL 129
Burris-Chi 118
Christenson-Phi .. 112
Fryman-Mon 112

Relief Runs
Hough-LA 20.5
Eastwick-Cin 16.9
Reed-Phi 14.8
Moffitt-SF 14.1
Forsch-Hou 13.8

Adjusted Relief Runs
Hough-LA 18.6
Eastwick-Cin 16.9
Moffitt-SF 15.5
Reed-Phi 15.4
Twitchell-Phi 12.3

Relief Ranking
Eastwick-Cin 31.8
Hough-LA 28.8
Moffitt-SF 21.0
Reed-Phi 20.1
Lavelle-SF 17.8

Total Pitcher Index
Denny-StL 3.1
Barr-SF 3.0
Rau-LA 2.4
Jones-SD 2.3
R.Reuschel-Chi ... 2.2

Total Baseball Ranking
Schmidt-Phi 6.4
Morgan-Cin 5.8
Foster-Cin 4.4
Maddox-Phi 3.9
Cey-LA 3.9

TEAM	G	W	L	PCT	GB	R	OR	AB	H	2B	3B	HR	BB	SO	AVG	OBP	SLG	PRO	PRO+	BR	/A	PF	CHI	RC	SB	CS	SBA	SBR
EAST																												
NY	159	97	62	.610		730	575	5555	1496	231	36	120	470	616	.269	.330	.389	.719	111	64	70	99	103	723	163	65	49	-9
BAL	162	88	74	.543	10.5	619	598	5457	1326	213	28	119	519	883	.243	.311	.358	.669	102	-32	7	94	102	612	150	61	55	-14
BOS	162	83	79	.512	15.5	716	660	5511	1448	257	53	134	500	832	.263	.327	.402	.729	100	80	0	112	98	709	95	70	56	-12
CLE	159	81	78	.509	16	615	615	5412	1423	189	38	85	479	631	.263	.324	.359	.683	101	-1	5	99	97	611	75	69	55	-11
DET	161	74	87	.460	24	609	709	5441	1401	207	38	101	450	730	.257	.318	.365	.683	96	-6	-30	104	97	611	107	59	52	-13
MIL	161	66	95	.410	32	570	655	5396	1326	170	38	88	511	909	.246	.314	.340	.654	92	-56	-43	98	98	575	62	61	54	-13
WEST																												
KC	162	90	72	.556		713	611	5540	1490	259	57	65	484	650	.269	.331	.371	.702	104	37	32	101	103	687	218	106	66	-7
OAK	161	87	74	.540	2.5	686	598	5353	1319	208	33	113	592	818	.246	.327	.361	.688	105	13	39	96	105	663	341	123	65	-1
MIN	162	85	77	.525	5	743	704	5574	1526	222	51	81	550	714	.274	.343	.375	.718	107	78	59	103	100	727	146	75	54	-9
TEX	162	76	86	.469	14	616	652	5555	1390	213	26	80	568	809	.250	.323	.341	.664	93	-31	-44	102	98	616	87	45	45	-13
CAL	162	76	86	.469	14	550	631	5385	1265	210	23	63	534	812	.235	.309	.318	.627	89	-104	-63	94	102	531	126	80	64	-13
CHI	161	64	97	.398	25.5	586	745	5532	1410	209	46	73	471	739	.255	.317	.349	.666	94	-35	-38	101	95	622	120	53	45	-10
TOT	967					7753		65711	16820	2588	467	1122	6128	9143	.256	.323	.361	.684							1690	867	66	-12

TEAM	CG	SH	SV	IP	H	H/G	HR	BB	SO	RAT	ERA	ERA+	OAV	OOB	PR	/A	PF	CPI	FA	E	DP	FW	PW	BW	SBW	DIF
EAST																										
NY	62	15	37	1455	1300	8.0	97	448	674	10.9	3.19	107	.269	.334	52	36	97	122	.980	126	141	.9	3.8	7.4	-.8	6.2
BAL	59	16	23	1469¹	1396	8.6	80	489	678	11.7	3.31	99	.289	.357	33	-7	93	131	.982	118	157	1.5	-.7	.7	-1.4	6.9
BOS	49	13	27	1458	1495	9.2	109	409	673	12.0	3.52	111	.295	.351	-1	62	111	127	.978	141	148	.2	6.6	-.0	-1.2	-3.6
CLE	30	17	46	1432	1361	8.6	80	533	928	12.1	3.47	101	.292	.369	7	3	99	132	.980	121	159	1.2	.3	.5	-1.1	.5
DET	55	12	20	1431¹	1426	9.0	101	550	738	12.6	3.87	96	.302	.378	-55	-25	105	128	.974	168	161	-1.4	-2.7	-3.2	-1.3	2.0
MIL	45	10	27	1435¹	1406	8.8	99	567	677	12.6	3.64	96	.300	.380	-19	-23	99	135	.975	152	160	-.5	-2.4	-4.6	-1.3	-5.7
WEST																										
KC	41	12	35	1472¹	1356	8.3	83	493	735	11.5	3.21	109	.278	.348	50	47	100	129	.978	139	147	.3	5.0	3.4	-.6	1.0
OAK	39	15	29	1459¹	1412	8.7	96	415	711	11.5	3.26	103	.284	.343	42	15	95	128	.977	144	130	-.0	1.6	4.1	.0	.8
MIN	29	11	23	1459	1421	8.8	89	610	762	12.8	3.69	97	.300	.384	-28	-15	102	133	.973	172	182	-1.6	-1.6	6.3	-.8	1.8
TEX	63	15	15	1472	1464	9.0	106	461	773	12.0	3.45	104	.295	.359	10	21	102	132	.976	156	142	-.7	2.2	-4.7	-1.3	-.6
CAL	64	15	17	1477¹	1323	8.1	95	553	992	11.7	3.36	99	.277	.356	26	-5	95	128	.977	150	139	-.3	-.5	-6.7	-1.3	3.8
CHI	54	10	22	1448	1460	9.1	87	600	802	13.0	4.25	84	.308	.390	-118	-110	101	120	.979	130	155	.7	-11.7	-4.0	-.9	-.6
TOT	590	161	321	17469		8.7				12.0	3.52		.256	.323					.977	1717	1821					

Runs		Hits		Doubles		Triples		Home Runs		Total Bases	
White-NY	104	Brett-KC	215	Otis-KC	40	Brett-KC	14	Nettles-NY	32	Brett-KC	298
Carew-Min	97	Carew-Min	200	McRae-KC	34	Garner-Oak	12	R.Jackson-Bal	27	Chambliss-NY	283
Rivers-NY	95	Chambliss-NY	188	Evans-Bos	34	Carew-Min	12	Bando-Oak	27	Rice-Bos	280
Brett-KC	94	Munson-NY	186	Carty-Cle	34	Poquette-KC	10			Carew-Min	280
		Rivers-NY	184	Brett-KC	34	Bostock-Min	9			Nettles-NY	277

Runs Batted In		Runs Produced		Bases On Balls		Batting Average		On Base Percentage		Slugging Average	
L.May-Bal	109	Carew-Min	178	Hargrove-Tex	97	Brett-KC	.333	McRae-KC	.412	R.Jackson-Bal	.502
Munson-NY	105	Munson-NY	167	Harrah-Tex	91	McRae-KC	.332	Hargrove-Tex	.401	Rice-Bos	.482
Yastrzemski-Bos	102	Hisle-Min	163	Grich-Bal	86	Carew-Min	.331	Carew-Min	.398	Nettles-NY	.475
		Otis-KC	161	White-NY	83	Bostock-Min	.323	Staub-Det	.392	Lynn-Bos	.467
				Staub-Det	83	LeFlore-Det	.316	Carty-Cle	.384	Carew-Min	.463

Production		Adjusted Production		Batter Runs		Adjusted Batter Runs		Clutch Hitting Index		Runs Created	
McRae-KC	.873	R.Jackson-Bal	158	Carew-Min	40.0	McRae-KC	38.4	Mayberry-KC	160	Brett-KC	114
Carew-Min	.861	McRae-KC	154	McRae-KC	38.8	Carew-Min	37.9	Rudi-Oak	152	Carew-Min	111
R.Jackson-Bal	.855	Tenace-Oak	150	Brett-KC	36.2	Brett-KC	35.7	Hisle-Min	144	McRae-KC	101
Brett-KC	.843	Carew-Min	147	Staub-Det	33.2	R.Jackson-Bal	32.4	Randle-Tex	138	Staub-Det	99
Lynn-Bos	.842	Brett-KC	145	Carty-Cle	29.8	Carty-Cle	30.5	L.May-Bal	137	White-NY	98

Total Average		Stolen Bases		Stolen Base Average		Stolen Base Runs		Fielding Runs		Total Player Rating	
McRae-KC	.862	North-Oak	75	Rivers-NY	86.0	Campaneris-Oak	9.0	White-KC	20.5	Nettles-NY	4.2
R.Jackson-Bal	.857	LeFlore-Det	58	Campaneris-Oak	81.8	Rivers-NY	8.7	Kuiper-Cle	20.0	Brett-KC	4.1
Tenace-Oak	.855	Campaneris-Oak	54	Baylor-Oak	81.3	Baylor-Oak	8.4	Brohamer-Chi	18.0	R.Jackson-Bal	3.8
Carew-Min	.854	Baylor-Oak	52	Bumbry-Bal	80.8	Bumbry-Bal	6.6	Nettles-NY	17.2	Grich-Bal	3.7
Brett-KC	.797	Patek-KC	51	R.Jackson-Bal	80.0	Patek-KC	6.3	Belanger-Bal	16.3	McRae-KC	3.6

Wins		Win Percentage		Games		Complete Games		Shutouts		Saves	
Palmer-Bal	22	Campbell-Min	.773	Campbell-Min	78	Fidrych-Det	24	Ryan-Cal	7	Lyle-NY	23
Tiant-Bos	21	Garland-Bal	.741	Fingers-Oak	70	Tanana-Cal	23	Blyleven-Min-Tex	6	LaRoche-Cle	21
Garland-Bal	20	Ellis-NY	.680	Lindblad-Oak	65	Palmer-Bal	23	Palmer-Bal	6	Fingers-Oak	20
		Fidrych-Det	.679	Lyle-NY	64			Blue-Oak	6	Campbell-Min	20
				LaRoche-Cle	61					Littell-KC	16

Innings Pitched		Fewest Hits/Game		Fewest BB/Game		Strikeouts		Strikeouts/Game		Ratio	
Palmer-Bal	315.0	Ryan-Cal	6.11	Bird-KC	1.41	Ryan-Cal	327	Ryan-Cal	10.35	Tanana-Cal	9.18
Hunter-NY	298.2	Tanana-Cal	6.62	Jenkins-Bos	1.85	Tanana-Cal	261	Eckersley-Cle	9.03	Fidrych-Det	9.81
Blue-Oak	298.1	Eckersley-Cle	7.00	Perry-Tex	1.87	Blyleven-Min-Tex	219	Tanana-Cal	8.15	Palmer-Bal	9.91
Blyleven-Min-Tex	297.2	Palmer-Bal	7.29	Blue-Oak	1.90	Eckersley-Cle	200	Blyleven-Min-Tex	6.62	Blue-Oak	10.02
Slaton-Mil	292.2	Brett-NY-Chi	7.67	Fidrych-Det	1.91	Hunter-NY	173	Campbell-Min	6.17	Perry-Tex	10.21

Earned Run Average		Adjusted ERA		Opponents' Batting Avg.		Opponents' On Base Pct.		Starter Runs		Adjusted Starter Runs	
Fidrych-Det	2.34	Fidrych-Det	159	Ryan-Cal	.195	Tanana-Cal	.261	Blue-Oak	38.6	Fidrych-Det	38.1
Blue-Oak	2.35	Blue-Oak	142	Tanana-Cal	.203	Fidrych-Det	.279	Palmer-Bal	35.1	Blue-Oak	33.1
Tanana-Cal	2.43	Tanana-Cal	137	Eckersley-Cle	.214	Blue-Oak	.280	Tanana-Cal	34.7	Tanana-Cal	28.5
Torrez-Oak	2.50	Torrez-Oak	134	Palmer-Bal	.224	Palmer-Bal	.282	Fidrych-Det	32.8	Palmer-Bal	26.5
Palmer-Bal	2.51	Palmer-Bal	130	Brett-NY-Chi	.233	Bird-KC	.283	Torrez-Oak	30.1	Tiant-Bos	26.2

Clutch Pitching Index		Relief Runs		Adjusted Relief Runs		Relief Ranking		Total Pitcher Index		Total Baseball Ranking	
Hartzell-Cal	124	Littell-KC	16.6	Hiller-Det	17.8	Hiller-Det	30.9	Fidrych-Det	5.1	Fidrych-Det	5.1
Travers-Mil	120	Fingers-Oak	15.6	Littell-KC	16.4	Fingers-Oak	25.5	Blue-Oak	3.3	Nettles-NY	4.2
Umbarger-Tex	118	Hiller-Det	15.3	Kern-Cle	14.6	Lyle-NY	24.0	Tanana-Cal	3.3	Brett-KC	4.1
Garland-Bal	116	Kern-Cle	15.0	Burgmeier-Min	14.1	Kern-Cle	23.2	Palmer-Bal	3.1	R.Jackson-Bal	3.8
Torrez-Oak	115	Lyle-NY	14.5	Thomas-Cle	14.0	Littell-KC	22.8	Torrez-Oak	2.7	Grich-Bal	3.7

TEAM	G	W	L	PCT	GB	R	OR	AB	H	2B	3B	HR	BB	SO	AVG	OBP	SLG	PRO	PRO+	BR	/A	PF	CHI	RC	SB	CS	SBA	SBR
EAST																												
PHI	162	101	61	.623		**847**	668	5546	1548	266	56	186	573	806	.279	.351	.448	.799	113	143	111	104	98	865	135	68	55	-12
PIT	162	96	66	.593	5	734	665	5662	1550	278	57	133	474	878	.274	.334	.413	.747	102	37	17	103	98	776	260	120	69	-4
STL	162	83	79	.512	18	737	688	5527	1490	252	56	96	489	823	.270	.332	.388	.720	99	-12	0	98	107	690	134	112	62	-3
CHI	162	81	81	.500	20	692	739	5604	1489	271	37	111	534	796	.266	.333	.387	.720	88	-10	-89	111	98	709	64	45	42	-11
MON	162	75	87	.463	26	665	736	5675	1474	294	50	138	498	877	.260	.320	.402	.722	100	-19	1	97	95	715	88	50	54	-16
NY	162	64	98	.395	37	587	663	5410	1319	227	30	88	529	887	.244	.315	.346	.661	87	-124	-91	95	103	577	98	81	60	-11
WEST																												
LA	162	98	64	.605		769	582	5589	1484	223	28	191	588	896	.266	.338	.418	.756	108	58	61	100	98	794	114	62	51	-11
CIN	162	88	74	.543	10	802	725	5524	1513	269	42	181	600	911	.274	.348	.436	.784	112	115	102	102	97	847	170	64	56	-13
HOU	162	81	81	.500	17	680	650	5530	1405	263	60	114	515	839	.254	.322	.385	.707	104	-40	-23	91	102	697	187	72	56	-11
SF	162	75	87	.463	23	673	711	5497	1392	227	41	134	568	842	.253	.326	.383	.709	95	-34	-31	100	100	683	90	59	51	-12
SD	162	69	93	.426	29	692	834	5602	1397	245	49	120	602	1057	.249	.325	.375	.700	103	-48	27	90	102	700	133	57	53	-14
ATL	162	61	101	.377	37	678	895	5534	1404	218	20	139	537	876	.254	.322	.376	.698	82	-57	-141	112	104	660	82	53	50	-13
TOT	972					8556		66700	17465	3033	526	1631	6487	10488	.262	.330	.396	.727							1555	843	65	-38

TEAM	CG	SH	SV	IP	H	H/G	HR	BB	SO	RAT	ERA	ERA+	OAV	OOB	PR	/A	PF	CPI	FA	E	DP	FW	PW	BW	SBW	DIF
EAST																										
PHI	31	7	**47**	1455²	1451	9.0	134	482	856	12.1	3.71	108	.262	.324	32	46	102	103	.981	120	168	1.3	4.7	**11.2**	-.9	3.7
PIT	25	**15**	39	1481²	1406	8.5	149	485	890	11.6	3.61	110	.251	.313	49	61	102	99	.977	145	137	-.0	6.2	1.7	-.0	7.3
STL	26	10	31	1446	1420	8.8	139	532	768	12.3	3.81	101	.260	.328	16	6	98	102	.978	139	**174**	.3	.6	.0	.0	1.1
CHI	16	10	44	1468	1500	9.2	128	489	**942**	12.3	4.01	109	.265	.326	-16	61	112	96	.977	153	147	-.5	6.2	-9.0	-.8	4.1
MON	31	11	33	1481	1426	8.7	135	579	856	12.3	4.01	95	.254	.327	-16	-33	97	94	.980	129	128	.8	-3.3	.1	-1.3	-2.3
NY	27	12	28	1433²	**1378**	8.7	118	490	911	11.9	3.77	99	.253	.319	21	-5	96	94	.978	134	132	.5	-.5	-9.2	-.8	-7.0
WEST																										
LA	34	13	39	1475¹	1393	8.5	119	**438**	930	**11.3**	**3.22**	119	.251	**.309**	112	98	98	104	.981	124	160	1.1	**9.9**	6.2	-.8	.6
CIN	33	12	32	1437¹	1469	9.2	156	544	868	12.8	4.21	93	.267	.336	-48	-45	101	100	**.984**	95	154	2.7	-4.6	10.3	-1.0	-.5
HOU	37	11	28	1465²	1384	**8.5**	**110**	545	871	12.0	3.54	101	**.250**	.321	60	4	91	99	.978	142	136	.0	.4	2.3	-.8	-2.0
SF	27	10	33	1458	1501	9.3	114	529	854	12.7	3.75	104	.267	.333	25	25	100	104	.972	179	136	-2.0	2.5	-3.1	-.9	-2.5
SD	6	5	44	1466¹	1556	9.6	160	673	827	13.8	4.43	80	.275	.355	-85	-145	91	**105**	.971	189	142	-2.5	-14.7	2.7	-1.1	3.5
ATL	28	5	31	1445¹	1581	9.8	169	701	915	14.5	4.85	92	.279	.362	-151	-64	114	101	.972	175	127	-1.7	-6.5	-14.3	-1.0	3.5
TOT	321	121	429	17514		9.0				12.5	3.91		.262	.330					.977	1724	1741					

Runs		Hits		Doubles		Triples		Home Runs		Total Bases	
Foster-Cin	124	Parker-Pit	215	Parker-Pit	44	Templeton-StL	18	Foster-Cin	52	Foster-Cin	388
Griffey-Cin	117	Rose-Cin	204	Cash-Mon	42	Schmidt-Phi	11	Burroughs-Atl	41	Parker-Pit	338
Schmidt-Phi	114	Templeton-StL	200	Hernandez-StL	41	Richards-SD	11	Luzinski-Phi	39	Luzinski-Phi	329
Morgan-Cin	113	Foster-Cin	197	Cromartie-Mon	41	Almon-SD	11	Schmidt-Phi	38	Garvey-LA	322
Parker-Pit	107	Garvey-LA	192					Garvey-LA	33	Schmidt-Phi	312

Runs Batted In		Runs Produced		Bases On Balls		Batting Average		On Base Percentage		Slugging Average	
Foster-Cin	149	Foster-Cin	221	Tenace-SD	125	Parker-Pit	.338	Smith-LA	.432	Foster-Cin	.631
Luzinski-Phi	130	Luzinski-Phi	190	Morgan-Cin	117	Templeton-StL	.322	Morgan-Cin	.420	Luzinski-Phi	.594
Garvey-LA	115	Schmidt-Phi	177	Smith-LA	104	Foster-Cin	.320	Tenace-SD	.417	Smith-LA	.576
Burroughs-Atl	114	Parker-Pit	174	Schmidt-Phi	104	Griffey-Cin	.318	Simmons-StL	.410	Schmidt-Phi	.574
		Garvey-LA	173	Cey-LA	93	Simmons-StL	.318	Parker-Pit	.399	Bench-Cin	.540

Production		Adjusted Production		Batter Runs		Adjusted Batter Runs		Clutch Hitting Index		Runs Created	
Foster-Cin	1.017	Smith-LA	168	Foster-Cin	56.0	Foster-Cin	54.6	Cey-LA	136	Foster-Cin	144
Smith-LA	1.008	Foster-Cin	165	Smith-LA	50.3	Smith-LA	50.6	Watson-Hou	131	Luzinski-Phi	132
Luzinski-Phi	.993	Luzinski-Phi	155	Luzinski-Phi	48.6	Luzinski-Phi	45.3	Bench-Cin	124	Parker-Pit	130
Schmidt-Phi	.972	Schmidt-Phi	151	Schmidt-Phi	45.8	Schmidt-Phi	42.4	Luzinski-Phi	124	Schmidt-Phi	129
Parker-Pit	.929	Hendrick-SD	148	Parker-Pit	42.0	Parker-Pit	39.8	Robinson-Pit	123	Smith-LA	129

Total Average		Stolen Bases		Stolen Base Average		Stolen Base Runs		Fielding Runs		Total Player Rating	
Smith-LA	1.121	Taveras-Pit	70	Bowa-Phi	91.4	Taveras-Pit	10.2	DeJesus-Chi	35.8	Schmidt-Phi	6.9
Morgan-Cin	1.054	Cedeno-Hou	61	McBride-StL-Phi	83.7	Cedeno-Hou	9.9	Trillo-Chi	30.1	Foster-Cin	6.1
Schmidt-Phi	1.046	Richards-SD	56	Morgan-Cin	83.1	Richards-SD	9.6	Schmidt-Phi	28.8	Parker-Pit	5.6
Luzinski-Phi	1.043	Moreno-Pit	53	Richards-SD	82.4	Morgan-Cin	8.7	Parker-Pit	28.1	Smith-LA	3.7
Foster-Cin	1.039	Morgan-Cin	49	Cedeno-Hou	81.3	Bowa-Phi	7.8	Tyson-StL	22.0	Hendrick-SD	3.5

Wins		Win Percentage		Games		Complete Games		Shutouts		Saves	
Carlton-Phi	23	Candelaria-Pit	.800	Fingers-SD	78	Niekro-Atl	20	Seaver-NY-Cin	7	Fingers-SD	35
Seaver-NY-Cin	21	Seaver-NY-Cin	.778	Tomlin-SD	76	Seaver-NY-Cin	19	Rogers-Mon	4	Sutter-Chi	31
		Christenson-Phi	.760	Spillner-SD	76	Rogers-Mon	17	R.Reuschel-Chi	4	Gossage-Pit	26
		John-LA	.741	Metzger-SD-StL	75	Carlton-Phi	17			Hough-LA	22
		Forsch-StL	.741			Richard-Hou	13				

Innings Pitched		Fewest Hits/Game		Fewest BB/Game		Strikeouts		Strikeouts/Game		Ratio	
Niekro-Atl	330.1	Seaver-NY-Cin	6.85	Candelaria-Pit	1.95	Niekro-Atl	262	Koosman-NY	7.62	Seaver-NY-Cin	9.13
Rogers-Mon	301.2	Richard-Hou	7.15	John-LA	2.04	Richard-Hou	214	Richard-Hou	7.21	Candelaria-Pit	9.72
Carlton-Phi	283.0	Carlton-Phi	7.28	Rau-LA	2.08	Rogers-Mon	206	Niekro-Atl	7.14	Hooton-LA	9.95
Richard-Hou	267.0	Hooton-LA	7.41	Barr-SF	2.15	Carlton-Phi	198	Seaver-NY-Cin	6.75	Carlton-Phi	10.24
Seaver-NY-Cin	261.1	Candelaria-Pit	7.69	Lemongello-Hou	2.18	Seaver-NY-Cin	196	Matlack-NY	6.55	Sutton-LA	10.45

Earned Run Average		Adjusted ERA		Opponents' Batting Avg.		Opponents' On Base Pct.		Starter Runs		Adjusted Starter Runs	
Candelaria-Pit	2.34	Candelaria-Pit	170	Seaver-NY-Cin	.209	Seaver-NY-Cin	.260	Candelaria-Pit	40.2	R.Reuschel-Chi	44.8
Seaver-NY-Cin	2.58	R.Reuschel-Chi	157	Richard-Hou	.218	Candelaria-Pit	.276	Carlton-Phi	39.9	Carlton-Phi	42.7
Hooton-LA	2.62	Carlton-Phi	151	Carlton-Phi	.223	Hooton-LA	.281	Seaver-NY-Cin	38.5	Candelaria-Pit	42.1
Carlton-Phi	2.64	Seaver-NY-Cin	149	Hooton-LA	.225	Carlton-Phi	.287	Hooton-LA	32.0	Seaver-NY-Cin	37.0
John-LA	2.78	Hooton-LA	146	Koosman-NY	.232	Sutton-LA	.291	R.Reuschel-Chi	31.5	Hooton-LA	29.9

Clutch Pitching Index		Relief Runs		Adjusted Relief Runs		Relief Ranking		Total Pitcher Index		Total Baseball Ranking	
Candelaria-Pit	126	Gossage-Pit	33.8	Sutter-Chi	36.3	Gossage-Pit	62.5	Carlton-Phi	5.7	Schmidt-Phi	6.9
John-LA	120	Sutter-Chi	30.6	Gossage-Pit	34.9	Sutter-Chi	54.0	R.Reuschel-Chi	5.6	Foster-Cin	6.1
Rooker-Pit	118	Lavelle-SF	24.4	Lavelle-SF	24.4	Lavelle-SF	35.3	Candelaria-Pit	4.9	Carlton-Phi	5.7
Lemongello-Hou	116	Garber-Phi	17.9	Garber-Phi	18.9	Garber-Phi	30.9	Seaver-NY-Cin	4.3	R.Reuschel-Chi	5.6
Rau-LA	114	Reed-Phi	16.0	Reed-Phi	17.2	G.Hernandez-Chi	21.7	Sutter-Chi	3.8	Parker-Pit	5.6

TEAM	G	W	L	PCT	GB	R	OR	AB	H	2B	3B	HR	BB	SO	AVG	OBP	SLG	PRO	PRO+	BR	/A	PF	CHI	RC	SB	CS	SBA	SBR
EAST																												
NY	162	100	62	.617		831	651	5605	1576	267	47	184	533	681	.281	.347	.444	.791	**115**	104	**112**	99	98	853	93	57	56	-16
BAL	161	97	64	.602	2.5	719	653	5494	1433	231	25	148	560	945	.261	.332	.393	.725	103	-22	23	94	102	711	90	51	48	-13
BOS	161	97	64	.602	2.5	859	712	5510	1551	258	56	**213**	528	905	.281	.349	**.465**	**.814**	107	**144**	58	112	98	**875**	66	47	49	-14
DET	162	74	88	.457	26	714	751	5604	1480	228	45	166	452	764	.264	.321	.410	.731	93	-24	-62	105	101	717	60	46	48	-14
CLE	161	71	90	.441	28.5	676	739	5491	1476	221	46	100	531	688	.269	.337	.380	.717	98	-30	-6	97	96	682	87	57	**64**	-11
MIL	162	67	95	.414	33	639	765	5517	1425	255	46	125	443	862	.258	.316	.389	.705	91	-72	-71	100	99	660	85	67	51	-10
TOR	161	54	107	.335	45.5	605	822	5418	1367	230	41	100	499	819	.252	.318	.365	.683	84	-105	-115	101	99	610	65	55	52	-14
WEST																												
KC	162	102	60	.630		822	651	5594	1549	**299**	**77**	146	522	687	.277	.343	.436	.779	110	82	76	101	100	835	170	87	63	-11
TEX	162	94	68	.580	8	767	657	5541	1497	265	39	135	596	904	.270	.345	.405	.750	102	34	26	101	98	780	154	85	57	**-8**
CHI	162	90	72	.556	12	844	771	5633	1568	254	52	192	559	**666**	.278	.347	.444	.791	114	107	108	100	99	858	42	44	44	-12
MIN	161	84	77	.522	17.5	**867**	776	5639	**1588**	273	60	123	563	754	**.282**	**.351**	.417	.768	109	71	82	99	105	827	105	65	60	-16
CAL	162	74	88	.457	28	675	695	5410	1380	233	40	131	542	880	.255	.327	.386	.713	96	-46	-17	96	100	681	159	89	60	**-8**
SEA	162	64	98	.395	38	624	855	5460	1398	218	33	133	426	769	.256	.314	.381	.695	88	-90	-82	99	100	643	110	67	53	-11
OAK	161	63	98	.391	38.5	605	749	5358	1284	176	37	117	516	910	.240	.311	.352	.663	81	-144	-133	99	**107**	589	176	89	63	-10
TOT	1131					10247		77274	20572	3408	644	2013	7270	11234	.266	.333	.405	.738							1462	936	61	-122

TEAM	CG	SH	SV	IP	H	H/G	HR	BB	SO	RAT	ERA	ERA+	OAV	OOB	PR	/A	PF	CPI	FA	E	DP	FW	PW	BW	SBW	DIF
EAST																										
NY	52	16	34	1449¹	1395	8.7	139	486	758	11.8	3.61	109	.254	.317	72	53	97	101	.979	132	151	.6	5.3	**11.1**	-.7	2.7
BAL	**65**	11	23	1451	1414	8.8	124	494	737	12.0	3.74	101	.260	.325	51	8	93	101	**.983**	106	**189**	**2.0**	.8	2.3	-.4	11.8
BOS	40	13	40	1428	1555	9.8	158	**378**	758	12.3	4.11	109	.278	.326	-8	60	111	102	.978	133	162	.5	6.0	5.8	-.5	4.8
DET	44	3	23	1457	1526	9.4	162	470	784	12.5	4.13	104	.270	.329	-11	25	106	100	.978	142	153	.0	2.5	-6.2	-.5	-2.8
CLE	45	8	30	1452¹	1441	8.9	136	550	876	12.5	4.10	96	.261	.331	-6	-25	97	96	.979	130	145	.7	-2.5	.6	-.2	-6.9
MIL	38	6	25	1431	1461	9.2	136	566	719	13.0	4.32	94	.268	.340	-41	-40	100	97	.978	139	165	.2	-4.0	-7.1	-.1	-3.1
TOR	40	3	20	1428¹	1538	9.7	152	623	771	13.7	4.57	92	.278	.353	-80	-59	103	101	.974	164	133	-1.2	-5.9	-11.4	-.5	-7.4
WEST																										
KC	41	15	**42**	1460²	**1377**	**8.5**	**110**	499	850	11.8	**3.52**	**115**	**.251**	.317	**87**	83	99	98	.978	137	145	.3	8.2	7.5	-.2	5.1
TEX	49	**17**	31	1472	1412	8.6	134	471	864	**11.7**	3.56	114	.254	**.316**	80	**84**	101	101	.982	117	156	1.5	**8.3**	2.6	.0	.5
CHI	34	3	40	1444²	1557	9.7	136	516	842	13.2	4.25	96	.276	.342	-30	-26	101	101	.974	159	125	-.9	-2.6	10.7	-.3	2.1
MIN	35	4	25	1442	1546	9.6	151	507	737	13.0	4.36	91	.278	.342	-47	-60	98	101	.978	143	184	-.0	-6.0	8.1	-.7	2.1
CAL	53	13	26	1437²	1383	8.7	136	572	**965**	12.5	3.72	105	.256	.332	54	30	96	**105**	.976	147	137	-.2	3.0	-1.7	.0	-8.1
SEA	18	1	31	1433	1508	9.5	194	578	785	13.5	4.83	85	.271	.346	-122	-114	101	96	.976	147	162	-.2	-11.3	-8.1	-.2	2.9
OAK	32	4	26	1436²	1459	9.1	145	560	788	12.8	4.04	100	.265	.335	2	-3	99	102	.970	190	136	-2.7	-.3	-13.2	-.1	-1.2
TOT	586	117	416	20223²		9.2				12.6	4.06		.266	.333					.977	1986	2143					

Runs		Hits		Doubles		Triples		Home Runs		Total Bases	
Carew-Min	128	Carew-Min	239	McRae-KC	54	Carew-Min	16	Rice-Bos	39	Rice-Bos	382
Fisk-Bos	106	LeFlore-Det	212	Jackson-NY	39	Rice-Bos	15	Nettles-NY	37	Carew-Min	351
Brett-KC	105	Rice-Bos	206	Lemon-Chi	38	Cowens-KC	14	Bonds-Cal	37	McRae-KC	330
		Bostock-Min	199	Carew-Min	38	Brett-KC	13	Scott-Bos	33	Cowens-KC	318
		Burleson-Bos	194			Bostock-Min	12	Jackson-NY	32	LeFlore-Det	310

Runs Batted In		Runs Produced		Bases On Balls		Batting Average		On Base Percentage		Slugging Average	
Hisle-Min	119	Carew-Min	214	Harrah-Tex	109	Carew-Min	.388	Carew-Min	.452	Rice-Bos	.593
Bonds-Cal	115	Cowens-KC	187	Singleton-Bal	107	Bostock-Min	.336	Singleton-Bal	.442	Carew-Min	.570
Rice-Bos	114	Hisle-Min	186	Hargrove-Tex	103	Singleton-Bal	.328	Hargrove-Tex	.424	Jackson-NY	.550
Hobson-Bos	112	Fisk-Bos	182	Gross-Oak	86	Rivers-NY	.326	Fisk-Bos	.408	Hisle-Min	.533
Cowens-KC	112	Bonds-Cal	181	Mayberry-KC	83	LeFlore-Det	.325	Page-Oak	.407	Brett-KC	.532

Production		Adjusted Production		Batter Runs		Adjusted Batter Runs		Clutch Hitting Index		Runs Created	
Carew-Min	1.022	Carew-Min	179	Carew-Min	67.0	Carew-Min	68.2	Wynegar-Min	141	Carew-Min	160
Rice-Bos	.972	Singleton-Bal	168	Rice-Bos	51.4	Singleton-Bal	53.3	Hisle-Min	133	Rice-Bos	136
Singleton-Bal	.949	Page-Oak	153	Singleton-Bal	48.5	Rice-Bos	41.6	Doyle-Bos	133	Singleton-Bal	124
Fisk-Bos	.929	Jackson-NY	151	Fisk-Bos	39.9	Page-Oak	38.4	Sundberg-Tex	133	McRae-KC	119
Page-Oak	.928	Thornton-Cle	149	Hargrove-Tex	37.8	Hargrove-Tex	37.0	Carty-Cle	133	Page-Oak	117

Total Average		Stolen Bases		Stolen Base Average		Stolen Base Runs		Fielding Runs		Total Player Rating	
Carew-Min	1.093	Patek-KC	53	Page-Oak	89.4	Page-Oak	9.6	Lemon-Chi	26.7	Carew-Min	6.3
Page-Oak	1.064	Page-Oak	42	Jackson-NY	85.0	Patek-KC	8.1	Sundberg-Tex	22.3	Page-Oak	4.5
Singleton-Bal	1.011	Remy-Cal	41	Harrah-Tex	84.4	Harrah-Tex	5.1	Belanger-Bal	20.7	Brett-KC	4.3
Jackson-NY	.997	Bonds-Cal	41	White-KC	82.1	White-KC	3.9	Smalley-Min	18.7	Bostock-Min	4.2
Harrah-Tex	.964	LeFlore-Det	39	Patek-KC	80.3			Campaneris-Tex	17.6	Singleton-Bal	4.0

Wins		Win Percentage		Games		Complete Games		Shutouts		Saves	
Palmer-Bal	20	Splittorff-KC	.727	Lyle-NY	72	Ryan-Cal	22	Tanana-Cal	7	Campbell-Bos	31
Leonard-KC	20	T.Johnson-Min	.696	T.Johnson-Min	71	Palmer-Bal	22	Leonard-KC	5	Lyle-NY	26
Goltz-Min	20	Guidry-NY	.696	Campbell-Bos	69	Leonard-KC	21	Guidry-NY	5	LaGrow-Chi	25
Ryan-Cal	19	Rozema-Det	.682	McClure-Mil	68	Garland-Cle	21	Blyleven-Tex	5	Kern-Cle	18
				LaGrow-Chi	66	Tanana-Cal	20			LaRoche-Cle-Cal	17

Innings Pitched		Fewest Hits/Game		Fewest BB/Game		Strikeouts		Strikeouts/Game		Ratio	
Palmer-Bal	319.0	Ryan-Cal	5.96	Rozema-Det	1.40	Ryan-Cal	341	Ryan-Cal	10.26	Blyleven-Tex	9.86
Goltz-Min	303.0	Blyleven-Tex	6.94	Jenkins-Bos	1.68	Leonard-KC	244	Tanana-Cal	7.65	Eckersley-Cle	10.01
Ryan-Cal	299.0	Palmer-Bal	7.42	Hartzell-Cal	1.81	Tanana-Cal	205	Guidry-NY	7.52	Guidry-NY	10.21
Leonard-KC	292.2	Guidry-NY	7.43	Eckersley-Cle	1.96	Palmer-Bal	193	Leonard-KC	7.50	Tanana-Cal	10.22
Garland-Cle	282.2	Tanana-Cal	7.50	Cleveland-Bos	2.03	Eckersley-Cle	191	Blyleven-Tex	6.98	Leonard-KC	10.24

Earned Run Average		Adjusted ERA		Opponents' Batting Avg.		Opponents' On Base Pct.		Starter Runs		Adjusted Starter Runs	
Tanana-Cal	2.54	Tanana-Cal	154	Ryan-Cal	.193	Eckersley-Cle	.278	Ryan-Cal	42.8	Ryan-Cal	38.0
Blyleven-Tex	2.72	Blyleven-Tex	150	Blyleven-Tex	.214	Blyleven-Tex	.279	Palmer-Bal	40.8	Tanana-Cal	36.9
Ryan-Cal	2.77	Ryan-Cal	141	Guidry-NY	.224	Guidry-NY	.284	Tanana-Cal	40.8	Blyleven-Tex	35.3
Guidry-NY	2.82	Guidry-NY	140	Tanana-Cal	.227	Leonard-KC	.285	Blyleven-Tex	34.8	Leonard-KC	32.2
Palmer-Bal	2.91	Rozema-Det	139	Leonard-KC	.227	Tanana-Cal	.286	Leonard-KC	33.0	Palmer-Bal	31.3

Clutch Pitching Index		Relief Runs		Adjusted Relief Runs		Relief Ranking		Total Pitcher Index		Total Baseball Ranking	
Slaton-Mil	118	Lyle-NY	28.8	Lyle-NY	27.0	Campbell-Bos	45.6	Tanana-Cal	4.0	Carew-Min	6.3
Rozema-Det	116	Torrealba-Oak	18.6	Campbell-Bos	23.8	Lyle-NY	43.4	Ryan-Cal	3.8	Page-Oak	4.5
Grimsley-Bal	110	LaGrow-Chi	17.5	Torrealba-Oak	18.1	Romo-Sea	28.1	Blyleven-Tex	3.7	Brett-KC	4.3
Splittorff-KC	108	Campbell-Bos	17.1	LaGrow-Chi	17.8	LaGrow-Chi	26.3	Palmer-Bal	3.3	Bostock-Min	4.2
Tanana-Cal	106	Coleman-Oak	15.6	Romo-Sea	16.2	T.Johnson-Min	22.8	Rozema-Det	3.1	Singleton-Bal	4.0

TEAM	G	W	L	PCT	GB	R	OR	AB	H	2B	3B	HR	BB	SO	AVG	OBP	SLG	PRO	PRO+	BR	/A	PF	CHI	RC	SB	CS	SBA	SBR
EAST																												
PHI	162	90	72	.556		708	586	5448	1404	248	32	133	552	866	.258	.331	.388	.719	106	49	43	101	101	715	152	58	54	-14
PIT	161	88	73	.547	1.5	684	637	5406	1390	239	**54**	115	480	874	.257	.323	.385	.708	99	21	-7	105	104	676	**213**	90	**63**	**-10**
CHI	162	79	83	.488	11	664	724	5532	**1461**	224	48	72	562	746	**.264**	.334	.361	.695	90	11	-68	112	99	673	110	58	48	**-10**
MON	162	76	86	.469	14	633	611	5530	1404	269	31	121	396	881	.254	.308	.379	.687	98	-26	-18	99	103	629	80	42	47	-15
STL	162	69	93	.426	21	600	657	5415	1351	263	44	79	420	**713**	.249	.306	.358	.664	92	-65	-55	99	**106**	583	97	42	47	-15
NY	162	66	96	.407	24	607	690	5433	1332	227	47	86	549	829	.245	.317	.352	.669	96	-46	-22	96	101	600	100	77	62	-13
WEST																												
LA	162	95	67	.586		**727**	573	5437	1435	251	27	**149**	610	818	**.264**	**.340**	**.402**	**.742**	**114**	98	100	100	96	**763**	137	52	46	-11
CIN	161	92	69	.571	2.5	710	688	5392	1378	**270**	32	136	**636**	899	.256	.337	.393	.730	110	75	75	100	97	730	137	58	56	-15
SF	162	89	73	.549	6	613	594	5364	1331	240	41	117	554	814	.248	.320	.374	.694	104	0	25	96	95	647	87	54	49	-12
SD	162	84	78	.519	11	591	598	5360	1349	208	42	75	536	848	.252	.323	.348	.671	101	-36	14	92	97	624	152	70	59	-13
HOU	162	74	88	.457	21	605	634	5458	1408	231	45	70	434	743	.258	.315	.355	.670	100	-48	0	93	103	608	178	59	50	-11
ATL	162	69	93	.426	26	600	750	5381	1313	191	39	123	550	874	.244	.317	.363	.680	86	-27	-98	111	98	608	90	65	57	-14
TOT	971					7742		65156	16556	2861	482	1276	6279	9905	.254	.323	.372	.694							1533	725	68	25

TEAM	CG	SH	SV	IP	H	H/G	HR	BB	SO	RAT	ERA	ERA+	OAV	OOB	PR	/A	PF	CPI	FA	E	DP	FW	PW	BW	SBW	DIF
EAST																										
PHI	38	9	29	1436¹	1343	8.4	118	**393**	813	**11.0**	3.33	107	.250	**.304**	38	37	100	99	**.983**	104	156	**2.0**	3.9	4.5	-1.7	.2
PIT	30	13	44	1444²	1366	8.5	103	499	880	11.8	3.41	108	.248	.315	25	45	104	98	.973	167	133	-1.4	4.8	-.7	**-1.3**	6.2
CHI	24	7	38	1455¹	1475	9.1	125	539	768	12.7	4.05	99	.264	.333	-76	-4	113	98	.978	144	154	-.2	-.4	-7.2	**-1.3**	7.1
MON	42	13	32	1446	1332	8.3	117	572	740	12.0	3.42	103	.249	.325	24	15	99	106	.979	134	150	.4	1.6	-1.9	-1.8	-3.3
STL	32	13	22	1437	**1300**	**8.1**	94	600	859	12.1	3.58	98	**.245**	.325	-1	-10	98	97	.978	136	155	.3	-1.1	-5.8	-1.8	-3.6
NY	21	7	26	1455¹	1447	8.9	114	531	775	12.4	3.87	90	.265	.333	-47	-62	98	101	.979	132	160	.5	-6.6	-2.3	-1.6	-5.0
WEST																										
LA	46	16	38	1440¹	1362	8.5	107	440	800	11.4	**3.12**	112	.250	.309	73	62	98	106	.978	140	138	.0	6.6	10.6	-1.4	-1.8
CIN	16	10	46	1448¹	1437	8.9	122	567	908	12.6	3.81	93	.260	.332	-37	-42	99	102	.978	134	120	.3	-4.4	7.9	-1.8	9.5
SF	42	17	29	1455	1385	8.5	84	453	840	11.5	3.30	104	.251	.311	43	23	96	98	.977	146	118	-.3	2.4	2.6	-1.5	4.7
SD	21	10	**55**	1433²	1385	8.7	**74**	483	744	11.8	3.28	101	.257	.320	47	7	93	104	.975	160	171	-1.0	.7	1.5	-1.6	3.4
HOU	**48**	17	23	1440¹	1328	8.3	86	578	**930**	12.1	3.63	91	.246	.323	-8	-51	93	94	.978	133	109	.4	-5.4	.0	-1.4	-.7
ATL	29	12	32	1440¹	1404	8.8	132	624	848	12.9	4.08	99	.256	.337	-80	-5	113	98	.975	153	126	-.6	-.5	-10.4	-1.7	1.2
TOT	389	144	414	17332²		8.6				12.0	3.58		.254	.323					.978	1683	1690					

Runs		Hits		Doubles		Triples		Home Runs		Total Bases	
DeJesus-Chi	104	Garvey-LA	202	Rose-Cin	51	Templeton-StL	13	Foster-Cin	40	Parker-Pit	340
Rose-Cin	103	Rose-Cin	198	Clark-SF	46	Richards-SD	12	Luzinski-Phi	35	Foster-Cin	330
Parker-Pit	102	Cabell-Hou	195	Simmons-StL	40	Parker-Pit	12	Parker-Pit	30	Garvey-LA	319
Foster-Cin	97	Parker-Pit	194	Parrish-Mon	39			Smith-LA	29	Clark-SF	318
Moreno-Pit	95	Bowa-Phi	192	Perez-Mon	38					Winfield-SD	293

Runs Batted In		Runs Produced		Bases On Balls		Batting Average		On Base Percentage		Slugging Average	
Foster-Cin	120	Parker-Pit	189	Burroughs-Atl	117	Parker-Pit	.334	Burroughs-Atl	.436	Parker-Pit	.585
Parker-Pit	117	Garvey-LA	181	Evans-SF	105	Garvey-LA	.316	Parker-Pit	.395	Smith-LA	.559
Garvey-LA	113	Foster-Cin	177	Tenace-SD	101	Cruz-Hou	.315	Tenace-SD	.394	Foster-Cin	.546
Luzinski-Phi	101	Clark-SF	163	Luzinski-Phi	100	Madlock-SF	.309	Smith-LA	.392	Clark-SF	.537
Clark-SF	98	Winfield-SD	161	Cey-LA	96	Winfield-SD	.308	Luzinski-Phi	.390	Burroughs-Atl	.529

Production		Adjusted Production		Batter Runs		Adjusted Batter Runs		Clutch Hitting Index		Runs Created	
Parker-Pit	.981	Smith-LA	164	Parker-Pit	52.9	Parker-Pit	49.9	Morgan-Cin	145	Parker-Pit	134
Burroughs-Atl	.965	Parker-Pit	163	Burroughs-Atl	50.1	Burroughs-Atl	42.8	Montanez-NY	139	Burroughs-Atl	116
Smith-LA	.951	Clark-SF	155	Luzinski-Phi	40.9	Luzinski-Phi	40.3	W.Robinson-Pit	136	Foster-Cin	115
Luzinski-Phi	.916	Winfield-SD	153	Foster-Cin	39.2	Foster-Cin	39.2	Reitz-StL	136	Luzinski-Phi	114
Foster-Cin	.909	Luzinski-Phi	152	Smith-LA	37.8	Clark-SF	38.5	Watson-Hou	128	Clark-SF	109

Total Average		Stolen Bases		Stolen Base Average		Stolen Base Runs		Fielding Runs		Total Player Rating	
Burroughs-Atl	1.042	Moreno-Pit	71	Cedeno-Hou	92.0	Lopes-LA	11.1	Trillo-Chi	28.9	Parker-Pit	5.2
Parker-Pit	1.025	Taveras-Pit	46	Lopes-LA	91.8	Moreno-Pit	8.1	Smith-SD	25.6	Clark-SF	4.2
Smith-LA	1.009	Lopes-LA	45	McBride-Phi	90.3	McBride-Phi	6.6	Templeton-StL	22.9	Lopes-LA	3.9
Luzinski-Phi	.957	DeJesus-Chi	41	Sexton-Hou	88.9			Thomas-SD	21.6	Foster-Cin	3.6
Foster-Cin	.893	Smith-SD	40	Bowa-Phi	84.4			Puhl-Hou	19.1	Winfield-SD	3.3

Wins		Win Percentage		Games		Complete Games		Shutouts		Saves	
Perry-SD	21	Perry-SD	.778	Tekulve-Pit	91	Niekro-Atl	22	Knepper-SF	6	Fingers-SD	37
Grimsley-Mon	20	Hooton-LA	.655	Littell-StL	72	Grimsley-Mon	19	Niekro-Atl	4	Tekulve-Pit	31
Niekro-Atl	19	Grimsley-Mon	.645	Moore-Chi	71	Richard-Hou	16	Halicki-SF	4	Bair-Cin	28
Hooton-LA	19	Blue-SF	.643	Moffitt-SF	70	Knepper-SF	16	Blyleven-Pit	4	Sutter-Chi	27
		John-LA	.630	Bair-Cin	70			Blue-SF	4	Garber-Phi-Atl	25

Innings Pitched		Fewest Hits/Game		Fewest BB/Game		Strikeouts		Strikeouts/Game		Ratio	
Niekro-Atl	334.1	Richard-Hou	6.28	Christenson-Phi	1.86	Richard-Hou	303	Richard-Hou	9.90	Swan-NY	9.72
Richard-Hou	275.1	Swan-NY	7.12	Barr-SF	1.93	Niekro-Atl	248	Seaver-Cin	7.83	Hooton-LA	9.80
Grimsley-Mon	263.0	Hooton-LA	7.47	R.Reuschel-Chi	2.00	Seaver-Cin	226	Vuckovich-StL	6.76	Halicki-SF	9.86
Perry-SD	260.2	Halicki-SF	7.51	Halicki-SF	2.04	Blyleven-Pit	182	Blyleven-Pit	6.72	Christenson-Phi	10.14
Knepper-SF	260.0	Knepper-SF	7.55	Sutton-LA	2.04	Montefusco-SF	177	Niekro-Atl	6.68	Rogers-Mon	10.36

Earned Run Average		Adjusted ERA		Opponents' Batting Avg.		Opponents' On Base Pct.		Starter Runs		Adjusted Starter Runs	
Swan-NY	2.43	Swan-NY	143	Richard-Hou	.196	Halicki-SF	.271	Knepper-SF	27.3	Niekro-Atl	43.3
Rogers-Mon	2.47	Rogers-Mon	143	Swan-NY	.219	Swan-NY	.277	Rogers-Mon	27.0	Rogers-Mon	25.7
Vuckovich-StL	2.54	Niekro-Atl	141	Halicki-SF	.221	Hooton-LA	.277	Swan-NY	26.4	Swan-NY	24.3
Knepper-SF	2.63	Vuckovich-StL	138	Hooton-LA	.226	Christenson-Phi	.284	Niekro-Atl	25.8	Knepper-SF	23.6
Hooton-LA	2.71	Knepper-SF	131	Seaver-Cin	.227	D.Robinson-Pit	.286	Perry-SD	24.5	Vuckovich-StL	21.4

Clutch Pitching Index		Relief Runs		Adjusted Relief Runs		Relief Ranking		Total Pitcher Index		Total Baseball Ranking	
Rau-LA	134	Tekulve-Pit	18.6	Bair-Cin	22.5	Bair-Cin	31.5	Niekro-Atl	5.8	Niekro-Atl	5.8
Vuckovich-StL	124	Garber-Phi-Atl	18.5	Tekulve-Pit	20.5	Tekulve-Pit	31.1	Carlton-Phi	3.1	Parker-Pit	5.2
Carlton-Phi	121	Bair-Cin	17.9	Bair-Cin	17.5	Garber-Phi-Atl	29.9	Denny-StL	2.8	Clark-SF	4.2
Jones-SD	114	Reed-Phi	16.2	Reed-Phi	16.1	Forster-LA	22.9	Rogers-Mon	2.7	Lopes-LA	3.9
Rogers-Mon	113	D'Acquisto-SD	14.9	D'Acquisto-SD	12.4	Fingers-SD	22.9	Swan-NY	2.7	Foster-Cin	3.6

TEAM	G	W	L	PCT	GB	R	OR	AB	H	2B	3B	HR	BB	SO	AVG	OBP	SLG	PRO	PRO+	BR	/A	PF	CHI	RC	SB	CS	SBA	SBR
EAST																												
NY	163	100	63	.613		735	582	5583	1489	228	38	125	505	695	.267	.332	.388	.720	104	14	30	98	105	720	98	42	40	-10
BOS	163	99	64	.607	1	796	657	5587	1493	270	46	172	582	835	.267	.339	.424	.763	102	96	21	111	100	793	74	51	56	-17
MIL	162	93	69	.574	6.5	804	650	5536	1530	265	38	173	520	805	.276	.342	.432	.774	115	114	111	100	100	822	95	53	49	-13
BAL	161	90	71	.559	9	659	633	5422	1397	248	19	154	552	864	.258	.329	.396	.725	109	18	59	94	95	691	75	61	55	-14
DET	162	86	76	.531	13.5	714	653	5601	1520	218	34	129	563	695	.271	.341	.392	.733	103	45	24	103	96	748	90	38	41	-12
CLE	159	69	90	.434	29	639	694	5365	1400	223	45	106	488	698	.261	.326	.379	.705	99	-18	-10	99	99	649	64	63	61	-17
TOR	161	59	102	.366	40	590	775	5430	1358	217	39	98	448	645	.250	.310	.359	.669	86	-92	-105	102	103	587	28	52	46	-11
WEST																												
KC	162	92	70	.568		743	634	5474	1469	305	59	98	498	644	.268	.333	.399	.732	102	34	16	103	104	739	216	84	65	-13
TEX	162	87	75	.537	5	692	632	5347	1353	216	36	132	624	779	.253	.335	.381	.716	100	11	9	100	100	696	196	91	58	-7
CAL	162	87	75	.537	5	691	666	5472	1417	226	28	108	539	682	.259	.333	.370	.703	100	-13	13	96	102	669	86	69	54	-11
MIN	162	73	89	.451	19	666	678	5522	1472	259	47	82	604	684	.267	.342	.375	.717	99	21	7	102	92	715	99	56	51	-13
CHI	161	71	90	.441	20.5	634	731	5393	1423	221	41	106	409	625	.264	.320	.379	.699	95	-34	-39	101	101	635	83	68	57	-13
OAK	162	69	93	.426	23	532	690	5321	1304	200	31	100	433	800	.245	.305	.351	.656	88	-116	-81	95	99	552	144	117	67	-4
SEA	160	56	104	.350	35	614	834	5358	1327	229	37	97	522	702	.248	.317	.359	.676	90	-72	-67	99	103	620	123	47	41	-10
TOT	1131					9509		76411	19952	3325	538	1680	7287	10153	.261	.329	.385	.714							1471	892	62	-93

TEAM	CG	SH	SV	IP	H	H/G	HR	BB	SO	RAT	ERA	ERA+	OAV	OOB	PR	/A	PF	CPI	FA	E	DP	FW	PW	BW	SBW	DIF
EAST																										
NY	39	16	36	1460²	1321	8.1	111	478	817	11.3	3.18	114	.243	.308	94	71	96	99	.982	113	134	1.5	7.3	3.1	-.3	6.9
BOS	57	15	26	1472²	1530	9.4	137	464	706	12.4	3.54	116	.269	.328	36	94	109	111	.977	146	171	-.3	9.7	2.2	-1.1	7.1
MIL	62	19	24	1435²	1442	9.0	109	398	577	11.8	3.65	103	.261	.316	17	16	100	95	.977	150	144	-.6	1.6	11.4	-.6	.2
BAL	65	16	33	1429	1340	8.4	107	509	754	11.7	3.56	98	.250	.317	31	-10	93	95	.982	110	166	1.6	-1.0	6.1	-.8	3.6
DET	60	12	21	1455²	1441	8.9	135	503	684	12.2	3.64	106	.262	.328	19	36	103	106	.981	118	177	1.2	3.7	2.5	-.5	-1.8
CLE	36	6	28	1407¹	1397	8.9	100	568	739	12.7	3.97	94	.261	.335	-32	-36	99	95	.980	123	142	.8	-3.7	-1.0	-1.1	-5.5
TOR	35	5	23	1429¹	1529	9.6	149	614	758	13.6	4.54	86	.278	.353	-123	-98	104	100	.979	131	163	.4	-10.1	-10.8	-.4	-.6
WEST																										
KC	53	14	33	1439	1350	8.4	108	478	657	11.6	3.44	111	.250	.315	51	61	102	98	.976	150	153	-.6	6.3	1.6	-.6	4.3
TEX	54	12	25	1456¹	1431	8.8	108	421	776	11.6	3.36	112	.259	.314	65	62	100	102	.976	153	140	-.8	6.4	.9	-.0	-.5
CAL	44	13	33	1455²	1382	8.5	125	599	892	12.4	3.65	99	.252	.329	18	-6	96	102	.978	136	136	.2	-.6	1.3	-.4	5.5
MIN	48	9	26	1459²	1468	9.1	100	520	703	12.5	3.69	103	.265	.332	11	20	102	102	.977	146	171	-.4	2.1	.7	-.6	-9.7
CHI	38	9	33	1409²	1380	8.8	128	586	710	12.8	4.21	90	.259	.337	-70	-64	101	94	.977	139	130	-.0	-6.6	-4.0	-.6	1.8
OAK	26	11	29	1433¹	1401	8.8	106	582	750	12.6	3.62	100	.258	.333	22	2	97	103	.971	179	145	-2.3	.2	-8.3	.3	-1.9
SEA	28	4	20	1419¹	1540	9.8	155	567	630	13.6	4.67	81	.280	.351	-143	-136	101	98	.978	141	174	-.2	-14.0	-6.9	-.3	-2.5
TOT	645	161	390	20163		8.9				12.4	3.76		.261	.329					.978	1935	2146					

Runs	Hits	Doubles	Triples	Home Runs	Total Bases
LeFlore-Det ... 126	Rice-Bos ... 213	Brett-KC ... 45	Rice-Bos ... 15	Rice-Bos ... 46	Rice-Bos ... 406
Rice-Bos ... 121	LeFlore-Det ... 198	McRae-KC ... 39	Ford-Min ... 10	Hisle-Mil ... 34	Murray-Bal ... 293
Baylor-Cal ... 103	Carew-Min ... 188	Fisk-Bos ... 39	Carew-Min ... 10	Baylor-Cal ... 34	Staub-Det ... 279
Thornton-Cle ... 97	Munson-NY ... 183	DeCinces-Bal ... 37	Yount-Mil ... 9	Thornton-Cle ... 33	Baylor-Cal ... 279
Hisle-Mil ... 96	Staub-Det ... 175	Ford-Min ... 36	Garr-Chi ... 9	Thomas-Mil ... 32	Thompson-Det ... 278

Runs Batted In	Runs Produced	Bases On Balls	Batting Average	On Base Percentage	Slugging Average
Rice-Bos ... 139	Rice-Bos ... 214	Hargrove-Tex ... 107	Carew-Min ... .333	Carew-Min ... .415	Rice-Bos ... .600
Staub-Det ... 121	Hisle-Mil ... 177	Singleton-Bal ... 98	Oliver-Tex ... .324	Singleton-Bal ... .410	Hisle-Mil ... .533
Hisle-Mil ... 115	LeFlore-Det ... 176	Kemp-Det ... 97	Rice-Bos ... .315	Hargrove-Tex ... .391	DeCinces-Bal ... .526
Thornton-Cle ... 105	Staub-Det ... 172	Thornton-Cle ... 93	Piniella-NY ... .314	Otis-KC ... .387	Otis-KC ... .525
	Thornton-Cle ... 169	Smalley-Min ... 85	Oglivie-Mil ... .303	Randolph-NY ... .385	Thornton-Cle ... .516

Production	Adjusted Production	Batter Runs	Adjusted Batter Runs	Clutch Hitting Index	Runs Created
Rice-Bos ... .973	Singleton-Bal ... 154	Rice-Bos ... 58.7	Rice-Bos ... 49.8	L.Johnson-Chi ... 137	Rice-Bos ... 147
Otis-KC ... .911	Rice-Bos ... 153	Hisle-Mil ... 36.3	Singleton-Bal ... 38.2	Chambliss-NY ... 137	LeFlore-Det ... 105
Hisle-Mil ... .909	Hisle-Mil ... 153	Thornton-Cle ... 35.6	Thornton-Cle ... 36.4	Staub-Det ... 131	Carew-Min ... 105
Thornton-Cle ... .898	Thornton-Cle ... 152	Otis-KC ... 35.2	Hisle-Mil ... 36.1	Bostock-Cal ... 129	Thompson-Det ... 104
Roberts-Sea ... .881	DeCinces-Bal ... 152	Singleton-Bal ... 34.0	Otis-KC ... 33.5	Whitaker-Det ... 128	Murray-Bal ... 104

Total Average	Stolen Bases	Stolen Base Average	Stolen Base Runs	Fielding Runs	Total Player Rating
Rice-Bos ... .973	LeFlore-Det ... 68	Cruz-Sea ... 85.5	Cruz-Sea ... 11.7	Belanger-Bal ... 33.8	Rice-Bos ... 5.2
Otis-KC ... .972	Cruz-Sea ... 59	Campaneris-Tex ... 84.6	LeFlore-Det ... 10.8	Bell-Cle ... 28.2	Smalley-Min ... 4.6
Hisle-Mil ... .907	Wills-Tex ... 52	Lowenstein-Tex ... 84.2	Wills-Tex ... 7.2	Yount-Mil ... 21.9	Otis-KC ... 4.0
Singleton-Bal ... .900	Dilone-Oak ... 50	Randolph-NY ... 83.7	Wilson-KC ... 6.6	Wills-Tex ... 21.3	Yount-Mil ... 3.9
Thornton-Cle ... .897	Wilson-KC ... 46	Rivers-NY ... 83.3	Randolph-NY ... 6.6	R.Miller-Cal ... 20.6	DeCinces-Bal ... 3.8

Wins	Win Percentage	Games	Complete Games	Shutouts	Saves
Guidry-NY ... 25	Guidry-NY ... .893	Lacey-Cal ... 74	Caldwell-Mil ... 23	Guidry-NY ... 9	Gossage-NY ... 27
Caldwell-Mil ... 22	Stanley-Bos ... .882	Heaverlo-Oak ... 69	Leonard-KC ... 20	Palmer-Bal ... 6	LaRoche-Cal ... 25
Palmer-Bal ... 21	Gura-KC ... .800	Sosa-Oak ... 68	Palmer-Bal ... 19	Caldwell-Mil ... 6	Stanhouse-Bal ... 24
Leonard-KC ... 21	Eckersley-Bos ... .714	Gossage-NY ... 63	Matlack-Tex ... 18	Tiant-Bos ... 5	Marshall-Min ... 21
	Caldwell-Mil ... .710				Hrabosky-KC ... 20

Innings Pitched	Fewest Hits/Game	Fewest BB/Game	Strikeouts	Strikeouts/Game	Ratio
Palmer-Bal ... 296.0	Guidry-NY ... 6.15	Jenkins-Tex ... 1.48	Ryan-Cal ... 260	Ryan-Cal ... 9.97	Guidry-NY ... 8.55
Leonard-KC ... 294.2	Ryan-Cal ... 7.02	Sorensen-Mil ... 1.60	Guidry-NY ... 248	Guidry-NY ... 8.16	Caldwell-Mil ... 9.79
Caldwell-Mil ... 293.1	Gura-KC ... 7.43	Caldwell-Mil ... 1.66	Leonard-KC ... 183	Kravec-Chi ... 6.83	Jenkins-Tex ... 9.83
Flanagan-Bal ... 281.1	Palmer-Bal ... 7.48	Matlack-Tex ... 1.70	Flanagan-Bal ... 167	Underwood-Tor ... 6.33	Gura-KC ... 10.03
Sorensen-Mil ... 280.2	Tiant-Bos ... 7.84	Rozema-Det ... 1.76	Eckersley-Bos ... 162	Knapp-Chi ... 6.02	Matlack-Tex ... 10.23

Earned Run Average	Adjusted ERA	Opponents' Batting Avg.	Opponents' On Base Pct.	Starter Runs	Adjusted Starter Runs
Guidry-NY ... 1.74	Guidry-NY ... 208	Guidry-NY ... .193	Guidry-NY ... .250	Guidry-NY ... 61.4	Guidry-NY ... 57.1
Matlack-Tex ... 2.27	Matlack-Tex ... 165	Ryan-Cal ... .220	Caldwell-Mil ... .274	Caldwell-Mil ... 45.7	Caldwell-Mil ... 45.5
Caldwell-Mil ... 2.36	Caldwell-Mil ... 159	Palmer-Bal ... .227	Jenkins-Tex ... .279	Matlack-Tex ... 44.9	Matlack-Tex ... 44.3
Palmer-Bal ... 2.46	Goltz-Min ... 153	Gura-KC ... .229	Matlack-Tex ... .284	Palmer-Bal ... 42.8	Palmer-Bal ... 34.0
Goltz-Min ... 2.49	Palmer-Bal ... 142	Tiant-Bos ... .234	Gura-KC ... .286	Goltz-Min ... 31.1	Eckersley-Bos ... 33.6

Clutch Pitching Index	Relief Runs	Adjusted Relief Runs	Relief Ranking	Total Pitcher Index	Total Baseball Ranking
Lee-Bos ... 130	Gossage-NY ... 26.2	Gossage-NY ... 24.0	Gossage-NY ... 44.7	Guidry-NY ... 6.6	Guidry-NY ... 6.6
Zahn-Min ... 129	Stanley-Bos ... 18.2	Stanley-Bos ... 23.7	Marshall-Min ... 37.2	Caldwell-Mil ... 5.2	Rice-Bos ... 5.2
Goltz-Min ... 125	Hiller-Det ... 14.6	Hiller-Det ... 15.7	Stanley-Bos ... 29.4	Matlack-Tex ... 5.0	Caldwell-Mil ... 5.2
Gale-KC ... 115	Marshall-Min ... 14.4	Marshall-Min ... 15.0	Hiller-Det ... 25.6	Palmer-Bal ... 3.8	Matlack-Tex ... 5.0
Eckersley-Bos ... 115	Sosa-Oak ... 13.6	Sosa-Oak ... 12.1	LaRoche-Cal ... 19.9	Goltz-Min ... 3.6	Smalley-Min ... 4.6

TEAM	G	W	L	PCT	GB	R	OR	AB	H	2B	3B	HR	BB	SO	AVG	OBP	SLG	PRO	PRO+	BR	/A	PF	CHI	RC	SB	CS	SBA	SBR
EAST																												
PIT	163	98	64	.605		**775**	643	5661	1541	264	52	148	483	855	.272	.333	**.416**	**.749**	105	68	35	105	101	**781**	180	66	54	-12
MON	160	95	65	.594	2	701	**581**	5465	1445	273	42	143	432	890	.264	.321	.408	.729	104	23	28	99	102	701	121	56	51	-13
STL	163	86	76	.531	12	731	693	5734	**1594**	**279**	**63**	100	460	838	**.278**	.335	.401	.736	106	46	40	101	98	757	116	69	58	-13
PHI	163	84	78	.519	14	683	718	5463	1453	250	53	119	602	764	.266	**.343**	.396	.739	104	63	41	103	91	743	128	76	57	-10
CHI	162	80	82	.494	18	706	707	5550	1494	250	43	135	478	762	.269	.331	.403	.734	96	40	-24	110	98	726	73	52	48	-12
NY	163	63	99	.389	35	593	706	5591	1399	255	41	74	498	817	.250	.315	.350	.665	90	-89	-63	96	99	615	135	79	62	-13
WEST																												
CIN	161	90	71	.559		731	644	5477	1445	266	31	132	**614**	902	.264	.340	.396	.736	106	55	50	101	99	741	99	47	43	-11
HOU	162	89	73	.549	1.5	583	582	5394	1382	224	52	49	461	**745**	.256	.317	.344	.661	91	-92	-53	94	102	591	**190**	95	**69**	-12
LA	162	79	83	.488	11.5	739	717	5490	1443	220	24	**183**	556	834	.263	.333	.412	.745	**110**	62	**72**	99	99	743	106	46	40	**-9**
SF	162	71	91	.438	19.5	672	751	5395	1328	192	36	125	580	925	.246	.322	.365	.687	99	-45	1	93	**106**	644	140	73	65	-16
SD	161	68	93	.422	22	603	681	5446	1316	193	63	93	534	770	.242	.313	.348	.661	91	-96	-55	94	103	600	100	58	47	-10
ATL	160	66	94	.413	23.5	669	763	5422	1389	220	28	126	490	818	.256	.320	.377	.697	89	-30	-79	107	105	654	98	50	52	-15
TOT	971					8186		66088	17229	2886	518	1427	6188	9920	.261	.327	.385	.712							1486	767	66	-13

TEAM	CG	SH	SV	IP	H	H/G	HR	BB	SO	RAT	ERA	ERA+	OAV	OOB	PR	/A	PF	CPI	FA	E	DP	FW	PW	BW	SBW	DIF
EAST																										
PIT	24	7	**52**	1493¹	1424	8.6	125	504	904	11.8	3.41	114	.253	.318	53	77	104	103	.979	134	163	.4	7.9	3.6	-1.1	6.2
MON	33	18	39	1447¹	1379	8.6	116	**450**	813	11.5	**3.14**	117	.252	.312	94	84	98	**107**	.979	131	123	.4	**8.7**	2.9	-1.2	4.2
STL	38	10	25	1486²	1449	8.8	127	501	788	11.9	3.72	101	.258	.320	1	6	101	97	.980	132	166	.5	.6	4.1	-1.2	.9
PHI	33	14	29	1441¹	1455	9.1	135	477	787	12.2	4.16	92	.266	.328	-68	-53	103	94	**.983**	106	148	**2.1**	-5.5	4.2	-.9	3.1
CHI	20	11	44	1446²	1500	9.3	127	521	**933**	12.8	3.88	106	.270	.337	-24	37	110	105	.975	159	163	-1.1	3.8	-2.5	-1.1	-.0
NY	16	10	36	1482²	1486	9.0	120	607	819	12.9	3.84	95	.266	.340	-18	-33	98	105	.978	140	**168**	.0	-3.4	-6.5	-1.2	-6.9
WEST																										
CIN	27	10	40	1440¹	1415	8.8	103	485	773	12.0	3.58	104	.259	.322	24	24	100	99	.980	124	152	.9	2.5	5.2	-1.0	2.0
HOU	**55**	**19**	31	1447²	**1278**	**7.9**	**90**	504	854	**11.2**	3.20	110	**.237**	**.305**	86	50	94	93	.978	138	146	.1	5.2	-5.5	-1.1	9.3
LA	30	6	34	1444	1425	8.9	101	555	811	12.5	3.83	95	.260	.331	15	-30	97	97	.981	118	123	1.3	-3.1	**7.4**	-.8	-6.8
SF	25	6	34	1436	1484	9.3	143	577	880	13.1	4.16	84	.268	.340	-68	-106	94	101	.974	163	138	-1.4	-10.9	.1	-1.5	3.7
SD	29	7	25	1453	1438	8.9	108	513	779	12.2	3.69	96	.262	.328	6	-26	95	101	.978	141	154	-.1	-2.7	-5.7	-.9	-3.1
ATL	32	3	34	1407²	1496	9.6	132	494	779	13.0	4.18	97	.272	.337	-70	-20	109	99	.970	183	139	-2.7	-2.1	-8.2	-1.4	.3
TOT	362	121	423	17426²		8.9				12.3	3.73		.261	.327					.978	1669	1783					

Runs
Hernandez-StL	116
Moreno-Pit	110
Schmidt-Phi	109
Parker-Pit	109
Lopes-LA	109

Hits
Templeton-StL	211
Hernandez-StL	210
Rose-Phi	208
Garvey-LA	204
Moreno-Pit	196

Doubles
Hernandez-StL	48
Cromartie-Mon	46
Parker-Pit	45
Reitz-StL	41
Rose-Phi	40

Triples
Templeton-StL	19
Moreno-Pit	12
McBride-Phi	12
Dawson-Mon	12

Home Runs
Kingman-Chi	48
Schmidt-Phi	45
Winfield-SD	34
Horner-Atl	33
Stargell-Pit	32

Total Bases
Winfield-SD	333
Parker-Pit	327
Kingman-Chi	326
Garvey-LA	322
Matthews-Atl	317

Runs Batted In
Winfield-SD	118
Kingman-Chi	115
Schmidt-Phi	114
Garvey-LA	110
Hernandez-StL	105

Runs Produced
Hernandez-StL	210
Winfield-SD	181
Schmidt-Phi	178
Parker-Pit	178
Garvey-LA	174

Bases On Balls
Schmidt-Phi	120
Tenace-SD	105
Lopes-LA	97
North-SF	96
Rose-Phi	95

Batting Average
Hernandez-StL	.344
Rose-Phi	.331
Knight-Cin	.318
Garvey-LA	.315
Horner-Atl	.314

On Base Percentage
Hernandez-StL	.421
Rose-Phi	.421
Tenace-SD	.407
Mazzilli-NY	.397
Winfield-SD	.396

Slugging Average
Kingman-Chi	.613
Schmidt-Phi	.564
Foster-Cin	.561
Winfield-SD	.558
Horner-Atl	.552

Production
Kingman-Chi	.960
Schmidt-Phi	.955
Winfield-SD	.954
Foster-Cin	.950
Hernandez-StL	.934

Adjusted Production
Winfield-SD	167
Foster-Cin	155
Schmidt-Phi	153
Hernandez-StL	152
Parrish-Mon	146

Batter Runs
Winfield-SD	47.4
Hernandez-StL	47.1
Schmidt-Phi	44.9
Parker-Pit	39.3
Kingman-Chi	37.8

Adjusted Batter Runs
Winfield-SD	52.0
Hernandez-StL	46.5
Schmidt-Phi	42.5
Parker-Pit	35.6
Foster-Cin	33.3

Clutch Hitting Index
Hebner-NY	148
Foli-NY-Pit	134
Luzinski-Phi	132
Flynn-NY	129
Hernandez-StL	127

Runs Created
Hernandez-StL	135
Winfield-SD	132
Parker-Pit	131
Schmidt-Phi	123
Matthews-Atl	118

Total Average
Schmidt-Phi	1.024
Winfield-SD	.988
Kingman-Chi	.972
Hernandez-StL	.961
Foster-Cin	.959

Stolen Bases
Moreno-Pit	77
North-SF	58
Taveras-Pit-NY	44
Lopes-LA	44
Scott-Mon	39

Stolen Base Average
Lopes-LA	91.7
Parker-Pit	83.3
Morgan-Cin	82.4
Royster-Atl	81.4
Smith-SD	80.0

Stolen Base Runs
Lopes-LA	10.8
Moreno-Pit	10.5
Royster-Atl	5.7
Morgan-Cin	4.8

Fielding Runs
Evans-SF	22.4
Smith-SD	20.4
Maddox-Phi	20.2
Hernandez-StL	18.8
Schmidt-Phi	18.4

Total Player Rating
Hernandez-StL	5.8
Winfield-SD	5.8
Schmidt-Phi	5.5
Parker-Pit	4.5
Templeton-StL	4.4

Wins
Niekro-Atl	21
Niekro-Hou	21
Richard-Hou	18
Reuschel-Chi	18
Carlton-Phi	18

Win Percentage
Seaver-Cin	.727
Niekro-Hou	.656
Martinez-StL	.652
Sutcliffe-LA	.630
Carlton-Phi	.621

Games
Tekulve-Pit	94
Romo-Pit	84
Jackson-Pit	72
Lavelle-SF	70
Garber-Atl	68

Complete Games
Niekro-Atl	23
Richard-Hou	19
Rogers-Mon	13
Carlton-Phi	13
Hooton-LA	12

Shutouts
Seaver-Cin	5
Rogers-Mon	5
Niekro-Hou	5
Richard-Hou	4
Carlton-Phi	4

Saves
Sutter-Chi	37
Tekulve-Pit	31
Garber-Atl	25
Sambito-Hou	22
Lavelle-SF	20

Innings Pitched
Niekro-Atl	342.0
Richard-Hou	292.1
Niekro-Hou	263.2
Jones-SD	263.0
Swan-NY	251.1

Fewest Hits/Game
Richard-Hou	6.77
Carlton-Phi	7.24
Niekro-Hou	7.54
Schatzeder-Mon	7.56
Andujar-Hou	7.79

Fewest BB/Game
Forsch-Hou	1.77
Candelaria-Pit	1.78
Hume-Cin	1.82
Lee-Mon	1.86
Swan-NY	2.04

Strikeouts
Richard-Hou	313
Carlton-Phi	213
Niekro-Atl	208
Blyleven-Pit	172
McGlothen-Chi	147

Strikeouts/Game
Richard-Hou	9.64
Carlton-Phi	7.64
Sanderson-Mon	7.39
Blyleven-Pit	6.52
Krukow-SF	6.50

Ratio
Forsch-Hou	9.62
Richard-Hou	9.88
Seaver-Cin	10.38
Sutton-LA	10.47
Carlton-Phi	10.61

Earned Run Average
Richard-Hou	2.71
Hume-Cin	2.76
Schatzeder-Mon	2.83
Hooton-LA	2.97
Niekro-Hou	3.00

Adjusted ERA
Hume-Cin	135
Richard-Hou	130
Schatzeder-Mon	129
Hooton-LA	122
Rogers-Mon	122

Opponents' Batting Avg.
Richard-Hou	.209
Carlton-Phi	.219
Schatzeder-Mon	.225
Niekro-Hou	.228
Andujar-Hou	.233

Opponents' On Base Pct.
Forsch-Hou	.275
Richard-Hou	.278
Seaver-Cin	.291
Sutton-LA	.291
Carlton-Phi	.292

Starter Runs
Richard-Hou	33.2
Niekro-Hou	21.3
Rogers-Mon	20.1
Fulgham-StL	19.5
Hooton-LA	17.9

Adjusted Starter Runs
Richard-Hou	26.0
Niekro-Atl	24.8
Fulgham-StL	20.0
Rogers-Mon	18.2
Bibby-Pit	16.3

Clutch Pitching Index
Hume-Cin	117
Lamp-Chi	114
Lee-Mon	113
Kobel-NY	112
Blyleven-Pit	112

Relief Runs
Sambito-Hou	19.9
Sosa-Mon	19.1
Hume-Cin	17.6
Minton-SF	17.0
Sutter-Chi	17.0

Adjusted Relief Runs
Sutter-Chi	21.3
Sosa-Mon	18.4
Sambito-Hou	17.6
Hume-Cin	17.6
Tekulve-Pit	16.9

Relief Ranking
Sutter-Chi	40.3
Sambito-Hou	35.6
Sosa-Mon	33.3
Tekulve-Pit	29.1
Littell-StL	25.6

Total Pitcher Index
Niekro-Atl	3.3
Sutter-Chi	2.4
Richard-Hou	2.4
Rogers-Mon	2.2
Reuschel-Chi	2.1

Total Baseball Ranking
Hernandez-StL	5.8
Winfield-SD	5.8
Schmidt-Phi	5.5
Parker-Pit	4.5
Templeton-StL	4.4

TEAM	G	W	L	PCT	GB	R	OR	AB	H	2B	3B	HR	BB	SO	AVG	OBP	SLG	PRO	PRO+	BR	/A	PF	CHI	RC	SB	CS	SBA	SBR
EAST																												
BAL	159	102	57	.642		757	582	5371	1401	258	24	181	608	847	.261	.339	.419	.758	106	25	52	96	98	758	99	49	54	-17
MIL	161	95	66	.590	8	807	722	5536	1552	291	41	185	549	745	.280	.347	.448	.795	**113**	95	95	100	94	**850**	100	53	50	-13
BOS	160	91	69	.569	11.5	841	711	5538	1567	**310**	34	**194**	512	708	**.283**	.347	**.456**	**.803**	109	**108**	66	106	97	848	60	43	46	-14
NY	160	89	71	.556	13.5	734	672	5421	1443	226	40	150	509	590	.266	.331	.406	.737	100	-20	-3	98	102	708	65	46	50	-15
DET	161	85	76	.528	18	770	738	5375	1446	221	35	164	575	814	.269	.342	.415	.757	99	24	0	103	101	754	176	86	**63**	-11
CLE	161	81	80	.503	22	760	805	5376	1388	206	29	138	**657**	786	.258	.344	.384	.728	95	-20	-23	100	103	720	143	90	59	**-7**
TOR	162	53	109	.327	50.5	613	862	5423	1362	253	34	95	448	663	.251	.313	.363	.676	81	-141	-149	101	103	602	75	56	49	-12
WEST																												
CAL	162	88	74	.543		**866**	768	5550	1563	242	43	164	589	843	.282	**.354**	.429	.783	**113**	83	**109**	97	101	842	100	53	52	-14
KC	162	85	77	.525	3	851	816	5653	**1596**	286	**79**	116	528	675	.282	.347	.422	.769	104	51	36	102	103	836	**207**	76	59	-12
TEX	162	83	79	.512	5	750	698	5562	1549	252	26	140	461	607	.278	.337	.409	.746	101	0	9	99	99	750	79	51	46	-11
MIN	162	82	80	.506	6	764	725	5544	1544	256	46	112	526	693	.278	.344	.402	.746	96	7	-22	104	99	770	66	45	49	-15
CHI	160	73	87	.456	14	730	748	5463	1505	290	33	127	454	668	.275	.335	.410	.745	100	-3	-3	100	99	726	97	62	56	-14
SEA	162	67	95	.414	21	711	820	5544	1490	250	52	132	515	725	.269	.304	.404	.738	96	-16	-28	102	96	733	126	52	48	-13
OAK	162	54	108	.333	34	573	860	5348	1276	188	32	108	482	751	.239	.304	.346	.650	79	-188	-148	95	**106**	552	104	69	59	-14
TOT	1128					10527		76704	20682	3529	548	2006	7413	10115	.270	.337	.408	.746							1497	831	64	-49

TEAM	CG	SH	SV	IP	H	H/G	HR	BB	SO	RAT	ERA	ERA+	OAV	OOB	PR	/A	PF	CPI	FA	E	DP	FW	PW	BW	SBW	DIF
EAST																										
BAL	52	**12**	30	1434¹	**1279**	8.0	133	467	786	**11.0**	3.26	123	.240	.303	151	118	95	100	.980	125	161	.8	**11.5**	5.1	-1.3	6.5
MIL	**61**	**12**	23	1439²	1563	9.8	162	**381**	580	12.3	4.03	103	.279	.327	29	21	99	105	.980	127	153	.7	2.0	9.3	-.9	3.4
BOS	47	11	29	1431¹	1487	9.4	133	463	731	12.5	4.03	110	.269	.330	29	61	105	100	.977	142	166	-.2	6.0	6.4	-1.0	-.2
NY	43	10	37	1432¹	1446	9.1	123	455	731	12.0	3.83	106	.267	.326	60	38	97	102	**.981**	122	183	1.0	3.7	-.3	-1.1	5.7
DET	25	5	37	1423¹	1429	9.0	167	547	802	12.8	4.27	101	.265	.338	-9	8	103	101	**.981**	120	184	**1.1**	.8	.0	-.7	3.3
CLE	28	7	32	1431²	1502	9.4	138	570	781	13.2	4.57	93	.272	.342	-56	-50	101	94	.978	134	149	.3	-4.9	-2.2	**-.3**	7.6
TOR	44	7	11	1417	1537	9.8	165	594	613	13.8	4.82	90	.281	.355	-95	-75	103	100	.975	159	187	-1.0	-7.3	-14.5	-.8	-4.3
WEST																										
CAL	46	9	33	1435²	1463	9.2	131	573	**820**	13.0	4.34	94	.266	.339	-19	-42	97	96	.978	135	172	.3	-4.1	**10.6**	-1.0	1.1
KC	42	7	27	1448¹	1477	9.2	165	536	640	12.7	4.45	96	.266	.334	-37	-30	101	95	.977	146	160	-.3	-2.9	3.5	-.8	4.5
TEX	26	10	**42**	1437	1371	8.6	135	532	773	12.1	4.36	107	.253	.323	56	45	98	97	.979	130	151	.6	4.4	.9	-.7	-3.2
MIN	31	6	33	1444¹	1590	9.9	128	452	721	12.8	4.13	106	.285	.340	13	39	104	**106**	.979	134	203	.4	3.8	-2.1	-1.1	.0
CHI	28	9	37	1409	1365	8.7	**114**	618	675	12.9	4.10	104	.255	.337	18	23	101	96	.972	173	142	-1.9	2.2	-.3	-1.0	-6.0
SEA	37	7	26	1438	1567	9.8	165	571	736	13.6	4.58	95	.280	.351	-57	-34	103	103	.978	141	170	.0	-3.3	-2.7	-.8	-7.1
OAK	41	4	20	1429¹	1606	10.1	147	654	726	14.5	4.75	85	.287	.367	-84	-111	96	105	.972	174	137	-1.9	-10.8	-14.4	-1.0	1.2
TOT	551	116	417	20051¹		9.3				12.8	4.22		.270	.337					.978	1962	2318					

Runs
Baylor-Cal 120
Brett-KC 119
Rice-Bos 117
Lynn-Bos 116
Lansford-Cal 114

Hits
Brett-KC 212
Rice-Bos 201
Bell-Tex 200
Molitor-Mil 188
Lansford-Cal 188

Doubles
Lemon-Chi 44
Cooper-Mil 44
Lynn-Bos 42
Brett-KC 42
Bell-Tex 42

Triples
Brett-KC 20
Molitor-Mil 16
Wilson-KC 13
Randolph-NY 13

Home Runs
Thomas-Mil 45
Rice-Bos 39
Lynn-Bos 39
Baylor-Cal 36
Singleton-Bal..... 35

Total Bases
Rice-Bos 369
Brett-KC 363
Lynn-Bos 338
Baylor-Cal 333
Singleton-Bal.... 304

Runs Batted In
Baylor-Cal 139
Rice-Bos 130
Thomas-Mil 123
Lynn-Bos 122
Porter-KC 112

Runs Produced
Baylor-Cal 223
Rice-Bos 208
Brett-KC 203
Lynn-Bos 199
Porter-KC 193

Bases On Balls
Porter-KC 121
Singleton-Bal.... 109
Thomas-Mil 98
Randolph-NY 95
Thornton-Cle 90

Batting Average
Lynn-Bos 333
Brett-KC 329
Downing-Cal 326
Rice-Bos 325
Oliver-Tex 323

On Base Percentage
Porter-KC 429
Lynn-Bos 426
Downing-Cal 420
Lezcano-Mil 420
Singleton-Bal.....409

Slugging Average
Lynn-Bos 637
Rice-Bos 596
Lezcano-Mil 573
Brett-KC 563
Jackson-NY 544

Production
Lynn-Bos 1.063
Lezcano-Mil 992
Rice-Bos 981
Kemp-Det..........946
Singleton-Bal.....942

Adjusted Production
Lynn-Bos 173
Lezcano-Mil 165
Singleton-Bal ... 158
Rice-Bos 152
Jackson-NY 151

Batter Runs
Lynn-Bos 62.1
Rice-Bos 50.2
Lezcano-Mil 44.6
Singleton-Bal ... 44.4
Brett-KC 42.8

Adjusted Batter Runs
Lynn-Bos 58.0
Singleton-Bal ... 47.5
Rice-Bos 45.6
Lezcano-Mil 44.6
Brett-KC 41.2

Clutch Hitting Index
Porter-KC 143
Bochte-Sea 127
Cerone-Tor 127
Ford-Cal 126
Sundberg-Tex 125

Runs Created
Lynn-Bos 147
Rice-Bos 138
Brett-KC 134
Singleton-Bal.... 127
Baylor-Cal 126

Total Average
Lynn-Bos 1.162
Lezcano-Mil 1.051
Rice-Bos 993
Singleton-Bal.....993
Porter-KC 982

Stolen Bases
Wilson-KC 83
LeFlore-Det 78
Cruz-Sea 49
Bumbry-Bal 37
Wills-Tex 35

Stolen Base Average
Wilson-KC 87.4
Otis-KC 85.7
LeFlore-Det 84.8
Cruz-Sea 84.5
Lowenstein-Bal ... 80.0

Stolen Base Runs
Wilson-KC 17.7
LeFlore-Det 15.0
Cruz-Sea 9.3
Otis-KC 6.0
Manning-Cle 4.2

Fielding Runs
Smalley-Min 33.1
Dent-NY 32.0
Mendoza-Sea 28.0
Burleson-Bos 22.1
Wilfong-Min 22.0

Total Player Rating
Smalley-Min 5.8
Brett-KC 5.3
Lynn-Bos 5.0
Porter-KC......... 4.1
Grich-Cal 3.9

Wins
Flanagan-Bal 23
John-NY 21
Koosman-Min 20
Guidry-NY 18

Win Percentage
Caldwell-Mil 727
Flanagan-Bal......719
Morris-Det 708
John-NY 700
Guidry-NY 692

Games
Marshall-Min 90
Monge-Cle 76
Kern-Tex 71
Lyle-Tex 67
Heaverlo-Oak 62

Complete Games
J.Martinez-Bal 18
Ryan-Cal 17
John-NY 17
Eckersley-Bos 17

Shutouts
Ryan-Cal 5
Leonard-KC 5
Flanagan-Bal 5
Stanley-Bos 4
Caldwell-Mil 4

Saves
Marshall-Min 32
Kern-Tex 29
Stanhouse-Bal.... 21
Lopez-Det 21
Monge-Cle 19

Innings Pitched
J.Martinez-Bal ... 292.1
John-NY 276.1
Flanagan-Bal 265.2
Koosman-Min 263.2
Jenkins-Tex 259.0

Fewest Hits/Game
Ryan-Cal 6.83
Kravec-Chi 7.49
Guidry-NY 7.73
Morris-Det 8.15
Baumgarten-Chi .. 8.26

Fewest BB/Game
McGregor-Bal 1.19
Caldwell-Mil 1.49
Sorensen-Mil 1.61
Stanley-Bos 1.83
John-NY 2.12

Strikeouts
Ryan-Cal 223
Guidry-NY 201
Flanagan-Bal 190
Jenkins-Tex 164
Koosman-Min 157

Strikeouts/Game
Ryan-Cal 9.01
Guidry-NY 7.65
Flanagan-Bal 6.44
Jenkins-Tex 5.70
Bannister-Sea ... 5.68

Ratio
McGregor-Bal 9.79
Guidry-NY 10.43
Flanagan-Bal 10.77
Leonard-KC 10.83
Eckersley-Bos ... 10.91

Earned Run Average
Guidry-NY 2.78
John-NY 2.96
Eckersley-Bos ... 2.99
Flanagan-Bal 3.08
Morris-Det 3.28

Adjusted ERA
Eckersley-Bos ... 148
Guidry-NY 147
John-NY 137
Morris-Det 132
Flanagan-Bal 130

Opponents' Batting Avg.
Ryan-Cal 212
Kravec-Chi 233
Guidry-NY 236
Baumgarten-Chi ...243
Morris-Det 244

Opponents' On Base Pct.
McGregor-Bal 275
Guidry-NY 294
Flanagan-Bal 297
Eckersley-Bos 298
Leonard-KC 299

Starter Runs
John-NY 38.4
Guidry-NY 37.7
Eckersley-Bos ... 33.6
Flanagan-Bal 33.5
Koosman-Min 24.5

Adjusted Starter Runs
Eckersley-Bos ... 39.0
John-NY 34.0
Guidry-NY 33.9
Koosman-Min 29.3
Flanagan-Bal 27.4

Clutch Pitching Index
Eckersley-Bos ... 115
Keough-Oak 114
McCatty-Oak 114
Travers-Mil 113
Koosman-Min 112

Relief Runs
Kern-Tex 42.0
Monge-Cle 26.4
Lopez-Det 25.5
Marshall-Min 24.8
Stoddard-Bal 16.2

Adjusted Relief Runs
Kern-Tex 40.9
Marshall-Min 27.4
Lopez-Det 27.0
Monge-Cle 26.9
Burgmeier-Bos ... 16.5

Relief Ranking
Kern-Tex 65.0
Marshall-Min 57.1
Monge-Cle 49.5
Lopez-Det 38.8
Drago-Bos 26.6

Total Pitcher Index
Eckersley-Bos 4.1
Kern-Tex 4.0
John-NY 3.7
Guidry-NY 3.3
Koosman-Min 3.2

Total Baseball Ranking
Smalley-Min 5.8
Brett-KC 5.3
Lynn-Bos 5.0
Eckersley-Bos 4.1
Porter-KC........ 4.1

1980 National League

TEAM	G	W	L	PCT	GB	R	OR	AB	H	2B	3B	HR	BB	SO	AVG	OBP	SLG	PRO	PRO+	BR	/A	PF	CHI	RC	SB	CS	SBA	SBR
EAST																												
PHI	162	91	71	.562		728	639	5625	1517	272	54	117	472	**708**	.270	.330	**.400**	.730	103	61	24	106	100	**736**	140	62	54	-13
MON	162	90	72	.556	1	694	629	5465	1407	250	61	114	547	865	.257	.327	.388	.715	104	36	35	100	101	709	237	82	60	-10
PIT	162	83	79	.512	8	666	646	5517	1469	249	38	116	452	760	.266	.325	.388	.713	102	27	17	102	98	686	209	102	63	**-6**
STL	162	74	88	.457	17	738	710	5608	**1541**	**300**	49	101	451	781	**.275**	**.331**	**.400**	**.731**	105	63	42	103	102	724	117	54	46	-10
NY	162	67	95	.414	24	611	702	5478	1407	218	41	61	501	840	.257	.322	.345	.667	94	-51	-32	97	102	601	158	99	**68**	-10
CHI	162	64	98	.395	27	614	728	5619	1411	251	35	107	471	912	.251	.311	.365	.676	87	-46	-94	107	100	627	93	64	48	-9
WEST																												
HOU	163	93	70	.571		637	**589**	5566	1455	231	**67**	75	540	755	.261	.328	.367	.695	**108**	2	**54**	92	96	688	194	74	61	-13
LA	163	92	71	.564	1	663	591	5568	1462	209	24	**148**	492	846	.263	.325	.388	.713	106	29	41	98	96	699	123	72	54	-10
CIN	163	89	73	.549	3.5	707	670	5516	1445	256	45	113	537	852	.262	.330	.386	.716	105	39	39	100	101	716	156	43	44	-13
ATL	161	81	80	.503	11	630	660	5402	1352	226	22	144	434	899	.250	.308	.380	.688	93	-26	-46	103	**104**	616	73	52	54	-16
SF	161	75	86	.466	17	573	634	5368	1310	199	44	80	509	840	.244	.311	.342	.653	90	-81	-66	98	102	571	100	58	52	-13
SD	163	73	89	.451	19.5	591	654	5540	1410	195	43	67	**563**	791	.255	.326	.342	.668	97	-47	-8	94	96	641	**239**	73	58	-12
TOT	973					7852		66272	17186	2856	523	1243	5969	9849	.259	.323	.374	.697							1839	835	69	51

TEAM	CG	SH	SV	IP	H	H/G	HR	BB	SO	RAT	ERA	ERA+	OAV	OOB	PR	/A	PF	CPI	FA	E	DP	FW	PW	BW	SBW	DIF
EAST																										
PHI	25	8	40	1480	1419	8.6	87	530	889	12.0	3.43	110	.254	.321	28	**58**	105	100	.979	136	136	.2	**6.1**	2.5	-1.8	2.9
MON	33	15	36	1456²	1447	8.9	100	460	823	11.9	3.48	102	.260	.319	19	14	99	102	.977	144	126	-.2	1.5	3.7	-1.5	5.5
PIT	25	8	**43**	1458¹	1422	8.8	110	**451**	832	11.7	3.58	102	.258	.317	3	9	101	99	.978	137	154	.2	1.0	1.8	**-1.1**	.1
STL	**34**	9	27	1447	1454	9.0	90	495	664	12.3	3.93	94	.265	.328	-53	-38	103	94	.981	122	**174**	1.0	-4.0	4.4	-1.5	-6.9
NY	17	9	33	1451¹	1473	9.1	140	510	886	12.4	3.85	92	.266	.330	-40	-48	99	104	.975	154	132	-.7	-5.1	-3.4	-1.5	-3.4
CHI	13	6	35	1479	1525	9.3	109	589	923	13.0	3.89	101	.271	.343	-47	4	109	106	.974	174	149	-1.7	.4	-9.9	-1.4	-4.4
WEST																										
HOU	31	18	41	1482²	1367	**8.3**	69	466	**929**	11.3	**3.10**	106	**.245**	**.306**	82	30	91	96	.978	140	145	.0	3.2	**5.7**	-1.8	4.4
LA	24	**19**	42	1472²	**1358**	**8.3**	105	480	835	11.3	3.25	108	.246	.308	58	41	97	100	.981	123	149	1.0	4.3	4.3	-1.5	2.4
CIN	30	12	37	1459¹	1404	8.7	113	506	833	11.9	3.85	93	.254	.318	-40	-44	99	92	**.983**	106	144	**1.9**	-4.6	4.1	-1.8	8.5
ATL	29	9	37	1428	1397	8.8	131	454	696	11.8	3.77	99	.257	.317	-26	-4	104	97	.975	162	156	-1.2	-.4	-4.9	-2.1	9.1
SF	27	10	35	1448¹	1446	9.0	92	492	811	12.2	3.46	102	.261	.325	23	13	98	104	.975	159	124	-1.0	1.4	-7.0	-1.8	2.9
SD	19	9	39	1466¹	1474	9.0	97	536	728	12.4	3.65	94	.266	.333	-8	-35	95	105	.980	132	157	.5	-3.7	-.8	-1.7	-2.2
TOT	307	132	445	17529²		8.8				12.0	3.60		.259	.323					.978	1689	1746					

Runs		Hits		Doubles		Triples		Home Runs		Total Bases	
Hernandez-StL	111	Garvey-LA	200	Rose-Phi	42	Scott-Mon	13	Schmidt-Phi	48	Schmidt-Phi	342
Schmidt-Phi	104	Richards-SD	193	Dawson-Mon	41	Moreno-Pit	13	Horner-Atl	35	Garvey-LA	307
Murphy-Atl	98	Hernandez-StL	191	Buckner-Chi	41	LeFlore-Mon	11	Murphy-Atl	33	Hernandez-StL	294
Dawson-Mon	96	Buckner-Chi	187	Knight-Cin	39	Herndon-SF	11	Carter-Mon	29	Baker-LA	291
				Hernandez-StL	39			Baker-LA	29	Murphy-Atl	290

Runs Batted In		Runs Produced		Bases On Balls		Batting Average		On Base Percentage		Slugging Average	
Schmidt-Phi	121	Hernandez-StL	194	Morgan-Hou	93	Buckner-Chi	.324	Hernandez-StL	.410	Schmidt-Phi	.624
Hendrick-StL	109	Schmidt-Phi	177	Driessen-Cin	93	Hernandez-StL	.321	Cedeno-Hou	.390	Clark-SF	.517
Garvey-LA	106	Dawson-Mon	166	Tenace-SD	92	Templeton-StL	.319	Clark-SF	.390	Murphy-Atl	.510
Carter-Mon	101	Simmons-StL	161	Schmidt-Phi	89	McBride-Phi	.309	Schmidt-Phi	.388	Simmons-StL	.505
Hernandez-StL	99	Griffey-Cin	161	Hernandez-StL	86	Cedeno-Hou	.309	Driessen-Cin	.382	Baker-LA	.503

Production		Adjusted Production		Batter Runs		Adjusted Batter Runs		Clutch Hitting Index		Runs Created	
Schmidt-Phi	1.012	Schmidt-Phi	169	Schmidt-Phi	56.5	Schmidt-Phi	52.7	Concepcion-Cin	135	Schmidt-Phi	137
Clark-SF	.907	Clark-SF	155	Hernandez-StL	43.3	Hernandez-StL	41.0	Montanez-SD-Mon	135	Hernandez-StL	122
Hernandez-StL	.904	Cedeno-Hou	150	Easler-Pit	37.2	Easler-Pit	36.5	McBride-Phi	131	Dawson-Mon	105
Simmons-StL	.885	Hernandez-StL	147	Clark-SF	31.1	Clark-SF	32.4	Cruz-Hou	130	Murphy-Atl	101
Murphy-Atl	.859	Simmons-StL	140	Simmons-StL	29.6	Cedeno-Hou	31.3	Youngblood-NY	127	Griffey-Cin	99

Total Average		Stolen Bases		Stolen Base Average		Stolen Base Runs		Fielding Runs		Total Player Rating	
Schmidt-Phi	1.095	LeFlore-Mon	97	Griffey-Cin	95.8	LeFlore-Mon	17.7	Smith-SD	40.8	Schmidt-Phi	7.8
Hernandez-StL	.915	Moreno-Pit	96	Mumphrey-SD	91.2	Mumphrey-SD	12.6	Templeton-StL	27.6	Smith-SD	4.7
Clark-SF	.906	Collins-Cin	79	LeFlore-Mon	83.6	Scott-Mon	11.1	Schmidt-Phi	23.2	Templeton-StL	4.7
Cedeno-Hou	.890	Scott-Mon	63	Maddox-Phi	83.3	Collins-Cin	11.1	Hubbard-Atl	19.2	Hernandez-StL	3.9
Simmons-StL	.872	Richards-SD	61	Scott-Mon	82.9	Moreno-Pit	9.0	Youngblood-NY	18.9	Dawson-Mon	3.9

Wins		Win Percentage		Games		Complete Games		Shutouts		Saves	
Carlton-Phi	24	Bibby-Pit	.760	Tidrow-Chi	84	Rogers-Mon	14	Reuss-LA	6	Sutter-Chi	28
Niekro-Hou	20	Reuss-LA	.750	Tekulve-Pit	78	Carlton-Phi	13	Rogers-Mon	4	Hume-Cin	25
Bibby-Pit	19	Carlton-Phi	.727	Hume-Cin	78	Niekro-Atl	11	Richard-Hou	4	Fingers-SD	23
Reuss-LA	18	Ruthven-Phi	.630	Camp-Atl	77	Niekro-Hou	11			Camp-Atl	22
Ruthven-Phi	17	Niekro-Hou	.625	Romo-Pit	74					Allen-NY	22

Innings Pitched		Fewest Hits/Game		Fewest BB/Game		Strikeouts		Strikeouts/Game		Ratio	
Carlton-Phi	304.0	Soto-Cin	5.96	Forsch-StL	1.38	Carlton-Phi	286	Soto-Cin	8.61	Sutton-LA	8.99
Rogers-Mon	281.0	Sutton-LA	6.91	Reuss-LA	1.57	Ryan-Hou	200	Carlton-Phi	8.47	Reuss-LA	9.14
Niekro-Atl	275.0	Carlton-Phi	7.19	Forsch-Hou	1.66	Soto-Cin	182	Ryan-Hou	7.70	Pastore-Cin	9.89
Reuschel-Chi	257.0	Seaver-Cin	7.50	Candelaria-Pit	1.93	Niekro-Atl	176	Blyleven-Pit	6.98	Carlton-Phi	9.92
Niekro-Hou	256.0	Reuss-LA	7.57	Sutton-LA	1.99	Blyleven-Pit	168	Welch-LA	5.94	Soto-Cin	10.02

Earned Run Average		Adjusted ERA		Opponents' Batting Avg.		Opponents' On Base Pct.		Starter Runs		Adjusted Starter Runs	
Sutton-LA	2.20	Carlton-Phi	162	Soto-Cin	.187	Sutton-LA	.258	Carlton-Phi	42.6	Carlton-Phi	49.0
Carlton-Phi	2.34	Sutton-LA	159	Sutton-LA	.211	Reuss-LA	.261	Sutton-LA	33.0	Sutton-LA	30.5
Reuss-LA	2.51	Reuss-LA	139	Carlton-Phi	.218	Pastore-Cin	.277	Reuss-LA	27.8	Reuss-LA	25.1
Blue-SF	2.97	Rogers-Mon	120	Seaver-Cin	.225	Carlton-Phi	.278	Ruhle-Hou	21.8	Rogers-Mon	18.3
Rogers-Mon	2.98	Blue-SF	119	Reuss-LA	.227	Soto-Cin	.279	Richard-Hou	21.5	Richard-Hou	17.5

Clutch Pitching Index		Relief Runs		Adjusted Relief Runs		Relief Ranking		Total Pitcher Index		Total Baseball Ranking	
Reuschel-Chi	119	McGraw-Phi	21.9	Caudill-Chi	24.5	McGraw-Phi	32.6	Carlton-Phi	5.3	Schmidt-Phi	7.8
Bomback-NY	116	Camp-Atl	20.3	McGraw-Phi	23.9	Camp-Atl	28.4	Sutton-LA	2.9	Carlton-Phi	5.3
Zachry-NY	114	Caudill-Chi	20.1	Camp-Atl	22.0	Hume-Cin	25.6	Reuss-LA	2.8	Smith-SD	4.7
Ruthven-Phi	112	Smith-Hou	19.1	Holland-SF	16.4	Sutter-Chi	25.5	Camp-Atl	2.8	Templeton-StL	4.7
Sanderson-Mon	111	Holland-SF	16.9	Smith-Hou	15.5	Fryman-Mon	20.1	McGraw-Phi	2.6	Hernandez-StL	3.9

TEAM	G	W	L	PCT	GB	R	OR	AB	H	2B	3B	HR	BB	SO	AVG	OBP	SLG	PRO	PRO+	BR	/A	PF	CHI	RC	SB	CS	SBA	SBR
EAST																												
NY	162	103	59	.636		820	662	5553	1484	239	34	189	643	739	.267	.346	.425	.771	111	79	91	98	100	820	86	36	38	-11
BAL	162	100	62	.617	3	805	640	5585	1523	258	29	156	587	766	.273	.344	.413	.757	107	52	59	99	102	788	111	38	50	-18
MIL	162	86	76	.531	17	811	682	5653	1555	**298**	36	**203**	455	745	.275	.332	**.448**	**.780**	115	78	**101**	97	100	**834**	131	56	53	-14
BOS	160	83	77	.519	19	757	767	5603	1588	297	36	162	475	720	.283	.343	.436	.779	106	**86**	48	105	93	810	79	48	48	-13
DET	163	84	78	.519	19	**830**	757	5648	1543	232	53	143	**645**	844	.273	.351	.409	.760	105	66	48	102	101	804	75	68	59	-14
CLE	160	79	81	.494	23	738	807	5470	1517	221	40	89	617	625	.277	**.355**	.381	.736	101	26	23	100	97	739	118	58	50	-12
TOR	162	67	95	.414	36	624	762	5571	1398	249	53	126	448	813	.251	.310	.383	.693	85	-91	-124	105	99	640	67	72	59	-13
WEST																												
KC	162	97	65	.599		809	694	5714	**1633**	266	**59**	115	508	709	**.286**	.348	.413	.761	107	62	56	101	100	826	**185**	43	42	-11
OAK	162	83	79	.512	14	686	642	5495	1424	212	35	137	506	824	.259	.324	.385	.709	100	-50	0	93	102	680	175	82	**66**	-14
MIN	161	77	84	.478	19.5	670	724	5530	1468	252	46	99	436	703	.265	.322	.381	.703	85	-64	-116	107	103	655	62	46	41	**-10**
TEX	163	76	85	.472	20.5	756	752	5690	1616	263	27	124	480	**589**	.284	.342	.405	.747	97	30	52	97	98	768	91	49	54	-17
CHI	162	70	90	.438	26	587	722	5444	1408	255	38	91	399	670	.259	.314	.370	.684	87	-103	-99	100	98	608	68	54	50	-13
CAL	160	65	95	.406	31	698	797	5443	1442	236	32	106	539	889	.265	.335	.378	.713	97	-32	-14	98	102	681	91	63	56	-14
SEA	163	59	103	.364	38	610	793	5489	1359	211	35	104	483	727	.248	.311	.356	.667	81	-135	-141	101	**104**	598	116	62	53	-12
TOT	1132					10201		77888	20958	3489	553	1844	7221	10363	.269	.334	.399	.733							1455	775	65	-28

TEAM	CG	SH	SV	IP	H	H/G	HR	BB	SO	RAT	ERA	ERA+	OAV	OOB	PR	/A	PF	CPI	FA	E	DP	FW	PW	BW	SBW	DIF
EAST																										
NY	29	**15**	50	1464¹	1433	8.8	**102**	463	845	11.8	3.58	109	.259	.319	73	54	97	98	.978	138	160	.0	5.4	9.1	-.9	8.4
BAL	42	10	41	1460	1438	8.9	134	507	789	12.1	3.64	108	.260	.325	63	50	98	104	**.985**	**95**	178	**2.4**	5.0	5.9	-1.6	7.3
MIL	48	14	30	1450	1530	9.5	137	**420**	575	12.3	3.71	104	.272	.326	52	26	96	**107**	.977	147	189	-.5	2.6	**10.1**	-1.2	-6.0
BOS	30	8	43	1441¹	1557	9.7	129	481	696	12.9	4.38	96	.279	.340	-55	-25	105	97	.977	149	206	-.7	-2.5	4.8	-1.1	2.5
DET	40	9	30	1467¹	1505	9.2	152	558	741	12.8	4.25	97	.267	.336	-35	-22	102	98	.979	133	165	.3	-2.2	4.8	-1.2	1.3
CLE	35	8	32	1428	1519	9.6	137	552	843	13.3	4.68	87	.274	.343	-103	-97	101	92	.983	105	143	1.8	-9.7	2.3	-1.0	5.6
TOR	39	9	23	1466	1523	9.3	135	635	705	13.4	4.19	103	.273	.350	-25	17	107	105	.979	133	206	.3	1.7	-12.4	-1.1	-2.5
WEST																										
KC	37	10	42	1459¹	1496	9.2	129	465	614	12.2	3.83	106	.266	.325	33	35	100	100	.978	141	150	-.2	3.5	5.6	-.9	8.0
OAK	**94**	9	13	1471²	**1347**	**8.2**	142	521	769	**11.6**	**3.46**	109	**.243**	**.312**	**93**	50	93	99	.979	130	115	.5	5.0	.0	-1.2	-2.2
MIN	35	9	30	1451	1502	9.3	120	468	744	12.4	3.93	**111**	.271	.331	16	68	108	100	.977	148	192	-.6	**6.8**	-11.6	-.8	2.7
TEX	35	6	25	1452	1561	9.7	119	519	**890**	13.1	4.02	97	.277	.342	1	-21	97	104	.977	147	169	-.5	-2.1	5.2	-1.5	-5.6
CHI	32	12	42	1435¹	1434	9.0	108	563	724	12.8	3.92	103	.263	.336	18	16	100	99	.973	171	162	-1.9	1.6	-9.9	-1.1	1.2
CAL	22	6	30	1428¹	1548	9.8	141	529	725	13.3	4.52	87	.278	.345	-76	-93	97	97	.978	134	144	.1	-9.3	-1.4	-1.2	-3.3
SEA	31	7	26	1457¹	1565	9.7	159	540	703	13.2	4.38	94	.277	.343	-55	-40	102	101	.977	149	189	-.6	-4.0	-14.1	-1.0	-2.4
TOT	549	132	457	20332		9.3				12.7	4.03		.269	.334					.978	1920	2368					

Runs		Hits		Doubles		Triples		Home Runs		Total Bases	
Wilson-KC	133	Wilson-KC	230	Yount-Mil	49	Wilson-KC	15	Oglivie-Mil	41	Cooper-Mil	335
Yount-Mil	121	Cooper-Mil	219	Oliver-Tex	43	Griffin-Tor	15	Jackson-NY	41	Oglivie-Mil	333
Bumbry-Bal	118	Rivers-Tex	210	Morrison-Chi	40	Washington-KC	11	Thomas-Mil	38	Murray-Bal	322
Henderson-Oak	111	Oliver-Tex	209	McRae-KC	39	Landreaux-Min	11	Armas-Oak	35	Yount-Mil	317
Trammell-Det	107	Bumbry-Bal	205	Evans-Bos	37	Yount-Mil	10	Murray-Bal	32	Oliver-Tex	315

Runs Batted In		Runs Produced		Bases On Balls		Batting Average		On Base Percentage		Slugging Average	
Cooper-Mil	122	Oliver-Tex	194	Randolph-NY	119	G.Brett-KC	.390	G.Brett-KC	.461	G.Brett-KC	.664
Oglivie-Mil	118	Cooper-Mil	193	Henderson-Oak	117	Cooper-Mil	.352	Randolph-NY	.429	Jackson-NY	.597
G.Brett-KC	118	Yount-Mil	185	Hargrove-Cle	111	Dilone-Cle	.341	Henderson-Oak	.422	Oglivie-Mil	.563
Oliver-Tex	117	Murray-Bal	184	Murphy-Oak	102	Rivers-Tex	.333	Hargrove-Cle	.421	Cooper-Mil	.539
Murray-Bal	116	G.Brett-KC	181	Harrah-Cle	98	Carew-Cal	.331	Thompson-Det-Cal	.402	Yount-Mil	.519

Production		Adjusted Production		Batter Runs		Adjusted Batter Runs		Clutch Hitting Index		Runs Created	
G.Brett-KC	1.124	G.Brett-KC	202	G.Brett-KC	64.8	G.Brett-KC	64.3	Kemp-Det	137	G.Brett-KC	135
Jackson-NY	.996	Jackson-NY	172	Jackson-NY	49.1	Jackson-NY	50.3	Manning-Cle	135	Cooper-Mil	126
Cooper-Mil	.931	Cooper-Mil	157	Cooper-Mil	42.9	Cooper-Mil	45.5	Aikens-KC	132	Jackson-NY	125
Oglivie-Mil	.930	Oglivie-Mil	156	Oglivie-Mil	39.2	Oglivie-Mil	41.7	G.Brett-KC	132	Oglivie-Mil	121
Singleton-Bal	.885	Singleton-Bal	143	Singleton-Bal	35.4	Singleton-Bal	36.2	Oliver-Tex	130	Henderson-Oak	120

Total Average		Stolen Bases		Stolen Base Average		Stolen Base Runs		Fielding Runs		Total Player Rating	
G.Brett-KC	1.258	Henderson-Oak	100	Otis-KC	94.1	Wilson-KC	17.7	Castino-Min	27.8	G.Brett-KC	6.6
Jackson-NY	1.060	Wilson-KC	79	Harrah-Cle	89.5	Henderson-Oak	14.4	Burleson-Bos	25.5	Henderson-Oak	6.2
Henderson-Oak	.973	Dilone-Cle	61	Kelly-Bal	88.9	Cruz-Sea	9.3	DeCinces-Bal	24.5	Oglivie-Mil	5.1
Randolph-NY	.952	Cruz-Sea	45	Wilson-KC	88.8	Dilone-Cle	7.5	Wilson-KC	24.4	Wilson-KC	4.9
Oglivie-Mil	.925	Bumbry-Bal	44	Cruz-Sea	86.5	Bumbry-Bal	6.6	Pryor-Chi	22.3	Bell-Tex	4.8

Wins		Win Percentage		Games		Complete Games		Shutouts		Saves	
Stone-Bal	25	Stone-Bal	.781	Quisenberry-KC	75	Langford-Oak	28	John-NY	6	Quisenberry-KC	33
Norris-Oak	22	May-NY	.750	Corbett-Min	73	Norris-Oak	24	Zahn-Min	5	Gossage-NY	33
John-NY	22	McGregor-Bal	.714	Monge-Cle	67	Keough-Oak	20	Stieb-Tor	4	Farmer-Chi	30
McGregor-Bal	20	Norris-Oak	.710	Lopez-Det	67	John-NY	16	McGregor-Bal	4	Stoddard-Bal	26
Leonard-KC	20	John-NY	.710			Gura-KC	16	Gura-KC	4	Burgmeier-Bos	24

Innings Pitched		Fewest Hits/Game		Fewest BB/Game		Strikeouts		Strikeouts/Game		Ratio	
Langford-Oak	290.0	Norris-Oak	6.81	Matlack-Tex	1.84	Barker-Cle	187	Barker-Cle	6.83	May-NY	9.39
Norris-Oak	284.1	May-NY	7.39	Splittorff-KC	1.90	Norris-Oak	180	May-NY	6.83	Norris-Oak	9.62
Gura-KC	283.1	Clancy-Tor	7.79	John-NY	1.90	Guidry-NY	166	Guidry-NY	6.80	Langford-Oak	10.58
Leonard-KC	280.1	Underwood-NY	7.84	Tanana-Cal	1.99	Leonard-KC	155	Bannister-Sea	6.41	Burns-Chi	10.59
John-NY	265.1	Keough-Oak	7.85	Langford-Oak	1.99	Bannister-Sea	155	Perry-Tex-NY	5.91	Eckersley-Bos	10.65

Earned Run Average		Adjusted ERA		Opponents' Batting Avg.		Opponents' On Base Pct.		Starter Runs		Adjusted Starter Runs	
May-NY	2.46	May-NY	159	Norris-Oak	.209	May-NY	.268	Norris-Oak	47.4	Norris-Oak	39.0
Norris-Oak	2.53	Norris-Oak	149	May-NY	.224	Norris-Oak	.272	Gura-KC	34.0	Gura-KC	34.5
Burns-Chi	2.84	Burns-Chi	142	Clancy-Tor	.233	Eckersley-Bos	.291	Burns-Chi	31.7	Burns-Chi	31.4
Keough-Oak	2.92	Gura-KC	137	Keough-Oak	.236	Burns-Chi	.295	Keough-Oak	31.0	May-NY	28.4
Gura-KC	2.95	Erickson-Min	134	Underwood-NY	.237	Bannister-Sea	.296	May-NY	30.6	Clancy-Tor	27.8

Clutch Pitching Index		Relief Runs		Adjusted Relief Runs		Relief Ranking		Total Pitcher Index		Total Baseball Ranking	
Sorensen-Mil	126	Corbett-Min	31.1	Corbett-Min	36.0	Corbett-Min	46.9	Norris-Oak	4.5	G.Brett-KC	6.6
Stanley-Bos	117	Burgmeier-Bos	22.4	Burgmeier-Bos	24.4	Burgmeier-Bos	33.2	Corbett-Min	4.0	Henderson-Oak	6.2
Keough-Oak	113	Gossage-NY	19.4	Garvin-Tor	18.5	Gossage-NY	26.8	Gura-KC	3.7	Oglivie-Mil	5.1
Trout-Chi	113	Darwin-Tex	17.1	Gossage-NY	18.1	Quisenberry-KC	26.3	Burns-Chi	3.2	Wilson-KC	4.9
Perry-Tex-NY	112	Garvin-Tor	16.0	Proly-Chi	15.6	Garvin-Tor	26.2	May-NY	2.9	Bell-Tex	4.8

TEAM	G	W	L	PCT	GB	R	OR	AB	H	2B	3B	HR	BB	SO	AVG	OBP	SLG	PRO	PRO+	BR	/A	PF	CHI	RC	SB	CS	SBA	SBR
EAST																												
STL	103	59	43	.578		464	417	3537	936	158	**45**	50	379	495	.265	.339	.377	.716	106	43	32	103	102	454	88	45	44	**-12**
MON	108	60	48	.556	2	443	394	3591	883	146	28	81	368	498	.246	.319	.370	.689	99	3	-1	101	**105**	435	**138**	40	48	-16
PHI	107	59	48	.551	2.5	**491**	472	3665	**1002**	165	25	69	372	**432**	**.273**	**.344**	**.389**	**.733**	109	66	**47**	104	100	**495**	103	46	49	-15
PIT	103	46	56	.451	13	407	425	3576	920	176	30	55	278	494	.257	.314	.369	.683	96	-8	-20	103	102	417	122	52	51	-14
NY	105	41	62	.398	18.5	348	432	3493	868	136	35	57	304	603	.248	.311	.356	.667	95	-25	-18	98	93	387	103	42	45	-13
CHI	106	38	65	.369	21.5	370	483	3546	838	138	29	57	342	611	.236	.306	.340	.646	84	-51	-69	104	103	368	72	41	48	-16
WEST																												
CIN	108	66	42	.611		464	440	3637	972	**190**	24	64	375	553	.267	.339	.385	.724	109	53	46	102	97	469	58	37	44	-14
LA	110	63	47	.573	4	450	356	3751	984	133	20	**82**	331	550	.262	.325	.374	.699	107	16	31	96	101	450	73	46	51	-16
HOU	110	61	49	.555	6	394	**331**	3693	948	160	35	45	340	488	.257	.321	.356	.677	103	-11	10	95	95	425	81	43	46	-14
SF	111	56	55	.505	11.5	427	414	3766	941	161	26	63	**386**	543	.250	.322	.357	.679	99	-7	1	98	99	431	89	50	52	-15
ATL	107	50	56	.472	15	395	416	3642	886	148	22	64	321	540	.243	.308	.349	.657	89	-40	-50	103	**105**	391	98	39	43	-13
SD	110	41	69	.373	26	382	455	3757	963	170	35	32	311	525	.256	.316	.346	.662	100	-32	0	93	96	400	83	62	**59**	-16
TOT	644					5035		43654	11141	1881	354	719	4107	6332	.255	.322	.364	.686							1108	543	67	7

TEAM	CG	SH	SV	IP	H	H/G	HR	BB	SO	RAT	ERA	ERA+	OAV	OOB	PR	/A	PF	CPI	FA	E	DP	FW	PW	BW	SBW	DIF
EAST																										
STL	11	5	**33**	943	902	8.6	52	290	388	11.5	3.63	98	.254	.314	-14	-7	102	91	**.981**	82	108	.5	-.8	3.4	**-1.3**	6.2
MON	20	12	23	975	902	8.3	58	**268**	520	11.0	3.30	106	.246	.301	21	21	100	92	.980	81	88	.7	2.3	-.1	-1.8	4.9
PHI	19	5	23	960¹	967	9.1	72	347	580	12.4	4.05	90	.266	.332	-59	-45	104	97	.980	86	90	.4	-4.8	**5.1**	-1.7	6.5
PIT	11	5	29	942	953	9.1	60	346	492	12.4	3.56	101	.266	.333	-7	3	103	107	.979	86	106	.3	.3	-2.1	-1.6	-1.9
NY	7	3	24	926¹	906	8.8	74	336	490	12.2	3.55	98	.258	.326	-5	-6	100	105	.968	130	89	-1.8	-.6	-1.9	-1.5	-4.6
CHI	6	2	20	956²	983	9.2	59	388	532	13.1	4.01	92	.269	.343	-55	-33	106	101	.974	113	103	-.9	-3.5	-7.4	-1.8	.2
WEST																										
CIN	25	14	20	965²	863	8.0	67	393	593	11.8	3.73	95	.241	.318	-25	-18	102	90	**.981**	80	99	.8	-1.9	4.9	-1.6	9.8
LA	**26**	**19**	24	997	904	8.2	54	302	603	11.0	3.01	110	.244	.304	53	34	95	100	.980	87	101	.5	3.7	3.3	-1.8	2.3
HOU	23	**19**	25	990	**842**	7.7	40	300	610	10.5	2.66	124	.231	.291	90	64	94	96	.980	87	81	.5	7.4	1.1	-1.6	-1.4
SF	8	9	**33**	1009¹	970	8.6	57	393	561	12.4	3.28	105	.255	.329	23	16	98	109	.977	102	102	-.2	1.7	.1	-1.7	.5
ATL	11	4	24	968	936	8.7	62	330	471	11.9	3.45	104	.257	.320	23	14	103	102	.976	102	93	-.4	1.5	-5.4	-1.5	2.7
SD	9	6	23	1002	1013	9.1	64	414	492	13.0	3.72	88	.268	.343	-25	-51	93	108	.977	102	**117**	-.2	-5.5	.0	-1.8	-6.5
TOT	176	103	301	11635¹		8.6				11.9	3.49		.255	.322					.978	1138	1177					

Runs		Hits		Doubles		Triples		Home Runs		Total Bases	
Schmidt-Phi	78	Rose-Phi	140	Buckner-Chi	35	Richards-SD	12	Schmidt-Phi	31	Schmidt-Phi	228
Rose-Phi	73	Buckner-Chi	131	Jones-SD	34	Reynolds-Hou	12	Dawson-Mon	24	Dawson-Mon	218
Dawson-Mon	71	Concepcion-Cin	129	Concepcion-Cin	28	Herr-StL	9	Kingman-NY	22	Foster-Cin	215
Hendrick-StL	67	Baker-LA	128	Hernandez-StL	27			Foster-Cin	22	Buckner-Chi	202
		Griffey-Cin	123	Chambliss-Atl	25			Hendrick-StL	18	Hendrick-StL	191

Runs Batted In		Runs Produced		Bases On Balls		Batting Average		On Base Percentage		Slugging Average	
Schmidt-Phi	91	Schmidt-Phi	138	Schmidt-Phi	73	Rose-Phi	.325	Schmidt-Phi	.439	Schmidt-Phi	.644
Foster-Cin	90	Foster-Cin	132	Morgan-SF	66	Baker-LA	.320	Hernandez-StL	.405	Dawson-Mon	.553
Buckner-Chi	75	Matthews-Phi	120	Hernandez-StL	61	Schmidt-Phi	.316	Matthews-Phi	.404	Foster-Cin	.519
Carter-Mon	68	Concepcion-Cin	119	Thompson-Pit	59	Buckner-Chi	.311	Raines-Mon	.394	Hendrick-StL	.485
		Garvey-LA	117	Matthews-Phi	59	Griffey-Cin	.311	Rose-Phi	.394	Buckner-Chi	.480

Production		Adjusted Production		Batter Runs		Adjusted Batter Runs		Clutch Hitting Index		Runs Created	
Schmidt-Phi	1.083	Schmidt-Phi	195	Schmidt-Phi	50.1	Schmidt-Phi	48.1	Matthews-Phi	147	Schmidt-Phi	102
Dawson-Mon	.923	Dawson-Mon	157	Dawson-Mon	28.8	Dawson-Mon	28.3	Concepcion-Cin	135	Dawson-Mon	83
Foster-Cin	.895	Foster-Cin	150	Foster-Cin	27.7	Foster-Cin	26.9	Buckner-Chi	134	Foster-Cin	81
Hernandez-StL	.868	Cey-LA	145	Hernandez-StL	24.6	Hernandez-StL	23.4	Carter-Mon	132	Hernandez-StL	73
Matthews-Phi	.855	Hernandez-StL	142	Matthews-Phi	22.0	Madlock-Pit	21.0	Scott-Mon	129	Matthews-Phi	71

Total Average		Stolen Bases		Stolen Base Average		Stolen Base Runs		Fielding Runs		Total Player Rating	
Schmidt-Phi	1.227	Raines-Mon	71	Lopes-LA	90.9	Raines-Mon	14.7	Smith-SD	25.9	Schmidt-Phi	6.9
Raines-Mon	1.034	Moreno-Pit	39	Lacy-Pit	88.9	Lacy-Pit	5.4	Schmidt-Phi	22.5	Dawson-Mon	4.6
Dawson-Mon	.989	Scott-Mon	30	Dawson-Mon	86.7	Dawson-Mon	5.4	Dawson-Mon	13.4	Foster-Cin	3.1
Matthews-Phi	.908			Raines-Mon	86.6	Scott-Mon	4.8	Flynn-NY	12.2	Raines-Mon	2.8
Foster-Cin	.898			Puhl-Hou	84.6	Lopes-LA	4.8	Trillo-Phi	10.8	Hernandez-StL	2.8

Wins		Win Percentage		Games		Complete Games		Shutouts		Saves	
Seaver-Cin	14	Seaver-Cin	.875	Lucas-SD	57	Valenzuela-LA	11	Valenzuela-LA	8	Sutter-StL	25
Valenzuela-LA	13	Carlton-Phi	.765	Minton-SF	55	Soto-Cin	10	Knepper-Hou	5	Minton-SF	21
Carlton-Phi	13	Ryan-Hou	.688	Tidrow-Chi	51	Carlton-Phi	10	Hooton-LA	4	Allen-NY	18
		Valenzuela-LA	.650	Hume-Cin	51	Reuss-LA	8			Camp-Atl	17
		Hooton-LA	.647	Sambito-Hou	49	Rogers-Mon	7				

Innings Pitched		Fewest Hits/Game		Fewest BB/Game		Strikeouts		Strikeouts/Game		Ratio	
Valenzuela-LA	192.1	Ryan-Hou	5.98	Perry-Atl	1.43	Valenzuela-LA	180	Carlton-Phi	8.48	Sutton-Hou	9.19
Carlton-Phi	190.0	Seaver-Cin	6.49	Reuss-LA	1.59	Carlton-Phi	179	Ryan-Hou	8.46	Valenzuela-LA	9.45
Soto-Cin	175.0	Valenzuela-LA	6.55	Sutton-Hou	1.64	Soto-Cin	151	Valenzuela-LA	8.42	Knepper-Hou	9.77
Seaver-Cin	166.1	Berenyi-Cin	6.93	Sorensen-StL	1.67	Ryan-Hou	140	Soto-Cin	7.77	Reuss-LA	9.96
Niekro-Hou	166.0	Blue-SF	7.00	Solomon-Pit	1.91	Gullickson-Mon	115	Berenyi-Cin	7.57	Hooton-LA	10.05

Earned Run Average		Adjusted ERA		Opponents' Batting Avg.		Opponents' On Base Pct.		Starter Runs		Adjusted Starter Runs	
Ryan-Hou	1.69	Ryan-Hou	195	Ryan-Hou	.188	Sutton-Hou	.268	Ryan-Hou	29.8	Ryan-Hou	26.5
Knepper-Hou	2.18	Knepper-Hou	151	Valenzuela-LA	.205	Valenzuela-LA	.271	Knepper-Hou	22.8	Carlton-Phi	25.6
Hooton-LA	2.28	Carlton-Phi	150	Seaver-Cin	.205	Knepper-Hou	.280	Carlton-Phi	22.7	Knepper-Hou	19.4
Reuss-LA	2.30	Hooton-LA	146	Berenyi-Cin	.211	Sanderson-Mon	.281	Valenzuela-LA	21.6	Seaver-Cin	18.7
Carlton-Phi	2.42	Reuss-LA	144	Blue-SF	.217	Ryan-Hou	.281	Reuss-LA	20.2	Valenzuela-LA	17.9

Clutch Pitching Index		Relief Runs		Adjusted Relief Runs		Relief Ranking		Total Pitcher Index		Total Baseball Ranking	
Mahler-Atl	124	Lucas-SD	14.9	Camp-Atl	15.2	Camp-Atl	29.3	Ryan-Hou	3.2	Schmidt-Phi	6.9
Solomon-Pit	124	Camp-Atl	14.5	Lucas-SD	12.6	Lucas-SD	21.7	Carlton-Phi	2.7	Dawson-Mon	4.6
Alexander-SF	122	Holland-SF	12.0	Holland-SF	11.4	Sambito-Hou	18.2	Seaver-Cin	2.5	Ryan-Hou	3.2
Blue-SF	112	Sambito-Hou	11.7	Sambito-Hou	10.3	Fryman-Mon	15.7	Valenzuela-LA	2.4	Foster-Cin	3.1
Zachry-NY	111	Reardon-NY-Mon	10.3	Reardon-NY-Mon	10.3	Holland-SF	14.0	Reuss-LA	2.4	Raines-Mon	2.8

TEAM	G	W	L	PCT	GB	R	OR	AB	H	2B	3B	HR	BB	SO	AVG	OBP	SLG	PRO	PRO+	BR	/A	PF	CHI	RC	SB	CS	SBA	SBR
EAST																												
MIL	109	62	47	.569		493	459	3743	961	173	20	96	300	461	.257	.317	.391	.708	108	9	32	95	108	451	39	36	40	-12
BAL	105	59	46	.562	1	429	437	3516	883	165	11	88	404	454	.251	.331	.379	.710	104	22	22	100	95	431	41	34	46	-16
NY	107	59	48	.551	2	421	343	3529	889	148	22	100	391	434	.252	.328	.391	.719	107	29	35	99	92	445	47	30	39	-13
DET	109	60	49	.550	2	427	404	3600	922	148	29	65	404	500	.256	.334	.368	.702	98	14	-1	104	94	442	61	37	49	-17
BOS	108	59	49	.546	2.5	519	481	3820	1052	168	17	90	378	520	.275	.343	.399	.742	106	65	36	106	99	514	32	31	39	-13
CLE	103	52	51	.505	7	431	442	3507	922	150	21	39	343	379	.263	.331	.351	.682	98	-10	-4	99	104	414	119	37	49	-17
TOR	106	37	69	.349	23.5	329	466	3521	797	137	23	61	284	556	.226	.288	.330	.618	73	-102	-128	106	104	326	66	57	54	-14
WEST																												
OAK	109	64	45	.587		458	403	3677	910	119	26	104	342	647	.247	.314	.379	.693	103	-7	14	95	105	438	98	47	47	-13
TEX	105	57	48	.543	5	452	389	3581	968	178	15	49	295	396	.270	.329	.369	.698	106	5	27	95	105	425	46	41	47	-15
CHI	106	54	52	.509	8.5	476	423	3615	982	135	27	76	322	518	.272	.338	.387	.725	110	41	50	98	100	471	86	44	48	-15
KC	103	50	53	.485	11	397	405	3560	952	169	29	61	301	419	.267	.327	.383	.710	104	17	20	99	90	437	100	53	52	-14
CAL	110	51	59	.464	13.5	476	453	3688	944	134	16	97	393	571	.256	.332	.380	.712	105	26	26	100	100	463	44	33	39	-13
SEA	110	44	65	.404	20	426	521	3780	950	148	13	89	329	553	.251	.316	.368	.684	93	-18	-36	104	98	441	100	50	56	-18
MIN	110	41	68	.376	23	378	486	3676	884	147	36	47	275	497	.240	.295	.338	.633	76	-86	-114	107	109	355	34	27	33	-11
TOT	750					6112		50813	13016	2119	305	1062	4761	6905	.256	.323	.373	.696							913	557	62	-59

TEAM	CG	SH	SV	IP	H	H/G	HR	BB	SO	RAT	ERA	ERA+	OAV	OOB	PR	/A	PF	CPI	FA	E	DP	FW	PW	BW	SBW	DIF
EAST																										
MIL	11	4	35	986	994	9.1	72	352	448	12.4	3.91	88	.265	.330	-27	-52	94	99	.982	79	135	.3	-5.5	3.4	-.8	10.1
BAL	25	10	23	939²	923	8.8	83	347	489	12.3	3.70	98	.260	.328	-4	-7	99	104	.983	68	114	.8	-.7	2.3	-1.2	5.4
NY	16	13	30	948	827	7.9	64	287	606	10.7	2.90	123	.235	.295	80	71	98	100	.982	72	100	.7	7.5	3.7	-.9	-5.4
DET	33	13	22	969	840	7.8	83	373	476	11.5	3.53	107	.235	.313	13	26	103	94	.984	67	109	1.0	2.7	-.1	-1.3	3.2
BOS	19	4	24	987¹	983	9.0	90	354	536	12.4	3.81	102	.261	.330	-16	6	106	103	.979	91	108	-.4	.6	3.8	-.9	1.9
CLE	33	10	13	931	989	9.6	67	311	569	12.7	3.88	94	.273	.333	-22	-26	99	102	.978	87	91	-.4	-2.7	-.4	-1.3	5.4
TOR	20	4	18	953	908	8.6	72	377	451	12.5	3.82	103	.252	.329	-16	13	108	97	.975	105	102	-1.3	1.4	-13.4	-1.0	-1.6
WEST																										
OAK	60	11	10	993²	883	8.0	80	370	505	11.6	3.30	106	.239	.313	39	19	95	101	.980	81	74	.2	2.0	1.5	-.9	6.7
TEX	23	13	18	940¹	851	8.1	67	322	488	11.4	3.40	102	.243	.310	27	7	95	95	.984	69	102	.7	.7	2.8	-1.1	1.3
CHI	20	8	23	940²	891	8.5	73	336	529	12.0	3.47	103	.251	.320	19	10	98	102	.979	87	113	-.3	1.0	5.2	-1.1	-3.9
KC	24	8	24	922¹	909	8.9	75	273	404	11.7	3.56	101	.259	.316	9	4	99	101	.982	72	94	.5	.4	2.1	-1.0	-3.5
CAL	27	8	19	971¹	958	8.9	81	323	426	12.1	3.70	99	.260	.323	-4	-5	100	102	.977	101	120	-.9	-.5	2.7	-.9	-4.4
SEA	10	5	23	997¹	1039	9.4	76	360	478	12.8	4.23	91	.271	.336	-63	-42	105	95	.979	91	122	-.3	-4.4	-3.8	-1.4	-.6
MIN	13	6	22	979²	1021	9.4	79	376	500	13.0	3.98	99	.271	.340	-34	-3	108	104	.978	96	103	-.6	-.3	-12.0	-.7	.0
TOT	334	117	304	13459¹		8.7				12.1	3.66		.256	.323					.980	1166	1487					

Runs
Henderson-Oak	89
Evans-Bos	84
Cooper-Mil	70
Harrah-Cle	64
Rivers-Tex	62

Hits
Henderson-Oak	135
Lansford-Bos	134
Wilson-KC	133
Cooper-Mil	133
Paciorek-Sea	132

Doubles
Cooper-Mil	35
Oliver-Tex	29
Paciorek-Sea	28
Dauer-Bal	27
G.Brett-KC	27

Triples
Castino-Min	9
Wilson-KC	7
Henderson-Oak	7
G.Brett-KC	7
Baines-Chi	7

Home Runs
Murray-Bal	22
Grich-Cal	22
Evans-Bos	22
Armas-Oak	22

Total Bases
Evans-Bos	215
Armas-Oak	211
Paciorek-Sea	206
Cooper-Mil	206
Murray-Bal	202

Runs Batted In
Murray-Bal	78
Armas-Oak	76
Oglivie-Mil	72
Evans-Bos	71
Winfield-NY	68

Runs Produced
Evans-Bos	133
Henderson-Oak	118
Cooper-Mil	118
Murray-Bal	113
Oglivie-Mil	111

Bases On Balls
Evans-Bos	85
Murphy-Oak	73
Kemp-Det	70
Henderson-Oak	64
Aikens-KC	62

Batting Average
Lansford-Bos	.336
Paciorek-Sea	.326
Cooper-Mil	.320
Henderson-Oak	.319
Hargrove-Cle	.317

On Base Percentage
Hargrove-Cle	.432
Evans-Bos	.418
Henderson-Oak	.411
Kemp-Det	.393
Lansford-Bos	.391

Slugging Average
Grich-Cal	.543
Murray-Bal	.534
Evans-Bos	.522
Paciorek-Sea	.509
Cooper-Mil	.495

Production
Evans-Bos	.940
Grich-Cal	.924
Murray-Bal	.897
Paciorek-Sea	.894
Lemon-Chi	.879

Adjusted Production
Grich-Cal	164
Evans-Bos	160
Murray-Bal	156
Lemon-Chi	155
Cooper-Mil	154

Batter Runs
Evans-Bos	39.8
Paciorek-Sea	28.4
Grich-Cal	28.3
Henderson-Oak	26.9
Murray-Bal	25.9

Adjusted Batter Runs
Evans-Bos	36.5
Henderson-Oak	29.5
Grich-Cal	28.3
Paciorek-Sea	26.4
Cooper-Mil	26.1

Clutch Hitting Index
Hargrove-Cle	150
Yastrzemski-Bos	150
Oglivie-Mil	149
Bell-Tex	144
Simmons-Mil	137

Runs Created
Evans-Bos	95
Henderson-Oak	81
Paciorek-Sea	76
Grich-Cal	73
Murray-Bal	70

Total Average
Evans-Bos	1.007
Grich-Cal	.917
Henderson-Oak	.899
Murray-Bal	.864
Paciorek-Sea	.846

Stolen Bases
Henderson-Oak	56
Cruz-Sea	43
LeFlore-Chi	36
Wilson-KC	34
Dilone-Cle	29

Stolen Base Average
Manning-Cle	89.3
Bannister-Cle	88.9
Cruz-Sea	84.3
Wilson-KC	81.0
Gibson-Det	77.3

Stolen Base Runs
Cruz-Sea	8.1
Manning-Cle	5.7
Wilson-KC	5.4
LeFlore-Chi	4.2

Fielding Runs
Bell-Tex	29.6
Yount-Mil	27.5
Wilson-KC	21.6
Burleson-Cal	21.0
Henderson-Oak	18.0

Total Player Rating
Henderson-Oak	5.0
Bell-Tex	4.7
Evans-Bos	4.2
Yount-Mil	4.2
Grich-Cal	4.1

Wins
Vuckovich-Mil	14
Morris-Det	14
McCatty-Oak	14
J.Martinez-Bal	14

Win Percentage
Vuckovich-Mil	.778
J.Martinez-Bal	.737
McGregor-Bal	.722
Guidry-NY	.688

Games
Corbett-Min	54
Fingers-Mil	47
Rawley-Sea	46
Easterly-Mil	44

Complete Games
Langford-Oak	18
McCatty-Oak	16
Morris-Det	15
Norris-Oak	12
Gura-KC	12

Shutouts
Medich-Tex	4
McCatty-Oak	4
Forsch-Cal	4
Dotson-Chi	4

Saves
Fingers-Mil	28
Gossage-NY	20
Quisenberry-KC	18
Corbett-Min	17
Saucier-Det	13

Innings Pitched
Leonard-KC	201.2
Morris-Det	198.0
Langford-Oak	195.1
McCatty-Oak	185.2
Stieb-Tor	183.2

Fewest Hits/Game
McCatty-Oak	6.79
Morris-Det	6.95
Guidry-NY	7.09
Darwin-Tex	7.09
Stewart-Bal	7.13

Fewest BB/Game
Honeycutt-Tex	1.20
Forsch-Cal	1.59
Gura-KC	1.83
Leonard-KC	1.83
Guidry-NY	1.84

Strikeouts
Barker-Cle	127
Burns-Chi	108
Leonard-KC	107
Blyleven-Cle	107
Guidry-NY	104

Strikeouts/Game
Barker-Cle	7.41
Guidry-NY	7.37
Bannister-Sea	6.30
Burns-Chi	6.20
Blyleven-Cle	6.04

Ratio
Guidry-NY	9.00
Gura-KC	9.30
Honeycutt-Tex	9.66
McCatty-Oak	9.84
Forsch-Cal	10.24

Earned Run Average
Stewart-Bal	2.32
McCatty-Oak	2.33
Lamp-Chi	2.41
John-NY	2.63
Burns-Chi	2.64

Adjusted ERA
Stewart-Bal	156
McCatty-Oak	149
Lamp-Chi	148
John-NY	136
Burns-Chi	135

Opponents' Batting Avg.
McCatty-Oak	.211
Guidry-NY	.214
Darwin-Tex	.218
Morris-Det	.218
Lamp-Chi	.222

Opponents' On Base Pct.
Guidry-NY	.257
Gura-KC	.269
Honeycutt-Tex	.272
McCatty-Oak	.279
Forsch-Cal	.289

Starter Runs
McCatty-Oak	27.5
Righetti-NY	18.8
Gura-KC	18.0
Burns-Chi	17.7
Lamp-Chi	17.6

Adjusted Starter Runs
McCatty-Oak	23.8
Righetti-NY	17.8
Gura-KC	17.1
Lamp-Chi	16.5
Burns-Chi	16.3

Clutch Pitching Index
Stewart-Bal	145
John-NY	129
Burns-Chi	121
Denny-Cle	119
McGregor-Bal	116

Relief Runs
Fingers-Mil	22.7
Gossage-NY	15.0
Quisenberry-KC	13.3
Saucier-Det	10.9
Corbett-Min	10.6

Adjusted Relief Runs
Fingers-Mil	20.7
Gossage-NY	14.5
Corbett-Min	13.4
Quisenberry-KC	13.0
Saucier-Det	11.5

Relief Ranking
Fingers-Mil	38.2
Gossage-NY	28.0
Saucier-Det	19.6
Quisenberry-KC	17.8
Corbett-Min	16.9

Total Pitcher Index
McCatty-Oak	2.6
Fingers-Mil	2.2
Gura-KC	1.9
Stieb-Tor	1.9
Lamp-Chi	1.9

Total Baseball Ranking
Henderson-Oak	5.0
Bell-Tex	4.7
Evans-Bos	4.2
Yount-Mil	4.2
Grich-Cal	4.1

TEAM	G	W	L	PCT	GB	R	OR	AB	H	2B	3B	HR	BB	SO	AVG	OBP	SLG	PRO	PRO+	BR	/A	PF	CHI	RC	SB	CS	SBA	SBR
EAST																												
STL	162	92	70	.568		685	**609**	5455	1439	239	**52**	67	569	805	.264	**.337**	.364	.701	100	24	17	101	99	682	**200**	91	**61**	**-8**
PHI	162	89	73	.549	3	664	654	5454	1417	245	25	112	506	831	.260	.325	.376	.701	99	14	0	102	99	654	128	76	55	-9
MON	162	86	76	.531	6	697	616	5557	1454	270	38	133	503	816	.262	.327	.396	.723	105	52	39	102	97	725	156	56	50	-12
PIT	162	84	78	.519	8	724	696	5614	**1535**	**272**	40	134	447	862	**.273**	.330	**.408**	**.738**	108	**80**	59	103	97	**745**	161	75	60	-13
CHI	162	73	89	.451	19	676	709	5531	1436	239	46	102	460	869	.260	.319	.375	.694	97	-3	-20	103	103	662	132	70	54	-10
NY	162	65	97	.401	27	609	723	5510	1361	227	26	97	456	1005	.247	.307	.350	.657	89	-74	-69	99	105	595	137	58	52	-13
WEST																												
ATL	162	89	73	.549		**739**	702	5507	1411	215	22	**146**	554	869	.256	.327	.383	.710	99	33	5	104	105	697	151	77	60	-12
LA	162	88	74	.543	1	691	612	5642	1487	222	32	138	528	**804**	.264	.330	.388	.718	**109**	47	**64**	98	95	735	151	56	48	-11
SF	162	87	75	.537	2	673	687	5499	1393	213	30	133	**607**	915	.253	.329	.376	.705	103	27	28	100	97	685	130	56	54	-15
SD	162	81	81	.500	8	675	658	5575	1435	217	**52**	81	429	877	.257	.313	.359	.672	99	-48	-12	95	**110**	626	165	77	59	-11
HOU	162	77	85	.475	12	569	620	5440	1342	236	48	74	435	830	.247	.305	.349	.654	95	-83	-34	92	101	578	140	61	51	-11
CIN	162	61	101	.377	28	545	661	5479	1375	228	34	82	470	817	.251	.313	.350	.663	89	-62	-75	102	92	588	131	69	58	-13
TOT	972					7947		66263	17085	2823	445	1299	5964	10300	.258	.322	.373	.695							1782	822	68	41

TEAM	CG	SH	SV	IP	H	H/G	HR	BB	SO	RAT	ERA	ERA+	OAV	OOB	PR	/A	PF	CPI	FA	E	DP	FW	PW	BW	SBW	DIF
EAST																										
STL	25	10	47	1465¹	1420	8.7	94	502	689	11.9	3.37	107	.257	.322	37	40	101	105	**.981**	124	169	.9	4.2	1.8	**-1.2**	5.3
PHI	**38**	13	33	1456¹	1395	8.6	86	472	**1002**	11.7	3.61	102	.254	.316	-1	9	102	93	**.981**	121	138	1.1	.9	.0	-1.3	7.2
MON	34	10	43	1460²	1371	8.4	110	**448**	936	11.3	3.31	**110**	.249	.308	46	**52**	101	99	.980	122	117	1.1	**5.5**	4.1	-1.6	-4.0
PIT	19	7	39	1466²	1434	8.8	118	521	933	12.2	3.81	97	.257	.323	-14	-17	103	96	.977	145	133	-.3	-1.8	6.2	-1.7	.6
CHI	9	7	43	1447¹	1510	9.4	125	452	764	12.4	3.92	95	.272	.330	-50	-29	104	102	.979	132	110	.5	-3.0	-2.1	-1.4	-1.9
NY	15	5	37	1447¹	1508	9.4	119	582	759	13.1	3.88	94	.272	.343	-44	-40	101	**109**	.972	175	134	-2.0	-4.2	-7.2	-1.7	-.8
WEST																										
ATL	15	11	**51**	1463	1484	9.1	126	502	813	12.4	3.82	98	.267	.330	-35	-14	104	103	.979	137	**186**	.2	-1.5	.5	-1.6	10.4
LA	37	**16**	28	1488¹	1356	**8.2**	**81**	468	932	**11.2**	3.26	106	**.243**	**.304**	56	34	96	92	.979	139	131	.0	3.6	**6.7**	-1.5	-1.9
SF	18	4	45	1465¹	1507	9.3	109	466	810	12.3	3.64	99	.269	.328	-5	-6	100	106	.973	173	125	-1.9	-.6	2.9	-1.9	7.5
SD	20	11	41	1476	1348	**8.2**	139	502	765	11.4	3.52	97	**.243**	.309	12	-16	95	96	.976	152	142	-.7	-1.7	-1.3	-1.5	5.1
HOU	37	**16**	31	1446²	**1338**	8.3	87	479	899	11.5	3.42	97	.246	.311	29	-15	92	94	.978	136	154	.3	-1.6	-3.6	-1.5	2.4
CIN	22	7	31	1460¹	1414	8.7	105	570	998	12.4	3.66	101	.257	.330	-9	6	103	102	.980	128	158	.7	.6	-7.9	-1.7	-11.7
TOT	289	117	469	17543¹		8.8				12.0	3.60		.258	.322					.978	1684	1697					

Runs		Hits		Doubles		Triples		Home Runs		Total Bases	
L.Smith-StL	120	Oliver-Mon	204	Oliver-Mon	43	Thon-Hou	10	Kingman-NY	37	Oliver-Mon	317
Murphy-Atl	113	Buckner-Chi	201	Kennedy-SD	42	Wilson-NY	9	Murphy-Atl	36	Guerrero-LA	308
Schmidt-Phi	108	Dawson-Mon	183	Dawson-Mon	37	Puhl-Hou	9	Schmidt-Phi	35	Murphy-Atl	303
Dawson-Mon	107	L.Smith-StL	182	Knight-Hou	36	Moreno-Pit	9	Horner-Atl	32	Dawson-Mon	303
Sandberg-Chi	103	Ray-Pit	182					Guerrero-LA	32	Buckner-Chi	290

Runs Batted In		Runs Produced		Bases On Balls		Batting Average		On Base Percentage		Slugging Average	
Oliver-Mon	109	Murphy-Atl	186	Schmidt-Phi	107	Oliver-Mon	.331	Schmidt-Phi	.407	Schmidt-Phi	.547
Murphy-Atl	109	Buckner-Chi	183	Thompson-Pit	101	Madlock-Pit	.319	Hernandez-StL	.404	Guerrero-LA	.536
Buckner-Chi	105	L.Smith-StL	181	Hernandez-StL	100	Durham-Chi	.312	Morgan-SF	.402	Durham-Chi	.521
Hendrick-StL	104	Oliver-Mon	177	Murphy-Atl	93	L.Smith-StL	.307	Thompson-Pit	.397	Oliver-Mon	.514
Clark-SF	103	Madlock-Pit	168	Clark-SF	90	Buckner-Chi	.306	Oliver-Mon	.394	Thompson-Pit	.511

Production		Adjusted Production		Batter Runs		Adjusted Batter Runs		Clutch Hitting Index		Runs Created	
Schmidt-Phi	.954	Schmidt-Phi	161	Schmidt-Phi	47.2	Schmidt-Phi	45.7	Hernandez-StL	150	Oliver-Mon	125
Guerrero-LA	.915	Guerrero-LA	157	Oliver-Mon	42.7	Guerrero-LA	42.0	Hendrick-StL	149	Guerrero-LA	120
Durham-Chi	.910	Oliver-Mon	149	Thompson-Pit	40.7	Oliver-Mon	41.3	DeJesus-Phi	133	Murphy-Atl	118
Oliver-Mon	.908	Lezcano-SD	149	Guerrero-LA	40.3	Thompson-Pit	38.5	Lezcano-SD	124	Schmidt-Phi	118
Thompson-Pit	.908	Durham-Chi	148	Murphy-Atl	37.8	Durham-Chi	36.0	Salazar-SD	124	Thompson-Pit	117

Total Average		Stolen Bases		Stolen Base Average		Stolen Base Runs		Fielding Runs		Total Player Rating	
Schmidt-Phi	1.026	Raines-Mon	78	Bailor-NY	87.0	Raines-Mon	13.8	O.Smith-StL	33.1	Schmidt-Phi	6.3
Guerrero-LA	.959	L.Smith-StL	68	Morgan-SF	85.7	Wilson-NY	7.8	Hubbard-Atl	19.9	Guerrero-LA	5.0
Thompson-Pit	.951	Moreno-Pit	60	Wiggins-SD	84.6	Wiggins-SD	6.3	Schmidt-Phi	18.8	Carter-Mon	4.9
Morgan-SF	.923	Wilson-NY	58	Matthews-Phi	84.0	Thon-Hou	6.3	Ramirez-Atl	16.5	Dawson-Mon	4.2
Durham-Chi	.917	S.Sax-LA	49	O.Smith-StL	83.3	Dawson-Mon	5.7	Salazar-SD	16.2	O.Smith-StL	4.1

Wins		Win Percentage		Games		Complete Games		Shutouts		Saves	
Carlton-Phi	23	Niekro-Atl	.810	Tekulve-Pit	85	Carlton-Phi	19	Carlton-Phi	6	Sutter-StL	36
Valenzuela-LA	19	Rogers-Mon	.704	Minton-SF	78	Valenzuela-LA	18	Niekro-Hou	5	Minton-SF	30
Rogers-Mon	19	Carlton-Phi	.676	Scurry-Pit	76	Niekro-Hou	16	Andujar-StL	5	Garber-Atl	30
Reuss-LA	18	Lollar-SD	.640	Reardon-Mon	75	Rogers-Mon	14			Reardon-Mon	26
		Forsch-StL	.625	Hernandez-Chi	75	Soto-Cin	13			Tekulve-Pit	20

Innings Pitched		Fewest Hits/Game		Fewest BB/Game		Strikeouts		Strikeouts/Game		Ratio	
Carlton-Phi	295.2	Ryan-Hou	7.05	Bird-Chi	1.41	Carlton-Phi	286	Soto-Cin	9.57	Soto-Cin	9.68
Valenzuela-LA	285.0	Soto-Cin	7.06	Hammaker-SF	1.44	Soto-Cin	274	Ryan-Hou	8.81	Niekro-Hou	9.77
Rogers-Mon	277.0	Lea-Mon	7.35	Andujar-StL	1.69	Ryan-Hou	245	Carlton-Phi	8.71	Andujar-StL	9.96
Niekro-Hou	270.0	Lollar-SD	7.43	Reuss-LA	1.77	Valenzuela-LA	199	Candelaria-Pit	6.85	Sutton-Hou	9.97
Andujar-StL	265.2	Niekro-Hou	7.47	Candelaria-Pit	1.91	Rogers-Mon	179	Welch-LA	6.72	Reuss-LA	10.04

Earned Run Average		Adjusted ERA		Opponents' Batting Avg.		Opponents' On Base Pct.		Starter Runs		Adjusted Starter Runs	
Rogers-Mon	2.40	Rogers-Mon	151	Ryan-Hou	.213	Soto-Cin	.273	Rogers-Mon	36.8	Rogers-Mon	38.0
Niekro-Hou	2.47	Andujar-StL	146	Soto-Cin	.215	Reuss-LA	.278	Niekro-Hou	34.0	Andujar-StL	33.8
Andujar-StL	2.47	Niekro-Hou	134	Lea-Mon	.222	Sutton-Hou	.279	Andujar-StL	33.3	Soto-Cin	25.9
Soto-Cin	2.79	Soto-Cin	132	Lollar-SD	.224	Niekro-Hou	.279	Soto-Cin	23.1	Niekro-Hou	25.5
Valenzuela-LA	2.87	Candelaria-Pit	126	Niekro-Hou	.229	Andujar-StL	.282	Valenzuela-LA	23.0	Valenzuela-LA	18.8

Clutch Pitching Index		Relief Runs		Adjusted Relief Runs		Relief Ranking		Total Pitcher Index		Total Baseball Ranking	
Camp-Atl	124	Minton-SF	24.2	Minton-SF	24.1	Minton-SF	37.9	Rogers-Mon	4.3	Schmidt-Phi	6.3
Jenkins-Chi	121	Scurry-Pit	21.5	Scurry-Pit	22.7	Garber-Atl	35.5	Andujar-StL	3.8	Guerrero-LA	5.0
Krukow-Phi	120	Reardon-Mon	18.6	Bedrosian-Atl	20.1	Reardon-Mon	27.6	Soto-Cin	2.7	Carter-Mon	4.9
Gale-SF	114	Bedrosian-Atl	18.1	Reardon-Mon	19.1	DeLeon-SD	24.8	Minton-SF	2.7	Rogers-Mon	4.3
Mura-StL	110	DeLeon-SD	17.8	Garber-Atl	18.5	Scurry-Pit	24.6	Valenzuela-LA	2.6	Dawson-Mon	4.2

TEAM	G	W	L	PCT	GB	R	OR	AB	H	2B	3B	HR	BB	SO	AVG	OBP	SLG	PRO	PRO+	BR	/A	PF	CHI	RC	SB	CS	SBA	SBR
EAST																												
MIL	163	95	67	.586		**891**	717	5733	1599	277	41	**216**	484	714	.279	.337	**.455**	**.792**	122	109	154	94	105	**865**	84	52	61	-20
BAL	163	94	68	.580	1	774	687	5557	1478	259	27	179	634	796	.266	.344	.419	.763	108	67	69	100	96	795	49	38	38	-10
BOS	162	89	73	.549	6	753	713	5596	1536	271	31	136	547	736	.274	.342	.407	.749	99	39	-3	106	98	755	42	39	51	-18
DET	162	83	79	.512	12	729	685	5590	1489	237	40	177	470	807	.266	.326	.418	.744	102	15	12	100	99	752	93	66	56	-13
NY	162	79	83	.488	16	709	716	5526	1417	225	37	161	590	719	.256	.331	.398	.729	100	-4	7	98	98	716	69	45	45	-13
TOR	162	78	84	.481	17	651	701	5526	1447	262	45	106	415	749	.262	.317	.383	.700	83	-69	-134	109	102	655	118	81	**64**	-13
CLE	162	78	84	.481	17	683	748	5559	1458	225	32	109	**651**	626	.262	.343	.373	.716	97	-12	-8	100	93	723	151	68	52	-10
WEST																												
CAL	162	93	69	.574		814	**670**	5532	1518	268	26	186	613	760	.274	**.350**	.433	.783	114	108	108	100	96	834	55	53	50	-13
KC	162	90	72	.556	3	784	717	5629	**1603**	295	58	132	442	758	**.285**	.340	.428	.768	108	67	66	100	99	802	133	48	49	-14
CHI	162	87	75	.537	6	786	710	5575	1523	266	52	136	533	866	.273	.340	.413	.753	106	43	43	100	102	784	136	58	54	-14
SEA	162	76	86	.469	17	651	712	5626	1431	259	33	130	456	806	.254	.313	.381	.694	86	-83	-103	103	102	657	131	82	60	-10
OAK	162	68	94	.420	25	691	819	5448	1286	211	27	149	582	948	.236	.312	.367	.679	89	-105	-73	96	**113**	644	**232**	87	59	**-8**
TEX	162	64	98	.395	29	590	749	5445	1354	204	26	115	447	750	.249	.309	.359	.668	87	-127	-91	95	102	593	63	45	43	-11
MIN	162	60	102	.370	33	657	819	5544	1427	234	44	148	474	887	.257	.319	.396	.715	92	-42	-61	103	98	676	38	33	43	-15
TOT	1135					10163		77886	20566	3493	519	2080	7338	10922	.264	.330	.402	.733							1394	795	64	-58

TEAM	CG	SH	SV	IP	H	H/G	HR	BB	SO	RAT	ERA	ERA+	OAV	OOB	PR	/A	PF	CPI	FA	E	DP	FW	PW	BW	SBW	DIF
EAST																										
MIL	34	6	**47**	1467¹	1514	9.3	152	511	717	12.5	3.98	95	.269	.333	15	-32	93	106	.980	125	**185**	.1	-3.2	**15.4**	-1.6	3.3
BAL	38	8	34	1462¹	1436	8.8	147	488	719	12.0	3.99	101	.257	**.319**	13	7	99	95	**.984**	101	140	1.4	.7	6.9	-.6	4.6
BOS	23	11	33	1453	1557	9.6	155	478	816	12.8	4.03	107	.275	.323	6	44	106	108	.981	121	172	.3	4.4	-.3	-1.4	5.0
DET	**45**	5	27	1451	**1371**	**8.5**	172	554	741	12.1	**3.80**	107	**.251**	.323	**43**	41	100	104	.981	117	165	.5	4.1	1.2	-.9	-2.9
NY	24	8	39	1459	1471	9.1	113	491	939	12.2	3.99	100	.263	.325	13	-1	99	95	.979	128	158	-.0	-.1	.7	-.9	-1.6
TOR	41	**13**	25	1443²	1428	8.9	147	493	776	12.1	3.95	**113**	.257	.320	20	**85**	110	97	.978	136	146	-.5	**8.5**	-13.4	-.9	3.3
CLE	31	9	30	1468¹	1433	8.8	122	589	882	12.5	4.11	99	.257	.330	-5	-4	100	94	.980	123	129	.2	-.4	-.8	-.6	-1.4
WEST																										
CAL	40	10	27	1464	1436	8.8	124	482	728	**12.0**	3.82	106	.258	.322	41	38	100	98	.983	108	171	1.0	3.8	10.8	-.9	-2.7
KC	16	12	45	1431	1443	9.1	163	471	650	12.2	4.08	100	.261	.322	-1	0	100	98	.979	127	140	-.0	.0	6.6	-1.0	3.4
CHI	30	10	41	1439	1502	9.4	**99**	**460**	753	12.4	3.87	104	.269	.328	33	26	99	100	.976	154	173	-1.5	2.6	4.3	-1.0	1.6
SEA	23	11	39	1476¹	1431	8.7	173	547	**1002**	12.3	3.88	109	.256	.325	32	59	100	104	.978	139	158	-.7	5.9	-10.3	-.6	.7
OAK	42	6	22	1456	1506	9.3	177	648	697	13.5	4.54	86	.267	.346	-76	-103	96	100	.974	160	140	-1.8	-10.3	-7.3	-.4	6.8
TEX	32	5	24	1431	1554	9.8	128	483	690	13.1	4.28	90	.280	.342	-33	-65	95	102	.981	121	169	.3	-6.5	-9.1	-.7	-1.0
MIN	26	7	30	1433	1484	9.3	208	643	812	13.4	4.72	90	.269	.346	-103	-76	104	101	.982	108	162	1.0	-7.6	-6.1	-1.1	-7.2
TOT	445	121	463	20335		9.1				12.5	4.07		.264	.330					.980	1768	2208					

Runs
Molitor-Mil	136
Yount-Mil	129
Evans-Bos	122
Henderson-Oak	119
Downing-Cal	109

Hits
Yount-Mil	210
Cooper-Mil	205
Molitor-Mil	201
Wilson-KC	194
McRae-KC	189

Doubles
Yount-Mil	46
McRae-KC	46
White-KC	45
DeCinces-Cal	42
Cowens-Sea	39

Triples
Wilson-KC	15
Herndon-Det	13
Yount-Mil	12
Mumphrey-NY	10

Home Runs
Thomas-Mil	39
R.Jackson-Cal	39
Winfield-NY	37
Oglivie-Mil	34

Total Bases
Yount-Mil	367
Cooper-Mil	345
McRae-KC	332
Evans-Bos	325
DeCinces-Cal	315

Runs Batted In
McRae-KC	133
Cooper-Mil	121
Thornton-Cle	116
Yount-Mil	114
Thomas-Mil	112

Runs Produced
Yount-Mil	214
McRae-KC	197
Cooper-Mil	193
Molitor-Mil	188
Evans-Bos	188

Bases On Balls
Henderson-Oak	116
Evans-Bos	112
Thornton-Cle	109
Hargrove-Cle	101
Murphy-Oak	94

Batting Average
Wilson-KC	.332
Yount-Mil	.331
Carew-Cal	.319
Murray-Bal	.316
Cooper-Mil	.313

On Base Percentage
Evans-Bos	.403
Harrah-Cle	.400
Henderson-Oak	.399
Carew-Cal	.399
Murray-Bal	.395

Slugging Average
Yount-Mil	.578
Winfield-NY	.560
Murray-Bal	.549
DeCinces-Cal	.548
McRae-KC	.542

Production
Yount-Mil	.962
Murray-Bal	.944
Evans-Bos	.937
DeCinces-Cal	.922
McRae-KC	.912

Adjusted Production
Yount-Mil	170
Murray-Bal	157
DeCinces-Cal	149
R.Jackson-Cal	147
McRae-KC	146

Batter Runs
Yount-Mil	50.3
Evans-Bos	48.5
Murray-Bal	42.5
DeCinces-Cal	38.1
Harrah-Cle	38.0

Adjusted Batter Runs
Yount-Mil	55.4
Evans-Bos	43.6
Murray-Bal	42.8
Harrah-Cle	38.4
DeCinces-Cal	38.1

Clutch Hitting Index
Otis-KC	160
Foli-Cal	143
Wathan-KC	138
McRae-KC	136
Luzinski-Chi	136

Runs Created
Yount-Mil	136
Evans-Bos	134
Harrah-Cle	123
McRae-KC	123
Cooper-Mil	118

Total Average
Evans-Bos	.976
Yount-Mil	.969
Murray-Bal	.957
Henderson-Oak	.934
Harrah-Cle	.931

Stolen Bases
Henderson-Oak	130
Garcia-Tor	54
J.Cruz-Sea	46
Molitor-Mil	41
Wilson-KC	37

Stolen Base Average
Sexton-Oak	100.0
Fisk-Chi	89.5
Dilone-Cle	86.8
Harrah-Cle	85.0
Brown-Sea	82.4

Stolen Base Runs
Henderson-Oak	13.8
Molitor-Mil	6.9
Dilone-Cle	6.9
J.Cruz-Sea	6.0
Wathan-KC	5.4

Fielding Runs
Bell-Tex	34.4
Almon-Chi	26.0
Bernazard-Chi	24.6
DeCinces-Cal	18.9
T.Cruz-Sea	17.1

Total Player Rating
Yount-Mil	6.5
DeCinces-Cal	5.2
Bell-Tex	5.1
Murray-Bal	4.0
Evans-Bos	3.8

Wins
Hoyt-Chi	19
Zahn-Cal	18
Vuckovich-Mil	18
Gura-KC	18

Win Percentage
Vuckovich-Mil	.750
Palmer-Bal	.750
Zahn-Cal	.692
Petry-Det	.625
Gura-KC	.600

Games
VandeBerg-Sea	78
F.Martinez-Sea	76
Quisenberry-KC	72
Caudill-Sea	70
Spillner-Cle	65

Complete Games
Stieb-Tor	19
Morris-Det	17
Langford-Oak	15
Hoyt-Chi	14

Shutouts
Stieb-Tor	5
Zahn-Cal	4
Forsch-Cal	4

Saves
Quisenberry-KC	35
Gossage-NY	30
Fingers-Mil	29
Caudill-Sea	26
Davis-Min	22

Innings Pitched
Stieb-Tor	288.1
Clancy-Tor	266.2
Morris-Det	266.1
Caldwell-Mil	258.0
J.Martinez-Bal	252.0

Fewest Hits/Game
Sutcliffe-Cle	7.25
Ujdur-Det	7.58
Righetti-NY	7.62
Palmer-Bal	7.73
Barker-Cle	7.76

Fewest BB/Game
John-NY-Cal	1.58
Eckersley-Bos	1.73
Hoyt-Chi	1.80
Haas-Mil	1.82
Langford-Oak	1.86

Strikeouts
Bannister-Sea	209
Barker-Cle	187
Righetti-NY	163
Guidry-NY	162
Tudor-Bos	146

Strikeouts/Game
Righetti-NY	8.02
Bannister-Sea	7.62
Beattie-Sea	7.31
Barker-Cle	6.88
Tudor-Bos	6.72

Ratio
Palmer-Bal	10.39
Eckersley-Bos	10.95
Stieb-Tor	10.96
Barker-Cle	11.11
Bannister-Sea	11.11

Earned Run Average
Sutcliffe-Cle	2.96
Stanley-Bos	3.10
Palmer-Bal	3.13
Petry-Det	3.22
Stieb-Tor	3.25

Adjusted ERA
Stanley-Bos	139
Stieb-Tor	138
Sutcliffe-Cle	138
Palmer-Bal	129
Beattie-Sea	127

Opponents' Batting Avg.
Sutcliffe-Cle	.226
Righetti-NY	.229
Ujdur-Det	.230
Palmer-Bal	.231
Barker-Cle	.232

Opponents' On Base Pct.
Palmer-Bal	.287
Eckersley-Bos	.297
Stieb-Tor	.299
Barker-Cle	.301
Clancy-Tor	.302

Starter Runs
Sutcliffe-Cle	26.8
Stieb-Tor	26.5
Palmer-Bal	23.7
Petry-Det	23.3
Vuckovich-Mil	18.2

Adjusted Starter Runs
Stieb-Tor	39.4
Sutcliffe-Cle	26.9
Petry-Det	23.0
Palmer-Bal	22.7
Clancy-Tor	22.6

Clutch Pitching Index
Vuckovich-Mil	131
Tudor-Bos	121
Dotson-Chi	118
Wilcox-Det	113
Stanley-Bos	110

Relief Runs
Spillner-Cle	23.5
Quisenberry-KC	22.9
Burgmeier-Bos	20.3
Gossage-NY	19.1
Caudill-Sea	18.3

Adjusted Relief Runs
Spillner-Cle	23.6
Quisenberry-KC	23.0
Burgmeier-Bos	23.0
Stanley-Bos	22.5
Caudill-Sea	20.1

Relief Ranking
Caudill-Sea	51.9
Spillner-Cle	43.2
Quisenberry-KC	37.4
Clear-Bos	34.6
Gossage-NY	29.0

Total Pitcher Index
Stieb-Tor	4.6
Quisenberry-KC	3.0
Sutcliffe-Cle	2.9
Petry-Det	2.9
Stanley-Bos	2.8

Total Baseball Ranking
Yount-Mil	6.5
DeCinces-Cal	5.2
Bell-Tex	5.1
Stieb-Tor	4.6
Murray-Bal	4.0

TEAM	G	W	L	PCT	GB	R	OR	AB	H	2B	3B	HR	BB	SO	AVG	OBP	SLG	PRO	PRO+	BR	/A	PF	CHI	RC	SB	CS	SBA	SBR
EAST																												
PHI	163	90	72	.556		696	635	5426	1352	209	45	125	**640**	906	.249	.331	.373	.704	102	17	25	99	101	676	143	75	56	-10
PIT	162	84	78	.519	6	659	648	5531	1460	238	29	121	497	873	.264	.327	.383	.710	100	17	0	103	96	682	124	77	58	-11
MON	163	82	80	.506	8	677	646	5611	1482	**297**	41	102	509	**733**	.264	.329	.386	.715	104	30	34	99	95	716	138	44	43	-12
STL	162	79	83	.488	11	679	710	5550	**1496**	262	**63**	83	543	879	.270	.337	.384	.721	**106**	47	**47**	100	94	725	**207**	89	**67**	-13
CHI	162	71	91	.438	19	701	719	5512	1436	272	42	140	470	868	.261	.322	**.401**	.723	101	35	3	105	100	707	84	40	37	-9
NY	162	68	94	.420	22	575	680	5444	1314	172	26	112	436	1031	.241	.301	.344	.645	84	-111	-104	99	107	562	141	64	63	-18
WEST																												
LA	163	91	71	.562		654	**609**	5440	1358	197	34	**146**	541	925	.250	.320	.379	.699	99	-5	-1	99	99	663	166	76	55	-9
ATL	162	88	74	.543	3	**746**	640	5472	1489	218	45	130	582	847	**.272**	**.344**	**.400**	**.744**	104	**91**	41	107	98	**744**	146	88	62	-10
HOU	162	85	77	.525	6	643	646	5502	1412	239	60	97	517	869	.257	.323	.375	.698	105	-6	35	94	97	673	164	95	61	**-7**
SD	163	81	81	.500	10	653	653	5527	1384	207	34	93	482	822	.250	.313	.351	.664	93	-73	-49	97	**110**	609	179	67	52	-10
SF	162	79	83	.488	12	687	697	5369	1324	206	30	142	619	990	.247	.328	.375	.703	104	11	32	97	102	662	140	78	60	-12
CIN	162	74	88	.457	17	623	710	5333	1274	236	35	107	588	1006	.239	.317	.356	.673	88	-48	-70	104	103	606	154	77	56	-10
TOT	974					7993		65717	16781	2753	484	1398	6424	10749	.255	.324	.376	.700							1786	870	67	14

TEAM	CG	SH	SV	IP	H	H/G	HR	BB	SO	RAT	ERA	ERA+	OAV	OOB	PR	/A	PF	CPI	FA	E	DP	FW	PW	BW	SBW	DIF
EAST																										
PHI	20	10	41	1461²	1429	8.8	111	464	**1092**	11.8	3.34	107	.256	.315	46	36	98	103	.976	152	117	-.7	3.8	2.6	-1.2	4.5
PIT	25	14	41	1462¹	1378	8.5	109	563	1061	12.1	3.55	104	.251	.323	12	24	102	99	**.982**	115	165	1.4	2.5	.0	-1.3	.3
MON	**38**	**15**	34	1471	1406	8.6	120	479	899	11.7	3.58	100	.254	.317	7	1	99	98	.981	116	130	1.4	.1	3.6	-1.4	-2.7
STL	22	10	27	1460²	1479	9.1	115	525	709	12.5	3.79	96	.266	.332	-26	-29	100	102	.976	152	173	-.8	-3.0	**4.9**	-1.5	-1.6
CHI	9	10	42	1428²	1496	9.4	117	498	807	12.7	4.08	93	.273	.337	-71	-45	105	100	**.982**	115	164	1.4	-4.7	.3	-1.1	-6.0
NY	18	7	33	1451	1384	8.6	97	615	717	12.5	3.68	99	.255	.333	-8	-8	100	100	.976	151	171	-.7	-.8	-10.9	-2.0	1.4
WEST																										
LA	27	12	40	1464	1336	8.2	97	495	1000	**11.4**	**3.10**	**116**	.244	**.309**	84	79	99	101	.974	168	132	-1.7	**8.3**	-.1	-1.1	4.6
ATL	18	4	**48**	1440²	1412	8.8	132	540	895	12.3	3.67	106	.259	.329	-7	34	107	**105**	.978	137	**176**	.1	3.6	4.3	-1.2	.2
HOU	22	14	**48**	1466¹	**1276**	**7.8**	**94**	570	904	11.5	3.45	99	**.236**	.312	28	-7	94	90	.977	147	165	-.5	-.7	3.7	**-.9**	2.4
SD	23	5	44	1467²	1389	8.5	144	528	850	11.9	3.62	96	.253	.321	1	-21	96	102	.979	129	135	.6	-2.2	-5.1	-1.2	7.8
SF	20	9	47	1445²	1431	8.9	127	520	881	12.3	3.70	96	.259	.326	-11	-26	97	101	.973	171	109	-1.9	-2.7	3.3	-1.4	.7
CIN	34	5	29	1441¹	1365	8.5	135	627	934	12.6	3.98	95	.252	.332	-57	-28	105	97	.981	**114**	121	**1.5**	-2.9	-7.3	-1.2	2.9
TOT	276	115	474	17461		8.6				12.1	3.63		.255	.324					.978	1667	1758					

Runs		Hits		Doubles		Triples		Home Runs		Total Bases	
Raines-Mon	133	Dawson-Mon	189	Ray-Pit	38	Butler-Atl	13	Schmidt-Phi	40	Dawson-Mon	341
Murphy-Atl	131	Cruz-Hou	189	Oliver-Mon	38	Moreno-Hou	11	Murphy-Atl	36	Murphy-Atl	318
Schmidt-Phi	104	Ramirez-Atl	185	Buckner-Chi	38	Green-StL	10	Guerrero-LA	32	Guerrero-LA	310
Dawson-Mon	104	Oliver-Mon	184	Carter-Mon	37	Dawson-Mon	10	Dawson-Mon	32	Thon-Hou	283
		Raines-Mon	183					Evans-SF	30	Schmidt-Phi	280

Runs Batted In		Runs Produced		Bases On Balls		Batting Average		On Base Percentage		Slugging Average	
Murphy-Atl	121	Murphy-Atl	216	Schmidt-Phi	128	Madlock-Pit	.323	Schmidt-Phi	.402	Murphy-Atl	.540
Dawson-Mon	113	Raines-Mon	193	Thompson-Pit	99	L.Smith-StL	.321	Hernandez-StL-NY	.398	Dawson-Mon	.539
Schmidt-Phi	109	Dawson-Mon	185	Raines-Mon	97	Cruz-Hou	.318	Murphy-Atl	.396	Guerrero-LA	.531
Guerrero-LA	103	Schmidt-Phi	173	Murphy-Atl	90	Hendrick-StL	.318	Raines-Mon	.395	Schmidt-Phi	.524
Kennedy-SD	98	Cruz-Hou	163	Morgan-Phi	89	Knight-Hou	.304	Madlock-Pit	.389	Evans-SF	.516

Production		Adjusted Production		Batter Runs		Adjusted Batter Runs		Clutch Hitting Index		Runs Created	
Murphy-Atl	.936	Schmidt-Phi	156	Murphy-Atl	46.2	Schmidt-Phi	44.1	Kennedy-SD	142	Murphy-Atl	131
Schmidt-Phi	.926	Evans-SF	151	Schmidt-Phi	43.2	Murphy-Atl	40.7	Garner-Hou	134	Raines-Mon	120
Guerrero-LA	.908	Guerrero-LA	150	Guerrero-LA	37.8	Guerrero-LA	38.2	McGee-StL	131	Guerrero-LA	118
Evans-SF	.896	Murphy-Atl	146	Evans-SF	33.0	Evans-SF	35.1	Concepcion-Cin	130	Schmidt-Phi	117
Dawson-Mon	.886	Cruz-Hou	143	Dawson-Mon	32.4	Dawson-Mon	32.8	Oliver-Mon	128	Dawson-Mon	113

Total Average		Stolen Bases		Stolen Base Average		Stolen Base Runs		Fielding Runs		Total Player Rating	
Murphy-Atl	1.014	Raines-Mon	90	Morgan-Phi	90.0	Raines-Mon	18.6	Sandberg-Chi	41.1	Schmidt-Phi	6.1
Schmidt-Phi	.986	Wiggins-SD	66	Murphy-Atl	88.2	Wiggins-SD	12.0	Schmidt-Phi	23.3	Thon-Hou	5.7
Raines-Mon	.959	S.Sax-LA	56	Raines-Mon	86.5	McGee-StL	6.9	Thon-Hou	20.8	Raines-Mon	5.6
Guerrero-LA	.935	Wilson-NY	54	Bailor-NY	85.7	Wilson-NY	6.6	Hubbard-Atl	20.7	Murphy-Atl	4.3
Evans-SF	.908	L.Smith-StL	43	Wiggins-SD	83.5	Murphy-Atl	6.6	Buckner-Chi	20.6	Guerrero-LA	4.3

Wins		Win Percentage		Games		Complete Games		Shutouts		Saves	
Denny-Phi	19	Denny-Phi	.760	Campbell-Chi	82	Soto-Cin	18	Rogers-Mon	5	Smith-Phi	29
Soto-Cin	17	Perez-Atl	.652	Tekulve-Pit	76	Rogers-Mon	13	Valenzuela-LA	4	Holland-Phi	25
Rogers-Mon	17	McWilliams-Pit	.652	Hernandez-Chi-Phi	74	Gullickson-Mon	10	McWilliams-Pit	4	Minton-SF	22
Gullickson-Mon	17	Candelaria-Pit	.652	Scherrer-Cin	73			Lea-Mon	4	Sutter-StL	21
Lea-Mon	16	McMurtry-Atl	.625	Minton-SF	73					Reardon-Mon	21

Innings Pitched		Fewest Hits/Game		Fewest BB/Game		Strikeouts		Strikeouts/Game		Ratio	
Carlton-Phi	283.2	Ryan-Hou	6.14	Hammaker-SF	1.67	Carlton-Phi	275	Carlton-Phi	8.73	Hammaker-SF	9.50
Soto-Cin	273.2	Soto-Cin	6.81	Ruthven-Phi-Chi	1.87	Soto-Cin	242	Ryan-Hou	8.39	Soto-Cin	10.10
Rogers-Mon	273.0	Welch-LA	7.24	Denny-Phi	1.97	McWilliams-Pit	199	Soto-Cin	7.96	Pena-LA	10.37
Niekro-Hou	263.2	Hammaker-SF	7.68	Reuss-LA	2.01	Valenzuela-LA	189	McWilliams-Pit	7.53	Welch-LA	10.54
Valenzuela-LA	257.0	Pena-LA	7.73	Candelaria-Pit	2.05	Ryan-Hou	183	Berenyi-Cin	7.29	Denny-Phi	10.61

Earned Run Average		Adjusted ERA		Opponents' Batting Avg.		Opponents' On Base Pct.		Starter Runs		Adjusted Starter Runs	
Hammaker-SF	2.25	Hammaker-SF	157	Ryan-Hou	.195	Hammaker-SF	.267	Denny-Phi	33.8	Soto-Cin	33.7
Denny-Phi	2.37	Denny-Phi	150	Soto-Cin	.208	Soto-Cin	.280	Soto-Cin	28.3	Denny-Phi	32.1
Welch-LA	2.65	Soto-Cin	141	Welch-LA	.222	Pena-LA	.285	Hammaker-SF	26.4	Hammaker-SF	24.6
Soto-Cin	2.70	Welch-LA	136	Hammaker-SF	.228	Welch-LA	.294	Welch-LA	22.2	Welch-LA	21.4
Pena-LA	2.75	Pena-LA	131	Pena-LA	.229	Denny-Phi	.294	Smith-Mon	19.6	McMurtry-Atl	19.8

Clutch Pitching Index		Relief Runs		Adjusted Relief Runs		Relief Ranking		Total Pitcher Index		Total Baseball Ranking	
Rhoden-Pit	119	Orosco-NY	26.3	Orosco-NY	26.3	Orosco-NY	52.2	Denny-Phi	3.8	Schmidt-Phi	6.1
Niekro-Atl	117	Smith-Chi	22.6	Smith-Chi	24.5	Smith-Chi	45.4	Soto-Cin	3.3	Thon-Hou	5.7
Reuss-LA	116	Tekulve-Pit	21.9	Tekulve-Pit	22.7	Tekulve-Pit	34.1	Orosco-NY	3.0	Raines-Mon	5.6
Denny-Phi	115	Niedenfuer-LA	18.1	Niedenfuer-LA	17.8	Howe-LA	33.3	Reuss-LA	2.8	Murphy-Atl	4.3
Knepper-Hou	111	Howe-LA	16.7	Howe-LA	16.4	Holland-Phi	23.8	Hammaker-SF	2.6	Guerrero-LA	4.3

TEAM	G	W	L	PCT	GB	R	OR	AB	H	2B	3B	HR	BB	SO	AVG	OBP	SLG	PRO	PRO+	BR	/A	PF	CHI	RC	SB	CS	SBA	SBR
EAST																												
BAL	162	98	64	.605		799	652	5546	1492	283	27	**168**	601	800	.269	**.343**	.421	.764	111	70	83	98	99	794	61	33	43	-15
DET	162	92	70	.568	6	789	679	5592	1530	283	53	156	508	831	.274	.338	.427	.765	111	67	86	97	99	799	93	53	55	-16
NY	162	91	71	.562	7	770	703	5631	1535	269	40	153	533	686	.273	.339	.416	.755	110	52	79	96	98	783	84	42	43	-12
TOR	162	89	73	.549	9	795	726	5581	1546	268	58	167	510	810	**.277**	.341	**.436**	**.777**	105	89	44	106	97	818	131	72	63	-15
MIL	162	87	75	.537	11	764	708	5620	**1556**	281	57	132	475	665	**.277**	.336	.418	.754	**114**	44	99	92	98	774	101	49	44	-11
BOS	162	78	84	.481	20	724	775	5590	1512	**287**	32	142	536	758	.270	.337	.409	.746	97	35	-17	107	94	749	30	26	37	-13
CLE	162	70	92	.432	28	704	785	5476	1451	249	31	86	**605**	691	.265	.341	.369	.710	91	-22	-49	104	99	687	109	71	**66**	-17
WEST																												
CHI	162	99	63	.611		**800**	650	5484	1439	270	42	157	527	888	.262	.332	.413	.745	100	26	0	104	**107**	762	165	50	43	-10
KC	163	79	83	.488	20	696	767	5598	1515	273	54	109	397	722	.271	.322	.397	.719	96	-30	-31	100	102	711	182	47	52	-16
TEX	163	77	85	.475	22	639	**609**	5610	1429	242	33	106	442	767	.255	.312	.366	.678	87	-107	-92	98	104	633	119	60	54	-13
OAK	162	74	88	.457	25	708	782	5516	1447	237	28	121	524	872	.262	.330	.381	.711	100	-33	9	94	102	694	**235**	98	64	**-8**
CAL	162	70	92	.432	29	722	779	5640	1467	241	22	.154	509	835	.260	.325	.393	.718	97	-28	-21	99	102	702	41	39	38	-10
MIN	162	70	92	.432	29	709	822	5601	1463	280	41	141	467	802	.261	.321	.401	.722	93	-22	-48	104	101	701	44	29	43	-16
SEA	162	60	102	.370	39	558	740	5336	1280	247	31	111	460	840	.240	.303	.360	.663	79	-134	-159	104	100	574	144	80	65	-14
TOT	1135					10177		77821	20662	3710	549	1903	7094	10967	.266	.330	.401	.731							1539	749	67	12

TEAM	CG	SH	SV	IP	H	H/G	HR	BB	SO	RAT	ERA	ERA+	OAV	OOB	PR	/A	PF	CPI	FA	E	DP	FW	PW	BW	SBW	DIF
EAST																										
BAL	36	**15**	38	1452¹	1451	9.0	130	452	774	11.9	3.63	109	.261	.318	70	52	97	104	.981	121	159	.5	5.2	8.3	-1.6	4.6
DET	42	9	28	1451	**1318**	**8.2**	170	522	875	11.6	3.80	103	**.241**	.311	41	16	96	96	.980	125	142	.3	1.6	8.6	-1.7	2.2
NY	**47**	12	32	1456²	1449	9.0	116	455	892	11.9	3.86	101	.259	.317	33	5	96	95	.978	139	157	-.5	.5	7.9	-1.3	3.4
TOR	43	8	32	1445¹	1434	8.9	145	517	835	12.4	4.12	104	.259	.327	-9	28	106	97	.981	115	148	.9	2.8	4.4	-1.6	1.5
MIL	35	10	43	1454	1513	9.4	133	491	689	12.6	4.02	93	.270	.332	6	-46	92	103	**.982**	113	162	**1.0**	-4.6	**9.9**	-1.2	.9
BOS	29	7	42	1446¹	1572	9.8	158	493	767	13.0	4.34	100	.279	.340	-44	1	107	104	.979	130	168	.0	.0	-1.7	-1.4	-1.7
CLE	34	8	25	1441²	1531	9.6	120	529	794	13.1	4.43	96	.275	.341	-59	-31	104	97	.980	122	174	.5	-3.1	-4.9	-1.8	-1.7
WEST																										
CHI	35	12	48	1445¹	1355	8.4	128	**447**	877	11.4	3.67	114	.248	**.308**	63	83	103	94	.981	120	158	.6	8.3	.0	-1.1	10.2
KC	19	8	**49**	1437²	1535	9.6	133	471	593	12.7	4.25	96	.273	.333	-30	-28	100	99	.974	165	178	-1.9	-2.8	-3.1	-1.7	7.4
TEX	43	11	32	1466²	1392	8.5	**97**	441	826	11.7	**3.31**	**121**	.251	.314	**121**	112	99	104	**.982**	113	151	**1.0**	**11.2**	-9.2	-1.4	-5.7
OAK	22	12	33	1454¹	1462	9.0	135	626	719	13.1	4.34	89	.262	.340	-45	-79	95	99	.974	157	157	-1.5	-7.9	-.9	**-.9**	2.3
CAL	39	7	23	1474	1636	10.0	130	496	668	13.2	4.31	91	.284	.343	-40	-48	99	104	.977	154	**190**	-1.3	-4.8	-2.1	-1.1	-1.7
MIN	20	5	39	1437	1559	9.8	163	580	748	13.6	4.67	91	.279	.351	-96	-66	105	102	.980	121	170	.5	-6.6	-4.8	-1.7	1.5
SEA	25	9	39	1418¹	1455	9.2	145	544	**910**	12.9	4.12	103	.268	.339	-9	21	105	**105**	.978	136	159	-.3	2.1	-15.9	-1.5	-5.4
TOT	469	133	503	20280²		9.2				12.5	4.06		.266	.330					.979	1831	2273					

Runs		**Hits**		**Doubles**		**Triples**		**Home Runs**		**Total Bases**	
Ripken-Bal	121	Ripken-Bal	211	Ripken-Bal	47	Yount-Mil	10	Rice-Bos	39	Rice-Bos	344
Murray-Bal	115	Boggs-Bos	210	Boggs-Bos	44	Herndon-Det	9	Armas-Bos	36	Ripken-Bal	343
Cooper-Mil	106	Whitaker-Det	206	Yount-Mil	42	Griffin-Tor	9	Kittle-Chi	35	Cooper-Mil	336
Henderson-Oak	105	Cooper-Mil	203	Parrish-Det	42	Gibson-Det	9	Murray-Bal	33	Murray-Bal	313
Moseby-Tor	104	Rice-Bos	191							Winfield-NY	307

Runs Batted In		**Runs Produced**		**Bases On Balls**		**Batting Average**		**On Base Percentage**		**Slugging Average**	
Rice-Bos	126	Cooper-Mil	202	Henderson-Oak	103	Boggs-Bos	.361	Boggs-Bos	.449	Brett-KC	.563
Cooper-Mil	126	Ripken-Bal	196	Singleton-Bal	99	Carew-Cal	.339	Henderson-Oak	.415	Rice-Bos	.550
Winfield-NY	116	Murray-Bal	193	Boggs-Bos	92	Whitaker-Det	.320	Carew-Cal	.411	Murray-Bal	.538
Parrish-Det	114	Winfield-NY	183	Thornton-Cle	87	Trammell-Det	.319	Murray-Bal	.398	Fisk-Chi	.518
Murray-Bal	111	Rice-Bos	177	Murray-Bal	86	Ripken-Bal	.318	Singleton-Bal	.395	Ripken-Bal	.517

Production		**Adjusted Production**		**Batter Runs**		**Adjusted Batter Runs**		**Clutch Hitting Index**		**Runs Created**	
Brett-KC	.949	Murray-Bal	158	Boggs-Bos	50.6	Murray-Bal	46.5	Simmons-Mil	145	Murray-Bal	133
Murray-Bal	.936	Brett-KC	157	Murray-Bal	44.9	Boggs-Bos	44.8	Murphy-Oak	135	Boggs-Bos	130
Boggs-Bos	.935	Yount-Mil	155	Rice-Bos	38.7	Yount-Mil	40.8	Franco-Cle	132	Ripken-Bal	120
Rice-Bos	.914	Boggs-Bos	147	Ripken-Bal	37.1	Ripken-Bal	38.7	Hargrove-Cle	130	Yount-Mil	115
Upshaw-Tor	.891	Ripken-Bal	145	Brett-KC	36.3	Brett-KC	36.1	Parrish-Det	127	Whitaker-Det	114

Total Average		**Stolen Bases**		**Stolen Base Average**		**Stolen Base Runs**		**Fielding Runs**		**Total Player Rating**	
Henderson-Oak	1.048	Henderson-Oak	108	Wilson-KC	88.1	Henderson-Oak	21.0	T.Cruz-Sea-Bal	24.7	Ripken-Bal	6.0
Murray-Bal	1.000	R.Law-Chi	77	R.Law-Chi	86.5	R.Law-Chi	15.9	Ward-Min	21.2	Henderson-Oak	5.7
Boggs-Bos	.964	Wilson-KC	59	Washington-KC	85.1	Wilson-KC	12.9	Dempsey-Bal	19.5	Boggs-Bos	5.1
Brett-KC	.964	J.Cruz-Sea-Chi	57	Henderson-Oak	85.0	J.Cruz-Sea-Chi	9.9	Brunansky-Min	18.8	Yount-Mil	4.4
Yount-Mil	.897	Sample-Tex	44			Sample-Tex	8.4	Fletcher-Chi	18.2	Murray-Bal	4.3

Wins		**Win Percentage**		**Games**		**Complete Games**		**Shutouts**		**Saves**	
Hoyt-Chi	24	Dotson-Chi	.759	Quisenberry-KC	69	Guidry-NY	21	Boddicker-Bal	5	Quisenberry-KC	45
Dotson-Chi	22	McGregor-Bal	.720	VandeBerg-Sea	68	Morris-Det	20	Stieb-Tor	4	Stanley-Bos	33
Guidry-NY	21	Hoyt-Chi	.706	Davis-Min	66	Stieb-Tor	14	Burns-Chi	4	Davis-Min	30
Morris-Det	20	Guidry-NY	.700	F.Martinez-Bal	65	Rawley-NY	13			Caudill-Sea	26
Petry-Det	19	Boddicker-Bal	.667	Stanley-Bos	64	McGregor-Bal	12			Ladd-Mil	25

Innings Pitched		**Fewest Hits/Game**		**Fewest BB/Game**		**Strikeouts**		**Strikeouts/Game**		**Ratio**	
Morris-Det	293.2	Boddicker-Bal	7.09	Hoyt-Chi	1.07	Morris-Det	232	Bannister-Chi	7.99	Hoyt-Chi	9.25
Stieb-Tor	278.0	Stieb-Tor	7.22	McGregor-Bal	1.56	Bannister-Chi	193	Morris-Det	7.11	Boddicker-Bal	9.70
Petry-Det	266.1	Conroy-Oak	7.82	John-Cal	1.88	Stieb-Tor	187	Righetti-NY	7.01	Morris-Det	10.51
Hoyt-Chi	260.2	Hough-Tex	7.82	Honeycutt-Tex	1.91	Righetti-NY	169	Conroy-Oak	6.21	Guidry-NY	10.57
McGregor-Bal	260.0	Dotson-Chi	7.84	Eckersley-Bos	1.99	Sutcliffe-Cle	160	Gott-Tor	6.16	Stieb-Tor	10.68

Earned Run Average		**Adjusted ERA**		**Opponents' Batting Avg.**		**Opponents' On Base Pct.**		**Starter Runs**		**Adjusted Starter Runs**	
Honeycutt-Tex	2.42	Honeycutt-Tex	165	Boddicker-Bal	.216	Hoyt-Chi	.262	Honeycutt-Tex	31.8	Stieb-Tor	38.8
Boddicker-Bal	2.77	Boddicker-Bal	143	Stieb-Tor	.219	Boddicker-Bal	.274	Stieb-Tor	31.4	Honeycutt-Tex	30.7
Stieb-Tor	3.04	Stieb-Tor	141	Conroy-Oak	.232	Morris-Det	.289	Boddicker-Bal	25.8	Dotson-Chi	25.6
Hough-Tex	3.18	Young-Sea	130	Bannister-Chi	.233	Guidry-NY	.291	McGregor-Bal	25.3	Boddicker-Bal	23.6
McGregor-Bal	3.18	Dotson-Chi	130	Morris-Det	.233	Stieb-Tor	.293	Hough-Tex	24.7	Hough-Tex	23.1

Clutch Pitching Index		**Relief Runs**		**Adjusted Relief Runs**		**Relief Ranking**		**Total Pitcher Index**		**Total Baseball Ranking**	
Honeycutt-Tex	139	Quisenberry-KC	32.7	Quisenberry-KC	32.9	Quisenberry-KC	41.0	Stieb-Tor	4.1	Ripken-Bal	6.0
Zahn-Cal	118	F.Martinez-Bal	19.6	Stanley-Bos	24.2	Stanley-Bos	39.4	Honeycutt-Tex	3.7	Henderson-Oak	5.7
Hurst-Bos	113	Stanley-Bos	19.6	F.Martinez-Bal	18.4	Gossage-NY	38.1	Quisenberry-KC	3.6	Boggs-Bos	5.1
Dotson-Chi	113	Gossage-NY	17.4	Barojas-Chi	16.6	F.Martinez-Bal	27.6	Dotson-Chi	3.2	Yount-Mil	4.4
McGregor-Bal	113	Lopez-Det	16.0	Gossage-NY	15.8	Lopez-Det	23.6	Boddicker-Bal	2.8	Murray-Bal	4.3

TEAM	G	W	L	PCT	GB	R	OR	AB	H	2B	3B	HR	BB	SO	AVG	OBP	SLG	PRO	PRO+	BR	/A	PF	CHI	RC	SB	CS	SBA	SBR
EAST																												
CHI	161	96	65	.596		**762**	658	5437	1415	240	47	136	**567**	967	.260	.333	.397	.730	101	78	18	109	104	729	154	66	54	-12
NY	162	90	72	.556	6.5	652	676	5438	1400	235	25	107	500	1001	.257	.322	.369	.691	101	1	10	99	100	645	149	54	50	-13
STL	162	84	78	.519	12.5	652	645	5433	1369	225	44	75	516	924	.252	.319	.351	.670	96	-34	-17	97	106	623	**220**	71	59	-13
PHI	162	81	81	.500	15.5	720	690	5614	1494	248	51	147	555	1084	**.266**	**.335**	**.407**	**.742**	112	102	91	102	93	**766**	186	60	50	-11
MON	161	78	83	.484	18	593	585	5439	1367	242	36	96	470	**782**	.251	.314	.362	.676	100	-31	-1	96	96	630	131	38	43	-13
PIT	162	75	87	.463	21.5	615	567	5537	1412	237	33	98	438	841	.255	.312	.363	.675	95	-36	-36	100	99	611	96	62	59	-16
WEST																												
SD	162	92	70	.568		686	634	5504	1425	207	42	109	472	810	.259	.320	.371	.691	100	0	1	100	105	645	152	68	54	-11
HOU	162	80	82	.494	12	693	630	5548	1465	222	**67**	79	494	837	.264	.326	.371	.697	109	14	61	93	102	679	105	61	53	-13
ATL	162	80	82	.494	12	632	655	5422	1338	234	27	111	555	896	.247	.319	.361	.680	90	-17	-64	107	99	623	140	85	**62**	-11
LA	162	79	83	.488	13	580	600	5399	1316	213	28	102	488	829	.244	.308	.348	.656	91	-67	-59	99	100	573	109	69	53	**-10**
CIN	162	70	92	.432	22	627	747	5498	1342	238	30	106	566	978	.244	.316	.356	.672	90	-33	-62	105	99	635	160	63	54	-13
SF	162	66	96	.407	26	682	807	5650	**1499**	229	26	112	528	980	.265	.330	.375	.705	107	31	53	97	97	686	126	76	58	-11
TOT	971					7894		65919	16842	2770	451	1278	6149	10929	.255	.321	.369	.691							1728	773	69	55

TEAM	CG	SH	SV	IP	H	H/G	HR	BB	SO	RAT	ERA	ERA+	OAV	OOB	PR	/A	PF	CPI	FA	E	DP	FW	PW	BW	SBW	DIF
EAST																										
CHI	19	8	50	1434	1458	9.2	99	**442**	879	12.1	3.75	104	.266	.324	-26	24	109	99	.981	121	137	1.1	2.5	1.9	-1.7	11.7
NY	12	15	50	1442²	1371	8.6	104	573	1028	12.3	3.60	98	.252	.326	-1	-10	99	101	.979	129	154	.7	-1.1	1.1	-1.8	10.2
STL	19	12	**51**	1449	1427	8.9	94	494	808	12.1	3.58	97	.262	.326	0	-18	97	103	**.982**	118	**184**	**1.3**	-1.9	-1.8	-1.8	7.2
PHI	11	6	35	1458¹	1416	8.7	101	448	904	11.6	3.62	100	.252	**.310**	-4	2	101	92	.975	161	112	-1.2	.2	**9.6**	-1.6	-6.9
MON	19	10	48	1431	1333	8.4	114	474	861	11.5	3.31	103	.248	.312	44	18	95	103	.978	132	147	.4	1.9	-.1	-1.8	-2.9
PIT	27	13	34	1470	1344	**8.2**	102	502	995	**11.4**	**3.11**	116	.245	**.310**	78	79	100	105	.980	128	142	.7	**8.3**	-3.8	-2.2	-9.1
WEST																										
SD	13	**17**	44	1460¹	**1327**	**8.2**	122	563	812	11.8	3.48	102	**.243**	.316	17	13	99	99	.978	138	144	.1	1.4	.1	-1.6	11.0
HOU	24	13	29	1449¹	1350	8.4	91	502	950	11.6	3.32	100	.248	.313	43	0	93	99	.979	133	160	.4	.0	6.4	-1.8	-6.0
ATL	17	7	49	1447	1421	8.7	122	525	859	12.1	3.57	98	.256	.324	2	45	107	105	.978	139	153	.0	4.7	-6.7	-1.6	2.5
LA	**39**	16	27	1460²	1381	8.5	**76**	499	**1033**	11.7	3.17	111	.250	.314	68	59	98	102	.975	163	146	-1.3	6.2	-6.2	**-1.5**	.9
CIN	25	6	25	1461¹	1445	8.9	128	578	946	12.6	4.16	91	.258	.330	-92	-61	105	94	.977	139	116	.0	-6.4	-6.5	-1.8	3.7
SF	9	7	38	1461	1589	9.8	125	549	854	13.4	4.39	80	.278	.345	-130	-143	98	99	.973	173	134	-1.9	-15.0	5.6	-1.6	-2.0
TOT	234	130	480	17424²		8.7				12.0	3.59		.255	.321					.978	1674	1729					

Runs		Hits		Doubles		Triples		Home Runs		Total Bases	
Sandberg-Chi	114	Gwynn-SD	213	Ray-Pit	38	Sandberg-Chi	19	Schmidt-Phi	36	Murphy-Atl	332
Wiggins-SD	106	Sandberg-Chi	200	Raines-Mon	38	Samuel-Phi	19	Murphy-Atl	36	Sandberg-Chi	331
Raines-Mon	106	Raines-Mon	192	Sandberg-Chi	36	Cruz-Hou	13	Carter-Mon	27	Samuel-Phi	310
Samuel-Phi	105	Samuel-Phi	191	Samuel-Phi	36			Strawberry-NY	26	Carter-Mon	290
Matthews-Chi	101	Cruz-Hou	187					Cey-Chi	25	Schmidt-Phi	283

Runs Batted In		Runs Produced		Bases On Balls		Batting Average		On Base Percentage		Slugging Average	
Schmidt-Phi	106	Sandberg-Chi	179	Matthews-Chi	103	Gwynn-SD	.351	Matthews-Chi	.417	Murphy-Atl	.547
Carter-Mon	106	Cruz-Hou	179	Hernandez-NY	97	Lacy-Pit	.321	Hernandez-NY	.415	Schmidt-Phi	.536
Murphy-Atl	100	Matthews-Chi	169	Schmidt-Phi	92	C.Davis-SF	.315	Gwynn-SD	.411	Sandberg-Chi	.520
Strawberry-NY	97	Schmidt-Phi	163	Thompson-Pit	87	Sandberg-Chi	.314	Raines-Mon	.395	C.Davis-SF	.507
Cey-Chi	97	Hernandez-NY	162	Raines-Mon	87	Ray-Pit	.312	Schmidt-Phi	.388	Durham-Chi	.505

Production		Adjusted Production		Batter Runs		Adjusted Batter Runs		Clutch Hitting Index		Runs Created	
Schmidt-Phi	.924	Schmidt-Phi	155	Murphy-Atl	43.8	Schmidt-Phi	40.1	Mumphrey-Hou	143	Sandberg-Chi	126
Murphy-Atl	.920	C.Davis-SF	149	Schmidt-Phi	41.2	Murphy-Atl	38.4	Davis-Chi	136	Raines-Mon	124
Sandberg-Chi	.889	Cruz-Hou	148	Sandberg-Chi	37.9	Hernandez-NY	36.5	Garvey-SD	135	Murphy-Atl	123
Durham-Chi	.877	Murphy-Atl	145	Hernandez-NY	35.5	Cruz-Hou	36.0	Matthews-Chi	135	Cruz-Hou	111
C.Davis-SF	.876	Hernandez-NY	145	Gwynn-SD	33.9	Gwynn-SD	34.0	Hernandez-NY	134	Carter-Mon	108

Total Average		Stolen Bases		Stolen Base Average		Stolen Base Runs		Fielding Runs		Total Player Rating	
Raines-Mon	.953	Raines-Mon	75	Dilone-Mon	93.1	Raines-Mon	16.5	O.Smith-StL	26.2	Sandberg-Chi	6.6
Murphy-Atl	.942	Samuel-Phi	72	Raines-Mon	88.2	Samuel-Phi	12.6	Sandberg-Chi	23.3	Hernandez-NY	5.0
Schmidt-Phi	.933	Wiggins-SD	70	Cedeno-Cin	86.4	Wilson-NY	8.4	Garner-Hou	23.1	Schmidt-Phi	5.0
Sandberg-Chi	.913	L.Smith-StL	50	VanSlyke-StL	84.8	Wiggins-SD	8.4	Hubbard-Atl	19.6	Raines-Mon	5.0
Matthews-Chi	.888			Stone-Phi	84.4	Redus-Cin	7.8	Anderson-LA	19.2	O.Smith-StL	4.7

Wins		Win Percentage		Games		Complete Games		Shutouts		Saves	
Andujar-StL	20	Sutcliffe-Chi	.941	Power-Cin	78	Soto-Cin	13	Pena-LA	4	Sutter-StL	45
Soto-Cin	18	Soto-Cin	.720	Lavelle-SF	77	Valenzuela-LA	12	Hershiser-LA	4	Smith-Chi	33
Gooden-NY	17	Gooden-NY	.654	Minton-SF	74	Andujar-StL	12	Andujar-StL	4	Orosco-NY	31
Sutcliffe-Chi	16	Show-SD	.625	Tekulve-Pit	72	Knepper-Hou	11			Holland-Phi	29
Niekro-Hou	16			Sutter-StL	71	Mahler-Atl	9			Gossage-SD	25

Innings Pitched		Fewest Hits/Game		Fewest BB/Game		Strikeouts		Strikeouts/Game		Ratio	
Andujar-StL	261.1	Gooden-NY	6.65	Gullickson-Mon	1.47	Gooden-NY	276	Gooden-NY	11.39	Gooden-NY	9.74
Valenzuela-LA	261.0	Soto-Cin	6.86	Candelaria-Pit	1.65	Valenzuela-LA	240	Ryan-Hou	9.65	Hershiser-LA	10.15
Niekro-Hou	248.1	DeLeon-Pit	6.88	Whitson-SD	2.00	Ryan-Hou	197	Valenzuela-LA	8.28	Andujar-StL	10.16
Rhoden-Pit	238.1	Ryan-Hou	7.01	Pena-LA	2.08	Soto-Cin	185	Berenyi-Cin-NY	7.27	Soto-Cin	10.35
Soto-Cin	237.1	Andujar-StL	7.51	Knepper-Hou	2.12	Carlton-Phi	163	DeLeon-Pit	7.16	Candelaria-Pit	10.39

Earned Run Average		Adjusted ERA		Opponents' Batting Avg.		Opponents' On Base Pct.		Starter Runs		Adjusted Starter Runs	
Pena-LA	2.48	Pena-LA	142	Gooden-NY	.202	Gooden-NY	.270	Pena-LA	24.5	Rhoden-Pit	23.3
Gooden-NY	2.60	Gooden-NY	136	Soto-Cin	.209	Hershiser-LA	.279	Gooden-NY	23.9	Pena-LA	23.2
Hershiser-LA	2.66	Hershiser-LA	133	Ryan-Hou	.211	Soto-Cin	.286	Rhoden-Pit	23.0	Gooden-NY	22.6
Rhoden-Pit	2.72	Rhoden-Pit	132	DeLeon-Pit	.214	Andujar-StL	.286	Hershiser-LA	19.6	Sutcliffe-Chi	20.3
Candelaria-Pit	2.72	Candelaria-Pit	132	Hershiser-LA	.225	Ryan-Hou	.288	Denny-Phi	19.5	Denny-Phi	20.3

Clutch Pitching Index		Relief Runs		Adjusted Relief Runs		Relief Ranking		Total Pitcher Index		Total Baseball Ranking	
McWilliams-Pit	130	Sutter-StL	27.9	Sutter-StL	26.3	Sutter-StL	44.8	Rhoden-Pit	3.9	Sandberg-Chi	6.6
Terrell-NY	124	Dawley-Hou	18.1	Lefferts-SD	16.9	Bedrosian-Atl	26.4	Mahler-Atl	2.9	Hernandez-NY	5.0
Candelaria-Pit	122	Lefferts-SD	17.1	Dawley-Hou	15.1	Dawley-Hou	22.6	Sutter-StL	2.8	Schmidt-Phi	5.0
Honeycutt-LA	117	Sisk-NY	13.0	Bedrosian-Atl	13.8	Orosco-NY	22.5	Sutcliffe-Chi	2.8	Raines-Mon	5.0
Trout-Chi	117	Andersen-Phi	12.1	Andersen-Phi	12.6	Power-Cin	22.1	Denny-Phi	2.8	O.Smith-StL	4.7

TEAM	G	W	L	PCT	GB	R	OR	AB	H	2B	3B	HR	BB	SO	AVG	OBP	SLG	PRO	PRO+	BR	/A	PF	CHI	RC	SB	CS	SBA	SBR
EAST																												
DET	162	104	58	.642		**829**	643	5644	1529	254	46	**187**	602	941	.271	.345	.432	.777	**113**	103	**108**	99	99	**843**	106	68	51	**-9**
TOR	163	89	73	.549	15	750	696	5687	1555	**275**	**68**	143	460	816	.273	.333	.421	.754	103	52	25	104	96	808	**193**	67	57	-13
NY	162	87	75	.537	17	758	679	5661	1560	**275**	32	130	534	**673**	.276	.342	.404	.746	110	47	75	96	97	773	62	38	40	-12
BOS	162	86	76	.531	18	810	764	5648	**1598**	259	45	181	500	842	**.283**	.343	**.441**	**.784**	109	48	102	98	97	832	38	25	38	-14
BAL	162	85	77	.525	19	681	667	5456	1374	234	23	160	**620**	884	.252	.331	.391	.722	101	-3	12	98	96	705	51	36	49	-18
CLE	163	75	87	.463	29	761	766	5643	1498	222	39	123	600	815	.265	.339	.384	.723	98	4	-8	102	103	732	126	77	61	-13
MIL	161	67	94	.416	36.5	641	734	5511	1446	232	36	96	432	**673**	.262	.319	.370	.689	93	-74	-46	96	103	621	52	57	48	-11
WEST																												
KC	162	84	78	.519		673	686	5543	1487	269	52	117	400	832	.268	.320	.399	.719	97	-22	-27	101	99	685	106	64	57	-14
CAL	162	81	81	.500	3	696	697	5470	1363	211	30	150	556	928	.249	.322	.381	.703	94	-45	-40	99	**104**	663	80	51	47	-12
MIN	162	81	81	.500	3	673	675	5562	1473	259	33	114	437	735	.265	.321	.385	.706	89	-44	-76	105	102	669	39	30	39	-13
OAK	162	77	85	.475	7	738	796	5457	1415	257	29	158	568	871	.259	.332	.404	.736	109	18	65	93	101	736	145	64	**62**	-17
SEA	162	74	88	.457	10	682	774	5546	1429	244	34	129	519	871	.258	.326	.384	.710	97	-31	-21	99	99	700	116	62	50	-10
CHI	162	74	88	.457	10	679	736	5513	1360	225	38	172	523	883	.247	.316	.395	.711	90	-36	-67	105	101	690	109	49	49	-14
TEX	161	69	92	.429	14.5	656	714	5569	1452	227	29	120	420	807	.261	.315	.377	.692	88	-74	-96	103	**104**	643	81	50	51	-15
TOT	1134					10027		77910	20539	3443	534	1980	7171	11571	.264	.329	.398	.727							1304	738	64	-51

TEAM	CG	SH	SV	IP	H	H/G	HR	BB	SO	RAT	ERA	ERA+	OAV	OOB	PR	/A	PF	CPI	FA	E	DP	FW	PW	BW	SBW	DIF
EAST																										
DET	19	8	51	1464	**1358**	8.3	130	489	914	11.5	3.49	112	.245	.310	81	69	98	98	.979	127	162	.3	**6.9**	**10.9**	-.5	5.4
TOR	34	10	33	1464	1433	8.8	140	528	875	12.3	3.86	106	.257	.325	21	38	103	99	.980	123	166	.6	3.8	2.5	-.9	2.0
NY	15	12	43	1465¹	1485	9.1	**120**	518	**992**	12.4	3.78	100	.264	.328	34	2	95	102	.977	142	**177**	-.5	.2	7.5	-.8	-.4
BOS	18	12	32	1442	1524	9.5	141	517	927	12.9	4.18	100	.269	.334	-29	-1	104	99	.977	143	128	-.6	-.1	7.9	-1.0	-1.2
BAL	**48**	**13**	32	1439¹	1393	8.7	137	512	714	12.1	3.71	104	.256	.322	44	25	97	102	**.981**	123	166	.5	2.5	1.2	-1.4	1.2
CLE	21	7	35	1467²	1523	9.3	141	545	803	12.8	4.26	96	.269	.336	-43	-27	102	98	.977	146	163	-.7	-2.7	-.8	-.9	-.8
MIL	13	7	41	1433	1532	9.6	137	480	785	12.8	4.06	95	.274	.334	-10	-33	96	103	.978	136	156	-.3	-3.3	-4.6	-.7	-4.6
WEST																										
KC	18	9	50	1444	1426	8.9	136	**433**	724	11.8	3.92	103	.258	.315	11	17	101	93	.979	131	157	.0	1.7	-2.7	-1.0	5.0
CAL	36	12	26	1458	1526	9.4	143	474	754	12.5	3.96	100	.270	.330	5	1	99	**104**	.980	128	170	.2	.1	-4.0	-.8	4.5
MIN	32	9	38	1437²	1489	8.9	159	463	713	12.1	3.85	109	.259	.321	22	56	105	101	.980	**120**	134	**.7**	5.6	-7.6	-.9	2.3
OAK	15	6	44	1430	1554	9.8	155	592	695	13.7	4.48	84	.277	.350	-77	-117	94	103	.975	146	159	-.8	-11.8	6.5	-1.3	3.3
SEA	26	4	35	1442	1497	9.3	138	619	972	13.5	4.31	93	.270	.347	-50	-51	100	102	.979	128	143	.2	-5.1	-2.1	-.6	.6
CHI	43	9	32	1454¹	1416	8.8	155	483	840	12.0	4.13	101	.256	.319	-23	4	104	93	**.981**	122	160	.6	.4	-6.7	-1.0	-.2
TEX	38	6	21	1438²	1443	9.0	148	518	863	12.5	3.91	106	.259	.326	13	37	104	101	.977	138	138	-.4	3.7	-9.7	-1.1	-4.1
TOT	398	124	513	20280		9.1				12.5	3.99		.264	.329					.979	1853	2179					

Runs
Evans-Bos 121
Henderson-Oak . . . 113
Boggs-Bos 109
Butler-Cle 108
Armas-Bos 107

Hits
Mattingly-NY 207
Boggs-Bos 203
Ripken-Bal 195
Winfield-NY 193

Doubles
Mattingly-NY 44
Parrish-Tex 42
Bell-Tor 39
Ripken-Bal 37
Evans-Bos 37

Triples
Moseby-Tor 15
Collins-Tor 15
Gibson-Det 10
Baines-Chi 10

Home Runs
Armas-Bos 43
Kingman-Oak 35
Thornton-Cle 33
Parrish-Det 33
Murphy-Oak 33

Total Bases
Armas-Bos 339
Evans-Bos 335
Ripken-Bal 327
Mattingly-NY 324
Easler-Bos 310

Runs Batted In
Armas-Bos 123
Rice-Bos 122
Kingman-Oak 118
Davis-Sea 116

Runs Produced
Evans-Bos 193
Rice-Bos 192
Winfield-NY 187
Armas-Bos 187

Bases On Balls
Murray-Bal 107
Davis-Sea 97
Evans-Bos 96
Thornton-Cle 91
Boggs-Bos 89

Batting Average
Mattingly-NY 343
Winfield-NY 340
Boggs-Bos 325
Bell-Tex 315
Trammell-Det 314

On Base Percentage
Murray-Bal 415
Boggs-Bos 409
Henderson-Oak 401
Winfield-NY 397
Davis-Sea 395

Slugging Average
Baines-Chi 541
Mattingly-NY 537
Evans-Bos 532
Armas-Bos 531
Hrbek-Min 522

Production
Evans-Bos 924
Mattingly-NY 923
Murray-Bal 923
Winfield-NY 912
Hrbek-Min 909

Adjusted Production
Mattingly-NY 159
Murray-Bal 157
Winfield-NY 156
Henderson-Oak . . . 147
Davis-Sea 147

Batter Runs
Murray-Bal 46.8
Evans-Bos 46.6
Mattingly-NY 41.3
Winfield-NY 38.4
Davis-Sea 37.5

Adjusted Batter Runs
Murray-Bal 48.6
Mattingly-NY 44.3
Evans-Bos 42.7
Winfield-NY 41.3
Davis-Sea 38.5

Clutch Hitting Index
Simmons-Mil 131
Kingman-Oak 130
Franco-Cle 127
Bell-Tex 123
Davis-Sea 122

Runs Created
Evans-Bos 132
Murray-Bal 130
Ripken-Bal 122
Mattingly-NY 120
Easler-Bos 118

Total Average
Murray-Bal 993
Henderson-Oak 971
Evans-Bos 942
Davis-Sea 928
Gibson-Det 926

Stolen Bases
Henderson-Oak 66
Collins-Tor 60
Butler-Cle 52
Pettis-Cal 48
Wilson-KC 47

Stolen Base Average
Wilson-KC 90.4
Tolleson-Tex 84.6
Perconte-Sea 82.9
Moseby-Tor 81.3
Collins-Tor 81.1

Stolen Base Runs
Wilson-KC 11.1
Collins-Tor 9.6
Henderson-Oak 9.0
Garcia-Tor 6.6
Moseby-Tor 6.3

Fielding Runs
Ripken-Bal 38.8
Puckett-Min 22.1
Cruz-Chi 22.1
Boggs-Bos 21.0
Bell-Tex 20.3

Total Player Rating
Ripken-Bal 8.7
Murray-Bal 4.8
Yount-Mil 4.8
Boggs-Bos 4.7
Mattingly-NY 4.6

Wins
Boddicker-Bal 20
Morris-Det 19
Blyleven-Cle 19
Viola-Min 18
Petry-Det 18

Win Percentage
Alexander-Tor 739
Blyleven-Cle 731
Petry-Det 692
Wilcox-Det 680

Games
Hernandez-Det 80
Quisenberry-KC . . . 72
Lopez-Det 71
Camacho-Cle 69
Caudill-Oak 68

Complete Games
Hough-Tex 17
Boddicker-Bal 16
Dotson-Chi 14
Blyleven-Cle 12
Beattie-Sea 12

Shutouts
Zahn-Cal 5
Ojeda-Bos 5

Saves
Quisenberry-KC . . . 44
Caudill-Oak 36
Hernandez-Det 32
Righetti-NY 31
Davis-Min 29

Innings Pitched
Stieb-Tor 267.0
Hough-Tex 266.0
Alexander-Tor . . . 261.2
Boddicker-Bal . . . 261.1
Viola-Min 257.2

Fewest Hits/Game
Stieb-Tor 7.25
Blyleven-Cle 7.49
Boddicker-Bal 7.51
Langston-Sea 7.52
Mason-Tex 7.76

Fewest BB/Game
Hoyt-Chi 1.64
Smithson-Min 1.93
Guidry-NY 2.02
Alexander-Tor 2.03
Haas-Mil 2.04

Strikeouts
Langston-Sea . . . 204
Stieb-Tor 198
Witt-Cal 196
Blyleven-Cle 170
Hough-Tex 164

Strikeouts/Game
Langston-Sea 8.16
Witt-Cal 7.15
Moore-Sea 6.71
Stieb-Tor 6.67
Berenguer-Det . . . 6.31

Ratio
Black-KC 10.30
Alexander-Tor . . . 10.32
Mason-Tex 10.35
Blyleven-Cle 10.43
Boddicker-Bal . . . 10.47

Earned Run Average
Boddicker-Bal . . . 2.79
Stieb-Tor 2.83
Blyleven-Cle 2.87
Niekro-NY 3.09
Zahn-Cal 3.12

Adjusted ERA
Stieb-Tor 145
Blyleven-Cle 143
Boddicker-Bal 139
Alexander-Tor 131
Viola-Min 131

Opponents' Batting Avg.
Stieb-Tor 221
Blyleven-Cle 224
Boddicker-Bal 228
Langston-Sea 230
Berenguer-Det . . .232

Opponents' On Base Pct.
Black-KC 283
Blyleven-Cle 287
Alexander-Tor 287
Mason-Tex 288
Seaver-Chi 290

Starter Runs
Boddicker-Bal . . . 34.9
Stieb-Tor 34.4
Blyleven-Cle 30.7
Alexander-Tor . . . 25.0
Black-KC 25.0

Adjusted Starter Runs
Stieb-Tor 37.5
Blyleven-Cle 33.3
Boddicker-Bal 31.4
Viola-Min 28.3
Alexander-Tor . . . 28.1

Clutch Pitching Index
Niekro-NY 125
Fontenot-NY 119
Cocanower-Mil . . . 114
Hurst-Bos 113
Burris-Oak 112

Relief Runs
Hernandez-Det . . . 32.2
Quisenberry-KC . . 19.4
Righetti-NY 17.7
Corbett-Cal 17.7
Camacho-Cle 17.3

Adjusted Relief Runs
Hernandez-Det . . . 31.1
Quisenberry-KC . . 19.9
Camacho-Cle 18.4
Corbett-Cal 17.5
Righetti-NY 15.6

Relief Ranking
Hernandez-Det . . . 39.9
Camacho-Cle 32.7
Quisenberry-KC . . 27.7
Righetti-NY 27.3
Caudill-Oak 25.9

Total Pitcher Index
Stieb-Tor 4.1
Boddicker-Bal 4.0
Blyleven-Cle 3.5
Hernandez-Det . . . 3.1
Black-KC 3.0

Total Baseball Ranking
Ripken-Bal 8.7
Murray-Bal 4.8
Yount-Mil 4.8
Boggs-Bos 4.7
Mattingly-NY 4.6

TEAM	G	W	L	PCT	GB	R	OR	AB	H	2B	3B	HR	BB	SO	AVG	OBP	SLG	PRO	PRO+	BR	/A	PF	CHI	RC	SB	CS	SBA	SBR
EAST																												
STL	162	101	61	.623		**747**	572	5467	1446	245	**59**	87	**586**	853	**.264**	**.338**	.379	**.717**	107	52	**57**	99	**105**	**733**	314	96	62	**-7**
NY	162	98	64	.605	3	695	**568**	5549	1425	239	35	134	546	872	.257	.326	.385	.711	107	31	47	98	99	691	117	53	46	-11
MON	161	84	77	.522	16.5	633	636	5429	1342	242	49	118	492	880	.247	.313	.375	.688	104	-18	19	94	101	633	169	77	**63**	-14
CHI	162	77	84	.478	23.5	686	729	5492	1397	239	28	**150**	562	937	.254	.326	.390	.716	95	40	-32	111	98	710	182	49	44	-11
PHI	162	75	87	.463	26	667	673	5477	1343	238	47	141	527	1095	.245	.314	.383	.697	97	0	-17	103	102	657	122	51	54	-16
PIT	161	57	104	.354	43.5	568	708	5436	1340	251	28	80	514	842	.247	.313	.347	.660	90	-63	-56	99	96	587	110	60	53	-13
WEST																												
LA	162	95	67	.586		682	579	5502	1434	226	28	129	539	846	.261	.330	.382	.712	**108**	38	**57**	97	97	704	136	58	52	-13
CIN	162	89	72	.553	5.5	677	666	5431	1385	249	34	114	576	856	.255	.329	.376	.705	98	26	-6	105	99	672	159	70	57	-12
SD	162	83	79	.512	12	650	622	5507	1405	241	28	.109	513	**809**	.255	.321	.368	.689	100	-8	1	99	100	645	60	39	41	-12
HOU	162	83	79	.512	12	706	691	5582	**1457**	261	42	121	477	873	.261	.322	.388	.710	107	25	44	97	103	684	96	56	58	-17
ATL	162	66	96	.407	29	632	781	5526	1359	213	28	126	553	849	.246	.317	.363	.680	97	-27	-66	106	99	622	72	52	47	-12
SF	162	62	100	.383	33	556	674	5420	1263	217	31	115	488	962	.233	.301	.348	.649	91	-92	-60	95	100	564	99	55	54	-15
TOT	971					7899		65818	16596	2861	437	1424	6373	10674	.252	.321	.374	.695							1636	716	70	61

TEAM	CG	SH	SV	IP	H	H/G	HR	BB	SO	RAT	ERA	ERA+	OAV	OOB	PR	/A	PF	CPI	FA	E	DP	FW	PW	BW	SBW	DIF
EAST																										
STL	**37**	20	44	1464	1343	8.3	**98**	453	798	11.2	3.10	114	.245	.306	79	69	98	102	**.983**	108	166	**1.7**	7.3	**6.0**	**-1.3**	6.3
NY	32	19	37	1488	1306	**7.9**	111	515	**1039**	11.1	3.11	111	.236	.303	79	57	96	99	.982	115	138	1.3	6.0	4.9	-1.7	6.5
MON	13	13	**53**	1457	1346	8.3	99	509	870	11.6	3.55	96	.246	.313	7	-25	94	93	.981	121	152	.8	-2.6	2.0	-2.0	5.3
CHI	20	8	42	1442[1]	1492	9.3	156	519	820	12.7	4.16	96	.270	.335	-90	-26	111	103	.979	134	150	.1	-2.7	-3.4	-1.7	4.2
PHI	24	9	30	1447	1424	8.9	115	596	899	12.7	3.68	100	.258	.333	-14	0	103	105	.978	139	142	-.2	.0	-1.8	-2.2	-1.8
PIT	15	6	29	1445[1]	1406	8.8	107	584	962	12.6	3.97	90	.255	.330	-61	-63	100	94	.979	133	127	.1	-6.6	-5.9	-1.9	-9.2
WEST																										
LA	**37**	**21**	36	1465	**1280**	**7.9**	102	462	979	**10.8**	**2.96**	117	**.234**	**.296**	102	83	97	98	.974	166	131	-1.8	**8.7**	**6.0**	-1.9	3.0
CIN	24	11	45	1451[1]	1347	8.4	131	535	910	11.8	3.71	102	.248	.317	-19	12	105	104	.980	122	142	.8	1.3	-.6	-1.8	8.8
SD	26	19	44	1451[1]	1399	8.7	127	**443**	727	11.6	3.40	104	.256	.315	29	20	98	**106**	.980	124	158	.7	2.1	.1	-1.8	.9
HOU	17	9	42	1458	1393	8.6	119	543	909	12.1	3.66	95	.253	.323	-11	-32	96	100	.976	152	159	-1.0	-3.4	4.6	-2.3	4.0
ATL	9	9	29	1457[1]	1512	9.3	134	642	776	13.5	4.19	92	.270	.349	-97	-56	107	104	.976	159	**197**	-1.4	-5.9	-6.9	-1.8	1.0
SF	13	5	24	1448	1348	8.4	125	572	985	12.1	3.61	95	.247	.321	-3	-28	96	99	.976	148	134	-.7	-2.9	-6.3	-2.1	-6.9
TOT	267	149	455	17474[2]		8.5				12.0	3.59		.252	.321					.979	1621	1796					

Runs		Hits		Doubles		Triples		Home Runs		Total Bases	
Murphy-Atl	118	McGee-StL	216	Parker-Cin	42	McGee-StL	18	Murphy-Atl	37	Parker-Cin	350
Raines-Mon	115	Parker-Cin	198	Wilson-Phi	39	Samuel-Phi	13	Parker-Cin	34	Murphy-Atl	332
McGee-StL	114	Gwynn-SD	197	Herr-StL	38	Raines-Mon	13	Schmidt-Phi	33	McGee-StL	308
Sandberg-Chi	113	Sandberg-Chi	186	Wallach-Mon	36	Garner-Hou	10	Guerrero-LA	33	Sandberg-Chi	307
Coleman-StL	107	Murphy-Atl	185			Coleman-StL	10	Carter-NY	32	Schmidt-Phi	292

Runs Batted In		Runs Produced		Bases On Balls		Batting Average		On Base Percentage		Slugging Average	
Parker-Cin	125	Herr-StL	199	Murphy-Atl	90	McGee-StL	.353	Guerrero-LA	.425	Guerrero-LA	.577
Murphy-Atl	111	Murphy-Atl	192	Schmidt-Phi	87	Guerrero-LA	.320	Scioscia-LA	.409	Parker-Cin	.551
Herr-StL	110	McGee-StL	186	Martinez-SD	87	Raines-Mon	.320	Raines-Mon	.407	Murphy-Atl	.539
Moreland-Chi	106	Parker-Cin	179	Rose-Cin	86	Gwynn-SD	.317	Rose-Cin	.398	Schmidt-Phi	.532
Wilson-Phi	102	Sandberg-Chi	170	Law-Mon	86	Parker-Cin	.312	Clark-StL	.397	Marshall-LA	.515

Production		Adjusted Production		Batter Runs		Adjusted Batter Runs		Clutch Hitting Index		Runs Created	
Guerrero-LA	1.002	Guerrero-LA	183	Guerrero-LA	52.8	Guerrero-LA	54.7	Herr-StL	155	Murphy-Atl	131
Murphy-Atl	.929	Raines-Mon	155	Murphy-Atl	47.6	Murphy-Atl	43.0	Pendleton-StL	151	Raines-Mon	124
Parker-Cin	.918	Clark-StL	151	Parker-Cin	42.5	Raines-Mon	41.6	Moreland-Chi	149	McGee-StL	123
Schmidt-Phi	.911	McGee-StL	148	Schmidt-Phi	38.5	Parker-Cin	38.8	Brooks-Mon	146	Guerrero-LA	121
Clark-StL	.899	Murphy-Atl	148	Raines-Mon	37.5	McGee-StL	37.3	Rose-Cin	144	Sandberg-Chi	117

Total Average		Stolen Bases		Stolen Base Average		Stolen Base Runs		Fielding Runs		Total Player Rating	
Guerrero-LA	1.086	Coleman-StL	110	Lopes-Chi	92.2	Coleman-StL	18.0	Hubbard-Atl	61.8	Guerrero-LA	6.0
Raines-Mon	1.022	Raines-Mon	70	Herr-StL	91.2	Raines-Mon	15.6	Wallach-Mon	36.7	Raines-Mon	5.6
Murphy-Atl	.960	McGee-StL	56	Raines-Mon	88.6	Lopes-Chi	11.7	Pendleton-StL	22.7	Hubbard-Atl	4.9
Schmidt-Phi	.927	Sandberg-Chi	54	VanSlyke-StL	85.0	Sandberg-Chi	9.6	McReynolds-SD	15.5	McGee-StL	4.7
McGee-StL	.920	Samuel-Phi	53	Davis-Cin	84.2	Herr-StL	7.5			Wallach-Mon	4.6

Wins		Win Percentage		Games		Complete Games		Shutouts		Saves	
Gooden-NY	24	Hershiser-LA	.864	Burke-Mon	78	Gooden-NY	16	Tudor-StL	10	Reardon-Mon	41
Tudor-StL	21	Gooden-NY	.857	M.Davis-SF	77	Valenzuela-LA	14	Gooden-NY	8	Smith-Chi	33
Andujar-StL	21	Smith-Mon	.783	Garrelts-SF	74	Tudor-StL	14	Valenzuela-LA	5	Smith-Hou	27
Browning-Cin	20	Darling-NY	.727	Carman-Phi	71	Cox-StL	10	Hershiser-LA	5	Power-Cin	27
Hershiser-LA	19	Tudor-StL	.724	Minton-SF	68	Andujar-StL	10			Gossage-SD	26

Innings Pitched		Fewest Hits/Game		Fewest BB/Game		Strikeouts		Strikeouts/Game		Ratio	
Gooden-NY	276.2	Fernandez-NY	5.71	Hoyt-SD	.86	Gooden-NY	268	Fernandez-NY	9.51	Tudor-StL	8.61
Tudor-StL	275.0	Gooden-NY	6.44	Eckersley-Chi	1.01	Soto-Cin	214	Gooden-NY	8.72	Gooden-NY	8.75
Valenzuela-LA	272.1	Hershiser-LA	6.72	Lynch-NY	1.27	Ryan-Hou	209	DeLeon-Pit	8.24	Eckersley-Chi	8.88
Andujar-StL	269.2	Tudor-StL	6.84	Tudor-StL	1.60	Valenzuela-LA	208	Ryan-Hou	8.11	Hershiser-LA	9.50
Mahler-Atl	266.2	Soto-Cin	6.87	Smith-Mon	1.66	Fernandez-NY	180	Soto-Cin	7.50	Smith-Mon	9.51

Earned Run Average		Adjusted ERA		Opponents' Batting Avg.		Opponents' On Base Pct.		Starter Runs		Adjusted Starter Runs	
Gooden-NY	1.53	Gooden-NY	226	Fernandez-NY	.181	Tudor-StL	.249	Gooden-NY	63.4	Gooden-NY	59.2
Tudor-StL	1.93	Tudor-StL	183	Gooden-NY	.201	Gooden-NY	.254	Tudor-StL	50.7	Tudor-StL	48.9
Hershiser-LA	2.03	Hershiser-LA	171	Hershiser-LA	.206	Eckersley-Chi	.255	Hershiser-LA	41.6	Hershiser-LA	38.5
Reuschel-Pit	2.27	Reuschel-Pit	157	Tudor-StL	.209	Hershiser-LA	.268	Valenzuela-LA	34.6	Valenzuela-LA	31.2
Welch-LA	2.31	Welch-LA	150	Soto-Cin	.211	Smith-Mon	.269	Reuschel-Pit	28.4	Reuschel-Pit	28.1

Clutch Pitching Index		Relief Runs		Adjusted Relief Runs		Relief Ranking		Total Pitcher Index		Total Baseball Ranking	
Darling-NY	120	Burke-Mon	16.0	Franco-Cin	17.6	Franco-Cin	28.8	Gooden-NY	7.8	Gooden-NY	7.8
Hawkins-SD	119	Gossage-SD	15.5	Carman-Phi	15.3	Gossage-SD	24.8	Tudor-StL	5.8	Guerrero-LA	6.0
Show-SD	119	Franco-Cin	15.5	Gossage-SD	15.0	Smith-Hou	24.7	Hershiser-LA	4.9	Tudor-StL	5.8
Reuss-LA	115	Garrelts-SF	15.2	Garrelts-SF	13.3	Carman-Phi	23.5	Valenzuela-LA	3.9	Raines-Mon	5.6
Gooden-NY	115	Carman-Phi	14.4	Burke-Mon	13.3	Power-Cin	22.5	Reuschel-Pit	3.9	Hershiser-LA	4.9

TEAM	G	W	L	PCT	GB	R	OR	AB	H	2B	3B	HR	BB	SO	AVG	OBP	SLG	PRO	PRO+	BR	/A	PF	CHI	RC	SB	CS	SBA	SBR
EAST																												
TOR	161	99	62	.615		759	**588**	5508	1482	281	**53**	158	503	807	.269	.334	.425	.759	103	43	24	103	98	767	144	77	60	-12
NY	161	97	64	.602	2	**839**	660	5458	1458	272	31	176	620	771	.267	.347	.425	.772	112	82	**99**	98	102	821	**155**	53	47	**-11**
DET	161	84	77	.522	15	729	688	5575	1413	254	45	202	526	926	.253	.321	.424	.745	102	8	13	99	97	765	75	41	47	-15
BAL	161	83	78	.516	16	818	764	5517	1451	234	22	**214**	604	908	.263	.338	**.430**	.768	112	64	84	97	102	794	69	43	48	-15
BOS	163	81	81	.500	18.5	800	720	5720	**1615**	**292**	31	162	562	816	**.282**	**.350**	.429	**.779**	107	**96**	64	104	93	**844**	66	27	36	-13
MIL	161	71	90	.441	28	690	802	5568	1467	250	44	101	462	746	.263	.322	.379	.701	91	-67	-63	100	103	666	69	34	49	-18
CLE	162	60	102	.370	39.5	729	861	5527	1465	254	31	116	492	817	.265	.327	.385	.712	94	-43	-37	99	106	681	132	72	60	-13
WEST																												
KC	162	91	71	.562		687	639	5500	1384	261	49	154	473	840	.252	.315	.401	.716	93	-46	-48	100	101	687	128	48	44	**-11**
CAL	162	90	72	.556	1	732	703	5442	1364	215	31	153	**648**	902	.251	.335	.386	.721	97	-16	-12	100	100	710	106	51	54	-16
CHI	163	85	77	.525	6	736	720	5470	1386	247	37	146	471	843	.253	.318	.392	.710	89	-54	-81	104	**109**	674	108	56	51	-13
MIN	162	77	85	.475	14	705	782	5509	1453	282	41	141	502	779	.264	.329	.407	.736	94	0	-41	106	96	729	68	44	46	-13
OAK	162	77	85	.475	14	757	787	5581	1475	230	34	155	508	861	.264	.327	.401	.728	105	-14	40	93	104	725	117	58	56	-15
SEA	162	74	88	.457	17	719	818	5521	1410	277	38	171	564	942	.255	.328	.412	.740	100	7	2	101	96	739	94	35	38	**-11**
TEX	161	62	99	.385	28.5	617	785	5361	1359	213	41	129	530	819	.253	.324	.381	.705	90	-53	-62	101	93	652	130	76	**67**	-16
TOT	1132					10317		77257	20182	3562	528	2178	7465	11777	.261	.330	.406	.735							1461	715	67	9

TEAM	CG	SH	SV	IP	H	H/G	HR	BB	SO	RAT	ERA	ERA+	OAV	OOB	PR	/A	PF	CPI	FA	E	DP	FW	PW	BW	SBW	DIF
EAST																										
TOR	18	9	47	1448	**1312**	8.2	147	484	823	11.3	3.31	127	.242	**.307**	135	145	102	107	.980	125	164	.2	**14.3**	2.4	-1.3	2.8
NY	25	9	**49**	1440¹	1373	8.6	157	518	907	11.9	3.69	109	.251	.317	73	50	97	104	.979	126	172	.2	4.9	**9.8**	-1.2	2.8
DET	31	**11**	40	1456	1313	**8.1**	141	556	943	11.7	3.78	108	**.240**	.313	58	46	98	94	.977	143	152	-.8	4.5	1.3	-1.5	.0
BAL	32	6	33	1427¹	1480	9.3	160	568	793	13.1	4.38	92	.269	.340	-36	-54	97	102	.979	129	168	-.0	-5.3	8.3	-1.5	1.1
BOS	35	8	29	1461¹	1487	9.2	130	540	913	12.7	4.06	106	.264	.332	14	36	103	101	.977	145	161	-.8	3.6	6.3	-1.4	-7.7
MIL	34	5	37	1437	1510	9.5	175	499	777	12.8	4.39	95	.270	.334	-38	-36	100	101	.977	142	153	-.7	-3.6	-6.2	-1.8	2.9
CLE	24	7	28	1421	1556	9.9	170	547	702	13.6	4.91	84	.280	.350	-121	-123	100	98	.977	141	161	-.6	-12.2	-3.7	-1.4	-3.2
WEST																										
KC	27	**11**	41	1461	1433	8.8	**103**	463	846	11.9	3.49	119	.256	.316	107	109	100	103	.980	127	160	.1	10.8	-4.7	-1.2	5.0
CAL	22	8	41	1457¹	1453	9.0	171	514	767	12.3	3.91	105	.262	.328	38	32	99	**108**	**.982**	112	**202**	1.0	3.2	-1.2	-1.6	7.7
CHI	20	8	39	1451²	1411	8.7	161	569	**1023**	12.8	4.07	106	.255	.329	12	40	104	101	**.982**	111	152	**1.1**	4.0	-8.0	-1.4	8.3
MIN	**41**	7	34	1426¹	1468	9.3	164	**462**	767	12.4	4.48	98	.268	.328	-52	-11	106	95	.980	120	139	.5	-1.1	-4.1	-1.4	-6.2
OAK	10	6	41	1453	1451	9.0	172	607	785	12.9	4.41	87	.258	.333	-42	-89	93	97	.977	140	137	-.6	-8.8	4.0	-1.5	3.0
SEA	23	8	30	1432	1456	9.2	154	637	868	13.4	4.68	90	.264	.345	-84	-73	102	96	.980	122	156	.4	-7.2	.2	-1.2	.8
TEX	18	5	33	1411²	1479	9.4	173	501	863	12.9	4.56	93	.268	.333	-64	-51	102	97	.980	120	145	.5	-5.0	-6.1	-1.6	-6.2
TOT	360	108	522	20184		9.0				12.5	4.15		.261	.330					.979	1803	2222					

Runs / Hits / Doubles / Triples / Home Runs / Total Bases

Runs		Hits		Doubles		Triples		Home Runs		Total Bases	
Henderson-NY	146	Boggs-Bos	240	Mattingly-NY	48	Wilson-KC	21	Evans-Det	40	Mattingly-NY	370
Ripken-Bal	116	Mattingly-NY	211	Buckner-Bos	46	Butler-Cle	14	Fisk-KC	37	Brett-KC	322
Murray-Bal	111	Buckner-Bos	201	Boggs-Bos	42	Puckett-Min	13	Balboni-KC	36	Bradley-Sea	319
Evans-Bos	110	Puckett-Min	199	Cooper-Mil	39	Fernandez-Tor	10	Mattingly-NY	35	Boggs-Bos	312
Brett-KC	108	Baines-Chi	198					J.Thomas-Sea	32	Murray-Bal	305

Runs Batted In / Runs Produced / Bases On Balls / Batting Average / On Base Percentage / Slugging Average

Runs Batted In		Runs Produced		Bases On Balls		Batting Average		On Base Percentage		Slugging Average	
Mattingly-NY	145	Mattingly-NY	217	Evans-Bos	114	Boggs-Bos	.368	Boggs-Bos	.452	Brett-KC	.585
Murray-Bal	124	Murray-Bal	204	Harrah-Tex	113	Brett-KC	.335	Brett-KC	.442	Mattingly-NY	.567
Winfield-NY	114	Ripken-Bal	200	Brett-KC	103	Mattingly-NY	.324	Harrah-Tex	.437	Barfield-Tor	.536
Baines-Chi	113	Henderson-NY	194	Henderson-NY	99	Henderson-NY	.314	Henderson-NY	.422	Murray-Bal	.523
Brett-KC	112	Winfield-NY	193	Boggs-Bos	96	Butler-Cle	.311	Murray-Bal	.387	Evans-Det	.519

Production / Adjusted Production / Batter Runs / Adjusted Batter Runs / Clutch Hitting Index / Runs Created

Production		Adjusted Production		Batter Runs		Adjusted Batter Runs		Clutch Hitting Index		Runs Created	
Brett-KC	1.028	Brett-KC	178	Brett-KC	63.4	Brett-KC	63.2	Thornton-Cle	146	Brett-KC	146
Mattingly-NY	.946	Henderson-NY	159	Boggs-Bos	54.8	Boggs-Bos	51.1	Meacham-NY	142	Boggs-Bos	143
Henderson-NY	.938	Mattingly-NY	159	Mattingly-NY	47.5	Mattingly-NY	49.6	Boone-Cal	136	Henderson-NY	138
Boggs-Bos	.929	Murray-Bal	150	Henderson-NY	45.5	Henderson-NY	47.3	Baylor-NY	134	Mattingly-NY	136
Murray-Bal	.910	Boggs-Bos	149	Murray-Bal	38.4	Murray-Bal	40.5	Buckner-Bos	132	Murray-Bal	122

Total Average / Stolen Bases / Stolen Base Average / Stolen Base Runs / Fielding Runs / Total Player Rating

Total Average		Stolen Bases		Stolen Base Average		Stolen Base Runs		Fielding Runs		Total Player Rating	
Henderson-NY	1.155	Henderson-NY	80	Perconte-Sea	93.9	Henderson-NY	18.0	Owen-Sea	26.8	Henderson-NY	7.1
Brett-KC	1.150	Pettis-Cal	56	Henderson-NY	88.9	Pettis-Cal	11.4	Buckner-Bos	25.4	Brett-KC	6.8
Gibson-Det	.953	Butler-Cle	47	Gibson-Det	88.2	Perconte-Sea	8.1	Barfield-Tor	17.3	Boggs-Bos	5.2
Boggs-Bos	.952	Wilson-KC	43	Pettis-Cal	86.2	Smith-KC	7.8	Gaetti-Min	16.2	Barfield-Tor	4.7
Murray-Bal	.938	Smith-KC	40	Smith-KC	85.1	Gibson-Det	6.6	Grich-Cal	15.0	Murray-Bal	4.2

Wins / Win Percentage / Games / Complete Games / Shutouts / Saves

Wins		Win Percentage		Games		Complete Games		Shutouts		Saves	
Guidry-NY	22	Guidry-NY	.786	Quisenberry-KC	84	Blyleven-Cle-Min	24	Blyleven-Cle-Min	5	Quisenberry-KC	37
Saberhagen-KC	20	Saberhagen-KC	.769	VandeBerg-Sea	76	Moore-Sea	14	Morris-Det	4	James-Chi	32
Viola-Min	18	Leibrandt-KC	.654	Righetti-NY	74	Hough-Tex	14	Burns-Chi	4	Moore-Cal	31
Burns-Chi	18	Higuera-Mil	.652	Hernandez-Det	74	Morris-Det	13			Hernandez-Det	31
				Nunez-Sea	70	Boyd-Bos	13				

Innings Pitched / Fewest Hits/Game / Fewest BB/Game / Strikeouts / Strikeouts/Game / Ratio

Innings Pitched		Fewest Hits/Game		Fewest BB/Game		Strikeouts		Strikeouts/Game		Ratio	
Blyleven-Cle-Min	293.2	Stieb-Tor	7.00	Haas-Mil	1.39	Blyleven-Cle-Min	206	Bannister-Chi	8.46	Saberhagen-KC	9.56
Boyd-Bos	272.1	Hough-Tex	7.12	Saberhagen-KC	1.45	Bannister-Chi	198	Hurst-Bos	7.42	Guidry-NY	9.90
Stieb-Tor	265.0	Petry-Det	7.16	Guidry-NY	1.46	Morris-Det	191	Burns-Chi	6.82	Key-Tor	10.16
Alexander-Tor	260.2	Morris-Det	7.42	Butcher-Min	1.86	Hurst-Bos	189	Morris-Det	6.69	Petry-Det	10.33
Guidry-NY	259.0	Higuera-Mil	7.88	Key-Tor	2.12	Witt-Cal	180	Tanana-Tex-Det	6.66	Hough-Tex	10.35

Earned Run Average / Adjusted ERA / Opponents' Batting Avg. / Opponents' On Base Pct. / Starter Runs / Adjusted Starter Runs

Earned Run Average		Adjusted ERA		Opponents' Batting Avg.		Opponents' On Base Pct.		Starter Runs		Adjusted Starter Runs	
Stieb-Tor	2.48	Stieb-Tor	170	Stieb-Tor	.213	Saberhagen-KC	.273	Stieb-Tor	49.1	Stieb-Tor	50.9
Leibrandt-KC	2.69	Leibrandt-KC	155	Hough-Tex	.215	Guidry-NY	.279	Leibrandt-KC	38.5	Leibrandt-KC	38.8
Saberhagen-KC	2.87	Saberhagen-KC	145	Petry-Det	.217	Key-Tor	.284	Saberhagen-KC	33.4	Blyleven-Cle-Min	35.4
Key-Tor	3.00	Key-Tor	140	Morris-Det	.225	Hough-Tex	.285	Blyleven-Cle-Min	32.3	Saberhagen-KC	33.8
Blyleven-Cle-Min	3.16	Seaver-Chi	136	Higuera-Mil	.235	Petry-Det	.285	Key-Tor	27.0	Seaver-Chi	30.5

Clutch Pitching Index / Relief Runs / Adjusted Relief Runs / Relief Ranking / Total Pitcher Index / Total Baseball Ranking

Clutch Pitching Index		Relief Runs		Adjusted Relief Runs		Relief Ranking		Total Pitcher Index		Total Baseball Ranking	
Leibrandt-KC	121	Moore-Cal	25.5	James-Chi	26.8	Moore-Cal	51.9	Stieb-Tor	6.1	Henderson-NY	7.1
Romanick-Cal	117	Quisenberry-KC	25.4	Quisenberry-KC	25.6	James-Chi	50.4	Leibrandt-KC	4.6	Brett-KC	6.8
Boddicker-Bal	115	James-Chi	24.7	Moore-Cal	25.0	Quisenberry-KC	46.9	Saberhagen-KC	3.8	Stieb-Tor	6.1
Alexander-Tor	114	Cliburn-Cal	22.6	Cliburn-Cal	22.2	Hernandez-Det	35.3	Blyleven-Cle-Min	3.5	Boggs-Bos	5.2
Stieb-Tor	112	Harris-Tex	21.1	Harris-Tex	22.1	Righetti-NY	32.2	Seaver-Chi	3.5	Barfield-Tor	4.7

TEAM	G	W	L	PCT	GB	R	OR	AB	H	2B	3B	HR	BB	SO	AVG	OBP	SLG	PRO	PRO+	BR	/A	PF	CHI	RC	SB	CS	SBA	SBR
EAST																												
NY	162	108	54	.667		**783**	578	5558	**1462**	261	31	148	631	968	**.263**	**.341**	**.401**	**.742**	**114**	84	104	97	101	**773**	118	48	47	-13
PHI	161	86	75	.534	21.5	739	713	5483	1386	266	39	154	589	1154	.253	.330	.400	.730	103	50	26	104	101	739	153	59	56	-15
STL	161	79	82	.491	28.5	601	611	5378	1270	216	48	58	568	905	.236	.311	.327	.638	82	-118	-111	99	109	584	**262**	78	58	-10
MON	161	78	83	.484	29.5	637	688	5508	1401	255	**50**	110	537	1016	.254	.324	.379	.703	100	0	6	99	94	676	193	95	62	**-8**
CHI	160	70	90	.438	37	680	781	5499	1409	258	27	**155**	508	966	.256	.321	.398	.719	96	21	-31	108	98	697	132	62	50	-10
PIT	162	64	98	.395	44	663	700	5456	1366	**273**	33	111	569	929	.250	.323	.374	.697	95	-11	-26	102	100	654	152	84	63	-12
WEST																												
HOU	162	96	66	.593		654	**569**	5441	1388	244	32	125	536	916	.255	.325	.381	.706	103	3	21	97	98	668	163	75	54	-9
CIN	162	86	76	.531	10	732	717	5536	1404	237	35	144	586	920	.254	.327	.387	.714	98	21	-8	104	104	712	177	53	50	-13
SF	162	83	79	.512	13	698	618	5501	1394	239	29	114	536	1087	.253	.324	.375	.699	104	-8	25	95	104	674	148	93	65	-10
SD	162	74	88	.457	22	656	723	5515	1442	239	25	136	484	917	.261	.323	.388	.711	104	9	23	98	97	671	96	68	51	-9
LA	162	73	89	.451	23	638	679	5471	1373	232	14	130	478	966	.251	.315	.370	.685	102	-41	5	93	102	639	155	67	57	-13
ATL	161	72	89	.447	23.5	615	719	5384	1348	241	24	138	538	**904**	.250	.321	.381	.702	93	-4	-41	106	93	646	93	76	57	-10
TOT	969					8096		65730	16643	2991	387	1523	6560	11648	.253	.324	.380	.704							1842	858	68	38

TEAM	CG	SH	SV	IP	H	H/G	HR	BB	SO	RAT	ERA	ERA+	OAV	OOB	PR	/A	PF	CPI	FA	E	DP	FW	PW	BW	SBW	DIF
EAST																										
NY	27	11	46	1484	1304	7.9	**103**	509	1083	11.2	3.11	114	.236	.304	**99**	69	95	98	.978	138	145	.1	7.2	**10.8**	-1.7	10.6
PHI	22	11	39	1451²	1473	9.1	130	553	874	12.7	3.85	100	.264	.333	-21	0	104	105	.978	137	157	.1	.0	2.7	-1.9	4.6
STL	17	4	46	1466¹	1364	8.4	135	**485**	761	11.5	3.37	108	.250	.314	56	43	98	**106**	**.981**	**123**	178	**.9**	4.5	-11.5	-1.4	6.0
MON	15	9	50	1466¹	1350	8.3	119	566	1051	12.0	3.78	98	.245	.320	-10	-14	99	93	.979	133	132	.3	-1.5	.6	**-1.2**	-.8
CHI	11	6	42	1445	1546	9.6	143	557	962	13.2	4.49	90	.278	.346	-124	-72	109	100	.980	124	147	.8	-7.5	-3.2	-1.4	1.3
PIT	17	9	30	1450²	1397	8.7	138	570	924	12.4	3.90	98	.254	.329	-30	-11	103	100	.978	143	134	-.2	-1.1	-2.7	-1.6	-11.4
WEST																										
HOU	18	**19**	51	1456¹	**1203**	7.4	116	523	**1160**	10.8	3.15	114	.225	.297	92	73	97	93	.979	130	108	.6	**7.6**	2.2	-1.3	5.9
CIN	14	8	45	1468	1465	9.0	136	524	924	12.3	3.91	99	.263	.329	-31	-6	104	101	.978	140	160	.0	-.6	-.8	-1.7	8.1
SF	18	10	35	1460¹	1264	7.8	121	591	992	11.6	3.33	106	.236	.315	61	30	95	101	.977	143	149	-.2	3.1	2.6	-1.4	-2.2
SD	13	7	32	1443¹	1406	8.8	150	607	934	12.7	3.99	92	.257	.334	-44	-54	98	102	.978	137	135	.2	-5.6	2.4	-1.3	-2.7
LA	**35**	14	25	1454¹	1428	8.8	115	499	1051	12.1	3.76	92	.256	.320	-7	-50	93	96	.971	181	118	-2.2	-5.2	.5	-1.7	.6
ATL	17	5	39	1424²	1443	9.1	117	576	932	12.9	3.97	100	.266	.339	-40	0	107	103	.978	141	**181**	-.1	.0	-4.3	-1.4	-2.8
TOT	224	113	480	17471		8.6				12.1	3.72		.253	.324					.978	1670	1744					

Runs		Hits		Doubles		Triples		Home Runs		Total Bases	
Hayes-Phi	107	Gwynn-SD	211	Hayes-Phi	46	Webster-Mon	13	Schmidt-Phi	37	Parker-Cin	304
Gwynn-SD	107	Sax-LA	210	Sax-LA	43	Samuel-Phi	12	Parker-Cin	31	Schmidt-Phi	302
Schmidt-Phi	97	Raines-Mon	194	Dunston-Chi	37	Raines-Mon	10	Davis-Hou	31	Gwynn-SD	300
Davis-Cin	97	Hayes-Phi	186	Bream-Pit	37	Coleman-StL	8	Murphy-Atl	29	Murphy-Atl	293
		Bass-Hou	184	Samuel-Phi	36					Hayes-Phi	293

Runs Batted In		Runs Produced		Bases On Balls		Batting Average		On Base Percentage		Slugging Average	
Schmidt-Phi	119	Hayes-Phi	186	Hernandez-NY	94	Raines-Mon	.334	Raines-Mon	.415	Schmidt-Phi	.547
Parker-Cin	116	Schmidt-Phi	179	Schmidt-Phi	89	Sax-LA	.332	Hernandez-NY	.414	Strawberry-NY	.507
Carter-NY	105	Parker-Cin	174	C.Davis-SD	84	Gwynn-SD	.329	Schmidt-Phi	.395	McReynolds-SD	.504
Davis-Hou	101	Hernandez-NY	164	Oberkfell-Atl	83	Bass-Hou	.311	Sax-LA	.391	Davis-Hou	.493
Hayes-Phi	98	Carter-NY	162	Doran-Hou	81	Hernandez-NY	.310	Gwynn-SD	.382	Bass-Hou	.486

Production		Adjusted Production		Batter Runs		Adjusted Batter Runs		Clutch Hitting Index		Runs Created	
Schmidt-Phi	.942	Schmidt-Phi	152	Schmidt-Phi	44.0	Schmidt-Phi	41.5	Carter-NY	154	Raines-Mon	130
Raines-Mon	.891	Raines-Mon	146	Raines-Mon	38.0	Raines-Mon	38.7	Herr-StL	135	Schmidt-Phi	122
Strawberry-NY	.871	Strawberry-NY	142	Hernandez-NY	32.2	Hernandez-NY	34.3	Pendleton-StL	133	Gwynn-SD	113
McReynolds-SD	.867	Hernandez-NY	141	Hayes-Phi	30.3	Sax-LA	31.4	Ray-Pit	132	Hayes-Phi	111
Hayes-Phi	.861	McReynolds-SD	140	Gwynn-SD	28.4	Gwynn-SD	30.0	Cruz-Hou	131	Sax-LA	110

Total Average		Stolen Bases		Stolen Base Average		Stolen Base Runs		Fielding Runs		Total Player Rating	
Raines-Mon	1.040	Coleman-StL	107	Dernier-Chi	93.1	Coleman-StL	23.7	Hubbard-Atl	41.0	Raines-Mon	5.5
Schmidt-Phi	.988	Davis-Cin	80	Raines-Mon	88.6	Davis-Cin	17.4	Pendleton-StL	24.5	Gwynn-SD	4.9
Strawberry-NY	.910	Raines-Mon	70	Coleman-StL	88.4	Raines-Mon	15.6	Bream-Pit	23.4	Hernandez-NY	4.4
Hernandez-NY	.873	Duncan-LA	48	Davis-Cin	87.9	Dernier-Chi	6.9	Dunston-Chi	20.3	Davis-Cin	4.4
McReynolds-SD	.848			Leonard-SF	84.2			Hernandez-NY	18.3	Hubbard-Atl	3.1

Wins		Win Percentage		Games		Complete Games		Shutouts		Saves	
Valenzuela-LA	21	Ojeda-NY	.783	Lefferts-SD	83	Valenzuela-LA	20	Scott-Hou	5	Worrell-StL	36
Krukow-SF	20	Gooden-NY	.739	McDowell-NY	75	Rhoden-Pit	12	Knepper-Hou	5	Reardon-Mon	35
Scott-Hou	18	Fernandez-NY	.727	Worrell-StL	74	Gooden-NY	12	Welch-LA	3	Smith-Hou	33
Ojeda-NY	18	Darling-NY	.714	Franco-Cin	74	Krukow-SF	10	Valenzuela-LA	3	Smith-Chi	31
		Krukow-SF	.690	Tekulve-Phi	73						

Innings Pitched		Fewest Hits/Game		Fewest BB/Game		Strikeouts		Strikeouts/Game		Ratio	
Scott-Hou	275.1	Scott-Hou	5.95	Eckersley-Chi	1.93	Scott-Hou	306	Scott-Hou	10.00	Scott-Hou	8.37
Valenzuela-LA	269.1	Youmans-Mon	5.96	Sanderson-Chi	1.96	Valenzuela-LA	242	Ryan-Hou	9.81	Krukow-SF	9.66
Knepper-Hou	258.0	Ryan-Hou	6.02	Krukow-SF	2.02	Youmans-Mon	202	Fernandez-NY	8.81	Ojeda-NY	9.90
Rhoden-Pit	253.2	Fernandez-NY	7.09	Welch-LA	2.10	Gooden-NY	200	Youmans-Mon	8.30	Gooden-NY	10.12
Gooden-NY	250.0	Gooden-NY	7.09	Ojeda-NY	2.15	Fernandez-NY	200	Valenzuela-LA	8.09	Rhoden-Pit	10.25

Earned Run Average		Adjusted ERA		Opponents' Batting Avg.		Opponents' On Base Pct.		Starter Runs		Adjusted Starter Runs	
Scott-Hou	2.22	Scott-Hou	162	Scott-Hou	.186	Scott-Hou	.244	Scott-Hou	45.7	Scott-Hou	42.1
Ojeda-NY	2.57	Ojeda-NY	138	Ryan-Hou	.188	Krukow-SF	.271	Ojeda-NY	27.7	Rhoden-Pit	28.0
Darling-NY	2.81	Rhoden-Pit	135	Youmans-Mon	.188	Ojeda-NY	.279	Rhoden-Pit	24.7	Ojeda-NY	23.3
Rhoden-Pit	2.84	Darling-NY	126	Gooden-NY	.215	Gooden-NY	.280	Gooden-NY	24.2	Ruffin-Phi	22.6
Gooden-NY	2.84	Cox-StL	125	Fernandez-NY	.216	Ryan-Hou	.285	Darling-NY	23.9	Gooden-NY	19.2

Clutch Pitching Index		Relief Runs		Adjusted Relief Runs		Relief Ranking		Total Pitcher Index		Total Baseball Ranking	
Dravecky-SD	115	Worrell-StL	18.8	Worrell-StL	17.9	Worrell-StL	43.5	Scott-Hou	4.6	Raines-Mon	5.5
Darling-NY	113	McGaffigan-Mon	16.9	McGaffigan-Mon	16.5	Smith-Chi	24.5	Rhoden-Pit	4.2	Gwynn-SD	4.9
Garrelts-SF	110	Horton-StL	16.4	Tekulve-Phi	15.6	Orosco-NY	23.1	Ojeda-NY	2.3	Hernandez-NY	4.8
Tudor-StL	109	Tekulve-Phi	14.4	Horton-StL	15.6	Garber-Atl	22.9	Darling-NY	2.1	Scott-Hou	4.6
Gullickson-Cin	109	McCullers-SD	14.2	McCullers-SD	13.2	Tekulve-Phi	22.3	Ruffin-Phi	2.0	Davis-Cin	4.4

TEAM	G	W	L	PCT	GB	R	OR	AB	H	2B	3B	HR	BB	SO	AVG	OBP	SLG	PRO	PRO+	BR	/A	PF	CHI	RC	SB	CS	SBA	SBR
EAST																												
BOS	161	95	66	.590		794	696	5498	1488	**320**	21	144	595	**707**	.271	.349	.415	.764	106	59	56	100	98	792	41	34	34	**-9**
NY	162	90	72	.556	5.5	797	738	5570	1512	275	23	188	645	911	.271	**.350**	**.430**	**.780**	**112**	**89**	**98**	99	94	**843**	139	48	59	-20
DET	162	87	75	.537	8.5	798	714	5512	1447	234	30	**198**	613	885	.263	.341	.424	.765	101	52	55	100	99	814	138	58	50	-12
TOR	163	86	76	.531	9.5	809	733	5716	1540	285	35	181	496	848	.269	.331	.427	.758	101	29	10	102	103	796	110	59	54	-14
CLE	163	84	78	.519	11.5	831	841	5702	**1620**	270	**45**	157	456	944	**.284**	.340	**.430**	.770	109	57	70	98	102	822	**141**	54	50	-13
MIL	161	77	84	.478	18	667	734	5461	1393	255	38	127	530	986	.255	.324	.385	.709	89	-58	-80	103	98	682	100	50	50	-14
BAL	162	73	89	.451	22.5	708	760	5524	1425	223	13	169	563	862	.258	.330	.395	.725	97	-27	-15	99	98	708	64	34	40	-13
WEST																												
CAL	162	92	70	.568		786	684	5433	1387	236	36	167	**671**	860	.255	.341	.404	.745	103	22	31	99	101	765	109	42	51	-17
TEX	162	87	75	.537	5	771	743	5529	1479	248	43	184	511	1088	.267	.333	.428	.761	102	37	19	102	99	761	103	85	**63**	-11
KC	162	76	86	.469	16	654	**673**	5561	1403	264	**45**	137	474	919	.252	.315	.390	.705	88	-76	-90	102	99	683	97	46	42	-10
OAK	162	76	86	.469	16	731	760	5435	1370	213	25	163	553	983	.252	.325	.390	.715	100	-47	8	93	106	700	139	61	59	-16
CHI	162	72	90	.444	20	644	699	5406	1335	197	34	121	487	940	.247	.313	.363	.676	80	-124	-146	103	**107**	614	115	54	48	-12
MIN	162	71	91	.438	21	741	839	5531	1446	257	39	196	501	977	.261	.327	.428	.755	97	21	2	103	97	756	81	61	56	-14
SEA	162	67	95	.414	25	718	835	5498	1392	243	41	158	572	1148	.253	.327	.399	.726	95	-27	-32	101	100	706	93	76	58	-11
TOT	1134					10449		77376	20237	3520	468	2290	7667	13058	.262	.332	.408	.740							1470	762	66	-15

TEAM	CG	SH	SV	IP	H	H/G	HR	BB	SO	RAT	ERA	ERA+	OAV	OOB	PR	/A	PF	CPI	FA	E	DP	FW	PW	BW	SBW	DIF
EAST																										
BOS	36	6	41	1429²	1469	9.2	167	**474**	1033	12.4	3.93	106	.266	.327	38	36	100	**106**	.979	129	146	-.2	3.5	5.5	**-.8**	6.4
NY	13	8	**58**	1443¹	1461	9.1	175	492	878	12.3	4.11	99	.262	.325	10	-3	98	100	.979	127	153	.0	-.3	**9.6**	-1.9	1.5
DET	33	12	38	1443²	1374	8.6	183	571	880	12.3	4.02	102	.250	.325	24	16	99	100	.982	108	163	1.1	1.6	5.4	-1.1	-1.1
TOR	16	12	44	1476	1467	8.9	164	487	1002	12.2	4.08	103	.260	.324	15	22	101	99	**.984**	100	150	**1.7**	2.2	1.0	-1.3	1.5
CLE	31	7	34	1447²	1548	9.6	167	605	744	13.7	4.58	91	.273	.349	-64	-69	99	101	.975	157	148	-1.7	-6.8	6.9	-1.2	5.8
MIL	29	12	32	1431²	1478	9.3	158	494	952	12.6	4.01	108	.266	.330	26	50	104	104	.976	146	146	-1.2	4.9	-7.9	-1.3	1.9
BAL	17	6	39	1436²	1451	9.1	177	535	954	12.6	4.30	96	.262	.330	-20	-27	99	98	.978	135	163	-.5	-2.7	-1.5	-1.2	-2.2
WEST																										
CAL	29	12	40	1456	1356	**8.4**	153	478	955	**11.5**	3.84	107	.247	**.311**	54	43	98	94	.983	107	156	1.2	4.2	3.0	-1.6	4.1
TEX	15	8	41	1450¹	1356	**8.4**	145	736	**1059**	13.2	4.11	105	.248	.342	10	31	103	100	.980	122	160	.3	3.0	1.9	-1.0	1.7
KC	24	**13**	31	1440²	1413	8.8	**121**	479	888	12.1	**3.82**	**111**	.257	.321	56	68	102	98	.980	123	153	.2	**6.7**	-8.8	-.9	-2.2
OAK	22	8	37	1433	**1334**	**8.4**	166	667	937	12.8	4.31	90	**.246**	.333	-21	-70	93	94	.978	135	120	-.5	-6.9	.8	-1.5	3.0
CHI	18	8	38	1442¹	1361	8.5	143	561	895	12.2	3.93	110	.250	.324	39	60	103	97	.981	117	142	.6	5.9	-14.4	-1.1	-.0
MIN	**39**	6	24	1432²	1579	9.9	200	503	937	13.4	4.77	90	.280	.344	-94	-73	103	101	.980	118	168	.5	-7.2	.2	-1.3	-2.3
SEA	33	5	27	1439²	1590	9.9	171	585	944	13.9	4.65	91	.282	.355	-76	-65	102	105	.975	156	191	-1.7	-6.4	-3.1	-1.0	-1.8
TOT	355	123	524	20203¹		9.0				12.7	4.18		.262	.332					.979	1780	2159					

Runs		Hits		Doubles		Triples		Home Runs		Total Bases	
Henderson-NY	130	Mattingly-NY	238	Mattingly-NY	53	Butler-Cle	14	Barfield-Tor	40	Mattingly-NY	388
Puckett-Min	119	Puckett-Min	223	Boggs-Bos	47	Sierra-Tex	10	Kingman-Oak	35	Puckett-in	365
Mattingly-NY	117	Fernandez-Tor	213	Rice-Bos	39	Fernandez-Tor	9	Gaetti-Min	34	Carter-Cle	341
Carter-Cle	108	Boggs-Bos	207	Buckner-Bos	39	Carter-Cle	9	Deer-Mil	33	Bell-Tor	341
				Barrett-Bos	39			Canseco-Oak	33	Barfield-Tor	329

Runs Batted In		Runs Produced		Bases On Balls		Batting Average		On Base Percentage		Slugging Average	
Carter-Cle	121	Carter-Cle	200	Boggs-Bos	105	Boggs-Bos	.357	Boggs-Bos	.455	Mattingly-NY	.573
Canseco-Oak	117	Mattingly-NY	199	Evans-Bos	97	Mattingly-NY	.352	P.Bradley-Sea	.406	Barfield-Tor	.559
Mattingly-NY	113	Rice-Bos	188	Randolph-NY	94	Puckett-Min	.328	Brett-KC	.404	Puckett-Min	.537
Rice-Bos	110	Puckett-Min	184	Jackson-Cal	92	Tabler-Cle	.326	Murray-Bal	.400	Bell-Tor	.532
		Bell-Tor	178	Evans-Det	91	Rice-Bos	.324	Mattingly-NY	.399	Gaetti-Min	.518

Production		Adjusted Production		Batter Runs		Adjusted Batter Runs		Clutch Hitting Index		Runs Created	
Mattingly-NY	.973	Mattingly-NY	163	Mattingly-NY	55.6	Mattingly-NY	56.7	Downing-Cal	132	Mattingly-NY	150
Boggs-Bos	.942	Boggs-Bos	156	Boggs-Bos	51.6	Boggs-Bos	51.3	Winfield-NY	132	Boggs-Bos	133
Barfield-Tor	.929	Barfield-Tor	145	Barfield-Tor	39.0	Barfield-Tor	37.1	Rice-Bos	128	Puckett-Min	127
Puckett-Min	.903	Puckett-Min	138	Puckett-Min	37.1	Puckett-Min	35.0	Murray-Bal	127	Barfield-Tor	122
Brett-KC	.885	Rice-Bos	137	Rice-Bos	32.6	Rice-Bos	32.4	Joyner-Cal	125	Carter-Cle	116

Total Average		Stolen Bases		Stolen Base Average		Stolen Base Runs		Fielding Runs		Total Player Rating	
Boggs-Bos	.987	Henderson-NY	87	Felder-Mil	88.9	Henderson-NY	15.3	Owen-Sea-Bos	31.9	Barfield-Tor	5.0
Mattingly-NY	.969	Pettis-Cal	50	Davis-Oak	87.1	Pettis-Cal	7.2	Reynolds-Sea	28.8	Boggs-Bos	4.3
Gibson-Det	.950	Cangelosi-Chi	50	Gibson-Det	85.0	Gibson-Det	6.6	Barfield-Tor	20.4	Mattingly-NY	3.8
Barfield-Tor	.931	Wilson-KC	34	Henderson-NY	82.9	Davis-Oak	5.7	Buckner-Bos	20.1	Ripken-Bal	3.8
Henderson-NY	.931	Gibson-Det	34			Wilson-KC	5.4	Gaetti-Min	19.0	Rice-Bos	3.7

Wins		Win Percentage		Games		Complete Games		Shutouts		Saves	
Clemens-Bos	24	Clemens-Bos	.857	Williams-Tex	80	Candiotti-Cle	17	Morris-Det	6	Righetti-NY	46
Morris-Det	21	Rasmussen-NY	.750	Righetti-NY	74	Blyleven-Min	16	Hurst-Bos	4	Aase-Bal	34
Higuera-Mil	20	Morris-Det	.724	Harris-Tex	73	Morris-Det	15	Higuera-Mil	4	Henke-Tor	27
Witt-Cal	18	Higuera-Mil	.645	Eichhorn-Tor	69	Higuera-Mil	15			Hernandez-Det	24
Rasmussen-NY	18	Witt-Cal	.643			Witt-Cal	14			Moore-Cal	21

Innings Pitched		Fewest Hits/Game		Fewest BB/Game		Strikeouts		Strikeouts/Game		Ratio	
Blyleven-Min	271.2	Clemens-Bos	6.34	Guidry-NY	1.78	Langston-Sea	245	Langston-Sea	9.21	Clemens-Bos	8.86
Witt-Cal	269.0	Rasmussen-NY	7.13	Boyd-Bos	1.89	Clemens-Bos	238	Hurst-Bos	8.62	Witt-Cal	9.84
Morris-Det	267.0	Witt-Cal	7.29	Blyleven-Min	1.92	Morris-Det	223	Clemens-Bos	8.43	Morris-Det	10.48
Moore-Sea	266.0	Hough-Tex	7.35	Wegman-Mil	1.95	Blyleven-Min	215	Correa-Tex	8.41	Rasmussen-NY	10.51
Clemens-Bos	254.0	Cowley-Chi	7.37	Sutton-Cal	2.13	Witt-Cal	208	Rijo-Oak	8.18	Sutton-Cal	10.61

Earned Run Average		Adjusted ERA		Opponents' Batting Avg.		Opponents' On Base Pct.		Starter Runs		Adjusted Starter Runs	
Clemens-Bos	2.48	Clemens-Bos	168	Clemens-Bos	.195	Clemens-Bos	.253	Clemens-Bos	47.8	Clemens-Bos	47.5
Higuera-Mil	2.79	Higuera-Mil	155	Rasmussen-NY	.217	Witt-Cal	.277	Witt-Cal	39.8	Higuera-Mil	42.4
Witt-Cal	2.84	Witt-Cal	144	Witt-Cal	.221	Morris-Det	.287	Higuera-Mil	38.2	Witt-Cal	37.8
Hurst-Bos	2.99	Hurst-Bos	139	Hough-Tex	.221	Sutton-Cal	.288	Morris-Det	26.9	Morris-Det	25.3
D.Jackson-KC	3.20	D.Jackson-KC	133	Correa-Tex	.223	Rasmussen-NY	.290	Hurst-Bos	22.9	Hurst-Bos	22.6

Clutch Pitching Index		Relief Runs		Adjusted Relief Runs		Relief Ranking		Total Pitcher Index		Total Baseball Ranking	
Hurst-Bos	123	Eichhorn-Tor	42.8	Eichhorn-Tor	43.6	Eichhorn-Tor	56.2	Clemens-Bos	4.9	Barfield-Tor	5.0
D.Jackson-KC	121	Righetti-NY	20.5	Righetti-NY	19.4	Righetti-NY	45.1	Eichhorn-Tor	4.5	Clemens-Bos	4.9
Higuera-Mil	119	Harris-Tex	16.7	Harris-Tex	18.2	Harris-Tex	33.8	Higuera-Mil	4.3	Eichhorn-Tor	4.5
Stieb-Tor	119	Clear-Mil	16.2	Clear-Mil	17.4	Clear-Mil	29.8	Witt-Cal	4.1	Boggs-Bos	4.3
Niekro-Cle	117	Mohorcic-Tex	14.7	Mohorcic-Tex	15.8	Plesac-Mil	27.9	Morris-Det	2.5	Higuera-Mil	4.3

TEAM	G	W	L	PCT	GB	R	OR	AB	H	2B	3B	HR	BB	SO	AVG	OBP	SLG	PRO	PRO+	BR	/A	PF	CHI	RC	SB	CS	SBA	SBR
EAST																												
STL	162	95	67	.586		798	693	5500	1449	252	49	94	**644**	933	.263	**.343**	.378	.721	95	-8	-22	102	**109**	740	**248**	72	56	-11
NY	162	92	70	.568	3	**823**	698	5601	**1499**	287	34	192	592	1012	**.268**	.341	**.434**	**.775**	117	81	119	95	100	**848**	159	49	47	-13
MON	162	91	71	.562	4	741	720	5527	1467	**310**	39	120	501	918	.265	.330	.401	.731	96	-5	-26	103	103	734	166	74	61	-13
PIT	162	80	82	.494	15	723	744	5536	1464	282	45	131	535	914	.264	.332	.403	.735	99	3	-1	101	98	741	140	58	49	-11
PHI	162	80	82	.494	15	702	749	5475	1390	248	**51**	169	587	1109	.254	.329	.410	.739	97	8	-15	103	95	736	111	49	50	-14
CHI	161	76	85	.472	18.5	720	801	5583	1475	244	33	**209**	504	1064	.264	.327	.432	.759	102	40	11	104	94	785	109	48	49	-14
WEST																												
SF	162	90	72	.556		783	**669**	5608	1458	274	32	205	511	1094	.260	.326	.430	.756	110	33	68	95	102	768	126	97	**66**	-10
CIN	162	84	78	.519	6	783	752	5560	1478	262	29	192	514	928	.266	.331	.427	.758	101	42	9	104	102	786	169	46	41	-10
HOU	162	76	86	.469	14	648	678	5485	1386	238	28	122	526	936	.253	.321	.373	.694	93	-77	-49	96	100	669	162	46	53	-17
LA	162	73	89	.451	17	635	675	5517	1389	236	23	125	445	923	.252	.311	.371	.682	88	-107	-88	97	104	627	128	59	53	-13
ATL	161	69	92	.429	20.5	747	829	5428	1401	284	24	152	641	**834**	.258	.341	.403	.744	98	28	-7	105	98	747	135	68	56	-12
SD	162	65	97	.401	25	668	763	5456	1419	209	48	113	577	992	.260	.334	.378	.712	98	-33	-6	96	96	693	198	91	62	**-9**
TOT	971					8771		66276	17275	3126	435	1824	6577	11657	.261	.331	.404	.734							1851	757	71	101

TEAM	CG	SH	SV	IP	H	H/G	HR	BB	SO	RAT	ERA	ERA+	OAV	OOB	PR	/A	PF	CPI	FA	E	DP	FW	PW	BW	SBW	DIF
EAST																										
STL	10	7	48	1466	1484	9.1	**129**	533	873	12.5	3.91	106	.265	.332	27	39	102	103	**.982**	116	172	.9	3.9	-2.2	-1.9	13.4
NY	16	7	**51**	1454	1407	8.7	135	510	1032	12.1	3.84	98	.254	.321	38	-10	93	97	.978	137	137	-.3	-1.0	**11.8**	-2.1	2.6
MON	16	8	50	1450[1]	1428	8.9	145	**446**	1012	11.8	3.92	107	.256	**.314**	26	**46**	103	95	.976	147	122	-.9	**4.6**	-2.6	-2.1	11.0
PIT	25	**13**	39	1445	1377	8.6	164	562	914	12.2	4.20	98	.253	.325	-18	-14	101	95	.980	123	147	.5	-1.4	-.0	-1.9	2.0
PHI	13	7	48	1448[1]	1453	9.0	167	587	877	12.9	4.18	101	.263	.337	-16	9	104	103	.980	121	137	.6	.9	-1.5	-2.2	1.2
CHI	11	5	48	1434[2]	1524	9.6	159	628	1024	13.7	4.55	94	.274	.351	-75	-44	105	103	.979	130	154	.0	-4.4	1.1	-2.2	1.0
WEST																										
SF	19	10	38	1471	1407	8.6	146	547	1038	12.1	**3.68**	105	.254	.325	**65**	27	94	**106**	.980	129	**183**	.1	2.7	6.8	-1.8	1.2
CIN	7	6	44	1453	1486	9.2	170	485	919	12.3	4.24	100	.267	.328	-26	0	104	99	.979	130	137	.0	.0	.9	-1.8	3.9
HOU	13	**13**	33	1441[1]	**1363**	8.5	141	525	**1137**	12.0	3.84	102	**.249**	.318	38	12	96	96	.981	116	113	.9	1.2	-4.9	-2.5	.3
LA	**29**	8	32	1455	1415	8.8	130	565	1097	12.4	3.72	107	.254	.326	58	40	97	103	.975	155	144	-1.3	4.0	-8.8	-2.1	.2
ATL	16	4	32	1427[2]	1529	9.6	163	587	837	13.6	4.63	94	.276	.349	-86	-44	107	101	**.982**	116	170	.8	-4.4	-.7	-2.0	-5.2
SD	14	10	33	1433[1]	1402	8.8	175	602	897	12.8	4.27	93	.255	.333	-30	-50	97	98	.976	147	135	-.9	-5.0	-.6	**-1.7**	-7.8
TOT	189	98	496	17379[2]		8.9				12.5	4.08		.261	.331					.979	1567	1751					

Runs
Raines-Mon	123
Coleman-StL	121
Davis-Cin	120
Gwynn-SD	119
Murphy-Atl	115

Hits
Gwynn-SD	218
Guerrero-LA	184
Smith-StL	182
Coleman-StL	180

Doubles
Wallach-Mon	42
Smith-StL	40
Galarraga-Mon	40

Triples
Samuel-Phi	15
Gwynn-SD	13
VanSlyke-Pit	11
McGee-StL	11
Coleman-StL	10

Home Runs
Dawson-Chi	49
Murphy-Atl	44
Strawberry-NY	39
Davis-Cin	37
Johnson-NY	36

Total Bases
Dawson-Chi	353
Samuel-Phi	329
Murphy-Atl	328
Strawberry-NY	310
Clark-SF	307

Runs Batted In
Dawson-Chi	137
Wallach-Mon	123
Schmidt-Phi	113
Clark-StL	106

Runs Produced
Wallach-Mon	186
Samuel-Phi	185
Davis-Cin	183
Smith-StL	179
Dawson-Chi	178

Bases On Balls
Clark-StL	136
Hayes-Phi	121
Murphy-Atl	115
Strawberry-NY	97
Raines-Mon	90

Batting Average
Gwynn-SD	.370
Guerrero-LA	.338
Raines-Mon	.330
Kruk-SD	.313
James-Atl	.312

On Base Percentage
Clark-StL	.461
Gwynn-SD	.450
Raines-Mon	.431
Guerrero-LA	.421
Murphy-Atl	.420

Slugging Average
Clark-StL	.597
Davis-Cin	.593
Strawberry-NY	.583
Clark-SF	.580
Murphy-Atl	.580

Production
Clark-StL	1.058
Murphy-Atl	1.000
Davis-Cin	.994
Strawberry-NY	.984
Gwynn-SD	.961

Adjusted Production
Clark-StL	174
Strawberry-NY	165
Gwynn-SD	160
Guerrero-LA	156
Clark-SF	155

Batter Runs
Clark-StL	54.3
Murphy-Atl	53.3
Gwynn-SD	49.6
Strawberry-NY	44.7
Raines-Mon	43.2

Adjusted Batter Runs
Clark-StL	53.0
Gwynn-SD	52.4
Murphy-Atl	49.3
Strawberry-NY	48.6
Guerrero-LA	44.5

Clutch Hitting Index
Herr-StL	200
McGee-StL	147
Pendleton-StL	142
Wallach-Mon	136
Kruk-SD	133

Runs Created
Murphy-Atl	143
Gwynn-SD	143
Strawberry-NY	132
Raines-Mon	132
Clark-StL	127

Total Average
Clark-StL	1.258
Davis-Cin	1.182
Raines-Mon	1.133
Murphy-Atl	1.106
Strawberry-NY	1.103

Stolen Bases
Coleman-StL	109
Gwynn-SD	56
Hatcher-Hou	53
Raines-Mon	50
Davis-Cin	50

Stolen Base Average
Sandberg-Chi	91.3
Raines-Mon	90.9
Davis-Cin	89.3
Hatcher-Hou	85.5
Coleman-StL	83.2

Stolen Base Runs
Coleman-StL	19.5
Raines-Mon	12.0
Davis-Cin	11.4
Hatcher-Hou	10.5
Gwynn-SD	9.6

Fielding Runs
Hubbard-Atl	28.2
Davis-Cin	21.7
Smith-StL	19.3
Hernandez-NY	17.7
Bonds-Pit	17.1

Total Player Rating
Davis-Cin	6.4
Gwynn-SD	5.8
Raines-Mon	5.5
Smith-StL	5.2
Murphy-Atl	5.0

Wins
Sutcliffe-Chi	18
Rawley-Phi	17
Scott-Hou	16
Hershiser-LA	16

Win Percentage
Gooden-NY	.682
Sutcliffe-Chi	.643
Welch-LA	.625
Rawley-Phi	.607
Z.Smith-Atl	.600

Games
Tekulve-Phi	90
Murphy-Cin	87
Williams-StL	85
J.Robinson-SF-Pit	81
McCullers-SD	78

Complete Games
Reuschel-Pit-SF	12
Valenzuela-LA	12
Hershiser-LA	10
Z.Smith-Atl	9
Scott-Hou	8

Shutouts
Reuschel-Pit-SF	4
Welch-LA	4

Saves
Bedrosian-Phi	40
Smith-Chi	36
Worrell-StL	33
Franco-Cin	32
McDowell-NY	25

Innings Pitched
Hershiser-LA	264.2
Welch-LA	251.2
Valenzuela-LA	251.0
Scott-Hou	247.2
Z.Smith-Atl	242.0

Fewest Hits/Game
Ryan-Hou	6.55
Scott-Hou	7.23
Welch-LA	7.30
Dunne-Pit	7.88
Darling-NY	7.93

Fewest BB/Game
Reuschel-Pit-SF	1.67
Heaton-Mon	1.72
Gullickson-Cin	2.13
Forsch-StL	2.26
Drabek-Pit	2.35

Strikeouts
Ryan-Hou	270
Scott-Hou	233
Welch-LA	196
Valenzuela-LA	190
Hershiser-LA	190

Strikeouts/Game
Ryan-Hou	11.48
Scott-Hou	8.47
Sebra-Mon	7.92
Gooden-NY	7.41
Darling-NY	7.24

Ratio
Reuschel-Pit-SF	10.19
Scott-Hou	10.25
Ryan-Hou	10.42
Welch-LA	10.51
Drabek-Pit	10.77

Earned Run Average
Ryan-Hou	2.76
Dunne-Pit	3.03
Hershiser-LA	3.06
Reuschel-Pit-SF	3.09
Gooden-NY	3.21

Adjusted ERA
Ryan-Hou	142
Dunne-Pit	136
Reuschel-Pit-SF	131
Hershiser-LA	130
Welch-LA	123

Opponents' Batting Avg.
Ryan-Hou	.199
Scott-Hou	.217
Welch-LA	.221
Darling-NY	.233
Dunne-Pit	.240

Opponents' On Base Pct.
Scott-Hou	.282
Ryan-Hou	.284
Reuschel-Pit-SF	.284
Welch-LA	.291
Drabek-Pit	.296

Starter Runs
Ryan-Hou	30.9
Hershiser-LA	30.0
Reuschel-Pit-SF	24.9
Welch-LA	24.1
Scott-Hou	23.3

Adjusted Starter Runs
Ryan-Hou	27.1
Hershiser-LA	26.6
Reuschel-Pit-SF	24.1
Welch-LA	20.9
Dunne-Pit	19.6

Clutch Pitching Index
LaCoss-SF	124
Cox-StL	120
Dravecky-SD-SF	113
Ruffin-Phi	112
Grant-SF-SD	111

Relief Runs
Burke-Mon	29.2
McGaffigan-Mon	22.5
Williams-Cin	20.9
J.Robinson-SF-Pit	16.9
Smith-Hou	16.2

Adjusted Relief Runs
Burke-Mon	30.5
McGaffigan-Mon	24.2
Williams-Cin	22.8
Worrell-StL	15.7
Franco-Cin	15.7

Relief Ranking
Franco-Cin	36.1
Burke-Mon	34.7
Worrell-StL	33.2
Smith-Chi	26.6
Bedrosian-Phi	25.3

Total Pitcher Index
Hershiser-LA	3.3
Burke-Mon	3.1
Reuschel-Pit-SF	2.9
Welch-LA	2.4
Williams-Cin	2.4

Total Baseball Ranking
Davis-Cin	6.4
Gwynn-SD	5.8
Raines-Mon	5.5
Smith-StL	5.2
Murphy-Atl	5.0

TEAM	G	W	L	PCT	GB	R	OR	AB	H	2B	3B	HR	BB	SO	AVG	OBP	SLG	PRO	PRO+	BR	/A	PF	CHI	RC	SB	CS	SBA	SBR
EAST																												
DET	162	98	64	.605		896	735	5649	1535	274	32	225	653	913	.272	.352	.451	.803	116	91	127	96	98	910	106	50	46	-12
TOR	162	96	66	.593	2	845	655	5635	1514	277	38	215	555	970	.269	.338	.446	.784	103	42	26	102	100	841	126	50	52	-15
MIL	162	91	71	.562	7	862	817	5625	1552	272	46	163	598	1040	.276	.349	.428	.777	102	40	18	103	101	852	176	74	59	-12
NY	162	89	73	.549	9	788	758	5511	1445	239	16	196	604	949	.262	.338	.418	.756	100	-5	4	99	100	773	105	43	42	-11
BOS	162	78	84	.481	20	842	825	5586	1554	273	26	174	606	825	.278	.355	.430	.785	104	61	39	103	97	855	77	45	52	-17
BAL	162	67	95	.414	31	729	880	5576	1437	219	20	211	524	939	.258	.324	.418	.742	97	-46	-24	97	98	736	69	45	46	-13
CLE	162	61	101	.377	37	742	957	5606	1476	267	30	187	489	977	.263	.326	.422	.748	95	-34	-38	101	98	772	140	54	54	-15
WEST																												
MIN	162	85	77	.525		786	806	5441	1422	258	35	196	523	898	.261	.330	.430	.760	95	-7	-34	104	102	757	113	65	55	-13
KC	162	83	79	.512	2	715	691	5499	1443	239	40	168	523	1034	.262	.330	.412	.742	92	-39	-57	102	97	747	125	43	44	-13
OAK	162	81	81	.500	4	806	789	5511	1432	263	33	199	593	1056	.260	.336	.428	.764	108	4	57	93	101	796	140	63	59	-16
SEA	162	78	84	.481	7	760	801	5508	1499	282	48	161	500	863	.272	.337	.428	.765	96	9	-30	105	96	788	174	73	55	-10
CHI	162	77	85	.475	8	748	746	5538	1427	283	36	173	487	971	.258	.321	.415	.736	90	-56	-74	102	103	737	138	52	49	-13
TEX	162	75	87	.463	10	823	849	5564	1478	264	35	194	567	1081	.266	.336	.430	.766	100	9	8	100	102	798	120	71	59	-13
CAL	162	75	87	.463	10	770	803	5570	1406	257	26	172	590	926	.252	.328	.401	.729	95	-64	-35	97	104	744	125	44	43	-12
TOT	1134					11112		77819	20620	3667	461	2634	7812	13442	.265	.336	.425	.761							1734	772	69	57

TEAM	CG	SH	SV	IP	H	H/G	HR	BB	SO	RAT	ERA	ERA+	OAV	OOB	PR	/A	PF	CPI	FA	E	DP	FW	PW	BW	SBW	DIF
EAST																										
DET	33	10	31	1456	1430	8.8	180	563	976	12.5	4.02	105	.255	.327	69	31	95	103	.980	122	147	.1	3.0	12.1	-1.5	3.4
TOR	18	8	43	1454	1323	8.2	158	567	1064	11.8	3.74	120	.243	.317	114	120	101	100	.982	111	148	.8	11.4	2.5	-1.8	2.1
MIL	28	6	45	1464	1548	9.5	169	529	1039	12.9	4.62	99	.271	.336	-27	-8	103	96	.976	145	155	-1.3	-.8	1.7	-1.5	11.9
NY	19	10	47	1446¹	1475	9.2	179	542	900	12.8	4.36	101	.265	.334	16	4	98	101	.983	102	155	1.3	.4	.4	-1.4	7.3
BOS	47	13	16	1436	1584	9.9	190	517	1034	13.4	4.77	95	.282	.346	-50	-37	102	102	.982	110	158	.8	-3.5	3.7	-2.0	-2.0
BAL	17	6	30	1439²	1555	9.7	226	547	870	13.3	5.01	88	.276	.343	-88	-97	99	98	.982	111	174	.8	-9.2	-2.3	-1.6	-1.6
CLE	24	8	25	1422²	1566	9.9	219	606	849	14.1	5.28	86	.278	.353	-130	-120	102	97	.975	153	128	-1.8	-11.4	-3.6	-1.8	-1.3
WEST																										
MIN	16	4	39	1427¹	1465	9.2	210	564	990	13.1	4.63	100	.265	.339	-27	-1	104	100	.984	98	147	1.6	-.0	-3.2	-1.6	7.4
KC	44	11	26	1424	1424	9.0	128	548	923	12.7	3.86	118	.261	.332	95	110	102	105	.979	131	151	-.5	10.5	-5.4	-1.6	-1.0
OAK	18	6	40	1445²	1442	9.0	176	531	1042	12.5	4.32	96	.258	.326	21	-31	93	96	.977	142	122	-1.1	-3.0	5.4	-1.9	.6
SEA	39	10	33	1430²	1503	9.5	199	497	919	12.8	4.49	105	.271	.334	-4	37	106	102	.980	122	150	.1	3.5	-2.9	-1.3	-2.4
CHI	29	12	37	1447²	1436	8.9	189	537	792	12.5	4.30	107	.259	.328	25	45	103	99	.981	116	174	.5	4.3	-7.1	-1.6	-.0
TEX	20	3	27	1444¹	1388	8.6	199	760	1103	13.7	4.63	97	.252	.349	-27	-25	100	100	.976	151	148	-1.7	-2.4	.8	-1.6	-1.1
CAL	20	7	36	1457¹	1481	9.1	212	504	941	12.5	4.38	98	.264	.328	12	-12	97	101	.981	117	162	.4	-1.1	-3.3	-1.5	-.4
TOT	372	114	475	20195²		9.2				12.9	4.46		.265	.336					.980	1731	2119					

Runs
Molitor-Mil	114
Bell-Tor	111
Whitaker-Det	110
Downing-Cal	110

Hits
Seitzer-KC	207
Puckett-Min	207
Trammell-Det	205
Boggs-Bos	200
Yount-Mil	198

Doubles
Molitor-Mil	41
Boggs-Bos	40

Triples
Wilson-KC	15
Polonia-Oak	10
P.Bradley-Sea	10
Yount-Mil	9

Home Runs
McGwire-Oak	49
Bell-Tor	47

Total Bases
Bell-Tor	369
McGwire-Oak	344
Puckett-Min	333
Trammell-Det	329
Boggs-Bos	324

Runs Batted In
Bell-Tor	134
Evans-Bos	123
McGwire-Oak	118
Joyner-Cal	117
Mattingly-NY	115

Runs Produced
Evans-Bos	198
Bell-Tor	198
Trammell-Det	186
Joyner-Cal	183
Yount-Mil	181

Bases On Balls
Evans-Bos	106
Downing-Cal	106
Boggs-Bos	105
Evans-Det	100
Butler-Cle	91

Batting Average
Boggs-Bos	.363
Molitor-Mil	.353
Trammell-Det	.343
Puckett-Min	.332
Mattingly-NY	.327

On Base Percentage
Boggs-Bos	.467
Molitor-Mil	.438
Evans-Bos	.422
Randolph-NY	.415
Trammell-Det	.406

Slugging Average
McGwire-Oak	.618
Bell-Tor	.605
Boggs-Bos	.588
Evans-Bos	.569
Molitor-Mil	.566

Production
Boggs-Bos	1.055
Molitor-Mil	1.004
McGwire-Oak	.992
Evans-Bos	.991
Bell-Tor	.962

Adjusted Production
Boggs-Bos	173
McGwire-Oak	168
Molitor-Mil	159
Trammell-Det	157
Evans-Bos	155

Batter Runs
Boggs-Bos	66.6
Evans-Bos	49.6
Molitor-Mil	44.8
McGwire-Oak	44.2
Trammell-Det	43.7

Adjusted Batter Runs
Boggs-Bos	64.4
McGwire-Oak	49.8
Trammell-Det	47.4
Evans-Bos	47.4
Molitor-Mil	43.0

Clutch Hitting Index
Griffin-Oak	132
Brock-Mil	132
Baines-Chi	130
Braggs-Mil	127
Tabler-Cle	127

Runs Created
Boggs-Bos	154
Trammell-Det	137
Evans-Bos	134
McGwire-Oak	131
Molitor-Mil	125

Total Average
Molitor-Mil	1.171
Boggs-Bos	1.169
Evans-Bos	1.059
McGwire-Oak	1.042
Trammell-Det	1.015

Stolen Bases
Reynolds-Sea	60
Wilson-KC	59
Redus-Chi	52
Molitor-Mil	45
Henderson-NY	41

Stolen Base Average
McDowell-Tex	92.3
Trammell-Det	91.3
Schofield-Cal	86.4
Moseby-Tor	84.8
Wilson-KC	84.3

Stolen Base Runs
Wilson-KC	11.1
Redus-Chi	9.0
Moseby-Tor	7.5
Molitor-Mil	7.5
Henderson-NY	7.5

Fielding Runs
Barrett-Bos	32.3
White-Cal	25.4
Salazar-KC	21.7
Manrique-Chi	18.9
Reynolds-Sea	18.8

Total Player Rating
Boggs-Bos	6.0
Molitor-Mil	4.9
Trammell-Det	4.7
Barrett-Bos	3.4
Henderson-NY	3.4

Wins
Stewart-Oak	20
Clemens-Bos	20
Langston-Sea	19

Win Percentage
Clemens-Bos	.690
Key-Tor	.680
Saberhagen-KC	.643
Higuera-Mil	.643

Games
Eichhorn-Tor	89
Williams-Tex	85
Mohorcic-Tex	74
Henke-Tor	72
Musselman-Tor	68

Complete Games
Clemens-Bos	18
Saberhagen-KC	15
Hurst-Bos	15
Langston-Sea	14
Higuera-Mil	14

Shutouts
Clemens-Bos	7
Saberhagen-KC	4

Saves
Henke-Tor	34
Righetti-NY	31
Reardon-Min	31
Plesac-Mil	23
Buice-Cal	17

Innings Pitched
Hough-Tex	285.1
Clemens-Bos	281.2
Langston-Sea	272.0
Blyleven-Min	267.0
Morris-Det	266.0

Fewest Hits/Game
Key-Tor	7.24
Hough-Tex	7.51
Morris-Det	7.68
Stewart-Oak	7.71
DeLeon-Chi	7.73

Fewest BB/Game
Long-Chi	1.49
Saberhagen-KC	1.86
Sutton-Cal	1.93
Bannister-Chi	1.93
Young-Oak	1.95

Strikeouts
Langston-Sea	262
Clemens-Bos	256
Higuera-Mil	240
Hough-Tex	223
Morris-Det	208

Strikeouts/Game
Langston-Sea	8.67
Higuera-Mil	8.25
Clemens-Bos	8.18
Bosio-Mil	7.94
Nieves-Mil	7.50

Ratio
Key-Tor	9.59
Bannister-Chi	10.43
Saberhagen-KC	10.68
Young-Oak	10.68
Viola-Min	10.80

Earned Run Average
Key-Tor	2.76
Viola-Min	2.90
Clemens-Bos	2.97
Saberhagen-KC	3.36
Morris-Det	3.38

Adjusted ERA
Key-Tor	163
Viola-Min	159
Clemens-Bos	153
Saberhagen-KC	135
Leibrandt-KC	134

Opponents' Batting Avg.
Key-Tor	.221
Hough-Tex	.223
Morris-Det	.228
Stewart-Oak	.229
DeLeon-Chi	.230

Opponents' On Base Pct.
Key-Tor	.273
Bannister-Chi	.286
Viola-Min	.294
Morris-Det	.294
Young-Oak	.295

Starter Runs
Key-Tor	49.2
Clemens-Bos	46.5
Viola-Min	43.6
Morris-Det	31.7
Saberhagen-KC	31.2

Adjusted Starter Runs
Key-Tor	50.3
Clemens-Bos	49.0
Viola-Min	48.1
Saberhagen-KC	34.0
Leibrandt-KC	30.6

Clutch Pitching Index
Viola-Min	115
Rhoden-NY	112
Terrell-Det	110
Blyleven-Min	109
Gubicza-KC	107

Relief Runs
Henke-Tor	20.5
Eckersley-Oak	18.3
Eichhorn-Tor	18.2
Thigpen-Chi	17.1
Plesac-Mil	16.3

Adjusted Relief Runs
Henke-Tor	20.9
Eichhorn-Tor	18.7
Thigpen-Chi	18.3
Plesac-Mil	17.3
Mohorcic-Tex	16.4

Relief Ranking
Plesac-Mil	32.9
Thigpen-Chi	29.6
Henke-Tor	29.2
Mohorcic-Tex	25.2
Eichhorn-Tor	22.4

Total Pitcher Index
Key-Tor	5.4
Viola-Min	4.8
Clemens-Bos	4.7
Leibrandt-KC	3.5
Saberhagen-KC	3.5

Total Baseball Ranking
Boggs-Bos	6.0
Key-Tor	5.4
Molitor-Mil	4.9
Viola-Min	4.8
Clemens-Bos	4.7

TEAM	G	W	L	PCT	GB	R	OR	AB	H	2B	3B	HR	BB	SO	AVG	OBP	SLG	PRO	PRO+	BR	/A	PF	CHI	RC	SB	CS	SBA	SBR
EAST																												
NY	160	100	60	.625		**703**	**532**	5408	1387	251	24	**152**	544	842	.256	**.328**	**.396**	**.724**	119	95	125	95	97	**717**	140	51	45	-11
PIT	160	85	75	.531	15	651	616	5379	1327	240	45	110	**553**	947	.247	.321	.369	.690	105	33	41	99	99	648	119	60	57	-15
MON	163	81	81	.500	20	628	592	5573	1400	260	**48**	107	454	1053	.251	.311	.373	.684	97	12	-17	105	97	636	189	89	**61**	**-9**
CHI	163	77	85	.475	24	660	694	5675	**1481**	262	46	113	403	910	**.261**	.312	.383	.695	100	31	2	105	94	673	120	46	43	-11
STL	162	76	86	.469	25	578	633	5518	1373	207	33	71	484	**827**	.249	.312	.337	.649	92	-46	-52	101	98	601	**234**	64	60	-16
PHI	162	65	96	.404	35.5	597	734	5403	1294	246	31	106	489	981	.239	.308	.355	.663	94	-21	-34	102	99	599	112	49	45	-11
WEST																												
LA	162	94	67	.584		628	544	5431	1346	217	25	99	437	947	.248	.308	.352	.660	99	-31	-11	97	**106**	590	131	46	51	-16
CIN	161	87	74	.540	7	641	596	5426	1334	246	25	122	479	922	.246	.311	.368	.679	97	6	-18	104	102	639	207	56	52	-13
SD	161	83	78	.516	11	594	583	5366	1325	205	35	94	494	892	.247	.313	.351	.664	98	-18	-6	98	99	594	123	50	49	-13
SF	162	83	79	.512	11.5	670	626	5450	1353	227	44	113	550	1023	.248	.321	.368	.689	108	32	59	96	101	650	121	78	**61**	-12
HOU	162	82	80	.506	12.5	617	631	5494	1338	239	31	96	474	840	.244	.308	.351	.659	98	-31	-6	96	103	604	198	71	54	-10
ATL	160	54	106	.338	39.5	555	741	5440	1319	228	28	96	432	848	.242	.301	.348	.649	87	-55	-85	105	99	549	95	69	56	-12
TOT	969					7522		65563	16277	2828	415	1279	5793	11032	.248	.313	.363	.675							1789	729	71	99

TEAM	CG	SH	SV	IP	H	H/G	HR	BB	SO	RAT	ERA	ERA+	OAV	OOB	PR	/A	PF	CPI	FA	E	DP	FW	PW	BW	SBW	DIF
EAST																										
NY	31	22	46	1439	**1253**	7.8	78	404	1100	10.6	2.91	111	**.234**	**.292**	86	49	93	97	**.981**	115	127	.9	5.3	**13.5**	-2.1	2.4
PIT	12	11	46	1440²	1349	8.4	108	469	790	11.6	3.47	98	.250	.313	-3	-10	99	101	.980	125	128	.3	-1.1	4.4	-2.5	3.8
MON	18	12	43	1482²	1310	8.0	122	476	923	11.1	3.08	**117**	.237	.302	59	**84**	104	**105**	.978	142	145	-.5	**9.1**	-1.8	**-1.9**	-4.9
CHI	30	10	29	1464¹	1494	9.2	115	490	897	12.4	3.84	94	.264	.326	-64	-38	105	102	.980	125	128	.5	-4.1	.2	-2.1	1.5
STL	17	14	42	1470²	1387	8.5	91	486	881	11.6	3.47	100	.251	.314	-3	0	101	99	**.981**	121	131	.6	.0	-5.6	-2.6	2.6
PHI	16	6	36	1433	1447	9.1	118	628	859	13.3	4.14	86	.264	.344	-110	-92	103	102	.976	145	139	-.7	-9.9	-3.7	-2.1	.9
WEST																										
LA	**32**	**24**	49	1463¹	1291	7.9	84	473	1029	11.0	2.96	112	.237	.300	78	59	97	102	.977	142	126	-.5	6.4	-1.2	-2.6	11.5
CIN	24	13	43	1455	1271	7.9	121	504	934	11.1	3.35	107	.236	.305	16	37	104	98	.980	125	131	.4	4.0	-1.9	-2.3	6.4
SD	30	9	39	1449²	1332	8.3	112	439	885	11.1	3.28	104	.246	.306	27	18	99	102	**.981**	120	**147**	.6	1.9	-.6	-2.3	2.9
SF	25	13	42	1462¹	1323	8.1	99	422	875	10.9	3.39	96	.242	.300	10	-20	95	93	.980	129	145	.2	-2.2	6.4	-2.2	-.2
HOU	21	15	40	1474²	1339	8.2	123	478	1049	11.3	3.41	97	.242	.307	6	-14	96	99	.978	138	124	-.3	-1.5	-.6	-2.0	5.4
ATL	14	4	25	1446	1481	9.2	108	524	810	12.7	4.09	90	.267	.336	-103	-66	107	100	.976	151	138	-1.1	-7.1	-9.2	-2.2	-6.4
TOT	270	153	480	17481¹		8.4				11.6	3.45		.248	.313					.979	1578	1609					

Runs		Hits		Doubles		Triples		Home Runs		Total Bases	
Butler-SF	109	Galarraga-Mon	184	Galarraga-Mon	42	VanSlyke-Pit	15	Strawberry-NY	39	Galarraga-Mon	329
Gibson-LA	106	Dawson-Chi	179	Palmeiro-Chi	41	Coleman-StL	10	Davis-Hou	30	Dawson-Chi	298
Clark-SF	102	Palmeiro-Chi	178	Sabo-Cin	40	Young-Hou	9	Galarraga-Mon	29	VanSlyke-Pit	297
VanSlyke-Pit	101	Sax-LA	175	Bream-Pit	37	Samuel-Phi	9	Clark-SF	29	Strawberry-NY	296
Strawberry-NY	101	Larkin-Cin	174			Butler-SF	9	McReynolds-NY	27	Clark-SF	292

Runs Batted In		Runs Produced		Bases On Balls		Batting Average		On Base Percentage		Slugging Average	
Clark-SF	109	Clark-SF	182	Clark-SF	100	Gwynn-SD	.313	Daniels-Cin	.400	Strawberry-NY	.545
Strawberry-NY	101	VanSlyke-Pit	176	Butler-SF	97	Palmeiro-Chi	.307	Butler-SF	.395	Galarraga-Mon	.540
VanSlyke-Pit	100	Strawberry-NY	163	Daniels-Cin	87	Dawson-Chi	.303	Clark-SF	.392	Clark-SF	.508
Bonilla-Pit	100	Bonilla-Pit	163	Johnson-NY	86	Galarraga-Mon	.302	Gibson-LA	.381	VanSlyke-Pit	.506
		Galarraga-Mon	162			Perry-Atl	.300	Gwynn-SD	.374	Dawson-Chi	.504

Production		Adjusted Production		Batter Runs		Adjusted Batter Runs		Clutch Hitting Index		Runs Created	
Strawberry-NY	.916	Strawberry-NY	168	Clark-SF	44.3	Clark-SF	47.3	Moreland-SD	142	Clark-SF	120
Clark-SF	.900	Clark-SF	163	Strawberry-NY	42.0	Strawberry-NY	45.3	Perry-Atl	129	Galarraga-Mon	114
Galarraga-Mon	.894	Gibson-LA	151	Galarraga-Mon	39.2	Galarraga-Mon	36.1	Doran-Hou	124	Strawberry-NY	111
Gibson-LA	.864	Bonds-Pit	147	Gibson-LA	33.8	Gibson-LA	35.8	Maldonado-SF	124	Gibson-LA	107
Daniels-Cin	.863	Galarraga-Mon	147	Daniels-Cin	33.2	Bonilla-Pit	33.2	Davis-Cin	123	VanSlyke-Pit	107

Total Average		Stolen Bases		Stolen Base Average		Stolen Base Runs		Fielding Runs		Total Player Rating	
Strawberry-NY	.957	Coleman-StL	81	McReynolds-NY	100.0	Smith-StL	11.7	Smith-StL	22.9	Smith-StL	4.9
Clark-SF	.955	Young-Hou	65	Davis-Cin	92.1	McGee-StL	8.7	Bream-Pit	20.9	Strawberry-NY	4.5
Gibson-LA	.929	Smith-StL	57	Gibson-LA	88.6	Davis-Cin	8.7	Sabo-Cin	18.8	Gibson-LA	4.5
Davis-Cin	.927	Sabo-Cin	46	McGee-StL	87.2	Coleman-StL	8.1	R.Alomar-SD	16.5	VanSlyke-Pit	4.4
Daniels-Cin	.924	Nixon-Mon	46	Smith-StL	86.4	Larkin-Cin	7.8	Templeton-SD	15.0	Larkin-Cin	4.4

Wins		Win Percentage		Games		Complete Games		Shutouts		Saves	
Jackson-Cin	23	Cone-NY	.870	Murphy-Cin	76	Jackson-Cin	15	Hershiser-LA	8	Franco-Cin	39
Hershiser-LA	23	Browning-Cin	.783	Robinson-Pit	75	Hershiser-LA	15	Leary-LA	6	Gott-Pit	34
Cone-NY	20	Jackson-Cin	.742	Agosto-Hou	75	Show-SD	13	Jackson-Cin	6	Worrell-StL	32
Reuschel-SF	19	Hershiser-LA	.742	Tekulve-Phi	70	Sutcliffe-Chi	12	Scott-Hou	5	Davis-SD	28
		Maddux-Chi	.692	Franco-Cin	70	Gooden-NY	10	Ojeda-NY	5	Bedrosian-Phi	28

Innings Pitched		Fewest Hits/Game		Fewest BB/Game		Strikeouts		Strikeouts/Game		Ratio	
Hershiser-LA	267.0	Fernandez-NY	6.11	B.Smith-Mon	1.45	Ryan-Hou	228	Ryan-Hou	9.33	Perez-Mon	8.81
Jackson-Cin	260.2	Perez-Mon	6.37	Mahler-Atl	1.52	Cone-NY	213	Fernandez-NY	9.10	Scott-Hou	9.18
Browning-Cin	250.2	Rijo-Cin	6.67	Reuschel-SF	1.54	DeLeon-StL	208	Rijo-Cin	8.89	Ojeda-NY	9.22
Mahler-Atl	249.0	Scott-Hou	6.67	Ojeda-NY	1.56	Scott-Hou	190	DeLeon-StL	8.31	Hershiser-LA	9.61
Maddux-Chi	249.0	Cone-NY	6.93	Tudor-StL-LA	1.87	Fernandez-NY	189	Cone-NY	8.29	Jackson-Cin	9.63

Earned Run Average		Adjusted ERA		Opponents' Batting Avg.		Opponents' On Base Pct.		Starter Runs		Adjusted Starter Runs	
Magrane-StL	2.18	Magrane-StL	160	Fernandez-NY	.191	Perez-Mon	.253	Hershiser-LA	35.3	Hershiser-LA	31.8
Cone-NY	2.22	Rijo-Cin	150	Perez-Mon	.196	Scott-Hou	.261	Cone-NY	31.6	Cone-NY	25.7
Hershiser-LA	2.26	Tudor-StL-LA	148	Scott-Hou	.204	Ojeda-NY	.264	Tudor-StL-LA	24.7	Jackson-Cin	24.7
Tudor-StL-LA	2.32	Hershiser-LA	147	Rijo-Cin	.209	Hershiser-LA	.271	Magrane-StL	23.3	Tudor-StL-LA	24.5
Rijo-Cin	2.39	Perez-Mon	147	Cone-NY	.213	Fernandez-NY	.274	Perez-Mon	21.0	Perez-Mon	24.1

Clutch Pitching Index		Relief Runs		Adjusted Relief Runs		Relief Ranking		Total Pitcher Index		Total Baseball Ranking	
Tudor-StL-LA	135	Franco-Cin	17.9	Franco-Cin	19.2	Franco-Cin	43.7	Hershiser-LA	4.3	Smith-StL	4.9
Rawley-Phi	122	Holton-LA	16.4	Holton-LA	15.3	Davis-SD	30.4	Magrane-StL	3.2	Strawberry-NY	4.5
Moyer-Chi	118	Pena-LA	16.1	Davis-SD	15.1	Myers-NY	24.7	Jackson-Cin	3.0	Gibson-LA	4.5
Robinson-SF	113	Davis-SD	15.7	Pena-LA	14.9	Pena-LA	22.7	J.Martinez-Mon	2.9	VanSlyke-Pit	4.4
J.Martinez-Mon	112	Myers-NY	13.0	Harris-Phi	14.3	Holton-LA	16.7	Tudor-StL-LA	2.8	Larkin-Cin	4.4

TEAM	G	W	L	PCT	GB	R	OR	AB	H	2B	3B	HR	BB	SO	AVG	OBP	SLG	PRO	PRO+	BR	/A	PF	CHI	RC	SB	CS	SBA	SBR
EAST																												
BOS	162	89	73	.549		**813**	689	5545	**1569**	310	39	124	623	728	**.283**	.360	.420	**.780**	113	**140**	**109**	104	94	842	65	36	46	-16
DET	162	88	74	.543	1	703	658	5433	1358	213	28	143	588	841	.250	.326	.378	.704	99	-19	7	96	103	673	87	42	48	-15
TOR	162	87	75	.537	2	763	680	5557	1491	271	47	**158**	521	935	.268	.334	.419	.753	108	68	65	100	98	771	107	36	43	-14
MIL	162	87	75	.537	2	682	**616**	5488	1409	258	26	113	439	911	.257	.316	.375	.691	92	-55	-60	101	**107**	648	**159**	55	**56**	-16
NY	161	85	76	.528	3.5	772	748	5592	1469	272	12	148	588	935	.263	.336	.395	.731	104	33	38	99	102	754	146	39	41	**-12**
CLE	162	78	84	.481	11	666	731	5505	1435	235	28	134	416	866	.261	.317	.387	.704	93	-34	-51	103	101	667	97	50	55	-17
BAL	161	54	107	.335	34.5	550	789	5358	1275	199	20	137	504	869	.238	.307	.359	.666	88	-100	-80	97	94	581	69	44	44	**-12**
WEST																												
OAK	162	104	58	.642		800	620	5602	1474	251	22	156	580	926	.263	.339	.399	.738	109	50	75	97	103	763	129	54	55	-16
MIN	162	91	71	.562	13	759	672	5510	1508	294	31	151	528	832	.274	.343	.421	.764	109	94	73	103	95	785	107	63	53	**-12**
KC	161	84	77	.522	19.5	704	648	5469	1419	275	40	121	486	944	.259	.324	.391	.715	98	-8	-14	101	102	696	137	54	50	-13
CAL	162	75	87	.463	29	714	771	5582	1458	258	31	124	469	819	.261	.324	.385	.709	100	-17	2	97	103	690	86	52	51	-14
CHI	161	71	90	.441	32.5	631	757	5449	1327	224	35	132	446	908	.244	.305	.370	.675	88	-91	-88	100	105	609	98	46	47	-13
TEX	161	70	91	.435	33.5	637	735	5479	1378	227	39	112	542	1022	.252	.323	.368	.691	90	-46	-62	102	97	661	130	57	55	-15
SEA	161	68	93	.422	35.5	664	744	5436	1397	271	27	148	461	787	.257	.319	.398	.717	94	-6	-36	104	97	673	95	61	53	-13
TOT	1131					9858		77005	19967	3558	425	1901	7191	12323	.259	.327	.391	.718							1512	689	69	40

TEAM	CG	SH	SV	IP	H	H/G	HR	BB	SO	RAT	ERA	ERA+	OAV	OOB	PR	/A	PF	CPI	FA	E	DP	FW	PW	BW	SBW	DIF
EAST																										
BOS	26	14	37	1426[1]	1415	8.9	143	493	**1085**	12.3	3.97	104	.258	.324	0	22	104	99	.984	93	123	1.6	2.2	**11.0**	-1.9	-4.9
DET	34	8	36	1445[2]	1361	8.5	150	497	890	11.8	3.71	103	.247	.314	40	16	96	99	.982	109	129	.6	1.6	.7	-1.8	5.9
TOR	16	**17**	47	1449	1404	8.7	143	528	904	12.4	3.80	104	.256	.327	27	21	99	**105**	.982	110	170	.6	2.1	6.6	-1.7	-1.6
MIL	30	8	51	1449[1]	1355	8.4	125	**437**	832	11.2	3.45	**115**	.247	**.305**	83	**85**	100	99	.981	120	146	-.0	**8.6**	-6.1	-1.9	5.4
NY	16	5	43	1456	1512	9.3	157	487	861	12.7	4.26	92	.267	.330	-47	-52	99	99	.978	134	161	-.9	-5.3	3.8	**-1.5**	8.3
CLE	35	10	46	1434	1501	9.4	120	442	812	12.4	4.16	99	.270	.328	-31	-7	104	97	.980	124	131	-.3	-.7	-5.2	-2.0	5.1
BAL	20	7	26	1416	1506	9.6	153	523	709	13.2	4.54	86	.274	.342	-90	-100	98	99	.980	119	172	.0	-10.1	-8.1	-1.5	-6.8
WEST																										
OAK	22	9	**64**	1489[1]	1376	8.3	116	553	983	11.8	**3.44**	110	.247	.318	87	56	95	104	.983	105	151	.9	5.7	7.6	-1.9	10.8
MIN	18	9	52	1431[2]	1457	9.2	146	453	897	12.3	3.93	104	.265	.326	5	22	103	104	**.986**	**84**	155	**2.1**	2.2	7.4	**-1.5**	-.2
KC	29	12	32	1428[1]	1415	8.9	102	465	886	12.1	3.65	109	.258	.320	49	52	101	100	.980	124	147	-.3	5.3	-1.4	-1.6	1.6
CAL	26	9	33	1455[2]	1503	9.3	135	568	817	13.1	4.32	89	.269	.341	-56	-73	97	101	.979	135	175	-.9	-7.4	.2	-1.7	3.8
CHI	11	9	43	1439	1467	9.2	138	533	754	12.7	4.12	96	.265	.334	-25	-24	100	101	.976	154	**177**	-2.1	-2.4	-8.9	-1.6	5.5
TEX	41	11	31	1438[2]	**1310**	**8.2**	129	654	912	12.6	4.05	101	**.243**	.331	-13	5	103	95	.979	131	145	-.7	.5	-6.3	-1.8	-2.2
SEA	28	11	28	1428	1385	8.7	144	558	981	12.5	4.15	100	.256	.329	-29	0	105	97	.980	123	168	-.2	.0	-3.6	-1.6	-7.0
TOT	352	139	569	20187		8.9				12.4	3.97		.259	.327					.981	1665	2150					

Runs
Boggs-Bos 128
Canseco-Oak 120
Henderson-NY 118
Molitor-Mil 115
Puckett-Min 109

Hits
Puckett-Min 234
Boggs-Bos 214
Greenwell-Bos 192
Yount-Mil 190
Molitor-Mil 190

Doubles
Boggs-Bos 45
Ray-Cal 42
Puckett-Min 42
Brett-KC 42
Fernandez-Tor 41

Triples
Yount-Mil 11
Wilson-KC 11
Reynolds-Sea 11
Greenwell-Bos 8

Home Runs
Canseco-Oak 42
McGriff-Tor 34
McGwire-Oak 32
Murray-Bal 28
Gaetti-Min 28

Total Bases
Puckett-Min 358
Canseco-Oak 347
Greenwell-Bos 313
Brett-KC 300
Carter-Cle 297

Runs Batted In
Canseco-Oak 124
Puckett-Min 121
Greenwell-Bos 119
Evans-Bos 111
Winfield-NY 107

Runs Produced
Puckett-Min 206
Canseco-Oak 202
Evans-Bos 186
Greenwell-Bos 183
Boggs-Bos 181

Bases On Balls
Boggs-Bos 125
Clark-NY 113
C.Ripken-Bal 102
Davis-Sea 95
Greenwell-Bos 87

Batting Average
Boggs-Bos 366
Puckett-Min 356
Greenwell-Bos 325
Winfield-NY 322
Molitor-Mil 312

On Base Percentage
Boggs-Bos 480
Greenwell-Bos 420
Davis-Sea 416
Winfield-NY 398
Henderson-NY 397

Slugging Average
Canseco-Oak 569
McGriff-Tor 552
Gaetti-Min 551
Puckett-Min 545
Greenwell-Bos 531

Production
Boggs-Bos 970
Canseco-Oak 963
Greenwell-Bos 950
McGriff-Tor 930
Winfield-NY 928

Adjusted Production
Canseco-Oak 172
Boggs-Bos 165
Winfield-NY 159
Greenwell-Bos 158
McGriff-Tor 156

Batter Runs
Boggs-Bos 65.8
Canseco-Oak 54.1
Greenwell-Bos . . . 53.4
Puckett-Min 45.5
Winfield-NY 43.4

Adjusted Batter Runs
Boggs-Bos 62.3
Canseco-Oak 57.0
Greenwell-Bos . . . 50.1
Winfield-NY 44.0
Puckett-Min 43.2

Clutch Hitting Index
Evans-Bos 139
Greenwell-Bos 132
Larkin-Min 131
Hall-Cle 128
Clark-NY 127

Runs Created
Boggs-Bos 140
Canseco-Oak 136
Greenwell-Bos 134
Puckett-Min 126
Brett-KC 119

Total Average
Boggs-Bos 1.043
Canseco-Oak 1.011
Greenwell-Bos . . . 1.000
McGriff-Tor 958
Henderson-NY 955

Stolen Bases
Henderson-NY 93
Pettis-Det 44
Molitor-Mil 41
Canseco-Oak 40

Stolen Base Average
Javier-Cal 95.2
Redus-Chi 92.9
Cotto-Sea 90.0
Henderson-NY . . . 87.7
Yount-Mil 84.6

Stolen Base Runs
Henderson-NY . . . 20.1
Pettis-Det 7.2
Redus-Chi 6.6

Fielding Runs
Guillen-Chi 42.6
Gruber-Tor 25.5
Schofield-Cal 20.8
Barfield-Tor 13.9
Puckett-Min 12.6

Total Player Rating
Canseco-Oak 6.0
Boggs-Bos 5.6
Greenwell-Bos 5.1
Puckett-Min 5.0
Henderson-NY 4.5

Wins
Viola-Min 24
Stewart-Oak 21
Gubicza-KC 20

Win Percentage
Viola-Min 774
Hurst-Bos 750
Gubicza-KC 714
Davis-Oak 696
Stieb-Tor 667

Games
Crim-Mil 70
Thigpen-Chi 68
Williams-Tex 67
Henneman-Det 65

Complete Games
Stewart-Oak 14
Clemens-Bos 14
Witt-Tex 13
Witt-Cal 12
Swindell-Cle 12

Shutouts
Clemens-Bos 8
Swindell-Cle 4
Stieb-Tor 4
Gubicza-KC 4

Saves
Eckersley-Oak 45
Reardon-Min 42
Jones-Cle 37
Thigpen-Chi 34
Plesac-Mil 30

Innings Pitched
Stewart-Oak 275.2
Gubicza-KC 269.2
Clemens-Bos 264.0
Langston-Sea 261.1
Saberhagen-KC . . 260.2

Fewest Hits/Game
Robinson-Det 6.33
Higuera-Mil 6.65
Stieb-Tor 6.82
Witt-Tex 6.92
Hough-Tex 7.21

Fewest BB/Game
Anderson-Min 1.65
Swindell-Cle 1.67
Alexander-Det 1.81
Bosio-Mil 1.88
Viola-Min 1.90

Strikeouts
Clemens-Bos 291
Langston-Sea 235
Viola-Min 193
Stewart-Oak 192
Higuera-Mil 192

Strikeouts/Game
Clemens-Bos 9.92
Langston-Sea 8.09
Witt-Tex 7.64
Higuera-Mil 7.60
Moore-Sea 7.16

Ratio
Higuera-Mil 9.22
Clemens-Bos 9.72
Robinson-Det . . . 10.26
Moore-Sea 10.31
Viola-Min 10.33

Earned Run Average
Anderson-Min 2.45
Higuera-Mil 2.45
Viola-Min 2.64
Gubicza-KC 2.70
Clemens-Bos 2.93

Adjusted ERA
Anderson-Min 166
Higuera-Mil 162
Viola-Min 154
Gubicza-KC 147
Clemens-Bos 140

Opponents' Batting Avg.
Robinson-Det 197
Higuera-Mil 207
Stieb-Tor 210
Witt-Tex 216
Clemens-Bos 220

Opponents' On Base Pct.
Higuera-Mil 265
Clemens-Bos 270
Robinson-Det 284
Moore-Sea 287
Swindell-Cle 287

Starter Runs
Higuera-Mil 38.2
Gubicza-KC 37.8
Viola-Min 37.5
Anderson-Min . . . 34.1
Clemens-Bos 30.3

Adjusted Starter Runs
Viola-Min 40.4
Higuera-Mil 38.5
Gubicza-KC 38.4
Anderson-Min . . . 36.5
Clemens-Bos 34.6

Clutch Pitching Index
Anderson-Min 138
Davis-Oak 121
Candiotti-Cle 116
Leibrandt-KC 116
Viola-Min 115

Relief Runs
Henneman-Det . . . 21.2
Jones-Cle 15.7
Harvey-Cal 15.5
Mirabella-Mil 15.4
Jackson-Sea 14.8

Adjusted Relief Runs
Henneman-Det . . . 19.7
Jones-Cle 17.1
Jackson-Sea 16.9
Mirabella-Mil 15.5
Harvey-Cal 14.6

Relief Ranking
Henneman-Det . . . 39.8
Jones-Cle 30.0
Harvey-Cal 28.1
Reardon-Min 26.4
Eckersley-Oak . . . 24.6

Total Pitcher Index
Gubicza-KC 4.5
Higuera-Mil 4.2
Viola-Min 4.2
Anderson-Min 4.1
Clemens-Bos 3.4

Total Baseball Ranking
Canseco-Oak 6.0
Boggs-Bos 5.6
Greenwell-Bos 5.1
Puckett-Min 5.0
Henderson-NY 4.5

TEAM	G	W	L	PCT	GB	R	OR	AB	H	2B	3B	HR	BB	SO	AVG	OBP	SLG	PRO	PRO+	BR	/A	PF	CHI	RC	SB	CS	SBA	SBR
EAST																												
CHI	162	93	69	.574		**702**	623	5513	**1438**	235	45	124	472	921	**.261**	.322	.387	**.709**	100	**54**	6	107	101	**685**	136	57	50	-12
NY	162	87	75	.537	6	683	595	5489	1351	**280**	21	**147**	504	934	.246	.313	.385	.698	110	30	60	95	102	676	158	53	51	-14
STL	164	86	76	.531	7	632	608	5492	1418	263	47	73	507	848	.258	**.323**	.363	.686	98	16	-4	103	97	652	155	54	51	-13
MON	162	81	81	.500	12	632	630	5482	1353	267	30	100	**572**	958	.247	.322	.361	.683	99	13	3	101	96	645	**160**	70	58	-13
PIT	164	74	88	.457	19	637	680	5539	1334	263	**53**	95	563	914	.241	.314	.359	.673	101	-12	10	97	100	629	155	69	54	**-11**
PHI	163	67	95	.414	26	629	735	5447	1324	215	36	123	558	926	.243	.316	.364	.680	100	1	1	100	99	634	106	50	48	-13
WEST																												
SF	162	92	70	.568		699	600	5469	1365	241	52	141	508	1071	.250	.318	**.390**	.708	**111**	50	**67**	97	102	683	87	54	53	-15
SD	162	89	73	.549	3	642	626	5422	1360	215	32	120	552	1013	.251	.321	.369	.690	102	22	21	100	98	644	136	67	56	-13
HOU	162	86	76	.531	6	647	669	5516	1316	239	28	97	530	860	.239	.308	.345	.653	95	-49	-26	97	**109**	606	144	62	53	-12
LA	160	77	83	.481	14	554	**536**	5465	1313	241	17	89	507	885	.240	.308	.339	.647	92	-60	-49	98	96	576	81	54	50	-13
CIN	162	75	87	.463	17	632	691	5520	1362	243	28	128	493	1028	.247	.312	.370	.682	96	1	-20	103	99	639	128	71	**59**	-13
ATL	161	63	97	.394	28	584	680	5463	1281	201	22	128	485	996	.234	.300	.350	.650	88	-63	-79	103	103	575	83	54	48	-12
TOT	973					7673		65817	16215	2903	411	1365	6251	11354	.246	.315	.365	.680							1529	715	68	30

TEAM	CG	SH	SV	IP	H	H/G	HR	BB	SO	RAT	ERA	ERA+	OAV	OOB	PR	/A	PF	CPI	FA	E	DP	FW	PW	BW	SBW	DIF
EAST																										
CHI	18	10	**55**	1460¹	1369	8.4	106	532	918	11.9	3.43	110	.249	.318	11	53	108	104	.980	124	130	.6	5.7	.6	-1.5	6.7
NY	24	12	38	1454¹	**1260**	7.8	115	532	**1108**	11.3	3.29	99	**.231**	.302	32	-4	93	95	.976	144	110	-.6	-.4	6.4	-1.8	2.3
STL	18	18	43	1461	1330	8.2	84	482	844	11.3	3.36	108	.243	.308	21	42	104	95	**.982**	112	134	1.4	4.5	-.4	-1.7	1.2
MON	20	13	35	1468²	1344	8.2	120	519	1059	11.6	3.48	102	.245	.313	3	8	101	101	.979	136	126	-.1	.9	.3	-1.7	.6
PIT	20	9	40	1487²	1394	8.4	121	539	827	11.9	3.64	92	.247	.316	-24	-47	96	98	.975	160	130	-1.4	-5.0	1.1	**-1.4**	-.2
PHI	10	10	33	1433¹	1408	8.8	127	613	899	12.9	4.04	88	.258	.336	-87	-79	101	101	.979	133	136	.1	-8.4	.1	-1.7	-4.1
WEST																										
SF	12	16	47	1457	1320	8.2	120	471	802	11.2	3.30	102	.243	.306	30	10	97	102	**.982**	114	135	1.2	1.1	**7.2**	-1.9	3.5
SD	21	11	52	1457¹	1359	8.4	133	481	933	11.5	3.38	103	.248	.311	18	18	100	106	.976	154	147	-1.1	1.9	2.2	-1.7	6.6
HOU	19	12	38	1479¹	1379	8.4	105	551	965	11.9	3.64	93	.247	.317	-24	-42	97	96	.977	142	121	-.4	-4.5	-2.8	-1.5	14.3
LA	**25**	**19**	36	1463¹	1278	7.9	95	504	1052	11.1	**2.95**	116	.237	.305	**89**	76	98	**107**	.981	118	**153**	.8	**8.1**	-5.2	-1.7	-5.1
CIN	16	9	37	1464¹	1404	8.6	125	559	981	12.3	3.73	96	.253	.325	-38	-21	103	102	.980	121	108	.8	-2.2	-2.1	-1.7	-.7
ATL	15	8	33	1447²	1370	8.5	114	**468**	966	11.5	3.70	99	.250	.311	-32	-8	104	94	.976	152	124	-1.1	-.9	-8.4	-1.5	-5.1
TOT	218	147	487	17534		8.3				11.7	3.49		.246	.315					.978	1610	1554					

Runs		Hits		Doubles		Triples		Home Runs		Total Bases	
Sandberg-Chi	104	Gwynn-SD	203	Wallach-Mon	42	Thompson-SF	11	Mitchell-SF	47	Mitchell-SF	345
Johnson-NY	104	Clark-SF	196	Guerrero-StL	42	Bonilla-Pit	10	Johnson-NY	36	Clark-SF	321
Clark-SF	104	R.Alomar-SD	184	Johnson-NY	41	VanSlyke-Pit	9	Davis-Hou	34	Johnson-NY	319
Mitchell-SF	100	Guerrero-StL	177	Clark-SF	38	Coleman-StL	9	Davis-Cin	34	Bonilla-Pit	302
Butler-SF	100	Sandberg-Chi	176	Bonilla-Pit	37	Clark-SF	9	Sandberg-Chi	30	Sandberg-Chi	301

Runs Batted In		Runs Produced		Bases On Balls		Batting Average		On Base Percentage		Slugging Average	
Mitchell-SF	125	Clark-SF	192	J.Clark-SD	132	Gwynn-SD	.336	L.Smith-Atl	.420	Mitchell-SF	.635
Guerrero-StL	117	Mitchell-SF	178	V.Hayes-Phi	101	Clark-SF	.333	J.Clark-SD	.413	Johnson-NY	.559
Clark-SF	111	Johnson-NY	169	Raines-Mon	93	L.Smith-Atl	.315	Clark-SF	.412	Clark-SF	.546
Johnson-NY	101	Guerrero-StL	160	Bonds-Pit	93	Grace-Chi	.314	Grace-Chi	.407	Davis-Cin	.541
Davis-Cin	101	Bonilla-Pit	158			Guerrero-StL	.311	Guerrero-StL	.398	L.Smith-Atl	.533

Production		Adjusted Production		Batter Runs		Adjusted Batter Runs		Clutch Hitting Index		Runs Created	
Mitchell-SF	1.027	Mitchell-SF	194	Mitchell-SF	62.1	Mitchell-SF	64.0	Guerrero-StL	154	Clark-SF	136
Clark-SF	.958	Clark-SF	177	Clark-SF	55.6	Clark-SF	57.6	J.Clark-SD	140	Mitchell-SF	136
L.Smith-Atl	.953	Johnson-NY	171	L.Smith-Atl	47.0	Johnson-NY	49.0	Murphy-Atl	134	Johnson-NY	127
Johnson-NY	.932	L.Smith-Atl	166	Johnson-NY	45.7	L.Smith-Atl	45.4	Hatcher-Hou-Pit	131	L.Smith-Atl	113
Davis-Cin	.916	Davis-Cin	154	Guerrero-StL	38.3	Guerrero-StL	36.1	Doran-Hou	127	Guerrero-StL	109

Total Average		Stolen Bases		Stolen Base Average		Stolen Base Runs		Fielding Runs		Total Player Rating	
Mitchell-SF	1.099	Coleman-StL	65	Doran-Hou	88.0	Coleman-StL	13.5	Pendleton-StL	30.2	Mitchell-SF	6.4
Johnson-NY	1.026	Samuel-Phi-NY	42	Biggio-Hou	87.5	Johnson-NY	7.5	Oquendo-StL	20.4	L.Smith-Atl	5.0
L.Smith-Atl	1.023	R.Alomar-SD	42	Coleman-StL	86.7	Raines-Mon	6.9	Foley-Mon	19.8	Clark-SF	4.8
Clark-SF	1.010	Raines-Mon	41	D.Martinez-Mon	85.2	Samuel-Phi-NY	5.4	Young-Hou	18.6	Bonilla-Pit	3.9
J.Clark-SD	.969	Johnson-NY	41	Johnson-NY	83.7	Doran-Hou	4.8	Scioscia-LA	17.7	Bonds-Pit	3.7

Wins		Win Percentage		Games		Complete Games		Shutouts		Saves	
Scott-Hou	20	Bielecki-Chi	.720	Williams-Chi	76	Hurst-SD	10	Belcher-LA	8	Davis-SD	44
Maddux-Chi	19	J.Martinez-Mon	.696	Dibble-Cin	74	Belcher-LA	10	Drabek-Pit	5	Williams-Chi	36
Magrane-StL	18	Reuschel-SF	.680	Parrett-Phi	72	Scott-Hou	9	Langston-Mon	4	Franco-Cin	32
Bielecki-Chi	18	Scott-Hou	.667	Dayley-StL	71	Magrane-StL	9	Hershiser-LA	4	Howell-LA	28
Reuschel-SF	17	Magrane-StL	.667	Agosto-Hou	71	Browning-Cin	9	Glavine-Atl	4	Burke-Mon	28

Innings Pitched		Fewest Hits/Game		Fewest BB/Game		Strikeouts		Strikeouts/Game		Ratio	
Hershiser-LA	256.2	DeLeon-StL	6.36	Robinson-SF	1.69	DeLeon-StL	201	Langston-Mon	8.92	Garrelts-SF	9.08
Browning-Cin	249.2	Fernandez-NY	6.44	Lilliquist-Atl	1.85	Belcher-LA	200	Fernandez-NY	8.12	DeLeon-StL	9.53
Hurst-SD	244.2	Howell-Phi	6.84	J.Martinez-Mon	1.90	Fernandez-NY	198	Belcher-LA	7.83	Scott-Hou	9.63
DeLeon-StL	244.2	Smoltz-Atl	6.92	Whitson-SD	1.90	Cone-NY	190	Cone-NY	7.78	Fernandez-NY	9.77
Drabek-Pit	244.1	Garrelts-SF	6.94	Glavine-Atl	1.94	Hurst-SD	179	DeLeon-StL	7.39	B.Smith-Mon	9.81

Earned Run Average		Adjusted ERA		Opponents' Batting Avg.		Opponents' On Base Pct.		Starter Runs		Adjusted Starter Runs	
Garrelts-SF	2.28	Garrelts-SF	148	DeLeon-StL	.197	Garrelts-SF	.260	Hershiser-LA	33.7	Hershiser-LA	31.4
Hershiser-LA	2.31	Hershiser-LA	148	Fernandez-NY	.198	Scott-Hou	.268	Garrelts-SF	26.1	Garrelts-SF	23.4
Langston-Mon	2.39	Langston-Mon	147	Smoltz-Atl	.212	DeLeon-StL	.269	Hurst-SD	22.0	Langston-Mon	22.3
Whitson-SD	2.66	Whitson-SD	132	Garrelts-SF	.212	Fernandez-NY	.272	Langston-Mon	21.6	Hurst-SD	22.0
Hurst-SD	2.69	Hurst-SD	130	Scott-Hou	.212	Smiley-Pit	.276	Whitson-SD	21.2	Maddux-Chi	21.5

Clutch Pitching Index		Relief Runs		Adjusted Relief Runs		Relief Ranking		Total Pitcher Index		Total Baseball Ranking	
Langston-Mon	135	Andersen-Hou	19.0	Lancaster-Chi	19.3	Davis-SD	29.7	Hershiser-LA	4.4	Mitchell-SF	6.4
Hershiser-LA	124	Lancaster-Chi	17.2	Andersen-Hou	18.0	Howell-LA	27.5	Maddux-Chi	3.1	L.Smith-Atl	5.0
Lilliquist-Atl	117	Davis-SD	17.0	Davis-SD	17.0	McDowell-NY-Phi	26.3	Garrelts-SF	2.6	Clark-SF	4.8
Maddux-Chi	115	Howell-LA	16.9	Dibble-Cin	16.6	Dibble-Cin	23.4	Langston-Mon	2.3	Hershiser-LA	4.4
Drabek-Pit	113	Landrum-Pit	16.5	Howell-LA	16.2	Landrum-Pit	19.4	Hurst-SD	2.3	Bonilla-Pit	3.9

TEAM	G	W	L	PCT	GB	R	OR	AB	H	2B	3B	HR	BB	SO	AVG	OBP	SLG	PRO	PRO+	BR	/A	PF	CHI	RC	SB	CS	SBA	SBR
EAST																												
TOR	162	89	73	.549		731	651	5581	1449	265	40	142	521	923	.260	.326	.398	.724	104	18	31	98	102	724	144	58	52	-13
BAL	162	87	75	.537	2	708	686	5440	1369	238	33	129	593	957	.252	.329	.379	.708	102	-5	16	97	102	678	118	55	51	-13
BOS	162	83	79	.512	6	774	735	5666	1571	326	30	108	643	755	.277	.355	.403	.758	106	106	60	106	93	802	56	35	41	-13
MIL	162	81	81	.500	8	707	679	5473	1415	235	32	126	455	791	.259	.321	.382	.703	97	-21	-14	99	106	677	165	62	60	-16
NY	161	74	87	.460	14.5	698	792	5458	1470	229	23	130	502	831	.269	.334	.391	.725	105	26	34	99	98	709	137	60	50	-11
CLE	162	73	89	.451	16	604	654	5463	1340	221	26	127	499	934	.245	.312	.365	.677	88	-71	-82	102	98	622	74	51	50	-14
DET	162	59	103	.364	30	617	816	5432	1315	198	24	116	585	899	.242	.320	.351	.671	91	-73	-57	98	100	616	103	50	50	-14
WEST																												
OAK	162	99	63	.611		712	576	5416	1414	220	25	127	562	855	.261	.334	.381	.715	104	12	36	96	101	687	157	55	52	-14
KC	162	92	70	.568	7	690	635	5475	1428	227	41	101	642	897	.261	.332	.373	.705	98	-8	-4	100	101	682	154	51	50	-14
CAL	162	91	71	.562	8	669	578	5545	1422	208	37	145	429	1011	.256	.313	.386	.699	97	-37	-24	98	103	663	89	40	44	-13
TEX	162	83	79	.512	16	695	714	5458	1433	260	46	122	503	989	.263	.329	.394	.723	101	18	6	102	98	694	101	49	53	-16
MIN	162	80	82	.494	19	740	738	5581	1542	278	35	117	483	743	.276	.338	.402	.740	101	53	6	107	98	751	111	53	50	-13
SEA	162	73	89	.451	26	694	728	5512	1417	237	29	134	489	838	.257	.323	.384	.707	94	-15	-37	103	102	679	81	55	52	-14
CHI	161	69	92	.429	29.5	693	750	5504	1493	262	36	94	464	873	.271	.331	.383	.714	103	4	20	98	100	696	97	52	50	-13
TOT	1133					9732		77004	20078	3404	457	1718	7277	12296	.261	.328	.384	.712							1587	726	69	41

TEAM	CG	SH	SV	IP	H	H/G	HR	BB	SO	RAT	ERA	ERA+	OAV	OOB	PR	/A	PF	CPI	FA	E	DP	FW	PW	BW	SBW	DIF
EAST																										
TOR	12	12	38	1467	1408	8.6	99	478	849	11.8	3.58	105	.255	.319	48	30	97	99	.980	127	164	-.1	3.1	3.2	-1.6	3.5
BAL	16	7	44	1448¹	1518	9.4	134	486	676	12.6	4.00	95	.271	.332	-19	-33	98	104	.986	87	163	2.3	-3.4	1.6	-1.6	7.1
BOS	14	9	42	1460¹	1448	8.9	131	548	1054	12.5	4.01	102	.260	.330	-19	15	106	99	.980	127	162	-.1	1.5	6.1	-1.6	-3.9
MIL	16	8	45	1432¹	1463	9.2	129	457	812	12.2	3.80	101	.264	.324	13	6	99	102	.975	155	164	-1.8	.6	-1.4	-1.9	4.5
NY	15	9	44	1414²	1550	9.9	150	521	787	13.4	4.50	86	.280	.346	-97	-100	100	102	.980	122	183	.1	-10.2	3.5	-1.7	1.5
CLE	23	13	38	1453	1423	8.8	107	452	844	11.8	3.65	109	.256	.315	37	50	102	96	.981	118	126	.4	5.1	-8.3	-1.7	-3.5
DET	24	4	26	1427¹	1514	9.5	150	652	831	13.9	4.53	84	.274	.355	-103	-113	98	103	.979	130	153	-.3	-11.5	-5.8	-1.7	-2.7
WEST																										
OAK	17	20	57	1448¹	1287	8.0	103	510	930	11.3	3.09	119	.238	.307	127	95	95	103	.979	129	159	-.2	9.7	3.7	-1.7	6.6
KC	27	13	38	1451²	1415	8.8	86	455	978	11.7	3.55	109	.256	.316	54	48	99	97	.982	114	139	.7	4.9	-.4	-1.7	7.6
CAL	32	20	38	1454¹	1384	8.6	113	465	897	11.6	3.28	116	.253	.314	97	86	98	107	.985	96	173	1.7	8.8	-2.4	-1.6	3.6
TEX	26	7	44	1434¹	1279	8.0	119	654	1112	12.4	3.91	101	.238	.326	-4	8	102	92	.978	136	137	-.6	.8	.6	-1.9	3.1
MIN	19	8	38	1429¹	1495	9.4	139	500	851	12.8	4.28	97	.269	.333	-63	-22	107	97	.982	107	141	1.1	-2.2	.6	-1.6	1.2
SEA	15	10	44	1438	1422	8.9	114	560	897	12.7	4.00	101	.259	.332	-18	4	104	98	.977	143	168	-1.1	.4	-3.8	-1.7	-1.9
CHI	9	5	46	1422	1472	9.3	144	539	778	12.9	4.23	90	.268	.338	-54	-66	98	101	.975	151	176	-1.6	-6.7	2.0	-1.6	-3.6
TOT	265	145	582	20181		9.0				12.4	3.88		.261	.328					.980	1742	2208					

Runs
R.Henderson-NY-Oak 113
Boggs-Bos 113
Yount-Mil 101
Sierra-Tex 101
McGriff-Tor 98

Hits
Puckett-Min 215
Sax-NY 205
Boggs-Bos 205
Yount-Mil 195

Doubles
Boggs-Bos 51
Puckett-Min 45
Reed-Bos 42
Bell-Tor 41
Yount-Mil 38

Triples
Sierra-Tex 14
White-Cal 13
Bradley-Bal 10

Home Runs
McGriff-Tor 36
Carter-Cle 35
McGwire-Oak 33
Jackson-KC 32
Esasky-Bos 30

Total Bases
Sierra-Tex 344
Yount-Mil 314
Carter-Cle 303
Mattingly-NY 301
Puckett-Min 295

Runs Batted In
Sierra-Tex 119
Mattingly-NY 113
Esasky-Bos 108
Jackson-KC 105
Carter-Cle 105

Runs Produced
Sierra-Tex 191
Yount-Mil 183
Bell-Tor 174
Mattingly-NY 169
Greenwell-Bos 168

Bases On Balls
R.Henderson-NY-Oak 126
McGriff-Tor 119
Boggs-Bos 107
Seitzer-KC 102
Davis-Sea 101

Batting Average
Puckett-Min .339
Lansford-Oak .336
Boggs-Bos .330
Yount-Mil .318
Franco-Tex .316

On Base Percentage
Boggs-Bos .434
Davis-Sea .428
R.Henderson-NY-Oak .413
McGriff-Tor .402
Evans-Bos .402

Slugging Average
Sierra-Tex .543
McGriff-Tor .525
Yount-Mil .511
Esasky-Bos .500
Davis-Sea .496

Production
McGriff-Tor .927
Davis-Sea .924
Yount-Mil .898
Sierra-Tex .895
Boggs-Bos .883

Adjusted Production
McGriff-Tor 162
Davis-Sea 155
Yount-Mil 152
Sierra-Tex 146
Baines-Chi-Tex 144

Batter Runs
McGriff-Tor 46.8
Boggs-Bos 46.6
Davis-Sea 44.2
Yount-Mil 41.2
Sierra-Tex 37.4

Adjusted Batter Runs
McGriff-Tor 48.2
Davis-Sea 42.0
Yount-Mil 41.9
Boggs-Bos 41.4
Sierra-Tex 36.2

Clutch Hitting Index
Brett-KC 141
Evans-Bos 132
Greenwell-Bos 131
Parker-Oak 131
Franco-Tex 130

Runs Created
Yount-Mil 125
Boggs-Bos 122
Sierra-Tex 122
McGriff-Tor 121
R.Henderson-NY-Oak 110

Total Average
McGriff-Tor .986
R.Henderson-NY-Oak .983
Davis-Sea .975
Yount-Mil .926
Boggs-Bos .882

Stolen Bases
R.Henderson-NY-Oak 77
Espy-Tex 45
White-Cal 44
Sax-NY 43
Pettis-Det 43

Stolen Base Average
Thurman-KC 100.0
Franco-Tex 87.5
Yount-Mil 86.4
Finley-Bal 85.0
R.Henderson-NY-Oak 84.6

Stolen Base Runs
R.Henderson-NY-Oak 14.7
Thurman-KC 4.8
Felder-Mil 4.8
Franco-Tex 4.5

Fielding Runs
Reynolds-Sea 27.0
Howell-Cal 21.9
Gruber-Tor 18.6
Fernandez-Tor 18.0
Gallego-Oak 18.0

Total Player Rating
R.Henderson-NY-Oak 4.8
Yount-Mil 4.4
Sierra-Tex 3.9
Puckett-Min 3.8
McGriff-Tor 3.6

Wins
Saberhagen-KC 23
Stewart-Oak 21
Moore-Oak 19
Davis-Oak 19
Ballard-Bal 18

Win Percentage
Saberhagen-KC .793
Blyleven-Cal .773
Davis-Oak .731
Stewart-Oak .700
Ballard-Bal .692

Games
Crim-Mil 76
Murphy-Bos 74
Rogers-Tex 73
Russell-Tex 71
Guetterman-NY 70

Complete Games
Saberhagen-KC 12
Morris-Det 10
Finley-Cal 9

Shutouts
Blyleven-Cal 5
Saberhagen-KC 4
McCaskill-Cal 4

Saves
Russell-Tex 38
Thigpen-Chi 34
Schooler-Sea 33
Plesac-Mil 33
Eckersley-Oak 33

Innings Pitched
Saberhagen-KC 262.1
Stewart-Oak 257.2
Gubicza-KC 255.0
Clemens-Bos 253.1
Milacki-Bal 243.0

Fewest Hits/Game
Ryan-Tex 6.09
Gordon-KC 6.74
Stieb-Tor 7.14
Saberhagen-KC 7.17
Moore-Oak 7.19

Fewest BB/Game
Key-Tor 1.13
Saberhagen-KC 1.48
Blyleven-Cal 1.64
Bosio-Mil 1.84
Witt-Cal 1.96

Strikeouts
Ryan-Tex 301
Clemens-Bos 230
Saberhagen-KC 193
Gubicza-KC 173
Bosio-Mil 173

Strikeouts/Game
Ryan-Tex 11.32
Gordon-KC 8.45
Clemens-Bos 8.17
Witt-Tex 7.69
Viola-Min 7.07

Ratio
Saberhagen-KC 8.71
Ryan-Tex 10.12
Blyleven-Cal 10.34
Moore-Oak 10.35
Key-Tor 10.67

Earned Run Average
Saberhagen-KC 2.16
Finley-Cal 2.57
Moore-Oak 2.61
Blyleven-Cal 2.73
McCaskill-Cal 2.93

Adjusted ERA
Saberhagen-KC 178
Finley-Cal 148
Moore-Oak 141
Blyleven-Cal 140
Clemens-Bos 131

Opponents' Batting Avg.
Ryan-Tex .187
Gordon-KC .210
Saberhagen-KC .217
Stieb-Tor .219
Moore-Oak .219

Opponents' On Base Pct.
Saberhagen-KC .252
Ryan-Tex .276
Moore-Oak .288
Blyleven-Cal .289
Bosio-Mil .291

Starter Runs
Saberhagen-KC 50.2
Moore-Oak 34.3
Blyleven-Cal 31.0
Finley-Cal 29.1
Bosio-Mil 24.2

Adjusted Starter Runs
Saberhagen-KC 49.2
Blyleven-Cal 29.1
Moore-Oak 28.8
Finley-Cal 27.6
Clemens-Bos 27.4

Clutch Pitching Index
Cerutti-Tor 130
Ballard-Bal 123
Finley-Cal 123
McCaskill-Cal 116
Davis-Oak 113

Relief Runs
Montgomery-KC 25.7
Olson-Bal 20.7
Lamp-Bos 19.5
Henke-Tor 19.4
Burns-Oak 17.6

Adjusted Relief Runs
Montgomery-KC 25.3
Lamp-Bos 22.2
Olson-Bal 19.8
Henke-Tor 18.3
Orosco-Cle 16.3

Relief Ranking
Jones-Cle 40.4
Russell-Tex 38.7
Montgomery-KC 35.9
Henke-Tor 29.6
Olson-Bal 28.9

Total Pitcher Index
Saberhagen-KC 5.5
Moore-Oak 3.3
Blyleven-Cal 3.3
Clemens-Bos 2.8
Gubicza-KC 2.7

Total Baseball Ranking
Saberhagen-KC 5.5
R.Henderson-NY-Oak 4.8
Yount-Mil 4.4
Sierra-Tex 3.9
Puckett-Min 3.8

TEAM	G	W	L	PCT	GB	R	OR	AB	H	2B	3B	HR	BB	SO	AVG	OBP	SLG	PRO	PRO+	BR	/A	PF	CHI	RC	SB	CS	SBA	SBR
EAST																												
PIT	162	95	67	.586		733	619	5388	1395	**288**	42	138	**582**	914	.259	**.334**	.405	**.739**	113	**64**	**91**	96	99	738	137	52	52	-15
NY	162	91	71	.562	4	**775**	613	5504	1410	278	21	**172**	536	851	.256	.326	**.408**	.734	109	48	63	98	**106**	748	110	33	39	-13
MON	162	85	77	.525	10	662	598	5453	1363	227	**43**	114	576	1024	.250	.325	.370	.695	97	-17	-12	99	99	672	**235**	99	**72**	-13
PHI	162	77	85	.475	18	646	729	5535	1410	237	27	103	**582**	915	.255	.329	.363	.692	96	-18	-14	100	96	675	108	35	33	**-8**
CHI	162	77	85	.475	18	690	774	5600	**1474**	240	36	136	406	869	.263	.316	.392	.708	91	-6	-66	109	102	695	151	50	60	-20
STL	162	70	92	.432	25	599	698	5462	1398	255	41	73	517	**844**	.256	.323	.358	.681	90	-45	-63	103	95	650	221	74	55	-10
WEST																												
CIN	162	91	71	.562		693	**597**	5525	1466	284	40	125	466	913	**.265**	.327	.399	.726	102	35	18	102	97	726	166	66	55	-12
LA	162	86	76	.531	5	728	685	5491	1436	222	27	129	538	952	.262	.331	.382	.713	108	17	55	94	104	699	141	65	54	-12
SF	162	85	77	.525	6	719	710	5573	1459	221	35	152	488	973	.262	.325	.396	.721	105	24	32	99	101	724	109	56	51	-13
SD	162	75	87	.463	16	673	673	5554	1429	243	35	123	509	902	.257	.323	.380	.703	97	-7	-17	102	99	682	138	59	54	-14
HOU	162	75	87	.463	16	573	656	5379	1301	209	32	94	548	997	.242	.315	.345	.660	88	-82	-69	98	97	596	179	83	61	-11
ATL	162	65	97	.401	26	682	821	5504	1376	263	26	162	473	1010	.250	.312	.396	.708	98	-7	-18	102	103	675	92	55	47	-11
TOT	972					8173		65968	16917	2967	405	1521	6221	11164	.256	.324	.383	.707							1787	727	71	100

TEAM	CG	SH	SV	IP	H	H/G	HR	BB	SO	RAT	ERA	ERA+	OAV	OOB	PR	/A	PF	CPI	FA	E	DP	FW	PW	BW	SBW	DIF
EAST																										
PIT	18	8	43	1447	1367	8.5	135	**413**	848	11.3	3.40	106	.250	.307	63	35	95	103	.979	134	125	-.4	3.6	**9.4**	-2.4	3.9
NY	18	**14**	41	1440	1339	8.4	119	444	**1217**	11.3	3.42	106	.245	**.306**	58	34	96	97	.978	132	107	-.3	3.5	6.5	-2.2	2.5
MON	18	11	50	1473¹	1349	**8.2**	127	510	991	11.6	**3.37**	111	**.244**	.313	**69**	63	99	103	.982	110	134	.9	6.5	-1.2	-2.2	.0
PHI	18	7	35	1449	1381	8.6	124	651	840	12.8	4.07	94	.253	.336	-44	-40	101	97	.981	117	**150**	.5	-4.1	-1.4	**-1.7**	2.7
CHI	13	7	42	1442²	1510	9.4	121	572	877	13.2	4.34	95	.271	.342	-87	-33	109	98	.980	124	136	.1	-3.4	-6.8	-2.9	9.0
STL	8	13	39	1443¹	1432	8.9	**98**	475	833	12.1	3.87	101	.260	.323	-13	6	103	95	.979	130	114	-.2	.6	-6.5	-1.9	-3.0
WEST																										
CIN	14	12	50	1456¹	**1338**	8.3	124	543	1029	11.8	3.39	**114**	.245	.317	64	77	102	105	**.983**	102	126	1.4	7.9	1.9	-2.1	.9
LA	29	12	29	1442	1364	8.5	137	478	1021	11.7	3.72	96	.248	.312	11	-25	94	96	.979	130	123	-.2	-2.6	5.7	-2.1	4.2
SF	14	6	45	1446¹	1477	9.2	131	553	788	12.8	4.08	91	.266	.335	-45	-57	98	101	**.983**	107	148	1.1	-5.9	3.3	-2.2	7.7
SD	21	12	35	1461²	1437	8.8	147	507	928	12.1	3.68	105	.258	.322	18	27	101	**106**	.977	141	141	-.8	2.8	-1.8	-2.3	-3.9
HOU	12	6	37	1450	1396	8.7	130	496	854	12.0	3.61	104	.254	.320	29	21	99	104	.978	131	124	-.3	2.2	-7.1	-2.0	1.2
ATL	17	8	30	1429²	1527	9.6	128	579	938	13.4	4.58	85	.275	.346	-124	-105	103	97	.974	158	133	-1.8	-10.8	-1.9	-2.0	.5
TOT	200	116	476	17381¹		8.8				12.2	3.79		.256	.324					.980	1516	1561					

Runs
Sandberg-Chi . . . 116
Bonilla-Pit 112
Butler-SF 108
Gant-Atl 107
Dykstra-Phi 106

Hits
Dykstra-Phi 192
Butler-SF 192
Sandberg-Chi . . . 188
Wallach-Mon 185
Larkin-Cin 185

Doubles
Jefferies-NY 40
Bonilla-Pit 39
Sabo-Cin 38
Wallach-Mon 37
Johnson-NY 37

Triples
Duncan-Cin 11
Gwynn-SD 10
L.Smith-Atl 9
Coleman-StL 9
Butler-SF 9

Home Runs
Sandberg-Chi 40
Strawberry-NY . . . 37
Mitchell-SF 35
Williams-SF 33
Bonds-Pit 33

Total Bases
Sandberg-Chi 344
Bonilla-Pit 324
Gant-Atl 310
Williams-SF 301
Wallach-Mon 295

Runs Batted In
Williams-SF 122
Bonilla-Pit 120
Carter-SD 115
Bonds-Pit 114
Strawberry-NY . . . 108

Runs Produced
Bonilla-Pit 200
Bonds-Pit 185
Williams-SF 176
Sandberg-Chi . . . 176
Carter-SD 170

Bases On Balls
J.Clark-SD 104
Bonds-Pit 93
Butler-SF 90
Dykstra-Phi 89
V.Hayes-Phi 87

Batting Average
McGee-StL 335
Murray-LA 330
Magadan-NY 328
Dykstra-Phi 325
Dawson-Chi 310

On Base Percentage
Magadan-NY 425
Dykstra-Phi 420
Murray-LA 417
Bonds-Pit 410
Butler-SF 401

Slugging Average
Bonds-Pit 565
Sandberg-Chi 559
Mitchell-SF 544
Gant-Atl 539
Justice-Atl 535

Production
Bonds-Pit 974
Murray-LA 936
Daniels-LA 923
Sandberg-Chi 918
Justice-Atl 909

Adjusted Production
Bonds-Pit 172
Murray-LA 165
Daniels-LA 160
Mitchell-SF 148
Magadan-NY 146

Batter Runs
Bonds-Pit 48.1
Murray-LA 44.7
Sandberg-Chi . . . 37.9
J.Clark-SD 36.5
Dykstra-Phi 34.3

Adjusted Batter Runs
Bonds-Pit 50.9
Murray-LA 48.7
J.Clark-SD 35.8
Daniels-LA 35.6
Dykstra-Phi 34.7

Clutch Hitting Index
Carter-SD 151
O.Smith-StL 132
Guerrero-StL 129
Williams-SF 128
Grace-Chi 128

Runs Created
Bonds-Pit 128
Sandberg-Chi . . . 124
Dykstra-Phi 121
Murray-LA 118
Gant-Atl 109

Total Average
Bonds-Pit 1.115
Daniels-LA 945
Murray-LA 945
Justice-Atl 941
Dykstra-Phi 941

Stolen Bases
Coleman-StL . . . 77
Yelding-Hou 64
Bonds-Pit 52
Butler-SF 51
Nixon-Mon 50

Stolen Base Average
Gibson-LA 92.9
Grissom-Mon . . . 91.7
Dawson-Chi 88.9
Davis-Cin 87.5
Dykstra-Phi 86.8

Stolen Base Runs
Coleman-StL . . . 12.9
Bonds-Pit 7.8
Nixon-Mon 7.2
Dykstra-Phi 6.9

Fielding Runs
Thompson-SF . . . 27.7
Grace-Chi 26.7
C.Hayes-Phi 23.6
Larkin-Cin 19.9
Lind-Pit 17.1

Total Player Rating
Bonds-Pit 6.5
Dykstra-Phi 4.9
Larkin-Cin 4.5
Murray-LA 4.5
Sandberg-Chi . . . 4.3

Wins
Drabek-Pit 22
Viola-NY 20
Martinez-LA 20
Gooden-NY 19

Win Percentage
Drabek-Pit 786
Martinez-LA 769
Gooden-NY 731
Viola-NY 625
Browning-Cin 625

Games
Agosto-Hou 82
Assenmacher-Chi . . 74
Harris-SD 73
McDowell-Phi . . . 72
Akerfelds-Phi 71

Complete Games
Martinez-LA 12
Hurst-SD 9
Drabek-Pit 9
Maddux-Chi 8

Shutouts
Morgan-LA 4
Hurst-SD 4

Saves
Franco-NY 33
Myers-Cin 31
L.Smith-StL 27
Smith-Hou 23
Lefferts-SD 23

Innings Pitched
Viola-NY 249.2
Maddux-Chi 237.0
Martinez-LA 234.1
Gooden-NY 232.2

Fewest Hits/Game
Fernandez-NY . . . 6.52
Rijo-Cin 6.90
Martinez-LA 7.34
Drabek-Pit 7.39
Darwin-Hou 7.52

Fewest BB/Game
Darwin-Hou 1.72
Whitson-SD 1.85
Leibrandt-Atl . . . 1.94
J.Martinez-Mon . . 1.95
Browning-Cin . . . 2.06

Strikeouts
Cone-NY 233
Martinez-LA 223
Gooden-NY 223
Viola-NY 182
Fernandez-NY . . . 181

Strikeouts/Game
Cone-NY 9.91
Fernandez-NY . . . 9.08
Gooden-NY 8.63
Martinez-LA 8.56
DeLeon-StL 8.08

Ratio
Darwin-Hou 9.46
Drabek-Pit 9.69
J.Martinez-Mon . . 9.80
Martinez-LA 10.06
Fernandez-NY . . . 10.14

Earned Run Average
Darwin-Hou 2.21
Smith-Mon-Pit . . 2.55
Whitson-SD 2.60
Viola-NY 2.67
Rijo-Cin 2.70

Adjusted ERA
Darwin-Hou 169
Whitson-SD 148
Smith-Mon-Pit . . 145
Rijo-Cin 144
Viola-NY 137

Opponents' Batting Avg.
Fernandez-NY 200
Rijo-Cin 212
Martinez-LA 220
Drabek-Pit 225
Darwin-Hou 225

Opponents' On Base Pct.
Darwin-Hou 267
Drabek-Pit 275
J.Martinez-Mon . . .275
Martinez-LA 279
Fernandez-NY 280

Starter Runs
Viola-NY 31.2
Whitson-SD 30.3
Smith-Mon-Pit . . 29.7
Darwin-Hou 28.5
Drabek-Pit 26.4

Adjusted Starter Runs
Whitson-SD 31.7
Smith-Mon-Pit . . 27.6
Darwin-Hou 27.6
Viola-NY 27.1
Rijo-Cin 25.7

Clutch Pitching Index
Gullickson-Hou . . . 121
Smith-Mon-Pit . . 118
Whitson-SD 115
Rasmussen-SD . . 114
Darwin-Hou 107

Relief Runs
Dibble-Cin 22.3
Brantley-SF 21.5
Harris-SD 19.4
Charlton-Cin . . . 18.0
Myers-Cin 16.5

Adjusted Relief Runs
Dibble-Cin 23.1
Brantley-SF 20.8
Harris-SD 19.4
Charlton-Cin . . . 19.4
Myers-Cin 17.3

Relief Ranking
Myers-Cin 31.8
Dibble-Cin 29.2
Harris-SD 28.2
Brantley-SF 27.6
L.Smith-StL 25.0

Total Pitcher Index
Whitson-SD 3.9
Smith-Mon-Pit . . 3.2
Drabek-Pit 3.1
Tudor-StL 3.0
Rijo-Cin 2.9

Total Baseball Ranking
Bonds-Pit 6.5
Dykstra-Phi 4.9
Larkin-Cin 4.5
Murray-LA 4.5
Sandberg-Chi . . . 4.3

TEAM	G	W	L	PCT	GB	R	OR	AB	H	2B	3B	HR	BB	SO	AVG	OBP	SLG	PRO	PRO+	BR	/A	PF	CHI	RC	SB	CS	SBA	SBR
EAST																												
BOS	162	88	74	.543		699	664	5516	**1502**	298	31	106	598	795	**.272**	**.346**	.395	.741	102	57	23	105	92	733	53	52	51	-14
TOR	162	86	76	.531	2	**767**	661	5589	1479	263	**50**	167	526	970	.265	.331	**.419**	**.750**	110	56	**69**	98	101	**769**	111	52	50	-13
DET	162	79	83	.488	9	750	754	5479	1418	241	32	**172**	634	952	.259	.339	.409	.748	108	**62**	65	100	98	754	82	57	53	-14
CLE	162	77	85	.475	11	732	737	5485	1465	266	41	110	458	836	.267	.327	.391	.718	98	-4	-14	102	107	694	107	52	50	-13
BAL	161	76	85	.472	11.5	669	698	5410	1328	234	22	132	**660**	962	.245	.332	.370	.702	98	-20	-4	98	98	676	94	52	51	-14
MIL	162	74	88	.457	14	732	760	5503	1408	247	36	128	519	821	.256	.324	.384	.708	100	-23	0	97	**108**	692	**164**	72	59	-13
NY	162	67	95	.414	21	603	749	5483	1322	208	19	147	427	1027	.241	.302	.366	.668	85	-108	-110	100	105	605	119	45	43	-11
WEST																												
OAK	162	103	59	.636		733	**570**	5433	1379	209	22	164	651	992	.254	.339	.391	.730	107	31	51	97	100	739	141	54	56	-16
CHI	162	94	68	.580	9	682	633	5402	1393	251	44	106	478	903	.258	.322	.379	.701	97	-34	-19	98	105	651	140	90	**62**	**-9**
TEX	162	83	79	.512	20	676	696	5469	1416	257	27	110	575	1054	.259	.333	.376	.709	96	-10	-22	102	98	688	115	48	44	-11
CAL	162	80	82	.494	23	690	706	5570	1448	237	27	147	566	1000	.260	.331	.391	.722	100	10	7	100	96	715	69	43	49	-16
SEA	162	77	85	.475	26	640	680	5474	1419	251	26	107	596	**749**	.259	.336	.373	.709	97	-6	-13	101	92	691	105	51	51	-14
KC	161	75	86	.466	27.5	707	709	5488	1465	**316**	44	100	498	879	.267	.331	.395	.726	104	14	29	98	101	706	107	62	55	-13
MIN	162	74	88	.457	29	666	729	5499	1458	281	39	100	445	**749**	.265	.326	.385	.711	91	-16	-64	107	99	673	96	53	49	-13
TOT	1133					9746		76800	19900	3559	460	1796	7631	12689	.259	.330	.388	.718							1503	783	66	-18

TEAM	CG	SH	SV	IP	H	H/G	HR	BB	SO	RAT	ERA	ERA+	OAV	OOB	PR	/A	PF	CPI	FA	E	DP	FW	PW	BW	SBW	DIF
EAST																										
BOS	15	13	44	1442	1439	9.0	**92**	519	997	12.5	3.72	110	.260	.329	29	57	104	100	.980	123	154	-.2	5.8	2.3	-1.3	.4
TOR	6	9	48	1454	1434	8.9	143	**445**	892	11.9	3.84	99	.259	.319	10	-7	97	99	**.986**	**86**	144	**2.0**	-.7	**7.0**	-1.2	-2.2
DET	15	12	45	1430[1]	1401	8.8	154	661	856	13.3	4.39	89	.258	.344	-76	-73	101	98	.979	131	178	-.7	-7.4	6.6	-1.3	.8
CLE	12	10	47	1427[1]	1491	9.4	163	518	860	12.9	4.26	93	.269	.336	-56	-44	102	102	.981	117	146	.2	-4.5	-1.4	-1.2	2.9
BAL	10	5	43	1435[1]	1445	9.1	161	537	776	12.5	4.04	95	.263	.331	-21	-34	98	103	.985	93	151	1.6	-3.5	-.4	-1.3	-.9
MIL	23	13	42	1445	1558	9.7	121	469	771	12.5	4.08	93	.275	.334	-27	-48	97	101	.976	149	152	-1.8	-4.9	.0	-1.2	.8
NY	15	6	41	1444[2]	1430	8.9	144	618	909	12.9	4.21	94	.261	.338	-49	-39	102	99	.980	126	164	-.4	-4.0	-11.2	-1.0	2.5
WEST																										
OAK	18	**16**	64	1456	**1287**	**8.0**	123	494	831	**11.2**	**3.18**	118	**.237**	.304	117	90	96	101	**.986**	87	152	**2.0**	**9.2**	5.2	-1.5	7.2
CHI	17	10	**68**	1449[1]	1313	8.2	106	548	914	11.8	3.61	106	.243	.317	47	34	98	95	.980	124	169	-.3	3.5	-1.9	**-.8**	12.5
TEX	**25**	9	36	1444[2]	1343	8.4	113	623	997	12.5	3.83	104	.247	.330	11	24	102	97	.979	133	161	-.8	2.4	-2.2	-1.0	3.6
CAL	21	13	42	1454	1482	9.2	106	544	944	12.8	3.79	103	.267	.336	17	17	100	**105**	.978	142	**186**	-1.4	1.7	.7	-1.5	-.6
SEA	21	7	41	1443[1]	1319	8.2	120	606	**1064**	12.3	3.69	107	.243	.324	34	43	101	97	.979	130	152	-.6	4.4	-1.3	-1.3	-5.1
KC	18	8	33	1420[2]	1449	9.2	116	560	1006	13.0	3.93	97	.263	.336	-4	-20	97	102	.980	122	161	-.2	-2.0	3.0	-1.2	-5.0
MIN	13	13	43	1435[2]	1509	9.5	134	489	872	12.7	4.12	102	.272	.334	-35	10	107	101	.983	101	161	1.1	1.0	-6.5	-1.2	-1.4
TOT	229	144	637	20182[1]		8.9				12.5	3.91		.259	.330					.981	1664	2231					

Runs	Hits	Doubles	Triples	Home Runs	Total Bases
R.Henderson-Oak . 119	Palmeiro-Tex 191	J.Reed-Bos 45	Fernandez-Tor 17	Fielder-Det 51	Fielder-Det 339
Fielder-Det 104	Boggs-Bos 187	Brett-KC 45	Sosa-Chi 10	McGwire-Oak 39	Gruber-Tor 303
Reynolds-Sea . . . 100	Kelly-NY 183	Calderon-Chi 44	Polonia-NY-Cal . . . 9	J.Canseco-Oak . . . 37	McGriff-Tor 295
Yount-Mil 98	Greenwell-Bos . . . 181	Boggs-Bos 44	Liriano-Tor-Min . . . 9	McGriff-Tor 35	K.Griffey-Sea 287
Phillips-Det 97		Harper-Min 42	Johnson-Chi 9	Gruber-Tor 31	Burks-Bos 286

Runs Batted In	Runs Produced	Bases On Balls	Batting Average	On Base Percentage	Slugging Average
Fielder-Det 132	Fielder-Det 185	McGwire-Oak 110	Brett-KC 329	R.Henderson-Oak . .441	Fielder-Det 592
Gruber-Tor 118	Gruber-Tor 179	Tettleton-Bal 106	R.Henderson-Oak . .325	McGriff-Tor 403	R.Henderson-Oak . .577
McGwire-Oak 108	Yount-Mil 158	Phillips-Det 99	Palmeiro-Tex 319	E.Martinez-Sea 399	J.Canseco-Oak 543
J.Canseco-Oak . . . 101	Burks-Bos 157	R.Henderson-Oak . . 97	Trammell-Det 304	Davis-Sea 393	McGriff-Tor 530
Sierra-Tex 96	McGwire-Oak 156	McGriff-Tor 94	Boggs-Bos 302	Brett-KC 392	Brett-KC 515

Production	Adjusted Production	Batter Runs	Adjusted Batter Runs	Clutch Hitting Index	Runs Created
R.Henderson-Oak 1.017	R.Henderson-Oak . 188	R.Henderson-Oak . 57.5	R.Henderson-Oak . 59.5	Leonard-Sea 150	R.Henderson-Oak . 137
Fielder-Det 972	Fielder-Det 169	Fielder-Det 51.3	Fielder-Det 51.7	Fletcher-Chi 131	McGriff-Tor 129
McGriff-Tor 932	McGriff-Tor 162	McGriff-Tor 45.5	McGriff-Tor 47.0	Sierra-Tex 130	McGwire-Oak 124
J.Canseco-Oak 917	J.Canseco-Oak . . . 158	Brett-KC 37.0	Brett-KC 38.6	Gaetti-Min 128	Brett-KC 106
Brett-KC 906	Brett-KC 155	J.Canseco-Oak . . . 34.3	J.Canseco-Oak . . . 36.1	Guillen-Chi 127	K.Griffey-Sea 103

Total Average	Stolen Bases	Stolen Base Average	Stolen Base Runs	Fielding Runs	Total Player Rating
R.Henderson-Oak 1.241	R.Henderson-Oak . . 65	Cotto-Sea 87.5	R.Henderson-Oak . 13.5	Espinoza-NY 21.1	R.Henderson-Oak . . 7.7
Fielder-Det 1.007	Sax-NY 43	R.Henderson-Oak . 86.7	Sax-NY 7.5	Reynolds-Sea 15.5	McGriff-Tor 4.5
McGriff-Tor 983	Kelly-NY 42	Molitor-Mil 85.7	Cole-Cle 6.6	Gaetti-Min 13.8	Fielder-Det 4.4
J.Canseco-Oak 943	Cole-Cle 40	Gantner-Mil 85.7	Wilson-Tor 4.5	Quintana-Bos 13.6	J.Canseco-Oak . . . 3.3
McGwire-Oak 903	Pettis-Tex 38	Wilson-Tor 85.2	Cotto-Sea 4.5	Gallego-Oak 13.3	Trammell-Det 3.2

Wins	Win Percentage	Games	Complete Games	Shutouts	Saves
Welch-Oak 27	Welch-Oak 818	Thigpen-Chi 77	Stewart-Oak 11	Stewart-Oak 4	Thigpen-Chi 57
Stewart-Oak 22	Clemens-Bos 778	Ward-Tor 73	Morris-Det 11	Clemens-Bos 4	Eckersley-Oak 48
Clemens-Bos 21	Stieb-Tor 750	Montgomery-KC . . 73		Perez-Chi 3	Jones-Cle 43
	Boddicker-Bos 680	Rogers-Tex 69		Morris-Det 3	Olson-Bal 37
		Henneman-Det . . . 69		Appier-KC 3	Righetti-NY 36

Innings Pitched	Fewest Hits/Game	Fewest BB/Game	Strikeouts	Strikeouts/Game	Ratio
Stewart-Oak 267.0	Ryan-Tex 6.04	Anderson-Min 1.86	Ryan-Tex 232	Ryan-Tex 10.24	Ryan-Tex 9.62
Morris-Det 249.2	Johnson-Sea 7.13	Swindell-Cle 1.97	Witt-Tex 221	Witt-Tex 8.96	Clemens-Bos 10.01
Welch-Oak 238.0	Clemens-Bos 7.61	Clemens-Bos 2.13	Hanson-Sea 211	Clemens-Bos 8.24	Wells-Tor 10.10
Hanson-Sea 236.0	Stewart-Oak 7.62	Knudson-Mil 2.14	Clemens-Bos 209	Gordon-KC 8.06	Hanson-Sea 10.49
Finley-Cal 236.0	Stieb-Tor 7.72	Wells-Tor 2.14	Langston-Cal 195	Hanson-Sea 8.05	Stewart-Oak 10.58

Earned Run Average	Adjusted ERA	Opponents' Batting Avg.	Opponents' On Base Pct.	Starter Runs	Adjusted Starter Runs
Clemens-Bos 1.93	Clemens-Bos 211	Ryan-Tex 188	Ryan-Tex 269	Clemens-Bos 50.1	Clemens-Bos 54.4
Finley-Cal 2.40	Finley-Cal 162	Johnson-Sea 216	Clemens-Bos 280	Stewart-Oak 39.9	Finley-Cal 39.3
Stewart-Oak 2.56	Stewart-Oak 146	Clemens-Bos 228	Wells-Tor 283	Finley-Cal 39.4	Stewart-Oak 34.8
Appier-KC 2.76	Appier-KC 138	Stieb-Tor 230	Hanson-Sea 289	Welch-Oak 25.3	Appier-KC 21.5
Stieb-Tor 2.93	Stieb-Tor 129	Stewart-Oak 231	Black-Cle-Tor 293	Appier-KC 23.6	Welch-Oak 20.7

Clutch Pitching Index	Relief Runs	Adjusted Relief Runs	Relief Ranking	Total Pitcher Index	Total Baseball Ranking
Finley-Cal 136	Farr-KC 27.1	Farr-KC 25.7	Eckersley-Oak 56.2	Clemens-Bos 6.2	R.Henderson-Oak . . 7.7
Appier-KC 121	Eckersley-Oak . . . 26.8	Eckersley-Oak . . . 25.4	Thigpen-Chi 48.3	Finley-Cal 4.0	Clemens-Bos 6.2
Clemens-Bos 118	Swift-Sea 21.5	Swift-Sea 22.3	Farr-KC 36.8	Stewart-Oak 3.6	McGriff-Tor 4.5
Welch-Oak 117	Thigpen-Chi 20.5	Thigpen-Chi 19.6	Jones-Cle 29.4	Farr-KC 2.7	Fielder-Det 4.4
Johnson-Bal 113	Nelson-Oak 19.4	Nelson-Oak 18.0	Olson-Bal 28.4	Stieb-Tor 2.5	Finley-Cal 4.0

The All-Time Leaders

The All-Time Leaders

This section is divided into two parts: lifetime leaders and single-season leaders. Both groups command our attention and convey the pleasures of the game, which lie as much in contemplation of the past as in experiencing the present: Henry Aaron, 755; Babe Ruth, 714; Willie Mays, 660—this is no mere aggregation of names and numbers, as in a telephone directory . . . it comprises the romance and lore of the home run, and of baseball itself. Jack Chesbro, 41, 1904; Bob Gibson, 1.12, 1968; Nolan Ryan, 373, 1973 . . . you can fill in the blanks that tell the story of pitching's most glorious seasons.

What follows are the all-time great achievements in 219 categories, both the traditional statistics and the new. For most of these we will give not the top 10 or 20 but the top 100, because some categories would otherwise be dominated by players of a certain era (for example, slugging average by batters of the 1920s and 1930s, earned run average by pitchers of 1900–1919). And for many stats we will offer a second kind of ranking, broken down into the five distinct eras of baseball, with the top 10 or 15 leaders in each. For example, breaking down single-season home runs this way would produce lists topped by these men:

1876–1892: Ned Williamson, 27, 1884
1893–1919: Babe Ruth, 29, 1919
1920–1941: Babe Ruth, 60, 1927
1942–1960: Ralph Kiner, 54, 1949
1961–1990: Roger Maris, 61, 1961

And for single-season Adjusted ERA (normalized to league average and adjusted for home-park factor), we get:

1876–1892: Tim Keefe, 294
(adjusted from actual 0.80), 1880
1893–1919: Dutch Leonard, 280
(adjusted from actual 0.96), 1914
1920–1941: Lefty Grove, 218
(adjusted from actual 2.06), 1931
1942–1960: Billy Pierce, 201
(adjusted from actual 1.97), 1955
1961–1990: Bob Gibson, 258
(adjusted from actual 1.12), 1968

This is quite a different lineup from the traditional list of ERA leaders (which relegates pre-1900 pitching to the shadows), where of the 15 top spots, 14 are accorded to pitchers active from 1905 to 1918. Is there a baseball fan alive who thinks that all the great pitchers were created in that 14-year span and that the mold was then broken?

But enough expostulation and fulmination. Let's set some ground rules, define some terms that may still be unfamiliar after you've browsed through the Player and Pitcher registers, and get on with the show.

To be eligible for a lifetime pitching category that is stated as an average, a man must have pitched 1,500 or more innings, or 750 or more innings if he is a relief pitcher, in the major leagues; for a counting statistic, he must simply have attained the necessary quantity to crack the list. For a single-season category expressed as an average, he must have pitched one inning per league scheduled game or have attained the necessary quantity (wins, strikeouts, saves) to head a counted list.

To be eligible for a lifetime batting category that is stated as an average, a man must have played in 1,000 or more games; for counting stats such as stolen bases, a Vince Coleman can take his place on the list despite his distance from 1,000 games played. For Pitcher Batting Average, the criterion is 1,500 innings pitched or 100 hits. And to reach the single-season batting lists, a man must have 3.1 plate appearances per scheduled game.

We provide tables of the top fielding performances, too, sorted by position as you would expect (and, in this second edition, including only games played at the position, rather than combining data from secondary positions under the dominant postion). But we go one step further and rank several *batting* categories by position, thus recognizing and illustrating the greater demands for fielding skill at such positions as shortstop, catcher, and second base, and the comparatively plentiful supply of batting talent in the outfield and at first base. As we establish a 1,000-game minimum for inclusion in all but a few batting and baserunning categories, we likewise establish for these positional rankings a minimum of 1,000 games played at the position.

For the three principal categories—Total Player Rating, Total Pitcher Index, and Total Baseball Ranking—we have introduced several variations. For example, TPR and TBR are shown 500 deep for lifetime leaders—sorted first by highest value; then alphabetically so that the reader may find a particular player without scanning 500 names; and last by the above-named eras, the top 25 in each. Total Pitcher Index is also sorted this way, but because far fewer pitchers than position players meet the longevity criteria, the lifetime groupings go 300 and 200 deep rather than 500 and 300. Ties are calculated to as many decimal places as needed to break them, but averages are shown to only three places. When two or more players are tied in an averaged category with a narrow base of data, such as a season's won-lost percentage, the reader can presume a numerical dead heat (and obviously this goes for counting stats, too—one man's 39 doubles are as good as another's). But where there is a tie for batting average, earned run average, or any of the sabermetric measures, the reader may assume that the man listed above the other(s) has the minutely higher average.

Here are the few stats carried in this section that are not carried in the Annual Record or Registers, with definitions where the terms are not self-explanatory (see Glossary for formulas):

Batting, Baserunning, Fielding

Runs (Scored) Per Game   Broken down by era
Home Run Percentage   Home runs per 100 at bats
Bases on Balls Percentage   Walks (most) per 100 at bats
At-Bats Per Strikeout   Broken down by era
Relative Batting Average   Normalized to league average
Isolated Power   Slugging average minus batting average
Extra Base Hits
Pinch Hits
Pinch Hit Batting Average
Pinch Hit Home Runs
Strikeout Percentage
Total Player Rating Per 150 Games   A new category, highlighting the achievements of modern players and those with comparatively short careers (though at least 1,000 games)
Total Chances Per Game   Broken down by position
Chances Accepted Per Game   Broken down by position
Putouts   Broken down by position

Putouts Per Game   Broken down by position
Assists   Broken down by position
Assists Per Game   Broken down by position
Double Plays   Broken down by position

Pitching

Wins Above Team   How many wins a pitcher garnered beyond those expected of an average pitcher for that team; the formula is weighted so that a pitcher on a good team has a chance to compete with pitchers on poor teams who otherwise would benefit from the larger potential spread between their team's won-lost percentage and their own; see Glossary for more information.
Wins Above League   A pitcher's won-lost record restated by adding his Pitching Wins above the league average to the record that a league-average pitcher would have had with the same number of decisions (for example, Tom Seaver goes 20–10 with 7 Pitching Wins; applying the 7 wins to a 15–15 mark in the same 30 decisions results in a WAL of 22–8).
Percentage of Team Wins
Relief Games
Pitchers' Batting Runs
Pitchers' Fielding Runs
Relief Wins   This statistic, like the relief stats below, now includes only games in relief rather than, as in the first edition, totals for any pitcher who averaged less than three innings per game.
Relief Losses
Relief Innings Pitched
Relief Points   Relief wins plus saves minus losses

Games

1	Pete Rose	3562
2	Carl Yastrzemski	3308
3	Hank Aaron	3298
4	Ty Cobb	3035
5	Stan Musial	3026
6	Willie Mays	2992
7	Rusty Staub	2951
8	Brooks Robinson	2896
9	Al Kaline	2834
10	Eddie Collins	2826
11	Reggie Jackson	2820
12	Frank Robinson	2808
13	Honus Wagner	2792
14	Tris Speaker	2789
15	Tony Perez	2777
16	Mel Ott	2730
17	Graig Nettles	2700
18	Darrell Evans	2687
19	Rabbit Maranville	2670
20	Joe Morgan	2649
21	Lou Brock	2616
22	Luis Aparicio	2599
23	Willie McCovey	2588
24	Paul Waner	2549
25	Ernie Banks	2528
26	Bill Buckner	2517
	Sam Crawford	2517
28	Dwight Evans	2505
29	Babe Ruth	2503
30	Dave Concepcion	2488
	Billy Williams	2488
32	Nap Lajoie	2480
33	Max Carey	2476
34	Rod Carew	2469
	Vada Pinson	2469
36	Ted Simmons	2456
37	Robin Yount	2449
38	Bill Dahlen	2443
39	Ron Fairly	2442
40	Harmon Killebrew	2435
41	Roberto Clemente	2433
42	Willie Davis	2429
43	Luke Appling	2422
44	Zach Wheat	2410
45	Mickey Vernon	2409
46	Buddy Bell	2405
47	Sam Rice	2404
	Mike Schmidt	2404
49	Mickey Mantle	2401
	Dave Winfield	2401
51	Eddie Mathews	2391
52	Jake Beckley	2386
53	Bobby Wallace	2383
54	Enos Slaughter	2380
55	George Davis	2368
	Al Oliver	2368
57	Nellie Fox	2367
58	Willie Stargell	2360
59	Jose Cruz	2353
60	Dave Parker	2334
61	Steve Garvey	2332
62	Bert Campaneris	2328
63	Frank White	2324
64	Charlie Gehringer	2323
65	Jimmie Foxx	2317
66	Frankie Frisch	2311
67	Harry Hooper	2309
68	Don Baylor	2292
	Ted Williams	2292
70	Goose Goslin	2287
71	Jimmy Dykes	2282
72	George Brett	2279
73	Carlton Fisk	2278
74	Cap Anson	2276
75	Lave Cross	2275
76	Bob Boone	2264
77	Chris Speier	2260
78	Rogers Hornsby	2259
79	Larry Bowa	2247
80	Ron Santo	2243
81	Fred Clarke	2242
82	Doc Cramer	2239
83	Red Schoendienst	2216
84	Al Simmons	2215
85	Joe Torre	2209
86	Tommy Corcoran	2200
87	Tony Taylor	2195
88	Richie Ashburn	2189
89	Bill Russell	2181
90	Chris Chambliss	2175
91	Joe Judge	2171
92	Charlie Grimm	2166
	Pee Wee Reese	2166
94	Lou Gehrig	2164
95	Bill Mazeroski	2163
96	Johnny Bench	2158
97	Tommy Leach	2156
98	Toby Harrah	2155
99	Harry Heilmann	2148
100	Duke Snider	2143

At Bats

1	Pete Rose	14053
2	Hank Aaron	12364
3	Carl Yastrzemski	11988
4	Ty Cobb	11434
5	Stan Musial	10972
6	Willie Mays	10881
7	Brooks Robinson	10654
8	Honus Wagner	10430
9	Lou Brock	10332
10	Luis Aparicio	10230
11	Tris Speaker	10195
12	Al Kaline	10116
13	Rabbit Maranville	10078
14	Frank Robinson	10006
15	Eddie Collins	9948
16	Reggie Jackson	9864
17	Tony Perez	9778
18	Rusty Staub	9720
19	Vada Pinson	9645
20	Nap Lajoie	9589
21	Sam Crawford	9570
22	Jake Beckley	9526
23	Robin Yount	9494
24	Paul Waner	9459
25	Mel Ott	9456
26	Roberto Clemente	9454
27	Ernie Banks	9421
28	Bill Buckner	9397
29	Max Carey	9363
30	Billy Williams	9350
31	Rod Carew	9315
32	Joe Morgan	9277
33	Sam Rice	9269
34	Nellie Fox	9232
35	Willie Davis	9174
36	Doc Cramer	9140
37	Frankie Frisch	9112
38	Zach Wheat	9106
39	Cap Anson	9101
40	Lave Cross	9072
41	Al Oliver	9049
42	Bill Dahlen	9031
	George Davis	9031
44	Buddy Bell	8995
45	Graig Nettles	8986
46	Darrell Evans	8973
47	Dave Winfield	8896
48	Charlie Gehringer	8860
49	Luke Appling	8856
	Dave Parker	8856
51	Steve Garvey	8835
52	Tommy Corcoran	8804
53	Harry Hooper	8785
54	Al Simmons	8759
55	Mickey Vernon	8731
56	Dwight Evans	8726
57	Dave Concepcion	8723
58	George Brett	8692
59	Bert Campaneris	8684
60	Ted Simmons	8680
61	Goose Goslin	8656
62	Bobby Wallace	8618
63	Willie Keeler	8591
64	Fred Clarke	8568
65	Eddie Mathews	8537
66	Red Schoendienst	8479
67	Jesse Burkett	8421
68	Larry Bowa	8418
69	Babe Ruth	8399
70	Richie Ashburn	8365
71	Mike Schmidt	8352
72	Bid McPhee	8291
73	George Sisler	8267
74	Jim Rice	8225
75	Don Baylor	8198
76	Willie McCovey	8197
77	Rogers Hornsby	8173
78	Jimmy Ryan	8164
79	Harmon Killebrew	8147
80	Ron Santo	8143
81	Jimmie Foxx	8134
82	Mickey Mantle	8102
83	Pee Wee Reese	8058
84	Carlton Fisk	8055
85	Jimmy Dykes	8046
86	George VanHaltren	8021
87	Lou Gehrig	8001
88	Eddie Murray	7997
89	Joe Kuhel	7984
90	Tommy Leach	7959
91	Enos Slaughter	7946
92	Orlando Cepeda	7927
	Willie Stargell	7927
94	Jose Cruz	7917
	Charlie Grimm	7917
96	Joe Judge	7898
97	Joe Torre	7874
98	Frank White	7859
99	Stuffy McInnis	7822
100	Roger Connor	7794

Runs

1	Ty Cobb	2245
2	Hank Aaron	2174
	Babe Ruth	2174
4	Pete Rose	2165
5	Willie Mays	2062
6	Stan Musial	1949
7	Lou Gehrig	1888
8	Tris Speaker	1882
9	Mel Ott	1859
10	Frank Robinson	1829
11	Eddie Collins	1819
12	Carl Yastrzemski	1816
13	Ted Williams	1798
14	Charlie Gehringer	1774
15	Jimmie Foxx	1751
16	Honus Wagner	1736
17	Jesse Burkett	1720
18	Cap Anson	1719
	Willie Keeler	1719
20	Billy Hamilton	1690
21	Bid McPhee	1678
22	Mickey Mantle	1677
23	Joe Morgan	1650
24	Jimmy Ryan	1642
25	George VanHaltren	1639
26	Paul Waner	1627
27	Al Kaline	1622
28	Roger Connor	1620
29	Fred Clarke	1619
30	Lou Brock	1610
31	Jake Beckley	1600
32	Ed Delahanty	1599
33	Bill Dahlen	1589
34	Rogers Hornsby	1579
35	Hugh Duffy	1552
36	Reggie Jackson	1551
37	Max Carey	1545
38	George Davis	1539
39	Frankie Frisch	1532
40	Dan Brouthers	1523
41	Tom Brown	1521
42	Sam Rice	1514
43	Eddie Mathews	1509
44	Al Simmons	1507
45	Mike Schmidt	1506
46	Nap Lajoie	1504
47	Harry Stovey	1492
48	Goose Goslin	1483
49	Arlie Latham	1478
50	Herman Long	1456
51	Jim O'Rourke	1446
52	Dwight Evans	1435
53	Robin Yount	1433
54	Harry Hooper	1429
55	Dummy Hoy	1426
56	Rod Carew	1424
57	Joe Kelley	1421
58	Roberto Clemente	1416
59	Billy Williams	1410
60	Monte Ward	1408
61	Mike Griffin	1405
62	Sam Crawford	1391
63	Joe DiMaggio	1390
64	Dave Winfield	1384
65	George Brett	1382
66	Vada Pinson	1366
67	Doc Cramer	1357
	King Kelly	1357
69	Tommy Leach	1355
70	Darrell Evans	1344
71	Pee Wee Reese	1338
72	Luis Aparicio	1335
73	Lave Cross	1333
74	George Gore	1327
75	Richie Ashburn	1322
76	Luke Appling	1319
77	Patsy Donovan	1318
78	Mike Tiernan	1313
79	Ernie Banks	1305
80	Jimmy Sheckard	1296
81	Kiki Cuyler	1295
82	Harry Heilmann	1291
83	Rickey Henderson	1290
84	Zach Wheat	1289
85	Heinie Manush	1287
86	George Sisler	1284
87	Harmon Killebrew	1283
88	Donie Bush	1280
89	Nellie Fox	1279
90	Fred Tenney	1278
91	Tony Perez	1272
92	Duke Snider	1259
93	Bobby Bonds	1258
94	Sam Thompson	1256
95	Rabbit Maranville	1255
96	Jim Rice	1249
97	Enos Slaughter	1247
98	Stan Hack	1239
	Bob Johnson	1239
100	2 players tied	1236

Runs per Game

1876-1892

1	George Gore	1.01
2	Harry Stovey	1.00
3	King Kelly	.93
4	Dan Brouthers	.91
5	Arlie Latham	.91
6	Sam Thompson	.89
7	Buck Ewing	.86
8	Tom Brown	.85
9	Hardy Richardson	.84
10	Tommy McCarthy	.84
11	Tip O'Neill	.83
12	Denny Lyons	.83
13	Curt Welch	.83
14	Jim O'Rourke	.82
15	Roger Connor	.81

1893-1919

1	Billy Hamilton	1.06
2	John McGraw	.93
3	Mike Griffin	.93
4	Hugh Duffy	.89
5	Mike Tiernan	.89
6	Ed Delahanty	.87
7	Cupid Childs	.83
8	Jesse Burkett	.83
9	George VanHaltren	.83
10	Jimmy Ryan	.82
11	Willie Keeler	.81
12	Dummy Hoy	.79
13	Herman Long	.78
14	Hughie Jennings	.77
15	Joe Kelley	.77

1920-1941

1	Lou Gehrig	.87
2	Babe Ruth	.87
3	Earle Combs	.82
4	Red Rolfe	.80
5	Charlie Gehringer	.76
6	Jimmie Foxx	.76
7	Hank Greenberg	.75
8	Earl Averill	.73
9	Max Bishop	.72
10	Lu Blue	.71
11	Mickey Cochrane	.70
12	Rogers Hornsby	.70
13	Kiki Cuyler	.69
14	Mel Ott	.68
15	Al Simmons	.68

1942-1960

1	Joe DiMaggio	.80
2	Ted Williams	.78
3	Dom DiMaggio	.75
4	Tommy Henrich	.70
5	Mickey Mantle	.70
6	Jackie Robinson	.69
7	Johnny Pesky	.68
8	Ralph Kiner	.66
9	Eddie Stanky	.64
10	Stan Musial	.64
11	George Case	.64
12	Eddie Mathews	.63
13	Larry Doby	.63
14	Charlie Keller	.62
15	Minnie Minoso	.62

1961-1990

1	Rickey Henderson	.80
2	Willie Mays	.69
3	Paul Molitor	.68
4	Wade Boggs	.68
5	Bobby Bonds	.68
6	Ron LeFlore	.67
7	Tim Raines	.66
8	Hank Aaron	.66
9	Frank Robinson	.65
10	Dick Allen	.63
11	Ryne Sandberg	.63
12	Mike Schmidt	.63
13	Brett Butler	.63
14	Joe Morgan	.62
15	Lou Brock	.62

Hits

#	Player	Hits
1	Pete Rose	4256
2	Ty Cobb	4190
3	Hank Aaron	3771
4	Stan Musial	3630
5	Tris Speaker	3514
6	Carl Yastrzemski	3419
7	Honus Wagner	3415
8	Eddie Collins	3310
9	Willie Mays	3283
10	Nap Lajoie	3242
11	Paul Waner	3152
12	Rod Carew	3053
13	Lou Brock	3023
14	Al Kaline	3007
15	Roberto Clemente	3000
16	Cap Anson	2995
17	Sam Rice	2987
18	Sam Crawford	2961
19	Frank Robinson	2943
20	Willie Keeler	2932
21	Jake Beckley	2930
	Rogers Hornsby	2930
23	Al Simmons	2927
24	Zach Wheat	2884
25	Frankie Frisch	2880
26	Mel Ott	2876
27	Babe Ruth	2873
28	Jesse Burkett	2850
29	Brooks Robinson	2848
30	Charlie Gehringer	2839
31	George Sisler	2812
32	Vada Pinson	2757
33	Luke Appling	2749
34	Robin Yount	2747
35	Al Oliver	2743
36	Goose Goslin	2735
37	Tony Perez	2732
38	Lou Gehrig	2721
39	Rusty Staub	2716
40	Bill Buckner	2715
41	Billy Williams	2711
42	George Brett	2707
43	Doc Cramer	2705
44	Luis Aparicio	2677
45	Fred Clarke	2672
46	Max Carey	2665
47	Nellie Fox	2663
48	George Davis	2660
	Harry Heilmann	2660
50	Ted Williams	2654
51	Jimmie Foxx	2646
52	Lave Cross	2645
53	Rabbit Maranville	2605
54	Steve Garvey	2599
55	Ed Delahanty	2597
56	Dave Parker	2592
57	Reggie Jackson	2584
58	Ernie Banks	2583
59	Richie Ashburn	2574
60	Willie Davis	2561
61	Dave Winfield	2548
62	George VanHaltren	2532
63	Heinie Manush	2524
64	Joe Morgan	2517
65	Buddy Bell	2514
66	Jimmy Ryan	2502
67	Mickey Vernon	2495
68	Ted Simmons	2472
69	Joe Medwick	2471
70	Roger Connor	2467
71	Harry Hooper	2466
72	Lloyd Waner	2459
73	Bill Dahlen	2457
74	Jim Rice	2452
75	Red Schoendienst	2449
76	Pie Traynor	2416
77	Mickey Mantle	2415
78	Stuffy McInnis	2405
79	Enos Slaughter	2383
80	Edd Roush	2376
81	Dwight Evans	2373
82	Joe Judge	2352
	Eddie Murray	2352
84	Orlando Cepeda	2351
85	Billy Herman	2345
86	Joe Torre	2342
87	Dave Concepcion	2326
	Jake Daubert	2326
89	Eddie Mathews	2315
90	Jim Bottomley	2313
91	Bobby Wallace	2309
92	Jim O'Rourke	2304
93	Kiki Cuyler	2299
	Charlie Grimm	2299
95	Dan Brouthers	2296
96	Joe Cronin	2285
97	Hugh Duffy	2282
98	Jimmy Dykes	2256
99	Ron Santo	2254
100	Patsy Donovan	2253

Doubles

#	Player	Doubles
1	Tris Speaker	792
2	Pete Rose	746
3	Stan Musial	725
4	Ty Cobb	724
5	Nap Lajoie	657
6	Carl Yastrzemski	646
7	Honus Wagner	640
8	Hank Aaron	624
9	Paul Waner	605
10	Charlie Gehringer	574
11	George Brett	559
12	Harry Heilmann	542
13	Rogers Hornsby	541
14	Joe Medwick	540
15	Al Simmons	539
16	Lou Gehrig	534
17	Al Oliver	529
18	Cap Anson	528
	Frank Robinson	528
20	Ted Williams	525
21	Willie Mays	523
22	Ed Delahanty	522
23	Joe Cronin	515
24	Babe Ruth	506
25	Tony Perez	505
26	Goose Goslin	500
	Dave Parker	500
28	Rusty Staub	499
29	Bill Buckner	498
	Al Kaline	498
	Sam Rice	498
	Robin Yount	498
33	Heinie Manush	491
34	Mickey Vernon	490
35	Mel Ott	488
36	Lou Brock	486
	Billy Herman	486
38	Vada Pinson	485
39	Hal McRae	484
40	Ted Simmons	483
41	Brooks Robinson	482
42	Zach Wheat	476
43	Dwight Evans	474
44	Jake Beckley	473
45	Frankie Frisch	466
46	Jim Bottomley	465
47	Reggie Jackson	463
48	Dan Brouthers	460
49	Sam Crawford	458
	Jimmie Foxx	458
51	Jimmy Dykes	453
52	Jimmy Ryan	451
53	George Davis	450
54	Joe Morgan	449
55	Rod Carew	445
56	George Burns	444
57	Dick Bartell	442
58	Roger Connor	441
59	Luke Appling	440
	Roberto Clemente	440
	Steve Garvey	440
62	Eddie Collins	437
63	Cesar Cedeno	436
	Joe Sewell	436
65	Wally Moses	435
66	Billy Williams	434
67	Joe Judge	433
	Dave Winfield	433
69	Red Schoendienst	427
70	Keith Hernandez	426
71	Buddy Bell	425
	Sherry Magee	425
	George Sisler	425
74	Willie Stargell	423
75	Max Carey	419
76	Orlando Cepeda	417
77	Cecil Cooper	415
78	Jim O'Rourke	414
79	Bill Dahlen	413
	Enos Slaughter	413
81	Joe Kuhel	412
82	Lave Cross	411
83	Mike Schmidt	408
84	Ernie Banks	407
	Ben Chapman	407
	Frank White	407
87	Eddie Murray	402
88	Earl Averill	401
	Marty McManus	401
90	Babe Herman	399
	Gee Walker	399
92	Chuck Klein	398
93	Doc Cramer	396
	Andre Dawson	396
	Gabby Hartnett	396
	Bob Johnson	396
	Chet Lemon	396
98	Willie Davis	395
99	3 players tied	394

Triples

#	Player	Triples
1	Sam Crawford	309
2	Ty Cobb	295
3	Honus Wagner	252
4	Jake Beckley	243
5	Roger Connor	233
6	Tris Speaker	222
7	Fred Clarke	220
8	Dan Brouthers	205
9	Joe Kelley	194
10	Paul Waner	191
11	Bid McPhee	188
12	Eddie Collins	186
13	Ed Delahanty	185
14	Sam Rice	184
15	Edd Roush	183
16	Jesse Burkett	182
17	Ed Konetchy	181
18	Buck Ewing	178
19	Rabbit Maranville	177
	Stan Musial	177
21	Harry Stovey	174
22	Goose Goslin	173
23	Tommy Leach	172
	Zach Wheat	172
25	Rogers Hornsby	169
26	Joe Jackson	168
27	Roberto Clemente	166
	Sherry Magee	166
29	Jake Daubert	165
	George Davis	165
31	Elmer Flick	164
	George Sisler	164
	Pie Traynor	164
34	Bill Dahlen	163
	Lou Gehrig	163
	Nap Lajoie	163
37	Mike Tiernan	162
38	George VanHaltren	161
39	Harry Hooper	160
	Heinie Manush	160
	Sam Thompson	160
42	Max Carey	159
	Joe Judge	159
44	Ed McKean	158
45	Kiki Cuyler	157
	Jimmy Ryan	157
47	Tommy Corcoran	155
48	Earle Combs	154
49	Jim Bottomley	151
	Harry Heilmann	151
51	Kip Selbach	149
	Al Simmons	149
53	Wally Pipp	148
	Enos Slaughter	148
55	Bobby Veach	147
56	Harry Davis	146
	Charlie Gehringer	146
58	Willie Keeler	145
59	Bobby Wallace	143
60	Lou Brock	141
61	Willie Mays	140
62	John Reilly	139
63	Tom Brown	138
	Willie Davis	138
	Frankie Frisch	138
	Jimmy Williams	138
67	Babe Ruth	136
	Jimmy Sheckard	136
	Elmer Smith	136
70	Lave Cross	135
	Pete Rose	135
72	Shano Collins	133
	Willie Wilson	133
74	Jim O'Rourke	132
	George Wood	132
76	Joe DiMaggio	131
	Buck Freeman	131
78	Buddy Myer	130
79	Oyster Burns	129
	Larry Gardner	129
81	Earl Averill	128
	Arky Vaughan	128
83	George Brett	127
	Vada Pinson	127
85	Hardy Richardson	126
86	Jimmie Foxx	125
87	John Anderson	124
	Cap Anson	124
	Hal Chase	124
	Frank Schulte	124
91	Larry Doyle	123
	Duke Farrell	123
93	Dummy Hoy	121
94	Mickey Vernon	120
95	Hugh Duffy	119
	Fred Pfeffer	119
97	Joe Cronin	118
	Chick Stahl	118
	Lloyd Waner	118
100	2 players tied	117

Triples (by era)

1876-1892

#	Player	Triples
1	Roger Connor	233
2	Dan Brouthers	205
3	Bid McPhee	188
4	Buck Ewing	178
5	Harry Stovey	174
6	Sam Thompson	160
7	John Reilly	139
8	Tom Brown	138
9	Jim O'Rourke	132
	George Wood	132
11	Oyster Burns	129
12	Hardy Richardson	126
13	Cap Anson	124
14	Fred Pfeffer	119
15	Bill Kuehne	115

1893-1919

#	Player	Triples
1	Sam Crawford	309
2	Ty Cobb	295
3	Honus Wagner	252
4	Jake Beckley	243
5	Tris Speaker	222
6	Fred Clarke	220
7	Joe Kelley	194
8	Eddie Collins	186
9	Ed Delahanty	185
10	Jesse Burkett	182
11	Ed Konetchy	181
12	Tommy Leach	172
	Zach Wheat	172
14	Joe Jackson	168
15	Sherry Magee	166

1920-1941

#	Player	Triples
1	Paul Waner	191
2	Sam Rice	184
3	Edd Roush	183
4	Rabbit Maranville	177
5	Goose Goslin	173
6	Rogers Hornsby	169
7	George Sisler	164
	Pie Traynor	164
9	Lou Gehrig	163
10	Heinie Manush	160
11	Max Carey	159
	Joe Judge	159
13	Kiki Cuyler	157
14	Earle Combs	154
15	2 players tied	151

1942-1960

#	Player	Triples
1	Stan Musial	177
2	Enos Slaughter	148
3	Joe DiMaggio	131
4	Mickey Vernon	120
5	Nellie Fox	112
6	Wally Moses	110
7	Richie Ashburn	109
8	Bill Bruton	102
	Jeff Heath	102
10	Phil Cavarretta	99
11	Dixie Walker	96
12	Bob Elliott	94
13	Bobby Doerr	89
14	Duke Snider	85
15	2 players tied	83

1961-1990

#	Player	Triples
1	Roberto Clemente	166
2	Lou Brock	141
3	Willie Mays	140
4	Willie Davis	138
5	Pete Rose	135
6	Willie Wilson	133
7	George Brett	127
	Vada Pinson	127
9	Robin Yount	116
10	Rod Carew	112
11	Garry Templeton	104
12	Larry Bowa	99
13	Hank Aaron	98
14	Joe Morgan	96
15	Jose Cruz	94

Home Runs

1	Hank Aaron	755
2	Babe Ruth	714
3	Willie Mays	660
4	Frank Robinson	586
5	Harmon Killebrew	573
6	Reggie Jackson	563
7	Mike Schmidt	548
8	Mickey Mantle	536
9	Jimmie Foxx	534
10	Willie McCovey	521
	Ted Williams	521
12	Ernie Banks	512
	Eddie Mathews	512
14	Mel Ott	511
15	Lou Gehrig	493
16	Stan Musial	475
	Willie Stargell	475
18	Carl Yastrzemski	452
19	Dave Kingman	442
20	Billy Williams	426
21	Darrell Evans	414
22	Duke Snider	407
23	Al Kaline	399
24	Graig Nettles	390
25	Johnny Bench	389
26	Frank Howard	382
	Jim Rice	382
28	Orlando Cepeda	379
	Dwight Evans	379
	Eddie Murray	379
	Tony Perez	379
32	Dale Murphy	378
	Dave Winfield	378
34	Norm Cash	377
35	Rocky Colavito	374
36	Gil Hodges	370
37	Ralph Kiner	369
38	Joe DiMaggio	361
39	Johnny Mize	359
40	Yogi Berra	358
41	Carlton Fisk	354
	Lee May	354
43	Dick Allen	351
44	George Foster	348
45	Andre Dawson	346
46	Ron Santo	342
47	Boog Powell	339
48	Don Baylor	338
49	Joe Adcock	336
50	Bobby Bonds	332
51	Hank Greenberg	331
52	Dave Parker	328
53	Willie Horton	325
54	Roy Sievers	318
55	Ron Cey	316
56	Reggie Smith	314
57	Gary Carter	313
58	Jack Clark	307
	Greg Luzinski	307
	Al Simmons	307
61	Fred Lynn	306
62	Rogers Hornsby	301
63	Chuck Klein	300
64	Rusty Staub	292
65	Jim Wynn	291
66	Del Ennis	288
	Bob Johnson	288
	Hank Sauer	288
69	Frank Thomas	286
70	Lance Parrish	285
71	Ken Boyer	282
72	George Brett	281
73	Ted Kluszewski	279
74	Rudy York	277
75	Roger Maris	275
76	Steve Garvey	272
77	George Scott	271
78	Joe Morgan	268
	Brooks Robinson	268
	Gorman Thomas	268
81	George Hendrick	267
82	Vic Wertz	266
83	Bobby Thomson	264
84	Bob Allison	256
	Larry Parrish	256
	Vada Pinson	256
87	John Mayberry	255
88	Larry Doby	253
	Joe Gordon	253
	Andy Thornton	253
91	Bobby Murcer	252
	Darryl Strawberry	252
	Joe Torre	252
94	Tony Armas	251
	Cy Williams	251
96	Brian Downing	248
	Goose Goslin	248
	Ted Simmons	248
99	Vern Stephens	247
100	Ken Singleton	246

Home Runs (by era)

1876-1892

1	Roger Connor	138
2	Sam Thompson	127
3	Harry Stovey	122
4	Dan Brouthers	106
5	Cap Anson	97
6	Fred Pfeffer	94
7	Jack Clements	77
8	Jerry Denny	74
9	Buck Ewing	71
10	Hardy Richardson	70
11	King Kelly	69
	John Reilly	69
13	George Wood	68
14	Oyster Burns	65
	Bug Holliday	65

1893-1919

1	Zach Wheat	132
2	Gavvy Cravath	119
3	Jimmy Ryan	118
	Tilly Walker	118
5	Ty Cobb	117
	Tris Speaker	117
7	Hugh Duffy	106
	Mike Tiernan	106
9	Ed Delahanty	101
	Honus Wagner	101
11	Sam Crawford	98
12	Frank Baker	96
13	Herman Long	92
	Frank Schulte	92
15	Jake Beckley	86

1920-1941

1	Babe Ruth	714
2	Jimmie Foxx	534
3	Mel Ott	511
4	Lou Gehrig	493
5	Hank Greenberg	331
6	Al Simmons	307
7	Rogers Hornsby	301
8	Chuck Klein	300
9	Bob Johnson	288
10	Cy Williams	251
11	Goose Goslin	248
12	Hack Wilson	244
13	Wally Berger	242
14	Dolph Camilli	239
15	Earl Averill	238

1942-1960

1	Mickey Mantle	536
2	Ted Williams	521
3	Eddie Mathews	512
4	Stan Musial	475
5	Duke Snider	407
6	Gil Hodges	370
7	Ralph Kiner	369
8	Joe DiMaggio	361
9	Johnny Mize	359
10	Yogi Berra	358
11	Joe Adcock	336
12	Roy Sievers	318
13	Del Ennis	288
	Hank Sauer	288
15	Frank Thomas	286

1961-1990

1	Hank Aaron	755
2	Willie Mays	660
3	Frank Robinson	586
4	Harmon Killebrew	573
5	Reggie Jackson	563
6	Mike Schmidt	548
7	Willie McCovey	521
8	Ernie Banks	512
9	Willie Stargell	475
10	Carl Yastrzemski	452
11	Dave Kingman	442
12	Billy Williams	426
13	Darrell Evans	414
14	Al Kaline	399
15	Graig Nettles	390

Home Run Percentage

1	Babe Ruth	8.50
2	Ralph Kiner	7.09
3	Harmon Killebrew	7.03
4	Ted Williams	6.76
5	Dave Kingman	6.62
6	Mickey Mantle	6.62
7	Jimmie Foxx	6.57
8	Mike Schmidt	6.56
9	Darryl Strawberry	6.46
10	Hank Greenberg	6.37
11	Willie McCovey	6.36
12	Lou Gehrig	6.16
13	Hank Aaron	6.11
14	Willie Mays	6.07
15	Hank Sauer	6.01
16	Eddie Mathews	6.00
17	Willie Stargell	5.99
18	Frank Howard	5.89
19	Frank Robinson	5.86
20	Bob Horner	5.77
21	Roy Campanella	5.76
22	Rocky Colavito	5.75
23	Gus Zernial	5.74
24	Gorman Thomas	5.73
25	Reggie Jackson	5.71
26	Dick Stuart	5.70
27	Duke Snider	5.68
28	Norm Cash	5.62
29	Johnny Mize	5.57
30	Dick Allen	5.54
31	Ernie Banks	5.43
32	Mel Ott	5.40
33	Roger Maris	5.39
34	Joe DiMaggio	5.29
35	Gil Hodges	5.26
36	Wally Post	5.24
37	Dale Murphy	5.17
38	Al Rosen	5.15
39	Hack Wilson	5.13
40	Bob Allison	5.09
41	Joe Adcock	5.09
42	Johnny Bench	5.08
43	Boog Powell	5.07
44	Jesse Barfield	5.07
45	Nate Colbert	5.06
46	Jack Clark	5.03
47	Charlie Keller	4.99
48	Roy Sievers	4.98
49	Cliff Johnson	4.97
50	Don Mincher	4.97
51	George Foster	4.96
52	Tony Armas	4.86
53	Andy Thornton	4.78
54	Orlando Cepeda	4.78
55	Kent Hrbek	4.78
56	Leon Wagner	4.77
57	Jim Lemon	4.76
58	Eddie Murray	4.74
59	Yogi Berra	4.74
60	Don Demeter	4.73
61	Larry Doby	4.73
62	Greg Luzinski	4.72
63	Bobby Bonds	4.71
64	Ted Kluszewski	4.71
65	Rudy York	4.70
66	Lance Parrish	4.70
67	Wally Berger	4.69
68	Howard Johnson	4.68
69	John Mayberry	4.68
70	Lee May	4.65
71	Jim Rice	4.64
72	Chuck Klein	4.63
73	Darrell Evans	4.61
74	Gene Tenace	4.58
75	Charlie Maxwell	4.56
76	Billy Williams	4.56
77	Frank Thomas	4.55
78	Tom Brunansky	4.53
79	Jim Ray Hart	4.49
80	Gary Roenicke	4.47
81	Dolph Camilli	4.46
82	Reggie Smith	4.46
83	George Bell	4.46
84	Woodie Held	4.45
85	Willie Horton	4.45
86	Andre Dawson	4.44
	Kirk Gibson	4.44
88	Oscar Gamble	4.44
89	Joe Carter	4.44
90	Joe Gordon	4.43
91	Fred Lynn	4.42
92	Hal Trosky	4.42
93	Ron Cey	4.41
94	Wes Covington	4.40
95	Carlton Fisk	4.39
96	Jim Wynn	4.37
97	Dale Long	4.37
98	Vic Wertz	4.36
99	Dwight Evans	4.34
100	Graig Nettles	4.34

Home Run Pctg. (by era)

1876-1892

1	Sam Thompson	2.12
2	Harry Stovey	1.99
3	Jack Clements	1.80
4	Roger Connor	1.77
5	Dan Brouthers	1.58
6	Jerry Denny	1.50
7	John Reilly	1.47
8	Denny Lyons	1.44
9	Charlie Bennett	1.44
10	Fred Pfeffer	1.43
11	Ned Williamson	1.41
12	Oyster Burns	1.40
13	Buck Ewing	1.32
14	George Wood	1.27
15	Hardy Richardson	1.24

1893-1919

1	Gavvy Cravath	3.01
2	Tilly Walker	2.33
3	Buck Freeman	1.95
4	Mike Tiernan	1.79
5	Fred Luderus	1.73
6	Frank Baker	1.60
7	Hugh Duffy	1.51
8	Charlie Hickman	1.48
9	Zach Wheat	1.45
10	Jimmy Ryan	1.45
11	Frank Schulte	1.41
12	Casey Stengel	1.40
13	Ed Delahanty	1.35
14	Mike Donlin	1.32
15	Chief Wilson	1.28

1920-1941

1	Babe Ruth	8.50
2	Jimmie Foxx	6.57
3	Hank Greenberg	6.37
4	Lou Gehrig	6.16
5	Mel Ott	5.40
6	Hack Wilson	5.13
7	Wally Berger	4.69
8	Chuck Klein	4.63
9	Dolph Camilli	4.46
10	Hal Trosky	4.42
11	Bob Johnson	4.16
12	Ken Williams	4.03
13	Earl Averill	3.75
14	Cy Williams	3.70
15	Rogers Hornsby	3.68

1942-1960

1	Ralph Kiner	7.09
2	Ted Williams	6.76
3	Mickey Mantle	6.62
4	Hank Sauer	6.01
5	Eddie Mathews	6.00
6	Roy Campanella	5.76
7	Gus Zernial	5.74
8	Duke Snider	5.68
9	Johnny Mize	5.57
10	Joe DiMaggio	5.29
11	Gil Hodges	5.26
12	Wally Post	5.24
13	Al Rosen	5.15
14	Joe Adcock	5.09
15	Charlie Keller	4.99

1961-1990

1	Harmon Killebrew	7.03
2	Dave Kingman	6.62
3	Mike Schmidt	6.56
4	Darryl Strawberry	6.46
5	Willie McCovey	6.36
6	Hank Aaron	6.11
7	Willie Mays	6.07
8	Willie Stargell	5.99
9	Frank Howard	5.89
10	Frank Robinson	5.86
11	Bob Horner	5.77
12	Rocky Colavito	5.75
13	Gorman Thomas	5.73
14	Reggie Jackson	5.71
15	Dick Stuart	5.70

Total Bases

1	Hank Aaron	6856
2	Stan Musial	6134
3	Willie Mays	6066
4	Ty Cobb	5855
5	Babe Ruth	5793
6	Pete Rose	5752
7	Carl Yastrzemski	5539
8	Frank Robinson	5373
9	Tris Speaker	5101
10	Lou Gehrig	5060
11	Mel Ott	5041
12	Jimmie Foxx	4956
13	Ted Williams	4884
14	Honus Wagner	4862
15	Al Kaline	4852
16	Reggie Jackson	4834
17	Rogers Hornsby	4712
18	Ernie Banks	4706
19	Al Simmons	4685
20	Billy Williams	4599
21	Tony Perez	4532
22	Mickey Mantle	4511
23	Roberto Clemente	4492
24	Nap Lajoie	4474
	Paul Waner	4474
26	Mike Schmidt	4404
27	George Brett	4363
28	Eddie Mathews	4349
29	Sam Crawford	4331
30	Goose Goslin	4325
31	Brooks Robinson	4270
32	Dave Winfield	4267
33	Vada Pinson	4264
34	Eddie Collins	4260
35	Charlie Gehringer	4257
36	Lou Brock	4238
37	Dave Parker	4222
38	Willie McCovey	4219
39	Willie Stargell	4190
40	Rusty Staub	4185
41	Robin Yount	4152
42	Jake Beckley	4147
43	Harmon Killebrew	4143
44	Jim Rice	4129
45	Dwight Evans	4128
46	Zach Wheat	4100
47	Al Oliver	4083
48	Cap Anson	4062
49	Harry Heilmann	4053
50	Rod Carew	3998
51	Joe Morgan	3962
52	Orlando Cepeda	3959
53	Sam Rice	3955
54	Eddie Murray	3949
55	Joe DiMaggio	3948
56	Steve Garvey	3941
57	Frankie Frisch	3937
58	George Sisler	3871
59	Darrell Evans	3866
60	Duke Snider	3865
61	Joe Medwick	3852
62	Bill Buckner	3833
63	Andre Dawson	3811
64	Ted Simmons	3793
65	Ed Delahanty	3792
66	Roger Connor	3788
67	Graig Nettles	3779
	Ron Santo	3779
69	Willie Davis	3778
70	Jesse Burkett	3759
71	Mickey Vernon	3741
72	Carlton Fisk	3738
73	Jim Bottomley	3737
74	Fred Clarke	3674
75	Heinie Manush	3665
76	George Davis	3659
77	Buddy Bell	3654
78	Johnny Bench	3644
79	Yogi Berra	3643
80	Johnny Mize	3621
	Jimmy Ryan	3621
82	Max Carey	3609
83	Enos Slaughter	3599
84	Don Baylor	3571
85	Willie Keeler	3563
86	Joe Torre	3560
87	Joe Cronin	3546
88	Luke Appling	3528
89	Chuck Klein	3522
90	Luis Aparicio	3504
91	Bob Johnson	3501
92	Lee May	3495
93	Dan Brouthers	3484
94	Dale Murphy	3483
95	Lave Cross	3467
96	Bill Dahlen	3448
97	Ken Boyer	3443
98	Reggie Smith	3439
99	Doc Cramer	3430
100	Cecil Cooper	3424

Runs Batted In

1	Hank Aaron	2297
2	Babe Ruth	2209
3	Lou Gehrig	1990
4	Stan Musial	1951
5	Ty Cobb	1937
6	Jimmie Foxx	1922
7	Willie Mays	1903
8	Cap Anson	1879
9	Mel Ott	1860
10	Carl Yastrzemski	1844
11	Ted Williams	1839
12	Al Simmons	1827
13	Frank Robinson	1812
14	Honus Wagner	1732
15	Reggie Jackson	1702
16	Tony Perez	1652
17	Ernie Banks	1636
18	Goose Goslin	1609
19	Nap Lajoie	1599
20	Mike Schmidt	1595
21	Rogers Hornsby	1584
	Harmon Killebrew	1584
23	Al Kaline	1583
24	Jake Beckley	1575
25	Willie McCovey	1555
26	Willie Stargell	1540
27	Harry Heilmann	1539
28	Joe DiMaggio	1537
29	Tris Speaker	1529
30	Sam Crawford	1525
31	Dave Winfield	1516
32	Mickey Mantle	1509
33	Billy Williams	1475
34	Rusty Staub	1466
35	Ed Delahanty	1464
36	Eddie Mathews	1453
37	Jim Rice	1451
38	George Davis	1437
39	Dave Parker	1434
40	Yogi Berra	1430
41	Charlie Gehringer	1427
42	Joe Cronin	1424
43	Jim Bottomley	1422
44	George Brett	1398
45	Ted Simmons	1389
46	Joe Medwick	1383
47	Johnny Bench	1376
48	Eddie Murray	1373
49	Orlando Cepeda	1365
50	Brooks Robinson	1357
51	Darrell Evans	1354
52	Dwight Evans	1346
53	Johnny Mize	1337
54	Duke Snider	1333
55	Ron Santo	1331
56	Al Oliver	1326
57	Roger Connor	1322
58	Graig Nettles	1314
	Pete Rose	1314
60	Mickey Vernon	1311
61	Paul Waner	1309
62	Steve Garvey	1308
63	Roberto Clemente	1305
64	Enos Slaughter	1304
65	Hugh Duffy	1302
66	Eddie Collins	1299
	Sam Thompson	1299
68	Dan Brouthers	1296
69	Del Ennis	1284
70	Bob Johnson	1283
71	Don Baylor	1276
	Hank Greenberg	1276
73	Gil Hodges	1274
74	Pie Traynor	1273
75	Zach Wheat	1248
76	Bobby Doerr	1247
77	Frankie Frisch	1244
	Lee May	1244
79	George Foster	1239
80	Bill Dahlen	1233
81	Andre Dawson	1231
	Carlton Fisk	1231
83	Bill Dickey	1210
	Dave Kingman	1210
85	Bill Buckner	1208
86	Chuck Klein	1201
	Robin Yount	1201
88	Bob Elliott	1195
89	Joe Kelley	1194
90	Tony Lazzeri	1191
91	Boog Powell	1187
92	Joe Torre	1185
93	Heinie Manush	1183
94	Gabby Hartnett	1179
95	Vic Wertz	1178
96	Sherry Magee	1176
97	George Sisler	1175
98	Vern Stephens	1174
99	Dale Murphy	1171
100	2 players tied	1170

Runs Batted In (by era)

1876-1892

1	Cap Anson	1879
2	Roger Connor	1322
3	Sam Thompson	1299
4	Dan Brouthers	1296
5	Fred Pfeffer	1019
6	Jim O'Rourke	1010
7	King Kelly	950
8	Buck Ewing	883
9	Monte Ward	867
10	Hardy Richardson	822
11	Deacon White	756
12	Paul Hines	751
13	Tom Burns	683
14	Sam Wise	672
15	2 players tied	667

1893-1919

1	Ty Cobb	1937
2	Honus Wagner	1732
3	Nap Lajoie	1599
4	Jake Beckley	1575
5	Tris Speaker	1529
6	Sam Crawford	1525
7	Ed Delahanty	1464
8	George Davis	1437
9	Hugh Duffy	1302
10	Eddie Collins	1299
11	Zach Wheat	1248
12	Bill Dahlen	1233
13	Joe Kelley	1194
14	Sherry Magee	1176
15	Bobby Veach	1166

1920-1941

1	Babe Ruth	2209
2	Lou Gehrig	1990
3	Jimmie Foxx	1922
4	Mel Ott	1860
5	Al Simmons	1827
6	Goose Goslin	1609
7	Rogers Hornsby	1584
8	Harry Heilmann	1539
9	Charlie Gehringer	1427
10	Joe Cronin	1424
11	Jim Bottomley	1422
12	Joe Medwick	1383
13	Paul Waner	1309
14	Bob Johnson	1283
15	Hank Greenberg	1276

1942-1960

1	Stan Musial	1951
2	Ted Williams	1839
3	Joe DiMaggio	1537
4	Mickey Mantle	1509
5	Eddie Mathews	1453
6	Yogi Berra	1430
7	Johnny Mize	1337
8	Duke Snider	1333
9	Mickey Vernon	1311
10	Enos Slaughter	1304
11	Del Ennis	1284
12	Gil Hodges	1274
13	Bobby Doerr	1247
14	Bob Elliott	1195
15	Vic Wertz	1178

1961-1990

1	Hank Aaron	2297
2	Willie Mays	1903
3	Carl Yastrzemski	1844
4	Frank Robinson	1812
5	Reggie Jackson	1702
6	Tony Perez	1652
7	Ernie Banks	1636
8	Mike Schmidt	1595
9	Harmon Killebrew	1584
10	Al Kaline	1583
11	Willie McCovey	1555
12	Willie Stargell	1540
13	Dave Winfield	1516
14	Billy Williams	1475
15	Rusty Staub	1466

Runs Batted In per Game

1	Sam Thompson	.92
2	Lou Gehrig	.92
3	Hank Greenberg	.92
4	Joe DiMaggio	.89
5	Babe Ruth	.88
6	Jimmie Foxx	.83
7	Cap Anson	.83
8	Al Simmons	.82
9	Ted Williams	.80
10	Ed Delahanty	.80
11	Hack Wilson	.79
12	Dan Brouthers	.77
13	Bob Meusel	.76
14	Hal Trosky	.75
15	Hugh Duffy	.75
16	Rudy York	.72
17	Harry Heilmann	.72
18	Jim Bottomley	.71
19	Johnny Mize	.71
20	Roy Campanella	.70
21	Goose Goslin	.70
22	Rogers Hornsby	.70
23	Earl Averill	.70
24	Joe Medwick	.70
25	Hank Aaron	.70
26	Jim Rice	.69
27	Ralph Kiner	.69
28	Bob Johnson	.69
29	Al Rosen	.69
30	Chuck Klein	.69
31	Tony Lazzeri	.68
32	Vern Stephens	.68
33	Mel Ott	.68
34	Don Mattingly	.68
35	Bill Dickey	.68
36	Del Ennis	.67
37	Yogi Berra	.67
38	Bob Horner	.67
39	Buck Ewing	.67
40	Joe Cronin	.67
41	Bobby Doerr	.67
42	Dick Stuart	.67
43	Wally Berger	.67
44	Mike Schmidt	.66
45	Roger Connor	.66
46	Darryl Strawberry	.66
47	Jake Beckley	.66
48	Pie Traynor	.66
49	Hughie Jennings	.65
50	Ken Williams	.65
51	King Kelly	.65
52	Willie Stargell	.65
53	Harmon Killebrew	.65
54	Charlie Keller	.65
55	Chick Hafey	.65
56	Ernie Banks	.65
57	Glenn Wright	.65
58	Jackie Jensen	.65
59	Frank Robinson	.65
60	Nap Lajoie	.64
61	Stan Musial	.64
62	Joe Kelley	.64
63	Eddie Murray	.64
64	Orlando Cepeda	.64
65	Babe Herman	.64
66	Jeff Heath	.64
67	Bobby Veach	.64
68	Dick Allen	.64
69	Ty Cobb	.64
70	Johnny Bench	.64
71	Dolph Camilli	.64
72	Willie Mays	.64
73	Irish Meusel	.64
74	Buck Freeman	.63
75	Larry Doby	.63
76	Vic Wertz	.63
77	Dave Winfield	.63
78	Joe Carter	.63
79	Patsy Tebeau	.63
80	Rocky Colavito	.63
81	George Kelly	.63
82	Gus Zernial	.63
83	Mickey Mantle	.63
84	George Foster	.63
85	Frank Baker	.63
86	George Bell	.63
87	Bill Terry	.63
88	Steve Brodie	.63
89	Hank Sauer	.63
90	Dave Kingman	.62
91	Joe Gordon	.62
92	Duke Snider	.62
93	Honus Wagner	.62
94	Frank McCormick	.62
95	Greg Luzinski	.62
96	Tommy Henrich	.62
97	Kent Hrbek	.62
98	Joe Vosmik	.62
99	Hardy Richardson	.62
100	Jack Rowe	.62

Walks

1	Babe Ruth	2056
2	Ted Williams	2019
3	Joe Morgan	1865
4	Carl Yastrzemski	1845
5	Mickey Mantle	1733
6	Mel Ott	1708
7	Eddie Yost	1614
8	Darrell Evans	1605
9	Stan Musial	1599
10	Pete Rose	1566
11	Harmon Killebrew	1559
12	Lou Gehrig	1508
13	Mike Schmidt	1507
14	Eddie Collins	1499
15	Willie Mays	1464
16	Jimmie Foxx	1452
17	Eddie Mathews	1444
18	Frank Robinson	1420
19	Hank Aaron	1402
20	Tris Speaker	1381
21	Reggie Jackson	1375
22	Willie McCovey	1345
23	Dwight Evans	1337
24	Luke Appling	1302
25	Al Kaline	1277
26	Ken Singleton	1263
27	Rusty Staub	1255
28	Ty Cobb	1249
29	Jim Wynn	1224
30	Pee Wee Reese	1210
31	Richie Ashburn	1198
32	Billy Hamilton	1187
33	Charlie Gehringer	1186
34	Donie Bush	1158
35	Max Bishop	1153
	Toby Harrah	1153
37	Harry Hooper	1136
38	Jimmy Sheckard	1135
39	Willie Randolph	1128
40	Jack Clark	1110
41	Ron Santo	1108
42	Rickey Henderson	1093
43	Lu Blue	1092
	Stan Hack	1092
45	Paul Waner	1091
46	Graig Nettles	1088
47	Bobby Grich	1087
48	Brian Downing	1077
49	Bob Johnson	1075
50	Harlond Clift	1070
	Keith Hernandez	1070
52	Bill Dahlen	1064
53	Joe Cronin	1059
54	Ron Fairly	1052
55	Billy Williams	1045
56	Norm Cash	1043
	Eddie Joost	1043
58	Roy Thomas	1042
59	Max Carey	1040
60	Rogers Hornsby	1038
61	Jim Gilliam	1036
62	Sal Bando	1031
63	Jesse Burkett	1029
64	Eddie Murray	1026
65	Rod Carew	1018
	Enos Slaughter	1018
67	Ron Cey	1012
68	Ralph Kiner	1011
69	Dummy Hoy	1004
70	Miller Huggins	1003
71	Roger Connor	1002
72	Boog Powell	1001
73	Eddie Stanky	996
74	Cupid Childs	991
75	Dave Winfield	988
76	Gene Tenace	984
77	Bid McPhee	981
78	Joe Kuhel	980
	Earl Torgeson	980
80	Augie Galan	979
81	Duke Snider	971
82	Bob Elliott	967
83	Mike Hargrove	965
	Joe Judge	965
	Buddy Myer	965
86	George Brett	964
87	Honus Wagner	963
88	Jimmy Dykes	958
89	Mickey Vernon	955
90	Cap Anson	952
91	Rocky Colavito	951
92	Goose Goslin	949
93	Dolph Camilli	947
94	Gil Hodges	943
95	Elmer Valo	942
96	Gary Matthews	940
97	Willie Stargell	937
	Arky Vaughan	937
99	Roy White	934
100	Dale Murphy	932

Walk Percentage

1	Ted Williams	20.76
2	Max Bishop	20.42
3	Babe Ruth	19.67
4	Eddie Stanky	18.80
5	Ferris Fain	18.70
6	Gene Tenace	18.31
7	Roy Cullenbine	18.03
8	Eddie Yost	18.01
9	Mickey Mantle	17.62
10	John McGraw	17.56
11	Charlie Keller	17.14
12	Joe Morgan	16.74
13	Earl Torgeson	16.47
14	Bernie Carbo	16.45
15	Roy Thomas	16.44
16	Ralph Kiner	16.26
17	Harmon Killebrew	16.06
18	Billy Hamilton	15.92
19	Lou Gehrig	15.86
20	Elmer Valo	15.78
21	Joe Ferguson	15.77
22	Harland Clift	15.74
23	Eddie Joost	15.69
24	Lu Blue	15.61
25	Jim Wynn	15.54
26	Rickey Henderson	15.38
27	Jack Clark	15.38
28	Mel Ott	15.30
29	Miller Huggins	15.29
30	Mike Schmidt	15.29
31	Darrell Evans	15.17
32	Jimmie Foxx	15.15
33	Joe Cunningham	15.12
34	Dolph Camilli	15.03
35	Cupid Childs	14.99
36	Ken Singleton	14.94
37	Elbie Fletcher	14.85
38	Merv Rettenmund	14.83
39	Mike Hargrove	14.78
40	Topsy Hartsel	14.72
41	Dwayne Murphy	14.66
42	Wayne Garrett	14.59
43	Jason Thompson	14.52
44	Eddie Mathews	14.47
45	Alvin Davis	14.36
46	Mickey Cochrane	14.22
47	Andy Thornton	14.20
48	Augie Galan	14.16
49	Gene Woodling	14.15
50	Willie McCovey	14.10
51	Hank Greenberg	14.09
52	Darrell Porter	14.04
53	Wade Boggs	14.03
54	Larry Doby	14.01
55	John Mayberry	13.92
56	John Briggs	13.87
57	Bill North	13.85
58	Donie Bush	13.84
59	Wally Schang	13.79
60	Roger Bresnahan	13.74
61	Paul Radford	13.71
62	Steve Braun	13.69
63	Norm Siebern	13.64
64	Bob Allison	13.64
65	Bobby Grich	13.63
66	Al Rosen	13.61
67	Toby Harrah	13.48
68	Lee Mazzilli	13.47
69	Norm Cash	13.46
70	Mike Jorgensen	13.46
71	Bob Johnson	13.45
72	Tommy Henrich	13.40
73	Willie Randolph	13.38
74	Rick Ferrell	13.38
75	Wayne Gross	13.36
76	Carl Yastrzemski	13.34
77	Grady Hatton	13.31
78	Dwight Evans	13.29
79	Lyn Lary	13.28
80	Ed Bailey	13.21
81	Jackie Robinson	13.17
82	Jack Graney	13.14
83	Brian Downing	13.13
84	Eddie Collins	13.10
85	Rick Monday	13.09
86	Don Mincher	13.08
87	Pee Wee Reese	13.06
88	Jeff Burroughs	13.05
89	Stan Hack	13.05
90	Gary Roenicke	13.04
91	Boog Powell	13.03
92	Jimmy Sheckard	12.99
93	Charlie Maxwell	12.98
94	Gorman Thomas	12.97
95	Darryl Strawberry	12.94
96	Andy Seminick	12.92
97	Don Buford	12.86
98	Luke Appling	12.82
99	John Milner	12.79
100	Ron Fairly	12.77

Strikeouts

1	Reggie Jackson	2597
2	Willie Stargell	1936
3	Mike Schmidt	1883
4	Tony Perez	1867
5	Dave Kingman	1816
6	Bobby Bonds	1757
7	Lou Brock	1730
8	Mickey Mantle	1710
9	Harmon Killebrew	1699
10	Dwight Evans	1643
11	Dale Murphy	1627
12	Lee May	1570
13	Dick Allen	1556
14	Willie McCovey	1550
15	Frank Robinson	1532
16	Willie Mays	1526
17	Rick Monday	1513
18	Greg Luzinski	1495
19	Eddie Mathews	1487
20	Frank Howard	1460
21	Dave Parker	1439
22	Jim Wynn	1427
23	Jim Rice	1423
24	George Foster	1419
25	George Scott	1418
26	Darrell Evans	1410
27	Carl Yastrzemski	1393
28	Hank Aaron	1383
29	Larry Parrish	1359
30	Ron Santo	1343
31	Gorman Thomas	1339
32	Babe Ruth	1330
33	Deron Johnson	1318
34	Willie Horton	1313
35	Jimmie Foxx	1311
36	Dave Winfield	1305
37	Johnny Bench	1278
	Bobby Grich	1278
39	Claudell Washington	1266
40	Lance Parrish	1255
41	Carlton Fisk	1251
42	Ken Singleton	1246
43	Duke Snider	1237
44	Ernie Banks	1236
45	Ron Cey	1235
46	Roberto Clemente	1230
47	Boog Powell	1226
48	Jack Clark	1221
49	Graig Nettles	1209
50	Tony Armas	1201
51	Andre Dawson	1199
52	Vada Pinson	1196
53	Dave Concepcion	1186
54	Orlando Cepeda	1170
55	Pete Rose	1143
56	Bert Campaneris	1142
57	Donn Clendenon	1140
58	Gil Hodges	1137
59	Jeff Burroughs	1135
	Leo Cardenas	1135
61	Jesse Barfield	1127
62	Bob Bailey	1126
63	Gary Matthews	1125
64	Fred Lynn	1116
65	Jim Fregosi	1097
	Robin Yount	1097
67	Joe Torre	1094
68	Lloyd Moseby	1092
69	Norm Cash	1091
70	Tony Taylor	1083
71	Tommy Harper	1080
72	Eddie Murray	1076
73	Don Baylor	1069
74	Johnny Callison	1064
75	Joe Adcock	1059
76	Doug Rader	1055
77	Garry Templeton	1054
78	Billy Williams	1046
79	Frank White	1035
80	Bob Allison	1033
81	Jose Cruz	1031
82	Reggie Smith	1030
83	Rod Carew	1028
84	Juan Samuel	1026
85	Darrell Porter	1025
86	Chet Lemon	1024
87	Al Kaline	1020
88	Ken Boyer	1017
89	Joe Morgan	1015
90	George Hendrick	1013
91	Keith Hernandez	1012
92	Larry Doby	1011
93	Amos Otis	1008
94	Steve Garvey	1003
95	Jeffrey Leonard	1000
96	Brian Downing	999
97	Gene Tenace	998
98	Brooks Robinson	990
	Willie Wilson	990
100	Chris Speier	988

At Bats per Strikeout

1	Joe Sewell	62.6
2	Lloyd Waner	44.9
3	Nellie Fox	42.7
4	Tommy Holmes	40.9
5	Andy High	33.8
6	Sam Rice	33.7
7	Frankie Frisch	33.5
8	Dale Mitchell	33.5
9	Johnny Cooney	31.5
10	Frank McCormick	30.3
11	Don Mueller	29.9
12	Billy Southworth	29.5
13	Rip Radcliff	28.9
14	Edd Roush	28.3
15	Pie Traynor	27.2
16	Doc Cramer	26.5
17	Carson Bigbee	26.0
18	Hank Severeid	25.5
19	George Sisler	25.3
20	Paul Waner	25.2
21	Sparky Adams	24.9
22	Lou Finney	24.9
23	Deacon White	24.8
24	Jack Rowe	24.8
25	Irish Meusel	24.6
26	Ezra Sutton	24.6
27	Red Schoendienst	24.5
28	Vic Power	24.5
29	Arky Vaughan	24.0
30	Felix Millan	23.9
31	Mickey Cochrane	23.8
32	Charlie Gehringer	23.8
33	Monte Ward	23.5
34	George Kell	23.4
35	George Cutshaw	23.2
36	Jack Tobin	23.1
37	Taffy Wright	23.1
38	Hughie Critz	23.1
39	Mark Koenig	22.5
40	Ernie Lombardi	22.3
41	Heinie Manush	22.2
42	Bobby Richardson	22.2
43	Jo-Jo Moore	22.0
44	Earl Sheely	21.8
45	Bill Dickey	21.8
46	Johnny Pesky	21.8
47	Rick Ferrell	21.8
48	Glenn Beckert	21.4
49	Dick Siebert	21.2
50	Eddie Waitkus	20.9
51	Max Flack	20.8
52	Bill Buckner	20.7
53	Dixie Walker	20.7
54	Everett Scott	20.7
55	Earle Combs	20.7
56	Paul Hines	20.6
57	Freddy Lindstrom	20.3
58	Mickey Owen	20.2
59	Joe Vosmik	20.1
60	Lou Boudreau	19.5
61	Milt Stock	19.5
62	Willard Marshall	19.3
63	Debs Garms	19.3
64	Charlie Grimm	19.3
65	Harry Rice	19.3
66	Skeeter Newsome	19.2
67	Curt Walker	19.1
68	Peanuts Lowrey	19.1
69	Charlie Jamieson	19.0
70	Muddy Ruel	19.0
71	Tommy Griffith	18.9
72	Tommy Thevenow	18.8
73	Joe Stripp	18.6
74	Joe DiMaggio	18.5
75	Bob Fothergill	18.5
76	Bing Miller	18.3
77	Riggs Stephenson	18.3
78	Yogi Berra	18.2
79	Tony Gwynn	18.2
80	Billy Herman	18.0
81	Lee Magee	18.0
82	Dave Cash	18.0
83	Elmer Valo	17.7
84	Heinie Groh	17.6
85	Luke Sewell	17.5
86	Rich Dauer	17.5
87	Buddy Lewis	17.4
88	Billy Goodman	17.2
89	Don Mattingly	17.1
90	Jim Gilliam	17.1
91	Harvey Kuenn	17.1
92	Gus Mancuso	17.1
93	Jimmy Wilson	17.1
94	Billy Cox	17.0
95	Ken Williams	16.9
96	George Case	16.9
97	Cecil Travis	16.9
98	Luke Appling	16.8
99	Jackie Hayes	16.8
100	Jackie Robinson	16.8

Batting Average

1	Ty Cobb	.366
2	Rogers Hornsby	.358
3	Joe Jackson	.356
4	Wade Boggs	.346
5	Ed Delahanty	.346
6	Tris Speaker	.345
7	Ted Williams	.344
8	Billy Hamilton	.344
9	Dan Brouthers	.342
10	Babe Ruth	.342
11	Harry Heilmann	.342
12	Pete Browning	.341
13	Willie Keeler	.341
14	Bill Terry	.341
15	George Sisler	.340
16	Lou Gehrig	.340
17	Jesse Burkett	.338
18	Nap Lajoie	.338
19	Riggs Stephenson	.336
20	Al Simmons	.334
21	John McGraw	.334
22	Paul Waner	.333
23	Eddie Collins	.333
24	Mike Donlin	.333
25	Stan Musial	.331
26	Sam Thompson	.331
27	Heinie Manush	.330
28	Tony Gwynn	.329
29	Cap Anson	.329
30	Rod Carew	.328
31	Honus Wagner	.327
32	Tip O'Neill	.326
33	Bob Fothergill	.325
34	Jimmie Foxx	.325
35	Earle Combs	.325
36	Joe DiMaggio	.325
37	Babe Herman	.324
38	Hugh Duffy	.324
39	Joe Medwick	.324
40	Edd Roush	.323
41	Sam Rice	.322
42	Ross Youngs	.322
43	Kiki Cuyler	.321
44	Charlie Gehringer	.320
45	Kirby Puckett	.320
46	Chuck Klein	.320
47	Pie Traynor	.320
48	Mickey Cochrane	.320
49	Ken Williams	.319
50	Earl Averill	.318
51	Arky Vaughan	.318
52	Roberto Clemente	.317
53	Don Mattingly	.317
54	Chick Hafey	.317
55	Joe Kelley	.317
56	Zach Wheat	.317
57	Roger Connor	.317
58	Lloyd Waner	.316
59	Frankie Frisch	.316
60	Goose Goslin	.316
61	George VanHaltren	.316
62	Bibb Falk	.314
63	Cecil Travis	.314
64	Hank Greenberg	.313
65	Jack Fournier	.313
66	Elmer Flick	.313
67	Bill Dickey	.313
68	Dale Mitchell	.312
69	Johnny Mize	.312
70	Joe Sewell	.312
71	Fred Clarke	.312
72	Barney McCosky	.312
73	Bing Miller	.312
74	George Brett	.311
75	Hughie Jennings	.311
76	Freddy Lindstrom	.311
77	Jackie Robinson	.311
78	Baby Doll Jacobson	.311
79	Taffy Wright	.311
80	Rip Radcliff	.311
81	Ginger Beaumont	.311
82	Mike Tiernan	.311
83	Denny Lyons	.310
84	Luke Appling	.310
85	Irish Meusel	.310
86	Elmer Smith	.310
87	Bobby Veach	.310
88	Jim O'Rourke	.310
89	John Stone	.310
90	Jim Bottomley	.310
91	Sam Crawford	.309
92	Bob Meusel	.309
93	Jack Tobin	.309
94	Spud Davis	.308
95	Richie Ashburn	.308
96	King Kelly	.308
97	Jake Beckley	.308
98	Stuffy McInnis	.307
99	Joe Vosmik	.307
100	Frank Baker	.307

Batting Average (by era)

1876-1892

1	Dan Brouthers	.342
2	Pete Browning	.341
3	Sam Thompson	.331
4	Cap Anson	.329
5	Tip O'Neill	.326
6	Roger Connor	.317
7	Denny Lyons	.310
8	Jim O'Rourke	.310
9	King Kelly	.308
10	Deacon White	.303
11	Henry Larkin	.303
12	Buck Ewing	.303
13	George Gore	.301
14	Paul Hines	.301
15	Oyster Burns	.300

1893-1919

1	Ty Cobb	.366
2	Joe Jackson	.356
3	Ed Delahanty	.346
4	Tris Speaker	.345
5	Billy Hamilton	.344
6	Willie Keeler	.341
7	Jesse Burkett	.338
8	Nap Lajoie	.338
9	John McGraw	.334
10	Eddie Collins	.333
11	Mike Donlin	.333
12	Honus Wagner	.327
13	Hugh Duffy	.324
14	Joe Kelley	.317
15	Zach Wheat	.317

1920-1941

1	Rogers Hornsby	.358
2	Babe Ruth	.342
3	Harry Heilmann	.342
4	Bill Terry	.341
5	George Sisler	.340
6	Lou Gehrig	.340
7	Riggs Stephenson	.336
8	Al Simmons	.334
9	Paul Waner	.333
10	Heinie Manush	.330
11	Bob Fothergill	.325
12	Jimmie Foxx	.325
13	Earle Combs	.325
14	Babe Herman	.324
15	Joe Medwick	.324

1942-1960

1	Ted Williams	.344
2	Stan Musial	.331
3	Joe DiMaggio	.325
4	Dale Mitchell	.312
5	Johnny Mize	.312
6	Barney McCosky	.312
7	Jackie Robinson	.311
8	Taffy Wright	.311
9	Richie Ashburn	.308
10	Johnny Pesky	.307
11	George Kell	.306
12	Dixie Walker	.306
13	Harvey Kuenn	.303
14	Tommy Holmes	.302
15	Enos Slaughter	.300

1961-1990

1	Wade Boggs	.346
2	Tony Gwynn	.329
3	Rod Carew	.328
4	Kirby Puckett	.320
5	Roberto Clemente	.317
6	Don Mattingly	.317
7	George Brett	.311
8	Matty Alou	.307
9	Ralph Garr	.306
10	Pedro Guerrero	.305
11	Hank Aaron	.305
12	Bill Madlock	.305
13	Tony Oliva	.304
14	Manny Mota	.304
15	Al Oliver	.303

Batting Average (by position)

First Base

1	Dan Brouthers	.342
2	Bill Terry	.341
3	George Sisler	.340
4	Lou Gehrig	.340
5	Cap Anson	.329
6	Rod Carew	.328
7	Jimmie Foxx	.325
8	Don Mattingly	.317
9	Roger Connor	.317
10	Hank Greenberg	.313

Second Base

1	Rogers Hornsby	.358
2	Nap Lajoie	.338
3	Eddie Collins	.333
4	Charlie Gehringer	.320
5	Frankie Frisch	.316
6	Cupid Childs	.306
7	Billy Herman	.304
8	Buddy Myer	.303
9	Del Pratt	.292
10	Tony Lazzeri	.292

Shortstop

1	Honus Wagner	.327
2	Arky Vaughan	.318
3	Joe Sewell	.312
4	Luke Appling	.310
5	Ed McKean	.302
6	Joe Cronin	.301
7	Lou Boudreau	.295
8	George Davis	.295
9	Glenn Wright	.294
10	Travis Jackson	.291

Third Base

1	Wade Boggs	.346
2	Pie Traynor	.320
3	George Brett	.311
4	Denny Lyons	.310
5	Frank Baker	.307
6	George Kell	.306
7	Bill Madlock	.305
8	Stan Hack	.301
9	Pinky Whitney	.295
10	Jimmy Collins	.294

Outfield

1	Ty Cobb	.366
2	Joe Jackson	.356
3	Ed Delahanty	.346
4	Tris Speaker	.345
5	Ted Williams	.344
6	Billy Hamilton	.344
7	Babe Ruth	.342
8	Harry Heilmann	.342
9	Willie Keeler	.341
10	Jesse Burkett	.338

Catcher

1	Mickey Cochrane	.320
2	Bill Dickey	.313
3	Spud Davis	.308
4	Ernie Lombardi	.306
5	Gabby Hartnett	.297
6	Manny Sanguillen	.296
7	Smoky Burgess	.295
8	Thurman Munson	.292
9	Hank Severeid	.289
10	Jack Clements	.286

Relative Batting Average

1	Ty Cobb	134.8
2	Joe Jackson	133.1
3	Wade Boggs	132.1
4	Pete Browning	131.6
5	Ted Williams	128.1
6	Dan Brouthers	127.8
7	Nap Lajoie	127.3
8	Rod Carew	127.0
9	Rogers Hornsby	126.2
10	Tony Gwynn	125.8
11	Tris Speaker	125.4
12	Tip O'Neill	125.3
13	Willie Keeler	124.5
14	Stan Musial	123.9
15	Mike Donlin	123.6
16	Honus Wagner	123.1
17	Billy Hamilton	122.7
18	Ed Delahanty	122.7
19	Cap Anson	122.7
20	Kirby Puckett	122.4
21	Jesse Burkett	121.7
22	Eddie Collins	121.6
23	Don Mattingly	121.1
24	Sam Thompson	121.1
25	Roberto Clemente	120.7
26	Tony Oliva	120.4
27	Harry Heilmann	119.4
28	Babe Ruth	119.2
29	George Sisler	118.9
30	George Brett	118.9
31	Sam Crawford	118.8
32	King Kelly	118.2
33	Jim O'Rourke	118.1
34	Matty Alou	117.9
35	Joe Medwick	117.8
36	Paul Waner	117.8
37	Elmer Flick	117.4
38	Roger Connor	117.4
39	Bill Terry	117.3
40	Lou Gehrig	117.2
41	Joe DiMaggio	117.1
42	Ginger Beaumont	117.0
43	Ralph Garr	116.7
44	Manny Mota	116.4
45	Dale Mitchell	116.3
46	Henry Larkin	116.3
47	John McGraw	116.2
48	Pedro Guerrero	116.2
49	Deacon White	116.0
50	Hank Aaron	116.0
51	Paul Hines	115.8
52	George Gore	115.7
53	Jackie Robinson	115.7
54	Pete Rose	115.6
55	Al Simmons	115.4
56	Frank Baker	115.4
57	Al Kaline	115.4
58	Bill Madlock	115.2
59	Arky Vaughan	115.1
60	Edd Roush	115.1
61	Al Oliver	115.1
62	Riggs Stephenson	115.0
63	Mickey Mantle	115.0
64	Johnny Mize	115.0
65	Zach Wheat	114.9
66	Tim Raines	114.9
67	Hugh Duffy	114.8
68	George Kell	114.8
69	Barney McCosky	114.7
70	Richie Ashburn	114.6
71	Hardy Richardson	114.6
72	Johnny Pesky	114.5
73	Harvey Kuenn	114.5
74	Rico Carty	114.4
75	Willie Mays	114.3
76	Fred Clarke	114.0
77	Heinie Manush	114.0
78	Cy Seymour	113.9
79	Paul Molitor	113.8
80	Jimmie Foxx	113.8
81	Joe Torre	113.8
82	Denny Lyons	113.6
83	Julio Franco	113.5
84	Cecil Cooper	113.5
85	Jim Rice	113.5
86	Frank Robinson	113.4
87	Tommy Davis	113.4
88	Taffy Wright	113.4
89	Minnie Minoso	113.1
90	Jimmy Wolf	113.0
91	Willie McGee	113.0
92	Tommy Holmes	113.0
93	Joe Kelley	112.9
94	Orlando Cepeda	112.9
95	Mickey Rivers	112.9
96	Bake McBride	112.8
97	Manny Sanguillen	112.8
98	Thurman Munson	112.8
99	John Reilly	112.7
100	Heinie Zimmerman	112.7

On Base Percentage

#	Player	
1	Ted Williams	.483
2	Babe Ruth	.474
3	John McGraw	.465
4	Billy Hamilton	.455
5	Lou Gehrig	.447
6	Wade Boggs	.440
7	Rogers Hornsby	.434
8	Ty Cobb	.432
9	Jimmie Foxx	.428
	Tris Speaker	.428
11	Ferris Fain	.425
12	Eddie Collins	.424
13	Max Bishop	.423
	Dan Brouthers	.423
	Joe Jackson	.423
	Mickey Mantle	.423
17	Mickey Cochrane	.419
18	Stan Musial	.418
19	Cupid Childs	.415
20	Jesse Burkett	.414
	Mel Ott	.414
22	Hank Greenberg	.412
23	Ed Delahanty	.411
	Roy Thomas	.411
25	Harry Heilmann	.410
	Charlie Keller	.410
	Jackie Robinson	.410
	Eddie Stanky	.410
29	Roy Cullenbine	.408
30	Denny Lyons	.407
	Riggs Stephenson	.407
32	Joe Cunningham	.406
	Arky Vaughan	.406
34	Rickey Henderson	.405
35	Charlie Gehringer	.404
	Paul Waner	.404
37	Pete Browning	.403
38	Lu Blue	.402
39	Mike Hargrove	.400
	Joe Kelley	.400
41	Luke Appling	.399
	Elmer Valo	.399
	Ross Youngs	.399
44	Joe DiMaggio	.398
	Ralph Kiner	.398
46	Richie Ashburn	.397
	Earle Combs	.397
	Roger Connor	.397
	Johnny Mize	.397
	Elmer Smith	.397
51	Cap Anson	.395
	Earl Averill	.395
	Rod Carew	.395
	Alvin Davis	.395
	Joe Morgan	.395
	Hack Wilson	.395
	Eddie Yost	.395
58	Stan Hack	.394
	Johnny Pesky	.394
60	Bob Johnson	.393
	Tim Raines	.393
	Wally Schang	.393
	Bill Terry	.393
	Ken Williams	.393
65	Jack Fournier	.392
	George Grantham	.392
	Tip O'Neill	.392
	Frank Robinson	.392
	Mike Tiernan	.392
70	Minnie Minoso	.391
	Joe Sewell	.391
	Ken Singleton	.391
	Gene Tenace	.391
74	Harlond Clift	.390
	Joe Cronin	.390
	Augie Galan	.390
77	Bernie Carbo	.389
	Hughie Jennings	.389
	Buddy Myer	.389
80	Dolph Camilli	.388
	Mike Griffin	.388
	Keith Hernandez	.388
	Honus Wagner	.388
	Gene Woodling	.388
85	Larry Doby	.387
	Goose Goslin	.387
	Tony Gwynn	.387
	Willie Mays	.387
	Earl Torgeson	.387
90	Kiki Cuyler	.386
	George Gore	.386
	Barney McCosky	.386
	Al Rosen	.386
94	Elmer Flick	.385
	Dummy Hoy	.385
	Willie Keeler	.385
	George VanHaltren	.385
98	7 players tied	.384

Slugging Average

1	Babe Ruth	.690
2	Ted Williams	.634
3	Lou Gehrig	.632
4	Jimmie Foxx	.609
5	Hank Greenberg	.605
6	Joe DiMaggio	.579
7	Rogers Hornsby	.577
8	Johnny Mize	.562
9	Stan Musial	.559
10	Willie Mays	.557
11	Mickey Mantle	.557
12	Hank Aaron	.555
13	Ralph Kiner	.548
14	Hack Wilson	.545
15	Chuck Klein	.543
16	Duke Snider	.540
17	Frank Robinson	.537
18	Al Simmons	.535
19	Dick Allen	.534
20	Earl Averill	.534
21	Mel Ott	.533
22	Babe Herman	.532
23	Ken Williams	.530
24	Willie Stargell	.529
25	Mike Schmidt	.527
26	Chick Hafey	.526
27	Hal Trosky	.522
28	Wally Berger	.522
29	Harry Heilmann	.520
30	Darryl Strawberry	.520
31	Dan Brouthers	.519
32	Charlie Keller	.518
33	Joe Jackson	.517
34	Willie McCovey	.515
35	Ty Cobb	.512
36	Eddie Mathews	.509
37	Jeff Heath	.509
38	Harmon Killebrew	.509
39	Bob Johnson	.506
40	Bill Terry	.506
41	Ed Delahanty	.505
42	Sam Thompson	.505
43	Joe Medwick	.505
44	Don Mattingly	.504
45	Jim Rice	.502
46	George Brett	.502
47	Tris Speaker	.500
48	Jim Bottomley	.500
49	Goose Goslin	.500
50	Roy Campanella	.500
51	Ernie Banks	.500
52	Orlando Cepeda	.499
53	Bob Horner	.499
54	Frank Howard	.499
55	Ted Kluszewski	.498
56	Bob Meusel	.497
57	Hank Sauer	.496
58	Pedro Guerrero	.496
59	Al Rosen	.495
60	Eddie Murray	.494
61	Kent Hrbek	.493
62	Billy Williams	.492
63	Ripper Collins	.492
64	Dolph Camilli	.492
65	Tommy Henrich	.491
66	Larry Doby	.490
67	Reggie Jackson	.490
68	Andre Dawson	.490
69	Dick Stuart	.489
70	Reggie Smith	.489
71	Gabby Hartnett	.489
72	Rocky Colavito	.489
73	Norm Cash	.488
74	Gil Hodges	.487
75	George Bell	.486
76	Bill Dickey	.486
77	Roger Connor	.486
78	Gus Zernial	.486
79	Joe Adcock	.485
80	Wally Post	.485
81	Fred Lynn	.484
82	Jack Fournier	.483
83	Rudy York	.483
84	Jack Clark	.483
85	Yogi Berra	.482
86	Charlie Gehringer	.480
87	George Foster	.480
88	Dave Winfield	.480
89	Al Kaline	.480
90	Heinie Manush	.479
91	Gavvy Cravath	.478
92	Dave Kingman	.478
93	Mickey Cochrane	.478
94	Greg Luzinski	.478
95	Dave Parker	.477
96	Tony Oliva	.476
97	Dale Murphy	.476
98	Roger Maris	.476
99	Johnny Bench	.476
100	Leon Durham	.475

Production

1	Babe Ruth	1.163
2	Ted Williams	1.116
3	Lou Gehrig	1.080
4	Jimmie Foxx	1.038
5	Hank Greenberg	1.017
6	Rogers Hornsby	1.010
7	Mickey Mantle	.979
8	Joe DiMaggio	.977
	Stan Musial	.977
10	Johnny Mize	.959
11	Mel Ott	.947
12	Ralph Kiner	.946
13	Ty Cobb	.944
	Willie Mays	.944
15	Dan Brouthers	.942
16	Joe Jackson	.940
	Hack Wilson	.940
18	Hank Aaron	.932
19	Harry Heilmann	.930
20	Frank Robinson	.929
21	Earl Averill	.928
	Charlie Keller	.928
	Tris Speaker	.928
24	Ken Williams	.924
25	Chuck Klein	.922
26	Duke Snider	.921
27	Ed Delahanty	.917
28	Babe Herman	.915
	Al Simmons	.915
30	Dick Allen	.914
31	Wade Boggs	.912
	Mike Schmidt	.912
33	Bob Johnson	.899
	Bill Terry	.899
35	Chick Hafey	.898
36	Mickey Cochrane	.897
37	Willie McCovey	.892
	Willie Stargell	.892
	Hal Trosky	.892
40	Eddie Mathews	.888
	Sam Thompson	.888
42	Goose Goslin	.887
	Billy Hamilton	.887
	Harmon Killebrew	.887
45	George Brett	.884
	Charlie Gehringer	.884
47	Roger Connor	.883
	Jackie Robinson	.883
49	Al Rosen	.882
50	Wally Berger	.881
	Darryl Strawberry	.881
52	Dolph Camilli	.880
	Riggs Stephenson	.880
54	Jeff Heath	.879
55	Larry Doby	.877
	Pedro Guerrero	.877
	Paul Waner	.877
58	Jack Fournier	.875
	John McGraw	.875
60	Tommy Henrich	.873
61	Don Mattingly	.872
62	Jim Bottomley	.869
	Pete Browning	.869
	Eddie Murray	.869
65	Bill Dickey	.868
66	Jack Clark	.867
	Joe Medwick	.867
68	Kent Hrbek	.866
69	Norm Cash	.865
70	Alvin Davis	.863
71	Roy Campanella	.861
72	Jesse Burkett	.860
	Kiki Cuyler	.860
74	Earle Combs	.859
	Al Kaline	.859
	Reggie Smith	.859
	Arky Vaughan	.859
78	Gabby Hartnett	.858
	Jim Rice	.858
80	Gavvy Cravath	.857
	Joe Cronin	.857
82	Heinie Manush	.856
	Billy Williams	.856
84	Honus Wagner	.855
85	George Grantham	.854
	Mike Tiernan	.854
87	Frank Howard	.853
88	Orlando Cepeda	.852
	Eddie Collins	.852
	Ripper Collins	.852
	Mike Donlin	.852
	Ted Kluszewski	.852
	Bob Meusel	.852
94	Rocky Colavito	.851
	Joe Kelley	.851
	Minnie Minoso	.851
97	Denny Lyons	.850
	Tip O'Neill	.850
99	Bob Nieman	.849
100	3 players tied	.848

Adjusted Production

1	Babe Ruth	209
2	Ted Williams	186
3	Lou Gehrig	182
4	Rogers Hornsby	176
5	Mickey Mantle	173
6	Dan Brouthers	171
7	Joe Jackson	169
8	Ty Cobb	167
9	Pete Browning	166
10	Jimmie Foxx	161
11	Hank Greenberg	157
	Willie Mays	157
	Johnny Mize	157
	Stan Musial	157
15	Hank Aaron	156
	Dick Allen	156
	Joe DiMaggio	156
	Tris Speaker	156
19	Roger Connor	155
	Ed Delahanty	155
	Mel Ott	155
22	Frank Robinson	154
23	Charlie Keller	152
24	Nap Lajoie	151
	Honus Wagner	151
26	Elmer Flick	150
27	Gavvy Cravath	149
28	Harry Heilmann	148
	Ralph Kiner	148
	Willie McCovey	148
	Sam Thompson	148
32	Mike Schmidt	147
	Willie Stargell	147
	Darryl Strawberry	147
35	Wade Boggs	145
	Eddie Mathews	145
	Hack Wilson	145
38	Sam Crawford	144
	Mike Donlin	144
	Pedro Guerrero	144
	Henry Larkin	144
42	Jack Fournier	143
	Frank Howard	143
	Harry Stovey	143
45	George Brett	142
	Jesse Burkett	142
	Billy Hamilton	142
	Harmon Killebrew	142
	Tip O'Neill	142
50	Jack Clark	141
	Eddie Collins	141
	Babe Herman	141
	Denny Lyons	141
	Eddie Murray	141
	Mike Tiernan	141
56	Wally Berger	140
	Jeff Heath	140
	Reggie Jackson	140
	Don Mattingly	140
60	Cap Anson	139
	Rickey Henderson	139
	Bob Johnson	139
63	Norm Cash	138
	Al Rosen	138
	Duke Snider	138
66	Oyster Burns	137
	Larry Doby	137
	King Kelly	137
	Sherry Magee	137
	John McGraw	137
	Gene Tenace	137
	Bill Terry	137
73	Reggie Smith	136
	Arky Vaughan	136
	Ken Williams	136
76	Frank Baker	135
	George Gore	135
	Chuck Klein	135
	Dave Winfield	135
80	Dolph Camilli	134
	Frank Chance	134
	Alvin Davis	134
	Charlie Hickman	134
	Paul Hines	134
	Al Kaline	134
	Joe Kelley	134
	Jim O'Rourke	134
	Boog Powell	134
89	Orlando Cepeda	133
	Fred Clarke	133
	Chick Hafey	133
	Joe Medwick	133
	Joe Morgan	133
	Bill Nicholson	133
	Paul Waner	133
96	9 players tied	132

Batting Runs

1	Babe Ruth	1322
2	Ted Williams	1166
3	Ty Cobb	1032
4	Stan Musial	983
5	Lou Gehrig	918
6	Hank Aaron	878
7	Rogers Hornsby	844
8	Tris Speaker	843
9	Willie Mays	827
10	Jimmie Foxx	803
	Mickey Mantle	803
12	Frank Robinson	773
13	Mel Ott	767
14	Honus Wagner	669
15	Dan Brouthers	648
16	Carl Yastrzemski	617
17	Eddie Collins	604
18	Mike Schmidt	592
19	Cap Anson	564
	Roger Connor	564
	Nap Lajoie	564
22	Ed Delahanty	550
23	Harmon Killebrew	532
24	Jesse Burkett	525
25	Willie McCovey	524
26	Johnny Mize	520
27	Harry Heilmann	517
28	Al Kaline	513
29	George Brett	509
30	Joe DiMaggio	507
31	Sam Crawford	505
32	Billy Hamilton	492
33	Paul Waner	491
34	Willie Stargell	483
35	Eddie Mathews	480
36	Dick Allen	470
37	Hank Greenberg	468
38	Reggie Jackson	466
39	Billy Williams	463
40	Joe Jackson	452
41	Duke Snider	441
42	Joe Morgan	438
43	Rod Carew	431
44	Pete Rose	416
45	Eddie Murray	414
46	Dwight Evans	410
47	Wade Boggs	405
48	Al Simmons	399
49	Fred Clarke	393
50	Joe Kelley	391
	Ralph Kiner	391
52	Norm Cash	390
53	Reggie Smith	379
54	Charlie Gehringer	376
	Sam Thompson	376
56	Chuck Klein	375
57	Pete Browning	368
58	Jim Rice	367
59	Bob Johnson	366
60	Arky Vaughan	361
61	Harry Stovey	360
62	Roberto Clemente	354
	Willie Keeler	354
	Joe Medwick	354
65	Dave Winfield	347
66	Jack Clark	346
67	Elmer Flick	345
	Ron Santo	345
69	Goose Goslin	341
70	Orlando Cepeda	337
71	Earl Averill	334
	Zach Wheat	334
73	Ken Singleton	332
74	Sherry Magee	329
75	Frank Howard	324
76	King Kelly	321
77	Rickey Henderson	320
78	Dolph Camilli	319
79	Rusty Staub	318
	Bill Terry	318
81	Jimmy Ryan	315
82	Keith Hernandez	310
	Mike Tiernan	310
84	Fred Lynn	309
85	Enos Slaughter	306
86	Boog Powell	305
	Hack Wilson	305
88	Babe Herman	304
89	Jim O'Rourke	303
90	Minnie Minoso	299
91	Joe Torre	298
92	Jake Beckley	297
	Rocky Colavito	297
	George Gore	297
95	John McGraw	295
96	Tony Perez	292
97	Greg Luzinski	291
98	Ernie Banks	288
	Hugh Duffy	288
100	Charlie Keller	287

Adjusted Batting Runs

1	Babe Ruth	1355
2	Ted Williams	1093
3	Ty Cobb	1018
4	Lou Gehrig	966
5	Stan Musial	930
6	Hank Aaron	903
7	Rogers Hornsby	859
8	Mickey Mantle	838
	Willie Mays	838
10	Tris Speaker	813
11	Mel Ott	773
12	Jimmie Foxx	768
13	Frank Robinson	754
14	Honus Wagner	652
15	Dan Brouthers	632
16	Eddie Collins	613
17	Nap Lajoie	567
18	Roger Connor	564
19	Ed Delahanty	561
	Mike Schmidt	561
21	Willie McCovey	538
22	Eddie Mathews	531
23	Harry Heilmann	527
24	Joe DiMaggio	522
25	Carl Yastrzemski	514
26	Johnny Mize	505
27	Jesse Burkett	504
28	Reggie Jackson	503
29	Harmon Killebrew	500
30	George Brett	497
31	Sam Crawford	487
32	Willie Stargell	485
33	Al Kaline	481
34	Paul Waner	474
35	Cap Anson	472
36	Joe Morgan	470
37	Dick Allen	469
38	Billy Hamilton	448
39	Eddie Murray	445
40	Hank Greenberg	440
	Joe Jackson	440
42	Rod Carew	414
43	Duke Snider	405
44	Billy Williams	401
45	Dave Winfield	394
46	Pete Browning	388
	Fred Clarke	388
48	Bob Johnson	381
49	Pete Rose	378
	Al Simmons	378
51	Wade Boggs	374
52	Ralph Kiner	373
53	Norm Cash	366
54	Sam Thompson	363
55	Roberto Clemente	362
56	Jack Clark	358
57	Arky Vaughan	356
58	Elmer Flick	352
59	Rickey Henderson	351
	Reggie Smith	351
61	Ken Singleton	350
62	Joe Kelley	349
63	Goose Goslin	348
64	Frank Howard	344
65	Dwight Evans	340
66	Charlie Gehringer	339
67	Orlando Cepeda	337
68	Zach Wheat	335
69	Rusty Staub	333
70	Bill Terry	332
71	Chuck Klein	330
72	Mike Tiernan	329
73	Sherry Magee	327
74	Joe Medwick	322
75	Harry Stovey	320
76	Jake Beckley	319
77	Babe Herman	318
	Keith Hernandez	318
79	Hack Wilson	310
80	Willie Keeler	309
	Boog Powell	309
82	Earl Averill	305
83	Jack Fournier	302
	Joe Torre	302
85	Jim O'Rourke	300
86	Jim Rice	299
87	Minnie Minoso	298
88	Charlie Keller	291
89	Rocky Colavito	290
90	Ron Santo	284
91	Pedro Guerrero	282
92	Jim Wynn	281
93	Fred Lynn	279
94	Larry Doby	278
95	Dolph Camilli	277
	John McGraw	277
97	Bobby Bonds	276
98	George Davis	273
99	Tony Perez	272
100	George VanHaltren	271

Batting Wins

1	Babe Ruth	127.5
2	Ted Williams	115.9
3	Ty Cobb	106.4
4	Stan Musial	99.7
5	Hank Aaron	91.1
6	Tris Speaker	86.1
7	Willie Mays	85.5
8	Lou Gehrig	85.4
9	Rogers Hornsby	84.9
10	Mickey Mantle	82.9
11	Frank Robinson	80.7
12	Mel Ott	76.2
13	Jimmie Foxx	75.3
14	Honus Wagner	69.0
15	Carl Yastrzemski	64.3
16	Eddie Collins	61.9
17	Mike Schmidt	61.8
18	Nap Lajoie	57.9
19	Dan Brouthers	56.7
20	Harmon Killebrew	55.8
21	Willie McCovey	54.9
22	Sam Crawford	53.7
23	Al Kaline	53.4
24	Johnny Mize	52.2
25	George Brett	51.3
26	Willie Stargell	51.0
27	Harry Heilmann	50.8
28	Dick Allen	50.0
29	Cap Anson	49.9
30	Roger Connor	49.3
31	Eddie Mathews	49.2
32	Joe DiMaggio	48.6
33	Billy Williams	48.6
34	Paul Waner	48.6
35	Ed Delahanty	48.5
36	Jesse Burkett	48.1
37	Reggie Jackson	47.9
38	Joe Jackson	47.4
39	Joe Morgan	45.9
40	Rod Carew	44.7
41	Hank Greenberg	44.5
42	Duke Snider	44.4
43	Pete Rose	43.9
44	Billy Hamilton	42.9
45	Eddie Murray	41.6
46	Dwight Evans	41.4
47	Norm Cash	41.1
48	Wade Boggs	40.4
49	Reggie Smith	40.3
50	Ralph Kiner	39.1
51	Fred Clarke	38.3
52	Al Simmons	37.4
53	Jim Rice	36.9
54	Roberto Clemente	36.8
55	Chuck Klein	36.7
56	Arky Vaughan	36.4
57	Ron Santo	36.3
58	Jack Clark	36.0
59	Joe Kelley	36.0
60	Joe Medwick	35.8
61	Sherry Magee	35.6
62	Dave Winfield	35.3
63	Bob Johnson	35.2
64	Elmer Flick	35.1
65	Charlie Gehringer	35.1
66	Orlando Cepeda	35.1
67	Frank Howard	34.4
68	Zach Wheat	34.4
69	Willie Keeler	34.2
70	Ken Singleton	34.0
71	Rusty Staub	33.3
72	Sam Thompson	32.6
73	Boog Powell	32.4
74	Keith Hernandez	32.4
75	Dolph Camilli	32.2
76	Pete Browning	32.1
77	Rickey Henderson	32.0
78	Goose Goslin	31.9
79	Harry Stovey	31.7
80	Joe Torre	31.4
81	Fred Lynn	31.1
82	Enos Slaughter	30.9
83	Earl Averill	30.8
84	Rocky Colavito	30.8
85	Bill Terry	30.8
86	Tony Perez	30.6
87	Minnie Minoso	30.3
88	Greg Luzinski	30.1
89	Ernie Banks	29.8
90	Gavvy Cravath	29.6
91	Hack Wilson	29.5
92	Babe Herman	29.5
93	Dale Murphy	29.0
94	Pedro Guerrero	29.0
95	Tony Oliva	28.9
96	King Kelly	28.8
97	Jack Fournier	28.8
98	Dave Parker	28.6
99	Charlie Keller	28.6
100	Bobby Bonds	28.4

Adjusted Batting Wins

1	Babe Ruth	130.7
2	Ted Williams	108.6
3	Ty Cobb	105.0
4	Stan Musial	94.3
5	Hank Aaron	93.7
6	Lou Gehrig	89.9
7	Willie Mays	86.6
8	Mickey Mantle	86.5
9	Rogers Hornsby	86.4
10	Tris Speaker	83.0
11	Frank Robinson	78.7
12	Mel Ott	76.8
13	Jimmie Foxx	72.0
14	Honus Wagner	67.3
15	Eddie Collins	58.6
16	Mike Schmidt	58.6
17	Nap Lajoie	58.2
18	Willie McCovey	56.4
19	Dan Brouthers	55.3
20	Eddie Mathews	54.4
21	Carl Yastrzemski	53.6
22	Harmon Killebrew	52.4
23	Sam Crawford	51.8
24	Harry Heilmann	51.7
25	Reggie Jackson	51.7
26	Willie Stargell	51.2
27	Johnny Mize	50.7
28	George Brett	50.1
29	Al Kaline	50.1
30	Joe DiMaggio	50.1
31	Dick Allen	49.8
32	Ed Delahanty	49.8
33	Roger Connor	49.3
34	Joe Morgan	49.2
35	Paul Waner	46.9
36	Jesse Burkett	46.2
37	Joe Jackson	46.1
38	Eddie Murray	44.7
39	Rod Carew	43.0
40	Billy Williams	42.1
41	Hank Greenberg	41.8
42	Cap Anson	41.8
43	Duke Snider	40.8
44	Dave Winfield	40.1
45	Pete Rose	39.9
46	Billy Hamilton	39.1
47	Norm Cash	38.6
48	Fred Clarke	37.9
49	Roberto Clemente	37.7
50	Reggie Smith	37.3
51	Wade Boggs	37.3
52	Ralph Kiner	37.3
53	Jack Clark	37.2
54	Bob Johnson	36.6
55	Frank Howard	36.6
56	Arky Vaughan	35.9
57	Elmer Flick	35.8
58	Ken Singleton	35.8
59	Al Simmons	35.4
60	Sherry Magee	35.4
61	Rickey Henderson	35.1
62	Orlando Cepeda	35.1
63	Rusty Staub	34.9
64	Zach Wheat	34.5
65	Dwight Evans	34.3
66	Pete Browning	33.8
67	Keith Hernandez	33.2
68	Boog Powell	32.8
69	Goose Goslin	32.6
70	Joe Medwick	32.6
71	Chuck Klein	32.3
72	Bill Terry	32.1
73	Joe Kelley	32.1
74	Joe Torre	31.8
75	Charlie Gehringer	31.7
76	Sam Thompson	31.5
77	Babe Herman	30.9
78	Jack Fournier	30.5
79	Minnie Minoso	30.2
80	Rocky Colavito	30.1
81	Jim Rice	30.1
82	Hack Wilson	30.0
83	Willie Keeler	29.9
84	Ron Santo	29.9
85	Jim Wynn	29.7
86	Pedro Guerrero	29.5
87	Jake Beckley	29.1
88	Charlie Keller	29.0
89	Bobby Bonds	28.6
90	Tony Perez	28.5
91	Mike Tiernan	28.5
92	Harry Stovey	28.2
93	Earl Averill	28.2
94	Fred Lynn	28.1
95	Dolph Camilli	28.0
96	Greg Luzinski	27.9
97	Larry Doby	27.7
98	Darrell Evans	27.5
99	Gavvy Cravath	27.3
100	Enos Slaughter	27.3

Runs Created

1	Babe Ruth	2838
2	Ty Cobb	2799
3	Stan Musial	2625
4	Hank Aaron	2550
5	Ted Williams	2538
6	Willie Mays	2372
7	Tris Speaker	2320
8	Lou Gehrig	2312
9	Mel Ott	2235
10	Pete Rose	2220
11	Honus Wagner	2218
12	Jimmie Foxx	2189
13	Carl Yastrzemski	2147
14	Frank Robinson	2126
15	Rogers Hornsby	2074
16	Mickey Mantle	2069
17	Eddie Collins	2054
18	Nap Lajoie	1895
19	Paul Waner	1853
20	Al Kaline	1846
21	Ed Delahanty	1828
22	Joe Morgan	1804
23	Jesse Burkett	1792
24	Charlie Gehringer	1781
25	Reggie Jackson	1772
26	Al Simmons	1770
27	Mike Schmidt	1757
28	Cap Anson	1751
29	Eddie Mathews	1738
30	Sam Crawford	1712
31	Billy Hamilton	1701
32	Goose Goslin	1700
33	Harry Heilmann	1690
34	Billy Williams	1671
35	George Brett	1669
36	Jake Beckley	1668
37	Willie Keeler	1667
38	Fred Clarke	1665
39	Roger Connor	1647
40	Willie McCovey	1638
41	George Davis	1624
42	Dan Brouthers	1622
43	Harmon Killebrew	1609
44	Joe DiMaggio	1606
45	Rod Carew	1595
46	Dwight Evans	1568
47	George VanHaltren	1560
48	Roberto Clemente	1557
49	Jimmy Ryan	1554
50	Zach Wheat	1539
51	Rusty Staub	1534
52	Willie Stargell	1531
53	Tony Perez	1523
54	Joe Kelley	1522
55	Ernie Banks	1513
56	Lou Brock	1512
57	Johnny Mize	1502
58	Hugh Duffy	1499
	Darrell Evans	1499
60	Sam Rice	1495
	Dave Winfield	1495
62	Luke Appling	1493
63	Bill Dahlen	1490
	George Sisler	1490
65	Duke Snider	1487
66	Eddie Murray	1481
67	Max Carey	1471
68	Frankie Frisch	1465
69	Robin Yount	1461
70	Enos Slaughter	1432
71	Joe Cronin	1426
72	Bob Johnson	1418
73	Dave Parker	1400
74	Vada Pinson	1394
75	Mickey Vernon	1387
76	Richie Ashburn	1386
77	Jim Bottomley	1384
78	Heinie Manush	1383
79	Jim Rice	1382
80	Ron Santo	1379
81	Chuck Klein	1378
82	Joe Medwick	1372
83	Earl Averill	1358
	Brooks Robinson	1358
85	Harry Hooper	1349
86	Al Oliver	1348
87	Orlando Cepeda	1338
88	Bid McPhee	1337
89	Kiki Cuyler	1336
90	Hank Greenberg	1331
91	Arky Vaughan	1323
92	Sherry Magee	1319
93	Joe Judge	1304
	Jimmy Sheckard	1304
95	Carlton Fisk	1301
96	Sam Thompson	1296
97	Lave Cross	1293
98	Dick Allen	1290
99	Dummy Hoy	1286
100	2 players tied	1284

Total Average

1	Babe Ruth	1.399
2	Ted Williams	1.320
3	Lou Gehrig	1.229
4	Billy Hamilton	1.191
5	John McGraw	1.151
6	Jimmie Foxx	1.143
7	Hank Greenberg	1.105
	Rogers Hornsby	1.105
9	Mickey Mantle	1.091
10	Ty Cobb	1.064
11	Dan Brouthers	1.061
12	Mel Ott	1.036
13	Ed Delahanty	1.035
14	Stan Musial	1.028
15	Joe DiMaggio	1.012
16	Tris Speaker	1.011
17	Joe Jackson	1.008
18	Ralph Kiner	1.006
19	Johnny Mize	1.005
	Hack Wilson	1.005
21	Charlie Keller	1.000
22	Rickey Henderson	.989
23	Willie Mays	.982
24	Mike Tiernan	.970
25	Harry Heilmann	.963
26	Frank Robinson	.961
27	Earl Averill	.957
28	Joe Kelley	.955
29	Denny Lyons	.954
	Mike Schmidt	.954
31	Roger Connor	.952
32	Mickey Cochrane	.947
33	Pete Browning	.946
34	Chuck Klein	.944
35	Ken Williams	.943
36	Babe Herman	.942
37	Hank Aaron	.940
	Eddie Collins	.940
	Honus Wagner	.940
40	Jesse Burkett	.939
	Jackie Robinson	.939
	Sam Thompson	.939
43	Tim Raines	.937
44	Duke Snider	.933
45	Wade Boggs	.931
46	Dick Allen	.930
	Hugh Duffy	.930
48	Dolph Camilli	.928
49	Harry Stovey	.923
50	Bob Johnson	.920
51	Darryl Strawberry	.917
52	Eddie Mathews	.916
53	Willie McCovey	.912
54	Charlie Gehringer	.910
	Harmon Killebrew	.910
	Joe Morgan	.910
	Elmer Smith	.910
58	Mike Donlin	.908
	Chick Hafey	.908
60	Mike Griffin	.905
61	Gavvy Cravath	.904
62	Elmer Flick	.903
	Al Simmons	.903
64	Kiki Cuyler	.901
	Goose Goslin	.901
66	Riggs Stephenson	.900
67	Bill Terry	.899
68	Cupid Childs	.898
69	Tip O'Neill	.897
70	Arky Vaughan	.894
71	Larry Doby	.893
	Tommy Henrich	.893
73	Frank Chance	.892
74	Willie Stargell	.889
	Hal Trosky	.889
76	Paul Waner	.888
77	Jack Fournier	.884
78	George Grantham	.882
79	Roy Cullenbine	.881
80	George VanHaltren	.880
81	Fred Clarke	.879
	Hughie Jennings	.879
83	Jack Clark	.878
84	Norm Cash	.875
	Al Rosen	.875
86	Oyster Burns	.873
87	George Brett	.872
88	Wally Berger	.870
89	Alvin Davis	.869
	Jeff Heath	.869
91	Jimmy Ryan	.868
92	Cap Anson	.867
93	Pedro Guerrero	.866
94	Dummy Hoy	.864
95	Jim Bottomley	.862
96	King Kelly	.861
97	Joe Cronin	.859
98	Harlond Clift	.858
	Tony Lazzeri	.858
	Eddie Murray	.858

Runs Produced

1	Ty Cobb	4065
2	Hank Aaron	3716
3	Babe Ruth	3669
4	Cap Anson	3501
5	Stan Musial	3425
6	Lou Gehrig	3385
7	Honus Wagner	3367
8	Pete Rose	3319
9	Willie Mays	3305
10	Tris Speaker	3294
11	Mel Ott	3208
	Carl Yastrzemski	3208
13	Jimmie Foxx	3139
14	Ted Williams	3116
15	Jake Beckley	3089
16	Eddie Collins	3071
17	Frank Robinson	3055
18	Al Simmons	3027
19	Nap Lajoie	3020
20	Charlie Gehringer	3017
21	Ed Delahanty	2962
22	George Davis	2903
23	Rogers Hornsby	2862
24	Goose Goslin	2844
25	Paul Waner	2822
26	Sam Crawford	2818
27	Al Kaline	2806
28	Roger Connor	2804
29	Hugh Duffy	2748
30	Bill Dahlen	2738
31	Dan Brouthers	2713
32	Reggie Jackson	2690
33	Frankie Frisch	2671
34	Mickey Mantle	2650
35	Harry Heilmann	2647
36	Jimmy Ryan	2617
37	Jesse Burkett	2597
38	George VanHaltren	2584
39	Fred Clarke	2567
40	Joe DiMaggio	2566
41	Sam Rice	2558
42	Mike Schmidt	2553
43	Joe Kelley	2550
44	Tony Perez	2545
45	Dave Winfield	2522
46	Joe Morgan	2515
47	George Brett	2499
48	Willie Keeler	2496
49	Joe Cronin	2487
50	Roberto Clemente	2481
51	Billy Williams	2459
52	Eddie Mathews	2450
53	Ernie Banks	2429
54	Sam Thompson	2428
55	Herman Long	2419
56	Robin Yount	2409
57	Jim O'Rourke	2406
58	Zach Wheat	2405
59	Dwight Evans	2402
60	Pie Traynor	2398
61	Luke Appling	2390
62	Billy Hamilton	2386
63	Enos Slaughter	2382
64	Jim Bottomley	2380
65	Joe Medwick	2376
66	Rusty Staub	2363
67	Lou Brock	2361
68	Heinie Manush	2360
69	George Sisler	2357
70	Rod Carew	2347
71	Mickey Vernon	2335
72	Dave Parker	2331
73	Brooks Robinson	2321
74	Jim Rice	2318
75	Al Oliver	2296
76	Harmon Killebrew	2294
77	Tommy Corcoran	2285
78	Darrell Evans	2284
79	Vada Pinson	2280
80	Max Carey	2276
81	Willie McCovey	2263
82	Willie Stargell	2260
83	Monte Ward	2249
84	Yogi Berra	2247
85	King Kelly	2238
86	Bob Johnson	2234
87	Kiki Cuyler	2232
88	Ted Simmons	2215
89	Sherry Magee	2205
90	Eddie Murray	2204
91	Duke Snider	2185
92	Steve Garvey	2179
93	Don Baylor	2174
94	Harry Hooper	2171
95	Doc Cramer	2162
96	Joe Kuhel	2154
97	Earl Averill	2150
98	Joe Judge	2147
	Joe Sewell	2147
100	Bobby Wallace	2144

Clutch Hitting Index

1	Cap Anson	139
2	Earl Sheely	136
	Pie Traynor	136
4	Duffy Lewis	135
	Bobby Veach	135
6	Sherry Magee	133
7	Kitty Bransfield	132
8	Sam Mertes	131
	Tommy Thevenow	131
10	Tommy Davis	130
	Chick Gandil	130
	Possum Whitted	130
13	Larry Gardner	129
	Stuffy McInnis	129
	Pinky Whitney	129
	Heinie Zimmerman	129
17	Red Smith	128
18	Bob Elliott	127
	Ted Simmons	127
	Patsy Tebeau	127
21	Rube Bressler	126
	Frank Chance	126
	Frank LaPorte	126
	Harry Steinfeldt	126
	Glenn Wright	126
26	Frank McCormick	125
	Dots Miller	125
	Red Murray	125
	Fred Pfeffer	125
	Enos Slaughter	125
	Gus Suhr	125
	Pat Tabler	125
33	Joe Cronin	124
	George Cutshaw	124
	Hughie Jennings	124
	Cookie Lavagetto	124
	Lee Tannehill	124
	Ned Williamson	124
	Taffy Wright	124
40	Tom Burns	123
	Gavvy Cravath	123
	Kid Elberfeld	123
	Del Ennis	123
	Ferris Fain	123
	Bob Fothergill	123
	Jackie Jensen	123
	Keith Moreland	123
	Luke Sewell	123
	Billy Sullivan	123
	Bobby Wallace	123
	Vic Wertz	123
	Deacon White	123
53	Frank Baker	122
	Frank Bowerman	122
	Roy Campanella	122
	Tony Cuccinello	122
	Art Fletcher	122
	Harry Heilmann	122
	Solly Hofman	122
	Willie Kamm	122
	Sam Mele	122
	Willie Montanez	122
	Muddy Ruel	122
	Joe Tinker	122
65	Lou Criger	121
	Ron Fairly	121
	Steve Kemp	121
	Tony Perez	121
	Boog Powell	121
	Ray Schalk	121
	Joe Sewell	121
	Riggs Stephenson	121
73	John Anderson	120
	Steve Brodie	120
	Tommy Corcoran	120
	Walt Dropo	120
	Bibb Falk	120
	Carl Furillo	120
	Mike Higgins	120
	George Kelly	120
	Tony Lazzeri	120
	Dan McGann	120
	Irish Meusel	120
	Mike Mowrey	120
	Del Pratt	120
	Dick Stuart	120
	Honus Wagner	120
	Bob Watson	120
89	13 players tied	119

Isolated Power

1	Babe Ruth	.348
2	Lou Gehrig	.292
3	Hank Greenberg	.292
4	Ted Williams	.289
5	Jimmie Foxx	.284
6	Ralph Kiner	.269
7	Mike Schmidt	.260
8	Mickey Mantle	.259
9	Darryl Strawberry	.257
10	Willie Mays	.256
11	Joe DiMaggio	.254
12	Harmon Killebrew	.252
13	Johnny Mize	.250
14	Hank Aaron	.250
15	Willie Stargell	.247
16	Willie McCovey	.245
17	Duke Snider	.244
18	Frank Robinson	.243
19	Dave Kingman	.242
20	Dick Allen	.242
21	Eddie Mathews	.238
22	Hack Wilson	.238
23	Charlie Keller	.231
24	Hank Sauer	.230
25	Mel Ott	.229
26	Stan Musial	.228
27	Reggie Jackson	.228
28	Dick Stuart	.225
29	Ernie Banks	.225
30	Frank Howard	.225
31	Roy Campanella	.224
32	Chuck Klein	.223
33	Gorman Thomas	.223
34	Rocky Colavito	.223
35	Bob Horner	.222
36	Wally Berger	.221
37	Gus Zernial	.221
38	Wally Post	.220
39	Hal Trosky	.219
40	Rogers Hornsby	.218
41	Norm Cash	.217
42	Bob Allison	.217
43	Roger Maris	.216
44	Earl Averill	.216
45	Jeff Heath	.216
46	Dolph Camilli	.215
47	Gil Hodges	.214
48	Jack Clark	.213
49	Jesse Barfield	.212
50	Ken Williams	.211
51	Al Rosen	.210
52	Bob Johnson	.210
53	Tommy Henrich	.209
54	Chick Hafey	.209
55	Dale Murphy	.209
56	Johnny Bench	.208
57	Roy Sievers	.208
58	Rudy York	.208
59	Joe Adcock	.208
60	Nate Colbert	.207
61	Babe Herman	.207
62	Andre Dawson	.207
63	Larry Doby	.207
64	George Foster	.206
65	Jim Rice	.204
66	Kent Hrbek	.204
67	Bobby Bonds	.203
68	Orlando Cepeda	.203
69	Billy Williams	.202
70	Greg Luzinski	.202
71	Cliff Johnson	.202
72	Reggie Smith	.202
73	Dwight Evans	.201
74	Fred Lynn	.201
75	Al Simmons	.201
76	Don Mincher	.201
77	Tony Armas	.200
78	George Bell	.200
79	Ted Kluszewski	.200
80	Eddie Murray	.200
81	Howard Johnson	.199
82	Leon Durham	.199
83	Jim Lemon	.198
84	Andy Thornton	.198
85	Bill Nicholson	.198
86	Dale Long	.198
87	Yogi Berra	.198
88	Joe Gordon	.197
89	Kirk Gibson	.196
90	Boog Powell	.196
91	Ripper Collins	.196
92	Don Demeter	.195
93	Joe Carter	.194
94	Dave Winfield	.193
95	Lance Parrish	.193
96	Tom Brunansky	.193
97	Lee May	.192
98	Vic Wertz	.192
99	Carlton Fisk	.192
100	Mack Jones	.192

Extra Base Hits

1	Hank Aaron	1477
2	Stan Musial	1377
3	Babe Ruth	1356
4	Willie Mays	1323
5	Lou Gehrig	1190
6	Frank Robinson	1186
7	Carl Yastrzemski	1157
8	Ty Cobb	1136
9	Tris Speaker	1131
10	Jimmie Foxx	1117
	Ted Williams	1117
12	Reggie Jackson	1075
13	Mel Ott	1071
14	Pete Rose	1041
15	Mike Schmidt	1015
16	Rogers Hornsby	1011
17	Ernie Banks	1009
18	Al Simmons	995
19	Honus Wagner	993
20	Al Kaline	972
21	George Brett	967
22	Tony Perez	963
23	Willie Stargell	953
24	Mickey Mantle	952
25	Billy Williams	948
26	Eddie Mathews	938
27	Dwight Evans	925
28	Goose Goslin	921
29	Willie McCovey	920
30	Paul Waner	909
31	Charlie Gehringer	904
32	Nap Lajoie	903
33	Dave Parker	901
34	Harmon Killebrew	887
	Dave Winfield	887
36	Joe DiMaggio	881
37	Harry Heilmann	876
38	Vada Pinson	868
39	Sam Crawford	865
40	Joe Medwick	858
41	Duke Snider	850
42	Roberto Clemente	846
43	Robin Yount	839
44	Rusty Staub	838
45	Jim Bottomley	835
46	Jim Rice	834
47	Andre Dawson	830
48	Al Oliver	825
49	Orlando Cepeda	823
50	Brooks Robinson	818
51	Joe Morgan	813
52	Roger Connor	812
53	Eddie Murray	810
54	Johnny Mize	809
55	Ed Delahanty	808
56	Joe Cronin	803
57	Jake Beckley	802
58	Johnny Bench	794
59	Carlton Fisk	792
60	Mickey Vernon	782
61	Hank Greenberg	781
62	Zach Wheat	780
63	Darrell Evans	779
	Bob Johnson	779
65	Ted Simmons	778
66	Lou Brock	776
67	Ron Santo	774
68	Chuck Klein	772
69	Dan Brouthers	771
70	Earl Averill	767
71	Heinie Manush	761
72	Steve Garvey	755
73	Dick Allen	750
74	Cap Anson	749
75	Graig Nettles	746
76	Hal McRae	741
77	Fred Lynn	737
78	Reggie Smith	734
79	Don Baylor	732
80	Dale Murphy	731
81	Enos Slaughter	730
82	Yogi Berra	728
83	Jimmy Ryan	726
84	Lee May	725
85	Bill Buckner	721
86	Sam Rice	716
87	Willie Davis	715
	Del Ennis	715
89	Gil Hodges	713
90	Frankie Frisch	709
91	Dave Kingman	707
92	Cecil Cooper	703
93	George Foster	702
94	Bobby Bonds	700
95	Gabby Hartnett	696
96	Cesar Cedeno	695
97	Bobby Doerr	693
98	George Sisler	691
99	Babe Herman	690
100	George Davis	688

Pinch Hits

1	Manny Mota	150
2	Smoky Burgess	145
3	Greg Gross	143
4	Jose Morales	123
5	Jerry Lynch	116
6	Red Lucas	114
7	Steve Braun	113
8	Terry Crowley	108
9	Gates Brown	107
10	Denny Walling	104
11	Mike Lum	103
12	Jim Dwyer	102
13	Rusty Staub	100
14	Larry Biittner	95
	Vic Davalillo	95
16	Jerry Hairston	94
17	Dave Philley	93
	Joel Youngblood	93
19	Jay Johnstone	92
20	Ed Kranepool	90
	Elmer Valo	90
22	Dave Collins	85
23	Jesus Alou	82
	Thad Bosley	82
	Kurt Bevacqua	82
	Tim McCarver	82

Pinch Hit Average

1	Tommy Davis	.320
2	Frenchy Bordagaray	.312
3	Frankie Baumholtz	.307
4	Rance Mulliniks	.304
5	Red Schoendienst	.303
6	Bob Fothergill	.300
7	Dave Philley	.299
8	Manny Mota	.297
9	Ted Easterly	.296
10	Harvey Hendrick	.295
11	Larry Herndon	.294
12	Terry Puhl	.294
13	Manny Sanguillen	.288
14	Ken Griffey	.287
15	Smoky Burgess	.286
16	Rick Miller	.286
17	Johnny Mize	.283
18	Bubba Morton	.281
19	Steve Braun	.281
20	Don Mueller	.280
21	Rusty Staub	.279
22	Mickey Vernon	.279
23	Thad Bosley	.278
24	Gene Woodling	.278
25	Bobby Adams	.277
26	Ed Kranepool	.277

Pinch Hit Home Runs

1	Cliff Johnson	20
2	Jerry Lynch	18
3	Gates Brown	16
	Smoky Burgess	16
	Willie McCovey	16
6	George Crowe	14
7	Joe Adcock	12
	Bob Cerv	12
	Jose Morales	12
	Graig Nettles	12
11	Jeff Burroughs	11
	Jay Johnstone	11
	Fred Whitfield	11
	Cy Williams	11
15	Jim Dwyer	10
	Mike Lum	10
	Ken McMullen	10
	Don Mincher	10
	Wally Post	10
	Champ Summers	10
	Jerry Turner	10
	Gus Zernial	10

Total Player Rating / 150g

1	Babe Ruth	6.47
2	Ted Williams	5.88
3	Nap Lajoie	5.58
4	Rickey Henderson	5.25
5	Rogers Hornsby	5.03
6	Mike Schmidt	4.99
7	Tris Speaker	4.65
8	Ty Cobb	4.48
9	Willie Mays	4.32
10	Honus Wagner	4.31
11	Wade Boggs	4.19
12	Joe Jackson	4.19
13	Lou Gehrig	4.19
14	Mickey Mantle	4.14
15	Hank Aaron	4.08
16	Tim Raines	4.02
17	Joe DiMaggio	3.82
18	Ed Delahanty	3.81
19	Frank Robinson	3.80
20	Eddie Collins	3.75
21	Stan Musial	3.71
22	Pete Browning	3.68
23	Dan Brouthers	3.63
24	Jimmie Foxx	3.52
25	Jackie Robinson	3.47
26	Mel Ott	3.34
27	Hughie Jennings	3.34
28	Jack Glasscock	3.33
29	George Davis	3.32
30	Frank Baker	3.27
31	Sam Thompson	3.25
32	Mickey Cochrane	3.23
33	Lou Boudreau	3.23
34	Cupid Childs	3.22
35	Hardy Richardson	3.21
36	Bill Dahlen	3.20
37	Arky Vaughan	3.18
38	Hank Greenberg	3.17
39	Darryl Strawberry	3.15
40	Buck Ewing	3.10
41	Bobby Grich	3.08
42	Joe Morgan	3.06
43	Roger Connor	3.05
44	Bobby Doerr	3.04
45	Johnny Mize	2.99
46	Eddie Mathews	2.97
47	Bob Johnson	2.95
48	Charlie Keller	2.92
49	George Brett	2.91
50	Tony Gwynn	2.90
51	Ryne Sandberg	2.89
52	Bid McPhee	2.89
53	Ozzie Smith	2.88
54	Elmer Flick	2.87
55	Bill Dickey	2.87
56	Dick Allen	2.83
57	Cal Ripken	2.83
58	Ralph Kiner	2.82
59	Eddie Murray	2.78
60	Joe Sewell	2.77
61	Gabby Hartnett	2.76
62	Charlie Gehringer	2.76
63	Denny Lyons	2.74
64	Joe Cronin	2.74
65	Roberto Clemente	2.74
66	Billy Hamilton	2.73
67	King Kelly	2.73
68	Keith Hernandez	2.71
69	Reggie Smith	2.70
70	Ron Santo	2.63
71	Bobby Bonds	2.56
72	Ferris Fain	2.55
73	Billy Herman	2.51
74	Joe Gordon	2.49
75	Jack Clark	2.49
76	Dave Bancroft	2.47
77	Bill Terry	2.46
78	Bill Mazeroski	2.45
79	Harry Stovey	2.45
80	Bobby Wallace	2.45
81	Frankie Frisch	2.45
82	Al Kaline	2.43
83	Roy Thomas	2.43
84	Gene Alley	2.42
85	Jim Wynn	2.41
86	Tony Oliva	2.40
87	Roy Campanella	2.40
88	Ray Chapman	2.37
89	Yogi Berra	2.36
90	Jack Fournier	2.35
91	John McGraw	2.35
92	Roy Cullenbine	2.34
93	Paul Molitor	2.33
94	Jesse Burkett	2.32
95	Dave Winfield	2.30
96	Norm Cash	2.29
97	Reggie Jackson	2.28
98	Pedro Guerrero	2.26
99	Willie McCovey	2.25
100	Kirby Puckett	2.24

Stolen Bases

1	Lou Brock	938
2	Rickey Henderson	936
3	Billy Hamilton	912
4	Ty Cobb	891
5	Eddie Collins	744
6	Arlie Latham	739
7	Max Carey	738
8	Honus Wagner	722
9	Joe Morgan	689
10	Tom Brown	657
11	Bert Campaneris	649
12	Tim Raines	634
13	George Davis	616
14	Willie Wilson	612
15	Dummy Hoy	594
16	Maury Wills	586
17	George VanHaltren	583
18	Hugh Duffy	574
19	Bid McPhee	568
20	Davey Lopes	557
21	Cesar Cedeno	550
22	Vince Coleman	549
23	Bill Dahlen	547
24	Monte Ward	540
25	Herman Long	534
26	Patsy Donovan	518
27	Jack Doyle	516
28	Harry Stovey	509
29	Luis Aparicio	506
	Fred Clarke	506
31	Willie Keeler	495
	Clyde Milan	495
33	Omar Moreno	487
34	Mike Griffin	473
35	Tommy McCarthy	468
36	Jimmy Sheckard	465
37	Ozzie Smith	464
38	Bobby Bonds	461
39	Ed Delahanty	455
	Ron LeFlore	455
41	Curt Welch	453
42	Joe Kelley	443
43	Sherry Magee	441
44	John McGraw	436
45	Tris Speaker	434
46	Mike Tiernan	428
47	Bob Bescher	427
48	Charlie Comiskey	419
	Frankie Frisch	419
50	Jimmy Ryan	418
51	Tommy Harper	408
52	Donie Bush	403
53	Frank Chance	401
54	Bill Lange	399
55	Willie Davis	398
56	Sam Mertes	396
57	Dave Collins	395
	Bill North	395
59	Jesse Burkett	389
60	Tommy Corcoran	387
61	Tom Daly	385
	Freddie Patek	385
63	George Burns	383
	Hugh Nicol	383
65	Fred Pfeffer	382
66	Walt Wilmot	381
67	Nap Lajoie	380
68	Steve Sax	376
69	Harry Hooper	375
	George Sisler	375
71	Jack Glasscock	372
72	King Kelly	368
73	Sam Crawford	366
	Tommy Dowd	366
75	Hal Chase	363
76	Paul Molitor	362
77	Tommy Leach	361
78	Hughie Jennings	359
	Fielder Jones	359
80	Brett Butler	358
81	Buck Ewing	354
82	Rod Carew	353
83	Tommy Tucker	352
84	Sam Rice	351
85	George Case	349
86	Lonnie Smith	347
87	Paul Radford	346
88	Julio Cruz	343
89	Amos Otis	341
90	John Anderson	338
	Willie Mays	338
92	Joe Tinker	336
93	Kip Selbach	334
94	Elmer Flick	330
95	Jose Cardenal	329
	Ned Hanlon	329
97	Monte Cross	328
	Kiki Cuyler	328
	Kid Gleason	328
100	Jim Fogarty	325

Stolen Base Average

1	Eric Davis	86.9
2	Tim Raines	85.7
3	Willie Wilson	83.7
4	Davey Lopes	83.0
5	Vince Coleman	82.7
6	Rickey Henderson	81.6
7	Julio Cruz	81.5
8	Joe Morgan	81.0
9	Ozzie Smith	80.7
10	Lenny Dykstra	80.2
11	Gary Redus	80.1
12	Mickey Mantle	80.1
13	Kirk Gibson	79.7
14	Enzo Hernandez	79.6
15	Andy VanSlyke	79.5
16	Joe Carter	79.3
17	R.J. Reynolds	79.0
18	Milt Thompson	78.9
19	Luis Aparicio	78.8
20	Amos Otis	78.6
21	Ryne Sandberg	78.3
22	Paul Molitor	78.2
23	Gary Pettis	78.1
24	Tommy Harper	77.9
25	Rudy Law	77.8
26	Bob Dernier	77.6
27	Miguel Dilone	77.4
28	Howard Johnson	77.0
29	Mookie Wilson	76.9
30	Barry Bonds	76.8
31	Hank Aaron	76.7
32	Willie Mays	76.6
33	Bert Campaneris	76.5
34	Ron LeFlore	76.2
35	George Case	76.2
36	Willie McGee	76.1
37	Billy Hatcher	76.1
38	Dick Howser	75.5
39	Cesar Cedeno	75.4
40	Lou Brock	75.3
41	Oddibe McDowell	75.2
42	Willie Davis	75.2
43	Andre Dawson	75.2
44	Larry Bowa	75.2
45	Bump Wills	75.1
46	Lloyd Moseby	74.9
47	Willie Randolph	74.9
48	Juan Samuel	74.8
49	Mickey Rivers	74.8
50	Dave Concepcion	74.7

Stolen Base Runs

1	Rickey Henderson	154
2	Tim Raines	127
3	Willie Wilson	112
4	Joe Morgan	110
5	Davey Lopes	99
6	Lou Brock	97
7	Vince Coleman	96
8	Bert Campaneris	75
9	Ozzie Smith	73
10	Luis Aparicio	70
11	Cesar Cedeno	58
12	Julio Cruz	56
13	Tommy Harper	53
14	Ron LeFlore	51
	Maury Wills	51
16	Eric Davis	49
17	Paul Molitor	48
18	Amos Otis	47
19	Gary Redus	44
20	Willie Davis	41
	Gary Pettis	41
22	Willie Mays	40
23	George Case	39
24	Mookie Wilson	38
25	Bobby Bonds	37
	Omar Moreno	37
	Freddie Patek	37
	Ryne Sandberg	37
29	Dave Collins	35
	Kirk Gibson	35
31	Miguel Dilone	33
32	Larry Bowa	32
33	Dave Concepcion	31
	Andre Dawson	31
	Willie McGee	31
	Juan Samuel	31
37	Rudy Law	29
	Andy VanSlyke	29
39	Hank Aaron	28
	Bob Dernier	28
41	Lloyd Moseby	27
42	Willie Randolph	26
	Mickey Rivers	26
	Lonnie Smith	26
	Frank Taveras	26
46	Lenny Dykstra	25
47	Mickey Mantle	23
48	Steve Sax	22
	Milt Thompson	22
50	4 players tied	21

Stolen Base Wins

1	Rickey Henderson	15.4
2	Tim Raines	13.3
3	Joe Morgan	11.5
4	Willie Wilson	11.2
5	Davey Lopes	10.2
6	Lou Brock	10.2
7	Vince Coleman	10.0
8	Bert Campaneris	7.9
9	Ozzie Smith	7.6
10	Luis Aparicio	7.3
11	Cesar Cedeno	6.1
12	Tommy Harper	5.6
13	Julio Cruz	5.6
14	Maury Wills	5.3
15	Ron LeFlore	5.2
16	Eric Davis	5.1
17	Amos Otis	4.9
18	Paul Molitor	4.8
19	Gary Redus	4.5
20	Willie Davis	4.3
21	Willie Mays	4.1
22	Gary Pettis	4.1
23	Mookie Wilson	4.0
24	George Case	3.9
25	Ryne Sandberg	3.9
26	Freddie Patek	3.8
27	Omar Moreno	3.8
28	Bobby Bonds	3.8
29	Dave Collins	3.6
30	Kirk Gibson	3.5
31	Miguel Dilone	3.4
32	Larry Bowa	3.3
33	Dave Concepcion	3.2
34	Andre Dawson	3.2
35	Juan Samuel	3.2
36	Willie McGee	3.2
37	Andy VanSlyke	3.0
38	Bob Dernier	2.9
39	Rudy Law	2.9
40	Hank Aaron	2.9
41	Frank Taveras	2.7
42	Lloyd Moseby	2.7
43	Lonnie Smith	2.7
44	Mickey Rivers	2.7
45	Willie Randolph	2.6
46	Lenny Dykstra	2.6
47	Mickey Mantle	2.4
48	Milt Thompson	2.3
49	Steve Sax	2.3
50	Gene Richards	2.2

Games

First Base
1. Jake Beckley — 2377
2. Mickey Vernon — 2237
3. Lou Gehrig — 2137
4. Charlie Grimm — 2131
5. Joe Judge — 2084
6. Ed Konetchy — 2073
7. Steve Garvey — 2059
8. Cap Anson — 2058
9. Joe Kuhel — 2057
10. Willie McCovey — 2045

Second Base
1. Eddie Collins — 2650
2. Joe Morgan — 2527
3. Nellie Fox — 2295
4. Charlie Gehringer — 2206
5. Frank White — 2150
6. Bid McPhee — 2126
7. Bill Mazeroski — 2094
8. Nap Lajoie — 2035
9. Willie Randolph — 1952
10. Bobby Doerr — 1852

Shortstop
1. Luis Aparicio — 2581
2. Larry Bowa — 2222
3. Luke Appling — 2218
4. Dave Concepcion — 2178
5. Rabbit Maranville — 2153
6. Bill Dahlen — 2132
7. Bert Campaneris — 2097
8. Tommy Corcoran — 2073
9. Roy McMillan — 2028
10. Pee Wee Reese — 2014

Third Base
1. Brooks Robinson — 2870
2. Graig Nettles — 2412
3. Mike Schmidt — 2212
4. Buddy Bell — 2183
5. Eddie Mathews — 2181
6. Ron Santo — 2130
7. Eddie Yost — 2008
8. Ron Cey — 1989
9. Aurelio Rodriguez — 1983
10. Sal Bando — 1896

Outfield
1. Ty Cobb — 2935
2. Willie Mays — 2843
3. Hank Aaron — 2760
4. Tris Speaker — 2698
5. Lou Brock — 2507
6. Al Kaline — 2488
7. Max Carey — 2421
8. Vada Pinson — 2403
9. Roberto Clemente — 2370
10. Zach Wheat — 2337

Catcher
1. Bob Boone — 2225
2. Carlton Fisk — 2044
3. Jim Sundberg — 1927
4. Al Lopez — 1918
5. Gary Carter — 1903
6. Rick Ferrell — 1806
7. Gabby Hartnett — 1793
8. Ted Simmons — 1772
9. Johnny Bench — 1744
10. Ray Schalk — 1727

Pitcher
1. Hoyt Wilhelm — 1070
2. Kent Tekulve — 1050
3. Lindy McDaniel — 987
4. Rollie Fingers — 944
5. Gene Garber — 931
6. Cy Young — 906
7. Sparky Lyle — 899
8. Jim Kaat — 898
9. Don McMahon — 874
10. Phil Niekro — 864

Fielding Average

First Base
1. Steve Garvey — .996
2. Wes Parker — .996
3. Don Mattingly — .995
4. Dan Driessen — .995
5. Jim Spencer — .995
6. Frank McCormick — .995
7. Keith Hernandez — .994
8. Vic Power — .994
9. Pete Rose — .994
10. Joe Adcock — .994

Second Base
1. Ryne Sandberg — .989
2. Tom Herr — .989
3. Rich Dauer — .987
4. Doug Flynn — .986
5. Marty Barrett — .986
6. Jerry Adair — .985
7. Jim Gantner — .985
8. Frank White — .984
9. Bobby Grich — .984
10. Lou Whitaker — .984

Shortstop
1. Tony Fernandez — .980
2. Larry Bowa — .980
3. Ozzie Smith — .978
4. Frank Duffy — .977
5. Cal Ripken — .977
6. Mark Belanger — .977
7. Alan Trammell — .977
8. Spike Owen — .976
9. Bucky Dent — .976
10. Roger Metzger — .976

Third Base
1. Brooks Robinson — .971
2. Ken Reitz — .970
3. George Kell — .969
4. Don Money — .968
5. Hank Majeski — .968
6. Don Wert — .968
7. Willie Kamm — .967
8. Heinie Groh — .967
9. Carney Lansford — .966
10. Clete Boyer — .965

Outfield
1. Terry Puhl — .993
2. Pete Rose — .991
3. Amos Otis — .991
4. Joe Rudi — .991
5. Mickey Stanley — .991
6. Don Demeter — .990
7. Brett Butler — .990
8. Jim Piersall — .990
9. Jim Landis — .989
10. Ken Berry — .989

Catcher
1. Bill Freehan — .993
2. Elston Howard — .993
3. Ron Hassey — .993
4. Jim Sundberg — .993
5. Joe Azcue — .992
6. Sherm Lollar — .992
7. Buddy Rosar — .992
8. Johnny Edwards — .992
9. Tom Haller — .992
10. Jerry Grote — .991

Pitcher
1. Don Mossi — .990
2. Gary Nolan — .990
3. Rick Rhoden — .989
4. Lon Warneke — .988
5. Jim Wilson — .988
6. Woodie Fryman — .988
7. Larry Gura — .986
8. Pete Alexander — .985
9. General Crowder — .984
10. Bill Monbouquette — .984

Total Chances per Game

First Base
1. Tom Jones — 11.38
2. George Stovall — 11.30
3. George Kelly — 11.09
4. Candy LaChance — 11.05
5. Wally Pipp — 11.05
6. Ed Konetchy — 11.04
7. George Burns — 10.92
8. Bill Terry — 10.91
9. Cap Anson — 10.86
10. Walter Holke — 10.83
11. Bill Phillips — 10.83
12. Fred Tenney — 10.83
13. Phil Todt — 10.83

Second Base
1. Joe Gerhardt — 7.11
2. Fred Pfeffer — 6.95
3. Fred Dunlap — 6.83
4. Bid McPhee — 6.70
5. Cub Stricker — 6.59
6. Lou Bierbauer — 6.50
7. Jack Burdock — 6.50
8. Cupid Childs — 6.32
9. Al Myers — 6.22
10. Ski Melillo — 6.16

Shortstop
1. Hughie Jennings — 6.69
2. Herman Long — 6.38
3. Dave Bancroft — 6.33
4. Bill Dahlen — 6.26
5. George Davis — 6.22
6. Rabbit Maranville — 6.10
7. Bobby Wallace — 6.10
8. Tommy Corcoran — 6.09
9. Kid Elberfeld — 6.07
10. Monte Cross — 6.06
11. Bones Ely — 6.06

Third Base
1. Jerry Denny — 4.21
2. Billy Shindle — 4.15
3. Billy Nash — 4.07
4. Arlie Latham — 4.04
5. Tommy Leach — 3.98
6. Denny Lyons — 3.98
7. Jimmy Collins — 3.89
8. Art Whitney — 3.82
9. Hick Carpenter — 3.81
10. Jimmy Austin — 3.74
11. Joe Mulvey — 3.74

Outfield
1. Taylor Douthit — 3.16
2. Richie Ashburn — 3.04
3. Johnny Mostil — 3.03
4. Dom DiMaggio — 2.99
5. Mike Kreevich — 2.95
6. Dwayne Murphy — 2.92
7. Sam Chapman — 2.91
8. Kirby Puckett — 2.89
9. Sam West — 2.88
10. Max Carey — 2.87

Catcher
1. Johnny Edwards — 6.98
2. Charlie Bennett — 6.87
3. John Roseboro — 6.83
4. Bill Freehan — 6.79
5. Joe Azcue — 6.72
6. John Bateman — 6.61
7. Mike Scioscia — 6.60
8. Jerry Grote — 6.53
9. Tony Pena — 6.45
10. Tim McCarver — 6.41

Pitcher
1. Nick Altrock — 3.72
2. Harry Howell — 3.61
3. Addie Joss — 3.60
4. Ed Walsh — 3.49
5. Nixey Callahan — 3.47
6. Willie Sudhoff — 3.31
7. George Mullin — 3.20
8. Barney Pelty — 3.20
9. Chick Fraser — 3.12
10. Red Donahue — 2.95
11. Ed Willett — 2.95

Chances Accepted per Game

First Base
1. Tom Jones — 11.21
2. George Stovall — 11.15
3. George Kelly — 11.00
4. Wally Pipp — 10.96
5. Ed Konetchy — 10.93
6. Candy LaChance — 10.87
7. Bill Terry — 10.82
8. George Burns — 10.77
9. Walter Holke — 10.75
10. Phil Todt — 10.74

Second Base
1. Joe Gerhardt — 6.49
2. Fred Pfeffer — 6.39
3. Bid McPhee — 6.33
4. Fred Dunlap — 6.32
5. Lou Bierbauer — 6.07
6. Ski Melillo — 6.00
7. Cub Stricker — 5.97
8. Jack Burdock — 5.93
9. Hughie Critz — 5.91
10. Frankie Frisch — 5.89

Shortstop
1. Hughie Jennings — 6.16
2. Dave Bancroft — 5.98
3. George Davis — 5.85
4. Rabbit Maranville — 5.81
5. Bill Dahlen — 5.80
6. Herman Long — 5.78
7. Bobby Wallace — 5.73
8. Travis Jackson — 5.67
9. Dick Bartell — 5.64
10. Tommy Corcoran — 5.63
11. Honus Wagner — 5.63

Third Base
1. Jerry Denny — 3.72
2. Billy Shindle — 3.70
3. Billy Nash — 3.65
4. Tommy Leach — 3.62
5. Jimmy Collins — 3.61
6. Arlie Latham — 3.52
7. Denny Lyons — 3.51
8. Lave Cross — 3.50
9. Jimmy Austin — 3.49
10. Ossie Vitt — 3.45

Outfield
1. Taylor Douthit — 3.07
2. Richie Ashburn — 2.98
3. Johnny Mostil — 2.94
4. Dom DiMaggio — 2.92
5. Mike Kreevich — 2.89
6. Dwayne Murphy — 2.88
7. Kirby Puckett — 2.86
8. Sam Chapman — 2.83
9. Sam West — 2.83
10. Max Carey — 2.77
11. Fred Schulte — 2.77

Catcher
1. Johnny Edwards — 6.92
2. John Roseboro — 6.76
3. Bill Freehan — 6.75
4. Joe Azcue — 6.67
5. Mike Scioscia — 6.51
6. John Bateman — 6.49
7. Charlie Bennett — 6.47
8. Jerry Grote — 6.47
9. Tony Pena — 6.38
10. Tim McCarver — 6.35

Pitcher
1. Nick Altrock — 3.59
2. Addie Joss — 3.47
3. Harry Howell — 3.45
4. Ed Walsh — 3.36
5. Nixey Callahan — 3.25
6. Willie Sudhoff — 3.11
7. George Mullin — 3.03
8. Barney Pelty — 3.00
9. Chick Fraser — 2.90
10. Red Donahue — 2.81
11. Christy Mathewson — 2.81

Putouts

First Base
1 Jake Beckley 23709
2 Ed Konetchy 21361
3 Cap Anson 20794
4 Charlie Grimm 20711
5 Stuffy McInnis 19962
6 Mickey Vernon 19808
7 Jake Daubert 19634
8 Lou Gehrig 19510
9 Joe Kuhel 19386
10 Joe Judge 19264

Second Base
1 Bid McPhee 6545
2 Eddie Collins 6526
3 Nellie Fox 6090
4 Joe Morgan 5742
5 Nap Lajoie 5496
6 Charlie Gehringer 5369
7 Bill Mazeroski 4974
8 Bobby Doerr 4928
9 Billy Herman 4780
10 Frank White 4740

Shortstop
1 Rabbit Maranville 5139
2 Bill Dahlen 4850
3 Dave Bancroft 4623
4 Honus Wagner 4576
5 Tommy Corcoran 4550
6 Luis Aparicio 4548
7 Luke Appling 4398
8 Herman Long 4225
9 Bobby Wallace 4142
10 Pee Wee Reese 4040

Third Base
1 Brooks Robinson 2697
2 Jimmy Collins 2372
3 Eddie Yost 2356
4 Lave Cross 2306
5 Pie Traynor 2289
6 Billy Nash 2219
7 Frank Baker 2154
8 Willie Kamm 2151
9 Eddie Mathews 2049
10 Puddin' Head Jones 2045

Outfield
1 Willie Mays 7095
2 Tris Speaker 6787
3 Max Carey 6363
4 Ty Cobb 6361
5 Richie Ashburn 6089
6 Hank Aaron 5539
7 Willie Davis 5449
8 Doc Cramer 5412
9 Vada Pinson 5097
10 Al Kaline 5035

Catcher
1 Bob Boone 11260
2 Gary Carter 10949
3 Carlton Fisk 10507
4 Bill Freehan 9941
5 Jim Sundberg 9767
6 John Roseboro 9291
7 Johnny Bench 9260
8 Johnny Edwards 8925
9 Ted Simmons 8906
10 Yogi Berra 8738

Pitcher
1 Phil Niekro 386
2 Fergie Jenkins 363
3 Gaylord Perry 349
4 Don Sutton 334
5 Tony Mullane 328
  Rick Reuschel 328
  Tom Seaver 328
8 Jim Galvin 324
9 Jack Morris 321
10 Robin Roberts 316

Putouts per Game

First Base
1 Tom Jones 10.53
2 Candy LaChance 10.48
3 George Stovall 10.45
4 George Kelly 10.37
5 Wally Pipp 10.33
6 Ed Konetchy 10.31
7 Bill Phillips 10.22
8 Walter Holke 10.20
9 Charlie Comiskey 10.15
10 Sid Farrar 10.13

Second Base
1 Joe Gerhardt 3.15
2 Bid McPhee 3.08
3 Fred Pfeffer 3.07
4 Fred Dunlap 3.03
5 Cub Stricker 3.02
6 Jack Burdock 2.82
7 Lou Bierbauer 2.74
8 Jerry Priddy 2.74
9 Bucky Harris 2.73
10 Nap Lajoie 2.71

Shortstop
1 Hughie Jennings 2.66
2 Dave Bancroft 2.47
3 Honus Wagner 2.43
4 Rabbit Maranville 2.39
5 Monte Cross 2.38
6 Heinie Wagner 2.38
7 George Davis 2.36
8 Herman Long 2.36
9 Kid Elberfeld 2.32
10 Dick Bartell 2.31
11 Ray Chapman 2.31

Third Base
1 Jerry Denny 1.61
2 Denny Lyons 1.55
3 Billy Nash 1.52
4 Jimmy Austin 1.43
5 Billy Shindle 1.43
6 Charlie Irwin 1.42
7 Jimmy Collins 1.41
8 Frank Baker 1.40
9 Tommy Leach 1.39
10 Hick Carpenter 1.37

Outfield
1 Taylor Douthit 3.01
2 Richie Ashburn 2.90
3 Johnny Mostil 2.83
4 Dom DiMaggio 2.82
5 Dwayne Murphy 2.82
6 Mike Kreevich 2.81
7 Kirby Puckett 2.78
8 Sam Chapman 2.74
9 Sam West 2.74
10 Gary Pettis 2.70
11 Fred Schulte 2.70

Catcher
1 Johnny Edwards 6.42
2 John Roseboro 6.30
3 Bill Freehan 6.29
4 Joe Azcue 6.14
5 Jerry Grote 6.00
6 Mike Scioscia 5.99
7 John Bateman 5.97
8 Tim McCarver 5.92
9 Tom Haller 5.85
10 Tony Pena 5.79

Pitcher
1 Mike Boddicker 0.80
2 Nick Altrock 0.78
3 Dave Foutz 0.78
4 Jack Morris 0.75
5 Dan Petry 0.74
6 Chick Fraser 0.73
7 Carl Morton 0.72
8 Dwight Gooden 0.70
9 Mel Stottlemyre 0.68
10 Nixey Callahan 0.66
11 Larry Corcoran 0.66
12 Dave Stieb 0.66
13 Walt Terrell 0.66

Assists

First Base
1 Keith Hernandez 1682
2 George Sisler 1529
3 Eddie Murray 1493
4 Mickey Vernon 1448
5 Fred Tenney 1363
6 Bill Buckner 1351
  Chris Chambliss 1351
8 Norm Cash 1317
9 Jake Beckley 1315
10 Joe Judge 1301

Second Base
1 Eddie Collins 7630
2 Charlie Gehringer 7068
3 Joe Morgan 6967
4 Bid McPhee 6905
5 Bill Mazeroski 6685
6 Nellie Fox 6373
7 Nap Lajoie 6262
8 Frank White 6250
9 Frankie Frisch 6026
10 Willie Randolph 5763

Shortstop
1 Luis Aparicio 8016
2 Bill Dahlen 7500
3 Rabbit Maranville 7354
4 Luke Appling 7218
5 Tommy Corcoran 7106
6 Larry Bowa 6857
7 Dave Concepcion 6594
8 Dave Bancroft 6561
9 Ozzie Smith 6535
10 Roger Peckinpaugh 6337

Third Base
1 Brooks Robinson 6205
2 Graig Nettles 5279
3 Mike Schmidt 5045
4 Buddy Bell 4925
5 Ron Santo 4581
6 Eddie Mathews 4322
7 Aurelio Rodriguez 4150
8 Ron Cey 4018
9 Sal Bando 3720
10 Lave Cross 3706

Outfield
1 Tris Speaker 448
2 Ty Cobb 392
3 Jimmy Ryan 375
4 Tom Brown 348
  George VanHaltren 348
6 Harry Hooper 344
7 Max Carey 339
8 Jimmy Sheckard 307
9 Clyde Milan 294
10 Orator Shaffer 289

Catcher
1 Deacon McGuire 1859
2 Ray Schalk 1811
3 Steve O'Neill 1698
4 Red Dooin 1590
5 Chief Zimmer 1580
6 Johnny Kling 1552
7 Ivey Wingo 1487
8 Wilbert Robinson 1454
9 Bill Bergen 1444
10 Wally Schang 1420

Pitcher
1 Cy Young 2014
2 Christy Mathewson 1503
3 Pete Alexander 1419
4 Jim Galvin 1382
5 Walter Johnson 1351
6 Burleigh Grimes 1252
7 George Mullin 1244
8 Jack Quinn 1240
9 Ed Walsh 1208
10 Eppa Rixey 1195

Assists per Game

First Base
1 Darrell Evans 0.88
2 Bill Buckner 0.87
3 Ferris Fain 0.84
4 Keith Hernandez 0.84
5 Vic Power 0.83
6 Pete O'Brien 0.80
7 Eddie Murray 0.79
8 Dick Siebert 0.79
9 George Sisler 0.78
10 Rudy York 0.77

Second Base
1 Hughie Critz 3.54
2 Frankie Frisch 3.42
3 Ski Melillo 3.38
4 Joe Gerhardt 3.35
5 Lou Bierbauer 3.34
6 Glenn Hubbard 3.34
7 Fred Pfeffer 3.33
8 Rogers Hornsby 3.31
9 Fred Dunlap 3.30
10 Jackie Hayes 3.30

Shortstop
1 Germany Smith 3.70
2 Art Fletcher 3.55
3 Bill Dahlen 3.52
4 Dave Bancroft 3.51
5 Hughie Jennings 3.51
6 Bones Ely 3.50
7 Travis Jackson 3.50
8 George Davis 3.49
9 Jack Glasscock 3.46
10 Bobby Wallace 3.46

Third Base
1 Terry Pendleton 2.36
2 Mike Schmidt 2.29
3 Bill Melton 2.27
4 Billy Shindle 2.27
5 Buddy Bell 2.26
6 Arlie Latham 2.26
7 Clete Boyer 2.24
8 Tommy Leach 2.23
9 Ossie Vitt 2.22
10 Jimmy Collins 2.20

Outfield
1 Orator Shaffer 0.35
2 Hugh Nicol 0.28
3 Paul Radford 0.25
4 Tommy McCarthy 0.23
5 Pop Corkhill 0.22
6 Jimmy Wolf 0.22
7 Sam Thompson 0.21
8 Tom Brown 0.20
9 Pete Hotaling 0.20
10 Jimmy Ryan 0.20
11 George VanHaltren 0.20
12 Curt Welch 0.20

Catcher
1 Bill Bergen 1.54
2 Duke Farrell 1.42
3 Lou Criger 1.37
4 Red Dooin 1.34
5 Johnny Kling 1.33
6 Bill Killefer 1.32
7 Bill Rariden 1.30
8 Oscar Stanage 1.29
9 Frank Bowerman 1.28
10 Chief Zimmer 1.28

Pitcher
1 Addie Joss 2.96
2 Harry Howell 2.84
3 Nick Altrock 2.81
4 Ed Walsh 2.81
5 Willie Sudhoff 2.73
6 Nixey Callahan 2.60
7 George Mullin 2.56
8 Ed Willett 2.54
9 Barney Pelty 2.51
10 Red Donahue 2.46

Double Plays

First Base

1	Mickey Vernon	2044
2	Joe Kuhel	1769
3	Charlie Grimm	1733
4	Chris Chambliss	1687
5	Eddie Murray	1673
6	Keith Hernandez	1654
7	Gil Hodges	1614
8	Lou Gehrig	1574
9	Jim Bottomley	1562
10	Jimmie Foxx	1528

Second Base

1	Bill Mazeroski	1706
2	Nellie Fox	1619
3	Bobby Doerr	1507
4	Joe Morgan	1505
5	Charlie Gehringer	1444
6	Willie Randolph	1398
7	Frank White	1382
8	Red Schoendienst	1368
9	Bobby Grich	1302
10	Eddie Collins	1215

Shortstop

1	Luis Aparicio	1553
2	Luke Appling	1424
3	Roy McMillan	1304
4	Dave Concepcion	1290
5	Larry Bowa	1265
6	Pee Wee Reese	1246
7	Dick Groat	1237
8	Phil Rizzuto	1217
9	Ozzie Smith	1200
10	Bert Campaneris	1186

Third Base

1	Brooks Robinson	618
2	Graig Nettles	470
3	Mike Schmidt	450
4	Buddy Bell	430
5	Aurelio Rodriguez	408
6	Ron Santo	395
7	Eddie Mathews	369
8	Ken Boyer	355
9	Sal Bando	345
	Eddie Yost	345

Outfield

1	Tris Speaker	139
2	Ty Cobb	107
3	Max Carey	86
4	Tom Brown	85
5	Harry Hooper	81
6	Jimmy Sheckard	80
7	Mike Griffin	75
8	Dummy Hoy	72
9	Jimmy Ryan	71
10	Fielder Jones	70

Catcher

1	Ray Schalk	226
2	Yogi Berra	175
	Steve O'Neill	175
4	Gabby Hartnett	163
5	Bob Boone	154
6	Jimmy Wilson	153
7	Wally Schang	149
8	Jim Sundberg	145
9	Gary Carter	144
10	Deacon McGuire	142

Pitcher

1	Phil Niekro	83
2	Warren Spahn	82
3	Freddie Fitzsimmons	79
4	Bob Lemon	78
5	Bucky Walters	76
6	Burleigh Grimes	74
7	Walter Johnson	72
8	Tommy John	69
9	Jim Kaat	65
10	Dizzy Trout	63

Fielding Runs

1	Nap Lajoie	370
2	Bill Mazeroski	362
3	Bill Dahlen	349
4	Bid McPhee	315
5	Fred Pfeffer	268
6	Mike Schmidt	265
7	George Davis	250
8	Jack Glasscock	248
9	Tris Speaker	246
10	Clete Boyer	233
	Ozzie Smith	233
12	Glenn Hubbard	228
13	Bobby Wallace	211
14	Joe Tinker	203
15	Dave Bancroft	198
16	Buddy Bell	195
17	Bobby Doerr	181
18	Dick Bartell	178
19	Mickey Doolan	177
20	Max Carey	172
21	George McBride	171
22	Mark Belanger	169
23	Aurelio Rodriguez	168
24	Joe Gerhardt	167
25	Lee Tannehill	166
26	Richie Ashburn	163
27	Art Fletcher	162
28	Darrell Evans	161
	Dal Maxvill	161
30	Roberto Clemente	159
	Rabbit Maranville	159
32	Germany Smith	156
33	Hughie Jennings	152
	Ski Melillo	152
35	Lou Bierbauer	151
	Frankie Frisch	151
	Brooks Robinson	151
38	Bobby Knoop	150
39	Fred Dunlap	149
	Keith Hernandez	149
41	Danny Richardson	148
42	Jim Hegan	146
43	Lave Cross	143
44	Bobby Wine	142
45	Billy Jurges	141
46	Jimmy Collins	140
47	Graig Nettles	138
	Ron Santo	138
49	Lou Boudreau	134
50	Hal Lanier	131
51	Bill Killefer	130
	Manny Trillo	130
53	Vic Power	128
54	Lou Criger	126
55	Gene Alley	125
56	Fred Tenney	123
	Al Weis	123
58	Terry Pendleton	120
59	Monte Ward	119
60	Harold Reynolds	118
61	Jerry Denny	117
	Everett Scott	117
63	Pop Snyder	115
64	Hobe Ferris	113
65	Hughie Critz	111
	Hardy Richardson	111
67	Bill Bergen	110
	Tommy Leach	110
	Joe Sewell	110
70	Johnny Callison	108
71	Tommy Corcoran	107
	Curt Welch	107
73	Ryne Sandberg	106
74	Travis Jackson	105
	Johnny Logan	105
76	Bill Buckner	103
	Eddie Miller	103
78	Honus Wagner	102
79	Roger Peckinpaugh	100
80	Rickey Henderson	99
81	Ozzie Guillen	98
82	Davy Force	97
	Herman Long	97
84	Jimmy Sheckard	96
85	Rocky Bridges	95
	Ed Brinkman	95
	Billy Shindle	95
88	Duke Farrell	93
89	Cupid Childs	92
	Johnny Edwards	92
	Ron Hansen	92
	Buddy Kerr	92
	Marty Marion	92
	Del Pratt	92
95	Harry Hooper	91
	Babe Pinelli	91
97	Rob Wilfong	90
	Chief Zimmer	90
99	4 players tied	89

Fielding Runs (by position)

First Base

1	Keith Hernandez	150
2	Fred Tenney	128
3	Vic Power	125
4	Bill Buckner	120
5	George Sisler	89
6	Darrell Evans	76
7	Bill Terry	67
8	Ed Konetchy	60
9	Ferris Fain	59
10	Norm Cash	57
	Eddie Murray	57

Second Base

1	Nap Lajoie	370
2	Bill Mazeroski	363
3	Bid McPhee	315
4	Fred Pfeffer	259
5	Glenn Hubbard	229
6	Bobby Doerr	180
7	Joe Gerhardt	153
8	Lou Bierbauer	152
9	Bobby Knoop	150
10	Fred Dunlap	149

Shortstop

1	Bill Dahlen	302
2	Jack Glasscock	251
3	Ozzie Smith	231
4	Joe Tinker	204
5	Dave Bancroft	200
6	George Davis	187
7	Rabbit Maranville	177
8	George McBride	173
9	Mickey Doolan	167
10	Mark Belanger	166

Third Base

1	Mike Schmidt	265
2	Clete Boyer	200
3	Buddy Bell	198
4	Aurelio Rodriguez	168
5	Brooks Robinson	151
6	Jimmy Collins	139
7	Graig Nettles	136
8	Ron Santo	135
9	Lave Cross	132
10	Terry Pendleton	121

Outfield

1	Tris Speaker	245
2	Max Carey	174
3	Richie Ashburn	163
4	Roberto Clemente	160
5	Johnny Callison	108
6	Jimmy Sheckard	105
7	Curt Welch	103
8	Mike Griffin	99
9	Ed Delahanty	98
10	Rickey Henderson	97

Catcher

1	Jim Hegan	145
2	Bill Killefer	131
3	Lou Criger	128
4	Bill Bergen	110
5	Johnny Edwards	93
	Chief Zimmer	93
7	Duke Farrell	92
8	Jim Sundberg	87
9	Rollie Hemsley	86
	Steve Yeager	86

Pitcher

1	Carl Mays	79
2	Ed Walsh	74
3	Freddie Fitzsimmons	65
	Christy Mathewson	65
5	Tommy John	63
6	Bob Lemon	61
7	Burleigh Grimes	58
8	Harry Gumbert	51
9	Harry Howell	49
10	Eddie Rommel	47

Fielding Wins

1	Nap Lajoie	38.0
2	Bill Mazeroski	37.7
3	Bill Dahlen	33.2
4	Mike Schmidt	27.7
5	Bid McPhee	27.4
6	Tris Speaker	25.1
7	Ozzie Smith	24.4
8	Clete Boyer	24.2
9	Glenn Hubbard	23.7
10	George Davis	23.5
11	Fred Pfeffer	23.4
12	Jack Glasscock	22.1
13	Joe Tinker	21.4
14	Bobby Wallace	21.3
15	Dave Bancroft	20.2
16	Buddy Bell	20.0
17	Mickey Doolan	18.9
18	George McBride	18.4
19	Lee Tannehill	18.0
20	Bobby Doerr	17.8
21	Mark Belanger	17.7
22	Max Carey	17.6
23	Dick Bartell	17.5
24	Aurelio Rodriguez	17.5
25	Art Fletcher	17.3
26	Dal Maxvill	17.1
27	Darrell Evans	16.6
28	Roberto Clemente	16.5
29	Richie Ashburn	16.3
30	Bobby Knoop	16.2
31	Rabbit Maranville	16.1
32	Brooks Robinson	15.9
33	Keith Hernandez	15.6
34	Joe Gerhardt	15.0
35	Bobby Wine	14.9
36	Frankie Frisch	14.8
37	Jim Hegan	14.6
38	Ron Santo	14.5
39	Billy Jurges	14.3
40	Graig Nettles	14.3
41	Ski Melillo	14.3
42	Bill Killefer	14.1
43	Hal Lanier	14.0
44	Manny Trillo	13.6
45	Jimmy Collins	13.5
46	Fred Dunlap	13.5
47	Lou Boudreau	13.5
48	Germany Smith	13.4
49	Hughie Jennings	13.4
50	Gene Alley	13.3
51	Lave Cross	13.1
52	Al Weis	13.1
53	Vic Power	13.1
54	Danny Richardson	12.9
55	Lou Bierbauer	12.8
56	Lou Criger	12.7
57	Terry Pendleton	12.5
58	Fred Tenney	12.2
59	Hobe Ferris	12.0
60	Everett Scott	11.9
61	Harold Reynolds	11.8
62	Bill Bergen	11.7
63	Tommy Leach	11.3
64	Johnny Callison	11.3
65	Ryne Sandberg	11.1
66	Hughie Critz	10.7
67	Bill Buckner	10.6
68	Johnny Logan	10.6
69	Honus Wagner	10.5
70	Eddie Miller	10.5
71	Monte Ward	10.5
72	Jerry Denny	10.4
73	Joe Sewell	10.4
74	Pop Snyder	10.3
75	Travis Jackson	10.1
76	Roger Peckinpaugh	10.1
77	Ed Brinkman	10.1
78	Rickey Henderson	9.9
79	Hardy Richardson	9.9
80	Jimmy Sheckard	9.8
81	Tommy Corcoran	9.8
82	Ozzie Guillen	9.8
83	Ron Hansen	9.7
84	Johnny Edwards	9.7
85	Rocky Bridges	9.6
86	Del Pratt	9.5
87	Marty Marion	9.4
88	Curt Welch	9.4
89	Harry Hooper	9.4
90	Buddy Kerr	9.3
91	Steve Yeager	9.2
92	Willie Miranda	9.0
93	Rob Wilfong	9.0
94	Doc Lavan	9.0
95	Alex Grammas	9.0
96	Jim Sundberg	8.9
97	Willie Mays	8.9
98	Davy Force	8.8
99	Julio Cruz	8.8
100	Rick Burleson	8.8

Total Player Rating

1	Babe Ruth	107.9
2	Nap Lajoie	92.2
3	Ty Cobb	90.6
4	Ted Williams	89.8
5	Hank Aaron	89.6
6	Tris Speaker	86.4
7	Willie Mays	86.2
8	Honus Wagner	80.3
9	Mike Schmidt	80.0
10	Rogers Hornsby	75.8
11	Stan Musial	74.9
12	Frank Robinson	71.2
13	Eddie Collins	70.6
14	Mickey Mantle	66.2
15	Mel Ott	60.8
16	Lou Gehrig	60.4
17	Rickey Henderson	56.3
18	Jimmie Foxx	54.3
19	Joe Morgan	54.0
20	George Davis	52.4
21	Bill Dahlen	52.1
22	Carl Yastrzemski	47.5
23	Eddie Mathews	47.3
24	Ed Delahanty	46.6
25	Al Kaline	46.0
26	Roberto Clemente	44.4
27	George Brett	44.2
	Joe DiMaggio	44.2
29	Reggie Jackson	42.9
30	Charlie Gehringer	42.7
31	Bobby Grich	41.2
32	Bid McPhee	41.1
33	Roger Connor	40.6
34	Dan Brouthers	40.5
35	Eddie Murray	39.5
36	Ron Santo	39.3
37	Willie McCovey	38.9
	Bobby Wallace	38.9
39	Joe Cronin	38.8
40	Jack Glasscock	38.5
	Arky Vaughan	38.5
42	Paul Waner	37.9
43	Bobby Doerr	37.8
44	Frankie Frisch	37.7
	Keith Hernandez	37.7
	Tim Raines	37.7
47	Johnny Mize	37.5
48	Wade Boggs	37.4
49	Joe Jackson	37.2
50	Ozzie Smith	37.0
51	Dave Winfield	36.8
52	Gabby Hartnett	36.6
	Bob Johnson	36.6
54	Robin Yount	36.3
55	Luke Appling	36.2
56	Reggie Smith	35.8
57	Lou Boudreau	35.4
	Bill Mazeroski	35.4
59	Joe Sewell	35.2
60	Darrell Evans	34.7
61	Frank Baker	34.3
62	Bill Dickey	34.2
63	Cap Anson	33.4
64	Yogi Berra	33.3
65	Dick Allen	33.0
66	Fred Clarke	32.6
67	Billy Herman	32.2
68	Jesse Burkett	32.0
	Jackie Robinson	32.0
70	Norm Cash	31.9
	Mickey Cochrane	31.9
72	Dave Bancroft	31.5
	Bobby Bonds	31.5
	Rod Carew	31.5
75	Cupid Childs	31.3
76	Harry Heilmann	31.0
77	Jim Wynn	30.8
78	Sam Crawford	30.7
	Fred Dunlap	30.7
80	Sam Thompson	30.5
81	Harmon Killebrew	30.4
82	Sherry Magee	30.3
83	Hank Greenberg	29.5
	Rusty Staub	29.5
85	Jack Clark	29.4
86	Zach Wheat	29.2
87	Billy Williams	29.1
88	Pete Browning	29.0
	Billy Hamilton	29.0
	Al Simmons	29.0
91	Hughie Jennings	28.6
92	Hardy Richardson	28.5
93	Elmer Flick	28.4
94	Dwight Evans	28.2
	Willie Stargell	28.2
	Bill Terry	28.2
97	Cal Ripken	27.8
98	Ralph Kiner	27.7
99	Buck Ewing	27.2
100	Max Carey	27.0

Total Player Rating

	Goose Goslin	27.0
	Joe Medwick	27.0
103	Andre Dawson	26.9
104	Tony Oliva	26.8
	Ryne Sandberg	26.8
106	Jim Rice	26.7
107	Richie Ashburn	26.5
	King Kelly	26.5
109	Stan Hack	26.3
110	Dick Bartell	26.2
	Buddy Bell	26.2
112	Joe Gordon	26.0
113	Carlton Fisk	25.8
	George Sisler	25.8
115	Jimmy Collins	25.6
116	Ernie Banks	25.3
117	Gary Carter	25.0
	Brooks Robinson	25.0
119	Graig Nettles	24.8
120	Duke Snider	24.4
121	Heinie Groh	24.3
	Harry Stovey	24.3
123	Jake Beckley	24.2
	Chuck Klein	24.2
	Fred Pfeffer	24.2
126	Rocky Colavito	24.1
127	Jack Fournier	24.0
128	Joe Kelley	23.9
	Paul Molitor	23.9
130	Dave Parker	23.8
	Jimmy Sheckard	23.8
	Roy Thomas	23.8
133	Joe Tinker	23.7
134	Minnie Minoso	23.6
135	Travis Jackson	23.3
	Darryl Strawberry	23.3
137	Cesar Cedeno	23.2
	Tony Gwynn	23.2
	Ed Konetchy	23.2
140	Johnny Bench	22.8
	Charlie Keller	22.8
142	Harlond Clift	22.4
143	Art Fletcher	22.0
144	Fred Lynn	21.6
145	George Foster	21.5
	Del Pratt	21.5
	Willie Randolph	21.5
148	Mike Griffin	21.2
149	Ron Cey	21.1
	Fred Tenney	21.1
151	Jose Cruz	21.0
152	Pedro Guerrero	20.8
	Charley Jones	20.8
154	Tommy Leach	20.7
155	Eric Davis	20.6
156	Denny Lyons	20.5
157	Pete Rose	20.3
158	Kiki Cuyler	20.2
159	Orlando Cepeda	20.0
	Miller Huggins	20.0
	Bill Joyce	20.0
162	Ferris Fain	19.6
	Joe Torre	19.6
164	Ken Singleton	19.5
165	Roy Campanella	19.4
166	Gene Alley	19.3
167	Frank Howard	19.2
168	Pie Traynor	19.0
169	Glenn Hubbard	18.8
	Eddie Stanky	18.8
171	Earl Averill	18.7
	Ted Simmons	18.7
173	Frank Chance	18.6
174	Roy Cullenbine	18.4
175	Ken Boyer	18.3
	Babe Herman	18.3
	Dale Murphy	18.3
	Alan Trammell	18.3
	Roy White	18.3
180	Bob Elliott	18.2
	Ken Williams	18.2
182	Gavvy Cravath	18.1
	Amos Otis	18.1
184	Wally Berger	18.0
	Art Devlin	18.0
	Larry Doby	18.0
187	Roger Bresnahan	17.9
188	George Gore	17.8
189	Jimmy Ryan	17.7
190	Lave Cross	17.5
	Chet Lemon	17.5
192	Wally Schang	17.4
193	Benny Kauff	17.3
194	Barry Bonds	17.2
	John McGraw	17.2
	Jim O'Rourke	17.2
197	Boog Powell	17.0
197	Paul Hines	16.8
199	Dolph Camilli	16.7
	Rico Carty	16.7

Total Player Rating

	Jocko Milligan	16.7
202	Ray Chapman	16.6
203	Bill Nicholson	16.5
204	Mike Hargrove	16.4
	Cy Seymour	16.4
206	Billy Nash	16.3
207	Roger Peckinpaugh	16.2
208	Kirby Puckett	16.0
209	Hack Wilson	15.9
210	Jesse Barfield	15.8
	George VanHaltren	15.8
212	Johnny Evers	15.7
	Hal McRae	15.7
214	Gil McDougald	15.6
	Dwayne Murphy	15.6
	Dave Orr	15.6
	Pee Wee Reese	15.6
	Rudy York	15.6
219	Johnny Callison	15.5
	Henry Larkin	15.5
221	Jim Fregosi	15.4
	Jeff Heath	15.4
	Kip Selbach	15.4
224	Chief Zimmer	15.3
225	Bob Allison	15.2
	Harry Davis	15.2
	Gil Hodges	15.2
	Tony Lazzeri	15.2
	Edd Roush	15.2
	Andy Thornton	15.2
231	Brian Downing	15.1
	Mike Tiernan	15.1
233	Duke Farrell	15.0
	Jimmy Williams	15.0
235	Enos Slaughter	14.8
	Vern Stephens	14.8
237	Ernie Lombardi	14.7
238	Kirk Gibson	14.6
239	Clete Boyer	14.5
	Augie Galan	14.5
	Sid Gordon	14.5
242	Doug DeCinces	14.4
	Johnny Logan	14.4
244	Mike Donlin	14.3
	Bobby Knoop	14.3
	Bobby Murcer	14.3
	Lou Whitaker	14.3
248	Ben Chapman	14.2
	Dave Johnson	14.2
	Willie Kamm	14.2
	Roy Smalley	14.2
252	Gene Tenace	14.1
253	Bobby Veach	14.0
254	Don Baylor	13.7
	Thurman Munson	13.7
	Tip O'Neill	13.7
257	Lance Parrish	13.6
	Roy Sievers	13.6
259	Don Mattingly	13.5
260	Tommy Henrich	13.3
261	Deacon McGuire	13.1
	Richie Zisk	13.1
263	Ken Keltner	13.0
	Kevin McReynolds	13.0
265	Will Clark	12.9
	Tony Fernandez	12.9
267	Mark Belanger	12.7
	Charlie Bennett	12.7
	Willie Keeler	12.7
	Orator Shaffer	12.7
	George Stone	12.7
272	Jerry Denny	12.6
	Kid Elberfeld	12.6
	Tony Perez	12.6
	Claude Ritchey	12.6
	Phil Rizzuto	12.6
	Ossee Schreckengost	12.6
278	Earle Combs	12.4
	Dal Maxvill	12.4
280	John Titus	12.3
281	Bill Freehan	12.2
282	Roger Maris	12.1
283	Jack Clements	12.0
	Lou Criger	12.0
285	Darrell Porter	11.9
	Red Smith	11.9
287	Jake Daubert	11.8
	Rick Ferrell	11.8
	Ron Hansen	11.8
	Ed McFarland	11.8
	Elmer Smith	11.8
292	Chief Meyers	11.7
	Al Rosen	11.7
294	Fred Carroll	11.6
	Tom Daly	11.6
	Greg Luzinski	11.6
	Ed Swartwood	11.6
	Cy Williams	11.6
299	Lonny Frey	11.5
300	Bill Melton	11.4

Total Player Rating

	Johnny Pesky	11.4
	Red Schoendienst	11.4
	Andy VanSlyke	11.4
	Curt Welch	11.4
305	Lonnie Smith	11.3
	Ned Williamson	11.3
	Jimmy Wolf	11.3
	Ross Youngs	11.3
309	Tony Cuccinello	11.2
	Oscar Gamble	11.2
311	Jackie Jensen	11.1
	Billy Jurges	11.1
	Sixto Lezcano	11.1
	Marty McManus	11.1
	Jerry Priddy	11.1
316	Jim Gentile	11.0
	Chick Hafey	11.0
	Joe Harris	11.0
	Mike Scioscia	11.0
	Al Weis	11.0
321	Charlie Hickman	10.9
	Larry Hisle	10.9
	Al Oliver	10.9
	Stan Spence	10.9
	Riggs Stephenson	10.9
	Dixie Walker	10.9
	Tim Wallach	10.9
	Deacon White	10.9
329	Monte Irvin	10.8
	Ben Oglivie	10.8
	Maury Wills	10.8
332	Harry Hooper	10.7
	Bill Lange	10.7
	Bob Watson	10.7
335	Jack Crooks	10.6
	Toby Harrah	10.6
	Kent Hrbek	10.6
338	Sam Rice	10.5
339	Oyster Burns	10.4
	Donie Bush	10.4
	Cecil Cooper	10.4
	Ken Griffey	10.4
	Tommy Holmes	10.4
	Cliff Johnson	10.4
345	Danny Murphy	10.3
346	Sal Bando	10.2
	Earl Battey	10.2
348	Alvin Davis	10.1
	Jimmy Dykes	10.1
	Whitey Kurowski	10.1
	Lee Tannehill	10.1
352	Bill Bradley	9.9
	Lefty O'Doul	9.9
	Cecil Travis	9.9
355	Heinie Zimmerman	9.8
356	Hugh Duffy	9.7
	Marty Marion	9.7
358	Tom Haller	9.6
359	Harold Baines	9.5
	Von Hayes	9.5
	Johnny Kling	9.5
	Dan McGann	9.5
	Harold Reynolds	9.5
	Vic Wertz	9.5
365	Nellie Fox	9.4
	Ken McMullen	9.4
	Doug Rader	9.4
	Andy Seminick	9.4
	Dickie Thon	9.4
	Pinky Whitney	9.4
	Sam Wise	9.4
372	Brett Butler	9.3
	Ripper Collins	9.3
	Dom DiMaggio	9.3
	Lenny Dykstra	9.3
	Hank Sauer	9.3
377	Frank Fennelly	9.2
	Topsy Hartsel	9.2
	Buck Herzog	9.2
	Rico Petrocelli	9.2
	Pete Reiser	9.2
382	Jimmy Barrett	9.1
	Rick Burleson	9.1
	Rabbit Maranville	9.1
	Danny Richardson	9.1
386	Johnny Bates	9.0
	Phil Cavarretta	9.0
	Dave Concepcion	9.0
	Don Mincher	9.0
390	Mickey Vernon	8.9
391	Vada Pinson	8.8
	Harry Steinfeldt	8.8
393	Herman Long	8.6
	John Romano	8.6
	Monte Ward	8.6
	Wes Westrum	8.6
397	Don Buford	8.5
	Freddy Lindstrom	8.5
	Mike Mitchell	8.5
400	Chili Davis	8.4

Total Player Rating

	Player	Rating
	Elbie Fletcher	8.4
	Fred Luderus	8.4
	Earl Torgeson	8.4
404	Happy Felsch	8.3
	Merv Rettenmund	8.3
	Socks Seybold	8.3
	Ernie Whitt	8.3
	Bump Wills	8.3
409	Larry Gardner	8.2
	Joe Gerhardt	8.2
	Eddie Miller	8.2
	Ken Phelps	8.2
	Gene Woodling	8.2
414	Joe Adcock	8.1
	Andy Pafko	8.1
	George Wood	8.1
417	George Burns	8.0
	Sherm Lollar	8.0
	George Selkirk	8.0
	Jim Sundberg	8.0
	Bill Sweeney	8.0
	Art Wilson	8.0
423	Glenn Davis	7.9
	Woodie Held	7.9
	Buddy Kerr	7.9
426	Phil Garner	7.8
	Solly Hemus	7.8
	Matty McIntyre	7.8
429	Hank Gowdy	7.6
	Harry Lumley	7.6
	Buddy Myer	7.6
432	Fielder Jones	7.5
	Gary Matthews	7.5
	Jim McTamany	7.5
	Rick Monday	7.5
	Ezra Sutton	7.5
437	Ginger Beaumont	7.4
	George Kell	7.4
439	Johnny Bassler	7.3
	Bernie Carbo	7.3
	Jim Fogarty	7.3
	Bake McBride	7.3
443	Luis Aparicio	7.2
	Phil Bradley	7.2
	Johnny Mostil	7.2
	Tom Tresh	7.2
	Bill White	7.2
448	Ron Hassey	7.1
	Jason Thompson	7.1
450	Dusty Baker	7.0
	Walker Cooper	7.0
	Chick Stahl	7.0
	Jake Stenzel	7.0
	Snuffy Stirnweiss	7.0
	John Stone	7.0
	Hank Thompson	7.0
457	Joe Ferguson	6.9
	Alex Kampouris	6.9
	Norm Siebern	6.9
460	Willie Horton	6.8
	Heinie Manush	6.8
462	Lyn Lary	6.7
	Terry Puhl	6.7
	Pop Smith	6.7
	Billy Werber	6.7
	Bobby Wine	6.7
467	Bobby Bonilla	6.6
	Bob Caruthers	6.6
	Dave Cash	6.6
	Del Ennis	6.6
	Ron Fairly	6.6
	George Hendrick	6.6
473	John Briggs	6.4
	Del Crandall	6.4
	Ival Goodman	6.4
	Joe Judge	6.4
	Heinie Peitz	6.4
	Mickey Rivers	6.4
479	Sid Bream	6.3
	Abner Dalrymple	6.3
	Stan Lopata	6.3
	Bill Skowron	6.3
483	Dave Anderson	6.2
	Larry Doyle	6.2
	Jim Essian	6.2
	Elston Howard	6.2
	Eddie Joost	6.2
488	George Bell	6.1
	Julio Franco	6.1
	Mike Grady	6.1
	Davey Lopes	6.1
	Charlie Maxwell	6.1
	Johnny Ray	6.1
	Emmett Seery	6.1
	Earl Smith	6.1
496	Jack Doyle	6.0
	Mike Easler	6.0
	Dummy Hoy	6.0
	Tim McCarver	6.0
500	10 players tied	5.9

Total Player Rating (alpha.)

Player	Rating
Hank Aaron	89.6
Joe Adcock	8.1
Dick Allen	33.0
Gene Alley	19.3
Bob Allison	15.2
Dave Anderson	6.2
Cap Anson	33.4
Luis Aparicio	7.2
Luke Appling	36.2
Richie Ashburn	26.5
Earl Averill	18.7
Harold Baines	9.5
Frank Baker	34.3
Dusty Baker	7.0
Dave Bancroft	31.5
Sal Bando	10.2
Ernie Banks	25.3
Jesse Barfield	15.8
Jimmy Barrett	9.1
Dick Bartell	26.2
Johnny Bassler	7.3
Johnny Bates	9.0
Earl Battey	10.2
Don Baylor	13.7
Ginger Beaumont	7.4
Jake Beckley	24.2
Mark Belanger	12.7
Buddy Bell	26.2
George Bell	6.1
Johnny Bench	22.8
Charlie Bennett	12.7
Wally Berger	18.0
Yogi Berra	33.3
Wade Boggs	37.4
Barry Bonds	17.2
Bobby Bonds	31.5
Bobby Bonilla	6.6
Lou Boudreau	35.4
Clete Boyer	14.5
Ken Boyer	18.3
Phil Bradley	7.2
Bill Bradley	9.9
Sid Bream	6.3
Roger Bresnahan	17.9
George Brett	44.2
John Briggs	6.4
Dan Brouthers	40.5
Pete Browning	29.0
Don Buford	8.5
Jesse Burkett	32.0
Rick Burleson	9.1
George Burns	8.0
Oyster Burns	10.4
Donie Bush	10.4
Brett Butler	9.3
Johnny Callison	15.5
Dolph Camilli	16.7
Roy Campanella	19.4
Bernie Carbo	7.3
Rod Carew	31.5
Max Carey	27.0
Fred Carroll	11.6
Gary Carter	25.0
Rico Carty	16.7
Bob Caruthers	6.6
Dave Cash	6.6
Norm Cash	31.9
Phil Cavarretta	9.0
Cesar Cedeno	23.2
Orlando Cepeda	20.0
Ron Cey	21.1
Frank Chance	18.6
Ray Chapman	16.6
Ben Chapman	14.2
Cupid Childs	31.3
Jack Clark	29.4
Will Clark	12.9
Fred Clarke	32.6
Roberto Clemente	44.4
Jack Clements	12.0
Harlond Clift	22.4
Ty Cobb	90.6
Mickey Cochrane	31.9
Rocky Colavito	24.1
Eddie Collins	70.6
Ripper Collins	9.3
Jimmy Collins	25.6
Earle Combs	12.4
Dave Concepcion	9.0
Roger Connor	40.6
Cecil Cooper	10.4
Walker Cooper	7.0
Del Crandall	6.4
Gavvy Cravath	18.1
Sam Crawford	30.7
Lou Criger	12.0
Joe Cronin	38.8
Jack Crooks	10.6
Lave Cross	17.5
Jose Cruz	21.0

Total Player Rating (alpha.)

Player	Rating
Tony Cuccinello	11.2
Roy Cullenbine	18.4
Kiki Cuyler	20.2
Bill Dahlen	52.1
Abner Dalrymple	6.3
Tom Daly	11.6
Jake Daubert	11.8
Alvin Davis	10.1
Chili Davis	8.4
Eric Davis	20.6
George Davis	52.4
Glenn Davis	7.9
Harry Davis	15.2
Andre Dawson	26.9
Ed Delahanty	46.6
Jerry Denny	12.6
Art Devlin	18.0
Bill Dickey	34.2
Larry Doby	18.0
Bobby Doerr	37.8
Mike Donlin	14.3
Brian Downing	15.1
Jack Doyle	6.0
Larry Doyle	6.2
Hugh Duffy	9.7
Fred Dunlap	30.7
Jimmy Dykes	10.1
Lenny Dykstra	9.3
Doug DeCinces	14.4
Dom DiMaggio	9.3
Joe DiMaggio	44.2
Mike Easler	6.0
Kid Elberfeld	12.6
Bob Elliott	18.2
Del Ennis	6.6
Jim Essian	6.2
Darrell Evans	34.7
Dwight Evans	28.2
Johnny Evers	15.7
Buck Ewing	27.2
Ferris Fain	19.6
Ron Fairly	6.6
Duke Farrell	15.0
Happy Felsch	8.3
Frank Fennelly	9.2
Joe Ferguson	6.9
Tony Fernandez	12.9
Rick Ferrell	11.8
Carlton Fisk	25.8
Art Fletcher	22.0
Elbie Fletcner	8.4
Elmer Flick	28.4
Jim Fogarty	7.3
George Foster	21.5
Jack Fournier	24.0
Nellie Fox	9.4
Jimmie Foxx	54.3
Julio Franco	6.1
Bill Freehan	12.2
Jim Fregosi	15.4
Lonny Frey	11.5
Frankie Frisch	37.7
Augie Galan	14.5
Oscar Gamble	11.2
Larry Gardner	8.2
Phil Garner	7.8
Lou Gehrig	60.4
Charlie Gehringer	42.7
Jim Gentile	11.0
Joe Gerhardt	8.2
Kirk Gibson	14.6
Jack Glasscock	38.5
Ival Goodman	6.4
Joe Gordon	26.0
Sid Gordon	14.5
George Gore	17.8
Goose Goslin	27.0
Hank Gowdy	7.6
Mike Grady	6.1
Hank Greenberg	29.5
Bobby Grich	41.2
Ken Griffey	10.4
Mike Griffin	21.2
Heinie Groh	24.3
Pedro Guerrero	20.8
Tony Gwynn	23.2
Stan Hack	26.3
Chick Hafey	11.0
Tom Haller	9.6
Billy Hamilton	29.0
Ron Hansen	11.8
Mike Hargrove	16.4
Toby Harrah	10.6
Joe Harris	11.0
Gabby Hartnett	36.6
Topsy Hartsel	9.2
Ron Hassey	7.1
Von Hayes	9.5
Jeff Heath	15.4
Harry Heilmann	31.0

Total Player Rating (alpha.)

Player	Rating
Woodie Held	7.9
Solly Hemus	7.8
Rickey Henderson	56.3
George Hendrick	6.6
Tommy Henrich	13.3
Babe Herman	18.3
Billy Herman	32.2
Keith Hernandez	37.7
Buck Herzog	9.2
Charlie Hickman	10.9
Paul Hines	16.8
Larry Hisle	10.9
Gil Hodges	15.2
Tommy Holmes	10.4
Harry Hooper	10.7
Rogers Hornsby	75.8
Willie Horton	6.8
Elston Howard	6.2
Frank Howard	19.2
Dummy Hoy	6.0
Kent Hrbek	10.6
Glenn Hubbard	18.8
Miller Huggins	20.0
Monte Irvin	10.8
Joe Jackson	37.2
Reggie Jackson	42.9
Travis Jackson	23.3
Hughie Jennings	28.6
Jackie Jensen	11.1
Cliff Johnson	10.4
Dave Johnson	14.2
Bob Johnson	36.6
Charley Jones	20.8
Fielder Jones	7.5
Eddie Joost	6.2
Bill Joyce	20.0
Joe Judge	6.4
Billy Jurges	11.1
Al Kaline	46.0
Willie Kamm	14.2
Alex Kampouris	6.9
Benny Kauff	17.3
Willie Keeler	12.7
George Kell	7.4
Charlie Keller	22.8
Joe Kelley	23.9
King Kelly	26.5
Ken Keltner	13.0
Buddy Kerr	7.9
Harmon Killebrew	30.4
Ralph Kiner	27.7
Chuck Klein	24.2
Johnny Kling	9.5
Bobby Knoop	14.3
Ed Konetchy	23.2
Whitey Kurowski	10.1
Nap Lajoie	92.2
Bill Lange	10.7
Henry Larkin	15.5
Lyn Lary	6.7
Tony Lazzeri	15.2
Tommy Leach	20.7
Chet Lemon	17.5
Sixto Lezcano	11.1
Freddy Lindstrom	8.5
Johnny Logan	14.4
Sherm Lollar	8.0
Ernie Lombardi	14.7
Herman Long	8.6
Stan Lopata	6.3
Davey Lopes	6.1
Fred Luderus	8.4
Harry Lumley	7.6
Greg Luzinski	11.6
Fred Lynn	21.6
Denny Lyons	20.5
Sherry Magee	30.3
Mickey Mantle	66.2
Heinie Manush	6.8
Rabbit Maranville	9.1
Marty Marion	9.7
Roger Maris	12.1
Eddie Mathews	47.3
Gary Matthews	7.5
Don Mattingly	13.5
Dal Maxvill	12.4
Charlie Maxwell	6.1
Willie Mays	86.2
Bill Mazeroski	35.4
Joe Medwick	27.0
Bill Melton	11.4
Chief Meyers	11.7
Eddie Miller	8.2
Jocko Milligan	16.7
Don Mincher	9.0
Minnie Minoso	23.6
Mike Mitchell	8.5
Johnny Mize	37.5
Paul Molitor	23.9
Rick Monday	7.5

Total Player Rating (alpha.)

Joe Morgan	54.0
Johnny Mostil	7.2
Thurman Munson	13.7
Bobby Murcer	14.3
Dale Murphy	18.3
Danny Murphy	10.3
Dwayne Murphy	15.6
Eddie Murray	39.5
Stan Musial	74.9
Buddy Myer	7.6
Bake McBride	7.3
Tim McCarver	6.0
Willie McCovey	38.9
Gil McDougald	15.6
Ed McFarland	11.8
Dan McGann	9.5
John McGraw	17.2
Deacon McGuire	13.1
Matty McIntyre	7.8
Marty McManus	11.1
Ken McMullen	9.4
Bid McPhee	41.1
Hal McRae	15.7
Kevin McReynolds	13.0
Jim McTamany	7.5
Billy Nash	16.3
Graig Nettles	24.8
Bill Nicholson	16.5
Lefty O'Doul	9.9
Tip O'Neill	13.7
Jim O'Rourke	17.2
Ben Oglivie	10.8
Tony Oliva	26.8
Al Oliver	10.9
Dave Orr	15.6
Amos Otis	18.1
Mel Ott	60.8
Andy Pafko	8.1
Dave Parker	23.8
Lance Parrish	13.6
Roger Peckinpaugh	16.2
Heinie Peitz	6.4
Tony Perez	12.6
Johnny Pesky	11.4
Rico Petrocelli	9.2
Fred Pfeffer	24.2
Ken Phelps	8.2
Vada Pinson	8.8
Darrell Porter	11.9
Boog Powell	17.0
Del Pratt	21.5
Jerry Priddy	11.1
Kirby Puckett	16.0
Terry Puhl	6.7
Doug Rader	9.4
Tim Raines	37.7
Willie Randolph	21.5
Johnny Ray	6.1
Pete Reiser	9.2
Merv Rettenmund	8.3
Harold Reynolds	9.5
Sam Rice	10.5
Jim Rice	26.7
Hardy Richardson	28.5
Danny Richardson	9.1
Cal Ripken	27.8
Claude Ritchey	12.6
Mickey Rivers	6.4
Phil Rizzuto	12.6
Brooks Robinson	25.0
Frank Robinson	71.2
Jackie Robinson	32.0
John Romano	8.6
Pete Rose	20.3
Al Rosen	11.7
Edd Roush	15.2
Babe Ruth	107.9
Jimmy Ryan	17.7
Ryne Sandberg	26.8
Ron Santo	39.3
Hank Sauer	9.3
Wally Schang	17.4
Mike Schmidt	80.0
Red Schoendienst	11.4
Ossee Schreckengost	12.6
Mike Scioscia	11.0
Emmett Seery	6.1
Kip Selbach	15.4
George Selkirk	8.0
Andy Seminick	9.4
Joe Sewell	35.2
Socks Seybold	8.3
Cy Seymour	16.4
Orator Shaffer	12.7
Jimmy Sheckard	23.8
Norm Siebern	6.9
Roy Sievers	13.6
Al Simmons	29.0
Ted Simmons	18.7
Ken Singleton	19.5

Total Player Rating (alpha.)

George Sisler	25.8
Bill Skowron	6.3
Enos Slaughter	14.8
Roy Smalley	14.2
Reggie Smith	35.8
Pop Smith	6.7
Earl Smith	6.1
Elmer Smith	11.8
Red Smith	11.9
Lonnie Smith	11.3
Ozzie Smith	37.0
Duke Snider	24.4
Tris Speaker	86.4
Stan Spence	10.9
Chick Stahl	7.0
Eddie Stanky	18.8
Willie Stargell	28.2
Rusty Staub	29.5
Harry Steinfeldt	8.8
Jake Stenzel	7.0
Vern Stephens	14.8
Riggs Stephenson	10.9
Snuffy Stirnweiss	7.0
George Stone	12.7
John Stone	7.0
Harry Stovey	24.3
Darryl Strawberry	23.3
Jim Sundberg	8.0
Ezra Sutton	7.5
Ed Swartwood	11.6
Bill Sweeney	8.0
Lee Tannehill	10.1
Gene Tenace	14.1
Fred Tenney	21.1
Bill Terry	28.2
Roy Thomas	23.8
Hank Thompson	7.0
Jason Thompson	7.1
Sam Thompson	30.5
Dickie Thon	9.4
Andy Thornton	15.2
Mike Tiernan	15.1
Joe Tinker	23.7
John Titus	12.3
Earl Torgeson	8.4
Joe Torre	19.6
Alan Trammell	18.3
Cecil Travis	9.9
Pie Traynor	19.0
Tom Tresh	7.2
Arky Vaughan	38.5
Bobby Veach	14.0
Mickey Vernon	8.9
George VanHaltren	15.8
Andy VanSlyke	11.4
Honus Wagner	80.3
Dixie Walker	10.9
Bobby Wallace	38.9
Tim Wallach	10.9
Paul Waner	37.9
Monte Ward	8.6
Bob Watson	10.7
Pee Wee Reese	15.6
Al Weis	11.0
Curt Welch	11.4
Billy Werber	6.7
Vic Wertz	9.5
Wes Westrum	8.6
Zach Wheat	29.2
Lou Whitaker	14.3
Deacon White	10.9
Roy White	18.3
Bill White	7.2
Pinky Whitney	9.4
Ernie Whitt	8.3
Billy Williams	29.1
Cy Williams	11.6
Jimmy Williams	15.0
Ken Williams	18.2
Ted Williams	89.8
Ned Williamson	11.3
Bump Wills	8.3
Maury Wills	10.8
Art Wilson	8.0
Hack Wilson	15.9
Bobby Wine	6.7
Dave Winfield	36.8
Sam Wise	9.4
Jimmy Wolf	11.3
George Wood	8.1
Gene Woodling	8.2
Jim Wynn	30.8
Carl Yastrzemski	47.5
Rudy York	15.6
Ross Youngs	11.3
Robin Yount	36.3
Chief Zimmer	15.3
Heinie Zimmerman	9.8
Richie Zisk	13.1

Total Player Rating (by era)

1876-1892

1	Bid McPhee	41.1
2	Roger Connor	40.6
3	Dan Brouthers	40.5
4	Jack Glasscock	38.5
5	Cap Anson	33.4
6	Fred Dunlap	30.7
7	Sam Thompson	30.5
8	Pete Browning	29.0
9	Hardy Richardson	28.5
10	Buck Ewing	27.2
11	King Kelly	26.5
12	Harry Stovey	24.3
13	Fred Pfeffer	24.2
14	Charley Jones	20.8
15	Denny Lyons	20.5
16	George Gore	17.8
17	Jim O'Rourke	17.2
18	Paul Hines	16.8
19	Jocko Milligan	16.7
20	Billy Nash	16.3
21	Dave Orr	15.6
22	Henry Larkin	15.5
23	Tip O'Neill	13.7
24	Charlie Bennett	12.7
	Orator Shaffer	12.7

1893-1919

1	Nap Lajoie	92.2
2	Ty Cobb	90.6
3	Tris Speaker	86.4
4	Honus Wagner	80.3
5	Eddie Collins	70.6
6	George Davis	52.4
7	Bill Dahlen	52.1
8	Ed Delahanty	46.6
9	Bobby Wallace	38.9
10	Joe Jackson	37.2
11	Frank Baker	34.3
12	Fred Clarke	32.6
13	Jesse Burkett	32.0
14	Cupid Childs	31.3
15	Sam Crawford	30.7
16	Sherry Magee	30.3
17	Zach Wheat	29.2
18	Billy Hamilton	29.0
19	Hughie Jennings	28.6
20	Elmer Flick	28.4
21	Jimmy Collins	25.6
22	Heinie Groh	24.3
23	Jake Beckley	24.2
24	Joe Kelley	23.9
25	2 players tied	23.8

1920-1941

1	Babe Ruth	107.9
2	Rogers Hornsby	75.8
3	Mel Ott	60.8
4	Lou Gehrig	60.4
5	Jimmie Foxx	54.3
6	Charlie Gehringer	42.7
7	Joe Cronin	38.8
8	Arky Vaughan	38.5
9	Paul Waner	37.9
10	Frankie Frisch	37.7
11	Gabby Hartnett	36.6
	Bob Johnson	36.6
13	Luke Appling	36.2
14	Joe Sewell	35.2
15	Bill Dickey	34.2
16	Billy Herman	32.2
17	Mickey Cochrane	31.9
18	Dave Bancroft	31.5
19	Harry Heilmann	31.0
20	Hank Greenberg	29.5
21	Al Simmons	29.0
22	Bill Terry	28.2
23	Max Carey	27.0
	Goose Goslin	27.0
	Joe Medwick	27.0

Total Player Rating (by era)

1942-1960

1	Ted Williams	89.8
2	Stan Musial	74.9
3	Mickey Mantle	66.2
4	Eddie Mathews	47.3
5	Joe DiMaggio	44.2
6	Bobby Doerr	37.8
7	Johnny Mize	37.5
8	Lou Boudreau	35.4
9	Yogi Berra	33.3
10	Jackie Robinson	32.0
11	Ralph Kiner	27.7
12	Richie Ashburn	26.5
13	Joe Gordon	26.0
14	Duke Snider	24.4
15	Minnie Minoso	23.6
16	Charlie Keller	22.8
17	Ferris Fain	19.6
18	Roy Campanella	19.4
19	Eddie Stanky	18.8
20	Roy Cullenbine	18.4
21	Bob Elliott	18.2
22	Larry Doby	18.0
23	Bill Nicholson	16.5
24	3 players tied	15.6

1961-1990

1	Hank Aaron	89.6
2	Willie Mays	86.2
3	Mike Schmidt	80.0
4	Frank Robinson	71.2
5	Rickey Henderson	56.3
6	Joe Morgan	54.0
7	Carl Yastrzemski	47.5
8	Al Kaline	46.0
9	Roberto Clemente	44.4
10	George Brett	44.2
11	Reggie Jackson	42.9
12	Bobby Grich	41.2
13	Eddie Murray	39.5
14	Ron Santo	39.3
15	Willie McCovey	38.9
16	Keith Hernandez	37.7
	Tim Raines	37.7
18	Wade Boggs	37.4
19	Ozzie Smith	37.0
20	Dave Winfield	36.8
21	Robin Yount	36.3
22	Reggie Smith	35.8
23	Bill Mazeroski	35.4
24	Darrell Evans	34.7
25	Dick Allen	33.0

Wins

1	Cy Young	511
2	Walter Johnson	417
3	Pete Alexander	373
	Christy Mathewson	373
5	Warren Spahn	363
6	Kid Nichols	361
7	Jim Galvin	360
8	Tim Keefe	342
9	Steve Carlton	329
10	John Clarkson	328
11	Eddie Plank	326
12	Don Sutton	324
13	Phil Niekro	318
14	Gaylord Perry	314
15	Tom Seaver	311
16	Charley Radbourn	309
17	Mickey Welch	307
18	Nolan Ryan	302
19	Lefty Grove	300
	Early Wynn	300
21	Tommy John	288
22	Robin Roberts	286
23	Fergie Jenkins	284
	Tony Mullane	284
25	Jim Kaat	283
26	Bert Blyleven	279
27	Red Ruffing	273
28	Burleigh Grimes	270
29	Jim Palmer	268
30	Bob Feller	266
	Eppa Rixey	266
32	Jim McCormick	265
33	Gus Weyhing	264
34	Ted Lyons	260
35	Red Faber	254
36	Carl Hubbell	253
37	Bob Gibson	251
38	Vic Willis	249
39	Jack Quinn	247
40	Joe McGinnity	246
41	Jack Powell	245
	Amos Rusie	245
43	Juan Marichal	243
44	Herb Pennock	240
45	Mordecai Brown	239
46	Clark Griffith	237
	Waite Hoyt	237
48	Whitey Ford	236
49	Charlie Buffinton	233
50	Sam Jones	229
	Luis Tiant	229
	Will White	229
53	George Mullin	228
54	Jim Bunning	224
	Jim Hunter	224
56	Paul Derringer	223
	Mel Harder	223
58	Hooks Dauss	222
	Jerry Koosman	222
60	Joe Niekro	221
61	Jerry Reuss	220
62	Bob Caruthers	218
	Earl Whitehill	218
64	Freddie Fitzsimmons	217
	Mickey Lolich	217
66	Wilbur Cooper	216
67	Stan Coveleski	215
	Jim Perry	215
69	Rick Reuschel	214
70	Chief Bender	212
71	Bobo Newsom	211
	Billy Pierce	211
73	Jesse Haines	210
74	Vida Blue	209
	Don Drysdale	209
	Milt Pappas	209
77	Eddie Cicotte	208
78	Bob Lemon	207
	Carl Mays	207
	Hal Newhouser	207
	Frank Tanana	207
82	Silver King	204
	Al Orth	204
84	Lew Burdette	203
	Jack Stivetts	203
86	Rube Marquard	201
	Charlie Root	201
88	George Uhle	200
89	Jack Chesbro	199
90	Jack Morris	198
	Bucky Walters	198
92	Larry French	197
	Bob Friend	197
	Jesse Tannehill	197
	Adonis Terry	197
	Dazzy Vance	197
97	Claude Osteen	196
	Bob Shawkey	196
99	Joe Bush	195
	Ed Walsh	195

Losses

1	Cy Young	316
2	Jim Galvin	308
3	Walter Johnson	279
4	Phil Niekro	274
5	Nolan Ryan	272
6	Gaylord Perry	265
7	Don Sutton	256
8	Jack Powell	254
9	Eppa Rixey	251
10	Robin Roberts	245
	Warren Spahn	245
12	Steve Carlton	244
	Early Wynn	244
14	Bert Blyleven	238
15	Jim Kaat	237
16	Gus Weyhing	232
17	Tommy John	231
18	Bob Friend	230
	Ted Lyons	230
20	Fergie Jenkins	226
21	Tim Keefe	225
	Red Ruffing	225
23	Bobo Newsom	222
24	Tony Mullane	220
25	Jack Quinn	218
26	Sam Jones	217
27	Jim McCormick	214
28	Red Faber	213
29	Paul Derringer	212
	Chick Fraser	212
	Burleigh Grimes	212
32	Mickey Welch	210
33	Jerry Koosman	209
34	Pete Alexander	208
	Kid Nichols	208
36	Tom Seaver	205
	Vic Willis	205
38	Joe Niekro	204
	Jim Whitney	204
40	George Mullin	196
	Frank Tanana	196
	Adonis Terry	196
43	Claude Osteen	195
	Charley Radbourn	195
45	Eddie Plank	194
46	Mickey Lolich	191
	Jerry Reuss	191
	Tom Zachary	191
49	Al Orth	189
	Rick Reuschel	189
51	Christy Mathewson	188
52	Mel Harder	186
53	Earl Whitehill	185
54	Jim Bunning	184
55	Joe Bush	183
	Larry Jackson	183
	Curt Simmons	183
58	Hooks Dauss	182
	Waite Hoyt	182
60	Murry Dickson	181
	Dutch Leonard	181
	Rick Wise	181
63	Lee Meadows	180
64	Pink Hawley	179
	Dolf Luque	179
66	John Clarkson	178
	Wilbur Cooper	178
68	Bill Dinneen	177
	Rube Marquard	177
70	Red Donahue	175
	Tom Hughes	175
72	Doyle Alexander	174
	Bob Gibson	174
	Jim Perry	174
	Amos Rusie	174
76	Luis Tiant	172
77	Larry French	171
78	Ted Breitenstein	170
	Camilo Pascual	170
80	Charlie Hough	169
	Billy Pierce	169
82	Red Ames	167
	Bert Cunningham	167
	Red Ehret	167
85	Don Drysdale	166
	Howard Ehmke	166
	Jim Hunter	166
	George Uhle	166
	Will White	166
90	Mark Baldwin	165
	Bump Hadley	165
	Si Johnson	165
93	Milt Gaston	164
	Win Mercer	164
	Milt Pappas	164
96	Bill Hutchinson	163
97	Jim Clancy	162
	Bob Feller	162
	Herb Pennock	162
100	2 players tied	161

Winning Percentage

1	Dwight Gooden	.721
2	Roger Clemens	.695
3	Dave Foutz	.690
4	Whitey Ford	.690
5	Bob Caruthers	.688
6	Lefty Grove	.680
7	Vic Raschi	.667
8	Larry Corcoran	.665
9	Christy Mathewson	.665
10	Sam Leever	.660
11	Sal Maglie	.657
12	Sandy Koufax	.655
13	Johnny Allen	.654
14	Ron Guidry	.651
15	Lefty Gomez	.649
16	John Clarkson	.648
17	Mordecai Brown	.648
18	Dizzy Dean	.644
19	Pete Alexander	.642
20	Jim Palmer	.638
21	Kid Nichols	.634
22	Deacon Phillippe	.634
23	Joe McGinnity	.634
24	Ed Reulbach	.632
25	Juan Marichal	.631
26	Mort Cooper	.631
27	Allie Reynolds	.630
28	Jesse Tannehill	.629
29	Ray Kremer	.627
30	Firpo Marberry	.627
31	Eddie Plank	.627
32	Tommy Bond	.627
33	Chief Bender	.625
34	Don Newcombe	.623
35	Nig Cuppy	.623
36	Addie Joss	.623
37	Fred Goldsmith	.622
38	Doc Crandall	.622
39	Carl Hubbell	.622
	Carl Mays	.622
41	Bob Feller	.621
42	Mel Parnell	.621
43	John Tudor	.619
44	Clark Griffith	.619
45	Bob Lemon	.618
46	Cy Young	.618
47	Bob Welch	.618
48	Monte Ward	.617
49	Urban Shocker	.615
50	Jeff Tesreau	.615
51	Jim Maloney	.615
52	Lon Warneke	.613
53	Charley Radbourn	.613
54	Gary Nolan	.611
55	Schoolboy Rowe	.610
56	Carl Erskine	.610
57	Ed Walsh	.607
58	Charlie Ferguson	.607
59	Dave McNally	.607
60	Hooks Wiltse	.607
61	John Candelaria	.606
62	Jack Stivetts	.606
63	Art Nehf	.605
64	Charlie Buffinton	.605
65	Orval Overall	.603
66	Tim Keefe	.603
67	Tom Seaver	.603
68	Stan Coveleski	.602
69	Preacher Roe	.602
70	Wes Ferrell	.601
71	Jack Chesbro	.601
72	J.R. Richard	.601
73	Walter Johnson	.599
74	Freddie Fitzsimmons	.598
75	Eddie Lopat	.597
76	Warren Spahn	.597
77	Herb Pennock	.597
78	Rip Sewell	.596
79	Ron Darling	.595
80	Mike Garcia	.594
81	Mickey Welch	.594
82	Pat Malone	.593
83	General Crowder	.592
84	Dave Stewart	.591
85	Harry Brecheen	.591
86	Jack Coombs	.591
87	Jim Bagby	.591
88	Bob Gibson	.591
89	Dutch Ruether	.591
90	Denny McLain	.590
91	Eddie Rommel	.590
92	Tiny Bonham	.589
93	Mike Cuellar	.587
94	Bill Bernhard	.586
95	Jeff Pfeffer	.585
96	Ed Stein	.585
97	Lew Burdette	.585
98	Amos Rusie	.585
99	Dazzy Vance	.585
100	Tommy Bridges	.584

Games

1	Hoyt Wilhelm	1070
2	Kent Tekulve	1050
3	Lindy McDaniel	987
4	Rollie Fingers	944
5	Gene Garber	931
6	Cy Young	906
7	Sparky Lyle	899
8	Jim Kaat	898
9	Don McMahon	874
10	Phil Niekro	864
11	Rich Gossage	853
12	Roy Face	848
13	Tug McGraw	824
14	Walter Johnson	802
15	Gaylord Perry	777
16	Don Sutton	774
17	Darold Knowles	765
18	Tommy John	760
19	Jack Quinn	756
20	Ron Reed	751
21	Warren Spahn	750
22	Tom Burgmeier	745
	Charlie Hough	745
	Gary Lavelle	745
25	Willie Hernandez	744
26	Steve Carlton	741
27	Nolan Ryan	740
28	Ron Perranoski	737
29	Ron Kline	736
30	Clay Carroll	731
31	Mike Marshall	723
32	Johnny Klippstein	711
33	Greg Minton	710
34	Stu Miller	704
35	Joe Niekro	702
36	Bill Campbell	700
37	Jim Galvin	697
38	Pete Alexander	696
39	Bob Miller	694
	Jeff Reardon	694
41	Grant Jackson	692
	Eppa Rixey	692
43	Early Wynn	691
44	Eddie Fisher	690
45	Ted Abernathy	681
46	Robin Roberts	676
47	Waite Hoyt	674
	Dan Quisenberry	674
49	Red Faber	669
50	Dave Giusti	668
51	Bert Blyleven	667
52	Fergie Jenkins	664
53	Bruce Sutter	661
54	Tom Seaver	656
55	Paul Lindblad	655
56	Wilbur Wood	651
57	Lee Smith	650
58	Sam Jones	647
	Dave LaRoche	647
60	Dutch Leonard	640
	Gerry Staley	640
62	Diego Segui	639
63	Bob Stanley	637
64	Christy Mathewson	635
65	Charlie Root	632
66	Jim Perry	630
67	Jerry Reuss	628
68	Lew Burdette	626
69	Murry Dickson	625
	Woodie Fryman	625
71	Red Ruffing	624
72	Eddie Plank	623
73	Kid Nichols	620
	Dick Tidrow	620
75	Herb Pennock	617
76	Burleigh Grimes	616
	Lefty Grove	616
78	Terry Forster	614
79	Jerry Koosman	612
80	Dennis Eckersley	604
81	Bob Friend	602
	Al Worthington	602
83	Elias Sosa	601
84	Tim Keefe	600
	Bobo Newsom	600
86	Ted Lyons	594
87	Pedro Borbon	593
88	Jim Bunning	591
89	Turk Farrell	590
90	Moe Drabowsky	589
91	Mickey Lolich	586
92	Billy Pierce	585
93	Doug Bair	584
	Jim Brewer	584
95	Mel Harder	582
	Pedro Ramos	582
97	Paul Derringer	579
98	Jack Powell	578
99	Bob Locker	576
100	Stan Bahnsen	574

Games Started

1	Cy Young	815
2	Don Sutton	756
3	Phil Niekro	716
4	Steve Carlton	709
5	Nolan Ryan	706
6	Tommy John	700
7	Gaylord Perry	690
8	Jim Galvin	682
9	Walter Johnson	665
	Warren Spahn	665
11	Bert Blyleven	661
12	Tom Seaver	647
13	Jim Kaat	625
14	Early Wynn	612
15	Robin Roberts	609
16	Pete Alexander	598
17	Fergie Jenkins	594
	Tim Keefe	594
19	Kid Nichols	561
20	Eppa Rixey	552
21	Christy Mathewson	551
22	Mickey Welch	549
23	Jerry Reuss	547
24	Red Ruffing	536
25	Eddie Plank	529
26	Rick Reuschel	528
27	Jerry Koosman	527
28	Jim Palmer	521
29	Frank Tanana	520
30	Jim Bunning	519
31	John Clarkson	518
32	Jack Powell	516
33	Tony Mullane	504
34	Charley Radbourn	503
	Gus Weyhing	503
36	Joe Niekro	500
37	Bob Friend	497
38	Mickey Lolich	496
39	Burleigh Grimes	495
40	Claude Osteen	488
41	Sam Jones	487
42	Jim McCormick	485
43	Bob Feller	484
	Ted Lyons	484
	Luis Tiant	484
46	Red Faber	483
	Bobo Newsom	483
48	Bob Gibson	482
49	Jim Hunter	476
50	Vida Blue	473
	Earl Whitehill	473
52	Vic Willis	471
53	Don Drysdale	465
	Milt Pappas	465
55	Doyle Alexander	464
56	Curt Simmons	461
57	Mike Torrez	458
58	Lefty Grove	457
	Juan Marichal	457
60	Rick Wise	455
61	Jim Perry	447
62	Paul Derringer	445
63	Jack Quinn	444
64	Whitey Ford	438
65	Mel Harder	433
66	Billy Pierce	432
67	Carl Hubbell	431
68	Larry Jackson	429
69	George Mullin	428
70	Amos Rusie	427
71	Freddie Fitzsimmons	426
72	Waite Hoyt	423
73	Bob Forsch	422
74	Herb Pennock	420
75	Bob Knepper	413
76	Ken Holtzman	410
77	Tom Zachary	409
78	Wilbur Cooper	408
	Jack Morris	408
80	Adonis Terry	406
81	Lee Meadows	404
	Camilo Pascual	404
83	Mike Flanagan	403
	Rube Marquard	403
85	Will White	401
86	Bucky Walters	398
87	Charlie Buffinton	396
	Dave McNally	396
	Jim Whitney	396
90	Al Orth	394
91	Steve Rogers	393
92	Paul Splittorff	392
93	Chick Fraser	389
94	Hooks Dauss	388
	Jesse Haines	388
96	Stan Coveleski	385
97	Larry French	384
98	Dave Stieb	382
99	Jim Clancy	381
	Joe McGinnity	381

Games Started (by era)

1876-1892

1	Jim Galvin	682
2	Tim Keefe	594
3	Mickey Welch	549
4	John Clarkson	518
5	Tony Mullane	504
6	Charley Radbourn	503
	Gus Weyhing	503
8	Jim McCormick	485
9	Adonis Terry	406
10	Will White	401
11	Charlie Buffinton	396
	Jim Whitney	396
13	Silver King	371
14	Bill Hutchinson	347
15	Jack Stivetts	333

1893-1919

1	Cy Young	815
2	Walter Johnson	665
3	Pete Alexander	598
4	Kid Nichols	561
5	Christy Mathewson	551
6	Eddie Plank	529
7	Jack Powell	516
8	Vic Willis	471
9	George Mullin	428
10	Amos Rusie	427
11	Rube Marquard	403
12	Al Orth	394
13	Chick Fraser	389
14	Hooks Dauss	388
15	Joe McGinnity	381

1920-1941

1	Eppa Rixey	552
2	Red Ruffing	536
3	Burleigh Grimes	495
4	Sam Jones	487
5	Ted Lyons	484
6	Red Faber	483
	Bobo Newsom	483
8	Earl Whitehill	473
9	Lefty Grove	457
10	Paul Derringer	445
11	Jack Quinn	444
12	Mel Harder	433
13	Carl Hubbell	431
14	Freddie Fitzsimmons	426
15	Waite Hoyt	423

1942-1960

1	Warren Spahn	665
2	Early Wynn	612
3	Robin Roberts	609
4	Bob Friend	497
5	Bob Feller	484
6	Curt Simmons	461
7	Whitey Ford	438
8	Billy Pierce	432
9	Dutch Leonard	375
10	Hal Newhouser	374
11	Lew Burdette	373
12	Bob Buhl	369
13	Vern Law	364
14	Bob Lemon	350

1961-1990

1	Don Sutton	756
2	Phil Niekro	716
3	Steve Carlton	709
4	Nolan Ryan	706
5	Tommy John	700
6	Gaylord Perry	690
7	Bert Blyleven	661
8	Tom Seaver	647
9	Jim Kaat	625
10	Fergie Jenkins	594
11	Jerry Reuss	547
12	Rick Reuschel	528
13	Jerry Koosman	527
14	Jim Palmer	521
15	Frank Tanana	520

Complete Games

1	Cy Young	749
2	Jim Galvin	639
3	Tim Keefe	554
4	Walter Johnson	531
	Kid Nichols	531
6	Mickey Welch	525
7	Charley Radbourn	489
8	John Clarkson	485
9	Tony Mullane	468
10	Jim McCormick	466
11	Gus Weyhing	448
12	Pete Alexander	438
13	Christy Mathewson	434
14	Jack Powell	422
15	Eddie Plank	410
16	Will White	394
17	Amos Rusie	392
18	Vic Willis	388
19	Warren Spahn	382
20	Jim Whitney	377
21	Adonis Terry	367
22	Ted Lyons	356
23	George Mullin	353
24	Charlie Buffinton	351
25	Chick Fraser	342
26	Clark Griffith	337
27	Red Ruffing	335
28	Silver King	329
29	Al Orth	324
30	Bill Hutchinson	321
31	Burleigh Grimes	314
	Joe McGinnity	314
33	Red Donahue	313
34	Guy Hecker	310
35	Bill Dinneen	306
36	Robin Roberts	305
37	Gaylord Perry	303
38	Ted Breitenstein	300
39	Bob Caruthers	298
	Lefty Grove	298
41	Pink Hawley	297
	Ed Morris	297
43	Mark Baldwin	296
44	Tommy Bond	295
45	Brickyard Kennedy	293
46	Eppa Rixey	290
	Early Wynn	290
48	Bill Donovan	289
	Bobby Mathews	289
50	Bert Cunningham	286
51	Wilbur Cooper	279
	Bob Feller	279
	Sadie McMahon	279
54	Jack Stivetts	278
	Jack Taylor	278
56	Charlie Getzien	277
57	Red Faber	273
58	Mordecai Brown	271
59	Frank Dwyer	270
	Jouett Meekin	270
61	Fergie Jenkins	267
62	Elton Chamberlain	264
	Matt Kilroy	264
64	Jesse Tannehill	263
65	Doc White	262
66	Jack Chesbro	261
	Rube Waddell	261
68	Red Ehret	260
	Carl Hubbell	260
70	Larry Corcoran	256
71	Chief Bender	255
	Bob Gibson	255
73	Steve Carlton	254
74	Frank Killen	253
75	Win Mercer	252
76	Paul Derringer	251
77	Sam Jones	250
	Ed Walsh	250
79	Eddie Cicotte	249
	Stump Weidman	249
81	Herb Pennock	247
82	Bobo Newsom	246
83	George Bradley	245
	Hooks Dauss	245
	Phil Niekro	245
86	Harry Howell	244
	Juan Marichal	244
	Monte Ward	244
89	Jack Quinn	243
90	Deacon Phillippe	242
	Bucky Walters	242
92	Bert Blyleven	241
	Sam Leever	241
94	Kid Gleason	240
95	Addie Joss	234
96	George Uhle	232
97	Carl Mays	231
	Tom Seaver	231
	Harry Staley	231
100	Earl Moore	230

Complete Games (by era)

1876-1892

1	Jim Galvin	639
2	Tim Keefe	554
3	Mickey Welch	525
4	Charley Radbourn	489
5	John Clarkson	485
6	Tony Mullane	468
7	Jim McCormick	466
8	Gus Weyhing	448
9	Will White	394
10	Jim Whitney	377
11	Adonis Terry	367
12	Charlie Buffinton	351
13	Silver King	329
14	Bill Hutchinson	321
15	Guy Hecker	310

1893-1919

1	Cy Young	749
2	Walter Johnson	531
	Kid Nichols	531
4	Pete Alexander	438
5	Christy Mathewson	434
6	Jack Powell	422
7	Eddie Plank	410
8	Amos Rusie	392
9	Vic Willis	388
10	George Mullin	353
11	Chick Fraser	342
12	Clark Griffith	337
13	Al Orth	324
14	Joe McGinnity	314
15	Red Donahue	313

1920-1941

1	Ted Lyons	356
2	Red Ruffing	335
3	Burleigh Grimes	314
4	Lefty Grove	298
5	Eppa Rixey	290
6	Wilbur Cooper	279
7	Red Faber	273
8	Carl Hubbell	260
9	Paul Derringer	251
10	Sam Jones	250
11	Herb Pennock	247
12	Bobo Newsom	246
13	Jack Quinn	243
14	Bucky Walters	242
15	George Uhle	232

1942-1960

1	Warren Spahn	382
2	Robin Roberts	305
3	Early Wynn	290
4	Bob Feller	279
5	Hal Newhouser	212
6	Billy Pierce	193
7	Dutch Leonard	192
8	Bob Lemon	188
9	Eddie Lopat	164
10	Bob Friend	163
	Curt Simmons	163
12	Lew Burdette	158
	Dizzy Trout	158
14	Whitey Ford	156
	Jim Tobin	156

1961-1990

1	Gaylord Perry	303
2	Fergie Jenkins	267
3	Bob Gibson	255
4	Steve Carlton	254
5	Phil Niekro	245
6	Juan Marichal	244
7	Bert Blyleven	241
8	Tom Seaver	231
9	Nolan Ryan	218
10	Jim Palmer	211
11	Mickey Lolich	195
12	Luis Tiant	187
13	Jim Hunter	181
14	Jim Kaat	180
15	Don Sutton	178

Shutouts

1	Walter Johnson	110
2	Pete Alexander	90
3	Christy Mathewson	79
4	Cy Young	76
5	Eddie Plank	69
6	Warren Spahn	63
7	Tom Seaver	61
8	Bert Blyleven	60
9	Nolan Ryan	59
10	Don Sutton	58
11	Ed Walsh	57
12	Jim Galvin	56
	Bob Gibson	56
14	Mordecai Brown	55
	Steve Carlton	55
16	Jim Palmer	53
	Gaylord Perry	53
18	Juan Marichal	52
19	Rube Waddell	50
	Vic Willis	50
21	Don Drysdale	49
	Fergie Jenkins	49
	Luis Tiant	49
	Early Wynn	49
25	Kid Nichols	48
26	Tommy John	46
	Jack Powell	46
28	Whitey Ford	45
	Addie Joss	45
	Phil Niekro	45
	Robin Roberts	45
	Red Ruffing	45
	Doc White	45
34	Babe Adams	44
	Bob Feller	44
36	Milt Pappas	43
37	Jim Hunter	42
	Bucky Walters	42
39	Mickey Lolich	41
	Hippo Vaughn	41
	Mickey Welch	41
42	Chief Bender	40
	Jim Bunning	40
	Larry French	40
	Sandy Koufax	40
	Claude Osteen	40
	Ed Reulbach	40
	Mel Stottlemyre	40
49	Tim Keefe	39
	Sam Leever	39
	Jerry Reuss	39
52	Stan Coveleski	38
	Billy Pierce	38
	Nap Rucker	38
55	Vida Blue	37
	John Clarkson	37
	Larry Jackson	37
	Eppa Rixey	37
	Steve Rogers	37
60	Tommy Bond	36
	Mike Cuellar	36
	Bob Friend	36
	Carl Hubbell	36
	Sam Jones	36
	Camilo Pascual	36
	Allie Reynolds	36
	Curt Simmons	36
	Will White	36
69	Joe Bush	35
	Jack Chesbro	35
	Eddie Cicotte	35
	Jack Coombs	35
	Wilbur Cooper	35
	Bill Donovan	35
	Burleigh Grimes	35
	Lefty Grove	35
	George Mullin	35
	Herb Pennock	35
	Charley Radbourn	35
80	Bill Doak	34
	Earl Moore	34
	Jesse Tannehill	34
83	Tommy Bridges	33
	Lew Burdette	33
	Dean Chance	33
	Mort Cooper	33
	Jerry Koosman	33
	Lefty Leifield	33
	Dutch Leonard	33
	Jim McCormick	33
	Dave McNally	33
	Hal Newhouser	33
	Bob Shawkey	33
	Virgil Trucks	33
95	Paul Derringer	32
	Joe McGinnity	32
	Jim Perry	32
	Frank Tanana	32
99	6 players tied	31

Saves

1	Rollie Fingers	341
2	Rich Gossage	307
3	Bruce Sutter	300
4	Jeff Reardon	287
5	Lee Smith	265
6	Dan Quisenberry	244
7	Sparky Lyle	238
8	Hoyt Wilhelm	227
9	Dave Righetti	224
10	Gene Garber	218
11	Dave Smith	199
12	Roy Face	193
13	Mike Marshall	188
14	Kent Tekulve	184
15	Johnny Franco	181
16	Tug McGraw	180
17	Ron Perranoski	179
18	Steve Bedrosian	178
19	Lindy McDaniel	172
20	Tom Henke	154
	Stu Miller	154
22	Don McMahon	153
23	Greg Minton	150
24	Ted Abernathy	148
	Bobby Thigpen	148
26	Willie Hernandez	147
27	Dennis Eckersley	145
	Dave Giusti	145
29	Clay Carroll	143
	Darold Knowles	143
31	Gary Lavelle	136
32	Jay Howell	133
33	Jim Brewer	132
	Bob Stanley	132
35	Ron Davis	130
36	Terry Forster	127
37	Bill Campbell	126
	Dave LaRoche	126
	Todd Worrell	126
40	John Hiller	125
	Roger McDowell	125
42	Dan Plesac	124
43	Jack Aker	123
44	Dick Radatz	122
45	Doug Jones	121
	Jesse Orosco	121
47	Tippy Martinez	115
48	Frank Linzy	111
49	Al Worthington	110
50	Fred Gladding	109
51	Wayne Granger	108
	Ron Kline	108
53	Johnny Murphy	107
54	Bill Caudill	106
55	Ron Reed	103
	John Wyatt	103
57	Tom Burgmeier	102
	Ellis Kinder	102
59	Firpo Marberry	101
60	Joe Hoerner	99
61	Al Hrabosky	97
	Tom Niedenfuer	97
63	Tim Burke	96
	Clem Labine	96
	Randy Moffitt	96
66	Bob Locker	95
67	Aurelio Lopez	93
68	Tom Hume	92
	Phil Regan	92
70	Mark Davis	91
71	Bill Henry	90
72	Donnie Moore	89
73	Jim Kern	88
74	Randy Myers	87
75	Ken Sanders	86
	Cecil Upshaw	86
77	Joe Sambito	84
	Mitch Williams	84
79	Mark Clear	83
	Turk Farrell	83
	Claude Raymond	83
	Elias Sosa	83
83	Don Aase	82
	Larry Sherry	82
85	Doug Bair	81
	Eddie Fisher	81
87	Pedro Borbon	80
	Eddie Watt	80
89	Grant Jackson	79
90	Al Holland	78
	Mike Schooler	78
92	Craig Lefferts	77
93	Joe Page	76
	Tim Stoddard	76
95	Neil Allen	75
	Ed Farmer	75
97	Jim Konstanty	74
98	Bob James	73
	Turk Lown	73
100	Ron Taylor	72

Innings Pitched

1	Cy Young	7354.2
2	Jim Galvin	5941.1
3	Walter Johnson	5923.2
4	Phil Niekro	5404.1
5	Gaylord Perry	5350.1
6	Don Sutton	5282.1
7	Warren Spahn	5243.2
8	Steve Carlton	5217.1
9	Pete Alexander	5189.1
10	Tim Keefe	5061.1
11	Kid Nichols	5057.1
12	Nolan Ryan	4989.1
13	Bert Blyleven	4837.0
14	Mickey Welch	4802.0
15	Tom Seaver	4782.2
16	Christy Mathewson	4781.0
17	Tommy John	4710.1
18	Robin Roberts	4688.2
19	Early Wynn	4564.0
20	John Clarkson	4536.1
21	Charley Radbourn	4535.1
22	Tony Mullane	4531.1
23	Jim Kaat	4530.1
24	Fergie Jenkins	4500.2
25	Eddie Plank	4495.2
26	Eppa Rixey	4494.2
27	Jack Powell	4389.0
28	Red Ruffing	4344.0
29	Gus Weyhing	4324.1
30	Jim McCormick	4275.2
31	Burleigh Grimes	4179.2
32	Ted Lyons	4161.0
33	Red Faber	4086.2
34	Vic Willis	3996.0
35	Jim Palmer	3948.0
36	Lefty Grove	3940.2
37	Jack Quinn	3920.1
38	Bob Gibson	3884.1
39	Sam Jones	3883.0
40	Jerry Koosman	3839.1
41	Bob Feller	3827.0
42	Amos Rusie	3769.2
43	Waite Hoyt	3762.1
44	Jim Bunning	3760.1
45	Bobo Newsom	3759.1
46	George Mullin	3686.2
47	Jerry Reuss	3669.2
48	Paul Derringer	3645.0
49	Mickey Lolich	3638.1
50	Bob Friend	3611.0
51	Carl Hubbell	3590.1
52	Joe Niekro	3584.0
53	Frank Tanana	3581.2
54	Herb Pennock	3571.2
55	Earl Whitehill	3564.2
56	Will White	3542.2
57	Rick Reuschel	3537.2
58	Adonis Terry	3514.0
59	Juan Marichal	3507.1
60	Jim Whitney	3496.1
61	Luis Tiant	3486.1
62	Wilbur Cooper	3480.0
63	Claude Osteen	3460.1
64	Jim Hunter	3449.1
65	Joe McGinnity	3441.0
66	Don Drysdale	3432.0
67	Mel Harder	3426.1
68	Charlie Buffinton	3404.0
69	Hooks Dauss	3390.2
70	Clark Griffith	3385.2
71	Doyle Alexander	3367.2
72	Chick Fraser	3355.2
73	Al Orth	3354.2
74	Curt Simmons	3348.1
75	Vida Blue	3343.1
76	Rube Marquard	3306.2
	Billy Pierce	3306.2
78	Jim Perry	3285.2
79	Larry Jackson	3262.2
80	Freddie Fitzsimmons	3223.2
81	Eddie Cicotte	3223.1
82	Dolf Luque	3220.1
83	Dutch Leonard	3218.1
84	Jesse Haines	3208.2
85	Red Ames	3198.1
86	Charlie Root	3197.1
87	Silver King	3190.2
88	Milt Pappas	3186.0
89	Mordecai Brown	3172.1
90	Whitey Ford	3170.1
91	Lee Meadows	3160.2
92	Larry French	3152.0
93	Rick Wise	3127.0
94	Tom Zachary	3126.1
95	George Uhle	3119.2
96	Charlie Hough	3107.2
97	Bucky Walters	3104.2
98	Joe Bush	3087.1
99	Bill Hutchinson	3083.0
100	Stan Coveleski	3082.0

Innings Pitched (by era)

1876-1892

1	Jim Galvin	5941.1
2	Tim Keefe	5061.1
3	Mickey Welch	4802.0
4	John Clarkson	4536.1
5	Charley Radbourn	4535.1
6	Tony Mullane	4531.1
7	Gus Weyhing	4324.1
8	Jim McCormick	4275.2
9	Will White	3542.2
10	Adonis Terry	3514.0
11	Jim Whitney	3496.1
12	Charlie Buffinton	3404.0
13	Silver King	3190.2
14	Bill Hutchinson	3083.0
15	Guy Hecker	2906.0

1893-1919

1	Cy Young	7354.2
2	Walter Johnson	5923.2
3	Pete Alexander	5189.1
4	Kid Nichols	5057.1
5	Christy Mathewson	4781.0
6	Eddie Plank	4495.2
7	Jack Powell	4389.0
8	Vic Willis	3996.0
9	Amos Rusie	3769.2
10	George Mullin	3686.2
11	Joe McGinnity	3441.0
12	Hooks Dauss	3390.2
13	Clark Griffith	3385.2
14	Chick Fraser	3355.2
15	Al Orth	3354.2

1920-1941

1	Eppa Rixey	4494.2
2	Red Ruffing	4344.0
3	Burleigh Grimes	4179.2
4	Ted Lyons	4161.0
5	Red Faber	4086.2
6	Lefty Grove	3940.2
7	Jack Quinn	3920.1
8	Sam Jones	3883.0
9	Waite Hoyt	3762.1
10	Bobo Newsom	3759.1
11	Paul Derringer	3645.0
12	Carl Hubbell	3590.1
13	Herb Pennock	3571.2
14	Earl Whitehill	3564.2
15	Wilbur Cooper	3480.0

1942-1960

1	Warren Spahn	5243.2
2	Robin Roberts	4688.2
3	Early Wynn	4564.0
4	Bob Feller	3827.0
5	Bob Friend	3611.0
6	Curt Simmons	3348.1
7	Billy Pierce	3306.2
8	Dutch Leonard	3218.1
9	Whitey Ford	3170.1
10	Lew Burdette	3067.1
11	Murry Dickson	3052.1
12	Hal Newhouser	2993.0
13	Bob Lemon	2850.0
14	Dizzy Trout	2725.2
15	Virgil Trucks	2682.1

1961-1990

1	Phil Niekro	5404.1
2	Gaylord Perry	5350.1
3	Don Sutton	5282.1
4	Steve Carlton	5217.1
5	Nolan Ryan	4989.1
6	Bert Blyleven	4837.0
7	Tom Seaver	4782.2
8	Tommy John	4710.1
9	Jim Kaat	4530.1
10	Fergie Jenkins	4500.2
11	Jim Palmer	3948.0
12	Bob Gibson	3884.1
13	Jerry Koosman	3839.1
14	Jim Bunning	3760.1
15	Jerry Reuss	3669.2

Hits per Game

1	Nolan Ryan	6.55
2	Sandy Koufax	6.79
3	J.R. Richard	6.88
4	Andy Messersmith	6.94
5	Hoyt Wilhelm	7.01
6	Sam McDowell	7.03
7	Ed Walsh	7.12
8	Bob Turley	7.18
9	Orval Overall	7.22
10	Jeff Tesreau	7.24
11	Ed Reulbach	7.24
12	Mario Soto	7.25
13	Addie Joss	7.30
14	Rich Gossage	7.37
15	Jim Maloney	7.39
16	Tom Seaver	7.47
17	Rube Waddell	7.48
18	Walter Johnson	7.49
19	Dwight Gooden	7.57
20	Bob Gibson	7.60
21	Don Wilson	7.61
22	Roger Clemens	7.62
23	Charlie Hough	7.63
24	Jim Palmer	7.63
25	Larry Cheney	7.68
26	Mordecai Brown	7.68
27	Sam Jones	7.68
28	Bob Feller	7.69
29	Johnny Vander Meer	7.69
30	Jim Hunter	7.72
31	Al Downing	7.72
32	Jim Scott	7.73
33	Bobby Bolin	7.79
34	Stan Williams	7.79
35	Rollie Fingers	7.80
36	Dean Chance	7.81
37	Frank Smith	7.82
38	Tug McGraw	7.83
39	Barney Pelty	7.84
40	Whitey Ford	7.85
41	Denny McLain	7.85
42	Bob Veale	7.87
43	Dave Stieb	7.89
44	Chief Bender	7.89
45	George McQuillan	7.89
46	Jack Coombs	7.89
47	Moe Drabowsky	7.90
48	Vida Blue	7.91
49	Nap Rucker	7.92
50	Tim Keefe	7.92
51	Allie Reynolds	7.92
52	Eddie Plank	7.92
53	Luis Tiant	7.94
54	Christy Mathewson	7.94
55	Rudy May	7.94
56	Ray Culp	7.95
57	Bill Donovan	7.99
58	Howie Camnitz	7.99
59	Don Sutton	7.99
60	Juan Pizarro	7.99
61	Mark Langston	8.01
62	Gary Bell	8.01
63	Earl Moore	8.02
64	Sonny Siebert	8.03
65	Lefty Tyler	8.03
66	Hal Newhouser	8.04
67	Fernando Valenzuela	8.04
68	Claude Hendrix	8.06
69	Steve Carlton	8.06
70	Hooks Wiltse	8.06
71	Mike Scott	8.06
72	Willie Mitchell	8.07
73	Larry Corcoran	8.08
74	Amos Rusie	8.08
75	Bill Singer	8.08
76	Bob Lemon	8.08
77	Stu Miller	8.09
78	Don Drysdale	8.09
79	Gary Nolan	8.09
80	Eddie Cicotte	8.09
81	Juan Marichal	8.09
82	Virgil Trucks	8.11
83	Hippo Vaughn	8.11
84	Doc White	8.12
85	Blue Moon Odom	8.12
86	Kirby Higbe	8.13
87	Jim Shaw	8.13
88	Mike Cuellar	8.13
89	Billy Pierce	8.14
90	Bob Welch	8.14
91	Mort Cooper	8.15
92	Red Ames	8.15
93	Vic Willis	8.16
94	Ron Darling	8.17
95	Harry Brecheen	8.17
96	Earl Wilson	8.17
97	Jim Bibby	8.18
98	Eddie Fisher	8.18
99	Jack Morris	8.18
100	Steve Barber	8.19

Home Runs Allowed

1	Robin Roberts	505
2	Fergie Jenkins	484
3	Phil Niekro	482
4	Don Sutton	472
5	Warren Spahn	434
6	Steve Carlton	414
7	Bert Blyleven	413
8	Gaylord Perry	399
9	Jim Kaat	395
10	Tom Seaver	380
11	Jim Hunter	374
12	Jim Bunning	372
	Frank Tanana	372
14	Mickey Lolich	347
15	Luis Tiant	346
16	Early Wynn	338
17	Doyle Alexander	324
18	Jack Morris	321
19	Juan Marichal	320
20	Pedro Ramos	315
21	Jim Perry	308
22	Charlie Hough	306
23	Jim Palmer	303
24	Murry Dickson	302
	Tommy John	302
26	Milt Pappas	298
27	Nolan Ryan	295
28	Jim Grant	292
29	Dennis Eckersley	291
30	Jerry Koosman	290
31	Lew Burdette	289
32	Bob Friend	286
33	Billy Pierce	284
34	Floyd Bannister	283
35	Don Drysdale	280
36	Jim Slaton	277
37	Joe Niekro	276
38	Vern Law	268
39	Dennis Martinez	265
40	Vida Blue	263
41	Rick Wise	261
42	Larry Jackson	259
43	Bob Gibson	257
44	Camilo Pascual	256
45	Mike McCormick	255
	Curt Simmons	255
47	Red Ruffing	254
48	Don Newcombe	252
49	Ken Holtzman	249
	Claude Osteen	249
51	Steve Renko	248
52	Jerry Reuss	245
53	Mike Flanagan	242
	Denny McLain	242
	Johnny Podres	242
56	Harvey Haddix	240
	Ray Sadecki	240
58	John Candelaria	239
59	Bob Buhl	238
60	Jim Clancy	236
	Earl Wilson	236
62	Scott McGregor	235
63	Joe Coleman	234
64	Jim Lonborg	233
	Frank Viola	233
66	Dave McNally	230
67	Whitey Ford	228
	Bob Knepper	228
69	Carl Hubbell	227
70	Ron Guidry	226
71	Don Cardwell	225
72	Bob Feller	224
73	Stan Bahnsen	223
	Ted Lyons	223
	Mike Torrez	223
76	Mike Cuellar	222
77	Ray Burris	221
	Rick Reuschel	221
79	Mike Caldwell	218
	Ron Kline	218
81	Bob Forsch	216
	Ralph Terry	216
83	Ned Garver	213
84	Bill Monbouquette	211
85	Bruce Hurst	210
	Herm Wehmeier	210
87	Joe Nuxhall	209
	Marty Pattin	209
	Wilbur Wood	209
90	Gary Bell	206
	Bobo Newsom	206
92	Dave Stieb	205
93	Larry Gura	204
	Sandy Koufax	204
	Dan Petry	204
	Milt Wilcox	204
97	Johnny Klippstein	203
98	Ross Grimsley	202
	Dennis Leonard	202
100	Juan Pizarro	201

Home Runs Allowed (by era)

1876-1892

1	John Clarkson	161
2	Jack Stivetts	131
3	Jim Galvin	122
4	Gus Weyhing	120
5	Charley Radbourn	117
6	Mickey Welch	106
7	Bill Hutchinson	104
8	Tony Mullane	97
9	Charlie Getzien	95
10	Harry Staley	92
11	Charlie Buffinton	87
12	Jim McCormick	84
13	Mark Baldwin	82
14	Jim Whitney	79
15	Adonis Terry	76

1893-1919

1	Pete Alexander	164
2	Kid Nichols	156
3	Cy Young	138
4	Jack Powell	110
5	Frank Dwyer	109
6	Rube Marquard	107
7	Walter Johnson	97
8	Brickyard Kennedy	93
9	Christy Mathewson	91
10	Hooks Dauss	87
11	Ad Gumbert	81
12	Kid Carsey	80
13	Ted Breitenstein	79
14	Bill Dinneen	78
15	2 players tied	76

1920-1941

1	Red Ruffing	254
2	Carl Hubbell	227
3	Ted Lyons	223
4	Bobo Newsom	206
5	Earl Whitehill	192
6	Charlie Root	187
7	Freddie Fitzsimmons	186
8	Tommy Bridges	181
9	Lon Warneke	175
10	George Blaeholder	173
	Syl Johnson	173
12	Bump Hadley	167
13	Jesse Haines	165
14	Larry French	164
15	Rube Walberg	163

1942-1960

1	Robin Roberts	505
2	Warren Spahn	434
3	Early Wynn	338
4	Pedro Ramos	315
5	Murry Dickson	302
6	Lew Burdette	289
7	Bob Friend	286
8	Billy Pierce	284
9	Vern Law	268
10	Curt Simmons	255
11	Don Newcombe	252
12	Johnny Podres	242
13	Harvey Haddix	240
14	Bob Buhl	238
15	Whitey Ford	228

1961-1990

1	Fergie Jenkins	484
2	Phil Niekro	482
3	Don Sutton	472
4	Steve Carlton	414
5	Bert Blyleven	413
6	Gaylord Perry	399
7	Jim Kaat	395
8	Tom Seaver	380
9	Jim Hunter	374
10	Jim Bunning	372
	Frank Tanana	372
12	Mickey Lolich	347
13	Luis Tiant	346
14	Doyle Alexander	324
15	Jack Morris	321

Walks

1	Nolan Ryan	2614
2	Steve Carlton	1833
3	Phil Niekro	1809
4	Early Wynn	1775
5	Bob Feller	1764
6	Bobo Newsom	1732
7	Amos Rusie	1704
8	Gus Weyhing	1566
9	Red Ruffing	1541
10	Bump Hadley	1442
11	Warren Spahn	1434
12	Earl Whitehill	1431
13	Tony Mullane	1408
14	Sam Jones	1396
15	Tom Seaver	1390
16	Charlie Hough	1382
17	Gaylord Perry	1379
18	Mike Torrez	1371
19	Walter Johnson	1362
20	Don Sutton	1343
21	Bob Gibson	1336
22	Chick Fraser	1332
23	Sam McDowell	1312
24	Jim Palmer	1311
25	Mark Baldwin	1307
26	Adonis Terry	1298
27	Mickey Welch	1297
28	Burleigh Grimes	1295
29	Bert Blyleven	1293
30	Kid Nichols	1268
31	Joe Bush	1263
32	Joe Niekro	1262
33	Allie Reynolds	1261
34	Tommy John	1259
35	Bob Lemon	1251
36	Hal Newhouser	1249
37	George Mullin	1238
38	Tim Keefe	1224
39	Cy Young	1219
40	Red Faber	1213
41	Vic Willis	1212
42	Ted Breitenstein	1203
43	Brickyard Kennedy	1201
44	Jerry Koosman	1198
45	Tommy Bridges	1192
46	John Clarkson	1191
47	Lefty Grove	1187
48	Vida Blue	1185
49	Billy Pierce	1178
50	Jack Stivetts	1155
51	Johnny Vander Meer	1132
52	Bill Hutchinson	1129
53	Jerry Reuss	1127
54	Ted Lyons	1121
	Bucky Walters	1121
56	Mel Harder	1118
57	Earl Moore	1108
58	Bob Buhl	1105
59	Luis Tiant	1104
60	Mickey Lolich	1099
61	Lefty Gomez	1095
62	Virgil Trucks	1088
63	Whitey Ford	1086
	Jack Morris	1086
65	Jim Kaat	1083
66	Eppa Rixey	1082
67	Eddie Plank	1072
68	Camilo Pascual	1069
69	Bob Turley	1068
70	Hooks Dauss	1067
71	Elton Chamberlain	1065
72	Bert Cunningham	1064
73	Curt Simmons	1063
74	Bill Donovan	1059
75	Murry Dickson	1058
	Jouett Meekin	1058
77	Vern Kennedy	1049
78	Dizzy Trout	1046
79	Howard Ehmke	1042
80	Wes Ferrell	1040
81	Tommy Byrne	1037
82	Red Ames	1034
83	Frank Tanana	1032
84	Rube Walberg	1031
85	Jack Powell	1021
86	Bob Shawkey	1018
87	Steve Renko	1010
88	Jim Slaton	1004
89	Joe Coleman	1003
	Waite Hoyt	1003
91	Jim Bunning	1000
92	Jim Perry	998
93	Fergie Jenkins	997
94	Kirby Higbe	979
95	Doyle Alexander	978
	Johnny Klippstein	978
97	Pink Hawley	974
98	Silver King	970
99	George Uhle	966
100	Rudy May	958

Fewest Walks per Game

1876-1892

1	Tommy Bond	0.58
2	George Bradley	0.67
3	Terry Larkin	0.71
4	Monte Ward	0.92
5	Fred Goldsmith	0.96
6	Jim Whitney	1.06
7	Bobby Mathews	1.11
8	Jim Galvin	1.13
9	Will White	1.26
10	Jack Lynch	1.39
11	Guy Hecker	1.51
12	Lee Richmond	1.53
13	Jim McCormick	1.58
14	Jumbo McGinnis	1.65
15	Ed Morris	1.67

1893-1919

1	Deacon Phillippe	1.25
2	Babe Adams	1.29
3	Addie Joss	1.41
4	Cy Young	1.49
5	Jesse Tannehill	1.56
6	Christy Mathewson	1.59
7	Nick Altrock	1.62
8	Pete Alexander	1.65
9	Noodles Hahn	1.69
10	Dick Rudolph	1.77
11	Al Orth	1.77
12	Slim Sallee	1.83
13	Bill Bernhard	1.83
14	Ed Siever	1.86
15	Ed Walsh	1.87

1920-1941

1	Red Lucas	1.61
2	Pete Donohue	1.80
3	Jess Barnes	1.80
4	Carl Hubbell	1.82
5	Curt Davis	1.85
6	Paul Derringer	1.88
7	Bill Swift	1.93
8	Sherry Smith	1.93
9	Watty Clark	1.97
10	Jack Quinn	1.97
11	Syl Johnson	2.03
12	Dizzy Dean	2.10
13	Art Nehf	2.13
14	Sloppy Thurston	2.15
15	Eppa Rixey	2.17

1942-1960

1	Tiny Bonham	1.67
2	Robin Roberts	1.73
3	Lew Burdette	1.84
4	Ken Raffensberger	1.88
5	Vern Law	2.01
6	Don Newcombe	2.05
7	Dutch Leonard	2.06
8	Hal Brown	2.08
9	Larry Jansen	2.09
10	Bob Purkey	2.17
11	Dick Donovan	2.21
12	Bob Friend	2.23
13	Don Mossi	2.24
14	Preacher Roe	2.37
15	Eddie Lopat	2.40

1961-1990

1	Fritz Peterson	1.73
2	Juan Marichal	1.82
3	Fergie Jenkins	1.99
4	Jim Barr	2.04
5	John Candelaria	2.06
6	Lary Sorensen	2.08
7	Dennis Eckersley	2.11
8	Bill Monbouquette	2.12
9	Ken Johnson	2.14
10	Jim Kaat	2.15
11	Bryn Smith	2.17
12	Ralph Terry	2.17
13	Scott McGregor	2.18
14	Gary Nolan	2.22
15	Mike Caldwell	2.23

Strikeouts

1	Nolan Ryan	5308
2	Steve Carlton	4136
3	Tom Seaver	3640
4	Bert Blyleven	3631
5	Don Sutton	3574
6	Gaylord Perry	3534
7	Walter Johnson	3509
8	Phil Niekro	3342
9	Fergie Jenkins	3192
10	Bob Gibson	3117
11	Jim Bunning	2855
12	Mickey Lolich	2832
13	Cy Young	2800
14	Warren Spahn	2583
15	Bob Feller	2581
16	Jerry Koosman	2556
17	Tim Keefe	2527
18	Christy Mathewson	2502
19	Don Drysdale	2486
20	Jim Kaat	2461
21	Frank Tanana	2459
22	Sam McDowell	2453
23	Luis Tiant	2416
24	Sandy Koufax	2396
25	Robin Roberts	2357
26	Early Wynn	2334
27	Rube Waddell	2316
28	Juan Marichal	2303
29	Lefty Grove	2266
30	Eddie Plank	2246
31	Tommy John	2245
32	Jim Palmer	2212
33	Pete Alexander	2198
34	Vida Blue	2175
35	Camilo Pascual	2167
36	Bobo Newsom	2082
37	Dazzy Vance	2045
38	Jim Hunter	2012
39	Rick Reuschel	2011
40	Billy Pierce	1999
41	Charlie Hough	1988
42	Red Ruffing	1987
43	Jack Morris	1980
44	John Clarkson	1978
45	Whitey Ford	1956
46	Dennis Eckersley	1938
47	Amos Rusie	1934
48	Jerry Reuss	1907
49	Kid Nichols	1868
50	Mickey Welch	1850
51	Charley Radbourn	1830
52	Tony Mullane	1803
53	Jim Galvin	1799
54	Hal Newhouser	1796
55	Ron Guidry	1778
56	Rudy May	1760
57	Fernando Valenzuela	1759
58	Joe Niekro	1747
59	Ed Walsh	1736
60	Bob Friend	1734
61	Joe Coleman	1728
	Milt Pappas	1728
63	Bob Welch	1714
64	Chief Bender	1711
65	Larry Jackson	1709
66	Jim McCormick	1704
67	Bob Veale	1703
68	Red Ames	1702
69	Charlie Buffinton	1700
70	Curt Simmons	1697
71	Floyd Bannister	1677
	Carl Hubbell	1677
73	Tommy Bridges	1674
74	Gus Weyhing	1665
75	Vic Willis	1651
76	Rick Wise	1647
77	Al Downing	1639
78	Mike Cuellar	1632
79	Chris Short	1629
80	Andy Messersmith	1625
81	Jack Powell	1621
	Steve Rogers	1621
83	Ray Sadecki	1614
84	Claude Osteen	1612
85	Hoyt Wilhelm	1610
86	Jim Maloney	1605
87	Ken Holtzman	1601
88	John Candelaria	1595
89	Rube Marquard	1593
90	Woodie Fryman	1587
91	Jim Perry	1576
92	Harvey Haddix	1575
93	Jim Whitney	1571
94	Dave Stieb	1557
95	Bill Donovan	1552
	Adonis Terry	1552
97	Dean Chance	1534
	Virgil Trucks	1534
99	Doyle Alexander	1528
100	Juan Pizarro	1522

Strikeouts per Game

1	Nolan Ryan	9.57
2	Sandy Koufax	9.28
3	Sam McDowell	8.86
4	Roger Clemens	8.47
5	J.R. Richard	8.37
6	Dwight Gooden	8.22
7	Mark Langston	8.16
8	Bob Veale	7.96
9	Jim Maloney	7.81
10	Rich Gossage	7.59
11	Sam Jones	7.54
12	Mario Soto	7.53
13	Bob Gibson	7.22
14	Steve Carlton	7.13
15	Rube Waddell	7.04
16	Mickey Lolich	7.01
17	Rollie Fingers	6.87
18	Tom Seaver	6.85
19	Jim Bunning	6.83
20	Bert Blyleven	6.76
21	Fernando Valenzuela	6.74
22	Juan Pizarro	6.73
23	Bobby Bolin	6.71
24	Ron Guidry	6.69
25	Ray Culp	6.69
26	Stan Williams	6.66
27	Camilo Pascual	6.65
28	Bob Turley	6.65
29	Don Wilson	6.60
30	Tug McGraw	6.59
31	Denny Lemaster	6.57
32	Andy Messersmith	6.56
33	Don Drysdale	6.52
34	Al Downing	6.50
35	Toad Ramsey	6.49
36	Floyd Bannister	6.49
37	Ron Darling	6.46
38	Bruce Hurst	6.46
39	Diego Segui	6.46
40	Dean Chance	6.43
41	Hoyt Wilhelm	6.43
42	Mike Scott	6.40
43	Fergie Jenkins	6.38
44	Moe Drabowsky	6.37
45	Earl Wilson	6.37
46	Harvey Haddix	6.34
47	Sonny Siebert	6.32
48	Chris Short	6.31
49	Frank Viola	6.27
50	Bill Singer	6.27
51	Luis Tiant	6.24
52	Turk Farrell	6.21
53	Dazzy Vance	6.20
54	Dennis Eckersley	6.20
55	Stu Miller	6.18
56	Frank Tanana	6.18
57	Clay Kirby	6.17
58	Gary Bell	6.15
59	Gary Peters	6.14
60	Bob Welch	6.14
61	Denny McLain	6.12
62	Don Sutton	6.09
63	Mike Krukow	6.07
64	Bob Feller	6.07
65	Joe Coleman	6.05
66	Fred Norman	6.05
67	Rudy May	6.04
68	Jerry Koosman	5.99
69	Rick Sutcliffe	5.97
70	Scott Sanderson	5.96
71	Danny Darwin	5.95
72	Gaylord Perry	5.94
73	Woodie Fryman	5.92
74	Dave Stewart	5.92
75	Juan Marichal	5.91
76	Steve Barber	5.89
77	Mike Boddicker	5.89
78	John Montefusco	5.89
79	John Candelaria	5.87
80	Mike Witt	5.86
81	Jack Morris	5.86
82	Vida Blue	5.85
83	Joey Jay	5.81
84	Don Robinson	5.81
85	Ray Sadecki	5.81
86	Jim O'Toole	5.79
87	Dave Giusti	5.78
88	Jon Matlack	5.77
89	Larry Dierker	5.76
90	Charlie Hough	5.76
91	Lindy McDaniel	5.73
92	Tony Cloninger	5.70
93	Johnny Podres	5.70
94	Jim Bibby	5.64
95	Billy O'Dell	5.61
96	Mike Moore	5.60
97	Gene Garber	5.60
98	Gary Nolan	5.58
99	Phil Niekro	5.57
100	Billy Hoeft	5.55

Ratio

1	Addie Joss	8.7
2	Ed Walsh	9.1
3	Monte Ward	9.4
4	Christy Mathewson	9.6
5	Tommy Bond	9.8
	Mordecai Brown	9.8
7	George Bradley	9.9
	Larry Corcoran	9.9
	Walter Johnson	9.9
10	Babe Adams	10.0
	Sandy Koufax	10.0
	Juan Marichal	10.0
	Ed Morris	10.0
	Rube Waddell	10.0
	Will White	10.0
16	Charlie Ferguson	10.1
	Tim Keefe	10.1
	Terry Larkin	10.1
	Deacon Phillippe	10.1
20	Pete Alexander	10.2
	Chief Bender	10.2
	Jim McCormick	10.2
	Eddie Plank	10.2
	Tom Seaver	10.2
	Cy Young	10.2
26	Nick Altrock	10.3
	Noodles Hahn	10.3
	Jim Hunter	10.3
	Charley Radbourn	10.3
	Doc White	10.3
	Jim Whitney	10.3
32	Tiny Bonham	10.4
	Bob Caruthers	10.4
	Roger Clemens	10.4
	Fred Goldsmith	10.4
	Dwight Gooden	10.4
	Fergie Jenkins	10.4
	Jumbo McGinnis	10.4
	George McQuillan	10.4
	Gary Nolan	10.4
	Don Sutton	10.4
	Hoyt Wilhelm	10.4
	Hooks Wiltse	10.4
44	Jack Chesbro	10.5
	Eddie Cicotte	10.5
	Guy Hecker	10.5
	Sam Leever	10.5
	Andy Messersmith	10.5
	Barney Pelty	10.5
	Dick Rudolph	10.5
	Jeff Tesreau	10.5
	George Winter	10.5
53	Rollie Fingers	10.6
	Dave Foutz	10.6
	Carl Hubbell	10.6
	Denny McLain	10.6
	Robin Roberts	10.6
	Frank Smith	10.6
59	John Candelaria	10.7
	Don Drysdale	10.7
	Dennis Eckersley	10.7
	Jim Galvin	10.7
	Ron Guidry	10.7
	Orval Overall	10.7
	Jim Palmer	10.7
	Ed Reulbach	10.7
	Slim Sallee	10.7
68	Mike Cuellar	10.8
	Bob Ewing	10.8
	Gaylord Perry	10.8
	Nap Rucker	10.8
	Dupee Shaw	10.8
	Mario Soto	10.8
	Warren Spahn	10.8
	Jesse Tannehill	10.8
	Jack Taylor	10.8
	Ralph Terry	10.8
78	Harry Brecheen	10.9
	John Clarkson	10.9
	Phil Douglas	10.9
	Eddie Fisher	10.9
	Bob Gibson	10.9
	Claude Hendrix	10.9
	Joe McGinnity	10.9
	Fritz Peterson	10.9
	Jim Scott	10.9
	Mike Scott	10.9
	Luis Tiant	10.9
	Fred Toney	10.9
	John Tudor	10.9
	Carl Weilman	10.9
92	14 players tied	11.0

Earned Run Average

#	Player	ERA
1	Ed Walsh	1.82
2	Addie Joss	1.89
3	Mordecai Brown	2.06
4	Monte Ward	2.10
5	Christy Mathewson	2.13
6	Rube Waddell	2.16
7	Walter Johnson	2.17
8	Orval Overall	2.24
9	Tommy Bond	2.25
10	Ed Reulbach	2.28
	Will White	2.28
12	Jim Scott	2.30
13	Eddie Plank	2.35
14	Larry Corcoran	2.36
15	Eddie Cicotte	2.38
	Ed Killian	2.38
	George McQuillan	2.38
18	Doc White	2.39
19	Nap Rucker	2.42
20	Terry Larkin	2.43
	Jim McCormick	2.43
	Jeff Tesreau	2.43
23	Chief Bender	2.46
24	Sam Leever	2.47
	Lefty Leifield	2.47
	Hooks Wiltse	2.47
27	Bob Ewing	2.49
	Hippo Vaughn	2.49
29	George Bradley	2.50
30	Hoyt Wilhelm	2.52
31	Noodles Hahn	2.55
32	Pete Alexander	2.56
	Slim Sallee	2.56
34	Deacon Phillippe	2.59
	Frank Smith	2.59
36	Ed Siever	2.60
37	Bob Rhoads	2.61
38	Tim Keefe	2.62
39	Red Ames	2.63
	Barney Pelty	2.63
	Vic Willis	2.63
	Cy Young	2.63
43	Claude Hendrix	2.65
44	Joe McGinnity	2.66
	Dick Rudolph	2.66
	Jack Taylor	2.66
47	Nick Altrock	2.67
	Charlie Ferguson	2.67
	Charley Radbourn	2.67
	Carl Weilman	2.67
51	Jack Chesbro	2.68
	Cy Falkenberg	2.68
53	Bill Donovan	2.69
	Fred Toney	2.69
55	Larry Cheney	2.70
56	Mickey Welch	2.71
57	Fred Goldsmith	2.73
58	Harry Howell	2.74
59	Howie Camnitz	2.75
	Whitey Ford	2.75
	Dummy Taylor	2.75
62	Babe Adams	2.76
	Sandy Koufax	2.76
	Dutch Leonard	2.76
65	Jeff Pfeffer	2.77
66	Jack Coombs	2.78
	Earl Moore	2.78
68	Tully Sparks	2.79
	Jesse Tannehill	2.79
70	Phil Douglas	2.80
71	John Clarkson	2.81
72	Ray Fisher	2.82
	Dwight Gooden	2.82
	Ed Morris	2.82
	George Mullin	2.82
76	Bob Caruthers	2.83
77	Dave Foutz	2.84
78	Andy Messersmith	2.86
	Jim Palmer	2.86
	Tom Seaver	2.86
81	Jim Galvin	2.87
	George Winter	2.87
83	Willie Mitchell	2.88
84	Roger Clemens	2.89
	Wilbur Cooper	2.89
	Stan Coveleski	2.89
	Juan Marichal	2.89
88	Rollie Fingers	2.90
89	Bob Gibson	2.91
90	Harry Brecheen	2.92
	Dean Chance	2.92
	Doc Crandall	2.92
	Rich Gossage	2.92
	Guy Hecker	2.92
	Carl Mays	2.92
	Jumbo McGinnis	2.92
97	Dave Davenport	2.93
98	Don Drysdale	2.95
	Kid Nichols	2.95
	Lefty Tyler	2.95

Earned Run Average (by era)

1876-1892

#	Player	ERA
1	Monte Ward	2.10
2	Tommy Bond	2.25
3	Will White	2.28
4	Larry Corcoran	2.36
5	Terry Larkin	2.43
	Jim McCormick	2.43
7	George Bradley	2.50
8	Tim Keefe	2.62
9	Charlie Ferguson	2.67
	Charley Radbourn	2.67
11	Mickey Welch	2.71
12	Fred Goldsmith	2.73
13	John Clarkson	2.81
14	Ed Morris	2.82
15	Bob Caruthers	2.83

1893-1919

#	Player	ERA
1	Ed Walsh	1.82
2	Addie Joss	1.89
3	Mordecai Brown	2.06
4	Christy Mathewson	2.13
5	Rube Waddell	2.16
6	Walter Johnson	2.17
7	Orval Overall	2.24
8	Ed Reulbach	2.28
9	Jim Scott	2.30
10	Eddie Plank	2.35
11	Eddie Cicotte	2.38
	Ed Killian	2.38
	George McQuillan	2.38
14	Doc White	2.39
15	Nap Rucker	2.42

1920-1941

#	Player	ERA
1	Wilbur Cooper	2.89
	Stan Coveleski	2.89
3	Carl Mays	2.92
4	Carl Hubbell	2.98
5	Dizzy Dean	3.03
6	Lefty Grove	3.06
7	Bob Shawkey	3.09
8	Red Faber	3.15
	Eppa Rixey	3.15
10	Urban Shocker	3.17
11	Lon Warneke	3.18
12	Art Nehf	3.20
13	Jess Barnes	3.22
14	George Mogridge	3.23
15	2 players tied	3.24

1942-1960

#	Player	ERA
1	Hoyt Wilhelm	2.52
2	Whitey Ford	2.75
3	Harry Brecheen	2.92
4	Mort Cooper	2.97
5	Max Lanier	3.01
6	Tiny Bonham	3.06
	Hal Newhouser	3.06
8	Warren Spahn	3.09
9	Sal Maglie	3.15
10	Eddie Lopat	3.21
11	Bob Lemon	3.23
	Dizzy Trout	3.23
13	Stu Miller	3.24
14	Bob Feller	3.25
	Dutch Leonard	3.25

1961-1990

#	Player	ERA
1	Sandy Koufax	2.76
2	Dwight Gooden	2.82
3	Andy Messersmith	2.86
	Jim Palmer	2.86
	Tom Seaver	2.86
6	Roger Clemens	2.89
	Juan Marichal	2.89
8	Rollie Fingers	2.90
9	Bob Gibson	2.91
10	Dean Chance	2.92
	Rich Gossage	2.92
12	Don Drysdale	2.95
13	Mel Stottlemyre	2.97
14	Bob Veale	3.07
15	Gary Nolan	3.08

Adjusted Earned Run Average

#	Player	AdjERA
1	Lefty Grove	148
2	Roger Clemens	146
	Walter Johnson	146
	Hoyt Wilhelm	146
5	Ed Walsh	145
6	Addie Joss	142
7	Mordecai Brown	139
	Kid Nichols	139
9	Cy Young	138
10	Christy Mathewson	136
11	Pete Alexander	135
	Rube Waddell	135
13	John Clarkson	134
14	Harry Brecheen	133
	Whitey Ford	133
16	Noodles Hahn	132
17	Sandy Koufax	131
18	Dizzy Dean	130
	Carl Hubbell	130
	Hal Newhouser	130
	Amos Rusie	130
22	Stan Coveleski	128
	Rich Gossage	128
24	Nig Cuppy	127
	Bob Gibson	127
	Sal Maglie	127
	Tom Seaver	127
28	Tommy Bridges	126
29	Lefty Gomez	125
	Tim Keefe	125
	Max Lanier	125
	Jim Palmer	125
	Mel Parnell	125
	Dave Stieb	125
	Dazzy Vance	125
36	Dave Foutz	124
	Dwight Gooden	124
	Urban Shocker	124
	Dizzy Trout	124
	John Tudor	124
41	Bob Caruthers	123
	Eddie Cicotte	123
	Mort Cooper	123
	Sam Leever	123
	Orval Overall	123
	Ed Reulbach	123
47	Larry Corcoran	122
	Bob Feller	122
	Silver King	122
	Juan Marichal	122
	Eddie Plank	122
	Eddie Rommel	122
53	Don Drysdale	121
	Charlie Ferguson	121
	Clark Griffith	121
	Andy Messersmith	121
	Jack Stivetts	121
58	Tiny Bonham	120
	Joe McGinnity	120
	Deacon Phillippe	120
	Charley Radbourn	120
	Jim Scott	120
	Hippo Vaughn	120
	Will White	120
65	Bert Blyleven	119
	Dean Chance	119
	Red Faber	119
	Rollie Fingers	119
	Ron Guidry	119
	Thornton Lee	119
	Bob Lemon	119
	Dutch Leonard	119
	Carl Mays	119
	Billy Pierce	119
	Nap Rucker	119
	Bobby Shantz	119
	Lon Warneke	119
78	Babe Adams	118
	Ted Lyons	118
	Jim McCormick	118
	Sadie McMahon	118
	Warren Spahn	118
	Monte Ward	118
	Vic Willis	118
85	Wes Ferrell	117
	Mike Garcia	117
	Dolf Luque	117
	Tony Mullane	117
	Gaylord Perry	117
	Toad Ramsey	117
	Bob Stanley	117
	Virgil Trucks	117
93	16 players tied	116

Adjusted ERA (by era)

1876-1892

#	Player	AdjERA
1	John Clarkson	134
2	Tim Keefe	125
3	Dave Foutz	124
4	Bob Caruthers	123
5	Larry Corcoran	122
	Silver King	122
7	Charlie Ferguson	121
	Jack Stivetts	121
9	Charley Radbourn	120
	Will White	120
11	Jim McCormick	118
	Sadie McMahon	118
	Monte Ward	118
14	Tony Mullane	117
	Toad Ramsey	117

1893-1919

#	Player	AdjERA
1	Walter Johnson	146
2	Ed Walsh	145
3	Addie Joss	142
4	Mordecai Brown	139
	Kid Nichols	139
6	Cy Young	138
7	Christy Mathewson	136
8	Pete Alexander	135
	Rube Waddell	135
10	Noodles Hahn	132
11	Amos Rusie	130
12	Nig Cuppy	127
13	4 players tied	123

1920-1941

#	Player	AdjERA
1	Lefty Grove	148
2	Dizzy Dean	130
	Carl Hubbell	130
4	Stan Coveleski	128
5	Tommy Bridges	126
6	Lefty Gomez	125
	Dazzy Vance	125
8	Urban Shocker	124
9	Eddie Rommel	122
10	Red Faber	119
	Thornton Lee	119
	Carl Mays	119
	Lon Warneke	119
14	Ted Lyons	118
15	2 players tied	117

1942-1960

#	Player	AdjERA
1	Hoyt Wilhelm	146
2	Harry Brecheen	133
	Whitey Ford	133
4	Hal Newhouser	130
5	Sal Maglie	127
6	Max Lanier	125
	Mel Parnell	125
8	Dizzy Trout	124
9	Mort Cooper	123
10	Bob Feller	122
11	Tiny Bonham	120
12	Bob Lemon	119
	Dutch Leonard	119
	Billy Pierce	119
	Bobby Shantz	119

1961-1990

#	Player	AdjERA
1	Roger Clemens	146
2	Sandy Koufax	131
3	Rich Gossage	128
4	Bob Gibson	127
	Tom Seaver	127
6	Jim Palmer	125
	Dave Stieb	125
8	Dwight Gooden	124
	John Tudor	124
10	Juan Marichal	122
11	Don Drysdale	121
	Andy Messersmith	121
13	4 players tied	119

Pitching Runs

1	Cy Young	753
2	Walter Johnson	705
3	Lefty Grove	595
4	Kid Nichols	531
5	Pete Alexander	484
6	Warren Spahn	470
7	Christy Mathewson	420
8	Tom Seaver	419
9	Amos Rusie	416
10	Tim Keefe	402
11	Carl Hubbell	393
12	Whitey Ford	386
13	Bob Feller	385
14	Jim Palmer	374
15	John Clarkson	368
16	Lefty Gomez	322
17	Ted Lyons	313
18	Gaylord Perry	311
19	Ed Walsh	310
	Hoyt Wilhelm	310
21	Charley Radbourn	298
22	Mordecai Brown	295
23	Red Faber	294
24	Bob Gibson	290
25	Nolan Ryan	287
26	Bert Blyleven	283
27	Dazzy Vance	281
28	Red Ruffing	272
29	Dutch Leonard	267
	Eddie Plank	267
31	Don Drysdale	266
32	Robin Roberts	264
33	Juan Marichal	262
34	Stan Coveleski	259
	Don Sutton	259
36	Hal Newhouser	257
37	Tommy Bridges	256
38	Bob Lemon	251
39	Billy Pierce	250
	Eppa Rixey	250
41	Dolf Luque	245
	Tony Mullane	245
43	Sandy Koufax	243
44	Rube Waddell	241
45	Steve Carlton	236
46	Clark Griffith	233
47	Carl Mays	217
48	Addie Joss	216
49	Bob Caruthers	214
	Tommy John	214
51	Jim McCormick	213
	Mickey Welch	213
53	Waite Hoyt	210
	Urban Shocker	210
55	Dave Stieb	209
56	Silver King	207
57	Nig Cuppy	201
	Ron Guidry	201
59	Eddie Cicotte	200
	Roger Clemens	200
61	Will White	198
62	Harry Brecheen	194
63	Phil Niekro	192
64	Mel Harder	190
65	Lon Warneke	188
66	Eddie Lopat	186
	Joe McGinnity	186
68	Dizzy Dean	185
69	Jim Bunning	179
	Eddie Rommel	179
71	Larry French	178
	Ed Morris	178
73	Dizzy Trout	177
74	Spud Chandler	176
75	Sam Leever	175
76	Freddie Fitzsimmons	174
	Mike Garcia	174
78	Sadie McMahon	173
79	Andy Messersmith	172
	Vic Willis	172
81	Early Wynn	170
82	Thornton Lee	169
83	Wilbur Cooper	168
	Ed Reulbach	168
85	Bob Welch	164
86	Jack Quinn	162
87	Babe Adams	161
88	Charlie Buffinton	160
89	Noodles Hahn	159
90	Jim Galvin	157
	Fergie Jenkins	157
92	Orel Hershiser	156
	Sal Maglie	156
	Firpo Marberry	156
95	Guy Hecker	154
96	Deacon Phillippe	153
97	Vida Blue	152
	Bucky Walters	152
99	Bob Shawkey	151
100	2 players tied	150

Adjusted Pitching Runs

1	Cy Young	819
2	Walter Johnson	662
3	Kid Nichols	653
4	Lefty Grove	643
5	Pete Alexander	522
6	John Clarkson	477
7	Tom Seaver	411
8	Christy Mathewson	403
9	Amos Rusie	381
10	Tim Keefe	371
11	Carl Hubbell	355
12	Bob Gibson	335
13	Bert Blyleven	331
14	Warren Spahn	330
15	Whitey Ford	315
	Jim Palmer	315
17	Hal Newhouser	305
	Gaylord Perry	305
19	Ted Lyons	302
20	Bob Feller	301
21	Phil Niekro	299
22	Tommy Bridges	291
23	Hoyt Wilhelm	289
24	Mordecai Brown	283
25	Steve Carlton	277
26	Stan Coveleski	276
27	Red Faber	274
28	Ed Walsh	270
29	Tony Mullane	267
30	Clark Griffith	266
	Dazzy Vance	266
32	Charley Radbourn	265
33	Eddie Plank	264
34	Fergie Jenkins	254
35	Silver King	253
36	Eppa Rixey	248
	Rube Waddell	248
38	Juan Marichal	247
	Jack Stivetts	247
40	Dave Stieb	245
41	Nig Cuppy	239
	Robin Roberts	239
43	Dizzy Trout	232
44	Don Drysdale	230
45	Lefty Gomez	229
	Billy Pierce	229
47	Urban Shocker	226
48	Dutch Leonard	224
49	Roger Clemens	222
50	Sandy Koufax	221
51	Eddie Rommel	217
52	Jim McCormick	213
53	Vic Willis	208
54	Bob Caruthers	207
	Addie Joss	207
	Joe McGinnity	207
57	Harry Brecheen	205
58	Jack Quinn	204
59	Nolan Ryan	203
60	Dolf Luque	200
61	Dizzy Dean	198
62	Eddie Cicotte	195
	Wes Ferrell	195
64	Bob Lemon	193
	Mickey Welch	193
66	Jim Bunning	192
67	Carl Mays	189
68	Lon Warneke	188
69	Noodles Hahn	186
70	Rick Reuschel	185
71	Sadie McMahon	184
72	Mel Harder	182
73	Will White	181
74	Wilbur Cooper	180
75	Tommy John	179
76	Frank Dwyer	177
77	Red Ruffing	174
78	Waite Hoyt	173
	Luis Tiant	173
80	Dennis Eckersley	172
	Thornton Lee	172
82	Larry French	171
83	Mel Parnell	170
84	Sam Leever	169
85	Bucky Walters	168
86	Ron Guidry	167
	Virgil Trucks	167
88	Babe Adams	161
89	Sal Maglie	160
90	Charlie Buffinton	158
	Jim Galvin	158
92	Ed Reulbach	156
93	Larry Jackson	155
94	Steve Rogers	154
95	Hippo Vaughn	152
96	Deacon Phillippe	150
	Joe Wood	150
98	Spud Chandler	149
	Dave Foutz	149
100	Dan Quisenberry	148

Pitching Wins

1	Walter Johnson	73.1
2	Cy Young	70.8
3	Lefty Grove	55.5
4	Pete Alexander	49.7
5	Warren Spahn	47.4
6	Kid Nichols	47.1
7	Christy Mathewson	44.2
8	Tom Seaver	43.8
9	Whitey Ford	39.3
10	Jim Palmer	38.8
11	Carl Hubbell	38.7
12	Bob Feller	37.5
13	Tim Keefe	36.1
14	Amos Rusie	35.8
15	Ed Walsh	33.4
16	John Clarkson	32.8
17	Gaylord Perry	32.6
18	Hoyt Wilhelm	31.9
19	Mordecai Brown	31.4
20	Bob Gibson	30.5
21	Nolan Ryan	29.9
22	Lefty Gomez	29.9
23	Ted Lyons	29.4
24	Bert Blyleven	29.1
25	Red Faber	28.9
26	Eddie Plank	28.3
27	Don Drysdale	27.7
28	Juan Marichal	27.6
29	Dazzy Vance	27.0
30	Don Sutton	26.9
31	Robin Roberts	26.6
32	Charley Radbourn	26.5
33	Dutch Leonard	26.4
34	Hal Newhouser	26.0
35	Stan Coveleski	25.9
36	Red Ruffing	25.6
37	Rube Waddell	25.3
38	Sandy Koufax	25.1
39	Eppa Rixey	25.1
40	Billy Pierce	25.1
41	Bob Lemon	25.0
42	Steve Carlton	24.7
43	Tommy Bridges	24.1
44	Dolf Luque	23.9
45	Addie Joss	23.4
46	Tommy John	22.1
47	Carl Mays	22.0
48	Tony Mullane	21.5
49	Eddie Cicotte	21.4
50	Dave Stieb	20.9
51	Clark Griffith	20.8
52	Urban Shocker	20.5
53	Waite Hoyt	20.2
54	Ron Guidry	20.1
55	Phil Niekro	20.0
56	Roger Clemens	19.9
57	Harry Brecheen	19.6
58	Jim McCormick	19.5
59	Mickey Welch	19.4
60	Lon Warneke	18.9
61	Bob Caruthers	18.8
62	Eddie Lopat	18.8
63	Jim Bunning	18.6
64	Joe McGinnity	18.6
65	Dizzy Dean	18.4
66	Will White	18.2
67	Andy Messersmith	18.2
68	Ed Reulbach	18.1
69	Mel Harder	18.1
70	Dizzy Trout	17.9
71	Silver King	17.8
72	Sam Leever	17.8
73	Vic Willis	17.6
74	Spud Chandler	17.6
75	Larry French	17.6
76	Wilbur Cooper	17.5
77	Mike Garcia	17.4
78	Early Wynn	17.2
79	Nig Cuppy	17.1
80	Freddie Fitzsimmons	17.1
81	Eddie Rommel	17.0
82	Bob Welch	17.0
83	Babe Adams	16.7
84	Fergie Jenkins	16.4
85	Orel Hershiser	16.3
86	Thornton Lee	16.3
87	Jack Quinn	16.1
88	Ed Morris	15.9
89	Vida Blue	15.9
90	Joe Wood	15.7
91	Sal Maglie	15.6
92	Noodles Hahn	15.6
93	Bucky Walters	15.4
94	Deacon Phillippe	15.4
95	Rich Gossage	15.4
96	Steve Rogers	15.3
97	Bob Shawkey	15.2
98	Rollie Fingers	15.1
99	Allie Reynolds	15.1
100	Jerry Koosman	15.1

Adjusted Pitching Wins

1	Cy Young	77.0
2	Walter Johnson	68.6
3	Lefty Grove	59.9
4	Kid Nichols	57.9
5	Pete Alexander	53.6
6	Tom Seaver	43.0
7	John Clarkson	42.6
8	Christy Mathewson	42.4
9	Bob Gibson	35.2
10	Carl Hubbell	35.0
11	Bert Blyleven	34.0
12	Tim Keefe	33.3
13	Warren Spahn	33.3
14	Amos Rusie	32.7
15	Jim Palmer	32.7
16	Whitey Ford	32.1
17	Gaylord Perry	32.0
18	Phil Niekro	31.2
19	Hal Newhouser	30.9
20	Mordecai Brown	30.1
21	Hoyt Wilhelm	29.7
22	Bob Feller	29.3
23	Ed Walsh	29.1
24	Steve Carlton	29.0
25	Ted Lyons	28.4
26	Eddie Plank	28.0
27	Stan Coveleski	27.6
28	Tommy Bridges	27.4
29	Red Faber	27.0
30	Fergie Jenkins	26.5
31	Rube Waddell	26.1
32	Juan Marichal	26.0
33	Dazzy Vance	25.6
34	Eppa Rixey	24.9
35	Dave Stieb	24.5
36	Robin Roberts	24.1
37	Don Drysdale	24.0
38	Clark Griffith	23.8
39	Charley Radbourn	23.6
40	Dizzy Trout	23.5
41	Tony Mullane	23.4
42	Billy Pierce	23.0
43	Sandy Koufax	22.9
44	Addie Joss	22.4
45	Dutch Leonard	22.1
46	Roger Clemens	22.1
47	Urban Shocker	22.1
48	Silver King	21.8
49	Vic Willis	21.3
50	Lefty Gomez	21.3
51	Nolan Ryan	21.1
52	Jack Stivetts	20.9
53	Eddie Cicotte	20.8
54	Harry Brecheen	20.7
55	Joe McGinnity	20.7
56	Eddie Rommel	20.6
57	Nig Cuppy	20.4
58	Jack Quinn	20.3
59	Jim Bunning	19.9
60	Dizzy Dean	19.7
61	Dolf Luque	19.5
62	Jim McCormick	19.5
63	Rick Reuschel	19.3
64	Bob Lemon	19.2
65	Carl Mays	19.1
66	Lon Warneke	18.9
67	Wilbur Cooper	18.7
68	Tommy John	18.5
69	Noodles Hahn	18.2
70	Bob Caruthers	18.2
71	Luis Tiant	18.2
72	Wes Ferrell	18.0
73	Mickey Welch	17.6
74	Dennis Eckersley	17.5
75	Mel Harder	17.3
76	Sam Leever	17.2
77	Bucky Walters	17.1
78	Virgil Trucks	16.9
79	Larry French	16.9
80	Ed Reulbach	16.8
81	Mel Parnell	16.8
82	Babe Adams	16.7
83	Ron Guidry	16.7
84	Will White	16.6
85	Waite Hoyt	16.6
86	Thornton Lee	16.6
87	Hippo Vaughn	16.5
88	Red Ruffing	16.4
89	Larry Jackson	16.1
90	Steve Rogers	16.1
91	Sal Maglie	16.0
92	Joe Wood	15.7
93	Sadie McMahon	15.7
94	Andy Messersmith	15.3
95	Don Sutton	15.2
96	John Tudor	15.2
97	Deacon Phillippe	15.1
98	Rich Gossage	15.1
99	Frank Dwyer	15.0
100	Spud Chandler	14.9

Opponents' Batting Average

1	Nolan Ryan	.203
2	Sandy Koufax	.205
3	Andy Messersmith	.212
	J.R. Richard	.212
5	Sam McDowell	.215
6	Hoyt Wilhelm	.216
7	Ed Walsh	.218
8	Mario Soto	.220
	Bob Turley	.220
10	Orval Overall	.222
11	Addie Joss	.223
	Jeff Tesreau	.223
13	Jim Maloney	.224
	Ed Reulbach	.224
15	Tim Keefe	.226
	Tom Seaver	.226
17	Roger Clemens	.227
	Larry Corcoran	.227
	Dwight Gooden	.227
	Rich Gossage	.227
	Walter Johnson	.227
22	Bob Gibson	.228
	Rube Waddell	.228
	Don Wilson	.228
25	Charlie Hough	.230
	Sam Jones	.230
	Jim Palmer	.230
28	Bobby Bolin	.231
	Bob Feller	.231
	Jim Hunter	.231
31	Mordecai Brown	.232
	Al Downing	.232
	Johnny Vander Meer	.232
	Stan Williams	.232
35	Larry Cheney	.233
36	Dean Chance	.234
	Denny McLain	.234
	Amos Rusie	.234
39	Ray Culp	.235
	Charlie Ferguson	.235
	Rollie Fingers	.235
	Whitey Ford	.235
	Dave Foutz	.235
	Ed Morris	.235
	Tony Mullane	.235
	Monte Ward	.235
47	Moe Drabowsky	.236
	Christy Mathewson	.236
	Toad Ramsey	.236
	Don Sutton	.236
	Luis Tiant	.236
	Bob Veale	.236
53	Vida Blue	.237
	Juan Marichal	.237
	Tug McGraw	.237
	Juan Pizarro	.237
	Frank Smith	.237
	Dave Stieb	.237
59	Rudy May	.238
	Allie Reynolds	.238
	Jim Scott	.238
	Sonny Siebert	.238
63	Gary Bell	.239
	Chief Bender	.239
	Bill Donovan	.239
	Don Drysdale	.239
	Jim McCormick	.239
	Hal Newhouser	.239
	Gary Nolan	.239
	Barney Pelty	.239
	Eddie Plank	.239
	Mike Scott	.239
73	Steve Carlton	.240
	Bob Caruthers	.240
	Mort Cooper	.240
	Mark Langston	.240
	Billy Pierce	.240
	Charley Radbourn	.240
	Bill Singer	.240
	Virgil Trucks	.240
	Fernando Valenzuela	.240
	Will White	.240
83	Howie Camnitz	.241
	John Clarkson	.241
	Jack Coombs	.241
	Kirby Higbe	.241
	Bob Lemon	.241
	Jumbo McGinnis	.241
	George McQuillan	.241
	Earl Moore	.241
	Mickey Welch	.241
	Hooks Wiltse	.241
93	10 players tied	.242

Opponents' On Base Pctg.

1	Monte Ward	.254
2	Addie Joss	.255
3	Tommy Bond	.262
	George Bradley	.262
5	Ed Walsh	.263
6	Larry Corcoran	.266
	Will White	.266
8	Terry Larkin	.267
9	Ed Morris	.269
10	Charlie Ferguson	.270
11	Tim Keefe	.271
	Jim McCormick	.271
13	Christy Mathewson	.272
14	Fred Goldsmith	.274
	Jumbo McGinnis	.274
16	Charley Radbourn	.275
	Jim Whitney	.275
18	Sandy Koufax	.276
19	Mordecai Brown	.278
	Guy Hecker	.278
	Juan Marichal	.278
22	Bob Caruthers	.279
23	Walter Johnson	.280
24	Dave Foutz	.281
25	Deacon Phillippe	.282
	Dupee Shaw	.282
27	Babe Adams	.283
	Jim Galvin	.283
	Rube Waddell	.283
	Cy Young	.283
31	Bobby Mathews	.285
	Tom Seaver	.285
33	Roger Clemens	.286
	Jack Lynch	.286
35	Pete Alexander	.287
	Dwight Gooden	.287
	Noodles Hahn	.287
	Jim Hunter	.287
	Gary Nolan	.287
	Don Sutton	.287
41	Chief Bender	.288
	Eddie Plank	.288
43	Nick Altrock	.289
	Tiny Bonham	.289
	John Clarkson	.289
	Fergie Jenkins	.289
	Andy Messersmith	.289
	Mickey Welch	.289
	Doc White	.289
	Hooks Wiltse	.289
51	Hoyt Wilhelm	.290
52	Charlie Buffinton	.291
	Carl Hubbell	.291
	Tony Mullane	.291
55	Henry Boyle	.292
	Jack Chesbro	.292
	Sam Leever	.292
	Denny McLain	.292
59	Dennis Eckersley	.293
	Robin Roberts	.293
	George Winter	.293
62	Don Drysdale	.294
	Ron Guidry	.294
	George McQuillan	.294
	Toad Ramsey	.294
	Jeff Tesreau	.294
67	Rollie Fingers	.295
	Frank Smith	.295
69	Kid Nichols	.296
	Jim Palmer	.296
	Barney Pelty	.296
	Mario Soto	.296
	Jesse Tannehill	.296
	Jack Taylor	.296
	Ralph Terry	.296
76	John Candelaria	.297
	Joe McGinnity	.297
	Gaylord Perry	.297
	Lee Richmond	.297
	Warren Spahn	.297
81	Harry Brecheen	.298
	Eddie Cicotte	.298
	Dizzy Dean	.298
	Orval Overall	.298
	Ed Reulbach	.298
	Dick Rudolph	.298
	Slim Sallee	.298
	Luis Tiant	.298
89	Jim Bunning	.299
	Mike Cuellar	.299
	Eddie Fisher	.299
	Bob Gibson	.299
	Hardie Henderson	.299
	Don Mossi	.299
	Don Newcombe	.299
	Mike Scott	.299
	Bryn Smith	.299
98	4 players tied	.300

Wins Above Team

1	Cy Young	100.1
2	Walter Johnson	90.3
3	Pete Alexander	81.9
4	Christy Mathewson	65.3
5	Lefty Grove	63.2
6	Tom Seaver	59.4
7	Jim McCormick	56.6
8	Jim Galvin	54.3
9	Charley Radbourn	50.6
10	Warren Spahn	46.3
11	Clark Griffith	46.1
12	Whitey Ford	44.7
13	Will White	44.0
14	Juan Marichal	39.1
15	Bob Feller	37.5
16	Mickey Welch	37.1
17	Phil Niekro	36.9
18	Ted Lyons	36.5
19	Tony Mullane	36.4
20	Amos Rusie	36.2
21	Eddie Plank	36.1
22	Jesse Tannehill	35.9
23	Charlie Buffinton	35.4
	Wes Ferrell	35.4
25	Steve Carlton	34.9
26	Kid Nichols	34.8
27	Carl Hubbell	34.7
28	Dazzy Vance	33.9
29	Joe McGinnity	32.7
30	Jim Devlin	32.5
31	Roger Clemens	32.4
32	Ed Walsh	32.0
33	Bob Gibson	31.5
34	Eddie Rommel	31.1
35	Ed Morris	31.0
36	Sandy Koufax	30.9
	Jim Palmer	30.9
38	Robin Roberts	30.6
39	Bob Caruthers	30.5
40	Urban Shocker	30.3
41	Guy Hecker	29.8
	Fergie Jenkins	29.8
	Sadie McMahon	29.8
44	Ron Guidry	29.7
45	Mordecai Brown	29.5
46	Addie Joss	28.7
47	Dwight Gooden	28.5
48	Dizzy Dean	27.7
49	Bobby Mathews	27.1
50	John Candelaria	27.0
	Schoolboy Rowe	27.0
52	Sam Leever	26.1
53	Jack Chesbro	25.7
	Rip Sewell	25.7
55	Frank Killen	25.6
56	Rick Reuschel	24.8
57	Red Lucas	24.7
	Herb Pennock	24.7
	Nap Rucker	24.7
60	Russ Ford	24.4
61	Gaylord Perry	24.2
62	Red Faber	24.1
63	Johnny Allen	23.9
64	Chief Bender	23.8
65	John Clarkson	23.7
66	Charlie Ferguson	23.6
	Noodles Hahn	23.6
68	Bob Welch	23.4
69	Tommy John	23.2
	Tim Keefe	23.2
	Firpo Marberry	23.2
	Joe Wood	23.2
73	Sal Maglie	23.1
74	Gus Weyhing	23.0
75	Burleigh Grimes	22.3
76	Bert Blyleven	22.2
	Carl Mays	22.2
78	Dave Stieb	22.1
79	Dutch Leonard	21.8
80	Claude Passeau	21.6
	George Uhle	21.6
82	Spud Chandler	21.4
	Jim Maloney	21.4
	Hippo Vaughn	21.4
	Bucky Walters	21.4
86	Hal Newhouser	21.2
	J.R. Richard	21.2
	Slim Sallee	21.2
	John Tudor	21.2
90	Freddie Fitzsimmons	21.1
91	Vida Blue	21.0
92	Babe Adams	20.9
93	Art Nehf	20.7
94	Allie Reynolds	20.6
	Luis Tiant	20.6
96	Lon Warneke	20.5
97	Ted Breitenstein	20.4
98	Stan Coveleski	20.3
	Orel Hershiser	20.3
100	Jim Hunter	20.2

Wins Above League

1	Cy Young	413.5
2	Walter Johnson	348.0
3	Jim Galvin	334.0
4	Warren Spahn	304.0
5	Phil Niekro	296.0
6	Pete Alexander	290.5
7	Don Sutton	290.0
8	Gaylord Perry	289.5
9	Nolan Ryan	287.0
10	Steve Carlton	286.5
11	Kid Nichols	284.5
12	Tim Keefe	283.5
13	Christy Mathewson	280.5
14	Early Wynn	272.0
15	Robin Roberts	265.5
16	Jim Kaat	260.0
	Eddie Plank	260.0
18	Tommy John	259.5
19	Bert Blyleven	258.5
	Eppa Rixey	258.5
	Mickey Welch	258.5
22	Tom Seaver	258.0
23	Fergie Jenkins	255.0
24	John Clarkson	253.0
25	Tony Mullane	252.0
	Charley Radbourn	252.0
27	Jack Powell	249.5
28	Red Ruffing	249.0
29	Gus Weyhing	248.0
30	Ted Lyons	245.0
31	Burleigh Grimes	241.0
32	Jim McCormick	239.5
33	Red Faber	233.5
34	Jack Quinn	232.5
35	Vic Willis	227.0
36	Sam Jones	223.0
37	Lefty Grove	220.5
38	Paul Derringer	217.5
39	Bobo Newsom	216.5
40	Jerry Koosman	215.5
41	Bob Feller	214.0
42	Bob Friend	213.5
43	Bob Gibson	212.5
	Joe Niekro	212.5
45	George Mullin	212.0
46	Jim Palmer	210.0
47	Waite Hoyt	209.5
	Amos Rusie	209.5
49	Jerry Reuss	205.5
50	Mel Harder	204.5
51	Jim Bunning	204.0
	Mickey Lolich	204.0
53	Carl Hubbell	203.5
54	Hooks Dauss	202.0
55	Rick Reuschel	201.5
	Frank Tanana	201.5
	Earl Whitehill	201.5
58	Herb Pennock	201.0
59	Luis Tiant	200.5
60	Will White	197.5
	Jim Whitney	197.5
62	Wilbur Cooper	197.0
63	Al Orth	196.5
	Adonis Terry	196.5
65	Claude Osteen	195.5
66	Jim Hunter	195.0
67	Jim Perry	194.5
68	Joe McGinnity	194.0
69	Chick Fraser	193.5
70	Charlie Buffinton	192.5
	Juan Marichal	192.5
72	Clark Griffith	191.5
73	Billy Pierce	190.0
74	Joe Bush	189.0
	Rube Marquard	189.0
76	Larry Jackson	188.5
	Tom Zachary	188.5
78	Curt Simmons	188.0
79	Don Drysdale	187.5
80	Dolf Luque	186.5
	Milt Pappas	186.5
82	Dutch Leonard	186.0
83	Vida Blue	185.0
84	Mordecai Brown	184.5
	Rick Wise	184.5
86	Doyle Alexander	184.0
	Larry French	184.0
	Jesse Haines	184.0
	Lee Meadows	184.0
90	George Uhle	183.0
91	Freddie Fitzsimmons	181.5
92	Charlie Root	180.5
93	Bucky Walters	179.0
94	Eddie Cicotte	178.5
	Stan Coveleski	178.5
	Silver King	178.5
	Hal Newhouser	178.5
98	Charlie Hough	177.5
99	Murry Dickson	176.5
100	Red Ames	175.0

Relief Games			Relief Wins			Relief Losses			Relief Innings Pitched		
1	Kent Tekulve	1050	1	Hoyt Wilhelm	124	1	Gene Garber	108	1	Hoyt Wilhelm	1871.0
2	Hoyt Wilhelm	1018	2	Lindy McDaniel	119	2	Hoyt Wilhelm	103	2	Lindy McDaniel	1694.0
3	Gene Garber	922	3	Rollie Fingers	107	3	Rollie Fingers	101	3	Rollie Fingers	1500.1
4	Lindy McDaniel	913	4	Rich Gossage	104	4	Mike Marshall	98	4	Gene Garber	1452.2
5	Rollie Fingers	907	5	Sparky Lyle	99	5	Kent Tekulve	90	5	Kent Tekulve	1436.1
6	Sparky Lyle	899	6	Roy Face	96	6	Lindy McDaniel	88	6	Sparky Lyle	1390.1
7	Don McMahon	872	7	Gene Garber	94	7	Roy Face	82	7	Rich Gossage	1383.1
8	Roy Face	821		Kent Tekulve	94	8	Rich Gossage	76	8	Tug McGraw	1301.1
9	Rich Gossage	816	9	Mike Marshall	92		Sparky Lyle	76	9	Don McMahon	1297.0
10	Tug McGraw	785	10	Don McMahon	90	10	Gary Lavelle	75	10	Mike Marshall	1259.1
11	Darold Knowles	757	11	Tug McGraw	89	11	Ron Perranoski	74	11	Tom Burgmeier	1248.2
12	Tom Burgmeier	742	12	Clay Carroll	88	12	Darold Knowles	71	12	Roy Face	1212.1
	Gary Lavelle	742	13	Bob Stanley	85		Bruce Sutter	71	13	Clay Carroll	1204.2
14	Ron Perranoski	736	14	Bill Campbell	80	14	Tug McGraw	69	14	Eddie Fisher	1186.0
15	Willie Hernandez	733		Gary Lavelle	80	15	Stu Miller	67	15	Bill Campbell	1177.1
16	Clay Carroll	703	16	Tom Burgmeier	79	16	Clay Carroll	66	16	Ron Perranoski	1170.2
	Greg Minton	703		Stu Miller	79		Don McMahon	66	17	Bob Stanley	1157.0
18	Mike Marshall	699		Ron Perranoski	79	18	Bill Campbell	65	18	Stu Miller	1095.2
19	Jeff Reardon	694	19	Johnny Murphy	73		Jeff Reardon	65	19	Greg Minton	1087.1
20	Bill Campbell	691	20	John Hiller	72	20	Greg Minton	62	20	Gary Lavelle	1077.2
21	Dan Quisenberry	674	21	Mark Clear	71	21	Bob Stanley	61	21	Darold Knowles	1052.1
22	Bruce Sutter	661		Dick Hall	71	22	John Hiller	60	22	Paul Lindblad	1043.1
23	Ted Abernathy	647	23	Willie Hernandez	70	23	Frank Linzy	57	23	Dan Quisenberry	1043.1
24	Lee Smith	644	24	Pedro Borbon	69		Lee Smith	57	24	Bruce Sutter	1042.1
25	Dave LaRoche	632	25	Bruce Sutter	68	25	Willie Hernandez	55	25	Johnny Klippstein	1039.2
26	Eddie Fisher	627	26	Al Hrabosky	64		Jesse Orosco	55	26	Pedro Borbon	1016.1
27	Paul Lindblad	623	27	Darold Knowles	63	27	Tom Burgmeier	53	27	Willie Hernandez	994.1
28	Stu Miller	611		Clem Labine	63		Ron Davis	53	28	Bob Miller	992.2
29	Grant Jackson	609		Dave LaRoche	63	29	Steve Bedrosian	52	29	Dave LaRoche	975.3
30	Elias Sosa	598	30	Jim Brewer	62		Jim Kern	52	30	Ted Abernathy	970.0
31	Bob Miller	595		Turk Farrell	62		Randy Moffitt	52	31	John Hiller	962.2
32	Pedro Borbon	589		Eddie Fisher	62	32	Turk Farrell	51	32	Jeff Reardon	943.2
33	Doug Bair	579		Grant Jackson	62		Eddie Fisher	51	33	Elias Sosa	905.0
34	Bob Locker	576		Paul Lindblad	62		Dave LaRoche	51	34	Dale Murray	901.1
35	Terry Forster	575		Frank Linzy	62		Claude Raymond	51	35	Doug Bair	889.1
36	Dave Smith	562		Jeff Reardon	62	36	Dale Murray	50	36	Terry Forster	888.0
37	Bob Stanley	552	37	Joe Heving	60		Al Worthington	50	37	Lee Smith	881.2
38	Johnny Klippstein	550	38	Johnny Klippstein	59	38	Jim Brewer	49	38	Bob Locker	879.0
39	Jim Brewer	549		Elias Sosa	59		Elias Sosa	49	39	Ron Reed	874.1
40	Jesse Orosco	547	40	Aurelio Lopez	58	40	Ted Abernathy	48	40	Jim Brewer	861.0
41	Al Hrabosky	544		Jesse Orosco	58		Mark Clear	48	41	Aurelio Lopez	860.0
	Tippy Martinez	544		Phil Regan	58	42	Don Elston	47	42	Dick Tidrow	857.2
43	Dave Giusti	535	43	Ted Abernathy	57		Ron Kline	47	43	Dave Giusti	854.2
44	Larry Andersen	533		Bob Locker	57		Dave Smith	47	44	Clem Labine	854.0
	Ron Kline	533		Greg Minton	57	45	Terry Forster	46	45	Grant Jackson	848.1
	Randy Moffitt	533	46	Mace Brown	56		Tom Hume	46	46	Al Worthington	838.0
	Al Worthington	533		Dan Quisenberry	56		Tom Niedenfuer	46	47	Diego Segui	829.0
48	Craig Lefferts	523		Gerry Staley	56		Dan Quisenberry	46	48	Ron Kline	827.2
49	Dale Murray	517	49	4 players tied	55	49	4 players tied	45	49	Tippy Martinez	823.1
50	Frank Linzy	514							50	Larry Andersen	814.1

Relief Points

1	Rollie Fingers	795
2	Rich Gossage	746
3	Bruce Sutter	665
4	Jeff Reardon	633
5	Hoyt Wilhelm	599
6	Sparky Lyle	598
7	Lee Smith	583
8	Dan Quisenberry	554
9	Gene Garber	516
10	Roy Face	496
11	Lindy McDaniel	494
12	Dave Righetti	492
13	Tug McGraw	469
14	Kent Tekulve	466
15	Mike Marshall	462
16	Dave Smith	457
17	Ron Perranoski	442
18	Johnny Franco	423
19	Don McMahon	420
20	Steve Bedrosian	412
21	Stu Miller	399
22	Clay Carroll	396
23	Willie Hernandez	379
24	Bob Stanley	373
25	Dave Giusti	363
26	Ted Abernathy	362
27	Gary Lavelle	357
28	Greg Minton	352
29	Bill Campbell	347
30	Darold Knowles	341
31	Tom Henke	340
32	Jim Brewer	339
33	John Hiller	336
34	Dave LaRoche	327
35	Dennis Eckersley	320
36	Johnny Murphy	317
37	Bobby Thigpen	311
38	Tom Burgmeier	309
	Jay Howell	309
40	Dick Radatz	305
41	Jesse Orosco	303
42	Terry Forster	302
43	Ron Davis	301
44	Tippy Martinez	300
45	Jack Aker	295
	Roger McDowell	295
47	Frank Linzy	289
48	Al Hrabosky	287
49	Fred Gladding	280
50	2 players tied	278

Relief Ranking

1	Hoyt Wilhelm	360
2	Rich Gossage	318
3	Bruce Sutter	214
4	Dan Quisenberry	208
5	Rollie Fingers	206
6	Kent Tekulve	203
7	Lee Smith	200
8	Mike Marshall	197
9	John Hiller	189
10	Sparky Lyle	181
11	Ellis Kinder	166
	Bob Stanley	166
13	Tug McGraw	163
14	Johnny Franco	163
15	Lindy McDaniel	160
16	Ron Perranoski	152
17	Gary Lavelle	150
18	Dave Righetti	147
19	Dave Smith	146
20	Stu Miller	145
21	Roy Face	143
22	Jeff Reardon	142
23	Gene Garber	141
24	Dennis Eckersley	137
	Jesse Orosco	137
26	Tom Henke	127
27	Clay Carroll	123
	Willie Hernandez	123
29	Lefty Grove	117
30	Doug Jones	114
31	Tom Burgmeier	113
32	Frank Linzy	110
33	Jim Brewer	108
34	Johnny Murphy	107
35	Bobby Thigpen	106
36	Ted Abernathy	104
37	Terry Forster	102
	Greg Minton	102
39	Bill Campbell	101
	Don McMahon	101
41	Jim Kern	100
42	Todd Worrell	98
43	Jim Brosnan	97
44	Tim Burke	92
	Al Worthington	92
46	Bill Caudill	91
	Eddie Rommel	91
48	Dan Plesac	91
49	Firpo Marberry	90
50	2 players tied	89

Relievers' Runs

1	Hoyt Wilhelm	261
2	Rich Gossage	175
3	Rollie Fingers	156
4	Dan Quisenberry	144
5	Kent Tekulve	128
6	Sparky Lyle	121
7	Tug McGraw	110
8	Clay Carroll	100
	Mike Marshall	100
	Ron Perranoski	100
11	John Hiller	99
	Gary Lavelle	99
	Don McMahon	99
14	Stu Miller	96
	Dave Smith	96
16	Lindy McDaniel	94
17	Bob Stanley	93
18	Bruce Sutter	91
19	Lee Smith	90
20	Greg Minton	88
	Jesse Orosco	88
22	Johnny Murphy	85
23	Dennis Eckersley	83
24	Ellis Kinder	82
25	Dave Righetti	81
26	Tom Henke	79
27	Tom Burgmeier	78
	Johnny Franco	78
29	Jeff Reardon	75
30	Willie Hernandez	74
31	Jim Brewer	73
32	Bobby Darwin	71
	Terry Forster	71
34	Tim Burke	70
	Bob Miller	70
36	Firpo Marberry	69
37	Dick Hall	66
	Waite Hoyt	66
	Ron Reed	66
	Gerry Staley	66
41	Grant Jackson	64
	Bob Locker	64
43	Roy Face	63
44	Gene Garber	62
	Marv Grissom	62
	Billy O'Dell	62
	Sammy Stewart	62
48	Mark Eichhorn	61
	Lefty Grove	61
50	Frank Linzy	60

Adjusted Relievers' Runs

1	Hoyt Wilhelm	245
2	Rich Gossage	171
3	Dan Quisenberry	148
4	Kent Tekulve	141
5	Bob Stanley	121
6	Rollie Fingers	120
7	Sparky Lyle	119
8	Bruce Sutter	116
9	John Hiller	115
10	Tug McGraw	113
	Lee Smith	113
12	Lindy McDaniel	108
13	Mike Marshall	103
14	Ellis Kinder	99
15	Clay Carroll	97
16	Gary Lavelle	96
17	Gene Garber	93
18	Tom Burgmeier	87
19	Johnny Franco	86
20	Don McMahon	85
21	Willie Hernandez	84
	Ron Perranoski	84
23	Stu Miller	83
	Jesse Orosco	83
25	Dave Smith	80
26	Terry Forster	78
	Tom Henke	78
28	Greg Minton	76
29	Dennis Eckerlsey	75
	Jeff Reardon	75
	Dave Righetti	75
32	Ron Reed	74
33	Tim Burke	70
34	Lefty Grove	67
35	Ted Abernathy	66
	Johnny Murphy	66
37	Danny Darwin	65
38	Grant Jackson	64
	Gerry Staley	64
40	Mark Eichhorn	63
	Waite Hoyt	63
42	Bill Campbell	61
	Roy Face	61
	Marv Grissom	61
	Bob Miller	61
46	Dick Hall	60
	Greg Harris	60
	Doug Jones	60
49	Frank Linzy	59
	Firpo Marberry	59

Clutch Pitching Index

1	Bob Rhoads	118
2	Ed Killian	116
3	Ed Siever	115
4	Will White	114
5	Ron Kline	113
	Bill Lee	113
7	Al Benton	112
	Eddie Lopat	112
	Bob Stanley	112
	Tom Zachary	112
11	Whitey Ford	111
	Lefty Leifield	111
	Win Mercer	111
	Preacher Roe	111
15	Bob Miller	110
	Bill Wight	110
17	Steve Blass	109
	Bob Buhl	109
	Max Butcher	109
	Dan Casey	109
	Max Lanier	109
	Sal Maglie	109
	Mel Parnell	109
	Bob Shaw	109
	Gerry Staley	109
	Dummy Taylor	109
	Geoff Zahn	109
28	Steve Barber	108
	Sheriff Blake	108
	Frank Dwyer	108
	Lefty Grove	108
	Carl Morton	108
	George Mullin	108
	Togie Pittinger	108
	Dizzy Trout	108
	Bob Veale	108
37	Nelson Briles	107
	Lloyd Brown	107
	Larry French	107
	Claude Osteen	107
	Eddie Rommel	107
	Dutch Ruether	107
	Eddie Smith	107
44	Jim Bagby	106
	Roger Craig	106
	Bill Duggleby	106
	Red Faber	106
	Mel Harder	106
	Joe Haynes	106
	Tommy John	106
	Bobby Mathews	106
	Cal McLish	106
	Jeff Pfeffer	106
	Howie Pollet	106
	Nap Rucker	106
	Jim Scott	106
	Sherry Smith	106
	Sloppy Thurston	106
	Steve Trout	106
	John Tudor	106
	Bucky Walters	106
62	Jack Curtis	105
	Ron Darling	105
	Murry Dickson	105
	Dick Ellsworth	105
	Bob Ewing	105
	Wes Ferrell	105
	Fred Frankhouse	105
	Gene Garber	105
	Mike Garcia	105
	Guy Hecker	105
	Ken Heintzelman	105
	Bruce Hurst	105
	Johnny Klippstein	105
	Thornton Lee	105
	Charlie Leibrandt	105
	Dutch Leonard	105
	Ted Lyons	105
	Tug McGraw	105
	Stu Miller	105
	Clarence Mitchell	105
	Shane Rawley	105
	Allie Reynolds	105
	Johnny Sain	105
	Jim Slaton	105
	Al Smith	105
	Hippo Vaughn	105
	Rube Waddell	105
	Lon Warneke	105
	Wilbur Wood	105
91	30 players tied	104

Pitcher Batting Runs

1	Red Ruffing	135
2	Bob Caruthers	110
3	Wes Ferrell	105
4	Walter Johnson	98
5	Red Lucas	97
6	George Uhle	93
7	George Mullin	90
8	Jim Whitney	89
9	Guy Hecker	87
10	Bob Lemon	86
11	Warren Spahn	82
12	Don Newcombe	81
13	Schoolboy Rowe	76
14	Babe Ruth	75
15	Jack Stivetts	72
16	Early Wynn	70
17	Bob Gibson	68
18	Al Orth	66
19	Carl Mays	62
20	Earl Wilson	60
21	Don Drysdale	59
22	Bucky Walters	58
23	Doc Crandall	57
	Christy Mathewson	57
	Gary Peters	57
26	Jesse Tannehill	55
27	Jim Tobin	54
28	Claude Hendrix	53
29	Burleigh Grimes	52
30	Ad Gumbert	51
31	Steve Carlton	50
32	Charlie Ferguson	49
	Bob Forsch	49
34	Joe Bush	48
	Tony Mullane	48
36	Dave Foutz	46
	Rick Rhoden	46
	Scott Stratton	46
39	Vern Law	45
	Dutch Ruether	45
	Adonis Terry	45
42	Don Larsen	44
43	Jim Kaat	43
	Jack Scott	43
45	Frank Killen	42
46	Tommy Byrne	40
	Wilbur Cooper	40
	Fred Hutchinson	40
49	Charley Radbourn	38
	Don Robinson	38
	Johnny Sain	38
52	Mickey McDermott	37
	Claude Osteen	37
	Sloppy Thurston	37
	Doc White	37
56	Ken Brett	36
	Clark Griffith	36
58	Jack Coombs	35
	Harvey Haddix	35
	Dolf Luque	35
61	Chief Bender	34
	Robin Roberts	34
	Jack Taylor	34
	Rick Wise	34
65	Win Mercer	33
	Art Nehf	33
	Ben Sanders	33
	Frank Smith	33
69	Ray Caldwell	32
	Hooks Dauss	32
	Jim Hunter	32
	Ted Lyons	32
	Dizzy Trout	32
74	Monte Ward	31
	Joe Wood	31
76	Al Maul	30
	Jouett Meekin	30
	Camilo Pascual	30
79	Ed Brandt	29
	Lew Burdette	29
	Jack Harshman	29
	Brickyard Kennedy	29
	Joe Nuxhall	29
	Urban Shocker	29
	Lefty Tyler	29
86	Eddie Lopat	28
	Jim Maloney	28
	Juan Pizarro	28
	Tom Seaver	28
	Fernando Valenzuela	28
	Lon Warneke	28
92	Charlie Buffinton	27
	Clarence Mitchell	27
	Bill Sherdel	27
95	Murry Dickson	26
	Ned Garver	26
	Frank Kitson	26
	Johnny Marcum	26
	Joe Shaute	26
	Elmer Smith	26

Pitcher Fielding Runs

1	Carl Mays	78
2	Ed Walsh	75
3	Freddie Fitzsimmons	66
4	Tommy John	63
	Christy Mathewson	63
6	Bob Lemon	62
7	Burleigh Grimes	59
8	Harry Gumbert	53
9	Harry Howell	49
10	Eddie Rommel	48
11	Willis Hudlin	46
	Jack Quinn	46
13	John Clarkson	44
	Jim Galvin	44
15	Bill Doak	42
16	Rick Reuschel	41
17	Nick Altrock	40
	Jack Russell	40
19	Mel Stottlemyre	39
	Dizzy Trout	39
21	Hooks Dauss	38
	Willie Sudhoff	38
23	Bobby Shantz	37
24	Randy Jones	36
25	Curt Davis	35
	Johnny Schmitz	35
27	Charlie Buffinton	34
	Murry Dickson	34
29	John Denny	33
	Gerry Staley	33
31	Hal Schumacher	32
	Sherry Smith	32
33	Tommy Bond	31
	Ben Cantwell	31
	Tony Mullane	31
36	Howard Ehmke	30
	Addie Joss	30
	Ed Willett	30
39	Tom Burgmeier	29
	Chick Fraser	29
	Sid Hudson	29
	Larry Jackson	29
	Bucky Walters	29
44	Lew Burdette	28
	Mike Caldwell	28
	Spud Chandler	28
	Matt Kilroy	28
	Claude Osteen	28
	Bob Purkey	28
50	Pete Alexander	27
	Guy Hecker	27
	Dennis Martinez	27
	George Mullin	27
	Dan Quisenberry	27
	Dave Stieb	27
56	Ted Abernathy	26
	Red Ames	26
	Nixey Callahan	26
	Dutch Leonard	26
	Frank Smith	26
	Bob Stanley	26
62	Don Drysdale	25
	Jean Dubuc	25
	Phil Niekro	25
65	Mike Boddicker	24
	Frank Corridon	24
	Whitey Ford	24
	Benny Frey	24
	Joe Horlen	24
	Frank Owen	24
	Fernando Valenzuela	24
	Monte Ward	24
	Vic Willis	24
74	Eldon Auker	23
	Jess Barnes	23
	Tom Brewer	23
	Kent Tekulve	23
	Doc White	23
79	Clint Brown	22
	Red Donahue	22
	Mel Harder	22
	Bill Hart	22
	Dennis Lamp	22
	Frank Linzy	22
	Jim McCormick	22
	Greg Minton	22
	Dan Petry	22
	Ed Reulbach	22
	Scott Stratton	22
90	Joaquin Andujar	21
	George Blaeholder	21
	Lloyd Brown	21
	Ray Fisher	21
	Ray Herbert	21
	Bill Lee	21
	Clarence Mitchell	21
	Wilcy Moore	21
	Amos Rusie	21
99	7 players tied	20

Pitcher Batting Average

1	Jack Stivetts	.297
2	George Uhle	.289
3	Charlie Ferguson	.288
4	Doc Crandall	.285
	Win Mercer	.285
6	Guy Hecker	.283
7	Bob Caruthers	.282
8	Red Lucas	.281
9	Wes Ferrell	.280
10	Jack Scott	.275
11	Scott Stratton	.274
12	Nixey Callahan	.273
	Ad Gumbert	.273
	Al Orth	.273
15	Don Newcombe	.271
16	Sloppy Thurston	.270
17	Red Ruffing	.269
18	Carl Mays	.268
19	Schoolboy Rowe	.263
20	George Mullin	.262
21	Brickyard Kennedy	.261
	Jim Whitney	.261
23	Dutch Ruether	.258
	Joe Shaute	.258
25	Lee Richmond	.257
26	Jesse Tannehill	.256
27	Joe Bush	.253
28	Clarence Mitchell	.252
	Jack Taylor	.252
30	Adonis Terry	.249
31	Ray Caldwell	.248
	Burleigh Grimes	.248
33	Amos Rusie	.247
34	Pete Donohue	.246
35	Charlie Buffinton	.245
	Johnny Sain	.245
37	Vern Kennedy	.244
38	Duke Esper	.243
	Jouett Meekin	.243
	Tony Mullane	.243
	Elam Vangilder	.243
	Bucky Walters	.243
43	Don Larsen	.242
	Bob Smith	.242
45	Pink Hawley	.241
	Claude Hendrix	.241
	Frank Killen	.241
48	Frank Kitson	.240
49	Wilbur Cooper	.239
50	Ed Crane	.238
	Rick Rhoden	.238
52	Tommy Bond	.236
	Ed Brandt	.236
	Jim McCormick	.236
55	Jack Coombs	.235
	Walter Johnson	.235
	Terry Larkin	.235
	Charley Radbourn	.235
59	Fritz Ostermueller	.234
60	Nig Cuppy	.233
	Clark Griffith	.233
	Ted Lyons	.233
	Sherry Smith	.233
64	Bob Lemon	.232
	Don Robinson	.232
66	Ben Cantwell	.231
	Murry Dickson	.231
68	Frank Dwyer	.230
	George Earnshaw	.230
	Jim Tobin	.230
71	Vic Aldridge	.229
72	George Bradley	.228
	Nels Potter	.228
	Ed Stein	.228
75	George Haddock	.227
	Dolf Luque	.227
	Bill Swift	.227
78	Jim Bagby	.226
	Jim Hunter	.226
	Kid Nichols	.226
	Tom Zachary	.226
82	Dizzy Dean	.225
	Frank Foreman	.225
84	Fred Goldsmith	.224
	Mickey Welch	.224
86	Hal Carlson	.223
	Larry Corcoran	.223
	George Hemming	.223
	Bill Sherdel	.223
	Jack Taylor	.223
	Lon Warneke	.223
92	Matt Kilroy	.222
	Gary Peters	.222
94	Van Mungo	.221
95	Sid Hudson	.220
96	Henry Boyle	.219
	John Clarkson	.219
	Whit Wyatt	.219
99	3 players tied	.218

Total Pitcher Index

#	Name	Index
1	Walter Johnson	80.2
2	Cy Young	79.9
3	Pete Alexander	64.3
4	Kid Nichols	62.2
5	Christy Mathewson	59.2
6	Lefty Grove	58.7
7	John Clarkson	52.1
8	Tom Seaver	50.4
9	Bob Gibson	44.7
10	Warren Spahn	43.0
11	Ed Walsh	40.8
12	Whitey Ford	38.3
13	Carl Hubbell	38.0
14	Hal Newhouser	37.8
15	Phil Niekro	37.6
16	Tim Keefe	37.2
17	Amos Rusie	37.0
18	Jim Palmer	36.4
19	Bob Lemon	35.7
20	Tony Mullane	35.6
21	Ted Lyons	35.5
	Carl Mays	35.5
23	Steve Carlton	35.4
24	Gaylord Perry	35.1
25	Mordecai Brown	34.7
26	Don Drysdale	34.6
27	Bert Blyleven	34.5
28	Dizzy Trout	33.8
29	Jack Stivetts	31.9
30	Fergie Jenkins	31.6
31	Bob Caruthers	30.9
32	Juan Marichal	30.7
33	Wes Ferrell	30.3
34	Clark Griffith	30.2
35	Charley Radbourn	30.1
36	Bucky Walters	29.1
37	Dave Stieb	29.0
38	Hoyt Wilhelm	28.7
39	Tommy Bridges	27.6
40	Tommy John	27.5
41	Eddie Plank	27.1
42	Stan Coveleski	27.0
43	Rick Reuschel	26.6
	Red Ruffing	26.6
45	Bob Feller	26.2
	Robin Roberts	26.2
47	Red Faber	25.7
48	Addie Joss	25.5
49	Burleigh Grimes	25.4
	Eddie Rommel	25.4
51	Silver King	25.0
	Jack Quinn	25.0
	Eppa Rixey	25.0
54	Dolf Luque	24.8
	Urban Shocker	24.8
56	Dazzy Vance	24.5
57	Eddie Cicotte	24.4
58	Harry Brecheen	23.5
	Guy Hecker	23.5
60	Nig Cuppy	23.4
	Freddie Fitzsimmons	23.4
62	Dutch Leonard	23.2
63	Rube Waddell	23.1
64	Roger Clemens	23.0
	Jim McCormick	23.0
	Lon Warneke	23.0
67	Billy Pierce	22.0
	Vic Willis	22.0
69	Charlie Buffinton	21.6
70	Jesse Tannehill	21.5
71	Spud Chandler	21.2
	Joe Wood	21.2
73	Jim Kaat	21.1
74	Wilbur Cooper	20.7
75	Larry Jackson	20.6
76	Joe McGinnity	20.4
77	Curt Davis	20.1
	Bobby Shantz	20.1
79	Dizzy Dean	19.9
80	Murry Dickson	19.6
81	Ed Reulbach	19.4
82	Don Newcombe	19.3
83	Luis Tiant	18.6
84	Hippo Vaughn	18.5
85	Mel Harder	18.4
	Orel Hershiser	18.4
	Sandy Koufax	18.4
	Steve Rogers	18.4
	Jim Whitney	18.4
90	Dave Foutz	18.2
	Mel Parnell	18.2
92	Babe Adams	18.0
	Dan Quisenberry	18.0
94	Ned Garver	17.9
	Eddie Lopat	17.9
	Mel Stottlemyre	17.9
	John Tudor	17.9
98	Andy Messersmith	17.8
	Doc White	17.8
100	Lefty Gomez	17.7

Total Pitcher Index

#	Name	Index
101	Thornton Lee	17.6
102	Noodles Hahn	17.5
	Jack Taylor	17.5
104	Ron Guidry	17.4
105	Charlie Ferguson	17.2
	Kent Tekulve	17.2
	Early Wynn	17.2
108	Claude Hendrix	17.1
	Claude Passeau	17.1
110	Jim Bunning	17.0
	Larry French	17.0
112	Frank Dwyer	16.9
	Dennis Eckersley	16.9
114	George Mullin	16.7
115	Hal Schumacher	16.5
116	Waite Hoyt	16.1
117	Schoolboy Rowe	16.0
118	Harry Howell	15.9
	Sam Leever	15.9
120	Bret Saberhagen	15.8
121	Jim Devlin	15.7
	Wilbur Wood	15.7
123	John Candelaria	15.6
124	Mickey Welch	15.5
125	Max Lanier	15.4
	Sadie McMahon	15.4
	Bob Stanley	15.4
	Virgil Trucks	15.4
129	Larry Corcoran	15.3
130	Dwight Gooden	15.1
131	Chief Bender	15.0
132	Sal Maglie	14.9
133	George Uhle	14.8
134	Mort Cooper	14.7
	Nolan Ryan	14.7
136	Jim Galvin	14.5
137	Deacon Phillippe	14.3
	Curt Simmons	14.3
139	Mike Garcia	14.1
	Bill Hutchinson	14.1
	Howie Pollet	14.1
142	Johnny Antonelli	14.0
	Charlie Hough	14.0
144	Fred Hutchinson	13.8
	Babe Ruth	13.8
146	Rich Gossage	13.6
	Jim Maloney	13.6
	Milt Pappas	13.6
149	Frank Lary	13.5
150	Jerry Koosman	13.3
	Bob Welch	13.3
	Will White	13.3
153	Bob Shawkey	13.2
	Frank Tanana	13.2
	Jim Tobin	13.2
156	John Hiller	13.1
157	Frank Killen	13.0
158	Jon Matlack	12.8
	Claude Osteen	12.8
	Sherry Smith	12.8
161	Don Sutton	12.7
162	Sparky Lyle	12.6
	Monte Ward	12.6
164	Ted Breitenstein	12.5
165	Tom Burgmeier	12.4
	Russ Ford	12.4
	Gene Garber	12.4
	Nap Rucker	12.4
169	Mike Marshall	12.3
	Stu Miller	12.3
	Bruce Sutter	12.3
172	Ben Sanders	12.2
173	Gary Peters	12.1
174	Rollie Fingers	11.9
175	Ewell Blackwell	11.8
	Jack Chesbro	11.8
	Jim Perry	11.8
178	Sonny Siebert	11.7
	Fernando Valenzuela	11.7
	Tom Zachary	11.7
181	Mike Boddicker	11.6
	Clay Carroll	11.6
	Jake Weimer	11.6
184	Dean Chance	11.5
	Harvey Haddix	11.5
186	Fritz Ostermueller	11.2
187	Bob Ewing	11.1
	Matt Kilroy	11.1
	Firpo Marberry	11.1
	Frank Sullivan	11.1
	Hooks Wiltse	11.1
192	Elton Chamberlain	11.0
	Lefty Leifield	11.0
	Lindy McDaniel	11.0
	Sam McDowell	11.0
	Orval Overall	11.0
	Frank Viola	11.0
198	Jimmy Key	10.9
199	Teddy Higuera	10.8
	Bob Rush	10.8

Total Pitcher Index

#	Name	Index
201	Hooks Dauss	10.7
	Tex Hughson	10.7
	Al Orth	10.7
	Camilo Pascual	10.7
205	Tommy Bond	10.6
	Bill Hands	10.6
	Art Nehf	10.6
	Jeff Pfeffer	10.6
209	Ellis Kinder	10.5
210	Al Brazle	10.4
	Mark Gubicza	10.4
	Van Mungo	10.4
	Charlie Root	10.4
214	Tug McGraw	10.3
215	Nixey Callahan	10.2
216	Rip Sewell	10.1
217	Joe Horlen	10.0
218	Johnny Sain	9.9
	Lee Smith	9.9
	Gerry Staley	9.9
221	Red Lucas	9.8
	Greg Minton	9.8
223	Joe Dobson	9.7
224	Johnny Allen	9.6
	Mark Baldwin	9.6
	Terry Forster	9.6
	Bill Lee	9.6
	Jack Morris	9.6
	Monte Pearson	9.6
	Rick Rhoden	9.6
231	Vida Blue	9.5
	Harry Coveleski	9.5
	Mike Cuellar	9.5
	Johnny Franco	9.5
	Gary Nolan	9.5
	Dave Righetti	9.5
237	Danny Darwin	9.4
	Ned Garvin	9.4
	Gary Lavelle	9.4
	Don Mossi	9.4
241	Watty Clark	9.3
	Doc Crandall	9.3
243	Red Ames	9.2
	Larry Jansen	9.2
245	Ed Morris	9.1
	Ron Perranoski	9.1
247	Frank Linzy	9.0
	Johnny Rigney	9.0
249	Clint Brown	8.9
	John Denny	8.9
	Pink Hawley	8.9
	Charlie Leibrandt	8.9
	Don McMahon	8.9
	Preacher Roe	8.9
255	Willis Hudlin	8.7
	Sam Jones	8.7
	Vern Law	8.7
	Slim Sallee	8.7
259	George Mogridge	8.6
260	Bob Friend	8.5
	Jesse Orosco	8.5
	Jim Scott	8.5
263	Johnny Schmitz	8.4
	Adonis Terry	8.4
265	Howard Ehmke	8.3
	Toad Ramsey	8.3
	Jeff Tesreau	8.3
	Lefty Tyler	8.3
269	Burt Hooton	8.2
	Bill Lee	8.2
	Billy Rhines	8.2
	Dave Rozema	8.2
273	Tim Burke	8.1
	Willie Hernandez	8.1
	Ray Kremer	8.1
	Bob Locker	8.1
	Herb Pennock	8.1
	Dutch Ruether	8.1
279	Tiny Bonham	8.0
	Joe Bush	8.0
	Frank Smith	8.0
282	Bill Doak	7.9
	Harry Gumbert	7.9
284	Lady Baldwin	7.8
	Bud Black	7.8
	Jesse Haines	7.8
	Lefty Stewart	7.8
288	Jack Harshman	7.7
	Reb Russell	7.7
	Whit Wyatt	7.7
291	Jim Barr	7.6
	Bump Hadley	7.6
	Darold Knowles	7.6
294	Jim Bagby	7.5
	Al Benton	7.5
	Joe Benz	7.5
	Paul Derringer	7.5
	Tom Henke	7.5
	Dave McNally	7.5
300	2 players tied	7.4

Total Pitcher Index (alpha.)

Name	Index
Babe Adams	18.0
Pete Alexander	64.3
Johnny Allen	9.6
Red Ames	9.2
Johnny Antonelli	14.0
Jim Bagby	7.5
Lady Baldwin	7.8
Mark Baldwin	9.6
Jim Barr	7.6
Chief Bender	15.0
Al Benton	7.5
Joe Benz	7.5
Bud Black	7.8
Ewell Blackwell	11.8
Vida Blue	9.5
Bert Blyleven	34.5
Mike Boddicker	11.6
Tommy Bond	10.6
Tiny Bonham	8.0
Al Brazle	10.4
Harry Brecheen	23.5
Ted Breitenstein	12.5
Tommy Bridges	27.6
Clint Brown	8.9
Mordecai Brown	34.7
Charlie Buffinton	21.6
Jim Bunning	17.0
Tom Burgmeier	12.4
Tim Burke	8.1
Joe Bush	8.0
Nixey Callahan	10.2
John Candelaria	15.6
Steve Carlton	35.4
Clay Carroll	11.6
Bob Caruthers	30.9
Elton Chamberlain	11.0
Dean Chance	11.5
Spud Chandler	21.2
Jack Chesbro	11.8
Eddie Cicotte	24.4
Watty Clark	9.3
John Clarkson	52.1
Roger Clemens	23.0
Wilbur Cooper	20.7
Mort Cooper	14.7
Larry Corcoran	15.3
Harry Coveleski	9.5
Stan Coveleski	27.0
Doc Crandall	9.3
Mike Cuellar	9.5
Nig Cuppy	23.4
Danny Darwin	9.4
Hooks Dauss	10.7
Curt Davis	20.1
Dizzy Dean	19.9
John Denny	8.9
Paul Derringer	7.5
Jim Devlin	15.7
Murry Dickson	19.6
Bill Doak	7.9
Joe Dobson	9.7
Don Drysdale	34.6
Frank Dwyer	16.9
Dennis Eckersley	16.9
Howard Ehmke	8.3
Bob Ewing	11.1
Red Faber	25.7
Bob Feller	26.2
Charlie Ferguson	17.2
Wes Ferrell	30.3
Rollie Fingers	11.9
Freddie Fitzsimmons	23.4
Whitey Ford	38.3
Russ Ford	12.4
Terry Forster	9.6
Dave Foutz	18.2
Johnny Franco	9.5
Larry French	17.0
Bob Friend	8.5
Jim Galvin	14.5
Gene Garber	12.4
Mike Garcia	14.1
Ned Garver	17.9
Ned Garvin	9.4
Bob Gibson	44.7
Lefty Gomez	17.7
Dwight Gooden	15.1
Rich Gossage	13.6
Clark Griffith	30.2
Burleigh Grimes	25.4
Lefty Grove	58.7
Mark Gubicza	10.4
Ron Guidry	17.4
Harry Gumbert	7.9
Harvey Haddix	11.5
Bump Hadley	7.6
Noodles Hahn	17.5
Jesse Haines	7.8
Bill Hands	10.6
Mel Harder	18.4

Total Pitcher Index (alpha.)

Jack Harshman	7.7
Pink Hawley	8.9
Guy Hecker	23.5
Claude Hendrix	17.1
Tom Henke	7.5
Willie Hernandez	8.1
Orel Hershiser	18.4
Teddy Higuera	10.8
John Hiller	13.1
Burt Hooton	8.2
Joe Horlen	10.0
Charlie Hough	14.0
Harry Howell	15.9
Waite Hoyt	16.1
Carl Hubbell	38.0
Willis Hudlin	8.7
Tex Hughson	10.7
Fred Hutchinson	13.8
Bill Hutchinson	14.1
Larry Jackson	20.6
Larry Jansen	9.2
Fergie Jenkins	31.6
Tommy John	27.5
Walter Johnson	80.2
Sam Jones	8.7
Addie Joss	25.5
Jim Kaat	21.1
Tim Keefe	37.2
Jimmy Key	10.9
Frank Killen	13.0
Matt Kilroy	11.1
Ellis Kinder	10.5
Silver King	25.0
Darold Knowles	7.6
Jerry Koosman	13.3
Sandy Koufax	18.4
Ray Kremer	8.1
Max Lanier	15.4
Frank Lary	13.5
Gary Lavelle	9.4
Vern Law	8.7
Thornton Lee	17.6
Bill Lee	8.2
Bill Lee	9.6
Sam Leever	15.9
Charlie Leibrandt	8.9
Lefty Leifield	11.0
Bob Lemon	35.7
Dutch Leonard	23.2
Frank Linzy	9.0
Bob Locker	8.1
Eddie Lopat	17.9
Red Lucas	9.8
Dolf Luque	24.8
Sparky Lyle	12.6
Ted Lyons	35.5
Sal Maglie	14.9
Jim Maloney	13.6
Firpo Marberry	11.1
Juan Marichal	30.7
Mike Marshall	12.3
Christy Mathewson	59.2
Jon Matlack	12.8
Carl Mays	35.5
Andy Messersmith	17.8
Stu Miller	12.3
Greg Minton	9.8
George Mogridge	8.6
Ed Morris	9.1
Jack Morris	9.6
Don Mossi	9.4
Tony Mullane	35.6
George Mullin	16.7
Van Mungo	10.4
Jim McCormick	23.0
Lindy McDaniel	11.0
Sam McDowell	11.0
Joe McGinnity	20.4
Tug McGraw	10.3
Don McMahon	8.9
Sadie McMahon	15.4
Dave McNally	7.5
Art Nehf	10.6
Don Newcombe	19.3
Hal Newhouser	37.8
Kid Nichols	62.2
Phil Niekro	37.6
Gary Nolan	9.5
Jesse Orosco	8.5
Al Orth	10.7
Claude Osteen	12.8
Fritz Ostermueller	11.2
Orval Overall	11.0
Jim Palmer	36.4
Milt Pappas	13.6
Mel Parnell	18.2
Camilo Pascual	10.7
Claude Passeau	17.1
Monte Pearson	9.6
Herb Pennock	8.1

Total Pitcher Index (alpha.)

Ron Perranoski	9.1
Gaylord Perry	35.1
Jim Perry	11.8
Gary Peters	12.1
Jeff Pfeffer	10.6
Deacon Phillippe	14.3
Billy Pierce	22.0
Eddie Plank	27.1
Howie Pollet	14.1
Jack Quinn	25.0
Dan Quisenberry	18.0
Charley Radbourn	30.1
Toad Ramsey	8.3
Ed Reulbach	19.4
Rick Reuschel	26.6
Billy Rhines	8.2
Rick Rhoden	9.6
Dave Righetti	9.5
Johnny Rigney	9.0
Eppa Rixey	25.0
Robin Roberts	26.2
Preacher Roe	8.9
Steve Rogers	18.4
Eddie Rommel	25.4
Charlie Root	10.4
Schoolboy Rowe	16.0
Dave Rozema	8.2
Nap Rucker	12.4
Dutch Ruether	8.1
Red Ruffing	26.6
Bob Rush	10.8
Amos Rusie	37.0
Reb Russell	7.7
Babe Ruth	13.8
Nolan Ryan	14.7
Bret Saberhagen	15.8
Johnny Sain	9.9
Slim Sallee	8.7
Ben Sanders	12.2
Johnny Schmitz	8.4
Hal Schumacher	16.5
Jim Scott	8.5
Tom Seaver	50.4
Rip Sewell	10.1
Bobby Shantz	20.1
Bob Shawkey	13.2
Urban Shocker	24.8
Sonny Siebert	11.7
Curt Simmons	14.3
Frank Smith	8.0
Lee Smith	9.9
Sherry Smith	12.8
Warren Spahn	43.0
Gerry Staley	9.9
Bob Stanley	15.4
Lefty Stewart	7.8
Dave Stieb	29.0
Jack Stivetts	31.9
Mel Stottlemyre	17.9
Frank Sullivan	11.1
Bruce Sutter	12.3
Don Sutton	12.7
Frank Tanana	13.2
Jesse Tannehill	21.5
Jack Taylor	17.5
Kent Tekulve	17.2
Adonis Terry	8.4
Jeff Tesreau	8.3
Luis Tiant	18.6
Jim Tobin	13.2
Dizzy Trout	33.8
Virgil Trucks	15.4
John Tudor	17.9
Lefty Tyler	8.3
George Uhle	14.8
Fernando Valenzuela	11.7
Dazzy Vance	24.5
Hippo Vaughn	18.5
Frank Viola	11.0
Rube Waddell	23.1
Ed Walsh	40.8
Bucky Walters	29.1
Monte Ward	12.6
Lon Warneke	23.0
Jake Weimer	11.6
Mickey Welch	15.5
Bob Welch	13.3
Doc White	17.8
Will White	13.3
Jim Whitney	18.4
Hoyt Wilhelm	28.7
Vic Willis	22.0
Hooks Wiltse	11.1
Joe Wood	21.2
Wilbur Wood	15.7
Whit Wyatt	7.7
Early Wynn	17.2
Cy Young	79.9
Tom Zachary	11.7

Total Pitcher Index (by era)

1876-1892

1	John Clarkson	52.1
2	Tim Keefe	37.2
3	Tony Mullane	35.6
4	Jack Stivetts	31.9
5	Bob Caruthers	30.9
6	Charley Radbourn	30.1
7	Silver King	25.0
8	Guy Hecker	23.5
9	Jim McCormick	23.0
10	Charlie Buffinton	21.6
11	Jim Whitney	18.4
12	Dave Foutz	18.2
13	Charlie Ferguson	17.2
14	Jim Devlin	15.7
15	Mickey Welch	15.5
16	Sadie McMahon	15.4
17	Larry Corcoran	15.3
18	Jim Galvin	14.5
19	Bill Hutchinson	14.1
20	Will White	13.3
21	Monte Ward	12.6
22	Ben Sanders	12.2
23	Matt Kilroy	11.1
24	Elton Chamberlain	11.0
25	Tommy Bond	10.6

1893-1919

1	Walter Johnson	80.2
2	Cy Young	79.9
3	Pete Alexander	64.3
4	Kid Nichols	62.2
5	Christy Mathewson	59.2
6	Ed Walsh	40.8
7	Amos Rusie	37.0
8	Mordecai Brown	34.7
9	Clark Griffith	30.2
10	Eddie Plank	27.1
11	Addie Joss	25.5
12	Eddie Cicotte	24.4
13	Nig Cuppy	23.4
14	Rube Waddell	23.1
15	Vic Willis	22.0
16	Jesse Tannehill	21.5
17	Joe Wood	21.2
18	Joe McGinnity	20.4
19	Ed Reulbach	19.4
20	Hippo Vaughn	18.5
21	Babe Adams	18.0
22	Doc White	17.8
23	Noodles Hahn	17.5
	Jack Taylor	17.5
25	Claude Hendrix	17.1

1920-1941

1	Lefty Grove	58.7
2	Carl Hubbell	38.0
3	Ted Lyons	35.5
	Carl Mays	35.5
5	Wes Ferrell	30.3
6	Bucky Walters	29.1
7	Tommy Bridges	27.6
8	Stan Coveleski	27.0
9	Red Ruffing	26.6
10	Red Faber	25.7
11	Burleigh Grimes	25.4
	Eddie Rommel	25.4
13	Jack Quinn	25.0
	Eppa Rixey	25.0
15	Dolf Luque	24.8
	Urban Shocker	24.8
17	Dazzy Vance	24.5
18	Freddie Fitzsimmons	23.4
19	Lon Warneke	23.0
20	Wilbur Cooper	20.7
21	Curt Davis	20.1
22	Dizzy Dean	19.9
23	Mel Harder	18.4
24	Lefty Gomez	17.7
25	Thornton Lee	17.6

Total Pitcher Index (by era)

1942-1960

1	Warren Spahn	43.0
2	Whitey Ford	38.3
3	Hal Newhouser	37.8
4	Bob Lemon	35.7
5	Dizzy Trout	33.8
6	Hoyt Wilhelm	28.7
7	Bob Feller	26.2
	Robin Roberts	26.2
9	Harry Brecheen	23.5
10	Dutch Leonard	23.2
11	Billy Pierce	22.0
12	Spud Chandler	21.2
13	Bobby Shantz	20.1
14	Murry Dickson	19.6
15	Don Newcombe	19.3
16	Mel Parnell	18.2
17	Ned Garver	17.9
	Eddie Lopat	17.9
19	Early Wynn	17.2
20	Max Lanier	15.4
	Virgil Trucks	15.4
22	Sal Maglie	14.9
23	Mort Cooper	14.7
24	Curt Simmons	14.3
25	2 players tied	14.1

1961-1990

1	Tom Seaver	50.4
2	Bob Gibson	44.7
3	Phil Niekro	37.6
4	Jim Palmer	36.4
5	Steve Carlton	35.4
6	Gaylord Perry	35.1
7	Don Drysdale	34.6
8	Bert Blyleven	34.5
9	Fergie Jenkins	31.6
10	Juan Marichal	30.7
11	Dave Stieb	29.0
12	Tommy John	27.5
13	Rick Reuschel	26.6
14	Roger Clemens	23.0
15	Jim Kaat	21.1
16	Larry Jackson	20.6
17	Luis Tiant	18.6
18	Orel Hershiser	18.4
	Sandy Koufax	18.4
	Steve Rogers	18.4
21	Dan Quisenberry	18.0
22	Mel Stottlemyre	17.9
	John Tudor	17.9
24	Andy Messersmith	17.8
25	Ron Guidry	17.4

Total Baseball Ranking

Rank	Name	Value
1	Babe Ruth	121.7
2	Nap Lajoie	92.2
3	Ty Cobb	90.6
4	Ted Williams	89.8
5	Hank Aaron	89.6
6	Tris Speaker	86.4
7	Willie Mays	86.2
8	Honus Wagner	80.6
9	Walter Johnson	80.2
10	Mike Schmidt	80.0
11	Cy Young	79.9
12	Rogers Hornsby	75.8
13	Stan Musial	74.9
14	Frank Robinson	71.2
15	Eddie Collins	70.6
16	Mickey Mantle	66.2
17	Pete Alexander	64.3
18	Kid Nichols	62.2
19	Mel Ott	60.8
20	Lou Gehrig	60.4
21	Christy Mathewson	59.2
22	Lefty Grove	58.7
23	Rickey Henderson	56.3
24	Jimmie Foxx	54.9
25	Joe Morgan	54.0
26	John Clarkson	52.1
	Bill Dahlen	52.1
28	George Davis	52.0
29	Tom Seaver	50.4
30	Carl Yastrzemski	47.5
31	Eddie Mathews	47.3
32	Ed Delahanty	46.6
33	Al Kaline	46.0
34	Bob Gibson	44.7
35	Roberto Clemente	44.4
36	George Brett	44.2
	Joe DiMaggio	44.2
38	Warren Spahn	43.0
39	Reggie Jackson	42.9
40	Charlie Gehringer	42.7
	Bobby Wallace	42.7
42	Bobby Grich	41.2
43	Bid McPhee	41.1
44	Ed Walsh	40.8
45	Roger Connor	40.6
46	Dan Brouthers	39.7
47	Eddie Murray	39.5
48	Ron Santo	39.3
49	Willie McCovey	38.9
50	Joe Cronin	38.8
51	Arky Vaughan	38.5
52	Jack Glasscock	38.4
53	Whitey Ford	38.3
54	Carl Hubbell	38.0
55	Paul Waner	37.9
56	Hal Newhouser	37.8
	Bobby Doerr	37.8
58	Frankie Frisch	37.7
	Keith Hernandez	37.7
	Tim Raines	37.7
61	Phil Niekro	37.6
62	Bob Caruthers	37.5
	Johnny Mize	37.5
64	Wade Boggs	37.4
65	Tim Keefe	37.2
	Joe Jackson	37.2
67	Amos Rusie	37.0
	Ozzie Smith	37.0
69	Dave Winfield	36.8
70	Tony Mullane	36.6
	Gabby Hartnett	36.6
	Bob Johnson	36.6
73	Jim Palmer	36.4
74	Robin Yount	36.3
75	Luke Appling	36.2
76	Reggie Smith	35.8
77	Bob Lemon	35.7
78	Ted Lyons	35.5
	Carl Mays	35.5
80	Steve Carlton	35.4
	Lou Boudreau	35.4
	Bill Mazeroski	35.4
83	Joe Sewell	35.2
84	Gaylord Perry	35.1
85	Mordecai Brown	34.7
	Darrell Evans	34.7
87	Don Drysdale	34.6
88	Bert Blyleven	34.5
89	Frank Baker	34.3
90	Bill Dickey	34.2
91	Dizzy Trout	33.8
92	Cap Anson	33.5
93	Yogi Berra	33.3
94	Dick Allen	33.0
95	Fred Clarke	32.6
96	Jack Stivetts	32.3
97	Billy Herman	32.2
98	Jackie Robinson	32.0
99	Norm Cash	31.9
	Mickey Cochrane	31.9

Total Baseball Ranking

Rank	Name	Value
101	Fergie Jenkins	31.6
102	Dave Bancroft	31.5
	Bobby Bonds	31.5
	Rod Carew	31.5
105	Cupid Childs	31.3
106	Harry Heilmann	31.0
107	Jim Wynn	30.8
108	Juan Marichal	30.7
	Sam Crawford	30.7
	Fred Dunlap	30.7
111	Sam Thompson	30.5
112	Harmon Killebrew	30.4
113	Charley Radbourn	30.3
114	Wes Ferrell	30.3
	Sherry Magee	30.3
116	Clark Griffith	30.2
117	Jesse Burkett	29.8
118	Hank Greenberg	29.5
	Rusty Staub	29.5
120	Jack Clark	29.4
121	Zach Wheat	29.2
122	Billy Williams	29.1
123	Dave Stieb	29.0
	Billy Hamilton	29.0
	Al Simmons	29.0
126	Pete Browning	28.9
127	Hoyt Wilhelm	28.7
128	Hughie Jennings	28.6
129	Hardy Richardson	28.5
130	Elmer Flick	28.4
131	Dwight Evans	28.2
	Willie Stargell	28.2
	Bill Terry	28.2
134	Bucky Walters	27.8
135	Cal Ripken	27.8
136	Ralph Kiner	27.7
137	Tommy Bridges	27.6
138	Tommy John	27.5
139	Buck Ewing	27.4
140	Eddie Plank	27.1
141	Stan Coveleski	27.0
	Max Carey	27.0
	Goose Goslin	27.0
	Joe Medwick	27.0
145	Andre Dawson	26.9
146	Tony Oliva	26.8
	Ryne Sandberg	26.8
148	Jim Rice	26.7
149	Rick Reuschel	26.6
	Red Ruffing	26.6
151	George Sisler	26.6
152	Richie Ashburn	26.5
	King Kelly	26.5
154	Stan Hack	26.3
155	Bob Feller	26.2
	Robin Roberts	26.2
	Dick Bartell	26.2
	Buddy Bell	26.2
159	Joe Gordon	26.0
160	Carlton Fisk	25.8
161	Red Faber	25.7
	Guy Hecker	25.7
163	Jimmy Collins	25.6
164	Addie Joss	25.5
165	Burleigh Grimes	25.4
	Eddie Rommel	25.4
167	Ernie Banks	25.3
168	Silver King	25.0
	Jack Quinn	25.0
	Eppa Rixey	25.0
	Gary Carter	25.0
	Brooks Robinson	25.0
173	Dolf Luque	24.8
	Urban Shocker	24.8
	Graig Nettles	24.8
176	Fred Pfeffer	24.7
177	Dazzy Vance	24.5
178	Eddie Cicotte	24.4
	Duke Snider	24.4
180	Rocky Colavito	24.3
181	Heinie Groh	24.3
182	Chuck Klein	24.2
183	Harry Stovey	24.2
184	Jake Beckley	24.1
185	Jack Fournier	24.0
186	Joe Kelley	23.9
	Paul Molitor	23.9
188	Dave Parker	23.8
	Jimmy Sheckard	23.8
	Roy Thomas	23.8
191	Joe Tinker	23.7
192	Minnie Minoso	23.6
193	Harry Brecheen	23.5
194	Nig Cuppy	23.4
	Freddie Fitzsimmons	23.4
196	Travis Jackson	23.3
	Darryl Strawberry	23.3
198	Dutch Leonard	23.2
	Cesar Cedeno	23.2
	Tony Gwynn	23.2

Total Baseball Ranking

Rank	Name	Value
	Ed Konetchy	23.2
202	Rube Waddell	23.1
203	Roger Clemens	23.0
	Jim McCormick	23.0
	Lon Warneke	23.0
206	Johnny Bench	22.8
	Charlie Keller	22.8
208	Harland Clift	22.4
209	Billy Pierce	22.0
	Vic Willis	22.0
	Art Fletcher	22.0
212	Fred Lynn	21.6
213	Jesse Tannehill	21.5
	George Foster	21.5
	Del Pratt	21.5
	Willie Randolph	21.5
217	Cy Seymour	21.3
218	Spud Chandler	21.2
	Joe Wood	21.2
	Mike Griffin	21.2
	Monte Ward	21.2
222	Jim Kaat	21.1
	Ron Cey	21.1
	Fred Tenney	21.1
225	Jose Cruz	21.0
226	Pedro Guerrero	20.8
	Charley Jones	20.8
228	Wilbur Cooper	20.7
	Tommy Leach	20.7
230	Larry Jackson	20.6
	Eric Davis	20.6
232	Denny Lyons	20.5
233	Charlie Buffinton	20.4
	Joe McGinnity	20.4
235	Pete Rose	20.3
236	Kiki Cuyler	20.2
237	Curt Davis	20.1
	Bobby Shantz	20.1
239	Orlando Cepeda	20.0
	Miller Huggins	20.0
	Bill Joyce	20.0
242	Dizzy Dean	19.9
243	Murry Dickson	19.6
	Ferris Fain	19.6
	Joe Torre	19.6
246	Ken Singleton	19.5
247	Ed Reulbach	19.4
	Roy Campanella	19.4
249	Don Newcombe	19.3
	Gene Alley	19.3
251	Frank Howard	19.2
252	Pie Traynor	19.0
253	Glenn Hubbard	18.8
	Eddie Stanky	18.8
255	Earl Averill	18.7
	Ted Simmons	18.7
257	Luis Tiant	18.6
	Frank Chance	18.6
259	Hippo Vaughn	18.5
260	Mel Harder	18.4
	Orel Hershiser	18.4
	Sandy Koufax	18.4
	Steve Rogers	18.4
	Jim Whitney	18.4
	Roy Cullenbine	18.4
266	Ken Boyer	18.3
	Babe Herman	18.3
	Dale Murphy	18.3
	Alan Trammell	18.3
	Roy White	18.3
271	Mel Parnell	18.2
	Bob Elliott	18.2
	Ken Williams	18.2
274	Roger Bresnahan	18.2
275	Gavvy Cravath	18.1
	Amos Otis	18.1
277	Babe Adams	18.0
	Dan Quisenberry	18.0
	Wally Berger	18.0
	Art Devlin	18.0
	Larry Doby	18.0
	Jimmy Ryan	18.0
283	Ned Garver	17.9
	Eddie Lopat	17.9
	Mel Stottlemyre	17.9
	John Tudor	17.9
287	Andy Messersmith	17.8
	Doc White	17.8
	George Gore	17.8
290	Lefty Gomez	17.7
291	Thornton Lee	17.6
292	Noodles Hahn	17.5
	Jack Taylor	17.5
	Lave Cross	17.5
	Chet Lemon	17.5
296	Ron Guidry	17.4
	Wally Schang	17.4
298	Benny Kauff	17.3
299	Charlie Ferguson	17.2
	Kent Tekulve	17.2

Total Baseball Ranking

Rank	Name	Value
	Early Wynn	17.2
	Barry Bonds	17.2
	John McGraw	17.2
304	Dave Foutz	17.1
	Claude Hendrix	17.1
	Claude Passeau	17.1
	Jim O'Rourke	17.1
308	Jim Bunning	17.0
	Larry French	17.0
	Boog Powell	17.0
	Elmer Smith	17.0
312	Frank Dwyer	16.9
	Dennis Eckersley	16.9
314	Paul Hines	16.8
315	George Mullin	16.7
	Dolph Camilli	16.7
	Rico Carty	16.7
	Jocko Milligan	16.7
319	Ray Chapman	16.6
320	Hal Schumacher	16.5
	Bill Nicholson	16.5
322	Mike Hargrove	16.4
323	Billy Nash	16.3
324	Roger Peckinpaugh	16.2
325	Waite Hoyt	16.1
326	Schoolboy Rowe	16.0
	Kirby Puckett	16.0
328	Sam Leever	15.9
	Hack Wilson	15.9
330	Bret Saberhagen	15.8
	Jesse Barfield	15.8
332	Jim Devlin	15.7
	Wilbur Wood	15.7
	Johnny Evers	15.7
	Hal McRae	15.7
336	John Candelaria	15.6
	Gil McDougald	15.6
	Dwayne Murphy	15.6
	Pee Wee Reese	15.6
	Rudy York	15.6
341	Mickey Welch	15.5
	Johnny Callison	15.5
	Henry Larkin	15.5
344	Max Lanier	15.4
	Sadie McMahon	15.4
	Bob Stanley	15.4
	Virgil Trucks	15.4
	Jim Fregosi	15.4
	Jeff Heath	15.4
	Kip Selbach	15.4
351	Larry Corcoran	15.3
	Dave Orr	15.3
	Chief Zimmer	15.3
354	Harry Howell	15.3
355	Bob Allison	15.2
	Harry Davis	15.2
	Gil Hodges	15.2
	Tony Lazzeri	15.2
	Edd Roush	15.2
	Andy Thornton	15.2
361	Dwight Gooden	15.1
	Brian Downing	15.1
363	Chief Bender	15.0
	Duke Farrell	15.0
	George VanHaltren	15.0
	Jimmy Williams	15.0
367	Sal Maglie	14.9
368	George Uhle	14.8
	Enos Slaughter	14.8
	Vern Stephens	14.8
371	Mort Cooper	14.7
	Nolan Ryan	14.7
	Ernie Lombardi	14.7
374	Kirk Gibson	14.6
375	Jim Galvin	14.5
	Clete Boyer	14.5
	Augie Galan	14.5
	Sid Gordon	14.5
379	Mike Tiernan	14.4
380	Doug DeCinces	14.4
	Johnny Logan	14.4
382	Deacon Phillippe	14.3
	Curt Simmons	14.3
	Bobby Knoop	14.3
	Bobby Murcer	14.3
	Lou Whitaker	14.3
387	Dave Johnson	14.2
	Willie Kamm	14.2
	Roy Smalley	14.2
390	Mike Garcia	14.1
	Bill Hutchinson	14.1
	Howie Pollet	14.1
	Gene Tenace	14.1
394	Johnny Antonelli	14.0
	Charlie Hough	14.0
	Bobby Veach	14.0
397	Mike Donlin	13.9
398	Fred Hutchinson	13.8
399	Don Baylor	13.7
	Ben Chapman	13.7

Total Baseball Ranking

	Thurman Munson	13.7
402	Rich Gossage	13.6
	Jim Maloney	13.6
	Milt Pappas	13.6
	Lance Parrish	13.6
	Roy Sievers	13.6
407	Frank Lary	13.5
	Don Mattingly	13.5
409	Jerry Koosman	13.3
	Bob Welch	13.3
	Will White	13.3
	Tommy Henrich	13.3
413	Bob Shawkey	13.2
	Frank Tanana	13.2
	Jim Tobin	13.2
416	John Hiller	13.1
	Deacon McGuire	13.1
	Richie Zisk	13.1
419	Tip O'Neill	13.1
420	Frank Killen	13.0
	Ken Keltner	13.0
	Kevin McReynolds	13.0
423	Will Clark	12.9
	Tony Fernandez	12.9
425	Jon Matlack	12.8
	Claude Osteen	12.8
	Sherry Smith	12.8
428	Don Sutton	12.7
	Mark Belanger	12.7
	Charlie Bennett	12.7
	Willie Keeler	12.7
	Orator Shaffer	12.7
	George Stone	12.7
434	Sparky Lyle	12.6
	Kid Elberfeld	12.6
	Tony Perez	12.6
	Claude Ritchey	12.6
	Phil Rizzuto	12.6
	Ossee Schreckengost	12.6
440	Ted Breitenstein	12.5
	Jerry Denny	12.5
442	Tom Burgmeier	12.4
	Russ Ford	12.4
	Gene Garber	12.4
	Nap Rucker	12.4
	Earle Combs	12.4
	Dal Maxvill	12.4
448	Mike Marshall	12.3
	Stu Miller	12.3
	Bruce Sutter	12.3
	John Titus	12.3
452	Ben Sanders	12.2
	Bill Freehan	12.2
454	Gary Peters	12.1
	Roger Maris	12.1
456	Jack Clements	12.0
	Lou Criger	12.0
458	Rollie Fingers	11.9
	Darrell Porter	11.9
	Red Smith	11.9
461	Ewell Blackwell	11.8
	Jack Chesbro	11.8
	Jim Perry	11.8
	Jake Daubert	11.8
	Rick Ferrell	11.8
	Ron Hansen	11.8
	Ed McFarland	11.8
468	Sonny Siebert	11.7
	Fernando Valenzuela	11.7
	Tom Zachary	11.7
	Chief Meyers	11.7
	Al Rosen	11.7
473	Mike Boddicker	11.6
	Clay Carroll	11.6
	Jake Weimer	11.6
	Fred Carroll	11.6
	Tom Daly	11.6
	Greg Luzinski	11.6
	Cy Williams	11.6
480	Dean Chance	11.5
	Harvey Haddix	11.5
	Lonny Frey	11.5
	Ed Swartwood	11.5
	Ned Williamson	11.5
485	Bill Melton	11.4
	Johnny Pesky	11.4
	Red Schoendienst	11.4
	Andy VanSlyke	11.4
489	Lonnie Smith	11.3
	Ross Youngs	11.3
491	Fritz Ostermueller	11.2
	Tony Cuccinello	11.2
	Oscar Gamble	11.2
	Charlie Hickman	11.2
495	11 players tied	11.1

Total Baseball Rank (alpha.)

Hank Aaron	89.6
Babe Adams	18.0
Pete Alexander	64.3
Dick Allen	33.0
Gene Alley	19.3
Bob Allison	15.2
Cap Anson	33.5
Johnny Antonelli	14.0
Luke Appling	36.2
Richie Ashburn	26.5
Earl Averill	18.7
Frank Baker	34.3
Dave Bancroft	31.5
Ernie Banks	25.3
Jesse Barfield	15.8
Dick Bartell	26.2
Don Baylor	13.7
Jake Beckley	24.1
Mark Belanger	12.7
Buddy Bell	26.2
Johnny Bench	22.8
Chief Bender	15.0
Charlie Bennett	12.7
Wally Berger	18.0
Yogi Berra	33.3
Ewell Blackwell	11.8
Bert Blyleven	34.5
Mike Boddicker	11.6
Wade Boggs	37.4
Barry Bonds	17.2
Bobby Bonds	31.5
Lou Boudreau	35.4
Clete Boyer	14.5
Ken Boyer	18.3
Harry Brecheen	23.5
Ted Breitenstein	12.5
Roger Bresnahan	18.2
George Brett	44.2
Tommy Bridges	27.6
Dan Brouthers	39.7
Mordecai Brown	34.7
Pete Browning	28.9
Charlie Buffinton	20.4
Jim Bunning	17.0
Tom Burgmeier	12.4
Jesse Burkett	29.8
Johnny Callison	15.5
Dolph Camilli	16.7
Roy Campanella	19.4
John Candelaria	15.6
Rod Carew	31.5
Max Carey	27.0
Steve Carlton	35.4
Clay Carroll	11.6
Fred Carroll	11.6
Gary Carter	25.0
Rico Carty	16.7
Bob Caruthers	37.5
Norm Cash	31.9
Cesar Cedeno	23.2
Orlando Cepeda	20.0
Ron Cey	21.1
Dean Chance	11.5
Frank Chance	18.6
Spud Chandler	21.2
Ray Chapman	16.6
Ben Chapman	13.7
Jack Chesbro	11.8
Cupid Childs	31.3
Eddie Cicotte	24.4
Jack Clark	29.4
Will Clark	12.9
Fred Clarke	32.6
John Clarkson	52.1
Roger Clemens	23.0
Roberto Clemente	44.4
Jack Clements	12.0
Harlond Clift	22.4
Ty Cobb	90.6
Mickey Cochrane	31.9
Rocky Colavito	24.3
Eddie Collins	70.6
Jimmy Collins	25.6
Earle Combs	12.4
Roger Connor	40.6
Wilbur Cooper	20.7
Mort Cooper	14.7
Larry Corcoran	15.3
Stan Coveleski	27.0
Gavvy Cravath	18.1
Sam Crawford	30.7
Lou Criger	12.0
Joe Cronin	38.8
Lave Cross	17.5
Jose Cruz	21.0
Tony Cuccinello	11.2
Roy Cullenbine	18.4
Nig Cuppy	23.4
Kiki Cuyler	20.2
Bill Dahlen	52.1

Total Baseball Rank (alpha.)

Tom Daly	11.6
Jake Daubert	11.8
Curt Davis	20.1
Eric Davis	20.6
George Davis	52.0
Harry Davis	15.2
Andre Dawson	26.9
Dizzy Dean	19.9
Ed Delahanty	46.6
Jerry Denny	12.5
Jim Devlin	15.7
Art Devlin	18.0
Bill Dickey	34.2
Murry Dickson	19.6
Larry Doby	18.0
Bobby Doerr	37.8
Mike Donlin	13.9
Brian Downing	15.1
Don Drysdale	34.6
Fred Dunlap	30.7
Frank Dwyer	16.9
Doug DeCinces	14.4
Joe DiMaggio	44.2
Dennis Eckersley	16.9
Kid Elberfeld	12.6
Bob Elliott	18.2
Darrell Evans	34.7
Dwight Evans	28.2
Johnny Evers	15.7
Buck Ewing	27.4
Red Faber	25.7
Ferris Fain	19.6
Duke Farrell	15.0
Bob Feller	26.2
Charlie Ferguson	17.2
Tony Fernandez	12.9
Wes Ferrell	30.3
Rick Ferrell	11.8
Rollie Fingers	11.9
Carlton Fisk	25.8
Freddie Fitzsimmons	23.4
Art Fletcher	22.0
Elmer Flick	28.4
Whitey Ford	38.3
Russ Ford	12.4
George Foster	21.5
Jack Fournier	24.0
Dave Foutz	17.1
Jimmie Foxx	54.9
Bill Freehan	12.2
Jim Fregosi	15.4
Larry French	17.0
Lonny Frey	11.5
Frankie Frisch	37.7
Augie Galan	14.5
Jim Galvin	14.5
Oscar Gamble	11.2
Gene Garber	12.4
Mike Garcia	14.1
Ned Garver	17.9
Lou Gehrig	60.4
Charlie Gehringer	42.7
Bob Gibson	44.7
Kirk Gibson	14.6
Jack Glasscock	38.4
Lefty Gomez	17.7
Dwight Gooden	15.1
Joe Gordon	26.0
Sid Gordon	14.5
George Gore	17.8
Goose Goslin	27.0
Rich Gossage	13.6
Hank Greenberg	29.5
Bobby Grich	41.2
Mike Griffin	21.2
Clark Griffith	30.2
Burleigh Grimes	25.4
Heinie Groh	24.3
Lefty Grove	58.7
Pedro Guerrero	20.8
Ron Guidry	17.4
Tony Gwynn	23.2
Stan Hack	26.3
Harvey Haddix	11.5
Noodles Hahn	17.5
Billy Hamilton	29.0
Ron Hansen	11.8
Mel Harder	18.4
Mike Hargrove	16.4
Gabby Hartnett	36.6
Jeff Heath	15.4
Guy Hecker	25.7
Harry Heilmann	31.0
Rickey Henderson	56.3
Claude Hendrix	17.1
Tommy Henrich	13.3
Babe Herman	18.3
Billy Herman	32.2
Keith Hernandez	37.7
Orel Hershiser	18.4

Total Baseball Rank (alpha.)

Charlie Hickman	11.2
John Hiller	13.1
Paul Hines	16.8
Gil Hodges	15.2
Rogers Hornsby	75.8
Charlie Hough	14.0
Frank Howard	19.2
Harry Howell	15.3
Waite Hoyt	16.1
Glenn Hubbard	18.8
Carl Hubbell	38.0
Miller Huggins	20.0
Fred Hutchinson	13.8
Bill Hutchinson	14.1
Larry Jackson	20.6
Joe Jackson	37.2
Reggie Jackson	42.9
Travis Jackson	23.3
Fergie Jenkins	31.6
Hughie Jennings	28.6
Tommy John	27.5
Walter Johnson	80.2
Dave Johnson	14.2
Bob Johnson	36.6
Charley Jones	20.8
Addie Joss	25.5
Bill Joyce	20.0
Jim Kaat	21.1
Al Kaline	46.0
Willie Kamm	14.2
Benny Kauff	17.3
Tim Keefe	37.2
Willie Keeler	12.7
Charlie Keller	22.8
Joe Kelley	23.9
King Kelly	26.5
Ken Keltner	13.0
Harmon Killebrew	30.4
Frank Killen	13.0
Ralph Kiner	27.7
Silver King	25.0
Chuck Klein	24.2
Bobby Knoop	14.3
Ed Konetchy	23.2
Jerry Koosman	13.3
Sandy Koufax	18.4
Nap Lajoie	92.2
Max Lanier	15.4
Henry Larkin	15.5
Frank Lary	13.5
Tony Lazzeri	15.2
Tommy Leach	20.7
Thornton Lee	17.6
Sam Leever	15.9
Bob Lemon	35.7
Chet Lemon	17.5
Dutch Leonard	23.2
Johnny Logan	14.4
Ernie Lombardi	14.7
Eddie Lopat	17.9
Dolf Luque	24.8
Greg Luzinski	11.6
Sparky Lyle	12.6
Fred Lynn	21.6
Ted Lyons	35.5
Denny Lyons	20.5
Sherry Magee	30.3
Sal Maglie	14.9
Jim Maloney	13.6
Mickey Mantle	66.2
Juan Marichal	30.7
Roger Maris	12.1
Mike Marshall	12.3
Eddie Mathews	47.3
Christy Mathewson	59.2
Jon Matlack	12.8
Don Mattingly	13.5
Dal Maxvill	12.4
Carl Mays	35.5
Willie Mays	86.2
Bill Mazeroski	35.4
Joe Medwick	27.0
Bill Melton	11.4
Andy Messersmith	17.8
Chief Meyers	11.7
Stu Miller	12.3
Jocko Milligan	16.7
Minnie Minoso	23.6
Johnny Mize	37.5
Paul Molitor	23.9
Joe Morgan	54.0
Tony Mullane	36.6
George Mullin	16.7
Thurman Munson	13.7
Bobby Murcer	14.3
Dale Murphy	18.3
Dwayne Murphy	15.6
Eddie Murray	39.5
Stan Musial	74.9
Jim McCormick	23.0

Total Baseball Rank (alpha.)

Player	Rank
Willie McCovey	38.9
Gil McDougald	15.6
Ed McFarland	11.8
Joe McGinnity	20.4
John McGraw	17.2
Deacon McGuire	13.1
Sadie McMahon	15.4
Bid McPhee	41.1
Hal McRae	15.7
Kevin McReynolds	13.0
Billy Nash	16.3
Graig Nettles	24.8
Don Newcombe	19.3
Hal Newhouser	37.8
Kid Nichols	62.2
Bill Nicholson	16.5
Phil Niekro	37.6
Tip O'Neill	13.1
Jim O'Rourke	17.1
Tony Oliva	26.8
Dave Orr	15.3
Claude Osteen	12.8
Fritz Ostermueller	11.2
Amos Otis	18.1
Mel Ott	60.8
Jim Palmer	36.4
Milt Pappas	13.6
Dave Parker	23.8
Mel Parnell	18.2
Lance Parrish	13.6
Claude Passeau	17.1
Roger Peckinpaugh	16.2
Tony Perez	12.6
Gaylord Perry	35.1
Jim Perry	11.8
Johnny Pesky	11.4
Gary Peters	12.1
Fred Pfeffer	24.7
Deacon Phillippe	14.3
Billy Pierce	22.0
Eddie Plank	27.1
Howie Pollet	14.1
Darrell Porter	11.9
Boog Powell	17.0
Del Pratt	21.5
Kirby Puckett	16.0
Jack Quinn	25.0
Dan Quisenberry	18.0
Charley Radbourn	30.3
Tim Raines	37.7
Willie Randolph	21.5
Pee Wee Reese	15.6
Ed Reulbach	19.4
Rick Reuschel	26.6
Jim Rice	26.7
Hardy Richardson	28.5
Cal Ripken	27.8
Claude Ritchey	12.6
Eppa Rixey	25.0
Phil Rizzuto	12.6
Robin Roberts	26.2
Brooks Robinson	25.0
Frank Robinson	71.2
Jackie Robinson	32.0
Steve Rogers	18.4
Eddie Rommel	25.4
Pete Rose	20.3
Al Rosen	11.7
Edd Roush	15.2
Schoolboy Rowe	16.0
Nap Rucker	12.4
Red Ruffing	26.6
Amos Rusie	37.0
Babe Ruth	121.7
Nolan Ryan	14.7
Jimmy Ryan	18.0
Bret Saberhagen	15.8
Ryne Sandberg	26.8
Ben Sanders	12.2
Ron Santo	39.3
Wally Schang	17.4
Mike Schmidt	80.0
Red Schoendienst	11.4
Ossee Schreckengost	12.6
Hal Schumacher	16.5
Tom Seaver	50.4
Kip Selbach	15.4
Joe Sewell	35.2
Cy Seymour	21.3
Orator Shaffer	12.7
Bobby Shantz	20.1
Bob Shawkey	13.2
Jimmy Sheckard	23.8
Urban Shocker	24.8
Sonny Siebert	11.7
Roy Sievers	13.6
Curt Simmons	14.3
Al Simmons	29.0
Ted Simmons	18.7
Ken Singleton	19.5

Total Baseball Rank (alpha.)

Player	Rank
George Sisler	26.6
Enos Slaughter	14.8
Roy Smalley	14.2
Sherry Smith	12.8
Reggie Smith	35.8
Elmer Smith	17.0
Red Smith	11.9
Lonnie Smith	11.3
Ozzie Smith	37.0
Duke Snider	24.4
Warren Spahn	43.0
Tris Speaker	86.4
Eddie Stanky	18.8
Bob Stanley	15.4
Willie Stargell	28.2
Rusty Staub	29.5
Vern Stephens	14.8
Dave Stieb	29.0
Jack Stivetts	32.3
George Stone	12.7
Mel Stottlemyre	17.9
Harry Stovey	24.2
Darryl Strawberry	23.3
Bruce Sutter	12.3
Don Sutton	12.7
Ed Swartwood	11.5
Frank Tanana	13.2
Jesse Tannehill	21.5
Jack Taylor	17.5
Kent Tekulve	17.2
Gene Tenace	14.1
Fred Tenney	21.1
Bill Terry	28.2
Roy Thomas	23.8
Sam Thompson	30.5
Andy Thornton	15.2
Luis Tiant	18.6
Mike Tiernan	14.4
Joe Tinker	23.7
John Titus	12.3
Jim Tobin	13.2
Joe Torre	19.6
Alan Trammell	18.3
Pie Traynor	19.0
Dizzy Trout	33.8
Virgil Trucks	15.4
John Tudor	17.9
George Uhle	14.8
Fernando Valenzuela	11.7
Dazzy Vance	24.5
Arky Vaughan	38.5
Hippo Vaughn	18.5
Bobby Veach	14.0
George VanHaltren	15.0
Andy VanSlyke	11.4
Rube Waddell	23.1
Honus Wagner	80.6
Bobby Wallace	42.7
Ed Walsh	40.8
Bucky Walters	27.8
Paul Waner	37.9
Monte Ward	21.2
Lon Warneke	23.0
Jake Weimer	11.6
Mickey Welch	15.5
Bob Welch	13.3
Zach Wheat	29.2
Lou Whitaker	14.3
Doc White	17.8
Will White	13.3
Roy White	18.3
Jim Whitney	18.4
Hoyt Wilhelm	28.7
Billy Williams	29.1
Cy Williams	11.6
Jimmy Williams	15.0
Ken Williams	18.2
Ted Williams	89.8
Ned Williamson	11.5
Vic Willis	22.0
Hack Wilson	15.9
Dave Winfield	36.8
Joe Wood	21.2
Wilbur Wood	15.7
Early Wynn	17.2
Jim Wynn	30.8
Carl Yastrzemski	47.5
Rudy York	15.6
Cy Young	79.9
Ross Youngs	11.3
Robin Yount	36.3
Tom Zachary	11.7
Chief Zimmer	15.3
Richie Zisk	13.1

Total Baseball Rank (by era)

1876-1892

	Player	Rank
1	John Clarkson	52.1
2	Bid McPhee	41.1
3	Roger Connor	40.6
4	Dan Brouthers	39.7
5	Jack Glasscock	38.4
6	Bob Caruthers	37.5
7	Tim Keefe	37.2
8	Tony Mullane	36.6
9	Cap Anson	33.5
10	Jack Stivetts	32.3
11	Fred Dunlap	30.7
12	Sam Thompson	30.5
13	Charley Radbourn	30.3
14	Pete Browning	28.9
15	Hardy Richardson	28.5
16	Buck Ewing	27.4
17	King Kelly	26.5
18	Guy Hecker	25.7
19	Silver King	25.0
20	Fred Pfeffer	24.7
21	Harry Stovey	24.2
22	Jim McCormick	23.0
23	Monte Ward	21.2
24	Charley Jones	20.8
25	Denny Lyons	20.5

1893-1919

	Player	Rank
1	Nap Lajoie	92.2
2	Ty Cobb	90.6
3	Tris Speaker	86.4
4	Honus Wagner	80.6
5	Walter Johnson	80.2
6	Cy Young	79.9
7	Eddie Collins	70.6
8	Pete Alexander	64.3
9	Kid Nichols	62.2
10	Christy Mathewson	59.2
11	Bill Dahlen	52.1
12	George Davis	52.0
13	Ed Delahanty	46.6
14	Bobby Wallace	42.7
15	Ed Walsh	40.8
16	Joe Jackson	37.2
17	Amos Rusie	37.0
18	Mordecai Brown	34.7
19	Frank Baker	34.3
20	Fred Clarke	32.6
21	Cupid Childs	31.3
22	Sam Crawford	30.7
23	Sherry Magee	30.3
24	Clark Griffith	30.2
25	Jesse Burkett	29.8

1920-1941

	Player	Rank
1	Babe Ruth	121.7
2	Rogers Hornsby	75.8
3	Mel Ott	60.8
4	Lou Gehrig	60.4
5	Lefty Grove	58.7
6	Jimmie Foxx	54.9
7	Charlie Gehringer	42.7
8	Joe Cronin	38.8
9	Arky Vaughan	38.5
10	Carl Hubbell	38.0
11	Paul Waner	37.9
12	Frankie Frisch	37.7
13	Gabby Hartnett	36.6
	Bob Johnson	36.6
15	Luke Appling	36.2
16	Ted Lyons	35.5
	Carl Mays	35.5
18	Joe Sewell	35.2
19	Bill Dickey	34.2
20	Billy Herman	32.2
21	Mickey Cochrane	31.9
22	Dave Bancroft	31.5
23	Harry Heilmann	31.0
24	Wes Ferrell	30.3
25	Hank Greenberg	29.5

Total Baseball Ranking (by era)

1942-1960

	Player	Rank
1	Ted Williams	89.8
2	Stan Musial	74.9
3	Mickey Mantle	66.2
4	Eddie Mathews	47.3
5	Joe DiMaggio	44.2
6	Warren Spahn	43.0
7	Whitey Ford	38.3
8	Hal Newhouser	37.8
	Bobby Doerr	37.8
10	Johnny Mize	37.5
11	Bob Lemon	35.7
12	Lou Boudreau	35.4
13	Dizzy Trout	33.8
14	Yogi Berra	33.3
15	Jackie Robinson	32.0
16	Hoyt Wilhelm	28.7
17	Ralph Kiner	27.7
18	Richie Ashburn	26.5
19	Bob Feller	26.2
	Robin Roberts	26.2
21	Joe Gordon	26.0
22	Duke Snider	24.4
23	Minnie Minoso	23.6
24	Harry Brecheen	23.5
25	Dutch Leonard	23.2

1961-1990

	Player	Rank
1	Hank Aaron	89.6
2	Willie Mays	86.2
3	Mike Schmidt	80.0
4	Frank Robinson	71.2
5	Rickey Henderson	56.3
6	Joe Morgan	54.0
7	Tom Seaver	50.4
8	Carl Yastrzemski	47.5
9	Al Kaline	46.0
10	Bob Gibson	44.7
11	Roberto Clemente	44.4
12	George Brett	44.2
13	Reggie Jackson	42.9
14	Bobby Grich	41.2
15	Eddie Murray	39.5
16	Ron Santo	39.3
17	Willie McCovey	38.9
18	Keith Hernandez	37.7
	Tim Raines	37.7
20	Phil Niekro	37.6
21	Wade Boggs	37.4
22	Ozzie Smith	37.0
23	Dave Winfield	36.8
24	Jim Palmer	36.4
25	Robin Yount	36.3

At Bats

1	Willie Wilson, 1980	705
2	Juan Samuel, 1984	701
3	Dave Cash, 1975	699
4	Matty Alou, 1969	698
5	Woody Jensen, 1936	696
6	Maury Wills, 1962	695
	Omar Moreno, 1979	695
8	Bobby Richardson, 1962	692
9	Kirby Puckett, 1985	691
10	Lou Brock, 1967	689
	Sandy Alomar, 1971	689
12	Dave Cash, 1974	687
	Tony Fernandez, 1986	687
14	Horace Clarke, 1970	686
15	Lloyd Waner, 1931	681
	Jo-Jo Moore, 1935	681
17	Pete Rose, 1973	680
	Frank Taveras, 1979	680
	Kirby Puckett, 1986	680
20	Harvey Kuenn, 1953	679
	Curt Flood, 1964	679
	Bobby Richardson, 1964	679
23	Dick Groat, 1962	678
24	Matty Alou, 1970	677
	Jim Rice, 1978	677
	Don Mattingly, 1986	677
27	Felix Millan, 1975	676
	Omar Moreno, 1980	676
29	Rennie Stennett, 1974	673
	Bill Buckner, 1985	673
31	Rabbit Maranville, 1922	672
	Tony Oliva, 1964	672
	Sandy Alomar, 1970	672
	Garry Templeton, 1979	672
35	Jack Tobin, 1921	671
36	Al Simmons, 1932	670
	Pete Rose, 1965	670
	Buddy Bell, 1979	670
39	Vada Pinson, 1965	669
	Larry Bowa, 1974	669
41	Buddy Lewis, 1937	668
	Brooks Robinson, 1961	668
	Ralph Garr, 1973	668
44	Carl Furillo, 1951	667
45	Billy Herman, 1935	666
	Zoilo Versalles, 1965	666
	Felipe Alou, 1966	666
	Dave Cash, 1976	666
	Ron LeFlore, 1978	666
	Paul Molitor, 1982	666
51	Tommy Davis, 1962	665
	Pete Rose, 1976	665
53	Taylor Douthit, 1930	664
	Bobby Richardson, 1965	664
	Don Kessinger, 1969	664
	Lou Brock, 1970	664
57	Jake Wood, 1961	663
	Bill Virdon, 1962	663
	Bobby Bonds, 1970	663
	Rick Burleson, 1977	663
	Cal Ripken, 1983	663
	Juan Samuel, 1985	663
	Joe Carter, 1986	663
64	Lloyd Waner, 1929	662
	Hughie Critz, 1930	662
	Richie Ashburn, 1949	662
	Granny Hamner, 1949	662
	Bobby Richardson, 1961	662
	Curt Flood, 1963	662
	Felipe Alou, 1968	662
	Pete Rose, 1975	662
72	Doc Cramer, 1933	661
	Doc Cramer, 1940	661
	Ken Hubbs, 1962	661
	Cecil Cooper, 1983	661
76	Tom Brown, 1892	660
	Doc Cramer, 1941	660
	Lou Brock, 1968	660
	Enos Cabell, 1978	660
80	Lloyd Waner, 1928	659
	Hughie Critz, 1932	659
	Red Schoendienst, 1947	659
	Billy Moran, 1962	659
	Zoilo Versalles, 1964	659
	Luis Aparicio, 1966	659
	Steve Garvey, 1975	659
	Warren Cromartie, 1979	659
88	Heinie Manush, 1933	658
	Doc Cramer, 1938	658
	Bill White, 1963	658
	Dave Cash, 1978	658
	Steve Garvey, 1980	658
	Julio Franco, 1984	658
94	Cesar Tovar, 1971	657
	Bill Buckner, 1982	657
	Jim Rice, 1984	657
	Kirby Puckett, 1988	657
98	9 players tied	656

Runs

1	Billy Hamilton, 1894	192
2	Tom Brown, 1891	177
	Babe Ruth, 1921	177
4	Tip O'Neill, 1887	167
	Lou Gehrig, 1936	167
6	Billy Hamilton, 1895	166
7	Willie Keeler, 1894	165
	Joe Kelley, 1894	165
9	Arlie Latham, 1887	163
	Babe Ruth, 1928	163
	Lou Gehrig, 1931	163
12	Willie Keeler, 1895	162
13	Hugh Duffy, 1890	161
14	Fred Dunlap, 1884	160
	Hugh Duffy, 1894	160
	Jesse Burkett, 1896	160
17	Hughie Jennings, 1895	159
18	Bobby Lowe, 1894	158
	Babe Ruth, 1920	158
	Babe Ruth, 1927	158
	Chuck Klein, 1930	158
22	John McGraw, 1894	156
	Rogers Hornsby, 1929	156
24	King Kelly, 1886	155
	Kiki Cuyler, 1930	155
26	Dan Brouthers, 1887	153
	Jesse Burkett, 1895	153
	Willie Keeler, 1896	153
29	Arlie Latham, 1886	152
	Mike Tiernan, 1889	152
	Harry Stovey, 1889	152
	Billy Hamilton, 1896	152
	Billy Hamilton, 1897	152
	Lefty O'Doul, 1929	152
	Woody English, 1930	152
	Al Simmons, 1930	152
	Chuck Klein, 1932	152
38	Babe Ruth, 1923	151
	Jimmie Foxx, 1932	151
	Joe DiMaggio, 1937	151
41	George Gore, 1886	150
	Babe Ruth, 1930	150
	Ted Williams, 1949	150
44	Herman Long, 1893	149
	Bill Dahlen, 1894	149
	Ed Delahanty, 1895	149
	Lou Gehrig, 1927	149
	Babe Ruth, 1931	149
49	Hub Collins, 1890	148
	Jake Stenzel, 1894	148
	Joe Kelley, 1895	148
	Joe Kelley, 1896	148
53	Mike Tiernan, 1889	147
	Hugh Duffy, 1893	147
	Ed Delahanty, 1894	147
	Ty Cobb, 1911	147
57	Darby O'Brien, 1889	146
	Tom Brown, 1890	146
	Hack Wilson, 1930	146
	Rickey Henderson, 1985	146
61	Jesse Burkett, 1893	145
	Cupid Childs, 1893	145
	Ed Delahanty, 1893	145
	Patsy Donovan, 1894	145
	Willie Keeler, 1897	145
	Nap Lajoie, 1901	145
	Harlond Clift, 1936	145
68	Hugh Duffy, 1889	144
	Billy Hamilton, 1889	144
	Ty Cobb, 1915	144
	Kiki Cuyler, 1925	144
	Charlie Gehringer, 1930	144
	Al Simmons, 1932	144
	Charlie Gehringer, 1936	144
	Hank Greenberg, 1938	144
76	Cupid Childs, 1894	143
	John McGraw, 1898	143
	Babe Ruth, 1924	143
	Babe Herman, 1930	143
	Lou Gehrig, 1930	143
	Earle Combs, 1932	143
	Red Rolfe, 1937	143
83	Mike Griffin, 1887	142
	Harry Stovey, 1890	142
	Jesse Burkett, 1901	142
	Paul Waner, 1928	142
	Ted Williams, 1946	142
88	Billy Hamilton, 1891	141
	Rogers Hornsby, 1922	141
	Ted Williams, 1942	141
91	Tom Poorman, 1887	140
	Jimmy Ryan, 1889	140
	Jim McTamany, 1890	140
	Mike Griffin, 1895	140
	Willie Keeler, 1899	140
	John McGraw, 1899	140
	Max Carey, 1922	140
	Earl Averill, 1931	140
99	9 players tied	139

Runs per Game

1876-1892

1	Ross Barnes, 1876	1.91
2	Fred Dunlap, 1884	1.58
3	George Gore, 1890	1.42
4	Tip O'Neill, 1887	1.35
5	King Kelly, 1886	1.31
6	Tom Brown, 1891	1.29
7	George Gore, 1886	1.27
8	Dan Brouthers, 1887	1.24
9	Orator Shaffer, 1884	1.23
10	Mike Tiernan, 1889	1.20
11	Harry Stovey, 1890	1.20
12	Arlie Latham, 1887	1.20
13	Harry Stovey, 1884	1.19
14	George Gore, 1882	1.18
15	George Gore, 1881	1.18

1893-1919

1	Billy Hamilton, 1894	1.49
2	Billy Hamilton, 1895	1.35
3	Billy Hamilton, 1893	1.34
4	Herman Long, 1894	1.32
5	Ed Delahanty, 1894	1.29
6	Ed Delahanty, 1895	1.28
7	Hugh Duffy, 1894	1.28
8	Willie Keeler, 1894	1.28
	Joe Kelley, 1894	1.28
10	John McGraw, 1894	1.26
11	Willie Keeler, 1895	1.24
12	Bill Dahlen, 1894	1.23
13	Jimmy Ryan, 1894	1.22
14	Willie Keeler, 1896	1.21
15	Hughie Jennings, 1895	1.21

1920-1941

1	Babe Ruth, 1921	1.16
2	Babe Ruth, 1920	1.11
3	Al Simmons, 1930	1.10
4	Lou Gehrig, 1936	1.08
5	Babe Ruth, 1928	1.06
6	Lou Gehrig, 1931	1.05
7	Jimmie Foxx, 1939	1.05
8	Babe Ruth, 1927	1.05
9	Babe Ruth, 1930	1.03
10	Babe Ruth, 1931	1.03
11	Chuck Klein, 1930	1.01
12	Rogers Hornsby, 1929	1.00
	Joe DiMaggio, 1937	1.00
14	Kiki Cuyler, 1930	.99
15	Babe Ruth, 1923	.99

1942-1960

1	Ted Williams, 1949	.97
2	Ted Williams, 1946	.95
3	Tommy Henrich, 1948	.95
4	Ted Williams, 1942	.94
5	Dom DiMaggio, 1950	.93
6	Ted Williams, 1948	.91
7	Johnny Mize, 1947	.89
8	Eddie Joost, 1949	.89
9	Mickey Mantle, 1954	.88
10	Johnny Pesky, 1950	.88
11	Mickey Mantle, 1956	.88
12	Stan Musial, 1948	.87
13	Goody Rosen, 1945	.87
	Dom DiMaggio, 1949	.87
15	Johnny Pesky, 1948	.87

1961-1990

1	Rickey Henderson, 1985	1.02
2	Paul Molitor, 1987	.97
3	Eric Davis, 1987	.93
4	Tim Raines, 1987	.88
5	Rickey Henderson, 1990	.88
6	Mickey Mantle, 1961	.86
7	Bobby Bonds, 1970	.85
8	Tim Raines, 1983	.85
9	Billy Williams, 1970	.85
10	Paul Molitor, 1982	.85
11	Rickey Henderson, 1986	.85
12	Robin Yount, 1980	.85
13	Rickey Henderson, 1988	.84
14	Willie Mays, 1961	.84
15	Frank Robinson, 1962	.83

Hits

1	George Sisler, 1920	257
2	Lefty O'Doul, 1929	254
	Bill Terry, 1930	254
4	Al Simmons, 1925	253
5	Rogers Hornsby, 1922	250
	Chuck Klein, 1930	250
7	Ty Cobb, 1911	248
8	George Sisler, 1922	246
9	Heinie Manush, 1928	241
	Babe Herman, 1930	241
11	Jesse Burkett, 1896	240
	Wade Boggs, 1985	240
13	Willie Keeler, 1897	239
	Rod Carew, 1977	239
15	Ed Delahanty, 1899	238
	Don Mattingly, 1986	238
17	Hugh Duffy, 1894	237
	Harry Heilmann, 1921	237
	Paul Waner, 1927	237
	Joe Medwick, 1937	237
21	Jack Tobin, 1921	236
22	Rogers Hornsby, 1921	235
23	Lloyd Waner, 1929	234
	Kirby Puckett, 1988	234
25	Joe Jackson, 1911	233
26	Nap Lajoie, 1901	232
	Earl Averill, 1936	232
28	Earle Combs, 1927	231
	Freddy Lindstrom, 1928	231
	Freddy Lindstrom, 1930	231
	Matty Alou, 1969	231
32	Stan Musial, 1948	230
	Tommy Davis, 1962	230
	Joe Torre, 1971	230
	Pete Rose, 1973	230
	Willie Wilson, 1980	230
37	Rogers Hornsby, 1929	229
38	Kiki Cuyler, 1930	228
	Stan Musial, 1946	228
40	Nap Lajoie, 1910	227
	Ty Cobb, 1912	227
	Rogers Hornsby, 1924	227
	Jim Bottomley, 1925	227
	Sam Rice, 1925	227
	Billy Herman, 1935	227
	Charlie Gehringer, 1936	227
47	Jesse Burkett, 1901	226
	Joe Jackson, 1912	226
	Bill Terry, 1929	226
	Chuck Klein, 1932	226
51	Tip O'Neill, 1887	225
	Jesse Burkett, 1895	225
	Ty Cobb, 1917	225
	Harry Heilmann, 1925	225
	Johnny Hodapp, 1930	225
	Bill Terry, 1932	225
57	George Sisler, 1925	224
	Joe Medwick, 1935	224
	Tommy Holmes, 1945	224
60	Frankie Frisch, 1923	223
	Lloyd Waner, 1927	223
	Paul Waner, 1928	223
	Chuck Klein, 1933	223
	Joe Medwick, 1936	223
	Hank Aaron, 1959	223
	Kirby Puckett, 1986	223
67	Sam Thompson, 1893	222
	Tris Speaker, 1912	222
	Eddie Collins, 1920	222
	Charlie Jamieson, 1923	222
71	Jesse Burkett, 1899	221
	Zach Wheat, 1925	221
	Lloyd Waner, 1928	221
	Heinie Manush, 1933	221
	Richie Ashburn, 1951	221
76	Pete Browning, 1887	220
	Billy Hamilton, 1894	220
	Kiki Cuyler, 1925	220
	Lou Gehrig, 1930	220
	Stan Musial, 1943	220
81	Ed Delahanty, 1893	219
	Willie Keeler, 1894	219
	Jimmy Williams, 1899	219
	Cy Seymour, 1905	219
	Chuck Klein, 1929	219
	Lefty O'Doul, 1932	219
	Paul Waner, 1937	219
	Ralph Garr, 1971	219
	Cecil Cooper, 1980	219
90	12 players tied	218

Doubles

1	Earl Webb, 1931	67
2	George Burns, 1926	64
	Joe Medwick, 1936	64
4	Hank Greenberg, 1934	63
5	Paul Waner, 1932	62
6	Charlie Gehringer, 1936	60
7	Tris Speaker, 1923	59
	Chuck Klein, 1930	59
9	Billy Herman, 1935	57
	Billy Herman, 1936	57
11	Joe Medwick, 1937	56
	George Kell, 1950	56
13	Ed Delahanty, 1899	55
	Gee Walker, 1936	55
15	Hal McRae, 1977	54
16	Tris Speaker, 1912	53
	Al Simmons, 1926	53
	Paul Waner, 1936	53
	Stan Musial, 1953	53
	Don Mattingly, 1986	53
21	Tip O'Neill, 1887	52
	Tris Speaker, 1921	52
	Tris Speaker, 1926	52
	Lou Gehrig, 1927	52
	Johnny Frederick, 1929	52
	Enos Slaughter, 1939	52
27	Hugh Duffy, 1894	51
	Nap Lajoie, 1910	51
	Baby Doll Jacobson, 1926	51
	George Burns, 1927	51
	Johnny Hodapp, 1930	51
	Beau Bell, 1937	51
	Joe Cronin, 1938	51
	Stan Musial, 1944	51
	Mickey Vernon, 1946	51
	Frank Robinson, 1962	51
	Pete Rose, 1978	51
	Wade Boggs, 1989	51
39	Tris Speaker, 1920	50
	Harry Heilmann, 1927	50
	Paul Waner, 1928	50
	Kiki Cuyler, 1930	50
	Chuck Klein, 1932	50
	Charlie Gehringer, 1934	50
	Odell Hale, 1936	50
	Ben Chapman, 1936	50
	Hank Greenberg, 1940	50
	Stan Musial, 1946	50
	Stan Spence, 1946	50
50	Ned Williamson, 1883	49
	Ed Delahanty, 1895	49
	Nap Lajoie, 1904	49
	George Sisler, 1920	49
	Heinie Manush, 1930	49
	Riggs Stephenson, 1932	49
	Hank Greenberg, 1937	49
	Robin Yount, 1980	49
58	Joe Kelley, 1894	48
	Nap Lajoie, 1901	48
	Nap Lajoie, 1906	48
	Tris Speaker, 1922	48
	Joe Sewell, 1927	48
	Babe Herman, 1930	48
	Dick Bartell, 1932	48
	Earl Averill, 1934	48
	Wally Moses, 1937	48
	Joe Medwick, 1939	48
	Stan Musial, 1943	48
	Keith Hernandez, 1979	48
	Don Mattingly, 1985	48
71	Harry Davis, 1905	47
	Ty Cobb, 1911	47
	George Burns, 1923	47
	Lou Gehrig, 1926	47
	Bob Meusel, 1927	47
	Lou Gehrig, 1928	47
	Heinie Manush, 1928	47
	Rogers Hornsby, 1929	47
	Chick Hafey, 1929	47
	Adam Comorosky, 1930	47
	Ed Morgan, 1930	47
	Charlie Gehringer, 1930	47
	Dale Alexander, 1931	47
	Eric McNair, 1932	47
	Joe Vosmik, 1935	47
	Joe Vosmik, 1937	47
	Joe Medwick, 1938	47
	Tommy Holmes, 1945	47
	Vada Pinson, 1959	47
	Wes Parker, 1970	47
	Pete Rose, 1975	47
	Fred Lynn, 1975	47
	Cal Ripken, 1983	47
	Wade Boggs, 1986	47
95	24 players tied	46

Triples

1	Chief Wilson, 1912	36
2	Dave Orr, 1886	31
	Heinie Reitz, 1894	31
4	Perry Werden, 1893	29
5	Harry Davis, 1897	28
6	George Davis, 1893	27
	Sam Thompson, 1894	27
	Jimmy Williams, 1899	27
9	John Reilly, 1890	26
	George Treadway, 1894	26
	Joe Jackson, 1912	26
	Sam Crawford, 1914	26
	Kiki Cuyler, 1925	26
14	Roger Connor, 1894	25
	Buck Freeman, 1899	25
	Sam Crawford, 1903	25
	Larry Doyle, 1911	25
	Tom Long, 1915	25
19	Ed McKean, 1893	24
	Ty Cobb, 1911	24
	Ty Cobb, 1917	24
22	Harry Stovey, 1884	23
	Sam Thompson, 1887	23
	Elmer Smith, 1893	23
	Dan Brouthers, 1894	23
	Nap Lajoie, 1897	23
	Ty Cobb, 1912	23
	Sam Crawford, 1913	23
	Earle Combs, 1927	23
	Adam Comorosky, 1930	23
	Dale Mitchell, 1949	23
32	Roger Connor, 1887	22
	Bid McPhee, 1890	22
	Jake Beckley, 1890	22
	Joe Visner, 1890	22
	Willie Keeler, 1894	22
	Kip Selbach, 1895	22
	John Anderson, 1898	22
	Honus Wagner, 1900	22
	Tommy Leach, 1902	22
	Sam Crawford, 1902	22
	Bill Bradley, 1903	22
	Elmer Flick, 1906	22
	Mike Mitchell, 1911	22
	Birdie Cree, 1911	22
	Tris Speaker, 1913	22
	Hi Myers, 1920	22
	Jake Daubert, 1922	22
	Paul Waner, 1926	22
	Earle Combs, 1930	22
	Snuffy Stirnweiss, 1945	22
52	Dave Orr, 1885	21
	Mike Tiernan, 1890	21
	Billy Shindle, 1890	21
	Tom Brown, 1891	21
	Ed Delahanty, 1892	21
	Sam Thompson, 1895	21
	Mike Tiernan, 1895	21
	Tom McCreery, 1896	21
	George Van Haltren, 1896	21
	Bobby Wallace, 1897	21
	Jimmy Williams, 1901	21
	Bill Keister, 1901	21
	Jimmy Williams, 1902	21
	Cy Seymour, 1905	21
	Frank Schulte, 1911	21
	Frank Baker, 1912	21
	Sam Crawford, 1912	21
	Vic Saier, 1913	21
	Joe Jackson, 1916	21
	Edd Roush, 1924	21
	Earle Combs, 1928	21
	Willie Wilson, 1985	21
74	36 players tied	20

Triples (by era)

1876-1892

1	Dave Orr, 1886	31
2	John Reilly, 1890	26
3	Harry Stovey, 1884	23
	Sam Thompson, 1887	23
5	Roger Connor, 1887	22
	Bid McPhee, 1890	22
	Jake Beckley, 1890	22
	Joe Visner, 1890	22
9	Dave Orr, 1885	21
	Mike Tiernan, 1890	21
	Billy Shindle, 1890	21
	Tom Brown, 1891	21
	Ed Delahanty, 1892	21
14	10 players tied	20

1893-1919

1	Chief Wilson, 1912	36
2	Heinie Reitz, 1894	31
3	Perry Werden, 1893	29
4	Harry Davis, 1897	28
5	George Davis, 1893	27
	Sam Thompson, 1894	27
	Jimmy Williams, 1899	27
8	George Treadway, 1894	26
	Joe Jackson, 1912	26
	Sam Crawford, 1914	26
11	Roger Connor, 1894	25
	Buck Freeman, 1899	25
	Sam Crawford, 1903	25
	Larry Doyle, 1911	25
	Tom Long, 1915	25

1920-1941

1	Kiki Cuyler, 1925	26
2	Earle Combs, 1927	23
	Adam Comorosky, 1930	23
4	Hi Myers, 1920	22
	Jake Daubert, 1922	22
	Paul Waner, 1926	22
	Earle Combs, 1930	22
8	Edd Roush, 1924	21
	Earle Combs, 1928	21
10	12 players tied	20

1942-1960

1	Dale Mitchell, 1949	23
2	Snuffy Stirnweiss, 1945	22
3	Stan Musial, 1943	20
	Stan Musial, 1946	20
	Willie Mays, 1957	20
6	Johnny Barrett, 1944	19
7	Stan Musial, 1948	18
	Minnie Minoso, 1954	18
9	Enos Slaughter, 1942	17
	Jim Gilliam, 1953	17
11	6 players tied	16

1961-1990

1	Willie Wilson, 1985	21
2	George Brett, 1979	20
3	Garry Templeton, 1979	19
	Juan Samuel, 1984	19
	Ryne Sandberg, 1984	19
6	Garry Templeton, 1977	18
	Willie McGee, 1985	18
8	Ralph Garr, 1974	17
	Tony Fernandez, 1990	17
10	Johnny Callison, 1965	16
	Willie Davis, 1970	16
	Rod Carew, 1977	16
	Paul Molitor, 1979	16
14	11 players tied	15

Home Runs

1	Roger Maris, 1961	61
2	Babe Ruth, 1927	60
3	Babe Ruth, 1921	59
4	Jimmie Foxx, 1932	58
	Hank Greenberg, 1938	58
6	Hack Wilson, 1930	56
7	Babe Ruth, 1920	54
	Babe Ruth, 1928	54
	Ralph Kiner, 1949	54
	Mickey Mantle, 1961	54
11	Mickey Mantle, 1956	52
	Willie Mays, 1965	52
	George Foster, 1977	52
14	Ralph Kiner, 1947	51
	Johnny Mize, 1947	51
	Willie Mays, 1955	51
	Cecil Fielder, 1990	51
18	Jimmie Foxx, 1938	50
19	Babe Ruth, 1930	49
	Lou Gehrig, 1934	49
	Lou Gehrig, 1936	49
	Ted Kluszewski, 1954	49
	Willie Mays, 1962	49
	Harmon Killebrew, 1964	49
	Frank Robinson, 1966	49
	Harmon Killebrew, 1969	49
	Andre Dawson, 1987	49
	Mark McGwire, 1987	49
29	Jimmie Foxx, 1933	48
	Harmon Killebrew, 1962	48
	Frank Howard, 1969	48
	Willie Stargell, 1971	48
	Dave Kingman, 1979	48
	Mike Schmidt, 1980	48
35	Babe Ruth, 1926	47
	Lou Gehrig, 1927	47
	Ralph Kiner, 1950	47
	Eddie Mathews, 1953	47
	Ted Kluszewski, 1955	47
	Ernie Banks, 1958	47
	Willie Mays, 1964	47
	Reggie Jackson, 1969	47
	Hank Aaron, 1971	47
	George Bell, 1987	47
	Kevin Mitchell, 1989	47
46	Babe Ruth, 1924	46
	Babe Ruth, 1929	46
	Babe Ruth, 1931	46
	Lou Gehrig, 1931	46
	Joe DiMaggio, 1937	46
	Eddie Mathews, 1959	46
	Orlando Cepeda, 1961	46
	Jim Gentile, 1961	46
	Harmon Killebrew, 1961	46
	Jim Rice, 1978	46
56	Ernie Banks, 1959	45
	Rocky Colavito, 1961	45
	Hank Aaron, 1962	45
	Harmon Killebrew, 1963	45
	Willie McCovey, 1969	45
	Johnny Bench, 1970	45
	Mike Schmidt, 1979	45
	Gorman Thomas, 1979	45
64	Jimmie Foxx, 1934	44
	Hank Greenberg, 1946	44
	Ernie Banks, 1955	44
	Hank Aaron, 1957	44
	Hank Aaron, 1963	44
	Willie McCovey, 1963	44
	Hank Aaron, 1966	44
	Harmon Killebrew, 1967	44
	Carl Yastrzemski, 1967	44
	Frank Howard, 1968	44
	Hank Aaron, 1969	44
	Frank Howard, 1970	44
	Willie Stargell, 1973	44
	Dale Murphy, 1987	44
78	Chuck Klein, 1929	43
	Johnny Mize, 1940	43
	Ted Williams, 1949	43
	Al Rosen, 1953	43
	Duke Snider, 1956	43
	Ernie Banks, 1957	43
	Dave Johnson, 1973	43
	Tony Armas, 1984	43
86	Rogers Hornsby, 1922	42
	Mel Ott, 1929	42
	Hal Trosky, 1936	42
	Ralph Kiner, 1951	42
	Duke Snider, 1953	42
	Gus Zernial, 1953	42
	Gil Hodges, 1954	42
	Duke Snider, 1955	42
	Roy Sievers, 1957	42
	Mickey Mantle, 1958	42
	Rocky Colavito, 1959	42
	Harmon Killebrew, 1959	42
	Dick Stuart, 1963	42
	Billy Williams, 1970	42
	Jose Canseco, 1988	42

Home Runs (by era)

1876-1892

1	Ned Williamson, 1884	27
2	Fred Pfeffer, 1884	25
3	Abner Dalrymple, 1884	22
4	Cap Anson, 1884	21
5	Sam Thompson, 1889	20
6	Billy O'Brien, 1887	19
	Bug Holliday, 1889	19
	Harry Stovey, 1889	19
9	Jerry Denny, 1889	18
10	Roger Connor, 1887	17
	Jimmy Ryan, 1889	17
12	Fred Pfeffer, 1887	16
	Jimmy Ryan, 1888	16
	Harry Stovey, 1891	16
	Mike Tiernan, 1891	16

1893-1919

1	Babe Ruth, 1919	29
2	Buck Freeman, 1899	25
3	Gavvy Cravath, 1915	24
4	Frank Schulte, 1911	21
5	Ed Delahanty, 1893	19
	Gavvy Cravath, 1913	19
	Gavvy Cravath, 1914	19
8	Hugh Duffy, 1894	18
	Sam Thompson, 1895	18
	Fred Luderus, 1913	18
	Vic Saier, 1914	18
12	5 players tied	17

1920-1941

1	Babe Ruth, 1927	60
2	Babe Ruth, 1921	59
3	Jimmie Foxx, 1932	58
	Hank Greenberg, 1938	58
5	Hack Wilson, 1930	56
6	Babe Ruth, 1920	54
	Babe Ruth, 1928	54
8	Jimmie Foxx, 1938	50
9	Babe Ruth, 1930	49
	Lou Gehrig, 1934	49
	Lou Gehrig, 1936	49
12	Jimmie Foxx, 1933	48
13	Babe Ruth, 1926	47
	Lou Gehrig, 1927	47
15	5 players tied	46

1942-1960

1	Ralph Kiner, 1949	54
2	Mickey Mantle, 1956	52
3	Ralph Kiner, 1947	51
	Johnny Mize, 1947	51
	Willie Mays, 1955	51
6	Ted Kluszewski, 1954	49
7	Ralph Kiner, 1950	47
	Eddie Mathews, 1953	47
	Ted Kluszewski, 1955	47
	Ernie Banks, 1958	47
11	Eddie Mathews, 1959	46
12	Ernie Banks, 1959	45
13	Hank Greenberg, 1946	44
	Ernie Banks, 1955	44
	Hank Aaron, 1957	44

1961-1990

1	Roger Maris, 1961	61
2	Mickey Mantle, 1961	54
3	Willie Mays, 1965	52
	George Foster, 1977	52
5	Cecil Fielder, 1990	51
6	Willie Mays, 1962	49
	Harmon Killebrew, 1964	49
	Frank Robinson, 1966	49
	Harmon Killebrew, 1969	49
	Andre Dawson, 1987	49
	Mark McGwire, 1987	49
12	5 players tied	48

Home Run Percentage

1	Babe Ruth, 1920	11.79
2	Babe Ruth, 1927	11.11
3	Babe Ruth, 1921	10.93
4	Mickey Mantle, 1961	10.51
5	Hank Greenberg, 1938	10.43
6	Roger Maris, 1961	10.34
7	Babe Ruth, 1928	10.07
8	Jimmie Foxx, 1932	9.91
9	Ralph Kiner, 1949	9.84
10	Mickey Mantle, 1956	9.76
11	Hack Wilson, 1930	9.57
12	Babe Ruth, 1926	9.49
	Hank Aaron, 1971	9.49
14	Jim Gentile, 1961	9.47
15	Babe Ruth, 1930	9.46
16	Willie Stargell, 1971	9.39
17	Willie Mays, 1965	9.32
18	Babe Ruth, 1929	9.22
19	Boog Powell, 1964	9.20
20	Willie McCovey, 1969	9.16
21	Ted Williams, 1957	9.05
22	Ralph Kiner, 1947	9.03
23	Dave Kingman, 1979	9.02
24	Babe Ruth, 1932	8.97
25	Cecil Fielder, 1990	8.90
26	Jimmie Foxx, 1938	8.85
27	Harmon Killebrew, 1969	8.83
28	Mark McGwire, 1987	8.80
29	Willie Mays, 1955	8.79
30	Mike Schmidt, 1980	8.76
31	Mike Schmidt, 1981	8.76
32	Harmon Killebrew, 1963	8.74
33	Johnny Mize, 1947	8.70
34	Babe Ruth, 1924	8.70
	Harmon Killebrew, 1962	8.70
36	Kevin Mitchell, 1989	8.66
37	Babe Ruth, 1922	8.62
38	Babe Ruth, 1931	8.61
39	Ralph Kiner, 1950	8.59
40	Reggie Jackson, 1969	8.56
41	Ted Kluszewski, 1954	8.55
42	Frank Robinson, 1966	8.51
43	Harmon Killebrew, 1961	8.50
44	Harmon Killebrew, 1964	8.49
45	Lou Gehrig, 1934	8.46
	Lou Gehrig, 1936	8.46
47	George Foster, 1977	8.46
48	Willie Stargell, 1973	8.43
49	Hank Greenberg, 1946	8.41
50	Eddie Mathews, 1954	8.40
51	Rocky Colavito, 1958	8.38
52	Jimmie Foxx, 1933	8.38
53	Joe Adcock, 1956	8.37
54	Jack Clark, 1987	8.35
55	Mike Schmidt, 1979	8.32
56	Eddie Mathews, 1955	8.22
57	Jimmie Foxx, 1934	8.16
58	Willie Mays, 1964	8.13
59	Eddie Mathews, 1953	8.12
60	Ted Williams, 1941	8.11
61	Frank Howard, 1969	8.11
62	Mickey Mantle, 1958	8.09
63	Gorman Thomas, 1979	8.08
64	Lou Gehrig, 1927	8.05
65	Harmon Killebrew, 1967	8.04
	Hank Aaron, 1969	8.04
67	Reggie Jackson, 1980	7.98
68	Mickey Mantle, 1962	7.96
69	Duke Snider, 1956	7.93
70	Darrell Evans, 1985	7.92
71	Ralph Kiner, 1951	7.91
72	Roy Campanella, 1953	7.90
73	Willie Mays, 1962	7.89
	Andre Dawson, 1987	7.89
75	Hank Sauer, 1954	7.88
76	Willie McCovey, 1970	7.88
77	Duke Snider, 1957	7.87
78	Orlando Cepeda, 1961	7.86
79	Babe Ruth, 1923	7.85
80	Roger Maris, 1960	7.82
81	Duke Snider, 1955	7.81
82	Dave Kingman, 1976	7.81
	Eric Davis, 1987	7.81
84	Willie McCovey, 1963	7.80
85	Harmon Killebrew, 1970	7.78
86	Frank Howard, 1970	7.77
	Dale Murphy, 1987	7.77
88	Eddie Mathews, 1959	7.74
89	Rogers Hornsby, 1925	7.74
90	Rocky Colavito, 1961	7.72
91	Mel Ott, 1929	7.71
92	George Bell, 1987	7.70
93	Harmon Killebrew, 1959	7.69
	Norm Cash, 1962	7.69
	Dave Johnson, 1973	7.69
	Jose Canseco, 1990	7.69
97	Ted Kluszewski, 1955	7.68
98	Cy Williams, 1923	7.66
	Norm Cash, 1961	7.66
100	Ernie Banks, 1959	7.64

Home Run Pctg.(by era)

1876-1892

1	Ned Williamson, 1884	6.47
2	Fred Pfeffer, 1884	5.35
3	Cap Anson, 1884	4.42
4	Abner Dalrymple, 1884	4.22
5	Billy O'Brien, 1887	4.19
6	Sam Thompson, 1889	3.75
7	Roger Connor, 1887	3.61
8	Dan Brouthers, 1884	3.52
9	Harry Stovey, 1889	3.42
10	Bug Holliday, 1889	3.37
11	Fred Pfeffer, 1887	3.34
12	Harry Stovey, 1883	3.33
13	Jerry Denny, 1889	3.11
14	Dan Brouthers, 1881	2.96
15	Mike Tiernan, 1891	2.95

1893-1919

1	Babe Ruth, 1919	6.71
2	Bill Joyce, 1894	4.79
3	Gavvy Cravath, 1915	4.60
4	Jack Clements, 1893	4.52
5	Buck Freeman, 1899	4.25
6	Gavvy Cravath, 1914	3.81
7	Jim Canavan, 1894	3.65
8	Frank Schulte, 1911	3.64
9	Gavvy Cravath, 1913	3.62
10	Bill Joyce, 1895	3.59
11	Sherry Magee, 1911	3.37
12	Vic Saier, 1914	3.35
13	Sam Thompson, 1895	3.35
14	Hugh Duffy, 1894	3.34
15	Ed Delahanty, 1893	3.19

1920-1941

1	Babe Ruth, 1920	11.79
2	Babe Ruth, 1927	11.11
3	Babe Ruth, 1921	10.93
4	Hank Greenberg, 1938	10.43
5	Babe Ruth, 1928	10.07
6	Jimmie Foxx, 1932	9.91
7	Hack Wilson, 1930	9.57
8	Babe Ruth, 1926	9.49
9	Babe Ruth, 1930	9.46
10	Babe Ruth, 1929	9.22
11	Babe Ruth, 1932	8.97
12	Jimmie Foxx, 1938	8.85
13	Babe Ruth, 1924	8.70
14	Babe Ruth, 1922	8.62
15	Babe Ruth, 1931	8.61

1942-1960

1	Ralph Kiner, 1949	9.84
2	Mickey Mantle, 1956	9.76
3	Ted Williams, 1957	9.05
4	Ralph Kiner, 1947	9.03
5	Willie Mays, 1955	8.79
6	Johnny Mize, 1947	8.70
7	Ralph Kiner, 1950	8.59
8	Ted Kluszewski, 1954	8.55
9	Hank Greenberg, 1946	8.41
10	Eddie Mathews, 1954	8.40
11	Rocky Colavito, 1958	8.38
12	Joe Adcock, 1956	8.37
13	Eddie Mathews, 1955	8.22
14	Eddie Mathews, 1953	8.12
15	Mickey Mantle, 1958	8.09

1961-1990

1	Mickey Mantle, 1961	10.51
2	Roger Maris, 1961	10.34
3	Hank Aaron, 1971	9.49
4	Jim Gentile, 1961	9.47
5	Willie Stargell, 1971	9.39
6	Willie Mays, 1965	9.32
7	Boog Powell, 1964	9.20
8	Willie McCovey, 1969	9.16
9	Dave Kingman, 1979	9.02
10	Cecil Fielder, 1990	8.90
11	Harmon Killebrew, 1969	8.83
12	Mark McGwire, 1987	8.80
13	Mike Schmidt, 1980	8.76
14	Mike Schmidt, 1981	8.76
15	Harmon Killebrew, 1963	8.74

Total Bases

1	Babe Ruth, 1921	457
2	Rogers Hornsby, 1922	450
3	Lou Gehrig, 1927	447
4	Chuck Klein, 1930	445
5	Jimmie Foxx, 1932	438
6	Stan Musial, 1948	429
7	Hack Wilson, 1930	423
8	Chuck Klein, 1932	420
9	Lou Gehrig, 1930	419
10	Joe DiMaggio, 1937	418
11	Babe Ruth, 1927	417
12	Babe Herman, 1930	416
13	Lou Gehrig, 1931	410
14	Rogers Hornsby, 1929	409
	Lou Gehrig, 1934	409
16	Joe Medwick, 1937	406
	Jim Rice, 1978	406
18	Chuck Klein, 1929	405
	Hal Trosky, 1936	405
20	Jimmie Foxx, 1933	403
	Lou Gehrig, 1936	403
22	Hank Aaron, 1959	400
23	George Sisler, 1920	399
	Babe Ruth, 1923	399
25	Jimmie Foxx, 1938	398
26	Lefty O'Doul, 1929	397
	Hank Greenberg, 1937	397
28	Al Simmons, 1925	392
	Bill Terry, 1930	392
	Al Simmons, 1930	392
31	Babe Ruth, 1924	391
32	Hank Greenberg, 1935	389
33	Babe Ruth, 1920	388
	George Foster, 1977	388
	Don Mattingly, 1986	388
36	Earl Averill, 1936	385
37	Hank Greenberg, 1940	384
38	Stan Musial, 1949	382
	Willie Mays, 1955	382
	Willie Mays, 1962	382
	Jim Rice, 1977	382
42	Rogers Hornsby, 1925	381
43	Babe Ruth, 1928	380
	Hank Greenberg, 1938	380
	Frank Robinson, 1962	380
46	Babe Ruth, 1930	379
	Ernie Banks, 1958	379
48	Rogers Hornsby, 1921	378
	Duke Snider, 1954	378
50	Willie Mays, 1954	377
51	Mickey Mantle, 1956	376
52	Hugh Duffy, 1894	374
	Babe Ruth, 1931	374
	Hal Trosky, 1934	374
	Tony Oliva, 1964	374
56	Rogers Hornsby, 1924	373
	Al Simmons, 1929	373
	Bill Terry, 1932	373
	Billy Williams, 1970	373
60	Lou Gehrig, 1932	370
	Duke Snider, 1953	370
	Hank Aaron, 1963	370
	Don Mattingly, 1985	370
64	Kiki Cuyler, 1925	369
	Ripper Collins, 1934	369
	Jimmie Foxx, 1936	369
	Hank Aaron, 1957	369
	Jim Rice, 1979	369
	George Bell, 1987	369
70	Johnny Mize, 1940	368
	Ted Williams, 1949	368
	Ted Kluszewski, 1954	368
73	Ty Cobb, 1911	367
	Ken Williams, 1922	367
	Heinie Manush, 1928	367
	Al Simmons, 1932	367
	Joe Medwick, 1936	367
	Joe DiMaggio, 1936	367
	Tommy Holmes, 1945	367
	Al Rosen, 1953	367
	Frank Robinson, 1966	367
	Robin Yount, 1982	367
83	Lou Gehrig, 1937	366
	Stan Musial, 1946	366
	Willie Mays, 1957	366
	Roger Maris, 1961	366
	Hank Aaron, 1962	366
88	Harry Heilmann, 1921	365
	Babe Ruth, 1926	365
	Chuck Klein, 1933	365
	Joe Medwick, 1935	365
	Kirby Puckett, 1986	365
93	Lou Gehrig, 1928	364
94	Dale Alexander, 1929	363
	Eddie Mathews, 1953	363
	George Brett, 1979	363
97	Jim Bottomley, 1928	362
98	4 players tied	361

Runs Batted In

1 Hack Wilson, 1930 190
2 Lou Gehrig, 1931 184
3 Hank Greenberg, 1937 ... 183
4 Lou Gehrig, 1927 175
  Jimmie Foxx, 1938 175
6 Lou Gehrig, 1930 174
7 Babe Ruth, 1921 171
8 Chuck Klein, 1930 170
  Hank Greenberg, 1935 ... 170
10 Jimmie Foxx, 1932 169
11 Joe DiMaggio, 1937 167
12 Sam Thompson, 1887 166
13 Sam Thompson, 1895 165
  Al Simmons, 1930 165
  Lou Gehrig, 1934 165
16 Babe Ruth, 1927 164
17 Babe Ruth, 1931 163
  Jimmie Foxx, 1933 163
19 Hal Trosky, 1936 162
20 Hack Wilson, 1929 159
  Lou Gehrig, 1937 159
  Ted Williams, 1949 159
  Vern Stephens, 1949 159
24 Al Simmons, 1929 157
25 Jimmie Foxx, 1930 156
26 Ken Williams, 1922 155
  Joe DiMaggio, 1948 155
28 Babe Ruth, 1929 154
  Joe Medwick, 1937 154
30 Babe Ruth, 1930 153
  Tommy Davis, 1962 153
32 Rogers Hornsby, 1922 ... 152
  Lou Gehrig, 1936 152
34 Mel Ott, 1929 151
  Lou Gehrig, 1932 151
  Al Simmons, 1932 151
37 Hank Greenberg, 1940 ... 150
38 Rogers Hornsby, 1929 ... 149
  George Foster, 1977 149
40 Johnny Bench, 1970 148
41 Cap Anson, 1886 147
42 Hardy Richardson, 1890 .. 146
  Ed Delahanty, 1893 146
  Babe Ruth, 1926 146
  Hank Greenberg, 1938 ... 146
46 Hugh Duffy, 1894 145
  Chuck Klein, 1929 145
  Ted Williams, 1939 145
  Al Rosen, 1953 145
  Don Mattingly, 1985 145
51 Walt Dropo, 1950 144
  Vern Stephens, 1950 144
53 Rogers Hornsby, 1925 ... 143
  Earl Averill, 1931 143
  Don Hurst, 1932 143
  Jimmie Foxx, 1936 143
  Ernie Banks, 1959 143
58 Lou Gehrig, 1928 142
  Babe Ruth, 1928 142
  Hal Trosky, 1934 142
  Roy Campanella, 1953 ... 142
  Orlando Cepeda, 1961 ... 142
  Roger Maris, 1961 142
64 Sam Thompson, 1894 141
  Ted Kluszewski, 1954 141
  Jim Gentile, 1961 141
  Willie Mays, 1962 141
68 Joe DiMaggio, 1938 140
  Rocky Colavito, 1961 140
  Harmon Killebrew, 1969 .. 140
71 Harry Heilmann, 1921 139
  Lou Gehrig, 1933 139
  Hank Greenberg, 1934 ... 139
  Jim Rice, 1978 139
  Don Baylor, 1979 139
76 Bob Meusel, 1925 138
  Goose Goslin, 1930 138
  Joe Medwick, 1936 138
  Zeke Bonura, 1936 138
  Johnny Mize, 1947 138
81 Ed Delahanty, 1899 137
  Babe Ruth, 1920 137
  Jim Bottomley, 1929 137
  Dale Alexander, 1929 137
  Chuck Klein, 1932 137
  Babe Ruth, 1932 137
  Johnny Mize, 1940 137
  Ted Williams, 1942 137
  Vern Stephens, 1948 137
  Joe Torre, 1971 137
  Andre Dawson, 1987 137
92 George Davis, 1897 136
  George Kelly, 1924 136
  Jim Bottomley, 1928 136
  Ed Morgan, 1930 136
  Duke Snider, 1955 136
  Frank Robinson, 1962 136
98 5 players tied 135

Runs Batted In per Game

1 Sam Thompson, 1894 .... 1.42
2 Sam Thompson, 1895 .... 1.39
3 Sam Thompson, 1887 .... 1.31
4 Hack Wilson, 1930 ...... 1.23
5 Al Simmons, 1930 ...... 1.20
6 Hank Greenberg, 1937 ... 1.19
7 Lou Gehrig, 1931 ...... 1.19
8 Cap Anson, 1886 ...... 1.18
9 Jimmie Foxx, 1938 ...... 1.17
10 Hugh Duffy, 1894 ...... 1.16
11 Dave Orr, 1890 ...... 1.16
12 Ed Delahanty, 1894 ...... 1.15
13 Babe Ruth, 1929 ...... 1.14
14 Lou Gehrig, 1930 ...... 1.13
15 Lou Gehrig, 1927 ...... 1.13
16 Babe Ruth, 1921 ...... 1.13
17 Babe Ruth, 1931 ...... 1.12
18 Hardy Richardson, 1890 .. 1.12
19 Hank Greenberg, 1935 ... 1.12
20 Ed Delahanty, 1893 ...... 1.11
21 Joe DiMaggio, 1937 ...... 1.11
22 Al Simmons, 1929 ...... 1.10
23 Jimmie Foxx, 1932 ...... 1.10
24 Jimmie Foxx, 1933 ...... 1.09
25 Chuck Klein, 1930 ...... 1.09
26 Babe Ruth, 1927 ...... 1.09
27 Oyster Burns, 1890 ...... 1.08
28 Hal Trosky, 1936 ...... 1.07
29 Lou Gehrig, 1934 ...... 1.07
30 Ed McKean, 1893 ...... 1.06
31 Hack Wilson, 1929 ...... 1.06
32 Walt Dropo, 1950 ...... 1.06
33 Babe Ruth, 1930 ...... 1.06
34 Buck Ewing, 1893 ...... 1.05
35 Lave Cross, 1894 ...... 1.05
36 Joe DiMaggio, 1939 ...... 1.05
37 George Davis, 1897 ...... 1.05
38 Dan Brouthers, 1894 ..... 1.04
39 Rogers Hornsby, 1925 ... 1.04
40 Jim O'Rourke, 1890 .... 1.04
41 Babe Ruth, 1932 ...... 1.03
42 Ted Williams, 1949 ...... 1.03
  Vern Stephens, 1949 ..... 1.03
44 Ed Delahanty, 1896 ...... 1.02
45 Steve Brodie, 1895 ...... 1.02
  Joe Kelley, 1895 .... 1.02
47 Jimmie Foxx, 1930 ...... 1.02
48 Hank Greenberg, 1940 ... 1.01
49 Ken Williams, 1922 ...... 1.01
  Joe DiMaggio, 1948 ..... 1.01
51 Lou Gehrig, 1937 ...... 1.01
52 Cap Anson, 1882 ...... 1.01
53 George Decker, 1894 ..... 1.01
54 George Brett, 1980 ...... 1.01
55 Joe DiMaggio, 1940 ...... 1.01
56 Mel Ott, 1929 ...... 1.01
57 Nap Lajoie, 1897 .... 1.00
  Al Simmons, 1931 ...... 1.00
59 Roger Connor, 1889 ..... .99
60 Tommy McCarthy, 1894 .. .99
61 Jake Beckley, 1890 ...... .99
62 Dan Brouthers, 1883 ..... .99
63 Joe Medwick, 1937 ...... .99
64 Rogers Hornsby, 1922 ... .99
65 Roy Campanella, 1953 ... .99
66 Jimmy Collins, 1897 ..... .99
67 Ed McKean, 1894 ...... .98
68 Bug Holliday, 1894 ...... .98
69 Lou Gehrig, 1936 ...... .98
70 Al Simmons, 1932 ...... .98
71 Walt Wilmot, 1894 ...... .98
72 Cap Anson, 1881 ...... .98
73 Chuck Klein, 1929 ...... .97
  Ted Williams, 1939 ...... .97
75 Heinie Reitz, 1894 ...... .97
76 Lou Gehrig, 1932 ...... .97
77 Vern Stephens, 1950 ..... .97
78 Joe DiMaggio, 1938 ...... .97
79 Babe Ruth, 1920 ...... .96
80 Cap Anson, 1885 ...... .96
81 Hugh Duffy, 1897 ...... .96
82 Sam Thompson, 1893 .... .96
83 Billy Nash, 1893 ...... .96
84 Babe Ruth, 1926 ...... .96
85 Harry Heilmann, 1929 .... .96
86 Tommy McCarthy, 1893 .. .96
87 Rogers Hornsby, 1929 ... .96
88 Hughie Jennings, 1895 ... .95
  Nap Lajoie, 1901 ...... .95
90 Don Hurst, 1932 ...... .95
91 Jim Gentile, 1961 ...... .95
92 Jack Doyle, 1894 ...... .95
93 Bill Dickey, 1937 ...... .95
94 Ted Kluszewski, 1954 .... .95
95 George Kelly, 1924 ...... .94
96 George Foster, 1977 ..... .94
97 Hank Greenberg, 1938 ... .94
98 Rudy York, 1938 ...... .94
99 Tommy Davis, 1962 ...... .94
100 2 players tied .... .94

Walks

1 Babe Ruth, 1923 170
2 Ted Williams, 1947 162
  Ted Williams, 1949 162
4 Ted Williams, 1946 156
5 Eddie Yost, 1956 151
6 Eddie Joost, 1949 149
7 Babe Ruth, 1920 148
  Eddie Stanky, 1945 148
  Jim Wynn, 1969 148
10 Jimmy Sheckard, 1911 ... 147
11 Mickey Mantle, 1957 146
12 Ted Williams, 1941 145
  Ted Williams, 1942 145
  Harmon Killebrew, 1969 .. 145
15 Babe Ruth, 1921 144
  Babe Ruth, 1926 144
  Eddie Stanky, 1950 144
  Ted Williams, 1951 144
19 Babe Ruth, 1924 142
20 Eddie Yost, 1950 141
21 Babe Ruth, 1927 138
22 Eddie Stanky, 1946 137
  Roy Cullenbine, 1947 137
  Ralph Kiner, 1951 137
  Willie McCovey, 1970 137
26 Jack Crooks, 1892 136
  Babe Ruth, 1930 136
  Ferris Fain, 1949 136
  Ted Williams, 1954 136
  Jack Clark, 1987 136
31 Babe Ruth, 1928 135
  Eddie Yost, 1959 135
33 Ferris Fain, 1950 133
34 Lou Gehrig, 1935 132
  Frank Howard, 1970 132
  Joe Morgan, 1975 132
  Jack Clark, 1989 132
38 Bob Elliott, 1948 131
  Eddie Yost, 1954 131
  Harmon Killebrew, 1967 .. 131
41 Babe Ruth, 1932 130
  Lou Gehrig, 1936 130
43 Eddie Yost, 1952 129
  Mickey Mantle, 1958 129
45 Max Bishop, 1929 128
  Max Bishop, 1930 128
  Babe Ruth, 1923 128
  Harmon Killebrew, 1970 .. 128
  Carl Yastrzemski, 1970 ... 128
  Mike Schmidt, 1983 128
51 Lu Blue, 1931 127
  Lou Gehrig, 1937 127
  Eddie Stanky, 1951 127
  Jim Wynn, 1976 127
55 Billy Hamilton, 1894 126
  Lu Blue, 1929 126
  Ted Williams, 1948 126
  Eddie Yost, 1951 126
  Mickey Mantle, 1961 126
  Darrell Evans, 1974 126
  Rickey Henderson, 1989 .. 126
62 Richie Ashburn, 1954 125
  Eddie Yost, 1960 125
  Gene Tenace, 1977 125
  Wade Boggs, 1988 125
66 John McGraw, 1899 124
  Norm Cash, 1961 124
  Eddie Mathews, 1963 124
  Darrell Evans, 1973 124
70 Bill Joyce, 1890 123
  Eddie Yost, 1953 123
  Ken Singleton, 1973 123
73 Jimmy Sheckard, 1912 ... 122
  Lou Gehrig, 1929 122
  Luke Appling, 1935 122
  Ralph Kiner, 1950 122
  Eddie Joost, 1952 122
  Mickey Mantle, 1962 122
  John Mayberry, 1973 122
80 Jack Crooks, 1893 121
  Topsy Hartsel, 1905 121
  Roy Cullenbine, 1941 121
  Luke Appling, 1949 121
  Willie McCovey, 1969 121
  Darrell Porter, 1979 121
  Von Hayes, 1987 121
87 Cupid Childs, 1893 120
  Eddie Lake, 1947 120
  Joe Morgan, 1974 120
  Mike Schmidt, 1979 120
91 14 players tied 119

Strikeouts

1 Bobby Bonds, 1970 189
2 Bobby Bonds, 1969 187
3 Rob Deer, 1987 186
4 Pete Incaviglia, 1986 185
5 Cecil Fielder, 1990 182
6 Mike Schmidt, 1975 180
7 Rob Deer, 1986 179
8 Dave Nicholson, 1963 175
  Gorman Thomas, 1979 ... 175
  Jose Canseco, 1986 175
11 Jim Presley, 1986 172
  Bo Jackson, 1989 172
13 Reggie Jackson, 1968 171
14 Gorman Thomas, 1980 ... 170
15 Andres Galarraga, 1990 .. 169
16 Juan Samuel, 1984 168
  Pete Incaviglia, 1987 168
18 Gary Alexander, 1978 166
  Steve Balboni, 1985 166
  Cory Snyder, 1987 166
21 Donn Clendenon, 1968 ... 163
22 Butch Hobson, 1977 162
  Juan Samuel, 1987 162
24 Dick Allen, 1968 161
  Reggie Jackson, 1971 161
26 Mickey Tettleton, 1990 ... 160
27 Bo Jackson, 1987 158
  Andres Galarraga, 1989 .. 158
  Rob Deer, 1989 158
  Jose Canseco, 1990 158
31 Dan Tartabull, 1986 157
  Jose Canseco, 1987 157
  Jim Presley, 1987 157
34 Tommie Agee, 1970 156
  Dave Kingman, 1982 156
  Reggie Jackson, 1982 156
  Tony Armas, 1984 156
38 Frank Howard, 1967 155
  Jeff Burroughs, 1975 155
40 Willie Stargell, 1971 154
  Larry Parrish, 1987 154
42 Dave Kingman, 1975 153
  Andres Galarraga, 1988 .. 153
  Rob Deer, 1988 153
  Pete Incaviglia, 1988 153
46 George Scott, 1966 152
  Larry Hisle, 1969 152
48 Don Lock, 1963 151
  Greg Luzinski, 1975 151
  Juan Samuel, 1988 151
51 Dick Allen, 1965 150
  Nate Colbert, 1970 150
  Ron Kittle, 1983 150
  Jesse Barfield, 1989 150
  Jesse Barfield, 1990 150
  Sammy Sosa, 1990 150
57 Billy Grabarkewitz, 1970 .. 149
  Mike Schmidt, 1976 149
  Fred McGriff, 1988 149
60 Bobby Bonds, 1973 148
  Mike Schmidt, 1983 148
  Gorman Thomas, 1983 ... 148
  Roberto Kelly, 1990 148
64 Rob Deer, 1990 147
65 Deron Johnson, 1971 146
  Nate Colbert, 1973 146
  Steve Balboni, 1986 146
  Jesse Barfield, 1986 146
  Bo Jackson, 1988 146
  Pete Incaviglia, 1990 146
71 Lee May, 1972 145
  Bobby Darwin, 1972 145
  Dale Murphy, 1978 145
  Jack Clark, 1989 145
75 Dick Stuart, 1963 144
  Bobby Knoop, 1966 144
  Dick Allen, 1969 144
78 Nelson Mathews, 1964 ... 143
  Byron Browne, 1966 143
  Rick Monday, 1968 143
  Gorman Thomas, 1982 ... 143
  Jesse Barfield, 1985 143
83 Harmon Killebrew, 1962 .. 142
  Donn Clendenon, 1966 ... 142
  Lee May, 1969 142
  Jim Wynn, 1969 142
  Reggie Jackson, 1969 142
  Cito Gaston, 1970 142
  Juan Samuel, 1986 142
  Dale Murphy, 1989 142
91 Jake Wood, 1961 141
  Frank Howard, 1968 141
  Bobby Bonds, 1977 141
  Reggie Jackson, 1984 141
  Dale Murphy, 1985 141
  Juan Samuel, 1985 141
  Dale Murphy, 1986 141
  Darryl Strawberry, 1986 .. 141
  Jesse Barfield, 1987 141
  Jack Clark, 1988 141

At Bats per Strikeout

1876-1892
1 Mike McGeary, 1876 .... 276.0
2 Cap Anson, 1878 .... 261.0
3 John Peters, 1876 .... 158.0
4 John Clapp, 1876 .... 149.0
5 Joe Start, 1877 .... 135.5
6 Joe Start, 1876 .... 132.0
7 Levi Meyerle, 1876 ..... 128.0
8 Jim Holdsworth, 1876 ... 120.5
9 Lon Knight, 1876 .... 120.0
10 Ezra Sutton, 1876 ...... 118.0
11 Bobby Mathews, 1876 ... 109.0
12 Paul Hines, 1876 .... 101.7
13 Deacon White, 1876 .... 101.0
14 Al Spalding, 1876 .... 97.3
15 Davy Force, 1876 .... 95.7

1893-1919
1 Jack Doyle, 1894 .... 140.7
2 Monte Ward, 1893 ...... 117.6
3 Willie Keeler, 1894 ..... 98.3
4 Joe Quinn, 1895 .... 90.5
5 Monte Ward, 1894 ...... 90.0
6 Joe Quinn, 1893 .... 78.1
7 Lave Cross, 1894 .... 75.6
8 Steve Brodie, 1894 ..... 71.6
9 Jack Glasscock, 1893 ... 69.7
10 Lave Cross, 1895 .... 66.9
11 Ed McKean, 1896 .... 63.4
12 Dummy Hoy, 1893 ...... 62.7
13 Patsy Donovan, 1893 ... 62.4
14 Farmer Vaughn, 1896 ... 61.9
15 Willie Keeler, 1896 ..... 60.4

1920-1941
1 Joe Sewell, 1932 .... 167.7
2 Joe Sewell, 1925 .... 152.0
3 Joe Sewell, 1929 .... 144.5
4 Joe Sewell, 1933 .... 131.0
5 Charlie Hollocher, 1922 ... 118.4
6 Stuffy McInnis, 1922 .... 107.4
7 Stuffy McInnis, 1924 .... 96.8
8 Joe Sewell, 1926 .... 96.3
9 Joe Sewell, 1927 .... 81.3
10 Pie Traynor, 1929 ...... 77.1
11 Sam Rice, 1929 .... 68.4
12 Tris Speaker, 1927 ..... 65.4
13 Joe Sewell, 1928 .... 65.3
14 Sam Rice, 1925 .... 64.9
15 Stuffy McInnis, 1921 ..... 64.9

1942-1960
1 Tommy Holmes, 1945 .... 70.7
2 Emil Verban, 1947 .... 67.5
3 Lou Boudreau, 1948 .... 62.2
4 Dale Mitchell, 1949 ..... 58.2
5 Tommy Holmes, 1944 .... 57.4
6 Dale Mitchell, 1952 ..... 56.8
7 Nellie Fox, 1958 .... 56.6
8 Tommy Holmes, 1942 .... 55.8
9 Jimmy Brown, 1942 ..... 55.1
10 Nellie Fox, 1951 .... 54.9
11 Lou Boudreau, 1947 .... 53.8
12 Nellie Fox, 1954 .... 52.6
13 Harvey Kuenn, 1954 .... 50.5
14 Don Mueller, 1955 ..... 50.4
15 Yogi Berra, 1950 .... 49.8

1961-1990
1 Nellie Fox, 1962 .... 51.8
2 Dave Cash, 1976 .... 51.2
3 Nellie Fox, 1961 .... 50.5
4 Tim Foli, 1979 .... 38.0
5 Matty Alou, 1970 .... 37.6
6 Felix Millan, 1974 ...... 37.0
7 Vic Power, 1961 .... 35.2
8 Nellie Fox, 1964 .... 34.0
9 Glenn Beckert, 1968 .... 32.2
10 Bill Buckner, 1980 ..... 32.1
11 Nellie Fox, 1963 .... 31.7
12 Tim Foli, 1981 .... 31.6
13 Bob Bailor, 1978 .... 29.6
14 Rich Dauer, 1980 ...... 29.3
15 Felix Millan, 1973 .... 29.0

Strikeout Percentage

1876-1892
1 Frank Meinke, 1884 .... 26.10
2 Jim Galvin, 1883 .... 24.53
3 Sam Wise, 1884 .... 24.41
4 Jim Galvin, 1879 .... 21.13
5 Charlie Bastian, 1885 ... 21.08
6 Will White, 1878 .... 20.81
7 Silver Flint, 1883 ...... 20.78
8 John Morrill, 1884 ...... 19.86
9 John Morrill, 1885 ...... 19.80
10 Charlie Bastian, 1886 ... 19.57
11 Jim Lillie, 1886 .... 19.23
12 Will White, 1879 ...... 19.05
13 John Morrill, 1886 ..... 18.84
14 Sam Wise, 1883 .... 18.23
15 Bill Crowley, 1884 ..... 18.18

1893-1919
1 Gus Williams, 1914 ..... 24.05
2 Grover Gilmore, 1914 ... 20.38
3 Gavvy Cravath, 1916 ... 19.87
4 Ed McDonald, 1912 .... 19.83
5 Art Wilson, 1914 .... 18.18
6 Gavvy Cravath, 1912 ... 17.66
7 Cozy Dolan, 1914 ...... 17.58
8 Max Carey, 1911 ...... 17.56
9 Danny Moeller, 1913 ... 17.49
10 Doug Baird, 1915 ...... 17.19
11 Al Boucher, 1914 ...... 17.05
12 Wally Pipp, 1915 ...... 16.91
13 Joe Agler, 1914 .... 16.85
14 Ray Powell, 1919 ...... 16.81
15 Cy Williams, 1917 ..... 16.67

1920-1941
1 Vince DiMaggio, 1938 .... 24.81
2 Vince DiMaggio, 1937 .... 22.52
3 Chet Ross, 1940 .... 22.32
4 Dolph Camilli, 1941 ..... 21.74
5 Joe Orengo, 1940 ...... 21.69
6 Jimmie Foxx, 1941 ..... 21.15
7 Boze Berger, 1935 ..... 21.04
8 Jimmie Foxx, 1936 ..... 20.34
9 Dolph Camilli, 1938 .... 19.84
10 Babe Ruth, 1922 .... 19.70
11 Babe Ruth, 1933 .... 19.61
12 Jimmy Dykes, 1922 ..... 19.56
13 Hank Greenberg, 1939 ... 19.00
14 Vince DiMaggio, 1941 ... 18.94
15 Dolph Camilli, 1939 ...... 18.94

1942-1960
1 Pancho Herrera, 1960 ... 26.56
2 Jim Lemon, 1956 .... 25.65
3 Dick Stuart, 1960 ...... 24.43
4 Frank Howard, 1960 .... 24.11
5 Harmon Killebrew, 1960 . 23.98
6 Jim Lemon, 1958 .... 23.95
7 Mickey Mantle, 1960 ... 23.72
8 Larry Doby, 1953 ...... 23.59
9 Pat Seerey, 1945 ...... 23.43
10 Mickey Mantle, 1959 ... 23.29
11 Mickey Mantle, 1958 ... 23.12
12 Wally Post, 1956 .... 23.01
13 Woodie Held, 1959 ..... 22.48
14 Gil Hodges, 1959 ...... 22.28
15 Norm Zauchin, 1955 ..... 22.01

1961-1990
1 Rob Deer, 1987 .... 39.24
2 Dave Nicholson, 1963 ... 38.98
3 Rob Deer, 1986 .... 38.41
4 Mickey Tettleton, 1990 . 36.04
5 Pete Incaviglia, 1986 ... 34.26
6 Rob Deer, 1989 .... 33.91
7 Rob Deer, 1990 .... 33.41
8 Bo Jackson, 1989 ...... 33.40
9 Gary Alexander, 1978 ... 33.33
10 Jack Clark, 1987 ...... 33.17
11 Pete Incaviglia, 1987 ... 33.01
12 Dick Allen, 1969 ...... 32.88
13 Jose Canseco, 1990 .... 32.85
14 Mike Schmidt, 1975 .... 32.03
15 Jack Clark, 1989 .... 31.87

Batting Average

1 Hugh Duffy, 1894 .... .440
2 Tip O'Neill, 1887 .... .435
3 Ross Barnes, 1876 .... .429
4 Nap Lajoie, 1901 .... .426
5 Willie Keeler, 1897 ...... .424
6 Rogers Hornsby, 1924 .... .424
7 George Sisler, 1922 ..... .420
8 Ty Cobb, 1911 .... .420
9 Fred Dunlap, 1884 ...... .412
10 Ty Cobb, 1912 .... .410
11 Ed Delahanty, 1899 ..... .410
12 Jesse Burkett, 1896 ..... .410
13 Jesse Burkett, 1895 ..... .409
14 Joe Jackson, 1911 ...... .408
15 Sam Thompson, 1894 ... .407
16 George Sisler, 1920 ..... .407
17 Ed Delahanty, 1894 ..... .407
18 Ted Williams, 1941 ..... .406
19 Billy Hamilton, 1894 ..... .404
20 Ed Delahanty, 1895 ..... .404
21 Rogers Hornsby, 1925 ... .403
22 Harry Heilmann, 1923 ... .403
23 Pete Browning, 1887 ..... .402
24 Rogers Hornsby, 1922 ... .401
25 Bill Terry, 1930 .... .401
26 Hughie Jennings, 1896 ... .401
27 Ty Cobb, 1922 .... .401
28 Cap Anson, 1881 .... .399
29 Lefty O'Doul, 1929 ..... .398
30 Harry Heilmann, 1927 ... .398
31 Rogers Hornsby, 1921 ... .397
32 Ed Delahanty, 1896 ..... .397
33 Jesse Burkett, 1899 ..... .396
34 Joe Jackson, 1912 ..... .395
35 Harry Heilmann, 1921 ... .394
36 Babe Ruth, 1923 .... .393
37 Harry Heilmann, 1925 ... .393
38 Babe Herman, 1930 ..... .393
39 Joe Kelley, 1894 .... .393
40 Sam Thompson, 1895 .... .392
41 John McGraw, 1899 ..... .391
42 Ty Cobb, 1913 .... .390
43 Fred Clarke, 1897 ...... .390
44 Al Simmons, 1931 ...... .390
45 George Brett, 1980 ..... .390
46 Tris Speaker, 1925 ..... .389
47 Bill Lange, 1895 .... .389
48 Billy Hamilton, 1895 ..... .389
49 Ty Cobb, 1921 .... .389
50 Ted Williams, 1957 ..... .388
51 King Kelly, 1886 .... .388
52 Rod Carew, 1977 .... .388
53 Luke Appling, 1936 ..... .388
54 Tris Speaker, 1920 ..... .388
55 Deacon White, 1877 .... .387
56 Al Simmons, 1925 ...... .387
57 Rogers Hornsby, 1928 ... .387
58 Tris Speaker, 1916 ..... .386
59 Willie Keeler, 1896 ..... .386
60 Chuck Klein, 1930 ..... .386
61 Lave Cross, 1894 ...... .386
    Hughie Jennings, 1895 ... .386
63 Willie Keeler, 1898 ..... .385
64 Arky Vaughan, 1935 .... .385
65 Rogers Hornsby, 1923 ... .384
66 Ty Cobb, 1919 .... .384
67 Nap Lajoie, 1910 ...... .384
68 Ty Cobb, 1910 .... .383
69 Jesse Burkett, 1897 ..... .383
70 Tris Speaker, 1912 ..... .383
71 Ty Cobb, 1917 .... .383
72 Ty Cobb, 1912 .... .383
73 Joe Jackson, 1920 ..... .382
74 Ty Cobb, 1918 .... .382
75 Honus Wagner, 1900 .... .381
76 Babe Herman, 1929 ..... .381
77 Joe DiMaggio, 1939 .... .381
78 Al Simmons, 1930 ...... .381
79 Paul Waner, 1927 ...... .380
80 Rogers Hornsby, 1929 ... .380
81 Billy Hamilton, 1893 ..... .380
82 Tris Speaker, 1923 ..... .380
83 Goose Goslin, 1928 .... .379
84 Freddy Lindstrom, 1930 .. .379
85 Willie Keeler, 1899 ..... .379
86 Lou Gehrig, 1930 .... .379
87 John Cassidy, 1877 ..... .378
88 Pete Browning, 1882 ..... .378
89 Ty Cobb, 1925 .... .378
90 Babe Ruth, 1924 .... .378
91 Sam Crawford, 1911 .... .378
92 Tris Speaker, 1922 ..... .378
93 Earl Averill, 1936 ...... .378
94 Babe Ruth, 1921 .... .378
95 Heinie Manush, 1928 .... .378
96 Heinie Manush, 1926 .... .378
97 Ed Delahanty, 1897 ..... .377
98 Willie Keeler, 1895 ..... .377
99 Ty Cobb, 1909 .... .377
100 Cy Seymour, 1905 .... .377

Batting Average (by era)

1876-1892
1 Tip O'Neill, 1887 .... .435
2 Ross Barnes, 1876 ...... .429
3 Fred Dunlap, 1884 ..... .412
4 Pete Browning, 1887 .... .402
5 Cap Anson, 1881 .... .399
6 King Kelly, 1886 .... .388
7 Deacon White, 1877 .... .387
8 John Cassidy, 1877 ..... .378
9 Pete Browning, 1882 .... .378
10 Dan Brouthers, 1883 .... .374
11 Pete Browning, 1890 .... .373
12 Dan Brouthers, 1889 .... .373
13 Dave Orr, 1890 .... .373
14 Sam Thompson, 1887 ... .372
15 Tommy Tucker, 1889 ..... .372

1893-1919
1 Hugh Duffy, 1894 .... .440
2 Nap Lajoie, 1901 ...... .426
3 Willie Keeler, 1897 ..... .424
4 Ty Cobb, 1911 .... .420
5 Ty Cobb, 1912 .... .410
6 Ed Delahanty, 1899 .... .410
7 Jesse Burkett, 1896 .... .410
8 Jesse Burkett, 1895 .... .409
9 Joe Jackson, 1911 ...... .408
10 Sam Thompson, 1894 ... .407
11 Ed Delahanty, 1894 .... .407
12 Billy Hamilton, 1894 .... .404
13 Ed Delahanty, 1895 .... .404
14 Hughie Jennings, 1896 ... .401
15 Ed Delahanty, 1896 ..... .397

1920-1941
1 Rogers Hornsby, 1924 ... .424
2 George Sisler, 1922 ..... .420
3 George Sisler, 1920 .... .407
4 Ted Williams, 1941 ..... .406
5 Rogers Hornsby, 1925 ... .403
6 Harry Heilmann, 1923 ... .403
7 Rogers Hornsby, 1922 ... .401
8 Bill Terry, 1930 .... .401
9 Ty Cobb, 1922 .... .401
10 Lefty O'Doul, 1929 ..... .398
11 Harry Heilmann, 1927 ... .398
12 Rogers Hornsby, 1921 ... .397
13 Harry Heilmann, 1921 ... .394
14 Babe Ruth, 1923 .... .393
15 Harry Heilmann, 1925 .... .393

1942-1960
1 Ted Williams, 1957 ..... .388
2 Stan Musial, 1948 ...... .376
3 Ted Williams, 1948 ..... .369
4 Stan Musial, 1946 ...... .365
5 Mickey Mantle, 1957 .... .365
6 Harry Walker, 1947 ..... .363
7 Dixie Walker, 1944 ..... .357
8 Stan Musial, 1943 ...... .357
9 Ted Williams, 1942 ..... .356
10 Phil Cavarretta, 1945 .... .355
11 Lou Boudreau, 1948 .... .355
12 Stan Musial, 1951 ...... .355
13 Hank Aaron, 1959 ...... .355
14 Billy Goodman, 1950 .... .354
15 Harvey Kuenn, 1959 ..... .353

1961-1990
1 George Brett, 1980 ...... .390
2 Rod Carew, 1977 .... .388
3 Tony Gwynn, 1987 ..... .370
4 Wade Boggs, 1985 ..... .368
5 Wade Boggs, 1988 ..... .366
6 Rico Carty, 1970 ...... .366
7 Rod Carew, 1974 ...... .364
8 Wade Boggs, 1987 ..... .363
9 Joe Torre, 1971 .... .363
10 Wade Boggs, 1983 ..... .361
11 Norm Cash, 1961 ...... .361
12 Rod Carew, 1975 ...... .359
13 Roberto Clemente, 1967 .. .357
14 Wade Boggs, 1986 ..... .357
15 Kirby Puckett, 1988 .... .356

Batting Average (by position)

First Base

1	George Sisler, 1922	.420
2	George Sisler, 1920	.407
3	Bill Terry, 1930	.401
4	Cap Anson, 1881	.399
5	Rod Carew, 1977	.388
6	Lou Gehrig, 1930	.379
7	Dan Brouthers, 1883	.374
8	Lou Gehrig, 1928	.374
9	Lou Gehrig, 1927	.373
10	Dan Brouthers, 1889	.373

Second Base

1	Ross Barnes, 1876	.429
2	Nap Lajoie, 1901	.426
3	Rogers Hornsby, 1924	.424
4	Fred Dunlap, 1884	.412
5	Rogers Hornsby, 1925	.403
6	Rogers Hornsby, 1922	.401
7	Rogers Hornsby, 1921	.397
8	Rogers Hornsby, 1928	.387
9	Nap Lajoie, 1910	.384
10	Rogers Hornsby, 1929	.380

Shortstop

1	Hughie Jennings, 1896	.401
2	Luke Appling, 1936	.388
3	Hughie Jennings, 1895	.386
4	Arky Vaughan, 1935	.385
5	Honus Wagner, 1905	.363
6	Hughie Jennings, 1897	.355
7	Honus Wagner, 1903	.355
8	Honus Wagner, 1908	.354
9	Honus Wagner, 1907	.350
10	Honus Wagner, 1904	.349

Third Base

1	John McGraw, 1899	.391
2	George Brett, 1980	.390
3	Lave Cross, 1894	.386
4	Freddy Lindstrom, 1930	.379
5	Heinie Zimmerman, 1912	.372
6	John McGraw, 1895	.369
7	Wade Boggs, 1985	.368
8	Denny Lyons, 1887	.367
9	Wade Boggs, 1988	.366
10	Pie Traynor, 1930	.366

Outfield

1	Hugh Duffy, 1894	.440
2	Tip O'Neill, 1887	.435
3	Willie Keeler, 1897	.424
4	Ty Cobb, 1911	.420
5	Ty Cobb, 1912	.410
6	Ed Delahanty, 1899	.410
7	Jesse Burkett, 1896	.410
8	Jesse Burkett, 1895	.409
9	Joe Jackson, 1911	.408
10	Sam Thompson, 1894	.407

Catcher

1	Cal McVey, 1877	.368
2	Mickey Cochrane, 1930	.357
3	Wilbert Robinson, 1894	.353
4	Spud Davis, 1933	.349
5	Mickey Cochrane, 1931	.349
6	Ernie Lombardi, 1938	.342
7	Gabby Hartnett, 1930	.339
8	Mickey Cochrane, 1932	.338
9	Ted Simmons, 1975	.332
10	Bill Dickey, 1937	.332

Relative Batting Average

1	Fred Dunlap, 1884	1.667
2	Ross Barnes, 1876	1.608
3	Tip O'Neill, 1887	1.564
4	Nap Lajoie, 1910	1.537
5	Ty Cobb, 1910	1.534
6	Pete Browning, 1882	1.526
7	Cap Anson, 1881	1.512
8	King Kelly, 1886	1.508
9	Ty Cobb, 1912	1.507
10	Roger Connor, 1885	1.506
11	Tris Speaker, 1916	1.506
12	Ty Cobb, 1917	1.501
13	Nap Lajoie, 1901	1.501
14	Nap Lajoie, 1904	1.499
15	Ty Cobb, 1911	1.493
16	Ty Cobb, 1909	1.493
17	Ted Williams, 1957	1.476
18	Ty Cobb, 1913	1.475
19	Ted Williams, 1941	1.472
20	Ty Cobb, 1918	1.469
21	George Gore, 1880	1.462
22	Rogers Hornsby, 1924	1.461
23	Rod Carew, 1977	1.458
24	Orator Shaffer, 1884	1.455
25	Dan Brouthers, 1885	1.455
26	Joe Jackson, 1911	1.452
27	Joe Jackson, 1912	1.451
28	Dan Brouthers, 1882	1.449
29	Dave Orr, 1884	1.448
30	George Brett, 1980	1.448
31	Ty Cobb, 1915	1.448
32	Pete Browning, 1887	1.446
33	Ty Cobb, 1916	1.445
34	Cap Anson, 1886	1.442
35	Pete Browning, 1885	1.439
36	Dan Brouthers, 1886	1.439
37	Honus Wagner, 1908	1.434
38	George Sisler, 1922	1.433
39	Cap Anson, 1882	1.428
40	Cy Seymour, 1905	1.425
41	Willie Keeler, 1897	1.422
42	Ed Delahanty, 1899	1.414
43	Wade Boggs, 1988	1.413
44	King Kelly, 1884	1.411
45	Joe Jackson, 1913	1.411
46	Rod Carew, 1974	1.408
47	Wade Boggs, 1985	1.407
48	Tris Speaker, 1912	1.406
49	Deacon White, 1877	1.405
50	Dan Brouthers, 1883	1.402
51	Jimmy Wolf, 1890	1.401
52	Stan Musial, 1948	1.400
53	George Stone, 1906	1.400
54	Cap Anson, 1888	1.399
55	George Sisler, 1920	1.398
56	Joe Torre, 1971	1.397
57	Hugh Duffy, 1894	1.394
58	Stan Musial, 1946	1.393
59	Ty Cobb, 1919	1.392
60	Rod Carew, 1975	1.391
61	Tommy Tucker, 1889	1.391
62	Nap Lajoie, 1906	1.390
63	John Reilly, 1884	1.389
64	Ed Swartwood, 1883	1.389
65	Harry Heilmann, 1923	1.389
66	Mickey Mantle, 1957	1.388
67	Willie Keeler, 1898	1.387
68	Honus Wagner, 1907	1.387
69	Roberto Clemente, 1967	1.385
70	George Sisler, 1917	1.383
71	Jim O'Rourke, 1884	1.383
72	Pete Browning, 1886	1.382
73	Tris Speaker, 1917	1.380
74	Ezra Sutton, 1884	1.380
75	Ty Cobb, 1907	1.379
76	Hick Carpenter, 1882	1.379
77	Roger Connor, 1886	1.378
78	Jesse Burkett, 1896	1.378
79	Paul Hines, 1879	1.377
80	Tony Gwynn, 1987	1.375
81	Pete Browning, 1884	1.374
82	Tris Speaker, 1913	1.374
83	Kirby Puckett, 1988	1.374
84	John Cassidy, 1877	1.373
85	Honus Wagner, 1905	1.372
86	Dave Orr, 1886	1.372
87	Rico Carty, 1970	1.372
88	George Hall, 1876	1.372
89	Eddie Collins, 1909	1.371
90	Tip O'Neill, 1888	1.370
91	Wade Boggs, 1987	1.370
92	Ty Cobb, 1922	1.370
93	Dan Brouthers, 1889	1.370
94	Cap Anson, 1880	1.368
95	Norm Cash, 1961	1.368
96	Jesse Burkett, 1899	1.367
97	Jesse Burkett, 1901	1.365
98	Hardy Richardson, 1886	1.365
99	Willie Keeler, 1904	1.365
100	Wade Boggs, 1986	1.365

On Base Percentage

1	Ted Williams, 1941	.551
2	John McGraw, 1899	.547
3	Babe Ruth, 1923	.545
4	Babe Ruth, 1920	.530
5	Ted Williams, 1957	.528
6	Billy Hamilton, 1894	.523
7	Ted Williams, 1954	.516
8	Babe Ruth, 1926	.516
9	Mickey Mantle, 1957	.515
10	Babe Ruth, 1924	.513
11	Babe Ruth, 1921	.512
12	Rogers Hornsby, 1924	.507
13	Joe Kelley, 1894	.502
14	John McGraw, 1900	.502
15	Hugh Duffy, 1894	.502
16	Ed Delahanty, 1895	.500
17	Ted Williams, 1942	.499
18	Ted Williams, 1947	.499
19	Rogers Hornsby, 1928	.498
20	Ted Williams, 1946	.497
21	Ted Williams, 1948	.497
22	Bill Joyce, 1894	.496
23	Babe Ruth, 1931	.495
24	Babe Ruth, 1930	.493
25	Arky Vaughan, 1935	.491
26	Ted Williams, 1949	.490
27	Billy Hamilton, 1895	.490
28	Billy Hamilton, 1893	.490
29	Tip O'Neill, 1887	.490
30	Rogers Hornsby, 1925	.489
	Babe Ruth, 1932	.489
32	Norm Cash, 1961	.488
33	Mickey Mantle, 1962	.488
34	Babe Ruth, 1927	.487
35	Ty Cobb, 1915	.486
36	Jesse Burkett, 1895	.486
37	Tris Speaker, 1920	.483
38	King Kelly, 1886	.483
39	Harry Heilmann, 1923	.481
40	Wade Boggs, 1988	.480
41	Billy Hamilton, 1898	.480
42	Tris Speaker, 1925	.479
	Ted Williams, 1956	.479
44	Ed Delahanty, 1894	.478
45	Lou Gehrig, 1936	.478
46	Billy Hamilton, 1896	.477
47	Cupid Childs, 1894	.475
48	John McGraw, 1898	.475
49	Harry Heilmann, 1927	.475
50	Tris Speaker, 1922	.474
51	Lou Gehrig, 1927	.474
52	Luke Appling, 1936	.474
53	Lou Gehrig, 1930	.473
54	Lou Gehrig, 1937	.473
55	Hughie Jennings, 1896	.472
56	Ed Delahanty, 1896	.472
57	John McGraw, 1897	.471
58	Joe Morgan, 1975	.471
59	Dan Brouthers, 1891	.471
60	Tris Speaker, 1916	.470
61	Bill Joyce, 1896	.470
62	Joe Kelley, 1896	.469
63	Tris Speaker, 1923	.469
64	Jimmie Foxx, 1932	.469
65	Jesse Burkett, 1897	.468
66	Ty Cobb, 1925	.468
67	Joe Jackson, 1911	.468
68	Lou Gehrig, 1928	.467
69	Ty Cobb, 1913	.467
70	George Sisler, 1922	.467
71	Mike Griffin, 1894	.467
72	Cupid Childs, 1896	.467
73	Mickey Mantle, 1956	.467
74	Wade Boggs, 1987	.467
75	Ty Cobb, 1911	.467
76	Dan Brouthers, 1890	.466
77	Lou Gehrig, 1935	.466
78	Lou Gehrig, 1934	.465
79	Lefty O'Doul, 1929	.465
80	Jimmie Foxx, 1939	.464
81	Tris Speaker, 1912	.464
82	Ed Delahanty, 1899	.464
83	Pete Browning, 1887	.464
84	Ted Williams, 1951	.464
85	Willie Keeler, 1897	.464
86	Bob Caruthers, 1887	.463
87	Cupid Childs, 1893	.463
88	Jimmie Foxx, 1929	.463
89	Hughie Jennings, 1897	.463
90	Jesse Burkett, 1899	.463
91	Nap Lajoie, 1901	.462
92	Ross Barnes, 1876	.462
	Jimmie Foxx, 1938	.462
	Ted Williams, 1958	.462
95	Dan Brouthers, 1889	.462
96	Ty Cobb, 1922	.462
97	Babe Ruth, 1928	.461
98	Jack Clark, 1987	.461
99	Eddie Collins, 1925	.461
100	Billy Hamilton, 1897	.461

Slugging Average

1	Babe Ruth, 1920	.847
2	Babe Ruth, 1921	.846
3	Babe Ruth, 1927	.772
4	Lou Gehrig, 1927	.765
5	Babe Ruth, 1923	.764
6	Rogers Hornsby, 1925	.756
7	Jimmie Foxx, 1932	.749
8	Babe Ruth, 1924	.739
9	Babe Ruth, 1926	.737
10	Ted Williams, 1941	.735
11	Babe Ruth, 1930	.732
12	Ted Williams, 1957	.731
13	Hack Wilson, 1930	.723
14	Rogers Hornsby, 1922	.722
15	Lou Gehrig, 1930	.721
16	Babe Ruth, 1928	.709
17	Al Simmons, 1930	.708
18	Lou Gehrig, 1934	.706
19	Mickey Mantle, 1956	.705
20	Jimmie Foxx, 1938	.704
21	Jimmie Foxx, 1933	.703
22	Stan Musial, 1948	.702
23	Babe Ruth, 1931	.700
24	Babe Ruth, 1929	.697
25	Lou Gehrig, 1936	.696
26	Rogers Hornsby, 1924	.696
27	Hugh Duffy, 1894	.694
28	Jimmie Foxx, 1939	.694
29	Tip O'Neill, 1887	.691
30	Mickey Mantle, 1961	.687
31	Chuck Klein, 1930	.687
32	Sam Thompson, 1894	.686
33	Hank Greenberg, 1938	.683
34	Rogers Hornsby, 1929	.679
35	Babe Herman, 1930	.678
36	Joe DiMaggio, 1937	.673
37	Babe Ruth, 1922	.672
38	Joe DiMaggio, 1939	.671
39	Hank Greenberg, 1940	.670
40	Hank Aaron, 1971	.669
41	Hank Greenberg, 1937	.668
42	Ted Williams, 1946	.667
43	Willie Mays, 1954	.667
44	Mickey Mantle, 1957	.665
45	George Brett, 1980	.664
46	Lou Gehrig, 1931	.662
47	Norm Cash, 1961	.662
48	Babe Ruth, 1932	.661
49	Willie Mays, 1955	.659
50	Ralph Kiner, 1949	.658
51	Chuck Klein, 1929	.657
52	Babe Ruth, 1919	.657
53	Willie McCovey, 1969	.656
54	Sam Thompson, 1895	.654
55	Jimmie Foxx, 1934	.653
56	Chick Hafey, 1930	.652
57	Ted Williams, 1949	.650
58	Bill Joyce, 1894	.648
59	Lou Gehrig, 1928	.648
60	Ted Williams, 1942	.648
61	Duke Snider, 1954	.647
62	Chuck Klein, 1932	.646
63	Jim Gentile, 1961	.646
64	Willie Stargell, 1973	.646
65	Willie Mays, 1965	.645
66	Mike Schmidt, 1981	.644
67	Hal Trosky, 1936	.644
68	Nap Lajoie, 1901	.643
69	Joe DiMaggio, 1941	.643
70	Lou Gehrig, 1937	.643
71	Ted Kluszewski, 1954	.642
72	Al Simmons, 1929	.642
73	Joe Medwick, 1937	.641
74	Al Simmons, 1931	.641
75	Ralph Kiner, 1947	.639
76	Rogers Hornsby, 1921	.639
77	Frank Robinson, 1966	.637
78	Jimmie Foxx, 1930	.637
79	Fred Lynn, 1979	.637
80	Hank Aaron, 1959	.636
81	Johnny Mize, 1940	.636
82	Jimmie Foxx, 1935	.636
83	Kevin Mitchell, 1989	.635
84	Mel Ott, 1929	.635
85	Ted Williams, 1954	.635
86	Ted Williams, 1947	.634
87	Chick Hafey, 1929	.632
88	George Sisler, 1920	.632
89	Rogers Hornsby, 1928	.632
90	Harry Heilmann, 1923	.632
	Dick Allen, 1966	.632
92	Ed Delahanty, 1896	.631
93	George Foster, 1977	.631
94	Jimmie Foxx, 1936	.631
95	Gabby Hartnett, 1930	.630
96	Jim Bottomley, 1928	.628
97	Hank Greenberg, 1935	.628
98	Duke Snider, 1955	.628
99	Willie Stargell, 1971	.628
100	Rogers Hornsby, 1923	.627

#	Production	Adjusted Production	Batting Runs	Adjusted Batting Runs
1	Babe Ruth, 1920 ... 1.378	Babe Ruth, 1920 ... 252	Babe Ruth, 1921 ... 119	Babe Ruth, 1923 ... 118
2	Babe Ruth, 1921 ... 1.358	Fred Dunlap, 1884 ... 249	Babe Ruth, 1923 ... 119	Babe Ruth, 1921 ... 117
3	Babe Ruth, 1923 ... 1.309	Babe Ruth, 1923 ... 238	Babe Ruth, 1920 ... 113	Babe Ruth, 1920 ... 110
4	Ted Williams, 1941 ... 1.286	Babe Ruth, 1921 ... 236	Ted Williams, 1941 ... 102	Lou Gehrig, 1927 ... 104
5	Babe Ruth, 1927 ... 1.259	Ted Williams, 1941 ... 232	Lou Gehrig, 1927 ... 101	Babe Ruth, 1927 ... 103
6	Ted Williams, 1957 ... 1.259	Pete Browning, 1882 ... 230	Babe Ruth, 1924 ... 101	Babe Ruth, 1924 ... 101
7	Babe Ruth, 1926 ... 1.253	Babe Ruth, 1927 ... 229	Babe Ruth, 1927 ... 101	Ted Williams, 1941 ... 100
8	Babe Ruth, 1924 ... 1.252	Babe Ruth, 1926 ... 228	Babe Ruth, 1926 ... 97	Babe Ruth, 1926 ... 99
9	Rogers Hornsby, 1925 ... 1.245	Ted Williams, 1957 ... 227	Jimmie Foxx, 1932 ... 97	Babe Ruth, 1931 ... 96
10	Lou Gehrig, 1927 ... 1.240	Lou Gehrig, 1927 ... 224	Ted Williams, 1946 ... 94	Rogers Hornsby, 1924 ... 96
11	Babe Ruth, 1930 ... 1.225	Babe Ruth, 1919 ... 224	Rogers Hornsby, 1924 ... 94	Rogers Hornsby, 1922 ... 94
12	Jimmie Foxx, 1932 ... 1.218	Babe Ruth, 1931 ... 223	Ted Williams, 1942 ... 93	Babe Ruth, 1930 ... 94
13	Rogers Hornsby, 1924 ... 1.203	Mickey Mantle, 1957 ... 223	Babe Ruth, 1931 ... 92	Jimmie Foxx, 1932 ... 93
14	Hugh Duffy, 1894 ... 1.196	Rogers Hornsby, 1924 ... 223	Ted Williams, 1947 ... 91	Lou Gehrig, 1930 ... 93
15	Babe Ruth, 1931 ... 1.195	Ross Barnes, 1876 ... 222	Stan Musial, 1948 ... 90	Lou Gehrig, 1934 ... 92
16	Lou Gehrig, 1930 ... 1.194	Babe Ruth, 1924 ... 221	Rogers Hornsby, 1922 ... 90	Ted Williams, 1946 ... 90
17	Rogers Hornsby, 1922 ... 1.181	Babe Ruth, 1930 ... 216	Ted Williams, 1957 ... 90	Ted Williams, 1942 ... 90
18	Tip O'Neill, 1887 ... 1.180	Ted Williams, 1942 ... 214	Babe Ruth, 1930 ... 90	Mickey Mantle, 1957 ... 90
19	Mickey Mantle, 1957 ... 1.179	Lou Gehrig, 1934 ... 213	Mickey Mantle, 1957 ... 89	Babe Ruth, 1928 ... 87
20	Hack Wilson, 1930 ... 1.177	Mickey Mantle, 1956 ... 213	Ted Williams, 1949 ... 89	Ted Williams, 1957 ... 86
21	Lou Gehrig, 1936 ... 1.174	Willie McCovey, 1969 ... 212	Lou Gehrig, 1930 ... 88	Mickey Mantle, 1956 ... 86
22	Mickey Mantle, 1956 ... 1.172	Ted Williams, 1946 ... 211	Tip O'Neill, 1887 ... 88	Lou Gehrig, 1936 ... 86
23	Lou Gehrig, 1934 ... 1.172	Mickey Mantle, 1961 ... 210	Rogers Hornsby, 1925 ... 87	Stan Musial, 1948 ... 86
24	Babe Ruth, 1928 ... 1.170	Babe Ruth, 1928 ... 210	Norm Cash, 1961 ... 86	Ted Williams, 1947 ... 86
25	Jimmie Foxx, 1938 ... 1.166	Rogers Hornsby, 1922 ... 210	Lou Gehrig, 1934 ... 86	Rogers Hornsby, 1925 ... 85
26	Ted Williams, 1946 ... 1.164	Ty Cobb, 1917 ... 210	Babe Ruth, 1928 ... 84	Lou Gehrig, 1931 ... 85
27	Jimmie Foxx, 1939 ... 1.158	George Hall, 1876 ... 208	Mickey Mantle, 1956 ... 83	Norm Cash, 1961 ... 84
28	Jimmie Foxx, 1933 ... 1.153	Rogers Hornsby, 1925 ... 208	Jimmie Foxx, 1933 ... 83	Ted Williams, 1949 ... 83
29	Stan Musial, 1948 ... 1.152	Tip O'Neill, 1887 ... 208	Lou Gehrig, 1936 ... 82	Jimmie Foxx, 1933 ... 82
30	Ted Williams, 1954 ... 1.151	Lou Gehrig, 1930 ... 207	Lou Gehrig, 1931 ... 80	Mickey Mantle, 1961 ... 80
31	Babe Ruth, 1932 ... 1.150	Honus Wagner, 1908 ... 206	Ty Cobb, 1911 ... 78	Lou Gehrig, 1928 ... 79
32	Norm Cash, 1961 ... 1.150	Babe Ruth, 1932 ... 206	Jimmie Foxx, 1938 ... 78	Tip O'Neill, 1887 ... 78
33	Ted Williams, 1942 ... 1.147	Nap Lajoie, 1904 ... 205	Hugh Duffy, 1894 ... 77	Willie McCovey, 1969 ... 77
34	Sam Thompson, 1894 ... 1.145	Ty Cobb, 1912 ... 204	Carl Yastrzemski, 1967 ... 76	Rogers Hornsby, 1928 ... 76
35	Bill Joyce, 1894 ... 1.143	Rogers Hornsby, 1928 ... 204	Mickey Mantle, 1961 ... 76	Rogers Hornsby, 1921 ... 76
36	Ted Williams, 1949 ... 1.141	Dan Brouthers, 1886 ... 204	Willie McCovey, 1969 ... 76	Babe Ruth, 1932 ... 75
37	Rogers Hornsby, 1929 ... 1.139	Jimmie Foxx, 1932 ... 203	Lou Gehrig, 1928 ... 76	Frank Robinson, 1966 ... 75
38	Mickey Mantle, 1961 ... 1.138	Roger Connor, 1885 ... 203	Ted Williams, 1948 ... 76	Hack Wilson, 1930 ... 75
39	Ted Williams, 1947 ... 1.133	George Brett, 1980 ... 203	Hack Wilson, 1930 ... 75	Ty Cobb, 1917 ... 75
40	Babe Herman, 1930 ... 1.132	Ty Cobb, 1910 ... 202	Nap Lajoie, 1901 ... 75	Ty Cobb, 1911 ... 74
41	Al Simmons, 1930 ... 1.130	Dave Orr, 1885 ... 201	Rogers Hornsby, 1921 ... 74	Rogers Hornsby, 1929 ... 74
42	Rogers Hornsby, 1928 ... 1.130	Frank Robinson, 1966 ... 200	Ty Cobb, 1917 ... 74	Jimmie Foxx, 1938 ... 74
43	Babe Ruth, 1929 ... 1.128	Dan Brouthers, 1885 ... 200	Rogers Hornsby, 1929 ... 74	Lou Gehrig, 1932 ... 73
44	George Brett, 1980 ... 1.124	Jimmie Foxx, 1933 ... 199	Frank Robinson, 1966 ... 74	Ed Delahanty, 1899 ... 73
45	Chuck Klein, 1930 ... 1.123	Dave Orr, 1884 ... 199	Lou Gehrig, 1937 ... 73	Lou Gehrig, 1937 ... 73
46	Hank Greenberg, 1938 ... 1.122	Ted Williams, 1947 ... 199	George Sisler, 1920 ... 73	Harry Heilmann, 1923 ... 72
47	Joe DiMaggio, 1939 ... 1.119	Lou Gehrig, 1935 ... 199	Tris Speaker, 1912 ... 73	Ted Williams, 1948 ... 72
48	Ed Delahanty, 1895 ... 1.117	Babe Ruth, 1929 ... 199	Rogers Hornsby, 1928 ... 72	Nap Lajoie, 1901 ... 72
49	Lou Gehrig, 1937 ... 1.116	Dick Allen, 1972 ... 199	Fred Dunlap, 1884 ... 72	Tris Speaker, 1923 ... 71
50	Lou Gehrig, 1928 ... 1.115	Norm Cash, 1961 ... 198	Stan Musial, 1949 ... 72	Carl Yastrzemski, 1967 ... 71
51	Babe Ruth, 1919 ... 1.114	Mickey Mantle, 1962 ... 198	Arky Vaughan, 1935 ... 72	Joe Jackson, 1911 ... 71
52	Willie McCovey, 1969 ... 1.114	Nap Lajoie, 1901 ... 198	Joe Jackson, 1911 ... 72	George Sisler, 1920 ... 71
53	Harry Heilmann, 1923 ... 1.113	Dan Brouthers, 1882 ... 198	Carl Yastrzemski, 1970 ... 72	Ty Cobb, 1912 ... 70
54	Ted Williams, 1948 ... 1.112	Nap Lajoie, 1910 ... 198	Ty Cobb, 1915 ... 72	Babe Ruth, 1919 ... 70
55	Lou Gehrig, 1931 ... 1.108	Ed Swartwood, 1882 ... 197	Babe Ruth, 1932 ... 71	Babe Herman, 1930 ... 70
56	Babe Ruth, 1922 ... 1.106	Lou Gehrig, 1928 ... 197	Ted Williams, 1954 ... 71	Fred Dunlap, 1884 ... 70
57	Nap Lajoie, 1901 ... 1.105	Stan Musial, 1948 ... 196	Tris Speaker, 1923 ... 71	Stan Musial, 1951 ... 70
58	Hank Greenberg, 1937 ... 1.105	Ty Cobb, 1918 ... 196	Stan Musial, 1946 ... 71	Jimmie Foxx, 1934 ... 70
59	Joe Kelley, 1894 ... 1.104	Ed Delahanty, 1899 ... 196	Ralph Kiner, 1951 ... 71	Hank Aaron, 1959 ... 70
60	Hank Greenberg, 1940 ... 1.103	Ty Cobb, 1913 ... 196	Harry Heilmann, 1923 ... 71	Arky Vaughan, 1935 ... 70
61	Ed Delahanty, 1896 ... 1.103	George Stone, 1906 ... 196	Joe Jackson, 1912 ... 70	Tris Speaker, 1912 ... 69
62	Jimmie Foxx, 1934 ... 1.102	Orator Shaffer, 1878 ... 196	Stan Musial, 1951 ... 70	Ralph Kiner, 1951 ... 69
63	Arky Vaughan, 1935 ... 1.098	Orator Shaffer, 1884 ... 195	Ed Delahanty, 1899 ... 70	Stan Musial, 1949 ... 68
64	Rogers Hornsby, 1921 ... 1.097	Mike Schmidt, 1981 ... 195	Ralph Kiner, 1949 ... 70	Hugh Duffy, 1894 ... 68
65	Jimmie Foxx, 1935 ... 1.096	Harry Heilmann, 1923 ... 195	Chuck Klein, 1933 ... 69	Rod Carew, 1977 ... 68
66	Mickey Mantle, 1962 ... 1.093	Kevin Mitchell, 1989 ... 194	Joe Medwick, 1937 ... 69	Ralph Kiner, 1949 ... 68
67	Harry Heilmann, 1927 ... 1.091	Ed Delahanty, 1896 ... 194	Hank Greenberg, 1940 ... 69	Jimmie Foxx, 1935 ... 68
68	Ralph Kiner, 1949 ... 1.089	Pete Browning, 1885 ... 193	Johnny Mize, 1939 ... 69	Ty Cobb, 1915 ... 68
69	Jimmie Foxx, 1929 ... 1.088	Lou Gehrig, 1936 ... 193	Babe Herman, 1930 ... 69	Joe Jackson, 1912 ... 68
70	Ty Cobb, 1911 ... 1.088	Ty Cobb, 1911 ... 193	Lou Gehrig, 1932 ... 69	Stan Musial, 1946 ... 68
71	Lefty O'Doul, 1929 ... 1.087	Ted Williams, 1954 ... 193	Lefty O'Doul, 1929 ... 69	Ed Delahanty, 1895 ... 68
72	Rogers Hornsby, 1923 ... 1.086	Joe Jackson, 1911 ... 192	Nap Lajoie, 1910 ... 68	Ed Delahanty, 1896 ... 67
73	Al Simmons, 1931 ... 1.085	Rogers Hornsby, 1921 ... 191	Chuck Klein, 1932 ... 68	Nap Lajoie, 1910 ... 67
74	Joe DiMaggio, 1937 ... 1.085	Cupid Childs, 1890 ... 191	Ed Delahanty, 1895 ... 68	Joe Medwick, 1937 ... 67
75	Sam Thompson, 1895 ... 1.085	Ty Cobb, 1909 ... 191	Ty Cobb, 1910 ... 68	Babe Ruth, 1929 ... 67
76	Ted Williams, 1956 ... 1.084	Hank Aaron, 1971 ... 190	Ty Cobb, 1912 ... 68	Mickey Mantle, 1958 ... 67
77	Mel Ott, 1929 ... 1.084	Joe Jackson, 1913 ... 190	Chuck Klein, 1930 ... 67	Carl Yastrzemski, 1970 ... 66
78	Joe DiMaggio, 1941 ... 1.083	Reggie Jackson, 1969 ... 190	Jimmie Foxx, 1935 ... 67	Lou Gehrig, 1935 ... 66
79	Willie Mays, 1954 ... 1.083	Deacon White, 1877 ... 190	Hank Greenberg, 1937 ... 67	Al Rosen, 1953 ... 65
80	Mike Schmidt, 1981 ... 1.083	Rogers Hornsby, 1920 ... 190	Rod Carew, 1977 ... 67	Joe DiMaggio, 1941 ... 65
81	Hank Aaron, 1971 ... 1.082	John Reilly, 1884 ... 190	Frank Robinson, 1962 ... 67	Rogers Hornsby, 1920 ... 65
82	George Sisler, 1920 ... 1.082	Joe Jackson, 1912 ... 190	Wade Boggs, 1987 ... 67	Honus Wagner, 1908 ... 65
83	Tris Speaker, 1922 ... 1.080	Cap Anson, 1881 ... 189	Babe Ruth, 1919 ... 67	Hank Greenberg, 1937 ... 65
84	Ralph Kiner, 1951 ... 1.079	Carl Yastrzemski, 1967 ... 189	Jimmie Foxx, 1934 ... 66	Reggie Jackson, 1969 ... 65
85	Tris Speaker, 1923 ... 1.079	Mickey Mantle, 1958 ... 189	Ed Delahanty, 1896 ... 66	Dick Allen, 1972 ... 65
86	Jim Gentile, 1961 ... 1.074	Frank Robinson, 1967 ... 189	Jimmie Foxx, 1939 ... 66	Billy Hamilton, 1894 ... 65
87	Duke Snider, 1954 ... 1.074	Ed Delahanty, 1895 ... 189	Dick Allen, 1972 ... 66	Lou Gehrig, 1933 ... 65
88	Lou Gehrig, 1932 ... 1.072	Ed Delahanty, 1902 ... 189	Hank Greenberg, 1938 ... 66	Ted Williams, 1954 ... 65
89	Bill Terry, 1930 ... 1.071	Willie Stargell, 1973 ... 189	Dan Brouthers, 1886 ... 66	Wade Boggs, 1987 ... 64
90	Jimmie Foxx, 1936 ... 1.071	Willie Stargell, 1971 ... 188	Cy Seymour, 1905 ... 66	George Brett, 1980 ... 64
91	Johnny Mize, 1939 ... 1.070	Jimmie Foxx, 1934 ... 188	Wade Boggs, 1988 ... 66	Frank Robinson, 1962 ... 64
92	Fred Dunlap, 1884 ... 1.069	King Kelly, 1879 ... 188	Tris Speaker, 1920 ... 66	Kevin Mitchell, 1989 ... 64
93	Jimmie Foxx, 1930 ... 1.066	Hank Aaron, 1959 ... 188	Harmon Killebrew, 1969 ... 66	Harmon Killebrew, 1969 ... 64
94	Ty Cobb, 1925 ... 1.066	Dan Brouthers, 1891 ... 188	Joe Jackson, 1913 ... 66	Johnny Mize, 1939 ... 64
95	Earl Averill, 1936 ... 1.065	Roger Connor, 1882 ... 188	Stan Musial, 1943 ... 66	Ty Cobb, 1910 ... 64
96	Chuck Klein, 1929 ... 1.065	Rogers Hornsby, 1923 ... 188	Hank Aaron, 1971 ... 65	Hank Aaron, 1963 ... 64
97	Ed Delahanty, 1894 ... 1.063	Dave Orr, 1886 ... 188	Honus Wagner, 1908 ... 65	Dan Brouthers, 1886 ... 64
98	Stan Musial, 1951 ... 1.063	Rickey Henderson, 1990 ... 188	George Brett, 1980 ... 65	Joe Jackson, 1913 ... 64
99	Willie Mays, 1955 ... 1.063	Arky Vaughan, 1935 ... 187	Willie Mays, 1965 ... 65	Jimmie Foxx, 1939 ... 63
100	Fred Lynn, 1979 ... 1.063	Ted Williams, 1949 ... 187	Tris Speaker, 1916 ... 65	George Brett, 1985 ... 63

Batting Wins

1 Babe Ruth, 1923 .... 11.5
2 Babe Ruth, 1921 .... 11.1
3 Babe Ruth, 1920 .... 11.0
4 Ted Williams, 1941 ...... 9.9
5 Ted Williams, 1946 ...... 9.9
6 Lou Gehrig, 1927 .... 9.6
7 Babe Ruth, 1927 .... 9.6
8 Babe Ruth, 1924 .... 9.5
9 Ted Williams, 1942 ...... 9.5
10 Ted Williams, 1947 ...... 9.4
11 Babe Ruth, 1926 .... 9.4
12 Rogers Hornsby, 1924 ... 9.3
13 Ted Williams, 1957 ...... 9.3
14 Mickey Mantle, 1957 ..... 9.2
15 Stan Musial, 1948 .... 9.0
16 Jimmie Foxx, 1932 ...... 8.9
17 Ted Williams, 1949 ...... 8.6
18 Norm Cash, 1961 .... 8.5
19 Babe Ruth, 1931 .... 8.5
20 Rogers Hornsby, 1922 ... 8.5
21 Carl Yastrzemski, 1967 ... 8.4
22 Ty Cobb, 1917 .... 8.3
23 Rogers Hornsby, 1925 ... 8.2
24 Mickey Mantle, 1956 ..... 8.2
25 Babe Ruth, 1928 .... 8.1
26 Babe Ruth, 1930 .... 8.1
27 Lou Gehrig, 1930 .... 8.0
28 Willie McCovey, 1969 .... 8.0
29 Lou Gehrig, 1934 .... 8.0
30 Frank Robinson, 1966 .... 7.9
31 Jimmie Foxx, 1933 .... 7.8
32 Ty Cobb, 1911 .... 7.7
33 Ty Cobb, 1915 .... 7.6
34 Nap Lajoie, 1910 .... 7.6
35 Mickey Mantle, 1961 ..... 7.6
36 Honus Wagner, 1908 ..... 7.5
37 Ty Cobb, 1910 .... 7.5
38 Stan Musial, 1946 .... 7.5
39 Dick Allen, 1972 .... 7.5
40 Carl Yastrzemski, 1970 ... 7.4
41 Lou Gehrig, 1931 .... 7.4
42 Rogers Hornsby, 1921 ... 7.3
43 Lou Gehrig, 1928 .... 7.3
44 Ted Williams, 1948 ...... 7.3
45 Ted Williams, 1954 ...... 7.3
46 Chuck Klein, 1933 .... 7.3
47 Tris Speaker, 1912 ...... 7.3
48 Lou Gehrig, 1936 .... 7.3
49 Ty Cobb, 1909 .... 7.2
50 Stan Musial, 1949 .... 7.2
51 Tris Speaker, 1916 ...... 7.1
52 Tip O'Neill, 1887 .... 7.1
53 Ralph Kiner, 1951 .... 7.1
54 George Sisler, 1920 ...... 7.1
55 Rogers Hornsby, 1928 ... 7.1
56 Jimmie Foxx, 1938 ...... 7.1
57 Joe Jackson, 1911 .... 7.1
58 Joe Jackson, 1912 .... 7.0
59 Stan Musial, 1951 .... 7.0
60 Hank Aaron, 1971 .... 7.0
61 Stan Musial, 1943 .... 7.0
62 Arky Vaughan, 1935 ..... 7.0
63 Joe Jackson, 1913 .... 7.0
64 Babe Ruth, 1919 .... 7.0
65 Ralph Kiner, 1949 .... 6.9
66 Harmon Killebrew, 1967 ... 6.9
67 Harmon Killebrew, 1969 ... 6.9
68 Johnny Mize, 1939 ...... 6.9
69 Nap Lajoie, 1904 .... 6.9
70 Tris Speaker, 1923 ...... 6.9
71 Willie Mays, 1965 .... 6.8
72 Harry Heilmann, 1923 .... 6.8
73 Hank Aaron, 1963 .... 6.8
74 Cy Seymour, 1905 .... 6.8
75 Joe Medwick, 1937 ...... 6.8
76 Nap Lajoie, 1901 .... 6.8
77 Ty Cobb, 1912 .... 6.8
78 Chuck Klein, 1932 .... 6.7
79 Rogers Hornsby, 1929 ... 6.7
80 Lou Gehrig, 1937 .... 6.7
81 Rogers Hornsby, 1920 ... 6.7
82 Joe Torre, 1971 .... 6.7
83 Hack Wilson, 1930 .... 6.7
84 Rod Carew, 1977 .... 6.7
85 Wade Boggs, 1988 ...... 6.7
86 Frank Robinson, 1962 .... 6.6
87 Kevin Mitchell, 1989 ..... 6.6
88 Mickey Mantle, 1958 ..... 6.6
89 Carl Yastrzemski, 1968 ... 6.6
90 Babe Ruth, 1932 .... 6.6
91 Billy Williams, 1972 ...... 6.6
92 Joe Morgan, 1976 .... 6.5
93 Reggie Jackson, 1969 .... 6.5
94 Hank Greenberg, 1940 ... 6.5
95 Johnny Mize, 1940 ...... 6.5
96 George Brett, 1980 ...... 6.5
97 Benny Kauff, 1914 ...... 6.4
98 Duke Snider, 1954 ...... 6.4
99 Ty Cobb, 1916 .... 6.4
100 Tris Speaker, 1920 .... 6.4

Adjusted Batting Wins

1 Babe Ruth, 1923 .... 11.4
2 Babe Ruth, 1921 .... 11.0
3 Babe Ruth, 1920 .... 10.7
4 Lou Gehrig, 1927 .... 9.8
5 Babe Ruth, 1927 .... 9.8
6 Ted Williams, 1941 ...... 9.7
7 Babe Ruth, 1926 .... 9.6
8 Babe Ruth, 1924 .... 9.5
9 Rogers Hornsby, 1924 ... 9.5
10 Ted Williams, 1946 ...... 9.5
11 Mickey Mantle, 1957 ..... 9.3
12 Ted Williams, 1942 ...... 9.2
13 Babe Ruth, 1931 .... 9.0
14 Ted Williams, 1957 ...... 8.9
15 Rogers Hornsby, 1922 ... 8.9
16 Ted Williams, 1947 ...... 8.9
17 Jimmie Foxx, 1932 ...... 8.6
18 Stan Musial, 1948 .... 8.6
19 Lou Gehrig, 1934 .... 8.5
20 Babe Ruth, 1930 .... 8.5
21 Mickey Mantle, 1956 ..... 8.4
22 Lou Gehrig, 1930 .... 8.4
23 Babe Ruth, 1928 .... 8.4
24 Norm Cash, 1961 .... 8.3
25 Ty Cobb, 1917 .... 8.3
26 Willie McCovey, 1969 .... 8.1
27 Ted Williams, 1949 ...... 8.0
28 Frank Robinson, 1966 .... 8.0
29 Rogers Hornsby, 1925 ... 8.0
30 Mickey Mantle, 1961 ..... 8.0
31 Lou Gehrig, 1931 .... 7.9
32 Carl Yastrzemski, 1967 ... 7.8
33 Jimmie Foxx, 1933 .... 7.8
34 Lou Gehrig, 1928 .... 7.6
35 Lou Gehrig, 1936 .... 7.6
36 Honus Wagner, 1908 ..... 7.5
37 Rogers Hornsby, 1921 ... 7.5
38 Nap Lajoie, 1910 .... 7.5
39 Rogers Hornsby, 1928 ... 7.5
40 Dick Allen, 1972 .... 7.4
41 Babe Ruth, 1919 .... 7.3
42 Ty Cobb, 1911 .... 7.3
43 Ty Cobb, 1915 .... 7.2
44 Stan Musial, 1946 .... 7.2
45 Ty Cobb, 1910 .... 7.1
46 Ty Cobb, 1912 .... 7.0
47 Hank Aaron, 1959 .... 7.0
48 Harry Heilmann, 1923 .... 7.0
49 Rogers Hornsby, 1920 ... 7.0
50 Stan Musial, 1951 .... 7.0
51 Ted Williams, 1948 ...... 7.0
52 Babe Ruth, 1932 .... 7.0
53 Joe Jackson, 1911 .... 7.0
54 Hank Aaron, 1963 .... 6.9
55 Nap Lajoie, 1904 .... 6.9
56 Mickey Mantle, 1958 ..... 6.9
57 Carl Yastrzemski, 1970 ... 6.9
58 Ty Cobb, 1909 .... 6.9
59 Tris Speaker, 1923 ...... 6.9
60 Tris Speaker, 1912 ...... 6.9
61 Ralph Kiner, 1951 .... 6.9
62 Kevin Mitchell, 1989 ..... 6.8
63 George Sisler, 1920 ...... 6.8
64 Reggie Jackson, 1969.... 6.8
65 Lou Gehrig, 1932 .... 6.8
66 Stan Musial, 1949 .... 6.8
67 Rod Carew, 1977 .... 6.8
68 Joe Jackson, 1912 .... 6.8
69 Joe Jackson, 1913 .... 6.8
70 Arky Vaughan, 1935 ..... 6.8
71 Ralph Kiner, 1949 .... 6.7
72 Rogers Hornsby, 1929 ... 6.7
73 Tris Speaker, 1916 ...... 6.7
74 Harmon Killebrew, 1969 .. 6.7
75 Ted Williams, 1954 ...... 6.7
76 Lou Gehrig, 1937 .... 6.7
77 Jimmie Foxx, 1938 ...... 6.7
78 Joe Medwick, 1937 ...... 6.7
79 Stan Musial, 1943 .... 6.7
80 Willie Mays, 1965 .... 6.6
81 Ed Delahanty, 1899 ...... 6.6
82 Hank Aaron, 1971 .... 6.6
83 Hack Wilson, 1930 .... 6.6
84 George Stone, 1906 ..... 6.6
85 Al Rosen, 1953 .... 6.6
86 Nap Lajoie, 1901 .... 6.5
87 Jimmie Foxx, 1934 ...... 6.5
88 George Brett, 1980 ...... 6.4
89 Johnny Mize, 1939 ...... 6.4
90 Joe Torre, 1971 .... 6.4
91 Frank Robinson, 1962 .... 6.4
92 Chuck Klein, 1933 .... 6.4
93 Frank Howard, 1969 ..... 6.4
94 Joe Morgan, 1976 .... 6.4
95 Jimmie Foxx, 1935 ...... 6.4
96 Joe DiMaggio, 1941 ..... 6.3
97 Willie Stargell, 1973 ..... 6.3
98 Wade Boggs, 1988 ...... 6.3
99 Babe Ruth, 1929 .... 6.3
100 Tip O'Neill, 1887 .... 6.3

Runs Created

1 Babe Ruth, 1921 238
2 Babe Ruth, 1923 223
3 Hugh Duffy, 1894 217
4 Babe Ruth, 1920 211
5 Jimmie Foxx, 1932 207
6 Ty Cobb, 1911 207
7 Billy Hamilton, 1894 206
8 Babe Ruth, 1924 205
9 Lou Gehrig, 1927 203
10 Ted Williams, 1941 202
11 Rogers Hornsby, 1922 ... 200
12 Babe Ruth, 1927 200
13 Lou Gehrig, 1936 199
14 Babe Ruth, 1926 196
15 Lou Gehrig, 1930 195
16 Lou Gehrig, 1934 195
17 Tip O'Neill, 1887 194
18 Ted Williams, 1949 193
19 Babe Ruth, 1931 192
20 Babe Ruth, 1930 191
21 Pete Browning, 1887 191
22 Stan Musial, 1948 191
23 Hack Wilson, 1930 189
24 Jimmie Foxx, 1938 189
25 Ted Williams, 1946 188
26 Mickey Mantle, 1956 188
27 Rogers Hornsby, 1925 ... 187
28 Ted Williams, 1947 186
29 Rogers Hornsby, 1924 ... 186
30 Chuck Klein, 1930 186
31 Lou Gehrig, 1931 185
32 Ted Williams, 1942 185
33 Jimmie Foxx, 1933 184
34 Rogers Hornsby, 1929 ... 183
35 Babe Herman, 1930 183
36 Babe Ruth, 1928 182
37 Lou Gehrig, 1937 181
38 Joe Kelley, 1894 181
39 Lefty O'Doul, 1929 180
40 Nap Lajoie, 1901 179
41 Mickey Mantle, 1957 178
42 Norm Cash, 1961 178
43 Hank Greenberg, 1937 ... 178
44 Joe Kelley, 1896 178
45 Billy Hamilton, 1895 177
46 George Sisler, 1920 176
47 Ed Delahanty, 1895 175
48 Benny Kauff, 1914 175
49 Ed Delahanty, 1899 175
50 Tris Speaker, 1912 175
51 Willie Keeler, 1897 175
52 Joe Jackson, 1911 175
53 Mickey Mantle, 1961 174
54 Ty Cobb, 1912 174
55 Stan Musial, 1949 173
56 Joe DiMaggio, 1937 173
57 Hank Greenberg, 1938 ... 172
58 Ted Williams, 1948 172
59 Chuck Klein, 1932 171
60 Hank Greenberg, 1940 ... 171
61 Ed Delahanty, 1896 170
62 Joe Medwick, 1937 170
63 Bill Terry, 1930 170
64 Stan Musial, 1951 169
65 Lou Gehrig, 1928 169
66 Rogers Hornsby, 1921 ... 169
67 Earl Averill, 1936 168
68 Jimmie Foxx, 1936 168
69 Lou Gehrig, 1932 168
70 Sam Thompson, 1895 ... 167
71 Ted Williams, 1957 167
72 Ed Delahanty, 1893 167
73 Stan Musial, 1953 166
74 Joe Jackson, 1912 166
75 Tris Speaker, 1923 166
76 Jesse Burkett, 1896 166
77 Jimmie Foxx, 1934 165
78 Ralph Kiner, 1951 165
79 Jake Stenzel, 1894 165
80 Ty Cobb, 1917 164
81 Jesse Burkett, 1895 164
82 Stan Musial, 1946 164
83 Ralph Kiner, 1949 163
84 Arky Vaughan, 1935 163
85 Jimmie Foxx, 1935 163
86 Al Simmons, 1930 163
87 Johnny Mize, 1939 162
88 Chuck Klein, 1933 162
89 George Sisler, 1922 162
90 Joe DiMaggio, 1941 162
91 Duke Snider, 1954 161
92 Hank Greenberg, 1935 ... 161
93 Duke Snider, 1953 161
94 Rod Carew, 1977 160
95 Bill Lange, 1895 160
96 Denny Lyons, 1887 160
97 Frank Robinson, 1962.... 160
98 Harry Heilmann, 1923 159
99 Billy Hamilton, 1896 159
100 Ty Cobb, 1909 159

Total Average

1 Babe Ruth, 1920 .... 1.797
2 Babe Ruth, 1921 .... 1.745
3 Ted Williams, 1941 ...... 1.688
4 Babe Ruth, 1923 .... 1.683
5 Hugh Duffy, 1894 .... 1.619
6 Babe Ruth, 1926 .... 1.606
7 Billy Hamilton, 1894 ..... 1.605
8 John McGraw, 1899 ..... 1.601
9 Ted Williams, 1957 ...... 1.599
10 Babe Ruth, 1927 .... 1.571
11 Babe Ruth, 1924 .... 1.558
12 Rogers Hornsby, 1925 ... 1.539
13 Mickey Mantle, 1957 ..... 1.534
14 Bill Joyce, 1894 .... 1.528
15 Ed Delahanty, 1895 ...... 1.517
16 Tip O'Neill, 1887 .... 1.514
17 Babe Ruth, 1930 .... 1.509
18 Joe Kelley, 1894 .... 1.503
19 Lou Gehrig, 1927 .... 1.500
20 Babe Ruth, 1931 .... 1.487
21 Ty Cobb, 1911 .... 1.464
22 Ted Williams, 1954 ...... 1.452
23 Jimmie Foxx, 1932 ...... 1.451
24 Billy Hamilton, 1895 ..... 1.443
25 Babe Ruth, 1932 .... 1.432
26 Ted Williams, 1946 ...... 1.431
27 Joe Kelley, 1896 .... 1.430
28 Lou Gehrig, 1936 .... 1.426
29 Mickey Mantle, 1956 ..... 1.426
30 Rogers Hornsby, 1924 ... 1.424
31 Pete Browning, 1887 .... 1.422
32 Hack Wilson, 1930 .... 1.411
33 Rogers Hornsby, 1928 ... 1.409
34 Sam Thompson, 1894 ... 1.409
35 Ed Delahanty, 1896 ...... 1.405
36 Babe Ruth, 1928 .... 1.405
37 Lou Gehrig, 1934 .... 1.401
38 Ted Williams, 1942 ...... 1.394
39 Jimmie Foxx, 1938 ...... 1.392
40 Ted Williams, 1947 ...... 1.391
41 Lou Gehrig, 1930 .... 1.389
42 Billy Hamilton, 1893 ..... 1.386
43 Mickey Mantle, 1962 ..... 1.385
44 Mickey Mantle, 1961 ..... 1.384
45 Bill Lange, 1895 .... 1.373
46 Bob Caruthers, 1887 ..... 1.368
47 King Kelly, 1886 .... 1.366
48 Babe Ruth, 1919 .... 1.358
49 Norm Cash, 1961 .... 1.358
50 Rogers Hornsby, 1922 ... 1.353
51 Babe Herman, 1930 ..... 1.351
52 Jimmie Foxx, 1933 ...... 1.348
53 Ted Williams, 1948 ...... 1.347
54 Ted Williams, 1949 ...... 1.347
55 Lou Gehrig, 1937 .... 1.339
56 Rogers Hornsby, 1929 ... 1.338
57 Ty Cobb, 1912 .... 1.328
58 Nap Lajoie, 1901 .... 1.324
59 Ty Cobb, 1910 .... 1.321
60 Jake Stenzel, 1894 ...... 1.320
61 Joe Morgan, 1976 .... 1.319
62 Arky Vaughan, 1935 ..... 1.317
63 Billy Hamilton, 1896 ..... 1.316
64 Ty Cobb, 1913 .... 1.310
65 Jimmie Foxx, 1934 ...... 1.310
66 Tris Speaker, 1912 ...... 1.310
67 Joe Jackson, 1911 .... 1.308
68 Bill Joyce, 1896 .... 1.306
69 Hank Greenberg, 1938 ... 1.306
70 Jimmie Foxx, 1939 ...... 1.304
71 Stan Musial, 1948 .... 1.298
72 Willie McCovey, 1969 .... 1.296
73 Ed Delahanty, 1894 ...... 1.290
74 Joe Kelley, 1895 .... 1.289
75 Jimmie Foxx, 1935 ...... 1.288
76 Babe Ruth, 1929 .... 1.288
77 Mel Ott, 1929 .... 1.287
78 Harry Heilmann, 1923 .... 1.284
79 Joe Morgan, 1975 .... 1.279
80 Benny Kauff, 1914 ...... 1.278
81 Hank Greenberg, 1937 ... 1.277
82 Chuck Klein, 1930 .... 1.274
83 Al Simmons, 1930 .... 1.272
84 Tris Speaker, 1922 ...... 1.272
85 Billy Hamilton, 1891 ..... 1.270
86 Sam Thompson, 1895 ... 1.269
87 Fred Clarke, 1897 .... 1.269
88 Lou Gehrig, 1931 .... 1.267
89 Harry Heilmann, 1927 .... 1.265
90 Jesse Burkett, 1895 ..... 1.265
91 Hughie Jennings, 1896 ... 1.263
92 Billy Hamilton, 1898 ..... 1.262
93 Willie Keeler, 1897 ...... 1.262
94 Jimmie Foxx, 1929 ...... 1.261
95 Jack Clark, 1987 .... 1.258
96 George Brett, 1980 ...... 1.258
97 Lou Gehrig, 1928 .... 1.256
98 Ted Williams, 1956 ...... 1.255
99 Bill Dahlen, 1896 .... 1.254
100 Bill Dahlen, 1894 .... 1.254

Runs Produced

1	Lou Gehrig, 1931	301
2	Babe Ruth, 1921	289
3	Chuck Klein, 1930	288
4	Hugh Duffy, 1894	287
5	Al Simmons, 1930	281
6	Hughie Jennings, 1895	280
	Hack Wilson, 1930	280
	Hank Greenberg, 1937	280
9	Sam Thompson, 1895	278
10	Lou Gehrig, 1927	277
11	Kiki Cuyler, 1930	276
	Lou Gehrig, 1930	276
13	Billy Hamilton, 1894	275
14	Ed Delahanty, 1894	274
15	Sam Thompson, 1887	273
16	Ed Delahanty, 1893	272
	Joe Kelley, 1895	272
	Joe DiMaggio, 1937	272
19	Joe Kelley, 1894	270
	Lou Gehrig, 1936	270
21	Ty Cobb, 1911	266
	Rogers Hornsby, 1929	266
	Babe Ruth, 1931	266
	Ted Williams, 1949	266
25	Jimmie Foxx, 1938	264
26	Ed Delahanty, 1899	263
27	Babe Ruth, 1927	262
	Jimmie Foxx, 1932	262
29	Al Simmons, 1932	260
	Lou Gehrig, 1937	260
31	Hardy Richardson, 1890	259
	Hugh Duffy, 1893	259
	Walt Wilmot, 1894	259
34	Dan Brouthers, 1894	256
	Bobby Lowe, 1894	256
	Jake Stenzel, 1894	256
	Nap Lajoie, 1901	256
38	Hack Wilson, 1929	255
	Lou Gehrig, 1932	255
	Hank Greenberg, 1935	255
41	Cap Anson, 1886	254
	Willie Keeler, 1894	254
	Lou Gehrig, 1928	254
	Babe Ruth, 1930	254
45	Harry Stovey, 1889	252
46	Rogers Hornsby, 1922	251
	Babe Ruth, 1928	251
	Earl Averill, 1931	251
	Chuck Klein, 1932	251
50	Charlie Gehringer, 1934	250
51	Hugh Duffy, 1897	248
52	John McGraw, 1894	247
	Mel Ott, 1929	247
54	Hughie Jennings, 1896	246
	Tris Speaker, 1923	246
	Jimmie Foxx, 1930	246
	Zeke Bonura, 1936	246
	Tommy Davis, 1962	246
59	Sam Thompson, 1893	245
	Bill Terry, 1930	245
	Lou Gehrig, 1933	245
	Charlie Gehringer, 1936	245
	Ted Williams, 1939	245
64	Steve Brodie, 1894	244
	Ed Delahanty, 1895	244
	Ed Delahanty, 1896	244
	Ken Williams, 1922	244
	Lou Gehrig, 1934	244
	Hal Trosky, 1936	244
70	Tom Brown, 1891	243
71	Dan Brouthers, 1887	242
	Ed McKean, 1895	242
	Lefty O'Doul, 1929	242
	Ted Williams, 1942	242
75	Lave Cross, 1894	241
	Bill Dahlen, 1894	241
	Babe Ruth, 1920	241
78	Dan Brouthers, 1892	240
	Joe Kelley, 1896	240
	Ty Cobb, 1915	240
	George Sisler, 1920	240
	Babe Ruth, 1923	240
	Joe Cronin, 1930	240
	Jimmie Foxx, 1933	240
85	Hughie Jennings, 1894	239
	Vern Stephens, 1950	239
87	George Davis, 1897	238
	Babe Ruth, 1926	238
	Babe Herman, 1930	238
	Hank Greenberg, 1940	238
91	Rogers Hornsby, 1925	237
	Al Simmons, 1929	237
	Joe DiMaggio, 1938	237
94	8 players tied	236

Clutch Hitting Index

1	Tom Herr, 1987	200
2	Ed Abbaticchio, 1907	194
3	Bill McClellan, 1878	193
4	George Davis, 1906	180
5	Sam Crawford, 1910	178
6	Frank LaPorte, 1914	176
7	Possum Whitted, 1920	176
8	Jack Barry, 1913	176
9	Heinie Reitz, 1896	176
10	George Stovall, 1911	176
11	John Sullivan, 1943	175
12	Cy Seymour, 1908	175
13	Fred Hartman, 1902	173
14	Cookie Lavagetto, 1941	173
15	Cap Anson, 1893	172
16	Farmer Vaughn, 1893	172
17	Pie Traynor, 1928	172
18	Larry Kopf, 1920	172
19	Stuffy McInnis, 1914	171
20	Cap Anson, 1880	171
21	Heinie Zimmerman, 1917	171
22	Sherry Magee, 1918	171
23	Bill Dahlen, 1904	170
24	Ned Williamson, 1885	170
	Clyde Barnhart, 1925	170
26	Cap Anson, 1881	169
27	Cap Anson, 1885	169
28	Joe Kelley, 1898	169
29	Larry Gardner, 1920	168
30	John Gochnauer, 1903	168
31	Cap Anson, 1882	167
	Maurice Van Robays, 1940	167
33	Jim O'Rourke, 1887	167
34	Monte Ward, 1881	167
35	Mike Higgins, 1938	167
36	Frank LaPorte, 1910	166
37	Bill Hague, 1878	166
38	Ross Youngs, 1921	166
39	Bob Ferguson, 1877	165
40	Deacon White, 1876	165
41	Johnny Berardino, 1941	165
42	Cap Anson, 1896	165
43	King Kelly, 1880	165
44	Larry Gardner, 1921	164
45	Bernie Friberg, 1924	164
46	Fred Pfeffer, 1886	164
47	Russ McKelvy, 1878	164
48	Steve Brodie, 1895	163
49	Tom Burns, 1888	163
50	Earl Sheely, 1931	163
	Harmon Killebrew, 1971	163
52	Kid Gleason, 1897	163
53	John Ganzel, 1901	163
54	Joe Gerhardt, 1879	162
	Mike Dorgan, 1886	162
	Sam Mertes, 1905	162
57	Sherry Magee, 1910	162
58	Art Croft, 1877	162
59	Dixie Walker, 1946	161
60	Joe Tinker, 1906	161
61	Enos Slaughter, 1952	161
62	Ed Konetchy, 1918	160
	Wally Pipp, 1923	160
64	Harry Swacina, 1914	160
65	Amos Otis, 1982	160
66	John Mayberry, 1976	160
67	Bill Brubaker, 1936	160
68	Jack Burdock, 1883	159
	Tommy Corcoran, 1904	159
70	George Davis, 1902	159
71	Fred Pfeffer, 1885	159
	Stuffy McInnis, 1918	159
	Milt Stock, 1923	159
74	Fred Pfeffer, 1882	159
75	Ed McKean, 1892	159
76	Del Pratt, 1916	158
77	Charlie Dexter, 1901	158
	Enos Slaughter, 1950	158
79	Steve Evans, 1910	158
80	Rudy York, 1946	158
81	Billy Nash, 1892	158
	Bobby Veach, 1915	158
	Irish Meusel, 1924	158
	Roy Schalk, 1945	158
85	Fred Hartman, 1898	158
86	Dixie Walker, 1945	157
87	Red Smith, 1918	157
	Glenn Wright, 1927	157
	Bob Elliott, 1945	157
90	Hugh Duffy, 1896	157
	Mike Mowrey, 1916	157
92	Bill Johnson, 1943	157
93	Denis Menke, 1969	157
94	Jim Nealon, 1906	156
95	Bid McPhee, 1896	156
	Gus Bell, 1959	156
	Tommy Davis, 1973	156
98	Art Fletcher, 1915	156
	Ray Bates, 1917	156
100	Sherry Magee, 1916	156

Isolated Power

1	Babe Ruth, 1920	.472
2	Babe Ruth, 1921	.469
3	Babe Ruth, 1927	.417
4	Lou Gehrig, 1927	.392
5	Babe Ruth, 1928	.386
6	Jimmie Foxx, 1932	.385
7	Babe Ruth, 1930	.373
8	Babe Ruth, 1923	.372
9	Mickey Mantle, 1961	.370
10	Hank Greenberg, 1938	.369
11	Hack Wilson, 1930	.368
12	Babe Ruth, 1926	.366
13	Babe Ruth, 1924	.361
14	Babe Ruth, 1922	.357
15	Jimmie Foxx, 1938	.356
16	Rogers Hornsby, 1925	.353
17	Mickey Mantle, 1956	.353
18	Babe Ruth, 1925	.353
19	Roger Maris, 1961	.351
20	Ralph Kiner, 1949	.348
21	Jimmie Foxx, 1933	.347
22	Willie Stargell, 1973	.347
23	Kevin Mitchell, 1989	.344
24	Lou Gehrig, 1934	.344
25	Jim Gentile, 1961	.344
26	Ted Williams, 1957	.343
27	Lou Gehrig, 1930	.343
28	Lou Gehrig, 1936	.342
29	Hank Aaron, 1971	.341
30	Willie Mays, 1955	.340
31	Mike Schmidt, 1980	.338
32	Willie McCovey, 1969	.336
33	Babe Ruth, 1919	.336
34	Jimmie Foxx, 1939	.334
35	Reggie Jackson, 1969	.333
36	Willie Stargell, 1971	.333
37	Hank Greenberg, 1937	.332
38	Hank Greenberg, 1940	.330
39	Ted Williams, 1941	.329
40	Mark McGwire, 1987	.329
41	Willie Mays, 1965	.328
42	Babe Ruth, 1931	.328
43	Mike Schmidt, 1981	.328
44	Hank Greenberg, 1946	.327
45	Joe DiMaggio, 1937	.327
46	Al Simmons, 1930	.327
47	Stan Musial, 1948	.326
48	Ralph Kiner, 1947	.326
49	Dave Kingman, 1979	.325
50	Ted Williams, 1946	.325
51	Eddie Mathews, 1953	.325
52	Willie McCovey, 1970	.323
53	Willie Mays, 1954	.322
54	Lou Gehrig, 1931	.321
55	Johnny Mize, 1940	.321
56	Frank Robinson, 1966	.321
57	Rogers Hornsby, 1922	.321
58	Duke Snider, 1955	.320
59	Babe Ruth, 1932	.319
60	Jimmie Foxx, 1934	.319
61	Ralph Kiner, 1951	.318
62	Ralph Kiner, 1950	.318
63	Harmon Killebrew, 1961	.318
64	Rocky Colavito, 1958	.317
65	Chick Hafey, 1930	.316
66	Boog Powell, 1964	.316
67	Ted Kluszewski, 1954	.316
68	Dick Allen, 1966	.315
69	Cecil Fielder, 1990	.314
70	Eddie Mathews, 1954	.313
71	Duke Snider, 1957	.313
72	Eddie Mathews, 1955	.313
73	Johnny Mize, 1947	.312
74	Willie Mays, 1964	.311
75	Willie Mays, 1962	.311
76	George Foster, 1977	.311
77	Mike Schmidt, 1979	.311
78	Jack Clark, 1987	.310
79	Hank Greenberg, 1939	.310
80	Harmon Killebrew, 1969	.308
81	Ted Williams, 1949	.307
82	Hank Aaron, 1969	.307
83	Duke Snider, 1954	.307
84	Mel Ott, 1929	.306
85	Duke Snider, 1956	.306
86	Joe Adcock, 1956	.306
87	Mickey Mantle, 1955	.306
88	Wally Berger, 1930	.305
89	Jim Bottomley, 1928	.304
90	Fred Lynn, 1979	.303
91	Harmon Killebrew, 1962	.303
92	Jimmie Foxx, 1930	.302
93	Chuck Klein, 1929	.302
94	Ernie Banks, 1958	.301
95	Norm Cash, 1961	.301
96	Chuck Klein, 1930	.301
97	Hank Greenberg, 1935	.300
98	Hal Trosky, 1936	.300
99	Ernie Banks, 1955	.300
100	Mike Schmidt, 1977	.300

Extra Base Hits

1	Babe Ruth, 1921	119
2	Lou Gehrig, 1927	117
3	Chuck Klein, 1930	107
4	Chuck Klein, 1932	103
	Hank Greenberg, 1937	103
	Stan Musial, 1948	103
7	Rogers Hornsby, 1922	102
8	Lou Gehrig, 1930	100
	Jimmie Foxx, 1932	100
10	Babe Ruth, 1920	99
	Babe Ruth, 1923	99
	Hank Greenberg, 1940	99
13	Hank Greenberg, 1935	98
14	Babe Ruth, 1927	97
	Hack Wilson, 1930	97
	Joe Medwick, 1937	97
17	Hank Greenberg, 1934	96
	Hal Trosky, 1936	96
	Joe DiMaggio, 1937	96
20	Lou Gehrig, 1934	95
	Joe Medwick, 1936	95
22	Rogers Hornsby, 1929	94
	Chuck Klein, 1929	94
	Babe Herman, 1930	94
	Jimmie Foxx, 1933	94
26	Jim Bottomley, 1928	93
	Al Simmons, 1930	93
	Lou Gehrig, 1936	93
29	Babe Ruth, 1924	92
	Lou Gehrig, 1931	92
	Jimmie Foxx, 1938	92
	Stan Musial, 1953	92
	Hank Aaron, 1959	92
	Frank Robinson, 1962	92
35	Babe Ruth, 1928	91
36	Rogers Hornsby, 1925	90
	Stan Musial, 1949	90
	Willie Mays, 1962	90
	Willie Stargell, 1973	90
40	Hal Trosky, 1934	89
	Duke Snider, 1954	89
42	Joe DiMaggio, 1936	88
43	Tris Speaker, 1923	87
	Kiki Cuyler, 1925	87
	Lou Gehrig, 1928	87
	Ripper Collins, 1934	87
	Charlie Gehringer, 1936	87
	Johnny Mize, 1940	87
	Willie Mays, 1954	87
	Robin Yount, 1982	87
	Kevin Mitchell, 1989	87
52	George Sisler, 1920	86
	Babe Ruth, 1930	86
	Wally Moses, 1937	86
	Johnny Mize, 1939	86
	Ted Williams, 1939	86
	Stan Musial, 1946	86
	Eddie Mathews, 1953	86
	Reggie Jackson, 1969	86
	Hal McRae, 1977	86
	Jim Rice, 1978	86
	Don Mattingly, 1985	86
	Don Mattingly, 1986	86
64	Tip O'Neill, 1887	85
	Hugh Duffy, 1894	85
	Chick Hafey, 1929	85
	Goose Goslin, 1930	85
	Lou Gehrig, 1932	85
	Lou Gehrig, 1933	85
	Earl Averill, 1934	85
	Hank Greenberg, 1938	85
	Rudy York, 1940	85
	Ted Williams, 1949	85
	Stan Musial, 1954	85
	Frank Robinson, 1966	85
	George Foster, 1977	85
	George Brett, 1979	85
78	Sam Thompson, 1895	84
	Ken Williams, 1922	84
	Al Simmons, 1929	84
	Ed Morgan, 1930	84
	Earl Webb, 1931	84
	Joe DiMaggio, 1941	84
	Duke Snider, 1953	84
	Tony Oliva, 1964	84
	Johnny Bench, 1970	84
	Jim Rice, 1979	84
88	Rogers Hornsby, 1921	83
	Lou Gehrig, 1926	83
	Dale Alexander, 1929	83
	Jimmie Foxx, 1930	83
	Earl Averill, 1932	83
	Lou Gehrig, 1937	83
	Ted Williams, 1946	83
	Ernie Banks, 1957	83
	Hank Aaron, 1961	83
	Jim Rice, 1977	83
	George Bell, 1987	83
99	14 players tied	82

Pinch Hits

1	Jose Morales, 1976	25
2	Dave Philley, 1961	24
	Vic Bavalillo, 1970	24
	Rusty Staub, 1983	24
5	Sam Leslie, 1932	22
	Red Schoendienst, 1962	22
	Wallace Johnson, 1988	22
8	Doc Miller, 1913	21
	Peanuts Lowrey, 1953	21
	Smoky Burgess, 1966	21
	Merv Rettenmund, 1977	21
12	Ed Coleman, 1936	20
	Frenchy Bordagaray, 1938	20
	Joe Frazier, 1954	20
	Smoky Burgess, 1965	20
	Ken Boswell, 1976	20
	Jerry Turner, 1978	20
	Thad Bosley, 1985	20
	Chris Chambliss, 1986	20
20	many players tied	19

Pinch Hit Average

1	Ed Kranepool, 1974	.486
2	Smead Jolley, 1931	.467
3	Frenchy Bordagaray, 1938	.465
4	Rick Miller, 1983	.457
5	Jose Pagan, 1969	.452
6	Elmer Valo, 1955	.452
7	Gates Brown, 1968	.450
8	Ted Easterly, 1912	.433
	Milt Thompson, 1985	.433
	Randy Bush, 1986	.433
11	Joe Cronin, 1943	.429
	Don Dillard, 1961	.429
13	Candy Maldonado, 1986	.425
14	Richie Ashburn, 1962	.419
	Dick Williams, 1962	.419
16	Merritt Ranew, 1963	.415
	Carl Taylor, 1969	.415
18	Kurt Bevacqua, 1983	.412
19	Jerry Turner, 1978	.408
20	Bob Bowman, 1958	.406
	Harry Spilman, 1986	.406
22	Frankie Baumholtz, 1955	.405
23	6 players tied	.400

Pinch Hit Home Runs

1	Johnny Frederick, 1932	6
2	Joe Cronin, 1943	5
	Butch Nieman, 1945	5
	Gene Freese, 1959	5
	Jerry Lynch, 1961	5
	Cliff Johnson, 1974	5
	Lee Lacy, 1978	5
	Jerry Turner, 1978	5
9	Ernie Lombardi, 1946	4
	Del Wilber, 1953	4
	Bill Taylor, 1955	4
	Bob Thurman, 1957	4
	Rip Repulski, 1958	4
	George Crowe, 1959	4
	George Crowe, 1960	4
	Johnny Blanchard, 1961	4
	Carl Sawatski, 1961	4
	Jerry Lynch, 1963	4
	Don Mincher, 1964	4
	Hal Breeden, 1973	4
	Mike Ivie, 1978	4
	Del Unser, 1979	4
	Jeff Burroughs, 1982	4
	Danny Heep, 1983	4
	Candy Maldonado, 1986	4
	Mark Carreon, 1989	4
	Tommy Gregg, 1990	4
	Ernest Riles, 1990	4

Total Player Rating / 150g

1	Fred Dunlap, 1884	12.03
2	Babe Ruth, 1923	10.36
3	Pete Browning, 1882	10.22
4	Mike Schmidt, 1981	10.15
5	Nap Lajoie, 1903	9.72
6	Nap Lajoie, 1901	9.62
7	Ross Barnes, 1876	9.55
8	Babe Ruth, 1921	9.47
9	Babe Ruth, 1920	9.30
10	Babe Ruth, 1927	8.84
11	Rickey Henderson, 1990	8.49
12	George Brett, 1980	8.46
13	Fred Pfeffer, 1884	8.44
14	Ted Williams, 1941	8.39
15	Ted Williams, 1942	8.30
16	Ty Cobb, 1917	8.29
17	Babe Ruth, 1924	8.24
18	Ted Williams, 1946	8.20
19	Mickey Mantle, 1957	8.13
20	George Sisler, 1920	8.08
21	Babe Ruth, 1919	8.08
22	Cal Ripken, 1984	8.06
23	Honus Wagner, 1906	8.03
24	Babe Ruth, 1926	7.99
25	Ted Williams, 1957	7.95
26	Lou Gehrig, 1927	7.94
27	Mickey Mantle, 1956	7.90
28	Nap Lajoie, 1906	7.89
29	Ted Williams, 1947	7.88
30	Rogers Hornsby, 1924	7.87
31	Jack Glasscock, 1882	7.86
32	Mike Schmidt, 1980	7.80
33	King Kelly, 1879	7.79
34	Tris Speaker, 1913	7.77
35	Babe Ruth, 1930	7.76
36	Rogers Hornsby, 1920	7.75
37	Ty Cobb, 1910	7.71
38	Ed Delahanty, 1896	7.68
39	Nap Lajoie, 1900	7.65
	Tris Speaker, 1912	7.65
41	Bob Ferguson, 1878	7.62
42	Hughie Jennings, 1896	7.62
43	Honus Wagner, 1903	7.56
44	Honus Wagner, 1905	7.55
45	Nap Lajoie, 1910	7.55
46	Cupid Childs, 1896	7.50
	Willie Mays, 1955	7.50
48	Stan Musial, 1948	7.45
	Ron Santo, 1966	7.45
50	Rickey Henderson, 1985	7.45
51	Hughie Jennings, 1895	7.44
52	Eric Davis, 1987	7.44
53	Rogers Hornsby, 1922	7.40
54	Ed Delahanty, 1893	7.39
55	Nap Lajoie, 1907	7.34
56	Lou Boudreau, 1944	7.30
57	Nap Lajoie, 1904	7.29
58	Buddy Bell, 1981	7.27
59	Dick Bartell, 1937	7.27
60	Cupid Childs, 1890	7.26
61	Ted Williams, 1949	7.26
62	Rogers Hornsby, 1917	7.24
63	Ty Cobb, 1911	7.19
	Joe Morgan, 1975	7.19
65	Hughie Jennings, 1897	7.18
66	Carl Yastrzemski, 1967	7.17
67	Benny Kauff, 1915	7.17
68	Nap Lajoie, 1908	7.17
69	Mickey Mantle, 1961	7.06
70	Ted Williams, 1954	7.05
71	Jimmie Foxx, 1933	7.05
72	Babe Ruth, 1931	7.03
73	Tris Speaker, 1914	7.03
74	Honus Wagner, 1907	6.97
75	Rickey Henderson, 1981	6.94
76	Honus Wagner, 1912	6.93
77	Ted Williams, 1948	6.90
78	Norm Cash, 1961	6.89
79	Stan Musial, 1943	6.78
	Willie Mays, 1965	6.78
81	Harlond Clift, 1937	6.77
82	Rogers Hornsby, 1929	6.73
83	Joe Jackson, 1912	6.72
	Babe Ruth, 1928	6.72
	Mike Schmidt, 1977	6.72
86	Stan Musial, 1951	6.71
87	Andre Dawson, 1981	6.70
88	Charley Jones, 1879	6.69
89	Arky Vaughan, 1935	6.68
90	George Sisler, 1922	6.65
91	Roger Peckinpaugh, 1919	6.64
92	Sam Barkley, 1884	6.63
93	Joe Jackson, 1911	6.63
94	Joe DiMaggio, 1939	6.63
95	Snuffy Stirnweiss, 1944	6.62
96	Willie Mays, 1958	6.61
97	George Brett, 1985	6.58
98	Charley Jones, 1877	6.58
99	Pedro Guerrero, 1985	6.57
100	Jackie Robinson, 1951	6.57

Stolen Bases

1	Hugh Nicol, 1887	138
2	Rickey Henderson, 1982	130
3	Arlie Latham, 1887	129
4	Lou Brock, 1974	118
5	Charlie Comiskey, 1887	117
6	Monte Ward, 1887	111
	Billy Hamilton, 1889	111
	Billy Hamilton, 1891	111
9	Vince Coleman, 1985	110
10	Arlie Latham, 1888	109
	Vince Coleman, 1987	109
12	Rickey Henderson, 1983	108
13	Vince Coleman, 1986	107
14	Tom Brown, 1891	106
15	Maury Wills, 1962	104
16	Pete Browning, 1887	103
	Hugh Nicol, 1888	103
18	Jim Fogarty, 1887	102
	Billy Hamilton, 1890	102
20	Rickey Henderson, 1980	100
21	Jim Fogarty, 1889	99
22	Billy Hamilton, 1894	98
23	Harry Stovey, 1890	97
	Billy Hamilton, 1895	97
	Ron LeFlore, 1980	97
26	Ty Cobb, 1915	96
	Omar Moreno, 1980	96
28	Bid McPhee, 1887	95
	Curt Welch, 1888	95
30	Mike Griffin, 1887	94
	Maury Wills, 1965	94
32	Tommy McCarthy, 1888	93
	Rickey Henderson, 1988	93
34	Darby O'Brien, 1889	91
35	Tim Raines, 1983	90
36	Curt Welch, 1887	89
	Herman Long, 1889	89
38	Tom Poorman, 1887	88
	Blondie Purcell, 1887	88
	Monte Ward, 1892	88
	Clyde Milan, 1912	88
42	Harry Stovey, 1888	87
	Arlie Latham, 1891	87
	Joe Kelley, 1896	87
	Rickey Henderson, 1986	87
46	Cub Stricker, 1887	86
47	Tommy Tucker, 1887	85
	Hub Collins, 1890	85
	Hugh Duffy, 1891	85
50	King Kelly, 1887	84
	Chippy McGarr, 1887	84
	Billy Sunday, 1890	84
	Bill Lange, 1896	84
54	Tommy McCarthy, 1890	83
	Billy Hamilton, 1896	83
	Ty Cobb, 1911	83
	Willie Wilson, 1979	83
58	Dummy Hoy, 1888	82
	John Reilly, 1888	82
60	Eddie Collins, 1910	81
	Vince Coleman, 1988	81
62	Emmett Seery, 1888	80
	Hugh Nicol, 1889	80
	Bob Bescher, 1911	80
	Rickey Henderson, 1985	80
	Eric Davis, 1986	80
67	Tom Brown, 1890	79
	Dave Collins, 1980	79
	Willie Wilson, 1980	79
70	Hugh Duffy, 1890	78
	Tom Brown, 1892	78
	John McGraw, 1894	78
	Ron LeFlore, 1979	78
	Tim Raines, 1982	78
75	Ted Scheffler, 1890	77
	Jimmy Sheckard, 1899	77
	Davey Lopes, 1975	77
	Omar Moreno, 1979	77
	Rudy Law, 1983	77
	Rickey Henderson, 1989	77
	Vince Coleman, 1990	77
82	Ed McKean, 1887	76
	Walt Wilmot, 1890	76
	Dusty Miller, 1896	76
	Ty Cobb, 1909	76
86	Yank Robinson, 1887	75
	George Van Haltren, 1891	75
	Clyde Milan, 1913	75
	Benny Kauff, 1914	75
	Bill North, 1976	75
	Tim Raines, 1984	75
92	Frank Fennelly, 1887	74
	Harry Stovey, 1887	74
	Walt Wilmot, 1894	74
	Fritz Maisel, 1914	74
	Lou Brock, 1966	74
97	7 players tied	73

Stolen Base Average

1	Kevin McReynolds, 1988	100.0
2	Max Carey, 1922	96.2
3	Ken Griffey, 1980	95.8
4	Stan Javier, 1988	95.2
5	Amos Otis, 1970	94.3
6	Jack Perconte, 1985	93.9
7	Miguel Dilone, 1984	93.1
	Bob Dernier, 1986	93.1
9	Kirk Gibson, 1990	92.9
10	Don Baylor, 1972	92.3
	Oddibe McDowell, 1987	92.3
12	Davey Lopes, 1985	92.2
13	Eric Davis, 1987	92.1
14	Bobby Bonds, 1969	91.8
	Davey Lopes, 1978	91.8
16	Davey Lopes, 1979	91.7
	Marquis Grissom, 1990	91.7
18	Jim Wynn, 1965	91.5
19	Larry Bowa, 1977	91.4
20	Ryne Sandberg, 1987	91.3
	Alan Trammell, 1987	91.3
22	Jerry Mumphrey, 1980	91.2
23	Tom Herr, 1985	91.2
24	Jack Smith, 1925	90.9
	Davey Lopes, 1981	90.9
	Tim Raines, 1987	90.9
27	Willie Wilson, 1984	90.4
28	Bake McBride, 1978	90.3
29	Henry Cotto, 1988	90.0
30	Mitchell Page, 1977	89.4
31	Tommy Harper, 1971	89.3
	Rick Manning, 1981	89.3
	Eric Davis, 1987	89.3
34	Maury Wills, 1962	88.9
	Jake Wood, 1962	88.9
	Tommy Harper, 1964	88.9
	Enzo Hernandez, 1972	88.9
	Dusty Baker, 1973	88.9
	Leon Lacy, 1981	88.9
	Rickey Henderson, 1985	88.9
41	Willie Wilson, 1980	88.8
42	Tim Raines, 1985	88.6
	Tim Raines, 1986	88.6
44	Bert Campaneris, 1969	88.6
	Kirk Gibson, 1988	88.6
46	Willie Mays, 1971	88.5
47	Vince Coleman, 1986	88.4
48	Dale Murphy, 1983	88.2
	Tim Raines, 1984	88.2
	Kirk Gibson, 1985	88.2

Stolen Base Runs

1	Vince Coleman, 1986	24
2	Maury Wills, 1962	23
3	Rickey Henderson, 1983 .	21
4	Rickey Henderson, 1988 .	20
5	Vince Coleman, 1987	20
6	Tim Raines, 1983	19
7	Vince Coleman, 1985	18
	Rickey Henderson, 1985 .	18
9	Willie Wilson, 1979	18
	Ron LeFlore, 1980	18
	Willie Wilson, 1980	18
12	Eric Davis, 1986	17
13	Tim Raines, 1984	17
14	Davey Lopes, 1975	16
	Rudy Law, 1983	16
16	Lou Brock, 1974	16
	Tim Raines, 1985	16
	Tim Raines, 1986	16
19	Rickey Henderson, 1986 .	15
20	Ron LeFlore, 1979	15
21	Tim Raines, 1981	15
	Rickey Henderson, 1989 .	15
23	Rickey Henderson, 1980 .	14
24	Max Carey, 1922	14
	Joe Morgan, 1975	14
26	Bert Campaneris, 1969 . . .	14
	Tim Raines, 1982	14
	Rickey Henderson, 1982 .	14
29	Vince Coleman, 1989	14
	Rickey Henderson, 1990 .	14
31	Davey Lopes, 1976	13
	Willie Wilson, 1983	13
	Vince Coleman, 1990	13
34	Mickey Rivers, 1975	13
	Joe Morgan, 1976	13
	Jerry Mumphrey, 1980 . . .	13
	Juan Samuel, 1984	13
38	Fritz Maisel, 1914	12
	Al Wiggins, 1983	12
	Tim Raines, 1987	12
41	Julio Cruz, 1978	12
	Davey Lopes, 1985	12
	Ozzie Smith, 1988	12
44	Lou Brock, 1966	11
	Lou Brock, 1968	11
	Gary Pettis, 1985	11
	Eric Davis, 1987	11
48	8 players tied	11

Stolen Base Wins

1	Vince Coleman, 1986	2.5
2	Maury Wills, 1962	2.3
3	Rickey Henderson, 1983 .	2.1
4	Rickey Henderson, 1988 .	2.0
5	Tim Raines, 1983	1.9
6	Vince Coleman, 1987	1.9
7	Vince Coleman, 1985	1.9
8	Ron LeFlore, 1980	1.9
9	Eric Davis, 1986	1.8
10	Rickey Henderson, 1985 .	1.8
11	Willie Wilson, 1980	1.8
12	Tim Raines, 1984	1.7
13	Willie Wilson, 1979	1.7
14	Davey Lopes, 1975	1.7
15	Tim Raines, 1985	1.6
16	Lou Brock, 1974	1.6
17	Tim Raines, 1986	1.6
18	Rudy Law, 1983	1.6
19	Tim Raines, 1981	1.6
20	Rickey Henderson, 1986 .	1.5
21	Rickey Henderson, 1989 .	1.5
22	Joe Morgan, 1975	1.5
23	Ron LeFlore, 1979	1.5
24	Tim Raines, 1982	1.4
25	Bert Campaneris, 1969 . . .	1.4
26	Vince Coleman, 1989	1.4
27	Rickey Henderson, 1980 .	1.4
28	Rickey Henderson, 1982 .	1.4
29	Rickey Henderson, 1990 .	1.4
30	Davey Lopes, 1976	1.4
31	Joe Morgan, 1976	1.3
32	Jerry Mumphrey, 1980 . . .	1.3
33	Max Carey, 1922	1.3
34	Vince Coleman, 1990	1.3
35	Fritz Maisel, 1914	1.3
36	Juan Samuel, 1984	1.3
37	Lou Brock, 1968	1.3
38	Willie Wilson, 1983	1.3
39	Mickey Rivers, 1975	1.3
40	Ozzie Smith, 1988	1.3
41	Al Wiggins, 1983	1.3
42	Davey Lopes, 1985	1.2
43	Julio Cruz, 1978	1.2
44	Lou Brock, 1966	1.2
45	Tim Raines, 1987	1.2
46	Davey Lopes, 1978	1.2
47	Dave Collins, 1980	1.2
	Rod Scott, 1980	1.2
49	Bobby Bonds, 1969	1.2
50	Tommy Harper, 1969	1.2

Fielding Average

First Base
1	Steve Garvey, 1984	1.000
2	Stuffy McInnis, 1921	.999
3	Frank McCormick, 1946 . .	.999
4	Steve Garvey, 1981	.999
5	Jim Spencer, 1973	.999
6	Wes Parker, 1968	.999
7	Eddie Murray, 1981	.999
8	Jim Spencer, 1976	.998
9	Jim Spencer, 1981	.998
10	Joe Judge, 1930	.998

Second Base
1	Bobby Grich, 1985	.997
2	Jose Oquendo, 1990	.996
3	Rob Wilfong, 1980	.995
4	Bobby Grich, 1973	.995
5	Frank White, 1988	.994
6	Jose Oquendo, 1989	.994
7	Jerry Adair, 1964	.994
8	Ryne Sandberg, 1986	.994
9	Tim Cullen, 1970	.994
10	Manny Trillo, 1982	.994

Shortstop
1	Cal Ripken, 1990	.996
2	Tony Fernandez, 1989	.992
3	Larry Bowa, 1979	.991
4	Ed Brinkman, 1972	.990
5	Cal Ripken, 1989	.990
6	Spike Owen, 1990	.989
7	Tony Fernandez, 1990	.989
8	Larry Bowa, 1972	.987
9	Ozzie Smith, 1987	.987
10	Larry Bowa, 1971	.987

Third Base
1	Don Money, 1974	.989
2	Hank Majeski, 1947	.988
3	Aurelio Rodriguez, 1978 . .	.987
4	Willie Kamm, 1933	.984
5	George Kell, 1946	.983
6	Heinie Groh, 1924	.983
7	Carney Lansford, 1979 . . .	.983
8	George Kell, 1950	.982
9	Pinky Whitney, 1937	.982
10	Buddy Bell, 1980	.981

Outfield
1	Danny Litwhiler, 1942	1.000
	Willard Marshall, 1951	1.000
	Tony Gonzalez, 1962	1.000
	Don Demeter, 1963	1.000
	Rocky Colavito, 1965	1.000
	Curt Flood, 1966	1.000
	Johnny Callison, 1968	1.000
	Mickey Stanley, 1968	1.000
	Ken Harrelson, 1968	1.000
	Ken Berry, 1969	1.000
	Mickey Stanley, 1970	1.000
	Roy White, 1971	1.000
	Al Kaline, 1971	1.000
	Ken Berry, 1972	1.000
	Carl Yastrzemski, 1977 . . .	1.000
	Terry Puhl, 1979	1.000
	Gary Roenicke, 1980	1.000
	Ken Landreaux, 1981	1.000
	Terry Puhl, 1981	1.000
	Ken Singleton, 1981	1.000
	Brian Downing, 1982	1.000
	John Lowenstein, 1982 . . .	1.000
	Brian Downing, 1982	1.000

Catcher
1	Spud Davis, 1939	1.000
	Buddy Rosar, 1946	1.000
	Lou Berberet, 1957	1.000
	Pete Daley, 1957	1.000
	Yogi Berra, 1958	1.000
	Rick Cerone, 1988	1.000
7	Joe Azcue, 1967	.999
8	Wes Westrum, 1950	.999
9	Thurman Munson, 1971 . .	.998
10	Rick Cerone, 1987	.998

Pitcher (92 chances accepted)
1	Kid Nichols, 1896	1.000
	Frank Owen, 1904	1.000
	Mordecai Brown, 1908 . . .	1.000
	Pete Alexander, 1913	1.000
	Walter Johnson, 1913	1.000
	Eppa Rixey, 1917	1.000
	Walter Johnson, 1917	1.000
	Hal Schumacher, 1935 . . .	1.000
	Larry Jackson, 1964	1.000
	Randy Jones, 1976	1.000
	Greg Maddux, 1990	1.000

Total Chances per Game

First Base
1	Joe Gerhardt, 1876	13.28
2	Jiggs Donahue, 1907	12.73
3	Oscar Walker, 1879	12.60
4	Joe Start, 1878	12.54
5	Tim Murnane, 1878	12.52
6	Joe Start, 1879	12.49
7	Jake Goodman, 1878	12.45
8	Herman Dehlman, 1876 . .	12.36
9	Phil Todt, 1926	12.36
10	Joe Start, 1877	12.35

Second Base
1	Thorny Hawkes, 1879	8.44
2	Chick Fulmer, 1879	8.34
3	Jack Burdock, 1878	8.30
4	Ed Somerville, 1876	8.28
5	Joe Gerhardt, 1877	8.12
6	Fred Pfeffer, 1884	8.08
7	Jack Burdock, 1879	7.88
8	Joe Quest, 1878	7.81
9	Pop Smith, 1885	7.74
10	Joe Quest, 1879	7.73

Shortstop
1	Herman Long, 1889	7.27
2	Hughie Jennings, 1895 . . .	7.16
3	Dave Bancroft, 1918	7.14
4	Phil Tomney, 1889	7.12
5	George Davis, 1899	7.08
6	Hughie Jennings, 1896 . . .	7.07
7	Hughie Jennings, 1897 . . .	7.03
8	Bobby Wallace, 1901	6.97
9	Monte Cross, 1897	6.97
10	Bill Dahlen, 1895	6.93

Third Base
1	Al Nichols, 1876	5.81
2	Bob Ferguson, 1877	5.61
3	Jumbo Davis, 1888	5.13
4	Cap Anson, 1876	5.03
5	Billy Shindle, 1892	4.93
6	Jack Gleason, 1882	4.90
7	Bill Bradley, 1900	4.87
8	George Bradley, 1880	4.84
9	Will Foley, 1877	4.79
10	Levi Meyerle, 1876	4.78

Outfield
1	Fred Treacey, 1876	4.39
2	Redleg Snyder, 1876	3.84
3	Charley Jones, 1877	3.77
4	Taylor Douthit, 1928	3.68
5	Mike Mansell, 1879	3.64
6	Richie Ashburn, 1951	3.64
7	Chet Lemon, 1977	3.60
8	Thurman Tucker, 1944	3.58
9	Kirby Puckett, 1984	3.57
10	Irv Noren, 1951	3.53

Catcher
1	Bill Holbert, 1883	10.63
2	Sam Trott, 1884	10.35
3	Bill Holbert, 1884	9.51
4	Jocko Milligan, 1884	9.40
5	Mert Hackett, 1884	9.35
6	Barney Gilligan, 1884	9.30
7	Mike Hines, 1883	9.27
8	George Baker, 1884	8.99
9	Jocko Milligan, 1885	8.82
10	Lew Brown, 1877	8.65

Pitcher
1	Harry Howell, 1905	5.42
2	Harry Howell, 1904	5.12
3	Will White, 1882	4.76
4	Ed Walsh, 1907	4.75
5	George Mullin, 1904	4.53
6	Tony Mullane, 1882	4.38
7	Red Donahue, 1902	4.37
8	Nick Altrock, 1905	4.37
9	Harry Howell, 1906	4.34
10	Jack Katoll, 1902	4.31

Chances Accepted per Game

First Base
1 Jiggs Donahue, 1907 .... 12.65
2 Joe Gerhardt, 1876 ..... 12.54
3 Phil Todt, 1926 .... 12.21
4 Joe Start, 1879 .... 12.15
5 George Burns, 1914 ..... 12.10
6 Stuffy McInnis, 1918 .... 12.10
7 George Stovall, 1908 .... 12.08
8 George Kelly, 1920 ...... 12.01
9 Joe Start, 1878 .... 12.00
10 Oscar Walker, 1879 ..... 11.92

Second Base
1 Jack Burdock, 1878 ..... 7.62
2 Thorny Hawkes, 1879 .... 7.56
3 Chick Fulmer, 1879 ..... 7.55
4 Fred Pfeffer, 1884 .... 7.29
5 Joe Gerhardt, 1877 ..... 7.21
6 Ed Somerville, 1876 ..... 7.20
7 Jack Burdock, 1879 ..... 7.18
8 Joe Quest, 1879 .... 7.16
9 Pop Smith, 1885 .... 7.13
10 Bid McPhee, 1886 .... 7.09

Shortstop
1 Hughie Jennings, 1895 ... 6.73
2 George Davis, 1899 ..... 6.69
3 Dave Bancroft, 1918 .... 6.62
4 Hughie Jennings, 1896 ... 6.56
5 Hughie Jennings, 1897 ... 6.55
6 Rabbit Maranville, 1919 .. 6.48
7 Bobby Wallace, 1901 .... 6.48
8 Monte Cross, 1897 ...... 6.41
9 Dave Bancroft, 1920 ..... 6.40
10 George Davis, 1900 ...... 6.39

Third Base
1 Bob Ferguson, 1877 ..... 4.71
2 Al Nichols, 1876 .... 4.53
3 Billy Shindle, 1892 .... 4.34
4 Jumbo Davis, 1888 ..... 4.33
5 Bill Bradley, 1900 .... 4.29
6 Cap Anson, 1876 .... 4.27
7 Joe Battin, 1883 .... 4.17
8 Bill Hague, 1878 .... 4.16
9 George Bradley, 1880 .... 4.14
10 Billy Shindle, 1888 ...... 4.13

Outfield
1 Fred Treacey, 1876 ...... 3.70
2 Taylor Douthit, 1928 ..... 3.62
3 Richie Ashburn, 1951 ... 3.59
4 Thurman Tucker, 1944 .. 3.55
5 Kirby Puckett, 1984 ..... 3.55
6 Chet Lemon, 1977 ...... 3.52
7 Irv Noren, 1951 .... 3.45
8 Richie Ashburn, 1949 .... 3.42
9 Carden Gillenwater, 1945 . 3.39
10 Sam West, 1935 .... 3.38

Catcher
1 Bill Holbert, 1883 .... 9.78
2 Sam Trott, 1884 .... 9.63
3 Jocko Milligan, 1884 .... 8.83
4 Bill Holbert, 1884 ...... 8.75
5 Mert Hackett, 1884 ..... 8.68
6 Barney Gilligan, 1884 ... 8.63
7 Duffy Dyer, 1972 .... 8.25
8 Jocko Milligan, 1885 .... 8.25
9 Mike Hines, 1883 .... 8.22
10 George Baker, 1884 ..... 8.06

Pitcher
1 Harry Howell, 1905 ..... 5.24
2 Harry Howell, 1904 ..... 4.97
3 Ed Walsh, 1907 .... 4.68
4 Will White, 1882 .... 4.56
5 Nick Altrock, 1905 ..... 4.32
6 George Mullin, 1904 .... 4.24
7 Tony Mullane, 1882 ..... 4.20
8 Willie Sudhoff, 1904 ..... 4.19
9 Red Donahue, 1902 ..... 4.14
10 Nick Altrock, 1904 ...... 4.13

Putouts

First Base
1 Jiggs Donahue, 1907 1846
2 George Kelly, 1920 1759
3 Phil Todt, 1926 1755
4 Wally Pipp, 1926 1710
5 Jiggs Donahue, 1906 1697
6 Candy LaChance, 1904 .. 1691
7 Tom Jones, 1907 1687
8 Ernie Banks, 1965 1682
9 Wally Pipp, 1922 1667
10 Lou Gehrig, 1927 1662

Second Base
1 Bid McPhee, 1886 529
2 Bobby Grich, 1974 484
3 Bucky Harris, 1922 483
4 Nellie Fox, 1956 478
5 Lou Bierbauer, 1889 472
6 Billy Herman, 1933 466
7 Bill Wambsganss, 1924 .. 463
8 Cub Stricker, 1887 461
9 Buddy Myer, 1935 460
10 Bill Sweeney, 1912 459

Shortstop
1 Hughie Jennings, 1895 ... 425
   Donie Bush, 1914 425
3 Joe Cassidy, 1905 408
4 Rabbit Maranville, 1914 .. 407
5 Dave Bancroft, 1922 405
   Eddie Miller, 1940 405
7 Monte Cross, 1898 404
8 Dave Bancroft, 1921 396
9 Mickey Doolan, 1906 395
10 Buck Weaver, 1913 392

Third Base
1 Denny Lyons, 1887 255
2 Jimmy Williams, 1899 ... 251
   Jimmy Collins, 1900 251
4 Jimmy Collins, 1898 243
   Willie Kamm, 1928 243
6 Willie Kamm, 1927 236
7 Frank Baker, 1913 233
8 Bill Coughlin, 1901 232
9 Ernie Courtney, 1905 ... 229
10 Jimmy Austin, 1911 228

Outfield
1 Taylor Douthit, 1928 547
2 Richie Ashburn, 1951 ... 538
3 Richie Ashburn, 1949 ... 514
4 Chet Lemon, 1977 512
5 Dwayne Murphy, 1980 ... 507
6 Dom DiMaggio, 1948 ... 503
   Richie Ashburn, 1956 ... 503
8 Richie Ashburn, 1957 ... 502
9 Richie Ashburn, 1953 ... 496
10 Richie Ashburn, 1958 495

Catcher
1 Johnny Edwards, 1969 ... 1135
2 Johnny Edwards, 1963 ... 1008
3 Randy Hundley, 1969 ... 978
4 Tony Pena, 1983 976
5 Bill Freehan, 1968 971
6 Gary Carter, 1985 956
7 Gary Carter, 1982 954
8 Bill Freehan, 1967 950
9 Johnny Bench, 1968 942
10 Elston Howard, 1964 939

Pitcher
1 Dave Foutz, 1886 57
2 Tony Mullane, 1882 54
3 George Bradley, 1876 50
   Guy Hecker, 1884 50
5 Mike Boddicker, 1984 ... 49
6 Larry Corcoran, 1884 ... 47
7 Al Spalding, 1876 45
   Ted Breitenstein, 1895 .. 45
9 Jim Devlin, 1876 44
   Dave Foutz, 1887 44
   Bill Hutchinson, 1890 44

Putouts per Game

First Base
1 Joe Gerhardt, 1876 ...... 12.30
2 Joe Start, 1879 .... 11.98
3 Joe Start, 1878 .... 11.79
4 Jiggs Donahue, 1907 ... 11.76
5 Joe Start, 1877 .... 11.73
6 Herman Dehlman, 1876 . 11.72
7 Joe Start, 1880 .... 11.63
8 Jake Goodman, 1878 ... 11.55
9 George Burns, 1914 .... 11.53
10 Oscar Walker, 1879 ..... 11.50

Second Base
1 Jack Burdock, 1878 ..... 4.08
2 Jack Burdock, 1880 ..... 3.81
3 Bid McPhee, 1886 ...... 3.78
4 Bid McPhee, 1884 ...... 3.71
5 Joe Quest, 1878 .... 3.68
6 Cub Stricker, 1887 ..... 3.66
7 Lou Bierbauer, 1889 .... 3.63
8 Jack Burdock, 1879 .... 3.61
9 Chick Fulmer, 1879 .... 3.59
10 Bob Ferguson, 1880 .... 3.59

Shortstop
1 Hughie Jennings, 1895 ... 3.24
2 Dave Bancroft, 1918 .... 2.97
3 Hughie Jennings, 1896 .. 2.90
4 Hughie Jennings, 1897 .. 2.89
5 George Davis, 1898 ..... 2.88
6 George Davis, 1899 ..... 2.88
7 Rabbit Maranville, 1919 . 2.76
8 Honus Wagner, 1913 ... 2.75
9 Kid Elberfeld, 1901 ..... 2.74
10 Buck Weaver, 1914 ...... 2.74

Third Base
1 Al Nichols, 1876 .... 2.16
2 Cap Anson, 1876 .... 2.05
3 Hick Carpenter, 1880 ... 2.03
4 Bob Ferguson, 1877 .... 1.95
5 Denny Lyons, 1887 ..... 1.86
6 Patsy Tebeau, 1890 .... 1.85
7 Cap Anson, 1877 .... 1.85
8 Joe Battin, 1876 .... 1.83
9 Jerry Denny, 1883 ...... 1.82
10 Frank Hankinson, 1881 .. 1.80

Outfield
1 Taylor Douthit, 1928 .... 3.55
2 Fred Treacey, 1876 ..... 3.54
3 Richie Ashburn, 1951 ... 3.49
4 Thurman Tucker, 1944 .. 3.45
5 Chet Lemon, 1977 ...... 3.44
6 Kirby Puckett, 1984 ..... 3.42
7 Richie Ashburn, 1949 ... 3.34
8 Irv Noren, 1951 .... 3.33
9 Sam West, 1935 .... 3.33
10 Jim Busby, 1952 .... 3.28

Catcher
1 Sam Trott, 1884 .... 8.18
2 Bill Holbert, 1883 .... 7.75
3 Duffy Dyer, 1972 .... 7.58
4 Johnny Edwards, 1969 .. 7.52
5 Barney Gilligan, 1884 ... 7.47
6 John Romano, 1964 .... 7.44
7 Johnny Edwards, 1964 .. 7.42
8 Joe Azcue, 1967 .... 7.40
9 John Roseboro, 1960 ... 7.36
10 Jerry Grote, 1971 .... 7.31

Pitcher
1 Mike Boddicker, 1984 ... 1.44
2 Oil Can Boyd, 1985 ..... 1.20
3 Nick Altrock, 1904 ...... 1.13
4 Greg Maddux, 1990 .... 1.11
5 Dave Foutz, 1887 ...... 1.10
6 Dwight Gooden, 1986 ... 1.09
7 Dan Petry, 1984 .... 1.09
8 Nat Hudson, 1888 ...... 1.08
   Al Nipper, 1986 .... 1.08
10 John Harkins, 1885 ...... 1.06
   Dan Petry, 1985 .... 1.06

Assists

First Base
1 Bill Buckner, 1985 184
2 Mark Grace, 1990 180
3 Sid Bream, 1986 166
4 Bill Buckner, 1983 161
5 Bill Buckner, 1982 159
6 Bill Buckner, 1986 157
7 Mickey Vernon, 1949 ... 155
8 Fred Tenney, 1905 152
   Eddie Murray, 1985 152
10 Ferris Fain, 1952 150

Second Base
1 Frankie Frisch, 1927 641
2 Hughie Critz, 1926 588
3 Rogers Hornsby, 1927 ... 582
4 Ski Melillo, 1930 572
5 Ryne Sandberg, 1983 ... 571
6 Rabbit Maranville, 1924 .. 568
7 Frank Parkinson, 1922 ... 562
8 Tony Cuccinello, 1936 ... 559
9 Johnny Hodapp, 1930 ... 557
10 Lou Bierbauer, 1892 555

Shortstop
1 Ozzie Smith, 1980 621
2 Glenn Wright, 1924 601
3 Dave Bancroft, 1920 598
4 Tommy Thevenow, 1926 .. 597
5 Ivan DeJesus, 1977 595
6 Cal Ripken, 1984 583
7 Whitey Wietelmann, 1943 . 581
8 Dave Bancroft, 1922 579
9 Rabbit Maranville, 1914 .. 574
10 Don Kessinger, 1968 573

Third Base
1 Graig Nettles, 1971 412
2 Graig Nettles, 1973 410
   Brooks Robinson, 1974 .. 410
4 Harland Clift, 1937 405
   Brooks Robinson, 1967 .. 405
6 Mike Schmidt, 1974 404
7 Doug DeCinces, 1982 ... 399
8 Clete Boyer, 1962 396
   Mike Schmidt, 1977 396
   Buddy Bell, 1982 396

Outfield
1 Orator Shaffer, 1879 50
2 Hugh Nicol, 1884 48
3 Hardy Richardson, 1881 .. 45
4 Tommy McCarthy, 1888 .. 44
   Chuck Klein, 1930 44
6 Charlie Duffee, 1889 43
   Jimmy Bannon, 1894 ... 43
8 Jim Fogarty, 1889 42
9 Orator Shaffer, 1883 41
   Jim Lillie, 1884 41

Catcher
1 Bill Rariden, 1915 238
2 Bill Rariden, 1914 215
3 Pat Moran, 1903 214
4 Oscar Stanage, 1911 212
   Art Wilson, 1914 212
6 Gabby Street, 1909 210
7 Frank Snyder, 1915 204
8 George Gibson, 1910 ... 203
9 Bill Bergen, 1909 202
   Claude Berry, 1914 202

Pitcher
1 Ed Walsh, 1907 227
2 Will White, 1882 223
3 Ed Walsh, 1908 190
4 Harry Howell, 1905 178
5 Tony Mullane, 1882 177
6 John Clarkson, 1885 174
7 John Clarkson, 1889 172
8 Jack Chesbro, 1904 166
9 George Mullin, 1904 163
10 Ed Walsh, 1911 160

Assists per Game

First Base
1	Mark Grace, 1990	1.18
2	Bill Buckner, 1986	1.14
3	Bill Buckner, 1985	1.14
4	Bill Buckner, 1983	1.12
5	Sid Bream, 1986	1.08
6	Ferris Fain, 1951	1.05
7	Ferris Fain, 1952	1.04
8	Fred Tenney, 1905	1.03
9	Keith Hernandez, 1983	1.02
10	Bob Robertson, 1971	1.02

Second Base
1	Joe Gerhardt, 1877	4.28
2	Frankie Frisch, 1927	4.19
3	Thorny Hawkes, 1879	4.13
4	Hughie Critz, 1933	4.07
5	Frank Parkinson, 1922	4.04
6	Joe Quest, 1879	3.99
7	Chick Fulmer, 1879	3.96
8	Ed Somerville, 1876	3.92
9	Ski Melillo, 1930	3.86
10	Glenn Hubbard, 1985	3.85

Shortstop
1	Germany Smith, 1885	4.21
2	Arthur Irwin, 1880	4.13
3	Art Fletcher, 1919	4.10
4	Bill Dahlen, 1895	4.09
5	Phil Tomney, 1889	4.05
6	Bobby Wallace, 1901	4.04
7	Jack Glasscock, 1887	4.04
8	Germany Smith, 1892	4.04
9	Henry Easterday, 1888	3.99
10	Dave Bancroft, 1920	3.99

Third Base
1	Jumbo Davis, 1888	2.96
2	Buddy Bell, 1981	2.93
3	George Bradley, 1880	2.89
4	Bill Hague, 1878	2.85
5	Billy Shindle, 1892	2.85
6	Bob Ferguson, 1877	2.77
7	Ned Williamson, 1879	2.76
8	Arlie Latham, 1884	2.75
9	Bill Bradley, 1900	2.75
10	Arlie Latham, 1891	2.74

Outfield
1	Orator Shaffer, 1879	0.69
2	Hardy Richardson, 1881	0.57
3	Hugh Nicol, 1884	0.55
4	King Kelly, 1878	0.51
5	John Cassidy, 1878	0.50
	King Kelly, 1880	0.50
7	King Kelly, 1883	0.46
8	Jake Evans, 1882	0.46
9	Orator Shaffer, 1878	0.44
10	Dick Higham, 1878	0.44

Catcher
1	Bill Holbert, 1884	2.41
2	Tom Daly, 1887	2.31
3	Bill Holbert, 1882	2.14
4	Pop Snyder, 1884	2.08
5	Bill Holbert, 1883	2.03
6	Buck Ewing, 1881	2.02
7	Pat Moran, 1903	2.00
	Charlie Reipschlager,	
8	1885	1.98
9	Connie Mack, 1888	1.92
10	King Kelly, 1888	1.92

Pitcher
1	Harry Howell, 1905	4.68
2	Harry Howell, 1904	4.21
3	Will White, 1882	4.13
4	Ed Walsh, 1907	4.05
5	Willie Sudhoff, 1904	3.85
6	Red Donahue, 1902	3.71
7	George Mullin, 1904	3.62
8	Frank Owen, 1904	3.51
9	Carl Mays, 1918	3.49
10	Nick Altrock, 1905	3.47

Double Plays

First Base
1	Ferris Fain, 1949	194
2	Ferris Fain, 1950	192
3	Donn Clendenon, 1966	182
4	Ron Jackson, 1979	175
5	Gil Hodges, 1951	171
6	Mickey Vernon, 1949	168
7	Ted Kluszewski, 1954	166
8	Rudy York, 1944	163
9	Donn Clendenon, 1965	161
	Rod Carew, 1977	161

Second Base
1	Bill Mazeroski, 1966	161
2	Jerry Priddy, 1950	150
3	Bill Mazeroski, 1961	144
4	Nellie Fox, 1957	141
	Dave Cash, 1974	141
6	Buddy Myer, 1935	138
	Bill Mazeroski, 1962	138
8	Jerry Coleman, 1950	137
	Jackie Robinson, 1951	137
	Red Schoendienst, 1954	137

Shortstop
1	Rick Burleson, 1980	147
2	Roy Smalley, 1979	144
3	Bobby Wine, 1970	137
4	Lou Boudreau, 1944	134
5	Spike Owen, 1986	133
6	Rafael Ramirez, 1982	130
7	Roy McMillan, 1954	129
8	Hod Ford, 1928	128
	Vern Stephens, 1949	128
	Gene Alley, 1966	128

Third Base
1	Graig Nettles, 1971	54
2	Harlond Clift, 1937	50
3	Johnny Pesky, 1949	48
	Paul Molitor, 1982	48
5	Sammy Hale, 1927	46
	Clete Boyer, 1965	46
	Gary Gaetti, 1983	46
8	Eddie Yost, 1950	45
	Frank Malzone, 1961	45
	Darrell Evans, 1974	45

Outfield
1	Happy Felsch, 1919	15
2	Jimmy Sheckard, 1899	14
3	Tom Brown, 1893	13
4	Tom Brown, 1886	12
	Tommy McCarthy, 1888	12
	Jimmy Bannon, 1894	12
	Mike Griffin, 1895	12
	Danny Green, 1899	12
	Cy Seymour, 1905	12
	Ginger Beaumont, 1907	12
	Ty Cobb, 1907	12
	Tris Speaker, 1909	12
	Jimmy Sheckard, 1911	12
	Tris Speaker, 1914	12
	Mel Ott, 1929	12

Catcher
1	Steve O'Neill, 1916	36
2	Frankie Hayes, 1945	29
3	Ray Schalk, 1916	25
	Yogi Berra, 1951	25
5	Jack Lapp, 1915	23
	Muddy Ruel, 1924	23
	Tom Haller, 1968	23
8	Steve O'Neill, 1914	22
	Bob O'Farrell, 1922	22
10	Gabby Hartnett, 1927	21
	Wes Westrum, 1950	21

Pitcher
1	Bob Lemon, 1953	15
2	Eddie Rommel, 1924	12
	Curt Davis, 1934	12
	Randy Jones, 1976	12
5	Scott Perry, 1919	11
	Tom Rogers, 1919	11
	Art Nehf, 1920	11
	Burleigh Grimes, 1925	11
	Gene Bearden, 1948	11
10	Nick Altrock, 1905	10
	Carl Mays, 1926	10
	Willis Hudlin, 1931	10
	Freddie Fitzsimmons, 1932	10
	Freddie Fitzsimmons, 1934	10
	Bucky Walters, 1939	10
	Dave Ferriss, 1945	10
	Bob Hooper, 1950	10
	Don Drysdale, 1958	10
	Dan Petry, 1983	10

Fielding Runs

1	Glenn Hubbard, 1985	61.8
2	Danny Richardson, 1892	57.6
3	Bill Mazeroski, 1963	56.7
4	Rabbit Maranville, 1914	51.8
5	Freddie Maguire, 1928	50.5
6	Nap Lajoie, 1908	49.3
7	Danny Richardson, 1891	49.1
8	Frankie Frisch, 1927	48.6
9	Hughie Critz, 1933	46.5
10	George Davis, 1899	46.3
11	Fred Pfeffer, 1884	45.8
12	Nap Lajoie, 1907	45.0
13	Dick Bartell, 1936	44.8
14	Ozzie Guillen, 1988	42.6
15	Dave Shean, 1910	42.5
	Lee Tannehill, 1911	42.5
17	Graig Nettles, 1971	42.3
18	Cupid Childs, 1896	42.2
19	Joe Gerhardt, 1890	41.5
20	Bid McPhee, 1889	41.1
	Bill Mazeroski, 1962	41.1
	Ryne Sandberg, 1983	41.1
23	Harlond Clift, 1937	41.0
	Glenn Hubbard, 1986	41.0
25	John Kerins, 1886	40.8
	Bill Mazeroski, 1966	40.8
	Ozzie Smith, 1980	40.8
28	Arlie Latham, 1884	40.1
	Nap Lajoie, 1903	40.1
30	Germany Smith, 1885	39.9
31	Lee Tannehill, 1906	39.6
32	Fred Pfeffer, 1888	39.4
33	Bob Allen, 1890	39.3
34	Dave Bancroft, 1920	39.0
35	Cal Ripken, 1984	38.8
36	Bobby Wallace, 1899	38.3
37	Everett Scott, 1921	38.1
38	Bill Dahlen, 1908	37.5
	Dick Bartell, 1937	37.5
	Dal Maxvill, 1970	37.5
41	Bobby Knoop, 1964	37.2
42	Al Weis, 1966	36.9
43	Billy Shindle, 1888	36.8
44	Tim Wallach, 1985	36.7
45	Lou Bierbauer, 1889	36.6
46	Clete Boyer, 1962	36.2
47	Harry Steinfeldt, 1900	35.9
	Miller Huggins, 1905	35.9
49	George Davis, 1898	35.8
	Tommy Leach, 1904	35.8
	Ivan DeJesus, 1977	35.8
52	Hughie Jennings, 1895	35.7
53	Billy Shindle, 1892	35.5
54	Eddie Collins, 1910	35.4
55	Freddie Patek, 1973	35.3
56	Bill Dahlen, 1895	35.2
57	Jack Glasscock, 1887	35.1
	Bobby Knoop, 1970	35.1
59	Tom Daly, 1887	34.9
	Jack Glasscock, 1889	34.9
61	Jimmy Bloodworth, 1941	34.7
62	Hughie Jennings, 1896	34.4
	Buddy Bell, 1982	34.4
64	Shorty Fuller, 1895	34.2
	Doc Lavan, 1916	34.2
66	Art Fletcher, 1915	34.1
67	Bid McPhee, 1893	34.0
68	Bill Mazeroski, 1964	33.9
69	Mark Belanger, 1978	33.8
70	Gene Alley, 1970	33.7
71	Buck Weaver, 1913	33.6
	Donie Bush, 1914	33.6
73	Leo Cardenas, 1969	33.5
74	Lave Cross, 1895	33.4
75	John Farrell, 1902	33.3
76	Pop Smith, 1885	33.2
77	Hughie Jennings, 1894	33.1
	Joe Cassidy, 1905	33.1
	Ski Melillo, 1931	33.1
	Roy Smalley, 1979	33.1
	Ozzie Smith, 1982	33.1
82	Lave Cross, 1899	32.9
	George McBride, 1908	32.9
	Red Schoendienst, 1952	32.9
	Red Schoendienst, 1954	32.9
86	Don Zimmer, 1958	32.6
87	Marty Barrett, 1987	32.3
88	Herman Long, 1889	32.2
89	Mickey Doolan, 1915	32.1
90	Germany Smith, 1887	32.0
	Wally Gerber, 1928	32.0
	Bucky Dent, 1979	32.0
93	Nap Lajoie, 1906	31.9
	Spike Owen, 1986	31.9
95	Pep Young, 1938	31.8
96	Lou Bierbauer, 1892	31.7
	Heinie Wagner, 1908	31.7
	Billy Jurges, 1932	31.7
99	Bill Dahlen, 1894	31.6
	Zoilo Versalles, 1962	31.6

Fielding Runs

First Base
1	Mark Grace, 1990	27
2	Bill Buckner, 1985	25
3	Chick Gandil, 1914	24
4	Sid Bream, 1986	24
5	Bill Buckner, 1983	22
6	Fred Tenney, 1905	21
7	Vic Power, 1960	21
8	Sid Bream, 1988	21
9	Jiggs Donahue, 1907	21
10	Jake Beckley, 1892	21

Second Base
1	Glenn Hubbard, 1985	62
2	Bill Mazeroski, 1963	57
3	Freddie Maguire, 1928	50
4	Frankie Frisch, 1927	49
5	Nap Lajoie, 1908	48
6	Hughie Critz, 1933	46
7	Fred Pfeffer, 1884	46
8	Danny Richardson, 1891	44
9	Nap Lajoie, 1907	43
10	Dave Shean, 1910	42

Shortstop
1	Rabbit Maranville, 1914	52
2	George Davis, 1899	46
3	Dick Bartell, 1936	45
4	Ozzie Guillen, 1988	43
5	Ozzie Smith, 1980	41
6	Germany Smith, 1885	40
7	Bob Allen, 1890	39
8	Dave Bancroft, 1920	39
9	Cal Ripken, 1984	39
10	Everett Scott, 1921	38

Third Base
1	Graig Nettles, 1971	42
2	Harlond Clift, 1937	41
3	Arlie Latham, 1884	40
4	Billy Shindle, 1892	38
5	Billy Shindle, 1888	37
6	Tim Wallach, 1985	37
7	Clete Boyer, 1962	36
8	Tommy Leach, 1904	36
9	Buddy Bell, 1982	35
10	Lave Cross, 1895	33

Outfield
1	Tommy McCarthy, 1888	30
2	Jim Fogarty, 1887	29
3	Dave Parker, 1977	28
4	Chuck Klein, 1930	28
5	Tris Speaker, 1914	28
6	Tom Brown, 1893	27
7	Chet Lemon, 1977	27
8	Richie Ashburn, 1957	27
9	Ed Delahanty, 1893	26
10	Mike Griffin, 1891	26

Catcher
1	Tom Daly, 1887	33
2	Duke Farrell, 1894	32
3	Bill Holbert, 1883	28
4	Connie Mack, 1892	25
5	George Mitterwald, 1970	24
6	Rollie Hemsley, 1934	24
7	Ray Berres, 1936	24
8	Jim Hegan, 1950	23
	Ossee Schreckengost, 1902	23
9		23
10	Cy Perkins, 1920	23

Pitcher
1	Ed Walsh, 1907	21
2	Harry Howell, 1905	16
3	Ed Walsh, 1911	14
4	Will White, 1882	13
5	Ed Walsh, 1908	12
6	John Clarkson, 1889	11
7	Carl Mays, 1926	11
8	Tony Mullane, 1882	11
9	Tommy Bond, 1880	10
10	Frank Smith, 1909	10

Fielding Wins

1 Glenn Hubbard, 1985 .... 6.5
2 Bill Mazeroski, 1963 ..... 6.2
3 Nap Lajoie, 1908 .... 5.6
4 Rabbit Maranville, 1914 . 5.6
5 Danny Richardson, 1892 . 5.3
6 Nap Lajoie, 1907 .... 5.0
7 Freddie Maguire, 1928 .. 4.9
8 Hughie Critz, 1933 ...... 4.9
9 Frankie Frisch, 1927 ..... 4.8
10 Graig Nettles, 1971 ..... 4.6
11 Dave Shean, 1910 .... 4.5
12 Danny Richardson, 1891 . 4.4
13 Dick Bartell, 1936 ...... 4.4
14 Lee Tannehill, 1906 ...... 4.4
15 Bill Dahlen, 1908 .... 4.3
16 Ozzie Smith, 1980 ...... 4.3
17 Ozzie Guillen, 1988 ..... 4.3
18 Ryne Sandberg, 1983 .... 4.3
19 Bill Mazeroski, 1966 ..... 4.3
20 Glenn Hubbard, 1986 .... 4.3
21 George Davis, 1899 ..... 4.2
22 Dave Bancroft, 1920 ..... 4.2
23 Lee Tannehill, 1911 ...... 4.2
24 Nap Lajoie, 1903 .... 4.2
25 Bill Mazeroski, 1962 ..... 4.1
26 Fred Pfeffer, 1884 .... 4.1
27 Al Weis, 1966 .... 4.0
28 Eddie Collins, 1910 ...... 3.9
29 Bobby Knoop, 1964 ..... 3.9
30 Cal Ripken, 1984 .... 3.9
31 Fred Pfeffer, 1888 ...... 3.9
32 Tim Wallach, 1985 ...... 3.9
33 Doc Lavan, 1916 .... 3.8
34 Art Fletcher, 1915 ...... 3.8
35 Tommy Leach, 1904 ..... 3.8
36 Harlond Clift, 1937 ...... 3.8
37 George McBride, 1908 ... 3.7
38 Dal Maxvill, 1970 ...... 3.7
39 Miller Huggins, 1905 .... 3.7
40 Dick Bartell, 1937 ...... 3.7
41 Donie Bush, 1914 .... 3.7
42 Arlie Latham, 1884 ...... 3.7
43 Joe Gerhardt, 1890 ..... 3.6
44 Bobby Knoop, 1970 ..... 3.6
45 Clete Boyer, 1962 ...... 3.6
46 Joe Cassidy, 1905 ...... 3.6
47 Ivan DeJesus, 1977 ..... 3.6
48 Freddie Patek, 1973 ..... 3.6
49 Heinie Wagner, 1908 .... 3.6
50 Germany Smith, 1885 ... 3.6
51 John Kerins, 1886 .... 3.6
52 Bill Mazeroski, 1964 ..... 3.6
53 Cupid Childs, 1896 ...... 3.6
54 Buck Weaver, 1913 ..... 3.6
55 Everett Scott, 1921 ...... 3.6
56 Joe Tinker, 1908 .... 3.5
57 Leo Cardenas, 1969 ..... 3.5
58 John Farrell, 1902 ...... 3.5
59 Nap Lajoie, 1906 .... 3.5
60 Bob Allen, 1890 .... 3.5
61 Mark Belanger, 1978 .... 3.5
62 Ozzie Smith, 1982 ...... 3.5
63 Bid McPhee, 1889 ...... 3.5
64 Bobby Wallace, 1899 .... 3.5
65 Mickey Doolan, 1915 .... 3.5
66 Buddy Bell, 1980 .... 3.4
67 Buck Herzog, 1915 ...... 3.4
68 Red Schoendienst, 1952 . 3.4
69 Brooks Robinson, 1967 .. 3.4
70 Billy Shindle, 1888 ...... 3.4
71 Horace Clarke, 1968 ..... 3.4
72 Nap Lajoie, 1916 .... 3.4
73 Jimmy Bloodworth, 1941 . 3.4
74 Gene Alley, 1970 .... 3.4
75 Freddie Patek, 1972 ..... 3.4
76 Bruno Betzel, 1916 ...... 3.3
77 George Davis, 1898 ..... 3.3
78 Ron Santo, 1967 .... 3.3
79 Johnny Evers, 1904 ..... 3.3
80 Buck Herzog, 1914 ...... 3.3
81 Don Zimmer, 1958 ...... 3.3
82 Billy Shindle, 1892 ...... 3.3
83 Jerry Terrell, 1974 ...... 3.3
84 Harry Steinfeldt, 1900 ... 3.3
85 Red Schoendienst, 1954 . 3.3
86 Roy Smalley, 1979 ...... 3.2
87 Terry Pendleton, 1989 ... 3.2
88 Ed Brinkman, 1970 ...... 3.2
89 Pep Young, 1938 .... 3.2
90 Rabbit Maranville, 1919 . 3.2
91 Zoilo Versalles, 1962 .... 3.2
92 Dave Bancroft, 1917 ..... 3.1
93 Spike Owen, 1986 ...... 3.1
94 Billy Jurges, 1932 ...... 3.1
95 Johnny Evers, 1907 ..... 3.1
96 Dal Maxvill, 1971 ...... 3.1
97 Hal Lanier, 1967 .... 3.1
   Bobby Wine, 1967 ...... 3.1
99 Bucky Dent, 1979 ...... 3.1
100 George McBride, 1912 ... 3.1

Total Player Rating

1 Babe Ruth, 1923 .... 10.5
2 Babe Ruth, 1921 .... 9.6
3 Babe Ruth, 1927 .... 8.9
4 Babe Ruth, 1920 .... 8.8
5 Cal Ripken, 1984 .... 8.7
6 Nap Lajoie, 1901 .... 8.4
  Ty Cobb, 1917 .... 8.4
  Babe Ruth, 1924 .... 8.4
9 George Sisler, 1920 ..... 8.3
  Ted Williams, 1942 ..... 8.3
11 Lou Gehrig, 1927 .... 8.2
  Ted Williams, 1946 ..... 8.2
  Ted Williams, 1947 ..... 8.2
14 Fred Dunlap, 1884 ...... 8.1
  Nap Lajoie, 1903 .... 8.1
  Babe Ruth, 1926 .... 8.1
17 Nap Lajoie, 1906 .... 8.0
  Nap Lajoie, 1910 .... 8.0
  Ted Williams, 1941 ..... 8.0
20 Mickey Mantle, 1956 .... 7.9
21 Tris Speaker, 1912 ..... 7.8
  Mickey Mantle, 1957 .... 7.8
  Mike Schmidt, 1980 ..... 7.8
24 Rogers Hornsby, 1920 ... 7.7
  Stan Musial, 1948 ...... 7.7
  Ron Santo, 1966 .... 7.7
  Carl Yastrzemski, 1967 .. 7.7
  Rickey Henderson, 1990 . 7.7
29 Honus Wagner, 1906 .... 7.6
  Rogers Hornsby, 1922 ... 7.6
  Willie Mays, 1955 ...... 7.6
32 Nap Lajoie, 1908 .... 7.5
  Rogers Hornsby, 1924 ... 7.5
  Babe Ruth, 1930 .... 7.5
  Ted Williams, 1949 ..... 7.5
36 Honus Wagner, 1905 .... 7.4
  Tris Speaker, 1914 ..... 7.4
38 Tris Speaker, 1913 ..... 7.3
  Lou Boudreau, 1944 .... 7.3
  Norm Cash, 1961 .... 7.3
41 Ty Cobb, 1910 .... 7.2
  Mickey Mantle, 1961 .... 7.2
43 Stan Musial, 1943 ...... 7.1
  Willie Mays, 1965 ...... 7.1
  Rickey Henderson, 1985 . 7.1
46 Ty Cobb, 1911 .... 7.0
  Rogers Hornsby, 1917 ... 7.0
  Babe Ruth, 1919 .... 7.0
  Rogers Hornsby, 1929 ... 7.0
  Jimmie Foxx, 1933 ..... 7.0
  Harlond Clift, 1937 ..... 7.0
  Ted Williams, 1957 ..... 7.0
  Joe Morgan, 1975 ...... 7.0
54 Joe Jackson, 1912 ..... 6.9
  Babe Ruth, 1928 .... 6.9
  Mike Schmidt, 1974 ..... 6.9
  Mike Schmidt, 1977 ..... 6.9
  Mike Schmidt, 1981 ..... 6.9
59 Nap Lajoie, 1904 .... 6.8
  Babe Ruth, 1931 .... 6.8
  Snuffy Stirnweiss, 1944 .. 6.8
  Stan Musial, 1951 ...... 6.8
  George Brett, 1985 ..... 6.8
64 Nap Lajoie, 1907 .... 6.7
  Honus Wagner, 1912 .... 6.7
  Rogers Hornsby, 1921 ... 6.7
  Jackie Robinson, 1951 .. 6.7
  Willie Mays, 1958 ...... 6.7
  Ron Santo, 1967 .... 6.7
70 Cupid Childs, 1896 ..... 6.6
  Hughie Jennings, 1896 .. 6.6
  Honus Wagner, 1907 .... 6.6
  Frankie Frisch, 1927 .... 6.6
  Chuck Klein, 1930 ...... 6.6
  Joe Cronin, 1930 .... 6.6
  Snuffy Stirnweiss, 1945 .. 6.6
  Hank Aaron, 1959 ...... 6.6
  Carl Yastrzemski, 1968 .. 6.6
  Reggie Jackson, 1969 ... 6.6
  George Brett, 1980 ..... 6.6
  Ryne Sandberg, 1984 ... 6.6
82 Ed Delahanty, 1893 ..... 6.5
  Hughie Jennings, 1895 .. 6.5
  Honus Wagner, 1903 .... 6.5
  Joe Jackson, 1911 ...... 6.5
  Ty Cobb, 1915 .... 6.5
  Benny Kauff, 1915 ...... 6.5
  Willie Mays, 1954 ...... 6.5
  Frank Robinson, 1966 ... 6.5
  Robin Yount, 1982 ...... 6.5
  Barry Bonds, 1990 ...... 6.5
92 Ty Cobb, 1909 .... 6.4
  Eddie Collins, 1910 ..... 6.4
  Jimmie Foxx, 1932 ..... 6.4
  Mike Schmidt, 1976 ..... 6.4
  Eric Davis, 1987 .... 6.4
  Kevin Mitchell, 1989 .... 6.4
98 10 players tied 6.3

Total Player Rating (alpha.)

Hank Aaron, 1959 .... 6.6
Barry Bonds, 1990 ...... 6.5
Lou Boudreau, 1944 ..... 7.3
George Brett, 1980 ..... 6.6
George Brett, 1985 ..... 6.8
Norm Cash, 1961 .... 7.3
Cupid Childs, 1896 ...... 6.6
Harlond Clift, 1937 ..... 7.0
Ty Cobb, 1909 .... 6.4
Ty Cobb, 1910 .... 7.2
Ty Cobb, 1911 .... 7.0
Ty Cobb, 1915 .... 6.5
Ty Cobb, 1917 .... 8.4
Eddie Collins, 1910 ..... 6.4
Joe Cronin, 1930 .... 6.6
Eric Davis, 1987 .... 6.4
Ed Delahanty, 1893 ..... 6.5
Fred Dunlap, 1884 ...... 8.1
Jimmie Foxx, 1932 ..... 6.4
Jimmie Foxx, 1933 ..... 7.0
Frankie Frisch, 1927 .... 6.6
Lou Gehrig, 1927 .... 8.2
Rickey Henderson, 1985 . 7.1
Rickey Henderson, 1990 . 7.7
Rogers Hornsby, 1917 ... 7.0
Rogers Hornsby, 1920 ... 7.7
Rogers Hornsby, 1921 ... 6.7
Rogers Hornsby, 1922 ... 7.6
Rogers Hornsby, 1924 ... 7.5
Rogers Hornsby, 1929 ... 7.0
Joe Jackson, 1911 ...... 6.5
Joe Jackson, 1912 ...... 6.9
Reggie Jackson, 1969 ... 6.6
Hughie Jennings, 1895 .. 6.5
Hughie Jennings, 1896 .. 6.5
Benny Kauff, 1915 ...... 6.5
Chuck Klein, 1930 ...... 6.6
Nap Lajoie, 1901 .... 8.4
Nap Lajoie, 1903 .... 8.1
Nap Lajoie, 1904 .... 6.8
Nap Lajoie, 1906 .... 8.0
Nap Lajoie, 1907 .... 6.7
Nap Lajoie, 1908 .... 7.5
Nap Lajoie, 1910 .... 8.0
Mickey Mantle, 1956 .... 7.9
Mickey Mantle, 1957 .... 7.8
Mickey Mantle, 1961 .... 7.2
Willie Mays, 1954 ...... 6.5
Willie Mays, 1955 ...... 7.6
Willie Mays, 1958 ...... 6.7
Willie Mays, 1965 ...... 7.1
Kevin Mitchell, 1989 .... 6.4
Joe Morgan, 1975 ...... 7.0
Stan Musial, 1943 ...... 7.1
Stan Musial, 1948 ...... 7.7
Stan Musial, 1951 ...... 6.8
Cal Ripken, 1984 .... 8.7
Jackie Robinson, 1951 .. 6.7
Frank Robinson, 1966 ... 6.5
Babe Ruth, 1919 .... 7.0
Babe Ruth, 1920 .... 8.8
Babe Ruth, 1921 .... 9.6
Babe Ruth, 1923 .... 10.5
Babe Ruth, 1924 .... 8.4
Babe Ruth, 1926 .... 8.1
Babe Ruth, 1927 .... 8.9
Babe Ruth, 1928 .... 6.9
Babe Ruth, 1930 .... 7.5
Babe Ruth, 1931 .... 6.8
Ryne Sandberg, 1984 ... 6.6
Ron Santo, 1966 .... 7.7
Ron Santo, 1967 .... 6.7
Mike Schmidt, 1974 ..... 6.9
Mike Schmidt, 1976 ..... 6.4
Mike Schmidt, 1977 ..... 6.9
Mike Schmidt, 1980 ..... 7.8
Mike Schmidt, 1981 ..... 6.9
George Sisler, 1920 ..... 8.3
Tris Speaker, 1912 ..... 7.8
Tris Speaker, 1913 ..... 7.3
Tris Speaker, 1914 ..... 7.4
Snuffy Stirnweiss, 1944 .. 6.8
Snuffy Stirnweiss, 1945 .. 6.6
Honus Wagner, 1903 .... 6.5
Honus Wagner, 1905 .... 7.4
Honus Wagner, 1906 .... 7.6
Honus Wagner, 1907 .... 6.6
Honus Wagner, 1912 .... 6.7
Ted Williams, 1941 ..... 8.0
Ted Williams, 1942 ..... 8.3
Ted Williams, 1946 ..... 8.2
Ted Williams, 1947 ..... 8.2
Ted Williams, 1949 ..... 7.5
Ted Williams, 1957 ..... 7.0
Carl Yastrzemski, 1967 .. 7.7
Carl Yastrzemski, 1968 ... 6.6
Robin Yount, 1982 ...... 6.5

Total Player Rating (by era)

1876-1892
1 Fred Dunlap, 1884 ...... 8.1
2 Fred Pfeffer, 1884 ...... 6.3
3 Cupid Childs, 1890 ..... 6.1
4 Jack Glasscock, 1889 ... 5.8
5 Dan Brouthers, 1892 ... 5.7
6 Tip O'Neill, 1887 .... 5.3
7 Hardy Richardson, 1886 .. 5.2
  Billy Nash, 1888 .... 5.2
9 King Kelly, 1886 .... 5.1
10 Bill Dahlen, 1892 ...... 5.0
11 John Kerins, 1886 .... 4.9
  Harry Stovey, 1889 ..... 4.9
13 Pete Browning, 1882 ... 4.7
  Jimmy Ryan, 1888 ..... 4.7
15 3 players tied 4.6

1893-1919
1 Nap Lajoie, 1901 .... 8.4
  Ty Cobb, 1917 .... 8.4
3 Nap Lajoie, 1903 .... 8.1
4 Nap Lajoie, 1906 .... 8.0
  Nap Lajoie, 1910 .... 8.0
6 Tris Speaker, 1912 ..... 7.8
7 Honus Wagner, 1906 .... 7.6
8 Nap Lajoie, 1908 .... 7.5
9 Honus Wagner, 1905 .... 7.4
  Tris Speaker, 1914 ..... 7.4
11 Tris Speaker, 1913 ..... 7.3
12 Ty Cobb, 1910 .... 7.2
13 Ty Cobb, 1911 .... 7.0
  Rogers Hornsby, 1917 ... 7.0
  Babe Ruth, 1919 .... 7.0

1920-1941
1 Babe Ruth, 1923 .... 10.5
2 Babe Ruth, 1921 .... 9.6
3 Babe Ruth, 1927 .... 8.9
4 Babe Ruth, 1920 .... 8.8
5 Babe Ruth, 1924 .... 8.4
6 George Sisler, 1920 ..... 8.3
7 Lou Gehrig, 1927 .... 8.2
8 Babe Ruth, 1926 .... 8.1
9 Ted Williams, 1941 ..... 8.0
10 Rogers Hornsby, 1920 ... 7.7
11 Rogers Hornsby, 1922 ... 7.6
12 Rogers Hornsby, 1924 ... 7.5
  Babe Ruth, 1930 .... 7.5
14 3 players tied 7.0

1942-1960
1 Ted Williams, 1942 ...... 8.3
2 Ted Williams, 1946 ...... 8.2
  Ted Williams, 1947 ...... 8.2
4 Mickey Mantle, 1956 .... 7.9
5 Mickey Mantle, 1957 .... 7.8
6 Stan Musial, 1948 ...... 7.7
7 Willie Mays, 1955 ...... 7.6
8 Ted Williams, 1949 ..... 7.5
9 Lou Boudreau, 1944 .... 7.3
10 Stan Musial, 1943 ...... 7.1
11 Ted Williams, 1957 ..... 7.0
12 Snuffy Stirnweiss, 1944 .. 6.8
  Stan Musial, 1951 ...... 6.8
14 Jackie Robinson, 1951 ... 6.7
  Willie Mays, 1958 .... 6.7

1961-1990
1 Cal Ripken, 1984 .... 8.7
2 Mike Schmidt, 1980 ..... 7.8
3 Ron Santo, 1966 .... 7.7
  Carl Yastrzemski, 1967 .. 7.7
  Rickey Henderson, 1990 . 7.7
6 Norm Cash, 1961 .... 7.3
7 Mickey Mantle, 1961 .... 7.2
8 Willie Mays, 1965 ...... 7.1
  Rickey Henderson, 1985 . 7.1
10 Joe Morgan, 1975 ...... 7.0
11 Mike Schmidt, 1974 ..... 6.9
  Mike Schmidt, 1977 ..... 6.9
  Mike Schmidt, 1981 ..... 6.9
14 George Brett, 1985 ..... 6.8
15 Ron Santo, 1967 .... 6.7

Wins

1	Charley Radbourn, 1884	59
2	John Clarkson, 1885	53
3	Guy Hecker, 1884	52
4	John Clarkson, 1889	49
5	Charley Radbourn, 1883	48
	Charlie Buffinton, 1884	48
7	Al Spalding, 1876	47
	Monte Ward, 1879	47
9	Jim Galvin, 1883	46
	Jim Galvin, 1884	46
	Matt Kilroy, 1887	46
12	George Bradley, 1876	45
	Jim McCormick, 1880	45
	Silver King, 1888	45
15	Mickey Welch, 1885	44
	Bill Hutchinson, 1891	44
17	Tommy Bond, 1879	43
	Will White, 1879	43
	Larry Corcoran, 1880	43
	Will White, 1883	43
21	Lady Baldwin, 1886	42
	Tim Keefe, 1886	42
	Bill Hutchinson, 1890	42
24	Tim Keefe, 1883	41
	Dave Foutz, 1886	41
	Ed Morris, 1886	41
	Jack Chesbro, 1904	41
28	Tommy Bond, 1877	40
	Tommy Bond, 1878	40
	Will White, 1882	40
	Bill Sweeney, 1884	40
	Bob Caruthers, 1885	40
	Bob Caruthers, 1889	40
	Ed Walsh, 1908	40
35	Monte Ward, 1880	39
	Mickey Welch, 1884	39
	Ed Morris, 1885	39
38	Toad Ramsey, 1886	38
	John Clarkson, 1887	38
	Kid Gleason, 1890	38
41	Jim Galvin, 1879	37
	Jim Whitney, 1883	37
	Tim Keefe, 1884	37
	Jack Lynch, 1884	37
	Toad Ramsey, 1887	37
	Bill Hutchinson, 1892	37
	Christy Mathewson, 1908	37
48	Jim McCormick, 1882	36
	Tony Mullane, 1884	36
	John Clarkson, 1886	36
	Sadie McMahon, 1890	36
	Cy Young, 1892	36
	Frank Killen, 1893	36
	Amos Rusie, 1894	36
	Walter Johnson, 1913	36
56	Jim Devlin, 1877	35
	Tony Mullane, 1883	35
	Larry Corcoran, 1884	35
	Tim Keefe, 1887	35
	Tim Keefe, 1888	35
	Ed Seward, 1888	35
	Silver King, 1889	35
	Sadie McMahon, 1891	35
	Kid Nichols, 1892	35
	Jack Stivetts, 1892	35
	Cy Young, 1895	35
	Joe McGinnity, 1904	35
68	Mickey Welch, 1880	34
	Larry Corcoran, 1883	34
	Ed Morris, 1884	34
	Will White, 1884	34
	Elmer Smith, 1887	34
	Scott Stratton, 1890	34
	Mark Baldwin, 1890	34
	George Haddock, 1891	34
	Kid Nichols, 1893	34
	Cy Young, 1893	34
	Joe Wood, 1912	34
79	Charley Radbourn, 1882	33
	Dave Foutz, 1885	33
	Henry Porter, 1885	33
	Mickey Welch, 1886	33
	Tony Mullane, 1886	33
	John Clarkson, 1888	33
	John Clarkson, 1891	33
	Amos Rusie, 1891	33
	Jack Stivetts, 1891	33
	Amos Rusie, 1893	33
	Jouett Meekin, 1894	33
	Cy Young, 1901	33
	Christy Mathewson, 1904	33
	Walter Johnson, 1912	33
	Pete Alexander, 1916	33
94	9 players tied	32

Wins (by era)

1876-1892

1	Charley Radbourn, 1884	59
2	John Clarkson, 1885	53
3	Guy Hecker, 1884	52
4	John Clarkson, 1889	49
5	Charley Radbourn, 1883	48
	Charlie Buffinton, 1884	48
7	Al Spalding, 1876	47
	Monte Ward, 1879	47
9	Jim Galvin, 1883	46
	Jim Galvin, 1884	46
	Matt Kilroy, 1887	46
12	George Bradley, 1876	45
	Jim McCormick, 1880	45
	Silver King, 1888	45
15	2 players tied	44

1893-1919

1	Jack Chesbro, 1904	41
2	Ed Walsh, 1908	40
3	Christy Mathewson, 1908	37
4	Frank Killen, 1893	36
	Amos Rusie, 1894	36
	Walter Johnson, 1913	36
7	Cy Young, 1895	35
	Joe McGinnity, 1904	35
9	Kid Nichols, 1893	34
	Cy Young, 1893	34
	Joe Wood, 1912	34
12	6 players tied	33

1920-1941

1	Jim Bagby, 1920	31
	Lefty Grove, 1931	31
3	Dizzy Dean, 1934	30
4	Dazzy Vance, 1924	28
	Lefty Grove, 1930	28
	Dizzy Dean, 1935	28
7	Pete Alexander, 1920	27
	Carl Mays, 1921	27
	Urban Shocker, 1921	27
	Eddie Rommel, 1922	27
	Dolf Luque, 1923	27
	George Uhle, 1926	27
	Bucky Walters, 1939	27
	Bob Feller, 1940	27
15	7 players tied	26

1942-1960

1	Hal Newhouser, 1944	29
2	Robin Roberts, 1952	28
3	Dizzy Trout, 1944	27
	Don Newcombe, 1956	27
5	Hal Newhouser, 1946	26
	Bob Feller, 1946	26
7	Hal Newhouser, 1945	25
	Dave Ferriss, 1946	25
	Mel Parnell, 1949	25
10	Johnny Sain, 1948	24
	Bobby Shantz, 1952	24
12	13 players tied	23

1961-1990

1	Denny McLain, 1968	31
2	Sandy Koufax, 1966	27
	Steve Carlton, 1972	27
	Bob Welch, 1990	27
5	Sandy Koufax, 1965	26
	Juan Marichal, 1968	26
7	12 players tied	25

Losses

1	John Coleman, 1883	48
2	Will White, 1880	42
3	Larry McKeon, 1884	41
4	George Bradley, 1879	40
	Jim McCormick, 1879	40
6	Henry Porter, 1888	37
	Kid Carsey, 1891	37
	George Cobb, 1892	37
9	Stump Weidman, 1886	36
	Bill Hutchinson, 1892	36
11	Jim Devlin, 1876	35
	Jim Galvin, 1880	35
	Fleury Sullivan, 1884	35
	Adonis Terry, 1884	35
	Hardie Henderson, 1885	35
	Red Donahue, 1897	35
17	Bobby Mathews, 1876	34
	Bob Barr, 1884	34
	Matt Kilroy, 1886	34
	Al Mays, 1887	34
	Mark Baldwin, 1889	34
	Amos Rusie, 1890	34
23	Harry McCormick, 1879	33
	Jim Whitney, 1881	33
	Lee Richmond, 1882	33
	Frank Mountain, 1883	33
	Jersey Bakely, 1888	33
28	Lee Richmond, 1880	32
	Hardie Henderson, 1883	32
	John Harkins, 1884	32
	Jim Whitney, 1885	32
	Jim Whitney, 1886	32
33	Sam Weaver, 1878	31
	Will White, 1879	31
	Charley Radbourn, 1886	31
	Dupee Shaw, 1886	31
	Billy Crowell, 1887	31
	Amos Rusie, 1892	31
39	Mickey Welch, 1880	30
	Jim McCormick, 1881	30
	Jim McCormick, 1882	30
	Bakely, 1884	30
	Jack Lynch, 1886	30
	Phenomenal Smith, 1887	30
	Toad Ramsey, 1888	30
	John Ewing, 1889	30
	Ed Beatin, 1890	30
	Ted Breitenstein, 1895	30
	Jim Hughey, 1899	30
50	Tommy Bond, 1880	29
	Jim Galvin, 1883	29
	John Healy, 1887	29
	Hank O'Day, 1888	29
	Bert Cunningham, 1888	29
	Red Ehret, 1889	29
	Silver King, 1891	29
	Bill Hart, 1896	29
	Jack Taylor, 1898	29
	Vic Willis, 1905	29
60	Jim McCormick, 1880	28
	Doc Landis, 1882	28
	Hank O'Day, 1884	28
	Hugh Daily, 1884	28
	Al Mays, 1886	28
	Gus Weyhing, 1887	28
	Mark Baldwin, 1891	28
	Duke Esper, 1893	28
	Bill Hill, 1896	28
69	Jim Galvin, 1879	27
	Tim Keefe, 1881	27
	Tim Keefe, 1883	27
	Charlie Buffinton, 1885	27
	Tony Mullane, 1886	27
	Toad Ramsey, 1886	27
	Toad Ramsey, 1887	27
	Park Swartzel, 1889	27
	Phil Knell, 1891	27
	Mark Baldwin, 1892	27
	Pink Hawley, 1894	27
	Chick Fraser, 1896	27
	Bill Hart, 1897	27
	Willie Sudhoff, 1898	27
	Bill Carrick, 1899	27
	Dummy Taylor, 1901	27
	George Bell, 1910	27
	Paul Derringer, 1933	27
87	19 players tied	26

Winning Percentage

1	Roy Face, 1959	.947
2	Rick Sutcliffe, 1984	.941
3	Ron Guidry, 1978	.893
	Freddie Fitzsimmons,	
4	1940	.889
5	Lefty Grove, 1931	.886
6	Preacher Roe, 1951	.880
7	Fred Goldsmith, 1880	.875
	Jim McCormick, 1884	.875
9	Joe Wood, 1912	.872
10	David Cone, 1988	.870
11	Orel Hershiser, 1985	.864
12	Billy Taylor, 1884	.862
	Bill Donovan, 1907	.862
	Whitey Ford, 1961	.862
15	Dwight Gooden, 1985	.857
	Roger Clemens, 1986	.857
17	Chief Bender, 1914	.850
18	Lefty Grove, 1930	.848
19	Tom Hughes, 1916	.842
	Emil Yde, 1924	.842
	Schoolboy Rowe, 1940	.842
	Sandy Consuegra, 1954	.842
	Ralph Terry, 1961	.842
	Ron Perranoski, 1963	.842
25	Lefty Gomez, 1934	.839
26	Bill Hoffer, 1895	.838
	Denny McLain, 1968	.838
28	Walter Johnson, 1913	.837
29	King Cole, 1910	.833
	Spud Chandler, 1943	.833
	Sandy Koufax, 1963	.833
32	Charley Radbourn, 1884	.831
33	Ed Reulbach, 1906	.826
	Elmer Riddle, 1941	.826
35	Jim Hughes, 1899	.824
	Jack Chesbro, 1902	.824
	Dazzy Vance, 1924	.824
38	Chief Bender, 1910	.821
	Bob Purkey, 1962	.821
40	Sal Maglie, 1950	.818
	Bob Welch, 1990	.818
42	Joe McGinnity, 1904	.814
43	Mordecai Brown, 1906	.813
	Russ Ford, 1910	.813
	Eddie Plank, 1912	.813
	Carl Hubbell, 1936	.813
47	Dizzy Dean, 1934	.811
48	Ed Reulbach, 1907	.810
	Doc Crandall, 1910	.810
	Johnny Allen, 1932	.810
	Ted Wilks, 1944	.810
	Phil Niekro, 1982	.810
53	General Crowder, 1928	.808
	Bobo Newsom, 1940	.808
	Tiny Bonham, 1942	.808
	Larry Jansen, 1947	.808
	Dave McNally, 1971	.808
	Jim Hunter, 1973	.808
59	Christy Mathewson, 1909	.806
	Howie Camnitz, 1909	.806
	Dave Ferriss, 1946	.806
	Juan Marichal, 1966	.806
63	Eddie Cicotte, 1919	.806
64	Mickey Welch, 1885	.800
	Ed Doheny, 1902	.800
	Sam Leever, 1905	.800
	Bert Humphries, 1913	.800
	Stan Coveleski, 1925	.800
	Firpo Marberry, 1931	.800
	Robin Roberts, 1952	.800
	Eddie Lopat, 1953	.800
	Don Newcombe, 1955	.800
	Jim Palmer, 1969	.800
	John Candelaria, 1977	.800
	Larry Gura, 1978	.800
76	Al Spalding, 1876	.797
77	Don Newcombe, 1956	.794
78	Jocko Flynn, 1886	.793
	Ellis Kinder, 1949	.793
	Sal Maglie, 1951	.793
	Bret Saberhagen, 1989	.793
82	Dutch Leonard, 1914	.792
	Sandy Koufax, 1964	.792
	Wally Bunker, 1964	.792
85	Fred Klobedanz, 1897	.788
	Bill James, 1914	.788
	Joe Bush, 1922	.788
88	Jouett Meekin, 1894	.786
	Lon Warneke, 1932	.786
	Tex Hughson, 1942	.786
	Ron Guidry, 1985	.786
	Doug Drabek, 1990	.786
93	Bob Caruthers, 1889	.784
94	George Mullin, 1909	.784
95	8 players tied	.783

Winning Percentage (by era)

1876-1892

1	Fred Goldsmith, 1880	.875
	Jim McCormick, 1884	.875
3	Billy Taylor, 1884	.862
4	Charley Radbourn, 1884 ..	.831
5	Mickey Welch, 1885......	.800
6	Al Spalding, 1876........	.797
7	Jocko Flynn, 1886	.793
8	Bob Caruthers, 1889	.784
9	Jack Manning, 1876	.783
10	Charlie Sweeney, 1884 ...	.774
11	Will White, 1882	.769
	Charlie Ferguson, 1886...	.769
13	John Clarkson, 1885	.768
14	Lady Baldwin, 1886	.764
15	2 players tied	.763

1893-1919

1	Joe Wood, 1912	.872
2	Bill Donovan, 1907	.862
3	Chief Bender, 1914	.850
4	Tom Hughes, 1916......	.842
5	Bill Hoffer, 1895	.838
6	Walter Johnson, 1913	.837
7	King Cole, 1910	.833
8	Ed Reulbach, 1906	.826
9	Jim Hughes, 1899	.824
	Jack Chesbro, 1902	.824
11	Chief Bender, 1910	.821
12	Joe McGinnity, 1904	.814
13	Mordecai Brown, 1906 ...	.813
	Russ Ford, 1910	.813
	Eddie Plank, 1912	.813

1920-1941

1	Freddie Fitzsimmons, 1940	.889
2	Lefty Grove, 1931	.886
3	Lefty Grove, 1930	.848
4	Emil Yde, 1924	.842
	Schoolboy Rowe, 1940...	.842
6	Lefty Gomez, 1934	.839
7	Elmer Riddle, 1941	.826
8	Dazzy Vance, 1924	.824
9	Carl Hubbell, 1936.......	.813
10	Dizzy Dean, 1934.......	.811
11	Johnny Allen, 1932	.810
12	General Crowder, 1928 ...	.808
	Bobo Newsom, 1940.....	.808
14	Stan Coveleski, 1925	.800
	Firpo Marberry, 1931.....	.800

1942-1960

1	Roy Face, 1959	.947
2	Preacher Roe, 1951	.880
3	Sandy Consuegra, 1954 ..	.842
4	Spud Chandler, 1943	.833
5	Sal Maglie, 1950	.818
6	Ted Wilks, 1944	.810
7	Tiny Bonham, 1942	.808
	Larry Jansen, 1947	.808
9	Dave Ferriss, 1946	.806
10	Robin Roberts, 1952	.800
	Eddie Lopat, 1953	.800
	Don Newcombe, 1955....	.800
13	Don Newcombe, 1956....	.794
14	Ellis Kinder, 1949	.793
	Sal Maglie, 1951	.793

1961-1990

1	Rick Sutcliffe, 1984	.941
2	Ron Guidry, 1978	.893
3	David Cone, 1988	.870
4	Orel Hershiser, 1985	.864
5	Whitey Ford, 1961	.862
6	Dwight Gooden, 1985	.857
	Roger Clemens, 1986	.857
8	Ralph Terry, 1961	.842
	Ron Perranoski, 1963	.842
10	Denny McLain, 1968	.838
11	Sandy Koufax, 1963	.833
12	Bob Purkey, 1962	.821
13	Bob Welch, 1990	.818
14	Phil Niekro, 1982	.810
15	2 players tied	.808

Games

1	Mike Marshall, 1974	106
2	Kent Tekulve, 1979	94
3	Mike Marshall, 1973	92
4	Kent Tekulve, 1978	91
5	Wayne Granger, 1969	90
	Mike Marshall, 1979	90
	Kent Tekulve, 1987	90
8	Mark Eichhorn, 1987	89
9	Wilbur Wood, 1968	88
10	Rob Murphy, 1987	87
11	Kent Tekulve, 1982	85
	Frank Williams, 1987	85
	Mitch Williams, 1987......	85
14	Ted Abernathy, 1965	84
	Enrique Romo, 1979	84
	Dick Tidrow, 1980	84
	Dan Quisenberry, 1985 ...	84
18	Ken Sanders, 1971	83
	Craig Lefferts, 1986......	83
20	Eddie Fisher, 1965	82
	Bill Campbell, 1983	82
	Juan Agosto, 1990	82
23	John Wyatt, 1964	81
	Dale Murray, 1976	81
	Jeff Robinson, 1987	81
26	Pedro Borbon, 1973	80
	Willie Hernandez, 1984 ...	80
	Mitch Williams, 1986	80
29	Dick Radatz, 1964	79
30	Hal Woodeshick, 1965 ...	78
	Ted Abernathy, 1968	78
	Bill Campbell, 1976	78
	Rollie Fingers, 1977......	78
	Tom Hume, 1980	78
	Kent Tekulve, 1980	78
	Greg Minton, 1982	78
	Ed Vande Berg, 1982....	78
	Ted Power, 1984	78
	Tim Burke, 1985	78
	Lance McCullers, 1987 ...	78
41	Bob Locker, 1967	77
	Wilbur Wood, 1970	77
	Charlie Hough, 1976	77
	Butch Metzger, 1976	77
	Rick Camp, 1980	77
	Gary Lavelle, 1984	77
	Mark Davis, 1985........	77
	Craig Lefferts, 1987......	77
	Bobby Thigpen, 1990	77
50	Will White, 1879	76
	Jim Galvin, 1883	76
	Charley Radbourn, 1883..	76
	Wilbur Wood, 1969	76
	Ron Herbel, 1970........	76
	Larry Hardy, 1974	76
	Rollie Fingers, 1974......	76
	Dan Spillner, 1977	76
	Dave Tomlin, 1977	76
	Sid Monge, 1979	76
	Rod Scurry, 1982........	76
	Tippy Martinez, 1982	76
	Kent Tekulve, 1983	76
	Ed Vande Berg, 1985	76
	Rob Murphy, 1988	76
	Mitch Williams, 1989	76
	Chuck Crim, 1989	76
67	Charley Radbourn, 1884 ..	75
	Guy Hecker, 1884	75
	Bill Hutchinson, 1892	75
	Ron Perranoski, 1969	75
	Rollie Fingers, 1975......	75
	Butch Metzger, 1977	75
	Dan Quisenberry, 1980 ...	75
	Willie Hernandez, 1982 ...	75
	Jeff Reardon, 1982	75
	Roger McDowell, 1986 ...	75
	Todd Worrell, 1987.......	75
	Juan Agosto, 1988	75
	Jeff Robinson, 1988	75
80	Jim McCormick, 1880	74
	Lee Richmond, 1880	74
	Jim Konstanty, 1950	74
	Bob Miller, 1964	74
	Ron Kline, 1965	74
	Dan McGinn, 1969.......	74
	Bob Lacey, 1978	74
	Enrique Romo, 1980	74
	Willie Hernandez, 1983 ...	74
	Greg Minton, 1984.......	74
	Scott Garrelts, 1985	74
	Willie Hernandez, 1985 ...	74
	Dave Righetti, 1985	74
	Johnny Franco, 1986	74
	Todd Worrell, 1986.......	74
	Dave Righetti, 1986	74
	Dale Mohorcic, 1987	74
	Rob Dibble, 1989	74
	Rob Murphy, 1989	74
	Paul Assenmacher, 1990 .	74
100	17 players tied	73

Games (by era)

1876-1892

1	Will White, 1879	76
	Jim Galvin, 1883	76
	Charley Radbourn, 1883..	76
4	Charley Radbourn, 1884..	75
	Guy Hecker, 1884	75
	Bill Hutchinson, 1892	75
7	Jim McCormick, 1880	74
	Lee Richmond, 1880	74
9	John Clarkson, 1889	73
10	Jim Galvin, 1884	72
11	Bill Hutchinson, 1890	71
12	Monte Ward, 1879	70
	Monte Ward, 1880	70
	John Clarkson, 1885	70
15	Matt Kilroy, 1887	69

1893-1919

1	Ed Walsh, 1908	66
2	Ed Walsh, 1912	62
3	Dave Davenport, 1916 ...	59
4	Amos Rusie, 1893.......	56
	Ted Breitenstein, 1894 ...	56
	Pink Hawley, 1895.......	56
	Ed Walsh, 1907	56
	Christy Mathewson, 1908.	56
	Ed Walsh, 1911	56
	Reb Russell, 1916	56
11	Frank Killen, 1893	55
	Joe McGinnity, 1903	55
	Jack Chesbro, 1904	55
	Dave Davenport, 1915 ...	55
15	3 players tied	54

1920-1941

1	Firpo Marberry, 1926.....	64
2	Clint Brown, 1939	61
3	Garland Braxton, 1927 ...	58
	Russ Van Atta, 1935.....	58
5	Eddie Rommel, 1923	56
	Firpo Marberry, 1927.....	56
	Hugh Mulcahy, 1937	56
8	Firpo Marberry, 1925.....	55
	Bump Hadley, 1931	55
	Jim Walkup, 1935	55
11	George Uhle, 1923	54
	Firpo Marberry, 1932.....	54
	Jack Russell, 1934	54
	Chubby Dean, 1939	54
	Clyde Shoun, 1940	54

1942-1960

1	Jim Konstanty, 1950	74
2	Hoyt Wilhelm, 1952	71
3	Ace Adams, 1943	70
	Mike Fornieles, 1960	70
5	Ellis Kinder, 1953	69
	Don Elston, 1958	69
7	Hoyt Wilhelm, 1953	68
	Roy Face, 1956	68
	Roy Face, 1960	68
10	Andy Karl, 1945	67
	Turk Lown, 1957	67
	Gerry Staley, 1959	67
13	6 players tied	65

1961-1990

1	Mike Marshall, 1974	106
2	Kent Tekulve, 1979	94
3	Mike Marshall, 1973	92
4	Kent Tekulve, 1978	91
5	Wayne Granger, 1969	90
	Mike Marshall, 1979	90
	Kent Tekulve, 1987	90
8	Mark Eichhorn, 1987	89
9	Wilbur Wood, 1968	88
10	Rob Murphy, 1987	87
11	Kent Tekulve, 1982	85
	Frank Williams, 1987	85
	Mitch Williams, 1987	85
14	4 players tied	84

Games Started

1	Will White, 1879	75
	Jim Galvin, 1883	75
3	Jim McCormick, 1880	74
4	Charley Radbourn, 1884..	73
	Guy Hecker, 1884	73
6	Jim Galvin, 1884	72
	John Clarkson, 1889	72
8	Bill Hutchinson, 1892	71
9	John Clarkson, 1885	70
10	Matt Kilroy, 1887	69
11	Jim Devlin, 1876	68
	Charley Radbourn, 1883 ..	68
	Tim Keefe, 1883	68
	Matt Kilroy, 1886	68
15	Monte Ward, 1880	67
	Jim McCormick, 1882	67
	Charlie Buffinton, 1884 ...	67
	Toad Ramsey, 1886	67
19	Jim Galvin, 1879	66
	Lee Richmond, 1880	66
	Bill Hutchinson, 1890	66
22	Mickey Welch, 1884	65
	Tony Mullane, 1884	65
	Silver King, 1888	65
25	George Bradley, 1876	64
	Tommy Bond, 1879	64
	Mickey Welch, 1880	64
	Will White, 1883	64
	Tim Keefe, 1886	64
	Toad Ramsey, 1887	64
31	Jim Whitney, 1881	63
	Ed Morris, 1885	63
	Ed Morris, 1886	63
	Amos Rusie, 1890	63
35	Will White, 1880	62
36	Jim Devlin, 1877	61
	John Coleman, 1883	61
	Hardie Henderson, 1885..	61
	Jersey Bakely, 1888	61
	Amos Rusie, 1892	61
41	Al Spalding, 1876........	60
	Jim McCormick, 1879	60
	Monte Ward, 1879	60
	Larry Corcoran, 1880	60
	Larry McKeon, 1884	60
	Bill Sweeney, 1884	60
47	Tommy Bond, 1878	59
	Frank Mountain, 1883	59
	Larry Corcoran, 1884	59
	Mickey Welch, 1886......	59
	John Clarkson, 1887	59
	Mark Baldwin, 1889	59
53	Tommy Bond, 1877	58
	Terry Larkin, 1879	58
	Jim McCormick, 1881	58
	Tim Keefe, 1884	58
	Hugh Daily, 1884	58
	Charley Radbourn, 1886..	58
	Bill Hutchinson, 1891	58
	Sadie McMahon, 1891 ...	58
61	Tommy Bond, 1880	57
	Dave Foutz, 1886	57
	Ed Seward, 1888	57
	Sadie McMahon, 1890 ...	57
	Mark Baldwin, 1890	57
	Amos Rusie, 1891	57
67	Bobby Mathews, 1876 ...	56
	Terry Larkin, 1877	56
	Terry Larkin, 1878	56
	Jim Whitney, 1883	56
	Lady Baldwin, 1886	56
	Tony Mullane, 1884	56
	Tim Keefe, 1887	56
	Matt Kilroy, 1889	56
	Silver King, 1890	56
	Jack Stivetts, 1891	56
77	George Derby, 1881	55
	Tony Mullane, 1882	55
	Adonis Terry, 1884	55
	Mickey Welch, 1885......	55
	John Clarkson, 1886	55
	Phenomenal Smith, 1887.	55
	Gus Weyhing, 1887	55
	Ed Morris, 1888	55
	Kid Gleason, 1890	55
86	George Bradley, 1879	54
	Harry McCormick, 1879 ..	54
	Jim Galvin, 1880	54
	Will White, 1882	54
	Henry Porter, 1885	54
	John Clarkson, 1888	54
	Henry Porter, 1888	54
	Ed Beatin, 1890	54
	Bob Barr, 1890	54
95	9 players tied	53

Games Started (by era)

1876-1892

1	Will White, 1879	75
	Jim Galvin, 1883	75
3	Jim McCormick, 1880	74
4	Charley Radbourn, 1884	73
	Guy Hecker, 1884	73
6	Jim Galvin, 1884	72
	John Clarkson, 1889	72
8	Bill Hutchinson, 1892	71
9	John Clarkson, 1885	70
10	Matt Kilroy, 1887	69
11	Jim Devlin, 1876	68
	Charley Radbourn, 1883	68
	Tim Keefe, 1883	68
	Matt Kilroy, 1886	68
15	4 players tied	67

1893-1919

1	Amos Rusie, 1893	52
2	Jack Chesbro, 1904	51
3	Ted Breitenstein, 1894	50
	Amos Rusie, 1894	50
	Ted Breitenstein, 1895	50
	Pink Hawley, 1895	50
	Frank Killen, 1896	50
8	Ed Walsh, 1908	49
9	Frank Killen, 1893	48
	Jouett Meekin, 1894	48
	Joe McGinnity, 1903	48
12	Cy Young, 1894	47
	Amos Rusie, 1895	47
	Jack Taylor, 1898	47
15	8 players tied	46

1920-1941

1	George Uhle, 1923	44
2	Pete Alexander, 1920	40
	Stan Coveleski, 1921	40
	George Uhle, 1922	40
	George Caster, 1938	40
	Bobo Newsom, 1938	40
	Bob Feller, 1941	40
8	Red Faber, 1920	39
	Red Faber, 1921	39
	Hooks Dauss, 1923	39
	Howard Ehmke, 1923	39
	George Earnshaw, 1930	39
	General Crowder, 1932	39
	Kirby Higbe, 1941	39
15	24 players tied	38

1942-1960

1	Bob Feller, 1946	42
	Bob Friend, 1956	42
3	Bill Voiselle, 1944	41
	Robin Roberts, 1953	41
5	Dizzy Trout, 1944	40
6	Johnny Sain, 1948	39
	Robin Roberts, 1950	39
	Warren Spahn, 1950	39
	Vern Bickford, 1950	39
	Robin Roberts, 1951	39
	Ron Kline, 1956	39
	Lew Burdette, 1959	39
13	10 players tied	38

1961-1990

1	Wilbur Wood, 1972	49
2	Wilbur Wood, 1973	48
3	Mickey Lolich, 1971	45
4	Phil Niekro, 1979	44
5	Wilbur Wood, 1975	43
	Phil Niekro, 1977	43
7	10 players tied	42

Complete Games

1	Will White, 1879	75
2	Charley Radbourn, 1884	73
3	Jim McCormick, 1880	72
	Jim Galvin, 1883	72
	Guy Hecker, 1884	72
6	Jim Galvin, 1884	71
7	Tim Keefe, 1883	68
	John Clarkson, 1885	68
	John Clarkson, 1889	68
10	Bill Hutchinson, 1892	67
11	Jim Devlin, 1876	66
	Charley Radbourn, 1883	66
	Matt Kilroy, 1886	66
	Toad Ramsey, 1886	66
	Matt Kilroy, 1887	66
16	Jim Galvin, 1879	65
	Jim McCormick, 1882	65
	Bill Hutchinson, 1890	65
19	Mickey Welch, 1880	64
	Will White, 1883	64
	Tony Mullane, 1884	64
	Silver King, 1888	64
23	George Bradley, 1876	63
	Charlie Buffinton, 1884	63
	Ed Morris, 1885	63
	Ed Morris, 1886	63
27	Mickey Welch, 1884	62
	Tim Keefe, 1886	62
29	Jim Devlin, 1877	61
	Toad Ramsey, 1887	61
31	Tommy Bond, 1879	60
	Jersey Bakely, 1888	60
33	Jim McCormick, 1879	59
	Monte Ward, 1880	59
	John Coleman, 1883	59
	Larry McKeon, 1884	59
	Hardie Henderson, 1885	59
38	Tommy Bond, 1877	58
	Monte Ward, 1879	58
	Will White, 1880	58
	Bill Sweeney, 1884	58
	Amos Rusie, 1892	58
43	Tommy Bond, 1878	57
	Terry Larkin, 1879	57
	Larry Corcoran, 1880	57
	Lee Richmond, 1880	57
	Jim McCormick, 1881	57
	Jim Whitney, 1881	57
	Frank Mountain, 1883	57
	Larry Corcoran, 1884	57
	Tim Keefe, 1884	57
	Charley Radbourn, 1886	57
	Ed Seward, 1888	57
54	Terry Larkin, 1878	56
	Hugh Daily, 1884	56
	Mickey Welch, 1886	56
	John Clarkson, 1887	56
	Amos Rusie, 1890	56
	Bill Hutchinson, 1891	56
60	Bobby Mathews, 1876	55
	Terry Larkin, 1877	55
	George Derby, 1881	55
	Mickey Welch, 1885	55
	Lady Baldwin, 1886	55
	Dave Foutz, 1886	55
	Tony Mullane, 1886	55
	Matt Kilroy, 1889	55
	Sadie McMahon, 1890	55
69	Al Spalding, 1876	54
	Jim Whitney, 1883	54
	Adonis Terry, 1884	54
	Tim Keefe, 1887	54
	Phenomenal Smith, 1887	54
	Ed Morris, 1888	54
	Mark Baldwin, 1889	54
	Kid Gleason, 1890	54
	Mark Baldwin, 1890	54
78	George Bradley, 1879	53
	Jack Lynch, 1884	53
	Bob Caruthers, 1885	53
	Henry Porter, 1885	53
	Gus Weyhing, 1887	53
	John Clarkson, 1888	53
	Henry Porter, 1888	53
	Ed Beatin, 1890	53
	Sadie McMahon, 1891	53
87	Will White, 1878	52
	Will White, 1882	52
	Will White, 1884	52
	Ed Seward, 1887	52
	Bob Barr, 1890	52
	Amos Rusie, 1891	52
93	Charley Radbourn, 1882	51
	Tony Mullane, 1882	51
	Larry Corcoran, 1883	51
	Fleury Sullivan, 1884	51
	Guy Hecker, 1885	51
	Gus Weyhing, 1891	51
99	10 players tied	50

Complete Games (by era)

1876-1892

1	Will White, 1879	75
2	Charley Radbourn, 1884	73
3	Jim McCormick, 1880	72
	Jim Galvin, 1883	72
	Guy Hecker, 1884	72
6	Jim Galvin, 1884	71
7	Tim Keefe, 1883	68
	John Clarkson, 1885	68
	John Clarkson, 1889	68
10	Bill Hutchinson, 1892	67
11	Jim Devlin, 1876	66
	Charley Radbourn, 1883	66
	Matt Kilroy, 1886	66
	Toad Ramsey, 1886	66
	Matt Kilroy, 1887	66

1893-1919

1	Amos Rusie, 1893	50
2	Jack Chesbro, 1904	48
3	Ted Breitenstein, 1894	46
	Ted Breitenstein, 1895	46
5	Amos Rusie, 1894	45
	Vic Willis, 1902	45
7	Cy Young, 1894	44
	Pink Hawley, 1895	44
	Frank Killen, 1896	44
	Joe McGinnity, 1903	44
11	Kid Nichols, 1893	43
12	7 players tied	42

1920-1941

1	Pete Alexander, 1920	33
	Burleigh Grimes, 1923	33
3	Red Faber, 1921	32
	George Uhle, 1926	32
5	Red Faber, 1922	31
	Wes Ferrell, 1935	31
	Bobo Newsom, 1938	31
	Bucky Walters, 1939	31
	Bob Feller, 1940	31
10	8 players tied	30

1942-1960

1	Bob Feller, 1946	36
2	Dizzy Trout, 1944	33
	Robin Roberts, 1953	33
4	Robin Roberts, 1952	30
5	Hal Newhouser, 1945	29
	Hal Newhouser, 1946	29
	Robin Roberts, 1954	29
8	Jim Tobin, 1942	28
	Jim Tobin, 1944	28
	Johnny Sain, 1948	28
	Bob Lemon, 1952	28
12	Bucky Walters, 1944	27
	Mel Parnell, 1949	27
	Vern Bickford, 1950	27
	Bobby Shantz, 1952	27

1961-1990

1	Juan Marichal, 1968	30
	Fergie Jenkins, 1971	30
	Steve Carlton, 1972	30
	Jim Hunter, 1975	30
5	Mickey Lolich, 1971	29
	Gaylord Perry, 1972	29
	Gaylord Perry, 1973	29
	Fergie Jenkins, 1974	29
9	Bob Gibson, 1968	28
	Denny McLain, 1968	28
	Bob Gibson, 1969	28
	Gaylord Perry, 1974	28
	Rick Langford, 1980	28
14	4 players tied	27

Shutouts

1	George Bradley, 1876	16
	Pete Alexander, 1916	16
3	Jack Coombs, 1910	13
	Bob Gibson, 1968	13
5	Tommy Bond, 1879	12
	Jim Galvin, 1884	12
	Ed Morris, 1886	12
	Pete Alexander, 1915	12
9	Charley Radbourn, 1884	11
	Dave Foutz, 1886	11
	Christy Mathewson, 1908	11
	Ed Walsh, 1908	11
	Walter Johnson, 1913	11
	Sandy Koufax, 1963	11
	Dean Chance, 1964	11
16	John Clarkson, 1885	10
	Cy Young, 1904	10
	Ed Walsh, 1906	10
	Joe Wood, 1912	10
	Dave Davenport, 1915	10
	Carl Hubbell, 1933	10
	Mort Cooper, 1942	10
	Bob Feller, 1946	10
	Bob Lemon, 1948	10
	Juan Marichal, 1965	10
	Jim Palmer, 1975	10
	John Tudor, 1985	10
28	Al Spalding, 1876	9
	Tommy Bond, 1878	9
	George Derby, 1881	9
	Cy Young, 1892	9
	Joe McGinnity, 1904	9
	Mordecai Brown, 1906	9
	Addie Joss, 1906	9
	Mordecai Brown, 1908	9
	Addie Joss, 1908	9
	Orval Overall, 1909	9
	Pete Alexander, 1913	9
	Walter Johnson, 1914	9
	Cy Falkenberg, 1914	9
	Babe Ruth, 1916	9
	Stan Coveleski, 1917	9
	Pete Alexander, 1919	9
	Bill Lee, 1938	9
	Bob Porterfield, 1953	9
	Luis Tiant, 1968	9
	Denny McLain, 1969	9
	Don Sutton, 1972	9
	Nolan Ryan, 1972	9
	Bert Blyleven, 1973	9
	Ron Guidry, 1978	9
52	Monte Ward, 1880	8
	Will White, 1882	8
	Charlie Buffinton, 1884	8
	Tim Keefe, 1888	8
	Ben Sanders, 1888	8
	John Clarkson, 1889	8
	Christy Mathewson, 1902	8
	Jack Chesbro, 1902	8
	Rube Waddell, 1904	8
	Christy Mathewson, 1905	8
	Ed Killian, 1905	8
	Lefty Leifield, 1906	8
	Rube Waddell, 1906	8
	Orval Overall, 1907	8
	Christy Mathewson, 1907	8
	Eddie Plank, 1907	8
	Mordecai Brown, 1909	8
	Christy Mathewson, 1909	8
	Ed Walsh, 1909	8
	Russ Ford, 1910	8
	Walter Johnson, 1910	8
	Reb Russell, 1913	8
	Jeff Tesreau, 1914	8
	Al Mamaux, 1915	8
	Jeff Tesreau, 1915	8
	Joe Bush, 1916	8
	Pete Alexander, 1917	8
	Jim Bagby, 1917	8
	Walter Johnson, 1917	8
	Hippo Vaughn, 1918	8
	Walter Johnson, 1918	8
	Carl Mays, 1918	8
	Babe Adams, 1920	8
	Hal Newhouser, 1945	8
	Steve Barber, 1961	8
	Camilo Pascual, 1961	8
	Whitey Ford, 1964	8
	Sandy Koufax, 1965	8
	Don Drysdale, 1968	8
	Juan Marichal, 1969	8
	Vida Blue, 1971	8
	Steve Carlton, 1972	8
	Wilbur Wood, 1972	8
	Fernando Valenzuela, 1981	8
	Dwight Gooden, 1985	8
	Orel Hershiser, 1988	8
	Roger Clemens, 1988	8
	Tim Belcher, 1989	8
100	88 players tied	7

Saves

1	Bobby Thigpen, 1990	57
2	Dennis Eckersley, 1990 ...	48
3	Dave Righetti, 1986	46
4	Dan Quisenberry, 1983	45
	Bruce Sutter, 1984	45
	Dennis Eckersley, 1988 ...	45
7	Dan Quisenberry, 1984 ...	44
	Mark Davis, 1989	44
9	Doug Jones, 1990	43
10	Jeff Reardon, 1988	42
11	Jeff Reardon, 1985	41
12	Steve Bedrosian, 1987	40
13	Johnny Franco, 1988	39
14	John Hiller, 1973	38
	Jeff Russell, 1989	38
16	Clay Carroll, 1972	37
	Rollie Fingers, 1978	37
	Bruce Sutter, 1979	37
	Dan Quisenberry, 1985 ...	37
	Doug Jones, 1988	37
	Gregg Olson, 1990	37
22	Bruce Sutter, 1982	36
	Bill Caudill, 1984	36
	Todd Worrell, 1986	36
	Lee Smith, 1987	36
	Mitch Williams, 1989	36
	Dave Righetti, 1990	36
28	Wayne Granger, 1970	35
	Sparky Lyle, 1972	35
	Rollie Fingers, 1977	35
	Dan Quisenberry, 1982 ...	35
	Jeff Reardon, 1986	35
33	Ron Perranoski, 1970	34
	Don Aase, 1986	34
	Tom Henke, 1987	34
	Jim Gott, 1988	34
	Bobby Thigpen, 1988	34
	Bobby Thigpen, 1989	34
39	Rich Gossage, 1980	33
	Dan Quisenberry, 1980 ...	33
	Bob Stanley, 1983	33
	Lee Smith, 1984	33
	Lee Smith, 1985	33
	Dave Smith, 1986	33
	Todd Worrell, 1987	33
	Dennis Eckersley, 1989 ...	33
	Dan Plesac, 1989	33
	Mike Schooler, 1989	33
	Johnny Franco, 1990	33
50	Jack Aker, 1966	32
	Mike Marshall, 1979	32
	Willie Hernandez, 1984 ...	32
	Bob James, 1985	32
	Johnny Franco, 1987	32
	Todd Worrell, 1988	32
	Johnny Franco, 1989	32
	Doug Jones, 1989	32
	Rick Aguilera, 1990	32
	Tom Henke, 1990	32
60	Ted Abernathy, 1965	31
	Ron Perranoski, 1969	31
	Ken Sanders, 1971	31
	Mike Marshall, 1973	31
	Bruce Sutter, 1977	31
	Bill Campbell, 1977	31
	Kent Tekulve, 1978	31
	Kent Tekulve, 1979	31
	Jesse Orosco, 1984	31
	Dave Righetti, 1984	31
	Willie Hernandez, 1985 ...	31
	Donnie Moore, 1985	31
	Lee Smith, 1986	31
	Jeff Reardon, 1987	31
	Dave Righetti, 1987	31
	Jeff Reardon, 1989	31
	Randy Myers, 1990	31
77	Dave Giusti, 1971	30
	Ed Farmer, 1980	30
	Gene Garber, 1982	30
	Greg Minton, 1982	30
	Rich Gossage, 1982	30
	Ron Davis, 1983	30
	Dan Plesac, 1988	30
	Mike Schooler, 1990	30
85	Luis Arroyo, 1961	29
	Dick Radatz, 1964	29
	Ron Kline, 1965	29
	Fred Gladding, 1969	29
	Lindy McDaniel, 1970	29
	Terry Forster, 1972	29
	Jim Kern, 1979	29
	Rollie Fingers, 1982	29
	Lee Smith, 1983	29
	Al Holland, 1984	29
	Ron Davis, 1984	29
	Jay Howell, 1985	29
	Dave Righetti, 1985	29
	Steve Bedrosian, 1986 ...	29
	Johnny Franco, 1986	29
	Lee Smith, 1988	29

Innings Pitched

1	Will White, 1879	680.0
2	Charley Radbourn, 1884 ..	678.2
3	Guy Hecker, 1884	670.2
4	Jim McCormick, 1880 ...	657.2
5	Jim Galvin, 1883	656.1
6	Jim Galvin, 1884	636.1
7	Charley Radbourn, 1883 ..	632.1
8	Bill Hutchinson, 1892	627.0
9	John Clarkson, 1885	623.0
10	Jim Devlin, 1876	622.0
11	John Clarkson, 1889	620.0
12	Tim Keefe, 1883	619.0
13	Bill Hutchinson, 1890	603.0
14	Jim McCormick, 1882 ...	595.2
15	Monte Ward, 1880	595.0
16	Jim Galvin, 1879	593.0
17	Lee Richmond, 1880	590.2
18	Matt Kilroy, 1887	589.1
19	Toad Ramsey, 1886	588.2
20	Monte Ward, 1879	587.0
	Charlie Buffinton, 1884 ..	587.0
22	Silver King, 1888	585.2
23	Matt Kilroy, 1886	583.0
24	Ed Morris, 1885	581.0
25	Will White, 1883	577.0
26	Mickey Welch, 1880	574.0
27	George Bradley, 1876 ...	573.0
28	Tony Mullane, 1884	567.0
29	Toad Ramsey, 1887	561.0
	Bill Hutchinson, 1891	561.0
31	Jim Devlin, 1877	559.0
32	Mickey Welch, 1884	557.1
33	Tommy Bond, 1879	555.1
	Ed Morris, 1886	555.1
35	Jim Whitney, 1881	552.1
36	Amos Rusie, 1890	548.2
37	Jim McCormick, 1879 ...	546.1
38	Tim Keefe, 1886	540.0
39	Hardie Henderson, 1885 ..	539.1
40	John Coleman, 1883	538.1
41	Bill Sweeney, 1884	538.0
42	Larry Corcoran, 1880	536.1
43	Tommy Bond, 1878	532.2
	Jersey Bakely, 1888	532.2
45	Amos Rusie, 1892	532.0
46	Tony Mullane, 1886	529.2
47	Al Spalding, 1876	528.2
48	Jim McCormick, 1881 ...	526.0
49	John Clarkson, 1887	523.0
50	Tommy Bond, 1877	521.0
51	Ed Seward, 1888	518.2
52	Will White, 1880	517.1
53	Larry Corcoran, 1884	516.2
54	Bobby Mathews, 1876 ...	516.0
55	Jim Whitney, 1883	514.0
56	Mark Baldwin, 1889	513.2
57	Terry Larkin, 1879	513.1
58	Larry McKeon, 1884	512.0
59	Charley Radbourn, 1886 ..	509.1
60	Sadie McMahon, 1890 ...	509.0
61	Terry Larkin, 1878	506.0
	Kid Gleason, 1890	506.0
63	Dave Foutz, 1886	504.0
64	Frank Mountain, 1883	503.0
	Sadie McMahon, 1891 ...	503.0
66	Terry Larkin, 1877	501.0
	Mark Baldwin, 1890	501.0
68	Hugh Daily, 1884	500.2
69	Amos Rusie, 1891	500.1
70	Mickey Welch, 1886	500.0
71	George Derby, 1881	494.2
72	Bob Barr, 1890	493.1
73	Tommy Bond, 1880	493.0
74	Mickey Welch, 1885	492.0
75	Tim Keefe, 1884	491.2
76	Phenomenal Smith, 1887 ..	491.1
77	George Bradley, 1879	487.0
	Jack Lynch, 1884	487.0
	Lady Baldwin, 1886	487.0
80	John Clarkson, 1888	483.1
81	Bob Caruthers, 1885	482.1
82	Amos Rusie, 1893	482.0
83	Henry Porter, 1885	481.2
84	Matt Kilroy, 1889	480.2
85	Will White, 1882	480.0
	Guy Hecker, 1885	480.0
	Ed Morris, 1888	480.0
88	Tim Keefe, 1887	478.2
89	Adonis Terry, 1884	476.0
90	Ed Beatin, 1890	474.1
91	Jim Galvin, 1881	474.0
	Charley Radbourn, 1882 ..	474.0
	Henry Porter, 1888	474.0
94	Larry Corcoran, 1883	473.2
95	Ed Seward, 1887	470.2
96	Gus Weyhing, 1892	469.2
97	Will White, 1878	468.0
98	John Clarkson, 1886	466.2
99	Gus Weyhing, 1887	466.1
100	Ed Walsh, 1908	464.0

Innings Pitched (by era)

1876-1892

1	Will White, 1879	680.0
2	Charley Radbourn, 1884 ..	678.2
3	Guy Hecker, 1884	670.2
4	Jim McCormick, 1880 ...	657.2
5	Jim Galvin, 1883	656.1
6	Jim Galvin, 1884	636.1
7	Charley Radbourn, 1883 ..	632.1
8	Bill Hutchinson, 1892	627.0
9	John Clarkson, 1885	623.0
10	Jim Devlin, 1876	622.0
11	John Clarkson, 1889	620.0
12	Tim Keefe, 1883	619.0
13	Bill Hutchinson, 1890	603.0
14	Jim McCormick, 1882 ...	595.2
15	Monte Ward, 1880	595.0

1893-1919

1	Amos Rusie, 1893	482.0
2	Ed Walsh, 1908	464.0
3	Jack Chesbro, 1904	454.2
4	Ted Breitenstein, 1894 ...	447.1
5	Pink Hawley, 1895	444.1
6	Amos Rusie, 1894	444.0
7	Joe McGinnity, 1903	434.0
8	Frank Killen, 1896	432.1
9	Ted Breitenstein, 1895 ...	429.2
10	Kid Nichols, 1893	425.0
11	Cy Young, 1893	422.2
12	Ed Walsh, 1907	422.1
13	Frank Killen, 1893	415.0
14	Cy Young, 1896	414.1
15	Vic Willis, 1902	410.0

1920-1941

1	Pete Alexander, 1920	363.1
2	George Uhle, 1923	357.2
3	Red Faber, 1922	352.0
4	Urban Shocker, 1922	348.0
5	Bob Feller, 1941	343.0
6	Jim Bagby, 1920	339.2
7	Carl Mays, 1921	336.2
8	Red Faber, 1921	330.2
	Burleigh Grimes, 1928 ..	330.2
10	Bobo Newsom, 1938	329.2
11	Wilbur Cooper, 1920	327.0
	Wilbur Cooper, 1921	327.0
	Burleigh Grimes, 1923 ...	327.0
	General Crowder, 1932 ...	327.0
15	Urban Shocker, 1921	326.2

1942-1960

1	Bob Feller, 1946	371.1
2	Dizzy Trout, 1944	352.1
3	Robin Roberts, 1953	346.2
4	Robin Roberts, 1954	336.2
5	Robin Roberts, 1952	330.0
6	Robin Roberts, 1951	315.0
7	Johnny Sain, 1948	314.2
8	Bob Friend, 1956	314.1
9	Hal Newhouser, 1945 ...	313.1
10	Bill Voiselle, 1944	312.2
11	Hal Newhouser, 1944 ...	312.1
12	Vern Bickford, 1950	311.2
13	Warren Spahn, 1951	310.2
14	Bob Lemon, 1952	309.2
15	Robin Roberts, 1955	305.0

1961-1990

1	Wilbur Wood, 1972	376.2
2	Mickey Lolich, 1971	376.0
3	Wilbur Wood, 1973	359.1
4	Steve Carlton, 1972	346.1
5	Gaylord Perry, 1973	344.0
6	Gaylord Perry, 1972	342.2
7	Phil Niekro, 1979	342.0
8	Denny McLain, 1968	336.0
9	Sandy Koufax, 1965	335.2
10	Phil Niekro, 1978	334.1
11	Wilbur Wood, 1971	334.0
12	Nolan Ryan, 1974	332.2
13	Phil Niekro, 1977	330.1
14	Gaylord Perry, 1970	328.2
15	Fergie Jenkins, 1974	328.1

Hits per Game

1	Nolan Ryan, 1972	5.26
2	Luis Tiant, 1968	5.30
3	Ed Reulbach, 1906	5.33
4	Dutch Leonard, 1914	5.57
5	Carl Lundgren, 1907	5.65
6	Sid Fernandez, 1985	5.71
7	Tommy Byrne, 1949	5.74
8	Dave McNally, 1968	5.77
9	Sandy Koufax, 1965	5.79
10	Russ Ford, 1910	5.83
11	Al Downing, 1963	5.84
12	Herb Score, 1956	5.85
13	Bob Gibson, 1968	5.85
14	Sam McDowell, 1965 ...	5.87
15	Ed Walsh, 1910	5.89
16	Mike Scott, 1986	5.95
17	Mario Soto, 1980	5.96
18	Floyd Youmans, 1986 ...	5.96
19	Nolan Ryan, 1977	5.96
20	Nolan Ryan, 1974	5.98
21	Nolan Ryan, 1981	5.98
22	Nolan Ryan, 1986	6.02
23	Sam McDowell, 1966 ...	6.02
24	Vida Blue, 1971	6.03
25	Walter Johnson, 1913 ...	6.03
26	Jim Bibby, 1973	6.04
27	Nolan Ryan, 1990	6.04
28	Pete Alexander, 1915 ...	6.05
29	Sam McDowell, 1968 ...	6.06
30	Joe Horlen, 1964	6.07
31	Andy Messersmith, 1969 .	6.08
32	Tim Keefe, 1880	6.09
33	Nolan Ryan, 1989	6.09
34	Stan Coveleski, 1917 ...	6.09
35	Jim Hunter, 1972	6.09
36	Nolan Ryan, 1976	6.11
37	Sid Fernandez, 1988 ...	6.11
38	Bob Turley, 1957	6.12
39	Bob Turley, 1955	6.13
40	Don Sutton, 1972	6.14
41	Nolan Ryan, 1983	6.14
42	Ron Guidry, 1978	6.15
43	Mordecai Brown, 1908 ...	6.17
44	Sandy Koufax, 1963	6.19
45	Jack Pfiester, 1906	6.21
46	Sandy Koufax, 1964	6.22
47	Charlie Sweeney, 1884 ..	6.23
	Roger Nelson, 1972	6.23
49	Herb Score, 1955	6.26
50	Cy Morgan, 1909	6.26
51	Dean Chance, 1964	6.27
52	Christy Mathewson, 1909.	6.28
	J.R. Richard, 1978	6.28
54	Art Fromme, 1909	6.28
55	Jack Coombs, 1910	6.32
56	Rube Waddell, 1905	6.33
57	Vean Gregg, 1911	6.33
58	Jeff Robinson, 1988	6.33
59	Larry Cheney, 1916	6.33
60	Walter Johnson, 1912 ...	6.33
61	Sonny Siebert, 1968	6.33
62	Allie Reynolds, 1943	6.34
63	Roger Clemens, 1986 ...	6.34
64	Willie Mitchell, 1913	6.35
65	Jose DeLeon, 1989	6.36
66	Pascual Perez, 1988	6.37
67	Dave Boswell, 1966	6.38
68	Harry Krause, 1909	6.38
69	Dutch Leonard, 1915 ...	6.38
70	Eddie Cicotte, 1917	6.39
71	Wayne Simpson, 1970 ...	6.39
72	Babe Ruth, 1916	6.40
73	Spec Shea, 1947	6.40
74	Ed Reulbach, 1905	6.41
75	Gaylord Perry, 1974	6.42
76	Eddie Fisher, 1965	6.42
77	Addie Joss, 1908	6.42
78	Mordecai Brown, 1906 ...	6.43
79	Luis Tiant, 1972	6.44
80	Frank Smith, 1908	6.44
81	Dwight Gooden, 1985 ...	6.44
82	Orval Overall, 1909	6.44
83	Sid Fernandez, 1989 ...	6.44
84	Denny McLain, 1968	6.46
85	Mordecai Brown, 1909 ...	6.46
86	Ray Caldwell, 1914	6.46
87	Fred Toney, 1915	6.47
88	Jim McCormick, 1884 ...	6.47
89	Dupee Shaw, 1884	6.47
90	Gary Peters, 1967	6.47
91	Walter Johnson, 1910 ...	6.47
92	Bob Turley, 1954	6.48
93	Ed Walsh, 1909	6.49
94	Guy Hecker, 1882	6.49
95	Frank Smith, 1910	6.49
96	Tom Seaver, 1981	6.49
97	Al Mamaux, 1915	6.51
98	Claude Hendrix, 1914 ...	6.51
	Jim Palmer, 1969	6.51
100	Sam Jones, 1955	6.52

Hits per Game (by era)

1876-1892

1	Tim Keefe, 1880	6.09
2	Charlie Sweeney, 1884	6.23
3	Jim McCormick, 1884	6.47
4	Dupee Shaw, 1884	6.47
5	Guy Hecker, 1882	6.49
6	Tim Keefe, 1888	6.55
7	Adonis Terry, 1888	6.69
8	Silver King, 1888	6.72
9	Tim Keefe, 1885	6.72
10	Frank Knauss, 1890	6.73
11	Ed Seward, 1888	6.73
12	Tony Mullane, 1892	6.77
13	Larry Corcoran, 1880	6.78
14	Mickey Welch, 1885	6.80
15	Cannonball Titcomb, 1888	6.81

1893-1919

1	Ed Reulbach, 1906	5.33
2	Dutch Leonard, 1914	5.57
3	Carl Lundgren, 1907	5.65
4	Russ Ford, 1910	5.83
5	Ed Walsh, 1910	5.89
6	Walter Johnson, 1913	6.03
7	Pete Alexander, 1915	6.05
8	Stan Coveleski, 1917	6.09
9	Mordecai Brown, 1908	6.17
10	Jack Pfiester, 1906	6.21
11	Cy Morgan, 1909	6.26
12	Christy Mathewson, 1909	6.28
13	Art Fromme, 1909	6.28
14	Jack Coombs, 1910	6.32
15	Rube Waddell, 1905	6.33

1920-1941

1	Johnny Vander Meer, 1941	6.84
2	Bob Feller, 1940	6.88
3	Bob Feller, 1939	6.89
4	Hal Schumacher, 1933	6.92
5	Dazzy Vance, 1924	6.94
6	Whit Wyatt, 1941	6.96
7	Bucky Walters, 1939	7.05
8	Johnny Vander Meer, 1938	7.07
9	Bucky Walters, 1940	7.11
10	Lefty Gomez, 1934	7.13
11	Ernie White, 1941	7.24
12	Dazzy Vance, 1928	7.26
13	Bump Hadley, 1931	7.26
14	Dolf Luque, 1920	7.28
15	Bob Feller, 1938	7.29

1942-1960

1	Tommy Byrne, 1949	5.74
2	Herb Score, 1956	5.85
3	Bob Turley, 1957	6.12
4	Bob Turley, 1955	6.13
5	Herb Score, 1955	6.26
6	Allie Reynolds, 1943	6.34
7	Spec Shea, 1947	6.40
8	Bob Turley, 1954	6.48
9	Sam Jones, 1955	6.52
10	Bob Turley, 1958	6.53
11	Hal Newhouser, 1946	6.61
12	Johnny Niggeling, 1943	6.66
13	Don Larsen, 1956	6.66
14	Whitey Ford, 1955	6.67
15	Mort Cooper, 1942	6.69

1961-1990

1	Nolan Ryan, 1972	5.26
2	Luis Tiant, 1968	5.30
3	Sid Fernandez, 1985	5.71
4	Dave McNally, 1968	5.77
5	Sandy Koufax, 1965	5.79
6	Al Downing, 1963	5.84
7	Bob Gibson, 1968	5.85
8	Sam McDowell, 1965	5.87
9	Mike Scott, 1986	5.95
10	Mario Soto, 1980	5.96
11	Floyd Youmans, 1986	5.96
12	Nolan Ryan, 1977	5.96
13	Nolan Ryan, 1974	5.98
14	Nolan Ryan, 1981	5.98
15	Nolan Ryan, 1986	6.02

Home Runs Allowed

1	Bert Blyleven, 1986	50
2	Robin Roberts, 1956	46
	Bert Blyleven, 1987	46
4	Pedro Ramos, 1957	43
5	Denny McLain, 1966	42
6	Robin Roberts, 1955	41
	Phil Niekro, 1979	41
8	Robin Roberts, 1957	40
	Ralph Terry, 1962	40
	Orlando Pena, 1964	40
	Phil Niekro, 1970	40
	Fergie Jenkins, 1979	40
	Jack Morris, 1986	40
14	Murry Dickson, 1948	39
	Pedro Ramos, 1961	39
	Jim Perry, 1971	39
	Jim Hunter, 1973	39
	Jack Morris, 1987	39
19	Warren Hacker, 1955	38
	Pedro Ramos, 1958	38
	Lew Burdette, 1959	38
	Jim Bunning, 1963	38
	Don Sutton, 1970	38
	Mickey Lolich, 1974	38
	Matt Keough, 1982	38
	Floyd Bannister, 1987	38
	Don Sutton, 1987	38
	Curt Young, 1987	38
29	Jim Bunning, 1959	37
	Earl Wilson, 1964	37
	Luis Tiant, 1969	37
	Fergie Jenkins, 1975	37
	Jack Morris, 1982	37
	Dan Petry, 1983	37
	Frank Viola, 1986	37
36	Larry Jansen, 1949	36
	Art Mahaffey, 1962	36
	Pete Richert, 1966	36
	Mickey Lolich, 1971	36
	Eddie Whitson, 1987	36
	Charlie Hough, 1987	36
	Tom Browning, 1988	36
43	Larry Corcoran, 1884	35
	Warren Hacker, 1953	35
	Robin Roberts, 1954	35
	Don Newcombe, 1955	35
	Jim Perry, 1960	35
	Roger Craig, 1962	35
	Robin Roberts, 1963	35
	Sammy Ellis, 1966	35
	Denny McLain, 1967	35
	Fergie Jenkins, 1973	35
	Mickey Lolich, 1973	35
	Mike Caldwell, 1983	35
	Mike Smithson, 1984	35
	Scott McGregor, 1986	35
	Scott Bankhead, 1987	35
	Bruce Hurst, 1987	35
59	Preacher Roe, 1950	34
	Johnny Sain, 1950	34
	Ken Raffensberger, 1950	34
	Robin Roberts, 1959	34
	Paul Foytack, 1959	34
	Juan Marichal, 1962	34
	Dick Ellsworth, 1964	34
	Bill Monbouquette, 1964	34
	Bob Gibson, 1965	34
	Jim Grant, 1965	34
	Earl Wilson, 1967	34
	Jim Hunter, 1969	34
	Mike Cuellar, 1970	34
	Gaylord Perry, 1973	34
	Rick Wise, 1975	34
	Frank Viola, 1983	34
	Danny Darwin, 1985	34
	Scott McGregor, 1985	34
	Ken Schrom, 1986	34
	Don Carman, 1987	34
	Mike Witt, 1987	34
80	Don Newcombe, 1956	33
	Camilo Pascual, 1956	33
	Jim Bunning, 1957	33
	Billy Pierce, 1958	33
	Mike McCormick, 1961	33
	Gene Conley, 1961	33
	Phil Regan, 1963	33
	Phil Ortega, 1965	33
	Jim Merritt, 1969	33
	Lew Krausse, 1970	33
	Jerry Garvin, 1977	33
	Dennis Leonard, 1979	33
	Bill Travers, 1979	33
	Rick Langford, 1982	33
	Ken Dixon, 1986	33
	Bill Gullickson, 1987	33
	Willie Fraser, 1988	33
97	26 players tied	32

Home Runs Allowed (by era)

1876-1892

1	Larry Corcoran, 1884	35
2	Charlie Getzien, 1889	27
3	Bill Hutchinson, 1891	26
4	Charlie Getzien, 1887	24
	John Healy, 1887	24
6	Jim Galvin, 1884	23
	Mark Baldwin, 1887	23
	Lev Shreve, 1888	23
9	Billy Serad, 1884	21
	John Clarkson, 1885	21
	Park Swartzel, 1889	21
	George Cobb, 1892	21
13	8 players tied	20

1893-1919

1	Frank Dwyer, 1894	27
	Jack Stivetts, 1894	27
3	Kid Nichols, 1894	23
4	Harry Staley, 1893	22
	Kid Carsey, 1894	22
6	Ted Breitenstein, 1894	21
7	Jack Stivetts, 1896	20
8	Tom Parrott, 1894	19
	Cy Young, 1894	19
10	Kid Gleason, 1893	18
	Al Orth, 1902	18
12	5 players tied	17

1920-1941

1	Lon Warneke, 1937	32
2	Phil Collins, 1934	30
	Bobo Newsom, 1938	30
4	Ray Kremer, 1930	29
	Lynn Nelson, 1938	29
6	George Earnshaw, 1932	28
	George Earnshaw, 1934	28
8	Roy Mahaffey, 1932	27
	Carl Hubbell, 1935	27
	Luke Hamlin, 1939	27
	Lynn Nelson, 1939	27
	Johnny Marcum, 1939	27
	Freddie Fitzsimmons,	
13	1930	26
	Gordon Rhodes, 1936	26
	Nels Potter, 1939	26

1942-1960

1	Robin Roberts, 1956	46
2	Pedro Ramos, 1957	43
3	Robin Roberts, 1955	41
4	Robin Roberts, 1957	40
5	Murry Dickson, 1948	39
6	Warren Hacker, 1955	38
	Pedro Ramos, 1958	38
	Lew Burdette, 1959	38
9	Jim Bunning, 1959	37
10	Larry Jansen, 1949	36
11	Warren Hacker, 1953	35
	Robin Roberts, 1954	35
	Don Newcombe, 1955	35
	Jim Perry, 1960	35
15	5 players tied	34

1961-1990

1	Bert Blyleven, 1986	50
2	Bert Blyleven, 1987	46
3	Denny McLain, 1966	42
4	Phil Niekro, 1979	41
5	Ralph Terry, 1962	40
	Orlando Pena, 1964	40
	Phil Niekro, 1970	40
	Fergie Jenkins, 1979	40
	Jack Morris, 1986	40
10	Pedro Ramos, 1961	39
	Jim Perry, 1971	39
	Jim Hunter, 1973	39
	Jack Morris, 1987	39
14	7 players tied	38

Walks

1	Amos Rusie, 1890	289
2	Mark Baldwin, 1889	274
3	Amos Rusie, 1892	267
4	Amos Rusie, 1891	262
5	Mark Baldwin, 1890	249
6	Jack Stivetts, 1891	232
7	Mark Baldwin, 1891	227
8	Phil Knell, 1891	226
9	Bob Barr, 1890	219
10	Amos Rusie, 1893	218
11	Cy Seymour, 1898	213
12	Gus Weyhing, 1889	212
13	Ed Crane, 1890	210
14	Bob Feller, 1938	208
15	Toad Ramsey, 1886	207
16	Elton Chamberlain, 1891	206
17	Mike Morrison, 1887	205
18	Henry Gruber, 1890	204
	Nolan Ryan, 1977	204
20	John Clarkson, 1889	203
21	Nolan Ryan, 1974	202
22	Bert Cunningham, 1890	201
23	Amos Rusie, 1894	200
24	Bill Hutchinson, 1890	199
25	Mark Baldwin, 1892	194
	Bob Feller, 1941	194
27	Bobo Newsom, 1938	192
28	Ted Breitenstein, 1894	191
29	Ed Crane, 1892	189
	Tony Mullane, 1893	189
31	Tony Mullane, 1891	187
	Bill Hutchinson, 1892	187
	Kid Gleason, 1893	187
34	Ed Beatin, 1890	186
35	Sam Jones, 1955	185
36	Tom Vickery, 1890	184
37	Nolan Ryan, 1976	183
38	Matt Kilroy, 1886	182
	Frank Killen, 1892	182
40	Willie McGill, 1893	181
	Bob Harmon, 1911	181
	Bob Turley, 1954	181
43	Jack Stivetts, 1890	179
	Gus Weyhing, 1890	179
	Tommy Byrne, 1949	179
46	Bill Hutchinson, 1891	178
	Ted Breitenstein, 1895	178
48	Bob Turley, 1955	177
49	Phenomenal Smith, 1887	176
	George Hemming, 1893	176
51	Silver King, 1892	174
52	Jack Stivetts, 1892	171
	Jouett Meekin, 1894	171
	Ed Stein, 1894	171
	Bump Hadley, 1932	171
56	Elton Chamberlain, 1892	170
	Cy Seymour, 1899	170
58	Willie McGill, 1891	168
	Gus Weyhing, 1892	168
	Brickyard Kennedy, 1893	168
	Elmer Myers, 1916	168
62	Toad Ramsey, 1887	167
	Gus Weyhing, 1887	167
	Darby O'Brien, 1889	167
	Kid Gleason, 1890	167
	Bill Daley, 1890	167
	Bobo Newsom, 1937	167
68	Tony Mullane, 1886	166
	Sadie McMahon, 1890	166
	Phil Knell, 1890	166
	Chick Fraser, 1896	166
72	Elton Chamberlain, 1889	165
	Dan Casey, 1890	165
	Kid Gleason, 1891	165
	John Wyckoff, 1915	165
76	Cy Seymour, 1897	164
	Earl Moore, 1911	164
	Phil Niekro, 1977	164
79	Mickey Welch, 1886	163
	Silver King, 1890	163
	Hank O'Day, 1890	163
	George Haddock, 1892	163
83	Johnny Vander Meer, 1943	162
	Nolan Ryan, 1973	162
85	John Sowders, 1890	161
	Kid Carsey, 1891	161
	Gus Weyhing, 1891	161
88	Tommy Byrne, 1950	160
89	George Hemming, 1894	159
	Amos Rusie, 1895	159
	Marty O'Toole, 1912	159
92	Joe Coleman, 1974	158
93	Matt Kilroy, 1887	157
	Bert Cunningham, 1888	157
	Pink Hawley, 1896	157
	Grover Lowdermilk, 1915	157
	Nolan Ryan, 1972	157
98	5 players tied	156

Fewest Walks/Game (by era)

1876-1892
1 George Zettlein, 1876 .... 0.23
2 Cherokee Fisher, 1876 ... 0.24
3 George Bradley, 1880 .... 0.28
4 Tommy Bond, 1876 ...... 0.29
5 Tommy Bond, 1879 ...... 0.39
6 Bobby Mathews, 1876 .... 0.42
7 Charlie Sweeney, 1884 ... 0.43
8 Guy Hecker, 1882 .... 0.43
9 Dale Williams, 1876....... 0.43
10 Al Spalding, 1876........ 0.44
11 Jim Galvin, 1879 .... 0.47
12 George Bradley, 1879 .... 0.48
13 Sam Weaver, 1878 ...... 0.49
14 Terry Larkin, 1879 ...... 0.53
15 Jim Devlin, 1876 .... 0.54

1893-1919
1 Christy Mathewson, 1913. 0.62
2 Christy Mathewson, 1914. 0.66
3 Cy Young, 1904 .... 0.69
4 Cy Young, 1906 .... 0.78
5 Babe Adams, 1919 ...... 0.79
6 Slim Sallee, 1919 .... 0.79
7 Slim Sallee, 1918 .... 0.82
8 Addie Joss, 1908 .... 0.83
9 Cy Young, 1905 .... 0.84
10 Deacon Phillippe, 1902 ... 0.86
11 Cy Young, 1901 .... 0.90
12 Deacon Phillippe, 1903 ... 0.90
13 Christy Mathewson, 1908. 0.97
14 Christy Mathewson, 1915. 0.97
15 Jesse Tannehill, 1902 .... 0.97

1920-1941
1 Babe Adams, 1920 ...... 0.62
2 Red Lucas, 1933 .... 0.74
3 Babe Adams, 1922 ...... 0.79
4 Pete Alexander, 1923 .... 0.89
5 Babe Adams, 1921 ...... 1.01
6 Paul Derringer, 1939 .... 1.05
7 Carl Hubbell, 1934 ...... 1.06
8 Bill Swift, 1932 .... 1.09
9 Pete Alexander, 1925 .... 1.11
10 Herb Pennock, 1930 .... 1.15
11 Red Lucas, 1932 .... 1.17
12 Pete Alexander, 1921 .... 1.18
13 Watty Clark, 1935 ...... 1.22
14 Pete Donohue, 1926 .... 1.23
15 Pete Alexander, 1922 .... 1.25

1942-1960
1 Tiny Bonham, 1942 ...... 0.96
2 Don Newcombe, 1959.... 1.09
3 Tiny Bonham, 1945 ...... 1.10
4 Lew Burdette, 1960 ...... 1.14
5 Lew Burdette, 1959 ...... 1.18
6 Robin Roberts, 1956 ..... 1.21
7 Robin Roberts, 1959 ..... 1.22
8 Robin Roberts, 1952 ..... 1.23
9 Hal Brown, 1960 .... 1.25
10 Ray Prim, 1945 .... 1.25
11 Robin Roberts, 1960 ..... 1.29
12 Fred Hutchinson, 1951 ... 1.29
13 Ted Lyons, 1942........ 1.30
14 Schoolboy Rowe, 1943 ... 1.31
15 Vern Law, 1960 .... 1.33

1961-1990
1 Lamarr Hoyt, 1985....... 0.86
2 Dennis Eckersley, 1985 ... 1.01
3 Gary Nolan, 1976 .... 1.02
4 Fergie Jenkins, 1971 ..... 1.02
5 Juan Marichal, 1966 ..... 1.05
6 Lamarr Hoyt, 1983 ...... 1.07
7 Lew Burdette, 1961 ...... 1.09
8 Jimmy Key, 1989 .... 1.13
9 Scott McGregor, 1979 ... 1.19
10 Jim Merritt, 1967 .... 1.19
11 Rick Honeycutt, 1981 .... 1.20
12 Vern Law, 1966 .... 1.22
13 Dick Donovan, 1963 ..... 1.22
14 Fritz Peterson, 1968 ..... 1.23
15 Fergie Jenkins, 1974 ..... 1.23

Strikeouts

1 Matt Kilroy, 1886 513
2 Toad Ramsey, 1886 499
3 Hugh Daily, 1884 483
4 Charley Radbourn, 1884.. 441
5 Charlie Buffinton, 1884 ... 417
6 Guy Hecker, 1884 385
7 Nolan Ryan, 1973 383
8 Sandy Koufax, 1965 382
9 Bill Sweeney, 1884 374
10 Jim Galvin, 1884 369
11 Mark Baldwin, 1889...... 368
12 Nolan Ryan, 1974 367
13 Tim Keefe, 1883........ 361
14 Toad Ramsey, 1887 355
15 Rube Waddell, 1904 349
16 Bob Feller, 1946 348
17 Hardie Henderson, 1884.. 346
18 Jim Whitney, 1883 345
   Mickey Welch, 1884...... 345
20 Amos Rusie, 1890 341
   Nolan Ryan, 1977 341
22 Amos Rusie, 1891 337
23 Tim Keefe, 1888........ 333
24 Nolan Ryan, 1972 329
25 Nolan Ryan, 1976 327
26 Ed Morris, 1886 326
27 Tony Mullane, 1884 325
   Sam McDowell, 1965 325
29 Tim Keefe, 1884........ 323
   Lady Baldwin, 1886 323
31 Sandy Koufax, 1966 317
32 Bill Hutchinson, 1892 316
33 Charley Radbourn, 1883.. 315
34 John Clarkson, 1886 313
   Walter Johnson, 1910 313
   J.R. Richard, 1979 313
37 Steve Carlton, 1972...... 310
38 Dupee Shaw, 1884 309
39 Larry McKeon, 1884 308
   John Clarkson, 1885 308
   Mickey Lolich, 1971...... 308
42 Sandy Koufax, 1963 306
   Mike Scott, 1986 306
44 Sam McDowell, 1970 304
45 Walter Johnson, 1912 303
   J.R. Richard, 1978 303
47 Ed Morris, 1884 302
   Rube Waddell, 1903 302
49 Vida Blue, 1971 301
   Nolan Ryan, 1989 301
51 Ed Morris, 1885 298
52 Tim Keefe, 1886........ 291
   Sadie McMahon, 1890 ... 291
   Roger Clemens, 1988 ... 291
55 Bill Hutchinson, 1890 289
   Jack Stivetts, 1890 289
   Tom Seaver, 1971 289
58 Amos Rusie, 1892 288
59 Rube Waddell, 1905 287
60 Jack Lynch, 1884........ 286
   Bobby Mathews, 1884 ... 286
   Bobby Mathews, 1885 ... 286
   Steve Carlton, 1980...... 286
   Steve Carlton, 1982...... 286
65 John Clarkson, 1889 284
66 Dave Foutz, 1886........ 283
   Sam McDowell, 1968 283
   Tom Seaver, 1970 283
69 Denny McLain, 1968 280
70 Jim Galvin, 1883 279
   Sam McDowell, 1969 279
72 Bob Veale, 1965 276
   Dwight Gooden, 1984 ... 276
74 Hal Newhouser, 1946 275
   Steve Carlton, 1983...... 275
76 Bob Gibson, 1970 274
   Fergie Jenkins, 1970 274
   Mario Soto, 1982 274
79 Fergie Jenkins, 1969 273
80 Larry Corcoran, 1884 272
   Mickey Welch, 1886...... 272
   Ed Seward, 1888 272
83 Mickey Lolich, 1969 271
84 Jim Whitney, 1884 270
   Bob Gibson, 1965 270
   Nolan Ryan, 1987 270
87 Ed Walsh, 1908 269
   Sandy Koufax, 1961 269
   Bob Gibson, 1969 269
   Frank Tanana, 1975 269
91 Larry Corcoran, 1880 268
   Bill Wise, 1884 268
   Jim Bunning, 1965 268
   Bob Gibson, 1968 268
   Dwight Gooden, 1985 268
96 Christy Mathewson, 1903. 267
97 Jim Maloney, 1963....... 265
98 Bob Emslie, 1884........ 264
   Luis Tiant, 1968 264
100 3 players tied 263

Strikeouts (by era)

1876-1892
1 Matt Kilroy, 1886 513
2 Toad Ramsey, 1886 499
3 Hugh Daily, 1884 483
4 Charley Radbourn, 1884.. 441
5 Charlie Buffinton, 1884.. 417
6 Guy Hecker, 1884 385
7 Bill Sweeney, 1884 374
8 Jim Galvin, 1884 369
9 Mark Baldwin, 1889...... 368
10 Tim Keefe, 1883........ 361
11 Toad Ramsey, 1887 355
12 Hardie Henderson, 1884.. 346
13 Jim Whitney, 1883 345
   Mickey Welch, 1884...... 345
15 Amos Rusie, 1890 341

1893-1919
1 Rube Waddell, 1904 349
2 Walter Johnson, 1910 313
3 Walter Johnson, 1912 303
4 Rube Waddell, 1903 302
5 Rube Waddell, 1905 287
6 Ed Walsh, 1908 269
7 Christy Mathewson, 1903. 267
8 Christy Mathewson, 1908. 259
9 Ed Walsh, 1910 258
   Joe Wood, 1912 258
11 Ed Walsh, 1911 255
12 Ed Walsh, 1912 254
13 Walter Johnson, 1913.... 243
14 Pete Alexander, 1915 241

1920-1941
1 Dazzy Vance, 1924 262
2 Bob Feller, 1940 261
3 Bob Feller, 1941 260
4 Bob Feller, 1939 246
5 Bob Feller, 1938 240
6 Van Mungo, 1936........ 238
7 Bobo Newsom, 1938..... 226
8 Dazzy Vance, 1925 221
9 Lefty Grove, 1930 209
10 Johnny Vander Meer, 1941 202
11 Dazzy Vance, 1928 200
12 Dizzy Dean, 1933........ 199
13 Dazzy Vance, 1923 197
14 Dizzy Dean, 1934........ 195
   Dizzy Dean, 1936........ 195

1942-1960
1 Bob Feller, 1946 348
2 Hal Newhouser, 1946 275
3 Herb Score, 1956........ 263
4 Don Drysdale, 1960 246
5 Herb Score, 1955........ 245
6 Don Drysdale, 1959 242
7 Sam Jones, 1958 225
8 Hal Newhouser, 1945 212
9 Bob Turley, 1955 210
10 Sam Jones, 1959 209
11 Jim Bunning, 1959 201
   Jim Bunning, 1960....... 201
13 Robin Roberts, 1953 198
   Sam Jones, 1955 198
15 Sandy Koufax, 1960 197

1961-1990
1 Nolan Ryan, 1973 383
2 Sandy Koufax, 1965 382
3 Nolan Ryan, 1974 367
4 Nolan Ryan, 1977 341
5 Nolan Ryan, 1972 329
6 Nolan Ryan, 1976 327
7 Sam McDowell, 1965 325
8 Sandy Koufax, 1966 317
9 J.R. Richard, 1979 313
10 Steve Carlton, 1972...... 310
11 Mickey Lolich, 1971...... 308
12 Sandy Koufax, 1963 306
   Mike Scott, 1986 306
14 Sam McDowell, 1970 304
15 J.R. Richard, 1978 303

Strikeouts per Game

1 Nolan Ryan, 1987 .... 11.48
2 Dwight Gooden, 1984 .... 11.39
3 Nolan Ryan, 1989 .... 11.32
4 Sam McDowell, 1965 .... 10.71
5 Nolan Ryan, 1973 .... 10.57
6 Sandy Koufax, 1962 ..... 10.55
7 Nolan Ryan, 1972 .... 10.43
8 Sam McDowell, 1966 .... 10.42
9 Nolan Ryan, 1976 .... 10.35
10 Nolan Ryan, 1977 .... 10.26
11 Sandy Koufax, 1965 ..... 10.24
12 Nolan Ryan, 1990 .... 10.24
13 Sandy Koufax, 1960 ..... 10.13
14 Mike Scott, 1986 .... 10.00
15 Nolan Ryan, 1978 .... 9.97
16 Nolan Ryan, 1974 .... 9.93
17 Roger Clemens, 1988 ... 9.92
18 David Cone, 1990 .... 9.91
19 J.R. Richard, 1978 ...... 9.90
20 Nolan Ryan, 1986 .... 9.81
21 Herb Score, 1955....... 9.70
22 Nolan Ryan, 1984 .... 9.65
23 J.R. Richard, 1979 ...... 9.64
24 Mario Soto, 1982 .... 9.57
25 Tom Griffin, 1969 ...... 9.56
26 Jim Maloney, 1963....... 9.53
27 Sid Fernandez, 1985 .... 9.51
28 Herb Score, 1956....... 9.49
29 Sandy Koufax, 1961 ..... 9.47
30 Sam McDowell, 1968 .... 9.47
31 Frank Tanana, 1975 ..... 9.41
32 Don Wilson, 1969 .... 9.40
33 Bob Veale, 1965 .... 9.34
34 Nolan Ryan, 1988 .... 9.33
35 Luis Tiant, 1967 .... 9.22
36 Mark Langston, 1986 .... 9.21
37 Luis Tiant, 1968 .... 9.20
38 Dave Boswell, 1966...... 9.19
39 Sam McDowell, 1964 .... 9.19
40 Sonny Siebert, 1965 ..... 9.11
41 Sid Fernandez, 1988 .... 9.10
42 Tom Seaver, 1971 ...... 9.08
43 Sid Fernandez, 1990 .... 9.08
44 Dennis Eckersley, 1976 .. 9.03
45 Nolan Ryan, 1979 ...... 9.01
46 Sandy Koufax, 1964 ..... 9.00
47 Sam McDowell, 1967 .... 8.99
48 Sam McDowell, 1970 .... 8.97
49 Bobby Witt, 1990 .... 8.96
50 Jim Maloney, 1964....... 8.92
51 Mark Langston, 1989 .... 8.92
52 Jose Rijo, 1988 .... 8.89
53 Sandy Koufax, 1963 ..... 8.86
54 Sandy Koufax, 1966 ..... 8.83
55 Sam McDowell, 1969 .... 8.81
56 Dupee Shaw, 1884 ...... 8.81
57 Sid Fernandez, 1986 ..... 8.81
58 Nolan Ryan, 1982 ...... 8.81
59 Tom Seaver, 1970 ...... 8.76
60 Al Downing, 1963 ...... 8.76
61 Bob Moose, 1969 ...... 8.74
62 Steve Carlton, 1983...... 8.73
63 Dwight Gooden, 1985 ... 8.72
64 Steve Carlton, 1982...... 8.71
65 Juan Pizarro, 1961 ..... 8.69
66 Mickey Lolich, 1969 ..... 8.69
67 Vida Blue, 1971 .... 8.68
68 Hugh Daily, 1884 .... 8.68
69 Mark Langston, 1987 .... 8.67
70 Bob Johnson, 1970 ..... 8.66
71 Jim Maloney, 1966....... 8.65
72 Dwight Gooden, 1990 ... 8.63
73 Bruce Hurst, 1986 ...... 8.62
74 Mario Soto, 1980 .... 8.61
75 Jim Maloney, 1965....... 8.60
76 Ramon Martinez, 1990 ... 8.56
77 Tom Seaver, 1972 ...... 8.55
78 Dick Selma, 1969 .... 8.54
79 Bob Veale, 1969 .... 8.49
80 Steve Carlton, 1981...... 8.48
81 Steve Carlton, 1980...... 8.47
82 Mike Scott, 1987 .... 8.47
83 Floyd Bannister, 1985 ... 8.46
84 Hal Newhouser, 1946 .... 8.46
85 Nolan Ryan, 1981 ...... 8.46
86 Nolan Ryan, 1975 ...... 8.45
87 Tom Gordon, 1989 ..... 8.45
88 Bob Feller, 1946 .... 8.43
89 Roger Clemens, 1986 ... 8.43
   Fernando Valenzuela,
90 1981 .... 8.42
91 Ed Correa, 1986........ 8.41
92 Sam Jones, 1956........ 8.40
93 Rube Waddell, 1903 ..... 8.39
94 Nolan Ryan, 1983 .... 8.39
95 Bob Gibson, 1970 ...... 8.39
96 Mickey Lolich, 1965 ..... 8.35
97 Don Sutton, 1966 .... 8.34
98 Jose DeLeon, 1988 ...... 8.31
99 Floyd Youmans, 1986 ... 8.30
100 Jim Bunning, 1965....... 8.29

Strikeouts per Game (by era)

1876-1892
1	Dupee Shaw, 1884	8.81
2	Hugh Daily, 1884	8.68
3	Matt Kilroy, 1886	7.92
4	Charlie Gagus, 1884	7.92
5	John Clarkson, 1884	7.78
6	Toad Ramsey, 1886	7.63
7	Jim Whitney, 1884	7.23
8	Mike Dorgan, 1884	7.17
9	Walter Burke, 1884	7.13
10	Hardie Henderson, 1884	7.09
11	Tim Keefe, 1888	6.90
12	Jim McCormick, 1884	6.90
13	Bob Black, 1884	6.80
14	Lady Baldwin, 1885	6.78
15	Jack Stivetts, 1889	6.71

1893-1919
1	Rube Waddell, 1903	8.39
2	Rube Waddell, 1904	8.20
3	Rube Waddell, 1905	7.86
4	Rube Marquard, 1911	7.68
5	Joe Wood, 1911	7.54
6	Walter Johnson, 1910	7.53
7	Walter Johnson, 1912	7.41
8	Rube Waddell, 1907	7.33
9	Rube Waddell, 1908	7.31
10	Dutch Leonard, 1914	7.05
11	Red Ames, 1906	6.90
12	Rube Waddell, 1902	6.84
13	Red Ames, 1905	6.78
14	Joe Wood, 1912	6.75
15	Orval Overall, 1908	6.68

1920-1941
1	Johnny Vander Meer, 1941	8.03
2	Bob Feller, 1938	7.78
3	Dazzy Vance, 1924	7.64
4	Dazzy Vance, 1925	7.50
5	Bob Feller, 1939	7.46
6	Dazzy Vance, 1926	7.46
7	Bob Feller, 1940	7.33
8	Van Mungo, 1936	6.87
9	Bob Feller, 1941	6.82
10	Van Mungo, 1937	6.82
11	Lefty Grove, 1926	6.77
12	Bill Hallahan, 1930	6.71
13	George Earnshaw, 1928	6.65
14	Red Ruffing, 1932	6.60
15	Lefty Grove, 1930	6.46

1942-1960
1	Sandy Koufax, 1960	10.13
2	Herb Score, 1955	9.70
3	Herb Score, 1956	9.49
4	Hal Newhouser, 1946	8.46
5	Bob Feller, 1946	8.43
6	Sam Jones, 1956	8.40
7	Herb Score, 1959	8.23
8	Don Drysdale, 1960	8.23
9	Sam Jones, 1958	8.10
10	Don Drysdale, 1959	8.05
11	Bob Turley, 1957	7.76
12	Camilo Pascual, 1956	7.73
13	Bob Turley, 1955	7.66
14	Stan Williams, 1960	7.60
15	Sam Jones, 1957	7.59

1961-1990
1	Nolan Ryan, 1987	11.48
2	Dwight Gooden, 1984	11.39
3	Nolan Ryan, 1989	11.32
4	Sam McDowell, 1965	10.71
5	Nolan Ryan, 1973	10.57
6	Sandy Koufax, 1962	10.55
7	Nolan Ryan, 1972	10.43
8	Sam McDowell, 1966	10.42
9	Nolan Ryan, 1976	10.35
10	Nolan Ryan, 1977	10.26
11	Sandy Koufax, 1965	10.24
12	Nolan Ryan, 1990	10.24
13	Mike Scott, 1986	10.00
14	Nolan Ryan, 1978	9.97
15	Nolan Ryan, 1974	9.93

Ratio

1	Guy Hecker, 1882	6.92
2	Jim McCormick, 1884	7.07
3	Walter Johnson, 1913	7.26
4	Charlie Sweeney, 1884	7.31
5	Addie Joss, 1908	7.31
6	Charlie Sweeney, 1884	7.41
7	Christy Mathewson, 1909	7.45
8	Ed Walsh, 1910	7.47
9	Dupee Shaw, 1884	7.53
10	George Bradley, 1880	7.53
11	Tim Keefe, 1880	7.54
12	Christy Mathewson, 1908	7.60
13	Henry Boyle, 1887	7.68
14	Mordecai Brown, 1908	7.72
15	Denny Driscoll, 1882	7.79
16	Cy Young, 1905	7.80
17	Guy Hecker, 1884	7.81
18	Pete Alexander, 1915	7.82
19	Sandy Koufax, 1965	7.83
20	Juan Marichal, 1966	7.88
21	Silver King, 1888	7.88
22	Bob Gibson, 1968	7.89
23	Roger Nelson, 1972	7.89
24	Dave McNally, 1968	7.91
25	Ed Walsh, 1908	7.91
26	Sandy Koufax, 1963	7.96
27	Luis Tiant, 1968	7.98
28	George Bradley, 1876	7.98
29	Jim Whitney, 1884	8.01
30	Mordecai Brown, 1909	8.04
31	Cy Young, 1908	8.07
32	Ed Morris, 1884	8.09
33	Tommy Bond, 1876	8.12
34	Doc White, 1906	8.12
35	Babe Adams, 1919	8.17
36	Russ Ford, 1910	8.17
37	Monte Ward, 1880	8.26
38	Lady Baldwin, 1885	8.28
39	Eddie Cicotte, 1917	8.28
40	Dutch Leonard, 1914	8.29
41	Charley Radbourn, 1884	8.30
42	Denny McLain, 1968	8.30
43	Jim Hunter, 1972	8.32
44	Pete Alexander, 1919	8.35
45	Juan Marichal, 1965	8.35
46	Don Sutton, 1972	8.35
47	Jack Lynch, 1884	8.35
48	Sandy Koufax, 1964	8.35
49	Mike Scott, 1986	8.37
50	Addie Joss, 1906	8.39
51	Christy Mathewson, 1905	8.42
52	Cy Young, 1904	8.43
53	Jack Chesbro, 1904	8.43
54	Tim Keefe, 1888	8.43
55	Larry Corcoran, 1880	8.44
56	Tim Keefe, 1884	8.48
57	Bill Bernhard, 1902	8.48
58	Tim Keefe, 1883	8.49
59	Reb Russell, 1916	8.51
60	Addie Joss, 1903	8.53
61	Mordecai Brown, 1906	8.53
62	Ron Guidry, 1978	8.55
63	Claude Hendrix, 1914	8.55
64	Warren Hacker, 1952	8.56
65	Pete Conway, 1888	8.56
	Barney Pelty, 1906	8.56
67	Bill Burns, 1908	8.56
68	John Clarkson, 1885	8.58
69	Walter Johnson, 1912	8.58
70	Joe Horlen, 1964	8.59
71	Ed Walsh, 1909	8.60
72	Perry Werden, 1884	8.60
73	Chief Bender, 1910	8.60
74	John Tudor, 1985	8.61
75	Charlie Buffinton, 1888	8.61
76	Walter Johnson, 1910	8.61
77	Addie Joss, 1909	8.64
78	Tom Seaver, 1971	8.64
79	Russ Ford, 1914	8.66
80	Ed Morris, 1885	8.67
81	Vida Blue, 1971	8.68
82	Frank Owen, 1904	8.69
83	Lady Baldwin, 1886	8.70
84	Larry Corcoran, 1882	8.70
85	Frank Smith, 1908	8.71
86	Tony Mullane, 1883	8.71
87	Bret Saberhagen, 1989	8.71
88	Christy Mathewson, 1907	8.71
89	Cy Young, 1903	8.72
90	Joe Horlen, 1967	8.72
91	Jim Devlin, 1876	8.73
92	Frank Smith, 1909	8.73
93	Mordecai Brown, 1907	8.73
94	Charlie Getzien, 1884	8.74
95	Cy Young, 1901	8.75
96	Dwight Gooden, 1985	8.75
97	Fred Anderson, 1917	8.78
98	Charlie Ferguson, 1886	8.78
99	Dick Hughes, 1967	8.78
100	Ray Caldwell, 1914	8.79

Earned Run Average

1	Tim Keefe, 1880	0.86
2	Dutch Leonard, 1914	0.96
3	Mordecai Brown, 1906	1.04
4	Bob Gibson, 1968	1.12
5	Christy Mathewson, 1909	1.14
6	Walter Johnson, 1913	1.14
7	Jack Pfiester, 1907	1.15
8	Addie Joss, 1908	1.16
9	Carl Lundgren, 1907	1.17
10	Denny Driscoll, 1882	1.21
11	Pete Alexander, 1915	1.22
12	George Bradley, 1876	1.23
13	Cy Young, 1908	1.26
14	Ed Walsh, 1910	1.27
15	Walter Johnson, 1918	1.27
16	Christy Mathewson, 1905	1.27
17	Guy Hecker, 1882	1.30
18	Jack Coombs, 1910	1.30
19	Mordecai Brown, 1909	1.31
20	Jack Taylor, 1902	1.33
21	Walter Johnson, 1910	1.35
22	George Bradley, 1880	1.38
23	Charley Radbourn, 1884	1.38
24	Mordecai Brown, 1907	1.39
25	Walter Johnson, 1912	1.39
26	Harry Krause, 1909	1.39
27	Ed Walsh, 1909	1.41
28	Ed Walsh, 1908	1.42
29	Ed Reulbach, 1905	1.42
30	Orval Overall, 1909	1.42
31	Christy Mathewson, 1908	1.43
32	Fred Anderson, 1917	1.44
33	Mordecai Brown, 1908	1.47
34	Rube Waddell, 1905	1.48
35	Joe Wood, 1915	1.49
36	Walter Johnson, 1919	1.49
37	Jack Pfiester, 1906	1.51
38	Monte Ward, 1878	1.51
39	Harry McCormick, 1882	1.52
40	Doc White, 1906	1.52
41	George McQuillan, 1908	1.53
42	Dwight Gooden, 1985	1.53
43	Eddie Cicotte, 1917	1.53
44	Will White, 1882	1.54
45	Jim McCormick, 1884	1.54
46	Charlie Sweeney, 1884	1.55
47	Cy Morgan, 1910	1.55
48	Walter Johnson, 1915	1.55
49	Pete Alexander, 1916	1.55
50	Howie Camnitz, 1908	1.56
51	Jim Devlin, 1876	1.56
52	Fred Toney, 1915	1.58
53	Eddie Cicotte, 1913	1.58
54	Rube Marquard, 1916	1.58
55	Tim Keefe, 1885	1.58
56	Chief Bender, 1910	1.58
57	Barney Pelty, 1906	1.59
58	Addie Joss, 1904	1.59
59	Ed Walsh, 1907	1.60
60	Luis Tiant, 1968	1.60
61	Joe McGinnity, 1904	1.61
62	Ray Collins, 1910	1.62
63	Rube Waddell, 1904	1.62
64	Howie Camnitz, 1909	1.62
65	Cy Young, 1901	1.62
66	Spud Chandler, 1943	1.64
67	Ernie Shore, 1915	1.64
68	Walter Johnson, 1908	1.64
69	Silver King, 1888	1.64
70	Ed Summers, 1908	1.64
71	Dean Chance, 1964	1.65
72	Ed Reulbach, 1906	1.65
73	Russ Ford, 1910	1.65
74	Chief Bender, 1909	1.66
75	Sam Leever, 1907	1.66
76	Carl Hubbell, 1933	1.66
77	Mickey Welch, 1885	1.66
78	Candy Cummings, 1876	1.67
79	Joe Wood, 1910	1.68
80	Tommy Bond, 1876	1.68
81	Billy Taylor, 1884	1.68
82	Ned Garvin, 1904	1.68
83	Ed Reulbach, 1907	1.69
84	Claude Hendrix, 1914	1.69
85	Bill Burns, 1908	1.69
86	Nolan Ryan, 1981	1.69
87	Jim McCormick, 1878	1.69
88	Orval Overall, 1907	1.70
89	Rube Foster, 1914	1.70
90	Addie Joss, 1909	1.71
91	Ed Killian, 1909	1.71
92	Walter Johnson, 1914	1.72
93	Doc White, 1909	1.72
94	Bill Doak, 1914	1.72
95	Addie Joss, 1906	1.72
	Pete Alexander, 1919	1.72
97	Sandy Koufax, 1966	1.73
98	Bob Ewing, 1907	1.73
99	Vic Willis, 1906	1.73
100	Sandy Koufax, 1964	1.74

Earned Run Average (by era)

1876-1892
1	Tim Keefe, 1880	0.86
2	Denny Driscoll, 1882	1.21
3	George Bradley, 1876	1.23
4	Guy Hecker, 1882	1.30
5	George Bradley, 1880	1.38
6	Charley Radbourn, 1884	1.38
7	Monte Ward, 1878	1.51
8	Harry McCormick, 1882	1.52
9	Will White, 1882	1.54
10	Jim McCormick, 1884	1.54
11	Charlie Sweeney, 1884	1.55
12	Jim Devlin, 1876	1.56
13	Tim Keefe, 1885	1.58
14	Silver King, 1888	1.64
15	Mickey Welch, 1885	1.66

1893-1919
1	Dutch Leonard, 1914	0.96
2	Mordecai Brown, 1906	1.04
3	Christy Mathewson, 1909	1.14
4	Walter Johnson, 1913	1.14
5	Jack Pfiester, 1907	1.15
6	Addie Joss, 1908	1.16
7	Carl Lundgren, 1907	1.17
8	Pete Alexander, 1915	1.22
9	Cy Young, 1908	1.26
10	Ed Walsh, 1910	1.27
11	Walter Johnson, 1918	1.27
12	Christy Mathewson, 1905	1.27
13	Jack Coombs, 1910	1.30
14	Mordecai Brown, 1909	1.31
15	Jack Taylor, 1902	1.33

1920-1941
1	Carl Hubbell, 1933	1.66
2	Pete Alexander, 1920	1.91
3	Dolf Luque, 1923	1.93
4	Lon Warneke, 1933	2.00
5	Lefty Grove, 1931	2.06
6	Dazzy Vance, 1928	2.09
7	Babe Adams, 1920	2.16
8	Hal Schumacher, 1933	2.16
9	Dazzy Vance, 1924	2.16
10	Burleigh Grimes, 1920	2.22
11	Elmer Riddle, 1941	2.24
12	Bill Walker, 1931	2.26
13	Wilcy Moore, 1927	2.28
14	Bucky Walters, 1939	2.29
15	Carl Hubbell, 1934	2.30

1942-1960
1	Spud Chandler, 1943	1.64
2	Mort Cooper, 1942	1.78
3	Hal Newhouser, 1945	1.81
4	Max Lanier, 1943	1.90
5	Hal Newhouser, 1946	1.94
6	Billy Pierce, 1955	1.97
7	Whitey Ford, 1958	2.01
8	Al Benton, 1945	2.02
9	Allie Reynolds, 1952	2.06
10	Ted Lyons, 1942	2.10
11	Howie Pollet, 1946	2.10
12	Spud Chandler, 1946	2.10
13	Warren Spahn, 1953	2.10
14	Dizzy Trout, 1944	2.12
15	Roger Wolff, 1945	2.12

1961-1990
1	Bob Gibson, 1968	1.12
2	Dwight Gooden, 1985	1.53
3	Luis Tiant, 1968	1.60
4	Dean Chance, 1964	1.65
5	Nolan Ryan, 1981	1.69
6	Sandy Koufax, 1966	1.73
7	Sandy Koufax, 1964	1.74
8	Ron Guidry, 1978	1.74
9	Tom Seaver, 1971	1.76
10	Sam McDowell, 1968	1.81
11	Vida Blue, 1971	1.82
12	Phil Niekro, 1967	1.87
13	Joe Horlen, 1964	1.88
14	Sandy Koufax, 1963	1.88
15	Luis Tiant, 1972	1.91

Adjusted Earned Run Average

1	Tim Keefe, 1880	294
2	Dutch Leonard, 1914	280
3	Bob Gibson, 1968	258
4	Walter Johnson, 1913	258
5	Mordecai Brown, 1906	255
6	Walter Johnson, 1912	239
7	Christy Mathewson, 1905	230
8	Dwight Gooden, 1985	226
9	Pete Alexander, 1915	225
10	Christy Mathewson, 1909	224
11	Lefty Grove, 1931	218
12	Cy Young, 1901	217
13	Jack Pfiester, 1907	216
14	Denny Driscoll, 1882	216
15	Walter Johnson, 1919	216
16	Walter Johnson, 1918	214
17	Carl Lundgren, 1907	213
18	Roger Clemens, 1990	211
19	Ed Reulbach, 1905	210
20	Ron Guidry, 1978	208
21	Addie Joss, 1908	206
22	Charley Radbourn, 1884	205
23	Jim McCormick, 1884	205
24	Jack Taylor, 1902	203
25	Billy Pierce, 1955	201
26	Dolf Luque, 1923	200
27	Dean Chance, 1964	199
28	Silver King, 1888	198
29	Spud Chandler, 1943	197
30	Al Maul, 1895	196
31	Cy Young, 1908	195
32	Nolan Ryan, 1981	195
33	Hal Newhouser, 1945	194
34	Mordecai Brown, 1909	194
35	Tom Seaver, 1971	194
36	Carl Hubbell, 1933	193
37	Mort Cooper, 1942	193
38	Monty Stratton, 1937	191
39	Lefty Gomez, 1937	191
40	Sandy Koufax, 1966	191
41	Ed Siever, 1902	191
42	Clark Griffith, 1898	191
43	Dazzy Vance, 1928	190
44	Guy Hecker, 1882	190
45	Vean Gregg, 1911	189
46	Lefty Grove, 1936	189
47	Ed Walsh, 1910	189
48	Amos Rusie, 1894	189
49	Walter Johnson, 1915	189
50	Hal Newhouser, 1946	189
51	Dazzy Vance, 1930	188
52	Billy Rhines, 1896	188
53	Wilbur Wood, 1971	188
54	Jack Stivetts, 1889	188
55	Joe Wood, 1915	187
56	Warren Spahn, 1953	187
57	Sandy Koufax, 1964	187
58	Lefty Grove, 1939	186
59	Eddie Cicotte, 1913	185
60	Walter Johnson, 1910	185
61	Luis Tiant, 1968	185
62	Lefty Grove, 1930	184
63	Hank Aguirre, 1962	184
64	Joe Horlen, 1964	184
65	Vida Blue, 1971	183
66	John Tudor, 1985	183
67	Harry Brecheen, 1948	183
68	Charlie Sweeney, 1884	183
69	Jack Coombs, 1910	183
70	Billy Rhines, 1890	182
71	Steve Carlton, 1972	182
72	Fred Toney, 1915	182
73	Russ Ford, 1914	181
74	Johnny Allen, 1937	181
75	Rube Waddell, 1905	180
76	Mordecai Brown, 1907	180
77	Orval Overall, 1909	179
78	Rube Waddell, 1902	179
79	Bret Saberhagen, 1989	178
80	Joe Wood, 1912	178
81	Phil Niekro, 1967	178
82	Max Lanier, 1943	177
83	Fred Anderson, 1917	177
84	Billy Taylor, 1884	177
85	Cy Young, 1892	176
86	Johnny Antonelli, 1954	176
87	Whitey Ford, 1958	176
88	Lefty Grove, 1935	176
89	Jack Pfiester, 1906	175
90	Harry McCormick, 1882	175
91	Eddie Cicotte, 1919	175
92	Claude Hendrix, 1914	175
93	Mel Harder, 1934	174
94	Lefty Gomez, 1934	174
95	George Bradley, 1876	174
96	Al Benton, 1945	174
97	Tom Seaver, 1973	174
98	Jim Devlin, 1876	174
99	Eddie Cicotte, 1917	174
100	Dazzy Vance, 1924	174

Adjusted ERA (by era)

1876-1892

1	Tim Keefe, 1880	294
2	Denny Driscoll, 1882	216
3	Charley Radbourn, 1884	205
4	Jim McCormick, 1884	205
5	Silver King, 1888	198
6	Guy Hecker, 1882	190
7	Jack Stivetts, 1889	188
8	Charlie Sweeney, 1884	183
9	Billy Rhines, 1890	182
10	Billy Taylor, 1884	177
11	Cy Young, 1892	176
12	Harry McCormick, 1882	175
13	George Bradley, 1876	174
14	Jim Devlin, 1876	174
15	Will White, 1882	173

1893-1919

1	Dutch Leonard, 1914	280
2	Walter Johnson, 1913	258
3	Mordecai Brown, 1906	255
4	Walter Johnson, 1912	239
5	Christy Mathewson, 1905	230
6	Pete Alexander, 1915	225
7	Christy Mathewson, 1909	224
8	Cy Young, 1901	217
9	Jack Pfiester, 1907	216
10	Walter Johnson, 1919	216
11	Walter Johnson, 1918	214
12	Carl Lundgren, 1907	213
13	Ed Reulbach, 1905	210
14	Addie Joss, 1908	206
15	Jack Taylor, 1902	203

1920-1941

1	Lefty Grove, 1931	218
2	Dolf Luque, 1923	200
3	Carl Hubbell, 1933	193
4	Monty Stratton, 1937	191
5	Lefty Gomez, 1937	191
6	Dazzy Vance, 1928	190
7	Lefty Grove, 1936	189
8	Dazzy Vance, 1930	188
9	Lefty Grove, 1939	186
10	Lefty Grove, 1930	184
11	Johnny Allen, 1937	181
12	Lefty Grove, 1935	176
13	Mel Harder, 1934	174
14	Lefty Gomez, 1934	174
15	Dazzy Vance, 1924	174

1942-1960

1	Billy Pierce, 1955	201
2	Spud Chandler, 1943	197
3	Hal Newhouser, 1945	194
4	Mort Cooper, 1942	193
5	Hal Newhouser, 1946	189
6	Warren Spahn, 1953	187
7	Harry Brecheen, 1948	183
8	Max Lanier, 1943	177
9	Johnny Antonelli, 1954	176
10	Whitey Ford, 1958	176
11	Al Benton, 1945	174
12	Hoyt Wilhelm, 1959	173
13	Ted Lyons, 1942	172

1961-1990

1	Bob Gibson, 1968	258
2	Dwight Gooden, 1985	226
3	Roger Clemens, 1990	211
4	Ron Guidry, 1978	208
5	Dean Chance, 1964	199
6	Nolan Ryan, 1981	195
7	Tom Seaver, 1971	194
8	Sandy Koufax, 1966	191
9	Wilbur Wood, 1971	188
10	Sandy Koufax, 1964	187
11	Luis Tiant, 1968	185
12	Hank Aguirre, 1962	184
13	Joe Horlen, 1964	184
14	Vida Blue, 1971	183
15	John Tudor, 1985	183

Pitching Runs

1	Amos Rusie, 1894	125.7
2	Charley Radbourn, 1884	120.6
3	Guy Hecker, 1884	108.0
4	Silver King, 1888	92.3
5	John Clarkson, 1889	89.2
6	Cy Young, 1901	84.2
7	Matt Kilroy, 1887	80.4
8	Pink Hawley, 1895	79.1
9	Silver King, 1890	78.9
10	Walter Johnson, 1912	78.7
11	Will White, 1883	77.7
12	Amos Rusie, 1893	77.1
13	Charley Radbourn, 1883	76.4
14	Dave Foutz, 1886	75.4
15	Lefty Grove, 1931	74.5
16	Dolf Luque, 1923	74.2
17	Jouett Meekin, 1894	73.9
18	Scott Stratton, 1890	72.3
19	Billy Rhines, 1890	71.7
20	Lefty Gomez, 1937	70.9
21	Jim Galvin, 1884	69.6
22	George Bradley, 1876	68.9
23	Walter Johnson, 1913	68.8
24	Cy Young, 1892	68.5
25	Kid Nichols, 1897	68.4
26	Lefty Grove, 1930	68.4
27	Dazzy Vance, 1930	67.9
28	Lefty Gomez, 1934	67.7
29	Elmer Smith, 1887	67.6
30	Sandy Koufax, 1966	67.5
31	John Clarkson, 1885	67.0
32	Red Faber, 1921	66.4
33	Toad Ramsey, 1886	65.9
34	Christy Mathewson, 1905	65.1
35	Warren Spahn, 1953	64.5
36	Pete Alexander, 1915	64.1
37	Ted Breitenstein, 1893	63.6
38	Kid Nichols, 1898	63.5
39	Amos Rusie, 1897	63.5
40	Kid Nichols, 1896	63.5
41	Dwight Gooden, 1985	63.4
42	Bob Gibson, 1968	63.1
43	Bob Caruthers, 1885	63.1
44	Bob Feller, 1940	63.0
45	Mickey Welch, 1885	63.0
46	Lefty Grove, 1936	62.8
47	Cy Young, 1894	62.7
48	Kid Nichols, 1890	62.7
49	Clark Griffith, 1898	62.6
50	Cy Young, 1895	62.5
51	Ed Morris, 1886	62.1
52	Ron Guidry, 1978	61.4
53	Cy Young, 1893	61.3
54	Carl Hubbell, 1934	61.3
55	Will White, 1882	61.3
56	Dean Chance, 1964	61.1
57	Tim Keefe, 1883	61.1
58	Claude Hendrix, 1914	61.0
59	Amos Rusie, 1890	61.0
60	Cy Young, 1902	60.8
61	Jim Palmer, 1975	60.6
62	Ed Seward, 1888	60.5
63	Thornton Lee, 1941	59.4
64	Dazzy Vance, 1928	59.2
65	Robin Roberts, 1953	59.1
66	Dazzy Vance, 1924	58.6
67	Charlie Ferguson, 1886	58.3
68	Bob Feller, 1939	58.3
69	Win Mercer, 1894	58.0
70	Lady Baldwin, 1886	57.9
71	Bucky Walters, 1939	57.8
72	Kid Nichols, 1895	57.8
73	Carl Hubbell, 1936	57.8
74	Ed Morris, 1885	57.7
75	Bill Hutchinson, 1890	57.5
76	Jesse Duryea, 1889	57.5
77	Carl Hubbell, 1933	57.5
78	Wilbur Wood, 1971	57.4
79	Guy Hecker, 1885	57.2
80	Tony Mullane, 1883	57.0
81	Vida Blue, 1971	57.0
82	Steve Carlton, 1972	56.9
83	John Clarkson, 1887	56.2
84	Walter Johnson, 1919	56.1
85	Sandy Koufax, 1965	56.0
86	Warren Spahn, 1947	55.7
87	Bill Hoffer, 1895	54.9
88	Tim Keefe, 1885	54.6
89	Bob Feller, 1946	54.5
90	Kid Nichols, 1893	54.5
91	Walter Johnson, 1918	54.3
92	Tom Seaver, 1971	54.3
93	Charlie Buffinton, 1884	54.2
94	Hal Newhouser, 1945	54.2
95	Joe Wood, 1912	53.9
96	Toad Ramsey, 1887	53.8
97	Mel Harder, 1934	53.6
98	Matt Kilroy, 1889	53.6
99	Red Ehret, 1890	53.4
100	Lefty Grove, 1932	53.2

Adjusted Pitching Runs

1	Amos Rusie, 1894	121.7
2	Charley Radbourn, 1884	109.3
3	Silver King, 1888	105.2
4	John Clarkson, 1889	99.5
5	Guy Hecker, 1884	95.0
6	Silver King, 1890	84.5
7	John Clarkson, 1885	82.0
8	Jim Galvin, 1884	80.5
9	John Clarkson, 1887	80.2
10	Jim Devlin, 1876	79.8
11	Walter Johnson, 1912	79.3
12	Cy Young, 1901	78.6
13	Toad Ramsey, 1886	78.5
14	Lefty Grove, 1931	78.2
15	Amos Rusie, 1893	76.6
16	Will White, 1883	75.4
17	Kid Nichols, 1897	74.9
18	Dave Foutz, 1886	74.8
19	Cy Young, 1892	73.7
20	Charley Radbourn, 1883	72.7
21	Cy Young, 1893	71.6
22	Scott Stratton, 1890	71.4
23	Kid Nichols, 1895	71.3
24	Billy Rhines, 1890	71.3
25	Kid Nichols, 1890	71.3
26	Cy Young, 1895	70.9
27	Kid Nichols, 1896	70.9
28	Lefty Grove, 1936	70.6
29	Jouett Meekin, 1894	70.3
30	Walter Johnson, 1913	69.5
31	Dolf Luque, 1923	69.3
32	Lefty Grove, 1930	69.1
33	Cy Young, 1894	69.0
34	Elmer Smith, 1887	68.4
35	Matt Kilroy, 1887	67.4
36	Kid Nichols, 1893	67.3
37	Kid Nichols, 1898	67.3
38	Tony Mullane, 1883	66.8
39	Ted Breitenstein, 1893	66.3
40	Pink Hawley, 1895	66.2
41	Dazzy Vance, 1930	66.0
42	Jack Stivetts, 1891	65.7
43	Lefty Gomez, 1937	65.5
44	Jim Devlin, 1877	65.4
45	Bob Caruthers, 1885	64.8
46	Red Faber, 1921	64.6
47	John Clarkson, 1886	63.7
48	Pete Alexander, 1915	63.7
49	Bill Hutchinson, 1890	63.5
50	Vic Willis, 1899	63.4
51	Tim Keefe, 1883	62.7
52	Christy Mathewson, 1905	62.4
53	Wilbur Wood, 1971	62.2
54	Steve Carlton, 1972	62.2
55	Lefty Grove, 1935	61.9
56	Clark Griffith, 1898	61.6
57	Cy Young, 1902	60.8
58	Bob Gibson, 1968	60.0
59	Kid Nichols, 1891	60.0
60	Cy Young, 1896	59.9
61	Toad Ramsey, 1887	59.7
62	Jesse Duryea, 1889	59.7
63	Will White, 1882	59.7
64	Hal Newhouser, 1945	59.4
65	Dwight Gooden, 1985	59.2
66	Elton Chamberlain, 1889	59.0
67	Matt Kilroy, 1889	58.7
68	Dazzy Vance, 1928	58.7
69	Dan Casey, 1887	58.4
70	Ed Morris, 1886	58.2
71	Lady Baldwin, 1886	58.1
72	Amos Rusie, 1897	57.9
73	Charlie Ferguson, 1886	57.9
74	George Bradley, 1876	57.9
75	Mark Baldwin, 1890	57.8
76	Thornton Lee, 1941	57.7
77	Cy Young, 1899	57.3
78	Ron Guidry, 1978	57.1
79	Bob Feller, 1940	57.1
80	Kid Gleason, 1890	57.0
81	Amos Rusie, 1890	56.9
82	Joe Wood, 1912	56.9
83	Nig Cuppy, 1895	56.7
84	Dizzy Trout, 1944	56.6
85	Bobo Newsom, 1940	56.5
86	Nig Cuppy, 1896	56.5
87	Sandy Koufax, 1966	56.3
88	Ed Seward, 1888	56.2
89	Robin Roberts, 1953	56.1
90	Tony Mullane, 1884	56.1
91	Guy Hecker, 1885	56.0
92	Win Mercer, 1894	55.8
93	Hal Newhouser, 1946	55.8
94	Ed Morris, 1885	55.8
95	Walter Johnson, 1919	55.5
96	Silver King, 1889	55.1
97	Mel Harder, 1934	55.0
98	Bucky Walters, 1939	54.8
99	Mickey Welch, 1885	54.7
100	Lefty Grove, 1932	54.6

Pitching Wins

#		
1	Charley Radbourn, 1884	10.8
2	Guy Hecker, 1884	9.9
3	Amos Rusie, 1894	9.6
4	Silver King, 1888	8.5
5	Walter Johnson, 1912	7.9
6	John Clarkson, 1889	7.7
7	Cy Young, 1901	7.6
8	Walter Johnson, 1913	7.3
9	Bob Gibson, 1968	7.2
10	Dolf Luque, 1923	7.1
11	Pete Alexander, 1915	7.1
12	Sandy Koufax, 1966	7.1
13	Lefty Grove, 1931	6.9
14	Will White, 1883	6.8
15	Christy Mathewson, 1905	6.8
16	Charley Radbourn, 1883	6.7
17	Dwight Gooden, 1985	6.7
18	Dave Foutz, 1886	6.6
19	Lefty Gomez, 1937	6.5
20	Matt Kilroy, 1887	6.5
21	Dean Chance, 1964	6.4
22	Pink Hawley, 1895	6.4
23	Billy Rhines, 1890	6.4
24	Scott Stratton, 1890	6.4
25	Cy Young, 1892	6.3
26	Claude Hendrix, 1914	6.3
27	Ron Guidry, 1978	6.3
28	Amos Rusie, 1893	6.3
29	John Clarkson, 1885	6.3
30	Lefty Gomez, 1934	6.3
31	Silver King, 1890	6.3
32	Jim Galvin, 1884	6.2
33	Warren Spahn, 1953	6.2
34	Red Faber, 1921	6.2
35	Jim Palmer, 1975	6.2
36	Lefty Grove, 1930	6.2
37	Wilbur Wood, 1971	6.2
38	Vida Blue, 1971	6.1
39	Steve Carlton, 1972	6.1
40	Carl Hubbell, 1933	6.1
41	George Bradley, 1876	6.1
42	Walter Johnson, 1918	6.1
43	Dazzy Vance, 1930	6.0
44	Carl Hubbell, 1934	6.0
45	Bob Feller, 1940	5.9
46	Kid Nichols, 1898	5.9
47	Mickey Welch, 1885	5.9
48	Sandy Koufax, 1965	5.9
49	Walter Johnson, 1919	5.9
50	Kid Nichols, 1897	5.9
51	Clark Griffith, 1898	5.8
52	Tom Seaver, 1971	5.8
53	Dazzy Vance, 1924	5.8
54	Hal Newhouser, 1945	5.8
55	Bucky Walters, 1939	5.8
56	Dazzy Vance, 1928	5.8
57	Toad Ramsey, 1886	5.8
58	Cy Young, 1902	5.8
59	Thornton Lee, 1941	5.8
60	Ed Walsh, 1908	5.8
61	Ed Walsh, 1910	5.7
62	Bob Feller, 1946	5.7
63	Robin Roberts, 1953	5.7
64	Bob Caruthers, 1885	5.7
65	Jouett Meekin, 1894	5.7
66	Carl Hubbell, 1936	5.6
67	Will White, 1882	5.6
68	Ed Seward, 1888	5.6
69	Kid Nichols, 1890	5.6
70	Lefty Grove, 1936	5.5
71	Jack Taylor, 1902	5.5
72	Walter Johnson, 1915	5.5
73	Warren Spahn, 1947	5.5
74	Elmer Smith, 1887	5.5
75	Mordecai Brown, 1906	5.5
76	Ed Morris, 1886	5.4
77	Amos Rusie, 1897	5.4
78	Mordecai Brown, 1909	5.4
79	Amos Rusie, 1890	5.4
80	Walter Johnson, 1910	5.4
81	Joe McGinnity, 1904	5.4
82	Joe Wood, 1912	5.4
83	Dizzy Trout, 1944	5.4
84	Kid Nichols, 1896	5.4
85	Tim Keefe, 1883	5.4
86	Bob Feller, 1939	5.4
87	Ed Reulbach, 1905	5.3
88	Hal Newhouser, 1946	5.3
89	John Tudor, 1985	5.3
90	Jack Coombs, 1910	5.3
91	Tom Seaver, 1973	5.3
92	Pete Alexander, 1920	5.3
93	Charlie Ferguson, 1886	5.3
94	Sandy Koufax, 1963	5.3
95	Pete Alexander, 1916	5.3
96	Lady Baldwin, 1886	5.2
97	Juan Marichal, 1969	5.2
98	Ted Breitenstein, 1893	5.2
99	Ed Morris, 1885	5.2
100	Bob Gibson, 1969	5.2

Adjusted Pitching Wins

#		
1	Charley Radbourn, 1884	9.8
2	Silver King, 1888	9.7
3	Amos Rusie, 1894	9.3
4	Guy Hecker, 1884	8.7
5	John Clarkson, 1889	8.6
6	Walter Johnson, 1912	7.9
7	John Clarkson, 1885	7.7
8	Walter Johnson, 1913	7.4
9	Lefty Grove, 1931	7.3
10	Jim Galvin, 1884	7.2
11	Cy Young, 1901	7.1
12	Pete Alexander, 1915	7.1
13	Jim Devlin, 1876	7.0
14	Bob Gibson, 1968	6.9
15	Toad Ramsey, 1886	6.9
16	Cy Young, 1892	6.8
17	John Clarkson, 1887	6.8
18	Silver King, 1890	6.7
19	Wilbur Wood, 1971	6.7
20	Steve Carlton, 1972	6.7
21	Dolf Luque, 1923	6.7
22	Will White, 1883	6.6
23	Dave Foutz, 1886	6.6
24	Christy Mathewson, 1905	6.5
25	Kid Nichols, 1897	6.4
26	Hal Newhouser, 1945	6.4
27	Charley Radbourn, 1883	6.3
28	Billy Rhines, 1890	6.3
29	Kid Nichols, 1890	6.3
30	Kid Nichols, 1893	6.3
31	Scott Stratton, 1890	6.3
32	Amos Rusie, 1893	6.3
33	Lefty Grove, 1930	6.3
34	Lefty Grove, 1936	6.2
35	Dwight Gooden, 1985	6.2
36	Red Faber, 1921	6.0
37	Kid Nichols, 1896	6.0
38	Lefty Gomez, 1937	6.0
39	Dizzy Trout, 1944	6.0
40	Sandy Koufax, 1966	5.9
41	Tony Mullane, 1883	5.9
42	Ron Guidry, 1978	5.9
43	Cy Young, 1893	5.9
44	Walter Johnson, 1918	5.9
45	Hal Newhouser, 1946	5.8
46	Bob Caruthers, 1885	5.8
47	Dazzy Vance, 1930	5.8
48	Jim Devlin, 1877	5.8
49	Walter Johnson, 1919	5.8
50	Lefty Grove, 1935	5.8
51	Kid Nichols, 1895	5.8
52	John Clarkson, 1886	5.8
53	Cy Young, 1902	5.8
54	Clark Griffith, 1898	5.8
55	Vic Willis, 1899	5.7
56	Cy Young, 1895	5.7
57	Dazzy Vance, 1928	5.7
58	Joe Wood, 1912	5.7
59	Jack Stivetts, 1891	5.7
60	Vida Blue, 1971	5.7
61	Bill Hutchinson, 1890	5.6
62	Gaylord Perry, 1972	5.6
63	Carl Hubbell, 1933	5.6
64	Tom Seaver, 1971	5.6
65	Pete Alexander, 1920	5.6
66	Thornton Lee, 1941	5.6
67	Elmer Smith, 1887	5.5
68	Roger Clemens, 1990	5.5
69	Kid Nichols, 1893	5.5
70	Tim Keefe, 1883	5.5
71	Mordecai Brown, 1906	5.5
72	Bucky Walters, 1939	5.5
73	Will White, 1882	5.5
74	Mort Cooper, 1942	5.5
75	Walter Johnson, 1915	5.5
76	Matt Kilroy, 1887	5.5
77	Cy Falkenberg, 1914	5.4
78	Pete Alexander, 1916	5.4
79	Ted Breitenstein, 1893	5.4
80	Dazzy Vance, 1924	5.4
81	Robin Roberts, 1953	5.4
82	Bob Feller, 1940	5.4
83	Jouett Meekin, 1894	5.4
84	Bill Hands, 1969	5.4
85	Kid Nichols, 1891	5.4
86	Pink Hawley, 1895	5.4
87	Joe McGinnity, 1904	5.3
88	Bobo Newsom, 1940	5.3
89	Dean Chance, 1964	5.3
90	Carl Hubbell, 1934	5.3
91	Bert Blyleven, 1973	5.3
92	Dizzy Dean, 1934	5.3
93	Cy Young, 1894	5.3
94	Ed Walsh, 1908	5.3
95	Walter Johnson, 1913	5.3
96	Claude Hendrix, 1914	5.3
97	Ed Reulbach, 1905	5.3
98	Curt Davis, 1934	5.3
99	Lady Baldwin, 1886	5.3
100	Charlie Ferguson, 1886	5.2

Opponents' Batting Average

#		
1	Luis Tiant, 1968	.168
2	Nolan Ryan, 1972	.171
3	Ed Reulbach, 1906	.175
4	Sandy Koufax, 1965	.179
5	Dutch Leonard, 1914	.180
6	Sid Fernandez, 1985	.181
7	Tim Keefe, 1880	.182
8	Dave McNally, 1968	.182
9	Tommy Byrne, 1949	.183
10	Al Downing, 1963	.184
11	Bob Gibson, 1968	.184
12	Charlie Sweeney, 1884	.185
13	Sam McDowell, 1965	.185
14	Carl Lundgren, 1907	.185
15	Herb Score, 1956	.186
16	Mike Scott, 1986	.186
17	Nolan Ryan, 1989	.187
18	Ed Walsh, 1910	.187
19	Mario Soto, 1980	.187
20	Walter Johnson, 1913	.187
21	Nolan Ryan, 1981	.188
22	Russ Ford, 1910	.188
23	Nolan Ryan, 1986	.188
24	Jim McCormick, 1884	.188
25	Dupee Shaw, 1884	.188
26	Nolan Ryan, 1990	.188
27	Guy Hecker, 1882	.188
28	Floyd Youmans, 1986	.188
29	Sam McDowell, 1966	.188
30	Sandy Koufax, 1963	.189
31	Sam McDowell, 1968	.189
32	Don Sutton, 1972	.189
33	Jim Hunter, 1972	.189
34	Vida Blue, 1971	.189
35	Nolan Ryan, 1974	.190
36	Andy Messersmith, 1969	.190
37	Joe Horlen, 1964	.190
38	Sid Fernandez, 1988	.191
39	Pete Alexander, 1915	.191
40	Sandy Koufax, 1964	.191
41	Jim Bibby, 1973	.192
42	Bob Turley, 1955	.193
43	Nolan Ryan, 1977	.193
44	Fred Beebe, 1908	.193
45	Ron Guidry, 1978	.193
46	Stan Coveleski, 1917	.194
47	Bob Turley, 1957	.194
48	Herb Score, 1955	.194
49	Jack Pfiester, 1906	.194
50	Mordecai Brown, 1908	.195
51	Nolan Ryan, 1976	.195
52	Nolan Ryan, 1983	.195
53	Dean Chance, 1964	.195
54	Roger Clemens, 1986	.195
55	Tim Keefe, 1888	.196
56	Walter Johnson, 1912	.196
57	Roger Nelson, 1972	.196
58	J.R. Richard, 1978	.196
59	Pascual Perez, 1988	.196
60	Jeff Robinson, 1988	.197
61	Jose DeLeon, 1989	.197
62	Dave Boswell, 1966	.197
63	Sandy Koufax, 1962	.197
64	Charlie Sweeney, 1884	.197
65	Addie Joss, 1908	.197
66	Sonny Siebert, 1968	.198
67	Sid Fernandez, 1989	.198
68	Tim Keefe, 1885	.198
69	Larry Cheney, 1916	.198
70	Wayne Simpson, 1970	.198
71	Larry Corcoran, 1880	.198
72	Orval Overall, 1909	.198
73	Gary Peters, 1967	.199
74	Jeff Tesreau, 1912	.199
75	Willie Mitchell, 1913	.199
76	Rube Waddell, 1905	.199
77	Adonis Terry, 1888	.199
78	Nolan Ryan, 1987	.199
79	Mordecai Brown, 1904	.199
80	Christy Mathewson, 1909	.200
81	Denny McLain, 1968	.200
82	Mickey Welch, 1885	.200
83	Bobby Bolin, 1968	.200
	Jim Palmer, 1969	.200
	Sid Fernandez, 1990	.200
86	Silver King, 1888	.200
87	Christy Mathewson, 1908	.200
88	Spec Shea, 1947	.200
89	Ed Seward, 1888	.200
90	Toad Ramsey, 1886	.201
91	Tony Mullane, 1892	.201
92	Art Fromme, 1909	.201
93	Babe Ruth, 1916	.201
94	Dwight Gooden, 1985	.201
95	Hal Newhouser, 1946	.201
96	Ed Reulbach, 1905	.201
97	Jack Coombs, 1910	.201
98	Frank Knauss, 1890	.201
99	Dwight Gooden, 1984	.202
100	Jim Maloney, 1963	.202

Opponents' On Base Pctg.

#		
1	Guy Hecker, 1882	.198
2	Jim McCormick, 1884	.202
3	Charlie Sweeney, 1884	.207
4	Dupee Shaw, 1884	.212
5	Charlie Sweeney, 1884	.212
6	Henry Boyle, 1884	.215
7	George Bradley, 1880	.216
8	Tim Keefe, 1880	.216
9	Walter Johnson, 1913	.217
10	Denny Driscoll, 1882	.218
11	Addie Joss, 1908	.218
12	Guy Hecker, 1884	.221
13	George Bradley, 1876	.221
14	Tommy Bond, 1876	.224
15	Christy Mathewson, 1908	.225
16	Jim Whitney, 1884	.225
17	Ed Walsh, 1910	.226
18	Silver King, 1888	.227
19	Ed Morris, 1884	.227
20	Sandy Koufax, 1965	.228
21	Christy Mathewson, 1909	.228
22	Sandy Koufax, 1963	.230
23	Juan Marichal, 1966	.230
24	Monte Ward, 1880	.232
25	Charley Radbourn, 1884	.232
26	Mordecai Brown, 1908	.232
27	Ed Walsh, 1908	.232
28	Jack Lynch, 1884	.233
29	Tim Keefe, 1883	.233
30	Lady Baldwin, 1885	.233
31	Luis Tiant, 1968	.233
32	Bob Gibson, 1968	.233
33	Pete Alexander, 1915	.234
34	Dave McNally, 1968	.234
35	Cy Young, 1905	.235
36	Perry Werden, 1884	.235
37	Tim Keefe, 1884	.235
38	Larry Corcoran, 1880	.236
39	Roger Nelson, 1972	.236
40	Jim Devlin, 1876	.237
41	Tony Mullane, 1883	.238
42	Tim Keefe, 1888	.239
43	Mordecai Brown, 1909	.239
44	John Clarkson, 1885	.240
45	Larry Corcoran, 1882	.240
46	Juan Marichal, 1965	.240
47	Cy Young, 1908	.240
48	Don Sutton, 1972	.240
49	Babe Adams, 1919	.241
50	Charlie Getzien, 1884	.241
51	Sandy Koufax, 1964	.241
52	Charley Radbourn, 1883	.241
53	Pete Conway, 1888	.242
54	Jim Hunter, 1972	.242
55	Ed Morris, 1885	.242
56	Billy Taylor, 1884	.243
57	Harry McCormick, 1882	.243
58	Charlie Buffinton, 1888	.243
59	Dave Foutz, 1884	.243
60	Denny McLain, 1968	.243
61	Mike Scott, 1986	.244
62	Lady Baldwin, 1886	.244
63	Will White, 1883	.244
64	Doc White, 1906	.244
65	Will White, 1882	.244
66	Jim Galvin, 1884	.244
67	Fred Goldsmith, 1880	.244
68	Russ Ford, 1910	.245
69	Charlie Buffinton, 1884	.245
70	Pete Alexander, 1919	.245
71	Christy Mathewson, 1905	.245
72	Charlie Ferguson, 1886	.245
73	Fred Corey, 1880	.246
74	Dutch Leonard, 1914	.246
75	Christy Mathewson, 1907	.247
76	Charlie Gagus, 1884	.247
77	Warren Hacker, 1952	.247
78	Tommy Bond, 1879	.248
79	Eddie Cicotte, 1917	.248
80	John Clarkson, 1884	.248
81	Jim McCormick, 1880	.248
82	Charley Radbourn, 1882	.248
83	Walter Johnson, 1912	.248
84	Henry Gruber, 1888	.249
85	Tony Mullane, 1884	.249
86	Cy Young, 1904	.249
87	Jack Chesbro, 1904	.249
88	Cannonball Titcomb, 1888	.249
89	Jumbo McGinnis, 1883	.249
90	John Tudor, 1985	.249
91	Tim Keefe, 1885	.249
92	Ben Sanders, 1888	.249
93	Ron Guidry, 1978	.250
94	Bill Bernhard, 1902	.250
95	Hugh Daily, 1884	.250
96	Addie Joss, 1903	.250
97	Frank Mountain, 1884	.250
98	Ed Seward, 1888	.250
99	Joe Horlen, 1964	.250
100	Jim Whitney, 1883	.250

Wins Above Team

1	George Bradley, 1876	22.5
2	Will White, 1879	21.5
3	Charley Radbourn, 1884	20.1
4	Jim McCormick, 1880	19.4
5	Guy Hecker, 1884	18.0
6	Jim Galvin, 1883	17.6
7	Jim Devlin, 1877	17.5
8	Charley Radbourn, 1883	15.7
9	Matt Kilroy, 1887	15.4
10	Jim Galvin, 1884	15.1
11	Jim Devlin, 1876	15.0
12	Charlie Buffinton, 1884	14.9
13	Walter Johnson, 1913	14.7
14	Jack Chesbro, 1904	14.0
15	Tony Mullane, 1884	13.9
16	Sadie McMahon, 1890	13.4
17	Will White, 1882	13.1
18	Ed Morris, 1885	12.9
19	Joe Wood, 1912	12.8
20	Bill Sweeney, 1884	12.7
	Ed Walsh, 1908	12.7
22	John Clarkson, 1889	12.1
23	Tommy Bond, 1879	12.0
24	Lefty Grove, 1931	11.8
25	Steve Carlton, 1972	11.7
26	Cy Young, 1901	11.6
27	Bill Hutchinson, 1891	11.4
	Denny McLain, 1968	11.4
29	Terry Larkin, 1878	11.2
	Mickey Welch, 1884	11.2
	Bob Caruthers, 1889	11.2
32	Henry Porter, 1885	11.0
	Bill Hoffer, 1895	11.0
	Christy Mathewson, 1908	11.0
35	Cy Young, 1902	10.9
36	Cy Young, 1895	10.7
37	Dazzy Vance, 1924	10.6
	Robin Roberts, 1952	10.6
	Ron Guidry, 1978	10.6
40	Bobby Mathews, 1876	10.5
	Dizzy Dean, 1934	10.5
42	Toad Ramsey, 1886	10.2
	Cy Young, 1892	10.2
	Joe McGinnity, 1904	10.2
	Eddie Rommel, 1922	10.2
46	Lefty Grove, 1930	10.1
47	Ed Morris, 1886	10.0
	Bill Donovan, 1907	10.0
49	Frank Mountain, 1883	9.9
	Eddie Cicotte, 1919	9.9
	Lefty Gomez, 1934	9.9
52	Kid Gleason, 1890	9.8
	Pete Alexander, 1915	9.8
	Hal Newhouser, 1944	9.8
55	Bobby Mathews, 1885	9.7
	Russ Ford, 1910	9.7
	Roger Clemens, 1986	9.7
58	Charlie Ferguson, 1886	9.6
	Pete Conway, 1888	9.6
	Eddie Plank, 1912	9.6
61	Pete Alexander, 1916	9.5
	Carl Hubbell, 1936	9.5
	Dwight Gooden, 1985	9.5
64	Jouett Meekin, 1894	9.4
	Walter Johnson, 1912	9.4
	Claude Hendrix, 1914	9.4
67	Joe McGinnity, 1900	9.3
	Sandy Koufax, 1963	9.3
69	Bert Cunningham, 1898	9.2
	Walter Johnson, 1911	9.2
	Bobby Shantz, 1952	9.2
	Don Newcombe, 1956	9.2
	Juan Marichal, 1966	9.2
	Bob Gibson, 1970	9.2
	Bob Welch, 1990	9.2
76	Tim Keefe, 1888	9.1
	Whitey Ford, 1961	9.1
78	Jim McCormick, 1882	9.0
	Cy Young, 1893	9.0
	Preacher Roe, 1951	9.0
81	Frank Killen, 1892	8.9
	Red Faber, 1921	8.9
83	Tim Keefe, 1883	8.8
	Tim Keefe, 1887	8.8
	Christy Mathewson, 1909	8.8
	Dolf Luque, 1923	8.8
87	Lee Richmond, 1881	8.7
	Frank Killen, 1893	8.7
	Jim Hughes, 1899	8.7
	Juan Marichal, 1963	8.7
	Juan Marichal, 1968	8.7
92	Jumbo McGinnis, 1882	8.6
	Jim McCormick, 1883	8.6
	Lefty Grove, 1933	8.6
	Bob Feller, 1946	8.6
	Roy Face, 1959	8.6
97	7 players tied	8.5

Wins Above League

1	Charley Radbourn, 1884	45.3
2	Guy Hecker, 1884	44.7
3	Charley Radbourn, 1883	42.8
4	Silver King, 1888	42.7
5	John Clarkson, 1889	42.6
6	John Clarkson, 1885	42.2
7	Jim Galvin, 1884	41.2
8	Jim Galvin, 1883	40.4
9	Bill Hutchinson, 1892	40.2
10	Jim McCormick, 1880	40.1
11	Jim Devlin, 1876	39.5
12	Tim Keefe, 1883	39.5
13	Will White, 1879	39.4
14	Toad Ramsey, 1886	39.4
15	Bill Hutchinson, 1890	39.1
16	Will White, 1883	39.1
17	Matt Kilroy, 1887	38.0
18	George Bradley, 1876	37.1
19	Toad Ramsey, 1887	36.8
20	Amos Rusie, 1890	36.6
21	Ed Morris, 1885	36.5
22	John Clarkson, 1887	36.3
23	Charlie Buffinton, 1884	36.3
24	Tony Mullane, 1884	36.1
25	Jim Devlin, 1877	35.8
26	Ed Morris, 1886	35.6
27	Jim McCormick, 1882	35.5
28	Dave Foutz, 1886	35.1
29	Lee Richmond, 1880	34.9
30	Tim Keefe, 1886	34.7
31	Monte Ward, 1880	34.5
32	Bill Hutchinson, 1891	34.3
33	Bill Sweeney, 1884	34.3
34	Monte Ward, 1879	34.3
35	Jim Galvin, 1879	34.0
36	Tommy Bond, 1879	34.0
37	Sadie McMahon, 1891	34.0
38	Amos Rusie, 1894	33.8
39	Mark Baldwin, 1890	33.6
40	Jim Whitney, 1883	33.3
41	Amos Rusie, 1893	33.3
42	Jack Stivetts, 1891	33.2
43	Al Spalding, 1876	33.1
44	Jim Whitney, 1881	33.0
45	Amos Rusie, 1892	32.9
46	Larry Corcoran, 1884	32.8
47	Ed Walsh, 1908	32.8
48	Lady Baldwin, 1886	32.8
49	Silver King, 1890	32.7
50	Mickey Welch, 1885	32.6
51	Mickey Welch, 1884	32.6
52	Kid Gleason, 1890	32.6
53	Bob Caruthers, 1885	32.3
54	John Clarkson, 1886	32.3
55	Ed Seward, 1888	32.2
56	Tommy Bond, 1877	32.1
57	Matt Kilroy, 1889	32.0
58	Will White, 1880	31.9
59	Mickey Welch, 1880	31.9
60	Pink Hawley, 1895	31.9
61	Matt Kilroy, 1886	31.8
62	Guy Hecker, 1885	31.5
63	Jack Chesbro, 1904	31.5
64	Sadie McMahon, 1890	31.5
65	Will White, 1882	31.5
66	Larry Corcoran, 1880	31.3
67	George Derby, 1881	31.2
68	Tommy Bond, 1878	31.1
69	Tim Keefe, 1884	31.1
70	Elmer Smith, 1887	31.0
71	Tony Mullane, 1883	30.9
72	Hugh Daily, 1884	30.9
73	Cy Young, 1893	30.9
74	Cy Young, 1892	30.8
75	Mark Baldwin, 1889	30.6
76	Jesse Duryea, 1889	30.6
77	Jim McCormick, 1879	30.5
78	Walter Johnson, 1912	30.4
79	Hardie Henderson, 1885	30.4
80	Scott Stratton, 1890	30.3
81	Larry Corcoran, 1883	30.3
82	Silver King, 1889	30.2
83	John Clarkson, 1891	29.9
84	Charley Radbourn, 1886	29.9
85	Charley Radbourn, 1882	29.9
86	Tim Keefe, 1887	29.9
87	Phil Knell, 1891	29.9
88	Tony Mullane, 1882	29.8
89	Joe McGinnity, 1903	29.8
90	Jersey Bakely, 1888	29.7
91	Amos Rusie, 1891	29.7
92	Kid Nichols, 1893	29.5
93	Henry Porter, 1885	29.5
94	Kid Nichols, 1890	29.3
95	Gus Weyhing, 1892	29.3
96	Gus Weyhing, 1889	29.0
97	Tony Mullane, 1886	29.0
98	Christy Mathewson, 1908	29.0
99	Jim McCormick, 1881	28.9
100	Walter Johnson, 1913	28.9

Relief Games

1	Mike Marshall, 1974	106
2	Kent Tekulve, 1979	94
3	Mike Marshall, 1973	92
4	Kent Tekulve, 1978	91
5	Wayne Granger, 1969	90
	Kent Tekulve, 1987	90
7	Mike Marshall, 1979	89
	Mark Eichhorn, 1987	89
9	Rob Murphy, 1987	87
10	Wilbur Wood, 1968	86
11	Kent Tekulve, 1982	85
	Frank Williams, 1987	85
13	Ted Abernathy, 1965	84
	Dick Tidrow, 1980	84
	Dan Quisenberry, 1985	84
	Mitch Williams, 1987	84
18	Ken Sanders, 1971	83
	Craig Lefferts, 1986	83
20	Eddie Fisher, 1965	82
	Bill Campbell, 1983	82
	Juan Agosto, 1990	82
23	John Wyatt, 1964	81
	Dale Murray, 1976	81
	Jeff Robinson, 1987	81
26	Pedro Borbon, 1973	80
	Willie Hernandez, 1984	80
	Mitch Williams, 1986	80
29	Dick Radatz, 1964	79
30	Hal Woodeshick, 1965	78
	Ted Abernathy, 1968	78
	Bill Campbell, 1976	78
	Rollie Fingers, 1977	78
	Tom Hume, 1980	78
	Kent Tekulve, 1980	78
	Greg Minton, 1982	78
	Ed Vande Berg, 1982	78
	Ted Power, 1984	78
	Tim Burke, 1985	78
	Lance McCullers, 1987	78
41	Bob Locker, 1967	77
	Wilbur Wood, 1970	77
	Charlie Hough, 1976	77
	Butch Metzger, 1976	77
	Rick Camp, 1980	77
	Gary Lavelle, 1984	77
	Craig Lefferts, 1987	77
	Bobby Thigpen, 1990	77
49	13 players tied	76

Relief Wins

1	Roy Face, 1959	18
2	John Hiller, 1974	17
	Bill Campbell, 1976	17
4	Jim Konstanty, 1950	16
	Ron Perranoski, 1963	16
	Dick Radatz, 1964	16
	Tom Johnson, 1977	16
8	Mace Brown, 1938	15
	Hoyt Wilhelm, 1952	15
	Luis Arroyo, 1961	15
	Dick Radatz, 1963	15
	Eddie Fisher, 1965	15
	Mike Marshall, 1974	15
	Dale Murray, 1975	15
15	Joe Page, 1947	14
	Joe Black, 1952	14
	Hersh Freeman, 1956	14
	Stu Miller, 1961	14
	Stu Miller, 1965	14
	Phil Regan, 1966	14
	Frank Linzy, 1969	14
	Mike Marshall, 1972	14
	Mike Marshall, 1973	14
	Ron Davis, 1979	14
	Mark Clear, 1982	14
	Jim Slaton, 1983	14
	Roger McDowell, 1986	14
	Mark Eichhorn, 1986	14
29	Earl Caldwell, 1946	13
	Joe Page, 1949	13
	Clyde King, 1951	13
	Lindy McDaniel, 1959	13
	Larry Sherry, 1960	13
	Gerry Staley, 1960	13
	Lindy McDaniel, 1963	13
	Al Hrabosky, 1975	13
	Rollie Fingers, 1976	13
	Bill Campbell, 1977	13
	Sparky Lyle, 1977	13
	Gary Lavelle, 1978	13
	Bob Stanley, 1978	13
	Ron Reed, 1979	13
	Jim Kern, 1979	13
	Aurelio Lopez, 1980	13
	Jesse Orosco, 1983	13
	Rich Gossage, 1983	13
47	29 players tied	12

Relief Losses

1	Gene Garber, 1979	16
2	Darold Knowles, 1970	14
	John Hiller, 1974	14
	Mike Marshall, 1975	14
	Mike Marshall, 1979	14
6	Wilbur Wood, 1970	13
	Rollie Fingers, 1978	13
	Skip Lockwood, 1978	13
9	Roy Face, 1956	12
	Roy Face, 1961	12
	Ken Sanders, 1971	12
	Mike Marshall, 1974	12
	Gene Garber, 1975	12
	Jim Willoughby, 1976	12
	Charlie Hough, 1977	12
	Mike Marshall, 1978	12
	Kent Tekulve, 1980	12
	Ken Howell, 1986	12
19	Nels Potter, 1949	11
	Frank Funk, 1961	11
	Dick Radatz, 1965	11
	Frank Linzy, 1966	11
	Wilbur Wood, 1968	11
	Wilbur Wood, 1969	11
	Mike Marshall, 1973	11
	Rollie Fingers, 1976	11
	Rich Gossage, 1978	11
	Dave Heaverlo, 1979	11
	Mark Clear, 1980	11
	Greg Minton, 1983	11
	Ron Davis, 1984	11
	Mark Davis, 1985	11
	Joe Boever, 1989	11
34	43 players tied	10

Relief Innings Pitched

1	Mike Marshall, 1974	208.1
2	Allan Russell, 1923	181.1
3	Mike Marshall, 1973	179.0
4	Bob Stanley, 1982	168.1
5	Bill Campbell, 1976	167.2
6	Andy Karl, 1945	166.2
7	Eddie Fisher, 1965	165.1
8	Lindy McDaniel, 1973	160.1
9	Hoyt Wilhelm, 1952	159.1
10	Dick Radatz, 1964	157.0
	Mark Eichhorn, 1986	157.0
12	Jim Konstanty, 1950	152.0
13	John Hiller, 1974	150.0
14	Tom Johnson, 1977	146.2
15	Garland Braxton, 1927	146.0
16	Bob Stanley, 1983	145.1
17	Hoyt Wilhelm, 1953	145.0
	Wilbur Wood, 1968	145.0
19	Wayne Granger, 1969	144.2
20	Steve Foucault, 1974	144.1
21	Hoyt Wilhelm, 1965	144.0
22	Jim Kern, 1979	143.0
23	Charlie Hough, 1976	142.2
24	Rich Gossage, 1975	141.2
25	Mike Marshall, 1979	140.2
26	Sammy Stewart, 1983	140.1
	Willie Hernandez, 1984	140.1
28	Bill Campbell, 1977	140.0
29	Jack Lamabe, 1963	139.2
30	Pedro Borbon, 1974	139.0
	Dan Quisenberry, 1983	139.0
32	Aurelio Lopez, 1984	137.2
33	Clay Carroll, 1966	137.1
34	Sparky Lyle, 1977	137.0
	Tom Hume, 1980	137.0
36	Dan Quisenberry, 1982	136.2
37	Ted Abernathy, 1965	136.1
	Ken Sanders, 1971	136.1
	Doug Corbett, 1980	136.1
40	Joe Page, 1949	135.1
41	Clay Carroll, 1968	135.0
	Kent Tekulve, 1978	135.0
43	Ted Abernathy, 1968	134.2
	Phil Regan, 1968	134.2
	Rollie Fingers, 1976	134.2
46	Bill Henry, 1959	134.1
	Dick Selma, 1970	134.1
	Rich Gossage, 1978	134.1
	Kent Tekulve, 1979	134.1
50	2 players tied	134.0

Relief Points

1	Bobby Thigpen, 1990	116
2	Dennis Eckersley, 1990	102
3	Dave Righetti, 1986	100
4	Dan Quisenberry, 1983	97
	Dan Quisenberry, 1984	97
6	Dennis Eckersley, 1988	96
7	Bruce Sutter, 1984	93
	Mark Davis, 1989	93
9	John Hiller, 1973	91
	Doug Jones, 1990	91
11	Steve Bedrosian, 1987	87
12	Johnny Franco, 1988	84
	Jeff Reardon, 1988	84
	Jeff Russell, 1989	84
15	Luis Arroyo, 1961	83
	Sparky Lyle, 1972	83
	Dan Quisenberry, 1980	83
	Bill Caudill, 1984	83
19	Clay Carroll, 1972	82
	Bruce Sutter, 1982	82
21	Dick Radatz, 1964	81
	Dan Quisenberry, 1982	81
	Dan Quisenberry, 1985	81
	Gregg Olson, 1990	81
25	Bruce Sutter, 1979	80
	Todd Worrell, 1986	80
27	Mike Marshall, 1973	79
	Bill Campbell, 1977	79
	Jim Kern, 1979	79
	Willie Hernandez, 1984	79
31	Jeff Reardon, 1985	78
32	Wayne Granger, 1970	77
	Rollie Fingers, 1977	77
	Lee Smith, 1984	77
35	Jack Aker, 1966	76
	Rich Gossage, 1980	76
	Greg Minton, 1982	76
	Jesse Orosco, 1984	76
	Lee Smith, 1985	76
	Todd Worrell, 1987	76
	Doug Jones, 1988	76
	Mitch Williams, 1989	76
43	Dave Righetti, 1985	75
	Jeff Reardon, 1986	75
	Johnny Franco, 1987	75
46	6 players tied	74

Relief Ranking

1	Jim Kern, 1979	65.0
2	John Hiller, 1973	64.9
3	Rich Gossage, 1977	62.5
4	Lindy McDaniel, 1960	57.5
5	Mike Marshall, 1979	56.2
6	Mark Eichhorn, 1986	56.2
7	Dennis Eckersley, 1990	56.2
8	Bruce Sutter, 1977	54.0
9	Ellis Kinder, 1953	53.6
10	Jesse Orosco, 1983	52.2
11	Donnie Moore, 1985	51.9
12	Bill Caudill, 1982	51.9
13	Dick Radatz, 1964	50.4
14	Bob James, 1985	50.4
15	Sid Monge, 1979	49.5
16	Dick Radatz, 1963	49.4
17	Bobby Thigpen, 1990	48.3
18	Rich Gossage, 1975	47.7
19	Doug Corbett, 1980	46.9
20	Dan Quisenberry, 1985	46.9
21	Mike Marshall, 1972	46.8
22	Bill Campbell, 1977	45.5
23	Lee Smith, 1983	45.4
24	Roy Face, 1962	45.2
25	Dave Righetti, 1986	45.1
26	Al Hrabosky, 1975	44.9
27	Bruce Sutter, 1984	44.8
28	Rich Gossage, 1978	44.7
29	Johnny Franco, 1988	43.8
30	Todd Worrell, 1986	43.5
31	Sparky Lyle, 1977	43.4
32	Dan Spillner, 1982	43.2
33	Tom Murphy, 1974	42.9
34	Stu Miller, 1965	42.7
35	Ken Sanders, 1971	41.6
36	Luis Arroyo, 1961	41.6
37	Ron Perranoski, 1969	41.3
38	Dan Quisenberry, 1983	41.0
39	Hoyt Wilhelm, 1964	40.7
40	Doug Jones, 1989	40.4
41	Joe Page, 1949	40.3
42	Bruce Sutter, 1979	40.3
43	Willie Hernandez, 1984	39.9
44	Jim Brewer, 1972	39.8
45	Mike Henneman, 1988	39.8
46	John Hiller, 1974	39.8
47	Dick Radatz, 1962	39.7
48	Ted Abernathy, 1967	39.7
49	Jim Konstanty, 1950	39.4
50	Bob Stanley, 1983	39.4

Relievers' Runs

1 Mark Eichhorn, 1986 . . . . . 42.8
2 Jim Kern, 1979 . . . . 42.0
3 Rich Gossage, 1977 . . . . . 33.8
4 John Hiller, 1973 . . . . 33.1
5 Dan Quisenberry, 1983 . . . 32.7
6 Willie Hernandez, 1984 . . . 32.2
7 Doug Corbett, 1980 . . . . . . 31.1
8 Bruce Sutter, 1977 . . . . 30.6
9 Rich Gossage, 1975 . . . . . 30.5
10 Tim Burke, 1987 . . . . 29.3
11 Sparky Lyle, 1977 . . . . 28.8
12 Lindy McDaniel, 1960 . . . . 28.6
13 Bob Lee, 1964 . . . . 28.4
14 Garland Braxton, 1927 . . . 28.2
15 Bruce Sutter, 1984 . . . . 27.9
16 Mike Marshall, 1974 . . . . . 27.7
17 Dennis Eckersley, 1990 . . . 26.8
18 Sid Monge, 1979 . . . . 26.4
19 Jesse Orosco, 1983 . . . . . . 26.3
20 Hoyt Wilhelm, 1965 . . . . . . 26.3
21 Rich Gossage, 1978 . . . . . 26.2
22 Jim Grant, 1970 . . . . 25.9
23 Phil Regan, 1966 . . . . 25.8
24 Jeff Montgomery, 1989 . . . 25.7
25 Ellis Kinder, 1953 . . . . 25.5
26 Aurelio Lopez, 1979 . . . . . 25.5
27 Donnie Moore, 1985 . . . . . 25.5
28 Dan Quisenberry, 1985 . . . 25.4
29 Ellis Kinder, 1951 . . . . 25.1
30 Jim Konstanty, 1950 . . . . . 25.0
31 Ted Abernathy, 1967 . . . . . 24.9
32 Mike Marshall, 1979 . . . . . 24.9
33 Sparky Lyle, 1974 . . . . 24.8
34 Bob James, 1985 . . . . 24.7
35 Rollie Fingers, 1973 . . . . . . 24.5
36 Gary Lavelle, 1977 . . . . 24.4
37 Dick Radatz, 1963 . . . . 24.4
38 Hoyt Wilhelm, 1954 . . . . . . 24.4
39 Greg Minton, 1982 . . . . 24.2
40 Joe Black, 1952 . . . . 24.2
41 Luis Arroyo, 1961 . . . . 24.2
42 Joe Page, 1949 . . . . 24.1
43 Dick Radatz, 1962 . . . . 24.0
44 Hoyt Wilhelm, 1964 . . . . . . 23.9
45 Dan Spillner, 1982 . . . . 23.5
46 Tom Murphy, 1974 . . . . 23.4
47 Ken Sanders, 1971 . . . . 23.4
48 Dick Radatz, 1964 . . . . 23.2
49 Joe Heving, 1933 . . . . 23.2
50 Dick Hyde, 1958 . . . . 23.1

Adjusted Relievers' Runs

1 Mark Eichhorn, 1986 . . . . . 43.6
2 Jim Kern, 1979 . . . . 40.9
3 John Hiller, 1973 . . . . 36.9
4 Bruce Sutter, 1977 . . . . 36.3
5 Doug Corbett, 1980 . . . . . . 36.0
6 Rich Gossage, 1977 . . . . . 34.9
7 Dan Quisenberry, 1983 . . . 32.9
8 Lindy McDaniel, 1960 . . . . 32.5
9 Rich Gossage, 1975 . . . . . 32.0
10 Willie Hernandez, 1984 . . . 31.1
11 Tim Burke, 1987 . . . . 30.5
12 Ellis Kinder, 1951 . . . . 29.3
13 Ted Abernathy, 1967 . . . . . 29.3
14 Ellis Kinder, 1953 . . . . 28.0
15 Mike Marshall, 1979 . . . . . 27.4
16 Dick Radatz, 1964 . . . . 27.3
17 Aurelio Lopez, 1979 . . . . . 27.0
18 Sparky Lyle, 1977 . . . . 27.0
19 Sid Monge, 1979 . . . . 26.9
20 Bob James, 1985 . . . . 26.8
21 Dick Radatz, 1963 . . . . 26.7
22 Jesse Orosco, 1983 . . . . . . 26.3
23 Bruce Sutter, 1984 . . . . 26.3
24 Dick Radatz, 1962 . . . . 26.2
25 Dan Quisenberry, 1985 . . . 25.6
26 Dennis Eckersley, 1990 . . . 25.4
27 Jeff Montgomery, 1989 . . . 25.3
28 Donnie Moore, 1985 . . . . . 25.0
29 Lee Smith, 1983 . . . . 24.5
30 Gary Lavelle, 1977 . . . . 24.4
31 Tom Burgmeier, 1980 . . . . 24.4
32 Bob Lee, 1964 . . . . 24.3
33 Bob Stanley, 1983 . . . . 24.2
34 Andy McGaffigan, 1987 . . . 24.2
35 Greg Minton, 1982 . . . . 24.1
36 Rich Gossage, 1978 . . . . . 24.0
37 Hoyt Wilhelm, 1954 . . . . . . 23.9
38 Tug McGraw, 1980 . . . . . . 23.9
39 Bill Campbell, 1977 . . . . . . 23.8
40 Dick Hyde, 1958 . . . . 23.7
41 Dan Spillner, 1982 . . . . 23.6
42 Ken Sanders, 1971 . . . . 23.5
43 Clay Carroll, 1966 . . . . 23.5
44 Jim Grant, 1970 . . . . 23.5
45 Tom Murphy, 1974 . . . . 23.4
46 Jim Konstanty, 1950 . . . . . 23.4
47 Bill Caudill, 1980 . . . . 23.3
48 Sparky Lyle, 1974 . . . . 23.2
49 Rob Dibble, 1990 . . . . 23.1
50 Dan Quisenberry, 1982 . . . 23.0

Percent of Team Wins (by era)

1876-1892

1 Will White, 1879 . . . . 100.0
Bobby Mathews, 1876 . . . 100.0
Jim Devlin, 1877 . . . . 100.0
Jim Devlin, 1876 . . . . 100.0
George Bradley, 1876 . . . . 100.0
6 Tommy Bond, 1878 . . . . . . 97.6
7 Terry Larkin, 1878 . . . . 96.7
8 Jim McCormick, 1880 . . . . 95.7
9 Tommy Bond, 1877 . . . . . . 95.2
10 Terry Larkin, 1877 . . . . 93.5
11 Al Spalding, 1876 . . . . 90.4
Jim Galvin, 1883 . . . . 88.5
13 Will White, 1880 . . . . 85.7
Jim McCormick, 1882 . . . . 85.7
15 Mickey Welch, 1880 . . . . . . 82.9

1893-1919

1 Ted Breitenstein, 1895 . . . . 48.7
2 Amos Rusie, 1893 . . . . . 4 48.5
3 Ted Breitenstein, 1894 . . . 48.2
4 Cy Young, 1893 . . . . 46.6
5 Ed Walsh, 1908 . . . . 45.5
Frank Killen, 1896 . . . . . . 45.5
7 Ted Breitenstein, 1896 . . . . 45.0
8 Jack Chesbro, 1904 . . . . . . 44.6
9 Frank Killen, 1893 . . . . 44.4
10 Pink Hawley, 1895 . . . . 43.7
11 Win Mercer, 1896 . . 1896 43.1
12 Noodles Hahn, 1901 . . . . . 42.3
13 Cy Young, 1901 . . . . 41.8
14 Cy Young, 1895 . . . . 41.6
15 Cy Young, 1902 . . . . 41.6

1920-1941

1 Eddie Rommel, 1922 . . . . . 41.5
2 Red Faber, 1921 . . . . 40.3
3 Buck Newsom, 1938 . . . . . 36.4
4 Jimmy Ring, 1923 . . . . 36.0
Pete Alexander, 1920 . . . . 36.0
6 Ted Lyons, 1930 . . . . 35.5
7 Curt Davis, 1934 . . . . 33.9
8 Urban Shocker, 1921 . . . . 33.3
Bob Feller, 1941 . . . . 33.3
Ed Morris, 1928 . . . . 33.3
11 Howard Ehmke, 1923 . . . . 32.8
12 Dazzy Vance, 1925 . . . . . . 32.4
Paul Derringer, 1935 . . . . 32.4
14 Wes Ferrell, 1935 . . . . 32.1
15 George Uhle, 1923 . . . . . . 31.7

1942-1960

1 Ned Garver, 1951 . . . . 38.5
2 Bob Feller, 1946 . . . . 38.2
3 Murry Dickson, 1952 . . . . . 33.3
4 Robin Roberts, 1952 . . . . . 32.2
5 Bill Voiselle, 1944 . . . . 31.3
6 Murry Dickson, 1951 . . . . . 31.3
7 Phil Marchildon, 1942 . . . . 30.9
8 Dizzy Trout, 1944 . . . . 30.7
9 Robin Roberts, 1954 . . . . . 30.7
10 Bobby Shantz, 1952 . . . . . 30.4
11 Ewell Blackwell, 1947 . . . . 30.1
12 Robin Roberts, 1955 . . . . . 29.9
13 Johnny Antonelli, 1956 . . . 29.9
14 Dave Ferriss, 1945 . . . . . . 29.6
15 2 players tied 29.0

1961-1990

1 Steve Carlton, 1972 . . . . . . 45.8
2 Gaylord Perry, 1972 . . . . . . 33.3
3 Nolan Ryan, 1974 . . . . 32.4
4 Phil Niekro, 1979 . . . . 31.8
5 Larry Jackson, 1964 . . . . . 31.6
6 Wilbur Wood, 1973 . . . . . . 31.2
7 Bob Gibson, 1970 . . . . 30.3
8 Randy Jones, 1976 . . . . . . 30.1
9 Denny McLain, 1968 . . . . . 30.1
10 Fergie Jenkins, 1974 . . . . . 29.8
11 Dave Stieb, 1981 . . . . 29.7
12 Juan Marichal, 1968 . . . . . 29.5
13 Sam McDowell, 1969 . . . . 29.0
14 Fergie Jenkins, 1971 . . . . . 28.9
Fernando Valenzuela,
15 1986 . . . . 28.8

Clutch Pitching Index

1 Henry Boyle, 1886 . . . . 159.8
2 Ned Garvin, 1904 . . . . 158.4
3 Mordecai Brown, 1903 . . . 157.1
4 Doc White, 1904 . . . . 152.0
5 Max Lanier, 1943 . . . . 150.8
6 Ed Summers, 1908 . . . . . . 148.0
7 Pete Schneider, 1917 . . . . 145.4
8 Sammy Stewart, 1981 . . . . 144.8
9 Jim McCormick, 1878 . . . . 144.4
10 Vic Willis, 1906 . . . . 144.3
11 Carl Lundgren, 1902 . . . . . 143.9
12 Andy Coakley, 1905 . . . . . . 143.6
Ed Willett, 1908 . . . . 143.6
14 Ed Killian, 1907 . . . . 142.8
15 Bill Burns, 1909 . . . . 142.4
16 Bob Rhoads, 1908 . . . . 142.1
Cy Morgan, 1910 . . . . 142.1
18 Fred Olmstead, 1910 . . . . . 141.6
19 Ben Tincup, 1914 . . . . 141.5
20 Dick Rudolph, 1919 . . . . . . 141.2
21 Sherry Smith, 1919 . . . . . . 141.1
22 Fred Blanding, 1913 . . . . . 140.8
23 Mal Eason, 1902 . . . . 140.4
24 Ed Poole, 1902 . . . . 139.7
25 Andy Coakley, 1908 . . . . . . 139.5
Bert Humphries, 1915 . . . . 139.5
27 Rick Honeycutt, 1983 . . . . 139.3
28 Doug Rau, 1976 . . . . 139.2
29 Sloppy Thurston, 1923 . . . 139.0
30 Al Benton, 1945 . . . . 138.7
Al Brazle, 1947 . . . . 138.7
32 Charlie Hodnett, 1884 . . . . 138.6
33 Joe McGinnity, 1908 . . . . . 138.3
34 Allan Anderson, 1988 . . . . 137.8
35 Andy Coakley, 1907 . . . . . . 136.7
36 Charlie Chech, 1905 . . . . . 136.5
37 Spud Chandler, 1942 . . . . . 136.2
Chuck Finley, 1990 . . . . . . 136.2
39 Ed Siever, 1904 . . . . 136.1
40 Mike O'Neill, 1904 . . . . 136.0
Red Faber, 1917 . . . . 136.0
42 King Cole, 1910 . . . . 135.8
43 Bob Buhl, 1957 . . . . 134.8
John Tudor, 1988 . . . . 134.8
45 Mark Langston, 1989 . . . . 134.7
46 Al Maul, 1895 . . . . 134.5
Doug Rau, 1978 . . . . 134.5
48 Stu Miller, 1959 . . . . 134.4
49 Ken Chase, 1940 . . . . 134.2
Dutch Leonard, 1948 . . . . 134.2
51 Harry Salisbury, 1879 . . . . 134.0
52 Mike Marshall, 1973 . . . . . 133.7
53 Bill Bernhard, 1904 . . . . . . 133.3
54 Joe Horlen, 1968 . . . . 133.1
55 Lon Knight, 1876 . . . . 133.0
56 Jim Pastorius, 1907 . . . . . . 132.9
57 Eddie Plank, 1911 . . . . 132.8
58 Art Nehf, 1928 . . . . 132.7
59 Gene Bearden, 1948 . . . . . 132.3
Hoyt Wilhelm, 1959 . . . . . . 132.3
61 Win Mercer, 1894 . . . . 132.1
Stan Baumgartner, 1924 . . 132.1
63 Ed Killian, 1909 . . . . 131.9
Bump Hadley, 1939 . . . . . . 131.9
65 Mordecai Brown, 1906 . . . 131.8
Lew Brockett, 1909 . . . . . 131.8
67 Lew Richie, 1908 . . . . 131.5
68 Mike Sullivan, 1892 . . . . . . 131.4
69 Buttons Briggs, 1904 . . . . . 131.3
Steve Blass, 1972 . . . . 131.3
71 Don Schwall, 1961 . . . . 131.1
72 Ted Lyons, 1942 . . . . 130.9
Bobby Shantz, 1957 . . . . . 130.9
74 Pete Vuckovich, 1982 . . . . 130.6
75 Bill Duggleby, 1905 . . . . . . 130.5
Lon Warneke, 1933 . . . . . . 130.5
Bill Lee, 1978 . . . . 130.5
78 Vive Lindaman, 1906 . . . . . 130.3
Chick Fraser, 1908 . . . . . . 130.3
Walt Dickson, 1914 . . . . . . 130.3
Hal McKain, 1929 . . . . 130.3
82 Larry Pape, 1911 . . . . 130.2
Hi Bithorn, 1942 . . . . 130.2
John Cerutti, 1989 . . . . . . 130.2
85 Vean Gregg, 1913 . . . . 130.1
86 Carl Lundgren, 1907 . . . . . 130.0
87 Rollie Naylor, 1920 . . . . . . 129.9
88 Will White, 1880 . . . . 129.7
89 Earl Moore, 1911 . . . . 129.6
Ruben Gomez, 1954 . . . . . 129.6
Larry McWilliams, 1984 . . . 129.6
92 Lefty Weinert, 1922 . . . . . . 129.4
93 Harry McIntire, 1907 . . . . . 129.3
Buster Brown, 1907 . . . . . 129.3
Tom Hughes, 1912 . . . . . . 129.3
Harry Moran, 1915 . . . . . . 129.3
Ned Garver, 1948 . . . . 129.3
98 4 players tied 129.2

Pitcher Batting Runs

1	Guy Hecker, 1884	26.2
2	Bob Caruthers, 1886	24.5
3	Jim Whitney, 1882	22.3
4	Wes Ferrell, 1935	21.5
5	Don Drysdale, 1965	20.2
6	Don Newcombe, 1955	20.1
7	Bob Caruthers, 1887	19.6
8	Guy Hecker, 1886	19.0
9	Jim Whitney, 1883	18.1
10	Wes Ferrell, 1931	17.8
11	Billy Taylor, 1884	17.4
12	Tony Mullane, 1884	16.9
13	Charlie Ferguson, 1885	16.8
14	Schoolboy Rowe, 1943	16.7
15	George Uhle, 1923	16.4
16	Babe Ruth, 1917	16.3
17	Warren Spahn, 1958	16.0
18	Walter Johnson, 1925	15.9
19	Scott Stratton, 1890	15.8
20	Bob Caruthers, 1889	15.7
21	Red Ruffing, 1930	15.6
22	Bob Lemon, 1950	15.6
23	Jack Stivetts, 1890	15.3
24	Jack Stivetts, 1892	15.1
25	Don Newcombe, 1959	15.1
26	Jack Bentley, 1923	14.8
27	Monte Ward, 1879	14.8
28	Bob Lemon, 1949	14.7
29	Red Lucas, 1930	14.7
30	Claude Hendrix, 1912	14.6
31	Babe Ruth, 1915	14.5
32	Doc Crandall, 1915	14.4
33	Dave Foutz, 1887	14.3
34	Frank Killen, 1893	14.2
35	Charlie Ferguson, 1887	14.1
36	Jim Tobin, 1942	14.0
37	Red Ruffing, 1936	13.8
38	Red Lucas, 1932	13.7
39	Robin Roberts, 1955	13.6
40	Terry Larkin, 1878	13.6
41	Elam Vangilder, 1922	13.4
42	Pete Conway, 1888	13.1
43	Babe Ruth, 1916	13.1
44	Joe Bush, 1924	13.0
45	Clark Griffith, 1901	13.0
46	Jack Coombs, 1911	13.0
47	Adonis Terry, 1890	12.9
48	Bucky Walters, 1939	12.7
49	Pink Hawley, 1895	12.7
50	Bob Lemon, 1948	12.6
51	Red Lucas, 1933	12.5
52	Cy Young, 1903	12.5
53	Schoolboy Rowe, 1935	12.5
54	Red Ruffing, 1932	12.5
55	Curt Davis, 1939	12.3
56	Scott Stratton, 1888	12.3
57	Red Ruffing, 1935	12.2
58	Bob Gibson, 1970	12.2
59	Red Ruffing, 1928	12.2
60	Jim Hunter, 1971	12.1
61	Wes Ferrell, 1936	11.9
62	Dizzy Trout, 1944	11.9
63	Joe Bowman, 1939	11.8
64	Charley Radbourn, 1883	11.8
65	Jouett Meekin, 1896	11.7
66	Fergie Jenkins, 1971	11.7
67	Johnny Sain, 1947	11.7
68	Adonis Terry, 1889	11.7
69	Dutch Ruether, 1921	11.6
70	Claude Hendrix, 1915	11.6
71	Erv Brame, 1929	11.5
72	Babe Ruth, 1918	11.5
73	Ad Gumbert, 1891	11.5
74	Jack Stivetts, 1896	11.5
75	George Van Haltren, 1888	11.3
76	George Mullin, 1904	11.3
77	Schoolboy Rowe, 1934	11.2
78	Charlie Ferguson, 1886	11.1
79	Bob Caruthers, 1891	11.0
80	Jim Whitney, 1887	11.0
81	Carl Mays, 1921	11.0
82	Tom Parrott, 1895	11.0
83	Jim Whitney, 1881	11.0
84	Mickey Welch, 1880	10.9
85	Charlie Buffinton, 1884	10.9
86	Jack Stivetts, 1894	10.9
87	Red Lucas, 1931	10.9
88	Dave Ferriss, 1945	10.9
89	Red Lucas, 1929	10.8
90	Red Ruffing, 1941	10.8
91	Erv Brame, 1930	10.8
92	Ad Gumbert, 1889	10.7
93	Fred Hutchinson, 1947	10.7
94	Joe Wood, 1912	10.6
95	Tim Keefe, 1884	10.6
96	Burleigh Grimes, 1928	10.6
97	Guy Hecker, 1887	10.5
98	Burleigh Grimes, 1920	10.5
99	Dick Burns, 1884	10.5
100	Blue Moon Odom, 1969	10.5

Pitcher Fielding Runs

1	Ed Walsh, 1907	21.0
2	Harry Howell, 1905	16.4
3	Ed Walsh, 1911	13.6
4	Will White, 1882	12.6
5	Ed Walsh, 1908	12.0
6	John Clarkson, 1889	10.9
7	Tony Mullane, 1882	10.6
	Carl Mays, 1926	10.6
9	Tommy Bond, 1880	9.9
	Frank Smith, 1909	9.9
11	Matt Kilroy, 1887	9.7
	Carl Mays, 1916	9.7
13	Nick Altrock, 1905	9.5
14	Sadie McMahon, 1890	9.4
	Harry Howell, 1904	9.4
	Elmer Stricklett, 1905	9.4
	Elmer Stricklett, 1906	9.4
18	Charlie Buffinton, 1888	9.1
	Randy Jones, 1976	9.1
20	John Clarkson, 1887	9.0
21	Curt Davis, 1934	8.9
22	Tony Mullane, 1884	8.8
	Ed Scott, 1900	8.8
	Carl Mays, 1918	8.8
	Bucky Walters, 1936	8.8
26	Mike Morrison, 1887	8.7
	Hooks Dauss, 1915	8.7
	Hooks Dauss, 1920	8.7
	Fred Newman, 1965	8.7
	Mel Stottlemyre, 1969	8.7
31	Park Swartzel, 1889	8.6
	Addie Joss, 1907	8.6
	Burleigh Grimes, 1925	8.6
34	Jack Taylor, 1898	8.4
35	Jim Galvin, 1887	8.3
	Ed Walsh, 1910	8.3
	Carl Mays, 1924	8.3
	Freddie Fitzsimmons, 1931	8.3
	Harry Gumbert, 1937	8.3
	Bob Lemon, 1953	8.3
	John Denny, 1978	8.3
42	Wilcy Moore, 1927	8.2
43	Matt Kilroy, 1889	8.1
	Christy Mathewson, 1911	8.1
	Gene Packard, 1914	8.1
	Carl Mays, 1917	8.1
	Eddie Rommel, 1924	8.1
	Bob Lemon, 1948	8.1
49	Harry Howell, 1907	7.9
	Harry Gumbert, 1938	7.9
51	George Mullin, 1904	7.8
	Christy Mathewson, 1908	7.8
	Mel Harder, 1933	7.8
54	Cy Young, 1895	7.7
	Jean Dubuc, 1913	7.7
56	Bob Caruthers, 1887	7.6
	Willie Sudhoff, 1898	7.6
58	Tommy Bond, 1879	7.5
	Cy Young, 1896	7.5
	Red Donahue, 1902	7.5
	Jack Quinn, 1910	7.5
	Russ Christopher, 1943	7.5
	Greg Maddux, 1990	7.5
64	Hal Schumacher, 1935	7.4
65	Ted Wingfield, 1925	7.3
66	Elmer Stricklett, 1907	7.2
	Ed Willett, 1910	7.2
68	Jim McCormick, 1883	7.1
	John Clarkson, 1885	7.1
	Doc White, 1908	7.1
	Eddie Cicotte, 1913	7.1
	Harry Coveleski, 1914	7.1
	Gene Krapp, 1915	7.1
	Freddie Fitzsimmons, 1932	7.1
75	Dave Foutz, 1885	7.0
	Bill Doak, 1915	7.0
	Willis Hudlin, 1929	7.0
	Jim Tobin, 1944	7.0
	Russ Christopher, 1945	7.0
	Larry Jackson, 1964	7.0
	Tommy John, 1973	7.0
82	Jim Galvin, 1881	6.9
	Larry McKeon, 1884	6.9
	Amos Rusie, 1894	6.9
	Cy Seymour, 1897	6.9
	Stan Coveleski, 1921	6.9
87	Charlie Buffinton, 1887	6.8
	Frank Owen, 1904	6.8
	Harry Howell, 1906	6.8
	Scott Perry, 1919	6.8
	Freddie Fitzsimmons, 1930	6.8
	Carl Hubbell, 1933	6.8
	Bob Lemon, 1952	6.8
	Bobby Shantz, 1957	6.8
	Tommy John, 1969	6.8
96	Carl Mays, 1920	6.7
	Mel Stottlemyre, 1965	6.7
	Fernando Arroyo, 1977	6.7
99	8 players tied	6.6

Total Pitcher Index

1	Guy Hecker, 1884	12.5
2	Silver King, 1888	11.8
3	Amos Rusie, 1894	10.9
4	Charley Radbourn, 1884	10.4
	John Clarkson, 1889	10.4
6	Walter Johnson, 1912	9.8
7	John Clarkson, 1885	9.5
	Bob Caruthers, 1886	9.5
	Walter Johnson, 1913	9.5
10	Scott Stratton, 1890	9.1
11	Tony Mullane, 1884	8.9
	Dave Foutz, 1886	8.9
	Christy Mathewson, 1905	8.9
	Dizzy Trout, 1944	8.9
15	Jim Devlin, 1876	8.7
	John Clarkson, 1887	8.7
17	Charley Radbourn, 1883	8.5
	Pete Alexander, 1915	8.5
19	Joe Wood, 1912	8.3
20	Jack Stivetts, 1891	8.1
21	Bucky Walters, 1939	8.0
22	Hal Newhouser, 1945	7.9
	Bob Gibson, 1968	7.9
24	Charlie Ferguson, 1886	7.8
	Cy Young, 1901	7.8
	Dwight Gooden, 1985	7.8
27	Will White, 1882	7.7
28	Steve Carlton, 1972	7.6
29	Lefty Grove, 1931	7.5
30	Walter Johnson, 1918	7.4
31	Jim Whitney, 1883	7.3
	Dolf Luque, 1923	7.3
33	Matt Kilroy, 1887	7.2
	Ed Walsh, 1908	7.2
35	Guy Hecker, 1886	7.1
	Matt Kilroy, 1889	7.1
	Silver King, 1890	7.1
	Cy Young, 1892	7.1
	Amos Rusie, 1893	7.1
	Kid Nichols, 1897	7.1
	Pete Alexander, 1916	7.1
	Wes Ferrell, 1935	7.1
	Wilbur Wood, 1971	7.1
44	Jim Devlin, 1877	7.0
	Jim Galvin, 1884	7.0
	Bob Caruthers, 1885	7.0
	Guy Hecker, 1885	7.0
	Kid Nichols, 1890	7.0
	Ed Walsh, 1910	7.0
	Carl Hubbell, 1933	7.0
51	Will White, 1883	6.9
	John Clarkson, 1886	6.9
	Cy Young, 1896	6.9
	Kid Nichols, 1898	6.9
	Jack Taylor, 1902	6.9
	Christy Mathewson, 1909	6.9
	Claude Hendrix, 1914	6.9
58	Amos Rusie, 1890	6.8
	Pink Hawley, 1895	6.8
	Jack Chesbro, 1904	6.8
	Walter Johnson, 1915	6.8
	Pete Alexander, 1920	6.8
63	Tim Keefe, 1883	6.7
	Tony Mullane, 1883	6.7
	Ed Walsh, 1907	6.7
	Fergie Jenkins, 1971	6.7
	Tom Seaver, 1971	6.7
68	Toad Ramsey, 1886	6.6
	Charlie Ferguson, 1887	6.6
	Walter Johnson, 1919	6.6
	Lefty Grove, 1930	6.6
	Curt Davis, 1934	6.6
	Lefty Grove, 1936	6.6
	Gaylord Perry, 1972	6.6
	Ron Guidry, 1978	6.6
76	Cy Young, 1895	6.5
	Mordecai Brown, 1906	6.5
	Thornton Lee, 1941	6.5
	Spud Chandler, 1943	6.5
80	Billy Rhines, 1890	6.4
	Christy Mathewson, 1908	6.4
	Walter Johnson, 1914	6.4
	Dazzy Vance, 1928	6.4
	Hal Newhouser, 1946	6.4
	Bob Lemon, 1948	6.4
	Juan Marichal, 1966	6.4
87	Kid Nichols, 1896	6.3
	Roger Clemens, 1990	6.3
89	Cy Young, 1893	6.2
	Nig Cuppy, 1896	6.2
	Clark Griffith, 1898	6.2
	Red Faber, 1921	6.2
	Lon Warneke, 1933	6.2
	Warren Spahn, 1953	6.2
	Bob Gibson, 1969	6.2
96	Charlie Buffinton, 1884	6.1
	Lady Baldwin, 1886	6.1
	Addie Joss, 1908	6.1
	Lefty Gomez, 1937	6.1
	Dave Stieb, 1985	6.1

Total Pitcher Index (alpha.)

Pete Alexander, 1915	8.5
Pete Alexander, 1916	7.1
Pete Alexander, 1920	6.8
Lady Baldwin, 1886	6.1
Mordecai Brown, 1906	6.5
Charlie Buffinton, 1884	6.1
Steve Carlton, 1972	7.6
Bob Caruthers, 1885	7.0
Bob Caruthers, 1886	9.5
Spud Chandler, 1943	6.5
Jack Chesbro, 1904	6.8
John Clarkson, 1885	9.5
John Clarkson, 1886	6.9
John Clarkson, 1887	8.7
John Clarkson, 1889	10.4
Roger Clemens, 1990	6.3
Nig Cuppy, 1896	6.2
Curt Davis, 1934	6.6
Jim Devlin, 1876	8.7
Jim Devlin, 1877	7.0
Red Faber, 1921	6.2
Charlie Ferguson, 1886	7.8
Charlie Ferguson, 1887	6.6
Wes Ferrell, 1935	7.1
Dave Foutz, 1886	8.9
Jim Galvin, 1884	7.0
Bob Gibson, 1968	7.9
Bob Gibson, 1969	6.2
Lefty Gomez, 1937	6.1
Dwight Gooden, 1985	7.8
Clark Griffith, 1898	6.2
Lefty Grove, 1930	6.6
Lefty Grove, 1931	7.5
Lefty Grove, 1936	6.6
Ron Guidry, 1978	6.6
Pink Hawley, 1895	6.8
Guy Hecker, 1884	12.5
Guy Hecker, 1885	7.0
Guy Hecker, 1886	7.1
Claude Hendrix, 1914	6.9
Carl Hubbell, 1933	7.0
Fergie Jenkins, 1971	6.7
Walter Johnson, 1912	9.8
Walter Johnson, 1913	9.5
Walter Johnson, 1914	6.4
Walter Johnson, 1915	6.8
Walter Johnson, 1918	7.4
Walter Johnson, 1919	6.6
Addie Joss, 1908	6.1
Tim Keefe, 1883	6.7
Matt Kilroy, 1887	7.2
Matt Kilroy, 1889	7.1
Silver King, 1888	11.8
Silver King, 1890	7.1
Thornton Lee, 1941	6.5
Bob Lemon, 1948	6.4
Dolf Luque, 1923	7.3
Juan Marichal, 1966	6.4
Christy Mathewson, 1905	8.9
Christy Mathewson, 1908	6.4
Christy Mathewson, 1909	6.9
Tony Mullane, 1883	6.7
Tony Mullane, 1884	8.9
Hal Newhouser, 1945	7.9
Hal Newhouser, 1946	6.4
Kid Nichols, 1890	7.0
Kid Nichols, 1896	6.3
Kid Nichols, 1897	7.1
Kid Nichols, 1898	6.9
Gaylord Perry, 1972	6.6
Charley Radbourn, 1883	8.5
Charley Radbourn, 1884	10.4
Toad Ramsey, 1886	6.6
Billy Rhines, 1890	6.4
Amos Rusie, 1890	6.8
Amos Rusie, 1893	7.1
Amos Rusie, 1894	10.9
Tom Seaver, 1971	6.7
Warren Spahn, 1953	6.2
Dave Stieb, 1985	6.1
Jack Stivetts, 1891	8.1
Scott Stratton, 1890	9.1
Jack Taylor, 1902	6.9
Dizzy Trout, 1944	8.9
Dazzy Vance, 1928	6.4
Ed Walsh, 1907	6.7
Ed Walsh, 1908	7.2
Ed Walsh, 1910	7.0
Bucky Walters, 1939	8.0
Lon Warneke, 1933	6.2
Will White, 1882	7.7
Will White, 1883	6.9
Jim Whitney, 1883	7.3
Joe Wood, 1912	8.3
Wilbur Wood, 1971	7.1
Cy Young, 1892	7.1
Cy Young, 1893	6.2
Cy Young, 1895	6.5
Cy Young, 1896	6.9
Cy Young, 1901	7.8

Total Pitcher Index (by era)

1876-1892
1 Guy Hecker, 1884 .... 12.5
2 Silver King, 1888 .... 11.8
3 Charley Radbourn, 1884 .. 10.4
  John Clarkson, 1889 ..... 10.4
5 John Clarkson, 1885 ..... 9.5
  Bob Caruthers, 1886 .... 9.5
7 Scott Stratton, 1890 ..... 9.1
8 Tony Mullane, 1884 ...... 8.9
  Dave Foutz, 1886 .... 8.9
10 Jim Devlin, 1876 .... 8.7
  John Clarkson, 1887 ..... 8.7
12 Charley Radbourn, 1883 .. 8.5
13 Jack Stivetts, 1891 ...... 8.1
14 Charlie Ferguson, 1886 ... 7.8
15 Will White, 1882 .... 7.7

1893-1919
1 Amos Rusie, 1894 .... 10.9
2 Walter Johnson, 1912 .... 9.8
3 Walter Johnson, 1913 .... 9.5
4 Christy Mathewson, 1905 . 8.9
5 Pete Alexander, 1915 .... 8.5
6 Joe Wood, 1912 .... 8.3
7 Cy Young, 1901 .... 7.8
8 Walter Johnson, 1918 .... 7.4
9 Ed Walsh, 1908 .... 7.2
10 Amos Rusie, 1893 .... 7.1
  Kid Nichols, 1897 .... 7.1
  Pete Alexander, 1916 .... 7.1
13 Ed Walsh, 1910 .... 7.0
14 5 players tied 6.9

1920-1941
1 Bucky Walters, 1939 ..... 8.0
2 Lefty Grove, 1931 .... 7.5
3 Dolf Luque, 1923 .... 7.3
4 Wes Ferrell, 1935 .... 7.1
5 Carl Hubbell, 1933 ...... 7.0
6 Pete Alexander, 1920 .... 6.8
7 Lefty Grove, 1930 .... 6.6
  Curt Davis, 1934 .... 6.6
  Lefty Grove, 1936 .... 6.6
10 Thornton Lee, 1941 ...... 6.5
11 Dazzy Vance, 1928 .... 6.4
12 Red Faber, 1921 .... 6.2
  Lon Warneke, 1933 ...... 6.2
14 Lefty Gomez, 1937 .... 6.1
15 Lefty Grove, 1935 .... 6.0

1942-1960
1 Dizzy Trout, 1944 .... 8.9
2 Hal Newhouser, 1945 .... 7.9
3 Spud Chandler, 1943 ..... 6.5
4 Hal Newhouser, 1946 .... 6.4
  Bob Lemon, 1948 .... 6.4
6 Warren Spahn, 1953 ..... 6.2
7 Robin Roberts, 1953 ..... 5.9
8 Hal Newhouser, 1944 .... 5.8
9 Mel Parnell, 1949 .... 5.7
10 Bobby Shantz, 1952 ...... 5.6
11 Mort Cooper, 1942 ...... 5.5
  Dizzy Trout, 1945 .... 5.5
  Johnny Antonelli, 1954 ... 5.5
14 Bob Lemon, 1949 .... 5.4
  Ned Garver, 1950 .... 5.4

1961-1990
1 Bob Gibson, 1968 .... 7.9
2 Dwight Gooden, 1985 .... 7.8
3 Steve Carlton, 1972 ..... 7.6
4 Wilbur Wood, 1971 ...... 7.1
5 Fergie Jenkins, 1971 ..... 6.7
  Tom Seaver, 1971 .... 6.7
7 Gaylord Perry, 1972 ..... 6.6
  Ron Guidry, 1978 .... 6.6
9 Juan Marichal, 1966 ..... 6.4
10 Roger Clemens, 1990 .... 6.3
11 Bob Gibson, 1969 .... 6.2
12 Dave Stieb, 1985 .... 6.1
13 Tom Seaver, 1973 .... 5.9
14 3 players tied 5.8

Total Baseball Ranking

1 Guy Hecker, 1884 .... 12.5
2 Silver King, 1888 .... 11.8
3 Amos Rusie, 1894 .... 10.9
4 Babe Ruth, 1923 .... 10.5
5 Charley Radbourn, 1884 .. 10.4
  John Clarkson, 1889 ..... 10.4
7 Walter Johnson, 1912 .... 9.8
8 Babe Ruth, 1921 .... 9.6
9 John Clarkson, 1885 ..... 9.5
  Bob Caruthers, 1886 .... 9.5
  Walter Johnson, 1913 .... 9.5
12 Scott Stratton, 1890 ..... 9.1
13 Tony Mullane, 1884 ...... 8.9
  Dave Foutz, 1886 .... 8.9
  Christy Mathewson, 1905 . 8.9
  Dizzy Trout, 1944 .... 8.9
  Babe Ruth, 1927 .... 8.9
18 Babe Ruth, 1920 .... 8.8
19 Jim Devlin, 1876 .... 8.7
  John Clarkson, 1887 ..... 8.7
  Cal Ripken, 1984 .... 8.7
22 Charley Radbourn, 1883 .. 8.5
  Pete Alexander, 1915 .... 8.5
24 Nap Lajoie, 1901 .... 8.4
  Ty Cobb, 1917 .... 8.4
  Babe Ruth, 1924 .... 8.4
27 Joe Wood, 1912 .... 8.3
  George Sisler, 1920 ...... 8.3
  Ted Williams, 1942 ...... 8.3
30 Lou Gehrig, 1927 .... 8.2
  Ted Williams, 1946 ...... 8.2
  Ted Williams, 1947 ...... 8.2
33 Jack Stivetts, 1891 ...... 8.1
  Fred Dunlap, 1884 .... 8.1
  Nap Lajoie, 1903 .... 8.1
  Babe Ruth, 1926 .... 8.1
37 Bucky Walters, 1939 ..... 8.0
  Nap Lajoie, 1906 .... 8.0
  Nap Lajoie, 1910 .... 8.0
  Ted Williams, 1941 ...... 8.0
41 Hal Newhouser, 1945 .... 7.9
  Bob Gibson, 1968 .... 7.9
  Mickey Mantle, 1956 ..... 7.9
44 Charlie Ferguson, 1886... 7.8
  Cy Young, 1901 .... 7.8
  Dwight Gooden, 1985 .... 7.8
  Tris Speaker, 1912 ...... 7.8
  Mickey Mantle, 1957 .... 7.8
  Mike Schmidt, 1980 ..... 7.8
50 Will White, 1882 .... 7.7
  Rogers Hornsby, 1920 ... 7.7
  Stan Musial, 1948 .... 7.7
  Ron Santo, 1966 .... 7.7
  Carl Yastrzemski, 1967 ... 7.7
  Rickey Henderson, 1990 . 7.7
56 Steve Carlton, 1972 ..... 7.6
  Honus Wagner, 1906 .... 7.6
  Rogers Hornsby, 1922 ... 7.6
  Willie Mays, 1955 .... 7.6
60 Lefty Grove, 1931 .... 7.5
  Nap Lajoie, 1908 .... 7.5
  Rogers Hornsby, 1924 ... 7.5
  Babe Ruth, 1930 .... 7.5
  Ted Williams, 1949 ...... 7.5
65 Walter Johnson, 1918 .... 7.4
  Honus Wagner, 1905 .... 7.4
  Tris Speaker, 1914 ...... 7.4
68 Jim Whitney, 1883 .... 7.3
  Dolf Luque, 1923 .... 7.3
  Tris Speaker, 1913 ...... 7.3
  Lou Boudreau, 1944 ..... 7.3
  Norm Cash, 1961 .... 7.3
73 Matt Kilroy, 1887 .... 7.2
  Ed Walsh, 1908 .... 7.2
  Ty Cobb, 1910 .... 7.2
  Mickey Mantle, 1961 ..... 7.2
77 Guy Hecker, 1886 .... 7.1
  Matt Kilroy, 1889 .... 7.1
  Silver King, 1890 .... 7.1
  Cy Young, 1892 .... 7.1
  Amos Rusie, 1893 .... 7.1
  Kid Nichols, 1897 .... 7.1
  Pete Alexander, 1916 .... 7.1
  Wes Ferrell, 1935 .... 7.1
  Wilbur Wood, 1971 ...... 7.1
  Stan Musial, 1943 .... 7.1
  Willie Mays, 1965 .... 7.1
  Rickey Henderson, 1985 . 7.1
89 15 players tied 7.0

Total Baseball Rank (alpha.)

Pete Alexander, 1915 .... 8.5
Pete Alexander, 1916 .... 7.1
Lou Boudreau, 1944 ..... 7.3
Steve Carlton, 1972 ..... 7.6
Bob Caruthers, 1886 .... 9.5
Norm Cash, 1961........ 7.3
John Clarkson, 1885 ..... 9.5
John Clarkson, 1887 ..... 8.7
John Clarkson, 1889 .... 10.4
Ty Cobb, 1910 .... 7.2
Ty Cobb, 1917 .... 8.4
Jim Devlin, 1876 .... 8.7
Fred Dunlap, 1884 .... 8.1
Charlie Ferguson, 1886... 7.8
Wes Ferrell, 1935 .... 7.1
Dave Foutz, 1886 .... 8.9
Lou Gehrig, 1927 .... 8.2
Bob Gibson, 1968 .... 7.9
Dwight Gooden, 1985 .... 7.8
Lefty Grove, 1931 .... 7.5
Guy Hecker, 1884 .... 12.5
Guy Hecker, 1886 .... 7.1
Rickey Henderson, 1985 . 7.1
Rickey Henderson, 1990 . 7.7
Rogers Hornsby, 1920 ... 7.7
Rogers Hornsby, 1922 ... 7.6
Rogers Hornsby, 1924 ... 7.5
Walter Johnson, 1912 .... 9.8
Walter Johnson, 1913 .... 9.5
Walter Johnson, 1918 .... 7.4
Matt Kilroy, 1887 .... 7.2
Matt Kilroy, 1889 .... 7.1
Silver King, 1888 .... 11.8
Silver King, 1890 .... 7.1
Nap Lajoie, 1901 .... 8.4
Nap Lajoie, 1903 .... 8.1
Nap Lajoie, 1906 .... 8.0
Nap Lajoie, 1908 .... 7.5
Nap Lajoie, 1910 .... 8.0
Dolf Luque, 1923 .... 7.3
Mickey Mantle, 1956 .... 7.9
Mickey Mantle, 1957 .... 7.8
Mickey Mantle, 1961 ..... 7.2
Christy Mathewson, 1905 . 8.9
Willie Mays, 1955 .... 7.6
Willie Mays, 1965 .... 7.1
Tony Mullane, 1884 ...... 8.9
Stan Musial, 1943 .... 7.1
Stan Musial, 1948 .... 7.7
Hal Newhouser, 1945 .... 7.9
Kid Nichols, 1897 .... 7.1
Charley Radbourn, 1883 .. 8.5
Charley Radbourn, 1884 .. 10.4
Cal Ripken, 1984 .... 8.7
Amos Rusie, 1893 .... 7.1
Amos Rusie, 1894 .... 10.9
Babe Ruth, 1920 .... 8.8
Babe Ruth, 1921 .... 9.6
Babe Ruth, 1923 .... 10.5
Babe Ruth, 1924 .... 8.4
Babe Ruth, 1926 .... 8.1
Babe Ruth, 1927 .... 8.9
Babe Ruth, 1930 .... 7.5
Ron Santo, 1966 .... 7.7
Mike Schmidt, 1980 ...... 7.8
George Sisler, 1920 ...... 8.3
Tris Speaker, 1912 ...... 7.8
Tris Speaker, 1913 ...... 7.3
Tris Speaker, 1914 ...... 7.4
Jack Stivetts, 1891 ...... 8.1
Scott Stratton, 1890 ..... 9.1
Dizzy Trout, 1944 .... 8.9
Honus Wagner, 1905 .... 7.4
Honus Wagner, 1906 .... 7.6
Ed Walsh, 1908 .... 7.2
Bucky Walters, 1939 ..... 8.0
Will White, 1882 .... 7.7
Jim Whitney, 1883 .... 7.3
Ted Williams, 1941 ...... 8.0
Ted Williams, 1942 ...... 8.3
Ted Williams, 1946 ...... 8.2
Ted Williams, 1947 ...... 8.2
Ted Williams, 1949 ...... 7.5
Joe Wood, 1912 .... 8.3
Wilbur Wood, 1971 ...... 7.1
Carl Yastrzemski, 1967 ... 7.7
Cy Young, 1892 .... 7.1
Cy Young, 1901 .... 7.8

Total Baseball Rank (by era)

1876-1892
1 Guy Hecker, 1884 .... 12.5
2 Silver King, 1888 .... 11.8
3 Charley Radbourn, 1884 .. 10.4
  John Clarkson, 1889 ..... 10.4
5 John Clarkson, 1885 ..... 9.5
  Bob Caruthers, 1886 .... 9.5
7 Scott Stratton, 1890 ..... 9.1
8 Tony Mullane, 1884 ...... 8.9
  Dave Foutz, 1886 .... 8.9
10 Jim Devlin, 1876 .... 8.7
  John Clarkson, 1887 ..... 8.7
12 Charley Radbourn, 1883 .. 8.5
13 Jack Stivetts, 1891 ...... 8.1
  Fred Dunlap, 1884 .... 8.1
15 Charlie Ferguson, 1886... 7.8

1893-1919
1 Amos Rusie, 1894 .... 10.9
2 Walter Johnson, 1912 .... 9.8
3 Walter Johnson, 1913 .... 9.5
4 Christy Mathewson, 1905 . 8.9
5 Pete Alexander, 1915 .... 8.5
6 Nap Lajoie, 1901 .... 8.4
  Ty Cobb, 1917 .... 8.4
8 Joe Wood, 1912 .... 8.3
9 Nap Lajoie, 1903 .... 8.1
10 Nap Lajoie, 1906 .... 8.0
  Nap Lajoie, 1910 .... 8.0
12 Cy Young, 1901 .... 7.8
  Tris Speaker, 1912 ...... 7.8
14 Honus Wagner, 1906 .... 7.6
15 Nap Lajoie, 1908 .... 7.5

1920-1941
1 Babe Ruth, 1923 .... 10.5
2 Babe Ruth, 1921 .... 9.6
3 Babe Ruth, 1927 .... 8.9
4 Babe Ruth, 1920 .... 8.8
5 Babe Ruth, 1924 .... 8.4
6 George Sisler, 1920 ...... 8.3
7 Lou Gehrig, 1927 .... 8.2
8 Babe Ruth, 1926 .... 8.1
9 Bucky Walters, 1939 ..... 8.0
  Ted Williams, 1941 ...... 8.0
11 Rogers Hornsby, 1920 ... 7.7
12 Rogers Hornsby, 1922 ... 7.6
13 Lefty Grove, 1931 .... 7.5
  Rogers Hornsby, 1924 ... 7.5
  Babe Ruth, 1930 .... 7.5

1942-1960
1 Dizzy Trout, 1944 .... 8.9
2 Ted Williams, 1942 ...... 8.3
3 Ted Williams, 1946 ...... 8.2
  Ted Williams, 1947 ...... 8.2
5 Hal Newhouser, 1945 .... 7.9
  Mickey Mantle, 1956 .... 7.9
7 Mickey Mantle, 1957 .... 7.8
8 Stan Musial, 1948 .... 7.7
9 Willie Mays, 1955 .... 7.6
10 Ted Williams, 1949 ...... 7.5
11 Lou Boudreau, 1944 ..... 7.3
12 Stan Musial, 1943 .... 7.1
13 Ted Williams, 1957 ...... 7.0
14 Snuffy Stirnweiss, 1944 .. 6.8
  Stan Musial, 1951 .... 6.8

1961-1990
1 Cal Ripken, 1984 .... 8.7
2 Bob Gibson, 1968 .... 7.9
3 Dwight Gooden, 1985 .... 7.8
  Mike Schmidt, 1980 ..... 7.8
5 Ron Santo, 1966 .... 7.7
  Carl Yastrzemski, 1967 ... 7.7
  Rickey Henderson, 1990 . 7.7
8 Steve Carlton, 1972 ..... 7.6
9 Norm Cash, 1961 .... 7.3
10 Mickey Mantle, 1961 ..... 7.2
11 Wilbur Wood, 1971 ...... 7.1
  Willie Mays, 1965 .... 7.1
  Rickey Henderson, 1985 . 7.1
14 Joe Morgan, 1975 .... 7.0
15 3 players tied 6.9

The Rosters

The Team Rosters

The Team Roster, like the three rosters that follow it, is offered as an adjunct to the five principal statistical sections of *Total Baseball:* the Player Register, the Pitcher Register, the Fielding Register, the Annual Record, and All-Time Leaders. Employed together, these rosters and registers give a thorough accounting of major league baseball records. And as we observe the 120th anniversary of professional league play, it can be said that these records are the very core of the game, the only imperishable remains of men who strode the fields of play yesterday or a hundred years ago.

The Team Roster lists the regular players, pitchers, key substitutes, and managers for all 2,073 team seasons in the history of professional league play since 1871. It does not contain the name of every man who played for every team in every year, for many teams have employed up to 50 or more players in a single season. The Team Roster allows the reader, by scanning its pages, to find who were the prominent players for a given team in a given year, or to track over time a team's personnel at a particular position (such as the "turnstile" at third base for the New York Mets since their inception). For a complete record of every one of the 13,490 major league players, consult the Player and Pitcher Registers.

Those included in a team roster are

- All managers
- All everyday players at eight positions, plus designated hitters
- Key utility or substitute players (unlimited, provided they have played in at least 60 percent of the scheduled games that year and are not listed as *regulars* at any position—that is, as having played at least 98 games during a 162-game season)
- Starting pitchers (the top five, provided they have pitched at least 60 percent of the innings that together would yield one inning per scheduled game—that is, 98 innings in a 162-game season)
- Relief pitchers (up to three, provided they have pitched at least 30 percent of the innings that would yield a rate of one inning per scheduled game—50 innings in a 162-game season; and provided that they averaged less than three innings pitched per appearance).

The yearly team rosters are grouped alphabetically by city. At the head of each city's entry is a listing of the leagues and years in which that city was represented in the top rank of baseball. The teams representing that city are grouped by league in the order shown at the head of the entry; the organizing principle is to present the teams in the order of the leagues' demise (excepting, of course, the National and American Leagues). Accordingly, for a city like Chicago, represented in all six major leagues, the teams would be presented in this order:

> National Association (last year, 1875)
> Union Association (last year, 1884)
> Players League (last year, 1890)
> American Association (last year, 1891)
> Federal League (last year, 1915)
> National League (first year, 1876)
> American League (first year, 1901)

The team and league abbreviations used in this section are found on the final pages of this book. Other abbreviations used in the Team Roster are these:

M	Manager
1B	First Base
2B	Second Base
SS	Shortstop
3B	Third Base
OF	Outfield
C	Catcher
DH	Designated Hitter
UT	Utility (substitute)
P	Pitcher
RP	Relief Pitcher

Altoona

ALT U 1884

ALT 1884 U

M	E. Curtis
1B	F. Harris
2B	C. Dougherty
SS	G. Smith
3B	H. Koons
OF	F. Shaffer
OF	J. Brown
OF	J. Murphy
C	J. Moore
P	J. Murphy

Atlanta

ATL N 1966-1990

ATL 1966 N

M	R. Bragan
M	W. Hitchcock
1B	F. Alou
2B	W. Woodward
SS	D. Menke
3B	E. Mathews
OF	H. Aaron
OF	R. Carty
OF	M. Jones
C	J. Torre
P	T. Cloninger
P	K. Johnson
P	D. Lemaster
RP	C. Carroll
RP	F. Olivo
RP	T. Abernathy

ATL 1967 N

M	W. Hitchcock
M	K. Silvestri
1B	F. Alou
2B	W. Woodward
SS	D. Menke
3B	C. Boyer
OF	H. Aaron
OF	M. Jones
OF	R. Carty
C	J. Torre
P	D. Lemaster
P	K. Johnson
P	P. Niekro
P	R. Jarvis
RP	R. Kelley
RP	C. Carroll
RP	J. Ritchie

ATL 1968 N

M	C. Harris
1B	D. Johnson
2B	F. Millan
SS	R. Jackson
3B	C. Boyer
OF	F. Alou
OF	H. Aaron
OF	M. Lum
C	J. Torre
UT	J. Francona
UT	O. Martinez
P	P. Niekro
P	R. Jarvis
P	R. Reed
P	K. Johnson
P	M. Pappas
RP	C. Upshaw
RP	J. Britton
RP	J. Raymond

ATL 1969 N

M	C. Harris
1B	O. Cepeda
2B	F. Millan
SS	R. Jackson
3B	C. Boyer
OF	H. Aaron
OF	F. Alou
OF	M. Lum
C	R. Didier
UT	R. Carty
P	P. Niekro
P	R. Reed
P	R. Jarvis
P	G. Stone
P	M. Pappas
RP	C. Upshaw
RP	G. Neibauer
RP	J. Raymond

ATL 1970 N

M	C. Harris
1B	O. Cepeda
2B	F. Millan
SS	R. Jackson
3B	C. Boyer
OF	R. Carty
OF	H. Aaron
OF	A. Gonzalez
C	J. Tillman
UT	G. Garrido
UT	M. Lum
P	R. Jarvis
P	P. Niekro
P	J. Nash
P	G. Stone
P	R. Reed
RP	J. Wilhelm
RP	R. Priddy

ATL 1971 N

M	C. Harris
1B	H. Aaron
2B	F. Millan
SS	M. Perez
3B	D. Evans
OF	R. Garr
OF	R. Jackson
OF	M. Lum
C	E. Williams
P	P. Niekro
P	R. Reed
P	G. Stone
P	R. Jarvis
P	T. Kelley
RP	C. Upshaw
RP	S. Barber
RP	R. Priddy

ATL 1972 N

M	C. Harris
M	E. Mathews
1B	H. Aaron
2B	F. Millan
SS	M. Perez
3B	D. Evans
OF	R. Garr
OF	J. Baker
OF	M. Lum
C	E. Williams
P	P. Niekro
P	R. Reed
P	R. Schueler
P	T. Kelley
P	G. Stone
RP	R. Jarvis
RP	C. Upshaw

ATL 1973 N

M	E. Mathews
1B	M. Lum
2B	D. Johnson
SS	M. Perez
3B	D. Evans
OF	J. Baker
OF	R. Garr
OF	H. Aaron
C	J. Oates
UT	R. Jackson
P	C. Morton
P	P. Niekro
P	R. Schueler
P	R. Harrison
P	R. Reed
RP	T. House

ATL 1974 N

M	E. Mathews
M	C. King
1B	D. Johnson
2B	M. Perez
SS	C. Robinson
3B	D. Evans
OF	J. Baker
OF	R. Garr
OF	R. Office
C	J. Oates
UT	H. Aaron
UT	M. Lum
P	P. Niekro
P	C. Morton
P	L. Capra
P	R. Reed
P	R. Harrison
RP	T. House
RP	M. Leon
RP	L. Krausse

ATL 1975 N

M	C. King
M	C. Ryan

ATL 1976 N

M	J. Bristol
1B	G. Montanez
2B	R. Gilbreath
SS	D. Chaney
3B	J. Royster
OF	J. Wynn
OF	K. Henderson
OF	R. Office
C	V. Correll
UT	D. May
UT	T. Paciorek
P	P. Niekro
P	R. Ruthven
P	J. Messersmith
P	C. Morton
P	F. LaCorte
RP	R. Moret
RP	P. Devine
RP	J. Dal Canton

ATL 1977 N

M	J. Bristol
M	R. Turner
M	V. Benson
M	J. Bristol
1B	G. Montanez
2B	R. Gilbreath
SS	P. Rockett
3B	A. Moore
OF	J. Burroughs
OF	G. Matthews
OF	R. Office
C	B. Pocoroba
UT	R. Bonnell
UT	J. Royster
P	P. Niekro
P	R. Ruthven
P	L. Capra
P	J. Messersmith
RP	D. Campbell
RP	M. Leon
RP	R. Camp

ATL 1978 N

M	R. Cox
1B	D. Murphy
2B	J. Royster
SS	D. Chaney
3B	J. Horner
OF	J. Burroughs
OF	R. Office
OF	G. Matthews
C	B. Pocoroba
UT	R. Beall
UT	R. Bonnell
UT	R. Gilbreath
P	P. Niekro
P	P. Hanna
P	M. Mahler
P	L. McWilliams
RP	E. Solomon
RP	H. Garber
RP	J. Easterly

ATL 1979 N

M	R. Cox
1B	D. Murphy
2B	G. Hubbard
SS	J. Frias
3B	J. Horner
OF	G. Matthews
OF	R. Bonnell
OF	J. Burroughs
C	B. Benedict
UT	M. Lum
UT	R. Office
UT	J. Royster
P	P. Niekro
P	E. Solomon
P	R. Matula
P	A. Brizzolara
P	M. Mahler
RP	H. Garber
RP	J. McLaughlin
RP	P. Devine

ATL 1980 N

M	R. Cox
1B	C. Chambliss
2B	G. Hubbard
SS	L. Gomez
3B	J. Horner
OF	D. Murphy
OF	G. Matthews
OF	J. Burroughs
C	B. Benedict
UT	J. Royster
P	P. Niekro
P	D. Alexander
P	T. Boggs
P	R. Matula
P	L. McWilliams
RP	R. Camp
RP	H. Garber
RP	P. Hanna

ATL 1981 N

M	R. Cox
1B	C. Chambliss
2B	G. Hubbard
SS	R. Ramirez
3B	J. Horner
OF	D. Murphy
OF	C. Washington
OF	R. Linares
C	B. Benedict
UT	J. Royster
P	G. Perry
P	T. Boggs
P	P. Niekro
P	R. Mahler
RP	J. Montefusco
RP	R. Camp
RP	H. Garber

ATL 1982 N

M	J. Torre
1B	C. Chambliss
2B	G. Hubbard
SS	R. Ramirez
3B	J. Horner
OF	D. Murphy
OF	C. Washington
OF	B. Butler
C	B. Benedict
UT	J. Royster
P	P. Niekro
P	R. Mahler
P	R. Camp
P	R. Walk
RP	S. Bedrosian
RP	H. Garber

ATL 1983 N

M	J. Torre
1B	C. Chambliss
2B	G. Hubbard
SS	R. Ramirez
3B	J. Horner
OF	D. Murphy
OF	B. Butler
OF	C. Washington
C	B. Benedict
P	J. McMurtry
P	P. Perez
P	P. Niekro
P	R. Camp
P	P. Falcone
RP	S. Bedrosian
RP	T. Forster
RP	D. Moore

ATL 1984 N

M	J. Torre
1B	C. Chambliss
2B	G. Hubbard
SS	R. Ramirez
3B	R. Johnson
OF	D. Murphy
OF	C. Washington
OF	B. Komminsk
C	B. Benedict
UT	G. Perry
P	R. Mahler
P	P. Perez
P	J. McMurtry
P	R. Camp
P	L. Barker
RP	H. Garber
RP	S. Bedrosian
RP	J. Dedmon

ATL 1985 N

M	G. Haas
M	R. Wine
1B	J. Horner

ATL 1986 N

M	C. Tanner
1B	J. Horner
2B	G. Hubbard
SS	A. Thomas
3B	K. Oberkfell
OF	D. Murphy
OF	O. Moreno
OF	T. Harper
C	O. Virgil
UT	C. Chambliss
UT	R. Ramirez
P	R. Mahler
P	D. Palmer
P	Z. Smith
P	D. Alexander
RP	J. Dedmon
RP	J. McMurtry
RP	H. Garber

ATL 1987 N

M	C. Tanner
1B	G. Perry
2B	G. Hubbard
SS	A. Thomas
3B	K. Oberkfell
OF	D. Murphy
OF	D. James
OF	G. Griffey
C	O. Virgil
UT	C. Chambliss
UT	B. Butler
C	B. Benedict
UT	J. Royster
P	P. Niekro
P	R. Mahler
P	R. Camp
RP	D. Campbell
RP	H. Garber

(ATL 1987 N continued)

P	R. Mahler
P	D. Palmer
P	D. Puleo
P	D. Alexander
RP	J. Acker
RP	J. Dedmon
RP	H. Garber

ATL 1988 N

M	C. Tanner
M	R. Nixon
1B	G. Perry
2B	R. Gant
SS	A. Thomas
3B	K. Oberkfell
OF	D. Murphy
OF	D. James
OF	A. Hall
C	O. Virgil
P	R. Mahler
P	P. Smith
P	T. Glavine
P	Z. Smith
P	D. Puleo
RP	C. Puleo
RP	J. Alvarez
RP	P. Assenmacher

ATL 1989 N

M	R. Nixon
1B	G. Perry
2B	H. Treadway
SS	A. Thomas
3B	J. Blauser
OF	D. Murphy
OF	L. Smith
OF	O. McDowell
C	J. Davis
UT	D. Evans
UT	W. Gregg
P	J. Smoltz
P	T. Glavine
P	D. Lilliquist
P	P. Smith
P	M. Clary
RP	J. Acker
RP	J. Boever
RP	M. Eichhorn

ATL 1990 N

M	R. Nixon
M	R. Cox
1B	D. Justice
2B	H. Treadway

(ATL 1990 N continued)

2B	G. Hubbard
SS	R. Ramirez
3B	K. Oberkfell
OF	D. Murphy
OF	T. Harper
C	C. Washington
C	R. Cerone
UT	C. Chambliss
UT	B. Komminsk
UT	G. Perry
P	R. Mahler
P	S. Bedrosian
P	Z. Smith
RP	R. Camp
RP	H. Garber
RP	H. Sutter

(ATL 1990 N continued)

SS	J. Blauser
3B	J. Presley
OF	R. Gant
OF	L. Smith
OF	D. Murphy
C	G. Olson
UT	W. Gregg
UT	M. Lemke
UT	O. McDowell
P	J. Smoltz
P	T. Glavine
P	C. Leibrandt
P	M. Clary
P	S. Avery
RP	A. Castillo
RP	R. Luecken
RP	M. Grant

Baltimore

MAR n 1873
BAL n 1872-1874
BAL U 1884
BAL a 1882-1889
BAL a 1890-1891
BAL N 1892-1899
BAL A 1901-1902
BAL F 1914-1915
BAL A 1954-1990

MAR 1873 n

M	W. Smith
1B	W. Lennon
2B	M. Simpson
SS	J. Smith
3B	H. Kohler
OF	W. French
OF	W. Stratton
OF	J. Sheppard
C	W. Smith
P	W. Stratton
P	F. Selman
P	Mc Doolan

BAL 1872 n

M	W. Craver
M	E. Mills
1B	E. Mills
2B	T. Carey
SS	J. Radcliff
3B	D. Force
OF	G. Hall
OF	T. York
OF	L. Pike
C	W. Craver
UT	R. Higham
P	R. Mathews
P	W. Fisher

BAL 1873 n

M	C. McVey
M	T. Carey
1B	E. Mills
2B	T. Carey
SS	J. Radcliff
3B	D. Force
OF	T. York
OF	L. Pike
OF	G. Hall
C	W. Craver
UT	C. McVey
P	W. Cummings
P	A. Brainard

BAL 1874 n

M	W. White
1B	C. Gould
2B	J. Manning
SS	L. Say
3B	W. White
OF	J. Ryan
OF	J. Deane
OF	C. Bielaski
C	C. Snyder
P	A. Brainard
P	J. Manning

BAL 1884 U

M	W. Henderson
1B	C. Levis
2B	J. Phelan
SS	L. Say
3B	W. Robinson
OF	J. Seery
OF	E. Cuthbert
C	B. Graham
C	E. Fusselback
P	W. Sweeney
P	T. Lee
P	A. Atkinson

BAL 1882 a

M	H. Myers
1B	C. Householder
2B	G. Pierce
SS	H. Myers
3B	J. Shetzline
OF	C. Waitt
OF	T. Brown
OF	J. Cline
C	E. Whiting
P	S. Landis
P	F. Nichols
P	E. Geis

BAL 1883 a

M	W. Barnie
1B	D. Stearns
2B	T. Manning
SS	L. Say
3B	J. McCormick
OF	J. Clinton
OF	D. Eggler
OF	D. Rowe
C	J. Kelly
P	J. Henderson
P	R. Emslie
P	J. Fox

BAL 1884 a

M	W. Barnie
1B	D. Stearns
2B	T. Manning
SS	J. Macullar
3B	J. Sommer
OF	J. Clinton
OF	T. York
OF	F. Gardner
C	S. Trott
P	R. Emslie
P	J. Henderson

BAL 1885 a

M	W. Barnie
1B	D. Stearns
2B	T. Manning
SS	J. Macullar
3B	M. Muldoon
OF	J. Sommer
OF	D. Casey
OF	E. Greer
C	W. Traffley
UT	T. Burns
P	J. Henderson
P	R. Emslie
P	J. Henry

BAL 1886 a

M	W. Barnie
1B	M. Scott
2B	M. Muldoon
SS	J. Macullar
3B	J. Davis
OF	J. Manning
OF	J. Sommer
OF	P. O'Connell
C	C. Fulmer
P	M. Kilroy
P	G. McGinnis
P	J. Henderson

BAL 1887 a

M	W. Barnie
1B	T. Tucker
2B	W. Greenwood
SS	T. Burns
3B	J. Davis
OF	W. Purcell
OF	M. Griffin
OF	J. Sommer
C	S. Trott
P	M. Kilroy
P	J. Smith

BAL 1888 a

M	W. Barnie
1B	T. Tucker
2B	W. Greenwood
SS	J. Farrell
3B	W. Shindle
OF	M. Griffin
OF	W. Purcell
OF	T. Burns
C	C. Fulmer
P	E. Cunningham
P	M. Kilroy
P	J. Smith

BAL 1889 a

M	W. Barnie

1B	T. Tucker
2B	J. Mack
SS	J. Farrell
3B	W. Shindle
OF	M. Hornung
OF	M. Griffin
OF	J. Sommer
C	E. Tate
P	M. Kilroy
P	F. Foreman
P	E. Cunningham

BAL 1890 a

M	W. Barnie
1B	T. Power
2B	J. Mack
SS	I. Ray
3B	P. Gilbert
OF	J. Sommer
OF	W. Johnson
OF	D. Long
C	G. Townsend
P	L. German
P	J. McMahon
P	M. O'Rourke
P	M. Morrison

BAL 1891 a

M	W. Barnie
1B	P. Werden
2B	S. Wise
SS	G. Van Haltren
3B	P. Gilbert
OF	W. Johnson
OF	C. Welch
OF	I. Ray
C	W. Robinson
P	J. McMahon
P	E. Cunningham
P	M. Madden
P	J. Healy

BAL 1892 N

M	G. Van Haltren
M	J. Waltz
M	E. Hanlon
1B	E. Sutcliffe
2B	J. Stricker
SS	T. O'Rourke
3B	W. Shindle
OF	G. Van Haltren
OF	H. Stovey
OF	C. Welch
C	W. Robinson
P	J. McMahon
P	G. Cobb
P	T. Vickery
P	C. Buffinton

BAL 1893 N

M	E. Hanlon
1B	H. Taylor
2B	H. Reitz
SS	J. McGraw
3B	W. Shindle
OF	J. Kelley
OF	G. Treadway
OF	J. Long
C	W. Robinson
P	J. McMahon
P	A. Mullane
P	W. Hawke
P	E. McNabb
P	K. Baker

BAL 1894 N

M	E. Hanlon
1B	D. Brouthers
2B	H. Reitz
SS	H. Jennings
3B	J. McGraw
OF	J. Kelley
OF	W. Brodie
OF	W. Keeler
C	W. Robinson
P	J. McMahon
P	W. Hawke
P	W. Gleason
P	A. Inks
P	A. Mullane

BAL 1895 N

M	E. Hanlon
1B	G. Carey
2B	W. Gleason
SS	H. Jennings
3B	J. McGraw
OF	J. Kelley
OF	W. Keeler
OF	W. Brodie
C	W. Robinson

P	W. Hoffer
P	G. Hemming
P	C. Esper
P	A. Clarkson
P	J. McMahon

BAL 1896 N

M	E. Hanlon
1B	J. Doyle
2B	H. Reitz
SS	H. Jennings
3B	J. Donnelly
OF	W. Brodie
OF	J. Kelley
OF	W. Keeler
C	W. Robinson
UT	W. Clarke
P	W. Hoffer
P	E. Pond
P	G. Hemming
P	J. McMahon
P	C. Esper

BAL 1897 N

M	E. Hanlon
1B	J. Doyle
2B	H. Reitz
SS	H. Jennings
3B	J. McGraw
OF	J. Stenzel
OF	J. Kelley
OF	W. Keeler
C	W. Clarke
P	J. Corbett
P	W. Hoffer
P	E. Pond
P	J. Nops

BAL 1898 N

M	E. Hanlon
1B	D. McGann
2B	De Montreville
SS	H. Jennings
3B	J. McGraw
OF	W. Keeler
OF	J. Kelley
OF	J. Holmes
C	W. Robinson
P	J. McJames
P	J. Hughes
P	A. Maul
P	J. Nops
P	F. Kitson

BAL 1899 N

M	J. McGraw
1B	G. LaChance
2B	De Montreville
SS	W. Keister
3B	J. McGraw
OF	S. Sheckard
OF	J. Holmes
OF	W. Brodie
C	W. Robinson
P	J. McGinnity
P	F. Kitson
P	J. Nops
P	H. Howell

BAL 1901 A

M	J. McGraw
1B	J. Hart
2B	J. Williams
SS	W. Keister
3B	J. McGraw
OF	J. Seymour
OF	J. Jackson
OF	W. Brodie
C	R. Bresnahan
UT	M. Donlin
UT	J. Dunn
P	J. McGinnity
P	H. Howell
P	F. Foreman
P	J. Nops

BAL 1902 A

M	J. McGraw
M	W. Robinson
1B	D. McGann
2B	J. Williams
SS	W. Gilbert
3B	R. Bresnahan
OF	A. Selbach
OF	J. Seymour
OF	H. Arndt
C	W. Robinson
P	J. McGinnity
P	H. Howell
P	L. Wiltse
P	C. Shields

P	J. Katoll

BAL 1914 F

M	F. Knabe
1B	H. Swacina
2B	F. Knabe
SS	M. Doolan
3B	M. Walsh
OF	V. Duncan
OF	B. Meyer
OF	G. Simmons
C	F. Jacklitsch
P	J. Quinn
P	G. Suggs
P	I. Wilhelm
P	F. Smith
P	W. Bailey

BAL 1915 F

M	F. Knabe
1B	H. Swacina
2B	F. Knabe
SS	M. Doolan
3B	M. Walsh
OF	V. Duncan
OF	S. McCandless
OF	G. Zinn
C	F. Owens
P	J. Quinn
P	G. Suggs
P	W. Bailey
P	C. Bender
P	A. Johnson

BAL 1954 A

M	J. Dykes
1B	E. Waitkus
2B	R. Young
SS	G. Hunter
3B	V. Stephens
OF	C. Diering
OF	C. Abrams
OF	J. Fridley
C	C. Courtney
UT	G. Coan
UT	R. Kennedy
UT	R. Kryhoski
P	R. Turley
P	J. Coleman
P	D. Larsen
P	D. Pillette
P	L. Kretlow
RP	R. Chakales
RP	M. Blyzka
RP	H. Fox

BAL 1955 A

M	P. Richards
1B	G. Triandos
2B	F. Marsh
SS	G. Miranda
3B	J. Causey
OF	C. Diering
OF	C. Abrams
OF	D. Philley
C	H. Smith
P	J. Wilson
P	E. Palica
P	R. Moore
P	W. Wight
RP	A. Schallock
RP	D. Johnson
RP	H. Dorish

BAL 1956 A

M	P. Richards
1B	R. Boyd
2B	W. Gardner
SS	G. Miranda
3B	G. Kell
OF	J. Francona
OF	R. Nieman
OF	R. Williams
C	G. Triandos
P	R. Moore
P	C. Johnson
P	W. Wight
P	H. Brown
P	E. Palica
RP	D. Ferrarese
RP	G. Zuverink
RP	W. Loes

BAL 1957 A

M	P. Richards
1B	R. Boyd
2B	W. Gardner
SS	G. Miranda
3B	G. Kell
OF	A. Pilarcik
OF	R. Nieman

OF	J. Busby
C	G. Triandos
UT	J. Francona
P	C. Johnson
P	R. Moore
P	W. Loes
P	H. Brown
P	W. O'Dell
RP	G. Zuverink
RP	K. Lehman
RP	A. Ceccarelli

BAL 1958 A

M	P. Richards
1B	R. Boyd
2B	W. Gardner
SS	G. Miranda
3B	B. Robinson
OF	A. Pilarcik
OF	E. Woodling
OF	J. Busby
C	G. Triandos
P	J. Harshman
P	W. O'Dell
P	A. Portocarrero
P	M. Pappas
P	C. Johnson
RP	G. Zuverink
RP	K. Lehman
RP	C. Beamon

BAL 1959 A

M	P. Richards
1B	R. Boyd
2B	W. Gardner
SS	A. Carrasquel
3B	B. Robinson
OF	W. Tasby
OF	E. Woodling
OF	A. Pilarcik
C	G. Triandos
UT	W. Klaus
UT	R. Nieman
P	J. Wilhelm
P	M. Pappas
P	W. O'Dell
P	J. Walker
P	H. Brown
RP	W. Loes
RP	E. Johnson

BAL 1960 A

M	P. Richards
1B	J. Gentile
2B	M. Breeding
SS	R. Hansen
3B	B. Robinson
OF	J. Brandt
OF	E. Woodling
OF	G. Stephens
C	G. Triandos
UT	A. Pilarcik
P	C. Estrada
P	M. Pappas
P	J. Fisher
P	S. Barber
P	H. Brown
RP	G. Jones

BAL 1961 A

M	P. Richards
M	C. Harris
1B	J. Gentile
2B	K. Adair
SS	R. Hansen
3B	B. Robinson
OF	J. Brandt
OF	R. Snyder
OF	D. Herzog
C	G. Triandos
UT	R. Williams
P	S. Barber
P	C. Estrada
P	J. Fisher
P	M. Pappas
P	H. Brown
RP	J. Wilhelm
RP	W. Stock

BAL 1962 A

M	W. Hitchcock
1B	J. Gentile
2B	M. Breeding
SS	K. Adair
3B	B. Robinson
OF	J. Brandt
OF	R. Snyder
OF	J. Powell
C	G. Triandos

UT	D. Herzog
UT	D. Nicholson
P	C. Estrada
P	M. Pappas
P	R. Roberts
P	J. Fisher
P	S. Barber
P	R. Hall
RP	R. Hall
RP	W. Hoeft
RP	J. Wilhelm

BAL 1963 A

M	W. Hitchcock
1B	J. Gentile
2B	K. Adair
SS	L. Aparicio
3B	B. Robinson
OF	J. Brandt
OF	R. Snyder
OF	J. Powell
C	J. Orsino
UT	R. Saverine
UT	A. Smith
P	S. Barber
P	R. Roberts
P	M. Pappas
P	M. McCormick
P	D. McNally
RP	S. Miller
RP	R. Hall
RP	W. Stock

BAL 1964 A

M	H. Bauer
1B	N. Siebern
2B	K. Adair
SS	L. Aparicio
3B	B. Robinson
OF	S. Bowens
OF	J. Brandt
OF	J. Powell
C	R. Brown
P	M. Pappas
P	W. Bunker
P	R. Roberts
P	D. McNally
P	S. Barber
RP	S. Miller
RP	H. Haddix
RP	R. Hall

BAL 1965 A

M	H. Bauer
1B	J. Powell
2B	K. Adair
SS	L. Aparicio
3B	B. Robinson
OF	C. Blefary
OF	P. Blair
OF	R. Snyder
C	R. Brown
UT	N. Siebern
P	M. Pappas
P	S. Barber
P	D. McNally
P	W. Bunker
P	R. Roberts
RP	S. Miller
RP	R. Hall
RP	D. Larsen

BAL 1966 A

M	H. Bauer
1B	J. Powell
2B	D. Johnson
SS	L. Aparicio
3B	B. Robinson
OF	F. Robinson
OF	P. Blair
OF	C. Blefary
C	A. Etchebarren
UT	R. Snyder
P	D. McNally
P	J. Palmer
P	E. Watt
P	W. Bunker
P	S. Barber
RP	M. Drabowsky
RP	S. Miller
RP	E. Fisher

BAL 1967 A

M	H. Bauer
1B	J. Powell
2B	D. Johnson
SS	L. Aparicio
3B	B. Robinson
OF	P. Blair
OF	F. Robinson
OF	C. Blefary
C	A. Etchebarren
UT	R. Snyder

P	T. Phoebus
P	P. Richert
P	W. Dillman
P	D. McNally
P	J. Hardin
RP	E. Watt
RP	M. Drabowsky
RP	E. Fisher

BAL 1968 A

M	H. Bauer
M	E. Weaver
1B	J. Powell
2B	D. Johnson
SS	M. Belanger
3B	B. Robinson
OF	P. Blair
OF	F. Robinson
OF	C. Blefary
C	A. Etchebarren
UT	D. Buford
P	D. McNally
P	J. Hardin
P	T. Phoebus
P	D. Leonhard
P	E. Brabender
RP	E. Watt
RP	P. Richert
RP	M. Drabowsky

BAL 1969 A

M	E. Weaver
1B	J. Powell
2B	D. Johnson
SS	M. Belanger
3B	B. Robinson
OF	P. Blair
OF	F. Robinson
OF	D. Buford
C	E. Hendricks
P	M. Cuellar
P	D. McNally
P	T. Phoebus
P	J. Palmer
P	J. Hardin
RP	D. Leonhard
RP	E. Watt
RP	M. Lopez

BAL 1970 A

M	E. Weaver
1B	J. Powell
2B	D. Johnson
SS	M. Belanger
3B	B. Robinson
OF	D. Buford
OF	P. Blair
OF	F. Robinson
C	E. Hendricks
UT	M. Rettenmund
P	J. Palmer
P	M. Cuellar
P	D. McNally
P	J. Hardin
P	T. Phoebus
RP	M. Lopez
RP	R. Hall
RP	E. Watt

BAL 1971 A

M	E. Weaver
1B	J. Powell
2B	D. Johnson
SS	M. Belanger
3B	B. Robinson
OF	P. Blair
OF	M. Rettenmund
OF	D. Buford
C	E. Hendricks
UT	F. Robinson
P	M. Cuellar
P	J. Palmer
P	D. Dobson
P	D. McNally
RP	G. Jackson

BAL 1972 A

M	E. Weaver
1B	J. Powell
2B	D. Johnson
SS	M. Belanger
3B	B. Robinson
OF	P. Blair
OF	D. Buford
OF	M. Rettenmund
C	J. Oates
UT	D. Baylor
UT	T. Crowley
UT	R. Grich
P	J. Palmer
P	P. Dobson
P	M. Cuellar

P	D. McNally
P	D. Alexander
RP	R. Harrison

BAL 1973 A

M	E. Weaver
1B	J. Powell
2B	R. Grich
SS	M. Belanger
3B	B. Robinson
OF	P. Blair
OF	D. Baylor
OF	R. Coggins
C	E. Williams
DH	H. Davis
UT	A. Bumbry
P	J. Palmer
P	M. Cuellar
P	D. McNally
P	D. Alexander
P	J. Jefferson
RP	R. Reynolds
RP	G. Jackson
RP	E. Watt

BAL 1974 A

M	E. Weaver
1B	J. Powell
2B	R. Grich
SS	M. Belanger
3B	B. Robinson
OF	P. Blair
OF	D. Baylor
OF	R. Coggins
C	E. Williams
DH	H. Davis
P	R. Grimsley
P	M. Cuellar
P	D. McNally
P	J. Palmer
P	D. Alexander
RP	R. Reynolds
RP	G. Jackson
RP	J. Jefferson

BAL 1975 A

M	E. Weaver
1B	L. May
2B	R. Grich
SS	M. Belanger
3B	B. Robinson
OF	K. Singleton
OF	P. Blair
OF	D. Baylor
C	D. Duncan
DH	H. Davis
UT	A. Bumbry
P	J. Palmer
P	M. Torrez
P	M. Cuellar
P	R. Grimsley
P	D. Alexander
RP	G. Jackson

BAL 1976 A

M	E. Weaver
1B	A. Muser
2B	R. Grich
SS	M. Belanger
3B	D. DeCinces
OF	P. Blair
OF	K. Singleton
OF	R. Jackson
C	D. Duncan
DH	L. May
UT	A. Bumbry
P	J. Palmer
P	M. Garland
P	R. May
P	R. Grimsley
P	M. Cuellar
RP	D. Miller

BAL 1977 A

M	E. Weaver
1B	L. May
2B	B. Smith
SS	M. Belanger
3B	D. DeCinces
OF	K. Singleton
OF	A. Bumbry
OF	H. Kelly
C	J. Dempsey
DH	E. Murray
UT	A. Muser
P	J. Palmer
P	R. May
P	M. Flanagan
P	R. Grimsley
P	J. Martinez
RP	F. Martinez

BAL 1978 A

M	E. Weaver
1B	E. Murray
2B	R. Dauer
SS	M. Belanger
3B	D. DeCinces
OF	K. Singleton
OF	L. Harlow
OF	C. Lopez
C	J. Dempsey
DH	L. May
UT	H. Kelly
P	J. Palmer
P	M. Flanagan
P	S. McGregor
RP	D. Stanhouse
RP	J. Kerrigan
RP	F. Martinez

BAL 1979 A

M	E. Weaver
1B	E. Murray
2B	R. Dauer
SS	A. Garcia
3B	D. DeCinces
OF	A. Bumbry
OF	K. Singleton
OF	G. Roenicke
C	J. Dempsey
DH	L. May
UT	M. Belanger
UT	J. Lowenstein
P	J. Martinez
P	M. Flanagan
P	S. Stone
P	S. McGregor
P	J. Palmer
RP	F. Martinez
RP	D. Stanhouse
RP	T. Stoddard

BAL 1980 A

M	E. Weaver
1B	E. Murray
2B	R. Dauer
SS	M. Belanger
3B	D. DeCinces
OF	A. Bumbry
OF	K. Singleton
OF	G. Roenicke
C	J. Dempsey
DH	T. Crowley
UT	A. Garcia
UT	J. Lowenstein
P	S. McGregor
P	S. Stone
P	M. Flanagan
P	J. Palmer
P	S. Stewart
RP	T. Stoddard
RP	F. Martinez
RP	D. Ford

BAL 1981 A

M	E. Weaver
1B	E. Murray
2B	R. Dauer
SS	M. Belanger
3B	D. DeCinces
OF	A. Bumbry
OF	G. Roenicke
OF	J. Lowenstein
C	J. Dempsey
DH	T. Crowley
UT	J. Dwyer
UT	K. Singleton
P	J. Martinez
P	S. McGregor
P	J. Palmer
P	M. Flanagan
P	S. Stewart
RP	F. Martinez
RP	D. Ford
RP	T. Stoddard

BAL 1982 A

M	E. Weaver
1B	E. Murray
2B	R. Dauer
SS	C. Ripken
3B	G. Gulliver
OF	A. Bumbry
OF	G. Roenicke
OF	D. Ford
C	J. Dempsey
DH	K. Singleton
UT	J. Lowenstein
UT	L. Sakata
P	J. Martinez
P	M. Flanagan
P	J. Palmer
P	S. McGregor
P	S. Stewart
RP	F. Martinez
RP	R. Grimsley
RP	T. Stoddard

BAL 1983 A

M	J. Altobelli
1B	E. Murray
2B	R. Dauer
SS	C. Ripken
3B	T. Cruz
OF	J. Shelby
OF	J. Lowenstein
OF	A. Bumbry
C	J. Dempsey
DH	K. Singleton
UT	J. Dwyer
UT	D. Ford
UT	G. Roenicke
P	S. McGregor
P	G. Davis
P	M. Boddicker
P	J. Martinez
P	M. Flanagan
RP	S. Stewart
RP	F. Martinez
RP	T. Stoddard

BAL 1984 A

M	J. Altobelli
1B	E. Murray
2B	R. Dauer
SS	C. Ripken
3B	W. Gross
OF	J. Shelby
OF	G. Roenicke
OF	M. Young
C	J. Dempsey
DH	K. Singleton
UT	A. Bumbry
UT	J. Lowenstein
P	M. Boddicker
P	M. Flanagan
P	G. Davis
P	S. McGregor
P	J. Martinez
RP	S. Stewart
RP	F. Martinez
RP	T. Underwood

BAL 1985 A

M	J. Altobelli
M	C. Ripken
M	E. Weaver
1B	E. Murray
2B	A. Wiggins
SS	C. Ripken
3B	F. Rayford
OF	F. Lynn
OF	L. Lacy
OF	M. Young
C	J. Dempsey
DH	L. Sheets
UT	J. Dwyer
UT	W. Gross
UT	G. Roenicke
P	S. McGregor
P	M. Boddicker
P	J. Martinez
P	G. Davis
P	K. Dixon
RP	S. Stewart
RP	N. Snell
RP	D. Aase

BAL 1986 A

M	E. Weaver
1B	E. Murray
2B	J. Bonilla
SS	C. Ripken
3B	F. Rayford
OF	J. Shelby
OF	L. Lacy
OF	F. Lynn
C	J. Dempsey
DH	L. Sheets
UT	J. Beniquez
UT	M. Young
P	M. Boddicker
P	S. McGregor
P	K. Dixon
P	M. Flanagan
P	G. Davis
RP	R. Bordi
RP	D. Aase
RP	N. Snell

BAL 1987 A

M	C. Ripken
1B	E. Murray
2B	W. Ripken
SS	C. Ripken
3B	C. Knight
OF	L. Sheets
OF	F. Lynn
OF	H. Gerhart
C	T. Kennedy
DH	M. Young
P	M. Boddicker
P	E. Bell
P	D. Schmidt
P	J. Habyan
P	K. Dixon
RP	M. Williamson
RP	T. Arnold
RP	T. Niedenfuer

BAL 1988 A

M	C. Ripken
M	F. Robinson
1B	J. Traber
2B	W. Ripken
SS	C. Ripken
3B	R. Gonzales
OF	J. Orsulak
OF	H. Gerhart
OF	F. Lynn
C	M. Tettleton
DH	E. Murray
UT	L. Sheets
P	J. Bautista
P	J. Tibbs
P	J. Ballard
P	M. Boddicker
P	D. Schmidt
RP	D. Sisk
RP	M. Thurmond
RP	T. Niedenfuer

BAL 1989 A

M	F. Robinson
1B	R. Milligan
2B	W. Ripken
SS	C. Ripken
3B	C. Worthington
OF	P. Bradley
OF	M. Devereaux
OF	J. Orsulak
C	M. Tettleton
DH	L. Sheets
P	R. Milacki
P	J. Ballard
P	D. Schmidt
P	P. Harnisch
RP	B. Holton
RP	M. Williamson
RP	M. Thurmond

BAL 1990 A

M	F. Robinson
1B	R. Milligan
2B	W. Ripken
SS	C. Ripken
3B	C. Worthington
OF	S. Finley
OF	J. Orsulak
OF	M. Devereaux
C	M. Tettleton
DH	S. Horn
P	P. Harnisch
P	D. Johnson
P	R. Milacki
P	J. Ballard
P	L. McDonald
RP	M. Williamson
RP	G. Olson
RP	J. Price

Boston

BOS n 1871-1875
BOS U 1884
BOS P 1890
BOS a 1891
BOS N 1876-1952
BOS A 1901-1990

BOS 1871 n

M	W. Wright
1B	C. Gould
2B	R. Barnes
SS	G. Wright
3B	H. Schafer
OF	H. Wright
OF	D. Birdsall
OF	J. Cone
C	C. McVey
P	A. Spalding

BOS 1872 n

M	W. Wright
1B	C. Gould
2B	R. Barnes
SS	G. Wright
3B	H. Schafer
OF	W. Wright
OF	F. Rogers
OF	A. Leonard
C	C. McVey
P	A. Spalding

BOS 1873 n

M	W. Wright
1B	J. O'Rourke
2B	R. Barnes
SS	G. Wright
3B	H. Schafer
OF	W. Wright
OF	A. Leonard
OF	R. Addy
C	J. White
P	A. Spalding

BOS 1874 n

M	W. Wright
1B	J. O'Rourke
2B	R. Barnes
SS	G. Wright
3B	H. Schafer
OF	C. McVey
OF	A. Leonard
OF	G. Hall
C	J. White
P	A. Spalding

BOS 1875 n

M	W. Wright
1B	C. McVey
2B	R. Barnes
SS	G. Wright
3B	H. Schafer
OF	A. Leonard
OF	J. Manning
OF	J. O'Rourke
C	J. White
P	A. Spalding

BOS 1884 U

M	T. Murnane
1B	T. Murnane
2B	T. O'Brien
SS	W. Hackett
3B	J. Irwin
OF	M. Slattery
OF	E. Crane
OF	F. Butler
C	L. Brown
P	W. Burke
P	F. Shaw
P	T. Bond

BOS 1890 P

M	M. Kelly
1B	D. Brouthers
2B	J. Quinn
SS	A. Irwin
3B	W. Nash
OF	T. Brown
OF	A. Richardson
OF	H. Stovey
C	M. Murphy
UT	M. Kelly
P	C. Radbourn
P	A. Gumbert
P	W. Daley
P	M. Kilroy

BOS 1891 a

M	A. Irwin
1B	D. Brouthers
2B	J. Stricker
SS	P. Radford
3B	C. Farrell
OF	T. Brown
OF	H. Duffy
OF	A. Richardson
C	M. Murphy
P	G. Haddock
P	C. Buffinton
P	J. O'Brien
P	W. Daley

BOS 1876 N

M	W. Wright
1B	T. Murnane
2B	J. Morrill
SS	G. Wright
3B	H. Schafer
OF	J. O'Rourke
OF	J. Manning
OF	A. Leonard
C	L. Brown
P	J. Borden
P	G. Bradley

BOS 1877 N

M	W. Wright
1B	J. White
2B	G. Wright
SS	E. Sutton
3B	J. Morrill
OF	J. O'Rourke
OF	A. Leonard
OF	T. Murnane
C	L. Brown
P	T. Bond

BOS 1878 N

M	W. Wright
1B	J. Morrill
2B	J. Burdock
SS	G. Wright
3B	E. Sutton
OF	A. Leonard
OF	J. Manning
OF	J. O'Rourke
C	C. Snyder
P	T. Bond

BOS 1879 N

M	W. Wright
1B	E. Cogswell
2B	J. Burdock
SS	E. Sutton
3B	J. Morrill
OF	C. Jones
OF	J. O'Rourke
OF	S. Houck
C	C. Snyder
P	T. Bond
P	C. Foley

BOS 1880 N

M	W. Wright
1B	J. Morrill
2B	J. Burdock
SS	E. Sutton
OF	J. O'Rourke
OF	C. Jones
OF	J. O'Rourke
C	P. Powers
P	T. Bond
P	C. Foley

BOS 1881 N

M	W. Wright
1B	J. Morrill
2B	J. Burdock
SS	R. Barnes
3B	E. Sutton
OF	M. Hornung
OF	W. Crowley
OF	F. Lewis
C	C. Snyder
P	J. Whitney
P	J. Fox

BOS 1882 N

M	J. Morrill
1B	J. Morrill
2B	J. Burdock
SS	S. Wise
3B	E. Sutton
OF	P. Hotaling
OF	M. Hornung
OF	W. Rowen
C	T. Deasley
P	J. Whitney
P	R. Mathews

BOS 1883 N

M	J. Burdock
M	J. Morrill
1B	J. Morrill
2B	J. Burdock
SS	S. Wise
3B	E. Sutton
OF	M. Hornung
OF	P. Radford
C	C. Buffinton
C	M. Hines
P	J. Whitney

BOS 1884 N

M	J. Morrill
1B	J. Morrill
2B	J. Burdock
SS	S. Wise
3B	E. Sutton
OF	M. Hornung
OF	W. Crowley
OF	J. Manning
C	M. Hackett
P	C. Buffinton
P	J. Whitney

BOS 1885 N

M	J. Morrill
1B	J. Morrill
2B	J. Burdock
SS	S. Wise
3B	E. Sutton
OF	J. Manning
OF	T. Poorman
OF	T. McCarthy
C	T. Gunning
P	J. Whitney
P	C. Buffinton
P	J. Davis

BOS 1886 N

M	J. Morrill
1B	S. Wise
2B	J. Burdock
SS	J. Morrill
3B	W. Nash
OF	R. Johnston
OF	M. Hornung
OF	T. Poorman
C	C. Daily
UT	E. Sutton
P	C. Radbourn
P	W. Stemmeyer

BOS 1887 N

M	M. Kelly
M	J. Morrill
1B	J. Morrill
2B	J. Burdock
SS	S. Wise
3B	W. Nash
OF	R. Johnston
OF	M. Hornung
OF	M. Kelly
C	E. Tate
UT	E. Sutton
P	C. Radbourn
P	M. Madden
P	R. Conway
P	W. Stemmeyer

BOS 1888 N

M	J. Morrill
1B	J. Morrill
2B	J. Quinn
SS	S. Wise
3B	W. Nash
OF	R. Johnston
OF	M. Hornung
OF	T. Brown
C	M. Kelly
P	J. Clarkson
P	W. Sowders
P	C. Radbourn
P	M. Madden

BOS 1889 N

M	J. Hart
1B	D. Brouthers
2B	A. Richardson
SS	J. Quinn
3B	W. Nash
OF	R. Johnston
OF	M. Kelly
OF	T. Brown
C	C. Bennett
P	J. Clarkson
P	C. Radbourn
P	M. Madden

BOS 1890 N

M	F. Selee
1B	T. Tucker
2B	C. Smith
SS	H. Long
3B	J. McGarr
OF	W. Brodie
OF	M. Sullivan
OF	P. Hines
C	C. Bennett
P	C. Nichols
P	J. Clarkson
P	C. Getzien

BOS 1891 N

M	F. Selee
1B	T. Tucker
2B	J. Quinn
SS	H. Long
3B	W. Nash
OF	H. Stovey
OF	W. Brodie
OF	R. Lowe
C	C. Bennett
P	J. Clarkson
P	C. Nichols
P	H. Staley
P	C. Getzien

BOS 1892 N

M	F. Selee
1B	T. Tucker
2B	J. Quinn
SS	H. Long
3B	W. Nash
OF	T. McCarthy
OF	H. Duffy
OF	R. Lowe
C	K. Kelly
P	C. Nichols
P	J. Stivetts
P	H. Staley
P	J. Clarkson

BOS 1893 N

M	F. Selee
1B	T. Tucker
2B	R. Lowe
SS	H. Long
3B	W. Nash
OF	H. Duffy
OF	S. Carroll
OF	T. McCarthy
C	C. Bennett
P	C. Nichols
P	J. Stivetts
P	H. Staley
P	H. Gastright

BOS 1894 N

M	F. Selee
1B	T. Tucker
2B	R. Lowe
SS	H. Long
3B	W. Nash
OF	J. Bannon
OF	T. McCarthy
OF	H. Duffy
C	C. Ganzel
P	C. Nichols
P	J. Stivetts
P	H. Staley
P	T. Lovett

BOS 1895 N

M	F. Selee
1B	T. Tucker
2B	R. Lowe
SS	H. Long
3B	W. Nash
OF	H. Duffy
OF	J. Bannon
OF	T. McCarthy
C	C. Ganzel
P	C. Nichols
P	J. Stivetts
P	P. Dolan
P	J. Sullivan

BOS 1896 N

M	F. Selee
1B	T. Tucker
2B	R. Lowe
SS	H. Long
3B	J. Collins
OF	W. Hamilton
OF	H. Duffy
OF	J. Bannon
C	M. Bergen
UT	F. Tenney
P	C. Nichols
P	J. Stivetts
P	J. Sullivan
P	F. Klobedanz

BOS 1897 N

M	F. Selee
1B	F. Tenney
2B	R. Lowe
SS	H. Long
3B	J. Collins
OF	H. Duffy
OF	W. Hamilton
OF	C. Stahl
C	M. Bergen
P	C. Nichols
P	F. Klobedanz
P	E. Lewis
P	J. Sullivan

BOS 1898 N

M	F. Selee
1B	F. Tenney
2B	R. Lowe
SS	H. Long
3B	J. Collins
OF	H. Duffy
OF	C. Stahl
OF	W. Hamilton
C	M. Bergen
P	C. Nichols
P	E. Lewis
P	V. Willis
P	F. Klobedanz

BOS 1899 N

M	F. Selee
1B	F. Tenney
2B	R. Lowe
SS	H. Long
3B	J. Collins
OF	C. Stahl
OF	H. Duffy
OF	W. Hamilton
C	M. Bergen
P	V. Willis
P	C. Nichols
P	E. Lewis
P	J. Meekin
P	F. Killen

BOS 1900 N

M	F. Selee
1B	F. Tenney
2B	R. Lowe
SS	H. Long
3B	J. Collins
OF	W. Hamilton
OF	C. Stahl
OF	J. Freeman
C	W. Clarke
P	W. Dinneen
P	V. Willis
P	C. Nichols
P	E. Lewis
P	C. Pittinger

BOS 1901 N

M	F. Selee
1B	F. Tenney
2B	De Montreville
SS	H. Long
3B	R. Lowe
OF	W. Hamilton
OF	J. Slagle
OF	D. Cooley
C	M. Kittridge
P	C. Nichols
P	W. Dinneen
P	V. Willis
P	C. Pittinger

BOS 1902 N

M	A.Buckenberger
1B	F. Tenney
2B	De Montreville
SS	H. Long
3B	L. Gremminger
OF	P. Carney
OF	D. Cooley
OF	W. Lush
C	M. Kittridge
P	V. Willis
P	C. Pittinger
P	M. Eason
P	J. Malarkey

BOS 1903 N

M	A.Buckenberger
1B	F. Tenney
2B	E. Abbaticchio
SS	H. Aubrey
3B	L. Gremminger
OF	D. Cooley
OF	C. Dexter
OF	P. Carney
C	P. Moran
UT	J. Stanley
P	C. Pittinger
P	V. Willis
P	J. Malarkey
P	W. Piatt

BOS 1904 N

M	A.Buckenberger
1B	F. Tenney
2B	F. Raymer
SS	E. Abbaticchio
3B	J. Delahanty
OF	P. Geier

OF	D. Cooley
OF	V. Cannell
C	T. Needham
UT	P. Moran
P	V. Willis
P	C. Pittinger
P	I. Wilhelm
P	T. Fisher
P	E. McNichol

BOS 1905 N

M	F. Tenney
1B	F. Tenney
2B	F. Raymer
SS	E. Abbaticchio
3B	H. Wolverton
OF	V. Cannell
OF	J. Delahanty
OF	P. Dolan
C	P. Moran
P	I. Young
P	V. Willis
P	C. Fraser
P	I. Wilhelm

BOS 1906 N

M	F. Tenney
1B	F. Tenney
2B	A. Strobel
SS	A. Bridwell
3B	D. Brain
OF	P. Dolan
OF	J. Bates
OF	G. Howard
C	T. Needham
P	I. Young
P	V. Lindaman
P	F. Pfeffer
P	A. Dorner

BOS 1907 N

M	F. Tenney
1B	F. Tenney
2B	C. Ritchey
SS	A. Bridwell
3B	D. Brain
OF	C. Beaumont
OF	J. Bates
OF	N. Randall
C	T. Needham
P	A. Dorner
P	V. Lindaman
P	I. Young
P	P. Flaherty
P	F. Pfeffer

BOS 1908 N

M	J. Kelley
1B	D. McGann
2B	C. Ritchey
SS	W. Dahlen
3B	W. Sweeney
OF	G. Browne
OF	C. Beaumont
OF	J. Bates
C	F. Bowerman
P	V. Lindaman
P	P. Flaherty
P	A. Dorner
P	G. Ferguson
P	T. McCarthy

BOS 1909 N

M	F. Bowerman
M	H. Smith
1B	F. Stem
2B	D. Shean
SS	J. Coffey
3B	W. Sweeney
OF	D. Becker
OF	C. Beaumont
OF	R. Thomas
C	G. Graham
UT	F. Beck
P	A. Mattern
P	G. Ferguson
P	O. White
P	L. Richie
P	C. Brown

BOS 1910 N

M	F. Lake
1B	B. Sharpe
2B	D. Shean
SS	W. Sweeney
3B	C. Herzog
OF	W. Collins
OF	F. Beck
OF	R. Miller
C	G. Graham
P	A. Mattern

P	C. Brown
P	S. Frock
P	C. Curtis
P	G. Ferguson

BOS 1911 N

M	F. Tenney
1B	F. Tenney
2B	W. Sweeney
SS	C. Herzog
3B	W. Ingerton
OF	R. Miller
OF	A. Kaiser
OF	M. Donlin
C	J. Kling
P	C. Brown
P	A. Mattern
P	G. Tyler
P	H. Perdue
P	O. Weaver

BOS 1912 N

M	J. Kling
1B	B. Houser
2B	W. Sweeney
SS	J. O'Rourke
3B	E. McDonald
OF	A. Campbell
OF	G. Jackson
OF	J. Titus
C	J. Kling
UT	A. Devlin
UT	J. Kirke
P	G. Tyler
P	O. Hess
P	H. Perdue
P	W. Dickson
P	E. Donnelly

BOS 1913 N

M	G. Stallings
1B	R. Myers
2B	W. Sweeney
SS	W. Maranville
3B	A. Devlin
OF	J. Connolly
OF	L. Mann
OF	J. Titus
C	W. Rariden
P	G. Tyler
P	R. Rudolph
P	O. Hess
P	H. Perdue
P	F. Pfeffer

BOS 1914 N

M	G. Stallings
1B	C. Schmidt
2B	J. Evers
SS	W. Maranville
3B	C. Deal
OF	L. Mann
OF	J. Connolly
OF	L. Gilbert
C	H. Gowdy
P	R. Rudolph
P	W. James
P	G. Tyler
P	R. Crutcher

BOS 1915 N

M	G. Stallings
1B	C. Schmidt
2B	J. Evers
SS	W. Maranville
3B	J. Smith
OF	S. Magee
OF	J. Moran
OF	J. Connolly
C	H. Gowdy
UT	E. Fitzpatrick
P	R. Rudolph
P	T. Hughes
P	D. Ragan
P	G. Tyler

BOS 1916 N

M	G. Stallings
1B	E. Konetchy
2B	J. Evers
SS	W. Maranville
3B	J. Smith
OF	S. Magee
OF	F. Snodgrass
OF	J. Wilhoit
C	H. Gowdy
P	R. Rudolph
P	G. Tyler
P	D. Ragan
P	J. Barnes
P	T. Hughes

BOS 1917 N

M	G. Stallings
1B	E. Konetchy
2B	J. Rawlings
SS	W. Maranville
3B	J. Smith
OF	J. Kelly
OF	R. Powell
OF	W. Rehg
C	W. Tragesser
P	J. Barnes
P	R. Rudolph
P	G. Tyler
P	A. Nehf
P	D. Ragan

BOS 1918 N

M	G. Stallings
1B	E. Konetchy
2B	C. Herzog
SS	J. Rawlings
3B	J. Smith
OF	A. Wickland
OF	R. Powell
OF	R. Massey
C	A. Wilson
P	A. Nehf
P	D. Ragan
P	R. Rudolph
P	B. Hearn
P	D. Fillingim

BOS 1919 N

M	G. Stallings
1B	W. Holke
2B	C. Herzog
SS	W. Maranville
3B	N. Boeckel
OF	R. Powell
OF	W. Cruise
OF	J. Riggert
C	H. Gowdy
UT	J. Smith
P	R. Rudolph
P	D. Fillingim
P	A. Nehf
P	R. Keating
P	A. Demaree

BOS 1920 N

M	G. Stallings
1B	W. Holke
2B	C. Pick
SS	W. Maranville
3B	N. Boeckel
OF	R. Powell
OF	L. Mann
OF	W. Cruise
C	G. O'Neil
P	J. Oeschger
P	J. Scott
P	D. Fillingim
P	H. McQuillan

BOS 1921 N

M	F. Mitchell
1B	W. Holke
2B	H. Ford
SS	W. Barbare
3B	N. Boeckel
OF	R. Powell
OF	W. Southworth
OF	W. Cruise
C	G. O'Neil
P	J. Oeschger
P	J. Watson
P	H. McQuillan
P	D. Fillingim
P	J. Scott

BOS 1922 N

M	F. Mitchell
1B	W. Holke
2B	W. Kopf
SS	H. Ford
3B	N. Boeckel
OF	R. Powell
OF	A. Nixon
C	G. O'Neil
UT	W. Barbare
P	J. Watson
P	F. Miller
P	R. Marquard
P	J. Oeschger
P	H. McQuillan
RP	T. McNamara
RP	E. Braxton

BOS 1923 N

M	F. Mitchell
1B	J. McInnis
2B	H. Ford
SS	R. Smith
3B	N. Boeckel
OF	W. Southworth
OF	A. Felix
OF	R. Powell
C	G. O'Neil
P	R. Marquard
P	J. Genewich
P	J. Barnes
P	J. Oeschger
P	T. McNamara
RP	D. Fillingim

BOS 1924 N

M	D. Bancroft
1B	J. McInnis
2B	J. Tierney
SS	R. Smith
3B	E. Padgett
OF	C. Stengel
OF	W. Cunningham
OF	F. Wilson
C	G. O'Neil
P	J. Barnes
P	J. Genewich
P	J. Cooney
P	T. McNamara
P	J. Yeargin

BOS 1925 N

M	D. Bancroft
1B	M. Burrus
2B	W. Gautreau
SS	D. Bancroft
3B	W. Marriott
OF	J. Welsh
OF	A. Felix
OF	D. Harris
C	F. Gibson
UT	B. Neis
P	J. Cooney
P	J. Barnes
P	L. Benton
P	J. Genewich
P	K. Graham
RP	R. Marquard
RP	A. Kamp

BOS 1926 N

M	D. Bancroft
1B	M. Burrus
2B	W. Gautreau
SS	D. Bancroft
3B	A. High
OF	E. Brown
OF	J. Welsh
OF	J. Smith
C	J. Taylor
P	L. Benton
P	J. Genewich
P	R. Smith
P	H. Wertz
P	G. Mogridge

BOS 1927 N

M	D. Bancroft
1B	J. Fournier
2B	W. Gautreau
SS	D. Bancroft
3B	A. High
OF	E. Brown
OF	J. Welsh
OF	L. Richbourg
C	J. Hogan
UT	E. Farrell
UT	G. Moore
P	R. Smith
P	K. Greenfield
P	J. Genewich
P	H. Wertz
P	C. Robertson
RP	G. Mogridge

BOS 1928 N

M	J. Slattery
M	R. Hornsby
1B	G. Sisler
2B	R. Hornsby
SS	E. Farrell
3B	L. Bell
OF	L. Richbourg
OF	E. Brown
OF	J. Smith
C	J. Taylor
P	R. Smith
P	E. Brandt
P	A. Delaney

P	K. Greenfield
RP	F. Edwards

BOS 1929 N

M	E. Fuchs
1B	G. Sisler
2B	F. Maguire
SS	W. Maranville
3B	L. Bell
OF	L. Richbourg
OF	G. Harper
OF	B. Clark
C	A. Spohrer
P	R. Smith
P	H. Seibold
P	P. Jones
P	E. Brandt
P	B. Cantwell

BOS 1930 N

M	W. McKechnie
1B	G. Sisler
2B	F. Maguire
SS	W. Maranville
3B	C. Chatham
OF	W. Berger
OF	L. Richbourg
OF	J. Welsh
C	A. Spohrer
P	H. Seibold
P	R. Smith
P	B. Cantwell
P	J. Zachary
P	E. Brandt
RP	B. Cunningham

BOS 1931 N

M	W. McKechnie
1B	E. Sheely
2B	F. Maguire
SS	W. Maranville
3B	W. Urbanski
OF	W. Berger
OF	R. Worthington
OF	E. Schulmerich
C	A. Spohrer
UT	L. Richbourg
P	E. Brandt
P	J. Zachary
P	H. Seibold
P	B. Cantwell
P	W. Sherdel
RP	H. Haid

BOS 1932 N

M	W. McKechnie
1B	C. Shires
2B	W. Maranville
SS	W. Urbanski
3B	W. Knothe
OF	W. Berger
OF	R. Worthington
OF	E. Schulmerich
C	A. Spohrer
UT	R. Moore
P	E. Brandt
P	W. Betts
P	R. Brown
P	J. Zachary
P	B. Cantwell
RP	F. Frankhouse
RP	B. Cunningham

BOS 1933 N

M	W. McKechnie
1B	B. Jordan
2B	W. Maranville
SS	W. Urbanski
3B	A. Whitney
OF	W. Berger
OF	R. Moore
OF	H. Lee
C	J. Hogan
P	E. Brandt
P	B. Cantwell
P	F. Frankhouse
P	W. Betts
P	J. Zachary

BOS 1934 N

M	W. McKechnie
1B	B. Jordan
2B	M. McManus
SS	W. Urbanski
3B	A. Whitney
OF	W. Berger
OF	H. Lee
OF	R. Thompson
C	A. Spohrer
UT	J. Hogan
UT	R. Moore

P	E. Brandt
P	F. Frankhouse
P	W. Betts
P	C. Rhem
P	B. Cantwell

BOS 1935 N

M	W. McKechnie
1B	B. Jordan
2B	L. Mallon
SS	W. Urbanski
3B	A. Whitney
OF	W. Berger
OF	H. Lee
OF	R. Thompson
C	A. Spohrer
UT	R. Moore
P	F. Frankhouse
P	B. Cantwell
P	R. Smith
P	E. Brandt
P	W. Betts
RP	L. Benton

BOS 1936 N

M	W. McKechnie
1B	B. Jordan
2B	A. Cuccinello
SS	W. Urbanski
3B	J. Coscarart
OF	H. Lee
OF	W. Berger
C	A. Lopez
UT	R. Thompson
P	D. Mac Fayden
P	J. Chaplin
P	J. Lanning
P	R. Reis
P	R. Smith

BOS 1937 N

M	W. McKechnie
1B	E. Fletcher
2B	A. Cuccinello
SS	W. Warstler
3B	G. English
OF	G. Moore
OF	V. DiMaggio
OF	D. Garms
C	A. Lopez
P	L. Fette
P	J. Turner
P	D. Mac Fayden
P	G. Bush
P	J. Lanning
RP	I. Hutchinson

BOS 1938 N

M	C. Stengel
1B	E. Fletcher
2B	A. Cuccinello
SS	W. Warstler
3B	J. Stripp
OF	V. DiMaggio
OF	J. Cooney
OF	M. West
C	R. Mueller
UT	D. Garms
P	J. Turner
P	L. Fette
P	D. Mac Fayden
P	I. Hutchinson
P	M. Shoffner

BOS 1939 N

M	C. Stengel
1B	J. Hassett
2B	A. Cuccinello
SS	E. Miller
3B	H. Majeski
OF	M. West
OF	J. Cooney
OF	D. Garms
C	A. Lopez
UT	A. Simmons
UT	H. Warstler
P	W. Posedel
P	D. Mac Fayden
P	J. Turner
P	L. Fette
P	M. Shoffner

BOS 1940 N

M	C. Stengel
1B	J. Hassett
2B	C. Rowell
SS	E. Miller
3B	S. Sisti
OF	C. Ross
OF	M. West

OF	J. Cooney
C	R. Berres
UT	E. Moore
P	R. Errickson
P	W. Posedel
P	J. Sullivan
P	M. Salvo
P	N. Strincevich
RP	A. Javery
RP	A. Piechota
RP	S. Coffman

BOS 1941 N

M	C. Stengel
1B	J. Hassett
2B	C. Rowell
SS	E. Miller
3B	S. Sisti
OF	M. West
OF	J. Cooney
OF	E. Moore
C	R. Berres
UT	P. Waner
P	J. Tobin
P	M. Salvo
P	A. Johnson
P	R. Errickson
P	A. Javery
RP	J. Hutchings
RP	F. Lamanna

BOS 1942 N

M	C. Stengel
1B	M. West
2B	S. Sisti
SS	E. Miller
3B	F. Fernandez
OF	T. Holmes
OF	P. Waner
OF	C. Ross
C	E. Lombardi
P	J. Tobin
P	A. Javery
P	L. Tost
P	M. Salvo
P	T. Earley
RP	J. Sain
RP	W. Donovan
RP	R. Errickson

BOS 1943 N

M	R. Coleman
M	C. Stengel
1B	J. McCarthy
2B	C. Ryan
SS	W. Wietelmann
3B	E. Joost
OF	T. Holmes
OF	C. Workman
OF	E. Nieman
C	P. Masi
UT	C. Ross
P	A. Javery
P	N. Andrews
P	C. Barrett
P	J. Tobin
P	M. Salvo
RP	D. Odom

BOS 1944 N

M	R. Coleman
1B	C. Etchison
2B	C. Ryan
SS	W. Wietelmann
3B	D. Phillips
OF	T. Holmes
OF	E. Nieman
OF	C. Workman
C	P. Masi
UT	M. Macon
P	J. Tobin
P	N. Andrews
P	A. Javery
P	C. Barrett
P	I. Hutchinson

BOS 1945 N

M	R. Coleman
M	A. Bissonette
1B	V. Shupe
2B	W. Wietelmann
SS	R. Culler
3B	C. Workman
OF	T. Holmes
OF	C. Gillenwater
OF	E. Nieman
C	P. Masi
P	J. Tobin
P	R. Logan
P	J. Hutchings
P	N. Andrews
P	H. Wright

RP	D. Hendrickson

BOS 1946 N

M	W. Southworth
1B	R. Sanders
2B	C. Ryan
SS	R. Culler
3B	F. Fernandez
OF	T. Holmes
OF	C. Rowell
OF	C. Gillenwater
C	P. Masi
UT	J. Hopp
P	J. Sain
P	M. Cooper
P	H. Wright
P	W. Lee
P	S. Johnson
RP	J. Wallace

BOS 1947 N

M	W. Southworth
1B	C. Torgeson
2B	C. Ryan
SS	R. Culler
3B	R. Elliott
OF	T. Holmes
OF	J. Hopp
OF	C. Rowell
C	P. Masi
P	W. Spahn
P	J. Sain
P	C. Barrett
P	W. Voiselle
P	S. Johnson
RP	C. Shoun
RP	H. Wright
RP	W. Lanfranconi

BOS 1948 N

M	W. Southworth
1B	C. Torgeson
2B	E. Stanky
SS	A. Dark
3B	R. Elliott
OF	T. Holmes
OF	J. Heath
OF	M. McCormick
C	P. Masi
P	J. Sain
P	W. Spahn
P	W. Voiselle
P	V. Bickford
P	C. Barrett
RP	R. Hogue
RP	C. Shoun

BOS 1949 N

M	W. Southworth
M	J. Cooney
1B	E. Fletcher
2B	E. Stanky
SS	A. Dark
3B	R. Elliott
OF	J. Russell
OF	T. Holmes
OF	M. Rickert
C	W. Salkeld
UT	S. Sisti
P	W. Spahn
P	J. Sain
P	V. Bickford
P	W. Voiselle
P	J. Antonelli
RP	N. Potter
RP	R. Hall
RP	R. Hogue

BOS 1950 N

M	W. Southworth
1B	C. Torgeson
2B	R. Hartsfield
SS	J. Kerr
3B	R. Elliott
OF	S. Jethroe
OF	S. Gordon
OF	T. Holmes
C	W. Cooper
UT	W. Marshall
P	V. Bickford
P	W. Spahn
P	J. Sain
P	R. Chipman
RP	R. Hogue
RP	J. Antonelli
RP	R. Hall

BOS 1951 N

M	W. Southworth
M	T. Holmes
1B	C. Torgeson

2B	R. Hartsfield
SS	J. Kerr
3B	R. Elliott
OF	S. Jethroe
OF	W. Marshall
OF	S. Gordon
C	W. Cooper
UT	S. Sisti
P	W. Spahn
P	M. Surkont
P	V. Bickford
P	J. Sain
P	C. Nichols
RP	D. Cole
RP	G. Estock
RP	R. Chipman

BOS 1952 N

M	T. Holmes
M	C. Grimm
1B	C. Torgeson
2B	J. Dittmer
SS	J. Logan
3B	E. Mathews
OF	S. Jethroe
OF	S. Gordon
OF	H. Daniels
C	W. Cooper
P	W. Spahn
P	J. Wilson
P	M. Surkont
P	V. Bickford
P	S. Burdette
RP	S. Jones

BOS 1901 A

M	J. Collins
1B	J. Freeman
2B	A. Ferris
SS	F. Parent
3B	J. Collins
OF	T. Dowd
OF	C. Hemphill
OF	C. Stahl
C	O.Schreckengost
P	D. Young
P	E. Lewis
P	G. Winter
P	F. Mitchell
P	G. Cuppy

BOS 1902 A

M	J. Collins
1B	G. LaChance
2B	A. Ferris
SS	F. Parent
3B	J. Collins
OF	J. Freeman
OF	C. Stahl
OF	P. Dougherty
C	L. Criger
P	D. Young
P	W. Dinneen
P	G. Winter
P	T. Sparks

BOS 1903 A

M	J. Collins
1B	G. LaChance
2B	A. Ferris
SS	F. Parent
3B	J. Collins
OF	J. Freeman
OF	P. Dougherty
OF	C. Stahl
C	L. Criger
UT	J. O'Brien
P	D. Young
P	W. Dinneen
P	T. Hughes
P	N. Gibson
P	G. Winter

BOS 1904 A

M	J. Collins
1B	G. LaChance
2B	A. Ferris
SS	F. Parent
3B	J. Collins
OF	C. Stahl
OF	J. Freeman
OF	A. Selbach
C	L. Criger
P	D. Young
P	W. Dinneen
P	J. Tannehill
P	N. Gibson
P	G. Winter

BOS 1905 A

M	J. Collins

1B	M. Grimshaw
2B	A. Ferris
SS	F. Parent
3B	J. Collins
OF	J. Burkett
OF	C. Stahl
OF	A. Selbach
C	L. Criger
UT	J. Freeman
P	D. Young
P	J. Tannehill
P	G. Winter
P	W. Dinneen
P	N. Gibson

BOS 1906 A

M	J. Collins
M	C. Stahl
1B	M. Grimshaw
2B	A. Ferris
SS	F. Parent
3B	J. Morgan
OF	C. Stahl
OF	J. Hoey
OF	J. Hayden
C	C. Armbruster
UT	J. Freeman
P	D. Young
P	J. Harris
P	W. Dinneen
P	G. Winter
P	J. Tannehill

BOS 1907 A

M	D. Young
M	G. Huff
M	R. Unglaub
M	J. McGuire
1B	R. Unglaub
2B	A. Ferris
SS	C. Wagner
3B	J. Knight
OF	D. Sullivan
OF	W. Congalton
OF	J. Barrett
C	L. Criger
UT	F. Parent
P	D. Young
P	G. Winter
P	D. Glaze
P	C. Pruiett
P	J. Tannehill

BOS 1908 A

M	J. McGuire
M	F. Lake
1B	G. Stahl
2B	A. McConnell
SS	C. Wagner
3B	H. Lord
OF	H. Gessler
OF	J. Thoney
OF	D. Sullivan
C	L. Criger
UT	C. Cravath
P	D. Young
P	E. Cicotte
P	H. Morgan
P	F. Burchell
P	G. Winter

BOS 1909 A

M	F. Lake
1B	G. Stahl
2B	A. McConnell
SS	C. Wagner
3B	H. Lord
OF	T. Speaker
OF	H. Niles
OF	H. Gessler
C	W. Carrigan
P	F. Arellanes
P	J. Wood
P	E. Cicotte
P	C. Chech

BOS 1910 A

M	P. Donovan
1B	G. Stahl
2B	W. Gardner
SS	C. Wagner
3B	H. Lord
OF	H. Hooper
OF	G. Lewis
OF	T. Speaker
C	W. Carrigan
UT	A. Ehgle
P	E. Cicotte
P	R. Collins
P	J. Wood
P	C. Hall
P	E. Karger

BOS 1911 A

M	P. Donovan
1B	A. Engle
2B	W. Gardner
SS	S. Yerkes
OF	T. Speaker
OF	H. Hooper
OF	G. Lewis
C	W. Carrigan
UT	A. Williams
P	J. Wood
P	E. Cicotte
P	R. Collins
P	L. Pape
P	C. Hall

BOS 1912 A

M	G. Stahl
1B	G. Stahl
2B	S. Yerkes
SS	C. Wagner
3B	W. Gardner
OF	G. Lewis
OF	T. Speaker
OF	H. Hooper
C	W. Carrigan
P	J. Wood
P	T. O'Brien
P	H. Bedient
P	R. Collins
P	C. Hall

BOS 1913 A

M	G. Stahl
M	W. Carrigan
1B	A. Engle
2B	S. Yerkes
SS	C. Wagner
3B	W. Gardner
OF	H. Hooper
OF	G. Lewis
OF	T. Speaker
C	W. Carrigan
P	H. Leonard
P	H. Bedient
P	R. Collins
P	J. Wood
P	E. Moseley

BOS 1914 A

M	W. Carrigan
1B	R. Hoblitzel
2B	S. Yerkes
SS	L. Scott
3B	W. Gardner
OF	T. Speaker
OF	G. Lewis
OF	H. Hooper
C	W. Carrigan
UT	H. Janvrin
P	R. Collins
P	H. Leonard
P	G. Foster
P	H. Bedient
P	E. Shore

BOS 1915 A

M	W. Carrigan
1B	R. Hoblitzel
2B	C. Wagner
SS	L. Scott
3B	W. Gardner
OF	G. Lewis
OF	T. Speaker
OF	H. Hooper
C	C. Thomas
UT	H. Janvrin
P	G. Foster
P	E. Shore
P	G. Ruth
P	H. Leonard
P	J. Wood

BOS 1916 A

M	W. Carrigan
1B	R. Hoblitzel
2B	J. Barry
SS	L. Scott
3B	W. Gardner
OF	G. Lewis
OF	H. Hooper
OF	C. Walker
C	C. Thomas
UT	H. Janvrin
P	G. Ruth
P	H. Leonard
P	C. Mays
P	E. Shore
P	G. Foster

BOS 1917 A

M	J. Barry
1B	R. Hoblitzel
2B	J. Barry
SS	L. Scott
3B	W. Gardner
OF	H. Hooper
OF	G. Lewis
OF	C. Walker
C	S. Agnew
P	G. Ruth
P	H. Leonard
P	C. Mays
P	E. Shore
P	G. Foster

BOS 1918 A

M	E. Barrow
1B	S. McInnis
2B	D. Shean
SS	L. Scott
3B	F. Thomas
OF	H. Hooper
OF	A. Strunk
OF	G. Whiteman
C	S. Agnew
UT	G. Ruth
UT	W. Schang
P	C. Mays
P	L. Bush
P	S. Jones
P	H. Leonard

BOS 1919 A

M	E. Barrow
1B	J. McInnis
2B	M. Shannon
SS	L. Scott
3B	O. Vitt
OF	H. Hooper
OF	G. Ruth
OF	B. Roth
C	W. Schang
P	S. Jones
P	H. Pennock
P	C. Mays
P	A. Russell
P	W. Hoyt

BOS 1920 A

M	E. Barrow
1B	J. McInnis
2B	M. McNally
SS	L. Scott
3B	E. Foster
OF	M. Menosky
OF	H. Hooper
OF	T. Hendryx
C	A. Walters
UT	W. Schang
P	S. Jones
P	L. Bush
P	H. Pennock
P	H. Harper
P	W. Hoyt

BOS 1921 A

M	H. Duffy
1B	J. McInnis
2B	D. Pratt
SS	L. Scott
3B	E. Foster
OF	J. Collins
OF	M. Menosky
OF	M. Leibold
C	H. Ruel
P	S. Jones
P	L. Bush
P	H. Pennock
P	A. Russell
P	E. Myers

BOS 1922 A

M	H. Duffy
1B	G. Burns
2B	D. Pratt
SS	J. Mitchell
3B	J. Dugan
OF	J. Collins
OF	M. Menosky
OF	J. Harris
C	H. Ruel
P	J. Quinn
P	H. Collins
P	H. Pennock
P	J. Ferguson
P	B. Karr
RP	C. Fullerton

BOS 1923 A

M	F. Chance
1B	G. Burns
2B	W. Fewster
SS	J. Mitchell
3B	H. Shanks
OF	J. Harris
OF	I. Flagstead
OF	R. Reichle
C	V. Picinich
UT	J. Collins
UT	N. McMillan
P	H. Ehmke
P	J. Quinn
P	J. Ferguson
P	W. Piercy
P	G. Murray
RP	F. O'Doul

BOS 1924 A

M	L. Fohl
1B	J. Harris
2B	W.Wambsganss
SS	E. Lee
3B	D. Clark
OF	I. Flagstead
OF	R. Veach
OF	I. Boone
C	S. O'Neill
P	H. Ehmke
P	J. Ferguson
P	J. Quinn
P	C. Fullerton
P	W. Piercy
RP	G. Murray

BOS 1925 A

M	L. Fohl
1B	P. Todt
2B	W.Wambsganss
SS	E. Lee
3B	J. Prothro
OF	I. Flagstead
OF	I. Boone
OF	R. Carlyle
C	V. Picinich
UT	E. Vache
P	H. Ehmke
P	F. Wingfield
P	C. Ruffing
P	P. Zahniser
P	J. Quinn
RP	C. Ross
RP	O. Fuhr

BOS 1926 A

M	L. Fohl
1B	P. Todt
2B	W. Regan
SS	E. Rigney
3B	F. Haney
OF	W. Jacobson
OF	I. Flagstead
OF	S. Rosenthal
C	L. Gaston
P	H. Wiltse
P	F. Wingfield
P	P. Zahniser
P	C. Ruffing
P	A. Welzer
RP	J. Russell

BOS 1927 A

M	W. Carrigan
1B	P. Todt
2B	W. Regan
SS	C. Myer
3B	W. Rogell
OF	I. Flagstead
OF	W. Shaner
OF	J. Tobin
C	G. Hartley
UT	H. Carlyle
UT	J. Rothrock
P	H. Wiltse
P	W. Harriss
P	A. Welzer
P	D. Mac Fayden
P	C. Ruffing

BOS 1928 A

M	W. Carrigan
1B	P. Todt
2B	W. Regan
SS	W. Gerber
3B	C. Myer
OF	D. Taitt
OF	I. Flagstead
OF	K. Williams
C	F. Hofmann
UT	W. Rogell

UT J. Rothrock
P C. Ruffing
P W. Morris
P J. Russell
P D. Mac Fayden
P W. Harriss
RP E. Settlemire
RP P. Simmons

BOS 1929 A

M W. Carrigan
1B P. Todt
2B W. Regan
SS H. Rhyne
3B R. Reeves
OF R. Scarritt
OF J. Rothrock
OF W. Barrett
C C. Berry
UT E. Bigelow
UT W. Narleski
P C. Ruffing
P N. Gaston
P J. Russell
P D. Mac Fayden
P W. Morris
RP E. Carroll

BOS 1930 A

M C. Wagner
1B P. Todt
2B W. Regan
SS H. Rhyne
3B O. Miller
OF T. Oliver
OF W. Webb
OF R. Scarritt
C C. Berry
UT C. Durst
P N. Gaston
P D. Mac Fayden
P H. Lisenbee
P J. Russell
P E. Durham
RP G. Smith

BOS 1931 A

M J. Collins
1B W. Sweeney
2B H. Warstler
SS H. Rhyne
3B O. Miller
OF W. Webb
OF T. Oliver
OF J. Rothrock
C C. Berry
UT U. Pickering
UT A. Van Camp
P J. Russell
P D. Mac Fayden
P W. Moore
P H. Lisenbee
P E. Durham

BOS 1932 A

M J. Collins
M M. McManus
1B D. Alexander
2B M. Olson
SS H. Warstler
3B U. Pickering
OF S. Jolley
OF T. Oliver
OF R. Johnson
C H. Tate
UT J. Watwood
P R. Weiland
P E. Durham
P R. Kline
P I. Andrews
RP W. Moore
RP J. Michaels
RP L. Boerner

BOS 1933 A

M M. McManus
1B D. Alexander
2B U. Hodapp
SS H. Warstler
3B M. McManus
OF R. Johnson
OF A. Cooke
OF S. Jolley
C R. Ferrell
UT W. Werber
P J. Rhodes
P R. Weiland
P L. Brown
P H. Johnson
P I. Andrews
RP J. Welch
RP R. Kline

BOS 1934 A

M S. Harris
1B E. Morgan
2B C. Cissell
SS L. Lary
3B W. Werber
OF R. Johnson
OF C. Reynolds
OF J. Solters
C R. Ferrell
UT M. Bishop
P J. Rhodes
P J. Welch
P F. Ostermueller
P W. Ferrell
P H. Johnson
RP H. Pennock

BOS 1935 A

M J. Cronin
1B E. Dahlgren
2B O. Melillo
SS J. Cronin
3B W. Werber
OF B. Almada
OF R. Johnson
OF A. Cooke
C R. Ferrell
P W. Ferrell
P R. Grove
P J. Rhodes
P J. Welch
P G. Walberg
RP J. Wilson
RP G. Hockette

BOS 1936 A

M J. Cronin
1B J. Foxx
2B O. Melillo
SS D. McNair
3B W. Werber
OF R. Cramer
OF A. Cooke
OF B. Almada
C R. Ferrell
P W. Ferrell
P R. Grove
P F. Ostermueller
P J. Marcum
P J. Wilson

BOS 1937 A

M J. Cronin
1B J. Foxx
2B D. McNair
SS J. Cronin
3B M. Higgins
OF R. Cramer
OF C. Mills
OF W. Chapman
C E. Desautels
P R. Grove
P J. Wilson
P L. Newsom
P J. Marcum
P A. McKain

BOS 1938 A

M J. Cronin
1B J. Foxx
2B R. Doerr
SS J. Cronin
3B M. Higgins
OF R. Cramer
OF J. Vosmik
OF W. Chapman
C E. Desautels
P J. Bagby
P J. Wilson
P F. Ostermueller
P R. Grove
P G. Dickman
RP A. McKain

BOS 1939 A

M J. Cronin
1B J. Foxx
2B R. Doerr
SS J. Cronin
3B J. Tabor
OF T. Williams
OF J. Vosmik
OF R. Cramer
C J. Peacock
UT L. Finney
P R. Grove
P J. Wilson
P F. Ostermueller
P E. Auker
P D. Galehouse

RP G. Dickman
RP J. Heving
RP J. Wade

BOS 1940 A

M J. Cronin
1B J. Foxx
2B R. Doerr
SS J. Cronin
3B J. Tabor
OF R. Cramer
OF T. Williams
OF D. DiMaggio
C E. Desautels
UT L. Finney
P J. Bagby
P J. Wilson
P R. Grove
P F. Ostermueller
P H. Hash
RP G. Dickman

BOS 1941 A

M J. Cronin
1B J. Foxx
2B R. Doerr
SS J. Cronin
3B J. Tabor
OF D. DiMaggio
OF T. Williams
OF L. Finney
C F. Pytlak
P H. Newsome
P M. Harris
P C. Wagner
P R. Grove
P J. Dobson

BOS 1942 A

M J. Cronin
1B J. Foxx
2B R. Doerr
SS J. Pesky
3B J. Tabor
OF D. DiMaggio
OF T. Williams
OF L. Finney
C W. Conroy
P C. Hughson
P C. Wagner
P J. Dobson
P H. Newsome
P T. Judd
RP M. Brown

BOS 1943 A

M J. Cronin
1B U. Lupien
2B R. Doerr
SS L. Newsome
3B J. Tabor
OF E. Fox
OF D. Culberson
OF G. Metkovich
C R. Partee
P C. Hughson
P L. Terry
P J. Dobson
P T. Judd
P H. Newsome
RP M. Brown

BOS 1944 A

M J. Cronin
1B L. Finney
2B R. Doerr
SS L. Newsome
3B J. Tabor
OF R. Johnson
OF E. Fox
OF G. Metkovich
C R. Partee
P C. Hughson
P G. Woods
P J. Bowman
P R. O'Neill
P D. Ryba
RP F. Barrett

BOS 1945 A

M J. Cronin
1B G. Metkovich
2B L. Newsome
SS E. Lake
3B J. Tobin
OF R. Johnson
OF D. Culberson
OF T. McBride
C R. Garbark
UT J. Lazor
P D. Ferriss

P J. Wilson
P R. O'Neill
P C. Hausmann
P D. Ryba
RP F. Barrett

BOS 1946 A

M J. Cronin
1B P. York
2B R. Doerr
SS J. Pesky
3B G. Russell
OF T. Williams
OF D. DiMaggio
OF G. Metkovich
C H. Wagner
P C. Hughson
P D. Ferriss
P M. Harris
P J. Dobson
P J. Bagby
RP E. Johnson
RP R. Klinger
RP C. Dreisewerd

BOS 1947 A

M J. Cronin
1B J. Jones
2B R. Doerr
SS J. Pesky
3B S. Dente
OF T. Williams
OF D. DiMaggio
OF S. Mele
C G. Tebbetts
P J. Dobson
P D. Ferriss
P C. Hughson
P D. Galehouse
P E. Johnson
RP J. Murphy
RP W. Zuber

BOS 1948 A

M J. McCarthy
1B W. Goodman
2B R. Doerr
SS V. Stephens
3B J. Pesky
OF D. DiMaggio
OF T. Williams
OF S. Spence
C G. Tebbetts
P J. Dobson
P M. Parnell
P J. Kramer
P E. Kinder
P D. Galehouse
RP E. Johnson

BOS 1949 A

M J. McCarthy
1B W. Goodman
2B R. Doerr
SS V. Stephens
3B J. Pesky
OF T. Williams
OF D. DiMaggio
OF A. Zarilla
C G. Tebbetts
P M. Parnell
P E. Kinder
P J. Dobson
P C. Stobbs
P J. Kramer
RP C. Hughson
RP E. Johnson

BOS 1950 A

M J. McCarthy
M S. O'Neill
1B W. Dropo
2B R. Doerr
SS V. Stephens
3B J. Pesky
OF D. DiMaggio
OF A. Zarilla
OF T. Williams
C G. Tebbetts
UT W. Goodman
P M. Parnell
P E. Kinder
P J. Dobson
P C. Stobbs
P M. McDermott

BOS 1951 A

M S. O'Neill
1B W. Dropo
2B R. Doerr
SS J. Pesky

3B V. Stephens
OF T. Williams
OF D. DiMaggio
OF C. Vollmer
UT W. Goodman
P M. Parnell
P R. Scarborough
P M. McDermott
P C. Stobbs
P W. Nixon
RP E. Kinder
RP J. Taylor
RP W. Masterson

BOS 1952 A

M L. Boudreau
1B R. Gernert
2B W. Goodman
SS J. Lipon
3B G. Kell
OF D. DiMaggio
OF W. Evers
OF M. Throneberry
C S. White
P M. Parnell
P M. McDermott
P P. Trout
P S. Hudson
P R. Brodowski
RP I. Delock
RP R. Scarborough

BOS 1953 A

M L. Boudreau
1B R. Gernert
2B W. Goodman
SS M. Bolling
3B G. Kell
OF J. Piersall
OF T. Williams
OF W. Evers
C S. White
P M. Parnell
P M. McDermott
P H. Brown
P S. Hudson
P W. Nixon
RP E. Kinder
RP I. Delock

BOS 1954 A

M L. Boudreau
1B H. Agganis
2B T. Lepcio
SS M. Bolling
3B G. Hatton
OF J. Jensen
OF J. Piersall
OF T. Williams
C S. White
UT W. Keough
UT V. Wertz
UT T. Williams
P F. Sullivan
P W. Nixon
P T. Brewer
P L. Kiely
P W. Henry
RP H. Brown
RP E. Kinder
RP S. Hudson

BOS 1955 A

M M. Higgins
1B N. Zauchin
2B W. Goodman
SS W. Klaus
3B G. Hatton
OF J. Jensen
OF J. Piersall
OF T. Williams
C S. White
UT G. Stephens
P F. Sullivan
P W. Nixon
P T. Brewer
P G. Susce
P I. Delock
RP L. Kiely
RP T. Hurd
RP E. Kinder

BOS 1956 A

M M. Higgins
1B J. Vernon
2B W. Goodman
SS D. Buddin
3B W. Klaus
OF J. Piersall
OF J. Jensen
OF T. Williams

C S. White
UT R. Gernert
UT G. Stephens
P T. Brewer
P F. Sullivan
P W. Nixon
P D. Sisler
P M. Parnell
RP I. Delock
RP T. Hurd

BOS 1957 A

M M. Higgins
1B R. Gernert
2B T. Lepcio
SS W. Klaus
3B F. Malzone
OF J. Piersall
OF J. Jensen
OF T. Williams
C S. White
UT G. Stephens
UT J. Vernon
P F. Sullivan
P T. Brewer
P W. Nixon
P J. Fornieles
P D. Sisler
RP I. Delock

BOS 1958 A

M M. Higgins
1B R. Gernert
2B W. Goodman
SS D. Buddin
3B F. Malzone
OF J. Jensen
OF J. Piersall
OF T. Williams
C S. White
UT G. Stephens
P T. Brewer
P F. Sullivan
P I. Delock
P D. Sisler
P J. Fornieles
RP M. Wall
RP L. Kiely

BOS 1959 A

M M. Higgins
M P. York
M W. Jurges
1B R. Gernert
2B W. Runnels
SS D. Buddin
3B F. Malzone
OF J. Jensen
OF G. Geiger
OF G. Stephens
C S. White
UT R. Keough
UT V. Wertz
UT T. Williams
P T. Brewer
P J. Casale
P F. Sullivan
P W.Monbouquette
P I. Delock
RP J. Fornieles
RP L. Kiely

BOS 1960 A

M W. Jurges
M D. Baker
M M. Higgins
1B V. Wertz
2B W. Runnels
SS D. Buddin
3B F. Malzone
OF W. Tasby
OF L. Clinton
OF T. Williams
C R. Nixon
UT E. Green
P W.Monbouquette
P T. Brewer
P F. Sullivan
P I. Delock
P B. Muffett
RP J. Fornieles
RP T. Sturdivant
RP T. Borland

BOS 1961 A

M M. Higgins
1B J. Vernon
2B W. Goodman
SS D. Buddin
3B W. Klaus
OF J. Piersall
OF J. Jensen
OF C. Yastrzemski
OF G. Geiger

OF J. Jensen
C J. Pagliaroni
P W.Monbouquette
P D. Conley
P D. Schwall
P I. Delock
P E. Stallard
RP J. Fornieles
RP B. Muffett
RP D. Hillman

BOS 1962 A

M M. Higgins
1B J. Runnels
2B C. Schilling
SS E. Bressoud
3B F. Malzone
OF C. Yastrzemski
OF G. Geiger
OF C. Hardy
C J. Pagliaroni
UT I. Clinton
P D. Conley
P R. Wilson
P D. Schwall
RP R. Radatz
RP J. Fornieles
RP A. Earley

BOS 1963 A

M J. Pesky
1B R. Stuart
2B C. Schilling
SS E. Bressoud
3B F. Malzone
OF C. Yastrzemski
OF L. Clinton
OF G. Geiger
C J. Tillman
UT R. Mejias
UT R. Nixon
P W.Monbouquette
P R. Wilson
P D. Morehead
P R. Heffner
RP J. Lamabe
RP R. Radatz
RP A. Earley

BOS 1964 A

M J. Pesky
M W. Herman
1B R. Stuart
2B J. Jones
SS E. Bressoud
3B F. Malzone
OF C. Yastrzemski
OF J. Thomas
OF A. Conigliaro
C J. Tillman
UT F. Mantilla
P W.Monbouquette
P R. Wilson
P J. Lamabe
P D. Morehead
RP R. Heffner
RP R. Radatz
RP W. Spanswick

BOS 1965 A

M W. Herman
1B J. Thomas
2B F. Mantilla
SS A. Petrocelli
3B F. Malzone
OF A. Conigliaro
OF C. Yastrzemski
OF L. Green
C J. Tillman
UT E. Bressoud
UT J. Jones
P R. Wilson
P W.Monbouquette
P D. Morehead
P J. Lonborg
P D. Bennett
RP R. Radatz
RP A. Earley
RP J. Ritchie

BOS 1966 A

M W. Herman
M J. Runnels
1B G. Scott
2B S. Smith
SS A. Petrocelli
3B J. Foy
OF C. Yastrzemski
OF A. Conigliaro
OF D. Demeter
C M. Ryan

UT	J. Jones
P	J. Lonborg
P	J. Santiago
P	D. Brandon
P	R. Wilson
RP	R. Stigman
RP	D. McMahon
RP	J. Wyatt

BOS 1967 A

M	R. Williams
1B	G. Scott
2B	M. Andrews
SS	A. Petrocelli
3B	J. Foy
OF	C. Yastrzemski
OF	C. Smith
OF	A. Conigliaro
C	M. Ryan
UT	J. Tartabull
P	J. Lonborg
P	A. Stange
P	G. Bell
P	D. Brandon
RP	J. Santiago
RP	J. Wyatt
RP	D. Osinski

BOS 1968 A

M	R. Williams
1B	G. Scott
2B	M. Andrews
SS	A. Petrocelli
3B	J. Foy
OF	C. Yastrzemski
OF	C. Smith
OF	K. Harrelson
C	J. Gibson
UT	J. Jones
P	R. Culp
P	G. Bell
P	R. Ellsworth
P	J. Santiago
P	J. Lonborg
RP	A. Stange
RP	A. Lyle
RP	W. Landis

BOS 1969 A

M	R. Williams
M	E. Popowski
1B	J. Jones
2B	M. Andrews
SS	A. Petrocelli
3B	G. Scott
OF	C. Yastrzemski
OF	C. Smith
OF	A. Conigliaro
C	J. Gibson
UT	J. Lahoud
UT	S. O'Brien
P	R. Culp
P	M. Nagy
P	W. Siebert
P	J. Lonborg
P	A. Stange
RP	V. Romo
RP	A. Lyle
RP	W. Landis

BOS 1970 A

M	E. Kasko
1B	C. Yastrzemski
2B	M. Andrews
SS	A. Petrocelli
3B	G. Scott
OF	A. Conigliaro
OF	C. Smith
OF	W. Conigliaro
C	G. Moses
P	R. Culp
P	W. Siebert
P	G. Peters
P	K. Brett
P	M. Nagy
RP	V. Romo
RP	A. Lyle

BOS 1971 A

M	E. Kasko
1B	G. Scott
2B	D. Griffin
SS	L. Aparicio
3B	A. Petrocelli
OF	C. Smith
OF	C. Yastrzemski
OF	W. Conigliaro
C	D. Josephson
UT	J. Lahoud
P	R. Culp
P	W. Siebert

P	G. Peters
P	J. Lonborg
RP	W. Lee
RP	B. Bolin
RP	K. Brett

BOS 1972 A

M	E. Kasko
1B	D. Cater
2B	D. Griffin
SS	L. Aparicio
3B	A. Petrocelli
OF	T. Harper
OF	C. Smith
OF	C. Yastrzemski
C	C. Fisk
UT	B. Oglivie
P	M. Pattin
P	W. Siebert
P	L. Tiant
P	J. Curtis
P	L. McGlothen
RP	G. Peters
RP	W. Lee
RP	L. Krausse

BOS 1973 A

M	E. Kasko
M	E. Popowski
1B	C. Yastrzemski
2B	D. Griffin
SS	L. Aparicio
3B	A. Petrocelli
OF	T. Harper
OF	R. Miller
OF	D. Evans
C	C. Fisk
DH	O. Cepeda
UT	C. Smith
P	W. Lee
P	L. Tiant
P	J. Curtis
P	M. Pattin
P	R. Moret
RP	B. Bolin

BOS 1974 A

M	D. Johnson
1B	C. Yastrzemski
2B	D. Griffin
SS	M. Guerrero
3B	A. Petrocelli
OF	D. Evans
OF	R. Miller
OF	J. Beniquez
C	B. Montgomery
DH	T. Harper
UT	R. Burleson
UT	B. Carbo
UT	C. Cooper
UT	R. McAuliffe
P	L. Tiant
P	W. Lee
P	R. Cleveland
P	R. Drago
P	R. Moret
RP	D. Segui

BOS 1975 A

M	D. Johnson
1B	C. Yastrzemski
2B	D. Griffin
SS	R. Burleson
3B	A. Petrocelli
OF	F. Lynn
OF	D. Evans
OF	B. Carbo
C	C. Fisk
DH	J. Rice
UT	C. Cooper
P	L. Tiant
P	W. Lee
P	R. Wise
P	R. Cleveland
P	R. Moret
RP	R. Drago
RP	D. Segui
RP	J. Burton

BOS 1976 A

M	D. Johnson
M	D. Zimmer
1B	C. Yastrzemski
2B	D. Doyle
SS	R. Burleson
3B	C. Hobson
OF	D. Evans
OF	F. Lynn
OF	R. Miller
C	C. Fisk
DH	J. Rice
UT	C. Cooper

P	L. Tiant
P	R. Wise
P	F. Jenkins
P	R. Cleveland
P	R. Pole
RP	J. Willoughby
RP	T. Murphy

BOS 1977 A

M	D. Zimmer
1B	G. Scott
2B	R. Doyle
SS	R. Burleson
3B	C. Hobson
OF	C. Yastrzemski
OF	F. Lynn
OF	R. Miller
C	C. Fisk
DH	J. Rice
P	F. Jenkins
P	R. Cleveland
P	L. Tiant
P	R. Stanley
P	R. Wise
RP	W. Campbell
RP	J. Willoughby

BOS 1978 A

M	D. Zimmer
1B	G. Scott
2B	J. Remy
SS	R. Burleson
3B	C. Hobson
OF	F. Lynn
OF	D. Evans
OF	C. Yastrzemski
C	C. Fisk
DH	J. Rice
P	D. Eckersley
P	M. Torrez
P	L. Tiant
P	W. Lee
P	J. Wright
RP	R. Stanley
RP	R. Drago
RP	T. Burgmeier

BOS 1979 A

M	D. Zimmer
1B	B. Watson
2B	J. Remy
SS	R. Burleson
3B	C. Hobson
OF	D. Evans
OF	F. Lynn
OF	J. Rice
C	G. Allenson
DH	C. Yastrzemski
P	M. Torrez
P	D. Eckersley
P	R. Stanley
P	S. Renko
P	C. Rainey
RP	R. Drago
RP	T. Burgmeier
RP	W. Campbell

BOS 1980 A

M	D. Zimmer
M	J. Pesky
1B	A. Perez
2B	D. Stapleton
SS	R. Burleson
3B	G. Hoffman
OF	D. Evans
OF	F. Lynn
OF	J. Rice
C	C. Fisk
DH	C. Yastrzemski
P	M. Torrez
P	D. Eckersley
P	R. Stanley
P	S. Renko
P	R. Drago
RP	T. Burgmeier

BOS 1981 A

M	R. Houk
1B	A. Perez
2B	J. Remy
SS	G. Hoffman
3B	C. Lansford
OF	J. Rice
OF	D. Evans
OF	R. Miller
C	R. Gedman
DH	C. Yastrzemski
UT	D. Stapleton
P	D. Eckersley
P	F. Tanana
P	M. Torrez
P	J. Tudor

P	R. Ojeda
RP	R. Stanley
RP	M. Clear
RP	T. Burgmeier

BOS 1982 A

M	R. Houk
1B	D. Stapleton
2B	G. Remy
SS	G. Hoffman
3B	C. Lansford
OF	D. Evans
OF	J. Rice
OF	R. Miller
C	G. Allenson
DH	C. Yastrzemski
UT	W. Boggs
P	D. Eckersley
P	J. Tudor
P	M. Torrez
P	R. Stanley
P	C. Rainey
RP	M. Clear
RP	T. Burgmeier
RP	L. Aponte

BOS 1983 A

M	R. Houk
1B	D. Stapleton
2B	G. Remy
3B	W. Boggs
OF	J. Rice
OF	A. Armas
OF	D. Evans
C	G. Allenson
DH	C. Yastrzemski
UT	R. Miller
UT	T. Nichols
P	J. Tudor
P	B. Hurst
P	D. Eckersley
P	R. Ojeda
P	M. Brown
RP	R. Stanley
RP	M. Clear
RP	L. Aponte

BOS 1984 A

M	R. Houk
1B	W. Buckner
2B	M. Barrett
SS	J. Gutierrez
3B	W. Boggs
OF	D. Evans
OF	J. Rice
OF	A. Armas
C	R. Gedman
DH	M. Easler
P	B. Hurst
P	R. Ojeda
P	D. Boyd
P	A. Nipper
P	W. Clemens
RP	R. Stanley
RP	M. Clear
RP	J. Johnson

BOS 1985 A

M	J. McNamara
1B	W. Buckner
2B	M. Barrett
SS	J. Gutierrez
3B	W. Boggs
OF	D. Evans
OF	J. Rice
OF	S. Lyons
C	R. Gedman
DH	M. Easler
UT	A. Armas
P	D. Boyd
P	B. Hurst
P	A. Nipper
P	R. Ojeda
RP	S. Crawford
RP	R. Stanley
RP	M. Clear

BOS 1986 A

M	J. McNamara
1B	W. Buckner
2B	M. Barrett
SS	E. Romero
3B	W. Boggs
OF	J. Rice
OF	D. Evans
OF	A. Armas
C	R. Gedman
DH	D. Baylor
P	W. Clemens
P	D. Boyd
P	B. Hurst

P	A. Nipper
P	G. Seaver
RP	R. Stanley
RP	S. Stewart
RP	S. Crawford

BOS 1987 A

M	J. McNamara
1B	D. Evans
2B	M. Barrett
SS	S. Owen
3B	W. Boggs
OF	E. Burks
OF	J. Rice
OF	M. Greenwell
C	M. Sullivan
DH	D. Baylor
P	W. Clemens
P	B. Hurst
P	A. Nipper
P	R. Stanley
P	J. Sellers
RP	W. Gardner
RP	C. Schiraldi
RP	S. Crawford

BOS 1988 A

M	J. McNamara
M	J. Morgan
1B	T. Benzinger
2B	M. Barrett
SS	J. Reed
3B	W. Boggs
OF	M. Greenwell
OF	E. Burks
OF	D. Evans
C	R. Gedman
DH	J. Rice
P	W. Clemens
P	B. Hurst
P	W. Gardner
P	D. Boyd
P	B. Smithson
RP	R. Stanley
RP	L. Smith
RP	D. Lamp

BOS 1989 A

M	J. Morgan
1B	N. Esasky
2B	M. Barrett
SS	L. Rivera
3B	W. Boggs
OF	M. Greenwell
OF	E. Burks
OF	K. Romine
C	R. Cerone
DH	D. Evans
UT	D. Heep
UT	J. Reed
P	W. Clemens
P	M. Boddicker
P	J. Dopson
P	B. Smithson
RP	D. Lamp
RP	R. Murphy
RP	R. Stanley

BOS 1990 A

M	J. Morgan
1B	C. Quintana
2B	J. Reed
SS	L. Rivera
3B	W. Boggs
OF	M. Greenwell
OF	E. Burks
OF	T. Brunansky
C	A. Pena
DH	D. Evans
P	W. Clemens
P	M. Boddicker
P	G. Harris
P	D. Kiecker
P	T. Bolton
RP	D. Lamp
RP	W. Gardner
RP	R. Murphy

Brooklyn

ECK n 1872
ATL n 1872-1875
BRO a 1884-1889
BRO a 1890
BRO P 1890
BRO F 1914-1915
BRO N 1890-1957

ECK 1872 n

M	J. Clinton

M	J. Wood
1B	A. Allison
2B	J. Nelson
SS	J. Snyder
3B	F. Fleet
OF	A. Gedney
OF	D. Patterson
OF	J. Snyder
C	D. Allison
UT	J. Clinton
P	A. Martin
P	G. Zettlein
P	J. McDermott
P	Malone

ATL 1872 n

M	R. Ferguson
1B	H. Dehlman
2B	J. Hall
SS	J. Burdock
3B	R. Ferguson
OF	J. Remsen
OF	A. Thake
OF	D. McDonald
C	T. Barlow
P	J. Britt

ATL 1873 n

M	R. Ferguson
1B	H. Dehlman
2B	J. Burdock
SS	R. Pearce
3B	R. Ferguson
OF	C. Pabor
OF	J. Remsen
OF	W. Boyd
C	T. Barlow
P	J. Britt

ATL 1874 n

M	R. Ferguson
1B	H. Dehlman
2B	J. Farrow
SS	R. Pearce
3B	R. Ferguson
OF	J. Chapman
OF	E. Booth
OF	R. Clack
C	J. Knowdell
P	T. Bond

ATL 1875 n

M	C. Pabor
M	W. Boyd
1B	F. Crane
2B	W. Boyd
SS	H. Kessler
3B	A. Nichols
OF	C. Pabor
OF	R. Clack
OF	P. McGee
C	J. Knowdell
P	J. Cassidy
P	J. Clinton
P	J. O'Neill

BRO 1884 a

M	G. Taylor
1B	C. Householder
2B	W. Greenwood
SS	W. Geer
3B	F. Warner
OF	J. Cassidy
OF	J. Remsen
OF	O. Walker
C	J. Corcoran
P	W. Terry
P	S. Kimber
P	J. Conway

BRO 1885 a

M	C. Hackett
M	C. Byrne
1B	W. Phillips
2B	G. Pinkney
SS	G. Smith
3B	W. McClellan
OF	C. Swartwood
OF	P. Hotaling
OF	J. Cassidy
C	J. Hayes
UT	W. Terry
P	H. Porter
P	J. Harkins

BRO 1886 a

M	C. Byrne

1B	W. Phillips
2B	W. McClellan
SS	G. Smith
3B	G. Pinkney
OF	C. Swartwood
OF	E. Burch
OF	J. McTamany
C	J. Peoples
P	H. Porter
P	J. Harkins
P	W. Terry
P	J. Henderson
P	S. Toole

BRO 1887 a

M	C. Byrne
1B	W. Phillips
2B	W. McClellan
SS	G. Smith
3B	G. Pinkney
OF	J. McTamany
OF	C. Swartwood
OF	E. Greer
C	J. Peoples
UT	W. Terry
P	H. Porter
P	J. Harkins
P	S. Toole
P	J. Henderson

BRO 1888 a

M	W. McGunnigle
1B	D. Orr
2B	J. Burdock
SS	G. Smith
3B	G. Pinkney
OF	W. O'Brien
OF	P. Radford
OF	D. Foutz
C	A. Bushong
UT	R. Caruthers
P	M. Hughes
P	W. Terry
P	A. Mays

BRO 1889 a

M	W. McGunnigle
1B	D. Foutz
2B	H. Collins
SS	G. Smith
3B	G. Pinkney
OF	J. Corkhill
OF	W. O'Brien
OF	T. Burns
C	J. Visner
P	R. Caruthers
P	W. Terry
P	T. Lovett
P	M. Hughes

BRO 1890 a

M	J. Kennedy
1B	W. O'Brien
2B	J. Gerhardt
SS	J. Nelson
3B	J. Davis
OF	J. Peltz
OF	H. Simon
OF	E. Daily
C	J. Toy
UT	F. Bowes
UT	H. Pitz
P	C. McCullough
P	M. Mattimore
P	C. Murphy

BRO 1890 P

M	J. Ward
1B	D. Orr
2B	L. Bierbauer
SS	J. Ward
3B	W. Joyce
OF	J. Seery
OF	J. McGeachey
OF	G. Andrews
C	T. Kinslow
UT	G. Van Haltren
P	A. Weyhing
P	J. Sowders
P	C. Murphy
P	G. Hemming

BRO 1914 F

M	W. Bradley
1B	R. Myers

2B A. Hofman
SS E. Gagnier
3B G. Wisterzil
OF L. Evans
OF A. Shaw
OF C. Cooper
C G. Land
UT G. Anderson
P T. Seaton
P E. Lafitte
P J. Finneran

BRO 1915 F
M L. Magee
M J. Ganzel
1B R. Myers
2B L. Magee
SS F. Smith
3B A. Halt
OF B. Kauff
OF G. Anderson
OF C. Cooper
C G. Land
P J. Finneran
P D. Marion
P T. Seaton
P J. Bluejacket
P W. Upham

BRO 1890 N
M W. McGunnigle
1B D. Foutz
2B H. Collins
SS G. Smith
3B G. Pinkney
OF T. Burns
OF W. O'Brien
OF W. Terry
C T. Daly
P T. Lovett

BRO 1891 N
M J. Ward
1B D. Foutz
2B H. Collins
SS J. Ward
3B G. Pinkney
OF M. Griffin
OF T. Burns
OF W. O'Brien
C T. Kinslow
P T. Lovett
P R. Caruthers
P G. Hemming
P W. Terry
P A. Inks

BRO 1892 N
M J. Ward
1B D. Brouthers
2B J. Ward
SS T. Corcoran
3B W. Joyce
OF T. Burns
OF M. Griffin
OF W. O'Brien
C C. Daily
UT T. Daly
P G. Haddock
P E. Stein
P W. Hart
P W. Kennedy

BRO 1893 N
M D. Foutz
1B D. Brouthers
2B D. Richardson
SS T. Corcoran
3B T. Daly
OF T. Burns
OF M. Griffin
OF D. Foutz
C T. Kinslow
UT G. Shoch
P W. Kennedy
P E. Stein
P G. Haddock
P D. Daub
P T. Lovett

BRO 1894 N
M D. Foutz
1B D. Foutz
2B T. Daly
SS T. Corcoran
3B W. Shindle
OF T. Burns
OF G. Treadway
OF M. Griffin
C T. Kinslow
P W. Kennedy

P E. Stein
P D. Daub
P H. Gastright

BRO 1895 N
M D. Foutz
1B G. LaChance
2B T. Daly
SS T. Corcoran
3B W. Shindle
OF M. Griffin
OF J. Anderson
OF G. Treadway
C J. Grim
P W. Kennedy
P E. Stein
P A. Gumbert
P D. Daub
P C. Lucid

BRO 1896 N
M D. Foutz
1B G. LaChance
2B T. Daly
SS T. Corcoran
3B W. Shindle
OF M. Griffin
OF T. McCarthy
OF F. Jones
C J. Grim
UT J. Anderson
P W. Kennedy
P H. Payne
P D. Daub
P B. Abbey
P E. Stein

BRO 1897 N
M W. Barnie
1B G. LaChance
2B G. Shoch
SS G. Smith
3B W. Shindle
OF F. Jones
OF M. Griffin
OF J. Anderson
C J. Grim
P W. Kennedy
P H. Payne
P J. Dunn
P C. Fisher
P D. Daub

BRO 1898 N
M W. Barnie
M M. Griffin
M C. Ebbets
1B G. LaChance
2B W. Hallman
SS G. Magoon
3B W. Shindle
OF F. Jones
OF M. Griffin
OF S. Sheckard
C J. Ryan
P W. Kennedy
P J. Dunn
P J. Yeager
P R. Miller
P J. McKenna

BRO 1899 N
M E. Hanlon
1B D. McGann
2B T. Daly
SS W. Dahlen
3B J. Casey
OF J. Kelley
OF W. Keeler
OF F. Jones
C C. Farrell
UT J. Anderson
P J. Dunn
P J. Hughes
P W. Kennedy
P J. McJames

BRO 1900 N
M E. Hanlon
1B H. Jennings
2B T. Daly
SS W. Dahlen
3B L. Cross
OF W. Keeler
OF F. Jones
OF S. Sheckard
C C. Farrell
UT J. Kelley
P J. McGinnity
P W. Kennedy
P F. Kitson

P H. Howell

BRO 1901 N
M E. Hanlon
1B J. Kelley
2B T. Daly
SS W. Dahlen
3B C. Irwin
OF W. Keeler
OF S. Sheckard
OF T. McCreery
C J. McGuire
P W. Donovan
P F. Kitson
P J. Hughes
P E. Newton
P J. McJames

BRO 1902 N
M E. Hanlon
1B T. McCreery
2B T. Flood
SS W. Dahlen
3B C. Irwin
OF P. Dolan
OF W. Keeler
OF S. Sheckard
C H. Hearne
P W. Donovan
P E. Newton
P F. Kitson
P J. Hughes
P R. Evans

BRO 1903 N
M E. Hanlon
1B J. Doyle
2B T. Flood
SS W. Dahlen
3B S. Strang
OF S. Sheckard
OF J. Dobbs
OF W. McCredie
C L. Ritter
P O. Jones
P H. Schmidt
P V. Garvin
P R. Evans
P W. Reidy

BRO 1904 N
M E. Hanlon
1B F. Dillon
2B A. Jordan
SS C. Babb
3B M. McCormick
OF H. Lumley
OF S. Sheckard
OF J. Dobbs
C W. Bergen
UT H. Gessler
P O. Jones
P J. Cronin
P V. Garvin
P E. Poole
P W. Scanlan

BRO 1905 N
M E. Hanlon
1B H. Gessler
2B C. Malay
SS P. Lewis
3B E. Batch
OF S. Sheckard
OF H. Lumley
OF J. Dobbs
C L. Ritter
P J. McIntire
P W. Scanlan
P E. Stricklett
P M. Eason
P O. Jones

BRO 1906 N
M P. Donovan
1B T. Jordan
2B C. Alperman
SS P. Lewis
3B J. Casey
OF W. Maloney
OF H. Lumley
OF J. McCarthy
C W. Bergen
UT J. Hummel
P E. Stricklett
P W. Scanlan
P J. McIntire
P M. Eason
P J. Pastorius

BRO 1907 N
M P. Donovan
1B J. Jordan
2B C. Alperman
SS P. Lewis
3B J. Casey
OF W. Maloney
OF H. Lumley
OF E. Batch
C L. Ritter
UT J. Hummel
P G. Rucker
P G. Bell
P E. Stricklett
P J. Pastorius
P J. McIntire

BRO 1908 N
M P. Donovan
1B T. Jordan
2B H. Pattee
SS P. Lewis
3B T. Sheehan
OF H. Lumley
OF A. Burch
OF W. Maloney
C W. Bergen
UT J. Hummel
P G. Rucker
P I. Wilhelm
P J. McIntire
P J. Pastorius
P G. Bell

BRO 1909 N
M H. Lumley
1B T. Jordan
2B C. Alperman
SS T. McMillan
3B J. Lennox
OF A. Burch
OF W. Clement
OF H. Lumley
C W. Bergen
UT J. Hummel
P G. Rucker
P G. Bell
P J. McIntire
P I. Wilhelm
P W. Scanlan

BRO 1910 N
M W. Dahlen
1B J. Daubert
2B J. Hummel
SS A. Smith
3B J. Lennox
OF Z. Wheat
OF W. Davidson
OF T. Dalton
C W. Bergen
UT A. Burch
P G. Rucker
P G. Bell
P E. Barger
P W. Scanlan
P E. Knetzer
RP F. Dessau

BRO 1911 N
M W. Dahlen
1B J. Daubert
2B J. Hummel
SS A. Tooley
3B E. Zimmerman
OF R. Coulson
OF Z. Wheat
OF W. Davidson
C W. Bergen
P G. Rucker
P E. Barger
P E. Knetzer
P W. Schardt
P W. Scanlan

BRO 1912 N
M W. Dahlen
1B J. Daubert
2B G. Cutshaw
SS A. Tooley
3B J. Smith
OF J. Moran
OF Z. Wheat
OF H. Northen
C L. Miller
UT J. Hummel
P D. Ragan
P E. Yingling
P W. Stack
P E. Knetzer

BRO 1913 N
M W. Dahlen
1B J. Daubert
2B G. Cutshaw
SS R. Fisher
3B J. Smith
OF Z. Wheat
OF J. Moran
OF C. Stengel
C L. Miller
P D. Ragan
P G. Rucker
P F. Allen
P C. Curtis
P E. Yingling

BRO 1914 N
M W. Robinson
1B J. Daubert
2B G. Cutshaw
SS R. Egan
3B J. Smith
OF Z. Wheat
OF C. Stengel
OF T. Dalton
C G. McCarty
P E. Pfeffer
P E. Reulbach
P D. Ragan
P R. Aitchison
P F. Allen

BRO 1915 N
M W. Robinson
1B J. Daubert
2B G. Cutshaw
SS O. O'Mara
3B J. Getz
OF H. Myers
OF Z. Wheat
OF C. Stengel
C L. Miller
P E. Pfeffer
P W. Dell
P J. Coombs
P G. Bell
P J. McIntire
P I. Wilhelm
P W. Scanlan

BRO 1916 N
M W. Robinson
1B J. Daubert
2B G. Cutshaw
SS I. Olson
3B H. Mowrey
OF Z. Wheat
OF C. Stengel
OF H. Myers
C J. Meyers
UT J. Johnston
P E. Pfeffer
P L. Cheney
P S. Smith
P R. Marquard
P J. Coombs

BRO 1917 N
M W. Robinson
1B J. Daubert
2B G. Cutshaw
SS I. Olson
3B H. Mowrey
OF C. Stengel
OF D. Hickman
OF Z. Wheat
C L. Miller
UT J. Johnston
UT H. Myers
P E. Pfeffer
P L. Cadore
P R. Marquard
P S. Smith
P L. Cheney

BRO 1918 N
M W. Robinson
1B J. Daubert
2B M. Doolan
SS I. Olson
3B O. O'Mara
OF H. Myers
OF Z. Wheat
OF J. Johnston
C L. Miller
P B. Grimes
P R. Marquard
P L. Cheney
P J. Coombs
P P. Robertson

BRO 1919 N
M W. Robinson
1B E. Konetchy
2B J. Johnston
SS I. Olson
3B L. Malone
OF Z. Wheat
OF H. Myers
OF T. Griffith
C E. Krueger
P E. Pfeffer
P L. Cadore
P A. Mamaux
P B. Grimes
P S. Smith

BRO 1920 N
M W. Robinson
1B E. Konetchy
2B P. Kilduff
SS I. Olson
3B J. Johnston
OF H. Myers
OF Z. Wheat
OF T. Griffith
C L. Miller
UT B. Neis
P B. Grimes
P L. Cadore
P E. Pfeffer
P A. Mamaux
P R. Marquard

BRO 1921 N
M W. Robinson
1B R. Schmandt
2B P. Kilduff
SS I. Olson
3B J. Johnston
OF Z. Wheat
OF H. Myers
OF T. Griffith
C L. Miller
UT B. Neis
P B. Grimes
P L. Cadore
P W. Ruether
P C. Mitchell
P S. Smith

BRO 1922 N
M W. Robinson
1B R. Schmandt
2B J. Johnston
SS I. Olson
3B A. High
OF Z. Wheat
OF H. Myers
OF T. Griffith
C J. DeBerry
UT B. Griffith
P W. Ruether
P B. Grimes
P C. Vance
P L. Cadore
P S. Smith
RP A. Mamaux

BRO 1923 N
M W. Robinson
1B J. Fournier
2B I. Olson
SS J. Johnston
3B A. High
OF T. Griffith
OF B. Neis
OF A. Bailey
C J. Taylor
UT Z. Wheat
P B. Grimes
P C. Vance
P W. Ruether
P L. Dickerman
P F. Henry
RP A. Decatur

BRO 1924 N
M W. Robinson
1B J. Fournier
2B A. High
SS J. Mitchell
3B M. Stock
OF Z. Wheat
OF J. Johnston
C L. Miller
OF T. Griffith
OF E. Brown
C J. Taylor
P B. Grimes
P C. Vance
P W. Ruether
P W. Doak
P A. Decatur

BRO 1925 N
M W. Robinson
1B J. Fournier
2B M. Stock
SS J. Mitchell
3B J. Johnston
OF E. Brown
OF Z. Wheat
OF E. Cox
C J. Taylor
P C. Vance
P B. Grimes
P W. Ehrhardt
P E. Osborne
P J. Petty
RP W. Hubbell

BRO 1926 N
M W. Robinson
1B F. Herman
2B M. Fewster
SS J. Butler
3B W. Marriott
OF A. Felix
OF E. Cox
OF Z. Wheat
C G. O'Neil
UT M. Jacobson
P J. Petty
P B. Grimes
P D. McWeeny
P R. McGraw
P C. Vance
RP W. Ehrhardt

BRO 1927 N
M W. Robinson
1B F. Herman
2B J. Partridge
SS J. Butler
3B R. Barrett
OF M. Carey
OF A. Statz
OF A. Felix
C J. DeBerry
UT H. Hendrick
P C. Vance
P J. Petty
P J. Elliott
P D. McWeeny
P W. Doak
RP W. Ehrhardt
RP W. Clark

BRO 1928 N
M W. Robinson
1B A. Bissonette
2B D. Flowers
SS D. Bancroft
3B H. Hendrick
OF R. Bressler
OF F. Herman
OF M. Carey
C J. DeBerry
P C. Vance
P D. McWeeny
P J. Petty
P W. Clark
P J. Elliott
RP R. Moss
RP W. Ehrhardt

BRO 1929 N
M W. Robinson
1B A. Bissonette
2B J. Moore
SS D. Bancroft
3B W. Gilbert
OF J. Frederick
OF F. Herman
OF R. Bressler
C V. Picinich
UT H. Hendrick
P W. Clark
P C. Vance
P R. Moss
P E. Dudley
P D. McWeeny
RP W. Moore
RP N. Ballou

BRO 1930 N
M W. Robinson
1B A. Bissonette
2B C. Finn
SS F. Wright
3B W. Gilbert
OF F. Herman
OF J. Frederick
OF R. Bressler
C A. Lopez

P	C. Vance
P	W. Clark
P	A. Luque
P	J. Elliott
P	R. Phelps

BRO 1931 N

M	W. Robinson
1B	A. Bissonette
2B	C. Finn
SS	G. Slade
3B	W. Gilbert
OF	F. Herman
OF	J. Frederick
OF	F. O'Doul
C	A. Lopez
P	W. Clark
P	C. Vance
P	R. Phelps
P	H. Thurston
P	F. Heimach
RP	J. Quinn
RP	W. Moore
RP	C. Day

BRO 1932 N

M	M. Carey
1B	G. Kelly
2B	A. Cuccinello
SS	F. Wright
3B	J. Stripp
OF	F. O'Doul
OF	L. Wilson
OF	D. Taylor
C	A. Lopez
UT	J. Frederick
P	W. Clark
P	V. Mungo
P	C. Vance
P	F. Heimach
P	H. Thurston
RP	J. Quinn
RP	W. Moore

BRO 1933 N

M	M. Carey
1B	S. Leslie
2B	A. Cuccinello
SS	F. Wright
3B	J. Stripp
OF	J. Frederick
OF	D. Taylor
OF	L. Wilson
C	A. Lopez
P	W. Beck
P	V. Mungo
P	R. Benge
P	O. Carroll
P	H. Thurston
RP	J. Shaute
RP	W. Ryan

BRO 1934 N

M	C. Stengel
1B	S. Leslie
2B	A. Cuccinello
SS	L. Frey
3B	J. Stripp
OF	L. Koenecke
OF	R. Boyle
OF	D. Taylor
C	A. Lopez
UT	J. Frederick
UT	J. Jordan
P	V. Mungo
P	R. Benge
P	E. Leonard
P	J. Babich
P	J. Zachary
RP	O. Carroll
RP	W. Beck

BRO 1935 N

M	C. Stengel
1B	S. Leslie
2B	A. Cuccinello
SS	L. Frey
3B	J. Stripp
OF	R. Boyle
OF	S. Bordagaray
OF	D. Taylor
C	A. Lopez
UT	J. Bucher
UT	J. Jordan
UT	L. Koenecke
P	V. Mungo
P	W. Clark
P	G. Earnshaw
P	J. Zachary
P	J. Babich
RP	L. Munns
RP	C. Vance

BRO 1936 N

M	C. Stengel
1B	J. Hassett
2B	J. Jordan
SS	L. Frey
3B	J. Stripp
OF	J. Cooney
OF	G. Watkins
OF	S. Bordagaray
C	R. Berres
UT	J. Bucher
UT	E. Phelps
P	V. Mungo
P	F. Frankhouse
P	E. Brandt
P	A. Butcher
P	W. Clark
RP	G. Jeffcoat
RP	T. Baker

BRO 1937 N

M	B. Grimes
1B	J. Hassett
2B	H. Lavagetto
SS	E. English
3B	J. Stripp
OF	H. Manush
OF	J. Cooney
OF	J. Winsett
C	E. Phelps
UT	G. Brack
UT	J. Bucher
P	A. Butcher
P	L. Hamlin
P	F. Frankhouse
P	W. Hoyt
P	V. Mungo
RP	G. Jeffcoat

BRO 1938 N

M	B. Grimes
1B	A. Camilli
2B	J. Hudson
SS	L. Durocher
3B	H. Lavagetto
OF	E. Koy
OF	G. Rosen
OF	J. Hassett
C	E. Phelps
P	L. Hamlin
P	F. Fitzsimmons
P	F. Pressnell
P	V. Tamulis
P	W. Posedel

BRO 1939 N

M	L. Durocher
1B	A. Camilli
2B	P. Coscarart
SS	L. Durocher
3B	H. Lavagetto
OF	E. Koy
OF	E. Moore
OF	A. Parks
C	E. Phelps
UT	J. Hudson
P	L. Hamlin
P	H. Casey
P	V. Tamulis
P	F. Pressnell
P	F. Fitzsimmons
RP	I. Hutchinson
RP	R. Evans

BRO 1940 N

M	L. Durocher
1B	A. Camilli
2B	P. Coscarart
SS	H. Reese
3B	H. Lavagetto
OF	J. Walker
OF	J. Medwick
OF	J. Vosmik
C	E. Phelps
P	J. Wyatt
P	L. Hamlin
P	V. Tamulis
P	H. Casey
P	J. Carleton
RP	F. Pressnell

BRO 1941 N

M	L. Durocher
1B	A. Camilli
2B	W. Herman
SS	H. Reese
3B	H. Lavagetto
OF	F. Walker
OF	H. Reiser
OF	J. Medwick
C	A. Owen

UT	J. Wasdell
P	W. Higbe
P	J. Wyatt
P	H. Casey
P	C. Davis
P	L. Hamlin

BRO 1942 N

M	L. Durocher
1B	A. Camilli
2B	W. Herman
SS	H. Reese
3B	J. Vaughan
OF	J. Medwick
OF	H. Reiser
OF	F. Walker
C	A. Owen
P	W. Higbe
P	J. Wyatt
P	C. Davis
P	L. French
P	E. Head
RP	H. Casey
RP	L. Webber

BRO 1943 N

M	L. Durocher
1B	A. Camilli
2B	W. Herman
SS	J. Vaughan
OF	F. Walker
OF	A. Galan
OF	P. Waner
C	A. Owen
P	W. Higbe
P	J. Wyatt
P	E. Head
P	C. Davis
P	L. Newsom
RP	L. Webber

BRO 1944 N

M	L. Durocher
1B	H. Schultz
2B	E. Stanky
SS	B. Bragan
3B	S. Bordagaray
OF	A. Galan
OF	F. Walker
OF	G. Rosen
C	A. Owen
UT	L. Olmo
P	H. Gregg
P	C. Davis
P	R. Melton
RP	L. Webber

BRO 1945 N

M	L. Durocher
1B	A. Galan
2B	E. Stanky
SS	E. Basinski
3B	S. Bordagaray
OF	F. Walker
OF	G. Rosen
OF	L. Olmo
C	M. Sandlock
P	H. Gregg
P	V. Lombardi
P	C. Davis
P	A. Herring
P	T. Seats
RP	C. King
RP	C. Buker

BRO 1946 N

M	L. Durocher
1B	E. Stevens
2B	E. Stanky
SS	H. Reese
3B	H. Lavagetto
OF	F. Walker
OF	C. Furillo
OF	H. Reiser
C	B. Edwards
UT	A. Galan
UT	D. Whitman
P	J. Hatten
P	W. Higbe
P	V. Lombardi
P	H. Behrman
P	H. Gregg
RP	H. Casey
RP	A. Herring
RP	R. Branca

BRO 1947 N

M	C. Sukeforth
M	B. Shotton
1B	J. Robinson
2B	E. Stanky

SS	H. Reese
3B	J. Jorgensen
OF	F. Walker
OF	C. Furillo
OF	H. Reiser
C	C. Edwards
P	R. Branca
P	J. Hatten
P	V. Lombardi
P	J. Taylor
RP	H. Gregg
RP	H. Behrman
RP	R. Barney

BRO 1948 N

M	L. Durocher
M	F. Blades
M	B. Shotton
1B	G. Hodges
2B	J. Robinson
SS	H. Reese
3B	W. Cox
OF	E. Hermanski
OF	C. Furillo
OF	M. Rackley
C	R. Campanella
UT	C. Edwards
P	R. Barney
P	R. Branca
P	J. Hatten
P	E. Roe
P	E. Palica
RP	H. Behrman
RP	P. Minner
RP	J. Ramsdell

BRO 1949 N

M	B. Shotton
1B	G. Hodges
2B	J. Robinson
SS	H. Reese
3B	W. Cox
OF	E. Snider
OF	C. Furillo
OF	E. Hermanski
C	R. Campanella
P	D. Newcombe
P	E. Roe
P	J. Hatten
P	R. Branca
P	J. Banta
RP	E. Palica
RP	P. Minner

BRO 1950 N

M	B. Shotton
1B	G. Hodges
2B	J. Robinson
SS	H. Reese
3B	W. Cox
OF	C. Furillo
OF	E. Snider
OF	E. Hermanski
C	R. Campanella
P	D. Newcombe
P	E. Roe
P	E. Palica
P	R. Branca
P	D. Bankhead

BRO 1951 N

M	C. Dressen
1B	G. Hodges
2B	J. Robinson
SS	H. Reese
3B	W. Cox
OF	C. Furillo
OF	E. Snider
OF	A. Pafko
C	R. Campanella
P	D. Newcombe
P	E. Roe
P	R. Branca
P	C. Erskine
RP	C. King
RP	C. Podbielan
RP	E. Palica

BRO 1952 N

M	C. Dressen
1B	G. Hodges
2B	J. Robinson
SS	H. Reese
3B	W. Cox
OF	E. Snider
OF	A. Pafko
OF	C. Furillo
C	R. Campanella
UT	G. Shuba
P	C. Erskine
P	W. Loes
P	B. Wade

P	E. Roe
P	C. Van Cuyk
RP	J. Black

BRO 1953 N

M	C. Dressen
1B	G. Hodges
2B	J. Gilliam
SS	H. Reese
3B	W. Cox
OF	E. Snider
OF	C. Furillo
OF	D. Thompson
C	R. Campanella
UT	J. Robinson
P	C. Erskine
P	R. Meyer
P	W. Loes
P	E. Roe
P	R. Milliken
RP	C. Labine
RP	B. Wade
RP	J. Hughes

BRO 1954 N

M	W. Alston
1B	G. Hodges
2B	J. Gilliam
SS	H. Reese
3B	D. Hoak
OF	C. Furillo
OF	E. Snider
OF	J. Robinson
C	R. Campanella
P	C. Erskine
P	R. Meyer
P	J. Podres
P	W. Loes
P	D. Newcombe
RP	C. Labine
RP	J. Hughes
RP	E. Palica

BRO 1955 N

M	W. Alston
1B	G. Hodges
2B	J. Gilliam
SS	H. Reese
3B	J. Robinson
OF	E. Snider
OF	C. Furillo
OF	E. Amoros
C	R. Campanella
UT	D. Hoak
P	D. Newcombe
P	C. Erskine
P	J. Podres
P	W. Loes
P	K. Spooner
RP	C. Labine
RP	E. Roebuck
RP	F. Bessent

BRO 1956 N

M	W. Alston
1B	G. Hodges
2B	J. Gilliam
SS	H. Reese
3B	R. Jackson
OF	E. Snider
OF	C. Furillo
OF	E. Amoros
C	R. Campanella
UT	J. Robinson
P	D. Newcombe
P	R. Craig
P	S. Maglie
P	C. Erskine
P	D. Drysdale
RP	C. Labine
RP	E. Roebuck
RP	F. Bessent

BRO 1957 N

M	W. Alston
1B	G. Hodges
2B	J. Gilliam
SS	C. Neal
3B	H. Reese
OF	G. Cimoli
OF	E. Snider
OF	C. Furillo
C	R. Campanella
UT	E. Amoros
P	D. Drysdale
P	J. Podres
P	D. McDevitt
P	R. Craig
RP	C. Labine
RP	E. Roebuck

Column 6 — Buffalo

Buffalo

BUF N 1879-1885
BUF P 1890
BUF F 1914-1915

BUF 1879 N

M	J. Clapp
1B	O. Walker
2B	C. Fulmer
SS	D. Force
3B	A. Richardson
OF	D. Eggler
OF	M. Hornung
OF	W. Crowley
C	J. Clapp
P	J. Galvin

BUF 1880 N

M	S. Crane
1B	T. Esterbrook
2B	D. Force
SS	M. Moynahan
3B	A. Richardson
OF	W. Crowley
OF	M. Hornung
OF	J. Rowe
P	J. Galvin
P	G. Weidman
P	T. Poorman

BUF 1881 N

M	J. O'Rourke
1B	C. Foley
2B	D. Force
SS	J. Peters
3B	J. O'Rourke
OF	A. Richardson
OF	D. Brouthers
OF	W. Purcell
C	J. Rowe
UT	J. White
P	J. Galvin
P	J. Lynch

BUF 1882 N

M	J. O'Rourke
1B	D. Brouthers
2B	A. Richardson
SS	D. Force
3B	J. White
OF	C. Foley
OF	W. Purcell
OF	J. O'Rourke
C	R. Campanella
UT	D. Hoak
P	D. Newcombe
P	C. Erskine
P	J. Podres
P	W. Loes
P	K. Spooner

BUF 1883 N

M	J. O'Rourke
1B	D. Brouthers
2B	A. Richardson
SS	D. Force
3B	J. White
OF	G. Shaffer
OF	J. O'Rourke
OF	J. Lillie
C	J. Rowe
P	J. Galvin
P	G. Derby

BUF 1884 N

M	J. O'Rourke
1B	D. Brouthers
2B	A. Richardson
SS	D. Force
3B	J. White
OF	J. Lillie
OF	J. O'Rourke
OF	D. Eggler
C	J. Rowe
UT	G. Myers
P	J. Galvin
P	W. Serad

BUF 1885 N

M	J. Galvin
M	J. Chapman
1B	D. Brouthers
2B	D. Force
SS	J. Rowe
3B	J. White
OF	J. Lillie
OF	W. Crowley
OF	A. Richardson
C	G. Myers
P	J. Galvin
P	W. Serad
P	P. Conway

P	P. Wood

BUF 1890 P

M	J. Rowe
M	J. Faatz
M	J. Rowe
1B	J. White
2B	S. Wise
SS	J. Rowe
3B	J. Irwin
OF	E. Beecher
OF	W. Hoy
OF	W. Halligan
C	C. Mack
P	G. Haddock
P	E. Cunningham
P	G. Keefe
P	J. Stafford

BUF 1914 F

M	H. Schlafly
1B	J. Agler
2B	T. Downey
SS	W. Louden
3B	F. Smith
OF	C. Hanford
OF	F. Delahanty
OF	C. McDonald
C	W. Blair
P	J. Anderson
P	E. Krapp
P	R. Ford
P	E. Moore
P	A. Schulz

BUF 1915 F

M	H. Schlafly
M	W. Blair
M	H. Lord
1B	H. Chase
2B	W. Louden
SS	W. Roach
3B	H. Lord
OF	T. Dalton
OF	A. Engle
OF	B. Meyer
C	W. Blair
UT	A. Hofman
P	A. Schulz
P	H. Bedient
P	J. Anderson
P	E. Krapp
P	R. Ford
RP	R. Marshall

California

CAL A 1965-1990

CAL 1965 A

M	W. Rigney
1B	V. Power
2B	R. Knoop
SS	J. Fregosi
3B	P. Schaal
OF	J. Cardenal
OF	W. Smith
OF	A. Pearson
C	R. Rodgers
UT	J. Adcock
P	F. Newman
P	W. Chance
P	M. Lopez
P	G. Brunet
P	R. May
RP	R. Lee
RP	A. Gatewood

CAL 1966 A

M	W. Rigney
1B	N. Siebern
2B	R. Knoop
SS	J. Fregosi
3B	P. Schaal
OF	J. Cardenal
OF	E. Kirkpatrick
OF	R. Reichardt
C	R. Rodgers
UT	T. Satriano
P	W. Chance
P	G. Brunet
P	M. Lopez
P	F. Newman
RP	J. Sanford
RP	R. Lee
RP	M. Rojas

CAL 1967 A

M	W. Rigney
1B	D. Mincher

2B R. Knoop	C A. Kusnyer	C T. Humphrey	OF F. Lynn	3B D. DeCinces	**CHI 1874 n**	OF W. Hoy
SS J. Fregosi	P L. Ryan	DH D. Baylor	C R. Boone	OF D. White	M F. Malone	C W. Sullivan
3B P. Schaal	P C. Wright	UT R. Jackson	DH D. Baylor	OF G. Pettis	M J. Wood	P R. Patterson
OF F. Reichardt	P R. May	P L. Ryan	UT R. Clark	OF J. Howell	1B J. Glenn	P C. Griffith
OF J. Hall	P J. Messersmith	P F. Tanana	P G. Zahn	C R. Boone	2B L. Meyerle	P J. Callahan
OF J. Cardenal	P R. Clark	P P. Hartzell	P K. Forsch	DH B. Downing	SS J. Peters	P J. Katoll
C R. Rodgers	RP L. Allen	P K. Brett	P M. Witt	P M. Witt	3B D. Force	P E. Harvey
P G. Brunet	RP E. Fisher	P W. Simpson	P S. Renko	P D. Sutton	OF E. Cuthbert	
P J. McGlothlin	RP S. Barber	RP D. Miller	P B. Kison	P W. Fraser	OF P. Hines	**CHI 1902 A**
P R. Clark		RP D. LaRoche	RP L. Sanchez	P J. Lazorko	OF F. Treacey	M C. Griffith
P J. Hamilton	**CAL 1973 A**	RP M. Barlow	RP A. Hassler	P J. Candelaria	C F. Malone	1B W. Isbell
RP M. Rojas	M B. Winkles		RP D. Corbett	RP D. Buice	UT J. Devlin	2B T. Daly
RP W. Kelso	1B M. Epstein	**CAL 1978 A**		RP C. Finley	P G. Zettlein	SS G. Davis
RP P. Cimino	2B S. Alomar	M D. Garcia	**CAL 1983 A**	RP G. Minton		3B S. Strang
	SS R. Meoli	M J. Fregosi	M J. McNamara		**CHI 1875 n**	OF F. Jones
CAL 1968 A	3B A. Gallagher	1B R. Fairly	1B R. Carew	**CAL 1988 A**	M J. Wood	OF E. Green
M W. Rigney	OF A. Berry	2B R. Grich	2B R. Grich	M O. Rojas	1B J. Devlin	OF S. Mertes
1B D. Mincher	OF V. Pinson	SS D. Chalk	SS T. Foli	M L. Stubing	2B P. Hines	C W. Sullivan
2B R. Knoop	OF L. Stanton	3B C. Lansford	3B D. DeCinces	1B W. Joyner	SS J. Peters	P J. Callahan
SS J. Fregosi	C J. Torborg	OF L. Bostock	OF F. Lynn	2B J. Ray	3B W. White	P R. Patterson
3B A. Rodriguez	DH F. Robinson	OF R. Miller	OF E. Valentine	SS R. Schofield	OF O. Bielaski	P W. Piatt
OF F. Reichardt	UT T. McCraw	OF J. Rudi	OF B. Downing	3B J. Howell	OF J. Glenn	P C. Griffith
OF R. Repoz	UT R. Oliver	C B. Downing	C R. Boone	OF C. Davis	OF W. Hastings	P V. Garvin
OF V. Davalillo	P L. Ryan	DH D. Baylor	DH R. Jackson	OF D. White	C R. Higham	
C R. Rodgers	P W. Singer	UT R. Jackson	UT R. Jackson	OF A. Armas	P G. Zettlein	**CHI 1903 A**
UT C. Hinton	P C. Wright	P F. Tanana	UT D. Sconiers	C R. Boone		M J. Callahan
UT T. Satriano	P R. May	P L. Ryan	P T. John	DH B. Downing	**CP 1884 U**	1B W. Isbell
P G. Brunet	RP S. Barber	P R. Knapp	P K. Forsch	P M. Witt	M E. Hengle	2B G. Magoon
P J. McGlothlin	RP D. Sells	P D. Aase	P G. Zahn	P W. Fraser	1B L. Schoeneck	SS L. Tannehill
P S. Ellis		P K. Brett	P M. Witt	P C. Finley	2B E. Hengle	3B J. Callahan
P C. Wright	**CAL 1974 A**	RP P. Hartzell	P B. Kison	P K. McCaskill	SS S. Matthias	OF F. Jones
P T. Murphy	M B. Winkles	RP D. LaRoche	RP L. Sanchez	P D. Petry	3B C. Householder	OF E. Green
RP M. Pattin	M D. Herzog	RP D. Miller	RP J. Curtis	RP S. Cliburn	OF J. Ellick	OF J. Holmes
RP J. Messersmith	M R. Williams			RP G. Minton	OF H. Wheeler	C J. Slattery
RP T. Burgmeier	1B J. Doherty	**CAL 1979 A**	**CAL 1984 A**	RP B. Harvey	OF H. Wheeler	P G. White
	2B R. Doyle	M J. Fregosi	M J. McNamara		C W. Krieg	P P. Flaherty
CAL 1969 A	SS D. Chalk	1B R. Carew	1B R. Carew	**CAL 1989 A**	UT C. Briggs	P R. Patterson
M W. Rigney	3B P. Schaal	2B R. Grich	2B R. Wilfong	M D. Rader	UT A. Suck	P F. Owen
M H. Phillips	OF J. Rivers	SS D. Campaneris	SS R. Schofield	1B W. Joyner	P H. Daily	
1B J. Spencer	OF L. Stanton	3B C. Lansford	3B D. DeCinces	2B J. Ray	P A. Atkinson	**CHI 1904 A**
2B S. Alomar	OF J. Lahoud	OF D. Ford	OF F. Lynn	SS R. Schofield	P J. Horan	M J. Callahan
SS J. Fregosi	C E. Rodriguez	OF R. Miller	OF G. Pettis	3B J. Howell		M F. Jones
3B A. Rodriguez	DH F. Robinson	OF J. Rudi	OF B. Downing	OF D. White	**CHI 1890 P**	1B J. Donahue
OF J. Johnstone	UT R. Oliver	C B. Downing	C R. Boone	OF C. Davis	M C. Comiskey	2B A. Dundon
OF F. Reichardt	UT R. Valentine	DH D. Baylor	DH R. Jackson	OF C. Washington	1B C. Comiskey	SS G. Davis
OF W. Voss	P L. Ryan	UT W. Aikens	UT J. Beniquez	C L. Parrish	2B N. Pfeffer	3B L. Tannehill
C J. Azcue	P F. Tanana	P C. Frost	UT R. Grich	DH B. Downing	SS C. Bastian	OF F. Jones
UT R. Repoz	P A. Hassler	P L. Ryan	P M. Witt	P R. Blyleven	3B E. Williamson	OF E. Green
P J. Messersmith	P R. Lange	P J. Barr	P R. Romanick	P M. Witt	OF J. O'Neill	OF J. Callahan
P T. Murphy	P W. Singer	P D. Aase	P G. Zahn	P K. McCaskill	OF H. Duffy	C W. Sullivan
P J. McGlothlin	RP C. Lockwood	P R. Knapp	P T. John	P C. Finley	OF J. Ryan	UT W. Isbell
P R. May		RP M. Clear	P J. Slaton	P J. Abbott	C C. Farrell	P F. Owen
P G. Brunet	**CAL 1975 A**	RP D. LaRoche	RP D. Corbett	RP W. Fraser	UT J. Boyle	P N. Altrock
RP E. Fisher	M R. Williams	RP M. Barlow	RP L. Sanchez	RP G. Minton	P M. Baldwin	P G. White
RP K. Tatum	1B B. Bochte		RP C. Kaufman	RP B. Harvey	P C. King	P F. Smith
RP J. Wilhelm	2B G. Remy	**CAL 1980 A**			P C. Bartson	P R. Patterson
	SS M. Miley	M J. Fregosi	**CAL 1985 A**	**CAL 1990 A**		
CAL 1970 A	3B D. Chalk	1B R. Carew	M G. Mauch	M D. Rader	**CHI 1914 F**	**CHI 1905 A**
M H. Phillips	OF J. Rivers	2B R. Grich	1B R. Carew	1B W. Joyner	M J. Tinker	M F. Jones
1B J. Spencer	OF L. Stanton	SS F. Patek	2B R. Grich	2B J. Ray	1B F. Beck	1B J. Donahue
2B S. Alomar	OF M. Nettles	3B C. Lansford	SS R. Schofield	SS R. Schofield	2B J. Farrell	2B A. Dundon
SS J. Fregosi	C E. Rodriguez	OF R. Miller	3B D. DeCinces	3B J. Howell	SS J. Tinker	SS G. Davis
3B K. McMullen	DH T. Harper	OF L. Harlow	OF G. Pettis	OF D. White	3B R. Zeider	3B L. Tannehill
OF A. Johnson	P F. Tanana	OF J. Rudi	OF B. Downing	OF D. Winfield	OF A. Wickland	OF F. Jones
OF R. Repoz	P E. Figueroa	C T. Donohue	OF R. Jones	OF A. Bichette	OF E. Zwilling	OF E. Green
OF J. Johnstone	P L. Ryan	DH J. Thompson	C R. Boone	C L. Parrish	OF M. Flack	OF J. Callahan
C J. Azcue	P W. Singer	P F. Tanana	DH R. Jackson	DH B. Downing	C A. Wilson	C W. Sullivan
P C. Wright	P A. Hassler	P D. Aase	UT J. Beniquez	UT C. Davis	P C. Hendrix	P F. Owen
P T. Murphy	RP D. Kirkwood	P A. Martinez	P M. Witt	UT D. Hill	P M. Fiske	P N. Altrock
P R. May	RP R. Scott	P R. Knapp	P R. Romanick	UT L. Polonia	P E. Lange	P F. Smith
P J. Messersmith		RP D. LaRoche	P K. McCaskill	P C. Finley	P C. Watson	P G. White
RP E. Fisher	**CAL 1976 A**	RP M. Clear	P J. Slaton	P M. Langston	P M. Prendergast	P E. Walsh
RP K. Tatum	M R. Williams	RP A. Hassler	RP D. Moore	P J. Abbott		
RP G. Garrett	M N. Sherry		RP S. Cliburn	P K. McCaskill	**CHI 1915 F**	**CHI 1906 A**
	1B B. Bochte	**CAL 1981 A**	RP P. Clements	P R. Blyleven	M J. Tinker	M F. Jones
CAL 1971 A	2B G. Remy	M J. Fregosi		RP M. Eichhorn	1B F. Beck	1B J. Donahue
M H. Phillips	SS D. Chalk	M G. Mauch	**CAL 1986 A**	RP W. Fraser	2B R. Zeider	2B W. Isbell
1B J. Spencer	3B R. Jackson	1B R. Carew	M G. Mauch	RP M. Fetters	SS J. Smith	SS G. Davis
2B S. Alomar	OF F. Torres	2B R. Grich	1B W. Joyner		3B H. Fritz	3B L. Tannehill
SS J. Fregosi	OF B. Bonds	SS R. Burleson	2B R. Wilfong	# Chicago	OF E. Zwilling	OF F. Jones
3B K. McMullen	OF L. Stanton	3B D. Hobson	SS R. Schofield		OF M. Flack	OF W. Hahn
OF A. Berry	C A. Etchebarren	OF D. Ford	3B D. DeCinces	CHI n 1871	OF L. Mann	OF W. O'Neill
OF R. Repoz	DH H. Davis	OF F. Lynn	OF G. Pettis	CHI n 1874-1875	C A. Wilson	C W. Sullivan
OF A. Gonzalez	UT D. Collins	OF B. Downing	OF B. Downing	CP U 1884	UT W. Fischer	P F. Owen
C J. Stephenson	UT W. Melton	C N. Ott	OF R. Jones	CHI P 1890	P G. McConnell	P N. Altrock
P C. Wright	P F. Tanana	DH D. Baylor	C R. Boone	CHI F 1914-1915	P C. Hendrix	P E. Walsh
P J. Messersmith	P L. Ryan	P G. Zahn	DH R. Jackson	CHI A 1901-1990	P M. Prendergast	P G. White
P T. Murphy	P G. Ross	P K. Forsch	UT R. Grich	CHI N 1876-1990	P M. Brown	P R. Patterson
P R. May	P P. Hartzell	P M. Witt	UT G. Hendrick		P D. Black	
RP E. Fisher	P D. Kirkwood	P S. Renko	P M. Witt	**CHI 1871 n**		**CHI 1907 A**
RP L. Allen	RP R. Drago	RP J. Jefferson	P K. McCaskill	M J. Wood	**CHI 1901 A**	M F. Jones
RP D. LaRoche		RP A. Hassler	P D. Sutton	1B H. McAtee	M C. Griffith	1B J. Donahue
	CAL 1977 A	RP D. Aase	P R. Romanick	2B J. Wood	1B W. Isbell	2B W. Isbell
CAL 1972 A	M N. Sherry		RP D. Corbett	SS E. Duffy	2B S. Mertes	SS G. Davis
M D. Rice	M D. Garcia	**CAL 1982 A**	RP D. Moore	3B E. Pinkham	SS F. Shugart	3B G. Rohe
1B R. Oliver	1B T. Solaita	M G. Mauch		OF F. Treacey	3B F. Hartman	OF W. Hahn
2B S. Alomar	2B G. Remy	1B R. Carew	**CAL 1987 A**	OF J. Simmons	P F. Jones	OF F. Jones
SS L. Cardenas	SS S. Mulliniks	2B B. Grich	M G. Mauch	OF T. Foley	OF H. McFarland	OF P. Dougherty
3B K. McMullen	3B D. Chalk	SS T. Foli	1B W. Joyner	C C. Hodes		C W. Sullivan
OF V. Pinson	OF B. Bonds	3B D. DeCinces	2B M. McLemore	UT M. King		P E. Walsh
OF L. Stanton	OF G. Flores	OF B. Downing	SS R. Schofield	P G. Zettlein		
OF A. Berry	OF J. Rudi	OF R. Jackson				

P F. Smith	**CHI 1914 A**	**CHI 1920 A**	**CHI 1926 A**	P C. Caraway	1B H. Bonura	**CHI 1943 A**
P G. White				P U. Faber	2B M. Hayes	
P N. Altrock	M J. Callahan	M W. Gleason	M E. Collins	P H. McKain	SS L. Appling	M J. Dykes
P R. Patterson	1B J. Fournier	1B J. Collins	1B E. Sheely	RP J. Moore	3B A. Piet	1B J. Kuhel
	2B R. Blackburne	2B E. Collins	2B E. Collins	RP E. Braxton	OF F. Walker	2B D. Kolloway
CHI 1908 A	SS G. Weaver	SS C. Risberg	SS W. Hunnefield		OF R. Radcliff	SS L. Appling
	3B J. Breton	3B G. Weaver	3B W. Kamm	**CHI 1932 A**	OF M. Kreevich	3B E. Hodgin
M F. Jones	OF J. Collins	OF J. Jackson	OF B. Falk		C J. Sewell	OF W. Moses
1B J. Donahue	OF C. Demmitt	OF O. Felsch	OF J. Mostil	M L. Fonseca	P L. Kennedy	OF T. Tucker
2B G. Davis	OF J. Bodie	OF H. Leibold	OF W. Barrett	1B L. Blue	P T. Lee	OF G. Curtright
SS F. Parent	C R. Schalk	C R. Schalk	C R. Schalk	2B M. Hayes	P T. Lyons	C M. Tresh
3B L. Tannehill	P J. Benz	P U. Faber	P T. Lyons	SS L. Appling	P J. Whitehead	P O. Grove
OF F. Jones	P E. Cicotte	P E. Cicotte	P A. Thomas	3B C. Selph	P M. Stratton	P E. Smith
OF P. Dougherty	P J. Scott	P C. Williams	P T. Blankenship	OF E. Funk	RP C. Brown	P J. Humphries
OF W. Hahn	P U. Faber	P R. Kerr	P U. Faber	OF R. Seeds		P W. Dietrich
C W. Sullivan	P E. Russell	P R. Wilkinson	P J. Edwards	OF R. Fothergill	**CHI 1938 A**	P L. Ross
UT J. Anderson	RP W. Lathrop			C F. Grube		RP G. Maltzberger
P E. Walsh		**CHI 1921 A**	**CHI 1927 A**	UT R. Kress	M J. Dykes	RP W. Swift
P F. Smith	**CHI 1915 A**			UT W. Sullivan	1B J. Kuhel	
P G. White		M W. Gleason	M R. Schalk	P T. Lyons	2B M. Hayes	**CHI 1944 A**
P F. Owen	M C. Rowland	1B E. Sheely	1B J. Clancy	P S. Jones	SS L. Appling	
P N. Altrock	1B J. Fournier	2B E. Collins	2B A. Ward	P N. Gaston	3B M. Owen	M J. Dykes
	2B E. Collins	SS E. Johnson	SS W. Hunnefield	P V. Frasier	OF M. Kreevich	1B H. Trosky
CHI 1909 A	SS G. Weaver	3B E. Mulligan	3B W. Kamm	P P. Gregory	OF G. Walker	2B L. Schalk
	3B R. Blackburne	OF B. Falk	OF W. Barrett	RP U. Faber	OF H. Steinbacher	SS J. Webb
M W. Sullivan	OF O. Felsch	OF A. Strunk	OF B. Falk		C J. Sewell	3B E. Hodgin
1B W. Isbell	OF J. Collins	OF H. Hooper	OF A. Metzler	**CHI 1933 A**	UT L. Berger	OF W. Moses
2B J. Atz	OF J. Murphy	C R. Schalk	C H. McCurdy		UT R. Radcliff	OF T. Tucker
SS F. Parent	C R. Schalk	UT J. Mostil	P A. Thomas	M L. Fonseca	P T. Lee	OF E. Carnett
3B L. Tannehill	P U. Faber	P U. Faber	P T. Lyons	1B R. Kress	P T. Lyons	C M. Tresh
OF P. Dougherty	P J. Scott	P R. Kerr	P T. Blankenship	2B M. Hayes	P M. Stratton	P W. Dietrich
OF W. Hahn	P J. Benz	P R. Wilkinson	P G. Connally	SS L. Appling	P J. Whitehead	P O. Grove
OF D. Altizer	P E. Russell	P C. Hodge	P U. Faber	3B J. Dykes	P J. Rigney	P E. Lopat
C W. Sullivan	P E. Cicotte	P D. McWeeny	RP W. Jacobs	OF G. Haas		P J. Humphries
UT W. Purtell			RP A. Cole	OF A. Simmons	**CHI 1939 A**	P J. Haynes
P F. Smith	**CHI 1916 A**	**CHI 1922 A**		OF E. Swanson		RP G. Maltzberger
P J. Scott			**CHI 1928 A**	C F. Grube	M J. Dykes	
P E. Walsh	M C. Rowland	M W. Gleason		P T. Lyons	1B J. Kuhel	**CHI 1945 A**
P W. Burns	1B J. Fournier	1B E. Sheely	M R. Schalk	P S. Jones	2B A. Bejma	
	2B E. Collins	2B E. Collins	M R. Blackburne	P N. Gaston	SS L. Appling	M J. Dykes
CHI 1910 A	SS Z. Terry	SS E. Johnson	1B J. Clancy	P E. Durham	3B D. McNair	1B M. Farrell
	3B G. Weaver	3B E. Mulligan	2B W. Hunnefield	P J. Miller	OF G. Walker	2B L. Schalk
M H. Duffy	OF J. Jackson	OF H. Hooper	SS C. Cissell	RP J. Heving	OF M. Kreevich	SS C. Michaels
1B A. Gandil	OF O. Felsch	OF B. Falk	3B W. Kamm	RP U. Faber	OF L. Rosenthal	3B A. Cuccinello
2B R. Zeider	OF J. Collins	OF J. Mostil	OF A. Metzler		C M. Tresh	OF W. Moses
SS R. Blackburne	C R. Schalk	C R. Schalk	OF J. Mostil	**CHI 1934 A**	UT R. Radcliff	OF J. Dickshot
3B W. Purtell	P E. Russell	P U. Faber	OF B. Falk		P T. Lee	OF O. Hockett
OF P. Dougherty	P C. Williams	P C. Robertson	C C. Crouse	M L. Fonseca	P J. Rigney	C M. Tresh
OF J. Collins	P U. Faber	P G. Leverett	P A. Thomas	M J. Dykes	P E. Smith	UT G. Curtright
OF P. Meloan	P E. Cicotte	P C. Hodge	P T. Lyons	1B H. Bonura	P T. Lyons	P T. Lee
C F. Payne	P J. Scott	P T. Blankenship	P G. Adkins	2B M. Hayes	P J. Knott	P O. Grove
P E. Walsh			P U. Faber	SS L. Appling	RP C. Brown	P E. Lopat
P G. White	**CHI 1917 A**	**CHI 1923 A**	P T. Blankenship	3B J. Dykes		P J. Humphries
P J. Scott			RP G. Connally	OF A. Simmons	**CHI 1940 A**	P W. Dietrich
P F. Olmstead	M C. Rowland	M W. Gleason		OF E. Swanson		RP J. Johnson
P I. Young	1B A. Gandil	1B E. Sheely	**CHI 1929 A**	OF G. Haas	M J. Dykes	
	2B E. Collins	2B E. Collins		C E. Madjeski	1B J. Kuhel	**CHI 1946 A**
CHI 1911 A	SS C. Risberg	SS H. McClellan	M R. Blackburne	P G. Earnshaw	2B J. Webb	
	3B G. Weaver	3B W. Kamm	1B C. Shires	P T. Lyons	SS L. Appling	M J. Dykes
M H. Duffy	OF O. Felsch	OF J. Mostil	2B J. Kerr	P N. Gaston	3B R. Kennedy	M T. Lyons
1B J. Collins	OF J. Jackson	OF H. Hooper	SS C. Cissell	P S. Jones	OF T. Wright	1B H. Trosky
2B A. McConnell	OF H. Leibold	OF B. Falk	3B W. Kamm	P L. Tietje	OF M. Kreevich	2B D. Kolloway
SS L. Tannehill	C R. Schalk	C R. Schalk	OF A. Metzler	RP J. Heving	OF J. Solters	SS L. Appling
3B H. Lord	P E. Cicotte	P C. Robertson	OF C. Reynolds	RP J. Wyatt	C M. Tresh	3B D. Lodigiani
OF M. McIntyre	P U. Faber	P U. Faber	OF C. Hoffman		UT L. Rosenthal	OF T. Tucker
OF F. Bodie	P C. Williams	P M. Cvengros	C M. Berg	**CHI 1935 A**	P J. Rigney	OF T. Wright
OF J. Callahan	P E. Russell	P E. Russell	UT J. Clancy		P T. Lee	OF R. Kennedy
C W. Sullivan	P D. Danforth	P G. Leverett	P A. Thomas	M J. Dykes	P E. Smith	C M. Tresh
P E. Walsh			P T. Lyons	1B H. Bonura	P T. Lyons	P E. Lopat
P J. Scott	**CHI 1918 A**	**CHI 1924 A**	P U. Faber	2B M. Hayes	P J. Knott	P O. Grove
P G. White			P H. McKain	SS L. Appling	RP C. Brown	P J. Haynes
P F. Lange	M C. Rowland	M J. Evers	P G. Adkins	3B J. Dykes	RP P. Appleton	P E. Smith
P F. Olmstead	1B A. Gandil	M E. Walsh		OF R. Radcliff		P F. Papish
	2B E. Collins	M E. Collins	**CHI 1930 A**	OF A. Simmons	**CHI 1941 A**	RP E. Caldwell
CHI 1912 A	SS G. Weaver	M J. Evers		OF G. Haas		RP R. Hamner
	3B F. McMullin	1B E. Sheely	M O. Bush	C J. Sewell	M J. Dykes	RP A. Hollingsworth
M J. Callahan	OF H. Leibold	2B E. Collins	1B J. Watwood	UT S. Washington	1B J. Kuhel	
1B R. Zeider	OF J. Collins	SS W. Barrett	2B J. Cissell	P J. Whitehead	2B W.Knickerbocker	**CHI 1947 A**
2B M. Rath	OF J. Murphy	3B W. Kamm	SS G. Mulleavy	P L. Kennedy	SS L. Appling	
SS G. Weaver	C R. Schalk	OF B. Falk	3B W. Kamm	P T. Lyons	3B D. Lodigiani	M T. Lyons
3B H. Lord	UT C. Risberg	OF H. Hooper	OF S. Jolley	P L. Tietje	OF T. Wright	1B P. York
OF F. Bodie	P E. Cicotte	OF J. Mostil	OF C. Reynolds	P S. Jones	OF M. Kreevich	2B D. Kolloway
OF J. Callahan	P F. Shellenback	C C. Crouse	OF E. Barnes	RP J. Wyatt	OF M. Hoag	SS L. Appling
OF J. Collins	P J. Benz	UT M. Archdeacon	C H. Tate		C M. Tresh	3B F. Baker
C W. Kuhn	P D. Danforth	P H. Thurston	P T. Lyons	**CHI 1936 A**	P T. Lee	OF D. Philley
P E. Walsh	P E. Russell	P T. Lyons	P C. Caraway		P E. Smith	OF R. Kennedy
P J. Benz		P U. Faber	P A. Thomas	M J. Dykes	P J. Rigney	OF T. Wright
P G. White	**CHI 1919 A**	P G. Connally	P U. Faber	1B H. Bonura	P T. Lyons	C M. Tresh
P F. Lange		P T. Blankenship	P F. Henry	2B M. Hayes	P W. Dietrich	UT C. Michaels
P E. Cicotte	M W. Gleason		RP E. Walsh	SS L. Appling		P E. Lopat
	1B A. Gandil	**CHI 1925 A**	RP H. McKain	3B J. Dykes	**CHI 1942 A**	P F. Papish
CHI 1913 A	2B E. Collins			OF M. Kreevich		P J. Haynes
	SS C. Risberg	M E. Collins	**CHI 1931 A**	OF R. Radcliff	M J. Dykes	P O. Grove
M J. Callahan	3B G. Weaver	1B E. Sheely		OF G. Haas	1B J. Kuhel	P R. Gillespie
1B H. Chase	OF J. Jackson	2B E. Collins	M O. Bush	C J. Sewell	2B D. Kolloway	RP E. Harrist
2B M. Rath	OF O. Felsch	SS I. Davis	1B L. Blue	UT A. Piet	SS L. Appling	RP P. Gebrian
SS G. Weaver	OF H. Leibold	3B W. Kamm	2B J. Kerr	P L. Kennedy	3B R. Kennedy	RP G. Maltzberger
3B H. Lord	C R. Schalk	OF J. Mostil	SS C. Cissell	P J. Whitehead	OF W. Moses	
OF J. Collins	P E. Cicotte	OF B. Falk	3B W. Sullivan	P M. Cain	OF M. Hoag	**CHI 1948 A**
OF F. Bodie	P C. Williams	OF H. Hooper	OF C. Reynolds	P T. Lyons	OF T. Wright	
OF W. Mattick	P R. Kerr	C R. Schalk	OF J. Watwood	P M. Stratton	C M. Tresh	M T. Lyons
C R. Schalk	P U. Faber	P T. Lyons	OF L. Fonseca	RP C. Brown	P J. Humphries	1B U. Lupien
P E. Russell	P G. Lowdermilk	P U. Faber	C H. Tate	RP R. Evans	P E. Smith	2B D. Kolloway
P J. Scott	RP D. Danforth	P T. Blankenship	UT L. Appling		P T. Lyons	SS C. Michaels
P E. Cicotte		P H. Thurston	UT R. Fothergill	**CHI 1937 A**	P W. Dietrich	3B L. Appling
P J. Benz		P C. Robertson	P V. Frasier		P L. Ross	OF D. Philley
P G. White		RP G. Connally	P A. Thomas	M J. Dykes	RP J. Haynes	OF T. Wright

OF J. Seerey
C A. Robinson
UT F. Baker
UT E. Hodgin
P W. Wight
P J. Haynes
P A. Gettel
P M. Pieretti
P R. Gumpert
RP H. Judson
RP F. Papish
RP O. Grove

CHI 1949 A

M J. Onslow
1B C. Kress
2B C. Michaels
SS L. Appling
3B F. Baker
OF D. Philley
OF G. Metkovich
OF H. Adams
C D. Wheeler
P W. Wight
P R. Gumpert
P W. Pierce
P R. Kuzava
P H. Judson
RP M. Pieretti
RP M. Surkont

CHI 1950 A

M J. Onslow
M J. Corriden
1B W. Robinson
2B J. Fox
SS A. Carrasquel
3B H. Majeski
OF D. Philley
OF G. Zernial
OF M. Rickert
C P. Masi
P W. Pierce
P W. Wight
P R. Cain
P R. Gumpert
P R. Scarborough
RP H. Judson
RP L. Aloma
RP M. Haefner

CHI 1951 A

M P. Richards
1B W. Robinson
2B J. Fox
SS A. Carrasquel
3B R. Dillinger
OF J. Busby
OF A. Zarilla
OF S. Minoso
C P. Masi
UT E. Stewart
P W. Pierce
P S. Rogovin
P K. Holcombe
P J. Dobson
P R. Gumpert
RP L. Aloma
RP M. Rotblatt

CHI 1952 A

M P. Richards
1B W. Robinson
2B J. Fox
SS A. Carrasquel
3B H. Rodriguez
OF S. Minoso
OF S. Mele
OF R. Coleman
C J. Lollar
P W. Pierce
P S. Rogovin
P J. Dobson
P M. Grissom
P C. Stobbs
RP H. Dorish
RP W. Kennedy

CHI 1953 A

M P. Richards
1B F. Fain
2B J. Fox
SS A. Carrasquel
3B R. Elliott
OF M. Rivera
OF S. Minoso
OF S. Mele
C J. Lollar
P W. Pierce
P V. Trucks
P J. Fornieles
P S. Rogovin

P S. Consuegra
RP H. Dorish
RP H. Bearden

CHI 1954 A

M P. Richards
M M. Marion
1B F. Fain
2B J. Fox
SS A. Carrasquel
3B C. Michaels
OF S. Minoso
OF M. Rivera
OF J. Groth
C J. Lollar
P V. Trucks
P R. Keegan
P W. Pierce
P J. Harshman
P S. Consuegra
RP H. Dorish
RP M. Martin

CHI 1955 A

M M. Marion
1B W. Dropo
2B J. Fox
SS A. Carrasquel
3B G. Kell
OF M. Rivera
OF S. Minoso
OF J. Busby
C J. Lollar
UT R. Nieman
P W. Pierce
P R. Donovan
P J. Harshman
P V. Trucks
P C. Johnson
RP S. Consuegra
RP M. Howell
RP M. Martin

CHI 1956 A

M M. Marion
1B W. Dropo
2B J. Fox
SS L. Aparicio
3B F. Hatfield
OF S. Minoso
OF L. Doby
OF M. Rivera
C J. Lollar
P W. Pierce
P R. Donovan
P J. Harshman
P J. Wilson
P R. Keegan
RP M. Howell

CHI 1957 A

M A. Lopez
1B C. Torgeson
2B J. Fox
SS L. Aparicio
3B J. Phillips
OF S. Minoso
OF L. Doby
OF J. Landis
C J. Lollar
UT S. Esposito
UT M. Rivera
P W. Pierce
P R. Donovan
P J. Wilson
P J. Harshman
P R. Keegan
RP G. Staley
RP M. Howell

CHI 1958 A

M A. Lopez
1B C. Torgeson
2B J. Fox
SS L. Aparicio
3B W. Goodman
OF J. Landis
OF A. Smith
OF M. Rivera
C J. Lollar
UT S. Esposito
P R. Donovan
P W. Pierce
P E. Wynn
P J. Wilson
P R. Moore
RP G. Staley
RP R. Shaw

CHI 1959 A

M A. Lopez

1B C. Torgeson
2B J. Fox
SS L. Aparicio
3B J. Phillips
OF J. Landis
OF A. Smith
OF M. Rivera
C J. Lollar
UT W. Goodman
P E. Wynn
P R. Shaw
P W. Pierce
P R. Donovan
P A. Latman
RP G. Staley
RP O. Lown

CHI 1960 A

M A. Lopez
1B R. Sievers
2B J. Fox
SS L. Aparicio
3B E. Freese
OF S. Minoso
OF J. Landis
OF A. Smith
C J. Lollar
P E. Wynn
P W. Pierce
P R. Shaw
P F. Baumann
P R. Kemmerer
RP G. Staley
RP R. Donovan
RP O. Lown

CHI 1961 A

M A. Lopez
1B R. Sievers
2B J. Fox
SS L. Aparicio
3B A. Smith
OF S. Minoso
OF J. Landis
OF F. Robinson
C J. Lollar
UT J. Martin
P J. Pizarro
P F. Baumann
P W. Pierce
P C. McLish
P R. Herbert
RP O. Lown
RP R. Kemmerer
RP D. Larsen

CHI 1962 A

M A. Lopez
1B J. Cunningham
2B J. Fox
SS L. Aparicio
3B A. Smith
OF F. Robinson
OF J. Landis
OF N. Hershberger
C J. Lollar
P R. Herbert
P J. Pizarro
P E. Fisher
P E. Wynn
P J. Buzhardt
RP D. Zanni
RP O. Lown

CHI 1963 A

M A. Lopez
1B T. McCraw
2B J. Fox
SS R. Hansen
3B P. Ward
OF F. Robinson
OF J. Landis
OF D. Nicholson
C J. Martin
UT C. Carreon
UT N. Hershberger
UT A. Weis
P G. Peters
P R. Herbert
P J. Pizarro
P J. Buzhardt
P J. Horlen
RP J. Wilhelm
RP J. Brosnan
RP F. Baumann

CHI 1964 A

M A. Lopez
1B T. McCraw
2B A. Weis
SS R. Hansen
3B P. Ward

OF F. Robinson
OF N. Hershberger
OF J. Landis
C J. Martin
UT D. Buford
UT D. Nicholson
P G. Peters
P J. Pizarro
P J. Horlen
P J. Buzhardt
P R. Herbert
RP J. Wilhelm
RP E. Fisher

CHI 1965 A

M A. Lopez
1B W. Skowron
2B D. Buford
SS R. Hansen
3B P. Ward
OF A. Berry
OF F. Robinson
OF D. Cater
C J. Martin
UT T. McCraw
UT J. Romano
UT A. Weis
P J. Horlen
P J. Buzhardt
P T. John
P G. Peters
P B. Howard
RP E. Fisher
RP J. Wilhelm
RP J. Locker

CHI 1966 A

M E. Stanky
1B T. McCraw
2B A. Weis
SS L. Elia
3B D. Buford
OF T. Agee
OF A. Berry
OF F. Robinson
C J. Romano
UT K. Adair
UT W. Skowron
P T. John
P J. Horlen
P G. Peters
P J. Buzhardt
P B. Howard
RP R. Locker
RP D. Higgins
RP J. Pizarro

CHI 1967 A

M E. Stanky
1B T. McCraw
2B J. Causey
SS R. Hansen
3B D. Buford
OF T. Agee
OF P. Ward
OF A. Berry
C J. Martin
UT W. Williams
P G. Peters
P J. Horlen
P T. John
P B. Howard
RP R. Locker
RP W. Wood
RP D. McMahon

CHI 1968 A

M E. Stanky
M J. Moss
M A. Lopez
M J. Moss
M A. Lopez
1B T. McCraw
2B S. Alomar
SS L. Aparicio
3B P. Ward
OF A. Berry
OF H. Davis
OF C. Bradford
C D. Josephson
P J. Horlen
P J. Fisher
P T. John
P G. Peters
P F. Carlos
RP W. Wood
RP J. Wilhelm
RP R. Locker

CHI 1969 A

M A. Lopez
M D. Gutteridge

1B G. Hopkins
2B R. Knoop
SS L. Aparicio
3B W. Melton
OF A. Berry
OF W. Williams
OF C. May
C E. Herrmann
UT P. Ward
UT J. Horlen
P J. Pizarro
P J. Horlen
P J. Buzhardt
P R. Herbert
RP J. Wilhelm
RP E. Fisher

CHI 1970 A

M D. Gutteridge
M M. Adair
M C. Tanner
1B G. Hopkins
2B R. Knoop
SS L. Aparicio
3B W. Melton
OF C. May
OF A. Berry
OF W. Williams
C E. Herrmann
UT T. McCraw
UT S. O'Brien
P T. John
P G. Janeski
P J. Horlen
RP W. Wood
RP J. Crider
RP D. Murphy

CHI 1971 A

M C. Tanner
1B C. May
2B M. Andrews
SS L. Alvarado
3B W. Melton
OF F. Reichardt
OF J. Johnstone
OF W. Williams
C E. Herrmann
UT C. McKinney
P W. Wood
P T. Bradley
P T. John
P C. Johnson
P J. Horlen
RP S. Kealey
RP V. Romo
RP T. Forster

CHI 1972 A

M C. Tanner
1B R. Allen
2B M. Andrews
SS R. Morales
3B E. Spiezio
OF C. May
OF H. Kelly
OF J. Johnstone
C E. Herrmann
UT L. Alvarado
UT F. Reichardt
P W. Wood
P T. Bradley
P S. Bahnsen
P D. Lemonds
RP T. Forster
RP R. Gossage
RP S. Kealey

CHI 1973 A

M C. Tanner
1B R. Allen
2B J. Orta
SS E. Leon
3B W. Melton
OF H. Kelly
OF J. Jeter
OF W. Sharp
C E. Herrmann
DH C. May
P W. Wood
P S. Bahnsen
P S. Stone
P T. Forster
P E. Fisher
RP C. Acosta
RP R. Gossage

CHI 1974 A

M C. Tanner
1B R. Allen
2B J. Orta
SS R. Dent

3B W. Melton
OF K. Henderson
OF C. May
OF W. Sharp
C E. Herrmann
DH H. Kelly
UT B. Downing
UT A. Muser
UT R. Santo
P W. Wood
P J. Kaat
P S. Bahnsen
P C. Johnson
RP T. Forster
RP L. Pitlock
RP R. Gossage

CHI 1975 A

M C. Tanner
1B C. May
2B J. Orta
SS R. Dent
3B W. Melton
OF K. Henderson
OF H. Kelly
OF N. Nyman
C B. Downing
DH D. Johnson
P J. Kaat
P W. Wood
P C. Osteen
P J. Jefferson
RP R. Gossage
RP D. Hamilton
RP D. Osborn

CHI 1976 A

M P. Richards
1B J. Spencer
2B J. Brohamer
SS R. Dent
3B K. Bell
OF C. Lemon
OF R. Garr
OF J. Orta
C B. Downing
DH H. Kelly
UT W. Stein
P R. Gossage
P C. Johnson
P K. Brett
P F. Barrios
P T. Forster
RP D. Hamilton
RP R. Carroll

CHI 1977 A

M R. Lemon
1B J. Spencer
2B J. Orta
SS A. Bannister
3B E. Soderholm
OF C. Lemon
OF R. Garr
OF R. Zisk
C J. Essian
DH O. Gamble
UT L. Johnson
P F. Barrios
P S. Stone
P K. Kravec
P R. Knapp
P W. Wood
RP L. LaGrow
RP D. Hamilton

CHI 1978 A

M R. Lemon
M L. Doby
1B M. Squires
2B J. Orta
SS D. Kessinger
3B E. Soderholm
OF R. Garr
OF C. Lemon
OF C. Washington
C W. Nahorodny
DH L. Johnson
UT R. Molinaro
P S. Stone
P K. Kravec
P F. Barrios
P W. Wood
RP J. Willoughby
RP L. LaGrow
RP R. Schueler

CHI 1979 A

M D. Kessinger
M A. LaRussa
1B M. Squires
2B A. Bannister

SS G. Pryor
3B K. Bell
OF C. Lemon
OF C. Washington
OF R. Torres
C M. May
DH J. Orta
UT R. Garr
UT L. Johnson
P K. Kravec
P R. Wortham
P R. Baumgarten
P S. Trout
RP R. Scarbery
RP M. Proly
RP E. Farmer

CHI 1980 A

M A. LaRussa
1B M. Squires
2B J. Morrison
SS T. Cruz
3B K. Bell
OF C. Lemon
OF H. Baines
OF W. Nordhagen
C B. Kimm
DH L. Johnson
UT R. Molinaro
UT R. Pryor
P R. Burns
P S. Trout
P R. Dotson
P R. Baumgarten
P D. Hoyt
RP M. Proly
RP E. Farmer
RP R. Wortham

CHI 1981 A

M A. LaRussa
1B M. Squires
2B A. Bernazard
SS W. Almon
3B J. Morrison
OF C. Lemon
OF R. LeFlore
OF H. Baines
C C. Fisk
DH G. Luzinski
UT R. Kuntz
UT W. Nordhagen
P R. Burns
P R. Dotson
P D. Lamp
P S. Trout
P R. Baumgarten
RP D. Hoyt
RP E. Farmer
RP K. Hickey

CHI 1982 A

M A. LaRussa
1B M. Squires
2B A. Bernazard
SS W. Almon
3B A. Rodriguez
OF H. Baines
OF S. Kemp
OF R. Law
C C. Fisk
DH G. Luzinski
UT V. Law
UT T. Paciorek
P D. Hoyt
P R. Dotson
P D. Lamp
P J. Koosman
P R. Burns
RP S. Barojas
RP K. Hickey
RP E. Escarrega

CHI 1983 A

M A. LaRussa
1B M. Squires
2B J. Cruz
SS J. Dybzinski
3B V. Law
OF H. Baines
OF R. Kittle
OF R. Law
C C. Fisk
DH G. Luzinski
UT S. Fletcher
UT J. Hairston
UT T. Paciorek
UT G. Walker
P D. Hoyt
P R. Dotson
P F. Bannister
P R. Burns
P J. Koosman

RP D. Lamp
RP R. Tidrow
RP S. Barojas

CHI 1984 A
M A. LaRussa
1B G. Walker
2B J. Cruz
SS S. Fletcher
3B V. Law
OF H. Baines
OF R. Law
OF R. Kittle
C C. Fisk
DH G. Luzinski
UT J. Hairston
UT T. Paciorek
UT M. Squires
P R. Dotson
P G. Seaver
P D. Hoyt
P F. Bannister
P R. Burns
RP R. Reed
RP J. Agosto
RP D. Spillner

CHI 1985 A
M A. LaRussa
1B G. Walker
2B J. Cruz
SS O. Guillen
3B T. Hulett
OF H. Baines
OF R. Law
OF D. Boston
C C. Fisk
DH R. Kittle
UT S. Fletcher
UT L. Salazar
P G. Seaver
P R. Burns
P F. Bannister
P W. Nelson
RP R. James
RP D. Spillner
RP J. Agosto

CHI 1986 A
M A. LaRussa
M D. Rader
M J. Fregosi
1B G. Walker
2B J. Cruz
SS O. Guillen
3B T. Hulett
OF H. Baines
OF J. Cangelosi
OF T. Nichols
C C. Fisk
DH R. Kittle
UT J. Hairston
P R. Dotson
P F. Bannister
P J. Cowley
P N. Allen
P J. Davis
RP W. Nelson
RP W. Dawley
RP D. Schmidt

CHI 1987 A
M J. Fregosi
1B G. Walker
2B F. Manrique
SS O. Guillen
3B T. Hulett
OF I. Calderon
OF G. Redus
OF K. Williams
C C. Fisk
DH H. Baines
UT D. Boston
UT D. Hill
P F. Bannister
P R. Dotson
P J. DeLeon
P W. Long
RP J. Winn
RP R. Thigpen
RP R. Searage

CHI 1988 A
M J. Fregosi
1B G. Walker
2B F. Manrique
SS O. Guillen
3B S. Lyons
OF D. Pasqua
OF D. Gallagher
OF D. Boston
C C. Fisk

DH H. Baines
P M. Perez
P J. Reuss
P W. Long
P D. LaPoint
P J. McDowell
RP R. Horton
RP R. Thigpen
RP J. Davis

CHI 1989 A
M J. Torborg
1B G. Walker
2B S. Lyons
SS O. Guillen
3B C. Martinez
OF D. Gallagher
OF I. Calderon
OF D. Boston
C C. Fisk
DH H. Baines
P M. Perez
P E. King
P S. Rosenberg
P J. Hibbard
P J. Reuss
RP S. Hillegas
RP D. Pall
RP R. Thigpen

CHI 1990 A
M J. Torborg
1B C. Martinez
2B S. Fletcher
SS O. Guillen
3B R. Ventura
OF S. Sosa
OF K. Johnson
OF I. Calderon
C C. Fisk
DH D. Pasqua
P J. Hibbard
P J. McDowell
P M. Perez
P E. King
RP W. Edwards
RP R. Thigpen
RP D. Pall

CHI 1876 N
M A. Spalding
1B C. McVey
2B R. Barnes
SS J. Peters
3B A. Anson
OF P. Hines
OF J. Glenn
OF O. Bielaski
C A. White
P A. Spalding

CHI 1877 N
M A. Spalding
1B A. Spalding
2B R. Barnes
SS J. Peters
3B A. Anson
OF P. Hines
OF J. Glenn
OF D. Eggler
C C. McVey
P G. Bradley
P L. Reis

CHI 1878 N
M R. Ferguson
1B J. Start
2B W. McClellan
SS R. Ferguson
3B F. Hankinson
OF J. Cassidy
OF J. Remsen
OF A. Anson
C W. Harbidge
P F. Larkin
P L. Reis

CHI 1879 N
M A. Anson
M F. Flint
1B A. Anson
2B J. Quest
SS J. Peters
3B E. Williamson
OF G. Shaffer
OF A. Dalrymple
OF G. Gore
C F. Flint
P L. Larkin
P F. Hankinson

CHI 1880 N
M A. Anson
1B A. Anson
2B J. Quest
SS T. Burns
3B E. Williamson
OF A. Dalrymple
OF G. Gore
OF M. Kelly
C F. Flint
P L. Corcoran
P F. Goldsmith

CHI 1881 N
M A. Anson
1B A. Anson
2B J. Quest
SS T. Burns
3B E. Williamson
OF A. Dalrymple
OF M. Kelly
OF G. Gore
C F. Flint
P L. Corcoran
P F. Goldsmith

CHI 1882 N
M A. Anson
1B A. Anson
2B T. Burns
SS M. Kelly
3B E. Williamson
OF G. Gore
OF A. Dalrymple
OF H. Nicol
C F. Flint
P F. Goldsmith
P L. Corcoran

CHI 1883 N
M A. Anson
1B A. Anson
2B N. Pfeffer
SS T. Burns
3B E. Williamson
OF G. Gore
OF M. Kelly
OF A. Dalrymple
C F. Flint
P L. Corcoran
P F. Goldsmith

CHI 1884 N
M A. Anson
1B A. Anson
2B N. Pfeffer
SS T. Burns
3B E. Williamson
OF A. Dalrymple
OF G. Gore
OF M. Kelly
C F. Flint
P F. Goldsmith
P L. Corcoran

CHI 1885 N
M A. Anson
1B A. Anson
2B N. Pfeffer
SS T. Burns
3B E. Williamson
OF A. Dalrymple
OF G. Gore
OF M. Kelly
C F. Flint
P L. Corcoran
P J. Clarkson
P J. McCormick

CHI 1886 N
M A. Anson
1B A. Anson
2B N. Pfeffer
SS E. Williamson
3B T. Burns
OF G. Gore
OF A. Dalrymple
OF J. Ryan
C F. Flint
P J. Clarkson
P J. McCormick
P J. Flynn

CHI 1887 N
M A. Anson
1B A. Anson
2B N. Pfeffer

SS E. Williamson
3B T. Burns
OF J. Ryan
OF M. Sullivan
OF W. Sunday
C T. Daly
P J. Clarkson
P M. Baldwin

CHI 1888 N
M A. Anson
1B A. Anson
2B N. Pfeffer
SS E. Williamson
3B T. Burns
OF J. Ryan
OF M. Sullivan
OF H. Duffy
C T. Daly
P A. Krock
P M. Baldwin
P J. Tener

CHI 1889 N
M A. Anson
1B A. Anson
2B N. Pfeffer
SS E. Williamson
3B T. Burns
OF G. Van Haltren
OF H. Duffy
OF J. Ryan
C C. Farrell
P W. Hutchinson
P J. Tener
P J. Dwyer
P A. Gumbert

CHI 1890 N
M A. Anson
1B A. Anson
2B R. Glenalvin
SS J. Cooney
3B T. Burns
OF W. Wilmot
OF S. Carroll
OF J. Andrews
C M. Kittridge
UT H. Earl
P W. Hutchinson
P J. Luby
P E. Stein
P M. Sullivan
P W. Coughlin

CHI 1891 N
M A. Anson
1B A. Anson
2B N. Pfeffer
SS J. Cooney
3B W. Dahlen
OF S. Carroll
OF W. Wilmot
OF J. Ryan
C M. Kittridge
P W. Hutchinson
P A. Gumbert
P J. Luby
P E. Stein

CHI 1892 N
M A. Anson
1B A. Anson
2B J. Canavan
SS W. Dahlen
3B W. Parrott
OF J. Ryan
OF S. Dungan
OF W. Wilmot
C W. Schriver
P W. Hutchinson
P A. Gumbert
P J. Luby

CHI 1893 N
M A. Anson
1B A. Anson
2B W. Lange
SS W. Dahlen
3B W. Parrott
OF S. Dungan
OF W. Wilmot
OF J. Ryan
C M. Kittridge
UT W. Decker
P W. Hutchinson
P W. McGill
P A. Mauck

CHI 1894 N
M A. Anson
1B A. Anson
2B W. Parrott
SS W. Dahlen
3B C. Irwin
OF W. Wilmot
OF W. Lange
OF J. Ryan
C W. Schriver
UT G. Decker
P C. Griffith
P W. McGill
P W. Terry
P C. Stratton

CHI 1895 N
M A. Anson
1B A. Anson
2B A. Stewart
SS W. Dahlen
3B W. Everett
OF W. Lange
OF W. Wilmot
OF J. Ryan
C T. Donahue
P C. Griffith
P W. Terry
P W. Hutchinson

CHI 1896 N
M A. Anson
1B A. Anson
2B N. Pfeffer
SS W. Dahlen
3B W. Everett
OF J. Ryan
OF W. Lange
OF G. Decker
C M. Kittridge
P C. Griffith
P D. Friend
P W. Terry
P H. Briggs

CHI 1897 N
M A. Anson
1B A. Anson
2B J. Connor
SS W. Dahlen
3B W. Everett
OF J. Ryan
OF W. Lange
OF G. Decker
C M. Kittridge
UT J. Callahan
UT W. McCormick
P C. Griffith
P D. Friend
P H. Briggs
P R. Denzer

CHI 1898 N
M T. Burns
1B W. Everett
2B J. Connor
SS W. Dahlen
3B W. McCormick
OF J. Ryan
OF W. Lange
OF S. Mertes
C T. Donahue
P C. Griffith
P J. Callahan
P W. Woods
P M. Kilroy

CHI 1899 N
M T. Burns
1B W. Everett
2B W. McCormick
SS De Montreville
3B H. Wolverton
OF J. Ryan
OF E. Green
OF S. Mertes
C T. Donahue
UT W. Lange
P J. Taylor
P C. Griffith
P J. Callahan
P V. Garvin

CHI 1900 N
M T. Loftus
1B J. Ganzel
2B C. Childs
SS W. McCormick
3B W. Bradley

OF J. McCarthy
OF J. Ryan
OF E. Green
C T. Donahue
UT S. Mertes
P J. Callahan
P C. Griffith
P V. Garvin
P J. Taylor
P J. Menefee

CHI 1901 N
M T. Loftus
1B J. Doyle
2B C. Childs
SS W. McCormick
3B F. Raymer
OF T. Hartsel
OF E. Green
OF F. Chance
C J. Kling
UT C. Dexter
P T. Hughes
P J. Taylor
P G. Waddell
P M. Eason

CHI 1902 N
M F. Selee
1B F. Chance
2B R. Lowe
SS J. Tinker
3B H. Schaefer
OF J. Slagle
OF D. Jones
OF J. Dobbs
C J. Kling
P J. Taylor
P W. Williams
P C. Lundgren
P R. Rhoads
P J. St. Vrain

CHI 1903 N
M F. Selee
1B F. Chance
2B J. Evers
SS J. Tinker
3B J. Casey
OF J. Slagle
OF D. Jones
OF R. Harley
C J. Kling
P J. Taylor
P J. Weimer
P R. Wicker
P C. Lundgren
P J. Menefee

CHI 1904 N
M F. Selee
1B F. Chance
2B J. Evers
SS J. Tinker
3B J. Casey
OF J. Slagle
OF J. McCarthy
OF D. Jones
C J. Kling
P J. Weimer
P H. Briggs
P C. Lundgren
P R. Wicker
P M. Brown

CHI 1905 N
M F. Selee
M F. Chance
1B F. Chance
2B J. Evers
SS J. Tinker
3B J. Casey
OF J. Slagle
OF W. Maloney
OF F. Schulte
C J. Kling
P E. Reulbach
P J. Weimer
P M. Brown
P R. Wicker
P C. Lundgren

CHI 1906 N
M F. Chance
1B F. Chance
2B J. Evers
SS J. Tinker
3B H. Steinfeldt
OF S. Sheckard
OF F. Schulte
OF J. Slagle

C J. Kling
P M. Brown
P J. Pfiester
P E. Reulbach
P C. Lundgren
P J. Taylor

CHI 1907 N
M F. Chance
1B F. Chance
2B J. Evers
SS J. Tinker
3B H. Steinfeldt
OF S. Sheckard
OF J. Slagle
OF F. Schulte
C J. Kling
UT A. Hofman
P O. Overall
P M. Brown
P C. Lundgren
P J. Pfiester
P E. Reulbach

CHI 1908 N
M F. Chance
1B F. Chance
2B J. Evers
SS J. Tinker
3B H. Steinfeldt
OF S. Sheckard
OF F. Schulte
OF J. Slagle
C J. Kling
UT A. Hofman
P M. Brown
P E. Reulbach
P J. Pfiester
P O. Overall
P C. Fraser

CHI 1909 N
M F. Chance
1B F. Chance
2B J. Evers
SS J. Tinker
3B H. Steinfeldt
OF A. Hofman
OF S. Sheckard
OF F. Schulte
C J. Archer
P M. Brown
P O. Overall
P E. Reulbach
P J. Pfiester
P F. Kroh

CHI 1910 N
M F. Chance
1B F. Chance
2B J. Evers
SS J. Tinker
3B H. Steinfeldt
OF F. Schulte
OF S. Sheckard
OF A. Hofman
C J. Kling
UT J. Archer
UT H. Zimmerman
P M. Brown
P L. Cole
P J. McIntire
P E. Reulbach
P O. Overall

CHI 1911 N
M F. Chance
1B V. Saier
2B H. Zimmerman
SS J. Tinker
3B J. Doyle
OF S. Sheckard
OF F. Schulte
OF A. Hofman
C J. Archer
P M. Brown
P L. Richie
P E. Reulbach
P L. Cole
P J. McIntire
RP E. Richter

CHI 1912 N
M F. Chance
1B V. Saier
2B H. Zimmerman
SS J. Tinker
3B H. Zimmerman
OF S. Sheckard
OF S. Sheckard
OF F. Schulte
OF T. Leach

C J. Archer
P L. Cheney
P J. Lavender
P L. Richie
P E. Reulbach
P C. Smith

CHI 1913 N

M J. Evers
1B V. Saier
2B J. Evers
SS A. Bridwell
3B H. Zimmerman
OF F. Schulte
OF T. Leach
OF M. Mitchell
C J. Archer
P L. Cheney
P J. Lavender
P A. Humphries
P G. Pearce
P C. Smith

CHI 1914 N

M H. O'Day
1B V. Saier
2B W. Sweeney
SS J. Corriden
3B H. Zimmerman
OF W. Good
OF T. Leach
OF F. Schulte
C R. Bresnahan
P L. Cheney
P J. Vaughn
P J. Lavender
P A. Humphries
P G. Pearce
RP K. Hageman

CHI 1915 N

M R. Bresnahan
1B V. Saier
2B H. Zimmerman
SS R. Fisher
3B A. Phelan
OF F. Williams
OF F. Schulte
OF W. Good
C J. Archer
P J. Vaughn
P J. Lavender
P G. Pearce
P A. Humphries
P G. Zabel

CHI 1916 N

M J. Tinker
1B V. Saier
2B F. Knabe
SS W. Wortman
3B H. Zimmerman
OF M. Flack
OF F. Williams
OF L. Mann
C J. Archer
UT R. Zeider
P J. Vaughn
P C. Hendrix
P J. Lavender
P G. McConnell
P E. Packard

CHI 1917 N

M F. Mitchell
1B F. Merkle
2B L. Doyle
SS W. Wortman
3B C. Deal
OF F. Williams
OF M. Flack
OF L. Mann
C A. Wilson
UT H. Wolter
UT R. Zeider
P J. Vaughn
P P. Douglas
P C. Hendrix
P A. Demaree
P P. Carter
RP M. Prendergast

CHI 1918 N

M F. Mitchell
1B F. Merkle
2B R. Zeider
SS C. Hollocher
3B C. Deal
OF L. Mann
OF G. Paskert
OF M. Flack

C W. Killefer
P J. Vaughn
P G. Tyler
P C. Hendrix
P P. Douglas

CHI 1919 N

M F. Mitchell
1B F. Merkle
2B C. Pick
SS C. Hollocher
3B C. Deal
OF M. Flack
OF G. Paskert
OF L. Mann
C W. Killefer
P J. Vaughn
P G. Alexander
P C. Hendrix
P E. Martin
P P. Douglas

CHI 1920 N

M F. Mitchell
1B F. Merkle
2B Z. Terry
SS C. Hollocher
3B C. Deal
OF G. Paskert
OF D. Robertson
OF M. Flack
C R. O'Farrell
UT T. Barber
P G. Alexander
P J. Vaughn
P C. Hendrix
P G. Tyler
P E. Martin

CHI 1921 N

M J. Evers
M W. Killefer
1B O. Grimes
2B Z. Terry
SS C. Hollocher
3B C. Deal
OF M. Flack
OF T. Barber
OF G. Maisel
C R. O'Farrell
UT J. Kelleher
P G. Alexander
P E. Martin
P A. Freeman
P V. Cheeves
P J. York

CHI 1922 N

M W. Killefer
1B O. Grimes
2B Z. Terry
SS C. Hollocher
3B M. Krug
OF L. Miller
OF A. Statz
OF B. Friberg
C R. O'Farrell
P V. Aldridge
P G. Alexander
P E. Osborne
P V. Cheeves
P P. Jones

CHI 1923 N

M W. Killefer
1B O. Grimes
2B G. Grantham
SS E. Adams
3B B. Friberg
OF A. Statz
OF L. Miller
OF C. Heathcote
C R. O'Farrell
P G. Alexander
P V. Aldridge
P A. Kaufmann
P E. Osborne
P H. Keen
RP F. Fussell

CHI 1924 N

M W. Killefer
1B H. Cotter
2B G. Grantham
SS E. Adams
3B B. Friberg
OF A. Statz
OF D. Grigsby
OF C. Heathcote
C C. Hartnett
P V. Aldridge

P H. Keen
P A. Kaufmann
P W. Jacobs
P G. Alexander

CHI 1925 N

M W. Killefer
M W. Maranville
M G. Gibson
1B C. Grimm
2B E. Adams
SS W. Maranville
3B H. Freigau
OF C. Heathcote
OF J. Brooks
OF T. Griffith
C C. Hartnett
P G. Alexander
P J. Blake
P A. Cooper
P A. Kaufmann
P G. Bush
RP H. Keen

CHI 1926 N

M J. McCarthy
1B C. Grimm
2B E. Adams
SS J. Cooney
3B H. Freigau
OF L. Wilson
OF C. Heathcote
OF J. Stephenson
C C. Hartnett
P C. Root
P J. Blake
P A. Kaufmann
P P. Jones
P G. Bush

CHI 1927 N

M J. McCarthy
1B C. Grimm
2B C. Beck
SS E. English
3B E. Adams
OF L. Wilson
OF J. Stephenson
OF W. Webb
C C. Hartnett
P C. Root
P J. Blake
P G. Bush
P H. Carlson
P J. Brillheart

CHI 1928 N

M J. McCarthy
1B C. Grimm
2B F. Maguire
SS E. English
3B C. Beck
OF L. Wilson
OF J. Stephenson
OF H. Cuyler
C C. Hartnett
P P. Malone
P J. Blake
P C. Root
P G. Bush
P A. Nehf
RP H. Carlson

CHI 1929 N

M J. McCarthy
1B C. Grimm
2B R. Hornsby
SS E. English
3B N. McMillan
OF L. Wilson
OF J. Stephenson
OF H. Cuyler
C J. Taylor
P C. Root
P G. Bush
P P. Malone
P J. Blake
P A. Nehf
RP M. Cvengros

CHI 1930 N

M J. McCarthy
M R. Hornsby
1B C. Grimm
2B C. Blair
SS E. English
3B L. Bell
OF H. Cuyler
OF L. Wilson
OF J. Stephenson
C C. Hartnett

P P. Malone
P G. Bush
P C. Root
P J. Blake
P A. Teachout
RP L. Nelson

CHI 1931 N

M R. Hornsby
1B C. Grimm
2B R. Hornsby
SS E. English
3B L. Bell
OF H. Cuyler
OF L. Wilson
OF D. Taylor
C C. Hartnett
P C. Root
P R. Smith
P P. Malone
P G. Bush
P L. Sweetland
RP F. May
RP A. Teachout

CHI 1932 N

M R. Hornsby
M C. Grimm
1B C. Grimm
2B W. Herman
SS W. Jurges
3B E. English
OF J. Stephenson
OF J. Moore
OF H. Cuyler
C C. Hartnett
P L. Warneke
P G. Bush
P P. Malone
P C. Root
P B. Grimes
RP F. May

CHI 1933 N

M C. Grimm
1B C. Grimm
2B W. Herman
SS W. Jurges
3B E. English
OF J. Demaree
OF F. Herman
OF J. Stephenson
C C. Hartnett
P L. Warneke
P G. Bush
P C. Root
P P. Malone
P L. Tinning

CHI 1934 N

M C. Grimm
1B C. Grimm
2B W. Herman
SS W. Jurges
3B S. Hack
OF H. Cuyler
OF F. Herman
OF C. Klein
C C. Hartnett
UT E. English
UT G. Stainback
P L. Warneke
P W. Lee
P G. Bush
P P. Malone
P J. Weaver

CHI 1935 N

M C. Grimm
1B P. Cavarretta
2B W. Herman
SS W. Jurges
3B S. Hack
OF A. Galan
OF C. Klein
OF J. Demaree
C C. Hartnett
P L. Warneke
P W. Lee
P L. French
P C. Root
P J. Carleton
RP F. Kowalik

CHI 1936 N

M C. Grimm
1B P. Cavarretta
2B W. Herman
SS W. Jurges
3B S. Hack
OF J. Demaree

OF A. Galan
OF E. Allen
C C. Hartnett
P W. Lee
P L. French
P L. Warneke
P J. Carleton
P C. Davis
RP C. Root
RP C. Bryant

CHI 1937 N

M C. Grimm
1B J. Collins
2B W. Herman
SS W. Jurges
3B S. Hack
OF J. Demaree
OF A. Galan
OF J. Marty
C C. Hartnett
UT P. Cavarretta
P W. Lee
P L. French
P J. Carleton
P C. Root
P L. Parmelee
RP C. Shoun

CHI 1938 N

M C. Grimm
M C. Hartnett
1B J. Collins
2B W. Herman
SS W. Jurges
3B S. Hack
OF C. Reynolds
OF J. Demaree
OF A. Galan
C C. Hartnett
P W. Lee
P C. Bryant
P L. French
P J. Carleton
P C. Root
RP J. Russell

CHI 1939 N

M C. Hartnett
1B G. Russell
2B W. Herman
SS R. Bartell
3B S. Hack
OF A. Galan
OF H. Leiber
OF J. Gleeson
C C. Hartnett
P W. Lee
P C. Passeau
P L. French
P C. Root
P V. Page
RP J. Russell
RP R. Lillard

CHI 1940 N

M C. Hartnett
1B P. Cavarretta
2B W. Herman
SS R. Mattick
3B S. Hack
OF W. Nicholson
OF J. Gleeson
OF H. Leiber
C A. Todd
UT N. Dallessandro
P C. Passeau
P L. French
P W. Lee
P V. Olsen
P J. Mooty
RP K. Raffensberger
RP V. Page

CHI 1941 N

M J. Wilson
1B E. Dahlgren
2B L. Stringer
SS R. Sturgeon
3B S. Hack
OF W. Nicholson
OF N. Dallessandro
OF P. Cavarretta
C C. McCullough
P C. Passeau
P V. Olsen
P W. Lee
P J. Mooty
P P. Erickson
RP F. Pressnell
RP V. Page

CHI 1942 N

M J. Wilson
1B P. Cavarretta
2B L. Stringer
SS L. Merullo
3B S. Hack
OF W. Nicholson
OF L. Novikoff
OF N. Dallessandro
C C. McCullough
UT G. Russell
P C. Passeau
P W. Lee
P H. Bithorn
P V. Olsen
P L. Fleming

CHI 1943 N

M J. Wilson
1B P. Cavarretta
2B E. Stanky
SS L. Merullo
3B S. Hack
OF W. Nicholson
OF H. Lowrey
OF L. Novikoff
C C. McCullough
P C. Passeau
P H. Bithorn
P S. Derringer
P H. Wyse
P E. Hanyzewski
RP R. Prim

CHI 1944 N

M J. Wilson
M R. Johnson
M C. Grimm
1B P. Cavarretta
2B D. Johnson
SS L. Merullo
3B S. Hack
OF W. Nicholson
OF A. Pafko
OF N. Dallessandro
C D. Williams
UT R. Hughes
P H. Wyse
P C. Passeau
P S. Derringer
P L. Fleming
P R. Chipman

CHI 1945 N

M C. Grimm
1B P. Cavarretta
2B D. Johnson
SS L. Merullo
3B S. Hack
OF W. Nicholson
OF A. Pafko
OF H. Lowrey
C T. Livingston
P H. Wyse
P C. Passeau
P S. Derringer
P R. Prim
P H. Borowy
RP R. Chipman

CHI 1946 N

M C. Grimm
1B E. Waitkus
2B D. Johnson
SS W. Jurges
3B S. Hack
OF H. Lowrey
OF M. Rickert
OF P. Cavarretta
C C. McCullough
UT W. Nicholson
UT R. Sturgeon
P J. Schmitz
P H. Wyse
P H. Borowy
P P. Erickson
P E. Kush

CHI 1947 N

M C. Grimm
1B E. Waitkus
2B D. Johnson
SS L. Merullo
3B H. Lowrey
OF W. Nicholson
OF A. Pafko
OF P. Cavarretta
C R. Scheffing
P J. Schmitz
P D. Lade
P H. Borowy

P P. Erickson
P H. Wyse
RP E. Kush
RP R. Meers

CHI 1948 N

M C. Grimm
1B E. Waitkus
2B H. Schenz
SS R. Smalley
3B A. Pafko
OF W. Nicholson
OF H. Jeffcoat
OF H. Lowrey
C R. Scheffing
UT P. Cavarretta
P J. Schmitz
P R. Meyer
P R. McCall
P H. Rush
P H. Borowy
RP A. Dobernic
RP E. Kush
RP R. Chipman

CHI 1949 N

M C. Grimm
M F. Frisch
1B H. Reich
2B E. Verban
SS R. Smalley
3B F. Gustine
OF H. Jeffcoat
OF H. Sauer
C A. Owen
UT P. Cavarretta
P J. Schmitz
P H. Rush
P E. Leonard
P W. Dubiel
P D. Lade
RP R. Chipman
RP J. Adkins
RP R. Muncrief

CHI 1950 N

M F. Frisch
1B P. Ward
2B W. Terwilliger
SS R. Smalley
3B W. Serena
OF A. Pafko
OF H. Sauer
OF R. Borkowski
C A. Owen
P R. Rush
P J. Schmitz
P P. Minner
P F. Hiller
P W. Dubiel
RP J. Vander Meer
RP E. Leonard
RP W. Voiselle

CHI 1951 N

M F. Frisch
M P. Cavarretta
1B K. Connors
2B E. Miksis
SS R. Smalley
3B R. Jackson
OF F. Baumholtz
OF H. Sauer
OF H. Jeffcoat
C F. Burgess
P R. Rush
P P. Minner
P C. McLish
P F. Hiller
P O. Lown
RP E. Leonard
RP W. Dubiel

CHI 1952 N

M P. Cavarretta
1B D. Fondy
2B E. Miksis
SS R. Smalley
3B R. Jackson
OF H. Sauer
OF F. Baumholtz
OF H. Jeffcoat
C M. Atwell
UT E. Hermanski
UT W. Serena
P R. Rush
P J. Klippstein
P W. Hacker
P P. Minner
P O. Lown
RP R. Schultz

RP E. Leonard

CHI 1953 N
- M P. Cavarretta
- 1B D. Fondy
- 2B E. Miksis
- SS R. Smalley
- 3B R. Jackson
- OF F. Baumholtz
- OF H. Kiner
- OF H. Sauer
- C C. McCullough
- UT H. Jeffcoat
- P W. Hacker
- P P. Minner
- P J. Klippstein
- P R. Rush
- P O. Lown
- RP E. Leonard

CHI 1954 N
- M S. Hack
- 1B D. Fondy
- 2B E. Baker
- SS E. Banks
- 3B R. Jackson
- OF H. Kiner
- OF H. Sauer
- OF R. Talbot
- C J. Garagiola
- P R. Rush
- P P. Minner
- P W. Hacker
- P J. Klippstein
- P H. Pollet
- RP J. Davis
- RP H. Jeffcoat
- RP W. Tremel

CHI 1955 N
- M S. Hack
- 1B D. Fondy
- 2B E. Baker
- SS E. Banks
- 3B R. Jackson
- OF E. Miksis
- OF J. King
- OF H. Sauer
- C H. Chiti
- UT F. Baumholtz
- UT R. Speake
- P S. Jones
- P R. Rush
- P W. Hacker
- P P. Minner
- P J. Davis
- RP H. Jeffcoat
- RP H. Pollet
- RP D. Hillman

CHI 1956 N
- M S. Hack
- 1B D. Fondy
- 2B E. Baker
- SS E. Banks
- 3B D. Hoak
- OF W. Moryn
- OF M. Irvin
- OF T. Whisenant
- C H. Landrith
- UT J. King
- UT E. Miksis
- P R. Rush
- P S. Jones
- P W. Hacker
- P C. Kaiser
- P J. Brosnan
- RP J. Davis
- RP O. Lown
- RP V. Valentinetti

CHI 1957 N
- M R. Scheffing
- 1B R. Long
- 2B R. Morgan
- SS J. Littrell
- 3B E. Banks
- OF W. Moryn
- OF R. Walls
- OF C. Tanner
- C C. Neeman
- UT J. Bolger
- UT R. Speake
- P M. Drabowsky
- P R. Drott
- P R. Rush
- P D. Elston
- P D. Hillman
- RP J. Brosnan
- RP O. Lown
- RP R. Littlefield

CHI 1958 N
- M R. Scheffing
- 1B R. Long
- 2B A. Taylor
- SS E. Banks
- 3B A. Dark
- OF R. Thomson
- OF W. Moryn
- OF R. Walls
- C S. Taylor
- P W. Phillips
- P G. Hobbie
- P R. Drott
- P D. Hillman
- P M. Drabowsky
- RP D. Elston
- RP W. Henry

CHI 1959 N
- M R. Scheffing
- 1B R. Long
- 2B A. Taylor
- SS E. Banks
- 3B A. Dark
- OF G. Altman
- OF R. Walls
- OF R. Thomson
- C S. Taylor
- UT R. Marshall
- UT W. Moryn
- P R. Anderson
- P G. Hobbie
- P D. Hillman
- P M. Drabowsky
- P A. Ceccarelli
- RP W. Henry
- RP D. Elston

CHI 1960 N
- M C. Grimm
- M L. Boudreau
- 1B E. Bouchee
- 2B G. Kindall
- SS E. Banks
- 3B R. Santo
- OF R. Ashburn
- OF R. Will
- OF G. Altman
- C M. Thacker
- UT F. Thomas
- UT D. Zimmer
- P G. Hobbie
- P R. Anderson
- P R. Ellsworth
- P D. Cardwell
- RP D. Elston
- RP S. Morehead
- RP M. Freeman

CHI 1961 N
- M A. Himsl
- M H. Craft
- M A. Himsl
- M E. Tappe
- M H. Craft
- M A. Himsl
- M E. Tappe
- M L. Klein
- M E. Tappe
- 1B E. Bouchee
- 2B D. Zimmer
- SS E. Banks
- 3B R. Santo
- OF B. Williams
- OF G. Altman
- OF A. Heist
- C R. Bertell
- UT R. Ashburn
- UT G. Kindall
- P D. Cardwell
- P G. Hobbie
- P R. Ellsworth
- P J. Curtis
- RP R. Anderson
- RP R. Drott
- RP D. Elston

CHI 1962 N
- M E. Tappe
- M L. Klein
- M C. Metro
- 1B E. Banks
- 2B K. Hubbs
- SS K. Rodgers
- 3B R. Santo
- OF B. Williams
- OF G. Altman
- OF L. Brock
- C R. Bertell
- P R. Buhl
- P R. Ellsworth
- P D. Cardwell

CHI 1963 N
- P C. Koonce
- P G. Hobbie
- RP R. Anderson
- RP G. Schultz
- RP D. Elston

CHI 1963 N
- M R. Kennedy
- 1B E. Banks
- 2B K. Hubbs
- SS K. Rodgers
- 3B R. Santo
- OF B. Williams
- OF L. Brock
- OF E. Burton
- C R. Bertell
- P R. Ellsworth
- P L. Jackson
- P R. Buhl
- P G. Hobbie
- P P. Toth
- RP L. McDaniel
- RP D. Elston
- RP J. Brewer

CHI 1964 N
- M R. Kennedy
- 1B E. Banks
- 2B J. Amalfitano
- SS K. Rodgers
- 3B R. Santo
- OF B. Williams
- OF B. Cowan
- OF L. Gabrielson
- C R. Bertell
- UT J. Stewart
- P L. Jackson
- P R. Ellsworth
- P R. Buhl
- P S. Burdette
- P E. Broglio
- RP L. McDaniel
- RP D. Elston
- RP S. Slaughter

CHI 1965 N
- M R. Kennedy
- M L. Klein
- 1B E. Banks
- 2B G. Beckert
- SS K. Rodgers
- 3B R. Santo
- OF B. Williams
- OF D. Landrum
- OF D. Clemens
- C V. Roznovsky
- UT J. Stewart
- P L. Jackson
- P R. Ellsworth
- P R. Buhl
- P C. Koonce
- RP T. Abernathy
- RP L. McDaniel
- RP R. Humphreys

CHI 1966 N
- M L. Durocher
- 1B E. Banks
- 2B G. Beckert
- SS D. Kessinger
- 3B R. Santo
- OF B. Williams
- OF B. Browne
- OF A. Phillips
- C C. Hundley
- P R. Ellsworth
- P K. Holtzman
- P F. Jenkins
- P W. Hands
- RP C. Koonce
- RP C. Hendley

CHI 1967 N
- M L. Durocher
- 1B E. Banks
- 2B G. Beckert
- SS D. Kessinger
- 3B R. Santo
- OF B. Williams
- OF A. Phillips
- OF T. Savage
- C C. Hundley
- P F. Jenkins
- P R. Nye
- P J. Niekro
- P R. Culp
- P W. Hands
- RP C. Hartenstein
- RP W. Stoneman
- RP C. Koonce

CHI 1968 N
- M L. Durocher
- 1B E. Banks
- 2B G. Beckert
- SS D. Kessinger
- 3B R. Santo
- OF B. Williams
- OF A. Phillips
- OF J. Hickman
- C C. Hundley
- P F. Jenkins
- P W. Hands
- P K. Holtzman
- P J. Niekro
- P R. Nye
- RP P. Regan
- RP J. Lamabe

CHI 1969 N
- M L. Durocher
- 1B E. Banks
- 2B G. Beckert
- SS D. Kessinger
- 3B R. Santo
- OF B. Williams
- OF J. Hickman
- OF D. Young
- C C. Hundley
- UT W. Smith
- P F. Jenkins
- P W. Hands
- P K. Holtzman
- P R. Selma
- RP P. Regan
- RP T. Abernathy
- RP R. Nye

CHI 1970 N
- M L. Durocher
- 1B J. Hickman
- 2B G. Beckert
- SS D. Kessinger
- 3B R. Santo
- OF B. Williams
- OF J. Callison
- OF C. James
- C C. Hundley
- P F. Jenkins
- P K. Holtzman
- P W. Hands
- P M. Pappas
- P G. Decker
- RP P. Regan
- RP J. Colborn

CHI 1971 N
- M L. Durocher
- 1B J. Pepitone
- 2B G. Beckert
- SS D. Kessinger
- 3B R. Santo
- OF B. Williams
- OF B. Davis
- OF J. Callison
- C C. Cannizzaro
- UT J. Hickman
- P F. Jenkins
- P M. Pappas
- P W. Hands
- P J. Pizarro
- RP P. Regan
- RP W. Bonham

CHI 1972 N
- M L. Durocher
- M C. Lockman
- 1B J. Hickman
- 2B G. Beckert
- SS D. Kessinger
- 3B R. Santo
- OF B. Williams
- OF J. Cardenal
- OF R. Monday
- C C. Hundley
- P F. Jenkins
- P B. Hooton
- P M. Pappas
- P W. Hands
- P R. Reuschel
- RP T. Phoebus
- RP J. Aker
- RP D. McGinn

CHI 1973 N
- M C. Lockman
- 1B J. Hickman
- 2B G. Beckert
- SS D. Kessinger
- 3B R. Santo
- OF R. Monday
- OF J. Cardenal
- OF B. Williams
- C C. Hundley
- UT G. Hiser
- UT P. Popovich
- P F. Jenkins
- P B. Hooton
- P R. Reuschel
- P M. Pappas
- P W. Bonham
- RP R. Locker
- RP B. Burris
- RP J. Aker

CHI 1974 N
- M C. Lockman
- M R. Marshall
- 1B A. Thornton
- 2B V. Harris
- SS D. Kessinger
- 3B B. Madlock
- OF J. Morales
- OF R. Monday
- OF J. Cardenal
- C S. Swisher
- UT B. Williams*
- P W. Bonham
- P R. Reuschel
- P B. Hooton
- P S. Stone
- RP K. Frailing
- RP D. LaRoche
- RP J. Todd

CHI 1975 N
- M R. Marshall
- 1B A. Thornton
- 2B J. Trillo
- SS D. Kessinger
- 3B B. Madlock
- OF J. Morales
- OF J. Cardenal
- OF R. Monday
- C S. Swisher
- UT R. LaCock
- P B. Burris
- P R. Reuschel
- P W. Bonham
- P S. Stone
- RP D. Knowles
- RP T. Dettore
- RP O. Zamora

CHI 1976 N
- M R. Marshall
- 1B R. LaCock
- 2B J. Trillo
- SS M. Kelleher
- 3B B. Madlock
- OF J. Morales
- OF J. Cardenal
- OF R. Monday
- C S. Swisher
- UT G. Mitterwald
- UT H. Wallis
- P R. Reuschel
- P B. Burris
- P W. Bonham
- P S. Renko
- RP P. Reuschel
- RP H. Sutter
- RP J. Coleman

CHI 1977 N
- M H. Franks
- 1B W. Buckner
- 2B J. Trillo
- SS I. DeJesus
- 3B S. Ontiveros
- OF B. Murcer
- OF J. Morales
- OF G. Gross
- C G. Mitterwald
- UT L. Biittner
- UT J. Cardenal
- UT E. Clines
- P R. Reuschel
- P B. Burris
- P W. Bonham
- P M. Krukow
- RP G. Hernandez
- RP H. Sutter
- RP P. Reuschel

CHI 1978 N
- M H. Franks
- 1B W. Buckner
- 2B J. Trillo
- SS I. DeJesus
- 3B S. Ontiveros
- OF B. Murcer
- OF G. Gross
- OF D. Kingman
- C D. Rader
- UT L. Biittner
- UT E. Clines
- P R. Reuschel
- P D. Lamp
- P B. Burris
- P D. Roberts
- P M. Krukow
- RP D. Moore
- RP H. Sutter
- RP L. McGlothen

CHI 1979 N
- M H. Franks
- M J. Amalfitano
- 1B W. Buckner
- 2B T. Sizemore
- SS I. DeJesus
- 3B S. Ontiveros
- OF J. Martin
- OF D. Kingman
- OF V. Thompson
- C B. Foote
- UT L. Biittner
- P R. Reuschel
- P L. McGlothen
- P D. Lamp
- P M. Krukow
- P K. Holtzman
- RP R. Tidrow
- RP H. Sutter
- RP G. Hernandez

CHI 1980 N
- M P. Gomez
- M J. Amalfitano
- 1B W. Buckner
- 2B M. Tyson
- SS I. DeJesus
- SS L. Randle
- 3B S. Dillard
- OF J. Martin
- OF M. Vail
- OF V. Thompson
- C T. Blackwell
- UT L. Biittner
- UT S. Dillard
- UT J. Figueroa
- UT M. Kelleher
- P R. Reuschel
- P M. Krukow
- P D. Lamp
- P L. McGlothen
- RP W. Caudill
- RP R. Tidrow
- RP G. Hernandez

CHI 1981 N
- M J. Amalfitano
- 1B W. Buckner
- 2B M. Tyson
- SS I. DeJesus
- 3B K. Reitz
- OF L. Durham
- OF S. Henderson
- OF J. Morales
- C J. Davis
- P M. Krukow
- P R. Martz
- P R. Reuschel
- P K. Kravec
- P J. Bird
- RP R. Tidrow
- RP W. Caudill
- RP L. Smith

CHI 1982 N
- M L. Elia
- 1B W. Buckner
- 2B E. Wills
- SS L. Bowa
- 3B R. Sandberg
- OF L. Durham
- OF G. Woods
- OF B. Moreland
- C J. Davis
- UT J. Johnstone
- UT J. Kennedy
- P F. Jenkins
- P J. Bird
- P D. Noles
- P R. Martz
- P A. Ripley
- RP L. Smith
- RP R. Tidrow
- RP W. Campbell

CHI 1983 N
- M L. Elia
- M C. Fox
- 1B W. Buckner
- 2B R. Sandberg
- SS L. Bowa
- 3B R. Cey
- OF B. Moreland
- OF M. Hall
- OF L. Durham
- C J. Davis
- P C. Rainey
- P S. Trout
- P F. Jenkins
- P R. Ruthven
- P D. Noles
- RP W. Campbell
- RP L. Smith
- RP C. Lefferts

CHI 1984 N
- M J. Frey
- 1B L. Durham
- 2B R. Sandberg
- SS L. Bowa
- 3B R. Cey
- OF G. Matthews
- OF R. Dernier
- OF B. Moreland
- C J. Davis
- UT H. Cotto
- P S. Trout
- P D. Eckersley
- P R. Sutcliffe
- P S. Sanderson
- P R. Ruthven
- RP L. Smith
- RP T. Stoddard
- RP R. Bordi

CHI 1985 N
- M J. Frey
- 1B L. Durham
- 2B R. Sandberg
- SS S. Dunston
- 3B R. Cey
- OF B. Moreland
- OF R. Dernier
- OF G. Matthews
- C J. Davis
- UT D. Lopes
- UT C. Speier
- P D. Eckersley
- P S. Fontenot
- P S. Trout
- P R. Sutcliffe
- P S. Sanderson
- RP L. Smith
- RP L. Sorensen
- RP G. Frazier

CHI 1986 N
- M J. Frey
- M J. Vukovich
- M E. Michael
- 1B L. Durham
- 2B R. Sandberg
- SS S. Dunston
- 3B R. Cey
- OF B. Moreland
- OF G. Matthews
- OF R. Dernier
- C J. Davis
- UT J. Mumphrey
- P D. Eckersley
- P R. Sutcliffe
- P S. Sanderson
- P S. Trout
- P E. Lynch
- RP L. Smith
- RP G. Hoffman
- RP D. Gumpert

CHI 1987 N
- M E. Michael
- M F. Lucchesi
- 1B L. Durham
- 2B R. Sandberg
- SS S. Dunston
- 3B B. Moreland
- OF A. Dawson
- OF D. Martinez
- OF J. Mumphrey
- C J. Davis
- UT B. Dayett
- UT J. Trillo
- P R. Sutcliffe
- P J. Moyer
- P G. Maddux
- P S. Sanderson
- P L. Lancaster
- RP E. Lynch
- RP L. Smith
- RP F. DiPino

CHI 1988 N

M	D. Zimmer
1B	M. Grace
2B	R. Sandberg
SS	S. Dunston
3B	V. Law
OF	R. Palmeiro
OF	A. Dawson
OF	D. Jackson
C	D. Berryhill
P	G. Maddux
P	R. Sutcliffe
P	J. Moyer
P	C. Schiraldi
P	J. Pico
RP	F. DiPino
RP	L. Lancaster

CHI 1989 N

M	D. Zimmer
1B	M. Grace
2B	R. Sandberg
SS	S. Dunston
3B	V. Law
OF	J. Walton
OF	A. Dawson
OF	J. Smith
C	D. Berryhill
UT	M. Webster
P	G. Maddux
P	R. Sutcliffe
P	M. Bielecki
P	S. Sanderson
P	P. Kilgus
RP	J. Pico
RP	S. Wilson
RP	M. Williams

CHI 1990 N

M	D. Zimmer
1B	M. Grace
2B	R. Sandberg
SS	S. Dunston
3B	L. Salazar
OF	A. Dawson
OF	D. Dascenzo
OF	J. Walton
C	J. Girardi
UT	D. Ramos
UT	J. Smith
P	G. Maddux
P	M. Harkey
P	M. Bielecki
P	S. Wilson
P	S. Boskie
RP	L. Lancaster
RP	P. Assenmacher
RP	J. Pico

Cincinnati

CIN N 1876-1880
CIN U 1884
CIN a 1882-1889
CIN a 1891
CIN N 1890-1990

CIN 1876 N

M	C. Gould
1B	C. Gould
2B	C. Sweasy
SS	H. Kessler
3B	W. Foley
OF	C. Jones
OF	E. Snyder
OF	D. Pierson
C	A. Booth
P	C. Dean
P	W. Fisher
P	E. Williams

CIN 1877 N

M	L. Pike
M	R. Addy
M	J. Manning
1B	C. Gould
2B	L. Pike
SS	J. Manning
3B	W. Foley
OF	R. Addy
OF	C. Jones
OF	E. Cuthbert
C	W. Hastings
UT	A. Booth
P	W. Cummings
P	R. Mathews
P	R. Mitchell

CIN 1878 N

M	C. McVey

1B	J. Sullivan
2B	J. Gerhardt
SS	W. Geer
3B	C. McVey
OF	C. Jones
OF	M. Kelly
OF	L. Pike
C	J. White
P	W. White
P	R. Mitchell

CIN 1879 N

M	J. White
M	C. McVey
1B	C. McVey
2B	J. Gerhardt
SS	R. Barnes
3B	W. Foley
OF	L. Dickerson
OF	P. Hotaling
OF	M. Kelly
C	J. White
P	W. White

CIN 1880 N

M	J. Clapp
1B	J. Reilly
2B	C. Smith
SS	L. Say
3B	W. Carpenter
OF	W. Purcell
OF	M. Mansell
OF	J. Manning
C	J. Clapp
P	W. White

CIN 1884 U

M	D. O'Leary
M	S. Crane
1B	M. Powell
2B	S. Crane
SS	R. Jones
3B	C. Barber
OF	L. Sylvester
OF	W. Harbridge
OF	W. Hawes
C	J. Kelly
UT	R. Burns
P	G. Bradley
P	J. McCormick

CIN 1882 a

M	C. Snyder
1B	D. Stearns
2B	J. McPhee
SS	C. Fulmer
3B	W. Carpenter
OF	J. Sommer
OF	J. Macullar
OF	H. Wheeler
C	C. Snyder
P	W. White
P	P. McCormick

CIN 1883 a

M	C. Snyder
1B	J. Reilly
2B	J. McPhee
SS	C. Fulmer
3B	W. Carpenter
OF	J. Sommer
OF	C. Jones
OF	J. Corkhill
C	C. Snyder
P	W. White
P	L. Deagle
P	P. McCormick

CIN 1884 a

M	W. White
M	C. Snyder
1B	J. Reilly
2B	J. McPhee
SS	J. Peoples
3B	W. Carpenter
OF	C. Jones
OF	J. Corkhill
OF	T. Mansell
C	C. Snyder
P	W. White
P	W. Mountjoy
P	A. Shallix

CIN 1885 a

M	O. Caylor
1B	J. Reilly
2B	J. McPhee
SS	F. Fennelly
3B	W. Carpenter
OF	C. Jones

OF	J. Corkhill
OF	J. Clinton
C	C. Snyder
P	W. White
P	L. McKeon
P	W. Mountjoy
P	G. Pechiney
P	A. Shallix

CIN 1886 a

M	O. Caylor
1B	J. Reilly
2B	J. McPhee
SS	F. Fennelly
3B	W. Carpenter
OF	C. Jones
OF	J. Corkhill
OF	F. Lewis
C	C. Baldwin
P	A. Mullane
P	G. Pechiney
P	L. McKeon

CIN 1887 a

M	G. Schmelz
1B	J. Reilly
2B	J. McPhee
SS	F. Fennelly
3B	W. Carpenter
OF	J. Corkhill
OF	H. Nicol
OF	G. Tebeau
C	C. Baldwin
P	E. Smith
P	A. Mullane
P	W. Serad

CIN 1888 a

M	G. Schmelz
1B	J. Reilly
2B	J. McPhee
SS	F. Fennelly
3B	W. Carpenter
OF	H. Nicol
OF	G. Tebeau
OF	J. Corkhill
C	J. Keenan
P	L. Viau
P	A. Mullane
P	E. Smith

CIN 1889 a

M	G. Schmelz
1B	J. Reilly
2B	J. McPhee
SS	O. Beard
3B	W. Carpenter
OF	J. Holliday
OF	G. Tebeau
OF	H. Nicol
C	J. Keenan
P	J. Duryea
P	L. Viau
P	A. Mullane
P	E. Smith

CIN 1891 a

M	M. Kelly
1B	J. Carney
2B	W. Robinson
SS	J. Canavan
3B	A. Whitney
OF	R. Johnston
OF	J. Seery
OF	G. Andrews
C	M. Kelly
P	J. Dwyer
P	E. Crane
P	W. Mains
P	W. McGill

CIN 1890 N

M	T. Loftus
1B	J. Reilly
2B	J. McPhee
SS	O. Beard
3B	C. Marr
OF	J. Holliday
OF	J. Knight
OF	H. Nicol
C	J. Harrington
P	W. Rhines
P	J. Duryea
P	F. Foreman
P	L. Viau

CIN 1891 N

M	T. Loftus
1B	J. Reilly
2B	J. McPhee

SS	G. Smith
3B	W. Latham
OF	J. Holliday
OF	C. Marr
OF	W. Halligan
C	J. Harrington
P	A. Mullane
P	W. Rhines
P	C. Radbourn
P	E. Crane

CIN 1892 N

M	C. Comiskey
1B	C. Comiskey
2B	J. McPhee
SS	G. Smith
3B	W. Latham
OF	J. Holliday
OF	J. O'Neill
OF	L. Browning
C	M. Murphy
P	E. Chamberlain
P	A. Mullane
P	J. Dwyer
P	M. Sullivan

CIN 1893 N

M	C. Comiskey
1B	C. Comiskey
2B	J. McPhee
SS	G. Smith
3B	W. Latham
OF	J. Holliday
OF	J. Canavan
OF	J. McCarthy
C	H. Vaughn
P	J. Dwyer
P	E. Chamberlain
P	M. Sullivan
P	T. Parrott
P	A. Mullane

CIN 1894 N

M	C. Comiskey
1B	C. Comiskey
2B	J. McPhee
SS	G. Smith
3B	W. Latham
OF	W. Hoy
OF	J. Holliday
OF	J. Canavan
C	M. Murphy
P	J. Dwyer
P	T. Parrott
P	E. Chamberlain
P	C. Fisher

CIN 1895 N

M	W. Ewing
1B	W. Ewing
2B	J. McPhee
SS	G. Smith
3B	W. Latham
OF	C. Miller
OF	W. Hoy
OF	G. Hogriever
C	H. Vaughn
P	J. Dwyer
P	W. Rhines
P	T. Parrott
P	F. Foreman
P	W. Phillips

CIN 1896 N

M	W. Ewing
1B	W. Ewing
2B	J. McPhee
SS	G. Smith
3B	C. Irwin
OF	C. Miller
OF	E. Burke
OF	W. Hoy
C	H. Peitz
UT	H. Vaughn
P	J. Dwyer
P	P. Ehret
P	F. Foreman
P	C. Fisher
P	W. Rhines

CIN 1897 N

M	W. Ewing
1B	J. Beckley
2B	J. McPhee
SS	C. Ritchey
3B	C. Irwin
OF	W. Hoy
OF	C. Miller
OF	E. Burke
C	H. Peitz
UT	T. Corcoran

P	T. Breitenstein
P	W. Rhines
P	J. Dwyer
P	P. Ehret
P	W. Dammann

CIN 1898 N

M	W. Ewing
1B	J. Beckley
2B	J. McPhee
SS	T. Corcoran
3B	C. Irwin
OF	C. Miller
OF	E. Smith
OF	A. McBride
C	H. Peitz
P	E. Hawley
P	T. Breitenstein
P	W. Hill
P	J. Dwyer
P	W. Dammann

CIN 1899 N

M	W. Ewing
1B	J. Beckley
2B	J. McPhee
SS	T. Corcoran
3B	C. Irwin
OF	A. Selbach
OF	E. Smith
OF	C. Miller
C	H. Peitz
UT	H. Steinfeldt
P	F. Hahn
P	E. Hawley
P	W. Phillips
P	T. Breitenstein
P	J. Taylor

CIN 1900 N

M	R. Allen
1B	J. Beckley
2B	J. Quinn
SS	T. Corcoran
3B	H. Steinfeldt
OF	J. Barrett
OF	A. McBride
OF	S. Crawford
C	H. Peitz
P	E. Scott
P	F. Hahn
P	E. Newton
P	W. Phillips
P	T. Breitenstein

CIN 1901 N

M	J. McPhee
1B	J. Beckley
2B	H. Steinfeldt
SS	G. Magoon
3B	C. Irwin
OF	R. Harley
OF	S. Crawford
OF	J. Dobbs
C	W. Bergen
P	F. Hahn
P	W. Phillips
P	E. Newton
P	A. Stimmel

CIN 1902 N

M	J. McPhee
M	F. Bancroft
M	J. Kelley
1B	J. Beckley
2B	H. Peitz
SS	T. Corcoran
3B	H. Steinfeldt
OF	S. Crawford
OF	W. Hoy
OF	J. Dobbs
C	W. Bergen
P	F. Hahn
P	W. Phillips
P	H. Thielman
P	E. Poole
P	G. Ewing

CIN 1903 N

M	J. Kelley
1B	J. Beckley
2B	T. Daly
SS	T. Corcoran
3B	H. Steinfeldt
OF	J. Seymour
OF	M. Donlin
OF	P. Dolan
C	H. Peitz
UT	J. Kelley
P	F. Hahn
P	G. Ewing

P	J. Sutthoff
P	E. Poole
P	C. Harper

CIN 1904 N

M	J. Kelley
1B	J. Kelley
2B	M. Huggins
SS	T. Corcoran
3B	H. Steinfeldt
OF	J. Seymour
OF	F. Odwell
OF	P. Dolan
C	G. Schlei
P	F. Hahn
P	C. Harper
P	W. Kellum
P	T. Walker
P	G. Ewing

CIN 1905 N

M	J. Kelley
1B	J. Barry
2B	M. Huggins
SS	T. Corcoran
3B	H. Steinfeldt
OF	J. Seymour
OF	F. Odwell
OF	J. Kelley
C	G. Schlei
P	O. Overall
P	G. Ewing
P	C. Chech
P	C. Harper
P	T. Walker

CIN 1906 N

M	E. Hanlon
1B	J. Deal
2B	M. Huggins
SS	T. Corcoran
3B	J. Delahanty
OF	J. Kelley
OF	F. Jude
OF	J. Seymour
C	G. Schlei
P	J. Weimer
P	G. Ewing
P	C. Fraser
P	R. Wicker
P	C. Hall

CIN 1907 N

M	E. Hanlon
1B	J. Ganzel
2B	M. Huggins
SS	J. Lobert
3B	H. Mowrey
OF	M. Mitchell
OF	A. Kruger
OF	F. Odwell
C	J. McLean
P	G. Ewing
P	A. Coakley
P	J. Weimer
P	R. Hitt
P	A. Mason

CIN 1908 N

M	J. Ganzel
1B	J. Ganzel
2B	M. Huggins
SS	R. Hulswitt
3B	J. Lobert
OF	J. Kane
OF	M. Mitchell
OF	G. Paskert
C	G. Schlei
UT	J. McLean
P	G. Ewing
P	R. Spade
P	A. Coakley
P	W. Campbell
P	J. Weimer

CIN 1909 N

M	C. Griffith
1B	R. Hoblitzel
2B	R. Egan
SS	T. Downey
3B	J. Lobert
OF	M. Mitchell
OF	R. Bescher
C	J. McLean
UT	G. Paskert
P	A. Fromme
P	H. Gaspar
P	J. Rowan
P	G. Ewing
P	W. Campbell

CIN 1910 N

M	C. Griffith
1B	R. Hoblitzel
2B	R. Egan
SS	T. McMillan
3B	J. Lobert
OF	R. Bescher
OF	M. Mitchell
OF	G. Paskert
C	J. McLean
UT	T. Downey
P	H. Gaspar
P	G. Suggs
P	J. Rowan
P	F. Beebe
P	W. Burns

CIN 1911 N

M	C. Griffith
1B	R. Hoblitzel
2B	R. Egan
SS	T. Downey
3B	E. Grant
OF	R. Bescher
OF	J. Bates
OF	M. Mitchell
C	J. McLean
P	G. Suggs
P	H. Gaspar
P	R. Keefe
P	A. Fromme
P	F. Smith

CIN 1912 N

M	H. O'Day
1B	R. Hoblitzel
2B	R. Egan
SS	J. Esmond
3B	A. Phelan
OF	M. Mitchell
OF	R. Bescher
OF	A. Marsans
C	J. McLean
UT	E. Grant
P	G. Suggs
P	J. Benton
P	A. Fromme
P	A. Humphries

CIN 1913 N

M	J. Tinker
1B	R. Hoblitzel
2B	H. Groh
SS	J. Tinker
3B	J. Dodge
OF	R. Bescher
OF	J. Bates
OF	A. Marsans
C	T. Clarke
P	G. Johnson
P	G. Suggs
P	E. Packard
P	L. Ames
P	M. Brown
RP	F. Harter

CIN 1914 N

M	C. Herzog
1B	R. Hoblitzel
2B	H. Groh
SS	C. Herzog
3B	J. Niehoff
OF	J. Moran
OF	B. Daniels
OF	G. Twombly
C	T. Clarke
UT	M. Gonzalez
P	L. Ames
P	J. Benton
P	P. Douglas
P	E. Yingling
P	P. Schneider

CIN 1915 N

M	C. Herzog
1B	F. Mollwitz
2B	W. Rodgers
SS	C. Herzog
3B	H. Groh
OF	T. Griffith
OF	W. Killefer
OF	T. Leach
C	I. Wingo
P	E. Dale
P	P. Schneider
P	F. Toney
P	J. Benton
P	C. Lear

CIN 1916 N
M C. Herzog
M I. Wingo
M C. Mathewson
1B H. Chase
2B W. Louden
SS C. Herzog
3B H. Groh
OF T. Griffith
OF A. Neale
OF E. Roush
C I. Wingo
P F. Toney
P P. Schneider
P A. Schulz
P C. Mitchell
P E. Knetzer

CIN 1917 N
M C. Mathewson
1B H. Chase
2B D. Shean
SS W. Kopf
3B H. Groh
OF E. Roush
OF A. Neale
OF T. Griffith
C I. Wingo
P F. Toney
P P. Schneider
P M. Regan
P C. Mitchell
P H. Eller

CIN 1918 N
M C. Mathewson
M H. Groh
1B H. Chase
2B L. Magee
SS R. Blackburne
3B H. Groh
OF T. Griffith
OF E. Roush
OF A. Neale
C I. Wingo
UT S. Magee
P H. Eller
P P. Schneider
P J. Ring
P F. Toney
P R. Bressler

CIN 1919 N
M P. Moran
1B J. Daubert
2B M. Rath
SS W. Kopf
3B H. Groh
OF A. Neale
OF E. Roush
OF R. Bressler
C I. Wingo
P H. Eller
P W. Ruether
P H. Sallee
P J. Ring
P R. Fisher

CIN 1920 N
M P. Moran
1B J. Daubert
2B M. Rath
SS W. Kopf
3B H. Groh
OF L. Duncan
OF A. Neale
OF E. Roush
C I. Wingo
P J. Ring
P W. Ruether
P H. Eller
P A. Luque
P R. Fisher

CIN 1921 N
M P. Moran
1B J. Daubert
2B S. Bohne
SS W. Kopf
3B H. Groh
OF L. Duncan
OF E. Roush
OF R. Bressler
C I. Wingo
P A. Luque
P E. Rixey
P R. Marquard
P P. Donohue
RP S. Napier

CIN 1922 N
M P. Moran
1B J. Daubert
2B S. Bohne
SS J. Caveney
3B R. Pinelli
OF G. Burns
OF L. Duncan
OF G. Harper
C E. Hargrave
P E. Rixey
P J. Couch
P A. Luque
P P. Donohue
P F. Keck
RP J. Gillespie

CIN 1923 N
M P. Moran
1B J. Daubert
2B S. Bohne
SS J. Caveney
3B R. Pinelli
OF G. Burns
OF L. Duncan
OF E. Roush
C E. Hargrave
P A. Luque
P E. Rixey
P P. Donohue
P J. Benton
RP F. Keck

CIN 1924 N
M J. Hendricks
1B J. Daubert
2B H. Critz
SS J. Caveney
3B R. Pinelli
OF E. Roush
OF W. Walker
OF G. Burns
C E. Hargrave
UT S. Bohne
UT R. Bressler
UT L. Duncan
P E. Rixey
P C. Mays
P P. Donohue
P A. Luque
P T. Sheehan
RP F. May

CIN 1925 N
M J. Hendricks
1B W. Holke
2B H. Critz
SS J. Caveney
3B R. Pinelli
OF W. Walker
OF E. Roush
OF W. Zitzmann
C E. Hargrave
UT R. Bressler
UT E. Smith
P P. Donohue
P A. Luque
P E. Rixey
P J. Benton
P F. May
RP H. Biemiller

CIN 1926 N
M J. Hendricks
1B W. Pipp
2B H. Critz
SS F. Emmer
3B C. Dressen
OF W. Walker
OF E. Roush
OF W. Christensen
C E. Hargrave
P P. Donohue
P C. Mays
P A. Luque
P E. Rixey
P F. May

CIN 1927 N
M J. Hendricks
1B W. Pipp
2B H. Critz
SS H. Ford
3B C. Dressen
OF W. Walker
OF R. Bressler
OF E. Allen
C E. Hargrave
P C. Lucas
P F. May
P A. Luque

CIN 1928 N
M J. Hendricks
1B G. Kelly
2B H. Critz
SS H. Ford
3B C. Dressen
OF E. Allen
OF W. Walker
OF W. Zitzmann
C V. Picinich
UT W. Pipp
P E. Rixey
P A. Luque
P R. Kolp
P C. Lucas
P P. Donohue
RP P. Appleton

CIN 1929 N
M J. Hendricks
1B G. Kelly
2B H. Critz
SS H. Ford
3B C. Dressen
OF E. Swanson
OF W. Walker
OF E. Allen
C J. Gooch
P C. Lucas
P E. Rixey
P F. May
P P. Donohue
P A. Luque
RP K. Ash
RP W. Ehrhardt

CIN 1930 N
M D. Howley
1B J. Stripp
2B H. Ford
SS L. Durocher
3B A. Cuccinello
OF W. Walker
OF R. Meusel
OF H. Heilmann
C C. Sukeforth
UT E. Swanson
P B. Frey
P C. Lucas
P L. Benton
P R. Kolp
P E. Rixey
RP S. Johnson
RP A. Campbell

CIN 1931 N
M D. Howley
1B H. Hendrick
2B A. Cuccinello
SS L. Durocher
3B J. Stripp
OF E. Crabtree
OF T. Douthit
OF E. Roush
C C. Sukeforth
UT H. Cullop
P S. Johnson
P C. Lucas
P L. Benton
P B. Frey
P E. Rixey

CIN 1932 N
M D. Howley
1B H. Hendrick
2B G. Grantham
SS L. Durocher
3B W. Gilbert
OF F. Herman
OF E. Crabtree
OF W. Roettger
C E. Lombardi
UT T. Douthit
P C. Lucas
P S. Johnson
P O. Carroll
P L. Benton
P R. Kolp
RP J. Ogden

CIN 1933 N
M O. Bush
1B J. Bottomley
2B J. Morrissey
SS O. Bluege
3B E. Adams
OF C. Hafey
OF H. Rice
OF J. Moore
C E. Lombardi
P S. Derringer
P C. Lucas
P S. Johnson
P L. Benton
P R. Kolp

CIN 1934 N
M R. O'Farrell
M B. Shotton
M C. Dressen
1B J. Bottomley
2B A. Piet
SS G. Slade
3B M. Koenig
OF C. Hafey
OF A. Comorosky
OF H. Pool
C E. Lombardi
P S. Derringer
P B. Frey
P S. Johnson
P A. Freitas
P A. Stout
RP J. Brennan
RP R. Kolp

CIN 1935 N
M C. Dressen
1B J. Bottomley
2B A. Kampouris
SS W. Myers
3B L. Riggs
OF I. Goodman
OF S. Byrd
OF F. Herman
C E. Lombardi
P S. Derringer
P A. Hollingsworth
P E. Schott
P A. Freitas
P S. Johnson

CIN 1936 N
M C. Dressen
1B L. Scarsella
2B A. Kampouris
SS W. Myers
3B L. Riggs
OF H. Cuyler
OF I. Goodman
OF F. Herman
C E. Lombardi
UT C. Chapman
UT T. Thevenow
P S. Derringer
P A. Hollingsworth
P E. Schott
P W. Hallahan
P B. Frey
RP J. Brennan

CIN 1937 N
M C. Dressen
M R. Wallace
1B B. Jordan
2B A. Kampouris
SS W. Myers
3B L. Riggs
OF I. Goodman
OF H. Cuyler
OF C. Hafey
C E. Lombardi
UT L. Scarsella
P L. Grissom
P S. Derringer
P R. Davis
P A. Hollingsworth
P E. Schott

CIN 1938 N
M W. McKechnie
1B F. McCormick
2B L. Frey
SS W. Myers
3B L. Riggs
OF H. Craft
OF I. Goodman
OF W. Berger
C E. Lombardi
P S. Derringer
P J. Vander Meer
P W. Walters
P R. Davis
P J. Weaver
RP E. Schott
RP J. Cascarella

CIN 1939 N
M W. McKechnie
1B F. McCormick
2B L. Frey
SS W. Myers
3B W. Werber
OF H. Craft
OF I. Goodman
OF W. Berger
C E. Lombardi
P W. Walters
P S. Derringer
P L. Moore
P L. Grissom
P E. Thompson

CIN 1940 N
M W. McKechnie
1B F. McCormick
2B L. Frey
SS W. Myers
3B W. Werber
OF I. Goodman
OF H. Craft
OF M. McCormick
C E. Lombardi
P W. Walters
P S. Derringer
P E. Thompson
P J. Turner
P L. Moore
RP J. Beggs
RP M. Shoffner
RP J. Hutchings

CIN 1941 N
M W. McKechnie
1B F. McCormick
2B L. Frey
SS E. Joost
3B W. Werber
OF H. Craft
OF M. McCormick
OF J. Gleeson
C E. Lombardi
P W. Walters
P S. Derringer
P J. Vander Meer
P E. Riddle
P J. Turner
RP L. Moore
RP J. Beggs

CIN 1942 N
M W. McKechnie
1B F. McCormick
2B L. Frey
SS E. Joost
3B B. Haas
OF M. Marshall
OF G. Walker
OF E. Tipton
C R. Lamanno
P R. Starr
P W. Walters
P J. Vander Meer
P S. Derringer
P E. Riddle
RP J. Beggs
RP C. Shoun

CIN 1943 N
M W. McKechnie
1B F. McCormick
2B L. Frey
SS E. Miller
3B S. Mesner
OF E. Tipton
OF M. Marshall
OF G. Walker
C R. Mueller
UT E. Crabtree
UT B. Haas
P J. Vander Meer
P E. Riddle
P W. Walters
P R. Starr
P C. Shoun
RP J. Beggs

CIN 1944 N
M W. McKechnie
1B F. McCormick
2B W. Williams
SS E. Miller
3B S. Mesner
OF E. Tipton
OF G. Walker
OF D. Clay
C R. Mueller
P W. Walters
P C. Shoun
P E. Heusser
P T. DeLa Cruz

CIN 1945 N
M W. McKechnie
1B F. McCormick
2B W. Williams
SS E. Miller
3B S. Mesner
OF D. Clay
OF A. Libke
OF E. Tipton
C A. Lakeman
UT G. Walker
P E. Heusser
P J. Bowman
P W. Walters
P H. Fox
P L. Kennedy
RP L. Lisenbee

CIN 1946 N
M W. McKechnie
1B B. Haas
2B R. Adams
SS E. Miller
3B G. Hatton
OF D. Clay
OF A. Libke
OF E. Lukon
C R. Mueller
UT L. Frey
P J. Vander Meer
P E. Blackwell
P J. Beggs
P E. Heusser
P W. Walters
RP C. Shoun
RP R. Malloy
RP C. Lambert

CIN 1947 N
M J. Neun
1B N. Young
2B B. Zientara
SS E. Miller
3B G. Hatton
OF F. Baumholtz
OF A. Galan
OF B. Haas
C R. Lamanno
P E. Blackwell
P J. Vander Meer
P K. Peterson
P E. Lively
P W. Walters
RP J. Hetki
RP H. Gumbert

CIN 1948 N
M J. Neun
M W. Walters
1B T. Kluszewski
2B R. Adams
SS T. Stallcup
3B G. Hatton
OF H. Sauer
OF J. Wyrostek
OF F. Baumholtz
C R. Lamanno
UT D. Litwhiler
P J. Vander Meer
P K.Raffensberger
P H. Fox
P H. Wehmeier
P E. Blackwell
RP H. Gumbert
RP W. Cress

CIN 1949 N
M W. Walters
M J. Sewell
1B T. Kluszewski
2B J. Bloodworth
SS T. Stallcup
3B G. Hatton
OF J. Wyrostek
OF L. Merriman
OF D. Litwhiler
C W. Cooper
UT R. Adams
P K.Raffensberger
P H. Fox
P H. Wehmeier
P J. Vander Meer
P E. Lively
RP E. Erautt
RP E. Blackwell
RP K. Peterson

CIN 1950 N
M J. Sewell
1B T. Kluszewski
2B C. Ryan
SS T. Stallcup
3B G. Hatton
OF J. Wyrostek
OF R. Usher
OF L. Merriman
C H. Howell
UT R. Adams
UT J. Adcock
P E. Blackwell
P K.Raffensberger
P H. Wehmeier
P H. Fox
P J. Ramsdell
RP F. Smith
RP E. Erautt
RP J. Hetki

CIN 1951 N
M J. Sewell
1B T. Kluszewski
2B C. Ryan
SS T. Stallcup
3B G. Hatton
OF J. Wyrostek
OF J. Adcock
OF L. Merriman
C H. Howell
UT R. Adams
UT R. Usher
P K.Raffensberger
P E. Blackwell
P H. Fox
P J. Ramsdell
P H. Wehmeier
RP H. Perkowski
RP F. Smith
RP E. Byerly

CIN 1952 N
M J. Sewell
M E. Brucker
M R. Hornsby
1B T. Kluszewski
2B G. Hatton
SS R. McMillan
3B R. Adams
OF W. Marshall
OF R. Borkowski
OF J. Adcock
C A. Seminick
P K.Raffensberger
P H. Perkowski
P H. Wehmeier
P E. Church
P F. Hiller
RP F. Smith
RP J. Nuxhall

CIN 1953 N
M R. Hornsby
M C. Mills
1B T. Kluszewski
2B E. Bridges
SS R. McMillan
3B R. Adams
OF J. Greengrass
OF D. Bell
OF W. Marshall
C A. Seminick
UT R. Borkowski
P H. Perkowski
P C. Podbielan
P K.Raffensberger
P J. Nuxhall
P F. Baczewski
RP F. Smith
RP H. Wehmeier
RP C. King

CIN 1954 N
M G. Tebbetts
1B T. Kluszewski
2B J. Temple
SS R. McMillan
3B R. Adams
OF D. Bell
OF J. Greengrass
OF W. Post
C A. Seminick
UT C. Harmon
P J. Fowler
P H. Valentine
P J. Nuxhall
P C. Podbielan
P F. Baczewski
RP H. Judson
RP F. Smith
RP J. Collum

CIN 1955 N
- M G. Tebbetts
- 1B T. Kluszewski
- 2B J. Temple
- SS R. McMillan
- 3B E. Bridges
- OF W. Post
- OF D. Bell
- OF S. Palys
- C F. Burgess
- UT C. Harmon
- P J. Nuxhall
- P J. Fowler
- P J. Klippstein
- P J. Collum
- P G. Staley
- RP R. Minarcin
- RP H. Freeman

CIN 1956 N
- M G. Tebbetts
- 1B T. Kluszewski
- 2B J. Temple
- SS R. McMillan
- 3B R. Jablonski
- OF F. Robinson
- OF D. Bell
- OF W. Post
- C L. Bailey
- P B. Lawrence
- P J. Klippstein
- P J. Nuxhall
- P J. Fowler
- P H. Jeffcoat
- RP H. Freeman
- RP T. Acker
- RP J. Black

CIN 1957 N
- M G. Tebbetts
- 1B G. Crowe
- 2B J. Temple
- SS R. McMillan
- 3B D. Hoak
- OF F. Robinson
- OF W. Post
- OF D. Bell
- C L. Bailey
- P B. Lawrence
- P H. Jeffcoat
- P J. Nuxhall
- P D. Gross
- P J. Klippstein
- RP T. Acker
- RP J. Fowler
- RP H. Freeman

CIN 1958 N
- M G. Tebbetts
- M J. Dykes
- 1B G. Crowe
- 2B J. Temple
- SS R. McMillan
- 3B D. Hoak
- OF F. Robinson
- OF D. Bell
- OF G. Lynch
- C L. Bailey
- UT F. Burgess
- UT A. Grammas
- UT R. Thurman
- P R. Purkey
- P H. Haddix
- P B. Lawrence
- P J. Nuxhall
- P D. Newcombe
- RP H. Jeffcoat
- RP W. Schmidt

CIN 1959 N
- M E. Smith
- M F. Hutchinson
- 1B F. Robinson
- 2B J. Temple
- SS E. Kasko
- 3B W. Jones
- OF V. Pinson
- OF D. Bell
- OF G. Lynch
- C L. Bailey
- UT F. Thomas
- P D. Newcombe
- P R. Purkey
- P J. Nuxhall
- P J. O'Toole
- RP O. Pena
- RP B. Lawrence
- RP W. Schmidt

CIN 1960 N
- M F. Hutchinson
- 1B F. Robinson
- 2B A. Martin
- SS R. McMillan
- 3B E. Kasko
- OF V. Pinson
- OF V. Pinson
- OF D. Bell
- OF W. Post
- C L. Bailey
- UT G. Lynch
- P R. Purkey
- P J. Hook
- P J. O'Toole
- P C. McLish
- RP J. Nuxhall
- RP J. Brosnan
- RP W. Henry

CIN 1961 N
- M F. Hutchinson
- 1B G. Coleman
- 2B D. Blasingame
- SS E. Kasko
- 3B E. Freese
- OF V. Pinson
- OF F. Robinson
- OF W. Post
- C G. Zimmerman
- UT D. Bell
- UT G. Lynch
- P J. O'Toole
- P J. Jay
- P R. Purkey
- P K. Hunt
- P J. Maloney
- RP J. Brosnan
- RP J. Hook
- RP S. Jones

CIN 1962 N
- M F. Hutchinson
- 1B G. Coleman
- 2B D. Blasingame
- SS L. Cardenas
- 3B E. Kasko
- OF F. Robinson
- OF V. Pinson
- OF W. Post
- C J. Edwards
- UT D. Johnson
- UT G. Lynch
- P R. Purkey
- P J. Jay
- P J. O'Toole
- P J. Maloney
- RP J. Klippstein
- RP J. Brosnan
- RP T. Wills

CIN 1963 N
- M F. Hutchinson
- 1B G. Coleman
- 2B P. Rose
- SS L. Cardenas
- 3B E. Freese
- OF V. Pinson
- OF F. Robinson
- OF T. Harper
- C J. Edwards
- P J. Maloney
- P J. O'Toole
- P J. Nuxhall
- P J. Tsitouris
- P J. Jay
- RP A. Worthington
- RP W. Henry

CIN 1964 N
- M F. Hutchinson
- M R. Sisler
- M F. Hutchinson
- M R. Sisler
- 1B D. Johnson
- 2B P. Rose
- SS L. Cardenas
- 3B S. Boros
- OF F. Robinson
- OF V. Pinson
- OF T. Harper
- C J. Edwards
- UT R. Keough
- P J. O'Toole
- P J. Maloney
- P R. Purkey
- P J. Jay
- P J. Tsitouris
- RP S. Ellis
- RP W. McCool
- RP W. Henry

CIN 1965 N
- M R. Sisler
- 1B A. Perez
- 2B P. Rose
- SS L. Cardenas
- 3B D. Johnson
- OF V. Pinson
- OF T. Harper
- OF F. Robinson
- C J. Edwards
- UT G. Coleman
- P S. Ellis
- P J. Maloney
- P J. Jay
- P J. Nuxhall
- P J. Tsitouris
- RP W. McCool
- RP T. Davidson
- RP R. Craig

CIN 1966 N
- M D. Heffner
- M J. Bristol
- 1B A. Perez
- 2B P. Rose
- SS L. Cardenas
- 3B T. Helms
- OF V. Pinson
- OF T. Harper
- OF D. Johnson
- C J. Edwards
- P J. Maloney
- P S. Ellis
- P M. Pappas
- P J. O'Toole
- P J. Nuxhall
- RP D. Nottebart
- RP W. McCool
- RP T. Davidson

CIN 1967 N
- M J. Bristol
- 1B L. May
- 2B T. Helms
- SS L. Cardenas
- 3B A. Perez
- OF V. Pinson
- OF P. Rose
- OF T. Harper
- C J. Edwards
- UT D. Johnson
- UT H. Ruiz
- P G. Nolan
- P M. Pappas
- P M. Queen
- P J. Maloney
- P S. Ellis
- RP T. Abernathy
- RP D. Nottebart
- RP G. Arrigo

CIN 1968 N
- M J. Bristol
- 1B L. May
- 2B T. Helms
- SS L. Cardenas
- 3B A. Perez
- OF P. Rose
- OF A. Johnson
- OF V. Pinson
- C J. Bench
- UT M. Jones
- P G. Culver
- P J. Maloney
- P G. Arrigo
- P G. Nolan
- RP T. Abernathy
- RP C. Carroll
- RP R. Lee

CIN 1969 N
- M J. Bristol
- 1B L. May
- 2B T. Helms
- SS W. Woodward
- 3B A. Perez
- OF P. Rose
- OF R. Tolan
- OF A. Johnson
- C J. Bench
- UT J. Stewart
- P J. Merritt
- P T. Cloninger
- P J. Maloney
- P J. Fisher
- P G. Nolan
- RP C. Carroll
- RP W. Granger
- RP P. Ramos

CIN 1970 N
- M G. Anderson
- 1B L. May
- 2B T. Helms
- SS D. Concepcion
- 3B P. Rose
- OF C. Geronimo
- 3B A. Perez
- OF P. Rose
- OF R. Tolan
- OF B. Carbo
- C J. Bench
- UT J. Stewart
- UT W. Woodward
- P G. Nolan
- P J. Merritt
- P J. McGlothlin
- P W. Simpson
- P T. Cloninger
- RP C. Carroll
- RP W. Granger
- RP D. Gullett

CIN 1971 N
- M G. Anderson
- 1B L. May
- 2B T. Helms
- SS D. Concepcion
- 3B A. Perez
- OF P. Rose
- OF G. Foster
- OF H. McRae
- C J. Bench
- UT B. Carbo
- UT W. Woodward
- P G. Nolan
- P D. Gullett
- P J. McGlothlin
- P R. Grimsley
- P W. Simpson
- RP W. Granger
- RP C. Carroll
- RP J. Gibbon

CIN 1972 N
- M G. Anderson
- 1B A. Perez
- 2B J. Morgan
- SS D. Concepcion
- 3B D. Menke
- OF P. Rose
- OF R. Tolan
- OF C. Geronimo
- C J. Bench
- P J. Billingham
- P R. Grimsley
- P G. Nolan
- P J. McGlothlin
- P D. Gullett
- RP T. Hall
- RP P. Borbon
- RP C. Carroll

CIN 1973 N
- M G. Anderson
- 1B A. Perez
- 2B J. Morgan
- SS D. Concepcion
- 3B D. Menke
- OF P. Rose
- OF C. Geronimo
- OF R. Tolan
- C J. Bench
- UT D. Chaney
- UT D. Driessen
- P J. Billingham
- P R. Grimsley
- P D. Gullett
- P F. Norman
- RP P. Borbon
- RP T. Hall
- RP C. Carroll

CIN 1974 N
- M G. Anderson
- 1B A. Perez
- 2B J. Morgan
- SS D. Concepcion
- 3B D. Driessen
- OF P. Rose
- OF C. Geronimo
- OF G. Foster
- C J. Bench
- UT D. Collins
- P J. Billingham
- P F. Norman
- P W. Bonham
- P P. Moskau
- RP T. Hume
- RP C. Bair
- RP T. Hall

CIN 1975 N
- M G. Anderson
- 1B A. Perez
- 2B J. Morgan
- SS D. Concepcion
- 3B P. Rose
- OF C. Geronimo
- OF G. Foster
- OF G. Griffey
- C J. Bench
- P G. Nolan
- P J. Billingham
- P F. Norman
- P D. Gullett
- P P. Darcy
- RP P. Borbon
- RP C. Carroll
- RP W. McEnaney

CIN 1976 N
- M G. Anderson
- 1B A. Perez
- 2B J. Morgan
- SS D. Concepcion
- 3B P. Rose
- OF G. Griffey
- OF G. Foster
- C J. Bench
- UT D. Driessen
- P G. Nolan
- P P. Zachry
- P F. Norman
- P J. Billingham
- P S. Alcala
- RP P. Borbon
- RP R. Eastwick
- RP W. McEnaney

CIN 1977 N
- M G. Anderson
- 1B D. Driessen
- 2B J. Morgan
- SS D. Concepcion
- 3B P. Rose
- OF G. Foster
- OF G. Griffey
- OF C. Geronimo
- C J. Bench
- P F. Norman
- P G. Seaver
- P J. Billingham
- P P. Moskau
- P D. Capilla
- RP P. Borbon
- RP D. Murray

CIN 1978 N
- M G. Anderson
- 1B D. Driessen
- 2B J. Morgan
- SS D. Concepcion
- 3B P. Rose
- OF G. Foster
- OF G. Griffey
- OF C. Geronimo
- C J. Bench
- UT D. Collins
- P G. Seaver
- P F. Norman
- P T. Hume
- P P. Moskau
- P W. Bonham
- RP M. Sarmiento
- RP C. Bair
- RP P. Borbon

CIN 1979 N
- M J. McNamara
- 1B D. Driessen
- 2B J. Morgan
- SS D. Concepcion
- 3B C. Knight
- OF C. Geronimo
- OF G. Foster
- OF G. Griffey
- C J. Bench
- UT D. Collins
- P G. Seaver
- P M. LaCoss
- P F. Norman
- P W. Bonham
- P P. Moskau
- RP T. Hume
- RP C. Bair
- RP P. Tomlin

CIN 1980 N
- M J. McNamara
- 1B D. Driessen
- 2B J. Kennedy
- SS D. Concepcion
- 3B C. Knight
- OF G. Foster
- OF D. Collins
- OF G. Griffey
- C J. Bench
- UT C. Geronimo
- UT R. Oester
- OF G. Foster
- OF G. Griffey
- C J. Bench
- P M. Soto
- P F. Pastore
- P C. Leibrandt
- P M. LaCoss
- P G. Seaver
- RP T. Hume
- RP C. Bair

CIN 1981 N
- M J. McNamara
- 1B D. Driessen
- 2B R. Oester
- SS D. Concepcion
- 3B C. Knight
- OF G. Foster
- OF G. Griffey
- OF D. Collins
- C J. Nolan
- P M. Soto
- P G. Seaver
- P F. Pastore
- P B. Berenyi
- P M. LaCoss
- RP T. Hume
- RP P. Moskau
- RP J. Price

CIN 1982 N
- M J. McNamara
- M R. Nixon
- 1B D. Driessen
- 2B R. Oester
- SS D. Concepcion
- 3B J. Bench
- OF P. Householder
- OF C. Cedeno
- OF E. Milner
- C A. Trevino
- UT L. Biittner
- P M. Soto
- P B. Berenyi
- P F. Pastore
- P R. Shirley
- P G. Seaver
- RP G. Harris
- RP J. Kern
- RP J. Price

CIN 1983 N
- M R. Nixon
- 1B D. Driessen
- 2B R. Oester
- SS D. Concepcion
- 3B N. Esasky
- OF E. Milner
- OF G. Redus
- OF P. Householder
- C D. Bilardello
- UT J. Bench
- UT C. Cedeno
- UT D. Walker
- P M. Soto
- P B. Berenyi
- P F. Pastore
- P C. Puleo
- P J. Price
- RP T. Power
- RP W. Scherrer
- RP R. Gale

CIN 1984 N
- M V. Rapp
- M P. Rose
- 1B D. Driessen
- 2B R. Oester
- SS D. Concepcion
- 3B N. Esasky
- OF D. Parker
- OF G. Redus
- OF E. Milner
- C B. Gulden
- UT C. Cedeno
- UT T. Foley
- UT W. Krenchicki
- P M. Soto
- P J. Russell
- P J. Price
- P J. Tibbs
- P F. Pastore
- RP T. Hume
- RP T. Power
- RP R. Owchinko

CIN 1985 N
- M P. Rose
- 1B P. Rose
- 2B R. Oester
- SS D. Concepcion
- 3B B. Bell
- OF D. Parker
- OF E. Milner
- OF G. Redus
- C D. Van Gorder
- UT N. Esasky
- P T. Browning
- P M. Soto
- P J. Tibbs
- P R. Robinson
- P J. Stuper
- RP J. Franco
- RP T. Power
- RP T. Hume

CIN 1986 N
- M P. Rose
- 1B N. Esasky
- 2B R. Oester
- SS K. Stillwell
- 3B B. Bell
- OF D. Parker
- OF E. Milner
- OF E. Davis
- C B. Diaz
- UT W. Venable
- P W. Gullickson
- P T. Browning
- P J. Denny
- P C. Welsh
- P M. Soto
- RP T. Power
- RP R. Robinson
- RP J. Franco

CIN 1987 N
- M P. Rose
- 1B N. Esasky
- 2B R. Oester
- SS B. Larkin
- 3B B. Bell
- OF D. Parker
- OF E. Davis
- OF T. Jones
- C B. Diaz
- UT D. Concepcion
- UT K. Daniels
- UT T. Francona
- UT K. Stillwell
- P T. Power
- P T. Browning
- P W. Gullickson
- P G. Hoffman
- P R. Robinson
- RP F. Williams
- RP R. Murphy
- RP J. Franco

CIN 1988 N
- M P. Rose
- M T. Helms
- M P. Rose
- 1B N. Esasky
- 2B H. Treadway
- SS B. Larkin
- 3B C. Sabo
- OF K. Daniels
- OF E. Davis
- OF P. O'Neill
- C B. Diaz
- UT D. Collins
- P D. Jackson
- P T. Browning
- P J. Rijo
- RP J. Franco
- RP R. Murphy
- RP T. Birtsas

CIN 1989 N
- M P. Rose
- M T. Helms
- 1B T. Benzinger
- 2B R. Oester
- SS B. Larkin
- 3B C. Sabo
- OF E. Davis
- OF P. O'Neill
- OF R. Roomes
- C J. Reed
- UT G. Griffey
- UT L. Quinones
- UT H. Winningham
- P T. Browning
- P R. Mahler
- P D. Jackson
- P J. Rijo
- P W. Scudder
- RP R. Dibble
- RP N. Charlton
- RP J. Franco

CIN 1990 N
- M L. Piniella
- 1B T. Benzinger
- 2B M. Duncan
- SS B. Larkin

3B C. Sabo
OF P. O'Neill
OF W. Hatcher
OF E. Davis
C J. Oliver
UT W. Morris
P T. Browning
P J. Rijo
P J. Armstrong
P R. Mahler
P D. Jackson
RP N. Charlton
RP R. Dibble
RP R. Myers

Cleveland

CLE n 1871-1872
CLE N 1879-1884
CLE a 1887-1888
CLE P 1890
CLE N 1889-1899
CLE A 1901-1990

CLE 1871 n
M C. Pabor
1B J. Carleton
2B C. Johnson
SS E. Kimball
3B E. Sutton
OF A. Allison
OF C. Pabor
OF E. White
C J. White
UT J. Bass
P A. Pratt

CLE 1872 n
M W. Hastings
M J. White
1B J. Simmons
2B C. Sweasy
SS J. Holdsworth
3B E. Sutton
OF C. Pabor
OF A. Allison
OF R. Wolters
C J. White
UT W. Hastings
P A. Pratt
P R. Wolters

CLE 1879 N
M J. McCormick
1B W. Phillips
2B J. Glasscock
SS T. Carey
3B F. Warner
OF C. Eden
OF G. Strief
OF W. Riley
C M. Kennedy
UT A. Gilligan
P J. McCormick
P R. Mitchell

CLE 1880 N
M J. McCormick
1B W. Phillips
2B F. Dunlap
SS J. Glasscock
3B F. Hankinson
OF G. Shaffer
OF P. Hotaling
OF E. Hanlon
C M. Kennedy
P J. McCormick
P F. Gardner

CLE 1881 N
M M. McGeary
M J. Clapp
1B W. Phillips
2B F. Dunlap
SS J. Glasscock
3B G. Bradley
OF G. Shaffer
OF J. Remsen
OF M. Moynahan
C J. Clapp
P J. McCormick
P E. Nolan

CLE 1882 N
M J. McCormick
M F. Dunlap
1B W. Phillips

2B F. Dunlap
SS J. Glasscock
3B M. Muldoon
OF G. Shaffer
OF T. Esterbrook
OF J. Richmond
C C. Briody
P J. McCormick
P G. Bradley

CLE 1883 N
M F. Bancroft
1B W. Phillips
2B F. Dunlap
SS J. Glasscock
3B M. Muldoon
OF T. York
OF P. Hotaling
OF J. Evans
C A. Bushong
P H. Daily
P J. McCormick
P W. Sawyer

CLE 1884 N
M C. Hackett
1B W. Phillips
2B G. Smith
SS J. Glasscock
3B M. Muldoon
OF P. Hotaling
OF J. Evans
OF W. Murphy
C A. Bushong
P J. Harkins
P J. McCormick

CLE 1887 a
M J. Williams
1B J. Toy
2B J. Stricker
SS E. McKean
3B P. Reccius
OF P. Hotaling
OF M. Allen
OF F. Mann
C C. Snyder
P W. Crowell
P M. Morrison
P H. Daily
P R. Gilks
P G. Pechiney

CLE 1888 a
M J. Williams
M T. Loftus
1B J. Faatz
2B J. Stricker
SS E. McKean
3B A. Alberts
OF P. Hotaling
OF R. Gilks
OF R. Hogan
C C. Zimmer
P E. Bakely
P J. O'Brien
P W. Crowell

CLE 1890 P
M H. Larkin
M O. Tebeau
1B H. Larkin
2B J. Stricker
SS E. Delahanty
3B O. Tebeau
OF L. Browning
OF J. McAleer
OF P. Radford
C E. Sutcliffe
P H. Gruber
P E. Bakely
P J. O'Brien
P W. McGill

CLE 1889 N
M T. Loftus
1B J. Faatz
2B J. Stricker
SS E. McKean
3B O. Tebeau
OF P. Radford
OF L. Twitchell
OF J. McAleer
C C. Zimmer
P J. O'Brien
P E. Beatin
P E. Bakely
P H. Gruber

CLE 1890 N
M G. Schmelz
M R. Leadley
1B W. Veach
2B J. Ardner
SS E. McKean
3B W. Smalley
OF G. Davis
OF R. Gilks
OF V. Dailey
C C. Zimmer
P E. Beatin
P J. Wadsworth
P D. Young
P E. Lincoln
P L. Viau

CLE 1891 N
M R. Leadley
M O. Tebeau
1B J. Virtue
2B C. Childs
SS E. McKean
3B O. Tebeau
OF J. McAleer
OF J. Burkett
OF J. Johnson
C C. Zimmer
P D. Young
P H. Gruber
P L. Viau

CLE 1892 N
M O. Tebeau
1B J. Virtue
2B C. Childs
SS E. McKean
3B G. Davis
OF J. McAleer
OF J. Burkett
OF J. O'Connor
C C. Zimmer
P D. Young
P G. Cuppy
P J. Clarkson
P G. Davies

CLE 1893 N
M O. Tebeau
1B J. Virtue
2B C. Childs
SS E. McKean
3B J. McGarr
OF J. Burkett
OF W. Ewing
OF J. McAleer
C C. Zimmer
UT J. O'Connor
P D. Young
P J. Clarkson
P G. Cuppy
P G. Hastings

CLE 1894 N
M O. Tebeau
1B O. Tebeau
2B C. Childs
SS E. McKean
3B J. McGarr
OF J. Burkett
OF H. Blake
OF J. McAleer
C C. Zimmer
UT J. O'Connor
P D. Young
P G. Cuppy
P J. Clarkson
P M. Sullivan

CLE 1895 N
M O. Tebeau
1B O. Tebeau
2B C. Childs
SS E. McKean
3B J. McGarr
OF J. McAleer
OF J. Burkett
OF H. Blake
C C. Zimmer
UT J. O'Connor
UT O. Tebeau
P D. Young
P G. Cuppy
P R. Wallace
P P. Knell

CLE 1896 N
M O. Tebeau
1B O. Tebeau
2B C. Childs
SS E. McKean
3B J. McGarr
OF J. Burkett
OF J. McAleer
OF H. Blake
C C. Zimmer
P D. Young
P G. Cuppy
P F. Wilson

CLE 1897 N
M O. Tebeau
1B O. Tebeau
2B C. Childs
SS E. McKean
3B R. Wallace
OF J. Burkett
OF L. Sockalexis
OF J. O'Connor
C C. Zimmer
P D. Young
P J. Powell
P G. Cuppy

CLE 1898 N
M O. Tebeau
1B O. Tebeau
2B C. Childs
SS E. McKean
3B R. Wallace
OF J. Burkett
OF H. Blake
OF J. McAleer
C L. Criger
UT J. O'Connor
P D. Young
P J. Powell
P F. Wilson
P G. Cuppy

CLE 1899 N
M L. Cross
M J. Quinn
1B T. Tucker
2B J. Quinn
SS R. Lochhead
3B S. Sullivan
OF T. Dowd
OF R. Harley
OF L. McAllister
C J. Sugden
P J. Hughey
P J. Knepper
P C. Bates
P F. Schmit
P J. Colliflower

CLE 1901 A
M J. McAleer
1B G. LaChance
2B E. Beck
SS F. Scheibeck
3B W. Bradley
OF O. Pickering
OF J. O'Brien
OF J. McCarthy
C R. Wood
P H. Dowling
P E. Moore
P W. Hart
P E. Scott
P J. Bracken

CLE 1902 A
M W. Armour
1B C. Hickman
2B N. Lajoie
SS J. Gochnauer
3B W. Bradley
OF E. Flick
OF H. Bay
OF J. McCarthy
C H. Bemis
P E. Moore
P A. Joss
P W. Bernhard
P C. Wright

CLE 1903 A
M W. Armour
1B C. Hickman
2B N. Lajoie
SS J. Gochnauer
3B W. Bradley
OF E. Flick
OF H. Bay
OF J. McCarthy
C H. Bemis
P A. Joss
P E. Moore
P W. Bernhard
P F. Donahue
P C. Wright

CLE 1904 A
M W. Armour
1B C. Hickman
2B N. Lajoie
SS T. Turner
3B W. Bradley
OF E. Flick
OF W. Lush
OF H. Bay
C H. Bemis
P W. Bernhard
P F. Donahue
P E. Moore
P A. Joss
P R. Rhoads

CLE 1905 A
M N. Lajoie
M W. Bradley
M N. Lajoie
1B C. Carr
2B N. Lajoie
SS T. Turner
3B W. Bradley
OF H. Bay
OF E. Flick
OF J. Jackson
C F. Buelow
UT G. Stovall
P A. Joss
P E. Moore
P R. Rhoads
P W. Bernhard
P F. Donahue

CLE 1906 A
M N. Lajoie
1B C. Rossman
2B N. Lajoie
SS T. Turner
3B W. Bradley
OF E. Flick
OF W. Congalton
OF J. Jackson
C H. Bemis
UT G. Stovall
P O. Hess
P R. Rhoads
P A. Joss
P W. Bernhard
P J. Townsend

CLE 1907 A
M N. Lajoie
1B G. Stovall
2B N. Lajoie
SS T. Turner
3B W. Bradley
OF W. Hinchman
OF E. Flick
OF J. Birmingham
C J. Clarke
P A. Joss
P G. Liebhardt
P R. Rhoads
P J. Thielman

CLE 1908 A
M N. Lajoie
1B G. Stovall
2B N. Lajoie
SS G. Perring
3B W. Bradley
OF J. Clarke
OF J. Birmingham
OF W. Hinchman
C J. Clarke
P A. Joss
P R. Rhoads
P G. Liebhardt
P C. Berger
P C. Chech

CLE 1909 A
M N. Lajoie
M J. McGuire
1B G. Stovall
2B N. Lajoie
SS C. Ball
3B W. Bradley
OF W. Hinchman
OF J. Birmingham
OF W. Good
C T. Easterly
P D. Young
P C. Berger
P A. Joss
P F. Falkenberg
P R. Rhoads

CLE 1910 A
M J. McGuire
1B G. Stovall
2B N. Lajoie
SS T. Turner
3B W. Bradley
OF J. Graney
OF J. Birmingham
OF B. Lord
C T. Easterly
P F. Falkenberg
P W. Mitchell
P D. Young
P E. Koestner
P F. Harkness

CLE 1911 A
M J. McGuire
M G. Stovall
1B G. Stovall
2B C. Ball
SS I. Olson
3B T. Turner
OF J. Jackson
OF J. Graney
OF J. Birmingham
C A. Fisher
UT T. Easterly
P S. Gregg
P E. Krapp
P W. Mitchell
P F. Blanding
P G. Kahler

CLE 1912 A
M H. Davis
M J. Birmingham
1B A. Griggs
2B N. Lajoie
SS R. Peckinpaugh
3B T. Turner
OF J. Jackson
OF J. Birmingham
OF J. Ryan
C S. O'Neill
UT I. Olson
P S. Gregg
P F. Blanding
P G. Kahler
P W. Mitchell
P W. Steen

CLE 1913 A
M J. Birmingham
1B W. Johnston
2B N. Lajoie
SS R. Chapman
3B I. Olson
OF J. Jackson
OF J. Graney
OF H. Leibold
C S. O'Neill
UT T. Turner
P S. Gregg
P F. Falkenberg
P W. Mitchell
P F. Blanding
P W. Steen

CLE 1914 A
M J. Birmingham
1B W. Johnston
2B N. Lajoie
SS R. Chapman
3B T. Turner
OF J. Graney
OF J. Jackson
OF H. Leibold
C S. O'Neill
P W. Mitchell
P W. Steen
P Z. Hagerman
P G. Morton
P F. Blanding

CLE 1915 A
M J. Birmingham
M L. Fohl
1B J. Kirke
2B W.Wambsganss
SS R. Chapman
3B W. Barbare
OF E. Smith
OF J. Graney
OF H. Leibold
C S. O'Neill
P G. Morton
P W. Mitchell
P Z. Hagerman
P S. Jones
P J. Walker
RP O. Harstad

CLE 1916 A
M L. Fohl
1B A. Gandil
2B I. Howard
SS W.Wambsganss
3B T. Turner
OF J. Graney
OF T. Speaker
OF R. Roth
C S. O'Neill
UT R. Chapman
P J. Bagby
P S. Coveleski
P G. Morton
P E. Klepfer
P F. Coumbe

CLE 1917 A
M L. Fohl
1B J. Harris
2B W.Wambsganss
SS R. Chapman
3B J. Evans
OF J. Graney
OF T. Speaker
OF R. Roth
C S. O'Neill
P J. Bagby
P S. Coveleski
P E. Klepfer
P G. Morton
P F. Coumbe

CLE 1918 A
M L. Fohl
1B W. Johnston
2B W.Wambsganss
SS R. Chapman
3B J. Evans
OF T. Speaker
OF R. Roth
OF J. Wood
C S. O'Neill
P S. Coveleski
P J. Bagby
P G. Morton
P F. Coumbe
P J. Enzmann

CLE 1919 A
M L. Fohl
M T. Speaker
1B W. Johnston
2B W.Wambsganss
SS R. Chapman
3B W. Gardner
OF T. Speaker
OF J. Graney
OF E. Smith
C S. O'Neill
RP S. Coveleski
P J. Bagby
P G. Morton
P E. Myers
P J. Uhle
RP T. Phillips

CLE 1920 A
M T. Speaker
1B W. Johnston
2B W.Wambsganss
SS R. Chapman
3B W. Gardner
OF T. Speaker
OF E. Smith
OF C. Jamieson
C S. O'Neill
P J. Bagby
P S. Coveleski
P R. Caldwell
P G. Morton

CLE 1921 A
M T. Speaker
1B W. Johnston
2B W.Wambsganss
SS J. Sewell
3B W. Gardner
OF C. Jamieson
OF T. Speaker
OF E. Smith
C S. O'Neill
P S. Coveleski
P G. Uhle
P J. Mails

P J. Bagby
P R. Caldwell

CLE 1922 A

M T. Speaker
1B J. McInnis
2B W.Wambsganss
SS J. Sewell
3B W. Gardner
OF C. Jamieson
OF J. Wood
OF T. Speaker
C S. O'Neill
P G. Uhle
P S. Coveleski
P G. Morton
P J. Mails
P J. Bagby
RP J. Lindsey

CLE 1923 A

M T. Speaker
1B F. Brower
2B W.Wambsganss
SS J. Sewell
3B W. Lutzke
OF C. Jamieson
OF T. Speaker
OF H. Summa
C S. O'Neill
P G. Uhle
P S. Coveleski
P J. Edwards
P J. Shaute
P G. Morton
RP G. Metivier
RP J. Boone

CLE 1924 A

M T. Speaker
1B G. Burns
2B W. Fewster
SS J. Sewell
3B W. Lutzke
OF C. Jamieson
OF T. Speaker
OF H. Summa
C G. Myatt
UT P. McNulty
P J. Shaute
P S. Smith
P S. Coveleski
P G. Uhle
RP G. Metivier

CLE 1925 A

M T. Speaker
1B G. Burns
2B W. Fewster
SS J. Sewell
3B W. Lutzke
OF C. Jamieson
OF P. McNulty
OF T. Speaker
C G. Myatt
UT F. Spurgeon
P S. Smith
P G. Uhle
P B. Karr
P J. Miller
P G. Buckeye

CLE 1926 A

M T. Speaker
1B G. Burns
2B F. Spurgeon
SS J. Sewell
3B W. Lutzke
OF H. Summa
OF T. Speaker
OF C. Jamieson
C L. Sewell
P G. Uhle
P E. Levsen
P J. Shaute
P S. Smith
P G. Buckeye

CLE 1927 A

M J. McCallister
1B G. Burns
2B L. Fonseca
SS J. Sewell
3B W. Lutzke
OF H. Summa
OF C. Jamieson
OF F. Eichrodt
C L. Sewell
P G. Hudlin
P J. Shaute
P G. Buckeye

P J. Miller
P G. Uhle

CLE 1928 A

M R. Peckinpaugh
1B L. Fonseca
2B H. Lind
SS J. Sewell
3B U. Hodapp
OF H. Summa
OF C. Jamieson
OF E. Langford
C L. Sewell
P J. Shaute
P G. Hudlin
P G. Uhle
P J. Miller
P G. Grant
RP W. Bayne
RP M. Harder

CLE 1929 A

M R. Peckinpaugh
1B L. Fonseca
2B U. Hodapp
SS J. Tavener
3B J. Sewell
OF H. Averill
OF B. Falk
OF C. Jamieson
C L. Sewell
UT E. Morgan
P G. Hudlin
P W. Ferrell
P J. Miller
P J. Shaute
P J. Miljus

CLE 1930 A

M R. Peckinpaugh
1B E. Morgan
2B U. Hodapp
SS J. Goldman
3B J. Sewell
OF H. Averill
OF R. Porter
OF C. Jamieson
C L. Sewell
P W. Ferrell
P G. Hudlin
P C. Brown
P M. Harder
P P. Appleton

CLE 1931 A

M R. Peckinpaugh
1B E. Morgan
2B U. Hodapp
SS E. Montague
3B W. Kamm
OF H. Averill
OF J. Vosmik
OF R. Porter
C J. Sewell
UT J. Burnett
P W. Ferrell
P G. Hudlin
P C. Brown
P M. Harder
RP P. Appleton

CLE 1932 A

M R. Peckinpaugh
1B E. Morgan
2B C. Cissell
SS J. Burnett
3B W. Kamm
OF J. Vosmik
OF H. Averill
OF R. Porter
C J. Sewell
P W. Ferrell
P C. Brown
P M. Harder
P G. Hudlin
P O. Hildebrand

CLE 1933 A

M R. Peckinpaugh
M B. Falk
M W. Johnson
1B E. Boss
2B A. Hale
SS W.Knickerbocker
3B W. Kamm
OF H. Averill
OF R. Porter
OF J. Vosmik
C R. Spencer
UT C. Cissell
P M. Harder

P O. Hildebrand
P W. Ferrell
P C. Brown
P G. Hudlin
RP G. Connally
RP B. Bean

CLE 1934 A

M W. Johnson
1B H. Trosky
2B A. Hale
SS W.Knickerbocker
3B W. Kamm
OF H. Averill
OF J. Vosmik
OF E. Rice
C F. Pytlak
P M. Pearson
P M. Harder
P O. Hildebrand
P G. Hudlin
P L. Brown
RP B. Bean
RP C. Brown

CLE 1935 A

M W. Johnson
M S. O'Neill
1B H. Trosky
2B L. Berger
SS W.Knickerbocker
3B A. Hale
OF J. Vosmik
OF H. Averill
OF M. Galatzer
C E. Phillips
P M. Harder
P G. Hudlin
P M. Pearson
P T. Lee
P O. Hildebrand
RP L. Brown
RP R. Winegarner
RP C. Brown

CLE 1936 A

M S. O'Neill
1B H. Trosky
2B R. Hughes
SS W.Knickerbocker
3B A. Hale
OF H. Averill
OF J. Vosmik
OF C. Weatherly
C W. Sullivan
P J. Allen
P M. Harder
P O. Hildebrand
P D. Galehouse
P L. Brown
RP T. Lee
RP G. Hudlin

CLE 1937 A

M S. O'Neill
1B H. Trosky
2B J. Kroner
SS L. Lary
3B A. Hale
OF H. Averill
OF J. Solters
OF B. Campbell
C F. Pytlak
UT R. Hughes
P M. Harder
P D. Galehouse
P G. Hudlin
P J. Allen
P R. Feller
RP L. Brown
RP J. Wyatt
RP J. Heving

CLE 1938 A

M O. Vitt
1B H. Trosky
2B A. Hale
SS L. Lary
3B K. Keltner
OF H. Averill
OF J. Heath
OF B. Campbell
C F. Pytlak
P R. Feller
P M. Harder
P J. Allen
P E. Whitehill
P G. Hudlin
RP J. Humphries
RP A. Milnar

CLE 1939 A

M O. Vitt
1B H. Trosky
2B A. Hale
SS J. Webb
3B K. Keltner
OF W. Chapman
OF B. Campbell
OF J. Heath
C R. Hemsley
UT O. Grimes
UT C. Weatherly
P R. Feller
P A. Milnar
P M. Harder
P J. Allen
P G. Hudlin
RP J. Dobson

CLE 1940 A

M O. Vitt
1B H. Trosky
2B R. Mack
SS L. Boudreau
3B K. Keltner
OF W. Chapman
OF C. Weatherly
OF R. Bell
C R. Hemsley
UT J. Heath
P R. Feller
P A. Milnar
P M. Harder
P A. Smith
P J. Allen
RP J. Dobson
RP H. Eisenstat

CLE 1941 A

M R. Peckinpaugh
1B H. Trosky
2B R. Mack
SS L. Boudreau
3B K. Keltner
OF J. Heath
OF G. Walker
OF C. Weatherly
C R. Hemsley
UT C. Campbell
P R. Feller
P A. Milnar
P A. Smith
P J. Bagby
RP C. Brown
RP J. Heving

CLE 1942 A

M L. Boudreau
1B L. Fleming
2B R. Mack
SS L. Boudreau
3B K. Keltner
OF J. Heath
OF O. Hockett
OF C. Weatherly
C O. Denning
P J. Bagby
P M. Harder
P A. Dean
P A. Smith
P A. Milnar
RP T. Ferrick
RP H. Eisenstat

CLE 1943 A

M L. Boudreau
1B M. Rocco
2B R. Mack
SS L. Boudreau
3B K. Keltner
OF O. Hockett
OF R. Cullenbine
OF J. Heath
C W. Rosar
P J. Bagby
P A. Smith
P A. Reynolds
P L. Kennedy
P M. Harder
RP J. Heving
RP M. Naymick

CLE 1944 A

M L. Boudreau
1B M. Rocco
2B R. Mack
SS L. Boudreau
3B K. Keltner
OF R. Cullenbine
OF O. Hockett
OF J. Seerey

C W. Rosar
P S. Gromek
P M. Harder
P A. Smith
P E. Klieman
P A. Reynolds
RP J. Heving
RP R. Poat
RP P. Calvert

CLE 1945 A

M L. Boudreau
1B M. Rocco
2B L. Meyer
SS L. Boudreau
3B D. Ross
OF J. Seerey
OF F. Mackiewicz
OF J. Heath
C F. Hayes
UT A. Cihocki
P S. Gromek
P A. Reynolds
P J. Bagby
P A. Smith
P E. Klieman
RP M. Center
RP J. Salveson

CLE 1946 A

M L. Boudreau
1B L. Fleming
2B L. Meyer
SS L. Boudreau
3B K. Keltner
OF H. Edwards
OF G. Case
OF J. Seerey
C J. Hegan
P R. Feller
P C. Embree
P A. Reynolds
P S. Gromek
RP R. Lemon
RP J. Krakauskas

CLE 1947 A

M L. Boudreau
1B W. Robinson
2B J. Gordon
SS L. Boudreau
3B K. Keltner
OF G. Metkovich
OF L. Mitchell
OF H. Edwards
C J. Hegan
UT L. Fleming
UT H. Peck
P R. Feller
P D. Black
P R. Lemon
P C. Embree
P A. Gettel
RP B. Stephens
RP E. Klieman
RP S. Gromek

CLE 1948 A

M L. Boudreau
1B W. Robinson
2B J. Gordon
SS L. Boudreau
3B K. Keltner
OF L. Mitchell
OF L. Doby
OF T. Tucker
C J. Hegan
P R. Lemon
P R. Feller
P H. Bearden
P S. Gromek
P S. Zoldak
RP E. Klieman
RP R. Christopher
RP D. Black

CLE 1949 A

M L. Boudreau
1B J. Vernon
2B J. Gordon
SS L. Boudreau
3B K. Keltner
OF L. Mitchell
OF L. Doby
OF R. Kennedy
C J. Hegan
P R. Lemon
P R. Feller
P E. Garcia
P E. Wynn
P J. Benton
RP L. Paige

RP F. Papish
RP S. Zoldak

CLE 1950 A

M L. Boudreau
1B L. Easter
2B J. Gordon
SS R. Boone
3B A. Rosen
OF R. Kennedy
OF L. Doby
OF L. Mitchell
C J. Hegan
P R. Lemon
P R. Feller
P E. Wynn
P E. Garcia
P S. Gromek
RP S. Zoldak
RP J. Benton
RP J. Flores

CLE 1951 A

M A. Lopez
1B L. Easter
2B R. Avila
SS R. Boone
3B A. Rosen
OF L. Doby
OF L. Mitchell
OF R. Kennedy
C J. Hegan
P E. Wynn
P R. Lemon
P E. Garcia
P R. Feller
P S. Gromek
RP L. Brissie

CLE 1952 A

M A. Lopez
1B L. Easter
2B R. Avila
SS R. Boone
3B A. Rosen
OF L. Doby
OF L. Mitchell
OF H. Simpson
C J. Hegan
P R. Lemon
P E. Garcia
P E. Wynn
P R. Feller
P S. Gromek
RP L. Brissie
RP M. Harris

CLE 1953 A

M A. Lopez
1B W. Glynn
2B R. Avila
SS R. Strickland
3B A. Rosen
OF L. Doby
OF L. Mitchell
OF R. Kennedy
C J. Hegan
P R. Lemon
P E. Garcia
P E. Wynn
P R. Feller
P D. Hoskins
RP R. Hooper

CLE 1954 A

M A. Lopez
1B W. Glynn
2B R. Avila
SS R. Strickland
3B A. Rosen
OF L. Doby
OF D. Philley
OF A. Smith
C J. Hegan
UT V. Wertz
P E. Wynn
P E. Garcia
P R. Lemon
P A. Houtteman
P R. Feller
RP D. Mossi
RP R. Narleski
RP H. Newhouser

CLE 1955 A

M A. Lopez
1B V. Wertz
2B R. Avila
SS G. Strickland

3B A. Rosen
OF L. Doby
OF A. Smith
OF R. Kiner
C J. Hegan
P E. Wynn
P H. Score
P R. Lemon
P E. Garcia
P A. Houtteman
RP R. Narleski
RP D. Mossi

CLE 1956 A

M A. Lopez
1B V. Wertz
2B R. Avila
SS A. Carrasquel
3B A. Rosen
OF J. Busby
OF A. Smith
OF R. Colavito
C J. Hegan
UT E. Woodling
P E. Wynn
P R. Lemon
P H. Score
P E. Garcia
RP D. Mossi
RP M. McLish
RP R. Narleski

CLE 1957 A

M M. Farrell
1B V. Wertz
2B R. Avila
SS A. Carrasquel
3B A. Smith
OF R. Colavito
OF E. Woodling
OF R. Maris
C J. Hegan
UT L. Raines
P E. Wynn
P E. Garcia
P D. Mossi
P R. Narleski
P C. McLish
RP L. Daley
RP R. Tomanek
RP S. Pitula

CLE 1958 A

M R. Bragan
M J. Gordon
1B J. Vernon
2B R. Avila
SS G. Hunter
3B W. Harrell
OF S. Minoso
OF R. Colavito
OF L. Doby
C R. Nixon
UT W. Moran
P C. McLish
P J. Grant
P R. Narleski
P G. Bell
P D. Ferrarese
RP D. Mossi

CLE 1959 A

M J. Gordon
1B V. Power
2B A. Martin
SS W. Held
3B G. Strickland
OF R. Colavito
OF S. Minoso
OF J. Piersall
C R. Nixon
UT J. Francona
P C. McLish
P G. Bell
P J. Grant
P H. Score
P J. Perry
RP E. Garcia

CLE 1960 A

M J. Gordon
M J. White
M J. Dykes
1B V. Power
2B K. Aspromonte
SS W. Held
3B J. Phillips
OF J. Francona
OF J. Piersall
OF H. Kuenn
C J. Romano
UT J. Temple

P	J. Perry
P	J. Grant
P	G. Bell
P	A. Latman
P	R. Stigman
RP	J. Klippstein
RP	D. Newcombe

CLE 1961 A

M	J. Dykes
M	M. Harder
1B	V. Power
2B	J. Temple
SS	W. Held
3B	J. Phillips
OF	W. Kirkland
OF	J. Francona
OF	J. Piersall
C	J. Romano
P	J. Grant
P	G. Bell
P	J. Perry
P	A. Latman
P	W. Hawkins
RP	L. Locke
RP	F. Funk
RP	R. Allen

CLE 1962 A

M	F. McGaha
M	M. Harder
1B	J. Francona
2B	G. Kindall
SS	W. Held
3B	J. Phillips
OF	W. Kirkland
OF	T. Cline
OF	C. Essegian
C	J. Romano
UT	A. Luplow
P	R. Donovan
P	P. Ramos
P	J. Perry
P	A. Latman
P	J. Grant
RP	G. Bell
RP	F. Funk

CLE 1963 A

M	G. Tebbetts
1B	F. Whitfield
2B	W. Held
SS	G. Kindall
3B	R. Alvis
OF	J. Francona
OF	W. Kirkland
OF	V. Davalillo
C	J. Azcue
UT	J. Adcock
UT	A. Luplow
P	J. Grant
P	R. Donovan
P	J. Kralick
P	P. Ramos
P	A. Latman
RP	G. Bell
RP	J. Walker
RP	T. Abernathy

CLE 1964 A

M	G. Strickland
M	G. Tebbetts
1B	R. Chance
2B	L. Brown
SS	R. Howser
3B	R. Alvis
OF	L. Wagner
OF	V. Davalillo
OF	J. Francona
C	J. Romano
UT	W. Held
UT	F. Whitfield
P	J. Kralick
P	S. McDowell
P	R. Donovan
P	W. Siebert
P	P. Ramos
RP	G. Bell
RP	D. McMahon
RP	T. Abernathy

CLE 1965 A

M	G. Tebbetts
1B	F. Whitfield
2B	P. Gonzalez
SS	L. Brown
3B	R. Alvis
OF	R. Colavito
OF	L. Wagner
OF	V. Davalillo
C	J. Azcue
UT	C. Hinton

UT	R. Howser
P	S. McDowell
P	L. Tiant
P	W. Siebert
P	R. Terry
P	A. Stange
RP	G. Bell
RP	J. Kralick
RP	D. McMahon

CLE 1966 A

M	G. Tebbetts
M	G. Strickland
1B	F. Whitfield
2B	P. Gonzalez
SS	L. Brown
3B	R. Alvis
OF	R. Colavito
OF	L. Wagner
OF	V. Davalillo
C	J. Azcue
UT	C. Hinton
UT	R. Salmon
P	G. Bell
P	W. Siebert
P	S. McDowell
P	S. Hargan
P	L. Tiant
RP	J. Kralick
RP	R. Radatz
RP	R. Allen

CLE 1967 A

M	J. Adcock
1B	A. Horton
2B	P. Gonzalez
SS	L. Brown
3B	R. Alvis
OF	C. Hinton
OF	V. Davalillo
OF	L. Wagner
C	J. Azcue
UT	A. Maye
UT	F. Whitfield
P	S. McDowell
P	S. Hargan
P	L. Tiant
P	W. Siebert
P	J. O'Donoghue
RP	O. Pena
RP	G. Culver
RP	S. Bailey

CLE 1968 A

M	A. Dark
1B	A. Horton
2B	V. Fuller
SS	L. Brown
3B	R. Alvis
OF	J. Cardenal
OF	T. Harper
OF	A. Maye
C	J. Azcue
UT	R. Salmon
UT	D. Sims
P	S. McDowell
P	L. Tiant
P	W. Siebert
P	S. Williams
P	S. Hargan
RP	E. Fisher
RP	M. Paul
RP	V. Romo

CLE 1969 A

M	A. Dark
1B	A. Horton
2B	V. Fuller
SS	L. Brown
3B	R. Alvis
OF	K. Harrelson
OF	J. Cardenal
OF	R. Snyder
C	D. Sims
UT	R. Scheinblum
P	S. McDowell
P	L. Tiant
P	S. Hargan
P	R. Ellsworth
RP	S. Williams
RP	M. Paul
RP	J. Pizarro

CLE 1970 A

M	A. Dark
1B	A. Horton
2B	E. Leon
SS	J. Heidemann
3B	G. Nettles
OF	V. Pinson
OF	T. Uhlaender
OF	R. Foster

C	R. Fosse
UT	C. Hinton
UT	D. Sims
P	S. McDowell
P	R. Hand
P	W. Chance
P	S. Hargan
RP	D. Higgins
RP	M. Paul
RP	P. Hennigan

CLE 1971 A

M	A. Dark
M	J. Lipon
1B	C. Chambliss
2B	E. Leon
SS	J. Heidemann
3B	G. Nettles
OF	V. Pinson
OF	T. Uhlaender
OF	R. Foster
C	R. Fosse
P	S. McDowell
P	S. Dunning
P	A. Foster
P	R. Lamb
P	S. Hargan
P	L. Tiant
RP	J. Kralick
RP	P. Hennigan
RP	E. Farmer

CLE 1972 A

M	K. Aspromonte
1B	C. Chambliss
2B	J. Brohamer
SS	F. Duffy
3B	G. Nettles
OF	D. Bell
OF	D. Unser
OF	A. Johnson
C	R. Fosse
UT	T. McCraw
P	G. Perry
P	F. Tidrow
P	M. Wilcox
P	R. Lamb
P	S. Dunning
RP	P. Hennigan
RP	E. Farmer
RP	M. Kilkenny

CLE 1973 A

M	K. Aspromonte
1B	C. Chambliss
2B	J. Brohamer
SS	F. Duffy
3B	D. Bell
OF	R. Torres
OF	L. Spikes
OF	G. Hendrick
C	D. Duncan
DH	O. Gamble
UT	J. Ellis
UT	J. Lowenstein
UT	W. Williams
P	G. Perry
P	F. Tidrow
P	M. Wilcox
P	T. Timmermann
P	B. Strom
RP	T. Hilgendorf
RP	R. Lamb
RP	J. Johnson

CLE 1974 A

M	K. Aspromonte
1B	J. Ellis
2B	J. Brohamer
SS	F. Duffy
3B	D. Bell
OF	L. Spikes
OF	G. Hendrick
OF	J. Lowenstein
C	D. Duncan
DH	O. Gamble
UT	R. Torres
P	G. Perry
P	J. Perry
P	F. Peterson
P	R. Bosman
RP	T. Buskey
RP	F. Beene
RP	M. Wilcox

CLE 1975 A

M	F. Robinson
1B	J. Powell
2B	D. Kuiper
SS	F. Duffy
3B	D. Bell
OF	G. Hendrick
OF	R. Manning

OF	L. Spikes
C	A. Ashby
DH	R. Carty
UT	O. Gamble
P	D. Eckersley
P	F. Peterson
P	D. Hood
P	R. Harrison
P	G. Perry
RP	D. LaRoche
RP	T. Buskey
RP	J. Brown

CLE 1976 A

M	F. Robinson
1B	J. Powell
2B	D. Kuiper
SS	F. Duffy
3B	D. Bell
OF	G. Hendrick
OF	R. Manning
OF	L. Spikes
C	A. Ashby
DH	R. Carty
UT	L. Blanks
P	P. Dobson
P	D. Eckersley
P	J. Brown
P	J. Bibby
P	M. Waits
P	J. Kern
RP	S. Thomas
RP	D. LaRoche

CLE 1977 A

M	F. Robinson
M	J. Torborg
1B	A. Thornton
2B	D. Kuiper
SS	F. Duffy
3B	D. Bell
OF	J. Norris
OF	L. Dade
OF	B. Bochte
C	F. Kendall
DH	R. Carty
UT	L. Blanks
P	M. Garland
P	D. Eckersley
P	J. Bibby
P	M. Waits
P	A. Fitzmorris
RP	D. Hood
RP	J. Kern

CLE 1978 A

M	J. Torborg
1B	A. Thornton
2B	D. Kuiper
SS	T. Veryzer
3B	D. Bell
OF	R. Manning
OF	J. Grubb
OF	L. Dade
C	G. Alexander
DH	B. Carbo
UT	J. Norris
P	M. Waits
P	R. Wise
P	M. Paxton
P	D. Hood
P	D. Clyde
RP	J. Kern
RP	I. Monge
RP	D. Spillner

CLE 1979 A

M	J. Torborg
M	D. Garcia
1B	A. Thornton
2B	D. Kuiper
SS	T. Veryzer
3B	C. Harrah
OF	R. Manning
OF	B. Bonds
OF	J. Norris
C	G. Alexander
DH	C. Johnson
UT	D. Hargrove
P	R. Wise
P	M. Waits
P	M. Paxton
P	D. Spillner
P	L. Barker
RP	I. Monge
RP	V. Cruz

CLE 1980 A

M	D. Garcia
1B	D. Hargrove
2B	J. Brohamer
SS	T. Veryzer

3B	C. Harrah
OF	R. Manning
OF	J. Orta
OF	M. Dilone
C	R. Hassey
DH	J. Charboneau
UT	J. Dybzinski
P	L. Barker
P	M. Waits
P	D. Spillner
P	M. Garland
P	R. Owchinko
RP	I. Monge
RP	M. Stanton
RP	V. Cruz

CLE 1981 A

M	D. Garcia
1B	D. Hargrove
2B	D. Kuiper
SS	T. Veryzer
3B	C. Harrah
OF	R. Manning
OF	J. Orta
OF	M. Dilone
C	R. Hassey
DH	A. Thornton
UT	A. Bannister
P	R. Blyleven
P	L. Barker
P	J. Denny
P	M. Waits
P	D. Spillner
RP	I. Monge
RP	M. Stanton

CLE 1982 A

M	D. Garcia
1B	D. Hargrove
2B	J. Perconte
SS	M. Fischlin
3B	C. Harrah
OF	R. Manning
OF	V. Hayes
OF	M. Dilone
C	R. Hassey
DH	A. Thornton
UT	A. Bannister
P	L. Barker
P	R. Sutcliffe
P	L. Sorensen
P	J. Denny
P	M. Waits
RP	D. Spillner
RP	E. Whitson
RP	E. Glynn

CLE 1983 A

M	M. Ferraro
M	P. Corrales
1B	D. Hargrove
2B	J. Trillo
SS	J. Franco
3B	C. Harrah
OF	G. Vukovich
OF	J. Thomas
OF	A. Bannister
C	R. Hassey
DH	A. Thornton
UT	P. Tabler
P	R. Sutcliffe
P	L. Sorensen
P	R. Blyleven
P	L. Barker
P	N. Heaton
RP	D. Spillner
RP	K. Anderson
RP	J. Easterly

CLE 1984 A

M	P. Corrales
1B	D. Hargrove
2B	A. Bernazard
SS	J. Franco
3B	B. Jacoby
OF	B. Butler
OF	G. Vukovich
OF	M. Castillo
C	G. Willard
DH	A. Thornton
UT	P. Tabler
P	R. Blyleven
P	N. Heaton
P	S. Comer
P	S. Farr
RP	E. Camacho
RP	T. Waddell
RP	J. Jeffcoat

CLE 1985 A

M	P. Corrales
1B	P. Tabler

2B	A. Bernazard
SS	J. Franco
3B	B. Jacoby
OF	B. Butler
OF	G. Vukovich
OF	J. Carter
C	G. Willard
DH	A. Thornton
UT	O. Nixon
P	N. Heaton
P	R. Blyleven
RP	V. Ruhle
RP	T. Waddell
RP	J. Easterly

CLE 1986 A

M	P. Corrales
1B	P. Tabler
2B	A. Bernazard
SS	J. Franco
3B	B. Jacoby
OF	B. Butler
OF	M. Hall
OF	J. Carter
C	A. Allanson
DH	A. Thornton
UT	O. Nixon
UT	J. Snyder
P	N. Heaton
P	R. Blyleven
P	V. Ruhle
RP	T. Candiotti
P	J. Niekro
P	K. Schrom
RP	S. Bailes
RP	R. Yett
RP	B. Oelkers

CLE 1987 A

M	P. Corrales
M	H. Edwards
1B	J. Carter
2B	A. Bernazard
SS	J. Franco
3B	B. Jacoby
OF	J. Snyder
OF	B. Butler
OF	M. Hall
C	C. Bando
DH	P. Tabler
P	T. Candiotti
P	K. Schrom
P	J. Niekro
P	S. Bailes
P	S. Carlton
RP	R. Yett
RP	D. Jones
RP	E. Vande Berg

CLE 1988 A

M	H. Edwards
1B	W. Upshaw
2B	J. Franco
SS	J. Bell
3B	B. Jacoby
OF	J. Carter
OF	J. Snyder
OF	M. Hall
C	A. Allanson
DH	R. Kittle
P	F. Swindell
P	T. Candiotti
P	J. Farrell
P	S. Bailes
P	R. Yett
RP	D. Jones
RP	D. Gordon
RP	B. Havens

CLE 1989 A

M	H. Edwards
M	J. Hart
1B	P. O'Brien
2B	J. Browne
SS	F. Fermin
3B	B. Jacoby
OF	J. Carter
OF	J. Snyder
OF	B. Komminsk
C	A. Allanson
DH	D. Clark
P	H. Black
P	J. Farrell
P	T. Candiotti
P	F. Swindell
P	S. Bailes
RP	D. Jones
RP	J. Orosco

CLE 1990 A

M	J. McNamara
1B	B. Jacoby
2B	J. Browne
SS	F. Fermin

3B	C. Baerga
OF	C. Maldonado
OF	J. Snyder
OF	M. Webster
C	S. Alomar
DH	J. James
P	F. Swindell
P	T. Candiotti
P	H. Black
P	S. Valdez
P	J. Farrell
RP	S. Olin
RP	D. Jones
RP	J. Orosco

Columbus

COL a 1883-1884
COL a 1889-1891

COL 1883 a

M	H. Phillips
1B	J. Field
2B	C. Smith
SS	J. Richmond
3B	W. Kuehne
OF	T. Brown
OF	H. Wheeler
OF	F. Mann
C	R. Kemmler
P	F. Mountain
P	E. Dundon
P	J. Valentine

COL 1884 a

M	G. Schmelz
1B	J. Field
2B	C. Smith
SS	J. Richmond
3B	W. Kuehne
OF	T. Brown
OF	F. Mann
OF	J. Cahill
C	R. Kemmler
UT	F. Carroll
P	E. Morris
P	F. Mountain

COL 1889 a

M	A. Buckenberger
1B	D. Orr
2B	W. Greenwood
SS	H. Easterday
3B	C. Marr
OF	J. McTamany
OF	E. Daily
OF	J. Johnson
C	J. O'Connor
P	M. Baldwin
P	W. Widner
P	H. Gastright
P	A. Mays

COL 1890 a

M	A. Buckenberger
M	G. Schmelz
M	J. Sullivan
1B	M. Lehane
2B	J. Crooks
SS	H. Easterday
3B	C. Reilly
OF	J. Johnson
OF	J. Sneed
OF	J. McTamany
C	J. O'Connor
P	H. Gastright
P	F. Knauss
P	J. Easton
P	E. Chamberlain
P	W. Widner

COL 1891 a

M	G. Schmelz
1B	M. Lehane
2B	J. Crooks
SS	W. Wheelock
3B	W. Kuehne
OF	C. Duffee
OF	J. Sneed
OF	J. McTamany
P	J. Donahue
P	J. Knell
P	H. Gastright
P	J. Dolan
P	J. Easton

Detroit

DET N 1881-1888
DET A 1901-1990

DET 1881 N
- M F. Bancroft
- 1B M. Powell
- 2B J. Gerhardt
- SS S. Houck
- 3B A. Whitney
- OF A. Knight
- OF G. Wood
- OF E. Hanlon
- C C. Bennett
- P G. Derby
- P G. Weidman
- P F. Mountain

DET 1882 N
- M F. Bancroft
- 1B M. Powell
- 2B J. Troy
- SS M. McGeary
- 3B J. Farrell
- OF G. Wood
- OF A. Knight
- OF E. Hanlon
- C C. Bennett
- P G. Weidman
- P G. Derby

DET 1883 N
- M J. Chapman
- 1B M. Powell
- 2B S. Trott
- SS S. Houck
- 3B J. Farrell
- OF G. Wood
- OF E. Hanlon
- OF G. Weidman
- C C. Bennett
- P G. Weidman
- P F. Shaw
- P D. Jones

DET 1884 N
- M J. Chapman
- 1B M. Scott
- 2B W. Geis
- SS F. Meinke
- 3B J. Farrell
- OF G. Wood
- OF E. Hanlon
- OF G. Weidman
- C C. Bennett
- P F. Shaw
- P C. Getzien
- P F. Brill

DET 1885 N
- M C. Morton
- M W. Watkins
- 1B W. McQuery
- 2B S. Crane
- SS M. Phillips
- 3B J. Donnelly
- OF E. Hanlon
- OF G. Wood
- OF S. Thompson
- C C. Bennett
- P G. Weidman
- P C. Getzien
- P C. Baldwin
- P D. Casey

DET 1886 N
- M W. Watkins
- 1B D. Brouthers
- 2B F. Dunlap
- SS J. Rowe
- 3B J. White
- OF E. Hanlon
- OF S. Thompson
- OF A. Richardson
- C C. Bennett
- P C. Baldwin
- P C. Getzien
- P P. Conway
- P W. Smith

DET 1887 N
- M W. Watkins
- 1B D. Brouthers
- 2B F. Dunlap
- SS J. Rowe
- 3B J. White
- OF S. Thompson
- OF E. Hanlon
- OF A. Richardson
- C C. Ganzel
- P C. Getzien
- P C. Baldwin
- P G. Weidman
- P P. Conway

DET 1888 N
- M W. Watkins
- M R. Leadley
- 1B D. Brouthers
- 2B A. Richardson
- SS J. Rowe
- 3B J. White
- OF L. Twitchell
- OF E. Hanlon
- OF C. Campau
- C C. Bennett
- UT C. Ganzel
- P C. Getzien
- P P. Conway
- P H. Gruber
- P E. Beatin

DET 1901 A
- M G. Stallings
- 1B F. Dillon
- 2B W. Gleason
- SS N. Elberfeld
- 3B J. Casey
- OF J. Barrett
- OF W. Nance
- OF J. Holmes
- C F. Buelow
- UT L. McAllister
- P R. Miller
- P E. Siever
- P J. Cronin
- P J. Yeager

DET 1902 A
- M J. Dwyer
- 1B F. Dillon
- 2B W. Gleason
- SS N. Elberfeld
- 3B J. Casey
- OF J. Barrett
- OF R. Harley
- OF J. Holmes
- C J. McGuire
- P G. Mercer
- P G. Mullin
- P E. Siever
- P R. Miller
- P J. Yeager

DET 1903 A
- M E. Barrow
- 1B C. Carr
- 2B G. Smith
- SS L. McAllister
- 3B J. Yeager
- OF S. Crawford
- OF J. Barrett
- OF W. Lush
- C J. McGuire
- P G. Mullin
- P W. Donovan
- P F. Kitson
- P C. Kisinger

DET 1904 A
- M E. Barrow
- M R. Lowe
- 1B C. Carr
- 2B R. Lowe
- SS C. O'Leary
- 3B L. Gremminger
- OF J. Barrett
- OF M. McIntyre
- OF S. Crawford
- C L. Drill
- UT C. Robinson
- P G. Mullin
- P E. Killian
- P W. Donovan
- P F. Kitson
- P J. Stovall

DET 1905 A
- M W. Armour
- 1B C. Lindsay
- 2B H. Schaefer
- SS C. O'Leary
- 3B W. Coughlin
- OF M. McIntyre
- OF S. Crawford
- OF D. Cooley
- C L. Drill
- P G. Mullin
- P E. Killian
- P W. Donovan
- P F. Kitson

DET 1906 A
- M W. Armour
- 1B C. Lindsay
- 2B H. Schaefer
- SS C. O'Leary
- 3B W. Coughlin
- OF M. McIntyre
- OF S. Crawford
- OF T. Cobb
- C C. Schmidt
- P G. Mullin
- P F. Donahue
- P E. Siever
- P W. Donovan
- P E. Killian

DET 1907 A
- M H. Jennings
- 1B C. Rossman
- 2B J. Downs
- SS C. O'Leary
- 3B W. Coughlin
- OF T. Cobb
- OF S. Crawford
- OF D. Jones
- C C. Schmidt
- UT H. Schaefer
- P G. Mullin
- P E. Killian
- P E. Siever
- P W. Donovan

DET 1908 A
- M H. Jennings
- 1B C. Rossman
- 2B J. Downs
- SS H. Schaefer
- 3B W. Coughlin
- OF M. McIntyre
- OF T. Cobb
- OF S. Crawford
- C C. Schmidt
- P O. Summers
- P G. Mullin
- P W. Donovan
- P R. Willett
- P E. Killian

DET 1909 A
- M H. Jennings
- 1B C. Rossman
- 2B H. Schaefer
- SS O. Bush
- 3B G. Moriarty
- OF T. Cobb
- OF S. Crawford
- OF M. McIntyre
- C C. Schmidt
- P G. Mullin
- P R. Willett
- P O. Summers
- P E. Killian
- P W. Donovan

DET 1910 A
- M H. Jennings
- 1B T. Jones
- 2B J. Delahanty
- SS O. Bush
- 3B G. Moriarty
- OF S. Crawford
- OF T. Cobb
- OF D. Jones
- C O. Stanage
- P G. Mullin
- P R. Willett
- P O. Summers
- P W. Donovan
- P R. Stroud

DET 1911 A
- M H. Jennings
- 1B J. Delahanty
- 2B C. O'Leary
- SS O. Bush
- 3B G. Moriarty
- OF S. Crawford
- OF T. Cobb
- OF D. Jones
- C O. Stanage
- UT D. Drake
- P G. Mullin
- P R. Willett
- P O. Summers
- P E. Lafitte
- P W. Donovan

DET 1912 A
- M H. Jennings
- 1B H. Heilmann
- 2B R. Young
- SS O. Bush
- 3B O. Vitt
- OF R. Veach
- OF T. Cobb
- OF S. Crawford
- OF T. Cobb
- OF D. Jones
- C O. Stanage
- P R. Willett
- P J. Dubuc
- P G. Mullin
- P J. Lake
- P R. Works

DET 1913 A
- M H. Jennings
- 1B D. Gainer
- 2B O. Vitt
- SS O. Bush
- 3B G. Moriarty
- OF S. Crawford
- OF R. Veach
- OF T. Cobb
- C O. Stanage
- P J. Dubuc
- P R. Willett
- P G. Dauss
- P M. Hall
- P J. Lake
- RP W. House

DET 1914 A
- M H. Jennings
- 1B G. Burns
- 2B M. Kavanagh
- SS O. Bush
- 3B G. Moriarty
- OF S. Crawford
- OF R. Veach
- OF T. Cobb
- C O. Stanage
- P H. Coveleski
- P G. Dauss
- P J. Dubuc
- P T. Cavet
- P M. Main

DET 1915 A
- M H. Jennings
- 1B G. Burns
- 2B R. Young
- SS O. Bush
- 3B O. Vitt
- OF S. Crawford
- OF T. Cobb
- OF R. Veach
- C O. Stanage
- UT M. Kavanagh
- P H. Coveleski
- P G. Dauss
- P J. Dubuc
- P B. Boland

DET 1916 A
- M H. Jennings
- 1B G. Burns
- 2B R. Young
- SS O. Bush
- 3B O. Vitt
- OF R. Veach
- OF T. Cobb
- OF S. Crawford
- C O. Stanage
- UT H. Heilmann
- P H. Coveleski
- P G. Dauss
- P J. Dubuc
- P W. James
- P G. Cunningham
- RP B. Boland

DET 1917 A
- M H. Jennings
- 1B G. Burns
- 2B R. Young
- SS O. Bush
- 3B O. Vitt
- OF R. Veach
- OF T. Cobb
- OF H. Heilmann
- C O. Stanage
- P G. Dauss
- P B. Boland
- P H. Ehmke
- P W. James
- P W. Mitchell

DET 1918 A
- M H. Jennings
- 1B H. Heilmann
- 2B R. Young
- SS O. Bush
- 3B O. Vitt
- OF R. Veach
- OF T. Cobb
- OF G. Harper
- C A. Yelle
- P G. Dauss
- P B. Boland
- P R. Kallio
- P G. Cunningham
- P W. James

DET 1919 A
- M H. Jennings
- 1B H. Heilmann
- 2B R. Young
- SS O. Bush
- 3B R. Jones
- OF R. Veach
- OF T. Cobb
- OF I. Flagstead
- C E. Ainsmith
- UT C. Shorten
- P G. Dauss
- P H. Ehmke
- P B. Boland
- P H. Leonard
- P Y. Ayers
- RP G. Cunningham

DET 1920 A
- M H. Jennings
- 1B H. Heilmann
- 2B R. Young
- SS O. Bush
- 3B R. Pinelli
- OF R. Veach
- OF T. Cobb
- OF C. Shorten
- C O. Stanage
- UT I. Flagstead
- P G. Dauss
- P H. Ehmke
- P J. Oldham
- P Y. Ayers
- P H. Leonard

DET 1921 A
- M T. Cobb
- 1B L. Blue
- 2B R. Young
- SS O. Bush
- 3B R. Jones
- OF R. Veach
- OF H. Heilmann
- OF T. Cobb
- C J. Bassler
- P H. Leonard
- P G. Dauss
- P J. Oldham
- P H. Ehmke
- P C. Holling

DET 1922 A
- M T. Cobb
- 1B L. Blue
- 2B G. Cutshaw
- SS E. Rigney
- 3B R. Jones
- OF R. Veach
- OF T. Cobb
- OF H. Heilmann
- C J. Bassler
- P H. Ehmke
- P H. Pillette
- P G. Dauss
- P J. Oldham
- P A. Olsen

DET 1923 A
- M T. Cobb
- 1B L. Blue
- 2B F. Haney
- SS E. Rigney
- 3B R. Jones
- OF T. Cobb
- OF H. Heilmann
- OF R. Veach
- C J. Bassler
- UT R. Fothergill
- UT H. Manush
- UT D. Pratt
- P G. Dauss
- P H. Pillette
- P K. Holloway
- P S. Johnson
- P A. Cole
- RP R. Francis

DET 1924 A
- M T. Cobb
- 1B L. Blue
- 2B D. Pratt
- SS E. Rigney
- 3B R. Jones
- OF T. Cobb
- OF H. Heilmann
- OF H. Manush
- C J. Bassler
- P E. Whitehill
- P U. Stoner
- P H. Collins
- P K. Holloway
- P G. Dauss

DET 1925 A
- M T. Cobb
- 1B L. Blue
- 2B J. O'Rourke
- SS J. Tavener
- 3B F. Haney
- OF H. Heilmann
- OF A. Wingo
- OF T. Cobb
- C J. Bassler
- UT H. Manush
- P E. Whitehill
- P G. Dauss
- P K. Holloway
- P U. Stoner
- P H. Collins
- RP J. Doyle

DET 1926 A
- M T. Cobb
- 1B L. Blue
- 2B C. Gehringer
- SS J. Tavener
- 3B J. Warner
- OF H. Heilmann
- OF H. Manush
- OF R. Fothergill
- C C. Manion
- UT J. Neun
- UT J. O'Rourke
- UT A. Wingo
- P E. Whitehill
- P S. Gibson
- P E. Wells
- P U. Stoner
- P K. Holloway

DET 1927 A
- M G. Moriarty
- 1B L. Blue
- 2B C. Gehringer
- SS J. Tavener
- 3B J. Warner
- OF H. Manush
- OF R. Fothergill
- OF H. Heilmann
- C C. Woodall
- UT M. McManus
- P E. Whitehill
- P U. Stoner
- P S. Gibson
- P K. Holloway
- P H. Collins
- RP G. Smith

DET 1928 A
- M G. Moriarty
- 1B W. Sweeney
- 2B C. Gehringer
- SS J. Tavener
- 3B M. McManus
- OF H. Rice
- OF H. Heilmann
- OF R. Fothergill
- C W. Hargrave
- P O. Carroll
- P E. Whitehill
- P V. Sorrell
- P E. Vangilder
- P U. Stoner
- RP G. Smith

DET 1929 A
- M S. Harris
- 1B D. Alexander
- 2B C. Gehringer
- SS H. Schuble
- 3B M. McManus
- OF R. Johnson
- OF H. Rice
- OF H. Heilmann
- C E. Phillips
- UT R. Fothergill
- P G. Uhle
- P E. Whitehill
- P V. Sorrell
- P O. Carroll
- RP J. Prudhomme
- RP U. Stoner

DET 1930 A
- M S. Harris
- 1B D. Alexander
- 2B C. Gehringer
- SS M. Koenig
- 3B M. McManus
- OF E. Funk
- OF R. Johnson
- OF J. Stone
- C R. Hayworth
- P G. Uhle
- P V. Sorrell
- P E. Whitehill
- P E. Hogsett
- P W. Hoyt
- RP C. Sullivan

DET 1931 A
- M S. Harris
- 1B D. Alexander
- 2B C. Gehringer
- SS W. Rogell
- 3B M. McManus
- OF R. Johnson
- OF J. Stone
- OF H. Walker
- C R. Hayworth
- UT M. Koenig
- UT J. Owen
- P E. Whitehill
- P V. Sorrell
- P G. Uhle
- P T. Bridges
- P A. Herring

DET 1932 A
- M S. Harris
- 1B H. Davis
- 2B C. Gehringer
- SS W. Rogell
- 3B H. Schuble
- OF J. Stone
- OF G. Walker
- OF W. Webb
- C R. Hayworth
- P E. Whitehill
- P V. Sorrell
- P J. Wyatt
- P T. Bridges
- P E. Hogsett

DET 1933 A
- M S. Harris
- M D. Baker
- 1B H. Greenberg
- 2B C. Gehringer
- SS W. Rogell
- 3B M. Owen
- OF J. Stone
- OF E. Fox
- OF G. Walker
- C R. Hayworth
- P F. Marberry
- P V. Sorrell
- P T. Bridges
- P C. Fischer
- P L. Rowe
- RP E. Hogsett
- RP A. Herring

DET 1934 A
- M G. Cochrane
- 1B H. Greenberg
- 2B C. Gehringer
- SS W. Rogell
- 3B M. Owen
- OF L. Goslin
- OF E. Fox
- OF J. White
- C G. Cochrane
- UT G. Walker
- P T. Bridges
- P L. Rowe
- P E. Auker
- P F. Marberry
- P V. Sorrell
- RP E. Hogsett

DET 1935 A
- M G. Cochrane
- 1B H. Greenberg
- 2B C. Gehringer
- SS W. Rogell
- 3B M. Owen
- OF L. Goslin
- OF E. Fox
- OF J. White
- C G. Cochrane
- UT G. Walker
- P L. Rowe
- P T. Bridges
- P A. Crowder
- P E. Auker
- P J. Sullivan

RP E. Hogsett

DET 1936 A
M G. Cochrane
1B J. Burns
2B C. Gehringer
SS W. Rogell
3B M. Owen
OF L. Goslin
OF A. Simmons
OF G. Walker
C R. Hayworth
P T. Bridges
P L. Rowe
P E. Auker
P V. Sorrell
P A. Lawson
RP C. Kimsey

DET 1937 A
M G. Cochrane
M D. Baker
M G. Cochrane
M D. Baker
M R. Perkins
1B H. Greenberg
2B C. Gehringer
SS W. Rogell
3B M. Owen
OF G. Walker
OF E. Fox
OF J. White
C P. York
P E. Auker
P T. Bridges
P A. Lawson
P J. Wade
P C. Poffenberger

DET 1938 A
M G. Cochrane
M D. Baker
1B H. Greenberg
2B C. Gehringer
SS W. Rogell
3B D. Ross
OF E. Fox
OF F. Walker
OF C. Morgan
C P. York
UT M. Christman
P L. Kennedy
P G. Gill
P E. Auker
P T. Bridges
P A. Lawson
RP G. Coffman
RP J. Wade

DET 1939 A
M D. Baker
1B H. Greenberg
2B C. Gehringer
SS F. Croucher
3B M. Higgins
OF W. McCosky
OF E. Fox
OF H. Averill
C G. Tebbetts
UT P. York
P L. Newsom
P T. Bridges
P L. Rowe
P P. Trout
P J. Benton
RP L. Thomas

DET 1940 A
M D. Baker
1B P. York
2B C. Gehringer
SS R. Bartell
3B M. Higgins
OF H. Greenberg
OF W. McCosky
OF E. Fox
C G. Tebbetts
UT B. Campbell
P L. Newsom
P T. Bridges
P L. Rowe
P J. Gorsica
P H. Newhouser
RP J. Benton
RP T. Seats
RP A. McKain

DET 1941 A
M D. Baker
1B P. York
2B C. Gehringer

SS F. Croucher
3B M. Higgins
OF B. Campbell
OF W. McCosky
OF R. Radcliff
C G. Tebbetts
UT G. Stainback
P L. Newsom
P H. Newhouser
P J. Gorsica
P J. Benton
P P. Trout
RP L. Thomas

DET 1942 A
M D. Baker
1B P. York
2B J. Bloodworth
SS W. Hitchcock
3B M. Higgins
OF W. McCosky
OF R. Cramer
OF R. Harris
C G. Tebbetts
P J. Benton
P P. Trout
P H. White
P H. Newhouser
P T. Bridges
RP R. Henshaw
RP J. Gorsica

DET 1943 A
M S. O'Neill
1B P. York
2B J. Bloodworth
SS R. Hoover
3B M. Higgins
OF R. Wakefield
OF R. Cramer
OF R. Harris
C P. Richards
P P. Trout
P V. Trucks
P H. Newhouser
P T. Bridges
P H. White
RP J. Gorsica
RP R. Henshaw

DET 1944 A
M S. O'Neill
1B P. York
2B E. Mayo
SS R. Hoover
3B M. Higgins
OF R. Cramer
OF J. Outlaw
OF R. Wakefield
C P. Richards
P P. Trout
P H. Newhouser
P J. Gentry
P F. Overmire
P J. Gorsica
RP W. Beck

DET 1945 A
M S. O'Neill
1B P. York
2B E. Mayo
SS J. Webb
3B R. Maier
OF R. Cullenbine
OF R. Cramer
OF J. Outlaw
C R. Swift
P H. Newhouser
P P. Trout
P J. Benton
P F. Overmire
P L. Mueller
RP W. Wilson
RP G. Caster

DET 1946 A
M S. O'Neill
1B H. Greenberg
2B J. Bloodworth
SS E. Lake
3B G. Kell
OF R. Wakefield
OF R. Cullenbine
OF W. Evers
C G. Tebbetts
P H. Newhouser
P P. Trout
P V. Trucks
P F. Hutchinson
P J. Benton

DET 1947 A
M S. O'Neill
1B R. Cullenbine
2B E. Mayo
SS E. Lake
3B G. Kell
OF W. Evers
OF P. Mullin
OF R. Wakefield
C R. Swift
UT V. Wertz
P H. Newhouser
P F. Hutchinson
P P. Trout
P V. Trucks
P F. Overmire
RP H. White
RP J. Gorsica

DET 1948 A
M S. O'Neill
1B G. Vico
2B E. Mayo
SS J. Lipon
3B G. Kell
OF W. Evers
OF P. Mullin
OF V. Wertz
C R. Swift
UT R. Wakefield
P H. Newhouser
P F. Hutchinson
P V. Trucks
P P. Trout
P A. Houtteman
RP F. Overmire
RP W. Pierce

DET 1949 A
M R. Rolfe
1B P. Campbell
2B C. Berry
SS J. Lipon
3B G. Kell
OF V. Wertz
OF W. Evers
OF J. Groth
C A. Robinson
UT D. Kolloway
UT E. Lake
UT P. Mullin
P H. Newhouser
P V. Trucks
P A. Houtteman
P T. Gray
P F. Hutchinson
RP P. Trout

DET 1950 A
M R. Rolfe
1B D. Kolloway
2B G. Priddy
SS J. Lipon
3B G. Kell
OF J. Groth
OF V. Wertz
OF W. Evers
C A. Robinson
P A. Houtteman
P F. Hutchinson
P H. Newhouser
P P. Trout
P T. Gray
RP H. White
RP P. Calvert

DET 1951 A
M R. Rolfe
1B R. Kryhoski
2B G. Priddy
SS J. Lipon
3B G. Kell
OF V. Wertz
OF J. Groth
OF W. Evers
C M. Ginsberg
UT P. Mullin
P T. Gray
P P. Trout
P F. Hutchinson
P V. Trucks
P R. Cain
RP H. Bearden
RP H. White

DET 1952 A
M R. Rolfe
M F. Hutchinson
1B W. Dropo
2B G. Priddy
SS C. Berry

3B F. Hatfield
OF J. Groth
OF V. Wertz
OF P. Mullin
C M. Ginsberg
P T. Gray
P A. Houtteman
P V. Trucks
P H. Newhouser
P W. Wight
RP H. White
RP R. Littlefield

DET 1953 A
M F. Hutchinson
1B W. Dropo
2B J. Pesky
SS H. Kuenn
3B R. Boone
OF R. Nieman
OF J. Delsing
OF D. Lund
C M. Batts
UT F. Hatfield
P W. Hoeft
P N. Garver
P T. Gray
P S. Gromek
P R. Branca
RP R. Marlowe
RP R. Herbert
RP D. Madison

DET 1954 A
M F. Hutchinson
1B W. Dropo
2B F. Bolling
SS H. Kuenn
3B R. Boone
OF W. Tuttle
OF A. Kaline
OF J. Delsing
C H. House
P S. Gromek
P N. Garver
P G. Zuverink
P W. Hoeft
P A. Aber
RP R. Marlowe
RP R. Herbert
RP R. Miller

DET 1955 A
M S. Harris
1B C. Torgeson
2B F. Hatfield
SS H. Kuenn
3B R. Boone
OF W. Tuttle
OF A. Kaline
OF J. Delsing
C H. House
UT J. Phillips
P F. Lary
P N. Garver
P W. Hoeft
P S. Gromek
RP W. Birrer
RP A. Aber
RP P. Foytack

DET 1956 A
M S. Harris
1B C. Torgeson
2B F. Bolling
SS H. Kuenn
3B R. Boone
OF A. Kaline
OF W. Tuttle
OF C. Maxwell
C H. House
P F. Lary
P P. Foytack
P W. Hoeft
P S. Gromek
P V. Trucks
RP D. Maas
RP A. Aber
RP W. Masterson

DET 1957 A
M J. Tighe
1B R. Boone
2B F. Bolling
SS H. Kuenn
3B R. Bertoia
OF A. Kaline
OF C. Maxwell
OF W. Tuttle
C H. House
P J. Bunning
P F. Lary

P D. Maas
P P. Foytack
P W. Hoeft
RP L. Sleater
RP H. Byrd

DET 1958 A
M J. Tighe
M H. Norman
1B B. Harris
2B F. Bolling
SS A. Martin
3B R. Bertoia
OF A. Kaline
OF H. Kuenn
OF C. Maxwell
C R. Wilson
P F. Lary
P P. Foytack
P J. Bunning
P W. Hoeft
P H. Moford
RP H. Aguirre
RP T. Morgan

DET 1959 A
M H. Norman
M J. Dykes
1B B. Harris
2B F. Bolling
SS E. Bridges
3B E. Yost
OF H. Kuenn
OF C. Maxwell
OF A. Kaline
C L. Berberet
P J. Bunning
P P. Foytack
P D. Mossi
P F. Lary
RP R. Narleski
RP T. Morgan
RP P. Burnside

DET 1960 A
M J. Dykes
M W. Hitchcock
M J. Gordon
1B N. Cash
2B F. Bolling
SS H. Fernandez
3B E. Yost
OF R. Colavito
OF A. Kaline
OF C. Maxwell
C L. Berberet
P F. Lary
P J. Bunning
P D. Mossi
P R. Bruce
P P. Burnside
RP H. Aguirre
RP P. Sisler
RP W. Fischer

DET 1961 A
M R. Scheffing
1B N. Cash
2B J. Wood
SS H. Fernandez
3B S. Boros
OF R. Colavito
OF W. Bruton
OF A. Kaline
C B. Brown
P F. Lary
P J. Bunning
P D. Mossi
P P. Foytack
P P. Regan
RP T. Fox
RP H. Aguirre

DET 1962 A
M R. Scheffing
1B N. Cash
2B J. Wood
SS H. Fernandez
3B S. Boros
OF R. Colavito
OF W. Bruton
OF A. Kaline
C B. Brown
UT R. McAuliffe
P J. Bunning
P H. Aguirre
P D. Mossi
P P. Regan
P P. Foytack
RP S. Jones
RP R. Kline

RP R. Nischwitz

DET 1963 A
M R. Scheffing
M C. Dressen
1B N. Cash
2B J. Wood
SS R. McAuliffe
3B J. Phillips
OF R. Colavito
OF A. Kaline
OF W. Bruton
C G. Triandos
UT W. Freehan
P J. Bunning
P H. Aguirre
P P. Regan
P M. Lolich
P D. Mossi
RP T. Fox
RP R. Anderson
RP T. Sturdivant

DET 1964 A
M C. Dressen
1B N. Cash
2B J. Lumpe
SS R. McAuliffe
3B D. Wert
OF A. Kaline
OF W. Brown
OF G. Thomas
C W. Freehan
UT W. Bruton
UT D. Demeter
P D. Wickersham
P M. Lolich
P H. Aguirre
P E. Rakow
P P. Regan
RP F. Gladding
RP L. Sherry
RP T. Fox

DET 1965 A
M R. Swift
M C. Dressen
1B N. Cash
2B J. Lumpe
SS R. McAuliffe
3B D. Wert
OF W. Horton
OF A. Kaline
OF D. Demeter
C W. Freehan
P M. Lolich
P D. McLain
P H. Aguirre
P D. Wickersham
P J. Sparma
RP L. Sherry
RP T. Fox
RP F. Gladding

DET 1966 A
M C. Dressen
M R. Swift
M F. Skaff
1B N. Cash
2B J. Lumpe
SS R. McAuliffe
3B D. Wert
OF W. Horton
OF A. Kaline
OF J. Northrup
C W. Freehan
UT J. Wood
P D. McLain
P M. Lolich
P R. Wilson
P D. Wickersham
P J. Podres
RP O. Pena
RP L. Sherry
RP F. Gladding

DET 1967 A
M E. Smith
1B N. Cash
2B R. McAuliffe
SS R. Oyler
3B D. Wert
OF J. Northrup
OF A. Kaline
OF M. Stanley
C W. Freehan
UT W. Horton
P R. Wilson
P D. McLain
P J. Sparma
P M. Lolich
RP D. Wickersham

RP F. Gladding
RP J. Hiller

DET 1968 A
M E. Smith
1B N. Cash
2B R. McAuliffe
SS R. Oyler
3B D. Wert
OF J. Northrup
OF W. Horton
OF M. Stanley
C W. Freehan
UT A. Kaline
P D. McLain
P R. Wilson
P M. Lolich
P J. Sparma
P J. Hiller
RP P. Dobson
RP D. Patterson

DET 1969 A
M E. Smith
1B N. Cash
2B R. McAuliffe
SS D. Tresh
3B D. Wert
OF J. Northrup
OF W. Horton
OF A. Kaline
C W. Freehan
UT M. Stanley
P D. McLain
P M. Lolich
P R. Wilson
P M. Kilkenny
RP P. Dobson
RP J. Hiller
RP T. Timmermann

DET 1970 A
M E. Smith
1B N. Cash
2B R. McAuliffe
SS C. Gutierrez
3B D. Wert
OF J. Northrup
OF M. Stanley
OF W. Horton
C W. Freehan
UT A. Kaline
UT E. Maddox
P M. Lolich
P J. Niekro
P L. Cain
P M. Kilkenny
P R. Wilson
RP J. Hiller
RP T. Timmermann
RP D. Patterson

DET 1971 A
M A. Martin
1B N. Cash
2B R. McAuliffe
SS E. Brinkman
3B A. Rodriguez
OF M. Stanley
OF A. Kaline
OF W. Horton
C W. Freehan
UT J. Northrup
P M. Lolich
P J. Coleman
P L. Cain
P J. Niekro
RP F. Scherman
RP W. Chance
RP M. Kilkenny

DET 1972 A
M A. Martin
1B N. Cash
2B R. McAuliffe
SS E. Brinkman
3B A. Rodriguez
OF M. Stanley
OF J. Northrup
OF W. Horton
C W. Freehan
UT W. Brown
UT A. Kaline
P M. Lolich
P J. Coleman
P T. Timmermann
P W. Fryman
RP C. Seelbach
RP F. Scherman
RP J. Niekro

DET 1973 A

M	A. Martin
M	J. Schultz
1B	N. Cash
2B	R. McAuliffe
SS	E. Brinkman
3B	A. Rodriguez
OF	M. Stanley
OF	J. Northrup
OF	W. Horton
C	W. Freehan
DH	W. Brown
P	M. Lolich
P	J. Coleman
P	J. Perry
P	W. Fryman
RP	J. Hiller
RP	F. Scherman
RP	L. LaGrow

DET 1974 A

M	R. Houk
1B	W. Freehan
2B	G. Sutherland
SS	E. Brinkman
3B	A. Rodriguez
OF	J. Northrup
OF	M. Stanley
OF	W. Horton
C	G. Moses
DH	A. Kaline
P	M. Lolich
P	J. Coleman
P	L. LaGrow
P	W. Fryman
RP	J. Hiller
RP	J. Ray

DET 1975 A

M	R. Houk
1B	L. Pierce
2B	G. Sutherland
SS	T. Veryzer
3B	A. Rodriguez
OF	R. LeFlore
OF	L. Roberts
OF	B. Oglivie
C	W. Freehan
DH	W. Horton
UT	D. Meyer
P	M. Lolich
P	J. Coleman
P	V. Ruhle
P	L. LaGrow
P	R. Bare
RP	J. Hiller

DET 1976 A

M	R. Houk
1B	J. Thompson
2B	P. Garcia
SS	T. Veryzer
3B	A. Rodriguez
OF	R. LeFlore
OF	D. Staub
OF	A. Johnson
C	B. Kimm
DH	W. Horton
UT	D. Meyer
UT	B. Oglivie
P	D. Roberts
P	M. Fidrych
P	V. Ruhle
P	R. Bare
P	J. Crawford
RP	J. Hiller
RP	S. Grilli

DET 1977 A

M	R. Houk
1B	J. Thompson
2B	R. Fuentes
SS	T. Veryzer
3B	A. Rodriguez
OF	R. LeFlore
OF	S. Kemp
OF	B. Oglivie
C	M. May
DH	D. Staub
P	D. Rozema
P	F. Arroyo
P	R. Sykes
P	D. Roberts
P	J. Crawford
RP	J. Hiller
RP	S. Foucault
RP	S. Grilli

DET 1978 A

M	R. Houk
1B	J. Thompson
2B	L. Whitaker
SS	A. Trammell
3B	A. Rodriguez
OF	S. Kemp
OF	R. LeFlore
OF	T. Corcoran
C	M. May
DH	D. Staub
P	J. Slaton
P	M. Wilcox
P	D. Rozema
P	J. Billingham
P	K. Young
RP	J. Hiller

DET 1979 A

M	J. Moss
M	R. Tracewski
M	G. Anderson
1B	J. Thompson
2B	L. Whitaker
SS	A. Trammell
3B	A. Rodriguez
OF	S. Kemp
OF	J. Morales
OF	R. LeFlore
C	L. Parrish
DH	D. Staub
P	J. Morris
P	M. Wilcox
P	J. Billingham
P	P. Underwood
P	D. Petry
RP	A. Lopez
RP	J. Hiller
RP	D. Tobik

DET 1980 A

M	G. Anderson
1B	R. Hebner
2B	L. Whitaker
SS	A. Trammell
3B	T. Brookens
OF	R. Peters
OF	A. Cowens
OF	S. Kemp
C	L. Parrish
DH	J. Summers
UT	J. Wockenfuss
P	J. Morris
P	M. Wilcox
P	D. Schatzeder
P	D. Petry
P	D. Rozema
RP	A. Lopez
RP	P. Underwood

DET 1981 A

M	G. Anderson
1B	R. Hebner
2B	L. Whitaker
SS	A. Trammell
3B	T. Brookens
OF	S. Kemp
OF	A. Cowens
OF	K. Gibson
C	L. Parrish
DH	J. Wockenfuss
UT	L. Jones
P	J. Morris
P	M. Wilcox
P	D. Petry
P	D. Rozema
P	D. Schatzeder
RP	A. Lopez
RP	D. Tobik
RP	K. Saucier

DET 1982 A

M	G. Anderson
1B	E. Cabell
2B	L. Whitaker
SS	A. Trammell
3B	T. Brookens
OF	L. Herndon
OF	C. Lemon
OF	G. Wilson
C	L. Parrish
DH	M. Ivie
P	J. Morris
P	D. Petry
P	M. Wilcox
P	G. Ujdur
P	P. Underwood
RP	D. Tobik
RP	D. Rucker
RP	E. Sosa

DET 1983 A

M	G. Anderson
1B	E. Cabell
2B	L. Whitaker
SS	A. Trammell
3B	T. Brookens
OF	C. Lemon
OF	G. Wilson
OF	L. Herndon
C	L. Parrish
DH	K. Gibson
UT	R. Leach
P	J. Morris
P	D. Petry
P	M. Wilcox
P	J. Berenguer
P	D. Rozema
RP	A. Lopez
RP	H. Bailey
RP	C. Bair

DET 1984 A

M	G. Anderson
1B	D. Bergman
2B	L. Whitaker
SS	A. Trammell
3B	H. Johnson
OF	C. Lemon
OF	K. Gibson
OF	L. Herndon
C	L. Parrish
DH	D. Evans
UT	T. Brookens
UT	B. Garbey
P	J. Morris
P	D. Petry
P	M. Wilcox
P	J. Berenguer
P	D. Rozema
RP	G. Hernandez
RP	A. Lopez
RP	C. Bair

DET 1985 A

M	G. Anderson
1B	D. Evans
2B	L. Whitaker
SS	A. Trammell
3B	T. Brookens
OF	C. Lemon
OF	K. Gibson
OF	L. Herndon
C	L. Parrish
DH	J. Grubb
P	J. Morris
P	D. Petry
P	C. Terrell
P	F. Tanana
RP	G. Hernandez
RP	A. Lopez
RP	W. Scherrer

DET 1986 A

M	G. Anderson
1B	D. Evans
2B	L. Whitaker
SS	A. Trammell
3B	D. Coles
OF	C. Lemon
OF	K. Gibson
OF	D. Collins
C	L. Parrish
DH	J. Grubb
UT	T. Brookens
UT	L. Herndon
UT	P. Sheridan
P	J. Morris
P	C. Terrell
P	F. Tanana
P	E. King
P	R. O'Neal
RP	G. Hernandez
RP	W. Campbell
RP	M. Thurmond

DET 1987 A

M	G. Anderson
1B	D. Evans
2B	L. Whitaker
SS	A. Trammell
3B	T. Brookens
OF	L. Herndon
OF	C. Lemon
OF	P. Sheridan
OF	K. Gibson
C	M. Nokes
DH	B. Madlock
P	J. Morris
P	C. Terrell
P	F. Tanana
P	D. Petry
P	J. Robinson
RP	E. King
RP	M. Henneman
RP	M. Thurmond

DET 1988 A

M	G. Anderson
1B	C. Knight
2B	L. Whitaker
SS	A. Trammell
3B	T. Brookens
OF	C. Lemon
OF	G. Pettis
OF	P. Sheridan
C	M. Nokes
DH	D. Evans
UT	D. Bergman
UT	L. Salazar
P	J. Morris
P	D. Alexander
P	C. Terrell
P	F. Tanana
P	J. Robinson
RP	P. Gibson
RP	M. Henneman
RP	G. Hernandez

DET 1989 A

M	G. Anderson
1B	D. Bergman
2B	L. Whitaker
SS	A. Trammell
3B	R. Schu
OF	G. Pettis
OF	C. Lemon
OF	K. Williams
C	M. Heath
DH	B. Moreland
UT	F. Lynn
UT	G. Ward
P	F. Tanana
P	D. Alexander
P	J. Morris
RP	P. Gibson
RP	M. Henneman
RP	F. Williams

DET 1990 A

M	G. Anderson
1B	C. Fielder
2B	L. Whitaker
SS	A. Trammell
3B	K. Phillips
OF	L. Moseby
OF	C. Lemon
OF	G. Ward
C	M. Heath
DH	D. Bergman
UT	L. Sheets
P	J. Morris
P	F. Tanana
P	D. Petry
P	J. Robinson
RP	P. Gibson
RP	M. Henneman
RP	J. Gleaton

Elizabeth

RES n 1873
RES 1873 n

M	J. Benjamin
1B	M. Campbell
2B	B. Laughlin
SS	F. Wordsworth
3B	Nevins
OF	H. Austin
OF	A. Allison
OF	E. Booth
C	D. Allison
UT	F. Fleet
P	H. Campbell

Fort Wayne

KEK n 1871
KEK 1871 n

M	W. Lennon
M	J. Deane
1B	J. Foran
2B	T. Carey
SS	W. Goldsmith
3B	F. Selman
OF	W. Kelly
OF	S. Armstrong
OF	E. Mincher
C	W. Lennon
P	R. Mathews

Hartford

HAR n 1874-1875
HAR N 1876-1877

HAR 1874 n

M	L. Pike
1B	E. Mills
2B	R. Addy
SS	T. Barlow
3B	W. Boyd
OF	J. Tipper
OF	L. Pike
OF	W. Barnie
C	W. Hastings
P	W. Fisher
P	W. Stearns

HAR 1875 n

M	R. Ferguson
1B	E. Mills
2B	J. Burdock
SS	T. Carey
3B	R. Ferguson
OF	T. York
OF	J. Remsen
OF	A. Allison
C	D. Allison
UT	W. Harbidge
P	W. Cummings
P	T. Bond

HAR 1876 N

M	R. Ferguson
1B	E. Mills
2B	J. Burdock
SS	T. Carey
3B	R. Ferguson
OF	J. Remsen
OF	T. York
OF	R. Higham
C	D. Allison
P	T. Bond
P	W. Cummings

HAR 1877 N

M	R. Ferguson
1B	J. Start
2B	J. Burdock
SS	T. Carey
3B	R. Ferguson
OF	J. Cassidy
OF	T. York
OF	J. Holdsworth
C	W. Harbidge
P	F. Larkin

Houston

HOU N 1962-1990

HOU 1962 N

M	H. Craft
1B	N. Larker
2B	J. Amalfitano
SS	R. Lillis
3B	R. Aspromonte
OF	R. Mejias
OF	C. Warwick
OF	A. Spangler
C	H. Smith
UT	J. Pendleton
P	R. Farrell
P	K. Johnson
P	R. Bruce
P	J. Golden
P	H. Woodeshick
RP	B. Tiefenauer
RP	D. McMahon
RP	R. Kemmerer

HOU 1963 N

M	H. Craft
1B	D. Staub
2B	E. Fazio
SS	R. Lillis
3B	R. Aspromonte
OF	C. Warwick
OF	H. Goss
OF	A. Spangler
C	J. Bateman
UT	J. Runnels
UT	J. Temple
P	K. Johnson
P	R. Farrell
P	D. Nottebart
P	R. Bruce
P	H. Brown

RP	H. Woodeshick
RP	D. McMahon
RP	J. Umbricht

HOU 1964 N

M	H. Craft
M	C. Harris
1B	W. Bond
2B	J. Fox
SS	E. Kasko
3B	R. Aspromonte
OF	A. Spangler
OF	A. Gaines
OF	J. White
C	G. Grote
UT	R. Lillis
P	K. Johnson
P	R. Bruce
P	R. Farrell
P	D. Nottebart
P	H. Brown
RP	J. Owens
RP	J. Raymond
RP	H. Woodeshick

HOU 1965 N

M	C. Harris
1B	W. Bond
2B	J. Morgan
SS	R. Lillis
3B	R. Aspromonte
OF	J. Wynn
OF	D. Staub
OF	A. Maye
C	R. Brand
UT	A. Gaines
P	R. Bruce
P	R. Farrell
P	D. Nottebart
P	L. Dierker
P	D. Giusti
RP	J. Raymond
RP	J. Owens
RP	R. Taylor

HOU 1966 N

M	G. Hatton
1B	C. Harrison
2B	J. Morgan
SS	R. Jackson
3B	R. Aspromonte
OF	D. Staub
OF	J. Wynn
OF	A. Maye
C	J. Bateman
UT	D. Nicholson
P	M. Cuellar
P	D. Giusti
P	L. Dierker
P	R. Farrell
P	R. Bruce
RP	J. Raymond
RP	R. Taylor
RP	J. Owens

HOU 1967 N

M	G. Hatton
1B	E. Mathews
2B	J. Morgan
SS	R. Jackson
3B	R. Aspromonte
OF	J. Wynn
OF	D. Staub
OF	R. Davis
C	J. Bateman
P	M. Cuellar
P	D. Giusti
P	D. Wilson
P	R. Belinsky
P	L. Dierker
RP	A. Latman
RP	C. Sembera
RP	D. Eilers

HOU 1968 N

M	G. Hatton
M	H. Walker
1B	D. Staub
2B	D. Menke
SS	H. Torres
3B	D. Rader
OF	J. Wynn
OF	N. Miller
OF	R. Davis
C	J. Bateman
UT	R. Aspromonte
P	D. Giusti
P	L. Dierker
P	D. Lemaster
P	D. Wilson

P	M. Cuellar
RP	J. Buzhardt
RP	J. Ray
RP	T. Dukes

HOU 1969 N

M	H. Walker
1B	C. Blefary
2B	J. Morgan
SS	D. Menke
3B	D. Rader
OF	J. Wynn
OF	N. Miller
OF	J. Alou
C	J. Edwards
P	L. Dierker
P	D. Lemaster
P	D. Wilson
P	T. Griffin
RP	J. Ray
RP	J. Billingham
RP	F. Gladding

HOU 1970 N

M	H. Walker
1B	R. Watson
2B	J. Morgan
SS	D. Menke
3B	D. Rader
OF	J. Wynn
OF	J. Alou
OF	C. Cedeno
C	J. Edwards
P	L. Dierker
P	J. Billingham
P	D. Wilson
P	D. Lemaster
P	T. Griffin
RP	J. Ray
RP	R. Cook
RP	J. Bouton

HOU 1971 N

M	H. Walker
1B	D. Menke
2B	J. Morgan
SS	R. Metzger
3B	D. Rader
OF	C. Cedeno
OF	J. Wynn
OF	J. Alou
C	J. Edwards
UT	R. Watson
P	D. Wilson
P	J. Billingham
P	K. Forsch
P	L. Dierker
P	W. Blasingame
RP	J. Ray
RP	G. Culver
RP	D. Lemaster

HOU 1972 N

M	H. Walker
M	F. Parker
M	L. Durocher
1B	L. May
2B	T. Helms
SS	R. Metzger
3B	D. Rader
OF	J. Wynn
OF	R. Watson
OF	C. Cedeno
C	J. Edwards
P	D. Wilson
P	L. Dierker
P	D. Roberts
P	J. Reuss
P	K. Forsch
RP	G. Culver
RP	T. Griffin
RP	J. Ray

HOU 1973 N

M	L. Durocher
1B	L. May
2B	T. Helms
SS	R. Metzger
3B	D. Rader
OF	R. Watson
OF	C. Cedeno
OF	J. Wynn
C	A. Jutze
P	J. Reuss
P	D. Roberts
P	D. Wilson
P	K. Forsch
P	T. Griffin
RP	J. Crawford
RP	J. Ray
RP	J. York

HOU 1974 N
M P. Gomez
1B L. May
2B T. Helms
SS R. Metzger
3B D. Rader
OF C. Cedeno
OF G. Gross
OF R. Watson
C M. May
UT R. Gallagher
UT L. Milbourne
P L. Dierker
P T. Griffin
P D. Wilson
P D. Roberts
P C. Osteen
RP K. Forsch
RP M. Cosgrove
RP F. Scherman

HOU 1975 N
M P. Gomez
M W. Virdon
1B R. Watson
2B R. Andrews
SS R. Metzger
3B D. Rader
OF C. Cedeno
OF G. Gross
OF W. Howard
C M. May
UT E. Cabell
UT J. Cruz
UT C. Johnson
P L. Dierker
P J. Richard
P D. Roberts
P D. Konieczny
P K. Forsch
RP J. Niekro
RP J. Crawford
RP W. Granger

HOU 1976 N
M W. Virdon
1B R. Watson
2B R. Andrews
SS R. Metzger
3B E. Cabell
OF C. Cedeno
OF J. Cruz
OF G. Gross
C E. Herrmann
UT C. Johnson
P J. Richard
P L. Dierker
P J. Andujar
P J. Niekro
RP K. Forsch
RP E. Pentz
RP G. Rondon

HOU 1977 N
M W. Virdon
1B R. Watson
2B A. Howe
SS R. Metzger
3B E. Cabell
OF J. Cruz
OF C. Cedeno
OF W. Howard
C J. Ferguson
UT J. Gonzalez
P J. Richard
P M. Lemongello
P J. Niekro
P J. Andujar
P F. Bannister
RP J. Sambito
RP E. Pentz
RP K. Forsch

HOU 1978 N
M W. Virdon
1B R. Watson
2B A. Howe
SS J. Sexton
3B E. Cabell
OF J. Cruz
OF T. Puhl
OF D. Walling
C L. Pujols
UT D. Bergman
P J. Richard
P M. Lemongello
P J. Niekro
P T. Dixon
P J. Andujar
RP K. Forsch
RP J. Sambito

HOU 1979 N
M W. Virdon
1B C. Cedeno
2B R. Landestoy
SS G. Reynolds
3B E. Cabell
OF J. Cruz
OF T. Puhl
OF J. Leonard
C A. Ashby
UT A. Howe
P J. Richard
P J. Niekro
P J. Andujar
P K. Forsch
P R. Williams
RP J. Sambito
RP R. Niemann

HOU 1980 N
M W. Virdon
1B A. Howe
2B J. Morgan
SS G. Reynolds
3B E. Cabell
OF J. Cruz
OF C. Cedeno
OF T. Puhl
C A. Ashby
UT R. Landestoy
UT D. Walling
P J. Niekro
P L. Ryan
P K. Forsch
P V. Ruhle
P J. Andujar
RP D. Smith
RP J. Sambito
RP F. LaCorte

HOU 1981 N
M W. Virdon
1B C. Cedeno
2B J. Pittman
SS G. Reynolds
3B A. Howe
OF J. Cruz
OF T. Puhl
OF A. Scott
C A. Ashby
P J. Niekro
P D. Sutton
P R. Knepper
P L. Ryan
P V. Ruhle
RP D. Smith
RP J. Sambito
RP F. LaCorte

HOU 1982 N
M W. Virdon
M R. Lillis
1B C. Knight
2B P. Garner
SS R. Thon
3B A. Howe
OF J. Cruz
OF T. Puhl
OF A. Scott
C A. Ashby
P J. Niekro
P L. Ryan
P D. Sutton
P R. Knepper
P V. Ruhle
RP M. LaCoss
RP F. LaCorte
RP D. Smith

HOU 1983 N
M R. Lillis
1B C. Knight
2B W. Doran
SS R. Thon
3B P. Garner
OF J. Cruz
OF T. Puhl
OF O. Moreno
C A. Ashby
UT D. Walling
P J. Niekro
P L. Ryan
P R. Knepper
P L. Ryan
P M. Scott
P M. LaCoss
RP V. Ruhle
RP W. Dawley
RP D. Smith

HOU 1984 N
M R. Lillis
1B E. Cabell
2B W. Doran
SS G. Reynolds
3B P. Garner
OF J. Cruz
OF J. Mumphrey
OF T. Puhl
C J. Bailey
UT K. Bass
P J. Niekro
P R. Knepper
P L. Ryan
P M. Scott
P M. LaCoss
RP W. Dawley
RP V. Ruhle
RP D. Smith

HOU 1985 N
M R. Lillis
1B G. Davis
2B W. Doran
SS G. Reynolds
3B P. Garner
OF K. Bass
OF J. Cruz
OF J. Mumphrey
C J. Bailey
UT D. Walling
P R. Knepper
P L. Ryan
P M. Scott
P J. Niekro
RP W. Dawley
RP D. Smith
RP F. DiPino

HOU 1986 N
M H. Lanier
1B G. Davis
2B W. Doran
SS R. Thon
3B D. Walling
OF K. Bass
OF J. Cruz
OF W. Hatcher
C A. Ashby
UT P. Garner
UT G. Reynolds
P M. Scott
P R. Knepper
P L. Ryan
P J. Deshaies
RP C. Kerfeld
RP A. Lopez
RP L. Andersen

HOU 1987 N
M H. Lanier
1B G. Davis
2B W. Doran
SS G. Reynolds
3B D. Walling
OF K. Bass
OF W. Hatcher
OF J. Cruz
C A. Ashby
P M. Scott
P L. Ryan
P D. Darwin
P R. Knepper
P J. Deshaies
RP L. Andersen
RP D. Smith
RP D. Meads

HOU 1988 N
M H. Lanier
1B G. Davis
2B W. Doran
SS R. Ramirez
3B D. Bell
OF K. Bass
OF G. Young
OF W. Hatcher
C A. Trevino
UT T. Puhl
P L. Ryan
P M. Scott
P J. Deshaies
P D. Darwin
P R. Knepper
RP J. Agosto
RP L. Andersen
RP D. Smith

HOU 1989 N
M A. Howe
1B G. Davis
2B W. Doran
SS R. Ramirez
3B K. Caminiti
OF G. Young
OF W. Hatcher
OF T. Puhl
C C. Biggio
UT G. Reynolds
P M. Scott
P J. Deshaies
P J. Clancy
P R. Knepper
P M. Portugal
RP D. Darwin
RP R. Forsch
RP L. Andersen

HOU 1990 N
M A. Howe
1B G. Davis
2B W. Doran
SS R. Ramirez
3B K. Caminiti
OF G. Wilson
OF E. Yelding
OF F. Stubbs
C C. Biggio
UT C. Candaele
P J. Deshaies
P M. Scott
P M. Portugal
P W. Gullickson
P D. Darwin
RP J. Agosto
RP J. Clancy
RP L. Andersen

Indianapolis

IND N 1878
IND a 1884
IND N 1887-1889
IND F 1914

IND 1878 N
M J. Clapp
1B A. Croft
2B J. Quest
SS F. Warner
3B E. Williamson
OF G. Shaffer
OF R. McKelvy
OF J. Clapp
C F. Flint
P E. Nolan
P J. McCormick
P T. Healey

IND 1884 a
M J. Gifford
M W. Watkins
1B J. Kerins
2B E. Merrill
SS M. Phillips
3B P. Callahan
OF J. Peltz
OF J. Weihe
OF J. Morrison
C J. Keenan
P L. McKeon
P R. Barr
P J. Aydelott
P A. McCauley

IND 1887 N
M G. Burnham
M F. Thomas
M H. Fogel
1B O. Schomberg
2B C. Bassett
SS J. Glasscock
3B J. Denny
OF J. Seery
OF J. McGeachey
OF J. Cahill
C G. Myers
P J. Healy
P H. Boyle
P L. Shreve

IND 1888 N
M H. Spence
1B T. Esterbrook
2B C. Bassett
SS J. Glasscock
3B J. Denny
OF J. Seery
OF P. Hines
OF J. McGeachey
C R. Buckley
P H. Boyle
P J. Healy
P L. Shreve
P W. Burdick

IND 1889 N
M F. Bancroft
M J. Glasscock
1B P. Hines
2B C. Bassett
SS J. Glasscock
3B J. Denny
OF J. McGeachey
OF J. Seery
OF M. Sullivan
C R. Buckley
P H. Boyle
P G. Getzien
P A. Rusie

IND 1914 F
M W. Phillips
1B C. Carr
2B F. LaPorte
SS J. Esmond
3B W. McKechnie
OF B. Kauff
OF A. Campbell
OF A. Scheer
C W. Rariden
P F. Falkenberg
P E. Moseley
P G. Kaiserling
P G. Mullin
P H. Billiard

Kansas City

KC U 1884
KC N 1886
KC a 1888-1889
KC F 1914-1915
KC A 1955-1967
KC A 1969-1990

KC 1884 U
M H. Wheeler
M M. Porter
M T. Sullivan
1B J. Sweeney
2B C. Berry
SS C. Cross
3B P. Sullivan
OF F. Shaffer
OF F. Wyman
OF B. McLaughlin
C C. Baldwin
P E. Hickman

KC 1886 N
M D. Rowe
1B W. McQuery
2B J. Myers
SS C. Bassett
3B J. Donnelly
OF J. Lillie
OF P. Radford
OF D. Rowe
C C. Briody
P G. Weidman
P J. Whitney

KC 1888 a
M D. Rowe
M S. Barkley
M W. Watkins
1B W. Phillips
2B S. Barkley
SS H. Easterday
3B J. Davis
OF J. McTamany
OF J. Cline
OF W. Hamilton
C J. Donahue
P H. Porter
P T. Sullivan
P W. Fagan
P F. Hoffman
P S. Toole

KC 1889 a
M W. Watkins
1B D. Stearns
2B S. Barkley
SS H. Long
3B J. Davis
OF W. Hamilton
OF J. Burns
OF J. Manning
C C. Hoover
P P. Swartzel
P J. Conway
P S. Sowders
P J. McCarty
P T. Sullivan

KC 1914 F
M G. Stovall
1B G. Stovall
2B W. Kenworthy
SS C. Goodwin
3B D. Perring
OF C. Chadbourne
OF E. Gilmore
OF A. Kruger
C T. Easterly
P E. Packard
P N. Cullop
P D. Stone
P B. Harris
P E. Henning

KC 1915 F
M G. Stovall
1B G. Stovall
2B W. Kenworthy
SS J. Rawlings
3B D. Perring
OF C. Chadbourne
OF A. Shaw
OF E. Gilmore
C T. Easterly
P N. Cullop
P E. Packard
P G. Johnson
P M. Main
P E. Henning

KC 1955 A
M L. Boudreau
1B V. Power
2B J. Finigan
SS J. DeMaestri
3B H. Lopez
OF G. Zernial
OF H. Simpson
OF W. Wilson
C J. Astroth
UT W. Renna
UT E. Slaughter
UT E. Valo
P A. Ditmar
P A. Kellner
P R. Shantz
P A. Ceccarelli
P A. Portocarrero
RP T. Gorman
RP W. Harrington

KC 1956 A
M L. Boudreau
1B V. Power
2B J. Finigan
SS J. DeMaestri
3B H. Lopez
OF H. Simpson
OF J. Groth
OF L. Skizas
C C. Thompson
UT G. Zernial
P A. Ditmar
P T. Gorman
P W. Burnette
P L. Kretlow
P W. Herriage
RP J. Crimian
RP R. Shantz
RP J. McMahan

KC 1957 A
M L. Boudreau
M H. Craft
1B V. Power
2B G. Hunter
SS J. DeMaestri
3B H. Lopez
OF G. Zernial
OF W. Held
OF R. Cerv
C H. Smith
UT L. Skizas
P N. Garver
P T. Morgan
P A. Kellner
P R. Terry
P J. Urban
RP V. Trucks
RP W. Burnette
RP M. McDermott

KC 1958 A
M H. Craft
1B V. Power
2B M. Baxes
SS J. DeMaestri
3B H. Lopez
OF W. Tuttle
OF R. Cerv
OF R. Maris
C H. Chiti
UT R. Martyn
UT H. Smith
P R. Terry
P N. Garver
P R. Herbert
P J. Urban
P R. Grim
RP T. Gorman
RP R. Tomanek
RP L. Daley

KC 1959 A
M H. Craft
1B K. Hadley
2B W. Terwilliger
SS J. DeMaestri
3B R. Williams
OF W. Tuttle
OF R. Cerv
OF R. Maris
C H. House
UT J. Lumpe
UT H. Smith
P L. Daley
P N. Garver
P R. Herbert
P J. Kucks
P R. Grim
RP W. Coleman
RP T. Sturdivant
RP M. Dickson

KC 1960 A
M R. Elliott
1B M. Throneberry
2B J. Lumpe
SS K. Hamlin
3B A. Carey
OF W. Tuttle
OF R. Snyder
OF N. Siebern
C P. Daley
UT H. Bauer
UT R. Williams
P R. Herbert
P L. Daley
P R. Hall
P N. Garver
P J. Kucks
P K. Johnson
RP M. Kutyna

KC 1961 A
M J. Gordon
M H. Bauer
1B N. Siebern
2B J. Lumpe
SS R. Howser
3B A. Causey
OF L. Posada
OF R. Del Greco
OF J. Hankins
C H. Sullivan
P J. Archer
P N. Bass
P J. Walker
P R. Shaw
P J. Nuxhall
RP E. Rakow
RP W. Kunkel
RP A. Ditmar

KC 1962 A
M H. Bauer
1B N. Siebern
2B J. Lumpe
SS R. Howser
3B E. Charles
OF G. Cimoli
OF R. Del Greco
OF M. Jimenez
C H. Sullivan
UT J. Causey
UT J. Tartabull
P E. Rakow
P D. Pfister
P J. Walker
P W. Fischer
P D. Segui
RP J. Wyatt
RP D. McDevitt

KC 1963 A
M E. Lopat
1B N. Siebern
2B J. Lumpe
SS J. Causey

3B E. Charles
OF G. Cimoli
OF R. Del Greco
OF J. Tartabull
C H. Edwards
UT C. Essegian
P D. Wickersham
P O. Pena
P E. Rakow
P M. Drabowsky
P D. Segui
RP E. Bowsfield
RP W. Fischer
RP J. Wyatt

KC 1964 A

M E. Lopat
M F. McGaha
1B J. Gentile
2B R. Green
SS J. Causey
3B E. Charles
OF R. Colavito
OF N. Mathews
OF J. Tartabull
C H. Edwards
UT G. Alusik
P O. Pena
P D. Segui
P J. O'Donoghue
P M. Drabowsky
RP J. Wyatt
RP E. Bowsfield
RP W. Stock

KC 1965 A

M F. McGaha
M H. Sullivan
1B K. Harrelson
2B R. Green
SS D. Campaneris
3B E. Charles
OF N. Hershberger
OF J. Landis
OF T. Reynolds
C W. Bryan
UT J. Causey
P F. Talbot
P R. Sheldon
P J. O'Donoghue
P D. Segui
P J. Hunter
RP W. Stock
RP J. Wyatt
RP J. Dickson

KC 1966 A

M A. Dark
1B K. Harrelson
2B R. Green
SS D. Campaneris
3B E. Charles
OF N. Hershberger
OF L. Stahl
OF J. Nossek
C P. Roof
UT D. Cater
UT R. Repoz
P L. Krausse
P J. Hunter
P J. Nash
P P. Lindblad
RP J. Aker
RP K. Sanders

KC 1967 A

M A. Dark
M L. Appling
1B R. Webster
2B J. Donaldson
SS D. Campaneris
3B R. Green
OF N. Hershberger
OF R. Monday
OF J. Gosger
C P. Roof
UT D. Cater
P J. Hunter
P J. Nash
P C. Dobson
P L. Krausse
P J. Odom
RP P. Lindblad
RP T. Pierce
RP J. Aker

KC 1969 A

M J. Gordon
1B M. Fiore
2B K. Adair
SS J. Hernandez
3B J. Foy

OF L. Piniella
OF H. Kelly
OF R. Oliver
C E. Rodriguez
UT E. Kirkpatrick
P W. Bunker
P R. Drago
P W. Butler
P R. Nelson
P J. Rooker
RP M. Drabowsky
RP T. Burgmeier
RP D. Wickersham

KC 1970 A

M C. Metro
M R. Lemon
1B R. Oliver
2B O. Rojas
SS J. Hernandez
3B P. Schaal
OF A. Otis
OF L. Piniella
OF H. Kelly
C E. Kirkpatrick
P R. Drago
P R. Johnson
P J. Rooker
P W. Butler
P D. Morehead
RP A. Fitzmorris
RP T. Burgmeier
RP T. Abernathy

KC 1971 A

M R. Lemon
1B G. Hopkins
2B O. Rojas
SS F. Patek
3B P. Schaal
OF A. Otis
OF L. Piniella
OF J. Keough
C J. May
UT E. Kirkpatrick
UT R. Oliver
P R. Drago
P M. Hedlund
P P. Splittorff
P J. Dal Canton
P A. Fitzmorris
RP J. York
RP T. Burgmeier
RP T. Abernathy

KC 1972 A

M R. Lemon
1B J. Mayberry
2B O. Rojas
SS F. Patek
3B P. Schaal
OF L. Piniella
OF A. Otis
OF R. Scheinblum
C E. Kirkpatrick
UT S. Hovley
P R. Drago
P P. Splittorff
P R. Nelson
P J. Dal Canton
P M. Hedlund
RP A. Fitzmorris
RP T. Abernathy
RP T. Burgmeier

KC 1973 A

M J. McKeon
1B J. Mayberry
2B O. Rojas
SS F. Patek
3B P. Schaal
OF A. Otis
OF L. Piniella
OF E. Kirkpatrick
C F. Healy
DH H. McRae
UT K. Bevacqua
UT S. Hovley
P P. Splittorff
P S. Busby
P R. Drago
P H. Garber
P J. Dal Canton
RP J. Bird
RP S. Mingori

KC 1974 A

M J. McKeon
1B J. Mayberry
2B O. Rojas
SS F. Patek
3B G. Brett

OF A. Otis
OF J. Wohlford
OF V. Pinson
C F. Healy
DH H. McRae
UT A. Cowens
UT F. White
P S. Busby
P P. Splittorff
P A. Fitzmorris
P J. Dal Canton
P M. Pattin
RP L. McDaniel
RP J. Bird
RP S. Mingori

KC 1975 A

M J. McKeon
M D. Herzog
1B J. Mayberry
2B O. Rojas
SS F. Patek
3B G. Brett
OF A. Otis
OF H. McRae
OF A. Cowens
C J. Martinez
DH H. Killebrew
UT V. Pinson
UT F. White
UT J. Wohlford
P S. Busby
P A. Fitzmorris
P D. Leonard
P M. Pattin
P P. Splittorff
RP J. Bird
RP L. McDaniel
RP S. Mingori

KC 1976 A

M D. Herzog
1B J. Mayberry
2B F. White
SS F. Patek
3B G. Brett
OF A. Otis
OF A. Cowens
OF T. Poquette
C J. Martinez
DH H. McRae
UT J. Wohlford
P D. Leonard
P A. Fitzmorris
P J. Bird
P P. Splittorff
P M. Pattin
RP M. Littell
RP S. Mingori

KC 1977 A

M D. Herzog
1B J. Mayberry
2B F. White
SS F. Patek
3B G. Brett
OF A. Cowens
OF A. Otis
OF T. Poquette
C D. Porter
DH H. McRae
UT J. Zdeb
P D. Leonard
P J. Colborn
P P. Splittorff
P A. Hassler
P M. Pattin
RP J. Bird
RP L. Gura
RP M. Littell

KC 1978 A

M D. Herzog
1B R. LaCock
2B F. White
SS F. Patek
3B G. Brett
OF A. Otis
OF A. Cowens
OF W. Wilson
C D. Porter
DH H. McRae
UT C. Hurdle
P D. Leonard
P P. Splittorff
P L. Gura
P R. Gale
RP J. Bird
RP M. Pattin
RP A. Hrabosky

KC 1979 A

M D. Herzog
1B R. LaCock
2B F. White
SS F. Patek
3B G. Brett
OF W. Wilson
OF A. Otis
OF A. Cowens
C D. Porter
DH H. McRae
UT U. Washington
P P. Splittorff
P L. Gura
P R. Gale
RP E. Rodriguez
RP A. Hrabosky

KC 1980 A

M J. Frey
1B W. Aikens
2B F. White
SS U. Washington
3B G. Brett
OF W. Wilson
OF C. Hurdle
OF A. Otis
C D. Porter
DH H. McRae
UT R. LaCock
UT J. Wathan
P L. Gura
P D. Leonard
P P. Splittorff
P R. Gale
P D. Martin
RP D. Quisenberry
RP M. Pattin

KC 1981 A

M J. Frey
M R. Howser
1B W. Aikens
2B F. White
SS U. Washington
3B G. Brett
OF W. Wilson
OF A. Otis
OF C. Geronimo
C J. Wathan
DH H. McRae
P D. Leonard
P L. Gura
P R. Gale
P P. Splittorff
P M. Jones
RP D. Quisenberry
RP D. Martin
RP K. Brett

KC 1982 A

M R. Howser
1B W. Aikens
2B F. White
SS U. Washington
3B G. Brett
OF J. Martin
OF W. Wilson
OF A. Otis
C J. Wathan
DH H. McRae
P L. Gura
P V. Blue
P P. Splittorff
P D. Leonard
RP D. Quisenberry
RP M. Armstrong
RP D. Hood

KC 1983 A

M R. Howser
1B W. Aikens
2B F. White
SS U. Washington
3B G. Brett
OF W. Wilson
OF P. Sheridan
OF A. Otis
C J. Wathan
DH H. McRae
P L. Gura
P H. Black
P P. Splittorff
P S. Renko
RP D. Quisenberry
RP M. Armstrong

KC 1984 A

M R. Howser
1B S. Balboni

2B F. White
SS O. Concepcion
3B G. Pryor
OF D. Motley
OF P. Sheridan
OF W. Wilson
C D. Slaught
DH H. McRae
UT G. Brett
UT J. Orta
UT J. Wathan
P H. Black
P M. Gubicza
P L. Gura
P B. Saberhagen
P C. Leibrandt
RP D. Quisenberry
RP T. Beckwith
RP M. Huismann

KC 1985 A

M R. Howser
1B S. Balboni
2B F. White
SS O. Concepcion
3B G. Brett
OF W. Wilson
OF L. Smith
OF D. Motley
C J. Sundberg
DH H. McRae
UT L. Jones
UT J. Orta
P C. Leibrandt
P B. Saberhagen
P D. Jackson
P H. Black
P M. Gubicza
RP D. Quisenberry
RP T. Beckwith
RP M. Jones

KC 1986 A

M R. Howser
M M. Ferraro
1B S. Balboni
2B F. White
SS A. Salazar
3B G. Brett
OF W. Wilson
OF L. Smith
OF A. Otis
C J. Sundberg
DH J. Orta
UT R. Biancalana
UT H. McRae
P C. Leibrandt
P D. Leonard
P D. Jackson
P M. Gubicza
P B. Saberhagen
RP H. Black
RP S. Farr
RP D. Quisenberry

KC 1987 A

M W. Gardner
M J. Wathan
1B G. Brett
2B F. White
SS A. Salazar
3B K. Seitzer
OF D. Tartabull
OF W. Wilson
OF V. Jackson
C J. Quirk
DH S. Balboni
P B. Saberhagen
P M. Gubicza
P C. Leibrandt
P D. Jackson
P H. Black
RP S. Farr
RP J. Gleaton
RP D. Quisenberry

KC 1988 A

M J. Wathan
1B G. Brett
2B F. White
SS K. Stillwell
3B K. Seitzer
OF W. Wilson
OF D. Tartabull
OF V. Jackson
C J. Quirk
DH W. Buckner
P M. Gubicza
P B. Saberhagen
P C. Leibrandt
P F. Bannister
RP S. Farr
RP J. Montgomery

KC 1989 A

M J. Wathan
1B G. Brett
2B F. White
SS K. Stillwell
3B K. Seitzer
OF J. Eisenreich
OF V. Jackson
OF W. Wilson
C R. Boone
DH D. Tartabull
UT P. Tabler
UT B. Wellman
P B. Saberhagen
P M. Gubicza
P T. Gordon
P C. Leibrandt
P L. Aquino
RP J. Montgomery
RP T. Leach
RP S. Farr

KC 1990 A

M J. Wathan
1B G. Brett
2B F. White
SS K. Stillwell
3B K. Seitzer
OF J. Eisenreich
OF W. Wilson
OF V. Jackson
C M. Macfarlane
DH G. Perry
P T. Gordon
P R. Appier
P B. Saberhagen
P G. Davis
RP S. Farr
RP J. Montgomery
RP S. Crawford

Keokuk

WES n 1875

WES 1875 n

M J. Simmons
1B J. Carbine
2B J. Miller
SS J. Hallinan
3B W. Goldsmith
OF C. Jones
OF J. Simmons
OF W. Riley
C J. Quinn
UT W. Barnie
P M. Golden

Los Angeles

LA A 1961-1964
LA N 1958-1990

LA 1961 A

M W. Rigney
1B S. Bilko
2B K. Aspromonte
SS J. Koppe
3B E. Yost
OF K. Hunt
OF L. Wagner
OF A. Pearson
C E. Averill
UT T. Kluszewski
UT J. Thomas
P K. McBride
P E. Grba
P E. Bowsfield
P R. Moeller
P R. Kline
RP J. Donohue
RP R. Duren
RP T. Morgan

LA 1962 A

M W. Rigney
1B J. Thomas
2B W. Moran
SS J. Koppe
3B F. Torres
OF A. Pearson
OF L. Wagner
OF G. Thomas
C R. Rodgers
P W. Chance
P W. Belinsky
P E. Grba
P D. Lee
P K. McBride

RP J. Fowler
RP R. Duren
RP J. Spring

LA 1963 A

M W. Rigney
1B J. Thomas
2B W. Moran
SS J. Fregosi
3B F. Torres
OF A. Pearson
OF L. Wagner
OF M. Perry
C R. Rodgers
C K. McBride
P W. Chance
P D. Osinski
P D. Lee
RP A. Navarro
RP J. Fowler
RP P. Foytack

LA 1964 A

M W. Rigney
1B J. Adcock
2B R. Knoop
SS J. Fregosi
3B F. Torres
OF W. Smith
OF L. Clinton
OF J. Piersall
C R. Rodgers
UT A. Pearson
UT T. Satriano
P W. Chance
P F. Newman
P A. Latman
P R. Belinsky
P K. McBride
P R. Lee
RP D. Osinski
RP D. Lee

LA 1958 N

M W. Alston
1B G. Hodges
2B C. Neal
SS D. Zimmer
3B R. Gray
OF C. Furillo
OF G. Cimoli
OF E. Snider
C J. Roseboro
UT J. Gilliam
UT N. Larker
P D. Drysdale
P J. Podres
P S. Koufax
P S. Williams
P C. Erskine
RP C. Labine
RP F. Kipp
RP J. Klippstein

LA 1959 N

M W. Alston
1B G. Hodges
2B C. Neal
SS D. Zimmer
3B J. Gilliam
OF W. Moon
OF D. Demeter
OF E. Snider
C J. Roseboro
UT R. Fairly
UT N. Larker
P D. Drysdale
P J. Podres
P S. Koufax
P R. Craig
P D. McDevitt
RP C. Labine
RP J. Fowler

LA 1960 N

M W. Alston
1B N. Larker
2B C. Neal
SS M. Wills
3B J. Gilliam
OF W. Moon
OF H. Howard
OF H. Davis
C J. Roseboro
UT G. Hodges
UT E. Snider
P D. Drysdale
P J. Podres
P S. Williams
P S. Koufax
P R. Craig

RP L. Sherry
RP E. Roebuck
RP D. McDevitt

LA 1961 N
M W. Alston
1B G. Hodges
2B C. Neal
SS M. Wills
3B J. Gilliam
OF W. Moon
OF W. Davis
OF H. Davis
C J. Roseboro
UT R. Fairly
UT N. Larker
P S. Koufax
P D. Drysdale
P S. Williams
P J. Podres
RP R. Craig
RP L. Sherry
RP R. Perranoski

LA 1962 N
M W. Alston
1B R. Fairly
2B L. Burright
SS M. Wills
3B J. Gilliam
OF W. Davis
OF H. Davis
OF F. Howard
C J. Roseboro
P D. Drysdale
P J. Podres
P S. Williams
P S. Koufax
RP E. Roebuck
RP R. Perranoski
RP L. Sherry

LA 1963 N
M W. Alston
1B R. Fairly
2B J. Gilliam
SS M. Wills
3B K. McMullen
OF W. Davis
OF H. Davis
OF F. Howard
C J. Roseboro
UT W. Moon
UT R. Tracewski
P D. Drysdale
P S. Koufax
P J. Podres
P R. Miller
RP R. Perranoski
RP L. Sherry

LA 1964 N
M W. Alston
1B R. Fairly
2B N. Oliver
SS M. Wills
3B J. Gilliam
OF W. Davis
OF H. Davis
OF F. Howard
C J. Roseboro
UT M. Parker
UT R. Tracewski
P D. Drysdale
P S. Koufax
P F. Ortega
P J. Moeller
RP R. Miller
RP R. Perranoski
RP J. Brewer

LA 1965 N
M W. Alston
1B M. Parker
2B J. Lefebvre
SS M. Wills
3B J. Kennedy
OF R. Fairly
OF W. Davis
OF L. Johnson
C J. Roseboro
UT J. Gilliam
P S. Koufax
P D. Drysdale
P C. Osteen
P J. Podres
RP R. Perranoski
RP R. Miller
RP H. Reed

LA 1966 N
M W. Alston
1B M. Parker
2B J. Lefebvre
SS M. Wills
3B J. Kennedy
OF W. Davis
OF L. Johnson
OF R. Fairly
C J. Roseboro
UT H. Davis
P S. Koufax
P D. Drysdale
P C. Osteen
P D. Sutton
RP P Regan
RP R. Miller
RP R. Perranoski

LA 1967 N
M W. Alston
1B M. Parker
2B R. Hunt
SS E. Michael
3B J. Lefebvre
OF W. Davis
OF R. Fairly
OF A. Ferrara
C J. Roseboro
UT R. Bailey
UT L. Johnson
P C. Osteen
P D. Drysdale
P D. Sutton
P W. Singer
P J. Brewer
RP R. Perranoski
RP P. Regan
RP R. Miller

LA 1968 N
M W. Alston
1B M. Parker
2B P. Popovich
SS Z. Versalles
3B R. Bailey
OF W. Davis
OF R. Fairly
OF L. Gabrielson
C T. Haller
UT J. Fairey
P W. Singer
P C. Osteen
P D. Drysdale
P D. Sutton
P M. Kekich
RP J. Grant
RP J. Brewer
RP J. Billingham

LA 1969 N
M W. Alston
1B M. Parker
2B T. Sizemore
SS M. Wills
3B W. Sudakis
OF W. Davis
OF W. Crawford
OF A. Kosco
C T. Haller
UT W. Russell
P C. Osteen
P W. Singer
P D. Sutton
P A. Foster
RP J. Brewer
RP P. Mikkelsen
RP J. Moeller

LA 1970 N
M W. Alston
1B M. Parker
2B T. Sizemore
SS M. Wills
3B B. Grabarkewitz
OF W. Davis
OF M. Mota
OF W. Crawford
C T. Haller
UT J. Lefebvre
P D. Sutton
P C. Osteen
P A. Foster
P J. Moeller
P G. Vance
RP J. Brewer
RP F. Norman
RP P. Mikkelsen

LA 1971 N
M W. Alston
1B M. Parker
2B J. Lefebvre
SS M. Wills
3B W. Davis
OF W. Davis
OF W. Crawford
OF W. Buckner
C D. Sims
UT R. Allen
UT R. Valentine
P D. Sutton
P A. Downing
P C. Osteen
P W. Singer
RP J. Brewer
RP P. Mikkelsen
RP J. Moeller

LA 1972 N
M W. Alston
1B M. Parker
2B L. Lacy
SS W. Russell
3B S. Garvey
OF W. Davis
OF M. Mota
OF F. Robinson
C C. Cannizzaro
UT W. Buckner
UT W. Crawford
UT R. Valentine
P D. Sutton
P C. Osteen
P A. Downing
P T. John
P W. Singer
RP J. Brewer
RP P. Mikkelsen
RP P. Richert

LA 1973 N
M W. Alston
1B W. Buckner
2B D. Lopes
SS W. Russell
3B R. Cey
OF W. Davis
OF W. Crawford
OF T. Paciorek
C J. Ferguson
UT S. Garvey
P D. Sutton
P C. Osteen
P T. John
P D. Rau
P R. Rhoden
RP C. Hough
RP J. Brewer
RP D. Rau

OF J. Baker
OF C. Smith
OF W. North
UT R. Monday
P B. Hooton
RP T. Forster
RP C. Rautzhan

LA 1974 N
M W. Alston
1B S. Garvey
2B D. Lopes
SS W. Russell
3B R. Cey
OF J. Wynn
OF W. Buckner
OF W. Crawford
C S. Yeager
UT J. Ferguson
P A. Messersmith
P D. Sutton
P D. Rau
P T. John
P A. Downing
RP M. Marshall
RP C. Hough

LA 1975 N
M W. Alston
1B S. Garvey
2B D. Lopes
SS W. Russell
3B R. Cey
OF J. Wynn
OF W. Crawford
OF W. Buckner
C S. Yeager
UT L. Lacy
P J. Messersmith
P D. Rau
P D. Sutton
P B. Hooton
P R. Rhoden
RP M. Marshall
RP C. Hough

LA 1976 N
M W. Alston
M T. Lasorda
1B S. Garvey
2B D. Lopes
SS W. Russell
3B R. Cey
OF W. Buckner
OF J. Baker
OF C. Smith
C S. Yeager
P D. Sutton
P D. Rau
P B. Hooton
P T. John
P R. Rhoden
RP C. Hough
RP M. Marshall
RP S. Wall

LA 1977 N
M T. Lasorda
1B S. Garvey
2B D. Lopes
SS W. Russell
3B R. Cey
OF J. Baker
OF C. Smith
OF R. Monday
C S. Yeager
P D. Sutton
P B. Hooton
P T. John
P R. Rhoden
P D. Rau
RP C. Hough
RP E. Sosa
RP M. Garman

LA 1978 N
M T. Lasorda
1B S. Garvey
2B D. Lopes
SS W. Russell
3B R. Cey
OF J. Baker
OF C. Smith
OF W. North
C S. Yeager
UT L. Lacy
UT R. Monday
P D. Sutton
P B. Hooton
P T. John
P D. Rau
P R. Rhoden
RP C. Hough
RP T. Forster
RP C. Rautzhan

LA 1979 N
M T. Lasorda
1B S. Garvey
2B D. Lopes
SS W. Russell
3B R. Cey
OF J. Baker
OF D. Thomas
OF G. Thomasson
C S. Yeager
UT J. Ferguson
P R. Sutcliffe
P D. Sutton
P B. Hooton
P J. Reuss
P C. Hough
RP D. Patterson

LA 1980 N
M T. Lasorda
1B S. Garvey
2B D. Lopes
SS W. Russell
3B R. Cey
OF J. Baker
OF R. Law
OF C. Smith
C S. Yeager
UT J. Johnstone
UT D. Thomas
P J. Reuss
P R. Welch
P D. Sutton
P B. Hooton
P D. Goltz
RP R. Sutcliffe
RP R. Castillo
RP S. Howe

LA 1981 N
M T. Lasorda
1B S. Garvey
2B D. Lopes
SS W. Russell
3B R. Cey
OF J. Baker
OF K. Landreaux
OF P. Guerrero
C M. Scioscia
UT D. Thomas
P F. Valenzuela
P J. Reuss
P B. Hooton
P R. Welch
RP D. Goltz
RP S. Howe
RP R. Castillo

LA 1982 N
M T. Lasorda
1B S. Garvey
2B S. Sax
SS W. Russell
3B R. Cey
OF J. Baker
OF P. Guerrero
OF K. Landreaux
C M. Scioscia
UT R. Monday
UT R. Roenicke
P F. Valenzuela
P J. Reuss
P R. Welch
P D. Stewart
P B. Hooton
RP S. Howe
RP T. Forster
RP T. Niedenfuer

LA 1983 N
M T. Lasorda
1B G. Brock
2B S. Sax
SS W. Russell
3B P. Guerrero
OF J. Baker
OF K. Landreaux
OF M. Marshall
C S. Yeager
UT D. Thomas
P F. Valenzuela
P J. Reuss
P R. Welch
P A. Pena
P B. Hooton
RP T. Niedenfuer
RP D. Stewart
RP T. Beckwith

LA 1984 N
M T. Lasorda
1B G. Brock
2B S. Sax
SS D. Anderson
3B G. Rivera
OF K. Landreaux
OF M. Marshall
OF C. Maldonado
C M. Scioscia
UT P. Guerrero
P F. Valenzuela
P A. Pena
P O. Hershiser
P F. Honeycutt
P R. Welch
RP B. Hooton
RP P. Zachry
RP K. Howell

LA 1985 N
M T. Lasorda
1B G. Brock
2B S. Sax
SS M. Duncan
3B D. Anderson
OF K. Landreaux
OF M. Marshall
OF C. Maldonado
C M. Scioscia
UT P. Guerrero
P F. Valenzuela
P O. Hershiser
P J. Reuss
P R. Welch
P F. Honeycutt
RP T. Niedenfuer
RP K. Howell
RP C. Diaz

LA 1986 N
M T. Lasorda
1B G. Brock
2B S. Sax
SS M. Duncan
3B B. Madlock
OF R. Williams
OF F. Stubbs
OF M. Marshall
C M. Scioscia
UT E. Cabell
UT K. Landreaux
UT W. Russell
P F. Valenzuela
P R. Welch
P O. Hershiser
P F. Honeycutt
RP K. Howell
RP T. Niedenfuer
RP E. Vande Berg

LA 1987 N
M T. Lasorda
1B F. Stubbs
2B S. Sax
3B M. Hatcher
OF J. Shelby
OF P. Guerrero
OF M. Marshall
C M. Scioscia
UT D. Anderson
UT K. Landreaux
P O. Hershiser
P R. Welch
P F. Valenzuela
P F. Honeycutt
RP T. Leary
RP A. Pena
RP B. Holton

LA 1988 N
M T. Lasorda
1B F. Stubbs
2B S. Sax
SS A. Griffin
3B J. Hamilton
OF K. Gibson
OF J. Shelby
OF M. Marshall
C M. Scioscia
UT D. Anderson
UT M. Davis
P O. Hershiser
P T. Leary
P T. Belcher
P F. Valenzuela
RP A. Pena
RP B. Holton
RP S. Crews

LA 1989 N
M T. Lasorda
1B E. Murray
2B W. Randolph
SS A. Griffin
3B J. Hamilton
OF M. Marshall
OF J. Shelby
OF J. Gonzalez
C M. Scioscia
P O. Hershiser
P T. Belcher
P F. Valenzuela
P M. Morgan
P T. Leary
RP J. Howell
RP A. Pena
RP S. Crews

LA 1990 N
M T. Lasorda
1B E. Murray
2B J. Samuel
SS A. Griffin
3B M. Sharperson
OF H. Brooks
OF K. Daniels
OF S. Javier
C M. Scioscia
UT J. Gonzalez
UT C. Gwynn
UT L. Harris
P R. Martinez
P M. Morgan
P F. Valenzuela
P T. Belcher
RP S. Crews
RP M. Hartley
RP J. Howell

Louisville

LOU 1876-1877
LOU a 1882-1891
LOU N 1892-1899

LOU 1876 N
M J. Chapman
1B J. Gerhardt
2B J. Gerhardt
SS C. Fulmer
3B W. Hague
OF W. Hastings
OF J. Ryan
OF A. Allison
C C. Snyder
P J. Devlin

LOU 1877 N
M J. Chapman
1B G. Latham
2B J. Gerhardt
SS W. Craver
3B W. Hague
OF G. Hall
OF G. Shaffer
OF W. Crowley
C C. Snyder
P J. Devlin

LOU 1882 a
M D. Mack
1B G. Hecker
2B L. Browning
SS D. Mack
3B W. Schenck
OF S. Maskrey
OF W. Wolf
OF J. Reccius
C D. Sullivan
P A. Mullane

LOU 1883 a
M J. Gerhardt
1B G. Latham
2B J. Gerhardt
SS J. Leary
3B J. Gleason
OF S. Maskrey
OF W. Wolf
OF L. Browning
C E. Whiting
P G. Hecker
P S. Weaver

LOU 1884 a
M M. Walsh
1B G. Latham
2B J. Gerhardt
SS T. McLaughlin
3B L. Browning
OF S. Maskrey
OF W. Wolf
OF W. Cline
C D. Sullivan
UT P. Reccius
P G. Hecker
P J. Driscoll
P L. Deagle

LOU 1885 a
M J. Hart
1B J. Kerins
2B T. McLaughlin
SS J. Miller
3B P. Reccius
OF L. Browning
OF W. Wolf
OF S. Maskrey
C J. Crotty
P G. Hecker
P N. Baker
P A. Mays
P T. Ramsey

LOU 1886 a
M J. Hart
1B J. Kerins
2B J. Mack
SS W. White
3B J. Werrick
OF W. Wolf
OF L. Browning
OF J. Strauss
C A. Cross
P T. Ramsey
P G. Hecker

LOU 1887 a
M J. Kelly
1B J. Kerins
2B J. Mack
SS W. White
3B J. Werrick
OF L. Browning
OF W. Wolf
OF H. Collins
C P. Cook
UT G. Hecker

P T. Ramsey
P E. Chamberlain

LOU 1888 a
M J. Kelly
M M. Davidson
M J. Kerins
M M. Davidson
1B S. Smith
2B J. Mack
SS W. Wolf
3B J. Werrick
OF L. Browning
OF H. Collins
OF J. Kerins
C P. Cook
P T. Ramsey
P E. Chamberlain
P J. Ewing

LOU 1889 a
M T. Esterbrook
M W. Wolf
M D. Shannon
M J. Chapman
1B G. Hecker
2B D. Shannon
SS P. Tomney
3B H. Raymond
OF W. Weaver
OF W. Wolf
OF L. Browning
C P. Cook
UT H. Vaughn
P P. Ehret
P J. Ewing
P T. Ramsey
P M. McDermott

LOU 1890 a
M J. Chapman
1B H. Taylor
2B T. Shinnick
SS P. Tomney
3B H. Raymond
OF C. Hamburg
OF W. Weaver
OF W. Wolf
C J. Ryan
P C. Stratton
P P. Ehret
P G. Meakim
P H. Goodall
P E. Daily

LOU 1891 a
M J. Chapman
1B H. Taylor
2B T. Shinnick
SS H. Jennings
3B O. Beard
OF W. Wolf
OF W. Weaver
OF P. Donovan
C J. Ryan
UT T. Cahill
P J. Fitzgerald
P J. Meekin
P P. Ehret
P C. Stratton
P J. Doran

LOU 1892 N
M J. Chapman
M N. Pfeffer
1B L. Whistler
2B N. Pfeffer
SS H. Jennings
3B W. Kuehne
OF T. Brown
OF W. Weaver
OF H. Taylor
C J. Grim
P C. Stratton
P A. Sanders
P F. Clausen
P J. Meekin
P A. Jones

LOU 1893 N
M W. Barnie
1B W. Brown
2B N. Pfeffer
SS T. O'Rourke
3B G. Pinkney
OF T. Brown
OF W. Weaver
OF L. Browning
C J. Grim
P G. Hemming
P C. Stratton

P W. Rhodes
P J. Menefee

LOU 1894 N
M W. Barnie
1B C. Lutenberg
2B N. Pfeffer
SS D. Richardson
3B J. Denny
OF T. Brown
OF F. Clarke
OF L. Twitchell
C J. Grim
P G. Hemming
P P. Knell
P J. Menefee
P J. Wadsworth

LOU 1895 N
M J. McCloskey
1B H. Spies
2B J. O'Brien
SS F. Shugart
3B J. Collins
OF F. Clarke
OF T. Gettinger
OF J. Wright
C J. Warner
P E. Cunningham
P A. Weyhing
P M. McDermott
P A. Inks

LOU 1896 N
M J. McCloskey
M W. McGunnigle
1B J. Rogers
2B J. O'Brien
SS J. Dolan
3B W. Clingman
OF F. Clarke
OF T. McCreery
OF C. Dexter
C G. Miller
P C. Fraser
P W. Hill
P E. Cunningham
P A. Herman

LOU 1897 N
M J. Rogers
M F. Clarke
1B P. Werden
2B J. Rogers
SS J. Stafford
3B W. Clingman
OF F. Clarke
OF T. McCreery
OF O. Pickering
C W. Wilson
P C. Fraser
P E. Cunningham
P W. Hill
P W. Magee

LOU 1898 N
M F. Clarke
1B J. Wagner
2B C. Ritchey
SS W. Clingman
OF F. Clarke
OF W. Hoy
OF C. Dexter
C M. Kittridge
P E. Cunningham
P W. Magee
P H. Dowling
P C. Fraser

LOU 1899 N
M F. Clarke
1B B. Kelley
2B C. Ritchey
SS W. Clingman
3B T. Leach
OF W. Hoy
OF F. Clarke
OF C. Dexter
C C. Zimmer
UT J. Wagner
P E. Cunningham
P C. Phillippe
P H. Dowling
P W. Woods

Middletown

MAN n 1872

MAN 1872 n
M J. Clapp
1B T. Murnane
2B E. Booth
SS J. O'Rourke
3B G. Fields
OF F. McCarton
OF J. Tipper
OF H. Allen
C J. Clapp
P C. Bentley
P F. Buttery

Milwaukee

MIL N 1878
MIL U 1884
MIL a 1891
MIL A 1901
MIL N 1953-1965
MIL A 1970-1990

MIL 1878 N
M J. Chapman
1B J. Goodman
2B J. Peters
SS W. Redmond
3B W. Foley
OF A. Dalrymple
OF M. Golden
OF W. Holbert
C C. Bennett
UT G. Creamer
P S. Weaver

MIL 1884 U
M T. Loftus
1B T. Griffin
2B J. Myers
SS T. Sexton
3B T. Morrissey
OF R. Hogan
OF S. Behel
OF C. Baldwin
C C. Broughton
P H. Porter
P E. Cushman

MIL 1891 a
M C. Cushman
1B J. Carney
2B J. Canavan
SS G. Shoch
3B A. Alberts
OF E. Burke
OF A. Dalrymple
OF H. Earl
C H. Vaughn
UT J. Grim
P G. Davies
P F. Killen
P J. Dwyer

MIL 1901 A
M H. Duffy
1B J. Anderson
2B W. Gilbert
SS W. Conroy
3B J. Burke
OF W. Hallman
OF H. Duffy
OF I. Waldron
C W. Maloney
UT W. Friel
P W. Reidy
P V. Garvin
P B. Husting
P T. Sparks
P E. Hawley

MIL 1953 N
M C. Grimm
1B J. Adcock
2B J. Dittmer
SS J. Logan
3B E. Mathews
OF W. Bruton
OF A. Pafko
OF S. Gordon
C D. Crandall
UT J. Pendleton
P W. Spahn
P S. Burdette
P R. Rush
P C. Willey
P J. Pizarro
RP D. Conley
RP D. McMahon
RP R. Trowbridge

MIL 1954 N
M C. Grimm
1B J. Adcock
2B D. O'Connell
SS J. Logan
3B E. Mathews
OF W. Bruton
OF A. Pafko
OF H. Aaron
C D. Crandall
P W. Spahn
P S. Burdette
P R. Buhl
P D. Conley
P J. Wilson
P C. Nichols
RP D. Jolly
RP E. Johnson
RP R. Crone

MIL 1955 N
M C. Grimm
1B G. Crowe
2B D. O'Connell
SS J. Logan
3B E. Mathews
OF H. Aaron
OF R. Thomson
C D. Crandall
UT C. Tanner
P W. Spahn
P S. Burdette
P R. Buhl
P D. Conley
P C. Nichols
RP E. Johnson
RP D. Jolly

MIL 1956 N
M C. Grimm
M F. Haney
1B J. Adcock
2B D. O'Connell
SS J. Logan
3B E. Mathews
OF H. Aaron
OF W. Bruton
OF R. Thomson
C D. Crandall
UT F. Torre
P W. Spahn
P S. Burdette
P R. Buhl
P R. Crone
P D. Conley
RP R. Trowbridge
RP E. Johnson

MIL 1957 N
M F. Haney
1B F. Torre
2B A. Schoendienst
SS J. Logan
3B E. Mathews
OF H. Aaron
OF J. Covington
OF W. Bruton
C D. Crandall
P W. Spahn
P S. Burdette
P R. Buhl
P D. Conley
P R. Trowbridge
RP W. Phillips
RP E. Johnson
RP D. McMahon

MIL 1958 N
M F. Haney
1B F. Torre
2B A. Schoendienst
SS J. Logan
3B E. Mathews
OF H. Aaron
OF W. Bruton
OF A. Pafko
C D. Crandall
UT J. Adcock
P W. Spahn
P S. Burdette
P R. Rush
P C. Willey
P J. Pizarro
RP D. Conley
RP D. McMahon
RP R. Trowbridge

MIL 1959 N
M F. Haney
1B J. Adcock
2B F. Mantilla
SS J. Logan
3B E. Mathews
OF H. Aaron
OF W. Bruton
OF J. Covington
C D. Crandall
UT F. Torre
P W. Spahn
P S. Burdette
P R. Buhl
P J. Jay
P J. Pizarro
RP D. McMahon

MIL 1960 N
M C. Dressen
1B J. Adcock
2B C. Cottier
SS J. Logan
3B E. Mathews
OF H. Aaron
OF W. Bruton
OF A. Spangler
C D. Crandall
UT J. Covington
P S. Burdette
P W. Spahn
P R. Buhl
P C. Willey
P J. Jay
RP D. McMahon
RP G. Brunet
RP R. Piche

MIL 1961 N
M C. Dressen
M G. Tebbetts
1B J. Adcock
2B F. Bolling
SS R. McMillan
3B E. Mathews
OF H. Aaron
OF F. Thomas
OF A. Maye
C J. Torre
P S. Burdette
P W. Spahn
P R. Buhl
P C. Willey
P D. Nottebart
RP D. McMahon

MIL 1962 N
M G. Tebbetts
1B J. Adcock
2B F. Bolling
SS R. McMillan
3B E. Mathews
OF H. Aaron
OF A. Maye
OF M. Jones
C D. Crandall
UT T. Aaron
P W. Spahn
P R. Shaw
P C. Hendley
P S. Burdette
P T. Cloninger
RP J. Curtis
RP C. Willey
RP D. Nottebart

MIL 1963 N
M R. Bragan
1B E. Oliver
2B F. Bolling
SS R. McMillan
3B E. Mathews
OF H. Aaron
OF A. Maye
OF M. Jones
C J. Torre
UT D. Menke
P W. Spahn
P D. Lemaster
P C. Hendley
P R. Shaw
P T. Cloninger
RP H. Fischer
RP J. Raymond
RP R. Piche

MIL 1964 N
M R. Bragan
1B E. Oliver
2B F. Bolling
SS D. Menke
3B E. Mathews
OF H. Aaron
OF A. Maye
OF R. Carty
C J. Torre
UT F. Alou
UT T. Cline
P T. Cloninger
P D. Lemaster
P W. Spahn
P H. Fischer
P R. Sadowski
RP B. Tiefenauer
RP W. Hoeft
RP F. Olivo

MIL 1965 N
M R. Bragan
1B F. Alou
2B F. Bolling
SS W. Woodward
3B E. Mathews
OF H. Aaron
OF M. Jones
OF T. Cline
C J. Torre
UT E. Oliver
P T. Cloninger
P W. Blasingame
P K. Johnson
P D. Lemaster
P R. Sadowski
RP W. O'Dell
RP D. Osinski
RP P. Niekro

MIL 1970 A
M J. Bristol
1B J. Hegan
2B T. Kubiak
SS R. Pena
3B T. Harper
OF D. Walton
OF R. Snyder
OF D. May
C P. Roof
UT G. McNertney
UT T. Savage
P M. Pattin
P L. Krausse
P C. Lockwood
P B. Bolin
P E. Brabender
RP K. Sanders
RP J. Gelnar

MIL 1971 A
M J. Bristol
1B J. Briggs
2B R. Theobald
SS F. Auerbach
3B T. Harper
OF D. May
OF W. Voss
OF J. Cardenal
C E. Rodriguez
UT A. Kosco
UT R. Pena
P M. Pattin
P W. Parsons
P C. Lockwood
P L. Krausse
P J. Slaton
RP K. Sanders
RP J. Morris
RP M. Lopez

MIL 1972 A
M J. Bristol
M R. McMillan
M D. Crandall
1B G. Scott
2B R. Theobald
SS F. Auerbach
3B M. Ferraro
OF D. May
OF J. Briggs
OF J. Lahoud
C E. Rodriguez
UT R. Heise
P J. Lonborg
P W. Parsons
P C. Lockwood
P J. Colborn
P K. Brett
RP K. Sanders
RP C. Stephenson
RP F. Linzy

MIL 1973 A
M D. Crandall
1B G. Scott
2B P. Garcia
SS T. Johnson
3B D. Money
OF D. May
OF J. Briggs
OF R. Coluccio
C D. Porter
DH O. Brown
P J. Colborn
P J. Slaton
P J. Bell
P C. Lockwood
P B. Champion
RP E. Rodriguez
RP C. Short
RP F. Linzy

MIL 1974 A
M D. Crandall
1B G. Scott
2B P. Garcia
SS R. Yount
3B D. Money
OF J. Briggs
OF R. Coluccio
OF D. May
C D. Porter
DH R. Mitchell
UT A. Berry
P J. Slaton
P C. Wright
P J. Colborn
P K. Kobel
P B. Champion
RP T. Murphy
RP E. Rodriguez
RP W. Travers

MIL 1975 A
M D. Crandall
M H. Kuenn
1B G. Scott
2B P. Garcia
SS R. Yount
3B D. Money
OF S. Lezcano
OF W. Sharp
OF J. Thomas
C D. Porter
DH H. Aaron
UT K. Bevacqua
P P. Broberg
P J. Slaton
P J. Colborn
P W. Travers
P T. Hausman
RP E. Rodriguez
RP T. Murphy

MIL 1976 A
M A. Grammas
1B G. Scott
2B T. Johnson
SS R. Yount
3B D. Money
OF S. Lezcano
OF V. Joshua
OF J. Thomas
C D. Porter
DH H. Aaron
P J. Slaton
P W. Travers
P J. Colborn
P G. Augustine
P E. Rodriguez
RP W. Castro
RP D. Frisella

MIL 1977 A
M A. Grammas
1B C. Cooper
2B D. Money
SS R. Yount
3B S. Bando
OF V. Joshua
OF J. Wohlford
OF S. Lezcano
C C. Moore
DH J. Quirk
P J. Slaton
P G. Augustine
P B. Haas
P E. Rodriguez
P L. Sorensen
RP S. Hinds
RP R. McClure
RP W. Castro

MIL 1978 A
M G. Bamberger
1B C. Cooper
2B P. Molitor
SS R. Yount
3B S. Bando
OF J. Thomas
OF S. Lezcano
OF B. Oglivie

C C. Moore
DH L. Hisle
UT D. Money
P R. Caldwell
P L. Sorensen
P G. Augustine
P W. Travers
P A. Replogle
RP W. Stein
RP R. McClure
RP W. Castro

MIL 1979 A
M G. Bamberger
1B C. Cooper
2B P. Molitor
SS R. Yount
3B S. Bando
OF J. Thomas
OF S. Lezcano
OF B. Oglivie
C C. Moore
DH R. Davis
P L. Sorensen
P R. Caldwell
P J. Slaton
P W. Travers
P B. Haas
RP G. Augustine
RP R. Cleveland
RP R. McClure

MIL 1980 A
M R. Rodgers
M G. Bamberger
M R. Rodgers
1B C. Cooper
2B P. Molitor
SS R. Yount
3B J. Gantner
OF J. Thomas
OF B. Oglivie
OF S. Lezcano
C C. Moore
DH R. Davis
P B. Haas
P R. Caldwell
P L. Sorensen
P W. Travers
P R. Cleveland
RP R. McClure
RP W. Castro
RP G. Augustine

MIL 1981 A
M R. Rodgers
1B C. Cooper
2B J. Gantner
SS R. Yount
3B D. Money
OF B. Oglivie
OF J. Thomas
OF M. Brouhard
C T. Simmons
DH L. Hisle
UT R. Howell
P P. Vuckovich
P R. Caldwell
P B. Haas
P J. Slaton
P R. Lerch
RP R. Fingers
RP R. Cleveland
RP J. Easterly

MIL 1982 A
M R. Rodgers
M H. Kuenn
1B C. Cooper
2B J. Gantner
SS R. Yount
3B P. Molitor
OF B. Oglivie
OF J. Thomas
OF C. Moore
C T. Simmons
DH R. Howell
P R. Caldwell
P P. Vuckovich
P B. Haas
P R. McClure
P J. Slaton
RP R. Fingers
RP D. Bernard

MIL 1983 A
M H. Kuenn
1B C. Cooper
2B J. Gantner
SS R. Yount
3B P. Molitor
OF C. Moore

OF B. Oglivie
OF R. Manning
C E. Yost
DH T. Simmons
P R. Caldwell
P D. Sutton
P B. Haas
P R. McClure
P C. Porter
RP J. Slaton
RP T. Tellmann
RP G. Augustine

MIL 1984 A
M R. Lachemann
1B C. Cooper
2B J. Gantner
SS R. Yount
3B E. Romero
OF B. Oglivie
OF D. James
OF R. Manning
C J. Sundberg
DH T. Simmons
P D. Sutton
P B. Haas
P J. Cocanower
P R. McClure
P R. Caldwell
RP P. Ladd
RP T. Tellmann
RP M. Waits

MIL 1985 A
M G. Bamberger
1B C. Cooper
2B J. Gantner
SS E. Riles
3B P. Molitor
OF R. Yount
OF B. Oglivie
OF P. Householder
C C. Moore
DH T. Simmons
P D. Darwin
P T. Higuera
P B. Burris
P B. Haas
P J. Cocanower
RP R. Gibson
RP R. McClure
RP R. Fingers

MIL 1986 A
M G. Bamberger
M T. Trebelhorn
1B W. Robidoux
2B J. Gantner
SS E. Riles
3B P. Molitor
OF R. Yount
OF R. Deer
OF R. Manning
C C. Moore
DH C. Cooper
UT B. Oglivie
P T. Higuera
P W. Wegman
P T. Leary
P J. Nieves
P D. Darwin
RP D. Plesac
RP M. Clear
RP B. Clutterbuck

MIL 1987 A
M T. Trebelhorn
1B G. Brock
2B J. Castillo
SS D. Sveum
3B E. Riles
OF R. Yount
OF R. Deer
OF G. Braggs
C W. Surhoff
DH C. Cooper
UT M. Felder
UT R. Manning
UT P. Molitor
P T. Higuera
P W. Wegman
P J. Nieves
P C. Bosio
RP C. Crim
RP D. Plesac
RP M. Clear

MIL 1988 A
M T. Trebelhorn
1B G. Brock
2B J. Gantner
SS D. Sveum

3B P. Molitor
OF R. Yount
OF R. Deer
OF J. Leonard
C W. Surhoff
DH T. Meyer
P T. Higuera
P W. Wegman
P C. Bosio
P D. August
P M. Birkbeck
RP C. Crim
RP O. Jones
RP P. Mirabella

MIL 1989 A
M T. Trebelhorn
1B G. Brock
2B J. Gantner
SS W. Spiers
3B P. Molitor
OF R. Yount
OF G. Braggs
OF R. Deer
C W. Surhoff
DH T. Meyer
UT M. Felder
P C. Bosio
P D. August
P T. Higuera
P M. Knudson
P J. Navarro
RP C. Crim
RP W. Krueger
RP D. Plesac

MIL 1990 A
M T. Trebelhorn
1B G. Brock
2B J. Gantner
SS W. Spiers
3B G. Sheffield
OF R. Yount
OF R. Deer
OF M. Felder
C W. Surhoff
DH D. Parker
UT P. Molitor
UT G. Vaughn
P T. Higuera
P M. Knudson
P J. Navarro
P R. Robinson
P C. Bosio
RP T. Edens
RP C. Crim
RP D. Plesac

Minnesota

MIN A 1961-1990

MIN 1961 A
M H. Lavagetto
M S. Mele
M H. Lavagetto
M S. Mele
1B H. Killebrew
2B A. Martin
SS Z. Versalles
3B B. Tuttle
OF L. Green
OF W. Allison
OF J. Lemon
C E. Battey
P P. Ramos
P C. Pascual
P J. Kralick
P J. Kaat
P D. Lee
RP W. Pleis
RP R. Moore

MIN 1962 A
M S. Mele
1B V. Power
2B B. Allen
SS Z. Versalles
3B R. Rollins
OF L. Green
OF H. Killebrew
OF W. Allison
C E. Battey
UT W. Tuttle
P J. Kaat
P C. Pascual
P J. Kralick
P R. Stigman
P J. Bonikowski
RP A. Stange
RP G. Maranda
RP R. Moore

MIN 1963 A
M S. Mele
1B V. Power
2B B. Allen
SS Z. Versalles
3B R. Rollins
OF W. Allison
OF J. Hall
OF H. Killebrew
C E. Battey
UT L. Green
P C. Pascual
P R. Stigman
P J. Kaat
P J. Perry
P A. Stange
RP W. Dailey
RP W. Pleis
RP G. Roggenburk

MIN 1964 A
M S. Mele
1B W. Allison
2B B. Allen
SS Z. Versalles
3B R. Rollins
OF P. Oliva
OF H. Killebrew
OF J. Hall
C E. Battey
UT D. Mincher
P C. Pascual
P J. Kaat
P R. Stigman
P J. Grant
RP G. Arrigo
RP A. Worthington
RP J. Perry

MIN 1965 A
M S. Mele
1B D. Mincher
2B J. Kindall
SS Z. Versalles
3B R. Rollins
OF P. Oliva
OF J. Hall
OF W. Allison
C E. Battey
UT H. Killebrew
UT H. Valdespino
P J. Grant
P J. Kaat
P J. Perry
P C. Pascual
P D. Boswell
RP A. Worthington
RP J. Klippstein
RP R. Stigman

MIN 1966 A
M S. Mele
1B D. Mincher
2B B. Allen
SS L. Cardenas
3B H. Killebrew
OF P. Oliva
OF J. Hall
OF T. Uhlaender
C E. Battey
UT C. Tovar
P J. Kaat
P J. Grant
P J. Perry
P D. Boswell
P J. Merritt
RP A. Worthington
RP J. Cimino
RP D. Siebler

MIN 1967 A
M S. Mele
M C. Ermer
1B H. Killebrew
2B R. Carew
SS Z. Versalles
3B R. Rollins
OF P. Oliva
OF W. Allison
OF T. Uhlaender
C G. Zimmerman
UT C. Tovar
P W. Chance
P J. Kaat
P J. Merritt
P D. Boswell
P J. Perry
RP A. Worthington
RP R. Kline

MIN 1968 A
M C. Ermer
1B V. Power
2B R. Carew
SS J. Hernandez
3B C. Tovar
OF T. Uhlaender
OF P. Oliva
OF W. Allison
C J. Roseboro
UT R. Clark
UT H. Killebrew
UT F. Quilici
P W. Chance
P J. Merritt
P J. Kaat
P J. Perry
RP R. Perranoski
RP A. Worthington
RP R. Miller

MIN 1969 A
M A. Martin
1B R. Reese
2B R. Carew
SS L. Cardenas
3B H. Killebrew
OF P. Oliva
OF T. Uhlaender
OF C. Tovar
C J. Roseboro
UT F. Quilici
P J. Perry
P D. Boswell
P J. Kaat
P T. Hall
RP R. Perranoski
RP R. Miller
RP R. Woodson

MIN 1970 A
M W. Rigney
1B R. Reese
2B D. Thompson
SS L. Cardenas
3B H. Killebrew
OF P. Oliva
OF C. Tovar
OF J. Holt
C G. Mitterwald
UT F. Quilici
P J. Perry
P J. Kaat
P R. Blyleven
P W. Zepp
RP T. Hall
RP S. Williams
RP R. Perranoski

MIN 1971 A
M W. Rigney
1B R. Reese
2B R. Carew
SS L. Cardenas
3B S. Braun
OF C. Tovar
OF P. Oliva
OF J. Holt
C G. Mitterwald
UT H. Killebrew
P R. Blyleven
P J. Perry
P J. Kaat
RP A. Corbin
RP T. Hall
RP S. Williams

MIN 1972 A
M W. Rigney
M F. Quilici
1B H. Killebrew
2B R. Carew
SS D. Thompson
3B E. Soderholm
OF A. Darwin
OF C. Tovar
OF S. Brye
C P. Roof
UT S. Braun
UT J. Nettles
UT R. Reese
P R. Blyleven
P R. Woodson
P J. Perry
P A. Corbin
P J. Kaat
RP D. LaRoche
RP W. Granger

MIN 1973 A
M F. Quilici
1B J. Lis
2B R. Carew
SS D. Thompson
3B S. Braun
OF L. Hisle
OF A. Darwin
OF J. Holt
C G. Mitterwald
DH P. Oliva
UT J. Terrell
P R. Blyleven
P J. Kaat
P G. Decker
P W. Hands
P R. Woodson
RP A. Corbin
RP E. Bane
RP W. Campbell

MIN 1974 A
M F. Quilici
1B C. Kusick
2B R. Carew
SS D. Thompson
3B E. Soderholm
OF A. Darwin
OF L. Hisle
OF S. Brye
C G. Borgmann
DH P. Oliva
UT S. Braun
UT H. Killebrew
UT J. Terrell
P R. Blyleven
P G. Decker
P D. Goltz
P V. Albury
P W. Hands
RP W. Campbell
RP T. Burgmeier

MIN 1975 A
M F. Quilici
1B C. Kusick
2B R. Carew
SS D. Thompson
3B E. Soderholm
OF D. Ford
OF S. Braun
OF L. Bostock
C G. Borgmann
DH P. Oliva
UT J. Terrell
P R. Blyleven
P J. Hughes
P D. Goltz
P V. Albury
RP W. Campbell
RP T. Burgmeier

MIN 1976 A
M G. Mauch
1B R. Carew
2B R. Randall
SS R. Smalley
3B M. Cubbage
OF L. Hisle
OF D. Ford
OF L. Bostock
C H. Wynegar
DH C. Kusick
UT S. Braun
P D. Goltz
P J. Hughes
P W. Singer
P S. Luebber
P P. Redfern
RP W. Campbell
RP T. Burgmeier
RP V. Albury

MIN 1977 A
M G. Mauch
1B R. Carew
2B R. Randall
SS R. Smalley
3B M. Cubbage
OF L. Bostock
OF D. Ford
OF L. Hisle
C H. Wynegar
DH C. Kusick
UT R. Chiles
P D. Goltz
P P.Thormodsgard
P G. Zahn
P P. Redfern
RP T. Johnson
RP R. Schueler
RP T. Burgmeier

MIN 1978 A
M G. Mauch
1B R. Carew
2B R. Randall
SS R. Smalley
3B M. Cubbage
OF D. Ford
OF H. Powell
OF W. Norwood
C H. Wynegar
DH G. Adams
UT J. Morales
UT J. Rivera
P R. Erickson
P G. Zahn
P D. Goltz
P G. Serum
RP M. Marshall

MIN 1979 A
M G. Mauch
1B R. Jackson
2B R. Wilfong
SS R. Smalley
3B J. Castino
OF K. Landreaux
OF J. Rivera
OF H. Powell
C H. Wynegar
DH J. Morales
UT G. Adams
P J. Koosman
P D. Goltz
P G. Zahn
P P. Hartzell
P R. Erickson
RP M. Marshall
RP P. Redfern
RP D. Jackson

MIN 1980 A
M G. Mauch
M J. Goryl
1B R. Jackson
2B R. Wilfong
SS R. Smalley
3B J. Castino
OF H. Powell
OF R. Sofield
OF K. Landreaux
C H. Wynegar
DH J. Morales
UT G. Adams
UT M. Cubbage
UT P. Mackanin
P J. Koosman
P G. Zahn
P R. Erickson
P D. Jackson
P P. Redfern
RP D. Corbett
RP J. Verhoeven

MIN 1981 A
M J. Goryl
M W. Gardner
1B D. Goodwin
2B R. Wilfong
SS R. Smalley
3B J. Castino
OF M. Hatcher
OF G. Ward
OF R. Engle
C S. Butera
DH G. Adams
UT P. Mackanin
UT H. Powell
P A. Williams
P P. Redfern
P F. Arroyo
P J. Koosman
P R. Erickson
RP D. Corbett
RP D. Cooper
RP J. Verhoeven

MIN 1982 A
M W. Gardner
1B K. Hrbek
2B J. Castino
SS R. Washington
3B G. Gaetti
OF G. Ward
OF T. Brunansky
OF R. Mitchell
C T. Laudner
DH R. Johnson
P R. Castillo
P B. Havens
P A. Williams
P F. Viola
P J. O'Connor

RP T. Felton
RP R. Davis
RP J. Pacella

MIN 1983 A

M W. Gardner
1B K. Hrbek
2B J. Castino
SS R. Washington
3B G. Gaetti
OF G. Ward
OF T. Brunansky
OF D. Brown
C R. Engle
DH R. Bush
UT M. Hatcher
P F. Viola
P K. Schrom
P A. Williams
P R. Castillo
RP R. Lysander
RP R. Davis
RP L. Whitehouse

MIN 1984 A

M W. Gardner
1B K. Hrbek
2B T. Teufel
SS A. Jimenez
3B G. Gaetti
OF T. Brunansky
OF K. Puckett
OF M. Hatcher
C R. Engle
DH R. Bush
P F. Viola
P B. Smithson
P J. Butcher
P K. Schrom
P E. Hodge
RP W. Filson
RP R. Davis
RP R. Lysander

MIN 1985 A

M W. Gardner
M R. Miller
1B K. Hrbek
2B T. Teufel
SS G. Gagne
3B G. Gaetti
OF K. Puckett
OF T. Brunansky
OF M. Hatcher
C M. Salas
DH R. Smalley
UT R. Bush
P B. Smithson
P F. Viola
P J. Butcher
P K. Schrom
P R. Blyleven
RP W. Filson
RP R. Davis
RP F. Eufemia

MIN 1986 A

M R. Miller
M J. Kelly
1B K. Hrbek
2B S. Lombardozzi
SS G. Gagne
3B G. Gaetti
OF K. Puckett
OF T. Brunansky
OF R. Bush
C M. Salas
DH R. Smalley
UT M. Hatcher
P R. Blyleven
P F. Viola
P B. Smithson
P N. Heaton
P M. Portugal
RP K. Atherton
RP R. Jackson
RP F. Pastore

MIN 1987 A

M J. Kelly
1B K. Hrbek
2B S. Lombardozzi
SS G. Gagne
3B G. Gaetti
OF K. Puckett
OF T. Brunansky
OF C. Gladden
C T. Laudner
DH R. Smalley
UT R. Bush
UT J. Davidson
UT A. Newman

P R. Blyleven
P F. Viola
P L. Straker
P B. Smithson
P J. Niekro
RP J. Berenguer
RP G. Frazier
RP J. Reardon

MIN 1988 A

M J. Kelly
1B K. Hrbek
2B S. Lombardozzi
SS G. Gagne
3B G. Gaetti
OF K. Puckett
OF C. Gladden
OF R. Bush
C T. Laudner
DH E. Larkin
UT J. Davidson
UT J. Moses
UT A. Newman
P F. Viola
P R. Blyleven
P A. Anderson
P C. Lea
P F. Toliver
RP J. Berenguer
RP K. Atherton
RP J. Reardon

MIN 1989 A

M J. Kelly
1B K. Hrbek
2B A. Newman
SS G. Gagne
3B G. Gaetti
OF K. Puckett
OF C. Gladden
OF R. Bush
C B. Harper
DH J. Dwyer
UT E. Larkin
UT T. Laudner
UT J. Moses
P A. Anderson
P F. Viola
P L. Smith
P S. Rawley
RP J. Berenguer
RP J. Reardon
RP G. Wayne

MIN 1990 A

M J. Kelly
1B K. Hrbek
2B A. Newman
SS G. Gagne
3B G. Gaetti
OF K. Puckett
OF C. Gladden
OF S. Mack
C B. Harper
DH E. Larkin
UT J. Moses
P A. Anderson
P K. Tapani
P L. Smith
P D. West
P M. Guthrie
RP J. Berenguer
RP T. Drummond
RP T. Leach

Montreal

MON N 1969-1990

MON 1969 N

M G. Mauch
1B R. Bailey
2B G. Sutherland
SS R. Wine
3B J. Laboy
OF D. Staub
OF M. Jones
OF A. Phillips
C R. Brand
UT T. Cline
P W. Stoneman
P J. Robertson
P M. Wegener
P G. Waslewski
P H. Reed
RP D. McGinn
RP D. Shaw
RP E. Face

MON 1970 N

M G. Mauch

1B R. Fairly
2B G. Sutherland
SS R. Wine
3B J. Laboy
OF D. Staub
OF M. Jones
OF A. Phillips
C J. Bateman
UT R. Bailey
UT M. Staehle
P C. Morton
P S. Renko
P W. Stoneman
P M. Wegener
RP D. McGinn
RP H. Reed
RP J. Raymond

MON 1971 N

M G. Mauch
1B R. Fairly
2B R. Hunt
SS R. Wine
3B R. Bailey
OF D. Staub
OF C. Day
OF J. Fairey
C J. Bateman
UT G. Sutherland
P W. Stoneman
P S. Renko
P C. Morton
P E. McAnally
P J. Strohmayer
RP M. Marshall
RP D. McGinn
RP H. Reed

MON 1972 N

M G. Mauch
1B M. Jorgensen
2B R. Hunt
SS T. Foli
3B R. Bailey
OF K. Singleton
OF C. Day
OF C. Mashore
C J. Boccabella
UT R. Fairly
UT R. Woods
P W. Stoneman
P M. Torrez
P C. Morton
P E. McAnally
P B. Moore
RP M. Marshall
RP J. Strohmayer
RP R. Walker

MON 1973 N

M G. Mauch
1B M. Jorgensen
2B R. Hunt
SS T. Foli
3B R. Bailey
OF K. Singleton
OF R. Fairly
OF R. Woods
C J. Boccabella
UT H. Breeden
UT C. Day
UT J. Frias
P S. Renko
P M. Torrez
P B. Moore
P E. McAnally
P S. Rogers
RP M. Marshall
RP R. Walker

MON 1974 N

M G. Mauch
1B M. Jorgensen
2B J. Cox
SS T. Foli
3B R. Hunt
OF W. Davis
OF K. Singleton
OF R. Bailey
C B. Foote
UT R. Fairly
UT L. Lintz
P S. Rogers
P S. Renko
P M. Torrez
P D. Blair
P E. McAnally
RP C. Taylor
RP R. Walker
RP J. Montague

MON 1975 N

M G. Mauch
1B M. Jorgensen
2B P. Mackanin
SS T. Foli
3B L. Parrish
OF J. Mangual
OF L. Biittner
OF G. Carter
C B. Foote
UT S. Renko
P S. Rogers
P S. Renko
P D. Warthen
P D. Blair
P W. Fryman
RP D. Murray
RP D. DeMola
RP F. Scherman

MON 1976 N

M K. Kuehl
M C. Fox
1B M. Jorgensen
2B P. Mackanin
SS T. Foli
3B L. Parrish
OF J. White
OF E. Valentine
OF D. Unser
C B. Foote
UT J. Morales
P S. Rogers
P W. Fryman
P D. Stanhouse
P D. Carrithers
RP D. Murray
RP S. Dunning
RP R. Lang

MON 1977 N

M R. Williams
1B A. Perez
2B D. Cash
SS C. Speier
3B L. Parrish
OF W. Cromartie
OF A. Dawson
OF E. Valentine
C G. Carter
UT D. Unser
P S. Rogers
P J. Brown
P D. Stanhouse
P W. Twitchell
P S. Bahnsen
RP J. Kerrigan
RP W. McEnaney
RP W. Atkinson

MON 1978 N

M R. Williams
1B A. Perez
2B D. Cash
SS C. Speier
3B L. Parrish
OF W. Cromartie
OF A. Dawson
OF E. Valentine
C G. Carter
UT D. Unser
P R. Grimsley
P S. Rogers
P D. Schatzeder
P R. May
P W. Twitchell
RP S. Bahnsen
RP D. Knowles
RP M. Garman

MON 1979 N

M R. Williams
1B A. Perez
2B R. Scott
SS C. Speier
3B L. Parrish
OF W. Cromartie
OF A. Dawson
OF E. Valentine
C G. Carter
P S. Rogers
P W. Lee
P S. Sanderson
P D. Schatzeder
P R. Grimsley
RP E. Sosa
RP R. May
RP S. Bahnsen

MON 1980 N

M R. Williams

1B W. Cromartie
2B R. Scott
SS C. Speier
3B L. Parrish
OF A. Dawson
OF R. LeFlore
OF R. Office
C G. Carter
UT J. White
P S. Rogers
P S. Sanderson
P W. Gullickson
P D. Palmer
P W. Lee
RP F. Norman
RP E. Sosa
RP S. Bahnsen

MON 1981 N

M R. Williams
M W. Fanning
1B W. Cromartie
2B R. Scott
SS C. Speier
3B L. Parrish
OF A. Dawson
OF T. Raines
OF J. White
C G. Carter
UT T. Wallach
P S. Rogers
P W. Gullickson
P S. Sanderson
P B. Burris
RP W. Lee
RP S. Bahnsen
RP W. Fryman

MON 1982 N

M W. Fanning
1B A. Oliver
2B R. Flynn
SS C. Speier
3B T. Wallach
OF A. Dawson
OF W. Cromartie
OF T. Raines
C G. Carter
P S. Rogers
P W. Gullickson
P S. Sanderson
P C. Lea
P B. Burris
RP J. Reardon
RP B. Smith
RP W. Fryman

MON 1983 N

M W. Virdon
1B A. Oliver
2B R. Flynn
SS C. Speier
3B T. Wallach
OF A. Dawson
OF T. Raines
OF W. Cromartie
C G. Carter
UT R. Francona
UT R. Little
P S. Rogers
P W. Gullickson
P C. Lea
P B. Smith
P B. Burris
RP J. Reardon
RP D. Schatzeder
RP R. James

MON 1984 N

M W. Virdon
M W. Fanning
1B T. Francona
2B R. Flynn
SS A. Salazar
3B T. Wallach
OF T. Raines
OF A. Dawson
OF J. Wohlford
C G. Carter
UT D. Thomas
P W. Gullickson
P C. Lea
P B. Smith
P S. Rogers
P D. Schatzeder
RP R. James
RP J. Reardon
RP G. Lucas

MON 1985 N

M R. Rodgers
1B D. Driessen

2B V. Law
SS R. Scott
3B T. Wallach
OF T. Raines
OF A. Dawson
OF H. Winningham
C M. Fitzgerald
UT T. Francona
P B. Smith
P W. Gullickson
P J. Hesketh
P D. Palmer
P D. Schatzeder
RP T. Burke
RP J. Reardon
RP R. St. Claire

MON 1986 N

M R. Rodgers
1B A. Galarraga
2B V. Law
SS H. Brooks
3B T. Wallach
OF T. Raines
OF M. Webster
OF A. Dawson
C D. Bilardello
UT W. Krenchicki
P F. Youmans
P J. Tibbs
P B. Smith
P J. Martinez
P A. McGaffigan
RP T. Burke
RP J. Reardon

MON 1987 N

M R. Rodgers
1B A. Galarraga
2B V. Law
SS H. Brooks
3B T. Wallach
OF M. Webster
OF T. Raines
OF H. Winningham
C M. Fitzgerald
UT D. Candaele
UT T. Foley
P N. Heaton
P R. Sebra
P B. Smith
P J. Martinez
P F. Youmans
RP A. McGaffigan
RP T. Burke
RP R. St. Claire

MON 1988 N

M R. Rodgers
1B A. Galarraga
2B T. Foley
SS L. Rivera
3B T. Wallach
OF H. Brooks
OF T. Raines
OF O. Nixon
C N. Santovenia
P J. Martinez
P B. Smith
P P. Perez
P J. Dopson
P B. Holman
RP J. Parrett
RP A. McGaffigan
RP T. Burke

MON 1989 N

M R. Rodgers
1B A. Galarraga
2B T. Foley
SS S. Owen
3B T. Wallach
OF H. Brooks
OF T. Raines
OF O. Nixon
C N. Santovenia
P J. Martinez
P B. Smith
P K. Gross
P P. Perez
P M. Langston
RP T. Burke
RP A. McGaffigan
RP Z. Smith

MON 1990 N

M R. Rodgers
1B A. Galarraga

2B D. DeShields
SS S. Owen
3B T. Wallach
OF L. Walker
OF T. Raines
OF D. Martinez
C M. Fitzgerald
UT O. Nixon
P J. Martinez
P D. Boyd
P K. Gross
P M. Gardner
P Z. Smith
RP W. Sampen
RP T. Burke
RP A. Hall

Newark

NEW F 1915

NEW 1915 F

M W. Phillips
M W. McKechnie
1B E. Huhn
2B F. LaPorte
SS J. Esmond
3B W. McKechnie
OF A. Scheer
OF E. Roush
OF A. Campbell
C W. Rariden
P E. Reulbach
P E. Moseley
P G. Kaiserling
P H. Moran
P F. Falkenberg

New Haven

NH n 1875

NH 1875 n

M C. Gould
M G. Latham
M C. Pabor
1B C. Gould
2B E. Somerville
SS S. Wright
3B H. Luff
OF J. Tipper
OF J. McKelvey
OF J. Ryan
C T. McGinley
UT W. Geer
P F. Nichols

New York

MUT n 1871-1875
NY N 1876
NY a 1883-1887
NY P 1890
NY N 1883-1957
NY N 1962-1990
NY A 1903-1990

MUT 1871 n

M R. Ferguson
1B J. Start
2B R. Higham
SS R. Pearce
3B R. Ferguson
OF D. Eggler
OF D. Patterson
OF J. Hatfield
C C. Mills
P R. Wolters

MUT 1872 n

M R. Pearce
M J. Hatfield
1B J. Start
2B J. Hatfield
SS R. Pearce
3B W. Boyd
OF D. Eggler
OF J. McMullin
OF G. Bechtel
C N. Hicks
UT C. Fulmer
P W. Cummings

MUT 1873 n

M J. Hatfield
M J. Start
1B J. Start

2B J. Nelson
SS J. Holdsworth
3B J. Hatfield
OF A. Gedney
OF D. Eggler
OF A. Martin
C N. Hicks
UT R. Higham
P R. Mathews

MUT 1874 n

M T. Carey
M R. Higham
1B J. Start
2B J. Nelson
SS T. Carey
3B J. Burdock
OF J. Remsen
OF J. Hatfield
OF D. Allison
C R. Higham
P R. Mathews

MUT 1875 n

M N. Hicks
1B J. Start
2B J. Nelson
SS J. Hallinan
3B J. Gerhardt
OF A. Gedney
OF E. Booth
OF J. Holdsworth
C N. Hicks
P R. Mathews

NY 1876 N

M W. Cammeyer
1B J. Start
2B W. Craver
SS J. Hallinan
3B A. Nichols
OF F. Treacey
OF E. Booth
OF J. Holdsworth
C N. Hicks
P R. Mathews

NY 1883 a

M J. Mutrie
1B S. Brady
2B S. Crane
SS J. Nelson
3B T. Esterbrook
OF E. Kennedy
OF J. Roseman
OF J. O'Rourke
C W. Holbert
P T. Keefe
P J. Lynch

NY 1884 a

M J. Mutrie
1B D. Orr
2B J. Troy
SS J. Nelson
3B T. Esterbrook
OF S. Brady
OF J. Roseman
OF E. Kennedy
C W. Holbert
P T. Keefe
P J. Lynch

NY 1885 a

M J. Gifford
1B D. Orr
2B T. Forster
SS J. Nelson
3B F. Hankinson
OF S. Brady
OF J. Roseman
OF E. Kennedy
C C. Reipschlager
P J. Lynch
P E. Cushman
P D. Crothers
P E. Begley
P J. Becannon

NY 1886 a

M J. Gifford
M R. Ferguson
1B D. Orr
2B T. Forster
SS J. Nelson
3B F. Hankinson
OF J. Roseman
OF S. Brady
OF S. Behel
C C. Reipschlager

P J. Lynch
P A. Mays
P E. Cushman

NY 1887 a

M R. Ferguson
M D. Orr
M O. Caylor
1B D. Orr
2B J. Gerhardt
SS P. Radford
3B F. Hankinson
OF W. O'Brien
OF C. Jones
OF J. Roseman
C W. Holbert
P A. Mays
P E. Cushman
P J. Lynch
P J. Shaffer
P G. Weidman

NY 1890 P

M W. Ewing
1B R. Connor
2B D. Shannon
SS D. Richardson
3B A. Whitney
OF J. O'Rourke
OF M. Slattery
OF G. Gore
C W. Ewing
P E. Crane
P H. O'Day
P J. Ewing
P T. Keefe

NY 1883 N

M J. Clapp
1B R. Connor
2B J. Troy
SS E. Caskin
3B F. Hankinson
OF P. Gillespie
OF M. Dorgan
OF J. Ward
C W. Ewing
P M. Welch
P J. O'Neill

NY 1884 N

M J. Price
M J. Ward
1B A. McKinnon
2B R. Connor
SS E. Caskin
3B F. Hankinson
OF P. Gillespie
OF M. Dorgan
OF J. Ward
C W. Ewing
UT D. Richardson
P M. Welch
P E. Begley

NY 1885 N

M J. Mutrie
1B R. Connor
2B J. Gerhardt
SS J. Ward
3B T. Esterbrook
OF J. O'Rourke
OF P. Gillespie
OF M. Dorgan
C W. Ewing
P M. Welch
P T. Keefe

NY 1886 N

M J. Mutrie
1B R. Connor
2B J. Gerhardt
SS J. Ward
3B T. Esterbrook
OF M. Dorgan
OF P. Gillespie
OF D. Richardson
C W. Ewing
UT J. O'Rourke
P T. Keefe
P M. Welch

NY 1887 N

M J. Mutrie
1B R. Connor
2B D. Richardson
SS J. Ward
3B W. Ewing
OF G. Gore
OF M. Tiernan

OF P. Gillespie
C W. Brown
UT J. O'Rourke
P T. Keefe
P M. Welch
P W. George

NY 1888 N

M J. Mutrie
1B R. Connor
2B D. Richardson
SS J. Ward
3B A. Whitney
OF M. Tiernan
OF M. Slattery
OF J. O'Rourke
C W. Ewing
P T. Keefe
P M. Welch
P L. Titcomb
P E. Crane

NY 1889 N

M J. Mutrie
1B R. Connor
2B D. Richardson
SS J. Ward
3B A. Whitney
OF J. O'Rourke
OF M. Tiernan
OF G. Gore
C W. Ewing
P M. Welch
P T. Keefe
P E. Crane
P H. O'Day

NY 1890 N

M J. Mutrie
1B L. Whistler
2B C. Bassett
SS J. Glasscock
3B J. Denny
OF M. Tiernan
OF J. Burkett
OF M. Hornung
C R. Buckley
UT A. Clarke
P A. Rusie
P M. Welch
P J. Sharrott

NY 1891 N

M J. Mutrie
1B R. Connor
2B D. Richardson
SS J. Glasscock
3B C. Bassett
OF M. Tiernan
OF G. Gore
OF J. O'Rourke
C R. Buckley
P A. Rusie
P J. Ewing
P M. Welch

NY 1892 N

M P. Powers
1B W. Ewing
2B E. Burke
SS W. Fuller
3B D. Lyons
OF M. Tiernan
OF J. O'Rourke
OF H. Lyons
C J. Boyle
P A. Rusie
P C. King
P E. Crane

NY 1893 N

M J. Ward
1B R. Connor
2B J. Ward
SS W. Fuller
3B G. Davis
OF E. Burke
OF M. Tiernan
OF J. Stafford
C J. Doyle
P A. Rusie
P M. Baldwin
P L. German

NY 1894 N

M J. Ward
1B J. Doyle
2B J. Ward
SS W. Fuller
3B G. Davis

OF G. Van Haltren
OF E. Burke
OF M. Tiernan
C C. Farrell
P A. Rusie
P J. Meekin
P H. Westervelt
P L. German
P W. Clarke

NY 1895 N

M G. Davis
M J. Doyle
M H. Watkins
1B J. Doyle
2B J. Stafford
SS W. Fuller
3B G. Davis
OF G. Van Haltren
OF M. Tiernan
OF E. Burke
C C. Farrell
P A. Rusie
P W. Clarke
P J. Meekin
P L. German

NY 1896 N

M A. Irwin
M W. Joyce
1B W. Clark
2B W. Gleason
SS F. Connaughton
3B G. Davis
OF G. Van Haltren
OF M. Tiernan
OF J. Stafford
C P. Wilson
P W. Clarke
P J. Meekin
P M. Sullivan
P E. Doheny

NY 1897 N

M W. Joyce
1B W. Clark
2B W. Gleason
SS G. Davis
3B W. Joyce
OF G. Van Haltren
OF M. Tiernan
OF J. Holmes
C J. Warner
P A. Rusie
P J. Meekin
P J. Seymour
P M. Sullivan
P E. Doheny

NY 1898 N

M W. Joyce
M A. Anson
M W. Joyce
1B W. Joyce
2B W. Gleason
SS G. Davis
3B F. Hartman
OF G. Van Haltren
OF M. Tiernan
OF J. Doyle
C J. Warner
P J. Seymour
P J. Meekin
P A. Rusie
P E. Doheny

NY 1899 N

M J. Day
M F. Hoey
1B J. Doyle
2B W. Gleason
SS G. Davis
3B F. Hartman
OF G. Van Haltren
OF T. O'Brien
C C. Foster
C J. Warner
UT P. Wilson
P W. Carrick
P J. Seymour
P E. Doheny
P J. Meekin
P C. Gettig

NY 1900 N

M W. Ewing
M G. Davis
1B J. Doyle
2B W. Gleason
SS G. Davis
3B C. Hickman

OF G. Van Haltren
OF A. Selbach
OF E. Smith
C F. Bowerman
P W. Carrick
P E. Hawley
P G. Mercer
P E. Doheny

NY 1901 N

M G. Davis
1B J. Ganzel
2B R. Nelson
SS G. Davis
3B S. Strang
OF G. Van Haltren
OF A. Selbach
OF A. McBride
C J. Warner
UT C. Hickman
P L. Taylor
P C. Mathewson
P W. Phyle

NY 1902 N

M H. Fogel
M G. Smith
M J. McGraw
1B D. McGann
2B G. Smith
SS J. Bean
3B W. Lauder
OF W. Brodie
OF J. Jones
OF G. Browne
C F. Bowerman
UT J. Dunn
P C. Mathewson
P L. Taylor
P R. Evans
P J. McGinnity
P T. Sparks

NY 1903 N

M J. McGraw
1B D. McGann
2B W. Gilbert
SS C. Babb
3B W. Lauder
OF G. Browne
OF S. Mertes
OF R. Bresnahan
C J. Warner
P J. McGinnity
P C. Mathewson
P L. Taylor
P J. Cronin
P R. Miller

NY 1904 N

M J. McGraw
1B D. McGann
2B W. Gilbert
SS W. Dahlen
3B A. Devlin
OF G. Browne
OF S. Mertes
OF R. Bresnahan
C J. Warner
P J. McGinnity
P C. Mathewson
P L. Taylor
P G. Wiltse
P L. Ames

NY 1905 N

M J. McGraw
1B D. McGann
2B W. Gilbert
SS W. Dahlen
3B A. Devlin
OF S. Mertes
OF M. Donlin
OF G. Browne
C R. Bresnahan
UT F. Bowerman
UT S. Strang
P C. Mathewson
P J. McGinnity
P L. Ames
P L. Taylor
P G. Wiltse

NY 1906 N

M J. McGraw
1B D. McGann
2B W. Gilbert
SS W. Dahlen
3B A. Devlin
OF G. Browne
OF W. Shannon

OF J. Seymour
C R. Bresnahan
UT F. Bowerman
UT S. Strang
P J. McGinnity
P C. Mathewson
P G. Wiltse
P L. Taylor
P L. Ames
RP G. Ferguson

NY 1907 N

M J. McGraw
1B D. McGann
2B L. Doyle
SS W. Dahlen
3B A. Devlin
OF W. Shannon
OF J. Seymour
OF G. Browne
C R. Bresnahan
UT F. Bowerman
UT S. Strang
P C. Mathewson
P J. McGinnity
P L. Ames
P G. Wiltse
P L. Taylor

NY 1908 N

M J. McGraw
1B F. Tenney
2B L. Doyle
SS A. Bridwell
3B A. Devlin
OF J. Seymour
OF M. Donlin
OF W. Shannon
C R. Bresnahan
P C. Mathewson
P G. Wiltse
P J. Crandall
P J. McGinnity
P L. Taylor

NY 1909 N

M J. McGraw
1B F. Tenney
2B L. Doyle
SS A. Bridwell
3B A. Devlin
OF J. Murray
OF W. O'Hara
OF H. McCormick
C G. Schlei
P C. Mathewson
P A. Raymond
P G. Wiltse
P L. Ames
P R. Marquard

NY 1910 N

M J. McGraw
1B F. Merkle
2B L. Doyle
SS A. Bridwell
3B A. Devlin
OF J. Murray
OF J. Devore
OF F. Snodgrass
C J. Meyers
P C. Mathewson
P L. Taylor
P G. Wiltse
P L. Drucke
P J. Crandall
P L. Ames

NY 1911 N

M J. McGraw
1B F. Merkle
2B L. Doyle
SS A. Bridwell
3B A. Devlin
OF F. Snodgrass
OF J. Devore
OF J. Murray
C J. Meyers
UT A. Fletcher
P C. Mathewson
P R. Marquard
P L. Ames
P J. Crandall
P G. Wiltse

NY 1912 N

M J. McGraw
1B F. Merkle
2B L. Doyle
SS A. Fletcher
3B C. Herzog
OF J. Murray

OF J. Devore
C J. Meyers
UT J. Devore
P C. Mathewson
P R. Marquard
P C. Tesreau
P L. Ames
P J. Crandall

NY 1913 N

M J. McGraw
1B F. Merkle
2B L. Doyle
SS A. Fletcher
3B C. Herzog
OF G. Burns
OF J. Murray
OF F. Snodgrass
C J. Meyers
UT A. Shafer
P C. Mathewson
P R. Marquard
P C. Tesreau
P A. Demaree
P A. Fromme
RP J. Crandall

NY 1914 N

M J. McGraw
1B F. Merkle
2B L. Doyle
SS A. Fletcher
3B M. Stock
OF G. Burns
OF R. Bescher
OF F. Snodgrass
C J. Meyers
P C. Tesreau
P C. Mathewson
P R. Marquard
P A. Demaree
P A. Fromme

NY 1915 N

M J. McGraw
1B F. Merkle
2B L. Doyle
SS A. Fletcher
3B J. Lobert
OF G. Burns
OF D. Robertson
OF F. Snodgrass
C J. Meyers
P C. Tesreau
P W. Perritt
P C. Mathewson
P R. Stroud
P R. Marquard
RP W. Ritter
RP F. Schupp

NY 1916 N

M J. McGraw
1B F. Merkle
2B L. Doyle
SS A. Fletcher
3B W. McKechnie
OF G. Burns
OF B. Kauff
OF D. Robertson
C W. Rariden
P C. Tesreau
P W. Perritt
P J. Benton
P J. Anderson
P F. Schupp

NY 1917 N

M J. McGraw
1B W. Holke
2B C. Herzog
SS A. Fletcher
3B H. Zimmerman
OF B. Kauff
OF G. Burns
OF D. Robertson
C W. Rariden
P F. Schupp
P H. Sallee
P W. Perritt
P J. Benton
P C. Tesreau

NY 1918 N

M J. McGraw
1B W. Holke
2B L. Doyle
SS A. Fletcher
3B H. Zimmerman
OF R. Youngs

OF G. Burns
OF B. Kauff
C G. McCarty
P W. Perritt
P C. Causey
P A. Demaree
P H. Sallee
P F. Toney

NY 1919 N
M J. McGraw
1B H. Chase
2B L. Doyle
SS A. Fletcher
3B H. Zimmerman
OF G. Burns
OF B. Kauff
OF R. Youngs
C G. McCarty
P J. Barnes
P J. Benton
P F. Toney
P J. Dubuc
P C. Causey

NY 1920 N
M J. McGraw
1B G. Kelly
2B L. Doyle
SS D. Bancroft
3B F. Frisch
OF G. Burns
OF R. Youngs
OF L. King
C F. Snyder
P J. Barnes
P A. Nehf
P F. Toney
P P. Douglas
P J. Benton

NY 1921 N
M J. McGraw
1B G. Kelly
2B J. Rawlings
SS D. Bancroft
3B F. Frisch
OF G. Burns
OF R. Youngs
OF E. Meusel
C F. Snyder
P A. Nehf
P J. Barnes
P F. Toney
P P. Douglas
P W. Ryan
RP H. Sallee

NY 1922 N
M J. McGraw
1B G. Kelly
2B F. Frisch
SS D. Bancroft
3B H. Groh
OF E. Meusel
OF R. Youngs
OF C. Stengel
C F. Snyder
P A. Nehf
P J. Barnes
P W. Ryan
P P. Douglas
P H. McQuillan
RP C. Jonnard
RP C. Causey
RP V. Barnes

NY 1923 N
M J. McGraw
1B G. Kelly
2B F. Frisch
SS D. Bancroft
3B H. Groh
OF R. Youngs
OF E. Meusel
OF W. Cunningham
C F. Snyder
UT T. Jackson
P H. McQuillan
P J. Scott
P A. Nehf
P J. Bentley
P W. Ryan
RP C. Jonnard
RP V. Barnes

NY 1924 N
M J. McGraw
M H. Jennings
M J. McGraw
1B G. Kelly

2B F. Frisch
SS T. Jackson
3B H. Groh
OF E. Meusel
OF R. Youngs
OF L. Wilson
C F. Snyder
UT W. Southworth
P V. Barnes
P J. Bentley
P H. McQuillan
P A. Nehf
P W. Dean
RP C. Jonnard

NY 1925 N
M J. McGraw
1B W. Terry
2B G. Kelly
SS T. Jackson
3B F. Lindstrom
OF R. Youngs
OF E. Meusel
OF W. Southworth
C F. Snyder
UT F. Frisch
P J. Scott
P V. Barnes
P K. Greenfield
P J. Bentley
P A. Nehf
RP W. Huntzinger

NY 1926 N
M J. McGraw
1B G. Kelly
2B F. Frisch
SS T. Jackson
3B F. Lindstrom
OF E. Meusel
OF R. Youngs
OF A. Tyson
C P. Florence
UT W. Terry
P J. Scott
P K. Greenfield
P F. Fitzsimmons
P V. Barnes
P J. Ring
RP L. Davies

NY 1927 N
M J. McGraw
M R. Hornsby
1B W. Terry
2B R. Hornsby
SS T. Jackson
3B F. Lindstrom
OF G. Harper
OF E. Roush
OF C. Mueller
C J. Taylor
UT A. Reese
P B. Grimes
P F. Fitzsimmons
P V. Barnes
P L. Benton
P F. Henry
RP D. Songer

NY 1928 N
M J. McGraw
1B W. Terry
2B A. Cohen
SS T. Jackson
3B F. Lindstrom
OF J. Welsh
OF M. Ott
OF F. O'Doul
C J. Hogan
UT A. Reese
P L. Benton
P F. Fitzsimmons
P J. Genewich
P C. Hubbell
P V. Aldridge

NY 1929 N
M J. McGraw
1B W. Terry
2B A. Cohen
SS T. Jackson
3B F. Lindstrom
OF M. Ott
OF E. Roush
OF F. Leach
C J. Hogan
UT R. O'Farrell
P C. Hubbell
P L. Benton
P F. Fitzsimmons
P W. Walker

P C. Mays
RP R. Judd

NY 1930 N
M J. McGraw
1B W. Terry
2B H. Critz
SS T. Jackson
3B F. Lindstrom
OF M. Ott
OF F. Leach
OF W. Roettger
C J. Hogan
UT R. O'Farrell
P W. Walker
P C. Hubbell
P F. Fitzsimmons
P H. Pruett
P C. Mitchell
RP J. Heving

NY 1931 N
M J. McGraw
1B W. Terry
2B W. Hunnefield
SS T. Jackson
3B J. Vergez
OF M. Ott
OF F. Leach
OF E. Allen
C J. Hogan
P F. Fitzsimmons
P C. Hubbell
P W. Walker
P C. Mitchell
P J. Berly

NY 1932 N
M J. McGraw
M W. Terry
1B W. Terry
2B H. Critz
SS E. Marshall
3B J. Vergez
OF M. Ott
OF F. Lindstrom
OF J. Moore
C J. Hogan
UT C. Fullis
P C. Hubbell
P F. Fitzsimmons
P W. Walker
P J. Mooney
P H. Bell
RP A. Luque
RP S. Gibson

NY 1933 N
M W. Terry
1B W. Terry
2B H. Critz
SS J. Ryan
3B J. Vergez
OF M. Ott
OF J. Moore
OF G. Davis
C A. Mancuso
P C. Hubbell
P H. Schumacher
P F. Fitzsimmons
P L. Parmelee
RP H. Bell
RP A. Luque
RP G. Spencer

NY 1934 N
M W. Terry
1B W. Terry
2B H. Critz
SS T. Jackson
3B J. Vergez
OF M. Ott
OF J. Moore
OF G. Watkins
C A. Mancuso
UT J. Ryan
P C. Hubbell
P H. Schumacher
P F. Fitzsimmons
P L. Parmelee
P J. Bowman
RP A. Smith
RP H. Bell

NY 1935 N
M W. Terry
1B W. Terry
2B M. Koenig
SS R. Bartell
3B T. Jackson
OF J. Moore

OF H. Leiber
OF M. Ott
C A. Mancuso
P C. Hubbell
P H. Schumacher
P L. Parmelee
P C. Castleman
P A. Smith
RP A. Stout
RP F. Gabler

NY 1936 N
M W. Terry
1B S. Leslie
2B B. Whitehead
SS R. Bartell
3B T. Jackson
OF J. Moore
OF M. Ott
OF H. Leiber
C A. Mancuso
UT J. Ripple
P C. Hubbell
P H. Schumacher
P A. Smith
P F. Gabler
P H. Gumbert
RP S. Coffman

NY 1937 N
M W. Terry
1B J. McCarthy
2B B. Whitehead
SS R. Bartell
3B L. Chiozza
OF J. Moore
OF J. Ripple
OF M. Ott
C H. Danning
P C. Hubbell
P C. Melton
P H. Schumacher
P H. Gumbert
P C. Castleman
RP A. Smith
RP S. Coffman

NY 1938 N
M W. Terry
1B J. McCarthy
2B A. Kampouris
SS R. Bartell
3B M. Ott
OF J. Ripple
OF J. Moore
OF H. Leiber
C H. Danning
P C. Melton
P H. Gumbert
P H. Schumacher
P C. Hubbell
P W. Lohrman
RP S. Coffman
RP W. Brown

NY 1939 N
M W. Terry
1B H. Bonura
2B B. Whitehead
SS W. Jurges
3B T. Hafey
OF J. Demaree
OF J. Moore
OF M. Ott
C H. Danning
P H. Gumbert
P C. Melton
P W. Lohrman
P H. Schumacher
P C. Hubbell
RP W. Brown
RP J. Lynn

NY 1940 N
M W. Terry
1B N. Young
2B A. Cuccinello
SS N. Witek
3B B. Whitehead
OF J. Moore
OF J. Demaree
OF M. Ott
C H. Danning
P H. Gumbert
P H. Schumacher
P C. Hubbell
P W. Lohrman
P C. Melton
RP W. Brown
RP R. Joiner

NY 1941 N
M W. Terry
1B N. Young
2B B. Whitehead
SS W. Jurges
3B R. Bartell
OF M. Ott
OF J. Rucker
OF J. Moore
C H. Danning
P H. Schumacher
P C. Melton
P C. Hubbell
P W. Lohrman
P R. Carpenter
RP R. Bowman
RP A. Adams
RP W. Brown

NY 1942 N
M M. Ott
1B J. Mize
2B N. Witek
SS W. Jurges
3B W. Werber
OF M. Ott
OF W. Marshall
OF H. Barna
C H. Danning
UT N. Young
P H. Schumacher
P R. Carpenter
P W. Lohrman
P C. Hubbell
P C. Melton
RP A. Adams

NY 1943 N
M M. Ott
1B J. Orengo
2B N. Witek
SS W. Jurges
3B R. Bartell
OF J. Rucker
OF M. Ott
OF J. Medwick
C A. Mancuso
UT S. Gordon
UT E. Lombardi
UT J. Maynard
P C. Melton
P J. Wittig
P V. Mungo
P R. Fischer
P K. Chase
RP A. Adams
RP W. Sayles

NY 1944 N
M M. Ott
1B P. Weintraub
2B G. Hausmann
SS J. Kerr
3B H. Luby
OF J. Rucker
OF J. Medwick
OF M. Ott
C E. Lombardi
UT N. Reyes
P W. Voiselle
P H. Feldman
P H. Pyle
P R. Fischer
RP A. Adams
RP A. Hansen

NY 1945 N
M M. Ott
1B P. Weintraub
2B G. Hausmann
SS J. Kerr
3B N. Reyes
OF M. Ott
OF J. Rucker
OF D. Gardella
C E. Lombardi
P W. Voiselle
P H. Feldman
P V. Mungo
P J. Brewer
P W. Emmerich
RP A. Adams
RP R. Fischer

NY 1946 N
M M. Ott
1B J. Mize
2B R. Blattner
SS J. Kerr
3B W. Rigney
OF W. Marshall

OF S. Gordon
OF G. Rosen
C W. Cooper
UT J. Graham
UT J. Rucker
UT N. Young
P G. Koslo
P M. Kennedy
P W. Voiselle
P K. Trinkle
P H. Schumacher
RP M. Budnick
RP E. Thompson

NY 1947 N
M M. Ott
1B J. Mize
2B W. Rigney
SS J. Kerr
3B J. Lohrke
OF W. Marshall
OF B. Thomson
OF S. Gordon
C W. Cooper
P L. Jansen
P G. Koslo
P M. Kennedy
P C. Hartung
RP K. Trinkle
RP J. Beggs

NY 1948 N
M M. Ott
M L. Durocher
1B J. Mize
2B W. Rigney
SS J. Kerr
3B S. Gordon
OF C. Lockman
OF W. Marshall
OF B. Thomson
C W. Cooper
UT J. Lohrke
P L. Jansen
P S. Jones
P R. Poat
P C. Hartung
P G. Koslo
RP A. Hansen
RP K. Trinkle

NY 1949 N
M L. Durocher
1B J. Mize
2B H. Thompson
SS J. Kerr
3B S. Gordon
OF B. Thomson
OF C. Lockman
OF W. Marshall
C W. Westrum
UT W. Rigney
P L. Jansen
P M. Kennedy
P G. Koslo
P S. Jones
P C. Hartung
RP W. Higbe
RP H. Behrman
RP A. Hansen

NY 1950 N
M L. Durocher
1B H. Gilbert
2B E. Stanky
SS A. Dark
3B H. Thompson
OF B. Thomson
OF C. Lockman
OF D. Mueller
C W. Westrum
UT M. Irvin
P L. Jansen
P S. Maglie
P S. Jones
P G. Koslo
P J. Hearn
RP J. Kramer
RP A. Hansen

NY 1951 N
M L. Durocher
1B C. Lockman
2B E. Stanky
SS A. Dark
3B H. Thompson
OF W. Mays
OF D. Mueller
OF M. Irvin
C W. Westrum
UT R. Thomson
P S. Maglie

P L. Jansen
P J. Hearn
P G. Koslo
RP G. Spencer
RP S. Jones
RP M. Kennedy

NY 1952 N
M L. Durocher
1B C. Lockman
2B D. Williams
SS A. Dark
3B R. Thomson
OF D. Mueller
OF H. Thompson
OF R. Elliott
C W. Westrum
P J. Hearn
P S. Maglie
P L. Jansen
P G. Koslo
P H. Lanier
RP J. Wilhelm
RP M. Kennedy
RP G. Spencer

NY 1953 N
M L. Durocher
1B C. Lockman
2B D. Williams
SS A. Dark
3B H. Thompson
OF R. Thomson
OF D. Mueller
OF M. Irvin
C W. Westrum
UT D. Spencer
P R. Gomez
P J. Hearn
P L. Jansen
P S. Maglie
P G. Koslo
RP J. Wilhelm
RP E. Corwin

NY 1954 N
M L. Durocher
1B C. Lockman
2B D. Williams
SS A. Dark
3B H. Thompson
OF D. Mueller
OF W. Mays
OF M. Irvin
C W. Westrum
P J. Antonelli
P R. Gomez
P S. Maglie
P J. Hearn
P D. Liddle
RP M. Grissom
RP J. Wilhelm
RP J. McCall

NY 1955 N
M L. Durocher
1B B. Harris
2B W. Terwilliger
SS A. Dark
3B H. Thompson
OF W. Mays
OF D. Mueller
OF C. Lockman
C R. Katt
UT R. Hofman
UT J. Rhodes
P J. Antonelli
P J. Hearn
P R. Gomez
P S. Maglie
P D. Liddle
RP J. Wilhelm
RP J. McCall
RP M. Grissom

NY 1956 N
M W. Rigney
1B W. White
2B A. Schoendienst
SS D. Spencer
3B F. Castleman
OF W. Mays
OF D. Mueller
OF J. Brandt
C W. Sarni
UT J. Rhodes
P J. Antonelli
P R. Gomez
P A. Worthington
P J. Hearn
P R. Littlefield
RP S. Ridzik

RP J. Wilhelm
RP M. Grissom

NY 1957 N

M W. Rigney
1B C. Lockman
2B D. O'Connell
SS D. Spencer
3B R. Jablonski
OF W. Mays
OF D. Mueller
OF H. Sauer
C V. Thomas
UT O. Virgil
P R. Gomez
P J. Antonelli
P C. Barclay
P S. Miller
P R. Crone
RP A. Worthington
RP M. Grissom
RP R. Monzant

NY 1962 N

M C. Stengel
1B M. Throneberry
2B C. Neal
SS E. Chacon
3B F. Mantilla
OF F. Thomas
OF J. Hickman
OF R. Ashburn
C C. Cannizzaro
UT J. Christopher
UT R. Kanehl
P R. Craig
P A. Jackson
P J. Hook
P R. Miller
RP N. Anderson
RP C. Moorhead
RP R. Daviault

NY 1963 N

M C. Stengel
1B T. Harkness
2B R. Hunt
SS R. Moran
3B C. Neal
OF E. Snider
OF F. Thomas
OF J. Hickman
C C. Coleman
UT R. Kanehl
P R. Craig
P A. Jackson
P C. Willey
P G. Cisco
P E. Stallard
RP L. Bearnarth
RP K. Mac Kenzie
RP D. Rowe

NY 1964 N

M C. Stengel
1B E. Kranepool
2B R. Hunt
SS R. McMillan
3B C. Smith
OF J. Christopher
OF J. Hickman
OF G. Altman
C J. Gonder
P J. Fisher
P E. Stallard
P A. Jackson
P G. Cisco
RP W. Wakefield
RP L. Bearnarth

NY 1965 N

M C. Stengel
M W. Westrum
1B E. Kranepool
2B C. Hiller
SS R. McMillan
3B C. Smith
OF J. Lewis
OF R. Swoboda
OF J. Christopher
C C. Cannizzaro
UT J. Hickman
UT R. Klaus
P J. Fisher
P A. Jackson
P W. Spahn
P G. Cisco
RP F. McGraw
RP T. Parsons
RP G. Kroll

NY 1966 N

M W. Westrum
1B E. Kranepool
2B R. Hunt
SS E. Bressoud
3B K. Boyer
OF C. Jones
OF A. Luplow
OF R. Swoboda
C G. Grote
UT C. Hiller
P J. Fisher
P D. Ribant
P R. Shaw
P R. Gardner
RP J. Hamilton
RP R. Selma
RP W. Hepler

NY 1967 N

M W. Westrum
M F. Parker
1B E. Kranepool
2B G. Buchek
SS D. Harrelson
3B E. Charles
OF H. Davis
OF C. Jones
OF R. Swoboda
C G. Grote
UT T. Reynolds
P T. Seaver
P J. Fisher
P D. Cardwell
P R. Shaw
RP R. Selma
RP R. Taylor
RP D. Shaw

NY 1968 N

M G. Hodges
1B E. Kranepool
2B P. Linz
SS D. Harrelson
3B E. Charles
OF C. Jones
OF T. Agee
OF R. Swoboda
C G. Grote
UT A. Shamsky
P G. Seaver
P J. Koosman
P D. Cardwell
P R. Selma
P L. Ryan
RP C. Koonce
RP R. Taylor
RP D. Frisella

NY 1969 N

M G. Hodges
1B E. Kranepool
2B K. Boswell
SS D. Harrelson
3B R. Garrett
OF T. Agee
OF C. Jones
OF R. Swoboda
C G. Grote
UT E. Gaspar
UT A. Shamsky
UT A. Weis
P G. Seaver
P J. Koosman
P G. Gentry
P D. Cardwell
P J. McAndrew
RP F. McGraw
RP C. Koonce
RP R. Taylor

NY 1970 N

M G. Hodges
1B D. Clendenon
2B K. Boswell
SS D. Harrelson
3B J. Foy
OF T. Agee
OF C. Jones
OF R. Swoboda
C G. Grote
UT R. Garrett
UT A. Shamsky
P G. Seaver
P J. Koosman
P G. Gentry
P J. McAndrew
P R. Sadecki
RP F. McGraw
RP R. Taylor
RP D. Frisella

NY 1971 N

M G. Hodges
1B E. Kranepool
2B K. Boswell
SS D. Harrelson
3B R. Staiger
OF C. Jones
OF T. Agee
OF K. Singleton
C G. Grote
UT C. Hiller
UT J. Fisher
UT D. Hahn
UT D. Marshall
P G. Seaver
P G. Gentry
P J. Koosman
P R. Sadecki
P L. Ryan
RP F. McGraw
RP D. Frisella
RP C. Williams

NY 1972 N

M L. Berra
1B E. Kranepool
2B K. Boswell
SS D. Harrelson
3B J. Fregosi
OF T. Agee
OF J. Milner
OF C. Jones
C D. Dyer
UT R. Garrett
UT T. Martinez
P G. Seaver
P J. Matlack
P G. Gentry
P J. Koosman
P J. McAndrew
RP F. McGraw
RP R. Sadecki
RP D. Frisella

NY 1973 N

M L. Berra
1B J. Milner
2B F. Millan
SS D. Harrelson
3B R. Garrett
OF D. Staub
OF C. Jones
OF D. Hahn
C G. Grote
UT E. Kranepool
P G. Seaver
P J. Koosman
P J. Matlack
P G. Stone
P R. Sadecki
RP F. McGraw
RP H. Parker

NY 1974 N

M L. Berra
1B J. Milner
2B F. Millan
SS D. Harrelson
3B R. Garrett
OF D. Staub
OF C. Jones
OF D. Hahn
C G. Grote
UT T. Martinez
P J. Matlack
P J. Koosman
P G. Seaver
P H. Parker
P R. Sadecki
RP R. Apodaca
RP F. McGraw
RP R. Miller

NY 1975 N

M L. Berra
M R. McMillan
1B E. Kranepool
2B F. Millan
SS M. Phillips
3B R. Garrett
OF D. Staub
OF D. Unser
OF D. Kingman
C G. Grote
UT J. Torre
P G. Seaver
P J. Koosman
P J. Matlack
P R. Tate
P H. Webb
RP R. Baldwin
RP R. Apodaca
RP T. Hall

NY 1976 N

M J. Frazier
1B E. Kranepool
2B F. Millan
SS D. Harrelson
3B R. Staiger
OF J. Milner
OF D. Kingman
OF B. Boisclair
C G. Grote
UT J. Torre
P G. Seaver
P J. Matlack
P J. Koosman
P M. Lolich
P C. Swan
RP C. Lockwood
RP R. Apodaca

NY 1977 N

M J. Frazier
M J. Torre
1B J. Milner
2B F. Millan
SS D. Harrelson
3B L. Randle
OF L. Mazzilli
OF S. Henderson
OF B. Boisclair
C J. Stearns
UT E. Kranepool
UT M. Vail
P J. Koosman
P A. Espinosa
P J. Matlack
P C. Swan
P P. Zachry
RP C. Lockwood
RP R. Myrick
RP R. Apodaca

NY 1978 N

M J. Torre
1B G. Montanez
2B R. Flynn
SS T. Foli
3B L. Randle
OF S. Henderson
OF L. Mazzilli
OF E. Maddox
C J. Stearns
UT B. Boisclair
UT J. Youngblood
P J. Koosman
P C. Swan
P A. Espinosa
P P. Zachry
P M. Bruhert
RP C. Lockwood
RP D. Murray
RP D. Bernard

NY 1979 N

M J. Torre
1B G. Montanez
2B R. Flynn
SS F. Taveras
3B R. Hebner
OF J. Youngblood
OF L. Mazzilli
OF S. Henderson
C J. Stearns
P C. Swan
P P. Falcone
P K. Kobel
RP N. Allen
RP D. Murray
RP A. Hassler

NY 1980 N

M J. Torre
1B L. Mazzilli
2B R. Flynn
SS F. Taveras
3B E. Maddox
OF S. Henderson
OF J. Youngblood
OF C. Washington
C A. Trevino
UT M. Jorgensen
P B. Burris
P P. Zachry
P M. Bomback
P C. Swan
RP T. Hausman
RP J. Reardon
RP N. Allen

NY 1981 N

M J. Torre

1B D. Kingman
2B R. Flynn
SS F. Taveras
3B H. Brooks
OF L. Mazzilli
OF W. Wilson
OF E. Valentine
C J. Stearns
UT M. Cubbage
UT M. Jorgensen
UT D. Staub
P P. Zachry
P M. Scott
P E. Lynch
P G. Harris
RP P. Falcone
RP N. Allen
RP D. Miller

NY 1982 N

M G. Bamberger
1B D. Kingman
2B W. Backman
SS R. Gardenhire
3B H. Brooks
OF W. Wilson
OF G. Foster
OF E. Valentine
C J. Stearns
UT M. Bailor
UT M. Jorgensen
UT D. Staub
P R. Puleo
P P. Falcone
P C. Swan
P M. Scott
P E. Lynch
RP J. Orosco
RP N. Allen

NY 1983 N

M G. Bamberger
M F. Howard
1B K. Hernandez
2B B. Giles
SS J. Oquendo
3B H. Brooks
OF G. Foster
OF W. Wilson
OF D. Strawberry
C R. Hodges
UT M. Bailor
UT D. Heep
UT D. Kingman
UT D. Staub
P G. Seaver
P M. Torrez
P E. Lynch
P C. Terrell
P C. Swan
RP J. Orosco
RP D. Sisk
RP R. Holman

NY 1984 N

M D. Johnson
1B K. Hernandez
2B W. Backman
SS J. Oquendo
3B H. Brooks
OF W. Wilson
OF D. Strawberry
OF G. Foster
C M. Fitzgerald
UT D. Heep
P D. Gooden
P C. Terrell
P R. Darling
P E. Lynch
P B. Berenyi
RP J. Orosco
RP B. Gaff
RP D. Sisk

NY 1985 N

M D. Johnson
1B K. Hernandez
2B W. Backman
SS R. Santana
3B H. Johnson
OF G. Foster
OF D. Strawberry
OF W. Wilson
C G. Carter
P D. Gooden
P R. Darling
P E. Lynch
P C. Fernandez
P R. Aguilera
RP R. McDowell
RP J. Orosco
RP D. Sisk

NY 1986 N

M D. Johnson
1B K. Hernandez
2B W. Backman
SS R. Santana
3B R. Knight
OF L. Dykstra
OF D. Strawberry
OF W. Wilson
C G. Carter
UT K. Mitchell
P D. Gooden
P R. Darling
P R. Ojeda
P C. Fernandez
P R. Aguilera
RP R. McDowell
RP J. Orosco
RP D. Sisk

NY 1987 N

M D. Johnson
1B K. Hernandez
2B T. Teufel
SS R. Santana
3B H. Johnson
OF D. Strawberry
OF W. McReynolds
OF L. Dykstra
C G. Carter
UT W. Wilson
P R. Darling
P D. Gooden
P C. Fernandez
P R. Aguilera
P J. Mitchell
RP T. Leach
RP R. McDowell
RP D. Sisk

NY 1988 N

M D. Johnson
1B K. Hernandez
2B W. Backman
SS K. Elster
3B H. Johnson
OF D. Strawberry
OF W. McReynolds
OF L. Dykstra
C G. Carter
UT D. Magadan
UT W. Wilson
P D. Gooden
P R. Darling
P D. Cone
P C. Fernandez
RP T. Leach
RP R. McDowell
RP R. Myers

NY 1989 N

M D. Johnson
1B D. Magadan
2B G. Jefferies
SS K. Elster
3B H. Johnson
OF W. McReynolds
OF D. Strawberry
OF J. Samuel
C B. Lyons
P D. Cone
P C. Fernandez
P R. Darling
P R. Ojeda
P D. Gooden
RP R. Myers
RP R. Aguilera
RP D. Aase

NY 1990 N

M D. Johnson
M B. Harrelson
1B D. Magadan
2B G. Jefferies
SS K. Elster
3B H. Johnson
OF D. Strawberry
OF W. McReynolds
OF D. Boston
C M. Sasser
P F. Viola
P D. Gooden
P D. Cone
P C. Fernandez
P R. Darling
RP A. Pena
RP J. Franco
RP W. Whitehurst

NY 1903 A

M C. Griffith
1B J. Ganzel
2B J. Williams
SS N. Elberfeld
3B W. Conroy
OF W. Keeler
OF H. McFarland
OF A. Davis
C H. Beville
P J. Chesbro
P J. Tannehill
P C. Griffith
P H. Howell
P W. Wolfe

NY 1904 A

M C. Griffith
1B J. Ganzel
2B J. Williams
SS N. Elberfeld
3B W. Conroy
OF W. Keeler
OF J. Anderson
OF P. Dougherty
C J. McGuire
UT D. Fultz
P J. Chesbro
P J. Powell
P A. Orth
P T. Hughes
P C. Griffith

NY 1905 A

M C. Griffith
1B H. Chase
2B J. Williams
SS N. Elberfeld
3B J. Yeager
OF W. Keeler
OF D. Fultz
OF P. Dougherty
C J. Kleinow
UT W. Conroy
P A. Orth
P J. Chesbro
P W. Hogg
P J. Powell
P C. Griffith

NY 1906 A

M C. Griffith
1B H. Chase
2B J. Williams
SS N. Elberfeld
3B F. LaPorte
OF W. Keeler
OF D. Hoffman
OF W. Conroy
C J. Kleinow
P A. Orth
P J. Chesbro
P W. Hogg
P W. Clarkson
P E. Newton

NY 1907 A

M C. Griffith
1B H. Chase
2B J. Williams
SS N. Elberfeld
3B J. Moriarty
OF D. Hoffman
OF W. Keeler
OF W. Conroy
C J. Kleinow
UT F. LaPorte
P A. Orth
P J. Chesbro
P J. Doyle
P W. Hogg
P E. Newton

NY 1908 A

M C. Griffith
M N. Elberfeld
1B H. Chase
2B J. Niles
SS C. Ball
3B W. Conroy
OF C. Hemphill
OF W. Keeler
OF G. Stahl
C J. Kleinow
UT J. Moriarty
P J. Chesbro
P J. Lake
P W. Manning
P W. Hogg
P A. Orth

NY 1909 A
- M G. Stallings
- 1B H. Chase
- 2B F. LaPorte
- SS J. Knight
- 3B J. Austin
- OF A. Engle
- OF C. Demmitt
- OF W. Keeler
- C J. Kleinow
- UT W. Cree
- UT N. Elberfeld
- P J. Warhop
- P J. Lake
- P W. Manning
- P L. Brockett
- P J. Doyle

NY 1910 A
- M G. Stallings
- M H. Chase
- 1B H. Chase
- 2B F. LaPorte
- SS J. Knight
- 3B J. Austin
- OF W. Cree
- OF H. Wolter
- OF C. Hemphill
- C E. Sweeney
- UT B. Daniels
- P R. Ford
- P J. Warhop
- P J. Quinn
- P J. Vaughn
- P T. Hughes

NY 1911 A
- M H. Chase
- 1B H. Chase
- 2B E. Gardner
- SS J. Knight
- 3B R. Hartzell
- OF W. Cree
- OF B. Daniels
- OF H. Wolter
- C W. Blair
- P R. Ford
- P R. Caldwell
- P J. Warhop
- P J. Quinn
- P R. Fisher

NY 1912 A
- M H. Wolverton
- 1B H. Chase
- 2B G. Simmons
- SS J. Martin
- 3B R. Hartzell
- OF B. Daniels
- OF G. Zinn
- OF W. Cree
- C E. Sweeney
- P R. Ford
- P J. Warhop
- P R. Caldwell
- P G. McConnell
- P J. Quinn

NY 1913 A
- M F. Chance
- 1B J. Knight
- 2B R. Hartzell
- SS R. Peckinpaugh
- 3B E. Midkiff
- OF W. Cree
- OF H. Wolter
- OF B. Daniels
- C E. Sweeney
- P R. Fisher
- P R. Ford
- P A. Schulz
- P G. McConnell
- P R. Caldwell

NY 1914 A
- M F. Chance
- M R. Peckinpaugh
- 1B C. Mullen
- 2B L. Boone
- SS R. Peckinpaugh
- 3B F. Maisel
- OF R. Hartzell
- OF L. Cook
- OF W. Cree
- C E. Sweeney
- P J. Warhop
- P R. Caldwell
- P R. Keating
- P R. Fisher
- P M. McHale

NY 1915 A
- M W. Donovan
- 1B W. Pipp
- 2B L. Boone
- SS R. Peckinpaugh
- 3B F. Maisel
- OF L. Cook
- OF H. High
- OF R. Hartzell
- C L. Nunamaker
- P R. Caldwell
- P R. Fisher
- P J. Warhop
- P C. Brown
- P E. Pieh

NY 1916 A
- M W. Donovan
- 1B W. Pipp
- 2B E. Gedeon
- SS R. Peckinpaugh
- 3B J. Baker
- OF L. Magee
- OF H. High
- OF F. Gilhooley
- C L. Nunamaker
- P J. Shawkey
- P G. Mogridge
- P R. Fisher
- P A. Russell
- P N. Cullop
- RP E. Love

NY 1917 A
- M W. Donovan
- 1B W. Pipp
- 2B F. Maisel
- SS R. Peckinpaugh
- 3B J. Baker
- OF E. Miller
- OF T. Hendryx
- OF H. High
- C L. Nunamaker
- P J. Shawkey
- P R. Caldwell
- P G. Mogridge
- P N. Cullop
- P U. Shocker

NY 1918 A
- M M. Huggins
- 1B W. Pipp
- 2B D. Pratt
- SS R. Peckinpaugh
- 3B J. Baker
- OF F. Gilhooley
- OF F. Bodie
- OF E. Miller
- C J. Hannah
- P G. Mogridge
- P E. Love
- P R. Caldwell
- P A. Russell
- P J. Finneran

NY 1919 A
- M M. Huggins
- 1B W. Pipp
- 2B D. Pratt
- SS R. Peckinpaugh
- 3B J. Baker
- OF G. Lewis
- OF F. Bodie
- OF S. Vick
- C H. Ruel
- P J. Quinn
- P J. Shawkey
- P H. Thormahlen
- P G. Mogridge
- P C. Mays

NY 1920 A
- M M. Huggins
- 1B W. Pipp
- 2B D. Pratt
- SS R. Peckinpaugh
- 3B A. Ward
- OF G. Lewis
- OF F. Bodie
- OF S. Vick
- C H. Ruel
- UT R. Meusel
- P C. Mays
- P J. Shawkey
- P J. Quinn
- P H. Collins
- P H. Thormahlen

NY 1921 A
- M M. Huggins
- 1B W. Pipp
- 2B A. Ward
- SS R. Peckinpaugh
- 3B J. Baker
- OF G. Ruth
- OF R. Meusel
- OF E. Miller
- C W. Schang
- P C. Mays
- P W. Hoyt
- P J. Shawkey
- P H. Collins
- P J. Quinn

NY 1922 A
- M M. Huggins
- 1B W. Pipp
- 2B A. Ward
- SS L. Scott
- 3B J. Dugan
- OF L. Witt
- OF R. Meusel
- OF G. Ruth
- C W. Schang
- P J. Shawkey
- P W. Hoyt
- P S. Jones
- P L. Bush
- P C. Mays
- RP G. Murray

NY 1923 A
- M M. Huggins
- 1B W. Pipp
- 2B A. Ward
- SS L. Scott
- 3B J. Dugan
- OF G. Ruth
- OF L. Witt
- OF R. Meusel
- C W. Schang
- P L. Bush
- P J. Shawkey
- P S. Jones
- P W. Hoyt
- P H. Pennock

NY 1924 A
- M M. Huggins
- 1B W. Pipp
- 2B A. Ward
- SS L. Scott
- 3B J. Dugan
- OF G. Ruth
- OF L. Witt
- OF R. Meusel
- C W. Schang
- P H. Pennock
- P L. Bush
- P W. Hoyt
- P J. Shawkey
- P S. Jones
- RP N. Gaston

NY 1925 A
- M M. Huggins
- 1B H. Gehrig
- 2B A. Ward
- SS P. Wanninger
- 3B J. Dugan
- OF E. Combs
- OF R. Meusel
- OF G. Ruth
- C B. Bengough
- P H. Pennock
- P S. Jones
- P U. Shocker
- P W. Hoyt
- P J. Shawkey
- P H. Johnson
- RP J. Ferguson

NY 1926 A
- M M. Huggins
- 1B H. Gehrig
- 2B A. Lazzeri
- SS M. Koenig
- 3B J. Dugan
- OF G. Ruth
- OF E. Combs
- OF R. Meusel
- C T. Collins
- UT B. Paschal
- P H. Pennock
- P U. Shocker
- P E. Combs
- P W. Hoyt
- P S. Jones
- P M. Thomas
- RP E. Braxton

NY 1927 A
- M M. Huggins
- 1B H. Gehrig
- 2B A. Lazzeri
- SS M. Koenig
- 3B J. Dugan
- OF E. Combs
- OF G. Ruth
- OF R. Meusel
- C T. Collins
- P W. Hoyt
- P W. Moore
- P H. Pennock
- P U. Shocker
- P W. Ruether

NY 1928 A
- M M. Huggins
- 1B H. Gehrig
- 2B A. Lazzeri
- SS M. Koenig
- 3B J. Dugan
- OF G. Ruth
- OF E. Combs
- OF R. Meusel
- C J. Grabowski
- UT L. Durocher
- P G. Pipgras
- P W. Hoyt
- P H. Pennock
- P H. Johnson
- P A. Shealy
- RP W. Moore

NY 1929 A
- M M. Huggins
- M A. Fletcher
- 1B H. Gehrig
- 2B A. Lazzeri
- SS L. Durocher
- 3B E. Robertson
- OF E. Combs
- OF G. Ruth
- OF R. Meusel
- C W. Dickey
- UT M. Koenig
- P G. Pipgras
- P W. Hoyt
- P E. Wells
- P H. Pennock
- P R. Sherid
- RP W. Moore

NY 1930 A
- M J. Shawkey
- 1B H. Gehrig
- 2B A. Lazzeri
- SS L. Lary
- 3B W. Chapman
- OF G. Ruth
- OF E. Combs
- OF H. Rice
- C W. Dickey
- P G. Pipgras
- P C. Ruffing
- P R. Sherid
- P H. Johnson
- P H. Pennock
- RP L. McEvoy

NY 1931 A
- M J. McCarthy
- 1B H. Gehrig
- 2B A. Lazzeri
- SS L. Lary
- 3B J. Sewell
- OF G. Ruth
- OF W. Chapman
- OF E. Combs
- C W. Dickey
- UT S. Byrd
- P V. Gomez
- P C. Ruffing
- P H. Johnson
- P H. Pennock
- P G. Pipgras

NY 1932 A
- M J. McCarthy
- 1B H. Gehrig
- 2B A. Lazzeri
- SS F. Crosetti
- 3B J. Sewell
- OF W. Chapman
- OF E. Combs
- OF G. Ruth
- C W. Dickey
- UT S. Byrd
- P V. Gomez
- P C. Ruffing
- P G. Pipgras
- P J. Allen
- P H. Pennock
- RP W. Brown

NY 1933 A
- M J. McCarthy
- 1B H. Gehrig
- 2B A. Lazzeri
- SS F. Crosetti
- 3B J. Sewell
- OF W. Chapman
- OF G. Ruth
- OF E. Combs
- C W. Dickey
- UT F. Walker
- P C. Ruffing
- P V. Gomez
- P J. Allen
- P R. Van Atta
- P D. Mac Fayden
- RP H. Pennock
- RP W. Moore

NY 1934 A
- M J. McCarthy
- 1B H. Gehrig
- 2B A. Lazzeri
- SS F. Crosetti
- 3B O. Saltzgaver
- OF W. Chapman
- OF G. Ruth
- OF S. Byrd
- C W. Dickey
- UT M. Hoag
- P V. Gomez
- P C. Ruffing
- P J. Murphy
- P J. Broaca
- P J. DeShong

NY 1935 A
- M J. McCarthy
- 1B H. Gehrig
- 2B A. Lazzeri
- SS F. Crosetti
- 3B R. Rolfe
- OF W. Chapman
- OF G. Selkirk
- OF J. Hill
- C W. Dickey
- P V. Gomez
- P C. Ruffing
- P J. Broaca
- P J. Allen
- P V. Tamulis
- RP J. Murphy
- RP J. DeShong
- RP P. Malone

NY 1936 A
- M J. McCarthy
- 1B H. Gehrig
- 2B A. Lazzeri
- SS F. Crosetti
- 3B R. Rolfe
- OF J. DiMaggio
- OF G. Selkirk
- OF A. Powell
- C W. Dickey
- P C. Ruffing
- P M. Pearson
- P J. Broaca
- P V. Gomez
- P I. Hadley

NY 1937 A
- M J. McCarthy
- 1B H. Gehrig
- 2B A. Lazzeri
- SS F. Crosetti
- 3B R. Rolfe
- OF J. DiMaggio
- OF M. Hoag
- OF A. Powell
- C W. Dickey
- P V. Gomez
- P C. Ruffing
- P I. Hadley
- P M. Pearson
- RP J. Murphy
- RP F. Makosky

NY 1938 A
- M J. McCarthy
- 1B H. Gehrig
- 2B J. Gordon
- SS F. Crosetti
- 3B R. Rolfe
- OF J. DiMaggio
- OF T. Henrich
- OF G. Selkirk

NY 1939 A
- M J. McCarthy
- 1B E. Dahlgren
- 2B J. Gordon
- SS F. Crosetti
- 3B R. Rolfe
- OF G. Selkirk
- OF J. DiMaggio
- OF C. Keller
- C W. Dickey
- UT T. Henrich
- P C. Ruffing
- P V. Gomez
- P I. Hadley
- P R. Donald
- P M. Pearson
- RP J. Murphy

NY 1940 A
- M J. McCarthy
- 1B E. Dahlgren
- 2B J. Gordon
- SS F. Crosetti
- 3B R. Rolfe
- OF C. Keller
- OF J. DiMaggio
- OF G. Selkirk
- C W. Dickey
- P C. Ruffing
- P M. Russo
- P S. Chandler
- P M. Breuer
- P R. Donald
- RP J. Murphy

NY 1941 A
- M J. McCarthy
- 1B J. Sturm
- 2B J. Gordon
- SS P. Rizzuto
- 3B R. Rolfe
- OF T. Henrich
- OF J. DiMaggio
- OF C. Keller
- C W. Dickey
- P M. Russo
- P C. Ruffing
- P S. Chandler
- P R. Donald
- P V. Gomez
- RP J. Murphy
- RP C. Stanceu
- RP N. Branch

NY 1942 A
- M J. McCarthy
- 1B B. Hassett
- 2B J. Gordon
- SS P. Rizzuto
- 3B F. Crosetti
- OF J. DiMaggio
- OF C. Keller
- OF T. Henrich
- C W. Dickey
- P E. Bonham
- P S. Chandler
- P C. Ruffing
- P H. Borowy
- P M. Breuer
- RP J. Murphy
- RP J. Lindell

NY 1943 A
- M J. McCarthy
- 1B N. Etten
- 2B J. Gordon
- SS F. Crosetti
- 3B W. Johnson
- OF C. Keller
- OF J. Lindell
- OF A. Metheny
- C W. Dickey
- P S. Chandler
- P E. Bonham
- P C. Wensloff
- P H. Borowy
- P R. Donald
- RP J. Murphy

NY 1944 A
- M J. McCarthy
- 1B N. Etten
- 2B G. Stirnweiss
- SS M. Milosevich
- 3B O. Grimes
- OF J. Lindell
- OF A. Metheny
- OF H. Martin
- C N. Garbark
- P H. Borowy
- P W. Dubiel
- P E. Bonham
- P R. Donald
- P W. Zuber

NY 1945 A
- M J. McCarthy
- 1B N. Etten
- 2B G. Stirnweiss
- SS F. Crosetti
- 3B O. Grimes
- OF A. Metheny
- OF H. Martin
- OF G. Stainback
- C N. Garbark
- P F. Bevens
- P E. Bonham
- P A. Gettel
- P W. Dubiel
- P H. Borowy
- RP K. Holcombe
- RP J. Turner

NY 1946 A
- M J. McCarthy
- M W. Dickey
- M J. Neun
- 1B N. Etten
- 2B J. Gordon
- SS P. Rizzuto
- 3B G. Stirnweiss
- OF C. Keller
- OF J. DiMaggio
- OF T. Henrich
- C A. Robinson
- UT J. Lindell
- P S. Chandler
- P F. Bevens
- P J. Page
- P R. Gumpert
- P E. Bonham

NY 1947 A
- M S. Harris
- 1B G. McQuinn
- 2B G. Stirnweiss
- SS P. Rizzuto
- 3B W. Johnson
- OF J. DiMaggio
- OF T. Henrich
- OF J. Lindell
- C A. Robinson
- P A. Reynolds
- P F. Shea
- P F. Bevens
- P S. Chandler
- P L. Newsom
- RP J. Page
- RP R. Gumpert

NY 1948 A
- M S. Harris
- 1B G. McQuinn
- 2B G. Stirnweiss
- SS P. Rizzuto
- 3B W. Johnson
- OF J. DiMaggio
- OF T. Henrich
- OF J. Lindell
- C C. Niarhos
- UT L. Berra
- UT R. Brown
- P A. Reynolds
- P E. Lopat
- P V. Raschi
- P F. Shea
- P T. Byrne
- RP J. Page
- RP F. Hiller

NY 1949 A
- M C. Stengel
- 1B T. Henrich
- 2B G. Coleman
- SS P. Rizzuto
- 3B B. Brown
- OF C. Mapes
- OF E. Woodling
- OF H. Bauer
- C L. Berra
- UT W. Johnson
- P V. Raschi
- P E. Lopat
- P A. Reynolds

P	T. Byrne
P	J. Sanford
RP	J. Page
RP	F. Shea
RP	C. Marshall

NY 1950 A

M	C. Stengel
1B	J. Collins
2B	G. Coleman
SS	P. Rizzuto
3B	W. Johnson
OF	J. DiMaggio
OF	E. Woodling
OF	H. Bauer
C	L. Berra
UT	R. Brown
UT	C. Mapes
P	V. Raschi
P	A. Reynolds
P	E. Lopat
P	T. Byrne
P	J. Sanford
RP	T. Ferrick
RP	J. Page

NY 1951 A

M	C. Stengel
1B	J. Collins
2B	G. Coleman
SS	P. Rizzuto
3B	R. Brown
OF	E. Woodling
OF	J. DiMaggio
OF	H. Bauer
C	L. Berra
UT	M. Mantle
UT	G. McDougald
UT	J. Mize
P	V. Raschi
P	E. Lopat
P	A. Reynolds
P	T. Morgan
P	F. Shea
RP	J. Ostrowski

NY 1952 A

M	C. Stengel
1B	J. Collins
2B	A. Martin
SS	P. Rizzuto
3B	G. McDougald
OF	M. Mantle
OF	H. Bauer
OF	E. Woodling
C	L. Berra
P	A. Reynolds
P	V. Raschi
P	E. Lopat
P	J. Sain
P	R. Kuzava
RP	J. McDonald
RP	R. Hogue

NY 1953 A

M	C. Stengel
1B	J. Collins
2B	A. Martin
SS	P. Rizzuto
3B	G. McDougald
OF	H. Bauer
OF	M. Mantle
OF	E. Woodling
C	L. Berra
UT	I. Noren
P	E. Ford
P	J. Sain
P	V. Raschi
P	E. Lopat
P	A. Reynolds
RP	R. Kuzava
RP	T. Gorman
RP	R. Scarborough

NY 1954 A

M	C. Stengel
1B	J. Collins
2B	G. McDougald
SS	P. Rizzuto
3B	A. Carey
OF	M. Mantle
OF	I. Noren
OF	H. Bauer
C	L. Berra
UT	G. Coleman
UT	E. Woodling
P	E. Ford
P	R. Grim
P	E. Lopat
P	A. Reynolds
P	T. Morgan
RP	J. Sain

NY 1955 A

M	C. Stengel
1B	W. Skowron
2B	G. McDougald
SS	G. Hunter
3B	A. Carey
OF	M. Mantle
OF	H. Bauer
OF	I. Noren
C	L. Berra
UT	J. Collins
UT	E. Howard
P	E. Ford
P	R. Turley
P	T. Byrne
P	J. Kucks
P	D. Larsen
RP	C. Konstanty
RP	T. Morgan
RP	T. Sturdivant

NY 1956 A

M	C. Stengel
1B	W. Skowron
2B	A. Martin
SS	G. McDougald
3B	A. Carey
OF	H. Bauer
OF	M. Mantle
OF	E. Howard
C	L. Berra
UT	J. Collins
P	E. Ford
P	J. Kucks
P	D. Larsen
P	T. Sturdivant
P	R. Turley
RP	T. Byrne
RP	R. Grim
RP	T. Morgan

NY 1957 A

M	C. Stengel
1B	W. Skowron
2B	R. Richardson
SS	G. McDougald
3B	A. Carey
OF	M. Mantle
OF	H. Bauer
OF	E. Howard
C	L. Berra
UT	A. Kubek
UT	E. Slaughter
P	T. Sturdivant
P	J. Kucks
P	R. Turley
P	B. Shantz
P	D. Larsen
RP	A. Ditmar
RP	T. Byrne
RP	R. Grim

NY 1958 A

M	C. Stengel
1B	W. Skowron
2B	G. McDougald
SS	A. Kubek
3B	A. Carey
OF	M. Mantle
OF	N. Siebern
OF	H. Bauer
C	L. Berra
UT	E. Howard
P	R. Turley
P	E. Ford
P	A. Ditmar
P	B. Shantz
P	J. Kucks
RP	R. Duren
RP	Z. Monroe

NY 1959 A

M	C. Stengel
1B	W. Skowron
2B	R. Richardson
SS	A. Kubek
3B	H. Lopez
OF	M. Mantle
OF	H. Bauer
OF	N. Siebern
C	L. Berra
UT	E. Howard
UT	G. McDougald
P	E. Ford
P	A. Ditmar
P	R. Turley
P	D. Maas
P	R. Terry
RP	J. Coates
RP	B. Shantz
RP	R. Duren

NY 1960 A

M	C. Stengel
1B	W. Skowron
2B	R. Richardson
SS	A. Kubek
3B	C. Boyer
OF	M. Mantle
OF	R. Maris
OF	H. Lopez
C	E. Howard
UT	L. Berra
UT	G. McDougald
P	A. Ditmar
P	E. Ford
P	R. Turley
P	R. Terry
P	J. Coates
RP	D. Maas
RP	B. Shantz
RP	J. Gabler

NY 1961 A

M	R. Houk
1B	W. Skowron
2B	R. Richardson
SS	A. Kubek
3B	C. Boyer
OF	R. Maris
OF	M. Mantle
OF	L. Berra
C	E. Howard
P	E. Ford
P	W. Stafford
P	R. Terry
P	R. Sheldon
P	J. Coates
RP	L. Arroyo

NY 1962 A

M	R. Houk
1B	W. Skowron
2B	R. Richardson
SS	T. Smith
3B	C. Boyer
OF	R. Maris
OF	M. Mantle
OF	H. Lopez
C	E. Howard
P	R. Terry
P	E. Ford
P	W. Stafford
P	J. Bouton
P	R. Sheldon
RP	J. Coates
RP	L. Daley
RP	M. Bridges

NY 1963 A

M	R. Houk
1B	J. Pepitone
2B	R. Richardson
SS	A. Kubek
3B	C. Boyer
OF	T. Tresh
OF	H. Lopez
OF	J. Reed
C	E. Howard
P	E. Ford
P	R. Terry
P	J. Bouton
P	A. Downing
P	S. Williams
RP	H. Reniff
RP	S. Hamilton

NY 1964 A

M	L. Berra
1B	J. Pepitone
2B	R. Richardson
SS	A. Kubek
3B	C. Boyer
OF	T. Tresh
OF	R. Maris
OF	M. Mantle
C	E. Howard
UT	P. Linz
UT	H. Lopez
P	J. Bouton
P	E. Ford
P	A. Downing
P	R. Terry
P	R. Sheldon
RP	P. Mikkelsen
RP	H. Reniff
RP	W. Stafford

NY 1965 A

M	J. Keane
1B	J. Pepitone
2B	R. Richardson
SS	A. Kubek
3B	C. Boyer
OF	T. Tresh
OF	M. Mantle
OF	R. Moschitto
C	E. Howard
UT	R. Barker
UT	P. Linz
UT	H. Lopez
P	M. Stottlemyre
P	E. Ford
P	A. Downing
P	J. Bouton
P	W. Stafford
RP	P. Ramos
RP	H. Reniff
RP	P. Mikkelsen

NY 1966 A

M	J. Keane
M	R. Houk
1B	J. Pepitone
2B	R. Richardson
SS	H. Clarke
3B	C. Boyer
OF	M. Mantle
OF	R. Maris
OF	T. Tresh
C	E. Howard
UT	R. White
P	M. Stottlemyre
P	F. Peterson
P	A. Downing
P	F. Talbot
P	J. Bouton
RP	H. Reniff
RP	P. Ramos
RP	S. Hamilton

NY 1967 A

M	R. Houk
1B	M. Mantle
2B	H. Clarke
SS	R. Amaro
3B	C. Smith
OF	J. Pepitone
OF	T. Tresh
OF	S. Whitaker
C	J. Gibbs
UT	W. Robinson
P	M. Stottlemyre
P	A. Downing
P	F. Peterson
P	F. Talbot
P	W.Monbouquette
RP	T. Tillotson
RP	H. Womack
RP	J. Verbanic

NY 1968 A

M	R. Houk
1B	M. Mantle
2B	H. Clarke
SS	T. Tresh
3B	R. Cox
OF	R. White
OF	W. Robinson
OF	A. Kosco
C	J. Gibbs
UT	J. Pepitone
P	M. Stottlemyre
P	S. Bahnsen
P	F. Peterson
P	S. Barber
P	F. Talbot
RP	J. Verbanic
RP	H. Womack
RP	L. McDaniel

NY 1969 A

M	R. Houk
1B	J. Pepitone
2B	H. Clarke
SS	E. Michael
3B	G. Kenney
OF	R. White
OF	B. Murcer
OF	R. Woods
C	J. Gibbs
P	M. Stottlemyre
P	F. Peterson
P	S. Bahnsen
P	W. Burbach
P	A. Downing
RP	L. McDaniel
RP	J. Aker
RP	S. Hamilton

NY 1970 A

M	R. Houk
1B	D. Cater
2B	H. Clarke
SS	E. Michael
3B	G. Kenney
OF	R. White
OF	B. Murcer
OF	C. Blefary
C	T. Munson
P	M. Stottlemyre
P	F. Peterson
P	S. Bahnsen
P	S. Kline
P	M. Kekich
RP	L. McDaniel
RP	R. Klimkowski
RP	J. Aker

NY 1971 A

M	R. Houk
1B	D. Cater
2B	H. Clarke
SS	E. Michael
3B	G. Kenney
OF	R. White
OF	B. Murcer
OF	F. Alou
C	T. Munson
P	F. Peterson
P	M. Stottlemyre
P	S. Bahnsen
P	S. Kline
P	M. Kekich
RP	L. McDaniel
RP	J. Aker

NY 1972 A

M	R. Houk
1B	R. Blomberg
2B	H. Clarke
SS	E. Michael
3B	C. Sanchez
OF	R. White
OF	B. Murcer
OF	J. Callison
C	T. Munson
UT	F. Alou
P	M. Stottlemyre
P	F. Peterson
P	S. Kline
P	M. Kekich
P	R. Gardner
RP	A. Lyle
RP	L. McDaniel
RP	F. Beene

NY 1973 A

M	R. Houk
1B	F. Alou
2B	H. Clarke
SS	E. Michael
3B	G. Nettles
OF	R. White
OF	B. Murcer
OF	M. Alou
C	T. Munson
DH	J. Hart
UT	R. Blomberg
P	M. Stottlemyre
P	G. Medich
P	F. Peterson
P	L. McDaniel
P	P. Dobson
RP	A. Lyle

NY 1974 A

M	W. Virdon
1B	C. Chambliss
2B	S. Alomar
SS	J. Mason
3B	G. Nettles
OF	B. Murcer
OF	E. Maddox
OF	L. Piniella
C	T. Munson
DH	R. Blomberg
UT	R. White
P	P. Dobson
P	G. Medich
P	R. Tidrow
P	R. May
P	M. Stottlemyre
RP	A. Lyle
RP	C. Upshaw
RP	M. Wallace

NY 1975 A

M	W. Virdon
M	A. Martin
1B	C. Chambliss
2B	S. Alomar
SS	J. Mason
3B	G. Nettles
OF	R. White
OF	B. Bonds
OF	E. Maddox
C	T. Munson
DH	E. Herrmann
UT	F. Stanley
P	J. Hunter
P	G. Medich
P	R. May
P	P. Dobson
P	L. Gura
RP	A. Lyle
RP	R. Tidrow

NY 1976 A

M	A. Martin
1B	C. Chambliss
2B	W. Randolph
SS	F. Stanley
3B	G. Nettles
OF	R. White
OF	J. Rivers
OF	O. Gamble
C	T. Munson
DH	C. May
UT	L. Piniella
P	J. Hunter
P	E. Figueroa
P	D. Ellis
P	K. Holtzman
P	D. Alexander
RP	A. Lyle
RP	R. Tidrow
RP	G. Jackson

NY 1977 A

M	A. Martin
1B	C. Chambliss
2B	W. Randolph
SS	B. Dent
3B	G. Nettles
OF	J. Rivers
OF	R. White
OF	R. Jackson
C	T. Munson
DH	C. May
UT	L. Piniella
P	E. Figueroa
P	M. Torrez
P	R. Guidry
P	D. Gullett
P	R. Tidrow
RP	A. Lyle
RP	K. Clay

NY 1978 A

M	A. Martin
M	R. Howser
M	R. Lemon
1B	C. Chambliss
2B	W. Randolph
SS	B. Dent
3B	G. Nettles
OF	J. Rivers
OF	R. Jackson
OF	L. Piniella
C	T. Munson
DH	C. Johnson
UT	R. White
P	R. Guidry
P	E. Figueroa
P	R. Tidrow
P	J. Beattie
P	J. Hunter
RP	R. Gossage
RP	A. Lyle
RP	K. Clay

NY 1979 A

M	R. Lemon
M	A. Martin
1B	C. Chambliss
2B	W. Randolph
SS	B. Dent
3B	G. Nettles
OF	R. Jackson
OF	L. Piniella
OF	B. Murcer
C	T. Munson
DH	J. Spencer
P	T. John
P	R. Guidry
P	L. Tiant
P	J. Hunter
P	E. Figueroa
RP	R. Davis
RP	K. Clay
RP	D. Hood

NY 1980 A

M	R. Howser
1B	R. Watson
2B	W. Randolph
SS	R. Dent
3B	G. Nettles

OF	R. Brown
OF	L. Piniella
OF	R. Jackson
C	R. Cerone
DH	R. Soderholm
UT	B. Murcer
UT	J. Spencer
P	T. John
P	R. Guidry
P	T. Underwood
P	R. May
P	L. Tiant
RP	R. Davis
RP	R. Gossage
RP	J. Bird

NY 1981 A

M	E. Michael
M	R. Lemon
1B	R. Watson
2B	W. Randolph
SS	R. Dent
3B	G. Nettles
OF	D. Winfield
OF	J. Mumphrey
OF	R. Jackson
C	R. Cerone
DH	B. Murcer
UT	O. Gamble
P	R. May
P	T. John
P	R. Guidry
P	D. Righetti
P	R. Reuschel
RP	R. Davis
RP	D. LaRoche
RP	R. Gossage

NY 1982 A

M	R. Lemon
M	E. Michael
M	C. King
1B	J. Mayberry
2B	W. Randolph
SS	R. Smalley
3B	G. Nettles
OF	D. Winfield
OF	G. Griffey
OF	J. Mumphrey
C	R. Cerone
DH	O. Gamble
UT	D. Collins
UT	L. Piniella
P	R. Guidry
P	T. John
P	D. Righetti
P	S. Rawley
P	M. Morgan
RP	G. Frazier
RP	R. May
RP	R. Gossage

NY 1983 A

M	A. Martin
1B	G. Griffey
2B	W. Randolph
SS	R. Smalley
3B	G. Nettles
OF	D. Winfield
OF	S. Kemp
OF	J. Mumphrey
C	H. Wynegar
DH	D. Baylor
UT	A. Robertson
P	R. Guidry
P	S. Rawley
P	D. Righetti
P	S. Shirley
P	S. Fontenot
RP	G. Frazier
RP	D. Murray
RP	R. Gossage

NY 1984 A

M	L. Berra
1B	D. Mattingly
2B	W. Randolph
SS	R. Meacham
3B	C. Harrah
OF	D. Winfield
OF	O. Moreno
OF	G. Griffey
C	H. Wynegar
DH	D. Baylor
P	P. Niekro
P	R. Guidry
P	S. Fontenot
P	D. Rasmussen
RP	R. Shirley
RP	J. Howell
RP	D. Righetti

NY 1985 A		NY 1990 A			RP R. Locker	OAK 1972 A			P P. Mitchell		UT J. Newman		OF J. Canseco		PHI n 1873-1875

NY 1985 A

- M L. Berra
- M A. Martin
- 1B D. Mattingly
- 2B W. Randolph
- SS R. Meacham
- 3B M. Pagliarulo
- OF D. Winfield
- OF R. Henderson
- OF G. Griffey
- C H. Wynegar
- DH D. Baylor
- P R. Guidry
- P P. Niekro
- P J. Cowley
- P E. Whitson
- P D. Rasmussen
- RP R. Shirley
- RP D. Righetti
- RP B. Fisher

NY 1986 A

- M L. Piniella
- 1B D. Mattingly
- 2B W. Randolph
- SS J. Tolleson
- 3B M. Pagliarulo
- OF R. Henderson
- OF D. Winfield
- OF D. Pasqua
- C H. Wynegar
- DH M. Easler
- P D. Rasmussen
- P R. Guidry
- P D. Drabek
- P R. Tewksbury
- P J. Niekro
- RP D. Righetti
- RP R. Shirley
- RP B. Fisher

NY 1987 A

- M L. Piniella
- 1B D. Mattingly
- 2B W. Randolph
- SS J. Tolleson
- 3B M. Pagliarulo
- OF D. Winfield
- OF G. Ward
- OF D. Pasqua
- C R. Cerone
- DH R. Kittle
- UT C. Washington
- P T. John
- P R. Rhoden
- P C. Hudson
- P D. Rasmussen
- P R. Guidry
- RP D. Righetti
- RP T. Stoddard
- RP P. Clements

NY 1988 A

- M A. Martin
- M L. Piniella
- 1B D. Mattingly
- 2B W. Randolph
- SS R. Santana
- 3B M. Pagliarulo
- OF D. Winfield
- OF R. Henderson
- OF C. Washington
- C D. Slaught
- DH J. Clark
- P R. Rhoden
- P T. John
- P R. Dotson
- P J. Candelaria
- P C. Hudson
- RP N. Allen
- RP D. Righetti
- RP S. Shields

NY 1989 A

- M G. Green
- M R. Dent
- 1B D. Mattingly
- 2B S. Sax
- SS A. Espinoza
- 3B M. Pagliarulo
- OF R. Kelly
- OF J. Barfield
- OF M. Hall
- C D. Slaught
- DH S. Balboni
- P M. Hawkins
- P J. Parker
- P D. LaPoint
- P C. Cary
- RP A. Guetterman
- RP L. McCullers
- RP E. Plunk

NY 1990 A

- M R. Dent
- M C. Merrill
- 1B D. Mattingly
- 2B S. Sax
- SS A. Espinoza
- 3B R. Velarde
- OF R. Kelly
- OF J. Barfield
- OF O. Azocar
- C R. Geren
- DH S. Balboni
- UT M. Hall
- P T. Leary
- P D. LaPoint
- P M. Hawkins
- P C. Cary
- P M. Witt
- RP G. Cadaret
- RP A. Guetterman
- RP J. Robinson

Oakland

OAK A 1968-1990

OAK 1968 A

- M R. Kennedy
- 1B D. Cater
- 2B J. Donaldson
- SS D. Campaneris
- 3B S. Bando
- OF R. Jackson
- OF R. Monday
- OF N. Hershberger
- C D. Duncan
- P J. Hunter
- P J. Odom
- P J. Nash
- P C. Dobson
- P L. Krausse
- RP D. Segui
- RP J. Aker
- RP E. Sprague

OAK 1969 A

- M H. Bauer
- M J. McNamara
- 1B D. Cater
- 2B R. Green
- SS D. Campaneris
- 3B S. Bando
- OF R. Jackson
- OF R. Monday
- OF T. Reynolds
- C P. Roof
- P J. Hunter
- P C. Dobson
- P J. Odom
- P L. Krausse
- P J. Nash
- RP R. Fingers
- RP J. Roland
- RP P. Lindblad

OAK 1970 A

- M J. McNamara
- 1B D. Mincher
- 2B R. Green
- SS D. Campaneris
- 3B S. Bando
- OF F. Alou
- OF R. Jackson
- OF R. Monday
- C F. Fernandez
- UT J. Rudi
- P C. Dobson
- P J. Hunter
- P D. Segui
- P J. Odom
- P R. Fingers
- RP J. Grant
- RP P. Lindblad
- RP M. Lachemann

OAK 1971 A

- M R. Williams
- 1B M. Epstein
- 2B R. Green
- SS D. Campaneris
- 3B S. Bando
- OF R. Jackson
- OF J. Rudi
- OF R. Monday
- C D. Duncan
- P V. Blue
- P J. Hunter
- P C. Dobson
- P D. Segui
- P J. Odom
- RP R. Fingers
- RP R. Locker
- RP D. Knowles

OAK 1972 A

- M R. Williams
- 1B M. Epstein
- 2B T. Cullen
- SS D. Campaneris
- 3B S. Bando
- OF J. Rudi
- OF R. Jackson
- OF A. Mangual
- C D. Duncan
- UT J. Hegan
- P J. Hunter
- P K. Holtzman
- P J. Odom
- P V. Blue
- P D. Hamilton
- RP R. Fingers
- RP J. Horlen
- RP R. Locker

OAK 1973 A

- M R. Williams
- 1B F. Tenace
- 2B R. Green
- SS D. Campaneris
- 3B S. Bando
- OF R. Jackson
- OF W. North
- OF J. Rudi
- C R. Fosse
- DH D. Johnson
- UT T. Kubiak
- P K. Holtzman
- P V. Blue
- P J. Hunter
- P J. Odom
- RP R. Fingers
- RP D. Knowles
- RP H. Pina

OAK 1974 A

- M A. Dark
- 1B F. Tenace
- 2B R. Green
- SS D. Campaneris
- 3B S. Bando
- OF J. Rudi
- OF W. North
- OF R. Jackson
- C R. Haney
- DH J. Alou
- UT T. Kubiak
- UT A. Mangual
- P J. Hunter
- P V. Blue
- P K. Holtzman
- P D. Hamilton
- P W. Abbott
- RP R. Fingers
- RP P. Lindblad
- RP J. Odom

OAK 1975 A

- M A. Dark
- 1B J. Rudi
- 2B P. Garner
- SS D. Campaneris
- 3B S. Bando
- OF C. Washington
- OF R. Jackson
- OF W. North
- C F. Tenace
- DH B. Williams
- UT J. Holt
- P V. Blue
- P K. Holtzman
- P R. Bosman
- P W. Abbott
- P S. Bahnsen
- RP R. Fingers
- RP J. Todd
- RP P. Lindblad

OAK 1976 A

- M C. Tanner
- 1B F. Tenace
- 2B P. Garner
- SS D. Campaneris
- 3B S. Bando
- OF W. North
- OF C. Washington
- OF J. Rudi
- C W. Haney
- DH B. Williams
- UT D. Baylor
- UT K. McMullen
- P V. Blue
- P J. Hunter
- P C. Dobson
- P D. Segui
- P J. Odom
- RP R. Fingers
- P P. Mitchell
- P R. Bosman
- RP R. Fingers
- RP P. Lindblad
- RP J. Todd

OAK 1977 A

- M J. McKeon
- M B. Winkles
- 1B R. Allen
- 2B M. Perez
- SS R. Picciolo
- 3B W. Gross
- OF M. Page
- OF A. Armas
- OF J. Tyrone
- C J. Newman
- DH M. Sanguillen
- UT R. Scott
- UT E. Williams
- P V. Blue
- P J. Langford
- P G. Medich
- RP J. Coleman
- RP R. Lacey
- RP P. Torrealba

OAK 1978 A

- M B. Winkles
- M J. McKeon
- 1B D. Revering
- 2B M. Edwards
- SS M. Guerrero
- 3B W. Gross
- OF M. Page
- OF M. Dilone
- OF A. Armas
- C J. Essian
- DH G. Alexander
- UT T. Duncan
- UT J. Newman
- P M. Keough
- P J. Johnson
- P J. Langford
- P P. Broberg
- P S. Renko
- RP D. Heaverlo
- RP R. Lacey
- RP E. Sosa

OAK 1979 A

- M R. Marshall
- 1B D. Revering
- 2B M. Edwards
- SS R. Picciolo
- 3B W. Gross
- OF D. Murphy
- OF L. Murray
- OF R. Henderson
- C J. Newman
- DH M. Page
- UT J. Essian
- P J. Langford
- P S. McCatty
- P M. Keough
- P M. Norris
- P C. Minetto
- RP D. Heaverlo
- RP D. Hamilton
- RP J. Todd

OAK 1980 A

- M A. Martin
- 1B D. Revering
- 2B D. McKay
- SS M. Guerrero
- 3B W. Gross
- OF D. Murphy
- OF A. Armas
- OF R. Henderson
- C J. Essian
- DH M. Page
- UT J. Newman
- P J. Langford
- P M. Norris
- P M. Keough
- P S. McCatty
- P B. Kingman
- RP R. Lacey

OAK 1981 A

- M A. Martin
- 1B J. Spencer
- 2B M. Babitt
- SS R. Picciolo
- 3B W. Gross
- OF A. Armas
- OF R. Henderson
- OF D. Murphy
- C M. Heath
- DH C. Johnson
- UT D. McKay
- UT J. Newman
- P J. Langford
- P S. McCatty
- P M. Norris
- P M. Keough
- P B. Kingman
- RP J. Jones
- RP R. Owchinko

OAK 1982 A

- M A. Martin
- 1B D. Meyer
- 2B R. Lopes
- SS F. Stanley
- 3B W. Gross
- OF D. Murphy
- OF R. Henderson
- OF A. Armas
- C M. Heath
- DH C. Johnson
- UT J. Burroughs
- P J. Langford
- P M. Keough
- P M. Norris
- P S. McCatty
- P B. Kingman
- RP T. Underwood
- RP R. Owchinko
- RP C. Beard

OAK 1983 A

- M S. Boros
- 1B W. Gross
- 2B D. Lopes
- SS K. Phillips
- 3B C. Lansford
- OF R. Henderson
- OF D. Murphy
- OF M. Davis
- C R. Kearney
- DH J. Burroughs
- UT W. Almon
- P M. Keough
- P J. Johnson
- P J. Langford
- P P. Broberg
- P S. Renko
- RP T. Underwood
- RP T. Burgmeier
- RP K. Atherton

OAK 1984 A

- M S. Boros
- M J. Moore
- 1B B. Bochte
- 2B J. Morgan
- SS K. Phillips
- 3B C. Lansford
- OF D. Murphy
- OF R. Henderson
- OF M. Davis
- C M. Heath
- DH D. Kingman
- UT W. Almon
- P B. Burris
- P L. Sorensen
- P S. McCatty
- P W. Krueger
- P C. Young
- RP K. Atherton
- RP W. Caudill
- RP T. Conroy

OAK 1985 A

- M J. Moore
- 1B B. Bochte
- 2B D. Hill
- SS A. Griffin
- 3B C. Lansford
- OF M. Davis
- OF D. Murphy
- OF D. Collins
- C M. Heath
- DH D. Kingman
- UT J. Baker
- P C. Codiroli
- P D. Sutton
- P W. Krueger
- P T. Birtsas
- RP K. Atherton
- RP J. Howell
- RP S. McCatty

OAK 1986 A

- M J. Moore
- M J. Newman
- M A. LaRussa
- 1B B. Bochte
- 2B K. Phillips
- SS A. Griffin
- 3B C. Lansford
- OF J. Canseco
- OF M. Davis
- OF D. Murphy
- C M. Tettleton
- DH D. Kingman
- UT D. Hill
- P C. Young
- P J. Rijo
- P J. Andujar
- P D. Stewart
- P E. Plunk
- RP W. Mooneyham
- RP S. Ontiveros
- RP J. Howell

OAK 1987 A

- M A. LaRussa
- 1B M. McGwire
- 2B K. Phillips
- SS A. Griffin
- 3B C. Lansford
- OF J. Canseco
- OF M. Davis
- OF L. Polonia
- C T. Steinbach
- DH R. Jackson
- P D. Stewart
- P C. Young
- P S. Ontiveros
- RP W. Nelson
- RP D. Eckersley
- RP E. Plunk

OAK 1988 A

- M A. LaRussa
- 1B M. McGwire
- 2B G. Hubbard
- SS W. Weiss
- 3B C. Lansford
- OF J. Canseco
- OF D. Henderson
- OF S. Javier
- C R. Hassey
- DH D. Baylor
- UT M. Gallego
- UT D. Parker
- UT T. Steinbach
- P D. Stewart
- P R. Welch
- P G. Davis
- P C. Young
- P T. Burns
- RP W. Nelson
- RP F. Honeycutt
- RP E. Plunk

OAK 1989 A

- M A. LaRussa
- 1B M. McGwire
- 2B K. Phillips
- SS M. Gallego
- 3B C. Lansford
- OF D. Henderson
- OF S. Javier
- OF R. Henderson
- C T. Steinbach
- DH D. Parker
- UT R. Hassey
- P D. Stewart
- P M. Moore
- P R. Welch
- P G. Davis
- P C. Young
- RP T. Burns
- RP W. Nelson
- RP F. Honeycutt

OAK 1990 A

- M A. LaRussa
- 1B M. McGwire
- 2B W. Randolph
- SS W. Weiss
- 3B C. Lansford
- OF R. Henderson
- OF D. Henderson
- OF D. Jose
- C T. Steinbach
- DH J. Canseco
- UT M. Gallego
- P D. Stewart
- P R. Welch
- P S. Sanderson
- P M. Moore
- P C. Young
- RP T. Burns
- RP W. Nelson
- RP D. Eckersley

Philadelphia

CEN n 1875

PHI n 1873-1875
ATH n 1871-1875
PHI N 1876
PHI U 1884
PHI P 1890
PHI a 1882-1891
PHI A 1901-1954
PHI N 1883-1990

CEN 1875 n

- M W. Craver
- 1B J. Abadie
- 2B E. Somerville
- SS W. Craver
- 3B G. Trenwith
- OF F. Warner
- OF F. Treacey
- OF C. Mason
- C T. McGinley
- P G. Bechtel

PHI 1873 n

- M F. Malone
- M J. Wood
- 1B D. Mack
- 2B J. Wood
- SS C. Fulmer
- 3B L. Meyerle
- OF F. Treacey
- OF E. Cuthbert
- OF G. Bechtel
- C F. Malone
- P G. Zettlein

PHI 1874 n

- M W. Craver
- 1B D. Mack
- 2B W. Craver
- SS C. Fulmer
- 3B J. Holdsworth
- OF D. Eggler
- OF T. York
- OF G. Bechtel
- C N. Hicks
- P W. Cummings

PHI 1875 n

- M M. McGeary
- M R. Addy
- 1B T. Murnane
- 2B L. Meyerle
- SS C. Fulmer
- 3B M. McGeary
- OF R. Addy
- OF J. McMullin
- OF F. Treacey
- C C. Snyder
- P W. Fisher
- P G. Zettlein
- P J. Borden

ATH 1871 n

- M J. McBride
- 1B W. Fisler
- 2B A. Reach
- SS J. Radcliff
- 3B L. Meyerle
- OF E. Cuthbert
- OF J. Sensenderfer
- OF G. Heubel
- C F. Malone
- UT G. Bechtel
- P J. McBride

ATH 1872 n

- M J. McBride
- 1B D. Mack
- 2B W. Fisler
- SS M. McGeary
- 3B A. Anson
- OF F. Treacey
- OF E. Cuthbert
- OF L. Meyerle
- C F. Malone
- P J. McBride

ATH 1873 n

- M J. McBride
- 1B A. Anson
- 2B W. Fisler
- SS M. McGeary
- 3B E. Sutton
- OF J. McMullin
- OF W. Fisher
- OF T. Murnane
- C J. Clapp
- P J. McBride

ATH 1874 n

M	J. McBride
1B	W. Fisler
2B	J. Battin
SS	M. McGeary
3B	E. Sutton
OF	J. McMullin
OF	A. Gedney
OF	A. Reach
C	J. Clapp
UT	A. Anson
P	J. McBride

ATH 1875 n

M	J. McBride
M	A. Anson
1B	W. Fisler
2B	W. Craver
SS	D. Force
3B	E. Sutton
OF	G. Hall
OF	D. Eggler
OF	G. Bechtel
C	J. Clapp
UT	A. Anson
P	J. McBride
P	A. Knight

PHI 1876 N

M	A. Wright
1B	E. Sutton
2B	W. Fisler
SS	D. Force
3B	L. Meyerle
OF	G. Hall
OF	D. Eggler
OF	W. Coon
C	F. Malone
P	A. Knight
P	G. Zettlein

PHI 1884 U

M	F. Malone
1B	J. McGuinness
2B	E. Peak
SS	H. Easterday
3B	J. McCormick
OF	W. Kienzle
OF	J. Flynn
OF	W. Hoover
C	T. Gillen
UT	J. Clements
P	E. Bakely
P	S. Weaver
P	Fisher

PHI 1890 P

M	J. Fogarty
M	C. Buffinton
1B	S. Farrar
2B	J. Pickett
SS	W. Shindle
3B	J. Mulvey
OF	G. Wood
OF	M. Griffin
OF	J. Fogarty
C	J. Milligan
UT	W. Hallman
P	A. Sanders
P	P. Knell
P	C. Buffinton
P	W. Husted
P	E. Cunningham

PHI 1882 a

M	G. Latham
1B	G. Latham
2B	J. Stricker
SS	L. Say
3B	R. Blakiston
OF	A. Birchall
OF	J. Dorgan
OF	J. Mansell
C	J. O'Brien
P	S. Weaver
P	W. Sweeney
P	F. Mountain

PHI 1883 a

M	A. Knight
1B	H. Stovey
2B	J. Stricker
SS	M. Moynahan
3B	G. Bradley
OF	G. Birchall
OF	A. Knight
OF	R. Blakiston
C	J. O'Brien
UT	F. Corey
P	R. Mathews

P	D. Jones
P	E. Bakely

PHI 1884 a

M	A. Knight
1B	H. Stovey
2B	J. Stricker
SS	S. Houck
3B	F. Corey
OF	A. Knight
OF	H. Larkin
OF	A. Birchall
C	J. Milligan
P	R. Mathews
P	W. Taylor
P	A. Atkinson

PHI 1885 a

M	H. Stovey
1B	H. Stovey
2B	J. Stricker
SS	S. Houck
3B	F. Corey
OF	H. Larkin
OF	J. Coleman
OF	W. Purcell
C	J. Milligan
P	R. Mathews
P	T. Lovett
P	E. Knouff
P	E. Cushman

PHI 1886 a

M	L. Simmons
M	W. Sharsig
1B	H. Stovey
2B	L. Bierbauer
SS	J. McGarr
3B	J. Gleason
OF	H. Larkin
OF	J. Coleman
OF	E. Greer
C	W. Robinson
UT	J. O'Brien
P	A. Atkinson
P	R. Mathews
P	W. Hart
P	T. Kennedy
P	J. Miller

PHI 1887 a

M	F. Bancroft
M	C. Mason
1B	J. Milligan
2B	L. Bierbauer
SS	J. McGarr
3B	D. Lyons
OF	T. Poorman
OF	H. Larkin
OF	H. Stovey
C	W. Robinson
P	E. Seward
P	A. Weyhing
P	A. Atkinson

PHI 1888 a

M	W. Sharsig
1B	H. Larkin
2B	L. Bierbauer
SS	W. Gleason
3B	D. Lyons
OF	C. Welch
OF	H. Stovey
OF	T. Poorman
C	W. Robinson
P	E. Seward
P	A. Weyhing
P	M. Mattimore

PHI 1889 a

M	W. Sharsig
1B	H. Larkin
2B	L. Bierbauer
SS	F. Fennelly
3B	D. Lyons
OF	H. Stovey
OF	W. Purcell
OF	C. Welch
C	W. Robinson
P	A. Weyhing
P	E. Seward
P	J. McMahon

PHI 1890 a

M	W. Sharsig
1B	J. O'Brien
2B	T. Shaffer
SS	B. Conroy
3B	D. Lyons
OF	W. Purcell
OF	C. Welch
OF	G. Shaffer
C	W. Robinson
P	J. McMahon
P	E. Green
P	E. Seward
P	C. Esper

PHI 1891 a

M	W. Sharsig
M	G. Wood
1B	H. Larkin
2B	W. Hallman
SS	T. Corcoran
3B	J. Mulvey
OF	G. Wood
OF	J. Corkhill
OF	J. McTamany
C	J. Milligan
UT	L. Cross
P	A. Weyhing
P	E. Chamberlain
P	W. Calihan

PHI 1901 A

M	C. Mack
1B	H. Davis
2B	N. Lajoie
SS	J. Dolan
3B	L. Cross
OF	D. Fultz
OF	R. Seybold
OF	M. McIntyre
C	M. Powers
P	C. Fraser
P	E. Plank
P	W. Bernhard
P	L. Wiltse
P	W. Piatt

PHI 1902 A

M	C. Mack
1B	H. Davis
2B	D. Murphy
SS	M. Cross
3B	L. Cross
OF	T. Hartsel
OF	R. Seybold
OF	D. Fultz
C	O.Schreckengost
P	E. Plank
P	G. Waddell
P	B. Husting
P	L. Wiltse
P	F. Mitchell

PHI 1903 A

M	C. Mack
1B	H. Davis
2B	D. Murphy
SS	M. Cross
3B	L. Cross
OF	O. Pickering
OF	R. Seybold
OF	T. Hartsel
C	O.Schreckengost
P	E. Plank
P	G. Waddell
P	C. Bender
P	W. Henley

PHI 1904 A

M	C. Mack
1B	H. Davis
2B	D. Murphy
SS	M. Cross
3B	L. Cross
OF	T. Hartsel
OF	R. Seybold
OF	O. Pickering
C	O.Schreckengost
P	G. Waddell
P	E. Plank
P	W. Henley
P	C. Bender

PHI 1905 A

M	C. Mack
1B	H. Davis
2B	D. Murphy
SS	J. Knight
3B	L. Cross
OF	T. Hartsel
OF	R. Seybold
OF	D. Hoffman
C	O.Schreckengost
P	E. Plank
P	G. Waddell
P	A. Coakley
P	C. Bender
P	W. Henley

PHI 1906 A

M	C. Mack
1B	H. Davis
2B	D. Murphy
SS	M. Cross
3B	J. Knight
OF	T. Hartsel
OF	B. Lord
OF	R. Seybold
C	O.Schreckengost
UT	H. Armbruster
P	G. Waddell
P	C. Bender
P	J. Dygert
P	E. Plank
P	J. Coombs

PHI 1907 A

M	C. Mack
1B	H. Davis
2B	D. Murphy
SS	S. Nicholls
3B	J. Collins
OF	R. Seybold
OF	T. Hartsel
OF	R. Oldring
C	O.Schreckengost
P	E. Plank
P	G. Waddell
P	J. Dygert
P	C. Bender
P	J. Coombs

PHI 1908 A

M	C. Mack
1B	H. Davis
2B	E. Collins
SS	S. Nicholls
3B	J. Collins
OF	T. Hartsel
OF	R. Oldring
OF	D. Murphy
C	O.Schreckengost
P	H. Vickers
P	E. Plank
P	J. Dygert
P	C. Bender
P	V. Schlitzer

PHI 1909 A

M	C. Mack
1B	H. Davis
2B	E. Collins
SS	J. Barry
3B	J. Baker
OF	D. Murphy
OF	R. Oldring
OF	R. Ganley
C	I. Thomas
P	E. Plank
P	C. Bender
P	H. Morgan
P	H. Krause
P	J. Coombs

PHI 1910 A

M	C. Mack
1B	H. Davis
2B	E. Collins
SS	J. Barry
3B	J. Baker
OF	D. Murphy
OF	R. Oldring
OF	T. Hartsel
C	J. Lapp
P	J. Coombs
P	H. Morgan
P	E. Plank
P	C. Bender
P	H. Krause

PHI 1911 A

M	C. Mack
1B	J. McInnis
2B	E. Collins
SS	J. Barry
3B	J. Baker
OF	D. Murphy
OF	B. Lord
OF	R. Oldring
C	I. Thomas
P	J. Coombs
P	E. Plank
P	H. Morgan
P	C. Bender
P	H. Krause

PHI 1912 A

M	C. Mack
1B	J. McInnis
2B	E. Collins
SS	J. Barry
3B	J. Baker
OF	A. Strunk
OF	R. Oldring
OF	B. Lord
C	J. Lapp
P	J. Coombs
P	E. Plank
P	C. Brown
P	B. Houck
P	C. Bender
RP	H. Pennock

PHI 1913 A

M	C. Mack
1B	J. McInnis
2B	E. Collins
SS	J. Barry
3B	J. Baker
OF	J. Murphy
OF	R. Oldring
OF	J. Walsh
C	J. Lapp
UT	A. Strunk
P	E. Plank
P	C. Bender
P	C. Brown
P	L. Bush
P	B. Houck

PHI 1914 A

M	C. Mack
1B	J. McInnis
2B	E. Collins
SS	J. Barry
3B	J. Baker
OF	J. Murphy
OF	A. Strunk
OF	R. Oldring
C	W. Schang
P	J. Shawkey
P	L. Bush
P	J. Wyckoff
P	E. Plank
P	C. Bender

PHI 1915 A

M	C. Mack
1B	J. McInnis
2B	N. Lajoie
SS	W. Kopf
3B	W. Schang
OF	A. Strunk
OF	J. Walsh
OF	R. Oldring
C	J. Lapp
P	J. Wyckoff
P	R. Bressler
P	L. Bush
P	T. Sheehan
P	T. Knowlson

PHI 1916 A

M	C. Mack
1B	J. McInnis
2B	N. Lajoie
SS	L. Witt
3B	C. Pick
OF	A. Strunk
OF	J. Walsh
OF	W. Schang
C	W. Meyer
P	E. Myers
P	L. Bush
P	H. Nabors
P	T. Sheehan

PHI 1917 A

M	C. Mack
1B	J. McInnis
2B	R. Grover
SS	L. Witt
3B	R. Bates
OF	A. Strunk
OF	F. Bodie
OF	C. Jamieson
C	W. Schang
P	L. Bush
P	A. Schauer
P	E. Myers
P	R. Johnson
P	W. Noyes

PHI 1918 A

M	C. Mack
1B	G. Burns
2B	J. Dykes
SS	J. Dugan
3B	W. Gardner
OF	C. Walker
OF	C. Jamieson
OF	M. Kopp
C	J. McAvoy
P	H. Perry
P	S. Gregg
P	W. Adams
P	J. Watson
P	E. Myers

PHI 1919 A

M	C. Mack
1B	G. Burns
2B	L. Witt
SS	J. Dugan
3B	F. Thomas
OF	C. Walker
OF	M. Kopp
OF	A. Strunk
C	R. Perkins
P	R. Naylor
P	W. Kinney
P	R. Johnson
P	H. Perry
P	T. Rogers

PHI 1920 A

M	C. Mack
1B	I. Griffin
2B	J. Dykes
SS	C. Galloway
3B	F. Thomas
OF	C. Walker
OF	F. Welch
OF	A. Strunk
C	R. Perkins
UT	J. Dugan
P	H. Perry
P	R. Naylor
P	W. Harriss
P	E. Rommel
P	R. Moore

PHI 1921 A

M	C. Mack
1B	J. Walker
2B	J. Dykes
SS	C. Galloway
3B	J. Dugan
OF	L. Witt
OF	C. Walker
OF	F. Welch
C	R. Perkins
P	E. Rommel
P	W. Harriss
P	R. Moore
P	R. Hasty
P	D. Keefe
RP	H. Freeman

PHI 1922 A

M	C. Mack
1B	J. Hauser
2B	R. Young
SS	C. Galloway
3B	J. Dykes
OF	C. Walker
OF	E. Miller
OF	F. Welch
C	R. Perkins
UT	F. McGowan
P	E. Rommel
P	W. Harriss
P	R. Hasty
P	F. Heimach
P	R. Naylor
RP	J. Sullivan
RP	C. Eckert

PHI 1923 A

M	C. Mack
1B	J. Hauser
2B	J. Dykes
SS	C. Galloway
3B	S. Hale
OF	W. Matthews
OF	E. Miller
OF	F. Welch
C	R. Perkins
UT	F. McGowan
P	E. Rommel
P	R. Hasty
P	W. Harriss
P	F. Heimach
P	R. Naylor

PHI 1924 A

M	C. Mack
1B	J. Hauser
2B	M. Bishop
SS	C. Galloway
3B	H. Riconda
OF	A. Simmons
OF	E. Miller
OF	W. Lamar
C	R. Perkins
UT	J. Dykes
UT	F. Welch
P	E. Rommel
P	F. Heimach
P	S. Baumgartner
P	D. Burns
P	S. Gray
RP	R. Hasty

PHI 1925 A

M	C. Mack
1B	J. Poole
2B	M. Bishop
SS	C. Galloway
3B	S. Hale
OF	A. Simmons
OF	W. Lamar
OF	E. Miller
C	G. Cochrane
UT	J. Dykes
P	E. Rommel
P	W. Harriss
P	S. Gray
P	R. Grove
P	G. Walberg

PHI 1926 A

M	C. Mack
1B	J. Poole
2B	M. Bishop
SS	C. Galloway
3B	J. Dykes
OF	A. Simmons
OF	W. Lamar
OF	W. French
C	G. Cochrane
UT	S. Hale
UT	J. Hauser
P	R. Grove
P	E. Rommel
P	J. Quinn
P	G. Walberg
P	S. Gray
RP	J. Pate

PHI 1927 A

M	C. Mack
1B	J. Dykes
2B	M. Bishop
SS	J. Boley
3B	S. Hale
OF	T. Cobb
OF	A. Simmons
OF	W. French
C	G. Cochrane
UT	E. Collins
P	R. Grove
P	G. Walberg
P	J. Quinn
P	H. Ehmke
P	E. Rommel
RP	J. Pate

PHI 1928 A

M	C. Mack
1B	J. Hauser
2B	M. Bishop
SS	J. Boley
3B	S. Hale
OF	E. Miller
OF	A. Simmons
OF	T. Cobb
C	G. Cochrane
UT	J. Foxx
P	R. Grove
P	G. Walberg
P	J. Quinn
P	E. Rommel
P	G. Earnshaw

PHI 1929 A

M	C. Mack
1B	J. Foxx
2B	M. Bishop
SS	J. Boley
3B	S. Hale
OF	E. Miller
OF	A. Simmons
OF	G. Haas
C	G. Cochrane
UT	J. Dykes
P	R. Grove
P	G. Walberg
P	G. Earnshaw
P	J. Quinn
P	W. Shores

PHI 1930 A

M	C. Mack
1B	J. Foxx
2B	M. Bishop
SS	J. Boley
3B	J. Dykes
OF	E. Miller
OF	A. Simmons
OF	G. Haas
C	G. Cochrane
P	G. Earnshaw
P	R. Grove
P	G. Walberg
P	W. Shores
P	L. Mahaffey
RP	J. Quinn

PHI 1931 A

M	C. Mack
1B	J. Foxx
2B	M. Bishop
SS	E. Williams
3B	J. Dykes
OF	E. Miller
OF	A. Simmons
OF	G. Haas
C	G. Cochrane
P	G. Walberg
P	R. Grove
P	G. Earnshaw
P	L. Mahaffey
P	E. Rommel

PHI 1932 A

M	C. Mack
1B	J. Foxx
2B	M. Bishop
SS	D. McNair
3B	J. Dykes
OF	A. Simmons
OF	G. Haas
OF	R. Cramer
C	G. Cochrane
UT	E. Miller
P	R. Grove
P	G. Walberg
P	G. Earnshaw
P	L. Mahaffey
P	A. Freitas
RP	L. Krausse

PHI 1933 A

M	C. Mack
1B	J. Foxx
2B	M. Bishop
SS	E. Williams
3B	M. Higgins
OF	R. Cramer
OF	R. Johnson
OF	P. Coleman
C	G. Cochrane
P	R. Grove
P	M. Cain
P	G. Walberg
P	L. Mahaffey
P	G. Earnshaw
RP	J. Peterson

PHI 1934 A

M	C. Mack
1B	J. Foxx
2B	H. Warstler
SS	D. McNair
3B	M. Higgins
OF	R. Cramer
OF	R. Johnson
OF	P. Coleman
C	C. Berry
P	J. Marcum
P	M. Cain
P	W. Dietrich
P	J. Cascarella
P	J. Benton

PHI 1935 A

M	C. Mack
1B	J. Foxx
2B	H. Warstler
SS	D. McNair
3B	M. Higgins
OF	R. Cramer
OF	R. Johnson
OF	W. Moses
C	P. Richards
UT	L. Finney
P	J. Marcum
P	W. Dietrich
P	G. Blaeholder
P	V. Wilshere
P	L. Mahaffey
RP	J. Benton

RP	G. Caster
RP	C. Lieber

PHI 1936 A

M	C. Mack
1B	L. Finney
2B	H. Warstler
SS	L. Newsome
3B	M. Higgins
OF	W. Moses
OF	R. Johnson
OF	G. Puccinelli
C	F. Hayes
UT	A. Dean
P	H. Kelley
P	J. Rhodes
P	L. Ross
P	H. Fink
RP	R. Gumpert

PHI 1937 A

M	C. Mack
M	E. Mack
1B	A. Dean
2B	R. Peters
SS	L. Newsome
3B	W. Werber
OF	W. Moses
OF	R. Johnson
OF	J. Hill
C	E. Brucker
P	G. Caster
P	H. Kelley
P	E. Smith
P	L. Thomas
P	L. Ross
RP	H. Fink
RP	G. Turbeville

PHI 1938 A

M	C. Mack
1B	L. Finney
2B	D. Lodigiani
SS	W. Ambler
3B	W. Werber
OF	R. Johnson
OF	W. Moses
OF	S. Chapman
C	F. Hayes
P	G. Caster
P	L. Thomas
P	L. Nelson
P	L. Ross
P	E. Smith

PHI 1939 A

M	C. Mack
M	E. Mack
1B	R. Siebert
2B	J. Gantenbein
SS	L. Newsome
3B	D. Lodigiani
OF	R. Johnson
OF	S. Chapman
OF	W. Moses
C	F. Hayes
UT	W. Ambler
UT	W. Miles
UT	W. Nagel
P	L. Nelson
P	N. Potter
P	L. Ross
P	W. Beckmann
P	G. Caster
RP	A. Dean

PHI 1940 A

M	C. Mack
1B	R. Siebert
2B	B. McCoy
SS	A. Brancato
3B	A. Rubeling
OF	R. Johnson
OF	W. Moses
OF	S. Chapman
C	F. Hayes
P	J. Babich
P	N. Potter
P	G. Caster
P	A. Dean
P	L. Ross
RP	E. Heusser

PHI 1941 A

M	C. Mack
1B	R. Siebert
2B	B. McCoy
SS	A. Brancato
3B	P. Suder
OF	S. Chapman
OF	W. McCosky
OF	R. Johnson

OF	W. Moses
C	F. Hayes
P	P. Marchildon
P	J. Knott
P	L. McCrabb
P	C. Harris
P	W. Beckmann

PHI 1942 A

M	C. Mack
1B	R. Siebert
2B	W.Knickerbocker
SS	P. Suder
3B	L. Blair
OF	R. Johnson
OF	E. Valo
OF	M. Kreevich
C	H. Wagner
UT	W. Miles
P	P. Marchildon
P	R. Wolff
P	C. Harris
P	R. Christopher
P	R. Fowler

PHI 1943 A

M	C. Mack
1B	R. Siebert
2B	P. Suder
SS	I. Hall
3B	E. Mayo
OF	J. White
OF	R. Estalella
OF	J. Welaj
C	H. Wagner
P	J. Flores
P	R. Wolff
P	C. Harris
P	D. Black
P	O. Arntzen

PHI 1944 A

M	C. Mack
1B	W. McGhee
2B	I. Hall
SS	E. Busch
3B	G. Kell
OF	R. Estalella
OF	R. Garrison
OF	J. White
C	F. Hayes
UT	R. Siebert
P	L. Newsom
P	R. Christopher
P	L. Hamlin
P	J. Flores
P	D. Black
RP	J. Berry

PHI 1945 A

M	C. Mack
1B	R. Siebert
2B	I. Hall
SS	E. Busch
3B	G. Kell
OF	R. Estalella
OF	H. Peck
OF	E. Smith
C	W. Rosar
P	L. Newsom
P	R. Christopher
P	J. Flores
P	W. Knerr
P	D. Black
RP	J. Berry

PHI 1946 A

M	C. Mack
1B	G. McQuinn
2B	E. Handley
SS	P. Suder
3B	H. Majeski
OF	S. Chapman
OF	E. Valo
OF	W. McCosky
C	W. Rosar
P	P. Marchildon
P	R. Fowler
P	J. Savage
P	J. Flores
P	W. Knerr

PHI 1947 A

M	C. Mack
1B	F. Fain
2B	P. Suder
SS	E. Joost
3B	H. Majeski
OF	S. Chapman
OF	W. McCosky
OF	E. Valo

C	W. Rosar
UT	G. Binks
P	P. Marchildon
P	R. Fowler
P	W. McCahan
P	J. Coleman
P	J. Flores
RP	R. Christopher

PHI 1948 A

M	C. Mack
1B	F. Fain
2B	P. Suder
SS	E. Joost
3B	H. Majeski
OF	W. McCosky
OF	S. Chapman
OF	E. Valo
C	W. Rosar
P	P. Marchildon
P	J. Coleman
P	R. Fowler
P	C. Scheib
P	L. Brissie
RP	C. Harris
RP	J. Savage

PHI 1949 A

M	C. Mack
1B	F. Fain
2B	P. Suder
SS	E. Joost
3B	H. Majeski
OF	S. Chapman
OF	E. Valo
OF	W. Moses
C	F. Guerra
P	A. Kellner
P	J. Coleman
P	L. Brissie
P	R. Fowler
P	C. Scheib
RP	C. Harris

PHI 1950 A

M	C. Mack
1B	F. Fain
2B	W. Hitchcock
SS	E. Joost
3B	R. Dillinger
OF	S. Chapman
OF	E. Valo
OF	P. Lehner
C	F. Guerra
P	L. Brissie
P	A. Kellner
P	R. Shantz
P	H. Wyse
P	R. Hooper
RP	C. Scheib

PHI 1951 A

M	J. Dykes
1B	F. Fain
2B	P. Suder
SS	E. Joost
3B	H. Majeski
OF	G. Zernial
OF	D. Philley
OF	E. Valo
C	J. Tipton
UT	L. Limmer
P	A. Kellner
P	R. Shantz
P	R. Hooper
P	C. Scheib
P	M. Martin
RP	J. Kucab

PHI 1952 A

M	J. Dykes
1B	F. Fain
2B	E. Kell
SS	E. Joost
3B	W. Hitchcock
OF	D. Philley
OF	G. Zernial
OF	E. Valo
C	J. Astroth
P	R. Shantz
P	A. Kellner
P	H. Byrd
P	C. Scheib
P	R. Hooper
RP	J. Kucab

PHI 1953 A

M	J. Dykes
1B	W. Robinson
2B	C. Michaels
SS	J. DeMaestri

3B	L. Babe
OF	D. Philley
OF	G. Zernial
OF	W. McGhee
C	J. Astroth
UT	P. Suder
P	H. Byrd
P	M. Fricano
P	A. Kellner
P	C. Bishop
P	R. Shantz
RP	M. Martin
RP	F. Fanovich

PHI 1954 A

M	E. Joost
1B	L. Limmer
2B	F. Jacobs
SS	J. DeMaestri
3B	J. Finigan
OF	W. Renna
OF	V. Power
OF	W. Wilson
C	J. Astroth
UT	D. Bollweg
UT	E. Valo
UT	G. Zernial
P	A. Portocarrero
P	A. Kellner
P	M. Fricano
P	R. Trice
P	J. Gray
RP	J. Dixon
RP	E. Burtschy
RP	A. Sima

PHI 1883 N

M	R. Ferguson
M	W. Purcell
1B	S. Farrar
2B	R. Ferguson
SS	W. McClellan
3B	W. Purcell
OF	J. Manning
OF	W. Harbidge
OF	F. Lewis
C	E. Gross
P	J. Coleman
P	A. Hagan

PHI 1884 N

M	W. Wright
1B	S. Farrar
2B	G. Andrews
SS	W. McClellan
3B	J. Mulvey
OF	J. Manning
OF	W. Purcell
OF	J. Fogarty
C	J. Crowley
P	C. Ferguson
P	W. Vinton
P	J. McElroy

PHI 1885 N

M	W. Wright
1B	S. Farrar
2B	J. Myers
SS	C. Bastian
3B	J. Mulvey
OF	J. Manning
OF	G. Andrews
OF	J. Fogarty
C	J. Clements
P	E. Daily
P	C. Ferguson
P	W. Vinton

PHI 1886 N

M	W. Wright
1B	S. Farrar
2B	C. Bastian
SS	A. Irwin
3B	J. Mulvey
OF	G. Andrews
OF	G. Wood
OF	J. Fogarty
C	J. McGuire
UT	E. Daily
P	C. Ferguson
P	D. Casey

PHI 1887 N

M	W. Wright
1B	S. Farrar
2B	B. McLaughlin
SS	A. Irwin
3B	J. Mulvey
OF	J. Fogarty
OF	G. Wood
OF	G. Andrews

C	J. Clements
P	D. Casey
P	C. Buffinton
P	C. Ferguson

PHI 1888 N

M	W. Wright
1B	S. Farrar
2B	C. Bastian
SS	A. Irwin
3B	J. Mulvey
OF	G. Andrews
OF	J. Fogarty
OF	G. Wood
C	J. Clements
P	C. Buffinton
P	D. Casey
P	A. Sanders
P	W. Gleason

PHI 1889 N

M	W. Wright
1B	S. Farrar
2B	J. Myers
SS	W. Hallman
3B	J. Mulvey
OF	S. Thompson
OF	J. Fogarty
OF	G. Wood
C	J. Clements
P	C. Buffinton
P	A. Sanders
P	W. Gleason
P	D. Casey

PHI 1890 N

M	W. Wright
M	J. Clements
M	A. Reach
M	R. Allen
M	W. Wright
1B	A. McCauley
2B	J. Myers
SS	R. Allen
3B	E. Mayer
OF	S. Thompson
OF	W. Hamilton
OF	E. Burke
C	J. Clements
P	W. Gleason
P	T. Vickery
P	J. Smith

PHI 1891 N

M	W. Wright
1B	W. Brown
2B	J. Myers
SS	R. Allen
3B	W. Shindle
OF	S. Thompson
OF	W. Hamilton
OF	E. Delahanty
C	J. Clements
P	W. Gleason
P	C. Esper
P	J. Thornton

PHI 1892 N

M	W. Wright
1B	R. Connor
2B	W. Hallman
SS	R. Allen
3B	C. Reilly
OF	S. Thompson
OF	W. Hamilton
OF	E. Delahanty
C	J. Clements
UT	L. Cross
P	A. Weyhing
P	W. Carsey
P	T. Keefe
P	C. Esper

PHI 1893 N

M	W. Wright
1B	J. Boyle
2B	W. Hallman
SS	R. Allen
3B	C. Reilly
OF	S. Thompson
OF	E. Delahanty
OF	W. Hamilton
C	J. Clements
UT	L. Cross
P	A. Weyhing
P	W. Carsey
P	T. Keefe
P	J. Taylor

PHI 1894 N

M	A. Irwin
1B	J. Boyle
2B	W. Hallman
SS	J. Sullivan
3B	L. Cross
OF	W. Hamilton
OF	S. Thompson
OF	E. Delahanty
C	J. Clements
UT	G. Turner
P	J. Taylor
P	W. Carsey
P	A. Weyhing
P	G. Harper

PHI 1895 N

M	A. Irwin
1B	J. Boyle
2B	W. Hallman
SS	J. Sullivan
3B	L. Cross
OF	W. Hamilton
OF	S. Thompson
OF	E. Delahanty
C	J. Clements
P	W. Carsey
P	J. Taylor
P	W. McGill
P	A. Orth

PHI 1896 N

M	W. Nash
1B	D. Brouthers
2B	W. Hallman
SS	W. Hulen
3B	W. Nash
OF	S. Thompson
OF	E. Delahanty
OF	D. Cooley
C	M. Grady
UT	L. Cross
P	J. Taylor
P	A. Orth
P	W. Carsey
P	J. Keener
P	W. McGill

PHI 1897 N

M	G. Stallings
1B	N. Lajoie
2B	L. Cross
SS	S. Gillen
3B	W. Nash
OF	D. Cooley
OF	E. Delahanty
OF	T. Dowd
C	J. Boyle
UT	P. Geier
P	J. Taylor
P	A. Orth
P	J. Fifield
P	G. Wheeler

PHI 1898 N

M	G. Stallings
M	W. Shettsline
1B	W. Douglass
2B	N. Lajoie
SS	M. Cross
3B	W. Lauder
OF	D. Cooley
OF	E. Delahanty
OF	E. Flick
C	E. McFarland
P	W. Piatt
P	F. Donahue
P	A. Orth
P	J. Fifield
P	G. Wheeler

PHI 1899 N

M	W. Shettsline
1B	D. Cooley
2B	N. Lajoie
SS	M. Cross
3B	W. Lauder
OF	E. Delahanty
OF	R. Thomas
OF	E. Flick
C	E. McFarland
UT	P. Chiles
P	W. Piatt
P	F. Donahue
P	C. Fraser
P	A. Orth
P	W. Bernhard

PHI 1900 N

M	W. Shettsline

1B	E. Delahanty
2B	N. Lajoie
SS	M. Cross
3B	H. Wolverton
OF	J. Slagle
OF	R. Thomas
OF	E. Flick
C	E. McFarland
P	A. Orth
P	F. Donahue
P	C. Fraser
P	W. Bernhard
P	W. Piatt

PHI 1901 N

M	W. Shettsline
1B	H. Jennings
2B	W. Hallman
SS	M. Cross
3B	H. Wolverton
OF	E. Flick
OF	R. Thomas
OF	E. Delahanty
C	E. McFarland
P	F. Donahue
P	A. Orth
P	W. Duggleby
P	G. White
P	J. Townsend

PHI 1902 N

M	W. Shettsline
1B	H. Jennings
2B	P. Childs
SS	R. Hulswitt
3B	W. Hallman
OF	R. Thomas
OF	J. Barry
OF	G. Browne
C	C. Dooin
UT	W. Douglass
P	G. White
P	W. Duggleby
P	H. Iburg
P	C. Fraser

PHI 1903 N

M	C. Zimmer
1B	W. Douglass
2B	W. Gleason
SS	R. Hulswitt
3B	H. Wolverton
OF	R. Thomas
OF	J. Barry
OF	W. Keister
C	F. Roth
P	W. Duggleby
P	C. Fraser
P	T. Sparks
P	F. Mitchell
P	J. McFetridge

PHI 1904 N

M	H. Duffy
1B	J. Doyle
2B	W. Gleason
SS	R. Hulswitt
3B	H. Wolverton
OF	J. Titus
OF	R. Thomas
OF	S. Magee
C	C. Dooin
UT	J. Lush
P	C. Fraser
P	W. Duggleby
P	T. Sparks
P	J. Sutthoff
P	J. McPherson

PHI 1905 N

M	H. Duffy
1B	W. Bransfield
2B	W. Gleason
SS	M. Doolan
3B	E. Courtney
OF	S. Magee
OF	J. Titus
OF	R. Thomas
C	C. Dooin
P	C. Pittinger
P	W. Duggleby
P	T. Sparks
P	F. Corridon
P	C. Nichols

PHI 1906 N

M	H. Duffy
1B	W. Bransfield
2B	W. Gleason
SS	M. Doolan
3B	E. Courtney
OF	S. Magee
OF	J. Titus
OF	R. Thomas
C	C. Dooin
P	T. Sparks
P	J. Lush
P	W. Duggleby
P	L. Richie
P	C. Pittinger

PHI 1907 N

M	W. Murray
1B	W. Bransfield
2B	F. Knabe
SS	M. Doolan
3B	E. Courtney
OF	J. Titus
OF	S. Magee
OF	R. Thomas
C	C. Dooin
P	F. Corridon
P	T. Sparks
P	L. Moren
P	C. Brown
P	L. Richie

PHI 1908 N

M	W. Murray
1B	W. Bransfield
2B	F. Knabe
SS	M. Doolan
3B	E. Grant
OF	W. Osborn
OF	J. Titus
OF	S. Magee
C	C. Dooin
P	G. McQuillan
P	T. Sparks
P	F. Corridon
P	L. Richie
P	L. Moren

PHI 1909 N

M	W. Murray
1B	W. Bransfield
2B	F. Knabe
SS	M. Doolan
3B	R. Byrne
OF	C. Cravath
OF	G. Whitted
OF	D. Becker
C	W. Killefer
UT	S. Magee
P	G. Alexander
P	E. Moore
P	L. Moren
P	G. McQuillan
P	F. Corridon
P	T. Sparks

PHI 1910 N

M	C. Dooin
1B	W. Bransfield
2B	F. Knabe
SS	M. Doolan
3B	E. Grant
OF	S. Magee
OF	J. Titus
OF	J. Bates
C	C. Dooin
P	E. Moore
P	G. Ewing
P	L. Moren
P	G. McQuillan
P	W. Stack

PHI 1911 N

M	C. Dooin
1B	F. Luderus
2B	F. Knabe
SS	M. Doolan
3B	J. Lobert
OF	G. Paskert
OF	S. Magee
OF	F. Beck
C	C. Dooin
UT	M. Walsh
P	G. Alexander
P	E. Moore
P	G. Chalmers
P	W. Burns

PHI 1912 N

M	C. Dooin
1B	F. Luderus
2B	F. Knabe
SS	M. Doolan
3B	J. Lobert
OF	G. Paskert
OF	S. Magee
OF	C. Cravath
C	W. Killefer
P	G. Alexander
P	T. Seaton
P	E. Moore
P	A. Brennan
P	E. Rixey
RP	W. Shultz

PHI 1913 N

M	C. Dooin
1B	F. Luderus
2B	F. Knabe
SS	M. Doolan
3B	J. Lobert
OF	C. Cravath
OF	S. Magee
OF	G. Paskert
C	W. Killefer
P	T. Seaton
P	G. Alexander
P	A. Brennan
P	E. Mayer
P	E. Rixey

PHI 1914 N

M	C. Dooin
1B	F. Luderus
2B	R. Byrne
SS	J. Martin
3B	J. Lobert
OF	C. Cravath
OF	G. Paskert
OF	D. Becker
C	W. Killefer
UT	S. Magee
P	G. Alexander
P	E. Mayer
P	A. Tincup
P	R. Marshall
P	J. Oeschger

PHI 1915 N

M	P. Moran
1B	F. Luderus
2B	J. Niehoff
SS	D. Bancroft
3B	R. Byrne
OF	C. Cravath
OF	G. Whitted
OF	D. Becker
C	W. Killefer
UT	G. Paskert
P	G. Alexander
P	E. Mayer
P	A. Demaree
P	E. Rixey
P	G. Chalmers

PHI 1916 N

M	P. Moran
1B	F. Luderus
2B	J. Niehoff
SS	D. Bancroft
3B	M. Stock
OF	G. Paskert
OF	G. Whitted
OF	C. Cravath
C	W. Killefer
P	G. Alexander
P	E. Rixey
P	A. Demaree
P	E. Mayer
P	C. Bender
RP	G. McQuillan

PHI 1917 N

M	P. Moran
1B	F. Luderus
2B	J. Niehoff
SS	D. Bancroft
3B	M. Stock
OF	G. Whitted
OF	C. Cravath
OF	G. Paskert
C	W. Killefer
P	G. Alexander
P	E. Rixey
P	J. Oeschger
P	E. Mayer
P	J. Lavender

PHI 1918 N

M	P. Moran
1B	F. Luderus
2B	M. McGaffigan
SS	D. Bancroft
3B	M. Stock
OF	M. Meusel
OF	C. Cravath
OF	F. Williams
C	J. Adams
P	M. Prendergast
P	C. Hogg
P	J. Oeschger
P	W. Jacobs
P	M. Watson
RP	F. Davis

PHI 1919 N

M	J. Coombs
M	C. Cravath
1B	F. Luderus
2B	E. Paulette
SS	D. Bancroft
3B	R. Blackburne
OF	E. Meusel
OF	F. Williams
OF	L. Callahan
C	J. Adams
P	G. Smith
P	H. Meadows
P	E. Rixey
P	C. Hogg
P	E. Packard

PHI 1920 N

M	C. Cravath
1B	E. Paulette
2B	J. Rawlings
SS	A. Fletcher
3B	R. Miller
OF	F. Williams
OF	E. Meusel
OF	C. Stengel
C	M. Wheat
UT	J. Miller
P	E. Rixey
P	G. Smith
P	H. Meadows
P	C. Causey
P	W. Hubbell

PHI 1921 N

M	W. Donovan
M	I. Wilhelm
1B	E. Konetchy
2B	J. Smith
SS	F. Parkinson
3B	R. Wrightstone
OF	F. Williams
OF	E. Meusel
OF	D. LeBourveau
C	F. Bruggy
P	J. Ring
P	G. Smith
P	W. Hubbell
P	H. Meadows
P	J. Winters

PHI 1922 N

M	I. Wilhelm
1B	R. Leslie
2B	F. Parkinson
SS	A. Fletcher
3B	J. Rapp
OF	F. Williams
OF	W. Walker
OF	C. Lee
C	W. Henline
UT	R. Wrightstone
P	J. Ring
P	H. Meadows
P	G. Smith
P	W. Hubbell
P	P. Weinert

PHI 1923 N

M	A. Fletcher
1B	W. Holke
2B	J. Tierney
SS	J. Sand
3B	R. Wrightstone
OF	W. Walker
OF	F. Williams
OF	J. Mokan
C	W. Henline
UT	C. Lee
P	J. Ring
P	C. Glazner
P	P. Weinert
P	C. Mitchell
P	R. Head
RP	W. Hubbell

PHI 1924 N

M	A. Fletcher
1B	W. Holke
2B	H. Ford
SS	J. Sand
3B	R. Wrightstone
OF	F. Williams
OF	G. Harper
OF	J. Mokan
C	W. Henline
UT	J. Wilson
P	J. Ring
P	H. Carlson
P	W. Hubbell
P	C. Mitchell
P	C. Glazner

PHI 1925 N

M	A. Fletcher
1B	N. Hawks
2B	B. Friberg
SS	J. Sand
3B	C. Huber
OF	G. Harper
OF	F. Williams
OF	G. Burns
C	J. Wilson
UT	L. Fonseca
P	J. Ring
P	H. Carlson
P	C. Mitchell
P	A. Decatur
P	E. Knight
RP	W. Betts
RP	J. Couch

PHI 1926 N

M	A. Fletcher
1B	J. Bentley
2B	B. Friberg
SS	J. Sand
3B	C. Huber
OF	J. Mokan
OF	F. Leach
OF	F. Williams
C	J. Wilson
UT	W. Henline
UT	A. Nixon
UT	R. Wrightstone
P	H. Carlson
P	W. Dean
P	C. Mitchell
P	C. Willoughby
P	F. Ulrich
RP	R. Pierce
RP	E. Baecht

PHI 1927 N

M	J. McInnis
1B	R. Wrightstone
2B	L. Thompson
SS	J. Sand
3B	B. Friberg
OF	F. Leach
OF	F. Williams
OF	C. Spalding
C	J. Wilson
P	J. Scott
P	J. Ferguson
P	F. Ulrich
P	H. Pruett
P	L. Sweetland
RP	C. Willoughby

PHI 1928 N

M	B. Shotton
1B	F. Hurst
2B	L. Thompson
SS	J. Sand
3B	A. Whitney
OF	D. Sothern
OF	F. Leach
OF	F. Williams
C	W. Lerian
P	R. Benge
P	J. Ring
P	L. Sweetland
P	R. McGraw
P	J. Ferguson

PHI 1929 N

M	B. Shotton
1B	F. Hurst
2B	L. Thompson
SS	T. Thevenow
3B	A. Whitney
OF	F. O'Doul
OF	C. Klein
OF	D. Sothern
C	W. Lerian
UT	V. Davis
UT	B. Friberg
P	C. Willoughby
P	L. Sweetland
P	R. Benge
P	P. Collins
RP	H. Elliott
RP	R. McGraw
RP	S. Dailey

PHI 1930 N

M	B. Shotton
1B	F. Hurst
2B	L. Thompson
SS	T. Thevenow
3B	A. Whitney
OF	C. Klein
OF	F. O'Doul
OF	D. Sothern
C	V. Davis
UT	B. Friberg
P	P. Collins
P	R. Benge
P	L. Sweetland
P	C. Willoughby
P	E. Collard
RP	H. Elliott
RP	W. Smythe

PHI 1931 N

M	B. Shotton
1B	F. Hurst
2B	L. Mallon
SS	R. Bartell
3B	A. Whitney
OF	C. Klein
OF	G. Brickell
OF	R. Arlett
C	V. Davis
UT	B. Friberg
P	J. Elliott
P	R. Benge
P	P. Collins
P	E. Dudley
P	F. Watt

PHI 1932 N

M	B. Shotton
1B	F. Hurst
2B	L. Mallon
SS	R. Bartell
3B	A. Whitney
OF	C. Klein
OF	H. Lee
OF	G. Davis
C	V. Davis
P	E. Holley
P	R. Benge
P	R. Hansen
P	P. Collins
P	C. Rhem

PHI 1933 N

M	B. Shotton
1B	F. Hurst
2B	J. Warner
SS	R. Bartell
3B	S. McLeod
OF	C. Klein
OF	C. Fullis
OF	E. Schulmerich
C	V. Davis
P	E. Holley
P	R. Hansen
P	J. Elliott
P	W. Moore
P	P. Collins
RP	A. Liska

PHI 1934 N

M	J. Wilson
1B	A. Camilli
2B	L. Chiozza
SS	R. Bartell
3B	W. Walters
OF	E. Allen
OF	J. Moore
OF	G. Davis
C	A. Todd
UT	J. Wilson
P	C. Davis
P	P. Collins
P	R. Hansen
P	S. Johnson
P	W. Moore
RP	R. Grabowski
RP	G. Darrow

PHI 1935 N

M	J. Wilson
1B	A. Camilli
2B	L. Chiozza
SS	M. Haslin
3B	J. Vergez
OF	E. Allen
OF	J. Moore
OF	G. Watkins
C	A. Todd
P	C. Davis
P	O. Jorgens
P	S. Johnson
P	J. Bivin
P	W. Walters
RP	J. Pezzullo
RP	R. Prim
RP	H. Mulcahy

PHI 1936 N

M	J. Wilson
1B	A. Camilli
2B	J. Gomez
SS	L. Norris
3B	A. Whitney
OF	C. Klein
OF	J. Moore
OF	E. Sulik
C	R. Grace
UT	L. Chiozza
P	W. Walters
P	L. Norris
P	J. Bowman
P	O. Jorgens
RP	S. Johnson
RP	E. Moore

PHI 1937 N

M	J. Wilson
1B	A. Camilli
2B	D. Young
SS	G. Scharein
3B	A. Whitney
OF	H. Martin
OF	M. Arnovich
OF	C. Klein
C	W. Atwood
UT	E. Brown
UT	J. Moore
UT	L. Norris
P	C. Passeau
P	W. Walters
P	W. LaMaster
P	H. Mulcahy
P	S. Johnson
RP	O. Jorgens
RP	H. Kelleher

PHI 1938 N

M	J. Wilson
M	J. Lobert
1B	P. Weintraub
2B	E. Mueller
SS	D. Young
3B	A. Whitney
OF	M. Arnovich
OF	C. Klein
OF	H. Martin
C	W. Atwood
UT	G. Scharein
P	H. Mulcahy
P	C. Passeau
P	A. Hollingsworth
P	A. Butcher
RP	P. Sivess
RP	A. Smith

PHI 1939 N

M	J. Prothro
1B	A. Suhr
2B	R. Hughes
SS	G. Scharein
3B	M. May
OF	M. Arnovich
OF	H. Martin
OF	J. Marty
C	V. Davis
UT	G. Brack
UT	E. Mueller
P	H. Mulcahy
P	W. Higbe
P	W. Beck
P	I. Pearson
P	S. Johnson
RP	W. Kerksieck

PHI 1940 N

M	J. Prothro
1B	A. Mahan
2B	H. Schulte
SS	R. Bragan
3B	M. May
OF	J. Marty
OF	C. Klein
OF	J. Rizzo
C	B. Warren
UT	E. Mueller
P	W. Higbe
P	H. Mulcahy
P	I. Pearson
P	S. Johnson
P	W. Beck

PHI 1941 N

M	J. Prothro
1B	N. Etten
2B	D. Murtaugh
SS	R. Bragan
3B	M. May
OF	D. Litwhiler
OF	J. Marty
OF	A. Benjamin
C	B. Warren
UT	T. Livingston
UT	J. Rizzo
P	J. Podgajny
P	T. Hughes
P	D. Blanton
P	S. Johnson
P	L. Grissom
RP	I. Pearson
RP	F. Hoerst
RP	W. Beck

PHI 1942 N

M	J. Lobert
1B	N. Etten
2B	A. Glossop
SS	R. Bragan
3B	M. May
OF	D. Litwhiler
OF	R. Northey
OF	E. Koy
C	B. Warren
UT	D. Murtaugh
UT	L. Waner
P	T. Hughes
P	R. Melton
P	S. Johnson
P	J. Podgajny
P	F. Hoerst
RP	I. Pearson
RP	S. Nahem
RP	W. Beck

PHI 1943 N

M	S. Harris
M	F. Fitzsimmons
1B	J. Wasdell
2B	D. Murtaugh
SS	G. Stewart
3B	M. May
OF	R. Northey
OF	E. Adams
OF	H. Triplett
C	T. Livingston
UT	E. Dahlgren
P	A. Gerheauser
P	J. Kraus
P	L. Rowe
P	T. Barrett
P	S. Johnson
RP	N. Kimball

PHI 1944 N

M	F. Fitzsimmons
1B	U. Lupien
2B	F. Mullen
SS	R. Hamrick
3B	G. Stewart
OF	R. Northey
OF	E. Adams
OF	J. Wasdell
C	R. Finley
UT	C. Letchas
P	K.Raffensberger
P	C. Schanz
P	T. Barrett
P	W. Lee
P	A. Gerheauser
RP	A. Karl

PHI 1945 N

M	F. Fitzsimmons
M	W. Chapman
1B	J. Wasdell
2B	F. Daniels
SS	E. Mott
3B	J. Antonelli
OF	V. DiMaggio
OF	H. Triplett
OF	V. Dinges
C	A. Seminick
UT	R. Monteagudo
P	T. Barrett
P	C. Schanz
P	C. Sproull
P	R. Mauney
RP	A. Karl

PHI 1946 N

M	W. Chapman
1B	F. McCormick
2B	E. Verban
SS	L. Newsome
3B	J. Tabor
OF	J. Wyrostek
OF	D. Ennis
OF	R. Northey
C	A. Seminick
P	K.Raffensberger
P	T. Judd
P	L. Rowe
P	C. Schanz
P	T. Hughes
RP	A. Karl
RP	R. Mulligan

PHI 1947 N

M	W. Chapman
1B	H. Schultz
2B	E. Verban
SS	L. Newsome
3B	L. Handley
OF	D. Ennis
OF	H. Walker
OF	J. Wyrostek
C	A. Seminick
P	E. Leonard
P	L. Rowe
P	T. Judd
P	K. Heintzelman
P	T. Hughes
RP	F. Schmidt

PHI 1948 N

M	W. Chapman
M	A. Cooke
M	E. Sawyer
1B	R. Sisler
2B	G. Hamner
SS	E. Miller
3B	B. Caballero
OF	D. Ennis
OF	R. Ashburn
OF	J. Blatnik
C	A. Seminick
UT	B. Haas
UT	H. Walker
P	E. Leonard
P	C. Simmons
P	W. Dubiel
P	L. Rowe
P	R. Roberts
RP	E. Heusser
RP	S. Nahem

PHI 1949 N

M	E. Sawyer
1B	R. Sisler
2B	E. Miller
SS	G. Hamner
3B	W. Jones
OF	D. Ennis
OF	R. Ashburn
OF	W. Nicholson
C	A. Seminick
P	K. Heintzelman
P	R. Roberts
P	R. Meyer
P	H. Borowy
P	C. Simmons
RP	C. Konstanty
RP	K. Trinkle
RP	L. Rowe

PHI 1950 N

M	E. Sawyer
1B	E. Waitkus
2B	M. Goliat
SS	G. Hamner
3B	W. Jones
OF	D. Ennis
OF	R. Ashburn
C	A. Seminick
P	R. Roberts
P	C. Simmons
P	R. Miller
P	R. Meyer
P	E. Church
RP	C. Konstanty

PHI 1951 N

M	E. Sawyer
1B	E. Waitkus
2B	B. Caballero
SS	G. Hamner
3B	W. Jones
OF	D. Ennis
OF	R. Ashburn
OF	B. Sisler
C	A. Seminick
P	R. Roberts
P	E. Church
P	R. Meyer
P	J. Thompson
P	K. Heintzelman
RP	C. Konstanty

PHI 1952 N

M	E. Sawyer
M	S. O'Neill
1B	E. Waitkus
2B	C. Ryan
SS	G. Hamner
3B	W. Jones
OF	R. Ashburn
OF	D. Ennis
OF	J. Wyrostek
C	F. Burgess
P	R. Roberts
P	R. Meyer
P	K. Drews
P	C. Simmons
P	S. Ridzik
RP	C. Konstanty
RP	A. Hansen

PHI 1953 N

M	S. O'Neill
1B	C. Torgeson
2B	G. Hamner
SS	T. Kazanski
3B	W. Jones
OF	R. Ashburn
OF	D. Ennis
OF	J. Wyrostek
C	F. Burgess
P	R. Roberts
P	C. Simmons
P	K. Drews
P	R. Meyer
RP	S. Ridzik
RP	A. Hansen

PHI 1954 N

M	S. O'Neill
M	T. Moore
1B	C. Torgeson
2B	G. Hamner
SS	R. Morgan
3B	W. Jones
OF	R. Ashburn
OF	D. Ennis
OF	C. Schell
C	F. Burgess
P	R. Roberts
P	C. Simmons
P	M. Dickson
P	R. Miller
P	H. Wehmeier
RP	S. Ridzik
RP	C. Konstanty

PHI 1955 N

M	E. Smith
1B	M. Blaylock
2B	R. Morgan
SS	R. Smalley
3B	W. Jones
OF	D. Ennis
OF	R. Ashburn
OF	J. Greengrass
C	A. Seminick
UT	G. Hamner
UT	S. Lopata
P	R. Roberts
P	M. Dickson
P	H. Wehmeier
P	C. Simmons
RP	J. Meyer
RP	R. Miller

PHI 1956 N

M	E. Smith
1B	M. Blaylock
2B	T. Kazanski
SS	G. Hamner
3B	W. Jones
OF	R. Ashburn
OF	D. Ennis
OF	E. Valo
C	S. Lopata
P	R. Roberts
P	H. Haddix
P	C. Simmons
P	S. Rogovin
P	S. Miller
RP	R. Miller
RP	J. Meyer
RP	R. Negray

PHI 1957 N

M	E. Smith
1B	E. Bouchee
2B	G. Hamner
SS	H. Fernandez
3B	W. Jones
OF	R. Ashburn
OF	E. Repulski
OF	H. Anderson
C	S. Lopata
UT	R. Bowman
P	R. Roberts
P	J. Sanford
P	C. Simmons
P	H. Haddix
P	D. Cardwell
RP	R. Farrell
RP	J. Hearn
RP	R. Miller

PHI 1958 N

M	E. Smith
M	E. Sawyer
1B	E. Bouchee
2B	S. Hemus
SS	H. Fernandez
3B	W. Jones
OF	R. Ashburn
OF	W. Post
OF	H. Anderson
C	S. Lopata
UT	T. Kazanski
P	R. Roberts
P	R. Semproch
P	J. Sanford
P	C. Simmons
P	D. Cardwell
RP	R. Farrell
RP	J. Meyer
RP	J. Hearn

PHI 1959 N

M	E. Sawyer
1B	E. Bouchee
2B	G. Anderson
SS	J. Koppe
3B	E. Freese
OF	R. Ashburn
OF	H. Anderson
OF	W. Post
C	C. Sawatski
UT	D. Philley
P	R. Roberts
P	P. Owens
P	D. Conley
P	D. Cardwell
P	R. Semproch
RP	J. Meyer
RP	H. Robinson
RP	W. Phillips

PHI 1960 N

M	E. Sawyer
M	A. Cohen
M	G. Mauch
1B	J. Herrera
2B	A. Taylor
SS	R. Amaro
3B	A. Dark
OF	K. Walters
OF	R. Del Greco
OF	J. Callison
C	J. Coker
UT	G. Curry
UT	B. Smith
P	R. Roberts
P	J. Buzhardt
P	D. Conley
P	J. Owens
P	G. Green
RP	C. Short
RP	R. Farrell
RP	R. Gomez

PHI 1961 N

M	G. Mauch
1B	J. Herrera
2B	A. Taylor
SS	R. Amaro
3B	C. Smith
OF	J. Callison
OF	A. Gonzalez
OF	D. Demeter
C	C. Dalrymple
UT	R. Malkmus
P	A. Mahaffey
P	J. Buzhardt
P	F. Sullivan
P	D. Ferrarese
P	G. Green
RP	J. Baldschun
RP	K. Lehman

PHI 1962 N

M	G. Mauch
1B	R. Sievers
2B	A. Taylor
SS	R. Wine
3B	D. Demeter
OF	J. Callison
OF	A. Gonzalez
OF	T. Savage
C	C. Dalrymple
UT	J. Covington
UT	W. Klaus
UT	F. Torre
P	A. Mahaffey
P	J. Hamilton
P	D. Bennett
P	C. McLish
P	C. Short
RP	J. Baldschun
RP	P. Brown
RP	W. Smith

PHI 1963 N

M	G. Mauch
1B	R. Sievers
2B	A. Taylor
SS	R. Wine
3B	R. Hoak
OF	J. Callison
OF	A. Gonzalez
OF	D. Demeter
C	C. Dalrymple
UT	R. Amaro
UT	J. Covington
P	C. McLish
P	R. Culp
P	C. Short
P	A. Mahaffey
P	G. Green
RP	J. Baldschun
RP	J. Klippstein
RP	R. Duren

PHI 1964 N

M	G. Mauch
1B	J. Herrnstein
2B	A. Taylor
SS	R. Wine
3B	R. Allen
OF	J. Callison
OF	A. Gonzalez
OF	J. Covington
C	C. Dalrymple
UT	R. Amaro
UT	O. Rojas
P	J. Bunning
P	C. Short
P	D. Bennett
P	A. Mahaffey
P	R. Culp
RP	J. Baldschun
RP	E. Roebuck
RP	R. Wise

PHI 1965 N

M	G. Mauch
1B	R. Stuart
2B	A. Taylor
SS	R. Wine
3B	R. Allen
OF	J. Callison
OF	A. Gonzalez
OF	A. Johnson
C	C. Dalrymple
UT	R. Amaro
UT	J. Covington
UT	O. Rojas
P	C. Short
P	J. Bunning
P	R. Culp
P	R. Herbert
P	R. Belinsky
RP	G. Wagner
RP	J. Baldschun
RP	E. Roebuck

PHI 1966 N

M	G. Mauch
1B	W. White
2B	O. Rojas
SS	R. Groat
3B	R. Allen
OF	J. Callison
OF	A. Gonzalez
OF	J. Brandt
C	C. Dalrymple
UT	A. Taylor
P	J. Bunning
P	C. Short
P	L. Jackson
P	R. Buhl
P	R. Culp
RP	D. Knowles
RP	R. Herbert

PHI 1967 N

M	G. Mauch
1B	W. White
2B	O. Rojas
SS	R. Wine
3B	R. Allen
OF	J. Callison
OF	A. Gonzalez
OF	D. Lock
C	C. Dalrymple
UT	J. Briggs
UT	G. Sutherland
UT	A. Taylor
P	J. Bunning
P	L. Jackson
P	C. Short
P	R. Wise
P	R. Ellsworth
RP	R. Farrell
RP	R. Hall
RP	G. Jackson

PHI 1968 N

M	G. Mauch
M	G. Myatt
M	R. Skinner
1B	W. White
2B	O. Rojas
SS	R. Pena
3B	A. Taylor
OF	R. Allen
OF	A. Gonzalez
OF	J. Callison
C	M. Ryan
UT	J. Briggs
UT	D. Lock
P	C. Short
P	L. Jackson
P	W. Fryman
P	R. Wise
P	J. James
RP	R. Farrell
RP	G. Wagner
RP	J. Boozer

PHI 1969 N

M	R. Skinner
M	G. Myatt
1B	R. Allen
2B	O. Rojas
SS	D. Money
3B	A. Taylor
OF	L. Hisle
OF	J. Callison
OF	J. Briggs
C	M. Ryan
UT	D. Johnson
UT	R. Joseph
UT	H. Stone
P	G. Jackson
P	W. Fryman
P	R. Wise
P	J. Johnson
P	B. Champion
RP	J. Boozer
RP	R. Farrell
RP	A. Raffo

PHI 1970 N

M	F. Lucchesi
1B	D. Johnson
2B	R. Doyle
SS	L. Bowa
3B	D. Money
OF	L. Hisle
OF	H. Stone
OF	J. Briggs
C	M. Ryan
UT	B. Browne
UT	A. Taylor
P	R. Wise
P	J. Bunning
P	C. Short
P	G. Jackson
P	B. Lersch
RP	R. Selma
RP	L. Palmer
RP	W. Wilson

PHI 1971 N

M	F. Lucchesi
1B	D. Johnson
2B	R. Doyle
SS	L. Bowa
3B	J. Vukovich
OF	G. Montanez
OF	R. Freed
OF	O. Gamble
C	J. McCarver
UT	D. Money
P	R. Wise
P	B. Lersch
P	C. Short
P	K. Reynolds
P	W. Fryman
RP	B. Champion
RP	D. Brandon
RP	J. Hoerner

PHI 1972 N

M	F. Lucchesi
M	P. Owens
1B	T. Hutton
2B	R. Doyle
SS	L. Bowa
3B	D. Money
OF	G. Luzinski
OF	G. Montanez
OF	W. Robinson
C	J. Bateman
UT	D. Johnson
P	S. Carlton
P	K. Reynolds
P	B. Champion
P	W. Fryman
RP	W. Twitchell
RP	D. Brandon
RP	B. Lersch

PHI 1973 N

M	D. Ozark
1B	G. Montanez
2B	R. Doyle
SS	L. Bowa
3B	M. Schmidt
OF	G. Luzinski
OF	D. Unser
OF	W. Robinson
C	R. Boone
UT	T. Hutton
UT	C. Tovar
P	S. Carlton
P	W. Twitchell
P	K. Brett
P	J. Lonborg
P	R. Ruthven
RP	B. Lersch
RP	G. Scarce
RP	D. Brandon

PHI 1974 N

M	D. Ozark
1B	G. Montanez
2B	D. Cash
SS	L. Bowa
3B	M. Schmidt
OF	D. Unser
OF	M. Anderson
OF	W. Robinson
C	R. Boone
P	S. Carlton
P	J. Lonborg
P	R. Ruthven
P	R. Schueler
P	W. Twitchell
RP	G. Scarce
RP	H. Garber

PHI 1975 N

M	D. Ozark
1B	R. Allen
2B	D. Cash
SS	L. Bowa
3B	M. Schmidt
OF	G. Luzinski
OF	M. Anderson
OF	J. Johnstone
C	R. Boone
UT	T. Hutton
UT	G. Maddox
P	S. Carlton
P	T. Underwood
P	L. Christenson
P	J. Lonborg
P	W. Twitchell
RP	H. Garber
RP	F. McGraw
RP	T. Hilgendorf

PHI 1976 N

M	D. Ozark
1B	R. Allen
2B	D. Cash
SS	L. Bowa
3B	M. Schmidt
OF	G. Maddox
OF	G. Luzinski
OF	J. Johnstone
C	R. Boone
UT	R. Martin
UT	R. Tolan
P	S. Carlton
P	J. Kaat
P	J. Lonborg

P L. Christenson
P T. Underwood
RP R. Reed
RP F. McGraw
RP H. Garber

PHI 1977 N
M D. Ozark
1B R. Hebner
2B T. Sizemore
SS L. Bowa
3B M. Schmidt
OF G. Luzinski
OF G. Maddox
OF J. Martin
C R. Boone
UT T. Hutton
UT J. Johnstone
P S. Carlton
P L. Christenson
P R. Lerch
P J. Kaat
P J. Lonborg
RP R. Reed
RP H. Garber
RP F. McGraw

PHI 1978 N
M D. Ozark
1B R. Hebner
2B T. Sizemore
SS L. Bowa
3B M. Schmidt
OF G. Maddox
OF G. Luzinski
OF A. McBride
C R. Boone
UT J. Martin
P S. Carlton
P L. Christenson
P R. Lerch
P R. Ruthven
P J. Kaat
RP R. Reed
RP F. McGraw
RP W. Brusstar

PHI 1979 N
M D. Ozark
M G. Green
1B P. Rose
2B J. Trillo
SS L. Bowa
3B M. Schmidt
OF A. McBride
OF G. Maddox
OF G. Luzinski
C R. Boone
UT G. Gross
P S. Carlton
P R. Lerch
P A. Espinosa
P R. Ruthven
P L. Christenson
RP R. Reed
RP F. McGraw
RP R. Eastwick

PHI 1980 N
M G. Green
1B P. Rose
2B J. Trillo
SS L. Bowa
3B M. Schmidt
OF G. Maddox
OF A. McBride
OF G. Luzinski
C R. Boone
UT G. Gross
UT L. Smith
P S. Carlton
P R. Ruthven
P R. Walk
P R. Lerch
RP F. McGraw
RP R. Reed
RP D. Noles

PHI 1981 N
M G. Green
1B P. Rose
2B J. Trillo
SS L. Bowa
3B M. Schmidt
OF G. Matthews
OF G. Maddox
OF A. McBride
C R. Boone
UT G. Gross
P S. Carlton
P R. Ruthven
P L. Christenson

P A. Espinosa
RP A. Lyle
RP M. Proly
RP R. Reed

PHI 1982 N
M P. Corrales
1B P. Rose
2B J. Trillo
SS I. DeJesus
3B M. Schmidt
OF G. Matthews
OF R. Dernier
OF G. Maddox
C B. Diaz
UT G. Gross
UT G. Vukovich
P S. Carlton
P L. Christenson
P M. Krukow
P R. Ruthven
RP R. Reed
RP E. Farmer
RP I. Monge

PHI 1983 N
M P. Corrales
M P. Owens
1B P. Rose
2B J. Morgan
SS I. DeJesus
3B M. Schmidt
OF G. Matthews
OF G. Gross
OF R. Dernier
C B. Diaz
UT V. Hayes
UT J. Lefebvre
P S. Carlton
P J. Denny
P C. Hudson
P M. Bystrom
RP R. Reed
RP G. Hernandez
RP A. Holland

PHI 1984 N
M P. Owens
1B L. Matuszek
2B J. Samuel
SS I. DeJesus
3B M. Schmidt
OF V. Hayes
OF G. Wilson
OF S. Lezcano
C O. Virgil
UT T. Corcoran
UT G. Gross
P S. Carlton
P J. Koosman
P C. Hudson
P J. Denny
P S. Rawley
RP K. Gross
RP A. Holland
RP L. Andersen

PHI 1985 N
M J. Felske
1B M. Schmidt
2B J. Samuel
SS L. Jeltz
3B R. Schu
OF G. Wilson
OF V. Hayes
OF G. Maddox
C O. Virgil
UT T. Corcoran
P J. Denny
P K. Gross
P S. Rawley
P C. Hudson
P J. Koosman
RP D. Carman
RP D. Rucker
RP L. Andersen

PHI 1986 N
M J. Felske
1B V. Hayes
2B J. Samuel
SS L. Jeltz
3B M. Schmidt
OF G. Wilson
OF M. Thompson
OF G. Redus
C J. Russell
UT R. Roenicke
P K. Gross
P S. Rawley
P B. Ruffin
P C. Hudson

RP D. Carman
RP K. Tekulve
RP T. Hume

PHI 1987 N
M J. Felske
M L. Elia
1B V. Hayes
2B J. Samuel
SS L. Jeltz
3B M. Schmidt
OF G. Wilson
OF M. Thompson
OF D. James
C L. Parrish
UT G. Gross
P S. Rawley
P D. Carman
P B. Ruffin
P K. Gross
RP M. Jackson
RP K. Tekulve
RP S. Bedrosian

PHI 1988 N
M L. Elia
M J. Vukovich
1B V. Hayes
2B J. Samuel
SS L. Jeltz
3B M. Schmidt
OF P. Bradley
OF D. James
OF M. Thompson
C L. Parrish
UT G. Gross
P K. Gross
P D. Carman
P S. Rawley
P D. Palmer
RP B. Ruffin
RP G. Harris
RP K. Tekulve

PHI 1989 N
M N. Leyva
1B P. Jordan
2B T. Herr
SS R. Thon
3B C. Hayes
OF V. Hayes
OF L. Dykstra
OF R. Dernier
C D. Daulton
C C. Ford
UT L. Jeltz
P K. Howell
P D. Carman
P B. Ruffin
P L. McWilliams
P D. Cook
RP J. Parrett
RP G. Harris
RP T. Frohwirth

PHI 1990 N
M N. Leyva
1B P. Jordan
2B T. Herr
SS R. Thon
3B C. Hayes
OF L. Dykstra
OF V. Hayes
OF J. Kruk
C D. Daulton
UT R. Ready
P P. Combs
P T. Mulholland
P B. Ruffin
P D. Cook
P J. DeJesus
RP D. Akerfelds
RP D. Carman
RP R. McDowell

Pittsburgh

CP U 1884
PIT a 1882-1886
PIT P 1890
PIT F 1914-1915
PIT N 1887-1990

CP 1884 U
M E. Hengle
1B L. Schoeneck
2B E. Hengle
SS S. Matthias
3B C. Householder
OF J. Ellick
OF C. Briggs

OF H. Wheeler
C W. Krieg
UT A. Suck
P H. Daily
P A. Atkinson
P J. Horan

PIT 1882 a
M A. Pratt
1B G. Lane
2B G. Strief
SS J. Peters
3B J. Battin
OF M. Mansell
OF C. Swartwood
OF J. Leary
C W. Taylor
P H. Salisbury
P J. Driscoll
P H. Arundel

PIT 1883 a
M A. Pratt
M O. Butler
M J. Battin
1B C. Swartwood
2B G. Creamer
SS D. Mack
3B J. Battin
OF M. Mansell
OF L. Dickerson
OF W. Taylor
C J. Hayes
P J. Driscoll
P R. Barr
P J. Neagle

PIT 1884 a
M D. McKnight
M R. Ferguson
M J. Battin
M G. Creamer
M H. Phillips
1B J. Knowles
2B G. Creamer
SS W. White
3B J. Battin
OF C. Swartwood
OF G. Miller
OF G. Taylor
C W. Colgan
P F. Sullivan
P J. Neagle

PIT 1885 a
M H. Phillips
1B J. Field
2B C. Smith
SS A. Whitney
3B W. Kuehne
OF T. Brown
OF F. Mann
OF C. Eden
C F. Carroll
P E. Morris
P P. Meegan
P H. O'Day
P J. Galvin

PIT 1886 a
M H. Phillips
1B O. Schomberg
2B S. Barkley
SS C. Smith
3B A. Whitney
OF F. Mann
OF T. Brown
OF E. Glenn
C F. Carroll
UT W. Kuehne
P E. Morris
P J. Galvin
P J. Handiboe

PIT 1890 P
M E. Hanlon
1B J. Beckley
2B W. Robinson
SS T. Corcoran
3B W. Kuehne
OF J. Visner
OF E. Hanlon
OF J. Fields
C F. Carroll
P H. Staley
P A. Maul
P J. Galvin
P E. Morris
P J. Tener

PIT 1914 F
M H. Gessler
M E. Oakes
1B H. Bradley
2B J. Lewis
SS E. Holly
3B J. Lennox
OF E. Oakes
OF J. Savage
OF D. Jones
C C. Berry
P E. Knetzer
P S. Camnitz
P W. Dickson
P E. Barger
P J. Walker

PIT 1915 F
M E. Oakes
1B E. Konetchy
2B S. Yerkes
SS M. Berghammer
3B H. Mowrey
OF E. Oakes
OF J. Kelly
OF J. Wickland
C C. Berry
P F. Allen
P E. Knetzer
P F. Rogge
P B. Hearn
P E. Barger

PIT 1887 N
M H. Phillips
1B S. Barkley
2B C. Smith
SS W. Kuehne
3B A. Whitney
OF J. Coleman
OF A. Dalrymple
OF T. Brown
C G. Miller
UT F. Carroll
P J. Galvin
P J. McCormick
P E. Morris

PIT 1888 N
M H. Phillips
1B J. Beckley
2B F. Dunlap
SS C. Smith
3B W. Kuehne
OF W. Sunday
OF J. Coleman
OF A. Dalrymple
C G. Miller
UT F. Carroll
P E. Morris
P J. Galvin
P H. Staley

PIT 1889 N
M H. Phillips
M F. Dunlap
M E. Hanlon
1B J. Beckley
2B F. Dunlap
SS J. Rowe
3B W. Kuehne
OF E. Hanlon
OF W. Sunday
OF A. Maul
C G. Miller
UT F. Carroll
P H. Staley
P J. Galvin
P E. Morris

PIT 1890 N
M G. Hecker
1B G. Hecker
2B S. LaRoque
SS E. Sales
3B G. Miller
OF W. Sunday
OF J. Kelty
OF J. Berger
C E. Decker
P K. Baker
P D. Anderson
P W. Sowders

PIT 1891 N
M E. Hanlon
M W. McGunnigle
1B J. Beckley
2B L. Bierbauer
SS F. Shugart

3B C. Reilly
OF E. Hanlon
OF F. Carroll
OF L. Browning
C C. Mack
UT G. Miller
P M. Baldwin
P C. King
P J. Galvin

PIT 1892 N
M A.Buckenberger
M T. Burns
M A.Buckenberger
1B J. Beckley
2B L. Bierbauer
SS F. Shugart
3B C. Farrell
OF E. Smith
OF P. Donovan
OF G. Miller
C C. Mack
P M. Baldwin
P P. Ehret
P W. Terry
P J. Galvin

PIT 1893 N
M A.Buckenberger
1B J. Beckley
2B L. Bierbauer
SS J. Glasscock
3B D. Lyons
OF E. Smith
OF P. Donovan
OF G. Van Haltren
C G. Miller
P F. Killen
P P. Ehret
P W. Terry
P A. Gumbert

PIT 1894 N
M A.Buckenberger
M C. Mack
1B J. Beckley
2B L. Bierbauer
SS J. Glasscock
3B D. Lyons
OF P. Donovan
OF J. Stenzel
OF E. Smith
C C. Mack
P P. Ehret
P A. Gumbert
P F. Killen
P T. Colcolough
P J. Menefee

PIT 1895 N
M C. Mack
1B J. Beckley
2B L. Bierbauer
SS M. Cross
3B W. Clingman
OF J. Stenzel
OF P. Donovan
OF E. Smith
C W. Merritt
P E. Hawley
P W. Hart
P J. Foreman
P F. Killen
P J. Gardner

PIT 1896 N
M C. Mack
1B J. Beckley
2B R. Padden
SS W. Ely
3B D. Lyons
OF P. Donovan
OF E. Smith
OF J. Stenzel
C J. Sugden
P F. Killen
P E. Hawley
P J. Hughey
P C. Hastings

PIT 1897 N
M P. Donovan
1B H. Davis
2B R. Padden
SS W. Ely
3B J. Hoffmeister
OF E. Smith
OF P. Donovan
OF W. Brodie
C J. Sugden
P F. Killen

P E. Hawley
P J. Hughey
P C. Hastings
P J. Gardner

PIT 1898 N
M W. Watkins
1B W. Clark
2B R. Padden
SS W. Ely
3B W. Grey
OF P. Donovan
OF J. McCarthy
OF T. O'Brien
C W. Schriver
P J. Tannehill
P W. Rhines
P J. Gardner
P F. Killen
P C. Hastings

PIT 1899 N
M W. Watkins
M P. Donovan
1B W. Clark
2B J. O'Brien
SS W. Ely
3B J. Williams
OF J. McCarthy
OF P. Donovan
OF C. Beaumont
C F. Bowerman
UT T. McCreery
P S. Leever
P J. Tannehill
P T. Sparks
P W. Hoffer
P J. Chesbro

PIT 1900 N
M F. Clarke
1B D. Cooley
2B C. Ritchey
SS W. Ely
3B J. Williams
OF C. Beaumont
OF J. Wagner
OF F. Clarke
C C. Zimmer
UT T. O'Brien
P C. Phillippe
P J. Tannehill
P S. Leever
P J. Chesbro
P G. Waddell

PIT 1901 N
M F. Clarke
1B W. Bransfield
2B C. Ritchey
SS W. Ely
3B T. Leach
OF C. Beaumont
OF F. Clarke
OF A. Davis
C C. Zimmer
UT J. Wagner
P C. Phillippe
P J. Chesbro
P J. Tannehill
P S. Leever

PIT 1902 N
M F. Clarke
1B W. Bransfield
2B C. Ritchey
SS W. Conroy
3B T. Leach
OF C. Beaumont
OF J. Wagner
C H. Smith
P J. Chesbro
P C. Phillippe
P J. Tannehill
P S. Leever
P E. Doheny

PIT 1903 N
M F. Clarke
1B W. Bransfield
2B C. Ritchey
SS J. Wagner
3B T. Leach
OF C. Beaumont
OF J. Sebring
OF F. Clarke
C E. Phelps
P C. Phillippe
P S. Leever
P E. Doheny

P W. Kennedy
P I. Wilhelm

PIT 1904 N

M F. Clarke
1B W. Bransfield
2B C. Ritchey
SS J. Wagner
3B T. Leach
OF C. Beaumont
OF J. Sebring
OF F. Clarke
C E. Phelps
P S. Leever
P P. Flaherty
P M. Lynch
P C. Phillippe
P C. Case

PIT 1905 N

M F. Clarke
1B G. Howard
2B C. Ritchey
SS J. Wagner
3B D. Brain
OF F. Clarke
OF C. Beaumont
OF O. Clymer
C H. Peitz
UT T. Leach
P C. Phillippe
P S. Leever
P C. Case
P M. Lynch
P P. Flaherty

PIT 1906 N

M F. Clarke
1B J. Nealon
2B C. Ritchey
SS J. Wagner
3B T. Sheehan
OF R. Ganley
OF F. Clarke
OF C. Beaumont
C G. Gibson
UT T. Leach
P V. Willis
P S. Leever
P A. Leifield
P C. Phillippe
P M. Lynch

PIT 1907 N

M F. Clarke
1B J. Nealon
2B E. Abbaticchio
SS J. Wagner
3B A. Storke
OF F. Clarke
OF E. Anderson
OF T. Leach
C G. Gibson
UT W. Hallman
P V. Willis
P A. Leifield
P S. Leever
P C. Phillippe
P S. Camnitz

PIT 1908 N

M F. Clarke
1B H. Swacina
2B E. Abbaticchio
SS J. Wagner
3B T. Leach
OF F. Clarke
OF J. Wilson
OF R. Thomas
C G. Gibson
P V. Willis
P N. Maddox
P S. Camnitz
P A. Leifield
P S. Leever

PIT 1909 N

M F. Clarke
1B W. Abstein
2B J. Miller
SS J. Wagner
3B W. Barbeau
OF J. Wilson
OF F. Clarke
OF T. Leach
C G. Gibson
P V. Willis
P S. Camnitz
P N. Maddox
P A. Leifield
P C. Phillippe

PIT 1910 N

M F. Clarke
1B J. Flynn
2B J. Miller
SS J. Wagner
3B R. Byrne
OF J. Wilson
OF T. Leach
OF F. Clarke
C G. Gibson
UT A. Campbell
P S. Camnitz
P C. Adams
P A. Leifield
P O. White
P C. Phillippe

PIT 1911 N

M F. Clarke
1B F. Hunter
2B J. Miller
SS J. Wagner
3B R. Byrne
OF J. Wilson
OF M. Carey
OF F. Clarke
C G. Gibson
UT T. Leach
UT W. McKechnie
P A. Leifield
P C. Adams
P S. Camnitz
P E. Steele
P C. Hendrix

PIT 1912 N

M F. Clarke
1B J. Miller
2B A. McCarthy
SS J. Wagner
3B R. Byrne
OF J. Wilson
OF M. Carey
OF M. Donlin
C G. Gibson
P C. Hendrix
P S. Camnitz
P M. O'Toole
P J. Robinson
P C. Adams

PIT 1913 N

M F. Clarke
1B J. Miller
2B J. Viox
SS J. Wagner
3B R. Byrne
OF J. Wilson
OF M. Carey
OF M. Mitchell
C M. Simon
P C. Adams
P C. Hendrix
P J. Robinson
P S. Camnitz
P M. O'Toole

PIT 1914 N

M F. Clarke
1B E. Konetchy
2B J. Viox
SS J. Wagner
3B H. Mowrey
OF M. Carey
OF J. Kelly
OF M. Mitchell
C G. Gibson
P C. Adams
P A. Cooper
P G. McQuillan
P R. Harmon
P J. Conzelman

PIT 1915 N

M F. Clarke
1B W. Johnston
2B J. Viox
SS J. Wagner
3B H. Baird
OF W. Hinchman
OF M. Carey
OF J. Collins
C G. Gibson
P R. Harmon
P A. Mamaux
P C. Adams
P A. Cooper
P E. Kantlehner
RP J. Conzelman

PIT 1916 N

M J. Callahan
1B W. Johnston
2B F. Farmer
SS J. Wagner
3B H. Baird
OF M. Carey
OF W. Hinchman
OF F. Schulte
C W. Schmidt
P A. Mamaux
P A. Cooper
P F. Miller
P R. Harmon
P E. Kantlehner

PIT 1917 N

M J. Callahan
M J. Wagner
M H. Bezdek
1B J. Wagner
2B J. Pitler
SS C. Ward
3B N. Boeckel
OF M. Carey
OF C. Bigbee
OF L. King
C W. Fischer
P A. Cooper
P W. Jacobs
P F. Miller
P B. Grimes
P R. Steele

PIT 1918 N

M H. Bezdek
1B F. Mollwitz
2B G. Cutshaw
SS J. Caton
3B W. McKechnie
OF M. Carey
OF C. Bigbee
OF W. Southworth
C W. Schmidt
P A. Cooper
P F. Miller
P R. Sanders
P E. Mayer
P R. Harmon

PIT 1919 N

M H. Bezdek
1B F. Mollwitz
2B G. Cutshaw
SS Z. Terry
3B W. Barbare
OF C. Bigbee
OF W. Southworth
OF C. Stengel
C W. Schmidt
P A. Cooper
P C. Adams
P F. Miller
P E. Hamilton
P H. Carlson

PIT 1920 N

M G. Gibson
1B C. Grimm
2B G. Cutshaw
SS J. Caton
3B G. Whitted
OF W. Southworth
OF C. Bigbee
OF M. Carey
C W. Schmidt
UT F. Nicholson
P A. Cooper
P C. Adams
P H. Carlson
P E. Hamilton
P C. Ponder

PIT 1921 N

M G. Gibson
1B C. Grimm
2B G. Cutshaw
SS W. Maranville
3B C. Barnhart
OF C. Bigbee
OF M. Carey
OF G. Whitted
C W. Schmidt
UT J. Tierney
P A. Cooper
P C. Glazner
P E. Hamilton
P C. Adams
P J. Morrison

PIT 1922 N

M G. Gibson
M W. McKechnie
1B C. Grimm
2B J. Tierney
SS W. Maranville
3B H. Traynor
OF M. Carey
OF C. Bigbee
OF E. Russell
C J. Gooch
P A. Cooper
P J. Morrison
P C. Glazner
P C. Adams
P E. Hamilton
RP M. Yellowhorse

PIT 1923 N

M W. McKechnie
1B C. Grimm
2B J. Rawlings
SS W. Maranville
3B H. Traynor
OF M. Carey
OF C. Bigbee
OF C. Barnhart
C W. Schmidt
UT E. Russell
P J. Morrison
P A. Cooper
P H. Meadows
P C. Adams
P E. Hamilton

PIT 1924 N

M W. McKechnie
1B C. Grimm
2B W. Maranville
SS F. Wright
3B H. Traynor
OF M. Carey
OF K. Cuyler
OF C. Barnhart
C J. Gooch
P A. Cooper
P R. Kremer
P J. Morrison
P H. Meadows
P E. Yde
RP E. Stone

PIT 1925 N

M W. McKechnie
1B G. Grantham
2B D. Moore
SS F. Wright
3B H. Traynor
OF H. Cuyler
OF C. Barnhart
OF M. Carey
C E. Smith
P H. Meadows
P R. Kremer
P V. Aldridge
P J. Morrison
P E. Yde
RP T. Sheehan

PIT 1926 N

M W. McKechnie
1B G. Grantham
2B R. Rhyne
SS F. Wright
3B H. Traynor
OF H. Cuyler
OF P. Waner
OF M. Carey
C E. Smith
P R. Kremer
P H. Meadows
P V. Aldridge
P E. Yde
P D. Songer

PIT 1927 N

M O. Bush
1B J. Harris
2B G. Grantham
SS F. Wright
3B H. Traynor
OF L. Waner
OF P. Waner
OF C. Barnhart
C J. Gooch
P H. Meadows
P C. Hill
P V. Aldridge
P R. Kremer
RP J. Morrison
RP M. Cvengros

PIT 1928 N

M O. Bush
1B G. Grantham
2B E. Adams
SS F. Wright
3B H. Traynor
OF L. Waner
OF P. Waner
OF G. Brickell
C C. Hargreaves
P B. Grimes
P C. Hill
P R. Kremer
P F. Fussell
P R. Dawson

PIT 1929 N

M O. Bush
M J. Ens
1B E. Sheely
2B G. Grantham
SS R. Bartell
3B H. Traynor
OF L. Waner
OF P. Waner
OF A. Comorosky
C C. Hargreaves
P B. Grimes
P E. Brame
P R. Kremer
P J. Petty
P S. Swetonic
RP C. Hill

PIT 1930 N

M J. Ens
1B A. Suhr
2B G. Grantham
SS R. Bartell
3B H. Traynor
OF L. Waner
OF P. Waner
OF A. Comorosky
C R. Hemsley
P R. Kremer
P L. French
P E. Brame
P G. Spencer
P H. Meine

PIT 1931 N

M J. Ens
1B A. Suhr
2B G. Grantham
SS T. Thevenow
3B H. Traynor
OF L. Waner
OF P. Waner
OF A. Comorosky
C E. Phillips
P H. Meine
P L. French
P R. Kremer
P G. Spencer
P E. Brame
RP J. Osborn

PIT 1932 N

M G. Gibson
1B A. Suhr
2B A. Piet
SS J. Vaughan
3B H. Traynor
OF P. Waner
OF L. Waner
OF A. Comorosky
C R. Grace
UT D. Barbee
P L. French
P W. Swift
P H. Meine
P W. Harris
P S. Swetonic
RP E. Brame

PIT 1933 N

M G. Gibson
1B A. Suhr
2B A. Piet
SS J. Vaughan
3B H. Traynor
OF P. Waner
OF F. Lindstrom
OF L. Waner
C R. Grace
P L. French
P W. Swift
P H. Meine
P S. Swetonic
P H. Smith
RP L. Chagnon

RP W. Harris

PIT 1934 N

M G. Gibson
M H. Traynor
1B A. Suhr
2B H. Lavagetto
SS J. Vaughan
3B H. Traynor
OF L. Waner
OF P. Waner
OF G. Brickell
C R. Grace
UT T. Thevenow
P L. French
P W. Swift
P R. Birkofer
P W. Hoyt
P C. Lucas
RP L. Chagnon
RP H. Smith

PIT 1935 N

M H. Traynor
1B A. Suhr
2B L. Young
SS J. Vaughan
3B H. Thevenow
OF F. Jensen
OF P. Waner
OF L. Waner
C T. Padden
P D. Blanton
P W. Swift
P G. Bush
P J. Weaver
P W. Hoyt

PIT 1936 N

M H. Traynor
1B A. Suhr
2B L. Young
SS J. Vaughan
3B W. Brubaker
OF F. Jensen
OF P. Waner
OF L. Waner
C T. Padden
P W. Swift
P D. Blanton
P J. Weaver
P C. Lucas
P M. Brown

PIT 1937 N

M H. Traynor
1B A. Suhr
2B L. Handley
SS J. Vaughan
3B W. Brubaker
OF P. Waner
OF L. Waner
OF F. Jensen
C A. Todd
UT L. Young
P D. Blanton
P R. Bauers
P E. Brandt
P W. Swift
P J. Bowman
RP M. Brown

PIT 1938 N

M H. Traynor
1B A. Suhr
2B L. Young
SS J. Vaughan
3B L. Handley
OF P. Waner
OF L. Waner
OF J. Rizzo
C A. Todd
P R. Bauers
P J. Tobin
P D. Blanton
P R. Klinger
P W. Swift
RP M. Brown

PIT 1939 N

M H. Traynor
1B E. Fletcher
2B L. Young
SS J. Vaughan
3B L. Handley
OF P. Waner
OF L. Waner
OF J. Rizzo
C R. Mueller
UT W. Brubaker
P R. Klinger

P M. Brown
P J. Bowman
P T. Sewell
P J. Tobin

PIT 1940 N

M F. Frisch
1B E. Fletcher
2B F. Gustine
SS J. Vaughan
3B L. Handley
OF R. Elliott
OF M. Van Robays
OF V. DiMaggio
C V. Davis
UT D. Garms
P T. Sewell
P J. Bowman
P M. Brown
P K. Heintzelman
P R. Klinger
RP R. Lanahan
RP D. Mac Fayden

PIT 1941 N

M F. Frisch
1B E. Fletcher
2B F. Gustine
SS J. Vaughan
3B L. Handley
OF V. DiMaggio
OF R. Elliott
OF M. Van Robays
C A. Lopez
P T. Sewell
P A. Butcher
P K. Heintzelman
P J. Lanning
P R. Klinger

PIT 1942 N

M F. Frisch
1B E. Fletcher
2B F. Gustine
SS P. Coscarart
3B R. Elliott
OF V. DiMaggio
OF J. Wasdell
OF J. Barrett
C A. Lopez
UT E. Phelps
UT M. Van Robays
P T. Sewell
P R. Klinger
P A. Butcher
P L. Dietz
P K. Heintzelman

PIT 1943 N

M F. Frisch
1B E. Fletcher
2B P. Coscarart
SS F. Gustine
3B R. Elliott
OF V. DiMaggio
OF J. Russell
OF J. Barrett
C A. Lopez
P T. Sewell
P R. Klinger
P A. Butcher
P W. Hebert
P H. Gornicki
RP W. Brandt

PIT 1944 N

M F. Frisch
1B E. Dahlgren
2B P. Coscarart
SS F. Gustine
3B R. Elliott
OF J. Russell
OF J. Barrett
OF V. DiMaggio
C A. Lopez
UT F. Colman
P T. Sewell
P F. Ostermueller
P A. Butcher
P N. Strincevich
P E. Roe
RP X. Rescigno

PIT 1945 N

M F. Frisch
1B E. Dahlgren
2B P. Coscarart
SS F. Gustine
3B R. Elliott
OF J. Russell
OF J. Barrett

OF A. Gionfriddo
C A. Lopez
UT L. Handley
UT W. Salkeld
P E. Roe
P N. Strincevich
P T. Sewell
P A. Butcher
P A. Gerheauser
RP X. Rescigno
RP A. Cuccurullo

PIT 1946 N
M F. Frisch
M V. Davis
1B E. Fletcher
2B F. Gustine
SS W. Cox
3B L. Handley
OF R. Kiner
OF J. Russell
OF R. Elliott
C A. Lopez
P F. Ostermueller
P N. Strincevich
P K. Heintzelman
P T. Sewell
P E. Bahr
RP A. Gerheauser

PIT 1947 N
M W. Herman
M W. Burwell
1B H. Greenberg
2B J. Bloodworth
SS W. Cox
3B F. Gustine
OF R. Kiner
OF J. Russell
OF W. Westlake
C H. Howell
UT C. Rikard
P W. Higbe
P F. Ostermueller
P E. Bonham
P E. Roe
P T. Sewell
RP N. Strincevich
RP B. Singleton

PIT 1948 N
M W. Meyer
1B E. Stevens
2B D. Murtaugh
SS S. Rojek
3B F. Gustine
OF R. Kiner
OF W. Westlake
OF F. Walker
C E. Fitzgerald
UT J. Hopp
UT C. Kluttz
P R. Chesnes
P E. Riddle
P V. Lombardi
P E. Bonham
P F. Ostermueller
RP W. Higbe
RP B. Singleton
RP M. Queen

PIT 1949 N
M W. Meyer
1B J. Hopp
2B R. Basgall
SS S. Rojek
3B P. Castiglione
OF R. Kiner
OF W. Westlake
OF D. Restelli
C C. McCullough
P M. Dickson
P W. Werle
P C. Chambers
P R. Chesnes
P V. Lombardi
RP T. Sewell

PIT 1950 N
M W. Meyer
1B J. Hopp
2B D. Murtaugh
SS S. Rojek
3B F. Fernandez
OF R. Kiner
OF W. Westlake
OF D. Bell
C C. McCullough
UT P. Castiglione
P C. Chambers
P M. Dickson
P W. Werle
P W. Macdonald
P V. Law
RP V. Lombardi
RP J. Walsh

PIT 1951 N
M W. Meyer
1B R. Kiner
2B D. Murtaugh
SS G. Strickland
3B P. Castiglione
OF D. Bell
OF G. Metkovich
OF W. Howerton
C C. McCullough
P M. Dickson
P M. Queen
P R. Friend
P H. Pollet
P V. Law
RP W. Werle
RP T. Wilks
RP J. Walsh

PIT 1952 N
M W. Meyer
1B A. Bartirome
2B J. Merson
SS R. Groat
3B P. Castiglione
OF R. Kiner
OF D. Bell
OF R. Del Greco
C J. Garagiola
UT C. Koshorek
UT G. Metkovich
P M. Dickson
P H. Pollet
P R. Friend
P F. Main
RP R. Kline
RP T. Wilks
RP P. LaPalme

PIT 1953 N
M F. Haney
1B P. Ward
2B J. O'Brien
SS E. O'Brien
3B D. O'Connell
OF F. Thomas
OF C. Abrams
OF C. Bernier
C M. Sandlock
UT R. Cole
UT P. Smith
P M. Dickson
P J. Lindell
P P. LaPalme
P R. Friend
P R. Hall
RP E. Face
RP J. Hetki
RP R. Bowman

PIT 1954 N
M F. Haney
1B R. Skinner
2B C. Roberts
SS G. Allie
3B R. Cole
OF F. Thomas
OF R. Hall
OF G. Lynch
C M. Atwell
UT S. Gordon
UT P. Ward
P M. Surkont
P R. Friend
P V. Law
P R. Littlefield
P R. Purkey
RP J. Hetki
RP E. Face

PIT 1955 N
M F. Haney
1B R. Long
2B J. O'Brien
SS R. Groat
3B E. Freese
OF F. Thomas
OF R. Clemente
OF G. Lynch
C J. Shepard
P V. Law
P R. Friend
P M. Surkont
P R. Kline
P R. Littlefield

PIT 1956 N
M R. Bragan
1B R. Long
2B W. Mazeroski
SS R. Groat
3B F. Thomas
OF R. Clemente
OF R. Walls
OF W. Virdon
C J. Shepard
UT R. Skinner
P R. Friend
P R. Kline
P V. Law
P G. Munger
RP E. Face
RP N. King
RP F. Waters

PIT 1957 N
M R. Bragan
M D. Murtaugh
1B D. Fondy
2B W. Mazeroski
SS R. Groat
3B E. Freese
OF W. Virdon
OF R. Clemente
OF R. Skinner
C H. Foiles
UT E. Baker
UT F. Thomas
P R. Friend
P R. Kline
P R. Purkey
P V. Law
RP L. Arroyo
RP E. Face
RP A. Swanson

PIT 1958 N
M D. Murtaugh
1B T. Kluszewski
2B W. Mazeroski
SS R. Groat
3B F. Thomas
OF W. Virdon
OF R. Skinner
OF R. Clemente
C H. Foiles
P R. Friend
P R. Kline
P V. Law
P C. Raydon
P G. Witt
RP E. Porterfield
RP E. Face
RP D. Gross

PIT 1959 N
M D. Murtaugh
1B R. Stuart
2B W. Mazeroski
SS R. Groat
3B D. Hoak
OF W. Virdon
OF R. Skinner
OF R. Clemente
C F. Burgess
UT R. Mejias
UT G. Nelson
P V. Law
P R. Friend
P H. Haddix
P R. Kline
RP B. Daniels
RP E. Face

PIT 1960 N
M D. Murtaugh
1B R. Stuart
2B W. Mazeroski
SS R. Groat
3B D. Hoak
OF R. Clemente
OF R. Skinner
OF W. Virdon
C F. Burgess
UT G. Cimoli
P R. Friend
P V. Law
P H. Haddix
P W. Mizell
RP E. Face
RP J. Gibbon
RP F. Green

PIT 1961 N
M D. Murtaugh
1B R. Stuart
2B W. Mazeroski
SS R. Groat
3B D. Hoak
OF W. Virdon
OF R. Clemente
OF R. Skinner
C F. Burgess
P R. Friend
P J. Gibbon
P H. Haddix
P E. Francis
P W. Mizell
RP C. Labine
RP E. Face
RP R. Shantz

PIT 1962 N
M D. Murtaugh
1B R. Stuart
2B W. Mazeroski
SS R. Groat
3B D. Hoak
OF W. Virdon
OF R. Clemente
OF R. Skinner
C F. Burgess
P R. Friend
P A. McBean
P E. Francis
P H. Haddix
P V. Law
RP T. Sturdivant
RP E. Face
RP D. Olivo

PIT 1963 N
M D. Murtaugh
1B D. Clendenon
2B W. Mazeroski
SS J. Schofield
3B R. Bailey
OF R. Clemente
OF W. Virdon
OF W. Stargell
C J. Pagliaroni
P R. Friend
P D. Cardwell
P D. Schwall
P J. Gibbon
RP A. McBean
RP T. Sisk
RP E. Francis

PIT 1964 N
M D. Murtaugh
1B D. Clendenon
2B W. Mazeroski
SS J. Schofield
3B R. Bailey
OF R. Clemente
OF W. Virdon
OF M. Mota
C J. Pagliaroni
UT E. Freese
UT G. Lynch
UT W. Stargell
P R. Veale
P R. Friend
P V. Law
P J. Gibbon
P S. Blass
RP A. McBean
RP E. Face
RP T. Butters

PIT 1965 N
M H. Walker
1B D. Clendenon
2B W. Mazeroski
SS L. Alley
3B R. Bailey
OF R. Clemente
OF W. Stargell
OF W. Virdon
C J. Pagliaroni
UT M. Mota
P R. Veale
P D. Cardwell
P R. Friend
P V. Law
P J. Gibbon
RP A. McBean
RP T. Sisk
RP D. Schwall

PIT 1966 N
M H. Walker
1B D. Clendenon
2B W. Mazeroski
SS L. Alley
3B R. Bailey
OF R. Clemente
OF M. Alou
OF W. Stargell
C J. Pagliaroni
UT M. Mota
UT R. Pagan
P R. Veale
P W. Fryman
P V. Law
P S. Blass
P T. Sisk
RP P. Mikkelsen
RP A. McBean
RP W. O'Dell

PIT 1967 N
M H. Walker
M D. Murtaugh
1B D. Clendenon
2B W. Mazeroski
SS L. Alley
3B M. Wills
OF R. Clemente
OF M. Alou
OF M. Mota
C J. May
UT W. Stargell
P T. Sisk
P R. Veale
P D. Ribant
P S. Blass
P W. Fryman
RP A. McBean
RP E. Pizarro
RP E. Face

PIT 1968 N
M L. Shepard
1B D. Clendenon
2B W. Mazeroski
SS L. Alley
3B M. Wills
OF M. Alou
OF R. Clemente
OF W. Stargell
C J. May
UT M. Mota
P R. Veale
P S. Blass
P A. McBean
P R. Moose
P J. Bunning
RP R. Kline
RP T. Sisk
RP J. Walker

PIT 1969 N
M L. Shepard
M A. Grammas
1B A. Oliver
2B W. Mazeroski
SS F. Patek
3B R. Hebner
OF M. Alou
OF R. Clemente
OF W. Stargell
C M. Sanguillen
UT J. Pagan
UT C. Taylor
P R. Veale
P D. Ellis
P S. Blass
P R. Moose
P J. Bunning
RP C. Hartenstein
RP J. Dal Canton
RP J. Gibbon

PIT 1970 N
M D. Murtaugh
1B R. Robertson
2B W. Mazeroski
SS L. Alley
3B R. Hebner
OF M. Alou
OF W. Stargell
OF R. Clemente
C M. Sanguillen
UT A. Oliver
P R. Veale
P D. Ellis
P S. Blass
P R. Moose
P J. Walker
RP D. Giusti
RP J. Dal Canton

PIT 1971 N
M D. Murtaugh
1B R. Robertson
2B D. Cash
SS L. Alley
3B R. Hebner
OF W. Stargell
OF R. Clemente
OF A. Oliver
C M. Sanguillen
UT E. Clines
UT V. Davalillo
P S. Blass
P D. Ellis
P R. Johnson
P J. Walker
P R. Moose
RP D. Giusti
RP J. Grant

PIT 1972 N
M W. Virdon
1B W. Stargell
2B D. Cash
SS L. Alley
3B R. Hebner
OF A. Oliver
OF V. Davalillo
OF R. Clemente
C M. Sanguillen
UT E. Clines
UT R. Robertson
UT R. Stennett
P S. Blass
P R. Moose
P N. Briles
P D. Ellis
P B. Kison
RP D. Giusti
RP R. Hernandez
RP R. Miller

PIT 1973 N
M W. Virdon
M D. Murtaugh
1B R. Robertson
2B D. Cash
SS C. Maxvill
3B R. Hebner
OF W. Stargell
OF A. Oliver
OF R. Zisk
C M. Sanguillen
UT M. May
UT R. Stennett
P N. Briles
P R. Moose
P D. Ellis
P J. Rooker
P J. Walker
RP D. Giusti
RP R. Johnson
RP R. Hernandez

PIT 1974 N
M D. Murtaugh
1B R. Robertson
2B R. Stennett
SS F. Taveras
3B R. Hebner
OF R. Zisk
OF W. Stargell
OF A. Oliver
C M. Sanguillen
UT E. Clines
UT E. Kirkpatrick
P J. Rooker
P J. Reuss
P K. Brett
P D. Ellis
P B. Kison
RP D. Giusti
RP R. Hernandez
RP J. Morlan

PIT 1975 N
M D. Murtaugh
1B W. Stargell
2B R. Stennett
SS F. Taveras
3B R. Hebner
OF A. Oliver
OF D. Parker
OF R. Zisk
C M. Sanguillen
P J. Reuss
P J. Rooker
P B. Kison
P D. Ellis
P J. Candelaria
RP L. Demery
RP D. Giusti
RP R. Moose

PIT 1976 N
M D. Murtaugh
1B W. Stargell
2B R. Stennett
SS F. Taveras
3B R. Hebner
OF R. Zisk
OF D. Parker
OF A. Oliver
C M. Sanguillen
UT E. Clines
P J. Candelaria
P J. Reuss
P J. Rooker
P B. Kison
P G. Medich
RP K. Tekulve
RP R. Moose
RP D. Giusti

PIT 1977 N
M C. Tanner
1B W. Robinson
2B R. Stennett
SS F. Taveras
3B P. Garner
OF D. Parker
OF A. Oliver
OF O. Moreno
C D. Dyer
UT N. Ott
P J. Candelaria
P J. Reuss
P J. Rooker
P B. Kison
P O. Jones
RP R. Gossage
RP K. Tekulve
RP G. Jackson

PIT 1978 N
M C. Tanner
1B W. Stargell
2B R. Stennett
SS F. Taveras
3B P. Garner
OF O. Moreno
OF D. Parker
OF W. Robinson
C N. Ott
UT J. Milner
P R. Blyleven
P R. Robinson
P J. Candelaria
P J. Rooker
P J. Bibby
RP K. Tekulve
RP G. Jackson
RP E. Whitson

PIT 1979 N
M C. Tanner
1B W. Stargell
2B R. Stennett
SS T. Foli
3B B. Madlock
OF O. Moreno
OF D. Parker
OF W. Robinson
C N. Ott
UT P. Garner
UT J. Milner
P R. Blyleven
P J. Candelaria
P B. Kison
P R. Robinson
P J. Bibby
RP K. Tekulve
RP E. Romo
RP G. Jackson

PIT 1980 N
M C. Tanner
1B J. Milner
2B P. Garner
SS T. Foli
3B B. Madlock
OF O. Moreno
OF D. Parker
OF M. Easler
C N. Ott
UT L. Lacy
UT W. Robinson
P J. Bibby
P J. Candelaria
P R. Blyleven
P R. Robinson
P R. Rhoden
RP E. Romo
RP K. Tekulve
RP G. Jackson

PIT 1981 N
M C. Tanner
1B J. Thompson
2B P. Garner

SS T. Foli
3B B. Madlock
OF O. Moreno
OF M. Easler
OF L. Lacy
C A. Pena
UT D. Berra
UT D. Parker
P R. Rhoden
P E. Solomon
P J. Bibby
P P. Perez
RP R. Scurry
RP K. Tekulve
RP E. Romo

PIT 1982 N

M C. Tanner
1B J. Thompson
2B J. Ray
SS D. Berra
3B B. Madlock
OF O. Moreno
OF M. Easler
OF L. Lacy
C A. Pena
P R. Rhoden
P D. Robinson
P J. Candelaria
P M. Sarmiento
P L. McWilliams
RP K. Tekulve
RP R. Scurry
RP E. Romo

PIT 1983 N

M C. Tanner
1B J. Thompson
2B J. Ray
SS D. Berra
3B B. Madlock
OF D. Parker
OF M. Easler
OF M. Wynne
C A. Pena
UT L. Lacy
UT L. Mazzilli
P R. Rhoden
P L. McWilliams
P J. Candelaria
P B. Tunnell
P J. DeLeon
RP C. Guante
RP K. Tekulve
RP M. Sarmiento

PIT 1984 N

M C. Tanner
1B J. Thompson
2B J. Ray
SS D. Berra
3B B. Madlock
OF M. Wynne
OF L. Lacy
OF D. Frobel
C A. Pena
UT L. Mazzilli
UT J. Morrison
P R. Rhoden
P L. McWilliams
P J. Tudor
P J. DeLeon
P J. Candelaria
RP D. Robinson
RP K. Tekulve
RP B. Tunnell

PIT 1985 N

M C. Tanner
1B J. Thompson
2B J. Ray
SS S. Khalifa
3B B. Madlock
OF J. Orsulak
OF M. Wynne
OF G. Hendrick
C A. Pena
P R. Rhoden
P R. Reuschel
P J. DeLeon
P B. Tunnell
P L. McWilliams
RP C. Guante
RP D. Robinson
RP J. Winn

PIT 1986 N

M J. Leyland
1B S. Bream
2B J. Ray
SS R. Belliard
3B J. Morrison

OF J. Orsulak
OF R. Reynolds
OF B. Bonds
C A. Pena
UT W. Almon
UT M. Diaz
P R. Rhoden
P R. Reuschel
P M. Bielecki
P R. Walk
P R. Kipper
RP L. McWilliams
RP J. Winn
RP C. Guante

PIT 1987 N

M J. Leyland
1B S. Bream
2B J. Ray
SS A. Pedrique
3B B. Bonilla
OF A. Van Slyke
OF B. Bonds
OF R. Reynolds
C M. LaValliere
UT J. Cangelosi
UT M. Diaz
P B. Fisher
P R. Reuschel
P D. Drabek
P M. Dunne
P R. Walk
RP J. Smiley
RP D. Robinson

PIT 1988 N

M J. Leyland
1B S. Bream
2B J. Lind
SS R. Belliard
3B B. Bonilla
OF A. Van Slyke
OF B. Bonds
OF R. Reynolds
C M. LaValliere
P D. Drabek
P R. Walk
P J. Smiley
P M. Dunne
P B. Fisher
RP J. Robinson
RP J. Gott
RP R. Kipper

PIT 1989 N

M J. Leyland
1B G. Redus
2B J. Lind
SS J. Bell
3B B. Bonilla
OF B. Bonds
OF A. Van Slyke
OF R. Reynolds
C A. Ortiz
UT J. Cangelosi
UT G. Wilson
P D. Drabek
P J. Smiley
P R. Walk
P N. Heaton
P R. Kramer
RP J. Robinson
RP R. Kipper
RP T. Landrum

PIT 1990 N

M J. Leyland
1B S. Bream
2B J. Lind
SS J. Bell
3B J. King
OF B. Bonds
OF B. Bonilla
OF A. Van Slyke
C M. LaValliere
UT W. Backman
P D. Drabek
P J. Smiley
P N. Heaton
P R. Kramer
RP J. Robinson
RP R. Kipper
RP T. Landrum

Providence

PRO N 1878-1885

PRO 1878 N

M T. York
1B T. Murnane

2B C. Sweasy
SS T. Carey
3B W. Hague
OF T. York
OF R. Higham
OF P. Hines
C L. Brown
P J. Ward
P F. Nichols
P H. Wheeler

PRO 1879 N

M G. Wright
1B J. Start
2B M. McGeary
SS G. Wright
3B W. Hague
OF P. Hines
OF T. York
OF J. O'Rourke
C L. Brown
P J. Ward
P R. Mathews

PRO 1880 N

M M. McGeary
M J. Ward
M M. Dorgan
1B J. Start
2B J. Farrell
SS J. Peters
3B G. Bradley
OF M. Dorgan
OF P. Hines
OF T. York
C E. Gross
P J. Ward

PRO 1881 N

M J. Farrell
M T. York
1B J. Start
2B J. Farrell
SS W. McClellan
3B J. Denny
OF T. York
OF P. Hines
OF J. Ward
C E. Gross
P C. Radbourn
P R. Mathews

PRO 1882 N

M W. Wright
1B J. Start
2B J. Farrell
SS G. Wright
3B J. Denny
OF P. Hines
OF T. York
OF J. Ward
C A. Gilligan
P C. Radbourn

PRO 1883 N

M W. Wright
1B J. Start
2B J. Farrell
SS A. Irwin
3B J. Denny
OF P. Hines
OF J. Cassidy
OF S. Carroll
C A. Gilligan
P C. Radbourn
P C. Sweeney

PRO 1884 N

M F. Bancroft
1B J. Start
2B J. Farrell
SS A. Irwin
3B J. Denny
OF S. Carroll
OF P. Hines
OF P. Radford
C A. Gilligan
P C. Radbourn
P C. Sweeney
P E. Conley

PRO 1885 N

M F. Bancroft
1B J. Start
2B J. Farrell
SS A. Irwin
3B J. Denny
OF S. Carroll

OF P. Hines
OF P. Radford
C A. Gilligan
UT C. Bassett
P C. Radbourn
P F. Shaw

Richmond

RIC a 1884

RIC 1884 a

M F. Moses
1B J. Powell
2B F. Larkin
SS W. Schenck
3B W. Nash
OF E. Glenn
OF R. Johnston
OF M. Mansell
C J. Hanna
P P. Meegan
P E. Dugan

Rochester

ROC a 1890

ROC 1890 a

M P. Powers
1B T. O'Brien
2B W. Greenwood
SS M. Phillips
3B J. Knowles
OF H. Lyons
OF T. Scheffler
OF T. Griffin
C J. McGuire
P R. Barr
P W. Calihan
P L. Titcomb
P R. Miller

Rockford

ROK n 1871

ROK 1871 n

M W. Hastings
2B D. Mack
SS C. Fulmer
3B A. Anson
OF G. Stires
OF G. Bird
OF R. Ham
C W. Hastings
UT R. Addy
P W. Fisher

St. Louis

STL n 1875
RS n 1875
STL N 1876-1877
STL U 1884
STL N 1885-1886
STL a 1882-1891
STL F 1914-1915
STL A 1902-1953
STL N 1892-1990

STL 1875 n

M R. Pearce
1B H. Dehlman
2B J. Battin
SS R. Pearce
3B W. Hague
OF E. Cuthbert
OF L. Pike
OF J. Chapman
C T. Miller
P G. Bradley
P J. Galvin

RS 1875 n

M C. Sweasy
1B C. Hautz
2B S. Sweasy
SS W. Redmon
3B J. McSorley
OF T. Oran
OF A. Croft
OF H. Morgan
C F. Flint
P J. Blong

STL 1876 N

M S. Graffen
M G. McManus
1B H. Dehlman
2B M. McGeary
SS D. Mack
3B J. Battin
OF E. Cuthbert
OF L. Pike
OF J. Blong
C J. Clapp
P G. Bradley

STL 1877 N

M G. McManus
1B H. Dehlman
2B M. McGeary
SS D. Force
3B J. Battin
3B M. Dorgan
OF J. Blong
OF J. Remsen
C J. Clapp
UT A. Croft
P F. Nichols

STL 1884 U

M T. Sullivan
M F. Dunlap
1B J. Quinn
2B F. Dunlap
SS M. Whitehead
3B J. Gleason
OF G. Shaffer
OF D. Rowe
OF H. Boyle
C G. Baker
P C. Sweeney
P W. Taylor
P P. Werden
P C. Hodnett

STL 1885 N

M F. Dunlap
M A. McKinnon
M F. Dunlap
1B A. McKinnon
2B F. Dunlap
SS J. Glasscock
3B E. Caskin
OF G. Shaffer
OF J. Seery
OF J. Quinn
C C. Briody
UT C. Sweeney
P H. Boyle
P J. Kirby
P J. Healy

STL 1886 N

M G. Schmelz
1B A. McKinnon
2B F. Dunlap
SS J. Glasscock
3B J. Denny
OF J. Seery
OF J. Cahill
OF J. McGeachey
C G. Myers
P J. Healy
P J. Kirby
P H. Boyle
P C. Sweeney

STL 1882 a

M E. Cuthbert
1B C. Comiskey
2B W. Smiley
SS W. Gleason
3B J. Gleason
OF O. Walker
OF E. Cuthbert
OF G. Seward
C T. Sullivan
P G. McGinnis
P J. Schappert
P C. Dorr

STL 1883 a

M T. Sullivan
M C. Comiskey
2B G. Strief
SS W. Gleason
3B W. Latham
OF H. Nicol
OF F. Lewis
OF T. Dolan
C T. Deasley

P A. Mullane
P G. McGinnis

STL 1884 a

M J. Williams
M C. Comiskey
1B C. Comiskey
2B J. Quest
SS W. Gleason
3B W. Latham
OF H. Nicol
OF F. Lewis
OF J. O'Neill
C T. Deasley
P G. McGinnis
P D. Foutz
P J. Davis

STL 1885 a

M C. Comiskey
1B C. Comiskey
2B S. Barkley
SS W. Gleason
3B W. Latham
OF C. Welch
OF H. Nicol
OF W. Robinson
C A. Bushong
P R. Caruthers
P D. Foutz
P G. McGinnis

STL 1886 a

M C. Comiskey
1B C. Comiskey
2B W. Robinson
SS W. Gleason
3B W. Latham
OF C. Welch
OF J. O'Neill
OF H. Nicol
C A. Bushong
P D. Foutz
P R. Caruthers
P N. Hudson
P G. McGinnis

STL 1887 a

M C. Comiskey
1B C. Comiskey
2B W. Robinson
SS W. Gleason
3B W. Latham
OF J. O'Neill
OF C. Welch
OF R. Caruthers
C J. Boyle
UT D. Foutz
P C. King

STL 1888 a

M C. Comiskey
1B C. Comiskey
2B W. Robinson
SS W. White
3B W. Latham
OF T. McCarthy
OF J. O'Neill
OF H. Lyons
C J. Boyle
P C. King
P N. Hudson
P E. Chamberlain
P J. Devlin
P E. Knouff

STL 1889 a

M C. Comiskey
1B C. Comiskey
2B W. Robinson
SS W. Fuller
3B W. Latham
OF T. McCarthy
OF J. O'Neill
OF C. Duffee
C J. Boyle
P C. King
P E. Chamberlain
P J. Stivetts

STL 1890 a

M T. McCarthy
M J. Kerins
M J. Roseman
M C. Campau
M T. McCarthy
M J. Gerhardt
1B E. Cartwright
2B W. Higgins
SS W. Fuller

3B C. Duffee
OF T. McCarthy
OF C. Campau
OF J. Roseman
C J. Munyan
P J. Stivetts
P T. Ramsey
P J. Hart
P W. Whitrock

STL 1891 a

M C. Comiskey
1B C. Comiskey
2B W. Eagan
SS W. Fuller
3B D. Lyons
OF W. Hoy
OF J. O'Neill
OF T. McCarthy
C J. Boyle
P J. Stivetts
P W. McGill
P C. Griffith
P J. Neale
P G. Rettger

STL 1914 F

M M. Brown
M F. Jones
1B H. Miller
2B J. Crandall
SS A. Bridwell
3B A. Boucher
OF J. Tobin
OF D. Drake
OF W. Miller
C M. Simon
UT J. Misse
P R. Groom
P D. Davenport
P H. Keupper
P R. Willett
P M. Brown
RP E. Herbert

STL 1915 F

M F. Jones
1B W. Borton
2B R. Vaughn
SS E. Johnson
3B C. Deal
OF J. Tobin
OF W. Miller
OF D. Drake
C G. Hartley
P D. Davenport
P J. Crandall
P E. Plank
P R. Groom
P C. Watson

STL 1902 A

M J. McAleer
1B J. Anderson
2B R. Padden
SS R. Wallace
3B W. McCormick
OF J. Burkett
OF J. Heidrick
OF C. Hemphill
C J. Sugden
P J. Powell
P F. Donahue
P C. Harper
P J. Sudhoff
P W. Reidy

STL 1903 A

M J. McAleer
1B J. Anderson
2B W. Friel
SS R. Wallace
3B H. Hill
OF J. Burkett
OF J. Heidrick
OF C. Hemphill
C M. Kahoe
P J. Powell
P J. Sudhoff
P E. Siever
P F. Donahue

STL 1904 A

M J. McAleer
1B T. Jones
2B R. Padden
SS R. Wallace
3B C. Moran
OF J. Burkett
OF J. Heidrick
OF C. Hemphill

C J. Sugden
P B. Pelty
P H. Howell
P F. Glade
P J. Sudhoff
P E. Siever

STL 1905 A

M J. McAleer
1B T. Jones
2B I. Rockenfield
SS R. Wallace
3B H. Gleason
OF G. Stone
OF B. Koehler
OF J. Frisk
C J. Sugden
UT C. Van Zandt
P H. Howell
P F. Glade
P B. Pelty
P J. Sudhoff
P J. Buchanan

STL 1906 A

M J. McAleer
1B T. Jones
2B P. O'Brien
SS R. Wallace
3B B. Hartzell
OF G. Stone
OF C. Hemphill
OF H. Niles
C W. Rickey
P H. Howell
P F. Glade
P B. Pelty
P J. Powell
P R. Smith

STL 1907 A

M J. McAleer
1B T. Jones
2B H. Niles
SS R. Wallace
3B J. Yeager
OF G. Stone
OF C. Hemphill
OF O. Pickering
C E. Spencer
P H. Howell
P B. Pelty
P J. Powell
P F. Glade
P W. Dinneen

STL 1908 A

M J. McAleer
1B T. Jones
2B J. Williams
SS R. Wallace
3B A. Ferris
OF G. Stone
OF D. Hoffman
OF R. Hartzell
C E. Spencer
P H. Howell
P G. Waddell
P J. Powell
P W. Dinneen
P B. Pelty

STL 1909 A

M J. McAleer
1B T. Jones
2B J. Williams
SS R. Wallace
3B A. Ferris
OF D. Hoffman
OF R. Hartzell
OF G. Stone
C L. Criger
UT A. Griggs
P J. Powell
P G. Waddell
P B. Pelty
P W. Bailey
P W. Graham

STL 1910 A

M J. O'Connor
1B P. Newnam
2B F. Truesdale
SS R. Wallace
3B R. Hartzell
OF G. Stone
OF A. Schweitzer
OF D. Hoffman
C J. Stephens
UT A. Griggs
P J. Lake

P W. Bailey
P B. Pelty
P R. Ray
P J. Powell

STL 1911 A

M R. Wallace
1B J. Black
2B F. LaPorte
SS R. Wallace
3B J. Austin
OF B. Shotton
OF W. Hogan
OF A. Schweitzer
C J. Clarke
P J. Lake
P J. Powell
P B. Pelty
P E. Hamilton
P A. Mitchell

STL 1912 A

M R. Wallace
M G. Stovall
1B G. Stovall
2B D. Pratt
SS R. Wallace
3B J. Austin
OF B. Shotton
OF W. Hogan
OF A. Compton
C J. Stephens
P E. Hamilton
P J. Powell
P G. Baumgardner
P M. Allison
P E. Brown

STL 1913 A

M G. Stovall
M J. Austin
M W. Rickey
1B G. Stovall
2B D. Pratt
SS M. Balenti
3B J. Austin
OF B. Shotton
OF A. Williams
OF J. Johnston
C S. Agnew
P G. Baumgardner
P C. Weilman
P A. Mitchell
P E. Hamilton
P W. Leverenz

STL 1914 A

M W. Rickey
1B J. Leary
2B D. Pratt
SS J. Lavan
3B J. Austin
OF B. Shotton
OF C. Walker
OF A. Williams
C S. Agnew
P E. Hamilton
P C. Weilman
P W. James
P G. Baumgardner
P W. Leverenz

STL 1915 A

M W. Rickey
1B J. Leary
2B D. Pratt
SS J. Lavan
3B J. Austin
OF B. Shotton
OF C. Walker
OF L. Walsh
C S. Agnew
UT I. Howard
P C. Weilman
P G. Lowdermilk
P E. Hamilton
P W. James
P E. Koob
RP E. Perryman

STL 1916 A

M F. Jones
1B G. Sisler
2B D. Pratt
SS J. Lavan
3B J. Austin
OF B. Shotton
OF A. Marsans
OF W. Miller
C H. Severeid
P D. Davenport

P C. Weilman
P E. Plank
P R. Groom
P E. Koob

STL 1917 A

M F. Jones
1B G. Sisler
2B D. Pratt
SS J. Lavan
3B J. Austin
OF W. Jacobson
OF B. Shotton
OF Y. Sloan
C H. Severeid
P D. Davenport
P A. Sothoron
P R. Groom
P E. Koob
P E. Plank

STL 1918 A

M F. Jones
M J. Austin
M J. Burke
1B G. Sisler
2B E. Gedeon
SS J. Austin
3B F. Maisel
OF J. Tobin
OF C. Demmitt
OF E. Smith
C L. Nunamaker
UT T. Hendryx
P A. Sothoron
P D. Davenport
P T. Rogers
P M. Gallia
P W. Wright
RP B. Houck

STL 1919 A

M J. Burke
1B G. Sisler
2B E. Gedeon
SS W. Gerber
3B J. Austin
OF J. Tobin
OF W. Jacobson
OF E. Smith
C H. Severeid
P A. Sothoron
P M. Gallia
P U. Shocker
P C. Weilman
P D. Davenport
RP E. Koob
RP W. Wright

STL 1920 A

M J. Burke
1B G. Sisler
2B E. Gedeon
SS W. Gerber
3B J. Austin
OF W. Jacobson
OF J. Tobin
OF K. Williams
C H. Severeid
UT E. Smith
P F. Davis
P U. Shocker
P A. Sothoron
P C. Weilman
P W. Burwell

STL 1921 A

M L. Fohl
1B G. Sisler
2B M. McManus
SS W. Gerber
3B F. Ellerbe
OF J. Tobin
OF K. Williams
OF W. Jacobson
C H. Severeid
P U. Shocker
P F. Davis
P E. Vangilder
P R. Kolp
P W. Bayne
RP W. Burwell

STL 1922 A

M L. Fohl
1B G. Sisler
2B M. McManus
SS W. Gerber
3B F. Ellerbe
OF K. Williams
OF J. Tobin

OF W. Jacobson
C H. Severeid
P U. Shocker
P E. Vangilder
P F. Davis
P R. Kolp
P W. Wright

STL 1923 A

M L. Fohl
M J. Austin
1B F. Schliebner
2B M. McManus
SS W. Gerber
3B E. Robertson
OF J. Tobin
OF W. Jacobson
OF K. Williams
C H. Severeid
P E. Vangilder
P U. Shocker
P D. Danforth
P R. Kolp
P F. Davis
RP C. Root

STL 1924 A

M G. Sisler
1B G. Sisler
2B M. McManus
SS W. Gerber
3B E. Robertson
OF W. Jacobson
OF J. Tobin
OF K. Williams
C H. Severeid
P U. Shocker
P D. Danforth
P E. Wingard
P F. Davis
P E. Vangilder
RP H. Pruett
RP G. Grant
RP W. Bayne

STL 1925 A

M G. Sisler
1B G. Sisler
2B M. McManus
SS R. LaMotte
3B E. Robertson
OF W. Jacobson
OF K. Williams
OF H. Rice
C L. Dixon
P N. Gaston
P L. Bush
P E. Vangilder
P F. Davis
P J. Giard

STL 1926 A

M G. Sisler
1B G. Sisler
2B O. Melillo
SS W. Gerber
3B M. McManus
OF H. Rice
OF E. Miller
OF K. Williams
C W. Schang
P J. Zachary
P N. Gaston
P E. Vangilder
P E. Wingard
P N. Ballou

STL 1927 A

M D. Howley
1B G. Sisler
2B O. Melillo
SS W. Gerber
3B J. O'Rourke
OF H. Rice
OF E. Miller
OF K. Williams
C W. Schang
P N. Gaston
P E. Vangilder
P S. Jones
P E. Wingard
P W. Stewart

STL 1928 A

M D. Howley
1B L. Blue
2B O. Brannan
SS R. Kress
3B J. O'Rourke
OF H. Manush
OF F. Schulte

OF G. McNeely
C W. Schang
P S. Gray
P A. Crowder
P J. Ogden
P G. Blaeholder
P W. Stewart
RP S. Coffman
RP H. Wiltse
RP E. Strelecki

STL 1929 A

M D. Howley
1B L. Blue
2B O. Melillo
SS R. Kress
3B J. O'Rourke
OF H. Manush
OF F. McGowan
OF F. Schulte
C W. Schang
P S. Gray
P A. Crowder
P G. Blaeholder
P H. Collins
P W. Stewart
RP C. Kimsey
RP S. Coffman

STL 1930 A

M W. Killefer
1B L. Blue
2B O. Melillo
SS R. Kress
3B J. O'Rourke
OF L. Goslin
OF F. Schulte
OF T. Gullic
C R. Ferrell
P W. Stewart
P S. Coffman
P G. Blaeholder
P H. Collins
P S. Gray
RP C. Kimsey
RP H. Holshouser

STL 1931 A

M W. Killefer
1B J. Burns
2B O. Melillo
SS J. Levey
3B R. Kress
OF L. Goslin
OF F. Schulte
OF T. Jenkins
C R. Ferrell
P W. Stewart
P S. Gray
P G. Blaeholder
P S. Coffman
P H. Collins
RP C. Kimsey
RP W. Stiles

STL 1932 A

M W. Killefer
1B J. Burns
2B O. Melillo
SS J. Levey
3B A. Scharein
OF L. Goslin
OF B. Campbell
OF F. Schulte
C R. Ferrell
P W. Stewart
P G. Blaeholder
P I. Hadley
P S. Gray
P W. Hebert
RP C. Kimsey

STL 1933 A

M W. Killefer
M A. Sothoron
M R. Hornsby
1B J. Burns
2B O. Melillo
SS J. Levey
3B A. Scharein
OF B. Campbell
OF S. West
OF C. Reynolds
C M. Shea
UT T. Gullic
P I. Hadley
P G. Blaeholder
P E. Wells
P R. Stiles
RP S. Gray
RP W. Hebert
RP H. McDonald

STL 1934 A

M R. Hornsby
1B J. Burns
2B O. Melillo
SS A. Strange
3B H. Clift
OF R. Pepper
OF B. Campbell
OF S. West
C R. Hemsley
UT A. Bejma
P L. Newsom
P G. Blaeholder
P I. Hadley
P S. Coffman
P I. Andrews
RP E. Wells
RP W. McAfee

STL 1935 A

M R. Hornsby
1B J. Burns
2B T. Carey
SS L. Lary
3B H. Clift
OF S. West
OF J. Solters
OF P. Coleman
C R. Hemsley
P I. Andrews
P J. Knott
P J. Walkup
P R. Van Atta
P M. Cain

STL 1936 A

M R. Hornsby
1B J. Bottomley
2B T. Carey
SS L. Lary
3B H. Clift
OF S. West
OF J. Solters
OF R. Bell
C R. Hemsley
P E. Hogsett
P J. Knott
P I. Andrews
P E. Caldwell
P A. Thomas
RP R. Van Atta
RP L. Mahaffey
RP G. Liebhardt

STL 1937 A

M R. Hornsby
M J. Bottomley
1B H. Davis
2B T. Carey
SS W. Knickerbocker
3B H. Clift
OF J. Vosmik
OF R. Bell
OF S. West
C R. Hemsley
UT E. Allen
P O. Hildebrand
P J. Knott
P E. Hogsett
P J. Walkup
P J. Bonetti

STL 1938 A

M C. Street
1B G. McQuinn
2B D. Heffner
SS R. Kress
3B H. Clift
OF R. Bell
OF C. Mills
OF B. Almada
C W. Sullivan
P L. Newsom
P H. Mills
P O. Hildebrand
P R. Van Atta
P J. Walkup
RP E. Cole
RP W. Cox

STL 1939 A

M F. Haney
1B G. McQuinn
2B J. Berardino
SS D. Heffner
3B H. Clift
OF M. Hoag
OF C. Laabs
OF J. Gallagher
C J. Glenn

UT W. Sullivan
P J. Kramer
P L. Kennedy
P W. Trotter
P A. Lawson
P H. Mills
RP J. Whitehead

STL 1940 A

M F. Haney
1B G. McQuinn
2B D. Heffner
SS J. Berardino
3B H. Clift
OF R. Radcliff
OF W. Judnich
OF C. Laabs
C R. Swift
P E. Auker
P L. Kennedy
P R. Harris
P J. Niggeling
P E. Bildilli
RP W. Trotter
RP G. Coffman
RP A. Lawson

STL 1941 A

M F. Haney
M L. Sewell
1B G. McQuinn
2B D. Heffner
SS J. Berardino
3B H. Clift
OF W. Judnich
OF R. Cullenbine
OF C. Laabs
C R. Ferrell
UT J. Grace
UT J. Lucadello
P E. Auker
P R. Muncrief
P D. Galehouse
P R. Harris
P J. Niggeling
RP J. Kramer
RP W. Trotter

STL 1942 A

M J. Sewell
1B G. McQuinn
2B O. Gutteridge
SS V. Stephens
3B H. Clift
OF C. Laabs
OF W. Judnich
OF G. McQuillen
C R. Ferrell
UT A. Criscola
P E. Auker
P J. Niggeling
P D. Galehouse
P A. Hollingsworth
P R. Muncrief
RP G. Caster

STL 1943 A

M J. Sewell
1B G. McQuinn
2B O. Gutteridge
SS V. Stephens
3B H. Clift
OF C. Laabs
OF M. Byrnes
OF M. Chartak
C F. Hayes
UT M. Christman
P O. Galehouse
P S. Sundra
P R. Muncrief
P N. Potter
P A. Hollingsworth
RP G. Caster

STL 1944 A

M J. Sewell
1B G. McQuinn
2B O. Gutteridge
SS V. Stephens
3B M. Christman
OF M. Byrnes
OF M. Kreevich
OF E. Moore
C F. Mancuso
UT A. Zarilla
P J. Kramer
P N. Potter
P R. Muncrief
P S. Jakucki
P D. Galehouse
RP G. Caster

STL 1945 A

- M J. Sewell
- 1B G. McQuinn
- 2B D. Gutteridge
- SS V. Stephens
- 3B M. Christman
- OF M. Byrnes
- OF E. Moore
- OF M. Kreevich
- C F. Mancuso
- UT L. Schulte
- P N. Potter
- P J. Kramer
- P S. Jakucki
- P A. Shirley
- P A. Hollingsworth
- RP S. Zoldak

STL 1946 A

- M J. Sewell
- M J. Taylor
- 1B C. Stevens
- 2B J. Berardino
- SS V. Stephens
- 3B M. Christman
- OF W. Judnich
- OF A. Zarilla
- OF J. Heath
- C F. Mancuso
- P J. Kramer
- P D. Galehouse
- P S. Zoldak
- P N. Potter
- P A. Shirley
- RP S. Ferens
- RP E. Kinder

STL 1947 A

- M H. Ruel
- 1B W. Judnich
- 2B J. Berardino
- SS V. Stephens
- 3B R. Dillinger
- OF J. Heath
- OF P. Lehner
- OF A. Zarilla
- C J. Moss
- UT R. Coleman
- P J. Kramer
- P E. Kinder
- P J. Sanford
- P R. Muncrief
- P S. Zoldak
- RP G. Moulder

STL 1948 A

- M J. Taylor
- 1B C. Stevens
- 2B G. Priddy
- SS E. Pellagrini
- 3B R. Dillinger
- OF A. Zarilla
- OF M. Platt
- OF P. Lehner
- C J. Moss
- UT S. Dente
- P J. Sanford
- P C. Fannin
- P N. Garver
- P W. Kennedy
- RP B. Stephens
- RP F. Biscan
- RP A. Widmar

STL 1949 A

- M J. Taylor
- 1B J. Graham
- 2B G. Priddy
- SS E. Pellagrini
- 3B R. Dillinger
- OF R. Kokos
- OF R. Sievers
- OF S. Spence
- C J. Lollar
- UT P. Lehner
- UT J. Moss
- UT M. Platt
- UT J. Sullivan
- P N. Garver
- P W. Kennedy
- P C. Fannin
- P A. Papai
- P J. Ostrowski
- RP T. Ferrick
- RP R. Starr

STL 1950 A

- M J. Taylor
- 1B D. Lenhardt
- 2B O. Friend
- SS T. Upton

STL 1950 A (cont.)

- 3B W. Sommers
- OF R. Kokos
- OF R. Coleman
- OF K. Wood
- C J. Lollar
- UT H. Arft
- UT R. Sievers
- P N. Garver
- P A. Widmar
- P F. Overmire
- P R. Starr
- P H. Dorish
- RP C. Marshall

STL 1951 A

- M J. Taylor
- 1B H. Arft
- 2B R. Young
- SS W. Jennings
- 3B F. Marsh
- OF J. Delsing
- OF K. Wood
- OF R. Coleman
- C J. Lollar
- P N. Garver
- P D. Pillette
- P T. Byrne
- P A. Widmar
- RP R. Mahoney
- RP L. Paige
- RP W. Kennedy

STL 1952 A

- M R. Hornsby
- M M. Marion
- 1B R. Kryhoski
- 2B R. Young
- SS J. DeMaestri
- 3B J. Dyck
- OF R. Nieman
- OF M. Rivera
- OF J. Delsing
- C C. Courtney
- P D. Pillette
- P T. Byrne
- P R. Cain
- P H. Bearden
- P N. Garver
- RP D. Madison

STL 1953 A

- M M. Marion
- 1B R. Kryhoski
- 2B R. Young
- SS G. Hunter
- 3B J. Dyck
- OF J. Groth
- OF V. Wertz
- OF R. Kokos
- C C. Courtney
- UT D. Lenhardt
- P D. Larsen
- P D. Pillette
- P R. Littlefield
- P H. Brecheen
- P R. Cain
- RP L. Paige
- RP M. Stuart
- RP M. Blyzka

STL 1892 N

- M J. Glasscock
- M J. Stricker
- M J. Crooks
- M G. Gore
- M R. Caruthers
- 1B P. Werden
- 2B J. Crooks
- SS J. Glasscock
- 3B G. Pinkney
- OF W. Brodie
- OF R. Caruthers
- OF S. Carroll
- C R. Buckley
- C W. Gleason
- P T. Breitenstein
- P E. Hawley
- P C. Getzien
- P W. Hawke

STL 1893 N

- M W. Watkins
- 1B P. Werden
- 2B J. Quinn
- SS J. Glasscock
- 3B J. Crooks
- OF T. Dowd
- OF W. Brodie
- OF C. Frank
- C H. Peitz
- P T. Breitenstein
- P W. Gleason

STL 1893 N (cont.)

- P E. Hawley
- P A. Clarkson

STL 1894 N

- M G. Miller
- 1B R. Connor
- 2B J. Quinn
- SS W. Ely
- 3B H. Peitz
- OF F. Shugart
- OF T. Dowd
- OF C. Frank
- C G. Miller
- P T. Breitenstein
- P E. Hawley
- P A. Clarkson

STL 1895 N

- M A. Buckenberger
- M C. Von Der Ahe
- M J. Quinn
- M L. Phelan
- 1B R. Connor
- 2B J. Quinn
- SS W. Ely
- 3B G. Miller
- OF D. Cooley
- OF T. Dowd
- OF T. Brown
- C H. Peitz
- P T. Breitenstein
- P P. Ehret
- P H. Staley
- P W. Kissinger
- P J. McDougal

STL 1896 N

- M H. Diddlebock
- M W. Latham
- M C. Von Der Ahe
- M R. Connor
- M T. Dowd
- 1B R. Connor
- 2B T. Dowd
- SS M. Cross
- 3B J. Myers
- OF T. Parrott
- OF W. Douglass
- OF G. Turner
- C E. McFarland
- P T. Breitenstein
- P W. Hart
- P F. Donahue
- P W. Kissinger

STL 1897 N

- M T. Dowd
- M H. Nicol
- M W. Hallman
- M C. Von Der Ahe
- 1B M. Grady
- 2B W. Hallman
- SS M. Cross
- 3B F. Hartman
- OF G. Turner
- OF R. Harley
- OF D. Lally
- C W. Douglass
- P F. Donahue
- P W. Hart
- P W. Carsey
- P J. Sudhoff

STL 1898 N

- M T. Hurst
- 1B G. Decker
- 2B J. Crooks
- SS G. Smith
- 3B L. Cross
- OF R. Harley
- OF T. Dowd
- OF J. Stenzel
- C J. Clements
- UT J. Quinn
- P J. Taylor
- P J. Sudhoff
- P J. Hughey
- P W. Carsey

STL 1899 N

- M O. Tebeau
- 1B O. Tebeau
- 2B C. Childs
- SS R. Wallace
- 3B L. Cross
- OF J. Heidrick
- OF J. Burkett
- OF H. Blake
- C L. Criger
- P J. Powell
- P D. Young

STL 1899 N (cont.)

- P J. Sudhoff
- P G. Cuppy

STL 1900 N

- M O. Tebeau
- M L. Heilbroner
- 1B D. McGann
- 2B W. Keister
- SS R. Wallace
- 3B J. McGraw
- OF J. Burkett
- OF P. Donovan
- OF J. Heidrick
- C L. Criger
- P D. Young
- P A. Jones
- P J. Powell
- P J. Sudhoff
- P J. Hughey

STL 1901 N

- M P. Donovan
- 1B D. McGann
- 2B R. Padden
- SS R. Wallace
- 3B A. Krueger
- OF J. Burkett
- OF P. Donovan
- OF J. Heidrick
- C J. Ryan
- UT A. Nichols
- P J. Powell
- P C. Harper
- P J. Sudhoff
- P E. Murphy

STL 1902 N

- M P. Donovan
- 1B N. Brashear
- 2B J. Farrell
- SS A. Krueger
- 3B F. Hartman
- OF G. Barclay
- OF H. Smoot
- OF P. Donovan
- C J. Ryan
- P M. O'Neill
- P S. Yerkes
- P E. Murphy
- P R. Wicker
- P C. Currie

STL 1903 N

- M P. Donovan
- 1B J. Hackett
- 2B J. Farrell
- SS D. Brain
- 3B J. Burke
- OF H. Smoot
- OF G. Barclay
- OF P. Donovan
- C J. O'Neill
- P C. McFarland
- P M. Brown
- P C. Currie
- P M. O'Neill
- P R. Rhoads

STL 1904 N

- M C. Nichols
- 1B J. Beckley
- 2B J. Farrell
- SS A. Shay
- 3B J. Burke
- OF H. Smoot
- OF W. Shannon
- OF G. Barclay
- C M. Grady
- UT D. Brain
- P J. Taylor
- P C. Nichols
- P C. McFarland
- P M. O'Neill
- P J. Corbett

STL 1905 N

- M C. Nichols
- M J. Burke
- M M. Robison
- 1B J. Beckley
- 2B H. Arndt
- SS G. McBride
- 3B J. Burke
- OF W. Shannon
- OF H. Smoot
- OF J. Dunleavy
- P J. Taylor
- P C. McFarland
- P J. Thielman
- P C. Brown

STL 1905 N (cont.)

- P A. Egan

STL 1906 N

- M J. McCloskey
- 1B J. Beckley
- 2B J. Bennett
- SS G. McBride
- 3B H. Arndt
- OF A. Burch
- OF H. Smoot
- OF W. Shannon
- C M. Grady
- UT A. Hoelskoetter
- P C. Brown
- P E. Karger
- P F. Beebe
- P J. Taylor
- P C. Druhot

STL 1907 N

- M J. McCloskey
- 1B E. Konetchy
- 2B J. Bennett
- SS E. Holly
- 3B R. Byrne
- OF J. Murray
- OF J. Barry
- OF J. Burnett
- C W. Marshall
- UT A. Hoelskoetter
- P U. McGlynn
- P E. Karger
- P F. Beebe
- P A. Fromme
- P J. Lush

STL 1908 N

- M J. McCloskey
- 1B E. Konetchy
- 2B W. Gilbert
- SS J. O'Rourke
- 3B R. Byrne
- OF J. Murray
- OF J. Delahanty
- OF A. Shaw
- C W. Ludwig
- UT R. Charles
- P A. Raymond
- P J. Lush
- P F. Beebe
- P E. Karger
- P H. Sallee

STL 1909 N

- M R. Bresnahan
- 1B E. Konetchy
- 2B R. Charles
- SS R. Hulswitt
- 3B R. Byrne
- OF G. Ellis
- OF L. Evans
- OF A. Shaw
- C E. Phelps
- UT J. Delahanty
- P F. Beebe
- P J. Lush
- P H. Sallee
- P R. Harmon
- P L. Backman
- RP S. Melter

STL 1910 N

- M R. Bresnahan
- 1B E. Konetchy
- 2B M. Huggins
- SS A. Hauser
- 3B H. Mowrey
- OF L. Evans
- OF G. Ellis
- OF E. Oakes
- C E. Phelps
- P R. Harmon
- P J. Lush
- P V. Willis
- P F. Corridon
- P L. Backman

STL 1911 N

- M R. Bresnahan
- 1B E. Konetchy
- 2B M. Huggins
- SS A. Hauser
- 3B H. Mowrey
- OF E. Oakes
- OF L. Evans
- OF G. Ellis
- C J. Bliss
- P R. Harmon
- P W. Steele
- P H. Sallee
- P R. Golden

STL 1911 N (cont.)

- P J. Geyer

STL 1912 N

- M R. Bresnahan
- 1B E. Konetchy
- 2B M. Huggins
- SS A. Hauser
- 3B H. Mowrey
- OF E. Oakes
- OF L. Evans
- OF L. Magee
- C I. Wingo
- UT G. Ellis
- P H. Sallee
- P R. Harmon
- P W. Steele
- P J. Geyer
- P J. Willis
- RP E. Woodburn

STL 1913 N

- M M. Huggins
- 1B E. Konetchy
- 2B M. Huggins
- SS C. O'Leary
- 3B H. Mowrey
- OF E. Oakes
- OF L. Magee
- OF L. Evans
- C I. Wingo
- UT G. Whitted
- P H. Sallee
- P R. Harmon
- P D. Griner
- P W. Perritt
- P W. Doak
- RP J. Geyer

STL 1914 N

- M M. Huggins
- 1B J. Miller
- 2B M. Huggins
- SS A. Butler
- 3B Z. Beck
- OF J. Wilson
- OF L. Magee
- OF A. Dolan
- C F. Snyder
- UT W. Cruise
- P W. Perritt
- P H. Sallee
- P W. Doak
- P D. Griner
- P H. Perdue

STL 1915 N

- M M. Huggins
- 1B J. Miller
- 2B M. Huggins
- SS A. Butler
- 3B C. Betzel
- OF T. Long
- OF R. Bescher
- OF J. Wilson
- C F. Snyder
- UT A. Dolan
- UT R. Hyatt
- P W. Doak
- P H. Sallee
- P H. Meadows
- P D. Griner
- P J. Robinson

STL 1916 N

- M M. Huggins
- 1B J. Miller
- 2B C. Betzel
- SS R. Corhan
- 3B R. Hornsby
- OF R. Bescher
- OF J. Smith
- OF J. Wilson
- C M. Gonzalez
- UT T. Long
- UT F. Snyder
- P H. Meadows
- P L. Ames
- P W. Doak
- P R. Steele
- P H. Jasper
- RP R. Williams

STL 1917 N

- M M. Huggins
- 1B E. Paulette
- 2B J. Miller
- SS R. Hornsby
- 3B H. Baird
- OF W. Cruise
- OF T. Long
- OF J. Smith

STL 1917 N (cont.)

- C F. Snyder
- UT C. Betzel
- UT M. Gonzalez
- P W. Doak
- P H. Meadows
- P L. Ames
- P M. Watson
- P E. Packard

STL 1918 N

- M J. Hendricks
- 1B E. Paulette
- 2B R. Fisher
- SS R. Hornsby
- 3B H. Baird
- OF E. Heathcote
- OF A. McHenry
- OF W. Cruise
- C M. Gonzalez
- P W. Doak
- P L. Ames
- P W. Sherdel
- P E. Packard
- P H. Meadows

STL 1919 N

- M W. Rickey
- 1B J. Miller
- 2B M. Stock
- SS J. Lavan
- 3B R. Hornsby
- OF J. Smith
- OF A. McHenry
- OF C. Heathcote
- C V. Clemons
- UT J. Schultz
- UT B. Shotton
- P W. Doak
- P M. Goodwin
- P O. Tuero
- P W. Sherdel
- P F. May

STL 1920 N

- M W. Rickey
- 1B J. Fournier
- 2B R. Hornsby
- SS J. Lavan
- 3B M. Stock
- OF A. McHenry
- OF C. Heathcote
- OF J. Smith
- C V. Clemons
- UT J. Schultz
- P J. Haines
- P W. Doak
- P F. Schupp
- P W. Sherdel
- P M. Goodwin

STL 1921 N

- M W. Rickey
- 1B J. Fournier
- 2B R. Hornsby
- SS J. Lavan
- 3B M. Stock
- OF A. McHenry
- OF J. Smith
- OF L. Mann
- C V. Clemons
- P J. Haines
- P W. Doak
- P W. Pertica
- P J. Walker
- P W. Sherdel
- RP L. North

STL 1922 N

- M W. Rickey
- 1B J. Fournier
- 2B R. Hornsby
- SS G. Toporcer
- 3B M. Stock
- OF J. Smith
- OF J. Schultz
- OF M. Flack
- C E. Ainsmith
- P E. Pfeffer
- P W. Sherdel
- P J. Haines
- P W. Doak
- P W. Pertica
- RP L. North
- RP C. Barfoot

STL 1923 N

- M W. Rickey
- 1B J. Bottomley
- 2B R. Hornsby
- SS H. Freigau
- 3B M. Stock

OF M. Flack
OF J. Smith
OF H. Myers
C E. Ainsmith
UT F. Blades
UT G. Toporcer
P J. Haines
P W. Sherdel
P F. Toney
P W. Doak
P E. Pfeffer
RP L. North

STL 1924 N
M W. Rickey
1B J. Bottomley
2B R. Hornsby
SS J. Cooney
3B H. Freigau
OF J. Smith
OF F. Blades
OF R. Holm
C M. Gonzalez
P J. Haines
P A. Sothoron
P W. Sherdel
P J. Stuart
P E. Dyer

STL 1925 N
M W. Rickey
M R. Hornsby
1B J. Bottomley
2B R. Hornsby
SS G. Toporcer
3B L. Bell
OF F. Blades
OF C. Hafey
OF C. Mueller
C R. O'Farrell
P J. Haines
P W. Sherdel
P C. Rhem
P A. Sothoron
P A. Reinhart

STL 1926 N
M R. Hornsby
1B J. Bottomley
2B R. Hornsby
SS T. Thevenow
3B L. Bell
OF T. Douthit
OF F. Blades
OF W. Southworth
C R. O'Farrell
P C. Rhem
P W. Sherdel
P J. Haines
P H. Keen
P G. Alexander
RP S. Johnson

STL 1927 N
M R. O'Farrell
1B J. Bottomley
2B F. Frisch
SS H. Schuble
3B L. Bell
OF T. Douthit
OF R. Holm
OF C. Hafey
C F. Snyder
P J. Haines
P G. Alexander
P W. Sherdel
P C. Rhem
P R. McGraw
RP H. Bell

STL 1928 N
M W. McKechnie
1B J. Bottomley
2B F. Frisch
SS W. Maranville
3B R. Holm
OF T. Douthit
OF C. Hafey
OF G. Harper
C J. Wilson
UT A. High
P W. Sherdel
P G. Alexander
P J. Haines
P C. Rhem
P C. Mitchell
RP H. Haid

STL 1929 N
M W. Southworth
M C. Street

M W. McKechnie
1B J. Bottomley
2B F. Frisch
SS C. Gelbert
3B A. High
OF T. Douthit
OF C. Hafey
OF E. Orsatti
C J. Wilson
P W. Sherdel
P S. Johnson
P J. Haines
P C. Mitchell
P H. Haid

STL 1930 N
M C. Street
1B J. Bottomley
2B F. Frisch
SS C. Gelbert
3B E. Adams
OF T. Douthit
OF C. Hafey
OF G. Watkins
C J. Wilson
P W. Hallahan
P S. Johnson
P J. Haines
P B. Grimes
P C. Rhem
RP H. Bell
RP J. Lindsey

STL 1931 N
M C. Street
1B J. Bottomley
2B F. Frisch
SS C. Gelbert
3B E. Adams
OF G. Watkins
OF C. Hafey
OF J. Martin
C J. Wilson
P W. Hallahan
P B. Grimes
P S. Derringer
P C. Rhem
P S. Johnson
RP J. Lindsey
RP A. Stout

STL 1932 N
M C. Street
1B J. Collins
2B J. Reese
SS C. Gelbert
3B D. Flowers
OF G. Watkins
OF E. Orsatti
OF J. Martin
C A. Mancuso
UT F. Frisch
P J. Dean
P S. Derringer
P J. Carleton
P W. Hallahan
P S. Johnson
RP J. Lindsey
RP A. Stout

STL 1933 N
M C. Street
M F. Frisch
1B J. Collins
2B F. Frisch
SS L. Durocher
3B J. Martin
OF J. Medwick
OF G. Watkins
OF E. Orsatti
C J. Wilson
P J. Dean
P J. Carleton
P W. Hallahan
P W. Walker
P J. Haines
RP S. Johnson

STL 1934 N
M F. Frisch
1B J. Collins
2B F. Frisch
SS L. Durocher
3B J. Martin
OF J. Rothrock
OF J. Medwick
OF E. Orsatti
C V. Davis
UT B. Whitehead
P J. Dean
P J. Carleton
P P. Dean

P W. Hallahan
P W. Walker
RP J. Haines
RP J. Mooney

STL 1935 N
M F. Frisch
1B J. Collins
2B F. Frisch
SS L. Durocher
3B J. Martin
OF J. Medwick
OF J. Rothrock
OF T. Moore
C W. DeLancey
UT V. Davis
UT B. Whitehead
P J. Dean
P P. Dean
P W. Walker
P W. Hallahan
P E. Heusser

STL 1936 N
M F. Frisch
1B J. Mize
2B S. Martin
SS L. Durocher
3B C. Gelbert
OF J. Medwick
OF T. Moore
OF J. Martin
C V. Davis
UT J. Collins
UT A. Ogrodowski
P J. Dean
P L. Parmelee
P J. Winford
P J. Haines
RP E. Heusser
RP G. Earnshaw

STL 1937 N
M F. Frisch
1B J. Mize
2B J. Brown
SS L. Durocher
3B D. Gutteridge
OF J. Medwick
OF J. Padgett
OF T. Moore
C A. Ogrodowski
UT S. Bordagaray
UT J. Martin
P R. Weiland
P L. Warneke
P J. Dean
P S. Johnson
P D. Ryba
RP R. Harrell

STL 1938 N
M F. Frisch
M M. Gonzalez
1B J. Mize
2B S. Martin
SS L. Myers
3B D. Gutteridge
OF J. Medwick
OF E. Slaughter
OF T. Moore
C A. Owen
UT J. Brown
UT D. Padgett
P R. Weiland
P W. McGee
P L. Warneke
P C. Davis
P R. Henshaw
RP C. Shoun
RP R. Harrell

STL 1939 N
M F. Blades
1B J. Mize
2B S. Martin
SS J. Brown
3B D. Gutteridge
OF E. Slaughter
OF J. Medwick
OF T. Moore
C A. Owen
P C. Davis
P M. Cooper
P R. Bowman
P L. Warneke
P W. McGee
RP C. Shoun

STL 1940 N
M F. Blades

M M. Gonzalez
M W. Southworth
1B J. Mize
2B J. Orengo
SS M. Marion
3B S. Martin
OF T. Moore
OF E. Slaughter
OF E. Koy
C A. Owen
UT J. Brown
P L. Warneke
P M. Cooper
P W. McGee
P C. Shoun
P R. Bowman
RP J. Russell

STL 1941 N
M W. Southworth
1B J. Mize
2B F. Crespi
SS M. Marion
3B J. Brown
OF T. Moore
OF E. Slaughter
OF J. Hopp
C A. Mancuso
UT D. Padgett
P L. Warneke
P E. White
P M. Cooper
P H. Lanier
P H. Gumbert
RP C. Shoun
RP I. Hutchinson

STL 1942 N
M W. Southworth
1B J. Hopp
2B F. Crespi
SS M. Marion
3B G. Kurowski
OF E. Slaughter
OF S. Musial
OF T. Moore
C W. Cooper
UT J. Brown
UT R. Sanders
P M. Cooper
P J. Beazley
P H. Gumbert
P H. Lanier
P E. White

STL 1943 N
M W. Southworth
1B R. Sanders
2B L. Klein
SS M. Marion
3B G. Kurowski
OF S. Musial
OF H. Walker
OF D. Litwhiler
C W. Cooper
P M. Cooper
P H. Lanier
P H. Krist
P H. Brecheen
P H. Gumbert
RP G. Munger

STL 1944 N
M W. Southworth
1B R. Sanders
2B E. Verban
SS M. Marion
3B G. Kurowski
OF S. Musial
OF D. Litwhiler
OF J. Hopp
C W. Cooper
P M. Cooper
P H. Lanier
P T. Wilks
P H. Brecheen
P A. Jurisich
RP S. Donnelly

STL 1945 N
M W. Southworth
1B R. Sanders
2B E. Verban
SS M. Marion
3B G. Kurowski
OF E. Adams
OF A. Schoendienst
OF J. Hopp
C J. O'Dea
UT A. Bergamo
P C. Barrett
P K. Burkhart

P S. Donnelly
P H. Brecheen
P G. Dockins
RP E. Byerly
RP A. Jurisich

STL 1946 N
M E. Dyer
1B S. Musial
2B A. Schoendienst
SS M. Marion
3B G. Kurowski
OF E. Slaughter
OF H. Walker
OF E. Dusak
C J. Garagiola
P H. Pollet
P H. Brecheen
P M. Dickson
P A. Brazle
P J. Beazley
RP T. Wilks
RP C. Barrett

STL 1947 N
M E. Dyer
1B S. Musial
2B A. Schoendienst
SS M. Marion
3B G. Kurowski
OF E. Slaughter
OF T. Moore
OF R. Northey
C D. Rice
UT C. Diering
UT E. Dusak
P M. Dickson
P G. Munger
P H. Brecheen
P H. Pollet
P A. Brazle
RP K. Burkhart
RP T. Wilks

STL 1948 N
M E. Dyer
1B V. Jones
2B A. Schoendienst
SS M. Marion
3B D. Lang
OF S. Musial
OF E. Slaughter
OF T. Moore
C D. Rice
UT E. Dusak
UT R. Northey
P M. Dickson
P H. Brecheen
P H. Pollet
P G. Munger
P A. Brazle
RP T. Wilks
RP J. Hearn
RP G. Staley

STL 1949 N
M E. Dyer
1B V. Jones
2B A. Schoendienst
SS M. Marion
3B E. Kazak
OF S. Musial
OF E. Slaughter
OF C. Diering
C D. Rice
P H. Pollet
P H. Brecheen
P A. Brazle
P G. Munger
P G. Staley
RP T. Wilks

STL 1950 N
M E. Dyer
1B G. Nelson
2B A. Schoendienst
SS M. Marion
3B T. Glaviano
OF E. Slaughter
OF W. Howerton
OF C. Diering
C D. Rice
UT S. Musial
P H. Pollet
P H. Lanier
P G. Staley
P A. Brazle
P H. Brecheen
RP F. Martin

STL 1951 N
M M. Marion
1B V. Jones
2B A. Schoendienst
SS S. Hemus
3B W. Johnson
OF E. Slaughter
OF S. Musial
OF H. Lowrey
C D. Rice
P G. Staley
P T. Poholsky
P H. Lanier
P H. Brecheen
P C. Chambers
RP A. Brazle
RP R. Bokelmann

STL 1952 N
M E. Stanky
1B R. Sisler
2B A. Schoendienst
SS S. Hemus
3B W. Johnson
OF E. Slaughter
OF S. Musial
OF H. Lowrey
C D. Rice
UT H. Rice
P G. Staley
P W. Mizell
P J. Presko
P C. Boyer
P H. Brecheen
RP A. Brazle
RP J. Yuhas

STL 1953 N
M E. Stanky
1B S. Bilko
2B A. Schoendienst
SS S. Hemus
3B R. Jablonski
OF S. Musial
OF E. Repulski
OF E. Slaughter
C D. Rice
UT H. Lowrey
P H. Haddix
P G. Staley
P W. Mizell
P J. Presko
P S. Miller
RP A. Brazle
RP H. White
RP C. Chambers

STL 1954 N
M E. Stanky
1B J. Cunningham
2B A. Schoendienst
SS A. Grammas
3B R. Jablonski
OF E. Repulski
OF S. Musial
OF W. Moon
C W. Sarni
UT S. Hemus
P H. Haddix
P V. Raschi
P B. Lawrence
P G. Staley
P T. Poholsky
RP A. Brazle
RP J. Presko
RP E. Deal

STL 1955 N
M E. Stanky
M H. Walker
1B S. Musial
2B A. Schoendienst
SS A. Grammas
3B K. Boyer
OF W. Virdon
OF E. Repulski
OF W. Moon
C W. Sarni
UT S. Hemus
P H. Haddix
P L. Jackson
P L. Arroyo
P T. Poholsky
P W. Schmidt
RP B. Lawrence
RP P. LaPalme

STL 1956 N
M F. Hutchinson
1B S. Musial
2B D. Blasingame

SS A. Dark
3B K. Boyer
OF E. Repulski
OF R. Del Greco
OF W. Moon
C H. Smith
P W. Mizell
P T. Poholsky
P M. Dickson
P H. Wehmeier
P W. Schmidt
RP L. McDaniel
RP L. Jackson
RP J. Collum

STL 1957 N
M F. Hutchinson
1B S. Musial
2B D. Blasingame
SS A. Dark
3B E. Kasko
OF W. Moon
OF D. Ennis
OF K. Boyer
C H. Smith
UT J. Cunningham
P L. Jackson
P L. McDaniel
P S. Jones
P H. Wehmeier
P W. Mizell
RP W. Schmidt
RP L. Merritt
RP H. Wilhelm

STL 1958 N
M F. Hutchinson
M S. Hack
1B S. Musial
2B D. Blasingame
SS E. Kasko
3B K. Boyer
OF C. Flood
OF D. Ennis
OF W. Moon
C H. Smith
UT J. Cunningham
UT G. Green
UT I. Noren
P S. Jones
P L. Jackson
P W. Mizell
P J. Brosnan
P J. Mabe
RP B. Muffett
RP P. Paine
RP W. Wight

STL 1959 N
M S. Hemus
1B S. Musial
2B D. Blasingame
SS A. Grammas
3B K. Boyer
OF G. Cimoli
OF J. Cunningham
OF C. Flood
C H. Smith
UT W. White
P L. Jackson
P W. Mizell
P E. Broglio
P G. Blaylock
RP L. McDaniel
RP M. Bridges

STL 1960 N
M S. Hemus
1B W. White
2B M. Javier
SS D. Spencer
3B K. Boyer
OF C. Flood
OF J. Cunningham
OF W. Moryn
C H. Smith
UT A. Grammas
UT S. Musial
P L. Jackson
P E. Broglio
P R. Sadecki
P C. Simmons
P R. Kline
RP L. McDaniel

STL 1961 N
M S. Hemus
M J. Keane
1B W. White
2B M. Javier
SS A. Grammas
3B K. Boyer

OF C. Flood
OF S. Musial
OF C. James
C J. Schaffer
UT J. Cunningham
UT D. Taussig
P R. Sadecki
P L. Jackson
P R. Gibson
P C. Simmons
P E. Broglio
RP L. McDaniel
RP A. Cicotte
RP R. Miller

STL 1962 N
M J. Keane
1B W. White
2B M. Javier
SS J. Gotay
3B K. Boyer
OF C. Flood
OF S. Musial
OF C. James
C E. Oliver
P L. Jackson
P R. Gibson
P E. Broglio
P R. Washburn
P C. Simmons
RP L. McDaniel
RP R. Shantz
RP D. Ferrarese

STL 1963 N
M J. Keane
1B W. White
2B M. Javier
SS R. Groat
3B K. Boyer
OF C. Flood
OF G. Altman
OF C. James
C J. McCarver
UT S. Musial
P R. Gibson
P E. Broglio
P C. Simmons
P R. Sadecki
P S. Burdette
RP R. Taylor
RP R. Shantz
RP E. Bauta

STL 1964 N
M J. Keane
1B W. White
2B M. Javier
SS R. Groat
3B K. Boyer
OF C. Flood
OF L. Brock
OF T. Shannon
C J. McCarver
P R. Gibson
P C. Simmons
P R. Sadecki
P R. Craig
RP R. Taylor
RP M. Cuellar
RP G. Schultz

STL 1965 N
M A. Schoendienst
1B W. White
2B M. Javier
SS R. Groat
3B K. Boyer
OF L. Brock
OF C. Flood
OF T. Shannon
C J. McCarver
UT P. Gagliano
P R. Gibson
P C. Simmons
P E. Stallard
P R. Sadecki
P R. Purkey
RP N. Briles
RP H. Woodeshick
RP D. Dennis

STL 1966 N
M A. Schoendienst
1B O. Cepeda
2B M. Javier
SS C. Maxvill
3B C. Smith
OF C. Flood
OF L. Brock
OF T. Shannon
C J. McCarver

UT G. Buchek
P R. Gibson
P A. Jackson
P R. Washburn
P N. Briles
P L. Jaster
RP J. Hoerner
RP H. Woodeshick
RP D. Dennis

STL 1967 N
M A. Schoendienst
1B O. Cepeda
2B M. Javier
SS C. Maxvill
3B T. Shannon
OF L. Brock
OF C. Flood
OF R. Maris
C J. McCarver
UT R. Tolan
P J. Hughes
P S. Carlton
P R. Washburn
P R. Gibson
P N. Briles
RP A. Jackson
RP R. Willis
RP J. Hoerner

STL 1968 N
M A. Schoendienst
1B O. Cepeda
2B M. Javier
SS C. Maxvill
3B T. Shannon
OF L. Brock
OF C. Flood
OF R. Maris
C J. McCarver
P R. Gibson
P N. Briles
P S. Carlton
P R. Washburn
P L. Jaster
RP R. Willis
RP R. Hughes
RP M. Nelson

STL 1969 N
M A. Schoendienst
1B J. Torre
2B M. Javier
SS C. Maxvill
3B T. Shannon
OF L. Brock
OF C. Flood
OF V. Pinson
C J. McCarver
P R. Gibson
P S. Carlton
P N. Briles
P R. Washburn
P C. Taylor
RP J. Grant
RP J. Hoerner

STL 1970 N
M A. Schoendienst
1B J. Hague
2B M. Javier
SS C. Maxvill
3B J. Torre
OF L. Brock
OF J. Cardenal
OF L. Lee
C T. Simmons
UT R. Allen
UT V. Davalillo
UT C. Taylor
P R. Gibson
P S. Carlton
P M. Torrez
P J. Reuss
P N. Briles
RP C. Taylor
RP F. Linzy
RP S. Campisi

STL 1971 N
M A. Schoendienst
1B J. Hague
2B M. Javier
SS C. Maxvill
3B J. Torre
OF L. Brock
OF M. Alou
OF J. Cruz
C T. Simmons
P S. Carlton
P R. Gibson
P R. Cleveland

P J. Reuss
RP C. Taylor
RP M. Drabowsky
RP F. Linzy

STL 1972 N
M A. Schoendienst
1B M. Alou
2B T. Sizemore
SS C. Maxvill
3B J. Torre
OF L. Brock
OF L. Melendez
OF J. Cruz
C T. Simmons
UT B. Carbo
UT E. Crosby
P R. Gibson
P R. Wise
P R. Cleveland
P A. Santorini
P S. Spinks
RP D. Segui

STL 1973 N
M A. Schoendienst
1B J. Torre
2B T. Sizemore
SS M. Tyson
3B K. Reitz
OF L. Brock
OF J. Cruz
OF L. Melendez
C T. Simmons
UT B. Carbo
UT J. McCarver
P R. Wise
P R. Cleveland
P A. Foster
P R. Gibson
RP D. Segui
RP R. Folkers
RP O. Pena

STL 1974 N
M A. Schoendienst
1B J. Torre
2B T. Sizemore
SS M. Tyson
3B K. Reitz
OF L. Brock
OF A. McBride
OF C. Smith
C T. Simmons
UT J. Cruz
P R. Gibson
P L. McGlothen
P J. Curtis
P A. Foster
P W. Siebert
RP R. Folkers
RP A. Hrabosky
RP M. Garman

STL 1975 N
M A. Schoendienst
1B C. Smith
2B T. Sizemore
SS M. Tyson
3B K. Reitz
OF L. Brock
OF A. McBride
OF L. Melendez
C T. Simmons
UT R. Fairly
P L. McGlothen
P R. Forsch
P R. Reed
P J. Curtis
P J. Denny
RP A. Hrabosky
RP M. Garman

STL 1976 N
M A. Schoendienst
1B K. Hernandez
2B M. Tyson
SS D. Kessinger
3B H. Cruz
OF L. Brock
OF W. Crawford
OF J. Mumphrey
C T. Simmons
UT V. Harris
P P. Falcone
P J. Denny
P L. McGlothen
P R. Forsch
P E. Rasmussen
RP A. Hrabosky
RP M. Wallace
RP W. Greif

STL 1977 N
M V. Rapp
1B K. Hernandez
2B M. Tyson
SS G. Templeton
3B K. Reitz
OF J. Mumphrey
OF L. Brock
OF H. Cruz
C T. Simmons
P E. Rasmussen
P R. Forsch
P J. Denny
P J. Urrea
P P. Falcone
RP C. Metzger
RP C. Carroll
RP A. Hrabosky

STL 1978 N
M V. Rapp
M J. Krol
M K. Boyer
1B K. Hernandez
2B M. Tyson
SS G. Templeton
3B K. Reitz
OF J. Morales
OF J. Mumphrey
OF G. Hendrick
C T. Simmons
P R. Forsch
P J. Denny
P P. Vuckovich
P S. Martinez
P J. Urrea
RP M. Littell
RP C. Schultz
RP A. Lopez

STL 1979 N
M K. Boyer
1B K. Hernandez
2B K. Oberkfell
SS G. Templeton
3B K. Reitz
OF A. Scott
OF G. Hendrick
OF J. Mumphrey
C T. Simmons
UT L. Brock
P P. Vuckovich
P R. Forsch
P S. Martinez
P J. Denny
P J. Fulgham
RP M. Littell
RP R. Thomas
RP W. McEnaney

STL 1980 N
M K. Boyer
M J. Krol
M D. Herzog
M A. Schoendienst
1B K. Hernandez
2B K. Oberkfell
SS G. Templeton
3B K. Reitz
OF G. Hendrick
OF A. Scott
OF L. Durham
C T. Simmons
UT D. Iorg
P P. Vuckovich
P R. Forsch
P R. Sykes
P S. Martinez
RP J. Kaat
RP D. Hood
RP J. Littlefield

STL 1981 N
M D. Herzog
1B K. Hernandez
2B T. Herr
SS G. Templeton
3B K. Oberkfell
OF G. Hendrick
OF T. Landrum
OF S. Lezcano
C D. Porter
UT D. Iorg
P L. Sorensen
P R. Forsch
P J. Martin
P S. Martinez
P H. Sutter
RP R. Shirley
RP J. Kaat

STL 1982 N
M D. Herzog
1B K. Hernandez
2B T. Herr
SS O. Smith
3B K. Oberkfell
OF L. Smith
OF G. Hendrick
OF W. McGee
C D. Porter
UT D. Iorg
UT M. Ramsey
P J. Andujar
P R. Forsch
P S. Mura
P D. LaPoint
P J. Stuper
RP H. Sutter
RP C. Bair
RP J. Kaat

STL 1983 N
M D. Herzog
1B G. Hendrick
2B T. Herr
SS O. Smith
3B K. Oberkfell
OF W. McGee
OF D. Green
OF L. Smith
C D. Porter
UT M. Ramsey
UT A. Van Slyke
P J. Andujar
P J. Stuper
P D. LaPoint
P R. Forsch
P N. Allen
RP H. Sutter
RP J. Lahti
RP D. Von Ohlen

STL 1984 N
M D. Herzog
1B D. Green
2B T. Herr
SS O. Smith
3B T. Pendleton
OF W. McGee
OF L. Smith
OF G. Hendrick
C D. Porter
UT T. Landrum
UT A. Van Slyke
P J. Andujar
P D. LaPoint
P D. Cox
P R. Horton
P K. Kepshire
RP H. Sutter
RP N. Allen
RP J. Lahti

STL 1985 N
M D. Herzog
1B J. Clark
2B T. Herr
SS O. Smith
3B T. Pendleton
OF V. Coleman
OF A. Van Slyke
OF W. McGee
C T. Nieto
P J. Tudor
P J. Andujar
P D. Cox
P K. Kepshire
P R. Forsch
RP R. Horton
RP J. Kaat
RP K. Dayley

STL 1986 N
M D. Herzog
1B J. Clark
2B T. Herr
SS O. Smith
3B T. Pendleton
OF V. Coleman
OF W. McGee
OF A. Van Slyke
C M. LaValliere
P R. Forsch
P D. Cox
P J. Tudor
P G. Mathews
P T. Conroy
RP T. Worrell
RP R. Horton
RP W. Perry

STL 1987 N
M D. Herzog
1B J. Clark
2B T. Herr
SS O. Smith
3B T. Pendleton
OF W. McGee
OF V. Coleman
OF C. Ford
C A. Pena
UT J. Morris
UT J. Oquendo
P D. Cox
P G. Mathews
P R. Forsch
P J. Magrane
P J. Tudor
RP H. Horton
RP W. Dawley
RP T. Worrell

STL 1988 N
M D. Herzog
1B J. Horner
2B L. Alicea
SS O. Smith
3B T. Pendleton
OF V. Coleman
OF W. McGee
C A. Pena
UT J. Oquendo
P J. DeLeon
P J. Magrane
P J. Tudor
P L. McWilliams
P R. Forsch
RP S. Terry
RP T. Worrell
RP K. Dayley

STL 1989 N
M D. Herzog
1B P. Guerrero
2B J. Oquendo
SS O. Smith
3B T. Pendleton
OF T. Brunansky
OF M. Thompson
OF V. Coleman
C A. Pena
P J. DeLeon
P J. Magrane
P K. Hill
P S. Terry
RP F. DiPino
RP D. Quisenberry
RP K. Dayley

STL 1990 N
M D. Herzog
M A. Schoendienst
M J. Torre
1B P. Guerrero
2B J. Oquendo
SS O. Smith
3B T. Pendleton
OF W. McGee
OF V. Coleman
OF M. Thompson
C T. Zeile
UT D. Collins
P J. Magrane
P J. DeLeon
P J. Tudor
P R. Tewksbury
P B. Smith
RP F. DiPino
RP K. Dayley
RP S. Terry

St. Paul

STP U 1884

STP 1884 U
M A. Thompson
1B S. Dunn
2B E. Hengle
SS J. Werrick
3B W. O'Brien
OF J. Tilley
OF J. Carroll
OF W. Barnes
C G. Ganzel
P J. Brown
P L. Galvin

San Diego

SD N 1969-1990

SD 1969 N
M P. Gomez
1B N. Colbert
2B J. Arcia
SS T. Dean
3B E. Spiezio
OF O. Brown
OF C. Gaston
OF A. Ferrara
C C. Cannizzaro
UT R. Pena
P C. Kirby
P J. Niekro
P A. Santorini
P R. Kelley
RP T. Sisk
RP G. Ross
RP F. Reberger

SD 1970 N
M P. Gomez
1B N. Colbert
2B D. Campbell
SS J. Arcia
3B E. Spiezio
OF C. Gaston
OF O. Brown
OF I. Murrell
C C. Cannizzaro
UT A. Ferrara
UT S. Huntz
P P. Dobson
P C. Kirby
P D. Coombs
P D. Roberts
RP R. Herbel
RP T. Dukes
RP G. Ross

SD 1971 N
M P. Gomez
1B N. Colbert
2B D. Mason
SS E. Hernandez
3B E. Spiezio
OF O. Brown
OF C. Gaston
OF L. Stahl
C L. Barton
UT D. Campbell
UT I. Murrell
P D. Roberts
P C. Kirby
P S. Arlin
P T. Phoebus
P F. Norman
RP A. Severinsen
RP R. Miller
RP R. Kelley

SD 1972 N
M P. Gomez
M D. Zimmer
1B N. Colbert
2B D. Thomas
SS E. Hernandez
3B D. Roberts
OF J. Morales
OF L. Lee
OF C. Gaston
C F. Kendall
UT J. Jeter
UT L. Stahl
P S. Arlin
P C. Kirby
P F. Norman
P R. Caldwell
P W. Greif
RP M. Corkins
RP G. Ross
RP E. Acosta

SD 1973 N
M D. Zimmer
1B N. Colbert
2B R. Morales
SS D. Thomas
3B D. Roberts
OF C. Gaston
OF J. Grubb
OF J. Morales
C F. Kendall
UT L. Lee
P W. Greif
P C. Kirby

P   S. Arlin
P   R. Troedson
P   R. Jones
RP   R. Caldwell
RP   M. Corkins
RP   V. Romo

SD 1974 N
M   J. McNamara
1B   W. McCovey
2B   D. Thomas
SS   E. Hernandez
3B   D. Roberts
OF   D. Winfield
OF   J. Grubb
OF   R. Tolan
C   F. Kendall
UT   N. Colbert
UT   C. Gaston
P   W. Greif
P   D. Freisleben
P   R. Jones
P   D. Spillner
RP   H. Hardy
RP   V. Romo
RP   D. Tomlin

SD 1975 N
M   J. McNamara
1B   W. McCovey
2B   R. Fuentes
SS   E. Hernandez
3B   T. Kubiak
OF   J. Grubb
OF   D. Winfield
OF   R. Tolan
C   F. Kendall
UT   M. Ivie
UT   G. Locklear
UT   H. Torres
P   R. Jones
P   J. McIntosh
P   D. Freisleben
P   D. Spillner
P   F. Folkers
RP   D. Frisella
RP   D. Tomlin
RP   W. Greif

SD 1976 N
M   J. McNamara
1B   M. Ivie
2B   R. Fuentes
SS   E. Hernandez
3B   D. Rader
OF   D. Winfield
OF   W. Davis
OF   J. Grubb
C   F. Kendall
UT   J. Turner
P   R. Jones
P   B. Strom
P   D. Freisleben
P   D. Spillner
RP   C. Metzger
RP   D. Tomlin
RP   R. Folkers

SD 1977 N
M   J. McNamara
M   R. Skinner
M   A. Dark
1B   M. Ivie
2B   R. Champion
SS   W. Almon
3B   T. Ashford
OF   D. Winfield
OF   G. Hendrick
OF   E. Richards
C   F. Tenace
UT   M. Rettenmund
UT   J. Turner
P   R. Shirley
P   R. Owchinko
P   T. Griffin
P   R. Jones
P   D. Freisleben
RP   R. Fingers
RP   D. Spillner
RP   R. Sawyer

SD 1978 N
M   R. Craig
1B   F. Tenace
2B   J. Gonzalez
SS   O. Smith
3B   W. Almon
OF   D. Winfield
OF   E. Richards
OF   O. Gamble
C   R. Sweet
UT   D. Thomas

UT   J. Turner
P   G. Perry
P   R. Jones
P   R. Owchinko
P   R. Shirley
P   E. Rasmussen
RP   R. Fingers
RP   J. D'Acquisto
RP   M. Lee

SD 1979 N
M   R. Craig
1B   F. Tenace
2B   J. Gonzalez
SS   O. Smith
3B   L. Dade
OF   D. Winfield
OF   E. Richards
OF   J. Turner
C   W. Fahey
UT   W. Almon
UT   K. Bevacqua
UT   D. Briggs
P   R. Jones
P   G. Perry
P   R. Shirley
P   E. Rasmussen
P   R. Owchinko
RP   J. D'Acquisto
RP   R. Fingers
RP   S. Mura

SD 1980 N
M   G. Coleman
1B   G. Montanez
2B   D. Cash
SS   O. Smith
3B   A. Rodriguez
OF   D. Winfield
OF   E. Richards
OF   J. Mumphrey
C   F. Tenace
P   J. Curtis
P   S. Mura
P   R. Wise
P   R. Jones
P   G. Lucas
RP   R. Shirley
RP   E. Rasmussen
RP   R. Fingers

SD 1981 N
M   F. Howard
1B   B. Perkins
2B   J. Bonilla
SS   O. Smith
3B   L. Salazar
OF   J. Jones
OF   E. Richards
OF   J. Lefebvre
C   T. Kennedy
UT   R. Bass
P   J. Eichelberger
P   S. Mura
P   C. Welsh
P   R. Wise
P   W. Lollar
RP   G. Lucas
RP   J. Curtis
RP   J. Littlefield

SD 1982 N
M   R. Williams
1B   B. Perkins
2B   T. Flannery
SS   G. Templeton
3B   L. Salazar
OF   J. Lezcano
OF   R. Jones
OF   E. Richards
C   T. Kennedy
UT   J. Lefebvre
P   W. Lollar
P   J. Montefusco
P   J. Eichelberger
P   E. Show
P   C. Welsh
RP   L. DeLeon
RP   G. Lucas
RP   F. Chiffer

SD 1983 N
M   R. Williams
1B   S. Garvey
2B   J. Bonilla
SS   G. Templeton
3B   L. Salazar
OF   R. Jones
OF   A. Wiggins
OF   G. Lezcano
C   T. Kennedy
P   E. Show

P   D. Dravecky
P   W. Lollar
P   E. Whitson
P   M. Hawkins
RP   L. DeLeon
RP   G. Lucas
RP   E. Sosa

SD 1984 N
M   R. Williams
1B   S. Garvey
2B   A. Wiggins
SS   G. Templeton
3B   G. Nettles
OF   A. Gwynn
OF   W. McReynolds
OF   C. Martinez
C   T. Kennedy
P   E. Show
P   W. Lollar
P   E. Whitson
P   M. Thurmond
P   D. Dravecky
RP   C. Lefferts
RP   R. Gossage
RP   G. Booker

SD 1985 N
M   R. Williams
1B   S. Garvey
2B   T. Flannery
SS   G. Templeton
3B   G. Nettles
OF   A. Gwynn
OF   W. McReynolds
OF   C. Martinez
C   T. Kennedy
P   E. Show
P   M. Hawkins
P   D. Dravecky
P   D. Hoyt
P   M. Thurmond
RP   C. Lefferts
RP   R. Gossage
RP   T. Stoddard

SD 1986 N
M   S. Boros
1B   S. Garvey
2B   T. Flannery
SS   G. Templeton
3B   G. Nettles
OF   A. Gwynn
OF   W. McReynolds
OF   W. Wynne
C   T. Kennedy
UT   J. Kruk
UT   C. Martinez
UT   L. Roberts
UT   J. Royster
P   M. Hawkins
P   D. Dravecky
P   D. Hoyt
P   E. Show
RP   L. McCullers
RP   C. Lefferts
RP   G. Walter

SD 1987 N
M   L. Bowa
1B   J. Kruk
2B   T. Flannery
SS   G. Templeton
3B   R. Ready
OF   A. Gwynn
OF   S. Jefferson
OF   S. Mack
C   B. Santiago
UT   C. Martinez
UT   M. Wynne
P   E. Whitson
P   E. Show
P   J. Jones
P   M. Hawkins
P   M. Grant
RP   L. McCullers
RP   D. Dravecky
RP   G. Booker

SD 1988 N
M   L. Bowa
M   J. McKeon
1B   B. Moreland
2B   R. Alomar
SS   G. Templeton
3B   J. Brown
OF   A. Gwynn
OF   M. Wynne
OF   C. Martinez
C   B. Santiago
UT   J. Kruk

UT   R. Ready
P   E. Show
P   M. Hawkins
P   E. Whitson
P   J. Jones
P   D. Rasmussen
RP   L. McCullers
RP   M. Grant
RP   M. Davis

SD 1989 N
M   J. McKeon
1B   J. Clark
2B   R. Alomar
SS   G. Templeton
3B   L. Salazar
OF   A. Gwynn
OF   M. Wynne
OF   D. James
C   B. Santiago
UT   C. Martinez
UT   L. Roberts
P   B. Hurst
P   E. Whitson
P   D. Rasmussen
P   C. Terrell
P   E. Show
RP   G. Harris
RP   M. Grant
RP   M. Davis

SD 1990 N
M   J. McKeon
M   G. Riddoch
1B   J. Clark
2B   R. Alomar
SS   G. Templeton
3B   M. Pagliarulo
OF   J. Carter
OF   A. Gwynn
OF   L. Roberts
C   B. Santiago
UT   P. Stephenson
P   E. Whitson
P   B. Hurst
P   A. Benes
P   D. Rasmussen
RP   G. Harris
RP   E. Show
RP   C. Schiraldi

San Francisco

SF N 1958-1990

SF 1958 N
M   W. Rigney
1B   O. Cepeda
2B   D. O'Connell
SS   D. Spencer
3B   J. Davenport
OF   W. Mays
OF   W. Kirkland
OF   F. Alou
C   R. Schmidt
P   J. Antonelli
P   R. Gomez
P   S. Miller
P   M. McCormick
P   R. Monzant
RP   A. Worthington
RP   M. Grissom

SF 1959 N
M   W. Rigney
1B   O. Cepeda
2B   D. Spencer
SS   E. Bressoud
3B   J. Davenport
OF   W. Mays
OF   W. Kirkland
OF   J. Brandt
C   H. Landrith
UT   F. Alou
P   J. Antonelli
P   S. Jones
P   M. McCormick
P   J. Sanford
RP   S. Miller
RP   A. Worthington

SF 1960 N
M   W. Rigney
M   T. Sheehan
1B   W. McCovey
2B   D. Blasingame
SS   E. Bressoud
3B   J. Davenport
OF   W. Mays
OF   W. Kirkland

OF   F. Alou
C   R. Schmidt
UT   J. Amalfitano
UT   O. Cepeda
P   M. McCormick
P   S. Jones
P   J. Sanford
P   W. O'Dell
RP   J. Antonelli
RP   S. Miller

SF 1961 N
M   A. Dark
1B   W. McCovey
2B   J. Amalfitano
SS   J. Pagan
3B   J. Davenport
OF   W. Mays
OF   F. Alou
OF   H. Kuenn
C   L. Bailey
UT   O. Cepeda
P   M. McCormick
P   J. Sanford
P   J. Marichal
P   S. Jones
P   W. Loes
RP   W. O'Dell
RP   S. Miller
RP   J. Duffalo

SF 1962 N
M   A. Dark
1B   O. Cepeda
2B   C. Hiller
SS   J. Pagan
3B   J. Davenport
OF   W. Mays
OF   F. Alou
OF   H. Kuenn
C   T. Haller
UT   J. Davenport
P   G. Perry
P   M. McCormick
P   J. Marichal
P   R. Sadecki
P   R. Herbel
RP   F. Linzy
RP   J. Gibbon
RP   L. McDaniel

SF 1963 N
M   A. Dark
1B   O. Cepeda
2B   C. Hiller
SS   J. Pagan
3B   J. Davenport
OF   W. Mays
OF   F. Alou
OF   W. McCovey
C   L. Bailey
UT   T. Haller
UT   H. Kuenn
P   J. Marichal
P   J. Sanford
P   W. O'Dell
P   J. Fisher
RP   B. Bolin
RP   W. Pierce
RP   G. Perry

SF 1964 N
M   A. Dark
1B   O. Cepeda
2B   H. Lanier
SS   J. Pagan
3B   J. Hart
OF   W. Mays
OF   J. Alou
OF   H. Kuenn
C   T. Haller
UT   M. Alou
UT   J. Davenport
UT   W. McCovey
P   J. Marichal
P   G. Perry
P   B. Bolin
P   C. Hendley
P   R. Herbel
RP   R. Shaw
RP   W. O'Dell
RP   J. Duffalo

SF 1965 N
M   H. Franks
1B   W. McCovey
2B   H. Lanier
SS   J. Schofield
3B   J. Hart
OF   W. Mays
OF   J. Alou
OF   M. Alou
C   T. Haller

OF   L. Gabrielson
UT   C. Peterson
UT   J. Davenport
P   J. Marichal
P   G. Perry
P   B. Shaw
P   R. Herbel
P   B. Bolin
P   J. Sanford
RP   F. Linzy
RP   M. Murakami

SF 1966 N
M   H. Franks
1B   W. McCovey
2B   H. Lanier
SS   R. Fuentes
3B   J. Hart
OF   W. Mays
OF   O. Brown
OF   J. Alou
C   T. Haller
UT   J. Davenport
P   J. Marichal
P   G. Perry
P   B. Bolin
P   R. Herbel
P   R. Sadecki
RP   L. McDaniel
RP   F. Linzy
RP   R. Priddy

SF 1967 N
M   H. Franks
1B   W. McCovey
2B   R. Fuentes
SS   H. Lanier
3B   J. Hart
OF   W. Mays
OF   J. Alou
OF   O. Brown
C   T. Haller
UT   J. Davenport
P   G. Perry
P   M. McCormick
P   J. Marichal
P   R. Sadecki
P   R. Herbel
RP   F. Linzy
RP   J. Gibbon
RP   L. McDaniel

SF 1968 N
M   H. Franks
1B   W. McCovey
2B   R. Hunt
SS   H. Lanier
3B   J. Davenport
OF   W. Mays
OF   J. Alou
OF   B. Bonds
C   R. Dietz
UT   T. Cline
UT   J. Hart
P   J. Marichal
P   G. Perry
P   R. Sadecki
P   M. McCormick
P   B. Bolin
RP   F. Linzy

SF 1969 N
M   C. King
1B   W. McCovey
2B   R. Hunt
SS   H. Lanier
3B   J. Davenport
OF   B. Bonds
OF   K. Henderson
OF   W. Mays
C   R. Dietz
UT   E. Burda
UT   D. Marshall
UT   D. Mason
P   G. Perry
P   J. Marichal
P   M. McCormick
P   B. Bolin
P   R. Sadecki
RP   F. Linzy
RP   R. Herbel

SF 1970 N
M   C. King
M   C. Fox
1B   W. McCovey
2B   R. Hunt
SS   H. Lanier
3B   A. Gallagher
OF   B. Bonds
OF   K. Henderson
OF   W. Mays
C   R. Dietz
UT   R. Fuentes
P   G. Perry

P   J. Marichal
P   R. Robertson
P   F. Reberger
RP   R. Bryant
RP   D. McMahon
RP   J. Johnson

SF 1971 N
M   C. Fox
1B   W. McCovey
2B   R. Fuentes
SS   C. Speier
3B   A. Gallagher
OF   B. Bonds
OF   K. Henderson
OF   W. Mays
C   R. Dietz
UT   H. Lanier
P   G. Perry
P   J. Marichal
P   J. Cumberland
P   R. Bryant
P   S. Stone
RP   J. Johnson
RP   D. McMahon
RP   R. Robertson

SF 1972 N
M   C. Fox
1B   W. McCovey
2B   R. Fuentes
SS   C. Speier
3B   A. Gallagher
OF   B. Bonds
OF   K. Henderson
OF   G. Maddox
C   D. Rader
UT   D. Kingman
P   R. Bryant
P   J. Barr
P   J. Marichal
P   S. McDowell
P   S. Stone
RP   J. Johnson
RP   R. Moffitt
RP   D. McMahon

SF 1973 N
M   C. Fox
1B   W. McCovey
2B   R. Fuentes
SS   C. Speier
3B   A. Gallagher
OF   B. Bonds
OF   G. Matthews
OF   G. Maddox
C   D. Rader
UT   D. Kingman
UT   G. Thomasson
P   R. Bryant
P   J. Barr
P   T. Bradley
P   J. Marichal
P   J. Willoughby
RP   E. Sosa
RP   R. Moffitt
RP   D. Carrithers

SF 1974 N
M   C. Fox
M   W. Westrum
1B   D. Kingman
2B   R. Fuentes
SS   C. Speier
3B   S. Ontiveros
OF   G. Matthews
OF   B. Bonds
OF   G. Maddox
C   D. Rader
UT   J. Goodson
UT   M. Phillips
UT   G. Thomasson
P   J. Barr
P   J. D'Acquisto
P   R. Caldwell
P   T. Bradley
P   R. Bryant
RP   R. Moffitt
RP   E. Sosa
RP   C. Williams

SF 1975 N
M   W. Westrum
1B   G. Montanez
2B   D. Thomas
SS   C. Speier
3B   S. Ontiveros
OF   B. Murcer
OF   V. Joshua
OF   G. Matthews
C   D. Rader
UT   C. Miller

UT G. Thomasson
P J. Montefusco
P J. Barr
P P. Falcone
P R. Caldwell
P E. Halicki
RP C. Williams
RP G. Lavelle
RP R. Moffitt

SF 1976 N
M W. Rigney
1B D. Evans
2B M. Perez
SS C. Speier
3B K. Reitz
OF G. Matthews
OF B. Murcer
OF L. Herndon
C D. Rader
UT G. Thomasson
P J. Montefusco
P J. Barr
P E. Halicki
P R. Dressler
P J. D'Acquisto
RP G. Lavelle
RP R. Caldwell
RP R. Moffitt

SF 1977 N
M J. Altobelli
1B W. McCovey
2B R. Andrews
SS T. Foli
3B B. Madlock
OF J. Clark
OF G. Thomasson
OF T. Whitfield
C M. Hill
UT D. Evans
UT D. Thomas
P E. Halicki
P J. Barr
P R. Knepper
P J. Montefusco
RP C. Williams
RP G. Lavelle
RP D. Heaverlo

SF 1978 N
M J. Altobelli
1B W. McCovey
2B B. Madlock
SS J. LeMaster
3B D. Evans
OF J. Clark
OF L. Herndon
OF T. Whitfield
C M. Hill
UT M. Ivie
P R. Knepper
P V. Blue
P J. Montefusco
P E. Halicki
P J. Barr
RP G. Lavelle
RP R. Moffitt
RP J. Curtis

SF 1979 N
M J. Altobelli
M J. Bristol
1B M. Ivie
2B J. Strain
SS J. LeMaster
3B D. Evans
OF J. Clark
OF W. North
OF L. Herndon
C D. Littlejohn
UT W. McCovey
UT T. Whitfield
P V. Blue
P R. Knepper
P J. Montefusco
P E. Halicki
P J. Curtis
RP G. Lavelle
RP T. Griffin
RP G. Minton

SF 1980 N
M J. Bristol
1B M. Ivie
2B R. Stennett
SS J. LeMaster
3B D. Evans
OF L. Herndon
OF J. Clark
OF W. North
C M. May

UT T. Whitfield
P V. Blue
P R. Knepper
P E. Whitson
P A. Ripley
P J. Montefusco
RP T. Griffin
RP G. Lavelle
RP G. Minton

SF 1981 N
M F. Robinson
1B E. Cabell
2B J. Morgan
SS J. LeMaster
3B D. Evans
OF J. Clark
OF L. Herndon
OF J. Martin
C M. May
P D. Alexander
P T. Griffin
P V. Blue
P E. Whitson
P A. Ripley
RP A. Holland
RP G. Minton
RP F. Breining

SF 1982 N
M F. Robinson
1B C. Smith
2B J. Morgan
SS J. LeMaster
3B D. Evans
OF J. Clark
OF C. Davis
OF J. Leonard
C M. May
UT D. Bergman
UT D. Kuiper
UT J. Wohlford
P W. Laskey
P C. Hammaker
P R. Gale
P D. Martin
RP F. Breining
RP A. Holland
RP J. Barr

SF 1983 N
M F. Robinson
1B D. Evans
2B B. Wellman
SS J. LeMaster
3B T. O'Malley
OF J. Leonard
OF C. Davis
OF J. Clark
C R. Brenly
UT J. Youngblood
P F. Breining
P M. Krukow
P C. Hammaker
P W. Laskey
P A. McGaffigan
RP G. Minton
RP D. Martin
RP J. Barr

SF 1984 N
M F. Robinson
M D. Ozark
1B V. Thompson
2B J. Trillo
SS J. LeMaster
3B J. Youngblood
OF J. Leonard
OF C. Davis
OF C. Gladden
C R. Brenly
UT J. Baker
P W. Laskey
P M. Krukow
P M. Davis
P J. Robinson
RP G. Minton
RP F. Williams
RP G. Lavelle

SF 1985 N
M J. Davenport
M R. Craig
1B D. Green
2B J. Trillo
SS J. Uribe
3B J. Brown
OF J. Leonard
OF C. Davis
OF C. Gladden
C R. Brenly
P D. LaPoint

P M. Krukow
P C. Hammaker
P J. Gott
P V. Blue
RP M. Davis
RP S. Garrelts
RP G. Minton

SF 1986 N
M R. Craig
1B W. Clark
2B R. Thompson
SS J. Uribe
3B J. Brown
OF C. Davis
OF C. Maldonado
OF C. Gladden
C R. Brenly
UT J. Youngblood
P M. Krukow
P M. LaCoss
P S. Garrelts
P V. Blue
RP J. Robinson
RP M. Davis
RP J. Berenguer

SF 1987 N
M R. Craig
1B W. Clark
2B R. Thompson
SS J. Uribe
3B K. Mitchell
OF C. Davis
OF J. Leonard
OF C. Maldonado
C R. Brenly
UT M. Aldrete
UT E. Milner
UT C. Speier
P K. Downs
P M. LaCoss
P C. Hammaker
P M. Krukow
P D. Dravecky
RP S. Garrelts
RP J. Robinson
RP J. Gott

SF 1988 N
M R. Craig
1B W. Clark
2B R. Thompson
SS J. Uribe
3B K. Mitchell
OF B. Butler
OF C. Maldonado
OF M. Aldrete
C R. Melvin
P R. Reuschel
P D. Robinson
P K. Downs
P C. Hammaker
P M. Krukow
RP S. Garrelts
RP C. Lefferts
RP J. Price

SF 1989 N
M R. Craig
1B W. Clark
2B R. Thompson
SS J. Uribe
3B E. Riles
OF B. Butler
OF K. Mitchell
OF C. Maldonado
C T. Kennedy
P R. Reuschel
P D. Robinson
P S. Garrelts
P M. LaCoss
RP C. Lefferts
RP J. Brantley
RP C. Hammaker

SF 1990 N
M R. Craig
1B W. Clark
2B R. Thompson
SS J. Uribe
3B M. Williams
OF B. Butler
OF K. Mitchell
OF M. Kingery
C T. Kennedy
P J. Burkett
P S. Garrelts
P D. Robinson
P T. Wilson
RP J. Brantley
RP S. Bedrosian

RP C. Hammaker

Seattle

SEA A 1969
SEA A 1977-1990

SEA 1969 A
M J. Schultz
1B D. Mincher
2B J. Donaldson
SS R. Oyler
3B T. Harper
OF H. Comer
OF H. Davis
OF S. Hovley
C G. McNertney
P E. Brabender
P M. Pattin
P F. Talbot
RP D. Segui
RP J. Gelnar
RP J. Bouton

SEA 1977 A
M D. Johnson
1B D. Meyer
2B J. Baez
SS G. Reynolds
3B W. Stein
OF R. Jones
OF S. Braun
OF L. Stanton
C G. Stinson
DH J. Bernhardt
UT D. Collins
UT C. Lopez
P W. Abbott
P J. Montague
P R. Pole
RP E. Romo
RP D. Segui
RP M. Kekich

SEA 1978 A
M D. Johnson
1B D. Meyer
2B J. Cruz
SS G. Reynolds
3B W. Stein
OF L. Roberts
OF R. Jones
OF J. Hale
C G. Stinson
DH L. Stanton
UT B. Bochte
P P. Mitchell
P W. Abbott
P F. Honeycutt
P T. House
P J. Colborn
RP S. Rawley
RP J. Todd
RP E. Romo

SEA 1979 A
M D. Johnson
1B B. Bochte
2B J. Cruz
SS M. Mendoza
3B D. Meyer
OF R. Jones
OF L. Roberts
OF J. Simpson
C L. Cox
DH W. Horton
UT L. Milbourne
UT T. Paciorek
P M. Parrott
P F. Honeycutt
P F. Bannister
P O. Jones
P W. Abbott
RP B. McLaughlin
RP J. Montague
RP S. Rawley

SEA 1980 A
M D. Johnson
M M. Wills
1B B. Bochte
2B J. Cruz
SS M. Mendoza
3B W. Cox
OF D. Meyer
OF J. Simpson
OF L. Roberts
C L. Cox
DH W. Horton
UT J. Anderson
UT L. Milbourne

UT T. Paciorek
P F. Bannister
P W. Abbott
P F. Honeycutt
P J. Beattie
P R. Dressler
RP S. Rawley
RP B. McLaughlin
RP D. Roberts

SEA 1981 A
M M. Wills
M R. Lachemann
1B B. Bochte
2B J. Cruz
SS J. Anderson
3B L. Randle
OF T. Paciorek
OF J. Simpson
OF J. Burroughs
C J. Narron
DH R. Zisk
UT G. Gray
UT D. Meyer
P W. Abbott
P F. Bannister
P K. Clay
P B. Clark
P M. Parrott
RP S. Rawley
RP L. Andersen
RP R. Drago

SEA 1982 A
M R. Lachemann
1B G. Gray
2B J. Cruz
SS T. Cruz
3B E. Castillo
OF A. Cowens
OF D. Henderson
OF B. Bochte
C R. Sweet
DH R. Zisk
UT J. Simpson
P F. Bannister
P G. Perry
P J. Beattie
P M. Moore
P W. Nelson
RP W. Caudill
RP L. Andersen
RP E. Vande Berg

SEA 1983 A
M R. Lachemann
M D. Crandall
1B P. Putnam
2B A. Bernazard
SS S. Owen
3B J. Allen
OF D. Henderson
OF S. Henderson
OF R. Nelson
C R. Sweet
DH R. Zisk
UT A. Cowens
P M. Young
P J. Beattie
P R. Stoddard
P B. Clark
P M. Moore
RP R. Thomas
RP W. Caudill
RP M. Stanton

SEA 1984 A
M D. Crandall
M C. Cottier
1B A. Davis
2B J. Perconte
SS S. Owen
3B J. Presley
OF A. Cowens
OF P. Bradley
OF D. Henderson
C R. Kearney
DH K. Phelps
UT R. Bonnell
UT S. Henderson
P M. Langston
P M. Moore
P J. Beattie
P M. Young
RP E. Vande Berg
RP R. Stoddard
RP C. Beard

SEA 1985 A
M C. Cottier
1B A. Davis
2B J. Perconte

SS S. Owen
3B J. Presley
OF P. Bradley
OF D. Henderson
OF A. Cowens
C R. Kearney
DH J. Thomas
P M. Moore
P M. Young
P M. Langston
P F. Wills
P W. Swift
RP R. Thomas
RP E. Nunez
RP E. Vande Berg

SEA 1986 A
M C. Cottier
M O. Martinez
M R. Williams
1B A. Davis
2B H. Reynolds
SS S. Owen
3B J. Presley
OF P. Bradley
OF D. Tartabull
OF J. Moses
C R. Kearney
DH J. Thomas
UT D. Henderson
UT K. Phelps
P M. Moore
P M. Langston
P M. Morgan
P W. Swift
RP M. Young
RP M. Huismann
RP A. Guetterman

SEA 1987 A
M R. Williams
1B A. Davis
2B H. Reynolds
SS R. Quinones
3B J. Presley
OF P. Bradley
OF M. Kingery
OF J. Moses
C S. Bradley
DH K. Phelps
P M. Langston
P M. Moore
P M. Morgan
P M. Bankhead
P A. Guetterman
RP J. Reed
RP W. Wilkinson
RP M. Trujillo

SEA 1988 A
M R. Williams
M J. Snyder
1B A. Davis
2B H. Reynolds
SS R. Quinones
3B J. Presley
OF M. Brantley
OF H. Cotto
OF G. Wilson
C S. Bradley
DH K. Phelps
UT S. Balboni
P M. Langston
P M. Moore
P W. Swift
P M. Bankhead
P M. Campbell
RP M. Jackson
RP J. Reed
RP M. Schooler

SEA 1989 A
M J. Lefebvre
1B A. Davis
2B H. Reynolds
SS O. Vizquel
3B J. Presley
OF G. Griffey
OF G. Briley
OF H. Cotto
C D. Valle
DH J. Leonard
UT S. Bradley
UT D. Coles
P M. Bankhead
P B. Holman
P R. Johnson
P W. Swift
P E. Hanson
RP J. Reed
RP M. Jackson
RP M. Schooler

SEA 1990 A
M J. Lefebvre
1B P. O'Brien
2B H. Reynolds
SS O. Vizquel
3B E. Martinez
OF K. Griffey
OF H. Cotto
OF G. Briley
C D. Valle
DH A. Davis
UT S. Bradley
UT J. Leonard
P E. Hanson
P M. Young
P R. Johnson
P B. Holman
RP W. Swift
RP M. Jackson
RP M. Schooler

Syracuse

SYR N 1879
SYR a 1890

SYR 1879 N
M M. Dorgan
M W. Holbert
M J. Macullar
1B W. Carpenter
2B J. Farrell
SS J. Macullar
3B J. Woodhead
OF M. Mansell
OF W. Purcell
OF J. Richmond
C W. Holbert
UT M. Dorgan
P P. McCormick

SYR 1890 a
M G. Frazer
M W. Fessenden
M G. Frazer
1B W. McQuery
2B C. Childs
SS B. McLaughlin
3B T. O'Rourke
OF W. Wright
OF W. Ely
OF P. Friel
C G. Briggs
P D. Casey
P J. Keefe
P M. Morrison
P E. Mars

Texas

TEX A 1972-1990

TEX 1972 A
M T. Williams
1B F. Howard
2B L. Randle
SS C. Harrah
3B D. Nelson
OF T. Ford
OF J. Lovitto
OF E. Maddox
C R. Billings
UT L. Biittner
P P. Broberg
P R. Bosman
P R. Hand
P M. Paul
P W. Gogolewski
RP P. Lindblad
RP J. Panther
RP R. Pina

TEX 1973 A
M D. Herzog
M D. Wilber
M A. Martin
1B J. Spencer
2B D. Nelson
SS J. Mason
3B C. Harrah
OF J. Burroughs
OF V. Harris
OF E. Maddox
C K. Suarez
DH A. Johnson
P J. Bibby
P J. Merritt
P W. Siebert
P P. Broberg
RP W. Gogolewski

RP M. Paul
RP J. Brown

TEX 1974 A
M A. Martin
1B D. Hargrove
2B D. Nelson
SS C. Harrah
3B L. Randle
OF J. Burroughs
OF C. Tovar
OF J. Lovitto
C J. Sundberg
DH J. Spencer
UT A. Johnson
P F. Jenkins
P J. Bibby
P J. Brown
P S. Hargan
P D. Clyde
RP S. Foucault

TEX 1975 A
M A. Martin
M F. Lucchesi
1B J. Spencer
2B L. Randle
SS C. Harrah
3B R. Howell
OF J. Burroughs
OF D. Hargrove
OF T. Grieve
C J. Sundberg
DH C. Tovar
P F. Jenkins
P S. Hargan
P G. Perry
P W. Hands
RP J. Umbarger
RP S. Foucault
RP S. Thomas

TEX 1976 A
M F. Lucchesi
1B D. Hargrove
2B L. Randle
SS C. Harrah
3B R. Howell
OF J. Burroughs
OF J. Beniquez
OF E. Clines
C J. Sundberg
DH T. Grieve
P G. Perry
P N. Briles
P R. Blyleven
P J. Umbarger
P S. Hargan
RP S. Foucault
RP M. Bacsik
RP J. Terpko

TEX 1977 A
M F. Lucchesi
M E. Stanky
M C. Ryan
M G. Hunter
1B D. Hargrove
2B E. Wills
SS D. Campaneris
3B C. Harrah
OF C. Washington
OF J. Beniquez
OF D. May
C J. Sundberg
DH W. Horton
P G. Perry
P D. Alexander
P R. Blyleven
P D. Ellis
P N. Briles
RP P. Devine
RP P. Lindblad
RP D. Knowles

TEX 1978 A
M G. Hunter
M P. Corrales
1B D. Hargrove
2B E. Wills
SS D. Campaneris
3B C. Harrah
OF J. Beniquez
OF B. Bonds
OF A. Oliver
C J. Sundberg
DH R. Zisk
P J. Matlack
P F. Jenkins
P D. Alexander
P G. Medich
P D. Ellis
RP R. Cleveland
RP L. Barker

TEX 1979 A
M P. Corrales
1B P. Putnam
2B E. Wills
SS N. Norman
3B D. Bell
OF R. Zisk
OF A. Oliver
OF W. Sample
C J. Sundberg
DH J. Ellis
UT J. Grubb
P F. Jenkins
P S. Comer
P G. Medich
P D. Alexander
RP J. Kern
RP A. Lyle
RP D. Rajsich

TEX 1980 A
M P. Corrales
1B P. Putnam
2B E. Wills
SS J. Frias
3B D. Bell
OF A. Oliver
OF J. Rivers
OF J. Norris
C J. Sundberg
DH R. Zisk
UT J. Grubb
UT D. Roberts
UT D. Staub
P J. Matlack
P G. Medich
P F. Jenkins
P G. Perry
RP D. Darwin
RP A. Lyle
RP J. Kern

TEX 1981 A
M D. Zimmer
1B P. Putnam
2B E. Wills
SS M. Mendoza
3B D. Bell
OF J. Rivers
OF L. Roberts
OF W. Sample
C J. Sundberg
DH A. Oliver
UT J. Grubb
P D. Darwin
P G. Medich
P F. Honeycutt
P F. Jenkins
P J. Matlack
RP S. Comer
RP D. Schmidt

TEX 1982 A
M D. Zimmer
M D. Johnson
1B D. Hostetler
2B M. Richardt
SS M. Wagner
3B D. Bell
OF G. Wright
OF L. Parrish
OF W. Sample
C J. Sundberg
DH L. Johnson
UT J. Grubb
P C. Hough
P F. Tanana
P F. Honeycutt
P J. Matlack
P G. Medich
RP S. Comer
RP D. Darwin
RP P. Mirabella

TEX 1983 A
M D. Rader
1B P. O'Brien
2B J. Tolleson
SS R. Dent
3B D. Bell
OF G. Wright
OF W. Sample
OF L. Parrish
C J. Sundberg
DH D. Hostetler
P C. Hough
P B. Smithson
P D. Darwin
P F. Honeycutt
P F. Tanana
RP J. Matlack
RP O. Jones

TEX 1984 A
M D. Rader
1B P. O'Brien
2B J. Tolleson
SS C. Wilkerson
3B D. Bell
OF G. Ward
OF W. Sample
OF G. Wright
C D. Scott
DH L. Parrish
UT J. Rivers
P C. Hough
P F. Tanana
P D. Darwin
P D. Stewart
P M. Mason
RP D. Schmidt
RP O. Jones

TEX 1985 A
M D. Rader
M R. Valentine
1B P. O'Brien
2B C. Harrah
SS C. Wilkerson
3B D. Bell
OF G. Ward
OF O. McDowell
OF G. Wright
C D. Slaught
DH C. Johnson
UT J. Tolleson
P C. Hough
P M. Mason
P B. Hooton
P D. Noles
RP G. Harris
RP D. Rozema
RP D. Schmidt

TEX 1986 A
M R. Valentine
1B P. O'Brien
2B C. Harrah
SS S. Fletcher
3B S. Buechele
OF O. McDowell
OF P. Incaviglia
OF R. Sierra
C D. Slaught
DH L. Parrish
UT G. Ward
UT C. Wilkerson
P C. Hough
P E. Correa
P J. Guzman
P R. Witt
P M. Mason
RP G. Harris
RP M. Williams
RP J. Russell

TEX 1987 A
M R. Valentine
1B P. O'Brien
2B J. Browne
SS S. Fletcher
3B S. Buechele
OF R. Sierra
OF P. Incaviglia
OF O. McDowell
C D. Slaught
DH L. Parrish
UT R. Brower
UT E. Petralli
P C. Hough
P J. Guzman
P R. Witt
P G. Harris
RP M. Williams
RP D. Mohorcic
RP J. Russell

TEX 1988 A
M R. Valentine
1B P. O'Brien
2B C. Wilkerson
SS S. Fletcher
3B S. Buechele
OF R. Sierra
OF O. McDowell
OF C. Espy
C E. Petralli
DH L. Parrish
UT P. Incaviglia
P C. Hough
P J. Guzman
P P. Kilgus
P J. Russell
P R. Witt
RP M. Williams
RP J. McMurtry
RP D. Mohorcic

TEX 1989 A
M R. Valentine
1B R. Palmeiro
2B J. Franco
SS S. Fletcher
3B S. Buechele
OF R. Sierra
OF C. Espy
OF P. Incaviglia
C C. Kreuter
C C. Cerone
DH H. Baines
UT J. Kunkel
UT R. Leach
P L. Ryan
P R. Witt
P J. Brown
P C. Hough
P J. Jeffcoat
RP K. Rogers
RP J. Russell
RP C. Guante

TEX 1990 A
M R. Valentine
1B R. Palmeiro
2B J. Franco
SS J. Huson
3B S. Buechele
OF R. Sierra
OF P. Incaviglia
OF G. Pettis
C E. Petralli
DH H. Baines
UT J. Daugherty
UT J. Kunkel
UT R. Stanley
P R. Witt
P C. Hough
P L. Ryan
P J. Brown
P J. Moyer
RP J. Jeffcoat
RP K. Rogers
RP B. Arnsberg

Toledo

TOL a 1884
TOL a 1890-1890

TOL 1884 a
M C. Morton
1B G. Lane
2B S. Barkley
SS J. Miller
3B E. Brown
OF C. Welch
OF T. Poorman
OF F. Olin
C M. Walker
P A. Mullane
P H. O'Day

TOL 1890 a
M C. Morton
1B P. Werden
2B T. Nicholson
SS F. Scheibeck
3B W. Alvord
OF C. Swartwood
OF W. Van Dyke
OF G. Tebeau
C H. Sage
P J. Healy
P E. Cushman
P F. Smith

Toronto

TOR A 1977-1990

TOR 1977 A
M R. Hartsfield
1B D. Ault
2B S. Staggs
SS H. Torres
3B R. Howell
OF A. Woods
OF S. Bowling
OF O. Velez
C A. Ashby
DH R. Fairly
UT R. Bailor
UT S. Ewing
P D. Lemanczyk
P T. Garvin
P J. Jefferson
RP P. Vuckovich
RP M. Willis
RP J. Johnson

TOR 1978 A
M R. Hartsfield
1B J. Mayberry
2B D. McKay
SS L. Gomez
3B R. Howell
OF R. Bosetti
OF R. Bailor
OF O. Velez
C R. Cerone
DH R. Carty
P J. Jefferson
P T. Underwood
P J. Clancy
P T. Garvin
P B. Moore
RP M. Willis
RP T. Murphy
RP J. Coleman

TOR 1979 A
M R. Hartsfield
1B J. Mayberry
2B D. Ainge
SS A. Griffin
3B R. Howell
OF R. Bosetti
OF A. Woods
OF R. Bailor
C R. Cerone
DH R. Carty
UT O. Velez
P T. Underwood
P P. Huffman
P D. Lemanczyk
P B. Moore
P D. Stieb
RP D. Freisleben
RP T. Buskey

TOR 1980 A
M R. Mattick
1B J. Mayberry
2B D. Garcia
SS A. Griffin
3B R. Howell
OF R. Bonnell
OF L. Moseby
OF R. Bailor
C L. Whitt
DH O. Velez
UT A. Woods
P J. Clancy
P D. Stieb
P P. Mirabella
P J. Jefferson
RP J. McLaughlin
RP T. Garvin
RP J. Kucek

TOR 1981 A
M R. Mattick
1B J. Mayberry
2B D. Garcia
SS A. Griffin
3B D. Ainge
OF L. Moseby
OF A. Woods
OF R. Bonnell
C L. Whitt
DH O. Velez
UT G. Iorg
P D. Stieb
P L. Leal
P J. Clancy
P J. Todd
P M. Bomback
RP R. Jackson
RP J. McLaughlin
RP T. Garvin

TOR 1982 A
M R. Cox
1B W. Upshaw
2B D. Garcia
SS A. Griffin
3B S. Mulliniks
OF L. Moseby
OF J. Barfield
OF R. Bonnell
C L. Whitt
DH D. Revering
UT G. Iorg
UT H. Powell
P D. Stieb
P J. Clancy
P L. Leal
P J. Gott
RP D. Murray
RP R. Jackson
RP J. McLaughlin

TOR 1983 A
M R. Cox
1B W. Upshaw
2B D. Garcia
SS A. Griffin
3B S. Mulliniks
OF L. Moseby
OF J. Barfield
OF R. Bonnell
C L. Whitt
DH C. Johnson
UT D. Collins
UT G. Iorg
UT J. Orta
P D. Stieb
P J. Clancy
P L. Leal
P J. Gott
P D. Alexander
RP J. Acker
RP R. Jackson
RP J. McLaughlin

TOR 1984 A
M R. Cox
1B W. Upshaw
2B D. Garcia
SS A. Griffin
3B S. Mulliniks
OF L. Moseby
OF J. Bell
OF D. Collins
C L. Whitt
DH C. Johnson
UT J. Barfield
UT G. Iorg
UT J. Martinez
P D. Stieb
P D. Alexander
P L. Leal
P J. Clancy
P J. Gott
RP R. Jackson
RP D. Lamp
RP J. Acker

TOR 1985 A
M R. Cox
1B W. Upshaw
2B D. Garcia
SS O. Fernandez
3B S. Mulliniks
OF J. Bell
OF J. Barfield
OF L. Moseby
C L. Whitt
DH J. Burroughs
UT G. Iorg
P D. Stieb
P D. Alexander
P J. Key
P J. Clancy
RP D. Lamp
RP J. Acker
RP G. Lavelle

TOR 1986 A
M J. Williams
1B W. Upshaw
2B D. Garcia
SS O. Fernandez
3B S. Mulliniks
OF J. Barfield
OF L. Moseby
OF J. Bell
C L. Whitt
DH C. Johnson
UT G. Iorg
UT R. Leach
P J. Key
P J. Clancy
P D. Stieb
P J. Cerutti
P D. Alexander
RP M. Eichhorn
RP T. Henke
RP D. Lamp

TOR 1987 A
M J. Williams
1B W. Upshaw
2B G. Iorg
SS O. Fernandez
3B K. Gruber
OF J. Barfield
OF J. Moseby
OF J. Bell
C L. Whitt
DH F. McGriff
UT R. Leach
UT S. Mulliniks
P J. Key
P J. Clancy
P D. Stieb
P J. Cerutti
RP M. Eichhorn
RP J. Nunez
RP T. Henke

TOR 1988 A
M J. Williams
1B F. McGriff
2B M. Lee
SS O. Fernandez
3B K. Gruber
OF J. Bell
OF J. Barfield
OF L. Moseby
C L. Whitt
DH S. Mulliniks
UT N. Liriano
P M. Flanagan
P D. Stieb
P J. Clancy
P J. Key
P T. Stottlemyre
RP J. Cerutti
RP R. Ward
RP T. Henke

TOR 1989 A
M J. Williams
M C. Gaston
1B F. McGriff
2B N. Liriano
SS O. Fernandez
3B K. Gruber
OF J. Bell
OF L. Moseby
OF J. Felix
C L. Whitt
DH S. Mulliniks
UT M. Lee
P J. Key
P D. Stieb
P J. Cerutti
P M. Flanagan
P T. Stottlemyre
RP R. Ward
RP T. Henke
RP D. Wells

TOR 1990 A
M C. Gaston
1B F. McGriff
2B M. Lee
SS O. Fernandez
3B K. Gruber
OF W. Wilson
OF J. Felix
OF J. Bell
C P. Borders
DH J. Olerud
P D. Stieb
P T. Stottlemyre
P D. Wells
P J. Key
P J. Cerutti
RP R. Ward
RP F. Wills
RP J. Acker

Troy

TRO n 1871-1872
TRO N 1879-1882

TRO 1871 n
M L. Pike
M W. Craver
1B W. Flynn
2B W. Craver
SS C. Flowers
3B E. Bellan
OF T. York
OF S. King
OF L. Pike
C M. McGeary
P J. McMullin

TRO 1872 n
M J. Wood
1B M. McAtee

2B	J. Wood
SS	E. Bellan
3B	D. Force
OF	S. King
OF	A. Martin
OF	A. Gedney
C	D. Allison
P	G. Zettlein

TRO 1879 N

M	H. Phillips
M	R. Ferguson
1B	D. Brouthers
2B	T. Hawkes
SS	E. Caskin
3B	J. Doscher
OF	J. Evans
OF	A. Hall
OF	T. Mansell
C	C. Reilley
P	G. Bradley
P	H. Salisbury
P	F. Goldsmith

TRO 1880 N

M	R. Ferguson
1B	E. Cogswell
2B	R. Ferguson
SS	E. Caskin
3B	R. Connor
OF	P. Gillespie
OF	J. Cassidy
OF	J. Evans
C	W. Holbert
P	M. Welch
P	T. Keefe

TRO 1881 N

M	R. Ferguson
1B	R. Connor
2B	R. Ferguson
SS	E. Caskin
3B	F. Hankinson
OF	P. Gillespie
OF	J. Cassidy
OF	J. Evans
C	W. Ewing
P	T. Keefe
P	M. Welch

TRO 1882 N

M	R. Ferguson
1B	J. Smith
2B	R. Ferguson
SS	N. Pfeffer
3B	W. Ewing
OF	J. Roseman
OF	P. Gillespie
OF	R. Connor
C	W. Holbert
P	T. Keefe
P	M. Welch

Washington

OLY n 1871-1872
NAT n 1872
WAS n 1873
WAS n 1875
WAS a 1884
WAS U 1884
WAS N 1886-1889
WAS a 1891
WAS N 1892-1899
WAS A 1901-1960
WAS A 1961-1971

OLY 1871 n

M	N. Young
1B	E. Mills
2B	A. Leonard
SS	D. Force
3B	F. Waterman
OF	G. Hall
OF	J. Glenn
OF	H. Berthrong
C	D. Allison
P	A. Brainard
P	W. Stearns

OLY 1872 n

M	N. Young
1B	W. Flynn
2B	T. Beals
SS	W. Goldsmith
3B	F. Waterman
OF	J. Glenn
OF	A. Robinson
OF	G. Heubel

C	F. Selman
P	A. Brainard

NAT 1872 n

M	J. Miller
1B	P. Hines
2B	J. Hollingshead
SS	J. Doyle
3B	W. White
OF	E. Mincher
OF	O. Bielaski
OF	S. Studley
C	W. Lennon
UT	D. Coughlin

WAS 1873 n

M	N. Young
1B	J. Glenn
2B	T. Beals
SS	J. Gerhardt
3B	W. White
OF	O. Bielaski
OF	P. Hines
OF	J. Hollingshead
C	C. Snyder
UT	J. Donnelly
P	W. Stearns
P	Greyson

WAS 1875 n

M	J. Hollingshead
M	W. Parks
1B	A. Allison
2B	S. Brady
SS	J. Dailey
3B	J. Doscher
OF	L. Ressler
OF	J. Hollingshead
OF	W. Parks
C	A. Thompson
P	W. Stearns

WAS 1884 a

M	J. Hollingshead
M	Bickerson
1B	W. Prince
2B	T. Hawkes
SS	F. Fennelly
3B	J. Gladman
OF	H. Mullin
OF	W. Morgan
OF	E. Trumbull
C	J. Humphries
P	R. Barr
P	J. Hamill

WAS 1884 U

M	M. Scanlon
1B	A. Joy
2B	T. Evers
SS	J. Halpin
3B	J. McCormick
OF	H. Moore
OF	W. Wise
OF	P. Baker
C	C. Fulmer
P	W. Wise
P	A. Voss
P	C. Gagus

WAS 1886 N

M	M. Scanlon
M	J. Gaffney
1B	P. Baker
2B	J. Farrell
SS	D. Force
3B	J. Knowles
OF	S. Carroll
OF	P. Hines
OF	E. Crane
C	A. Gilligan
P	F. Shaw
P	R. Barr
P	W. Madigan
P	F. Gilmore

WAS 1887 N

M	J. Gaffney
1B	W. O'Brien
2B	J. Myers
SS	J. Farrell
3B	J. Donnelly
OF	P. Hines
OF	S. Carroll
OF	E. Daily
C	C. Mack
P	J. Whitney
P	H. O'Day
P	F. Gilmore

P	F. Shaw

WAS 1888 N

M	W. Hewett
M	T. Sullivan
1B	W. O'Brien
2B	J. Myers
SS	G. Shoch
3B	J. Donnelly
OF	W. Hoy
OF	W. Wilmot
OF	E. Daily
C	C. Mack
P	H. O'Day
P	J. Whitney
P	W. Widner
P	G. Keefe
P	F. Gilmore

WAS 1889 N

M	J. Morrill
M	A. Irwin
1B	J. Carney
2B	S. Wise
SS	A. Irwin
3B	J. Irwin
OF	W. Hoy
OF	W. Wilmot
OF	E. Beecher
C	T. Daly
UT	C. Mack
P	A. Ferson
P	G. Haddock
P	G. Keefe
P	H. O'Day
P	J. Healy

WAS 1891 a

M	S. Trott
M	C. Snyder
M	D. Shannon
M	T. Griffin
1B	W. McQuery
2B	T. Dowd
SS	G. Hatfield
3B	W. Alvord
OF	L. Murphy
OF	E. Beecher
OF	P. Hines
C	J. McGuire
P	W. Carsey
P	F. Foreman
P	E. Bakely

WAS 1892 N

M	W. Barnie
M	A. Irwin
M	D. Richardson
1B	H. Larkin
2B	T. Dowd
SS	D. Richardson
3B	W. Robinson
OF	W. Hoy
OF	C. Duffee
OF	P. Radford
C	J. McGuire
P	F. Killen
P	B. Abbey
P	P. Knell
P	J. Duryea
P	J. Meekin

WAS 1893 N

M	J. O'Rourke
1B	H. Larkin
2B	S. Wise
SS	J. Sullivan
3B	J. Mulvey
OF	W. Hoy
OF	P. Radford
OF	J. O'Rourke
C	C. Farrell
P	C. Esper
P	A. Maul
P	J. Meekin
P	J. Duryea

WAS 1894 N

M	G. Schmelz
1B	E. Cartwright
2B	F. Ward
SS	F. Scheibeck
3B	W. Joyce
OF	C. Abbey
OF	A. Selbach
OF	W. Hassamaer
C	J. McGuire
UT	P. Radford
P	G. Mercer
P	A. Maul
P	C. Esper

P	M. Sullivan
P	O. Stocksdale

WAS 1895 N

M	G. Schmelz
1B	E. Cartwright
2B	J. Crooks
SS	F. Scheibeck
3B	W. Joyce
OF	C. Abbey
OF	A. Selbach
OF	W. Hassamaer
C	J. McGuire
P	G. Mercer
P	V. Anderson
P	O. Stocksdale
P	A. Maul
P	J. Malarkey

WAS 1896 N

M	G. Schmelz
1B	E. Cartwright
2B	J. O'Brien
SS	De Montreville
3B	W. Joyce
OF	A. Selbach
OF	T. Brown
OF	W. Lush
C	J. McGuire
P	G. Mercer
P	J. McJames
P	L. German
P	C. King

WAS 1897 N

M	G. Schmelz
M	T. Brown
1B	T. Tucker
2B	J. O'Brien
SS	De Montreville
3B	C. Reilly
OF	A. Selbach
OF	T. Brown
OF	C. Abbey
C	J. McGuire
UT	G. Wrigley
P	G. Mercer
P	J. McJames
P	J. Swaim
P	C. King
P	L. German

WAS 1898 N

M	T. Brown
M	J. Doyle
M	J. McGuire
M	A. Irwin
1B	J. Doyle
2B	H. Reitz
SS	G. Wrigley
3B	J. Smith
OF	J. Gettman
OF	A. Selbach
OF	J. Anderson
C	J. McGuire
UT	C. Farrell
P	A. Weyhing
P	G. Mercer
P	W. Dinneen
P	F. Killen
P	J. Swaim

WAS 1899 N

M	A. Irwin
1B	D. McGann
2B	F. Bonner
SS	R. Padden
3B	C. Atherton
OF	J. Freeman
OF	J. Slagle
OF	J. O'Brien
C	J. McGuire
UT	G. Mercer
P	A. Weyhing
P	W. Dinneen
P	A. McFarlan

WAS 1901 A

M	J. Manning
1B	M. Grady
2B	J. Farrell
SS	W. Clingman
3B	W. Coughlin
OF	S. Dungan
OF	C. Foster
OF	I. Waldron
C	W. Clarke
P	W. Carrick
P	W. Lee
P	C. Patten
P	G. Mercer

WAS 1902 A

M	T. Loftus
1B	G. Carey
2B	J. Doyle
SS	W. Ely
3B	W. Coughlin
OF	J. Ryan
OF	E. Delahanty
OF	W. Lee
C	W. Clarke
UT	W. Keister
P	A. Orth
P	C. Patten
P	W. Carrick
P	J. Townsend

WAS 1903 A

M	T. Loftus
1B	W. Clarke
2B	W. McCormick
SS	C. Moran
3B	W. Coughlin
OF	A. Selbach
OF	J. Ryan
OF	W. Lee
C	M. Kittridge
UT	C. Robinson
P	C. Patten
P	A. Orth
P	H. Wilson
P	J. Townsend
P	E. Dunkle

WAS 1904 A

M	M. Kittridge
M	P. Donovan
1B	G. Stahl
2B	W. McCormick
SS	J. Cassidy
3B	H. Hill
OF	P. Donovan
OF	W. O'Neill
OF	F. Huelsman
C	M. Kittridge
P	C. Patten
P	J. Townsend
P	A. Jacobson
P	W. Wolfe
P	T. Hughes

WAS 1905 A

M	G. Stahl
1B	G. Stahl
2B	C. Hickman
SS	J. Cassidy
3B	H. Hill
OF	C. Jones
OF	F. Huelsman
OF	J. Anderson
C	M. Heydon
UT	G. Nill
P	C. Patten
P	T. Hughes
P	J. Townsend
P	W. Wolfe
P	A. Jacobson

WAS 1906 A

M	G. Stahl
1B	G. Stahl
2B	H. Schlafly
SS	D. Altizer
3B	L. Cross
OF	J. Anderson
OF	C. Jones
OF	C. Hickman
C	H. Wakefield
P	F. Falkenberg
P	C. Patten
P	C. Smith
P	T. Hughes
P	F. Kitson

WAS 1907 A

M	J. Cantillon
1B	J. Anderson
2B	J. Delahanty
SS	D. Altizer
3B	W. Shipke
OF	R. Ganley
OF	C. Jones
OF	O. Clymer
C	J. Warner
P	C. Smith
P	C. Patten
P	F. Falkenberg
P	T. Hughes
P	W. Johnson

WAS 1908 A

M	J. Cantillon
1B	F. Freeman
2B	J. Delahanty
SS	G. McBride
3B	W. Shipke
OF	R. Ganley
OF	J. Milan
OF	O. Pickering
C	C. Street
UT	O. Clymer
P	T. Hughes
P	W. Johnson
P	C. Smith
P	B. Keeley
P	W. Burns

WAS 1909 A

M	J. Cantillon
1B	J. Donahue
2B	J. Delahanty
SS	G. McBride
3B	W. Conroy
OF	J. Milan
OF	G. Browne
OF	J. Lelivelt
C	C. Street
UT	R. Unglaub
P	W. Johnson
P	R. Groom
P	W. Gray
P	C. Smith
P	T. Hughes

WAS 1910 A

M	J. McAleer
1B	R. Unglaub
2B	W. Killefer
SS	G. McBride
3B	N. Elberfeld
OF	H. Gessler
OF	J. Milan
OF	J. Lelivelt
C	C. Street
UT	W. Conroy
P	W. Johnson
P	R. Groom
P	W. Gray
P	E. Walker
P	F. Reisling

WAS 1911 A

M	J. McAleer
1B	H. Schaefer
2B	W. Cunningham
SS	G. McBride
3B	W. Conroy
OF	J. Milan
OF	H. Gessler
OF	C. Walker
C	C. Street
UT	N. Elberfeld
P	W. Johnson
P	R. Groom
P	T. Hughes
P	E. Walker
P	W. Gray

WAS 1912 A

M	C. Griffith
1B	A. Gandil
2B	R. Morgan
SS	G. McBride
3B	E. Foster
OF	J. Milan
OF	D. Moeller
OF	H. Shanks
C	J. Henry
P	W. Johnson
P	R. Groom
P	T. Hughes
P	J. Cashion

WAS 1913 A

M	C. Griffith
1B	A. Gandil
2B	R. Morgan
SS	G. McBride
3B	E. Foster
OF	J. Milan
OF	D. Moeller
OF	H. Shanks
C	J. Henry
P	W. Johnson
P	R. Groom
P	J. Boehling
P	J. Engel
P	T. Hughes

WAS 1914 A

M	C. Griffith
1B	A. Gandil
2B	R. Morgan
SS	G. McBride
3B	E. Foster
OF	D. Moeller
OF	H. Shanks
OF	J. Milan
C	J. Henry
P	W. Johnson
P	Y. Ayers
P	J. Shaw
P	J. Boehling
P	J. Bentley
RP	H. Harper

WAS 1915 A

M	C. Griffith
1B	A. Gandil
2B	R. Morgan
SS	G. McBride
3B	E. Foster
OF	J. Milan
OF	D. Moeller
OF	H. Shanks
C	J. Henry
P	W. Johnson
P	M. Gallia
P	J. Boehling
P	Y. Ayers
P	J. Shaw

WAS 1916 A

M	C. Griffith
1B	J. Judge
2B	R. Morgan
SS	G. McBride
3B	E. Foster
OF	J. Milan
OF	H. Shanks
OF	D. Moeller
C	J. Henry
P	W. Johnson
P	M. Gallia
P	H. Harper
P	Y. Ayers
P	J. Boehling

WAS 1917 A

M	C. Griffith
1B	J. Judge
2B	R. Morgan
SS	H. Shanks
3B	E. Foster
OF	E. Rice
OF	J. Milan
OF	M. Menosky
C	E. Ainsmith
UT	J. Leonard
P	W. Johnson
P	J. Shaw
P	M. Gallia
P	Y. Ayers
P	G. Dumont

WAS 1918 A

M	C. Griffith
1B	J. Judge
2B	R. Morgan
SS	J. Lavan
3B	E. Foster
OF	J. Milan
OF	B. Shotton
OF	F. Schulte
C	E. Ainsmith
UT	H. Shanks
P	W. Johnson
P	H. Harper
P	J. Shaw
P	Y. Ayers

WAS 1919 A

M	C. Griffith
1B	J. Judge
2B	H. Janvrin
SS	H. Shanks
3B	E. Foster
OF	E. Rice
OF	M. Menosky
OF	J. Milan
C	V. Picinich
UT	E. Gharrity
P	J. Shaw
P	W. Johnson
P	H. Harper
P	E. Erickson

WAS 1920 A

M	C. Griffith

1B	J. Judge
2B	S. Harris
SS	J. O'Neill
3B	F. Ellerbe
OF	E. Rice
OF	R. Roth
OF	J. Milan
C	E. Gharrity
UT	H. Shanks
P	J. Zachary
P	E. Erickson
P	J. Shaw
P	H. Courtney
P	W. Johnson

WAS 1921 A

M	G. McBride
1B	J. Judge
2B	S. Harris
SS	J. O'Rourke
3B	H. Shanks
OF	E. Rice
OF	E. Miller
OF	J. Milan
C	E. Gharrity
P	G. Mogridge
P	W. Johnson
P	J. Zachary
P	H. Courtney
RP	A. Schacht

WAS 1922 A

M	J. Milan
1B	J. Judge
2B	S. Harris
SS	R. Peckinpaugh
3B	R. LaMotte
OF	E. Rice
OF	F. Brower
OF	L. Goslin
C	E. Gharrity
P	W. Johnson
P	G. Mogridge
P	R. Francis
P	J. Zachary
P	E. Erickson

WAS 1923 A

M	O. Bush
1B	J. Judge
2B	S. Harris
SS	R. Peckinpaugh
3B	O. Bluege
OF	L. Goslin
OF	E. Rice
OF	H. Leibold
C	H. Ruel
UT	J. Evans
P	W. Johnson
P	G. Mogridge
P	J. Zachary
P	A. Russell
P	P. Zahniser

WAS 1924 A

M	S. Harris
1B	J. Judge
2B	S. Harris
SS	R. Peckinpaugh
3B	O. Bluege
OF	E. Rice
OF	L. Goslin
OF	H. Leibold
C	H. Ruel
P	W. Johnson
P	G. Mogridge
P	J. Zachary
P	F. Marberry
P	J. Martina
RP	A. Russell
RP	B. Speece

WAS 1925 A

M	S. Harris
1B	J. Judge
2B	S. Harris
SS	R. Peckinpaugh
3B	O. Bluege
OF	E. Rice
OF	L. Goslin
OF	G. McNeely
C	H. Ruel
UT	J. Harris
P	S. Coveleski
P	W. Johnson
P	W. Ruether
P	J. Zachary
RP	F. Marberry
RP	S. Gregg
RP	A. Russell

WAS 1926 A

M	S. Harris
1B	J. Judge
2B	S. Harris
SS	C. Myer
3B	O. Bluege
OF	E. Rice
OF	L. Goslin
OF	G. McNeely
C	H. Ruel
UT	J. Harris
P	W. Johnson
P	S. Coveleski
P	W. Ruether
P	A. Crowder
P	W. Ogden
RP	F. Marberry
RP	W. Morrell
RP	J. Ferguson

WAS 1927 A

M	S. Harris
1B	J. Judge
2B	S. Harris
SS	R. Reeves
3B	O. Bluege
OF	L. Goslin
OF	E. Rice
OF	T. Speaker
C	H. Ruel
P	H. Lisenbee
P	H. Thurston
P	I. Hadley
P	W. Johnson
P	J. Zachary
RP	F. Marberry
RP	E. Braxton
RP	B. Burke

WAS 1928 A

M	S. Harris
1B	J. Judge
2B	S. Harris
SS	R. Reeves
3B	O. Bluege
OF	E. Rice
OF	L. Goslin
OF	S. West
C	H. Ruel
UT	E. Barnes
P	I. Hadley
P	S. Jones
P	E. Braxton
P	F. Marberry
P	N. Gaston

WAS 1929 A

M	W. Johnson
1B	J. Judge
2B	C. Myer
SS	J. Cronin
3B	M. Hayes
OF	E. Rice
OF	L. Goslin
OF	S. West
C	H. Tate
P	F. Marberry
P	I. Hadley
P	E. Braxton
P	L. Brown
P	S. Jones

WAS 1930 A

M	W. Johnson
1B	J. Judge
2B	C. Myer
SS	J. Cronin
3B	O. Bluege
OF	E. Rice
OF	S. West
OF	H. Manush
C	R. Spencer
P	I. Hadley
P	A. Crowder
P	L. Brown
P	F. Marberry
P	S. Jones

WAS 1931 A

M	W. Johnson
1B	J. Kuhel
2B	C. Myer
SS	J. Cronin
3B	O. Bluege
OF	H. Manush
OF	S. West
OF	E. Rice
C	R. Spencer
P	L. Brown
P	A. Crowder
P	F. Marberry
P	C. Fischer
P	I. Hadley

WAS 1932 A

M	W. Johnson
1B	J. Kuhel
2B	C. Myer
SS	J. Cronin
3B	O. Bluege
OF	H. Manush
OF	S. West
OF	C. Reynolds
C	R. Spencer
UT	E. Rice
P	A. Crowder
P	M. Weaver
P	L. Brown
P	F. Marberry
P	A. Thomas

WAS 1933 A

M	J. Cronin
1B	J. Kuhel
2B	C. Myer
SS	J. Cronin
3B	O. Bluege
OF	H. Manush
OF	F. Schulte
OF	L. Goslin
C	J. Sewell
P	A. Crowder
P	E. Whitehill
P	W. Stewart
P	M. Weaver
P	A. Thomas
RP	J. Russell
RP	B. Burke
RP	W. McAfee

WAS 1934 A

M	J. Cronin
1B	J. Kuhel
2B	C. Myer
SS	J. Cronin
3B	C. Travis
OF	F. Schulte
OF	H. Manush
OF	J. Stone
C	E. Phillips
UT	O. Bluege
UT	D. Harris
P	E. Whitehill
P	M. Weaver
P	R. Burke
P	W. Stewart
P	A. Thomas
RP	J. Russell
RP	A. McColl

WAS 1935 A

M	S. Harris
1B	J. Kuhel
2B	C. Myer
SS	O. Bluege
3B	C. Travis
OF	A. Powell
OF	J. Stone
OF	H. Manush
C	W. Bolton
P	E. Whitehill
P	I. Hadley
P	L. Newsom
P	E. Linke
RP	J. Russell
RP	L. Pettit

WAS 1936 A

M	S. Harris
1B	J. Kuhel
2B	O. Bluege
SS	C. Travis
3B	J. Lewis
OF	J. Stone
OF	W. Chapman
OF	C. Reynolds
C	W. Bolton
UT	R. Kress
P	L. Newsom
P	J. DeShong
P	E. Whitehill
P	P. Appleton
P	J. Cascarella
RP	J. Russell

WAS 1937 A

M	S. Harris
1B	J. Kuhel
2B	C. Myer
SS	C. Travis
3B	J. Lewis
OF	J. Stone
OF	A. Simmons
OF	B. Almada
C	R. Ferrell
P	J. DeShong
P	W. Ferrell
P	M. Weaver
P	P. Appleton
P	E. Linke
RP	S. Cohen

WAS 1938 A

M	S. Harris
1B	H. Bonura
2B	C. Myer
SS	C. Travis
3B	J. Lewis
OF	A. Simmons
OF	G. Case
OF	S. West
C	R. Ferrell
UT	T. Wright
P	E. Leonard
P	P. Appleton
P	K. Chase
P	W. Ferrell
P	H. Kelley
RP	E. Hogsett

WAS 1939 A

M	S. Harris
1B	J. Vernon
2B	J. Bloodworth
SS	C. Travis
3B	J. Lewis
OF	T. Wright
OF	G. Case
OF	S. West
C	R. Ferrell
P	E. Leonard
P	K. Chase
P	J. Krakauskas
P	J. Haynes
P	A. Carrasquel
RP	P. Appleton
RP	W. Masterson

WAS 1940 A

M	S. Harris
1B	H. Bonura
2B	J. Bloodworth
SS	J. Pofahl
3B	C. Travis
OF	G. Case
OF	G. Walker
OF	J. Lewis
C	R. Ferrell
P	E. Leonard
P	K. Chase
P	S. Hudson
P	W. Masterson
P	J. Krakauskas
RP	J. Haynes
RP	A. Carrasquel

WAS 1941 A

M	S. Harris
1B	J. Vernon
2B	J. Bloodworth
SS	C. Travis
3B	G. Archie
OF	R. Cramer
OF	G. Case
OF	J. Lewis
C	J. Early
P	E. Leonard
P	S. Hudson
P	K. Chase
P	S. Sundra
P	A. Anderson
RP	A. Carrasquel
RP	W. Zuber
RP	W. Masterson

WAS 1942 A

M	S. Harris
1B	J. Vernon
2B	E. Clary
SS	J. Sullivan
3B	R. Estalella
OF	S. Spence
OF	G. Case
OF	B. Campbell
C	J. Early
P	S. Hudson
P	L. Newsom
P	E. Wynn
P	A. Carrasquel
P	W. Masterson

WAS 1943 A

M	O. Bluege
1B	J. Vernon
2B	G. Priddy
SS	J. Sullivan
3B	E. Clary
OF	S. Spence
OF	G. Case
OF	R. Johnson
C	J. Early
P	E. Wynn
P	E. Leonard
P	M. Candini
P	M. Haefner
P	A. Carrasquel

WAS 1944 A

M	O. Bluege
1B	J. Kuhel
2B	G. Myatt
SS	J. Sullivan
3B	D. Torres
OF	S. Spence
OF	G. Case
OF	A. Powell
C	R. Ferrell
P	E. Leonard
P	M. Haefner
P	E. Wynn
P	J. Niggeling
P	R. Wolff
RP	W. LeFebvre

WAS 1945 A

M	O. Bluege
1B	J. Kuhel
2B	G. Myatt
SS	D. Torres
3B	H. Clift
OF	G. Binks
OF	G. Case
OF	J. Lewis
C	R. Ferrell
P	R. Wolff
P	M. Haefner
P	M. Pieretti
P	E. Leonard
P	J. Niggeling
RP	C. Ullrich

WAS 1946 A

M	O. Bluege
1B	J. Vernon
2B	G. Priddy
SS	W. Hitchcock
3B	C. Travis
OF	S. Spence
OF	J. Lewis
OF	J. Grace
C	A. Evans
P	M. Haefner
P	L. Newsom
P	E. Leonard
P	R. Scarborough
P	S. Hudson
RP	M. Pieretti

WAS 1947 A

M	O. Bluege
1B	J. Vernon
2B	G. Priddy
SS	M. Christman
3B	E. Yost
OF	S. Spence
OF	J. Lewis
OF	J. Grace
C	A. Evans
UT	S. Robertson
P	W. Masterson
P	E. Wynn
P	M. Haefner
P	R. Scarborough
P	S. Hudson
RP	M. Candini
RP	T. Ferrick
RP	S. Cary

WAS 1948 A

M	J. Kuhel
1B	J. Vernon
2B	A. Kozar
SS	M. Christman
3B	E. Yost
OF	G. Coan
OF	E. Stewart
OF	E. Wooten
C	J. Early
P	E. Wynn
P	W. Masterson
P	R. Scarborough
P	S. Hudson
P	M. Haefner
RP	D. Thompson
RP	M. Candini

WAS 1949 A

M	J. Kuhel
1B	W. Robinson
2B	A. Kozar
SS	S. Dente
3B	E. Yost
OF	C. Vollmer
OF	E. Stewart
OF	G. Coan
C	A. Evans
UT	J. Lewis
P	S. Hudson
P	R. Scarborough
P	P. Calvert
P	M. Harris
P	L. Hittle
RP	J. Haynes
RP	R. Welteroth

WAS 1950 A

M	S. Harris
1B	J. Vernon
2B	C. Michaels
SS	S. Dente
3B	E. Yost
OF	I. Noren
OF	E. Stewart
OF	S. Mele
C	A. Evans
UT	G. Coan
P	S. Hudson
P	R. Kuzava
P	C. Marrero
P	S. Consuegra
P	J. Haynes
RP	M. Harris
RP	J. Pearce

WAS 1951 A

M	S. Harris
1B	J. Vernon
2B	C. Michaels
SS	J. Runnels
3B	E. Yost
OF	G. Coan
OF	I. Noren
OF	S. Mele
C	F. Guerra
P	C. Marrero
P	S. Consuegra
P	D. Johnson
P	S. Hudson
P	E. Porterfield
RP	M. Harris
RP	J. Haynes

WAS 1952 A

M	S. Harris
1B	J. Vernon
2B	F. Baker
SS	J. Runnels
3B	E. Yost
OF	J. Jensen
OF	J. Busby
OF	G. Coan
C	N. Grasso
P	E. Porterfield
P	C. Marrero
P	F. Shea
P	W. Masterson
P	J. Moreno
RP	S. Consuegra
RP	D. Johnson
RP	T. Ferrick

WAS 1953 A

M	S. Harris
1B	J. Vernon
2B	W. Terwilliger
SS	J. Runnels
3B	E. Yost
OF	J. Busby
OF	J. Jensen
OF	C. Vollmer
C	E. Fitzgerald
P	E. Porterfield
P	W. Masterson
P	F. Shea
P	C. Stobbs
P	C. Marrero
RP	J. Dixon
RP	A. Sima
RP	J. Lane

WAS 1954 A

M	S. Harris
1B	J. Vernon
2B	W. Terwilliger
SS	J. Runnels
3B	E. Yost
OF	J. Busby
OF	R. Sievers
OF	T. Umphlett
C	E. Fitzgerald
P	E. Porterfield
P	M. McDermott
P	J. Schmitz
P	C. Stobbs
P	D. Stone
RP	C. Pascual
RP	C. Keriazakos
RP	V. Stewart

WAS 1955 A

M	C. Dressen
1B	J. Vernon
2B	J. Runnels
SS	J. Valdivielso
3B	E. Yost
OF	R. Sievers
OF	T. Umphlett
OF	C. Paula
C	E. Fitzgerald
UT	J. Oravetz
P	D. Stone
P	E. Porterfield
P	J. Schmitz
P	M. McDermott
P	C. Stobbs
RP	P. Ramos
RP	T. Abernathy
RP	P. Shea

WAS 1956 A

M	C. Dressen
1B	R. Sievers
2B	J. Runnels
SS	J. Valdivielso
3B	E. Yost
OF	J. Lemon
OF	H. Herzog
OF	K. Olson
C	C. Courtney
UT	L. Berberet
P	C. Stobbs
P	C. Pascual
P	P. Ramos
P	D. Stone
P	R. Wiesler
RP	H. Griggs
RP	R. Chakales
RP	C. Grob

WAS 1957 A

M	C. Dressen
M	H. Lavagetto
1B	J. Runnels
2B	H. Plews
SS	E. Bridges
3B	E. Yost
OF	J. Lemon
OF	R. Sievers
OF	R. Usher
C	L. Berberet
UT	J. Becquer
P	P. Ramos
P	C. Stobbs
P	C. Pascual
P	R. Kemmerer
RP	T. Clevenger
RP	R. Hyde
RP	E. Byerly

WAS 1958 A

M	H. Lavagetto
1B	N. Zauchin
2B	K. Aspromonte
SS	E. Bridges
3B	E. Yost
OF	A. Pearson
OF	J. Lemon
OF	R. Sievers
C	C. Courtney
UT	B. Chrisley
UT	H. Plews
P	P. Ramos
P	R. Kemmerer
P	C. Pascual
P	H. Griggs
P	V. Valentinetti
RP	T. Clevenger
RP	R. Hyde

WAS 1959 A

M	H. Lavagetto
1B	R. Sievers
2B	R. Bertoia
SS	W. Consolo
3B	H. Killebrew
OF	W. Allison

OF	J. Lemon
OF	M. Throneberry
C	H. Naragon
UT	J. Becquer
P	C. Pascual
P	P. Ramos
P	R. Kemmerer
P	W. Fischer
RP	T. Clevenger
RP	H. Griggs
RP	C. Stobbs

WAS 1960 A

M	H. Lavagetto
1B	J. Becquer
2B	W. Gardner
SS	J. Valdivielso
3B	R. Bertoia
OF	J. Lemon
OF	W. Allison
OF	L. Green
C	E. Battey
UT	W. Consolo
UT	D. Dobbek
UT	H. Killebrew
P	P. Ramos
P	D. Lee
P	C. Pascual
P	J. Kralick
RP	T. Clevenger
RP	C. Stobbs
RP	H. Woodeshick

WAS 1961 A

M	J. Vernon
1B	R. Long
2B	C. Cottier
SS	O. Veal
3B	D. O'Connell
OF	W. Tasby
OF	R. Keough
OF	C. Hinton
C	G. Green
UT	J. King
UT	E. Woodling
P	J. McClain
P	B. Daniels
P	R. Donovan
P	E. Hobaugh
P	P. Burnside
RP	M. Kutyna

RP	J. Klippstein
RP	D. Sisler

WAS 1962 A

M	J. Vernon
1B	H. Bright
2B	C. Cottier
SS	K. Hamlin
3B	R. Johnson
OF	C. Hinton
OF	J. Piersall
OF	J. King
C	K. Retzer
UT	W. Hicks
P	D. Stenhouse
P	F. Rudolph
P	T. Cheney
P	B. Daniels
P	C. Osteen
RP	S. Hamilton
RP	M. Kutyna
RP	E. Hobaugh

WAS 1963 A

M	J. Vernon
M	E. Yost
M	G. Hodges
1B	L. Osborne
2B	C. Cottier
SS	E. Brinkman
3B	D. Zimmer
OF	D. Lock
OF	C. Hinton
OF	J. King
C	K. Retzer
UT	S. Minoso
UT	R. Phillips
P	C. Osteen
P	F. Rudolph
P	B. Daniels
P	T. Cheney
P	J. Duckworth
RP	R. Kline
RP	P. Burnside
RP	E. Roebuck

WAS 1964 A

M	G. Hodges
1B	W. Skowron

2B	D. Blasingame
SS	E. Brinkman
3B	J. Kennedy
OF	D. Lock
OF	C. Hinton
OF	J. King
C	T. Brumley
UT	R. Phillips
UT	F. Valentine
UT	D. Zimmer
P	C. Osteen
P	L. Narum
P	B. Daniels
P	A. Koch
RP	S. Ridzik
RP	J. Hannan
RP	R. Kline

WAS 1965 A

M	G. Hodges
1B	R. Nen
2B	D. Blasingame
SS	E. Brinkman
3B	K. McMullen
OF	F. Howard
OF	D. Lock
OF	W. Held
C	T. Brumley
UT	K. Hamlin
UT	J. King
UT	W. Kirkland
P	P. Richert
P	F. Ortega
P	L. Narum
P	M. McCormick
P	B. Daniels
RP	S. Ridzik
RP	R. Kline
RP	F. Kreutzer

WAS 1966 A

M	G. Hodges
1B	R. Nen
2B	R. Saverine
SS	E. Brinkman
3B	K. McMullen
OF	F. Valentine
OF	F. Howard

OF	D. Lock
C	P. Casanova
UT	J. King
UT	W. Kirkland
P	P. Richert
P	M. McCormick
P	F. Ortega
P	J. Hannan
RP	J. Cox
RP	R. Humphreys
RP	R. Kline

WAS 1967 A

M	G. Hodges
1B	M. Epstein
2B	B. Allen
SS	E. Brinkman
3B	K. McMullen
OF	F. Howard
OF	F. Valentine
OF	C. Peterson
C	P. Casanova
UT	H. Allen
UT	T. Cullen
UT	R. Nen
P	F. Ortega
P	C. Pascual
P	R. Moore
P	J. Coleman
P	F. Bertaina
RP	D. Knowles
RP	R. Priddy
RP	R. Humphreys

WAS 1968 A

M	J. Lemon
1B	M. Epstein
2B	B. Allen
SS	R. Hansen
3B	K. McMullen
OF	D. Unser
OF	F. Howard
OF	E. Stroud
C	P. Casanova
P	J. Coleman
P	C. Pascual
P	J. Hannan

P	R. Bosman
P	F. Bertaina
RP	D. Higgins
RP	R. Humphreys

WAS 1969 A

M	T. Williams
1B	M. Epstein
2B	B. Allen
SS	E. Brinkman
3B	K. McMullen
OF	D. Unser
OF	F. Howard
OF	H. Allen
C	P. Casanova
UT	G. Alyea
UT	T. Cullen
UT	E. Stroud
P	J. Coleman
P	R. Bosman
P	J. Cox
P	J. Hannan
P	R. Moore
RP	J. Shellenback
RP	D. Higgins
RP	D. Knowles

WAS 1970 A

M	T. Williams
1B	M. Epstein
2B	T. Cullen
SS	E. Brinkman
3B	A. Rodriguez
OF	F. Howard
OF	E. Stroud
OF	D. Unser
C	P. Casanova
UT	B. Allen
UT	F. Reichardt
P	R. Bosman
P	J. Coleman
P	J. Cox
P	J. Hannan
P	G. Brunet
RP	D. Knowles
RP	J. Grzenda
RP	H. Pina

WAS 1971 A

M	T. Williams
1B	D. Mincher
2B	T. Cullen
SS	C. Harrah
3B	D. Nelson
OF	D. Unser
OF	E. Maddox
OF	F. Howard
C	P. Casanova
UT	B. Allen
UT	R. Billings
UT	T. McCraw
P	R. Bosman
P	D. McLain
P	P. Broberg
P	W. Gogolewski
P	J. Shellenback
RP	J. Cox
RP	P. Lindblad
RP	D. Riddleberger

Wilmington

WIL U 1884

WIL 1884 U

M	J. Simmons
1B	E. Snyder
2B	C. Bastian
SS	H. Myers
3B	J. Say
OF	T. Lynch
OF	J. Munce
OF	Fisher
C	A. Cusick
P	J. Murphy
P	E. Nolan
P	D. Casey
P	E. Bakely

Worcester

WOR N 1880-1882

WOR 1880 N

M	F. Bancroft
1B	J. Sullivan
2B	G. Creamer
SS	A. Irwin
3B	A. Whitney
OF	G. Wood
OF	A. Knight
OF	H. Stovey
C	C. Bennett
P	J. Richmond

WOR 1881 N

M	M. Dorgan
M	H. Stovey
1B	H. Stovey
2B	G. Creamer
SS	A. Irwin
3B	W. Carpenter
OF	L. Dickerson
OF	P. Hotaling
OF	F. Corey
C	A. Bushong
P	J. Richmond
P	P. McCormick

WOR 1882 N

M	F. Brown
M	T. Bond
M	J. Chapman
1B	H. Stovey
2B	G. Creamer
SS	A. Irwin
3B	F. Mann
OF	J. Evans
OF	J. Hayes
OF	J. Clinton
C	A. Bushong
UT	F. Corey
P	J. Richmond
P	F. Mountain

The Manager Roster

This section details the managerial record of every man who ever held the reins of a major league club from 1871 through 1990. For many years, the assignment of wins and losses was thought a relatively simple task—almost as simple as identifying the managers themselves. In recent years, however, Richard Topp and Robert Tiemann wondered how it was that "managers" who never set foot on the field to lead their charges or even accompanied their clubs on road trips could be regarded as managers at all, at least in the commonly understood sense of field manager rather than business manager. Topp and Tiemann wondered how John McGraw, for example, could be credited as manager of the New York Giants for all of 1924 when a knee injury kept him from the bench for seven weeks: Somebody else must have run the team, they figured, so why not credit that man as interim manager?

That there were record-keeping errors in the 1870s or even the early 1900s may strike the average fan as unsurprising, but the incorrect assignment of decisions to helmsmen has been characteristic of every decade, up to and including the 1980s. Tiemann and Topp undertook a complete review of managerial records dating back to the National Association and found that the records published in previous baseball encyclopedias were wrong—so wrong that they had to be refigured from scratch. Here are the criteria they established for their groundbreaking study:

1. *Definition* A manager is the person designated by the club ownership to run the club on the field.
2. *Absences* When the regular manager is unable to be with the team for 30 or more days, the assistant in charge during his absence should be credited with the team's record from the time the absence begins until the regular manager returns to active duty.
3. *Interim manager* When a manager is removed, either by resignation or by being fired, and his designated replacement is not present to replace him, the assistant temporarily in charge of the team shall be credited with the team's record during the interim.
4. *Head coaches* From 1961 through 1964, the Chicago Cubs had a "panel of coaches" rather than a single manager. One of these coaches was designated *head coach* for a period of time; and that coach is credited with the team's record during his term as head coach.
5. *Captains* During the early years of professional baseball, the man who had the title of "manager" often served merely as the club's business manager, while the captain (a player) was responsible for the team on the field. Some captains were also managers. Each ambiguous situation is judged according to its particular circumstances, but in general the captain, rather than the manager, is credited with the team's record if the manager did not travel with the team or did not have previous baseball experience.
6. *Suspended games* If a game was suspended when one man was managing the team and was completed on a later date when another man was managing, the second manager is credited if the game was suspended before five innings were completed. If the game was suspended after five or more innings were played, then:

(a) credit the first manager with a win if the team was leading at the point of suspension and maintained the lead to win the game; or
(b) credit the first manager with a loss if the team was losing at the point of suspension and remained behind to lose the game; or
(c) credit the second manager with a win (or tie) if the team was losing at the point of suspension but came back to tie the score or win the game; or
(d) credit the second manager with a loss if the team was winning at the point of suspension but then lost the lead and/or game; or
(e) credit the second manager with the win or loss if the score was tied at the point of suspension.

7. *Protested games* If a protest was granted and the game was ordered resumed from the point of protest, then the same rules used for suspended games apply. If a protested game of at least five innings' duration was ordered replayed in its entirety, then no win or loss is credited, but both managers are credited with a no-decision game.
8. *Forfeited games* All forfeited games are counted as games managed, even if the game did not start or if it did not go five innings.
9. *Split seasons* In 1892 the National League played a split season, the winners meeting for the championship. In 1981, because of a players' strike, the National and American Leagues played split seasons. The managers' totals will have entries for each half-season.
10. *Replacement clubs* In the American Association (1882–1891), there were three instances in which one club dropped out and was replaced by another club. In 1884 Richmond replaced Washington; in 1890 Baltimore replaced Brooklyn; and in 1891 Milwaukee replaced Cincinnati. In each case, the new club inherited the old club's record. Therefore, the manager of the new club is credited with starting in the position (standing) in which the old club finished.

In the Union Association (1884), when a new club

replaced an old one, the new club started with a 0–0 record rather than inheriting the old club's record, except in the case of the Chicago franchise, which moved to Pittsburgh. Therefore, all such Union Association managers are credited with a finish as if their teams had begun their season at the beginning of the league season. The finish for each manager is his club's standing in the eight-team league when (a) he left the job, (b) his club dropped out of the league, or (c) his club finished the season. The clubs that dropped out were Altoona (replaced by Kansas City); Philadelphia (replaced by Wilmington); Wilmington (replaced by St. Paul); and Pittsburgh (replaced by Milwaukee).

In a typical entry in the Manager Roster (a hypothetical entry has been created below), the column marked STANDING will, in cases where a team has had only one manager throughout the year, show the team's final standing (in the example below, see the entry for 1972). In the case of a manager who began the season but was replaced midway, however, the figure on the left of the column shows the team's standing when he departed and the figure on the right shows the team's final standing (in the example below, see the entry for 1976). In the case of a manager who finished the season but did not begin it, the team's standing when he took over is shown on the left and the final standing on the right (see the entry for 1978). In the case of a manager who began when the season was already under way but who failed to finish, the figure on the left of the column shows the team's standing when he took over; the middle figure shows the team's standing when he departed; and a third figure shows the team's final standing (see the entry for 1977). The figure in the next column represents the number of wins predicted by the team's runs scored and runs allowed, with about ten extra runs being required for each win beyond .500. Last, the number of wins in the A-E column, which may be a positive figure or a negative figure, reflects the extent to which a manager may have stretched (or hindered) his available talent. The bottom line of a manager's entry provides his career totals, beginning at the left with the number of years, full or partial, in which he managed a major league club. The symbols shown in the sample entry are explained after the example.

Whenever a manager served two or more teams in the same year, the totals for each club are shown separately (see the entry above for 1973). The split seasons of 1892 and 1981 are indicated with separate records for each half. A figure to the right of the year indicates first half or second half (see entry above for 1981).

TM/L	Team and League
G	Games managed (including ties)
W	Wins
L	Losses
PCT	Percentage of games won
M/Y	Manager/Year (The latter figure indicates how many managers the team employed that year, while the former indicates the chronological position of the manager whose entry it is; "2/5," for example, would mean that this manager was the second of the team's five managers during that year.)
W-EXP	Expected Wins Calculated for the team based on its actual runs scored and allowed, not its predicted runs scored and runs allowed. A team that allows exactly as many runs as it scores is predicted to play .500 ball. The equation for expected wins is:

$$\frac{\text{Runs Scored} - \text{Runs Allowed} + 81}{\text{Runs Per Win}}$$

A-E	Actual Wins Minus Expected Wins (A measure of the extent to which a team outperformed or underperformed its talent; for a single season or two a high figure may be attributable to chance, but over time one must credit good managing.)
E	Eastern Division
W	Western Division
*	Indicates playing manager; for vital statistics, consult the player or pitcher register
▲	Tied for first place, involved in league or division playoff
●	Tied for position in standings
◆	League Championship Series win
★	World Series win

The team and league abbreviations used in this section are found on the final pages of this book. For a prose account of the history of managers (and coaches), see the feature article by Fred Stein.

YEAR	TM/L	G	W	L	PCT	STANDING			M/Y	W-EXP	A-E
Blow, Josiah H. "Joe"											
1969	Det-A*	134	71	63	.530	3 E	3 E		1/2	66.8	4.2
1971	Tex-A*	23	9	14	.391	6 W	6 W		3/3	12.0	-3.0
1972	Tex-A	161	84	76	.525	2 W				79.1	4.9
1973	Tex-A	95	44	51	.463	4 W	3 W		1/2	44.2	-0.2
1973	NY-A	56	30	26	.535	3 E	3 E		2/2	28.7	1.3
1974	NY-A	159	97	62	.610	★◆1 E				82.8	14.2
1975	NY-A	162	100	62	.617	◆1 E				90.0	10.0
1976	NY-A	94	52	42	.553	3 E ▲◆1E			1/3	53.8	-1.8
1977	Bos-A	95	55	40	.579	4 E	4 E	2 E	2/3	50.4	4.6
1978	Oak-A	152	83	69	.546	5 W ●2 W			2/2	75.2	7.8
1979	Oak-A	60	37	23	.617	1 W	2 W		1/2	33.0	4.0
1980	Oak-A	49	27	22	.551	2 W	3 W		2/2	27.4	-0.4
1981(1)	Oak-A	62	24	38	.387	6 W				32.4	-7.6
1981(2)	Oak-A	100	44	56	.440	5 W				57.0	-13.0
1982	NY-A	162	91	71	.562	3 E				81.5	10.5
1983	NY-A	145	91	54	.628	7 E	2 E		2/2	84.0	7.0
	14	1709	939	769	.550					898.3	42.5

Adair, Marion Danne "Bill"

YEAR	TM/L	G	W	L	PCT	STANDING			M/Y	W-EXP	A-E
1970	Chi-A	10	4	6	.400	6 W	6 W	6 W	2/3	3.8	0.2

Adcock, Joseph Wilbur "Joe"

YEAR	TM/L	G	W	L	PCT	STANDING			M/Y	W-EXP	A-E
1967	Cle-A	162	75	87	.463	8				75.0	0.0

Addy, Robert Edward "Bob"

YEAR	TM/L	G	W	L	PCT	STANDING			M/Y	W-EXP	A-E
1875	Phi-n*	7	3	4	.429	4	5		2/2	4.3	-1.3
1877	Cin-N*	24	5	19	.208	6	6	6	2/3	5.3	-0.3
	2	31	8	23	.258						-1.6

Allen, Robert Gilman "Bob"

YEAR	TM/L	G	W	L	PCT	STANDING			M/Y	W-EXP	A-E
1890	Phi-N*	35	25	10	.714	3	2	3	4/5	20.2	4.8
1900	Cin-N*	144	62	77	.446	7				65.5	-3.5
	2	179	87	87	.500						1.3

Alston, Walter Emmons

YEAR	TM/L	G	W	L	PCT	STANDING			M/Y	W-EXP	A-E
1954	Bro-N	154	92	62	.597	2				80.6	11.4
1955	Bro-N	154	98	55	.641	★1				96.4	1.6
1956	Bro-N	154	93	61	.604	1				89.2	3.8
1957	Bro-N	154	84	70	.545	3				87.3	-3.3
1958	LA-N	154	71	83	.461	7				67.8	3.2
1959	LA-N	156	88	68	.564	▲★1				81.5	6.5
1960	LA-N	154	82	72	.532	4				84.3	-2.3
1961	LA-N	154	89	65	.578	2				80.7	8.3
1962	LA-N	165	102	63	.618	▲2				96.7	5.3
1963	LA-N	163	99	63	.611	★1				91.0	8.0
1964	LA-N	164	80	82	.494	●6				85.7	-5.7
1965	LA-N	162	97	65	.599	★1				90.9	6.1
1966	LA-N	162	95	67	.586	1				94.4	0.6
1967	LA-N	162	73	89	.451	8				72.3	0.7
1968	LA-N	162	76	86	.469	●7				76.2	-0.2
1969	LA-N	162	85	77	.525	4 W				90.2	-5.2
1970	LA-N	161	87	74	.540	2 W				87.0	-0.0
1971	LA-N	162	89	73	.549	2 W				89.2	-0.2
1972	LA-N	155	85	70	.548	3 W				83.9	1.1
1973	LA-N	162	95	66	.590	2 W				92.4	2.6
1974	LA-N	162	102	60	.630	♦1 W				105.6	-3.6
1975	LA-N	162	88	74	.543	2 W				93.7	-5.7
1976	LA-N	158	90	68	.570	2 W	2 W		1/2	86.1	3.9
	23	3658	2040	1613	.558						36.8

Altobelli, Joseph "Joe"

YEAR	TM/L	G	W	L	PCT	STANDING			M/Y	W-EXP	A-E
1977	SF-N	162	75	87	.463	4 W				77.1	-2.1
1978	SF-N	162	89	73	.549	3 W				83.1	5.9
1979	SF-N	140	61	79	.436	4 W	4 W		1/2	63.1	-2.1
1983	Bal-A	162	98	64	.605	★1 E				95.7	2.3
1984	Bal-A	162	85	77	.525	5 E				82.5	2.5
1985	Bal-A	55	29	26	.527	4 E	4 E		1/3	29.3	-0.3
	6	843	437	406	.518						6.3

Amalfitano, John Joseph "Joey"

YEAR	TM/L	G	W	L	PCT	STANDING			M/Y	W-EXP	A-E
1979	Chi-N	7	2	5	.286	5 E	5 E		2/2	3.5	-1.5
1980	Chi-N	72	26	46	.361	6 E	6 E		2/2	30.7	-4.7
1981(1)	Chi-N	54	15	37	.288	6 E					
(2)	Chi-N	52	23	28	.451	5 E				39.5	-1.5
	3	185	66	116	.363						-7.8

Anderson, George Lee "Sparky"

YEAR	TM/L	G	W	L	PCT	STANDING			M/Y	W-EXP	A-E
1970	Cin-N	162	102	60	.630	♦1 W				90.4	11.6
1971	Cin-N	162	79	83	.488	●4 W				81.6	-2.6
1972	Cin-N	154	95	59	.617	♦1 W				92.7	2.3
1973	Cin-N	162	99	63	.611	1 W				93.4	5.6
1974	Cin-N	163	98	64	.605	2 W				95.8	2.2
1975	Cin-N	162	108	54	.667	★1 W				106.7	1.3
1976	Cin-N	162	102	60	.630	★1 W				103.2	-1.2
1977	Cin-N	162	88	74	.543	2 W				88.5	-0.5
1978	Cin-N	161	92	69	.571	2 W				82.7	9.3
1979	Det-A	106	56	50	.528	5 E	5 E		3/3	55.1	0.9
1980	Det-A	163	84	78	.519	5 E				88.0	-4.0
1981(1)	Det-A	57	31	26	.544	4 E					
(2)	Det-A	52	29	23	.558	●2 E				57.0	3.0
1982	Det-A	162	83	79	.512	4 E				85.5	-2.5
1983	Det-A	162	92	70	.568	2 E				92.0	0.0
1984	Det-A	162	104	58	.642	★1 E				99.5	4.5
1985	Det-A	161	84	77	.522	3 E				84.6	-0.6
1986	Det-A	162	87	75	.537	3 E				89.2	-2.2
1987	Det-A	162	98	64	.605	1 E				96.2	1.8
1988	Det-A	162	88	74	.543	2 E				85.7	2.3
1989	Det-A	162	59	103	.364	7 E				60.9	-1.9
1990	Det-A	162	79	83	.488	3 E				80.6	-1.6
	21	3285	1837	1446	.560						27.7

Anson, Adrian Constantine "Cap"

YEAR	TM/L	G	W	L	PCT	STANDING			M/Y	W-EXP	A-E
1875	Ath-n*	8	4	4	.667	2	2		2/2	4.9	-0.9
1879	Chi-N*	64	41	21	.661	2	4		1/2	32.9	8.1
1880	Chi-N*	86	67	17	.798	1				63.0	4.0
1881	Chi-N*	84	56	28	.667	1				57.4	-1.4
1882	Chi-N*	84	55	29	.655	1				64.3	-9.3
1883	Chi-N*	98	59	39	.602	2				60.8	-1.8
1884	Chi-N*	113	62	50	.554	●4				71.4	-9.4
1885	Chi-N*	113	87	25	.777	1				88.1	-1.1
1886	Chi-N*	126	90	34	.726	1				92.5	-2.5
1887	Chi-N*	127	71	50	.587	3				68.9	2.1
1888	Chi-N*	136	77	58	.570	2				74.5	2.5
1889	Chi-N*	136	67	65	.508	3				70.5	-3.5
1890	Chi-N*	139	84	53	.613	2				82.5	1.5
1891	Chi-N*	137	82	53	.607	2				76.6	5.4
1892(1)	Chi-N*	71	31	39	.443	8					
(2)	Chi-N*	76	39	37	.513	7				63.2	6.8
1893	Chi-N*	128	56	71	.441	9				59.8	-3.8
1894	Chi-N*	137	57	75	.432	8				64.1	-7.1
1895	Chi-N*	133	72	58	.554	4				66.0	6.0
1896	Chi-N*	132	71	57	.555	5				65.4	5.6
1897	Chi-N*	138	59	73	.447	9				60.7	-1.7
1898	NY-N	22	9	13	.409	6	7	7	2/3	11.5	-2.5
	21	2288	1296	947	.578						-3.2

Appling, Lucius Benjamin "Luke"

YEAR	TM/L	G	W	L	PCT	STANDING			M/Y	W-EXP	A-E
1967	KC-A	40	10	30	.250	10	10		2/2	16.5	-6.5

Armour, William Clark "Bill"

YEAR	TM/L	G	W	L	PCT	STANDING			M/Y	W-EXP	A-E
1902	Cle-A	137	69	67	.507	5				69.8	-0.8
1903	Cle-A	140	77	63	.550	3				76.1	0.9
1904	Cle-A	154	86	65	.570	4				93.8	-7.8
1905	Det-A	154	79	74	.516	3				66.5	12.5
1906	Det-A	151	71	78	.477	6				65.6	5.4
	5	736	382	347	.524						10.3

Aspromonte, Kenneth Joseph "Ken"

YEAR	TM/L	G	W	L	PCT	STANDING			M/Y	W-EXP	A-E
1972	Cle-A	156	72	84	.462	5 E				72.4	-0.4
1973	Cle-A	162	71	91	.438	6 E				66.6	4.4
1974	Cle-A	162	77	85	.475	4 E				77.7	-0.7
	3	480	220	260	.458						3.3

Austin, James Philip "Jimmy"

YEAR	TM/L	G	W	L	PCT	STANDING			M/Y	W-EXP	A-E
1913	StL-A*	8	2	6	.250	7	7	8	2/3	3.3	-1.3
1918	StL-A*	16	7	9	.438	6	6	5	2/3	7.7	-0.7
1923	StL-A*	51	22	29	.431	3	5		2/2	24.4	-2.4
	3	75	31	44	.413						-4.5

Baker, Delmer David "Del"

YEAR	TM/L	G	W	L	PCT	STANDING			M/Y	W-EXP	A-E
1933	Det-A	2	2	0	1.000	5	5		2/2	1.0	1.0
1937	Det-A	54	34	20	.630	3	3	2	2/5	29.9	4.1
	Det-A	10	7	3	.700	2	2	2	4/5	5.5	1.5
1938	Det-A	57	37	19	.661	5	4			30.2	6.8
1939	Det-A	155	81	73	.526	5				85.1	-4.1
1940	Det-A	155	90	64	.584	1				92.9	-2.9
1941	Det-A	155	75	79	.487	●4				71.4	3.6
1942	Det-A	156	73	81	.474	5				77.2	-4.2
1960	Bos-A	7	2	5	.286	8	8	7	2/3	3.0	-1.0
	8	751	401	344	.538						4.7

Bamberger, George Irvin

YEAR	TM/L	G	W	L	PCT	STANDING			M/Y	W-EXP	A-E
1978	Mil-A	162	93	69	.574	3 E				96.4	-3.4
1979	Mil-A	161	95	66	.590	2 E				88.8	6.2
1980	Mil-A	92	47	45	.511	2 E	4 E 3 E		2/3	53.2	-6.2
1982	NY-N	162	65	97	.401	6 E				69.1	-4.1
1983	NY-N	46	16	30	.348	6 E	6 E		1/2	19.8	-3.8
1985	Mil-A	161	71	90	.441	6 E				69.5	1.5
1986	Mil-A	152	71	81	.467	6 E	6 E		1/2	69.6	1.4
	7	936	458	478	.489						-8.3

Bancroft, David James "Dave"

YEAR	TM/L	G	W	L	PCT	STANDING			M/Y	W-EXP	A-E
1924	Bos-N*	154	53	100	.346	8				47.8	5.2
1925	Bos-N*	153	70	83	.458	5				67.5	2.5
1926	Bos-N*	153	66	86	.434	7				66.4	-0.4
1927	Bos-N*	155	60	94	.390	7				65.1	-5.1
	4	615	249	363	.407						2.2

Bancroft, Frank Carter

YEAR	TM/L	G	W	L	PCT	STANDING			M/Y	W-EXP	A-E
1880	Wor-N	85	40	43	.482	5				45.7	-5.7
1881	Det-N	84	41	43	.488	4				42.9	-1.9
1882	Det-N	86	42	41	.506	6				34.0	8.0
1883	Cle-N	100	55	42	.567	4				51.8	3.2
1884	Pro-N	114	84	28	.750	1				83.3	0.7
1885	Pro-N	110	53	57	.482	4				46.0	7.0
1887	Phi-a	55	26	29	.473	6	5		1/2	27.6	-1.6
1889	Ind-N	68	25	43	.368	7	7		1/2	30.8	-5.8
1902	Cin-N	16	9	7	.563	6	6	4	2/3	8.8	0.2
	9	718	375	333	.530						4.1

Barkley, Samuel E. "Sam"

YEAR	TM/L	G	W	L	PCT	STANDING			M/Y	W-EXP	A-E
1888	KC-a*	57	21	36	.368	8	8	8	2/3	16.2	4.8

Barnie, William Harrison "Billy"

YEAR	TM/L	G	W	L	PCT	STANDING			M/Y	W-EXP	A-E
1883	Bal-a*	96	28	68	.292	8				25.1	2.9
1884	Bal-a	108	63	43	.594	6				64.1	-1.1
1885	Bal-a	110	41	68	.376	8				41.7	-0.7
1886	Bal-a	139	48	83	.366	8				42.4	5.6
1887	Bal-a	141	77	58	.570	3				77.0	0.0
1888	Bal-a	137	57	80	.416	5				56.8	0.2
1889	Bal-a	139	70	65	.519	5				67.1	2.9
1890	Bal-a	38	15	19	.441	8				16.0	-1.0
1891	Bal-a	139	71	64	.526	3				72.0	-1.0
1892(1)	Was-N	2	0	2	.000	●11	7		1/2	0.8	-0.8
1893	Lou-N	126	50	75	.400	11				47.6	2.4
1894	Lou-N	131	36	94	.277	12				39.3	-3.3
1897	Bro-N	136	61	71	.462	●6				62.3	-1.3
1898	Bro-N	35	15	20	.429	9	10		1/3	13.5	1.5
	14	1477	632	810	.438						6.1

Barrow, Edward Grant "Ed"

YEAR	TM/L	G	W	L	PCT	STANDING			M/Y	W-EXP	A-E
1903	Det-A	137	65	71	.478	5				71.0	-6.0

YEAR	TM/L	G	W	L	PCT	STANDING			M/Y	W-EXP	A-E
1904	Det-A	84	32	46	.410	7	7		1/2	31.9	0.1
1918	Bos-A	126	75	51	.595	★1				73.8	1.2
1919	Bos-A	138	66	71	.482	6				69.8	-3.8
1920	Bos-A	154	72	81	.471	5				71.6	0.4
	5	639	310	320	.492						-8.1

Barry, John Joseph "Jack"

YEAR	TM/L	G	W	L	PCT	STANDING			M/Y	W-EXP	A-E
1917	Bos-A*	157	90	62	.592	2				88.0	2.0

Battin, Joseph V. "Joe"

YEAR	TM/L	G	W	L	PCT	STANDING			M/Y	W-EXP	A-E
1883	Pit-a*	13	2	11	.154	7	7		3/3	4.2	-2.2
1884	Pit-a*	13	6	7	.462	11	10	10	3/5	2.9	3.1
	Pit-U*	6	1	5	.167	5	5		1/2	2.7	-1.7
	2	32	9	23	.281						-0.9

Bauer, Henry Albert "Hank"

YEAR	TM/L	G	W	L	PCT	STANDING			M/Y	W-EXP	A-E
1961	KC-A*	102	35	67	.343	8	●9		2/2	39.9	-4.9
1962	KC-A	162	72	90	.444	9				72.2	-0.2
1964	Bal-A	163	97	65	.599	3				93.2	3.8
1965	Bal-A	162	94	68	.580	3				87.9	6.1
1966	Bal-A	160	97	63	.606	★1				95.9	1.1
1967	Bal-A	161	76	85	.472	●6				87.2	-11.2
1968	Bal-A	80	43	37	.538	3	2		1/2	44.7	-1.7
1969	Oak-A	149	80	69	.537	2 W	2 W		1/2	80.3	-0.3
	8	1139	594	544	.522						-7.2

Benjamin, John W.

YEAR	TM/L	G	W	L	PCT	STANDING			M/Y	W-EXP	A-E
1873	Res-n	23	2	21	.087	8				-3.0	5.0

Benson, Vernon Adair "Vern"

YEAR	TM/L	G	W	L	PCT	STANDING			M/Y	W-EXP	A-E
1977	Atl-N	1	1	0	1.000	6 W	6 W	6 W	3/4	0.4	0.6

Berra, Lawrence Peter "Yogi"

YEAR	TM/L	G	W	L	PCT	STANDING			M/Y	W-EXP	A-E
1964	NY-A	164	99	63	.611	1				97.3	1.7
1972	NY-N	156	83	73	.532	3 E				72.4	10.6
1973	NY-N	161	82	79	.509	◆1 E				82.7	-0.7
1974	NY-N	162	71	91	.438	5 E				72.9	-1.9
1975	NY-N	109	56	53	.514	3 E	●3 E		1/2	56.0	-0.0
1984	NY-A	162	87	75	.537	3 E				89.0	-2.0
1985	NY-A	16	6	10	.375	7 E	2 E		1/2	9.7	-3.7
	7	930	484	444	.522						4.0

Bezdek, Hugo Frank

YEAR	TM/L	G	W	L	PCT	STANDING			M/Y	W-EXP	A-E
1917	Pit-N	91	30	59	.337	8	8		3/3	35.8	-5.8
1918	Pit-N	126	65	60	.520	4				68.6	-3.6
1919	Pit-N	139	71	68	.511	4				70.2	0.8
	3	356	166	187	.470						-8.6

Bickerson

YEAR	TM/L	G	W	L	PCT	STANDING			M/Y	W-EXP	A-E
1884	Was-a	1	0	1	.000	12	12		2/2	0.2	-0.2

Birmingham, Joseph Leo "Joe"

YEAR	TM/L	G	W	L	PCT	STANDING			M/Y	W-EXP	A-E
1912	Cle-A*	28	21	7	.750	6	5		2/2	13.9	7.1
1913	Cle-A*	155	86	66	.566	3				86.6	-0.6
1914	Cle-A*	157	51	102	.333	8				58.3	-7.3
1915	Cle-A	28	12	16	.429	6	7		1/2	11.4	0.6
	4	368	170	191	.471						-0.2

Bissonette, Adelphia Louis "Del"

YEAR	TM/L	G	W	L	PCT	STANDING			M/Y	W-EXP	A-E
1945	Bos-N	60	25	34	.424	7	6		2/2	29.2	-4.2

Blackburne, Russell Aubrey "Lena"

YEAR	TM/L	G	W	L	PCT	STANDING			M/Y	W-EXP	A-E
1928	Chi-A	80	40	40	.500	6	5		2/2	36.4	3.6
1929	Chi-A*	152	59	93	.388	7				59.8	-0.8
	2	232	99	133	.427						2.8

Blades, Francis Raymond "Ray"

YEAR	TM/L	G	W	L	PCT	STANDING			M/Y	W-EXP	A-E
1939	StL-N	155	92	61	.601	2				91.0	1.0
1940	StL-N	39	14	24	.368	6	3		1/3	20.2	-6.2
1948	Bro-N	1	1	0	1.000	5	5	3	2/3	0.5	0.5
	3	195	107	85	.557						-4.7

Blair, Walter Allen "Walter"

YEAR	TM/L	G	W	L	PCT	STANDING			M/Y	W-EXP	A-E
1915	Buf-F*	2	1	1	.500	8	8	6	2/3	0.9	0.1

Bluege, Oswald Louis "Ossie"

YEAR	TM/L	G	W	L	PCT	STANDING			M/Y	W-EXP	A-E
1943	Was-A	153	84	69	.549	2				83.9	0.1
1944	Was-A	154	64	90	.416	8				69.4	-5.4
1945	Was-A	156	87	67	.565	2				83.5	3.5
1946	Was-A	155	76	78	.494	4				66.9	9.1
1947	Was-A	154	64	90	.416	7				57.5	6.5
	5	772	375	394	.488						13.7

Bond, Thomas Henry "Tommy"

YEAR	TM/L	G	W	L	PCT	STANDING			M/Y	W-EXP	A-E
1882	Wor-N*	6	2	4	.333	8	8	8	2/3	1.3	0.7

Boros, Stephen "Steve"

YEAR	TM/L	G	W	L	PCT	STANDING			M/Y	W-EXP	A-E
1983	Oak-A	162	74	88	.457	4 W				73.7	0.3
1984	Oak-A	44	20	24	.455	5 W	4 W		1/2	20.5	-0.5
1986	SD-N	162	74	88	.457	4 W				74.1	-0.1
	3	368	168	200	.457						-0.3

Bottomley, James Leroy "Jim"

YEAR	TM/L	G	W	L	PCT	STANDING			M/Y	W-EXP	A-E
1937	StL-A*	78	21	56	.273	7	8		2/2	24.7	-3.7

Boudreau, Louis "Lou"

YEAR	TM/L	G	W	L	PCT	STANDING			M/Y	W-EXP	A-E
1942	Cle-A*	156	75	79	.487	4				69.7	5.3
1943	Cle-A*	153	82	71	.536	3				79.0	3.0
1944	Cle-A*	155	72	82	.468	●5				73.5	-1.5
1945	Cle-A*	147	73	72	.503	5				73.5	-0.5
1946	Cle-A*	156	68	86	.442	6				66.0	2.0
1947	Cle-A*	157	80	74	.519	4				87.4	-7.4
1948	Cle-A*	156	97	58	.626	▲★1				104.7	-7.7
1949	Cle-A*	154	89	65	.578	3				87.6	1.4
1950	Cle-A*	155	92	62	.597	4				91.9	0.1
1952	Bos-A*	154	76	78	.494	6				78.0	-2.0
1953	Bos-A	153	84	69	.549	4				79.0	5.0
1954	Bos-A	156	69	85	.448	4				74.2	-5.2
1955	KC-A	155	63	91	.409	6				51.1	11.9
1956	KC-A	154	52	102	.338	8				56.3	-4.3
1957	KC-A	104	36	67	.350	8	7		1/2	41.2	-5.2
1960	Chi-N	139	54	83	.394	7	7		2/2	55.9	-1.9
	16	2404	1162	1224	.487						-6.9

Bowa, Lawrence Robert "Larry"

YEAR	TM/L	G	W	L	PCT	STANDING			M/Y	W-EXP	A-E
1987	SD-N	162	65	97	.401	6 W				71.4	-6.4
1988	SD-N	46	16	30	.348	5 W	3 W		1/2	23.3	-7.3
	2	208	81	127	.389						-13.8

Bowerman, Frank Eugene "Frank"

YEAR	TM/L	G	W	L	PCT	STANDING			M/Y	W-EXP	A-E
1909	Bos-N*	76	22	54	.289	8	8		1/2	24.2	-2.2

Boyd, William J. "Bill"

YEAR	TM/L	G	W	L	PCT	STANDING			M/Y	W-EXP	A-E
1875	Atl-n*	2	0	2	.000	12	12		2/2	-0.2	0.2

Boyer, Kenton Lloyd "Ken"

YEAR	TM/L	G	W	L	PCT	STANDING			M/Y	W-EXP	A-E
1978	StL-N	143	62	81	.434	6 E	5 E		3/3	66.1	-4.1
1979	StL-N	163	86	76	.531	3 E				84.9	1.1
1980	StL-N	51	18	33	.353	6 E	4 E		1/4	26.4	-8.4
	3	357	166	190	.466						-11.3

Bradley, William Joseph "Bill"

YEAR	TM/L	G	W	L	PCT	STANDING			M/Y	W-EXP	A-E
1905	Cle-A	41	20	21	.488	●1	2	5	2/3	19.9	0.1
1914	Bro-F*	157	77	77	.500	5				75.5	1.5
	2	198	97	98	.497						1.6

Bragan, Robert Randall "Bobby"

YEAR	TM/L	G	W	L	PCT	STANDING			M/Y	W-EXP	A-E
1956	Pit-N	157	66	88	.429	7				70.1	-4.1
1957	Pit-N	104	36	67	.350	7	●7		1/2	43.8	-7.8
1958	Cle-A	67	31	36	.463	6	4		1/2	36.1	-5.1
1963	Mil-N	163	84	78	.519	6				88.9	-4.9
1964	Mil-N	162	88	74	.543	5				86.7	1.3
1965	Mil-N	162	86	76	.531	5				88.8	-2.8
1966	Atl-N	112	52	59	.468	7	5		1/2	62.3	-10.3
	7	927	443	478	.481						-33.8

Bresnahan, Roger Philip

YEAR	TM/L	G	W	L	PCT	STANDING			M/Y	W-EXP	A-E
1909	StL-N*	154	54	98	.355	7				60.8	-6.8
1910	StL-N*	153	63	90	.412	7				68.5	-5.5
1911	StL-N*	158	75	74	.503	5				67.1	7.9
1912	StL-N*	153	63	90	.412	6				60.1	2.9
1915	Chi-N*	157	73	80	.477	4				71.1	1.9
	5	775	328	432	.432						0.5

Bristol, James David "Dave"

YEAR	TM/L	G	W	L	PCT	STANDING			M/Y	W-EXP	A-E
1966	Cin-N	77	39	38	.506	8	7		2/2	38.0	1.0
1967	Cin-N	162	87	75	.537	4				85.6	1.4
1968	Cin-N	163	83	79	.512	4				82.8	0.2
1969	Cin-N	163	89	73	.549	3 W				83.9	5.1
1970	Mil-A	163	65	97	.401	●4 W				66.7	-1.7
1971	Mil-A	161	69	92	.429	6 W				72.1	-3.1
1972	Mil-A	30	10	20	.333	6 E	6 E		1/3	12.8	-2.8
1976	Atl-N	162	70	92	.432	6 W				72.6	-2.6
1977	Atl-N	29	8	21	.276	6 W	6 W		1/4	10.8	-2.8
	Atl-N	131	52	79	.397	6 W	6 W		4/4	48.6	3.4
1979	SF-N	22	10	12	.455	4 W	4 W		2/2	9.9	0.1
1980	SF-N	161	75	86	.466	5 W				73.8	1.2
	11	1424	657	764	.462						-0.5

Brown, Freeman

YEAR	TM/L	G	W	L	PCT	STANDING			M/Y	W-EXP	A-E
1882	Wor-N	41	9	32	.220	8	8		1/3	9.1	-0.1

Brown, Mordecai Peter Centennial "Three Finger"

YEAR	TM/L	G	W	L	PCT	STANDING			M/Y	W-EXP	A-E
1914	StL-F*	114	50	63	.442	7	8		1/2	46.1	3.9

Brown, Thomas T. "Tom"

YEAR	TM/L	G	W	L	PCT	STANDING			M/Y	W-EXP	A-E
1897	Was-N*	99	52	46	.531	11	●6		2/2	48.2	3.8
1898	Was-N*	38	12	26	.316	11	11		1/4	13.6	-1.6
	2	137	64	72	.471						2.2

Brucker, Earle Francis Sr

YEAR	TM/L	G	W	L	PCT	STANDING			M/Y	W-EXP	A-E
1952	Cin-N	5	3	2	.600	7	7	6	2/3	2.4	0.6

Buckenberger, Albert C. "Al"

YEAR	TM/L	G	W	L	PCT	STANDING			M/Y	W-EXP	A-E
1889	Col-a	140	60	78	.435	6				56.5	3.5
1890	Col-a	80	39	41	.488	5	2		1/3	51.9	-12.9
1892(1)	Pit-N	29	15	14	.517	7	6		1/2		
(2)	Pit-N	66	38	27	.585	10	4		2/2	47.3	5.7
1893	Pit-N	131	81	48	.628	2				81.3	-0.3
1894	Pit-N	110	53	55	.491	7	7		1/2	52.9	0.1
1895	StL-N	50	16	34	.320	11	11		1/4	16.0	-0.0
1902	Bos-N	142	73	64	.533	3				74.6	-1.6
1903	Bos-N	140	58	80	.420	6				57.0	1.0
1904	Bos-N	155	55	98	.359	7				49.1	5.9
	9	1043	488	539	.475						1.3

Buffinton, Charles G. "Charlie"

YEAR	TM/L	G	W	L	PCT	STANDING			M/Y	W-EXP	A-E
1890	Phi-P*	116	61	54	.530	5	5		2/2	63.6	-2.6

Burdock, John Joseph "Jack"

YEAR	TM/L	G	W	L	PCT	STANDING			M/Y	W-EXP	A-E
1883	Bos-N*	54	30	24	.556	4	1		1/2	37.4	-7.4

YEAR	TM/L	G	W	L	PCT	STANDING			M/Y	W-EXP	A-E
Burke, James Timothy "Jimmy"											
1905	StL-N*	90	34	56	.378	7	6	6	2/3	32.8	1.2
1918	StL-A	61	29	31	.483	6	5		3/3	28.8	0.2
1919	StL-A	140	67	72	.482	5				65.9	1.1
1920	StL-A	154	76	77	.497	4				79.4	-3.4
	4	445	206	236	.466						-0.9
Burnham, George Walter "Watch"											
1887	Ind-N	28	6	22	.214	8	8		1/3	7.7	-1.7
Burns, Thomas Everett "Tom"											
1892(1)	Pit-N*	47	22	25	.468	7	6		2/2		
(2)	Pit-N*	13	5	7	.417	10	4		1/2	29.7	-2.7
1898	Chi-N	152	85	65	.567	4				89.2	-4.2
1899	Chi-N	152	75	73	.507	8				78.6	-3.6
	3	364	187	170	.524						-10.5
Burwell, William Edwin "Bill"											
1947	Pit-N	1	1	0	1.000	8	●7		2/2	0.5	0.5
Bush, Owen Joseph "Donie"											
1923	Was-A*	155	75	78	.490	4				73.9	1.1
1927	Pit-N	156	94	60	.610	1				92.4	1.6
1928	Pit-N	152	85	67	.559	4				88.5	-3.5
1929	Pit-N	119	67	51	.568	2	2		1/2	67.7	-0.7
1930	Chi-A	154	62	92	.403	7				62.6	-0.6
1931	Chi-A	156	56	97	.366	8				54.8	1.2
1933	Cin-N	153	58	94	.382	8				59.8	-1.8
	7	1045	497	539	.480						-2.7
Butler, Ormond Hook											
1883	Pit-a	53	17	36	.321	6	6	7	2/3	17.3	-0.3
Byrne, Charles H. "Charlie"											
1885	Bro-a	75	38	37	.507	7	●5		2/2	36.0	2.0
1886	Bro-a	141	76	61	.555	3				68.5	7.5
1887	Bro-a	138	60	74	.448	6				65.8	-5.8
	3	354	174	172	.503						3.7
Callahan, James Joseph "Jim"											
1903	Chi-A*	138	60	77	.438	7				58.3	1.7
1904	Chi-A*	42	23	18	.561	4	3		1/2	24.1	-1.1
1912	Chi-A*	158	78	76	.506	4				76.2	1.8
1913	Chi-A*	153	78	74	.513	5				74.8	3.2
1914	Chi-A	157	70	84	.455	●6				68.5	1.5
1916	Pit-N	157	65	89	.422	6				65.3	-0.3
1917	Pit-N	61	20	40	.333	8	8		1/3	24.1	-4.1
	7	866	394	458	.462						2.7
Cammeyer, William Henry "Bill"											
1876	NY-N	57	21	35	.375	6				14.7	6.3
Campau, Charles Columbus "Count"											
1890	StL-a	42	27	14	.659	5	2	3	4/6	24.1	2.9
Cantillon, Joseph D. "Joe"											
1907	Was-A	154	49	102	.325	8				55.6	-6.6
1908	Was-A	155	67	85	.441	7				69.0	-2.0
1909	Was-A	156	42	110	.276	8				43.9	-1.9
	3	465	158	297	.347						-10.4
Carey, Max George											
1932	Bro-N	154	81	73	.526	3				77.5	3.5
1933	Bro-N	157	65	88	.425	6				68.4	-3.4
	2	311	146	161	.476						0.1
Carey, Thomas John "Tom"											
1873	Bal-n*	24	14	9	.609	3	3		2/2	16.9	-2.9
1874	Mut-n*	25	13	12	.520	2	2		1/2	16.4	-3.4
	2	49	27	21	.563						-6.3
Carrigan, William Francis "Bill"											
1913	Bos-A*	70	40	30	.571	5	4		2/2	36.0	4.0
1914	Bos-A*	159	91	62	.595	2				85.4	5.6
1915	Bos-A*	155	101	50	.669	★1				94.0	7.0
1916	Bos-A*	156	91	63	.591	★1				85.2	5.8
1927	Bos-A	154	51	103	.331	8				51.7	-0.7
1928	Bos-A	154	57	96	.373	8				58.2	-1.2
1929	Bos-A	155	58	96	.377	8				57.3	0.7
	7	1003	489	500	.494						21.2
Caruthers, Robert Lee "Bob"											
1892(2)	StL-N*	50	16	32	.333	12	11		3/3	17.5	-1.5
Cavarretta, Philip Joseph "Phil"											
1951	Chi-N*	74	27	47	.365	7	8		2/2	30.4	-3.4
1952	Chi-N*	155	77	77	.500	5				76.7	0.3
1953	Chi-N*	155	65	89	.422	7				57.3	7.7
	3	384	169	213	.442						4.6
Caylor, Oliver Perry "O.P."											
1885	Cin-a	112	63	49	.563	2				62.1	0.9
1886	Cin-a	141	65	73	.471	5				70.5	-5.5
1887	NY-a	100	35	60	.368	7	7		3/3	27.6	7.4
	3	353	163	182	.472						2.7
Chance, Frank Leroy											
1905	Chi-N*	90	55	33	.625	4	3		2/2	58.5	-3.5
1906	Chi-N*	155	116	36	.763	1				112.7	3.3
1907	Chi-N*	155	107	45	.704	★1				97.9	9.1
1908	Chi-N*	158	99	55	.643	★1				95.7	3.3
1909	Chi-N*	155	104	49	.680	2				105.1	-1.1
1910	Chi-N*	154	104	50	.675	1				99.8	4.2
1911	Chi-N*	158	92	62	.597	2				92.3	-0.3
1912	Chi-N*	153	91	59	.607	3				83.6	7.4
1913	NY-A*	153	57	94	.377	7				60.6	-3.6
1914	NY-A*	137	60	74	.448	7	●6		1/2	65.8	-5.8
1923	Bos-A	154	61	91	.401	8				53.6	7.4
	11	1622	946	648	.593						20.5
Chapman, John Curtis "Jack"											
1876	Lou-N*	69	30	36	.455	5				26.6	3.4
1877	Lou-N	61	35	25	.583	2				34.8	0.2
1878	Mil-N	61	15	45	.250	6				18.0	-3.0
1882	Wor-N	37	7	30	.189	8	8		3/3	8.2	-1.2
1883	Det-N	101	40	58	.408	7				37.9	2.1
1884	Det-N	114	28	84	.250	8				28.9	-0.9
1885	Buf-N	88	31	57	.352	7	7		2/2	25.3	5.7
1889	Lou-a	7	1	6	.143	8	8		4/4	1.5	-0.5
1890	Lou-a	136	88	44	.667	1				87.5	0.5
1891	Lou-a	139	54	83	.394	7				52.9	1.1
1892(1)	Lou-N	54	21	33	.389	10	11		1/2		
	11	867	350	501	.411						7.5
Chapman, William Benjamin "Ben"											
1945	Phi-N*	85	28	57	.329	8	8		2/2	25.2	2.8
1946	Phi-N*	155	69	85	.448	5				61.8	7.2
1947	Phi-N	155	62	92	.403	●7				66.8	-4.8
1948	Phi-N	79	37	42	.468	7	6		1/3	32.2	4.8
	4	474	196	276	.415						10.1
Chase, Harold Homer "Hal"											
1910	NY-A*	14	10	4	.714	3	2		2/2	7.7	2.3
1911	NY-A*	153	76	76	.500	6				72.0	4.0
	2	167	86	80	.518						6.3
Clapp, John Edgar											
1872	Man-n*	24	5	19	.208	8				4.1	0.9
1878	Ind-N*	63	24	36	.400	5				26.7	-2.7
1879	Buf-N*	79	46	32	.590	3				41.8	4.2
1880	Cin-N*	82	21	59	.262	8				22.6	-1.6
1881	Cle-N*	74	32	41	.438	6	7		2/2	34.6	-2.6
1883	NY-N*	98	46	50	.479	6				43.8	2.2
	6	420	174	237	.423						0.3
Clarke, Fred Clifford											
1897	Lou-N*	92	35	54	.393	9	11		2/2	32.9	2.1
1898	Lou-N*	154	70	81	.464	9				65.6	4.4
1899	Lou-N*	156	75	77	.493	9				80.9	-5.9
1900	Pit-N*	140	79	60	.568	2				81.1	-2.1
1901	Pit-N*	140	90	49	.647	1				93.2	-3.2
1902	Pit-N*	142	103	36	.741	1				103.9	-0.9
1903	Pit-N*	141	91	49	.650	1				87.1	3.9
1904	Pit-N*	156	87	66	.569	4				85.2	1.8
1905	Pit-N*	155	96	57	.627	2				89.3	6.7
1906	Pit-N*	154	93	60	.608	3				93.7	-0.7
1907	Pit-N*	157	91	63	.591	2				90.8	0.2
1908	Pit-N*	155	98	56	.636	●2				90.3	7.7
1909	Pit-N*	154	110	42	.724	★1				103.6	6.4
1910	Pit-N*	154	86	67	.562	3				84.9	1.1
1911	Pit-N*	156	85	69	.552	3				96.4	-11.4
1912	Pit-N	153	93	58	.616	2				94.5	-1.5
1913	Pit-N*	155	78	71	.523	4				83.8	-5.8
1914	Pit-N*	158	69	85	.448	7				72.7	-3.7
1915	Pit-N*	157	73	81	.474	5				81.2	-8.2
	19	2829	1602	1181	.576						-9.2
Clements, John J. "Jack"											
1890	Phi-N*	19	13	6	.684	1	2	3	2/5	11.0	2.0
Clinton, James Lawrence "Jim"											
1872	Eck-n*	11	0	11	.000	10	9		1/2	-1.2	1.2
Cobb, Tyrus Raymond "Ty"											
1921	Det-A*	154	71	82	.464	6				79.3	-8.3
1922	Det-A*	155	79	75	.513	3				80.4	-1.4
1923	Det-A*	155	83	71	.539	2				85.5	-2.5
1924	Det-A*	156	86	68	.558	3				81.9	4.1
1925	Det-A*	156	81	73	.526	4				83.7	-2.7
1926	Det-A*	157	79	75	.513	6				73.5	5.5
	6	933	479	444	.519						-5.3
Cochrane, Gordon Stanley "Mickey"											
1934	Det-A*	154	101	53	.656	1				99.8	1.2
1935	Det-A*	152	93	58	.616	★1				99.1	-6.1
1936	Det-A*	154	83	71	.539	2				81.4	1.6
1937	Det-A*	29	16	13	.552	3	2		1/5	16.1	-0.1
	Det-A*	47	26	20	.565	3	2	2	3/5	25.5	0.5
1938	Det-A	98	47	51	.480	5	4		1/2	52.9	-5.9
	5	634	366	266	.579						-8.8
Cohen, Andrew Howard "Andy"											
1960	Phi-N	1	1	0	1.000	●6	●4	8	2/3	0.4	0.6
Coleman, Gerald Francis "Jerry"											
1980	SD-N	163	73	89	.451	6 W				74.2	-1.2
Coleman, Robert Hunter "Bob"											
1943	Bos-N	46	21	25	.457	6	6		1/2	18.0	3.0
1944	Bos-N	155	65	89	.422	6				68.5	-3.5
1945	Bos-N	94	42	51	.452	7	6		1/2	46.1	-4.1

YEAR	TM/L	G	W	L	PCT	STANDING			M/Y	W-EXP	A-E
	3	295	128	165	.437						-4.6

Collins, Edward Trowbridge Sr. "Eddie"

YEAR	TM/L	G	W	L	PCT	STANDING			M/Y	W-EXP	A-E
1925	Chi-A*	154	79	75	.513	5				80.8	-1.8
1926	Chi-A*	155	81	72	.529	5				83.0	-2.0
	2	309	160	147	.521						-3.8

Collins, James Joseph "Jimmy"

YEAR	TM/L	G	W	L	PCT	STANDING			M/Y	W-EXP	A-E
1901	Bos-A*	138	79	57	.581	2				82.4	-3.4
1902	Bos-A*	138	77	60	.562	3				74.8	2.2
1903	Bos-A*	141	91	47	.659	★1				89.9	1.1
1904	Bos-A*	157	95	59	.617	1				93.3	1.7
1905	Bos-A*	153	78	74	.513	4				77.6	0.4
1906	Bos-A*	115	35	79	.307	8	8		1/2	37.3	-2.3
	6	842	455	376	.548						-0.3

Collins, John Francis "Shano"

YEAR	TM/L	G	W	L	PCT	STANDING			M/Y	W-EXP	A-E
1931	Bos-A	153	62	90	.408	6				58.8	3.2
1932	Bos-A	55	11	44	.200	8	8		1/2	15.4	-4.4
	2	208	73	134	.353						-1.2

Comiskey, Charles Albert "Charlie"

YEAR	TM/L	G	W	L	PCT	STANDING			M/Y	W-EXP	A-E
1883	StL-a*	19	12	7	.632	2	2		2/2	12.1	-0.1
1884	StL-a*	25	16	7	.696	5	4		2/2	13.8	2.2
1885	StL-a*	112	79	33	.705	1				76.3	2.7
1886	StL-a*	139	93	46	.669	1				101.3	-8.3
1887	StL-a*	138	95	40	.704	1				97.5	-2.5
1888	StL-a*	137	92	43	.681	1				95.7	-3.7
1889	StL-a*	141	89	46	.659	2				91.9	-1.9
1890	Chi-P*	138	75	62	.547	4				78.5	-3.5
1891	StL-a*	139	85	51	.625	2				86.9	-1.9
1892(1)	Cin-N*	77	44	31	.587	4					
(2)	Cin-N*	78	38	37	.507	8				78.4	3.6
1893	Cin-N*	131	65	63	.508	•6				59.2	5.8
1894	Cin-N*	134	55	75	.423	10				51.5	3.5
	12	1408	838	541	.608						-4.1

Connor, Roger

YEAR	TM/L	G	W	L	PCT	STANDING			M/Y	W-EXP	A-E
1896	StL-N*	46	8	37	.178	11	11	11	4/5	12.3	-4.3

Cooke, Allen Lindsey "Dusty"

YEAR	TM/L	G	W	L	PCT	STANDING			M/Y	W-EXP	A-E
1948	Phi-N	13	6	6	.500	7	6	6	2/3	4.9	1.1

Coombs, John Wesley "Jack"

YEAR	TM/L	G	W	L	PCT	STANDING			M/Y	W-EXP	A-E
1919	Phi-N	63	18	44	.290	8	8		1/2	22.3	-4.3

Cooney, John Walter "Johnny"

YEAR	TM/L	G	W	L	PCT	STANDING			M/Y	W-EXP	A-E
1949	Bos-N	46	20	25	.444	4	4		2/2	22.1	-2.1

Corrales, Patrick "Pat"

YEAR	TM/L	G	W	L	PCT	STANDING			M/Y	W-EXP	A-E
1978	Tex-A	1	1	0	1.000	•2 W	•2 W		2/2	0.5	0.5
1979	Tex-A	162	83	79	.512	3 W				86.2	-3.2
1980	Tex-A	163	76	85	.472	4 W				80.9	-4.9
1982	Phi-N	162	89	73	.549	2 E				82.1	6.9
1983	Phi-N	86	43	42	.506	1 E	♦1 E		1/2	45.9	-2.9
	Cle-A	62	30	32	.484	7 E	7 E		2/2	27.9	2.1
1984	Cle-A	163	75	87	.463	6 E				80.5	-5.5
1985	Cle-A	162	60	102	.370	7 E				68.4	-8.4
1986	Cle-A	163	84	78	.519	5 E				80.1	3.9
1987	Cle-A	87	31	56	.356	7 E	7 E		1/2	32.8	-1.8
	9	1211	572	634	.474						-13.2

Corriden, John Michael Sr. "Red"

YEAR	TM/L	G	W	L	PCT	STANDING			M/Y	W-EXP	A-E
1950	Chi-A	125	52	72	.419	8	6		2/2	51.9	0.1

Cottier, Charles Keith "Chuck"

YEAR	TM/L	G	W	L	PCT	STANDING			M/Y	W-EXP	A-E
1984	Sea-A	27	15	12	.556	7 W	•5 W		2/2	12.0	3.0
1985	Sea-A	162	74	88	.457	6 W				71.4	2.6
1986	Sea-A	28	9	19	.321	6 W	7 W		1/3	12.0	-3.0
	3	217	98	119	.452						2.6

Cox, Robert Joseph "Bobby"

YEAR	TM/L	G	W	L	PCT	STANDING			M/Y	W-EXP	A-E
1978	Atl-N	162	69	93	.426	6 W				65.4	3.6
1979	Atl-N	160	66	94	.412	6 W				70.6	-4.6
1980	Atl-N	161	81	80	.503	4 W				77.3	3.7
1981(1)	Atl-N	55	25	29	.463	4 W				50.7	-0.7
(2)	Atl-N	52	25	27	.481	5 W				50.7	-0.7
1982	Tor-A	162	78	84	.481	•6 E				75.8	2.2
1983	Tor-A	162	89	73	.549	4 E				87.8	1.2
1984	Tor-A	163	89	73	.549	2 E				86.4	2.6
1985	Tor-A	161	99	62	.615	1 E				98.2	0.8
1990	Atl-N	97	40	57	.412	6 W	6 W		2/2	40.3	-0.3
	9	1335	661	672	.496						8.4

Craft, Harry Francis

YEAR	TM/L	G	W	L	PCT	STANDING			M/Y	W-EXP	A-E
1957	KC-A	50	23	27	.460	8	7		2/2	20.0	3.0
1958	KC-A	156	73	81	.474	7				69.8	3.2
1959	KC-A	154	66	88	.429	7				69.3	-3.3
1961	Chi-N	12	4	8	.333	•6	7	7	2/9	5.2	-1.2
	Chi-N	4	3	1	.750	7	7	7	5/9	1.7	1.3
1962	Hou-N	162	64	96	.400	8				66.8	-2.8
1963	Hou-N	162	66	96	.407	9				60.8	5.2
1964	Hou-N	149	61	88	.409	9	9		1/2	60.6	0.4
	7	849	360	485	.426						6.0

Craig, Roger Lee

YEAR	TM/L	G	W	L	PCT	STANDING			M/Y	W-EXP	A-E
1978	SD-N	162	84	78	.519	4 W				80.2	3.8
1979	SD-N	161	69	93	.422	5 W				72.2	-4.2
1985	SF-N	18	6	12	.333	6 W	6 W		2/2	7.6	-1.6
1986	SF-N	162	83	79	.512	3 W				89.4	-6.4
1987	SF-N	162	90	72	.556	1 W				92.4	-2.4
1988	SF-N	162	83	79	.512	4 W				85.7	-2.7
1989	SF-N	162	92	70	.568	♦1 W				91.5	0.5
1990	SF-N	162	85	77	.525	3 W				81.9	3.1
	8	1151	591	560	.513						-9.9

Crandall, Delmar Wesley "Del"

YEAR	TM/L	G	W	L	PCT	STANDING			M/Y	W-EXP	A-E
1972	Mil-A	124	54	70	.435	6 E	6 E		3/3	52.8	1.2
1973	Mil-A	162	74	88	.457	5 E				78.7	-4.7
1974	Mil-A	162	76	86	.469	5 E				79.6	-3.4
1975	Mil-A	161	67	94	.416	5 E	5 E		1/2	68.9	-1.9
1983	Sea-A	89	34	55	.382	7 W	7 W		2/2	33.9	0.1
1984	Sea-A	135	59	76	.437	7 W	•5 W		1/2	59.8	-0.8
	6	833	364	469	.437						-9.7

Crane, Samuel Newhall "Sam"

YEAR	TM/L	G	W	L	PCT	STANDING			M/Y	W-EXP	A-E
1880	Buf-N*	84	24	58	.293	7				24.6	-0.6
1884	Cin-U*	70	49	21	.700	5	3		2/2	49.2	-0.2
	2	154	73	79	.480						-0.8

Cravath, Clifford Carlton "Gavvy"

YEAR	TM/L	G	W	L	PCT	STANDING			M/Y	W-EXP	A-E
1919	Phi-N*	75	29	46	.387	8	8		2/2	27.0	2.0
1920	Phi-N*	153	62	91	.405	8				61.0	1.0
	2	228	91	137	.399						2.9

Craver, William H. "Bill"

YEAR	TM/L	G	W	L	PCT	STANDING			M/Y	W-EXP	A-E
1871	Tro-n*	25	12	12	.500	7	6		2/2	11.4	0.6
1872	Bal-n*	41	27	13	.675	2	2		1/2	29.6	-2.6
1874	Phi-n*	58	29	29	.500	4				32.6	-3.6
1875	Cen-n*	14	2	12	.143	11				1.7	0.3
	4	138	70	66	.515						-5.3

Creamer, George W.

YEAR	TM/L	G	W	L	PCT	STANDING			M/Y	W-EXP	A-E
1884	Pit-a*	8	0	8	.000	10	10	10	4/5	1.8	-1.8

Cronin, Joseph Edward "Joe"

YEAR	TM/L	G	W	L	PCT	STANDING			M/Y	W-EXP	A-E
1933	Was-A*	153	99	53	.651	1				93.6	5.4
1934	Was-A*	155	66	86	.434	7				68.7	-2.7
1935	Bos-A*	154	78	75	.510	4				75.1	2.9
1936	Bos-A*	155	74	80	.481	6				78.0	-4.0
1937	Bos-A*	154	80	72	.526	5				80.3	-0.3
1938	Bos-A*	150	88	61	.591	2				88.1	-0.1
1939	Bos-A*	152	89	62	.589	2				84.1	4.9
1940	Bos-A*	154	82	72	.532	•4				81.2	0.8
1941	Bos-A*	155	84	70	.545	2				87.7	-3.7
1942	Bos-A*	152	93	59	.612	2				92.8	0.2
1943	Bos-A*	155	68	84	.447	7				71.2	-3.2
1944	Bos-A*	156	77	77	.500	4				83.3	-6.3
1945	Bos-A*	157	71	83	.461	7				69.1	1.9
1946	Bos-A	156	104	50	.675	1				96.9	7.1
1947	Bos-A	157	83	71	.539	3				82.1	0.9
	15	2315	1236	1055	.540						3.7

Crooks, John Charles

YEAR	TM/L	G	W	L	PCT	STANDING			M/Y	W-EXP	A-E
1892(1)	StL-N*	47	24	22	.522	11	9		3/3		
(2)	StL-N*	15	3	11	.214	12	11		1/3	21.9	5.1

Cross, Lafayette Napoleon "Lave"

YEAR	TM/L	G	W	L	PCT	STANDING			M/Y	W-EXP	A-E
1899	Cle-N*	38	8	30	.211	12	12		1/2	3.3	4.7

Curtis, Edwin R. "Ed"

YEAR	TM/L	G	W	L	PCT	STANDING			M/Y	W-EXP	A-E
1884	Alt-U	25	6	19	.240	6				1.7	4.3

Cushman, Charles H. "Charlie"

YEAR	TM/L	G	W	L	PCT	STANDING			M/Y	W-EXP	A-E
1891	Mil-a	36	21	15	.583	5				24.5	-3.5

Cuthbert, Edgar Edward "Ned"

YEAR	TM/L	G	W	L	PCT	STANDING			M/Y	W-EXP	A-E
1882	StL-a*	80	37	43	.463	5				31.3	5.7

Dahlen, William Frederick "Bill"

YEAR	TM/L	G	W	L	PCT	STANDING			M/Y	W-EXP	A-E
1910	Bro-N*	156	64	90	.416	6				62.9	1.1
1911	Bro-N*	154	64	86	.427	7				62.1	1.9
1912	Bro-N	153	58	95	.379	7				66.3	-8.3
1913	Bro-N	152	65	84	.436	6				72.6	-7.6
	4	615	251	355	.414						-12.9

Dark, Alvin Ralph

YEAR	TM/L	G	W	L	PCT	STANDING			M/Y	W-EXP	A-E
1961	SF-N	155	85	69	.552	3				88.7	-3.7
1962	SF-N	165	103	62	.624	▲1				100.8	2.2
1963	SF-N	162	88	74	.543	3				89.7	-1.7
1964	SF-N	162	90	72	.556	4				88.5	1.5
1966	KC-A	160	74	86	.463	7				70.8	3.2
1967	KC-A	121	52	69	.430	10	10		1/2	50.0	2.0
1968	Cle-A	162	86	75	.534	3				81.9	4.1
1969	Cle-A	161	62	99	.385	6 E				65.2	-3.2
1970	Cle-A	162	76	86	.469	5 E				78.3	-2.3
1971	Cle-A	103	42	61	.408	6 E	6 E		1/2	37.7	4.3
1974	Oak-A	162	90	72	.556	★1 W				96.0	-6.0
1975	Oak-A	162	98	64	.605	1 W				96.7	1.3
1977	SD-N	113	48	65	.425	4 W	5 W		3/3	46.8	1.2
	13	1950	994	954	.510						2.9

Davenport, James Houston "Jim"

YEAR	TM/L	G	W	L	PCT	STANDING			M/Y	W-EXP	A-E
1985	SF-N	144	56	88	.389	6 W	6 W		1/2	60.6	-4.6

Davidson, Mordecai H.

YEAR	TM/L	G	W	L	PCT	STANDING			M/Y	W-EXP	A-E
1888	Lou-a	3	1	2	.333	8	8	7	2/4	1.1	-0.1
	Lou-a	90	34	52	.395	8	7		4/4	32.7	1.3

Davis, George Stacey

YEAR	TM/L	G	W	L	PCT	STANDING			M/Y	W-EXP	A-E
1895	NY-N*	33	16	17	.485	8	9		1/3	16.9	-0.9

YEAR	TM/L	G	W	L	PCT	STANDING			M/Y	W-EXP	A-E
1900	NY-N*	78	39	37	.513	8	8		2/2	32.5	6.5
1901	NY-N*	141	52	85	.380	7				47.6	4.4
	3	252	107	139	.435						10.0

Davis, Harry H

YEAR	TM/L	G	W	L	PCT	STANDING			M/Y	W-EXP	A-E
1912	Cle-A*	127	54	71	.432	6	5		1/2	62.2	-8.2

Davis, Virgil Lawrence "Spud"

1946	Pit-N	3	1	2	.333	7	7		2/2	1.3	-0.3

Day, John B.

1899	NY-N	66	29	35	.453	9	10		1/2	26.9	2.1

Deane, John Henry "Harry"

1871	Kek-n*	5	2	3	.400	7	8		2/2	0.6	1.4

Dent, Russell Earl "Bucky"

1989	NY-A	40	18	22	.450	6 E	5 E		2/2	17.7	0.3
1990	NY-A	49	18	31	.367	7 E	7 E		1/2	19.9	-1.9
	2	89	36	53	.404						-1.6

Dickey, William Malcolm "Bill"

1946	NY-A*	105	57	48	.543	2	3	3	2/3	62.4	-5.4

Diddlebock, Henry H. "Harry"

1896	StL-N	17	7	10	.412	10	11		1/5	4.6	2.4

Doby, Lawrence Eugene "Larry"

1978	Chi-A	87	37	50	.425	5 W	5 W		2/2	38.1	-1.1

Donovan, Patrick Joseph "Patsy"

1897	Pit-N*	135	60	71	.458	8				51.2	8.8
1899	Pit-N*	131	69	58	.543	10	7		2/2	69.0	0.0
1901	StL-N*	142	76	64	.543	4				79.6	-3.6
1902	StL-N*	140	56	78	.418	6				48.8	7.2
1903	StL-N*	139	43	94	.314	8				40.0	3.0
1904	Was-A*	139	37	97	.276	8	8		2/2	37.3	-0.3
1906	Bro-N*	153	66	86	.434	5				61.7	4.3
1907	Bro-N*	153	65	83	.439	5				64.9	0.1
1908	Bro-N	154	53	101	.344	7				59.7	-6.7
1910	Bos-A	158	81	72	.529	4				84.5	-3.5
1911	Bos-A	153	78	75	.510	5				80.3	-2.3
	11	1597	684	879	.438						6.9

Donovan, William Edward "Bill"

1915	NY-A*	154	69	83	.454	5				75.6	-6.6
1916	NY-A*	156	80	74	.519	4				78.8	1.2
1917	NY-A	155	71	82	.464	6				72.6	-1.6
1921	Phi-N	87	25	62	.287	8	8		1/2	27.3	-2.3
	4	552	245	301	.449						-9.3

Dooin, Charles Sebastian "Red"

1910	Phi-N*	157	78	75	.510	4				80.1	-2.1
1911	Phi-N*	153	79	73	.520	4				74.9	4.1
1912	Phi-N*	152	73	79	.480	5				74.2	-1.2
1913	Phi-N*	159	88	63	.583	2				81.4	6.6
1914	Phi-N*	154	74	80	.481	6				73.3	0.7
	5	775	392	370	.514						8.0

Dorgan, Michael Cornelius "Mike"

1879	Syr-N*	43	17	26	.395	6	7		1/3	10.9	6.1
1880	Pro-N*	39	26	12	.684	3	2		3/3	24.7	1.3
1881	Wor-N*	56	24	32	.429	7	8		1/2	22.9	1.1
	3	138	67	70	.489						8.6

Dowd, Thomas Jefferson "Tom"

1896	StL-N*	63	25	38	.397	11	11		5/5	17.2	7.8
1897	StL-N*	29	6	22	.214	12	12		1/4	5.1	0.9
	2	92	31	60	.341						8.8

Doyle, John Joseph "Jack"

1895	NY-N*	64	32	31	.508	8	9	9	2/3	32.2	-0.2
1898	Was-N*	17	8	9	.471	11	10	11	2/4	6.1	1.9
	2	81	40	40	.500						1.7

Dressen, Charles Walter "Chuck"

1934	Cin-N	60	21	39	.350	8	8		3/3	21.7	-0.7
1935	Cin-N	154	68	85	.444	6				64.0	4.0
1936	Cin-N	154	74	80	.481	5				73.3	0.7
1937	Cin-N	130	51	78	.395	8	8		1/2	56.3	-5.3
1951	Bro-N	158	97	60	.618	▲2				96.2	0.8
1952	Bro-N	155	96	57	.627	1				93.8	2.2
1953	Bro-N	155	105	49	.682	1				101.5	3.5
1955	Was-A	154	53	101	.344	8				57.9	-4.9
1956	Was-A	155	59	95	.383	7				51.4	7.6
1957	Was-A	20	4	16	.200	8	8		1/2	7.4	-3.4
1960	Mil-N	154	88	66	.571	2				83.6	4.4
1961	Mil-N	130	71	58	.550	3	4		1/2	69.2	1.8
1963	Det-A	102	55	47	.539	9	●5		2/2	50.8	4.2
1964	Det-A	163	85	77	.525	4				83.2	1.8
1965	Det-A	120	65	55	.542	3	4		2/2	66.2	-1.2
1966	Det-A	26	16	10	.615	3	3		1/3	13.3	2.7
	16	1990	1008	973	.509						18.2

Duffy, Hugh

1901	Mil-A*	139	48	89	.350	8				51.2	-3.2
1904	Phi-N*	155	52	100	.342	8				54.4	-2.4
1905	Phi-N*	155	83	69	.546	4				86.9	-3.9
1906	Phi-N*	154	71	82	.464	4				72.4	-1.4
1910	Chi-A	156	68	85	.444	6				73.8	-5.8
1911	Chi-A	154	77	74	.510	4				85.2	-8.2

YEAR	TM/L	G	W	L	PCT	STANDING			M/Y	W-EXP	A-E
1921	Bos-A	154	75	79	.487	5				74.2	0.8
1922	Bos-A	154	61	93	.396	8				59.8	1.2
	8	1221	535	671	.444						-22.9

Dunlap, Frederick C. "Fred"

1882	Cle-N*	80	42	36	.538	8	5		2/2	38.2	3.8
1884	StL-U*	83	66	16	.805	1	1		2/2	70.3	-4.3
1885	StL-N*	50	21	29	.420	5	8		1/3	15.5	5.5
	StL-N*	22	9	11	.450	8	8		3/3	6.2	2.8
1889	Pit-N*	17	7	10	.412	6	7	5	2/3	7.6	-0.6
	4	252	145	102	.587						7.1

Durocher, Leo Ernest

1939	Bro-N*	157	84	69	.549	3				82.9	1.1
1940	Bro-N*	156	88	65	.575	2				84.3	3.7
1941	Bro-N*	157	100	54	.649	1				99.2	0.8
1942	Bro-N	155	104	50	.675	2				101.5	2.5
1943	Bro-N*	153	81	72	.529	3				80.7	0.3
1944	Bro-N	155	63	91	.409	7				63.4	-0.4
1945	Bro-N*	155	87	65	.565	3				83.8	3.2
1946	Bro-N	157	96	60	.615	▲2				91.8	4.2
1948	Bro-N	73	35	37	.486	5	3		1/3	39.6	-4.6
	NY-N	79	41	38	.519	4	5		2/2	43.3	-2.3
1949	NY-N	153	73	81	.474	5				81.3	-8.3
1950	NY-N	154	86	68	.558	3				86.2	-0.2
1951	NY-N	157	98	59	.624	▲1				92.5	5.5
1952	NY-N	154	92	62	.597	2				85.4	6.6
1953	NY-N	155	70	84	.455	5				79.0	-9.0
1954	NY-N	154	97	57	.630	★1				95.9	1.1
1955	NY-N	154	80	74	.519	3				79.9	0.1
1966	Chi-N	162	59	103	.364	10				64.5	-5.5
1967	Chi-N	162	87	74	.540	3				88.7	-1.7
1968	Chi-N	163	84	78	.519	3				81.1	2.9
1969	Chi-N	163	92	70	.568	2 E				92.4	-0.4
1970	Chi-N	162	84	78	.519	2 E				93.6	-9.6
1971	Chi-N	162	83	79	.512	●3 E				79.8	3.2
1972	Chi-N	91	46	44	.511	4 E	2 E		1/2	52.3	-6.3
	Hou-N	31	16	15	.516	2 W	2 W		3/3	17.0	-1.0
1973	Hou-N	162	82	80	.506	4 W				81.9	0.1
	24	3739	2008	1709	.540						-14.0

Dwyer, John Francis "Frank"

1902	Det-A	137	52	83	.385	7				58.4	-6.4

Dyer, Edwin Hawley "Eddie"

1946	StL-N	156	98	58	.628	▲★1				95.7	2.3
1947	StL-N	156	89	65	.578	2				91.5	-2.5
1948	StL-N	155	85	69	.552	2				86.6	-1.6
1949	StL-N	157	96	58	.623	2				92.2	3.8
1950	StL-N	153	78	75	.510	5				78.8	-0.8
	5	777	446	325	.578						1.2

Dykes, James Joseph "Jimmy"

1934	Chi-A*	138	49	88	.358	8	8		2/2	48.6	0.4
1935	Chi-A*	153	74	78	.487	5				74.8	-0.8
1936	Chi-A*	153	81	70	.536	3				79.6	1.4
1937	Chi-A*	154	86	68	.558	3				81.8	4.2
1938	Chi-A*	149	65	83	.439	6				69.9	-4.9
1939	Chi-A*	155	85	69	.552	4				78.7	6.3
1940	Chi-A	155	82	72	.532	●4				83.3	-1.3
1941	Chi-A	156	77	77	.500	3				75.9	1.1
1942	Chi-A	148	66	82	.446	6				66.3	-0.3
1943	Chi-A	155	82	72	.532	4				74.7	7.3
1944	Chi-A	154	71	83	.461	7				64.2	6.8
1945	Chi-A	150	71	78	.477	6				70.6	0.4
1946	Chi-A	30	10	20	.333	7	5		1/2	14.3	-4.3
1951	Phi-A	154	70	84	.455	6				76.1	-6.1
1952	Phi-A	155	79	75	.513	4				71.1	7.9
1953	Phi-A	157	59	95	.383	7				60.4	-1.4
1954	Bal-A	154	54	100	.351	7				56.7	-2.7
1958	Cin-N	41	24	17	.585	8	4		2/2	22.5	1.5
1959	Det-A	137	74	63	.540	8	4		2/2	66.8	7.2
1960	Det-A	96	44	52	.458	6	6		1/3	47.3	-3.3
	Cle-A	58	26	32	.448	4	4		3/3	28.0	-2.0
1961	Cle-A	160	77	83	.481	5	5		1/2	78.5	-1.5
	21	2962	1406	1541	.477						15.7

Ebbets, Charles Hercules "Charlie"

1898	Bro-N	110	38	68	.358	9	10		3/3	40.8	-2.8

Edwards, Howard Rodney "Doc"

1987	Cle-A	75	30	45	.400	7 E	7 E		2/2	28.3	1.7
1988	Cle-A	162	78	84	.481	6 E				74.4	3.6
1989	Cle-A	143	65	78	.455	6 E	6 E		1/2	66.7	-1.7
	3	380	173	207	.455						3.6

Elberfeld, Norman Arthur "Kid"

1908	NY-A*	98	27	71	.276	6	8		2/2	31.4	-4.4

Elia, Lee Constantine

1982	Chi-N	162	73	89	.451	5 E				77.6	-4.6
1983	Chi-N	123	54	69	.439	5 E	5 E		1/2	60.1	-6.1
1987	Phi-N	101	51	50	.505	5 E	●4 E		2/2	47.6	3.4
1988	Phi-N	153	60	92	.395	6 E	6 E		1/2	62.5	-2.5
	4	539	238	300	.442						-9.8

YEAR	TM/L	G	W	L	PCT	STANDING			M/Y	W-EXP	A-E
Ellick, Joseph J. "Joe"											
1884	Pit-U*	13	6	6	.500	5	5		2/2	5.4	0.6
Elliott, Robert Irving "Bob"											
1960	KC-A	155	58	96	.377	8				62.8	-4.8
Ens, Jewel Winklemeyer											
1929	Pit-N	35	21	14	.600	2	2		2/2	20.1	0.9
1930	Pit-N	154	80	74	.519	5				73.8	6.2
1931	Pit-N	155	75	79	.487	5				71.4	3.6
3		344	176	167	.513						10.8
Ermer, Calvin Coolidge "Cal"											
1967	Min-A	114	66	46	.589	6	●2		2/2	62.1	3.9
1968	Min-A	162	79	83	.488	7				82.8	-3.8
2		276	145	129	.529						0.1
Esterbrook, Thomas Jefferson "Dude"											
1889	Lou-a*	10	2	8	.200	7	8		1/4	2.2	-0.2
Evers, John Joseph "Johnny"											
1913	Chi-N*	155	88	65	.575	3				85.6	2.4
1921	Chi-N	96	41	55	.427	6	7		1/2	41.6	-0.6
1924	Chi-A	21	10	11	.476	6			1/4	9.7	0.3
	Chi-A	103	41	61	.402	8			4/4	47.0	-6.0
5		375	180	192	.484						-3.9
Ewing, William "Buck"											
1890	NY-P*	132	74	57	.565	3				76.8	-2.8
1895	Cin-N*	132	66	64	.508	8				69.0	-3.0
1896	Cin-N*	128	77	50	.606	3				78.3	-1.3
1897	Cin-N*	134	76	56	.576	4				71.3	4.7
1898	Cin-N	157	92	60	.605	3				84.6	7.4
1899	Cin-N	157	83	67	.553	6				83.0	0.0
1900	NY-N	63	21	41	.339	8	8		1/2	26.5	-5.5
7		903	489	395	.553						-0.5
Faatz, Jayson S. "Jay"											
1890	Buf-P*	34	9	24	.273	8	8	8	2/3	8.6	0.4
Falk, Bibb August											
1933	Cle-A	1	1	0	1.000	5	5	4	2/3	0.5	0.5
Fanning, William James "Jim"											
1981(2)	Mon-N	27	16	11	.593	2 E	1 E		2/2	14.8	1.2
1982	Mon-N	162	86	76	.531	3 E				89.5	-3.5
1984	Mon-N	30	14	16	.467	5 E	5 E		2/2	15.2	-1.2
3		219	116	103	.530						-3.5
Farrell, John A. "Jack"											
1881	Pro-N*	51	24	27	.471	4	2		1/2	26.7	-2.7
Farrell, Major Kerby "Kerby"											
1957	Cle-A	153	76	77	.497	6				72.5	3.5
Felske, John Frederick											
1985	Phi-N	162	75	87	.463	5 E				80.4	-5.4
1986	Phi-N	161	86	75	.534	2 E				83.1	2.9
1987	Phi-N	61	29	32	.475	5 E	●4 E		1/2	28.7	0.3
3		384	190	194	.495						-2.2
Ferguson, Robert V. "Bob"											
1871	Mut-n*	33	16	17	.485	4				15.7	0.3
1872	Atl-n*	37	9	28	.243	6				2.3	6.7
1873	Atl-n*	55	17	37	.315	6				13.5	3.5
1874	Atl-n*	56	22	33	.400	6				15.4	6.6
1875	Har-n*	86	54	28	.659	3				60.8	-6.8
1876	Har-N*	69	47	21	.691	3				49.9	-2.9
1877	Har-N*	60	31	27	.534	3				31.7	-0.7
1878	Chi-N*	61	30	30	.500	4				33.5	-3.5
1879	Tro-N*	30	7	22	.241	8	8		2/2	6.8	0.2
1880	Tro-N*	83	41	42	.494	4				37.1	3.9
1881	Tro-N*	85	39	45	.464	5				39.1	-0.1
1882	Tro-N*	85	35	48	.422	7				33.3	1.7
1883	Phi-N*	17	4	13	.235	8	8		1/2	2.1	1.9
1884	Pit-a*	42	11	31	.262	9	11	10	2/5	9.4	1.6
1886	NY-a	120	48	70	.407	8	7		2/2	47.7	0.3
1887	NY-a	30	6	24	.200	8	7		1/3	8.7	-2.7
16		949	417	516	.447						9.8
Ferraro, Michael Dennis "Mike"											
1983	Cle-A	100	40	60	.400	7 E	7 E		1/2	45.1	-5.1
1986	KC-A	74	36	38	.486	4 W	●3 W		2/2	36.1	-0.1
2		174	76	98	.437						-5.1
Fessenden, Wallace Clifton											
1890	Syr-a	11	4	7	.364	7	7	6	2/3	4.5	-0.5
Fitzsimmons, Frederick Landis "Freddie"											
1943	Phi-N	65	26	38	.406	7	7		2/2	27.4	-1.4
1944	Phi-N	154	61	92	.399	8				63.7	-2.7
1945	Phi-N	69	18	51	.261	8	8		1/2	20.4	-2.4
3		288	105	181	.367						-6.5
Fletcher, Arthur "Art"											
1923	Phi-N	155	50	104	.325	8				53.8	-3.8
1924	Phi-N	152	55	96	.364	7				59.1	-4.1
1925	Phi-N	153	68	85	.444	●6				66.0	2.0
1926	Phi-N	152	58	93	.384	8				55.7	2.3
1929	NY-A	11	6	5	.545	2	2		2/2	6.3	-0.3
5		623	237	383	.382						-4.0
Flint, Frank Sylvester "Silver"											
1879	Chi-N*	19	5	12	.294	2	4		2/2	9.0	-4.0
Fogarty, James G. "Jim"											
1890	Phi-P*	16	7	9	.438	5	5		1/2	8.9	-1.9
Fogel, Horace S.											
1887	Ind-N	70	20	49	.290	8	8		3/3	18.9	1.1
1902	NY-N	44	18	23	.439	4	8		1/3	14.1	3.9
2		114	38	72	.345						5.0
Fohl, Leo Alexander "Lee"											
1915	Cle-A	127	45	79	.363	6	7		2/2	50.6	-5.6
1916	Cle-A	157	77	77	.500	6				80.0	-3.0
1917	Cle-A	156	88	66	.571	3				81.6	6.4
1918	Cle-A	129	73	54	.575	2				69.8	3.2
1919	Cle-A	78	44	34	.564	3	2		1/2	44.7	-0.7
1921	StL-A	154	81	73	.526	3				76.1	4.9
1922	StL-A	154	93	61	.604	2				98.5	-5.5
1923	StL-A	103	52	49	.515	3	5		1/2	48.4	3.6
1924	Bos-A	157	67	87	.435	7				70.4	-3.4
1925	Bos-A	152	47	105	.309	8				49.5	-2.5
1926	Bos-A	154	46	107	.301	8				49.3	-3.3
11		1521	713	792	.474						-5.8
Fonseca, Lewis Albert "Lew"											
1932	Chi-A*	152	49	102	.325	7				54.0	-5.0
1933	Chi-A*	151	67	83	.447	6				62.5	4.5
1934	Chi-A	15	4	11	.267	8	8		1/2	5.3	-1.3
3		318	120	196	.380						-1.8
Foutz, David Luther "Dave"											
1893	Bro-N*	130	65	63	.508	●6				58.1	6.9
1894	Bro-N*	135	70	61	.534	5				66.6	3.4
1895	Bro-N*	134	71	60	.542	●5				68.3	2.7
1896	Bro-N*	133	58	73	.443	●9				59.0	-1.0
4		532	264	257	.507						12.1
Fox, Charles Francis "Charlie"											
1970	SF-N	120	67	53	.558	4 W	3 W		2/2	60.3	6.7
1971	SF-N	162	90	72	.556	1 W				87.4	2.6
1972	SF-N	155	69	86	.445	5 W				78.8	-9.8
1973	SF-N	162	88	74	.543	3 W				84.7	3.3
1974	SF-N	76	34	42	.447	5 W	5 W		1/2	33.7	0.3
1976	Mon-N	34	12	22	.353	6 E	6 E		2/2	12.4	-0.4
1983	Chi-N	39	17	22	.436	5 E	5 E		2/2	19.1	-2.1
7		748	377	371	.504						0.5
Franks, Herman Louis											
1965	SF-N	163	95	67	.586	2				90.5	4.5
1966	SF-N	161	93	68	.578	2				85.7	7.3
1967	SF-N	162	91	71	.562	2				92.1	-1.1
1968	SF-N	163	88	74	.543	2				89.0	-1.0
1977	Chi-N	162	81	81	.500	4 E				76.3	4.7
1978	Chi-N	162	79	83	.488	3 E				74.8	4.2
1979	Chi-N	155	78	77	.503	5 E	5 E		1/2	77.4	0.6
7		1128	605	521	.537						19.2
Frazer, George Kasson											
1890	Syr-a	71	31	40	.437	7	6		1/3	29.0	2.0
	Syr-a	46	20	25	.444	7	6		3/3	18.4	1.6
Frazier, Joseph Filmore "Joe"											
1976	NY-N	162	86	76	.531	3 E				89.7	-3.7
1977	NY-N	45	15	30	.333	6 E	6 E		1/2	20.2	-5.2
2		207	101	106	.488						-8.9
Fregosi, James Louis "Jim"											
1978	Cal-A	117	62	55	.530	3 W	●2 W		2/2	60.4	1.6
1979	Cal-A	162	88	74	.543	1 W				90.3	-2.3
1980	Cal-A	160	65	95	.406	6 W				70.3	-5.3
1981(1)	Cal-A	47	22	25	.468	4 W	4 W		1/2	24.5	-2.5
1986	Chi-A	96	45	51	.469	5 W	5 W		3/3	44.6	0.4
1987	Chi-A	162	77	85	.475	5 W				81.2	-4.2
1988	Chi-A	161	71	90	.441	5 W				67.6	3.4
7		905	430	475	.475						-8.9
Frey, James Gottfried "Jim"											
1980	KC-A	162	97	65	.599	◆1 W				92.3	4.7
1981(1)	KC-A	50	20	30	.400	5 W					
(2)	KC-A	20	10	10	.500	●2 W	1 W		1/2	34.4	-4.4
1984	Chi-N	161	96	65	.596	1 E				91.0	5.0
1985	Chi-N	162	77	84	.478	4 E				76.1	0.9
1986	Chi-N	56	23	33	.411	5 E	5 E		1/3	24.5	-1.5
5		611	323	287	.530						4.6
Frisch, Frank Francis "Frankie"											
1933	StL-N*	63	36	26	.581	5	5		2/2	34.3	1.7
1934	StL-N*	154	95	58	.621	★1				90.5	4.5
1935	StL-N*	154	96	58	.623	2				96.9	-0.9
1936	StL-N*	155	87	67	.565	●2				77.1	9.9
1937	StL-N*	157	81	73	.526	4				82.4	-1.4
1938	StL-N	139	63	72	.467	6	6		1/2	67.9	-4.9
1940	Pit-N	156	78	76	.506	4				79.4	-1.4
1941	Pit-N	156	81	73	.526	4				81.8	-0.8
1942	Pit-N	151	66	81	.449	5				68.6	-2.6
1943	Pit-N	157	80	74	.519	4				83.7	-3.7
1944	Pit-N	158	90	63	.588	2				84.7	5.3
1945	Pit-N	155	82	72	.532	4				83.6	-1.6

YEAR	TM/L	G	W	L	PCT	STANDING			M/Y	W-EXP	A-E
1946	Pit-N	152	62	89	.411	7	7		1/2	63.3	-1.3
1949	Chi-N	104	42	62	.404	7	8		2/2	39.8	2.2
1950	Chi-N	154	64	89	.418	7				63.7	0.3
1951	Chi-N	81	35	45	.438	7	8		1/2	32.9	2.1
	16	2246	1138	1078	.514						7.3

Fuchs, Emil Edmund "Judge"

1929	Bos-N	154	56	98	.364	8				56.2	-0.2

Gaffney, John H.

1886	Was-N	43	15	25	.375	8			2/2	9.0	6.0
1887	Was-N	126	46	76	.377	7				41.6	4.4
	2	169	61	101	.377						10.4

Galvin, James Francis "Jim"

1885	Buf-N*	24	7	17	.292	7	7		1/2	6.9	0.1

Ganzel, John Henry

1908	Cin-N*	155	73	81	.474	5				70.6	2.4
1915	Bro-F	35	17	18	.486	7	7		2/2	16.9	0.1
	2	190	90	99	.476						2.5

Garcia, David "Dave"

1977	Cal-A	81	35	46	.432	5 W	5 W		2/2	39.5	-4.5
1978	Cal-A	45	25	20	.556	3 W	●2 W		1/2	23.2	1.8
1979	Cle-A	66	38	28	.576	6 E	6 E		2/2	31.2	6.8
1980	Cle-A	160	79	81	.494	6 E				73.3	5.7
1981(1)	Cle-A	50	26	24	.520	6 E					
(2)	Cle-A	53	26	27	.491	5 E				50.4	1.6
1982	Cle-A	162	78	84	.481	●6 E				74.4	3.6
	6	617	307	310	.498						14.9

Gardner, William Frederick "Billy"

1981(1)	Min-A	20	6	14	.300	6 W	7 W		2/2		
(2)	Min-A	53	24	29	.453	4 W				28.8	1.2
1982	Min-A	162	60	102	.370	7 W				64.9	-4.9
1983	Min-A	162	70	92	.432	5 W				70.0	0.0
1984	Min-A	162	81	81	.500	2 W				80.8	0.2
1985	Min-A	62	27	35	.435	6 W	4 W		1/2	28.1	-1.1
1987	KC-A	126	62	64	.492	4 W	2 W		1/2	64.9	-2.9
	6	747	330	417	.442						-7.4

Gaston, Clarence Edwin "Cito"

1989	Tor-A	126	77	49	.611	6 E	1 E		2/2	69.4	7.6
1990	Tor-A	162	86	76	.531	2 E				91.7	-5.7
	2	288	163	125	.566						1.9

Gerhardt, John Joseph "Joe"

1883	Lou-a*	98	52	45	.536	5				48.7	3.3
1890	StL-a*	38	20	16	.556	2	3		6/6	21.1	-1.1
	2	136	72	61	.541						2.2

Gessler, Harry Homer "Doc"

1914	Pit-F	11	3	8	.273	8	7		1/2	4.8	-1.8

Gibson, George C. "Moon"

1920	Pit-N	155	79	75	.513	4				74.5	4.5
1921	Pit-N	154	90	63	.588	2				86.6	3.4
1922	Pit-N	65	32	33	.492	5	●3		1/2	37.6	-5.6
1925	Chi-N	26	12	14	.462	7	8		3/3	12.2	-0.2
1932	Pit-N	154	86	68	.558	2				76.0	10.0
1933	Pit-N	154	87	67	.565	2				82.0	5.0
1934	Pit-N	51	27	24	.529	4	5		1/2	26.2	0.8
	7	759	413	344	.546						17.9

Gifford, James H. "Jim"

1884	Ind-a	87	25	60	.294	10	11		1/2	21.5	3.5
1885	NY-a	108	44	64	.407	7				39.5	4.5
1886	NY-a	17	5	12	.294	8	7		1/2	6.9	-1.9
	3	212	74	136	.352						6.1

Glasscock, John Wesley "Jack"

1889	Ind-N*	67	34	32	.515	7	7		2/2	29.9	4.1
1892(1)	StL-N*	4	1	3	.250	10	9		1/3		
	2	71	35	35	.500						4.1

Gleason, William J. "Kid"

1919	Chi-A	140	88	52	.629	1				83.6	4.4
1920	Chi-A	154	96	58	.623	2				89.6	6.4
1921	Chi-A	154	62	92	.403	7				60.4	1.4
1922	Chi-A	155	77	77	.500	5				77.0	0.0
1923	Chi-A	156	69	85	.448	7				72.1	-3.1
	5	759	392	364	.519						9.3

Gomez, Pedro W. [Martinez] "Preston"

1969	SD-N	162	52	110	.321	6 W				50.5	1.5
1970	SD-N	162	63	99	.389	6 W				70.3	-7.3
1971	SD-N	161	61	100	.379	6 W				66.2	-5.2
1972	SD-N	11	4	7	.364	4 W	6 W		1/2	4.1	-0.1
1974	Hou-N	162	81	81	.500	4 W				83.2	-2.2
1975	Hou-N	127	47	80	.370	6 W	6 W		1/2	59.7	-12.7
1980	Chi-N	90	38	52	.422	6 E	6 E		1/2	38.4	-0.4
	7	875	346	529	.395						-26.5

Gonzalez, Miguel Angel "Mike"

1938	StL-N	17	8	8	.500	6	6		2/2	8.0	-0.0
1940	StL-N	6	1	5	.167	6	7	3	2/3	3.2	-2.2
	2	23	9	13	.409						-2.2

Gordon, Joseph Lowell "Joe"

1958	Cle-A	86	46	40	.535	6	4		2/2	46.4	-0.4
1959	Cle-A	154	89	65	.578	2				86.9	2.1
1960	Cle-A	95	49	46	.516	4	4		1/3	45.9	3.1
	Det-A	57	26	31	.456	6	6		3/3	28.1	-2.1
1961	KC-A	60	26	33	.441	8	●9		1/2	23.1	2.9
1969	KC-A	163	69	93	.426	4 W				70.1	-1.1
	5	615	305	308	.498						4.6

Gore, George F.

1892(2)	StL-N*	16	6	9	.400	12	12	11	2/3	5.5	0.5

Goryl, John Albert "Johnny"

1980	Min-A	36	23	13	.639	4 W	3 W		2/2	16.8	6.2
1981(1)	Min-A	37	11	25	.306	6 W	7 W		1/2		
	2	73	34	38	.472						6.2

Gould, Charles Harvey "Charlie"

1875	NH-n*	23	2	21	.087	11	8		1/3	1.9	0.1
1876	Cin-N*	65	9	56	.138	8				3.6	5.4
	2	88	11	77	.125						5.5

Gowdy, Henry Morgan "Hank"

1946	Cin-N	4	3	1	.750	6	6		2/2	1.9	1.1

Graffen, Samuel Mason "Mase"

1876	StL-N	56	39	17	.696	2	2		1/2	41.3	-2.3

Grammas, Alexander Peter "Alex"

1969	Pit-N	5	4	1	.800	3 E	3 E		2/2	2.7	1.3
1976	Mil-A	161	66	95	.410	6 E				71.3	-5.3
1977	Mil-A	162	67	95	.414	6 E				68.2	-1.2
	3	328	137	191	.418						-5.1

Green, George Dallas "Dallas"

1979	Phi-N	30	19	11	.633	5 E	4 E		2/2	14.3	4.7
1980	Phi-N	162	91	71	.562	★1 E				90.2	0.8
1981(1)	Phi-N	55	34	21	.618	1 E					
(2)	Phi-N	52	25	27	.481	3 E				55.4	3.6
1989	NY-A	121	56	65	.463	6 E	5 E		1/2	53.5	2.5
	4	420	225	195	.536						11.5

Griffin, Michael Joseph "Mike"

1898	Bro-N*	4	1	3	.250	9	9	10	2/3	1.5	-0.5

Griffin, Tobias Charles "Sandy"

1891	Was-a*	6	2	4	.333	8	8		4/4	1.6	0.4

Griffith, Clark Calvin

1901	Chi-A*	137	83	53	.610	1				85.3	-2.3
1902	Chi-A*	138	74	60	.552	4				74.2	-0.2
1903	NY-A*	136	72	62	.537	4				67.6	4.4
1904	NY-A*	155	92	59	.609	2				83.5	8.5
1905	NY-A*	152	71	78	.477	6				70.7	0.3
1906	NY-A*	155	90	61	.596	2				86.5	3.5
1907	NY-A*	152	70	78	.473	5				67.8	2.2
1908	NY-A	57	24	32	.429	6	8		1/2	17.9	6.1
1909	Cin-N*	157	77	76	.503	4				77.3	-0.3
1910	Cin-N*	156	75	79	.487	5				70.4	4.6
1911	Cin-N	159	70	83	.458	6				74.1	-4.1
1912	Was-A*	154	91	61	.599	2				88.2	2.8
1913	Was-A*	155	90	64	.584	2				80.8	9.2
1914	Was-A*	158	81	73	.526	3				83.1	-2.1
1915	Was-A	155	85	68	.556	4				85.4	-0.4
1916	Was-A	159	76	77	.497	7				75.7	0.3
1917	Was-A	158	74	79	.484	5				73.9	0.1
1918	Was-A	130	72	56	.563	3				69.7	2.3
1919	Was-A	142	56	84	.400	7				66.0	-10.0
1920	Was-A	153	68	84	.447	6				68.5	-0.5
	20	2918	1491	1367	.522						24.5

Grimes, Burleigh Arland

1937	Bro-N	155	62	91	.405	6				60.9	1.1
1938	Bro-N	151	69	80	.463	7				73.9	-4.9
	2	306	131	171	.434						-3.8

Grimm, Charles John "Charlie"

1932	Chi-N*	55	37	18	.673	2	1		2/2	30.6	6.4
1933	Chi-N*	154	86	68	.558	3				88.9	-2.9
1934	Chi-N*	152	86	65	.570	3				82.2	3.8
1935	Chi-N*	154	100	54	.649	1				101.5	-1.5
1936	Chi-N*	154	87	67	.565	●2				92.4	-5.4
1937	Chi-N	154	93	61	.604	2				89.4	3.6
1938	Chi-N	81	45	36	.556	3	1		1/2	46.8	-1.8
1944	Chi-N	146	74	69	.517	8	4		3/3	74.6	-0.6
1945	Chi-N	155	98	56	.636	1				98.3	-0.3
1946	Chi-N	155	82	71	.536	3				81.3	0.7
1947	Chi-N	155	69	85	.448	6				60.9	8.1
1948	Chi-N	155	64	90	.416	8				65.7	-1.7
1949	Chi-N	50	19	31	.380	7	8		1/2	19.1	-0.1
1952	Bos-N	120	51	67	.432	7	7		2/2	52.2	-1.2
1953	Mil-N	157	92	62	.597	2				92.4	-0.4
1954	Mil-N	154	89	65	.578	3				89.1	-0.1
1955	Mil-N	154	85	69	.552	2				84.4	0.6
1956	Mil-N	46	24	22	.522	5	2		1/2	27.4	-3.4
1960	Chi-N	17	6	11	.353	7	7		1/2	6.9	-0.9
	19	2368	1287	1067	.547						2.8

Groh, Henry Knight "Heinie"

1918	Cin-N*	10	7	3	.700	4	3		2/2	5.3	1.7

Gutteridge, Donald Joseph "Don"

YEAR	TM/L	G	W	L	PCT		STANDING		M/Y	W-EXP	A-E
1969	Chi-A	145	60	85	.414	4 W	5 W		2/2	63.4	-3.4
1970	Chi-A	136	49	87	.360	6 W	6 W		1/3	52.1	-3.1
	2	281	109	172	.388						-6.5

Haas, George Edwin "Eddie"

YEAR	TM/L	G	W	L	PCT		STANDING		M/Y	W-EXP	A-E
1985	Atl-N	121	50	71	.413	5 W	5 W		1/2	49.2	0.8

Hack, Stanley Camfield "Stan"

YEAR	TM/L	G	W	L	PCT		STANDING		M/Y	W-EXP	A-E
1954	Chi-N	154	64	90	.416	7				70.6	-6.6
1955	Chi-N	154	72	81	.471	6				67.6	4.4
1956	Chi-N	157	60	94	.390	8				65.4	-5.4
1958	StL-N	10	3	7	.300	5	●5		2/2	4.4	-1.4
	4	475	199	272	.423						-9.1

Hackett, Charles M. "Charlie"

YEAR	TM/L	G	W	L	PCT		STANDING		M/Y	W-EXP	A-E
1884	Cle-N	113	35	77	.313	7				32.0	3.0
1885	Bro-a	37	15	22	.405	7	●5		1/2	17.7	-2.7
	2	150	50	99	.336						0.3

Hallman, William Wilson "Bill"

YEAR	TM/L	G	W	L	PCT		STANDING		M/Y	W-EXP	A-E
1897	StL-N*	50	13	36	.265	12	12	12	3/4	8.9	4.1

Haney, Fred Girard

YEAR	TM/L	G	W	L	PCT		STANDING		M/Y	W-EXP	A-E
1939	StL-A	156	43	111	.279	8				50.1	-7.1
1940	StL-A	156	67	87	.435	6				65.4	1.6
1941	StL-A	44	15	29	.341	7	●6		1/2	20.4	-5.4
1953	Pit-N	154	50	104	.325	8				51.6	-1.6
1954	Pit-N	154	53	101	.344	8				48.4	4.6
1955	Pit-N	154	60	94	.390	8				55.8	4.2
1956	Mil-N	109	68	40	.630	5	2		2/2	64.3	3.7
1957	Mil-N	155	95	59	.617	★1				93.0	2.0
1958	Mil-N	154	92	62	.597	1				91.3	0.7
1959	Mil-N	157	86	70	.551	▲2				88.3	-2.3
	10	1393	629	757	.454						0.4

Hanlon, Edward Hugh "Ned"

YEAR	TM/L	G	W	L	PCT		STANDING		M/Y	W-EXP	A-E
1889	Pit-N*	46	26	18	.591	7	5		3/3	19.8	6.2
1890	Pit-P*	131	60	68	.469	6				59.3	0.7
1891	Pit-N*	78	31	47	.397	8	8		1/2	35.5	-4.5
1892(1)	Bal-N*	56	17	39	.304	12	12		3/3		
(2)	Bal-N*	77	26	46	.361	10				45.7	-2.7
1893	Bal-N	130	60	70	.462	8				59.0	1.0
1894	Bal-N	129	89	39	.695	1				90.9	-1.9
1895	Bal-N	132	87	43	.669	1				95.8	-8.8
1896	Bal-N	132	90	39	.698	1				92.7	-2.7
1897	Bal-N	136	90	40	.692	2				90.1	-0.1
1898	Bal-N	154	96	53	.644	2				103.8	-7.8
1899	Bro-N	150	101	47	.682	1				95.8	5.2
1900	Bro-N	142	82	54	.603	1				76.6	5.4
1901	Bro-N	137	79	57	.581	3				81.8	-2.8
1902	Bro-N	141	75	63	.543	2				73.9	1.1
1903	Bro-N	139	70	66	.515	5				66.6	3.4
1904	Bro-N	154	56	97	.366	6				63.4	-7.4
1905	Bro-N	155	48	104	.316	8				45.0	3.0
1906	Cin-N	155	64	87	.424	6				70.0	-6.0
1907	Cin-N	156	66	87	.431	6				77.3	-11.3
	19	2530	1313	1164	.530						-29.8

Harder, Melvin Leroy "Mel"

YEAR	TM/L	G	W	L	PCT		STANDING		M/Y	W-EXP	A-E
1961	Cle-A	1	1	0	1.000	5	5		2/2	0.5	0.5
1962	Cle-A	2	2	0	1.000	6	6		2/2	0.9	1.1
	2	3	3	0	1.000						1.6

Harrelson, Derrel McKinley "Bud"

YEAR	TM/L	G	W	L	PCT		STANDING		M/Y	W-EXP	A-E
1990	NY-N	120	71	49	.592	4 E	2 E		2/2	72.3	-1.3

Harris, Chalmer Luman "Lum"

YEAR	TM/L	G	W	L	PCT		STANDING		M/Y	W-EXP	A-E
1961	Bal-A	27	17	10	.630	3	3		2/2	15.3	1.7
1964	Hou-N	13	5	8	.385	9	9		2/2	5.3	-0.3
1965	Hou-N	162	65	97	.401	9				65.8	-0.8
1968	Atl-N	163	81	81	.500	5				76.9	4.1
1969	Atl-N	162	93	69	.574	1 W				87.3	5.7
1970	Atl-N	162	76	86	.469	5 W				77.5	-1.5
1971	Atl-N	162	82	80	.506	3 W				75.2	6.8
1972	Atl-N	105	47	57	.452	4 W	4 W		1/2	45.0	2.0
	8	956	466	488	.488						17.7

Harris, Stanley Raymond "Bucky"

YEAR	TM/L	G	W	L	PCT		STANDING		M/Y	W-EXP	A-E
1924	Was-A*	156	92	62	.597	★1				91.4	0.6
1925	Was-A*	152	96	55	.636	1				90.7	5.3
1926	Was-A*	152	81	69	.540	4				78.8	2.2
1927	Was-A*	157	85	69	.552	3				82.0	3.0
1928	Was-A*	155	75	79	.487	4				78.3	-3.3
1929	Det-A*	155	70	84	.455	6				76.8	-6.8
1930	Det-A	154	75	79	.487	5				72.4	2.6
1931	Det-A	154	61	93	.396	7				59.1	1.9
1932	Det-A	153	76	75	.503	5				76.6	-0.6
1933	Det-A	153	73	79	.480	5	5		1/2	74.9	-1.9
1934	Bos-A	153	76	76	.500	4				80.2	-4.2
1935	Was-A	154	67	86	.438	6				69.3	-2.3
1936	Was-A	153	82	71	.536	4				84.6	-2.6
1937	Was-A	158	73	80	.477	6				68.6	4.4
1938	Was-A	152	75	76	.497	5				70.2	4.8
1939	Was-A	153	65	87	.428	6				66.9	-1.9
1940	Was-A	154	64	90	.416	7				62.9	1.1
1941	Was-A	156	70	84	.455	●6				70.3	-0.3
1942	Was-A	151	62	89	.411	7				59.7	2.3
1943	Phi-N	92	38	52	.422	7	7		1/2	38.5	-0.5
1947	NY-A	155	97	57	.630	★1				99.9	-2.9
1948	NY-A	154	94	60	.610	3				98.6	-4.6
1950	Was-A	155	67	87	.435	5				65.1	1.9
1951	Was-A	154	62	92	.403	7				68.0	-6.0
1952	Was-A	157	78	76	.506	5				75.9	2.1
1953	Was-A	152	76	76	.500	5				83.5	-7.5
1954	Was-A	155	66	88	.429	6				72.1	-6.1
1955	Det-A	154	79	75	.513	5				88.5	-9.5
1956	Det-A	155	82	72	.532	5				85.7	-3.7
	29	4408	2157	2218	.493						-32.5

Hart, James Aristotle "Jim"

YEAR	TM/L	G	W	L	PCT		STANDING		M/Y	W-EXP	A-E
1885	Lou-a	112	53	59	.473	●5				52.8	0.2
1886	Lou-a	138	66	70	.485	4				70.4	-4.4
1889	Bos-N	133	83	45	.648	2				82.2	0.8
	3	383	202	174	.537						-3.4

Hart, John Henry

YEAR	TM/L	G	W	L	PCT		STANDING		M/Y	W-EXP	A-E
1989	Cle-A	19	8	11	.421	6 E	6 E		2/2	8.9	-0.9

Hartnett, Charles Leo "Gabby"

YEAR	TM/L	G	W	L	PCT		STANDING		M/Y	W-EXP	A-E
1938	Chi-N*	73	44	27	.620	3	1		2/2	41.0	3.0
1939	Chi-N*	156	84	70	.545	4				81.6	2.4
1940	Chi-N*	154	75	79	.487	5				81.6	-6.6
	3	383	203	176	.536						-1.2

Hartsfield, Roy Thomas

YEAR	TM/L	G	W	L	PCT		STANDING		M/Y	W-EXP	A-E
1977	Tor-A	161	54	107	.335	7 E				58.6	-4.6
1978	Tor-A	161	59	102	.366	7 E				61.4	-2.4
1979	Tor-A	162	53	109	.327	7 E				56.2	-3.2
	3	484	166	318	.343						-10.3

Hastings, Winfield Scott "Scott"

YEAR	TM/L	G	W	L	PCT		STANDING		M/Y	W-EXP	A-E
1871	Rok-n*	25	4	21	.160	9				8.8	-4.8
1872	Cle-n*	20	6	14	.300	5	7		1/2	5.1	0.9
	2	45	10	35	.222						-3.9

Hatfield, John Van Buren

YEAR	TM/L	G	W	L	PCT		STANDING		M/Y	W-EXP	A-E
1872	Mut-n*	40	24	14	.632	4	3		2/2	27.6	-3.6
1873	Mut-n*	28	11	17	.393	5	4		1/2	15.6	-4.6
	2	68	35	31	.530						-8.1

Hatton, Grady Edgebert

YEAR	TM/L	G	W	L	PCT		STANDING		M/Y	W-EXP	A-E
1966	Hou-N	163	72	90	.444	8				72.2	-0.2
1967	Hou-N	162	69	93	.426	9				69.0	-0.0
1968	Hou-N	61	23	38	.377	10	10		1/2	27.1	-4.1
	3	386	164	221	.426						-4.3

Hecker, Guy Jackson

YEAR	TM/L	G	W	L	PCT		STANDING		M/Y	W-EXP	A-E
1890	Pit-N*	138	23	113	.169	8				15.5	7.5

Heffner, Donald Henry "Don"

YEAR	TM/L	G	W	L	PCT		STANDING		M/Y	W-EXP	A-E
1966	Cin-N	83	37	46	.446	8	7		1/2	41.0	-4.0

Heilbroner, Louis Wilbur "Louie"

YEAR	TM/L	G	W	L	PCT		STANDING		M/Y	W-EXP	A-E
1900	StL-N	50	23	25	.479	7	●5		2/2	23.9	-0.9

Helms, Tommy Vann

YEAR	TM/L	G	W	L	PCT		STANDING		M/Y	W-EXP	A-E
1988	Cin-N	27	12	15	.444	4 W	4 W	2 W	2/3	14.3	-2.3
1989	Cin-N	37	16	21	.432	●4 W	5 W		2/2	17.1	-1.1
	2	64	28	36	.438						-3.4

Hemus, Solomon Joseph "Solly"

YEAR	TM/L	G	W	L	PCT		STANDING		M/Y	W-EXP	A-E
1959	StL-N*	154	71	83	.461	7				68.5	2.5
1960	StL-N	155	86	68	.558	3				79.4	6.6
1961	StL-N	75	33	41	.446	6	5		1/2	38.7	-5.7
	3	384	190	192	.497						3.3

Henderson, William C. "Bill"

YEAR	TM/L	G	W	L	PCT		STANDING		M/Y	W-EXP	A-E
1884	Bal-U	106	58	47	.552	4				55.5	2.5

Hendricks, John Charles "Jack"

YEAR	TM/L	G	W	L	PCT		STANDING		M/Y	W-EXP	A-E
1918	StL-N	133	51	78	.395	8				56.5	-5.5
1924	Cin-N	153	83	70	.542	4				83.9	-0.9
1925	Cin-N	153	80	73	.523	3				81.3	-1.3
1926	Cin-N	157	87	67	.565	2				86.7	0.3
1927	Cin-N	153	75	78	.490	5				75.5	-0.5
1928	Cin-N	153	78	74	.513	5				72.1	5.9
1929	Cin-N	155	66	88	.429	7				69.7	-3.7
	7	1057	520	528	.496						-5.7

Hengle, Edward S. "Ed"

YEAR	TM/L	G	W	L	PCT		STANDING		M/Y	W-EXP	A-E
1884	Chi-U	74	34	39	.466	5				41.3	-0.3

Herman, William Jennings Bryan "Billy"

YEAR	TM/L	G	W	L	PCT		STANDING		M/Y	W-EXP	A-E
1947	Pit-N*	155	61	92	.399	8	●7		1/2	69.6	-8.6
1964	Bos-A	2	2	0	1.000	8	8		2/2	0.9	1.1
1965	Bos-A	162	62	100	.383	9				68.8	-6.8
1966	Bos-A	146	64	82	.438	9	9		1/2	66.0	-2.0
	4	465	189	274	.408						-16.3

Herzog, Charles Lincoln "Buck"

YEAR	TM/L	G	W	L	PCT		STANDING		M/Y	W-EXP	A-E
1914	Cin-N*	157	60	94	.390	8				63.8	-3.8
1915	Cin-N*	160	71	83	.461	7				69.1	1.9
1916	Cin-N*	84	34	49	.410	8	●7		1/3	34.7	-0.7
	3	401	165	226	.422						-2.6

Herzog, Dorrel Norman Elvert "Whitey"

YEAR	TM/L	G	W	L	PCT		STANDING		M/Y	W-EXP	A-E
1973	Tex-A	138	47	91	.341	6 W	6 W		1/3	49.9	-2.9
1974	Cal-A	4	2	2	.500	6 W	6 W	6 W	2/3	1.9	0.1

YEAR	TM/L	G	W	L	PCT	STANDING	M/Y	W-EXP	A-E
1975	KC-A	66	41	25	.621	2 W 2 W	2/2	35.6	5.4
1976	KC-A	162	90	72	.556	1 W		91.7	-1.7
1977	KC-A	162	102	60	.630	1 W		98.0	4.0
1978	KC-A	162	92	70	.568	1 W		92.2	-0.2
1979	KC-A	162	85	77	.525	2 W		84.3	0.7
1980	StL-N	73	38	35	.521	6 E 5 E 4 E	3/4	37.8	0.2
1981(1)	StL-N	51	30	20	.600	2 E			
(2)	StL-N	52	29	23	.558	2 E		55.8	3.2
1982	StL-N	162	92	70	.568	★1 E		89.1	2.9
1983	StL-N	162	79	83	.488	4 E		77.8	1.2
1984	StL-N	162	84	78	.519	3 E		81.7	2.3
1985	StL-N	162	101	61	.623	◆1 E		99.4	1.6
1986	StL-N	161	79	82	.491	3 E		79.4	-0.4
1987	StL-N	162	95	67	.586	◆1 E		91.4	3.6
1988	StL-N	162	76	86	.469	5 E		75.0	1.0
1989	StL-N	164	86	76	.531	3 E		83.6	2.4
1990	StL-N	80	33	47	.412	6 E 6 E	1/3	34.8	-1.8
	18	2409	1281	1125	.532				21.6

Hewett, Walter F.

YEAR	TM/L	G	W	L	PCT	STANDING	M/Y	W-EXP	A-E
1888	Was-N	40	10	29	.256	8 8	1/2	12.2	-2.2

Hicks, Nathaniel Woodhull "Nat"

1875	Mut-n*	71	30	38	.441	7		25.1	4.9

Higgins, Michael Franklin "Pinky"

1955	Bos-A	154	84	70	.545	4		87.2	-3.2
1956	Bos-A	155	84	70	.545	4		79.8	4.2
1957	Bos-A	154	82	72	.532	3		82.3	-0.3
1958	Bos-A	155	79	75	.513	3		77.6	1.4
1959	Bos-A	73	31	42	.425	8 8	1/3	37.9	-6.9
1960	Bos-A	105	48	57	.457	8 7	3/3	44.7	3.3
1961	Bos-A	163	76	86	.469	6		74.8	1.2
1962	Bos-A	160	76	84	.475	8		75.1	0.9
	8	1119	560	556	.502				0.6

Higham, Richard "Dick"

1874	Mut-n*	40	29	11	.725	2 2	2/2	26.2	2.8

Himsl, Avitus Bernard "Vedie"

1961	Chi-N	11	5	6	.455	6 ●6	1/9	4.7	0.3
	Chi-N	17	5	12	.294	7 7 7	3/9	7.3	-2.3
	Chi-N	4	0	3	.000	7 7 7	6/9	1.3	-1.3

Hitchcock, William Clyde "Billy"

1960	Det-A	1	1	0	1.000	6 6 6	2/3	0.5	0.5
1962	Bal-A	162	77	85	.475	7		78.1	-1.1
1963	Bal-A	162	86	76	.531	4		83.5	2.5
1966	Atl-N	51	33	18	.647	7 5	2/2	28.6	4.4
1967	Atl-N	159	77	82	.484	7 7	1/2	78.6	-1.6
	5	535	274	261	.512				4.8

Hodges, Gilbert Raymond "Gil"

1963	Was-A	121	42	79	.347	10 10	3/3	42.6	-0.6
1964	Was-A	162	62	100	.383	9		64.7	-2.7
1965	Was-A	162	70	92	.432	8		67.3	2.7
1966	Was-A	159	71	88	.447	8		68.4	2.6
1967	Was-A	161	76	85	.472	●6		70.9	5.1
1968	NY-N	163	73	89	.451	9		77.8	-4.8
1969	NY-N	162	100	62	.617	★1 E		91.1	8.9
1970	NY-N	162	83	79	.512	3 E		87.8	-4.8
1971	NY-N	162	83	79	.512	●3 E		85.3	-2.3
	9	1414	660	753	.467				4.1

Hoey, Frederick C. "Fred"

1899	NY-N	87	31	55	.360	9 10	2/2	36.2	-5.2

Holbert, William H. "Bill"

1879	Syr-N*	1	0	1	.000	6 6 7	2/3	0.3	-0.3

Hollingshead, John Samuel "Holly"

1875	Was-n*	20	4	16	.200	8 10	1/2	-2.4	6.4
1884	Was-a	62	12	50	.194	12 12	1/2	10.8	1.2
	2	82	16	66	.195				7.6

Holmes, Thomas Francis "Tommy"

1951	Bos-N*	95	48	47	.505	5 4	2/2	51.3	-3.3
1952	Bos-N	35	13	22	.371	7 7	1/2	15.5	-2.5
	2	130	61	69	.469				-5.8

Hornsby, Rogers

1925	StL-N*	115	64	51	.557	8 4	2/2	62.0	2.0
1926	StL-N*	156	89	65	.578	★1		90.5	-1.5
1927	NY-N*	33	22	10	.688	4 3	2/2	17.9	4.1
1928	Bos-N*	122	39	83	.320	7 7	2/2	42.2	-3.2
1930	Chi-N*	4	4	0	1.000	2 2	2/2	2.3	1.7
1931	Chi-N*	156	84	70	.545	3		88.3	-4.3
1932	Chi-N*	99	53	46	.535	2 1	1/2	55.2	-2.2
1933	StL-A*	54	19	33	.365	8 8	3/3	21.0	-2.0
1934	StL-A*	154	67	85	.441	6		63.8	3.2
1935	StL-A*	155	65	87	.428	7		56.5	8.5
1936	StL-A*	155	57	95	.375	7		53.5	3.5
1937	StL-A*	78	25	52	.325	7 8	1/2	24.7	0.3
1952	StL-A	51	22	29	.431	8 7	1/2	21.1	0.9
	Cin-N	51	27	24	.529	7 6	3/3	24.0	3.0
1953	Cin-N	147	64	82	.438	6 6	1/2	66.2	-2.2
	14	1530	701	812	.463				11.9

Houk, Ralph George "Ralph"

YEAR	TM/L	G	W	L	PCT	STANDING	M/Y	W-EXP	A-E
1961	NY-A	163	109	53	.673	★1		102.7	6.3
1962	NY-A	162	96	66	.593	★1		94.5	1.5
1963	NY-A	161	104	57	.646	1		98.4	5.6
1966	NY-A	140	66	73	.475	10 10	2/2	69.4	-3.4
1967	NY-A	163	72	90	.444	9		69.8	2.2
1968	NY-A	164	83	79	.512	5		81.6	1.4
1969	NY-A	162	80	81	.497	5 E		77.7	2.3
1970	NY-A	163	93	69	.574	2 E		88.2	4.8
1971	NY-A	162	82	80	.506	4 E		81.7	0.3
1972	NY-A	155	79	76	.510	4 E		80.9	-1.9
1973	NY-A	162	80	82	.494	4 E		84.3	-4.3
1974	Det-A	162	72	90	.444	6 E		65.8	6.2
1975	Det-A	159	57	102	.358	6 E		57.3	-0.3
1976	Det-A	161	74	87	.460	5 E		70.0	4.0
1977	Det-A	162	74	88	.457	4 E		77.3	-3.3
1978	Det-A	162	86	76	.531	5 E		87.3	-1.3
1981(1)	Bos-A	56	30	26	.536	5 E			
(2)	Bos-A	52	29	23	.558	●2 E		57.7	1.3
1982	Bos-A	162	89	73	.549	3 E		85.0	4.0
1983	Bos-A	162	78	84	.481	6 E		76.0	2.0
1984	Bos-A	162	86	76	.531	4 E		85.4	0.6
	20	3157	1619	1531	.514				27.8

Howard, Frank Oliver

1981(1)	SD-N	56	23	33	.411	6 W			
(2)	SD-N	54	18	36	.333	6 W		47.1	-6.1
1983	NY-N	116	52	64	.448	6 E 6 E	2/2	49.9	2.1
	2	226	93	133	.412				-4.0

Howe, Arthur Henry "Art"

1989	Hou-N	162	86	76	.531	3 W		78.7	7.3
1990	Hou-N	162	75	87	.463	●4 W		72.0	3.0
	2	324	161	163	.497				10.4

Howley, Daniel Philip "Dan"

1927	StL-A	155	59	94	.386	7		59.8	-0.8
1928	StL-A	154	82	72	.532	3		79.9	2.1
1929	StL-A	154	79	73	.520	4		78.0	1.0
1930	Cin-N	154	59	95	.383	7		58.7	0.3
1931	Cin-N	154	58	96	.377	8		61.7	-3.7
1932	Cin-N	155	60	94	.390	8		62.4	-2.4
	6	926	397	524	.431				-3.5

Howser, Richard Dalton "Dick"

1978	NY-A	1	0	1	.000	3 E 4 E ▲★1E	2/3	0.6	-0.6
1980	NY-A	162	103	59	.636	1 E		96.7	6.3
1981(2)	KC-A	33	20	13	.606	●2 W 1 W	2/2	16.2	3.8
1982	KC-A	162	90	72	.556	2 W		87.6	2.4
1983	KC-A	163	79	83	.488	2 W		73.9	5.1
1984	KC-A	162	84	78	.519	1 W		79.7	4.3
1985	KC-A	162	91	71	.562	★1 W		86.0	5.0
1986	KC-A	88	40	48	.455	4 W ●3 W	1/2	42.9	-2.9
	8	933	507	425	.544				23.4

Huff, George A.

1907	Bos-A	8	2	6	.250	●4 6 7	2/4	3.4	-1.4

Huggins, Miller James

1913	StL-N*	153	51	99	.340	8		51.5	-0.5
1914	StL-N*	157	81	72	.529	3		78.5	2.5
1915	StL-N*	157	72	81	.471	6		75.3	-3.3
1916	StL-N*	153	60	93	.392	●7		59.4	0.6
1917	StL-N	154	82	70	.539	3		72.0	10.0
1918	NY-A	126	60	63	.488	4		63.4	-3.4
1919	NY-A	141	80	59	.576	3		77.3	2.7
1920	NY-A	154	95	59	.617	3		97.3	-2.3
1921	NY-A	153	98	55	.641	1		98.4	-0.4
1922	NY-A	154	94	60	.610	1		91.1	2.9
1923	NY-A	152	98	54	.645	★1		95.6	2.4
1924	NY-A	153	89	63	.586	2		88.7	0.3
1925	NY-A	156	69	85	.448	7		70.4	-1.4
1926	NY-A	155	91	63	.591	1		89.7	1.3
1927	NY-A	155	110	44	.714	★1		112.4	-2.4
1928	NY-A	154	101	53	.656	★1		96.6	4.4
1929	NY-A	143	82	61	.573	2 2	1/2	82.0	0.0
	17	2570	1413	1134	.555				13.5

Hunter, Gordon William "Billy"

1977	Tex-A	93	60	33	.645	5 W 2 W	4/4	52.9	7.1
1978	Tex-A	161	86	75	.534	●2 W ●2 W	1/2	86.8	-0.8
	2	254	146	108	.575				6.4

Hurst, Timothy Carroll "Tim"

1898	StL-N	154	39	111	.260	12		40.6	-1.6

Hutchinson, Frederick Charles "Fred"

1952	Det-A*	83	27	55	.329	8 8	2/2	31.0	-4.0
1953	Det-A*	158	60	94	.390	6		55.6	4.4
1954	Det-A	155	68	86	.442	5		68.5	-0.5
1956	StL-N	156	76	78	.494	4		75.0	1.0
1957	StL-N	154	87	67	.565	2		84.1	2.9
1958	StL-N	144	69	75	.479	5 ●5	1/2	63.9	5.1
1959	Cin-N	74	39	35	.527	7 ●5	2/2	38.2	0.8
1960	Cin-N	154	67	87	.435	6		71.7	-4.7
1961	Cin-N	154	93	61	.604	1		82.7	10.3
1962	Cin-N	162	98	64	.605	3		92.6	5.4

YEAR	TM/L	G	W	L	PCT	STANDING	M/Y	W-EXP	A-E
1963	Cin-N	162	86	76	.531	5		86.9	-0.9
1964	Cin-N	100	54	45	.545	3 •2	1/4	55.8	-1.8
	Cin-N	10	6	4	.600	4 3 •2	3/4	5.6	0.4
	12	1666	830	827	.501				18.5

Irwin, Arthur Albert

YEAR	TM/L	G	W	L	PCT	STANDING	M/Y	W-EXP	A-E
1889	Was-N*	76	28	45	.384	8 8	2/2	23.2	4.8
1891	Bos-a*	139	93	42	.689	1		97.8	-4.8
1892(1)	Was-N	74	35	39	.473	•11 7	2/2	44.0	2.0
(2)	Was-N	34	11	21	.344	11 12	1/2		
1894	Phi-N*	132	71	57	.555	4		77.1	-6.1
1895	Phi-N	133	78	53	.595	3		74.0	4.0
1896	NY-N	90	36	53	.404	10 7	1/2	45.0	-9.0
1898	Was-N	30	10	19	.345	11 11	4/4	10.4	-0.4
1899	Was-N	155	54	98	.355	11		54.4	-0.4
	8	863	416	427	.493				-9.9

Jennings, Hugh Ambrose "Hughie"

YEAR	TM/L	G	W	L	PCT	STANDING	M/Y	W-EXP	A-E
1907	Det-A*	153	92	58	.613	1		92.2	-0.2
1908	Det-A	154	90	63	.588	1		87.3	2.7
1909	Det-A*	158	98	54	.645	1		95.2	2.8
1910	Det-A	155	86	68	.558	3		87.2	-1.2
1911	Det-A	154	89	65	.578	2		82.1	6.9
1912	Det-A*	154	69	84	.451	6		71.0	-2.0
1913	Det-A	153	66	87	.431	6		67.2	-1.2
1914	Det-A	157	80	73	.523	4		76.2	3.8
1915	Det-A	156	100	54	.649	2		95.3	4.7
1916	Det-A	155	87	67	.565	3		84.9	2.1
1917	Det-A	155	78	75	.510	4		83.1	-5.1
1918	Det-A*	128	55	71	.437	7		54.4	0.6
1919	Det-A	140	80	60	.571	4		74.1	5.9
1920	Det-A	155	61	93	.396	7		59.5	1.5
1924	NY-N	44	32	12	.727	3 1	2/3	28.0	4.0
	15	2171	1163	984	.542				25.4

Johnson, Darrell Dean

YEAR	TM/L	G	W	L	PCT	STANDING	M/Y	W-EXP	A-E
1974	Bos-A	162	84	78	.519	3 E		84.6	-0.6
1975	Bos-A	160	95	65	.594	♦1 E		88.5	6.5
1976	Bos-A	86	41	45	.477	5 E 3 E	1/2	46.1	-5.1
1977	Sea-A	162	64	98	.395	6 W		58.1	5.9
1978	Sea-A	160	56	104	.350	7 W		58.1	-2.1
1979	Sea-A	162	67	95	.414	6 W		70.4	-3.4
1980	Sea-A	105	39	65	.375	6 W 7 W	1/2	40.0	-1.0
1982	Tex-A	66	26	40	.394	6 W 6 W	2/2	26.2	-0.2
	8	1063	472	590	.444				0.1

Johnson, David Allen "Dave"

YEAR	TM/L	G	W	L	PCT	STANDING	M/Y	W-EXP	A-E
1984	NY-N	162	90	72	.556	2 E		78.5	11.5
1985	NY-N	162	98	64	.605	2 E		94.6	3.4
1986	NY-N	162	108	54	.667	★1 E		102.2	5.8
1987	NY-N	162	92	70	.568	2 E		93.2	-1.2
1988	NY-N	160	100	60	.625	1 E		98.5	1.5
1989	NY-N	162	87	75	.537	2 E		90.4	-3.4
1990	NY-N	42	20	22	.476	4 E 2 E	1/2	25.3	-5.3
	7	1012	595	417	.588				12.2

Johnson, Roy J

YEAR	TM/L	G	W	L	PCT	STANDING	M/Y	W-EXP	A-E
1944	Chi-N	1	0	1	.000	8 8 4	2/3	0.5	-0.5

Johnson, Walter Perry

YEAR	TM/L	G	W	L	PCT	STANDING	M/Y	W-EXP	A-E
1929	Was-A	153	71	81	.467	5		71.6	-0.6
1930	Was-A	154	94	60	.610	2		96.0	-2.0
1931	Was-A	156	92	62	.597	3		91.5	0.5
1932	Was-A	154	93	61	.604	3		88.7	4.3
1933	Cle-A	99	48	51	.485	5 4	3/3	48.5	-0.5
1934	Cle-A	154	85	69	.552	3		81.8	3.2
1935	Cle-A	96	46	48	.489	5 3	1/2	49.2	-3.2
	7	966	529	432	.550				1.7

Jones, Fielder Allison

YEAR	TM/L	G	W	L	PCT	STANDING	M/Y	W-EXP	A-E
1904	Chi-A*	114	66	47	.584	4 3	2/2	66.4	-0.4
1905	Chi-A*	158	92	60	.605	2		94.6	-2.6
1906	Chi-A*	154	93	58	.616	★1		88.3	4.7
1907	Chi-A*	157	87	64	.576	3		88.7	-1.7
1908	Chi-A*	156	88	64	.579	3		83.9	4.1
1914	StL-F*	40	12	26	.316	7 8	2/2	15.5	-3.5
1915	StL-F*	159	87	67	.565	2		88.9	-1.4
1916	StL-A	158	79	75	.513	5		81.8	-2.8
1917	StL-A	155	57	97	.370	7		57.9	-0.9
1918	StL-A	46	22	24	.478	6 5	1/3	22.1	-0.1
	10	1297	683	582	.540				-5.0

Joost, Edwin David "Eddie"

YEAR	TM/L	G	W	L	PCT	STANDING	M/Y	W-EXP	A-E
1954	Phi-A*	156	51	103	.331	8		43.8	7.2

Joyce, William Michael "Bill"

YEAR	TM/L	G	W	L	PCT	STANDING	M/Y	W-EXP	A-E
1896	NY-N*	43	28	14	.667	10 7	2/2	21.2	6.8
1897	NY-N*	138	83	48	.634	3		83.1	-0.1
1898	NY-N*	43	22	21	.512	6 7	1/3	22.5	-0.5
	NY-N*	92	46	39	.541	7 7	3/3	44.4	1.6
	3	316	179	122	.595				7.7

Jurges, William Frederick "Billy"

YEAR	TM/L	G	W	L	PCT	STANDING	M/Y	W-EXP	A-E
1959	Bos-A	80	44	36	.550	8 5	3/3	41.5	2.5
1960	Bos-A	42	15	27	.357	8 7	1/3	17.9	-2.9
	2	122	59	63	.484				-0.4

Kasko, Edward Michael "Eddie"

YEAR	TM/L	G	W	L	PCT	STANDING	M/Y	W-EXP	A-E
1970	Bos-A	162	87	75	.537	3 E		87.3	-0.3
1971	Bos-A	162	85	77	.525	3 E		83.5	1.5
1972	Bos-A	155	85	70	.548	2 E		79.6	5.4
1973	Bos-A	161	88	73	.547	2 E 2 E	1/2	89.8	-1.8
	4	640	345	295	.539				4.8

Keane, John Joseph "Johnny"

YEAR	TM/L	G	W	L	PCT	STANDING	M/Y	W-EXP	A-E
1961	StL-N	80	47	33	.587	6 5	2/2	41.8	5.2
1962	StL-N	163	84	78	.519	6		92.1	-8.1
1963	StL-N	162	93	69	.574	2		93.3	-0.3
1964	StL-N	162	93	69	.574	★1		87.5	5.5
1965	NY-A	162	77	85	.475	6		81.8	-4.8
1966	NY-A	20	4	16	.200	10 10	1/2	10.0	-6.0
	6	749	398	350	.532				-8.5

Kelley, Joseph James "Joe"

YEAR	TM/L	G	W	L	PCT	STANDING	M/Y	W-EXP	A-E
1902	Cin-N*	60	34	26	.567	6 4	3/3	33.0	1.0
1903	Cin-N*	141	74	65	.532	4		79.8	-5.8
1904	Cin-N*	157	88	65	.575	3		92.3	-4.3
1905	Cin-N*	155	79	74	.516	5		80.2	-1.2
1908	Bos-N*	156	63	91	.409	6		67.6	-4.6
	5	669	338	321	.513				-14.8

Kelly, Jay Thomas "Tom"

YEAR	TM/L	G	W	L	PCT	STANDING	M/Y	W-EXP	A-E
1986	Min-A	23	12	11	.522	7 W 6 W	2/2	10.2	1.8
1987	Min-A	162	85	77	.525	♦1 W		79.1	5.9
1988	Min-A	162	91	71	.562	2 W		89.8	1.2
1989	Min-A	162	80	82	.494	5 W		81.2	-1.2
1990	Min-A	162	74	88	.457	7 W		74.6	-0.6
	5	671	342	329	.510				7.2

Kelly, John O.

YEAR	TM/L	G	W	L	PCT	STANDING	M/Y	W-EXP	A-E
1887	Lou-a	139	76	60	.559	4		76.5	-0.5
1888	Lou-a	39	10	29	.256	8 7	1/4	14.8	-4.8
	2	178	86	89	.491				-5.3

Kelly, Michael Joseph "King"

YEAR	TM/L	G	W	L	PCT	STANDING	M/Y	W-EXP	A-E
1887	Bos-N*	95	49	43	.533	5 5	1/2	48.5	0.5
1890	Bos-P*	133	81	48	.628	1		82.9	-1.9
1891	Cin-a*	102	43	57	.430	6		41.8	1.2
	3	330	173	148	.539				-0.1

Kennedy, James C. "Jim"

YEAR	TM/L	G	W	L	PCT	STANDING	M/Y	W-EXP	A-E
1890	Bro-a	100	26	73	.263	8		28.8	-2.8

Kennedy, Robert Daniel "Bob"

YEAR	TM/L	G	W	L	PCT	STANDING	M/Y	W-EXP	A-E
1963	Chi-N	162	82	80	.506	7		80.1	1.9
1964	Chi-N	162	76	86	.469	8		73.3	2.7
1965	Chi-N	58	24	32	.429	9 8	1/2	24.8	-0.8
1968	Oak-A	163	82	80	.506	6		83.9	-1.9
	4	545	264	278	.487				1.9

Kerins, John Nelson

YEAR	TM/L	G	W	L	PCT	STANDING	M/Y	W-EXP	A-E
1888	Lou-a*	7	3	4	.429	8 8 7	3/4	2.7	0.3
1890	StL-a*	17	9	8	.529	4 4 3	2/6	10.0	-1.0
	2	24	12	12	.500				-0.6

Kessinger, Donald Eulon "Don"

YEAR	TM/L	G	W	L	PCT	STANDING	M/Y	W-EXP	A-E
1979	Chi-A	106	46	60	.434	5 W 5 W	1/2	51.8	-5.8

Killefer, William Lavier "Bill"

YEAR	TM/L	G	W	L	PCT	STANDING	M/Y	W-EXP	A-E
1921	Chi-N*	57	23	34	.404	6 7	2/2	24.7	-1.7
1922	Chi-N	156	80	74	.519	5		73.5	6.5
1923	Chi-N	154	83	71	.539	4		82.1	0.9
1924	Chi-N	154	81	72	.529	5		76.4	4.6
1925	Chi-N	75	33	42	.440	7 8	1/3	35.2	-2.2
1930	StL-A	154	64	90	.416	6		64.6	-0.6
1931	StL-A	154	63	91	.409	5		63.2	-0.2
1932	StL-A	154	63	91	.409	6		62.1	0.9
1933	StL-A	91	34	57	.374	8 8	1/3	36.7	-2.7
	9	1149	524	622	.457				5.6

King, Clyde Edward

YEAR	TM/L	G	W	L	PCT	STANDING	M/Y	W-EXP	A-E
1969	SF-N	162	90	72	.556	2 W		89.0	1.0
1970	SF-N	42	19	23	.452	4 W 3 W	1/2	21.1	-2.1
1974	Atl-N	64	38	25	.603	4 W 3 W	2/2	35.7	2.3
1975	Atl-N	134	58	76	.433	5 W 5 W	1/2	53.4	4.6
1982	NY-A	62	29	33	.468	•5 E 5 E	3/3	30.7	-1.7
	5	464	234	229	.505				4.1

Kittridge, Malachi J.

YEAR	TM/L	G	W	L	PCT	STANDING	M/Y	W-EXP	A-E
1904	Was-A*	18	1	16	.059	8 8	1/2	4.7	-3.7

Klein, Louis Frank "Lou"

YEAR	TM/L	G	W	L	PCT	STANDING	M/Y	W-EXP	A-E
1961	Chi-N	11	5	6	.455	7 7 7	8/9	4.7	0.3
1962	Chi-N	30	12	18	.400	9 9 9	2/3	11.4	0.6
1965	Chi-N	106	48	58	.453	9 8	2/2	47.0	1.0
	3	147	65	82	.442				1.9

Kling, John "Johnny"

YEAR	TM/L	G	W	L	PCT	STANDING	M/Y	W-EXP	A-E
1912	Bos-N*	155	52	101	.340	8		60.6	-8.6

Knabe, Franz Otto "Otto"

YEAR	TM/L	G	W	L	PCT	STANDING	M/Y	W-EXP	A-E
1914	Bal-F*	160	84	70	.545	3		78.8	5.2
1915	Bal-F*	155	47	107	.305	8		55.4	-8.4
	2	315	131	177	.425				-3.2

Knight, Alonzo P. "Lon"

YEAR	TM/L	G	W	L	PCT	STANDING	M/Y	W-EXP	A-E
1883	Phi-a*	98	66	32	.673	1		63.4	2.6
1884	Phi-a*	108	61	46	.570	7		67.1	-6.1

YEAR	TM/L	G	W	L	PCT	STANDING			M/Y	W-EXP	A-E
		2	206	127	78	.620					-3.5

Krol, John Thomas "Jack"

YEAR	TM/L	G	W	L	PCT	STANDING			M/Y	W-EXP	A-E
1978	StL-N	2	1	1	.500	6 E	6 E	5 E	2/3	0.9	0.1
1980	StL-N	1	0	1	.000	6 E	6 E	4 E	2/4	0.5	-0.5
		2	3	1	2	.333					-0.4

Kuehl, Karl Otto

YEAR	TM/L	G	W	L	PCT	STANDING			M/Y	W-EXP	A-E
1976	Mon-N	128	43	85	.336	6 E	6 E		1/2	46.8	-3.8

Kuenn, Harvey Edward

YEAR	TM/L	G	W	L	PCT	STANDING			M/Y	W-EXP	A-E
1975	Mil-A	1	1	0	1.000	5 E	5 E		2/2	0.4	0.6
1982	Mil-A	116	72	43	.626	5 E	♦1 E		2/2	69.3	2.7
1983	Mil-A	162	87	75	.537	5 E				86.6	0.4
		3	279	160	118	.576					3.7

Kuhel, Joseph Anthony "Joe"

YEAR	TM/L	G	W	L	PCT	STANDING			M/Y	W-EXP	A-E
1948	Was-A	154	56	97	.366	7				54.6	1.4
1949	Was-A	154	50	104	.325	8				49.3	0.7
		2	308	106	201	.345					2.1

Lachemann, Rene George

YEAR	TM/L	G	W	L	PCT	STANDING			M/Y	W-EXP	A-E
1981(1)	Sea-A	33	15	18	.455	7 W	6 W		2/2		
(2)	Sea-A	52	23	29	.442	5 W				34.9	3.1
1982	Sea-A	162	76	86	.469	4 W				74.7	1.3
1983	Sea-A	73	26	47	.356	7 W	7 W		1/2	27.8	-1.8
1984	Mil-A	161	67	94	.416	7 E				71.0	-4.0
		4	481	207	274	.430					-1.4

Lajoie, Napoleon "Nap"

YEAR	TM/L	G	W	L	PCT	STANDING			M/Y	W-EXP	A-E
1905	Cle-A*	58	37	21	.638	●1	5		1/3	28.2	8.8
	Cle-A*	56	19	36	.345	2	5		3/3	26.7	-7.7
1906	Cle-A*	157	89	64	.582	3				96.6	-7.6
1907	Cle-A*	158	85	67	.559	4				76.6	8.4
1908	Cle-A*	157	90	64	.584	2				90.0	-0.0
1909	Cle-A*	114	57	57	.500	4	6		1/2	53.6	3.4
		5	700	377	309	.550					5.3

Lake, Frederick Lovett "Fred"

YEAR	TM/L	G	W	L	PCT	STANDING			M/Y	W-EXP	A-E
1908	Bos-A	40	22	17	.564	6	5		2/2	21.0	1.0
1909	Bos-A	152	88	63	.583	3				80.6	7.4
1910	Bos-N*	157	53	100	.346	8				54.1	-1.1
		3	349	163	180	.475					7.3

Lanier, Harold Clifton "Hal"

YEAR	TM/L	G	W	L	PCT	STANDING			M/Y	W-EXP	A-E
1986	Hou-N	162	96	66	.593	1 W				90.3	5.7
1987	Hou-N	162	76	86	.469	3 W				77.9	-1.9
1988	Hou-N	162	82	80	.506	5 W				79.5	2.5
		3	486	254	232	.523					6.4

Larkin, Henry E. "Ted"

YEAR	TM/L	G	W	L	PCT	STANDING			M/Y	W-EXP	A-E
1890	Cle-P*	79	34	45	.430	7	7		1/2	30.9	3.1

LaRussa, Anthony "Tony"

YEAR	TM/L	G	W	L	PCT	STANDING			M/Y	W-EXP	A-E
1979	Chi-A	54	27	27	.500	5 W	5 W		2/2	26.4	0.6
1980	Chi-A	162	70	90	.438	5 W				65.8	4.2
1981(1)	Chi-A	53	31	22	.585	3 W					
(2)	Chi-A	53	23	30	.434	6 W				58.5	-4.5
1982	Chi-A	162	87	75	.537	3 W				88.5	-1.5
1983	Chi-A	162	99	63	.611	1 W				96.0	3.0
1984	Chi-A	162	74	88	.457	●5 W				75.2	-1.2
1985	Chi-A	163	85	77	.525	3 W				82.6	2.4
1986	Chi-A	64	26	38	.406	6 W	5 W		1/3	29.7	-3.7
	Oak-A	79	45	34	.570	7 W	●3 W		3/3	38.1	6.9
1987	Oak-A	162	81	81	.500	3 W				82.6	-1.6
1988	Oak-A	162	104	58	.642	♦1 W				99.2	4.8
1989	Oak-A	162	99	63	.611	★1 W				95.5	3.5
1990	Oak-A	162	103	59	.636	♦1 W				98.2	4.8
		12	1762	954	805	.542					17.6

Lasorda, Thomas Charles "Tom"

YEAR	TM/L	G	W	L	PCT	STANDING			M/Y	W-EXP	A-E
1976	LA-N	4	2	2	.500	2 W	2 W		2/2	2.2	-0.2
1977	LA-N	162	98	64	.605	♦1 W				100.4	-2.4
1978	LA-N	162	95	67	.586	♦1 W				97.3	-2.3
1979	LA-N	162	79	83	.488	3 W				83.2	-4.2
1980	LA-N	163	92	71	.564	▲2 W				89.3	2.7
1981(1)	LA-N	57	36	21	.632	★1 W					
(2)	LA-N	53	27	26	.509	4 W				65.4	-2.4
1982	LA-N	162	88	74	.543	2 W				89.4	-1.4
1983	LA-N	163	91	71	.562	1 W				85.9	5.1
1984	LA-N	162	79	83	.488	4 W				78.8	0.2
1985	LA-N	162	95	67	.586	1 W				92.1	2.9
1986	LA-N	162	73	89	.451	5 W				76.7	-3.7
1987	LA-N	162	73	89	.451	4 W				76.8	-3.8
1988	LA-N	162	94	67	.584	★1 W				89.9	4.1
1989	LA-N	160	77	83	.481	4 W				82.1	-5.1
1990	LA-N	162	86	76	.531	2 W				85.4	0.6
		15	2220	1185	1033	.534					-9.7

Latham, George Warren "Juice"

YEAR	TM/L	G	W	L	PCT	STANDING			M/Y	W-EXP	A-E
1875	NH-n*	18	4	14	.222	11	8	8	2/3	1.5	2.5
1882	Phi-a*	75	41	34	.547	2				39.1	1.9
		2	93	45	48	.484					4.4

Latham, Walter Arlington "Arlie"

YEAR	TM/L	G	W	L	PCT	STANDING			M/Y	W-EXP	A-E
1896	StL-N*	3	0	3	.000	10	10	11	2/5	0.8	-0.8

Lavagetto, Harry Arthur "Cookie"

YEAR	TM/L	G	W	L	PCT	STANDING			M/Y	W-EXP	A-E
1957	Was-A	134	51	83	.381	8	8		2/2	49.3	1.7
1958	Was-A	156	61	93	.396	8				56.8	4.2
1959	Was-A	154	63	91	.409	8				68.6	-5.6
1960	Was-A	154	73	81	.474	5				74.6	-1.6
1961	Min-A	49	19	30	.388	8	7		1/4	22.4	-3.4
	Min-A	10	4	6	.400	9	9	7	3/4	4.6	-0.6
		5	657	271	384	.414					-5.3

Leadley, Robert H. "Bob"

YEAR	TM/L	G	W	L	PCT	STANDING			M/Y	W-EXP	A-E
1888	Det-N	40	19	19	.500	3	5		2/2	21.5	-2.5
1890	Cle-N	58	23	33	.411	7	7		2/2	20.2	2.8
1891	Cle-N	68	34	34	.500	4	5		1/2	31.8	2.2
		3	166	76	86	.469					2.5

Lefebvre, James Kenneth "Jim"

YEAR	TM/L	G	W	L	PCT	STANDING			M/Y	W-EXP	A-E
1989	Sea-A	162	73	89	.451	6 W				77.6	-4.6
1990	Sea-A	162	77	85	.475	5 W				76.8	0.2
		2	324	150	174	.463					-4.4

Lemon, James Robert "Jim"

YEAR	TM/L	G	W	L	PCT	STANDING			M/Y	W-EXP	A-E
1968	Was-A	161	65	96	.404	10				64.9	0.1

Lemon, Robert Granville "Bob"

YEAR	TM/L	G	W	L	PCT	STANDING			M/Y	W-EXP	A-E
1970	KC-A	110	46	64	.418	5 W	●4 W		2/2	48.3	-2.3
1971	KC-A	161	85	76	.528	2 W				84.6	0.4
1972	KC-A	154	76	78	.494	4 W				80.9	-4.9
1977	Chi-A	162	90	72	.556	3 W				87.9	2.1
1978	Chi-A	74	34	40	.459	5 W	5 W		1/2	32.4	1.6
	NY-A	68	48	20	.706	4 E	▲★1E		3/3	40.7	7.3
1979	NY-A	65	34	31	.523	4 E	4 E		2/2	35.0	-1.0
1981(2)	NY-A	25	11	14	.440	4 E	6 E		2/2	14.5	-3.5
1982	NY-A	14	6	8	.429	●4 E	5 E		1/3	6.9	-0.9
		8	833	430	403	.516					-1.4

Lennon, William F. "Bill"

YEAR	TM/L	G	W	L	PCT	STANDING			M/Y	W-EXP	A-E
1871	Kek-n*	14	5	9	.357	7	8		1/2	1.8	3.2

Leyland, James Richard "Jim"

YEAR	TM/L	G	W	L	PCT	STANDING			M/Y	W-EXP	A-E
1986	Pit-N	162	64	98	.395	6 E				77.2	-13.2
1987	Pit-N	162	80	82	.494	●4 E				78.9	1.1
1988	Pit-N	160	85	75	.531	2 E				83.7	1.3
1989	Pit-N	164	74	88	.457	5 E				76.4	-2.4
1990	Pit-N	162	95	67	.586	1 E				92.8	2.2
		5	810	398	410	.493					-11.1

Leyva, Nicolas Tomas "Nick"

YEAR	TM/L	G	W	L	PCT	STANDING			M/Y	W-EXP	A-E
1989	Phi-N	163	67	95	.414	6 E				70.0	-3.0
1990	Phi-N	162	77	85	.475	●4 E				72.5	4.5
		2	325	144	180	.444					1.5

Lillis, Robert Perry "Bob"

YEAR	TM/L	G	W	L	PCT	STANDING			M/Y	W-EXP	A-E
1982	Hou-N	51	28	23	.549	5 W	5 W		2/2	23.7	4.3
1983	Hou-N	162	85	77	.525	3 W				80.7	4.3
1984	Hou-N	162	80	82	.494	●2 W				87.6	-7.6
1985	Hou-N	162	83	79	.512	●3 W				82.5	0.5
		4	537	276	261	.514					1.5

Lipon, John Joseph "Johnny"

YEAR	TM/L	G	W	L	PCT	STANDING			M/Y	W-EXP	A-E
1971	Cle-A	59	18	41	.305	6 E	6 E		2/2	21.6	-3.6

Lobert, John Bernard "Hans"

YEAR	TM/L	G	W	L	PCT	STANDING			M/Y	W-EXP	A-E
1938	Phi-N	2	0	2	.000	8	8		2/2	0.6	-0.6
1942	Phi-N	151	42	109	.278	8				40.8	1.2
		2	153	42	111	.275					0.6

Lockman, Carroll Walter "Whitey"

YEAR	TM/L	G	W	L	PCT	STANDING			M/Y	W-EXP	A-E
1972	Chi-N	65	39	26	.600	4 E	2 E		2/2	37.7	1.3
1973	Chi-N	161	77	84	.478	5 E				76.1	0.9
1974	Chi-N	93	41	52	.441	5 E	6 E		1/2	37.6	3.4
		3	319	157	162	.492					5.5

Loftus, Thomas Joseph "Tom"

YEAR	TM/L	G	W	L	PCT	STANDING			M/Y	W-EXP	A-E
1884	Mil-U	12	8	4	.667	2				8.1	-0.1
1888	Cle-a	71	30	38	.441	8	6		2/2	25.3	4.7
1889	Cle-N	136	61	72	.459	6				60.5	0.5
1890	Cin-N	134	77	55	.583	4				77.2	-0.2
1891	Cin-N	138	56	81	.409	7				55.1	0.9
1900	Chi-N	146	65	75	.464	●5				58.7	6.3
1901	Chi-N	140	53	86	.381	6				57.5	-4.5
1902	Was-A	138	61	75	.449	6				60.4	0.6
1903	Was-A	140	43	94	.314	8				41.7	1.3
		9	1055	454	580	.439					9.6

Lopat, Edmund Walter "Eddie"

YEAR	TM/L	G	W	L	PCT	STANDING			M/Y	W-EXP	A-E
1963	KC-A	162	73	89	.451	8				71.6	1.4
1964	KC-A	52	17	35	.327	10	10		1/2	19.1	-2.1
		2	214	90	124	.421					-0.7

Lopez, Alfonso Ramon "Al"

YEAR	TM/L	G	W	L	PCT	STANDING			M/Y	W-EXP	A-E
1951	Cle-A	155	93	61	.604	2				87.6	5.4
1952	Cle-A	155	93	61	.604	2				92.8	0.2
1953	Cle-A	155	92	62	.597	2				91.3	0.7
1954	Cle-A	156	111	43	.721	1				102.7	8.3
1955	Cle-A	154	93	61	.604	2				87.0	6.0
1956	Cle-A	155	88	66	.571	2				90.6	-2.6
1957	Chi-A	155	90	64	.584	2				91.8	-1.8
1958	Chi-A	155	82	72	.532	2				79.0	3.0
1959	Chi-A	156	94	60	.610	1				85.6	8.4
1960	Chi-A	154	87	67	.565	3				89.5	-2.5
1961	Chi-A	163	86	76	.531	4				84.9	1.1
1962	Chi-A	162	85	77	.525	5				86.1	-1.1
1963	Chi-A	162	94	68	.580	2				96.2	-2.2

YEAR	TM/L	G	W	L	PCT	STANDING	M/Y	W-EXP	A-E
1964	Chi-A	162	98	64	.605	2		96.9	1.1
1965	Chi-A	162	95	67	.586	2		91.1	3.9
1968	Chi-A	11	6	5	.545	9 9 ●8	3/5	5.0	1.0
	Chi-A	36	15	21	.417	9 ●8	5/5	16.3	-1.3
1969	Chi-A	17	8	9	.471	4 W 5 W	1/2	7.4	0.6
	17	2425	1410	1004	.584				28.3

Lord, Harry Donald

YEAR	TM/L	G	W	L	PCT	STANDING	M/Y	W-EXP	A-E
1915	Buf-F*	110	60	49	.550	8 6	3/3	49.9	10.1

Lowe, Robert Lincoln "Bobby"

YEAR	TM/L	G	W	L	PCT	STANDING	M/Y	W-EXP	A-E
1904	Det-A*	78	30	44	.405	7 7	2/2	30.3	-0.3

Lucchesi, Frank Joseph

YEAR	TM/L	G	W	L	PCT	STANDING	M/Y	W-EXP	A-E
1970	Phi-N	161	73	88	.453	5 E		66.3	6.7
1971	Phi-N	162	67	95	.414	6 E		66.9	0.1
1972	Phi-N	76	26	50	.342	6 E 6 E	1/2	30.9	-4.9
1975	Tex-A	67	35	32	.522	4 W 3 W	2/2	32.7	2.3
1976	Tex-A	162	76	86	.469	●4 W		77.1	-1.1
1977	Tex-A	62	31	31	.500	●3 W 2 W	1/4	35.3	-4.3
1987	Chi-N	25	8	17	.320	5 E 6 E	2/2	11.3	-3.3
	7	715	316	399	.442				-4.4

Lumley, Harry G

YEAR	TM/L	G	W	L	PCT	STANDING	M/Y	W-EXP	A-E
1909	Bro-N*	155	55	98	.359	6		55.6	-0.6

Lyons, Theodore Amar "Ted"

YEAR	TM/L	G	W	L	PCT	STANDING	M/Y	W-EXP	A-E
1946	Chi-A	125	64	60	.516	7 5	2/2	59.1	4.9
1947	Chi-A	155	70	84	.455	6		65.4	4.6
1948	Chi-A	154	51	101	.336	8		50.4	0.6
	3	434	185	245	.430				10.1

Mack, Cornelius Alexander "Connie"

YEAR	TM/L	G	W	L	PCT	STANDING	M/Y	W-EXP	A-E
1894	Pit-N*	23	12	10	.545	7 7	2/2	10.8	1.2
1895	Pit-N*	135	71	61	.538	7		68.1	2.9
1896	Pit-N*	131	66	63	.512	6		68.5	-2.5
1901	Phi-A	137	74	62	.544	4		71.9	2.1
1902	Phi-A	137	83	53	.610	2		81.0	2.0
1903	Phi-A	137	75	60	.556	2		75.7	-0.7
1904	Phi-A	155	81	70	.536	5		81.7	-0.7
1905	Phi-A	152	92	56	.622	1		88.5	3.5
1906	Phi-A	149	78	67	.538	4		74.6	3.4
1907	Phi-A	150	88	57	.607	2		80.4	7.6
1908	Phi-A	157	68	85	.444	6		67.7	0.3
1909	Phi-A	153	95	58	.621	2		99.5	-4.5
1910	Phi-A	155	102	48	.680	★1		101.0	1.0
1911	Phi-A	152	101	50	.669	★1		100.7	0.3
1912	Phi-A	153	90	62	.592	3		87.8	2.2
1913	Phi-A	153	96	57	.627	★1		96.6	-0.6
1914	Phi-A	158	99	53	.651	1		99.2	-0.2
1915	Phi-A	154	43	109	.283	8		42.3	0.7
1916	Phi-A	154	36	117	.235	8		41.5	-5.5
1917	Phi-A	154	55	98	.359	8		59.2	-4.2
1918	Phi-A	130	52	76	.406	8		50.0	2.0
1919	Phi-A	140	36	104	.257	8		40.8	-4.8
1920	Phi-A	156	48	106	.312	8		49.3	-1.3
1921	Phi-A	155	53	100	.346	8		54.0	-1.0
1922	Phi-A	155	65	89	.422	7		65.1	-0.1
1923	Phi-A	153	69	83	.454	6		66.2	2.8
1924	Phi-A	152	71	81	.467	5		67.0	4.0
1925	Phi-A	153	88	64	.579	2		87.1	0.9
1926	Phi-A	150	83	67	.553	3		86.1	-3.1
1927	Phi-A	155	91	63	.591	2		87.9	3.1
1928	Phi-A	153	98	55	.641	2		97.4	0.6
1929	Phi-A	151	104	46	.693	★1		102.1	1.9
1930	Phi-A	154	102	52	.662	★1		95.0	7.0
1931	Phi-A	153	107	45	.704	1		98.4	8.6
1932	Phi-A	154	94	60	.610	2		97.5	-3.5
1933	Phi-A	152	79	72	.523	3		77.5	1.5
1934	Phi-A	153	68	82	.453	5		68.1	-0.1
1935	Phi-A	149	58	91	.389	8		59.8	-1.8
1936	Phi-A	154	53	100	.346	8		47.1	5.9
1937	Phi-A	120	39	80	.328	7 7	1/2	48.0	-9.0
1938	Phi-A	154	53	99	.349	8		55.1	-2.1
1939	Phi-A	62	25	37	.403	6 7	1/2	19.7	5.3
1940	Phi-A	154	54	100	.351	8		55.9	-1.9
1941	Phi-A	154	64	90	.416	8		65.0	-1.0
1942	Phi-A	154	55	99	.357	8		51.5	3.5
1943	Phi-A	155	49	105	.318	8		53.4	-4.4
1944	Phi-A	155	72	82	.468	●5		69.3	2.7
1945	Phi-A	153	52	98	.347	8		59.1	-7.1
1946	Phi-A	155	49	105	.318	8		60.8	-11.8
1947	Phi-A	156	78	76	.506	5		79.0	-1.0
1948	Phi-A	154	84	70	.545	4		76.4	7.6
1949	Phi-A	154	81	73	.526	5		77.1	3.9
1950	Phi-A	154	52	102	.338	8		54.3	-2.3
	53	7755	3731	3948	.486				13.4

Mack, Dennis Joseph "Denny"

YEAR	TM/L	G	W	L	PCT	STANDING	M/Y	W-EXP	A-E
1882	Lou-a*	80	42	38	.525	3		48.7	-6.7

Mack, Earle Thaddeus

YEAR	TM/L	G	W	L	PCT	STANDING	M/Y	W-EXP	A-E
1937	Phi-A	34	15	17	.469	7 7	2/2	12.9	2.1
1939	Phi-A	91	30	60	.333	6 7	2/2	28.6	1.4
	2	125	45	77	.369				3.5

Macullar, James F. "Jimmy"

YEAR	TM/L	G	W	L	PCT	STANDING	M/Y	W-EXP	A-E
1879	Syr-N*	27	5	21	.192	6 7	3/3	6.6	-1.6

Magee, Leo Christopher "Lee"

YEAR	TM/L	G	W	L	PCT	STANDING	M/Y	W-EXP	A-E
1915	Bro-F*	118	53	64	.453	7 7	1/2	56.5	-3.5

Malone, Ferguson G. "Fergy"

YEAR	TM/L	G	W	L	PCT	STANDING	M/Y	W-EXP	A-E
1873	Phi-n*	10	8	2	.800	2 2	1/2	6.8	1.2
1874	Chi-n*	36	18	18	.500	4 5	1/2	15.1	2.9
1884	Phi-U*	67	21	46	.313	7		23.1	-2.1
	3	113	47	66	.416				2.0

Manning, James H. "Jimmy"

YEAR	TM/L	G	W	L	PCT	STANDING	M/Y	W-EXP	A-E
1901	Was-A	138	61	73	.455	6		58.8	2.2

Manning, John E. "Jack"

YEAR	TM/L	G	W	L	PCT	STANDING	M/Y	W-EXP	A-E
1877	Cin-N*	20	7	12	.368	6 6	3/3	4.2	2.8

Maranville, Walter James Vincent "Rabbit"

YEAR	TM/L	G	W	L	PCT	STANDING	M/Y	W-EXP	A-E
1925	Chi-N*	53	23	30	.434	7 7 8	2/3	24.8	-1.8

Marion, Martin Whitford "Marty"

YEAR	TM/L	G	W	L	PCT	STANDING	M/Y	W-EXP	A-E
1951	StL-N	155	81	73	.526	3		78.2	2.8
1952	StL-A*	104	42	61	.408	8 7	2/2	42.7	-0.7
1953	StL-A*	154	54	100	.351	8		54.3	-0.3
1954	Chi-A	9	3	6	.333	3 3	2/2	5.7	-2.7
1955	Chi-A	155	91	63	.591	3		94.5	-3.5
1956	Chi-A	154	85	69	.552	3		91.1	-6.1
	6	731	356	372	.489				-10.5

Marshall, Rufus James "Jim"

YEAR	TM/L	G	W	L	PCT	STANDING	M/Y	W-EXP	A-E
1974	Chi-N	69	25	44	.362	5 E 6 E	2/2	27.9	-2.9
1975	Chi-N	162	75	87	.463	●5 E		69.8	5.2
1976	Chi-N	162	75	87	.463	4 E		68.8	6.2
1979	Oak-A	162	54	108	.333	7 W		52.0	2.0
	4	555	229	326	.413				10.5

Martin, Alfred Manuel "Billy"

YEAR	TM/L	G	W	L	PCT	STANDING	M/Y	W-EXP	A-E
1969	Min-A	162	97	65	.599	1 W		98.5	-1.5
1971	Det-A	162	91	71	.562	2 E		86.8	4.2
1972	Det-A	156	86	70	.551	1 E		83.0	3.0
1973	Det-A	134	71	63	.530	3 E 3 E	1/2	64.2	6.8
	Tex-A	23	9	14	.391	6 W 6 W	3/3	8.3	0.7
1974	Tex-A	161	84	76	.525	2 W		79.2	4.8
1975	Tex-A	95	44	51	.463	4 W 3 W	1/2	46.4	-2.4
	NY-A	56	30	26	.536	3 E 3 E	2/2	31.5	-1.5
1976	NY-A	159	97	62	.610	♦1 E		95.7	1.3
1977	NY-A	162	100	62	.617	★1 E		98.9	1.1
1978	NY-A	94	52	42	.553	3 E ▲★1E	1/3	56.3	-4.3
1979	NY-A	95	55	40	.579	4 E 4 E	2/2	51.2	3.8
1980	Oak-A	162	83	79	.512	2 W		85.6	-2.6
1981(1)	Oak-A	60	37	23	.617	1 W			
(2)	Oak-A	49	27	22	.551	2 W		60.4	3.6
1982	Oak-A	162	68	94	.420	5 W		68.4	-0.4
1983	NY-A	162	91	71	.562	3 E		87.7	3.3
1985	NY-A	145	91	54	.628	7 E 2 E	2/2	88.4	2.6
1988	NY-A	68	40	28	.588	2 E 5 E	1/2	35.0	5.0
	16	2267	1253	1013	.553				27.5

Martinez, Orlando [Oliva] "Marty"

YEAR	TM/L	G	W	L	PCT	STANDING	M/Y	W-EXP	A-E
1986	Sea-A	1	0	1	.000	6 W 6 W 7 W	2/3	0.4	-0.4

Mason, Charles E. "Charlie"

YEAR	TM/L	G	W	L	PCT	STANDING	M/Y	W-EXP	A-E
1887	Phi-a	82	38	40	.487	6 5	2/2	39.1	-1.1

Mathews, Edwin Lee "Eddie"

YEAR	TM/L	G	W	L	PCT	STANDING	M/Y	W-EXP	A-E
1972	Atl-N	50	23	27	.460	4 W 4 W	2/2	21.6	1.4
1973	Atl-N	162	76	85	.472	5 W		82.9	-6.9
1974	Atl-N	99	50	49	.505	4 W 3 W	1/2	56.1	-6.1
	3	311	149	161	.481				-11.6

Mathewson, Christopher "Christy"

YEAR	TM/L	G	W	L	PCT	STANDING	M/Y	W-EXP	A-E
1916	Cin-N*	69	25	43	.368	8 ●7	3/3	28.4	-3.4
1917	Cin-N	157	78	76	.506	4		75.9	2.1
1918	Cin-N	120	61	57	.517	4 3	1/2	62.3	-1.3
	3	346	164	176	.482				-2.7

Mattick, Robert James "Bobby"

YEAR	TM/L	G	W	L	PCT	STANDING	M/Y	W-EXP	A-E
1980	Tor-A	162	67	95	.414	7 E		66.8	0.2
1981(1)	Tor-A	58	16	42	.276	7 E			
(2)	Tor-A	48	21	27	.438	7 E		38.0	-1.0
	2	268	104	164	.388				-0.8

Mauch, Gene William

YEAR	TM/L	G	W	L	PCT	STANDING	M/Y	W-EXP	A-E
1960	Phi-N	152	58	94	.382	●4 8	3/3	60.8	-2.8
1961	Phi-N	155	47	107	.305	8		55.7	-8.7
1962	Phi-N	161	81	80	.503	7		75.1	5.9
1963	Phi-N	162	87	75	.537	4		88.0	-3.1
1964	Phi-N	162	92	70	.568	●2		87.4	4.6
1965	Phi-N	162	85	76	.528	6		79.1	5.9
1966	Phi-N	162	87	75	.537	4		86.9	0.1
1967	Phi-N	162	82	80	.506	5		84.4	-2.4
1968	Phi-N	54	27	27	.500	●6 ●7	1/3	24.3	2.7
1969	Mon-N	162	52	110	.321	6 E		59.5	-7.5
1970	Mon-N	162	73	89	.451	6 E		69.1	3.9
1971	Mon-N	162	71	90	.441	5 E		69.4	1.6
1972	Mon-N	156	70	86	.449	5 E		67.3	2.7
1973	Mon-N	162	79	83	.488	4 E		77.5	1.5
1974	Mon-N	161	79	82	.491	4 E		81.0	-2.0
1975	Mon-N	162	75	87	.463	●5 E		71.5	3.5

YEAR	TM/L	G	W	L	PCT	STANDING			M/Y	W-EXP	A-E
1976	Min-A	162	85	77	.525	3 W				84.9	0.1
1977	Min-A	161	84	77	.522	4 W				89.0	-5.0
1978	Min-A	162	73	89	.451	4 W				79.8	-6.8
1979	Min-A	162	82	80	.506	4 W				84.9	-2.9
1980	Min-A	125	54	71	.432	4 W	3 W		1/2	58.2	-4.2
1981(1)	Cal-A	13	9	4	.692	4 W	4 W		2/2		
(2)	Cal-A	50	20	30	.400	7 W				32.9	-3.9
1982	Cal-A	162	93	69	.574	1 W				95.3	-2.3
1985	Cal-A	162	90	72	.556	2 W				83.9	6.1
1986	Cal-A	162	92	70	.568	1 W				91.2	0.8
1987	Cal-A	162	75	87	.463	●6 W				77.8	-2.8
	26	3942	1902	2037	.483						-12.9

McAleer, James Robert "Jimmy"

YEAR	TM/L	G	W	L	PCT	STANDING			M/Y	W-EXP	A-E
1901	Cle-A*	138	55	82	.401	7				53.6	1.4
1902	StL-A*	140	78	58	.574	2				69.2	8.8
1903	StL-A	139	65	74	.468	6				66.7	-1.7
1904	StL-A	156	65	87	.428	6				62.0	3.0
1905	StL-A	156	54	99	.353	8				65.6	-11.6
1906	StL-A	154	76	73	.510	5				81.4	-5.4
1907	StL-A*	155	69	83	.454	6				74.5	-5.5
1908	StL-A	155	83	69	.546	4				83.1	-0.1
1909	StL-A	154	61	89	.407	7				59.3	1.7
1910	Was-A	157	66	85	.437	7				69.8	-3.8
1911	Was-A	154	64	90	.416	7				62.9	1.1
	11	1658	736	889	.453						-12.3

McBride, George Florian

YEAR	TM/L	G	W	L	PCT	STANDING			M/Y	W-EXP	A-E
1921	Was-A	154	80	73	.523	4				73.2	6.8

McBride, James Dickson "Dick"

YEAR	TM/L	G	W	L	PCT	STANDING			M/Y	W-EXP	A-E
1871	Ath-n*	28	21	7	.750	1				20.9	0.1
1872	Ath-n*	47	30	14	.682	4				35.1	-5.1
1873	Ath-n*	52	28	23	.549	5				30.7	-2.7
1874	Ath-n*	56	33	23	.589	3				35.2	-2.2
1875	Ath-n*	69	49	18	.731	2	2		1/2	55.1	-6.1
	5	252	161	85	.654						-16.0

McCallister, John "Jack"

YEAR	TM/L	G	W	L	PCT	STANDING			M/Y	W-EXP	A-E
1927	Cle-A	153	66	87	.431	6				66.9	-0.9

McCarthy, Joseph Vincent "Joe"

YEAR	TM/L	G	W	L	PCT	STANDING			M/Y	W-EXP	A-E
1926	Chi-N	155	82	72	.532	4				85.3	-3.3
1927	Chi-N	153	85	68	.556	4				85.3	-0.3
1928	Chi-N	154	91	63	.591	3				87.1	3.9
1929	Chi-N	156	98	54	.645	1				96.1	1.9
1930	Chi-N	152	86	64	.573	2	2		1/2	85.8	0.2
1931	NY-A	155	94	59	.614	2				103.3	-9.3
1932	NY-A	156	107	47	.695	★1				102.1	4.9
1933	NY-A	152	91	59	.607	2				89.3	1.7
1934	NY-A	154	94	60	.610	2				93.6	0.4
1935	NY-A	149	89	60	.597	2				92.4	-3.4
1936	NY-A	155	102	51	.667	★1				105.9	-3.9
1937	NY-A	157	102	52	.662	★1				105.5	-3.5
1938	NY-A	157	99	53	.651	★1				99.5	-0.5
1939	NY-A	152	106	45	.702	★1				114.5	-8.5
1940	NY-A	155	88	66	.571	3				91.1	-3.1
1941	NY-A	156	101	53	.656	★1				96.5	4.5
1942	NY-A	154	103	51	.669	1				107.3	-4.3
1943	NY-A	155	98	56	.636	★1				90.6	7.4
1944	NY-A	154	83	71	.539	3				82.9	0.1
1945	NY-A	152	81	71	.533	4				83.2	-2.2
1946	NY-A	35	22	13	.629	2	3		1/3	20.8	1.2
1948	Bos-A	155	96	59	.619	▲2				94.8	1.2
1949	Bos-A	155	96	58	.623	2				98.6	-2.6
1950	Bos-A	59	31	28	.525	4	3		1/2	36.9	-5.9
	24	3487	2125	1333	.615						-23.6

McCarthy, Thomas Francis "Tommy"

YEAR	TM/L	G	W	L	PCT	STANDING			M/Y	W-EXP	A-E
1890	StL-a*	22	11	11	.500	4	3		1/6	12.9	-1.9
	StL-a*	5	4	1	.800	2	2	3	5/6	2.9	1.1

McCloskey, John Joseph

YEAR	TM/L	G	W	L	PCT	STANDING			M/Y	W-EXP	A-E
1895	Lou-N	133	35	96	.267	12				33.4	1.6
1896	Lou-N	19	2	17	.105	12	12		1/2	5.2	-3.2
1906	StL-N	154	52	98	.347	7				59.5	-7.5
1907	StL-N	155	52	101	.340	8				54.7	-2.7
1908	StL-N	154	49	105	.318	8				46.9	2.1
	5	615	190	417	.313						-9.7

McCormick, James "Jim"

YEAR	TM/L	G	W	L	PCT	STANDING			M/Y	W-EXP	A-E
1879	Cle-N*	82	27	55	.329	6				27.5	-0.5
1880	Cle-N*	85	47	37	.560	3				47.1	-0.1
1882	Cle-N*	4	0	4	.000	8	5		1/2	2.0	-2.0
	3	171	74	96	.435						-2.6

McGaha, Fred Melvin "Mel"

YEAR	TM/L	G	W	L	PCT	STANDING			M/Y	W-EXP	A-E
1962	Cle-A	160	78	82	.488	6	6		1/2	73.7	4.3
1964	KC-A	111	40	70	.364	10	10		2/2	40.3	-0.3
1965	KC-A	26	5	21	.192	10	10		1/2	10.2	-5.2
	3	297	123	173	.416						-1.2

McGeary, Michael Henry "Mike"

YEAR	TM/L	G	W	L	PCT	STANDING			M/Y	W-EXP	A-E
1875	Phi-n*	63	34	27	.557	4	5		1/2	37.8	-3.8
1880	Pro-N*	16	8	7	.533	4	2		1/3	9.7	-1.7
1881	Cle-N*	11	4	7	.364	6	7		1/2	5.2	-1.2
	3	90	46	41	.529						-6.7

McGraw, John Joseph

YEAR	TM/L	G	W	L	PCT	STANDING			M/Y	W-EXP	A-E
1899	Bal-N*	152	86	62	.581	4				86.9	-0.9
1901	Bal-A*	135	68	65	.511	5				67.4	0.6
1902	Bal-A*	58	26	31	.456	7	8		1/2	23.5	2.5
	NY-N*	65	25	38	.397	8	8		3/3	21.7	3.3
1903	NY-N*	142	84	55	.604	2				85.6	-1.6
1904	NY-N*	158	106	47	.693	1				105.4	0.6
1905	NY-N*	155	105	48	.686	★1				105.0	0.0
1906	NY-N*	153	96	56	.632	2				88.7	7.3
1907	NY-N	155	82	71	.536	4				83.8	-1.8
1908	NY-N	157	98	56	.636	●2				99.1	-1.1
1909	NY-N	158	92	61	.601	3				85.0	7.0
1910	NY-N	155	91	63	.591	2				92.4	-1.4
1911	NY-N	154	99	54	.647	1				98.6	0.4
1912	NY-N	154	103	48	.682	1				100.6	2.4
1913	NY-N	156	101	51	.664	1				94.3	6.7
1914	NY-N	156	84	70	.545	2				87.2	-3.2
1915	NY-N	155	69	83	.454	8				71.1	-2.1
1916	NY-N	155	86	66	.566	4				86.5	-0.5
1917	NY-N	158	98	56	.636	1				97.3	0.7
1918	NY-N	124	71	53	.573	2				69.3	1.7
1919	NY-N	140	87	53	.621	2				84.6	2.4
1920	NY-N	155	86	68	.558	2				91.8	-5.8
1921	NY-N	153	94	59	.614	1				96.1	-2.1
1922	NY-N	156	93	61	.604	★1				95.7	-2.7
1923	NY-N	153	95	58	.621	★1				93.1	1.9
1924	NY-N	29	16	13	.552	3	1		1/3	18.4	-2.4
	NY-N	81	45	35	.563	1	1		3/3	50.9	-5.9
1925	NY-N	152	86	66	.566	2				79.3	6.7
1926	NY-N	151	74	77	.490	5				75.0	-1.0
1927	NY-N	122	70	52	.574	4	3		1/2	68.3	1.7
1928	NY-N	155	93	61	.604	2				92.1	0.9
1929	NY-N	152	84	67	.556	3				92.9	-8.9
1930	NY-N	154	87	67	.565	3				89.8	-2.8
1931	NY-N	153	87	65	.572	2				93.0	-6.0
1932	NY-N	40	17	23	.425	8	●6		1/2	21.2	-4.2
	33	4801	2784	1959	.587						-7.6

McGuire, James Thomas "Deacon"

YEAR	TM/L	G	W	L	PCT	STANDING			M/Y	W-EXP	A-E
1898	Was-N*	70	21	47	.309	10	11	11	3/4	24.3	-3.3
1907	Bos-A*	112	45	61	.425	8	7		4/4	45.2	-0.2
1908	Bos-A*	115	53	62	.461	6	5		1/2	61.8	-8.8
1909	Cle-A	41	14	25	.359	4	6		2/2	18.3	-4.3
1910	Cle-A*	161	71	81	.467	5				64.0	7.0
1911	Cle-A	17	6	11	.353	7	3		1/2	8.3	-2.3
	6	516	210	287	.423						-12.0

McGunnigle, William Henry "Bill"

YEAR	TM/L	G	W	L	PCT	STANDING			M/Y	W-EXP	A-E
1888	Bro-a	143	88	52	.629	2				87.0	1.0
1889	Bro-a	140	94	43	.686	1				93.4	-0.4
1890	Bro-N	129	86	43	.667	1				87.7	-1.7
1891	Pit-N	59	24	33	.421	8	8		2/2	25.9	-1.9
1896	Lou-N	115	36	76	.321	12	12		2/2	30.9	5.1
	5	586	328	247	.570						2.1

McInnis, John Phalen "Stuffy"

YEAR	TM/L	G	W	L	PCT	STANDING			M/Y	W-EXP	A-E
1927	Phi-N*	155	51	103	.331	8				55.9	-4.9

McKechnie, William Boyd "Bill"

YEAR	TM/L	G	W	L	PCT	STANDING			M/Y	W-EXP	A-E
1915	New-F*	102	54	45	.545	6	5		2/2	51.2	2.8
1922	Pit-N	90	53	36	.596	5	●3		2/2	51.5	1.5
1923	Pit-N	154	87	67	.565	3				85.7	1.3
1924	Pit-N	153	90	63	.588	3				90.4	-0.4
1925	Pit-N	153	95	58	.621	★1				94.6	0.4
1926	Pit-N	157	84	69	.549	3				84.4	-0.4
1928	StL-N	154	95	59	.617	1				93.8	1.2
1929	StL-N	63	34	29	.540	4	4		3/3	32.5	1.5
1930	Bos-N	154	70	84	.455	6				63.5	6.5
1931	Bos-N	156	64	90	.416	7				61.2	2.8
1932	Bos-N	155	77	77	.500	5				76.4	0.6
1933	Bos-N	156	83	71	.539	4				79.4	3.6
1934	Bos-N	152	78	73	.517	4				72.4	5.6
1935	Bos-N	153	38	115	.248	8				49.3	-11.3
1936	Bos-N	157	71	83	.461	6				68.4	2.6
1937	Bos-N	152	79	73	.520	5				78.5	0.5
1938	Cin-N	151	82	68	.547	4				83.9	-1.9
1939	Cin-N	156	97	57	.630	1				94.5	2.5
1940	Cin-N	155	100	53	.654	★1				95.5	4.5
1941	Cin-N	154	88	66	.571	3				82.6	5.4
1942	Cin-N	154	76	76	.500	4				74.0	2.0
1943	Cin-N	155	87	67	.565	2				84.2	2.8
1944	Cin-N	155	89	65	.578	3				81.0	8.0
1945	Cin-N	154	61	93	.396	7				60.2	0.8
1946	Cin-N	152	64	86	.427	6	6		1/2	69.8	-5.8
	25	3647	1896	1723	.524						37.3

McKeon, John Aloysius "Jack"

YEAR	TM/L	G	W	L	PCT	STANDING			M/Y	W-EXP	A-E
1973	KC-A	162	88	74	.543	2 W				81.3	6.7
1974	KC-A	162	77	85	.475	5 W				81.5	-4.5
1975	KC-A	96	50	46	.521	2 W	2 W		1/2	51.7	-1.7
1977	Oak-A	53	26	27	.491	●5 W	7 W		1/2	21.6	4.4
1978	Oak-A	123	45	78	.366	1 W	6 W		2/2	48.4	-3.4
1988	SD-N	115	67	48	.583	5 W	3 W		2/2	58.4	8.6
1989	SD-N	162	89	73	.549	2 W				82.7	6.3

YEAR	TM/L	G	W	L	PCT	STANDING	M/Y	W-EXP	A-E
1990	SD-N	80	37	43	.463	4 W 5 W	1/2	40.0	-3.0
	8	953	479	474	.503				13.4

McKinnon, Alexander J. "Alex"

YEAR	TM/L	G	W	L	PCT	STANDING	M/Y	W-EXP	A-E
1885	StL-N*	39	6	32	.158	5 8 8	2/3	11.8	-5.8

McKnight, Dennis Hamar "Denny"

YEAR	TM/L	G	W	L	PCT	STANDING	M/Y	W-EXP	A-E
1884	Pit-a	12	4	8	.333	9 10	1/5	2.7	1.3

McManus, George

YEAR	TM/L	G	W	L	PCT	STANDING	M/Y	W-EXP	A-E
1876	StL-N	8	6	2	.750	2 2	2/2	5.9	0.1
1877	StL-N	60	28	32	.467	4		26.8	1.2
	2	68	34	34	.500				1.3

McManus, Martin Joseph "Marty"

YEAR	TM/L	G	W	L	PCT	STANDING	M/Y	W-EXP	A-E
1932	Bos-A*	99	32	67	.323	8 8	2/2	27.8	4.2
1933	Bos-A*	149	63	86	.423	7		68.9	-5.9
	2	248	95	153	.383				-1.7

McMillan, Roy David

YEAR	TM/L	G	W	L	PCT	STANDING	M/Y	W-EXP	A-E
1972	Mil-A	2	1	1	.500	6 E 6 E 6 E	2/3	0.9	0.1
1975	NY-N	53	26	27	.491	3 E ●3 E	2/2	27.2	-1.2
	2	55	27	28	.491				-1.1

McNamara, John Francis

YEAR	TM/L	G	W	L	PCT	STANDING	M/Y	W-EXP	A-E
1969	Oak-A	13	8	5	.615	2 W 2 W	2/2	7.0	1.0
1970	Oak-A	162	89	73	.549	2 W		90.1	-1.1
1974	SD-N	162	60	102	.370	6 W		51.2	8.8
1975	SD-N	162	71	91	.438	4 W		66.8	4.2
1976	SD-N	162	73	89	.451	5 W		71.0	2.0
1977	SD-N	48	20	28	.417	4 W 5 W	1/3	19.9	0.1
1979	Cin-N	161	90	71	.559	1 W		89.4	0.6
1980	Cin-N	163	89	73	.549	3 W		84.8	4.2
1981(1)	Cin-N	56	35	21	.625	2 W			
(2)	Cin-N	52	31	21	.596	2 W		56.5	9.5
1982	Cin-N	92	34	58	.370	6 W 6 W	1/2	38.8	-4.8
1983	Cal-A	162	70	92	.432	●5 W		75.4	-5.4
1984	Cal-A	162	81	81	.500	●2 W		80.9	0.1
1985	Bos-A	163	81	81	.500	5 E		88.9	-7.9
1986	Bos-A	161	95	66	.590	◆1 E		90.2	4.8
1987	Bos-A	162	78	84	.481	5 E		82.6	-4.6
1988	Bos-A	85	43	42	.506	4 E 1 E	1/2	48.9	-5.9
1990	Cle-A	162	77	85	.475	4 E		80.5	-3.5
	17	2290	1125	1163	.492				2.3

McPhee, John Alexander "Bid"

YEAR	TM/L	G	W	L	PCT	STANDING	M/Y	W-EXP	A-E
1901	Cin-N	142	52	87	.374	8		44.8	7.2
1902	Cin-N	65	27	37	.422	6 4	1/3	35.2	-8.2
	2	207	79	124	.389				-0.9

McVey, Calvin Alexander "Cal"

YEAR	TM/L	G	W	L	PCT	STANDING	M/Y	W-EXP	A-E
1873	Bal-a*	32	19	13	.594	2 3	1/2	23.5	-4.5
1878	Cin-N*	61	37	23	.617	2		34.9	2.1
1879	Cin-N*	63	34	28	.548	4 5	2/2	32.4	1.6
	3	156	90	64	.584				-0.9

Mele, Sabath Anthony "Sam"

YEAR	TM/L	G	W	L	PCT	STANDING	M/Y	W-EXP	A-E
1961	Min-A	7	2	5	.286	8 9 7	2/4	3.2	-1.2
	Min-A	95	45	49	.479	9 7	4/4	42.9	2.1
1962	Min-A	163	91	71	.562	2		89.4	1.6
1963	Min-A	161	91	70	.565	3		97.5	-6.5
1964	Min-A	163	79	83	.488	●6		87.0	-8.0
1965	Min-A	162	102	60	.630	1		98.9	3.1
1966	Min-A	162	89	73	.549	2		89.9	-0.9
1967	Min-A	50	25	25	.500	6 ●2	1/2	27.7	-2.7
	7	963	524	436	.546				-12.4

Merrill, Carl Harrison "Stump"

YEAR	TM/L	G	W	L	PCT	STANDING	M/Y	W-EXP	A-E
1990	NY-A	113	49	64	.434	7 E 7 E	2/2	45.9	3.1

Metro, Charles "Charlie"

YEAR	TM/L	G	W	L	PCT	STANDING	M/Y	W-EXP	A-E
1962	Chi-N	112	43	69	.384	9 9	3/3	42.5	0.5
1970	KC-A	52	19	33	.365	5 W ●4 W	1/2	22.8	-3.8
	2	164	62	102	.378				-3.3

Meyer, William Adam "Billy"

YEAR	TM/L	G	W	L	PCT	STANDING	M/Y	W-EXP	A-E
1948	Pit-N	156	83	71	.539	4		77.7	5.3
1949	Pit-N	154	71	83	.461	6		69.3	1.7
1950	Pit-N	154	57	96	.373	8		59.8	-2.8
1951	Pit-N	155	64	90	.416	7		62.1	1.0
1952	Pit-N	155	42	112	.273	8		48.3	-6.3
	5	774	317	452	.412				-0.2

Michael, Eugene Richard "Gene"

YEAR	TM/L	G	W	L	PCT	STANDING	M/Y	W-EXP	A-E
1981(1)	NY-A	56	34	22	.607	◆1 E			
(2)	NY-A	26	14	12	.538	4 E 6 E	1/2	47.7	0.3
1982	NY-A	86	44	42	.512	●4 E ●5 E 5 E	2/3	42.6	1.4
1986	Chi-N	102	46	56	.451	5 E 5 E	3/3	44.6	1.4
1987	Chi-N	136	68	68	.500	5 E 6 E	1/2	61.3	6.7
	4	406	206	200	.507				9.7

Milan, Jesse Clyde "Clyde"

YEAR	TM/L	G	W	L	PCT	STANDING	M/Y	W-EXP	A-E
1922	Was-A*	154	69	85	.448	6		71.3	-2.3

Miller, George Frederick

YEAR	TM/L	G	W	L	PCT	STANDING	M/Y	W-EXP	A-E
1894	StL-N*	133	56	76	.424	9		50.8	5.2

Miller, Joseph Wick "Joe"

YEAR	TM/L	G	W	L	PCT	STANDING	M/Y	W-EXP	A-E
1872	Nat-n*	11	0	11	.000	11		-1.2	1.2

Miller, Raymond Roger "Ray"

YEAR	TM/L	G	W	L	PCT	STANDING	M/Y	W-EXP	A-E
1985	Min-A	100	50	50	.500	6 W 4 W	2/2	45.3	4.7
1986	Min-A	139	59	80	.424	7 W 6 W	1/2	61.4	-2.4
	2	239	109	130	.456				2.3

Mills, Colonel Buster "Buster"

YEAR	TM/L	G	W	L	PCT	STANDING	M/Y	W-EXP	A-E
1953	Cin-N	8	4	4	.500	6 6	2/2	3.6	0.4

Mills, Everett

YEAR	TM/L	G	W	L	PCT	STANDING	M/Y	W-EXP	A-E
1872	Bal-n*	17	8	6	.571	2 2	2/2	10.3	-2.3

Mitchell, Frederick Francis "Fred"

YEAR	TM/L	G	W	L	PCT	STANDING	M/Y	W-EXP	A-E
1917	Chi-N	157	74	80	.481	5		75.3	-1.3
1918	Chi-N	131	84	45	.651	1		80.8	3.2
1919	Chi-N	140	75	65	.536	3		75.7	-0.7
1920	Chi-N	154	75	79	.487	●5		75.3	-0.3
1921	Bos-N	153	79	74	.516	4		78.9	0.1
1922	Bos-N	154	53	100	.346	8		54.2	-1.2
1923	Bos-N	155	54	100	.351	7		61.0	-7.0
	7	1044	494	543	.476				-7.2

Moore, Jackie Spencer

YEAR	TM/L	G	W	L	PCT	STANDING	M/Y	W-EXP	A-E
1984	Oak-A	118	57	61	.483	5 W 4 W	2/2	54.9	2.1
1985	Oak-A	162	77	85	.475	●4 W		78.1	-1.1
1986	Oak-A	73	29	44	.397	●6 W ●3 W	1/3	35.2	-6.2
	3	353	163	190	.462				-5.2

Moore, Terry Bluford

YEAR	TM/L	G	W	L	PCT	STANDING	M/Y	W-EXP	A-E
1954	Phi-N	77	35	42	.455	3 4	2/2	40.8	-5.8

Moran, Patrick Joseph "Pat"

YEAR	TM/L	G	W	L	PCT	STANDING	M/Y	W-EXP	A-E
1915	Phi-N	153	90	62	.592	1		90.4	-0.4
1916	Phi-N	154	91	62	.595	2		87.0	4.0
1917	Phi-N	155	87	65	.572	2		84.8	2.2
1918	Phi-N	125	55	68	.447	6		53.1	1.9
1919	Cin-N	140	96	44	.686	★1		90.0	6.0
1920	Cin-N	154	82	71	.536	3		84.0	-2.0
1921	Cin-N	153	70	83	.458	6		73.3	-3.3
1922	Cin-N	156	86	68	.558	2		85.8	0.2
1923	Cin-N	154	91	63	.591	2		85.0	6.0
	9	1344	748	586	.561				14.6

Morgan, Joseph Michael "Joe"

YEAR	TM/L	G	W	L	PCT	STANDING	M/Y	W-EXP	A-E
1988	Bos-A	77	46	31	.597	4 E 1 E	2/2	44.3	1.7
1989	Bos-A	162	83	79	.512	3 E		84.8	-1.8
1990	Bos-A	162	88	74	.579	1 E		84.6	3.4
	3	401	217	174	.555				3.2

Moriarty, George Joseph

YEAR	TM/L	G	W	L	PCT	STANDING	M/Y	W-EXP	A-E
1927	Det-A	156	82	71	.536	4		80.2	1.8
1928	Det-A	154	68	86	.442	6		71.3	-3.3
	2	310	150	157	.489				-1.5

Morrill, John Francis

YEAR	TM/L	G	W	L	PCT	STANDING	M/Y	W-EXP	A-E
1882	Bos-N*	85	45	39	.536	●3		47.4	-2.4
1883	Bos-N*	44	33	11	.750	4 1	2/2	30.5	2.5
1884	Bos-N*	116	73	38	.658	2		76.1	-3.1
1885	Bos-N*	113	46	66	.411	5		50.2	-4.2
1886	Bos-N*	118	56	61	.479	5		58.1	-2.1
1887	Bos-N*	32	12	17	.414	5 5	2/2	15.3	-3.3
1888	Bos-N*	137	70	64	.522	4		71.9	-1.9
1889	Was-N*	51	13	38	.255	8 8	1/2	16.2	-3.2
	8	696	348	334	.510				-17.7

Morton, Charles Hazen "Charlie"

YEAR	TM/L	G	W	L	PCT	STANDING	M/Y	W-EXP	A-E
1884	Tol-a*	110	46	58	.442	8		41.4	4.6
1885	Det-N*	38	7	31	.184	8 6	1/2	16.7	-9.7
1890	Tol-a	134	68	64	.515	4		70.6	-2.6
	3	282	121	153	.442				-7.8

Moses, Felix I.

YEAR	TM/L	G	W	L	PCT	STANDING	M/Y	W-EXP	A-E
1884	Ric-a	46	12	30	.286	12		11.8	0.2

Moss, John Lester "Les"

YEAR	TM/L	G	W	L	PCT	STANDING	M/Y	W-EXP	A-E
1968	Chi-A	2	0	2	.000	9 9 ●8	2/5	0.9	-0.9
	Chi-A	34	12	22	.353	9 9 ●8	4/5	15.4	-3.4
1979	Det-A	53	27	26	.509	5 E 5 E	1/3	27.5	-0.5
	2	89	39	50	.438				-4.8

Murnane, Timothy Hayes "Tim"

YEAR	TM/L	G	W	L	PCT	STANDING	M/Y	W-EXP	A-E
1884	Bos-U*	111	58	51	.532	5		61.6	-3.6

Murray, William Jeremiah "Billy"

YEAR	TM/L	G	W	L	PCT	STANDING	M/Y	W-EXP	A-E
1907	Phi-N	149	83	64	.565	3		77.7	5.3
1908	Phi-N	155	83	71	.539	4		84.2	-1.2
1909	Phi-N	154	74	79	.484	5		76.3	-2.3
	3	458	240	214	.529				1.9

Murtaugh, Daniel Edward "Danny"

YEAR	TM/L	G	W	L	PCT	STANDING	M/Y	W-EXP	A-E
1957	Pit-N	51	26	25	.510	7 ●7	2/2	21.7	4.3
1958	Pit-N	154	84	70	.545	2		82.7	1.3
1959	Pit-N	155	78	76	.506	4		74.0	4.0
1960	Pit-N	155	95	59	.617	★1		91.5	3.5
1961	Pit-N	154	75	79	.487	6		78.9	-3.9
1962	Pit-N	161	93	68	.578	4		88.8	4.2
1963	Pit-N	162	74	88	.457	8		77.9	-3.9
1964	Pit-N	162	80	82	.494	●6		83.9	-3.9
1967	Pit-N	79	39	39	.500	6 6	2/2	38.3	0.7
1970	Pit-N	162	89	73	.549	1 E		87.7	1.3
1971	Pit-N	162	97	65	.599	★1 E		100.4	-3.4
1973	Pit-N	26	13	13	.500	2 E 3 E	2/2	13.2	-0.2
1974	Pit-N	162	88	74	.543	1 E		90.6	-2.6

YEAR	TM/L	G	W	L	PCT	STANDING	M/Y	W-EXP	A-E
1975	Pit-N	161	92	69	.571	1 E		96.2	-4.2
1976	Pit-N	162	92	70	.568	2 E		89.1	2.9
	15	2068	1115	950	.540				0.2

Mutrie, James J. "Jim"

YEAR	TM/L	G	W	L	PCT	STANDING	M/Y	W-EXP	A-E
1883	NY-a	97	54	42	.563	4		57.1	-3.1
1884	NY-a	112	75	32	.701	1		82.5	-7.5
1885	NY-N	112	85	27	.759	2		87.3	-2.3
1886	NY-N	124	75	44	.630	3		72.2	2.8
1887	NY-N	129	68	55	.553	4		69.6	-1.6
1888	NY-N	138	84	47	.641	1		84.3	-0.3
1889	NY-N	131	83	43	.659	1		82.2	0.8
1890	NY-N	135	63	68	.481	6		66.9	-3.9
1891	NY-N	136	71	61	.538	3		69.9	1.1
	9	1114	658	419	.611				-14.1

Myatt, George Edward "George"

YEAR	TM/L	G	W	L	PCT	STANDING	M/Y	W-EXP	A-E
1968	Phi-N	1	1	0	1.000	•6 5 •7	2/3	0.5	0.5
1969	Phi-N	54	19	35	.352	5 E 5 E	2/2	23.6	-4.6
	2	55	20	35	.364				-4.0

Myers, Henry C.

YEAR	TM/L	G	W	L	PCT	STANDING	M/Y	W-EXP	A-E
1882	Bal-a*	74	19	54	.260	6		14.2	4.8

Nash, William Mitchell "Billy"

YEAR	TM/L	G	W	L	PCT	STANDING	M/Y	W-EXP	A-E
1896	Phi-N*	130	62	68	.477	8		64.9	-2.9

Neun, John Henry "Johnny"

YEAR	TM/L	G	W	L	PCT	STANDING	M/Y	W-EXP	A-E
1946	NY-A	14	8	6	.571	3 3	3/3	8.3	-0.3
1947	Cin-N	154	73	81	.474	5		69.7	3.3
1948	Cin-N	100	44	56	.440	7 7	1/2	39.1	4.9
	3	268	125	143	.466				7.8

Newman, Jeffrey Lynn "Jeff"

YEAR	TM/L	G	W	L	PCT	STANDING	M/Y	W-EXP	A-E
1986	Oak-A	10	2	8	.200	•6 W 7 W •3 W	2/3	4.8	-2.8

Nichols, Charles Augustus "Kid"

YEAR	TM/L	G	W	L	PCT	STANDING	M/Y	W-EXP	A-E
1904	StL-N*	155	75	79	.487	5		77.8	-2.8
1905	StL-N*	14	5	9	.357	7 6	1/3	5.1	-0.1
	2	169	80	88	.476				-2.9

Nicol, Hugh

YEAR	TM/L	G	W	L	PCT	STANDING	M/Y	W-EXP	A-E
1897	StL-N	40	8	32	.200	12 12 12	2/4	7.3	0.7

Nixon, Russell Eugene "Russ"

YEAR	TM/L	G	W	L	PCT	STANDING	M/Y	W-EXP	A-E
1982	Cin-N	70	27	43	.386	6 W 6 W	2/2	29.5	-2.5
1983	Cin-N	162	74	88	.457	6 W		71.9	2.1
1988	Atl-N	121	42	79	.347	6 W 6 W	2/2	45.7	-3.7
1989	Atl-N	161	63	97	.394	6 W		69.7	-6.7
1990	Atl-N	65	25	40	.385	6 W 6 W	1/2	27.0	-2.0
	5	579	231	347	.400				-12.8

Norman, Henry Willis Patrick "Bill"

YEAR	TM/L	G	W	L	PCT	STANDING	M/Y	W-EXP	A-E
1958	Det-A	105	56	49	.533	8 5	2/2	56.3	-0.3
1959	Det-A	17	2	15	.118	8 4	1/2	8.3	-6.3
	2	122	58	64	.475				-6.6

Oakes, Ennis Telfair "Rebel"

YEAR	TM/L	G	W	L	PCT	STANDING	M/Y	W-EXP	A-E
1914	Pit-F*	143	61	78	.439	8 7	2/2	60.6	0.4
1915	Pit-F*	156	86	67	.562	3		84.1	1.9
	2	299	147	145	.503				2.3

O'Connor, John Joseph "Jack"

YEAR	TM/L	G	W	L	PCT	STANDING	M/Y	W-EXP	A-E
1910	StL-A*	158	47	107	.305	8		45.1	1.9

O'Day, Henry Francis "Hank"

YEAR	TM/L	G	W	L	PCT	STANDING	M/Y	W-EXP	A-E
1912	Cin-N	155	75	78	.490	4		69.9	5.1
1914	Chi-N	156	78	76	.506	4		73.5	4.5
	2	311	153	154	.498				9.6

O'Farrell, Robert Arthur "Bob"

YEAR	TM/L	G	W	L	PCT	STANDING	M/Y	W-EXP	A-E
1927	StL-N*	153	92	61	.601	2		85.3	6.7
1934	Cin-N*	91	30	60	.333	8 8	1/3	32.5	-2.5
	2	244	122	121	.502				4.2

O'Leary, Daniel "Dan"

YEAR	TM/L	G	W	L	PCT	STANDING	M/Y	W-EXP	A-E
1884	Cin-U*	35	20	15	.571	5 3	1/2	24.6	-4.6

O'Neill, Stephen Francis "Steve"

YEAR	TM/L	G	W	L	PCT	STANDING	M/Y	W-EXP	A-E
1935	Cle-A	60	36	23	.610	5 3	2/2	30.9	5.1
1936	Cle-A	157	80	74	.519	5		82.3	-2.3
1937	Cle-A	156	83	71	.539	4		81.6	1.4
1943	Det-A	155	78	76	.506	5		84.8	-6.8
1944	Det-A	156	88	66	.571	2		85.2	2.8
1945	Det-A	155	88	65	.575	★1		83.8	4.2
1946	Det-A	155	92	62	.597	2		91.4	0.6
1947	Det-A	158	85	69	.552	2		84.4	0.6
1948	Det-A	154	78	76	.506	5		74.4	3.6
1950	Bos-A	95	63	32	.663	4 3	2/2	59.5	3.5
1951	Bos-A	154	87	67	.565	3		84.5	2.5
1952	Phi-N	91	59	32	.648	6 4	2/2	52.1	6.9
1953	Phi-N	156	83	71	.539	•3		82.0	1.0
1954	Phi-N	77	40	37	.519	3 4	1/2	40.8	-0.8
	14	1879	1040	821	.559				22.2

Onslow, John James "Jack"

YEAR	TM/L	G	W	L	PCT	STANDING	M/Y	W-EXP	A-E
1949	Chi-A	154	63	91	.409	6		68.1	-5.1
1950	Chi-A	31	8	22	.267	8 6	1/2	12.6	-4.6
	2	185	71	113	.386				-9.7

O'Rourke, James Henry "Jim"

YEAR	TM/L	G	W	L	PCT	STANDING	M/Y	W-EXP	A-E
1881	Buf-N*	83	45	38	.542	3		40.9	4.1
1882	Buf-N*	84	45	39	.536	•3		45.5	-0.5
1883	Buf-N*	98	52	45	.536	5		51.8	0.2
1884	Buf-N*	115	64	47	.577	3		62.0	2.0
1893	Was-N*	130	40	89	.310	12		39.2	0.8
	5	510	246	258	.488				6.7

Orr, David L. "Dave"

YEAR	TM/L	G	W	L	PCT	STANDING	M/Y	W-EXP	A-E
1887	NY-a*	8	3	5	.375	8 7 7	2/3	2.3	0.7

Ott, Melvin Thomas "Mel"

YEAR	TM/L	G	W	L	PCT	STANDING	M/Y	W-EXP	A-E
1942	NY-N*	154	85	67	.559	3		83.8	1.2
1943	NY-N*	156	55	98	.359	8		60.2	-5.2
1944	NY-N*	155	67	87	.435	5		68.1	-1.1
1945	NY-N*	154	78	74	.513	5		72.8	5.2
1946	NY-N*	154	61	93	.396	8		69.5	-8.5
1947	NY-N*	155	81	73	.526	4		83.5	-2.5
1948	NY-N	76	37	38	.493	4 5	1/2	41.1	-4.1
	7	1004	464	530	.467				-14.9

Owens, Paul Francis

YEAR	TM/L	G	W	L	PCT	STANDING	M/Y	W-EXP	A-E
1972	Phi-N	80	33	47	.412	6 E 6 E	2/2	32.5	0.5
1983	Phi-N	77	47	30	.610	1 E ♦1 E	2/2	41.5	5.5
1984	Phi-N	162	81	81	.500	4 E		84.1	-3.1
	3	319	161	158	.505				2.9

Ozark, Daniel Leonard "Danny"

YEAR	TM/L	G	W	L	PCT	STANDING	M/Y	W-EXP	A-E
1973	Phi-N	162	71	91	.438	6 E		73.2	-2.2
1974	Phi-N	162	80	82	.494	3 E		78.4	1.6
1975	Phi-N	162	86	76	.531	2 E		85.1	0.9
1976	Phi-N	162	101	61	.623	1 E		103.3	-2.3
1977	Phi-N	162	101	61	.623	1 E		98.6	2.4
1978	Phi-N	162	90	72	.556	1 E		94.0	-4.0
1979	Phi-N	133	65	67	.492	5 E 4 E	1/2	63.1	1.9
1984	SF-N	56	24	32	.429	6 W 6 W	2/2	23.7	0.3
	8	1161	618	542	.533				-1.4

Pabor, Charles Henry "Charlie"

YEAR	TM/L	G	W	L	PCT	STANDING	M/Y	W-EXP	A-E
1871	Cle-n*	29	10	19	.345	7		8.4	1.6
1875	Atl-n*	42	2	40	.048	12 12	1/2	-3.3	5.3
	NH-n*	6	1	5	.167	8 8	3/3	0.5	0.5
	2	77	13	64	.169				7.5

Parker, Francis James "Salty"

YEAR	TM/L	G	W	L	PCT	STANDING	M/Y	W-EXP	A-E
1967	NY-N	11	4	7	.364	10 10	2/2	4.2	-0.2
1972	Hou-N	1	1	0	1.000	2 W 2 W	2/3	0.5	0.5
	2	12	5	7	.417				0.3

Parks, William Robert "Bill"

YEAR	TM/L	G	W	L	PCT	STANDING	M/Y	W-EXP	A-E
1875	Was-n*	8	1	7	.125	8 10	2/2	-1.0	2.0

Pearce, Richard J. "Dickey"

YEAR	TM/L	G	W	L	PCT	STANDING	M/Y	W-EXP	A-E
1872	Mut-n*	16	10	6	.625	4 3	1/2	11.6	-1.6
1875	StL-n*	72	39	29	.574	4		35.6	3.4
	2	88	49	35	.583				1.8

Peckinpaugh, Roger Thorpe

YEAR	TM/L	G	W	L	PCT	STANDING	M/Y	W-EXP	A-E
1914	NY-A*	20	10	10	.500	7 •6	2/2	9.8	0.2
1928	Cle-A	155	62	92	.403	7		62.0	0.0
1929	Cle-A	152	81	71	.533	3		74.2	6.8
1930	Cle-A	154	81	73	.526	4		74.8	6.2
1931	Cle-A	155	78	76	.506	4		81.7	-3.7
1932	Cle-A	153	87	65	.572	4		85.1	1.9
1933	Cle-A	51	26	25	.510	5 4	1/3	25.0	1.0
1941	Cle-A	155	75	79	.487	•4		77.9	-2.9
	8	995	500	491	.505				9.5

Perkins, Ralph Foster "Cy"

YEAR	TM/L	G	W	L	PCT	STANDING	M/Y	W-EXP	A-E
1937	Det-A	15	6	9	.400	2 2	5/5	8.3	-2.3

Pesky, John Michael "Johnny"

YEAR	TM/L	G	W	L	PCT	STANDING	M/Y	W-EXP	A-E
1963	Bos-A	161	76	85	.472	7		76.6	-0.6
1964	Bos-A	160	70	90	.438	8 8	1/2	69.7	0.3
1980	Bos-A	5	1	4	.200	3 E 4 E	2/2	2.5	-1.5
	3	326	147	179	.451				-1.8

Pfeffer, Nathaniel Frederick "Fred"

YEAR	TM/L	G	W	L	PCT	STANDING	M/Y	W-EXP	A-E
1892(1)	Lou-N*	23	9	14	.391	10 11	2/2		
(2)	Lou-N*	77	33	42	.440	9		39.2	2.8

Phelan, Lewis G. "Lew"

YEAR	TM/L	G	W	L	PCT	STANDING	M/Y	W-EXP	A-E
1895	StL-N	45	11	30	.268	11 11	4/4	13.1	-2.1

Phillips, Harold Ross "Lefty"

YEAR	TM/L	G	W	L	PCT	STANDING	M/Y	W-EXP	A-E
1969	Cal-A	124	60	63	.488	6 W 3 W	2/2	51.0	9.0
1970	Cal-A	162	86	76	.531	3 W		81.1	4.9
1971	Cal-A	162	76	86	.469	4 W		73.5	2.5
	3	448	222	225	.497				16.4

Phillips, Horace B.

YEAR	TM/L	G	W	L	PCT	STANDING	M/Y	W-EXP	A-E
1879	Tro-N	47	12	34	.261	8 8	1/2	10.8	1.2
1883	Col-a	97	32	65	.330	6		32.4	-0.4
1884	Pit-a	35	9	24	.273	10 10	5/5	7.4	1.6
1885	Pit-a	111	56	55	.505	3		56.3	-0.3
1886	Pit-a	140	80	57	.584	2		83.7	-3.7
1887	Pit-N	125	55	69	.444	6		50.3	4.7
1888	Pit-N	139	66	68	.493	6		62.1	3.9
1889	Pit-N	71	28	43	.394	6 5	1/3	31.9	-3.9
	8	765	338	415	.449				3.1

Phillips, William Corcoran "Bill"

YEAR	TM/L	G	W	L	PCT	STANDING	M/Y	W-EXP	A-E
1914	Ind-F	157	88	65	.575	1		90.6	-2.6

YEAR	TM/L	G	W	L	PCT	STANDING			M/Y	W-EXP	A-E
1915	New-F	53	26	27	.491	6	5		1/2	27.4	-1.4
	2	210	114	92	.553						-4.0

Pike, Lipman Emanuel "Lip"

YEAR	TM/L	G	W	L	PCT	STANDING			M/Y	W-EXP	A-E
1871	Tro-n*	4	1	3	.250	7	6		1/2	1.9	-0.9
1874	Har-n*	54	17	37	.315	7				19.0	-3.0
1877	Cin-N*	14	3	11	.214	6	6		1/3	3.1	-0.1
	3	72	21	51	.292						-4.0

Piniella, Louis Victor "Lou"

YEAR	TM/L	G	W	L	PCT	STANDING		M/Y	W-EXP	A-E
1986	NY-A	162	90	72	.556	2 E			86.8	3.2
1987	NY-A	162	89	73	.549	4 E			83.9	5.1
1988	NY-A	93	45	48	.484	2 E	5 E	2/2	47.9	-2.9
1990	Cin-N	162	91	71	.562	★1 W			91.2	-0.2
	4	579	315	264	.544					5.3

Popowski, Edward Joseph "Eddie"

YEAR	TM/L	G	W	L	PCT	STANDING		M/Y	W-EXP	A-E
1969	Bos-A	9	5	4	.556	3 E	3 E	2/2	4.5	0.5
1973	Bos-A	1	1	0	1.000	2 E	2 E	2/2	0.6	0.4
	2	10	6	4	.600					0.9

Porter, Matthew S. "Matt"

YEAR	TM/L	G	W	L	PCT	STANDING			M/Y	W-EXP	A-E
1884	KC-U*	16	3	13	.188	8	8	8	2/3	2.5	0.5

Powers, Patrick Thomas "Pat"

YEAR	TM/L	G	W	L	PCT	STANDING	M/Y	W-EXP	A-E
1890	Roc-a	133	63	63	.500	5		62.8	0.2
1892(1)	NY-N	74	31	43	.419	10			
(2)	NY-N	79	40	37	.519	6		74.1	-3.1
	2	286	134	143	.484				-2.9

Pratt, Albert George "Al"

YEAR	TM/L	G	W	L	PCT	STANDING		M/Y	W-EXP	A-E
1882	Pit-a	79	39	39	.500	4			39.9	-0.9
1883	Pit-a	32	12	20	.375	6	7	1/3	10.4	1.6
	2	111	51	59	.464					0.6

Price, James L. "Jim"

YEAR	TM/L	G	W	L	PCT	STANDING		M/Y	W-EXP	A-E
1884	NY-N	100	56	42	.571	4	●4	1/2	54.5	1.5

Prothro, James Thompson "Doc"

YEAR	TM/L	G	W	L	PCT	STANDING	M/Y	W-EXP	A-E
1939	Phi-N	152	45	106	.298	8		45.6	-0.6
1940	Phi-N	153	50	103	.327	8		49.6	0.4
1941	Phi-N	155	43	111	.279	8		46.7	-3.7
	3	460	138	320	.301				-3.9

Purcell, William Aloysius "Blondie"

YEAR	TM/L	G	W	L	PCT	STANDING		M/Y	W-EXP	A-E
1883	Phi-N*	82	13	68	.160	8	8	2/2	10.0	3.0

Quilici, Francis Ralph "Frank"

YEAR	TM/L	G	W	L	PCT	STANDING		M/Y	W-EXP	A-E
1972	Min-A	84	41	43	.488	3 W	3 W	2/2	42.1	-1.1
1973	Min-A	162	81	81	.500	3 W			85.6	-4.6
1974	Min-A	163	82	80	.506	3 W			81.4	0.6
1975	Min-A	159	76	83	.478	4 W			78.3	-2.3
	4	568	280	287	.494					-7.5

Quinn, Joseph J. "Joe"

YEAR	TM/L	G	W	L	PCT	STANDING			M/Y	W-EXP	A-E
1895	StL-N*	40	11	28	.282	11	11	11	3/4	12.5	-1.5
1899	Cle-N*	116	12	104	.103	12	12		2/2	10.0	2.0
	2	156	23	132	.148						0.6

Rader, Douglas Lee "Doug"

YEAR	TM/L	G	W	L	PCT	STANDING			M/Y	W-EXP	A-E
1983	Tex-A	163	77	85	.475	3 W				84.3	-7.3
1984	Tex-A	161	69	92	.429	7 W				74.5	-5.5
1985	Tex-A	32	9	23	.281	7 W	7 W		1/2	12.6	-3.6
1986	Chi-A	2	1	1	.500	6 W	5 W	5 W	2/3	0.9	0.1
1989	Cal-A	162	91	71	.562	3 W				90.8	0.2
1990	Cal-A	162	80	82	.494	4 W				79.4	0.6
	6	682	327	354	.480						-15.5

Rapp, Vernon Fred "Vern"

YEAR	TM/L	G	W	L	PCT	STANDING		M/Y	W-EXP	A-E
1977	StL-N	162	83	79	.512	3 E			86.0	-3.0
1978	StL-N	17	6	11	.353	6 E	5 E	1/3	7.9	-1.9
1984	Cin-N	121	51	70	.421	5 W	5 W	1/2	51.3	-0.3
	3	300	140	160	.467					-5.1

Reach, Alfred James "Al"

YEAR	TM/L	G	W	L	PCT	STANDING			M/Y	W-EXP	A-E
1890	Phi-N	11	4	7	.364	2	3	3	3/5	6.4	-2.4

Rice, Delbert "Del"

YEAR	TM/L	G	W	L	PCT	STANDING	M/Y	W-EXP	A-E
1972	Cal-A	155	75	80	.484	5 W		68.1	6.9

Richards, Paul Rapier

YEAR	TM/L	G	W	L	PCT	STANDING		M/Y	W-EXP	A-E
1951	Chi-A	155	81	73	.526	4			84.1	-3.1
1952	Chi-A	156	81	73	.526	3			81.6	-0.6
1953	Chi-A	156	89	65	.578	3			89.8	-0.8
1954	Chi-A	146	91	54	.628	3	3	1/2	91.5	-0.5
1955	Bal-A	156	57	97	.370	7			54.7	2.3
1956	Bal-A	154	69	85	.448	6			63.0	6.0
1957	Bal-A	154	76	76	.500	5			77.0	-1.0
1958	Bal-A	154	74	79	.484	6			70.4	3.6
1959	Bal-A	155	74	80	.481	6			69.4	4.6
1960	Bal-A	154	89	65	.578	2			84.9	4.1
1961	Bal-A	136	78	57	.578	3	3	1/2	76.7	1.3
1976	Chi-A	161	64	97	.398	6 W			63.9	0.1
	12	1837	923	901	.506					15.9

Richardson, Daniel "Danny"

YEAR	TM/L	G	W	L	PCT	STANDING		M/Y	W-EXP	A-E
1892(2)	Was-N*	43	12	31	.279	11	12	2/2	17.9	-5.9

Rickey, Wesley Branch "Branch"

YEAR	TM/L	G	W	L	PCT	STANDING		M/Y	W-EXP	A-E
1913	StL-A	12	5	6	.455	7	8	3/3	4.6	0.4
1914	StL-A*	159	71	82	.464	5			66.2	4.8
1915	StL-A	159	63	91	.409	6			59.7	3.3

YEAR	TM/L	G	W	L	PCT	STANDING			M/Y	W-EXP	A-E
1919	StL-N	138	54	83	.394	7				58.7	-4.7
1920	StL-N	155	75	79	.487	●5				76.3	-1.3
1921	StL-N	154	87	66	.569	3				88.8	-1.8
1922	StL-N	154	85	69	.552	●3				81.0	4.0
1923	StL-N	154	79	74	.516	5				77.9	1.1
1924	StL-N	154	65	89	.422	6				76.0	-11.0
1925	StL-N	38	13	25	.342	8	4		1/2	20.5	-7.5
	10	1277	597	664	.473						-12.7

Riddoch, Gregory Lee "Greg"

YEAR	TM/L	G	W	L	PCT	STANDING		M/Y	W-EXP	A-E
1990	SD-N	82	38	44	.463	4 W	5 W	2/2	41.0	-3.0

Rigney, William Joseph "Bill"

YEAR	TM/L	G	W	L	PCT	STANDING		M/Y	W-EXP	A-E
1956	NY-N	154	67	87	.435	6			65.1	1.9
1957	NY-N	154	69	85	.448	6			71.1	-2.1
1958	SF-N	154	80	74	.519	3			79.9	0.1
1959	SF-N	154	83	71	.539	3			86.4	-3.4
1960	SF-N	58	33	25	.569	2	5	1/2	30.6	2.4
1961	LA-A	162	70	91	.435	8			76.6	-6.6
1962	LA-A	162	86	76	.531	3			82.2	3.8
1963	LA-A	161	70	91	.435	9			73.7	-3.7
1964	LA-A	162	82	80	.506	5			80.2	1.8
1965	Cal-A	162	75	87	.463	7			76.2	-1.2
1966	Cal-A	162	80	82	.494	6			76.8	3.2
1967	Cal-A	161	84	77	.522	5			78.3	5.7
1968	Cal-A	162	67	95	.414	8			67.6	-0.6
1969	Cal-A	39	11	28	.282	6 W	3 W	1/2	16.2	-5.2
1970	Min-A	162	98	64	.605	1 W			95.5	2.5
1971	Min-A	160	74	86	.463	5 W			78.3	-4.3
1972	Min-A	70	36	34	.514	3 W	3 W	1/2	35.1	0.9
1976	SF-N	162	74	88	.457	4 W			71.3	2.7
	18	2561	1239	1321	.484					-2.0

Ripken, Calvin Edwin Sr. "Cal"

YEAR	TM/L	G	W	L	PCT	STANDING			M/Y	W-EXP	A-E
1985	Bal-A	1	1	0	1.000	4 E	4 E	4 E	2/3	0.5	0.5
1987	Bal-A	162	67	95	.414	6 E				66.6	0.4
1988	Bal-A	6	0	6	.000	7 E	7 E		1/2	2.1	-2.1
	3	169	68	101	.402						-1.2

Robinson, Frank

YEAR	TM/L	G	W	L	PCT	STANDING		M/Y	W-EXP	A-E
1975	Cle-A*	159	79	80	.497	4 E			78.0	1.0
1976	Cle-A*	159	81	78	.509	4 E			79.5	1.5
1977	Cle-A*	57	26	31	.456	5 E	5 E	1/2	26.2	-0.2
1981(1)	SF-N	59	27	32	.458	5 W				
(2)	SF-N	52	29	23	.558	3 W			56.9	-0.9
1982	SF-N	162	87	75	.537	3 W			79.6	7.4
1983	SF-N	162	79	83	.488	5 W			80.0	-1.0
1984	SF-N	106	42	64	.396	6 W	6 W	1/2	44.9	-2.9
1988	Bal-A	155	54	101	.348	7 E	7 E	2/2	53.6	0.4
1989	Bal-A	162	87	75	.537	2 E			83.3	3.7
1990	Bal-A	162	76	85	.472	5 E			77.5	-1.5
	10	1395	667	727	.478					7.6

Robinson, Wilbert

YEAR	TM/L	G	W	L	PCT	STANDING		M/Y	W-EXP	A-E
1902	Bal-A*	83	24	57	.296	7	8	2/2	33.5	-9.5
1914	Bro-N	154	75	79	.487	5			77.4	-2.4
1915	Bro-N	154	80	72	.526	3			73.3	6.7
1916	Bro-N	156	94	60	.610	1			90.1	3.9
1917	Bro-N	156	70	81	.464	7			70.0	-0.0
1918	Bro-N	127	57	69	.452	5			50.9	6.1
1919	Bro-N	141	69	71	.493	5			71.3	-2.3
1920	Bro-N	155	93	61	.604	1			91.3	1.7
1921	Bro-N	152	77	75	.507	5			74.6	2.4
1922	Bro-N	155	76	78	.494	6			75.9	0.1
1923	Bro-N	155	76	78	.494	6			78.2	-2.2
1924	Bro-N	154	92	62	.597	2			81.2	10.8
1925	Bro-N	153	68	85	.444	●6			69.2	-1.2
1926	Bro-N	155	71	82	.464	6			68.1	2.9
1927	Bro-N	154	65	88	.425	6			68.0	-3.0
1928	Bro-N	155	77	76	.503	6			79.1	-2.1
1929	Bro-N	153	70	83	.458	6			64.3	5.7
1930	Bro-N	154	86	68	.558	4			89.3	-3.3
1931	Bro-N	153	79	73	.520	4			76.8	2.2
	19	2819	1399	1398	.500					16.4

Robison, Matthew Stanley "Stanley"

YEAR	TM/L	G	W	L	PCT	STANDING		M/Y	W-EXP	A-E
1905	StL-N	50	19	31	.380	6	6	3/3	18.2	0.8

Rodgers, Robert Leroy "Bob"

YEAR	TM/L	G	W	L	PCT	STANDING		M/Y	W-EXP	A-E
1980	Mil-A	47	26	21	.553	2 E	3 E	1/3	27.2	-1.2
	Mil-A	23	13	10	.565	4 E	3 E	3/3	13.3	-0.3
1981(1)	Mil-A	56	31	25	.554	3 E				
(2)	Mil-A	53	31	22	.585	1 E			58.0	4.0
1982	Mil-A	47	23	24	.489	5 E	♦1 E	1/2	28.3	-5.3
1985	Mon-N	161	84	77	.522	3 E			80.2	3.8
1986	Mon-N	161	78	83	.484	4 E			75.2	2.8
1987	Mon-N	162	91	71	.562	3 E			83.1	7.9
1988	Mon-N	163	81	81	.500	3 E			84.9	-3.9
1989	Mon-N	162	81	81	.500	4 E			81.2	-0.2
1990	Mon-N	162	85	77	.525	3 E			87.9	-2.9
	9	1197	624	572	.522					4.7

Rogers, James F. "Jim"

YEAR	TM/L	G	W	L	PCT	STANDING		M/Y	W-EXP	A-E
1897	Lou-N*	44	17	24	.415	9	11	1/2	15.2	1.8

Rojas, Octavio Victor "Cookie"

YEAR	TM/L	G	W	L	PCT	STANDING		M/Y	W-EXP	A-E
1988	Cal-A	154	75	79	.487	4 W	4 W	1/2	71.6	3.4

YEAR	TM/L	G	W	L	PCT	STANDING			M/Y	W-EXP	A-E
Rolfe, Robert Abial "Red"											
1949	Det-A	155	87	67	.565	4				86.6	0.4
1950	Det-A	157	95	59	.617	2				88.8	6.2
1951	Det-A	154	73	81	.474	5				71.5	1.5
1952	Det-A	73	23	49	.319	8	8		1/2	27.2	-4.2
4		539	278	256	.521						3.9
Rose, Peter Edward "Pete"											
1984	Cin-N*	41	19	22	.463	5 W	5 W		2/2	17.4	1.6
1985	Cin-N*	162	89	72	.553	2 W				81.6	7.4
1986	Cin-N*	162	86	76	.531	2 W				82.5	3.5
1987	Cin-N	162	84	78	.519	2 W				84.0	-0.0
1988	Cin-N	23	11	12	.478	4 W	2 W		1/3	12.2	-1.2
	Cin-N	111	64	47	.577	4 W	2 W		3/3	58.9	5.1
1989	Cin-N	125	59	66	.472	●4 W	5 W		1/2	57.7	1.3
6		786	412	373	.525						17.7
Roseman, James John "Chief"											
1890	StL-a*	15	7	8	.467	4	5	3	3/6	8.8	-1.8
Rowe, David E. "Dave"											
1886	KC-N*	126	30	91	.248	7				26.1	3.9
1888	KC-a*	50	14	36	.280	8	8		1/3	14.2	-0.2
2		176	44	127	.257						3.7
Rowe, John Charles "Jack"											
1890	Buf-P*	81	22	58	.275	8	8		1/3	20.9	1.1
	Buf-P*	19	5	14	.263	8	8		3/3	5.0	0.0
Rowland, Clarence Henry "Pants"											
1915	Chi-A	156	93	61	.604	3				99.2	-6.2
1916	Chi-A	155	89	65	.578	2				88.7	0.3
1917	Chi-A	156	100	54	.649	★1				98.5	1.5
1918	Chi-A	124	57	67	.460	6				63.2	-6.2
4		591	339	247	.578						-10.6
Ruel, Herold Dominic "Muddy"											
1947	StL-A	154	59	95	.383	8				58.5	0.5
Runnels, James Edward "Pete"											
1966	Bos-A	16	8	8	.500	9	9		2/2	7.2	0.8
Ryan, Cornelius Joseph "Connie"											
1975	Atl-N	27	9	18	.333	5 W	5 W		2/2	10.8	-1.8
1977	Tex-A	6	2	4	.333	3 W	5 W	2 W	3/4	3.4	-1.4
2		33	11	22	.333						-3.2
Sawyer, Edwin Milby "Eddie"											
1948	Phi-N	63	23	40	.365	6	6		3/3	25.7	-2.7
1949	Phi-N	154	81	73	.526	3				76.4	4.6
1950	Phi-N	157	91	63	.591	1				87.0	4.0
1951	Phi-N	154	73	81	.474	5				77.4	-4.4
1952	Phi-N	63	28	35	.444	6	4		1/2	36.1	-8.1
1958	Phi-N	70	30	40	.429	8	8		2/2	30.6	-0.6
1959	Phi-N	155	64	90	.416	8				64.1	-0.1
1960	Phi-N	1	0	1	.000	●6	8		1/3	0.4	-0.4
8		817	390	423	.480						-7.7
Scanlon, Michael B. "Mike"											
1884	Was-U	114	47	65	.420	6				46.3	0.7
1886	Was-N	82	13	67	.162	8	8		1/2	18.0	-5.0
2		196	60	132	.313						-4.3
Schalk, Raymond William "Ray"											
1927	Chi-A*	153	70	83	.458	5				71.9	-1.9
1928	Chi-A*	75	32	42	.432	6	5		1/2	33.7	-1.7
2		228	102	125	.449						-3.6
Scheffing, Robert Boden "Bob"											
1957	Chi-N	156	62	92	.403	●7				67.4	-5.4
1958	Chi-N	154	72	82	.468	●5				75.4	-3.4
1959	Chi-N	155	74	80	.481	●5				75.5	-1.5
1961	Det-A	163	101	61	.623	2				97.7	3.3
1962	Det-A	161	85	76	.528	4				87.1	-2.1
1963	Det-A	60	24	36	.400	9	●5		1/2	29.9	-5.9
6		849	418	427	.495						-15.1
Schlafly, Harry Linton "Larry"											
1914	Buf-F*	156	80	71	.530	4				77.4	2.6
1915	Buf-F	41	13	28	.317	8	6		1/3	18.8	-5.8
2		197	93	99	.484						-3.2
Schmelz, Gustavius Heinrich "Gus"											
1884	Col-a	110	69	39	.639	2				66.3	2.7
1886	StL-N	126	43	79	.352	6				45.3	-2.3
1887	Cin-a	136	81	54	.600	2				80.2	0.8
1888	Cin-a	137	80	54	.597	4				78.1	1.9
1889	Cin-a	141	76	63	.547	4				80.7	-4.7
1890	Cle-N	78	21	55	.276	7	7		1/2	27.4	-6.4
	Col-a	57	38	13	.745	5	2		2/3	33.1	4.9
1891	Col-a	138	61	76	.445	6				61.6	-0.6
1894	Was-N	132	45	87	.341	11				47.5	-2.5
1895	Was-N	133	43	85	.336	10				47.2	-4.2
1896	Was-N	133	58	73	.443	●9				57.0	1.0
1897	Was-N	36	9	25	.265	11	●6		1/2	16.7	-7.7
11		1357	624	703	.470						-17.2
Schoendienst, Albert Fred "Red"											
1965	StL-N	162	80	81	.497	7				83.9	-3.9
1966	StL-N	162	83	79	.512	6				80.3	2.7
1967	StL-N	161	101	60	.627	★1				95.3	5.7
1968	StL-N	162	97	65	.599	1				94.1	2.9
1969	StL-N	162	87	75	.537	4 E				87.2	-0.2
1970	StL-N	162	76	86	.469	4 E				80.7	-4.7
1971	StL-N	163	90	72	.556	2 E				85.0	5.0
1972	StL-N	156	75	81	.481	4 E				74.5	0.5
1973	StL-N	162	81	81	.500	2 E				85.3	-4.3
1974	StL-N	161	86	75	.534	2 E				84.1	1.9
1975	StL-N	163	82	80	.506	●3 E				78.2	3.8
1976	StL-N	162	72	90	.444	5 E				76.6	-4.6
1980	StL-N	37	18	19	.486	5 E	4 E		4/4	19.1	-1.1
1990	StL-N	24	13	11	.542	6 E	6 E	6 E	2/3	10.4	2.6
14		1999	1041	955	.522						6.2
Schultz, Joseph Charles Jr. "Joe"											
1969	Sea-A	163	64	98	.395	6 W				64.8	-0.8
1973	Det-A	28	14	14	.500	3 E	3 E		2/2	13.4	0.6
2		191	78	112	.411						-0.3
Selee, Frank Gibson											
1890	Bos-N	134	76	57	.571	5				82.5	-6.5
1891	Bos-N	140	87	51	.630	1				86.3	0.7
1892(1)	Bos-N	75	52	22	.703	1					
(2)	Bos-N	77	50	26	.658	2				95.3	6.7
1893	Bos-N	131	86	43	.667	1				81.7	4.3
1894	Bos-N	133	83	49	.629	3				82.1	0.9
1895	Bos-N	133	71	60	.542	●5				72.2	-1.2
1896	Bos-N	132	74	57	.565	4				74.0	0.0
1897	Bos-N	135	93	39	.705	1				96.5	-3.5
1898	Bos-N	152	102	47	.685	1				99.3	2.7
1899	Bos-N	153	95	57	.625	2				96.4	-1.4
1900	Bos-N	142	66	72	.478	4				72.6	-6.6
1901	Bos-N	140	69	69	.500	5				66.3	2.7
1902	Chi-N	143	68	69	.496	5				71.7	-3.7
1903	Chi-N	139	82	56	.594	3				78.4	3.6
1904	Chi-N	156	93	60	.608	2				85.7	7.3
1905	Chi-N	65	37	28	.569	4	3		1/2	43.2	-6.2
16		2180	1284	862	.598						-0.2
Sewell, James Luther "Luke"											
1941	StL-A	113	55	55	.500	7	●6		2/2	51.1	3.9
1942	StL-A*	151	82	69	.543	3				84.8	-2.8
1943	StL-A	153	72	80	.474	6				75.1	-3.1
1944	StL-A	154	89	65	.578	1				87.1	1.9
1945	StL-A	154	81	70	.536	3				80.9	0.1
1946	StL-A	125	53	71	.427	7	7		1/2	54.6	-1.6
1949	Cin-N	3	1	2	.333	7	7		2/2	1.2	-0.2
1950	Cin-N	153	66	87	.431	6				68.5	-2.5
1951	Cin-N	155	68	86	.442	6				65.5	2.5
1952	Cin-N	98	39	59	.398	7	6		1/3	46.1	-7.1
10		1259	606	644	.485						-9.0
Shannon, Daniel W. "Dan"											
1889	Lou-a*	58	10	46	.179	8	8	8	3/4	12.1	-2.1
1891	Was-a*	51	15	34	.306	7	8	8	3/4	13.0	2.0
2		109	25	80	.238						-0.1
Sharsig, William A. "Bill"											
1886	Phi-a	41	22	17	.564	6	6		2/2	15.3	6.7
1888	Phi-a	137	81	52	.609	3				88.1	-7.1
1889	Phi-a	138	75	58	.564	3				74.5	0.5
1890	Phi-a	132	54	78	.409	7				45.4	8.6
1891	Phi-a	18	6	11	.353	7	4		1/2	8.8	-2.8
5		466	238	216	.524						5.9
Shawkey, James Robert "Bob"											
1930	NY-A	154	86	68	.558	3				90.8	-4.8
Sheehan, Thomas Clancy "Tom"											
1960	SF-N	98	46	50	.479	2	5		2/2	50.6	-4.6
Shepard, Lawrence William "Larry"											
1968	Pit-N	163	80	82	.494	6				86.9	-6.9
1969	Pit-N	157	84	73	.535	3 E	3 E		1/2	85.8	-1.8
2		320	164	155	.514						-8.6
Sherry, Norman Burt "Norm"											
1976	Cal-A	66	37	29	.561	6 W	●4 W		2/2	29.3	7.7
1977	Cal-A	81	39	42	.481	5 W	5 W		1/2	39.5	-0.5
2		147	76	71	.517						7.2
Shettsline, William Joseph "Bill"											
1898	Phi-N	104	59	44	.573	●8	6		2/2	54.0	5.0
1899	Phi-N	154	94	58	.618	3				91.8	2.2
1900	Phi-N	141	75	63	.543	3				70.7	4.3
1901	Phi-N	140	83	57	.593	2				82.8	0.2
1902	Phi-N	138	56	81	.409	7				51.2	4.8
5		677	367	303	.548						16.5
Shotton, Burton Edwin "Burt"											
1928	Phi-N	152	43	109	.283	8				48.7	-5.7
1929	Phi-N	154	71	82	.464	5				65.1	5.9
1930	Phi-N	156	52	102	.338	8				56.4	-4.4
1931	Phi-N	155	66	88	.429	6				63.2	2.8
1932	Phi-N	154	78	76	.506	4				81.4	-3.4
1933	Phi-N	156	60	92	.395	7				60.7	-0.7
1934	Cin-N	1	1	0	1.000	8	8	8	2/3	0.4	0.6
1947	Bro-N	153	92	60	.605	●1	1		2/2	86.3	5.7

YEAR	TM/L	G	W	L	PCT	STANDING			M/Y	W-EXP	A-E
1948	Bro-N	81	48	33	.593	5	3		3/3	44.5	3.5
1949	Bro-N	156	97	57	.630	1				98.8	-1.8
1950	Bro-N	155	89	65	.578	2				88.6	0.4
	11	1469	697	764	.477						3.0

Silvestri, Kenneth Joseph "Ken"

YEAR	TM/L	G	W	L	PCT	STANDING			M/Y	W-EXP	A-E
1967	Atl-N	3	0	3	.000	7	7		2/2	1.5	-1.5

Simmons, Joseph S. "Joe"

YEAR	TM/L	G	W	L	PCT	STANDING			M/Y	W-EXP	A-E
1875	Wes-n	13	1	12	.077	13				2.5	-1.5
1884	Wil-U	18	2	16	.111	8				0.8	1.2
	2	31	3	28	.097						-0.2

Simmons, Lewis "Lew"

YEAR	TM/L	G	W	L	PCT	STANDING			M/Y	W-EXP	A-E
1886	Phi-a	98	41	55	.427	6	6		1/2	37.7	3.3

Sisler, George Harold

YEAR	TM/L	G	W	L	PCT	STANDING			M/Y	W-EXP	A-E
1924	StL-A*	153	74	78	.487	4				72.3	1.7
1925	StL-A*	154	82	71	.536	3				76.0	6.0
1926	StL-A*	155	62	92	.403	7				61.4	0.6
	3	462	218	241	.475						8.3

Sisler, Richard Allan "Dick"

YEAR	TM/L	G	W	L	PCT	STANDING			M/Y	W-EXP	A-E
1964	Cin-N	6	3	3	.500	3	4	●2	2/4	3.4	-0.4
	Cin-N	47	29	18	.617	3	●2		4/4	26.5	2.5
1965	Cin-N	162	89	73	.549	4				92.8	-3.8
	2	215	121	94	.563						-1.7

Skaff, Francis Michael "Frank"

YEAR	TM/L	G	W	L	PCT	STANDING			M/Y	W-EXP	A-E
1966	Det-A	79	40	39	.506	2	3		3/3	40.5	-0.5

Skinner, Robert Ralph "Bob"

YEAR	TM/L	G	W	L	PCT	STANDING			M/Y	W-EXP	A-E
1968	Phi-N	107	48	59	.449	5	●7		3/3	48.2	-0.2
1969	Phi-N	108	44	64	.407	5 E	5 E		1/2	47.2	-3.2
1977	SD-N	1	1	0	1.000	4 W	4 W	5 W	2/3	0.4	0.6
	3	216	93	123	.431						-2.7

Slattery, John Terrence "Jack"

YEAR	TM/L	G	W	L	PCT	STANDING			M/Y	W-EXP	A-E
1928	Bos-N	31	11	20	.355	7	7		1/2	10.7	0.3

Smith, Edward Mayo "Mayo"

YEAR	TM/L	G	W	L	PCT	STANDING			M/Y	W-EXP	A-E
1955	Phi-N	154	77	77	.500	4				77.9	-0.9
1956	Phi-N	154	71	83	.461	5				70.0	1.0
1957	Phi-N	156	77	77	.500	5				73.5	3.5
1958	Phi-N	84	39	45	.464	8	8		1/2	36.7	2.3
1959	Cin-N	80	35	45	.438	7	●5		1/2	41.3	-6.3
1967	Det-A	163	91	71	.562	●2				91.3	-0.3
1968	Det-A	164	103	59	.636	★1				101.2	1.8
1969	Det-A	162	90	72	.556	2 E				91.6	-1.6
1970	Det-A	162	79	83	.488	4 E				74.4	4.6
	9	1279	662	612	.520						4.0

Smith, George Henry "Heinie"

YEAR	TM/L	G	W	L	PCT	STANDING			M/Y	W-EXP	A-E
1902	NY-N*	32	5	27	.156	4	8	8	2/3	11.0	-6.0

Smith, Harry Thomas

YEAR	TM/L	G	W	L	PCT	STANDING			M/Y	W-EXP	A-E
1909	Bos-N*	79	23	54	.299	8	8		2/2	24.6	-1.6

Smith, William J. "Bill"

YEAR	TM/L	G	W	L	PCT	STANDING			M/Y	W-EXP	A-E
1873	Mar-n*	5	0	5	.000	9				-3.9	3.9

Snyder, Charles N. "Pop"

YEAR	TM/L	G	W	L	PCT	STANDING			M/Y	W-EXP	A-E
1882	Cin-a*	80	55	25	.688	1				61.6	-6.6
1883	Cin-a*	98	61	37	.622	3				71.6	-10.6
1884	Cin-a*	40	24	14	.632	5	5		2/2	26.5	-2.5
1891	Was-a*	70	23	46	.333	6	7	8	2/4	18.3	4.7
	4	288	163	122	.572						-14.9

Snyder, James Robert "Jim"

YEAR	TM/L	G	W	L	PCT	STANDING			M/Y	W-EXP	A-E
1988	Sea-A	105	45	60	.429	6 W	7 W		2/2	47.2	-2.2

Sothoron, Allen Sutton

YEAR	TM/L	G	W	L	PCT	STANDING			M/Y	W-EXP	A-E
1933	StL-A	8	2	6	.250	8	8	8	2/3	3.2	-1.2

Southworth, William Harrison "Billy"

YEAR	TM/L	G	W	L	PCT	STANDING			M/Y	W-EXP	A-E
1929	StL-N*	90	43	45	.489	4	4		1/3	45.3	-2.3
1940	StL-N	111	69	40	.633	7	3		3/3	57.9	11.1
1941	StL-N	155	97	56	.634	2				91.4	5.6
1942	StL-N	156	106	48	.688	★1				106.1	-0.1
1943	StL-N	157	105	49	.682	1				99.6	5.4
1944	StL-N	157	105	49	.682	★1				106.8	-1.8
1945	StL-N	155	95	59	.617	2				94.7	0.3
1946	Bos-N	154	81	72	.529	4				80.5	0.5
1947	Bos-N	154	86	68	.558	3				85.1	0.9
1948	Bos-N	154	91	62	.595	1				92.4	-1.4
1949	Bos-N	111	55	54	.505	4	4		1/2	53.6	1.4
1950	Bos-N	156	83	71	.539	4				81.7	1.3
1951	Bos-N	60	28	31	.475	5	4		1/2	31.8	-3.8
	13	1770	1044	704	.597						17.1

Spalding, Albert Goodwill "Al"

YEAR	TM/L	G	W	L	PCT	STANDING			M/Y	W-EXP	A-E
1876	Chi-N*	66	52	14	.788	1				63.1	-11.1
1877	Chi-N*	60	26	33	.441	5				28.7	-2.7
	2	126	78	47	.624						-13.9

Speaker, Tristram E "Tris"

YEAR	TM/L	G	W	L	PCT	STANDING			M/Y	W-EXP	A-E
1919	Cle-A*	61	40	21	.656	3	2		2/2	35.0	5.0
1920	Cle-A*	154	98	56	.636	★1				97.7	0.3
1921	Cle-A*	154	94	60	.610	2				96.6	-2.6
1922	Cle-A*	155	78	76	.506	4				72.4	5.6
1923	Cle-A*	153	82	71	.536	3				89.5	-7.5
1924	Cle-A*	153	67	86	.438	6				71.0	-4.0
1925	Cle-A*	155	70	84	.455	6				73.7	-3.7
1926	Cle-A*	154	88	66	.571	2				89.8	-1.8
	8	1139	617	520	.543						-8.7

Spence, Harrison L. "Harry"

YEAR	TM/L	G	W	L	PCT	STANDING			M/Y	W-EXP	A-E
1888	Ind-N	136	50	85	.370	7				55.2	-5.2

Stahl, Charles Sylvester "Chick"

YEAR	TM/L	G	W	L	PCT	STANDING			M/Y	W-EXP	A-E
1906	Bos-A*	40	14	26	.350	8	8		2/2	13.1	0.9

Stahl, Garland "Jake"

YEAR	TM/L	G	W	L	PCT	STANDING			M/Y	W-EXP	A-E
1905	Was-A*	154	64	87	.424	7				68.6	-4.6
1906	Was-A*	151	55	95	.367	7				59.3	-4.3
1912	Bos-A*	154	105	47	.691	★1				101.9	3.1
1913	Bos-A*	81	39	41	.488	5	4		1/2	41.2	-2.2
	4	540	263	270	.493						-8.0

Stallings, George Tweedy

YEAR	TM/L	G	W	L	PCT	STANDING			M/Y	W-EXP	A-E
1897	Phi-N*	134	55	77	.417	10				62.5	-7.5
1898	Phi-N	46	19	27	.413	●8	6		1/2	24.1	-5.1
1901	Det-A	136	74	61	.548	3				71.8	2.2
1909	NY-A	153	74	77	.490	5				75.8	-1.8
1910	NY-A	142	78	59	.569	3	2		1/2	75.3	2.7
1913	Bos-N	154	69	82	.457	5				70.5	-1.5
1914	Bos-N	158	94	59	.614	★1				88.3	5.7
1915	Bos-N	157	83	69	.546	2				80.1	2.9
1916	Bos-N	158	89	63	.586	3				86.6	2.4
1917	Bos-N	158	72	81	.471	6				74.7	-2.7
1918	Bos-N	124	53	71	.427	7				57.0	-4.0
1919	Bos-N	140	57	82	.410	6				58.6	-1.6
1920	Bos-N	153	62	90	.408	7				60.2	1.8
	13	1813	879	898	.495						-6.7

Stanky, Edward Raymond "Eddie"

YEAR	TM/L	G	W	L	PCT	STANDING			M/Y	W-EXP	A-E
1952	StL-N*	154	88	66	.571	3				81.8	6.2
1953	StL-N*	157	83	71	.539	●3				82.4	0.6
1954	StL-N	154	72	82	.468	6				77.8	-5.8
1955	StL-N	36	17	19	.472	5	7		1/2	15.6	1.4
1966	Chi-A	163	83	79	.512	4				87.6	-4.6
1967	Chi-A	162	89	73	.549	4				85.8	3.2
1968	Chi-A	79	34	45	.430	9	8		1/5	35.7	-1.7
1977	Tex-A	1	1	0	1.000	●3 W	3 W	2 W	2/4	0.6	0.4
	8	906	467	435	.518						-0.3

Start, Joseph "Joe"

YEAR	TM/L	G	W	L	PCT	STANDING			M/Y	W-EXP	A-E
1873	Mut-n*	25	18	7	.720	5	4		2/2	13.9	4.1

Stengel, Charles Dillon "Casey"

YEAR	TM/L	G	W	L	PCT	STANDING			M/Y	W-EXP	A-E
1934	Bro-N	153	71	81	.467	6				71.6	-0.6
1935	Bro-N	154	70	83	.458	5				71.1	-1.1
1936	Bro-N	156	67	87	.435	7				68.0	-1.0
1938	Bos-N	153	77	75	.507	5				69.8	7.2
1939	Bos-N	152	63	88	.417	7				66.3	-3.3
1940	Bos-N	152	65	87	.428	7				63.8	1.2
1941	Bos-N	156	62	92	.403	7				63.8	-1.8
1942	Bos-N	150	59	89	.399	7				60.0	-1.0
1943	Bos-N	107	47	60	.439	6	6		2/2	41.9	5.1
1949	NY-A	155	97	57	.630	★1				95.7	1.3
1950	NY-A	155	98	56	.636	★1				97.8	0.2
1951	NY-A	154	98	56	.636	★1				94.5	3.5
1952	NY-A	154	95	59	.617	★1				94.7	0.3
1953	NY-A	151	99	52	.656	★1				101.0	-2.0
1954	NY-A	155	103	51	.669	2				101.4	1.6
1955	NY-A	154	96	58	.623	1				96.7	-0.7
1956	NY-A	154	97	57	.630	★1				98.8	-1.8
1957	NY-A	154	98	56	.636	1				96.8	1.2
1958	NY-A	155	92	62	.597	★1				95.6	-3.6
1959	NY-A	155	79	75	.513	3				81.1	-2.1
1960	NY-A	155	97	57	.630	1				89.0	8.0
1962	NY-N	161	40	120	.250	10				48.1	-8.1
1963	NY-N	162	51	111	.315	10				51.8	-0.8
1964	NY-N	163	53	109	.327	10				59.4	-6.4
1965	NY-N	96	31	64	.326	10	10		1/2	31.1	-0.1
	25	3766	1905	1842	.508						-4.8

Stovall, George Thomas

YEAR	TM/L	G	W	L	PCT	STANDING			M/Y	W-EXP	A-E
1911	Cle-A*	139	74	62	.544	7	3		2/2	66.1	7.9
1912	StL-A*	117	41	74	.357	8	7		2/2	41.1	-0.1
1913	StL-A*	135	50	84	.373	7	8		1/3	56.1	-6.1
1914	KC-F*	154	67	84	.444	6				71.5	-4.5
1915	KC-F*	153	81	72	.529	4				76.1	4.9
	5	698	313	376	.454						2.1

Stovey, Harry Duffield

YEAR	TM/L	G	W	L	PCT	STANDING			M/Y	W-EXP	A-E
1881	Wor-N*	27	8	18	.308	7	8		2/2	10.6	-2.6
1885	Phi-a*	113	55	57	.491	4				62.1	-7.1
	2	140	63	75	.457						-9.7

Street, Charles Evard "Gabby"

YEAR	TM/L	G	W	L	PCT	STANDING			M/Y	W-EXP	A-E
1929	StL-N	1	1	0	1.000	4	4	4	2/3	0.5	0.5
1930	StL-N	154	92	62	.597	1				96.4	-4.4
1931	StL-N*	154	101	53	.656	★1				96.8	4.2
1932	StL-N	156	72	82	.468	●6				73.7	-1.7
1933	StL-N	91	46	45	.505	5	5		1/2	50.3	-4.3
1938	StL-A	156	55	97	.362	7				57.3	-2.3
	6	712	367	339	.520						-8.0

Stricker, John A. "Cub"

YEAR	TM/L	G	W	L	PCT		STANDING		M/Y	W-EXP	A-E
1892(1)	StL-N*	23	6	17	.261	10	11	9	2/3	8.4	-2.4

Strickland, George Bevan

1964	Cle-A	73	33	39	.458	8	●6		1/2	35.8	-2.8
1966	Cle-A	39	15	24	.385	3	5		2/2	19.2	-4.2
	2	112	48	63	.432						-7.0

Stubing, Lawrence George "Moose"

1988	Cal-A	8	0	8	.000	4 W	4 W		2/2	3.7	-3.7

Sukeforth, Clyde Leroy

1947	Bro-N	2	2	0	1.000	●1	1		1/2	1.1	0.9

Sullivan, Haywood Cooper

1965	KC-A	136	54	82	.397	10	10		2/2	53.1	0.9

Sullivan, James Patrick "Pat"

1890	Col-a	3	2	1	.667	5	5	2	3/3	1.9	0.1

Sullivan, Timothy Paul "Ted"

1883	StL-a	79	53	26	.671	2	2		1/2	50.3	2.7
1884	StL-U	31	28	3	.903	1	1		1/2	26.6	1.4
	KC-U*	62	13	46	.220	8	8		3/3	9.1	3.9
1888	Was-N	96	38	57	.400	8	8		2/2	29.8	8.2
	3	268	132	132	.500						16.2

Sullivan, William Joseph Sr. "Billy"

1909	Chi-A*	159	78	74	.513	4				79.6	-1.6

Sweasy, Charles James "Charlie"

1875	RS-n*	19	4	15	.211	9				0.6	3.4

Swift, Robert Virgil "Bob"

1965	Det-A	42	24	18	.571	3	4		1/2	23.2	0.8
1966	Det-A	57	32	25	.561	3	2	3	2/3	29.2	2.8
	2	99	56	43	.566						3.6

Tanner, Charles William "Chuck"

1970	Chi-A	16	3	13	.188	6 W	6 W		3/3	6.1	-3.1
1971	Chi-A	162	79	83	.488	3 W				83.2	-4.2
1972	Chi-A	154	87	67	.565	2 W				80.1	6.9
1973	Chi-A	162	77	85	.475	5 W				75.5	1.5
1974	Chi-A	163	80	80	.500	4 W				76.2	3.8
1975	Chi-A	161	75	86	.466	5 W				75.5	-0.5
1976	Oak-A	161	87	74	.540	2 W				89.8	-2.8
1977	Pit-N	162	96	66	.593	2 E				88.0	8.0
1978	Pit-N	161	88	73	.547	2 E				85.4	2.6
1979	Pit-N	163	98	64	.605	★1 E				94.4	3.6
1980	Pit-N	162	83	79	.512	3 E				83.1	-0.1
1981(1)	Pit-N	49	25	23	.521	4 E					
(2)	Pit-N	54	21	33	.389	6 E				49.1	-3.1
1982	Pit-N	162	84	78	.519	4 E				83.8	0.2
1983	Pit-N	162	84	78	.519	2 E				82.2	1.8
1984	Pit-N	162	75	87	.463	6 E				86.3	-11.3
1985	Pit-N	161	57	104	.354	6 E				65.6	-8.6
1986	Atl-N	161	72	89	.447	6 W				69.7	2.3
1987	Atl-N	161	69	92	.429	5 W				72.6	-3.6
1988	Atl-N	39	12	27	.308	6 W	6 W		1/2	14.7	-2.7
	19	2738	1352	1381	.495						-9.6

Tappe, Elvin Walter "El"

1961	Chi-N	2	2	0	1.000	7	7	7	4/9	0.9	1.1
	Chi-N	79	35	43	.449	7	7	7	7/9	33.5	1.5
	Chi-N	16	5	11	.313	7	7		9/9	6.9	-1.9
1962	Chi-N	20	4	16	.200	9	9		1/3	7.6	-3.6
	2	117	46	70	.397						-2.9

Taylor, George J.

1884	Bro-a	109	40	64	.385	9				36.3	3.7

Taylor, James Wren "Zack"

1946	StL-A	31	13	17	.433	7	7		2/2	13.2	-0.2
1948	StL-A	155	59	94	.386	6				59.4	-0.4
1949	StL-A	155	53	101	.344	7				53.9	-0.9
1950	StL-A	154	58	96	.377	7				55.4	2.6
1951	StL-A	154	52	102	.338	8				50.9	1.1
	5	649	235	410	.364						2.2

Tebbetts, George Robert "Birdie"

1954	Cin-N	154	74	80	.481	5				73.7	0.3
1955	Cin-N	154	75	79	.487	5				84.5	-9.5
1956	Cin-N	155	91	63	.591	3				88.5	2.5
1957	Cin-N	154	80	74	.519	4				73.8	6.2
1958	Cin-N	113	52	61	.460	8	4		1/2	62.1	-10.1
1961	Mil-N	25	12	13	.480	3	4		2/2	13.4	-1.4
1962	Mil-N	162	86	76	.531	5				87.6	-1.6
1963	Cle-A	162	79	83	.488	●5				74.0	5.0
1964	Cle-A	91	46	44	.511	8	●6		2/2	44.8	1.2
1965	Cle-A	162	87	75	.537	5				86.3	0.7
1966	Cle-A	123	66	57	.537	3	5		1/2	60.5	5.5
	11	1455	748	705	.515						-1.3

Tebeau, Oliver Wendell "Patsy"

1890	Cle-P*	52	21	30	.412	7	7		2/2	20.0	1.0
1891	Cle-N*	73	31	40	.437	4	5		2/2	33.2	-2.2
1892(1)	Cle-N*	74	40	33	.548	5					
(2)	Cle-N*	79	53	23	.697	1				97.9	-4.9
1893	Cle-N*	129	73	55	.570	3				75.0	-2.0
1894	Cle-N*	130	68	61	.527	6				67.4	0.6

1895	Cle-N*	132	84	46	.646	2				81.7	2.3
1896	Cle-N*	135	80	48	.625	2				81.2	-1.2
1897	Cle-N*	132	69	62	.527	5				73.9	-4.9
1898	Cle-N*	156	81	68	.544	5				79.2	1.8
1899	StL-N*	155	84	67	.556	5				83.1	0.9
1900	StL-N*	92	42	50	.457	7	●5		1/2	45.8	-3.8
	11	1339	726	583	.555						-12.2

Tenney, Frederick "Fred"

1905	Bos-N*	156	51	103	.331	7				48.5	2.5
1906	Bos-N*	152	49	102	.325	8				48.1	0.9
1907	Bos-N*	152	58	90	.392	7				57.7	0.3
1911	Bos-N*	156	44	107	.291	8				46.4	-2.4
	4	616	202	402	.334						1.3

Terry, William Harold "Bill"

1932	NY-N*	114	55	59	.482	8	●6		2/2	60.5	-5.5
1933	NY-N*	156	91	61	.599	★1				89.4	1.6
1934	NY-N*	153	93	60	.608	2				94.4	-1.4
1935	NY-N*	156	91	60	.595	3				85.9	5.1
1936	NY-N*	154	92	62	.597	1				89.2	2.8
1937	NY-N	152	95	57	.625	1				89.2	5.8
1938	NY-N	152	83	67	.553	3				81.9	1.1
1939	NY-N	151	77	74	.510	5				77.3	-0.3
1940	NY-N	152	72	80	.474	6				76.4	-4.4
1941	NY-N	156	74	79	.484	5				72.6	1.4
	10	1496	823	661	.555						6.3

Thomas, Frederick L. "Fred"

1887	Ind-N	29	11	18	.379	8	8	8	2/3	7.9	3.1

Thompson, Andrew M. "A. M."

1884	Stp-U	9	2	6	.250	7				0.7	1.3

Tighe, John Thomas "Jack"

1957	Det-A	154	78	76	.506	4				77.0	1.0
1958	Det-A	49	21	28	.429	8	5		1/2	26.3	-5.3
	2	203	99	104	.488						-4.3

Tinker, Joseph Bert "Joe"

1913	Cin-N*	156	64	89	.418	7				65.2	-1.2
1914	Chi-F*	158	87	67	.565	2				88.6	-1.6
1915	Chi-F*	156	86	66	.566	1				87.1	-1.1
1916	Chi-N*	156	67	86	.438	5				74.1	-7.1
	4	626	304	308	.497						-10.9

Torborg, Jeffrey Allen "Jeff"

1977	Cle-A	104	45	59	.433	5 E	5 E		2/2	47.9	-2.9
1978	Cle-A	159	69	90	.434	6 E				73.8	-4.8
1979	Cle-A	95	43	52	.453	6 E	6 E		1/2	44.9	-1.9
1989	Chi-A	161	69	92	.429	7 W				74.8	-5.8
1990	Chi-A	162	94	68	.580	2 W				86.2	7.8
	5	681	320	361	.470						-7.6

Torre, Joseph Paul "Joe"

1977	NY-N*	117	49	68	.419	6 E	6 E		2/2	52.6	-3.6
1978	NY-N	162	66	96	.407	6 E				72.2	-6.2
1979	NY-N	163	63	99	.389	6 E				69.0	-6.0
1980	NY-N	162	67	95	.414	5 E				71.4	-4.4
1981(1)	NY-N	52	17	34	.333	5 E					
(2)	NY-N	53	24	28	.462	4 E				42.3	-1.3
1982	Atl-N	162	89	73	.549	1 W				84.7	4.3
1983	Atl-N	162	88	74	.543	2 W				91.9	-3.9
1984	Atl-N	162	80	82	.494	●2 W				78.6	1.4
1990	StL-N	58	24	34	.414	6 E	6 E		3/3	25.2	-1.2
	9	1253	567	683	.454						-20.8

Tracewski, Richard Joseph "Dick"

1979	Det-A	2	2	0	1.000	5 E	5 E	5 E	2/3	1.0	1.0

Traynor, Harold Joseph "Pie"

1934	Pit-N*	100	47	52	.475	4	5		2/2	50.9	-3.9
1935	Pit-N*	153	86	67	.562	4				86.1	-0.1
1936	Pit-N	156	84	70	.545	4				85.3	-1.3
1937	Pit-N*	154	86	68	.558	3				82.9	3.1
1938	Pit-N	152	86	64	.573	2				82.8	3.2
1939	Pit-N	153	68	85	.444	6				71.0	-3.0
	6	868	457	406	.530						-1.9

Trebelhorn, Thomas Lynn "Tom"

1986	Mil-A	9	6	3	.667	6 E	6 E		2/2	4.1	1.9
1987	Mil-A	162	91	71	.562	3 E				85.2	5.8
1988	Mil-A	162	87	75	.537	●3 E				88.0	-1.0
1989	Mil-A	162	81	81	.500	4 E				83.9	-2.9
1990	Mil-A	162	74	88	.457	6 E				78.2	-4.2
	5	657	339	318	.516						-0.4

Trott, Samuel W. "Sam"

1891	Was-a	12	4	7	.364	6	9		1/4	2.9	1.1

Turner, Robert Edward "Ted"

1977	Atl-N	1	0	1	.000	6 W	6 W	6 W	2/4	0.4	-0.4

Unglaub, Robert Alexander "Bob"

1907	Bos-A*	29	9	20	.310	6	8	7	3/4	12.4	-3.4

Valentine, Robert John "Bobby"

1985	Tex-A	129	53	76	.411	7 W	7 W		2/2	50.8	2.2
1986	Tex-A	162	87	75	.537	2 W				83.7	3.3
1987	Tex-A	162	75	87	.463	●6 W				78.6	-3.6

YEAR	TM/L	G	W	L	PCT	STANDING			M/Y	W-EXP	A-E
1988	Tex-A	161	70	91	.435	6 W				70.4	-0.4
1989	Tex-A	162	83	79	.512	4 W				79.1	3.9
1990	Tex-A	162	83	79	.512	3 W				78.9	4.1
6		938	451	487	.481						9.4

Van Haltren, George Edward

YEAR	TM/L	G	W	L	PCT	STANDING			M/Y	W-EXP	A-E
1892(1)	Bal-N*	11	1	10	.091	12	12		1/3	3.9	-2.9

Vernon, James Barton "Mickey"

YEAR	TM/L	G	W	L	PCT	STANDING			M/Y	W-EXP	A-E
1961	Was-A	161	61	100	.379	●9				64.4	-3.4
1962	Was-A	162	60	101	.373	10				68.2	-8.2
1963	Was-A	40	14	26	.350	10	10		1/3	14.1	-0.1
3		363	135	227	.373						-11.7

Virdon, William Charles "Bill"

YEAR	TM/L	G	W	L	PCT	STANDING			M/Y	W-EXP	A-E
1972	Pit-N	155	96	59	.619	1 E				96.8	-0.8
1973	Pit-N	136	67	69	.493	2 E	3 E		1/2	68.9	-1.9
1974	NY-A	162	89	73	.549	2 E				86.1	2.9
1975	NY-A	104	53	51	.510	3 E	3 E		1/2	58.4	-5.4
	Hou-N	35	17	17	.500	6 W	6 W		2/2	16.0	1.0
1976	Hou-N	162	80	82	.494	3 W				77.6	2.4
1977	Hou-N	162	81	81	.500	3 W				84.1	-3.1
1978	Hou-N	162	74	88	.457	5 W				77.9	-3.9
1979	Hou-N	162	89	73	.549	2 W				81.1	7.9
1980	Hou-N	163	93	70	.571	▲1 W				86.8	6.2
1981(1)	Hou-N	57	28	29	.491	3 W				62.4	-1.4
(2)	Hou-N	53	33	20	.623	1 W					-1.4
1982	Hou-N	111	49	62	.441	5 W	5 W		1/2	51.6	-2.6
1983	Mon-N	163	82	80	.506	3 E				84.3	-2.3
1984	Mon-N	131	64	67	.489	5 E	5 E		1/2	66.2	-2.2
13		1918	995	921	.519						-3.2

Vitt, Oscar Joseph "Ossie"

YEAR	TM/L	G	W	L	PCT	STANDING			M/Y	W-EXP	A-E
1938	Cle-A	153	86	66	.566	3				82.0	4.0
1939	Cle-A	154	87	67	.565	3				86.3	0.7
1940	Cle-A	155	89	65	.578	2				84.4	4.6
3		462	262	198	.570						9.3

Von Der Ahe, Christian Frederick Wilhelm "Chris"

YEAR	TM/L	G	W	L	PCT	STANDING			M/Y	W-EXP	A-E
1895	StL-N	1	1	0	1.000	11	11	11	2/4	0.3	0.7
1896	StL-N	2	0	2	.000	10	11	11	3/5	0.5	-0.5
1897	StL-N	14	2	12	.143	12	12		4/4	2.5	-0.5
3		17	3	14	.176						-0.4

Vukovich, John Christopher

YEAR	TM/L	G	W	L	PCT	STANDING			M/Y	W-EXP	A-E
1986	Chi-N	2	1	1	.500	5 E	5 E	5 E	2/3	0.9	0.1
1988	Phi-N	9	4	5	.444	6 E	6 E		2/2	3.7	0.3
2		11	5	6	.455						0.4

Wagner, Charles F. "Heinie"

YEAR	TM/L	G	W	L	PCT	STANDING			M/Y	W-EXP	A-E
1930	Bos-A	154	52	102	.338	8				57.1	-5.1

Wagner, John Peter "Honus"

YEAR	TM/L	G	W	L	PCT	STANDING			M/Y	W-EXP	A-E
1917	Pit-N*	5	1	4	.200	8	8	8	2/3	2.0	-1.0

Walker, Harry William

YEAR	TM/L	G	W	L	PCT	STANDING			M/Y	W-EXP	A-E
1955	StL-N*	118	51	67	.432	5	7		2/2	51.2	-0.2
1965	Pit-N	163	90	72	.556	3				91.3	-1.3
1966	Pit-N	162	92	70	.568	3				93.0	-1.0
1967	Pit-N	84	42	42	.500	6	6		1/2	41.2	0.8
1968	Hou-N	101	49	52	.485	10	10		2/2	44.9	4.1
1969	Hou-N	162	81	81	.500	5 W				81.8	-0.8
1970	Hou-N	162	79	83	.488	4 W				79.1	-0.1
1971	Hou-N	162	79	83	.488	●4 W				83.0	-4.0
1972	Hou-N	121	67	54	.554	2 W	2 W		1/3	66.3	0.7
9		1235	630	604	.511						-1.9

Wallace, Roderick John "Bobby"

YEAR	TM/L	G	W	L	PCT	STANDING			M/Y	W-EXP	A-E
1911	StL-A*	152	45	107	.296	8				51.6	-6.6
1912	StL-A*	40	12	27	.308	8	7		1/2	13.9	-1.9
1937	Cin-N	25	5	20	.200	8	8		2/2	10.9	-5.9
3		217	62	154	.287						-14.4

Walsh, Edward Augustine "Ed"

YEAR	TM/L	G	W	L	PCT	STANDING			M/Y	W-EXP	A-E
1924	Chi-A	3	1	2	.333	6			2/4	1.4	-0.4

Walsh, Michael John "Mike"

YEAR	TM/L	G	W	L	PCT	STANDING			M/Y	W-EXP	A-E
1884	Lou-a	110	68	40	.630	3				68.7	-0.7

Walters, William Henry "Bucky"

YEAR	TM/L	G	W	L	PCT	STANDING			M/Y	W-EXP	A-E
1948	Cin-N*	53	20	33	.377	7	7		2/2	20.7	-0.7
1949	Cin-N	153	61	90	.404	7	7		1/2	61.4	-0.4
2		206	81	123	.397						-1.2

Waltz, John J.

YEAR	TM/L	G	W	L	PCT	STANDING			M/Y	W-EXP	A-E
1892(1)	Bal-N	8	2	6	.250	12	12	12	2/3	2.9	-0.9

Ward, John Montgomery "Monte"

YEAR	TM/L	G	W	L	PCT	STANDING			M/Y	W-EXP	A-E
1880	Pro-N*	32	18	13	.581	4	3	2	2/3	20.1	-2.1
1884	NY-N*	16	6	8	.429	4	●4		2/2	7.8	-1.8
1890	Bro-P*	133	76	56	.576	2				71.7	4.3
1891	Bro-N*	137	61	76	.445	6				63.6	-2.6
1892(1)	Bro-N*	78	51	26	.662	2					
(2)	Bro-N*	80	44	33	.571	3				95.7	-0.7
1893	NY-N*	136	68	64	.515	5				73.9	-5.9
1894	NY-N*	139	88	44	.667	2				78.8	9.2
7		751	412	320	.563						0.4

Wathan, John David

YEAR	TM/L	G	W	L	PCT	STANDING			M/Y	W-EXP	A-E
1987	KC-A	36	21	15	.583	4 W	2 W		2/2	18.5	2.5
1988	KC-A	161	84	77	.522	3 W				86.3	-2.3
1989	KC-A	162	92	70	.568	2 W				86.8	5.2
1990	KC-A	161	75	86	.466	6 W				80.3	-5.3
4		520	272	248	.523						0.1

Watkins, Harvey L.

YEAR	TM/L	G	W	L	PCT	STANDING			M/Y	W-EXP	A-E
1895	NY-N	35	18	17	.514	9	9		3/3	17.9	0.1

Watkins, William Henry "Bill"

YEAR	TM/L	G	W	L	PCT	STANDING			M/Y	W-EXP	A-E
1884	Ind-a*	23	4	18	.182	10	11		2/2	5.6	-1.6
1885	Det-N	70	34	36	.486	8	6		2/2	30.8	3.2
1886	Det-N	126	87	36	.707	2				88.0	-1.0
1887	Det-N	127	79	45	.637	1				83.0	-4.0
1888	Det-N	94	49	44	.527	3	5		1/2	52.7	-3.7
	KC-a	25	8	17	.320	8	8		3/3	7.1	0.9
1889	KC-a	139	55	82	.401	7				53.9	1.1
1893	StL-N	135	57	75	.432	10				58.6	-1.6
1898	Pit-N	151	72	76	.486	8				67.9	4.1
1899	Pit-N	24	7	15	.318	10	7		1/2	11.9	-4.9
9		914	452	444	.504						-7.6

Weaver, Earl Sidney

YEAR	TM/L	G	W	L	PCT	STANDING			M/Y	W-EXP	A-E
1968	Bal-A	82	48	34	.585	3	2		2/2	45.8	2.2
1969	Bal-A	162	109	53	.673	◆1 E				108.8	0.2
1970	Bal-A	162	108	54	.667	★1 E				103.5	4.5
1971	Bal-A	158	101	57	.639	◆1 E				101.4	-0.4
1972	Bal-A	154	80	74	.519	3 E				87.8	-7.8
1973	Bal-A	162	97	65	.599	1 E				101.3	-4.3
1974	Bal-A	162	91	71	.562	1 E				86.0	5.0
1975	Bal-A	159	90	69	.566	2 E				93.4	-3.4
1976	Bal-A	162	88	74	.543	2 E				83.3	4.7
1977	Bal-A	161	97	64	.602	●2 E				87.3	9.7
1978	Bal-A	161	90	71	.559	4 E				83.3	6.7
1979	Bal-A	159	102	57	.642	◆1 E				97.6	4.4
1980	Bal-A	162	100	62	.617	2 E				97.6	2.4
1981(1)	Bal-A	54	31	23	.574	2 E					
(2)	Bal-A	51	28	23	.549	4 E				51.7	7.3
1982	Bal-A	163	94	68	.580	2 E				89.7	4.3
1985	Bal-A	105	53	52	.505	4 E	4 E		3/3	55.9	-2.9
1986	Bal-A	162	73	89	.451	7 E				75.8	-2.8
17		2541	1480	1060	.583						29.9

Westrum, Wesley Noreen "Wes"

YEAR	TM/L	G	W	L	PCT	STANDING			M/Y	W-EXP	A-E
1965	NY-N	68	19	48	.284	10	10		2/2	21.9	-2.9
1966	NY-N	161	66	95	.410	9				62.5	3.5
1967	NY-N	151	57	94	.377	10	10		1/2	57.4	-0.4
1974	SF-N	86	38	48	.442	5 W	5 W		2/2	38.1	-0.1
1975	SF-N	161	80	81	.497	3 W				79.2	0.8
5		627	260	366	.415						0.9

Wheeler, Harry Eugene

YEAR	TM/L	G	W	L	PCT	STANDING			M/Y	W-EXP	A-E
1884	KC-U*	4	0	4	.000	8	8		1/3	0.6	-0.6

White, James Laurie "Deacon"

YEAR	TM/L	G	W	L	PCT	STANDING			M/Y	W-EXP	A-E
1872	Cle-n*	2	0	2	.000	5	7		2/2	0.5	-0.5
1879	Cin-N*	18	9	9	.500	4	5		1/2	9.4	-0.4
2		20	9	11	.450						-0.9

White, Joyner Clifford "Jo-Jo"

YEAR	TM/L	G	W	L	PCT	STANDING			M/Y	W-EXP	A-E
1960	Cle-A	1	1	0	1.000	4	4	4	2/3	0.5	0.5

White, William Henry "Will"

YEAR	TM/L	G	W	L	PCT	STANDING			M/Y	W-EXP	A-E
1884	Cin-a*	72	44	27	.620	5			1/2	49.6	-5.6

White, William Warren "Warren"

YEAR	TM/L	G	W	L	PCT	STANDING			M/Y	W-EXP	A-E
1874	Bal-n*	47	9	38	.191	8				2.4	6.6

Wilber, Delbert Quentin "Del"

YEAR	TM/L	G	W	L	PCT	STANDING			M/Y	W-EXP	A-E
1973	Tex-A	1	1	0	1.000	6 W	6 W	6 W	2/3	0.4	0.6

Wilhelm, Irvin Key "Kaiser"

YEAR	TM/L	G	W	L	PCT	STANDING			M/Y	W-EXP	A-E
1921	Phi-N*	67	26	41	.388	8	8		2/2	21.0	5.0
1922	Phi-N	154	57	96	.373	7				59.9	-2.9
2		221	83	137	.377						2.1

Williams, James A. "Jimmy"

YEAR	TM/L	G	W	L	PCT	STANDING			M/Y	W-EXP	A-E
1884	StL-a	85	51	33	.607	5	4		1/2	50.5	0.5
1887	Cle-a	133	39	92	.298	8				34.6	4.4
1888	Cle-a	64	20	44	.313	8	6		1/2	23.8	-3.8
3		282	110	169	.394						1.1

Williams, James Francis "Jimy"

YEAR	TM/L	G	W	L	PCT	STANDING			M/Y	W-EXP	A-E
1986	Tor-A	163	86	76	.531	4 E				88.4	-2.4
1987	Tor-A	162	96	66	.593	2 E				99.7	-3.7
1988	Tor-A	162	87	75	.537	●3 E				89.3	-2.3
1989	Tor-A	36	12	24	.333	6 E	1 E		1/2	19.8	-7.8
4		523	281	241	.538						-16.3

Williams, Richard Hirschfeld "Dick"

YEAR	TM/L	G	W	L	PCT	STANDING			M/Y	W-EXP	A-E
1967	Bos-A	162	92	70	.568	1				92.3	-0.3
1968	Bos-A	162	86	76	.531	4				81.3	4.7
1969	Bos-A	153	82	71	.536	3 E	3 E		1/2	77.2	4.8
1971	Oak-A	161	101	60	.627	1 W				94.1	6.9
1972	Oak-A	155	93	62	.600	★1 W				94.4	-1.4
1973	Oak-A	162	94	68	.580	★1 W				95.7	-1.7
1974	Cal-A	84	36	48	.429	6 W	6 W		3/3	39.8	-3.8
1975	Cal-A	161	72	89	.447	6 W				70.7	1.3
1976	Cal-A	96	39	57	.406	6 W	●4 W		1/2	42.7	-3.7
1977	Mon-N	162	75	87	.463	5 E				73.8	1.2
1978	Mon-N	162	76	86	.469	4 E				83.4	-7.4
1979	Mon-N	160	95	65	.594	2 E				92.7	2.3
1980	Mon-N	162	90	72	.556	2 E				87.8	2.2
1981(1)	Mon-N	55	30	25	.545	3 E					
(2)	Mon-N	26	14	12	.538	2 E	1 E		1/2	44.5	-0.5

YEAR	TM/L	G	W	L	PCT	STANDING			M/Y	W-EXP	A-E
1982	SD-N	162	81	81	.500	4 W				82.8	-1.8
1983	SD-N	163	81	81	.500	4 W				81.0	0.0
1984	SD-N	162	92	70	.568	♦1 W				86.5	5.5
1985	SD-N	162	83	79	.512	●3 W				84.0	-1.0
1986	Sea-A	133	58	75	.436	6 W	7 W		3/3	57.2	0.8
1987	Sea-A	162	78	84	.481	4 W				77.0	1.0
1988	Sea-A	56	23	33	.411	6 W	7 W		1/2	25.2	-2.2
	21	3023	1571	1451	.520						7.0

Williams, Theodore Samuel "Ted"

1969	Was-A	162	86	76	.531	4 E				86.2	-0.2
1970	Was-A	162	70	92	.432	6 E				74.4	-4.4
1971	Was-A	159	63	96	.396	5 E				66.1	-3.1
1972	Tex-A	154	54	100	.351	6 W				58.2	-4.2
	4	637	273	364	.429						-11.8

Wills, Maurice Morning "Maury"

1980	Sea-A	58	20	38	.345	6 W	7 W		2/2	22.3	-2.3
1981(1)	Sea-A	25	6	18	.250	7 W	6 W		1/2		
	2	83	26	56	.317						-2.3

Wilson, James "Jimmie"

1934	Phi-N*	149	56	93	.376	7				63.1	-7.1
1935	Phi-N*	156	64	89	.418	7				58.8	5.2
1936	Phi-N*	154	54	100	.351	8				63.2	-9.2
1937	Phi-N*	155	61	92	.399	7				62.9	-1.9
1938	Phi-N*	149	45	103	.304	8	8		1/2	45.7	-0.7
1941	Chi-N	155	70	84	.455	6				76.6	-6.6
1942	Chi-N	155	68	86	.442	6				69.2	-1.2
1943	Chi-N	154	74	79	.484	5				79.9	-5.9
1944	Chi-N	10	1	9	.100	8	4		1/3	5.2	-4.2
	9	1237	493	735	.401						-31.7

Wine, Robert Paul Sr. "Bobby"

1985	Atl-N	41	16	25	.390	5 W	5 W		2/2	16.7	-0.7

Wingo, Ivey Brown

1916	Cin-N*	2	1	1	.500	8	8	●7	2/3	0.8	0.2

Winkles, Bobby Brooks

1973	Cal-A	162	79	83	.488	4 W				78.0	1.0
1974	Cal-A	75	30	44	.405	6 W	6 W		1/3	35.1	-5.1
1977	Oak-A	108	37	71	.343	●5 W	7 W		2/2	44.0	-7.0
1978	Oak-A	39	24	15	.615	1 W	6 W		1/2	15.3	8.7
	4	384	170	213	.444						-2.5

Wolf, William Van Winkle "Chicken"

1889	Lou-a*	65	14	51	.215	8	8	8	2/4	14.0	-0.0

Wolverton, Harry Sterling

1912	NY-A*	153	50	102	.329	8				55.5	-5.5

Wood, George A.

1891	Phi-a*	125	67	55	.549	7	4		2/2	62.8	4.2

Wood, James Leon "Jimmy"

1871	Chi-n*	28	19	9	.679	2				18.2	0.8
1872	Tro-n*	25	15	10	.600	5				18.2	-3.2
	Eck-n*	18	3	15	.167	10	9		2/2	-2.0	5.0
1873	Phi-n*	43	28	15	.651	2	2		2/2	29.1	-1.1
1874	Chi-n	23	10	13	.435	4	5		2/2	9.6	0.4
1875	Chi-n	69	30	37	.448	6				30.2	-0.2
	5	206	105	99	.515						1.7

Wright, Alfred Hector "Al"

1876	Phi-N	60	14	45	.237	7				17.5	-3.5

Wright, George

1879	Pro-N*	85	59	25	.702	1				64.9	-5.9

Wright, William Henry "Harry"

1871	Bos-n*	31	20	10	.667	3				21.2	-1.2
1872	Bos-n*	48	39	8	.830	1				45.0	-6.0
1873	Bos-n*	60	43	16	.729	1				48.2	-5.2
1874	Bos-n*	71	52	18	.743	1				58.9	-6.9
1875	Bos-n*	82	71	8	.899	1				78.2	-7.2
1876	Bos-N*	70	39	31	.557	4				36.7	2.3
1877	Bos-N*	61	42	18	.700	1				44.0	-2.0
1878	Bos-N*	60	41	19	.683	1				35.7	5.3
1879	Bos-N	84	54	30	.643	2				61.5	-7.5
1880	Bos-N	86	40	44	.476	6				38.2	1.8
1881	Bos-N	83	38	45	.458	6				35.4	2.6
1882	Pro-N	84	52	32	.619	2				52.3	-0.3
1883	Pro-N	98	58	40	.592	3				67.1	-9.1
1884	Phi-N	113	39	73	.348	6				32.3	6.7
1885	Phi-N	111	56	54	.509	3				55.2	0.8
1886	Phi-N	119	71	43	.623	4				69.0	2.0
1887	Phi-N	128	75	48	.610	2				78.4	-3.4
1888	Phi-N	132	69	61	.531	3				67.8	1.2
1889	Phi-N	130	63	64	.496	3				63.0	0.0
1890	Phi-N	22	14	8	.636	1	3		1/5	12.7	1.3
	Phi-N	46	22	23	.489	2	3		5/5	26.0	-4.0
1891	Phi-N	138	68	69	.496	4				67.0	1.0
1892(1)	Phi-N	77	46	30	.605	3					
(2)	Phi-N	78	41	36	.532	5				92.6	-5.6
1893	Phi-N	133	72	57	.558	4				78.2	-6.2
	23	2145	1225	885	.581						-39.7

York, Preston Rudolph "Rudy"

1959	Bos-A	1	0	1	.000	8	8	5	2/3	0.5	-0.5

York, Thomas J. "Tom"

1878	Pro-N*	62	33	27	.550	3				31.4	1.6
1881	Pro-N*	34	23	10	.697	4	2		2/2	17.3	5.7
	2	96	56	37	.602						7.3

Yost, Edward Frederick "Eddie"

1963	Was-A	1	0	1	.000	10	10	10	2/3	0.4	-0.4

Young, Denton True "Cy"

1907	Bos-A*	6	3	3	.500	●4	7		1/4	2.6	0.4

Young, Nicholas Ephraim "Nick"

1871	Oly-n	32	15	15	.500	5				15.5	-0.5
1872	Oly-n	9	2	7	.222	10				-1.1	3.1
1873	Was-n	39	8	31	.205	7				5.8	2.2
	3	80	25	53	.321						4.7

Zimmer, Charles Louis "Chief"

1903	Phi-N*	139	49	86	.363	7				55.9	-6.9

Zimmer, Donald William "Don"

1972	SD-N	142	54	88	.380	4 W	6 W		2/2	53.0	1.0
1973	SD-N	162	60	102	.370	6 W				57.6	-2.4
1976	Bos-A	76	42	34	.553	5 E	3 E		2/2	40.7	1.3
1977	Bos-A	161	97	64	.602	●2 E				94.6	2.4
1978	Bos-A	163	99	64	.607	▲2 E				95.5	3.5
1979	Bos-A	160	91	69	.569	3 E				92.5	-1.5
1980	Bos-A	155	82	73	.529	3 E	4 E		1/2	76.6	5.4
1981(1)	Tex-A	55	33	22	.600	2 W					
(2)	Tex-A	50	24	26	.480	3 W				59.2	-2.2
1982	Tex-A	96	38	58	.396	6 W	6 W		1/2	38.2	-0.2
1988	Chi-N	163	77	85	.475	4 E				77.5	-0.5
1989	Chi-N	162	93	69	.574	1 E				89.3	3.7
1990	Chi-N	162	77	85	.475	●4 E				72.6	4.4
	12	1707	867	839	.508						19.7

Biographical Data for Managers Not Appearing in Player/Pitcher Registers

BILL ADAIR Adair, Marion Danne   b: 2/10/13, Mobile, Ala.

BILL ARMOUR Armour, William Clark   b: 9/3/1869, Homestead, Pa.   d: 12/2/22, Minneapolis, Minn.

FRANK BANCROFT Bancroft, Frank Carter   b: 5/9/1846, Lancaster, Mass.   d: 3/30/21, Cincinnati, Ohio

ED BARROW Barrow, Edward Grant "Cousin Ed"   b: 5/10/1868, Springfield, Ill.   d: 12/15/53, Port Chester, N.Y.

JOHN BENJAMIN Benjamin, John W.   b: 1835, Elizabeth, N.J.   d: 11/14/1895, Elizabeth, N.J.

HUGO BEZDEK Bezdek, Hugo Frank   b: 4/1/1884, Prague, Czechoslovakia   d: 9/19/52, Atlantic City, N.J.

BICKERSON Bickerson

DAVE BRISTOL Bristol, James David   b: 6/23/33, Macon, Ga.

FREEMAN BROWN Brown, Freeman   b: 1/31/1845, Hubbardstown, Mass   d: 12/27/16, Worcester, Mass.

AL BUCKENBERGER Buckenberger, Albert C.   b: 1/31/1861, Detroit, Mich.   d: 7/1/17, Syracuse, N.Y.

GEORGE BURNHAM Burnham, George Walter "Watch"   b: 5/20/1860, Albion, Mich.   d: 11/18/02, Detroit, Mich.

ORMOND BUTLER Butler, Ormond Hook   b: 11/1854, West Virginia   d: 9/12/15, Mt.Hope, Md.

CHARLIE BYRNE Byrne, Charles H.   b: 9/1843, New York, N.Y.   d: 1/4/1898, New York, N.Y.

BILL CAMMEYER Cammeyer, William Henry   b: 3/20/1821, New York, N.Y.   d: 9/4/1898, New York, N.Y.

JOE CANTILLON Cantillon, Joseph D. "Pongo Joe"   b: 8/19/1861, Janesville, Wis.   d: 1/31/30, Hickman, Ky.

O. P. CAYLOR Caylor, Oliver Perry   b: 12/17/1849, Near Dayton, Ohio   d: 10/19/1897, Winona, Minn.

ED CURTIS Curtis, Edwin R.

CHARLIE CUSHMAN Cushman, Charles H.   b: 5/25/1850, New York, N.Y.   d: 6/29/09, Milwaukee, Wis.

MORDECAI DAVIDSON Davidson, Mordecai H.   b: 11/30/1846, Port Washington, O   d: 9/6/40, Louisville, Ky.

JOHN DAY Day, John B.   b: 9/23/47, Colchester, Mass.   d: 1/25/25, Cliffside, N.J.

HARRY DIDDLEBOCK Diddlebock, Henry H.   b: 6/27/1854, Philadelphia, Pa.   d: 2/5/1900, Philadelphia, Pa.

CHARLIE EBBETS Ebbets, Charles Hercules   b: 10/29/1859, New York, N.Y.   d: 4/18/25, New York, N.Y.

WALLACE FESSENDEN Fessenden, Wallace Clifton   b: Watertown, Mass.

HORACE FOGEL Fogel, Horace S.   b: 3/2/1861, Macungie, Pa.   d: 11/15/28, Philadelphia, Pa.

GEORGE FRAZER Frazer, George Kasson   b: 1/7/1861, Syracuse, N.Y.   d: 2/5/13, Philadelphia, Pa.

JIM FREY Frey, James Gottfried   b: 5/26/31, Cleveland, Ohio

JUDGE FUCHS Fuchs, Emil Edmund   b: 4/17/1878, Hamburg, Germany   d: 12/5/61, Boston, Mass.

JOHN GAFFNEY Gaffney, John H.   b: 6/29/1855, Roxbury, Mass.   d: 8/8/13, New York, N.Y.

DAVE GARCIA Garcia, David   b: 9/15/20, E.St.Louis, Mo.

JIM GIFFORD Gifford, James H.   b: 10/18/1845, Warren, N.Y.   d: 12/19/01, Columbus, Ohio

MASE GRAFFEN Graffen, Samuel Mason   b: 1845, Philadelphia, Pa.   d: 11/18/1883, Silver City, N.Mex.

CHARLIE HACKETT Hackett, Charles M.   b: 1855, Lee, Mass.   d: 8/1/1898, Holyoke, Mass.

JIM HART Hart, James Aristotle   b: 7/10/1855, Fairview, Pa.   d: 7/18/19, Chicago, Ill.

JOHN HART Hart, John Henry (born John Henry Reen)   b: 7/21/48, Tampa, Fla.

LOUIE HEILBRONER Heilbroner, Louis Wilbur   b: 7/4/1861, Ft.Wayne, Ind.   d: 12/21/33, Ft.Wayne, Ind.

BILL HENDERSON Henderson, William C.

ED HENGLE Hengle, Edward S.   b: Chicago, Ill.

WALTER HEWETT Hewett, Walter F.   b: 1861, Washington, D.C.   d: 10/7/44, Washington, D.C.

VEDIE HIMSL Himsl, Avitus Bernard   b: 4/2/17, Plevna, Mont.

FRED HOEY Hoey, Frederick C.   b: New York, N.Y.   d: 12/7/33, Paris, France

GEORGE HUFF Huff, George A. "Gee"   b: 6/11/1872, Champaign, Ill.   d: 10/1/36, Champaign, Ill.

TIM HURST Hurst, Timothy Carroll   b: 6/30/1865, Ashland, Pa.   d: 6/4/15, Pottsville, Pa.

JOHNNY KEANE Keane, John Joseph   b: 11/3/11, St.Louis, Mo.   d: 1/6/67, Houston, Tex.

JIM KENNEDY Kennedy, James C.   b: 1867, New York, N.Y.   d: 4/20/04, Brighton Beach, N.Y.

JACK KROL Krol, John Thomas   b: 7/5/36, Chicago, Ill.

KARL KUEHL Kuehl, Karl Otto   b: 9/9/37, Monterey Park, Cal.

BOB LEADLEY Leadley, Robert H.   b: 1858, Brooklyn, N.Y.

JIM LEYLAND Leyland, James Richard   b: 12/15/44, Toledo, Ohio

NICK LEYVA Leyva, Nicolas Tomas   b: 8/16/53, Ontario, Cal.

FRANK LUCCHESI Lucchesi, Frank Joseph   b: 4/24/27, San Francisco, Cal.

JACK McCALLISTER McCallister, John   b: 1/19/1879, Marietta, Ohio   d: 10/18/46, Columbus, Ohio

JOE McCARTHY McCarthy, Joseph Vincent "Marse Joe"   b: 4/21/1887, Philadelphia, Pa.   d: 1/13/78, Buffalo, N.Y.

JOHN McCLOSKEY McCloskey, John Joseph "Honest John"   b: 4/4/1862, Louisville, Ky.   d: 11/17/40, Louisville, Ky.

MEL McGAHA McGaha, Fred Melvin   b: 9/26/26, Bastrop, La.

JACK McKEON McKeon, John Aloysius   b: 11/23/30, South Amboy, N.J.

DENNY McKNIGHT McKnight, Dennis Hamar   b: 1847, Pittsburgh, Pa.   d: 5/5/1900, Pittsburgh, Pa.

GEORGE McMANUS McManus, George   b: 1846, Ireland   d: 10/2/18, New York, N.Y.

JOHN McNAMARA McNamara, John Francis   b: 6/4/32, Sacramento, Cal.

STUMP MERRILL Merrill, Carl Harrison   b: 2/25/44, Brunswick, Me.

RAY MILLER Miller, Raymond Roger   b: 4/30/45, Takoma Park, Md.

FELIX MOSES Moses, Felix I.   b: Richmond, Va.

BILLY MURRAY Murray, William Jeremiah   b: 4/13/1864, Peabody, Mass.   d: 3/25/37, Youngstown, Ohio

JIM MUTRIE Mutrie, James J. "Truthful Jim"   b: 6/13/1851, Chelsea, Mass.   d: 1/24/38, New York, N.Y.

PAUL OWENS Owens, Paul Francis   b: 2/7/24, Salamanca, N.Y.

DANNY OZARK Ozark, Daniel Leonard   b: 11/26/23, Buffalo, N.Y.

LEW PHELAN Phelan, Lewis G.

LEFTY PHILLIPS Phillips, Harold Ross   b: 6/16/19, Los Angeles, Cal.   d: 6/12/72, Fullerton, Cal.

HORACE PHILLIPS Phillips, Horace B.   b: 5/14/1853, Salem, Ohio

EDDIE POPOWSKI Popowski, Edward Joseph   b: 8/20/13, Sayerville, N.J.

PAT POWERS Powers, Patrick Thomas   b: 6/27/1860, Trenton, N.J.   d: 8/29/25, Belmar, N.J.

JIM PRICE Price, James L.   b: 1847, New York, N.Y.

VERN RAPP Rapp, Vernon Fred   b: 5/11/28, St.Louis, Mo.

GREG RIDDOCH Riddoch, Gregory Lee   b: 7/17/45, Greeley, Colo.

CAL RIPKEN Ripken, Calvin Edwin Sr.   b: 12/17/35, Aberdeen, Md.

STAN ROBISON Robison, Matthew Stanley   b: 3/30/1859, Pittsburgh, Pa.   d: 3/24/11, Cleveland, Ohio

PANTS ROWLAND Rowland, Clarence Henry   b: 2/12/1879, Platteville, Wis.   d: 5/17/69, Chicago, Ill.

EDDIE SAWYER Sawyer, Edwin Milby   b: 9/10/10, Westerly, R.I.

MIKE SCANLON Scanlon, Michael B.   b: 1847, Cork, Ireland   d: 1/18/29, Washington, D.C.

GUS SCHMELZ Schmelz, Gustavius Heinrich   b: 9/26/1850, Columbus, Ohio   d: 10/13/25, Columbus, Ohio

FRANK SELEE Selee, Frank Gibson   b: 10/26/1859, Amherst, N.Y.   d: 7/5/09, Denver, Colo.

BILL SHARSIG Sharsig, William A. b: 1855, Philadelphia, Pa. d: 2/1/02, Philadelphia, Pa.
LARRY SHEPARD Shepard, Lawrence William b: 4/3/19, Lakewood, Ohio
BILL SHETTSLINE Shettsline, William Joseph b: 10/25/1863, Philadelphia, Pa. d: 2/22/33, Philadelphia, Pa.
LEW SIMMONS Simmons, Lewis b: 8/27/1838, New Castle, Pa. d: 9/2/11, Jamestown, Pa.
HARRY SPENCE Spence, Harrison L. b: 1858, Virginia d: 5/17/08, Chicago, Ill.
PAT SULLIVAN Sullivan, James Patrick d: 5/22/1898
GEORGE TAYLOR Taylor, George J. b: 11/22/1853, New York
FRED THOMAS Thomas, Frederick L. b: Indiana
JACK TIGHE Tighe, John Thomas b: 8/9/13, Kearny, N.J.
TOM TREBELHORN Trebelhorn, Thomas Lynn b: 1/27/48, Portland, Ore.
TED TURNER Turner, Robert Edward b: 11/19/38, Cincinnati, Ohio
CHRIS VON DER AHE Von Der Ahe, Christian Frederick Wilhelm b: 11/7/1851, Hille, Germany d: 6/7/13, St.Louis, Mo.
MIKE WALSH Walsh, Michael John b: 4/29/1850, Ireland d: 2/2/29, Louisville, Ky.
JOHN WALTZ Waltz, John J.
HARVEY WATKINS Watkins, Harvey L.
EARL WEAVER Weaver, Earl Sidney b: 8/14/30, St.Louis, Mo.
JIMMY WILLIAMS Williams, James Andrews b: 1/3/1848, Columbus, Ohio d: 10/24/18, N.Hempstead, N.Y.
BOBBY WINKLES Winkles, Bobby Brooks b: 3/11/30, Tuckerman, Ark.
AL WRIGHT Wright, Alfred Hector b: 3/30/1842, Cedar Grove, N.J. d: 4/20/05, New York, N.Y.
NICK YOUNG Young, Nicholas Ephraim b: 9/12/1840, Amsterdam, N.Y. d: 10/31/16, Washington, D.C.

The Coach Roster

I n an age of ever greater specialization in baseball, coaches have become increasingly important to the successful management of a team. The need for such assistance did not occur to any manager until John McGraw took on Arlie Latham as baseball's first full-time coach in 1909; today, teams employ separate coaches for first base, third base, pitching, the bullpen, hitting, baserunning, strength, conditioning, and more. Some coaches, like Charlie Lau and Roger Craig, have achieved fame exceeding that of the managers under whom they served. But coaches leave no statistical trail by which to track them. Players and pitchers have official records, and so do managers, but the accomplishments of coaches (and umpires) have until now resided largely in memory.

In the first edition of *Total Baseball,* the Coach Roster that follows represented a first attempt in a baseball encyclopedia to recognize these foot soldiers, who too often serve as scapegoats when a team fails but are invisible when it succeeds. We offered the roster in full knowledge that there were gaps and probably gaffes in our research; we hoped that our readers would advise us of omissions so that we could improve this roster in future editions of *Total Baseball*—and they have. A new feature is the addition of not only many names, but also full biographical data for all coaches who did not play at the major-league level and so are absent from the Registers.

The principal sources of the data herein are, for 1921–1939, the *Baseball Blue Book*; for 1940–1981, the *Baseball Register*; and for years since 1982, the *American League Red Book* and the *National League Green Book*. We have done our best to reconcile the many differences among the lists. The team and league abbreviations used in the Coach Roster are found on the final pages of this book.

For a prose account of the history of coaches (and managers), see the feature article by Fred Stein.

Aaron, Tommie Lee   Atl-N 1979-83
Abbott, Spencer   Was-A 1935
Adair, James A. "Jimmy"   Chi-A 1951-52,
Bal-A 1957-61, Hou-N 1962-65
Adair, K. Jerry   Oak-A 1972-74, Cal-A 1975
Adair, Marion D. "Bill"   Mil-N 1962, Atl-N 1967,
Chi-A 1970, Mon-N 1976
Adams, Charles D. "Red"   LA-N 1969-80
Adams, Robert H. "Bobby"   Chi-N 1961-64
Aguirre, Henry J. "Hank"   Chi-N 1972-74
Aker, Jackie D. "Jack"   Cle-A 1985-87
Alomar, Santos C. "Sandy"   SD-N 1986-90
Alou, Felipe R.   Mon-N 1979-80, 1984
Alou, Jesus M. R.   Hou-N 1979
Altobelli, Joseph S. "Joe"   NY-A 1981-82, 1986,
Chi-N 1988-90
Altrock, Nicholas "Nick"   Was-A 1912-53
Amalfitano, J. Joseph "Joey"   Chi-N 1967-71,
SF-N 1972-75, SD-N 1976-77, Chi-N 1978-80,
Cin-N 1982, LA-N 1983-90
Amaro, Ruben   Phi-N 1980-81, Chi-N 1983-86
Anderson, George L. "Sparky"   SD-N 1969
Appling, Lucius B. "Luke"   Det-A 1960,
Cle-A 1960-61, Bal-A 1963, KC-A 1964-67,
Chi-A 1970-71
Auferio, Anthony P. "Tony"   StL-N 1973
Austin, James P. "Jimmy"   StL-A 1923-32,
Chi-A 1933-40
Babe, Loren R.   NY-A 1967, Chi-A 1980-81,
1983
Bader, Lore V.   Bos-N 1926
Baker, Delmer D. "Del"   Det-A 1933-38,
Cle-A 1943-44, Bos-A 1945-48, 1953-60
Baker, Eugene W. "Gene"   Pit-N 1963
Baker, Floyd W.   Min-A 1961-64
Baker, Johnnie B. "Dusty"   SF-N 1988-90
Baker, William P. "Bill"   Chi-A 1950
Bamberger, George I.   Bal-A 1968-77
Bancroft, David J. "Dave"   NY-N 1930-32
Bando, Salvatore L. "Sal"   Mil-A 1980-81
Banks, Ernest "Ernie"   Chi-N 1967-69, 1972-73
Bartell, Richard W. "Dick"   Det-A 1949-52,
Cin-N 1954-55
Bartirome, Anthony J. "Tony"   Atl-N 1986-88
Basgall, Romanus "Monty"   LA-N 1973-86
Bassler, John L. "Johnny"   Cle-A 1938-40,
StL-A 1941
Baylor, Don E.   Mil-A 1990
Bauer, Henry A. "Hank"   Bal-A 1963
Bearnarth, Lawrence D. "Larry"   Mon-N 1976,
1985-90
Beck, Walter W. "Boom-Boom"   Was-A 1957-59
Becker, Joseph E. "Joe"   Bro-N 1955-57,
LA-N 1958-64, StL-N 1965-66, Chi-N 1967-70
Bedell, Howard W. "Howie"   KC-A 1984,
SE-A 1988
Bender, Charles A. "Chief"   Cin-N 1919,
Chi-A 1925-26, NY-N 1931, Phi-A 1951-53
Bengough, Bernard O. "Benny"
Was-A 1940-43, Bos-N 1945,
Phi-N 1946-58
Benson, Vernon A. "Vern"   StL-N 1961-64,
NY-A 1965-66, Cin-N 1966-69, StL-N 1970-75,
Atl-N 1976-77, SF-N 1980
Berardino, Richard J. "Dick"   Bos-A 1989-90
Berg, Morris "Moe"   Bos-A 1940-41
Beringer, Carroll J. "C. B."   LA-N 1967-72,
Phi-N 1973-78
Berra, Lawrence P. "Yogi"
NY-A 1963, NY-N 1965-71, NY-A 1976-83,
Hou-N 1986-89
Berres, Raymond F. "Ray"   Chi-A 1949-66,
1968-69
Berry, Charles F. "Charlie"   Phi-A 1936-40
Bevington, Terry Paul   Chi-A 1989-90
Bissonette, Adelphia L. "Del"   Bos-N 1945,
Pit-N 1946
Blackburn, Wayne C.   Det-A 1963-64
Blackburne, Russell A. "Lena"   Chi-A 1927-28,
StL-A 1930, Phi-A 1933-40, 1942-43
Blades, F. Raymond "Ray"   StL-N 1930-32,
Cin-N 1942, Bro-N 1947-48, StL-N 1951,
Chi-N 1953-56
Blaylock, Gary N.   KC-A 1984-87
Bloomfield, Gordon L. "Jack"   SD-N 1974,
Chi-N 1975-76
Bluege, Oswald L. "Ossie"   Was-A 1940-42
Bonds, Bobby L.   Cle-A 1984-87
Boros, Stephen "Steve"   KC-A 1975-79,
Mon-N 1981-82
Bosman, Richard A. "Dick"   Chi-A 1986-87
Bottomley, James L. "Jim"   StL-A 1937
Bowa, Lawrence R. "Larry"   Phi-N 1988-90

Boyer, Cletis L. "Clete"   Oak-A 1980-85,
NY-A 1988
Boyer, Cloyd V.   NY-A 1977, Atl-N 1978-81,
KC-A 1982-83
Boyer, Kenton L. "Ken"   StL-N 1971-72
Bragan, James A. "Jimmy"   Cin-N 1967-69,
Mon-N 1970-72, Mil-A 1976-77
Bragan, Robert R. "Bobby"   LA-N 1960,
Hou-N 1962
Braun, Stephen R. "Steve"   StL-N 1990
Brecheen, Harry D.   Bal-A 1954-67
Breeden, H. Scott   Cin-N 1986-89
Bresnahan, Roger P.   NY-N 1925-28,
Det-A 1930-31
Brewer, James T. "Jim"   Mon-N 1977-79
Bridges, Everett L. "Rocky"   LA-N 1962-63,
Cal-A 1968-71, SF-N 1985
Bridges, Thomas J. "Tommy"   Det-A 1946,
Cin-N 1951
Brinkman, Edwin A. "Ed"   Det-A 1979,
SD-N 1981, Chi-A 1983-88
Bristol, J. David "Dave"   Cin-N 1966,
Mon-N 1973-75, SF-N 1978-79, Phi-N 1982-85,
1988, Cin-N 1989
Brown, Jackie G.   Tex-A 1979-82
Brown, James R. "Jimmy"   Bos-N 1949-51
Brown, Mace S.   Bos-A 1965
Brown, William J. "Gates"   Det-A 1978-84
Brucker, Earle F., Sr.   Phi-A 1941-49,
StL-A 1950, Cin-N 1952
Bryant, Claiborne H. "Clay"   LA-N 1961,
Cle-A 1967, 1974
Bryant, Donald R. "Don"   Bos-A 1974-76,
Sea-A 1977-80
Buford, Donald A. "Don"   SF-N 1981-84
Bumbry, Alonza B. "Al"   Bos-A 1988-90
Burdette, S. Lewis "Lew"   Atl-N 1972-73
Burgess, Thomas R. "Tom"   NY-N 1977,
Atl-N 1978
Burke, James T. "Jimmy"   Bos-A 1921-23,
Chi-N 1926-30, NY-A 1931-33
Burkett, Jesse C.   NY-N 1921
Burns, George J.   NY-N 1931
Burns, John I. "Jack"   Bos-A 1955-59
Burris, B. Ray   Mil-A 1990
Burwell, William E. "Bill"   Bos-A 1944,
Pit-N 1947-48, 1958-62
Busby, James F. "Jim"   Bal-A 1961,
Hou-N 1962, 1963-67, Atl-N 1968-75,
Chi-A 1976, Sea-A 1977-78
Butler, John S. "Johnny"   Chi-A 1932
Camacho, Joseph G. "Joe"   Was-A 1969-71,
Tex-A 1972
Camilli, Douglas J. "Doug"   Was-A 1968-69,
Bos-A 1970-73
Cannizzaro, Christopher J. "Chris"
Atl-N 1976-78
Carey, Max G.   Pit-N 1930
Carey, Thomas F. "Tom"   Bos-A 1946-47
Carisch, Frederick B. "Fred"   Det-A 1923-24
Carnevale, Daniel J. "Danny"   KC-A 1970
Carrion, Leonel S,   Mon-N 1988
Carter, Richard J. "Dick"   Phi-N 1959-60
Case, George W.   Was-A 1961-63, Min-A 1968
Cavarretta, Philip J. "Phil"   Det-A 1961-63,
NY-N 1978
Cepeda, Orlando M.   Chi-A 1980
Chambliss, C. Christopher "Chris"   NY-A 1988
Chandler, Spurgeon F. "Spud"   KC-A 1957-58
Chapman, W. Benjamin "Ben"   Cin-N 1952
Chesbro, John D. "Jack"   Was-A 1924
Cisco, Galen B.   KC-A 1971-79,
Mon-N 1980-84, SD-N 1985-87, Tor-A 1988,
1990
Clark, Ronald B. "Ron"   Chi-A 1988-90
Clarke, Thomas A. "Tommy"   NY-N 1932-35,
1938
Clary, Ellis   Was-A 1955-60, Tor-A 1989
Clear, E. Robert "Bob"   Cal-A 1976-87
Clines, Eugene A. "Gene"   Chi-N 1979-81,
Hou-N 1988, Sea-A 1989-90
Cluck, Robert A. "Bob"   Hou-N 1979, 1990
Clymer, William J. "Bill"   Cin-N 1925
Cochrane, Gordon S. "Mickey"   Phi-A 1950
Cohen, Andrew H. "Andy"   Phi-N 1960
Colavito, Rocco D. "Rocky"   Cle-A 1973,
1976-78, KC-A 1982-83
Cole, Richard R. "Dick"   Chi-N 1961
Coleman, Joseph H. "Joe"   Cal-A 1988-90
Coleman, Robert H. "Bob"   Bos-A 1926,
Det-A 1932, Bos-N 1943
Collins, Edward T. "Eddie"   Phi-A 1931-32
Collins, James A. "Ripper"   Chi-N 1961-63

Combs, Earle B.   NY-A 1936-44, StL-A 1947,
Bos-A 1948-52, Phi-N 1954
Combs, Merrill R. "Merl"   Tex-A 1974-75
Comer, Stephen M. "Steve"   Cle-A 1987
Connor, Mark P.   NY-A 1984-85, 1986-87, 1990
Connors, William J. "Billy"   KC-A 1980-81,
Chi-N 1982-86, Sea-A 1987-88, NY-A 1989-90
Conroy, William E. "Wid"   Phi-N 1922
Consolo, William A. "Billy"   Det-A 1979-90
Cooke, Allen L. "Dusty"   Phi-N 1948-52
Coombs, John W. "Jack"   Det-A 1920
Cooney, John W. "Johnny"   Bos-A 1940-42,
1946-49, 1950-52, Mil-N 1953-55,
Chi-A 1957-64
Cooper, W. Walker   StL-N 1957, KC-A 1960
Corrales, Patrick "Pat"   Tex-A 1975-78,
NY-A 1989, Atl-N 1990
Corriden, John M., Sr. "Red"   Chi-N 1932-40,
Bro-N 1941-46, NY-A 1947-48, Chi-A 1950
Cottier, Charles K. "Chuck"   NY-N 1979-81,
Sea-A 1982-84, Chi-N 1988-90
Courtney, Clinton D. "Clint"   Hou-N 1965
Cox, Larry E.   Chi-N 1988-89
Cox, Robert J. "Bobby"   NY-A 1977
Crabtree, Estel C.   Cin-N 1943-44
Craft, Harry F.   KC-A 1955-57, Chi-N 1960-61
Craig, Roger L.   SD-N 1969-72, Hou-N 1974-75,
SD-N 1976-77, Det-A 1980-84
Cramer, Roger M. "Doc"   Det-A 1948,
Chi-A 1951-53
Crandall, Delmar W. "Del"   Cal-A 1977
Crandall, J. Otis "Doc"   Pit-N 1931-34
Cravath, Clifford C. "Gavvy"   Phi-N 1923
Cresse, Mark E.   LA-N 1977-90
Crosetti, Frank P. J. "Frankie"   NY-A 1947-68,
Sea-A 1969, Min-A 1970-71
Crowley, Terrence M. "Terry"   Bal-A 1985-88
Cubbage, Michael L. "Mike"   NY-N 1990
Cuccinello, Anthony F. "Tony"   Cin-N 1949-51,
Cle-A 1952-56, Chi-A 1957-66, Det-A 1967-68,
Chi-A 1969
Culp, Benjamin B. "Benny"   Phi-N 1946-47
Cunningham, Joseph R. "Joe"   StL-N 1982
Cunningham, William A. "Bill"   Chi-A 1932
Cuyler, Hazen S. "Kiki"   Chi-N 1941-43,
Bos-A 1949
Dahlgren, Ellsworth T. "Babe"   KC-A 1964
Dal Canton, J. Bruce   Chi-A 1978, Atl-N 1987-90
Daly, Thomas D. "Tom"   Bos-A 1933-46
Dark, Alvin R.   Chi-N 1965, 1977
Dauer, Richard F. "Rich"   Cle-A 1990
Davenport, James H. "Jim"   SF-N 1970,
SD-N 1974-75, SF-N 1976-82, 1984,
Phi-N 1986-87, Cle-A 1989
Davis, Harry H.   Phi-A 1913-19
Davis, H. Thomas "Tommy"   Sea-A 1981
Davis, R. Brandon "Brandy"   Phi-N 1972
Davis, Virgil L. "Spud"   Pit-N 1942-46,
Chi-N 1950-53
Deal, Ellis F. "Cot"   Cin-N 1959-60,
Hou-N 1962-64, NY-A 1965, KC-A 1966-67,
Cle-A 1970-71, Det-A 1973-74, Hou-N 1983-85
DeMars, William L. "Billy"   Phi-N 1969-81,
Mon-N 1982-84, Cin-N 1985-87
Dean, Jay H. "Dizzy"   Chi-N 1941
DeMeritt, Martin G. "Marty"   SF-N 1989
Demeter, Stephen "Steve"   Pit-N 1985
Devlin, Arthur M. "Art"   Bos-N 1926, 1928
Dews, Robert W. "Bobby"   Atl-N 1979-81, 1985
Dickey, William M. "Bill"   NY-A 1949-57, 1960
Didier, Robert D. "Bob"   Oak-A 1984-86,
Sea-A 1989-90
DiMaggio, Joseph P. "Joe"   Oak-A 1968-69
Dobson, Patrick E. "Pat"   Mil-A 1982-84,
SD-N 1988-90
Doby, Lawrence E. "Larry"   Mon-N 1971-73,
Cle-A 1974, Mon-N 1976, Chi-A 1977-78
Doerr, Robert P. "Bobby"   Bos-A 1967-69,
Tor-A 1977-81
Dolan, Albert J. "Cozy"   NY-N 1922-24
Donnelly, Richard F. "Rich"   Tex-A 1980,
1983-85, Pit-N 1986-90
Doolan, Michael J. "Mickey"   Chi-N 1926-28,
Cin-N 1930-32
Dorish, Harry "Fritz"   Bos-A 1963,
Atl-N 1968-71
Douglas, Otis W.   Cin-N 1961-62
Down, Richard J. "Rick"   Cal-A 1987-88
Drabowsky, Myron W. "Moe"   Chi-A 1986
Dressen, Charles W. "Chuck"   Bro-N 1939-42,
1943-46, NY-A 1947-48, LA-N 1958-59
Dubuc, Jean J.   Det-A 1930-31
Duffy, Hugh   Bos-A 1932

Dugey, Oscar J. Chi-N 1921-24
Duncan, David E. "Dave" Cle-A 1978-81,
  Sea-A 1982, Chi-A 1983-86, Oak-A 1986-90
Dunlop, Harry A. KC-A 1969-75, Chi-N 1976,
  Cin-N 1979-82, SD-N 1983-86
Durocher, Leo E. LA-N 1961-64
Dusan, Eugene P. "Gene" NY-N 1983
Dyer, Don R. "Duffy" Chi-N 1983,
  Mil-A 1989-90
Dykes, James J. "Jimmy" Phi-A 1949-50,
  Cin-N 1955-58, Pit-N 1959, Mil-N 1962,
  KC-A 1963-64
Earnshaw, George L. Phi-N 1949-50
Easter, L. Luke Cle-A 1969
Edwards, Howard R. "Doc" Phi-N 1970-72,
  Cle-A 1985-87, NY-N 1990
Egan, Arthur A. "Ben" Bro-N 1925, Chi-A 1926
Egan, Richard W. "Dick" Tex-A 1988-89
Elia, Lee C. Phi-N 1980-81, 1985-87,
  NY-A 1989
Elliott, Robert I. "Bob" LA-A 1961
Ellis, Samuel J. "Sammy" NY-A 1982, 1983-84,
  1986, Chi-A 1989-90
Emery, Calvin W. "Cal" Chi-A 1988
Ens, Jewel W. Pit-N 1926-29, Det-A 1932,
  Cin-N 1933, Bos-N 1934, Pit-N 1935-39,
  Cin-N 1941
Ermer, Calvin C. "Cal" Bal-A 1962,
  Mil-A 1970-71, Oak-A 1977
Estrada, Charles L. "Chuck" Tex-A 1973,
  SD-N 1978-81, Cle-A 1983
Etchebarren, Andrew A. "Andy" Cal-A 1977,
  Mil-A 1985-90
Evans, Darrell W. NY-A 1990
Evers, John J. "Johnny" NY-N 1920,
  Chi-A 1922-23, Bos-N 1929-32
Evers, Walter A. "Hoot" Cle-A 1970
Ezell, Glenn W. Tex-A 1983-85, KC-A 1989-90
Faber, Urban C. "Red" Chi-A 1946-48
Fahey, William R. "Bill" SF-N 1986-90
Falk, Bibb A. Cle-A 1933, Bos-A 1934
Fanning, W. James "Jim" Atl-N 1967
Farrell, M. Kerby Chi-A 1966-69, Cle-A 1970-71
Felske, John F. Tor-A 1980-81, Phi-N 1984
Ferguson, Joseph V. "Joe" Tex-A 1986-87,
  LA-N 1988-89
Ferraro, Michael D. "Mike" NY-A 1979-82,
  KC-A 1984-86, NY-A 1987-88, 1989-90
Ferrell, Richard B. "Rick" Was-A 1946-49,
  Det-A 1950-53
Ferrick, Thomas J. "Tom" Cin-N 1954-58,
  Phi-N 1959, Det-A 1960-63, KC-A 1964-65
Ferriss, David M. "Dave" Bos-A 1955-59
Fischer, William C. "Bill" Cin-N 1979-83,
  Bos-A 1985-90
Fitzgerald, Edward R. "Ed" Cle-A 1960,
  KC-A 1961, Min-A 1962-64
Fitzgerald, Joseph P. "Joe" Was-A 1947-56
Fitzpatrick, John A. Pit-N 1953-56,
  Mil-N 1958-59
Fitzsimmons, Frederick "Freddie" Bro-N 1942,
  Bos-N 1948, NY-N 1949-53, 1954-55,
  Chi-N 1957-59, KC-A 1960, Chi-N 1966
Fletcher, Arthur "Art" NY-A 1927-45
Flowers, D'Arcy R. "Jake" Pit-N 1940-45,
  Bos-N 1946, Cle-A 1951-52
Foli, Timothy J. "Tim" Tex-A 1986-87
Ford, Edward C. "Whitey" NY-A 1968, 1974-75
Fowler, J. Arthur "Art" LA-N 1964, Min-A 1969,
  Det-A 1971-73, Tex-A 1973-75, NY-A 1977-79,
  Oak-A 1980-82, NY-A 1983, 1988
Fox, Charles F. "Charlie" SF-N 1965-68,
  NY-A 1989
Fox, J. Nelson "Nellie" Hou-N 1965, 1966-67,
  Was-A 1968-71, Tex-A 1972
Franks, Herman L. NY-N 1949-55, SF-N 1958,
  1964, Chi-N 1970
Fraser, Charles C. "Chick" Pit-N 1923
Frey, James G. "Jim" Bal-A 1970-79,
  NY-N 1982-83
Friend, Owen L. KC-A 1969
Frisch, Frank F. "Frankie" NY-N 1949
Funk, Franklin R. "Frank" SF-N 1976,
  Sea-A 1980-81, 1983-84, KC-A 1988-90
Galan, August J. "Augie" Phi-A 1954
Galante, Matthew "Matt" Hou-N 1985-90
Garcia, David "Dave" SD-N 1970-73,
  Cle-A 1975-76, Cal-A 1977, Cle-A 1979,
  Mil-A 1983-84
Gardner, William F. "Billy" Bos-A 1965-66,
  Mon-N 1977-78, Min-A 1981
Garner, Philip M. "Phil" Hou-N 1989-90
Garrett, H. Adrian KC-A 1988-90

Garrison, R. Ford Cin-N 1953
Gaston, Clarence E. "Cito" Tor-A 1982-89
Gebhard, Robert H. "Bob" Mon-N 1982
Gehringer, Charles L. "Charlie" Det-A 1942
Gernert, Richard E. "Dick" Tex-A 1975-76
Gharrity, E. Patrick "Patsy" Was-A 1929-32,
  Cle-A 1933-35
Gibson, George C. Was-A 1923, Chi-N 1925
Gibson, Robert "Bob" NY-N 1981,
  Atl-N 1982-84
Gilbert, Andrew "Andy" SF-N 1972-75
Gilliam, James W. "Jim" LA-N 1965-78
Gladding, Fred E. Det-A 1976-78
Gleason, William J. "Kid" Phi-N 1908-11,
  Chi-A 1912-17, Phi-A 1926-32
Gleeson, James J. "Jim" KC-A 1957,
  NY-A 1964
Gomez, Pedro "Preston" LA-N 1965-68,
  Hou-N 1973, StL-N 1976, LA-N 1977-79,
  Cal-A 1981-84
Gonzalez, Miguel A. "Mike" StL-N 1934-46
Gooch, John B. "Johnny" Pit-N 1937-39
Goodman, William D. "Billy" Atl-N 1968-70
Gordon, Joseph L. "Joe" Det-A 1956
Goryl, John A. "Johnny" Min-A 1968-69,
  1979-80, Cle-A 1982-88
Gowdy, Henry M. "Hank" Bos-N 1929-37,
  Cin-N 1938-42, 1945-46, NY-N 1947-48
Graff, Milton E. "Milt" Pit-N 1985
Grammas, Alexander P. "Alex" Pit-N 1965-69,
  Cin-N 1970-75, 1978, Atl-N 1979,
  Det-A 1980-90
Grimes, Burleigh A. KC-A 1955
Grimm, Charles J. "Charlie" Chi-N 1941,
  1961-62
Grissom, Marvin E. "Marv"
  LA-N 1961-65, Cal-A 1966, Chi-A 1967-68,
  Cal-A 1969, Min-A 1970-71, Chi-N 1975-76,
  Cal-A 1977-78
Grodzicki, John "Johnny" Det-A 1979
Guerrero, Epifanio O. "Epy" Tor-A 1981
Gutteridge, Donald J. "Don" Chi-A 1955-66,
  1968-69
Haas, G. Edward "Eddie" Atl-N 1974-77, 1984
Haas, George W. "Mule" Chi-A 1940-46
Hack, Stanley C. "Stan" StL-N 1957-58
Hacker, Richard W. "Rich" StL-N 1986-90
Haddix, Harvey NY-N 1966-67, Cin-N 1969,
  Bos-A 1971, Cle-A 1975-78, Pit-N 1979-84
Haines, Jesse J. Bro-N 1938
Hairston, Samuel "Sammy" Chi-A 1978
Haller, Thomas F. "Tom" SF-N 1977-79
Hamilton, Steve A. Chi-A 1975
Hancken, Morris M. "Buddy" Hou-N 1968-72
Haney, Fred G. Mil-N 1956
Haney, W. Larry Mil-A 1978-90
Hansen, Ronald L. "Ron" Mil-A 1980-83,
  Mon-N 1985-89
Harder, Melvin L. "Mel" Cle-A 1947, 1949-63,
  NY-N 1964, Chi-N 1965, Cin-N 1966-68,
  KC-A 1969
Hargrove, D. Michael "Mike" Cle-A 1990
Harmon, Thomas "Tom" Chi-N 1982
Harper, Tommy Bos-A 1980-84, Mon-N 1990
Harrah, Colbert D. "Toby" Tex-A 1989-90
Harrelson, Derrel M. "Bud" NY-N 1982,
  1985-90
Harris, C. Luman "Lum" Chi-A 1951-54,
  Bal-A 1955-61, Hou-N 1962-64
Hart, John H. Bal-A 1988
Hartenstein, Charles O. "Chuck" Cle-A 1979,
  Mil-A 1987-89
Hartley, Grover A. Cle-A 1928-30,
  Pit-N 1931-33, StL-A 1934-36, NY-N 1946
Hartnett, Charles L. "Gabby" Chi-N 1938,
  NY-N 1941, KC-A 1965
Hartsfield, Roy T. LA-N 1969-72, Atl-N 1973
Hatfield, Fred J. Det-A 1977-78
Hatton, Grady E. Chi-N 1960, Hou-N 1973-74
Haynes, Joseph W. "Joe" Was-A 1953-55
Hayworth, Raymond H. "Ray" Bro-N 1945
Hebner, Richard J. "Richie" Bos-A 1989-90
Heffner, Donald H. "Don" KC-A 1958-60,
  Det-A 1961, Min-A 1964-65, Cal-A 1967-68
Hegan, James E. "Jim" NY-A 1960-73,
  Det-A 1974-78, NY-A 1979-80
Heilmann, Harry E. Cin-N 1932
Heist, Alfred M. "Al" Hou-N 1966-67,
  SD-N 1980
Helms, Tommy V. Tex-A 1981-82,
  Cin-N 1983-89
Hemsley, Ralston B. "Rollie" Phi-A 1954,
  Was-A 1961-62

Hemus, Solomon J. "Solly" NY-N 1962-63,
  Cle-A 1964-65
Hendricks, Elrod J. Bal-A 1978-90
Henrich, Thomas D. "Tommy" NY-A 1951,
  NY-N 1957, Det-A 1958-59
Herman, Floyd C. "Babe" Pit-N 1951
Herman, William J. "Billy" Bro-N 1952-57,
  Mil-N 1958-59, Bos-A 1960-64, Cal-A 1967,
  SD-N 1978-79
Herzog, Dorrel N. "Whitey" KC-A 1965,
  NY-N 1966, Cal-A 1974-75
Hiatt, Jack E Chi-N 1981
High, Andrew A. "Andy" Bro-N 1937-38
Hill, Marc K. Hou-N 1988
Hiller, Charles J. "Chuck" Tex-A 1973,
  KC-A 1976-79, StL-N 1981-83, SF-N 1985,
  NY-N 1990
Hilton, J. David "Dave" Mil-A 1987-88
Himsl, Avitus B. "Vedie" Chi-N 1960-64
Hinchman, William W. "Bill" Pit-N 1923
Hines, Benjamin T. "Ben" Sea-A 1984,
  LA-N 1986, 1988-90
Hitchcock, William C. "Billy" Det-A 1955-60,
  Atl-N 1966
Hoak, Donald A. "Don" Phi-N 1967
Hofman, Robert G. "Bobby" KC-A 1966-67,
  Was-A 1968, Oak-A 1969-70, Cle-A 1971-72,
  Oak-A 1974-75, 1978
Hofmann, Fred StL-A 1938-49
Holke, Walter H. StL-A 1940
Hollingsworth, Albert W. "Al" StL-N 1957-58
Holt, Golden D. "Goldie" Pit-N 1948-50,
  Chi-N 1961-64
Holmquist, Douglas L. "Doug" NY-A 1984,
  1985
Hopp, John L. "Johnny" Det-A 1954,
  StL-N 1956
Hornsby, Rogers Chi-N 1958-59, NY-N 1962
Horton, Willie W. NY-A 1985, Chi-A 1986
Hoscheit, Vernard A. "Vern" Bal-A 1968,
  Oak-A 1969-74, Cal-A 1976, NY-N 1984-87
Houk, Ralph G. NY-A 1954, 1958-60
House, Thomas R. "Tom" Tex-A 1985-90
Howard, Elston G. NY-A 1969-79
Howard, Frank O. Mil-A 1977-80,
  NY-N 1982-83, 1984, Mil-A 1985-86,
  Sea-A 1987-88, NY-A 1989
Howe, Arthur H. "Art" Tex-A 1985-88
Howley, Daniel P. "Dan" Bos-A 1919,
  Det-A 1921-22
Howser, Richard D. "Dick" NY-A 1969-78
Hriniak, Walter J. "Walt" Mon-N 1974-75,
  Bos-A 1977-88, Chi-A 1989-90
Hudlin, G. Willis Det-A 1957-59
Hudson, Sidney C. "Sid" Was-A 1961-65,
  1968-71, Tex-A 1972, 1977-78
Hulswitt, Rudolph E. "Rudy" Bos-A 1931-33
Hundley, C. Randolph "Randy" Chi-N 1977
Hunter, Frederick C. "Newt" Phi-N 1928-31,
  1933
Hunter, G. William "Billy" Bal-A 1964-77
Isaac, Luis Cle-A 1987-90
Jackson, Alvin N. "Al" Bos-A 1977-79,
  Bal-A 1989-90
Jackson, Grant D. Pit-N 1984-85
Jackson, Roland T. "Sonny" Atl-N 1982-83
Jackson, Travis C. NY-N 1939-40, 1947-48
Jansen, Lawrence J. "Larry" NY-N 1954,
  SF-N 1961-71, Chi-N 1972-73
Jaramillo, Rudolph "Rudy" Hou-N 1990
Jennings, Hugh A. "Hughie" NY-N 1921-25
Johnson, Darrell D. StL-N 1960-61, Bal-A 1962,
  Bos-A 1968-69, Tex-A 1981-82
Johnson, Deron R. Cal-A 1979-80, NY-N 1981,
  Phi-N 1982-84, Sea-A 1985-86, Chi-A 1987,
  Cal-A 1989-90
Johnson, Roy J. Chi-N 1935-39, 1944-53
Johnson, Sylvester W. "Syl" Phi-N 1937-40
Johnston, James H. "Jimmy" Bro-N 1931
Jones, Clarence W. Atl-N 1985, 1988-90
Jones, Gordon B. Hou-N 1966-67
Jones, Grover W. "Deacon" Hou-N 1976-82,
  SD-N 1984-87
Jones, Joseph C. "Joe" KC-A 1987
Jonnard, Clarence J. "Bubber" Phi-N 1935,
  NY-N 1942-46
Judge, Joseph I. "Joe" Was-A 1945-46
Jurges, William F. "Billy" Chi-N 1947-48,
  Was-A 1956-59
Kaat, James L. "Jim" Cin-N 1984-85
Kahn, Louis "Lou" StL-N 1955
Katt, Raymond F. "Ray" StL-N 1959-60,
  Cle-A 1962

Kaufmann, Anthony C. "Tony" StL-N 1947-50
Keane, John J. "Johnny" StL-N 1959-61
Keefe, David E. "Dave" Phi-A 1940-49
Keely, Robert W. "Bob" Bos-N 1946-52, Mil-N 1953-57
Kelleher, Michael D. "Mick" Pit-N 1986
Kelley, Joseph J. "Joe" Bro-N 1926
Kelly, Bernard F. "Mike" Chi-A 1930-31, Chi-N 1934, Bos-N 1937-39, Pit-N 1940-41
Kelly, George L. Cin-N 1935-37, Bos-N 1938-43, Cin-N 1947-48
Kelly, J. Thomas "Tom" Min-A 1983-86
Kennedy, Robert D. "Bob" Chi-N 1962-64, Atl-N 1967
Kerr, John F. Was-A 1935
Kerrigan, Joseph T. "Joe" Mon-N 1983-86
Killefer, William L. "Bill" StL-N 1926, StL-A 1927-29, Bro-N 1939, Phi-A 1942
Kim, Wendell K. SF-N 1989-90
Kimm, Bruce E. Cin-N 1984-88, Pit-N 1989
King, Clyde E. Cin-N 1959, Pit-N 1965-67, NY-A 1981, 1988
Kissell, George M. StL-N 1969-75
Kittle, Hubert M. "Hub" Hou-N 1971-75, StL-N 1981-83
Klein, Charles H. "Chuck" Phi-N 1942-45
Klein, Louis F. "Lou" Chi-N 1960-65
Kluszewski, Theodore B. "Ted" Cin-N 1970-78
Knoop, Robert F. "Bobby" Chi-A 1977-78, Cal-A 1979-90
Knowles, Darold D. StL-N 1983, Phi-N 1989-90
Koenig, Fred Carl Cal-A 1970-71, StL-N 1976, Tex-A 1977-82, Chi-N 1983, Cle-A 1985-86
Kress, Ralph "Red" Det-A 1940, NY-N 1946-49, Cle-A 1953-60, LA-N 1961, NY-N 1962
Krol, John T. "Jack" StL-N 1977-80, SD-N 1981-86
Kuehl, Karl O. Min-A 1977-82
Kuenn, Harvey E. Mil-A 1971-82
Kuntz, Russell J. "Rusty" Sea-A 1989-90
Kusnyer, Arthur W. "Art" Chi-A 1980-87, Oak-A 1989-90
Lachemann, Marcel E. Cal-A 1984-90
Lachemann, Rene G. Bos-A 1985-86, Oak-A 1987-90
Lakeman, Albert W. "Al" Bos-A 1963-64, 1967-69
Lamont, Gene W. Pit-N 1986-90
Land, Grover C. Cin-N 1926-28, Chi-N 1929
Landestoy, Rafael S. Mon-N 1989
Landrith, Hobert N. "Hobie" Was-A 1964
Lanier, Harold C. "Hal" StL-N 1981-85, Phi-N 1990
LaRoche, David E. "Dave" Chi-A 1989-90
LaRussa, Anthony "Tony" Chi-A 1978
Lasorda, Thomas C. "Tommy" LA-N 1973-76
Latham, W. Arlington "Arlie" Cin-N 1900, NY-N 1909
Lau, Charles R. "Charlie" Bal-A 1969, Oak-A 1970, KC-A 1971-74, 1975-78, NY-A 1979-81, Chi-A 1982-83
Lauder, William "Billy" Chi-A 1925
Lavagetto, Harry A. "Cookie" Bro-N 1951-53, Was-A 1955-57, NY-N 1962-63, SF-N 1964-67
Law, Vernon S. "Vern" Pit-N 1968-69
Lazzeri, Anthony M. "Tony" Chi-N 1938
Lefebvre, James K. "Jim" LA-N 1978-79, SF-N 1980-82, Oak-A 1987-88
Leifield, Albert P. "Lefty" StL-A 1920-23, Bos-A 1924-26, Det-A 1927-28
Lemon, James R. "Jim" Min-A 1965-67, 1981-84
Lemon, Robert G. "Bob" Cle-A 1960, Phi-N 1961, Cal-A 1967-68, KC-A 1970, NY-A 1976
Lenhardt, Donald E. "Don" Bos-A 1970-73
Leonard, Emil J. "Dutch" Chi-N 1954-56
Leppert, Donald G. "Don" Pit-N 1968-76, Tor-A 1977-79, Hou-N 1980-85
Lett, James C. "Jim" Cin-N 1988-89
Levy, Leonard Pit-N 1957-63
Lewis, George E. "Duffy" Bos-N 1931-35
Lewis, Johnny J. StL-N 1973-76, 1985-89
Leyland, James R. "Jim" Chi-A 1982-85
Leyva, Nicolas T. "Nick" StL-N 1984-88
Lillis, Robert P. "Bob" Hou-N 1967, 1973-82, SF-N 1986-90
Lipon, John J. "Johnny" Cle-A 1968-71
Litwhiler, Daniel W. "Danny" Cin-N 1951
Llenas, Winston S. Tor-A 1988
Lobe, William C. "Bill" Cle-A 1951-56

Lobert, John B. "Hans" Phi-N 1934-41, Cin-N 1943-44
Lockman, Carroll W. "Whitey" Cin-N 1960, SF-N 1961-64, Chi-N 1966
Lodigiani, Dario A. KC-A 1961-62
Lollar, J. Sherman "Sherm" Bal-A 1964-67, Oak-A 1968
Long, R. Dale NY-A 1963
Lonnett, Joseph P. "Joe" Chi-A 1971-75, Oak-A 1976, Pit-N 1977-84
Lopat, Edmund W. "Ed" NY-A 1960, Min-A 1961, KC-A 1962
Lopes, David E. "Davey" Tex-A 1988-90
Lowe, Q. V. "Q. V." Chi-N 1972
Lowrey, Harry L. "Peanuts" Phi-N 1960-66, SF-N 1967-68, Mon-N 1969, Chi-N 1970-71, Cal-A 1972, Chi-N 1977-79, 1981
Lucchesi, Frank J. Tex-A 1974-75, 1979-80
Lum, Michael K. "Mike" Chi-A 1985, KC-A 1988-89
Lumpe, Jerry D. Oak-A 1971
Lund, Donald A. "Don" Det-A 1957-58
Luque, Adolfo "Dolf" NY-N 1935-38, 1941-45
Lutz, R. Joseph "Joe" Cle-A 1972-73
Lyons, Edward H. "Eddie" Min-A 1976
Lyons, Theodore A. "Ted" Det-A 1949-53, Bro-N 1954
Macha, Kenneth E. "Ken" Mon-N 1986-90
Mack, Earle T. Phi-A 1924-50
MacKenzie, H. Gordon "Gordy" KC-A 1980-81, Chi-N 1982, SF-N 1986-88
Maglie, Salvatore A. "Sal" Bos-A 1960-62, 1966-67, Sea-A 1969
Mahoney, James T. "Jim" Chi-A 1972-76, Sea-A 1985-86
Majtyka, LeRoy W. "Roy" Atl-N 1988-90
Malmberg, Harry W. Bos-A 1963-64
Maloof, Jack G. SD-N 1990
Maltzberger, Gordon R. Min-A 1962-64
Mancuso, August R. "Gus" Cin-N 1950
Mantle, Mickey C. NY-A 1970
Manuel, Charles F. "Charlie" Cle-A 1988-89
Manush, Henry E. "Heinie" Was-A 1953-54
Marion, Martin W. "Marty" StL-A 1952, Chi-A 1954
Marshall, R. James "Jim" Chi-N 1974
Martin, Alfred M. "Billy" Min-A 1965-68, Tex-A 1974
Martin, Fred T. Chi-N 1961-64, Chi-A 1979
Martin, John L. "Pepper" Chi-N 1956
Martin, Joseph C. "J. C." Chi-N 1974
Martinez, Jose KC-A 1980-87, Chi-N 1988-90
Martinez, Orlando "Marty" Sea-A 1984-86
Mathews, Edwin L. "Eddie" Atl-N 1971-72
Mathews, Henry "Harry" Cle-A 1926-27, NY-A 1929
Mathewson, Christopher "Christy" NY-N 1919-21
Maxvill, C. Dallan "Dal" Oak-A 1975, NY-N 1978, StL-N 1979-80, Atl-N 1982-84
May, Lee A. KC-A 1984-86, Cin-N 1988-89
May, Milton S. "Milt" Pit-N 1987-90
Mayberry, John C. KC-A 1989-90
Mayo, Edward J. "Eddie" Bos-A 1951, Phi-N 1952-54
Mays, Willie H. NY-N 1974-79
Mazeroski, William S. "Bill" Pit-N 1973, Sea-A 1979-80
Mazzone, Leo D. Atl-N 1985, 1990
McBride, George F. Det-A 1925-26, 1929
McBride, Kenneth F. "Ken" Mil-A 1975
McCallister, John "Jack" Cle-A 1920-26, Bos-A 1930
McCormick, Frank A. Cin-N 1956-57
McCrabb, Lester W. "Les" Phi-A 1950-54
McCraw, Tommy L. Cle-A 1975, 1979-82, SF-N 1983-85, Bal-A 1989-90
McCullough, Clyde E. Was-A 1960, Min-A 1961, NY-N 1963, SD-N 1982
McDermott, Maurice J. "Mickey" Cal-A 1968
McDonnell, Robert A. "Maje" Phi-N 1951-57
McGaha, F. Melvin "Mel" Cle-A 1961, KC-A 1963-64, Hou-N 1968-70
McGinnity, Joseph J. "Joe" Bro-N 1926
McGuire, James T. "Deacon" Det-A 1911-16
McKay, David L. "Dave" Oak-A 1984-90
McKechnie, William B. "Bill" Pit-N 1922, StL-N 1927, Cle-A 1947-49, Bos-A 1952-53
McKee, J. R. Pit-N 1947
McKeon, John A. "Jack" Oak-A 1978
McLaren, John L. Tor-A 1986-90
McLish, Calvin C. "Cal" Phi-N 1965-66, Mon-N 1969-75, Mil-A 1976-82

McMahon, Donald J. "Don" SF-N 1973-75, Min-A 1976-77, SF-N 1980-82, Cle-A 1983-85
McMillan, Roy D. Mil-A 1970-72, NY-N 1973-76
McNamara, John F. Oak-A 1968-69, SF-N 1971-73, Cal-A 1978
McNeely, G. Earl StL-A 1931, Was-A 1936-37
McNertney, Gerald E. "Jerry" Bos-A 1988
McRae, Harold A. "Hal" KC-A 1987, Mon-N 1990
Mele, Sabath A. "Sam" Was-A 1959-60, Min-A 1961
Melillo, Oscar D. "Ski" StL-N 1938, Cle-A 1939-40, 1942, 1945-48, 1950, Bos-A 1952-53, Cle-A 1955-56
Mendoza, Mario Bal-A 1988
Menke, Denis J. Tor-A 1980-81, Hou-N 1983-88, Phi-N 1989-90
Merkle, Frederick C. "Fred" NY-A 1925-26
Merrill, Carl H. "Stump" NY-A 1985, 1986-87
Metro, Charles "Charlie" Chi-N 1962, Chi-A 1965, Oak-A 1982
Meusel, Emil F. "Irish" NY-N 1930
Meyer, Bernhard "Benny" Phi-N 1924-26, Det-A 1928-30
Michael, Eugene R. "Gene" NY-A 1976-77, 1978, 1984-86, 1988, 1989
Milan, J. Clyde Was-A 1928-29, 1938-52
Miller, Dyar K Chi-A 1987-88
Miller, Edmund J. "Bing" Bos-A 1937, Det-A 1938-41, Chi-A 1942-49, Phi-A 1950-53
Miller, L. Otto Bro-N 1926-36
Miller, Raymond R. "Ray" Bal-A 1978-85, Pit-N 1987-90
Miller, Robert L. "Bob" Tor-A 1977-79, SF-N 1985
Milliken, Robert F. "Bob" StL-N 1965-70, 1976
Mills, Arthur G. "Art" Det-A 1944-48
Mills, C. Buster Cle-A 1946, Chi-A 1947-50, Cin-N 1953, Bos-A 1954
Minoso, S. Orestes "Minnie" Chi-A 1976-78, 1980-81
Mitchell, Clarence E. NY-N 1932-33
Mitterwald, George E. Oak-A 1979-82, NY-A 1988
Mize, John R. "Johnny" KC-A 1961
Monbouquette, William C. "Bill" NY-N 1982-83, NY-A 1985
Monchak, Alex "Al" Chi-A 1971-75, Oak-A 1976, Pit-N 1977-84, Atl-N 1986-88
Moon, Wallace W. "Wally" SD-N 1969
Moore, Jackie S. Mil-A 1970-72, Tex-A 1973-74, 1975-76, Tor-A 1977-79, Tex-A 1980, Oak-A 1981-84, Mon-N 1987-89, Cin-N 1990
Moore, Terry B. StL-N 1949-52, 1956-58
Morales, Jose M. SF-N 1986-88, Cle-A 1990
Morales, Richard A. "Rich" Atl-N 1986-87
Morgan, Joseph M. "Joe" Pit-N 1972, Bos-A 1985-88
Morgan, Tom S. Cal-A 1972-74, SD-N 1975, NY-A 1979, Cal-A 1981-83
Morgan, Vernon T. "Vern" Min-A 1969-75
Moses, Wallace "Wally" Phi-A 1952-54, Phi-N 1955-58, Cin-N 1959-60, NY-A 1961-62, 1966, Det-A 1967-70
Moss, J. Lester "Les" Chi-A 1967-68, 1970, Chi-N 1981, Hou-N 1982-84, 1985-89
Mota, Manuel R. "Manny" LA-N 1980-89
Mozzali, Maurice J. "Mo" StL-N 1977-78
Mueller, Ray C. NY-N 1956, Chi-N 1957
Muffett, Billy A. StL-N 1967-70, Cal-A 1974-77, Det-A 1985-90
Mulcahy, Hugh N. Chi-A 1970
Mull, Jack L. SF-N 1985
Mulleavy, Gregory T. "Greg" Bro-N 1957, LA-N 1958-60, 1962-64
Mullin, Patrick J. "Pat" Det-A 1963-66, Cle-A 1967, Mon-N 1979-81
Murphy, Daniel F. "Danny" Phi-A 1921-24, Phi-N 1927
Murtaugh, Daniel E. "Danny" Pit-N 1956-57
Muser, Anthony J. "Tony" Mil-A 1985-89
Myatt, George E. Was-A 1950-54, Chi-A 1955-56, Chi-N 1957-59, Mil-N 1960-61, Det-A 1962-63, Phi-N 1964-72
Napoleon, Edward G. "Ed" Cle-A 1983-85, KC-A 1987-88, Hou-N 1989
Naragon, Harold R. "Hal" Min-A 1963-66, Det-A 1967-69
Narron, Samuel "Sam" Pit-N 1952-64
Neale, A. Earle "Greasy" StL-N 1929
Nelson, David E. "Dave" Chi-A 1981-84
Neun, John H. "Johnny" NY-A 1944-46

Newman, Jeffrey L. "Jeff" Oak-A 1986
Niarhos, C. Gus KC-A 1962-64
Niehoff, J. Albert "Bert" NY-N 1929
Nixon, Russell E. "Russ" Cin-N 1976-82,
Mon-N 1984-85, Atl-N 1986-87
Noren, Irving A. "Irv" Oak-A 1971-74,
Chi-N 1975
Norman, H. Willis P. "Bill" StL-A 1952-53
Northey, Ronald J. "Ron" Pit-N 1961-63
Nossek, Joseph R. "Joe" Mil-A 1973-75,
Min-A 1976, Cle-A 1977-81, KC-A 1982-83,
Chi-A 1984-85, 1986
Nottle, Edward W. "Ed" Oak-A 1983
Oates, Johnny L. Chi-N 1984-87,
Bal-A 1989-90
O'Brien, Edward J. "Eddie" Sea-A 1969
Oceak, Frank J. Pit-N 1958-64, Cin-N 1965,
Pit-N 1970-72
O'Connell, Daniel F. "Danny" Was-A 1963-64
Okrie, Leonard J. "Len" Bos-A 1961-62,
1965-66, Det-A 1970
Oldis, Robert C. "Bob" Phi-N 1964-66,
Min-A 1968, Mon-N 1969
O'Leary, Charles T. "Charley" StL-N 1913,
NY-A 1921-30, Chi-N 1931-33, StL-A 1934-37
Oliva, Pedro "Tony" Min-A 1976-78, 1985-90
Oliver, David J. "Dave" Tex-A 1987-90
Oliver, Thomas N. "Tom" Phi-A 1951-53,
Bal-A 1954
Olson, Ivan M. "Ivy" Bro-N 1924, 1930-31,
NY-N 1932
O'Neil, G. Michael "Mickey" Cle-A 1930
O'Neil, John S. "Buck" Chi-N 1962
O'Neill, Stephen F. "Steve" Cle-A 1935,
Det-A 1941, Cle-A 1949, Bos-A 1950
Onslow, John J. "Jack" Pit-N 1925-26,
Was-A 1927, StL-N 1928, Phi-N 1931-32,
Bos-A 1934
Osborn, Donald E. "Don" Pit-N 1963-64,
1970-72, 1974-76
Osteen, Claude W. StL-N 1977-80,
Phi-N 1982-88
Otero, Regino J. "Regie" Cin-N 1959-65,
Cle-A 1966
Otis, Amos J. SD-N 1988-90
Ott, N. Edward "Ed" Hou-N 1989-90
Overmire, Frank "Stubby" Det-A 1963-66
Owen, Arnold M. "Mickey" Bos-A 1955-56
Owens, James P. "Jim" Hou-N 1967-72
Ozark, Daniel L. "Danny" LA-N 1965-72,
1980-82, SF-N 1983-84
Pacheco, Antonio A. "Tony" Cle-A 1974,
Hou-N 1976-79, 1982
Paepke, Jack LA-N 1961-64, Cal-N 1965-66
Pafko, Andrew "Andy" Mil-N 1960-62
Pagan, Jose A. Pit-N 1974-78
Page, Philippe R. "Phil" Cin-N 1947-52
Paige, Leroy O. "Satchell" Atl-N 1968-69
Parker, Francis J. "Salty" SF-N 1958-61,
Cle-A 1962, LA-A 1964, Cal-N 1965-66,
NY-N 1967, Hou-N 1968-72, Cal-A 1973-74
Pascual, Camilo A. Min-A 1978-80
Pattin, Martin W. "Marty" Tor-A 1989
Paul, Michael G. "Mike" Oak-A 1987-88,
Sea-A 1989-90
Pavlick, Gregory M. "Greg" NY-N 1985-86,
1988-90
Peitz, Henry C. "Heinie" StL-N 1913
Pennock, Herbert J. "Herb" Bos-A 1936-39
Pepitone, Joseph A. "Joe" NY-A 1982
Perez, Atanacio R. "Tony" Cin-N 1987-90
Perkins, Ralph F. "Cy" NY-A 1932-33,
Det-A 1934-39, Phi-N 1946-54
Perlozzo, Samuel B. "Sam" NY-N 1987-89,
Cin-N 1990
Perranoski, Ronald P. "Ron" LA-N 1981-90
Pesky, John M. "Johnny" Pit-N 1965-67,
Bos-A 1975-84
Peterson, Eric H. "Rick" Pit-N 1984-85
Phillips, Harold R. "Lefty" LA-N 1965-68,
Cal-A 1969
Phillips, Richard E. "Dick" SD-N 1980
Picciolo, Robert M. "Rob" SD-N 1990
Piche, Ronald J. "Ron" Mon-N 1976
Picinich, Valentine J. "Val" Cin-N 1934
Piersall, James A. "Jimmy" Tex-A 1975
Pignatano, Joseph B. "Joe" Was-A 1965-67,
NY-N 1968-81, Atl-N 1982-85
Piniella, Louis V. "Lou" NY-A 1984-85
Pinson, Vada E. Sea-A 1977-80, Chi-A 1981,
Sea-A 1982-83, Det-A 1985-90
Pitler, Jacob A. "Jake" Bro-N 1947-57
Plaza, Ronald C. "Ron" Sea-A 1969,

Cin-N 1978-83, Oak-A 1986
Plummer, William F. "Bill" Sea-A 1982-83,
1988-90
Podres, John J. "Johnny" SD-N 1973,
Bos-A 1980, Min-A 1981-85
Pole, Richard H. "Dick" Chi-N 1988-90
Pollet, Howard J. "Howie" StL-N 1959-64,
Hou-N 1965
Popowski, Edward J. "Eddie" Bos-A 1967-76
Posedel, William J. "Bill" Pit-N 1949-53,
StL-N 1954-57, Phi-N 1958, SF-N 1959-60,
Oak-A 1968-72, SD-N 1974
Queen, Melvin D. "Mel" Cle-A 1982
Quilici, Francis R. "Frank" Min-A 1971-72
Quirk, James P. "Jamie" StL-N 1984
Rader, Douglas L. "Doug" SD-N 1979,
Chi-A 1986-87
Ragan, D. C. Patrick "Pat" Phi-N 1924
Randall, Robert L. "Bobby" Min-A 1980
Rapp, Vernon F. "Vern" Mon-N 1979-83
Reese, Harold H. "Pee Wee" LA-N 1959
Reese, James H. "Jimmie" Cal-A 1973-90
Regan, Philip R. "Phil" Sea-A 1984-86
Reiser, Harold P. "Pete" LA-N 1960-64,
Chi-N 1966-69, Cal-A 1970-71, Chi-N 1972-73
Renick, W. Richard "Rick" KC-A 1981,
Mon-N 1985-86, Min-A 1987-90
Resinger, Grover S. Atl-N 1966, Chi-A 1967-68,
Det-A 1969-70, Cal-A 1975-76
Rettenmund, Mervin W. "Merv" Cal-A 1980-82,
Tex-A 1983-85, Oak-A 1989-90
Reyes, Benjamin "Cananea" Sea-A 1981
Reynolds, Tommie D Oak-A 1989-90
Rice, Delbert "Del" LA-N 1962-64,
Cal-A 1965-66, Cle-A 1967
Ricketts, David W. "Dave" Pit-N 1971-73,
StL-N 1974-75, 1978-90
Riddle, John L. "Johnny" Pit-N 1948-50,
StL-N 1952-55, Mil-N 1956-57, Cin-N 1958,
Phi-N 1959
Riddoch, Gregory L. "Greg" SD-N 1987-90
Riggleman, James D. "Jim" StL-N 1989-90
Rigney, William J. "Bill" SD-N 1975
Ripken, Calvin E., Sr. "Cal" Bal-A 1976-86,
1989-90
Rippelmeyer, Raymond R. "Ray"
Phi-N 1970-78
Roarke, Michael T. "Mike" Det-A 1965-66,
Cal-A 1967-69, Det-A 1970, Chi-N 1978-80,
StL-N 1984-90
Roberts, David W. "Dave" Cle-A 1987
Robertson, Sherrard A. "Sherry" Min-A 1970
Robinson, Brooks C. Bal-A 1977
Robinson, Frank Cal-A 1977, Bal-A 1978-80,
1985-87
Robinson, Warren G. "Sheriff" NY-N 1964,
1965-67, 1972
Robinson, Wilbert NY-N 1911-13
Robinson, William H. "Bill" NY-N 1984-89
Robinson, W. Edward "Eddie" Bal-A 1957-59
Robson, Thomas J. "Tom" Tex-A 1986-90
Rodgers, Robert L. "Bob" Min-A 1970-74,
SF-N 1976, Mil-N 1978-80
Rojas, Octavio V. "Cookie" Chi-N 1978-81
Rolfe, Robert A. "Red" NY-A 1946
Rommel, Edwin A. "Eddie" Phi-A 1933-34
Roof, Phillip A. "Phil" SD-N 1978,
Sea-A 1983-88, Chi-N 1990
Root, Charles H. "Charlie" Chi-N 1951-53,
Mil-N 1956-57, Chi-N 1960
Roseboro, John J. Was-A 1971, Cal-A 1972-74
Rosenbaum, Glen O. Chi-A 1973-75, 1986-88
Roth, Francis C. "Frank" Pit-N 1917,
NY-A 1921-22, Cle-A 1923-25, Chi-A 1927
Rothschild, Lawrence L. "Larry" Cin-N 1990
Roush, Edd J Cin-N 1938
Rowe, Donald H. "Don" Chi-A 1988
Rowe, Kenneth D. "Ken" Bal-A 1985-86
Rowe, Lynwood T. "Schoolboy" Det-A 1954-55
Rowe, Ralph E. Min-A 1972-75, Bal-A 1981-84
Ruberto, John E. "Sonny" StL-N 1977-78
Rudi, Joseph O. "Joe" Oak-A 1986-87
Rudolph, Richard "Dick" Bos-N 1921-27
Ruel, Herold D. "Muddy" Chi-A 1935-45,
Cle-A 1948-50
Ruffing, Charles H. "Red" NY-N 1962
Runnels, James E. "Pete" Bos-A 1965-66
Runnells, Thomas W. "Tommy" Mon-N 1990
Russell, William E. "Bill" LA-N 1987-90
Ruth, George H. "Babe" Bro-N 1938
Ryan, Cornelius J. "Connie" Mil-N 1957,
Atl-N 1971, 1973-75, Tex-A 1977-79
Ryan, John B. "Jack" Bos-A 1923-27

Ryan, Michael J. "Mike" Phi-N 1980-89
Ryba, Dominic J. "Mike" StL-N 1951-54
Sain, John F. "Johnny" KC-A 1959,
NY-A 1961-63, Min-A 1965-66, Det-A 1967-69,
Chi-A 1971-75, Atl-N 1977, 1985-86
Sanford, John A. "Jack" Cle-A 1968-69
Sandt, Thomas J. "Tommy" Pit-N 1987-90
Sauer, Henry J. "Hank" SF-N 1959
Saul, James A. "Jim" Chi-N 1975-76,
Oak-A 1979
Scarborough, Ray W. Bal-A 1968
Schacht, Alexander "Al" Was-A 1925-34,
Bos-A 1935-36
Schaefer, Robert W. "Bob" KC-A 1988-90
Schaffer, Jimmie R. "Jim" Tex-A 1978,
KC-A 1980-88
Schalk, Raymond W. "Ray" Chi-A 1930-31
Schang, Walter H. "Wally" Cle-A 1936-38
Scheffing, Robert B. "Bob" StL-N 1952-53,
Chi-N 1954-55, Mil-N 1960
Scherger, George R. Cin-N 1970-78, 1982-86
Schoendienst, Albert F. "Red" StL-N 1963-64,
Oak-A 1977-78, StL-N 1979-89
Schreiber, Paul F. NY-A 1942, Bos-A 1947-58
Schueler, Ronald R. "Ron" Chi-A 1979-82,
Oak-A 1983-84, Pit-N 1986
Schulte, John C. "Johnny" Chi-N 1933,
NY-A 1934-48, Bos-A 1949-50
Schultz, George W. "Barney" StL-N 1971-75,
Chi-N 1977
Schultz, Joseph C., Jr. "Joe" StL-A 1949,
StL-N 1963-68, KC-A 1970, Det-A 1971-76
Seminick, Andrew W. "Andy" Phi-N 1957-58,
1967-69
Sewell, J. Luther "Luke" Cle-A 1939-41,
Cin-N 1949
Sewell, Joseph W. "Joe" NY-A 1934-35
Sewell, Truett B. "Rip" Pit-N 1948
Shanks, Howard S. "Howie" Cle-A 1928-32
Shaughnessy, Francis J. "Shag" Det-A 1928
Shaw, Robert J. "Bob" Mil-A 1973
Shawkey, J. Robert "Bob" NY-A 1929
Shea, Mervyn D. "Merv" Det-A 1939-42,
Phi-N 1944-45, Chi-N 1949
Sheehan, Thomas J. "Tom" Cin-N 1935-37,
Bos-N 1944
Shellenback, Frank V. StL-A 1939,
Bos-A 1940-44, Det-A 1946-47, NY-N 1950-55
Shellenback, James P. "Jim" Min-A 1983
Shepard, Robert E. "Bert" Was-A 1946
Shepard, Lawrence W. "Larry" Phi-N 1967,
Cin-N 1970-78, SF-N 1979
Sherry, Lawrence "Larry" Pit-N 1977-78,
Cal-A 1979-80
Sherry, Norman B. "Norm" Cal-A 1970-71,
1976, Mon-N 1978-81, SD-N 1982-84,
SF-N 1986-90
Shore, Raymond E. "Ray" Cin-N 1963-67
Shotton, Burton E. "Burt" StL-N 1923-25,
Cin-N 1934, Cle-A 1942-45
Showalter, William N. "Buck" NY-A 1990
Sievers, Roy E. Cin-N 1966
Silvera, Charles A. "Charlie" Min-A 1969,
Det-A 1971-73, Tex-A 1973-75
Silvestri, Kenneth J. "Ken" Phi-N 1959-60,
Mil-N 1963-65, Atl-N 1966-75, Chi-A 1976,
1982
Simmons, Aloysius H. "Al" Phi-A 1940-42,
1944-49, Cle-A 1950-51
Sisler, George H. Bos-N 1930
Sisler, Richard A. "Dick" Cin-N 1961-64,
StL-N 1966-70, SD-N 1975-76, NY-N 1979-80
Sisti, Sebastian D. "Sibby" Sea-A 1969
Skaff, Francis M. "Frank" Bal-A 1954,
Det-A 1965-66, 1970
Skinner, Robert R. "Bob" SD-N 1970-73,
Pit-N 1974-76, SD-N 1977, Cal-A 1978,
Pit-N 1979-85, Atl-N 1986-88
Slattery, John T. "Jack" Bos-N 1918-19
Slider, Rachel W. "Rac" Bos-A 1987-90
Smith, Alfred J. "Al" NY-N 1933
Smith, Billy F. Tor-A 1984-88
Smith, Harold R. "Hal" StL-N 1962,
Pit-N 1965-67, Cin-N 1968-69, Mil-N 1976-77
Smith, Richard P. "Red" Chi-N 1945-48
Snitker, Brian G. Atl-N 1985, 1988-90
Snyder, Francis E. "Frank" NY-N 1933-41
Snyder, James R. "Jim" Chi-N 1987,
Sea-A 1988
Sommers, Dennis J. "Denny" NY-N 1977-78,
Cle-A 1980-85, SD-N 1988-90
Sothoron, Allen S. StL-N 1927-28,
StL-A 1932-33

Southworth, William H. "Billy" NY-N 1933
Spahn, Warren E. NY-N 1965, Cle-A 1972-73
Spalding, Charles H. "Dick" Phi-N 1934-36,
  Chi-N 1941-43
Spangler, Albert D. "Al" Chi-N 1970-71, 1974
Sparks, Joseph E. "Joe" Chi-A 1979,
  Cin-N 1984, Mon-N 1989, NY-A 1990
Spencer, H. Thomas "Tom" Cle-A 1988-89
Squires, Michael L. "Mike" Tor-A 1989-90
Staller, George W. Bal-A 1962, 1969-75
Stanage, Oscar H. Pit-N 1927-31
Stange, A. Lee Bos-A 1972-74, Min-A 1975,
  Oak-A 1977-79, Bos-A 1981-84
Stanky, Edward R. "Eddie" Chi-A 1957-58
Stargell, Wilver D. "Willie" Pit-N 1985,
  Atl-N 1986-88
Starrette, Herman P. "Herm" Atl-N 1974-76,
  SF-N 1977-78, Phi-N 1979-81, SF-N 1983-84,
  Mil-A 1985-86, Chi-N 1987, Bal-A 1988
Staub, Daniel J. "Rusty" NY-N 1982
Stearns, John H. NY-A 1989
Stelmaszek, Richard F. "Rick" Min-A 1981-90
Stengel, Charles D. "Casey" Bro-N 1932-33
Stevens, Edward L. "Ed" SD-N 1981
Stock, Milton J. "Milt" Chi-N 1944-48,
  Bro-N 1949-50, Pit-N 1951-52
Stock, Wesley G. "Wes" KC-A 1967,
  Mil-N 1970-72, Oak-A 1972-76, Sea-A 1977-81,
  Oak-A 1984-86
Stottlemyre, Melvin L. "Mel" NY-N 1984-90
Stratton, Monty F. Chi-A 1939-41
Street, Charles E. "Gabby" StL-N 1929,
  StL-A 1937
Strickland, George B. Min-A 1962,
  Cle-A 1963-69, KC-A 1970-72
Stubing, Lawrence G. "Moose" Cal-A 1985-88,
  1989-90
Such, Richard S. "Dick" Tex-A 1983-85,
  Min-A 1985-90
Sugden, Joseph "Joe" StL-N 1921-25,
  Phi-N 1926-27
Sukeforth, Clyde L. Bro-N 1943-51,
  Pit-N 1952-57
Sullivan, John P. KC-A 1979, Atl-N 1980-81,
  Tor-A 1982-90
Summers, John J. "Champ" NY-A 1989-90
Susce, George C. M. Cle-A 1941-47, 1948-49,
  Bos-A 1950-54, KC-A 1955-56, Mil-A 1958-59,
  Was-A 1961-67, 1969-71, Tex-A 1972
Sweeney, William J. "Bill" Det-A 1947-48
Sweet, Ricky J. "Rick" Sea-A 1984
Swift, Robert V. "Bob" Det-A 1953-54,
  KC-A 1957-59, Was-A 1960, Det-A 1963-66
Tannehill, Jesse N. Phi-N 1920
Tappe, Elvin W. "El" Chi-N 1959-63
Taylor, Antonio N. "Tony" Phi-N 1977-79,
  1988-89
Taylor, James W. "Zack" Bro-N 1936,
  StL-A 1941-46, Pit-N 1947
Temple, John E. "Johnny" Cin-N 1964
Tenace, F. Gene Hou-N 1986-87, Tor-A 1990
Terwilliger, W. Wayne Was-A 1969-71,
  Tex-A 1972, 1981-85, Min-A 1986-90
Testa, Nicholas "Nick" SF-N 1958
Thomas, George E. Bos-A 1970
Thomas, Ira F. Phi-A 1914-17, 1925-26

Thomas, J. Leroy "Lee" StL-N 1972, 1983
Thomas, Roy A. StL-N 1922
Thompson, Charles L. "Tim" StL-N 1981
Tiefenauer, Bobby G. Phi-N 1979
Tighe, John T. "Jack" Det-A 1942, 1955-56
Tincup, A. Ben Bro-N 1940
Tobin, John T. "Jack" StL-A 1949-51
Tolan, Robert "Bobby" SD-N 1980-83,
  Sea-A 1987
Torborg, Jeffrey A. "Jeff" Cle-A 1975-77,
  NY-A 1979-88
Torchia, Anthony L. "Tony" Bos-A 1985
Tracewski, Richard J. "Dick" Det-A 1972-90
Trebelhorn, Thomas L. "Tom" Mil-A 1984, 1986
Trucks, Virgil O. Pit-N 1963
Turley, Robert L. "Bob" Bos-A 1964
Turner, James R. "Jim" NY-A 1949-59,
  Cin-N 1961-65, NY-A 1966-73
Turner, Terrence L. "Terry" StL-N 1924
Uhle, George E. Cle-A 1936-37, Chi-N 1940,
  Was-A 1944
Unser, Delbert B. "Del" Phi-N 1985-88
Valentine, Robert J. "Bobby" NY-N 1983-85
Valo, Elmer W. Cle-A 1963-64
Van Ornum, John C. SF-N 1981-84
Vernon, James B. "Mickey" Pit-N 1960, 1964,
  StL-N 1965, Mon-N 1977-78, Mil-A 1982
Vincent, Albert L. "Al" Det-A 1943-44,
  Bal-A 1955-59, Phi-N 1961-63, KC-A 1966-67
Virdon, William C. "Bill" Pit-N 1968-71, 1986
Virgil, Osvaldo Jose Sr. "Ozzie" SF-N 1969-72,
  1974-75, Mon-N 1976-81, SD-N 1982-85,
  Sea-A 1986-88
Vukovich, John C. Chi-N 1982-87, Phi-N 1988,
  1989-90
Wagner, Charles F. "Heinie" Bos-A 1916-19,
  1927-29
Wagner, Charles T. "Charley" Bos-A 1970
Wagner, John P. "Honus" Pit-N 1933-51
Walker, Albert B. "Rube" LA-N 1958,
  Was-A 1965-67, NY-N 1968-81, Atl-N 1982-84
Walker, Fred "Dixie" StL-N 1953, 1955,
  Mil-N 1963-65
Walker, Gerald H. "Gee" Cin-N 1946
Walker, Harry W. StL-N 1959-62
Walker, Jerry A. NY-A 1981-82, Hou-N 1983-85
Walker, Verlon L. Chi-N 1961-70
Wallace, Roderick J. "Bobby" Cin-N 1926
Walls, R. Lee Oak-A 1979-82, NY-A 1983
Walsh, Edward A. "Ed" Chi-A 1923-25,
  1928-30
Walters, William H. "Bucky" Bos-N 1950-52,
  Mil-N 1953-55, NY-N 1956-57
Walton, James R. "Jim" Mil-A 1973-75
Waner, Paul G. Phi-N 1965
Ward, John F. "Jay" NY-A 1987
Ward, Peter T. "Pete" Atl-N 1978
Wares, Clyde E. "Buzzy" StL-N 1930-35,
  1937-51
Warner, Harry C. Tor-A 1977-79, 1980,
  Mil-A 1981-82
Wathan, John D. KC-A 1986
Watson, Robert J. "Bob" Oak-A 1986-88
Weaver, Earl S. Bal-A 1968
Webb, William J. "Billy" Chi-A 1935-39

West, Samuel F. "Sam" Was-A 1947-49
Westrum, Wesley N. "Wes" SF-N 1958-63,
  NY-N 1964-65, SF-N 1968-71
Whisenant, T. Peter "Pete" Cin-N 1961-62
White, Ernest D. "Ernie" Bos-A 1947-48,
  NY-N 1963
White, Joyner C. "Jo-Jo" Cle-A 1958-60,
  Det-A 1960, KC-A 1961-62, Mil-A 1963-65,
  Atl-N 1966, KC-A 1969
White, Roy H. NY-A 1983-84, 1986
Whitehill, Earl O. Cle-A 1941, Phi-N 1943
Widmar, Albert J. "Al" Phi-N 1962-64, 1968-69,
  Mil-A 1973-74, Tor-A 1980-88, 1989
Wietelmann, William F. "Whitey"
  Cin-N 1966-67, SD-N 1969-79
Wilber, Delbert Q. "Del" Chi-A 1955-56,
  Was-A 1970, Tex-A 1973
Wiley, Mark E. Bal-A 1987, Cle-A 1988-90
Wilhelm, Irvin K. "Kaiser" Phi-N 1921
Wilks, Theodore "Ted" KC-A 1961
Williams, Billy L. Chi-N 1980-82,
  Oak-A 1983-85, Chi-N 1986-87
Williams, David C. "Davey" NY-N 1956-57
Williams, Donald E. "Don" SD-N 1977-80
Williams, James B. "Jimmy" Hou-N 1975,
  Bal-A 1981-87
Williams, James F. "Jimy" Tor-A 1980-85,
  Atl-N 1990
Williams, Otto G. Det-A 1925, StL-N 1926,
  StL-A 1927, Cin-N 1930
Williams, Richard H. "Dick" Mon-N 1970
Williams, Stanley W. "Stan" Bos-A 1975-76,
  Chi-A 1977-78, NY-A 1980-81, 1982,
  Cin-N 1984, NY-A 1987, 1988, Cin-N 1990
Williams, Walter A. "Walt" Chi-A 1988
Wilson, James "Jimmy" Cin-N 1939-40,
  1944-46
Wiltse, George L. "Hooks" NY-A 1925
Wine, Robert P. Sr. "Bobby" Phi-N 1972-83,
  Atl-N 1985, 1988-90
Winegarner, Ralph L. StL-A 1948-51
Wingo, Ivey B. Cin-N 1928-29, 1936
Winkles, Bobby B. Cal-A 1972, Oak-A 1974-75,
  SF-N 1976-77, Chi-A 1979-81, Mon-N 1986-88
Wolgamot, C. Earl Cle-A 1931-33
Woodall, C. Lawrence "Larry" Bos-A 1942-48
Woodling, Eugene R. "Gene" Bal-A 1964-67
Worthington, Allan F. "Al" Min-A 1972-73
Wright, Melvin J. "Mel" Chi-N 1963-64, 1971,
  Pit-N 1973, NY-A 1974-75, Hou-N 1976-82
Wyatt, J. Whitlow "Whit" Phi-N 1955-57,
  Mil-N 1958-65, Atl-N 1966-67
Wynn, Early Cle-A 1964-66, Min-A 1967-69
York, P. Rudolph "Rudy" Bos-A 1959-62
Yost, Edward F. "Eddie" LA-N 1962,
  Was-A 1963-67, NY-N 1968-76, Bos-A 1977-84
Zarilla, Allen L. "Al" Was-A 1971
Zeller, Barton W. "Bart" StL-N 1970
Zimmer, Donald W. "Don" Mon-N 1971,
  SD-N 1972, Bos-A 1974-76, NY-A 1983,
  Chi-N 1984-86, NY-A 1986, SF-N 1987
Zimmer, Thomas J. "Tom" StL-N 1976
Zimmerman, Gerald R. "Gerry" Min-A 1967,
  Mon-N 1969-75, Min-A 1976-80
Zwilling, Edward H. "Dutch" Cle-A 1941

Biographical Data for Coaches Not Appearing in the Player/Pitcher Registers or Manager Roster

SPENCER ABBOTT Abbott, Spencer b: 8/27/1877, Chicago, Ill. d: 12/18/51, Washington, D.C. (1B)
TONY AUFERIO Auferio, Anthony Patrick b: 6/13/47, Orange, N.J. BR/TR, 5'10", 185 lbs. (3B)
DICK BERARDINO Berardino, Richard J. b: 7/2/37, Cambridge, Mass. BR/TR, 6'1", 190 lbs. (OF)
C. B. BERINGER Beringer, Carroll James b: 8/14/28, Bellwood, Neb. BR/TR, 6', 195 lbs. (P)
TERRY BEVINGTON Bevington, Terry Paul b: 7/7/56, Akron, Ohio BR/TR, 6'2", 190 lbs. (C)
WAYNE BLACKBURN Blackburn, Wayne Clark b: 7/10/16, My.Joy, Ohio BL/TR, 5'10", 165 lbs. (OF-3B-2B)
JACK BLOOMFIELD Bloomfield, Gordon Leigh b: 8/7/32, Monti Alto, Tex. BL/TR, 6'2", 185 lbs. (2B)
JIMMY BRAGAN Bragan, James Alton b: 3/12/29, Birmingham, Ala. BR/TR, 6', 198 lbs. (2B)
SCOTT BREEDEN Breeden, Harold Scott b: 9/17/37, Charlottesville, Va. BR/TR, 6'2", 210 lbs. (P)
JOE CAMACHO Camacho, Joseph Gomes b: 5/29/28, New Bedford, Mass. BR/TR, 6', 185 lbs. (SS-2B)
DANNY CARNEVALE Carnevale, Daniel Joseph b: 2/8/18, Buffalo, N.Y. BR/TR, 6', 195 lbs. (SS)
LEONEL CARRION Carrion, Leonel Santiago (Matheus) b: 2/15/52, Maracaibo, Venez. BR/TR, 5'11", 185 lbs. (OF)
DICK CARTER Carter, Richard Joseph b: 8/31/16, Philadelphia, Pa. d: 9/11/69, Philadelphia, Pa. BR/TR, 5'10", 190 lbs. (P-OF)
BOB CLEAR Clear, Elwood Robert b: 12/14/27, Denver, Colo. BR/TR, 5'10", 170 lbs. (P)
BOB CLUCK Cluck, Robert Alton b: 1/10/46, San Diego, Cal. BL/TL, 6'2", 195 lbs. (P)
MARK CONNOR Connor, Mark Peter b: 5/27/49, Brooklyn, N.Y. BR/TR, 6'3", 195 lbs. (P)
MARK CRESSE Cresse, Mark Emery b: 9/21/51, St.Albans, N.Y. BR/TR, 6'3", 220 lbs. (C)
MARTY DeMERRITT DeMerritt, Martin Gordon b: 3/4/53, San Francisco, Cal. BR/TR, 6'2.5", 205 lbs. (P)
BOBBY DEWS Dews, Robert Walter b: 3/23/38, Clinton, Iowa BR/TR, 6'1", 175 lbs. (SS)
RICH DONNELLY Donnelly, Richard Francis b: 8/3/46, Steubenville, Ohio BL/TR, 6', 185 lbs. (C)
OTIS DOUGLAS Douglas, Otis W. b: 7/25/11, Reedville, Va. d: 3/21/89, Kilmarnock, Va. BR/TR, 6'1", 230 lbs. (DNP)

RICK DOWN Down, Richard John   b: 12/14/50, Wyandotte, Mich.   BR/TR, 5'11", 220 lbs.   (OF)
HARRY DUNLOP Dunlop, Harry Alexander   b: 9/6/33, Sacramento, Cal.   BL/TR, 6'3", 200 lbs.   (C)
GENE DUSAN Dusan, Eugene Paul   b: 11/9/49, Los Angeles, Cal.   BB/TR, 6', 200 lbs.   (C)
GLENN EZZELL Ezzell, Glenn Wayne   b: 10/29/44, Kentwood, La.   BR/TR, 6', 190 lbs.   (C)
JOE FITZGERALD Fitzgerald, Joseph Patrick   b: 3/17/1897, Washington, D.C.   d: 8/29/67, Orlando, Fla.   BR/TR, 5'11", 200 lbs.   (C)
JOHN FITZPATRICK Fitzpatrick, John Arthur   b: 3/9/ 19, 04La Salle, Ill.   BR/TR, 6'1.5", 185 lbs.   (C)
MATT GALANTE Galante, Matthew Joseph   b: 3/2/44, Brooklyn, N.Y.   BR/TR, 5'6", 175 lbs.   (2B)
EPY GUERRERO Guerrero, Epifanio Obdulio (Abud)   b: 1/3/42, Santo Domingo, D.R.   BR/TR, 5'11", 168 lbs.   (OF)
TOM HARMON Harmon, Thomas Harold   b: 12/16/48, Lubbock, Tex.   BL/TR, 5'11", 185 lbs.   (OF)
BEN HINES Hines, Benjamin Thortan   b: 11/7/35, Yeager, Okla.   BR/TR, 5'11", 205 lbs.   (3B-C)
GOLDIE HOLT Holt, Golden Desmond   b: 3/22/02, Enlo, Tex.   BR/TR, 5'7.5", 165 lbs.   (3B-OF-2B)
DOUG HOLMQUIST Holmquist, Douglas Leonard   b: 10/4/41, Bridgeport, Conn.   d: 2/27/88, Altamonte Springs, Fla.   BR/TR, 6'2", 195 lbs.   (C)
VERN HOSCHEIT Hoscheit, Vernard Arthur   b: 4/1/22, Brunswick, Neb.   BR/TR, 5'9", 185 lbs.   (C)
LUIS ISAAC Isaac, Luis (Aponte)   b: 6/19/46, Rio Piedras, P.R.   BR/TR, 5'11.5", 195 lbs.   (C)
RUDY JARAMILLO Jaramillo, Rudolph   b: 9/20/50, Beeville, Tex.   BL/TR, 5'11", 180 lbs.   (OF)
JOE JONES Jones, Joseph Carmack   b: 12/13/41, Lebanon, Tenn.   BR/TR, 5'9", 155 lbs.   (2B)
LOU KAHN Kahn, Louis   b: 12/4/16, St.Louis, Mo.   BR/TR, 5'11", 195 lbs.   (C)
MIKE KELLY Kelly, Bernard Francis   b: 5/1/1896, Indianapolis, Ind.   d: 10/23/68, Indianapolis, Ind.   BR/TR, 6', 198 lbs.   (1B)
WENDELL KIM Kim, Wendell Kealohapauloe   b: 3/9/51, Honolulu, Hawaii   BR/TR, 5'5", 160 lbs.   (2B)
GEORGE KISSELL Kissell, George Marshall   b: 9/9/21, Watertown, N.Y.   BR/TR, 5'8", 175 lbs.   (3B)
HUB KITTLE Kittle, Hubert Milton   b: 2/19/17, Los Angeles, Cal.   BR/TR, 6'1", 195 lbs.   (P)
FRED KOENIG Koenig, Fred Carl   b: 4/27/31, St.Louis, Mo.   BR/TR, 6'3", 200 lbs.   (1B-3B)
JIM LETT Lett, James Curtis   b: 1/3/51, Charleston, W.Va.   BR/TR, 6'2", 185 lbs.   (3B)
LENNY LEVY Levy, Leonard Howard   b: 6/11/13, Pittsburgh, Pa.   BR/TR, 5'10.5", 190 lbs.   (C)
BILL LOBE Lobe, William Charles   b: 3/24/12, Cleveland, Ohio   d: 1/7/69, Cleveland, Ohio   BR/TR, 5'9.5", 178 lbs.   (C)
Q. V. LOWE Lowe, Q. V.   b: 1/15/45, Red Level, Ala.   BR/TR, 6'1", 185 lbs.   (P)
ROY MAJTYKA Majtyka, Le Roy W.   b: 6/1/39, Buffalo, N.Y.   BR/TR, 5'11", 170 lbs.   (2B)
JACK MALOOF Maloof, Jack Garth   b: 10/12/49, Redlands, Cal.   BL/TR, 6', 175 lbs.   (1B-OF)
HARRY MATHEWS Mathews, Henry
LEO MAZZONE Mazzone, Leo David   b: 10/16/48, Keyser, W.Va.   BL/TL, 5'10", 185 lbs.   (P)
MAJE McDONNELL McDonnell, Robert A.   b: 7/20/20, Philadelphia, Pa.   BR/TR, 5'6", 135 lbs.   (P)
J. R. McKEE McKee, J. R.
JOHN McLAREN McLaren, John Lowell   b: 9/29/51, Galveston, Tex.   BR/TR, 6', 200 lbs.   (C)
MO MOZZALI Mozzali, Maurice Joseph   b: 12/12/22, Louisville, Ky.   d: 3/2/87, Lakeland, Fla.   BL/TL, 5'10", 160 lbs.   (1B)
JACK MULL Mull, Jack Leroy   b: 9/29/43, Chambersburg, Pa.   BR/TR, 5'10", 188 lbs.   (C)
ED NAPOLEON Napoleon, Edward George   b: 9/17/37, Baltimore, Md.   BR/TR, 5'8", 165 lbs.   (OF-3B-1B)
ED NOTTLE Nottle, Edward William   b: 10/22/39, Philadelphia, Pa.   BR/TR, 5'10", 180 lbs.   (P)
FRANK OCEAK Oceak, Frank John "Fez"   b: 9/8/12, Pocahontas, Va.   d: 3/19/83, Johnstown, Pa.   BR/TR, 5'9", 172 lbs.   (2B)
BUCK O'NEIL O'Neil, John Jordan   b: 11/13/11, Carrabelle, Fla.   BR/TR, 6'2", 190 lbs.   (1B)
DON OSBORN Osborn, Donald Edwin   b: 6/3/08, Sandpoint, Idaho   d: 3/23/79, Torrance, Cal.   BR/TR, 6', 185 lbs.   (P)
TONY PACHECO Pacheco, Antonio Aristides   b: 8/9/27, Havana, Cuba   d: 87, Miami, Fla.   BR/TR, 6', 190 lbs.   (2B)
JACK PAEPKE Paepke, Jack   b: 8/8/ 28, 22Provo, Utah   BR/TR, 6'2.5", 220 lbs.   (C-P)
GREG PAVLICK Pavlick, Gregory Michael   b: 3/10/50, Washington, D.C.   BR/TR, 6'3", 205 lbs.   (P)
RICK PETERSON Peterson, Eric Harding   b: 10/30/54, Brunswick, N.J.   BL/TL, 6', 175 lbs.   (P)
RON PLAZA Plaza, Ronald Charles   b: 8/24/34, Passaic, N.J.   BL/TR, 6', 180 lbs.   (3B)
GROVER RESINGER Resinger, Grover S   b: 10/20/15, St.Louis, Mo.   d: 1/11/86, St.Louis, Mo.   BR/TR, 5'9", 180 lbs.   (3B)
CANANEA REYES Reyes, Benjamin (Chavez)   b: 2/18/37, Nacosari, Sonora, Mexico   BR/TR, 5'10", 180 lbs.   (OF)
GREG RIDDOCH Riddoch, Gregory Lee   b: 7/17/45, Greeley, Colo.   BR/TR, 5'11", 178 lbs.   (SS)
JIM RIGGLEMAN Riggleman, James David   b: 11/9/52, Fort Dix, N.J.   BR/TR, 5'11", 175 lbs.   (3B)
SHERIFF ROBINSON Robinson, Warren Grant   b: 9/8/21, Cambridge, Md.   BR/TR, 6'1", 195 lbs.   (C)
GLEN ROSENBAUM Rosenbaum, Glen Otis   b: 6/14/36, Union Mills, Ind.   BR/TR, 5'11", 180 lbs.   (P)
RALPH ROWE Rowe, Ralph Emanuel   b: 7/14/24, Newberry, S.C.   BL/TR, 5'6", 160 lbs.   (OF)
JIM SAUL Saul, James Allen   b: 11/24/39, Bristol, Va.   BL/TR, 6'3", 210 lbs.   (C)
BOB SCHAEFER Schaefer, Robert Wald   b: 5/22/44, Putnam, Conn.   BL/TR, 5'11", 180 lbs.   (SS)
GEORGE SCHERGER Scherger, George Richard   b: 11/20/20, Dickinson, N.D.   BR/TR, 5'8", 183 lbs.   (2B)
BUCK SHOWALTER Showalter, William Nathaniel   b: 5/23/57, DeFuniak Springs, Fla   BL/TL, 5'10", 185 lbs.   (1B-OF)
RAC SLIDER Slider, Rachel W.   b: 12/23/33, Simms, Tex.   BL/TR, 5'8", 160 lbs.   (SS)
BILLY SMITH Smith, Billy Franklin   b: 1/14/30, High Point, N.C.   BL/TL, 5'9", 160 lbs.   (1B-OF)
BRIAN SNITKER Snitker, Brian Gerald   b: 10/17/55, Decatur, Ill.   BR/TR, 6'1", 192 lbs.   (C)
DENNY SOMMERS Sommers, Dennis James   b: 7/12/40, New London, Wis.   BL/TR, 6'2", 205 lbs.   (C)
JOE SPARKS Sparks, Joseph Everett   b: 3/15/38, McComas, W.Va.   BL/TR, 6', 195 lbs.   (3B-2B)
TONY TORCHIA Torchia, Anthony Lewis   b: 12/13/43, Chicago, Ill.   BR/TL, 5'10", 180 lbs.   (1B-OF)
JOHN VanORNUM Van Ornum, John Clayton   b: 10/20/39, Pasadena, Cal.   BR/TR, 5'11", 175 lbs.   (C)
AL VINCENT Vincent, Albert Linder   b: 12/23/06, Birmingham, Ala.   BR/TR, 5'9.5", 170 lbs.   (2B)
VERLON WALKER Walker, Verlon Lee "Rube"   b: 3/7/29, Lenoir, N.C.   d: 3/24/71, Chicago, Ill.   BL/TR, 6', 210 lbs.   (C)
JIM WALTON Walton, James Robert   b: 9/5/35, Shattuck, Okla.   BR/TR, 6'2", 190 lbs.   (P)
HARRY WARNER Warner, Harry Clinton   b: 12/11/28, Reeders, Pa.   BL/TR, 6'2", 215 lbs.   (1B)
DON WILLIAMS Williams, Donald Ellis   b: 12/24/37, Paragould, Ark.   BR/TR, 5'10", 185 lbs.   (SS)
JIMMY WILLIAMS Williams, James Bernard   b: 5/15/26, Toronto, Ont., Can.   BR/TR, 5'10", 180 lbs.   (OF)
EARL WOLGAMOT Wolgamot, Clinton Earl   b: 12/ 21, 95Fairbank, Iowa   d: 4/25/70, Independence, Iowa   BR/TR, 5'8", 155 lbs.   (C)

The Umpire Roster

The men in blue have been rebuked and scorned since the Knickerbockers cavorted on the Elysian Fields of Hoboken. The first to incur an umpire's wrath in return was Knickerbocker player Davis, fined six cents for swearing, perhaps understandably since his team was being trounced by the New York Club, 23–1. The name of the umpire in that historic game of June 19, 1846—the first match game under Alexander Cartwright's new rules—was not recorded. Ever since, a handful of researchers have scrambled to find out who umpired the league games of baseball's early history.

Larry Gerlach, who knows more about umpires and umpiring than anybody (see his feature article in Part 1 of this volume), has created the Umpire Roster that follows. The basis of his roster is the list compiled by S. C. Thompson in the 1930s and 1940s, but his research has corrected several errors and omissions in that list and has scrupulously brought the umpire roster up to date. In *Total Baseball 1* he hoped that "by the next edition we will have finished a complete re-study of the umpire roster. . . . I am going to try to fashion a biographical encyclopedia of major league umpires—vital statistics; minor and major league service; All-Star, World Series, Playoff games; special achievements; and so on. One of the more frustrating things about the Turkin/Thompson roster (and even ours) is how years of service are noted in terms of seasons; it really is misleading to identify someone as working from 1980–1987 when he may have broken into the majors on September 24, 1980."

The data presented here does not meet those lofty goals, but it is vastly increased and improved, as well as reorganized. Umpires are now divided not only by league but also by: regular, league-employed umpires; substitutes; player-umpires, pressed into emergency service; and those subs used during the recent strikes. New leads continue to flow in, especially about the early days, when umpires were not assigned by the leagues but were supplied by the teams, recruited from among the fans in attendance (this explains why so many given names are lacking for pre-1900 arbiters), or, not infrequently, plucked from the team's reserve players. An instance of this last practice occurred as late as 1935, when Chicago White Sox outfielder Jocko Conlan was recruited to fill in for umpire Red Ormsby in a game between the Sox and the St. Louis Browns. Conlan, of course, went on to a Hall of Fame career as a man in blue.

But the story of umpires and umpiring is better told in Gerlach's essay in Part 1. Let's call the roll.

NATIONAL ASSOCIATION UMPIRES

National Association (1871-75)

Addy, Robert E., 1875
Allison, Arthur A., 1872, 1874
Allison, Douglas L., 1872-73, 1875
Allison, H., 1874
Alston, David, 1871-72, 1875
Annan, —, 1873
Arnold, Willis S., 1875
Barlow, Thomas H., 1875
Barnes, Roscoe C., 1874
Barrett, William, 1872, 1874
Barron, James, 1875
Barrows, Frederick, 1872
Batt, Thomas, 1871
Battin, Joseph V., 1874
Beals, Thomas J., 1874-75
Beardslee, J. J., 1871-73
Bechtel, George A., 1874
Beck, W. S., 1872
Bielaski, Oscar, 1874-75
Bigelow, W. J., 1875
Birdsall, David S., 1873-74
Blair, William J., 1873
Blodgett, C. W., 1875
Boake, J. L., 1871
Bomeisler, Theodore, 1871-75
Bonse, N., 1871
Bordman, Frederick, 1875
Boyd, William J., 1873, 1875
Bradley, George H., 1875
Brainard, Asa, 1872, 1875
Briggs, —, 1874
Brown, William, 1872, 1875
Bryant, —, 1875
Buck, —, 1871
Bunce, Joshua, 1874
Burdock, John J., 1872-74
Bush, A. M., 1871
Carey, Thomas J., 1873, 1875
Cassidy, Joseph P., 1875
Cavanaugh, J. H., 1875
Chandler, Moses E., 1872, 1874
Chapman, John C., 1871-74
Clapp, John E., 1874-75
Clifton, —, 1872
Clinton, James L., 1873
Clinton, John L., 1875
Collins, Daniel T., 1875
Cone, J. F., 1873-75
Cope, Elias, 1871
Craver, William H., 1873
Cuthbert, Edgar E., 1875
Daniels, Charles F., 1874-75
Daubney, Thomas, 1871
David, L. N., 1874
Dawson, —, 1871
Dean, Harry J., 1871
Deane, Henry C., 1874
Dehlman, Harmon J., 1873-75
Demorest, —, 1872-73
Dobson, H. A., 1871
Dole, William Carrington, 1875
Dornlach, D. E., 1872
Douglass, Benjamin F., 1875
Draper, John H., 1871
Ellis, William R., 1871-72, 1875
English, John W., 1874-75
Erby, Frederick, 1872
Evans, George, 1872
Fellows, T. E., 1871
Fenoe, —, 1872
Ferguson, Robert V., 1871-75

Fisher, William C., 1871, 1875
Foley, Thomas J., 1874-75
Force, David W., 1873
Fulmer, Charles J., 1872-75
Garrigan, —, 1873
Geer, William H., 1874-75
Gerhardt, Joseph J., 1875
Ginn, —, 1875
Glenn, John W., 1874
Glover, Frank, 1873
Goodwin, J. C., 1871-72
Gould, Charles H., 1874-75
Graham, —, 1872
Halback, A. C. N., 1873-74
Hall, George W., 1873-75
Hall, James, 1872
Hanford, Charles, 1874
Hastings, Winfield S., 1871-74
Hatfield, John V. B., 1872-73
Hayhurst, Elias H., 1875
Haynie, James L., 1871
Hegeman, William H., 1871
Helm, J., 1871-72
Heubel, George A., 1875
Higham, Richard, 1873-75
Hodes, Charles, 1874
Hodges, A. D., 1874-75
Holly, Samuel J., 1871
Hooper, Michael H., 1872-74
Hosworth, —, 1872-74
Howard, —, 1872
Hynan, —, 1871
Jennings, Alfred, 1873
Kahn, S. L., 1875
Keerl, George W., 1872
Kent, John, 1875
Knight, G. H., 1875
Kohler, Henry, 1873
Lamb, Harry, 1875
Laughlin, Benjamin, 1873
Lennon, William F., 1871-72
Leonard, —, 1872
Leonard, Andrew, 1872-73, 1875
Leroy, Isaac, 1871
Locke, Marshall, 1873-74
Lowell, John A., 1872-73
Lush, M. R., 1871, 1873
MacDiarmed, Thomas, 1872
Mack, Dennis J., 1871-75
Malone, —, 1875
Marion, S. H., 1873
Martin, Alphonse C., 1871, 1873, 1875
Martin, Lewis G., 1871, 1873-74
Mathews, Robert T., 1871, 1873-75
Mawny, J. H., 1871
Maxwell, Cortez, 1875
Mays, —, 1871
McCrea, —, 1872
McDonald, James F., 1872
McGeary, Michael H., 1872, 1875
McLean, Harry, 1871, 1873
McLean, William B., 1872-75
McMahon, W., 1871
McMullen, John F., 1874
McVey, Calvin A., 1875
Miller, Joseph W., 1872-73
Mills, Charles, 1871-72
Mincher, Edward J., 1872, 1875
Mincher, William E., 1875
Mitchell, C. L., 1874
Mitchell, F. B., 1875
Mosely, M., 1873
Murdock, —, 1872
Murnane, Timothy H., 1873-75
Nelson, J., 1872
Nichols, A. N., 1871
Norton, F., 1872
O'Brien, P., 1875
Pabor, Charles H., 1875

Parks, William R., 1875
Patterson, Daniel T., 1872, 1874
Pearce, Richard S., 1872
Pearson, S. W., 1872
Phelps, Cornelius C., 1874
Pike, Jacob Emanuel, 1875
Porter, —, 1874
Powers, W., 1872-73, 1875
Pratt, Thomas J., 1871-73
Quinn, Patrick, 1875
Radcliffe, John J., 1873
Rastall, J. N., 1872
Reach, Albert J., 1872-75
Reed, Hugh, 1871, 1873-74
Remsen, John J., 1873-74
Robinson, A. V., 1872
Robinson, Miley, 1873
Rogers, Morton, 1871-72
Ryan, John J., 1872, 1875
Sawyer, D., 1871
Schafer, Harry C., 1875
Schroeder, —, 1875
Schuester, John A., 1874-75
Sears, —, 1873
Selman, Frank C., 1873
Sensenderfer, John P. J., 1872-75
Simmons, Joseph S., 1871, 1874
Smith, Eb, 1872
Smith, George, 1872
Smith, Gustavus, 1872, 1875
Snyder, —, 1875
Stahl, G., 1875
Stanwood, —, 1872
Sutton, Ezra B., 1875
Swandell, John M., 1871-73
Sweasy, Charles J., 1871, 1873-74
Tate, William, 1874
Tighe, Edward, 1871
Treacy, Frederick, 1871, 1873, 1875
Tyler, C. T., 1871-74
Urell, E., 1873
Van Delft, —, 1875
Voltz, Edward, 1871-72
Walk, Frank, 1871
Walsh, Michael F., 1875
Wardell, —, 1874
Waterman, Frederick A., 1873
Weaver, C., 1873
Weigel, W. H., 1873-74
White, H. F., 1873
White, Warren W., 1874-75
Whiting, R., 1872
Wiggins, —, 1875
Wildey, John, 1871
Willard, Gardner, 1871
Wood, James B., 1871
Worth, Adam, 1875
Woulfe, —, 1871
Wright, George, 1871
Wright, William H., 1875
York, Thomas J., 1874
Young, Nicholas E., 1871-75

REGULAR UMPIRES

National League (1876-   )

Baker, William P. "Bill", 1957
Ballanfant, E. Lee, 1936-57
Barlick, Albert J. "Al", 1940-43, 1946-55, 1958-71
Barnes, Ronald "Ron", 1990
Barr, George M., 1932-49
Bates, —, 1877
Battin, Joseph V. "Joe", 1891
Bausewine, George, 1905
Betts, William G., 1894-96,

1898-99
Betz, Edwin J., 1961
Bigelow, —, 1877
Boggess, Lynton R. "Dusty", 1944-48, 1950-62
Boles, Charles, 1877
Bond, Thomas H. "Tommy", 1883, 1885
Bonin, Gregory "Greg", 1986-90
Bradley, George H. "Foghorn", 1877, 1879-83
Brady, —, 1877
Brady, Jackson, 1887
Bransfield, William E. "Kitty", 1917
Brennan, William T. "Bill", 1909-13, 1921
Brocklander, Fred W., 1979-90
Brockway, John, 1877, 1879
Brown, Thomas T. "Tom", 1898-99, 1901-02
Brunton, Thomas H., 1879
Budding, —, 1877
Bunce, Joshua, 1877
Burkhart, W. Kenneth "Ken", 1957-73
Burnham, George W., 1883
Burns, John S., 1884
Burns, Thomas E. "Tom", 1892
Burtis, L. W., 1876-77
Bush, Garner C., 1911-12
Byron, William J. "Bill" or "Lord", 1913-19
Callahan, Edward J., 1881
Campbell, Daniel "Dan", 1894-96
Campbell, William M. "Bill", 1939-40
Cantillon, Joseph D. "Joe", 1902
Carey, S., 1879
Carpenter, William B. "Bill", 1897, 1904, 1906-07
Chandler, Moses E., 1877
Clarke, Robert M., 1930-31
Cockill, George W., 1915
Colgan, Harry W., 1901
Colosi, Nicholas "Nick", 1968-82
Conahan, —, 1896
Conlan, John B. "Jocko", 1941-64
Connolly, Thomas H. "Tommy", 1898-1900
Conway, John H., 1906
Crawford, Gerald J. "Jerry", 1976-90
Crawford, Henry C. "Shag", 1956-75
Curry, Wesley "Wes", 1885-86, 1889, 1898
Cusack, Stephen P., 1909
Cushman, Charles H. "Charley", 1885
Dailey, John J., 1882
Dale, Jerry P., 1970-85
Daniels, Charles F., 1876-80, 1887-88
Darling, Gary R., 1988-90
Dascoli, Frank, 1948-62
Davidson, David L. "Satch", 1969-84
Davidson, Robert A. "Bob", 1983-90
Davis, Gerald "Gerry", 1985-90
Day, —, 1879
Decker, Stewart M., 1883-85, 1888
Delmore, Victor "Vic", 1956-59
DeMuth, Dana A., 1986-90
Dezelan, Frank J., 1966-71
Dixon, Hal H., 1953-59
Donatelli, August J. "Augie", 1950-73

Donnelly, Charles H., 1931-32
Donohue, Michael R., 1930
Doscher, John H. Sr. "Herm", 1879-81, 1887
Doyle, John J. "Jack", 1911
Draper, John H., 1877
Ducharme, —, 1876-77
Dunlap, Frederick C. "Fred", 1879
Dunn, John, 1879
Dunn, Thomas P. "Tom", 1939-46
Dunnigan, Joseph, 1881-82
Eagan, John J., 1878, 1886
Ellick, Joseph J. "Joe", 1886
Emslie, Robert D. "Bob", 1891-1924
Engel, Robert A. "Bob", 1965-90
Engeln, William R. "Bill", 1952-56
Feber, Fred W., 1879
Fessenden, Wallace C. "Wally", 1889-90
Fields, Stephen H. "Steve", 1979-82
Finneran, William F., 1911-12, 1924
Forman, Allen S. "Al", 1962-65
Fountain, Edward G., 1879
Frary, Ralph, 1911
Froemming, Bruce N., 1971-90
Furlong, William E., 1877-79
Fyfe, Lee C., 1920
Gaffney, John H., 1884-86
Geer, William H. "Billy", 1879
Gillean, Thomas, 1879-80
Gleason, John D., 1877
Gleason, William G. "Bill", 1877
Goetz, Lawrence J. "Larry", 1936-57
Gore, Arthur J. "Artie", 1947-56
Gorman, Thomas D. "Tom", 1951-76
Gregg, Eric E., 1977-90
Guglielmo, A. Augie, 1952
Guthrie, William J. "Bill", 1913-15
Hallion, Thomas F. "Tom", 1986-90
Harris, Lannie D., 1979-85
Harrison, Peter A. "Pete", 1916-20
Hart, Eugene F. "Bob", 1920-28
Harvey, H. Douglas "Doug", 1962-77, 1979-90
Hastings, W. Scott, 1877
Hautz, Charles A., 1876, 1879
Henderson, J. Harding "Hardie", 1895-96
Hengle, Edward S. "Ed", 1887
Henline, Walter J. "Butch", 1945-48
Heuble, George A., 1876
Higham, Richard "Dick", 1881-82
Hirschbeck, Mark, 1988-90
Hoagland, Willard A., 1894
Hodges, A. D., 1876-77, 1879
Hohn, William J. "Bill", 1987-90
Holland, John A., 1887
Hunt, John T., 1895, 1898-99
Hurst, Timothy C. "Tim", 1891-97
Jackowski, William A. "Bill", 1952-68
Jeffers, W. W., 1881

Johnson, Harry S., 1914
Johnstone, James E. "Jim", 1903-12
Jorda, Louis D. "Lou", 1927-31, 1940-52
Joyce, C. E., 1879
Julian, Joseph O., 1878
Kelley, W. W., 1877
Kelly, John O., 1882
Kennedy, Charles, 1904
Kibler, John W., 1963-89
Klem, William J. "Bill", 1905-41
Landes, Stanley A. "Stan", 1955-72
Lane, Frank, 1883
Latham, W. Arlington "Arlie", 1899
Layne, Jerry B., 1989-90
Libby, Stephen A., 1880
Lincoln, Frederick H., 1914, 1917
Lynch, Thomas J. "Tom", 1888-99
Macullar, James F. "Jimmy", 1892
Magee, Sherwood R. "Sherry", 1928
Magerkurth, George L., 1929-47
Mahoney, Michael J., 1892
Malone, Ferguson G. "Fergy", 1884
Manassau, Alfred S. "Al", 1899
Marsh, Randall G. "Randy", 1983-90
McCormick, William J. "Barry", 1919-29
McDermott, Michael J. "Sandy", 1890, 1897
McDonald, James F., 1895, 1897-99
McElwee, Harvey, 1877
McFarland, Horace, 1896-97
McGrew, Harry T. "Ted", 1930-31, 1933-34
McLaughlin, Edward J., 1929
McLaughlin, Michael, 1893
McLaughlin, Peter J., 1924-28
McLean, William B. "Billy", 1876-80, 1882-84
McMater, —, 1877
McQuaid, John H., 1889-94
McSherry, John P., 1971-90
Meagher, John, 1877
Miller, George E., 1879
Mills, Abraham G., 1877
Mitchell, Charles, 1892
Montague, —, 1877
Montague, Edward M. "Ed", 1976-90
Moran, August "Augie", 1903-04, 1910-11, 1918
Moran, Charles B. "Charlie", 1917-39
Mullin, John, 1909
Nash, William M. "Billy", 1901
O'Connor, Arthur, 1914
Odlin, Albert F., 1883
O'Hara, —, 1915
O'Leary, Daniel, 1879
Olsen, Andrew H. "Andy", 1968-8l
O'Sullivan, John J., 1922
Owens, Clarence B. "Brick", 1908, 1912-13
Pallone, David M. "Dave", 1979-88
Parker, George L., 1936-38
Pearce, Richard J. "Dicky", 1878, 1882
Pears, Frank, 1897, 1905
Pelekoudas, Christos G. "Chris", 1960-75
Pfirman, Charles H. "Cy", 1922-36

Pierce, Grayson S. "Gracie", 1886-87
Pinelli, Ralph A. "Babe", 1935-56
Poncino, Larry L., 1986-88
Powell, Jack, 1923-24, 1933
Powers, Philip J. "Phil", 1881, 1886-91
Pratt, Albert G. "Al", 1879
Pratt, Thomas J. "Tom", 1886
Pryor, J. Paul, 1961-8l
Pulli, Frank V., 1972-90
Quest, Joseph L. "Joe", 1886-87
Quick, James E. "Jim", 1976-90
Quigley, Ernest C. "Ernie", 1913-37
Quinn, William H. "Billy", 1877
Rapuano, Edward "Ed", 1990
Reardon, John E. "Beans", 1926-49
Reliford, Charles "Charlie", 1989-90
Rennert, Laurence H. "Dutch", 1973-90
Rigler, Charles "Cy", 1906-22, 1924-35
Riley, William J., 1880
Rippley, T. Steven "Steve", 1985-90
Robb, Douglas W. "Scotty", 1948-52
Roberts, Leonard W. "Lenny", 1953-55
Rudderham, John E., 1908
Runge, Paul E., 1973-90
Ryan, Walter, 1946
Scott, James "Jim", 1930-31
Sears, John W. "Ziggy", 1934-45
Secory, Frank E., 1952-70
Sentelle, Leopold T. "Paul", 1922-23
Seward, George E., 1876-79
Sheridan, John F. "Jack", 1892
Smith, Vincent A. "Vinnie", 1957-65
Smith, William W. "Billy", 1898-99
Snyder, Charles N. "Pop", 1892-93
Stage, Charles W. "Billy", 1894
Stambaugh, Calvin G., 1877-79
Stark, Albert D. "Dolly", 1928-35, 1937-39, 1942
Steiner, Melvin J. "Mel", 1961-72
Steinfeldt, Harry M., 1905
Stello, Richard J. "Dick", 1969-87
Sternburg, Paul, 1909
Stewart, William J. "Bill", 1933-54
Stockdale, M. J., 1915
Sudol, Edward L. "Ed", 1957-77
Sullivan, David F. "Dave", 1882
Sullivan, Jeremiah "Jerry", 1887
Sullivan, T. P., 1880
Summer, James G., 1876-77
Swartwood, C. Edward "Ed", 1894, 1898-1900
Sweasy, Charles J. "Charlie", 1879
Sweeney, James M. "Jim", 1924-26
Tata, Terry A., 1973-90
Tremblay, Richard H. "Dick", 1971
Truby, Harry G., 1909

Valentine, John G., 1887-88
Van Court, Eugene, 1884
Vargo, Edward P. "Ed", 1960-83
Venzon, Anthony "Tony", 1957-71
Walker, William E., 1876-78
Walsh, Francis D. "Frank", 1961-63
Walsh, Frank, 1877
Walsh, Michael F. "Mike", 1876, 1878-80
Warneke, Lonnie "Lon", 1949-55
Warner, Albert "Al", 1898-1900
Weidman, George E. "Stump", 1896
Wendelstedt, Harry H., 1966-90
West, Joseph H. "Joe", 1976, 1978-90
Westervelt, Frederick E., 1922
Weyer, Lee H., 1961, 1963-88
Wheeler, Robert, 1879
Wickham, Daniel "Dan", 1990
Wilbur, Charles E., 1879
Williams, Arthur "Art", 1972-77
Williams, Charles H. "Charlie", 1978, 1983-90
Williams, James A., 1879
Williams, William G. "Bill", 1963-87
Wilson, Frank, 1923-28
Wilson, John A., 1887
Winters, Michael "Mike", 1990
Wise, Samuel W. "Sam", 1889, 1893
Wood, George A., 1898
York, Thomas J. "Tom", 1886
Young, John W., 1879
Zacharias, Thomas, 1890

American Association (1882-91)

Barnum, George W., 1890
Bauers, Albert J. "Al", 1887
Becannon, William H., 1883
Bradley, George H. "Foghorn", 1886
Brennan, John E., 1884
Butler, Ormond H., 1883
Carey, Thomas J. "Tom", 1882
Clinton, James L. "Jim", 1886
Connell, Terence G., 1884
Connelly, John M., 1885, 1887
Connelly, William, 1884
Curry, Wesley "Wes", 1887, 1890
Cuthbert, Edgar E. "Ned", 1887
Dailey, John J., 1884
Daniels, Charles F., 1883-85, 1889
Davis, James J. "Jumbo", 1891
DeVinney, P. H. "Dan", 1884
Doscher, John H. Sr. "Herm", 1888, 1890
Emslie, Robert D. "Bob", 1890
Ferguson, Robert V. "Bob", 1886-89, 1891
Gaffney, John H., 1888-89
Gleason, William G. "Bill", 1891
Goldsmith, Frederick E. "Fred", 1888-89
Griffith, E. A., 1884
Hautz, Charles A.

"Charlie", 1882
Holland, John A., 1884
Holland, Willard A., 1889
Hurley, Daniel "Dan", 1887
Jones, Charles W. "Charley", 1891
Kelly, John O., 1883-86
Kerins, John A. "Jack", 1889-91
Knight, Alonzo P. "Lon", 1887
Lawler, John F., 1884
Mack, Dennis J. "Denny", 1886
Mahoney, M. J., 1891
McLaughlin, Thomas, 1891
McNichol, Robert T., 1883
McQuade, John H., 1886-88
O'Brien, Frank, 1890
Pratt, Albert G. "Al", 1883
Quinn, A. J., 1886
Riley, William J., 1882
Ross, Robert T., 1882
Seward, George E., 1884
Simmons, Joseph S. "Joe", 1882
Sommer, Benjamin, 1883
Sullivan, Jeremiah "Jerry", 1887
Sullivan, Theodore P. "Ted", 1887
Taylor, Walter, 1890
Toole, Stephen J. "Steve", 1890
Tunnison, William, 1885-86
Valentine, John G., 1884-87
Walsh, Michael F. "Mike", 1882-83, 1885-86
York, Thomas J. "Tom", 1886
Young, Benjamin F. "Ben", 1886

Union Association (1884)

Crawford, Alexander, 1884
DeVinney, P. H. "Dan", 1884
Dutton, Patrick J., 1884
Hengle, Emory J. "Moxie", 1884
Holland, John A., 1884
Hooper, Michael H., 1884
Jennings, Alfred G. "Al", 1884
Jordan, —, 1884
Mapledoram, Blake A., 1884
McCaffrey, Harry C., 1884
Seward, George E., 1884
Stearns, D. Eckford "Ecky", 1884
Sullivan, David F. "Dave", 1884

Players League (1890)

Barnes, Roscoe C. "Ross", 1890
Ferguson, Robert V. "Bob", 1890
Gaffney, John H., 1890
Gunning, Thomas F. "Tom", 1890
Holbert, William H. "Bill", 1890
Jones, Charles W. "Charley", 1890
Knight, Alonzo P. "Lon", 1890
Leach, Henry, 1890
Matthews, John, 1890
Pierce, Grayson S. "Gracie", 1890
Sheridan, John F., 1890
Snyder, Charles N. "Pop", 1890

American League (1901-   )

Adams, John H., 1903
Anthony, G. Merlyn, 1969-75
Ashford, Emmett L., 1966-70
Avants, Nick R., 1969-71
Barnett, Lawrence R. "Larry", 1968-90
Barry, Daniel "Dan", 1928
Basil, Stephen J. "Steve", 1936-42
Berry, Charles F. "Charlie", 1942-62
Boyer, James M. "Jim", 1944-50
Bremigan, Nicholas G. "Nick", 1974-88
Brinkman, Joseph N. "Joe", 1973-90
Campbell, William M. "Bick", 1928-31
Cantillon, Joseph "Joe", 1901
Carrigan, H. Sam, 1961-65
Carpenter, William B., 1904
Caruthers, Robert L. "Bob", 1902-03
Cederstrom, Gary, 1989-90
Chill, Oliver P. "Ollie", 1914-16, 1919-22
Chylak, Nestor L., 1954-78
Clark, Alan M. "Al", 1976-90
Coble, G. Drew, 1983-90
Colliflower, James H., 1910
Connolly, Thomas H. "Tommy", 1901-31
Connor, Thomas "Tom", 1905-06
Cooney, Terrance J. "Terry", 1975-90
Cousins, Derryl, 1979-90
Craft, Terry, 1989-90
Deegan, William E. J. "Bill", 1970-80
Denkinger, Donald A. "Don", 1968-90
DiMuro, Louis J. "Lou", 1963-80
Dinneen, William H. "Bill", 1909-37
Donnelly, Charles H., 1934-35
Doyle, Walter J., 1963
Drummond, Calvin T. "Cal", 1960-69
Duffy, James F. "Jim", 1951-55
Dwyer, J. Francis "Frank", 1904
Egan, John J. "Rip", 1903
Eldridge, Clarence E., 1914-15
Evans, James B. "Jim", 1971-90
Evans, William G. "Billy", 1906-27
Ferguson, Charles A., 1913
Flaherty, John F. "Red", 1953-73
Ford, R. Dale, 1975-90
Frantz, Arthur F. "Art", 1969-77
Friel, William E. "Bill", 1920
Froese, Grover A., 1952-53
Garcia, Richard R. "Rich", 1975-90
Geisel, Harry C., 1925-42
Goetz, Russell L. "Russ", 1968-83
Grieve, William T. T. "Bill", 1938-55
Guthrie, William J. "Bill", 1922, 1928-32
Haller, William E. "Bill", 1961, 1963-82
Hart, Robert F. "Bertie", 1912-13
Hart, William F. "Bill", 1901
Haskell, John E., 1901

Hassett, James E., 1903
Hayes, Gerald, 1925-26
Hendry, Eugene "Ted", 1978-90
Hickox, Edward "Ed", 1990
Hildebrand, George A., 1912-34
Hirschbeck, John F., 1984-90
Holmes, Howard E., 1923-24
Honochick, G. James "Jim", 1949-73
Hubbard, R. Cal, 1936-51, 1954-62
Hurley, Edwin H. "Eddie", 1947-65
Hurst, Timothy C. "Tim", 1905-09
Johnson, Mark S., 1984-90
Johnston, Charles E., 1936-37
Johnstone, James E. "Jim", 1902
Jones, Nicholas I. "Red", 1944-49
Joyce, James A. "Jim", 1989-90
Kaiser, Kenneth J. "Ken", 1977-90
Kelly, Thomas B., 1905
King, Charles F., 1904
Kinnamon, William E. "Bill", 1960-69
Kolls, Louis C., 1933-40
Kosc, Gregory J. "Greg", 1976-90
Kunkel, William G. "Bill", 1968-84
Linsalata, Joseph N. "Joe", 1961-62
Luciano, Ronald M. "Ron", 1968-80
Maloney, George P., 1969-83
Mannassau, Alfred S., 1901
Marberry, Frederick "Firpo", 1935
McCarthy, John "Jack", 1905
McClelland, Timothy R. "Tim", 1984-90
McCormick, William J. "Barry", 1917
McCoy, Larry S., 1970-90
McGowan, William A. "Bill", 1925-54
McGreevy, Edward, 1912-13
McKean, James G. "Jim", 1974-90
McKinley, William F. "Bill", 1946-65
Meriwether, Julius "Chuck", 1988-90
Merrill, E. Durwood, 1977-90
Morgenweck, Henry C. "Hank", 1972-75
Moriarty, George J., 1917-26, 1929-40
Morrison, Daniel G. "Dan", 1984-90
Mullaney, Dominic J., 1915
Mullin, John, 1911-12
Nallin, Richard F. "Dick", 1915-32
Napp, Larry A., 1951-74
Neudecker, Jerome A. "Jerry", 1965-85
O'Brien, Joseph "Joe", 1912, 1914
Odom, James C. "Jim", 1965-74
O'Donnell, James M. "Jake", 1968-71
O'Loughlin, Frank H. "Silk", 1902-18
Ormsby, Emmett T. "Red", 1923-41
Owens, Clarence B. "Brick", 1916-37

Palermo, Stephen M. "Steve", 1977-90
Paparella, Joseph J. "Joe", 1946-65
Parker, Harley P., 1911
Parks, Dallas F., 1979-83
Passarella, Arthur M. "Art", 1941-42, 1945-53
Perrine, Fred "Bull", 1909-12
Phillips, David R. "Dave", 1971-90
Pipgras, George W., 1938-46
Quinn, John A., 1935-42
Reed, Rick A., 1984-90
Reilly, Michael E. "Mike", 1978-90
Rice, John L., 1955-73
Robb, Douglas W. "Scotty", 1952-53
Rodriguez, Armando H., 1974-75
Roe, John "Rocky", 1982-90
Rommel, Edwin A. "Eddie", 1938-59
Rowland, Clarence H. "Pants", 1923-27
Rue, Joseph W. "Joe", 1938-47
Runge, Edward P. "Ed", 1954-70
Salerno, Alexander J. "Al", 1961-68
Schwarts, Harry C., 1960-62
Scott, Dale A., 1986-90
Sheridan, John F. "Jack", 1901-14
Shulock, John R., 1979-90
Smith, W. Alaric "Al", 1960-65
Soar, A. Henry "Hank", 1950-73
Spenn, Frederick C. "Fred", 1979-80
Springstead, Martin J. "Marty", 1965-86
Stafford, John H., 1907
Stevens, John W. "Johnny", 1948-71
Stewart, Ernest D., 1941-45
Stewart, Robert W. "Bob", 1959-70
Summers, William R. "Bill", 1933-59
Tabacchi, Frank T., 1956-59
Tschida, Timothy J. "Tim", 1986-90
Umont, Frank W., 1954-73
Valentine, William T. "Bill", 1963-68
Van Graflan, Roy, 1927-33
Voltaggio, Vito H. "Vic", 1977-90
Wallace, Roderick J. "Bobby", 1915-16
Walsh, Edward A. "Ed", 1922
Weafer, Harold L. "Hal", 1943-47
Welke, Timothy J. "Tim", 1985-90
Westervelt, Frederick E., 1911-12
Wilson, Frank, 1921-22
Young, Larry E., 1985-90

Federal League (1914-15)

Anderson, Oliver O. "Ollie", 1914
Brennan, William T. "Bill", 1914-15
Bush, Garnet C., 1914
Corcoran, Thomas W. "Tommy", 1915
Cross, Montford M. "Monte", 1914
Cusack, Stephen P., 1914

Finneran, William E., 1915
Fyfe, Louis, 1915
Goeckel, E., 1914
Howell, H. Harry, 1915
Johnstone, James E. "Jim", 1915
Kane, Stephen J., 1914
Langden, Joseph, 1915
Mannassau, Alfred S. "Al", 1914
McCormick, William J. "Barry", 1914-15
Mullin, John, 1915
O'Brien, Joseph "Joe", 1915
Quisser, —, 1914
Shannon, William P. "Spike", 1914-15
Stocksdale, Otis H., 1915
Van Sickle, Charles F., 1914
Westervelt, Frederick E., 1915
Wilhelm, Irving K. "Kaiser", 1915

SUBSTITUTE UMPIRES

National League (1876-   )

Allen, Hezekiah "Ham", 1876
Ayers, —, 1876
Baker, Charles, 1884
Barker, Alfred L., 1881
Barnie, William S. "Billy", 1882
Barnum, George W., 1896
Barton, —, 1876
Beard, Oliver P. "Ollie", 1894
Becannon, James M., 1885
Behle, Frank, 1896, 1901
Berger, Frederick, 1886
Bittman, Henry "Red", 1892, 1894-95, 1897
Blakiston, Robert J. "Bob", 1884
Blodgett, C. W., 1876
Bredburg, George W., 1877-79
Brennan, John E. "Jack", 1887
Brown, Samuel W., 1907
Bullymore, Charles L., 1882
Burke, —, 1892
Burlingame, Frank A., 1878
Campbell, Al, 1886
Caruthers, Robert L. "Bob", 1886
Chapman, John C. "Jack", 1876
Chill, Oliver P. "Ollie", 1916
Cheffer, —, 1876
Chipman, Harry F., 1883
Cohen, —, 1893
Collins, Daniel T. "Dan", 1876
Cone, J. F. "Fred", 1876-77
Connell, Terence G., 1885, 1887
Connolly, John M., 1885
Crandall, Robert, 1876-78
Cray, P. C., 1893
Cross, John A., 1876
Cudworth, Al, 1880
Curren, Peter, 1876
Daniels, —, 1885
Deane, J. Henry "Harry", 1876
Devinney, P. H. "Dan", 1876-77
Dyler, John F., 1892, 1897
Earle, William M. "Billy", 1892
Eason, Malcolm W. "Mal", 1901
Eustace, —, 1904
Evans, Jacob "Jake", 1886
Fenno, Norman, 1876
Fisher, William C.

"Cherokee", 1876
Flaherty, —, 1882
Flynn, John A. "Jocko", 1893
Fouser, William C., 1876
Fulmer, Charles J. "Chick", 1881
Ganzel, Charles W. "Charlie", 1901
Gifford, James H., 1881
Glenn, John W., 1880
Goldsmith, Frederick E. "Fred", 1886
Griffiths, —, 1884
Gross, Edward M., 1881
Guinney, Daniel, 1882
Hardie, Louis W. "Lou", 1887
Hartley, John "Jack", 1894
Hatfield, John V. B., 1876
Hawes, William A., 1880-82
Hegeman, William H., 1881
Heydler, John A., 1895-97
Hickey, James L., 1882
Hogan, —, 1897
Hogriever, George C., 1893
Hornung, M. Joseph "Joe", 1892
Howard, C. F., 1884
Hurll, George, 1876
Jevne, Frederick "Fred", 1892, 1894
Jose, —, 1889
Kane, Stephen J., 1906
Kecher, W. H., 1910
Keenan, James W. "Jim", 1893
Kennedy, —, 1893
Kennedy, Michael J., 1884
Kenney, John, 1876-77
Kerins, John A. "Jack", 1888
Kipp, Eden, 1881
Kling, William "Bill", 1892
Klusman, William F. "Billy", 1893
Knight, Alonzo P. "Lon", 1876, 1888
Lally, Bud, 1896
Laney, B., 1884
Lanigan, Charles, 1908
Laughlin, —, 1876
Lawler, Michael H., 1882
Long, William H. "Billy", 1893
Lynch, F. G., 1892
Maddox, Charles, 1882
Maloney, James "Jim", 1893
Manning, —, 1881
Mapledoram, Blake A., 1886
Martin, Alphonse C. "Phonney", 1876
Mason, Charles E. "Charlie", 1876
Mathews, Robert T. "Bobby", 1876
Mayer, —, 1893
McCaffrey, Harry, 1885-86
McCrum, —, 1892
McGee, —, 1876
McGinnis, —, 1910
McGinty, —, 1897
McKinney, —, 1883
McLeod, —, 1895
McMullen, John F., 1876
Mears, Charles W., 1894
Medart, William, 1876-77
Megrue, Cliff, 1876
Morrill, John F., 1891, 1896
Morris, Edward, 1897
Morris, John S., 1876
Muir, Thomas, 1876
Mullen, Peter C., 1893
Murnane, Timothy H. "Tim", 1886
Murphy, Henry, 1880
Murphy, Martin W., 1886
Murray, Jeremiah J. "Miah", 1886
Myers, Henry C., 1890
Nicol, Hugh N., 1894

O'Brien, William, 1876
Orr, David L. "Dave", 1891
Osborne, William, 1876
Pfeffer, Nathaniel F. "Nate", 1897
Phelan, —, 1896
Pierce, —, 1893
Pike, Lipman E. "Lip", 1890
Power, Charles B., 1893
Power, Thomas E., 1894-95
Quincy, W., 1893
Quinn, Joseph C. "Joe", 1881
Quinn, P. J., 1876
Redheffer, —, 1895
Reid, William A., 1882
Reilly, Charles, 1880
Remsen, John J. "Jack", 1880
Rhodes, Eugene A., 1887
Richards, J. E., 1880
Ritchie, F., 1876
Rocap, Adam, 1876
Roll, —, 1876
Rowe, John C. "Jack", 1881
Rudderham, Francis F. "Frank", 1907
Schurer, —, 1896
Seward, Edward W. "Ed", 1892
Sick, —, 1884
Simmons, Joseph S. "Joe", 1876
Skelly, —, 1880
Skinner, S. A., 1886
Smith, —, 1876
Sneeden, —, 1895
Stafford, John H. "Jack", 1906
Strief, George A., 1880
Sullivan, —, 1889
Supple, —, 1906
Sutton, Ezra B., 1876
Tilden, Otis, 1876
Tindall, —, 1890
Toole, Stephen J. "Steve", 1888
Tuthill, Benjamin "Ben", 1895
Twitchell, Lawrence G. "Larry", 1894
Wade, Ben F., 1880
Walters, —, 1892-93
Walton, G. W., 1876
Warren, L. B., 1876
Weeden, —, 1889-90
West, —, 1885
West, George, 1878
West, Milton D. "Buck", 1890
White, George F., 1876-78
White, W. Warren, 1876
Williams, Elisha A. "Dale", 1876
Wolf, William V. "Jimmy", 1893, 1895-97
Wood, James B. "Jimmy", 1876
Wright, William H. "Harry", 1876-77, 1885
Wycoff, —, 1892

American Association (1882-91)

Arnold, Frank W., 1889
Austin, Ed, 1890
Barnie, William S. "Billy", 1882, 1884, 1887
Battin, Joseph V. "Joe", 1882, 1886
Bell, Frank G., 1889
Bittman, Henry P. "Red", 1889
Blogg, Wesley C. "Wes", 1886
Bloom, —, 1887
Burdock, John J. "Jack", 1887
Burkalow, Isaac, 1888
Burns, —, 1882

Butler, Charles, 1889
Campbell, Daniel "Dan", 1890
Carlin, William J. "Billy", 1885
Connell, J., 1885
Cornell, —, 1884
Crandall, Robert, 1882
Creighton, —, 1889-90
Critchley, Morris A. "Morrie", 1884-85
Curry, Frank, 1884, 1886
Daniels, Lawrence, 1887
Devine, W. James "Jim", 1890
Devlin, Charles "Charlie", 1888
Dolan, Thomas J. "Tom", 1890-91
Dow, Clarence, 1891
Dugan, —, 1887
Duke, Martin F., 1890
Dunlevy, Hugh, 1887
Dyler, John F., 1883
Ellick, Joseph J. "Joe", 1888-89
Ewing, William "Buck", 1882
Fell, —, 1885
Fountain, Henry V., 1888
Galvin, James F. "Jim", 1885
Geer, William H. "Billy", 1887
Gill, Thomas H. "Tommy", 1886
Helburn, Hugo, 1887
Henderson, J. Harding "Hardie", 1889
Hengle, Edward S. "Ed", 1889
Hicks, Nathaniel W. "Nat", 1885
Holliday, James W. "Bug", 1888
Irwin, —, 1882
Irwin, John, 1885
Jennings, Alfred "Al", 1882, 1884-85
Julian, Joseph O., 1888
Kelly, William, 1884
Kleinbacker, —, 1886
Levis, Charles H. "Charlie", 1882
Lilly, J., 1884
Little, —, 1884
Loughlin, —, 1885
Loughlin, William, 1882
Lyons, Toby A., 1891
Lyston, William E., 1890
Magner, John T., 1882
Malone, J. R., 1888
Marshall, —, 1887
Mathews, Robert T. "Bobby", 1888
McCartney, Joseph, 1882
McCormick, —, 1888
McGee, Patrick, 1882, 1884
McGinnis, George W. "Jumbo", 1888-89
McIntosh, —, 1882
McLaughlin, William, 1882
McLean, William B. "Billy", 1882
McQuade, James H., 1891
Medart, William, 1887
Miller, Charles A., 1884
Mitchell, —, 1887
Morgan, Henry W., 1884
Morton, Charles H. "Charlie", 1884
Mullen, Peter C., 1891
O'Dea, Lawrence, 1890
Paasch, William, 1887-89
Parker, —, 1887
Phillips, Horace B., 1882
Pike, Lipman. E. "Lip", 1887
Quinn, William H., 1884-85
Ramsey, Dick, 1887
Reeder, James E., 1884
Reising, Charles, 1882

Rice, —, 1885
Robb, John, 1886
Ruhl, Gus, 1882
Ryan, John, 1882
Selman, Frank C., 1882
Sherman, —, 1890
Simpson, Lew, 1884
Skinner, —, 1884, 1886
Smith, George, 1887
Sneed, Jonathon L., 1885
Sullivan, David F. "Dave", 1884
Talbot, —, 1887
Tinney, —, 1882
West, —, 1885, 1887
Wood, George A., 1886
Wright, —, 1884
Young, Joseph, 1890

Union Association (1884)

Adler, —, 1884
Burlingame, F. A., 1884
Donovan, E. S., 1884
Furlong, William E. "Bill", 1884
Hudson, Vincent D., 1884
Lee, Thomas F., 1884
McGunningle, William H. "Bill", 1884
McManaway, D., 1884
McMinimum, Dennis, 1884
Montgomery, —, 1884
Powers, Charles B., 1884
Timblin, —, 1884
Torry, —, 1884

American League (1901-   )

Betts, William G., 1903
Brown, Thomas T. "Tom", 1907
Kerin, John, 1908
Kerins, John A., 1903
Mace, Harry L., 1903
Pears, Frank, 1903
Quigley, Ernest C. "Ernie", 1906

Federal League (1914-15)

Murphy, J. A., 1914

ACTIVE PLAYERS WHO UMPIRED

National League (1876-   )

Abbey, Charles S. "Charlie", 1897
Abbott, H. Frederick "Fred", 1905
Andrews, G. Edward "Ed", 1889
Arundel, John T. "Tug", 1888
Baker, Philip "Phil", 1889
Baldwin, Marcus E. "Mark", 1892
Bannon, James H. "Jimmy", 1894
Beatin, Ebenezer "Ed", 1889
Beck, Erwin T. "Erve", 1902
Beckley, Jacob P. "Jake", 1906
Beebe, Fred L., 1907
Berger, John H. "Tun", 1891
Bonner, Frank J., 1894
Boyle, Henry J., 1886
Boyle, John A. "Jack", 1892, 1897
Breitenstein, Theodore P. "Ted", 1900
Briody, Charles F. "Fatty", 1881
Brown, Willard, 1891
Buelow, Charles J. "Charlie", 1901
Buffinton, Charles G.

"Charlie", 1883, 1888-89, 1892
Burdock, John J. "Jack", 1881
Burns, Thomas P. "Oyster", 1895
Bushong, Albert J. "Doc", 1880, 1890
Butler, Richard H. "Dick", 1897
Carrick, William M. "Bill", 1900
Carroll, Frederick H. "Fred", 1889
Carsey, Wilfred "Kid", 1894, 1896
Casey, Daniel M. "Dan", 1888
Caskin, Edward J. "Ed", 1884
Cassidy, John P., 1882
Chamberlain, Elton P., 1894
Chance, Frank L., 1902
Clack, Robert H. "Bobby", 1876
Clarke, Arthur F. "Artie", 1890
Clarke, William J. "Boileryard", 1893-94, 1896
Clarkson, Arthur H. "Dad", 1893-96
Clarkson, John G., 1888, 1892-93
Clements, John J. "Jack", 1892
Coleman, John F., 1884
Coogan, Daniel G. "Dan", 1895
Crane, Edward N. "Ed", 1892
Crane, Samuel N. "Sam", 1886
Crolius, Frederick J. "Fred", 1901
Cronin, John J. "Jack", 1902-03
Cross, Lafayette N. "Lave", 1892
Cunningham, Elmer E. "Bert", 1896-97, 1900
Cuppy, George M., 1894
Cusick, Andrew D. "Tony", 1886-87
Daily, Cornelius F. "Con", 1886, 1891, 1894, 1896
Daly, Thomas P. "Tom", 1901
Darling, Conrad "Dell", 1887
Dealy, Patrick E. "Pat", 1886
Dexter, Charles D. "Charlie", 1896-97
Donahue, Francis R. "Red", 1897
Donahue, Timothy C. "Tim", 1895-96
Donlin, Michael J. "Mike", 1900
Donnelly, James B. "Jim", 1896
Donovan, William E. "Bill", 1902
Dooin, Charles S. "Red", 1904
Douglass, William B. "Klondike", 1903
Dowse, Thomas J. "Tom", 1890
Duggleby, William J. "Bill", 1905
Dwyer, J. Francis "Frank", 1889, 1893-94, 1896-97
Ehret, Philip S. "Phil", 1892, 1896-97
Farrell, Charles A. "Duke", 1901-02
Ferguson, Charles J. "Charlie", 1886
Ferguson, Robert V. "Bob", 1879

Flaherty, Patrick J. "Patsy", 1904-07
Force, David W. "Davy", 1881
Foreman, Frank I., 1895
Foreman, John D. "Brownie", 1896
Foster, Clarence F. "Pop", 1900
Freeman, John F. "Buck", 1900
Galvin, James F. "Jim", 1881
Gardner, James A. "Jim", 1899
George, William M. "Bill", 1889
German, Lester S. "Les", 1895
Gleason, William J. "Kid", 1890, 1892
Grady, Michael W. "Mike", 1895
Graves, Frank M., 1886
Griffith, Clark C., 1894-95
Grim, John H., 1892, 1895-96
Gruber, Henry J., 1889
Gumbert, Addison C. "Ad", 1892, 1895
Gunning, Thomas F. "Tom", 1884-85
Gunson, Joseph B. "Joe", 1892
Hackett, Mortimer M. "Mert", 1886
Haddock, George S., 1889
Hallman, William W. "Bill", 1903
Hanlon, Edward H. "Ned", 1892
Hart, William F. "Bill", 1896
Hatfield, Gilbert "Gil", 1889
Healy, John J., 1887
Hemming, George E., 1895-96
Hines, Michael P. "Mike", 1884
Holliday, James W. "Bug", 1897
Howe, John "Shorty", 1890
Hyatt, R. Hamilton "Ham", 1912
Irwin, Arthur A., 1881
Jacklitsch, Fred L., 1901
Jennings, Hugh A. "Hughie", 1893, 1900
Jones, Henry M., 1890
Kahoe, Michael J. "Mike", 1905
Karger, Edwin "Ed", 1906
Keefe, Timothy J. "Tim", 1880-82, 1884-85, 1887, 1892
Kelley, Joseph J. "Joe", 1904
Kellum, Winford A. "Win", 1905
Kelly, Michael J. "King", 1892-93
Killen, Frank B., 1896-97
Kinslow, Thomas F. "Tom", 1892
Kittridge, Malachi J., 1890, 1899
Kitson, Frank R., 1902
Kling, John G. "Johnny", 1901
Knell, Philip H. "Phil", 1895
Knowles, James "Jimmy", 1892
Krieg, William F. "Bill", 1887
Leever, Samuel W. "Sam", 1900, 1904
Lindeman, Vivian A. "Vive", 1907
Lundgren, Carl L., 1905-06
Maloney, William J. "Billy", 1902
Manning, James H. "Jim", 1886
Mathewson, Christopher "Christy", 1901, 1907

Mcaleer, James R. "Jim", 1893
McAllister, Lewis W. "Sport", 1899
McCarthy, Thomas F. M. "Tommy", 1896
McCauley, Allen A. "Al", 1890
McCauley, Patrick M. "Pat", 1896
McCormick, James "Jim", 1885
McFarland, Edward W. "Ed", 1896
McGann, Dennis L. "Dan", 1903
McGarr, James B. "Chippy", 1895
McGinnity, Joseph J. "Joe", 1900
McGuire, James T. "Deacon", 1886, 1894, 1896, 1901
McKinnon, Alexander J. "Alex", 1886
McMahon, John H. "Sadie", 1893
Meekin, Jouette, 1895-96
Menefee, John "Jock", 1903
Mertes, Samuel B. "Sam", 1905
Miller, George F. "Doggie", 1893, 1896
Miller, Joseph H., 1884
Moran, Patrick J. "Pat", 1901
Mullane, Anthony J. "Tony", 1893
Mulvey, Joseph H. "Joe", 1895
Murphy, Morgan E., 1893, 1896, 1898
Murphy, William H. "Yale", 1895, 1897
Myers, George D., 1886
Needham, Thomas J. "Tom", 1904, 1907
Newton, Eustace J. "Doc", 1902
Nichols, Charles A. "Kid", 1900-01
Nolan, Edward S. "The Only", 1881
Noonan, Peter J. "Pete", 1906-07
O'Brien, John F. "Darby", 1889
O'Connor, John J. "Jack", 1893, 1901
O'Day, Henry F. "Hank", 1888-89
O'Neill, Michael J. "Mike", 1904
O'Rourke, James H. "Jim", 1893
Orth, Albert L. "Al", 1901
Overall, Orval, 1905, 1910
Peitz, Henry C. "Heinie", 1901, 1906
Phelps, Edward J. "Ed", 1912
Phillippe, Charles L. "Deacon", 1903
Quinn, Joseph J. "Joe", 1894, 1896
Reilly, Charles T. "Charlie", 1892, 1894-95
Reitz, Henry P. "Heinie", 1895
Rhines, William P. "Billy", 1891, 1896
Richardson, A. Harding "Hardie", 1892
Richmond, J. Lee, 1883
Robinson, Wilbert, 1898
Ryan, James E. "Jimmy", 1892
Sanders, A. Bennett "Ben", 1889
Schmidt, Henry M., 1903
Schriver, William F. "Pop", 1901

Serad, William T. "Billy", 1884
Smith, A. Edgar, 1883
Smith, Charles M. "Pop", 1881
Smith, Edgar E., 1890
Smith, George H. "Heinie", 1901
Smith, Harry T., 1903
Smith, William E. "Bill", 1886
Sommers, Joseph A. "Joe", 1889
Staley, Harry E., 1892, 1895
Stearns, D. Eckford "Ecky", 1881
Stein, Edward F. "Ed", 1890, 1894, 1896
Stivetts, John C. "Jack", 1894
Stocksdale, Otis H., 1895
Stricker, John A. "Cub", 1892
Stricklett, Elmer E., 1907
Sugden, Joseph "Joe", 1897
Sullivan, James E. "Jim", 1896
Sullivan, Martin C. "Marty", 1889
Sullivan, Michael J. "Mike", 1897
Sullivan, Thomas J. "Sleeper", 1881
Sutcliffe, Elmer E. "Sy", 1889, 1892
Tannehill, Jesse N., 1897, 1901-02
Tate, Edward C. "Pop", 1888
Taylor, John B. "Jack", 1899
Taylor, John W. "Jack", 1901, 1905
Tener, John K., 1889
Terry, William J. "Adonis", 1892, 1895-96
Tiernan, Michael J. "Mike", 1895
Vaughn, Harry F. "Farmer", 1892, 1899
Viau, Leon "Lee", 1891
Vickery, Thomas G. "Tom", 1890
Walker, Thomas W. "Tom", 1905
Wall, Joseph F. "Joe", 1901
Wallace, Roderick J. "Bobby", 1895
Ward, John M. "Monte", 1888
Warner, John J. "Jack", 1896-97, 1903
Weaver, William B. "Farmer", 1893
Weimer, Jacob W. "Jake", 1905, 1907
Welch, Michael F. "Mickey", 1881-82, 1885-86, 1888
Weyhing, August "Gus", 1899-1900
Whistler, Lewis "Lew", 1891
White, Guy H. "Doc", 1901-02
White, James L. "Deacon", 1880
Whitney, James E. "Jim", 1884, 1886
Wilhelm, Irving K. "Kaiser", 1904-05
Williamson, Edward N. "Ned", 1880
Willis, Victor G. "Vic", 1903
Wilmot, Walter R. "Walt", 1897
Wilson, Frank A. "Zeke", 1896, 1899
Wilson, Parke A. 1894-96, 1899

Wilson, William G. "Bill", 1890
Yeager, George J., 1901
Young, Denton T. "Cy", 1896
Young, Irving M. "Irv", 1905, 1907
Zimmer, Charles L. "Chief", 1889

American Association (1882-91)

Baldwin, Clarence G. "Kid", 1887
Becannon, James M. "Buck", 1884
Bond, Thomas H. "Tommy", 1884
Booth, Amos S., 1882
Boyle, John A. "Jack", 1888
Brennan, John G. "Jack", 1888
Briody, Charles F. "Fatty", 1888
Burns, Thomas P. "Oyster", 1888
Bushong, Albert J. "Doc", 1888-89
Carsey, Wilfred "Kid", 1891
Cassidy, John P., 1884
Chamberlain, Elton P., 1887, 1891
Cross, Lafayette N. "Lave", 1889
Crowell, William T. "Billy", 1888
Darling, Conrad "Dell", 1891
Donahue, James A. "Jim", 1888
Easton, John S. "Jack", 1891
Ehret, Philip S. "Phil", 1890
Ewing, John, 1889
Fulmer, Charles J. "Chick", 1888
Ganzel, Charles W. "Charlie", 1886
Goldsby, Walton H. "Walt", 1888
Greenwood, William F. "Bill", 1884
Griffith, Clark C., 1891
Gunning, Thomas F. "Tom", 1888-89
Healy, John J., 1890
Hecker, Guy J., 1888
Herr, Edward J. "Ed", 1888
Higgins, William E. "Bill", 1890
Holbert, William H. "Bill", 1888
Johnston, Richard F. "Dick", 1884
Keefe, Timothy J. "Tim", 1884
Keenan, James W. "Jim", 1887-88
Kilroy, Matthew A. "Matt", 1887
Kirby, John F., 1888
Knell, Philip L. "Phil", 1891
Latham, George W. "Juice", 1884
Lynch, John H. "Jack", 1884
Macullar, James F. "Jimmy", 1888
Mattimore, Michael J. "Mike", 1888
Mays, Albert C. "Al", 1887
McCarthy, Thomas F. M. "Tommy", 1889
McKelvy, Russell E. "Russ", 1882
McMahon, John J. "Sadie", 1890
McSorley, John B. "Trick", 1884
Merrill, Edward M. "Ed", 1884

Mountain, Frank H., 1884
Mullane, Anthony J. "Tony", 1888
Murphy, Joseph A. "Joe", 1887
O'Brien, William D. "Darby", 1887-88
O'Connor, John J. "Jack", 1889
O'Day, Henry F. "Hank", 1884
Peoples, James E. "Jimmy", 1888-89
Pierce, Grayson S. "Gracie", 1882
Sage, Harry, 1890
Serad, William I. "Billy", 1888
Smith, Charles M. "Pop", 1882, 1886
Smith, Frederick C. "Fred", 1890
Smith, John F. "Phenomenal", 1888
Snyder, Charles N. "Pop", 1886
Sommer, Joseph J. "Joe", 1888
Sprague, Charles W. "Charlie", 1890
Stivetts, John C. "Jack", 1891
Sweeney, Charles J. "Charley", 1887
Sylvester, Louis J. "Lou", 1888
Terry, William J. "Adonis", 1884, 1888
Townsend, George H., 1890
Traffley, William F. "Bill", 1884
Vaughn, Harry F. "Farmer", 1891
Weyhing, August "Gus", 1891
Wheeler, Harry E., 1882
Zimmer, Charles L. "Chief", 1888

Union Association (1884)

Bradley, George W., 1884
Callahan, Edward J. "Ed", 1884
Carroll, Patrick "Pat", 1884
Cuthbert, Edgar H. "Ned", 1884
Kelly, John F., 1884
McLaughlin, James C. "Jim", 1884
Oberbeck, Henry A., 1884
Wheeler, Harry E., 1884
Williams, Washington J. "Wash", 1884

Players League (1890)

Bakely, Edward E. "Ed", 1890
Carney, John J., 1890
Comiskey, Charles A. "Charlie", 1890
Daily, Cornelius F. "Con", 1890
Gumbert, Addison C. "Ad", 1890
Haddock, George S., 1890
Hallman, William W. "Bill", 1890
Keefe, Timothy J. "Tim", 1890
Kelly, Michael "King", 1890
Madden, Michael J. "Kid", 1890
Milligan, John "Jocko", 1890
O'Day, Henry "Hank", 1890
Tener, John K., 1890

American League (1901-)

Bernhard, William H. "Bill", 1903
Beville, H. Monte, 1903-04
Conlan, John B. "Jocko", 1935
Coughlin, William P. "Bill", 1904
Cronin, John J. "Jack", 1901
Davis, —, 1903
Donahue, Francis R. "Red", 1903, 1906
Donovan, William E. "Bill", 1903, 1906
Drill, Lewis L. "Lew", 1903-04
Flaherty, Patrick J. "Patsy", 1903
Griffith, Clark C., 1903
Howell, H. Harry, 1904, 1906
Kittridge, Malachi J., 1905
Leppert, Donald G. "Don", 1978
McAllister, Lewis W. "Sport", 1902
Moore, Earl A., 1903
Patten, Case L., 1903
Pelty, Barney, 1906
Powers, Michael R. "Mike", 1902
Schreckengost, Ossee F., 1903
Warner, John J. "Jack", 1908
White, Guy H. "Doc", 1903
Winter, George L., 1903, 1905
Young, Denton T. "Cy", 1903
Zimmerman, Gerald R. "Jerry", 1978

UMPIRES DURING STRIKES

National League (1876-   )

Anderson, Lewis E. "Andy", 1978-79
Andress, William J. "Bill", 1979
Baird, John, 1979
Barston, Michael "Mike", 1979
Baswell, Jack S., 1979
Beck, Robert "Bob", 1979
Bendekovits, Joseph "Joe", 1979
Betcher, Ralph A., 1976
Blandford, Fred, 1970
Bovey, Terry R., 1979, 1984
Campagna, Frank J., 1979, 1984
Cavanaugh, Richard P. "Dick", 1979, 1984
Cohen, Alfred A. "Al", 1976
Cote, Emilien, 1979
Cuneo, James "Jim", 1978-79
Deniston, Shannon W. "Shan", 1979
Dierking, Roger A., 1978
Edwards, Larry, 1978
Fick, Jerry D., 1978-79
Fisher, Frank, 1979, 1984
Fleming, Thomas E. "Tom", 1979
Fowler, A. Wheeler, 1978
Freels, Robert L. "Bob", 1979
Grimsley, John, 1970
Grinder, Scott, 1976
Grooms, Roger C., 1979
Grygiel, George R., 1970
Guckert, Elmer, 1976
Hadry, Merrill A., 1979
Hamil, Ray, 1979
Hansen, Howard, 1978-79

Hantak, H. Robert "Bob", 1979
Henry, William "Bill", 1979
Hutson, Ronald "Ron", 1979
Jeffers, Ronald L. "Ron", 1979
Jones, James "Jim", 1979
Jumper, Howard, 1979
Lauzon, Jacques, 1979
Lawson, William R. "Bill", 1979
Loeber, Gerald G. "Jerry", 1979
Lospitalier, Philip A. "Phil", 1979
Lupo, Charles "Charlie", 1978-79
Maher, Robert J. "Bob", 1979, 1984
Mauer, Boyd, 1978-79
Melton, David "Dave", 1978
Miller, Marvin G. "Bud", 1979
Mills, Greg, 1979
Morgenweck, Henry C. "Hank", 1970
Mrvos, Joseph S. "Joe", 1979
Myers, Joseph "Joe", 1979
Negri, Peter "Pete", 1979
Nelson, Robert "Bob", 1979
Norris, Edward E. "Ed", 1978-79
Oliger, Edward C. "Ed", 1979
Patch, Tony D., 1978-79
Perez, J. Ray, 1979
Pomponi, Joseph L. "Joe", 1979, 1984
Rains, James "Jim", 1978-79
Riccio, Dennis R., 1979
Riccio, L. Leonard "Len", 1979
Roth, Roy, 1978-79
Rountree, Henry J. "Hank", 1978-79
Schaller, Cliff, 1978-79
Schleyer, John, 1979
Schratz, Joseph "Joe", 1979
Schroeder, Robert L. "Bobby", 1978-79
Scott, James "Jim", 1978-79
Sharkey, Michael E. "Mick", 1978-79
Sharp, Robert C. "Bob", 1979
Siroka, Harold L., 1979
Slattery, Donald L. "Don", 1979
Slickenmeyer, David W. "Dave", 1979, 1984
Smail, Harry F., 1979
Spinelli, Michel, 1979
Stansell, B. Jack, 1979
Stewart, John, 1979, 1984
Strey, Murray W., 1978-79
Telford, Thomas "Tom", 1979
Tillman, Henry T. "Hank", 1978-79
Treitel, Leslie J. "Les", 1978-79
Tremblay, Richard H. "Dick", 1979
Urlage, Richard C. "Dick", 1979
Waller, James "Jim", 1979
Williams, Dale, 1978-79

American League (1901-   )

Berry, Charles F. "Charlie", 1970
Bible, Jonathan D. "Jon", 1984
Bishop, Homer L., 1979

Borga, Steven A. "Steve", 1979
Briscese, Michael L. "Mike", 1979
Brown, Buddy Lee "Bud", 1979
Brown, Douglas D. "Doug", 1979
Brown, Jeff, 1978-79
Camp, John W., 1979
Campbell, Robert "Bob", 1979
Christal, W. Randle "Randy", 1984
Clegg, Richard "Dick", 1979
Clement, Robert F. "Bob", 1978-79
Contant, Alan, 1978-79
Cossey, Douglas C. "Doug", 1978-79, 1984
Cuneo, James "Jim", 1979
Davidson, Dale F., 1979
Deegan, William E. "Bill", 1970, 1984
Denny, Richard, 1984
Dreke, Roy, 1979
Driscoll, Joseph M. "Joe", 1978
Dunne, James "Jim", 1978-79
Easley, Harold L., 1979
Eshelman, George R., 1979
Farmer, Michael "Mike", 1979

Farnsworth, Harry, 1979
Feaser, Richard L. "Dick", 1979
Fitzpatrick, Michael N. "Mike", 1979
Follmer, William A. "Bill", 1979
Forman, Allen S. "Al", 1978-79
Fuchs, Lester, 1978-79
Gallagher, Lawrence E. "Larry", 1979
George, Edward "Ed", 1979
Giard, Robert "Bob", 1978
Gustafson, G. David "Dave", 1978
Hafner, William F. "Bill", 1979
Hadry, Merrill A., 1979
Heitzer, Richard "Dick", 1979
Henry, William E. "Bill", 1979
Ivory, William J. "Bill", 1979
Jackson, Charles L., 1979
James, John F. "Johnny", 1978-79
Jones, Robert G. "Bob", 1979, 1984
Jordan, Harold E., 1984
Kavulich, Joseph "Joe", 1978-79
Keister, R. Wayne, 1978-79
Kelly, Eugene C. "Gene", 1979

Kirby, Kenneth "Ken", 1979
LaPierre, Richard, 1979
Laude, William F. "Bill", 1978-79
Lazar, Richard R. "Richie", 1978-79
Levet, Jay, 1979
Loeber, Gerald G. "Jerry", 1979
Lospitalier, Philip A. "Phil", 1979
Lupo, Charles "Charlie", 1979
Mabbot, Frederick J. "Fred", 1979
Mackin, John F., 1979
Marino, James H. "Jimmy", 1979
Mauer, Boyd, 1979
McNally, James "Jim", 1979
Merritt, Clarence, 1979
Miller, Gale, 1979
Miller, John A. "Jack", 1979
Moyer, Robert "Bob", 1979
Mulcahy, James "Jim", 1979
Nelson, Richard "Dick", 1979
Nothhnagel, Carl L., 1984
Novack, Lester A. "Les", 1979
O'Brien, James D. "Jim", 1979
O'Connor, James "Jim",

1978-79
O'Connor, Thomas M. "Tom", 1979
O'Dell, Mikel R. "Mike", 1984
Panas, Richard J. "Rich", 1978-79
Patch, Tony D., 1979
Perez, David A. "Dave", 1979
Phipps, George H. "Jerry", 1978-79
Pratt, Lester, 1979
Purduski, Al J., 1979
Ravashiere, Thomas "Tom", 1979
Riccio, L. Leonard "Len", 1979
Rice, Robert W. "Bob", 1979
Robinson, William N. "Bill", 1978-79
Roesner, Robert A. "Bob", 1978-79
Roth, Roy, 1979
Runchey, Richard D. "Dick", 1979, 1984
Satchell, Darold L., 1970
Sawchuk, Joseph W. "Joe", 1978-79
Scheel, Alfred M. "Al", 1979
Schirmer, Donald A. "Don", 1979

Schulte, Donald E. "Don", 1979
Shaw, A. Duane, 1979
Shewmake, James B. "Jim", 1978
Siroka, Harold L., 1979
Slattery, Donald L. "Don", 1979
Slickenmeyer, David W. "Dave", 1979
Sprincz, William "Bill", 1978-79
Stevens, John W. "Johnny", 1970
Sweeney, George P., 1979
Swenson, Charles H., 1979
Taylor, Joe Bob, 1979
Terlop, Russell F. "Russ", 1979
Theilander, Theodore "Ted", 1979
Thompson, Michael G. "Mike", 1978-79
Tillman, Henry "Hank", 1979
Trimmer, Harry, 1979
Turner, Leo I., 1978
Urchak, Woody J., 1978-79
Williams, Dale, 1979
Zirbel, Lawrence A. "Larry", 1979, 1984
Zivic, Richard J. "Dick", 1984
Zuccaro, Amerigo J. "Rico", 1978-79

The Owners and Officials Roster

Major League Baseball dates its inception from 1876 with the formation of the National League, not 1871, the founding date of the National Association. Because the latter year marks the beginning of professional league play, *Total Baseball* includes NA player records with those of the MLB-recognized leagues; however, it is undeniable that something dramatic occurred in 1876 that altered forevermore the character of professional baseball: the division of the game into two classes, labor and management.

The National Association of Professional Base Ball Players was an outgrowth of the amateur association of the same name, in which baseball clubs were formed as organizations devoted to social intercourse and fraternal competition. Amateur clubs were organized along the same lines as today's Elks or Odd Fellows, with elected officials and dues-paying members. As players of special skill were invited into these clubs, their dues might be forgiven or "emoluments" offered—no-show jobs or under-the-table payments. The abuses of the amateur system of the mid-1860s led to the declaration by several clubs of their openly professional status; players would sometimes draw salaries and as often would share in gate receipts. By the end of the decade gambling and game-fixing were rife.

Despite the formation of the National Association, these evils continued largely unabated into the 1870s. A monopolization of talent, largely in Boston, rendered Western clubs uncompetitive, and spectator rowdyism spawned by gambling interest, and the open sale of hard liquor burdened the new league. Clubs were admitted into the NA for paltry fees and fulfilled their schedules half-heartedly. Some of the member clubs had active presidents who functioned much as owners later would; other clubs were "cooperative nines," managed by the players themselves; still others were hybrids, born of civic boosterism. By 1876, the odd amalgam of the NA, presided over by Brooklyn Atlantics star Bob Ferguson, was failing.

Thus in 1876 William Hulbert, president of the Chicago club, combined with seven other team representatives to form the National League, a circuit run entirely by owners. Since then, fan interest has focused on the players, of course, and to a lesser extent on the managers, coaches, and umpires. But it can be said with some justice that while the on-field personnel and personalities "are" the game, it is the club owners, presidents, and league officials who make the game possible and ensure its continuity.

The Owners and Officials Roster that follows represents a first attempt in a baseball encyclopedia to recognize these individuals. As we did with the Coach Roster in the first edition of *Total Baseball,* we offer this section in full knowledge that there are gaps and probably gaffes in our research; we hope that our readers will advise us of omissions so that we can improve the roster in future editions. (The names of National Association club presidents and officials are listed below despite our understanding that these individuals were, by and large, not owners in the sense used after 1876.)

For a prose account of the history of owners and officials, see the articles by David Voigt and by Steve Mann and David Pietrusza.

Commissioners, Major League Baseball

1920–1944	Kenesaw M. Landis
1945–1951	Albert B. Chandler
1951–1965	Ford C. Frick
1965–1968	William D. Eckert
1969–1984	Bowie K. Kuhn
1984–1989	Peter Ueberroth
1989	A. Bartlett Giamatti
1989–1990	Francis T. Vincent, Jr.

National Association

Association President

1871	James W. Kerns
1872–1875	Robert W. Ferguson

Club Presidents and/or NA Convention Delegates

Baltimore Lord Baltimores

1872	—
1873	R. C. Hall
1874	C. A. Hadel

Baltimore Marylands

1873	W. J. Smith

Boston Red Stockings

1871	Ivers Whitney Adams
1872	Col. Charles H. Porter
1873–1875	Nathan Taylor Appolonio

Brooklyn Atlantics

1872–1873	Robert W. Ferguson
1874	—
1875	B. Van Delft

Brooklyn Eckfords

1872	William H. Ray

Chicago White Stockings

1871	J. M. Thatcher
1874	Mr. Gassette
	George W. Gage
1875	William A. Hulbert

Cleveland Forest City

1871	J. F. Evans
1872	H. C. Doolittle

Elizabeth Resolutes

1873	Charles N. Garrighan

Fort Wayne Kekiongas

1871	George J. E. Mayers

Hartford Dark Blues

1874	G. B. Hubbell
1875	Morgan G. Bulkeley

Keokuk Westerns

1875	W. Trimble

Middletown Mansfields

1872	B. Douglass, Jr.
	T. W. Ratcliff

New Haven Elm City

1875	W. S. Arnold

New York Mutuals

1871–1872	Alexander V. Davidson
1873	Robert Mathews
1874	Alexander V. Davidson
1875	William H. Cammeyer

Philadelphia Athletics

1871	James W. Kerns
1872–1873	E. H. Hayhurst
1874	D. F. Houston
1875	George W. Thompson
	C. Spering

Philadelphia White Stockings

1873	Frank McBride
1874	D. L. Reid
1875	George Concannon

Philadelphia Centennials

1875	E. H. Hayhurst

Rockford Forest City

1871	Hiram Waldo

St. Louis Brown Stockings

1875	C. O. Bishop

St. Louis Red Stockings

1875	A. Blong

Troy Haymakers

1871	J. W. Scofield
1872	C. C. Clark

Washington Nationals

1872	Mr. Millar
	R. Hough

Washington Olympics

1871	Nicholas E. Young
1872	Mr. Pike

Washington

1873	Nicholas E. Young
1875	D. W. Bruce
	A. F. Childs

National League

Presidents

1876	Morgan G. Bulkeley
1877–1882	William A. Hulbert
1882	Arthur H. Soden
1883–1884	Abraham G. Mills
1885–1902	Nicholas E. Young
1903–1909	Harry C. Pulliam
1909	John A. Heydler
1910–1913	Thomas J. Lynch
1913–1918	John K. Tener
1918–1934	John A. Heydler
1934–1951	Ford C. Frick
1951–1969	Warren C. Giles
1970–1986	Charles S. Feeney
1986–1989	A. Bartlett Giamatti
1989–1990	William White

Vice Presidents

1929–1932	Barney Dreyfuss
1933–1936	Charles A. Stoneham
1936–1947	Samuel Breadon
1947–1966	Philip K. Wrigley
1966–1969	Horace C. Stoneham
1970–1986	John J. McHale
1987–1990	Phyllis Collins

Club Presidents

Atlanta

1966	John J. McHale
1967–1972	William C. Bartholomay
1973–1975	Daniel J. Donahue
1976–1986	R. E. (Ted) Turner
1987–1990	William C. Bartholomay (Ch. of Bd.)

Baltimore

1892	Harry B. Von der Horst
1893–1899	Edward H. Hanlon

Boston (to Milwaukee)

1876	Nathan Taylor Appolonio
1907–1909	George B. Dovey
1909–1910	John S. Dovey
1911	W. Hepburn Russell
1912	John M. Ward
1913–1915	James E. Gaffney
1916–1918	Percy D. Haughton
1919–1922	George W. Grant
1923	Christopher Mathewson
1924	J. A. Robert Quinn
1925	Christopher Mathewson
1926	J. A. Robert Quinn
1927–1935	Emil E. Fuchs
1936–44	J. A. Robert Quinn
1945–1956	Louis R. Perini

Brooklyn (to L.A.)

1890–1897	Charles H. Byrne
1898–1925	Charles H. Ebbets
1925	Edward J. McKeever
1925–1929	Wilbert Robinson
1930–1932	Frank B. York
1933–1938	Stephen W. McKeever
1939–1942	Leland S. MacPhail, Sr.
1943–1950	W. Branch Rickey

1950–1957	Walter F. O'Malley

Buffalo

1879–1880	E. B. Smith
1880	John B. Sage
1881–1885	Josiah Jewett

Chicago

1876–1881	William A. Hulbert
1882–1891	Albert G. Spalding
1892–1905	James A. Hart
1906–1913	Charles W. Murphy
1914–1915	Charles H. Thomas
1916–1918	Charles H. Weeghman
1919	Fred F. Mitchell
1919–1933	William L. Veeck, Sr.
1934	William M. Walker
1934–1977	Philip K. Wrigley
1977–1981	William J. Hagenah, Jr.
1982–1983	Andrew J. McKenna (Ch. of Bd.)
1984	James E. Finks (Pres./CEO)
1985–1987	Dallas Green
1988	John W. Madigan (Ch. of Bd.)
1989–1990	Donald C. Grenesko

Cincinnati

1876–1877	Josiah L. Keck
1878–1879	J. Wayne Neff
1880	Justus Thorner

Cincinnati

1890	Aaron A. Stern
1891–1902	John T. Brush
1902–1927	August Hermann
1928–1929	C. J. McDiarmid
1930–1933	Sidney Weil
1934–1946	Powel Crosley, Jr.
1946–1951	Warren C. Giles
1951–1961	Powel Crosley, Jr.
1961–1966	William O. DeWitt
1967–1973	Francis L. Dale
1973–1978	Robert L. Howsam
1979–1983	Richard Wagner
1984–1985	Robert L. Howsam (Pres./CEO)
1986–1990	Marge Schott

Cleveland

1879–1881	J. Ford Evans
1882–1884	C. H. Bulkley

Cleveland

1889–1898	Frank D. Robison
1899	M. Stanley Robison

Detroit

1881–1884	William G. Thompson
1885–1886	Joseph H. Marsh
1887–1888	Fred K. Stearns
1888	Charles W. Smith

Hartford

1876–1877	Morgan G. Bulkeley

Houston

1962	Craig Cullinan, Jr.
1963–1971	Roy Hofheinz
1972–1973	Reuben W. Askanase
1974–1975	T. H. Neyland
1976	Sidney L. Shlenker
1976–1980	Talbot M. Smith
1981–1985	Albert L. Rosen
1986–1987	Dick Wagner
1988	Fred Stanley
1980–1990	Dr. John J. McMullen (Ch. of Bd.)

Indianapolis

1878	William D. Perritt

Indianapolis

1887–1889	John T. Brush

Kansas City

1886	Joseph J. Heim

Los Angeles

1958–1969	Walter F. O'Malley
1970–1990	Peter O'Malley

Louisville

1876–1877	Walter N. Haldeman

Louisville

1892	T. Hunt Stucky
1893–1896	Fred Drexler

1897–1899	Harry C. Pulliam
1899	Barney Dreyfuss

Milwaukee

1878	J. R. Kaine

Milwaukee Braves (to Atlanta Braves)

1953–1956	Louis R. Perini
1957–1961	Joseph F. Cairnes
1962–1966	John J. McHale

Montreal Expos

1969–1986	John J. McHale
1987–1990	Claude R. Brochu (Pres./CEO)
1969–1990	Charles R. Bronfman (Ch. of Bd.)

Mutual Club (N.Y.)

1876	William H. Cammeyer

New York Giants (to San Francisco)

1883–1892	John B. Day
1893–1894	C. C. Van Cott
1895–1902	Andrew Freedman
1903–1912	John T. Brush
1912–1918	Harry N. Hempstead
1919–1935	Charles A. Stoneham
1936–1957	Horace C. Stoneham

New York Mets

1962–1966	George M. Weiss
1967	Vaughan P. Devine
1968–1975	Mrs. Joan W. Payson
1976–1979	Mrs. Lorinda de Roulet
1980–1990	Fred Wilpon (Pres./CEO)

Philadelphia Athletics

1876	Thomas J. Smith

Philadelphia Phillies

1883–1902	Alfred J. Reach
1903–1904	James Potter
1905–1908	William J. Shettsline
1909	Israel W. Durham
1909–1912	Horace S. Fogel
1912	Alfred D. Wiler
1913	William H. Locke
1913–1930	William F. Baker
1931–1932	L. Charles Ruch
1933–1942	Gerald P. Nugent
1943	William D. Cox
1943–1972	Robert M. Carpenter, Jr.
1973–1981	Robert M. Carpenter III
1982–1990	Bill Giles (Pres./General Partner)

Pittsburgh

1887–1890	William A. Nimick
1891	J. Palmer O'Neill
1892	William C. Temple
1893	Albert C. Buckenberger
1894–1897	William W. Kerr
1898	William H. Watkins
1899	William W. Kerr
1900–1932	Barney Dreyfuss
1932–1946	William E. Benswanger
1946–1950	Frank E. McKinney
1951–1969	John W. Galbreath
1970–1985	Daniel M. Galbreath
1986–1987	Malcolm Prine
1988–1990	Carl F. Barger
1988–1990	Douglas D. Danforth (Chairman/CEO)

Providence

1878	John D. Thurston
1879–1881	Henry J. Root
1882–1883	Henry B. Winship
1884–1885	Henry J. Root

St. Louis Brown Stockings

1876–1877	John R. Lucas

St. Louis Maroons

1885–1886	Henry V. Lucas

St. Louis Cardinals

1892–1897	Chris Von der Ahe
1898	Benjamin S. Muckenfuss
1899–1906	Frank D. Robison
1907–1910	M. Stanley Robison
1911–1912	E. A. Steininger
1912	James C. Jones
1913–1916	Schuyler P. Britton
1916	Mrs. Schuyler P. Britton
1917–1919	W. Branch Rickey

1920–1947	Samuel Breadon
1947–1949	Robert E. Hannegan
1949–1952	Fred M. Saigh, Jr.
1953–1989	August A. Busch, Jr.
1990	Fred L. Kuhlmann (Pres./CEO)

San Diego

1969–1977	Emil J. Bavasi
1977–1980	Ray A. Kroc
1981–1983	Ray A. Kroc (owner)
1980–1987	Ballard F. Smith, Jr.
1988	Chub Feeney
1990	Dick Freeman
1984–1990	Joan Kroc (owner)

San Francisco

1958–1975	Horace C. Stoneham
1976–1985	Robert A. Lurie
1976–1990	Robert A. Lurie (owner)
1986–1990	Al Rosen

Syracuse

1879	Hamilton S. White

Troy

1879–1880	Gardner Earl
1881–1882	A. L. Hotchkin
1882	Francis N. Mann

Washington

1886–1888	Robert C. Hewitt
1889	Walter F. Hewitt

Washington

1892–1899	George W. Wagner

Worcester

1880–1882	Elbert B. Pratt

American Association

League Presidents

1882–1885	H. D. McKnight
1886–1889	Wheeler C. Wyckoff
1890	Zach Phelps
1891	Louis Kramer
	Ed Renau
	Zach Phelps

Club Presidents

Baltimore

1882	H. C. Myers (?)
1883	William Barnie (?)
1884	H. T. Houck
1885–1887	William Barnie
1888	Harry Von der Horst
1889	William Barnie
1891	Harry Von der Horst

Boston

1891	Charles A. Prince

Brooklyn

1884–1889	Charles H. Byrne

Brooklyn–Baltimore

1890	James M. Kennedy
	Wm. Barnie (?)

Cincinnati

1882	Justus Thorner
1883–1884	Aaron S. Stern
1885	George L. Herancourt
1886	John Hauck
1887–1889	Aaron S. Stern

Cincinnati-Milwaukee

1891	Albert Johnson

Cleveland

1887–1888	Frank Robison

Columbus

1883–1884	H. T. Crittendon (?)
1889–1891	Conrad Born, Jr.

Indianapolis

1884	Joseph Schwabacher

Kansas City

1888	Joseph J. Heim
1889	John W. Speas

Louisville

1882–1883	J. H. Pank
1884	William L. Jackson, Jr.
1885–1887	Zach Phelps
1888	W. L. Lyons
1889	M. H. Davidson
1890	Lawrence S. Parsons
1891	Julian B. Hart

New York

1883–1884	John B. Day
1885	Frank Rhouer
1886–1887	Erastus Wiman

Philadelphia

1882	Lew Simmons (?)
1883–1886	William Sharsig
1887	Lew Simmons
1888–1890	H. C. Pennypacker
1891	J. Earle Wagner

Pittsburgh

1882–1883	H. D. McKnight
1884	E. E. Converse
1885–1886	William A. Nimick

Richmond

1884	W. C. Seddon

Rochester

1890	Henry Brinker

St. Louis

1882–1891	Chris Von der Ahe

Syracuse

1890	George K. Frazier

Toledo

1884	W. J. Colburn
1890	V. H. Ketcham

Washington

1884	L. Moxley
1891	H. B. Bennett

Union Association

League Presidents

1883	H. B. Bennett
	Henry V. Lucas
1883–1885	Henry V. Lucas

Club Presidents

Altoona

1884	W. W. Rich

Baltimore

1884	J. W. Lowe

Boston

1884	Frank E. Winslow

Chicago-Pittsburgh

1884	A. H. Henderson

Cincinnati

1884	Justus Thorner

Kansas City

1884	Americus V. McKim

Milwaukee

1884	Charles Kippen (?)

Philadelphia

1884	Thomas J. Pratt

St. Louis

1884	H. V. Lucas

St. Paul

1884	A. M. Thompson (?)

Washington

1884	H. B. Bennett

Wilmington

1884	John T. West

Players League

League President

1890	Col. Edward A. McAlpin

Club Presidents

Boston

1890	Col. Charles H. Porter

Brooklyn

1890	Wendell Goodwin

Buffalo

1890	Moses Shire

Chicago

1890	John Addison

Cleveland

1890	Albert L. Johnson

New York

1890	Cornelius Van Cott

Philadelphia

1890	H. M. Love

Pittsburgh

1890	William McCallin

American League

Presidents

1901–1927	B. Bancroft Johnson
1927–1931	Ernest S. Barnard
1931–1959	William Harridge
1959–1973	Joseph E. Cronin
1974–1984	Leland S. MacPhail, Jr.
1984–1990	Robert W. Brown, M.D.

Vice Presidents

1901–1916	Charles W. Somers
1917–1919	Charles A. Comiskey
1921–1935	Frank J. Navin
1935–1938	Jacob Ruppert
1939–1955	Clark C. Griffith
1955–1976	Thomas A. Yawkey
1976–1982	Calvin R. Griffith
1983–1984	Calvin R. Griffith
	John Fetzer
	Gene Autry
1985	John Fetzer and Gene Autry
1986–1989	Calvin R. Griffith
	John Fetzer
	Gene Autry
1990	John Fetzer and Gene Autry

Club Presidents

Baltimore (to New York)

1901	Sidney W. Frank
1902	John J. Mahon

Baltimore

1954–1955	Clarence W. Miles
1956–1959	James Keelty, Jr.
1960–1965	Leland S. MacPhail, Jr.
1966–1979	Jerold C. Hoffberger (Ch. of Bd.)
1980–1982	Jerold C. Hoffberger (as Pres.)
1983–1988	Edward B. Williams (Ch. of Bd./Pres.)
1989–1990	Larry Lucchino

Boston

1901–1902	Charles W. Somers
1903–1904	Henry J. Killilea
1904–1911	John I. Taylor
1912–1913	James R. McAleer
1913–1916	Joseph J. Lannin
1917–1923	Harry H. Frazee
1923–1932	John A. Quinn
1933–1976	Thomas A. Yawkey
1977–1988	Jean R. Yawkey (majority owner)
1989	John L. Harrington

California (includes Los Angeles, 1961–64)

1961–1974	Robert Reynolds
1975–1977	Arthur E. Patterson
1977–1990	Gene Autry (owner/president)

Chicago

1901–1931	Charles A. Comiskey
1932–1939	J. Louis Comiskey
1940	Harry Grabiner (VP)
1941–1956	Mrs. Grace Comiskey
1957–1958	None
1959–1961	William L. Veeck, Jr.
1961–1969	Arthur C. Allyn, Jr.
1970–1975	John W. Allyn
1976–1980	William L. Veeck, Jr.
1981–1990	Eddie Einhorn
1981–1990	Jerry M. Reinsdorf (Chairman)

Cleveland

1901–1909	John F. Kilfoyl
1910–1915	Charles W. Somers
1916–1922	James C. Dunn
1922–1927	Ernest S. Barnard
1928–1946	Alva Bradley
1946–1949	William L. Veeck, Jr.
1950–1952	Ellis W. Ryan
1953–1962	Myron H. Wilson, Jr.
1963–1971	Gabriel H. Paul
1972–1975	Nick Mileti
1975–1977	Alva T. Bonda
1978–1983	F. J. (Steve) O'Neill
1983–1986	Patrick J. O'Neill (Chairman)
1978–1985	Gabriel H. Paul
1986	Peter Bavasi
1987–1990	Richard E. Jacobs (Ch. of Bd.)
1988–1990	Hank Peters

Detroit

1901	James D. Burns
1902–1903	Samuel F. Angus
1904–1907	William H. Yawkey
1908–1935	Frank J. Navin
1936–1952	Walter O. Briggs, Sr.
1952–1956	Walter O. Briggs, Jr.
1957	Frederick A. Knorr
1957–1959	Harvey R. Hansen
1960	William O. DeWitt
1961–1989	John E. Fetzer (Chairman)
1978–1989	James Campbell
1984–1990	Thomas S. Monaghan
1990	Glenn E. (Bo) Schembechler

Kansas City A's (to Oakland)

1955–1959	Arnold Johnson
1960	Parke Carroll (VP)
1961–1967	Charles O. Finley

Kansas City Royals

1969–1981	Ewing Kauffman
1982–1990	Joe Burke

Milwaukee (to St. Louis)

1901	Matthew Killilea

Milwaukee Brewers

1970–1990	Allan H. Selig

Minnesota

1961–1984	Calvin R. Griffith (Chairman/Pres.)
1985–1986	Howard T. Fox, Jr.
1987–1989	Jerry Bell
1985–1990	Carl Pohlad (owner)

New York

1903–1906	Joseph W. Gordon
1903–1915	Frank J. Farrell and William S. Devery (owners)
1907–1914	Frank J. Farrell
1915–1938	Jacob Ruppert
1939–1944	Edward G. Barrow
1945–1947	Leland S. MacPhail, Sr.
1948–1966	Daniel R. Topping
1966–1973	Michael Burke
1973–1977	Gabriel H. Paul
1978–1980	Albert Rosen
1980–1990	George M. Steinbrenner (Ch. of Bd.)
1990	Robert Nederland

Oakland

1968–1980	Charles O. Finley
1981–1987	Roy Eisenhardt
1981–1990	Walter J. Haas (owner)

Philadelphia (to Kansas City)

1901–1921	Benjamin F. Shibe

1922–1935	Thomas S. Shibe
1936	John D. Shibe
1937–1954	Connie Mack

Seattle Pilots (to Milwaukee)

1969	Dewey Soriano

Seattle Mariners

1977–1979	Danny Kaye and Lester Smith
1980–1983	Daniel F. O'Brien
1981–1989	George L. Argyros (Ch. of Bd./CEO)
1984–1989	Charles G. Armstrong
1990	Jeff Smulyan (Ch. of Bd.)

St. Louis (to Baltimore)

1902	Ralph T. Orthwein
1903–1915	Robert L. Hedges
1916–1933	Philip D. Ball
1934–1936	Louis B. Von Weise
1937–1945	Donald L. Barnes
1946–1948	Richard C. Muckerman
1949–1951	William O. DeWitt
1951–1953	William L. Veeck, Jr.

Texas

1972–1974	Robert E. Short
1974	Robert W. Brown, M.D.
1975–1980	Bradford G. Corbett
1980–1987	Eddie Chiles (Owner/Ch. of Bd./CEO)
1984–1990	Michael H. Stone

Toronto

1977–1981	Peter Bavasi
1977–1988	R. Howard Webster (Ch. of Bd.)
1989–1990	Paul Beeston

Washington (to Minnesota)

1901–1903	Frederick Postal
1904	Thomas J. Loftus
1904	Harry B. Lambert
1905–1912	Thomas C. Noyes
1920–1955	Clark C. Griffith
1956–1960	Calvin R. Griffith

Washington

1961–1962	Elwood R. Quesada
1963–1967	James M. Johnston (Ch. of Bd.)
1968	James H. Lemon (Ch. of Bd.)
1969–1971	Robert E. Short

Federal League

League Presidents

1914–1915	James A. Gilmore

Club Presidents

Baltimore

1914–1915	Carrol W. Rasin

Brooklyn

1914–1915	Robert B. Ward

Buffalo

1914	Walter F. Mullen
	William E. Robertson
1915	William E. Robertson

Chicago

1914–1915	Charles A. Weeghman

Indianapolis

1914	J. E. Krause

Kansas City

1914	C. C. Madison
1915	Charles Baird
	Conrad H. Mann

Newark

1915	P. T. Powers
	Harry Sinclair

Pittsburgh

1914	John R. Barbour
1915	Edward W. Gwinner

St. Louis

1914	E. A. Steininger
1915	Lloyd H. Rickart

Home-Road Statistics

Home–Road Statistics

This section consists of two parts, each illustrating the powerful effects a ballpark can have on batting and pitching performance. (Parks affect fielding and baserunning as well, but to a far lesser degree.) The first component is a summary of the won-lost records and run-scoring characteristics of every park for all years of the four most significant major leagues—the American and National leagues and the American and National associations. The second is a breakdown of the home-road records for all teams in all leagues since 1871; detailed here are the won-lost records, runs scored and allowed; home runs hit and allowed; and a variety of hitting and pitching factors that are helpful for evaluation of a team and, by extension, its players.

What is the definition of success at home and on the road? Every team is expected to win more games at home than it does on the road, to the extent that if it only breaks even on the road it is thought to have a shot at the pennant. No matter whether its home park favors hitters or pitchers, a home team should be able to take advantage of the park's peculiarities better than the visiting team can. The Houston Astros may score fewer (and the Boston Red Sox more) runs at home than they do on the road, but their *differential* between runs scored and runs allowed will be greater than their run differential on the road. Greater run differential means more wins.

Almost anybody, it seems, can play .500 ball at home (in the NL of 1983, for example, only one team had a losing record on its own turf). This is somewhat deceptive, for while .500 is the average of all games played, and a team that goes 81–81 is thus defined as average, .500 is not the average at home nor, for that matter, away. The table below, which gives the home park won-lost records of all major leagues since 1900, shows the home average to be .543. The inverse, .457, is the average road record in this century.

If the average home winning percentage is .543, then an average team (81–81) should be expected to go 44–37 at home and 37–44 on the road. Until 1987, only four teams with road records that were below average—that is, 37–44—ever won the pennant, and none went on to win the World Series. Then the Minnesota Twins took the American League flag with a regular-season road mark of 29–52, by far the worst ever for a pennant or division winner, and then proceeded to lose all three World Series road games while winning all four at home. We are not likely to see such a performance again.

Just as runs scored and runs allowed may predict won-lost records, as discussed in the Introduction to the Annual Record, so we can move backward from won-lost records (the actual home-park norm of 44–37, which is between 5 and 10 percent better than the theoretical norm of 41–40) to examine runs scored and runs allowed. Runs (and home runs) per inning at home are indeed accumulated at a rate per inning about 10 percent higher than on the road, but the game and season totals presented in this section fall short of that mark. The reason: since the number of innings played at home is about 5 percent lower than on the road (leading home teams do not bat in the bottom half of final innings), total runs and homers are in actuality only about 5 percent higher.

Home Park Won-Lost Records

National League

Years	W	L	Pct.
1900–10 ('01 AL)	3489	2995	.538
1911–20	3189	2775	.537
1921–30	3360	2770	.548
1931–40	3353	2760	.549
1941–50	3319	2823	.540
1951–60 ('61 NL)	3681	3098	.543
1961–68 ('62 NL)	3075	2591	.543
1969–76	4088	3638	.529
1977–90	7200	6058	.543
	40,902	34,658	.541

American League

Years	W	L	Pct.
1900–10 ('01 AL)	3345	2530	.569
1911–20	3201	2754	.537
1921–30	3344	2787	.545
1931–40	3349	2753	.549
1941–50	3383	2754	.551
1951–60 ('61 NL)	3291	2863	.535
1961–68 ('62 NL)	3462	3003	.535
1969–76	4142	3568	.537
1977–90	8434	7061	.544
	43,146	36,102	.544

Federal League

Years	W	L	Pct.
1914–15	660	560	.541

Major League

Years	W	L	Pct.
1900–90	84,708	71,320	.543

Detailed technical information about the formulas and calculations behind Park Factor, as applied to teams as well as individuals, will be found in the Glossary. For the general reader, suffice it to say that all factors and ratings related to home-park effects are calculated by comparing runs scored and allowed per inning at home to runs scored and allowed per inning on the road. The same holds true for home runs.

Adjustments such as the Run Rating for Batters (RB) and the Home Run rating for Batters (HRB) are made to team measures of batting strength to take into account the fact that a team's batters do not have to face its own pitchers. Innings are estimated from the number of games and games won (leading home teams not batting in the final inning).

For additional useful information about home-road differences, we refer the reader to the Annual Record and the Glossary. For a key to the team and league abbreviations used throughout this section, flip to the last pages of this volume.

Other abbreviations follow.

TM	Team
LG	League
W	Wins
L	Losses
T	Ties
R	Runs
OR	Opponents' Runs
HR	Home Runs
OHR	Opponents' Home Runs

HRF   Home Run Factor (A measure of the home runs hit in a given ballpark, with 100 representing the average home park and the highest figure above that representing the best home-run park.)

HRB   Home Run Batter Rating (A measure of a team's home-run ability, taking into account the HRF and the fact that its batters do not face its own pitchers, with 100 representing the average and the highest figure above that representing the best.)

HRP   Home Run Pitcher Rating (A measure of a team's ability to prevent home runs, taking into account the HRF and the fact that its pitchers do not face its own batters, with 100 representing the average and the lowest figure beneath that representing the best.)

RF   Run Factor (A measure of the runs scored in a given ballpark compared to other ballparks, with 100 representing the average home park and the highest figure above that representing the best hitters' park.)

RB   Run Rating for Batters (A measure of a team's run-scoring ability, taking into account the HRF and the fact that its batters do not face its own pitchers, with 100 representing the average and the highest figure above that representing the best.)

RP   Run Rating for Pitchers (A measure of a team's run-prevention ability, taking into account the HRF and the fact that its pitchers do not face its own batters, with 100 representing the average and the lowest figure beneath that representing the best.)

BPF   Batting Park Factor (Equivalent to the Park Factor shown in the batters' section of the team statistics in the Annual Record; above 100 means batters benefited from playing half their games in a good hitting park.)

PPF   Pitching Park Factor (Equivalent to the Park Factor shown in the pitchers' section of the team statistics in the Annual Record; above 100 means a pitcher was hurt by playing half his games in a good hitting park.)

PARK	TM	LG	YEARS	RF	HRF	HOME W	L	T	R	OR	HR	OHR	ROAD W	L	T	R	OR	HR	OHR
AMERICAN LEAGUE																			
Oriole Park	BAL	A	1901–1902	115	125	72	56	2	821	736	28	29	46	97	3	654	862	29	22
Memorial Stadium	BAL	A	1954–1990	93	90	1654	1262	9	11933	10919	2410	2182	1481	1455	0	12658	12225	2714	2400
Huntington Avenue Grounds	BOS	A	1901–1911	102	174	464	357	10	3494	3075	220	173	386	424	14	3229	3201	105	120
Fenway Park (I)	BOS	A	1912–1933	96	52	834	821	15	6818	7274	180	359	679	983	16	6743	8007	476	557
Fenway Park (II)	BOS	A	1934–1990	114	112	2640	1823	16	23498	20658	4031	3565	2081	2386	12	19371	19613	3492	3291
Chavez Ravine	CAL	A	1965–1965	92	65	46	34	0	265	254	36	35	29	53	0	262	315	56	56
Anaheim Stadium	CAL	A	1966–1990	92	98	1028	970	0	7912	7928	1481	1591	918	1071	2	8305	8746	1524	1589
South Side Park (II)	CHI	A	1901–1909	89	34	433	235	21	2811	1987	33	32	311	340	13	2598	2659	71	115
Comiskey/White Sox Park	CHI	A	1910–1990	97	86	3346	2917	32	26768	26375	2811	3464	2871	3416	34	26920	27823	3351	3992
League Park (I)	CLE	A	1901–1909	96	65	385	281	13	2846	2379	66	60	313	351	8	2614	2763	106	85
League Park (II)	CLE	A	1910–1931	107	67	906	761	15	8158	7759	287	295	781	884	19	7368	7574	416	451
League/Municipal shared	CLE	A	1932–1946	95	73	667	495	7	5485	4939	558	418	532	598	12	5300	5495	710	592
League Park (II)				110	96	408	280	2	3706	3224	443	312							
Municipal Stadium				77	40	259	215	5	1779	1715	115	106							
Municipal/Cleveland Stadium	CLE	A	1947–1990	99	112	1858	1609	7	14882	14725	3101	2999	1619	1848	9	14932	15139	2772	2694
Bennett Park	DET	A	1901–1911	107	97	483	327	15	3727	3284	105	93	375	438	13	3199	3364	99	106
Navin Field	DET	A	1912–1937	102	93	1089	891	9	10250	9715	631	727	939	1031	22	9832	9783	751	709
Briggs/Tiger Stadium	DET	A	1938–1990	105	128	2336	1842	16	19403	18119	4053	3913	1990	2167	18	17917	17739	3184	3038
Municipal Stadium (I)	KC	A	1955–1967	106	108	452	575	2	4267	5067	767	1086	377	649	5	3837	4917	713	995
Municipal Stadium (II)	KC	A	1969–1972	100	65	159	159	1	1211	1227	137	175	136	185	0	1169	1277	216	268
Royals Stadium	KC	A	1973–1990	103	75	843	581	1	6680	5846	885	880	683	748	0	6097	6193	1176	1191
Wrigley Field	LA	A	1961–1961	127	199	46	36	0	447	421	122	126	24	55	1	297	363	67	54
Chavez Ravine	LA	A	1962–1964	86	52	124	119	0	851	900	106	125	114	128	0	1008	1017	228	213
Lloyd Street Grounds	MIL	A	1901–1901	92	94	32	37	1	342	373	15	14	16	52	1	299	455	11	19
County Stadium	MIL	A	1970–1990	97	88	870	797	1	7165	7126	1324	1298	746	924	1	7265	7512	1477	1486
Metropolitan Stadium	MIN	A	1961–1981	108	110	910	759	5	7698	7026	1424	1443	809	853	2	6929	6680	1325	1270
Humphrey Metrodome	MIN	A	1982–1990	110	104	402	330	0	3518	3483	674	777	287	439	0	2918	3399	630	746
Hilltop Park	NY	A	1903–1912	116	161	400	344	8	3299	3270	134	122	334	415	19	2702	3082	58	104
Polo Grounds (IV)	NY	A	1913–1922	101	197	416	335	10	3312	2916	332	292	358	378	6	3055	2945	190	119
Yankee Stadium (I)	NY	A	1923–1973	91	103	2553	1410	16	19607	14741	3654	2408	2168	1790	26	20696	17497	3532	2427
Shea Stadium	NY	A	1974–1975	92	92	90	69	0	638	571	92	106	82	81	0	714	640	119	102
Yankee Stadium (II)	NY	A	1976–1990	95	97	709	472	0	5450	4759	1124	954	598	589	0	5555	5269	1173	993
Oakland Coliseum	OAK	A	1968–1990	88	88	1038	796	1	7527	6883	1525	1397	876	953	0	8176	8166	1683	1625
Columbia Park	PHI	A	1901–1908	107	107	383	189	11	2758	2120	128	63	256	321	14	2228	2406	107	75
Shibe Park/Connie Mack Stadium	PHI	A	1909–1954	102	125	1763	1707	31	16091	16918	1809	1901	1484	2031	23	15436	17179	1458	1531
Sportsman's Park (III)	STL	A	1902–1908	93	102	275	243	12	1906	1793	59	73	215	300	10	1849	2087	57	71
Sportsman's Park (IV)	STL	A	1909–1966	108	137	1615	1796	40	15888	17694	1680	2004	1309	2126	34	13902	17169	1217	1509
Sicks Stadium	SEA	A	1969–1969	100	125	34	47	1	329	399	74	93	30	51	0	310	400	51	79
Kingdome	SEA	A	1977–1990	105	136	505	608	0	4775	5405	1063	1208	432	667	2	4296	5250	741	899
Arlington Stadium	TEX	A	1972–1990	99	95	774	733	0	6393	6524	1083	1179	643	857	4	6228	6753	1168	1212
Exhibition Stadium	TOR	A	1977–1988	107	106	480	462	0	4243	4319	798	914	414	529	2	3890	4147	810	803
Skydome	TOR	A	1989–1990	95	111	90	72	0	715	649	157	132	85	77	0	783	663	152	110
American League Park (I)	WAS	A	1901–1903	104	214	100	103	4	1015	1065	67	98	65	139	5	811	1187	30	47
American League Park (II)	WAS	A	1904–1910	92	45	224	297	16	1709	2048	31	31	157	380	10	1671	2418	65	72
Griffith Stadium (I)	WAS	A	1911–1955	93	39	1840	1601	38	15190	14988	528	784	1526	1886	24	15564	16609	1411	1870
Griffith Stadium (II)	WAS	A	1956–1961	101	99	192	272	1	1858	2361	364	449	180	287	2	1859	2291	409	411
R.F.K. Stadium	WAS	A	1962–1971	96	96	363	441	0	2906	3356	616	715	316	491	1	2928	3580	652	735
NATIONAL LEAGUE																			
Atlanta/Fulton County Stadium	ATL	N	1966–1990	113	139	984	996	4	8689	9153	1891	1893	854	1141	3	7503	8379	1452	1275
Union Park	BAL	N	1892–1899	109	46	378	168	15	4106	2775	72	54	266	279	11	3392	3254	114	158
South End Grounds (I)	BOS	N	1876–1893	103	101	623	327	16	6232	4289	296	200	479	467	16	5099	5194	230	265
South End Grounds (II)	BOS	N	1894–1914	110	200	807	718	28	7847	7453	517	535	610	917	27	6382	7477	209	314
Braves Field	BOS	N	1915–1952	89	67	1411	1430	23	10995	11822	893	1001	1188	1739	27	12211	14098	1281	1633
Washington Park (II)	BRO	N	1890–1890	98	80	58	16	0	547	303	27	9	28	27	0	337	318	16	18
Eastern Park	BRO	N	1891–1897	89	88	293	182	11	3026	2567	117	117	188	281	6	2831	3282	114	145
Washington Park (III)	BRO	N	1898–1912	96	82	554	556	17	4460	4647	168	155	436	662	20	4314	5092	184	206
Ebbets Field	BRO	N	1913–1957	102	110	1974	1452	34	16255	14838	1960	1931	1683	1750	24	15474	15118	1750	1786
Riverside Park	BUF	N	1879–1883	104	35	123	87	3	1278	1068	12	12	89	125	2	997	1285	31	38
Olympic Park (I)	BUF	N	1884–1885	112	95	56	56	3	674	717	36	33	46	65	0	521	668	26	44
23rd Street Grounds	CHI	N	1876–1877	125	69	42	18	0	558	299	3	5	36	29	1	432	333	5	8
Lake Front Park (I)	CHI	N	1878–1882	109	78	150	56	2	1443	875	21	16	104	81	5	1056	916	16	28
Lake Front Park (II)	CHI	N	1882–1884	121	480	75	30	0	908	566	142	72	46	59	0	605	621	13	32
West Side Park (I)	CHI	N	1885–1890	121	300	267	123	6	2934	1994	318	230	209	162	10	2069	1916	92	86
South Side Park (I)	CHI	N	1891–1893	104	109	118	87	3	1297	1092	68	54	90	113	1	1000	1247	50	60
West Side Park (II)	CHI	N	1894–1915	101	90	1008	635	28	8152	6881	334	246	816	750	35	7402	6967	360	263
Wrigley Field	CHI	N	1916–1990	106	116	3142	2711	30	26610	26001	4305	4148	2594	3208	32	23949	25227	3636	3575
Avenue Grounds	CIN	N	1876–1879	86	147	64	65	2	681	766	18	11	40	93	1	666	1043	5	15
Bank Street Grounds	CIN	N	1880–1880	103	341	14	25	1	163	216	5	8	7	34	2	131	256	2	2
League Park (I)	CIN	N	1890–1893	99	125	158	123	5	1630	1378	86	84	122	144	6	1294	1590	54	75
League Park (II)	CIN	N	1894–1901	105	61	349	217	12	3532	3113	100	108	214	319	14	2778	3224	142	182
Palace of the Fans	CIN	N	1902–1911	108	58	410	355	14	3436	3108	84	62	326	412	14	2848	2993	121	122
Redland/Crosley Field	CIN	N	1912–1969	99	86	2441	2043	26	19346	18722	2315	2155	1961	2484	26	18426	19751	2475	2654
Riverfront Stadium	CIN	N	1970–1990	103	107	948	718	2	7438	6819	1391	1337	877	793	1	7211	6775	1345	1231
Kennard Street Park	CLE	N	1879–1884	94	39	132	139	3	1226	1310	17	23	110	160	5	1209	1471	45	58
National League Park	CLE	N	1889–1890	95	54	63	72	3	710	696	21	20	42	88	4	570	855	25	48
League Park (I)	CLE	N	1891–1899	107	38	361	198	7	3822	2958	56	68	272	406	17	3566	4263	164	234
Recreation Park	DET	N	1881–1888	100	108	248	179	8	2602	2146	153	95	178	258	9	2245	2621	111	124
Hartford Ball Club Grounds	HAR	N	1876–1876	106	0	23	9	8	220	107	0	0	24	12	1	209	154	2	2
Union Grounds (Brooklyn)	HAR	N	1877–1877	71	107	19	8	2	167	92	2	1	12	19	0	174	219	2	2
Colt Stadium	HOU	N	1962–1964	86	64	117	125	2	750	898	98	119	79	163	0	801	1087	139	194
Astrodome	HOU	N	1965–1990	89	61	1164	911	0	7981	7509	945	994	882	1194	2	8321	9109	1513	1662
South Street Park	IND	N	1878–1878	68	62	10	17	1	106	115	1	1	14	19	2	187	213	2	2
Athletic Park (I)	IND	N	1887–1887	99	98	24	39	1	349	456	19	28	13	50	0	278	507	14	32
Athletic Park (II)	IND	N	1888–1889	111	275	63	71	1	823	780	77	94	46	89	1	595	842	19	43
Association Park	KC	N	1886–1886	124	40	19	42	1	301	456	9	4	11	49	4	193	420	10	23
Memorial Coliseum	LA	N	1958–1961	113	146	172	137	0	1474	1430	346	397	158	151	0	1296	1291	257	254
Chavez Ravine/Dodger Stadium	LA	N	1962–1990	88	86	1346	974	0	8949	7714	1522	1407	1182	1136	6	9858	9120	1817	1600
Louisville Baseball Park	LOU	N	1876–1877	133	675	36	25	2	368	326	13	6	29	36	2	251	307	2	1

PARK	TM	LG	YEARS	RF	HRF	HOME W	L	T	R	OR	HR	OHR	ROAD W	L	T	R	OR	HR	OHR
Eclipse Park (I)	LOU	N	1892–1892	82	35	37	31	2	309	286	7	3	26	58	0	340	518	11	23
Eclipse Park (II)	LOU	N	1893–1899	93	123	202	233	12	2422	2727	130	136	154	361	4	2604	3770	114	134
Milwaukee Base-ball Grounds	MIL	N	1878–1878	126	35	7	18	0	127	177	1	0	8	27	1	129	209	1	3
County Stadium	MIL	N	1953–1965	87	82	602	414	7	4408	3694	998	776	544	476	1	4977	4424	1232	951
Jarry Park	MON	N	1969–1976	106	119	285	356	0	2519	2927	461	519	269	378	1	2347	2792	382	442
Olympic Stadium	MON	N	1977–1990	98	86	611	495	0	4554	4201	713	764	531	572	2	4482	4461	884	838
Union Grounds (Brooklyn)	NY	N	1876–1876	78	646	13	20	0	143	207	2	7	8	15	1	117	205	0	1
Polo Grounds (I)	NY	N	1883–1888	92	71	234	112	12	2111	1418	87	46	186	161	12	1973	1905	100	89
Polo Grounds (II)	NY	N	1889–1890	98	54	84	42	3	874	583	26	17	62	69	6	769	820	51	35
Polo Grounds (III)	NY	N	1891–1910	97	134	876	564	38	7662	6329	377	280	686	736	27	7029	7160	227	255
Polo Grounds (IV)	NY	N	1911–1957	97	170	2107	1465	24	16910	14434	3146	2524	1832	1749	29	16953	15529	1763	1603
Polo Grounds (IV)	NY	N	1962–1963	110	162	56	105	0	611	891	154	213	35	126	1	507	831	81	141
Shea Stadium	NY	N	1964–1990	94	99	1103	1049	5	8143	8110	1445	1550	970	1183	2	8407	8902	1470	1545
Jefferson Street Grounds	PHI	N	1876–1876	114	55	10	24	1	259	309	4	0	4	21	0	119	225	3	2
Recreation Park	PHI	N	1883–1886	95	32	102	117	5	1115	1286	21	21	81	134	3	1013	1435	42	84
Philadelphia Baseball Grounds	PHI	N	1887–1894	102	96	353	200	6	3889	2735	185	117	230	276	13	2871	3201	136	157
Baker Bowl	PHI	N	1895–1937	114	159	1607	1577	25	16007	16788	1619	1392	1288	1913	35	13361	15589	903	1000
Shibe Park/Connie Mack Stadium	PHI	N	1938–1970	96	89	1211	1350	13	10001	11185	1552	1731	1062	1516	7	10096	11829	1702	1971
Veteran's Stadium	PHI	N	1971–1990	105	110	882	708	3	7108	6650	1333	1191	717	870	1	6293	6737	1156	1134
Recreation Park	PIT	N	1887–1890	79	14	122	117	7	1229	1138	15	12	83	204	3	1249	2230	81	144
Exposition Park	PIT	N	1891–1908	99	65	813	502	9	7058	5714	226	103	641	604	32	6376	6196	246	244
Forbes Field	PIT	N	1909–1969	102	69	2593	2113	35	21368	20076	1847	1929	2162	2508	38	20019	20318	2534	2924
Three Rivers Stadium	PIT	N	1970–1990	100	94	941	724	1	7286	6492	1193	1138	802	863	3	7036	6822	1302	1192
Messer Street Grounds	PRO	N	1878–1885	91	61	244	115	4	2033	1363	44	28	194	163	5	2004	1765	54	66
Grand Avenue Park	STL	N	1876–1877	77	65	44	16	0	327	182	1	2	29	35	0	344	365	2	3
Union Park	STL	N	1885–1886	87	58	50	67	4	503	575	19	14	29	84	3	435	731	19	35
Sportsman's Park (I)	STL	N	1892–1892	92	241	37	36	2	379	380	32	32	19	58	3	324	542	13	15
Robison Field	STL	N	1893–1919	97	110	885	1063	39	8222	9495	385	424	691	1268	25	7718	10290	275	451
Sportsman's Park (IV)	STL	N	1920–1965	106	104	2133	1429	28	18069	15545	2306	2266	1810	1730	24	16384	15239	2191	2221
Busch Stadium	STL	N	1966–1990	101	80	1073	921	5	8227	7888	917	1132	990	997	1	8120	7854	1156	1400
Jack Murphy Stadium	SD	N	1969–1990	90	92	846	908	1	6396	6963	1051	1307	710	1036	1	6694	7948	1136	1388
Seals Stadium	SF	N	1958–1959	94	97	86	68	0	702	625	165	151	77	77	0	730	686	172	154
Candlestick Park	SF	N	1960–1990	97	97	1390	1083	0	10512	9690	2094	1795	1164	1311	5	10463	10542	2133	1880
Newell Park	SYR	N	1879–1879	80	53	11	22	1	115	200	1	2	11	26	0	160	257	4	2
Putnam Grounds	TRO	N	1879–1879	94	96	12	27	2	191	263	3	6	7	29	0	130	281	1	7
Haymakers' Grounds	TRO	N	1880–1881	113	479	44	39	1	426	453	9	15	36	48	0	365	413	1	4
Troy Ball Clubs Grounds	TRO	N	1882–1882	93	57	22	20	0	238	217	7	2	13	28	2	192	305	5	11
Swampdoodle Grounds	WAS	N	1886–1889	90	91	96	141	3	1136	1362	71	66	67	196	1	1023	1865	54	102
Boundary Field	WAS	N	1892–1899	99	126	264	270	11	3413	3347	222	139	146	427	7	2805	4359	116	184
Worcester Driving Park Grounds	WOR	N	1880–1882	118	151	55	69	2	703	777	21	25	35	90	1	498	737	10	20

AMERICAN ASSOCIATION

PARK	TM	LG	YEARS	RF	HRF	HOME W	L	T	R	OR	HR	OHR	ROAD W	L	T	R	OR	HR	OHR
Newington Park	BAL	A	1882–1882	94	98	9	25	1	138	225	2	7	10	29	0	134	287	2	8
Oriole Park	BAL	A	1883–1890	98	75	240	181	18	2689	2263	72	39	159	303	7	2168	3179	62	95
Union Park	BAL	A	1891–1891	102	49	44	24	2	481	354	13	8	27	40	2	367	442	17	25
Congress Street Grounds	BOS	A	1891–1891	93	170	51	17	2	518	299	37	22	42	25	2	507	379	15	20
Washington Park (I)	BRO	A	1884–1889	99	132	241	149	10	2555	1971	91	72	169	205	9	2045	2360	52	67
Ridgewood Park	BRO	A	1890–1890	100	41	15	22	1	220	252	4	3	11	51	0	272	481	9	18
Ban Street Grounds	CIN	A	1882–1883	101	279	68	24	0	648	293	29	18	48	38	0	498	388	10	6
League Park (I)	CIN	A	1884–1889	104	185	262	144	2	2796	1947	165	93	171	190	10	2012	2148	63	65
Pendleton Park	CIN	A	1891–1891	122	215	24	20	0	290	282	21	9	19	37	1	250	354	7	11
National League Park (II)	CLE	A	1887–1888	101	48	56	65	3	749	807	10	19	33	109	2	632	1132	16	53
Recreation Park (I)	COL	A	1883–1884	83	120	56	45	1	480	490	28	22	45	59	1	579	628	27	16
Recreation Park (II)	COL	A	1889–1891	83	56	117	84	2	1169	859	26	27	83	125	7	1148	1454	46	55
Seventh Street Park	IND	A	1884–1884	98	120	16	39	1	244	377	13	15	13	39	2	219	378	7	15
Association Park (I)	KC	A	1888–1888	124	124	23	34	4	330	392	15	10	20	55	0	249	502	4	22
Exposition Park	KC	A	1889–1889	121	55	35	35	0	523	518	8	17	20	47	2	329	512	10	34
Eclipse Park (I)	LOU	A	1882–1891	95	66	357	240	12	3709	2955	83	66	217	397	8	3054	4055	91	138
Athletic Field	MIL	A	1891–1891	140	383	11	5	0	172	82	11	5	5	10	0	56	74	2	1
Polo Grounds (I) West Diamond	NY	A	1883–1885	87	52	100	50	5	905	580	24	13	73	88	1	854	936	25	50
St. George Cricket Grounds	NY	A	1886–1887	89	72	55	67	5	658	750	20	19	42	104	2	715	1108	19	43
Oakdale Park	PHI	A	1882–1882	127	325	21	18	0	236	220	3	11	20	16	0	166	166	2	2
Jefferson Street Grounds	PHI	A	1883–1890	104	84	322	189	10	3689	2780	122	70	197	275	8	2559	3164	102	109
Athletic Park	PHI	A	1891–1891	105	72	43	26	3	465	366	29	9	30	40	1	354	427	26	26
Expositon Park (I)	PIT	A	1882–1883	95	110	35	49	0	477	493	22	6	35	57	1	470	646	9	19
Recreation Park	PIT	A	1884–1886	92	26	101	86	2	990	864	6	10	65	104	3	774	1043	17	39
Allen Pasture	RIC	A	1884–1884	101	117	5	15	2	96	142	3	8	7	15	2	98	153	4	5
Culver Field (I)	ROC	A	1890–1890	82	57	40	22	1	348	252	13	4	23	41	6	361	458	18	15
Sportsman's Park (I)	STL	A	1882–1891	116	201	459	178	6	4739	2929	214	145	322	254	13	3182	2972	91	75
Star Park (II)	SYR	A	1890–1890	83	19	30	30	0	321	320	2	4	25	42	1	373	501	12	24
League Park	TOL	A	1884–1884	107	33	28	25	2	270	267	3	2	18	33	4	193	305	5	10
Speranza Park	TOL	A	1890–1890	104	143	40	27	1	422	316	17	11	28	37	1	316	374	7	12
Athletic Park	WAS	A	1884–1884	82	37	10	20	0	137	181	3	4	2	31	0	111	300	3	17
Boundary Field	WAS	A	1891–1891	98	88	28	40	4	389	519	13	18	16	51	0	300	547	6	26

NATIONAL ASSOCIATION

PARK	TM	LG	YEARS	RF	HRF	HOME W	L	T	R	OR	HR	OHR	ROAD W	L	T	R	OR	HR	OHR
Jefferson Street Grounds	ATH	N	1871–1875	109	102	104	28	5	1516	834	23	4	61	58	3	1013	930	10	14
Capitoline Grounds	ATL	N	1872–1872	147	205	6	12	0	153	265	0	4	3	16	0	84	208	0	2
Union Grounds	ATL	N	1873–1875	78	93	30	53	2	464	641	8	14	11	59	0	335	795	1	18
Newington Park	BAL	N	1872–1874	102	285	46	26	3	799	544	22	5	32	53	2	689	846	5	6
South End Grounds (I)	BOS	N	1871–1875	109	170	120	23	1	1714	806	36	4	105	37	6	1513	951	19	6
Centennial Grounds	CEN	N	1875–1875	93	0	0	7	0	25	77	0	0	2	5	0	45	61	0	0
Union Base-Ball Grounds	CHI	N	1871–1871	119	98	13	3	0	196	135	6	3	6	6	0	106	106	4	3
23rd Street Grounds	CHI	N	1874–1875	101	27	34	26	1	439	373	1	1	24	42	1	358	523	2	6
National Association Grounds	CLE	N	1871–1872	95	286	5	15	0	165	227	4	13	11	20	0	258	368	3	6
Union Grounds	ECK	N	1872–1872	77	21	3	11	0	75	167	0	1	0	15	0	77	246	0	5
Hartford Ball Club Grounds	HAR	N	1874–1875	116	25	39	28	2	533	397	1	1	31	37	2	395	417	3	5
Hamilton Field	KEK	N	1871–1871	110	0	5	4	0	78	112	0	0	2	8	0	59	131	2	5
Mansfield Club Grounds	MAN	N	1872–1872	99	23	4	7	0	130	133	1	0	1	12	0	90	215	0	5
Newington Park	MAR	N	1873–1873	85	0	0	1	0	3	24	0	0	0	5	0	23	128	0	4

PARK	TM	LG	YEARS	RF	HRF	HOME							ROAD						
						W	L	T	R	OR	HR	OHR	W	L	T	R	OR	HR	OHR
Union Grounds (Brooklyn)	MUT	N	1871–1875	94	163	93	53	3	1209	835	21	9	58	69	2	868	1027	5	11
Nationals Grounds	NAT	N	1872–1872	154	0	0	7	0	65	135	0	0	0	4	0	15	55	0	2
Hamilton Park	NH	N	1875–1875	76	87	3	25	0	89	215	1	3	4	15	0	81	182	1	2
Olympics Grounds	OLY	N	1871–1872	111	244	9	11	0	197	218	5	2	8	11	2	167	225	1	2
Jefferson Street Grounds	PHI	N	1873–1875	106	48	54	30	1	760	527	8	0	48	47	1	712	673	6	13
Waverly Fairgrounds	RES	N	1873–1873	92	0	0	8	0	34	101	0	0	2	13	0	64	198	0	8
Agricultural Society Fair Gnds	ROK	N	1871–1871	91	0	3	4	0	72	66	0	0	1	17	0	159	221	3	3
Red Stocking Base Ball Park	RS	N	1875–1875	87	0	3	11	0	50	108	0	0	1	4	0	10	53	0	0
Grand Avenue Park	STL	N	1875–1875	78	53	21	12	1	183	135	0	1	18	17	1	203	234	0	2
Haymakers' Grounds	TRO	N	1871–1872	108	123	13	15	1	326	327	7	3	15	10	0	298	226	4	3
Olympics Grounds	WAS	N	1873–1873	102	45	6	12	0	157	208	3	1	2	19	0	126	277	0	10
Olympics Grounds	WAS	N	1875–1875	108	0	2	10	0	45	158	0	0	3	13	0	62	180	0	6
Perry Park	WES	N	1875–1875	113	0	1	7	0	30	57	0	0	0	5	0	15	31	0	0

TM	HOME								ROAD								ALL															
	G	W	L	T	R	OR	HR	OHR	G	W	L	T	R	OR	HR	OHR	G	W	L	T	R	OR	HR	OHR	HRF	HRB	HRP	RF	RB	RP	BPF	PPF
1871 NATIONAL ASSOCIATION																																
ATH	15	12	3	0	184	125	3	0	13	9	4	0	192	141	6	3	28	21	7	0	376	266	9	3	32	273	70	84	139	103	93	89
BOS	18	12	5	1	230	168	2	1	13	8	5	0	171	135	1	1	31	20	10	1	401	303	3	2	109	44	32	96	126	99	98	95
CHI	16	13	3	0	196	135	6	3	12	6	6	0	106	106	4	3	28	19	9	0	302	241	10	6	98	201	134	117	90	77	111	109
CLE	13	3	10	0	119	162	4	10	16	7	9	0	130	179	3	3	29	10	19	0	249	341	7	13	235	99	147	109	80	106	103	107
KEK	9	5	4	0	78	112	0	0	10	2	8	0	59	131	2	5	19	7	12	0	137	243	2	5	0	100	100	108	68	113	102	108
MUT	19	12	7	0	178	127	0	4	14	4	10	0	124	186	1	3	33	16	17	0	302	313	1	7	76	19	118	74	102	105	88	88
OLY	13	8	5	0	163	113	5	2	19	7	10	2	147	190	1	2	32	15	15	2	310	303	6	4	270	52	46	118	87	83	110	110
ROK	7	3	4	0	72	66	0	0	18	1	17	0	159	221	3	3	25	4	21	0	231	287	3	3	0	100	100	92	96	107	95	97
TRO	17	7	9	1	200	231	4	3	12	6	6	0	151	131	2	1	29	13	15	1	351	362	6	4	153	84	54	106	116	116	101	101
1872 NATIONAL ASSOCIATION																																
ATH	28	22	4	2	371	171	3	1	19	8	10	1	168	178	1	2	47	30	14	3	539	349	4	3	92	86	74	107	113	83	105	102
ATL	18	6	12	0	153	265	0	4	19	3	16	0	84	208	0	2	37	9	28	0	237	473	0	6	187	0	109	141	58	113	117	124
BAL	29	20	7	2	321	189	12	3	29	15	12	2	296	245	2	0	58	35	19	4	617	434	14	3	476	86	11	96	115	83	100	97
BOS	21	20	1	0	249	87	2	0	27	19	7	1	272	149	5	0	48	39	8	1	521	236	7	0	56	164	0	106	109	52	108	102
CLE	7	2	5	0	46	65	0	3	15	4	11	0	128	189	0	3	22	6	16	0	174	254	0	6	190	0	208	75	95	133	86	89
ECK	14	3	11	0	75	167	0	1	15	0	15	0	77	246	0	5	29	3	26	0	152	413	0	6	22	0	298	78	68	163	85	93
MAN	11	4	7	0	130	133	1	0	13	1	12	0	90	215	0	5	24	5	19	0	220	348	1	5	25	214	209	99	108	156	94	99
MUT	29	20	8	1	263	144	2	0	27	14	12	1	260	218	2	2	56	34	20	2	523	362	4	2	50	103	37	82	108	76	94	91
NAT	7	0	7	0	65	135	0	0	4	0	4	0	15	55	0	2	11	0	11	0	80	190	0	2	0	100	100	147	57	142	117	127
OLY	7	1	6	0	34	105	0	0	2	1	1	0	20	35	0	0	9	2	7	0	54	140	0	0	0	100	100	73	98	203	79	88
TRO	12	6	6	0	126	96	3	0	13	9	4	0	147	95	2	2	25	15	10	0	273	191	5	2	83	233	90	100	116	84	102	99
1873 NATIONAL ASSOCIATION																																
ATH	27	21	6	0	298	165	3	0	25	7	17	1	176	238	1	3	52	28	23	1	474	403	4	3	72	71	45	104	97	86	103	102
ATL	29	14	14	1	215	228	6	4	26	3	23	0	151	321	0	3	55	17	37	1	366	549	6	7	241	33	70	84	83	117	91	95
BAL	26	19	6	1	363	178	9	1	31	15	16	0	281	273	3	3	57	34	22	1	644	451	12	4	181	111	51	116	116	84	109	105
BOS	32	24	8	0	444	238	11	0	28	19	8	1	295	222	2	3	60	43	16	1	739	460	13	5	203	94	59	116	123	83	110	104
MAR	1	0	1	0	3	24	0	0	5	0	5	0	23	128	0	4	6	0	6	0	26	152	0	4	0	100	100	86	54	278	77	99
MUT	31	22	9	0	286	170	6	1	22	7	15	0	138	215	0	4	53	29	24	0	424	385	6	5	121	62	81	93	88	86	99	98
PHI	27	22	5	0	283	185	3	0	26	14	12	0	243	211	3	3	53	36	17	0	526	396	6	3	52	120	45	101	107	84	103	100
RES	8	0	8	0	34	101	0	0	15	2	13	0	64	198	0	8	23	2	21	0	98	299	0	8	0	100	100	93	51	139	92	103
WAS	18	6	12	0	157	208	3	1	21	2	19	0	126	277	0	10	39	8	31	0	283	485	3	11	48	162	242	102	84	134	97	103
1874 NATIONAL ASSOCIATION																																
ATH	29	21	8	0	275	183	6	3	26	12	14	0	166	161	0	2	55	33	22	0	441	344	6	5	294	37	66	123	92	76	114	111
ATL	29	15	13	1	170	164	0	5	27	7	20	0	131	285	1	11	56	22	33	1	301	449	1	16	42	27	392	76	85	115	88	92
BAL	20	7	13	0	115	177	1	0	27	2	25	0	112	328	0	3	47	9	38	0	227	505	1	4	89	30	83	88	75	142	89	98
BOS	36	27	9	0	411	194	11	1	35	25	9	1	324	221	7	0	71	52	18	1	735	415	18	1	157	197	11	109	128	79	107	100
CHI	28	18	10	0	228	174	1	1	31	10	21	0	190	306	2	6	59	28	31	0	418	480	3	7	30	106	164	91	102	111	94	96
HAR	30	13	17	0	244	242	1	1	23	3	20	0	127	229	1	1	53	16	37	0	371	471	2	2	77	43	43	102	93	118	98	102
MUT	35	27	8	0	307	173	6	3	30	15	15	0	193	204	2	0	65	42	23	0	500	377	8	3	287	69	16	105	96	77	105	103
PHI	25	16	9	0	246	166	1	0	33	13	20	0	230	262	2	4	58	29	29	0	476	428	3	4	24	114	62	109	107	95	105	103
1875 NATIONAL ASSOCIATION																																
ATH	38	28	7	3	388	190	8	0	39	25	13	1	311	212	2	4	77	53	20	4	699	402	10	4	136	169	92	115	136	83	108	104
ATL	27	1	26	0	79	249	2	5	17	1	16	0	53	189	0	4	44	2	42	0	132	438	2	9	104	69	331	82	57	174	87	95
BOS	37	37	0	0	380	119	10	0	45	34	8	3	451	224	4	2	82	71	8	3	831	343	14	2	195	183	42	95	166	72	100	92
CEN	7	0	7	0	25	77	0	0	7	2	5	0	45	61	0	0	14	2	12	0	70	138	0	0	0	100	100	93	88	165	92	98
CHI	33	16	16	1	211	199	0	0	36	14	21	1	168	217	0	0	69	30	37	2	379	416	0	0	0	100	100	114	83	91	107	108
HAR	39	26	11	2	289	155	0	0	47	28	17	2	268	188	2	4	86	54	28	4	557	343	2	4	0	100	100	118	95	60	112	109
MUT	35	12	21	2	175	221	7	1	36	18	17	1	153	204	0	2	71	30	38	3	328	425	7	3	330	48	58	112	71	90	106	108
NH	28	3	25	0	89	215	1	3	19	4	15	0	81	182	1	2	47	7	40	0	170	397	2	5	88	81	183	77	71	154	86	92
PHI	33	16	16	1	231	176	4	0	37	21	15	1	239	200	1	6	70	37	31	2	470	376	5	6	66	178	138	104	106	86	103	101
RS	14	3	11	0	50	108	0	0	5	1	4	0	10	53	0	0	19	4	15	0	60	161	0	0	0	100	100	88	51	151	90	98
STL	34	21	12	1	183	135	0	0	36	18	17	1	203	234	0	3	70	39	29	2	386	369	0	3	55	0	80	79	100	93	91	90
WES	8	1	7	0	30	57	0	0	5	0	5	0	15	31	0	0	13	1	12	0	45	88	0	0	0	100	100	111	52	99	105	110
WAS	12	2	10	0	45	158	0	0	16	3	13	0	62	180	0	6	28	5	23	0	107	338	0	6	0	100	100	107	65	187	96	106
1882 AMERICAN ASSOCIATION																																
BAL	35	9	25	1	138	225	2	7	39	10	29	0	134	287	2	8	74	19	54	1	272	512	4	15	98	56	168	95	77	129	92	102
CIN	42	31	11	0	270	130	0	5	38	24	14	0	219	138	5	2	80	55	25	0	489	268	5	7	70	55	90	103	108	65	109	100
LOU	39	26	13	0	215	129	0	0	41	16	25	0	230	229	9	6	80	42	38	0	445	358	9	6	0	100	100	82	115	94	94	90
PHI	39	21	18	0	236	220	3	11	36	20	16	0	166	166	2	2	75	41	34	0	402	386	5	13	236	43	75	122	92	89	112	111
PIT	35	17	18	0	185	172	12	3	44	22	21	1	239	241	6	1	79	39	39	1	424	413	18	4	210	126	32	95	106	103	97	97
STL	44	24	20	0	253	262	7	2	36	13	23	0	150	236	4	5	80	37	43	0	403	498	11	7	84	131	91	107	95	116	100	104
1883 AMERICAN ASSOCIATION																																
BAL	49	18	31	0	300	395	4	6	47	10	37	0	173	342	1	6	96	28	68	0	473	737	5	12	128	28	70	122	79	119	107	113
CIN	50	37	13	0	378	163	29	13	48	24	24	0	279	250	5	4	98	61	37	0	657	413	34	17	315	103	65	100	113	76	103	98
COL	47	18	29	0	198	283	5	8	50	14	36	0	276	376	10	8	97	32	65	0	474	659	15	16	78	118	131	79	98	130	87	91
LOU	48	29	19	0	282	229	4	0	50	23	26	1	282	334	10	7	98	52	45	1	564	563	14	7	27	154	47	88	108	106	94	94
NY	48	30	17	0	273	189	3	4	49	24	25	0	225	216	3	8	97	54	42	1	498	405	6	12	68	51	89	107	83	70	108	105
PHI	50	37	13	0	402	258	9	8	48	29	19	0	318	289	11	14	98	66	32	0	720	547	20	22	69	187	196	106	125	99	103	99
PIT	49	18	31	0	292	321	10	3	49	13	36	0	231	405	3	18	98	31	67	0	523	726	13	21	64	141	162	95	100	132	94	98
STL	49	35	14	0	298	197	5	3	49	30	19	0	251	211	2	4	98	65	33	0	549	408	7	7	130	38	41	108	90	70	108	105
1884 AMERICAN ASSOCIATION																																
BAL	57	42	13	2	371	224	21	8	51	21	30	0	264	292	11	8	108	63	43	2	635	516	32	16	134	132	74	97	113	94	99	97
BRO	52	23	26	3	263	265	9	8	57	17	38	2	213	379	7	12	109	40	64	5	476	644	16	20	97	81	98	97	87	113	98	100
CIN	57	40	16	1	439	233	31	20	55	28	25	2	315	279	5	7	112	68	41	3	754	512	36	27	335	71	68	110	121	86	106	103
COL	55	38	16	1	282	207	23	14	55	31	23	1	303	252	17	8	110	69	39	2	585	459	40	22	145	164	93	90	105	84	97	95
IND	56	16	39	1	244	377	13	15	54	13	39	0	219	378	7	15	110	29	78	3	463	700	20	30	118	92	137	98	83	131	97	101
LOU	56	41	14	1	278	145	4	2	54	27	26	1	295	280	13	7	110	68	40	2	573	425	17	9	31	121	66	74	114	83	89	87
NY	55	42	9	4	370	179	11	4	57	33	23	1	364	244	11	11	112	75	32	5	734	423	22	15	74	123	80	96	125	75	100	96
PHI	54	38	16	0	438	268	12	4	54	23	30	1	262	278	14	12	108	61	46	1	700	546	26	16	64	162	95	129	107	88	114	113
PIT	56	18	37	0	225	350	1	4	54	12	41	0	182	375	1	21	110	30	78	0	407	725	2	25	23	28	173	97	73	125	97	101
RIC	22	5	15	2	96	142	3	8	24	7	15	2	98	153	4	6	46	12	30	4	194	295	7	14	116	81	151	101	82	120	99	102
STL	54	38	15	1	383	256	6	10	56	29	25	2	275	281	5	6	110	67	40	3	658	537	11	16	147	44	61	119	104	87	110	108
TOL	55	28	25	2	270	267	3	2	55	18	33	4	193	305	5	10	110	46	58	6	463	572	8	12	35	64	73	107	77	95	104	105
WAS	30	10	20	0	137	181	3	4	33	2	31	0	111	300	3	17	63	12	51	0	248	481	6	21	39	103	226	83	88	153	88	93

1885 AMERICAN ASSOCIATION

TM	HOME								ROAD								ALL															
	G	W	L	T	R	OR	HR	OHR	G	W	L	T	R	OR	HR	OHR	G	W	L	T	R	OR	HR	OHR	HRF	HRB	HRP	RF	RB	RP	BPF	PPF
BAL	54	29	25	0	360	296	11	2	56	12	43	1	182	388	6	10	110	41	68	1	542	684	17	12	85	98	65	115	83	105	106	109
BRO	58	36	22	0	386	308	9	14	54	17	37	0	238	342	5	13	112	53	59	0	624	650	14	27	116	71	130	109	96	102	104	105
CIN	56	35	21	0	358	269	17	17	56	28	28	0	284	307	9	7	112	63	49	0	642	576	26	24	187	100	90	106	100	92	104	103
LOU	56	37	19	0	334	259	16	4	56	16	40	0	228	339	3	9	112	53	59	0	562	598	19	13	153	69	62	104	89	94	102	103
NY	52	28	24	0	262	212	10	5	56	16	40	0	265	476	11	31	108	44	64	0	527	688	21	36	41	240	267	71	111	129	84	86
PHI	57	33	23	1	449	330	18	9	56	22	34	0	315	362	12	2	113	55	57	1	764	692	30	11	170	114	40	111	118	110	103	102
PIT	57	37	20	0	342	242	3	3	54	19	35	0	206	295	2	11	111	56	55	0	548	537	5	14	47	43	83	109	83	84	106	106
STL	55	44	11	0	319	160	6	5	57	35	22	0	358	301	11	7	112	79	33	0	677	461	17	12	68	100	75	79	119	82	93	89

1886 AMERICAN ASSOCIATION

TM	G	W	L	T	R	OR	HR	OHR	G	W	L	T	R	OR	HR	OHR	G	W	L	T	R	OR	HR	OHR	HRF	HRB	HRP	RF	RB	RP	BPF	PPF
BAL	66	30	31	5	320	315	2	2	73	18	52	3	298	560	6	23	139	48	83	8	618	875	8	25	17	93	155	83	89	115	90	94
BRO	69	43	25	1	453	364	9	7	72	33	36	3	379	462	7	10	141	76	61	4	832	826	16	17	99	75	79	102	104	103	100	100
CIN	71	40	31	0	472	380	32	16	70	25	42	3	406	484	13	9	141	65	73	3	878	864	45	25	188	151	96	95	115	113	96	96
LOU	69	37	30	2	484	402	19	9	69	29	40	0	345	395	1	7	138	66	70	2	829	797	20	16	266	38	53	117	98	95	108	108
NY	65	30	33	2	336	352	10	9	72	23	49	0	290	415	8	14	137	53	82	2	626	767	18	23	95	94	114	106	78	93	104	106
PHI	71	37	32	2	434	468	13	11	68	26	40	2	337	472	8	24	139	63	72	4	771	940	21	35	74	140	197	106	97	116	100	103
PIT	76	46	29	1	423	272	2	3	64	34	28	2	386	373	14	7	140	80	57	3	809	645	16	10	22	106	94	80	112	91	92	90
STL	70	52	18	0	546	286	13	7	69	41	28	0	398	307	7	6	139	93	46	0	944	593	20	13	145	75	53	116	107	72	111	106

1887 AMERICAN ASSOCIATION

TM	G	W	L	T	R	OR	HR	OHR	G	W	L	T	R	OR	HR	OHR	G	W	L	T	R	OR	HR	OHR	HRF	HRB	HRP	RF	RB	RP	BPF	PPF
BAL	68	42	21	5	500	328	16	6	73	35	37	1	470	536	15	10	141	77	58	6	970	864	31	16	96	104	57	90	110	97	96	94
BRO	75	36	38	1	514	470	18	14	63	24	36	3	398	448	7	13	138	60	74	4	912	918	25	27	128	73	85	98	102	103	98	99
CIN	71	45	26	0	517	386	24	16	65	36	28	1	376	360	13	12	136	81	54	1	893	746	37	28	140	110	89	112	91	79	108	106
CLE	61	22	37	2	375	481	2	7	72	17	55	0	354	619	12	27	133	39	92	2	729	1100	14	34	29	72	174	101	86	122	97	103
LOU	70	46	23	1	561	409	14	15	69	30	37	2	394	450	13	16	139	76	60	3	955	859	27	31	99	97	110	112	97	90	107	106
NY	62	25	34	3	322	398	10	10	76	19	55	2	425	693	11	29	138	44	89	5	747	1091	21	39	63	104	154	80	95	128	88	92
PHI	70	41	27	2	502	404	18	11	67	23	42	2	387	492	11	18	137	64	69	4	889	896	29	29	96	107	99	99	100	99	100	
STL	73	58	15	0	679	381	26	16	65	37	25	3	453	372	13	3	138	95	40	3	1132	753	39	19	204	90	39	115	113	80	109	105

1888 AMERICAN ASSOCIATION

TM	G	W	L	T	R	OR	HR	OHR	G	W	L	T	R	OR	HR	OHR	G	W	L	T	R	OR	HR	OHR	HRF	HRB	HRP	RF	RB	RP	BPF	PPF
BAL	56	30	26	0	285	276	7	11	81	27	54	0	361	503	12	12	137	57	80	0	646	779	19	23	107	77	94	94	96	109	96	98
BRO	76	53	20	3	451	267	18	10	67	35	32	0	307	312	7	5	143	88	52	3	758	579	25	15	183	65	43	103	97	78	105	102
CIN	79	55	24	0	467	317	24	5	58	25	30	3	277	311	8	14	137	80	54	3	744	628	32	19	98	129	93	99	102	91	101	99
CLE	63	34	28	1	374	326	8	12	72	16	54	2	278	513	4	26	135	50	82	3	652	839	12	38	78	69	166	100	97	118	97	100
KC	57	23	34	0	330	392	15	10	75	20	55	0	249	502	4	22	132	43	89	0	579	894	19	32	121	83	127	121	81	118	106	112
LOU	61	27	30	4	324	303	1	4	78	21	57	0	362	567	13	24	139	48	87	4	686	870	14	28	19	76	175	87	107	126	91	93
PHI	74	54	20	0	505	253	20	8	62	27	32	3	320	338	11	6	136	81	52	3	825	591	31	14	133	106	53	98	115	88	101	97
STL	82	60	21	1	525	284	22	13	55	32	22	1	264	215	14	6	137	92	43	2	789	499	36	19	117	138	76	113	97	68	111	106

1889 AMERICAN ASSOCIATION

TM	G	W	L	T	R	OR	HR	OHR	G	W	L	T	R	OR	HR	OHR	G	W	L	T	R	OR	HR	OHR	HRF	HRB	HRP	RF	RB	RP	BPF	PPF
BAL	67	41	23	3	436	314	10	4	72	29	42	1	355	481	10	23	139	70	65	4	791	795	20	27	49	79	77	97	95	94	100	99
BRO	70	50	18	2	488	297	28	19	70	43	26	1	510	417	19	14	140	93	44	3	998	714	47	33	137	105	77	88	123	91	96	92
CIN	74	47	26	1	543	362	37	19	67	29	37	1	354	407	15	16	141	76	63	2	897	769	52	35	152	104	80	107	99	88	105	103
COL	69	36	33	0	407	350	13	11	71	24	45	2	376	573	23	22	140	60	78	2	783	923	36	33	58	121	83	103	116	91	92	
KC	70	35	35	0	523	518	8	17	69	20	47	2	329	512	10	34	139	55	82	2	852	1030	18	51	59	68	159	118	94	113	106	109
LOU	65	18	47	0	330	473	10	18	75	9	64	2	302	617	12	25	140	27	111	2	632	1090	22	43	86	65	116	98	78	125	96	102
PHI	73	46	22	5	506	347	16	13	65	29	36	0	380	440	27	22	138	75	58	5	886	787	43	35	56	154	130	94	108	98	98	96
STL	71	51	18	2	581	317	45	28	70	39	27	4	372	367	13	11	141	90	45	6	953	684	58	39	243	86	64	119	98	75	112	109

1890 AMERICAN ASSOCIATION

TM	G	W	L	T	R	OR	HR	OHR	G	W	L	T	R	OR	HR	OHR	G	W	L	T	R	OR	HR	OHR	HRF	HRB	HRP	RF	RB	RP	BPF	PPF
BAL	22	8	11	3	117	115	1	0	16	7	8	1	65	77	1	3	38	15	19	4	182	192	2	3	20	77	48	116	77	82	109	110
BRO	38	15	22	1	220	252	4	3	62	11	51	0	272	481	9	18	100	26	73	1	492	733	13	21	44	112	132	100	95	128	97	101
COL	71	47	22	2	453	246	9	8	69	32	33	4	377	369	7	12	140	79	55	6	830	615	16	20	89	69	83	93	108	82	99	96
LOU	74	57	13	4	513	275	8	8	62	31	31	0	307	304	7	10	136	88	44	4	820	579	15	18	82	68	80	109	99	75	107	104
PHI	72	36	36	0	453	452	16	4	60	18	42	0	240	493	8	11	132	54	78	0	693	945	24	17	96	102	78	102	95	128	97	101
ROC	63	40	22	1	348	252	13	4	70	23	41	0	361	458	18	15	133	63	63	7	709	710	31	19	60	169	97	83	105	101	92	92
STL	72	45	25	2	551	396	42	31	67	33	33	1	313	341	6	7	139	78	58	3	864	737	48	38	357	78	72	131	94	84	116	114
SYR	60	30	30	0	321	320	2	4	68	25	42	1	373	501	12	24	128	55	72	1	694	821	14	28	21	103	187	84	108	123	90	92
TOL	68	40	27	1	422	316	17	11	66	28	37	1	316	374	7	12	134	68	64	2	738	690	24	23	137	83	87	104	96	91	103	102

1891 AMERICAN ASSOCIATION

TM	G	W	L	T	R	OR	HR	OHR	G	W	L	T	R	OR	HR	OHR	G	W	L	T	R	OR	HR	OHR	HRF	HRB	HRP	RF	RB	RP	BPF	PPF
BAL	70	44	24	2	481	354	13	8	69	27	40	2	367	442	17	25	139	71	64	4	848	796	30	33	52	113	109	102	103	98	101	100
BOS	70	51	17	2	518	299	37	22	69	42	25	2	507	379	15	20	139	93	42	4	1025	678	52	42	157	108	98	94	128	89	99	94
CIN	44	24	20	0	290	282	21	9	57	19	37	1	250	354	7	11	101	43	57	1	540	636	28	20	190	70	59	119	85	98	109	111
COL	63	34	29	0	309	263	4	8	75	27	47	1	395	512	16	21	138	61	76	1	704	775	20	29	41	68	104	77	99	103	89	90
LOU	71	39	32	0	388	331	7	6	68	15	51	2	309	540	10	27	139	54	83	2	697	871	17	33	36	79	112	82	97	115	90	92
MIL	21	16	5	0	172	82	11	5	15	5	10	0	56	74	2	1	36	21	15	0	228	156	13	6	291	59	29	134	82	67	120	118
PHI	72	43	26	3	465	366	29	9	71	30	40	1	354	427	26	26	143	73	66	4	819	793	55	35	74	173	109	105	95	93	100	101
STL	73	52	21	0	604	390	42	30	65	33	30	2	348	341	16	20	138	85	51	2	952	731	58	50	166	118	113	126	101	83	114	111
WAS	72	28	40	4	389	519	13	18	67	16	51	0	300	547	6	26	139	44	91	4	689	1066	19	44	89	57	119	98	89	131	95	101

1884 UNION ASSOCIATION

TM	G	W	L	T	R	OR	HR	OHR	G	W	L	T	R	OR	HR	OHR	G	W	L	T	R	OR	HR	OHR	HRF	HRB	HRP	RF	RB	RP	BPF	PPF
ALT	18	6	12	0	73	156	0	2	7	0	7	0	17	60	2	1	25	6	19	0	90	216	2	3	27	99	190	110	56	140	101	109
BAL	50	29	21	0	372	312	12	16	56	29	26	1	304	318	5	8	106	58	47	1	676	630	17	24	219	71	101	122	102	97	110	110
BOS	58	34	23	1	346	260	7	5	53	24	28	1	290	297	12	12	111	58	51	2	636	557	19	17	48	167	144	95	103	91	98	97
CHI	35	20	14	1	177	159	2	2	39	14	25	0	183	252	8	9	74	34	39	1	360	411	10	11	28	143	150	87	93	102	94	94
CIN	52	35	17	0	382	239	18	12	53	34	19	0	325	241	8	5	105	69	36	0	707	480	26	17	216	109	72	113	110	77	108	105
KC	36	11	23	2	150	205	3	6	46	5	40	1	159	414	3	8	82	16	63	3	309	619	6	14	101	51	111	78	80	140	87	91
MIL	12	8	4	0	53	35	0	1	0	0	0	0	0	0	0	0	12	8	4	0	53	35	0	1	0	100	100	0	100	100	54	54
PHI	34	13	21	0	223	249	4	1	33	8	25	0	192	296	3	6	67	21	46	0	415	545	7	7	55	102	79	93	119	151	93	95
PIT	5	1	4	0	22	29	0	1	14	6	7	1	56	42	0	0	19	7	11	1	78	71	0	1	0	100	100	139	62	62	122	122
STL	56	50	6	0	461	179	10	4	58	44	13	1	426	250	22	5	114	94	19	1	887	429	32	9	58	227	78	102	133	68	104	98
STP	0	0	0	0	0	0	0	0	9	2	6	1	24	57	0	1	9	2	6	1	24	57	0	1	0	100	100	0	100	100	54	54
WAS	65	36	27	2	382	318	4	10	49	11	38	0	192	362	0	6	114	47	65	2	574	680	4	16	164	13	71	95	90	110	97	98
WIL	7	1	6	0	16	46	1	4	11	1	10	0	19	68	1	0	18	2	16	0	35	114	2	4	501	48	37	107	34	103	103	109

1890 PLAYERS LEAGUE

TM	G	W	L	T	R	OR	HR	OHR	G	W	L	T	R	OR	HR	OHR	G	W	L	T	R	OR	HR	OHR	HRF	HRB	HRP	RF	RB	RP	BPF	PPF
BOS	70	48	21	1	602	383	42	38	60	33	27	0	386	384	12	11	130	81	48	1	988	767	54	49	241	78	71	110	102	84	107	104
BRO	66	46	19	1	564	410	20	7	67	30	37	0	398	480	14	19	133	76	56	1	962	890	34	26	85	89	66	112	99	93	106	105
BUF	65	23	42	0	425	498	7	20	69	13	54	2	367	698	13	47	134	36	96	2	792	1196	20	67	50	75	203	91	95	133	92	97
CHI	70	46	23	1	504	345	18	12	68	29	39	0	381	425	13	15	138	75	62	1	885	770	31	27	104	70	62	102	89	79	104	103

TM	HOME								ROAD								ALL														
	G	W	L	T	R	OR	HR	OHR	G	W	L	T	R	OR	HR	OHR	G	W	L	T	R	OR	HR	OHR	HRF	HRB	HRP	RF	RB	RP	BPF	PPF
CLE	62	31	30	1	416	403	10	15	69	24	45	0	433	623	17	30	131	55	75	1	849	1026	27	45	62	87	132	87	104	119	92	94
NY	66	47	19	0	628	404	35	21	66	27	38	1	389	477	31	16	132	74	57	1	1017	881	66	37	117	155	94	117	102	92	109	107
PHI	65	35	30	0	482	418	20	15	67	33	33	1	465	434	29	18	132	68	63	1	947	852	49	33	79	135	97	103	102	93	102	101
PIT	65	37	28	0	435	356	21	15	63	23	40	0	398	535	14	17	128	60	68	0	833	891	35	32	110	84	79	84	104	109	92	92

1914 FEDERAL LEAGUE

TM	HOME								ROAD								ALL														
	G	W	L	T	R	OR	HR	OHR	G	W	L	T	R	OR	HR	OHR	G	W	L	T	R	OR	HR	OHR	HRF	HRB	HRP	RF	RB	RP	BPF	PPF
BAL	83	53	26	4	350	298	25	15	77	31	44	2	295	330	7	19	160	84	70	6	645	628	32	34	136	65	78	97	99	97	99	99
BRO	80	47	32	1	358	335	27	13	77	30	45	2	304	342	15	18	157	77	77	3	662	677	42	31	114	101	80	103	102	104	101	101
BUF	79	47	29	3	345	300	21	18	76	33	42	1	275	302	17	27	155	80	71	4	620	602	38	45	87	116	132	107	93	91	104	104
CHI	75	41	34	0	248	208	30	19	82	46	33	3	373	309	22	24	157	87	67	3	621	517	52	43	115	134	115	76	105	89	91	89
IND	80	53	23	4	439	339	14	8	77	35	42	0	323	283	19	21	157	88	65	4	762	622	33	29	57	113	93	121	106	89	111	108
KC	76	38	37	1	322	306	28	21	78	29	47	2	322	377	11	16	154	67	84	3	644	683	39	37	167	76	79	93	107	112	95	96
PIT	75	37	37	1	297	307	11	10	79	27	49	3	308	391	23	29	154	64	86	4	605	698	34	39	46	132	140	91	102	114	94	96
STL	76	31	44	1	304	368	13	23	78	31	45	2	261	329	13	15	154	62	89	3	565	697	26	38	126	64	88	114	85	102	106	108

1915 FEDERAL LEAGUE

TM	HOME								ROAD								ALL														
	G	W	L	T	R	OR	HR	OHR	G	W	L	T	R	OR	HR	OHR	G	W	L	T	R	OR	HR	OHR	HRF	HRB	HRP	RF	RB	RP	BPF	PPF
BAL	75	24	51	0	299	419	29	36	79	23	56	0	251	341	7	16	154	47	107	0	550	760	36	52	235	67	104	121	87	115	107	111
BRO	74	34	40	0	315	324	20	11	79	36	42	1	332	349	16	16	153	70	82	1	647	673	36	27	103	114	88	100	112	116	98	98
BUF	77	37	40	0	290	324	21	21	76	37	38	1	284	310	19	14	153	74	78	1	574	634	40	35	122	120	105	102	98	106	100	101
CHI	78	44	32	2	310	252	21	10	77	42	34	1	330	286	29	23	155	86	66	3	640	538	50	33	62	207	140	92	110	95	97	95
KC	77	46	31	0	274	249	15	19	76	35	41	0	273	302	13	10	153	81	72	0	547	551	28	29	138	76	76	91	96	97	97	97
NEW	79	40	39	0	267	271	4	2	76	40	33	3	318	291	13	13	155	80	72	3	585	562	17	15	25	84	62	87	104	101	94	94
PIT	77	45	31	1	292	269	4	10	79	41	36	2	300	255	16	27	156	86	67	3	592	524	20	37	37	89	163	104	95	85	104	102
STL	82	43	34	5	334	280	12	15	77	44	33	0	300	247	11	7	159	87	67	5	634	527	23	22	135	60	54	105	99	84	105	102

1876 NATIONAL LEAGUE

TM	HOME								ROAD								ALL														
	G	W	L	T	R	OR	HR	OHR	G	W	L	T	R	OR	HR	OHR	G	W	L	T	R	OR	HR	OHR	HRF	HRB	HRP	RF	RB	RP	BPF	PPF
BOS	36	19	17	0	253	200	5	3	34	20	14	0	218	250	4	4	70	39	31	0	471	450	9	7	96	182	148	93	121	116	95	94
CHI	31	25	6	0	352	143	3	1	35	27	8	0	272	114	5	5	66	52	14	0	624	257	8	6	50	229	153	141	130	59	125	113
CIN	30	6	24	0	119	243	2	2	35	3	32	0	119	336	2	7	65	9	56	0	238	579	4	9	53	135	214	90	70	150	89	100
HAR	32	23	9	0	220	107	0	0	37	24	12	1	209	154	2	2	69	47	21	1	429	261	2	2	0	100	100	106	98	62	108	103
LOU	33	15	16	2	149	154	6	3	36	15	20	1	131	190	0	0	69	30	36	3	280	344	6	3	0	100	102	66	80	104	106	
NY	33	13	20	0	143	207	2	7	24	8	15	1	117	205	0	1	57	21	35	1	260	412	2	8	384	10	63	80	90	135	87	93
PHI	35	10	24	1	259	309	4	0	25	4	21	0	119	225	3	2	60	14	45	1	378	534	7	2	59	188	56	112	103	145	99	105
STL	30	24	6	0	150	58	1	1	34	21	13	0	236	171	1	2	64	45	19	0	386	229	2	3	80	43	59	62	118	69	88	82

1877 NATIONAL LEAGUE

TM	HOME								ROAD								ALL														
	G	W	L	T	R	OR	HR	OHR	G	W	L	T	R	OR	HR	OHR	G	W	L	T	R	OR	HR	OHR	HRF	HRB	HRP	RF	RB	RP	BPF	PPF
BOS	32	27	5	0	260	110	0	1	29	15	13	1	159	153	4	4	61	42	18	1	419	263	4	5	14	119	271	108	110	77	108	101
CHI	29	17	12	0	206	156	0	4	31	9	21	1	160	219	0	3	60	26	33	1	366	375	0	7	133	0	124	101	110	111	98	99
CIN	30	12	17	1	157	201	4	1	28	3	25	0	134	284	2	3	58	15	42	1	291	485	6	4	92	168	121	81	110	163	82	90
HAR	29	19	8	2	167	92	2	1	31	12	19	0	174	219	2	1	60	31	27	2	341	311	4	2	106	87	48	74	116	100	89	87
LOU	30	21	9	0	219	172	7	3	31	14	16	1	120	117	2	1	61	35	25	1	339	289	9	4	246	122	63	154	74	66	132	130
STL	30	20	10	0	177	124	0	1	30	8	22	0	108	194	1	1	60	28	32	0	285	318	1	2	54	21	58	99	82	90	102	103

1878 NATIONAL LEAGUE

TM	HOME								ROAD								ALL														
	G	W	L	T	R	OR	HR	OHR	G	W	L	T	R	OR	HR	OHR	G	W	L	T	R	OR	HR	OHR	HRF	HRB	HRP	RF	RB	RP	BPF	PPF
BOS	30	23	7	0	171	104	1	3	30	18	12	0	127	137	1	3	60	41	19	0	298	241	2	6	102	58	145	105	89	75	108	105
CHI	35	17	18	0	226	210	2	2	26	13	12	1	145	121	1	2	61	30	30	1	371	331	3	4	99	77	103	118	108	97	108	106
CIN	34	25	8	1	190	126	4	2	27	12	15	0	143	155	1	0	61	37	23	1	333	281	5	2	294	59	15	87	111	98	95	93
IND	28	10	17	1	106	115	1	1	35	14	19	2	187	213	2	2	63	24	36	3	293	328	3	3	66	84	84	72	102	112	87	88
MIL	25	7	18	0	127	177	1	0	36	8	27	1	129	209	1	3	61	15	45	1	256	386	2	3	39	93	59	121	78	110	107	114
PRO	32	17	13	2	182	170	4	2	30	16	14	0	171	167	4	3	62	33	27	2	353	337	8	5	83	260	182	98	113	109	98	97

1879 NATIONAL LEAGUE

TM	HOME								ROAD								ALL														
	G	W	L	T	R	OR	HR	OHR	G	W	L	T	R	OR	HR	OHR	G	W	L	T	R	OR	HR	OHR	HRF	HRB	HRP	RF	RB	RP	BPF	PPF
BOS	42	29	13	0	308	165	11	2	42	25	17	0	254	183	9	7	84	54	30	0	562	348	20	9	84	312	159	109	117	78	107	101
BUF	40	23	16	1	223	204	1	0	39	23	16	0	167	161	1	3	79	46	32	1	390	365	2	3	27	58	36	124	81	77	114	113
CHI	43	29	13	1	264	191	2	0	40	17	20	3	173	219	1	5	83	46	33	4	437	410	3	5	34	83	62	108	94	90	105	104
CIN	37	21	16	0	215	196	8	6	44	22	21	1	270	268	0	5	81	43	37	1	485	464	8	11	259	46	102	92	119	114	95	94
CLE	42	15	27	0	167	236	2	1	40	12	28	0	155	225	2	3	82	27	55	0	322	461	4	4	59	67	59	99	75	103	99	103
PRO	42	34	8	0	323	143	9	4	43	25	17	1	289	212	3	5	85	59	25	1	612	355	12	9	157	118	105	98	134	83	101	94
SYR	34	11	22	1	115	200	1	2	37	11	26	0	160	257	4	2	71	22	48	1	275	457	5	4	57	83	84	83	82	128	89	95
TRO	41	12	27	2	191	263	3	6	36	7	29	0	130	281	1	7	77	19	56	2	321	544	4	13	96	64	181	95	84	134	93	100

1880 NATIONAL LEAGUE

TM	HOME								ROAD								ALL														
	G	W	L	T	R	OR	HR	OHR	G	W	L	T	R	OR	HR	OHR	G	W	L	T	R	OR	HR	OHR	HRF	HRB	HRP	RF	RB	RP	BPF	PPF
BOS	43	25	17	1	213	190	14	1	43	15	27	1	203	265	6	1	86	40	44	2	416	455	20	2	187	160	23	87	113	121	92	93
BUF	44	13	29	2	173	233	1	1	41	11	29	1	159	269	2	9	85	24	58	3	332	502	3	10	18	101	176	88	92	132	91	96
CHI	43	37	5	1	284	148	1	0	43	30	12	1	254	169	3	8	86	67	17	2	538	317	4	8	11	154	98	105	127	80	105	98
CIN	40	14	25	1	163	216	5	8	43	7	34	2	131	256	2	2	83	21	59	3	294	472	7	10	262	54	68	102	77	116	99	105
CLE	43	23	19	1	182	168	2	1	42	24	18	0	205	169	5	3	85	47	37	1	387	337	7	4	40	119	70	93	98	87	99	97
PRO	44	31	12	1	210	116	4	2	43	21	20	2	209	183	4	5	87	52	32	3	419	299	8	7	69	121	100	84	108	79	96	92
TRO	41	20	21	0	204	257	5	6	42	21	21	0	188	181	0	2	83	41	42	0	392	438	5	8	357	17	50	124	92	100	110	112
WOR	42	24	17	1	247	186	5	6	43	16	26	1	165	184	3	7	85	40	43	2	412	370	8	13	111	107	163	123	91	84	112	111

1881 NATIONAL LEAGUE

TM	HOME								ROAD								ALL														
	G	W	L	T	R	OR	HR	OHR	G	W	L	T	R	OR	HR	OHR	G	W	L	T	R	OR	HR	OHR	HRF	HRB	HRP	RF	RB	RP	BPF	PPF
BOS	41	19	22	0	151	180	2	4	42	19	23	0	197	230	3	5	83	38	45	0	348	410	5	9	79	58	100	81	90	104	91	93
BUF	41	25	16	0	241	206	2	0	42	20	22	1	199	242	10	9	83	45	38	1	440	448	12	9	12	273	105	104	103	105	101	101
CHI	42	32	10	0	309	186	7	6	42	24	18	0	241	194	5	8	84	56	28	0	550	380	12	14	102	135	154	114	118	86	108	103
CLE	42	20	22	0	190	185	3	4	43	16	26	1	201	229	4	5	85	36	48	1	391	414	7	9	81	79	99	90	94	99	96	96
DET	42	23	19	0	252	213	14	4	42	18	24	0	188	216	3	4	84	41	43	0	440	429	17	8	215	100	68	113	96	95	106	106
PRO	43	23	20	0	209	194	4	2	42	24	17	1	240	232	7	3	85	47	37	1	449	426	11	5	62	130	66	86	112	107	93	92
TRO	43	24	18	1	222	196	4	9	42	15	27	0	177	232	1	2	85	39	45	1	399	428	5	11	301	25	51	99	92	98	100	101
WOR	42	19	22	1	240	253	7	4	41	13	28	1	170	239	0	7	83	32	50	2	410	492	7	11	142	52	102	114	92	109	105	107

1882 NATIONAL LEAGUE

TM	HOME								ROAD								ALL														
	G	W	L	T	R	OR	HR	OHR	G	W	L	T	R	OR	HR	OHR	G	W	L	T	R	OR	HR	OHR	HRF	HRB	HRP	RF	RB	RP	BPF	PPF
BOS	43	27	15	1	263	191	8	7	42	18	24	0	209	220	7	3	85	45	39	1	472	411	15	10	139	77	50	103	99	88	103	102
BUF	39	26	13	0	286	184	5	7	45	19	26	0	214	278	13	9	84	45	39	0	500	462	18	16	66	131	130	109	106	99	104	103
CHI	45	35	10	0	360	140	9	8	39	20	19	0	243	213	6	5	84	55	29	0	603	353	15	13	130	80	70	97	130	83	101	95
CLE	42	21	19	2	175	170	6	7	42	21	21	0	227	240	14	15	84	42	40	2	402	410	20	22	48	188	205	76	99	100	90	92
DET	43	24	18	1	221	238	14	10	43	18	23	2	186	252	5	9	86	42	41	3	407	490	19	19	158	89	98	104	86	101	102	104
PRO	42	30	12	0	247	172	6	6	42	22	20	0	216	184	5	6	84	52	32	0	463	356	11	12	109	65	70	105	96	76	106	103
TRO	42	22	20	0	238	217	7	2	43	13	28	2	192	305	5	11	85	35	48	2	430	522	12	13	60	102	87	94	99	116	95	97
WOR	42	12	30	0	216	338	9	15	42	6	36	0	163	314	7	6	84	18	66	0	379	652	16	21	163	83	98	111	83	134	100	107

TM	HOME								ROAD								ALL															
	G	W	L	T	R	OR	HR	OHR	G	W	L	T	R	OR	HR	OHR	G	W	L	T	R	OR	HR	OHR	HRF	HRB	HRP	RF	RB	RP	BPF	PPF
1883 NATIONAL LEAGUE																																
BOS	49	41	8	0	391	190	21	3	49	22	27	0	277	267	13	8	98	63	35	0	668	457	34	11	114	200	80	107	110	80	106	102
BUF	49	36	13	0	355	241	3	4	49	16	32	1	258	335	5	8	98	52	45	1	613	576	8	12	57	64	90	101	108	102	100	99
CHI	49	36	13	0	410	254	11	6	49	23	26	0	269	287	2	15	98	59	39	0	679	541	13	21	101	88	134	118	109	91	109	106
CLE	49	31	18	0	248	203	0	4	51	24	24	3	227	240	8	3	100	55	42	3	475	443	8	7	41	45	74	101	79	74	104	104
DET	51	23	26	2	264	280	12	9	50	17	32	1	260	371	1	13	101	40	58	3	524	651	13	22	138	63	121	85	99	118	91	94
NY	49	28	19	2	292	262	20	15	49	18	31	0	238	315	4	4	98	46	50	2	530	577	24	19	307	71	62	100	94	101	100	101
PHI	50	9	40	1	224	439	0	1	49	8	41	0	222	449	3	19	99	17	81	1	446	888	3	20	5	20	212	94	86	156	90	99
PRO	49	34	15	0	330	186	10	5	49	24	25	0	304	250	11	7	98	58	40	0	634	436	21	12	86	143	88	95	111	80	101	96
1884 NATIONAL LEAGUE																																
BOS	56	40	16	0	328	181	14	4	60	33	22	5	356	288	22	26	116	73	38	5	684	469	36	30	44	125	83	88	110	77	98	93
BUF	58	37	18	3	409	311	23	20	56	27	29	0	292	314	16	26	114	64	47	3	701	625	39	46	100	99	115	113	104	95	107	105
CHI	56	39	17	0	498	312	131	66	56	23	33	0	336	334	11	17	112	62	50	0	834	646	142	83	402	121	104	118	124	101	108	104
CLE	56	22	34	0	264	348	4	6	57	13	43	1	194	368	12	29	113	35	77	1	458	716	16	35	27	66	116	107	72	107	102	108
DET	58	18	38	2	228	347	14	16	56	10	46	0	215	389	17	20	114	28	84	2	443	736	31	36	78	85	97	91	76	118	93	99
NY	58	34	22	2	378	261	8	4	58	28	28	2	315	362	15	24	116	62	50	4	693	623	23	28	34	89	81	96	111	101	98	97
PHI	57	19	37	1	281	388	1	1	56	20	36	0	268	436	13	37	113	39	73	1	549	824	14	38	4	90	137	93	96	136	92	97
PRO	57	45	11	1	329	164	4	6	57	39	17	1	336	224	17	20	114	84	28	2	665	388	21	26	31	70	90	92	104	64	102	96
1885 NATIONAL LEAGUE																																
BOS	57	21	35	1	245	283	7	5	56	25	31	0	283	306	15	21	113	46	66	1	528	589	22	26	35	166	166	89	101	111	94	95
BUF	57	19	38	0	265	406	13	13	55	19	36	0	229	354	10	18	112	38	74	0	494	760	23	31	89	119	152	108	90	130	99	105
CHI	57	43	14	0	458	269	47	27	56	44	11	1	377	200	7	10	113	87	25	1	835	469	54	37	309	108	98	123	132	79	114	106
DET	52	29	23	0	294	228	13	8	56	12	44	0	220	355	12	10	108	41	67	0	514	583	25	18	101	116	86	97	100	109	97	99
NY	55	45	10	0	362	178	7	6	57	40	17	0	329	192	9	5	112	85	27	0	691	370	16	11	99	68	48	109	114	66	109	102
PHI	55	29	26	0	277	244	7	7	56	27	28	1	236	267	13	11	111	56	54	1	513	511	20	18	63	109	101	105	90	90	104	104
PRO	54	30	24	0	203	218	3	1	56	23	33	0	239	313	3	17	110	53	57	0	442	531	6	18	23	73	87	81	89	104	91	93
STL	58	23	33	2	215	262	6	4	53	13	39	1	175	332	2	11	111	36	72	3	390	594	8	15	72	44	70	86	78	111	92	97
1886 NATIONAL LEAGUE																																
BOS	58	32	25	1	354	280	15	8	60	24	36	0	303	379	9	25	118	56	61	1	657	659	24	33	73	102	118	96	110	109	97	97
CHI	62	52	10	0	539	275	45	34	64	38	24	2	364	281	8	15	126	90	34	2	903	556	53	49	274	82	94	128	117	78	116	110
DET	60	48	12	0	441	255	37	10	66	39	24	3	388	283	16	10	126	87	36	3	829	538	53	20	180	113	52	114	115	79	110	104
KC	62	19	42	1	301	456	9	4	64	11	49	4	193	420	10	23	126	30	91	5	494	876	19	27	43	96	96	121	70	117	106	114
NY	63	47	12	4	327	195	10	4	61	28	32	1	366	363	11	19	124	75	44	5	693	558	21	23	49	96	83	73	123	98	89	85
PHI	62	45	14	3	333	215	13	12	57	26	29	2	287	283	13	17	119	71	43	5	620	498	26	29	80	97	106	91	102	83	98	96
STL	63	27	34	2	288	313	13	10	63	16	45	2	260	399	17	24	126	43	79	4	548	712	30	34	58	126	130	91	88	110	95	98
WAS	65	19	42	4	245	372	13	12	60	9	50	1	200	420	10	22	125	28	92	5	445	792	23	34	73	89	119	90	73	122	93	100
1887 NATIONAL LEAGUE																																
BOS	63	39	21	3	466	322	29	17	64	22	39	3	367	471	24	38	127	61	60	6	833	793	53	55	78	132	128	96	111	106	98	97
CHI	64	44	18	2	540	347	67	44	63	27	32	4	278	372	13	11	127	71	50	6	818	719	80	55	317	74	56	130	89	83	116	115
DET	61	43	17	1	502	306	25	20	66	36	28	2	467	405	30	32	127	79	45	3	969	711	55	52	82	129	121	102	124	94	102	97
IND	64	24	39	1	349	456	19	28	63	13	50	0	278	507	14	32	127	37	89	1	627	963	33	60	98	71	121	99	84	123	96	102
NY	63	36	26	1	439	340	21	8	66	32	29	5	378	377	27	19	129	68	55	6	817	717	48	27	69	110	62	108	99	89	105	103
PHI	64	38	23	3	438	321	25	22	64	37	25	2	453	380	22	26	128	75	48	5	891	701	47	48	99	98	99	93	117	95	98	95
PIT	66	31	34	1	336	336	6	4	59	24	35	0	285	421	14	35	125	55	69	1	621	757	20	39	20	89	109	86	88	104	93	96
WAS	63	27	32	4	329	349	29	19	63	19	44	0	271	466	18	28	126	46	76	4	600	815	47	47	102	97	98	92	83	107	95	99
1888 NATIONAL LEAGUE																																
BOS	68	36	30	2	365	315	23	16	69	34	34	1	304	305	33	20	137	70	64	3	669	620	56	36	77	148	102	112	102	95	106	105
CHI	70	43	27	0	438	336	50	44	66	34	31	1	294	323	27	19	136	77	58	1	732	659	77	63	174	144	117	116	110	102	107	106
DET	68	40	26	2	400	279	24	18	66	28	37	1	321	350	27	26	134	68	63	3	721	629	51	44	79	143	124	99	121	107	98	97
IND	66	31	35	0	328	302	27	40	70	19	50	1	270	426	7	24	136	50	85	1	598	728	34	64	195	53	106	95	103	120	95	98
NY	70	44	23	3	313	182	21	9	68	40	24	4	347	296	34	18	138	84	47	7	660	478	55	27	60	155	82	78	115	85	92	89
PHI	66	37	29	0	313	268	6	12	66	32	32	2	222	241	10	14	132	69	61	2	535	509	16	26	78	41	66	122	78	76	114	113
PIT	70	37	30	3	280	234	0	1	69	29	38	2	254	346	14	22	139	66	68	5	534	580	14	23	3	29	109	86	91	96	94	95
WAS	66	26	38	2	260	318	17	25	70	22	48	0	222	410	13	25	136	48	86	2	482	728	30	50	113	69	109	96	82	117	96	101
1889 NATIONAL LEAGUE																																
BOS	68	48	17	3	455	272	24	14	65	35	28	2	371	352	18	27	133	83	45	5	826	624	42	41	84	98	93	98	104	82	102	98
CHI	69	37	30	2	450	398	54	52	67	30	35	2	416	417	25	19	136	67	65	4	866	815	79	71	200	116	102	99	110	105	99	98
CLE	68	33	35	0	353	341	8	13	68	28	37	3	302	379	17	23	136	61	72	3	655	720	25	36	56	63	90	101	81	88	102	103
IND	69	32	36	1	495	478	50	54	66	27	39	0	325	416	12	19	135	59	75	1	820	894	62	73	250	71	90	121	95	104	109	110
NY	63	47	15	1	513	311	18	15	68	36	28	4	422	396	34	23	131	83	43	5	935	707	52	38	67	130	102	109	116	91	105	102
PHI	68	43	24	1	467	347	27	12	62	20	40	2	274	402	17	21	130	63	64	3	741	749	44	33	94	96	74	108	92	95	104	105
PIT	70	40	28	2	388	307	6	2	64	21	43	0	337	492	36	40	134	61	71	2	725	799	42	42	11	194	133	79	106	113	89	90
WAS	56	24	29	3	302	323	12	10	71	17	54	0	330	569	13	27	127	41	83	3	632	892	25	37	71	67	84	88	95	123	92	95
1890 NATIONAL LEAGUE																																
BOS	66	43	23	0	435	284	20	11	68	33	34	1	328	308	11	16	134	76	57	1	763	592	31	27	116	86	79	115	92	74	111	108
BRO	74	58	16	0	547	303	27	9	55	28	27	0	337	318	16	18	129	86	43	0	884	621	43	27	82	154	106	98	121	92	100	96
CHI	74	48	24	2	509	369	55	29	65	36	29	0	340	323	12	12	139	84	53	2	849	692	67	41	246	106	80	115	99	84	109	107
CIN	73	50	23	0	470	323	19	25	61	27	32	2	283	309	8	17	134	77	55	2	753	632	27	42	140	69	108	111	92	81	108	106
CLE	70	30	37	3	357	355	13	7	66	14	51	1	268	476	8	25	136	44	88	4	625	831	21	32	59	91	109	90	89	113	94	97
NY	66	37	27	2	361	272	8	2	69	26	41	2	347	424	17	12	135	63	68	4	708	696	25	14	39	105	50	87	100	97	95	94
PHI	76	54	22	0	554	378	14	10	57	24	32	1	269	329	9	12	133	78	54	1	823	707	23	22	88	73	72	115	99	91	108	107
PIT	40	14	25	1	225	261	3	5	98	9	88	1	373	971	17	47	138	23	113	2	598	1232	20	52	33	90	170	87	98	154	88	95
1891 NATIONAL LEAGUE																																
BOS	73	51	20	2	527	328	34	33	67	36	31	0	320	330	20	18	140	87	51	2	847	658	54	51	152	119	112	119	96	79	112	109
BRO	72	41	31	0	438	383	11	19	65	20	45	0	327	438	12	21	137	61	76	0	765	821	23	40	83	69	113	97	104	111	97	98
CHI	67	43	22	2	467	343	39	30	70	39	31	0	366	387	21	23	137	82	53	2	833	730	60	53	153	136	126	112	103	92	106	105
CIN	67	26	41	0	296	328	19	17	71	30	40	1	350	463	21	23	138	56	81	1	646	791	40	40	87	118	117	83	93	110	91	93
CLE	69	40	28	1	484	426	4	6	72	25	46	1	352	462	18	18	141	65	74	2	836	888	22	24	32	76	91	114	102	108	105	106
NY	69	39	28	2	377	302	28	15	67	32	33	2	377	409	18	12	136	71	61	4	754	711	46	27	133	104	66	98	107	101	94	93
PHI	69	35	34	0	372	350	8	3	69	33	35	1	384	423	13	20	138	68	69	1	756	773	21	29	55	72	92	91	104	106	95	95
PIT	66	32	34	0	379	316	14	9	71	23	46	2	300	428	15	22	137	55	80	2	679	744	29	31	69	94	92	102	89	95	101	102
1892 NATIONAL LEAGUE																																
BAL	78	28	46	4	472	486	13	14	74	18	55	1	307	534	17	37	152	46	101	5	779	1020	30	51	49	135	193	105	100	129	100	102

TM	HOME								ROAD								ALL															
	G	W	L	T	R	OR	HR	OHR	G	W	L	T	R	OR	HR	OHR	G	W	L	T	R	OR	HR	OHR	HRF	HRB	HRP	RF	RB	RP	BPF	PPF
BOS	76	54	21	1	490	344	20	27	76	48	27	1	372	305	14	14	152	102	48	2	862	649	34	41	162	78	89	123	98	76	113	111
BRO	78	51	24	3	485	340	14	8	80	44	35	1	450	393	16	18	158	95	59	4	935	733	30	26	69	99	81	101	114	92	101	99
CHI	68	37	31	0	292	278	9	9	79	33	45	1	343	457	17	26	147	70	76	1	635	735	26	35	51	106	128	84	93	103	92	93
CIN	80	45	32	3	440	352	29	21	75	37	36	2	326	379	15	18	155	82	68	5	766	731	44	39	138	103	97	105	93	90	103	103
CLE	79	54	24	1	483	281	4	4	74	39	32	1	372	332	22	24	153	93	56	4	855	613	26	28	18	128	133	103	106	78	103	101
LOU	70	37	31	2	309	286	7	3	84	26	58	0	340	518	11	23	154	63	89	2	649	804	18	26	37	86	82	84	91	107	92	93
NY	79	42	36	1	452	382	26	12	74	29	44	1	359	444	13	20	153	71	80	2	811	826	39	32	107	106	92	97	106	108	98	98
PHI	81	55	26	0	512	322	34	8	74	32	40	2	348	368	16	16	155	87	66	2	860	690	50	24	119	123	68	107	103	86	104	103
PIT	87	52	34	1	477	363	32	14	68	28	39	1	325	433	6	14	155	80	73	2	802	796	38	28	169	67	67	88	109	109	94	94
STL	75	37	36	2	379	380	32	32	80	19	58	3	324	542	13	15	155	56	94	5	703	922	45	47	215	82	88	93	94	119	95	97
WAS	70	34	36	0	404	379	23	22	83	24	57	2	327	490	14	18	153	58	93	2	731	869	37	40	156	85	93	111	90	105	105	106

1893 NATIONAL LEAGUE

TM	G	W	L	T	R	OR	HR	OHR	G	W	L	T	R	OR	HR	OHR	G	W	L	T	R	OR	HR	OHR	HRF	HRB	HRP	RF	RB	RP	BPF	PPF
BAL	60	36	24	0	451	404	16	9	70	24	46	0	369	489	11	20	130	60	70	0	820	893	27	29	94	73	74	114	90	98	107	108
BOS	65	49	15	1	557	350	48	41	66	37	28	1	451	445	17	25	131	86	43	2	1008	795	65	66	199	113	125	104	114	92	103	101
BRO	67	43	24	0	393	348	24	17	63	22	39	2	382	497	21	24	130	65	63	2	775	845	45	41	87	129	117	81	101	108	91	91
CHI	73	38	34	1	538	471	20	15	55	18	37	0	291	403	12	11	128	56	71	1	829	874	32	26	112	77	64	108	93	101	104	104
CIN	66	37	27	2	424	375	19	21	65	28	36	1	335	439	10	17	131	65	63	3	759	814	29	38	141	61	82	102	87	93	101	102
CLE	70	47	22	1	579	440	10	9	59	26	33	0	397	399	22	26	129	73	55	1	976	839	32	35	36	133	137	108	110	97	104	103
LOU	53	24	28	1	329	367	3	14	73	26	47	0	430	575	16	24	126	50	75	1	759	942	19	38	60	53	124	95	96	115	96	98
NY	71	49	20	2	571	390	48	19	65	19	44	2	370	455	13	17	136	68	64	4	941	845	61	36	188	95	72	106	101	93	103	103
PHI	66	43	22	1	559	351	45	13	67	29	35	3	452	490	35	17	133	72	57	4	1011	841	80	30	113	190	80	99	116	98	100	98
PIT	73	54	19	0	593	417	25	8	58	27	29	1	377	349	12	21	131	81	48	2	970	766	37	29	82	105	84	111	104	86	106	105
STL	72	40	30	2	424	405	7	14	63	17	45	1	321	424	3	24	135	57	75	3	745	829	10	38	69	32	104	97	85	94	99	100
WAS	49	21	27	1	281	298	8	7	81	19	62	0	441	734	15	47	130	40	89	1	722	1032	23	54	41	102	153	81	97	124	89	92

1894 NATIONAL LEAGUE

TM	G	W	L	T	R	OR	HR	OHR	G	W	L	T	R	OR	HR	OHR	G	W	L	T	R	OR	HR	OHR	HRF	HRB	HRP	RF	RB	RP	BPF	PPF
BAL	67	52	15	0	626	378	13	9	62	37	24	1	545	442	20	22	129	89	39	1	1171	820	33	31	52	85	75	97	124	90	99	96
BOS	63	44	19	0	672	519	77	70	70	39	30	1	550	483	26	19	133	83	49	1	1222	1002	103	89	301	105	87	127	111	93	113	111
BRO	68	42	24	2	512	452	22	15	66	28	37	1	509	555	20	26	134	70	61	3	1021	1007	42	41	80	88	83	89	110	108	94	94
CHI	67	35	30	2	625	513	26	13	68	22	45	1	416	553	39	30	135	57	75	3	1041	1066	65	43	59	153	100	116	96	100	108	108
CIN	67	38	28	1	512	515	43	45	65	17	47	1	398	570	18	40	132	55	75	2	910	1085	61	85	141	97	141	102	93	110	100	101
CLE	59	35	24	0	511	411	8	18	71	33	37	1	421	485	29	36	130	68	61	1	932	896	37	54	51	86	136	121	89	85	111	111
LOU	61	24	37	0	317	366	16	7	69	12	57	0	375	635	26	32	130	36	94	0	692	1001	42	39	46	117	89	76	83	113	88	91
NY	69	49	17	3	477	362	29	21	68	39	27	2	463	427	14	16	137	88	44	5	940	789	43	37	158	58	53	95	94	80	100	98
PHI	69	48	20	1	674	398	26	31	60	23	37	0	469	568	14	31	129	71	57	1	1143	966	40	62	110	74	115	91	127	109	95	94
PIT	75	46	28	1	559	475	26	11	57	19	37	1	396	497	22	28	132	65	65	2	955	972	48	39	58	122	94	89	104	108	94	94
STL	66	34	32	0	429	438	30	16	67	22	44	1	342	516	24	32	133	56	76	1	771	954	54	48	84	113	97	102	78	95	101	103
WAS	62	32	30	0	476	463	35	20	70	13	57	0	406	659	24	39	132	45	87	0	882	1122	59	59	97	118	114	98	94	115	98	100

1895 NATIONAL LEAGUE

TM	G	W	L	T	R	OR	HR	OHR	G	W	L	T	R	OR	HR	OHR	G	W	L	T	R	OR	HR	OHR	HRF	HRB	HRP	RF	RB	RP	BPF	PPF
BAL	67	54	12	1	581	293	10	8	65	33	31	1	428	353	15	23	132	87	43	2	1009	646	25	31	49	86	95	110	108	72	107	104
BOS	67	48	19	0	537	363	50	38	65	23	41	1	370	463	4	18	132	71	60	1	907	826	54	56	314	50	80	105	101	94	103	102
BRO	66	43	22	1	444	334	22	20	67	28	38	1	423	500	17	21	133	71	60	2	867	834	39	41	112	91	96	87	106	101	94	94
CHI	69	43	26	0	477	439	32	23	64	29	32	3	389	415	23	15	133	72	58	3	866	854	55	38	131	117	83	106	96	95	103	103
CIN	65	42	22	1	528	404	8	7	67	24	42	1	375	450	28	32	132	66	64	2	903	854	36	39	27	144	144	115	96	92	108	107
CLE	60	47	13	0	423	274	5	10	71	37	33	1	494	446	24	23	131	84	46	1	917	720	29	33	41	88	117	90	110	87	97	95
LOU	59	19	38	2	328	447	14	12	74	16	58	0	370	643	20	28	133	35	96	2	698	1090	34	40	68	101	110	94	85	125	95	99
NY	67	40	27	0	424	376	14	8	65	26	38	1	428	458	18	26	132	66	65	1	852	834	32	34	51	112	103	89	104	101	95	94
PHI	73	51	21	1	653	455	42	16	60	27	32	1	415	502	19	20	133	78	53	2	1068	957	61	36	121	130	88	100	122	113	99	98
PIT	67	44	21	2	422	334	9	3	67	27	40	0	389	453	17	14	134	71	61	2	811	787	26	17	41	89	50	91	96	92	96	96
STL	67	25	41	1	411	491	26	35	68	14	51	3	336	541	12	29	135	39	92	4	747	1032	38	64	142	77	130	102	84	113	100	102
WAS	69	31	34	4	523	521	39	33	63	12	51	0	314	527	16	22	132	43	85	4	837	1048	55	55	160	103	110	110	92	115	103	105

1896 NATIONAL LEAGUE

TM	G	W	L	T	R	OR	HR	OHR	G	W	L	T	R	OR	HR	OHR	G	W	L	T	R	OR	HR	OHR	HRF	HRB	HRP	RF	RB	RP	BPF	PPF
BAL	67	49	16	2	528	310	8	4	65	41	23	1	467	352	15	18	132	90	39	3	995	662	23	22	38	103	82	101	122	84	102	99
BOS	67	42	24	1	510	371	23	39	65	32	33	0	350	390	13	18	132	74	57	1	860	761	36	57	181	80	119	115	99	90	108	107
BRO	65	35	28	2	298	298	13	19	68	23	45	0	394	466	15	20	133	58	73	2	692	764	28	39	95	85	116	74	99	107	87	88
CHI	68	42	24	2	470	427	19	16	64	29	33	2	345	372	15	14	132	71	57	4	815	799	34	30	113	94	84	117	94	93	108	108
CIN	66	51	15	0	450	292	6	1	62	26	35	1	333	328	14	26	128	77	50	1	783	620	20	27	18	141	97	106	96	78	105	103
CLE	64	43	19	2	445	315	9	4	71	37	29	5	395	335	19	23	135	80	48	7	840	650	28	27	37	124	95	116	94	75	110	108
LOU	64	25	37	2	326	471	24	38	70	13	56	1	327	526	13	10	134	38	93	3	653	997	37	48	249	69	76	100	83	121	98	102
NY	66	39	26	1	438	371	21	14	67	25	41	1	391	450	19	15	133	64	67	2	829	821	40	33	94	122	102	98	105	104	99	99
PHI	69	42	27	0	530	448	30	24	61	20	41	0	360	443	19	15	130	62	68	0	890	891	49	39	135	126	102	107	110	112	102	102
PIT	66	35	31	0	369	335	5	2	65	31	32	2	418	406	22	16	131	66	63	2	787	741	27	18	20	135	78	85	107	101	93	93
STL	62	27	34	1	322	374	25	18	69	13	56	0	271	555	12	22	131	40	90	1	593	929	37	40	134	95	106	92	80	118	95	98
WAS	68	38	29	1	462	395	30	12	65	20	44	1	356	525	15	12	133	58	73	2	818	920	45	24	142	104	62	93	108	119	95	96

1897 NATIONAL LEAGUE

TM	G	W	L	T	R	OR	HR	OHR	G	W	L	T	R	OR	HR	OHR	G	W	L	T	R	OR	HR	OHR	HRF	HRB	HRP	RF	RB	RP	BPF	PPF
BAL	69	51	15	3	470	293	4	7	67	39	25	3	494	381	15	11	136	90	40	6	964	674	19	18	44	75	83	87	127	91	95	92
BOS	67	54	12	1	573	307	26	26	68	39	27	2	452	358	19	13	135	93	39	3	1025	665	45	39	160	118	99	112	120	82	107	103
BRO	70	38	29	3	456	412	11	19	66	23	42	1	346	433	13	15	136	61	71	4	802	845	24	34	100	78	108	104	98	104	102	102
CHI	67	36	30	1	444	405	16	15	71	23	43	5	388	489	22	15	138	59	73	6	832	894	38	30	89	127	104	102	103	109	100	101
CIN	68	49	18	1	444	345	4	3	66	27	38	1	319	360	18	15	134	76	56	2	763	705	22	18	22	114	92	112	90	84	107	107
CLE	65	49	16	0	477	306	8	11	67	20	46	1	296	374	8	21	132	69	62	1	773	680	16	32	70	66	117	119	89	81	111	110
LOU	68	34	31	3	343	402	26	23	66	18	47	1	326	457	14	16	134	52	78	4	669	859	40	39	150	106	92	89	112	95	97	
NY	75	51	19	5	495	347	16	12	62	32	29	1	400	348	15	14	137	83	48	6	895	695	31	26	82	109	93	95	113	90	98	96
PHI	67	32	34	1	381	357	17	6	67	23	43	1	371	435	23	22	134	55	77	2	752	792	40	28	53	181	115	91	100	104	96	96
PIT	65	38	27	0	354	363	10	5	70	22	44	4	322	472	15	17	135	60	71	4	676	835	25	22	53	108	84	97	87	105	98	100
STL	60	18	41	1	273	467	20	41	72	11	61	0	315	616	11	13	132	29	102	1	588	1083	31	54	254	67	101	93	81	141	93	99
WAS	68	40	26	2	434	372	28	13	67	21	45	1	347	421	8	14	135	61	71	3	781	793	36	27	171	79	72	103	97	99	101	102

1898 NATIONAL LEAGUE

TM	G	W	L	T	R	OR	HR	OHR	G	W	L	T	R	OR	HR	OHR	G	W	L	T	R	OR	HR	OHR	HRF	HRB	HRP	RF	RB	RP	BPF	PPF
BAL	76	58	15	3	505	268	4	1	78	38	38	2	428	355	8	16	154	96	53	5	933	623	12	17	23	97	76	103	119	82	103	100
BOS	79	62	15	2	510	272	45	22	73	40	32	1	362	342	8	15	152	102	47	3	872	614	53	37	240	112	108	104	111	82	104	101
BRO	74	30	41	3	319	367	10	15	75	24	50	1	319	444	7	19	149	54	91	4	638	811	17	34	96	74	139	91	92	114	95	96
CHI	89	58	31	0	520	378	10	4	63	27	34	2	308	301	8	13	152	85	65	2	828	679	18	17	50	106	89	105	105	90	103	102
CIN	89	58	28	3	521	423	2	0	68	34	32	2	310	317	17	13	157	92	60	5	831	740	19	16	14	125	132	115	97	89	108	107
CLE	58	37	19	2	268	212	5	1	98	44	49	5	462	471	13	25	156	81	68	7	730	683	18	26	29	131	95	89	99	90	96	95
LOU	79	43	34	2	410	368	24	25	75	27	47	1	318	465	8	8	154	70	81	3	728	833	32	33	250	73	74	94	99	112	96	98
NY	76	45	28	3	423	322	18	10	81	32	45	4	414	478	16	11	157	77	73	7	837	800	34	21	110	126	81	90	114	108	95	94
PHI	81	49	31	1	452	371	13	9	69	29	40	0	371	413	20	14	150	78	71	1	823	784	33	23	57	177	128	90	117	113	94	94

	HOME								ROAD								ALL															
TM	G	W	L	T	R	OR	HR	OHR	G	W	L	T	R	OR	HR	OHR	G	W	L	T	R	OR	HR	OHR	HRF	HRB	HRP	RF	RB	RP	BPF	PPF
PIT	74	39	34	1	314	308	6	3	78	33	42	3	320	386	8	11	152	72	76	4	634	694	14	14	52	76	64	93	86	93	98	98
STL	66	20	44	2	285	424	8	15	88	19	67	2	286	505	5	17	154	39	111	4	571	929	13	32	132	47	109	115	72	112	106	110
WAS	80	34	44	2	418	471	29	17	75	17	57	1	286	468	7	12	155	51	101	3	704	939	36	29	202	85	85	108	89	117	102	105
1899 NATIONAL LEAGUE																																
BAL	77	50	25	2	473	343	4	2	75	36	37	2	354	348	13	11	152	86	62	4	827	691	17	13	26	92	62	113	96	82	108	106
BOS	80	53	26	1	460	346	32	33	73	42	31	0	398	299	7	11	153	95	57	1	858	645	39	44	279	66	82	106	102	78	105	103
BRO	78	61	16	1	510	315	13	18	72	40	31	1	382	343	14	14	150	101	47	2	892	658	27	32	104	94	109	106	108	83	105	102
CHI	85	44	39	2	429	415	14	14	67	31	34	2	383	348	13	6	152	75	73	4	812	763	27	20	115	86	61	92	107	101	96	96
CIN	88	57	29	2	543	416	2	7	68	26	38	4	313	354	11	19	156	83	67	6	856	770	13	26	25	67	148	111	97	91	106	105
CLE	42	9	33	0	152	352	3	5	112	11	101	0	377	959	9	38	154	20	134	0	529	1252	12	43	46	64	149	87	75	154	89	96
LOU	63	33	28	2	369	306	23	17	92	42	49	1	458	469	17	16	155	75	77	3	827	775	40	33	166	108	92	106	100	93	103	103
NY	75	35	38	2	382	394	7	6	77	25	52	0	352	469	16	13	152	60	90	2	734	863	23	19	48	103	87	96	95	110	97	99
PHI	83	58	25	0	503	353	11	3	71	36	33	2	413	390	20	14	154	94	58	2	916	743	31	17	38	160	78	93	117	97	97	95
PIT	84	49	34	1	475	381	12	8	70	27	39	4	359	384	15	19	154	76	73	5	834	765	27	27	51	130	121	96	105	98	99	98
STL	87	50	33	4	480	446	38	33	68	34	34	0	339	293	9	8	155	84	67	4	819	739	47	41	275	79	70	114	93	84	108	107
WAS	79	34	44	1	415	448	30	15	76	20	54	2	328	535	17	20	155	54	98	3	743	983	47	35	114	150	119	95	96	123	96	98
1900 NATIONAL LEAGUE																																
BOS	73	42	29	2	507	420	40	43	69	24	43	2	271	319	8	16	142	66	72	4	778	739	48	59	254	80	111	140	85	84	120	120
BRO	73	43	26	4	452	394	15	15	69	39	28	2	364	328	11	15	142	82	54	6	816	722	26	30	109	77	89	114	102	92	108	106
CHI	77	45	30	2	337	329	12	5	69	20	45	4	298	422	21	16	146	65	75	6	635	751	33	21	44	139	86	84	91	105	93	94
CIN	63	27	34	2	255	309	12	9	81	35	43	3	448	436	21	19	144	62	77	5	703	745	33	28	70	117	99	83	99	107	92	93
NY	71	38	31	2	393	375	13	8	70	22	47	1	320	448	10	18	141	60	78	3	713	823	23	26	76	83	87	98	100	113	97	99
PHI	70	45	23	2	434	353	13	7	71	30	40	1	376	438	16	22	141	75	63	3	810	791	29	29	57	122	108	99	113	110	98	98
PIT	70	42	28	0	359	315	14	7	70	37	32	1	374	297	12	17	140	79	60	1	733	612	26	24	76	94	82	101	98	83	103	101
STL	72	40	31	1	382	317	23	18	70	25	44	1	361	431	13	19	142	65	75	2	743	748	36	37	120	103	109	87	108	108	93	93
1901 NATIONAL LEAGUE																																
BOS	70	41	29	0	297	298	18	17	70	28	40	2	234	258	10	12	140	69	69	2	531	556	28	29	148	78	83	118	73	77	112	112
BRO	68	43	25	0	400	303	13	6	69	36	32	1	344	297	19	12	137	79	57	1	744	600	32	18	66	133	78	111	111	92	106	103
CHI	70	30	39	1	293	357	7	10	70	23	47	0	285	342	11	17	140	53	86	1	578	699	18	27	63	77	110	102	89	105	100	102
CIN	72	27	43	2	279	409	23	33	70	25	44	1	282	409	15	18	142	52	87	3	561	818	38	51	151	116	146	96	90	125	95	100
NY	71	30	38	3	255	350	8	11	70	22	47	1	289	405	11	13	141	52	85	4	544	755	19	24	79	72	89	86	91	122	91	95
PHI	69	46	23	0	349	247	11	6	71	37	34	0	319	296	13	13	140	83	57	0	668	543	24	19	71	95	73	101	100	84	103	100
PIT	69	45	24	0	372	255	15	8	71	45	25	1	404	279	14	12	140	90	49	1	776	534	29	20	93	102	72	97	119	86	101	96
STL	72	40	31	1	392	338	21	20	70	36	33	1	400	351	18	19	142	76	64	2	792	689	39	39	107	139	139	96	125	111	97	95
1902 NATIONAL LEAGUE																																
BOS	72	42	27	3	283	230	13	11	70	31	37	2	289	286	1	4	142	73	64	5	572	516	14	15	321	40	63	88	106	97	95	94
BRO	69	45	23	1	277	210	8	2	72	30	40	2	287	309	11	8	141	75	63	3	564	519	19	10	58	195	100	87	107	98	95	94
CHI	70	31	38	1	228	249	1	3	71	37	31	3	302	252	5	7	141	68	69	4	530	501	6	10	37	60	111	89	98	94	96	95
CIN	70	35	35	0	353	305	11	8	71	35	35	1	280	261	7	8	141	70	70	1	633	566	18	16	124	134	124	120	103	93	110	108
NY	71	24	44	3	214	297	7	7	68	24	44	0	187	293	1	9	139	48	88	3	401	590	8	16	127	54	114	100	73	102	100	104
PHI	69	29	39	1	264	351	1	6	69	27	42	0	220	298	4	6	138	56	81	1	484	649	5	12	72	44	107	115	84	108	105	109
PIT	71	56	15	0	410	207	9	2	71	47	21	3	365	233	10	2	142	103	36	3	775	440	19	4	95	141	35	105	130	80	105	98
STL	70	28	38	4	262	336	3	7	70	28	40	2	255	359	7	9	140	56	78	6	517	695	10	16	65	99	157	97	98	126	95	99
1903 NATIONAL LEAGUE																																
BOS	68	31	35	2	283	314	11	19	72	27	45	0	295	385	14	11	140	58	80	2	578	699	25	30	122	132	150	93	90	106	96	98
BRO	73	40	33	0	359	361	8	9	66	30	33	3	308	321	7	9	139	70	66	3	667	682	15	18	97	81	95	103	99	101	101	102
CHI	73	45	28	0	345	285	2	7	66	37	28	1	350	314	7	6	139	82	56	1	695	599	9	13	66	51	80	88	110	97	95	93
CIN	76	41	35	0	440	389	12	7	65	33	30	2	325	267	16	28	141	74	65	2	765	656	28	15	71	171	102	117	104	90	109	107
NY	70	41	27	2	368	296	9	10	72	43	28	1	361	271	11	10	142	84	55	3	729	567	20	20	95	108	108	108	81	106	103	
PHI	61	25	33	3	250	298	9	6	78	24	53	1	367	440	3	15	139	49	86	4	617	738	12	21	104	67	102	87	100	117	92	94
PIT	70	46	24	0	393	327	17	5	71	45	25	1	400	286	17	3	141	91	49	1	793	613	34	8	112	157	43	107	113	90	105	101
STL	69	22	45	2	248	393	7	13	70	21	49	0	257	402	1	13	139	43	94	2	505	795	8	26	135	34	112	97	79	118	96	102
1904 NATIONAL LEAGUE																																
BOS	79	34	45	0	269	363	13	10	76	21	53	2	222	386	11	14	155	55	98	2	491	749	24	24	89	120	119	99	84	121	96	102
BRO	76	31	44	1	234	287	3	11	78	25	53	0	263	327	12	16	154	56	97	1	497	614	15	27	54	84	161	90	87	104	95	98
CHI	78	49	27	2	303	240	6	10	78	44	33	1	296	277	16	6	156	93	60	3	599	517	22	16	76	105	87	96	98	86	100	99
CIN	79	49	27	3	409	295	12	7	78	39	38	1	286	252	9	7	157	88	65	4	695	547	21	14	116	83	58	125	98	80	114	111
NY	84	56	26	2	397	258	23	30	74	50	21	3	347	218	8		158	106	47	5	744	476	31	36	262	81	81	104	115	77	105	100
PHI	73	28	43	2	269	348	7	7	82	24	57	1	302	436	16	15	155	52	100	3	571	784	23	22	53	135	132	93	102	133	93	97
PIT	78	48	30	0	338	286	5	2	78	39	36	3	337	306	10	11	156	87	66	3	675	592	15	13	37	100	71	98	111	99	99	98
STL	76	39	36	1	298	280	14	15	79	36	43	0	304	315	10	8	155	75	79	1	602	595	24	23	154	88	83	97	100	99	99	99
1905 NATIONAL LEAGUE																																
BOS	76	29	46	1	234	344	14	14	80	22	57	1	234	387	3	22	156	51	103	2	468	731	17	36	114	73	145	97	76	112	97	102
BRO	77	29	47	1	273	379	16	16	78	19	57	2	233	428	13	8	155	48	104	3	506	807	29	24	142	108	87	98	83	125	96	102
CHI	81	54	25	2	365	212	7	4	74	38	36	0	302	230	5	10	155	92	61	2	667	442	12	14	71	61	64	100	100	70	105	100
CIN	79	50	28	1	438	330	12	2	76	29	46	1	297	368	15	20	155	79	74	2	735	698	27	22	42	191	117	110	111	108	103	103
NY	76	54	21	1	377	234	33	19	79	51	27	1	401	271	6		155	105	48	2	778	505	39	25	317	75	58	97	121	83	101	96
PHI	76	39	36	1	353	314	8	9	79	44	33	2	355	288	8	12	155	83	69	3	708	602	16	21	90	73	92	107	107	93	104	102
PIT	78	49	28	1	362	287	4	1	77	47	29	1	330	283	18	11	155	96	57	2	692	570	22	12	19	156	72	105	105	88	104	102
STL	77	32	45	0	245	342	13	10	77	26	51	0	290	392	7	18	154	58	96	0	535	734	20	28	92	97	126	87	93	122	91	95
1906 NATIONAL LEAGUE																																
BOS	76	28	47	1	218	329	11	16	76	21	55	0	190	320	5	8	152	49	102	1	408	649	16	24	180	76	110	104	75	113	100	106
BRO	76	31	44	1	191	287	9	5	77	35	42	0	305	338	16	10	153	66	86	1	496	625	25	15	57	206	133	77	104	129	86	90
CHI	79	56	21	2	345	214	7	6	76	60	15	1	360	167	13	6	155	116	36	3	705	381	20	12	71	141	95	104	120	69	107	102
CIN	78	36	40	2	316	333	10	10	77	28	47	2	217	249	6	4	155	64	87	4	533	582	16	14	175	73	61	130	83	91	115	116
NY	75	51	24	0	309	239	9	8	78	45	32	1	316	271	6	9	153	96	56	1	625	510	15	13	151	75	65	99	114	96	100	97
PHI	77	37	40	0	226	270	2	5	77	34	42	1	302	294	10	13	154	71	82	1	528	564	12	18	33	106	172	85	104	111	92	93
PIT	77	49	27	1	325	232	4	8	77	44	33	0	298	238	8	5	154	93	60	1	623	470	12	13	94	75	82	104	109	85	104	101
STL	77	28	48	1	241	313	6	10	77	24	50	3	229	294	4	7	154	52	98	4	470	607	10	17	136	53	87	104	85	106	101	104
1907 NATIONAL LEAGUE																																
BOS	74	31	42	1	253	304	14	20	78	27	48	3	249	348	8	8	152	58	90	4	502	652	22	28	192	94	110	98	102	128	95	99
BRO	77	37	38	2	223	232	9	10	76	28	45	3	223	290	9	6	153	65	83	5	446	522	18	16	121	93	82	88	91	104	94	96
CHI	76	54	19	3	282	198	2	5	79	53	26	0	290	192	11	6	155	107	45	3	572	390	13	11	47	80	89	105	102	73	106	102

Team Home-Road Statistics

	HOME								ROAD								ALL															
TM	G	W	L	T	R	OR	HR	OHR	G	W	L	T	R	OR	HR	OHR	G	W	L	T	R	OR	HR	OHR	HRF	HRB	HRP	RF	RB	RP	BPF	PPF
CIN	81	43	36	2	287	227	3	5	75	23	51	1	239	292	12	11	156	66	87	3	526	519	15	16	35	117	139	90	105	103	95	95
NY	77	45	30	2	317	250	19	19	78	37	41	0	257	260	4	6	155	82	71	2	574	510	23	25	284	63	75	110	103	94	105	104
PHI	75	45	30	0	265	247	2	4	74	38	34	2	247	229	10	9	149	83	64	2	512	476	12	13	34	90	115	106	97	91	104	103
PIT	77	47	29	1	330	258	7	3	80	44	34	2	304	252	12	9	157	91	63	3	634	510	19	12	53	133	82	110	113	94	105	102
STL	79	31	47	1	223	289	9	10	76	21	54	1	196	317	10	10	155	52	101	2	419	606	19	20	91	115	120	95	83	115	96	100
1908 NATIONAL LEAGUE																																
BOS	78	35	42	1	295	328	13	20	78	28	49	1	242	294	4	9	156	63	91	2	537	622	17	29	211	56	98	113	100	113	104	106
BRO	77	27	50	0	179	243	16	3	77	26	51	0	198	273	12	14	154	53	101	0	377	516	28	17	74	178	105	89	77	102	95	99
CHI	78	47	30	1	294	264	9	15	80	52	25	3	330	197	10	5	158	99	55	4	624	461	19	20	154	83	77	109	112	86	106	102
CIN	77	40	37	0	260	272	8	7	78	33	44	1	229	272	6	12	155	73	81	1	489	544	14	19	86	81	103	106	92	102	103	104
NY	80	52	25	3	343	235	10	11	77	46	31	0	309	221	10	15	157	98	56	3	652	456	20	26	84	122	151	106	120	88	104	100
PHI	78	43	34	1	251	213	0	3	77	40	37	0	253	232	11	5	155	83	71	1	504	445	11	8	21	53	94	95	98	88	100	98
PIT	77	42	35	0	227	255	12	4	78	56	21	1	358	214	13	12	155	98	56	1	585	469	25	16	69	159	100	88	118	100	95	92
STL	77	28	49	0	185	295	9	11	77	21	56	0	186	331	8	5	154	49	105	0	371	626	17	16	142	75	67	92	78	122	94	100
1909 NATIONAL LEAGUE																																
BOS	76	27	47	2	219	326	11	9	79	18	61	0	216	357	4	14	155	45	108	2	435	683	15	23	111	76	114	97	80	118	96	102
BRO	79	34	45	0	238	311	12	9	76	21	53	2	206	316	4	22	155	55	98	2	444	627	16	31	79	111	178	100	79	107	99	103
CHI	77	47	29	1	281	199	8	0	78	57	20	1	354	191	12	6	155	104	49	2	635	390	20	6	49	131	31	92	111	73	100	95
CIN	80	39	38	3	282	299	5	2	76	38	38	0	324	300	17	3	156	77	76	3	606	599	22	5	36	143	46	90	113	112	94	94
NY	77	44	33	0	298	294	19	23	81	48	28	5	325	252	7	6	158	92	61	5	623	546	26	29	264	79	81	108	103	92	105	103
PHI	77	40	37	0	266	279	6	10	77	34	42	1	250	239	6	13	154	74	79	1	516	518	12	23	86	71	125	110	86	86	106	106
PIT	78	56	21	1	354	237	10	6	75	54	21	0	345	210	15	6	153	110	42	1	699	447	25	12	77	143	77	104	119	80	105	99
STL	76	26	48	2	271	387	9	12	78	28	50	0	312	344	6	10	154	54	98	2	583	731	15	22	127	71	101	101	107	130	96	99
1910 NATIONAL LEAGUE																																
BOS	78	29	48	1	292	396	25	25	79	24	52	3	203	305	6	11	157	53	100	4	495	701	31	36	236	64	82	129	68	94	114	118
BRO	80	39	39	2	255	287	9	5	76	25	51	0	242	336	16	12	156	64	90	2	497	623	25	17	50	119	81	89	83	101	95	98
CHI	77	58	19	0	354	231	18	9	77	46	31	0	358	268	16	9	154	104	50	0	712	499	34	18	109	118	67	96	114	83	101	96
CIN	77	39	37	1	320	341	6	8	79	36	42	1	300	343	17	19	156	75	79	2	620	684	23	27	43	116	138	105	98	106	101	102
NY	79	52	26	1	352	255	20	17	76	39	37	0	363	312	11	13	155	91	63	1	715	567	31	30	141	96	96	89	120	98	95	92
PHI	78	40	36	2	333	290	12	18	79	38	39	2	341	349	10	18	157	78	75	4	674	639	22	36	107	81	126	93	111	106	96	95
PIT	76	46	30	0	365	308	17	8	78	40	37	1	290	268	16	12	154	86	67	1	655	576	33	20	93	125	80	121	94	85	112	110
STL	76	35	41	0	312	316	3	14	77	28	49	0	327	402	12	16	153	63	90	0	639	718	15	30	64	64	134	88	114	125	91	93
1911 NATIONAL LEAGUE																																
BOS	75	19	54	2	391	536	28	47	81	25	53	3	308	485	9	29	156	44	107	5	699	1021	37	76	184	68	139	120	98	136	103	109
BRO	74	31	42	1	247	303	10	11	80	33	44	3	292	356	18	16	154	64	86	4	539	659	28	27	69	79	78	92	82	98	97	99
CHI	84	49	32	3	380	306	26	13	73	43	30	0	377	301	28	13	157	92	62	3	757	607	54	26	85	140	74	90	114	94	97	94
CIN	82	38	42	2	331	317	5	6	77	32	41	4	351	389	16	30	159	70	83	6	682	706	21	36	25	89	126	84	106	109	92	92
NY	75	49	25	1	357	267	25	13	79	50	29	0	399	275	16	20	154	99	54	1	756	542	41	33	111	97	81	99	108	81	102	98
PHI	76	42	34	0	352	357	48	26	77	37	39	1	306	312	12	17	153	79	73	1	658	669	60	43	216	90	80	114	91	92	107	108
PIT	78	48	29	1	393	246	29	6	77	37	40	0	351	311	20	30	155	85	69	1	744	557	49	36	72	151	102	96	108	83	101	97
STL	79	36	38	5	343	380	11	12	79	39	36	4	328	365	15	27	158	75	74	9	671	745	26	39	58	84	113	104	95	104	101	102
1912 NATIONAL LEAGUE																																
BOS	79	31	47	1	407	471	22	28	76	21	54	1	286	390	13	15	155	52	101	2	693	861	35	43	155	76	91	119	90	109	107	110
BRO	76	33	43	0	303	368	17	20	77	25	52	0	348	386	15	25	153	58	95	0	651	754	32	45	93	96	128	92	97	110	95	97
CHI	77	46	29	2	394	347	22	18	75	45	30	0	362	321	21	15	152	91	59	2	756	668	43	33	108	115	91	106	104	93	104	102
CIN	77	45	32	0	309	311	7	2	78	30	46	2	347	411	14	26	155	75	78	2	656	722	21	28	25	110	88	85	100	108	92	93
NY	76	49	25	2	387	302	31	21	78	54	23	1	436	269	16	15	154	103	48	3	823	571	47	36	160	99	81	102	112	81	104	99
PHI	75	34	41	0	318	352	25	26	77	39	38	0	352	336	18	17	152	73	79	0	670	688	43	43	141	103	103	100	95	98	100	101
PIT	76	45	31	0	347	275	15	10	76	48	27	1	404	290	24	18	152	93	58	1	751	565	39	28	63	130	97	92	108	85	99	95
STL	77	37	40	0	354	414	14	9	76	26	50	0	305	416	13	22	153	63	90	0	659	830	27	31	67	92	95	104	94	115	99	102
1913 NATIONAL LEAGUE																																
BOS	77	34	40	3	298	337	14	12	77	35	42	0	343	353	18	25	154	69	82	3	641	690	32	37	63	104	112	92	106	113	95	96
BRO	77	29	47	1	296	343	20	14	75	36	37	2	299	270	19	11	152	65	84	3	595	613	39	33	88	108	92	108	91	93	104	105
CHI	76	51	25	0	372	278	37	20	79	37	40	2	348	352	22	19	155	88	65	2	720	630	59	39	138	127	92	98	113	101	99	97
CIN	78	32	44	2	307	380	15	13	78	32	45	1	300	337	12	27	156	64	89	3	607	717	27	40	74	83	109	106	92	107	102	104
NY	81	54	23	4	367	250	22	22	75	47	28	0	317	265	8	16	156	101	51	4	684	515	30	38	158	55	75	100	103	80	112	111
PHI	78	43	33	2	361	366	51	23	81	45	30	6	332	270	12	17	159	88	63	8	693	636	73	40	177	130	83	123	95	87	112	111
PIT	79	41	35	3	324	277	13	6	76	37	36	3	349	308	22	20	155	78	71	6	673	585	35	26	47	121	84	90	109	97	96	94
STL	74	25	48	1	239	346	8	20	79	26	51	2	289	409	7	37	153	51	99	3	528	755	15	57	70	52	156	89	90	123	92	97
1914 NATIONAL LEAGUE																																
BOS	79	51	25	3	339	279	17	16	79	43	34	2	318	269	18	22	158	94	59	5	657	548	35	38	85	115	122	106	104	89	104	102
BRO	79	45	34	0	342	306	17	17	75	30	45	0	280	312	14	19	154	75	79	0	622	618	31	36	98	96	110	103	104	104	101	101
CHI	76	46	30	0	318	281	22	20	80	32	46	2	287	357	20	17	156	78	76	2	605	638	42	37	117	119	106	98	103	107	98	99
CIN	77	34	42	1	290	328	4	5	80	26	52	2	240	323	12	25	157	60	94	3	530	651	16	30	28	78	118	111	84	101	105	107
NY	80	43	36	1	316	288	16	24	76	41	34	1	356	288	14	23	156	84	70	2	672	576	30	47	103	94	138	91	118	103	96	94
PHI	78	48	30	0	377	321	50	16	76	26	50	0	274	366	12	10	154	74	80	0	651	687	62	26	235	100	56	105	109	116	100	101
PIT	77	39	36	2	234	214	3	6	81	30	49	2	269	326	15	21	158	69	85	4	503	540	18	27	29	73	114	81	90	95	92	93
STL	79	42	34	3	285	280	20	14	78	39	38	1	273	260	13	12	157	81	72	4	558	540	33	26	129	82	68	104	89	87	104	103
1915 NATIONAL LEAGUE																																
BOS	78	49	27	2	280	263	3	5	79	34	42	3	302	282	14	18	157	83	69	5	582	545	17	23	28	85	118	95	104	98	98	97
BRO	78	51	26	1	299	263	9	14	76	29	46	1	237	297	5	15	154	80	72	2	536	560	14	29	111	47	93	102	95	99	101	102
CHI	77	42	34	1	296	314	31	16	79	31	46	2	274	306	22	12	156	73	80	3	570	620	53	28	135	162	94	107	99	106	102	103
CIN	79	39	37	1	265	295	6	7	81	32	46	3	251	290	9	21	160	71	83	6	516	585	15	28	48	75	115	105	87	97	103	104
NY	76	37	38	1	275	270	15	20	79	32	45	2	307	358	9	20	155	69	83	3	582	628	24	40	121	81	129	86	114	121	91	92
PHI	76	49	27	0	313	235	46	18	77	41	35	1	276	228	12	8	153	90	62	1	589	463	58	26	255	111	61	110	99	80	107	104
PIT	79	40	37	2	290	241	8	6	77	33	44	0	267	279	16	15	156	73	81	2	557	520	24	21	47	113	97	95	100	94	99	98
STL	81	42	36	3	320	303	11	10	76	30	45	1	270	298	9	20	157	72	81	4	590	601	20	30	71	87	117	102	103	105	100	100
1916 NATIONAL LEAGUE																																
BOS	78	41	31	6	224	207	6	4	80	48	32	0	318	246	16	20	158	89	63	6	542	453	22	24	31	112	104	81	106	92	93	91
BRO	78	50	27	1	300	233	19	9	78	44	33	1	285	238	9	15	156	94	60	2	585	471	28	24	115	82	75	103	105	87	103	100
CHI	79	37	41	1	309	317	34	22	77	30	45	2	211	224	12	10	156	67	86	3	520	541	46	32	208	96	73	133	82	85	119	117
CIN	78	32	44	0	242	312	4	10	79	28	49	2	263	305	10	25	155	60	93	2	505	617	14	35	44	66	146	100	96	115	98	101
NY	78	47	30	1	291	229	21	23	77	39	36	2	306	275	21	18	155	86	66	3	597	504	42	41	111	143	139	90	117	101	96	93

TM	HOME								ROAD								ALL															
	G	W	L	T	R	OR	HR	OHR	G	W	L	T	R	OR	HR	OHR	G	W	L	T	R	OR	HR	OHR	HRF	HRB	HRP	RF	RB	RP	BPF	PPF
PHI	79	50	29	0	281	233	29	17	75	41	33	1	300	256	13	11	154	91	62	1	581	489	42	28	166	102	75	90	114	98	96	94
PIT	78	37	40	1	268	298	9	5	79	28	49	2	216	288	11	19	157	65	89	3	484	586	20	24	50	93	91	111	85	101	105	107
STL	76	36	40	0	251	295	12	15	77	24	53	0	225	334	13	16	153	60	93	0	476	629	25	31	94	88	106	98	94	119	97	100

1917 NATIONAL LEAGUE

TM	HOME								ROAD								ALL															
	G	W	L	T	R	OR	HR	OHR	G	W	L	T	R	OR	HR	OHR	G	W	L	T	R	OR	HR	OHR	HRF	HRB	HRP	RF	RB	RP	BPF	PPF
BOS	77	35	42	0	240	269	13	3	80	37	39	4	296	283	9	16	157	72	81	4	536	552	22	19	69	105	77	92	100	103	96	97
BRO	78	36	38	4	270	288	14	14	78	34	43	1	241	271	11	18	156	70	81	5	511	559	25	32	97	105	130	107	90	97	104	105
CHI	77	35	42	0	273	305	11	14	80	39	38	3	279	262	6	20	157	74	80	3	552	567	17	34	100	70	128	109	96	98	104	105
CIN	80	39	38	3	279	296	10	3	77	39	38	0	322	315	16	17	157	78	76	3	601	611	26	20	41	153	98	88	118	119	92	93
NY	80	50	28	2	294	220	21	17	78	48	28	2	341	237	18	12	158	98	56	4	635	457	39	29	121	142	109	89	117	88	97	93
PHI	76	46	29	1	297	270	26	20	78	41	36	1	281	230	12	5	154	87	65	2	578	500	38	25	229	96	58	113	99	87	108	106
PIT	79	25	53	1	232	307	2	4	78	26	50	2	232	288	7	10	157	51	103	3	464	595	9	14	37	45	72	100	84	105	100	103
STL	78	38	38	2	266	302	15	15	76	44	32	0	265	265	11	14	154	82	70	2	531	567	26	29	115	99	110	104	96	102	102	102

1918 NATIONAL LEAGUE

TM	HOME								ROAD								ALL															
	G	W	L	T	R	OR	HR	OHR	G	W	L	T	R	OR	HR	OHR	G	W	L	T	R	OR	HR	OHR	HRF	HRB	HRP	RF	RB	RP	BPF	PPF
BOS	52	23	29	0	163	183	5	2	72	30	42	0	261	286	8	12	124	53	71	0	424	469	13	14	51	104	85	88	99	109	94	95
BRO	54	33	21	0	173	185	4	12	72	24	48	0	187	278	6	10	126	57	69	0	360	463	10	22	128	53	108	102	79	97	101	104
CHI	76	50	26	0	300	235	9	5	55	34	19	2	238	158	12	8	131	84	45	2	538	393	21	13	55	154	101	100	112	84	102	98
CIN	71	46	24	1	298	256	9	5	58	22	36	0	232	240	6	14	129	68	60	1	530	496	15	19	61	117	130	97	117	111	97	96
NY	56	35	21	0	204	181	9	13	68	36	32	0	276	234	4	7	124	71	53	0	480	415	13	20	207	51	78	93	109	96	98	96
PHI	57	27	29	1	220	261	19	13	68	28	39	1	210	246	6	9	125	55	68	2	430	507	25	22	212	93	93	121	88	102	109	111
PIT	69	41	27	1	270	232	9	4	57	24	33	0	196	180	6	9	126	65	60	1	466	412	15	13	74	99	84	109	96	86	106	105
STL	73	32	40	1	241	280	14	7	58	19	38	1	213	247	13	9	131	51	78	2	454	527	27	16	77	173	111	90	103	117	93	95

1919 NATIONAL LEAGUE

TM	HOME								ROAD								ALL															
	G	W	L	T	R	OR	HR	OHR	G	W	L	T	R	OR	HR	OHR	G	W	L	T	R	OR	HR	OHR	HRF	HRB	HRP	RF	RB	RP	BPF	PPF
BOS	68	29	38	1	231	265	11	9	72	28	44	0	234	298	13	20	140	57	82	1	465	563	24	29	67	117	128	98	93	110	98	100
BRO	69	36	33	0	243	227	12	10	72	33	38	1	282	286	13	11	141	69	71	1	525	513	25	21	96	95	81	88	109	106	94	94
CHI	71	40	31	0	232	190	11	7	69	35	34	0	222	217	10	7	140	75	65	0	454	407	21	14	103	74	51	95	89	80	100	99
CIN	71	52	19	0	315	189	10	5	69	44	25	0	262	212	10	16	140	96	44	0	577	401	20	21	60	99	91	105	107	78	105	101
NY	69	46	23	0	310	209	28	17	71	41	30	0	295	261	12	17	140	87	53	0	605	470	40	34	150	124	117	98	119	95	100	96
PHI	71	26	44	1	307	378	29	24	67	21	46	0	203	321	13	16	138	47	90	1	510	699	42	40	156	133	133	118	96	128	104	108
PIT	70	40	30	0	273	218	8	7	69	31	38	0	199	248	9	16	139	71	68	0	472	466	17	23	62	83	100	107	88	88	105	105
STL	69	34	35	0	240	244	9	10	69	20	48	1	223	308	9	15	138	54	83	1	463	552	18	25	80	78	102	91	98	113	94	96

1920 NATIONAL LEAGUE

TM	HOME								ROAD								ALL															
	G	W	L	T	R	OR	HR	OHR	G	W	L	T	R	OR	HR	OHR	G	W	L	T	R	OR	HR	OHR	HRF	HRB	HRP	RF	RB	RP	BPF	PPF
BOS	74	36	37	1	271	292	5	11	79	26	53	0	252	378	18	28	153	62	90	1	523	670	23	39	40	98	165	95	90	111	96	99
BRO	78	49	29	0	360	291	17	14	77	44	32	1	300	237	11	11	155	93	61	1	660	528	28	25	134	70	64	118	97	79	111	108
CHI	77	43	34	0	322	302	19	15	77	32	45	0	297	333	15	22	154	75	79	0	619	635	34	37	93	111	118	99	103	105	99	99
CIN	77	42	34	1	281	238	5	1	77	40	37	0	358	331	13	25	154	82	71	1	639	569	18	26	18	121	89	78	117	105	90	88
NY	80	45	35	0	334	282	31	33	75	41	33	1	348	261	15	11	155	86	68	1	682	543	46	44	199	97	88	96	112	91	99	99
PHI	77	32	45	0	339	380	50	30	76	30	46	0	226	334	14	5	153	62	91	0	565	714	64	35	296	99	50	122	85	106	109	112
PIT	78	42	35	1	276	263	6	4	77	37	40	0	254	289	10	21	155	79	75	1	530	552	16	25	35	79	91	98	85	89	101	101
STL	76	38	38	0	330	332	10	10	79	37	41	1	345	350	22	20	155	75	79	1	675	682	32	30	53	124	119	99	112	113	98	98

1921 NATIONAL LEAGUE

TM	HOME								ROAD								ALL															
	G	W	L	T	R	OR	HR	OHR	G	W	L	T	R	OR	HR	OHR	G	W	L	T	R	OR	HR	OHR	HRF	HRB	HRP	RF	RB	RP	BPF	PPF
BOS	74	42	32	0	332	292	20	18	79	37	42	0	389	405	41	36	153	79	74	0	721	697	61	54	56	133	121	86	111	106	93	92
BRO	78	41	37	0	360	361	32	23	74	36	38	0	307	320	27	23	152	77	75	0	667	681	59	46	104	98	79	108	91	93	105	105
CHI	73	32	44	0	345	434	23	37	77	32	45	0	323	339	14	30	153	64	89	0	668	773	37	67	131	56	97	116	89	101	107	108
CIN	76	40	36	0	321	306	5	2	77	30	47	0	297	343	15	35	153	70	83	0	618	649	20	37	16	74	69	87	91	101	101	101
NY	79	53	26	0	407	321	47	46	74	41	33	0	433	316	28	33	153	94	59	0	840	637	75	79	137	114	121	93	123	97	97	94
PHI	76	29	47	0	326	485	67	49	78	22	56	0	291	434	21	30	154	51	103	0	617	919	88	79	197	100	101	111	86	121	102	107
PIT	76	45	31	0	343	295	13	10	78	45	32	1	349	300	24	27	154	90	63	1	692	595	37	37	50	81	76	102	95	83	103	101
STL	78	48	29	1	397	307	43	25	76	39	37	0	412	374	40	36	154	87	66	1	809	681	83	61	89	156	119	89	121	104	95	93

1922 NATIONAL LEAGUE

TM	HOME								ROAD								ALL															
	G	W	L	T	R	OR	HR	OHR	G	W	L	T	R	OR	HR	OHR	G	W	L	T	R	OR	HR	OHR	HRF	HRB	HRP	RF	RB	RP	BPF	PPF
BOS	76	32	43	1	287	373	6	15	78	21	57	0	309	449	26	42	154	53	100	1	596	822	32	57	34	65	119	89	83	109	94	98
BRO	78	44	34	0	380	326	25	35	77	32	44	1	363	428	31	39	155	76	78	1	743	754	56	74	86	92	118	89	101	102	95	95
CHI	76	39	37	0	344	382	22	37	80	41	37	2	427	426	20	40	156	80	74	2	771	808	42	77	103	63	108	91	104	109	95	96
CIN	79	48	29	2	378	297	8	13	77	38	39	0	388	380	37	33	156	86	68	2	766	677	45	49	31	91	111	88	103	92	96	94
NY	79	51	27	1	439	333	48	38	77	42	34	1	413	325	32	33	156	93	61	2	852	658	80	71	126	106	97	103	106	84	104	100
PHI	77	35	41	1	449	517	95	60	77	22	55	0	289	403	21	29	154	57	96	1	738	920	116	89	243	95	89	131	84	103	113	117
PIT	78	45	33	0	439	390	22	16	77	40	36	1	426	346	30	36	155	85	69	1	865	736	52	52	60	97	91	106	108	94	103	101
STL	77	42	35	0	446	414	59	31	77	43	34	0	417	405	48	30	154	85	69	0	863	819	107	61	114	152	94	105	111	106	101	100

1923 NATIONAL LEAGUE

TM	HOME								ROAD								ALL															
	G	W	L	T	R	OR	HR	OHR	G	W	L	T	R	OR	HR	OHR	G	W	L	T	R	OR	HR	OHR	HRF	HRB	HRP	RF	RB	RP	BPF	PPF
BOS	77	22	55	0	291	429	7	27	78	32	45	1	345	369	25	37	155	54	100	1	636	798	32	64	58	54	113	100	85	104	100	102
BRO	78	37	40	1	348	383	26	27	77	39	38	0	405	358	36	28	155	76	78	1	753	741	62	55	84	97	88	95	102	101	98	98
CHI	77	46	31	0	402	354	63	57	77	37	40	0	354	350	27	29	154	83	71	0	756	704	90	86	188	93	92	107	97	91	104	103
CIN	78	46	32	0	337	300	6	4	76	45	31	0	371	329	39	24	154	91	63	0	708	629	45	28	17	98	66	91	97	87	98	96
NY	77	47	30	0	408	362	41	53	76	48	28	0	446	317	44	29	153	95	58	0	854	679	85	82	124	119	112	101	114	93	101	98
PHI	75	20	55	0	418	597	76	77	80	30	49	1	330	411	36	23	155	50	104	1	748	1008	112	100	223	110	92	136	88	114	114	118
PIT	77	47	30	0	381	322	16	9	77	40	37	0	405	374	33	44	154	87	67	0	786	696	49	53	36	112	99	92	109	98	97	95
STL	78	42	35	1	335	320	22	27	76	37	39	0	411	412	41	43	154	79	74	1	746	732	63	70	60	118	131	80	111	109	90	90

1924 NATIONAL LEAGUE

TM	HOME								ROAD								ALL															
	G	W	L	T	R	OR	HR	OHR	G	W	L	T	R	OR	HR	OHR	G	W	L	T	R	OR	HR	OHR	HRF	HRB	HRP	RF	RB	RP	BPF	PPF
BOS	76	28	48	0	254	366	9	8	78	25	52	1	266	434	16	41	154	53	100	1	520	800	25	49	33	67	94	91	79	115	94	99
BRO	77	46	31	0	342	338	26	30	77	46	31	0	375	337	46	28	154	92	62	0	717	675	72	58	79	126	108	97	104	98	99	98
CHI	78	46	31	1	373	341	33	68	76	35	41	0	325	358	33	21	154	81	72	1	698	699	66	89	166	89	100	102	99	99	101	101
CIN	76	43	33	0	311	283	3	3	77	40	37	0	338	296	33	27	153	83	70	0	649	579	36	30	11	87	79	96	93	84	101	99
NY	77	51	26	0	385	272	51	40	77	42	34	1	472	369	44	37	154	93	60	1	857	641	95	77	112	150	126	81	134	104	91	88
PHI	76	26	49	1	369	483	58	64	76	29	47	0	307	366	36	20	152	55	96	1	676	849	94	84	188	114	93	121	91	111	108	111
PIT	77	49	28	0	393	293	19	17	76	41	35	0	331	295	24	25	153	90	63	0	724	588	43	42	76	75	73	108	98	82	106	104
STL	77	40	37	0	419	359	32	37	77	25	52	0	321	391	35	32	154	65	89	0	740	750	67	69	102	108	111	107	103	105	102	103

1925 NATIONAL LEAGUE

TM	HOME								ROAD								ALL															
	G	W	L	T	R	OR	HR	OHR	G	W	L	T	R	OR	HR	OHR	G	W	L	T	R	OR	HR	OHR	HRF	HRB	HRP	RF	RB	RP	BPF	PPF
BOS	76	37	39	0	315	383	15	14	77	33	44	0	393	419	26	53	153	70	83	0	708	802	41	67	40	78	102	88	97	109	94	95
BRO	77	40	37	0	383	407	25	41	76	28	48	0	403	459	39	49	153	68	85	0	786	866	64	75	90	83	91	108	118	94	95	95
CHI	77	37	40	0	367	359	57	63	77	31	46	0	356	414	29	39	154	68	86	0	723	773	86	102	160	83	99	94	95	101	97	98
CIN	76	44	32	0	334	285	10	5	77	36	41	0	356	358	34	30	153	80	73	0	690	643	44	35	26	81	57	89	92	86	97	97
NY	76	47	29	0	362	334	55	40	76	33	44	0	374	368	59	34	152	86	66	0	736	702	114	73	102	143	97	95	97	93	99	98
PHI	77	38	39	0	488	547	73	74	76	30	46	0	324	383	27	43	153	68	85	0	812	930	100	117	182	89	109	136	90	102	116	118
PIT	77	52	25	0	481	342	27	31	76	43	33	0	431	373	51	50	153	95	58	0	912	715	78	81	61	122	128	102	116	94	102	99

TM	|HOME G	W	L	T	R	OR	HR	OHR	|ROAD G	W	L	T	R	OR	HR	OHR	|ALL G	W	L	T	R	OR	HR	OHR	HRF	HRB	HRP	RF	RB	RP	BPF	PPF
STL	76	48	28	0	449	359	66	41	77	29	48	0	379	405	43	45	153	77	76	0	828	764	109	86	120	126	105	104	105	98	102	101

1926 NATIONAL LEAGUE

TM	|HOME G	W	L	T	R	OR	HR	OHR	|ROAD G	W	L	T	R	OR	HR	OHR	|ALL G	W	L	T	R	OR	HR	OHR	HRF	HRB	HRP	RF	RB	RP	BPF	PPF
BOS	77	43	34	0	296	266	4	5	76	23	52	1	328	453	12	41	153	66	86	1	624	719	16	46	19	60	111	73	106	116	86	88
BRO	76	38	38	0	314	331	23	26	79	33	44	2	309	374	17	24	155	71	82	2	623	705	40	50	120	65	80	98	89	99	99	101
CHI	78	49	28	1	377	295	38	17	77	33	44	0	305	307	28	21	155	82	72	1	682	602	66	38	110	109	68	108	91	82	106	105
CIN	77	53	23	1	372	259	8	8	80	34	44	2	375	392	27	32	157	87	67	3	747	651	35	40	31	90	97	88	111	97	95	93
NY	76	43	33	0	333	317	45	43	75	31	44	0	330	351	28	27	151	74	77	0	663	668	73	70	147	114	110	95	99	100	98	98
PHI	76	33	42	1	392	470	51	42	76	25	51	0	295	430	24	26	152	58	93	1	687	900	75	68	166	105	100	115	96	122	103	107
PIT	79	49	28	2	446	374	17	16	78	35	41	2	323	315	27	35	157	84	69	4	769	689	44	51	56	102	111	123	96	87	112	111
STL	79	47	30	2	411	359	54	42	77	42	35	0	406	319	36	34	156	89	65	2	817	678	90	76	129	149	131	104	113	96	102	100

1927 NATIONAL LEAGUE

TM	|HOME G	W	L	T	R	OR	HR	OHR	|ROAD G	W	L	T	R	OR	HR	OHR	|ALL G	W	L	T	R	OR	HR	OHR	HRF	HRB	HRP	RF	RB	RP	BPF	PPF
BOS	74	32	41	1	296	339	5	10	81	28	53	0	355	432	32	33	155	60	94	1	651	771	37	43	28	78	107	89	98	114	93	95
BRO	74	34	39	1	266	296	20	35	80	31	49	0	275	323	19	28	154	65	88	1	541	619	39	63	122	59	90	101	75	84	103	104
CHI	78	50	28	0	398	315	37	19	75	35	40	0	352	346	37	31	153	85	68	0	750	661	74	50	82	135	94	99	107	96	100	99
CIN	80	45	35	0	348	320	3	11	73	30	43	0	295	333	26	25	153	75	78	0	643	653	29	36	28	59	97	97	92	93	100	100
NY	74	49	25	0	389	342	62	49	81	43	37	1	428	378	47	28	155	92	62	1	817	720	109	77	152	152	110	100	115	103	100	98
PHI	78	34	43	1	375	429	32	46	77	17	60	0	303	474	25	38	155	51	103	1	678	903	57	84	117	91	127	100	99	127	96	100
PIT	79	48	31	0	406	345	25	23	77	46	29	2	411	314	29	35	156	94	60	2	817	659	54	58	77	100	105	102	112	93	102	99
STL	80	55	25	0	433	354	55	51	73	37	36	0	321	311	29	21	153	92	61	0	754	665	84	72	175	104	87	113	100	90	107	106

1928 NATIONAL LEAGUE

TM	|HOME G	W	L	T	R	OR	HR	OHR	|ROAD G	W	L	T	R	OR	HR	OHR	|ALL G	W	L	T	R	OR	HR	OHR	HRF	HRB	HRP	RF	RB	RP	BPF	PPF
BOS	76	25	51	0	309	448	24	62	77	25	52	0	322	430	28	38	153	50	103	0	631	878	52	100	125	64	111	100	90	120	97	101
BRO	77	41	35	1	330	296	31	25	78	36	41	1	335	344	35	34	155	77	76	2	665	640	66	59	84	90	81	94	92	89	99	99
CHI	77	52	25	0	335	264	40	18	77	39	38	0	379	351	52	38	154	91	63	0	714	615	92	56	68	139	87	85	105	91	95	93
CIN	78	44	33	1	324	318	3	17	75	34	41	0	324	368	29	41	153	78	74	1	648	686	32	58	30	49	114	91	94	99	96	97
NY	77	51	26	0	411	315	80	46	78	42	35	1	396	338	38	31	155	93	61	1	807	653	118	77	169	112	80	101	109	90	102	99
PHI	75	26	49	0	360	521	54	67	77	17	60	0	300	436	31	42	152	43	109	0	660	957	85	109	153	93	116	117	89	123	104	109
PIT	77	47	30	0	479	356	16	14	75	38	37	0	358	348	36	51	152	85	67	0	837	704	52	65	37	103	113	114	109	95	107	105
STL	77	42	35	0	367	336	62	51	77	53	24	0	440	300	51	35	154	95	59	0	807	636	113	86	128	133	104	97	112	91	100	97

1929 NATIONAL LEAGUE

TM	|HOME G	W	L	T	R	OR	HR	OHR	|ROAD G	W	L	T	R	OR	HR	OHR	|ALL G	W	L	T	R	OR	HR	OHR	HRF	HRB	HRP	RF	RB	RP	BPF	PPF
BOS	77	34	43	0	318	403	11	39	77	22	55	0	339	473	22	64	154	56	98	0	657	876	33	103	60	43	122	89	85	109	94	97
BRO	77	42	35	0	371	413	53	48	76	28	48	0	384	475	46	44	153	70	83	0	755	888	99	92	109	101	95	91	98	112	94	96
CHI	78	52	25	0	490	374	76	41	78	46	29	3	492	384	63	36	156	98	54	4	982	758	139	77	117	131	79	100	116	93	101	98
CIN	78	38	39	1	356	356	7	18	77	28	49	0	330	404	27	43	155	66	88	1	686	760	34	61	38	45	84	96	83	91	99	100
NY	77	39	37	1	418	374	79	59	75	45	30	0	479	335	57	43	152	84	67	1	897	709	136	102	130	129	101	96	110	90	100	97
PHI	76	39	37	0	503	580	86	74	78	32	45	1	394	452	67	49	154	71	82	1	897	1032	153	123	134	146	120	126	99	112	110	112
PIT	76	45	31	0	471	382	28	37	78	43	34	1	433	398	32	58	154	88	65	1	904	780	60	95	77	72	106	105	106	93	103	102
STL	77	43	32	2	414	386	48	50	77	35	42	0	417	420	52	51	154	78	74	2	831	806	100	101	96	110	111	96	102	100	98	98

1930 NATIONAL LEAGUE

TM	|HOME G	W	L	T	R	OR	HR	OHR	|ROAD G	W	L	T	R	OR	HR	OHR	|ALL G	W	L	T	R	OR	HR	OHR	HRF	HRB	HRP	RF	RB	RP	BPF	PPF
BOS	77	39	38	0	329	401	29	51	77	31	46	0	364	434	37	66	154	70	84	0	693	835	66	117	80	66	110	92	82	96	97	99
BRO	76	49	27	0	438	336	73	66	78	37	41	0	433	402	49	49	154	86	68	0	871	738	122	115	138	92	88	96	99	85	100	98
CHI	79	51	26	2	538	454	93	62	77	39	38	0	460	416	78	49	156	90	64	2	998	870	171	111	117	141	97	110	107	95	105	103
CIN	77	37	40	0	300	368	20	21	77	22	55	0	365	489	54	54	154	59	95	0	665	857	74	75	41	88	90	79	84	105	90	93
NY	78	47	31	0	468	395	91	63	76	40	36	0	491	419	52	54	154	87	67	0	959	814	143	117	135	108	94	94	112	97	98	96
PHI	77	35	42	0	543	644	72	72	79	17	60	2	401	555	54	70	156	52	102	2	944	1199	126	142	115	108	120	121	100	124	106	109
PIT	77	42	35	0	433	454	26	51	77	38	39	0	458	474	60	77	154	80	74	0	891	928	86	128	60	96	142	96	105	109	97	98
STL	77	53	24	0	541	383	52	50	77	39	38	0	463	401	52	37	154	92	62	0	1004	784	104	87	114	85	72	107	109	88	105	102

1931 NATIONAL LEAGUE

TM	|HOME G	W	L	T	R	OR	HR	OHR	|ROAD G	W	L	T	R	OR	HR	OHR	|ALL G	W	L	T	R	OR	HR	OHR	HRF	HRB	HRP	RF	RB	RP	BPF	PPF
BOS	78	36	41	1	278	318	16	24	78	28	49	1	255	362	18	42	156	64	90	2	533	680	34	66	69	66	115	96	77	96	99	102
BRO	76	46	29	1	363	317	46	22	77	33	44	0	318	356	25	34	153	79	73	1	681	673	71	56	115	106	89	102	98	97	101	101
CHI	77	50	27	0	414	311	40	22	79	34	43	2	414	399	44	41	156	84	70	2	828	710	84	54	86	144	97	93	124	108	96	94
CIN	77	38	39	1	312	328	6	3	77	20	57	0	280	414	15	48	154	58	96	0	592	742	21	51	16	84	98	92	91	110	95	98
NY	78	50	27	1	379	274	80	47	75	37	38	0	389	325	21	24	153	87	65	1	768	599	101	71	225	95	79	90	116	94	96	93
PHI	76	40	36	0	391	423	53	33	79	26	52	1	293	405	28	46	155	66	88	1	684	828	81	75	123	120	116	117	93	110	106	109
PIT	78	44	33	1	343	327	25	16	77	31	46	0	293	364	16	39	155	75	79	1	636	691	41	55	76	77	92	100	91	98	100	101
STL	78	54	24	0	439	320	31	29	76	47	29	0	376	294	29	36	154	101	53	0	815	614	60	65	92	103	110	111	111	86	107	103

1932 NATIONAL LEAGUE

TM	|HOME G	W	L	T	R	OR	HR	OHR	|ROAD G	W	L	T	R	OR	HR	OHR	|ALL G	W	L	T	R	OR	HR	OHR	HRF	HRB	HRP	RF	RB	RP	BPF	PPF
BOS	77	44	33	0	299	285	27	20	78	33	44	1	350	370	36	41	155	77	77	1	649	655	63	61	65	91	85	84	98	98	93	93
BRO	78	44	34	0	378	353	59	31	76	37	39	0	374	394	51	41	154	81	73	0	752	747	110	72	96	137	95	94	111	110	96	96
CHI	77	53	24	0	390	303	32	33	77	37	40	0	330	330	37	33	154	90	64	0	720	633	69	68	92	86	85	105	98	87	104	103
CIN	77	33	44	0	270	344	11	11	78	27	50	1	305	371	36	58	155	60	94	1	575	715	47	69	26	94	115	92	84	102	96	99
NY	77	37	40	0	362	359	78	71	77	35	42	0	393	347	38	41	154	72	82	0	755	706	116	112	169	109	108	97	108	102	99	98
PHI	77	45	32	0	507	429	86	71	77	33	44	0	337	367	36	36	154	78	76	0	844	796	122	107	190	105	96	128	106	102	112	111
PIT	76	45	31	0	352	338	22	25	78	41	37	0	349	373	26	61	154	86	68	0	701	711	48	86	59	79	120	99	100	101	99	100
STL	79	42	35	2	354	357	36	38	77	30	47	0	330	360	40	38	156	72	82	2	684	717	76	76	93	95	100	95	99	100	99	101

1933 NATIONAL LEAGUE

TM	|HOME G	W	L	T	R	OR	HR	OHR	|ROAD G	W	L	T	R	OR	HR	OHR	|ALL G	W	L	T	R	OR	HR	OHR	HRF	HRB	HRP	RF	RB	RP	BPF	PPF
BOS	77	45	31	1	265	230	27	26	79	38	40	1	287	301	27	28	156	83	71	2	552	531	54	54	99	92	92	88	93	89	96	96
BRO	80	36	41	3	306	352	33	29	77	29	47	1	311	343	29	22	157	65	88	4	617	695	62	51	114	98	82	96	103	114	97	98
CHI	79	55	24	0	334	239	40	32	75	31	44	0	312	297	32	19	154	86	68	0	646	536	72	51	129	109	78	91	109	92	97	95
CIN	79	37	42	0	264	321	5	10	74	21	52	1	232	322	29	37	153	58	94	1	496	643	34	47	23	88	131	98	83	104	98	102
NY	77	48	27	2	298	241	55	44	79	43	34	2	338	274	27	17	156	91	61	4	636	515	82	61	200	95	70	92	104	86	99	96
PHI	72	32	40	0	355	437	45	46	80	28	52	0	252	323	15	41	152	60	92	0	607	760	60	87	163	81	124	142	86	105	118	121
PIT	77	50	27	0	332	272	12	13	77	37	40	0	335	347	27	41	154	87	67	0	667	619	39	54	40	99	122	90	115	108	95	94
STL	77	46	31	0	347	315	18	25	77	36	40	1	340	294	39	30	154	82	71	1	687	609	57	55	66	116	119	104	110	99	102	100

1934 NATIONAL LEAGUE

TM	|HOME G	W	L	T	R	OR	HR	OHR	|ROAD G	W	L	T	R	OR	HR	OHR	|ALL G	W	L	T	R	OR	HR	OHR	HRF	HRB	HRP	RF	RB	RP	BPF	PPF
BOS	75	40	35	0	280	280	36	27	77	38	38	1	403	434	47	51	152	78	73	1	683	714	83	78	69	121	110	72	112	116	86	86
BRO	77	43	33	1	390	355	40	38	76	28	48	0	358	440	39	43	153	71	81	1	748	795	79	81	94	98	100	93	111	116	95	95
CHI	77	47	30	0	347	301	53	44	75	39	35	1	358	338	48	36	152	86	65	1	705	639	101	80	112	117	95	92	102	93	98	96
CIN	78	30	47	1	331	406	17	24	74	22	52	0	259	395	38	37	152	52	99	1	590	801	55	61	54	81	94	104	82	108	101	105
NY	75	49	26	0	363	254	75	43	78	44	34	0	397	329	51	32	153	93	60	0	760	583	126	75	141	126	81	91	108	85	98	95
PHI	71	35	36	0	384	400	28	72	78	21	57	0	291	394	28	54	149	56	93	0	675	794	56	126	127	66	134	120	89	104	108	111
PIT	78	45	32	1	421	369	22	38	73	29	44	0	314	344	30	40	151	74	76	1	735	713	52	78	82	69	100	111	98	96	105	105
STL	77	48	29	0	451	363	56	43	77	47	29	1	348	293	48	34	154	95	58	1	799	656	104	77	119	114	87	124	97	82	114	111

TM	HOME								ROAD								ALL															
	G	W	L	T	R	OR	HR	OHR	G	W	L	T	R	OR	HR	OHR	G	W	L	T	R	OR	HR	OHR	HRB	HRP	HRF	RF	RB	RP	BPF	PPF
1935 NATIONAL LEAGUE																																
BOS	75	25	50	0	309	381	34	41	78	13	65	0	266	471	41	40	153	38	115	0	575	852	75	81	94	93	100	95	84	118	96	100
BRO	77	38	38	1	349	346	32	43	77	32	45	0	362	421	27	45	154	70	83	1	711	767	59	88	103	70	101	90	105	111	94	95
CHI	77	56	21	0	426	264	43	40	77	44	33	0	421	333	45	45	154	100	54	0	847	597	88	85	95	110	107	94	118	87	99	95
CIN	76	41	35	0	331	320	18	18	78	27	50	1	315	452	55	47	154	68	85	1	646	772	73	65	39	119	111	88	96	111	93	95
NY	79	50	27	2	386	302	84	66	77	41	35	1	384	373	39	40	156	91	62	3	770	675	123	106	169	110	100	91	109	97	96	95
PHI	79	35	43	1	416	499	52	68	77	29	46	2	269	372	40	38	156	64	89	3	685	871	92	106	140	95	105	132	81	102	114	117
PIT	77	46	31	0	398	340	32	25	76	40	36	0	345	307	34	38	153	86	67	0	743	647	66	63	81	86	81	111	96	85	107	105
STL	77	53	24	0	441	298	39	27	77	43	34	0	388	327	47	41	154	96	58	0	829	625	86	68	78	114	92	104	110	86	104	100
1936 NATIONAL LEAGUE																																
BOS	79	35	43	1	292	339	26	23	78	36	40	2	339	376	41	46	157	71	83	3	631	715	67	69	59	110	110	88	90	101	95	96
BRO	79	37	40	2	360	397	15	46	77	30	47	0	302	355	18	39	156	67	87	2	662	752	33	85	103	43	101	110	86	96	105	106
CHI	77	50	27	0	404	290	34	41	77	37	40	0	351	313	42	35	154	87	67	0	755	603	76	76	98	102	102	105	99	82	105	102
CIN	76	42	34	0	358	350	24	21	78	32	46	0	364	410	58	30	154	74	80	0	722	760	82	51	56	128	91	94	103	108	96	97
NY	78	52	26	0	378	296	68	54	76	40	36	0	364	325	29	21	154	92	62	0	742	621	97	75	204	83	65	97	102	87	100	98
PHI	78	30	48	0	408	499	69	56	76	24	52	0	318	375	34	31	154	54	100	0	726	874	103	87	167	102	90	122	92	109	108	111
PIT	76	46	30	0	375	342	23	25	80	38	40	2	429	376	37	49	156	84	70	2	804	718	60	74	62	97	113	95	112	102	98	96
STL	77	43	33	1	363	386	38	43	78	44	34	0	432	408	50	46	155	87	67	1	795	794	88	89	88	127	130	92	115	115	94	94
1937 NATIONAL LEAGUE																																
BOS	76	43	33	0	252	224	26	15	76	36	40	0	327	332	37	45	152	79	73	0	579	556	63	60	53	107	93	75	94	90	90	90
BRO	76	36	39	1	336	389	20	30	79	26	52	1	280	383	17	38	155	62	91	2	616	772	37	68	94	47	82	111	84	103	104	107
CHI	78	46	32	0	412	361	47	48	76	47	29	0	399	321	49	43	154	93	61	0	811	682	96	91	102	126	120	105	114	98	103	100
CIN	80	28	51	1	268	347	13	14	75	28	47	0	344	360	60	24	155	56	98	1	612	707	73	38	33	119	84	83	96	110	91	93
NY	75	50	25	0	353	288	76	57	77	45	32	0	379	314	35	28	152	95	57	0	732	602	111	85	191	99	79	97	107	90	100	98
PHI	74	29	45	0	379	481	65	69	81	32	47	2	345	388	38	47	155	61	92	2	724	869	103	116	157	108	122	123	96	113	108	111
PIT	78	46	32	0	360	332	13	28	76	40	36	0	344	314	34	43	154	86	68	0	704	646	47	71	56	73	112	103	99	92	102	101
STL	80	45	33	2	406	379	52	51	77	36	40	1	383	354	42	44	157	81	73	3	789	733	94	95	113	114	115	102	111	104	100	100
1938 NATIONAL LEAGUE																																
BOS	75	45	30	0	233	241	12	19	78	32	45	1	328	377	42	47	153	77	75	1	561	618	54	66	39	93	119	73	95	102	88	89
BRO	74	31	41	2	319	349	38	44	77	38	39	0	385	361	23	44	151	69	80	2	704	710	61	88	123	73	103	94	110	111	96	96
CHI	77	44	33	0	349	326	24	41	77	45	30	2	364	272	41	30	154	89	63	2	713	598	65	71	93	85	94	106	100	85	105	103
CIN	77	43	34	0	344	323	50	31	74	39	34	1	379	311	60	44	151	82	68	1	723	634	110	75	78	167	120	94	111	99	98	96
NY	73	43	30	0	365	297	89	58	79	40	37	2	340	340	36	29	152	83	67	2	705	637	125	87	208	107	80	105	102	93	103	102
PHI	75	26	48	1	286	439	18	40	76	19	57	0	264	401	22	36	151	45	105	1	550	840	40	76	99	53	94	107	82	119	100	106
PIT	78	44	33	1	348	330	22	22	74	42	31	1	359	300	43	49	152	86	64	2	707	630	65	71	49	115	122	99	105	95	100	99
STL	81	36	41	4	414	425	58	45	75	35	39	1	311	296	33	32	156	71	80	5	725	721	91	77	138	96	84	123	94	93	111	111
1939 NATIONAL LEAGUE																																
BOS	73	37	35	1	254	272	13	14	79	26	53	0	318	387	43	49	152	63	88	1	572	659	56	63	34	97	107	82	93	104	92	93
BRO	78	51	27	0	385	329	41	49	79	33	42	4	323	316	37	44	157	84	69	4	708	645	78	93	111	91	106	112	95	87	107	106
CHI	80	44	34	2	379	343	44	35	76	40	36	0	345	335	47	39	156	84	70	2	724	678	91	74	89	116	97	101	104	98	101	100
CIN	81	55	25	1	404	307	48	39	75	42	32	1	363	288	50	42	156	97	57	2	767	595	98	81	90	126	107	102	107	86	103	100
NY	74	41	33	0	360	315	84	58	77	36	41	0	343	370	32	28	151	77	74	0	703	685	116	84	208	93	74	99	106	103	99	99
PHI	74	29	44	1	288	384	19	49	78	16	62	0	265	472	30	57	152	45	106	1	553	856	49	106	83	69	138	95	88	127	94	99
PIT	77	35	42	0	339	365	22	29	76	33	43	0	327	356	41	41	153	68	85	0	666	721	63	70	64	92	103	101	98	105	100	101
STL	79	51	27	1	431	317	63	42	76	41	34	1	348	316	35	34	155	92	61	2	779	633	98	76	140	97	80	108	107	90	105	103
1940 NATIONAL LEAGUE																																
BOS	75	35	40	0	328	352	25	30	77	30	47	0	295	393	34	53	152	65	87	0	623	745	59	83	67	83	110	101	95	110	99	101
BRO	81	41	37	3	369	358	40	55	75	47	28	0	328	263	53	46	156	88	65	3	697	621	93	101	91	115	124	113	94	85	108	106
CHI	77	40	37	0	333	316	40	32	77	35	42	0	348	320	46	42	154	75	79	0	681	636	86	74	84	107	93	97	101	95	100	99
CIN	77	55	21	1	352	240	47	36	78	45	32	1	355	288	42	37	155	100	53	2	707	528	89	73	107	97	82	95	103	79	101	98
NY	76	33	43	0	323	339	61	75	76	39	37	0	340	320	30	35	152	72	80	0	663	659	91	110	184	77	91	100	99	99	100	100
PHI	79	24	55	0	232	403	33	50	74	26	48	0	262	347	42	42	153	50	103	0	494	750	75	92	92	93	111	96	76	109	97	102
PIT	75	40	34	1	390	354	26	22	81	38	42	1	419	429	50	50	156	78	76	2	809	783	76	72	55	109	101	95	124	120	95	95
STL	77	41	36	0	368	364	69	47	79	43	33	3	379	335	50	36	156	84	69	3	747	699	119	83	133	117	86	105	107	101	102	101
1941 NATIONAL LEAGUE																																
BOS	76	32	44	0	276	321	17	28	80	30	48	2	316	399	31	47	156	62	92	2	592	720	48	75	63	77	115	88	96	114	93	95
BRO	79	52	25	2	421	282	55	40	78	48	29	1	379	299	46	41	157	100	54	3	800	581	101	81	108	131	109	103	116	88	103	99
CHI	77	38	39	0	311	306	37	20	78	32	45	1	355	364	62	40	155	70	84	1	666	670	99	60	60	164	105	88	109	109	94	94
CIN	79	45	34	0	308	273	27	27	75	43	32	0	308	291	37	34	154	88	66	0	616	564	64	61	75	96	93	94	96	88	99	98
NY	78	38	39	1	360	358	68	69	78	36	40	2	307	348	27	21	156	74	79	3	667	706	95	90	231	78	70	108	98	103	103	104
PHI	76	23	52	1	255	384	34	37	79	20	59	0	246	409	30	42	155	43	111	1	501	793	64	79	100	87	104	99	79	118	97	103
PIT	78	45	32	1	346	336	20	28	78	36	41	1	344	307	36	38	156	81	73	2	690	643	56	66	68	86	102	104	102	96	103	102
STL	79	53	24	2	405	324	37	53	76	44	32	0	329	265	33	32	155	97	56	2	734	589	70	85	129	84	97	117	102	84	110	107
1942 NATIONAL LEAGUE																																
BOS	70	33	36	1	250	271	36	34	80	26	53	1	265	374	32	48	150	59	89	2	515	645	68	82	99	109	126	93	93	111	95	98
BRO	79	57	22	0	381	250	30	35	78	47	28	1	361	260	32	38	155	104	50	1	742	510	62	73	92	96	111	100	121	87	102	97
CHI	78	36	41	1	298	318	36	27	77	32	45	0	293	347	39	43	155	68	86	1	591	665	75	70	78	127	117	95	102	113	96	98
CIN	78	38	39	1	264	276	30	23	76	38	37	1	263	269	36	24	154	76	76	2	527	545	66	47	88	99	74	99	87	89	101	102
NY	79	47	31	1	376	296	80	67	75	38	36	1	299	304	29	27	154	85	67	2	675	600	109	94	211	104	93	106	109	99	103	101
PHI	74	23	51	1	182	340	18	31	77	19	58	0	212	366	26	30	151	42	109	1	394	706	44	61	90	68	92	99	119	94	101	
PIT	77	41	34	2	333	301	15	21	74	25	47	2	252	330	39	41	151	66	81	4	585	631	54	62	46	108	127	104	98	105	101	102
STL	78	60	17	1	419	229	31	24	78	46	31	1	336	253	29	25	156	106	48	2	755	482	60	49	103	82	69	111	114	78	108	103
1943 NATIONAL LEAGUE																																
BOS	77	38	39	0	247	327	25	34	76	30	46	0	218	285	14	32	153	68	85	0	465	612	39	66	122	66	109	110	73	93	106	109
BRO	77	46	31	0	389	323	21	30	76	35	41	0	327	351	18	29	153	81	72	0	716	674	39	59	106	72	104	103	119	113	100	99
CHI	75	36	38	1	292	300	24	19	79	38	41	0	340	300	28	34	154	74	79	1	632	600	52	53	75	112	110	98	105	101	99	98
CIN	78	48	29	1	282	280	17	15	76	39	38	0	326	263	26	23	154	87	67	1	608	543	43	38	68	90	81	95	100	91	99	98
NY	77	34	43	0	291	326	63	52	79	21	55	3	267	387	18	28	156	55	98	3	558	713	81	80	212	93	103	96	95	117	96	99
PHI	78	33	43	2	269	314	29	17	79	31	47	1	302	362	37	41	157	64	90	3	571	676	66	59	64	155	133	89	99	114	93	96
PIT	78	47	30	1	364	296	20	15	79	33	44	2	305	309	22	29	157	80	74	3	669	605	42	44	72	88	88	108	104	95	104	103
STL	81	58	21	2	355	243	33	17	76	47	28	1	324	232	37	16	157	105	49	3	679	475	70	33	91	127	65	103	105	76	105	100
1944 NATIONAL LEAGUE																																
BOS	78	38	40	0	293	307	51	44	77	27	49	1	300	367	28	36	155	65	89	1	593	674	79	80	138	92	96	89	96	106	95	96

Team Home-Road Statistics

TM	HOME G	W	L	T	R	OR	HR	OHR	ROAD G	W	L	T	R	OR	HR	OHR	ALL G	W	L	T	R	OR	HR	OHR	HRF	HRB	HRP	RF	RB	RP	BPF	PPF
BRO	77	37	39	1	372	413	27	34	78	26	52	0	318	419	29	41	155	63	91	1	690	832	56	75	89	83	107	106	106	124	99	102
CHI	78	35	42	1	346	342	33	40	79	40	37	2	356	327	38	35	157	75	79	3	702	669	71	75	101	98	103	102	104	100	101	100
CIN	78	45	33	0	253	252	14	23	77	44	32	1	320	285	37	37	155	89	65	1	573	537	51	60	53	86	107	85	91	86	95	95
NY	75	39	36	0	372	382	75	86	80	28	51	1	310	391	18	30	155	67	87	1	682	773	93	116	269	69	91	112	100	112	104	105
PHI	79	29	49	1	271	346	20	21	75	32	43	0	268	312	35	28	154	61	92	1	539	658	55	49	64	89	82	100	82	98	100	103
PIT	81	49	28	4	399	357	23	31	77	41	35	1	345	305	47	34	158	90	63	5	744	662	70	65	67	111	109	110	105	95	105	104
STL	77	54	22	1	360	230	39	14	80	51	27	2	412	260	61	41	157	105	49	3	772	490	100	55	58	171	95	94	115	77	101	95

1945 NATIONAL LEAGUE

TM	HOME G	W	L	T	R	OR	HR	OHR	ROAD G	W	L	T	R	OR	HR	OHR	ALL G	W	L	T	R	OR	HR	OHR	HRF	HRB	HRP	RF	RB	RP	BPF	PPF
BOS	75	36	38	1	411	395	68	63	79	31	47	1	310	333	33	36	154	67	85	2	721	728	101	99	177	105	105	126	93	95	112	113
BRO	78	48	30	1	387	347	29	34	77	39	37	1	408	377	28	40	155	87	67	1	795	724	57	74	93	82	103	94	120	111	96	95
CHI	76	49	26	1	330	253	24	17	79	49	30	0	405	279	33	40	155	98	56	1	735	532	57	57	62	95	89	91	107	81	99	95
CIN	77	36	41	0	267	307	25	23	77	25	52	0	269	387	31	47	154	61	93	0	536	694	56	70	64	97	112	88	83	104	94	97
NY	78	47	30	1	366	325	83	47	76	31	44	1	302	375	31	38	154	78	74	2	668	700	114	85	166	116	99	100	98	102	100	100
PHI	77	22	55	0	261	450	23	28	77	24	53	0	287	415	33	33	154	46	108	0	548	865	56	61	78	85	93	99	83	123	96	102
PIT	79	45	34	0	407	352	31	25	76	37	38	1	346	334	41	36	155	82	72	1	753	686	72	61	73	113	97	107	105	97	103	102
STL	78	48	29	1	368	286	28	29	77	47	30	0	388	297	36	41	155	95	59	1	756	583	64	70	76	100	107	96	109	87	100	97

1946 NATIONAL LEAGUE

TM	HOME G	W	L	T	R	OR	HR	OHR	ROAD G	W	L	T	R	OR	HR	OHR	ALL G	W	L	T	R	OR	HR	OHR	HRF	HRB	HRP	RF	RB	RP	BPF	PPF
BOS	77	45	31	1	300	268	14	31	77	36	41	0	330	324	30	45	154	81	72	1	630	592	44	76	63	76	127	89	109	103	95	94
BRO	79	56	22	1	374	273	20	22	78	40	38	0	327	297	35	36	157	96	60	1	701	570	55	58	62	92	97	103	110	92	103	100
CHI	77	44	33	0	291	260	24	30	78	38	38	2	335	321	32	28	155	82	71	2	626	581	56	58	93	80	83	87	108	101	94	93
CIN	77	35	42	0	267	289	37	39	79	32	45	2	256	281	28	31	156	67	87	2	523	570	65	70	126	81	87	105	82	88	104	105
NY	77	38	39	0	340	336	76	75	77	23	54	0	272	349	45	39	154	61	93	0	612	685	121	114	162	107	144	135	107	99	109	102
PHI	78	41	36	1	280	335	38	34	77	29	49	0	280	370	42	39	155	69	85	1	560	705	80	73	89	122	113	94	96	118	95	98
PIT	78	37	40	1	303	342	24	23	77	26	51	0	249	326	36	27	155	63	91	1	552	668	60	50	75	92	80	108	87	103	103	106
STL	78	49	29	0	370	288	39	36	78	49	29	0	342	257	42	27	156	98	58	0	712	545	81	63	109	109	87	110	108	86	107	103

1947 NATIONAL LEAGUE

TM	HOME G	W	L	T	R	OR	HR	OHR	ROAD G	W	L	T	R	OR	HR	OHR	ALL G	W	L	T	R	OR	HR	OHR	HRF	HRB	HRP	RF	RB	RP	BPF	PPF
BOS	77	50	27	0	332	289	29	39	77	36	41	0	369	333	56	54	154	86	68	0	701	622	85	93	65	89	100	90	103	93	97	95
BRO	78	52	25	1	409	343	37	57	77	42	35	0	365	325	46	47	155	94	60	1	774	668	83	104	101	74	90	108	104	92	105	103
CHI	79	36	43	0	280	384	29	51	76	33	42	1	287	338	42	55	155	69	85	1	567	722	71	106	81	70	101	101	79	98	101	104
CIN	77	42	35	0	318	330	48	47	77	31	46	0	363	425	47	55	154	73	81	0	681	755	95	102	94	88	94	84	107	116	91	92
NY	76	45	31	0	417	380	131	75	79	36	42	1	413	381	90	47	155	81	73	1	830	761	221	122	146	167	100	104	117	108	101	99
PHI	77	38	38	1	309	323	24	43	78	24	54	0	280	364	36	55	155	62	92	1	589	687	60	98	76	59	93	99	83	95	100	102
PIT	79	32	45	2	384	437	55	87	77	30	47	0	360	380	61	68	156	62	92	2	744	817	156	155	130	127	128	106	103	112	101	102
STL	77	46	31	0	400	331	45	49	79	43	34	2	380	303	70	57	156	89	65	2	780	634	115	106	79	113	108	109	103	86	106	104

1948 NATIONAL LEAGUE

TM	HOME G	W	L	T	R	OR	HR	OHR	ROAD G	W	L	T	R	OR	HR	OHR	ALL G	W	L	T	R	OR	HR	OHR	HRF	HRB	HRP	RF	RB	RP	BPF	PPF
BOS	76	45	31	0	349	297	32	40	78	46	31	1	390	287	63	53	154	91	62	1	739	584	95	93	67	103	105	99	107	87	102	99
BRO	78	36	41	1	352	386	43	68	77	48	29	0	392	281	48	51	155	84	70	1	744	667	91	119	110	84	105	108	104	94	104	103
CHI	78	35	42	1	282	323	38	34	77	29	48	0	315	383	49	55	155	64	90	1	597	706	87	89	71	95	95	86	104	108	93	95
CIN	77	32	45	0	312	398	68	52	76	32	44	0	276	354	36	52	153	64	89	0	588	752	104	104	128	85	89	109	84	104	103	106
NY	77	37	40	0	366	374	89	82	78	41	36	1	414	330	75	40	155	78	76	1	780	704	164	122	142	134	99	101	114	104	100	98
PHI	76	32	44	0	276	332	32	44	79	34	44	1	315	397	59	51	155	66	88	1	591	729	91	95	74	95	102	89	91	110	94	97
PIT	80	47	31	2	384	370	69	64	76	36	40	0	322	329	39	56	156	83	71	2	706	699	108	120	128	88	100	109	98	97	104	104
STL	77	44	33	0	359	327	47	43	78	41	36	1	383	319	58	60	155	85	69	1	742	646	105	103	80	110	108	100	107	95	101	99

1949 NATIONAL LEAGUE

TM	HOME G	W	L	T	R	OR	HR	OHR	ROAD G	W	L	T	R	OR	HR	OHR	ALL G	W	L	T	R	OR	HR	OHR	HRF	HRB	HRP	RF	RB	RP	BPF	PPF
BOS	77	43	34	0	344	328	40	40	80	32	45	3	362	391	63	70	157	75	79	3	706	719	103	110	66	104	109	94	103	104	97	97
BRO	78	48	29	1	431	335	86	73	78	49	28	1	448	316	66	59	156	97	57	2	879	651	152	132	125	118	104	101	122	94	101	98
CHI	77	33	44	0	285	365	53	38	77	28	49	0	308	408	44	66	154	61	93	0	593	773	97	104	84	91	94	91	90	113	94	97
CIN	78	35	42	1	326	349	50	54	78	27	50	1	301	421	36	70	156	62	92	2	627	770	86	124	97	75	103	93	93	111	96	98
NY	79	43	34	2	404	331	94	78	77	30	47	0	332	362	53	54	156	73	81	2	736	693	147	132	146	102	95	102	102	97	101	101
PHI	77	40	37	0	336	326	61	35	77	41	36	0	326	342	61	69	154	81	73	0	662	668	122	104	77	120	100	99	94	95	100	101
PIT	77	36	41	0	341	397	77	75	77	35	42	0	340	363	49	67	154	71	83	0	681	760	126	142	126	98	111	104	97	106	101	102
STL	79	51	26	2	427	325	48	33	78	45	32	1	339	291	54	54	157	96	58	3	766	616	102	87	77	94	80	117	97	80	110	108

1950 NATIONAL LEAGUE

TM	HOME G	W	L	T	R	OR	HR	OHR	ROAD G	W	L	T	R	OR	HR	OHR	ALL G	W	L	T	R	OR	HR	OHR	HRF	HRB	HRP	RF	RB	RP	BPF	PPF
BOS	79	46	31	2	343	294	59	45	77	37	40	0	442	442	89	84	156	83	71	2	785	736	148	129	62	132	115	73	126	118	86	85
BRO	78	48	30	0	458	386	110	96	77	41	35	1	389	338	84	67	155	89	65	1	847	724	194	163	130	126	108	113	110	96	106	104
CHI	78	35	42	1	352	411	79	63	76	29	47	0	291	361	82	67	154	64	89	1	643	772	161	130	93	121	101	111	85	100	105	107
CIN	76	38	38	0	355	373	52	81	77	28	49	0	299	361	47	54	153	66	87	0	654	734	99	145	117	67	94	109	88	97	105	106
NY	76	44	32	0	362	290	84	67	78	42	36	0	373	353	49	73	154	86	68	0	735	643	133	140	124	86	92	94	104	92	98	97
PHI	78	47	30	1	348	279	58	53	79	44	33	2	374	345	67	69	157	91	63	3	722	624	125	122	85	95	92	90	101	89	97	96
PIT	77	33	44	0	370	447	81	79	77	24	52	1	311	410	57	73	154	57	96	1	681	857	138	152	118	93	102	110	92	113	103	106
STL	76	47	29	0	389	303	50	43	77	31	46	0	304	367	52	76	153	78	75	0	693	670	102	119	76	85	93	104	94	92	103	103

1951 NATIONAL LEAGUE

TM	HOME G	W	L	T	R	OR	HR	OHR	ROAD G	W	L	T	R	OR	HR	OHR	ALL G	W	L	T	R	OR	HR	OHR	HRF	HRB	HRP	RF	RB	RP	BPF	PPF
BOS	78	42	35	1	367	310	59	37	77	34	43	0	356	352	71	59	155	76	78	1	723	662	130	96	75	113	85	95	107	99	98	97
BRO	78	49	29	0	412	316	100	81	80	48	31	1	443	356	84	69	158	97	60	1	855	672	184	150	120	133	111	95	124	100	98	95
CHI	77	32	45	0	304	364	45	59	78	30	47	1	310	386	58	66	155	62	92	1	614	750	103	125	86	86	103	97	91	109	97	100
CIN	77	35	42	0	289	320	44	46	78	33	44	1	270	347	44	73	155	68	86	1	559	667	88	119	80	77	98	99	80	94	101	103
NY	78	50	28	0	399	308	115	89	79	48	31	0	382	333	64	59	157	98	59	0	781	641	179	148	157	109	94	101	110	92	102	99
PHI	77	38	39	0	312	305	43	50	77	35	42	0	336	339	65	60	154	73	81	0	648	644	108	110	77	94	97	92	97	97	97	97
PIT	78	32	45	1	388	465	72	84	77	32	45	0	301	380	65	73	155	64	90	1	689	845	137	157	109	106	119	119	93	112	107	109
STL	79	44	34	1	370	323	44	56	76	37	39	0	313	348	51	63	155	81	73	1	683	671	95	119	86	79	96	101	98	96	101	101

1952 NATIONAL LEAGUE

TM	HOME G	W	L	T	R	OR	HR	OHR	ROAD G	W	L	T	R	OR	HR	OHR	ALL G	W	L	T	R	OR	HR	OHR	HRF	HRB	HRP	RF	RB	RP	BPF	PPF
BOS	77	31	45	1	257	314	48	44	78	33	44	1	312	337	62	62	155	64	89	2	569	651	110	106	77	108	104	90	93	104	95	97
BRO	80	45	33	2	389	324	76	78	75	51	24	0	386	279	77	43	155	96	57	2	775	603	153	121	119	126	100	102	118	95	101	98
CHI	77	42	35	0	329	316	51	40	78	35	42	1	299	315	56	61	155	77	77	1	628	631	107	101	81	103	96	106	94	94	103	103
CIN	77	38	39	0	318	319	43	43	77	31	46	0	297	340	61	68	154	69	85	0	615	659	104	111	69	109	114	99	96	102	99	100
NY	77	50	27	0	369	327	103	74	77	42	35	0	353	312	48	47	154	92	62	0	722	639	151	121	170	99	84	105	110	99	102	101
PHI	76	47	29	0	318	269	42	43	78	40	38	0	339	283	51	52	154	87	67	0	657	552	93	95	87	86	87	98	101	87	101	99
PIT	77	23	54	0	261	414	45	72	78	19	58	1	254	379	47	61	155	42	112	1	515	793	92	133	106	80	110	105	80	117	100	105
STL	77	48	29	0	343	291	46	59	77	40	37	0	334	339	51	60	154	88	66	0	677	630	97	119	96	88	105	96	108	101	98	97

1953 NATIONAL LEAGUE

TM	HOME G	W	L	T	R	OR	HR	OHR	ROAD G	W	L	T	R	OR	HR	OHR	ALL G	W	L	T	R	OR	HR	OHR	HRF	HRB	HRP	RF	RB	RP	BPF	PPF
BRO	78	60	17	1	517	333	110	82	77	45	32	0	438	356	98	87	155	105	49	1	955	689	208	169	104	141	118	107	125	94	104	99
CHI	77	43	34	0	351	417	74	69	78	22	55	1	282	418	63	82	155	65	89	1	633	835	137	151	99	92	100	109	83	107	103	106
CIN	78	38	39	1	367	391	89	96	77	30	47	0	347	397	77	83	155	68	86	1	714	788	166	179	111	108	116	100	98	107	99	100

	HOME								ROAD								ALL															
TM	G	W	L	T	R	OR	HR	OHR	G	W	L	T	R	OR	HR	OHR	G	W	L	T	R	OR	HR	OHR	HRF	HRB	HRP	RF	RB	RP	BPF	PPF
MIL	79	45	31	3	332	260	51	44	78	47	31	0	406	329	105	63	157	92	62	3	738	589	156	107	60	121	91	82	105	86	94	92
NY	77	38	39	0	395	345	109	81	78	32	45	1	373	402	67	65	155	70	84	1	768	747	176	146	137	98	85	97	106	104	98	98
PHI	78	48	29	1	363	304	63	65	78	35	42	1	353	362	52	73	156	83	71	2	716	666	115	138	102	74	88	94	98	92	99	98
PIT	77	26	51	0	338	460	53	88	77	24	53	0	284	427	46	80	154	50	104	0	622	887	99	168	108	65	104	109	83	114	102	106
STL	78	48	30	0	420	321	65	58	79	35	41	3	348	392	75	81	157	83	71	3	768	713	140	139	82	101	99	102	101	95	101	101
1954 NATIONAL LEAGUE																															
BRO	77	45	32	0	380	393	101	92	77	47	30	0	398	347	85	72	154	92	62	0	778	740	186	164	121	125	112	104	109	105	101	100
CHI	77	40	37	0	366	385	86	59	77	24	53	0	334	381	73	72	154	64	90	0	700	766	159	131	99	114	96	104	99	107	101	102
CIN	77	41	36	0	380	407	94	105	77	33	44	0	349	356	53	64	154	74	80	0	729	763	147	169	156	83	95	110	100	104	104	104
MIL	77	43	34	0	285	251	43	29	77	46	31	0	385	305	96	77	154	89	65	0	670	556	139	106	45	133	102	81	102	87	93	91
NY	76	53	23	0	387	254	120	67	78	44	34	0	345	296	66	46	154	97	57	0	732	550	186	113	159	100	66	104	99	77	105	102
PHI	78	39	39	0	315	305	47	60	76	36	40	0	344	309	55	73	154	75	79	0	659	614	102	133	83	79	100	93	95	89	99	98
PIT	77	31	46	0	277	422	22	42	77	22	55	0	280	423	54	86	154	53	101	0	557	845	76	128	48	71	115	98	82	118	97	102
STL	77	33	44	0	386	431	57	90	77	39	38	0	413	359	62	80	154	72	82	0	799	790	119	170	103	87	118	105	113	112	100	100
1955 NATIONAL LEAGUE																															
BRO	77	56	21	0	461	318	119	85	77	42	34	1	396	332	82	83	154	98	55	1	857	650	201	168	122	115	100	108	118	93	104	101
CHI	77	43	33	1	348	322	80	62	77	29	48	0	278	391	84	91	154	72	81	1	626	713	164	153	83	114	106	100	90	101	100	101
CIN	77	46	31	0	425	341	102	91	77	29	48	0	336	343	79	70	154	75	79	0	761	684	181	161	125	102	92	111	103	94	106	104
MIL	77	46	31	0	342	297	75	51	77	39	38	0	401	371	107	87	154	85	69	0	743	668	182	138	68	136	105	85	115	104	93	92
NY	79	44	35	0	362	327	95	91	75	36	39	0	340	346	74	64	154	80	74	0	702	673	169	155	124	95	88	96	102	99	98	98
PHI	77	46	31	0	371	309	76	78	77	31	46	0	304	357	56	83	154	77	77	0	675	666	132	161	109	79	95	103	95	94	102	102
PIT	75	36	39	0	298	337	34	48	79	24	55	0	262	430	57	94	154	60	94	0	560	767	91	142	60	71	103	96	83	109	97	101
STL	77	41	36	0	358	362	84	92	77	27	50	0	296	395	59	93	154	68	86	0	654	757	143	185	113	86	109	103	93	106	100	102
1956 NATIONAL LEAGUE																															
BRO	77	52	25	0	369	300	102	89	77	41	36	0	351	301	77	82	154	93	61	0	720	601	179	171	118	110	107	103	107	92	103	100
CHI	80	39	38	3	335	328	78	77	77	21	56	0	262	380	64	84	157	60	94	3	597	708	142	161	100	93	104	98	91	106	98	101
CIN	77	51	26	0	426	346	128	75	78	40	37	1	349	312	93	66	155	91	63	1	775	658	221	141	126	128	87	117	109	95	108	106
MIL	77	47	29	1	344	265	77	53	78	45	33	0	365	304	100	80	155	92	62	1	709	569	177	133	76	130	101	94	109	90	99	96
NY	77	37	40	0	269	306	94	86	77	30	47	0	271	344	51	58	154	67	87	0	540	650	145	144	152	74	75	94	85	100	97	99
PHI	77	40	37	0	337	335	61	74	77	31	46	0	331	403	60	98	154	71	83	0	668	738	121	172	87	88	118	92	109	118	94	95
PIT	78	35	43	0	301	328	49	45	79	31	45	3	287	325	61	97	157	66	88	3	588	653	110	142	63	89	105	103	86	95	102	103
STL	78	43	34	1	358	328	58	73	78	33	44	1	320	370	66	82	156	76	78	2	678	698	124	155	90	85	104	99	104	106	99	99
1957 NATIONAL LEAGUE																															
BRO	77	43	34	0	383	348	84	88	77	41	36	0	307	243	63	56	154	84	70	0	690	591	147	144	137	84	82	128	88	76	116	114
CHI	78	31	46	1	301	353	81	68	78	31	46	1	327	369	66	76	156	62	92	2	628	722	147	144	103	97	95	94	95	108	96	98
CIN	77	45	32	0	417	410	118	101	77	35	42	0	330	371	69	78	154	80	74	0	747	781	187	179	141	108	106	116	105	109	105	106
MIL	78	45	32	1	312	289	75	51	77	50	27	0	460	324	124	73	155	95	59	1	772	613	199	124	67	158	107	79	125	104	90	88
NY	77	37	40	0	353	341	99	86	77	32	45	0	290	360	58	64	154	69	85	0	643	701	157	150	142	87	86	105	93	101	102	103
PHI	78	38	39	1	299	322	60	60	78	39	38	1	324	334	57	79	156	77	77	2	623	656	117	139	90	82	95	95	93	97	98	99
PIT	77	36	41	0	273	321	20	53	78	26	51	1	313	375	72	105	155	62	92	1	586	696	92	158	45	80	143	88	92	107	94	96
STL	77	42	35	0	356	348	64	70	77	45	32	0	381	318	68	70	154	87	67	0	737	666	132	140	98	90	95	101	109	99	101	99
1958 NATIONAL LEAGUE																															
CHI	77	35	42	0	350	381	101	72	77	37	40	0	359	344	81	70	154	72	82	0	709	725	182	142	112	115	93	103	104	106	100	101
CIN	77	40	37	0	364	337	71	86	77	36	41	0	331	284	52	62	154	76	78	0	695	621	123	148	131	71	84	112	96	86	107	106
LA	77	39	38	0	359	405	92	101	77	32	45	0	309	356	80	72	154	71	83	0	668	761	172	173	122	108	107	112	94	106	105	106
MIL	77	48	29	0	291	207	72	48	77	44	33	0	384	334	95	77	154	92	62	0	675	541	167	125	73	128	98	73	112	91	89	87
PHI	77	35	42	0	318	397	59	77	77	34	43	0	346	365	65	71	154	69	85	0	664	762	124	148	99	84	98	100	100	112	98	100
PIT	77	49	28	0	323	260	41	40	77	35	42	0	339	347	93	83	154	84	70	0	662	607	134	123	50	116	110	87	103	95	95	94
STL	77	39	38	0	329	381	62	88	77	33	44	0	290	323	49	70	154	72	82	0	619	704	111	158	122	68	93	113	86	96	106	108
SF	77	44	33	0	363	354	85	88	77	36	41	0	364	344	85	78	154	80	74	0	727	698	170	166	106	114	112	101	107	104	100	100
1959 NATIONAL LEAGUE																															
CHI	77	38	39	0	336	329	87	76	78	36	41	1	337	359	76	76	155	74	80	1	673	688	163	152	107	109	103	97	100	102	98	99
CIN	77	43	34	0	423	367	101	84	77	31	46	0	341	371	60	78	154	74	80	0	764	738	161	162	128	98	101	109	109	106	103	103
LA	78	46	32	0	363	333	82	90	78	42	36	0	342	337	66	67	156	88	68	0	705	670	148	157	126	91	95	103	101	96	102	101
MIL	79	49	29	1	350	274	83	64	78	37	41	0	374	349	94	64	157	86	70	1	724	623	177	128	93	123	93	87	111	97	95	93
PHI	78	37	40	1	316	354	55	66	77	27	50	0	283	371	58	84	155	64	90	1	599	725	113	150	85	85	108	100	88	104	99	102
PIT	77	47	30	0	348	334	47	53	78	31	46	1	303	346	65	81	155	78	76	1	651	680	112	134	72	89	103	106	92	96	103	104
STL	77	42	35	0	366	359	64	64	77	29	48	0	275	366	54	73	154	71	83	0	641	725	118	137	100	81	92	111	90	101	105	106
SF	77	42	35	0	339	271	80	63	77	41	36	0	366	342	87	76	154	83	71	0	705	613	167	139	89	123	104	88	109	96	95	94
1960 NATIONAL LEAGUE																															
CHI	79	33	44	2	331	390	52	78	77	27	50	0	303	386	67	74	156	60	94	2	634	776	119	152	90	97	121	101	98	117	98	101
CIN	77	37	40	0	314	347	75	68	77	30	47	0	326	345	65	66	154	67	87	0	640	692	140	134	107	105	101	98	100	107	98	99
LA	77	42	35	0	379	334	89	97	77	40	37	0	283	259	37	57	154	82	72	0	662	593	126	154	177	69	86	127	88	80	115	114
MIL	77	51	26	0	342	270	90	56	77	37	40	0	382	388	80	74	154	88	66	0	724	658	170	130	96	135	107	82	123	112	91	89
PHI	77	31	46	0	300	373	54	74	77	28	49	0	246	318	45	59	154	59	95	0	546	691	99	133	118	70	91	115	78	96	107	110
PIT	78	52	25	1	362	287	51	36	77	43	34	0	372	306	69	69	155	95	59	1	734	593	120	105	66	109	94	96	112	93	99	97
STL	77	51	26	0	361	308	78	64	78	35	42	1	278	308	60	63	155	86	68	1	639	616	138	127	115	98	91	114	90	87	108	108
SF	77	45	32	0	296	256	46	34	79	34	43	2	375	375	84	73	156	79	75	2	671	631	130	107	56	124	102	78	114	107	90	89
1961 NATIONAL LEAGUE																															
CHI	78	40	37	1	372	391	102	81	78	24	53	1	317	409	74	84	156	64	90	2	689	800	176	165	113	111	106	104	98	111	100	102
CIN	77	47	30	0	345	355	70	75	77	46	31	0	365	298	88	72	154	93	61	0	710	653	158	147	93	110	104	106	98	91	104	103
LA	77	45	32	0	373	358	83	109	77	44	33	0	362	339	74	58	154	89	65	0	735	697	157	167	139	91	93	105	103	99	102	101
MIL	77	45	32	0	324	280	84	72	78	38	39	1	388	376	104	81	155	83	71	1	712	656	188	153	87	135	114	82	111	102	92	91
PHI	78	22	55	1	256	408	43	77	77	25	52	0	328	388	60	78	155	47	107	1	584	796	103	155	86	74	107	91	89	117	94	98
PIT	77	38	39	0	338	338	49	54	77	37	40	0	356	337	79	67	154	75	79	0	694	675	128	121	73	95	93	98	100	98	99	99
STL	78	48	29	1	413	362	54	69	77	32	45	0	290	306	49	67	155	80	74	1	703	668	103	136	104	66	85	124	88	85	113	113
SF	77	45	32	0	371	316	97	77	78	40	37	1	402	339	86	75	155	85	69	1	773	655	183	152	109	118	100	95	112	97	98	96
1962 NATIONAL LEAGUE																															
CHI	81	32	49	0	333	456	71	94	81	27	54	0	299	371	55	65	162	59	103	0	632	827	126	159	131	76	94	114	82	105	106	109
CIN	81	58	23	0	456	294	95	68	81	40	41	0	346	391	72	81	162	98	64	0	802	685	167	149	107	112	102	103	108	94	102	100
HOU	82	32	48	2	268	340	44	41	80	32	48	0	324	377	61	72	162	64	96	2	592	717	105	113	64	87	91	85	88	105	93	95
LA	83	54	29	0	409	289	47	39	82	48	34	0	433	408	93	76	165	102	63	0	842	697	140	115	54	120	101	85	124	103	93	91
MIL	81	49	32	0	374	307	93	74	81	37	44	0	356	358	88	77	162	86	76	0	730	665	181	151	101	125	107	96	102	93	99	98

	HOME								ROAD								ALL														
TM	G	W	L	T	R	OR	HR	OHR	G	W	L	T	R	OR	HR	OHR	G	W	L	T	R	OR	HR	OHR	HRF	HRB	HRP	RF	RB	RP	BPF	PPF
NY	80	22	58	0	335	510	93	120	81	18	62	1	282	438	46	72	161	40	120	1	617	948	139	192	165	73	101	114	82	121	104	108
PHI	80	46	34	0	341	346	70	66	81	35	46	0	364	413	72	89	161	81	80	0	705	759	142	155	87	107	115	91	103	110	95	95
PIT	81	51	30	0	358	315	48	56	80	42	38	0	348	311	60	62	161	93	68	0	706	626	108	118	86	79	86	102	96	86	102	101
STL	81	44	37	0	407	362	64	83	82	40	41	1	367	302	73	66	163	84	78	1	774	664	137	149	107	92	98	115	98	85	108	107
SF	82	61	21	0	479	299	109	74	83	42	41	0	399	391	95	74	165	103	62	0	878	690	204	148	110	133	100	101	118	95	101	99

1963 NATIONAL LEAGUE

	HOME								ROAD								ALL														
TM	G	W	L	T	R	OR	HR	OHR	G	W	L	T	R	OR	HR	OHR	G	W	L	T	R	OR	HR	OHR	HRF	HRB	HRP	RF	RB	RP	BPF	PPF
CHI	81	43	38	0	298	302	63	70	81	39	42	0	272	276	64	49	162	82	80	0	570	578	127	119	116	97	91	109	88	89	105	105
CIN	81	46	35	0	344	300	65	46	81	40	41	0	304	294	57	71	162	86	76	0	648	594	122	117	88	107	102	107	101	93	104	103
HOU	81	44	37	0	236	268	25	34	81	22	59	0	228	372	37	61	162	66	96	0	464	640	62	95	62	62	90	85	82	108	92	95
LA	81	53	28	0	296	248	42	43	82	46	35	1	344	302	68	68	163	99	63	1	640	550	110	111	66	106	108	88	108	94	95	94
MIL	82	45	36	1	341	307	68	81	81	39	42	0	336	296	71	68	163	84	78	1	677	603	139	149	105	114	121	101	108	97	101	100
NY	81	34	47	0	276	381	61	93	81	17	64	0	225	393	35	69	162	51	111	0	501	774	96	162	139	67	110	104	82	121	99	104
PHI	81	45	36	0	340	282	61	60	81	42	39	0	302	296	65	53	162	87	75	0	642	578	126	113	103	92	104	101	92	103	102	102
PIT	81	42	39	0	275	295	47	42	81	32	49	0	292	300	61	57	162	74	88	0	567	595	108	99	77	98	91	96	93	97	99	99
STL	81	53	28	0	429	311	79	70	81	40	41	0	318	317	49	54	162	93	69	0	747	628	128	124	139	87	86	115	112	97	107	106
SF	81	50	31	0	363	289	101	64	81	38	43	0	362	352	96	62	162	88	74	0	725	641	197	126	104	161	109	93	123	110	96	94

1964 NATIONAL LEAGUE

	HOME								ROAD								ALL														
TM	G	W	L	T	R	OR	HR	OHR	G	W	L	T	R	OR	HR	OHR	G	W	L	T	R	OR	HR	OHR	HRF	HRB	HRP	RF	RB	RP	BPF	PPF
CHI	81	40	41	0	337	397	85	87	81	36	45	0	312	327	60	57	162	76	86	0	649	724	145	144	140	102	101	113	95	104	105	106
CIN	82	47	34	1	331	294	62	59	81	45	36	0	329	272	68	53	163	92	70	1	660	566	130	112	100	106	93	103	98	85	103	102
HOU	81	41	40	0	246	290	29	44	81	25	56	0	249	338	41	61	162	66	96	0	495	628	70	105	73	66	95	91	79	98	96	98
LA	81	41	40	0	259	259	26	38	83	39	42	2	355	313	53	50	164	80	82	2	614	572	79	88	66	73	84	81	101	95	92	91
MIL	81	45	36	0	405	356	89	78	81	43	38	0	398	388	70	82	162	88	74	0	803	744	159	160	109	132	98	128	119	97	96	96
NY	82	33	48	1	298	363	58	61	81	20	61	0	271	413	45	69	163	53	109	1	569	776	103	130	101	85	105	94	92	121	95	98
PHI	81	46	35	0	352	298	59	61	81	46	35	0	341	334	71	68	162	92	70	0	693	632	130	129	88	115	115	97	108	99	99	98
PIT	81	42	39	0	340	315	55	31	81	38	43	0	323	321	66	61	162	80	82	0	663	636	121	92	70	116	87	101	101	97	101	101
STL	81	48	33	0	386	378	59	81	81	45	36	0	329	274	50	52	162	93	69	0	715	652	109	133	133	79	93	124	98	90	112	111
SF	81	44	37	0	314	299	86	63	81	46	35	0	342	288	79	55	162	90	72	0	656	587	165	118	111	130	96	98	101	91	100	99

1965 NATIONAL LEAGUE

	HOME								ROAD								ALL														
TM	G	W	L	T	R	OR	HR	OHR	G	W	L	T	R	OR	HR	OHR	G	W	L	T	R	OR	HR	OHR	HRF	HRB	HRP	RF	RB	RP	BPF	PPF
CHI	83	40	41	2	330	380	79	94	81	32	49	0	305	343	55	60	164	72	90	2	635	723	134	154	139	85	96	106	94	106	102	103
CIN	81	49	32	0	450	352	108	69	81	40	41	0	375	352	75	67	162	89	73	0	825	704	183	136	122	125	98	110	122	106	104	102
HOU	81	36	45	0	250	313	25	32	81	29	52	0	319	398	72	91	162	65	97	0	569	711	97	123	37	106	132	79	98	120	89	91
LA	81	50	31	0	268	218	26	41	81	47	34	0	340	303	52	86	162	97	65	0	608	521	78	127	52	78	120	78	102	88	91	90
MIL	81	44	37	0	366	331	98	75	81	42	39	0	342	302	98	48	162	86	76	0	708	633	196	123	117	138	90	108	104	94	104	103
NY	82	29	52	1	258	380	50	81	82	21	60	1	237	372	57	66	164	50	112	2	495	752	107	147	104	80	106	102	75	109	100	104
PHI	80	45	35	0	312	300	77	55	82	40	41	1	342	367	61	61	162	85	76	1	654	667	144	116	105	105	87	90	106	107	95	95
PIT	82	49	32	1	334	284	37	38	81	41	40	0	341	296	74	51	163	90	72	1	675	580	111	89	62	97	83	97	103	90	100	98
STL	81	42	39	0	379	361	68	103	81	38	42	1	328	313	41	63	162	80	81	1	707	674	109	166	154	66	98	114	102	97	106	106
SF	81	51	30	0	365	327	81	81	82	44	37	1	317	266	78	56	163	95	67	1	682	593	159	137	121	110	95	119	94	83	111	109

1966 NATIONAL LEAGUE

	HOME								ROAD								ALL														
TM	G	W	L	T	R	OR	HR	OHR	G	W	L	T	R	OR	HR	OHR	G	W	L	T	R	OR	HR	OHR	HRF	HRB	HRP	RF	RB	RP	BPF	PPF
ATL	82	43	38	1	394	335	119	82	81	42	39	0	388	348	88	47	163	85	77	1	782	683	207	129	141	124	79	98	119	105	99	97
CHI	81	32	49	0	342	410	80	100	81	27	54	0	302	399	60	84	162	59	103	0	644	809	140	184	120	95	122	105	97	119	100	103
CIN	79	46	33	0	417	372	91	93	81	30	51	0	275	330	58	60	160	76	84	0	692	702	149	153	151	88	90	129	92	95	114	114
HOU	81	45	36	0	318	317	48	48	82	27	54	1	294	378	64	82	163	72	90	1	612	695	112	130	68	96	107	96	94	105	97	99
LA	81	53	28	0	286	220	43	36	81	42	39	0	320	270	65	48	162	95	67	0	606	490	108	84	73	86	69	88	94	78	97	95
NY	81	32	49	0	276	372	51	94	80	34	46	0	311	389	47	72	161	66	95	0	587	761	98	166	117	67	108	91	95	120	94	97
PHI	81	48	33	0	354	319	52	65	81	39	42	0	342	321	65	72	162	87	75	0	696	640	117	137	87	90	105	102	104	96	101	100
PIT	81	46	35	0	384	317	48	48	81	46	35	0	375	324	110	77	162	92	70	0	759	641	158	125	54	144	123	101	114	98	101	99
STL	81	43	38	0	274	288	48	64	81	40	41	0	297	289	60	66	162	83	79	0	571	577	108	130	90	81	97	96	86	87	100	100
SF	81	47	34	0	317	312	91	77	80	46	34	0	358	314	90	63	161	93	68	0	675	626	181	140	108	128	101	94	105	98	97	97

1967 NATIONAL LEAGUE

	HOME								ROAD								ALL														
TM	G	W	L	T	R	OR	HR	OHR	G	W	L	T	R	OR	HR	OHR	G	W	L	T	R	OR	HR	OHR	HRF	HRB	HRP	RF	RB	RP	BPF	PPF
ATL	81	48	33	0	352	316	91	74	81	29	52	0	279	324	67	44	162	77	85	0	631	640	158	118	141	121	91	109	97	99	104	105
CHI	84	49	34	1	366	332	70	90	78	38	40	1	336	292	58	52	162	87	74	1	702	624	128	142	131	104	111	103	111	100	101	100
CIN	81	49	32	0	343	287	57	66	81	38	43	0	261	276	52	35	162	87	75	0	604	563	109	101	136	85	76	116	89	84	109	108
HOU	81	46	35	0	337	315	31	32	81	23	58	0	289	427	62	88	162	69	93	0	626	742	93	120	44	122	145	91	108	125	93	95
LA	81	42	39	0	241	230	36	35	81	31	50	0	278	365	46	58	162	73	89	0	519	595	82	93	70	87	95	75	96	106	88	89
NY	78	36	42	0	258	307	44	61	84	25	59	0	240	365	39	63	162	61	101	0	498	672	83	124	108	73	105	99	81	106	99	102
PHI	80	45	35	0	320	292	48	44	82	37	45	0	292	289	55	42	162	82	80	0	612	581	103	86	99	92	78	107	94	90	104	104
PIT	81	49	32	0	370	321	43	49	82	32	49	1	309	372	48	59	163	81	81	1	679	693	91	108	88	87	101	102	109	111	100	100
STL	81	49	32	0	326	301	53	54	80	52	28	0	369	256	62	43	161	101	60	0	695	557	115	97	102	103	88	100	111	91	101	99
SF	82	51	31	0	333	271	65	59	80	40	40	0	319	280	75	54	162	91	71	0	652	551	140	113	95	131	109	99	104	89	101	99

1968 NATIONAL LEAGUE

	HOME								ROAD								ALL														
TM	G	W	L	T	R	OR	HR	OHR	G	W	L	T	R	OR	HR	OHR	G	W	L	T	R	OR	HR	OHR	HRF	HRB	HRP	RF	RB	RP	BPF	PPF
ATL	81	41	40	0	241	241	42	43	82	40	41	1	273	308	38	44	163	81	81	1	514	549	80	87	104	87	94	85	99	105	93	94
CHI	82	47	34	1	363	332	83	83	81	37	44	0	249	279	47	55	163	84	78	1	612	611	130	138	152	120	129	126	97	98	112	112
CIN	82	40	41	1	377	400	55	66	81	43	38	0	313	273	51	48	163	83	79	1	690	673	106	114	118	112	119	127	112	108	111	111
HOU	81	42	39	0	279	269	22	30	81	30	51	0	231	319	44	38	162	72	90	0	510	588	66	68	65	85	91	99	93	105	99	100
LA	81	41	40	0	212	215	25	24	81	35	46	0	258	294	42	41	162	76	86	0	470	509	67	65	61	90	87	79	94	100	91	91
NY	82	32	49	1	224	270	49	50	81	41	40	0	249	229	32	37	163	73	89	1	473	499	81	87	135	76	82	101	83	87	102	103
PHI	81	38	43	0	274	297	52	46	81	38	43	0	269	318	48	45	162	76	86	0	543	615	100	91	104	111	102	97	100	112	97	99
PIT	81	40	41	0	289	268	33	30	82	40	41	1	294	264	47	43	163	80	82	1	583	532	80	73	73	101	93	101	103	95	101	100
STL	81	47	34	0	267	218	31	35	81	50	31	0	316	254	42	47	162	97	65	0	583	472	73	82	77	92	102	87	110	91	95	93
SF	81	42	39	0	299	242	60	32	82	46	35	1	300	287	48	54	163	88	74	1	599	529	108	86	93	126	101	94	110	98	98	96

1969 NATIONAL LEAGUE

	HOME								ROAD								ALL														
TM	G	W	L	T	R	OR	HR	OHR	G	W	L	T	R	OR	HR	OHR	G	W	L	T	R	OR	HR	OHR	HRF	HRB	HRP	RF	RB	RP	BPF	PPF
ATL	81	50	31	0	360	321	77	84	81	43	38	0	331	310	64	60	162	93	69	0	691	631	141	144	128	103	104	106	102	93	104	103
CHI	82	49	32	1	387	321	84	64	81	43	38	0	333	290	58	54	163	92	70	1	720	611	142	118	128	100	85	112	102	88	107	105
CIN	81	50	31	0	407	373	97	74	82	39	42	1	391	395	74	75	163	89	73	1	798	768	171	149	115	131	117	101	122	118	99	98
HOU	81	52	29	0	371	313	47	43	81	29	52	0	305	355	57	68	162	81	81	0	676	668	104	111	74	98	102	103	101	100	101	101
LA	81	50	31	0	325	258	41	55	81	35	46	0	320	303	56	67	162	85	77	0	645	561	97	122	80	88	109	94	100	88	99	97
MON	81	24	57	0	288	421	73	87	81	28	53	0	294	370	52	58	162	52	110	0	582	791	125	145	138	87	99	104	88	117	100	103
NY	82	52	30	0	312	270	56	59	80	48	32	0	320	271	53	60	162	100	62	0	632	541	109	119	101	89	96	96	83	100	99	99
PHI	81	30	51	0	317	378	75	64	81	33	48	0	328	367	62	70	162	63	99	0	645	745	137	134	104	111	109	99	100	114	98	99
PIT	81	47	34	0	324	322	41	33	81	41	40	0	401	330	78	63	162	88	74	0	725	652	119	96	55	122	101	90	116	106	95	94
STL	80	42	38	0	273	273	41	43	82	45	37	0	322	267	49	56	162	87	75	0	595	540	90	99	84	79	85	96	91	83	100	100
SD	81	28	53	0	239	358	47	47	81	24	57	0	229	388	52	66	162	52	110	0	468	746	99	113	80	90	100	95	74	113	97	100
SF	81	52	29	0	362	317	77	61	81	38	43	0	351	319	59	59	162	90	72	0	713	636	136	120	116	102	92	102	107	97	101	100

TM	HOME								ROAD								ALL															
	G	W	L	T	R	OR	HR	OHR	G	W	L	T	R	OR	HR	OHR	G	W	L	T	R	OR	HR	OHR	HRF	HRB	HRP	RF	RB	RP	BPF	PPF

1970 NATIONAL LEAGUE

TM	G	W	L	T	R	OR	HR	OHR	G	W	L	T	R	OR	HR	OHR	G	W	L	T	R	OR	HR	OHR	HRF	HRB	HRP	RF	RB	RP	BPF	PPF
ATL	81	42	39	0	395	398	92	119	81	34	47	0	341	374	68	66	162	76	86	0	736	772	160	185	150	95	105	110	96	101	104	105
CHI	80	46	34	0	471	394	109	92	82	38	44	0	335	285	70	51	162	84	78	0	806	679	179	143	161	99	79	138	92	79	120	118
CIN	81	57	24	0	416	334	100	58	81	45	36	0	359	347	91	60	162	102	60	0	775	681	191	118	106	131	84	107	102	90	104	103
HOU	81	44	37	0	350	351	51	64	81	35	46	0	394	412	78	67	162	79	83	0	744	763	129	131	81	100	104	88	109	111	93	94
LA	81	39	42	0	310	316	35	82	80	48	32	0	439	368	52	82	161	87	74	0	749	684	87	164	88	67	121	78	114	106	90	89
MON	80	39	41	0	363	385	77	91	82	34	48	0	324	422	59	71	162	73	89	0	687	807	136	162	128	86	101	102	94	109	100	102
NY	82	44	38	0	374	314	63	75	80	39	41	0	321	316	57	60	162	83	79	0	695	630	120	135	114	80	88	105	91	84	104	103
PHI	80	40	40	0	293	337	48	63	81	33	48	0	301	393	53	69	161	73	88	0	594	730	101	132	92	75	96	92	85	103	96	98
PIT	82	50	32	0	356	315	43	41	80	39	41	0	373	349	87	65	162	89	73	0	729	664	130	106	56	114	98	92	103	95	97	96
STL	81	34	47	0	377	418	51	44	81	42	39	0	367	329	62	58	162	76	86	0	744	747	113	102	80	87	79	113	96	96	106	106
SD	81	31	50	0	312	393	68	56	81	32	49	0	369	395	104	93	162	63	99	0	681	788	172	149	64	152	132	92	98	112	95	96
SF	81	48	33	0	413	386	84	77	81	38	43	0	418	440	81	79	162	86	76	0	831	826	165	156	101	118	113	94	119	118	96	96

1971 NATIONAL LEAGUE

TM	G	W	L	T	R	OR	HR	OHR	G	W	L	T	R	OR	HR	OHR	G	W	L	T	R	OR	HR	OHR	HRF	HRB	HRP	RF	RB	RP	BPF	PPF
ATL	82	43	39	0	366	384	96	90	80	39	41	0	277	315	57	62	162	82	80	0	643	699	153	152	146	110	111	121	92	100	110	111
CHI	81	44	37	0	363	342	74	70	81	39	42	0	274	306	54	62	162	83	79	0	637	648	128	132	122	101	105	120	91	94	110	110
CIN	81	46	35	0	303	251	69	51	81	33	48	0	283	330	69	61	162	79	83	0	586	581	138	112	93	125	103	91	96	95	96	96
HOU	81	39	42	0	256	263	18	27	81	40	41	0	329	304	53	48	162	79	83	0	585	567	71	75	47	77	88	83	100	97	93	92
LA	81	42	39	0	324	286	43	56	81	47	34	0	339	301	52	54	162	89	73	0	663	587	95	110	94	84	97	96	106	95	99	98
MON	80	36	44	0	304	366	50	68	82	35	46	1	318	363	38	65	162	71	90	1	622	729	88	133	115	72	106	100	99	115	99	100
NY	81	44	37	0	281	256	48	50	81	39	42	0	307	294	50	50	162	83	79	0	588	550	98	100	98	85	87	90	96	91	96	96
PHI	81	34	47	0	296	353	73	80	81	33	48	0	262	335	50	52	162	67	95	0	558	688	123	132	143	89	95	107	86	104	103	105
PIT	80	52	28	0	393	279	66	49	82	45	37	0	395	320	88	59	162	97	65	0	788	599	154	108	82	146	107	98	126	98	99	97
STL	82	45	36	1	376	358	38	49	81	45	36	0	363	341	57	55	163	90	72	1	739	699	95	104	79	90	100	103	115	110	101	100
SD	81	33	48	0	233	296	42	43	80	28	52	0	253	314	54	50	161	61	100	0	486	610	96	93	81	91	89	92	80	99	96	98
SF	81	51	30	0	372	300	71	58	81	39	42	0	334	344	69	70	162	90	72	0	706	644	140	128	94	127	117	100	112	103	100	99

1972 NATIONAL LEAGUE

TM	G	W	L	T	R	OR	HR	OHR	G	W	L	T	R	OR	HR	OHR	G	W	L	T	R	OR	HR	OHR	HRF	HRB	HRP	RF	RB	RP	BPF	PPF
ATL	78	36	41	1	339	392	86	88	77	34	43	0	289	338	58	67	155	70	84	1	628	730	144	155	133	112	121	113	99	114	105	106
CHI	77	46	31	0	392	305	83	63	79	39	39	1	293	262	50	49	156	85	70	1	685	567	133	112	146	94	82	126	99	83	114	112
CIN	76	42	34	0	300	266	58	59	78	53	25	0	407	291	66	70	154	95	59	0	707	557	124	129	90	118	122	85	125	102	93	91
HOU	77	41	36	0	367	355	58	56	76	43	33	0	341	281	76	58	153	84	69	0	708	636	134	114	86	129	113	114	112	101	106	105
LA	75	41	34	0	267	221	46	37	80	44	36	0	317	306	52	46	155	85	70	0	584	527	98	83	92	88	75	85	103	93	94	93
MON	78	35	43	0	252	324	50	56	78	35	43	0	261	285	41	47	156	70	86	0	513	609	91	103	118	72	81	104	82	96	102	104
NY	78	41	37	0	254	264	45	56	78	42	36	0	274	314	60	62	156	83	73	0	528	578	105	118	84	100	112	89	91	99	95	96
PHI	79	28	51	0	246	316	49	57	77	31	46	0	257	319	49	60	156	59	97	0	503	635	98	117	94	89	105	94	85	106	97	99
PIT	78	49	29	0	351	259	53	34	77	47	30	0	340	253	57	56	155	96	59	0	691	512	110	90	79	108	87	103	111	84	103	100
STL	77	40	37	0	298	308	31	38	79	35	44	0	270	292	39	49	156	75	81	0	568	600	70	87	82	66	81	109	89	94	105	105
SD	80	26	54	0	217	315	41	64	73	32	41	0	271	350	61	57	153	58	95	0	488	665	102	121	81	101	120	79	93	124	88	91
SF	77	34	43	0	336	321	86	65	78	35	43	0	326	328	64	65	155	69	86	0	662	649	150	130	116	124	110	101	110	108	100	100

1973 NATIONAL LEAGUE

TM	G	W	L	T	R	OR	HR	OHR	G	W	L	T	R	OR	HR	OHR	G	W	L	T	R	OR	HR	OHR	HRF	HRB	HRP	RF	RB	RP	BPF	PPF
ATL	81	40	40	1	460	437	118	87	81	36	45	0	339	337	88	57	162	76	85	1	799	774	206	144	136	137	98	129	105	102	113	113
CHI	80	41	39	0	327	356	66	72	81	36	45	0	287	299	51	56	161	77	84	0	614	655	117	128	127	80	87	116	85	90	108	109
CIN	81	50	31	0	330	287	47	67	81	49	32	0	411	334	90	60	162	99	63	0	741	621	137	135	75	119	123	85	118	101	93	92
HOU	81	41	40	0	315	322	58	53	81	41	40	0	366	350	76	58	162	82	80	0	681	672	134	111	84	111	94	90	107	106	95	95
LA	81	50	31	0	338	271	63	62	81	45	35	1	337	294	47	67	162	95	66	1	675	565	110	129	110	81	94	98	100	85	100	99
MON	81	43	38	0	364	353	63	70	81	36	45	0	304	349	62	58	162	79	83	0	668	702	125	128	110	92	94	109	95	100	104	104
NY	81	43	38	0	314	283	39	61	80	39	41	0	294	305	46	66	161	82	79	0	608	588	85	127	89	70	101	99	91	88	101	100
PHI	81	38	43	0	358	381	78	80	81	33	48	0	284	336	56	51	162	71	91	0	642	717	134	131	141	86	84	117	88	98	108	109
PIT	81	41	40	0	334	301	72	42	81	39	42	0	370	392	82	68	162	80	82	0	704	693	154	110	78	134	96	84	114	112	92	92
STL	81	43	38	0	290	255	27	30	81	38	43	0	353	348	48	75	162	81	81	0	643	603	75	105	49	79	101	79	106	99	91	90
SD	81	31	50	0	273	355	51	80	81	29	52	0	275	415	61	77	162	60	102	0	548	770	112	157	94	91	124	90	87	118	94	97
SF	81	47	34	0	395	363	85	79	81	41	40	0	344	339	76	66	162	88	74	0	739	702	161	145	115	118	107	110	105	100	105	104

1974 NATIONAL LEAGUE

TM	G	W	L	T	R	OR	HR	OHR	G	W	L	T	R	OR	HR	OHR	G	W	L	T	R	OR	HR	OHR	HRF	HRB	HRP	RF	RB	RP	BPF	PPF
ATL	81	46	35	0	337	290	65	44	82	42	39	1	324	273	55	53	163	88	74	1	661	563	120	97	102	110	90	106	93	80	105	104
CHI	81	32	49	0	344	424	67	72	81	34	47	0	325	402	43	50	162	66	96	0	669	826	110	122	142	85	95	104	99	120	100	102
CIN	82	50	31	1	389	295	74	62	81	48	33	0	387	336	61	64	163	98	64	1	776	631	135	126	108	123	116	95	117	97	98	96
HOU	81	46	35	0	330	293	58	35	81	35	46	0	323	339	52	49	162	81	81	0	653	632	110	84	93	105	81	95	99	96	98	98
LA	81	52	29	0	355	250	68	51	81	50	31	0	443	311	71	61	162	102	60	0	798	561	139	112	92	137	112	83	128	93	93	90
MON	80	42	38	0	356	329	50	49	81	37	44	0	306	328	36	50	161	79	82	0	662	657	86	99	115	75	86	108	95	94	104	104
NY	81	36	45	0	279	325	43	49	81	35	46	0	293	321	53	50	162	71	91	0	572	646	96	99	90	94	97	98	86	96	99	100
PHI	81	46	35	0	378	337	55	56	81	34	47	0	298	364	40	55	162	80	82	0	676	701	95	111	115	82	96	107	97	101	103	104
PIT	81	52	29	0	380	303	41	32	81	36	45	0	371	354	67	61	162	88	74	0	751	657	114	93	64	130	105	95	114	101	98	96
STL	81	44	37	0	356	329	45	46	80	42	38	0	321	314	38	51	161	86	75	0	677	643	83	97	101	77	89	106	98	93	104	103
SD	81	36	45	0	272	381	47	54	81	24	57	0	269	449	52	70	162	60	102	0	541	830	99	124	83	104	126	90	87	127	93	97
SF	81	37	44	0	340	398	50	61	81	35	46	0	294	325	43	55	162	72	90	0	634	723	93	116	111	83	102	117	88	99	108	109

1975 NATIONAL LEAGUE

TM	G	W	L	T	R	OR	HR	OHR	G	W	L	T	R	OR	HR	OHR	G	W	L	T	R	OR	HR	OHR	HRF	HRB	HRP	RF	RB	RP	BPF	PPF
ATL	80	37	43	0	280	350	58	63	81	30	51	0	303	389	49	38	161	67	94	0	583	739	107	101	135	90	83	92	92	115	95	97
CHI	81	42	39	0	392	427	54	71	81	33	48	0	320	400	41	59	162	75	87	0	712	827	95	130	122	85	113	112	102	118	104	105
CIN	81	64	17	0	457	275	70	52	81	44	37	0	383	311	54	60	162	108	54	0	840	586	124	112	108	116	107	107	120	87	104	101
HOU	81	37	44	0	313	338	40	43	81	27	53	1	351	373	44	63	162	64	97	1	664	711	84	106	78	93	113	90	105	112	94	95
LA	81	49	32	0	319	221	64	52	81	39	42	0	329	313	54	52	162	88	74	0	648	534	118	104	109	110	98	86	103	85	95	93
MON	81	39	42	0	326	375	53	57	81	36	45	0	275	315	45	45	162	75	87	0	601	690	98	102	120	87	90	117	83	94	108	109
NY	81	42	39	0	294	301	52	48	81	40	41	0	352	324	49	51	162	82	80	0	646	625	101	99	100	98	96	89	101	99	95	95
PHI	81	51	30	0	401	326	72	47	81	35	46	0	334	368	53	64	162	86	76	0	735	694	125	111	102	121	109	104	108	103	101	101
PIT	80	52	28	0	348	270	67	41	81	40	41	0	364	295	71	38	161	92	69	0	712	565	138	79	101	132	79	96	108	87	99	97
STL	82	45	36	1	351	352	46	39	81	37	44	0	311	337	35	59	163	82	80	1	662	689	81	98	90	83	97	107	95	99	103	103
SD	81	38	43	0	279	338	33	38	81	33	48	0	273	345	45	61	162	71	91	0	552	683	78	99	68	90	111	99	83	101	100	101
SF	81	46	35	0	346	335	36	37	80	34	46	0	313	336	48	55	161	80	81	0	659	671	84	92	72	95	103	103	98	99	102	102

1976 NATIONAL LEAGUE

TM	G	W	L	T	R	OR	HR	OHR	G	W	L	T	R	OR	HR	OHR	G	W	L	T	R	OR	HR	OHR	HRF	HRB	HRP	RF	RB	RP	BPF	PPF
ATL	81	34	47	0	338	401	43	56	81	36	45	0	282	299	39	30	162	70	92	0	620	700	82	86	138	75	76	124	87	96	111	112
CHI	81	42	39	0	355	385	71	84	81	33	48	0	256	343	34	39	162	75	87	0	611	728	105	123	193	78	90	121	86	102	109	111
CIN	81	49	32	0	426	337	73	46	81	53	28	0	431	296	68	54	162	102	60	0	857	633	141	100	99	155	114	106	129	98	103	100
HOU	82	46	36	0	277	264	30	27	80	34	46	0	348	393	36	55	162	80	82	0	625	657	66	82	63	89	103	73	113	117	86	87
LA	81	49	32	0	296	265	42	48	81	43	38	0	312	278	49	46	162	92	70	0	608	543	91	93	102	108	96	95	85	100	99	
MON	80	27	53	0	266	374	45	41	82	28	54	0	265	360	49	48	162	55	107	0	531	734	94	89	90	106	101	103	82	111	100	103
NY	82	45	37	0	269	245	43	43	80	41	39	0	346	293	59	54	162	86	76	0	615	538	102	97	76	126	121	80	104	92	92	91

TM	HOME G	W	L	T	R	OR	HR	OHR	ROAD G	W	L	T	R	OR	HR	OHR	ALL G	W	L	T	R	OR	HR	OHR	HRF	HRB	HRP	RF	RB	RP	BPF	PPF
PHI	81	53	28	0	424	277	63	49	81	48	33	0	346	280	47	49	162	101	61	0	770	557	110	98	117	110	100	112	111	83	107	105
PIT	81	47	34	0	366	302	54	44	81	45	36	0	342	328	56	51	162	92	70	0	708	630	110	95	93	124	108	100	109	98	100	99
STL	81	37	44	0	335	346	27	40	81	35	46	0	294	325	36	51	162	72	90	0	629	671	63	91	78	76	107	108	94	100	104	104
SD	80	42	38	0	254	271	30	38	82	31	51	0	316	391	34	49	162	73	89	0	570	662	64	87	85	74	98	77	100	114	88	90
SF	81	40	41	0	314	352	44	32	81	34	47	0	281	334	41	36	162	74	88	0	595	686	85	68	98	90	73	107	89	102	103	104

1977 NATIONAL LEAGUE

TM	HOME G	W	L	T	R	OR	HR	OHR	ROAD G	W	L	T	R	OR	HR	OHR	ALL G	W	L	T	R	OR	HR	OHR	HRF	HRB	HRP	RF	RB	RP	BPF	PPF
ATL	81	40	41	0	416	488	97	111	81	21	60	0	262	407	42	58	162	61	101	0	678	895	139	169	189	70	87	130	83	110	113	115
CHI	81	46	35	0	411	402	69	82	81	35	46	0	281	337	42	46	162	81	81	0	692	739	111	128	162	62	70	128	85	91	114	115
CIN	81	48	33	0	408	355	83	83	81	40	41	0	394	370	98	73	162	88	74	0	802	725	181	156	98	137	120	100	113	103	100	99
HOU	81	46	35	0	309	291	40	33	81	35	46	0	371	359	74	77	162	81	81	0	680	650	114	110	51	111	103	83	103	99	93	92
LA	81	51	30	0	386	273	96	65	81	47	34	0	383	309	95	54	162	98	64	0	769	582	191	119	108	134	87	97	108	83	100	98
MON	81	38	43	0	329	362	66	65	81	37	44	0	336	374	72	70	162	75	87	0	665	736	138	135	93	105	103	97	95	104	98	99
NY	79	35	44	0	282	297	46	56	83	29	54	0	305	366	42	62	162	64	98	0	587	663	88	118	102	63	83	90	86	96	96	97
PHI	81	60	21	0	453	299	101	63	81	41	40	0	394	369	85	71	162	101	61	0	847	668	186	134	106	133	99	100	118	95	100	98
PIT	81	58	23	0	396	315	64	76	81	38	43	0	338	350	69	73	162	96	66	0	734	665	133	149	100	99	110	104	100	92	103	102
STL	83	52	31	0	379	314	41	53	79	31	48	0	358	374	55	86	162	83	79	0	737	688	96	137	66	87	120	91	108	101	96	95
SD	81	35	46	0	299	368	53	70	81	34	47	0	393	466	67	90	162	69	93	0	692	834	120	160	79	100	130	79	111	131	88	89
SF	81	38	43	0	353	371	62	56	81	37	44	0	320	340	72	58	162	75	87	0	673	711	134	114	91	101	88	108	90	95	104	105

1978 NATIONAL LEAGUE

TM	HOME G	W	L	T	R	OR	HR	OHR	ROAD G	W	L	T	R	OR	HR	OHR	ALL G	W	L	T	R	OR	HR	OHR	HRF	HRB	HRP	RF	RB	RP	BPF	PPF
ATL	81	39	42	0	364	400	87	89	81	30	51	0	236	350	36	43	162	69	93	0	600	750	123	132	201	76	84	126	82	103	112	114
CHI	82	44	38	0	393	387	41	76	80	35	45	0	271	337	31	49	162	79	83	0	664	724	72	125	138	58	96	122	93	101	110	111
CIN	80	49	31	0	379	338	74	61	81	43	38	0	331	350	62	60	161	92	69	0	710	688	136	122	111	124	113	107	108	105	103	102
HOU	81	50	31	0	327	254	30	29	81	24	57	0	278	380	40	57	162	74	88	0	605	634	70	86	63	81	94	89	100	103	95	95
LA	81	54	27	0	361	272	78	59	81	41	40	0	366	301	71	48	162	95	67	0	727	573	149	107	115	131	97	96	114	91	99	97
MON	80	41	39	0	299	283	46	49	82	35	47	0	334	328	75	68	162	76	86	0	633	611	121	117	70	134	132	91	102	99	96	95
NY	80	33	47	0	295	340	37	60	82	33	49	0	312	350	49	54	162	66	96	0	607	690	86	114	96	83	108	98	96	108	98	99
PHI	82	54	28	0	405	279	80	70	80	36	44	0	303	307	53	48	162	90	72	0	708	586	133	118	140	104	94	109	103	88	105	104
PIT	81	55	26	0	389	310	57	61	80	33	47	0	295	327	58	42	161	88	73	0	684	637	115	103	115	101	90	110	101	95	105	105
STL	81	37	44	0	289	307	29	32	81	32	49	0	311	350	50	51	162	69	93	0	600	657	79	94	56	95	109	90	98	106	95	96
SD	81	50	31	0	291	245	31	23	81	34	47	0	300	353	44	51	162	84	78	0	591	598	75	74	59	88	82	83	100	99	92	92
SF	81	50	31	0	291	244	47	30	81	39	42	0	322	350	70	54	162	89	73	0	613	594	117	84	64	132	96	81	104	100	91	91

1979 NATIONAL LEAGUE

TM	HOME G	W	L	T	R	OR	HR	OHR	ROAD G	W	L	T	R	OR	HR	OHR	ALL G	W	L	T	R	OR	HR	OHR	HRF	HRB	HRP	RF	RB	RP	BPF	PPF
ATL	79	34	45	0	359	425	73	80	81	32	49	0	310	338	53	52	160	66	94	0	669	763	126	132	142	90	93	121	91	102	109	110
CHI	81	45	36	0	423	370	79	72	81	35	46	0	283	337	56	55	162	80	82	0	706	707	135	127	132	98	93	125	91	93	112	112
CIN	80	48	32	0	360	298	71	53	81	42	39	0	371	346	61	50	161	90	71	0	731	644	132	103	113	104	83	94	111	98	97	96
HOU	81	52	29	0	269	234	15	31	81	37	44	0	314	348	34	59	162	89	73	0	583	582	49	90	52	51	93	78	95	94	90	90
LA	81	46	35	0	389	341	106	55	81	33	48	0	350	376	77	46	162	79	83	0	739	717	183	101	127	133	78	100	109	106	100	99
MON	81	56	25	0	378	275	68	51	79	39	40	0	323	306	75	65	160	95	65	0	701	581	143	116	85	132	109	102	101	86	102	101
NY	82	28	53	1	267	354	30	58	81	35	46	0	326	352	44	62	163	63	99	1	593	706	74	120	82	67	107	90	91	107	95	96
PHI	81	43	38	0	332	342	52	72	82	41	40	1	351	376	67	63	163	84	78	1	683	718	119	135	97	102	115	95	103	107	97	97
PIT	81	48	33	0	399	339	74	77	82	50	31	1	376	304	74	48	163	98	64	1	775	643	148	125	124	112	94	110	107	90	106	104
STL	82	42	39	1	379	372	48	65	81	44	37	0	352	321	52	62	163	86	76	1	731	693	100	127	98	85	105	110	102	97	105	104
SD	81	39	42	0	287	335	36	47	80	29	51	0	316	346	57	61	161	68	93	0	603	681	93	108	71	91	106	93	92	103	96	97
SF	81	38	43	0	298	361	53	61	81	33	48	0	374	390	72	82	162	71	91	0	672	751	125	143	75	123	138	87	106	118	92	93

1980 NATIONAL LEAGUE

TM	HOME G	W	L	T	R	OR	HR	OHR	ROAD G	W	L	T	R	OR	HR	OHR	ALL G	W	L	T	R	OR	HR	OHR	HRF	HRB	HRP	RF	RB	RP	BPF	PPF
ATL	80	50	30	0	352	297	84	79	81	31	50	0	278	363	60	52	161	81	80	0	630	660	144	131	142	119	108	102	96	100	101	101
CHI	81	37	44	0	338	385	54	62	81	27	54	0	276	343	53	47	162	64	98	0	614	728	107	109	113	98	99	114	88	104	106	108
CIN	82	44	37	1	356	349	66	70	81	45	36	0	351	321	47	43	163	89	73	1	707	670	113	113	144	90	89	104	106	101	102	101
HOU	81	55	26	0	329	255	26	22	82	38	44	0	308	334	49	47	163	93	70	0	637	589	75	69	53	91	82	93	99	92	98	97
LA	82	55	27	0	327	272	82	58	81	37	44	0	336	319	66	47	163	92	71	0	663	591	148	105	121	129	94	92	104	94	97	96
MON	80	51	29	0	357	286	51	40	82	39	43	0	337	343	63	60	162	90	72	0	694	629	114	100	78	124	109	98	107	98	99	98
NY	82	38	44	0	306	336	35	80	80	29	51	0	305	366	26	60	162	67	95	0	611	702	61	140	126	53	115	93	98	111	96	97
PHI	81	49	32	0	398	334	64	44	81	42	39	0	330	305	53	43	162	91	71	0	728	639	117	87	112	105	80	115	104	92	107	106
PIT	81	47	34	0	355	322	63	53	81	36	45	0	311	324	53	57	162	83	79	0	666	646	116	110	105	110	105	106	99	96	103	103
STL	81	41	40	0	396	357	41	42	81	33	48	0	342	353	60	48	162	74	88	0	738	710	101	90	78	108	98	107	110	106	103	102
SD	81	45	36	0	295	274	29	33	82	28	53	1	296	380	38	64	163	73	89	1	591	654	67	97	63	80	108	86	97	105	93	94
SF	81	44	37	0	283	293	24	41	80	31	49	0	290	341	56	51	161	75	86	0	573	634	80	92	62	92	112	91	92	101	96	96

1981 NATIONAL LEAGUE

TM	HOME G	W	L	T	R	OR	HR	OHR	ROAD G	W	L	T	R	OR	HR	OHR	ALL G	W	L	T	R	OR	HR	OHR	HRF	HRB	HRP	RF	RB	RP	BPF	PPF
ATL	50	22	27	1	182	195	37	41	57	28	29	0	213	221	27	21	107	50	56	1	395	416	64	62	172	82	76	99	95	100	99	100
CHI	58	27	30	1	239	254	41	38	48	11	35	2	131	229	24	30	106	38	65	3	370	483	57	59	164	68	75	111	84	111	104	106
CIN	54	32	22	0	226	230	26	41	54	34	20	0	238	210	38	26	108	66	42	0	464	440	64	67	105	105	108	103	109	104	101	100
HOU	51	31	20	0	166	106	16	9	59	30	29	0	228	225	29	31	110	61	49	0	394	331	45	40	51	96	76	72	105	85	88	87
LA	56	33	23	0	221	171	37	34	54	30	24	0	229	185	45	20	110	63	47	0	450	356	82	54	106	129	87	93	107	86	98	96
MON	56	38	18	0	255	170	39	23	52	22	30	0	188	224	42	36	108	60	48	0	443	394	81	58	77	154	112	97	106	96	99	98
NY	52	24	27	1	186	207	30	38	53	17	35	1	162	225	27	36	105	41	62	2	348	432	57	74	108	96	121	102	84	103	101	102
PHI	55	36	19	0	295	261	41	39	52	23	29	0	196	211	28	33	107	59	48	0	491	472	69	72	122	105	110	127	104	101	112	112
PIT	51	22	28	1	189	207	29	29	52	24	28	0	218	218	26	31	103	46	56	1	407	425	55	60	103	95	103	93	105	110	96	96
STL	53	32	21	0	244	218	22	26	50	27	22	1	220	199	28	24	103	59	43	1	464	417	50	52	86	93	97	105	113	103	102	101
SD	55	20	35	0	168	223	9	27	55	21	34	0	214	232	23	37	110	41	69	0	382	455	32	64	61	62	126	87	95	112	93	95
SF	53	29	24	0	218	204	28	19	58	27	31	0	209	210	35	38	111	56	55	0	427	414	63	57	72	119	103	109	94	91	105	105

1982 NATIONAL LEAGUE

TM	HOME G	W	L	T	R	OR	HR	OHR	ROAD G	W	L	T	R	OR	HR	OHR	ALL G	W	L	T	R	OR	HR	OHR	HRF	HRB	HRP	RF	RB	RP	BPF	PPF
ATL	81	42	39	0	388	387	95	86	81	47	34	0	351	315	51	40	162	89	73	0	739	702	146	126	185	96	82	115	104	99	107	107
CHI	81	38	43	0	352	371	53	62	81	35	46	0	324	338	49	63	162	73	89	0	676	709	102	125	102	95	114	108	99	103	103	104
CIN	81	33	48	0	296	325	37	47	81	28	53	0	249	336	45	58	162	61	101	0	545	661	82	105	82	83	104	104	80	96	102	104
HOU	81	43	38	0	290	294	31	26	81	34	47	0	279	326	43	61	162	77	85	0	569	620	74	87	57	88	96	97	87	94	99	100
LA	81	43	38	0	321	283	57	35	81	45	36	0	370	329	81	46	162	88	74	0	691	612	138	81	74	142	88	110	109	95	94	94
MON	81	40	41	0	335	352	59	65	81	46	35	0	362	264	74	45	162	86	76	0	697	616	133	110	104	121	101	109	100	89	105	104
NY	81	33	48	0	307	357	48	60	81	32	49	0	302	366	49	59	162	65	97	0	609	723	97	119	99	91	110	98	93	109	98	100
PHI	81	51	30	0	301	307	57	46	81	38	43	0	363	347	55	40	162	89	73	0	664	654	112	86	108	98	76	87	107	106	94	94
PIT	81	46	35	0	391	394	77	65	81	42	39	0	333	302	57	53	162	88	74	0	724	696	134	118	126	110	98	121	99	95	110	110
STL	81	46	35	0	338	325	27	48	81	46	35	0	347	284	40	46	162	92	70	0	685	609	67	94	89	64	89	105	100	90	103	102
SD	81	43	38	0	316	286	33	76	81	38	43	0	359	372	48	63	162	81	81	0	675	658	81	139	98	77	127	84	111	108	92	92
SF	81	45	36	0	319	312	55	54	81	42	39	0	354	375	78	55	162	87	75	0	673	687	133	109	84	133	113	88	109	111	94	94

1983 NATIONAL LEAGUE

TM	HOME G	W	L	T	R	OR	HR	OHR	ROAD G	W	L	T	R	OR	HR	OHR	ALL G	W	L	T	R	OR	HR	OHR	HRF	HRB	HRP	RF	RB	RP	BPF	PPF
ATL	80	46	34	0	394	327	66	71	82	42	40	0	352	313	64	61	162	88	74	0	746	640	130	132	112	107	108	111	106	92	106	104

	HOME								ROAD								ALL															
TM	G	W	L	T	R	OR	HR	OHR	G	W	L	T	R	OR	HR	OHR	G	W	L	T	R	OR	HR	OHR	HRF	HRB	HRP	RF	RB	RP	BPF	PPF
CHI	81	43	38	0	384	341	71	69	81	28	53	0	317	378	69	48	162	71	91	0	701	719	140	117	117	112	94	103	104	107	101	101
CIN	81	36	45	0	331	360	52	64	81	38	43	0	292	350	55	71	162	74	88	0	623	710	107	135	92	97	120	106	91	103	103	104
HOU	82	46	36	0	294	278	26	28	80	39	41	0	349	368	71	66	162	85	77	0	643	646	97	94	41	115	115	79	108	108	90	90
LA	80	48	32	0	316	296	74	49	83	43	39	1	338	313	72	48	163	91	71	1	654	609	146	97	106	119	82	98	98	92	100	99
MON	81	46	35	0	341	325	40	56	82	36	45	1	336	321	62	64	163	82	80	1	677	646	102	120	79	97	114	102	100	95	102	101
NY	82	41	41	0	300	329	63	53	80	27	53	0	275	351	49	44	162	68	94	0	575	680	112	97	119	87	76	97	88	102	99	100
PHI	82	50	31	1	361	310	61	61	81	40	41	0	335	325	64	50	163	90	72	1	696	635	125	111	106	104	93	101	103	95	101	100
PIT	81	41	40	0	335	336	60	63	81	43	38	0	324	312	61	46	162	84	78	0	659	648	121	109	114	97	87	105	96	95	103	103
STL	81	44	37	0	334	350	38	58	81	35	46	0	345	360	45	57	162	79	83	0	679	710	83	115	94	73	99	97	104	109	98	98
SD	82	47	34	1	350	299	53	82	81	34	47	0	303	354	40	62	163	81	81	1	653	653	93	144	127	71	106	98	99	98	99	99
SF	81	43	38	0	346	356	73	67	81	36	45	0	341	341	69	60	162	79	83	0	687	697	142	127	108	119	107	103	103	104	101	101

1984 NATIONAL LEAGUE

	HOME								ROAD								ALL															
TM	G	W	L	T	R	OR	HR	OHR	G	W	L	T	R	OR	HR	OHR	G	W	L	T	R	OR	HR	OHR	HRF	HRB	HRP	RF	RB	RP	BPF	PPF
ATL	81	38	43	0	328	376	53	72	81	42	39	0	304	279	58	50	162	80	82	0	632	655	111	122	114	99	107	119	88	90	110	110
CHI	80	51	29	0	414	360	86	70	81	45	36	0	348	298	50	29	161	96	65	0	762	658	136	99	186	91	64	120	106	93	110	109
CIN	81	39	42	0	356	381	58	73	81	31	50	0	271	366	48	55	162	70	92	0	627	747	106	128	124	91	107	113	90	106	106	107
HOU	81	43	38	0	309	292	18	29	81	37	44	0	384	338	61	62	162	80	82	0	693	630	79	91	40	98	123	84	114	104	92	92
LA	81	40	41	0	287	321	49	40	81	39	42	0	293	279	53	36	162	79	83	0	580	600	102	76	100	93	71	106	85	88	104	104
MON	81	39	42	0	266	260	45	56	80	39	41	0	327	325	51	58	161	78	83	0	593	585	96	114	92	95	111	81	99	98	91	91
NY	81	48	33	0	336	327	56	47	81	42	39	0	316	349	51	57	162	90	72	0	652	676	107	104	96	102	99	100	99	102	100	100
PHI	81	39	42	0	353	369	79	45	81	42	39	0	367	323	68	56	162	81	81	0	720	690	147	101	100	138	98	105	108	103	102	101
PIT	81	41	40	0	282	263	48	44	81	34	47	0	333	304	50	58	162	75	87	0	615	567	98	102	86	99	102	86	99	92	94	94
STL	81	44	37	0	327	310	29	42	81	40	41	0	325	335	46	52	162	84	78	0	652	645	75	94	74	79	99	97	100	99	99	99
SD	81	48	33	0	344	300	60	61	81	44	37	0	342	334	49	61	162	92	70	0	686	634	109	122	110	98	110	96	106	98	98	98
SF	81	35	46	0	340	393	55	63	81	31	50	0	342	414	57	62	162	66	96	0	682	807	112	125	98	108	119	96	108	126	96	98

1985 NATIONAL LEAGUE

	HOME								ROAD								ALL															
TM	G	W	L	T	R	OR	HR	OHR	G	W	L	T	R	OR	HR	OHR	G	W	L	T	R	OR	HR	OHR	HRF	HRB	HRP	RF	RB	RP	BPF	PPF
ATL	81	32	49	0	336	431	65	80	81	34	47	0	296	350	61	54	162	66	96	0	632	781	126	134	122	97	101	116	90	109	106	108
CHI	81	41	39	1	399	423	98	104	81	36	45	0	287	306	52	52	162	77	84	1	686	729	150	156	180	92	95	134	90	95	116	117
CIN	81	47	34	0	347	359	49	65	81	42	38	1	330	307	65	66	162	89	72	1	677	666	114	131	88	102	117	110	98	96	105	105
HOU	81	44	37	0	333	338	47	48	81	39	42	0	373	353	74	71	162	83	79	0	706	691	121	119	68	121	120	93	112	109	96	96
LA	81	48	33	0	310	258	47	54	81	47	34	0	372	321	82	48	162	95	67	0	682	579	129	102	80	117	98	84	111	96	93	92
MON	81	44	37	0	300	289	45	45	80	40	40	0	333	347	73	54	161	84	77	0	633	636	118	99	72	113	99	87	103	104	94	94
NY	81	51	30	0	344	254	58	58	81	47	34	0	351	314	76	53	162	98	64	0	695	568	134	111	92	117	99	92	109	90	97	95
PHI	81	41	40	0	350	338	72	57	81	34	47	0	317	335	69	58	162	75	87	0	667	673	141	115	101	118	98	92	105	99	100	102
PIT	80	35	45	0	314	347	39	53	81	22	59	0	254	361	41	54	161	57	104	0	568	708	80	107	97	68	89	106	84	104	103	104
STL	81	54	27	0	358	255	36	39	81	47	34	0	389	317	51	59	162	101	61	0	747	572	87	98	71	84	93	89	119	93	96	93
SD	81	44	37	0	321	323	63	77	81	39	42	0	329	299	46	50	162	83	79	0	650	622	109	127	141	77	88	102	97	93	102	101
SF	81	38	43	0	265	307	58	67	81	24	57	0	291	367	57	58	162	62	100	0	556	674	115	125	107	94	101	87	91	108	93	95

1986 NATIONAL LEAGUE

	HOME								ROAD								ALL															
TM	G	W	L	T	R	OR	HR	OHR	G	W	L	T	R	OR	HR	OHR	G	W	L	T	R	OR	HR	OHR	HRF	HRB	HRP	RF	RB	RP	BPF	PPF
ATL	81	41	40	0	331	360	77	71	80	31	49	0	284	359	61	46	161	72	89	0	615	719	138	117	132	94	79	105	90	104	102	103
CHI	80	42	38	0	394	399	89	79	80	28	52	0	286	382	66	64	160	70	90	0	680	781	155	143	125	110	103	116	95	109	107	108
CIN	81	43	38	0	383	377	86	73	81	43	38	0	349	340	58	63	162	86	76	0	732	717	144	136	128	99	95	110	104	102	104	104
HOU	81	52	29	0	327	289	49	56	81	44	37	0	327	280	76	60	162	96	66	0	654	569	125	116	79	107	102	102	94	83	103	102
LA	81	46	35	0	326	290	57	46	81	27	54	0	312	389	73	69	162	73	89	0	638	679	130	115	74	117	104	88	101	106	94	95
MON	80	36	44	0	296	347	42	56	81	42	39	0	341	341	68	63	161	78	83	0	637	688	110	119	77	96	106	96	97	104	98	98
NY	81	55	26	0	379	251	77	47	81	53	28	0	404	327	71	56	162	108	54	0	783	578	148	103	100	115	82	89	121	91	96	93
PHI	80	49	31	0	413	344	86	49	81	37	44	0	326	369	68	81	161	86	75	0	739	713	154	130	93	128	108	110	105	102	104	104
PIT	81	31	50	0	331	357	49	75	81	33	48	0	332	343	62	63	162	64	98	0	663	700	111	138	98	88	108	101	98	103	100	101
STL	81	42	39	0	321	303	27	63	80	37	43	0	280	308	31	72	161	79	82	0	601	611	58	135	87	49	108	104	87	88	103	103
SD	81	43	38	0	339	319	80	78	81	31	50	0	317	404	56	72	162	74	88	0	656	723	136	150	121	98	108	92	102	111	95	96
SF	81	46	35	0	345	275	50	61	81	37	44	0	353	343	64	60	162	83	79	0	698	618	114	121	90	93	99	90	108	96	96	95

1987 NATIONAL LEAGUE

	HOME								ROAD								ALL															
TM	G	W	L	T	R	OR	HR	OHR	G	W	L	T	R	OR	HR	OHR	G	W	L	T	R	OR	HR	OHR	HRF	HRB	HRP	RF	RB	RP	BPF	PPF
ATL	81	42	39	0	421	450	82	88	80	27	53	0	326	379	70	75	161	69	92	0	747	829	152	163	113	95	101	119	95	104	108	109
CHI	80	40	40	0	381	389	114	90	81	36	45	0	339	412	95	69	161	76	85	0	720	801	209	159	123	125	97	103	98	108	101	102
CIN	81	42	39	0	396	401	94	97	81	42	39	0	387	351	98	73	162	84	78	0	783	752	192	170	111	122	108	107	104	100	103	103
HOU	81	47	34	0	334	268	51	46	81	29	52	0	314	410	71	95	162	76	86	0	648	678	122	141	60	102	111	84	97	99	93	93
LA	81	40	41	0	280	306	52	56	81	33	48	0	355	369	73	74	162	73	89	0	635	675	125	130	75	92	96	82	95	100	92	92
MON	81	48	33	0	401	371	62	74	81	43	38	0	340	349	58	71	162	91	71	0	741	720	120	145	106	76	91	112	95	93	106	106
NY	81	49	32	0	407	335	93	63	81	43	38	0	416	363	99	72	162	92	70	0	823	698	192	135	93	130	94	114	98	97	98	97
PHI	81	43	38	0	385	373	80	78	81	37	44	0	317	376	89	89	162	80	82	0	702	749	169	167	90	119	117	108	92	98	104	105
PIT	81	47	34	0	404	363	71	84	81	33	48	0	319	381	60	80	162	80	82	0	723	744	131	164	110	82	102	109	95	98	104	104
STL	81	49	32	0	387	339	42	60	81	46	35	0	411	354	52	69	162	95	67	0	798	693	94	129	86	65	88	96	111	97	98	97
SD	81	37	44	0	338	357	60	97	81	28	53	0	330	406	53	78	162	65	97	0	668	763	113	175	117	69	104	94	95	107	97	98
SF	81	46	35	0	373	312	118	72	81	44	37	0	410	357	87	74	162	90	72	0	783	669	205	146	117	123	92	91	111	96	96	95

1988 NATIONAL LEAGUE

	HOME								ROAD								ALL															
TM	G	W	L	T	R	OR	HR	OHR	G	W	L	T	R	OR	HR	OHR	G	W	L	T	R	OR	HR	OHR	HRF	HRB	HRP	RF	RB	RP	BPF	PPF
ATL	79	28	51	0	295	391	48	64	81	26	55	0	260	350	48	44	160	54	106	0	555	741	96	108	120	83	91	112	86	112	104	107
CHI	82	39	42	1	346	373	58	71	81	38	43	0	314	321	55	44	163	77	85	1	660	694	113	115	125	95	94	110	100	105	104	105
CIN	80	45	35	0	333	312	75	71	81	42	39	0	308	284	47	50	161	87	74	0	641	596	122	121	147	94	94	110	97	91	105	105
HOU	81	44	37	0	293	282	33	50	81	38	43	0	324	349	63	73	162	82	80	0	617	631	96	123	63	110	142	87	105	107	93	93
LA	81	45	36	0	316	297	49	38	81	49	31	1	312	247	50	46	162	94	67	1	628	544	99	84	92	95	81	110	94	82	106	105
MON	81	43	38	0	333	304	47	62	82	38	43	1	295	288	60	60	163	81	81	1	628	592	107	122	93	104	118	110	94	89	105	105
NY	80	56	24	0	313	218	67	34	80	44	36	0	390	314	85	44	160	100	60	0	703	532	152	78	81	156	85	78	126	97	90	88
PHI	81	38	42	0	327	361	62	64	81	27	54	0	270	373	44	54	162	65	96	0	597	734	106	118	124	89	99	105	94	113	101	103
PIT	81	43	38	0	326	298	56	50	79	42	37	0	325	318	54	58	160	85	75	0	651	616	110	108	93	108	106	95	107	102	98	97
STL	81	41	40	0	314	318	29	39	81	35	46	0	264	315	42	52	162	76	86	0	578	633	71	91	74	75	95	108	88	96	104	105
SD	81	47	34	0	303	267	56	56	80	36	44	0	291	316	38	56	161	83	78	0	594	583	94	112	116	81	97	93	98	96	97	97
SF	81	45	36	0	318	284	58	42	81	38	43	0	352	342	55	57	162	83	79	0	670	626	113	99	90	111	97	88	114	107	94	93

1989 NATIONAL LEAGUE

	HOME								ROAD								ALL															
TM	G	W	L	T	R	OR	HR	OHR	G	W	L	T	R	OR	HR	OHR	G	W	L	T	R	OR	HR	OHR	HRF	HRB	HRP	RF	RB	RP	BPF	PPF
ATL	79	33	46	0	309	334	55	61	82	30	51	1	275	346	73	53	161	63	97	1	584	680	128	114	95	116	105	106	90	104	102	104
CHI	81	48	33	0	381	334	61	64	81	45	36	0	321	289	63	42	162	93	69	0	702	623	124	106	118	100	85	116	101	91	108	107
CIN	81	38	43	0	312	377	59	50	81	37	44	0	320	314	69	54	162	75	87	0	632	691	128	125	105	111	108	107	96	104	103	104
HOU	82	47	35	0	340	344	42	50	80	39	41	0	307	325	55	55	162	86	76	0	647	669	97	100	83	92	100	105	99	102	102	103
LA	81	44	37	0	253	244	37	46	79	33	46	0	301	292	52	49	160	77	83	0	554	536	89	95	81	86	92	83	95	92	93	93
MON	81	44	37	0	336	309	55	60	81	37	44	0	296	321	45	60	162	81	81	0	632	630	100	120	109	84	100	104	97	97	102	102
NY	81	51	30	0	333	275	78	56	81	36	45	0	316	314	60	59	162	87	75	0	683	595	147	115	105	127	102	92	111	98	96	95
PHI	81	38	42	1	321	376	61	67	82	29	53	0	308	359	62	60	163	67	95	1	629	735	123	127	105	106	109	104	97	112	101	102
PIT	81	39	42	0	296	313	45	62	83	35	46	2	341	367	50	59	164	74	88	2	637	680	95	121	100	83	103	89	105	111	94	94

	HOME								ROAD								ALL															
TM	G	W	L	T	R	OR	HR	OHR	G	W	L	T	R	OR	HR	OHR	G	W	L	T	R	OR	HR	OHR	HRF	HRB	HRP	RF	RB	RP	BPF	PPF
STL	83	46	35	2	319	308	27	36	81	40	41	0	313	300	46	48	164	86	76	2	632	608	73	84	68	73	85	100	97	94	101	100
SD	81	46	35	0	324	312	66	82	81	43	38	0	318	314	54	51	162	89	73	0	642	626	120	133	137	91	98	101	100	98	101	101
SF	81	53	28	0	368	255	63	61	81	39	42	0	331	345	78	59	162	92	70	0	699	600	141	120	92	130	113	93	113	98	97	96

1990 NATIONAL LEAGUE

	HOME								ROAD								ALL															
TM	G	W	L	T	R	OR	HR	OHR	G	W	L	T	R	OR	HR	OHR	G	W	L	T	R	OR	HR	OHR	HRF	HRB	HRP	RF	RB	RP	BPF	PPF
ATL	81	37	44	0	352	427	85	70	81	28	53	0	330	394	77	58	162	65	97	0	682	821	162	128	112	121	97	106	99	117	101	103
CHI	81	39	42	0	372	437	75	73	81	38	43	0	318	332	61	48	162	77	85	0	690	774	136	121	132	93	82	121	93	103	109	110
CIN	81	46	35	0	334	312	70	73	81	45	36	0	359	285	55	51	162	91	71	0	693	597	125	124	132	85	84	101	100	87	102	100
HOU	81	49	32	0	298	271	35	47	81	26	55	0	275	385	59	83	162	75	87	0	573	656	94	130	60	93	125	87	90	101	94	95
LA	81	47	34	0	351	323	54	73	81	39	42	0	377	362	75	64	162	86	76	0	728	685	129	137	92	106	113	92	111	105	96	95
MON	81	47	34	0	328	268	48	62	81	38	43	0	334	330	66	65	162	85	77	0	662	598	114	127	85	96	108	91	101	92	97	96
NY	81	52	29	0	397	280	86	52	81	39	42	0	378	333	86	67	162	91	71	0	775	613	172	119	92	142	101	96	115	93	99	97
PHI	81	41	40	0	311	367	47	67	81	36	45	0	335	362	56	57	162	77	85	0	646	729	103	124	101	81	96	97	97	108	98	99
PIT	81	49	32	0	351	299	59	63	81	46	35	0	382	320	79	72	162	95	67	0	733	619	138	135	83	120	118	94	110	94	98	96
STL	81	34	47	0	319	366	43	47	81	36	45	0	280	332	30	51	162	70	92	0	599	698	73	98	109	53	71	110	84	97	105	106
SD	81	37	44	0	342	348	63	78	81	38	43	0	331	325	60	69	162	75	87	0	673	673	123	147	108	95	111	104	97	97	102	102
SF	81	49	32	0	380	340	81	70	81	36	45	0	339	370	71	61	162	85	77	0	719	710	152	131	113	113	99	102	105	104	100	100

1901 AMERICAN LEAGUE

	HOME								ROAD								ALL															
TM	G	W	L	T	R	OR	HR	OHR	G	W	L	T	R	OR	HR	OHR	G	W	L	T	R	OR	HR	OHR	HRF	HRB	HRP	RF	RB	RP	BPF	PPF
BAL	66	40	25	1	430	367	11	11	69	28	40	1	330	383	13	10	135	68	65	2	760	750	24	21	100	82	73	115	98	98	107	107
BOS	69	49	20	0	383	252	21	17	69	30	37	2	376	356	11	16	138	79	57	2	759	608	37	33	117	122	111	89	106	87	97	94
CHI	71	49	21	1	441	285	14	11	66	34	32	0	378	346	18	16	137	83	53	1	819	631	32	27	72	132	113	95	113	90	99	96
CLE	69	29	39	1	321	403	0	12	69	26	43	0	346	428	12	9	138	55	82	1	667	831	12	21	60	39	91	93	95	115	95	98
DET	70	42	27	1	438	369	15	10	66	32	34	0	303	325	14	12	136	74	61	1	741	694	29	22	92	104	81	119	92	88	110	109
MIL	70	32	37	1	342	373	15	14	69	16	52	1	299	455	11	19	139	48	89	2	641	828	26	33	94	95	116	93	91	113	95	98
PHI	66	42	24	0	410	352	15	9	71	32	38	1	395	409	20	11	137	74	62	1	805	761	35	20	85	126	78	102	110	104	100	100
WAS	68	31	35	2	333	375	17	36	70	30	38	2	349	396	16	15	138	61	73	4	682	771	33	51	160	102	135	98	94	105	98	100

1902 AMERICAN LEAGUE

	HOME								ROAD								ALL															
TM	G	W	L	T	R	OR	HR	OHR	G	W	L	T	R	OR	HR	OHR	G	W	L	T	R	OR	HR	OHR	HRF	HRB	HRP	RF	RB	RP	BPF	PPF
BAL	64	32	31	1	391	369	17	18	77	18	57	2	324	479	16	12	141	50	88	3	715	848	33	30	140	85	76	111	103	118	102	104
BOS	71	43	27	1	348	284	24	15	67	34	33	0	316	316	18	12	138	77	60	1	664	600	42	27	120	116	79	96	99	91	99	98
CHI	71	48	19	4	371	238	5	2	67	26	41	0	304	364	9	28	138	74	60	4	675	602	14	30	20	103	111	88	106	95	95	94
CLE	65	40	25	0	357	257	15	7	72	29	42	1	329	410	18	19	137	69	67	1	686	667	33	26	69	122	91	93	107	102	97	96
DET	68	35	33	0	312	286	13	8	69	17	50	2	254	371	9	12	137	52	83	2	566	657	22	20	100	65	59	96	86	97	99	100
PHI	73	56	17	0	477	330	19	12	64	27	36	1	298	306	19	21	137	83	53	1	775	636	38	33	72	144	124	116	105	90	108	106
STL	73	49	21	3	350	289	16	14	67	29	37	1	269	318	13	22	140	78	58	4	619	607	29	36	81	101	119	101	88	87	102	102
WAS	68	40	28	0	407	341	35	38	70	21	47	2	300	449	12	18	138	61	75	2	707	790	47	56	210	97	119	102	106	117	98	100

1903 AMERICAN LEAGUE

	HOME								ROAD								ALL															
TM	G	W	L	T	R	OR	HR	OHR	G	W	L	T	R	OR	HR	OHR	G	W	L	T	R	OR	HR	OHR	HRF	HRB	HRP	RF	RB	RP	BPF	PPF
BOS	70	49	20	1	395	266	35	12	71	42	27	2	313	238	13	11	141	91	47	3	708	504	48	23	179	141	85	120	109	82	112	107
CHI	70	41	28	1	284	244	5	2	68	19	49	0	232	369	9	21	138	60	77	1	516	613	14	23	25	127	123	86	100	114	92	94
CLE	74	49	25	0	364	256	11	5	66	28	38	0	275	323	20	11	140	77	63	0	639	579	31	16	50	175	97	94	115	107	96	95
DET	65	37	28	0	279	222	5	7	72	28	43	1	288	317	7	12	137	65	71	1	567	539	12	19	73	59	88	93	105	99	97	96
NY	67	41	26	0	301	269	10	6	69	31	36	2	278	304	8	13	136	72	62	2	579	573	18	19	81	88	87	101	104	103	100	100
PHI	67	44	21	2	323	238	17	8	70	31	39	0	274	281	15	12	137	75	60	2	597	519	32	20	98	141	93	105	102	91	104	102
STL	70	38	32	0	250	228	7	15	69	27	42	0	250	297	5	11	139	65	74	0	500	525	12	26	129	45	92	87	93	96	95	95
WAS	71	29	40	2	275	349	15	24	69	14	54	1	162	342	2	14	140	43	94	3	437	691	17	38	199	42	110	115	71	109	105	111

1904 AMERICAN LEAGUE

	HOME								ROAD								ALL															
TM	G	W	L	T	R	OR	HR	OHR	G	W	L	T	R	OR	HR	OHR	G	W	L	T	R	OR	HR	OHR	HRF	HRB	HRP	RF	RB	RP	BPF	PPF
BOS	81	49	30	2	325	240	18	18	76	46	29	1	283	226	8	13	157	95	59	3	608	466	26	31	151	109	134	105	104	83	105	101
CHI	78	50	27	1	297	226	0	2	78	39	38	1	303	256	14	11	156	89	65	2	600	482	14	13	9	69	156	95	110	90	99	97
CLE	78	44	31	3	329	242	14	2	76	42	34	0	318	240	13	8	154	86	65	3	647	482	27	10	77	150	58	100	117	90	102	98
DET	79	34	40	5	237	295	3	4	83	28	50	5	268	332	8	12	162	62	90	10	505	627	11	16	40	74	101	93	92	111	95	98
NY	75	46	29	0	321	288	22	25	80	46	30	4	277	238	5	4	155	92	59	4	598	526	27	29	357	62	61	124	97	87	112	111
PHI	79	47	31	1	308	235	19	8	76	34	39	3	249	268	12	5	155	81	70	4	557	503	31	13	144	126	58	101	99	91	102	101
STL	78	32	43	3	231	288	2	14	78	33	44	1	250	316	8	11	156	65	87	4	481	604	10	25	85	55	131	92	92	112	95	98
WAS	78	23	52	3	221	350	3	2	79	15	61	3	216	393	7	17	157	38	113	6	437	743	10	19	23	103	124	93	85	135	93	99

1905 AMERICAN LEAGUE

	HOME								ROAD								ALL															
TM	G	W	L	T	R	OR	HR	OHR	G	W	L	T	R	OR	HR	OHR	G	W	L	T	R	OR	HR	OHR	HRF	HRB	HRP	RF	RB	RP	BPF	PPF
BOS	77	44	32	1	296	281	21	20	76	34	42	0	283	283	8	13	153	78	74	1	579	564	29	33	173	113	136	101	102	100	100	100
CHI	82	50	29	3	300	207	5	2	76	42	31	3	312	244	6	9	158	92	60	6	612	451	11	11	47	76	62	87	109	83	97	93
CLE	77	40	37	0	290	284	5	13	78	36	41	1	277	303	13	10	155	76	78	1	567	587	18	23	81	100	132	100	100	103	100	100
DET	76	45	30	1	267	275	5	5	78	34	44	0	245	327	8	6	154	79	74	1	512	602	13	11	76	70	61	98	92	106	98	100
NY	75	40	35	0	316	303	15	15	77	31	43	3	270	319	8	11	152	71	78	3	586	622	23	26	150	98	112	107	103	108	102	103
PHI	74	50	23	1	337	247	12	12	78	42	33	3	286	245	12	9	152	92	56	4	623	492	24	21	119	117	103	115	102	83	109	106
STL	79	34	42	3	250	267	5	7	77	20	57	0	261	341	11	12	156	54	99	3	511	608	16	19	53	104	124	84	98	113	91	93
WAS	77	33	42	2	289	340	10	4	77	31	45	1	270	283	12	8	154	64	87	3	559	623	22	12	72	125	71	111	95	104	104	106

1906 AMERICAN LEAGUE

	HOME								ROAD								ALL															
TM	G	W	L	T	R	OR	HR	OHR	G	W	L	T	R	OR	HR	OHR	G	W	L	T	R	OR	HR	OHR	HRF	HRB	HRP	RF	RB	RP	BPF	PPF
BOS	77	22	54	1	230	364	10	22	78	27	51	0	232	342	3	15	155	49	105	1	462	706	13	37	161	59	162	102	83	120	98	104
CHI	79	54	23	2	275	180	2	1	75	39	35	1	295	280	5	10	154	93	58	3	570	460	7	11	21	77	78	78	111	91	92	89
CLE	79	47	30	2	351	229	4	8	78	42	34	2	312	253	8	8	157	89	64	4	663	482	12	16	77	74	99	102	112	85	103	99
DET	78	42	34	2	315	317	4	5	73	29	44	0	203	282	6	5	151	71	78	2	518	599	10	14	59	73	97	118	85	99	108	110
NY	76	53	23	0	398	294	14	8	79	37	38	4	246	249	3	13	155	90	61	4	644	543	17	21	137	79	108	139	94	82	120	118
PHI	73	48	23	2	285	211	21	4	76	30	44	2	276	331	11	5	149	78	67	4	561	542	32	9	151	143	50	87	111	105	94	93
STL	76	40	34	2	272	225	12	10	78	36	39	3	286	273	8	4	154	76	73	5	558	498	20	14	170	86	58	92	101	91	98	97
WAS	75	33	41	1	260	288	7	5	76	22	54	0	258	376	19	10	151	55	95	1	518	664	26	15	45	209	141	88	103	127	91	94

1907 AMERICAN LEAGUE

	HOME								ROAD								ALL															
TM	G	W	L	T	R	OR	HR	OHR	G	W	L	T	R	OR	HR	OHR	G	W	L	T	R	OR	HR	OHR	HRF	HRB	HRP	RF	RB	RP	BPF	PPF
BOS	78	34	41	3	249	270	12	11	77	25	49	3	215	288	6	11	155	59	90	6	464	558	18	22	127	132	162	101	81	96	101	103
CHI	79	48	29	2	316	222	0	5	78	39	35	4	272	252	5	8	157	87	64	6	588	474	5	13	42	37	135	102	99	82	104	101
CLE	82	46	31	5	267	226	7	5	76	39	36	1	263	299	4	3	158	85	67	6	530	525	11	8	149	63	47	84	99	98	93	93
DET	79	50	27	2	373	265	3	3	74	42	31	1	321	267	8	4	153	92	58	3	694	532	11	7	51	102	75	102	122	97	101	98
NY	75	33	40	2	331	372	10	7	77	37	38	2	274	293	5	7	152	70	78	4	605	665	15	14	137	99	98	123	100	109	109	110
PHI	73	50	20	3	324	235	14	6	77	38	37	2	258	276	8	6	150	88	57	5	582	511	22	12	143	144	89	110	100	90	106	104
STL	76	36	40	0	261	262	5	11	79	33	43	3	281	293	4	6	155	69	83	3	542	555	9	17	153	58	99	95	98	100	98	98
WAS	75	27	47	1	228	310	1	3	79	22	55	2	278	381	11	7	154	49	102	3	506	691	12	10	25	114	145	86	100	130	90	94

1908 AMERICAN LEAGUE

	HOME								ROAD								ALL															
TM	G	W	L	T	R	OR	HR	OHR	G	W	L	T	R	OR	HR	OHR	G	W	L	T	R	OR	HR	OHR	HRF	HRB	HRP	RF	RB	RP	BPF	PPF
BOS	77	37	40	2	273	249	9	9	78	38	39	1	291	264	5	9	155	75	79	1	564	513	14	18	125	87	112	96	107	99	98	97
CHI	78	51	25	2	271	184	1	4	78	37	39	2	266	286	2	7	156	88	64	4	537	470	3	11	59	24	82	85	107	93	94	93
CLE	78	51	26	1	305	223	8	7	79	39	38	2	263	234	10	9	157	90	64	3	568	457	18	16	83	137	124	107	99	82	106	103

TM	HOME								ROAD								ALL															
	G	W	L	T	R	OR	HR	OHR	G	W	L	T	R	OR	HR	OHR	G	W	L	T	R	OR	HR	OHR	HRF	HRB	HRP	RF	RB	RP	BPF	PPF
DET	78	44	33	1	315	300	6	6	76	46	30	0	332	247	13	6	154	90	63	1	647	547	19	12	65	154	112	104	121	104	101	99
NY	77	30	47	0	234	352	11	16	78	21	56	1	225	361	2	10	155	51	103	1	459	713	13	26	194	57	126	100	90	132	95	101
PHI	78	46	30	2	294	272	11	4	79	22	55	2	192	290	10	6	157	68	85	4	486	562	21	10	95	141	74	116	83	96	107	110
STL	78	46	31	1	292	234	12	2	77	37	38	2	252	249	8	5	155	83	69	3	544	483	20	7	106	124	50	104	99	89	103	102
WAS	78	43	32	3	249	237	2	8	77	24	53	0	230	302	6	8	155	67	85	3	479	539	8	16	73	61	122	91	95	104	95	97

1909 AMERICAN LEAGUE

TM	HOME								ROAD								ALL															
	G	W	L	T	R	OR	HR	OHR	G	W	L	T	R	OR	HR	OHR	G	W	L	T	R	OR	HR	OHR	HRF	HRB	HRP	RF	RB	RP	BPF	PPF
BOS	75	47	28	0	329	295	18	13	77	41	35	1	268	255	2	5	152	88	63	1	597	550	20	18	317	60	74	120	105	98	109	108
CHI	81	42	34	5	256	201	1	3	78	36	40	2	236	262	3	5	159	78	74	7	492	463	4	8	52	33	68	90	93	88	97	96
CLE	77	39	37	1	262	259	2	1	78	32	45	1	231	273	8	8	155	71	82	2	493	532	10	9	21	121	90	104	91	97	102	103
DET	78	57	19	2	377	246	12	9	80	41	35	4	289	247	7	7	158	98	54	6	666	493	19	16	146	112	99	118	111	86	110	106
NY	77	41	35	1	338	263	11	9	76	33	42	1	252	324	5	12	153	74	77	2	590	587	16	21	114	118	154	103	113	113	99	99
PHI	76	49	27	0	293	200	9	4	77	46	31	0	312	208	12	5	153	95	58	0	605	408	21	9	81	165	80	98	113	80	102	97
STL	79	40	37	2	242	235	4	6	75	21	52	2	199	340	6	10	154	61	89	4	441	575	10	16	62	95	141	85	92	114	92	94
WAS	77	27	48	2	197	271	5	2	79	15	62	2	183	385	4	10	156	42	110	4	380	656	9	12	53	96	95	84	80	126	90	96

1910 AMERICAN LEAGUE

TM	HOME								ROAD								ALL															
	G	W	L	T	R	OR	HR	OHR	G	W	L	T	R	OR	HR	OHR	G	W	L	T	R	OR	HR	OHR	HRF	HRB	HRP	RF	RB	RP	BPF	PPF
BOS	80	51	28	1	338	262	32	21	78	30	44	4	300	302	11	9	158	81	72	5	638	564	43	30	216	151	116	98	112	101	99	97
CHI	79	41	37	1	233	198	2	2	77	27	48	2	224	281	5	14	156	68	85	3	457	479	7	16	23	74	114	85	86	88	95	95
CLE	80	39	36	5	278	330	4	2	81	32	45	4	270	327	5	8	161	71	81	9	548	657	9	10	50	63	58	102	94	110	100	102
DET	78	46	31	1	346	306	18	21	77	40	37	0	333	276	10	13	155	86	68	1	679	582	28	34	155	133	158	105	118	103	102	100
NY	77	49	25	3	343	284	13	6	79	39	38	2	283	273	7	10	156	88	63	5	626	557	20	16	113	100	84	114	103	93	107	106
PHI	78	57	19	2	339	211	9	0	77	45	29	3	334	230	10	8	155	102	48	5	673	441	19	8	54	133	44	98	117	81	102	97
STL	79	26	51	2	229	359	4	3	79	21	56	2	222	384	8	11	158	47	107	4	451	743	12	14	39	95	96	96	83	129	94	100
WAS	77	38	35	4	265	252	3	7	80	28	50	2	236	298	6	12	157	66	85	6	501	550	9	19	61	59	118	100	87	94	101	102

1911 AMERICAN LEAGUE

TM	HOME								ROAD								ALL															
	G	W	L	T	R	OR	HR	OHR	G	W	L	T	R	OR	HR	OHR	G	W	L	T	R	OR	HR	OHR	HRF	HRB	HRP	RF	RB	RP	BPF	PPF
BOS	76	39	37	0	328	312	20	15	77	39	38	0	352	331	15	6	153	78	75	0	680	643	35	21	156	111	66	96	97	93	99	98
CHI	78	40	37	1	341	299	8	13	76	37	37	2	378	325	12	9	154	77	74	3	719	624	20	22	98	80	87	90	105	93	97	95
CLE	77	46	30	1	368	344	7	4	79	34	43	2	323	368	13	13	156	80	73	3	691	712	20	17	47	105	83	105	93	96	103	103
DET	76	51	25	0	468	403	21	15	78	38	40	0	363	373	9	13	154	89	65	0	831	776	30	28	156	92	94	119	108	103	108	107
NY	75	36	40	1	365	422	14	14	76	40	36	1	319	302	11	12	153	76	76	1	684	724	25	26	117	94	97	121	88	92	111	111
PHI	75	54	20	1	384	253	11	5	77	47	30	0	477	348	24	12	152	101	50	1	861	601	35	17	50	181	97	83	132	96	93	88
STL	78	25	53	0	296	396	9	10	74	20	54	0	271	416	8	18	152	45	107	0	567	812	17	28	71	86	126	94	85	117	95	100
WAS	77	39	38	0	323	356	11	21	77	25	52	0	302	410	5	18	154	64	90	0	625	766	16	39	132	57	131	95	91	109	97	99

1912 AMERICAN LEAGUE

TM	HOME								ROAD								ALL															
	G	W	L	T	R	OR	HR	OHR	G	W	L	T	R	OR	HR	OHR	G	W	L	T	R	OR	HR	OHR	HRF	HRB	HRP	RF	RB	RP	BPF	PPF
BOS	78	57	20	1	417	286	10	10	76	48	27	1	382	258	19	8	154	105	47	2	799	544	29	18	76	167	118	108	109	78	107	102
CHI	78	34	43	1	276	340	11	12	80	44	33	3	362	306	6	14	158	78	76	4	638	646	17	26	115	81	120	95	92	93	99	99
CLE	76	40	35	1	344	327	4	6	79	35	43	1	332	353	8	9	155	75	78	2	676	680	12	15	64	70	88	102	97	98	101	101
DET	76	37	39	0	344	370	8	6	78	32	45	1	376	407	11	10	154	69	84	1	720	777	19	16	71	112	95	94	111	119	95	96
NY	76	31	44	1	352	423	14	16	77	19	58	0	278	419	4	12	153	50	102	1	630	842	18	28	168	67	111	109	91	118	101	105
PHI	78	45	32	1	381	342	11	6	75	45	30	0	398	316	11	6	153	90	62	1	779	658	22	12	97	109	64	99	116	100	99	97
STL	79	27	50	2	287	379	6	11	78	26	51	1	265	385	13	6	157	53	101	3	552	764	19	17	88	98	92	99	80	107	99	103
WAS	78	45	32	1	335	289	13	12	76	46	29	1	363	292	7	12	154	91	61	2	698	581	20	24	125	92	112	95	103	88	99	97

1913 AMERICAN LEAGUE

TM	HOME								ROAD								ALL															
	G	W	L	T	R	OR	HR	OHR	G	W	L	T	R	OR	HR	OHR	G	W	L	T	R	OR	HR	OHR	HRF	HRB	HRP	RF	RB	RP	BPF	PPF
BOS	75	41	34	0	328	312	3	0	76	38	37	1	303	298	14	6	151	79	71	1	631	610	17	6	17	139	29	107	103	100	103	103
CHI	77	40	37	0	216	233	5	4	76	38	37	1	272	265	19	6	153	78	74	1	488	498	24	10	39	151	86	85	85	87	95	95
CLE	79	45	31	3	336	284	4	9	76	41	35	0	297	252	12	10	155	86	66	3	633	536	16	19	60	93	120	108	98	85	106	104
DET	76	34	42	0	312	368	9	5	77	32	45	0	312	348	15	8	153	66	87	0	624	716	24	13	64	139	82	103	105	118	99	101
NY	75	27	47	1	265	339	5	20	78	30	47	1	264	329	3	11	153	57	94	2	529	668	8	31	166	32	109	104	87	107	101	104
PHI	76	50	26	0	388	271	19	14	77	46	31	0	406	321	14	10	153	96	57	0	794	592	33	24	134	148	112	94	137	106	96	92
STL	77	31	46	0	247	309	13	11	78	26	50	2	281	333	5	10	155	57	96	2	528	642	18	21	149	69	86	92	91	108	95	98
WAS	79	43	35	1	297	318	9	29	76	47	29	0	299	243	10	6	155	90	64	1	596	561	19	35	198	80	103	109	93	87	106	105

1914 AMERICAN LEAGUE

TM	HOME								ROAD								ALL															
	G	W	L	T	R	OR	HR	OHR	G	W	L	T	R	OR	HR	OHR	G	W	L	T	R	OR	HR	OHR	HRF	HRB	HRP	RF	RB	RP	BPF	PPF
BOS	79	44	31	4	270	247	3	5	80	47	31	2	318	264	15	13	159	91	62	6	588	511	18	18	32	133	155	92	104	92	98	96
CHI	81	43	37	1	271	285	7	4	76	27	47	2	216	275	12	11	157	70	84	3	487	560	19	15	48	141	108	105	82	93	103	105
CLE	79	32	47	0	289	380	4	3	78	19	55	4	249	329	6	7	157	51	102	4	538	709	10	10	56	66	62	111	92	117	102	106
DET	78	42	35	1	315	318	11	9	79	38	38	3	300	300	14	8	157	80	73	4	615	618	25	17	93	140	101	106	105	106	102	102
NY	78	36	40	2	278	259	8	24	79	34	44	1	260	291	4	6	157	70	84	3	538	550	12	30	252	42	83	98	94	96	100	100
PHI	78	51	24	3	354	247	17	13	80	48	29	3	395	282	5	12	158	99	53	6	749	529	29	18	166	120	74	93	133	99	97	93
STL	81	42	36	3	271	298	11	14	78	29	46	3	252	316	6	6	159	71	82	6	523	614	17	20	178	66	74	97	92	106	98	100
WAS	77	40	33	4	282	246	8	7	81	41	40	0	290	273	10	13	158	81	73	4	572	519	18	20	72	116	123	99	98	90	101	100

1915 AMERICAN LEAGUE

TM	HOME								ROAD								ALL															
	G	W	L	T	R	OR	HR	OHR	G	W	L	T	R	OR	HR	OHR	G	W	L	T	R	OR	HR	OHR	HRF	HRB	HRP	RF	RB	RP	BPF	PPF
BOS	76	55	20	1	323	221	5	4	79	46	30	3	345	278	9	14	155	101	50	4	668	499	14	18	45	100	110	93	110	84	99	96
CHI	79	54	24	1	353	236	9	4	76	39	37	0	364	273	16	10	155	93	61	1	717	509	25	14	52	160	93	91	120	89	98	93
CLE	77	27	50	0	277	362	7	9	77	30	45	2	262	308	13	10	154	57	95	2	539	670	20	19	71	115	114	109	85	103	104	106
DET	77	51	26	0	416	318	11	7	79	49	28	2	362	279	12	7	156	100	54	2	778	597	23	14	99	110	71	117	116	92	109	105
NY	82	37	43	2	306	303	28	32	72	32	40	0	278	285	3	9	154	69	83	2	584	588	31	41	307	64	105	95	98	98	98	98
PHI	77	20	55	2	285	457	9	18	77	23	54	0	260	431	7	3	154	43	109	2	545	888	16	21	219	57	55	104	93	141	96	103
STL	76	35	38	3	237	315	6	4	83	28	53	2	284	364	13	14	159	63	91	5	521	679	19	21	55	117	130	93	86	109	96	99
WAS	77	48	28	1	277	235	2	2	78	37	40	1	292	256	10	10	155	85	68	2	569	491	12	12	23	88	88	96	92	80	101	99

1916 AMERICAN LEAGUE

TM	HOME								ROAD								ALL															
	G	W	L	T	R	OR	HR	OHR	G	W	L	T	R	OR	HR	OHR	G	W	L	T	R	OR	HR	OHR	HRF	HRB	HRP	RF	RB	RP	BPF	PPF
BOS	78	49	28	1	252	205	1	1	78	42	35	1	298	275	13	9	156	91	63	2	550	480	14	10	10	118	101	83	103	90	94	92
CHI	77	49	28	0	326	254	9	5	78	40	37	1	275	243	8	9	155	89	65	1	601	497	17	14	86	100	82	112	97	83	108	106
CLE	78	44	33	1	323	293	4	9	79	33	44	2	307	309	12	7	157	77	77	3	630	602	16	16	72	95	106	101	109	105	100	99
DET	77	49	28	0	350	313	7	8	78	38	39	1	320	282	10	4	155	87	67	1	670	595	17	12	108	88	63	111	113	101	104	103
NY	79	46	31	2	306	277	22	22	77	34	43	0	271	284	13	15	156	80	74	2	577	561	35	37	144	183	194	102	99	97	101	101
PHI	76	23	53	0	231	399	15	17	78	13	64	1	216	377	4	9	154	36	117	1	447	776	19	26	208	66	99	105	80	130	98	105
STL	79	45	32	2	290	238	7	10	79	34	43	2	298	307	7	3	158	79	75	4	588	545	14	15	135	65	66	89	107	99	95	94
WAS	81	49	28	4	294	248	6	1	78	27	49	2	242	295	6	13	159	76	77	6	536	543	12	14	39	111	82	97	92	93	100	100

1917 AMERICAN LEAGUE

TM	HOME								ROAD								ALL															
	G	W	L	T	R	OR	HR	OHR	G	W	L	T	R	OR	HR	OHR	G	W	L	T	R	OR	HR	OHR	HRF	HRB	HRP	RF	RB	RP	BPF	PPF
BOS	80	45	33	2	293	245	3	4	77	45	29	3	262	209	11	8	157	90	62	5	555	454	14	12	39	108	106	110	90	75	108	106
CHI	79	56	21	2	327	204	7	3	77	44	33	0	329	260	11	7	156	100	54	2	656	464	18	10	58	129	74	90	118	87	98	93
CLE	77	43	34	0	317	314	5	8	79	45	32	2	267	229	8	9	156	88	66	2	584	543	13	17	81	85	109	127	90	84	114	113
DET	76	34	41	1	285	303	5	5	78	44	34	0	354	274	20	7	154	78	75	1	639	577	25	12	41	193	129	97	116	107	98	96
NY	75	35	40	0	269	292	19	24	80	36	42	2	255	266	8	4	155	71	82	2	524	558	27	28	282	97	81	112	87	92	107	107

	HOME								ROAD								ALL															
TM	G	W	L	T	R	OR	HR	OHR	G	W	L	T	R	OR	HR	OHR	G	W	L	T	R	OR	HR	OHR	HRF	HRB	HRP	RF	RB	RP	BPF	PPF
PHI	76	29	47	0	264	319	11	17	78	26	51	1	265	372	6	6	154	55	98	1	529	691	17	23	202	73	89	93	101	127	94	97
STL	78	31	46	1	252	337	7	11	77	26	51	0	258	350	8	8	155	57	97	1	510	687	15	19	108	89	108	95	95	123	95	98
WAS	81	42	36	3	264	255	1	3	76	32	43	1	279	311	3	9	157	74	79	4	543	566	4	12	34	33	92	84	103	107	92	93

1918 AMERICAN LEAGUE

	HOME								ROAD								ALL															
TM	G	W	L	T	R	OR	HR	OHR	G	W	L	T	R	OR	HR	OHR	G	W	L	T	R	OR	HR	OHR	HRF	HRB	HRP	RF	RB	RP	BPF	PPF
BOS	70	49	21	0	272	165	2	3	56	26	30	0	202	215	13	6	126	75	51	0	474	380	15	9	24	192	167	86	109	90	95	93
CHI	56	30	26	0	216	194	4	4	68	27	41	0	241	252	4	5	124	57	67	0	457	446	8	9	107	64	71	101	101	98	100	100
CLE	62	38	22	2	274	219	1	4	67	35	32	0	230	228	8	5	129	73	54	2	504	447	9	9	45	79	109	115	99	90	108	107
DET	58	28	29	1	221	246	2	6	70	27	42	1	255	311	11	4	128	55	71	2	476	557	13	10	67	109	112	99	106	121	97	99
NY	67	37	29	1	251	237	10	22	59	23	34	2	242	238	10	3	126	60	63	3	493	475	20	25	189	148	130	91	114	110	94	94
PHI	68	35	32	1	256	273	15	8	62	17	44	1	156	265	7	5	130	52	76	2	412	538	22	13	158	136	89	111	82	106	104	108
STL	53	23	30	0	178	195	1	7	70	35	34	1	248	253	4	4	123	58	64	1	426	448	5	11	127	38	79	98	95	100	99	100
WAS	74	41	32	1	268	238	1	6	56	31	24	1	193	174	3	4	130	72	56	2	461	412	4	10	79	36	83	104	93	84	104	103

1919 AMERICAN LEAGUE

	HOME								ROAD								ALL															
TM	G	W	L	T	R	OR	HR	OHR	G	W	L	T	R	OR	HR	OHR	G	W	L	T	R	OR	HR	OHR	HRF	HRB	HRP	RF	RB	RP	BPF	PPF
BOS	66	35	30	1	233	241	10	3	72	31	41	0	331	311	23	13	138	66	71	1	564	552	33	16	43	145	68	82	108	107	91	91
CHI	70	48	22	0	344	279	5	11	70	40	30	0	323	255	20	14	140	88	52	0	667	534	25	25	51	97	115	108	111	91	105	102
CLE	69	44	25	0	340	276	12	4	70	40	30	0	296	261	13	15	139	84	55	0	636	537	25	19	62	102	69	112	105	91	107	104
DET	70	46	24	0	307	243	10	14	70	34	36	0	311	335	13	21	140	80	60	0	618	578	23	35	74	90	129	87	116	108	93	92
NY	73	46	25	2	326	255	33	30	68	34	34	0	252	251	12	17	141	80	59	2	578	506	45	47	180	106	118	107	94	85	106	104
PHI	70	21	49	0	266	400	29	31	70	15	55	0	191	342	6	13	140	36	104	0	457	742	35	44	244	62	88	118	75	116	106	112
STL	70	40	30	0	280	249	19	23	70	27	42	1	253	318	12	12	140	67	72	1	533	567	31	35	160	81	88	93	96	101	97	98
WAS	72	32	40	0	265	282	2	5	70	24	44	2	268	288	22	15	142	56	84	2	533	570	24	20	20	101	125	95	94	99	98	99

1920 AMERICAN LEAGUE

	HOME								ROAD								ALL															
TM	G	W	L	T	R	OR	HR	OHR	G	W	L	T	R	OR	HR	OHR	G	W	L	T	R	OR	HR	OHR	HRF	HRB	HRP	RF	RB	RP	BPF	PPF
BOS	76	41	35	0	327	300	3	14	78	31	46	1	323	398	19	25	154	72	81	1	650	698	22	39	43	54	114	90	93	98	96	97
CHI	77	52	25	0	381	298	18	10	77	44	33	0	413	367	19	35	154	96	58	0	794	665	37	45	56	111	112	90	113	97	96	94
CLE	78	51	27	0	441	330	20	10	76	47	29	0	416	312	15	21	154	98	56	0	857	642	35	31	84	79	69	104	113	88	104	100
DET	78	32	46	0	336	452	12	24	77	29	47	1	316	381	18	22	155	61	93	1	652	833	30	46	89	67	100	109	86	106	103	106
NY	77	49	28	0	424	308	71	36	77	46	31	0	414	321	44	12	154	95	59	0	838	629	115	48	173	189	83	101	112	87	102	99
PHI	77	25	50	2	254	401	35	40	79	23	56	0	304	433	9	16	156	48	106	2	558	834	44	56	241	52	71	90	80	114	94	99
STL	78	40	38	0	473	415	31	33	76	36	39	1	324	351	19	20	154	76	77	1	797	766	50	53	149	88	93	124	97	95	111	111
WAS	76	37	38	1	343	386	5	7	77	31	46	0	380	416	31	44	153	68	84	1	723	802	36	51	18	135	180	93	104	114	95	96

1921 AMERICAN LEAGUE

	HOME								ROAD								ALL															
TM	G	W	L	T	R	OR	HR	OHR	G	W	L	T	R	OR	HR	OHR	G	W	L	T	R	OR	HR	OHR	HRF	HRB	HRP	RF	RB	RP	BPF	PPF
BOS	77	41	36	0	332	333	3	16	77	34	43	0	336	363	14	37	154	75	79	0	668	696	17	53	40	35	112	96	85	88	100	100
CHI	77	37	40	0	378	399	13	20	77	25	52	0	305	459	22	32	154	62	92	0	683	858	35	52	64	69	99	101	87	107	99	102
CLE	77	51	26	0	467	330	15	10	77	43	34	0	458	382	27	33	154	94	60	0	925	712	42	43	45	96	88	97	118	94	99	96
DET	77	37	40	0	433	412	19	28	77	34	42	1	450	440	39	43	154	71	82	1	883	852	58	71	60	123	151	95	117	113	96	96
NY	78	53	25	0	500	355	83	34	75	45	30	0	448	353	51	17	153	98	55	0	948	708	134	51	155	176	75	104	118	91	103	99
PHI	77	28	47	2	353	464	65	59	78	25	53	0	304	430	17	26	155	53	100	2	657	894	82	85	233	79	90	109	80	105	103	107
STL	77	43	34	0	423	434	42	43	77	38	39	0	412	411	25	28	154	81	73	0	835	845	67	71	149	91	97	104	105	106	101	101
WAS	76	46	30	0	358	332	14	13	78	34	43	1	346	406	28	38	154	80	73	1	704	738	42	51	45	97	107	95	91	94	99	99

1922 AMERICAN LEAGUE

	HOME								ROAD								ALL															
TM	G	W	L	T	R	OR	HR	OHR	G	W	L	T	R	OR	HR	OHR	G	W	L	T	R	OR	HR	OHR	HRF	HRB	HRP	RF	RB	RP	BPF	PPF
BOS	73	31	42	0	280	344	6	17	81	30	51	0	318	425	39	31	154	61	93	0	598	769	45	48	39	78	108	93	85	106	96	99
CHI	77	43	34	0	351	335	10	21	78	34	43	1	340	356	35	36	155	77	77	1	691	691	45	57	48	83	115	100	93	93	101	101
CLE	80	44	35	1	423	424	12	20	75	34	41	0	345	393	20	31	155	78	76	1	768	817	32	58	55	62	104	107	102	108	102	103
DET	77	43	34	0	426	370	15	32	78	36	41	0	402	421	39	30	155	79	75	1	828	791	54	62	72	90	110	98	115	111	98	97
NY	77	50	27	0	387	291	53	48	77	44	33	0	371	327	42	25	154	94	60	1	758	618	95	73	143	123	95	99	102	85	101	99
PHI	78	38	39	1	388	437	80	82	77	27	50	0	317	393	31	25	155	65	89	1	705	830	111	107	230	107	99	112	92	106	104	106
STL	77	54	23	0	471	314	70	41	77	39	38	0	396	329	28	30	154	93	61	0	867	643	98	71	173	106	87	108	112	87	106	102
WAS	79	40	39	0	329	295	15	3	75	29	46	0	321	411	30	46	154	69	85	0	650	706	45	49	25	130	87	82	98	104	92	93

1923 AMERICAN LEAGUE

	HOME								ROAD								ALL															
TM	G	W	L	T	R	OR	HR	OHR	G	W	L	T	R	OR	HR	OHR	G	W	L	T	R	OR	HR	OHR	HRF	HRB	HRP	RF	RB	RP	BPF	PPF
BOS	78	37	40	1	327	402	11	15	76	24	51	1	257	407	23	33	154	61	91	2	584	809	34	48	48	81	109	105	78	104	102	106
CHI	75	30	45	0	327	348	13	24	81	39	40	2	365	393	29	25	156	69	85	2	692	741	42	49	76	80	97	96	94	100	98	99
CLE	78	42	36	0	455	393	22	16	75	40	35	0	433	353	37	20	153	82	71	0	888	746	59	36	67	121	80	104	120	103	101	99
DET	77	45	32	0	400	351	21	31	78	38	39	1	431	390	20	27	155	83	71	1	831	741	41	58	111	70	95	94	116	105	97	95
NY	76	46	30	0	407	329	62	50	76	52	24	0	416	293	43	18	152	98	54	0	823	622	105	68	168	152	97	105	109	85	104	101
PHI	75	34	41	0	345	360	28	32	78	35	42	1	316	401	25	36	153	69	83	1	661	761	53	68	102	99	123	102	90	102	100	102
STL	78	40	36	2	377	364	50	44	76	34	42	0	311	356	32	15	154	74	78	2	688	720	82	59	174	112	76	107	90	94	104	105
WAS	79	43	34	2	363	339	7	16	76	32	44	0	357	408	19	40	155	75	78	2	720	747	26	56	41	65	131	89	103	106	95	95

1924 AMERICAN LEAGUE

	HOME								ROAD								ALL															
TM	G	W	L	T	R	OR	HR	OHR	G	W	L	T	R	OR	HR	OHR	G	W	L	T	R	OR	HR	OHR	HRF	HRB	HRP	RF	RB	RP	BPF	PPF
BOS	77	41	36	0	402	391	8	17	80	26	51	3	335	415	22	26	157	67	87	3	737	806	30	43	57	69	103	108	91	99	104	105
CHI	77	37	39	1	403	414	13	23	77	29	48	0	390	444	28	29	154	66	87	1	793	858	41	52	66	98	126	98	107	114	97	98
CLE	75	37	38	0	374	375	13	18	78	30	48	0	381	439	28	25	153	67	86	0	755	814	41	43	64	96	106	95	103	110	97	97
DET	78	45	33	0	427	393	17	28	78	41	35	2	422	403	18	17	156	86	68	2	849	796	35	55	101	70	105	100	110	104	99	99
NY	78	45	32	1	397	324	57	46	75	44	31	0	401	343	41	13	153	89	63	1	798	667	98	59	167	158	91	95	106	90	99	97
PHI	75	36	39	0	328	391	32	24	77	35	42	0	357	387	31	19	152	71	81	0	685	778	63	43	113	120	86	99	91	102	99	101
STL	78	41	36	1	426	445	44	49	75	33	42	0	343	364	23	19	153	74	78	1	769	809	67	68	186	99	96	116	94	98	107	108
WAS	79	47	30	2	371	280	1	7	77	45	32	0	384	333	21	27	156	92	62	2	755	613	22	34	18	50	115	91	99	82	98	96

1925 AMERICAN LEAGUE

	HOME								ROAD								ALL															
TM	G	W	L	T	R	OR	HR	OHR	G	W	L	T	R	OR	HR	OHR	G	W	L	T	R	OR	HR	OHR	HRF	HRB	HRP	RF	RB	RP	BPF	PPF
BOS	75	28	47	0	309	441	10	28	77	19	58	0	330	481	31	39	152	47	105	0	639	922	41	67	58	73	125	94	85	117	95	99
CHI	77	44	33	0	366	378	13	32	77	35	42	0	445	392	25	37	154	79	75	0	811	770	38	69	75	63	111	90	106	102	96	95
CLE	77	37	39	1	421	430	23	19	78	33	45	0	361	387	29	22	155	70	84	1	782	817	52	41	85	79	64	113	91	95	106	107
DET	77	43	34	0	451	399	18	36	79	38	39	2	452	430	32	34	156	81	73	2	903	829	50	70	86	78	108	109	112	104	99	98
NY	79	42	36	1	354	356	54	56	77	27	49	1	352	418	56	22	156	69	85	2	706	774	110	78	131	149	104	91	91	98	96	97
PHI	77	51	26	0	435	351	35	37	76	37	38	1	396	362	41	23	153	88	64	1	831	713	76	60	110	109	87	103	102	89	103	101
STL	78	45	32	1	503	501	73	73	76	37	39	0	397	405	37	26	154	82	71	1	900	906	110	99	196	119	102	119	104	105	108	108
WAS	76	53	22	1	408	298	13	13	76	43	33	0	421	372	43	36	152	96	55	1	829	670	56	49	36	116	107	91	107	89	98	95

1926 AMERICAN LEAGUE

	HOME								ROAD								ALL															
TM	G	W	L	T	R	OR	HR	OHR	G	W	L	T	R	OR	HR	OHR	G	W	L	T	R	OR	HR	OHR	HRF	HRB	HRP	RF	RB	RP	BPF	PPF
BOS	77	25	51	1	288	438	9	16	77	21	56	1	274	397	23	29	154	46	107	1	562	835	32	45	50	75	107	105	76	108	101	106
CHI	79	47	31	1	332	294	8	19	76	34	41	1	398	371	24	28	155	81	72	2	730	665	32	47	53	72	111	81	109	100	92	90
CLE	80	49	31	0	376	301	11	19	74	39	35	0	362	311	16	30	154	88	66	0	738	612	27	49	64	62	104	95	102	86	100	97
DET	81	39	41	1	380	445	16	38	76	40	34	2	413	385	20	20	157	79	75	3	793	830	36	58	123	62	90	98	110	115	97	97
NY	75	50	25	0	417	326	58	33	80	41	38	1	430	387	63	21	155	91	63	1	847	713	121	56	112	222	117	98	116	100	99	97
PHI	71	44	27	0	365	314	34	27	79	39	40	1	312	256	27	11	150	83	67	0	677	570	61	38	163	90	55	128	82	70	118	115
STL	79	40	39	0	375	429	53	64	76	22	53	1	307	416	19	22	155	62	92	1	682	845	72	86	224	85	99	105	92	112	101	103

TM	HOME								ROAD								ALL														RB	RP	BPF	PPF
	G	W	L	T	R	OR	HR	OHR	G	W	L	T	R	OR	HR	OHR	G	W	L	T	R	OR	HR	OHR	HRF	HRB	HRP	R						
WAS	74	42	30	2	373	378	4	15	78	39	39	0	429	383	39	30	152	81	69	2	802	761	43	45	32	97	143	9?3		114	109	98	97

1927 AMERICAN LEAGUE

TM	G	W	L	T	R	OR	HR	OHR	G	W	L	T	R	OR	HR	OHR	G	W	L	T	R	OR	HR	OHR	HRF	HRB	HRP	R	RB	RP	BPF	PPF
BOS	78	29	49	0	299	409	5	29	76	22	54	0	298	447	23	27	154	51	103	0	597	856	28	56	68	56	117	92	83	114	95	99
CHI	75	38	37	0	337	343	6	22	78	32	46	0	325	365	30	33	153	70	83	0	662	708	36	55	49	77	135	102	86	91	102	103
CLE	77	35	42	0	333	367	10	11	76	31	45	0	335	399	16	26	153	66	87	0	668	766	26	37	52	61	79	94	91	103	97	99
DET	78	44	32	2	467	433	25	28	78	38	39	1	378	372	26	24	156	82	71	3	845	805	51	52	106	89	90	117	102	98	108	107
NY	77	57	19	1	479	267	83	30	78	53	25	0	496	332	75	12	155	110	44	1	975	599	158	42	129	251	79	94	128	84	100	94
PHI	77	50	27	0	412	327	26	36	78	41	36	1	429	399	30	29	155	91	63	1	841	726	56	65	107	101	115	92	14	100	97	95
STL	78	38	38	2	440	457	42	57	77	21	56	0	284	447	13	22	155	59	94	2	724	904	55	79	226	60	87	117	89	109	106	109
WAS	79	51	28	0	416	308	10	19	78	34	41	3	366	422	19	34	157	85	69	0	782	730	29	53	58	64	111	92	05	98	97	96

1928 AMERICAN LEAGUE

TM	G	W	L	T	R	OR	HR	OHR	G	W	L	T	R	OR	HR	OHR	G	W	L	T	R	OR	HR	OHR	HRF	HRB	HRP	R	RB	RP	BPF	PPF
BOS	74	26	47	1	283	363	10	15	80	31	49	0	306	407	28	34	154	57	96	1	589	770	38	49	46	79	103	97	2	104	98	101
CHI	78	37	40	1	316	369	11	28	77	35	42	0	340	356	13	38	155	72	82	1	656	725	24	66	78	45	111	97	98	99	100	
CLE	77	29	48	0	366	443	10	15	78	33	44	1	308	387	24	37	155	62	92	1	674	830	34	52	44	75	108	114	104	106	108	
DET	77	36	41	0	382	400	33	26	77	32	45	0	362	404	29	32	154	68	86	0	744	804	62	58	97	104	98	101	104	99	100	
NY	77	52	25	0	400	301	69	36	77	49	28	0	494	384	64	23	154	101	53	0	894	685	133	59	119	205	103	83	105	92	89	
PHI	77	52	25	0	430	295	54	33	76	46	30	0	399	320	35	33	153	98	55	0	829	615	89	66	124	134	106	101	85	103	99	
STL	77	44	33	0	398	389	51	64	77	38	39	0	374	353	12	29	154	82	72	0	772	742	63	93	229	60	96	107	98	104	103	
WAS	80	37	43	0	363	378	16	12	75	38	36	1	355	327	24	28	155	75	79	1	718	705	40	40	54	83	79	102	94	102	101	

1929 AMERICAN LEAGUE

TM	G	W	L	T	R	OR	HR	OHR	G	W	L	T	R	OR	HR	OHR	G	W	L	T	R	OR	HR	OHR	HRF	HRB	HRP	R	RB	RP	BPF	PPF
BOS	78	32	45	1	328	399	11	36	77	26	51	0	277	404	17	42	155	58	96	1	605	803	28	78	80	41	105	103	77	99	102	105
CHI	76	35	41	0	306	366	19	41	76	24	52	0	321	426	18	43	155	59	93	0	627	792	37	84	97	51	107	90	87	95	97	
CLE	76	44	32	0	359	363	27	21	76	37	39	0	358	373	35	35	158	71	0		717	736	62	56	72	95	85	99	94	96	100	101
DET	77	38	39	0	476	453	57	33	78	32	45	1	450	475	53	40	158	84	1		926	928	110	73	98	149	105	101	123	97	97	
NY	77	49	28	0	463	362	69	55	77	39	38	0	436	413	73	28	154	66	0		899	775	142	83	120	180	111	98	118	104	99	97
PHI	74	57	16	1	484	302	72	47	77	47	30	0	417	313	50	26	154	46	1		901	615	122	73	154	133	84	112	110	79	109	104
STL	77	41	36	0	370	341	22	58	77	38	37	2	363	372	24	42	159	73	2		733	713	46	100	118	59	116	97	93	100	100	
WAS	78	37	40	1	376	390	10	17	75	34	41	0	354	386	38	31	151	81	1		730	776	48	48	41	80	92	99	96	100	100	

1930 AMERICAN LEAGUE

TM	G	W	L	T	R	OR	HR	OHR	G	W	L	T	R	OR	HR	OHR	G	W	L	T	R	OR	HR	OHR	HRF	HRB	HRP	R	RB	RP	BPF	PPF
BOS	76	30	46	0	287	354	15	31	78	22	56	0	325	460	32	44		102	0		612	814	47	75	64	64	102	84	79	101	93	96
CHI	78	34	44	0	393	457	25	42	76	28	48	0	336	427	38	32		92	0		729	884	63	74	93	76	88	106	85	101	103	105
CLE	77	44	33	0	494	469	34	46	77	37	40	0	396	446	38	39		73	0		890	915	72	85	104	84	97	113	102	105	105	105
DET	78	45	33	0	441	419	45	48	76	30	46	0	342	414	37	38		79	0		783	833	82	86	118	90	93	109	105	105	105	
NY	76	47	29	0	471	390	69	5?	78	39	39	0	591	508	83	39		68	0		1062	898	152	93	104	184	122	83	142	123	105	106
PHI	76	58	18	0	4??	329	76	4?	78	44	34	0	466	422	49	35		52	0		951	751	125	84	145	121	87	96	115	93	90	87
STL	78	38	40	0	432	475	35	7?	76	26	50	0	319	4??	40	52		90	0		751	886	75	124	111	91	138	117	83	97	99	96
WAS	77	56	21	0	474	300	17	15	77	38	39	0	418	389	40	37		60	0		892	689	57	52	45	86	79	97	106	84	108	110

1931 AMERICAN LEAGUE

TM	G	W	L	T	R	OR	HR	OHR	G	W	L	T	R	OR	HR	OHR	G	W	L	T	R	OR	HR	OHR	HRF	HRB	HRP	R	RB	RP	BPF	PPF
BOS	80	39	40	1	332	362	11	29	73	23	50	?	293	438	26	25		90	1		625	800	37	54	73	56	83	87	85	106	94	96
CHI	77	31	45	1	341	421	11	45	79	25	52	?	363	518	16	37		97	3		704	939	27	82	106	36	100	89	95	122	92	96
CLE	76	45	31	0	503	405	38	32	79	33	5	1	382	428	33	32		76	1		885	833	71	64	110	92	84	114	104	100	106	
DET	77	36	41	0	349	432	19	43	77	25	4?	1	302	404	24	36		93	0		651	836	43	79	102	60	103	108	79	99	106	107
NY	77	51	25	1	545	337	84	39	78	4?	34	1	522	423	71	28		59	2		1067	760	155	67	123	194	95	96	137	102	93	
PHI	75	60	15	0	446	289	61	37	78	47	30	1	412	337	57	3?		45	1		858	626	118	73	110	160	106	104	104	79	105	93
STL	77	39	38	0	407	425	42	48	77	24	53	0	315	445	34	36		91	0		722	870	76	84	123	97	106	107	89	105	101	
WAS	79	55	22	2	453	308	13	24	77	37	40	0	390	38?	?6	49		62	2		843	691	49	73	46	89	132	97	105	88	101	98

1932 AMERICAN LEAGUE

TM	G	W	L	T	R	OR	HR	OHR	G	W	L	T	R	OR	HR	OHR	G	W	L	T	R	OR	HR	OHR	HRF	HRB	HRP	R	RB	RP	BPF	PPF
BOS	77	27	50	0	?95	439	18	31	??	?1	53	1	367	507	26	48	15	111	0		566	915	53	79	61	72	105	96	73	111	97	102
CHI	77	28	49	0	?00	390	10	36	??	44	32	0	385	346	42	52	15?	102	1		667	897	36	88	60	49	116	78	97	124	87	91
PHI	77	6?	1?	2	423	39?	?	75	34	41	0	376	388	51	37	15?	65	1		845	747	78	70	88	91	83	115	97	87	108		91
STL	77	51	26	0	482	?06	?	80	77	43	34	2	520	424	79	49	153	75	2		799	787	80	89	86	97	109	103	98	102	107	
WAS	75	33	42	0	385	428	?	56	79	30	49	0	409	346	63	32	156	47	2		1002	724	160	93	102	180	115	88	129	97	95	102
WAS	77	51	26	0	431	325	21	77	42	35	0	409	391	40	47	154	60	0		981	752	172	112	179	146	96	126	106	85	114	

1933 AMERICAN LEAGUE

TM	G	W	L	T	R	OR	HR	OHR	G	W	L	T	R	OR	HR	OHR	G	W	L	T	R	OR	HR	OHR	HRF	HRB	HRP	R	RB	RP	BPF	PPF
BOS	72	32	40	0	341	???	23	35	77	31	46	0					154	61	0		840	716	61		73	58	84	99	96	105	91	100
CHI	77	35	41	1	355	426	20	42	74	32	42	0	359	381	27	40	149	86	0		700	758	50	75	93	69	99	103	93	100	101	
CLE	77	45	32	0	353	341	22	24	74	30	44	0	328	388	23	43	151	83	1		683	814	43	85	91	60	111	104	90	104	101	102
DET	78	43	35	0	394	382	27	36	77	32	44	1	301	328	28	36	15?	76	0		654	669	50	60	72	75	87	105	83	85	105	103
NY	75	51	23	1	421	324	79	26	77	40	36	1	328	351	30	48	155	79	1		722	733	57	84	82	82	115	111	87	89	107	107
PHI	76	46	29	1	414	387	82	50	76	33	43	0	461	466	57	27	15?	59	2		927	768	144	66	103	186	96	83	134	114	91	88
STL	77	30	46	1	389	480	43	16	76	25	50	1	280	340	21	28	15?	72	1		875	853	139	77	147	151	88	88	126	123	92	91
WAS	76	46	30	0	358	338	14	16	77	53	23	1	492	327	46	48	15?	96	2		669	820	64	96	191	59	82	130	76	91	115	117

1934 AMERICAN LEAGUE

TM	G	W	L	T	R	OR	HR	OHR	G	W	L	T	R	OR	HR	OHR	G	W	L	T	R	OR	HR	OHR	HRF	HRB	HRP	R	RB	RP	BPF	PPF
BOS	77	42	35	0	447	405	23	24	76	34	41	1	373	370	28	46	15?	53	1		850	665	60	64	36	109	118	89	115	94	96	93
CHI	75	29	46	0	370	464	47	82	78	24	53	1	334	482	24	57	1?	76	1		820	775	51	70	66	71	90	111	99	94	106	105
CLE	78	47	31	0	435	362	45	34	76	38	38	0	379	401	55	36	1?	99	1		704	946	71	139	151	69	128	104	90	117	99	103
DET	80	54	26	0	479	345	28	34	77	44	27	0	426	394	46	54	15?	53	0		814	763	100	70	87	121	89	100	103	97	100	100
NY	77	53	24	0	416	275	75	34	77	41	36	0	426	394	60	37	154	94	0		842	669	135	71	112	145	84	87	112	91	96	94
PHI	76	34	42	2	371	410	81	48	77	41	36	2	393	428	63	36	15?	68	2		764	838	144	84	126	150	94	96	100	109	97	98
STL	76	36	39	1	356	405	35	60	78	31	46	1	318	395	27	34	1?	67	3		674	800	62	94	148	59	84	108	82	96	104	106
WAS	76	34	40	2	368	397	14	26	79	32	46	1	361	409	37	48	1?		3		729	806	51	74	52	72	106	102	91	99	101	102

1935 AMERICAN LEAGUE

TM	G	W	L	T	R	OR	HR	OHR	G	W	L	T	R	OR	HR	OHR	G	W	L	T	R	OR	HR	OHR	HRF	HRB	HRP	R	RB	RP	BPF	PPF
BOS	79	41	37	1	393	404	26	29	75	37	38	0	325	328	43	38	154	78	1		718	732	69	67	68	95	94	114	85	86	108	108
CHI	77	42	34	1	418	396	50	61	76	32	44	0	320	354	24	44	153	74	1		738	750	74	105	149	71	101	116	87	88	109	109
CLE	77	48	29	0	340	340	53	30	79	34	42	3	385	399	40	38	156	82	3		776	739	93	68	108	102	78	97	98	94	99	
DET	79	53	25	1	467	304	45	33	77	43	40	0	452	361	61	48	154	96	1		919	665	106	72	106	102	91	99	103	99	97	93
NY	74	41	33	0	341	294	60	51	75	48	27	0	477	338	44	40	149	89	0		818	632	104	91	130	114	102	82	115	93	93	
PHI	72	30	42	0	369	414	63	39	77	28	49	0	341	455	49	34	149	58	0		710	869	112	73	125	122	84	103	93	92	97	93
STL	76	31	44	1	374	513	36	49	79	34	43	2	344	417	37	61	154	67	3		718	930	73	92	108	84	130	114	86	107	106	
WAS	77	37	39	1	388	414	5	28	77	30	47	0	435	489	7	67	154	32	1		823	903	89	40	47	139	88	115	124	91		

	HOME								ROAD								ALL														
TM	G	W	L	T	R	OR	HR	OHR	G	W	L	T	R	OR	HR	OHR	G	W	L	T	R	OR	HR	OHR	HRF	HRB	HRP	RF	RB	RP	BPF	PPF

1936 AMERICAN LEAGUE

TM	G	W	L	T	R	OR	HR	OHR	G	W	L	T	R	OR	HR	OHR	G	W	L	T	R	OR	HR	OHR	HRF	HRB	HRP	RF	RB	RP	BPF	PPF
BOS	77	47	29	1	437	360	38	31	78	27	51	0	338	404	48	47	155	74	80	1	775	764	86	78	76	100	91	107	83	82	106	106
CHI	75	43	32	0	453	419	23	55	78	38	38	2	467	454	37	49	153	81	70	2	920	873	60	104	95	65	108	99	107	102	99	99
CLE	81	49	30	2	535	433	73	33	76	31	44	1	386	429	50	40	157	80	74	3	921	862	123	73	109	117	76	110	97	93	105	105
DET	77	44	33	0	448	399	51	58	77	39	38	0	473	472	43	42	154	83	71	0	921	871	94	100	124	90	94	91	111	105	95	95
NY	77	56	21	0	492	311	82	41	78	46	30	2	573	420	100	43	155	102	51	2	1065	731	182	84	90	201	106	85	128	92	95	90
PHI	77	31	46	0	383	531	43	77	77	22	54	1	331	514	29	54	154	53	100	1	714	1045	72	131	135	67	114	106	81	114	100	105
STL	77	31	43	3	443	552	47	63	78	26	52	0	361	512	32	52	155	57	95	3	804	1064	79	115	126	75	105	112	88	113	103	107
WAS	77	42	35	0	433	380	16	27	76	40	36	0	456	439	46	46	153	82	71	0	889	799	62	73	50	80	101	93	105	96	98	96

1937 AMERICAN LEAGUE

TM	G	W	L	T	R	OR	HR	OHR	G	W	L	T	R	OR	HR	OHR	G	W	L	T	R	OR	HR	OHR	HRF	HRB	HRP	RF	RB	RP	BPF	PPF
BOS	74	44	29	1	420	368	5?	43	80	36	43	1	401	407	47	49	154	80	72	2	821	775	100	92	107	96	89	105	99	94	103	102
CHI	77	47	30	0	397	365	39	62	77	39	38	0	383	365	28	53	154	86	68	0	780	730	67	115	122	61	100	102	94	89	103	102
CLE	78	50	28	0	430	329	4?	22	78	33	43	2	387	439	55	39	156	83	71	2	817	768	103	61	77	109	66	93	103	97	97	97
DET	77	49	28	0	521	448	9?	58	78	40	37	1	414	393	59	44	155	89	65	1	935	841	150	102	140	125	90	119	106	97	109	108
NY	79	57	20	2	520	298	9?4	41	78	45	32	1	459	373	80	51	157	102	52	3	979	671	174	92	103	168	98	99	117	84	102	97
PHI	79	27	50	2	333	419	5?	47	75	27	47	1	366	435	43	58	154	54	97	3	699	854	94	105	92	99	109	89	93	110	94	96
STL	78	25	51	2	385	513	39	74	78	21	57	0	330	510	32	69	156	46	108	2	715	1023	71	143	108	71	131	104	89	121	99	103
WAS	80	43	35	2	376	381	14	30	78	30	45	3	381	460	33	66	158	73	80	5	757	841	47	96	47	61	116	89	98	106	94	96

1938 AMERICAN LEAGUE

TM	G	W	L	T	R	OR	HR	OHR	G	W	L	T	R	OR	HR	OHR	G	W	L	T	R	OR	HR	OHR	HRF	HRB	HRP	RF	RB	RP	BPF	PPF
BOS	75	52	23	0	481	356		67	52	75	36	38	1	421	395	31	50	75	88	61	1	902	751	98	102	140	74	82	103	109	93	102	100
CHI	73	33	39	1	326	364		24	41	76	32	44	0	383	388	43	60	49	65	83	1	709	752	67	101	68	74	108	93	91	96	98	98
CLE	76	46	30	0	425	363		54	35	77	40	36	1	422	419	59	63	86	66	1	847	782	113	100	76	120	104	96	105	97	99	98
DET	79	48	31	0	447	392		83	60	76	36	39	1	415	403	54	55	84	70	1	862	795	137	110	128	109	92	99	103	96	100	99
NY	79	55	22	2	524	342		112	43	78	44	31	3	442	368	62	57	99	53	5	966	710	174	85	141	125	70	106	109	83	105	102
PHI	76	28	47	1	378	48?		55	64	78	25	52	1	348	470	43	54	53	99	2	726	956	92	142	99	95	130	106	87	111	101	104
STL	77	31	43	3	385	48?		52	62	79	24	54	1	370	475	40	56	55	97	4	755	962	92	132	104	84	115	104	90	112	100	103
WAS	78	44	33	1	412	41?	3	33	27	74	31	43	0	402	460	52	62	75	76	1	814	873	85	92	52	106	107	92	105	112	95	96

1939 AMERICAN LEAGUE

TM	G	W	L	T	R	OR	HR	OHR	G	W	L	T	R	OR	HR	OHR	G	W	L	T	R	OR	HR	OHR	HRF	HRB	HRP	RF	RB	RP	BPF	PPF
BOS	75	42	32	1	458			45	57	39	77	47	30	0	432	350	67	52	89	62	1	890	795	124	77	95	125	83	117	104	94	108	107
CHI	77	50	27	0	414			66	38	51	78	35	42	1	341	371	2?5	85	69	1	755	737	64	99	119	57	86	110	88	86	107	106
CLE	77	44	33	0	363			47	30	33	77	43	34	0	434	353	5?4	87	67	0	797	700	85	75	68	95	88	92	101	91	98	96
DET	78	42	35	1	461			434	66	65	77	39	38	0	388	328	65	81	73	1	849	762	124	104	128	110	92	120	95	110		110
NY	77	52	25	0	382			261	84	48	75	54	20	1	585	295	62	106	45	1	967	556	166	85	109	160	90	75	133	84		85
PHI	76	28	48	0	354			523	45	83	77	27	49	1	357	499	66	55	97	1	711	1022	98	148	107	103	145	102	92	126	97	102
STL	78	18	59	1	372			561	47	80	78	25	52	1	361	474	66	43	113	2	733	1035	91	133	34	84	116	108	90	121	100	105
WAS	77	37	39	1	326			337	11	19	76	28	48	0	376	460	63	65	87	1	702	797	44	75				98	109	90	91

1940 AMERICAN LEAGUE

TM	G	W	L	T	R	OR	HR	OHR	G	W	L	T	R	OR	HR	OHR	G	W	L	T	R	OR	HR	OHR	HRF	HRB	HRP	RF	RB	RP	BPF	PPF
BOS	79	45	34	0	46?		421	73	64	75	37	38	0	404	404	54	82	72	0	81?	825	145	124	95	136	119	104	113	108	101	100
CHI	78	41	36	1	35?	7	363	36	65	77	41	36	0	378	309	55	82	72	1	735	672	73	111	116	50	121	102	81	100	90	93	92
CLE	82	51	30	1	35?	0	281	37	27	73	38	35	0	360	356	55	90	64	1	888	7?4	102	147	97	75	121	103	86	111	109
DET	79	50	29	0	5?	2	389	82	64	76	40	35	1	376	328	55	88	66	0	817	671		119	111	132	108	90	90	96	99
NY	76	52	24	0	4?	14	284	83	63	79	36	42	1	403	387	55	88	54	100	0	703	932	1	135	92	102	128	97	97	123	95	99
PHI	71	29	42	0	3?	36	409	44	62	83	25	58	0	367	523	54	67	87	2	757	882		89	85	92	106	106	108
STL	77	37	39	1	4?	19	460	68	68	79	30	48	1	338	422	67	90	0	665	811	52		62	100	94	111	93	95
WAS	77	36	41	0	3?	16	368	19	28	77	28	49	0	349	443	154												

1941 AMERICAN LEAGUE

TM	G	W	L	T	R	OR	HR		G	W	L	T	R	OR	HR		G	W	L	T	R	OR	HR								BPF	PPF
BOS	77	47	30	0	461	371	70	51	78	37	40	1	404	379	155	84	70	2	638	?0	124	88	90	118	87	97	114	101	103	101
CHI	79	38	39		288	297	17	40	77	39	38	0	350	352	156	77	77	1	677	668	47	89	73	57	104	83	92	94	93	94
CLE	77	42	35		340	322	45	35	78	33	44	1	337	346	155	75	79	1	686	743	71	88	116	84	98	91	90	101	100
DET	77	43	34		381	377	51	44	78	32	45	1	305	366	155	75	79	1	830	631	151	135	73	74	12	88	94	106	107
NY	78	51	26	1	396	295	76	44	78	50	27	1	434	336	156	101	53	2	713	840		108	157	141	95	102	103	95
PHI	77	36	41	0	373	432	43	75	77	28	49	0	340	408	154	64	90	3	765	823	91	120	97	100	101
STL	79	40	37	2	407	408	49	63	78	30	47	1	358	415	157	70	84	3	728	798	52	75
WAS	78	40	37	1	367	387	13	19	78	30	47	1	368	411	156	70												91	104	100

1942 AMERICAN LEAGUE

TM	G	W	L	T	R	OR	HR		G	W	L	T	R	OR	HR		G	W	L	T	R	OR									BPF	PPF
BOS	77	53	24		0	403	299	54	33	75	40	35	0	358	295	152	93	59	0	761	594	103	95	105	103	105	113	91	93
CHI	70	35	35		0	256	275	6	31	78	31	47	0	282	334	148	66	82	0	538	609	50	74	69	65	88	96	86	107
CLE	80	39	39		2	266	308	20	24	76	36	40	0	245	285	156	75	79	1	590	559	76	60	61	78	121	123	82	99
DET	77	43	34		0	344	302	50	40	79	30	47	2	407	281	156	73	81	2	589	587	108	71	127	144	101	121	96
NY	77	58	19		0	394	226	62	39	77	45	32	0	300	386	154	103	55	0	801	801	33	89	93	53	128	98	87
PHI	76	25	51		0	249	415	16	42	78	30	48	0	354	287	154	55	99	0	549	637	98	63	124
STL	77	40	37		0	376	350	55	37	74	42	32	0	314	408	151	82	0	730	817	40	50
WAS	77	35	42		0	339	409	13	11	74	27	47	0	314	408	151	62			653

1943 AMERICAN LEAGUE

TM	G	W	L	T	R	OR	HR		G	W	L	T	R	OR	HR		G	W	L	T	R	OR										
BOS	77	39	36		2	293	312	29	25	78	29	48	1	270	295	28	68	84	3	563	607	57	61	87	104	109	90	97	103	104
CHI	76	40	36		0	264	311	20	25	79	42	36	1	309	283	13	72	82	1	573	594	33	54	55	115	82	109	99	96	94
CLE	77	44	33		0	269	247	16	21	76	38	38	0	331	330	39	31	82	71	1	600	577	77	51	120	115	94	90	115	96	94
DET	78	44	33		1	345	284	45	26	77	33	44	1	348	301	40	27	78	76	1	669	542	100	73	97	45	94	101	100	101	100	101
NY	77		54	23	0	321	241	60	36	76	22	54	0	236	330	12	37	155	49	105		497	717	26	74	170	102	122	108	108	98	104	102
PHI	79		27	51	1	261	387	14	36	76	22	54	1	277	314	29	23	153	72	80	1	594	604	78	48	36	106
STL	77		44	33	0	319	290	49	51	76	28	47	1	321	288	38	34	153	84		666	595	47
WAS	76		44	32	0	345	307	9	14	77	40	37	1	321		24	35	154											98	119	110	98	97

1944 AMERICAN LEAGUE

TM	G	W	L	T	R	OR	HR		G	W	L	T	R	OR	HR		G	W	L	T	R	OR										
BOS	77		47	30	1	389	311	48	34	78	30	47	1	350	365	21	32	156	77	77	2	739	676	69	66	145	95					
CHI	77		41	36	0	302	304	11	24	77	30	47	0	241	358	12	44	154	71	83	0	543	662	23	68	65	52	129
CLE	78		39	38	1	345	328	27	16	77	33	44	0	298	349	13	18	155	72	82	1	643	677	40	39	140	82
DET	78		43	34	1	325	318	38	21	78	45	32	1	333	263	22	18	156	88	66	2	658	581	60	39	128	62
NY	78		47	31	0	388	307	58	45	76	36	40	0	286	310	38	37	154	83	71	0	674	617	96	99	62
PHI	76		39	37	0	277	272	45	24	79	33	45	1	248	324	18	18	155	72	82	1	525	594	36	54	112
STL			54	23	0	368	272	45	24	77	35	42	0	306	396	24	35	154	64	90	0	592	664	33	48	40
WAS		1	37	0	286	268	9	13	77	24	54	0																	97	111	92	104	114	95	96

...EAGUE 1 306 299 22 28 79 29 48 2 293 375 28 30 157 71 83 3 599 674 50 58 88 97 111 92 104 114 95 96

TM	HOME								ROAD								ALL															
	G	W	L	T	R	OR	HR	OHR	G	W	L	T	R	OR	HR	OHR	G	W	L	T	R	OR	HR	OHR	HRF	HRB	HRP	RF	RB	RP	BPF	PPF
CHI	74	44	29	1	305	277	8	34	76	27	49	0	291	356	14	29	150	71	78	1	596	633	22	63	100	42	110	93	107	112	95	96
CLE	77	44	33	0	292	273	27	15	70	29	39	2	265	275	38	24	147	73	72	2	557	548	65	39	65	150	96	96	99	97	99	98
DET	76	50	26	0	333	285	43	28	79	38	39	2	300	280	34	20	155	88	65	2	633	565	77	48	132	121	80	110	99	89	106	105
NY	76	48	28	0	395	297	65	51	76	33	43	0	281	309	28	15	152	81	71	0	676	606	93	66	223	111	76	115	106	97	107	106
PHI	77	39	35	3	265	270	16	21	76	13	63	0	229	368	17	34	153	52	98	3	494	638	33	55	73	72	110	88	89	110	94	96
STL	76	47	27	2	353	291	32	33	78	34	43	1	244	257	31	26	154	81	70	3	597	548	63	59	115	110	104	127	86	81	115	114
WAS	78	46	31	1	278	255	1	6	78	41	36	1	344	307	26	36	156	87	67	2	622	562	27	42	13	59	136	84	110	101	93	92

1946 AMERICAN LEAGUE

TM	HOME								ROAD								ALL															
	G	W	L	T	R	OR	HR	OHR	G	W	L	T	R	OR	HR	OHR	G	W	L	T	R	OR	HR	OHR	HRF	HRB	HRP	RF	RB	RP	BPF	PPF
BOS	78	61	16	1	469	315	65	44	78	43	34	1	323	279	44	45	156	104	50	2	792	594	109	89	121	121	104	128	109	86	114	111
CHI	79	40	38	1	272	290	17	46	76	34	42	0	290	305	20	34	155	74	80	1	562	595	37	80	110	43	86	92	92	97	97	97
CLE	77	36	41	0	231	264	25	36	79	32	45	2	306	374	54	48	156	68	86	2	537	638	79	84	64	114	127	77	96	111	88	90
DET	79	48	30	1	391	300	75	68	76	44	32	0	313	267	33	29	155	92	62	1	704	567	108	97	194	90	82	114	103	86	108	105
NY	77	47	30	0	342	262	68	34	77	40	37	0	342	285	68	32	154	87	67	0	684	547	136	66	102	163	88	97	109	90	100	98
PHI	78	31	46	1	297	351	21	38	77	18	59	0	232	329	19	45	155	49	105	1	529	680	40	83	90	51	99	110	80	101	104	107
STL	77	35	41	1	313	344	46	29	79	31	47	1	308	366	38	44	156	66	88	2	621	710	84	73	94	105	91	99	100	113	98	100
WAS	76	38	38	0	253	343	16	25	79	38	40	1	355	363	44	56	155	76	78	1	608	706	60	81	46	97	130	88	104	120	92	94

1947 AMERICAN LEAGUE

TM	HOME								ROAD								ALL															
	G	W	L	T	R	OR	HR	OHR	G	W	L	T	R	OR	HR	OHR	G	W	L	T	R	OR	HR	OHR	HRF	HRB	HRP	RF	RB	RP	BPF	PPF
BOS	81	49	30	2	421	355	61	39	76	34	41	1	299	314	42	45	157	83	71	3	720	669	103	84	107	115	98	116	102	97	108	107
CHI	75	32	43	0	244	322	20	31	80	38	41	1	309	339	33	45	155	70	84	1	553	661	53	76	72	70	98	94	89	104	97	99
CLE	78	38	39	1	314	279	52	51	79	42	35	2	373	309	60	43	157	80	74	3	687	588	112	94	101	133	114	90	110	96	96	94
DET	80	46	31	3	370	345	62	47	78	39	38	1	344	297	41	32	158	85	69	4	714	642	103	79	138	99	78	108	105	95	104	103
NY	77	55	22	0	392	242	54	49	78	42	35	1	402	326	61	46	155	97	57	1	794	568	115	95	99	140	119	91	128	95	97	92
PHI	78	39	38	1	296	324	33	41	78	39	38	1	337	290	28	44	156	78	76	2	633	614	61	85	102	70	95	99	98	95	100	100
STL	77	29	48	0	286	401	52	57	77	30	47	0	278	343	38	46	154	59	95	0	564	744	90	103	124	98	111	108	87	110	102	105
WAS	77	36	41	0	244	326	10	20	77	28	49	0	252	349	32	43	154	64	90	0	496	675	42	63	43	63	98	95	80	105	97	101

1948 AMERICAN LEAGUE

TM	HOME								ROAD								ALL															
	G	W	L	T	R	OR	HR	OHR	G	W	L	T	R	OR	HR	OHR	G	W	L	T	R	OR	HR	OHR	HRF	HRB	HRP	RF	RB	RP	BPF	PPF
BOS	78	55	23	0	481	336	60	43	77	41	36	0	426	384	61	40	155	96	59	0	907	720	121	83	102	134	97	101	124	101	100	97
CHI	76	27	48	1	278	378	21	36	78	24	53	1	281	436	34	53	154	51	101	2	559	814	55	89	69	73	112	93	81	112	95	100
CLE	79	48	30	1	398	272	77	41	77	49	28	0	442	296	78	41	156	97	58	1	840	568	155	82	98	175	102	91	116	82	99	94
DET	77	39	38	0	327	355	39	61	77	39	38	0	373	371	39	31	154	78	76	0	700	726	78	92	136	77	85	93	100	103	96	97
NY	77	50	27	0	413	315	70	54	77	44	33	0	444	318	69	40	154	94	60	0	857	633	139	94	113	151	107	97	118	90	100	96
PHI	77	36	41	0	347	396	33	47	77	48	29	0	382	339	35	39	154	84	70	0	729	735	68	86	107	74	90	103	99	99	101	102
STL	76	34	42	0	363	451	29	64	79	25	52	2	308	398	34	39	155	59	94	2	671	849	63	103	126	65	97	116	87	106	106	109
WAS	78	29	48	1	312	419	11	24	76	27	49	0	266	377	20	57	154	56	97	1	578	796	31	81	47	48	109	108	77	102	103	107

1949 AMERICAN LEAGUE

TM	HOME								ROAD								ALL															
	G	W	L	T	R	OR	HR	OHR	G	W	L	T	R	OR	HR	OHR	G	W	L	T	R	OR	HR	OHR	HRF	HRB	HRP	RF	RB	RP	BPF	PPF
BOS	77	61	16	0	514	310	71	43	78	35	42	1	382	357	60	39	155	96	58	1	896	667	131	82	116	124	82	113	115	90	107	103
CHI	77	32	45	0	327	353	15	52	77	31	46	0	321	384	28	56	154	63	91	0	648	737	43	108	81	49	115	96	92	103	98	99
CLE	77	49	28	0	319	263	61	42	77	40	37	0	356	311	51	40	154	89	65	0	675	574	112	82	112	108	82	89	96	83	98	96
DET	78	50	27	1	402	350	57	60	77	37	40	0	349	305	31	42	155	87	67	1	751	655	88	102	148	72	85	112	96	85	108	106
NY	78	54	23	1	419	304	72	53	77	43	34	0	410	333	43	45	155	97	57	1	829	637	115	98	135	100	89	98	114	91	100	97
PHI	77	52	25	0	389	326	42	42	77	29	48	0	337	399	40	63	154	81	73	0	726	725	82	105	84	95	116	98	102	102	99	99
STL	77	36	41	0	394	426	69	56	78	17	60	1	273	487	48	57	155	53	101	1	667	913	117	113	116	115	113	106	92	122	100	104
WAS	77	26	51	0	254	426	20	14	77	24	53	0	330	442	61	65	154	50	104	0	584	868	81	79	29	133	117	88	88	126	91	96

1950 AMERICAN LEAGUE

TM	HOME								ROAD								ALL															
	G	W	L	T	R	OR	HR	OHR	G	W	L	T	R	OR	HR	OHR	G	W	L	T	R	OR	HR	OHR	HRF	HRB	HRP	RF	RB	RP	BPF	PPF
BOS	77	55	22	0	625	427	100	67	77	39	38	0	402	377	61	54	154	94	60	0	1027	804	161	121	139	111	88	131	114	94	114	111
CHI	79	35	42	2	316	352	52	55	77	25	52	0	309	397	41	52	156	60	94	2	625	749	93	107	109	71	81	92	82	96	97	99
CLE	77	49	28	0	386	297	102	57	78	43	34	1	420	357	62	63	155	92	62	1	806	654	164	120	126	118	93	91	105	87	98	95
DET	81	50	30	1	405	346	60	72	76	45	29	2	432	367	54	69	157	95	59	3	837	713	114	141	102	93	113	91	110	95	97	95
NY	77	53	24	0	440	333	78	51	78	45	32	1	474	358	81	67	155	98	56	1	914	691	159	118	91	138	106	96	118	92	99	96
PHI	77	29	48	0	314	406	45	67	77	23	54	0	356	507	55	71	154	52	102	0	670	913	100	138	89	89	119	84	97	126	90	93
STL	74	27	47	0	368	484	52	69	80	31	49	0	316	432	54	60	154	58	96	0	684	916	106	129	111	84	99	118	83	107	107	111
WAS	78	35	42	1	347	407	18	28	77	32	45	0	343	406	58	71	155	67	87	1	690	813	76	99	38	84	112	99	89	103	99	101

1951 AMERICAN LEAGUE

TM	HOME								ROAD								ALL															
	G	W	L	T	R	OR	HR	OHR	G	W	L	T	R	OR	HR	OHR	G	W	L	T	R	OR	HR	OHR	HRF	HRB	HRP	RF	RB	RP	BPF	PPF
BOS	75	50	25	0	460	348	80	65	79	37	42	0	344	377	47	35	154	87	67	0	804	725	127	100	169	90	72	116	104	96	108	106
CHI	78	39	38	1	334	310	28	47	77	42	35	0	380	334	58	62	155	81	73	1	714	644	86	109	65	97	124	90	103	94	97	95
CLE	77	53	24	0	324	249	76	42	78	40	37	1	372	345	64	44	155	93	61	1	696	594	140	86	110	123	81	84	103	89	94	93
DET	77	36	41	0	358	402	58	60	77	37	40	0	327	339	46	42	154	73	81	0	685	741	104	102	128	87	85	112	91	97	106	107
NY	78	56	22	0	366	258	72	43	76	42	34	0	432	363	68	49	154	98	56	0	798	621	140	92	98	134	93	80	123	98	91	88
PHI	79	38	41	0	406	407	54	59	75	32	43	0	330	338	48	50	154	70	84	0	736	745	102	109	108	94	100	113	97	98	106	106
STL	77	24	53	0	327	486	41	66	77	28	49	0	284	396	45	65	154	52	102	0	611	882	86	131	96	86	125	115	82	113	105	109
WAS	76	32	44	0	319	362	13	35	78	30	48	0	353	402	41	70	154	62	92	0	672	764	54	110	45	67	134	93	99	110	95	97

1952 AMERICAN LEAGUE

TM	HOME								ROAD								ALL															
	G	W	L	T	R	OR	HR	OHR	G	W	L	T	R	OR	HR	OHR	G	W	L	T	R	OR	HR	OHR	HRF	HRB	HRP	RF	RB	RP	BPF	PPF
BOS	77	50	27	0	406	309	68	49	77	26	51	0	262	349	45	58	154	76	78	0	668	658	113	107	112	109	106	115	96	97	107	107
CHI	79	44	33	2	305	276	42	39	77	37	40	0	305	292	38	47	156	81	73	2	610	568	80	86	94	81	86	96	94	88	100	99
CLE	77	49	28	0	333	260	72	43	78	44	33	1	430	346	76	51	155	93	61	1	763	606	148	94	94	155	105	81	130	106	91	88
DET	77	32	45	0	284	366	55	59	79	18	59	2	273	372	38	52	156	50	104	2	557	738	103	111	132	89	97	101	86	110	99	103
NY	77	49	28	0	345	264	64	48	77	46	31	0	382	293	65	46	154	95	59	0	727	557	129	94	102	130	99	92	115	91	98	95
PHI	78	45	32	1	382	403	55	60	77	34	43	0	282	320	34	53	155	79	75	1	664	723	89	113	126	80	100	124	92	100	111	112
STL	78	42	35	1	321	346	47	52	77	22	55	0	283	387	35	59	155	64	90	1	604	733	82	111	103	83	108	98	96	114	97	100
WAS	78	42	35	1	299	292	13	18	79	36	41	2	299	316	37	60	157	78	76	3	598	608	50	78	35	71	101	98	91	92	100	100

1953 AMERICAN LEAGUE

TM	HOME								ROAD								ALL															
	G	W	L	T	R	OR	HR	OHR	G	W	L	T	R	OR	HR	OHR	G	W	L	T	R	OR	HR	OHR	HRF	HRB	HRP	RF	RB	RP	BPF	PPF
BOS	76	38	38	1	335	354	57	59	77	46	31	0	321	278	44	33	153	84	69	0	656	632	101	92	144	75	67	115	89	85	109	108
CHI	78	41	36	1	349	328	30	56	78	48	29	1	367	264	44	57	156	89	65	2	716	592	74	113	87	70	104	107	97	82	106	103
CLE	78	53	24	1	379	272	90	46	77	39	38	0	391	355	70	46	155	92	62	1	770	627	160	92	115	133	83	88	117	97	95	93
DET	79	30	47	2	369	462	55	97	79	30	47	0	326	461	53	57	158	60	94	4	695	923	108	154	131	89	112	104	101	129	98	102
NY	77	50	27	0	347	255	64	39	74	49	25	0	454	292	75	55	151	99	52	0	801	547	139	94	80	143	101	81	128	93	93	88
PHI	78	27	50	1	299	447	49	74	79	32	45	2	333	352	67	47	157	59	95	3	632	799	116	121	107	102	105	108	89	108	102	105
STL	77	23	54	0	281	447	58	64	77	31	46	0	274	331	54	37	154	54	100	0	555	778	112	101	127	90	80	116	76	102	107	111
WAS	75	39	36	0	305	283	10	31	77	37	40	0	382	331	59	81	152	76	76	0	687	614	69	112	33	84	152	86	107	97	94	93

1954 AMERICAN LEAGUE

TM	HOME								ROAD								ALL															
	G	W	L	T	R	OR	HR	OHR	G	W	L	T	R	OR	HR	OHR	G	W	L	T	R	OR	HR	OHR	HRF	HRB	HRP	RF	RB	RP	BPF	PPF
BAL	77	32	45	0	235	313	19	23	77	22	55	0	248	355	33	33	154	54	100	0	483	668	52	78	50	66	91	91	79	105	95	99
BOS	79	38	39	2	357	384	69	70	77	31	46	0	343	344	54	48	156	69	85	2	700	728	123	118	127	107	102	104	107	111	100	10*
CHI	78	45	32	1	327	294	39	51	77	49	28	0	384	227	55	43	155	94	60	1	711	521	94	94	93	93	94	101	106	80	103	1*

Team Home-Road Statistics

TM	HOME								ROAD								ALL														
	G	W	L	T	R	OR	HR	OHR	G	W	L	T	R	OR	HR	OHR	G	W	L	T	R	OR	HR	OHR	HRF	HRB	HRP	RF	RB	RP	BPF	PPF
CLE	77	59	18	0	376	252	78	57	79	52	25	2	370	252	78	32	156	111	43	2	746	504	156	89	125	134	80	105	108	76	106	101
DET	77	35	42	0	285	336	44	80	78	33	44	1	299	328	46	58	155	68	86	1	584	664	90	138	117	85	122	100	90	101	100	101
NY	78	54	23	1	388	274	68	42	77	49	28	0	417	289	65	44	155	103	51	1	805	563	133	86	101	126	86	95	125	92	99	94
PHI	77	29	47	1	260	467	44	85	79	22	56	1	282	408	50	56	156	51	103	2	542	875	94	141	119	88	122	105	84	128	98	105
WAS	78	37	41	0	320	335	27	27	77	29	47	1	312	345	54	52	155	66	88	1	632	680	81	79	53	98	97	98	99	106	98	99
1955 AMERICAN LEAGUE																																
BAL	79	30	47	2	249	335	15	42	77	27	50	0	291	419	39	61	156	57	97	2	540	754	54	103	58	52	100	81	87	116	90	93
BOS	78	47	31	0	470	395	84	79	76	37	39	0	285	257	53	49	154	84	70	0	755	652	137	128	146	93	88	146	88	78	124	122
CHI	77	49	28	0	357	262	54	47	78	42	35	1	368	295	62	64	155	91	63	1	725	557	116	111	84	104	99	96	104	83	101	98
CLE	77	49	28	0	343	318	84	58	77	44	33	0	355	283	64	53	154	93	61	0	698	601	148	111	119	111	87	104	98	86	104	102
DET	77	46	31	0	386	301	81	59	77	33	44	0	389	357	49	67	154	79	75	0	775	658	130	126	118	99	99	93	117	101	97	95
KC	76	33	43	0	333	477	70	110	79	30	48	1	305	434	51	65	155	63	91	1	638	911	121	175	149	86	116	111	92	125	101	106
NY	77	52	25	0	378	248	89	44	77	44	33	0	384	321	86	64	154	96	58	0	762	569	175	108	91	153	100	91	114	88	98	94
WAS	77	28	49	0	282	357	20	25	77	25	52	0	316	432	60	74	154	53	101	0	598	789	80	99	36	94	114	86	96	122	91	94
1956 AMERICAN LEAGUE																																
BAL	77	41	36	0	275	315	35	39	77	28	49	0	296	390	56	60	154	69	85	0	571	705	91	99	66	78	84	87	85	102	94	96
BOS	78	43	34	1	408	388	68	64	77	41	36	0	372	363	71	66	155	84	70	1	780	751	139	130	96	105	99	106	105	102	103	102
CHI	77	46	31	0	403	320	69	47	78	39	38	1	373	314	59	71	154	85	69	0	776	634	128	118	91	99	91	105	104	87	104	102
CLE	77	46	31	0	340	287	71	61	78	42	35	1	372	294	82	55	155	88	66	1	712	581	153	116	99	112	88	97	97	81	101	99
DET	78	37	40	1	359	357	75	77	77	45	32	0	430	342	75	63	155	82	72	1	789	699	150	140	108	108	101	93	113	102	97	95
KC	77	22	55	0	305	449	62	113	77	30	47	0	314	382	50	74	154	52	102	0	619	831	112	187	132	76	117	106	86	111	101	105
NY	77	49	28	0	412	303	88	48	77	48	29	0	445	328	102	66	154	97	57	0	857	631	190	114	84	152	98	95	121	93	99	95
WAS	77	32	45	0	354	481	63	95	78	27	50	1	298	443	49	76	155	59	95	1	652	924	112	171	122	77	112	111	89	120	102	107
1957 AMERICAN LEAGUE																																
BAL	77	42	33	2	283	248	36	30	77	34	43	0	314	340	51	65	154	76	76	2	597	588	87	95	60	83	85	83	99	97	93	93
BOS	77	44	33	0	408	360	72	67	77	38	39	0	313	308	81	49	154	82	72	0	721	668	153	116	106	115	90	120	100	94	110	109
CHI	77	45	32	0	347	263	40	59	78	45	32	1	360	303	66	65	155	90	64	1	707	566	106	124	80	90	105	95	109	89	99	97
CLE	77	40	37	0	348	384	71	74	76	36	40	0	334	338	69	56	153	76	77	0	682	722	140	130	112	104	97	106	104	109	102	102
DET	77	45	32	0	351	304	71	86	77	33	44	0	263	310	45	61	154	78	76	0	614	614	116	147	140	76	95	112	87	88	107	107
KC	77	37	40	0	294	344	91	77	77	22	54	1	269	366	75	76	154	59	94	1	563	710	166	153	109	128	120	99	88	107	99	102
NY	77	48	29	0	316	241	60	51	77	50	27	0	407	293	85	59	154	98	56	0	723	534	145	110	80	123	98	83	118	91	94	90
WAS	77	28	49	0	304	415	60	79	77	27	50	0	299	393	51	70	154	55	99	0	603	808	111	149	111	84	108	102	95	122	98	102
1958 AMERICAN LEAGUE																																
BAL	78	46	31	1	248	256	46	36	76	28	48	0	273	319	62	70	154	74	79	1	521	575	108	106	64	99	94	85	87	94	94	95
BOS	77	49	28	0	384	350	73	65	78	30	47	1	313	341	82	56	155	79	75	1	697	691	155	121	101	115	93	112	103	102	105	105
CHI	77	47	30	0	318	282	47	68	78	35	42	1	316	333	54	84	155	82	72	1	634	615	101	152	86	83	119	95	100	97	98	98
CLE	76	42	34	0	324	293	72	59	77	35	42	0	370	342	89	64	153	77	76	0	694	635	161	123	88	130	104	89	115	107	94	93
DET	77	43	34	0	348	306	59	79	77	34	43	0	311	300	50	54	154	77	77	0	659	606	109	133	127	73	86	106	99	92	104	103
KC	78	43	34	1	365	363	88	96	78	30	47	1	277	350	50	54	156	73	81	2	642	713	138	150	161	80	86	114	93	103	105	107
NY	78	44	33	1	362	318	78	62	77	48	29	0	397	259	86	54	155	92	62	1	759	577	164	116	100	122	91	103	114	90	103	99
WAS	78	33	44	1	269	373	49	80	78	28	49	1	284	374	72	76	156	61	93	2	553	747	121	156	88	98	124	97	88	115	97	100
1959 AMERICAN LEAGUE																																
BAL	78	38	39	1	260	299	53	50	77	36	41	0	291	322	56	61	155	74	80	1	551	621	109	111	88	82	83	91	84	94	97	98
BOS	77	43	34	0	404	356	62	66	77	32	45	0	322	340	63	69	154	75	79	0	726	696	125	135	97	93	100	113	102	99	106	105
CHI	78	47	30	1	313	272	44	61	78	47	30	1	356	316	53	68	156	94	60	2	669	588	97	129	89	73	95	89	102	91	97	95
CLE	77	43	34	0	346	316	84	74	77	46	31	0	399	330	83	74	154	89	65	0	745	646	167	148	101	124	112	93	115	102	97	95
DET	77	41	36	0	401	411	95	105	77	35	42	0	312	321	65	72	154	76	78	0	713	732	160	177	138	102	112	124	96	98	111	111
KC	77	37	40	0	362	386	58	80	77	29	48	0	319	374	59	68	154	66	88	0	681	760	117	148	107	84	103	106	100	110	101	103
NY	77	40	37	0	293	305	63	45	78	39	38	1	394	342	90	75	155	79	75	1	687	647	153	120	69	131	104	84	109	104	93	92
WAS	77	34	43	0	307	360	83	68	77	29	48	0	312	341	80	55	154	63	91	0	619	701	163	123	109	114	88	101	92	103	100	102
1960 AMERICAN LEAGUE																																
BAL	77	44	33	0	332	313	50	52	77	45	32	0	350	293	73	65	154	89	65	0	682	606	123	117	77	100	96	101	99	89	102	101
BOS	77	36	41	0	347	413	65	69	77	29	48	0	311	362	59	58	154	65	89	0	658	775	124	127	112	86	87	110	94	109	103	105
CHI	77	51	26	0	379	298	57	54	77	36	41	0	362	319	55	73	154	87	67	0	741	617	112	127	89	87	96	100	108	92	101	99
CLE	77	39	38	0	315	351	62	84	77	37	40	0	352	342	65	77	154	76	78	0	667	693	127	161	102	95	117	96	101	104	98	98
DET	77	40	37	0	322	323	78	85	77	31	46	0	311	321	72	56	154	71	83	0	633	644	150	141	123	101	94	101	92	94	102	102
KC	78	34	43	1	327	369	58	79	77	24	53	0	288	387	52	81	155	58	96	1	615	756	110	160	100	82	114	100	92	110	99	101
NY	77	55	22	0	350	273	92	52	78	42	35	1	396	354	101	71	155	97	57	1	746	627	193	123	88	150	102	87	116	100	94	92
WAS	77	32	45	0	336	366	75	74	77	41	36	0	336	330	72	56	154	73	81	0	672	696	147	130	114	101	90	104	98	101	102	102
1961 AMERICAN LEAGUE																																
BAL	82	48	33	1	320	283	61	46	81	47	34	0	371	305	88	63	163	95	67	1	691	588	149	109	73	108	81	90	96	83	97	96
BOS	82	50	31	1	401	386	63	91	81	26	55	0	328	406	49	76	163	76	86	1	729	792	112	167	119	67	96	105	97	105	102	103
CHI	81	53	28	0	411	320	80	55	82	33	48	1	354	406	58	103	163	86	76	1	765	726	138	158	86	99	107	98	105	100	99	99
CLE	81	40	41	0	342	380	74	98	80	38	42	0	395	372	76	80	161	78	83	0	737	752	150	178	108	97	112	93	105	107	96	97
DET	82	50	31	1	389	324	90	95	81	51	30	0	452	347	90	75	163	101	61	1	841	671	180	170	111	112	106	90	119	97	96	94
KC	80	33	47	0	365	434	33	61	82	28	53	0	318	429	57	80	162	61	100	0	683	863	90	141	72	66	102	107	91	113	102	104
LA	82	46	36	1	447	421	122	126	80	24	55	1	297	363	67	54	162	70	91	1	744	784	189	180	181	90	83	124	90	96	111	112
MIN	81	36	44	1	380	423	92	89	80	34	46	0	327	355	75	74	161	70	90	1	707	778	167	163	117	102	100	114	91	99	106	107
NY	81	65	16	0	411	251	112	59	82	44	37	1	416	361	128	78	163	109	53	1	827	612	240	137	87	166	101	89	117	88	96	93
WAS	79	33	46	0	288	366	34	53	82	28	54	0	330	410	85	78	161	61	100	0	618	776	119	131	57	93	109	91	89	109	95	97
1962 AMERICAN LEAGUE																																
BAL	82	44	38	0	328	299	66	65	80	33	47	0	324	381	90	82	162	77	85	0	652	680	156	147	76	113	108	88	96	99	95	95
BOS	79	39	40	0	369	377	72	76	81	37	44	0	338	379	74	83	160	76	84	0	707	756	146	159	97	97	105	106	97	104	102	103
CHI	81	43	38	0	315	319	36	58	81	42	39	0	392	339	56	65	162	85	77	0	707	658	92	123	80	63	84	88	103	97	95	94
CLE	81	43	38	0	348	350	103	89	81	37	44	0	334	395	77	85	162	80	82	0	682	745	180	174	116	108	106	96	97	105	98	99
DET	82	49	33	0	448	368	117	91	79	36	43	0	310	324	92	78	161	85	76	0	758	692	209	169	116	126	105	121	95	88	111	110
KC	81	39	42	0	387	423	64	118	81	33	48	0	358	414	52	81	162	72	90	0	745	837	116	199	131	66	107	104	103	115	100	101
LA	81	40	41	0	357	368	50	50	81	46	35	0	361	338	87	68	162	86	76	0	718	706	137	118	67	101	90	104	98	96	102	102
MIN	82	45	36	1	417	378	97	97	81	46	35	0	381	335	88	69	163	91	71	1	798	713	185	166	120	109	98	109	105	95	105	104
NY	80	50	30	0	369	306	92	67	82	46	36	0	448	374	107	79	162	96	66	0	817	680	199	146	90	135	102	86	121	103	94	92
WAS	80	27	53	0	293	364	65	79	82	33	48	1	306	352	67	72	162	60	101	1	599	716	132	151	104	83	94	101	83	97	101	102
…ERICAN LEAGUE																																
		48	33	0	311	268	72	56	81	38	43	0	333	353	74	81	162	86	76	0	644	621	146	137	84	106	99	86	104	100	94	93

	HOME								ROAD								ALL															
TM	G	W	L	T	R	OR	HR	OHR	G	W	L	T	R	OR	HR	OHR	G	W	L	T	R	OR	HR	OHR	HRF	HRB	HRP	RF	RB	RP	BPF	PPF
BOS	80	44	36	0	383	346	95	73	81	32	49	0	283	358	76	79	161	76	85	0	666	704	171	152	108	111	100	113	95	101	106	106
CHI	82	49	33	0	362	272	63	46	80	45	35	0	321	272	51	54	162	94	68	0	683	544	114	100	102	73	65	105	99	81	104	102
CLE	81	41	40	0	308	341	88	87	81	38	43	0	327	361	81	89	162	79	83	0	635	702	169	176	103	114	118	95	99	109	97	98
DET	81	47	34	0	395	339	94	109	81	32	49	0	305	364	54	86	162	79	83	0	700	703	148	195	139	84	111	109	102	103	104	104
KC	81	36	45	0	326	390	52	87	81	37	44	0	289	314	43	69	162	73	89	0	615	704	95	156	121	58	91	116	87	98	107	108
LA	81	39	42	0	264	306	24	44	80	31	49	0	333	354	71	76	161	70	91	0	597	660	95	120	48	80	108	83	99	109	91	92
MIN	81	48	33	0	377	306	112	99	80	43	37	0	390	296	113	63	161	91	70	0	767	602	225	162	117	143	105	99	116	94	100	98
NY	80	58	22	0	367	246	88	55	81	46	35	0	347	301	100	60	161	104	57	0	714	547	188	115	93	128	83	98	108	85	101	98
WAS	80	31	49	0	286	406	63	82	82	25	57	0	292	406	75	94	162	56	106	0	578	812	138	176	88	100	125	100	89	121	98	101

1964 AMERICAN LEAGUE

	HOME								ROAD								ALL															
TM	G	W	L	T	R	OR	HR	OHR	G	W	L	T	R	OR	HR	OHR	G	W	L	T	R	OR	HR	OHR	HRF	HRB	HRP	RF	RB	RP	BPF	PPF
BAL	82	49	32	1	351	296	79	64	81	48	33	0	328	271	83	65	163	97	65	1	679	567	162	129	97	104	85	107	98	83	105	103
BOS	81	45	36	0	393	382	100	87	81	27	54	0	295	411	86	91	162	72	90	0	688	793	186	178	104	120	116	108	102	117	102	103
CHI	81	52	29	0	306	213	43	42	81	46	35	0	336	288	63	82	162	98	64	0	642	501	106	124	62	84	93	86	103	81	95	93
CLE	82	41	40	1	365	351	84	82	82	38	43	1	324	342	80	72	164	79	83	2	689	693	164	154	108	101	95	107	101	101	103	103
DET	82	46	35	1	340	320	85	89	81	39	42	0	359	358	72	75	163	85	77	1	699	678	157	164	115	94	98	92	111	108	96	95
KC	81	26	55	0	330	455	107	132	82	31	50	1	291	381	59	88	163	57	105	1	621	836	166	220	153	86	114	115	90	117	105	108
LA	81	45	36	0	230	226	32	31	81	37	44	0	314	325	70	69	162	82	80	0	544	551	102	100	48	85	83	74	93	94	89	89
MIN	82	40	41	1	386	336	115	88	81	39	42	0	351	342	106	93	163	79	83	1	737	678	221	181	101	145	122	102	110	103	101	100
NY	81	50	31	0	363	290	69	56	83	49	32	2	367	287	93	73	164	99	63	2	730	577	162	129	80	113	92	103	106	86	103	101
WAS	81	31	50	0	294	380	71	95	81	31	50	0	284	353	54	77	162	62	100	0	578	733	125	172	122	73	98	104	87	108	101	103

1965 AMERICAN LEAGUE

	HOME								ROAD								ALL															
TM	G	W	L	T	R	OR	HR	OHR	G	W	L	T	R	OR	HR	OHR	G	W	L	T	R	OR	HR	OHR	HRF	HRB	HRP	RF	RB	RP	BPF	PPF
BAL	79	46	33	0	302	282	62	71	83	48	35	0	339	296	63	49	162	94	68	0	641	578	125	120	123	82	77	98	100	91	100	99
BOS	81	34	47	0	375	433	94	88	81	28	53	0	294	358	71	70	162	62	100	0	669	791	165	158	124	109	105	120	97	113	107	109
CAL	80	46	34	0	265	254	36	35	82	29	53	0	262	315	56	56	162	75	87	0	527	569	92	91	67	77	76	93	85	90	98	98
CHI	81	48	33	0	288	241	45	51	81	47	34	0	359	314	80	71	162	95	67	0	647	555	125	122	67	107	107	81	110	96	92	90
CLE	82	52	30	0	342	287	90	58	80	35	45	0	321	326	66	71	162	87	75	0	663	613	156	129	105	110	94	96	106	98	98	97
DET	81	47	34	0	362	310	96	85	81	42	39	0	318	292	66	52	162	89	73	0	680	602	162	137	146	96	82	110	101	91	105	104
KC	81	33	48	0	301	365	47	68	81	26	55	0	284	390	63	93	162	59	103	0	585	755	110	161	75	94	132	98	95	119	97	100
MIN	81	51	30	0	379	308	67	89	81	51	30	0	395	292	83	77	162	102	60	0	774	600	150	166	99	113	123	101	120	95	101	98
NY	83	40	43	0	320	306	77	63	79	37	42	0	291	298	72	63	162	77	85	0	611	604	149	126	99	109	93	101	95	94	101	101
WAS	81	36	45	0	302	366	62	86	81	34	47	0	289	355	74	74	162	70	92	0	591	721	136	160	99	101	117	103	92	111	100	102

1966 AMERICAN LEAGUE

	HOME								ROAD								ALL															
TM	G	W	L	T	R	OR	HR	OHR	G	W	L	T	R	OR	HR	OHR	G	W	L	T	R	OR	HR	OHR	HRF	HRB	HRP	RF	RB	RP	BPF	PPF
BAL	79	48	31	0	375	296	85	65	81	49	32	0	380	305	90	62	160	97	63	0	755	601	175	127	102	127	96	101	120	98	101	98
BOS	81	40	41	0	374	397	80	97	81	32	49	0	281	334	65	67	162	72	90	0	655	731	145	164	129	94	104	122	95	105	109	110
CAL	81	42	39	0	303	315	54	67	81	38	43	0	301	328	68	69	162	80	82	0	604	643	122	136	89	94	104	98	97	102	99	100
CHI	81	45	36	0	273	217	31	36	82	38	43	1	301	300	56	65	163	83	79	1	574	517	87	101	59	76	87	84	96	87	94	93
CLE	81	41	40	0	283	300	82	65	81	40	41	0	291	286	73	64	162	81	81	0	574	586	155	129	107	109	92	101	90	91	101	102
DET	81	42	39	0	360	374	97	101	81	46	35	0	359	324	82	84	162	88	74	0	719	698	179	185	118	125	128	107	112	108	102	102
KC	81	42	39	0	284	292	18	27	79	32	47	0	280	356	52	79	160	74	86	0	564	648	70	106	36	74	107	89	97	109	94	95
MIN	81	49	32	0	375	311	94	83	81	40	41	0	288	270	50	56	162	89	73	0	663	581	144	139	157	80	80	121	94	84	111	110
NY	82	35	46	1	302	280	74	63	78	35	43	0	309	332	88	61	160	70	89	1	611	612	162	124	88	126	100	87	105	105	94	94
WAS	78	42	36	0	273	292	62	84	81	29	52	0	284	367	64	70	159	71	88	0	557	659	126	154	111	90	108	91	95	110	95	96

1967 AMERICAN LEAGUE

	HOME								ROAD								ALL															
TM	G	W	L	T	R	OR	HR	OHR	G	W	L	T	R	OR	HR	OHR	G	W	L	T	R	OR	HR	OHR	HRF	HRB	HRP	RF	RB	RP	BPF	PPF
BAL	77	35	42	0	283	275	64	49	84	41	43	0	371	317	74	67	161	76	85	0	654	592	138	116	88	123	105	89	116	106	95	94
BOS	81	49	32	0	408	355	90	88	81	43	38	0	314	259	68	54	162	92	70	0	722	614	158	142	140	113	101	130	105	91	115	113
CAL	83	53	30	0	288	276	56	59	78	31	47	0	279	311	58	59	161	84	77	0	567	587	114	118	93	99	102	91	100	103	96	96
CHI	82	49	33	0	243	222	38	38	80	40	40	0	288	269	51	49	162	89	73	0	531	491	89	87	76	81	80	83	95	88	94	93
CLE	81	36	45	0	274	316	76	69	81	39	42	0	285	297	55	51	162	75	87	0	559	613	131	120	131	94	87	101	93	101	100	101
DET	82	52	29	1	360	272	83	79	81	39	42	0	323	315	69	72	163	91	71	1	683	587	152	151	113	122	122	99	114	99	99	98
KC	81	37	44	0	288	320	19	38	80	25	55	0	245	340	50	87	161	62	99	0	533	660	69	125	43	80	140	101	90	109	100	102
MIN	81	52	29	0	372	292	70	63	83	39	42	2	299	298	61	52	164	91	71	2	671	590	131	115	119	98	87	113	103	93	107	106
NY	82	43	38	1	268	271	60	47	81	29	52	0	254	350	40	63	163	72	90	1	522	621	100	110	102	81	89	89	92	107	94	96
WAS	80	40	40	0	277	332	57	54	81	36	45	0	273	305	58	59	161	76	85	0	550	637	115	113	96	98	96	106	90	103	102	104

1968 AMERICAN LEAGUE

	HOME								ROAD								ALL															
TM	G	W	L	T	R	OR	HR	OHR	G	W	L	T	R	OR	HR	OHR	G	W	L	T	R	OR	HR	OHR	HRF	HRB	HRP	RF	RB	RP	BPF	PPF
BAL	80	47	33	0	288	248	57	54	82	44	38	0	291	249	76	47	162	91	71	0	579	497	133	101	94	123	97	102	103	89	102	101
BOS	81	46	35	0	325	299	58	61	81	40	41	0	289	312	67	54	162	86	76	0	614	611	125	115	99	115	107	104	111	110	101	101
CAL	81	32	49	0	229	299	49	66	81	35	46	0	269	316	34	65	162	67	95	0	498	615	83	131	113	71	109	90	96	116	94	96
CHI	81	36	45	0	225	273	29	47	81	31	50	0	238	254	42	50	162	67	95	0	463	527	71	97	83	69	93	100	83	94	101	102
CLE	81	43	37	1	246	262	36	56	81	43	38	0	270	242	39	42	162	86	75	1	516	504	75	98	112	64	80	100	93	91	101	101
DET	81	56	25	0	348	254	107	75	83	47	34	2	323	238	78	54	164	103	59	2	671	492	185	129	138	143	104	110	113	85	106	103
MIN	81	41	40	0	299	290	50	51	81	38	43	0	263	256	55	41	162	79	83	0	562	546	105	92	105	92	81	112	96	94	106	106
NY	82	39	42	1	268	268	56	50	82	44	37	1	268	263	53	49	164	83	79	2	536	531	109	99	104	95	87	101	95	94	101	101
OAK	83	44	38	1	296	258	38	58	80	38	42	0	273	286	56	66	163	82	80	1	569	544	94	124	78	96	125	96	104	100	98	98
WAS	81	34	47	0	257	300	53	53	80	31	49	0	267	365	71	65	161	65	96	0	524	665	124	118	78	129	124	87	105	129	91	94

1969 AMERICAN LEAGUE

	HOME								ROAD								ALL															
TM	G	W	L	T	R	OR	HR	OHR	G	W	L	T	R	OR	HR	OHR	G	W	L	T	R	OR	HR	OHR	HRF	HRB	HRP	RF	RB	RP	BPF	PPF
BAL	81	60	21	0	402	251	82	51	81	49	32	0	377	266	93	66	162	109	53	0	779	517	175	117	86	135	93	103	113	78	104	100
BOS	81	46	35	0	392	391	105	78	81	41	40	0	351	345	92	77	162	87	75	0	743	736	197	155	108	140	113	112	107	106	105	105
CAL	81	43	38	0	277	305	49	65	82	28	53	1	251	347	39	61	163	71	91	1	528	652	88	126	113	59	83	98	80	97	99	101
CHI	81	41	40	0	352	387	61	80	81	27	54	0	273	336	51	66	162	68	94	0	625	723	112	146	118	75	96	118	87	100	108	110
CLE	81	33	48	0	276	341	56	60	80	29	51	0	297	376	63	74	161	62	99	0	573	717	119	134	84	95	106	90	92	113	94	96
DET	81	46	35	0	361	305	104	72	81	44	37	0	340	296	78	56	162	90	72	0	701	601	182	128	129	115	84	105	102	89	103	102
KC	82	36	45	1	301	362	39	63	81	33	48	0	285	326	59	73	163	69	93	1	586	688	98	136	77	79	109	106	86	99	103	104
MIN	81	57	24	0	414	298	79	61	81	40	41	0	376	320	84	58	162	97	65	0	790	618	163	119	100	118	88	103	117	93	102	100
NY	80	48	32	0	284	245	44	51	82	32	49	1	278	342	50	67	162	80	81	1	562	587	94	118	84	73	90	88	89	92	95	96
OAK	81	49	32	0	330	315	73	70	81	39	42	0	410	363	75	93	162	88	74	0	740	678	148	163	87	118	128	85	121	112	92	91
SEA	82	34	47	1	329	399	74	93	81	30	51	0	310	400	51	79	163	64	98	1	639	799	125	172	123	82	111	100	97	120	98	100
WAS	81	47	34	0	353	290	77	62	81	39	42	0	341	354	71	73	162	86	76	0	694	644	148	135	97	109	100	93	108	101	97	96

1970 AMERICAN LEAGUE

	HOME								ROAD								ALL															
TM	G	W	L	T	R	OR	HR	OHR	G	W	L	T	R	OR	HR	OHR	G	W	L	T	R	OR	HR	OHR	HRF	HRB	HRP	RF	RB	RP	BPF	PPF
BAL	81	59	22	0	386	256	88	58	81	49	32	0	406	318	91	81	162	108	54	0	792	574	179	139	87	132	104	91	121	90	97	94
BOS	81	52	29	0	455	382	117	75	81	35	46	0	331	340	86	81	162	87	75	0	786	722	203	156	114	131	105	123	105	98	111	110
CAL	81	43	38	0	287	274	41	59	81	43	38	0	344	356	73	95	162	86	76	0	631	630	114	154	62	97	129	82	102	102	91	91
CHI	84	31	53	0	346	469	78	97	78	25	53	0	287	353	45	94	162	56	106	0	633	822	123	164	138	70	94	115	89	112	106	108
CLE	81	43	38	0	386	370	133	103	81	33	48	0	263	305	50	60	162	76	86	0	649	675	183	165	195	82	80	129	83	87	115	115
DET	81	42	39	0	348	379	86	86	81	37	44	0	318	352	62	67	162	79	83	0	666	731	148	153	130	89	92	108	96	104	103	104
KC	79	35	44	0	305	331	46	48	83	30	53	0	306	374	51	90	162	65	97	0	611	705	97	138	71	79	105	97	92	105	98	100

	HOME								ROAD								ALL														
TM	G	W	L	T	R	OR	HR	OHR	G	W	L	T	R	OR	HR	OHR	G	W	L	T	R	OR	HR	OHR	HRF	HRB	HRP	RF	RB	RP	BPF	PPF
MIL	81	38	42	1	313	362	68	72	82	27	55	0	300	389	58	74	163	65	97	1	613	751	126	146	106	84	96	98	92	111	98	100
MIN	81	51	30	0	366	285	66	53	81	47	34	0	378	320	87	77	162	98	64	0	744	605	153	130	75	119	102	95	112	93	98	97
NY	81	53	28	0	317	257	60	40	82	40	41	1	363	355	51	90	163	93	69	1	680	612	111	130	74	89	96	83	109	98	92	91
OAK	81	49	32	0	337	265	83	56	81	40	41	0	341	328	88	78	162	89	73	0	678	593	171	134	85	127	101	91	104	92	97	96
WAS	81	40	41	0	303	330	72	61	81	30	51	0	323	359	66	78	162	70	92	0	626	689	138	139	92	99	99	93	96	105	96	97

1971 AMERICAN LEAGUE

TM	G	W	L	T	R	OR	HR	OHR	G	W	L	T	R	OR	HR	OHR	G	W	L	T	R	OR	HR	OHR	HRF	HRB	HRP	RF	RB	RP	BPF	PPF
BAL	77	53	24	0	374	254	78	67	81	48	33	0	368	276	80	58	158	101	57	0	742	530	158	125	111	124	100	104	118	87	103	100
BOS	80	47	33	0	375	338	88	75	82	38	44	0	316	329	73	61	162	85	77	0	691	667	161	136	122	118	101	112	104	101	106	105
CAL	81	35	46	0	233	297	39	55	81	41	40	0	278	279	57	46	162	76	86	0	511	576	96	101	92	78	83	95	83	93	98	99
CHI	81	39	42	0	278	310	60	53	81	40	41	0	339	287	78	47	162	79	83	0	617	597	138	100	91	114	85	94	101	98	98	97
CLE	81	29	52	0	297	400	62	99	81	31	50	0	246	347	47	55	162	60	102	0	543	747	109	154	149	73	97	114	82	110	106	108
DET	81	54	27	0	352	289	90	70	81	37	44	0	349	356	89	56	162	91	71	0	701	645	179	126	110	138	100	92	117	108	96	95
KC	81	44	37	0	296	277	23	36	80	41	39	0	307	289	57	48	161	85	76	0	603	566	80	84	58	76	86	96	98	93	99	98
MIL	82	34	48	0	282	319	46	64	79	35	44	0	252	290	58	66	161	69	92	0	534	609	104	130	86	91	112	105	83	94	103	104
MIN	79	37	42	0	332	356	57	71	81	37	44	0	322	314	59	68	160	74	86	0	654	670	116	139	103	94	111	110	102	104	104	104
NY	81	44	37	0	327	297	39	61	81	38	43	0	321	344	58	65	162	82	80	0	648	641	97	126	83	85	109	94	107	106	97	97
OAK	81	46	35	0	325	300	84	74	80	55	25	0	366	264	76	57	161	101	60	0	691	564	160	131	117	120	100	99	110	92	100	99
WAS	81	35	46	0	268	296	34	59	78	28	50	0	269	364	52	73	159	63	96	0	537	660	86	132	73	82	123	86	95	114	92	94

1972 AMERICAN LEAGUE

TM	G	W	L	T	R	OR	HR	OHR	G	W	L	T	R	OR	HR	OHR	G	W	L	T	R	OR	HR	OHR	HRF	HRB	HRP	RF	RB	RP	BPF	PPF
BAL	77	38	39	0	240	211	44	40	77	42	35	0	279	219	56	45	154	80	74	0	519	430	100	85	85	110	95	91	100	84	98	96
BOS	78	52	26	0	373	303	71	49	77	33	44	0	267	317	53	52	155	85	70	0	640	620	124	101	112	119	100	113	112	111	105	105
CAL	80	44	36	0	221	218	30	31	75	31	44	0	233	315	48	59	155	75	80	0	454	533	78	90	55	104	115	77	97	110	88	90
CHI	78	55	23	0	341	252	65	44	76	32	44	0	225	286	43	50	154	87	67	0	566	538	108	94	114	103	92	113	99	96	106	106
CLE	77	43	34	0	263	261	59	79	79	29	50	0	209	258	32	44	156	72	84	0	472	519	91	123	173	68	91	113	81	89	107	108
DET	78	44	34	0	312	288	68	67	78	42	36	0	246	226	54	34	156	86	70	0	558	514	122	101	148	102	82	125	91	85	113	112
KC	77	44	33	0	309	257	29	28	77	32	45	0	271	288	49	57	154	76	78	0	580	545	78	85	56	102	108	101	108	102	100	100
MIL	79	37	42	0	243	286	36	45	77	28	49	0	250	309	52	71	156	65	91	0	493	595	88	116	66	111	141	92	96	114	95	97
MIN	74	42	32	0	299	255	52	54	80	35	45	0	238	280	41	51	154	77	77	0	537	535	93	105	122	87	97	114	94	94	107	107
NY	77	46	31	0	270	219	53	37	78	33	45	0	287	308	50	50	155	79	76	0	557	527	103	87	92	109	92	85	113	106	92	92
OAK	77	48	29	0	287	210	68	52	78	45	33	0	317	247	66	44	155	93	62	0	604	457	134	96	111	130	96	91	116	90	97	94
TEX	77	31	46	0	235	288	33	41	77	23	54	0	226	340	23	51	154	54	100	0	461	628	56	92	98	58	91	92	92	121	94	97

1973 AMERICAN LEAGUE

TM	G	W	L	T	R	OR	HR	OHR	G	W	L	T	R	OR	HR	OHR	G	W	L	T	R	OR	HR	OHR	HRF	HRB	HRP	RF	RB	RP	BPF	PPF
BAL	81	50	31	0	408	284	63	60	81	47	34	0	346	277	56	64	162	97	65	0	754	561	119	124	103	90	94	111	101	77	107	105
BOS	81	48	33	0	390	339	83	83	81	41	40	0	348	308	64	75	162	89	73	0	738	647	147	158	118	106	114	111	101	89	106	105
CAL	81	43	38	0	316	294	41	49	81	36	45	0	313	363	55	52	162	79	83	0	629	657	93	104	85	76	85	91	95	98	96	96
CHI	81	40	41	0	329	368	56	58	81	37	44	0	323	337	55	52	162	77	85	0	652	705	111	110	106	82	81	105	92	99	102	103
CLE	81	34	47	0	320	427	92	100	81	37	44	0	360	399	66	72	162	71	91	0	680	826	158	172	134	107	116	98	101	121	97	99
DET	81	47	34	0	329	332	86	71	81	38	43	0	313	342	71	83	162	85	77	0	642	674	157	154	102	122	120	101	92	96	101	101
KC	81	48	33	0	422	404	54	61	81	40	41	0	333	348	60	53	162	88	74	0	755	752	114	114	102	86	86	120	100	100	109	109
MIL	81	40	41	0	349	343	73	52	81	34	47	0	359	388	72	67	162	74	88	0	708	731	145	119	90	117	97	93	107	110	96	96
MIN	81	37	44	0	357	386	56	60	81	44	37	0	381	306	64	55	162	81	81	0	738	692	120	115	98	93	89	107	103	97	104	103
NY	81	50	31	0	359	263	74	42	81	30	51	0	282	347	57	58	162	80	82	0	641	610	131	109	94	103	86	99	92	88	101	100
OAK	81	50	31	0	313	253	70	70	81	44	37	0	445	362	77	73	162	94	68	0	758	615	147	143	95	118	115	73	125	104	87	85
TEX	81	35	46	0	321	408	47	51	81	22	59	0	298	436	63	79	162	57	105	0	619	844	110	130	70	101	116	98	92	122	97	100

1974 AMERICAN LEAGUE

TM	G	W	L	T	R	OR	HR	OHR	G	W	L	T	R	OR	HR	OHR	G	W	L	T	R	OR	HR	OHR	HRF	HRB	HRP	RF	RB	RP	BPF	PPF
BAL	81	46	35	0	281	293	48	46	81	45	36	0	378	319	68	55	162	91	71	0	659	612	116	101	78	112	100	84	107	100	93	92
BOS	81	46	35	0	375	348	58	66	81	38	43	0	321	313	51	60	162	84	78	0	696	661	109	126	111	91	105	113	98	94	107	106
CAL	81	36	45	0	291	287	46	47	82	32	49	1	327	370	49	54	163	68	94	1	618	657	95	101	91	86	90	84	100	106	92	93
CHI	82	46	34	2	360	365	66	43	81	34	46	1	324	356	69	60	163	80	80	3	684	721	135	103	85	127	98	105	101	106	102	102
CLE	81	40	41	0	338	349	72	92	81	37	44	0	324	345	59	46	162	77	85	0	662	694	131	138	149	96	96	102	99	103	101	101
DET	81	36	45	0	335	412	74	84	81	36	45	0	285	356	51	46	162	72	90	0	620	768	131	148	127	104	116	114	88	107	106	108
KC	81	40	41	0	355	353	38	42	81	37	44	0	312	309	51	49	162	77	85	0	667	662	89	91	81	84	86	112	95	94	106	106
MIL	81	40	41	0	342	329	58	69	81	36	45	0	305	331	62	57	162	76	86	0	647	660	120	126	106	104	108	105	95	97	102	103
MIN	82	48	33	1	365	317	60	56	81	34	47	0	308	352	51	59	163	82	80	1	673	669	111	115	104	95	98	102	100	99	101	101
NY	81	47	34	0	315	295	42	50	81	42	39	0	356	328	59	54	162	89	73	0	671	623	101	104	83	95	99	90	106	99	96	95
OAK	81	49	32	0	345	265	69	43	81	41	40	0	344	286	63	47	162	90	72	0	689	551	132	90	102	112	79	98	103	84	100	99
TEX	80	42	38	0	321	340	43	57	81	42	38	1	369	358	56	69	161	84	76	1	690	698	99	126	83	96	121	93	109	110	96	96

1975 AMERICAN LEAGUE

TM	G	W	L	T	R	OR	HR	OHR	G	W	L	T	R	OR	HR	OHR	G	W	L	T	R	OR	HR	OHR	HRF	HRB	HRP	RF	RB	RP	BPF	PPF
BAL	77	44	33	0	282	231	46	45	82	46	36	0	400	322	78	65	159	90	69	0	682	553	124	110	70	118	107	78	109	90	91	89
BOS	81	47	34	0	427	399	74	83	79	48	31	0	369	310	60	62	160	95	65	0	796	709	134	145	124	100	107	118	107	95	109	108
CAL	81	35	46	0	294	349	24	52	80	37	43	0	334	374	31	51	161	72	89	0	628	723	55	123	75	51	108	90	96	109	95	96
CHI	81	42	39	0	350	359	42	54	80	33	47	0	305	344	52	53	161	75	86	0	655	703	94	107	91	79	90	107	91	98	103	104
CLE	80	41	39	0	331	367	79	85	79	38	41	0	357	336	74	51	159	79	80	0	688	703	153	136	126	114	100	99	101	103	99	100
DET	80	31	49	0	301	421	63	83	79	26	53	0	269	365	62	54	159	57	102	0	570	786	125	137	120	96	102	110	80	108	104	106
KC	81	51	30	0	377	309	46	45	81	40	41	0	333	340	72	63	162	91	71	0	710	649	118	108	70	111	103	102	100	92	102	101
MIL	81	36	45	0	348	398	72	63	81	32	49	0	327	394	74	70	162	68	94	0	675	792	146	133	93	124	114	102	97	112	100	101
MIN	82	39	43	0	401	410	75	88	77	37	40	0	323	326	46	49	159	76	83	0	724	736	121	137	153	79	88	115	99	100	107	107
NY	78	43	35	0	323	276	50	56	82	40	42	0	358	312	60	48	160	83	77	0	681	588	110	104	103	88	83	95	100	88	99	98
OAK	81	54	27	0	366	247	75	43	81	44	37	0	392	359	76	59	162	98	64	0	758	606	151	102	89	128	89	84	118	95	93	91
TEX	80	39	41	0	349	366	52	70	82	40	42	0	365	367	82	53	162	79	83	0	714	733	134	123	93	112	105	100	103	106	99	100

1976 AMERICAN LEAGUE

TM	G	W	L	T	R	OR	HR	OHR	G	W	L	T	R	OR	HR	OHR	G	W	L	T	R	OR	HR	OHR	HRF	HRB	HRP	RF	RB	RP	BPF	PPF
BAL	81	42	39	0	280	306	58	38	81	46	35	0	339	292	61	42	162	88	74	0	619	598	119	80	94	129	90	94	97	95	98	97
BOS	81	46	35	0	408	352	71	61	81	37	44	0	308	308	63	49	162	83	79	0	716	660	134	109	117	134	110	121	99	93	110	110
CAL	81	38	43	0	249	284	24	35	81	38	43	0	301	347	39	60	162	76	86	0	550	631	63	95	61	83	121	83	92	104	92	93
CHI	80	35	45	0	300	369	31	34	81	29	52	0	286	376	42	53	161	64	97	0	586	745	73	87	70	92	106	101	92	114	99	101
CLE	79	44	35	0	311	295	40	43	80	37	43	0	304	320	45	37	159	81	78	0	615	615	85	80	102	90	85	99	97	96	100	100
DET	80	36	44	0	305	381	51	62	81	38	43	0	304	328	50	46	161	74	87	0	609	709	101	101	125	96	96	109	91	105	103	105
KC	81	49	32	0	368	287	37	35	81	41	40	0	345	324	28	48	162	90	72	0	713	611	65	83	96	70	87	99	110	96	100	98
MIL	81	36	45	0	292	321	45	43	80	30	50	0	278	334	43	56	161	66	95	0	570	655	88	99	88	101	112	98	89	101	99	100
MIN	81	44	37	0	368	348	34	52	81	41	40	0	375	356	47	37	162	85	77	0	743	704	81	89	102	85	92	98	116	111	98	98
NY	80	45	35	0	349	294	67	51	79	52	27	0	381	281	53	46	159	97	62	0	730	575	120	97	117	120	100	97	115	93	99	97
OAK	81	51	30	0	353	284	56	57	80	36	44	0	333	314	57	39	161	87	74	0	686	598	113	96	115	114	96	98	107	94	100	98
TEX	81	39	42	0	319	330	40	57	81	37	44	0	297	322	40	49	162	76	86	0	616	652	80	106	108	83	107	104	93	98	102	103

1977 AMERICAN LEAGUE

TM	G	W	L	T	R	OR	HR	OHR	G	W	L	T	R	OR	HR	OHR	G	W	L	T	R	OR	HR	OHR	HRF	HRB	HRP	RF	RB	RP	BPF	PPF
BAL	81	54	27	0	356	269	74	62	80	43	37	0	363	384	74	62	161	97	64	0	719	653	148	124	100	102	87	85	107	96	93	92

TM	HOME								ROAD								ALL															
	G	W	L	T	R	OR	HR	OHR	G	W	L	T	R	OR	HR	OHR	G	W	L	T	R	OR	HR	OHR	HRF	HRB	HRP	RF	RB	RP	BPF	PPF
BOS	80	51	29	0	495	407	124	95	81	46	35	0	364	305	89	63	161	97	64	0	859	712	213	158	143	124	93	134	100	84	117	116
CAL	81	39	42	0	320	321	69	65	81	35	46	0	355	374	62	71	162	74	88	0	675	695	131	136	100	90	94	88	97	100	95	95
CHI	81	48	33	0	434	370	85	58	81	42	39	0	410	401	107	78	162	90	72	0	844	771	192	136	79	149	108	100	116	106	99	99
CLE	81	37	44	0	339	357	54	66	80	34	46	0	337	382	46	70	161	71	90	0	676	739	100	136	101	69	92	95	95	103	98	98
DET	81	39	42	0	369	401	81	100	81	35	46	0	345	350	85	62	162	74	88	0	714	751	166	162	121	107	102	109	93	97	105	105
KC	81	55	26	0	408	320	56	50	81	47	34	0	414	331	90	60	162	102	60	0	822	651	146	110	73	113	89	99	112	90	100	99
MIL	81	37	44	0	305	365	49	54	81	30	51	0	334	400	76	82	162	67	95	0	639	765	125	136	66	104	112	91	91	108	95	96
MIN	80	48	32	0	469	376	61	79	81	36	45	0	398	400	62	72	161	84	77	0	867	776	123	151	106	84	101	107	115	105	103	102
NY	81	55	26	0	412	305	84	63	81	45	36	0	419	346	100	76	162	100	62	0	831	651	184	139	86	137	106	95	115	92	98	97
OAK	81	35	46	0	302	347	58	69	80	28	52	0	303	402	59	76	161	63	98	0	605	749	117	145	92	85	104	90	87	106	95	97
SEA	81	29	52	0	303	419	75	103	81	35	46	0	321	436	58	91	162	64	98	0	624	855	133	194	117	87	124	95	88	118	96	98
TEX	81	44	37	0	369	368	62	78	81	50	31	0	398	289	73	56	162	94	68	0	767	657	135	134	109	90	88	108	100	86	105	104
TOR	80	25	55	0	297	444	45	94	81	29	52	0	308	378	55	58	161	54	107	0	605	822	100	152	120	65	93	107	81	108	103	105

1978 AMERICAN LEAGUE

TM	HOME								ROAD								ALL															
	G	W	L	T	R	OR	HR	OHR	G	W	L	T	R	OR	HR	OHR	G	W	L	T	R	OR	HR	OHR	HRF	HRB	HRP	RF	RB	RP	BPF	PPF
BAL	81	51	30	0	316	258	74	42	80	39	41	0	343	375	80	65	161	90	71	0	659	633	154	107	81	143	100	81	108	103	91	90
BOS	82	59	23	0	445	334	94	72	81	40	41	0	351	323	78	65	163	99	64	0	796	657	172	137	115	134	109	114	108	91	107	106
CAL	81	50	31	0	371	316	56	58	81	37	44	0	320	350	52	67	162	87	75	0	691	666	108	125	96	92	105	103	100	97	102	101
CHI	80	38	42	0	342	349	56	58	81	33	48	0	292	382	50	70	161	71	90	0	634	731	106	128	96	91	108	103	93	106	101	102
CLE	78	42	36	0	319	287	50	37	81	27	54	0	320	407	56	63	159	69	90	0	639	694	106	100	77	101	93	87	103	110	93	94
DET	81	47	34	0	395	338	74	78	81	39	42	0	319	315	55	57	162	86	76	0	714	653	129	135	133	93	97	115	97	90	108	107
KC	81	56	25	0	434	264	43	44	81	36	45	0	309	370	55	64	162	92	70	0	743	634	98	108	75	93	100	103	107	92	102	101
MIL	81	54	27	0	446	318	94	50	81	39	42	0	358	332	79	59	162	93	69	0	804	650	173	109	105	140	92	111	111	92	106	104
MIN	81	38	43	0	322	308	44	39	81	35	46	0	344	370	38	63	162	73	89	0	666	678	82	102	83	75	89	89	104	105	94	94
NY	81	55	26	0	358	275	68	59	82	45	37	0	377	307	57	52	163	100	63	0	735	582	125	111	118	94	84	95	109	87	99	97
OAK	80	38	42	0	281	330	52	51	82	31	51	0	251	360	48	55	162	69	93	0	532	690	100	106	102	82	86	102	78	99	101	102
SEA	81	32	49	0	343	423	58	93	79	24	55	0	271	411	39	62	160	56	104	0	614	834	97	155	139	69	107	107	89	119	102	104
TEX	82	52	30	0	348	289	62	49	80	35	45	0	344	343	70	59	162	87	75	0	692	632	132	108	85	118	98	91	106	97	96	96
TOR	81	37	44	0	334	366	50	75	80	22	58	0	256	409	48	74	161	59	102	0	590	775	98	149	100	84	123	102	87	112	100	102

1979 AMERICAN LEAGUE

TM	HOME								ROAD								ALL															
	G	W	L	T	R	OR	HR	OHR	G	W	L	T	R	OR	HR	OHR	G	W	L	T	R	OR	HR	OHR	HRF	HRB	HRP	RF	RB	RP	BPF	PPF
BAL	79	55	24	0	369	259	74	57	80	47	33	0	388	323	107	76	159	102	57	0	757	582	181	133	75	145	110	91	105	82	97	96
BOS	80	51	29	0	470	357	121	59	80	40	40	0	371	354	73	74	160	91	69	0	841	711	194	133	121	121	88	114	105	90	107	106
CAL	81	49	32	0	408	339	71	55	81	39	42	0	458	429	93	76	162	88	74	0	866	768	164	131	76	128	104	86	124	111	93	92
CHI	79	33	46	0	349	401	56	60	81	40	41	0	381	347	71	54	160	73	87	0	730	748	127	114	95	90	82	105	96	98	102	103
CLE	81	47	34	0	428	409	87	72	80	34	46	0	332	396	51	66	161	81	80	0	760	805	138	138	131	82	84	112	95	101	106	106
DET	80	46	34	0	394	323	101	74	81	39	42	0	376	415	63	93	161	85	76	0	770	738	164	167	113	108	112	93	107	102	96	96
KC	81	46	35	0	462	421	53	81	81	39	42	0	389	395	63	84	162	85	77	0	851	816	116	165	92	85	118	112	107	103	105	105
MIL	81	52	29	0	401	362	91	81	80	43	37	0	406	360	94	81	161	95	66	0	807	722	185	162	98	132	117	99	107	97	100	99
MIN	81	39	42	0	415	390	67	61	81	43	38	0	349	335	45	67	162	82	80	0	764	725	112	128	113	72	83	116	93	89	109	108
NY	81	51	30	0	360	308	77	59	79	38	41	0	374	364	73	64	160	89	71	0	734	672	150	123	98	106	88	90	103	95	96	95
OAK	81	31	50	0	262	371	46	65	81	23	58	0	311	489	62	82	162	54	108	0	573	860	108	147	77	85	113	79	86	125	89	91
SEA	81	36	45	0	371	404	88	94	81	31	50	0	340	416	44	71	162	67	95	0	711	820	132	165	151	72	92	101	94	107	100	101
TEX	81	44	37	0	382	335	69	63	81	39	42	0	368	363	71	72	162	83	79	0	750	698	140	135	93	100	97	98	99	93	100	99
TOR	81	32	49	0	345	432	50	74	81	21	60	0	268	430	45	91	162	53	109	0	613	862	95	165	90	70	117	108	78	108	103	106

1980 AMERICAN LEAGUE

TM	HOME								ROAD								ALL															
	G	W	L	T	R	OR	HR	OHR	G	W	L	T	R	OR	HR	OHR	G	W	L	T	R	OR	HR	OHR	HRF	HRB	HRP	RF	RB	RP	BPF	PPF
BAL	81	50	31	0	397	319	75	81	81	50	31	0	408	321	81	53	162	100	62	0	805	640	156	134	116	110	94	100	110	89	101	99
BOS	81	36	45	0	370	420	79	74	79	47	32	0	387	347	83	55	160	83	77	0	757	767	162	129	108	120	97	105	103	104	102	102
CAL	81	30	51	0	330	403	49	76	79	35	44	0	368	394	57	65	160	65	95	0	698	797	106	141	99	82	107	93	101	114	96	97
CHI	81	37	42	2	281	350	41	37	81	33	48	0	306	372	50	71	162	70	90	2	587	722	91	108	66	84	94	93	83	101	97	98
CLE	79	44	35	0	400	389	55	66	81	35	46	0	338	418	34	71	160	79	81	0	738	807	89	137	117	63	96	100	100	109	102	103
DET	82	43	38	1	440	404	77	95	81	41	40	0	390	353	66	57	163	84	78	1	830	757	143	152	135	94	97	111	107	98	105	105
KC	81	49	32	0	397	335	47	51	81	48	33	0	412	359	68	78	162	97	65	0	809	694	115	129	69	103	114	96	113	98	98	97
MIL	82	40	42	0	368	336	90	65	80	46	34	0	443	346	113	72	162	86	76	0	811	682	203	137	83	169	119	88	117	101	94	93
MIN	80	44	36	0	392	361	51	63	81	33	48	0	278	363	48	57	161	77	84	0	670	724	99	120	109	72	86	117	84	92	109	109
NY	81	53	28	0	409	315	91	47	81	50	31	0	411	347	98	55	162	103	59	0	820	662	189	102	92	147	83	97	113	93	99	98
OAK	81	46	35	0	337	277	58	57	81	37	44	0	349	365	79	85	162	83	79	0	686	642	137	142	72	122	125	87	100	93	94	94
SEA	81	36	45	0	340	389	74	99	82	23	58	1	270	404	30	60	163	59	103	1	610	793	104	159	180	54	86	107	80	103	103	105
TEX	80	39	41	0	380	365	58	57	83	37	44	2	376	387	66	62	163	76	85	2	756	752	124	119	93	96	92	101	103	102	100	100
TOR	81	35	46	0	311	386	56	75	81	32	49	0	313	376	70	60	162	67	95	0	624	762	126	135	100	96	102	100	86	103	100	101

1981 AMERICAN LEAGUE

TM	HOME								ROAD								ALL															
	G	W	L	T	R	OR	HR	OHR	G	W	L	T	R	OR	HR	OHR	G	W	L	T	R	OR	HR	OHR	HRF	HRB	HRP	RF	RB	RP	BPF	PPF
BAL	55	33	22	0	231	217	49	47	50	26	24	0	198	220	39	36	105	59	46	0	429	437	88	83	116	110	104	98	101	103	99	99
BOS	53	30	23	0	278	247	52	47	55	29	26	0	241	234	38	43	108	59	49	0	519	481	90	90	125	106	107	114	111	104	106	106
CAL	54	26	28	0	244	233	48	39	56	25	31	0	232	220	49	42	110	51	59	0	476	453	97	81	99	126	107	108	102	98	104	104
CHI	49	25	24	0	215	198	31	33	57	29	28	0	261	225	45	40	106	54	52	0	476	423	76	73	88	106	103	99	110	99	100	99
CLE	54	25	29	0	210	216	19	33	49	27	22	0	221	226	20	34	103	52	51	0	431	442	39	67	88	56	94	87	111	113	93	93
DET	55	32	23	0	241	196	43	44	54	28	26	0	186	208	22	39	109	60	49	0	427	404	65	83	137	69	91	109	91	87	105	105
KC	47	19	28	0	163	197	17	27	56	31	25	0	234	208	44	48	103	50	53	0	397	405	61	75	59	99	128	97	95	98	99	99
MIL	49	28	21	0	203	203	33	29	60	34	26	0	290	256	63	43	109	62	47	0	493	459	96	72	74	138	110	92	115	108	96	95
MIN	61	24	36	1	213	292	25	47	49	17	32	0	165	194	22	32	110	41	68	1	378	486	47	79	105	59	95	110	80	101	105	106
NY	51	32	19	0	203	154	47	24	56	27	29	0	218	189	53	40	107	59	48	0	421	343	100	64	85	142	92	97	96	79	100	99
OAK	56	35	21	0	234	183	57	46	53	29	24	0	224	220	47	34	109	64	45	0	458	403	104	80	120	123	96	90	108	96	96	95
SEA	57	20	37	0	226	271	52	53	53	24	28	1	200	250	37	23	110	44	65	1	426	521	89	76	154	91	74	102	95	115	100	101
TEX	56	32	24	0	232	168	21	24	49	25	24	0	220	221	28	43	105	57	48	0	452	389	49	67	58	86	111	81	117	101	91	90
TOR	53	17	36	0	172	272	34	41	53	20	33	0	157	194	27	31	106	37	69	0	329	466	61	72	125	72	84	122	69	95	111	113

1982 AMERICAN LEAGUE

TM	HOME								ROAD								ALL															
	G	W	L	T	R	OR	HR	OHR	G	W	L	T	R	OR	HR	OHR	G	W	L	T	R	OR	HR	OHR	HRF	HRB	HRP	RF	RB	RP	BPF	PPF
BAL	82	53	28	1	397	330	87	87	81	41	40	0	377	357	92	60	163	94	68	1	774	687	179	147	113	113	93	99	106	95	100	99
BOS	81	49	32	0	434	370	67	82	81	40	41	0	319	343	69	73	162	89	73	0	753	713	136	155	105	90	101	120	94	90	110	110
CAL	81	52	29	0	414	322	99	69	81	41	40	0	400	348	87	55	162	93	69	0	814	670	186	124	118	114	78	99	112	94	100	99
CHI	80	49	31	0	383	332	51	43	82	38	44	0	403	378	85	56	162	87	75	0	786	710	136	99	70	103	78	95	111	101	97	97
CLE	81	41	40	0	342	377	44	64	81	36	45	0	341	371	60	58	162	78	84	0	683	748	109	122	96	74	82	101	94	102	100	101
DET	81	47	34	0	378	328	108	100	81	36	45	0	351	357	69	72	162	83	79	0	729	685	177	172	143	99	97	100	100	95	100	100
KC	81	56	25	0	431	318	61	64	81	34	47	0	353	399	71	99	162	90	72	0	784	717	132	163	75	103	123	100	108	99	100	99
MIL	82	48	34	0	431	319	89	64	81	47	33	1	460	398	127	88	163	95	67	1	891	717	216	152	72	169	123	84	130	106	94	92
MIN	81	37	44	0	351	401	81	110	81	23	58	0	306	418	67	98	162	60	102	0	657	819	148	208	113	96	132	102	90	111	100	102
NY	81	42	39	0	346	338	73	55	81	37	44	0	363	378	88	58	162	79	83	0	709	716	161	113	88	113	81	93	101	102	96	96
OAK	81	36	45	0	328	398	71	83	81	32	49	0	363	421	78	94	162	68	94	0	691	819	149	177	89	108	126	92	100	117	95	96
SEA	81	42	39	0	356	388	78	104	81	34	47	0	295	324	52	69	162	76	86	0	651	712	130	173	145	72	94	118	82	89	109	110
TEX	81	38	43	0	286	333	43	66	81	26	55	0	304	416	72	62	162	64	98	0	590	749	115	128	82	83	94	86	88	109	93	94

TM	G	W	L	T	R	OR	HR	OHR	G	W	L	T	R	OR	HR	OHR	G	W	L	T	R	OR	HR	OHR	HRF	HRB	HRP	RF	RB	RP	BPF	PPF
			HOME									ROAD												ALL								
TOR	81	44	37	0	353	379	62	70	81	34	47	0	298	322	44	77	162	78	84	0	651	701	106	147	108	68	93	116	83	89	109	109

1983 AMERICAN LEAGUE

TM	G	W	L	T	R	OR	HR	OHR	G	W	L	T	R	OR	HR	OHR	G	W	L	T	R	OR	HR	OHR	HRF	HRB	HRP	RF	RB	RP	BPF	PPF
BAL	81	50	31	0	389	328	79	66	81	48	33	0	410	324	89	64	162	98	64	0	799	652	168	130	96	126	99	99	110	91	100	99
BOS	81	38	43	0	373	390	65	76	81	40	41	0	351	385	77	82	162	78	84	0	724	775	142	158	89	112	124	103	99	105	101	102
CAL	81	35	46	0	368	354	86	67	81	35	46	0	354	425	68	63	162	70	92	0	722	779	154	130	115	105	90	93	104	111	96	96
CHI	81	55	26	0	432	306	84	64	81	44	37	0	368	344	73	64	162	99	63	0	800	650	157	128	109	110	92	105	107	88	103	102
CLE	81	36	45	0	367	424	48	71	81	34	47	0	337	361	38	49	162	70	92	0	704	785	86	120	132	54	74	111	92	102	105	106
DET	81	48	33	0	377	314	83	87	81	44	37	0	412	365	73	83	162	92	70	0	789	679	156	170	109	112	121	90	114	99	96	94
KC	82	45	36	1	381	369	50	66	81	34	47	0	315	398	59	67	163	79	83	1	696	767	109	133	91	83	100	103	94	103	101	102
MIL	81	52	29	0	356	305	64	57	81	35	46	0	408	403	68	76	162	87	75	0	764	708	132	133	85	105	105	83	115	107	92	91
MIN	81	37	44	0	389	427	56	91	81	33	48	0	320	395	85	72	162	70	92	0	709	822	141	163	93	109	125	112	93	107	105	106
NY	81	51	30	0	398	323	67	55	81	40	41	0	372	380	86	61	162	91	71	0	770	703	153	116	85	120	94	97	108	99	99	98
OAK	81	42	39	0	348	367	60	54	81	32	49	0	360	415	61	81	162	74	88	0	708	782	121	135	81	99	108	92	102	112	96	96
SEA	81	30	51	0	281	369	64	80	81	30	51	0	277	371	47	65	162	60	102	0	558	740	111	145	124	73	94	99	77	101	99	101
TEX	81	44	37	0	326	294	45	33	82	33	48	1	313	315	61	64	163	77	85	1	639	609	106	97	65	93	82	100	86	83	101	101
TOR	81	48	33	0	437	385	101	84	81	41	40	0	358	341	66	61	162	89	73	0	795	726	167	145	142	102	90	117	101	93	108	108

1984 AMERICAN LEAGUE

TM	G	W	L	T	R	OR	HR	OHR	G	W	L	T	R	OR	HR	OHR	G	W	L	T	R	OR	HR	OHR	HRF	HRB	HRP	RF	RB	RP	BPF	PPF
BAL	81	44	37	0	319	306	82	59	81	41	40	0	362	361	78	78	162	85	77	0	681	667	160	137	91	119	102	88	101	99	94	94
BOS	81	41	40	0	456	413	100	76	81	45	36	0	354	351	81	65	162	86	76	0	810	764	181	141	119	117	93	122	102	97	110	110
CAL	81	37	44	0	341	364	79	83	81	44	37	0	355	333	71	60	162	81	81	0	696	697	150	143	122	96	91	102	96	96	101	101
CHI	81	43	38	0	394	389	103	77	81	31	50	0	285	347	69	78	162	74	88	0	679	736	172	155	120	110	102	121	85	93	110	111
CLE	81	41	39	1	411	399	65	73	82	34	48	0	350	367	58	68	163	75	87	1	761	766	123	141	110	82	94	113	100	100	106	106
DET	82	53	29	0	406	295	85	69	80	51	29	0	423	348	102	61	162	104	58	0	829	643	187	130	94	136	97	91	121	95	96	94
KC	81	44	37	0	344	326	48	59	81	40	41	0	329	360	69	77	162	84	78	0	673	686	117	136	75	94	109	98	95	96	99	99
MIL	81	38	43	0	286	344	42	68	80	29	51	0	355	390	54	69	161	67	94	0	641	734	96	137	88	72	101	84	98	112	92	93
MIN	81	47	34	0	372	337	63	77	81	34	47	0	301	338	51	82	162	81	81	0	673	675	114	159	105	79	108	110	89	89	106	106
NY	81	51	30	0	372	292	62	49	81	36	45	0	386	387	68	71	162	87	75	0	758	679	130	120	81	101	92	87	113	101	94	93
OAK	81	44	37	0	356	344	77	72	81	33	48	0	382	452	81	83	162	77	85	0	738	796	158	155	91	118	116	85	113	120	91	92
SEA	81	42	39	0	357	394	68	82	81	32	49	0	325	380	61	56	162	74	88	0	682	774	129	138	125	81	85	106	93	105	102	103
TEX	80	34	46	0	327	357	55	70	81	35	46	0	329	357	65	78	161	69	92	0	656	714	120	148	89	91	110	100	92	100	100	101
TOR	81	49	32	0	387	339	59	78	82	40	41	1	363	357	84	62	163	89	73	1	750	696	143	140	96	102	101	102	103	96	101	101

1985 AMERICAN LEAGUE

TM	G	W	L	T	R	OR	HR	OHR	G	W	L	T	R	OR	HR	OHR	G	W	L	T	R	OR	HR	OHR	HRF	HRB	HRP	RF	RB	RP	BPF	PPF
BAL	81	45	36	0	414	374	103	87	80	38	42	0	404	390	111	73	161	83	78	0	818	764	214	160	102	138	105	98	113	106	99	98
BOS	81	43	37	1	415	357	73	64	82	38	44	0	385	363	89	66	163	81	81	1	800	720	162	130	90	107	88	104	105	96	102	101
CAL	79	49	30	0	370	331	75	93	83	41	42	0	362	372	78	78	162	90	72	0	732	703	153	171	113	93	103	101	98	95	101	101
CHI	81	45	36	0	359	361	74	83	82	40	41	1	377	359	72	78	163	85	77	1	736	720	146	161	106	91	99	99	99	97	100	100
CLE	81	38	43	0	380	379	52	76	81	22	59	0	349	482	64	94	162	60	102	0	729	861	116	170	81	83	118	91	105	122	94	95
DET	81	44	37	0	386	368	108	93	80	40	40	0	343	320	94	48	161	84	77	0	729	688	202	141	136	111	76	112	93	88	106	106
KC	82	50	32	0	357	317	67	43	80	41	39	0	330	322	87	60	162	91	71	0	687	639	154	103	75	110	75	101	91	85	102	101
MIL	80	40	40	0	368	416	50	86	81	31	50	0	322	386	51	89	161	71	90	0	690	802	101	175	98	66	111	110	90	104	105	106
MIN	84	49	35	0	407	393	71	83	78	28	50	0	298	389	70	81	162	77	85	0	705	782	141	164	95	93	107	107	92	102	103	104
NY	80	58	22	0	411	288	92	67	81	39	42	0	428	372	84	90	161	97	64	0	839	660	176	157	94	118	105	90	120	95	96	94
OAK	79	43	36	0	348	347	66	71	83	34	49	0	409	440	89	101	162	77	85	0	757	787	155	172	77	113	124	87	111	114	93	93
SEA	83	42	41	0	360	389	92	78	79	32	47	0	359	429	79	76	162	74	88	0	719	818	171	154	104	108	98	91	103	116	94	95
TEX	80	37	43	0	356	406	76	102	81	25	56	0	261	379	53	71	161	62	99	0	617	785	129	173	139	70	92	117	77	98	108	110
TOR	80	54	26	0	396	264	75	78	81	45	36	0	363	324	83	69	161	99	62	0	759	588	158	147	103	100	94	99	103	81	101	99

1986 AMERICAN LEAGUE

TM	G	W	L	T	R	OR	HR	OHR	G	W	L	T	R	OR	HR	OHR	G	W	L	T	R	OR	HR	OHR	HRF	HRB	HRP	RF	RB	RP	BPF	PPF
BAL	79	37	42	0	348	362	91	98	83	36	47	0	360	398	78	79	162	73	89	0	708	760	169	177	124	93	97	98	96	102	99	99
BOS	81	51	30	0	389	350	55	85	80	44	36	0	405	346	89	82	161	95	66	0	794	696	144	167	83	96	113	98	107	95	100	99
CAL	82	50	32	0	371	335	88	84	80	42	38	0	415	349	79	69	162	92	70	0	786	684	167	153	113	95	88	91	109	96	96	95
CHI	81	41	40	0	341	335	51	63	81	31	50	0	303	364	70	80	162	72	90	0	644	699	121	143	77	82	97	101	85	92	101	101
CLE	81	45	35	1	403	415	80	80	82	39	43	0	428	426	77	87	163	84	78	1	831	841	157	167	99	96	102	97	113	115	98	98
DET	81	49	32	0	403	310	96	83	81	38	43	0	395	404	102	100	162	87	75	0	798	714	198	183	90	129	120	90	112	101	95	95
KC	81	45	36	0	342	317	60	46	81	31	50	0	312	356	77	75	162	76	86	0	654	673	137	121	71	97	84	98	88	90	100	100
MIL	80	41	39	0	338	375	63	79	81	36	45	0	329	359	64	79	161	77	84	0	667	734	127	158	100	78	95	104	88	96	102	103
MIN	81	43	38	0	426	439	116	107	81	28	53	0	315	400	80	93	162	71	91	0	741	839	196	200	126	107	111	118	91	103	108	109
NY	80	41	39	0	384	396	93	96	82	49	33	0	413	342	95	79	162	90	72	0	797	738	188	175	111	110	102	106	104	96	103	103
OAK	83	47	36	0	363	349	75	81	79	29	50	0	368	411	88	85	162	76	86	0	731	760	163	166	86	107	109	88	105	109	94	94
SEA	82	41	41	0	410	427	97	99	80	26	54	0	308	408	61	72	162	67	95	0	718	835	158	171	138	80	88	112	91	106	105	106
TEX	81	51	30	0	374	343	87	61	81	36	45	0	397	400	97	84	162	87	75	0	771	743	184	145	83	122	97	91	108	104	95	95
TOR	81	42	39	0	415	389	87	89	82	44	37	1	394	344	94	75	163	86	76	1	809	733	181	164	105	107	98	110	103	93	105	104

1987 AMERICAN LEAGUE

TM	G	W	L	T	R	OR	HR	OHR	G	W	L	T	R	OR	HR	OHR	G	W	L	T	R	OR	HR	OHR	HRF	HRB	HRP	RF	RB	RP	BPF	PPF
BAL	82	31	51	0	351	456	110	125	80	36	44	0	378	424	101	101	162	67	95	0	729	880	211	226	111	108	114	97	94	112	98	99
BOS	80	50	30	0	436	383	86	75	82	28	54	0	406	442	88	115	162	78	84	0	842	825	174	190	82	103	109	99	107	105	99	99
CAL	81	38	43	0	377	405	88	116	81	37	44	0	393	398	84	96	162	75	87	0	770	803	172	212	112	87	106	99	98	102	99	100
CHI	81	38	43	0	394	414	72	90	81	39	42	0	354	332	101	99	162	77	85	0	748	746	173	189	82	101	110	116	87	86	109	109
CLE	81	35	46	0	373	519	94	118	81	26	55	0	369	438	93	101	162	61	101	0	742	957	187	219	107	97	112	108	91	115	103	105
DET	81	54	27	0	442	338	125	101	81	44	37	0	454	397	100	79	162	98	64	0	896	735	225	180	125	106	86	93	116	97	97	96
KC	81	46	35	0	375	349	73	57	81	37	44	0	340	342	95	71	162	83	79	0	715	691	168	128	80	97	75	106	87	84	104	104
MIL	81	48	33	0	440	420	72	79	81	43	38	0	422	397	91	90	162	91	71	0	862	817	163	169	85	93	96	105	106	101	102	102
MIN	81	56	25	0	411	348	106	92	81	29	52	0	375	458	90	118	162	85	77	0	786	806	196	210	96	108	114	92	104	105	96	96
NY	81	51	30	0	401	346	98	88	81	38	43	0	387	412	98	91	162	89	73	0	788	758	196	179	99	104	96	94	102	98	98	97
OAK	81	42	39	0	363	351	88	75	81	39	42	0	443	438	111	101	162	81	81	0	806	789	199	176	78	118	105	82	112	109	91	91
SEA	81	40	41	0	403	400	103	115	81	38	43	0	357	401	58	84	162	78	84	0	760	801	161	199	148	68	85	105	93	98	103	103
TEX	81	43	38	0	426	447	93	111	81	32	49	0	397	402	101	88	162	75	87	0	823	849	194	199	107	100	102	108	100	103	104	104
TOR	81	52	29	0	425	319	101	83	81	44	37	0	420	336	114	75	162	96	66	0	845	655	215	158	98	114	86	99	105	83	101	99

1988 AMERICAN LEAGUE

TM	G	W	L	T	R	OR	HR	OHR	G	W	L	T	R	OR	HR	OHR	G	W	L	T	R	OR	HR	OHR	HRF	HRB	HRP	RF	RB	RP	BPF	PPF
BAL	80	34	46	0	286	354	70	77	81	20	61	0	264	435	67	76	161	54	107	0	550	789	137	153	102	101	112	92	83	115	95	97
BOS	81	53	28	0	456	360	68	73	81	36	45	0	357	329	56	70	162	89	73	0	813	689	124	143	112	86	99	118	105	91	109	108
CAL	81	35	46	0	333	368	58	71	81	40	41	0	381	403	66	64	162	75	87	0	714	771	124	135	99	91	99	90	107	115	94	95
CHI	81	40	41	0	311	373	56	64	80	31	49	0	320	384	77	74	161	71	90	0	631	757	132	138	79	109	115	96	92	109	97	99
CLE	81	44	37	0	353	359	62	52	81	34	47	0	313	372	72	68	162	78	84	0	666	731	134	120	82	107	96	103	93	101	101	102
DET	81	50	31	0	328	303	83	76	81	38	43	0	375	355	60	74	162	88	74	0	703	658	143	150	118	97	102	88	106	99	94	94
KC	80	44	36	0	359	330	55	37	81	40	41	0	345	318	66	65	161	84	77	0	704	648	121	102	73	103	85	105	97	90	103	103
MIL	81	47	34	0	354	310	60	65	81	40	41	0	328	306	53	60	162	87	75	0	682	616	113	125	110	78	86	105	93	85	103	103
MIN	81	47	34	0	402	354	76	79	81	44	37	0	357	318	75	67	162	91	71	0	759	672	151	146	109	107	103	112	101	90	106	105

	HOME								ROAD								ALL														
TM	G	W	L	T	R	OR	HR	OHR	G	W	L	T	R	OR	HR	OHR	G	W	L	T	R	OR	HR	OHR	HRF	HRB	HRP	RF	RB	RP	BPF	PPF
NY	80	46	34	0	378	345	77	75	81	39	42	0	394	403	71	82	161	85	76	0	772	748	148	157	101	110	116	93	115	111	96	95
OAK	81	54	27	0	362	294	67	47	81	50	31	0	438	326	89	69	162	104	58	0	800	620	156	116	75	130	98	88	119	94	95	93
SEA	81	37	44	0	362	405	97	81	80	31	49	0	302	339	51	63	161	68	93	0	664	744	148	144	147	87	88	116	88	98	107	108
TEX	81	38	43	0	336	368	58	67	80	32	48	0	301	367	54	62	161	70	91	0	637	735	112	129	105	80	92	103	90	102	101	102
TOR	81	45	36	0	371	344	78	73	81	42	39	0	392	336	80	70	162	87	75	0	763	680	158	143	101	116	106	99	108	98	100	99

1989 AMERICAN LEAGUE

	HOME								ROAD								ALL														
TM	G	W	L	T	R	OR	HR	OHR	G	W	L	T	R	OR	HR	OHR	G	W	L	T	R	OR	HR	OHR	HRF	HRB	HRP	RF	RB	RP	BPF	PPF
BAL	81	47	34	0	347	338	61	65	81	40	41	0	361	348	68	69	162	87	75	0	708	686	129	134	93	110	114	97	103	100	99	98
BOS	81	46	35	0	419	374	52	70	81	37	44	0	355	361	56	61	162	83	79	0	774	735	108	131	104	87	103	110	106	102	105	104
CAL	81	52	29	0	317	285	73	75	81	39	42	0	352	293	72	38	162	91	71	0	669	578	145	113	132	103	78	94	98	85	99	98
CHI	80	35	45	0	301	365	36	58	81	34	47	0	392	385	58	86	161	69	92	0	693	750	94	144	67	93	139	87	108	117	93	93
CLE	81	41	40	0	319	332	56	51	81	32	49	0	285	322	71	56	162	73	89	0	604	654	127	107	85	111	95	106	84	90	104	104
DET	81	38	43	0	321	389	74	77	81	21	60	0	296	427	42	73	162	59	103	0	617	816	116	150	127	83	109	97	91	118	97	99
KC	81	55	26	0	335	288	38	26	81	37	44	0	355	347	63	60	162	92	70	0	690	635	101	86	54	106	87	90	104	96	96	95
MIL	81	45	36	0	344	321	69	54	81	36	45	0	363	358	57	75	162	81	81	0	707	679	126	129	94	107	108	93	105	101	97	96
MIN	81	45	36	0	387	404	59	69	81	35	46	0	353	334	58	70	162	80	82	0	740	738	117	139	100	96	113	114	100	99	106	106
NY	81	41	40	0	373	419	64	88	80	33	47	0	325	373	66	62	161	74	87	0	698	792	130	150	115	101	114	111	97	109	104	105
OAK	81	54	27	0	370	284	65	51	81	45	36	0	342	292	62	52	162	99	63	0	712	576	127	103	103	101	83	104	99	81	103	102
SEA	81	40	41	0	353	386	68	67	81	33	48	0	341	342	66	47	162	73	89	0	694	728	134	114	117	100	85	107	97	101	103	104
TEX	81	45	36	0	352	371	75	63	81	38	43	0	343	343	47	56	162	83	79	0	695	714	122	119	131	85	85	105	98	100	102	103
TOR	81	46	35	0	330	308	64	50	81	43	38	0	401	343	78	49	162	89	73	0	731	651	142	99	91	119	86	87	112	101	94	93

1990 AMERICAN LEAGUE

	HOME								ROAD								ALL														
TM	G	W	L	T	R	OR	HR	OHR	G	W	L	T	R	OR	HR	OHR	G	W	L	T	R	OR	HR	OHR	HRF	HRB	HRP	RF	RB	RP	BPF	PPF
BAL	80	40	40	0	320	337	74	82	81	36	45	0	349	361	58	79	161	76	85	0	669	698	132	161	114	98	119	94	100	104	97	97
BOS	81	51	30	0	394	318	61	44	81	37	44	0	305	346	45	48	162	88	74	0	699	664	106	92	112	76	67	109	95	91	105	105
CAL	81	42	39	0	360	354	89	55	81	38	43	0	330	352	58	51	162	80	82	0	690	706	147	106	129	98	74	104	97	99	102	102
CHI	80	49	31	0	345	315	41	53	82	45	37	0	337	318	65	53	162	94	68	0	682	633	106	106	83	87	90	104	95	89	103	102
CLE	81	41	40	0	363	373	52	86	81	36	45	0	369	364	58	77	162	77	85	0	732	737	110	163	102	87	125	100	105	106	100	100
DET	81	39	42	0	372	399	92	75	81	40	41	0	378	355	80	79	162	79	83	0	750	754	172	154	105	133	121	105	106	106	102	102
KC	81	45	36	0	370	342	42	46	80	30	50	0	337	367	58	70	161	75	86	0	707	709	100	116	69	92	105	100	103	103	100	100
MIL	81	39	42	0	356	374	60	59	81	35	46	0	376	386	68	62	162	74	88	0	732	760	128	121	92	103	98	96	108	112	97	97
MIN	81	41	40	0	373	380	46	69	81	33	48	0	293	349	54	65	162	74	88	0	666	729	100	134	96	79	105	115	89	97	107	108
NY	81	37	44	0	296	361	64	78	81	30	51	0	307	388	83	66	162	67	95	0	603	749	147	144	95	119	117	94	90	110	97	98
OAK	81	51	30	0	321	244	69	52	81	52	29	0	412	326	95	71	162	103	59	0	733	570	164	123	75	145	112	79	116	92	91	89
SEA	81	38	43	0	310	341	49	60	81	39	42	0	330	339	58	60	162	77	85	0	640	680	107	120	93	86	96	97	93	98	99	99
TEX	82	47	35	0	354	348	64	59	80	36	44	0	322	348	46	54	162	83	79	0	676	696	110	113	118	77	80	102	96	99	101	101
TOR	81	44	37	0	385	341	93	82	81	42	39	0	382	320	74	61	162	86	76	0	767	661	167	143	127	116	100	103	108	94	102	101

Appendices

Rules and Scoring

Dennis Bingham and Thomas R. Heitz

The chronologies presented here trace the evolution of baseball's playing and scoring rules from those governing the first properly organized baseball club (1845) to the present major league clubs (through 1990).

Playing Rules

As a starting point, the rules of the 1845 Knickerbocker Base Ball Club of New York City are provided. During earlier decades, rules had been published for popular bat-and-ball and baserunning games played by eighteenth- and early nineteenth-century youths (indeed, some basic baseball principles can be traced back for centuries), but the codified Knickerbocker rules serve as a direct link to the rules of today. Their rules were the model for the hundreds of organized amateur clubs that sprang up in the 1850s. Following the 1845 rules is an outline listing the significant rule changes made in the next twelve years.

In 1858, several baseball clubs, including the old Knickerbockers, met to establish the National Association of Base-Ball Players and, in the process, greatly expanded, refined, and polished the rule book. Although the association was composed primarily of amateurs, this rule book became the core of every rule book for every baseball league that followed. These rules are set forth in their entirety and are followed by changes to the rules under annual headings through 1990.

The first major league, the National Association of Professional Base-Ball Players, was formed in 1871 and used essentially the same rule book as its predecessor. In 1876 the National League dethroned the professional players' association and adopted their rule book, with their amendments to the rules noted under that year's heading.

Rule differences for subsequent major leagues are also listed in the chronology and are noted under the annual heading in which they were introduced, e.g. Union Association (1884) and Players League (1890.)

In most cases, the actual text of a new rule or change has been taken verbatim from original sources. However, to reduce verbiage, the references to section numbering and headings, which have varied widely over the years, have been deleted along with other extraneous spacing and punctuation. In many cases, primarily in the early years, the wording has been slightly changed to convey the meaning of the rule more clearly. In a few cases the technical wording of complex rules has been summarized for ease of reading. Researchers requiring precise quotations of rules are advised to consult original sources, e.g., the *Spalding* and *Reach Baseball Guides*.

Headings have been added to each of the changes under the annual headings to assist the reader. By consulting the index and headings, readers may follow the evolution of any one particular rule through the years.

The chronology does not include *all* changes to the playing rules—only those of significance and substance. Numerous minor changes in wording not affecting meaning, or changes in punctuation and spelling which had no purpose other than gram-matical correctness, have been ignored. Also, the chronology includes only those rules and regulations found in the official baseball rule book, not those found in other baseball documents such as league constitutions and the Basic Agreement. Thus rules and subject matter that may have been dropped from the early rule books, such as those concerning player eligibility and discipline, may still govern baseball for years later but had been inserted in the league's constitution.

In some instances, significant rule changes affecting umpires and little-used rules regarding suspended games or batting out of order have been summarized or simply alluded to in the interests of brevity. The scoring rules are presented in a separate section of this appendix because of their length and special interest.

Baseball's rules continue to evolve in the twentieth century despite the perception of many that "the game remains pretty much the same as it always has been." The most far-reaching revision of baseball's playing rules came in 1950 when the entire code was virtually rewritten. Additional changes and refinements were added throughout the 1950s, and it is the rules of 1950 for the most part that we use today.

The rules of baseball are commonly considered the means of keeping the game in that delicate balance between offense and defense with neither side enjoying a marked advantage. This balance is the dynamic force of competition, which drives the game and ultimately creates interest and motivation for players and spectators alike.

But changes to the playing rules can also be categorized in terms of response to various social, economic, and technological factors as well as to the need for competitive balance. For example, when the uncouth language of hard-bitten nineteenth-century players became offensive to female rooters, appropriate rules were adopted (in an attempt) to modify player behavior. Likewise, gloves were introduced gradually in the 1870s and 1880s to protect the players' catching hands from injury. However, when glove design clearly departed from the goal of protection and extended to aiding in the catching process, effectively making the glove an extension of the hand, it became necessary to invoke standards for gloves in the rules.

In terms of competitive balance, perhaps the most striking evolution is that of the pitching rules, which have undergone a remarkable transformation from the days of simple under-handed hurling from a boxlike enclosure to today's complex series of physical motions from which almost any deviation is likely to elicit a call of "balk."

In many cases, the introduction of a playing rule followed several years of development on the field of play. Like state and federal legislative bodies, baseball's rule-making authorities are often slow to respond to changing conditions or perhaps justifiably cautious about making such changes before the effects are fully understood. For example, there is no mention of pitching mounds in the playing rules until 1903, when the maximum elevation was fixed at 15 inches. However, pitching mounds were in general use many years prior to 1903 and may have come into vogue as early as the 1880s. The lifting of restrictions on the angle of pitching delivery in 1884 made overhanded throwing legal, and it was not long before the hurlers realized the mechanical advantages of stepping off a short incline as they directed the ball toward the plate. Presumably, by 1903 the lack of uniformity in certain parks had become a problem, and so the rules set a standard.

Another point that should be kept in mind while reading this chronology is that just because a particular rule is "in the book" doesn't necessarily mean that it was (or is) always enforced.

The researcher is advised to scan the Index to Playing Rule Changes prior to consulting the chronology.

Scoring Rules

The chronology presented after that of the playing rules traces the evolution of professional baseball's scoring rules from 1877 through 1990.

Clubs, sportswriters, and fans had been keeping score and compiling statistics for decades, but the scoring rules of 1877 are presented as a starting point, in their entirety, because they are the first official scoring rules included in the rule book. Thereafter changes to the scoring rules are noted under annual headings.

In most cases, as with the playing rules, the actual text of a new scoring rule or change has been taken verbatim from original sources.

The scoring rules are at the heart of baseball's accountability to itself and to the millions of fans who follow the game day by day. Through the use of these rules the daily performance of players and teams is described and measured in a uniform and meaningful way. Baseball is unique in publishing the performance records of its key personnel, and in so doing it subjects the individual, the team, and its management to the scrutiny and judgment of anyone who has the price of a daily newspaper.

Like the playing rules, they have evolved from a rather primitive code to a complex, legalistic document. The scoring rules have been transformed over the decades from the simple recording of hits, outs, errors, and assists in the 1870s into a highly technical set of rules and guidelines used to record every significant offensive and defensive event that transpires on the field of play.

While the collection of such statistics as "caught stealing" did not commence until later years, still baseball's major performance records can be traced in an unbroken skein well back into the nineteenth century. As a result, no other professional sport can claim such a rich resource of historical statistics.

The researcher is advised to scan the Index to Scoring Rule Changes prior to consulting the chronology.

Playing Rules for 1845

1. Members must strictly observe the time agreed upon for exercise, and be punctual in their attendance.
2. When assembled for exercise, the President, or in his absence the Vice-President, shall appoint an Umpire, who shall keep the game in a book provided for that purpose, and note all violations of the By-Laws and Rules during the time of exercise.
3. The presiding officer shall designate two members as Captains, who shall retire and make the match to be played, observing at the same time that the players put opposite to each other should be as nearly equal as possible; the choice of sides to be then tossed for, and the first in hand to be decided in like manner.
4. The bases shall be from "home" to second base, forty-two paces; from first to third base, forty-two paces, equidistant.
5. No stump match shall be played on a regular day of exercise.
6. If there should not be a sufficient number of members of the Club present at the time agreed upon to commence exercise, gentlemen not members may be chosen in to make up the match, which shall not be broken up to take in members that may afterwards appear; but, in all cases, members shall have the

preference, when present, at the making of a match.
7. If members appear after the game is commenced they may be chosen in if mutually agreed upon.
8. The game to consist of twenty-one counts, or aces; but at the conclusion an equal number of hands must be played.
9. The ball must be pitched, and not thrown, for the bat.
10. A ball knocked out of the field, or outside the range of the first or third base, is foul.
11. Three balls being struck at and missed and the last one caught, is a hand out; if not caught is considered fair, and the striker bound to run.
12. If a ball be struck, or tipped, and caught, either flying or on the first bound, it is a hand out.
13. A player running the bases shall be out, if the ball is in the hands of an adversary on the base, or the runner is touched with it before he makes his base; it being understood, however, that in no instance is a ball to be thrown at him.
14. A player running who shall prevent an adversary from catching or getting the ball before making his base, is a hand out.
15. Three hands out, all out.
16. Players must take their strike in regular turn.
17. All disputes and differences relative to the game, to be decided by the Umpire, from which there is no appeal.
18. No ace or base can be made on a foul strike.
19. A runner cannot be put out in making one base, when a balk is made by the pitcher.
20. But one base allowed when a ball bounds out of the field when struck.

Rule Changes 1846-57

In 1848 a rule was amended declaring that the batter-runner was out if the ball was held on first base before he reached it; previously, the rule applied the situation to *all* bases. By 1852, the captains of each club had been given the authority to position each player in the field, which could not be changed without their consent, and that each club member would take turns as umpire.

The 1854 rule book included the following: "When a fair ball is struck and the striker not put out, the first base must be vacated as well as the next base or bases if similarly occupied; players may be put out, under these circumstances, in the same manner as when running to first base." In other words, the force out had been introduced.

The dimensions of the ball had also been established—from 5½ to 6 ounces in weight and from 2¾ to 3½ inches in diameter. A player was also now called out if he *intentionally* prevented an opponent from catching the ball.

A major rule change was made in 1857 when it was determined that nine complete innings would constitute a game rather than the first team to score 21 runs at the end of equal innings.

Playing Rules for 1858

Section 1. The ball. The ball must weigh not less than six nor more than six and one-quarter ounces avoirdupois. It must measure not less than ten nor more than ten and a quarter inches in circumference. It must be composed of India rubber and yarn, and covered with leather, and in all match games shall be furnished by the challenging club, and become the property of the winning club as a trophy of victory.
Section 2. The bat. The bat must be round and must not exceed two and a half inches in diameter in the thickest part. It must be made of wood and may be of any length to suit the striker.
Section 3. The bases. The bases must be four in number, placed at equal distances from each other, and securely fastened upon the four corners of a square whose sides are respectively thirty yards. They must be so constructed as to be distinctly seen by the

umpire, and must cover a space equal to one square foot of surface. The first, second, and third bases shall be canvas bags, painted white, and filled with sand or sawdust; the home base and pitcher's points to each marked with a flat circular iron plate, painted or enameled white.

Section 4. Position of the bases. The base from which the ball is struck shall be designated the home base and must be directly opposite the second base; the first base must always be that upon the right hand, and the third base that upon the left hand side of the striker when occupying the position at the home base.

Section 5. The pitcher's position. The pitcher's position shall be designated by a line four yards in length, drawn at right angles to a line from home to the second base, having its center upon that line, at a fixed iron plate placed at a point fifteen yards from the home base. The pitcher must deliver the ball as near as possible over the center of said base, and for the striker.

Section 6. Delivering the ball. The ball must be pitched, not jerked or thrown, to the bat; and whenever the pitcher draws back his hand, or moves with the apparent purpose or pretension to deliver the ball, he shall so deliver it, and must have neither foot in advance of the line at the time of delivering the ball; and if he fails in either of these particulars, then it shall be declared a balk.

Section 7. Balking. When a balk is made by the pitcher, every player running the bases is entitled to one base without being put out.

Section 8. Foul and fair hit balls. If the ball, from a stroke of the bat, is caught behind the range of home and the first base or home and the third base, without having touched the ground, or first touches the ground behind those bases, it shall be termed foul and must be so declared by the umpire unasked. If the ball first touches the ground, either upon or in front of the range of those bases, it shall be considered fair.

Section 9. Scoring a run. A player making the home base shall be entitled to score one run.

Section 10. Running on third strike. If three balls are struck at and missed, and the last one is not caught flying or upon the first bound, it shall be considered fair and the striker must attempt to make his run.

How batsmen are put out.

Section 11. Caught foul ball. The striker is out if a foul ball is caught, either before touching the ground or upon the first bound;

Section 12. Three strikes. Or if three balls are struck at and missed, and the last is caught either before touching the ground or upon the first bound;

Section 13. Caught fair ball. Or if a fair ball is struck, and the ball is caught without having touched the ground or upon the first bound;

Section 14. At first base. Or if a fair ball is struck, and the ball is held by an adversary on the first base before the striker touches the base;

Section 15. Touched with ball. Or if, at any time, he is touched by the ball while in play in the hands of an adversary, without some part of his person being on a base.

Section 16. Running on fair and foul balls. No ace or base can be made upon a foul ball, nor when a fair ball has been caught without touching the ground; and the ball shall, in both instances, be considered dead and not in play until it shall first have been settled in the hands of the pitcher; in either case the players running the bases shall return to them, and shall not be put out in so running unless the ball has been first pitched to the striker.

Section 17. The batsman's position. The striker must stand on a line drawn through the center of the home base, not exceeding in length three feet from either side thereof, and parallel with the line occupied by the pitcher. He shall be considered the striker until he has made the first base. Players must strike in regular rotation and, after the first inning is played, the turn commences

with the player who stands on the list next to the one who lost the third hand.

Section 18. Forced off a base. Players must take their bases in the order of striking; and when a fair ball is struck, and not caught flying nor on the first bound, the first base must be vacated, as also the second and third bases if they are occupied at the same time. Players may be put out at any base, under these circumstances, in the same manner as the striker when running to the first base.

Section 19. Running out of line of bases. Players running the bases must, as far as possible, keep upon the direct line between the bases; and should any player run three feet out of this line, for the purpose of avoiding the ball in the hands of an adversary, he shall be declared out.

Section 20. Interfering with fielder. Any player who shall intentionally prevent an adversary from catching or fielding the ball, shall be declared out.

Section 21. Obstructing baserunners. If the player is prevented from making a base by the intentional obstruction of an adversary, he shall be entitled to that base and not be put out.

Section 22. Illegally stopping the ball. If an adversary stops the ball with his hat or cap, or takes it from the hands of a party not engaged in the game, no player can be put out unless the ball shall first have been settled in the hands of the pitcher.

Section 23. Caught fly balls. If a ball, from the strike of a bat, is held under any other circumstances than as enumerated in Section 22, and without having touched the ground more than once, the striker is out.

Section 24. No run scored. If two hands are already out, no player running home at the time a ball is struck can make an ace if the striker is put out.

Section 25. End of innings. An inning must be concluded at the time the third hand is put out.

Section 26. The game. The game shall consist of nine innings to each side, when, should the number of runs be equal, the play shall be continued until a majority of runs, upon an equal number of innings shall be declared, which shall conclude the game.

Section 27. Eligible players. In playing all matches, nine players from each club shall constitute a full field, and they must have been regular members of the club which they represent, and of no other club, for thirty days prior to the match. No change or substitution shall be made after the game has been commenced, unless for reason of illness or injury. Position of players and choice of innings shall be determined by captains previously appointed for that purpose by the respective clubs.

Section 28. Duties of the umpire. The umpire shall take care that the regulations respecting the ball, bats, bases, and the pitcher's and striker's positions are strictly observed. He shall keep a record of the game in a book prepared for the purpose; he shall be the judge of fair and unfair play, and shall determine all disputes and differences which may occur during the game; he shall take especial care to declare all foul balls and balks immediately upon their occurrence, unasked, and in a distinct and audible manner.

Section 29. Selection of umpire/scorers. In all matches, the umpire shall be selected by the captains of the respective sides, and shall perform all the duties enumerated in Section 28, except recording the game, which shall be done by two scorers, one of whom shall be appointed by each of the contending clubs.

Section 30. Betting prohibited. No person engaged in a match, either as umpire, scorer, or player, shall be directly or indirectly interested in any bet upon the game. Neither umpire, scorer, nor player shall be changed during a match, unless with the consent of both parties, except for a violation of this law and except as provided in Section 27, and then the umpire may dismiss any transgressor.

Section 31. Suspending and completing game. The umpire in any match shall determine when play shall be suspended; and if the game cannot be concluded, it shall be decided by the last even innings, provided five innings have been played, and the party having the greatest number of runs shall be declared the winner.

Section 32. Special ground rules. Clubs may adopt such rules respecting balls knocked beyond or outside of the bounds of the field, as the circumstances of the ground may demand and these rules shall govern all matches played upon the ground, provided that they are distinctly made known to every player and umpire previous to the commencement of the game.

Section 33. Interfering with participants. No person shall be permitted to approach or to speak with the umpire, scorers, or players, or in any manner to interrupt or interfere during the progress of the game, unless by special request of the umpire.

Section 34. Eligible umpires and scorers. No person shall be permitted to act as umpire or scorer in any match, unless he shall be a member of a base ball club governed by these rules.

Section 35. Forfeited game. Whenever a match shall have been determined upon between two clubs, play shall be called at the exact hour appointed; and should either party fail to produce their players within fifteen minutes thereafter, the party so failing shall admit a defeat.

Section 36. Ineligible players. No person who may be in arrears to any club he may have belonged to previous to the one he is then a member of shall be competent to play in a match unless such arrears are paid.

Section 37. Calling strikes. Should a striker stand at the bat without striking at good balls repeatedly pitched to him, for the purpose of delaying the game or of giving advantage to a player, the umpire, after warning him, shall call one strike, and if he persists in such action, two and three strikes. When three strikes are called, he shall be subject to the same rules as if he had struck at the three balls.

Chronology of Rule Changes 1859-1990

1859

Ball The ball must weigh 5¾ to 6 ounces and measure 9¾ to 10 inches in circumference.

Player/Eligible No person who receives compensation for his services as a player shall be competent to play in any match.

Game/Number Every match shall be decided by a single game.

Note: In previous years, a series of games often determined the winner of a "match."

Runner/Advancing Caught fly balls which do not touch the ground are no longer considered dead balls.

Note: With this amendment it was understood that runners, following caught fly balls, could now advance after returning to their original base. This, however, was not as yet written into the rules.

1860

Game/Number Every match shall be decided by a single game unless otherwise mutually agreed upon by the contesting clubs.

Runner/Returning Runners, returning to their bases following foul balls and caught fly balls not touching the ground, may be put out in the same manner as the batter when running to first base.

Note: At the 1857 meeting of baseball clubs, the progressive Knickerbockers proposed that in order to retire the batter the ball must be caught on the fly and not on one bounce. It became a hotly debated topic during the next several conventions but, although it gained more support each year, the "fly rule" continued to be defeated when put to a vote. In 1860, however, the "fly game" was allowed if both contesting clubs agreed. This concession was not officially written into the rule book.

1861

Ball The ball must weigh 5½ to 5¾ ounces and measure 9½ to 9¾ inches in circumference.

Foul Ball If the ball, from the stroke of the bat, first touches the ground, the person of a player, or any object behind the range of home and first or home and third base, it shall be a foul ball.

Grounds A line connecting home and first base and home and third base shall be marked by chalk, or other suitable material, so as to be distinctly seen by the umpire.

Runner Players running the bases must make them in the following order: first, second, third, and home, and in returning must reverse this order.

Umpire The umpire, before leaving the grounds, must declare the winning club and record his decision in the scorebooks of the two clubs.

1862

There were no changes to the playing rules this year.

1863

Base on Balls When three "balls" have been called, the striker is entitled to first base, and each player occupying a base is entitled to one base without being put out.

Note: In actuality it took more than three balls to be awarded first base; see 1863, *Strike Zone.*

Pitcher/Delivery If the pitcher, at the time of delivery, has either foot off the ground or in advance of the front line of his position, it shall be declared a balk.

Pitcher/Position The pitcher's position shall be two lines, each twelve feet in length, with the front line forty-five feet and the back line forty-eight feet distant from home base.

Note: This introduces the pitcher's box, which replaces the single twelve-foot line.

Runner/Advancing Runners, after returning to their respective bases, may advance immediately after a fair fly ball has been settled in the hands of a fielder.

Note: This put into words what had been understood for the past four years; see 1859 rule.

Runner/Bases Each runner must touch each base in making the circuit.

Note: Runners were previously allowed to go around or near the bases.

Strike Zone Should the pitcher repeatedly fail to deliver "fair" balls, for the purpose of delaying the game or for any cause, the umpire, after warning him, shall call one "ball"; and if the pitcher persists, two and three balls.

1864

Batter/Caught Fly A batted ball in foul territory must be caught on the fly to be declared an out.

Note: The "fly game" has been adopted; fair balls caught on one bounce are no longer outs.

1865

Interference/Spectator If a ball is stopped by any person not engaged in the game, no player may be put out unless the ball has first been settled in the hands of the pitcher.

Umpire The umpire is no longer responsible for keeping a record of the game in the scorebook.

Note: This amendment corrects a contradiction in earlier rule books in which one rule held the umpire responsible for keeping score and another rule instructed the umpire not to perform the duty.

1866

Bases First, second, and third bases shall be canvas bags, painted white and filled with some soft material.

Game/Legal Any game played in contravention of National Association rules shall be considered null and void and shall not be counted in the list of games won or lost; unless a game is delayed by rain beyond the appointed start. Any game may be put off by mutual consent of the two clubs. No game shall be commenced in the rain.

Game/Number Every game shall be decided by the best two games out of three, unless a single game is mutually agreed upon by the two clubs.

Pitcher/Position The back line of the pitcher's box is moved back one foot, increasing the length to 4 feet while remaining 12 feet in width.

1867

Batter/Position The batter, when in the act of striking, shall not step forward or backward but must stand on the three-foot line drawn through the center of home base.

Batter-Runner The batter shall be considered a baserunner as soon as he hits a fair ball.

Dead Ball Any pitch on which a "balk" or "ball" has been called is considered a dead ball, and the batter cannot be put out if he hits such a ball. Dead balls are returned to play when the ball has been settled in the hands of the pitcher while he stands within the pitcher's box.

Forfeited Game A club failing to produce their players within thirty minutes of the start of the game shall admit a defeat. The opposing club receives a win and is entitled to nine runs, and the game is counted in the list of games played. The game shall not be forfeited if the club fails to play because of the recent death of one of its members and there hasn't been sufficient time to notify the opposing club.

Pitcher/Delivery The pitcher must deliver the ball as near as possible over the center of home base and fairly for the striker.

The ball must be pitched, not jerked or thrown, to the bat. The ball shall be considered jerked if the pitcher's arm touches his person when the arm is swung forward to deliver the ball; and it is a throw if the arm is bent at the elbow at an angle from the body or horizontally from the shoulder when the arm is swung forward in delivery. A pitched ball is one delivered with arm straight and swinging perpendicularly and free from the body.

Note: The word *perpendicular* was used in the rule but the word *parallel* was intended. This error would be repeated for several years.

Pitcher/Position The pitcher's box is reduced in size to six feet in width and four feet in length.

Player/Eligible All players who play baseball for money, place, or emolument are regarded as professional players and shall not take part in any game. Any club giving compensation to a player or having knowledge that one of their players is playing for compensation shall be expelled from the National Association. Any club engaging in a game with an expelled club shall also forfeit membership.

Run Scored If there are two outs, no player can score a run if the batter is put out by a legal catch, forced between home and first base, or the ball is held by an adversary on first base before the batter reaches it.

Strikeout The batter is out if three balls are swung at and missed and the last one is caught either on the fly or on the first bound; provided the pitches are not those on which "balks" or "balls" have been called, or if the batter swings for the purpose of willfully striking out.

Strike Zone All pitches striking the ground in front of home base, over the head of the batter, or to the side opposite to that which the batter swings from, shall be considered unfair "balls."

Substitute An umpire, scorer, or player shall not be changed during a game except for reason of illness or injury and with the consent of both clubs; or when the umpire dismisses a transgressor for violation of the rules.

Umpire The umpire must declare when a player is out and in what position and manner.

Note: For example, if a batter is out on a caught fly to center, the umpire must yell, "Striker is out on the fly by the center fielder." This rule lasted only one year.

1868

Ball The ball must weigh from 5 to $5\frac{1}{4}$ ounces and measure from $9\frac{1}{4}$ to $9\frac{1}{2}$ inches in circumference.

The challenging club must furnish a ball with the size, weight, and maker's name on it.

Bases The base-bag shall be considered the base and not the part to which it is or should be fastened.

Note: This rule was dropped in 1876.

The home plate and pitcher's points must be flat plates, painted white.

Bat The bat shall not exceed forty inches in length.

Batter/Position The batter, when about to strike the ball, must stand astride the three-foot line which is drawn through the center of home base and parallel with the front line of the pitcher's box.

The batter must not take any backward step when striking at the ball. The penalty is the calling of "foul strike," and when three such strikes are called, the batter is out. The batter is also out if he hits such a "strike" and the ball is caught, either fair or foul. No base may be run, but the baserunner is allowed to return to his base without being put out.

Catch If a fair ball is held by a fielder before touching the ground after it has rebounded from the hands or person of another player, it shall be considered a catch. A foul ball, if similarly held but touches the ground once, is also a catch.

Dead Ball No base may be run or player put out on a dead ball. If the batter hits a pitch on which a "balk" or "ball" has been called, no "strike" or foul ball shall be called, or a player put out; except bases may be taken on balks and calls of ball three.

Forfeited Game Any club failing to take their positions within five minutes after the umpire calls "play" shall forfeit the game.

Game/Rain No game shall be started when rain is falling and no game shall be continued when rain has fallen for five minutes.

Game/Scheduled When a challenge has been accepted for a series of games, each of the three games must be played at least within fifteen days of the previous game. The first game is played on the grounds of the challenger, the second game on the grounds of the challenged, and the third game, if necessary, on grounds mutually agreed upon. When a first-nine match is to be played, the clubs must play their recognized first nine, as far as practicable.

Note: This rule was dropped the next season.

Game/"Time" When the umpire calls "play," the game must begin at once. When the umpire calls "time," play shall be suspended until he calls "play" again. When the umpire "calls" a game, it shall end, but when he merely suspends play for any stated period, it may be resumed at the point at which it was suspended, provided it does not extend to the next day.

Obstruction If a runner is prevented from making a base by the intentional obstruction of an adversary, he shall be entitled to that base and not be put out. Any obstruction that could readily have been avoided shall be considered intentional.

Pitcher/Delivery   The pitcher is no longer required to keep both feet on the ground when delivering the ball.

Player   Every player taking part in a regular match game, no matter how many innings have been played, shall be, in the meaning of these rules, considered a member of the club with which he plays.

Runner/Bases   If a runner fails to touch each base, he shall be declared out unless he returns to the base before the ball is held on it.

Run Scored   When there are two outs, no runner may score if the batter is put out.

Substitute   No player may be substituted after the third inning except in cases of illness and injury.

Umpire/Decisions   Only the captain of each club is allowed to appeal for the reversal of a decision by the umpire. No decision by the umpire shall be reversed by the testimony of any player; and no decision whatever shall be reversed except for a palpable infringement of the rules, and then only on an appeal by the captain.

Umpire/Scorer   The umpire shall require that the game be recorded by a scorer for each of the contesting clubs.
Note: This rule was dropped from the rule book in 1874.

1869

Ball   In the first and third games of a series the ball shall be furnished by the challenging club, and in the second game by the challenged club.

Base on Balls   When the batter is awarded first base after three called balls, no other runner shall take a base unless he is obliged to vacate the base he occupies.

Bat   The bat shall not exceed forty-two inches in length.

Batter/Fails to Bat   Any player failing to take his turn at bat, unless for reason of illness or injury or by consent of the opposing captain, shall be declared out.
Note: In 1870, the rule was amended: Any player failing to bat "after the umpire has called for the striker . . . shall be declared out."

Catch   It is not a catch if the ball is caught after touching any object [fence, building, tree] other than a player, even if the ball does not touch the ground.

Club/Eligible   Any club willfully infringing any rule shall be suspended for a period not to exceed one year for the first offense, and expulsion from membership for the second offense, after trial by the judiciary committee.

Forfeited Game   No game shall be forfeited because of the failure of the umpire to discharge his duties or for failing to declare the winning club of a match.
There must be at least a two-day notice for postponement of a game because of the death of a club member or the club is liable to forfeit.

Game/Drawn   If the score is tied at the end of nine innings, the captains may mutually agree to consider the game a draw. In case of no such agreement, the club refusing to continue play shall forfeit the ball.

Game/Winner   If the game cannot be continued, it shall be decided by the score of the last equal innings and the club having the greater number of runs is the winner; unless one club has completed their inning and the other club has exceeded their opponent's score in their uncompleted inning, in which case the club with the higher score is the winner. But no game shall be considered as played unless five innings on each side have been completed.

Pitcher/Delivery   When about to deliver the ball or at the actual time of delivery, the pitcher cannot have either foot outside the pitcher's box.

Pitcher/Position   The pitcher's box is enlarged to a six-foot square.

Player/Eligible   Players must not have been members of any other National Association club (college clubs excepted) for sixty days immediately prior to the game.
All players who play baseball for money or who at any time receive compensation for their services as players shall be considered professional players; and all others shall be regarded as amateur players.
Note: This rule officially recognized two distinct classes of players—professional and amateur—and permitted the participation of professional players.

Runner/Forced   No baserunner shall be forced to vacate a base unless as provided in these rules.
Note: This amendment prevented a runner, not forced to vacate his own base, from forcing another to vacate his base. For example, if a runner attempts to steal third base, changes his mind before reaching third, and returns to second base to find the runner from first now standing on the bag, the original runner still has the right to the base.

Run Scored   When there are two outs, no runner may score a run if the batter or player running the bases is put out before touching first base.

Strike Zone   Balls and strikes may not be called unless there has first been issued a warning and they may not be called until the pitch has crossed the plate. All "balls" *must* be called by the umpire after the pitcher has been warned of the penalty. One warning for each batter shall suffice.

Substitute/Runner   No player shall be allowed to have a substitute run the bases for him except in cases of illness or injury.

1870

Ball   The challenged club must supply the means of ascertaining the size and weight of the ball furnished by the other club.
Note: This rule was dropped in 1871 and replaced with the previous rule requiring the challenging club to furnish a ball on which its size, weight, and the name of the manufacturer is stamped.

Base on Balls   Any player awarded a base on balls is allowed to advance, at his own risk, beyond the base awarded him.
Note: This rule was inexplicably left out of the 1871 rule book but was back in 1872.

Dead Ball   Called "balls" not hit by the batter are no longer dead balls, and any base can be run or player put out on such pitches.

Fair Ball   If the ball, from the stroke of the bat, first touches the ground, the person of a player or any other object, either upon or in front of the foul lines, it shall be declared a fair ball.

Forfeited Game   All games in which any rule is infringed shall be considered forfeited games and shall be recorded as games won by a score of 9 to 0 against the club infringing the rules.
No forfeit shall be declared if a club fails to play a game because of the recent death of one of its members.
Note: The requirement of two days notice has been dropped.

Grounds   The lines of the batter's and pitcher's positions must be marked with chalk or other suitable material so as to be distinctly seen by the umpire.

Runner/Forced   The moment the player running to first base is out, other baserunners previously forced to vacate their bases shall cease to be forced and may return to their bases.

Note: In 1872 the rule was amended and clarified that runners could still be put out in returning to their base.

Strike Zone The umpire no longer issues a warning before calling a pitch, but "balls" and "strikes" may not be called on the first pitch delivered.

All pitches which are not within the fair reach of the striker, such as pitches over the striker's head, on the ground in front of home base, to the side opposite to that the batsman strikes from, or which hit the striker while he is standing in his proper position, are considered unfair "balls" and must be called whenever delivered (except for the first pitch).

Umpire/Decisions No decision given by the umpire shall be reversed by the testimony of any player, and the umpire shall not be guided in his decisions by any such testimony.

1871

The rule book is adopted by the National Association of Professional Base-Ball Players.

Ball The ball must weigh from 5 to 5¼ ounces and must measure exactly 9¼ inches in circumference.

Batter/Position The batter must stand at least one foot from home base 'and astride the three-foot line drawn through the center of home base. When striking at the ball, he may take a forward step but must keep one foot behind the line.

Dead Ball It is a dead ball whenever a pitch touches the umpire, or is accidentally stopped by him.

Game/Legal Under no circumstances shall a game be considered played unless five innings have been completed. Should darkness or rain prevent the continuing of the game before the end of the fifth inning, the umpire shall declare "no game."

Note: This made clearer what had long been understood by most.

Grounds No fence may be erected within ninety feet of home base, unless the fence marks the boundary line of the field. Baserunners are entitled to one base whenever the ball passes the catcher and touches a fence located closer than ninety feet behind home base.

Pitcher/Delivery The penalty for pitches thrown, jerked, or delivered other than with a straight arm swinging perpendicular [parallel] to the body shall be the calling of a "ball." If, after a warning by the umpire, three men are awarded first base in one inning on such called balls, the game shall be declared a forfeit.

Player/Eligible Players who have been constitutionally expelled from another club for dishonorable conduct shall not be permitted to play in any game played during the year they were expelled.

Player/Position The fielders may take any position in the field their captain may choose to assign them.

Note: This rule made it clear that the captains could position their players anywhere in the field they wished, including foul territory. The rule, with an obvious omission, was rectified in 1874 with the added phrase, "with the exception of the pitcher, who must occupy his appointed position."

Runner/Advancing Baserunners, on caught fly balls, may advance after they return to their original base after the ball has been settled momentarily in the hands of the pitcher. Baserunners shall not be entitled to any base touched after a fair fly ball has been hit and prior to the catch being made.

Runner/Fielder When a fielder, holding the ball, tags a runner who is off a base but the ball is knocked out of his hand by the runner, the runner is still out.

Runner/Overrunning First A baserunner touching and overrunning first base shall be allowed to return at once to the base

without being put out, provided he does not attempt to make second base.

Strike Zone The batter is allowed to call for either a "high" or "low" pitch, and the pitcher must deliver the ball as required. A "high" ball is one pitched between the waist and the shoulder of the batter; a "low" ball is one pitched between the knee and the waist. Should the batter refuse to swing at balls pitched over the home base and within the specified reach of the bat, it shall be a called "strike." All pitches over the home base that are between the batter's knee and shoulder are considered "fair" pitches.

No strike shall be called when the pitch is struck at for the purpose of willfully striking out.

Note: This sentence was deleted from the rules in 1874.

No strike shall be called on the first pitch delivered unless the batter swings at the pitch.

Note: This one was dropped in 1875.

Substitute/Runner No player shall be allowed to have a substitute run the bases for him, except for illness or injury, unless by special consent of the opposing captain.

1872

Ball The ball must weigh from 5 to 5¼ ounces and measure from 9 to 9¼ inches in circumference.

Note: These are the dimensions of today's ball.

The ball shall contain one ounce of vulcanized rubber in mold form.

If the ball becomes ripped, out of shape, or, in the umpire's opinion, unfit for play, the umpire shall call for a new ball at the end of a complete inning.

Bases Home base shall be made of white marble or stone and fixed in the ground so as to be even with the surface.

Bat A batter shall be privileged to use his own private bat exclusively. No player of the opposing club shall have any claim to the use of the bat except by consent of the owner.

Note: This rule was dropped in 1874.

Batter/Illegal Act The batter is out if he willfully "balks" [interferes with] the catcher.

Batter/Position When striking at the ball, the batter is allowed to make a backward step as well as a forward step as long as he keeps one foot on either side of the line.

Coach The umpire shall require members of the side at bat to remain a reasonable distance (at least fifteen feet) from the foul lines while directing the movements of baserunners to prevent the interference of fielders. If a club persists in infringing this rule, the umpire shall declare a forfeit.

Dead Balls Foul balls are dead and are not in play until the ball has been settled in the hands of the pitcher, no matter in what part of the field the pitcher may happen to be.

Forfeited Game It is not a forfeit if a club fails to play because of the death of a club member or because of an unavoidable accident.

Note: This rule was dropped in 1876.

Game/Drawn Clubs are no longer allowed to mutually agree to call a game a draw. Drawn games may only be declared if, after five or more innings, the game is prevented from being continued because of darkness, rain, or other cause, and the score is equal on the even innings played.

Game/Rain Should rain begin to fall during a game, the umpire must promptly note the time and should the rain continue to fall for five minutes, the umpire shall suspend play and the game shall not continue until, in the umpire's opinion, the ground is fit for fair fielding.

Interference/Offensive Any player who designedly [*willfully* and *intentionally* are used in subsequent years] lets the ball hit him or kicks the ball while at bat or running the bases, thus preventing an opponent from holding or fielding the ball, shall be declared out. Any baserunner who, in any way, prevents a fielder from catching a batted fly ball, fair or foul, shall be called out.

Pitcher/Delivery   The pitcher must deliver the ball while within the lines of his position and must remain within them until the ball has left his hand. He shall not make any motion to deliver the ball while outside the box.

Whenever the pitcher delivers the pitch with an overhand or roundarm throw, the umpire shall call a "foul balk." Should the pitcher persist in such action, the umpire, after warning him of the penalty, shall declare the game forfeited. Baserunners are awarded one base on "foul balks" as on any other balk.

Note: This rule legalized the jerk, wrist snap, and bent-elbow deliveries and, thus, the curveball. It was now legal for the pitcher to snap his wrist as long as he kept his hand, while in the forward motion, below the hip.

Pitcher/Position   Iron plates must be placed at each end of the front line of the pitcher's box.

Player/Eligible   Any player who has willfully broken a written engagement to a club shall not be eligible to play in any game during the year the engagement was made. No engagement shall be considered binding unless made in writing and signed by at least two witnesses. This rule shall be binding unless rescinded by the judiciary committee.

Runner/Overrunning First   A runner may overrun first base without being put out if, after touching first, he runs straight down the line or to the right of the bag. Should he turn to the left or attempt to make second base, he shall be at risk of being put out.

Strike Zone   All pitches that come within one foot of the batter shall be called "balls."

All pitches that are sent in over home base at the height called for by the batter and are not delivered with an overhand throw or round-arm delivery as in cricket are "fair" pitches. Should the batter fail to call either a "high" or "low" pitch, no "ball" shall be called for "fair" pitches.

A "low" ball is a pitch between the waist of the batter and one foot from the ground.

Substitute/Runner   No player shall be allowed a substitute in running the bases, except for illness or injury, unless by special consent of the opposing captain; and in such case the captain shall select the player to run as substitute.

Umpire/Duties   The umpire is required to call all foul balls, while the ball is still in the air, as soon as he sees the ball is falling in foul territory.

Umpire/Replacing   The umpire shall not be changed during the game, unless with the consent of both captains, except for illness or injury or for violation of the rules.

1873

Interference/Spectator   If a ball is stopped in any way by a person not engaged in the game, no player can be put out until the ball has been first settled in the hands of the pitcher while he stands within the lines of his position.

Fielder/Illegal Act   If a fielder stops the ball with his hat or cap, no player can be put out and each baserunner shall be entitled to one base.

1874

Ball   The yarn used in the composition of the ball must be woolen.

The visiting club furnishes the ball for a series of games; the home team when only a single game is played.

Base   Home base must have one corner facing the pitcher's position.

Base on Balls   Note: In 1874 there were two classifications of base on balls. See explanation under *Strike Zone*.

Bat   The bat must be made wholly of wood.

Note: This made it clear that the bat must be made entirely of wood. Any metal or other material on it renders it illegal.

Batter/Fails to Bat   Any batter refusing to bat within three minutes after the umpire has called for him shall be declared out.

Batter/Position   The batter's position shall be a space on either side of home base, six feet long by three feet wide, which extends three feet in front and three feet behind the line drawn through the center of home base, and its nearest line one foot from home base. Batters must stand within this position when in the act of striking the ball.

Note: This introduces the batter's box.

Batter/Runner   When the batsman has fairly struck a fair ball, he shall vacate his position and is considered a baserunner until he is put out or scores his run.

Batting Order   The batsmen must take their positions in the order in which they are named on the scorebook.

Any batsman failing to take his position in the order of striking, unless by reason of illness or injury or by consent of the opposing captain, shall be declared out, unless the error is discovered before a fair ball has been hit or the batter is put out.

Catch   Should the umpire be unable to see whether a catch has been fairly made, he shall be privileged to appeal to the bystanders and render his decision according to the fairest testimony at command.

Coach/Offensive Team   The umpire shall require members of the batting side, who are not at bat or running the bases, to keep at a distance of at least fifty feet from the foul lines, or farther if the umpire desires. The captain and one assistant only are permitted to approach the foul lines, and not nearer than fifteen feet, to coach baserunners. If a club persists in infringing this rule, the umpire shall declare a forfeit.

Dead Ball   All pitches that touch the striker's bat without being swung at, or touch the batter while he is standing in his box, or which hit the umpire, shall be considered dead balls. No base shall be run or run scored on such balls. Pitches that strike the umpire are not dead balls unless the ball passes the catcher.

Should the batter swing at or hit any pitch on which a "ball" has been called, the umpire shall disregard his call and render his decision on the swing or hit made. It is not a dead ball.

Fielder/Illegal Act   Should any fielder stop the ball with his hat, cap, or any other part of his dress, the umpire shall call "dead ball" and the ball shall not be in play again until the umpire calls "ball in play." Baserunners are entitled to the base they were running for.

Forfeited Game   Any game in which the umpire declares any section of these rules to have been willfully violated, he shall at once declare the game a forfeit.

Gambling   Any player who shall, in any way, be interested in any bet or wager on the game in which he takes part, either as umpire, player, or scorer, or who purchases or has purchased for him any "pool" or chance, sold or given away, on the game in which he takes part, he shall be dishonorably expelled from both his club and the association [league in 1876]. Umpires, players, and scorers who have wagers on any other association [league] game shall be suspended for the season.

Ground Rules   Before calling "play," the umpire shall ask the home field captain whether there are any special ground rules and shall take note of such rules and see that they are enforced, provided they do not conflict with any regular rules of the game. Should the umpire not be notified of any ground rules, the rules shall not be enforced.

Note: This last sentence was dropped from the 1876 rule book.

Grounds The foul ball lines shall be unlimited in length and shall run from the center of home base through the center of first and third bases to the foul ball posts, which shall be located at the boundary of the field and within the range of home and first base, and home and third base. Said lines shall be marked from base to base with chalk, or some other white substance, so as to be plainly seen by the umpire.

Interference/Spectator Should the ball be willfully stopped by any outside person not engaged in the game, the ball shall be dead until settled in the hands of the pitcher while standing in his box. Baserunners at the time shall be entitled to the base they were running for.

Pitcher/Delivery The ball must be delivered with the arm swinging nearly perpendicular [parallel] to the side of the body.

Should the pitcher deliver the ball by an overhand throw, outward swing of the arm, roundarm bowling, or any other swing other than nearly perpendicular to the body, it shall be a "foul balk." When a foul balk is called, the umpire shall warn the pitcher of the penalty and should three foul balks be called in one inning, the umpire shall declare a forfeit.

If the pitcher makes any motion to deliver the ball and fails to do so—except if the ball is accidentally dropped—the umpire shall call a balk.

Pitcher/Position Each corner of the pitcher's box must be marked by a flat six-inch square iron plate.

Player/Eligible Players must not have been members of any other club in the association for sixty days prior to the date of the game, unless their previous club has disbanded and their contract with such club has been canceled.

The rules of 1874 also include other rules concerning contracts including disciplinary actions for players who violate them.

Runner A player running the bases shall be considered holding a base—entitled to occupy it—until he has regularly touched the next base in order.

Note: This new rule is inaccurate because it neglects to mention the important exception of runners forced off their base. This correction would not be made until 1880.

Runner/Foul Ball In the case of a foul ball, the baserunner returning to touch the base must remain on it until the ball is held by the pitcher, no matter in what part of the field the pitcher happens to be.

Runner/Overrunning First The batter may overrun first base without risk of being put out provided he makes no attempt to run to second base and returns at once to first base.

Run Scored No run shall score unless the home base is touched before three players have been put out; and if the third player is put out before reaching first base, the run shall not be scored.

Spectators No person not engaged in the game shall be permitted to occupy any position within the lines of the field, or in any way interrupt the umpire during the game.

Strike Zone There are now two classifications of unfair pitches: "balls" and "wide balls."

"Balls" are pitches not at the height called for by the batter ("high" or "low") or are not exactly over home base. "Wide balls" are pitches that are out of the reach of the striker's bat, such as those that hit the ground or the batter, or are over the batter's head. The umpire shall call every third "ball." When three "balls" [actually nine pitches] have been called, the batter is awarded first base. With the exception of the first pitch, all

"wides" are called in the order of their delivery. When three "wides" have been called, the batter is awarded first base.

Note: When you consider that one type of base on balls required three (and sometimes four) pitches, while another required nine pitches—not to mention calling strikes—it's no wonder they started paying the unfortunate umpire of 1874. "Wide balls" as a special classification of unfair pitches lasted only one year and was dropped from the rule book in 1875.

Substitute No player not in position on the field or ready to bat after the close of the third inning and before the start of the fourth, shall be substituted for another player, except in running the bases.

Substitute/Runner A player serving as substitute for another in running the bases must cross the batter's position in front of home base, and must not start to run until the batter strikes at the ball.

Note: This clarified the position in which the substitute runner must stand. In previous years, substitute runners often ran behind the batter and interfered with the catcher.

Umpire/Decisions The umpire shall render no decision except when appealed to by a player, unless expressly required to do so by the rules of the game, as in calling "balls," etc.

No player shall be permitted to converse with the umpire during the game, except to make a legal appeal for his decision in giving a player out.

No decision by the umpire on any point of play in baserunning shall be reversed upon the testimony of any player. But if it is shown by the two captains that the umpire has misinterpreted the rules or has given an erroneous decision, the umpire shall be allowed to reverse his decision.

Umpire/Payment The umpire may receive compensation for his services as the clubs deem advisable, provided he receives the same amount from both clubs.

Note: This was dropped from the rule book in 1876.

Umpire/Replacing The umpire shall not be changed during the game, except for illness or injury, or by consent of both captains if the umpire has willfully violated the written rules of the game.

Should the umpire fail to enforce any section of the rules or should he interpret the rules other than the express letter of the rule, he shall cease to be eligible to act in the position and shall at once be dismissed.

Note: This last paragraph was dropped from the 1876 rule book.

1875

Ball When the ball becomes out of shape, cut or ripped to expose the yarn, or in any way injured to be unfit for fair use, the umpire, at the close of an even inning at the request of either captain, shall call for a new ball.

Base The corner of home base facing the pitcher's position must touch the intersection of the foul lines.

Note: This places home base entirely in foul territory.

Base on Balls See *Strike Zone*.

Batter/Position The batsman's position is six feet long by three feet wide, extending two feet in front of and four feet behind the center of home base. Its nearest line is one foot from home base.

Note: With the placement of home base in foul territory, the batter's box has also been moved back.

Should the batter step outside the batter's box while striking the ball, the umpire shall call "foul strike," and two such foul strikes shall put the batter out. All baserunners are allowed to return to their original base.

Game/Rain After rain has fallen for five minutes, the umpire shall suspend play at the request of either captain.

Strike Zone All pitches not over home base or at the height called for by the batter are considered unfair "balls." Every third consecutive "ball" must be called by the umpire. When three "balls" [nine pitches] have been called, the batter is awarded first base.

Note: The term *wide balls* has been dropped from the rule book. In 1876, the word *consecutive* was dropped.

Umpire The umpire shall not enter the infield while the ball is in play.

1876

The National League is founded and adopts the rule book.

Ball In all regular match games, the balls are furnished by the home club. Should any ball used in a game prove, on examination by the umpire, to be illegal in size, weight, or materials, balls of the same manufacture shall not be used thereafter in regular match games.

The rubber used in the composition of the ball must weigh not more than one ounce.

Should the ball be lost during a game, the umpire, at the expiration of five minutes, shall call for a new ball.

Batter/Position If the batter steps outside the batter's box when he strikes at the ball, the umpire shall call "foul balk and out" and baserunners shall return to their original base.

Fielder/Illegal Act Baserunners are entitled to two bases for any fair hit ball stopped or caught by a fielder with his hat, cap, or any part of his dress. The ball is dead.

Foul Ball See *Runner/Advancing.*

Game/Rain If a game cannot be concluded, it shall be decided by the score of the last equal innings played, unless one club has completed an inning and the other club has equalled or exceeded their opponent's score in an incomplete inning, in which case the game shall be decided by the total score.

Obstruction If a baserunner is prevented from making a base by the obstruction of an adversary, he shall be entitled to that base and shall not be put out.

Pitcher/Delivery It shall be a balk if the pitcher unnecessarily delays the game by not delivering the ball.

Player/Eligible Many rules and regulations concerning eligibility of players, contracts, and disciplinary actions are removed from the rule book.

Player/Illegal Act No manager, captain, or player shall address the audience except in case of necessary explanation. Any manager, captain, or player who uses abusive, threatening, or improper language to the audience shall be punished by suspension from play for twenty days and forfeiture of his salary for such period.

Rules No section of these rules shall be construed as conflicting with or affecting any article of the league's constitution.

Runner/Advancing Following caught fly balls, runners may advance after returning to their original base. On all other foul balls, including foul balls caught on one bounce, runners may not advance but may return to their original base without being put out.

Run Scored If the third out is forced out or is put out before reaching first base, no run shall be scored.

Strikeout Should the batter, with two strikes, not swing at the next "good ball," the umpire shall not call a "strike" but warn him by calling "good ball." But should the batter swing and miss or fail to swing at the next good ball, "three strikes" must be called and the batter must run to first as in the case of hitting a fair ball.

Strike Zone The batsman, on taking his position, must call for a "high," "low," or "fair" pitch, and the umpire shall notify the pitcher to deliver the ball as required; such call cannot be changed after the first pitch is delivered.

Substitute No player taking part in the game shall be replaced by another after the start of the fourth inning, except in running the bases.

Umpire No player shall be permitted to converse with the umpire during the game, except the two captains and then only to appeal a misinterpretation of the rules or an erroneous decision.

1877

Ball No ball is to be used except those furnished by the secretary of the league.

Bases First, second, and third bases must cover a space equal to 15 inches square.

Home base is to be placed entirely into fair territory with two of its sides forming part of the foul lines.

Batter/Fails to Bat Any batsman who fails to take his position at bat within one minute after the umpire has called for him shall be out.

Batter/Position The batter's box is six feet long by three feet wide with the line of home base running through its center.

Note: This arrangement permitted a batter to stand three feet in front of or three feet behind home base.

Coach See *Grounds.*

Foul/Fair Balls A batted ball striking in foul territory and then in fair is fair; a batted ball striking fair and then foul is foul.

Game The home club shall first take the bat.

Game/Rain Should rain continue to fall for 10 minutes (following suspension of play) the game shall terminate.

Grounds Lines parallel to the foul lines and 15 feet back are to be drawn to delineate a boundary for the captain and one assistant to coach baserunners. Lines parallel to the foul lines and 50 feet back are to be drawn to delineate a boundary for players on the batting side.

Note: In the rules of 1880, these lines are referred to as the "Captain's Lines" and the "Players' Lines" respectively.

Interference/Offensive When a fielder occupies the basepath in the act of fielding a ball, the baserunner shall run out of the path and behind the fielder to avoid interference.

A baserunner struck by a batted ball is out.

A baserunner, from home to first base, shall not run inside the foul line or more than three feet outside of it, or he shall be declared out.

Player/Expulsion Any player who shall, in any way, be interested in any bet or wager on any league game or who shall purchase or have purchased for him any "pool" or chance, sold or given away, shall be expelled.

The club is entitled to the best services of the player, and players who become indifferent or careless in play or who become unable to render satisfactory service to the club from any cause may have their salaries suspended or their contracts canceled.

Players conspiring against the interest of their clubs or who "manifest a disposition" to obstruct club management may be expelled.

Note: These three rules were removed from the rule book in 1878.

Runner/Fielder A baserunner who knocks the ball out of the hand of a fielder while in the act of running to a base is no longer out.

Strike Zone A "low" pitch is one thrown belt high or below the belt and above the knee. A "high" pitch is one above the belt to the shoulder.

A ball pitched and called "dead" by reason of having struck the umpire shall be counted as one of nine called balls entitling the batter to a base if it is also an "unfair" ball.

Substitute No substitution is to be made after the start of the second inning except in cases of illness or injury.

1878

Batting Order The batsmen must take their positions in the order in which they are directed by their captain, and after each player has had one time at bat, the order established shall not be changed during the game.

Batter/Position The batter must actually hit the ball while outside the batter's box to commit a "foul strike" and be called out.

Game The club that bats first shall be determined by the two captains.

Grounds The foul lines shall be continued to the limits of the field beyond and back of home base. This triangular area shall be for the exclusive use of the catcher, umpire, and batsman; and no offensive player (except the batsman) shall occupy it.

Note: In the rules of 1880, these lines are referred to as the "Catcher's Lines."

Pitcher/Delivery The pitcher's hand must pass below the waist in delivering the ball.

Substitute/Runner No player shall be allowed a substitute in running the bases except for illness or injury incurred in the game then being played, and then such substitute shall take the player's place only after the latter has reached first base.

1879

Ball The "Spalding League Ball" is adopted as the official ball, which is indicated in the footnotes of some rule books.

Base on Balls Note: The amount of unfair pitches is still the same for the awarding of a base on balls but, to everyone's delight, the terminology is finally changed from "every third ball must be called" to "every ball must be called." The result is the same, nine "balls" and the batter is awarded first base.

Batting Order After the first inning, the first striker in each inning shall be the batsman whose name follows that of the last man who has completed his turn (time) at bat in the preceding inning.

Pitcher/Delivery The pitcher, when taking his position to deliver the ball, must face the batter.

Pitcher/Illegal Act If a pitcher delivers the ball to intentionally strike the batter, in the judgment of the umpire, the umpire shall fine the pitcher not less than $10 nor more than $50.

Pitcher/Position The pitcher's box is now four feet wide and six feet long.

1880

Appeal/Runner A baserunner who fails to touch intervening bases when returning to a base shall not be declared out unless the opposing captain appeals to the umpire before the pitcher delivers the ball to the batter.

Base on Balls A base on balls is awarded to the batter when eight balls have been called by the umpire.

Grounds The ground must be an enclosed field sufficient in size to enable each player to play in his position as required by the rules.

Interference/Offensive No run can be scored if a baserunner is declared out for being hit with a fair hit batted ball.

Runner/Returning The baserunner is out if he fails to return to the base he occupied after a foul fly has been caught and the runner is touched with the ball or the ball is returned to the base the runner occupied before he returns.

Strikeout The batter becomes a runner immediately when three strikes have been called by the umpire.

The batter is out when the umpire calls three strikes and the catcher momentarily holds the ball before it touches the ground, or any other object other than a fielder, provided the fielder has not caught it in his hat.

Umpire No player except the captain or his assistant shall address the umpire concerning any point of play. Violators are subject to a fine.

1881

Base on Balls A batter is awarded first base after seven balls are called by the umpire.

Forfeited Game Every club shall furnish sufficient police force upon its own grounds to preserve order. In the event of a crowd entering the field during the progress of a game, and interfering with play in any manner, the visiting club may refuse to play further until the field is cleared; if the ground is not cleared within 15 minutes, the visiting club is entitled to a forfeit by a score of 9–0, regardless of the number of innings played.

Pitcher/Position The pitcher's box is to be fifty feet from the center of home base.

Security See *Forfeited Game*.

Spectators No person shall be allowed upon any part of the field during the progress of the game, in addition to the nine players on each side and the umpire, except such officers of the law who are present in uniform to preserve the peace.

Substitute A substitute is not permitted unless a player is disabled by injury or illness in the game being played.

Substitute/Runner A player shall not have a substitute run the bases for him.

Umpire/Decisions The umpire shall *not* reverse his decision on any point of play upon the testimony of any player or bystander.

1882

The American Association begins its first season and makes several modifications to the rule book to meet its own needs and wants. Among the rules not included in the AA rule book are the prohibition of liquor being sold on club grounds, and the fining of pitchers who, in the umpire's judgment, purposely hit batters with pitched balls. Other changes and amendments particular to the AA are noted below.

Ball Should the ball become so injured as to be unfit for fair use in the opinion of the umpire, on being appealed to by either captain, a new ball shall be called for by the umpire at the end of an even inning.

Note: The AA's rule doesn't require an appeal by a captain.

Ball (American Association) The ball must be stamped "American Association." Each ball shall be enclosed in a paper box and sealed by the manufacturer. The seal shall not be broken except by the umpire in the presence of the two captains after "play" has been called.

Note: The AA selected the Mahn Sporting Company's ball as its official ball.

Batter The two players following the batsman, in the order in which they are named on the scorebook, must be ready with bat in hand to promptly take their position as batsmen.

Note: This rule was not adopted by the AA.

Game/"Time" The umpire shall suspend play for an accident to himself or a player; but in case of an accident to a fielder, time shall not be called until the ball is returned and held by the pitcher standing in his position.

Note: The AA rule book does not include this important exception.

Grounds/Bench   The players' bench must be furnished by the home club and placed on a portion of the ground outside the players' lines. It must be twelve feet in length and fastened to the ground. Bat racks sufficient in size to hold twenty bats are to be adjacent to the players' bench.

Note: This is not in the AA rule book.

Grounds/Three-Foot Line   The three-foot line area, in which the batter-runner must run to avoid interference, must be marked on the field.

Note: The rules of the AA do not require the actual markings.

Interference/Offensive   A baserunner is out if he obstructs a fielder attempting to field a batted ball; provided that if two or more fielders attempt to field the ball and the runner comes in contact with one of them, the umpire shall determine which fielder is entitled to the benefit of the rule and shall not call the runner out for coming in contact with the other fielder.

Note: This provision isn't included in the AA rules.

The batter is out if he plainly attempts to hinder the catcher from catching the ball, without effort to make a fair hit.

Note: Not outlined in the AA rules.

Interference/Spectator   A "blocked ball" is a batted or thrown ball that is stopped or handled by any person not engaged in the game. Whenever a block is called, baserunners may run the bases without being put out until the ball is returned to and held by the pitcher standing in his position. Exception: When the person not engaged in the game retains possession of the ball or throws or kicks it beyond reach of fielders, the umpire should call time and require baserunners to stop at the last base touched by them.

Note: The AA does not use the term *blocked ball* and uses the following rule for spectator interference: "If a batted or thrown ball is stopped by any person not engaged in the game, the ball shall not be considered in play until it is held by the pitcher standing in his position. The baserunner shall be entitled to take one base."

Spectators   Spectators hissing or hooting at the umpire are to be promptly ejected from the grounds.

1883

Ball   In calling for a new ball, replacing one unfit for fair play, the umpire may call for one "at once" and does not have to wait until the end of the inning.

Note: The AA here still requires the umpire to wait until the close of an inning before calling for a new ball.

Ball (American Association)   The ball must be manufactured by A. J. Reach, according to the specifications, and stamped "American Association."

Note: The Mahn ball was found unsatisfactory.

Batter/Caught Foul   A batted ball in foul territory must be caught on the fly to be declared an out.

Note: Foul balls caught on one bounce are no longer outs. The AA refuses to go along with the rule and continues with the one-bound foul flyout.

Batting Order   The batter is out if he fails to take his position at bat in the order of batting, unless the error is discovered and the proper batsman takes his position before a fair hit has been made. In such case, the "balls" and "strikes" called will be counted in the time at bat of the proper batsman.

Note: This last sentence is not included in the AA rule book.

Pitcher/Delivery   A fair ball is a ball delivered by the pitcher, while wholly within the lines of his position, and while facing the

batsman and his hand, in delivering the ball, must not pass above the line of his shoulder.

When the umpire has called two "foul balks," the batter and all baserunners are awarded one base. Three foul balks in one inning no longer constitutes a forfeited game.

Note: The AA discards the term "foul balk."

Runner/Overrunning First   In the American Association a runner touching and overrunning first base is at risk of being put out while off the base if he turns to the left from the foul line while returning to the bag.

Runner/Returning   A baserunner who fails to return to his base at a run following a foul ball is liable to be put out by being touched by the ball while off his base.

Substitute/Runner   The American Association allows a substitute to run the bases for a player if the player is injured in the game being played and the opposing club consents to the use of a substitute runner.

Umpire   Umpires are to be salaried employees.

1884

In 1884 the Union Association became operational and adopted virtually the same rule book used by the American Association. The few exceptions include the additional rule requiring foul balls to be caught on the fly to record an out, and the Wright & Ditson ball as the league's official ball. The Union Association folded after one season.

Base on Balls   The batter is awarded a base on balls after six balls have been called by the umpire. Note: The AA and UA retain the seven-ball base on balls.

Bat Boy/Girl   The American Association allows "a person to take charge of the bats of each club" to be on the playing field.

Note: Not in the UA rule book.

Fair/Foul Balls   When a batted ball passes outside the grounds, the umpire shall declare it fair should it disappear within, or foul should it disappear outside of the range of the foul lines.

Note: This is not found in the AA and UA rule books.

Hit by Pitch   The American Association adds the following rule: If a batsman be solidly hit by a ball from the pitcher when he evidently cannot avoid the same, he shall be given his base by the umpire.

Note: The PA is the first league to award a batter first base for being hit with a pitch; not in the UA rule book.

Pitcher/Delivery   All restrictions on the delivery of the ball are lifted except that the pitcher must be entirely within the lines of his position and must face the batter.

Note: The overhanded delivery was thus permitted for the first time. The AA and UA kept the shoulder-high delivery.

1885

Bases   The home base may be made of white rubber or stone.

Note: In the AA, home base must be made of white rubber only.

Bat   The handle of the bat may be wound with twine not to exceed 18 inches from the end.

Note: No such rule in the AA rule book.

The bat must be round except that a portion of the surface on one side may be flat.

Note: The AA nixed this one also.

Batter/Position   The batter's box is now six feet long by four feet wide with its nearest line six inches from home base.

Note: The AA keeps the six by three foot box that is one foot from the plate.

Game   The American Association gives the option of which club bats first to the home team captain.

Grounds/Fence   A fair batted ball that goes over the fence at a distance less than 210 feet from home base shall entitle the batsman to two bases. A distinctive line shall be marked on the fence at this point.

Note: This is not in the AA rule book.

Grounds/Three-Foot Line   The American Association requires the marking of the three-foot area in which the batsman must run to avoid interference.

Home Run/Double   See *Grounds/Fence.*

Pitcher/Delivery   The pitcher must have both feet touching the ground while making any one of the series of motions he is accustomed to make in the delivery of the ball. A violation of this rule shall be a "foul balk" and two foul balks entitles the batter and each runner to one base.

Note: The AA doesn't require their pitchers to keep both feet on the ground during delivery.

A balk is made whenever the pitcher, when about to deliver the ball to the bat while standing in his position, makes any one of the series of actions he habitually makes in delivery, and he fails to deliver the ball to the bat.

Uniforms (American Association)   Every club shall be required to adopt a neat and attractive uniform for its players, and shall at all times be required to present the same upon the field in a clean and attractive condition.

1886

Ball   Should the ball be knocked outside of the enclosure or lost during the game, the umpire shall call at once for another ball.

Bat/Handle   A granulated substance may be applied to the bat handle not to exceed 18 inches from the end.

Batter/Position   The batter's box is returned to the six foot long by three foot wide area, one foot from home base.

Base on Balls   It's back to seven balls to be awarded a base on balls.

Pitcher/Delivery   The pitcher is no longer required to keep both feet on the ground while delivering the ball.

Note: The term "foul balk" is dropped from the rules.

Pitcher/Position   The pitcher's lines must be straight lines forming a box seven feet long by four feet wide.

1887

The National League and the American Association agree to be governed by the same rule book after several rules are rewritten.

Ball   In all games, the ball or balls played with shall be furnished by the home club, and the last ball in play becomes the property of the winning club. Each ball to be used in championship games shall be examined, measured, and weighed by the Secretary of the Association, enclosed in a paper box, and sealed with the seal of the Secretary, which seal shall not be broken except by the umpire in the presence of the captains of the two contesting nines after play has been called.

Note: The Spalding and Reach balls respectively remain the official balls of the National League and the American Association.

For each championship game, two balls shall be furnished by the home club to the umpire for use. When the ball in play is batted over the fence or stands, onto foul ground out of sight of the players, the other ball shall be immediately put into play by the umpire. As often as one of the two in use shall be lost, a new one must be substituted, so that the umpire may at all times, after the game begins, have two for use. The moment the umpire delivers the alternate ball to the catcher or pitcher, it comes into play, and shall not be exchanged until it, in turn, passes out of sight onto foul ground.

Base on Balls   The batter is entitled to one base when five balls have been called by the umpire.

Bases   Home base must be made of whitened rubber.

Second base shall be upon its corner of the infield, and the center of the first and third bases shall be on lines running to and from second base and 7½ inches from the foul lines, providing that each base shall be entirely within the foul lines.

Batter/Position   The batter's box is again made four feet wide by six feet long.

Coach/Position   The captain's or coacher's lines must be 15 feet from and parallel with the foul lines and should commence 75 feet distant from the catcher's line. Should the captain or coacher willfully fail to remain in said bounds, he shall be fined by the umpire $5 for each such offense, except upon an appeal by the captain from the umpire's decision upon a misinterpretation of the rules.

The captains and coachers are restricted in coaching to the baserunner only, and are not allowed to address any remarks except to the baserunner, and then only in words of necessary direction; no player shall use language which will, in any manner, refer to or reflect upon a player of the opposing club or the audience. To enforce the above, the captain of the opposing side may call the attention of the umpire to the offense and upon a repetition of the same the club shall be debarred from further coaching during the game.

Foul Ball   See last paragraph under *Strike Zone.*

Game   The choice of innings is given to the home team captain.

No game is to be begun later than two hours before sunset.

The players of each club in a match game shall be nine in number, and in no case shall less than nine men be allowed to play on each side.

Game/Rain   The home club captain shall be the sole judge of the fitness of the ground for beginning a game after rain.

Game/"Time"   The umpire may call "timeout" to enforce order in case of annoyance from spectators.

Grounds/Foul Lines   The foul lines must be drawn in straight lines from the outer corner of home base along the outer edges of the first and third bases to the boundaries of the ground.

Note: Also see *Coach* for "Coacher's Lines."

Hit by Pitch   The batter is entitled to take first base if his person or clothing is hit by a ball from the pitcher, unless in the umpire's opinion he intentionally permitted himself to be hit.

Interference/Offensive   The baserunner is out if he intentionally interferes with a thrown ball.

Pitcher/Delivery   The pitcher shall take his position facing the batsman, with both feet squarely on the ground, the right foot on the rear line of the "box," his left foot in advance of the right, and to the left of an imaginary line from his right foot to the center of the home base. He shall not raise his right foot, unless in the act of delivering the ball, nor make more than one step in such delivery. He shall hold the ball, before delivery, fairly in front of his body, and in sight of the umpire. In the case of a lefthanded pitcher, the above words "left" and "right" are to be reversed. When the pitcher feigns to throw the ball to a base, he must resume the above position and pause momentarily before delivering the ball to the bat.

Any motion made by the pitcher to deliver the ball to the bat without delivering it is a balk, and shall be held to include any and every accustomed motion with the hands, arms, or feet, or position of the body assumed by the pitcher in his delivery of the ball, and any motion calculated to deceive a baserunner, except the ball be accidentally dropped.

It is a balk if the ball be held by the pitcher so long as to delay the game unnecessarily. It is a balk if the pitcher makes any motion to deliver the ball to the bat when any part of his person is upon grounds outside of the lines of his position, including all preliminary motions with the hands, arms, and feet. The batter becomes a baserunner after any illegal delivery of a ball by the pitcher.

Pitcher/Position The pitcher's box is now 5½ feet long by four feet wide.

Player/Illegal Act No umpire, manager, captain, or player shall address the audience during the progress of a game, except in case of necessary explanation.

Runner/Overrunning First If the baserunner overruns first base and turns to his left from the foul line, he may be put out in returning to the base or in attempting to advance.

Runner/Returning Baserunners need not return to their bags on the run following a foul ball etc., provided they do not unnecessarily delay the game.

Spectators No person shall be allowed upon any part of the field during the progress of a game, in addition to the players in uniform, the manager on each side, and the umpire; except such officers of the law as may be present in uniform, and such officials of the home club as may be necessary to preserve the peace.

Strikeout The batter is out after four strikes are declared by the umpire.

Strike Zone The batter can no longer call for a "high" or "low" pitch.

A "fair" ball (strike) is defined as a legally pitched ball that passes over home base "not lower than the batsman's knee, nor higher than his shoulder."

A strike is called when the batter makes any obvious attempt to make a foul hit.

Umpire/Decisions No one except the captains of the contending teams can question an umpire's decision; no player other than a captain can approach or address the umpire unless required to do so. Violators may be fined $10.

The umpire cannot reverse his decision by the testimony of a player or spectator. However, the umpire may consult a player on the question before rendering his decision.

Uniforms/Shoes Every club shall be required to adopt uniforms for its players. Each player shall be required to present himself upon the field during the game in a neat and clean condition, but no player shall attach anything to the sole or heel of his shoes other than the ordinary baseball shoe plate.

1888

Interference/Offensive If a fair hit ball strikes the baserunner before touching a fielder, the runner shall be declared out—however, in such case, no base shall be run unless forced by the batter becoming a baserunner, and no run shall be scored.

Note: In 1890, the rule was amended with the additional phrase, "and no other baserunner put out." This clarified that the batter could not be thrown out nor any possible double play could be made on such a play.

Strikeout The batter is out after three strikes are declared by the umpire.

The batter is out if, while making the third strike, the ball hits his person or clothing.

1889

Base on Balls A batter is entitled to take first base when four balls have been called by the umpire.

Foul Tip A foul tip is defined as a foul hit not rising above the batter's head and caught by the catcher playing within 10 feet of home base. In the case of a foul tip, the batter is not out and any baserunners may return to their bases without being put out.

Pitcher/Delivery The pitcher shall take his position facing the batsman with both feet square on the ground, one foot on the rear line of the "box." He shall not raise either foot, unless in the act of delivering the ball, nor make more than one step in such delivery. He shall hold the ball, before the delivery fairly in front of his body, and in sight of the umpire. When the pitcher feigns to throw the ball to a base, he must resume the above position and pause momentarily before delivering the ball to the bat.

Substitute One player, whose name shall be printed on the scorecard as an extra player, may be substituted at the end of any complete inning by either club, but the player retired shall not thereafter participate in the game. In addition thereto, a substitute may be allowed at any time in place of a player disabled in the game then being played, by reason of illness or injury, of the nature and extent of which the umpire shall be the sole judge.

Substitute/Runner The baserunner shall not have a substitute run for him, except by consent of the captains of the contesting teams.

1890

In 1890, the Players League was in operation for its one and only season, for which they adopted the rule book and made several modifications.

Ball The Players League used the "Keefe ball" as its official ball.

Ball/Defacing At no time shall the ball be intentionally discolored by rubbing it with the soil or otherwise.

Note: This rule was not in the Players League rule book.

Forfeited Game (Players League) If a club fails to begin play within one minute after the umpire calls "play" at the start of the game, unless such delay is unavoidable, the game shall be declared a forfeit.

If the club fails to resume play within five minutes after the umpire has called "play" (following suspension of play), the game shall be declared a forfeit.

Note: The NL and AA rule book allowed for just the opposite before declaring a forfeit—five minutes at the start of the game, one minute after suspended play.

Pitcher/Delivery The Players League deleted the following line from its rule book: "He [the pitcher] shall not raise either foot, unless in the act of delivering the ball."

Note: See 1889 *Pitcher/Delivery*.

Pitcher/Position (Players League) The pitcher's lines must be six feet long by four feet wide, its forward line distant fifty-one feet from the center of home base. Each corner of the "box" must be marked by a wooden peg.

Substitute Two players, whose names shall be printed on the scorecard as extra players, may be substituted at any time by either club, but no player so retired shall thereafter participate in the game.

Note: The Players League applied this rule but required the substitution to be made at the end of a complete inning.

Umpire (Players League) There shall be two umpires at every championship game; one shall stand behind the bat and the other shall stand in the field.

Note: Leave it to the players to understand the importance of having at least two umpires on the field of play.

1891

Substitute Each team is required to have one or more substitutes available.

1892

Coach A team is permitted to have not more than two coaches who may be one player participating in the game and any other player under contract to the club.

Coaches are not to use language which in any manner refers to or reflects upon spectators.

Dead/Live Ball A legally delivered fair ball that touches the bat of the batter in his position shall be considered a batted ball and in play.

Forfeited Game A forfeit shall be declared if a team resorts to dilatory practices in order to gain time, for the purpose of having the game called on account of darkness or rain or for any reason whatsoever.

Game "No Game" shall be declared by the umpire if he shall terminate play on account of rain or darkness before five innings on each side are completed, except in a case when the game is called, the club second at bat shall have more runs at the end of its fourth inning than the club first at bat made in its five innings, then the umpire shall award the game to the club having made the greatest number of runs, and it shall be a game and be so counted in the championship record.

Grounds/Fence A fair batted ball that goes over the fence shall entitle the batter to a home run; except that should it go over the fence at a distance less than 235 feet from home base, the batter is entitled to only two bases. A distinctive line is to be marked on the fence showing the required point.

Hit by Pitch The batter becomes a baserunner if, while he be a batsman, his person—excepting hands or forearm, which makes it a dead ball—or clothing be hit by a ball from the pitcher, unless, in the opinion of the umpire, he intentionally permits himself to be so hit.

Home Run/Double See *Grounds/Fence.*

Interference/Offensive The batter is out if he attempts to hinder the catcher from fielding or throwing the ball by stepping outside the lines of his position or otherwise obstructing or interfering with the catcher.

Player/Bench Players' benches must be located at least 25 feet back of the players' lines.

1893

Bat The bat must be made wholly of hard wood except that the handle may be wound with twine, or a granulated substance applied, not to exceed 18 inches from the end. It must be round, not to exceed 2½ inches in diameter in the thickest part, and must not exceed 42 inches in length.

Note: Bats with a flat side are now illegal.

Batting Order The batsmen must take their positions within the batsmen's lines in the order in which they are named in the batting order, which batting order must be submitted by the captains of the opposing teams to the umpire before the game, and when approved by him this batting order must be followed except in the case of a substitute player, in which case the substitute must take the place of the original player in the batting order. After the first inning the first striker (batter) in each inning shall be the batsman whose name follows that of the last man who has completed his turn—time at bat—in the preceding inning.

Pitcher/Delivery The pitcher shall take his position facing the batter with both feet square on the ground, and in front of the pitcher's plate but in the act of delivering the ball one foot must be in contact with the pitcher's plate.

A balk is any motion in delivering the ball to the bat by the pitcher while not in the required position.

Pitcher/Position The pitcher's boundary shall be marked by a white rubber plate 12 inches long and 4 inches wide so fixed in the ground as to be even with the surface at the distance of *60 feet 6 inches* from the outer corner of the home plate, so that a line drawn from the center of the home base and the center of the second base shall give 6 inches on either side.

1894

Foul Ball See *Strike Zone.*

Grounds Detailed directions are included in the rules of 1894 for laying out a baseball diamond.

Strike Zone A strike is called when the batter makes a foul hit, other than a foul tip, while attempting a bunt hit that falls or rolls upon foul ground between home base and first or third bases.

1895

Bat The bat cannot exceed 2¾ inches in diameter.

Batting Order The batsman is out if he fails to take his position at the bat in his order of batting, unless the error be discovered and the proper batsman takes his position before a time "at bat" recorded; and in such case the balls and strikes called must be counted in the time "at bat" of the proper batsman, and only the proper batsman shall be declared out. This rule shall not take effect unless the out is declared before the ball is delivered to the succeeding batsman, and no runs shall be scored or bases run, and further, no outs shall be counted other than that of the proper batsman.

Foul Tip A strike is called when a ball is tipped by the batter and caught by the catcher within the 10-foot lines.

Glove The catcher and first baseman are permitted to wear a glove or mitt of any size, shape or weight. All other players are restricted to the use of a glove or mitt weighing not over 10 ounces, and measuring in circumference around the palm of the hand not over 14 inches.

Infield Fly The batter is out if he hits a fly ball that can be handled by an infielder while first and second bases are occupied, or first, second, and third, with only one out. If the third strike is called (on attempted bunt in foul territory) the umpire shall declare infield or outfield hit.

Pitcher/Position The pitcher's plate is enlarged to 24 by 6 inches.

Strike Zone See *Foul Tip.*

Umpire Umpires may assess fines of $25 to $100 for specified misconduct by players.

1896

Ball The home club shall have at least a dozen regulation balls on the field ready for use on the call of the umpire during each game.

Game/Rain The choice of innings shall be given to the captain of the home club, who shall also be the sole judge of the fitness of the ground for beginning a game after rain, but after play has been called by the umpire he alone shall be the judge as to the fitness of the ground for resuming play after the game has been suspended on account of rain.

Pitcher/Delivery The pitcher is no longer required to hold the ball before the delivery fairly in front of his body and in the sight of the umpire.

Player/Bench No one is to occupy the players' bench under any circumstances except the club president, managers, and players in uniform.

Player/Illegal Act Players guilty of indecent or vulgar language or conduct shall be removed from the game and fined $25.

Umpire Umpires may assess fines of $5 to $10 for specified misconduct; repeat violators are to be fined $25.

1897

Ball/Defaced At no time shall the ball be intentionally discolored by rubbing it with the soil or otherwise. In the event of a new ball being intentionally discolored, or otherwise injured by a player, the umpire shall, upon appeal from the captain of the opposite side, forthwith demand the return of that ball and shall substitute another new ball and impose a fine of $5 upon the offending player.

Bunt A bunt hit is a ball delivered by the pitcher to the batsman who, while standing within the lines of his position, makes a deliberate attempt to hit the ball so slowly within the infield that it cannot be fielded in time to retire the batsman. If such a bunt hit goes to foul ground a strike shall be called by the umpire.

Defense/Illegal Act See *Ball/Defacing.*

Fair/Foul Ball A fair hit is a ball batted by the batsman— while he is standing within the lines of his position—that first touches "fair" ground, or the person of a player or the umpire while standing on fair ground, and then settles on fair ground before passing the line of first or third base.

A foul hit is a similarly batted ball that first touches "foul" ground or the person of a player or the umpire while standing on foul ground.

Should such "fair hit" ball bound or roll to foul ground before passing the line of first or third base and settle on foul ground, it shall be declared by the umpire a foul ball.

Should such "foul hit" ball bound or roll to fair ground and settle there before passing the line of first or third base, it shall be declared by the umpire a "fair ball."

Foul Tip A foul tip is a ball batted by the batsman while standing within the lines of his position that goes foul sharp from the bat to the catcher's hands.

Obstruction The baserunner shall be entitled, without being put out, to take a base in the following cases: (1) If he be prevented from making a base by the obstruction of an adversary, unless the latter be a fielder having the ball in his hand ready to meet the baserunner; (2) If the fielder stop or catch a batted ball with his hat or any part of his uniform except his gloved hand.

Runner/Bases The baserunner must touch each base in regular order, viz., first, second, third, and home bases, and when obliged to return (except on a foul hit) must retouch the base or bases in reverse order. He shall only be considered as holding a base after touching it, and shall then be entitled to hold such base until he has legally touched the next base in order or has been legally forced to vacate it for a succeeding baserunner. However, no baserunner shall score a run to count in the game until the baserunner preceding him in the batting list (provided there has been such a baserunner who has not been put out in that inning) shall have first touched home base without being put out.

Substitute In every championship game, each side shall be required to have present on the field, in uniform, a sufficient number of substitute players to carry out the provision which requires that not less than nine players shall occupy the field in any inning of a game.

Umpire The umpire shall not address the spectators at any time, except in case of necessary explanation of misunderstood decision or points of play.

Umpire/Decisions No decision, rendered by the umpire, shall be reversed by him in which the question of an error of judgment is alone involved.

Should the umpire render any decision based on an illegal interpretation of any rule of the game, the same shall be reversed on the appeal of either of the two captains, but not otherwise.

1898

Batting Order The batsman is out if he fails to take his position at the bat in his order of batting, unless the error be discovered and the proper batsman takes his position before a time "at bat" is recorded, and, in such case, the balls and strikes called must be counted in the time "at bat" of the proper batsman, and only the proper batsman shall be declared out, and no runs shall be scored or bases run because of any act of the improper batsman. Provided, this rule shall not take effect unless the out is declared before the ball is delivered to the succeeding batsman. Should the batsman declared out by this rule be sufficient to retire the side, the proper batsman the next inning is the player who would have come to bat had the players been out by ordinary play.

Pitcher/Delivery A balk shall be: (1) Any motion made by the pitcher to deliver the ball to the bat without delivering it; (2) Any delivery of the ball to the bat while his pivot foot is not in contact with the pitcher's plate; (3) Any motion in delivering the ball to the bat by the pitcher while not in the position required by the rules; (4) The holding of the ball by the pitcher so long as, in the opinion of the umpire, to delay the game unnecessarily; (5) Standing in position and making any motion to pitch without having the ball in his possession, except in the case of a "block ball"; (6) The making of any motion the pitcher habitually makes in his method of delivery, without his immediately delivering the ball to the bat; (7) If the pitcher feigns to throw the ball to a base and does not resume his legal position and pause momentarily before delivering the ball to the bat. When the pitcher feigns to throw the ball to a base he must resume the required position and pause momentarily before delivering the ball to the bat.

Player/Illegal Act Players in uniform shall not be permitted to occupy seats in the stands or to stand among the spectators.

Umpire The rules of 1898 describe in detail the responsibilities of each umpire in games where two umpires are assigned.

1899

Catcher/Position The catcher must stand within the lines of his position whenever the pitcher delivers the ball to the bat.

Foul Tip A foul tip by the batter, caught by the catcher while standing within the lines of his position is a strike.

Game If the umpire calls "Game" on account of darkness or rain at any time after five innings have been completed, the score shall be that of the last equal innings played, but if the side second at bat shall have scored in an unequal number of innings or before the completion of its unfinished inning one or more runs than the side first at bat, the score of the game shall be the total number of runs made.

Interference/Defensive The batter becomes a baserunner if the catcher interferes with him, preventing him from striking the ball.

Pitcher/Delivery In addition to the rules for "balk" promulgated in 1898, the rules of 1899 state: A balk shall be: (1) The throwing of the ball by the pitcher to any base to catch the baserunner without first stepping directly towards said base immediately before throwing the ball; (2) Any delivery of the ball to the bat by the pitcher while his pivot foot is not in contact with the pitcher's plate, and he is not facing the batsman; (3) If the pitcher delivers the ball to the bat when the catcher is standing outside the lines of the catcher's position as defined by the rules.

The batter becomes a baserunner when a balk is called by the umpire.

Player/Bench The players' benches must be furnished by the home club and placed upon a portion of the ground not less than 25 feet outside of the players' lines. One such bench shall be for the exclusive use of the visiting club, and one for the exclusive use of the home club. The benches must be covered by a roof and closed at the back and each end; a space, however, not more than six inches wide may be left just under the roof for ventilation. All players of the side at bat must be seated on their bench, except such as are legally assigned to coach baserunners, and also the batsman, except when called to the bat by the umpire, and under no circumstances shall the umpire permit any person, except managers and players in uniform to occupy seats on the benches.

Strike Zone See *Foul Tip.*

Substitute In any championship game, each side shall be required to have present on the field, in uniform, conforming to the suits worn by their teammates, a sufficient number of substitute players to carry out the provision which requires that not less than nine players shall occupy the field in any innings of a game.

Uniforms Every club shall adopt uniforms for its players, and the suit of each team shall conform in color and style. No player who shall attach anything to the sole or heel of his shoes other than the ordinary baseball shoe plate, or who shall appear in a uniform not conforming to the suits of the other members of his team, shall be permitted to take part in the game.

1900

Bases The shape of home base is changed from a 12-inch square to a five-sided shape, 17 inches wide.

Pitcher/Delivery The batter does not become a runner when the pitcher balks in throwing to pick off a runner on the bases.

Any motion made by the pitcher to deliver the ball to the bat or to first base without delivering it is a balk.

Note: This rule previously specified "any base."

1901

The American League begins operation and adopts the rule book with only a few modifications.

Catcher/Position The catcher must stand within the lines of his position whenever the pitcher delivers the ball to the bat and within 10 feet of the home base.

Note: This rule was adopted by the National League in 1901. The American League adopted the rule in 1902.

Foul Ball A foul hit ball not caught on the fly is a strike unless two strikes have already been called.

Note: This rule was used by the National League in 1901 and 1902. The American League adopted the rule in 1903. See 1902 summary for further elaboration of this rule by the National League.

A "bunt hit" which sends the ball to foul ground either directly or by bounding or rolling from fair ground to foul ground and which settles on foul ground is a strike.

Infield Fly The batter is out if he hits a fly ball that can be handled by an infielder while first and second bases are occupied, or first, second, and third, unless two hands are out. In such case the umpire shall, as soon as the ball is hit, declare infield or outfield hit.

Pitcher/Delivery If the ball is thrown by the pitcher to any player other than the catcher (except to retire a baserunner) and the batsman is standing in his proper position ready to strike at a pitched ball, each ball so delivered shall be called a ball.

The umpire shall call a ball on the pitcher each time he delays the game by failing to deliver the ball to the batsman when in position for a longer period than 20 seconds.

Strike See *Foul Ball.*

1902

Foul Ball A strike is a foul hit ball not caught on the fly unless two strikes have already been called, which falls or settles on foul ground inside or on the line of the territory described by lines

drawn from first and third bases at right angles with an imaginary line drawn from home to second base and extending on each side to the limit of the playing field.

Note: National League rule only.

A strike is any intention or effort to hit the ball to foul ground outside of the lines of the territory described by lines drawn from first and third bases at right angles with an imaginary line drawn from home to second base and extending on each side to the limit of the playing field.

The batter is out if after two strikes have been called the batter obviously attempts to make a foul hit.

Hit by Pitch The batsman becomes a baserunner if while he be a batsman, without making any attempt to strike at the ball, his person or clothing be hit by a ball from the pitcher, unless in the opinion of the umpire he plainly avoids making any effort to get out of the way of the ball from the pitcher and thereby permits himself to be so hit.

Pitcher/Delivery The umpire shall call a ball on the pitcher each time he delays the game by failing to deliver the ball to the batsman when in position for a longer period than 20 seconds, excepting that in the case of the first batsman in each inning, the pitcher may occupy not more than one minute in delivering [warm-up pitches] not to exceed five balls to a baseman.

If the ball is thrown by the pitcher to any player other than the catcher (except to retire a baserunner) after the batter is standing in his position ready to strike at a pitched ball each ball so delivered will be called a ball.

Strike/Strikeout See *Foul Ball.*

1903

Pitcher/Position The pitcher's box shall be no more than 15 inches higher than the baselines and home plate. The baselines and home plate shall be on a perfect level, and the slope from the pitcher's box towards the baselines and home plate shall be gradual.

Note: In 1904, the phrase "pitcher's box" was deleted from this rule and replaced by the phrase "pitcher's plate."

Umpire The rules of 1903 contain an extensive reorganization and rewriting of the rules pertaining to umpires.

1904

Ball Two regulation balls of the make adopted by the league of which the contesting clubs are members shall be delivered by the home club to the umpire at or before the hour for the commencement of a championship game. If the ball first placed in play be batted or thrown out of the grounds or into one of the stands for spectators or, in the judgment of the umpire, become unfit for play from any cause, the umpire shall at once deliver the alternate ball to the pitcher and another legal ball shall be supplied to him, so that he shall at all times have in his control one or more alternate balls to substitute for the ball in play in any of the contingencies above set forth. Provided, however, that all balls batted or thrown out of the ground or into a stand, shall, when returned to the field, be given into the custody of the umpire immediately and become alternate balls, and so long as he has in his possession two or more alternate balls, he shall not call for a new ball to replace a ball that has gone out of play. The alternate balls shall become the ball in play in the order in which they were delivered to the umpire.

Bunt A bunt hit is a legally batted ball, not swung at, but met with the bat and tapped slowly within the infield by the batsman with the expectation of reaching first base before the ball can be fielded to that base. If the attempt to bunt result in a foul, a strike shall be called by the umpire.

Coach/Illegal Act The baserunner is out if, before two hands are out and while third base is occupied, the coacher stationed near that base shall run in the direction of home base on or near the baseline while a fielder is making or trying to make a play on a batted ball not caught on the fly, or on a thrown ball, and thereby draws a throw to home base. The baserunner entitled to third base shall be declared out by the umpire for the coacher's interference with and prevention of the legitimate play.

Note: In 1914, the words "on a fly ball" were inserted in this rule.

Dead/Live Ball   Immediately upon the delivery to him of the alternate ball by the umpire, the pitcher shall take his position and on the call of "Play," by the umpire, it shall become the ball in play. Provided, however, that play shall not be resumed with the alternate ball when a fair batted ball or a ball thrown by a fielder goes out of the ground or into a stand for spectators until the baserunners have completed the circuit of the bases unless compelled to stop at second or third base in compliance with a ground rule.

Grounds/Fences   To obviate the necessity for ground rules, the shortest distance from a fence or stand on fair territory to home base should be 235 feet and from home base to the grandstand 90 feet.

Interference/Offensive   The baserunner is out if one or more members of the team at bat stand or collect at or around a base for which a baserunner is trying, thereby confusing the fielding side and adding to the difficulty of making such play. The baserunner shall be declared out for the interference of his teammate or teammates.

The players of the side at bat must speedily abandon their bench and hasten to another part of the field when by remaining upon or near it they or any of them would interfere with a fielder in an attempt to catch or handle a thrown ball.

Player   The players of each club, actively engaged in a game at one time, shall be nine in number, one of whom shall act as captain; and in no case shall more or less than nine men be allowed to play on a side in a game.

Note: The previous rule read, "in no case shall less than nine men be allowed to play."

Runner   The baserunner is out if he touch home base before a baserunner preceding him in the batting order, if there be such preceding baserunner, lose his right to third base.

Uniform   Every club shall adopt two uniforms for its players, one to be worn in games at home and the other in games abroad, and the suits of each of the uniforms of a team shall conform in color and style.

1905

There were no changes in the playing rules this year.

1906

Bunt   A bunt hit is a legally batted ball, not swung at, but met with the bat and tapped slowly within the infield by the batsman. If the attempt to bunt result in a foul not legally caught, a strike shall be called by the umpire.

Game/Rain   The choice of innings shall be given to the captain of the home club, who shall be the sole judge of the fitness of the ground for beginning a game after a rain; but, after play has been called by the umpire, he alone shall be the judge as to the fitness of the ground for resuming play after the game has been suspended on account of rain, and when time is so called the groundskeeper and sufficient assistants shall be under the control of the umpire for the purpose of putting the ground in proper shape for play, under penalty of forfeiture of the game by the home team.

Ground/Foul Lines   Foul lines are to be clearly visible from any part of the diamond, and no wood or other hard substance shall be used in the construction of such lines.

1907

Ball/Defaced   In the event of a ball being intentionally discolored by rubbing it with the soil or otherwise by any player except the pitcher, or otherwise damaged by any player, the umpire shall, upon appeal by the captain of the opposite side, forthwith demand the return of that ball and substitute for it another legal ball and impose a fine of $5 on the offending player.

Batter/Awarded Bases   The baserunner shall be entitled to advance one base without liability to be put out if, while the batsman, he becomes a baserunner by reason of "four balls" or for being hit by a pitched ball, or for being interfered with by the catcher in striking at a pitched ball.

Batter/Position   The batter is out if he steps from one batsman's box to the other after the pitcher has taken his position.

Batter/Runner   The batter becomes a baserunner if a fair hit ball strike the person or clothing of the umpire or a baserunner on fair ground.

Defense/Illegal Act   See *Ball/Defaced*.

Game/Legal   If the umpire calls a game at any time after five innings have been completed, the score shall be that of the last equal innings played, except that if the side second at bat shall have scored in an unequal number of innings, or before the completion of the unfinished inning, at least one run more than the side first at bat, the score of the game shall be the total number of runs each team has made.

Game/Rain   If the game be called by the umpire on account of darkness, rain, fire, panic, or for other cause which puts patrons or players in peril, the game shall terminate.

Interference/Offensive   The baserunner is out if with one or no one out and a baserunner on third base, the batsman interferes with a play being made at home plate.

See also *Batter/Runner*.

Interference/Umpire   See *Batter/Runner*.

Pitcher/Delivery   A fairly delivered ball is a ball pitched or thrown to the bat by the pitcher while standing in his position and facing the batsman that passes over any portion of the home base, before touching the ground, not lower than the batsman's knee, nor higher than his shoulder. For every such fairly delivered ball, the umpire shall call one strike.

An unfairly delivered ball is a ball delivered to the bat by the pitcher while standing in his position and facing the batsman that does not pass over any portion of the home base between the batsman's shoulder and knees, or that touches the ground before passing home base, unless struck at by the batsman. For every unfairly delivered ball the umpire shall call one ball.

Runner/Illegal Act   The baserunner is out if he passes a baserunner who is caught between two bases. He shall be declared out immediately upon passing the preceding baserunner.

1908

Ball/Defacing   The rule prohibiting the discoloring of the ball by rubbing it with the soil was amended to include the pitcher as well as all players.

1909

Dead/Live Ball   In case of a foul strike, foul hit ball not legally caught, dead ball, interference with the fielder or batsman, or a fair hit ball touching a baserunner, the ball shall not be considered in play until it be held by the pitcher standing in his position and the umpire shall have called "Play."

Fair/Foul Ball   A fair hit is a legally batted ball that settles on fair ground between home and first base or between home and third base or that is on fair ground when bounding to the outfield past first or third base or that first falls on fair territory beyond first or third base or that, while on or over fair ground, touches the person of the umpire or a player.

A foul hit is a legally batted ball that settles on foul territory between home and first base or home and third base or that bounds past first or third base in foul territory or that falls on foul territory beyond first or third base or while on or over foul ground, touches the person of the umpire or a player.

Ground Rules Before the commencement of a game the umpire shall see that the rules governing all the materials of the game are strictly observed. He shall ask the captain of the home club whether there are any special ground rules, and if there be, he shall acquaint himself with them, advise the captain of the visiting team of their scope, and see that each is duly enforced, provided that it does not conflict with any of these rules, and are acceptable to the captain of the visiting team. If the latter object to a proposed ground rule, the umpire shall have authority to adopt or reject it.

Pitcher When the umpire announces the pitcher prior to commencement of the game, the player announced must pitch until the first batsman has either been put out or has reached first base.

Player/Ejected In the event of removal of player or manager by the umpire, he shall go direct to the club house and remain there during progress of the game, or leave the grounds; and a failure to do so will warrant a forfeiture of the game by the umpire.

Relief Pitcher In event of the pitcher being taken from the game by either manager or captain, the player substituted for him shall continue to pitch until the batsman then at bat has either been put out or has reached first base.

1910

Batter/Awarded Bases The baserunner shall be entitled, without liability to be put out, to advance a base if, while the batsman, he becomes a baserunner by reason of "four balls" or for being hit by a pitched ball, or if a fair hit ball strike the person or clothing of the umpire or a baserunner on fair ground.

Batter/Position The batter is out if he steps from one batsman's box to the other while the pitcher is in his position ready to pitch.

An illegally batted ball is a ball batted by the batsman when either or both of his feet are upon the ground outside the lines of the batsman's position.

Note: This rule replaced the term "foul strike."

Batting Order The batting order of each team must be on the scorecard and must be delivered before the game by its captain to the umpire at home plate, who shall submit it to the inspection of the captain of the other side. The batting order delivered to the umpire must be followed throughout the game unless a player be substituted for another, in which case the substitute must take the place in the batting order of the retired player.

Dead/Live Ball In case of an illegally batted ball, a balk, foul hit ball not legally caught, dead ball, interference with the fielder or batsman, or a fair hit ball striking a baserunner or umpire before touching a fielder, the ball shall not be considered in play until it be held by the pitcher standing in his position, and the umpire shall have called "Play."

Fielder/Illegal Act If the fielder stop or catch a batted ball with his cap, glove, or any part of his uniform, while detached from its proper place on his person, the runner or runners shall be entitled to three bases.

Ground Rules/Spectators In case of spectators overflowing on the playing field, the home captain shall make special ground rules to cover balls batted or thrown into the crowd, provided such rules be acceptable to the captain of the visiting club. If the latter object, then the umpire shall have full authority to make and enforce such special rules, and he shall announce the scope of same to the spectators.

Interference/Offensive The baserunner shall return to his base without liability to be put out if the umpire declares the batsman or another baserunner out for interference.

Interference/Umpire If a thrown or pitched ball strike the person or clothing of an umpire on foul ground the ball shall be considered in play and the runner or runners shall be entitled to all the bases they can make.

The baserunner shall return to his base without liability to be put out if the umpire be struck by a fair hit ball before touching a fielder; in which case no base shall be run unless necessitated by the batsman becoming a baserunner, and no run shall be scored unless all the bases are occupied.

Pitcher/Delivery An unfairly delivered ball is a ball delivered to the bat by the pitcher while standing in his position and facing the batsman that does not pass over any portion of the home base between the batsman's shoulder and knees, or that touches the ground before passing home base, unless struck at by the batsman; or, with the bases unoccupied, any ball delivered by the pitcher while either foot is not in contact with the pitcher's plate. For every unfairly delivered ball the umpire shall call one ball.

Player/Position The players of the team not at bat may be stationed at any points of the field on fair ground their captain may elect, regardless of their respective positions, except that the pitcher, while in the act of delivering the ball to the bat must take his position as defined in the rules and the catcher likewise must be within the lines of his position and within 10 feet of home base whenever the pitcher delivers the ball to the bat.

Relief Pitcher In event of the pitcher being taken from his position by either manager or captain, the player substituted for him shall continue to pitch until the batsman then at bat has either been put out or has reached first base.

Runner/Awarded Bases In all cases where there are no spectators on the playing field, and where a thrown ball goes into a stand for spectators, or over or through any fence surrounding the playing field, into the players' bench (whether the ball rebounds into the field or not), the runner or runners shall be entitled to two bases. The umpire in awarding such bases shall be governed by the position of the runner or runners at the time the throw is made.

Substitute Whenever one player is substituted for another, whether as batsman, baserunner, or fielder, the captain of the side making the change must immediately notify the umpire, who in turn must announce the same to the spectators. A fine of $5 shall be assessed by the umpire against the captain for each violation of this rule, and the president of the League shall impose a similar fine against the umpire who, after having been notified of a change, fails to make proper announcement. Play shall be suspended while announcement is being made, and the player substituted shall become actively engaged in the game immediately upon his captain's notice of the change to the umpire.

Umpire The rules of 1910 contain new provisions for umpires and describe the respective duties of the Umpire-in-Chief and the Field Umpire.

1911

Ball Cork-center balls are used for the first time as regulation balls in all games.

1912-13
There were no changes in the playing rules in these years.

1914
The Federal League begins operation and adopts virtually the

entire rule book. The Victor Sporting Goods Company provides the new league's official ball. The Federal League folded after the 1915 season.

Ball League presidents are no longer required to examine, measure, and weigh baseballs for use in championship games.

Coach A coach may address words of assistance and direction to the baserunners and to the batter.

Coach/Illegal Acts If, while third base is occupied, the coacher stationed near that base shall run in the direction of home base on or near the base line while a fielder is making or trying to make a play on a batted ball not caught on the fly or on a thrown ball or a fly ball [see note below], and thereby draws a throw to home base, the baserunner entitled to third base shall be declared out by the umpire for the coacher's interference with and prevention of the legitimate play.

Note: This rule was first adopted in 1904 but did not include the phrase "or a fly ball."

If a coach at third base touch or hold a baserunner at third base or a baserunner who is rounding third base for home plate, such baserunner is out.

Fielder/Illegal Acts The baserunner is entitled to advance a base without liability to be put out if the fielder stop or catch a batted ball or a thrown ball with his cap, glove, or any part of his uniform, while detached from its proper place on his person, the runner or runners shall be entitled to three bases if a batted ball or to two bases if a thrown ball.

Home Run/Double See *Runner/Bases.*

Interference/Offensive The batter is out if he obstructs or interferes with the catcher except when he does so with a runner on third base (with one out or no one out) in which case the baserunner is out.

Interference/Umpire The baserunner shall return to his base without liability to be put out if the person or clothing of the umpire, while stationed back of the bat, interfere with the catcher in an attempt to throw.

The baserunner is entitled to advance a base if a thrown or pitched ball strike the person or clothing of an umpire. The ball shall be considered in play and the baserunner or runners shall be entitled to all the bases they can make.

Note: Under the previous rule only balls striking the umpire in foul territory entitled the baserunner to advance.

Pitcher/Delivery The pitcher is permitted to have his feet on top of the pitcher's plate or in front of the plate preliminary to pitching.

Runner/Awarded Bases In all cases where there are no spectators on the playing field, and where a thrown ball goes into a stand for spectators or over or through any fence surrounding the playing field or into the players' bench (whether the ball rebounds into the field or not) or remains in the meshes of a wire screen protecting the spectators, the runner or runners shall be entitled to two bases. The umpire in awarding such bases shall be governed by the position of the runner or runners at the time the throw is made.

Runner/Bases A batter who hits a home run or a ground-rule double must touch all of the bases in regular order.

1915–19

There were no changes in the playing rules in these years.

1920

Ball The President of the League of which the contesting clubs are members shall specify the number of baseballs which the home club must deliver to the umpire prior to the hour set for the commencement of a championship game, and all of such baseballs shall be of the regulation make adopted by the league.

The seal on boxes of new balls is not to be broken by the umpire except prior to game time and for the purpose of inspecting the ball and removing the gloss therefrom.

Ball Defacing In event of the ball being intentionally discolored by any player, either by rubbing it with the soil, or by applying rosin, paraffin, licorice, or any other foreign substance to it, or otherwise intentionally damaging or roughening the same with sandpaper or emery paper, or other substance, the umpire shall forthwith demand the return of that ball and substitute for it another legal ball, and the offending player shall be disbarred from further participation in the game. If, however, the umpire cannot detect the violator of this rule, and the ball is delivered to the bat by the pitcher, then the latter shall be at once removed from the game, and as an additional penalty shall be automatically suspended for a period of 10 days.

At no time during the progress of the game shall the pitcher be allowed to: (1) Apply a foreign substance of any kind to the ball; (2) Expectorate either on the ball or his glove; (3) Rub the ball on his glove, person, or clothing; (4) Deface the ball in any manner; (5) or to deliver what is called the "shine" ball, "spit" ball, "mud" ball, or "emery" ball. For violation of any part of this rule the umpire shall at once order the pitcher from the game, and in addition he shall be automatically suspended for a period of 10 days, on notice from the president of the League.

Note: In adopting the foregoing rule against "freak" deliveries on February 9, 1920, it was understood and agreed that all bona fide spitball pitchers would be certified to the respective presidents of the National and American leagues at least 10 days prior to April 14, 1920, and that the pitchers so certified would be exempt from the operation of the rule, as far as it related to the spitball only.

Batter/Awarded Bases The baserunner shall be entitled to advance one base if, while the batsman, he becomes a baserunner by reason of "four balls" or for being hit by a pitched ball or for being interfered with by the catcher in striking at a pitched ball or if a fair hit ball strike the person or clothing of the umpire or a baserunner on fair ground before touching a fielder. Provided, that if a fair hit ball strike the umpire after having passed a fielder or having been touched by a fielder, the ball shall be considered in play. Also, if a fair hit ball strike the umpire on foul ground, the ball shall be in play.

Catcher/Position It shall be illegal for the catcher to leave his natural position immediately and directly back of the plate for the purpose of aiding the pitcher to intentionally give a base on balls to a batsman. If the catcher shall move out of position prior to the time of the ball leaving the pitcher's hand, all runners on bases shall be entitled to advance one base.

Also see *Interference/Defensive.*

Coach See *Interference/Offensive.*

Dead Ball The baserunner shall return to his base without liability to be put out if the umpire declares a dead ball, unless it also be the fourth unfair ball, and he be thereby forced to take the next base as provided in the rules. Provided, such fourth unfair ball shall not be called if the umpire declare the ball "dead" because of a pitched ball accidentally hitting the bat.

Fair/Foul Ball A fair or foul fly must be judged according to the relative position of the ball and the foul line, and not as to whether the fielder is on fair or foul ground at the time he touches the ball.

Fielder See *Runner Tagged.*

Force Out A force out can be made only when a baserunner legally loses the right to the base he occupies by reason of the batsman becoming a baserunner, and he is thereby obliged to advance.

Game/Doubleheader Whenever necessity demands that two

games be played in one afternoon, the first game shall be the regularly scheduled game for that day.

Game/Drawn A drawn game shall be declared by the umpire if the score is equal on the last even inning played when he terminates play in accordance with the rules after five or more equal innings have been played by each team. But if the side that went second to bat is at bat when the game is terminated, and has scored the same number of runs as the other side, the umpire shall declare the game drawn without regard to the score of the last equal inning. Provided, that if the side last at bat shall, before the completion of the fifth inning, equal the score made by the opposing side in five complete innings then the game shall be declared as legally drawn, and the individual and team averages shall be incorporated in the Official Playing Records.

Game/Legal "No Game" shall be declared by the umpire if he terminates play in accordance with the rules before five innings are completed by each team. Provided, however, that if the club second at bat shall have made more runs at the end of its fourth inning, or before the completion of its fifth inning, than the club first at bat made in five completed innings of a game so terminated, the umpire shall award the game to the club having made the greater number of runs, and it shall count as a legal game in the championship record.

Game/"Time" The rules of 1920 contain several new provisions governing the calling of "Time" by the umpire, the most important of which is the following: That in case of an accident to a player or players in attempting to make a play on either a batted or a thrown ball, "Time" shall not be called until, in the judgment of the umpire, no further play is possible.

Hit by Pitch A "dead" ball is a ball delivered to the bat by the pitcher, not struck at by the batsman, that touches any part of the batsman's person or clothing while he is standing in his position or a wildly pitched ball which the batsman plainly makes an attempt to dodge to avoid being hit, but which ball accidentally hits his bat.

Home Run/Game-Ending If a batsman, in the last half of the final inning of any game, hit a home run over the fence or into a stand, all runners on the bases at the time, as well as the batsman, shall be entitled to score, and in such event all bases must be touched in order, and the final score of the game shall be the total number of runs made.

Infield Fly If, before two hands are out, while first and second or first, second, and third bases are occupied, he hit a fair fly ball, other than a line drive, that can be handled by an infielder, the batter is out. In such case, the umpire shall, as soon as the ball be hit, declare it an infield or outfield hit; but the runners may be off their bases or advance at the risk of the ball being caught, the same as on any other fly ball. Provided, that with first and second bases occupied, with less than two out, any attempt to bunt which results in a fair fly ball shall not be regarded as an infield fly.

Interference/Defensive In the event a baserunner is trying to score from third base on a pitched ball or the "squeeze" play, a "balk" and also an "interference" should be called if the catcher runs out in front of the plate to catch the ball; the runner shall be allowed to score and the batsman entitled to first base. The same penalties must be imposed in case the catcher pushes the batsman out of the way or tips his bat.

Interference/Offensive The baserunner is out if, in the judgment of the umpire, the coacher at third base by touching or holding the runner physically assists him in returning to or leaving third base. The runner, however, should not be declared out if no play is being made.

The baserunner shall be entitled to advance one base if a thrown ball strike a coacher on foul ground and the ball shall be considered in play. Provided, that if in the opinion of the umpire

the coacher intentionally interfere with such thrown ball, the runner or runners must return to the last bases touched, and the coacher penalized by removal from the playing field.

The baserunner is *not* out if a fair hit ball goes through an infielder, and hits a runner immediately back of him. The umpire must be convinced that the ball passed through the infield and that no other infielder had the chance to make a play on the ball. If, in the judgment of the umpire, the runner deliberately and intentionally kicks such a hit ball, on which the infielder has missed a play, then the runner must be called out for interference.

Interference/Umpire See *Batter/Awarded Bases.*

Pitcher/Delivery The following prohibitions were added to the previous balk rule in 1920:

A balk shall be: Making any motion to pitch while standing in his position without having the ball in his possession; or, regardless of whether he makes any motion to pitch or not, if the pitcher takes a legal position on the rubber without the ball in his possession, or if he takes a position off the rubber and feints to deliver the ball to the bat.

A balk shall be: After the pitcher has taken position, with both hands holding the ball in front of him, he cannot take either hand off the ball except in the act of delivering the ball to the batsman or in throwing to bases.

A balk shall be: If, with one or more runners on bases, the pitcher, in the act of delivering the ball to the batsman or in throwing to first base, drop the ball, either intentionally or accidentally, the umpire shall call it a "balk" and advance runner or runners. No penalty shall be imposed if, with no one on bases, the pitcher drop the ball while delivering it to the batsman.

If the pitcher steps off the rubber, after being in position, for the purpose either of drying his hands or rubbing his eyes, or for other reasons, and it is a legitimate action not understood or interpreted by the umpire to deceive the baserunner, then the umpire shall call "Time."

In case a balk is called, the ball shall be considered "dead" when announcement is made, and no play can be made until the runner or runners reach the base or bases to which they are entitled.

If, with no one on base, the pitcher deliver the ball while off the rubber, the umpire shall call a "ball" whether it goes over the plate fair or not. If, however, the batsman strikes at such illegally delivered ball it counts either for a strike or whatever play may follow.

Pitcher/Illegal Act See *Ball/Defacing.*

Player/Position The players of the team not at bat may be stationed at any points of the field on fair ground their captain may elect, regardless of their respective positions, except that the pitcher, while in the act of delivering the ball to the bat must take his position and the catcher must be within the lines of his position, and within 10 feet of home base, whenever the pitcher delivers the ball to the bat; nor shall the catcher leave his natural position immediately and directly back of the plate for the purpose of aiding the pitcher to intentionally give a base on balls to a batsman.

Runner/Advancing A baserunner who holds his base on a fly ball shall have the right to advance the moment such fly ball touches the hands of a fielder.

Runner/Bases The failure of a preceding runner to touch a base (and who is declared out therefore) shall not affect the status of a succeeding runner who touches each base in proper order.

Runner/Illegal Act A baserunner having acquired legal title to a base cannot run bases in reverse order for the purpose either of confusing the fielders or making a travesty of the game. A runner violating this rule is out if touched with the ball, or the ball held on the base said runner was entitled to hold.

Runner/Returning   In case a runner is being run down between bases, and the following runner occupies the same base the first runner has left, the second man cannot be put out while holding said base. If the first runner, however, returns safely to the base he left, and both runners are then occupying the same base, the second runner is the man out, if touched with the ball.

Runner/Tagged   The baserunner is out if at any time while the ball is in play, he be touched by the ball in the hands of a fielder, unless some part of his person be touching the base he is entitled to occupy; provided, however, that the ball be held by the fielder after touching him, unless the baserunner deliberately knock it out of his hand. The ball must be firmly held by the fielder after touching the runner. The ball cannot be juggled, even though the fielder may retain possession of the ball and prevent same from dropping to the ground.

Substitute   When a substitution is made but no announcement of the substitution is made as required by the rules the substitute will nevertheless be considered in the game as follows: if a pitcher, when he takes his place on the rubber; if a batter, when he takes his place in the batsman's box; if a fielder, when he takes the place of the fielder substituted for; if a runner, when the substitute replaces him on the base he is holding, and any play made by such unannounced substitute shall be legal under the rules.

Umpire   The rules of 1920 contain various new provisions governing umpires and their respective duties.

1921

Pitcher   Note: By concurrent action of the National and American leagues taken at their respective annual meetings held in New York in December 1920, it was agreed that all bona fide spitball pitchers then remaining in the National and American leagues be exempt from the operation of the rule against the use of the spitball during the balance of their major league careers. The pitchers so exempted were: National League—William Doak, Phil Douglas, Dana Fillingim, Ray Fisher, Marvin Goodwin, Burleigh Grimes, Clarence Mitchell, and Richard Rudolph (8). American League—A. W. Ayers, Ray Caldwell, Stanley Coveleskie, Urban Faber, H. B. Leonard, Jack Quinn, Allan Russell, Urban Shocker, and Allan Sothoron (9).

1922–25

There were no changes to the playing rules in these years.

1926

Batter/Awarded Bases   A fair batted ball that goes over the fence or into a stand shall entitle the batsman to a home run, unless it should pass out of the ground or into a stand at a distance less than 250 feet from the home base, in which case the batsman shall be entitled to two bases only. In either event the batsman must touch the bases in regular order. The point at which a fence or stand is less than 250 feet from the home base shall be plainly indicated by a white or black sign or mark for the umpire's guidance.

Pitcher/Legal Act   Under the supervision and control of the umpire, the pitcher may use to dry his hands a small, finely meshed sealed bag containing powdered rosin, furnished by the League.

Note: This rule was first adopted by the National League only.

1927–30

There were no changes to the playing rules in these years.

1931

Batter   The rules of 1931 provide new wording for the rule

governing when the batter is out without changing the substance of the rule.

Batter/Awarded Bases   A fair hit ball that bounds into a stand or over a fence shall be a two-base hit.

Note: There is no reference to distance in this rule and any fair hit ball bounding over the fence or into the stand is a two-base hit.

Coach   See *Interference/Offensive.*

Dead Ball   The rules of 1931 merge two previous rules governing dead balls in one differently worded rule without changing the substance of the old rules.

Fair/Foul Ball   When a batted ball passes outside the playing field the umpire shall decide it fair or foul according to where it leaves the playing field.

Game   The rules of 1931 merge four previous rules governing regulation games in one differently worded rule without changing the substance of the old rules.

Game/Legal   "No game" shall be declared by the umpire if he terminates play in accordance with the rules before five innings have been completed by each team; but if the team last at bat is at bat in the last half of the fifth inning and has equaled before the completion of that inning the score of the side first at bat, the umpire shall declare the game "legally drawn" in accordance with the rules. If the team second at bat shall have made more runs at the end of its fourth inning or before the completion of its fifth inning, than the team first at bat has made in five completed innings of a game so terminated, the umpire shall award the game to the team having made the greater number of runs, and it shall count as a legal game in the championship record.

Glove/Pitcher   The pitcher's glove must be uniform in color.

Interference/Offensive   The players or coachers of the side at bat must immediately vacate any space occupied by them if it is needed by a fielder attempting to handle a batted or thrown ball.

The baserunner is out if, in running the last half of the distance from home base to first base, while the ball is being fielded to first base, he run outside the three-foot lines and, in the opinion of the umpire, interferes with the fielder taking the throw at first base; except that he may run outside the three-foot lines to avoid a fielder attempting to field a batted ball.

Obstruction   The baserunner shall advance one base if he be prevented from making a base by the obstruction of a fielder, except when a fielder is trying to field a batted ball unless the latter has the ball in his hand ready to touch the baserunner. The ball is still in play so far as other baserunners are concerned.

Pitcher/Delivery   Preliminary to pitching, the pitcher shall take his position facing the batsman, with both feet squarely on the ground and on top of the pitcher's plate, or one foot on top of the pitcher's plate and the other foot in contact with same, or one foot in front of the pitcher's plate and the other foot on top of same, and in the act of delivering the ball to the batsman he must keep one foot in contact with the pitcher's plate. He shall not raise either foot until in the act of delivering the ball to the batsman, or in throwing to a base; nor may he make more than one step in such delivery. With a runner on first base or on second base, the pitcher must face the batsman with both hands holding the ball in front of him. If he indulges in a preliminary stretch by raising his arms above his head or out in front, he must return to a natural pitcher's position and stop before starting his delivery of the ball to the batsman.

Runner/Awarded Bases   In all cases where there are no spectators on the playing field and where a thrown ball goes into a stand for spectators or over or through any fence surrounding the playing field or into the players' bench (whether the ball rebounds into the field or not) or remains in the meshes of a wire screen protecting the spectators, the runner or runners shall be entitled to two bases. When the throw is made by an infielder, the umpire, in awarding such bases, shall be governed by the position of the runner or runners at the time the ball was pitched; when the throw is made by an outfielder, the award shall be governed by the position of the runner or runners at the time the throw was made.

The baserunner shall advance one base without liability to be put out if a ball delivered by the pitcher pass the catcher and touch any fence or building within 60 feet of the home base. The ball shall be dead in such case.

Runner/Bases The baserunner is out if, when advancing bases or obliged to return to a base while the ball is in play, he fail to touch the intervening base or bases, if any, in the regular or reverse order, as the case may be, he may be put out by the ball being held by a fielder on any base he failed to touch or by being touched by the ball in the hand of a fielder in the same manner as in running to first base; provided, that the baserunner shall not be out in such case if the ball be delivered to the bat by the pitcher before the fielder hold it on said base or touch the baserunner with it; however, after a fly ball other than a foul tip be legally caught by a fielder, the baserunner who complies with this rule can only be retired by the ball being held by a fielder on the base occupied by the runner when such ball was batted or by being touched by the ball in the hand of the fielder.

The failure of a preceding runner to touch a base (and who is declared out therefore) shall not affect the status of a succeeding runner who touches each base in proper order; except that, after two are out, a succeeding runner cannot score a run when a preceding runner is declared out for failing to touch a base as provided in the rules. This exception also applies to a batsman who hits the ball out of the playing field for an apparent home run.

Substitute Substitutions shall not be in effect until the manager or captain of the team making the change notifies the umpire.

Substitute/Runner The manager or the captain of the opposing team must consent before a runner can be substituted for another baserunner.

Note: Previously this rule referred only to the captain. Throughout the rules of 1931, wherever authority or decision-making authority is granted to the captain, the words "or manager" have been added.

Uniform Glass buttons or polished metal must not be used on a uniform.

1932–38

There were no changes to the playing rules in these years.

1939

Batter/Caught Fly The baserunner is out if, having made a fair hit while batsman, such fair hit ball be caught by a fielder before touching the ground or any object other than a fielder; provided, it be not caught in a fielder's hat, cap, protector, pocket, or other part of his uniform.

Fielder/Drops Fly Ball If, before two are out, while first and second or first, second, and third bases are occupied, an outfielder, in the judgment of the umpire, intentionally drops a fly ball or a line drive, he shall immediately rule the ball has been caught.

Note: Baserunners are obliged to "tag up" after the out has been declared before they can advance.

Gloves The catcher may wear a leather glove or mitt of any size, shape or weight.

The first baseman may wear a leather glove or mitt not more than 12 inches from top to bottom and not more than 8 inches wide across the palm, with thumb and palm connected by leather lacing of not more than 4 inches from thumb to palm, which lacing shall not be enlarged, extended or reinforced by any process or material whatever.

Every other player is restricted to the use of a leather glove weighing not over 10 ounces and measuring not over 14 inches around the palm. The pitcher's glove must be uniform in color.

Pitcher/Delivery Preliminary to pitching, the pitcher shall take his position facing the batsman with both feet squarely on the ground, but his pivot foot must be on or in front in contact with the pitcher's plate; his other foot may be directly behind or in front (not on the side) of the pitcher's plate, and in the act of delivering the ball to the batsman he must keep one foot in contact with the pitcher's plate. He shall not raise either foot until in the act of delivering the ball to the batsman or in throwing to a base; nor may he make more than one step in such delivery. With a runner on first base or second base, the pitcher must face the batsman with both hands holding the ball in front of him. If he indulges in a preliminary stretch by raising his arms above his head or out in front, he must return to a natural pitcher's position and stop before starting his delivery of the ball to the batsman.

Note: After pitcher takes legal position for delivery of ball to batsman, he can take but one step and that must be forward.

A balk will be called (entitling the runner or runners to advance one base) if the pitcher makes any delivery of the ball to the bat while his pivot foot is back of and not in contact with the pitcher's plate.

1940

Bat The bat must be made entirely of hardwood in one piece.

Coach No fines are to be assessed for violations of the coaching rules.

Dead Ball A batted or thrown ball touched, stopped, or handled by a person not engaged in the game is dead and not in play. If a fair hit, the batsman making the hit shall be entitled to two bases and each baserunner shall be entitled to advance two bases. If a thrown ball, each baserunner shall be entitled to advance in accordance with the rules governing a thrown ball.

Note: This rule replaces the rule regarding "blocked balls."

Fielder See *Runner/Tagged.*

Fielder/Drops Fly Ball See *Runner/Advancing.*

Foul Ball A foul hit is a legally batted ball that settles on foul territory between home and first base or home and third base or that bounds past first or third base on or over foul territory or that falls on foul territory beyond first or third base or, while on or over foul ground, touches the person of the umpire or a player or any object foreign to the natural ground. A foul fly must be judged according to the relative position of the ball and the foul line, and not as to whether the fielder is on foul or fair ground at the time he touches the ball.

Game/Doubleheader No club or clubs shall engage in more than two championship games within a period of one day.

Game/Start No inning of any night game shall be started after 11:50 P.M. standard time.

Grounds The ball ground must be enclosed. To obviate the necessity for ground rules, the shortest distance from a fence or stand on fair territory to the home base should be 250 feet and from home base to the grandstand 60 feet.

Grounds/Foul Lines The foul lines are to be continued until they reach the boundary lines of the ground and not less than 10 feet above the top of the fence or stand. The foul lines are to be made, on the playing field, of lime, chalk, or other powder or paint.

Infield Fly The batter is out if, before two are out, while first and second or first, second, and third bases are occupied, he hit a fair fly ball, other than a line drive, that can reasonably be caught by an infielder. In such case, the umpire shall declare it an infield fly. However, the runners may be off their bases or advance at the risk of the ball being caught, the same as on any other fly ball; but if hit by the ball while standing on base, that baserunner shall not be called out, but the ball is dead and the batsman shall be called out and if the baserunner be hit while off base, both that baserunner and the batsman shall be called out and the ball is dead. Provided, that, with first and second bases occupied or first, second, and third bases occupied, with less than two out, any attempt to bunt which results in a fair fly ball shall not be regarded as an infield fly.

Interference/Defensive   The batter becomes a baserunner if the catcher interferes with him, unless he makes a safe hit.

The baserunner is entitled to advance one base if the catcher interferes with the batsman while a baserunner is attempting to steal a base.

Interference/Offensive   If one or more members of the team at bat stand or collect at or around a base for which a baserunner is trying, thereby confusing the team in the field and adding to the difficulty of making such play or if a batsman or baserunner who has just been retired obstructs or interferes with any following play being made on a baserunner, the baserunner shall be declared out for the interference of his teammate or teammates.

The baserunner is out if, after having hit or bunted a ball to fair territory, his bat again hits the ball on or over fair territory and deflects its course. Other baserunners cannot advance.

Pitcher/Delivery   Preliminary to pitching, the pitcher shall take his position facing the batsman with his pivot foot always on or in front of and in contact with the pitcher's plate. In the act of delivering the ball to the batsman, the pitcher's other foot is free, except that he cannot step to either side of the pitcher's plate. He shall not raise either foot until in the act of delivering the ball to the batsman or in throwing to a base. With a runner on first or second base, the pitcher must face the batsman with both hands holding the ball in front of him. If he raises his arms above his head or out in front he must return to a natural pitcher's position and stop before starting the delivery of the ball to the batsman.

Note: After pitcher takes legal position for delivery of ball to batsman, he may take one step backward and one step forward, but not to either side.

It is a balk if the pitcher, in the act of delivering the ball to the batsman or in throwing to first base, drop the ball, either intentionally or accidentally.

Note: With no one on base, it is not a balk if the pitcher drops the ball while delivering it to the batsman.

A balk (entitling the runner or runners to advance one base) shall be called for: (1) Throwing the ball by the pitcher to any base to catch the baserunner without first stepping directly toward such base in the act of making such throw; or throwing or feinting to throw to an unoccupied base; (2) Making any motion of the arm, shoulder, hip, knee, foot, or body the pitcher habitually makes in his method of delivery, without immediately delivering the ball to the bat.

Runner/Advancing   A baserunner who holds his base on a fly ball shall have the right to advance the moment such fly ball touches the person or uniform of a fielder.

The baserunner may "tag up" and advance if, before two are out, while first, or first and second, or first, second, and third bases are occupied, any player, in the judgment of the umpire, intentionally drops a fly ball or a line drive, the umpire shall immediately rule the ball has been caught.

Runner/Awarded Bases   In all cases where there are no spectators on the playing field, and where a thrown ball goes into a stand for spectators, or over or through any fence surrounding the playing field, or into the players' bench (whether the ball

rebounds into the field or not), or remains in the meshes of a wire screen protecting the spectators, the runner or runners shall be entitled to two bases. When a first throw made by an infielder, the umpire, in awarding such bases, shall be governed by the position of the runner or runners at the time the ball was pitched; when the throw is made by an outfielder or is the result of any following plays or attempted plays, the award shall be governed by the position of the runner or runners at the time the last throw was made.

Runner/Overrunning First   The baserunner is permitted to "overslide" as well as overrun first base without liability to be put out.

Runner/Tagged   The baserunner is out if at any time while the ball is in play, he be touched by the ball in the hand of a fielder, unless some part of his person be touching the base he is entitled to occupy; provided, however, that the ball be held by the fielder after touching him, unless the baserunner deliberately knock it out of his hand. The ball must be firmly held by the fielder after touching the runner. The ball cannot be juggled, even though the fielder may regain possession of the ball and prevent same from dropping to the ground.

Note: The previous rule read: "even though the fielder may *retain* possession of the ball."

Trainer   Trainers are permitted to occupy the players' bench.

Trainer/Umpire   Umpires are given authority over trainers.

Umpire   The rules of 1940 describe the procedures to be used when more than two umpires are assigned.

The Umpire-in-Chief is to make all decisions regarding batters.

1941

There were no changes to the playing rules this year.

1942

Game/Start   No inning of any night game shall be started after 12:50 A.M. war time.

1943–48

There were no changes to the playing rules in these years.

1949

Catcher/Position   The catcher must stand with both feet inside the catcher's lines until the ball leaves the pitcher's hand.

Coach   First base coaches as well as third base coaches must refrain from touching or holding the runner physically or the runner is out.

Foul/Fair Ball   A foul fly must be judged according to the relative position of the ball and the foul line, including the foul pole, and not as to whether the fielder is on foul or fair ground at the time he touches the ball.

Game/Start   No inning of any night game shall be started after 12:50 A.M. local city time.

Pitcher/Delivery   No balk can be committed with all bases empty.

Player/Illegal Act   No manager, captain, coach, or player shall address the spectators before or during a game except in reply to a request for information about the progress or state of the game or to give the name of a player.

1950

Bases   The home plate and the pitcher's plate shall be of whitened rubber, anchored in the ground, even with its surface. The home plate, with beveled edges, shall be level with the baselines. The pitcher's plate shall be on a mound 15 inches higher than home plate. The slope from the pitcher's plate to the baselines shall be gradual.

First, second, and third bases shall be approved bags of white canvas, securely anchored in the ground. They shall be 15 inches square and not less than three, nor more than five inches thick and shall be filled with soft material.

Bat The bat shall be round, not over 2¾ inches in diameter at the thickest part, not more than 42 inches in length, and entirely of hard, solid wood in one piece. Twine may be wound around it or a granulated substance applied to it, for a distance of 18 inches from the end of the handle, but not elsewhere.

Batter/Awarded Bases Each runner including the batter-runner may, without liability of being put out, advance to home base, scoring a run, if a fair ball goes over the field fence in flight and he touch all bases legally; or if a fair ball which, in the umpire's judgment, would have cleared the field fence in flight, is deflected by the act of a defensive player in throwing his glove, cap, or any article of his apparel, the runner shall be awarded a home run.

The rules of 1950 include various new provisions for baserunners when balls are hit or thrown into the stands.

The batter becomes a baserunner when a fair ball, after touching the ground, bounds into the stands or passes through or under a fence or through or under a scoreboard or through or under shrubbery or vines on the fence, in which case the batter and the baserunners shall be entitled to advance two bases.

The batter becomes a baserunner when any fair ball which, either before or after striking the ground, passes through or under a fence or through or under a scoreboard or through any opening in the fence or scoreboard or through or under shrubbery or vines on the fence, in which case the batter and the baserunners shall be entitled to two bases.

The batter becomes a baserunner when any bounding fair ball is deflected by the fielder into the stands or over or under a fence on fair or foul ground, in which case the batter and all baserunners shall be entitled to advance two bases.

The batter becomes a baserunner when any fair fly ball is deflected by the fielder into the stands or over the fence into foul territory, in which case the batter shall be entitled to advance to second base; but if deflected into the stands or over the fence in fair territory, the batter shall be entitled to a home run.

Batter/Illegal Act The batter is out for illegal action when he fails to take his position in the batter's box promptly. If he persists in unwarranted delay in taking his position the umpire shall direct the pitcher to deliver the ball to the bat and every such pitch shall be called "strike" by the umpire. If he enters the batter's box in the interval between any such pitches, the ball and strike count shall continue regularly, but if he has not entered the batter's box when three strikes are called he shall be declared "out."

Catch A catch is the act of a defensive player in receiving, and holding firmly in his hand or glove, a batted or thrown ball. It is not a catch, however, if simultaneously or immediately following his contact with the ball, he collide with a player or with a wall or if he fall down, and as a result of such collision or falling, drops the ball. If the player has made the catch and drops the ball while in the act of making a throw following the catch, the ball shall be adjudged to have been caught. In establishing the validity of the catch, the player shall hold the ball long enough to prove that he has complete control of the ball and that his release of the ball is voluntary and intentional.

Dead/Live Ball See *Game/"Time."*

Definitions Rule Two of the rules of 1950 includes the definitions of 69 baseball terms as used in the rules. Several of the key definitions are quoted throughout this year's rule entries.

Fair Territory Fair territory is that part of the playing field

within, and including the first and third baselines, from home base to the bottom of the playing field fence and perpendicularly upwards. All foul lines are in fair territory.

Foul Tip A foul tip is a ball batted by the batter that goes sharp and direct from the bat to the catcher's hands and is legally caught. It is not a foul tip unless caught and any foul tip that is caught is a strike, and the ball is in play. It is not a catch if it is a rebound from any part of the catcher's equipment other than the catcher's glove or hand.

Game Baseball is a game between two teams of nine players, each with adequate substitutes, coaches, and trainers, under direction of a manager, played in accordance with these rules, under jurisdiction of an umpire or umpires on an enclosed field.

The object of each team is to win by scoring the more runs.

A game consists of nine innings, except as otherwise provided, and an inning is that portion of the game during which each team shall play both offensively and defensively.

The winner of the game shall be that team which shall have scored, in accordance with these rules, the greater number of runs at the conclusion of a regulation game.

Game/Doubleheader The rules of 1950 include a series of new provisions governing the conduct of doubleheaders.

Game/Rain The manager of the home team shall be the sole judge of the fitness of the playing field for the beginning of any game other than the second game of a doubleheader. Exception: Any league may permanently authorize its president to suspend the application of this rule as to that league during the closing weeks of its championship season in order to ensure that the championship is decided each year on its merits. When the postponement of, and possible failure to play, a game in the final series of a championship season between any two teams might affect the final standing of any club in the league, the president, on appeal from any league member, may assume the authority granted the home team manager by this rule.

Game/Start The players of the home team shall take their defensive positions, the first batter of the visiting team shall take his position in the batter's box, the umpire shall call "Play," and the game shall proceed.

The rules of 1950 include a series of new provisions governing the preliminaries before championship games.

Game/"Time" The ball is dead when the umpire-in-chief suspends play by calling "Time" when a manager requests "Time" for a substitution or for conference with his player.

The ball is dead when the umpire-in-chief suspends play by calling "Time" when a fielder, after catching a fly ball, falls into a bench, dugout, or stand or falls across ropes into a crowd (when spectators are on the field), and baserunners may advance one base without liability to be put out.

Note: If player after making the catch steps into the dugout but does not fall, the ball is alive and in play and runners may advance at their own peril.

After the umpire calls "Play" the ball is alive and in play and remains alive and in play until for legal cause, or at the umpire's call of "Time" suspending play, the ball becomes dead. While the ball is dead no player may be put out, no bases may be run, and no runs may be scored, except that runners may advance as legally provided.

Glove/Fielder Each player, other than the first baseman and the catcher, is restricted to the use of a leather glove not more than twelve inches long nor more than eight inches wide, measured from the base of the thumb crotch to the outside edge of the glove. The space between the thumb and the forefinger shall not exceed 4½ inches at the top nor more than 3½ inches at the base of the thumb crotch. The webbing may be standard leather or lacing and shall not be enlarged, extended, or reinforced by any process or materials whatever. The webbing cannot be constructed of wound or wrapped lacing to make a net type of trap. The glove may be of any weight.

Glove/First Baseman   The first baseman may wear a leather glove or mitt not more than 12 inches long from top to bottom and not more than eight inches wide across the palm, measured from base of thumb crotch to outer edge of the mitt. The space between the thumb section and the finger section of the mitt shall not exceed four inches at the top of the mitt and 3½ inches at the base of the thumb crotch. The mitt shall be constructed so that this space is permanently fixed and cannot be enlarged, extended, widened, or deepened by the use of any materials or process whatever. The web of the mitt shall measure not more than five inches from its top to the base of the thumb crotch. The web may be either a lacing, lacing through leather tunnels, or a center piece of leather which may be an extension of the palm connected to the mitt with lacing and constructed so that it will not exceed the above-mentioned measurements. The webbing cannot be constructed of wound or wrapped lacing or deepened to make a net type of trap.

Glove/Pitcher   The pitcher's glove shall be uniform in color and cannot be white or gray.

Home Run   See *Batter/Awarded Bases*.

Infield Fly   An infield fly is an out called by the umpire on the batter—if, before two are out, while first and second or first, second, and third bases are occupied, he hit a fair fly ball, other than a line drive, that in the judgment of the umpire can reasonably be caught by an infielder. Where a defensive player who normally plays in the outfield places himself in the infield, he shall for the purpose of the infield fly rule be considered an infielder. In such case, the umpire shall declare it an infield fly. However, the runners may be off their bases or advance at the risk of the ball being caught, the same as on any other fly ball. If a runner is hit by the ball while standing on base, he shall not be called out, but the ball is dead and the batter shall be called out; but if a baserunner is hit while off base, both he and the batter shall be called out and the ball is dead. Provided, that, with first and second bases occupied, or first, second, and third bases occupied, before two are out, any attempt to bunt which results in a fair fly ball shall not be regarded as an infield fly.

Interference/Offensive   The rules of 1950 include several new provisions describing the circumstances under which a baserunner is out for interference.

The batter is out when a preceding runner shall, in the umpire's judgment, intentionally interfere with the play of a defensive player who is attempting to catch a thrown ball or to throw the ball in an attempt to complete any play.

The batter is out when with two out, a runner on third base, and two strikes on the batter, the runner attempts to steal home base on a legal pitch and the ball strikes the runner in the strike zone. The umpire shall call "strike three," the batter is out and the run shall not count; with less than two out the umpire shall call "strike three," the ball is dead, and the run counts.

The batter is out when after striking or bunting the ball he intentionally strikes the ball a second time, or strikes it with a thrown bat or deflects its course in any manner while running to first base. The ball is dead and no runners may advance. If the runner drops his bat and the ball rolls against the bat and, in the umpire's judgment, there was no intention to interfere with the course of the ball, the ball is alive and in play.

Obstruction   A batter who has become a runner is entitled to unimpeded progress as he advances around the bases. Whenever a defensive player impedes the runner in any way, unless he is attempting to field a batted ball or has the ball in his possession, the umpire shall call "obstruction," the ball shall remain in play, and all runners shall be permitted to advance, without liability to be put out, to the bases which, in the judgment of the umpire, the runners would have reached had obstruction not been called.

In a "run-down" play, if the runner's progress is impeded by any defensive player who does not have the ball in his possession, the umpire shall call "obstruction" and the runner shall be entitled to occupy the base he is attempting to reach when the obstruction occurred.

Pitcher/Delivery   There are two legal pitching positions: The "Wind-up" position and the "Set" position. Either position may be used at any time.

Pivot Foot   The pitcher's pivot foot is that foot which is in contact with the pitcher's plate as he delivers the pitch.

Set Position   Set position is the pitcher's position when he stands facing the batter with his entire pivot foot on or in front of and in contact with, and not off the end of the pitcher's plate, and his other foot in front of the pitcher's plate, holding the ball in both hands in front of his body and coming to a complete stop of at least one second.

Wind-up Position   Wind-up position is the pitcher's position when he stands facing the batter, his pivot foot on or in front of and touching the pitcher's plate, and the other foot free.

From the set position, the pitcher may deliver the ball to the batter, throw to a base, or step backward off the pitcher's plate with his pivot foot. Before assuming set position the pitcher may elect to make any natural preliminary motion such as that known as "the stretch." But if he so elects, he must come to set position before delivering the ball to the batter. After assuming set position, any natural motion associated with his delivery of the ball to the batter commits him to the pitch without alteration or interruption.

If there is a runner or runners it is a balk if the pitcher delivers the pitch from "set position" without coming to a stop of one full second.

Pitcher/Illegal Act   The pitcher shall not be allowed to pitch at a batter's head, and if, in the umpire's opinion, such violation occurs, he shall call "Time" and warn the pitcher and the manager of the defensive team that another such pitch will mean the immediate expulsion of the pitcher from the game. If such pitch is repeated, the umpire shall inflict the penalty as follows: The pitcher shall be removed from the game and from the grounds. The president of the League shall impose such fine and suspension as his judgment warrants.

See also *Pitcher/Uniform*.

Pitcher/Illegal Pitches   If the pitcher makes an illegal pitch with the bases unoccupied it shall be called a ball, unless the batter shall make a fair hit or reaches first base on an error or otherwise.

The pitcher shall not be allowed to pitch the "quick return ball." Whenever such pitch is attempted the umpire shall call "Time." If the offense is repeated the umpire shall call each such repeated offense a "ball," unless the batter reaches first base on a fair hit, an error, or otherwise, and no other runner is forced by his reaching first base, in which case the play proceeds.

Pitcher-Infielder   If the pitcher removes his pivot foot from contact with the pitcher's plate by stepping backward with that foot, he thereby becomes an infielder and, if his subsequent throw to a base, when off the pitcher's plate, goes into a stand or over, through, or under a fence or into a bench or dugout (whether the ball rebounds or not) or remains in the meshes of a wire screen protecting the spectators, the ball is dead and all runners shall be entitled to advance two bases.

Pitcher/Pick-Off   At any time during the pitcher's preliminary movements and until his natural pitching motion commits him to the pitch, he may throw to any base provided he step directly toward such base before making the throw.

Pitcher/Position   See *Bases* for pitcher's plate.

Pitcher/Uniform   The pitcher shall not be allowed to wear a garment with ragged, frayed or slit sleeves, and shall not be permitted to attach tape or other material of a color different from his uniform or glove to his glove or clothing.

Pitcher/Warm-Ups When a pitcher takes his position at the beginning of each inning or when he relieves another pitcher, he shall be permitted to pitch not to exceed eight preparatory pitches to his catcher during which play shall be suspended. Such preparatory pitches shall not consume more than one minute of time.

Player/Illegal Acts Players in uniform shall not address nor mingle with spectators, nor sit in the stands before or during a game. No manager, captain, coacher, or player shall address any spectator before or during a game. Players of opposing teams shall not fraternize at any time while in uniform. Penalty: The president of the league shall impose fines for violation of this rule at his discretion.

No manager, player, substitute, coacher, trainer, or batboy shall at any time, whether from the bench, the coacher's box, or on the playing field, or elsewhere call "Time," or employ any other word or phrase while the ball is alive and in play for the obvious purpose of confusing an umpire or an opposing player.

Except the batter, or a runner attempting to score, no offensive player shall cross the catcher's lines when the ball is in play.

Runner/Out The baserunner is out if, after he has acquired legal possession of a base, he or that base is tagged while he is running the bases in reverse order for the purpose of confusing the defense or making a travesty of the game. No runner may advance in this situation in the event of an error on this play by the defensive team.

The baserunner is out if, in running or sliding for home base, he fails to touch home base and makes no attempt to return to the base, when a defensive player holds the ball in his hand while touching home base and appeals to the umpire for the decision.

Strike Zone The strike zone is that space over home plate which is between the batter's armpits and the top of his knees when he assumes his natural stance.

Substitute A player or players may be substituted during a game at any time the ball is dead. A substituted player shall bat in the replaced player's position in the team's batting order. A player once removed from a game shall not re-enter that game. If a substitute enters the game in place of a manager, the manager may thereafter go to the coaching lines at his discretion. When two or more substitute players of the defensive team enter the game at the same time, the manager, or his designated representative, shall, immediately before they take their position as defensive players, designate to the umpire-in-chief such players' positions in the team's batting order and the umpire-in-chief shall so notify the official scorer. If this information is not immediately given to the umpire-in-chief, he shall have authority to designate the substitutes' places in the batting order.

Substitute/Runner A player whose name is on his team's batting order may not become a substitute runner for another member of his team.

Umpire Each umpire is the representative of the president of the league, the president of the National Association and the Commissioner of Baseball.

The umpire-in-chief shall enforce the rules from the moment he receives the batting order from the manager of the home team until termination of the game. This shall include control of ground crews, newsmen, and photographers, and any other persons whose duties require their presence upon the field.

1951–53

There were no changes to the playing rules in these years.

1954

Bat The bat shall be a smooth, rounded stick not more than

2¾inches in diameter at the thickest part and not more than 42 inches in length. The bat shall be one piece of solid wood or formed from a block of wood consisting of two or more pieces of wood bonded together with an adhesive in such a way that the grain direction of all pieces is essentially parallel to the length of the bat. Any such laminated bat shall contain only wood or adhesive, except for a clear finish.

For a distance of 18 inches from the end by which the bat is gripped, it may be roughened or wrapped with tape or twine.

Note: Approval of the laminated bat is experimental for the 1954 season, and no laminated bat shall be used in a professional game until the manufacturer has secured approval from the Rules Committee of his design and method of manufacture. In giving or withholding such approval, the Rules Committee will be guided by comparison of the laminated bat with one-piece solid wood bats. Laminated bats which are inferior to one-piece solid wood bats in safety or durability will not be approved. A design or method of manufacture which produces a "loaded" or "freak" type of bat or which produces a substantially greater reaction or distance factor than one-piece solid wood bats will not be approved.

Batter/Illegal Act See *Interference/Offensive.*

Catch A catch is the act of a fielder in getting secure possession in his hand or glove of a ball in flight and firmly holding it; providing he does not use his cap, protector, pocket, or any other part of his uniform in getting possession.

Dead/Live Ball See *Game/"Time."*

Definitions Rules Two and Three of the rules of 1954 contain several new definitions of key baseball terms as used in the rules.

Fielder/Drops Fly Ball The batter is out when, with less than two out and first, first and second, first and third, or first, second, and third bases occupied, a fielder intentionally drops a fair fly ball or line drive. Runners need not re-touch and may advance at their own peril.

Fielder/Illegal Act No fielder shall take a position in the batter's line of vision, and with deliberate unsportsmanlike intent, act in a manner to distract the batter.

Game The rules of 1954 contain a series of new provisions governing suspended games.

Game/"Time" After the umpire calls "Play" the ball is alive and in play and remains alive and in play until for legal cause, or at the umpire's call of "Time" suspending play, the ball becomes dead. While the ball is dead no player may be put out, no bases may be run, and no runs may be scored, except that runners may advance one or more bases as the result of acts which occurred while the ball was alive (such as, but not limited to, a balk, an overthrow, interference, or a home run or other fair hit out of the playing field).

Gloves/Equipment Members of the offensive team shall carry all gloves and other equipment off the field and to the dugout while their team is at bat. No equipment shall be left lying on the field, either in fair or foul territory.

Interference/Defensive Defensive interference is an illegal act by a fielder which hinders or prevents a batter from hitting a pitch.

Interference/Offensive The batter is out after hitting or bunting a fair ball, when his bat hits the ball a second time in fair territory. The ball is dead and no runners may advance. If the batter-runner drops his bat and the ball rolls against the bat in fair territory and, in the umpire's judgment, there was no intention to interfere with the course of the ball, the ball is alive and in play.

The batter is out after hitting or bunting a foul ball, when he intentionally deflects the course of the ball in any manner while running to first base. The ball is dead and no runners may advance.

The batter is out when his fair ball touches him before touching a fielder.

It is interference by a batter or runner when he intentionally deflects the course of a foul ball in any manner.

Interference/Spectator The batter is out when spectator interference clearly prevents a fielder from catching his fly ball.

Spectator interference occurs when a spectator reaches out of the stands, or goes on the playing field and touches a live ball. When there is spectator interference with any thrown ball, except a throw by the pitcher, the ball shall be dead at the moment of interference and the umpire shall impose such penalties as in his opinion will nullify the act of interference.

Pitcher/Delivery In the event a balk is called, the ball is dead, and each runner shall advance one base without liability to be put out unless the batter hits the pitch on which the balk is made, in which case the manager of the offensive team may elect to accept either the balk penalty or the result of the batter's action.

Pitcher/Illegal Pitch A quick return pitch is a pitch made with obvious intent to catch a batter off balance.

Pitcher/Starter The pitcher named in the batting order handed the umpire-in-chief shall pitch to the first batter or any substitute batter until the batter is put out or reaches first base, unless the pitcher sustains injury or illness which, in the judgment of the umpire-in-chief, incapacitates him from pitching.

If the pitcher is replaced, the substitute pitcher shall pitch to the batter then at bat, or any substitute batter, until such batter is retired or reaches first base, or until the offensive team is retired, unless the substitute pitcher sustains injury or illness which, in the umpire-in-chief's judgment, incapacitates him for further play as a pitcher.

Relief Pitcher See above, *Pitcher/Starter.*

Runner The rules of 1954 include several new provisions awarding baserunners additional bases in various circumstances.

Squeeze Play Squeeze play is a term to designate a play when a team, with a runner on third base, attempts to score that runner by means of a bunt.

Triple Play A triple play is a play by the defense in which three offensive players are legally put out as a result of continuous action, providing there is no error between the putouts.

Umpire The umpire's authority to act in legal manner on all matters pertaining to a game shall not be questioned. The umpire shall have power to make decisions on any points not specifically covered in the rules.

Wild Pitch A wild pitch is one so high, so low, or so wide of the plate that it cannot be handled with ordinary effort by the catcher.

1955

Ball The ball shall be a sphere formed by yarn wound around a small core of cork, rubber or similar material, covered with two strips of white horsehide, tightly stitched together. It shall weigh not less than 5 nor more than 5¼ ounces avoirdupois and measure not less than 9 nor more than 9¼ inches in circumference.

Batter/Position (Illegal) An illegally batted ball is one hit by the batter with one or both feet outside of the batter's box.

Batting Order The umpire-in-chief shall make certain that the original and copies of the respective batting orders are identical, and then tender a copy of each batting order to the opposing manager. The copy retained by the umpire shall be the official batting order. The tender of the batting order by the umpire shall establish the batting orders. Thereafter, no substitutions shall be made by either manager, except as provided in the rules.

Catcher/Position The catcher shall stand with both feet within the lines of the catcher's box, directly back of the plate, until the ball leaves the pitcher's hand. The intent of this rule is to deter the giving of intentional bases on balls. If the catcher has either foot outside his box when the pitcher delivers the ball, it is a balk.

Dead/Live Ball See *Game/"Time."*

Interference/Defensive The batter becomes a runner and is entitled to first base when the catcher or any other fielder interferes with him, unless the batter reaches first base on a hit, an error, or otherwise, and all other runners advance at least one base, in which case the play proceeds without reference to the interference.

Interference/Offensive It is interference by a batter or runner when any member or members of the offensive team stand or gather around any base to which a runner is advancing, to confuse, hinder, or add to the difficulty of the fielders. Such runner shall be declared out for the interference of his teammate or teammates.

It is interference by a batter or runner when any batter or runner who has just been retired hinders or impedes any following play being made on a runner. Such runner shall be declared out for the interference of his teammate.

Forfeited Game A game shall be forfeited in favor of the opposing team when a team is unable or refuses to place nine players on the field.

Game The rules of 1955 include new provisions for determining a suspended game and its resumption.

Game/Rain The manager of the home team shall be the sole judge as to whether a game shall be started because of unsuitable weather conditions or the unfit condition of the playing field, except for the second game of a doubleheader.

Game/"Time" The ball becomes dead when the umpire-in-chief suspends play by calling "Time" when an accident incapacitates a player or umpire, or if it is necessary to remove a player or spectator from the grounds. The umpire shall not call "Time" because of an accident to player or umpire during a play, until in his judgment, no further action is possible in that play, unless an accident to a runner is such as to prevent him from proceeding to a base to which he is legally entitled, as on a home run hit out of the playing field, or an award of one or more bases, in which case a substitute runner shall be permitted to complete the play.

Pitcher/Delivery When the bases are unoccupied, the pitcher shall deliver the ball to the batter within 20 seconds after taking his pitching position. Each time the pitcher delays the game by violating this rule, the umpire shall call "Ball."

1956

There were no changes to the playing rules this year.

1957

The rules of 1957 contain new wording and explanation for the rules governing a batter who bats out of order.

Ball/Defacing See *Pitcher/Illegal Act.*

Batter/Position The batter shall take his position in the batter's box promptly when it is his time at bat.

The batter shall not leave his position in the batter's box after the pitcher comes to the Set Position, or starts his windup. Penalty: If the pitcher pitches, the umpire shall call "Ball" or "Strike," as the case may be.

Catcher/Position When the ball is put in play at the start of or during a game, all fielders other than the catcher shall be on fair territory. The catcher shall station himself directly back of the plate. He may leave his position at any time to catch a pitch or make a play except that when the batter is being given an intentional base on balls, the catcher must stand with both feet within the lines of the catcher's box until the ball leaves the pitcher's hand. Penalty: Balk.

Coach The offensive team shall station two coaches on the field during its term at bat, one near first base and one near third base. Failure to place two coaches on the field shall subject the manager to fine or suspension or both by the league president.

Coaches shall be limited to two in number and shall (1) be in team uniform; (2) remain within the coach's box at all times; and (3) address players of their own team only. Penalty: The offending coach shall be removed from the game, and shall leave the playing field.

Game When the winning run is scored in the last half-inning of a regulation game, or in the last half of an extra inning, as the result of a base on balls, hit batsman, or any other play with the bases full which forces the runner on third to advance, the umpire shall not declare the game ended until the runner forced to advance from third has touched home base and the batter-runner has touched first base. Penalty: If the runner on third refuses to advance to and touch home base in a reasonable time, the umpire shall disallow the run, call out the offending player, and order the game resumed. If, with less than two out, the batter-runner refuses to advance to and touch first base, the run shall count, but the offending player shall be called out.

The rules of 1957 include a rewording of the rules governing suspended games and the resumption of suspended games.

Game/Doubleheader A league may adopt a rule providing that one game of a doubleheader shall be seven innings in length. In such games, any of these rules applying to the ninth inning shall apply to the seventh inning.

The second game of a doubleheader shall start 20 minutes after the first game is completed, unless a longer interval (not to exceed 30 minutes) is declared by the umpire-in-chief and announced to the opposing managers at the end of the first game. Exception: If the league president has approved a request of the home club for a longer interval between games for some special event, the umpire-in-chief shall declare such longer interval and announce it to the opposing managers. The umpire-in-chief of the first game shall be the timekeeper controlling the interval between games.

Hit by Pitch The batter becomes a runner and is entitled to first base without liability to be put out (provided he advances to and touches first base) when he is touched by a pitched ball which he is not attempting to hit unless: (1) The ball is in the strike zone when it touches the batter, or (2) The batter makes no attempt to avoid being touched by the ball.

Note: If the ball is in the strike zone when it touches the batter, it shall be called a strike, whether or not the batter tries to avoid the ball. If the ball is outside the strike zone when it touches the batter, it shall be called a ball if he makes no attempt to avoid being touched.

Infield Fly An infield fly is a fair fly ball (not including a line drive nor an attempted bunt) which can be caught by an infielder with ordinary effort when first and second, or first, second, and third bases are occupied, before two are out. The pitcher, catcher, and any outfielder who stations himself in the infield on the play shall be considered infielders for the purpose of this rule.

When it seems apparent that a batted ball will be an infield fly, the umpire shall immediately declare "Infield Fly" for the benefit of the runners. If the ball is near the baselines, the umpire shall declare "Infield Fly, if Fair."

The ball is alive and runners may advance at the risk of the ball being caught, or re-touch and advance after the ball is touched, the same as on any fly ball. If the hit becomes a foul ball, it is treated the same as any foul.

Note: If a declared infield fly is allowed to fall untouched to the ground, and bounces foul, it is a foul ball. If a declared infield fly falls untouched to the ground outside the baseline, and bounces fair, it is an infield fly.

Interference/Defensive If, with a runner on third base and trying to score by means of a squeeze play or a steal, the catcher or any other fielder steps on, or in front of home base without possession of the ball, or touches the batter or his bat, the pitcher shall be charged with a balk, the batter shall be awarded first base on the interference, and the ball is dead.

Each runner, other than the batter, may without liability to be put out, advance one base when he is attempting to steal a base, if the batter is interfered with by the catcher or any other fielder.

Note: When a runner is entitled to a base without liability to be put out, while the ball is in play, or under any rule in which the ball is in play after the runner reaches the base to which he is entitled, and the runner fails to touch the base to which he is entitled before attempting to advance to the next base, the runner shall forfeit his exemption from liability to be put out, and he may be put out by tagging the base or by tagging the runner before he returns to the missed base.

Obstruction In a rundown play, if the runner is obstructed by any fielder who does not have the ball in his possession (unless the fielder is in the act of fielding the ball), the umpire shall call "Obstruction" and the runner shall be entitled to occupy the base he is attempting to reach when the obstruction occurs. If such base is held by a following runner, any following runner forced to vacate his base by the obstructed runner's return shall be permitted to return to his last-held base without liability to be put out.

Pitcher/Delivery When the bases are unoccupied, the pitcher shall deliver the ball to the batter within 20 seconds after he receives the ball. Each time the pitcher delays the game by violating this rule, the umpire shall call "Ball."

Note: The intent of this rule is to avoid unnecessary delays. The umpire shall insist that the catcher return the ball promptly to the pitcher, and that the pitcher take his position on the rubber promptly. Obvious delay by the pitcher should instantly be penalized by the umpire.

If there is a runner or runners it is a balk if the pitcher, while giving an intentional base on balls, pitches when the catcher is not in the catcher's box.

If there is a runner or runners it is a balk if the pitcher makes an illegal pitch.

Pitcher/Illegal Act The pitcher shall not (1) apply a foreign substance of any kind to the ball; (2) expectorate either on the ball or his glove; (3) rub the ball on his glove, person, or clothing; (4) deface the ball in any manner; (5) deliver what is called the "shine" ball, "spit" ball, "mud" ball or "emery" ball. The pitcher, of course, is allowed to rub the ball between his bare hands. Penalty: For violation of any part of this rule, the umpire shall immediately disqualify the pitcher, and the league president shall suspend the pitcher for a period of 10 days. If a pitch is delivered in violation of this rule, it shall be treated as an illegal pitch.

Player/Illegal Act Players in uniform shall not address nor mingle with spectators, nor sit in the stands before, during, or after a game. No manager, captain, coach, or player shall address any spectator before or during a game.

Players of opposing teams shall not fraternize at any time while in uniform. Penalty: The league president shall impose fines for violation of this rule at his discretion.

Player/Position See *Catcher/Position.*

Relief Pitcher If an improper substitution is made for the pitcher, the umpire shall direct the proper pitcher to return to the game until the provisions of this rule are fulfilled. If the improper pitcher is permitted to pitch, any play that results is legal. The improper pitcher becomes the proper pitcher as soon as he makes his first pitch to the batter, or as soon as any runner is retired.

Strike Zone A strike is a legal pitch when so called by the umpire which (a) is struck at by the batter and is missed; (b) enters the strike zone in flight and is not struck at; (c) is fouled by the batter when he has less than two strikes; (d) is bunted foul; (e) touches the batter as he strikes at it; (f) touches the batter in flight in the strike zone; or (g) becomes a foul tip. Note: (f) was added to the former rule and definition.

Touch/Definition To touch a player or umpire is to touch any part of his body, clothing, or his equipment.

Umpire Each umpire has authority to disqualify any player, coach, manager, or substitute for objecting to decisions or for unsportsmanlike conduct or language, and to remove such disqualified person from the playing field. If an umpire disqualifies a player while a play is in progress, the disqualification shall not take effect until no further action is possible in that play.

Each umpire has authority at his discretion to remove from the playing field (1) any person whose duties permit his presence on the field, such as ground-crew members, ushers, photographers, newsmen, broadcasting-crew members, etc., or (2) any spectator or other person not authorized to be on the playing field.

Umpire/Decisions If different decisions should be made on one play by different umpires, the umpire-in-chief shall call all the umpires into consultation, with no manager or player present. After consultation, the umpire-in-chief (unless another umpire may have been designated by the league president) shall determine which decision shall prevail, based on which umpire was in best position and which decision was most likely correct. Play shall proceed as if only the final decision had been made.

1958

Appeal/Runner Any runner shall be called out, on appeal, when (a) after a fly ball is caught, he fails to re-touch his base before he or his base is tagged; (b) with the ball in play, while advancing or returning to a base, he fails to touch each base in order before he, or a missed base is tagged; (c) he overruns or overslides first base and fails to return to the base immediately, and he or the base is tagged; (d) he fails to touch home base and makes no attempt to return to that base, and home base is tagged. Any appeal under this rule must be made before the next legal pitch. If the violation occurs during a play which ends a half-inning, the appeal must be made before the defensive team leaves the field.

Note: Appeal plays may require an umpire to recognize an apparent "fourth out." If the third out is made during a play in which an appeal play is sustained on another runner, the appeal play decision takes precedence in determining the out. If there is more than one appeal during a play that ends a half-inning, the defense may elect to take the out that gives it the advantage. If the third out on appeal is a force play or failure of the batter-runner to touch first base, no runs can score on the play. Otherwise runs made before the appeal is sustained shall count. For the purposes of this rule, the defensive team has "left the field" when the pitchers and all infielders have left fair territory on their way to the bench or clubhouse.

1959

Grounds Any playing field constructed by a professional club after June 1, 1958, shall provide a minimum distance of 325 feet from home base to the nearest fence, stand, or other obstruction on the right and left field foul lines, and a minimum distance of 400 feet to the center field fence. No existing playing fields shall be remodeled after June 1, 1958, in such manner as to reduce the distance from home base to the foul poles and to the center field fence below the minimum distances.

Interference/Spectator When there is spectator interference with any thrown ball, the ball shall be dead at the moment of interference, and the umpire shall impose such penalties as in his opinion will nullify the act of interference.

Runner/Awarded Bases The runner is entitled to advance one base, if a ball, pitched to the batter, or thrown by the pitcher from his position on the pitcher's plate to a base to catch a runner, goes into a stand, or players' bench, or over or through a field fence or backstop. The ball is dead.

Note: If such a wild pitch is ball four, the batter-runner is entitled to first base only.

Each runner, including the batter-runner, may advance two bases, if a fair ball bounces or is deflected into the stands outside the first or third base foul lines; or if it goes through or under a field fence, or through or under a scoreboard, or through or under shrubbery or vines on the fence; or if it sticks in such fence, scoreboard, shrubbery, or vines.

1960–62

There were no changes to the playing rules in these years.

1963

Interference/Offensive Offensive interference is an act by the team at bat which interferes with, obstructs, impedes, hinders, or confuses any fielder attempting to make a play. If the umpire declares the batter, batter-runner, or a runner out for interference, all other runners shall return to the last base that was, in the judgment of the umpire, legally touched at the time of the interference.

Pitcher/Delivery Wind-up Position The pitcher shall stand facing the batter, his entire pivot foot on, or in front of and touching and not off the end of the pitcher's plate, and the other foot free. From this position any natural movement associated with his delivery of the ball to the batter commits him to the pitch without interruption or alteration. He shall not raise either foot from the ground, except that in his actual delivery of the ball to the batter, he may take one step backward, and one step forward with his free foot.

Note: When a pitcher holds the ball with both hands in front of his body, with his entire pivot foot on, or in front of and touching but not off the end of the pitcher's plate, and his other foot free, he will be considered in a Windup Position.

If there is a runner, or runners, it is a balk when the pitcher, after coming to a legal pitching position, removes one hand from the ball other than in an actual pitch, or in throwing to a base.

Pitcher/Warm-Up Pitches When a pitcher takes his position at the beginning of each inning, or when he relieves another pitcher, he shall be permitted to pitch not to exceed eight preparatory pitches to his catcher during which play shall be suspended. A league by its own action may limit the number of preparatory pitches to less than eight preparatory pitches. Such preparatory pitches shall not consume more than one minute of time. If a sudden emergency causes a pitcher to be summoned into the game without any opportunity to warm up, the umpire-in-chief shall allow him as many pitches as the umpire deems necessary.

Runner A runner acquires the right to an unoccupied base when he touches it before he is out. He is then entitled to it until he is put out, or forced to vacate it for another runner.

Unless two are out, the status of a following runner is not affected by a preceding runner's failure to touch or re-touch a base. If, upon appeal, the preceding runner is the third out, no runners following him shall score. If such third out is the result of a force play, neither preceding nor following runners shall score.

Strike Zone The strike zone is that space over home plate which is between the top of the batter's shoulders and his knees when he assumes his natural stance. The umpire shall determine the strike zone according to the batter's usual stance when he swings at a pitch.

1964

Bat No colored bat may be used in a professional game unless approved by the rules committee.

Interference/Defensive The batter becomes a runner and is entitled to first base when the catcher or any fielder interferes with him. If a play follows the interference, the manager of the offense may advise the plate umpire that he elects to decline the interference penalty and accept the play. Such election shall be made immediately at the end of the play. However, if the batter reaches first base on a hit, an error, a base on balls, a hit batsman, or otherwise, and all other runners advance at least one base, the play proceeds without reference to the interference.

Interference/Offensive It is interference by a batter or a runner when a batter-runner willfully and deliberately interferes with a batted ball or a fielder in the act of fielding a batted ball, with the obvious intent to break up a double play. The ball is dead. The umpire shall call the batter-runner out for interference and also call out the next preceding runner for the action of his teammate. In no event may bases be run or runs scored because of such action by a runner.

It is interference by a batter or a runner when, in the judgment of the umpire, a baserunner willfully and deliberately interferes with a batted ball or a fielder in the act of fielding a batted ball with the obvious intent to break up a double play. The ball is dead. The umpire shall call the runner out for interference and also call out the batter-runner because of the action of his teammate. In no event may bases be run or runs scored because of such action by a runner.

Pitcher/Delivery *The Set Position* Set Position shall be indicated by the pitcher when he stands facing the batter with his entire pivot foot on, or in front of, and in contact with, and not off the end of the pitcher's plate, and his other foot in front of the pitcher's plate, holding the ball in both hands in front of his body and coming to a complete stop. From such Set Position he may deliver the ball to the batter, throw to a base or step backward off the pitcher's plate with his pivot foot. Before assuming Set Position, the pitcher may elect to make any natural preliminary motion such as that known as "the stretch." But, if he so elects, he shall come to Set Position before delivering the ball to the batter. After assuming Set Position any natural motion associated with his delivery of the ball to the batter commits him to the pitch without alteration or interruption.

Uniforms Any part of an undershirt exposed to view shall be of a uniform solid color for all players on a team. Any player other than the pitcher may have numbers, letters, insignia attached to the sleeve of an undershirt.

1965

Glove/Catcher The catcher may wear a leather glove or mitt no more than 38 inches in circumference, nor more than 15½ inches from top to bottom. Such limits shall include all lacing and any leather band or facing attached to the outer edge of the mitt. The space between the thumb section and the finger section of the mitt shall not exceed six inches at the top of the mitt and four inches at the base of the thumb crotch. The web shall measure not more than seven inches across the top or more than six inches from its top to the base of the thumb crotch. The web may be either a lacing or lacing through leather tunnels, or a center piece of leather which may be an extension of the palm, connected to the mitt with lacing and constructed so that it will not exceed any of the above mentioned requirements. The glove may be of any weight.

Interference/Offensive It is interference by a batter or runner if a batter-runner willfully and deliberately interferes with a batted ball or a fielder in the act of fielding a batted ball.

Runner/Bases Any runner shall be called out, on appeal, when with the ball in play, while advancing or returning to a base, he fails to touch each base in order before he, or a missed base, is tagged. Approved Ruling: (1) No runner may return to touch a missed base after a following runner has scored. (2) When the ball is dead, no runner may return to touch a missed base or one he has left after he has advanced to and touched a base beyond the missed base.

1966

There were no changes to the playing rules this year.

1967

Catch A catch is the act of a fielder in getting secure possession in his hand or glove of a ball in flight and firmly holding it; providing he does not use his cap, protector, pocket, or any other part of his uniform in getting possession. It is not a catch, however, if simultaneously or immediately following his contact with the ball, he collides with a player, or with a wall, or if he falls down, and as a result of such collision or falling, drops the ball. It is not a catch if a fielder touches a fly ball which then hits a member of the offensive team or an umpire and then is caught by another defensive player. If the fielder has made the catch and drops the ball while in the act of making a throw following the catch, the ball shall be adjudged to have been caught. In establishing the validity of the catch, the fielder shall hold the ball long enough to prove that he has complete control of the ball and that his release of the ball is voluntary and intentional.

Coach/Manager See *Pitcher/Visits*.

Interference/Offensive It is interference by a batter or runner when, in the judgment of the umpire, a batter-runner willfully and deliberately interferes with a batted ball or a fielder in the act of fielding a batted ball, with the obvious intent to break up a double play. The ball is dead. The umpire shall call the batter-runner out for interference and shall also call out the runner who had advanced closest to the home plate regardless where the double play might have been possible. In no event shall bases be run because of such interference.

The players, coaches, or any member of an offensive team shall vacate any space (including both dugouts) needed by a fielder who is attempting to field a batted or thrown ball. Penalty: Interference shall be called and the batter or runner on whom the play is being made shall be declared out.

The batter becomes a runner when a fair ball, after having passed a fielder other than the pitcher, or after having been touched by a fielder, including the pitcher, shall touch an umpire or runner on fair territory.

Interference/Umpire See above, *Interference/Offensive*.

Pitcher/Delivery Pitchers shall take signs from the catcher while standing on the rubber.

The ball becomes dead and runners advance one base, or return to their bases, without liability to be put out when a balk is committed.

Pitcher/Visits A professional league shall adopt the following rule pertaining to the visit of the manager or coach to the pitcher: (a) This rule limits the number of trips a manager or coach may make to any one pitcher in any one inning; (b) A second trip to the same pitcher in the same inning will cause the pitcher's automatic removal; (c) The manager or coach is prohibited from making a second visit to the mound while the same batter is at bat; but (d) If a pinch-hitter is substituted for this batter, the manager or coach may make a second visit to the mound, but must remove the pitcher.

A manager or coach is considered to have concluded his visit to the mound when he leaves the 18-foot circle surrounding the pitcher's rubber.

Runner A runner acquires the right to an unoccupied base

when he touches it before he is out. He is then entitled to it until he is put out, or forced to vacate it for another runner legally entitled to that base.

1968

Ball/Defaced　See *Pitcher/Illegal Act.*

Coach　See *Interference/Offensive.*

Interference/Offensive　The ball becomes dead and runners advance one base or return to their bases without liability to be put out when a base coach intentionally interferes with a thrown ball. Runners return to the base last legally touched.

Pitcher/Illegal Act　The pitcher shall not (1) bring his pitching hand in contact with his mouth or lips. Penalty: For violating this part of this rule the umpire shall warn the pitcher and if this action is repeated the umpire shall immediately disqualify the pitcher; (2) apply a foreign substance of any kind to the ball; (3) expectorate on the ball, his pitching hand, or his glove; (4) rub the ball on his glove, person, or clothing; (5) deface the ball in any manner; (6) deliver what is called the "shine" ball, "spit" ball, "mud" ball, or "emery" ball. The pitcher, of course, is allowed to rub the ball between his bare hands. Penalty: For violation of any part of this rule the umpire shall immediately disqualify the pitcher.

1969

Game　A game called at the end of a completed inning with the score tied after nine innings shall be a suspended game.

Pitcher/Position　The pitcher's plate shall be 10 inches above the level of home plate. The degree of slope from a point six inches in front of the pitcher's plate to a point six feet toward home plate shall be one inch to one foot, and such degree of slope shall be uniform.

Runner/Advancing　Any runner is out when he fails to re-touch his base after a fair or foul ball is legally caught before he or his base is tagged by a fielder. He shall not be called out for failure to re-touch his base after the first following pitch, or any play or attempted play. This is an appeal play.

Strike Zone　The strike zone is that space over home plate which is between the batter's armpits and the top of his knees when he assumes his natural stance. The umpire shall determine the strike zone according to the batter's usual stance when he swings at a pitch.

1970

There were no changes to the playing rules this year.

1971

Helmet　All players shall use some type of protective helmet while at bat.

1972

Appeal　An appeal is not to be interpreted as a play or an attempted play.

Successive appeals may not be made on a runner at the same base. If the defensive team on its first appeal errs, a request for a second appeal on the same runner at the same base shall not be allowed by the umpire.

Game/Suspended　A game may be suspended to be completed at a future date by reason of light failure or malfunction of a mechanical field device, e.g., automatic tarpaulin or water-removal equipment.

1973

Designated Hitter　Any league may elect to use the Designated Hitter (DH) rule as follows: (1) A hitter may be designated to bat for the starting pitcher and all subsequent pitchers in any game without otherwise affecting the status of the pitcher or pitcher in the game. A DH for the pitcher must be selected prior to the game and must be included in the lineup cards presented to the umpire-in-chief; (2) It is not mandatory that a club designate a hitter for the pitcher, but failure to do so prior to the game precludes the use of a DH for that game; (3) Pinch hitters for a DH may be used. Any substitute hitter for a DH becomes the DH. A replaced DH shall not re-enter the game in any capacity; (4) The DH may be used defensively, continuing to bat in the same position in the batting order, but the pitcher must then bat in the place of the substituted defensive player, unless more than one substitution is made, and the manager then must designate their spots in the batting order; (5) A runner may be substituted for the DH and the runner assumes the role of DH; (6) A DH is "locked" into the batting order. No multiple substitutions may be made that will alter the batting rotation of the DH; (7) Once the game-pitcher is switched from the mound to a defensive position this move shall terminate the DH role for the remainder of the game; (8) Once the game-pitcher bats for the DH this move shall terminate the DH's role for the remainder of the game. The game pitcher may only pinch-hit for the DH; (9) Once a DH assumes a defensive position this move shall terminate the DH role for the remainder of the game.

Note: The DH rule was adopted only by the American League.

Game　In all protested games, the decision of the league president shall be final.

1974

Ball/Defaced　See *Pitcher/Illegal Act.*

Helmet　All players are required to wear batting helmets with ear flaps.

Pitcher/Illegal Act　If, in his judgment, the umpire determines that a foreign substance has been applied to the ball, he shall (a) call the pitch a ball, warn the pitcher and have announced by the public address system the reason for the action; (b) in the case of a second offense by the same pitcher any time later in the game, the pitcher shall be disqualified from the game and may additionally be subject to such action as may be imposed by the league office; (c) if a play follows the violation called by the umpire, the manager of the offensive team may advise the plate umpire that he elects to decline the penalty and accept the play. Such election shall be made immediately at the end of the play. However, if a batter reaches first base on a hit, an error, a base on balls, a hit batsman, or otherwise, and no other runner is put out before advancing at least one base, the play shall proceed without reference to the violation; (d) even though the offense elects to take the play, the violation shall be recognized and the penalties in (a) and (b) will still be in effect; (e) the umpire shall be the sole judge on whether any portion of this rule has been violated.

1975

Ball　The ball can be covered with white cowhide as well as horsehide.

Bat　Cupped Bats　An indentation in the end of the bat up to one inch in depth is permitted and may be no wider than two inches and no less than one inch in diameter. The indentation must be curved with no foreign substance added.

Bat/Illegal　A batter is out for illegal action when he hits a fair ball with a filled, doctored, or flat-surfaced bat in which event he shall be immediately ejected from the game and suspended by his league president for three days.

Fielder/Drops Fly Ball　A batter is out when an infielder intentionally drops a fair fly ball or line drive, with first, first and second, first and third, or first, second, and third bases occupied before two are out. The ball is dead and runner or runners shall return to their original base or bases. Approved Ruling: In this situation, the batter is not out if the infielder permits the ball to drop untouched to the ground, except when the infield fly rule applies.

Game   A game may be suspended if local law prohibits the use of lights and it is too dark to continue.

Infield Fly   See *Fielder/Drops Fly Ball.*

Pitcher/Illegal Act   The pitcher shall not have on his person, or in his possession, any foreign substance. For such infraction of this section the penalty shall be immediate ejection from the game.

Runner/Advancing   Any runner shall be called out, on appeal, when after a fly ball is caught, he fails to re-touch his original base before he or his original base is tagged.

Runner/Awarded Bases   Each runner, including the batter-runner, may advance one base if a ball, pitched to the batter, or thrown by the pitcher from his position on the pitcher's plate to a base to catch a runner, goes into a stand or a bench, or over or through a field fence or backstop. The ball is dead. Approved Ruling: When a wild pitch or passed ball goes through or by the catcher, or deflects off the catcher, and goes directly into the dugout, stands, above the break, or any area where the ball is dead, the awarding of bases shall be one base. One base shall also be awarded if the pitcher, while in contact with the rubber, throws to a base, and the throw goes directly into the stands or into any area where the ball is dead.

   If, however, the pitched or thrown ball goes through or by the catcher or through the fielder, and remains on the playing field, and is subsequently kicked or deflected into the dugout, stands or other area where the ball is dead, the awarding of bases shall be two bases from position of runners at the time of the pitch or throw.

1976

Bat   The bat handle, for not more than 18 inches from the end, may be covered or treated with any material (including pine tar) to improve the grip. Any such material, including pine tar, which extends past the 18-inch limitation, in the umpire's judgment, shall cause the bat to be removed from the game. No such material shall improve the reaction or distance factor of the bat.

Bat/Illegal   The batter is out for illegal action when he uses or attempts to use a bat that, in the umpire's judgment, has been altered or tampered with in such a way to improve the distance factor or cause an unusual reaction on the baseball. This includes, bats that are filled, flat-surfaced, nailed, hollowed, grooved, or covered with a substance such as paraffin, wax, etc. No advancement on the bases will be allowed and any out or outs made during a play shall stand. In addition to being called out, the player shall be ejected from the game and may be subject to additional penalties as determined by the league president.

Designated Hitter   A Designated Hitter (DH) may not pinch run.

   Once a pinch hitter bats for any player in the batting order and then enters the game to pitch, this move shall terminate the DH role for the remainder of the game.

   A substitute for the DH need not be announced until it is the DH's turn to bat.

Player/Illegal Act   No manager, player, substitute, coach, trainer, or batboy shall at any time, whether from the bench, the coach's box or on the playing field, or elsewhere make intentional contact with the umpire in any manner.

Umpire   See *Player/Illegal Act.*

Uniform/Shoes   No player shall attach anything to the heel or toe of his shoe other than the ordinary shoe plate or toe plate. Shoes with pointed spikes similar to golf or track shoes shall not be worn.

1977

There were no changes to the playing rules this year.

1978

Designated Hitter   In the event of interleague competition between clubs of leagues using the Designated Hitter rule and clubs of leagues not using the Designated Hitter rule, the rule will be used as follows: (1) In exhibition games, the rule will be used or not used as is the practice of the home team; (2) In All-Star Games, the rule will only be used if both teams and both leagues so agree; (3) In World Series play, the rule will be used every other year. It will not be used in 1977, but will be used in 1978, etc.

Pitcher/Illegal Act   The pitcher shall not intentionally pitch at the batter. If, in the umpire's judgment, such a violation occurs, the umpire shall warn the pitcher and his manager that another such pitch will mean immediate expulsion of the pitcher. At the same time the umpire shall warn the opposing manager that such an infraction by his pitcher shall result in that pitcher's expulsion. If, in the umpire's judgment, there is another such pitch during the game by any pitcher, the umpire shall eject the pitcher from the game. If, in the umpire's judgment circumstances warrant, one or both teams may be officially "warned" prior to the game or an actual violation during the game in progress. League presidents may take additional action under the rules.

   Note: To pitch at a batter's head is unsportsmanlike and highly dangerous. It should be—and is—condemned by everybody. Umpires should act without hesitation in enforcement of this rule.

1979

There were no changes to the playing rules this year.

1980

Game   The rules of 1980 include several amendments to the rules governing suspended games and protested games.

Substitute/Fielder   If no announcement of a substitution is made, the substitute shall be considered as having entered the game when, if a fielder, he reaches the position usually occupied by the fielder he has replaced and play commences.

1981

Designated Hitter   The Designated Hitter (DH) named in the starting lineup must come to bat at least one time, unless the opposing club changes pitchers.

1982

Pitcher   Under extreme weather conditions a pitcher may warm his throwing hand by blowing on it provided both managers and umpires have agreed to this before the game begins.

1983

Helmet   All players shall use some type of protective helmet while at bat. All players in National Association Leagues shall wear a double ear-flap helmet while at bat. All players entering the major leagues commencing with the 1983 championship season and every succeeding season thereafter must wear a single ear-flap helmet (or at the player's option, a double ear-flap helmet), except those players who were in the major leagues during the 1982 season, and who, as recorded in that season, objected to wearing a single ear-flap helmet. If the umpire observes any violation of these rules, he shall direct the violation to be corrected. If the violation is not corrected within a reasonable time, in the umpire's judgment, the umpire shall eject the offender from the game.

1984

Bat   The bat handle, for not more than 18 inches from its end, may be covered or treated with any material or substance to improve the grip. Any such material or substance, which extends past the 18-inch limitation, shall cause the bat to be removed from the game.

1985

Uniform   No part of the uniform shall include patches or designs relating to commercial advertisements.

A league may provide that the uniforms of its member teams include the names of its players on their backs. Any name other than the last name of the player must be approved by the league president. If adopted, all uniforms for a team must have the names of its players.

1986

Designated Hitter   The Designated Hitter (DH) rule will be used or not used in World Series or exhibition games according to the practice of the home team.

1987

There were no changes to the playing rules this year.

1988

Bases   Home base shall be marked by a five-sided slab of whitened rubber. It shall be a 17-inch square with two of the corners removed so that one edge is 17 inches long, two adjacent sides are 8½ inches and the remaining two sides are 12 inches and set at an angle to make a point. It shall be set in the ground with the point at the intersection of the lines extending from home base to first base and to third base; with the 17-inch edge facing the pitcher's plate, and the two 12-inch edges coinciding with the first and third baselines. The top edges of home base shall be beveled and the base shall be fixed in the ground level with the ground surface.

Helmet   All catchers shall wear a catcher's protective helmet, while fielding their position.

All bat/ballboys or girls shall wear a protective helmet while performing their duties.

Pitcher/Delivery   The Set Position   Preparatory to coming to a set position, the pitcher shall have one hand by his side.

Set Position is assumed by the pitcher when he stands facing the batter with his entire pivot foot on, and parallel to, the pitcher's plate, or in front of, parallel to, and in contact with, the pitcher's plate. The non-pivot foot must be on the ground in front of the pitcher's plate. The pitcher must hold the ball in both hands in front of his body and come to a single complete and discernible stop before throwing the ball. A complete stop shall not be construed as occurring because of a change in direction of the hands and arms.

From such set position he must deliver the ball to the batter, throw to a base, or step backward off the pitcher's plate with his pivot foot.

Before assuming set position, the pitcher may elect to make any natural preliminary motion such as that known as "the stretch." But if he so elects, he shall come to a set position before delivering the ball to the batter. After assuming set position, any natural motion associated with his delivery of the ball to the batter commits him to the pitch without alteration or interruption.

The pitcher, following his stretch, must (a) hold the ball in both hands in front of his body and (b) come to a complete and discernible stop, with both feet on the ground. This must be enforced. Umpires should watch this closely, and should immediately call a "balk" for any violation.

Pitcher/Illegal Act   The pitcher shall not intentionally pitch at the batter. If, in the umpire's judgment, such a violation occurs,

the umpire may elect either to: (1) expel the pitcher, or the manager and the pitcher, from the game, or; (2) may warn the pitcher and the manager of both teams that another such pitch will result in the immediate expulsion of that pitcher (or a replacement) and the manager. If, in the umpire's judgment, and circumstances warrant, both teams may be officially "warned" prior to the game or at any time during the game. League presidents may take additional action under the rules.

1989

Bat   The bat shall be a smooth, *round* stick not more than 2¾ inches in diameter at the thickest part and not more than 42 inches in length. The bat shall be one piece of solid wood.

Note: No laminated or experimental bats shall be used in a professional game (either championship or exhibition games) until the manufacturer has secured approval from the Rules Committee of his design and methods of manufacture.

Pitcher/Delivery   The Set Position   Set Position shall be indicated by the pitcher when he stands facing the batter with his entire pivot foot on, or in front of, and in contact with, and not off the end of the pitcher's plate, and his other foot in front of the pitcher's plate, holding the ball in both hands in front of his body and coming to a complete stop. From such Set Position he may deliver the ball to the batter, throw to a base, or step backward off the pitcher's plate with his pivot foot. Before assuming Set Position, the pitcher may elect to make any natural preliminary motion such as that known as "the stretch." But if he so elects, he shall come to Set Position before delivering the ball to the batter. After assuming Set Position, any natural motion associated with his delivery of the ball to the batter commits him to the pitch without alteration or interruption.

Preparatory to coming to a set position, the pitcher shall have one hand on his side; from this position he shall go to his set position as defined above without interruption and in one continuous motion.

The whole width of the foot in contact with the rubber must be on the rubber. A pitcher cannot pitch from off the end of the rubber with just the side of his foot touching the rubber.

The pitcher, following his stretch, must (a) hold the ball in both hands in front of his body and (b) come to a complete stop. This must be enforced. Umpires should watch this closely. Pitchers are constantly attempting to "beat the rule" in their efforts to hold runners on bases and in cases where the pitcher fails to make a complete "stop" called for in the rules, the umpire should immediately call a "balk."

1990

There were no changes to the playing rules this year.

Index to Playing Rule Changes 1845–1990

Note: Dates shown following an entry refer to the year a rule change or amendment was adopted. Rule changes and summaries of rules are to be found in the chronology.

Alcoholic beverages prohibited 1881; 1882
Appeal play, fourth out on 1958
Appeal plays 1958; 1965; 1969; 1972; 1975
Balk (*See also* Pitcher, delivery by) 1845; 1858; 1863; 1867; 1868; 1872; 1873; 1876; 1883; 1885; 1886; 1887; 1900; 1910; 1920; 1939; 1940; 1949; 1950; 1954; 1955; 1957; 1963; 1988; 1989
Ball 1846–57; 1858; 1859; 1861; 1868; 1871; 1872; 1874; 1876; 1877; 1879; 1882; 1883; 1887; 1890; 1904; 1911; 1914; 1920; 1955; 1975
Ball, furnishing of 1858; 1868; 1869; 1870; 1874; 1876; 1877; 1887; 1896; 1904; 1920
Ball, intentional discoloring or defacing (*See also* Pitcher, freak deliveries by) 1890; 1897; 1907; 1908; 1920

Ball, replacing lost or damaged 1872; 1875; 1882; 1883; 1886; 1887; 1904; 1907

Balls, pitched (*See* Strike Zone)

Base on balls 1863; 1869; 1870; 1874; 1875; 1879; 1880; 1881; 1884; 1886; 1887; 1889; 1907; 1910; 1920; 1957

Base on balls, intentional 1920; 1955

Base (plate), Home 1845; 1858; 1868; 1872; 1874; 1875; 1877; 1885; 1887; 1900; 1950; 1988

Bases 1845; 1856; 1866; 1868; 1877; 1887; 1950

Bases, position of, distance between 1845; 1858; 1874; 1875; 1877; 1887

Bat 1858; 1868; 1869; 1872; 1874; 1885; 1886; 1893; 1895; 1940; 1950: 1954; 1964; 1975; 1976; 1984; 1989

Bat, colored, cupped, laminated 1954; 1964; 1975; 1989

Bat handle 1885; 1886; 1893; 1950; 1954; 1976; 1984

Batter, ball accidentally hits bat of 1874; 1920

Batter, ball hits bat a second time by 1940; 1950; 1954

Batter becomes baserunner 1845; 1858; 1863; 1869; 1870; 1874; 1875; 1879; 1880; 1881; 1884; 1886; 1887; 1889; 1892; 1899; 1902; 1907; 1910; 1920; 1931; 1940; 1950; 1955; 1957; 1964; 1967

Batter failing or refusing to bat (*See also* Batter out of batting order) 1869; 1874; 1877; 1950

Batter hit by pitch (*See* Hit by Pitch)

Batter, intentional effort to hit foul ball by 1887; 1902

Batter is out 1845; 1858; 1864; 1868; 1869; 1874; 1876; 1877; 1880; 1882; 1883; 1888; 1892; 1895; 1898; 1901; 1907; 1910; 1914; 1920; 1931; 1950; 1954; 1957; 1975; 1976

Batter out of batter's box (*See also* Batter's Box) 1868; 1976; 1878; 1910; 1955; 1957

Batter out of turn (*See also* Batting Order) 1874; 1883; 1895; 1898; 1957

Batter's Box 1858; 1867; 1868; 1870; 1871; 1872; 1874; 1875; 1876; 1877; 1878; 1885; 1886; 1887; 1907; 1910; 1955; 1957

Batting Order 1845; 1858; 1874; 1878; 1879; 1883; 1893; 1895; 1898; 1910; 1950; 1955

Bat, use of illegal 1975; 1976

Blocked ball (*See* Interference by spectators)

Bunt 1894; 1897; 1901; 1904; 1906; 1950; 1954

Captain (*See* Manager)

Catch, definition of legal 1845; 1858; 1864; 1868; 1869; 1874; 1880; 1883; 1950; 1954; 1967

Catcher 1878; 1882; 1892; 1895; 1899; 1901; 1907; 1920; 1939; 1940; 1949; 1950; 1954; 1955; 1957; 1963; 1964; 1965; 1967; 1975; 1988

Catcher's Box 1878; 1901

Catcher's interference (*See* Interference by catcher)

Catcher's mitt (*See* Glove, restrictions on)

Club, eligible 1867; 1869

Coaches, number of required 1957

Coach hit by thrown ball (*See also* Interference by coach) 1920

Coach, no fines for rule violations to be assessed to 1940

Coach required to be in uniform 1957

Coach, restrictions on 1872; 1874; 1887; 1892; 1904; 1914; 1920; 1940; 1949; 1957; 1967

Coach's Box 1872; 1874; 1877; 1887

Coach's interference (*See* Interference by coach)

Coach, use of offensive language by 1887, 1892

Contract, player's 1872; 1874; 1876; 1877

Darkness (*See* Game, delayed or terminated)

Dead Ball 1858; 1867; 1868; 1871; 1874; 1876; 1909; 1910; 1920; 1931; 1940; 1950; 1954; 1955; 1957; 1959; 1964; 1965; 1967; 1968; 1975

Death of player prevents game 1867; 1869; 1870; 1872

Defensive interference, definition of (*See also* Interference) 1964

Definitions of terms used in rules as special section 1950

Designated Hitter (DH) rule 1973; 1976; 1978; 1980; 1986

Dimensions of field (*See* Grounds, layout of)

Doubleheader 1920; 1940; 1950; 1957

Dugout, bench, player's area 1877; 1882; 1892; 1896; 1899; 1904; 1950

Emery Ball (*See* Pitcher, freak deliveries by)

Equipment, while at bat removal from field of 1954

Fair and Foul Balls 1845; 1858; 1861; 1867; 1870; 1876; 1877; 1884; 1887; 1894; 1897; 1901; 1902; 1904; 1906; 1909; 1910; 1920; 1931; 1940

Fair territory, definition of 1950

Fences on grounds 1871; 1885; 1892; 1904; 1940; 1959

Fielder distracting batter 1954

Fielder, legal catch by (*See* Catch, definition of legal)

First baseman's mitt (*See* Glove, restrictions on)

Force out (*See also* Runner forced to vacate base) 1846-57; 1858; 1920; 1958; 1963

Forfeited game 1858; 1868; 1869; 1870; 1872; 1874; 1881; 1890; 1892; 1906; 1909; 1955

Foul fly 1845; 1864; 1876; 1883; 1940; 1949

Foul lines 1861; 1874; 1876; 1877; 1887; 1906; 1940; 1950

Foul tip 1889; 1895; 1897; 1899; 1950

Gambling 1858; 1874; 1877

Game, "called" (no game) 1858; 1868; 1871; 1892; 1920; 1931

Game, choice of innings 1845; 1877; 1878; 1885; 1887; 1896; 1906

Game, commencement of 1866; 1868; 1887; 1896; 1906; 1940; 1942; 1949; 1950

Game, complete (official) 1845; 1846-57; 1858; 1859; 1860; 1866; 1868; 1869; 1871; 1876; 1892; 1907; 1920; 1931; 1957

Game, delayed or terminated (rain, darkness, locust, etc.) 1866; 1868; 1871; 1872; 1875; 1876; 1877; 1887; 1892; 1899; 1906; 1907; 1950

Game, drawn (tie game) 1869; 1872; 1876; 1920; 1931; 1969

Game of baseball defined 1950

Game, preliminaries 1845; 1858; 1874; 1893; 1904; 1909; 1910; 1940; 1950; 1955

Game, suspended 1907; 1931; 1954; 1957; 1969; 1972; 1975; 1980

Game winner defined 1845; 1846-57; 1858; 1869; 1876; 1892; 1899; 1907; 1920; 1931; 1950; 1957

Glass buttons or polished metal not to be used on uniforms 1931

Gloves, restrictions on 1895; 1931; 1939; 1950; 1965

Gloves, while at bat removal from field of 1954

"Ground rule" double 1885; 1892; 1914; 1926; 1931

Ground rules 1858; 1874; 1876; 1904; 1909; 1910; 1940

Grounds, fitness of (*See also* League President, Manager or Umpire as judge of fitness of grounds) 1872; 1880; 1887; 1896; 1906; 1950; 1955

Groundskeeper/Grounds Crew 1906; 1950; 1957

Grounds, layout of 1845; 1858; 1861; 1870; 1871; 1875; 1874; 1877; 1878; 1880; 1882; 1885; 1887; 1892; 1894; 1904; 1940; 1959

Helmet, bat/ballboys and girls 1988

Helmet, batter 1971; 1974; 1983

Helmet, catcher 1988

Hit by Pitch 1884; 1887; 1888; 1892; 1902; 1907; 1910; 1920; 1957

Home Base (plate) (*See* Base, Home)

Home run 1885; 1892; 1914; 1920; 1926; 1931; 1950; 1955

Illegally batted ball (*See* Batter out of batter's box)

Infield fly rule 1895; 1901; 1920; 1940; 1950; 1954; 1957; 1975

Inning, definition of 1845; 1858; 1950

Interference by batter 1845; 1846-57; 1872; 1877; 1882; 1892; 1907; 1910; 1914; 1931; 1950; 1954; 1955; 1965; 1967

Interference by catcher 1899; 1907; 1920; 1940; 1954; 1955; 1957; 1964

Interference by coach 1904; 1914; 1920; 1931; 1967; 1968

Interference by fielder 1954; 1955; 1957; 1964

Interference by retired runner 1940; 1955

Interference by runner 1845; 1846-57; 1872; 1880; 1882; 1887; 1888; 1910; 1920; 1931; 1940; 1950; 1954; 1955; 1963; 1964; 1965; 1967

Interference by spectators 1858; 1865; 1873; 1874; 1881; 1882; 1954; 1959

Interference by teammates 1867; 1904; 1931; 1940; 1950; 1955

Interference by umpire 1877; 1907; 1910; 1914; 1920; 1967

League President as judge of fitness of ground 1950

Malfunction of mechanical field devices 1972

Manager appealing for new ball 1875; 1882

Manager appealing to or addressing umpire (See Umpire, addressing the)

Manager as coach (See Coach, restrictions on)

Manager as judge of fitness of ground 1887

Manager may elect balk penalty or result of play 1954

Manager may elect freak delivery penalty or result of play 1974

Manager may elect interference penalty or result of play 1964

Manager's authority to call game a draw 1869

Manager's authority to position players 1846-57; 1858; 1871

Manager's choice of innings (See Game, choice of innings)

Manager's consent to replace umpire 1872; 1875

Manager selects opponent's substitute runner 1872; 1883; 1889

Mud Ball (See Pitcher, freak deliveries by)

Newsmen and photographers 1950; 1957

No changes in the playing rules 1862; 1905; 1912; 1913; 1915; 1916; 1917; 1918; 1919; 1921; 1922; 1923; 1924; 1925; 1927; 1928; 1930; 1932; 1933; 1934; 1935; 1936; 1937; 1938; 1941; 1943; 1944; 1945; 1946; 1947; 1948; 1951; 1952; 1953; 1956; 1960; 1961; 1962; 1966; 1970; 1977; 1979; 1987; 1990.

Objective of baseball club 1950

Obstruction 1858; 1868; 1876; 1897; 1931; 1950; 1957

Offensive interference, definition of (See also Interference) 1963

Pitcher allowed to warm up 1902; 1950; 1963

Pitcher attempting pickoff 1898; 1899; 1900; 1901; 1902; 1950; 1959; 1963; 1975

Pitcher, delivery by 1845; 1858; 1863; 1867; 1868; 1869; 1871; 1872; 1874; 1876; 1878; 1879; 1883; 1884; 1885; 1887; 1889; 1890; 1893; 1898; 1899; 1900; 1901;1902; 1904; 1910; 1914; 1920; 1931; 1939; 1940; 1949; 1950; 1954; 1955; 1957; 1963; 1964; 1968; 1988; 1989

Pitcher, disqualification of 1957; 1968; 1974; 1975; 1978; 1988

Pitcher, elevation of mound of 1903; 1950; 1969

Pitcher, failure to deliver pitch within 20 seconds by 1901; 1902; 1955; 1957

Pitcher, freak delivery by 1920; 1921; 1957; 1968; 1974

Pitcher, illness or injury to 1954

Pitcher, improper substitution for 1957

Pitcher intentionally throwing at batter 1879; 1978; 1988

Pitcher must face first batter when announced 1909; 1954

Pitcher permitted to blow on throwing hand in cold weather 1982

Pitcher permitted to use rosin bag 1926

Pitcher prohibited from bringing pitching hand in contact with mouth or lips 1968

Pitcher prohibited from possessing foreign substance 1975

Pitcher, removal from game of 1920

Pitcher, restrictions on visits by manager or coach to 1967

Pitcher's glove 1931; 1950

Pitchers of spitball certified and exempted from rule prohibiting freak deliveries for balance of career 1920; 1921

Pitcher's plate/box, distance from home base of 1858; 1863; 1881; 1890; 1893

Pitcher's position, box, plate, rubber 1858; 1863; 1866; 1867; 1869; 1870; 1872; 1874; 1881; 1886; 1887; 1893; 1895; 1903; 1910; 1914; 1939; 1950

Pitcher's uniform, restrictions on 1950; 1964

Pitcher to take signs from catcher while standing on rubber 1967

Pivot foot, definition of 1950

Player, eligible 1845; 1858; 1859; 1867; 1868; 1869; 1871; 1872; 1874; 1876

Player, expulsion 1877

Players conspiring against club 1877

Players except catcher to be in fair territory when play begins 1957

Players' positions 1846–57; 1858; 1871; 1879; 1910; 1920; 1957

Players prohibited from fraternizing with opponents while in uniform 1950; 1957

Players prohibited from mingling with spectators 1876; 1898; 1950; 1957

Players prohibited from using vulgar language 1896

Professional players 1867; 1869

Protested game 1973

Quick return pitch 1950; 1954

Rain (See Game, delayed or terminated)

Relief pitcher 1909, 1910, 1954, 1957

Runner acquires right to a base 1874; 1963; 1967

Runner advancing after caught fly ball 1858; 1859; 1863; 1871; 1876; 1920; 1940; 1958

Runner attempting to steal a base 1940

Runner caught in rundown 1920; 1950; 1957

Runner failing to re-touch a base 1969; 1975

Runner failing to touch a base 1863; 1868; 1876; 1920; 1931; 1957; 1963; 1965

Runner failing to touch home base 1950; 1958

Runner forced to vacate a base (See also Force out) 1858; 1869; 1870

Runner hit by batted ball 1877; 1880; 1888; 1890; 1909; 1910; 1920

Runner hit by batted ball not out if passes through fielder 1920

Runner hit by pitch in strike zone while attempting steal of home 1950

Runner is out 1845; 1846–57; 1858; 1876; 1877; 1880; 1890; 1904; 1907; 1909; 1910; 1914; 1920; 1939; 1940; 1958; 1965; 1969; 1975

Runner knocks ball from fielder's hand 1871; 1877

Runner may advance without liability to be put out 1845; 1858; 1863; 1867; 1868; 1871; 1872; 1873; 1876; 1881; 1882; 1883; 1885; 1886; 1887; 1897; 1900; 1907; 1910; 1914; 1920; 1931; 1939; 1940; 1949; 1950; 1954; 1955; 1957; 1959; 1963; 1967; 1968; 1975; 1988; 1989

Runner not affected by preceding runner's failure to touch a base 1963

Runner out of baseline 1858; 1876; 1931

Runner overruns first base 1871; 1872; 1874; 1876; 1883; 1887; 1940

Runner passing preceding runner 1897; 1904; 1907

Runner refusing to advance 1957

Runner returning to base 1858; 1859; 1860; 1874; 1876; 1880; 1883; 1887; 1889; 1897; 1910; 1914; 1931

Runner running bases in reverse order 1861; 1920; 1950

Run scored 1858; 1867; 1868; 1969; 1974; 1876; 1880; 1890; 1897; 1920; 1950

Security 1881; 1887

Set position, definition of 1950; 1964; 1988

Shine Ball (See Pitcher, freak deliveries by)

Shoes, player's 1887; 1899; 1976

Spectator interference (See Interference by spectators)

Spectators 1858; 1874; 1876; 1881; 1882; 1883; 1884; 1887; 1897; 1898; 1910; 1914; 1931; 1940; 1949; 1950; 1954; 1955; 1957; 1959

Spectators hissing or booing the umpire 1882

Spectators overflowing playing field 1910

Spitball (See Pitcher, freak deliveries by)

Squeeze play, definition of 1954

Strikeout 1845; 1858; 1867; 1876; 1880; 1887; 1888; 1902

Strikes (See Strike zone)

Strike zone 1858; 1863; 1867; 1869; 1870; 1871; 1872; 1874; 1875; 1876; 1877; 1880; 1887; 1888; 1894; 1895; 1899; 1901; 1902; 1904; 1906; 1907; 1909; 1910; 1920; 1950; 1954; 1955; 1957; 1963; 1969

Substitution 1858; 1868; 1869; 1871; 1872; 1874; 1876; 1877;

1878; 1881; 1889; 1890; 1891; 1893; 1897; 1899; 1909; 1910; 1920; 1931; 1950; 1957; 1976; 1980

Substitution for batter 1893; 1910; 1954; 1955

Substitution for designated hitter (*See* Designated Hitter rule)

Substitution for fielder 1980

Substitution for pitcher (*See* Relief Pitcher)

Substitution for runner 1869; 1871; 1872; 1874; 1878; 1881; 1889; 1910; 1931; 1950; 1955; 1976

"Time" called during game (*See also* Dead Ball) 1868; 1882; 1887; 1920; 1950; 1954; 1955

Touch, definition of 1957

Trainers 1940

Tripleheaders prohibited 1940

Triple play, definition of 1954

Umpire, accident to 1867; 1872; 1874; 1882; 1955

Umpire addressing spectators 1874; 1881; 1887; 1897; 1910

Umpire, addressing the 1858; 1874; 1876; 1880; 1882; 1887

Umpire, appealing to (*See also* Appeal plays) 1868; 1874; 1875; 1876; 1880; 1882; 1887; 1897; 1907

Umpire, appealing to spectators for assistance by 1874; 1881

Umpire as judge of fitness of grounds 1872; 1887; 1896; 1906; 1950

Umpire as paid employee 1874; 1883; 1884

Umpire assessing fines 1879; 1880; 1887; 1895; 1896; 1910

Umpire, authority to accept or reject ground rules by 1874; 1909

Umpire, authority to disqualify and remove personnel from field 1867; 1882; 1909; 1957

Umpire, calling foul balls by (*See also* Fair and Foul Balls) 1858; 1872

Umpire, calling pitch too early by 1874

Umpire consulting player before decision 1887

Umpire hit by batted ball 1907; 1910; 1920; 1967

Umpire hit by pitched or thrown ball 1877; 1910; 1914

Umpire, intentional contact prohibited with 1976

Umpire interference (*See* Interference by umpire)

Umpire, keeping score of game by 1845; 1858; 1865; 1867

Umpire, position of 1875; 1878; 1890

Umpire, replacing of 1867; 1872; 1874

Umpire reversing decision 1868; 1870; 1874; 1881; 1887; 1897

Umpire, selection of 1845; 1846-57; 1858

Umpires, procedure when decisions are in conflict by 1957

Umpires, system using two (Umpire-in-Chief) 1890; 1940; 1950; 1958

Umpire, uniform of 1885

Umpire, various responsibilities of 1845; 1858; 1861; 1867; 1868; 1869; 1872; 1874; 1876; 1879

Wild pitch, definition of 1954

Windup position, definition of 1950; 1963

Winner of game (*See* Game winner defined)

Scoring Rules for 1877

Batting

Section 1. The first item in the tabulated score, after the player's name and position, shall be the number of times he has been at bat during the game. Any time or times where the player has been sent to base on called balls shall not be included in this column.

Section 2. In the second column should be set down the runs made by each player.

Section 3. In the third column should be placed the first-base hits made by each player. A base hit should be scored in the following cases:

When the ball from the bat strikes the ground between the foul lines and out of the reach of the fielders.

When a hit is partially or wholly stopped by a fielder in motion, but such player cannot recover himself in time to handle the ball before the striker reaches first base.

When the ball is hit so sharply to an infielder that he cannot handle it in time to put out a man. In case of doubt over this class of hits, score a base hit and exempt the fielder from the charge of an error.

When a ball is hit so slowly toward a fielder that he cannot reach it before the batsman is safe.

Section 4. In the fourth column should be placed to the credit of each player the total bases made off his hits. The unit, or base, consists in getting from any one base to any other base without being put out, and the striker is to be credited not only with the number of bases which he himself makes after a hit, but, in addition, with those safely made by every other player who is on base at the time he runs toward first. It should be understood that a base or bases made off an error of a fielder count toward the score of the player who ran from home base toward first base when the error was made. All the bases made off such error, whether by the striker or by some other player then on base, shall go to the credit of the striker. The striker shall be credited with a base when he is sent to base on called balls, and, in addition, with all the bases made by other players who may be advanced on the play under the rules.

A base or bases shall be given to the runner for a successful steal, whether made on an error of his opponents, or without error.

Bases shall not be given to a striker when any player, other than himself, shall be put out on his strike.

Fielding

Section 5. The number of opponents put out by each player shall be set down in the fifth column. Where a striker is given out by the umpire for a foul strike or because he struck out of his turn, the putout shall be scored to the catcher.

Section 6. The number of times a player assists shall be set down in the sixth column. An assist should be given to each player who handles the ball in a runout or other play of the kind.

An assist should be given to the pitcher when a batsman fails to hit the ball on the third strike.

An assist should be given to the pitcher in each case where the batsman is declared out for making a foul strike or striking out of turn.

An assist should be given to a player who makes a play in time to put a runner out, even if the player who should complete the play fails, through no fault of the player assisting.

An assist should not be given to a player who muffs the ball, or allows it to bound off his body toward a player who then assists or puts out a player.

And, generally, an assist should be given to each player who handles the ball from the time it leaves the bat until it reaches the player who makes the putout, or in case of a thrown ball, to each player who throws or handles it cleanly, and in such way that a putout results, or would result, if no error were made by the receiver.

Section 7. An error should be given for each misplay, which allows the striker or baserunner to make one or more bases, when perfect play would have insured his being put out. In scoring errors off batted balls, see Sec. 3 of this Article.

Chronology of Scoring Rules 1878-1990

1878

Assist An assist is no longer denied a player who has a ball bounce off him toward another player who then makes an assist or putout.

On-Base In the fourth column should be placed to the credit of each player the number of times he reaches first base during the game, whether upon hits, errors, called balls, or in any other way he is not put out.

Total Bases The statistic crediting players with total bases is dropped from the rule book (Section 4 in 1877).

1879
There were no changes to the scoring rules this year.

1880

Base Hit Score a base hit when a ball is hit so slowly toward a fielder that he cannot handle it in time to put out a man.

Total Bases In the fourth column should be placed to the credit of each player the total bases run during the game. In scoring "bases run" where a player has reached first base as the result of the putting out of another player, such first base shall not be credited to the striker as one of the bases run by him.

Total Chances In the seventh column should be placed the "total chances offered" to retire players, which should include each perfect play, as well as each misplay or failure to accept a chance to retire a batsman or baserunner. "Chances offered" should not include "passed balls," "called balls," or "wild pitches." In scoring "chances offered" off batted balls, see Sec. 3 of the Scoring Rules.

Note: This rule does not appear in the scoring rules following 1880.

1881

Total Bases In the fourth column should be placed to the credit of each player the total bases made by him off his hits.

1882

In 1882 the American Association was founded, adopted the rule book, and made the following addition and deletion for their scoring rules:

Assist (American Association) An assist should be given to the pitcher on every chance offered to the catcher for a putout on a foul ball.

Total Bases (American Association) Total bases were not credited to the player's record.

1883

Assist The pitcher is no longer credited with an assist when the batsman fails to hit the ball on the third strike, or when the batsman is declared out for making a foul strike or for striking out of turn.

Assist (American Association) An assist should be given to the pitcher when a batsman fails to hit the ball on the third strike.

An assist should be given to the pitcher in each case where the batsman is declared out for making a foul strike, or striking out of turn. Such assistance is to be placed in the summary of the score.

Note: These two rules were dropped by the AA in 1884.

Error An error should be given to the pitcher when the batsman is given first base on "called balls."

Scoring Summary In the summary of the game should be credited to the pitcher the number of times a batsman fails to hit the ball on the third strike.

Scoring Summary (American Association) The summary shall contain: (1) The number of earned runs made by each side; (2) The number of two-base hits made by each player; (3) The number of three-base hits made by each player; (4) The number of home runs made by each player; (5) The number of men on each side left on bases; (6) The number of double and triple plays made by each side; (7) The number of men struck out by each pitcher; (8) The number of men given base on balls by each

pitcher; (9) The number of passed balls by each catcher; (10) The number of wild pitches by each pitcher; (11) The time of game; (12) The name of the umpire.

1884
In 1884 the Union Association was formed and adopted the same scoring rules used by the American Association, with the exception that the new league credited assists to the pitcher for strikeouts, batters called out for batting out of turn, and batters striking the ball while out of the batter's box. The Union Association existed for one season.

Scoring Summary (American Association) The number of men given bases from being hit by pitched balls is added to the summary.

Note: The Union Association did not include this in their summary.

Strikeout (American Association) A strikeout should be given to the pitcher when a batsman fails to hit the ball on the third strike, and in each case where the batsman is declared out for making a foul strike, or striking out of turn.

1885

Assist An assist shall be given the pitcher when the batsman fails to hit the ball on the third strike, and the same shall also be entered in the summary under the head of "struck out."

Note: This rule was dropped in 1889.

Error Wild pitches and passed balls shall be charged to the pitcher and catcher respectively in the error column, and shall also appear in the summary.

Note: This rule was dropped in 1886.

Error (American Association) An error shall be given for each misplay which allows the striker or baserunner to make one or more bases, when perfect play would have insured his being put out; except that wild pitches, bases on called balls, bases on the batsman being struck by a pitched ball, balks, and passed balls shall not be included in said column.

Note: The National League adopted this rule in 1887 and added the term "illegal pitched ball" to the exceptions. The phrase "bases on called balls" was deleted from the exceptions in 1888 only.

1886

Stolen Base Bases stolen by players shall appear to their credit in the summary of the game.

1887
In 1887 the National League and the American Association agreed to use the same scoring rules.

Assist An assist shall be given the pitcher when the batsman fails to hit the ball on the fourth [third in 1888] strike, and the same shall be entered in the summary under the head of "struck out."

Note: This rule was dropped in 1889.

Base Hit A base hit is to be scored when the batsman is awarded a base on balls.

Note: This rule was dropped in 1888.

Scoring Summary The summary shall contain: (1) The number of earned runs made by each side; (2) The number of two-base hits made by each player; (3) The number of three-base hits made by each player; (4) The number of home runs made by each player; (5) The number of double and triple plays made by each side, with the names of the players assisting in the same; (6) The number of men given bases on called balls by each pitcher; (7) The number of men given bases from being hit by pitched balls; (8) The number of passed balls by each catcher; (9) The number of wild pitches by each pitcher; (10) The time of the game; (11) The name of the umpire.

Stolen Base   In the fourth column shall be scored bases stolen, and shall include every base made after first base has been reached by a baserunner, except those made by reason of, or with the aid of, a "battery" error, or by batting, "balks" or by being forced off. In short, shall include all bases made by a "clean steal," or through a wild throw or muff of the ball by a fielder who is directly trying to put the baserunner out while attempting to steal a base.

Time at Bat   The first item in the tabulated score, after the player's name and position, shall be the number of times he has been at bat during the game. Any time or times where the player has been sent to base by being hit by a pitched ball or by the pitcher's illegal delivery, shall not be included in this column.

1888

Base Hit   In all cases where a baserunner is retired by being hit by a batted ball, the batsman should be credited with a base hit.

That when a player reaches first base through an error of judgment such as two fielders allowing the ball to drop between them, the batter shall not be credited with a base hit, nor the fielder charged with an error, but it shall be scored as an unaccepted chance, and the batter shall be charged with a time at the bat.

Note: This rule was dropped in 1889.

Earned Run   An earned run shall be scored every time the player reaches the home base unaided by errors before chances have been offered to retire the side, but bases on balls, though summarized as errors, shall be credited as factors in earned runs.

Note: This rule was deleted in 1898 but reappears in 1917. Also see 1912.

Stolen Base   In the fourth column shall be scored bases stolen, and shall be governed as follows: Any attempt to steal a base must go to the credit of the baserunner, but any manifest error is to be charged to the fielder making the same. If the baserunner advances another base he shall not be credited with a stolen base, and the fielder allowing the advancement is also to be charged with an error. If a baserunner makes a start and a battery error is made, the runner secures the credit of a stolen base, and the battery error is scored against the player making it. Should a baserunner overrun a base and then be put out, he should receive the credit for the stolen base.

Time at Bat   The first item in the tabulated score, after the player's name and position, shall be the number of times he has been at bat during the game. At any time or times where the player has been sent to base by being hit by a pitched ball, by the pitcher's illegal delivery, or by a base on balls shall not be included in this column.

1889

Base Hit   A base hit should be scored when a batted ball hits the person or clothing of the umpire as provided in the playing rules.

Earned Run   An earned run shall be scored every time the player reaches the home base unaided by errors before chances have been offered to retire the side.

Note: See entries under 1888, 1912, and 1917.

Sacrifice   In the fourth column shall be placed sacrifice hits, which shall be credited to the batsman, who when but one man is out advances a runner on base on a fly to the outfield or a ground hit, which results in putting out the batsman, or would so result if handled without error.

Scoring Summary   The number of bases stolen is added to the scoring summary.

1890

Assist   Assistances on strikes are not to be included in the record of fielding assistances.

Earned Run   Earned runs should be charged against the pitcher only on the basis of base hits made off the pitching, and should not include stolen bases or bases scored in any other way.

1891

Scoring Summary   The number of runs batted in by base hits by each batsman is added to the scoring summary.

1892

Stolen Base   The following sentence is added to the 1888 rule for scoring stolen bases: If a baserunner advances a base on a fly out, or gains two bases on a single base hit, or an infield out, or attempted out, he shall be credited with a stolen base, provided there is a possible chance and a palpable attempt made to retire him.

Note: This sentence was dropped from the rule in 1897.

1893

There were no changes to the scoring rules this year.

1894

Sacrifice   A sacrifice hit is to be credited to the batsman who advances a runner with no one out or one out by a bunt sacrifice which results in putting out the batsman.

Note: Previously the rule applied only with one out. See 1889.

Time at Bat   The batter is not charged with a time at bat for a sacrifice hit purposely made to the infield which advances a runner without resulting in a putout except to the batsman.

1895–6

There were no changes to the scoring rules in these years.

1897

Earned Run   An earned run shall be scored every time the player reaches the home base by the aid of base hits only before chances have been offered to retire the side.

Note: See entries under 1888, 1912 and 1917.

Sacrifice   In the fourth column shall be placed the sacrifice hits, which shall be credited to the batsman who, when no one is out or when but one man is out, advances a runner a base by a bunt hit, which results in putting out the batsman, or would so result if the ball were handled without error.

Scoring Summary   The summary shall contain: (1) The number of earned runs made off each pitcher; (2) The number of two-base hits made by each player; (3) The number of three-base hits made by each player; (4) The number of home runs made by each player; (5) The number of bases stolen by each player; (6) The number of double and triple plays made by each side and the names of the players assisting in the same; (7) The number of men given bases on called balls by each pitcher and the names of the players who were thus given bases; (8) The number of men given bases from being hit by pitched balls by each pitcher and the names of the players who are thus given bases; (9) The number of men struck out by each pitcher and the names of the players struck out; (10) The number of passed balls by each catcher; (11) The number of wild pitches by each pitcher; (12) The number of baserunners left on bases by each side; (13) The number of innings each pitcher played; (14) The number of base hits made off each pitcher; (15) The number of bases on balls given by each pitcher; (16) The number of batsmen hit by each pitcher; (17) The number of batsmen struck out by each pitcher [Note: This requirement apparently duplicates Sec. 9 above]; (18) The number of baserunners of each side who reached first base by fielding errors; (19) The time it took to play the game; (20) The condition of the weather; (21) The condition of the playing field; (22) The name of the umpire.

Stolen Base   The rule regarding stolen bases is now the same as that used between 1888 through 1891. Additional language adopted in 1892 and included through 1896 has been deleted. See 1892.

Time at Bat   The first item in the tabulated score, after the player's name and position, shall be the number of times he has been at bat during the game. The time or times when the player has been sent to base by being hit by a pitched ball, by the pitcher's illegal delivery, or by a base on balls, or has made a sacrifice hit which was manifestly intentional, shall not be included in this column.

1898

Assist   Assists should be credited to every player who handles the ball in the play which results in a baserunner being called out for interference or for running out of line.

Base Hit   A base hit should be scored when a ball is hit with such force to an infielder that he cannot handle it in time to put out the batsman. In case of doubt over this class of hits, score a base hit and exempt the fielder from the charge of an error.

In no case shall a base hit be scored when a baserunner has been forced out by the play.

Error   An error shall be given in the seventh column for each misplay which allows the striker or baserunner to make one or more bases when perfect play would have insured his being put out, except that "wild pitches," "bases on balls," bases on the batsman being struck by a "pitched ball," or in case of illegal pitched balls, balks and passed balls, all of which comprise battery errors, shall not be included in said column. In scoring errors of batted balls see Sec. 3 of this rule.

An error shall not be scored against the catcher for a wild throw to prevent a stolen base, unless the baserunner advances an extra base because of the error.

No error shall be scored against an infielder who attempts to complete a double play, unless the throw is so wild that an additional base is gained.

Putout   The number of opponents put out by each player shall be set down in the fifth column. Where a batsman is given out by the umpire for a foul strike, or where the batsman fails to bat in proper order, the putout shall be scored to the catcher. In all cases of "out" for interference, running out of line, or infield fly dropped, the "out" should be credited to the player who would have made the play but for the action of the baserunner or batsman.

Scoring Summary   The summary shall contain: (1) The score made in each inning of the game; (2) The number of bases stolen by each player; (3) The number of two-base hits made by each player; (4) The number of three-base hits made by each player; (5) The number of home runs made by each player; (6) The number of double and triple plays made by each side and the names of the players assisting in the same; (7) The number of innings each pitcher pitched in; (8) The number of base hits made off each pitcher; (9) The number of times the pitcher strikes out the opposing batsmen; (10) The number of times the pitcher gives bases on balls; (11) The number of wild pitches charged to the pitcher; (12) The number of times the pitcher hits batsmen with pitched ball; (13) The number of passed balls by each catcher; (14) The time of the game; (15) The names and positions of each umpire.

Stolen Base   A stolen base shall be credited to the baserunner whenever he reaches the base he attempts to steal unaided by a fielding or by a battery error or a hit by the batsman.

Time at Bat   The first item in the tabulated score, after the player's name and position, shall be the number of times he has been at bat during the game. No time at bat shall be scored if the batsman be hit by a pitched ball while standing in his position,

and after trying to avoid being so hit, or in case of the pitcher's illegal delivery of the ball to the bat which gives the batsman his base, or when he intentionally hits the ball to the field, purposely to be put out, or if he is given first base on called balls.

1899–1903

There were no changes to the scoring rules in these years.

1904

Assist   The number of times, if any, each player assists in putting out an opponent shall be set down in the sixth column. An assist should be given to each player who handles the ball in aiding in a run-out or any other play of the kind, except the one who completes it.

Note: The rule remains unchanged except to clarify that the fielder completing a run-down play by making the putout is not to be credited with an assist even if he handled the ball prior to receiving it again to make the putout. But see the entry under 1910.

Base Hit   A base hit should be scored when the ball is hit so slowly toward a fielder that he cannot handle it in time to put out the batsman or force out a baserunner.

Note: The phrase "or force out a baserunner" has been added to the original rule. See 1878.

Error   An error shall be given in the seventh column for each misplay which prolongs the time at bat of the batsman or allows a baserunner to make one or more bases when perfect play would have insured his being put out. But a wild pitch, a base on balls, a base awarded to a batsman by being struck by a pitched ball, an illegal pitch, a balk and a passed ball, each of which is a battery and not a fielding error, shall not be included in the seventh column.

In case a baserunner advance a base through the failure of a baseman to stop or try to stop a ball accurately thrown to his base, he shall be charged with an error and not the player who made such throw, provided there were occasion for it. If such throw be made to second base, the scorer shall determine whether the second baseman or shortstop shall be charged with an error.

Putout   The number of opponents, if any, put out by each player shall be set down in the fifth column. Where the batsman is given out by the umpire for a foul strike, or fails to bat in proper order, the putout shall be scored to the catcher. In cases of the baserunner being declared "out" for interference, running out of line, or on an infield fly, the "out" should be credited to the player who would have made the play but for the action of the baserunner or the announcement of the umpire.

Note: The phrase "or the announcement of the umpire" has been added in place of "or batsman." See 1898.

Sacrifice   In the fourth column shall be placed the sacrifice hits. A sacrifice hit shall be credited to the batsman who, when no one is out or when but one man is out, advances a runner a base by a bunt hit, which results in the batsman being put out before reaching first, or would so result if it were handled without error.

Note: The phrase "before reaching first" has been added to the rule. See 1889.

Scoring Summary   The scoring summary is to include the total runs by each side as well as the score made in each inning.

Stolen Base   A stolen base shall be credited to the baserunner whenever he advances a base unaided by a base hit, a putout, a fielding or a battery error.

Time at Bat   The first item in the tabulated score, after the player's name and position, shall be the number of times he has been at bat during the game, but the exceptions made in rule 82 must not be included.

Note: See rule 82 below.

"A Time at Bat" is the term at-bat of a batsman. It begins when he takes his position, and continues until he is put out or becomes a baserunner. But a time at bat shall not be charged against a batsman who is awarded first base by the umpire for being hit by a pitched ball or for the illegal delivery of the pitcher, or on called balls, or when he makes a sacrifice hit.

1905–06

There were no changes to the scoring rules in these years.

1907

Base Hit In all cases where a baserunner is retired by being hit by a batted ball, unless batted by himself, the batsman should be credited with a base hit.

Game Played All appearances by a player in a championship game count as a game played in the American League, which prior to 1907 had not so credited the appearances of pinch hitters, pinch runners, and defensive substitutes in most cases. See 1912 for National League.

1908

Sacrifice A sacrifice hit shall be credited to the batsman who, when no one is out or when but one man is out, advances a runner a base by a bunt hit, which results in the batsman being put out before reaching first, or would so result if it were handled without error. A sacrifice hit shall also be credited to a batsman who, when no one is out or when but one man is out, hits a fly ball that is caught but results in a run being scored.

1909

Double Play A double play shall mean any two continuous putouts that take place between the time the ball leaves the pitcher's hands until it is returned to him again standing in the pitcher's box.

Error In case a runner advances a base through the failure of a baseman to stop or try to stop a ball accurately thrown to his base, the latter shall be charged with an error and not the player who made such throw, provided there was occasion for it. If such throw be made to second base, the scorer shall determine whether the second baseman or shortstop shall be charged with an error.

An error shall be given in the sixth column for each misplay which prolongs the time at bat of the batsman or allows a baserunner to make one or more bases when perfect play would have insured his being put out. But a base on balls, a base awarded to a batsman by being struck by a pitched ball, an illegal pitch, a balk, a passed ball or wild pitch, unless such wild pitch or passed ball be on the third strike and allow the batter to reach first base, shall not be included in the sixth column. In case of a wild pitch or a passed ball allowing the batter to reach first base, the pitcher or the catcher, as the case may be, shall be charged with an error.

In event of a fielder dropping a fly but recovering the ball in time to force a batter at another base, he shall be exempted from an error, the play being scored as a "force-out."

Putout The number of opponents, if any, put out by each player shall be set down in the fourth column. Where the batsman is given out by the umpire for a foul strike, or fails to bat in proper order, or is declared out on third bunt strike, the putout shall be scored to the catcher. In cases of the baserunner being declared "out" for interference, running out of line, or on an infield fly, the "out" should be credited to the player who would have made the play but for the action of the baserunner or the announcement of the umpire.

Sacrifice A sacrifice hit shall be credited to the batsman who, when no one is out or when but one man is out, advances a runner a base by a bunt hit, which results in the batsman being put out

before reaching first, or would so result if it were handled without error. A sacrifice hit shall also be credited to a batsman who, when no one is out or when but one man is out, hits a fly ball that is caught but results in a run being scored, or would in the judgment of the scorer so result if caught.

Scoring Summary The summary shall contain: (1) The score made in each inning of the game and the total runs of each side in the game; (2) The number of stolen bases, if any, by each player; (3) The number of sacrifice hits, if any, made by each player; (4) The number of sacrifice flies, if any, made by each player; (5) The number of two-base hits, if any, made by each player; (6) The number of three-base hits, if any, made by each player; (7) The number of home runs, if any, made by each player; (8) The number of double and triple plays, if any, made by each club and the players participating in same; (9) The number of innings each pitcher pitched in; (10) The number of base hits, if any, made off each pitcher and the number of legal at-bats scored against each pitcher; (11) The number of times, if any, the pitcher strikes out the opposing batsmen; (12) The number of times, if any, the pitcher gives bases on balls; (13) The number of wild pitches, if any, charged against the pitcher; (14) The number of times, if any, the pitcher hits a batsman with a pitched ball, the name or names of the batsman or batsmen so hit to be given; (15) The number of passed balls by each catcher; (16) The time of the game; (17) The name of the umpire or umpires.

Stolen Base A stolen base shall be credited to the baserunner whenever he advances a base unaided by a base hit, a putout, a fielding or a battery error, subject to the following exceptions: (1) In event of a double steal being attempted from bases one and two to bases two and three, where either is thrown out, the other shall not be credited with a stolen base; (2) In event of a baserunner being touched out after sliding over a base, he shall not be regarded as having stolen the base in question; (3) In event of a baserunner making his start to steal a base prior to a battery error, he shall be credited with a stolen base; (4) In event of a palpable muff of a ball thrown by the catcher, when the baserunner is clearly blocked, the infielder making the muff shall be charged with an error and the baserunner shall not be credited with a stolen base.

1910

Assist The number of times, if any, each player assists in putting out an opponent shall be set down in the fifth column. An assist should be given to each player who handles the ball in aiding in a run-out or any other play of the kind, even though he complete the play by making the putout.

Note: Compare to the 1904 rule.

Error An error shall be given in the sixth column for each misplay which prolongs the time at bat of the batsman or allows a baserunner to make one or more bases when perfect play would have insured his being put out. But a base on balls, a base awarded to a batsman by being struck by a pitched ball, a balk, a passed ball, or wild pitch shall not be included in the sixth column.

Passed Ball A passed ball is a legally delivered ball that the catcher should hold or control with ordinary effort, but his failure to do so enables the batsman, who becomes a baserunner on such pitched ball, to reach first base or a baserunner to advance.

Stolen Base In event of a double or triple steal being attempted, where either runner is thrown out, the other or others shall not be credited with a stolen base.

Wild Pitch A wild pitch is a legally delivered ball, so high, low or wide of the plate that the catcher cannot or does not stop and control it with ordinary effort, and as a result the batsman, who becomes a baserunner on such pitched ball, reaches first base or a baserunner advances.

1911

There were no changes to the scoring rules this year.

1912

Earned Run An earned run is charged to the pitcher every time a player scores by the aid of safe hits, sacrifice hits, bases on balls, hit batters, wild pitches, and balks before fielding chances have been offered to retire the side.

Note: This rule is not included in the scoring rules for 1912 but earned runs were compiled in the official pitching records of the National League (1912) and American League (1913). The earned run scoring rule does not appear in the scoring rules until 1917.

Game Played All appearances by a player in a championship game count as a game played in the National League, which prior to 1912 had not so credited the appearances of pinch hitters, pinch runners, and defensive substitutes, with certain exceptions.

1913

There were no changes to the scoring rules this year.

1914

Assist The number of times, if any, each player assists in putting out an opponent shall be set down in the fifth column. One assist and no more shall be given to each player who handles the ball in aiding in a run-out or any other play of the kind even though he complete the play by making the putout.

Note: Compare to 1910 and 1904.

Base Hit A base hit should be scored when the ball from the bat strikes the ground on or within the foul lines and out of reach of the fielders, provided the batter reaches first base safely.

When a fielder, after handling a batted ball, elects to try to retire a baserunner instead of the batter, the play is known as a "fielder's choice." In case the runner is retired, or would be retired but for an error, the batter shall be charged with a time at bat, but no hit. If the runner is not retired, and no error is made, the batter shall be charged with a time at bat, but no hit, provided he swung at the ball, and shall be credited with a sacrifice hit, provided he bunted the ball; if, however, in the judgment of the scorer, the batter could not have been retired at first base by perfect fielding, he shall be credited with a base hit.

Error In event of a baserunner making his start to steal a base prior to a battery error, he shall be credited with a stolen base and the battery error shall also be charged.

An error shall not be scored against the catcher or an infielder who attempts to complete a double play, unless the throw be so wild that an additional base be gained. This, however, does not exempt from an error a player who drops a thrown ball when by holding it he would have completed a double play.

An error shall be given in the sixth column for each misplay which prolongs the time at bat of the batsman or prolongs the life of the baserunner or allows a baserunner to make one or more bases when perfect play would have insured his being put out. But a base on balls, a base awarded to a batsman by being struck with a pitched ball, a balk, a passed ball, or wild pitch shall not be included in the sixth column.

Note: The phrase "or prolongs the life of the baserunner" has been added to the existing rule.

Fielder's Choice See *Base Hit*.

Sacrifice A sacrifice hit shall also be credited to a batsman who, when no one is out or when but one man is out, hits a fly ball that is caught but results in a run being scored on the catch, or would in the judgment of the scorer so result if caught.

1915–16

There were no changes to the scoring rules in these years.

1917

Earned Run A run earned off the pitcher shall be scored every time a player reaches home base by the aid of safe hits, sacrifice hits, stolen bases, bases on balls, hit batsmen, wild pitches, and balks, before fielding chances have been offered to retire the side.

The pitcher shall be given the benefit of doubt whenever fielding errors are made and in determining the base to which a runner should have been held with perfect support on part of fielders. A fielding error made by the pitcher shall be considered the same as any other fielding error. No run can be earned that scores as a result of the batsman having reached first base on a fielding error or passed ball; nor can any run be earned after the fielding side has failed to accept chances offered to retire the side.

Percentage To determine the pitcher's percentage for the season, the total number of runs earned off his pitching shall be divided by the total number of innings he has pitched; then multiplied by nine, to find his average effectiveness for a complete game.

1918–19

There were no changes to the scoring rules in these years.

1920

Error An error shall be charged to the first baseman if, on receiving a throw in ample time to retire the batsman, he fail to touch first base.

An error shall be charged to the catcher if he drop a third strike, allowing the runner to reach first base; except this rule is not to apply in case of a wild pitch.

Game Ending Hit If, in the last half of the final inning, with the winning run on base, the batsman drives home that run, credit shall be given him for as many bases on his hit as the runner advances; except, however, that in case of the batsman driving a fair ball out of the playing field, he shall receive credit for a home run.

Percentage To determine the percentage of games won and lost, divide the total number of games won and lost into the number won.

To determine batting averages, divide the total "Times at Bat" into the total number of base hits.

To determine fielding averages, divide the total of putouts, assists, and errors into the total of putouts and assists.

In all cases where the remaining fraction is one-half or over, a point is added to the average.

Sacrifice A sacrifice hit shall also be credited to a batsman who, when no one is out or when but one man is out, hits a fly ball that is caught but results in a run being scored on the catch, or would in the judgment of the scorer so result if caught; but no distinction shall be made in the summary as between bunted or fly-ball sacrifices.

Scoring Summary The scoring summary is to include sacrifice flies (within the category of sacrifice hits) and the number of runs batted in by each batsman.

Stolen Base No stolen base shall be credited to a runner who is allowed to advance without any effort being made to stop him.

Wild Pitch See *Error*, second paragraph.

1921–25

There were no changes to the scoring rules in these years.

1926

Error   See *Wild Pitch.*

Passed Ball   The catcher shall be charged with a passed ball when a baserunner is enabled to advance by the catcher's failure to hold or control a legally delivered ball that should have been held or controlled with ordinary effort.

Wild Pitch   An error shall be charged to the pitcher if he make a wild pitch for the third strike, and the batsman reach first base; in such case the pitcher shall not have credit for a strikeout.

A wild pitch is a legally delivered ball, so high, low, or wide of the plate that the catcher cannot or does not stop and control it with ordinary effort, and as a result the batsman reaches first base or a baserunner advances.

1927–30

There were no changes to the scoring rules in these years.

1931

Assist   Credit an assist to a player who, by deflecting a batted ball with his glove or any part of his body, aids in retiring the batsman or another baserunner.

Credit an assist to each player who handles and throws the ball in such a way that a putout would have resulted except for the error of a teammate.

Do not credit an assist to a fielder who makes a bad throw, even when a runner trying to advance on it is subsequently retired. A play that follows an error is a new play and the player making an error is not entitled to an assist unless he takes part in the new play.

Do not credit an assist to the pitcher when, in legally delivering the ball to the batsman, he helps to retire a runner attempting to steal home.

Base Hit   A base hit shall be scored in the following cases: (1) When a fair hit is made, as defined in the Playing Rules, and the batsman reaches first base safely; (2) When a fair hit ball is partially or wholly stopped by a fielder in motion, but such player cannot recover himself in time to field the ball to first before the batsman reaches that base, or to some other base in time to force out another runner; (3) When a ball is hit with such force to an infielder or pitcher that he cannot handle it in time to put out the batsman or force out a baserunner; except when the ball is recovered by another fielder in time to retire the batsman or force out a baserunner. In case of doubt over this kind of hit, a base hit should be scored and the fielder be exempted from the charge of an error.

Earned Run   A run earned off the pitcher shall be scored every time a player reaches home base by the aid of safe hits, sacrifice hits, stolen bases, putouts, bases on balls, hit batsman, wild pitches, or balks, before fielding chances have been offered to retire the side.

The pitcher shall be given the benefit of doubt whenever fielding errors are made and in determining the base to which a runner should have been held with perfect support on part of fielders. A fielding error made by the pitcher shall be considered the same as any other fielding error. No run can be earned that scores as a result of the batsman having reached first base on a catcher's interference, a fielding error, or passed ball; nor can any run be earned after the fielding side has failed to accept chances offered to retire the side.

Note: The phrase "catcher's interference" has been added to the prior rule. See entry for 1917.

Error   An error, but not a passed ball, shall be charged to the catcher if he drops or misses a third strike, allowing the batsman to reach first base. Credit the pitcher with a strikeout.

An error shall be charged to the first baseman (or the pitcher or second baseman when covering first base) if, on receiving a throw in ample time to retire the batsman, he does not touch first base as required by rule. The same rule shall be followed with respect to any fielder covering any other base on a force play.

Forfeited Game   In a regulation game which the umpire shall declare forfeited after four and one-half innings have been played, all individual and team averages shall be incorporated in the official playing records.

Game-Ending Hit   If, in the last half of the final inning, with the winning run on base, the batsman drives home that run, credit shall be given him for as many bases as, in the judgment of the official scorer, he would have made under normal conditions; the number, however, not to exceed the number of bases advanced by the runner; except when the batsman drives a fair ball out of the playing field, he shall receive credit for a home run, provided he legally touches each base in proper order.

Hit by Pitch   When a batsman is hit by what would have been the fourth called ball, it shall be scored as a "hit by pitcher."

Passed Ball   See *Error.*

Percentage   In determining averages where the remaining fraction is one-half or over, a full point is to be added to the average.

Putout   The number of opponents, if any, put out by each player shall be set down in the fourth column. When the batsman is called out by the umpire for an illegally batted ball, or for a foul third strike bunt, or for being hit by his own batted ball, or for interference with the catcher, or for failing to bat in proper turn, the putout shall be credited to the catcher. When a baserunner is declared out on an infield fly, the putout shall be credited to the player who would have made the play except for the action of the runner or the announcement of the umpire. When a baserunner is declared out because of being hit by a batted ball, the putout shall be credited to the fielder nearest to the ball at the time of the occurrence.

Run Batted In   Runs batted in should include runs scored on safe hits (including home runs), sacrifice hits, infield outs, and when the run is forced over by reason of batsman becoming a baserunner. With less than two out, if an error is made on a play on which a runner from third would ordinarily score, credit the batsman with a run batted in.

Stolen Base   In the event of a palpable muff of a ball thrown by the catcher, when, in the judgment of the scorer, the baserunner would have been out if the ball had been held, the infielder making the muff shall be charged with an error and the baserunner shall not be credited with a stolen base.

When a wild pitch or a passed ball occurs after a runner has started to steal, do not credit the runner with a stolen base but charge the wild pitch or passed ball.

Do not give a stolen base to a runner who has started to steal and the pitcher balks.

Time at Bat   A "Time at Bat" is the term at bat of a batsman. It begins when he takes his position, and continues until he is put out or becomes a baserunner. But a time at bat shall not be charged against a batsman who is awarded first base by the umpire for being hit by a pitched ball, or on called balls, or when he makes a sacrifice hit, or for interference by the catcher.

Note: This rule is Rule 69, Sec. 5, of the Playing Rules.

The first item in the tabulated score, after the player's name and position, shall be the number of times he has been at bat during the game, but the exceptions made in Rule 69, Sec. 5, must not be included.

Note: See above entry for Rule 69, Sec. 5, of the Playing Rules.

Wild Pitch   A wild pitch is a legally delivered ball, so high, low, or wide of the plate that the catcher cannot or does not stop and control it with ordinary effort, and as a result the batsman reaches first base or a baserunner advances. Any pitched ball that strikes the ground before reaching the home plate and

passes the catcher, allowing runners to advance, shall be scored
as a wild pitch.

1932–38

There were no changes to the scoring rules in these years.

1939

Base Hit/Value In event of a batsman oversliding second or
third bases and being tagged by the opposing fielder when said
batsman is attempting to stretch a single into a two-base hit or a
two-base hit into a three-base hit, the play should be scored the
same as when a baserunner attempts to steal, overslides the base
and is tagged out. In other words, the batsman oversliding second base and is tagged out shall be credited only with a single,
while one who overslides third base and is tagged out shall be
credited only with a two-base hit.

Earned Run A wild pitch which is a third strike is to be used in
determining earned runs charged to the pitcher.

Run Batted In The batsman shall not be credited with driving
in a run when a runner scores as he hits into a force infield double
play or a double play in which the first baseman picks up a fair
hit ground ball, touches first base and then throws to second
retiring the runner who had been on first, said runner not being
forced, has to be tagged out.

Sacrifice A sacrifice hit also shall be credited to the batsman
who, when no one is out or when but one man is out, hits a fly ball
that is caught but which results in a baserunner scoring, or would
have scored a runner if said fly ball had not been dropped for an
error, in the judgment of the scorer; but no distinction shall be
made in the summary as between bunted or fly ball sacrifices.

1940

Base Hit In all cases where a baserunner is retired by being hit
by a batted ball, unless batted by himself, the batsman should be
credited with a base hit, except if the runner is hit by an infield
fly, the play should be scored as provided in the Playing Rules
(Sec. 8 of Rule 44).

Earned Run A run earned off the pitcher shall be scored every
time a player reaches home base by the aid of safe hits, sacrifice
hits, stolen bases, putouts, bases on balls, hit batsman, wild
pitches, or balks, even though the wild pitch be a third strike,
before fielding chances have been offered to retire the team. The
preceding pitcher, and not a relieving pitcher shall be charged
with runs scored by any runners on base when such relief pitcher
entered the game. The relieving pitcher shall not be charged
with his first batsman reaching first base if such batsman had
any advantage because of poor pitching by the preceding
pitcher. With the count two or three balls and one or no strikes,
or three balls and two strikes, charge preceding pitcher if batsman reaches first base, but credit relieving pitcher if batsman is
retired. With count one or two balls and two strikes, charge
relieving pitcher if batsman reaches first base and credit him if
batsman is retired.

Forfeited Game In a regulation game which the umpire shall
declare forfeited after four and one-half innings have been
played, all individual and team averages shall be incorporated in
the official playing records, except that no pitcher shall be
credited with a victory or charged with a loss in said game.

1941–49

There were no changes to the scoring rules in these years.

1950

Assist An assist shall be credited to each player who throws or
deflects a batted or thrown ball in such a way that a putout
results, or would have resulted except for a subsequent error by a
teammate, but only one assist and no more shall be credited to

each player who throws or deflects the ball in a rundown play
which results in a putout, or would have resulted in a putout,
except for a subsequent error.

Credit an assist to each player who throws or deflects the ball
during a play which results in a baserunner being called out for
interference, or for running out of line.

Do not credit an assist to a pitcher when, in legally delivering
the ball to a batter, he helps to retire a baserunner attempting to
steal home.

Situations will arise in which a wild throw shall be scored as an
assist and not as an error while on some plays a wild throw shall
be scored both as an assist and as an error.

Note: The scoring rules for 1950 then present four detailed
examples illustrating the application of the assist provisions.

Base Hit A base hit shall be scored under these circumstances:
(1) When a batter reaches first base (or any succeeding base)
safely on a legally batted ball which settles on fair ground or
strikes a fence behind fair ground before being touched by a
fielder, or which clears a fence behind fair territory; (2) When a
batter reaches first base after hitting a ball with such force, or so
slowly, that the pitcher or fielder attempting to make a play with
it has no opportunity to do so; (3) When a batter reaches first
base safely on a batted ball which strikes either first base, second, or third base before being touched by a fielder and bounces
away from the reach of the fielder; (4) When a batter reaches
first base safely on a legally batted ball which has not been
touched by a fielder and which is in fair territory when it bounds
into the outfield unless in the scorer's judgment it could have
been handled with ordinary effort; (5) When a legally batted ball
which has not been touched by a fielder becomes "dead" by
reason of touching the person or clothing of a runner or umpire,
except that when a runner is called out for having been struck by
an "infield fly" the batter shall not be credited with a hit; (6)
When, in the scorer's judgment, the batter could not have been
retired at first base by perfect fielding, when the fielder fails in an
attempt to retire a preceding baserunner; (7) Always give the
batter the benefit of the doubt. A safe course to follow being to
score a hit when exceptionally good fielding of a batted ball fails
to result in a putout; (8) In no case shall a base hit be scored
when a runner is forced out by a batted ball, or would have been
forced out except for a fielding error. Nor shall a hit be scored
when an infield batted ball results in another runner, who is
attempting to advance one base, being retired, whether forced
out or not; (9) Score the play as a "fielder's choice" when a
fielder uses a batted ball to retire a preceding baserunner, or
would have retired one with ordinary effort except for a fielding
error, charging the batter with time at bat, but no hit.

Base Hit/Value Whether a safe hit shall be scored as a one-
base hit, two-base hit or a three-base hit when no error or putout
results shall be determined as follows:

It is a one-base hit if the batter stops at first base; it is a two-
base hit if the batter stops at second base; it is a three-base hit if
the batter stops at third base, but note this exception: the batter
must, if attempting to take two or three bases on a safe hit by
sliding, hold the last base to which he advances. If he overslides
and is tagged out before getting back to the base safely he shall
be given credit for only as many bases as he safely attained. If he
overslides second base and is tagged out he shall be given a one-
base hit; if he overslides third base and is tagged out, he shall be
given a two-base hit. If he runs past second base after reaching
that base on his feet, attempts to return and is tagged out, he
shall be given credit for a one-base hit. If he runs past third base
after reaching that base on his feet, attempts to return and is
tagged out, he shall be given credit for a three-base hit.

If a batter is awarded three bases on a batted or bunted ball
because a fielder has touched the ball with his glove, cap, or any
other part of his uniform while such article is detached from its
proper place on his person, the scorer's judgment shall dictate
whether the batter shall be given credit for a one-base hit, a two-

base hit, a three-base hit, or a home run. If the scorer believes the fielder could have, by ordinary effort, kept the hit from being good for more than one, two, or three bases he shall score it as a one-base hit or as a two-base hit or as a three-base hit and charge the fielder with an error. If, however, the scorer believes the hit would have been a legitimate home run, despite illegal use of equipment, he shall so score it if the batter touches all bases in the proper order.

In no instance shall the batter be credited with a two-base hit or a three-base hit if he fail to advance a preceding runner whose advance is necessary to permit the batter to reach second or third base. Example: Runner on first, batter makes a long hit and reaches second but runner is thrown out at third. Score a one-base hit and credit batter with reaching second on the play.

Should a batter, after making a safe hit, be called out for having failed to touch a base, the last base he reached safely shall determine if his hit is scored as a one-base hit, a two-base hit, or a three-base hit. If he is called out for missing second base, the hit shall be scored as a one-base hit. If he is called out for missing third base, his hit shall be scored as a two-base hit. If he is tagged out after missing home base, his hit shall be scored as a three-base hit. If he is called out for missing first base, he shall be charged with a time at bat but no hit.

When a batter ends a game with a safe hit, other than a home run, which drives in as many runs as are necessary to put his team in the lead, he shall be credited with only as many bases on his hit as are advanced by the runner who scores the winning run, and then only if the batter runs out his hit for as many bases as are advanced by the runner who scores the winning run, touching each base in the proper order.

If a batter ends a game with a home run out of the playing field and touches all the bases in their proper order, his run, and also the runs of all other runners who were on base when the home run was hit, shall count in the final score even though this gives the team last at bat a winning margin in excess of one run.

Base on Balls   A base on balls shall be scored whenever a batter is awarded first base by the umpire because of four balls having been pitched outside the strike zone, but when the fourth such ball strike the batter it shall be scored as a "hit batter."

Championship   To be eligible for the individual batting championship of any minor league, a player must have appeared in at least two-thirds of the games played by his team. Thus, if a team plays 154 games, a player must appear in 102 games. If his team plays 150 games he must appear in 100. If his team plays 140 games he must appear in 93, etc.

To be eligible for the individual batting championship of a major league, a player must be credited with at least 400 official "times at bat."

Double Play   A double play is any two successive putouts which take place between the time a ball leaves a pitcher's hand and is returned to him while he is standing in the pitcher's box.

Earned Run   An earned run is a run for which the pitching is held accountable.

An earned run shall be scored every time a player reaches home base by the aid of safe hits, sacrifices, stolen bases, putouts, bases on balls, hit batters, balks, or wild pitches (even though a wild pitch be a third strike which enables a batter to reach first base), before fielding chances have been offered to retire the offensive team.

Since a wild pitch on which a batter reaches first base is the pitcher's fault, solely, even though it is scored as a fielding error, it shall be disregarded as an error and considered as a wild pitch in computing earned runs and is the only instance in which an error is so disregarded.

In computing earned runs, any type of fielding error made by a pitcher (other than the one mentioned in the preceding two paragraphs) shall be considered in the same light as an error by any other fielder.

Whenever a fielding error occurs the pitcher shall be given the benefit of the doubt in determining to which bases any baserunners would have advanced had the fielding by the defensive team been errorless.

No run can be earned which scores as a result of a batter having reached first base safely because of a catcher's interference, or because of any fielding error, except a wild pitch.

When pitchers are changed during an inning, the preceding pitcher, and not the relieving pitcher, shall be charged with any earned or unearned runs scored by any runners on base when such relief pitcher entered the game. There is, however, this exception: If the action of any batter to whom the relieving pitcher pitches results in the retirement of a runner left on base by the preceding pitcher, the batter whose action resulted in the retirement of that runner shall be considered as having been left on base by the preceding pitcher and any run scored by such runner shall be charged to the preceding pitcher.

A relieving pitcher shall not be held accountable for the first batter to whom he pitches reaching first base if that batter had a decided advantage because of ineffective pitching by the pitcher whom the relieving pitcher succeeded. Thus, if the count is two or three balls and one or no strikes, or if the count is three balls and two strikes when pitchers are changed, and the batter reaches first base safely, charge that batter to the pitcher who was replaced. If such a batter is retired, or would have been retired except for a fielding error, the batter shall be credited to the relieving pitcher. Likewise, if such a batter hits into a force-out or into a fielder's choice on which a runner is retired, or would have been retired except for a fielding error, credit the action of such a batter to the relieving pitcher. (The foregoing sentence is not to be construed as affecting or conflicting with the exception noted.) If pitchers are changed when the count is two balls and one or no strikes, or one ball and one or no strikes, the relieving pitcher shall be held accountable for whatever the batter does.

Error   An error shall be scored for each misplay (fumble, muff, or wild throw) which prolongs the time at bat of a batter, or which prolongs the life of a runner, or which permits a runner to advance one or more bases when perfect play would have resulted in the batter or the runner being retired.

Certain misplays by the catcher and pitcher known as "passed balls" and "wild pitches" are not errors but items for the summary and are defined elsewhere in these rules.

Errors are not charged when a batter is awarded first base because of a base on balls, or for being struck by a pitched ball, or if a runner, or runners, advance because of a passed ball or because of the pitcher making a balk or a wild pitch, except: If a batter swings at a wild pitch for his third strike and thereby is enabled to reach first base, it shall be scored as a strikeout and also as an error for the pitcher and not a wild pitch; when a catcher muffs a third strike, thereby permitting a batter to reach first base, it shall be scored as an error for the catcher, not a passed ball, and as a strikeout.

No error shall be charged against the catcher or any other player for making a wild throw in attempting to prevent a stolen base or any other advance by a runner, unless the scorer is convinced such wild throw permitted the runner to advance one or more bases. If the wild throw permits a runner to advance an extra base, or bases, one error shall be charged to the player making the wild throw.

When any player throws wildly in attempting to complete a double play, or a triple play, no error shall be scored unless the throw is so wild that at least one additional base is gained. However, if a fielder muff a thrown ball which, if held, would have completed a double play or a triple play, score an error for the player who drops the ball.

An error shall be scored against any player who, on receiving a thrown ball in ample time to retire a batter or any other baserunner on a force play, does not touch the base as required by the rules.

When a runner advances because of the failure of a fielder to stop, or try to stop, an accurately thrown ball, the fielder failing to stop the ball shall be charged with an error and not the player making the throw, provided there was occasion for the throw. If such throw be made to second base the scorer shall determine whether it was the duty of the second baseman or the shortstop to stop the ball, and he shall charge the error to the negligent player.

No error shall be scored if any fielder, after dropping a fly ball, a line drive or a thrown ball recovers the ball in time to force out a runner at another base.

Accurately directed throws, especially from the outfield, which strike a baserunner or an umpire, or which take an unnatural bounce and permit a baserunner or baserunners to advance, shall be scored as errors for the player making the throw, even though it appears to be doing an injustice to the thrower. Every base advanced by a baserunner must be accounted for.

Game-Ending Hit   See last two paragraphs, *Base Hit/Value.*

Hit by Pitch   See *Base on Balls.*

Innings Pitched   In giving a pitcher credit for the number of innings pitched divide each inning into three parts. Thus, if a pitcher is replaced, with one opponent out, in the sixth inning the pitcher so replaced shall be credited with having pitched 5⅓ innings. If a pitcher is replaced with none out in the opposing team's sixth inning he shall be credited with having pitched 5 innings and a notation made to the effect that there were none out in the sixth inning.

Passed Ball   A catcher shall be charged with a passed ball when a runner, or runners, advance because of the catcher's failure to hold or to control a legally pitched ball which should have been held or controlled with ordinary effort.

Percentage   To determine a pitcher's earned run prevention average for a season, the total number of earned runs charged against his pitching shall be divided by the total number of innings he has pitched, then multiplied by nine to find his average effectiveness for a complete game.

(a) To determine the percentage of games won and lost divide the total number of games won and lost into the number won.

(b) To determine a batting average, divide the total "times at bat" into the total number of safe hits.

(c) To determine a slugging percentage, divide the total "times at bat" into the total bases of all safe hits.

(d) To determine a fielding average, divide the total of putouts, assists, and errors into the total of putouts and assists.

Putout   A putout shall be recorded each time a defensive player catches a fly ball, whether fair or foul, a line drive or a thrown ball which retires a batter or runner, or when a fielder tags a runner with the ball when the runner is off the base to which he legally is entitled.

Automatic putouts shall be credited to the catcher as follows: (1) When a batter is called out by the umpire for an illegally batted ball; when a batter is called out by the umpire for bunting foul for his third strike; when a batter is called out by an umpire for being struck by his own batted ball; when a batter is called out by an umpire for interfering with the catcher; when a batter is called out by an umpire for failing to bat in his proper turn. (Note exception in 10.14 (a).) (2) Other automatic putouts shall be credited as follows: (3) When a batter is called out on an infield fly which is not caught, the putout shall be credited to the fielder whom the scorer believes could have made the putout; (4) When a runner is called out for being struck by a fair ball (including an infield fly) the putout shall be credited to the fielder nearest the ball; (5) When a runner is declared out by an umpire for running out of line to avoid being tagged by the ball in the hands of a fielder, the putout shall be credited to the fielder whom the runner avoided; (6) When a runner is declared out by the umpire for having interfered with a fielder, credit the putout

to the fielder with whom the runner interfered, unless the fielder was in the act of throwing the ball when interfered with, in which case the putout shall be credited to the fielder for whom the throw was intended, and the fielder whose throw was interfered with shall be credited with an assist.

Relief Pitcher   See last two paragraphs, *Earned Run.*

Runs Batted In   A run batted in is a run which reaches home base safely because of a safe hit, sacrifice hit, infield putout or outfield putout, or which is forced over home plate by reason of the batter being struck by a pitched ball, or being awarded a base on balls, or being awarded first base because of interference by the catcher. If a batter hit a home run with the bases empty, score both a home run and a run batted in. If, with less than two out, an error is made on a play on which a runner from third base ordinarily would score and does score, credit the batter with a run batted in.

The batter shall not be credited with a run batted in if a run scores when he hits into a force double play, or into a double play in which the first baseman fields a fair hit ground ball, touches first base ahead of the batter for an out, then throws to second or third base, retiring a second runner who has to be tagged.

Sacrifice   Score a sacrifice if, with less than two out, the batter advances one or more runners with a bunt and is retired at first base, or would have been retired except for a fielding error. In case a runner is forced out at any base on a bunt, it shall be scored as a time at bat but no sacrifice.

Scorer   The scorer is an actual official of the game he is scoring, is an accredited representative of the league, is entitled to the respect and dignity of his office and shall be accorded full protection by the president of the league.

The scorer shall report to the President of the league any indignity expressed by manager, player, club employee or club official in the course of, or as the result of, the discharge of his duties.

To promote uniformity in keeping the records of championship games, scorers shall conform to the instructions of this scoring code.

Scoring Summary   In making a box score of a game, each player's name and the fielding position or positions he has played shall be listed in the order in which he batted, or would have batted if the game ends before he gets to bat, followed by a tabulated record of each player's batting and fielding. (a) The first column shall show the number of times each player batted during the game, but no time at bat shall be charged against a player when he is awarded first base on four called balls, for being hit by a pitched ball, or because of being interfered with by the catcher, or for being obstructed by the catcher or any other player, while en route to first base. A sacrifice also exempts a player from being charged with a time at bat. (b) The second column shall show the number of runs, if any, made by each player. (c) The third column shall show the number of safe hits, if any, made by each player. (d) The fourth column shall show the number of putouts, if any, made by each player. (e) The fifth column shall show the number of fielding assists, if any, made by each player. (f) The sixth column shall show the number of fielding errors, if any, made by each player. (g) All players inserted into each team's lineup as substitute batters or substitute runners shall be so designated by special symbols plus notations at the bottom of their team's tabulated record. The symbols a, b, c, d, etc., are recommended. It also is recommended that the notations should describe what the extra batters did, such as—a-Singled for _____ in sixth inning; b-Flied out for _____ in third inning;c-Forced _____ for _____ in seventh inning; d-Grounded out for _____ in ninth inning. (h) The score by innings of each team follows the box score tabulations and precedes the summary in which should be listed the following items in this order: (1) Runs batted in; (2) Two-base hits; (3) Three-base hits; (4) Home runs, together with the names of the pitchers off whom hit; (5) Stolen bases; (6) Sacrifices; (7) Double plays; (8) Triple plays; (9) Number of runners left on base by each team; (10) Number of bases on balls issued by each pitcher; (11) Number of batters struck out by each pitcher. These shall be listed as "strikeouts"; (12) Number of hits and runs (also earned runs) allowed by each pitcher (if one or both teams use more than one pitcher), together with the number of innings pitched by each pitcher. If a team uses only one pitcher, list the number of earned runs he allowed; (13) The names of any hit batters together with the names of the pitchers who hit them, if a team uses more than one pitcher; (14) The number of wild pitches made; (15) The number of passed balls made by the catchers; (16) The name of the winning pitcher, if the winning team uses more than one pitcher; (17) The name of the losing pitcher, if the losing team uses more than one pitcher; (18) The names of the umpires, listed in this order: (a) plate umpire; (b) first base umpire; (c) second base umpire; (d) third base umpire; (19) The time of game with any delays for rain, fog, snow, light failure or violent wind storm deducted; (20) All individual and team records of any forfeited or tied game which has reached or exceeded legal length when ended shall become a part of the official averages except that no pitcher shall be credited with a victory or charged with a defeat; (21) A box score is in balance (or proved) when the total of a team's times at bat, bases on balls received, hit batters, sacrifices and batters awarded first base because of interference or obstruction equals the total of that team's runs, players left on base, and the other team's putouts.

Stolen Base A stolen base shall be credited to a runner whenever he advances one base unaided by a base hit, a putout, a forceout, a fielder's choice, a passed ball, a wild pitch or a balk, subject to the following exceptions:

If a double or triple steal is attempted and one runner is thrown out before reaching and holding the base he is attempting to steal, no other runner shall be credited with a stolen base;

A runner who is touched out after oversliding a base shall not be regarded as having stolen that base.

If it is the scorer's judgment that a palpable muff of a thrown ball prevents a runner who is attempting to steal from being retired, it shall be scored as an error for the player muffing the throw, an assist for the player throwing the ball, and not a stolen base.

No stolen base shall be scored when a runner advances solely because of the defensive team's indifference to his advancement.

If a runner advances while the defensive team, unsuccessfully, is attempting to retire another runner who, in attempting to steal, evades being put out in a rundown play and returns to the base he originally occupied, a stolen base shall be credited to the runner who so advances.

If a runner has started for a succeeding base before the pitcher delivers the ball and the pitch results in a wild pitch or a passed ball, credit the runner with a stolen base with this exception: If another runner also advances because of the pitch becoming a wild pitch or passed ball, the wild pitch or passed ball also shall be scored.

If a runner, attempting to steal, is well advanced toward the base he is attempting to steal and a balk is called on the pitcher, credit the runner with a stolen base and do not score the balk unless another runner who is not attempting to steal is advanced by the balk.

Note: This paragraph was dropped in 1951.

Squeeze Play "Squeeze play" is the term designating a play when a team, with a runner on third base, attempts to score that runner by means of a bunt. It also is a "squeeze play" if an attempt is made to score a runner from second base by means of a bunt.

Strikeout A strikeout shall be scored whenever a pitcher delivers three legal pitches at which the batter swings and misses, or which the umpire decrees are strikes even though the batter may reach first base safely after the third strike by reason of a wild pitch or the catcher's failure to hold the ball.

A strikeout shall be scored whenever a batter bunts foul when there are two strikes against him, except that should the bunt result in a foul fly caught by the catcher or any other player it shall not be scored as a strikeout but as a regular foul-fly putout.

When a batter goes out of the game with two strikes against him and the substitute batter completes a strikeout, score it as a strikeout for the first batter. If the substitute batter completes the turn at bat in any other manner, score the action as having been that of the substitute batter.

Substitute Batter See last paragraph, *Strikeout.*

Triple Play A triple play is any three successive putouts which take place between the time a ball leaves a pitcher's hand and is returned to him while he is standing in the pitcher's box.

Wild Pitch A wild pitch shall be scored when a legally delivered ball is so high, or so wide, or so low that the catcher does not stop and control the ball by ordinary effort and, as a result, a runner, or runners, advance.

Any legally pitched ball which strikes the ground before reaching home plate and passes the catcher, permitting a runner, or runners, to advance shall be scored as a wild pitch.

Winning and Losing Pitcher Determining the winning and losing pitcher of a game often calls for much careful consideration.

Do not give the starting pitcher credit for a game won, even if the score is in his favor, unless he has pitched at least five innings when replaced.

The five-inning rule to determine a winning pitcher shall be in effect for all games of six or more innings. When a game is called after five innings of play the starting pitcher must have pitched at least four innings to be credited with the victory. If the starting pitcher is replaced (except in a five-inning game) before he has pitched five complete innings when his team is ahead, remains ahead to win, and more than one relief pitcher is used by his team, the scorer shall credit the victory (as among all relieving pitchers) to the pitcher whom the scorer considers to have done the most effective pitching. If, in a five-inning game, the starting pitcher is replaced before pitching four complete innings when his team is ahead, remains ahead to win, and more than one relief pitcher is used by his team, the scorer shall credit the victory (as among all relieving pitchers) to the pitcher whom the scorer considers to have done the most effective pitching.

Regardless of how many innings the first pitcher has pitched, he shall be charged with the loss of the game if he is replaced when his team is behind in the score, and his team thereafter fails to either tie the score or gain the lead.

If a pitcher retires from the game for a substitute batter, or a substitute runner, after pitching five or more innings and his team scores enough runs in the inning in which he is replaced to take the lead, those runs shall be credited to his benefit. Thus, if a pitcher is removed for a substitute batter or a substitute baserunner in any inning after the pitcher has pitched at least five complete innings and during the inning in which he is removed his team assumes the lead, he shall be credited with the victory if his team remains ahead until the finish of the game.

Examples: If the pitcher of the team first at bat is removed in the first half of the sixth inning for a substitute batter, or a substitute runner, and his team gains the lead in that inning and the relieving pitcher holds the lead through the last half of the ninth inning, the pitcher who was removed shall be credited with the victory; if the pitcher of the team last at bat is removed in the last half of the fifth inning for a substitute batter, or a substitute runner, and his team gains the lead in that inning with the relieving pitcher holding the lead through the ninth inning, the pitcher who was removed shall be credited with the victory.

1951

Base Hit   When a batter apparently hits safely and a runner who is obliged to advance by reason of the batter becoming a baserunner misses touching the first base to which he is advancing and is called out on appeal, charge the batter with a time at bat but no hit.

Caught Stealing   When records are kept of players caught stealing by catchers, credit the catcher with preventing a stolen base each time he traps a runner off any base with a thrown ball and, as a result of such throw, the runner is retired or would have been except for a subsequent error by any fielder, including the catcher. Runners who are retired in rundown plays started by the catcher trapping a runner off any base, or whose baserunning life is prolonged by an error after they have been trapped off base by the catcher, are to be included among those prevented from stealing by the catcher.

Championship   To be designated as the leader of his league's pitchers in the minimum average number of earned runs allowed, a pitcher is required to pitch at least as many innings as the number of games scheduled for each team in his league. (This would be 154 innings in a major league.)

Error   If a batter is awarded first base by an umpire because of interference by the catcher, charge the catcher with an error; if an umpire awards a runner or runners one or more bases because of interference or obstruction by any defensive player, charge the player who committed the interference or obstruction with one error, no matter how many bases the runner or runners are advanced.

An error is to be charged when a fielder, in violation of the playing rules, touches a thrown ball with his cap, glove, or uniform while such article is detached from its proper place.

Sacrifice   Score a sacrifice if, with less than two out, the batter advances one or more runners with a bunt and is retired at first base, or would have been retired except for a fielding error. In case a runner is forced out at any base on a bunt, it shall be scored as a time at bat but no sacrifice. Also score a sacrifice if, with less than two out, the fielders handle a bunted ball without error in attempting to force a preceding runner but fail to do so. Exception: When such an attempt is made to turn a bunt into a force-out of a preceding runner and fails and it is the scorer's judgment that perfect play would not have retired the batter at first base, it shall be scored as a one-base hit and not as a sacrifice.

Shutout   No pitcher shall be credited with pitching a shutout unless he pitches the complete game. When two or more pitchers combine to pitch a shutout, a notation to that effect should be included in the league's official pitching records.

Stolen Base   See *Caught Stealing*; also see 1950 *Stolen Base* entry.

Time at Bat   See *Base Hit*.

Winning and Losing Pitcher   Determining the winning and losing pitcher of a game in which a team uses more than one pitcher often calls for careful consideration. Scorers can be guided by these rules: (1) Credit the starting pitcher with a game won only if he has pitched at least five complete innings and his team not only is in the lead when he is replaced but remains in the lead the remainder of the game; (2) They "must pitch five complete innings" rule in respect to the starting pitcher shall be in effect for all games of six or more innings. When a game is ended after five innings of play the starting pitcher must have pitched at least four complete innings to be credited with a victory. As stated in 10.16 (a), the starting pitcher in a five-inning game can be credited with a victory only if his team is in the lead when he is replaced (after pitching at least four complete innings) and his

team remains in the lead to the finish of the game; (3) Except in a five-inning game (when they "must pitch at least four complete innings" rule applies) if the winning team uses more than two pitchers and the starting pitcher has not pitched at least five complete innings the victory shall be awarded one of the relieving pitchers on this basis: (a) Once the opposing team assumes the lead, all pitchers who have pitched for the winning team up to that point are excluded from being credited with the victory with the exception that if the pitcher against whose pitching the opposing team gained the lead continues to pitch until his team regains the lead which it holds to the finish of the game that pitcher would be the winning pitcher; (b) If, after the starting pitcher is replaced before pitching at least five complete innings, the opposing team does not tie the score or take the lead, credit the victory to the relief pitcher deemed by the scorer to have done the most effective pitching; (c) Whenever the score is tied, the game becomes a new contest insofar as determining the winning and losing pitchers are concerned; (d) With one exception, no pitcher can be credited with a victory unless he is the pitcher of record when his team assumes a lead and maintains the lead to the finish of the game; (e) The exception to the foregoing is: Do not credit a game won to a relief pitcher who pitches briefly and ineffectively and is the pitcher of record when his team assumes a lead which it maintains over a period of innings to the finish of the game. If a succeeding relief pitcher pitches effectively in helping to maintain his team in the lead credit such relief pitcher with the victory.

1952

Championship   The individual batting champion of any league shall be the player with the highest batting average, if he is credited with as many or more times at bat as the number of games scheduled for one club in his league during the season, multiplied by 2.6. However, if there is any player in a league with fewer than the required number of times at bat whose average would be the highest if he were charged with this required at-bat total, then that player shall be awarded the batting championship.

Putout   When a runner is declared out by an umpire for running out of line to avoid being tagged by the ball in the hands of a fielder, the putout shall be credited to the fielder whom the runner avoided; when a runner is called out for passing another runner, credit the putout to the fielder nearest the spot at which the violation took place.

1953

There were no changes to the scoring rules this year.

1954

Double Play   A double play is a play by the defense in which two offensive players are legally put out as a result of continuous action, providing there is no error between putouts.

Sacrifice   The following section was added to the rule regarding sacrifice bunts and flies: Also score a sacrifice if, with less than two out, the batter hits a fair fly ball which is caught, and a runner scores after the catch, or is dropped for an error, and a runner scores, if in the scorer's judgment, the runner could have scored after the catch had the fly been caught.

Scorer   To promote uniformity in keeping the records of championship games, scorers shall conform to the instructions of this scoring code, but in no case shall the scorer's decisions conflict with the playing rules.

Scoring Summary   Sacrifice flies and bunts are to be listed separately in the scoring summary.

1955

Assist   Mere ineffective contact with the ball shall not be considered an assist. "Deflect" shall mean to slow down or change the direction of the ball and thereby effectively assist in retiring a batter or runner.

Do not credit an assist to the pitcher when, as the result of a legal pitch caught by the catcher, a runner is retired, as when the catcher picks a runner off base, throws out a runner trying to steal or tags a runner trying to steal home.

Do not credit an assist to a fielder whose wild throw permits a runner to advance, even though the runner subsequently is retired as a result of a continuous play. A play which follows an error is a new play, and the player making an error is not entitled to an assist unless he takes part in the new play.

Base Hit A base hit shall be scored when a batter reaches first base safely on a fair ball which takes an unnatural bounce so that a fielder cannot handle it with ordinary effort, or which strikes the pitcher's plate or any base (including home plate) before being touched by a fielder and bounces so that a fielder cannot handle it with ordinary effort.

A base hit shall be scored when the fielder throws to another base in an unsuccessful attempt to retire a preceding runner, and in the scorer's judgment the batter-runner would not have been retired at first base by perfect fielding.

A base hit shall not be scored when a fielder fails in an attempt to retire a preceding runner, and in the scorer's judgment the batter-runner could have been retired at first base.

A base hit shall not be scored when a fielder handles a batted ball and retires a preceding runner, or would have retired one with ordinary effort except for a fielding error. Charge the batter with a time at bat but no hit.

Note: This shall not apply if the fielder merely looks toward or feints toward another base before attempting to make the putout at first base.

Base Hit/Value Whether a safe hit shall be scored as a one-base hit, two-base hit, or three-base hit when no error or putout results, shall be determined as follows: When, with one or more runners on base, the batter advances more than one base on a safe hit and the defensive team makes an attempt to retire a preceding runner, the scorer shall determine whether the batter made a legitimate two-base hit or three-base hit, or whether he advanced beyond first base on the fielder's choice.

Note: The rules of 1955 include a series of examples to illustrate the application of this rule for the guidance of the scorer.

When the batter attempts to make a two-base hit or a three-base hit by sliding, he must hold the last base to which he advances. If he overslides and is tagged out before getting back to the base safely, he shall be credited with only as many bases as he attained safely. If he overslides second base and is tagged out, he shall be credited with a one-base hit; if he overslides third base and is tagged out he shall be credited with a two-base hit.

Note: If the batter overruns second or third base and is tagged out trying to return, he shall be credited with the last base he touched. If he runs past second base after reaching that base on his feet, attempts to return and is tagged out, he shall be credited with a two-base hit. If he runs past third base after reaching that base on his feet, attempts to return and is tagged out, he shall be credited with a three-base hit.

Subject to provisions of the playing rules, when the batter ends a game with a safe hit which drives in as many runs as are necessary to put his team in the lead, he shall be credited with only as many bases on his hit as are advanced by the runner who scores the winning run, and then only if the batter runs out his hit for as many bases as are advanced by the runner who scores the winning run, touching each base in proper order.

Note: Apply this rule even when the batter is theoretically entitled to more bases because of being awarded an "automatic" extra-base hit under various provisions of the playing rules.

Base on Balls A base on balls shall be scored whenever a batter is awarded first base because of four balls having been pitched outside the strike zone, but when the fourth such ball strikes the

batter it shall be scored as a "hit batter."

Note: The scoring rules contain detailed instructions for charging runners who receive a base on balls when the pitcher is changed in mid-batter.

Batter/Out of Turn When a player bats out of turn, and is put out, and the proper batter is called out before the ball is pitched to the next batter, charge the proper batter with a time at bat and score the putout and any assists the same as if the correct batting order had been followed. If an improper batter becomes a runner by reason of a hit, error, fielder's choice, hit batter, base on balls, interference or obstruction, and the proper batter is called out for having missed his turn at bat, charge the proper batter with a time at bat, credit the putout to the catcher, and ignore everything entering into the improper batter's safe arrival on base. If more than one batter bats out of turn in succession, score all plays just as they occur, skipping the turn at bat of the player or players who first missed batting in the proper order.

Box Score A box score is in balance (or proved) when the total of the team's times at bat, bases on balls received, hit batters, sacrifice bunts, sacrifice flies, and batters awarded first base because of interference or obstruction, equals the total of that team's runs, players left on base, and the opposing team's putouts.

Caught Stealing Do not credit the catcher with a man "caught stealing" when he traps a runner off base after fielding a batted ball or on any play started by another fielder.

Championship The individual fielding champions shall be the fielders with the highest fielding average at each position, subject to the following: (1) A catcher must have participated as a catcher in at least 90 games (80 games in leagues playing schedules of 140 games or less); (2) An infielder or outfielder must have participated at his position in at least 100 games (90 games in leagues playing schedules of 140 games or less); (3) A pitcher must have pitched in at least as many innings as the number of games scheduled for each club in his league that season.

Earned Run The scoring rules of 1955 contain detailed provisions for charging runners and runs to starting pitchers and relief pitchers where pitching changes are made in mid-batter.

No run can be earned which scores as a result of the batter reaching first base (1) on a hit or otherwise after his time at bat is prolonged by a muffed foul fly; (2) because of interference or obstruction; or (3) because of any fielding error, except for a wild pitch charged as an error.

Error Slow handling of the ball which does not involve mechanical misplay shall not be construed as an error.

An error shall be charged against any fielder when he muffs a foul fly, to prolong the time at bat of the batter, whether the batter subsequently reaches first base or is retired.

If a runner advances on a throw by a fielder, and in the scorer's judgment there was no occasion for the throw, an error shall be charged to the fielder making the unnecessary throw.

An error shall be charged against any fielder whose throw takes an unnatural bounce, or strikes a base or the pitcher's plate, or strikes a runner, a fielder or an umpire, thereby permitting any runner to advance.

Note: Apply this rule even when it appears to be an injustice to a fielder whose throw was accurately directed. Every base advanced by a runner must be accounted for.

When an umpire awards the batter or any runner or runners one or more bases because of interference or obstruction, charge the fielder who committed the interference or obstruction with one error, no matter how many bases the batter, or runner or runners, may be advanced.

No error shall be charged against the catcher when he makes a wild throw in attempting to prevent a stolen base, unless such wild throw permits the base stealer to advance one or more extra bases, or in the scorer's judgment permits another runner to advance one or more bases. Charge only one error on such a wild throw, regardless of the number of bases advanced by the runner or runners.

No error shall be charged against any fielder when he makes a wild throw in attempting to prevent a runner's advance, unless in the scorer's judgment such wild throw permits the runner to advance beyond the base he would have reached had the throw not been wild, or permits any other runner to advance one or more bases beyond the base he would have reached had the throw not been wild. Charge only one error on such wild throw, regardless of the number of bases advanced by the runner or runners.

See also *Wild Pitch*.

Fielder's choice   Fielder's choice is the act of a fielder who handles a fair grounder and, instead of throwing to first base to retire the batter-runner, throws to another base in an attempt to retire a preceding runner. The term is also used by scorers (1) to account for the advance of the batter-runner who takes one or more extra bases when the fielder who handles his safe hit attempts to retire a preceding runner; and (2) to account for the advance of a runner (other than by stolen base or error) while a fielder is attempting to retire another runner.

Note: This definition appears in the Playing Rules for 1955.

Game-Ending Hit   See last paragraph, *Base Hit/Value*.

Putout   When a runner is called out for running the bases in reverse order, credit the putout to the fielder covering the base he left in starting his reverse run. Do not credit any assist on such plays.

When the batter-runner is called out because of interference by a preceding runner, credit the putout to the first baseman. If the fielder interfered with was in the act of throwing the ball, credit him with an assist, but credit only one assist on any one play.

Run Batted In   A run batted in is a run which reaches home base safely because of a safe hit, a sacrifice bunt, a sacrifice fly, a putout via a foul fly, an infield putout, or a fielder's choice; or which is forced over home plate by reason of the batter being struck by a pitched ball, or being awarded a base on balls, or being awarded first base because of interference or obstruction. If a batter hits a home run always score the home run as a run batted in. Also count all other runs which score ahead of the batter who hit the home run as runs batted in. If, with less than two out, an error is made on a play on which a runner from third base ordinarily would score and does score, credit the batter with a run batted in.

Sacrifice   Score a sacrifice bunt when, with less than two outs, the fielders handle a bunted ball without error in an unsuccessful attempt to retire a preceding runner advancing one base. Exception: When an attempt to turn a bunt into a putout of a preceding runner fails, and in the scorer's judgment perfect play would not have retired the batter at first base, the batter shall be credited with a one-base hit and not a sacrifice.

Do not score a sacrifice bunt when a runner is retired attempting to advance one base on a bunt. Charge the batter with a time at bat.

Scorer   The Official Scorer shall keep records of each game as outlined in the scoring rules. He shall have sole authority to make all decisions involving judgment, such as whether a batter's advance to first base is the result of a hit or an error. In no event shall a scorer make a decision conflicting with the Official Playing Rules or with an umpire's decision.

Scoring Summary   The scoring summary shall contain: (1) Number of runners left on base by each team. This total shall include all runners who get on base by any means and who do not score and are not put out. Include in this total a batter-runner whose batted ball results in another runner being retired for the

third out; (2) Total number of bases on balls issued by each pitcher and a separate listing of the number of intentional bases on balls issued by each pitcher.

The scoring rules of 1955 also include detailed instructions for notations to the tabulated game records. It is recommended that letters a, b, c, d, etc., be used in the notations as symbols for substitute batters and that numerals 1, 2, 3, 4, etc., be used as symbols for substitute runners. Also the instructions detail notations needed when a substitute is announced but removed for another substitute before he actually enters the game.

Stolen Base   A stolen base shall be credited to a runner whenever he advances one base unaided by a base hit, a putout, an error, a force-out, a fielder's choice, a passed ball, a wild pitch or a balk, subject to the following: When a runner, attempting to steal, evades being put out in a rundown play and advances to the next base without the aid of an error, credit the runner with a stolen base. If another runner also advances on the play, credit both runners with stolen bases. If a runner advances while another runner, attempting to steal, evades being put out in a rundown play and returns safely, without the aid of an error, to the base he originally occupied, credit a stolen base to the runner who advances.

Strikeout   A strikeout shall be scored whenever a pitcher delivers three legal pitches at which the batter swings and misses, or which the umpire decrees are strikes. A strikeout shall be scored even though the batter reaches first base safely after the third strike because of an error by the pitcher or catcher as defined in the scoring rules.

Wild Pitch   When the batter's fourth called ball is a wild pitch and as a result (1) the batter-runner advances to a base beyond first base; (2) any runner, forced to advance by reason of the batter becoming a runner, advances more than one base; or (3) any runner, not forced to advance by reason of the batter becoming a runner, advances one or more bases, score the base on balls and also an error for the pitcher and do not score a wild pitch.

When the batter swings at a wild pitch for his third strike and thereby is enabled to reach first base, score a strikeout and also an error for the pitcher, and do not score a wild pitch.

When the batter swings at a wild pitch for his third strike or when the catcher muffs a third strike, if the catcher recovers the ball and throws out the batter-runner trying to reach first base, but another runner or runners advance, score the strikeout and error the same as if the batter had reached first base. Credit an assist to the catcher, and a putout to the fielder taking the throw at first base.

Winning and Losing Pitcher   In some non-championship games (such as the Major League All-Star Game) it is provided in advance that each pitcher shall work a stated number of innings, usually two or three. In such games, it is customary to credit the victory to the pitcher of record, whether starter or reliever, when the winning team takes a lead which it maintains to the end of the game, unless such pitcher is knocked out after the winning team has a commanding lead, and the scorer believes a subsequent pitcher is entitled to credit for the victory.

1956

Base Hit   A base hit should be scored when the fielder unsuccessfully attempts to retire a preceding runner, and, in the scorer's judgment, the batter-runner would not have been retired at first base by perfect fielding.

Also see *Time at Bat*.

Run Batted In   The batter shall not be credited with a run batted in if a run scores when he grounds into a force double play, or grounds into a double play in which the first out is made at first base and the second out made by tagging a runner who was originally forced, attempting to advance one base.

Time at Bat   When a fielder handles a batted ball and retires a preceding runner who is attempting to advance one base, or would have retired one with ordinary effort except for a fielding error, charge the batter with a time at bat but no hit.

1957

Base Hit A base hit shall be scored when a batter reaches first base safely on a fair ball hit with such force, or so slowly, that any fielder attempting to make a play with it has no opportunity to do so.

Note: A hit shall be scored if the fielder attempting to handle the ball cannot make a play, even if such fielder deflects the ball from or cuts off another fielder who could have retired a runner.

Also see *Time at Bat*.

Championship To assure uniformity in establishing the batting, pitching and fielding championship of professional leagues, such champions shall meet the following minimum performance standards: The individual batting champion shall be the player with the highest batting average, provided he is credited with as many or more total appearances at the plate in league championship games as the number of games scheduled for each club in the league that season, multiplied by 3.1. Total appearances at the plate shall include official times at bat, plus bases on balls, times hit by pitcher, sacrifice hits, sacrifice flies and times awarded first base because of interference or obstruction.

Earned Run An earned run shall be scored every time a runner reaches home base by the aid of safe hits, sacrifice bunts, a sacrifice fly, stolen bases, putouts, fielder's choices, bases on balls, hit batters, balks or wild pitches (including a wild pitch on third strike which permits a batter to reach first base) before fielding chances have been offered to retire the offensive team.

Note: A wild pitch is solely the pitcher's fault, and contributes to an earned run just as a base on balls or a balk.

No run can be earned which scores as a result of the batter reaching base (1) on a hit or otherwise after his time at bat is prolonged by a muffed foul fly; (2) because of interference or obstruction; or (3) because of any fielding error.

An error by the pitcher is treated exactly the same as an error by any other fielder in computing earned runs.

Error No error shall be charged to any fielder who permits a foul fly to fall safe with a runner on third base before two are out, if in the scorer's judgment the fielder deliberately refuses the catch in order that the runner on third shall not score after the catch.

Because the pitcher and catcher handle the ball much more than other fielders, certain misplays on pitched balls are called "wild pitches" and "passed balls," and are defined elsewhere in the scoring rules. No error shall be charged when a wild pitch or passed ball is scored. No error shall be charged when the batter is awarded first base on four called balls or because he was touched by a pitched ball, or when he reaches first base as the result of a wild pitch or passed ball. When the third strike is a wild pitch, permitting the batter to reach first base, score a strikeout and a wild pitch. When the third strike is a passed ball, permitting the batter to reach first base, score a strikeout and a passed ball.

Passed Ball See second paragraph, *Error*.

Run Batted In Scorer's judgment must determine whether a run batted in shall be credited for a run which scores when a fielder holds the ball, or throws to a wrong base. Ordinarily, if the runner keeps going, credit a run batted in; if the runner stops and takes off again when he notices the misplay, credit the run as scored on a fielder's choice.

Scorer The league president shall appoint an official scorer for each league championship game. The official scorer shall observe the game from a position in the press box. The scorer shall have sole authority to make all decisions involving judgment, such as whether a batter's advance to first base is the result of a hit or an error. He shall communicate such decisions to the press box and broadcasting booths by hand signals or over the press box loudspeaker system, and shall advise the public address announcer of such decisions if requested.

After each game, including drawn, forfeited and called games, the scorer shall prepare a report, on a form prescribed by the league president, listing the date of the game, where it was played, the names of the competing clubs and the umpires, the full score of the game, and all records of individual players compiled according to the system specified in these Official Scoring Rules. He shall forward this report to the league office within 36 hours after the game ends. He shall forward the report of any suspended game within 36 hours after the game has been completed, or after it becomes an official game because it cannot be completed, as provided by the Official Playing Rules.

To achieve uniformity in keeping the records of championship games, the scorer shall conform strictly to the Official Scoring Rules.

If the teams change sides before three men are put out, the scorer shall immediately inform the umpire of the mistake.

If the game is protested or suspended, the scorer shall make note of the exact situation at the time of the protest or suspension, including the score, the number of outs, the position of any runners, and the ball and strike count on the batter.

Note: It is important that a suspended game resume with exactly the same situation as existed at the time of suspension. If a protested game is ordered replayed from the point of protest, it must be resumed with exactly the situation that existed just before the protested play.

The scorer shall not make any decision conflicting with the Official Playing Rules or with an umpire's decision.

The scorer shall not call the attention of the umpire or of any member of either team to the fact that a player is batting out of turn.

The scorer is an official representative of the league, and is entitled to the respect and dignity of his office, and shall be accorded full protection by the league president. The scorer shall report to the president any indignity expressed by any manager, player, club employee or club officer in the course of, or as the result of, the discharge of his duties.

The umpire-in-chief shall inform the official scorer of the official batting order, and any changes in the lineups and batting order, on request.

Wild Pitch See second paragraph, *Error*.

Winning and Losing Pitcher Regardless of how many innings the first pitcher has pitched, he shall be charged with the loss of the game if he is replaced when his team is behind in the score, and his team thereafter fails either to tie the score or gain the lead.

1958

Championship The individual fielding champions shall be the fielders with the highest fielding average at each position, provided: (1) A catcher must have participated as a catcher in at least one-half the number of games scheduled for each club in his league that season; (2) An infielder or outfielder must have participated at his position in at least two-thirds of the number of games scheduled for each club in his league that season; (3) A pitcher must have pitched at least as many innings as the number of games scheduled for each club in his league that season.

Percentage To compute the pitcher's earned run average, multiply the total earned runs charged against his pitching by 9, and divide the result by the total number of innings he pitched.

Sacrifice Score a sacrifice fly when, before two are out, the batter hits a fair fly ball which: (1) is caught, and a runner scores after the catch, or (2) is dropped, and a runner scores, if, in the scorer's judgment, the runner could have scored after the catch had the fly been caught.

Note: Score a sacrifice fly in accordance with the scoring rules even though another runner is forced out by reason of the batter becoming a runner.

1959–64

There were no changes to the scoring rules in these years.

1965

Championship   To qualify for the fielding championship at his position a pitcher must have pitched at least as many innings as the number of games scheduled for each club in his league that season. Exception: If another pitcher has a fielding average as high or higher, and has handled more total chances in a lesser number of innings, he shall be the fielding champion.

1966

There were no changes to the scoring rules this year.

1967

Championship   The individual batting champion shall be the player with the highest batting average, provided he is credited with as many or more total appearances at the plate in league championship games as the number of games scheduled for each club in his league that season, multiplied by 3.1. Exception: However, if there is any player with fewer than the required number of plate appearances whose average would be highest if he were charged with the required number of plate appearances or official at-bats, then that player shall be awarded the batting championship.

Error   Mental mistakes or misjudgments are not to be scored as errors unless specifically covered in the rules.

No error shall be charged against any fielder when, after fumbling a ground ball or dropping a fly ball, a line drive or a thrown ball, he recovers the ball in time to force out a runner at any base.

Sacrifice   Do not score a sacrifice bunt when, in the judgment of the scorer, the batter is bunting for a base hit and not solely for the purpose of advancing a runner or runners. Charge the batter with a time at bat.

Note: In applying this rule always give the batter the benefit of the doubt.

Stolen Base   When a runner, attempting to steal, or after being picked off base, evades being put out in a rundown play and advances to the next base without the aid of an error, credit the runner with a stolen base. If another runner also advances on the play, credit both runners with stolen bases. If a runner advances while another runner, attempting to steal, evades being put out in a rundown play and returns safely, without the aid of an error, to the base he originally occupied, credit a stolen base to the runner who advances.

1968

There were no changes to the scoring rules this year.

1969

Double Play/Triple Play   Credit participation in the double play or triple play to each fielder who earns a putout or an assist when two or three players are put out between the time a pitch is delivered and the time the ball next becomes dead or is next in possession of the pitcher in pitching position, unless an error or misplay intervenes between putouts.

Note: Credit the double play or triple play also if an appeal play after the ball is in possession of the pitcher results in an additional putout.

Earned Run   An earned run is a run for which the pitcher is held accountable. In determining earned runs, the inning should be reconstructed without the errors and passed balls, and the benefit of the doubt should always be given to the pitcher in determining which bases would have been reached by errorless play.

When pitchers are changed during an inning, the relief pitcher shall not have the benefit of previous chances for outs not accepted in determining earned runs.

Note: It is the intent of this rule to prevent relief pitchers from not being charged with earned runs for which they are solely responsible.

Error   When an umpire awards the batter or any runner or runners one or more bases because of interference or obstruction, charge the fielder who committed the interference or obstruction with one error, no matter how many bases the batter, or runner or runners, may be advanced.

Note: Do not charge an error if obstruction does not change the play in the opinion of the scorer.

Relief Pitcher   See *Earned Run*, second paragraph.

Sacrifice   Do not score a sacrifice bunt when, in the judgment of the scorer, the batter is bunting *primarily* for a base hit and not for the purpose of advancing a runner or runners. Charge the batter with a time at bat.

Note: In applying this rule always give the batter the benefit of the doubt.

Note: The rule is the same as that appearing in the 1967 scoring rules with the addition of the word *primarily*.

Save   Credit a save to a relief pitcher who enters a game with his team in the lead if he holds the lead the remainder of the game, provided he is not credited with the victory. A relief pitcher cannot be credited with a save if he does not finish the game unless he is removed for a pinch hitter or pinch runner. When more than one relief pitcher qualifies for a save under the provisions of this rule, credit the save to the relief pitcher judged by the scorer to have been the most effective. Only one save can be credited in any game.

1970–72

There were no changes to the scoring rules in these years.

1973

Save   A pitcher shall be credited with a save when, in entering a game as a relief pitcher, he finds the potential tying or winning run either on base or at the plate or pitches at least three or more effective innings and, in either case, preserves the lead.

1974

Hitting/Playing Streaks   A consecutive hitting streak shall not be terminated if the plate appearance results in a base on balls, hit batsman, defensive interference or a sacrifice bunt.

A sacrifice fly shall terminate the streak.

A consecutive-game hitting streak shall not be terminated if all the player's plate appearances (one or more) result in a base on balls, hit batsman, defensive interference or a sacrifice bunt. The streak shall terminate if the player has a sacrifice fly and no hit.

A consecutive-game playing streak shall be extended if the player plays one half-inning on defense, or if he completes a time at bat by reaching base or being put out. A pinch-running appearance only shall not extend the streak. If a player is ejected from a game by an umpire before he can comply with the requirements of this rule, his streak shall continue.

Suspended Game   For the purpose of the scoring rules, all performances in the completion of a suspended game shall be considered as occurring on the original date of the game.

1975

Sacrifice   Score a sacrifice fly when, before two are out, the batter hits a fly ball or a line drive handled by an outfielder or an infielder running in the outfield which: (1) is caught, and a runner scores after the catch, or (2) is dropped, and a runner scores, if in the scorer's judgment the runner could have scored after the catch had the fly been caught.

Note: Score a sacrifice fly in accordance with the scoring rules even though another runner is forced out by reason of the batter becoming a runner.

Save Credit a pitcher with a save when he meets all three of the following conditions: (1) He is the finishing pitcher in a game won by his club; and (2) He is not the winning pitcher; and (3) He qualifies under one of the following conditions: (a) He enters the game with a lead of no more than three runs and pitches for at least one inning; or (b) He enters the game with the potential tying run either on base, or at bat, or on deck (that is, the potential tying run is either already on base or is one of the first two batsmen he faces); or (c) He pitches effectively for at least three innings. No more than one save may be credited in each game.

1976

Base on Balls See *Strikeout*.

Earned Run An earned run is a run for which the pitcher is held accountable. In determining earned runs, the inning should be reconstructed without the errors (which includes catcher's interference) and passed balls, and the benefit of the doubt should always be given to the pitcher in determining which bases would have been reached by errorless play.

When pitchers are changed during an inning, the relief pitcher shall not be charged with any run (earned or unearned) scored by a runner who was on base at the time he entered the game, nor for runs scored by any runner who reaches base on a fielder's choice which puts out a runner left on base by the preceding pitcher.

Note: It is the intent of this rule to charge each pitcher with the number of runners he put on base, rather than with the individual runners. When a pitcher puts runners on base and is relieved, he shall be charged with all runs subsequently scored up to and including the number of runners he left on base when he left the game, unless such runners are put out without action by the batter, i.e., caught stealing, picked off base, or called out for interference when a batter-runner does not reach first base on the play. Exception: The pitcher walks batter A and is relieved. The relief pitcher allows B to single, but runner A is out trying for third. Runner B takes second on the throw. Batter C singles, scoring runner B. Charge the run to the relief pitcher rather than the preceding pitcher.

Game Played When a player listed in the starting lineup for the visiting club is substituted for before he plays defensively, he shall not receive credit in the defensive statistics (fielding), unless he actually plays that position during a game. All such players, however, shall be credited with one game played (in batting statistics) as long as they are announced into the game or listed on the official lineup card.

Percentage For purposes of earned run average calculations and innings pitched totals, innings pitched shall be rounded off to the nearest whole inning. Examples: 200⅓ innings becomes 200; 200⅔ becomes 201.

Note: This standard was changed in 1982 and fractions were no longer rounded off but counted for their full value. Also see rule addition under 1981.

Relief Pitcher See *Earned Run*, second paragraph.

Scoring Summary The name of a pitcher credited with a save is to be shown on the scoring summary.

Strikeout When the batter leaves the game with two strikes against him, and the substitute batter completes a strikeout, charge the strikeout and the time at bat to the first batter. If the substitute batter completes the turn at bat in any other manner,

including a base on balls, score the action as having been that of the substitute batter.

Substitute Batter See *Strikeout*.

1977

Base on Balls Intentional base on balls shall be scored when the pitcher makes no attempt to throw the last pitch to the batter into the strike zone but purposely throws the ball wide to the catcher outside the catcher's box.

1978

There were no changes to the scoring rules this year.

1979

Caught Stealing A runner shall be charged as "caught stealing" if he is put out, or would have been put out by errorless play, when he (1) tries to steal; (2) is picked off a base and tries to advance (any move toward the next base shall be considered an attempt to advance); (3) overslides while stealing.

Note: In those instances where a pitched ball eludes the catcher and the runner is put out trying to advance, no caught stealing shall be charged.

Earned Run An earned run is a run for which the pitcher is held accountable. In determining earned runs, the inning should be reconstructed without the errors (which include catcher's interference) and passed balls, and the benefit of the doubt should always be given to the pitcher in determining which bases would have been reached by errorless play. For the purpose of determining earned runs, an intentional base on balls, regardless of the circumstances, shall be construed in exactly the same manner as any other base on balls.

Scorer The official scorer must make all decisions concerning judgment calls within twenty-four (24) hours after a game has been officially concluded. No judgment decision shall be changed thereafter except, upon immediate application to the league president, the scorer may request a change, citing the reasons for such. In all cases the official scorer is not permitted to make a scoring decision which is in conflict with the scoring rules.

1980

Run Batted In Game-winning RBI is credited for the RBI that gives a club the lead it never relinquishes.

Note: There does not have to be a game-winning RBI in every game and all game-winning RBIs must conform to the scoring rule governing RBIs.

1981

Percentage For purposes of earned run average calculations and innings pitched totals, do not round off the fraction where a pitcher has only ⅓ of an inning for the entire season. In such cases carry his total for innings pitched as ⅓.

1982

Percentage Earned run averages shall be calculated on the basis of total innings pitched, including fractional innings. Example: 9⅓ innings pitched and three earned runs is an earned run average of 2.89 (3 ER times 9 divided by 9⅓ equals 2.89).

1983

Championship The individual batting champion or slugging champion shall be the player with the highest batting average or slugging percentage, provided he is credited with as many or more total appearances at the plate in League championship games as the number of games scheduled for each club in his League that season, multiplied by 3.1 in the case of a major league player. Exception: However, if there is any player with fewer than the required number of plate appearances or official at-bats, but who, when credited with an out for each of his deficient at-bats, still has the highest average, then that player shall be awarded the batting championship or slugging championship.

1984

Percentage   To compute on-base percentage, divide the total of hits, all bases on balls, and hit by pitch, by the total of at-bats, all bases on balls, hit by pitch, and sacrifice flies.

Note: For the purpose of computing on-base percentage, ignore being awarded first base on interference or obstruction.

1985–88

There were no changes to the scoring rules this year.

1989

Run Batted In   The game-winning RBI is dropped from the rule book.

1990

There were no changes to the scoring rules this year.

Index to Scoring Rule Changes 1877–1990

Note: Dates shown following an entry refer to the year a rule change or amendment was adopted. Rule changes and summaries of rules are to be found in the chronology.

All-Star Game, determining winning pitcher of   1955
Assist   1877; 1882; 1883; 1885; 1887; 1890; 1897; 1904; 1910; 1914; 1931; 1950; 1955
Assist, mere ineffective contact with ball not to be   1955
Assist not to be scored on strikes   1890
Assist scored or not scored to pitcher   1877; 1882; 1883; 1885; 1887; 1890; 1931; 1950; 1955
Assist scored to each player handling ball   1877; 1897; 1904; 1910; 1914; 1931; 1950
Assist scored to player deflecting ball   1931; 1950
Assist scored to player even when putout is not completed   1877
Assist, wild throw scored as   1950
Base Hit, determining value of   1920; 1931; 1939; 1950; 1955
Base Hit scored when batted ball strikes base, home plate, or pitcher's plate   1950; 1955
Base Hit scored when batter receives base on balls   1887
Base Hit, when or when *not* to score   1877; 1880; 1881; 1887; 1888; 1889; 1898; 1904; 1907; 1914; 1931; 1940; 1950; 1951; 1955; 1956; 1957; 1967
Base on Balls   1877; 1883; 1885; 1887; 1888; 1897; 1898; 1904; 1909; 1910; 1912; 1914; 1917; 1931; 1940; 1950; 1955; 1957; 1979; 1984
Base on balls scored as error charged to pitcher   1883
Bases run, scoring of total ("Total Bases")   1877; 1878; 1880; 1881; 1882
Batter batting ball illegally ("Foul strike", out of batter's box)   1883; 1884; 1898; 1904; 1909; 1931; 1950
Batter batting out of turn   1877; 1883; 1884; 1904; 1909; 1931; 1950; 1955
Batter entitled to benefit of doubt   1950
Batter out on bunt foul for third strike   1931
Batter out when struck with own batted ball   1931
Batter, scoring when substitute completes time at bat for   1950; 1955; 1976
Batter, time at bat charged or not charged to   1877; 1887; 1888; 1894; 1897; 1898; 1904; 1914; 1931; 1950; 1951; 1955
Battery Error   1887; 1888; 1898; 1904; 1909; 1914
Batting Average, computing of   1920; 1950
Batting Championship, eligibility for   1950; 1952; 1957; 1967; 1983
Batting Order (*See* Batter batting out of turn)
Box Score, balanced   1955
Box Score, detailed form and contents of   1950

Catcher's automatic putouts (*See* Putouts automatic to catcher)
Caught Stealing, when to score   1951; 1955; 1979
Chances offered, scoring of   1880
Double (*See* Base Hit, determining value of)
Double Play, determining and effect of   1909; 1914; 1939; 1950; 1954; 1955; 1956; 1969
Double Steal   1909; 1910
Earned Run Average Championship, eligibility for   1951
Earned Run Average, computing of   1917; 1950; 1958; 1976; 1981; 1982
Earned Run, pitcher receives benefit of the doubt on determining   1917; 1931; 1950; 1969; 1979
Earned Run, when to score   1888; 1889; 1890; 1897; 1912; 1917; 1931; 1940; 1950; 1955; 1957; 1969; 1976; 1979
Error   1877; 1883; 1885; 1887; 1888; 1898; 1904; 1909; 1910; 1914; 1917; 1920; 1926; 1931; 1950; 1951; 1955 1957; 1967; 1969
Error allowing batter to advance   1877; 1887; 1898; 1931
Error allowing runner to advance   1877; 1887; 1898; 1904; 1909; 1910; 1914; 1950; 1955
Error charged to baseman failing to stop thrown ball   1904; 1909; 1931; 1950
Error charged or not charged to catcher (*See* also Battery Error)   1885; 1909; 1914; 1920; 1931; 1950; 1951; 1955
Error charged or not charged to fielder   1877; 1887; 1888; 1950; 1951; 1955; 1957; 1969
Error charged or not charged to pitcher (*See* also Battery Error)   1883; 1885; 1909; 1917; 1926; 1931; 1950; 1955; 1957
Error charged to fielder making unnecessary throw   1955
Error charged to fielder on throw that takes unnatural bounce or which strikes obstacle   1950; 1955
Error charged to first baseman   1920; 1931; 1950
Error charged to infielder   1898; 1914; 1931; 1950
Error charged to second baseman   1931
Error charged when ball touched with detached cap, glove, etc.   1950; 1951
Error, mental mistakes and misjudgments not to be scored as   1967
Error not to be charged to fielder allowing foul fly to drop with runner on third and less than two out   1957
Error prolonging life of runner   1914;   1950
Error prolonging time at bat of batter   1904; 1909; 1910; 1914; 1950; 1955
Error, slow handling of ball not involving mechanical misplay is not to be construed as   1955
Error, wild throw scored as   1950
Fielder's Choice, scoring of   1914; 1950; 1955; 1957
Fielding Average, computing of   1920; 1950
Fielding Championship, eligibility for   1955; 1958; 1965
Force Out, scoring of and effect of   1898; 1904; 1909; 1931; 1939; 1950; 1955; 1967
Forfeited Game   1931; 1940; 1957
Forfeited Game, no victory or loss to pitcher in   1940
Game-Ending Hit (*See* Base Hit, determining value of)
Game Played (*See* Player, appearances in game by)
Game-Winning Run Batted In, scoring of   1980; 1989
Hit by Pitch   1885; 1887; 1888; 1897; 1898; 1904; 1909; 1910; 1912; 1914; 1917; 1931; 1940; 1950; 1957; 1984
Hitting Streak, termination of consecutive game   1974
Home Run, scoring of (*See* also Base Hit, determining value of)   1920; 1931; 1950
Infield Fly, scoring of dropped   1898; 1904; 1909; 1931; 1940; 1950
Innings Pitched   1950
Intentional Base on Balls, scoring and effect of   1977; 1979
Interference by runner   1898; 1904; 1909; 1950; 1955
Interference, defensive   1931; 1950; 1951; 1955; 1957; 1969; 1979; 1984

Interference with catcher, scoring when batter is out for   1931; 1950

Interference with fielder   1950

No changes to the scoring rules   1879; 1882; 1884; 1893; 1895; 1896; 1899; 1900; 1901; 1902; 1903; 1905; 1906; 1911; 1913; 1915; 1916; 1918; 1919; 1921; 1922; 1923; 1924; 1925; 1927; 1928; 1929; 1930; 1932; 1933; 1934; 1935; 1936; 1937; 1938; 1941; 1942; 1943; 1944; 1945; 1946; 1947; 1948; 1949; 1953; 1959; 1960; 1961; 1962; 1963; 1964; 1966; 1968; 1970; 1971; 1972; 1978; 1985; 1986; 1987; 1988; 1990

Obstruction, scoring of   1951; 1955; 1957; 1969; 1984

Official playing records   1931; 1940

On-Base Percentage, computing of   1984

Passed Ball, definition of   1910; 1926

Passed Ball, scoring and effect of   1880; 1882; 1885; 1887; 1898; 1904; 1909; 1910; 1914; 1926; 1931; 1950; 1957; 1969; 1979

Percentages, computing of statistics and   1917; 1920; 1931; 1950; 1951; 1958; 1974; 1976; 1982; 1984

Pitcher, illegal delivery by   1887; 1888; 1897; 1898; 1904; 1909

Pitcher, mention of balk committed by   1885; 1887; 1898; 1904; 1909; 1910; 1912; 1914; 1917; 1931; 1940; 1950; 1951; 1955; 1957

Player, appearances in game by   1907; 1912; 1976

Player, recording number of times first base reached by   1878

Player, recording runs made by each   1877

Playing Streak, termination of consecutive game   1974

Putout automatic to catcher   1931; 1950

Putout automatic to fielder (interference, runner hit by batted ball, etc.)   1898; 1904; 1909; 1931

Putout scored to catcher   1877; 1882; 1898; 1904; 1909; 1931; 1950; 1955

Putout, scoring of   1877; 1882; 1898; 1904; 1909; 1914; 1931; 1950; 1952; 1955

Run Batted In, game-winning (See Game-Winning Run Batted In)

Run Batted In, when to score   1891; 1931; 1939; 1950; 1955; 1956; 1957

Relief Pitcher, determining runs charged to   1940; 1950; 1955; 1969; 1976

Runner failing to touch a base   1950; 1951

Runner hit by batted ball   1888; 1901; 1931; 1940; 1950

Runner passing a preceding runner   1952

Runner running bases in reverse order   1955

Runner running out of base line   1898; 1904; 1909; 1950; 1952

Runner overrunning a base   1888; 1950; 1955

Runner oversliding a base   1909; 1939; 1950; 1955; 1979

Runner stealing a base (See Stolen Base, scoring of)

Sacrifice flies and hits listed separately   1954

Sacrifice Fly   1889; 1908; 1909; 1912; 1914; 1917; 1920; 1931; 1939; 1940; 1954; 1957; 1958; 1975; 1984

Sacrifice Hit (bunt)   1889; 1894; 1897; 1898; 1904; 1908; 1909; 1912; 1917; 1920; 1931; 1939; 1940; 1950; 1951; 1955; 1957; 1967; 1969; 1984

Sacrifices   1889; 1894; 1897; 1898; 1904; 1908; 1909; 1912; 1914; 1917; 1920; 1931; 1939; 1940; 1950; 1951; 1954; 1955; 1957; 1958; 1967; 1969; 1975; 1984

Saves, crediting of   1969; 1973; 1975

Scorer as league official   1950; 1957

Scorer changing decision   1979

Scorer, duties of   1950; 1954; 1955; 1957; 1979

Scorer's decisions not to conflict with playing or scoring rules   1950; 1954; 1955; 1957; 1979

Scorer's decisions not to conflict with umpire's decisions   1955; 1957

Scorer's duty if batter bats out of turn   1957

Scorer's duty if game is protested or suspended   1957

Scorer's duty if sides change before three are out   1957

Scorer's reporting of abuse to league president   1950

Scorer's seating position to observe the game   1957

Scoring Summary   1877; 1880; 1881; 1884; 1885; 1886; 1887; 1888; 1889; 1890; 1891; 1897; 1898; 1904; 1909; 1910; 1914; 1920; 1950; 1954; 1955; 1976

Shutout, crediting of   1951

Slugging Championship, eligibility for   1983

Slugging Percentage, computing of   1950

Squeeze Play, definition of   1950

Stolen Base, detailed description of   1950

Stolen Base, indifference of defensive team to   1950

Stolen Base, scoring of   1886; 1887; 1888; 1889; 1890; 1892; 1897; 1898; 1904; 1909; 1914; 1917; 1920; 1931; 1940; 1950; 1951; 1955; 1957; 1967

Streaks, consecutive game hitting and playing   1974

Strikeout   1883; 1884; 1885; 1887; 1888; 1926; 1931; 1939; 1940; 1950; 1955; 1957; 1976

Substitute completes time at bat for batter, scoring when   1950; 1955; 1976

Time at Bat (See Batter, time at bat charged or not charged to)

Triple (See Base Hit, determining value of)

Triple Play   1950; 1969

Triple steal   1910; 1950

Umpire, batted ball hitting   1889; 1950

Umpire-in-Chief to inform scorer of batting order and changes   1957

Wild Pitch, definition of   1910; 1926; 1931; 1950

Wild Pitch, scoring of   1880; 1882; 1885; 1887; 1898; 1904; 1909; 1910; 1912; 1914; 1917; 1920; 1926; 1931; 1939; 1940; 1950; 1955; 1957

Wild throw scored as both error and assist   1950

Wild throw, scoring of   1898; 1914; 1931; 1950; 1955

Winning and Losing Pitcher, determining   1950; 1951; 1955; 1957

Won-Lost percentage, computing of   1920; 1950

Forfeit and No-Decision Games

A forfeited game is one in which the umpire, having observed any one of a number of specified flagrant violations of the rules, declares the game over and awards the decision to the offended team by a score of 9–0. Such games are relatively rare in major league history, but they have provided scoring problems—whether to award wins and losses to the contending pitchers, whether to include batting, fielding, and pitching statistics in the player and team records, and whether to count such games as victories/defeats for the opposing manager. This section details the conclusions the editors have reached regarding how the totals for these forfeit games should be recorded, if at all; in some cases reference is made to the Macmillan *Baseball Encyclopedia* to illustrate differences between how a game has been previously regarded and how it is counted in *Total Baseball*. We follow with an evaluation of no-decision games, that is, games that were terminated without a win or loss awarded to either club.

Forfeit Games

All forfeit games show the winner listed first. For games in which no win or loss was awarded, the appended comment "no game" means it was not a regulation game; otherwise, the loser was ahead at the time of forfeit. In those cases in which the team that was ahead at the time of forfeit won, and the game was a regulation game, the appended comment is "OK" followed by the score. In a game noted as "OK," a win and loss should be awarded to individual pitchers. The research of Frank Williams into early scoring practices has shown that the rules of the day indicated that in some years tied forfeit games should also have wins and losses awarded to the pitchers.

In the lists below, the victorious team is presented first. If that team was the home team, it is followed by "vs" and the visiting team; if the visiting team was victorious, it is presented first, followed by "at" and the name of the home team. For a key to the abbreviations used in these tables, see the last page of the book. The official score of all these games is 9–0.

Year	Date	League	Teams	Notes
1871	May 11	NA	Chi at Cle	Game OK, Chi ahead 18–10
	May 17	NA	Oly at Rok	Later ruled a forfeit because Rok used ineligible player Scott Hastings
	May 23	NA	Kek vs Rok	Later ruled a forfeit because Rok used ineligible player Scott Hastings
	June 5	NA	Ath vs Rok	Later ruled a forfeit because Rok used ineligible player Scott Hastings
	June 15	NA	Ath vs Rok	Later ruled a forfeit because Rok used ineligible player Scott Hastings

Year	Date	League	Teams	Notes
	June 19	NA	Tro vs Kek	Kek ahead 6–3, no pitcher win/loss
1872	Aug. 31	NA	Ath vs Eck	Game OK, score tied 5–5
1874	Sept. 28	NA	Ath vs Chi	Game OK, Ath ahead 15–7
1875	May 29	NA	Was vs NH	Game OK, Was ahead 11–10
1876	Aug. 21	N	StL vs Chi	Game OK, StL ahead 7–6
1877	May 15	N	Cin vs Lou	Lou ahead 8–5 (game later thrown out)
1880	Sept. 10	N	Buf vs Cin	Score tied 11–11 (game later thrown out, however Macmillan counted it as a tie; counted as a tie in *Total Baseball*, since Tattersall stats included it, and these do not have day-by-day breakdowns)
1882	June 29	A	StL vs Lou	No game (later thrown out; however, it was counted as a no-game forfeit by Macmillan, which did not count either the StL vs Lou tie (6–6) on Oct 3 or the StL vs Lou win (6–2) on Oct 5, which were treated as if they were exhibition games. They should have been counted, and *Total Baseball* does.)
	Aug. 16	N	Cle at Wor	No game (game later thrown out)
1883	July 4	N	Phi vs Pro	Game OK, Pro ahead 11–9 in AM game (Pro had to leave for PM game in NY after 7 innings), no pitcher win/loss
	July 27	AA	NY vs Phi	No game (game later thrown out)
	Aug. 1	N	Bos at Cle	Game OK, Bos ahead 10–3
1884	May 31	AA	Cin at Was	Game OK, Cin ahead 6–0
	July 5	U	Bal vs Cin	No game (umpire late, Cin refused to play)
	Aug. 11	N	Buf at Chi	No game (1st game; argument in first inning; the second game, a makeup, ended in a 6–6 tie)
	Aug. 22	U	StL at KC	Game OK, KC ahead 6–3, no pitcher win/loss
	Aug. 23	N	Bos vs Det	Game OK, Bos ahead 7–5 (Macmillan gave no win or loss in this game, should be Whitney-W, Meinke-L)
	Aug. 25	U	Bos vs Wil	No game (1st game; Wil arrived late)
	Aug. 30	AA	Tol at StL	Game OK, Tol ahead 2–1 (PM game)
	Sept. 8	U	Was vs Pit	No game (Pit failed to appear)
	Sept. 20	U	Was vs Cin	No game (Cin failed to appear)
	Sept. 24	AA	Tol vs Ric	No game (Ric failed to appear)
	Sept. 24	A	Bal at Pit	Game OK, Bal ahead 8–6
	Oct. 11	U	StL vs Was	No game (Was refused to continue)
	Oct. 11	U	Bos at Cin	No game
1886	July 30	N	Det at Was	Game OK, Det ahead 13–9 (Macmillan gave no win or loss in this game. Win should go to Hardy Richardson in relief, loss to George Keefe; Getzien started for Det but left in the 5th behind 9–6. Det got 7 in 7th. There is some controversy on this game because a lot of runs were scored before the game was actually forfeited)
	Sept. 29	N	Was vs StL	Score tied 2–2
	Oct. 7	N	Was vs KC	No game (1st game, AM)
	Oct. 8	N	Was vs KC	No game (1st game, AM)
	Oct. 9	N	Was vs KC	No game (1st game, AM; KC refused to play morning games on these three dates)
1887	Apr. 30	AA	Lou vs Cin	No game (Cin arrived late)
	June 27	N	Det vs NY	No game (1st game; game thrown out on Aug. 14)
	July 3	AA	Lou at StL	No game

Year	Date	League	Teams	Notes
	July 22	AA	Phi vs Cle	Game OK, Cle ahead 6–4 (no pitcher win/loss)
	Aug. 12	AA	NY at Phi	Game OK, NY ahead 9–7
1888	May 31	N	NY vs Pit	No game (Pit did not appear)
	July 14	AA	KC vs Bro	Game OK, KC ahead 5–4
	Sept. 12	N	Chi vs NY	Game OK, Chi ahead 8–2 (Macmillan awarded no win or loss in this game, should be Krock-W, Keefe-L)
	Oct. 13	N	Phi vs Chi	No game (Chi did not appear; Macmillan has extra win for Phi, extra loss for Pit—they counted a Phi win over Pit May 5 which was later thrown out; Buffington should have one less win, Morris one less loss; *Total Baseball* counts stats for May 5th game except for wins and losses)
1889	May 5	AA	Phi at Bro	Game OK, Phi ahead 11–1
	June 24	AA	Bro vs Col	No game (1st game; Col refused to play with sub ump; second game was played)
	Sept. 7	AA	Bro vs StL	StL ahead 4–2 (this forfeit later overruled and given back to StL as normal game)
	Sept. 8	AA	Bro vs StL	No game (StL did not appear)
	Sept. 26	AA	Cle vs Was	No game (Washington's train delayed; game later thrown out, played on Sept 28)
1890	Apr. 20	AA	Lou vs StL	No game
	Apr. 24	N	Bos vs NY	Game OK, score tied 2–2
	June 17	N	Pit vs Cle	No game (train delay; game later thrown out)
	July 2	AA	Phi at Tol	Game OK; score tied 5–5
	July 27	AA	Col vs Bro	Game OK; Bro ahead 13–8 (no pitcher win/loss)
	Aug. 3	AA	Syr vs Lou	No game
	Aug. 5	AA	Tol vs Roc	Game OK, Tol ahead 7–3
	Sept. 2	N	Chi at Bos	No game (1st game; umpire late, game not started; later forfeited to Bos and then thrown out)
	Sept. 21	AA	Stl at Roc	Game OK (2nd game), StL ahead 10–3
1891	Apr. 8	AA	StL vs Cin	No game, tied 7–7 (overruled and replayed on Apr. 13; counted by Macmillan and *Total Baseball* as a tie)
	Sept. 12	AA	StL vs Bos	Game OK, StL ahead 4–2
	Sept. 20	AA	Lou vs Phi	No game; Phi refused to continue (2nd game)
	Sept. 25	N	Chi vs Pit	Game OK, score tied 4–4
	Sept. 25	AA	StL at Lou	
	Oct. 2	AA	StL vs Lou	(These two games were exhibitions but were counted by Macmillan and *Total Baseball 1* but should not have been. Meekin beat McGill, 7–4, in the first one, McGill beat Fitzgerald, 13–8, in the second)
	Oct. 5	AA	Was vs Bal	Game OK, Bal ahead 4–1, no pitcher win/loss (counted as a win for Bal in Macmillan; there should be win for Healy or loss for Foreman)
1892	Apr. 20	N	NY at Bal	Game OK, Balt ahead 6–5, no pitcher win/loss
	Apr. 23	N	Lou at Chi	Game OK, Chi ahead 4–2, no pitcher win/loss (Macmillan has extra loss for Chi, extra win for NY. They gave a loss to Luby on Apr. 23 and a win to King on Apr. 20, although the opposing team pitcher in each case had his decision removed)
	May 10	N	Pit vs NY	No game (NY refused to play in rain)
	May 21	N	Cle vs StL	No game (1st game; StL arrived late)
	Aug. 16	N	Pit vs Was	Game OK, score tied 2–2
	Sept. 22	N	Pit vs Chi	No game (Chi trying to delay for rain)
	Oct. 12	N	Pit vs Cle	No game (Cle did not appear)
1893	May 25	N	Lou vs Chi	No game (Chi did not appear)
	Sept. 16	N	Cle vs Bal	Game OK, Cle ahead 15–11
1894	May 1	N	Bro vs Was	Game OK, Was ahead 2–1; no pitcher win/loss (Macmillan gave a loss (and shutout!) to Stephens of Was in this game)
	May 26	N	Pit at Cle	Game OK, Pit ahead 12–3
	July 17	N	Phi vs Bos	Game OK, Phi ahead 12–2

Year	Date	League	Teams	Notes
	Aug. 3	N	Lou vs Chi	No game (Chi refused to play)
	Sept. 5	N	Was vs StL	Game OK, Washington ahead 7–4
1895	May 23	N	Bro at Lou	No game
	Aug. 28	N	Bal vs Pit	No game (1st game; Pit arrived late)
1896	May 13	N	Bos at Chi	Game OK, score tied 4–4
	July 24	N	Bal vs StL	Game OK, Bal ahead 13–8
1897	May 3	N	NY at Was	No game
	June 1	N	NY vs Pit	Game OK, Pit ahead 7–4, no pitcher win/loss
	June 4	N	Phi vs Pit	No game
	July 24	N	Cle vs Phi	Game OK, Phi ahead 4–3, no pitcher win/loss
	Aug. 1	N	StL vs Lou	Lou ahead 5–4 (2nd game, later thrown out)
	Aug. 4	N	Lou vs Cle	No game (1st game; Cle refused to continue)
	Sept. 8	N	Was vs Cle	No game (2nd game)
	Sept. 10	N	Bal vs Lou	Game OK, Bal ahead 6–5
1898	July 25	N	Bal vs NY	No game (NY refused to continue)
	Sept. 16	N	Phi vs Chi	(1st game) Chi ahead 2–1 (Macmillan gave Donahue, Phi a win in this game, but this was not a regulation game and should have no stats counted)
1899	May 19	N	StL vs NY	Game OK, NY ahead 10–9, no pitcher win/loss
	June 16	N	Bro at NY	No game
	Oct. 14	N	Bro vs Bal	No game (1st game)
1900	June 22	N	Bro at Phi	Game OK, Bro ahead 20–13
	Sept. 19	N	Bro vs StL	No game (StL refused to continue)
1901	May 2	A	Det at Chi	Game OK, Det ahead 7–5
	May 13	NL	NY vs Bro	Game OK, score tied 7–7
	May 31	AL	Det vs Bal	Game OK, score tied 5–5
	June 9	NL	NY at Cin	Game OK, NY ahead 25–13
	July 23	AL	Cle vs Was	Game OK, score tied 4–4
	Aug. 21	AL	Det vs Bal	No game (crowd swarmed on field)
1902	June 16	NL	Pit at Bos	No game (Bos trying to delay for rain)
	June 28	AL	Bos vs Bal	Game OK, Bos ahead 9–4
	July 17	AL	StL at Bal	No game (Bal did not appear)
1903	Aug. 8	AL	Det at Cle	Game OK, Det ahead 6–5
1904	Oct. 4	NL	StL at NY	No game (2nd game; NY refused to continue)
1905	Aug. 5	NL	Pit vs NY	Game OK, score tied 5–5
	Aug. 22	AL	Was at Det	Game OK, Washington ahead 2–1
1906	June 9	NL	Pit vs Phi	Game OK, Pit ahead 7–1
	July 2	AL	NY at Phi	Game OK, NY ahead 5–1
	Aug. 7	NL	Chi at NY	No game (umpire not allowed into park)
	Sept. 3	AL	NY vs Phi	Game OK (2nd game, score tied 3–3)
1907	Apr. 11	NL	Phi at NY	Game OK, Phi ahead 3–0
	Oct. 5	NL	StL vs Chi	No game (1st game, Chi refused to continue)
1909	Oct. 4	NL	NY vs Phi	No game (2nd game, score tied 1–1 in 4th inning; this was not a regulation game but was included in the official stats)
1913	July 6	NL	StL at Chi	No game (2nd game, Chi tried to stall so that curfew would be invoked; this was not a regulation game but was included in the official stats)
1914	June 26	AL	Phi vs Was	No game (1st game, Washington refused to continue)
1916	July 18	NL	Bro at Chi	Game OK, score tied 4–4
1917	Sept. 9	AL	Chi vs Cle	Game OK, score tied 3–3
1918	July 20	AL	Cle at Phi	Game OK (2nd game, Cle ahead 9–1)
1920	Aug. 20	AL	Chi at Phi	Game OK (2nd game, Chi ahead 5–2)
1924	June 13	AL	NY at Det	Game OK, NY ahead 10–6
1925	Apr. 26	AL	Cle at Chi	Game OK, Cle ahead 7–2
1937	June 6	NL	StL vs Phi	No game (2nd game, Phi tried to stall so that curfew would be invoked)
1941	Aug. 15	AL	Bos at Was	Game OK, Washington ahead 6–3, no pitcher win/loss
1942	Sept. 26	NL	Bos at NY	Game OK (2nd game, NY ahead 5–2, no pitcher win/loss)
1949	Aug. 21	NL	NY at Phi	Game OK (2nd game, NY ahead 4–2)
1954	July 18	NL	Phi at StL	No game (2nd game, StL tried to stall for darkness)

Year	Date	League	Teams	Notes
1971	Sept. 30	AL	NY at Was	Game OK (Washington ahead 7–5, no pitcher win/loss; this was the last game in Washington and fans vandalized the field in the 9th)
1974	June 4	AL	Tex at Cle	Game OK, scored tied 5–5 (crowd invaded field)
1977	Sept. 15	AL	Tor vs Bal	Game OK, Tor ahead 4–0 (Bal refused to continue)
1979	July 12	AL	Det at Chi	No game (2nd game, crowd littered field between games)

No-Decision Games

In the National Association of 1871–75, no-decision games were counted in the records by researcher Michael Stagno and thus are adopted in *Total Baseball.* In the National League of 1876–1890, no-decision games were counted by researcher John Tattersall and thus were adopted by the Macmillan *Baseball Encyclopedia* and *Total Baseball.* In the ensuing period, covered by ICI research and the computer printouts that ICI deposited at the Hall of Fame, protested games were not counted. Although they may have been included in the official averages, source data for these has been lost. In the 1910–19 period, protested games were not counted at all. From 1920–90, protested games were counted. Because of the effect these games had on the records of the teams' managers, the managers are listed. For more on this, see the Introduction to the Manager Roster, criterion number 7.

This list of no-decision games does not include protests that were upheld in which the game was resumed from the point of protest; it includes only those games that were thrown out entirely. These games did ultimately come to a decision.

Year	Date	League	Teams	Notes/Managers
This was counted by Michael Stagno:				
1872	May 20	NA	Ath at Bal	Game disallowed (McBride–Craver)
These were counted by Tattersall:				
1877	May 15	NL	Lou at Cin	Forfeit to Cin overruled (Chapman–Pike)
1880	Sept. 10	NL	Cin at Buf	Forfeit to Buf overruled; this game counted as a tie with all stats in by Macmillan (Clapp–Crane)
1887	Sept. 23	NL	Bos at Chi	Second game
1887	Sept. 24	NL	Bos at Chi	First and second games; these two games plus the one of the day before were ties replayed without proper consent; counted as no-decisions but included in averages by Tattersall and Macmillan (Morrill–Anson)
	July 4	NL	Bos at Det	2nd game was a 4½-inning, 7–7 tie; since it did not go five innings, it should not have counted in the records, but it was included by Tattersall and Macmillan. It was not protested (Kelly–Watkins)

Year	Date	League	Teams	Notes/Managers
1888	May 5	NL	Phi at Pit	Phi ahead 4–3; this game counted by Tattersall and Macmillan as a win for Phi (Wright–Phillips)
These were not counted by Macmillan:				
1888	June 10	AA	Bal at Phi	(Barnie–Sharsig)
1890	July 10, 11, 12	PL	Pit at Bos	Three games in which Bos used Gil Hatfield, on loan from NY, against league rules (Hanlon–Kelly)
1891	Apr. 8	AA	Cin at StL	Forfeit overruled (Kelly–Comiskey)
1894	Apr. 26	NL	Phi at Bro	(Irwin–Foutz)
	May 23	NL	Pit at Chi	Forfeit overruled (Buckenberger–Anson)
	Aug. 18	NL	Chi at NY	1st game (Anson–Ward)
	Aug. 25	NL	Lou at NY	1st game (Barnie–Ward)
	Aug. 27	NL	Cin at Phi	1st game (Comiskey–Irwin)
	Sept. 6	NL	Cin at Phi	1st game (Comiskey–Irwin)
1895	June 1	NL	Pit at Bro	(Mack–Foutz)
	July 14	NL	Cle at StL	(Schmelz–Selee)
	Aug. 12	NL	Was at Bos	(Tebeau–Quinn)
1897	June 3	NL	Lou at NY	1st game (Rogers–Joyce)
	Aug. 1	NL	Lou at StL	2nd game (Clarke–Hallman)
1899	May 3	NL	Lou at Pit	(Clarke–Watkins)
	May 30	NL	NY at Cin	PM game (Ewing–Day)
1902	May 7	NL	NY at Chi	(Fogel–Selee)
	May 8	NL	NY at Chi	Pitching distance too short; this game and the one above may have been included in the official averages, but no record exists (Fogel–Selee)
These were not counted in the official averages or by Macmillan:				
1911	May 30	NL	Chi at Pit	1st game (Chance–Clarke)
1912	Oct. 2	NL	Pit at Chi	(Clarke–Chance)
1914	May 14	FL	Chi at Buf	(Tinker–Schafly)
	June 19	FL	Chi at Bal	(Tinker–Knabe)
	Sept. 3	AL	Cle at Chi	2nd game (Fohl–Rowland)
	Aug. 17	NL	Chi at Pit	1st game; Benton pitched for Pit (Bresnahan–Clarke)
1917	Apr. 17	NL	Bos at Phi	(Stallings–Moran)
	Aug. 19	AL	Was vs Det	(Griffith–Jennings)
1918	Apr. 29	NL	StL at Cin	(Hendricks–Mathewson)
	June 3	NL	StL at Bro	(Hendricks–Robinson)
These were counted by both the offical averages and Macmillan:				
1909	Apr. 23	NL	Cin at Pit	(Griffith–Clarke)
1924	July 15	NL	NY at Chi	(McGraw–Killefer)
1924	July 28	AL	Bos at StL	Individual data counted, team data not counted; Macmillan originally took out the individual records; later editions have added the batting records, but omitted the pitching records (Fohl–Sisler)
1932	Aug. 19	AL	NY at Det	All data counted except in the games-played column in official records; games played added by Macmillan (McCarthy–Harris)
1937	Aug. 6	AL	NY vs Cle	(McCarthy–O'Neill)
1938	May 14	NL	StL vs Cin	(7–6, this game later declared a tie)
1939	Sept. 12	AL	Chi at Was	(Dykes–Harris)
1940	June 20	AL	Chi vs NY	(Dykes–McCarthy)
1947	July 20	NL	Bro vs StL	(3–2, this game later declared a tie)

Pitcher Lifetime Fielding

Pitcher Defense is a column entry in the Pitcher Register, but pitchers are not included in the Fielding Register because even those who hurl the most innings handle so few chances per season (and of course we are subject to space limitations). All the same over the course of a career a pitcher may pile up some meaningful fielding totals, and his Fielding Runs may show that he saved (or cost) himself some extra wins. Look, for example, at the fine records of Carl Mays or Tommy John and the unimpressive totals of Nolan Ryan or Jim Bunning.

The column heads below are the same as those used in the Fielding Register, with the exception of Innings Pitched (IP), which we thought a useful addition. The criterion for inclusion in this list is 1,500 innings or 500 games.

Pitcher	PCT	G	PO	A	E	DP	FR	IP
Ted Abernathy	.950	681	92	304	21	16	27	1146
Babe Adams	.976	482	58	648	17	17	-32	2995
Vic Aldridge	.969	248	26	354	12	19	-8	1599
Doyle Alexander	.961	561	264	521	32	36	12	3367
Pete Alexander	.985	696	189	1419	25	50	25	5189
Johnny Allen	.957	352	104	366	21	24	6	1951
Nick Altrock	.964	218	169	612	29	23	38	1515
Red Ames	.937	533	107	1000	74	25	24	3197
Larry Andersen	.911	534	83	132	21	13	4	822
Joaquin Andujar	.915	405	142	437	54	28	20	2154
Johnny Antonelli	.952	377	72	342	21	24	-2	1992
Eldon Auker	.967	333	120	460	20	38	22	1964
Jim Bagby	.956	303	122	359	22	38	13	1668
Jim Bagby	.962	316	115	411	21	18	-12	1822
Stan Bahnsen	.942	574	154	414	35	26	9	2527
Doug Bair	.956	584	72	123	9	9	1	909
Jersey Bakely	.862	215	74	369	71	14	-8	1782
Mark Baldwin	.904	347	175	552	77	10	-4	2811
Floyd Bannister	.971	379	82	258	10	12	-19	2325
Steve Barber	.926	466	106	372	38	31	8	2000
Jess Barnes	.976	422	138	748	22	37	22	2571
Jim Barr	.954	454	148	388	26	22	18	2065
Steve Bedrosian	.952	552	52	105	8	11	-8	990
Gary Bell	.963	519	141	278	16	30	-5	2015
Chief Bender	.947	459	173	809	55	24	-8	3017
Ray Benge	.959	346	59	317	16	16	-18	1877
Al Benton	.939	455	97	301	26	18	-2	1689
Rube Benton	.963	437	75	680	29	23	3	2518
Larry Benton	.962	455	93	469	22	33	-11	2297
Bill Bernhard	.950	231	83	560	34	19	7	1792
Jim Bibby	.938	340	88	216	20	16	-8	1722
Jack Billingham	.966	476	133	344	17	21	2	2231
George Blaeholder	.944	338	141	469	36	33	22	1913
Sheriff Blake	.972	304	55	401	13	24	8	1620
Steve Blass	.960	282	137	251	16	19	3	1599
Vida Blue	.967	502	127	427	19	21	-24	3344
Bert Blyleven	.969	667	282	649	30	47	-8	4836
Mike Boddicker	.951	273	216	308	27	34	24	1802
Bobby Bolin	.949	495	87	190	15	6	-14	1576
Tommy Bond	.927	322	159	667	65	21	31	2779
Tiny Bonham	.966	231	63	165	8	15	-25	1553
Pedro Borbon	.928	593	54	152	16	8	0	1026
Hank Borowy	.975	314	85	350	11	22	4	1715
Dick Bosman	.968	306	119	213	11	12	-5	1591
Henry Boyle	.912	207	83	311	38	10	-7	1712
George Bradley	.896	287	164	509	78	15	11	2404
Ed Brandt	.977	378	78	512	14	19	2	2268
Harry Brecheen	.983	318	78	376	8	22	4	1905
Ted Breitenstein	.942	379	244	690	57	24	19	2965
Ken Brett	.966	349	104	263	13	18	9	1526
Jim Brewer	.947	584	30	150	10	10	-7	1041
Tom Brewer	.967	241	125	343	16	22	24	1509
Tommy Bridges	.962	424	144	469	24	23	-10	2827
Nelson Briles	.966	452	131	263	14	17	-12	2112
Hal Brown	.977	358	93	243	8	23	-7	1681
Lloyd Brown	.969	404	99	427	17	24	21	1693
Mordecai Brown	.966	481	171	843	36	43	2	3171
Charlie Buffinton	.916	414	172	851	94	30	35	3403
Bob Buhl	.974	457	211	461	18	32	9	2587
Jim Bunning	.962	591	206	372	23	20	-48	3759
Lew Burdette	.970	626	245	622	27	55	28	3067
Tom Burgmeier	.970	745	124	293	13	36	28	1258
Ray Burris	.952	480	157	300	23	16	-2	2190
Guy Bush	.974	542	138	643	21	38	16	2721
Joe Bush	.969	489	208	839	34	50	20	3088
Max Butcher	.975	334	98	402	13	25	10	1787
Mike Caldwell	.976	475	116	499	15	39	27	2407
Ray Caldwell	.960	343	80	523	25	17	-20	2242
Nixey Callahan	.936	195	127	506	43	21	27	1602
Howie Camnitz	.947	326	63	486	31	8	-21	2086
Bill Campbell	.957	700	119	172	13	11	2	1229
John Candelaria	.973	467	58	332	11	16	-12	2447
Ben Cantwell	.967	316	95	463	19	33	29	1533
Don Cardwell	.957	410	164	394	25	25	10	2122
Tex Carleton	.968	293	93	334	14	23	3	1607
Hal Carlson	.971	377	74	497	17	18	2	2002
Steve Carlton	.952	741	109	724	42	36	-29	5217
Clay Carroll	.971	731	60	310	11	24	17	1353
Kid Carsey	.911	294	109	578	67	22	18	2222
Bob Caruthers	.927	340	192	580	61	15	15	2829
Dan Casey	.896	201	67	339	47	8	1	1681
Elton Chamberlain	.913	321	105	463	54	5	-13	2522
Dean Chance	.936	406	111	373	33	31	6	2148
Larry Cheney	.924	313	55	501	46	8	-2	1880
Jack Chesbro	.943	392	102	829	56	28	-1	2898
Eddie Cicotte	.942	502	127	998	69	36	13	3223
Jim Clancy	.950	418	182	292	25	30	-6	2429
Watty Clark	.976	355	54	384	11	12	1	1748
John Clarkson	.894	531	221	1143	162	44	43	4537
Roger Clemens	.974	206	122	139	7	5	-9	1512
Reggie Cleveland	.935	428	121	227	24	14	-7	1809
Tony Cloninger	.938	352	114	279	26	20	-3	1768
Jim Colborn	.958	301	114	274	17	18	9	1597
Joe Coleman	.955	484	179	351	25	22	-4	2572
Rip Collins	.967	311	90	437	18	20	8	1712
Gene Conley	.944	276	78	241	19	17	-8	1589
Jack Coombs	.966	354	151	512	23	22	-22	2321
Wilbur Cooper	.956	517	102	785	41	27	-29	3482
Mort Cooper	.952	295	50	270	16	20	-22	1843
Larry Corcoran	.910	277	182	498	67	13	11	2393
Stan Coveleski	.972	450	174	851	29	45	18	3081
Roger Craig	.956	368	120	274	18	21	7	1537
Doc Crandall	.962	302	76	432	20	17	5	1547
Ed Crane	.842	204	72	307	71	7	-8	1550
General Crowder	.984	402	56	387	7	22	-23	2344
Mike Cuellar	.949	453	108	453	30	33	-2	2807
Ray Culp	.944	322	135	237	22	15	-11	1897
Bert Cunningham	.887	341	197	676	111	25	16	2727
Nig Cuppy	.950	302	94	552	34	16	10	2284
Jack Curtis	.964	438	66	260	12	21	0	1641
Ron Darling	.943	240	123	275	24	30	14	1518
Danny Darwin	.947	488	117	220	19	15	-9	1914
Hooks Dauss	.968	538	99	1128	41	25	39	3391
Dave Davenport	.943	259	25	407	26	11	-12	1538

Pitcher	PCT	G	PO	A	E	DP	FR	IP
Curt Davis	.973	429	146	616	21	39	36	2324
Dizzy Dean	.960	317	76	283	15	15	-25	1966
John Denny	.952	325	179	451	32	46	34	2149
Paul Derringer	.969	579	153	656	26	30	-21	3646
Murry Dickson	.968	625	236	668	30	54	34	3053
Larry Dierker	.950	356	152	287	23	16	-11	2335
Bill Dietrich	.951	366	95	369	24	22	-3	2004
Bill Dinneen	.943	391	133	800	56	19	-15	3075
Bill Doak	.960	453	103	934	43	33	42	2782
Joe Dobson	.977	414	126	341	11	24	-5	2172
Pat Dobson	.958	414	142	289	19	14	-6	2119
Red Donahue	.953	368	127	905	51	22	23	2975
Pete Donohue	.952	344	71	499	29	23	2	2112
Dick Donovan	.960	345	144	336	20	25	6	2020
Bill Donovan	.943	378	174	654	50	20	-38	2966
Richard Dotson	.972	305	116	269	11	25	3	1858
Phil Douglas	.948	299	61	521	32	18	12	1709
Al Downing	.961	405	72	368	18	23	-2	2269
Moe Drabowsky	.961	589	100	222	13	14	-6	1640
Dick Drago	.964	519	83	268	13	33	-5	1876
Don Drysdale	.937	518	188	686	59	55	25	3432
Bill Duggleby	.936	240	86	541	43	15	15	1732
Frank Dwyer	.935	365	204	577	54	28	-2	2809
George Earnshaw	.936	319	71	371	30	17	-4	1916
Dennis Eckersley	.948	604	186	320	28	17	-20	2815
Howard Ehmke	.958	427	143	853	44	35	32	2821
Red Ehret	.882	362	104	598	94	19	-5	2755
Dock Ellis	.952	345	173	287	23	26	-2	2129
Dick Ellsworth	.957	407	120	437	25	29	14	2157
Carl Erskine	.948	335	105	262	20	20	-4	1719
Duke Esper	.945	237	68	382	26	8	1	1734
Bob Ewing	.955	291	93	539	30	15	-19	2302
Red Faber	.946	669	130	1108	71	33	10	4086
Roy Face	.958	848	104	212	14	15	-2	1375
Cy Falkenberg	.941	330	100	727	52	26	10	2276
Turk Farrell	.952	590	64	212	14	9	-18	1704
Bob Feller	.963	570	146	510	25	28	-34	3828
Charlie Ferguson	.919	183	99	310	36	12	5	1515
Wes Ferrell	.975	374	122	532	17	30	6	2623
Rollie Fingers	.963	944	108	253	14	23	1	1701
Eddie Fisher	.956	690	107	262	17	17	3	1540
Jack Fisher	.969	400	157	312	15	18	2	1977
Ray Fisher	.946	278	75	610	39	13	20	1755
Freddie Fitzsimmons	.977	513	237	942	28	79	65	3225
Mike Flanagan	.980	420	77	401	10	22	-4	2637
Whitey Ford	.961	498	173	630	33	49	22	3171
Frank Foreman	.883	229	70	324	52	8	-11	1726
Ken Forsch	.944	521	134	305	26	24	1	2125
Bob Forsch	.973	498	234	405	18	35	3	2795
Terry Forster	.951	614	48	243	15	18	16	1105
Dave Foutz	.925	251	195	408	49	22	19	1998
Fred Frankhouse	.961	402	108	476	24	30	18	1889
Chick Fraser	.930	433	315	938	94	31	29	3355
Larry French	.951	570	124	628	39	40	-9	3152
Bob Friend	.969	602	228	630	27	40	5	3612
Woodie Fryman	.988	625	97	389	6	25	1	2413
Denny Galehouse	.959	375	104	320	18	20	-8	2003
Jim Galvin	.914	697	324	1382	161	43	44	5941
Gene Garber	.967	931	159	280	15	23	18	1509
Mike Garcia	.972	428	134	359	14	27	1	2176
Ned Garver	.961	402	203	469	27	41	17	2477
Milt Gaston	.956	355	106	460	26	36	1	2106
Charlie Getzien	.893	296	135	434	68	13	-13	2540
Bob Gibson	.949	528	291	484	42	46	-20	3885
Dave Giusti	.964	668	134	264	15	11	2	1718
Kid Gleason	.906	299	163	476	66	16	1	2389
Fred Goldsmith	.882	189	96	351	60	5	8	1609
Dave Goltz	.954	353	152	287	21	26	0	2039
Lefty Gomez	.957	368	56	393	20	20	-21	2503
Dwight Gooden	.947	211	147	225	21	22	9	1524
Rich Gossage	.925	853	67	169	19	10	-20	1636
Jim Grant	.966	571	162	376	19	40	-1	2441
Sam Gray	.927	379	81	399	38	22	-8	1953
Clark Griffith	.942	453	179	863	64	22	9	3387
Burleigh Grimes	.954	616	225	1252	71	74	58	4181
Ross Grimsley	.970	345	60	357	13	14	3	2039
Steve Gromek	.966	447	126	248	13	20	-18	2065
Bob Groom	.938	367	98	685	52	18	-1	2337
Lefty Grove	.954	616	65	722	38	26	-25	3940
Ron Guidry	.981	368	107	307	8	19	-10	2393
Bill Gullickson	.957	280	124	191	14	14	-15	1837
Ad Gumbert	.919	262	111	435	48	12	1	1985
Harry Gumbert	.979	508	129	670	17	42	51	2156
Larry Gura	.986	403	107	369	7	32	13	2046
Moose Haas	.963	266	143	191	13	21	-6	1655
Harvey Haddix	.957	453	115	358	21	24	-4	2236
George Haddock	.908	204	90	395	49	12	10	1580
Bump Hadley	.962	528	140	573	28	30	-2	2946
Noodles Hahn	.912	242	101	447	53	16	-14	2021
Jesse Haines	.966	555	107	651	27	32	-19	3208
Bill Hallahan	.925	324	67	330	32	19	-8	1740
Earl Hamilton	.965	410	124	612	27	29	-3	2341
Bill Hands	.948	374	140	297	24	12	2	1951
Mel Harder	.954	582	209	734	45	38	23	3426
Steve Hargan	.937	354	130	272	27	25	11	1631
Bob Harmon	.965	321	88	620	26	22	16	2054
Slim Harriss	.955	349	35	521	26	20	13	1751
Bill Hart	.923	206	90	461	46	18	21	1583
Pink Hawley	.921	393	129	688	70	19	0	3011
Joe Haynes	.966	379	83	283	13	12	-4	1580
John Healy	.867	227	57	340	61	10	-10	1874
Jim Hearn	.954	396	106	355	22	33	13	1704
Guy Hecker	.935	334	215	633	59	17	27	2906
Ken Heintzelman	.977	319	37	267	7	23	-8	1502
George Hemming	.930	204	81	330	31	10	-2	1587
Hardie Henderson	.864	210	107	307	65	14	1	1787
Claude Hendrix	.962	360	77	724	32	22	13	2372
Bill Henry	.970	527	48	115	5	9	-7	914
Ray Herbert	.975	407	126	389	13	41	21	1884
Willie Hernandez	.983	744	58	169	4	12	4	1046
Kirby Higbe	.972	418	92	285	11	17	-19	1953
John Hiller	.958	545	45	136	8	5	-11	1241
Billy Hoeft	.952	505	87	249	17	19	-13	1848
Al Hollingsworth	.966	315	67	297	13	16	-2	1519
Ken Holtzman	.958	451	117	471	26	27	0	2868
Rick Honeycutt	.946	491	83	393	27	19	18	1923
Burt Hooton	.971	480	165	373	16	21	-2	2652
Joe Horlen	.973	361	159	421	16	17	23	2003
Charlie Hough	.971	745	205	466	20	35	8	3106
Art Houtteman	.963	325	105	339	17	28	19	1556
Harry Howell	.958	340	208	964	52	22	49	2567
Waite Hoyt	.966	674	153	842	35	41	-2	3763
Al Hrabosky	.907	545	20	58	8	4	-15	721
Carl Hubbell	.967	535	155	824	33	55	17	3591
Willis Hudlin	.959	491	150	734	38	54	46	2613
Sid Hudson	.955	380	151	514	31	41	31	2181
Tom Hughes	.924	399	96	675	63	19	-23	2642
Tom Hume	.973	543	60	195	7	11	8	1086
Jim Hunter	.959	500	225	319	23	16	-40	3449
Bruce Hurst	.968	303	81	283	12	13	2	1928
Bill Hutchinson	.916	375	138	664	74	17	4	3083
Grant Jackson	.934	692	55	170	16	12	-10	1359
Larry Jackson	.960	558	257	656	38	46	28	3262
Larry Jansen	.977	291	138	335	11	31	9	1767
Joey Jay	.959	310	105	221	14	15	-5	1547
Fergie Jenkins	.954	664	363	660	49	45	7	4498
Tommy John	.963	760	237	1028	49	69	63	4708
Ken Johnson	.963	334	93	322	16	19	5	1737
Si Johnson	.970	492	56	404	14	21	-19	2280
Syl Johnson	.965	542	63	291	13	13	-41	2167
Walter Johnson	.969	802	276	1351	52	72	-43	5924
Randy Jones	.970	305	114	465	18	30	35	1932
Sam Jones	.933	322	84	209	21	12	-15	1644
Sam Jones	.954	647	196	874	52	48	-7	3884
Addie Joss	.965	286	146	845	36	20	31	2327
Jim Kaat	.947	898	262	744	56	65	12	4529
Tim Keefe	.888	600	260	1062	167	28	12	5061
Alex Kellner	.955	321	83	280	17	27	-10	1851
Vern Kennedy	.961	344	98	439	22	28	11	2025
Brickyard Kennedy	.940	405	123	767	57	29	16	3021
Frank Killen	.896	321	96	612	82	14	5	2511
Ed Killian	.952	213	82	455	27	10	-10	1599
Matt Kilroy	.892	303	156	599	91	12	28	2435
Silver King	.932	398	146	640	57	22	-6	3190
Clay Kirby	.896	261	79	172	29	12	-14	1550
Bruce Kison	.965	380	140	297	16	27	13	1809
Frank Kitson	.941	303	75	550	39	7	-13	2217
Ron Kline	.959	736	147	319	20	24	0	2078
Johnny Klippstein	.966	711	106	324	15	23	-2	1970
Bob Knepper	.949	445	103	451	30	32	4	2708
Jack Knott	.948	325	45	286	18	17	-4	1557
Darold Knowles	.919	765	51	276	29	16	20	1091
Ray Kolp	.973	383	86	351	12	22	-5	1688
Jerry Koosman	.943	612	116	582	42	36	-8	3839
Dave Koslo	.965	348	75	307	14	23	0	1591
Sandy Koufax	.954	397	64	228	14	13	-37	2325
Jack Kramer	.956	322	73	298	17	23	0	1639
Ray Kremer	.974	308	37	331	10	12	-27	1955
Mike Krukow	.949	369	146	284	23	27	-7	2190
Clem Labine	.956	513	97	207	14	15	10	1079
Mike LaCoss	.957	397	122	303	19	24	10	1692
Dennis Lamp	.964	567	122	337	17	25	24	1712
Mark Langston	.937	233	72	239	21	20	2	1597
Max Lanier	.959	327	78	324	17	25	4	1618
Terry Larkin	.884	176	59	268	43	2	-12	1567
Dave LaRoche	.960	647	48	144	8	5	-2	1049
Don Larsen	.952	412	92	244	17	22	-1	1548
Frank Lary	.962	350	174	351	21	23	6	2161
Gary Lavelle	.942	745	48	181	14	11	2	1086
Vern Law	.972	483	212	453	19	41	6	2673
Thornton Lee	.929	374	67	428	38	21	-8	2331
Bill Lee	.934	462	163	662	58	37	16	2862

Pitcher	PCT	G	PO	A	E	DP	FR	IP
Bill Lee	.947	416	83	415	28	24	20	1944
Sam Leever	.956	388	83	659	34	11	-14	2661
Craig Lefferts	.972	528	38	99	4	11	-3	762
Charlie Leibrandt	.960	300	108	323	18	18	15	1735
Lefty Leifield	.960	296	85	558	27	23	12	1839
Denny Lemaster	.960	357	78	232	13	9	-14	1788
Bob Lemon	.969	460	263	709	31	78	61	2849
Dennis Leonard	.947	312	135	292	24	28	-6	2188
Dutch Leonard	.965	640	174	719	32	41	25	3220
Dutch Leonard	.945	331	53	432	28	8	-38	2191
Paul Lindblad	.978	655	56	205	6	11	2	1214
Frank Linzy	.970	516	51	236	9	17	22	817
Bob Locker	.948	576	77	216	16	11	17	878
Mickey Lolich	.935	586	100	448	38	16	-31	3640
Jim Lonborg	.954	425	189	268	22	18	-16	2464
Eddie Lopat	.968	340	100	468	19	30	9	2439
Turk Lown	.961	504	74	198	11	16	6	1032
Red Lucas	.981	396	109	516	12	33	-4	2543
Dolf Luque	.958	550	188	786	43	36	11	3221
Sparky Lyle	.923	899	54	198	21	12	-6	1391
Jack Lynch	.846	220	80	306	70	4	-9	1916
Ted Lyons	.958	594	219	943	51	57	18	4162
Danny MacFayden	.951	465	118	635	39	38	10	2706
Sal Maglie	.974	303	96	280	10	26	-3	1722
Rick Mahler	.960	369	153	325	20	31	14	1886
Pat Malone	.964	357	63	311	14	14	-18	1915
Jim Maloney	.957	302	100	232	15	10	-15	1849
Firpo Marberry	.965	551	92	370	17	29	-16	2066
Juan Marichal	.949	471	291	577	47	27	8	3506
Rube Marquard	.951	536	63	697	39	27	-35	3309
Mike Marshall	.963	723	105	283	15	25	22	1387
Tippy Martinez	.958	546	58	145	9	13	6	835
Dennis Martinez	.966	460	213	497	25	44	28	2712
Walt Masterson	.921	399	92	281	32	19	-2	1648
Bobby Mathews	.845	323	97	452	101	11	-13	2734
Christy Mathewson	.972	635	281	1503	52	41	65	4782
Jon Matlack	.952	361	68	346	21	14	-8	2363
Jakie May	.977	410	53	321	9	17	-11	1563
Rudy May	.927	535	87	382	37	18	-11	2621
Carl Mays	.968	490	174	1138	44	56	79	3022
Bob McClure	.932	568	30	147	13	12	-6	1066
Jim McCormick	.923	492	263	922	99	28	23	4276
Mike McCormick	.976	484	102	394	12	26	-1	2381
Lindy McDaniel	.963	987	127	447	22	28	20	2140
Sam McDowell	.925	425	79	328	33	23	-16	2492
Jumbo McGinnis	.862	186	49	337	62	8	-4	1594
Joe McGinnity	.919	465	202	929	100	25	6	3441
Tug McGraw	.927	824	75	219	23	16	-5	1516
Scott McGregor	.980	356	119	317	9	18	3	2140
Harry McIntire	.939	237	38	439	31	16	-6	1651
Denny McLain	.966	280	154	212	13	15	-10	1885
Cal McLish	.975	352	131	302	11	27	12	1609
Don McMahon	.964	874	83	187	10	12	-4	1313
Sadie McMahon	.916	321	101	664	70	24	18	2634
Dave McNally	.961	424	97	417	21	37	-7	2730
George McQuillan	.963	273	53	390	17	10	-8	1577
Hugh McQuillan	.921	279	52	404	39	24	1	1562
Larry McWilliams	.965	370	85	275	13	22	8	1558
Lee Meadows	.947	490	84	850	52	39	5	3160
Doc Medich	.950	312	114	286	21	12	-5	1996
Jouett Meekin	.905	324	117	457	60	17	-21	2603
Win Mercer	.903	331	166	609	83	19	9	2467
Andy Messersmith	.917	344	136	318	41	15	-5	2230
Russ Meyer	.962	319	69	257	13	19	-2	1531
Bob Miller	.952	694	106	335	22	27	17	1552
Stu Miller	.972	704	152	341	14	35	17	1694
Greg Minton	.965	710	95	261	13	17	23	1131
Clarence Mitchell	.972	390	104	615	21	42	21	2217
Willie Mitchell	.904	276	63	344	43	10	-28	1633
Vinegar Bend Mizell	.934	268	79	217	21	14	-9	1528
Randy Moffitt	.922	534	53	101	13	7	-2	782
George Mogridge	.960	398	127	638	32	35	15	2266
Bill Monbouquette	.984	343	155	266	7	19	-4	1961
John Montefusco	.944	298	82	187	16	8	-13	1650
Earl Moore	.920	388	66	627	60	17	-39	2776
Mike Moore	.949	295	170	299	25	17	14	1898
Ed Morris	.891	311	97	477	70	14	-7	2678
Jack Morris	.967	430	321	333	22	31	-5	3043
Johnny Morrison	.963	297	19	318	13	12	-12	1536
Carl Morton	.975	255	182	249	11	15	9	1649
Guy Morton	.900	317	35	414	50	10	-12	1630
Don Mossi	.990	460	69	239	3	28	-1	1548
Tony Mullane	.918	555	328	1041	123	41	32	4531
George Mullin	.947	487	229	1244	82	30	29	3686
Van Mungo	.960	364	99	448	23	22	4	2111
Dale Murray	.920	518	58	206	23	14	14	901
Art Nehf	.976	451	142	749	22	48	19	2708
Don Newcombe	.963	344	159	313	18	27	-5	2154
Hal Newhouser	.971	488	135	611	22	40	15	2993
Bobo Newsom	.958	600	112	534	28	32	-35	3762
Kid Nichols	.952	620	311	1031	67	34	-12	5057
Joe Niekro	.969	702	253	532	25	41	7	3585
Phil Niekro	.972	864	386	878	37	83	24	5404
Gary Nolan	.990	250	95	189	3	11	-14	1675
Fred Norman	.919	403	64	232	26	12	-15	1938
Joe Nuxhall	.932	526	95	341	32	31	-14	2304
Hank O'Day	.907	201	76	333	42	9	2	1652
Billy O'Dell	.963	479	88	252	13	11	-13	1815
Blue Moon Odom	.904	295	141	243	41	21	5	1507
Joe Oeschger	.959	365	64	447	22	19	-7	1818
Jesse Orosco	.981	551	33	119	3	9	0	791
Al Orth	.932	440	172	957	83	18	7	3356
Claude Osteen	.971	541	159	699	26	37	27	3459
Fritz Ostermueller	.954	390	108	373	23	15	-1	2069
Jim O'Toole	.938	270	80	223	20	10	-11	1615
Orval Overall	.941	217	64	401	29	10	-4	1532
Jim Palmer	.962	558	292	577	34	53	2	3948
Milt Pappas	.969	520	245	486	23	38	5	3187
Mel Parnell	.971	289	69	327	12	27	4	1752
Camilo Pascual	.973	529	210	507	20	26	13	2930
Claude Passeau	.977	444	130	583	17	44	11	2718
Case Patten	.930	270	146	568	54	16	-7	2063
Marty Pattin	.966	475	123	274	14	16	-6	2038
Barney Pelty	.938	266	131	666	53	26	18	1909
Herb Pennock	.973	617	101	824	26	45	-8	3571
Ron Perranoski	.937	737	45	222	18	12	4	1176
Gaylord Perry	.970	777	349	877	38	58	15	5352
Jim Perry	.960	630	191	506	29	33	-1	3287
Gary Peters	.966	359	111	312	15	27	-2	2081
Fritz Peterson	.963	355	116	429	21	44	15	2217
Dan Petry	.981	330	243	314	11	35	22	1980
Jeff Pfeffer	.963	347	58	549	23	21	-19	2408
Deacon Phillippe	.956	372	93	624	33	17	-15	2608
Billy Pierce	.956	585	123	487	28	32	-21	3305
Togie Pittinger	.927	262	93	528	49	13	-4	2040
Juan Pizarro	.969	488	74	299	12	15	-9	2036
Eddie Plank	.971	623	229	1108	40	37	-30	4497
Johnny Podres	.956	440	80	313	18	24	-15	2266
Howie Pollet	.960	403	82	396	20	32	-2	2105
Henry Porter	.891	207	50	375	52	4	4	1794
Bob Porterfield	.960	318	80	280	15	15	3	1567
Nels Potter	.957	349	98	307	18	18	3	1685
Jack Powell	.938	578	127	967	72	34	-60	4388
Bob Purkey	.966	386	184	464	23	32	28	2115
Jack Quinn	.968	756	139	1240	45	40	45	3922
Dan Quisenberry	.965	674	97	264	13	22	26	1042
Charley Radbourn	.915	528	228	951	110	39	11	4535
Ken Raffensberger	.960	396	71	335	17	17	-17	2152
Pat Ragan	.959	283	56	411	20	16	-3	1610
Pedro Ramos	.977	582	146	328	11	33	-7	2355
Toad Ramsey	.752	248	44	280	107	5	-32	2101
Vic Raschi	.977	269	84	259	8	20	-10	1820
Shane Rawley	.958	469	80	307	17	22	3	1871
Jeff Reardon	.917	694	36	63	9	3	-18	944
Ron Reed	.975	751	170	340	13	25	-4	2477
Phil Regan	.976	551	90	200	7	15	-2	1373
Steve Renko	.948	451	161	316	26	18	-9	2493
Ed Reulbach	.946	399	136	814	54	37	20	2633
Rick Reuschel	.972	553	328	666	29	39	39	3539
Jerry Reuss	.948	628	170	603	42	38	6	3670
Allie Reynolds	.935	434	111	349	32	22	-21	2492
Flint Rhem	.944	294	33	389	25	25	-2	1726
Billy Rhines	.930	249	88	433	39	15	3	1901
Bob Rhoads	.958	218	81	509	26	23	1	1691
Rick Rhoden	.989	413	173	386	6	23	4	2593
J.R. Richard	.939	238	113	195	20	6	-8	1606
Lee Richmond	.886	191	50	317	47	6	-1	1583
Dave Righetti	.936	522	27	119	10	8	-11	1136
Jimmy Ring	.967	389	78	659	25	30	12	2353
Eppa Rixey	.978	692	131	1195	30	56	19	4494
Dave Roberts	.967	445	83	383	16	23	14	2098
Robin Roberts	.967	676	316	601	31	45	-36	4689
Don Robinson	.962	479	103	203	12	10	-13	1776
Preacher Roe	.975	333	90	295	10	26	-9	1916
Steve Rogers	.958	399	237	462	31	37	12	2839
Eddie Rommel	.968	500	159	810	32	51	47	2557
Jim Rooker	.948	319	80	282	20	22	-1	1811
Charlie Root	.976	632	95	506	15	21	-37	3197
Schoolboy Rowe	.974	382	97	421	14	24	3	2218
Nap Rucker	.966	336	55	625	24	18	-5	2375
Dick Rudolph	.970	279	79	624	22	19	16	2048
Dutch Ruether	.970	309	60	494	17	30	-9	2124
Red Ruffing	.968	624	153	677	27	51	-39	4342
Bob Rush	.955	417	171	428	28	24	4	2409
Amos Rusie	.897	462	176	876	121	35	21	3769
Jack Russell	.964	557	132	610	28	30	39	2051
Dick Ruthven	.916	355	149	298	41	19	-2	2109
Nolan Ryan	.896	740	210	513	84	25	-55	4990
Ray Sadecki	.878	563	62	312	52	23	-32	2500
Johnny Sain	.963	412	127	371	19	18	-1	2125
Slim Sallee	.973	476	86	661	21	17	-22	2822
Scott Sanderson	.958	343	112	186	13	10	-17	1826

Pitcher	PCT	G	PO	A	E	DP	FR	IP
Jack Sanford	.959	388	122	365	21	19	4	2047
Johnny Schmitz	.963	366	113	483	23	43	34	1812
Hal Schumacher	.971	391	154	646	24	34	31	2483
Jim Scott	.940	317	54	571	40	18	1	1891
Jack Scott	.956	356	62	399	21	15	-11	1816
Mike Scott	.952	345	156	298	23	12	2	2062
Tom Seaver	.960	656	328	692	42	54	5	4782
Diego Segui	.956	639	128	243	17	11	-6	1808
Rip Sewell	.954	390	142	445	28	27	7	2119
Bobby Shantz	.976	537	174	468	16	48	33	1936
Joe Shaute	.963	360	87	356	17	12	-14	1819
Dupee Shaw	.901	211	63	330	43	10	-7	1763
Jim Shaw	.933	287	71	330	29	18	-20	1599
Bob Shaw	.945	430	114	299	24	16	1	1779
Bob Shawkey	.954	488	146	697	41	22	4	2938
Bill Sherdel	.955	514	77	540	29	25	-24	2710
Urban Shocker	.980	412	155	599	15	22	-10	2681
Chris Short	.965	501	112	359	17	22	-5	2324
Eric Show	.929	309	71	202	21	10	-13	1603
Sonny Siebert	.949	399	159	329	26	28	4	2152
Ed Siever	.934	203	72	422	35	13	-8	1508
Curt Simmons	.965	569	127	514	23	26	-17	3348
Bill Singer	.923	322	95	310	34	7	-11	2174
Jim Slaton	.959	496	180	378	24	36	-1	2683
Al Smith	.961	356	55	367	17	26	6	1663
Bryn Smith	.949	310	115	242	19	20	4	1540
Dave Smith	.917	563	42	80	11	6	-6	761
Eddie Smith	.948	282	56	290	19	16	-3	1596
Frank Smith	.963	354	176	782	37	22	25	2274
Lee Smith	.984	650	41	81	2	7	-10	920
Bob Smith	.981	435	118	539	13	37	13	2247
Sherry Smith	.959	373	91	686	33	27	30	2053
Lary Sorensen	.950	346	151	263	22	23	4	1736
Vic Sorrell	.958	280	68	321	17	17	-5	1671
Elias Sosa	.946	601	52	123	10	4	-5	918
Allen Sothoron	.871	264	66	312	56	3	-25	1584
Mario Soto	.931	297	95	203	22	8	-15	1731
Warren Spahn	.955	750	222	999	58	82	12	5246
Tully Sparks	.934	313	107	544	46	20	-21	2337
Dan Spillner	.956	556	81	157	11	10	-12	1493
Paul Splittorff	.975	429	125	450	15	49	13	2555
Gerry Staley	.971	640	146	481	19	33	34	1981
Harry Staley	.927	283	56	455	40	17	-10	2270
Bob Stanley	.952	637	122	357	24	38	27	1708
Ed Stein	.943	216	110	355	28	8	4	1664
Dave Stewart	.938	393	146	174	21	18	-13	1826
Lefty Stewart	.973	279	68	370	12	18	3	1724
Dave Stieb	.972	390	254	453	20	41	28	2667
Jack Stivetts	.924	388	166	584	62	17	-3	2888
Chuck Stobbs	.977	459	116	301	10	21	-4	1921
Steve Stone	.945	320	125	254	22	13	-1	1789
Mel Stottlemyre	.969	360	242	570	26	38	40	2662
Scott Stratton	.938	231	120	483	40	19	22	1893
Willie Sudhoff	.938	279	106	760	57	22	38	2086
George Suggs	.972	245	74	521	17	20	17	1652
Frank Sullivan	.978	351	121	275	9	30	1	1732
Rick Sutcliffe	.975	357	176	322	13	18	8	2129
Bruce Sutter	.963	661	90	145	9	9	-1	1040
Don Sutton	.968	774	334	613	31	42	-31	5282
Bill Swift	.961	336	41	231	11	11	-25	1637
Frank Tanana	.982	541	195	549	14	35	10	3579
Jesse Tannehill	.953	358	110	837	47	29	18	2751
Jack Taylor	.898	270	101	579	77	19	20	2078
Jack Taylor	.954	310	127	738	42	24	11	2617
Dummy Taylor	.945	274	95	509	35	15	2	1916
Kent Tekulve	.970	1050	92	327	13	17	23	1436
Walt Terrell	.978	250	163	237	9	33	10	1631
Ralph Terry	.967	338	150	235	13	16	-9	1850
Adonis Terry	.903	440	244	722	104	15	8	3513
Jeff Tesreau	.955	247	52	440	23	19	0	1679
Tommy Thomas	.975	398	56	372	11	21	-24	2177
Sloppy Thurston	.968	288	71	390	15	18	8	1542
Luis Tiant	.946	573	221	389	35	31	-25	3486
Dick Tidrow	.963	620	97	212	12	10	-12	1748
Jim Tobin	.965	287	96	479	21	27	19	1899
Fred Toney	.959	336	57	555	26	14	-11	2206
Mike Torrez	.944	494	223	472	41	38	6	3042
Dizzy Trout	.944	521	193	645	50	63	42	2726
Steve Trout	.946	301	77	310	22	28	17	1501
Virgil Trucks	.955	517	156	420	27	14	-7	2684
John Tudor	.974	281	85	321	11	27	10	1796
Bob Turley	.971	310	88	211	9	16	-14	1710
Lefty Tyler	.954	323	117	672	38	25	21	2228
George Uhle	.960	513	175	624	33	42	-18	3120
Tom Underwood	.898	379	49	180	26	13	-13	1587
Fernando Valenzuela	.964	331	164	451	23	28	24	2348
Dazzy Vance	.975	442	126	570	18	29	-13	2967
Johnny Vander Meer	.944	346	82	404	29	30	-6	2104
Elam Vangilder	.962	367	67	384	18	24	-8	1714
Hippo Vaughn	.918	390	92	740	74	17	-6	2731
Bob Veale	.936	397	37	270	21	19	-17	1926
Frank Viola	.934	307	60	251	22	10	-15	2109
Rube Waddell	.909	407	169	740	91	16	-20	2963
Rube Walberg	.948	544	113	558	37	18	-2	2645
Ed Walsh	.963	430	233	1208	56	32	74	2965
Bucky Walters	.974	428	153	746	24	76	27	3104
Monte Ward	.932	292	169	574	54	20	25	2462
Lon Warneke	.988	445	126	538	8	31	-6	2781
Herm Wehmeier	.930	361	87	259	26	16	-14	1804
Stump Weidman	.885	279	143	444	76	9	-1	2319
Carl Weilman	.947	239	59	444	28	19	1	1521
Mickey Welch	.874	564	217	705	133	23	-48	4801
Bob Welch	.960	396	203	320	22	26	-3	2514
Gus Weyhing	.881	538	201	743	128	27	-42	4324
Doc White	.960	427	234	960	50	25	24	3041
Will White	.887	403	117	715	106	10	-17	3542
Earl Whitehill	.949	541	166	701	47	31	-12	3562
Jim Whitney	.900	413	123	769	99	24	15	3496
Eddie Whitson	.948	439	118	265	21	16	-14	2163
Bill Wight	.909	347	45	355	40	16	8	1562
Milt Wilcox	.947	394	122	357	27	30	11	2015
Hoyt Wilhelm	.978	1070	114	373	11	17	-1	2253
Ed Willett	.949	274	72	695	41	18	29	1773
Stan Williams	.944	482	109	246	21	20	-6	1763
Vic Willis	.954	513	271	1124	67	29	24	3997
Don Wilson	.922	266	93	191	24	12	-15	1748
Jim Wilson	.988	257	94	235	4	13	-5	1540
Earl Wilson	.945	338	183	295	28	19	4	2052
Hooks Wiltse	.953	357	123	579	35	19	7	2111
George Winter	.927	220	94	488	46	21	0	1656
Rick Wise	.982	506	206	504	13	46	13	3125
Mike Witt	.950	330	145	291	23	21	0	2063
Wilbur Wood	.977	651	84	523	14	26	17	2684
Al Worthington	.948	602	82	229	17	12	7	1245
Clyde Wright	.962	329	108	344	18	30	18	1729
Whit Wyatt	.956	360	74	316	18	15	-8	1761
Early Wynn	.967	691	193	670	29	47	-29	4566
Cy Young	.939	906	229	2014	146	40	13	7356
Tom Zachary	.967	533	83	773	29	27	4	3128
Geoff Zahn	.945	304	87	326	24	19	8	1848

Notes on Contributors

Paul D. Adomites was born and raised in Pittsburgh, and lives there now, although he has also lived in Oregon, Florida, and New York. He was publications director for the Society for American Baseball Research (SABR) from 1987–1990. He is the founder and continuing editor of *The SABR Review of Books* and a writer on topics as diverse as ethnic cooking and the history of technology. His book, *The Bridges of Pittsburgh,* is nearing publication.

Larry Amman was born and raised in the suburbs of Detroit. He graduated from Wayne State University with a B.A. in history and political science in 1967, then served in the U.S. Army Intelligence in Vietnam and Germany. Although he has lived in Washington, D.C., for the last ten years, the Detroit Tigers remain his favorite team. He has published several articles on the Tigers, and has compiled all their game-winning RBIs from 1901–1980. He is currently employed as a travel agent.

Dennis Bingham is editor of the Chicago Police Department's Publications Section, a freelance cartoonist, and an umpire for several adult and youth baseball leagues in the Chicago area. (His umpiring partner is often his father, Bill, who taught him the rules.) Bingham served as a historical adviser for the movie *Eight Men Out,* in which he also played a bit part as umpire Billy Evans. He was associate editor of the SABR publication *Baseball in Chicago* and has headed the rules section of SABR's Umpires and Rules Committee since its formation. A White Sox fan, Bingham lives with his wife, Diane, and sons Sean and Kevin on Chicago's South Side.

Bob Carroll, a former teacher, is presently a freelance writer and illustrator living in North Huntingdon, Pennsylvania. He is the founder and executive director of the Professional Football Researchers Association (PFRA). He is also a longtime member of SABR. He is the author of *The Hidden Game of Football* and *The Football Abstract* (both with Pete Palmer and John Thorn), *The Whole Baseball Catalogue* (with Thorn), *100 Greatest Running Backs, The Official Baseball Hall of Fame Fun & Fact Sticker Book* (with Mark Rucker), *This Year in Baseball 1990,* and *The Official Major League Baseball Way to Play Baseball.* He has also written numerous sports-related articles for magazines, including *The National Pastime, Sport, Sports Heritage, Sports History,* and *The Saturday Evening Post.*

Merritt Clifton, an award-winning veteran environmental journalist, is news editor for *The Animals' Agenda,* an international magazine of animal rights and ecology. Clifton also is author of numerous works on "outlaw" baseball, especially as played in Quebec, Vermont, Japan, and Mexico, and *Relative Baseball,* a pioneering sabermetric study. Having recently relocated from Quebec to Connecticut, he would like to find a team that plays Saturdays or Sundays and could use an experienced righthander.

Eliot Cohen founded *Major League Monthly,* a forum for baseball opinion and research, in 1985. A graduate of Yale and Stanford, Cohen also edits the annual *Who's Who in Baseball* and covers New York teams for United Press International. His book reviews appear in publications ranging from *The New York Times* to *The SABR Review of Books.* Formerly a city planner in his native New York and a U.S. diplomat in Tanzania, Cohen wrote on consumer issues, urban planning, and international relations before specializing in baseball. Cohen lives in Washington, D.C., with his wife, Lynn Ferenc.

Harrington E. Crissey, Jr., better known as "Kit" to his acquaintances, was born in Schenectady, New York, and currently lives in Philadelphia. He received a B.A. degree in Latin literature from the University of Rochester and a master of education degree from Temple University. He currently teaches Latin to Philadelphia public school children and English as a second language to foreign adults. Crissey holds the rank of commander in the Naval Reserve. A Boston Red Sox fan, he participates actively in the Society for American Baseball Research and is the author of three books about baseball during World War Two, one of which covers baseball and the Navy.

L. Robert Davids, retired writer and historian, was born in rural Iowa in 1926. He graduated from the University of Missouri (BJ '49; MA '51) and received his Ph.D. from Georgetown University in 1961. He served in the Army Air Corps from 1944–1946 and worked for the U.S. Government in Washington, D.C., from 1951–1981. Davids organized SABR in 1971, served four years as president, and edited SABR publications from 1971–1983. He was a freelance writer for *The Sporting News* from 1951–1965, published *Baseball Briefs* from 1971–1975 and 1981–1990, and produced *Insider's Baseball* (Scribners) in 1983.

Bill Deane is senior research associate at the National Baseball Library in Cooperstown, New York. He has written for numerous baseball publications, including *Baseball Digest, Street & Smith's, The National Pastime,* and *The Bill James Baseball Abstract.* Born in Poughkeepsie, New York, in 1957, he now resides in Fly Creek, New York, with his wife, Pam, and daughter, Sarah.

Cappy Gagnon joined SABR in 1977 and has written articles for its *Baseball Research Journal* on Roger Bresnahan, Ed Reulbach, and the subject of "batting eye." He has also made numerous presentations at SABR national conventions and regional meetings. Additionally, he has written for the Greenwood Press's *Baseball Biographical Encyclopedia, Baseball Digest,* and the *Baseball Quarterly Review,* and is in the midst of writing *Anson to Yaz,* a book about the 65 major leaguers who attended Notre Dame. (Gagnon began this research more than 20 years ago.) On the board of directors of SABR since 1984, Gagnon served two terms as president.

Larry R. Gerlach is professor of history at the University of Utah. He is a member of the editorial board of *Baseball History,* and chair of the Umpires and Rules Committee of SABR. His publications include *The Men in Blue: Conversations with Umpires* (1980).

Stanley Grosshandler was born in Youngstown, Ohio, and attended the University of Cincinnati and the College of Wooster where he played football. He received his M.D. from Ohio State and served in the Army. Grosshandler has written over 250 articles on sports history and has been a member of SABR, where he has held several offices, since 1971. He presently resides in Raleigh, North Carolina, and teaches at North Carolina

State University and the University of North Carolina. He and his wife, Mary, have five children.

Gary Hailey is a Washington, D.C., attorney and the author of "Anatomy of a Murder: The Federal League and the Courts," which appeared in the Spring 1985 issue of *The National Pastime.* He is a native of Joplin, Missouri, and a graduate of Rice University and Harvard Law School. Although he now realizes that he will never achieve his childhood ambition of playing center field for the New York Yankees, he still daydreams about one day being the Yankees' general counsel.

Stephen S. Hall, of New York City, is the author of *Invisible Frontiers,* a popular history of the origins of biotechnology. An award-winning science and travel writer, he has published in *Hippocrates, The New York Times Magazine, Smithsonian,* and *GEO,* where his definitive article on baseball in Italy appeared.

Barry Halper, born in Newark, New Jersey, in 1939, is the president of Halper Bros., Inc., a paper products company based in Edison, New Jersey. He began collecting baseball material sixteen years ago and now holds the largest single collection of baseball memorabilia, surpassing even Cooperstown's. His collection includes over one million baseball cards and 964 player uniforms. Halper and his wife, Sharon, have three children and reside in Livingston, New Jersey.

Tom Heitz, born in Kansas City, Missouri, in 1940, has been a lifelong baseball fan. He learned the National Pastime from his father, a law professor and Little League coach, and from Harry Caray, the voice of the St. Louis Cardinals. Heitz received his formal education at the University of Kansas (B.A., 1962), the University of Missouri at Kansas City School of Law (J.D., 1965), and the University of Washington, where he studied library science under renowned law librarian Marian Gallagher. Heitz left the legal profession in 1983 to become librarian at the National Baseball Hall of Fame in Cooperstown, New York.

Bob Hoie has long been an active member of the Society for American Baseball Research, receiving the Society's Bob Davids Award for meritorious service in 1987. He was a principal contributor to *Minor League Baseball Stars,* volumes 1 and 2, and is now working on volume 3. A native of Los Angeles and a fan of the Pacific Coast League Angels until their demise in 1957, Hoie is an urban planner for Los Angeles County.

John B. Holway has written for numerous magazines and newspapers, including *American Heritage, The Sporting News, The New York Times,* and the Washington *Post.* He is the author of *Voices from the Great Black Leagues, Blackball Stars,* and, with John Thorn, *The Pitcher.* He has written about Ted Williams, whom he saw in 1941, the Negro leagues, which he saw in 1944, Japanese baseball, which he saw in 1948, and pitching, which he has spent a lifetime swinging at and missing. He won *Spitball* magazine's Casey Award and SABR's Bob Davids Award, both in 1990.

Frederick Ivor-Campbell turned to baseball research and writing five years ago after many years in religious publishing (editor/writer, Gospel Light Publications, California), public information (Barrington College, Rhode Island), and college teaching (English, at the University of Rhode Island and King's College, New York). He has written baseball history and biography for several periodicals and reference works. Among his current projects are a book portraying Old Hoss Radbourn as an epic hero and research to uncover the full story of how baseball became America's national game. Ivor-Campbell lives with his wife, Alma, in Warren, Rhode Island.

Clifford S. Kachline, following a stint as sports editor of the North Penn *Reporter* of Lansdale, Pennsylvania, joined the editorial staff of *The Sporting News* at age 21 in April 1943. He remained there for 24 years. Besides writing for *TSN,* for 20 years he was the compiler and editor of the *Official Baseball Guide* and *The Dope Book.* Kachline left *TSN* in May 1967 to become public relations director of the North American Soccer League; he then served as Baseball Hall of Fame historian (1969–1982), and then, until his retirement in 1985, as the first executive director of the Society for American Baseball Research.

Jack Kavanagh is enjoying a happy retirement working as a sports historian/writer after a career in advertising and broadcast management, capped by a veer to final employment as an administrator of services for the handicapped. Married 45 years, with a son and daughter and five grandchildren, he lives in Rhode Island in busy disarray.

Jack Lang has reported on major league baseball for forty-two years, starting in 1946 when he covered the Brooklyn Dodgers for the Long Island *Press.* Lang's last 13 years on the beat were for the New York *Daily News,* where he was the senior major league baseball writer in 1987 when he retired. In 1966 he began conducting the annual Hall of Fame election and was elected Secretary-Treasurer of the Baseball Writers Association of America, where he conducted the annual Most Valuable Player, Cy Young, Rookie, and Manager polls for the BBWAA. In 1987 Lang himself was elected to the Hall of Fame when he was named winner of the J. G. Taylor Spink Award for meritorious contributions to baseball writing. He has served as a member of the Major League Scoring Rules Committee and was appointed in 1990 by Commissioner Fay Vincent to the Committee for Statistical Accuracy. Although semiretired, Lang still serves as Executive Secretary of the BBWAA and is a columnist and contributing editor for *SportsTicker.*

Philip J. Lowry is author of *Green Cathedrals,* the definitive study of all ballparks ever used for Major League and Negro League games since 1871. He has served on the Board of Directors and as Ballparks Chair and Negro Leagues Chair for SABR. Phil received a B.A. degree from Harvard College, served in the U.S. Army airborne for six years as an infantry captain, and now resides in San Diego with his wife, Ellen, and their two young children, Evan and Megan.

Bill Madden majored in journalism at the University of South Carolina and launched his sportswriting career at United Press International in New York in 1970. From 1980–1988, Madden was *The Daily News*'s New York Yankees beat writer. He became that publication's national baseball columnist in 1989. In 1990 he collaborated on the best-selling book, *Damned Yankees.* In his years at *The Daily News* he was responsible for breaking numerous baseball stories, including the National League's surprise election of Bill White as its president in February 1989. In addition to writing for *The Daily News,* Madden also has contributed freelance articles to numerous sports publications and currently writes a semiweekly sports collecting column for *The Sporting News.*

Steve Mann is president of the Baseball Analysis Company, a major league consulting and software development firm that he cofounded in 1982. In 1979, Steve became baseball's first professional statistical analyst when he took on that role for the Houston Astros. From 1982 through 1986, his company represented 13 big league clubs in salary arbitration under the auspices of Tal Smith Enterprises. In the 1987–1988 arbitration campaign, the company swung its salary services over to the players and their representatives. Steve earned a B.A. from the University of Pennsylvania (1968) and a doctorate in educational philosophy at Temple University (1980).

Yoichi Nagata holds a B.A. from Osaka University in Japan and an M.A. from the University of Pennsylvania. He has been a freelance sports journalist, writing numerous articles on sports for Japanese magazines. He is an avid baseball fan of the now-defunct Nishitetsu Lions of Fukuoka and of the Philadelphia Phillies. His first book on Japanese-American baseball players is due out in 1991.

Joseph M. Overfield was born in 1916 in Buffalo, where he has lived all his life, except for three years in the Air Force in World War Two. Historian for the Buffalo Bisons and a member of the Buffalo Baseball Hall of Fame Committee, he wrote *100 Seasons of Buffalo Baseball* in 1985, and has written for *Baseball Digest, The Sporting News,* Buffalo's *Courier-Express* and *News, Niagara Frontier,* and SABR's *Baseball Research Journal* and *The National Pastime.* Overfield was honored in 1986 by SABR for his contributions to minor league history. He is now semiretired after 51 years with a Buffalo real-estate title firm.

Pete Palmer is the former editor of the Barnes *Official Encyclopedia of Baseball.* He began compiling his historical and analytical data in the mid-1960s, and from 1978–1987 he was chairman of SABR's statistical analysis committee. In that time he also served as a consultant for the Sports Information Center, the official statisticians of the American League. He is currently on the board of directors of Project Scoresheet. Palmer has contributed articles to *Sport, Sports Heritage, The National Pastime,* and *Baseball Research Journal.* He is coauthor, with John Thorn, of *The Hidden Game of Baseball* and *The Baseball Record Book;* with Thorn and Bob Carroll, of *The Hidden Game of Football* and *The Football Abstract;* and with Thorn and Eliot Cohen of *The Baseball Annual 1990.* He won SABR's prestigious Bob Davids Award in 1989.

Dick Perez, artist-in-residence at Perez-Steele Galleries in Fort Washington, Pennsylvania, is the official artist for the National Baseball Hall of Fame, the Philadelphia Phillies, and the Donruss Company. He created the National League Centennial logo and the cover for the 1983 World Series program. Mr. Perez's works are central pieces in private, corporate, and institutional collections in this country and abroad. His portrait of Grover Cleveland Alexander is in the private collection of President Ronald Reagan. He created the illustrations for the title page and part-title pages of *Total Baseball.*

David Pietrusza is the author of *Baseball's Canadian-American League* and *Baseball's Major Leagues.* He served as a research consultant for *Ballparks of North America* and contributed chapters to *The Empire State of Baseball.* He is a member of the Society for American Baseball Research's By-Laws, Ballparks, and Minor Leagues committees. A resident of Scotia, New York, Pietrusza has written for *The National Pastime, Ballparks Bulletin,* and *Baseball Research Journal.* A former member of the Amsterdam (N.Y.) City Council, Pietrusza holds an M.A. in history and has a torn rotator cuff.

Bruce L. Prentice was born and raised in Toronto, Ontario, Canada, and was a top amateur baseball player before turning to coaching and instruction. In the late 1970s he assisted the introduction of the first high school baseball programs in Canada. He was founder of Canada's first college baseball program at Seneca College in Toronto and was an area scout for the Blue Jays from 1980–1986. Prentice is the owner and operator of Proway Baseball Schools, the founder and president of the Canadian Baseball Hall of Fame and Museum, and was instrumental in forming the World Baseball Hall of Fame in 1989.

Rob Ruck is an assistant professor of history at Chatham College in Pittsburgh. He is the coauthor of *Steve Nelson, American Radical* and author of *Sandlot Seasons: Sport in Black Pittsburgh.* His book on baseball in the Dominican Republic is due out in June 1991.

Debra A. Shattuck is a captain in the U.S. Air Force and an assistant professor of history at the U.S. Air Force Academy. Born in Lorain, Ohio, in 1959, she received her B.A. in history from Cedarville College in 1981 and her M.A. in history from Brown University in 1988. Her master's thesis was on female baseball players in the United States, 1866–1954. She lives with her husband and three children in Colorado Springs, Colorado.

Fred Stein's avid interest in baseball goes back to the 1930s, when he discovered the wonders of the game from a bleacher seat in the Polo Grounds. Subsequently, he was an infantryman in World War Two, a student at Penn State, and an employee of the U.S. departments of Agriculture and Commerce before his retirement in 1979. Since then, he has been an environmental consultant, has published books on the New York and San Francisco Giants, and has contributed baseball articles to a number of publications. A transplanted New York City native, he has resided in the northern Virginia area since 1951.

John Thorn is the author/editor of many baseball books, including *The Game for All America, The Armchair Books of Baseball, The National Pastime, The Pitcher* (with John Holway), and, with Pete Palmer, *The Hidden Game of Baseball* and *The Baseball Record Book;* with Palmer and Bob Carroll he coauthored *The Hidden Game of Football* and *The Football Abstract;* and with Carroll he produced *The Whole Baseball Catalogue.* He also has written for several periodicals, among them *The Sporting News, Sport,* and *American Heritage.* Thorn founded *The National Pastime,* an annual publication of the Society for American Baseball Research.

Robert Tiemann is chairman of the nineteenth-century research committee of the Society for American Baseball Research and is the author of *Cardinal Classics* and *Dodger Classics.* He heads a SABR research project that is reconstructing from newspaper play-by-play accounts much of the missing data for the National Association of 1871–1875. With Rich Topp, Tiemann shared a SABR award for his redevelopment of the Manager Roster as it appears in *Total Baseball.*

Richard Topp is an "accountant-turned-historian" from Chicago. A member of the Society for American Baseball Research since 1975, he served for many years as chairman of its biographical committee; beginning in 1989, he assumed SABR's presidency. Topp has compiled the most extensive biographical data file on major league players since 1871, and his research has appeared in numerous books and newspapers across the nation. In 1988 he shared with Bob Tiemann of St. Louis an award given by SABR for his research on managers; this research informs the Manager Roster in *Total Baseball.*

Jules Tygiel is a professor of history at San Francisco State University. He is the author of *Baseball's Great Experiment: Jackie Robinson and his Legacy* (Oxford University Press, 1983; Vintage Paperback edition, 1984) and has contributed articles to many periodicals.

David Quentin Voigt is a baseball historian and a professor at Albright College in Reading, Pennsylvania, where he teaches a popular course entitled Baseball in American Culture. Over the years he has written seven books and more than a hundred articles on the subject of baseball. His major works include *American Baseball,* a three-volume history; *Baseball: An Illustrated History,* a single volume published in 1987 by the Pennsylvania State University Press; and *America Through Baseball.* A past president of SABR, Voigt and his wife, Virginia, a teacher, reside in Shillington, Pennsylvania.

With appreciation to these readers of *Total Baseball 1* who sent in corrections or made suggestions on how to improve the second edition:

Larry Amman, Ray Andreotti, Mel Bailey, Craig Barbarino, Edgar K. Beatty, James M. Beck, Joseph R. Bender, Robert Beukelher, John Booth, Jim Bostain, Therese R. Brown, J. Paul Browne, Bob Cambris, Kevin A. Carleton, Bob Carroll, Anthony M. Chieco, Ken Coleman, Steve Cooper, Owen Curtis, Clay Davenport, L. Robert Davids, Bill Deane, Harold Dellinger, Ted D. DeVries, Don Dewey, Raymond A. DiSanto, Sam Elfand, Don Elliott, John Emerson, Eddie Epstein, Kenneth Fink, Robert L. Franz, Andrew Fussner, Cam Gibson, Steven Goldberg, Ray Gonzalez, Dan Greenia, Bill Haber, Rod Hay, Bob Hoie, Fred Ivor-Campbell, Tom Jennings, Bill Jensen, Warren Johnson, Cliff Kachline, James Kaufman, Dave Kemp, Larry Kempster, Randall Kleinman, Jack Lang, Ron Liebman, Jerry Malloy, James F. Maxfield, Bob McConnell, Joe M. McGowan, David Molnar, George S. Moskal, Frank J. Mueller, Neil Munro, Thomas L. Nester, Dave Nichols, Tom O'Brien, Yoshio Ohno, S. Mark Parker, Paul E. Pennebaker, Peretz Perl, Dave Pietrusza, Mike Post, Jorgen Rasmussen, Allan Rausch, Andrew Richardson, John Rickert, John M. Roca, Winslow Rogers, Tom Ruane, Bill Rubenstein, David Schermer, Leon Schmerhold, John Schwartz, Alfred Secondi, Sy Siegel, Richard Siegelman, Al Smith, David M. Snyder, David Stephan, Mike Sparks, Lyle Spatz, Dean Sullivan, Issac Thorn, Richard Topp, Stephen Toth, T. Brook Treakle III, Jim Troisi, Jim Tuttle, Jim Vail, Cullen P. Vane, David Vincent, Joseph M. Wayman, Jim Weigand, Bernard Weisberger, Christopher Williams, Frank Williams, Joseph C. Williams, Ralph Winnie, Jim Wright, and Ed Yerha.

Glossary of Statistical Terms

This Glossary contains definitions of the statistical terms and measures carried in Part 2 of *Total Baseball* that may be unfamiliar to the average baseball fan or that represent what today might seem odd scoring practices. The Glossary will also be of value to the advanced fan who wishes to know more about the mathematical and theoretical foundations of certain statistics. Also included at the end of this section are the team and league abbreviations used in this book.

/A "Adjusted"; means that the statistic to the immediate left of this mark has been normalized to league average and adjusted for home park factor. Stats that are normalized in this book are Batting Runs, Production, Batting Average, On Base Percentage, Slugging Average, Earned Run Average, and Pitcher Runs.

Assist Although credited to pitchers on strikeouts in some of baseball's early years, not counted as such in this volume.

Assist Average Assists divided by games played. Stat created by Philadelphia baseball writer Al Wright in 1875.

At-Bats Charged to batters on sacrifice hits, 1889–1894; on sacrifice-fly situations, 1931–1938 and 1940–1953; bases on balls, 1876, 1887. However, we did not count at-bats for bases on balls.

Average and Over Early form of expressing averages for base hits, runs, and outs. The average of a batter with 23 hits in six games would be not 3.83 but 3–5 (an average of 3 with an overage, or remainder, of 5); borrowed from cricket.

Average Bases Allowed A pitcher's total bases allowed, divided by his innings pitched—what might be termed Opponents' Slugging Average. Created by Alfred P. Berry in 1951.

Average Batting (Pitching, Fielding) Skill The great philosophical as well as statistical puzzler: after one has normalized a player's performance to that of his league, how does one compare one season's league average with that of another far removed in time? Does a .266 batting average in the National League of 1902 mean the same thing as a .266 batting average in the American League of 1977?

Bases on Balls Counted as an out for batters in 1876 and as a hit for batters in 1887, but as neither throughout this book. Awarded for a varying number of errant pitches since 1876, from nine in that year to the current four (standardized in 1889). (After 1887, the batter was no longer allowed to specify strike zone as waist to shoulders or waist to shins.)

Bases on Balls Percentage Batters' stat: most walks per 100 at-bats.

Bases on Balls Per Game Game defined as nine innings; league-leading pitchers calculated on basis of lowest mark; computed as bases on balls times nine, divided by innings.

Base-Out Percentage Barry Codell's stat for measuring complete offensive performance, in which the elements of the numerator represent bases gained while the events in the denominator represent outs produced (sacrifices and sacrifice flies appear in both because they achieve both—gaining a base for the team while costing it an out). The formula:

$$\frac{\text{Total Bases} + \text{Walks} + \text{HBP} + \text{Steals} + \text{Sacrifices} + \text{Sacrifice Flies}}{\text{At-bats} - \text{Hits} + \text{Caught Stealing} + \text{GIDP} + \text{Sac.} + \text{Sac. Flies}}$$

(GIDP, in the equation above, stands for Grounded Into Double Play; HBP for Hit By Pitch.)

Batters Facing Pitcher Unavailable before 1909 in the National League and 1908 in the American; for earlier years, constructed from available data in this manner: subtract league base hits from league at-bats, divide by league innings pitched, multiply by the pitcher's innings, and add his hits allowed, walks, hit by pitch, and sacrifice hits, if available. Abbreviated as BFP.

Batter's Park Factor The Park Factor shown in the batters' section of the team statistics in the Annual Record, Player Register, and Home-Road Statistics. Above 100 means batters benefited from playing half their games in a good hitting park. Abbreviated as BPF or, in what are clearly batters' stats (as in the Player Register) simply as PF. See entry for *Park Factor* for an exhaustive explanation of the computation.

Battery Errors In baseball's early years, wild pitches, passed balls, and hit batsmen were lumped together in the statistical summary of a game as *battery errors* and were charged against the fielding percentage of the pitcher or catcher. Such battery errors have been removed from individual and team stats for this book.

Batting Average Calculated as base hits divided by at-bats ever since its first appearance in print in 1874. In 1876 walks were counted as at-bats, and in 1887 they were counted as at-bats and as hits. For this book, batting averages are computed in uniform fashion throughout baseball history. Abbreviated in Part 2 of this volume as AVG, although it is also commonly abbreviated BA.

Batting Runs The Linear Weights measure of runs contributed *beyond* those of a league-average batter or team, such league average defined as zero. The formula depends upon the run values for each offensive event that resulted from Pete Palmer's 1978 computer simulation of all major league games played since 1901. Run values change marginally with changing conditions of play (an out costs a team more in a hitters' year, such as 1930, than in a pitchers' year, such as 1908), and they differ slightly up and down the batting order (a homer is not worth as much to the leadoff hitter as it is to the fifth-place batter; a walk is worth more for the man batting second than for the man batting eighth); however, these differences have been averaged out historically in the figures below.

$$\text{Runs} = (.47)1B + (.78)2B + (1.09)3B + (1.40)HR + (.33)(BB + HB) - (.25)(AB - H) - (.50)OOB$$

(An out is considered to be a hitless at-bat and its value is set so that the sum of all events times their frequency is zero, thus establishing zero as the baseline, or norm, for performance.)

Some events one might expect to see included in this formula but that do not appear are sacrifices, sacrifice hits, grounded into double plays, and reached on error. The last is not known for most years and in the official statistics is indistinguishable from outs on base (OOB). The sacrifice has values that essentially cancel one another, trading an out for an advanced base which, often as not, leaves the team in a situation with poorer run potential than it had before the sacrifice. The sacrifice fly has dubious run value because it is entirely dependent on a situation not under the batter's control: while a single or a walk or a hit by pitch always has potential run value, a long fly does not unless a man happens to be poised at third base. Last, the grounded into double play is to a far greater extent a function of one's

2622 Glossary of Statistical Terms

place in the batting order than it is of poor speed or failure in the clutch, and thus it does not find a home in a formula applicable to all batters. It is no accident that Hank Aaron, who ran well for most of his long career and wasn't too shabby in the clutch, hit into more DPs than anyone else, nor that Roberto Clemente, Al Kaline, and Frank Robinson, who fit the same description, are also among the ten "worst" in this department.

The Batting Runs formula can be condensed by eliminating the components for steals, caught stealing, and outs on base. Outs on base (calculated as *Hits + Walks + Hit Batsman − Left on Base − Runs − Caught Stealing*) is meaningful only for teams, not individuals. We eliminate steals from the formula in those years in which caught-stealing figures are not available, but the surviving data for the early years indicate that few of the men with high base-stealing totals exceeded the break-even point of 66.7 percent by a margin large enough to produce even one additional Batting Win. A further condensation that we have used for our historical data, as indicated in the formula above, involves setting the value of a single at .47 runs and each extra base at .31, making a double .78, a triple 1.09, and a homer 1.40. (This tends to even out the fluctuations in run values for base hits and extra bases over time: a double, for example, was in fact worth .82 runs from 1901–1920, .80 runs from 1941–1960, and .77 runs from 1961–1977.) Subtract the hits from the total bases and multiply the resulting extra bases by .31 and the hits by .47. This may introduce small variations from a more rigorous formula that includes differing run values for the differing periods or even for single years (generally amounting to a fraction of a run), but the calculation is much snappier for those without a complete computer database at the ready.

The Batting Runs formula may be long, even in its condensed form, but it calls for only addition, subtraction, and multiplication and thus is as simple as Slugging Average, whose incorrect weights (1, 2, 3, and 4) it revises and expands upon. Each event has a value and frequency, just as in Slugging Average, yet in Batting Runs outs are treated as offensive events with a run value of their own (albeit a negative one). Just as the run potential for a team in a given half-inning is boosted by a man reaching base, it is diminished by a man being retired; not only has he failed to brighten the situation on the bases but he has deprived his team of the services of a man further down the order who might have come up in this half-inning, either with men on base and/or with scores already in.

The Batting Runs stat treats every offensive event in terms of its impact upon the team—an *average* team, so that a man does not benefit in his individual record for having the good fortune to bat cleanup with the Red Sox or suffer for batting cleanup with the White Sox. The relationship of individual performance to team play is stated poorly or not at all in conventional baseball statistics. In Batting Runs it is crystal clear.

Recognizing that some readers will wish to keep track of batting performance by compiling Batting Runs themselves over the course of a season and that they may be frustrated by the difficulty of separating out pitcher batting or of calculating the (At-Bats − Hits) factor for the league, we advise that using the fixed value of −.25 for outs will tend to work quite well if you wish to include pitcher batting performance, and a fixed value of −.27 will serve if you wish to exclude it. Actually, any fixed value will suffice in midseason; it's only when all the numbers are in and you care to compare this year's results with last year's (or, e.g., with those of the 1927 Yankees) that more precision is desirable. At that point the value of the out may be calculated by the more ambitious among you, but, ideally, your newspaper or the sporting press will provide accurate Batting Runs figures. (Who, after all, calculates ERA for himself?) Batting Runs are abbreviated as BR.

Batting Wins Adjusted Batting Runs divided by the number of runs required to create an additional win beyond average (see *Runs Per Win*). That average is defined as a team record of .500 because a league won-lost average must be .500, or as an individual record of zero because the value of the out for a given year is calculated to establish a baseline of zero. Abbreviated as BW.

Calculated Stat One or more counting stats (see below) subjected to a mathematical process such as averaging.

Chances Accepted Total chances for putouts and assists, minus errors.

Clutch Hitting Index Calculated for individuals, actual RBIs over expected RBIs, adjusted for league average and slot in batting order; 100 is a league-average performance. The spot in the batting order is figured as

$$5 - (9 \times BFPGP - BFPGT)$$

where BFPGP is the batters facing pitcher per game for the player, or plate appearances divided by games, and BFPGT is the batters facing pitcher per game of the entire team.

Expected RBIs are calculated as

$$(.25 \text{ singles} + .50 \text{ doubles} + .75 \text{ triples} + 1.75 \text{ homers}) \times$$
$$LGAV \times EXPSL$$

where LGAV (league average) = league RBIs divided by (.25 singles + .50 doubles + .75 triples + 1.75 homers), and EXPSL (expected RBI by slot number) = .88 for the leadoff batter, and for the remaining slots, descending to ninth, .90, .98, 1.08, 1.08, 1.04, 1.04, 1.04, and 1.02.

Calculated for teams, Clutch Hitting Index is actual runs scored over Batting Runs. Abbreviated as CHI.

Clutch Pitching Index Expected runs allowed over actual runs allowed, with 100 being a league-average performance. Expected runs are figured on the basis of the pitcher's opposing at-bats, hits, walks, and hit batsmen (doubles and triples estimated at league average). Abbreviated as CPI.

Counting Stat A raw figure that tells how many of an item have been accumulated, as opposed to a calculated or derived figure such as an average.

Differential The difference between a team's actual won-lost record and that predicted by the total of its Pitching Wins, Batting Wins, Fielding Wins, and Stolen Base Wins; this measure indicates the extent to which a team outperformed or underperformed its talent. Abbreviated as DIF.

Earned Run Average Calculated as earned runs times nine, divided by innings pitched. For a few years after being introduced as an official stat in the National League in 1912 and the American League in 1913, runs aided by stolen bases were not counted as earned (see Chronology of Scoring Rules in Appendix 1, Rules and Scoring). For years before 1912, ERA has been constructed from raw data, but for some teams in some seasons, earned runs cannot be identified with perfect certainty. For those teams, we use the estimating procedure created by Information Concepts, Inc., of assigning to those runs whose earned/unearned status is unknown the percentage of earned runs to runs that characterize the team's known runs. In *Total Baseball*, we have created an Adjusted ERA by normalizing to the league average—which is done by dividing the league average ERA by the individual ERA—and then factoring in home park.

Expected Wins Calculated for the team based on its actual runs scored and allowed, not its predicted runs scored and allowed. A team that allows exactly as many runs as it scores is predicted to play .500 ball. The equation for expected wins is:

$$\frac{\text{Runs Scored} - \text{Runs Allowed} + 81}{\text{Runs Per Win}}$$

Abbreviated as W−EXP.

Fielding Average Defined as putouts and assists divided by the total of putouts, assists, and errors. The weakness of this stat is that it values a player with minimal range but good hands over another player who may accept many more chances but mishandle a few of these. Abbreviated as FA. See *Range Factor, Total Chances*.

Fielding Runs The Linear Weights measure of runs saved *beyond* what a league-average player at that position might have saved, defined as zero; this stat is calculated to take account of the particular demands of the different positions.

For second basemen, shortstops, and third basemen, the formula begins by calculating the league average for the position, in this fashion:

$$\text{AVG} \begin{array}{c} \text{pos.} \\ \text{lg.} \end{array} = \left(\frac{.20\,(PO + 2A - E + DP)\text{ league at position}}{PO\text{ league total} - K\text{ league total}} \right)$$

where A = assists, PO = putouts, E = errors, DP = double plays, and K = strikeouts. Then we estimate the number of innings for each player at each position based upon each player's entire fielding record and his number of plate appearances. So, if the team played 1,500 innings and one player was calculated to have played 1,000 of those innings at a given position, his Fielding Runs (FR) would be calculated as:

$$FR = .20\,(PO + 2A - E + DP)\text{ player} - \text{avg. pos. lg.} \times \left(\begin{array}{c} PO \\ \text{team} \end{array} - \begin{array}{c} K \\ \text{team} \end{array} \right) \frac{\text{innings, player}}{\text{innings, team}}$$

Assists are doubly weighted because more fielding skill is generally required to get one than to record a putout.

For catchers, the above formula is modified by removing strikeouts from their formulas and subtracting not only errors but also passed balls divided by two. Also incorporated in the catcher's Fielding Runs is one tenth of the adjusted Pitching Runs for the team, times the percentage of games behind the plate by that catcher.

For pitchers, the above formula is modified to subtract individual pitcher strikeouts from the total number of potential outs (otherwise, exceptional strikeout pitchers like Nolan Ryan or Bob Feller would see their Fielding Runs artificially depressed). Also, pitchers' chances are weighted less than infielders' assists because a pitcher's style may produce fewer ground balls. Thus the formula for pitchers is .10(PO + 2A − E + DP), whereas for second basemen, shortstops, and third basemen it is .20(PO + 2A − E + DP).

For first basemen, because putouts and double plays require so little skill in all but the odd case, these plays are eliminated, leaving only .20(2A − E) in the numerator.

For outfielders, the formula becomes .20(PO + 4A − E + 2DP). The weighting for assists is boosted here because a good outfielder can prevent runs through the threat of assists that are never made; for them, unlike infielders, the assist is essentially an elective play, like the stolen base. Outfielders' Fielding Runs are subject to some degree of error because outfielders sometimes switch fields within a game or season (Babe Ruth, for example, was positioned in the field that required the lesser range—right field in Yankee Stadium, left field in most road parks). Also, short distances to left- or right-field walls in some parks tend to depress putout totals.

Fielding Runs are abbreviated as FR.

Fielding Wins Fielding Runs divided by the number of runs required to create an additional win beyond average. That average is defined as a team record of .500 because a league won-lost average must be .500. Abbreviated as FW. See *Runs Per Win*.

Games Behind Figured by adding the difference in wins between a trailing team and the leader to the difference in losses, and dividing by two. Thus a team that is three games behind may trail by three in the win column and three in the loss column, or four and two, or any other combination of wins and losses totaling six. Abbreviated as GB.

Game-Winning Run Batted In Credited to the batter who drives in a run that gives his club a lead that it never relinquishes, no matter when that run is driven in nor what the final score is. Introduced in 1980 as an official stat, the GWRBI has met with deserved scorn and is not recorded in this volume.

Grounded into Double Play Erratically recorded on an official basis, this stat tends to be overvalued by the general public as an indicator of rally-killing ineptitude. Instead, it is largely a function of high totals of at-bats, which tend to be accumulated by the game's best players, not its worst. Abbreviated as GIDP.

Hands Out The original 1840s scoring term for batters producing

outs either at the plate or on the bases. On a force out, the runner retired on the bases would be charged with a hand out, not the batter. Also called Hands Lost, and abbreviated as HO or HL.

Hit by Pitch A batter struck by a pitched ball was not awarded first base until 1884 in the American Association and 1887 in the National League. Reconstruction of stats for batters and pitchers in the years 1903–1908 is in process. Abbreviated as HBP.

Hits Bases on balls originally counted as hits in 1887, but are recorded in this volume as neither hits nor at-bats.

Home Run Batter Rating A measure of a team's home-run ability, taking into account its Home Run Factor (see below) and its not having to face its own pitchers. The average mark is represented as 100 and the highest figure above that indicates the best. Abbreviated as HRB, it is computed by comparing homers scored and allowed per inning at home and on the road. Innings are estimated from the number of games and the number of games won (allowing for a leading home team not batting in the ninth). The team figure thus obtained is then compared to the league average.

Home Run Factor A measure of the home runs hit in a given ballpark, with 100 representing the average home park and the highest figure above that representing the best home-run park. Computed in the same manner as Home Run Batter Rating (see above). Abbreviated as HRF.

Home Run Percentage Home runs per 100 at-bats.

Home Run Pitcher Rating A measure of a team's ability to prevent home runs, taking into account the Home Run Factor (see above) of the park and the team's not having to face its own batters. The average mark is represented as 100, and the lowest figure beneath that indicates the best.

Home Runs When is a home run not a home run? Before 1920, not if it came with men on base in the ultimate inning and created a margin of victory greater than one run. A ruling of the Special Baseball Records Committee in 1969 reversed its earlier decision that had made home runs of 37 disputed final-inning, game-winning base hits. In accordance with the practice of the day, such a hit, even if it sailed out of the park, would be credited with only as many bases as necessary to plate the winning run. Thus Babe Ruth's "715th home run," hit on July 8, 1918, to win a game against Cleveland, remained a triple, and Jimmy Collins and Sherry Magee were each deprived of two home runs.

Innings Pitched Until 1976 official baseball practice was to lop off fractional innings for individuals; from that point until 1982, fractional innings were rounded off to the next highest inning. Since then fractional innings have been kept for individuals and teams. In this volume fractional innings are supplied for all individuals and all teams in all years. Those men who took a turn on the mound but failed to retire a batter are credited with no innings pitched and, if they allowed a runner or runners to score, an ERA of infinity.

Intentional Bases on Balls Recorded only since 1955.

Isolated Power Total bases minus hits, divided by at-bats; in other words, Slugging Average minus Batting Average. Appears to have been created by Allan Roth and Branch Rickey in the early 1950s.

League-Average Replacement Player That model player who performs at precisely the league average, creating a baseline against which to measure others.

Linear Weights A system created by Pete Palmer to measure all the events on a ballfield in terms of runs. At the root of this system, as with other sabermetric figures such as Runs Created, is the knowledge that wins and losses are what the game of baseball is about, that wins and losses are proportional in some way to runs scored and runs allowed, and that runs in turn are proportional to the events that go into their making.

Normalizing Restating a figure as a ratio by comparing it to the league average, or norm.

On Base Percentage Created by Roth and Rickey in its current form—hits plus walks plus hit by pitch, divided by at-bats plus walks plus hit by pitch—in the early 1950s, although there were nineteenth-century forebears such as "Reached First Base." When OBP, as it is abbreviated, was adopted as an official stat in 1984, the denominator was expanded to include sacrifice flies. The effect is to penalize a batter in his on base percentage by giving him a plate appearance while at the same time crediting him in his batting average by deleting the plate appearance. In this book we calculate OBP without considering sacrifice flies, which in any event are calculable on a continuing basis only since 1954.

On Base plus Slugging See *Production.*

Opponents' Batting Average Hits allowed divided by at-bats allowed (or, if at-bats allowed is unknown, then at-bats equals hits plus inning times "K," where "K" is the league average of at-bats minus hits, all over innings). Abbreviated as OAV.

Opponents' On Base Percentage For years before 1908 in the American League and 1909 in the National League, the number of batters facing a pitcher has been constructed from the available raw data. We have subtracted league base hits from league at-bats, divided by league innings pitched, multiplied by the pitcher's innings, and added his hits and walks allowed and hit by pitch and sacrifices, if available. Abbreviated as OOB.

Outs Until 1883, included catching a ball on one bounce in foul ground. Not credited after three strikes in 1887, when the rule was "four strikes and yer out"—as it was, in fact, from 1871–1881, when batters commonly received "warning pitches" rather than called strikes.

Outs Per Game The 1860s successor to Hands Out (see above), it joined with Runs Per Game to form the batting record before the rise of professional league play.

Park Factor Calculated separately for batters and pitchers. Above 100 signifies a park favorable to hitters; below 100 signifies a park favorable to pitchers. The computation of PF is admittedly daunting, and what follows is probably of interest to the merest handful of readers, but we feel obliged to state the mathematical underpinnings for those few who may care. For this second edition of *Total Baseball*, we use a three-year average Park Factor for players and teams unless they change home parks. Then a two-year average is used, unless the park existed for only one year. Then a one-year mark is used. If a team started up in Year 1, played two years in the first park, one in the next, and three in the park after that and then stopped play, the average would be as follows (where F*n* is the one-year park factor for year *n*):

Year 1 and 2 = (F1 + F2)/2	Year 4 = (F4 + F5)/2
Year 3 = F3	Year 5 = (F4 + F5 + F6)/3
	Year 6 = (F5 + F6)/2

Step 1. Find games, losses, and runs scored and allowed for each team at home and on the road. Take runs per game scored and allowed at home over runs per game scored and allowed on the road. This is the initial figure, but we must make two corrections to it.

Step 2. The first correction is for innings pitched at home and on the road. This is a bit complicated, so the mathematically faint of heart may want to head back at this point. First, find the team's home winning percentage (wins at home over games at home). Do the same for road games. Calculate the Innings Pitched Corrector (IPC) shown below. If it is greater than 1, this means the innings pitched on the road are higher because the other team is batting more often in the last of the ninth. This rating is divided by the Innings Pitched Corrector, like so:

$$\text{IPC} = \frac{(18.5 - \text{Wins at home / Games at home})}{(18.5 - \text{Losses on road / Games on road})}$$

Note: 18.5 is the average number of half-innings per game if the home team always bats in the ninth.

Step 3. Make corrections for the fact that the other road parks' total difference from the league average is offset by the park rating of the club that is being rated. Multiply rating by this Other Parks Corrector (OPC):

$$\text{OPC} = \frac{\text{No. of teams}}{\text{No. of teams} - 1 + \text{Run Factor, team}}$$

(Note that this OPC differs from that presented earlier in *The Hidden Game of Baseball*, for in preparing the pre-1900 data for *Total Baseball*, we discovered that for some parks with extreme characteristics, like Chicago's Lake Front Park of 1884, which had a Home Run Factor of nearly 5, the earlier formula produced wrong results. For parks with factors of 1.5 or less, either formula works well.)

Example. In 1982, Atlanta scored 388 runs and allowed 387 runs at home in 81 games, and scored 351 and allowed 315 on the road in 81 games. The initial factor is $(775/81) \div (666/81) = 1.164$. The Braves' home record was 42–39, or .519, and their road record was 47–34, or .580. Thus the IPC $= (18.5 - .519) \div (18.5 - .420) = .995$. The team rating is now $1.164/.995 = 1.170$. The OPC $= (12) \div (12 - 1 + 1.170) = .986$. The final runs-allowed rating is $1.170 \times .986$, or 1.154.

We warned you it wouldn't be easy!

The batter adjustment factor is composed of two parts, one the park factor and the other the fact that a batter does not have to face his own team's pitchers. The initial correction takes care of only the second factor. Start with the following (SF = Scoring Factor, previously determined [for Atlanta, 1.154], and SF1 = Scoring Factor of the other clubs [NT = number of teams]):

$$1 - \frac{\text{SF} - 1}{\text{NT} - 1}$$

Next is an iterative process in which the initial team pitching rating is assumed to be 1, and the following factors are employed:

RHT, RAT = Runs per game scored at home (H) and away (A), by team
OHT, OAT = Runs per game allowed at home, away, by team
RAL = Runs per game by both teams

Now, with the Team Pitching Rating (TPR) = 1, we proceed to calculate Team Batting Rating (TBR):

$$\text{TBR} = \left(\frac{\text{RAT}}{\text{SF1}} + \frac{\text{RHT}}{\text{SF}} \right) \left(1 + \frac{\text{TPR} - 1}{\text{NT} - 1} \right) \Big/ \text{RAL}$$

$$\text{TPR} = \left(\frac{\text{OAT}}{\text{SF1}} + \frac{\text{OHT}}{\text{SF}} \right) \left(1 + \frac{\text{TBR} - 1}{\text{NT} - 1} \right) \Big/ \text{RAL}$$

The last two steps are repeated three more times. The final Batting Corrector, or Batters' Park Factor (BPF) is

$$\text{BPF} = \frac{(\text{SF} + \text{SF1})}{\left(2 \times \left[1 + \dfrac{\text{TPR} - 1}{\text{NT} - 1} \right] \right)}$$

Similarly, the final Pitching Corrector, or Pitchers' Park Factor (PPF) is

$$\text{PPF} = \frac{(\text{SF} + \text{SF1})}{\left(2 \times \left[1 + \dfrac{\text{TBR} - 1}{\text{NT} - 1} \right] \right)}$$

Now an example, using the 1982 Atlanta Braves once again.

$$\text{RHT} = \frac{388}{81} = 4.79 \qquad \text{RAT} = \frac{351}{81} = 4.33$$

$$\text{OHT} = \frac{387}{81} = 4.78 \qquad \text{OAT} = \frac{315}{81} = 3.89$$

$$\text{RAL} = \frac{7947}{972} = 8.18 \qquad \text{NT} = 12$$

$$SF = 1.154 \qquad SF1 = 1 - \left(\frac{1.154 - 1}{11} \right) = .986$$

$$TBR = \left(\frac{4.33}{.986} + \frac{4.79}{1.154} \right) \left(1 + \frac{1 - 1}{11} \right) \Big/ 8.18 = 1.044$$

$$TPR = \left(\frac{3.89}{.986} + \frac{4.78}{1.154} \right) \left(1 + \frac{1.044 - 1}{11} \right) \Big/ 8.18 = .993$$

Repeating these steps gives a TBR of 1.04 and a TPR of .97. The Batters' Park Factor is

$$BPF = \frac{(1.170 + .986)}{\left(2 \times \left[1 + \frac{.99 - 1}{11} \right] \right)} = 1.07$$

This is not a great deal removed from taking the original ratio,

$$\frac{1.170 + 1}{2}, \text{ which is } 1.08.$$

The Pitchers' Park Factor may be calculated in analogous fashion.

To apply the Batters' Park Factor to Batting Runs, one must use this formula:

$$\frac{BR}{corr.} = \frac{BR}{uncorr.} - \frac{Runs\,(league)}{\underset{league}{(AB + BB + HBP)}} \times (BPF - 1) \times \underset{player\,or\,team}{(AB + BB + HBP)}$$

For example, if a player produces 20 runs above average in 700 plate appearances with a Batters' Park Factor of 1.10, and the league average of runs produced per plate appearance is .11, this means that the player's uncorrected Batting Runs is 20 over the zero point of 700 × .11 (77 runs). In other words, 77 runs is the average run contribution expected of this batter were he playing in an average home park. But because his Batters' Park Factor is 1.10, which means his home park was 10 percent kinder to hitters (than the average), you would really expect an average run production of 1.1 × 77, or 85 runs. Thus the player whose uncorrected Batting Runs is 97 with a BF of 1.1 is only +12 runs rather than +20, and 12 is his Park Adjusted Batting Runs (in the Player Register, BR/A):

$$12 = 20 - .11 \times (1.10 - 1) \times 700$$

Percentage of Team Wins A simple but deceiving measure of a good pitcher's contribution to a bad club; in this, it shares the virtues and flaws of Ted Oliver's Weighted Rating System and, to a lesser degree, our own Wins Above Team (both of which see). Steve Carlton had the highest single-season rating in this century when, in 1972, he went 27–10 for a Phillie club that won only 59 games. Yet his mark of 45.8 percent of his team's wins would not make the top 100 list of seasons since 1876, making this stat nearly useless for historical analysis.

Pitcher Defense Abbreviated as PD. See *Fielding Runs*.

Pitchers' Park Factor The same as the Park Factor shown in the pitchers' section of the team statistics portion of the Annual Record and in the Pitcher Register; above 100 means a pitcher was hurt by playing half his games in a good hitting park. See *Park Factor*.

Pitcher Strikeouts Made tougher or easier by cyclically varying rules and conditions. For instance, foul tips did not count as strikes for many years, even when deliberate, as with bunts; fouls caught on a bounce were outs until 1883; the ball-strike count underwent much experimentation until settling at four balls and three strikes in 1889; not to mention the high-low strike zone, warning pitches, varying pitching distances, and restricted deliveries. It helps to know some history before rattling off stats to prove this or that, but normalizing a stat to its league helps, even with counting stats such as strikeouts.

Pitching Runs The Linear Weights measure of runs saved *beyond*

what a league-average pitcher or team might have saved, defined as zero. The math is simple: *Pitching Runs = Innings Pitched × (League ERA/9) − Earned Runs Allowed.* An alternate version is: *Innings Pitched/9 × (Individual ERA − League ERA).* Abbreviated as PR.

Pitching Wins Park Adjusted Pitching Runs divided by the number of runs required to create an additional win beyond average. That average is defined as a team record of .500 because a league won-lost average must be .500. Abbreviated as PW. See *Pitching Runs*, above, and *Runs Per Win*.

Player Win Averages The title of a 1970 book issued by the Mills brothers, Harlan and Eldon, as well as the name of their overall method of determining not only the *what* of baseball statistics but also the *when*, or clutch element. Computerizing complete play-by-play data for a full season for their book, they assigned "Win Points"—reflective of that event's potential impact on the team's prospects of victory—to *every* event on a baseball field.

Positional Adjustment A key factor in the Total Player Rating that addresses the relative worth to a ball club of the defensive positions. A man who bats .270, hits 25 homers, and drives in 80 runs may be an average performer in left field, no matter how good his glove; but credit those batting stats to a shortstop or second baseman and you have a star, because the defensive demands of the position are so much greater. To balance the abundance of good-hitting outfielders or first basemen against the scarcity of such players at catcher or shortstop, we created a positional adjustment expressed in terms of the average batting skill needed to hold down a major league spot at that position.

To determine the average defensive skill required of a position, simply subtract the average batting skill at that position from his Total Player Rating. This may seem strange at first glance, but it does put, for example, shortstops and left fielders on the same footing. Let's say that last year all National League outfielders accounted for 360 Batting Runs. Dividing that figure by 3 (for left, center, and right fields), we get 120 per outfield post. The positional adjustment, or factor for average defensive skill, for a left fielder who played in all 162 games would be 162 × 120/1,944, where 1,944 is the number of games played in the league by all left fielders (or any other position, obviously). Thus an outfielder who played in all his team's games would have 10 runs subtracted from the sum of his Batting Runs, Stolen Base Runs, and Fielding Runs. If all National League shortstops last year accounted for 84 Batting Runs below average, the adjustment for a shortstop would be figured in the same way, multiplying his games played by −84/1,944, or −7 runs, meaning that 7 runs (minus a minus 7) would be *added* to his Total Player Rating.

Production On Base Percentage plus Slugging Average: a simple but elegant measure of batting prowess, in that the weaknesses of one-half of the formulation, On Base Percentage, are countered by the strengths of the other, Slugging Average, and vice versa. When PRO, as it is abbreviated, is adjusted for home park and normalized to league average to become PRO⁺, the calculation is modified slightly to create a baseline of 100 for a league-average performance. For PRO⁺, the calculation is

$$\frac{\text{Player On Base Pct.}}{\text{League On Base Pct.}} + \frac{\text{Player Slugging Avg.}}{\text{League Slugging Avg.}} - 1$$

This produces a figure with a decimal point—an above-average figure, like 1.46, or a below-average figure, like 0.82. For ease of display, in this book we drop the decimal and express these as 146 and 82.

Putout Average Putouts divided by games played; a stat created by Philadelphia baseball writer Al Wright in 1875.

Quality Start A game started in which a pitcher lasts for six innings or more and allows three runs or less.

Ratio Hits allowed plus walks allowed per nine innings. Abbreviated as RAT.

RBI Opportunities An official American League stat for the first three weeks of 1918, until the league saw how much work it involved and scrapped it. Still a good idea, sort of, and the folks at the Elias Sports Bureau have tracked this type of "situational stat" since 1975.

Reached First Base A precursor of the On Base Percentage, this stat was introduced as an official National League measure in 1879, its one and only year of existence. It included times reached via hits, walks, and errors, but not hit by pitch because putting their bodies on the line did not yet, in 1879, send batters to first base. Trivia: the league leader in this stat's lone year of life was Paul Hines, with 193.

Relative Batting Average Pioneered by David Shoebotham in a *Baseball Research Journal* article in 1976, this was the first traditional stat normalized to league average so as to permit cross-era comparison. Most folks who have employed this measure simply divide individual batting average by league batting average. Shoebotham's original computation was more precise:

$$\text{RBA} = \frac{\text{player's hits}}{\text{player's AB}} \Big/ \frac{\text{league hits} - \text{player's hits}}{\text{league AB} - \text{player's AB}}$$

In this manner a player's own performance would not be compared with itself.

Relief Points Relief wins plus saves minus losses was the original formula used as the basis for the Rolaids Company's annual award to the top reliever in each league. Recently the formula has been changed to include a debit for blown saves.

Relief Ranking Takes *Relief Runs* (which see), adjusts them for home park, then weights them by a factor (F in the formula below) reflecting the greater value of the innings pitched by a bullpen "closer." Relief Runs, which weights all innings identically, will tend to benefit long and middle relievers who are effective over many innings, while Relief Ranking—which is reserved for those men who pitch less than three innings per game over a season or career—will tend to benefit relievers who may have fewer innings but who have more saves and decisions. The formula is

$$(\text{Relief Runs}) \times F \text{ where the Factor} = \frac{9(\text{Wins} + \text{Losses} + \text{Saves}/4)}{\text{IP}}$$

Relief Runs Identical to Pitching Runs but confined to relief pitchers, defined as those who average less than three innings per appearance. Abbreviated as RR. See *Relief Ranking*.

Run Batted In Though widely regarded as a good measure of a batter's overall productivity and value to his team, the RBI is extremely situation-dependent, denying equal access to opportunity on the basis of a player's team, slot in the batting order, and particularly the men surrounding him in the batting order.

Run Factor A measure of the run scoring in a given ballpark compared to other ballparks, with 100 representing the average home park and the highest figure above that representing the best hitters' park. Abbreviated as RF, it is computed on the basis of comparing runs scored and allowed per inning at home and on the road. Innings are estimated from the number of games and games won, allowing for the home team not batting in the final inning of a game in which it leads. The resulting Run Factor is then compared to the league average.

Run Rating for Batters A measure of a team's run-scoring ability, taking into account the park's *Run Factor* (see above) and the team's batters not having to face its own pitchers, with 100 representing the average and the highest figure above that representing the best. Abbreviated as RB.

Run Rating for Pitchers A measure of a team's run-prevention ability, taking into account the *Run Factor* (see above) and the team's pitchers not having to face its own batters, with 100 representing the average and the lowest figure beneath that representing the best. Abbreviated as RP.

Runs Created Bill James's formulation for run contribution from a variety of batting and baserunning events. Many different formulas are used, depending upon data available. In its basic expression, the formula is:

$$\frac{(\text{Hits} + \text{Walks}) \, (\text{Total Bases})}{\text{At-Bats} + \text{Walks}}$$

The essence of this formulation is that the ability to get on base and the ability to push baserunners around fairly describes offensive ability. James later refined the formula with a "stolen base version":

$$\frac{(\text{Hits} + \text{Walks} - \text{Caught Stealing}) \, (\text{Total Bases} + .55 \times \text{Stolen Bases})}{\text{At-Bats} + \text{Walks}}$$

Next came the "technical version": a longer formulation, presented below using the standard abbreviations for the various offensive events (the two elements multiplied in the numerator are referred to below as "A" and "B," and the denominator is referred to as "C"):

$$\frac{(\text{H} + \text{BB} + \text{HBP} - \text{CS} - \text{GIDP}) \, (\text{TB} + .26[\text{BB} - \text{IBB} + \text{HBP}] + .52[\text{SH} + \text{SF} + \text{SB}])}{\text{AB} + \text{BB} + \text{HBP} + \text{SH} + \text{SF}}$$

From this technical version (Tech-1), James spun off 13 additional technical versions. "The reason that we have to do this," he wrote in *The Bill James Historical Baseball Abstract*, "is that the data set changes and evolves rapidly throughout the century, or at least up until about 1955, when the progress of evolution in statistical information came to a temporary halt (it stopped moving forward until Bill James and Pete Palmer came around, about twenty years later). In 1900 we have no data for how many times a player grounded into a double play, how many times he was hit by a pitch, how many of his walks might have been intentional, how many times he was caught stealing, or how many sacrifice flies he hit." Accordingly, James adjusted his Runs Created formula to fit the available data; some versions, such as Tech-3, cover as much as a decade in a given league, while others, such as Tech-4, are in force for only a single league season. In *Total Baseball*, we have computed Runs Created values for all players since 1876 using the version most applicable to the period, with the single exception of Tech-9, which James applied only to the American League of 1916 but which we use for 1914–1916 in the AL and 1915–1916 in the NL because we have discovered additional caught-stealing data. (For those players whose careers began before 1900, James used the Tech-11 formula "to estimate how many runs they had created," but appended a note saying that "these estimates were of indeterminate accuracy.")

Here are the formulas for Runs Created (RC) technical versions 2–14 (Tech-1 was used for both leagues in 1955–1988):

Tech-2 (1954)
Factors A and C of Tech-1 remain the same, while Part B simply drops Intentional Bases on Balls.

Tech-3 (AL 1940–1953; NL 1951–1953)
Factor A remains the same, while SF is dropped from Factor C; Factor B changes to: 1.025 TB + .26(BB + HBP) + .52(SH + SB).

Tech-4 (AL 1939)
Factors A and C remain the same, while B becomes: TB + .26(BB + HBP) + .52(SH + SB).

Tech-5 (AL 1931–1938)
Factors B and C remain the same, while A becomes: .96(H + BB + HBP − CS).

Tech-6 (AL 1928–1930, 1920–1926; NL 1920–1925)
Factors A and C remain the same, while B changes only in the value placed on the sacrifice hit and stolen base, which declines from .52 to .51.

Tech-7 (AL 1927; NL 1926–1930)
C remains the same, while A changes to: .93(H + BB + HBP), and B becomes: TB + .26(BB + HBP) + .46(SH).

Tech-8 (AL 1913, 1917–1919; NL 1913–1914, 1917–1919)
C remains the same, while A becomes: H + W + HBP − .02(AB), and B becomes: TB + .85(SH + SB).

Tech-9 (AL 1914–1916; NL 1915–1916)
B and C remain the same, while A becomes: H + BB + HBP − CS.

Tech-10 (AL, NL 1908–1912)
A and C remain the same, while B becomes: 1.025(TB + SB) + .75(SH).

Tech-11 (AL, NL 1900–1907)
B and C remain the same, while A becomes: H + BB + HBP.

Tech-12 (NL 1939–1950)
A Factor: H + BB + HBP − GIDP
B Factor: TB + .26(BB +HBP) + .52(SH)

Tech-13 (NL 1933–1938)
A and C remain the same as above, while B becomes: 1.025(TB) + .26(BB + HBP) + .52(SH)

Tech-14 (NL 1931–1932)
B and C remain the same, but A becomes: .95(H + BB + HBP).

Runs Per Game With its mate *Outs Per Game* (which see), this was the precursor, in the 1860s, of the batting average; by the end of that decade it gave way to Hits Per Game.

Runs Per Win Branch Rickey and Allan Roth first stated the proportional nature of runs and wins in their 1954 article in *Life*. Since then the point has been expanded upon by George Lindsey, Pete Palmer, Bill James, and every sabermetrician worth his salt: the point being that just as runs scored and allowed are the key to victory in a given game, so are they the key to success over the course of a season and the predictors of won-lost record with a surprising degree of precision. In 1982, Palmer wrote in *The National Pastime*, "My work showed that as a rough rule of thumb, each additional ten runs scored (or ten less runs allowed) produced one extra win. . . . However, breaking the teams into groups showed that high-scoring teams needed more runs to produce a win. This runs-per-win factor I determined to be ten times the square root of the average number of runs scored per inning by both teams. Thus in normal play, when 4.5 runs per game are scored by each club, each team scores .5 runs per inning—totaling one run, the square root of which is one, times ten."

For *Total Baseball*, we have improved the Runs Per Win figure used in calculating the overall win figures in the Total Player Rating and the Total Pitcher Index. Rather than using 10 times the square root of the average number of runs scored per inning by both teams, we use adjusted runs per inning based on what the player or pitcher rating is. A hitter will increase the figure by adding in his rating over the number of games played, while a pitcher will have his rating subtracted. Say the average number of runs scored per inning is 1, as in the model above; then Runs Per Win = 10. Take a pitcher who allows 45 runs less than average in 25 games. This lowers the runs per game by 1.8, or runs per inning by .2, so the new Runs Per Win figure is 10 times the square root of the average number of runs scored per inning by both teams, *minus the pitcher's rating*. So we take from the one run per inning the .2 run saved by the pitcher, giving a result of 0.8. Ten times the square root of 0.8 is 8.9, so the pitcher gets 45/8.9, or 5.1, wins instead of 4.5. A hitter with plus 45 runs in 150 games, or .3 runs per game, contributes .03 runs per inning. His Runs Per Win is now 10 times the square root of the average number of runs scored per inning *plus the batter's rating*. So we add to the 1 run per inning the .03 runs added by the batter, giving a result of 10.1. Ten times the square root of 10.1 gives the batter 4.4 wins. (This method makes makes more of a difference in pitching because the runs are contributed over fewer games. With the same run contribution—45 beyond average—the pitcher gains 0.7 wins over the batter. This is because when the total number of runs scored is lowered, the value of each run is greater).

Runs Produced Runs batted in plus runs scored minus home runs.

Sabermetrics Defined by Bill James, who coined the term in honor of the Society for American Baseball Research, as "the search for objective knowledge about baseball" and, earlier, as "the

mathematical and statistical analysis of baseball records."

SABR Pronounced "saber," this is the acronym for the Society for American Baseball Research, the organization that has, since its founding by Bob Davids in 1971, steadily advanced the state of baseball knowledge.

Sacrifice Fly First recognized as an event in 1908 but indistinguishable in the official records from sacrifice hits until 1954. There has been much flip-flopping since 1930 on whether to credit the sacrifice flier with an at-bat or an RBI or whether a fly ball that advances a runner to a base other than home plate also should exempt a man from an at-bat.

Sacrifice Hits Invented in the 1860s, recorded since 1889; sacrificer charged with an at-bat until 1895. Sabermetricians frown on the strategy because all the studies show that the trading of an out for a base advanced is a losing strategy—lowering the run expectations of the team that attempts it—in all but the most unusual of cases . . . even if the sacrifice "succeeds."

Sacrifice Hits Allowed Computed officially in the National League in 1916, in the American in 1922; what it signified about anything is unclear.

Save Created by Jerry Holtzman of the Chicago *Sun-Times*, the save began to be reported by *The Sporting New* on a regular basis in 1960. The major leagues adopted the save in 1969, at which time it was credited to a reliever who finished a game that his team won. In 1973 the save was redefined so that a reliever had not only to finish the game but also to find the potential tying or winning run on base or at the plate, or, alternately, to pitch the final three innings of a victorious contest. In 1975 the rule was liberalized to include a reliever's appearance of one inning or more in which he protects a lead of three runs or less; or he enters the game with the tying or winning run on base, at bat, or on deck; or he pitches three innings to the game's conclusion. In this book, the 1969 definition is applied to all games before 1969; otherwise the rule in force at the time prevails. Abbreviated as SV.

Shutouts On an individual basis, credited only to pitchers of complete-game scoreless victories; former practice was to credit combined shutouts to the starting pitcher if he had pitched most of the way. Abbreviated as SH.

Situational Stats How does a batter perform with the bases loaded? At night? On artificial turf? With no one on base? After the seventh inning when his team is tied or trails? That kind of stuff, now the specialty of Project Scoresheet and the Elias Sports Bureau.

Slugging Average Total bases divided by at-bats; combines nicely with On Base Percentage to create *Production* (which see). Abbreviated as SLG.

Starter Runs Identical to *Pitching Runs* (which see) but confined to starting pitchers, defined as those who average more than three innings per appearance. Abbreviated as SR.

Stolen Base Average Stolen bases divided by attempts; its computation is dependent upon the availability of caught-stealing numbers. Abbreviated as SBA.

Stolen Base Runs For teams, the Linear Weights measure of runs contributed *beyond* what a league-average basestealing team might have gained, defined as zero; for individuals, Stolen Base Runs are calculated on the basis of the 66.7 percent success rate that sabermetric studies have shown to be the break-even point for producing runs beyond the average. Availability dependent upon caught stealing data as with Stolen Base Average. The formula is simple: .30(Stolen Bases) − .60(Caught Stealing). A man who steals two bases in three attempts is merely spinning his wheels in terms of value to his team, and even a man who succeeds at an 80 percent clip will have to steal a lot of bases—about 65—to create just one win beyond average. Abbreviated as SBR.

Stolen Base Wins Stolen Base Runs divided by the number of runs required to create an additional win beyond average. Those runs are generally around around 10—historically in the range of 9–11. Abbreviated as SBW. See *Runs Per Win*.

Stolen Bases Recorded since 1886, but until 1898 steals are thought to have included a variety of daring baserunning exploits, such as going from first to third on a single or advancing an extra base on an out. Abbreviated as SB.

Strikeouts Varying rules concerning the strike zone, the foul strike, and the warning pitch—not to mention the fourth strike of 1887—all contribute to making the cross-era comparison of strikeout accomplishments a very sticky business. Abbreviated as SO.

Strikeout Percentage A batters' stat: fewest strikeouts per 100 at bats.

Total Average Tom Boswell's formulation for offensive contribution from a variety of batting and baserunning events; as with Runs Created, we have calculated Total Average to make use of the maximum available data in a given year. The concept of the numerator is bases gained, that of the denominator is outs made:

$$\frac{\text{Total Bases} + \text{Steals} + \text{Walks} + \text{HBP}}{\text{At-Bats} - \text{Hits} + \text{Caught Stealing} + \text{GIDP}}$$

Abbreviated as TA. See *Base-Out Percentage*.

Total Baseball Ranking The "MVP" of statistics, this ranks pitchers and position players by their total wins contributed in all their endeavors, revealing the most valuable performers in a given year. Abbreviated as TBR, it is not a computed stat but a sorting of players and pitchers by, respectively, their Total Batter Rating and Total Pitcher Index.

Total Bases Average Henry Chadwick's measure that divided total bases by games played; a forerunner of the Slugging Average.

Total Bases Run A silly stat of one year's duration, 1880, this was sort of an RBI in reverse, from the runner's perspective. Also called "Bases Touched," it was nothing more than that and signified nothing about individual talent. Trivia: the National League's leader in 1880 was Abner Dalrymple, with 501 bases touched.

Total Chances Putouts plus assists plus errors; in other words, total chances offered, not total chances accepted.

Total Pitcher Index The sum of a pitcher's Pitching Runs, Batting Runs (in the AL since 1973, 0), and Fielding Runs, all divided by the Runs Per Win factor for that year (generally around 10, historically in the 9–11 range); abbreviated as TPI. See *Runs Per Win*.

Total Player Rating The sum of a player's Adjusted Batting Runs, Fielding Runs, and Base Stealing Runs, minus his positional adjustment, all divided by the Runs Per Win factor for that year (generally around 10, historically in the 9–11 range). See *Runs Per Win*.

Triple Crown Long regarded as consisting of batting average, home runs, and RBIs, but was not always so. In the early years of this century, newspapers spoke of Ty Cobb shooting for the "triple crown" of batting average, runs, and hits.

Weighted Average The next step in statistical sophistication after first, counting and, next, averaging. Chadwick's Total Bases Average was probably the first weighted average, in that it assigned values of 1 to a single, 2 to a double, 3 to a triple, and 4 to a home run.

Weighted Rating System Ted Oliver's invention, promoted in a 1944 self-published booklet called *Kings of the Mound*. We have modified Oliver's pioneering effort to create *Wins Above Team* (see below), which entry presents a discussion of Oliver's effort.

Win Points See *Player Win Averages*.

Wins Above League A pitcher's won-lost record restated by adding his Pitching Wins above the league average to the record that a league-average pitcher would have had with his number of decisions. Example: Tom Seaver has a hard-luck season, going only 16–14 despite a 1.76 ERA and five Pitching Wins; applying the five wins to a league-average 15–15 mark in the same 30 decisions results in a WAL of 20-10.

Wins Above Team How many wins a pitcher garnered beyond those expected of an average pitcher for that team. As the editors of this volume, in their earlier *Hidden Game of Baseball*, modified Ted Oliver's *Weighted Rating System* (see above), they now improve this statistic thanks to Bill Deane's corrective for its tendency to overvalue the contributions of good pitchers on awful teams.

Oliver's Weighted Rating System for pitchers was motivated by the inadequacies of both the won-lost percentage and the ERA when it came to evaluating pitchers laboring for poor teams. The Oliver formula, ingenious if flawed, was: pitcher's won-lost percentage minus the team's won-lost percentage—after removing the pitcher's decisions from the team's record—then multiplying the difference by the pitcher's number of decisions. Here is an example of the Oliver method as applied to Bobby Castillo, who in 1982 pitched very well in going 13–11 for a very bad Minnesota club (60–102; without him, 47–91):

$$\left(\frac{13}{24} - \frac{47}{138}\right) \times 24$$

or

$$(.542 - .341) \times 24$$

or

$$.201 \times 24 = 4.824$$

The figure of 4.824 would have been represented by Ted Oliver as "4,824 points"; he did not seem to recognize that had he retained the decimal point, his rating would have been expressed directly in *wins*. Thus the number of wins Castillo accounted for in his 24 decisions that an average Minnesota pitcher would *not* have gained was 4.8.

Thanks to a key modification of our earlier formula for Wins Above Team, abbreviated as WAT, we now propose the following: calculate the pitcher's won-lost percentage and the team's winning percentage after his decisions have been set aside. If the pitcher's percentage is higher, then WAT is

$$\text{Pitcher decisions} \times \left(\frac{\text{Pitcher pct.} - \text{Team pct.}}{2 - 2 \times \text{Team pct.}}\right)$$

If the pitcher's percentage is lower, then WAT is

$$\text{Pitcher decisions} \times \left(\frac{\text{Pitcher pct.} - \text{Team pct.}}{2 \times \text{Team pct.}}\right)$$

Won-lost percentage Computed as wins over decisions.

Team and League Abbreviations

These are the 144 franchises, seven principal leagues, and their abbreviations as used throughout this book.

NATIONAL ASSOCIATION, 1871–1875 (shown as n or NA)

Abbrev.	First	Last	Team
ATH n	1871	1875	Philadelphia Athletics
ATL n	1872	1875	Brooklyn Atlantics
BAL n	1872	1874	Baltimore Lord Baltimores
BOS n	1871	1875	Boston Red Stockings
CEN n	1875	1875	Philadelphia Centennials
CHI n	1871	1871	Chicago White Stockings
CHI n	1874	1875	Chicago White Stockings
CLE n	1871	1872	Cleveland Forest City
ECK n	1872	1872	Brooklyn Eckfords
HAR n	1874	1875	Hartford Dark Blues
KEK n	1871	1871	Fort Wayne Kekiongas
MAN n	1872	1872	Middletown (Conn.) Mansfields
MAR n	1873	1873	Baltimore Marylands
MUT n	1871	1875	New York Mutuals
NAT n	1872	1872	Washington, D.C., Nationals
NH n	1875	1875	New Haven Elm City
OLY n	1871	1872	Washington, D.C., Olympics
PHI n	1873	1875	Philadelphia White Stockings
RES n	1873	1873	Elizabeth (N.J.) Resolutes
ROK n	1871	1871	Rockford (Ill.) Forest City
RS n	1875	1875	St. Louis Red Stockings
STL n	1875	1875	St. Louis Brown Stockings
TRO n	1871	1872	Troy Haymakers
WAS n	1873	1873	Washington Washingtons
WAS n	1875	1875	Washington Washingtons
WES n	1875	1875	Keokuk (Iowa) Westerns

NATIONAL LEAGUE, 1876– (shown as N or NL)

Abbrev.	First	Last	Team
ATL N	1966		Atlanta
BAL N	1892	1899	Baltimore
BOS N	1876	1952	Boston (transferred to Milwaukee)
BRO N	1890	1957	Brooklyn (transferred to Los Angeles)
BUF N	1879	1885	Buffalo
CHI N	1876		Chicago
CIN N	1876	1880	Cincinnati
CIN N	1890		Cincinnati
CLE N	1879	1884	Cleveland
CLE N	1889	1899	Cleveland
DET N	1881	1888	Detroit
HAR N	1876	1877	Hartford (played in Brooklyn in 1877)
HOU N	1962		Houston
IND N	1878	1878	Indianapolis
IND N	1887	1889	Indianapolis
KC N	1886	1886	Kansas City
LA N	1958		Los Angeles
LOU N	1876	1877	Louisville
LOU N	1892	1899	Louisville
MIL N	1878	1878	Milwaukee
MIL N	1953	1965	Milwaukee (transferred to Atlanta)
MON N	1969		Montreal
NY N	1876	1876	New York (played in Brooklyn)
NY N	1883	1957	New York (transferred to San Francisco)
NY N	1962		New York
PHI N	1876	1876	Philadelphia
PHI N	1883		Philadelphia
PIT N	1887		Pittsburgh
PRO N	1878	1885	Providence
STL N	1876	1877	St. Louis
STL N	1885	1886	St. Louis
STL N	1892		St. Louis
SD N	1969		San Diego
SF N	1958		San Francisco
SYR N	1879	1879	Syracuse
TRO N	1879	1882	Troy (N.Y.)
WAS N	1886	1889	Washington, D.C.
WAS N	1892	1899	Washington, D.C.
WOR N	1880	1882	Worcester (Mass.)

AMERICAN ASSOCIATION, 1882-1891 (shown as a or AA)

Abbrev.	First	Last	Team
BAL a	1882	1889	Baltimore
BAL a	1890	1890	Baltimore (combined with Brooklyn, shown as BB)
BAL a	1891	1891	Baltimore (transferred to National League)
BOS a	1891	1891	Boston
BRO a	1884	1889	Brooklyn (transferred to National League)
BRO a	1890	1890	Brooklyn (combined with Baltimore, shown as BB)
CIN a	1882	1889	Cincinnati (transferred to National League)
CIN a	1891	1891	Cincinnati
CLE a	1887	1888	Cleveland (transferred to National League)
COL a	1883	1884	Columbus (Ohio)
COL a	1889	1891	Columbus (Ohio)
IND a	1884	1884	Indianapolis
KC a	1888	1889	Kansas City
LOU a	1882	1891	Louisville (transferred to National League)
MIL a	1891	1891	Milwaukee
NY a	1883	1887	New York
PHI a	1882	1891	Philadelphia
PIT a	1882	1886	Pittsburgh (transferred to National League)
RIC a	1884	1884	Richmond
ROC a	1890	1890	Rochester
STL a	1882	1891	St. Louis (transferred to National League)
SYR a	1890	1890	Syracuse
TOL a	1884	1884	Toledo
TOL a	1890	1890	Toledo
WAS a	1884	1884	Washington, D.C.
WAS a	1891	1891	Washington, D.C. (transferred to National League)

UNION ASSOCIATION, 1884 (shown as U or UA)

Abbrev.	First	Last	Team
ALT U	1884	1884	Altoona (Pa.)
BAL U	1884	1884	Baltimore
BOS U	1884	1884	Boston
CHI U	1884	1884	Chicago (combined with Pittsburgh, shown as CP)
CIN U	1884	1884	Cincinnati
KC U	1884	1884	Kansas City
MIL U	1884	1884	Milwaukee
PHI U	1884	1884	Philadelphia
PIT U	1884	1884	Pittsburgh (combined with Chicago, shown as CP)
STL U	1884	1884	St. Louis
STP U	1884	1884	St. Paul (Minn.)
'WAS U	1884	1884	Washington, D.C.
WIL U	1884	1884	Wilmington (Del.)

PLAYERS LEAGUE, 1890 (shown as P or PL)

Abbrev.	First	Last	Team
BOS P	1890	1890	Boston
BRO P	1890	1890	Brooklyn
BUF P	1890	1890	Buffalo
CHI P	1890	1890	Chicago
CLE P	1890	1890	Cleveland
NY P	1890	1890	New York
PHI P	1890	1890	Philadelphia
PIT P	1890	1890	Pittsburgh

AMERICAN LEAGUE, 1901– (shown as A or AL)

Abbrev.	First	Last	Team
BAL A	1901	1902	Baltimore (replaced by New York)
BAL A	1954		Baltimore
BOS A	1901		Boston
CAL A	1965		California
CHI A	1901		Chicago
CLE A	1901		Cleveland
DET A	1901		Detroit
KC A	1955	1967	Kansas City (transferred to Oakland)
KC A	1969		Kansas City
LA A	1961	1964	Los Angeles (transferred to California)
MIL A	1901	1901	Milwaukee (replaced by St. Louis)
MIL A	1970		Milwaukee
MIN A	1961		Minnesota
NY A	1903		New York
OAK A	1968		Oakland
PHI A	1901	1954	Philadelphia (transferred to Kansas City)
STL A	1902	1953	St. Louis (transferred to Baltimore)
SEA A	1969	1969	Seattle (transferred to Milwaukee)
SEA A	1977		Seattle
TEX A	1972		Texas
TOR A	1977		Toronto
WAS A	1901	1960	Washington, D.C. (transferred to Minnesota)
WAS A	1961	1971	Washington, D.C. (transferred to Texas)

FEDERAL LEAGUE, 1914-1915 (shown as F or FL)

Abbrev.	First	Last	Team
BAL F	1914	1915	Baltimore
BRO F	1914	1915	Brooklyn
BUF F	1914	1915	Buffalo
CHI F	1914	1915	Chicago
IND F	1914	1914	Indianapolis (transferred to Newark)
KC F	1914	1915	Kansas City
NEW F	1915	1915	Newark
PIT F	1914	1915	Pittsburgh
STL F	1914	1915	St. Louis